# IMMUNE SYSTEM

LORRIE KLOSTERMAN

**mc Marshall Cavendish**
Benchmark

Marshall Cavendish Benchmark
99 White Plains Road
Tarrytown, New York 10591
www.marshallcavendish.us

Editor: Karen Ang
Publisher: Michelle Bisson
Art Director: Anahid Hamparian
Series Designer: Kay Petronio

Library of Congress Cataloging-in-Publication Data

Klosterman, Lorrie.
 Immune system / by Lorrie Klosterman.
   p. cm. -- (The amazing human body)
 Includes bibliographical references and index.
 Summary: "Discusses the parts that make up the human immune system, what can go wrong, how to treat
those illnesses and diseases, and how to stay healthy."--Provided by publisher.
 ISBN 978-0-7614-3054-4
 1. Immune system--Juvenile literature. I. Title.
QR181.8.K66 2009
616.07'9--dc22
2007050439

Front cover image: A magnified image of human immune cells killing a parasitic worm called microfilaria.
Title page: Microscopic pollen that has been inhaled can cause an immune response. This response appears as an allergic reaction.
Back cover: White blood cells

 = cells from a tonsil, an organ that is part of the immune system

Photo research by Tracey Engel

Front cover photo: Eye of Science / Photo Researchers, Inc.
The photographs in this book are used by permission and through the courtesy of:
 *Superstock:* Image Source Black, 1, 4; Purestock, 22, back cover. *Alamy:* Peter Arnold, Inc., 6; PHOTOTAKE Inc., 9, 12, 19, 24, 29,
30; Medical-on-Line, 10, 21, 32; Nucleus Medical Art, Inc., 18, 20; Scott Camazine, 39; Bubbles Photography, 50; Leslie Garland
Picture Library, 65; Olivier DIGOIT, 68. *Visuals Unlimited:* Dr. Dennis Kunkel, 7, 11; Dr. David Phillips, 15; Science VU/ W. J. Johnson,
41. *Shutterstock:* 63; Sebastian Kaulitzki, 8; Michael Pettigrew, 25; Christophe Testi, 36; Scott Rothstein, 43; Christy Thompson, 44;
Franziska Richter, 52; Denis Pepin, 56, 60; Margie Hurwich, 58; Radu Razvan, 61; Ana Blazic, 62; 63; eAlisa, 64; icyimage, 66. *Photo
Researchers, Inc:* Omikron, 13; CNRI, 14; Tim Vernon, LTH NHS Trust, 26; Anatomical Travelogue, 27; Phanie, 28; David M. Phillips, 34;
Andrew Paul Leonard, 38; Pr. M. Brauner, 42; Eye of Science, 45; Dr. Kari Lounatmaa, 46; Stem Jems, 48; John Vavosi, 51; BSIP, 54;
Coneyl Jay, 55; SPL, 57. *CORBIS:* Karen Kasmauski, 33. *AP/Wide World Photos:* 67. *Getty Images:* Justin Sullivan, 69.

Printed in China
123456

# CONTENTS

# 1

# *What Is the Immune System?*

**E**very day millions of people enjoy the benefits of good health. We go to school and to work, play with friends, enjoy sports, movies, and many other activities, outdoors and in. We do not often realize that our immune systems are working nonstop to keep us healthy. In fact, many people do not know what the immune system is.

The immune system is a collection of cells and organs that protect us from illness and disease, and allow us to recover when we do get sick. The main activity of the immune system is to destroy pathogens, or germs, which are disease-causing microorganisms, such as bacteria, viruses, and parasites. Another important activity of the immune system is to rid the body of its own cells that have become damaged or abnormal.

◄ *A healthy immune system protects you from microorganisms like these* Streptococci *bacteria, which can make you sick.*

*Immune cells called macrophages destroy invading germs and other foreign substances that do not belong in the body.*

Most of the time, the immune system goes about its job invisibly. But sometimes we notice—when it is dealing with pathogens or other internal problems that have gotten out of hand. For example, a fever, sore throat, cough, and muscle aches are common symptoms of the flu, an illness caused by viruses that have settled into the airways. It usually takes several days, perhaps weeks, for the immune system to get rid of the viruses and for symptoms to disappear. For each of the times we get symptoms of illness, though, there probably have been dozens or even hundreds of other times that our immune systems removed microorganisms before they became plentiful enough to make us feel sick.

Our knowledge of the immune system has blossomed in the last several decades. And yet, there *is* still a lot of mystery and confusion about what this system is and what it *does*. Even science books and classes about the human body sometimes gloss over the immune system. Why?

It has not been easy to study the immune system. Immune cells, like other cells of the body, are invisible to the naked eye. You can only see them with powerful microscopes. Immune cells are among the least numerous cells in the body. Their activities depend on releasing a variety of important chemicals, but the amounts they release are so small that it is hard to detect and study them. Researchers have made remarkable progress in revealing the immune system and how it works, but many questions remain. Fortunately, there are some simple basics that everybody deserves to know about how the immune system works.

Immune cells can be compared to players on a sports team. On a football team, players each have different skills and responsibilities. Similarly, there are several types of immune cells with different jobs to do. A football team will not succeed without each player doing his part. But the players also must communicate and work together as a group. Immune cells, too, carry out their own tasks, but make a very effective germ-fighting team. The cells even communicate with each other in the form of chemicals,

*The cells and organs of the immune system work together to fight illness and disease.*

called cytokines. Cells release these chemicals that influence the behavior of other cells. Unlike a typical sports team, the immune system team has millions of players spread out over a very large playing field: the entire human body!

## WHITE BLOOD CELLS

*Under a very strong microscope, healthy red blood cells look like small round disks.*

Immune cells were first described centuries ago, when curious scientists looked at one of the easiest bits of the human body to study: a drop of blood. In the 1600s, Dutch scientist Antonie van Leeuwenhoek, built excellent microscopes so he could magnify things up to three hundred times their real size. He was shocked to find that blood, instead of being a red liquid, was made of red disklike objects in an amber-colored liquid. (This liquid is now called serum, or plasma). The small red objects were red blood cells. Blood cells were later were found to be packed with an iron-containing red pigment called hemoglobin, which carries oxygen for all the body's cells to use.

But there were other cells among the red ones. They had no pigment, so they were transparent. In fact, they were not discovered until the late 1800s. German scientist Paul Ehrlich had been experimenting with dyes, adding colors to bits of tissue (collections of cells) from animals and people, just as dyes are used to color fabrics. Ehrlich—who is now considered one of the "fathers of modern medicine" for his many discoveries—found that certain dyes revealed many other cell types among the red blood cells. The new cells were named white blood cells (WBCs) because without the aid of dyes, the microscope's bright light easily passed through them. Another name for these cells is leukocytes. (*Leuko* is Greek for white, *cyte* refers to cell.)

Ehrlich saw that the nucleus—the place where a cell's genetic material, or DNA, resides—in some of the WBCs was spherical. In other cells the nucleus was shaped like a barbell, or a flower with a few fat petals. He also noticed that some WBCs had a grainy appearance because of hundreds of tiny spheres, or granules, in the cells. Other cells looked clear instead of grainy. The WBCs with a grainy appearance are called granulocytes. Those that look clear are called agranulocytes. (The prefix *a* means "without.")

## Granulocytes

Ehrlich saw that granulocytes are not all alike. Some had granules that glistened like tiny beads of pinkish-orange glass when treated with an acidic dye called eosin. Those cells were named eosinophils (*phil* means "loving"). The granules in other granulocytes took on the bluish-purple color of certain

*White blood cells with a grainy appearance are called granulocytes.*

basic dyes. Those cells were named basophils. Finally, many cells had small granules, some of which turned bluish and others pink. Those cells were named neutrophils because they reacted to both basic and acidic dyes.

Early medical researchers noticed that granulocytes were more abundant in the blood of sick people. A person infected with parasites, such as hookworms that live in the intestine, had many more eosinophils than usual. Someone with an illness caused by bacteria, such as a kidney infection, had an abundance of neutrophils. Someone who suffered with hay fever or other allergies often had many basophils in their blood. It seemed that there had to be a connection between illnesses and granules. But what that connection was remained a mystery until researchers managed to study these tiny objects in the last few decades.

It turns out that the granules are droplets of chemicals which aid the cells in doing their jobs. For example, neutrophil granules contain enzymes that break up proteins—including proteins that make up germs. Neutrophils release these enzymes into their surroundings, which helps destroy the pathogens. Some of the enzymes, called defensins, create holes in bacteria that cause them to "leak" and die.

Basophil          Neutrophil          Eosinophil

*The three kinds of granulocytes have different jobs within the immune system.*

The granules in basophils contain a lot of histamine, a chemical with multiple effects on the body's own cells. For instance, histamine improves blood flow to an area of germ invasion. That, in turn, delivers more WBCs and helpful pathogen-fighting substances to the infected area. Eosinophils and the chemicals in their granules are especially good at destroying parasitic worms, such as tapeworms or pinworms, which are much larger than an immune cell.

## Agranulocytes

Agranulocytes may seem rather dull compared to cells filled with brightly colored granules. But their tasks are mighty. Agranulocytes can be divided into lymphocytes and monocytes.

Lymphocytes are the smallest of all the white blood cells. Under the microscope, they first seem a little boring, but they are very busy cells once they come into contact with something that is not a normal part of the body. Some of the lymphocytes are called B-lymphocytes, or B-cells for short. B-cells make tiny structures called antibodies. Antibodies attach to the surfaces of microorganisms and other foreign invaders. That makes these invaders harmless—or nearly so. Antibodies also work their way out of the bloodstream and settle in among cells throughout the body, such as in the digestive tract, where they defend against germs that are swallowed. Antibodies also are plentiful in saliva, mother's milk, and other secretions.

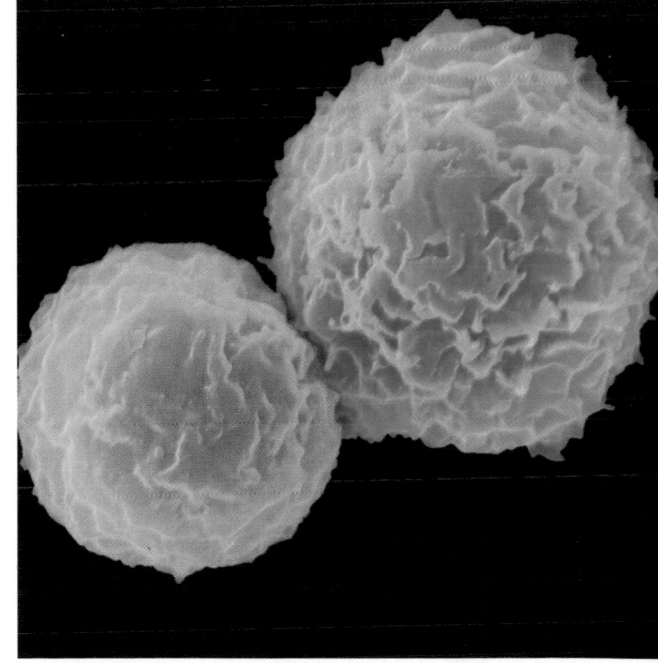

*The immune cell on the left is a T-cell, while the larger one on the right is a B-cell. Both are important in the body's immune response.*

Another group of lymphocytes, the T-lymphocytes, or T-cells for short, are very important in fighting viruses and cancer. With these illnesses, some of the body's own cells become abnormal. T-cells are specialists in recognizing "self" cells that are damaged—as in a viral infection—or mutated or changed cells—as in cancer. Some of the T-cells attach directly to the abnormal cells and destroy them. Those are called cytotoxic ("cell-killing") T-cells. Another kind of T-cell releases chemicals when it comes into contact with an abnormal cell. Those are helper T-cells, which are like a coach for the immune system team. T-cell chemicals flow out

E. coli *bacteria (orange) that has invaded the body is being destroyed by two different types of white blood cell—a monocyte (green) and a macrophage (blue).*

to other immune cells and cause the cells to work better, like a message saying, "There's an invader here, get rid of it!"

One more type of agranulocyte is the monocyte. Monocytes are thought to transform into another type of immune cell, the macrophage, by leaving the bloodstream and getting into tissues. Macrophages are excellent at cleaning up microorganisms and injured or dead cells. (*Macro* means "large" and *phage* means "eater.") They might be compared to the body's garbage collectors—they get rid of everything that is not needed, or at least they try. Macrophages do this by taking bacteria and parts of other cells inside themselves and breaking them into pieces. This process of killing cells by ingesting and killing cells is called phagocytosis.

0 sec.  10 sec.  20 sec.  30 sec.  40 sec.  50 sec.  60 sec.  70 sec.

*These magnified images show a macrophage (blue) destroying a bacterium (green). Within seventy seconds, the bacterium has been completely engulfed by the white blood cell.*

# THE LIFE CYCLE OF AN IMMUNE CELL

Many of the cells in our bodies live for a few months or a few years, and then die. Fortunately, new cells replace them and carry on their tasks. Immune cells die and are replaced, too. Some immune cells live for a few months, though others appear to live for many years—perhaps for a person's entire lifetime. Those that die are replaced by cells that are made inside bones, especially the long bones of the legs. Bone marrow, as a bone's interior is called, is alive with cells that can produce new immune cells over and over, all through a person's life. These are called stem cells. Each stem cell is something like a queen bee in a hive who lays all the eggs that will become new bees.

The newly made immune cells spend a while in the bone marrow, where they develop into various granulocytes and agranulocytes. They then move out into the bloodstream and many settle into tissues and lymph organs. An immune cell becomes most active when it encounters a pathogen or other unfamiliar substance. In its efforts to deal with the foreign item, many of the immune cells die. But thanks to stem cells, new immune cells are always developing to replace them.

*The magnified photo shows different types of blood cells—red and white—being formed in bone marrow.*

## IMMUNE CELLS EVERYWHERE

White blood cells are just some of the body's immune cell team. Millions—possibly billions—of immune cells live full-time in almost every area of the body. For instance, cells that act like macrophages live among the neurons in the brain, helping to keep that very important organ free of pathogens. The digestive tract is rich in immune cells, which sit among the other cells that absorb digested food. The deeper layers of skin have immune cells ready to respond to foreign materials that might break through the skin's surface layers. The moist tissues of the airways—the nose, throat, bronchi, and lungs—also have several kinds of immune cells that can deal with inhaled substances.

Additionally, WBCs in the bloodstream can squeeze through small openings in blood vessels and gather in areas of the body that are injured

*A neutrophil passes through a small opening in the wall of a tiny blood vessel.*

# WHITE BLOOD CELLS AT A GLANCE

Use this chart as a quick reference for the different types of WBCs.

| Granuloctyes | | | |
|---|---|---|---|
| basophils | | | Release chemicals—mostly histamine-increasing blood flow to the site of germ invasion. More WBCs and other immune cells can travel through the blood to fight the infection. Basophils releasing too much histamine also cause the symptoms of an allergic reaction. |
| eosinophils | | | Release chemicals that are toxic to parasites and other invaders. These chemicals also cause symptoms of asthma and allergic reactions. |
| neutrophils | | | Travel to infected areas to engulf and destroy foreign invaders. Neutrophils are phagocytes. |
| Agranuloctyes | | | |
| Monocytes | | | |
| | macrophages | | Engulf, ingest, and destroy foreign invaders. Some macrophages surround the germ, while others use long projectile-like "arms" to grab the germs. Use small parts of the germ to stimulate other immune cells into action. |
| Lymphocytes | | | |
| | B-cells | | Produce antibodies that attach to viruses and other invaders. These "marked" invaders are then destroyed by other immune cells. Some B-cells are "memory cells" that help the immune system remember how to fight foreign invaders that have infected the body before. |
| | T-cells | | |
| | | cytotoxic T-cells | Identify damaged or infected cells and then destroy them. |
| | | helper T-cells | Identify damaged or infected cells and release chemicals that alert the immune system. |

or infected. In fact, injured tissues release chemicals that attract WBCs from the bloodstream. Neutrophils are the first to accumulate because they are the most numerous type of WBC in the blood. Other immune cells accumulate over days and even weeks.

Sometimes so many WBCs collect at one place that the site becomes visible to the naked eye. For instance, pimples, which often appear on the faces of teenagers as they mature into adults, have a white center of WBCs. These cells are fighting bacteria that have collected in a pore, which is a tiny opening that is a natural part of the skin. As another example, people and also pets sometimes get an abscess, or a painful lump, just beneath the skin, where bacteria have gotten in and WBCs have accumulated in huge numbers to fight the infection. Abscesses usually break open after a few weeks, releasing WBCs and fluid, or a doctor may need to help clean them out.

## IMMUNE ORGANS

Certain organs of the body are part of the immune system because they are home to many immune cells. The largest of these is the spleen. It is about the size of an open hand, cupping the lower left side of the stomach. The spleen is rich in WBCs of several kinds, and red blood cells, too. Many blood vessels course through the spleen, making it an especially important place where pathogens are removed from the blood. The WBCs also remove parts of old red blood cells and other cellular debris. And though people can survive without a spleen—which sometimes gets badly injured, as in a traffic accident, and must be removed—this organ does a good deal of the body's "housecleaning" tasks.

Another immune organ is the thymus, or thymus gland. Most people have never heard of it. The thymus is located in the middle of the chest, near the heart. In the first few years of a person's life, certain WBCs finish their development within the thymus. Without spending some time

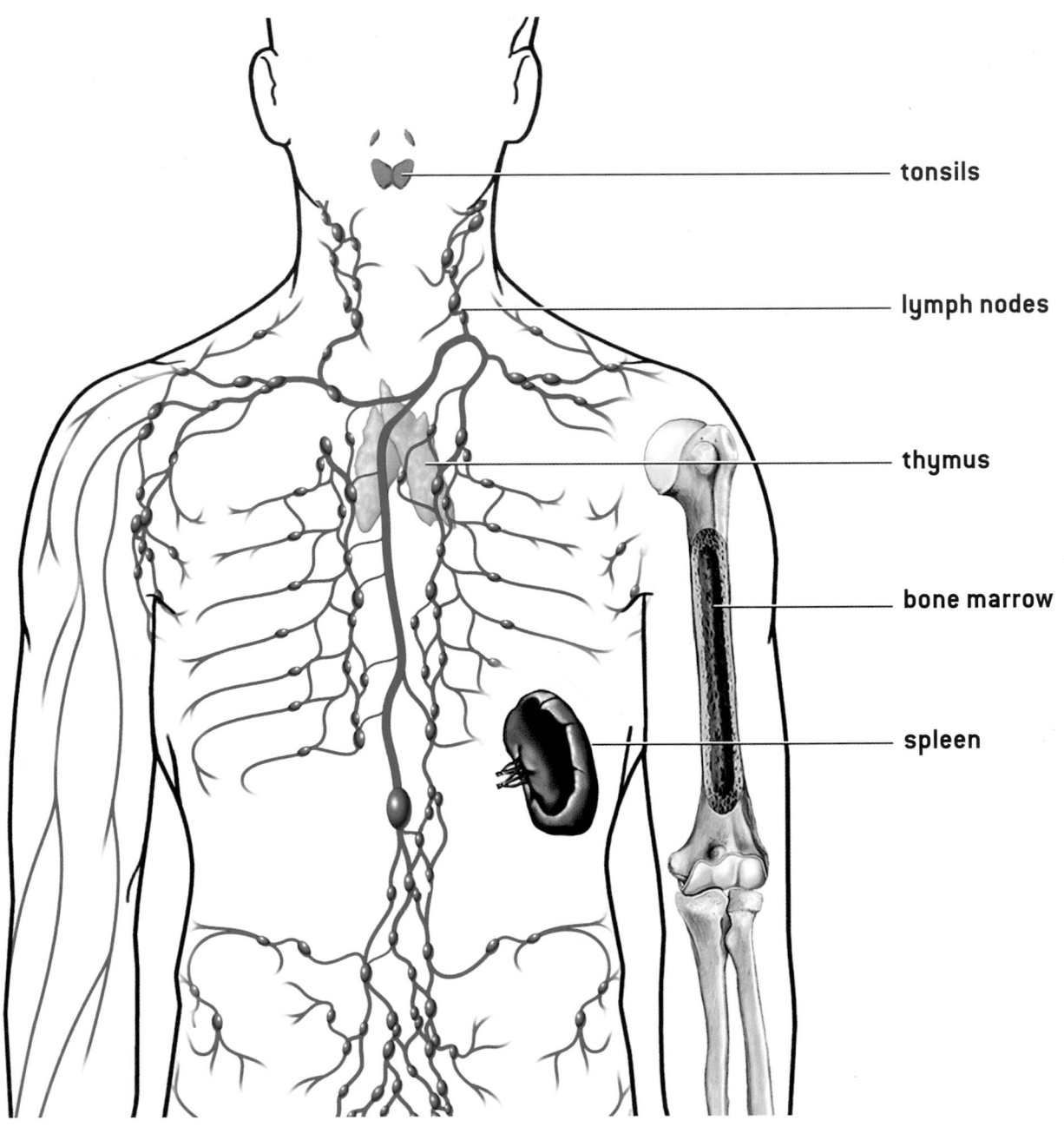

tonsils

lymph nodes

thymus

bone marrow

spleen

*The immune system is also made up of many organs found in different parts of the body.*

there, in contact with thymus cells, the immune cells will not work properly later. Those cells are the T-cells (T stands for thymus). The thymus becomes much smaller as a person gets older, because most of the T-cells eventually move out into the bloodstream and to other parts of the body.

Tonsils are also immune organs. There are several tonsils around the throat. One pair is easy to see, at the back of the throat on both sides. Tonsils provide a place where WBCs reside, and help prevent pathogens and other microscopic substances that are swallowed or inhaled from getting deeper into the body.

Lymph nodes are small immune organs about the size of a pea or kidney bean, sometimes larger. Like the spleen, they are

*Sometimes when a person is very sick, his or her tonsils will become swollen as part of the body's immune response.*

home to WBCs. We each have hundreds of lymph nodes throughout the body. Sometimes a person first notices a lymph node by feeling a tiny round lump just beneath the skin in the armpit or groin region, where the legs meet the torso. The lymph nodes are spaced along a network of tubes called lymph vessels. Together, the lymph nodes and vessels look

*There are many lymph nodes located around your neck and face.*

something like strings of beads. The vessels collect fluid that leaks out of blood vessels. This fluid, known as lymph, travels along lymph vessels and passes in and out of lymph nodes. The lymph is cleaned by WBCs. The lymph then flows back into large blood vessels near the heart and rejoins the bloodstream.

All of these organs and cells are often referred to as the lymphatic system, because of the lymph nodes and lymph vessels. The lymphatic system and immune system are basically the same. And while most people probably have never heard of "lymph," the immune system as a whole is getting more popular all the time. Many are realizing that it keeps us alive, just as much as our hearts and brains and kidneys do.

*When a lymph node becomes swollen from immune activity—such as this node in the neck—it can sometimes be felt through the skin.*

# 2

# How the Immune System Works

Our bodies are constantly in contact with bacteria, viruses, and parasites. Most of these microorganisms are harmless to us because they cannot live on, or in, our bodies. They need different surroundings to thrive, such as soil, or a certain kind of animal, or a plant. Some, though, can make us ill if they get into our bodies. But first, pathogens have to get past the skin and other defenses.

*A computer-generated image shows white blood cells traveling through a blood vessel.*

# THE FIRST LINES OF DEFENSE: SKIN AND SECRETIONS

The skin is a very effective barrier to microorganisms, thanks to its many layers of surface cells, which are dead. In fact, a healthy person's skin is covered with bacteria which, as long as they stay on the outside, are no threat to health.

Microorganisms live harmlessly just inside the body, too, in its various openings, such as the mouth, nose, urethra (the tube that carries urine from the bladder outside the body), and vagina (the portion of the female reproductive tract that connects the uterus, or womb, with the outside of the body). The cells that line these openings provide a barrier, as the skin does, which prevents the microscopic intruders from settling deeper into underlying tissues. In addition, these areas each create moist secretions that keep microorganism numbers low. Saliva, the moist substance constantly produced by salivary glands around and inside the mouth, is slightly

*Some microorganisms are harmless to the body and actually take part in healthy and necessary reactions. These probiotic organisms—as they are sometimes called—are usually ignored by the immune system.*

acidic and contains bacteria-killing enzymes and antibodies. Urine rinses bacteria out of the urethra regularly and is acidic, as are the natural secretions of the vagina, which keep microorganism populations low.

## When First-line Defenses Fail

The skin and the body's secretions are good barriers, but not perfect ones. A cut, scrape, burn, animal bite, or other break in the skin becomes a point of entry for microorganisms. If the wound is not cleaned well, and kept clean until it heals, pathogens can settle in and multiply. Pathogens also can be "injected" beneath the protective layers of skin by biting animals, such as mosquitoes, fleas, or ticks. People who inject illegal drugs are much more likely to become ill from microorganisms that are present on unclean skin, needles, or syringes. In addition, bacteria, viruses, yeast, or parasites can sometimes flourish beyond what is normal in the body's openings.

*Dangerous invaders can be introduced into the body when the skin is cut or pierced. Mosquitoes often pass along germs when they drink the blood of animals.*

Those microorganisms can work their way deeper into the body. Also, the digestive tract—in spite of saliva and the stomach's digestive enzymes and harsh acids—can sometimes become a home to disease-causing invaders that are swallowed. Fortunately, when any of these defenses has failed to keep back microorganisms, the immune system gets to work.

## THE IMMUNE SYSTEM IN ACTION

Imagine the immune cells of a healthy person. White blood cells are going around in the bloodstream. A variety of immune cells are stationed full time in the lungs, brain, skin, tonsils, intestine—virtually everywhere, nestled among other types of cells. Still, other immune cells are tucked away in lymph nodes, tonsils, and the spleen. What happens when a pathogen enters the scene?

Someone with a cold has sneezed. Tiny droplets of saliva become airborne, carrying millions of cold-causing viruses. Someone nearby

*Millions of germs can be passed along through a sneeze or a cough. This is why it is important to always cover your nose or mouth when sneezing or coughing.*

*This illustration shows a harmful microorganism (yellow ball) on the lining of a person's respiratory tract (the path used for breathing). Membranes in this tract produce fluid (called mucus) that may kill the germ. This is one example of the immune system's first line of defense.*

inhales some droplets, which stick to the moist linings of the nose and throat. The viruses then attach to cells. Portions of the viruses stay on the outside, while other components move inside the cells, where they use the cells' materials to make thousands more viruses. The newly made viruses burst out of the cells and move on to infect others. In a few days, even before the person feels sick, millions of viruses may have been produced. (That is why people can unknowingly spread pathogens to others, even before having the symptoms of a cold.)

*The adenovirus is a type of virus that can cause infections in the eyes and the respiratory and digestive systems.*

The immune system reacts to this invasion when immune cells in the tonsils, nose, or throat bump into whole viruses, or notice that nearby cells have parts of viruses stuck to their surfaces. The immune cells then each get busy doing their specific jobs. Macrophages engulf and destroy the viruses. Neutrophils arrive from the bloodstream and settle into throat areas to release pathogen-destroying chemicals. Cytotoxic T-cells latch onto cells that are infected with viruses and destroy them, ending their role as virus factories. B-lymphocytes produce antibodies that attach to the viruses. Helper T-cells release chemicals that signal the other kinds of immune cells to do their jobs better and faster. Immune cells also make copies of themselves to amplify their response. This is like bringing thousands of new team members onto the field!

During all of this, the person may get a sore throat, runny nose, cough, and feel tired. These cold symptoms are due in part to damage done by the virus. However, the immune cells' activities also cause swelling, tenderness, extra production of secretions (a runny nose), and other physical reactions. Fevers—which occur when the body's temperature is higher than normal—are also symptoms of many illnesses. Part of the purpose of a fever is to make it too hot for invading cells to reproduce and survive. When the immune system has cleared the viruses and infected cells, symptoms subside and healing takes over.

Infections with bacteria, instead of viruses, trigger a similar reaction to the scenario above. However, bacteria do not take over cells, as viruses do. Instead, they easily make copies of themselves wherever they settle, between cells or in the body's secretions. So cytotoxic T-cells probably are not as important in defense against bacteria. Macrophages, on the other hand, are major players in cleaning up bacteria, and can engulf many, once they notice them. And, as an example of how immune

*A phagocyte (blue) is engulfing bacteria (green) that are attacking the linings of the lungs.*

cells work as a team, macrophages grab hold of bacteria better if they are coated with antibodies produced by B-cells. In addition, cytokines produced by helper T-cells enhance the activities of both the macrophages and B-cells.

## Immune Cells Lend Their Helping Hands

Most immune cells need to come into direct contact with unfamiliar substances to become "activated" and do their job. This activation step is very important. To understand how this works, think of an immune cell as a person with many hands. Imagine the person sits all day, eyes closed, picking up a variety of objects. The hands become familiar with

*Some macrophages have cellular projections that reach out to grab invading germs.*

the feel of these objects. Then, if a new object is picked up, the hands notice something has changed. In response, the person tries to destroy it because it does not belong.

Similarly, an immune cell has many proteins on its surface, which are in contact with things around the cell. When the proteins touch something unfamiliar, the cell becomes activated to help destroy the unfamiliar thing. A macrophage will try to devour the item, neutrophils will release enzymes from their granules, B-cells will make antibodies, and so on. Many immune cells become activated as a pathogen multiplies and spreads.

## CONTINUED PROTECTION

Most people do not get sick as often as they could thanks to immunity provided by the immune system. Immunity, or "being immune," means that a certain pathogen does not make the person sick. This happens when the immune system comes across a pathogen it has already fought off before. The system can eliminate it again, faster and more completely, so that symptoms of illness do not arise.

Immunity happens because of memory cells. These are immune cells that react to a pathogen and continue to live for many months or years afterward, or even for a person's lifetime. (Many other immune cells appear to die in the process of fighting pathogens and are replaced by new ones.) Memory cells are able to react more quickly to the same pathogen the next time they encounter it, and they also make millions of cells like themselves that do the same. Antibodies, too, help with immunity. Some linger for a long time and help fight later infections by the same pathogen.

Memory cells and antibodies explain why someone who has been sick with measles or mumps, for instance, will not get sick with those again. The pathogen may show up, but the immune system will wipe it out before symptoms appear. Lifelong immunity does not apply to all illnesses.

Sometimes it lasts for a few years. Sometimes it does not even last a year—or so it seems. People get colds and flu year after year, because the viruses that cause them can change enough in a year that memory cells no longer recognize them.

Immunity can be created artificially by vaccination. Vaccination, or immunization, means giving weakened pathogens to a healthy person by injection, through nasal sprays, or in medications that can be swallowed. These shots or medications, called vaccines, activate the immune system to fight off the pathogen and make memory cells and antibodies. If the person is later exposed to the real pathogen, the memory cells help the

*Thanks to discoveries made by researchers, such as Paul Erlich, scientists have been able to develop vaccines and other treatments that kill or prevent dangerous illnesses.*

immune system destroy it quickly. Unfortunately, vaccines only work for some illnesses. But scientists continue to find ways to strengthen the immune system and build up a person's immunity to diseases.

There are many more intricate details than these about immune cells, their chemicals, and actions. Immunologists—experts in the immune system—are collecting information all the time, and must frequently update their understanding about how the system works. Each new discovery brings more questions.

*Over the years, progress in technology has helped to create vaccines that can target specific diseases. This scientist is manufacturing a vaccine that may prevent deadly smallpox infections.*

# When the Immune System Fails

For most of us, the immune system quietly does its work quite well. And if it worked perfectly, people would never get the flu, colds, measles, skin infections, tapeworms, malaria, or any of the hundreds of illnesses that are caused by bacteria, viruses, parasites, fungus, and other invaders. But we do get sick. Sometimes it is a shortcoming of the immune system. Sometimes the pathogen is especially harmful. In other cases, it is a combination of several problems.

◀ *Good and bad bacteria survive on the surface of your skin. Sometimes the harmful bacteria enters the body and causes illness. Usually, the immune system works to eradicate the germs and heal your body.*

*Babies have some immunities from their mother—either from when they were inside of her or when they drink her milk. But because their immune systems are not fully developed, they are more likely to get very sick from illnesses that an average adult can fight off.*

## IMMUNE SYSTEMS OF THE YOUNG AND THE OLD

When a baby is born, its immune system is not fully developed. For the first several months of life, the baby has help from its mother's immune system. Antibodies from the mother crossed from her bloodstream into the baby's before birth. But these wear out in about six months. If the baby is nursing, it will get more antibodies and other immune-boosting substances from the mother's milk. Eventually, though, it is up to the baby's own immune system to take over completely.

Although immune cells of a young person are ready to deal with thousands of pathogens, their immune systems will get better at destroying pathogens as it gains practice doing so. For a while, though, it takes longer to vanquish invaders than it would for an older child or adults. This is one reason why infants and young children tend to get sick more often than older people, and why they also tend to get high fevers more readily (Fevers are a response to infections.) In the later decades of life, the immune systems get weaker.

For these reasons, doctors are especially concerned for the very young and the elderly when an illness is passing through a community, such as the flu or food poisoning. Special care and attention is given to protect and aid these people.

## A WEAKENED IMMUNE SYSTEM

A person's immune system can be ineffective for reasons other than age. Someone who does not get enough good food, especially fruits and vegetables with a lot of vitamins and minerals, will have trouble keeping all their defenses healthy, including skin, secretions, and immune cells. Chronic diseases, which are illnesses that last for years, use a good deal of the body's energy, leaving less for fighting pathogens. Examples include cancer and diabetes. Certain types of medications, such as steroids and cancer treatments, also interfere with immune cell activity.

Genetic defects can also cause immune system weakness. These defects are passed along in genetic material from parent to child. For example, some people are born with very few or none of the B-cells that make antibodies. Others are born without T-lymphocytes, so that the important activities of cytotoxic and helper T-cells are missing. Infections are much more common in these people, even though they have other kinds of immune cells to do some of the germ fighting.

Every so often, a baby is born with a genetic mutation in the stem cells that should be making B- and T-cells. As a result, there are neither B- nor

T-lymphocytes. This condition, called severe combined immunodeficiency disease (SCID), soon leads to multiple infections and death within a few years. Fortunately, two medical treatments can help repair the situation. Bone marrow transplants put healthy stem cells from another person—usually a relative—into the patient's marrow, where the donated cells make colonies of lymphocytes. A gene therapy treatment puts normal genes into the patient's own stem cells to replace the mutated genes. For at least a dozen people, this has created their own functioning lymphocytes.

*A magnified image shows a stem cell taken from bone marrow. Scientists are trying to find ways to use stem cells to repair or replace cells that are not working properly.*

*Once-healthy cells that have become infected with AIDS (blue) are destroyed as copies of the virus (pink) burst from the host cells.*

## AIDS

Sometimes a person's immune system does not work well because the immune cells themselves are being attacked by pathogens. This sort of problem used to be rare. But now the world is in the middle of a global epidemic known as AIDS. AIDS stands for acquired immunodeficiency syndrome. Acquired means something that happened after birth (as opposed to a genetic mutation a person was born with). Syndrome refers to a collection of symptoms. These symptoms of AIDS vary from person to person, but all relate to poor immune cell function, or immunodeficiency. Most people who die of AIDS succumb to infections, especially pneumonia or tuberculosis, caused by microorganisms that invade the lungs.

What an AIDS victim has "acquired" is a virus called HIV, human immunodeficiency virus. (There are actually several different forms of this virus that make people sick). The virus enters and destroys several kinds of cells. Unfortunately, helper T-lymphocytes are among them.

Medications have been created to control the number of HIV viruses in the body. This helps some people live for years longer than they would without the medications. Unfortunately, not everyone can afford these medications, especially in the world's poorest nations. In addition, medications do not always work for long, because the viruses can change their form and survive anyway. A very big challenge with AIDS medications is that none of them can get rid of the virus permanently, since HIV, like all viruses, gets into a cell's inner workings—and its DNA—permanently.

Dozens of studies around the globe are now testing treatments to build up a healthy person's defenses to HIV. Hopefully some will work to prevent the millions of deaths—about 40 million worldwide in 2006—that result each year from HIV and AIDS.

## Cancer and the Immune System

Medical researchers suspect that cancer is due, in part, to a fault in the immune system. They think that normally our immune systems are busily destroying abnormal cells that show up from time to time—ones with mutated DNA that can lead to cancer. If such cells are not destroyed, they can sometimes make millions of copies of themselves and spread, crowding out healthy cells and taking over areas of the body. That is cancer.

Cancer research has focused a lot on treatments, but fortunately scientists are turning their attention to the immune system to understand why mutated cells escape the immune system in the first place. They also are testing new ways to get a patient's immune system to do better at destroying cancer cells that have already formed. For instance, certain cancers are associated with viral infection, probably because the viruses get into cells' DNA and mutate it—a prelude to those cells behaving like cancer cells.

*A macrophage (purple) is engulfing cancer cells (pink). In most cases, however, immune cells cannot kill enough cancer cells to completely heal the body. Additional medical treatment is needed to try to cure or treat cancer.*

Vaccinations against the viruses might help. An example is a new vaccine against human papilloma viruses, which are very common viruses and often harmless. But they appear to be a key step in cervical cancer (cancer of the lower part of the uterus), which about 11,000 women in the U.S. get each year. The vaccine's creators suggest that all girls should get the vaccine, but there is great controversy about requiring them to do so.

Another unique vaccine approach is the "personalized vaccine," that is being studied to treat a type of skin cancer called melanoma once it has already developed. The vaccine is made for each patient from his or her own cancer cells, which have been modified in the lab and injected back into the person. For some people this activates the immune cells to destroy

*A colored X ray shows tumors (orange), which are collections of cancerous cells, invading the lung. When tumors have become too large and have spread throughout most of the body, there is usually nothing that the immune system can do to help treat the cancer.*

the cancer cells. These and other fascinating approaches to helping out the immune system are offering hope to people whose immune systems are not doing as well as they could.

## FOOD-BORNE ILLNESSES

Sometimes the immune system fails when it is overwhelmed by quickly spreading bacteria or bacteria that are stronger than immune cells. Often, the body is introduced to these kinds of bacteria through food and beverages. This is commonly called food poisoning.

Harmful bacteria in food can cause severe digestive problems, such as painful cramps, vomiting, and diarrhea. Many thousands of people in the

# FOOD TIPS

You can prevent food poisoning by doing the following:

* Separate raw meats (including seafood and eggs) from other foods in the refrigerator

* Designate a cutting board for raw foods only

* Keep uncooked meat juices off of surfaces, utensils, hands, and cleaning cloths (use disposable ones or paper towels).

* Cook meats to temperatures that will kill bacteria. To be sure, use a meat thermometer that is inserted into the meat.

* Always refrigerate foods that are meant to be cold. When on a picnic or if you are traveling, keep foods cool using an ice pack or a cooler.

* Rinse all fresh fruits and vegetables before eating—even those with skins—before peeling and cooking. This also applies to packaged vegetables that claim to be "prewashed."

* When traveling to some foreign countries or regions—especially to tropical places—be careful about how foods and drinks are prepared and served. Fruits and vegetables should be avoided unless they have thick skins, like bananas or oranges. Avoid ice cubes or other products made from local water. Drink bottled or purified water, canned juice, or hot coffee or tea instead.

* Be careful about the water you drink. Never drink from a pond, puddle, or stream where the water is not moving. When you are camping or staying outdoors, bring your own water. If you must use water you collect from outdoors, boil it or use special water purifying tablets before drinking it.

*Using a meat thermometer can help you determine if you have cooked meat to a safe temperature.*

*Meat that is not properly cooked can still contain harmful food-borne germs that can make you sick.*

United States get food poisoning each year, and several dozens die from it. One particular type of bacteria known as *Escherichia coli,* or *E. coli* for short, has caused most cases of food poisoning in the United States in recent decades. These bacteria live harmlessly in the digestive tracts of cattle, deer, goats, pigs, and sheep, and are abundant in the animals' fecal waste. When the animals are killed for meat, bacteria can get on the meat. Milk that has not been pasteurized to kill germs can also sicken people with *E. coli. Salmonella* is another kind of bacteria—especially from poultry and raw eggs—that causes food poisoning.

Pathogens from human feces can contaminate food, too. For instance, a worker at a restaurant or food-packing plant might use the toilet without washing his or her hands afterward, and then handle the food. The germs on their hands are transferred to your food, and then put into your body.

The germs multiply and you become ill. Even fruits and vegetables, which normally do not harbor bacteria, can be contaminated this way.

To avoid food poisoning, meats and eggs must be well cooked to destroy germs. In addition, in the kitchen, foods that will be eaten raw must be kept away from surfaces and utensils that touch raw meat. Fruits and vegetables should be washed before eating. Careful and frequent hand washing when preparing or eating food is also a good idea. You cannot prevent yourself from coming into contact with all bacteria, but you can limit your amount of exposure.

*These parasitic* Trichinella spiralis *worms—found in raw or undercooked pork—can cause an illness called Trichinosis. Thoroughly cooking pork may prevent Trichinosis infections.*

# SUPER BUGS

Super bugs are not insects. They are bacteria that survive many kinds of bacteria-killing medicines called antibiotics. Antibiotics are specially designed to break apart bacteria or to keep them from multiplying. But bacteria change over time into forms that resist the effects of antibiotics. For instance, certain antibiotics stick to structures inside bacteria, called ribosomes, which make the bacteria's proteins. Ribosomes then cannot work properly, and the bacteria die. Bacteria have become resistant by acquiring slightly different ribosomes to which antibiotics no longer can stick.

This methicillin-resistant Staphylococcus aureus (MRSA) bacterium is immune to most types of antibiotic drugs.

Unfortunately, resistant forms of many disease-causing bacteria are becoming more plentiful, and some are super bugs. These bacteria are resistant to many or all antibiotic drugs. Scientists constantly create new antibiotics to tackle drug-resistant bacteria. Yet bacteria eventually become resistant to these, too. It is now clear that humans have a role to play in this problem. Frequent use of antibiotics actually helps create resistant bacteria. When the bacteria that are susceptible to the antibiotics die off, resistant ones flourish. Doctors realize they must stop giving antibiotics for simple infections that the immune system usually can handle, and must not give them for viral infections, since antibiotics do not harm viruses. Similarly, patients need to understand that antibiotics cannot cure all illnesses. Sometimes the body just needs time to fight off the illness on its own, as in a common cold or certain types of the flu.

Another big contributor to bacterial resistance is the widespread practice of feeding antibiotics to cows, pigs, chickens, and other food animals. These livestock are raised in crowded conditions, so antibiotics are given in order to prevent illness from spreading among them. Many nations have banned this practice, or plan to.

## MRSA

One superbug that has been in the news recently is methicillin-resistant *Staphylococcus aureus*, or MRSA. Staph (*Staphylococcus*) bacteria are common on the skin and membranes of most people. Some staph germs are harmless, while others can cause infections—sometimes deadly ones. Regular staph infections can be treated with some general antibiotics. However, MRSA bacteria are immune to the effects of most antibiotics. A MRSA infection usually appears as skin or tissue infections, and sometimes pneumonia (a serious respiratory infection). Scientists and doctors have found that only extremely strong antibiotics can fight MRSA infections.

MRSA was in the U.S. news because doctors were finding more cases of MRSA in students. There were even a few deaths from severe untreated MRSA infections. Students and other people who spend a lot of time in common areas with a lot of people, such as gyms, classrooms, dormitories, and hospitals get more exposure to the bacteria, which may lead to the infections.

However, there is no reason to panic. Experts have advised gyms, schools, and other institutions that the key to fighting MRSA is cleanliness. Properly disinfecting athletic equipment, desks, and other surfaces can help stop the spread of MRSA. Students and athletes—and other people who come into contact with a lot of people—should wash their hands regularly. Gym lockers should be cleaned out and disinfected often, and people should not keep using the same unwashed sweaty gym clothes they use for practice or workouts. Maintaining overall health will also help. If you eat right, get enough sleep, practice good hygiene, and go to the doctor when you get sick, the chances of getting MRSA are very slim.

# 4

# When the Immune System Does Too Much

It may seem impossible for the immune system to be too active. But sometimes it is. An overactive immune system causes problems that range from annoying to life-threatening. In most cases a foreign substance gets the problem started.

## ALLERGIES

How can something as harmless as a walk outdoors in spring or petting a cat become a miserable experience? For millions of people, things like pollen or animal fur trigger an allergic reaction. Within minutes of

A magnified image shows mast cells. These immune cells play an important part in overactive immune responses. One example of too many mast cells causing problems is an allergic reaction.

exposure to these things, physical symptoms appear, including itchy skin, sneezing, coughing, runny nose, watery eyes, abdominal cramps, or worse. The tendency to have an allergy is inherited. But it is also common for somebody to have an allergic reaction to something that his or her parents are not allergic to.

A substance that causes reactions like these is called an allergen. The most common allergens are dust mites, cockroach droppings, pet dander (a combination of fur and dried saliva that collects indoors), and pollen. Some foods and food additives are allergens for some people. So are chemicals in lotions, perfumes, cleansers, and other common household and personal care items. Even medications trigger allergic reactions in some people.

*Allergic skin rashes are the result of a very strong immune response. Skin rashes often cause itching or burning. Usually, medication can be used to treat the rash and its cause.*

Yet the allergens themselves do no—or very little—harm. Instead, a type of immune cell known as a mast cell is stirring up a lot of fuss. (A mast cell is very similar to a basophil.) Mast cells are present in many of the body's tissues. When they encounter a foreign substance they release histamine. In an allergic person, mast cells are especially reactive, releasing excessive amounts of the chemical. Histamine has many actions. It makes blood vessels leak, allowing fluid to escape into tissues, which contributes to runny nose, watery eyes, congestion, sneezing, and coughing. Histamine from mast cells in the skin causes skin itching, swelling, and redness. Excessive histamine in the digestive tract causes painful cramps.

Those allergy symptoms are troublesome, but histamine also causes tiny muscles around the airways—the tubes that carry air in and out of

*This illustration shows a white blood cell's reaction to allergens. The allergens (green) have attached to the white blood cells' antibodies (yellow, Y-shaped structures). As a result, granules (purple) release a lot of histamine (red spheres) into the bloodstream. Too much histamine can lead to an allergic reaction like swelling or itching in different parts of the body.*

the lungs—to tighten. That narrows the space within the tubes. So mast cells in the airways of allergic people can, through histamine, make breathing difficult, or even impossible. In addition, an allergen that gets into the bloodstream is likely to activate mast cells in many places at once, creating a health crisis called anaphylactic shock. The problem is that so much fluid leaks out of blood vessels at once that blood volume falls and not enough oxygen can travel to vital organs, such as the kidneys or brain.

In these ways, histamine turns something as harmless as enjoying a bouquet of flowers, eating a peanut, being stung by a bee (bee venom contains allergens), or taking a common medication such as penicillin, into a life-threatening situation. An injection of the medication epinephrine, if given right away, can usually remedy the situation. It opens airways and improves blood delivery to vital organs. People who know they have a serious allergy carry epinephrine shots with them at all times.

## ASTHMA

Asthma is an illness in which airways suddenly narrow, making breathing extremely difficult for many minutes, sometimes as long as an hour. These periods are called "asthma attacks." For some people, asthma attacks are an allergic reaction to something they inhaled. For other people, asthma is triggered by cold air, stress, exercise, and other things. Like allergies, mast cells and histamine are thought to be the culprits behind this reaction. Not surprisingly, people who have allergies are more likely to have asthma than people without allergies.

*Medication given through an inhaler can help treat the symptoms of an asthma attack.*

A device called an inhaler helps with asthma attacks. It has a plastic tube to be placed in the mouth and a reservoir of medicine, which is sprayed out and breathed into the airways. The medicine relaxes airway muscles within moments.

Asthma has becoming more common around the world in the last few decades, especially among children. About one of every ten children in the United States—nearly seven million kids—has asthma. One possible explanation for the increase is that people are spending more time indoors where they are exposed to indoor allergens as well as chemicals that irritate the airways, such as tobacco smoke and manmade chemicals that get into the air from furnishings, cleaners, and other products. Kids in particular have been spending more time indoors watching TV, using the computer, and playing video games over the last few decades, just when asthma has been increasing.

## AUTOIMMUNE DISEASES

Autoimmune diseases are ones in which the immune system damages healthy cells (*auto* means "self" in Greek). Antibodies are thought to play a major role in autoimmunity. One way they cause trouble is when many antibodies collect in one place. Rheumatoid arthritis is a disease in which antibodies collect in joint capsules, which are fluid-filled sacs that surround the ends of two bones that meet each other. This causes painful, irreversible joint damage. A type of kidney disease known as glomerulonephritis sometimes can be traced to antibody buildup as well.

Antibodies lead to damage because, besides attaching to pathogens, they also stimulate other immune responses. Those other responses then do the damage. For instance, macrophages engulf pathogens much better if antibodies are attached to the pathogen. So wherever antibodies have settled, macrophages are likely to be attempting to engulf them—and

*The hand on the left is deformed from inflammation caused by rheumatoid arthritis. The hand on the right is healthy and free of arthritis.*

whatever else the antibodies are stuck to. In this way, antibodies can get carried away and damage the body's own cells.

In addition, antibodies interact with a group of proteins called complement proteins. These proteins destroy pathogens, and also attract other immune cells, such as neutrophils, to the area where the antibodies are. Neutrophils release chemicals that damage whatever is nearby, including "self" cells.

For some autoimmune diseases, antibodies appear to attach directly to healthy cells as though they were foreign objects. Rheumatic heart disease is an example. Antibodies latch on to cells inside the heart, marking it as "foreign." Immune cells then mistakenly damage it. Another example is juvenile diabetes, also known as type 1 diabetes, in which the pancreas is attacked. The pancreas is an oblong organ near the stomach, which produces the hormone insulin. Insulin is essential for the proper usage of sugars. But in type 1 diabetes, the immune system has destroyed the insulin-producing cells. After that, injections of insulin are required throughout life.

Medical researchers are not sure why autoimmunity happens to some people and not to others. Viruses, bacteria, medications, food additives, or other manmade chemicals are suspected to play a role. What may happen is that parts of these get attached to cells in such a way that the immune system can no longer tell its own cells from invaders.

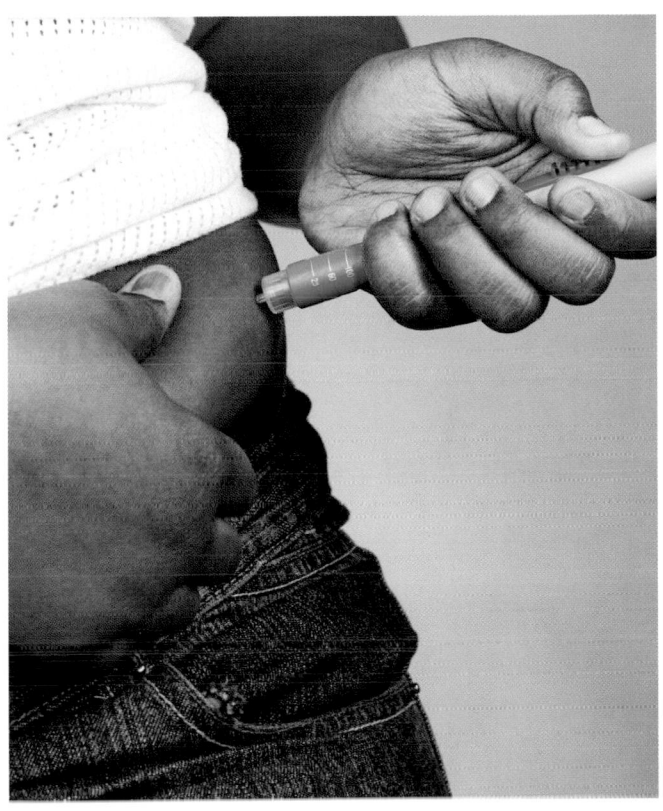

*People with certain types of diabetes need to have insulin shots to control the body's blood sugar balance.*

## TRANSPLANT REJECTION

A person who receives a transplanted organ or other body materials from another person, such as blood or bone marrow, is going to have an immune reaction to it. This is because every person has proteins on their cells that are like cellular fingerprints. Even though human cells are very similar to each other, nobody—except identical twins—will have the exact same collection of proteins. As a result, the immune system will attack any human materials that carry a different set of proteins. The result is rejection, or destruction, of the transplant.

*Different types of medications have been developed to help the body's immune system. Some boost immune cell production, while some may limit it.*

Doctors work hard to prevent transplant rejection. The first step is to carefully compare the proteins on the cells from the patient with those on the cells of donor cells. Then the doctors must decide if the proteins match closely enough. Fortunately, some people's proteins are similar enough to be worth a try. Usually, though, the patient receiving the transplant must take immune-suppressing medications for the rest of his or her life. These medications weaken immune cells and prevent transplant rejection, but they also leave the patient with a poor immune response to pathogens. This also increases their risk of getting serious infections of all kinds.

# WHITE BLOOD CELL COUNT AND LEUKEMIA

In the blood of a healthy person, white blood cells are a small minority compared to red blood cells. In a single drop there are usually about 6,000 granulocytes compared to about five or six *million* red blood cells! In that same drop there are usually about 1,500 agranulocytes.

The number of WBCs in a blood sample changes, though, when a person has some kind of infection. WBCs become more abundant as the immune system surges into action. For a person who feels ill but does not know why, a "high white count," or more WBCs than normal, is a clue for a doctor that an infection is underway somewhere in the body. The types of WBCs that are most numerous can help determine what the infection is.

But for some people, abundant WBCs are a sign of leukemia. Leukemia is an illness in which immune cells become abnormally plentiful even though there is no infection to fight. This happens because stem cells in bone marrow produce more immune cells than necessary. Genetic mutations, toxins, radiation, and viruses are common causes. And though it sounds like a good thing to have lots of immune cells, those produced in leukemia do not function well and soon crowd out normal immune cells. This leaves the person vulnerable to life-threatening illnesses. Medical treatments are increasingly successful at controlling those infections and eliminating or subduing the abnormal immune cells.

*This blood sample taken from a person with leukemia has too many lymphocytes (blue). One negative effect of having too many lymphocytes is that red blood cells and other white blood cells are outnumbered and cannot function properly.*

# 5

# Building a Good Immune System

Nowadays, more people are realizing that having a healthy immune system is a top priority. A healthy immune system means cells and organs get what they need and are ready to deal with pathogens efficiently. Another step is prevention—keeping exposure to pathogens low, even by simply washing your hands a few times a day.

## THE BASICS: NUTRITION, EXERCISE, AND SLEEP

The immune system works best if we make healthy choices. Eating nutritious foods every day provides nutrients to keep up strong skin and

*Washing your hands regularly is one of the most important things you can do to help prevent illness.*

*The right amount of fruits and vegetables in your diet can strengthen your immune system. A well-balanced diet will also help other body systems stay healthy.*

secretions that are the first barriers against invaders. Fresh vegetables and fruits will help keep immune cells well-stocked with essential vitamins and minerals they need to do their jobs. A good balance of food types is important, too. For instance, antibodies are made of protein, and people who eat a lot of carbohydrates (pasta, potatoes, breads, snack foods, sugars, sodas) would help their immune systems by substitute some of those for protein-rich grains, legumes (beans, lentils), nuts, or lean meats.

Exercise is good for the immune system, too. It gets the heart pumping and blood flowing, which helps to circulate white blood cells everywhere.

Immune cells that are already living outside of the bloodstream, in tissues throughout the body, benefit from good blood circulation, too. In addition, lymph fluid moves along lymph vessels much better when muscles nearby are squeezing and relaxing. Good lymph flow gives immune cells in lymph nodes a chance to destroy pathogens.

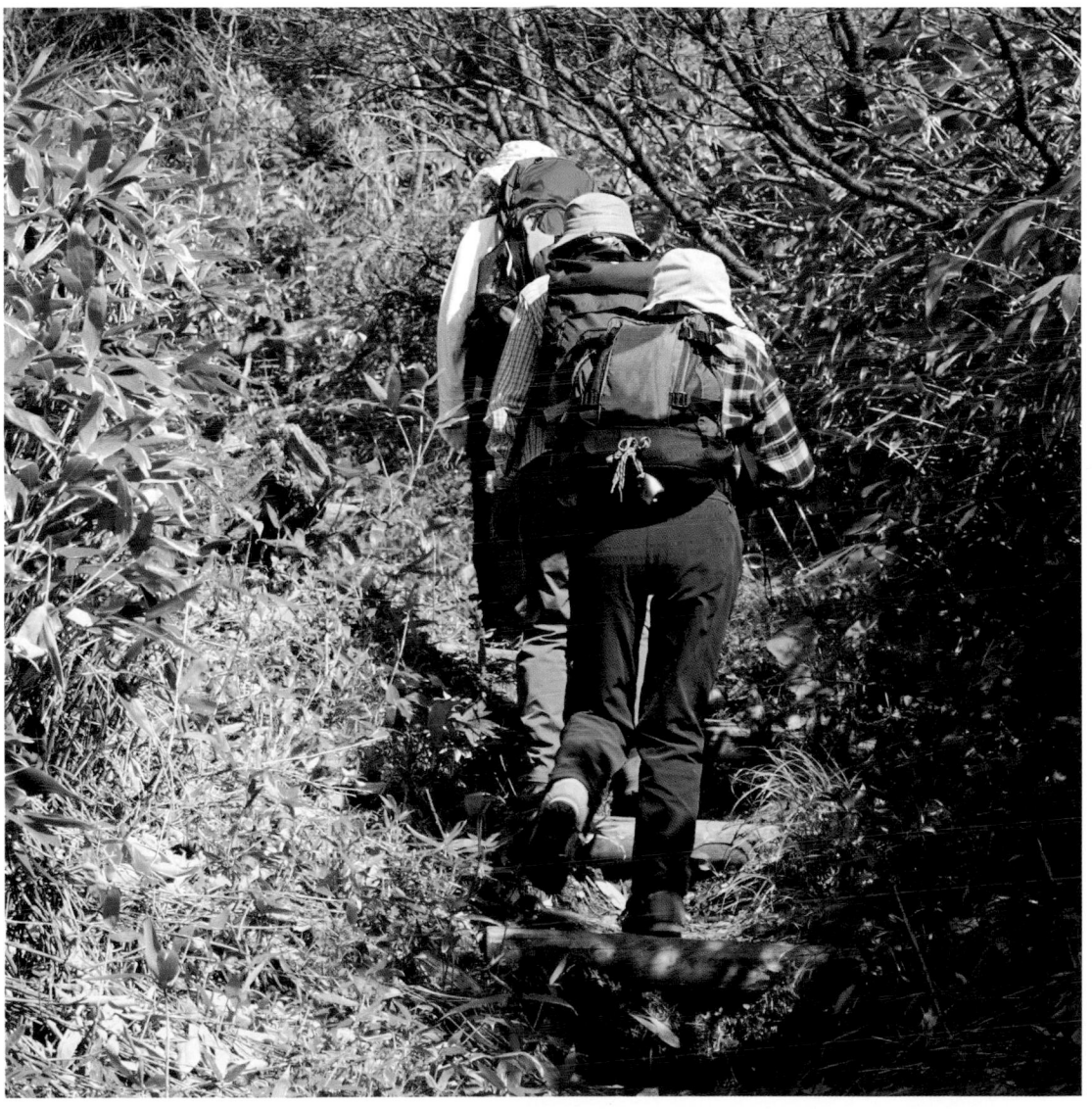

*Regular exercise is essential for good health. Working out at the gym or going for a run are good ways to get your heart pumping. But a brisk walk or a hike are also good forms of exercise.*

Sleep is important, too. A sleeping body can continue clearing pathogens and repairing any damage instead of using energy and nutrients to carry out wakeful activities. If you do not get enough sleep, you are more likely to get sick because your immune system—along with other body systems—are not functioning as well.

*Getting enough sleep is important for your overall health. Quick naps wherever you happen to be when you are tired are not good enough. You should be getting several hours' worth of restful sleep with your body in a comfortable position.*

## KEEPING CLEAN

Your body and everything around you is covered in bacteria—good and bad—and other germs. There is no way to get rid of all the bacteria, and you would not want to. But that does not mean you should not try to stay away from or wash off some of the germs. You can help your immune system by lowering your body's exposure to germs.

*Handwashing must be done properly in order to be effective. Some experts say that you should wash your hands with soap and water for at least twenty seconds or for as long as it takes you to sing the Happy Birthday song.*

### On Your Body

You should wash your hands frequently, and always before eating or preparing food. This prevents you from getting or spreading food-borne illnesses. Whenever you apply makeup, lotion, or touch your face, be sure your hands are clean. The moist tissues in your face, such as around your eyes, nose, and mouth, are easy entry points for germs. If you have been around someone who has a cold, the flu, or another contagious illness, wash your hands well and try not to touch your face until you do. Cold viruses often spread from the hands to the face.

*E. coli* and other germs can come from human fecal matter. That is why you should always wash your hands after using the bathroom or after changing a baby's diaper. Animals, such as livestock or pets, harbor a number of germs that can make you sick. Always wash your hands after touching an animal or its blood, saliva, urine, or feces.

Some people love to walk around barefoot outside. Usually, this is fine, but sometimes you can pick up certain germs or parasites from the

# NATURAL IMMUNE BOOSTERS

The shelves of natural foods stores, grocery stores, and pharmacies are brimming with products claiming to be immune-boosting supplements. Some of these are nutrient boosters that would aid any living cell. Others, though, contain ingredients that have been used for centuries as immunity boosters in countries like China and India.

People in these countries, as well as native people in many parts of the world, have survived for thousands of years without phar-maceuticals (medications made mostly in the laboratory by drug companies). Unfortunately, many have died of illnesses that modern drugs are excellent at treating. But their use of natural foods and other ingredients have also helped them to stay healthy without drugs. Many people in the United States are interested in—and are trying—remedies from these other cultures, in the form of dried plants to make teas, or in concentrated extracts or pills. Not a lot of these natural remedies have been tested for effectiveness in the same strict ways that pharmaceutical medications have. But as their popularity increases, natural remedies are being carefully studied by scientists.

However, natural remedies are not the answer for everyone. Taking too much of anything can be dangerous for the body. And some people with certain health conditions should be careful about what natural supplements they are taking. When in doubt, talk to a doctor, medical professional, or nutritionist when it comes to natural remedies.

*Some experts believe that drinking green tea is a good way to stay healthy.*

ground. These parasites and germs can then enter your body or be spread to other parts of your body. When spending time outdoors—especially if you walked around barefoot—be sure to wash your feet and legs well. If you have any sores, cuts, or blisters on your feet, you are better off wearing shoes outside and slippers around the house. Germs can enter the body through open wounds. This is also true for injuries on other parts of your body. Bandages or other forms of coverings will keep your cuts clean and dry and prevent germs from causing infections.

## Cleaning Your Surroundings

You can use germ-killing soaps where pathogens are known to collect. These include places in the kitchen where raw meat has been prepared or handled and bathrooms, especially around the toilet and sinks. You may be surprised to learn that everyday objects like doorknobs, computer accessories, such as keyboards and mice, and phones are also places where pathogens can collect. Obviously, you cannot—and should not—avoid using those items just because there may be germs. It is a good idea, however, to clean them with germ-killing cleaners every now and then.

If someone in your family has been sick, it is important to clean the items they have used or touched. If they were staying in a bedroom most of the time, open the window to let fresh air in. Throw away all used tissues or napkins, and wash bed linens and clothes with hot water and laundry soap. Keeping your environment clean can make a big difference in staying healthy.

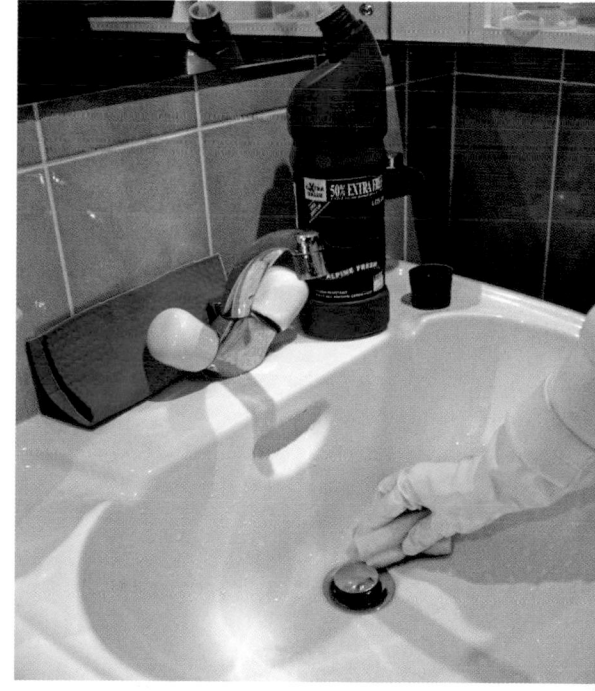

*Sinks, tubs, and other surfaces you touch can collect germs and other harmful material. Regular cleaning with effective detergents can help prevent illness.*

*Some vaccinations are required in order for children to attend school or participate in other activities.*

## VACCINES

Most children in the United States and in some other countries get a series of vaccinations when they are young, to create immunity for several of the most dangerous illnesses. Some adults get immunizations, too, against seasonal illnesses such as the flu, or to pathogens they might encounter through their type of work. Students who are entering college in the United States are now required to have vaccinations to protect them from bacterial meningitis. This is a potentially deadly infection of the brain and spinal cord that is easily passed among people who live close together, as in a college dorm. Some vaccinations must be repeated every few years to boost the immune system's group of memory cells. The tetanus vaccination is an example. Most people should receive a tetanus shot every ten years.

# EDIBLE VACCINES?

A fascinating new approach to making vaccines is getting plant cells to make them. Vaccines usually are prepared in chicken eggs, which serve as germ-free, nutrient-rich incubators. But this takes a long time and the eggs and vaccines can get contaminated. So far, researchers have been able to get plants—spinach, Swiss chard, and petunias so far—to make bits of flu viruses. The plant parts can then be extracted, purified, and made into vaccines.

Taking this one step further, virus-containing potatoes have been developed, which are simply eaten to deliver their vaccine. It will be a while before we can simply chow down on foods instead of getting a shot to boost our immunity. But these novel approaches to strengthening the immune system will undoubtedly offer more appealing and practical way to produce vaccines than using eggs and animals to do the job.

*These scientists from the University of Virginia are experimenting with ways to use plant parts to make vaccines.*

New vaccines are always being tested to protect against the most serious communicable diseases that can easily be spread from person to person. Sometimes a vaccine causes a severe reaction and sickens or even kills the recipient. This is rare, however, and most medical experts agree that it is important to immunize as many people as possible to control those pathogens that can kill or permanently harm millions of people.

## THE BODY-MIND CONNECTION

Can our thoughts influence our health? Ancient civilizations had no doubt this was so, and many cultures outside the United States believe this today. Modern doctors, however, had put that notion aside because antibiotics and other medicines proved so effective on their own. Now there is growing acceptance once again that thoughts and feelings—belonging to the realm of the mind—play a role in illness and health. Several studies of sick patients have shown that mood and attitude can influence how serious the patients' symptoms are, how quickly they recover, and even how long they survive.

Studies of a different kind are suggesting how this can be so. These studies probe the intricate microscopic and chemical relations among cells. There is a network—both chemical and physical—that links brain

Scientists continue to test new procedures and chemical combinations to create vaccines that can help prevent some of the world's most dangerous diseases.

cells to immune cells. Both kinds of cells release chemicals that serve as communication signals to each other and influence one another's activities.

For instance, it is typical for people who are stressed or anxious or depressed to get sick more often. It may be that these problems, which involve chemical changes in the brain, directly inhibit immune cells through the brain-immune cell network. In addition, mental or physical stress increases the release of a hormone, cortisol, from the adrenal gland. Cortisol puts the brakes on immune cell activities, which may also lead to sickness.

*As part of their medical treatment, these cancer patients are meditating through yoga exercises.*

If there is in fact a mind-body connection to immunity, then there are some simple solutions to helping your immune system. Trying to avoid stressful situations, or relieving stress may decrease your chances of getting sick. Using relaxing exercises such as yoga or other forms of meditation may also help relieve the stress and strengthen all parts of your body.

The natural actions of a healthy immune system give us needed protection against germs most of the time. When we do get sick, the immune system ensures our recovery and sets the stage for healing. Sometimes we need an artificial boost to prevent or overcome illnesses that are severe, such as vaccines or medications. Thanks to years of research and experimentation, doctors and immunologists have come up with remarkable strategies to help us keep our immune systems healthy.

# Glossary

**agranulocytes**—White blood cells that have no granules in them.

**antibody**—A protein made by B-cells that attaches to a pathogen or other foreign substance that gets into the body.

**asthma**—A disease in which the airways suddenly narrow, making breathing difficult. Some cases of asthma are caused by the immune system's strong reaction to inhaled substances.

**bacteria**—Single-celled organisms that live virtually everywhere on earth, including on humans and inside them. Some types are human pathogens.

**B-lymphocyte (B-cell)**—An immune cell that makes antibodies.

**cytokine**—One of the many chemicals cells use to communicate with one another.

**cytotoxic T-cell**—An immune cell that destroys infected or cancerous cells of the body.

**germ**—A microorganism that causes infections and illnesses. Certain bacteria, viruses, and parasites are the most common pathogens.

**granulocyte**—A type of white blood cell that has tiny spheres, or granules, in it. Basophils, eosinophils, and neutrophils are the granulocytes found in the bloodstream.

**helper T-cell**—An immune cell that releases several chemicals that improve the abilities of other immune cells to do their jobs.

**histamine**—A chemical released by certain cells, especially mast cells and basophils, which can cause harmful changes in the body if too much is released.

**immune cells**—The collection of WBCs in the bloodstream and in immune organs, plus cells scattered throughout the body, which recognize and remove foreign substances.

**immune system**—The body's team of immune cells and immune organs (spleen, tonsils, thymus, lymph nodes) that work together to destroy foreign substance and keep a person disease free.

**infection**—The presence of harmful bacteria, viruses, parasites, or other microorganisms in the body.

**lymph nodes**—Small, spherical organs throughout the body in which white blood cells live.

**lymphocyte**—A type of white blood cell that does not have granules in it. B-cells and T-cells are the main types of lymphocytes.

**macrophage**—An immune cell that engulfs and destroys pathogens, dead cells, or substances not familiar to the body.

**mast cell**—A type of immune cell found in many areas of the body, and which releases histamine in response to a foreign substance.

**microorganism**—A tiny life form, only visible with the microscope. Bacteria and viruses are examples.

**monocyte**—A cell in the blood that becomes a macrophage when it leaves the blood vessel.

**mutation**—A change in a cell's DNA that makes it abnormal.

**pathogen**—A microorganism that causes infections and illnesses. Certain bacteria, viruses, and parasites are the most common pathogens. Sometimes called germs.

**spleen**—An immune organ near the stomach in which millions of immune cells live.

**stem cells**—Cells that are continually dividing to make more cells that go on to develop into specific cell types. Stem cells in bone marrow provide all the cells that will become white blood cells and red blood cells.

**thymus**—An organ near the heart in which young immune cells mature into T-lymphocytes.

**tissue**—a group of similar cells, such as muscle cells, brain cells, or skin cells.

**T-lymphocyte (T-cell)**—An immune cell that spends some time during its development in the thymus gland.

**tonsil**—One of several small organs at the back of the throat in which immune cells live and help keep pathogens from getting further into the body.

**vaccine**—A preparation of killed, weakened, or fully infectious microbes that is given to provide protection from a particular disease or illness.

**virus**—A microscopic entity that thrives inside the cells of living things; some viruses are human pathogens.

**white blood cells (WBCs)**—Immune cells found in the blood, but which form in bone marrow and can settle outside the bloodstream in lymph nodes, spleen, and elsewhere.

# Find Out More

## Books

Bjorklund, Ruth. *Food-Borne Illnesses*. Tarrytown, NY: Marshall Cavendish Benchmark, 2006.

De la Bédoyère, Guy. *The Discovery of Penicillin*. London: Evans, 2005.

Donnellan, William L. *The Miracle of Immunity*. Tarrytown, NY: Benchmark Books, 2003.

Farrell, Jeanette. *Invisible Allies: Microbes that Shape Our Lives*. New York : Farrar, Straus, and Giroux, 2005.

Goldsmith, Connie. *Invisible Invaders: New and Dangerous Infectious Disease*. Minneapolis. MN: Twenty-First Century Books, 2006.

——. *Superbugs Strike Back: When Antibiotics Fail*. Minneapolis. MN: Twenty-First Century Books, 2007.

Hicks, Terry Allan. *Allergies*. Tarrytown, NY: Marshall Cavendish Benchmark, 2006.

——. *The Common Cold*. Tarrytown, NY: Marshall Cavendish Benchmark, 2006.

Klosterman, Lorrie. *Leukemia*. Tarrytown, NY: Marshall Cavendish Benchmark, 2006.

Snedden, Robert. *Fighting Infectious Diseases*. Portsmouth, NH: Heinemann, 2007.

Walker, Pam and Elaine Wood. *The Immune System*. San Diego, CA: Lucent Books, 2003.

## Web Sites

How Your Immune System Works
http://www.howstuffworks.com/immune-system.htm

The Immune System
http://www.kidshealth.org/teen/your_body/body_basics/immune.html

The Immune System
http://www.niaid.nih.gov/final/immun/immun.htm

Infectious Disease Basics
http://www.mayoclinic.com/health/infectious-disease/ID00024

An Ounce of Prevention Keeps the Germs Away
http://www.cdc.gov/ncidod/op/_resources/OOP%20Brochure%2012.20.05.pdf

Questions & Answers about MRSA
http://www.cdc.gov/Features/MRSAinSchools/

SUPERBUGS: Protecting the Power of Antibiotics
http://www.cdcfoundation.org/healththreats/AntibioticResistance.aspx

Your Immune System
http://kids.jdrf.org/index.cfm?fuseaction=home.viewpage&page_
id=4B312651-5004-D739-A52F211666036011

# Bibliography

Antigenics. "Oncophage Personalized Melanoma Vaccine." Antigenics, Inc. http://www.melanomavaccine.com/oncophage.html

Division of Bacterial and Mycotic Diseases. "*Escherichia coli* O157:H7." CDC. http://www.cdc.gov/ncidod/dbmd/diseaseinfo/escherichiacoli_g.htm

Division of Bacterial and Mycotic Diseases. "Salmonellosis." CDC. http://www.cdc.gov/ncidod/dbmd/diseaseinfo/salmonellosis_g.htm

Division of Diabetes Translation. "Diabetes Fact Sheet." CDC. http://www.cdc.gov/diabetes/pubs/general.htm#what

Early, P. J. "Antibiotic Resistant 'Superbug' on the Rise." Medical College of Wisconsin. http://healthlink.mcw.edu/article/1031002378.html

Marieb, Elaine N., *Human Anatomy and Physiology*. 6th ed. Redwood City, CA: Benjamin Cummings, 2003.

*Science News*. "Edible Vaccine Spawns Antibodies to Virus." *Science News* 158, no. 4 (July 22, 2000): 54. http://www.sciencenews.org/articles/20000722/fob6.asp

Selim, Jocelyn. "Spinach Fights the Flu." DiscoverMagazine.com. http://www.discover.com/issues/feb-05/rd/spinach-fights-the-flu

Springhouse. *Pathophysiology Made Incredibly Easy!* 3rd ed. Philadelphia: Lippincott Williams & Wilkins, 2006.

Sternberg, Esther M., and Philip W. Gold. "The Mind-Body Interaction in Disease." Scientific American, Inc. http://www.sciamdigital.com/index.cfm?fa=Products.ViewIssuePreview&ARTICLEID_CHAR=D5325A53-BACA-4335-88E8-5E5F74B9158

# Index

Page numbers in **boldface** are illustrations and tables.

. . . . . . . . . . . . . . . . . . . . . . . . . . . . . . . . . . . . . . . . .

## About the Author

Lorrie Klosterman is a science writer and educator who earned a Bachelor of Science degree from Oregon State University and a Doctoral Degree from the University of California at Berkeley, both in the field of zoology (the study of animal life, including humans). She has taught courses in human health and disease to college and nursing students for several years, and writes about health for a magazine in New York's Hudson Valley. Lorrie Klosterman has also written several health-related books for young adults. Her greatest joy comes from experiencing and learning about the amazing world of animals and plants, and sharing those experiences with others.

# ProQuest Statistical Abstract of the United States 2020

# ProQuest Statistical Abstract
# of the United States 2020

Issued December 2019

Published by Rowman & Littlefield
A wholly owned subsidiary of The Rowman & Littlefield Publishing Group, Inc.
4501 Forbes Boulevard, Suite 200, Lanham, Maryland 20706
www.rowman.com, 800-462-6420
6 Tinworth Street, London SE11 5AL, United Kingdom

ISBN 13: 978-1-64143-392-1

Suggested Citation:
ProQuest LLC. ProQuest Statistical Abstract of the United States, 2020. (8th ed.) Bethesda, MD 2019

# Preface

The *Statistical Abstract of the United States,* published since 1878, is the best-known statistical reference publication in the country. As a comprehensive collection of statistics on the social, political, and economic conditions of the United States, it is a snapshot of America and its people. In the spring of 2011, the Census Bureau terminated their Statistical Compendia program and production of the *Statistical Abstract.* Since 2012, ProQuest has taken responsibility for curating the data found in this valuable statistical reference tool and publishing it in this print edition and an expanded online edition.

The *ProQuest Statistical Abstract of the United States* is designed to serve as a convenient volume for statistical reference and as a guide to other statistical publications and sources. The latter function is served by the introductory text to each section; source citations appearing below each table; and Appendix I, which is comprised of the *Guide to Sources of Statistics,* including a list of international statistical abstracts, and the *Guide to State Statistical Abstracts.*

**Contents**—This volume includes a selection of data from many statistical sources, both government and private, as indicated in the source citations at the bottom of every table. Data are obtained from a variety of resources including PDF documents, Excel data packages, and complex databases. Publications cited as source reports usually contain additional statistical detail and more comprehensive discussions of definitions and concepts. Data not available in written publications issued by the contributing agency, but obtained from data files available on the internet or unpublished records are also identified in the source notes. More information on the subjects covered in the tables may generally be obtained from the source.

Except as indicated, figures are for the United States as presently constituted. Although emphasis in the *ProQuest Statistical Abstract* is primarily given to national data, many tables present data for regions and individual states and a smaller number for metropolitan areas and cities. "Appendix II, Metropolitan and Micropolitan Statistical Areas: Concepts, Components, and Population," presents explanatory text, a complete current listing, and 2018 population data for metropolitan and micropolitan areas defined as of September 2018. Statistics for the Commonwealth of Puerto Rico and for Island Areas of the United States are included in many state tables and are supplemented by information in Section 29.

Statistics in this edition are generally for the most recent year or period available, as of early September 2019. Each year over 1,400 tables are reviewed and evaluated, new tables of current interest are added, continuing series are updated, and less timely data are condensed or eliminated. Text notes and appendices are revised as appropriate.

**Changes in this edition**—This year ProQuest introduces approximately 40 new tables, presenting data on topics including drug overdose deaths by drug type and user characteristics, physician use of electronic medical records, disability prevalence among adults, education certificates, use of alternative voting methods, TSA checkpoint screenings and firearm discoveries, characteristics of farmers, household energy consumption, use of ride hailing services, cyberbullying, private nonprofit businesses, research and development spending and employment, active shooter incidents, the working poor, and public school counselors, psychologists, and social workers. For a complete list of new tables, see "New Tables," p. xi.

**Online edition**—*ProQuest Statistical Abstract* is also available in an online edition. This dynamic edition features table-specific capabilities for narrowing results by source, data date, subject, and type of data breakdown. Importantly, the online edition is updated with new statistical content on a monthly basis, enabling users to regularly access new and revised data. The online product functions as a repository for additional back year's data that cannot fit into the print publication. Users will find spreadsheets that correspond to each table in the book. In many cases, these spreadsheets present expanded coverage of the data shown in print. It is available as a stand-alone product or as a part of ProQuest's Statistical Premium Collection (see inside back cover for details).

**Limitations of the data**—The contents of this volume were taken from many sources. All data from censuses, surveys, and administrative records are subject to error arising from a number of factors including the following: sampling variability (for statistics based on samples), reporting errors in the data for individual units, incomplete coverage, nonresponse, and imputation and processing errors (see also Appendix III). ProQuest cannot accept responsibility for the accuracy or limitations of the data presented here; however, selection of the material and its proper presentation is the responsibility of ProQuest.

**For additional information on data presented**—Please consult the source publications available in local libraries and on the internet, or contact the agency or organization indicated in the source notes.

# Contents

[Numbers following subject are page numbers]

# New and Deleted Tables for the 2020 Edition

## New Tables for 2020

# Tables Deleted Since the 2019 Edition of the Statistical Abstract

[Tables are deleted for several reasons, including: source data has been discontinued, source data was monographic and new data is not expected to be available, data is believed to no longer be reliable, and data was previously unpublished and cannot be replicated. Some tables have been replaced with tables illustrating similar content. Where applicable, please see reference to new table number]

| 2019 Table | Section and Table Title | Replaced by... |
|---|---|---|
| | **Section 2: Births, Deaths, Marriages, and Divorces** | |
| Table 82........ | Live Births, Birth Rates, and Fertility Rates by Hispanic Origin: 2010 to 2016 | |
| Table 130...... | Death Rates From Human Immunodeficiency Virus (HIV/AIDS) Disease by Sex, Age, and Race/Ethnicity: 1990 to 2016 | |
| | **Section 3: Health and Nutrition** | |
| Table 156...... | Medicaid and Children's Health Insurance Program (CHIP)—Summary by State: 2010 to 2013 | Table 158 |
| Table 189...... | Hospital Emergency Department Visits by Sex and Diagnosis: 2015 | Table 192 |
| Table 208...... | Injury and Poisoning Episodes by Age and Sex: 2014 | Table 213 |
| Table 242...... | Nutrition—Nutrients in Foods Available for Civilian Consumption Per Capita Per Day: 1970 to 2010 | |
| Table 243...... | Nutrients Available for Consumption from Major Food Groups Per Capita Per Day: 2010 | |
| | **Section 4: Education** | |
| Table 274...... | Private School Teachers, Base Salary, and Additional Income by Selected Characteristics: 2012 | |
| Table 275...... | Education and Certification Qualifications of Public High School Teachers: 2012 | Table 277 |
| Table 276...... | Teacher Stayers, Movers, and Leavers by Selected Characteristics: 2013 | |
| Table 277...... | Public School Employment by Occupation, Sex, and Race: 2010 and 2012 | |
| Table 280...... | Average Salary and Wages Paid in Public School Systems: 1985 to 2011 | |
| Table 289...... | General Educational Development (GED) Credentials Issued: 1980 to 2013 | |
| Table 322...... | Associate's Degrees and Certificates Below the Associate's Degree Level by Field and Sex: 2015 | Tables 322, 323 |
| | **Section 8: State and Local Government Finances and Employment** | |
| Table 495...... | City Government Employment and Payroll—Largest Cities: 2000 to 2015 | |
| Table 496...... | County Government Employment and Payroll—Largest Counties: 2010 to 2015 | |
| | **Section 9: Federal Government Finances and Employment** | |
| Table 520...... | Federal Civilian Employment and Annual Payroll by Branch: 1970 to 2014 | |
| Table 523...... | Federal Civilian Employment by Branch and Agency: 1990 to 2014 | |
| | **Section 10: National Security and Veterans Affairs** | |
| Table 535...... | U.S. Active Duty Military Deaths by Manner of Death: 1980 to 2012 | Table 538 |
| Table 548...... | Homeland Security Funding by Agency: Fiscal Years 2010 to 2016 | |
| Table 556...... | Coast Guard Migrant Interdictions by Nationality of Alien: 1990 to 2015 | |
| | **Section 11: Social Insurance and Human Services** | |
| Table 596...... | Support Provided on Behalf of Children Under Age 21 Living in Another Household by Gender of Provider: 2010 | |
| | **Section 15: Business Enterprise** | |
| Table 778...... | Corporations by Receipt-Size Class and Industry: 2013 | |
| Table 779...... | Corporations by Asset-Size Class and Industry: 2013 | |
| Table 791...... | Number of Active Establishments by Firm Age and Size: 2014 | Table 794 |
| | **Section 18: Forestry, Fishing, and Mining** | |
| Table 941...... | Federal Offshore Leasing, Exploration, Production, and Revenue: 1990 to 2016 | |
| | **Section 23: Transportation** | |
| Table 1090..... | Passenger Airline Cost Indexes: 1980 to 2014 | |
| Table 1093..... | Top 25 Domestic Airline Markets—Average Daily Passengers: 2014 | |
| Table 1140..... | Transit Ridership in Selected Urbanized Areas: 2013 | |
| | **Section 24: Information and Communication** | |
| Table 1174..... | Cellular Telephone Activities and Applications Among Adults by Cell Phone User Characteristics: 2015 | |
| Table 1187..... | Public Library Technology Services and Resources Available for Patrons: 2014 | |
| | **Section 27: Accommodation, Food Services, and Other Services** | |
| Table 1300..... | Lodging Industry Summary: 1990 to 2014 | |
| Table 1302..... | Commercial and Noncommercial Restaurant Groups—Food and Drink Sales: 2013 to 2017 | |
| | **Section 29: Puerto Rico and the Island Areas** | |
| Table 1341..... | Prisoners in Custody of Correctional Authorities in U.S. Territories and Commonwealths: 2005 to 2016 | |
| | **Section 30: International Statistics** | |
| Table 1410..... | Foreign Exchange Rates by Country and Currency: 2017 | |

# Guide to Tabular Presentation

## Example of Table Structure

### Table 1294. Top 20 U.S. Gateway Airports for Nonstop International Air Travel Passengers: 2018

[238,605 represents 238,605,000. International passengers are residents of any country traveling nonstop to and from the United States on U.S. and foreign carriers. The data cover all passengers arriving and departing from U.S. airports on nonstop commercial international flights with 60 seats or more]

| Gateway airport | Airport code | Passengers, (1,000) | Gateway airport | Airport code | Passengers, (1,000) |
|---|---|---|---|---|---|
| **Total, all airports**......................... | **(X)** | **238,605** | Fort Lauderdale, FL....................... | FLL | 8,455 |
| Total, top 20 airports........................ | (X) | 210,648 | Dallas-Ft. Worth, TX.................... | DFW | 8,390 |
| Top 20, percentage of total.............. | (X) | 88.3 | Washington (Dulles), DC............... | IAD | 7,865 |
| | | | Boston, MA................................. | BOS | 7,243 |
| New York (JFK), NY........................ | JFK | 33,302 | Orlando, FL................................. | MCO | 6,401 |
| Los Angeles, CA............................ | LAX | 25,824 | Honolulu, HI................................ | HNL | 5,332 |
| Miami, FL..................................... | MIA | 21,078 | Seattle-Tacoma, WA..................... | SEA | 5,275 |
| San Francisco, CA.......................... | SFO | 13,965 | Philadelphia, PA.......................... | PHL | 3,861 |
| Newark, NJ................................... | EWR | 13,792 | Detroit, MI.................................. | DTW | 3,751 |
| Chicago (O'Hare), IL....................... | ORD | 13,600 | Las Vegas, NV............................. | LAS | 3,618 |
| Atlanta, GA.................................. | ATL | 12,318 | Charlotte, NC.............................. | CLT | 3,125 |
| Houston (G. Bush), TX.................... | IAH | 10,485 | Minneapolis-St. Paul, MN.............. | MSP | 2,968 |

X Not applicable.

Source: U.S. Department of Transportation, Research and Innovative Technology Administration, Bureau of Transportation Statistics, Office of Airline Information, "T-100 International Segment data," <http://www.transtats.bts.gov/Fields.asp?Table_ID=261>, accessed June 2019.

*Headnotes* immediately below table titles provide information important for correct interpretation or evaluation of the table as a whole or for a major segment of it.

*Footnotes* below the bottom rule of tables give information relating to specific items or figures within the table.

*Unit indicators* show the *specified quantities* in which data items are presented. They are used for two primary reasons. Sometimes data are not available in absolute form and are estimates (as in the case of many surveys). In other cases we round the numbers in order to save space to show more data, as in the case above.

When a table presents data with more than one unit indicator, they are found in the headnotes and column headings (Tables 4 and 28), spanner (Table 37), stub (Table 27), or unit column (Table 250). When the data in a table are shown in the same unit indicator, it is shown as the first part of the headnote (Table 2). If no unit indicator is shown, data presented are in absolute form (Table 1).

*Vertical rules* are used to separate independent sections of a table (Table 1), or in tables where the stub is continued into one or more additional columns (Table 2).

**Averages**—An average is a single number or value that is often used to represent the "typical value" of a group of numbers. It is regarded as a measure of "location" or "central tendency" of a group of numbers.

The *arithmetic mean* is the type of average used most frequently. It is derived by summing the individual item values of a particular group and dividing the total by the number of items. The arithmetic mean is often referred to as simply the "mean" or "average."

The *median* of a group of numbers is the middle number or value when each item in the group is arranged according to size (lowest to highest or vice versa); it generally has the same number of items above it as well as below it. If there is an even number of items in the group, the median is taken to be the average of the two middle numbers.

*Per capita* (or per person) quantities—a per capita figure represents an average computed for every person in a specified group (or population). It is derived by taking the total for an item (such as income, taxes, or retail sales) and dividing it by the number of persons in the specified population.

**Index numbers**—An index number is the measure of difference or change, usually expressed as a percent, relating one quantity (the variable) of a specified kind to another quantity of the same kind. Index numbers are widely used to express changes in prices over periods of time, but may also be used to express differences between related subjects for a single point in time.

To compute a price index, a base year or period is selected. The base year price (of the commodity or service) is then designated as the base or reference price to which the prices for other years or periods are related. Many price indexes use the year 1982 as the base year; in tables this is shown as "1982 = 100." A method expressing the price relationship is: The price of a set of one or more items for a related year (e.g. 1990) **divided by** the price of the same set of items for the base year (e.g. 1982). The result multiplied by 100 provides the index number. When 100 is subtracted from the index number, the result equals the percent change in price from the base year.

**Average annual percent change**—Unless otherwise stated in the *Abstract* (as in Section 1, Population), average annual percent change is computed by use of a *compound interest formula*. This formula assumes that the rate of change is constant throughout a specified compounding period (1 year for average annual rates of change). The formula is similar to that used to compute the balance of a savings account that receives compound interest. According to this formula, at the end of a compounding period the amount of accrued change (e.g., school enrollment or bank interest) is added to the amount that existed at the beginning of the period. As a result, over time (e.g., with each year or quarter), the same rate of change is applied to a larger and larger figure.

The *exponential formula,* which is based on continuous compounding, is often used to measure population change. It is preferred by population experts, because they view population and population-related subjects as changing without interruption, ever ongoing. Both exponential and compound interest formulas assume a constant rate of change. The former, however, applies the amount of change continuously to the base rather than at the end of each compounding period. When the average annual rates are small (e.g., less than 5 percent), both formulas give virtually the same results. For an explanation of these two formulas as they relate to population, see U.S. Census Bureau, *The Methods and Materials of Demography,* Vol. 2, 3d printing (rev.), 1975.

**Current and constant dollars**—Statistics in some tables in a number of sections are expressed in both current and constant dollars (see, e.g., Table 696 in Section 13, Income, Expenditures, Poverty, and Wealth). Current dollar figures reflect actual prices or costs prevailing during the specified year(s). Constant dollar figures are estimates representing an effort to remove the effects of price changes from statistical series reported in dollar terms. In general, constant dollar series are derived by dividing current dollar estimates by the appropriate price index for the appropriate period (e.g., the Consumer Price Index). The result is a series as it would presumably exist if prices were the same throughout, as in the base year—in other words, as if the dollar had constant purchasing power. Any changes in this constant dollar series would reflect only changes in real volume of output, income, expenditures, or other measure.

## Explanation of Symbols

The following symbols, used in the tables throughout this book, are explained in condensed form in footnotes to the tables where they appear:

— Represents zero or rounds to less than half the unit of measurement shown.

B Base figure too small to meet statistical standards for reliability of a derived figure.

D Figure withheld to avoid disclosure pertaining to a specific organization or individual.

NA Data not enumerated, tabulated, or otherwise available separately.

P Data are preliminary or projected.

S Figure does not meet publication standards for reasons other than that covered by symbol B, above.

X Figure not applicable because column heading and stub line make entry impossible, absurd, or meaningless.

Z Entry would amount to less than half the unit of measurement shown.

In many tables, details will not add to the totals shown because of rounding.

# Section 1
# Population

This section presents statistics on the growth, distribution, and characteristics of the U.S. population. The principal source of these data is the U.S. Census Bureau, which conducts a decennial census of population, a monthly population survey, a program of population estimates and projections, and a number of other periodic surveys.

**Decennial censuses**—The U.S. Constitution provides for a census of the population every 10 years, primarily to establish a basis for apportionment of members of the House of Representatives among the states. For over a century after the first census in 1790, the census organization was a temporary one, created only for each decennial census. In 1902, the Census Bureau was established as a permanent federal agency, responsible for enumerating the population and also for compiling statistics on other population and housing characteristics.

Historically, the enumeration of the population has been a complete (100 percent) count. That is, an attempt is made to account for every person, for each person's residence, and for other characteristics (sex, age, family relationships, etc.). In the twentieth century, the questions were divided between a "short" and "long" form. Only a subset of the population was required to answer the long-form questions. The most recent census consisted only of a short form, which included basic questions about age, sex, race, Hispanic origin, household relationship, and owner/renter status. After the 2000 Census, the long form became the American Community Survey (ACS) and continues to collect long-form-type information. The ACS includes not only the basic short-form questions, but also detailed questions about population and housing characteristics. It is a nationwide, continuous sample survey designed to provide communities with reliable and timely demographic, housing, social, and economic data every year. Since its start, the ACS has been providing a continuous stream of updated information for states and local areas. Sample data may be used with confidence where large numbers are involved and assumed to indicate trends and relationships where small numbers are involved.

**Current Population Survey (CPS)**—The CPS sample is a probability sample designed primarily to produce national and state estimates of labor force characteristics of the civilian non-institutional population 16 years of age and older. The sample consists of independent samples in each state and the District of Columbia, and each state sample is specifically tailored to the demographic and labor market conditions that prevail in that particular state. About 60,000 housing units are required in order to meet the national and State reliability criteria, drawn from 824 sample areas.

The CPS also serves as a vehicle for inquiries on other subjects. Using CPS data, the Census Bureau issues a series of publications under the general title of *Current Population Reports*.

Estimates of population characteristics based on the CPS will not agree with the counts from the census because the CPS and the census use different procedures for collecting and processing the data for racial groups, the Hispanic population, and other topics. Caution should also be used when comparing estimates for various years because of the periodic introduction of changes into the CPS. Beginning in January 1994, a number of changes were introduced into the CPS that affect all data comparisons with prior years. These changes included the results of a major redesign of the survey questionnaire and collection methodology and the introduction of 1990 census population controls, adjusted for the estimated undercount. Beginning with the 2001 CPS Annual Demographic Supplement, the independent estimates used as control totals for the CPS are based on civilian population benchmarks consistent with Census 2000. In 2003 the name of the March supplement was changed to Annual Social and Economic Supplement (ASEC). Beginning with the 2012 March CPS supplement, the estimates are based on Census 2010 population controls. These changes in population controls had relatively little impact on derived measures such as means, medians, and percent distribution, but did have a significant impact on levels.

In 2002, the ASEC incorporated a significant sample expansion. The sample was expanded primarily to improve state estimates of children's health insurance coverage (CHIP). This sample increase of 19,000 households added to the regular sample of 72,500 households and the Hispanic sample of 6,500 gives a total sample size of about 98,000 households. The 2014 CPS ASEC included redesigned questions for income and health insurance coverage. All of the approximately 98,000 addresses were selected to receive the improved set of health insurance coverage items. The improved income questions were implemented using a split panel design. Approximately 68,000 addresses were selected to receive a set of income questions similar to those used in the 2013 CPS ASEC. The remaining 30,000 addresses were selected to receive the redesigned income questions.

**Population estimates and projections**—Each year, the United States Census Bureau produces and publishes estimates of the population for the nation, states, counties, state/county equivalents, and Puerto Rico. With each annual release of population estimates, the Population Estimates Program revises and updates the entire time series of estimates from April 1, 2010 to July 1 of the current year, which is referred to as the vintage year. "Vintage" denotes an entire time series created with a consistent population starting point and methodology. The release of a new vintage of estimates supersedes any previous series and incorporates the most up-to-date input data and methodological improvements.

Estimates of the United States population are derived by updating the resident population enumerated in Census 2010 with information on the components of population change: births, deaths, and net international migration. The population estimates base reflects changes to the decennial census population due to the Count Question Resolution program, geographic program revisions, and modifications to the 2010 Census race categories for consistency with the race categories in input data.

Registered births and deaths are estimated from data supplied by the National Center for Health Statistics and the Federal-State Cooperative for Population Estimates (FSCPE). The net international migration component consists of four parts: (1) the net international migration of the foreign born, (2) the net migration of natives to and from the United States, (3) the net migration between the United States and Puerto Rico, and (4) the net overseas movement of the Armed Forces population. Data from the ACS are used to estimate the annual net migration of the foreign-born population. The estimated net migration of the native-born population is produced using the foreign-census method which utilized data from over 80 countries. This work compares estimates of the United States born or United States citizen population living overseas measured by population registers and censuses in other countries at two consecutive time periods. The residual was used to develop estimates of net native migration. Estimates for net migration between Puerto Rico and the U.S. are derived from the ACS and the Puerto Rico Community Survey. Estimates of the net overseas movement of the Armed Forces are derived from data collected by the Defense Manpower Data Center.

Estimates for state and county areas are based on the same components of change data and sources as the national estimates with the addition of net internal migration. Estimates of net internal migration are derived from federal income tax returns from the Internal Revenue Service; group quarters data from the branches of the military, the Department of Veterans Affairs, and the FSCPE; and Medicare data from the Centers for Medicare and Medicaid Services.

Population estimates and projections are available on the Census Bureau Web site, see <http://www.census.gov>. These estimates and projections are consistent with official decennial census figures with no adjustment for estimated net census coverage. For details on methodology, see "Methodology for the United States Population Estimates: Vintage 2018," <https://www.census.gov/programs-surveys/popest/technical-documentation/methodology.html>.

**Immigration**—Immigration (migration to a country) is one component of international migration; the other component is emigration (migration *from* a country). In its simplest form, international migration is defined as any movement across a national border. In the United States, federal statistics on international migration are produced primarily by the U.S. Census Bureau and the Office of Immigration Statistics of the U.S. Department of Homeland Security (DHS).

The Census Bureau collects data used to estimate international migration through its decennial censuses and numerous surveys of the U.S. population.

The Office of Immigration Statistics publishes immigration data in annual flow reports and the *Yearbook of Immigration Statistics*. Data for these publications are collected from several administrative data sources including the DS-230 *Application for Immigrant Visa and Alien Registration*, the DS-260 *Electronic Application for Immigrant Visa and Alien Registration* of the U.S. Department of State (used by applicants living abroad), and the I-485 *Application to Register Permanent Residence or Adjust Status* of U.S. Citizenship and Immigration Services (USCIS) for applicants living in the United States.

An immigrant, or lawful permanent resident (LPR), is a foreign national who has been granted lawful permanent residence in the United States. New arrivals are foreign nationals living abroad who apply for an immigrant visa at a consular office of the Department of State, while individuals adjusting status are already living in the United States and file an application for adjustment of status to lawful permanent residence with USCIS. Individuals adjusting status include refugees, asylees, and various classes of nonimmigrants. A refugee is a person outside his or her country of nationality who is unable or unwilling to return to his or her country of nationality because of persecution or a well-founded fear of persecution. An asylee is a person who meets the definition of refugee and is already present in the United States or is seeking admission at a port of entry. Refugees are required to apply for LPR ("green card") status one year after being admitted, and asylees may apply for green card status one year after their grant of asylum.

Nonimmigrants are foreign nationals granted temporary entry into the United States. The major activities for which nonimmigrant admission is authorized include temporary visits for business or pleasure, academic or vocational study, temporary employment, and to act as a representative of a foreign government or international organization. DHS collects information on the characteristics of a proportion of nonimmigrant admissions, those recorded on the I-94/I-94W arrival and departure records.

U.S. immigration law gives preferential immigration status to persons with a close family relationship with a U.S. citizen or legal permanent resident, persons with needed job skills, persons who qualify as refugees or asylees, and persons who are from countries with relatively low levels of immigration to the United States (diversity immigrants). Immigration to the United States can be divided into two general categories: (1) classes of admission subject to the annual worldwide limitation and (2) classes of admission exempt from worldwide limitations. Numerical limits are imposed on visas issued and not on admissions. In 2017, the annual limit for family-sponsored preferences was 226,000 and the limit for employment-based preferences was 140,000 plus any unused visas in the family-sponsored preference classes from the previous year, of which there were zero from 2016.

The Diversity Visa Program is available to nationals of countries with fewer than 50,000 persons granted LPR status during the preceding five years in the employment-based and family-sponsored preferences and immediate relative classes of admission. The annual diversity visa limit has been 50,000 since 1999.

The number of persons who may be admitted to the United States as refugees each year is established by the President in consultation with Congress. The ceiling was originally set at 110,000 for 2017, but reset to 50,000 through a pair of Executive Orders. There is no numerical limit on the number of persons who can be granted asylum status in a year.

Classes of admission exempt from the worldwide limitation include immediate relatives of U.S. citizens, refugees and asylees adjusting to permanent residence, and other various classes of special immigrants.

**Metropolitan and micropolitan areas**—Metropolitan and micropolitan statistical areas (metro and micro areas) are geographic entities delineated by the U.S. Office of Management and Budget (OMB) for use by Federal statistical agencies in collecting, tabulating, and publishing Federal statistics. These areas are the result of the application of published standards to Census Bureau data. Generally, the areas are delineated using the most recent set of standards following each decennial census. Between censuses, the delineations are updated annually to reflect the most recent Census Bureau population estimates. Areas based on the 2010 standards and Census Bureau data were last delineated in September 2018.

The term "Core Based Statistical Area" (CBSA) is a collective term for both metro and micro areas. A metro area contains a core urban area of 50,000 or more population, and a micro area contains an urban core of at least 10,000 (but less than 50,000) population. Each metro or micro area consists of one or more counties and includes the counties containing the core urban area, as well as any adjacent counties that have a high degree of social and economic integration (as measured by commuting to work) with the urban core.

**Urban and rural**—The Census Bureau's urban-rural classification is fundamentally a delineation of geographical areas, identifying both individual urban areas and the rural areas of the nation. The Census Bureau's urban areas represent densely developed territory, and encompass residential, commercial, and other non-residential urban land uses.

For the 2010 Census, an urban area comprises a densely settled core of census tracts and/or census blocks that meet minimum population density requirements, along with adjacent territory containing non-residential urban land uses as well as territory with low population density included to link outlying densely settled territory with the densely settled core. To qualify as an urban area, the territory identified according to criteria must encompass at least 2,500 people, at least 1,500 of which reside outside institutional group quarters. The Census Bureau identifies two types of urban areas: Urbanized Areas of 50,000 or more people; and Urban Clusters of at least 2,500 and less than 50,000 people. "Rural" encompasses all population, housing, and territory not included within an urban area. For Census 2010, many more geographic entities, including metropolitan areas, counties, and places, contain both urban and rural territory, population, and housing units.

**Residence**—In determining residence, the Census Bureau counts each person as an inhabitant of a usual place of residence (i.e., the place where one lives and sleeps most of the time). While this place is not necessarily a person's legal residence or voting residence, the use of these different bases of classification would produce the same results in the vast majority of cases.

**Race**—Census 2000 and 2010 adhere to the federal standards for collecting and presenting data on race and ethnicity as established by the OMB in October 1997. Starting with Census 2000, the OMB requires federal agencies to use a minimum of five race categories: White, Black or African American, American Indian or Alaska Native, Asian, and Native Hawaiian or Other Pacific Islander. Additionally, to collect data on individuals of mixed race parentage, respondents were allowed to select one or more races. For

respondents who did not identify with any of these five race categories, the OMB approved and included a sixth category—"Some other race" on the Census 2000 and 2010 questionnaire. The Census 2000 and 2010 question on race included 15 separate response categories and three areas where respondents could write in a more specific race group. The response categories and write-in answers can be combined to create the five minimum OMB race categories plus "Some other race." People who responded to the question on race by indicating only one race are referred to as the *race alone* population, or the group that reported only one race category. Six categories make up this population: White alone, Black or African American alone, American Indian and Alaska Native alone, Asian alone, Native Hawaiian and Other Pacific Islander alone, and Some other race alone. Individuals who chose more than one of the six race categories are referred to as the *Two or More Races* population, or as the group that reported more than one race. Additionally, respondents who reported one race together with those who reported the same race plus one or more other races are combined to create the race alone or in *combination* categories. For example, the *White alone or in combination group* consists of those respondents who reported only White or who reported White combined with one or more other race groups, such as "White and Black or African American," or "White and Asian and American Indian and Alaska Native." Another way to think of the group who reported White alone or in combination is as the total number of people who identified entirely or partially as White. This group is also described as people who reported White, whether or not they reported any other race.

The *alone or in combination* categories are tallies of *responses* rather than *respondents*. That is, the alone or in combination categories are not mutually exclusive. Individuals who reported two races were counted in two separate and distinct alone or in combination race categories, while those who reported three races were counted in three categories, and so on. Consequently, the sum of all alone or in combination categories equals the number of races reported, which exceeds the total population.

The racial categories included in the census questionnaire generally reflect a social definition of race recognized in this country and not an attempt to define race biologically, anthropologically, or genetically. It is also recognized that the categories of the race item include racial and national origin or sociocultural groups. For example, data are available for the American Indian and Alaska Native tribes. A detailed explanation of race can be found at <https://www.census.gov/prod/cen2010/doc/sf1.pdf>.

Data for the population by race for April 1, 2000 and 2010, (shown in Tables 7, 9, and 10) are modified counts and are not comparable to Census 2000 and 2010 race categories. These numbers were computed using Census 2000 and 2010 data by race and had been modified to be consistent with the 1997 OMB's "Revisions to the Standards for the Classification of Federal Data on Race and Ethnicity," (Federal Register Notice, Vol. 62, No 210, October 1997). A detailed explanation of the race modification procedure appears at <https://www.census.gov/programs-surveys/popest/technical-documentation/research/modified-race-data.html>.

In the CPS and other household sample surveys conducted through personal interview, respondents are asked to classify their race as: (1) White; (2) Black or African American; (3) American Indian or Alaska Native; (4) Asian; or (5) Native Hawaiian or Other Pacific Islander. Beginning January 2003, respondents were allowed to report more than one race to indicate their mixed racial heritage.

**Hispanic population**—People who identify with the terms "Hispanic" or "Latino" are those who classify themselves in one of the specific Hispanic or Latino categories listed on the decennial census questionnaire and various Census Bureau survey questionnaires – "Mexican, Mexican American, Chicano" or "Puerto Rican" or "Cuban" – as well as those who indicate that they are "another Hispanic, Latino, or Spanish origin." Origin can be viewed as the heritage, nationality group, lineage, or country of birth of the person or the person's ancestors before their arrival in the United States.

Traditional and current data collection and classification treat race and Hispanic origin as two separate and distinct concepts in accordance with guidelines from the OMB. People who are Hispanic may be of any race and people in each race group may be either Hispanic or Not Hispanic. Also, each person has two attributes, their race (or races) and whether or not they are Hispanic. The overlap of race and Hispanic origin is the main comparability issue. For example, Black Hispanics (Hispanic Blacks) are included in both the number of Blacks and in the number of Hispanics. For further information, see <http://www.census.gov/population/www/socdemo/compraceho.html>.

**Foreign-born and native populations**—The Census Bureau separates the U.S. resident population into two groups based on whether or not a person was a U.S. citizen or U.S. national at the time of birth. Anyone born in the United States, Puerto Rico, or a U.S. Island Area (such as Guam), or born abroad to a U.S. citizen parent is a U.S. citizen at the time of birth and consequently included in the *native population*. The term *foreign-born population* refers to anyone who is not a U.S. citizen or a U.S. national at birth. This includes naturalized U.S. citizens, legal permanent resident aliens (immigrants), temporary migrants (such as foreign students), humanitarian migrants (such as refugees), and people illegally present in the United States. The Census Bureau provides a variety of demographic, social, economic, geographic, and housing information on the foreign-born population in the United States at <https://www.census.gov/topics/population/foreign-born.html>.

**Mobility status**—The U.S. population is classified according to mobility status on the basis of a comparison between the place of residence of each individual at the time of the survey or census and the place of residence at a specified earlier date. Nonmovers are all persons who were living in the same house or apartment at the end of the period as at the beginning of the period. Movers are all persons who were living in a different house or apartment at the end of the period than at the beginning of the period. Movers are further classified as to whether they were living in the same or different county, state, or region, or were movers from abroad. Movers from abroad include all persons whose place of residence was outside the United States (including Puerto Rico, other U.S. Island Area, or a foreign country) at the beginning of the period.

**Living arrangements**—Living arrangements refer to residency in households or in group quarters. A "household" comprises all persons who occupy a "housing unit," that is, a house, an apartment or other group of rooms, or a single room that constitutes "separate living quarters." A household includes the related family members and all the unrelated persons, if any, such as lodgers, foster children, or employees who share the housing unit. A person living alone or a group of unrelated persons sharing the same housing unit is also counted as a household. See text, Section 20, Construction and Housing, for definition of housing unit.

All persons not living in housing units are classified as living in group quarters. These individuals may be institutionalized, e.g., under care or custody in juvenile facilities, jails, correctional centers, hospitals, or nursing homes; or they may be residents in noninstitutional group quarters such as college dormitories, group homes, or military barracks.

**Householder**—The householder is the person, or one of the people, in whose name the home is owned, being bought, or rented. If a home is owned or rented jointly by a married couple, either spouse may be listed first. Two types of householders are distinguished: a family householder and a nonfamily householder. A family householder is a householder living with one or more people related to him or her by birth, marriage, or adoption. The householder and all people in the household related to him or her are family members. A family household may contain people not related to the householder, but those people are not included as part of the householder's family in census tabulations. Thus, the number of family households is equal to the number of families, but family households may include more members than do families.

**Nonfamily**—A nonfamily householder is a householder living alone or with nonrelatives only.

**Subfamily**—A subfamily is a married couple with or without children, or a single parent with one or more own never-married children under 18 years old, who does not maintain their own household, but lives in the home of someone else (the householder). Subfamilies are divided into "related" and "unrelated" subfamilies. A related subfamily is related to, but does not include, the householder or the spouse of the householder. Members of a related subfamily are also members of the family with whom they live. The number of related subfamilies, therefore, is not included in the count of families. An unrelated subfamily may include persons such as guests, lodgers, or resident employees and their spouses and/or children; none of whom is related to the householder. The number of unrelated subfamily members is included in the total number of household members, but is not included in the count of family members.

**Married couple**—A married couple is defined as a husband and wife living together in the same household, with or without children and other relatives.

**Statistical reliability**—For a discussion of statistical collection and estimation, sampling procedures, and measures of statistical reliability applicable to Census Bureau data, see Appendix III.

Figure 1.1
**Percent Change in Population for States: April 1, 2000 to April 1, 2010**

Percent change
in population

- 18.0 or more
- 12.0 to 17.9
- 6.0 to 11.9
- 0.0 to 5.9
- Population decline

*U.S. percent = 9.7*

Source: Chart prepared by U.S. Census Bureau.

## Mean Center of Population for the United States: 1790 to 2010

## Median Center of Population for the United States: 1880 to 2010

# Table 1. Population and Area: 1790 to 2010

[Area figures represent area on indicated date including in some cases considerable areas not then organized or settled, and not covered by the census. Area data include Alaska beginning in 1870 and Hawaii beginning in 1900. Total area figures for 1790 to 1970 have been recalculated on the basis of the remeasurement of states and counties for the 1980 census, but not on the basis of subsequent censuses. The land and water area figures for past censuses have not been adjusted and are not strictly comparable with the total area data for comparable dates because the land areas were derived from different base data, and these values are known to have changed with the construction of reservoirs, draining of lakes, etc. Density figures are based on land area measurements as reported in earlier censuses]

| Census date | Resident population | | | | Area (square miles) | | |
| --- | --- | --- | --- | --- | --- | --- | --- |
| | Number | Per square mile of land area | Increase over preceding census | | Total | Land | Water [1] |
| | | | Number | Percent | | | |
| 1790 (Aug. 2)....... | 3,929,214 | 4.5 | (X) | (X) | 891,364 | 864,746 | 24,065 |
| 1800 (Aug. 4)....... | 5,308,483 | 6.1 | 1,379,269 | 35.1 | 891,364 | 864,746 | 24,065 |
| 1810 (Aug. 6)....... | 7,239,881 | 4.3 | 1,931,398 | 36.4 | 1,722,685 | 1,681,828 | 34,175 |
| 1820 (Aug. 7)....... | 9,638,453 | 5.5 | 2,398,572 | 33.1 | 1,792,552 | 1,749,462 | 38,544 |
| 1830 (June 1)...... | 12,866,020 | 7.4 | 3,227,567 | 33.5 | 1,792,552 | 1,749,462 | 38,544 |
| 1840 (June 1)...... | 17,069,453 | 9.8 | 4,203,433 | 32.7 | 1,792,552 | 1,749,462 | 38,544 |
| 1850 (June 1)...... | 23,191,876 | 7.9 | 6,122,423 | 35.9 | 2,991,655 | 2,940,042 | 52,705 |
| 1860 (June 1)...... | 31,443,321 | 10.6 | 8,251,445 | 35.6 | 3,021,295 | 2,969,640 | 52,747 |
| 1870 (June 1)...... | [2] 39,818,449 | [2] 11.2 | 8,375,128 | 26.6 | 3,612,299 | 3,540,705 | 68,082 |
| 1880 (June 1)...... | 50,189,209 | 14.2 | 10,370,760 | 26.0 | 3,612,299 | 3,540,705 | 68,082 |
| 1890 (June 1)...... | 62,979,766 | 17.8 | 12,790,557 | 25.5 | 3,612,299 | 3,540,705 | 68,082 |
| 1900 (June 1)...... | 76,212,168 | 21.5 | 13,232,402 | 21.0 | 3,618,770 | 3,547,314 | 67,901 |
| 1910 (Apr. 15)..... | 92,228,496 | 26.0 | 16,016,328 | 21.0 | 3,618,770 | 3,547,045 | 68,170 |
| 1920 (Jan. 1)....... | 106,021,537 | 29.9 | 13,793,041 | 15.0 | 3,618,770 | 3,546,931 | 68,284 |
| 1930 (Apr. 1)........ | 123,202,624 | 34.7 | 17,181,087 | 16.2 | 3,618,770 | 3,554,608 | 60,607 |
| 1940 (Apr. 1)........ | 132,164,569 | 37.2 | 8,961,945 | 7.3 | 3,618,770 | 3,554,608 | 60,607 |
| 1950 (Apr. 1)....... | 151,325,798 | 42.6 | 19,161,229 | 14.5 | 3,618,770 | 3,552,206 | 63,005 |
| 1960 (Apr. 1)....... | 179,323,175 | 50.6 | 27,997,377 | 18.5 | 3,618,770 | 3,540,911 | 74,212 |
| 1970 (Apr. 1)....... | 203,302,031 | 57.5 | 23,978,856 | 13.4 | 3,618,770 | 3,536,855 | 78,444 |
| 1980 (Apr. 1)....... | [3] 226,542,199 | 64.0 | 23,240,168 | 11.4 | 3,618,770 | 3,539,289 | 79,481 |
| 1990 (Apr. 1)....... | [4] 248,718,302 | 70.3 | 22,176,103 | 9.8 | [5] 3,717,796 | 3,536,278 | [5] 181,518 |
| 2000 (Apr. 1)....... | [6] 281,424,603 | 79.6 | 32,706,301 | 13.1 | 3,794,083 | 3,537,438 | 256,645 |
| 2010 (Apr. 1)....... | [7] 308,746,065 | 87.4 | 27,321,462 | 9.7 | 3,796,742 | 3,531,905 | 264,837 |

X Not applicable. [1] Data for 1790 to 1980 cover inland water only. Data for 1990 comprise Great Lakes, inland, and coastal water. Data for 2000 and 2010 comprise Great Lakes, inland, territorial, and coastal water. [2] Revised to include adjustments for underenumeration in southern states; unrevised number is 38,558,371 (10.9 per square mile). [3] Total population count has been revised since the 1980 census publications. Numbers by age, race, Hispanic origin, and sex have not been corrected. [4] The April 1, 1990, census count Includes count question resolution corrections processed through December 1997, and does not include adjustments for census coverage errors. [5] Data reflect corrections made after publication of the results. [6] Reflects modifications to the Census 2000 population as documented in the Count Question Resolution program. [7] Reflects modifications to the Census 2010 population as documented in the Count Question Resolution program (updated February 11, 2014).

Source: U.S. Census Bureau, *Notes and Errata, 2010 Census of Population and Housing*, SF/10-1, 2014; 2000 Census of Population and Housing, *Population and Housing Unit Counts, United States Summary*, Series PHC-3-1, and *Notes and Errata*, (2000), SF/01-ER; *Areas of the United States: 1940*; Area data for 1990: unpublished data from TIGER ®; and Davis, Warren, personal correspondence, U.S. Census Bureau, 23 June 2006.

# Table 2. Population: 1970 to 2018

[In thousands (205,052 represents 205,052,000). Estimates as of July 1. Civilian population excludes Armed Forces. For basis of estimates, see text, this section]

| Year | Resident population, including Armed Forces overseas | Resident population | Civilian population | Year | Resident population, including Armed Forces overseas | Resident population | Civilian population |
| --- | --- | --- | --- | --- | --- | --- | --- |
| 1970........ | 205,052 | 203,984 | 201,895 | 1995........ | 266,557 | 266,278 | 264,927 |
| 1972........ | 209,896 | 209,284 | 207,511 | 1996........ | 269,667 | 269,394 | 268,108 |
| 1973........ | 211,909 | 211,357 | 209,600 | 1997........ | 272,912 | 272,647 | 271,394 |
| 1974........ | 213,854 | 213,342 | 211,636 | 1998........ | 276,115 | 275,854 | 274,633 |
| 1975........ | 215,973 | 215,465 | 213,789 | 1999........ | 279,295 | 279,040 | 277,841 |
| 1976........ | 218,035 | 217,563 | 215,894 | 2000........ | (NA) | 282,162 | (NA) |
| 1977........ | 220,239 | 219,760 | 218,106 | 2001........ | (NA) | 284,969 | (NA) |
| 1978........ | 222,585 | 222,095 | 220,467 | 2002........ | (NA) | 287,625 | (NA) |
| 1979........ | 225,055 | 224,567 | 222,969 | 2003........ | (NA) | 290,108 | (NA) |
| 1980........ | 227,726 | 227,225 | 225,621 | 2004........ | (NA) | 292,805 | (NA) |
| 1981........ | 229,966 | 229,466 | 227,818 | 2005........ | (NA) | 295,517 | (NA) |
| 1982........ | 232,188 | 231,664 | 229,995 | 2006........ | (NA) | 298,380 | (NA) |
| 1983........ | 234,307 | 233,792 | 232,097 | 2007........ | (NA) | 301,231 | (NA) |
| 1984........ | 236,348 | 235,825 | 234,110 | 2008........ | (NA) | 304,094 | (NA) |
| 1985........ | 238,466 | 237,924 | 236,219 | 2009........ | (NA) | 306,772 | (NA) |
| 1986........ | 240,651 | 240,133 | 238,412 | 2010........ | 309,746 | 309,326 | 308,091 |
| 1987........ | 242,804 | 242,289 | 240,550 | 2011........ | 311,997 | 311,580 | 310,362 |
| 1988........ | 245,021 | 244,499 | 242,817 | 2012........ | 314,211 | 313,874 | 312,634 |
| 1989........ | 247,342 | 246,819 | 245,131 | 2013........ | 316,359 | 316,058 | 314,815 |
| 1990........ | 250,132 | 249,623 | 247,983 | 2014........ | 318,662 | 318,386 | 317,160 |
| 1991........ | 253,493 | 252,981 | 251,370 | 2015........ | 320,978 | 320,743 | 319,546 |
| 1992........ | 256,894 | 256,514 | 254,929 | 2016........ | 323,291 | 323,071 | 321,869 |
| 1993........ | 260,255 | 259,919 | 258,446 | 2017........ | 325,368 | 325,147 | 323,957 |
| 1994........ | 263,436 | 263,126 | 261,714 | 2018........ | 327,404 | 327,167 | 325,981 |

NA Not available.

Source: U.S. Census Bureau, Population Division, data prior to 2010, <http://www.census.gov/programs-surveys/popest.html>; and 2010 to 2018, "Monthly Population Estimates for the United States: April 1, 2010 to December 1, 2019 (NA-EST2018-01)," <https://www.census.gov/data/tables/time-series/demo/popest/2010s-national-total.html>, accessed December 2018.

# Table 3. Resident Population Projections and Components of Change: 2017 to 2060

[In thousands, except as indicated (325,511 represents 325,511,000). As of July 1. The 2017 National Projections are based on the July 1, 2016 population estimates, which are based on the 2010 Census. The projections were produced using a cohort-component method and are based on assumptions about future births, deaths, and net international migration. More information on methodology and assumptions is available at <https://www.census.gov/programs-surveys/popproj/technical-documentation/methodology.html>]

| Year | Population | | | Components of change | | | |
|---|---|---|---|---|---|---|---|
| | Total | Numeric change | Percent change [1] | Natural increase | Births | Deaths | Net international migration [2] |
| 2017 | 325,511 | 2,384 | 0.7 | 1,387 | 4,054 | 2,667 | 997 |
| 2018 | 327,892 | 2,381 | 0.7 | 1,379 | 4,075 | 2,696 | 1,002 |
| 2019 | 330,269 | 2,377 | 0.7 | 1,371 | 4,095 | 2,724 | 1,006 |
| 2020 | 332,639 | 2,370 | 0.7 | 1,360 | 4,112 | 2,752 | 1,010 |
| 2021 | 334,998 | 2,359 | 0.7 | 1,345 | 4,126 | 2,781 | 1,014 |
| 2022 | 337,342 | 2,344 | 0.7 | 1,326 | 4,137 | 2,811 | 1,017 |
| 2023 | 339,665 | 2,323 | 0.7 | 1,302 | 4,146 | 2,844 | 1,021 |
| 2024 | 341,963 | 2,298 | 0.7 | 1,274 | 4,152 | 2,878 | 1,025 |
| 2025 | 344,234 | 2,271 | 0.7 | 1,241 | 4,156 | 2,915 | 1,030 |
| 2026 | 346,481 | 2,247 | 0.7 | 1,205 | 4,160 | 2,954 | 1,042 |
| 2027 | 348,695 | 2,214 | 0.6 | 1,166 | 4,162 | 2,996 | 1,048 |
| 2028 | 350,872 | 2,177 | 0.6 | 1,123 | 4,163 | 3,040 | 1,054 |
| 2029 | 353,008 | 2,136 | 0.6 | 1,077 | 4,163 | 3,086 | 1,059 |
| 2030 | 355,101 | 2,093 | 0.6 | 1,028 | 4,162 | 3,134 | 1,064 |
| 2031 | 357,147 | 2,047 | 0.6 | 978 | 4,161 | 3,184 | 1,069 |
| 2032 | 359,147 | 1,999 | 0.6 | 926 | 4,161 | 3,235 | 1,073 |
| 2033 | 361,099 | 1,952 | 0.5 | 875 | 4,161 | 3,287 | 1,077 |
| 2034 | 363,003 | 1,905 | 0.5 | 824 | 4,163 | 3,339 | 1,081 |
| 2035 | 364,862 | 1,859 | 0.5 | 774 | 4,166 | 3,391 | 1,085 |
| 2036 | 366,676 | 1,814 | 0.5 | 726 | 4,170 | 3,444 | 1,088 |
| 2037 | 368,448 | 1,772 | 0.5 | 681 | 4,175 | 3,495 | 1,091 |
| 2038 | 370,179 | 1,731 | 0.5 | 637 | 4,182 | 3,545 | 1,094 |
| 2039 | 371,871 | 1,693 | 0.5 | 596 | 4,189 | 3,592 | 1,096 |
| 2040 | 373,528 | 1,657 | 0.5 | 558 | 4,196 | 3,638 | 1,098 |
| 2041 | 375,152 | 1,624 | 0.4 | 523 | 4,204 | 3,681 | 1,100 |
| 2042 | 376,746 | 1,594 | 0.4 | 492 | 4,213 | 3,720 | 1,102 |
| 2043 | 378,314 | 1,568 | 0.4 | 465 | 4,222 | 3,757 | 1,104 |
| 2044 | 379,861 | 1,547 | 0.4 | 442 | 4,232 | 3,790 | 1,105 |
| 2045 | 381,390 | 1,529 | 0.4 | 424 | 4,243 | 3,819 | 1,106 |
| 2046 | 382,907 | 1,517 | 0.4 | 410 | 4,254 | 3,844 | 1,107 |
| 2047 | 384,415 | 1,508 | 0.4 | 400 | 4,267 | 3,867 | 1,108 |
| 2048 | 385,918 | 1,502 | 0.4 | 394 | 4,279 | 3,885 | 1,108 |
| 2049 | 387,419 | 1,501 | 0.4 | 392 | 4,292 | 3,900 | 1,109 |
| 2050 | 388,922 | 1,503 | 0.4 | 394 | 4,304 | 3,910 | 1,110 |
| 2051 | 390,431 | 1,509 | 0.4 | 399 | 4,316 | 3,918 | 1,110 |
| 2052 | 391,947 | 1,516 | 0.4 | 406 | 4,328 | 3,922 | 1,110 |
| 2053 | 393,473 | 1,526 | 0.4 | 415 | 4,339 | 3,924 | 1,111 |
| 2054 | 395,009 | 1,537 | 0.4 | 426 | 4,349 | 3,924 | 1,111 |
| 2055 | 396,557 | 1,548 | 0.4 | 437 | 4,359 | 3,922 | 1,112 |
| 2056 | 398,118 | 1,560 | 0.4 | 448 | 4,368 | 3,920 | 1,112 |
| 2057 | 399,691 | 1,573 | 0.4 | 460 | 4,376 | 3,916 | 1,113 |
| 2058 | 401,277 | 1,586 | 0.4 | 471 | 4,383 | 3,912 | 1,115 |
| 2059 | 402,874 | 1,598 | 0.4 | 482 | 4,390 | 3,909 | 1,116 |
| 2060 | 404,483 | 1,609 | 0.4 | 491 | 4,397 | 3,906 | 1,118 |

[1] Percent change from immediate preceding year. For 2017, change from 2016. [2] Net international migration includes the international migration of both native and foreign-born populations. Specifically, it includes: (a) the net international migration of the foreign born and (b) the net international migration of the native born, including migration to and from Puerto Rico.

Source: U.S. Census Bureau, 2017 National Population Projections Tables, "Table 1. Projected population size and births, deaths, and migration: 2016 to 2060 (NP2017-T1)," September 2018, <https://www.census.gov/programs-surveys/popproj/data/tables.html>, accessed September 2018.

# Table 4. Components of Population Change: 2010 to 2018

[In thousands, except as indicated (308,758 represents 308,758,000). Resident population]

| Period | Population as of beginning of period | Net increase | | Births | Deaths | Net international migration [2] | Population as of end of period |
|---|---|---|---|---|---|---|---|
| | | Total | Percent [1] | | | | |
| April 1, 2010 to July 1, 2010 [3] | 308,758 | 568 | 0.2 | 988 | 599 | 179 | 309,326 |
| July 1, 2010 to July 1, 2011 | 309,326 | 2,254 | 0.7 | 3,973 | 2,512 | 793 | 311,580 |
| July 1, 2011 to July 1, 2012 | 311,580 | 2,294 | 0.7 | 3,937 | 2,502 | 859 | 313,874 |
| July 1, 2012 to July 1, 2013 | 313,874 | 2,184 | 0.7 | 3,941 | 2,608 | 851 | 316,058 |
| July 1, 2013 to July 1, 2014 | 316,058 | 2,329 | 0.7 | 3,963 | 2,582 | 948 | 318,386 |
| July 1, 2014 to July 1, 2015 | 318,386 | 2,356 | 0.7 | 3,992 | 2,700 | 1,064 | 320,743 |
| July 1, 2015 to July 1, 2016 | 320,743 | 2,329 | 0.7 | 3,963 | 2,703 | 1,069 | 323,071 |
| July 1, 2016 to July 1, 2017 | 323,071 | 2,076 | 0.6 | 3,902 | 2,779 | 953 | 325,147 |
| July 1, 2017 to July 1, 2018 | 325,147 | 2,020 | 0.6 | 3,856 | 2,814 | 979 | 327,167 |

[1] Percent of population at beginning of period. [2] Net international migration includes the international migration of both native and foreign-born populations. Specifically, it includes: (a) the net international migration of the foreign born, (b) the net migration between the United States and Puerto Rico, (c) the net migration of natives to and from the United States, and (d) the net movement of the Armed Forces population between the United States and overseas. [3] The April 1, 2010 population estimates base reflects changes from the Count Question Resolution program and geographic program revisions.

Source: U.S. Census Bureau, Population Division, "Population, population change, and estimated components of population change: April 1, 2010 to July 1, 2018 (NST-EST2018-alldata)," <https://www.census.gov/data/tables/time-series/demo/popest/2010s-national-total.html>, accessed December 2018.

# Table 5. Components of Population Change by Race and Hispanic Origin: 2010 to 2018

[In thousands (18,409 represents 18,409,000). Resident population. Covers period April 1, 2010 to July 1, 2018. The April 1, 2010 population estimates base reflects changes to the Census 2010 population from the Count Question Resolution program and geographic program revisions. Responses of "Some Other Race" from the 2010 Census are modified. This results in differences between the population for specific race categories shown for the 2010 Census population in this table versus those in the original 2010 Census data. Minus sign (-) indicates decrease]

| Race and Hispanic origin | April 1, 2010 to July 1, 2018 | | | | |
|---|---|---|---|---|---|
| | Net increase | Natural increase | Births | Deaths | Net international migration [1] |
| **Total**............................................. | **18,409** | **10,715** | **32,515** | **21,800** | **7,694** |
| One race............................................. | 16,447 | 8,953 | 30,566 | 21,613 | 7,494 |
| White............................................. | 8,194 | 5,042 | 23,424 | 18,382 | 3,152 |
| Black or African American............................ | 3,550 | 2,405 | 4,971 | 2,566 | 1,145 |
| American Indian and Alaska Native.................... | 408 | 367 | 527 | 159 | 41 |
| Asian............................................. | 4,171 | 1,056 | 1,546 | 491 | 3,115 |
| Native Hawaiian and Other Pacific Islander............. | 125 | 84 | 98 | 15 | 41 |
| Two or more races................................... | 1,962 | 1,762 | 1,949 | 187 | 200 |
| Race alone or in combination: [2] | | | | | |
| White............................................. | 10,005 | 6,683 | 25,217 | 18,534 | 3,322 |
| Black or African American............................ | 4,625 | 3,397 | 6,026 | 2,628 | 1,227 |
| American Indian and Alaska Native.................... | 735 | 667 | 921 | 254 | 68 |
| Asian............................................. | 4,937 | 1,706 | 2,258 | 551 | 3,230 |
| Native Hawaiian and Other Pacific Islander............. | 260 | 201 | 237 | 36 | 58 |
| Hispanic [3]......................................... | 9,393 | 7,008 | 8,421 | 1,413 | 2,385 |
| White alone, not Hispanic............................ | 220 | -840 | 16,255 | 17,095 | 1,060 |

[1] Net international migration includes the international migration of both native and foreign-born populations. Specifically, it includes: (a) the net international migration of the foreign born, (b) the net migration between the United States and Puerto Rico, (c) the net migration of natives to and from the United States, and (d) the net movement of the Armed Forces population between the United States and overseas. [2] In combination with one or more other races. The sum of the five race groups adds to more than the total population because individuals may report more than one race. [3] Hispanic origin is considered an ethnicity, not a race. Persons of Hispanic origin may be of any race.

Source: U.S. Census Bureau, Population Division, "Estimates of the Components of Resident Population Change by Race and Hispanic Origin for the United States: April 1, 2010 to July 1, 2018," <http://factfinder.census.gov>, accessed June 2019.

# Table 6. Resident Population by Sex and Age: 2000 to 2018

[In thousands, except as indicated (281,425 represents 281,425,000). As of April 1, except 2017 and 2018 as of July 1. Excludes Armed Forces overseas]

| Age | 2000 [1] | | | 2010 [1] | | | 2017 | | | 2018 | | |
|---|---|---|---|---|---|---|---|---|---|---|---|---|
| | Total | Male | Female | Total | Male | Female | Total | Male | Female | Total | Male | Female |
| **Total**................. | **281,425** | **138,056** | **143,368** | **308,758** | **151,789** | **156,969** | **325,147** | **160,126** | **165,021** | **327,167** | **161,129** | **166,039** |
| Under 5 years........ | 19,176 | 9,811 | 9,365 | 20,201 | 10,319 | 9,882 | 19,892 | 10,173 | 9,719 | 19,810 | 10,132 | 9,678 |
| 5 to 9 years.......... | 20,550 | 10,523 | 10,026 | 20,349 | 10,390 | 9,959 | 20,305 | 10,369 | 9,936 | 20,196 | 10,316 | 9,880 |
| 10 to 14 years........ | 20,528 | 10,520 | 10,008 | 20,677 | 10,580 | 10,097 | 20,766 | 10,600 | 10,166 | 20,880 | 10,659 | 10,221 |
| 15 to 19 years........ | 20,219 | 10,391 | 9,828 | 22,042 | 11,305 | 10,737 | 21,103 | 10,783 | 10,320 | 21,097 | 10,775 | 10,322 |
| 20 to 24 years........ | 18,963 | 9,688 | 9,275 | 21,588 | 11,015 | 10,572 | 22,066 | 11,319 | 10,747 | 21,874 | 11,202 | 10,672 |
| 25 to 29 years........ | 19,382 | 9,799 | 9,583 | 21,103 | 10,637 | 10,467 | 23,336 | 11,886 | 11,450 | 23,562 | 12,019 | 11,543 |
| 30 to 34 years........ | 20,511 | 10,322 | 10,189 | 19,963 | 9,997 | 9,966 | 21,938 | 11,074 | 10,865 | 22,136 | 11,192 | 10,944 |
| 35 to 39 years........ | 22,707 | 11,319 | 11,388 | 20,180 | 10,043 | 10,138 | 21,190 | 10,597 | 10,594 | 21,564 | 10,790 | 10,773 |
| 40 to 44 years........ | 22,442 | 11,130 | 11,313 | 20,892 | 10,395 | 10,497 | 19,591 | 9,726 | 9,865 | 19,714 | 9,797 | 9,917 |
| 45 to 49 years........ | 20,093 | 9,890 | 10,203 | 22,709 | 11,210 | 11,500 | 20,916 | 10,358 | 10,558 | 20,747 | 10,264 | 10,483 |
| 50 to 54 years........ | 17,586 | 8,608 | 8,978 | 22,299 | 10,934 | 11,365 | 21,348 | 10,494 | 10,853 | 20,885 | 10,277 | 10,607 |
| 55 to 59 years........ | 13,469 | 6,509 | 6,961 | 19,665 | 9,524 | 10,141 | 21,960 | 10,677 | 11,283 | 21,941 | 10,669 | 11,272 |
| 60 to 64 years........ | 10,806 | 5,137 | 5,669 | 16,818 | 8,078 | 8,741 | 19,942 | 9,535 | 10,407 | 20,332 | 9,730 | 10,602 |
| 65 to 74 years........ | 18,391 | 8,303 | 10,088 | 21,714 | 10,097 | 11,617 | 29,633 | 13,853 | 15,780 | 30,492 | 14,246 | 16,246 |
| 75 to 84 years........ | 12,361 | 4,879 | 7,482 | 13,062 | 5,477 | 7,585 | 14,691 | 6,402 | 8,288 | 15,394 | 6,735 | 8,659 |
| 85 years and over. .. | 4,240 | 1,227 | 3,013 | 5,495 | 1,790 | 3,705 | 6,470 | 2,280 | 4,191 | 6,545 | 2,326 | 4,219 |
| 5 to 13 years......... | 37,026 | 18,964 | 18,062 | 36,860 | 18,834 | 18,026 | 36,947 | 18,865 | 18,081 | 36,908 | 18,849 | 18,059 |
| 14 to 17 years........ | 16,093 | 8,285 | 7,808 | 17,121 | 8,792 | 8,329 | 16,745 | 8,547 | 8,198 | 16,681 | 8,509 | 8,172 |
| 18 to 24 years........ | 27,141 | 13,873 | 13,268 | 30,674 | 15,663 | 15,011 | 30,549 | 15,658 | 14,891 | 30,457 | 15,593 | 14,864 |
| 18 years and over. .. | 209,130 | 100,996 | 108,133 | 234,576 | 113,843 | 120,733 | 251,564 | 122,541 | 129,023 | 253,768 | 123,638 | 130,130 |
| 55 years and over. .. | 59,267 | 26,055 | 33,212 | 76,755 | 34,966 | 41,789 | 92,696 | 42,747 | 49,949 | 94,704 | 43,706 | 50,998 |
| 65 years and over. .. | 34,992 | 14,410 | 20,582 | 40,271 | 17,364 | 22,907 | 50,794 | 22,535 | 28,259 | 52,431 | 23,307 | 29,124 |
| 75 years and over. .. | 16,601 | 6,106 | 10,495 | 18,557 | 7,267 | 11,290 | 21,161 | 8,682 | 12,479 | 21,939 | 9,061 | 12,878 |
| Median age (years).. | 35.3 | 34.0 | 36.5 | 37.2 | 35.8 | 38.5 | 38.0 | 36.8 | 39.4 | 38.2 | 36.9 | 39.5 |

[1] The April 1, 2000 and April 1, 2010 population estimates bases reflect changes to the Census 2000 and Census 2010 population from the Count Question Resolution program and geographic program revisions.

Source: U.S. Census Bureau, Current Population Reports, P25-1095; "Intercensal Estimates of the United States Population by Age and Sex, 1990-2000: All Months," September 2002, <https://www.census.gov/data/tables/time-series/demo/popest/intercensal-national.html>; and "PEPAGESEX: Annual Estimates of the Resident Population for Selected Age Groups by Sex for the United States, States, Counties, and Puerto Rico Commonwealth and Municipios: April 1, 2010 to July 1, 2018," <https://factfinder.census.gov>, accessed June 2019.

# Table 7. Resident Population by Sex, Race, and Hispanic Origin: 2000 to 2018

[281,425 represents 281,425,000. Data shown are modified race counts; see text, this section]

| Characteristic | Number (1,000) | | | | | Percent change | |
| --- | --- | --- | --- | --- | --- | --- | --- |
| | 2000 [1] (April) | 2010 [1] (April) | 2016 (July) | 2017 (July) | 2018 (July) | 2000 to 2010 | 2010 to 2018 |
| **BOTH SEXES** | | | | | | | |
| **Total**.................................... | **281,425** | **308,758** | **323,071** | **325,147** | **327,167** | **9.7** | **6.0** |
| One race......................... | 277,527 | 301,774 | 314,602 | 316,440 | 318,221 | 8.7 | 5.5 |
| White........................... | 228,106 | 241,945 | 248,439 | 249,305 | 250,139 | 6.1 | 3.4 |
| Black or African American.......... | 35,705 | 40,254 | 43,003 | 43,410 | 43,804 | 12.7 | 8.8 |
| American Indian and Alaska Native........ | 2,664 | 3,740 | 4,055 | 4,102 | 4,148 | 40.4 | 10.9 |
| Asian........................... | 10,589 | 15,160 | 18,335 | 18,838 | 19,331 | 43.2 | 27.5 |
| Native Hawaiian and Other Pacific Islander.......... | 463 | 675 | 770 | 785 | 799 | 45.9 | 18.5 |
| Two or more races.................. | 3,898 | 6,984 | 8,469 | 8,707 | 8,946 | 79.2 | 28.1 |
| Race alone or in combination with one or more races: | | | | | | | |
| White........................... | (NA) | 248,076 | 255,939 | 257,025 | 258,081 | (NA) | 4.0 |
| Black or African American.......... | (NA) | 43,217 | 46,775 | 47,314 | 47,842 | (NA) | 10.7 |
| American Indian and Alaska Native........ | (NA) | 6,139 | 6,704 | 6,790 | 6,874 | (NA) | 12.0 |
| Asian........................... | (NA) | 17,677 | 21,433 | 22,029 | 22,613 | (NA) | 27.9 |
| Native Hawaiian and Other Pacific Islander.......... | (NA) | 1,333 | 1,531 | 1,562 | 1,592 | (NA) | 19.5 |
| Not Hispanic........................ | 246,118 | 258,279 | 265,499 | 266,440 | 267,296 | 4.9 | 3.5 |
| One race......................... | 242,712 | 252,675 | 258,748 | 259,507 | 260,181 | 4.1 | 3.0 |
| White........................... | 195,577 | 197,326 | 197,794 | 197,699 | 197,546 | 0.9 | 0.1 |
| Black or African American.......... | 34,314 | 37,926 | 40,243 | 40,580 | 40,902 | 10.5 | 7.8 |
| American Indian and Alaska Native........ | 2,097 | 2,263 | 2,387 | 2,403 | 2,417 | 7.9 | 6.8 |
| Asian........................... | 10,357 | 14,662 | 17,759 | 18,249 | 18,729 | 41.6 | 27.7 |
| Native Hawaiian and Other Pacific Islander.......... | 367 | 497 | 566 | 576 | 586 | 35.4 | 17.9 |
| Two or more races.................. | 3,406 | 5,605 | 6,750 | 6,933 | 7,115 | 64.5 | 26.9 |
| Race alone or in combination with one or more races: | | | | | | | |
| White........................... | (NA) | 202,237 | 203,766 | 203,840 | 203,857 | (NA) | 0.8 |
| Black or African American.......... | (NA) | 40,287 | 43,225 | 43,663 | 44,086 | (NA) | 9.4 |
| American Indian and Alaska Native........ | (NA) | 4,042 | 4,303 | 4,339 | 4,374 | (NA) | 8.2 |
| Asian........................... | (NA) | 16,795 | 20,381 | 20,950 | 21,507 | (NA) | 28.1 |
| Native Hawaiian and Other Pacific Islander.......... | (NA) | 1,020 | 1,164 | 1,187 | 1,208 | (NA) | 18.4 |
| Hispanic [2]........................ | 35,306 | 50,479 | 57,573 | 58,707 | 59,872 | 43.0 | 18.6 |
| One race......................... | 34,815 | 49,099 | 55,854 | 56,933 | 58,040 | 41.0 | 18.2 |
| White........................... | 32,530 | 44,619 | 50,645 | 51,606 | 52,593 | 37.2 | 17.9 |
| Black or African American.......... | 1,391 | 2,328 | 2,760 | 2,830 | 2,902 | 67.4 | 24.6 |
| American Indian and Alaska Native........ | 566 | 1,476 | 1,668 | 1,699 | 1,730 | 160.6 | 17.2 |
| Asian........................... | 232 | 498 | 576 | 589 | 602 | 114.2 | 20.9 |
| Native Hawaiian and Other Pacific Islander.......... | 95 | 177 | 204 | 209 | 213 | 85.9 | 20.1 |
| Two or more races.................. | 491 | 1,380 | 1,719 | 1,774 | 1,832 | 180.8 | 32.8 |
| Race alone or in combination with one or more races: | | | | | | | |
| White........................... | (NA) | 45,839 | 52,174 | 53,185 | 54,224 | (NA) | 18.3 |
| Black or African American.......... | (NA) | 2,930 | 3,550 | 3,651 | 3,756 | (NA) | 28.2 |
| American Indian and Alaska Native........ | (NA) | 2,097 | 2,402 | 2,451 | 2,500 | (NA) | 19.2 |
| Asian........................... | (NA) | 881 | 1,051 | 1,079 | 1,107 | (NA) | 25.5 |
| Native Hawaiian and Other Pacific Islander.......... | (NA) | 312 | 366 | 375 | 384 | (NA) | 23.0 |
| **MALE** | | | | | | | |
| **Total**.................................... | **138,056** | **151,789** | **159,088** | **160,126** | **161,129** | **9.9** | **6.2** |
| One race......................... | 136,146 | 148,362 | 154,904 | 155,820 | 156,701 | 9.0 | 5.6 |
| White........................... | 112,478 | 119,703 | 123,137 | 123,580 | 124,002 | 6.4 | 3.6 |
| Black or African American.......... | 16,972 | 19,208 | 20,591 | 20,792 | 20,986 | 13.2 | 9.3 |
| American Indian and Alaska Native........ | 1,333 | 1,890 | 2,045 | 2,067 | 2,089 | 41.8 | 10.6 |
| Asian........................... | 5,128 | 7,219 | 8,741 | 8,983 | 9,219 | 40.8 | 27.7 |
| Native Hawaiian and Other Pacific Islander.......... | 235 | 343 | 391 | 398 | 405 | 45.8 | 18.2 |
| Two or more races.................. | 1,910 | 3,426 | 4,184 | 4,306 | 4,428 | 79.4 | 29.2 |
| Race alone or in combination with one or more races: | | | | | | | |
| White........................... | (NA) | 122,721 | 126,853 | 127,409 | 127,943 | (NA) | 4.3 |
| Black or African American.......... | (NA) | 20,635 | 22,431 | 22,698 | 22,961 | (NA) | 11.3 |
| American Indian and Alaska Native........ | (NA) | 3,055 | 3,337 | 3,379 | 3,421 | (NA) | 12.0 |
| Asian........................... | (NA) | 8,468 | 10,289 | 10,578 | 10,861 | (NA) | 28.3 |
| Native Hawaiian and Other Pacific Islander.......... | (NA) | 668 | 769 | 784 | 799 | (NA) | 19.7 |
| Not Hispanic........................ | 119,894 | 126,169 | 129,999 | 130,472 | 130,894 | 5.2 | 3.7 |
| Hispanic [2]........................ | 18,162 | 25,620 | 29,089 | 29,654 | 30,234 | 41.1 | 18.0 |
| **FEMALE** | | | | | | | |
| **Total**.................................... | **143,368** | **156,969** | **163,983** | **165,021** | **166,039** | **9.5** | **5.8** |
| One race......................... | 141,381 | 153,411 | 159,698 | 160,620 | 161,520 | 8.5 | 5.3 |
| White........................... | 115,628 | 122,242 | 125,303 | 125,724 | 126,138 | 5.7 | 3.2 |
| Black or African American.......... | 18,733 | 21,047 | 22,412 | 22,619 | 22,818 | 12.4 | 8.4 |
| American Indian and Alaska Native........ | 1,331 | 1,850 | 2,010 | 2,035 | 2,058 | 39.0 | 11.3 |
| Asian........................... | 5,461 | 7,941 | 9,594 | 9,855 | 10,112 | 45.4 | 27.3 |
| Native Hawaiian and Other Pacific Islander.......... | 227 | 332 | 379 | 387 | 394 | 45.9 | 18.8 |
| Two or more races.................. | 1,987 | 3,558 | 4,285 | 4,402 | 4,519 | 79.0 | 27.0 |
| Race alone or in combination with one or more races: | | | | | | | |
| White........................... | (NA) | 125,355 | 129,087 | 129,616 | 130,138 | (NA) | 3.8 |
| Black or African American.......... | (NA) | 22,582 | 24,344 | 24,616 | 24,881 | (NA) | 10.2 |
| American Indian and Alaska Native........ | (NA) | 3,084 | 3,367 | 3,411 | 3,453 | (NA) | 12.0 |
| Asian........................... | (NA) | 9,209 | 11,144 | 11,451 | 11,752 | (NA) | 27.6 |
| Native Hawaiian and Other Pacific Islander.......... | (NA) | 665 | 762 | 778 | 793 | (NA) | 19.3 |
| Not Hispanic........................ | 126,224 | 132,110 | 135,500 | 135,968 | 136,401 | 4.7 | 3.2 |
| Hispanic [2]........................ | 17,144 | 24,859 | 28,483 | 29,053 | 29,638 | 45.0 | 19.2 |

NA Not available. [1] The April 1, 2000 and 2010 population estimates base reflect changes to the Census 2000 and 2010 population from the Count Question Resolution program and geographic program revisions. [2] Persons of Hispanic origin may be of any race.

Source: U.S. Census Bureau, Population Division, "Table 2. Intercensal Estimates of the Resident Population by Sex, Race, and Hispanic Origin for the United States: April 1, 2000 to July 1, 2010 (US-EST00INT-02)," September 2011, <https://www.census.gov/data/tables/time-series/demo/popest/intercensal-2000-2010-national.html>; and National Population by Characteristics: 2010-2018, Datasets, "Monthly Population Estimates by Age, Sex, Race, and Hispanic Origin for the United States: April 1, 2010 to July 1, 2018," <https://www2.census.gov/programs-surveys/popest/datasets/2010-2018/national/asrh>; accessed June 2019.

# Table 8. Resident Population Projections by Sex and Age: 2020 to 2060

[In thousands, except as indicated (332,639 represents 332,639,000). As of July 1. The 2017 National Projections are based on the July 1, 2016 population estimates, which are based on the 2010 Census. The projections were produced using a cohort-component method and are based on assumptions about future births, deaths, and net international migration. More information on methodology and assumptions is available at <https://www.census.gov/programs-surveys/popproj/technical-documentation/methodology.htm>]

| Age | 2020 Total | 2020 Male | 2020 Female | 2025 | 2030 | 2035 | 2040 | 2045 | 2050 | 2060 | Percent distribution 2020 | 2030 | 2040 | 2050 | 2060 |
|---|---|---|---|---|---|---|---|---|---|---|---|---|---|---|---|
| Total.......... | 332,639 | 163,904 | 168,735 | 344,234 | 355,101 | 364,862 | 373,528 | 381,390 | 388,922 | 404,483 | 100.0 | 100.0 | 100.0 | 100.0 | 100.0 |
| **FIVE-YEAR AGE GROUPS** | | | | | | | | | | | | | | | |
| Under 5 years........ | 20,439 | 10,446 | 9,993 | 20,868 | 20,976 | 20,993 | 21,105 | 21,319 | 21,610 | 22,144 | 6.1 | 5.9 | 5.7 | 5.6 | 5.5 |
| 5 to 9 years......... | 20,200 | 10,325 | 9,875 | 20,721 | 21,163 | 21,283 | 21,311 | 21,432 | 21,653 | 22,261 | 6.1 | 6.0 | 5.7 | 5.6 | 5.5 |
| 10 to 14 years....... | 20,770 | 10,604 | 10,166 | 20,489 | 21,019 | 21,471 | 21,599 | 21,634 | 21,761 | 22,288 | 6.2 | 5.9 | 5.8 | 5.6 | 5.5 |
| 15 to 19 years....... | 21,038 | 10,732 | 10,306 | 21,221 | 20,960 | 21,507 | 21,974 | 22,114 | 22,159 | 22,527 | 6.3 | 5.9 | 5.9 | 5.7 | 5.6 |
| 20 to 24 years....... | 21,899 | 11,199 | 10,701 | 21,910 | 22,146 | 21,929 | 22,510 | 23,005 | 23,168 | 23,384 | 6.6 | 6.2 | 6.0 | 6.0 | 5.8 |
| 25 to 29 years....... | 23,512 | 12,029 | 11,483 | 22,792 | 22,863 | 23,152 | 22,978 | 23,593 | 24,115 | 24,387 | 7.1 | 6.4 | 6.2 | 6.2 | 6.0 |
| 30 to 34 years....... | 22,979 | 11,649 | 11,330 | 24,147 | 23,480 | 23,593 | 23,919 | 23,775 | 24,412 | 25,155 | 6.9 | 6.6 | 6.4 | 6.3 | 6.2 |
| 35 to 39 years....... | 21,922 | 10,990 | 10,932 | 24,326 | 24,527 | 23,899 | 24,041 | 24,391 | 24,268 | 25,470 | 6.6 | 6.9 | 6.4 | 6.2 | 6.3 |
| 40 to 44 years....... | 20,430 | 10,168 | 10,262 | 22,063 | 23,501 | 24,725 | 24,129 | 24,294 | 24,664 | 25,218 | 6.1 | 6.6 | 6.5 | 6.3 | 6.2 |
| 45 to 49 years....... | 20,105 | 9,947 | 10,157 | 20,412 | 22,061 | 23,519 | 24,760 | 24,196 | 24,382 | 24,680 | 6.0 | 6.2 | 6.6 | 6.3 | 6.1 |
| 50 to 54 years....... | 20,510 | 10,110 | 10,401 | 19,855 | 20,197 | 21,858 | 23,336 | 24,590 | 24,064 | 24,681 | 6.2 | 5.7 | 6.2 | 6.2 | 6.1 |
| 55 to 59 years....... | 21,772 | 10,599 | 11,173 | 20,100 | 19,506 | 19,891 | 21,562 | 23,057 | 24,327 | 24,087 | 6.5 | 5.5 | 5.8 | 6.3 | 6.0 |
| 60 to 64 years....... | 21,011 | 10,092 | 10,919 | 21,105 | 20,144 | 19,046 | 19,478 | 21,154 | 22,664 | 23,525 | 6.3 | 5.7 | 5.2 | 5.8 | 5.8 |
| 65 to 69 years....... | 18,030 | 8,492 | 9,538 | 19,978 | 18,542 | 18,753 | 18,312 | 18,792 | 20,460 | 23,269 | 5.4 | 5.2 | 4.9 | 5.3 | 5.8 |
| 70 to 74 years....... | 14,759 | 6,837 | 7,922 | 16,662 | 18,779 | 18,779 | 17,567 | 17,217 | 17,744 | 20,884 | 4.4 | 5.3 | 4.7 | 4.6 | 5.2 |
| 75 to 79 years....... | 10,053 | 4,502 | 5,551 | 13,001 | 14,768 | 16,526 | 16,827 | 15,837 | 15,592 | 17,725 | 3.0 | 4.2 | 4.5 | 4.0 | 4.4 |
| 80 to 84 years....... | 6,508 | 2,765 | 3,743 | 8,136 | 10,609 | 12,147 | 13,690 | 14,035 | 13,317 | 13,779 | 2.0 | 3.0 | 3.7 | 3.4 | 3.4 |
| 85 to 89 years....... | 3,943 | 1,529 | 2,414 | 4,496 | 5,695 | 7,518 | 8,707 | 9,911 | 10,252 | 9,808 | 1.2 | 1.6 | 2.3 | 2.6 | 2.4 |
| 90 to 94 years....... | 2,017 | 684 | 1,333 | 2,105 | 2,455 | 3,173 | 4,269 | 5,033 | 5,817 | 5,957 | 0.6 | 0.7 | 1.1 | 1.5 | 1.5 |
| 95 to 99 years....... | 649 | 184 | 465 | 729 | 784 | 945 | 1,257 | 1,740 | 2,106 | 2,666 | 0.2 | 0.2 | 0.3 | 0.5 | 0.7 |
| 100 years and over... | 92 | 21 | 71 | 120 | 140 | 156 | 196 | 270 | 386 | 589 | (Z) | (Z) | 0.1 | 0.1 | 0.1 |
| **SPECIAL AGE CATEGORIES** | | | | | | | | | | | | | | | |
| 5 to 13 years........ | 36,780 | 18,789 | 17,992 | 37,074 | 38,051 | 38,453 | 38,568 | 38,715 | 39,049 | 40,090 | 11.1 | 10.7 | 10.3 | 10.0 | 9.9 |
| 14 to 17 years....... | 16,748 | 8,545 | 8,203 | 16,712 | 16,625 | 17,217 | 17,457 | 17,527 | 17,566 | 17,903 | 5.0 | 4.7 | 4.7 | 4.5 | 4.4 |
| 18 to 24 years....... | 30,380 | 15,526 | 14,854 | 30,554 | 30,612 | 30,519 | 31,369 | 31,943 | 32,126 | 32,467 | 9.1 | 8.6 | 8.4 | 8.3 | 8.0 |
| 16 years and over.... | 267,049 | 130,396 | 136,653 | 278,019 | 287,784 | 296,814 | 305,159 | 312,637 | 319,519 | 333,323 | 80.3 | 81.0 | 81.7 | 82.2 | 82.4 |
| 18 years and over.... | 258,672 | 126,125 | 132,547 | 269,580 | 279,449 | 288,199 | 296,397 | 303,829 | 310,697 | 324,346 | 77.8 | 78.7 | 79.4 | 79.9 | 80.2 |
| 15 to 44 years....... | 131,781 | 66,768 | 65,013 | 135,459 | 137,476 | 138,804 | 139,551 | 141,173 | 142,786 | 146,140 | 39.6 | 38.7 | 37.4 | 36.7 | 36.1 |
| 55 years and over.... | 98,834 | 45,705 | 53,129 | 106,432 | 112,208 | 116,934 | 121,865 | 127,046 | 132,665 | 142,289 | 29.7 | 31.6 | 32.6 | 34.1 | 35.2 |
| 65 years and over.... | 56,052 | 25,014 | 31,037 | 65,226 | 73,138 | 77,997 | 80,827 | 82,835 | 85,675 | 94,676 | 16.9 | 20.6 | 21.6 | 22.0 | 23.4 |
| 75 years and over.... | 23,262 | 9,685 | 13,577 | 28,587 | 34,451 | 40,465 | 44,946 | 46,826 | 47,470 | 50,524 | 7.0 | 9.7 | 12.0 | 12.2 | 12.5 |
| 85 years and over.... | 6,701 | 2,418 | 4,283 | 7,450 | 9,074 | 11,793 | 14,430 | 16,953 | 18,561 | 19,019 | 2.0 | 2.6 | 3.9 | 4.8 | 4.7 |
| Median age (years) [1].. | 38.5 | 37.2 | 39.8 | 39.3 | 40.1 | 41.0 | 41.5 | 41.9 | 42.3 | 42.9 | (X) | (X) | (X) | (X) | (X) |

X Not applicable. Z Less than 0.05 percent. [1] For definition of median, see Guide to Tabular Presentation.

Source: U.S. Census Bureau, 2017 National Population Projections Tables, "Table 2. Projected age and sex composition of the population" and "Table 3. Detailed age and sex composition of the population," September 2018, <https://www.census.gov/programs-surveys/popproj/data/tables.html>, accessed September 2018.

## Table 9. Resident Population by Race, Hispanic Origin, and Age: 2010 and 2018

[In thousands, except as indicated (308,758 represents 308,758,000). 2010 data as of April 1 and 2018 data as of July 1]

| Age | Total 2010[1] | Total 2018 | White alone 2010[1] | White alone 2018 | Black or African American alone 2010[1] | Black or African American alone 2018 | American Indian, Alaska Native alone 2010[1] | American Indian, Alaska Native alone 2018 | Asian alone 2010[1] | Asian alone 2018 | Native Hawaiian, Other Pacific Islander alone 2010[1] | Native Hawaiian, Other Pacific Islander alone 2018 | Two or more races 2010[1] | Two or more races 2018 | Hispanic origin[2] 2010[1] | Hispanic origin[2] 2018 | Not Hispanic White alone 2010[1] | Not Hispanic White alone 2018 |
|---|---|---|---|---|---|---|---|---|---|---|---|---|---|---|---|---|---|---|
| **Total** | 308,758 | 327,167 | 241,945 | 250,139 | 40,254 | 43,804 | 3,740 | 4,148 | 15,160 | 19,331 | 675 | 799 | 6,984 | 8,946 | 50,479 | 59,872 | 197,326 | 197,546 |
| **FIVE-YEAR AGE GROUPS** | | | | | | | | | | | | | | | | | | |
| Under 5 years | 20,201 | 19,810 | 14,691 | 14,161 | 3,055 | 3,018 | 330 | 317 | 948 | 1,056 | 59 | 62 | 1,119 | 1,196 | 5,114 | 5,172 | 10,307 | 9,767 |
| 5 to 9 years | 20,349 | 20,196 | 15,044 | 14,493 | 3,013 | 3,068 | 321 | 323 | 972 | 1,083 | 56 | 60 | 944 | 1,169 | 4,791 | 5,256 | 10,885 | 9,994 |
| 10 to 14 years | 20,677 | 20,880 | 15,399 | 15,169 | 3,155 | 3,122 | 318 | 334 | 922 | 1,117 | 54 | 61 | 829 | 1,075 | 4,525 | 5,279 | 11,449 | 10,615 |
| 15 to 19 years | 22,042 | 21,097 | 16,347 | 15,476 | 3,573 | 3,176 | 340 | 324 | 999 | 1,148 | 60 | 58 | 723 | 915 | 4,532 | 4,975 | 12,387 | 11,143 |
| 20 to 24 years | 21,588 | 21,874 | 16,247 | 15,964 | 3,240 | 3,365 | 319 | 326 | 1,149 | 1,341 | 66 | 61 | 566 | 817 | 4,322 | 4,839 | 12,468 | 11,730 |
| 25 to 29 years | 21,103 | 23,562 | 16,061 | 17,057 | 2,912 | 3,730 | 300 | 346 | 1,279 | 1,656 | 64 | 70 | 488 | 702 | 4,311 | 4,877 | 12,269 | 12,794 |
| 30 to 34 years | 19,963 | 22,136 | 15,185 | 16,387 | 2,744 | 3,144 | 275 | 310 | 1,284 | 1,680 | 56 | 70 | 420 | 546 | 4,125 | 4,552 | 11,534 | 12,392 |
| 35 to 39 years | 20,180 | 21,564 | 15,473 | 16,129 | 2,707 | 2,985 | 261 | 294 | 1,334 | 1,607 | 49 | 66 | 357 | 484 | 3,856 | 4,479 | 12,018 | 12,185 |
| 40 to 44 years | 20,892 | 19,714 | 16,342 | 14,852 | 2,752 | 2,675 | 251 | 263 | 1,188 | 1,477 | 45 | 54 | 314 | 393 | 3,442 | 4,108 | 13,250 | 11,202 |
| 45 to 49 years | 22,709 | 20,747 | 18,103 | 15,919 | 2,902 | 2,747 | 255 | 255 | 1,105 | 1,426 | 43 | 50 | 302 | 350 | 3,022 | 3,761 | 15,387 | 12,553 |
| 50 to 54 years | 22,299 | 20,885 | 18,009 | 16,352 | 2,753 | 2,730 | 228 | 243 | 1,004 | 1,213 | 37 | 45 | 268 | 301 | 2,442 | 3,265 | 15,813 | 13,424 |
| 55 to 59 years | 19,665 | 21,941 | 16,144 | 17,535 | 2,246 | 2,725 | 177 | 236 | 863 | 1,117 | 28 | 42 | 207 | 287 | 1,841 | 2,750 | 14,476 | 15,068 |
| 60 to 64 years | 16,818 | 20,332 | 14,089 | 16,483 | 1,715 | 2,375 | 134 | 197 | 703 | 1,005 | 21 | 34 | 156 | 238 | 1,372 | 2,141 | 12,839 | 14,557 |
| 65 to 69 years | 12,436 | 17,087 | 10,564 | 14,084 | 1,181 | 1,819 | 89 | 145 | 483 | 837 | 14 | 26 | 105 | 175 | 949 | 1,566 | 9,694 | 12,666 |
| 70 to 74 years | 9,278 | 13,405 | 7,911 | 11,304 | 865 | 1,250 | 60 | 101 | 361 | 609 | 9 | 18 | 72 | 124 | 700 | 1,117 | 7,266 | 10,286 |
| 75 to 79 years | 7,318 | 9,267 | 6,341 | 7,879 | 625 | 825 | 39 | 63 | 255 | 410 | 6 | 11 | 51 | 79 | 511 | 741 | 5,867 | 7,199 |
| 80 to 84 years | 5,744 | 6,127 | 5,079 | 5,229 | 430 | 532 | 25 | 38 | 171 | 272 | 4 | 7 | 35 | 49 | 351 | 496 | 4,752 | 4,772 |
| 85 years and over | 5,495 | 6,545 | 4,918 | 5,665 | 386 | 517 | 19 | 34 | 140 | 276 | 3 | 6 | 30 | 47 | 271 | 499 | 4,666 | 5,201 |
| **SPECIAL AGE CATEGORIES** | | | | | | | | | | | | | | | | | | |
| Under 18 years | 74,182 | 73,399 | 54,746 | 53,007 | 11,317 | 11,076 | 1,168 | 1,166 | 3,411 | 3,934 | 203 | 219 | 3,337 | 3,997 | 17,131 | 18,701 | 39,890 | 36,953 |
| Under 5 years | 20,201 | 19,810 | 14,691 | 14,161 | 3,055 | 3,018 | 330 | 317 | 948 | 1,056 | 59 | 62 | 1,119 | 1,196 | 5,114 | 5,172 | 10,307 | 9,767 |
| 5 to 13 years | 36,860 | 36,908 | 27,331 | 26,608 | 5,530 | 5,580 | 576 | 592 | 1,707 | 1,974 | 99 | 110 | 1,617 | 2,045 | 8,426 | 9,517 | 20,002 | 18,437 |
| 14 to 17 years | 17,121 | 16,681 | 12,724 | 12,238 | 2,732 | 2,478 | 263 | 258 | 756 | 904 | 45 | 47 | 601 | 757 | 3,591 | 4,012 | 9,582 | 8,749 |
| 18 to 64 years | 194,305 | 201,337 | 152,388 | 152,972 | 25,450 | 27,785 | 2,339 | 2,599 | 10,338 | 12,993 | 436 | 514 | 3,354 | 4,474 | 30,566 | 36,752 | 125,192 | 120,469 |
| 18 to 24 years | 30,674 | 30,457 | 22,982 | 22,257 | 4,719 | 4,674 | 459 | 457 | 1,579 | 1,811 | 92 | 84 | 844 | 1,174 | 6,154 | 6,820 | 17,606 | 16,295 |
| 25 to 44 years | 82,138 | 86,976 | 63,061 | 64,424 | 11,114 | 12,534 | 1,087 | 1,212 | 5,084 | 6,421 | 214 | 260 | 1,578 | 2,125 | 15,734 | 18,016 | 49,070 | 48,572 |
| 45 to 64 years | 81,492 | 83,904 | 66,345 | 66,290 | 9,617 | 10,578 | 793 | 930 | 3,675 | 4,761 | 130 | 170 | 932 | 1,175 | 8,678 | 11,916 | 58,515 | 55,602 |
| 65 years and over | 40,271 | 52,431 | 34,812 | 44,161 | 3,488 | 4,944 | 232 | 382 | 1,410 | 2,404 | 36 | 67 | 293 | 475 | 2,782 | 4,418 | 32,244 | 40,124 |
| 85 years and over | 5,495 | 6,545 | 4,918 | 5,665 | 386 | 517 | 19 | 34 | 140 | 276 | 3 | 6 | 30 | 47 | 271 | 499 | 4,666 | 5,201 |
| 16 years and over | 243,288 | 262,141 | 193,656 | 203,275 | 30,361 | 33,989 | 2,706 | 3,110 | 12,130 | 15,847 | 495 | 604 | 3,939 | 5,316 | 35,154 | 43,163 | 162,310 | 165,001 |
| 18 years and over | 234,576 | 253,768 | 187,200 | 197,132 | 28,937 | 32,728 | 2,571 | 2,981 | 11,749 | 15,397 | 471 | 581 | 3,647 | 4,949 | 33,348 | 41,171 | 157,436 | 160,594 |
| 15 to 44 years | 125,768 | 129,946 | 95,655 | 95,865 | 17,928 | 19,075 | 1,746 | 1,862 | 7,232 | 8,909 | 341 | 379 | 2,867 | 3,857 | 24,589 | 27,831 | 73,925 | 71,445 |
| Median age (years)[3] | 37.2 | 38.2 | 39.0 | 40.1 | 32.0 | 33.8 | 29.0 | 31.6 | 35.1 | 36.8 | 28.3 | 31.9 | 19.1 | 20.7 | 27.3 | 29.5 | 42.0 | 43.6 |

[1] The April 1, 2010 population estimates base reflects changes to the Census 2010 population from the Count Question Resolution program and geographic program revisions. [2] Hispanic origin is considered an ethnicity, not a race. Persons of Hispanic origin may be of any race. [3] For definition of median, see Guide to Tabular Presentation.

Source: U.S. Census Bureau, "Annual Estimates of the Resident Population by Sex, Age, Race, and Hispanic Origin for the United States and States: April 1, 2010 to July 1, 2018," <http://factfinder.census.gov>, accessed June 2019.

# Table 10. Resident Population by Race, Hispanic Origin, and Single Years of Age: 2018

[In thousands, except as indicated (327,167 represents 327,167,000). As of July 1. For derivation of estimates, see text, this section]

| Age | Total | Race | | | | | | Hispanic origin [1] | Non-Hispanic White alone |
|---|---|---|---|---|---|---|---|---|---|
| | | White alone | Black or African American alone | American Indian, Alaska Native alone | Asian alone | Native Hawaiian and Other Pacific Islander alone | Two or more races | | |
| Total............. | 327,167 | 250,139 | 43,804 | 4,148 | 19,331 | 799 | 8,946 | 59,872 | 197,546 |
| Under 5 years old............. | 19,810 | 14,161 | 3,018 | 317 | 1,056 | 62 | 1,196 | 5,172 | 9,767 |
| Under 1 year old............. | 3,848 | 2,757 | 586 | 62 | 195 | 12 | 237 | 1,008 | 1,902 |
| 1 year old............. | 3,913 | 2,801 | 595 | 62 | 205 | 12 | 237 | 1,023 | 1,933 |
| 2 years old............. | 3,991 | 2,852 | 608 | 64 | 214 | 13 | 241 | 1,051 | 1,958 |
| 3 years old............. | 4,037 | 2,878 | 615 | 64 | 224 | 13 | 242 | 1,051 | 1,985 |
| 4 years old............. | 4,021 | 2,872 | 614 | 65 | 219 | 12 | 239 | 1,040 | 1,989 |
| 5 to 9 years old............. | 20,196 | 14,493 | 3,068 | 323 | 1,083 | 60 | 1,169 | 5,256 | 9,994 |
| 5 years old............. | 4,010 | 2,863 | 611 | 64 | 223 | 12 | 236 | 1,036 | 1,981 |
| 6 years old............. | 4,015 | 2,879 | 611 | 65 | 215 | 12 | 233 | 1,043 | 1,988 |
| 7 years old............. | 4,059 | 2,927 | 614 | 63 | 210 | 12 | 233 | 1,071 | 2,005 |
| 8 years old............. | 4,056 | 2,911 | 613 | 65 | 218 | 12 | 236 | 1,060 | 2,003 |
| 9 years old............. | 4,055 | 2,912 | 618 | 65 | 217 | 12 | 230 | 1,047 | 2,017 |
| 10 to 14 years old............. | 20,880 | 15,169 | 3,122 | 334 | 1,117 | 61 | 1,075 | 5,279 | 10,615 |
| 10 years old............. | 4,184 | 3,010 | 638 | 67 | 225 | 13 | 231 | 1,081 | 2,083 |
| 11 years old............. | 4,203 | 3,039 | 637 | 68 | 221 | 13 | 224 | 1,082 | 2,109 |
| 12 years old............. | 4,168 | 3,032 | 623 | 67 | 220 | 12 | 214 | 1,060 | 2,117 |
| 13 years old............. | 4,157 | 3,033 | 614 | 67 | 225 | 12 | 206 | 1,039 | 2,135 |
| 14 years old............. | 4,167 | 3,055 | 610 | 65 | 226 | 12 | 199 | 1,018 | 2,171 |
| 15 to 19 years old............. | 21,097 | 15,476 | 3,176 | 324 | 1,148 | 58 | 915 | 4,975 | 11,143 |
| 15 years old............. | 4,141 | 3,041 | 607 | 64 | 227 | 12 | 190 | 1,002 | 2,170 |
| 16 years old............. | 4,131 | 3,033 | 619 | 64 | 220 | 11 | 184 | 991 | 2,171 |
| 17 years old............. | 4,242 | 3,109 | 642 | 65 | 231 | 12 | 184 | 1,001 | 2,237 |
| 18 years old............. | 4,320 | 3,163 | 661 | 66 | 235 | 12 | 182 | 1,004 | 2,287 |
| 19 years old............. | 4,264 | 3,129 | 647 | 65 | 235 | 12 | 176 | 977 | 2,278 |
| 20 to 24 years old............. | 21,874 | 15,964 | 3,365 | 326 | 1,341 | 61 | 817 | 4,839 | 11,730 |
| 20 years old............. | 4,274 | 3,130 | 652 | 65 | 244 | 12 | 171 | 967 | 2,286 |
| 21 years old............. | 4,293 | 3,144 | 652 | 64 | 255 | 12 | 167 | 961 | 2,304 |
| 22 years old............. | 4,335 | 3,173 | 654 | 64 | 269 | 12 | 163 | 959 | 2,334 |
| 23 years old............. | 4,439 | 3,233 | 688 | 65 | 281 | 13 | 160 | 971 | 2,382 |
| 24 years old............. | 4,534 | 3,284 | 720 | 67 | 293 | 13 | 157 | 981 | 2,425 |
| 25 to 29 years old............. | 23,562 | 17,057 | 3,730 | 346 | 1,656 | 70 | 702 | 4,877 | 12,794 |
| 25 years old............. | 4,606 | 3,329 | 742 | 69 | 303 | 13 | 151 | 985 | 2,465 |
| 26 years old............. | 4,729 | 3,418 | 758 | 71 | 319 | 13 | 149 | 1,000 | 2,542 |
| 27 years old............. | 4,814 | 3,479 | 768 | 71 | 339 | 15 | 143 | 990 | 2,616 |
| 28 years old............. | 4,802 | 3,480 | 755 | 69 | 347 | 15 | 135 | 976 | 2,628 |
| 29 years old............. | 4,611 | 3,351 | 707 | 66 | 348 | 14 | 125 | 927 | 2,542 |
| 30 to 34 years old............. | 22,136 | 16,387 | 3,144 | 310 | 1,680 | 70 | 546 | 4,552 | 12,392 |
| 30 years old............. | 4,501 | 3,302 | 664 | 64 | 339 | 14 | 118 | 920 | 2,497 |
| 31 years old............. | 4,422 | 3,263 | 637 | 62 | 333 | 14 | 112 | 907 | 2,467 |
| 32 years old............. | 4,434 | 3,289 | 626 | 62 | 335 | 14 | 108 | 913 | 2,488 |
| 33 years old............. | 4,461 | 3,319 | 623 | 61 | 338 | 14 | 106 | 919 | 2,512 |
| 34 years old............. | 4,318 | 3,214 | 595 | 60 | 335 | 13 | 101 | 893 | 2,429 |
| 35 to 39 years old............. | 21,564 | 16,129 | 2,985 | 294 | 1,607 | 66 | 484 | 4,479 | 12,185 |
| 35 years old............. | 4,376 | 3,265 | 601 | 61 | 334 | 14 | 102 | 907 | 2,467 |
| 36 years old............. | 4,367 | 3,264 | 599 | 60 | 331 | 14 | 99 | 908 | 2,464 |
| 37 years old............. | 4,313 | 3,234 | 594 | 58 | 317 | 13 | 97 | 895 | 2,445 |
| 38 years old............. | 4,391 | 3,285 | 617 | 60 | 320 | 13 | 96 | 920 | 2,474 |
| 39 years old............. | 4,116 | 3,082 | 574 | 55 | 304 | 12 | 89 | 849 | 2,334 |
| 40 to 44 years old............. | 19,714 | 14,852 | 2,675 | 263 | 1,477 | 54 | 393 | 4,108 | 11,202 |
| 40 years old............. | 4,031 | 3,033 | 553 | 54 | 295 | 11 | 86 | 843 | 2,287 |
| 41 years old............. | 3,986 | 3,000 | 545 | 54 | 294 | 11 | 83 | 835 | 2,260 |
| 42 years old............. | 3,866 | 2,908 | 524 | 52 | 293 | 11 | 78 | 819 | 2,182 |
| 43 years old............. | 3,980 | 3,003 | 537 | 52 | 301 | 11 | 75 | 824 | 2,269 |
| 44 years old............. | 3,851 | 2,908 | 517 | 51 | 294 | 10 | 72 | 788 | 2,203 |
| 45 to 49 years old............. | 20,747 | 15,919 | 2,747 | 255 | 1,426 | 50 | 350 | 3,761 | 12,553 |
| 45 years old............. | 3,904 | 2,947 | 531 | 51 | 294 | 10 | 71 | 775 | 2,254 |
| 46 years old............. | 4,074 | 3,102 | 549 | 51 | 292 | 10 | 71 | 766 | 2,416 |
| 47 years old............. | 4,301 | 3,311 | 570 | 52 | 285 | 10 | 72 | 760 | 2,631 |
| 48 years old............. | 4,350 | 3,361 | 570 | 52 | 286 | 10 | 71 | 755 | 2,685 |
| 49 years old............. | 4,118 | 3,199 | 527 | 49 | 268 | 9 | 65 | 704 | 2,568 |
| 50 to 54 years old............. | 20,885 | 16,352 | 2,730 | 243 | 1,213 | 45 | 301 | 3,265 | 13,424 |
| 50 years old............. | 4,026 | 3,124 | 529 | 48 | 255 | 9 | 61 | 684 | 2,511 |
| 51 years old............. | 4,025 | 3,148 | 526 | 47 | 235 | 9 | 59 | 656 | 2,559 |
| 52 years old............. | 4,094 | 3,197 | 544 | 48 | 238 | 9 | 59 | 648 | 2,616 |
| 53 years old............. | 4,333 | 3,403 | 569 | 50 | 241 | 9 | 61 | 652 | 2,818 |
| 54 years old............. | 4,406 | 3,480 | 563 | 50 | 243 | 9 | 60 | 624 | 2,920 |
| 55 to 59 years old............. | 21,941 | 17,535 | 2,725 | 236 | 1,117 | 42 | 287 | 2,750 | 15,068 |
| 55 years old............. | 4,394 | 3,482 | 553 | 49 | 242 | 9 | 60 | 594 | 2,949 |
| 56 years old............. | 4,377 | 3,496 | 545 | 48 | 221 | 9 | 58 | 569 | 2,985 |
| 57 years old............. | 4,423 | 3,549 | 544 | 47 | 216 | 8 | 58 | 545 | 3,059 |
| 58 years old............. | 4,453 | 3,558 | 555 | 48 | 226 | 8 | 57 | 545 | 3,069 |
| 59 years old............. | 4,294 | 3,451 | 527 | 44 | 211 | 8 | 54 | 496 | 3,005 |

See footnotes at end of table.

| Age | Total | Race | | | | | | Hispanic origin [1] | Non-Hispanic White alone |
|-----|-------|------|--|--|--|--|--|--------------------|-------------------------|
| | | White alone | Black or African American alone | American Indian, Alaska Native alone | Asian alone | Native Hawaiian and Other Pacific Islander alone | Two or more races | | |
| 60 to 64 years old............ | 20,332 | 16,483 | 2,375 | 197 | 1,005 | 34 | 238 | 2,141 | 14,557 |
| 60 years old................ | 4,259 | 3,438 | 509 | 43 | 211 | 7 | 52 | 468 | 3,017 |
| 61 years old................ | 4,203 | 3,400 | 500 | 42 | 204 | 7 | 50 | 451 | 2,995 |
| 62 years old................ | 4,043 | 3,271 | 476 | 40 | 202 | 7 | 48 | 429 | 2,886 |
| 63 years old................ | 4,000 | 3,249 | 461 | 38 | 201 | 6 | 46 | 414 | 2,875 |
| 64 years old................ | 3,826 | 3,126 | 429 | 35 | 188 | 6 | 42 | 378 | 2,785 |
| 65 to 69 years old............ | 17,087 | 14,084 | 1,819 | 145 | 837 | 26 | 175 | 1,566 | 12,666 |
| 65 years old................ | 3,670 | 3,014 | 398 | 33 | 179 | 6 | 40 | 351 | 2,696 |
| 66 years old................ | 3,516 | 2,901 | 374 | 30 | 170 | 5 | 36 | 325 | 2,606 |
| 67 years old................ | 3,399 | 2,800 | 367 | 29 | 163 | 5 | 35 | 313 | 2,517 |
| 68 years old................ | 3,308 | 2,718 | 354 | 28 | 170 | 5 | 34 | 301 | 2,445 |
| 69 years old................ | 3,194 | 2,652 | 325 | 26 | 155 | 5 | 31 | 275 | 2,402 |
| 70 to 74 years old............ | 13,405 | 11,304 | 1,250 | 101 | 609 | 18 | 124 | 1,117 | 10,286 |
| 70 years old................ | 3,144 | 2,634 | 306 | 24 | 146 | 4 | 30 | 263 | 2,395 |
| 71 years old................ | 3,261 | 2,780 | 287 | 24 | 136 | 4 | 30 | 249 | 2,554 |
| 72 years old................ | 2,392 | 2,004 | 228 | 19 | 115 | 4 | 23 | 216 | 1,808 |
| 73 years old................ | 2,345 | 1,968 | 223 | 18 | 110 | 3 | 22 | 204 | 1,782 |
| 74 years old................ | 2,263 | 1,917 | 206 | 16 | 101 | 3 | 20 | 185 | 1,747 |
| 75 to 79 years old............ | 9,267 | 7,879 | 825 | 63 | 410 | 11 | 79 | 741 | 7,199 |
| 75 years old................ | 2,294 | 1,964 | 199 | 15 | 93 | 3 | 19 | 175 | 1,804 |
| 76 years old................ | 1,978 | 1,681 | 176 | 14 | 89 | 2 | 17 | 156 | 1,538 |
| 77 years old................ | 1,786 | 1,513 | 162 | 12 | 81 | 2 | 15 | 145 | 1,380 |
| 78 years old................ | 1,666 | 1,407 | 153 | 12 | 78 | 2 | 14 | 138 | 1,280 |
| 79 years old................ | 1,543 | 1,313 | 136 | 10 | 70 | 2 | 13 | 126 | 1,197 |
| 80 to 84 years old............ | 6,127 | 5,229 | 532 | 38 | 272 | 7 | 49 | 496 | 4,772 |
| 80 years old................ | 1,452 | 1,237 | 127 | 10 | 65 | 2 | 12 | 117 | 1,129 |
| 81 years old................ | 1,311 | 1,117 | 114 | 8 | 59 | 1 | 11 | 107 | 1,019 |
| 82 years old................ | 1,224 | 1,044 | 108 | 8 | 54 | 1 | 10 | 99 | 952 |
| 83 years old................ | 1,144 | 979 | 98 | 7 | 50 | 1 | 9 | 93 | 893 |
| 84 years old................ | 996 | 853 | 85 | 6 | 44 | 1 | 8 | 80 | 779 |
| 85 to 89 years old............ | 3,899 | 3,376 | 307 | 21 | 163 | 4 | 28 | 301 | 3,096 |
| 85 years old................ | 933 | 801 | 78 | 5 | 41 | 1 | 7 | 72 | 735 |
| 86 years old................ | 857 | 741 | 68 | 5 | 36 | 1 | 6 | 66 | 680 |
| 87 years old................ | 782 | 680 | 60 | 4 | 32 | 1 | 6 | 61 | 624 |
| 88 years old................ | 715 | 621 | 55 | 4 | 30 | 1 | 5 | 56 | 569 |
| 89 years old................ | 611 | 532 | 46 | 3 | 25 | 1 | 4 | 47 | 489 |
| 90 to 94 years old............ | 1,959 | 1,705 | 149 | 10 | 79 | 2 | 14 | 145 | 1,571 |
| 90 years old................ | 540 | 471 | 40 | 3 | 22 | (Z) | 4 | 40 | 433 |
| 91 years old................ | 462 | 403 | 35 | 2 | 18 | (Z) | 3 | 34 | 371 |
| 92 years old................ | 382 | 332 | 30 | 2 | 15 | (Z) | 3 | 29 | 306 |
| 93 years old................ | 320 | 278 | 25 | 2 | 13 | (Z) | 2 | 24 | 256 |
| 94 years old................ | 255 | 222 | 20 | 1 | 11 | (Z) | 2 | 19 | 204 |
| 95 to 99 years old............ | 593 | 508 | 50 | 3 | 27 | 1 | 4 | 45 | 467 |
| 95 years old................ | 198 | 171 | 16 | 1 | 9 | (Z) | 1 | 15 | 157 |
| 96 years old................ | 151 | 130 | 12 | 1 | 7 | (Z) | 1 | 11 | 119 |
| 97 years old................ | 113 | 97 | 9 | 1 | 5 | (Z) | 1 | 8 | 89 |
| 98 years old................ | 78 | 66 | 7 | (Z) | 4 | (Z) | 1 | 6 | 60 |
| 99 years old................ | 53 | 44 | 5 | (Z) | 3 | (Z) | (Z) | 4 | 41 |
| 100 years old and over....... | 94 | 76 | 11 | 1 | 6 | (Z) | 1 | 8 | 68 |
| Median age (years) [2]........ | 38.2 | 40.1 | 33.8 | 31.6 | 36.8 | 31.9 | 20.7 | 29.5 | 43.6 |

Z Less than 500. [1] Persons of Hispanic origin may be of any race. [2] For definition of median, see Guide to Tabular Presentation.

Source: U.S. Census Bureau, Population Division, "Annual Estimates of the Resident Population by Sex, Single Year of Age, Race, and Hispanic Origin for the United States: April 1, 2010 to July 1, 2018," <http://factfinder.census.gov>, accessed June 2019.

# Table 11. Resident Population Projections by Race, Hispanic Origin, and Age: 2020

[In thousands (332,639 represents 332,639,000). As of July 1. The 2017 National Projections are based on the July 1, 2016 population estimates, which are based on the 2010 Census. The projections were produced using a cohort-component method and are based on assumptions about future births, deaths, and net international migration. More information on methodology and assumptions is available at <https://www.census.gov/programs-surveys/popproj/technical-documentation/methodology.html>]

| Age group | Total | White alone | Black or African American alone | American Indian/ Alaska Native alone | Asian alone | Native Hawaiian/ Other Pacific Islander alone | Two or more races | Hispanic origin [1] | Not Hispanic, White alone |
|---|---|---|---|---|---|---|---|---|---|
| Total.................... | 332,639 | 253,280 | 44,734 | 4,232 | 20,009 | 813 | 9,570 | 62,313 | 198,571 |
| Under 5 years............... | 20,439 | 14,363 | 3,197 | 317 | 1,142 | 55 | 1,364 | 5,126 | 10,025 |
| 5 to 9 years................ | 20,200 | 14,452 | 3,064 | 322 | 1,113 | 62 | 1,187 | 5,278 | 9,948 |
| 10 to 14 years.............. | 20,770 | 14,978 | 3,133 | 333 | 1,125 | 62 | 1,139 | 5,380 | 10,355 |
| 15 to 19 years.............. | 21,038 | 15,413 | 3,105 | 326 | 1,169 | 59 | 966 | 5,144 | 10,939 |
| 20 to 24 years.............. | 21,899 | 16,024 | 3,297 | 326 | 1,330 | 59 | 863 | 5,068 | 11,585 |
| 25 to 29 years.............. | 23,512 | 17,004 | 3,706 | 346 | 1,627 | 67 | 763 | 5,096 | 12,530 |
| 30 to 34 years.............. | 22,979 | 16,853 | 3,395 | 324 | 1,736 | 72 | 598 | 4,739 | 12,696 |
| 35 to 39 years.............. | 21,922 | 16,378 | 3,008 | 300 | 1,663 | 68 | 505 | 4,559 | 12,362 |
| 40 to 44 years.............. | 20,430 | 15,335 | 2,806 | 274 | 1,525 | 59 | 432 | 4,269 | 11,558 |
| 45 to 49 years.............. | 20,105 | 15,270 | 2,691 | 256 | 1,478 | 50 | 360 | 3,926 | 11,756 |
| 50 to 54 years.............. | 20,510 | 15,950 | 2,672 | 241 | 1,287 | 46 | 314 | 3,428 | 12,874 |
| 55 to 59 years.............. | 21,772 | 17,283 | 2,738 | 240 | 1,173 | 44 | 295 | 2,978 | 14,609 |
| 60 to 64 years.............. | 21,011 | 16,932 | 2,518 | 210 | 1,056 | 37 | 258 | 2,391 | 14,783 |
| 65 to 69 years.............. | 18,030 | 14,798 | 1,971 | 158 | 881 | 27 | 195 | 1,767 | 13,200 |
| 70 to 74 years.............. | 14,759 | 12,358 | 1,429 | 114 | 697 | 20 | 141 | 1,278 | 11,195 |
| 75 to 79 years.............. | 10,053 | 8,535 | 896 | 69 | 452 | 12 | 88 | 830 | 7,775 |
| 80 to 84 years.............. | 6,508 | 5,542 | 571 | 42 | 293 | 7 | 53 | 543 | 5,042 |
| 85 to 89 years.............. | 3,043 | 2,401 | 325 | 22 | 162 | 4 | 30 | 313 | 3,111 |
| 90 to 94 years.............. | 2,017 | 1,765 | 152 | 10 | 75 | 2 | 14 | 148 | 1,627 |
| 95 to 99 years.............. | 649 | 568 | 50 | 3 | 23 | (Z) | 4 | 43 | 527 |
| 100 years and over......... | 92 | 78 | 9 | (Z) | 4 | (Z) | 1 | 6 | 73 |
| SPECIAL CATEGORIES | | | | | | | | | |
| 5 to 13 years................ | 36,780 | 26,383 | 5,573 | 588 | 2,013 | 112 | 2,112 | 9,588 | 18,180 |
| 14 to 17 years............... | 16,748 | 12,242 | 2,461 | 264 | 921 | 48 | 812 | 4,172 | 8,625 |
| 18 to 24 years............... | 30,380 | 22,243 | 4,565 | 455 | 1,803 | 83 | 1,232 | 7,110 | 16,022 |
| 16 years and over........... | 267,049 | 206,436 | 34,725 | 3,193 | 16,400 | 622 | 5,673 | 45,479 | 166,102 |
| 18 years and over........... | 258,672 | 200,292 | 33,503 | 3,064 | 15,933 | 599 | 5,282 | 43,427 | 161,740 |
| 16 to 64 years.............. | 210,998 | 159,390 | 29,322 | 2,775 | 13,814 | 549 | 5,147 | 40,550 | 123,550 |
| 55 years and over........... | 98,834 | 81,260 | 10,660 | 868 | 4,814 | 153 | 1,078 | 10,298 | 71,943 |
| 65 years and over........... | 56,052 | 47,046 | 5,404 | 418 | 2,585 | 73 | 526 | 4,929 | 42,551 |
| 75 years and over........... | 23,262 | 19,890 | 2,003 | 146 | 1,008 | 26 | 190 | 1,884 | 18,156 |
| 85 years and over........... | 6,701 | 5,813 | 536 | 35 | 263 | 6 | 48 | 511 | 5,339 |

Z Less than 500. [1] Hispanic origin is considered an ethnicity, not a race. Persons of Hispanic origin may be of any race.

Source: U.S. Census Bureau, 2017 National Population Projections Datasets, "Table 1. Projected Population by Single Year of Age, Sex, Race, and Hispanic Origin for the United States: 2016 to 2060," September 2018, <https://census.gov/programs-surveys/popproj/data/datasets.html>, accessed September 2018.

# Table 12. Resident Population Projections for Native and Foreign-Born Populations by Age Group: 2020 to 2060

[In thousands (332,639 represents 332,639,000). As of July 1. Based on 2017 National Projections, see headnote Table 11]

| Nativity and age group | 2020 | 2025 | 2030 | 2035 | 2040 | 2045 | 2050 | 2055 | 2060 |
|---|---|---|---|---|---|---|---|---|---|
| Total population.............. | 332,639 | 344,234 | 355,101 | 364,862 | 373,528 | 381,390 | 388,922 | 396,557 | 404,483 |
| Under 18 years...................... | 73,967 | 74,654 | 75,652 | 76,664 | 77,131 | 77,561 | 78,225 | 79,148 | 80,137 |
| Under 5 years....................... | 20,439 | 20,868 | 20,976 | 20,993 | 21,106 | 21,319 | 21,610 | 21,914 | 22,144 |
| 5 to 13 years....................... | 36,780 | 37,074 | 38,051 | 38,453 | 38,568 | 38,715 | 39,049 | 39,532 | 40,090 |
| 14 to 17 years...................... | 16,748 | 16,712 | 16,625 | 17,217 | 17,457 | 17,527 | 17,566 | 17,701 | 17,903 |
| 18 to 64 years...................... | 202,621 | 204,354 | 206,311 | 210,201 | 215,571 | 220,995 | 225,023 | 227,794 | 229,670 |
| 18 to 24 years...................... | 30,380 | 30,554 | 30,612 | 30,519 | 31,369 | 31,943 | 32,126 | 32,229 | 32,467 |
| 25 to 44 years...................... | 88,843 | 92,328 | 94,370 | 95,368 | 95,067 | 96,054 | 97,459 | 98,727 | 100,230 |
| 45 to 64 years...................... | 83,398 | 81,472 | 81,329 | 84,314 | 89,135 | 92,998 | 95,437 | 96,838 | 96,973 |
| 65 years and over................... | 56,052 | 65,226 | 73,138 | 77,997 | 80,827 | 82,835 | 85,675 | 89,615 | 94,676 |
| Native population.............. | 285,936 | 293,965 | 301,318 | 307,758 | 313,372 | 318,497 | 323,612 | 329,123 | 335,150 |
| Under 18 years...................... | 71,353 | 72,145 | 73,115 | 74,088 | 74,469 | 74,825 | 75,425 | 76,294 | 77,235 |
| Under 5 years....................... | 20,153 | 20,592 | 20,689 | 20,697 | 20,801 | 21,006 | 21,292 | 21,591 | 21,815 |
| 5 to 13 years....................... | 35,462 | 35,780 | 36,770 | 37,123 | 37,194 | 37,303 | 37,603 | 38,059 | 38,592 |
| 14 to 17 years...................... | 15,738 | 15,772 | 15,656 | 16,268 | 16,475 | 16,516 | 16,530 | 16,644 | 16,828 |
| 18 to 64 years...................... | 166,549 | 166,637 | 167,354 | 170,136 | 174,634 | 179,178 | 182,350 | 184,223 | 185,264 |
| 18 to 24 years...................... | 27,225 | 27,470 | 27,588 | 27,433 | 28,233 | 28,732 | 28,837 | 28,873 | 29,053 |
| 25 to 44 years...................... | 72,200 | 75,428 | 77,224 | 77,935 | 77,366 | 78,041 | 79,107 | 79,984 | 81,113 |
| 45 to 64 years...................... | 67,124 | 63,740 | 62,542 | 64,767 | 69,036 | 72,404 | 74,406 | 75,367 | 75,098 |
| 65 years and over................... | 48,034 | 55,182 | 60,849 | 63,535 | 64,268 | 64,494 | 65,838 | 68,606 | 72,652 |
| Foreign-born population...... | 46,703 | 50,270 | 53,783 | 57,104 | 60,156 | 62,894 | 65,310 | 67,434 | 69,333 |
| Under 18 years...................... | 2,614 | 2,509 | 2,537 | 2,576 | 2,662 | 2,736 | 2,800 | 2,854 | 2,902 |
| Under 5 years....................... | 285 | 275 | 286 | 296 | 305 | 312 | 319 | 324 | 329 |
| 5 to 13 years....................... | 1,319 | 1,294 | 1,280 | 1,330 | 1,374 | 1,413 | 1,446 | 1,473 | 1,498 |
| 14 to 17 years...................... | 1,010 | 940 | 970 | 949 | 982 | 1,011 | 1,036 | 1,057 | 1,075 |
| 18 to 64 years...................... | 36,072 | 37,717 | 38,957 | 40,066 | 40,936 | 41,817 | 42,673 | 43,571 | 44,406 |
| 18 to 24 years...................... | 3,155 | 3,084 | 3,024 | 3,086 | 3,136 | 3,211 | 3,289 | 3,356 | 3,415 |
| 25 to 44 years...................... | 16,643 | 16,900 | 17,146 | 17,433 | 17,701 | 18,013 | 18,352 | 18,744 | 19,117 |
| 45 to 64 years...................... | 16,273 | 17,732 | 18,787 | 19,547 | 20,099 | 20,593 | 21,031 | 21,472 | 21,875 |
| 65 years and over................... | 8,017 | 10,044 | 12,289 | 14,462 | 16,559 | 18,341 | 19,837 | 21,009 | 22,024 |

Source: U.S. Census Bureau, 2017 National Population Projections Tables, "Table 2. Projected age and sex composition of the population," "Table 9. Age composition of the native-born population," and "Table 10. Age composition of the foreign-born population," September 2018, <https://www.census.gov/programs-surveys/popproj/data/tables.html>, accessed September 2018.

# Table 13. Resident Population Projections by Race/Ethnicity and Hispanic Origin: 2020 to 2060

[In thousands, except as indicated (332,639 represents 332,639,000). As of July 1. Data shown are modified race counts; see text, this section. The 2017 National Projections are based on the July 1, 2016 population estimates, which are based on the 2010 Census. The projections were produced using a cohort-component method and are based on assumptions about future births, deaths, and net international migration. More information on methodology and assumptions is available at <https://www.census.gov/programs-surveys/popproj/technical-documentation/methodology.html>]

| Characteristic | 2020 | 2025 | 2030 | 2035 | 2040 | 2045 | 2050 | 2060 |
|---|---|---|---|---|---|---|---|---|
| **Total** | **332,639** | **344,234** | **355,101** | **364,862** | **373,528** | **381,390** | **388,922** | **404,483** |
| One race | 323,069 | 333,181 | 342,432 | 350,454 | 357,252 | 363,105 | 368,473 | 379,228 |
| White | 253,280 | 258,778 | 263,453 | 267,057 | 269,578 | 271,249 | 272,486 | 275,014 |
| Black or African American | 44,734 | 46,906 | 49,009 | 51,002 | 52,919 | 54,814 | 56,725 | 60,690 |
| American Indian and Alaska Native | 4,232 | 4,452 | 4,663 | 4,859 | 5,038 | 5,199 | 5,341 | 5,583 |
| Asian | 20,009 | 22,181 | 24,394 | 26,579 | 28,718 | 30,806 | 32,850 | 36,815 |
| Native Hawaiian/Other Pacific Islander | 813 | 865 | 913 | 958 | 999 | 1,038 | 1,071 | 1,125 |
| Two or more races | 9,570 | 11,053 | 12,669 | 14,408 | 16,276 | 18,285 | 20,450 | 25,255 |
| Race alone or in combination: [1] | | | | | | | | |
| White | 261,811 | 268,702 | 274,901 | 280,151 | 284,447 | 288,035 | 291,344 | 298,488 |
| Black or African American | 49,137 | 52,177 | 55,248 | 58,303 | 61,383 | 64,550 | 67,855 | 74,984 |
| American Indian and Alaska Native | 7,052 | 7,485 | 7,910 | 8,316 | 8,699 | 9,060 | 9,404 | 10,059 |
| Asian | 23,522 | 26,253 | 29,074 | 31,916 | 34,764 | 37,614 | 40,476 | 46,250 |
| Native Hawaiian/Other Pacific Islander | 1,642 | 1,784 | 1,928 | 2,073 | 2,220 | 2,368 | 2,518 | 2,823 |
| **Not Hispanic** | **270,326** | **275,750** | **280,293** | **283,632** | **285,912** | **287,564** | **289,125** | **293,267** |
| One race | 262,710 | 266,968 | 270,242 | 272,225 | 273,055 | 273,150 | 273,030 | 273,450 |
| White | 198,571 | 198,751 | 197,992 | 196,105 | 193,210 | 189,671 | 185,954 | 179,162 |
| Black or African American | 41,702 | 43,548 | 45,322 | 46,978 | 48,550 | 50,098 | 51,664 | 54,949 |
| American Indian and Alaska Native | 2,445 | 2,514 | 2,575 | 2,623 | 2,659 | 2,683 | 2,701 | 2,722 |
| Asian | 19,393 | 21,516 | 23,678 | 25,810 | 27,895 | 29,928 | 31,917 | 35,779 |
| Native Hawaiian/Other Pacific Islander | 599 | 639 | 676 | 710 | 741 | 769 | 795 | 839 |
| Two or more races | 7,616 | 8,783 | 10,051 | 11,407 | 12,857 | 14,415 | 16,094 | 19,816 |
| Race alone or in combination: [1] | | | | | | | | |
| White | 205,358 | 206,638 | 207,078 | 206,480 | 204,970 | 202,923 | 200,821 | 197,620 |
| Black or African American | 45,184 | 47,720 | 50,263 | 52,759 | 55,247 | 57,769 | 60,462 | 66,233 |
| American Indian and Alaska Native | 4,457 | 4,645 | 4,822 | 4,978 | 5,112 | 5,233 | 5,347 | 5,572 |
| Asian | 22,366 | 24,959 | 27,630 | 30,308 | 32,975 | 35,630 | 38,285 | 43,607 |
| Native Hawaiian/Other Pacific Islander | 1,246 | 1,351 | 1,456 | 1,559 | 1,662 | 1,763 | 1,865 | 2,071 |
| **Hispanic [2]** | **62,313** | **68,484** | **74,807** | **81,230** | **87,616** | **93,826** | **99,798** | **111,216** |
| One race | 60,359 | 66,214 | 72,189 | 78,229 | 84,197 | 89,956 | 95,442 | 105,777 |
| White | 54,709 | 60,026 | 65,461 | 70,952 | 76,367 | 81,578 | 86,532 | 95,852 |
| Black or African American | 3,033 | 3,358 | 3,687 | 4,024 | 4,368 | 4,715 | 5,060 | 5,740 |
| American Indian and Alaska Native | 1,787 | 1,938 | 2,088 | 2,236 | 2,380 | 2,515 | 2,640 | 2,862 |
| Asian | 616 | 666 | 716 | 769 | 823 | 878 | 933 | 1,036 |
| Native Hawaiian/Other Pacific Islander | 214 | 226 | 237 | 248 | 259 | 268 | 277 | 286 |
| Two or more races | 1,954 | 2,270 | 2,618 | 3,000 | 3,419 | 3,871 | 4,355 | 5,439 |
| Race alone or in combination: [1] | | | | | | | | |
| White | 56,454 | 62,064 | 67,823 | 73,671 | 79,477 | 85,112 | 90,523 | 100,869 |
| Black or African American | 3,953 | 4,457 | 4,985 | 5,545 | 6,135 | 6,753 | 7,393 | 8,751 |
| American Indian and Alaska Native | 2,594 | 2,840 | 3,089 | 3,339 | 3,587 | 3,827 | 4,057 | 4,487 |
| Asian | 1,156 | 1,294 | 1,444 | 1,608 | 1,789 | 1,984 | 2,191 | 2,642 |
| Native Hawaiian/Other Pacific Islander | 396 | 433 | 472 | 514 | 558 | 605 | 653 | 752 |
| PERCENT DISTRIBUTION | | | | | | | | |
| **Total** | **100.0** | **100.0** | **100.0** | **100.0** | **100.0** | **100.0** | **100.0** | **100.0** |
| One race | 97.1 | 96.8 | 96.4 | 96.1 | 95.6 | 95.2 | 94.7 | 93.8 |
| White | 76.1 | 75.2 | 74.2 | 73.2 | 72.2 | 71.1 | 70.1 | 68.0 |
| Black or African American | 13.5 | 13.6 | 13.8 | 14.0 | 14.2 | 14.4 | 14.6 | 15.0 |
| American Indian and Alaska Native | 1.3 | 1.3 | 1.3 | 1.3 | 1.4 | 1.4 | 1.4 | 1.4 |
| Asian | 6.0 | 6.4 | 6.9 | 7.3 | 7.7 | 8.1 | 8.5 | 9.1 |
| Native Hawaiian/Other Pacific Islander | 0.2 | 0.3 | 0.3 | 0.3 | 0.3 | 0.3 | 0.3 | 0.3 |
| Two or more races | 2.9 | 3.2 | 3.6 | 4.0 | 4.4 | 4.8 | 5.3 | 6.2 |
| **Not Hispanic** | **81.3** | **80.1** | **78.9** | **77.7** | **76.5** | **75.4** | **74.3** | **72.5** |
| One race | 79.0 | 77.6 | 76.1 | 74.6 | 73.1 | 71.6 | 70.2 | 67.6 |
| White | 59.7 | 57.7 | 55.8 | 53.8 | 51.7 | 49.7 | 47.8 | 44.3 |
| Black or African American | 12.5 | 12.7 | 12.8 | 12.9 | 13.0 | 13.1 | 13.3 | 13.6 |
| American Indian and Alaska Native | 0.7 | 0.7 | 0.7 | 0.7 | 0.7 | 0.7 | 0.7 | 0.7 |
| Asian | 5.8 | 6.3 | 6.7 | 7.1 | 7.5 | 7.9 | 8.2 | 8.9 |
| Native Hawaiian/Other Pacific Islander | 0.2 | 0.2 | 0.2 | 0.2 | 0.2 | 0.2 | 0.2 | 0.2 |
| Two or more races | 2.3 | 2.6 | 2.8 | 3.1 | 3.4 | 3.8 | 4.1 | 4.9 |
| **Hispanic [2]** | **18.7** | **19.9** | **21.1** | **22.3** | **23.5** | **24.6** | **25.7** | **27.5** |
| One race | 18.2 | 19.2 | 20.3 | 21.4 | 22.5 | 23.6 | 24.5 | 26.2 |
| White | 16.5 | 17.4 | 18.4 | 19.5 | 20.4 | 21.4 | 22.3 | 23.7 |
| Black or African American | 0.9 | 1.0 | 1.0 | 1.1 | 1.2 | 1.2 | 1.3 | 1.4 |
| American Indian and Alaska Native | 0.5 | 0.6 | 0.6 | 0.6 | 0.6 | 0.7 | 0.7 | 0.7 |
| Asian | 0.2 | 0.2 | 0.2 | 0.2 | 0.2 | 0.2 | 0.2 | 0.3 |
| Native Hawaiian/Other Pacific Islander | 0.1 | 0.1 | 0.1 | 0.1 | 0.1 | 0.1 | 0.1 | 0.1 |
| Two or more races | 0.6 | 0.7 | 0.7 | 0.8 | 0.9 | 1.0 | 1.1 | 1.3 |

[1] In combination with one or more other races. The sum of the five race groups adds to more than the total population because individuals may report more than one race. The original race data from Census 2010 are modified to eliminate the "some other race" category. [2] Persons of Hispanic origin may be of any race.

Source: U.S. Census Bureau, 2017 National Population Projections Datasets, "Table 1. Projected Population by Single Year of Age, Sex, Race, and Hispanic Origin for the United States: 2016 to 2060," September 2018, <https://census.gov/programs-surveys/popproj/data/datasets.html>, accessed September 2018.

# Table 14. Resident Population by Region and State: 1990 to 2018

[In thousands (248,791 represents 248,791,000). 1990, 2000, and 2010 data as of April 1, data for other years as of July 1. Insofar as possible, population shown for all years is that of present area of state. See Appendix III]

| State and region | 1990, estimates base [1] | 2000, estimates base [2] | 2010, estimates base [3] | 2013 | 2014 | 2015 | 2016 | 2017 | 2018 |
|---|---|---|---|---|---|---|---|---|---|
| **United States** | **248,791** | **281,425** | **308,758** | **316,058** | **318,386** | **320,743** | **323,071** | **325,147** | **327,167** |
| Northeast | 50,828 | 53,595 | 55,318 | 55,908 | 56,016 | 56,048 | 56,059 | 56,073 | 56,111 |
| Midwest | 59,669 | 64,397 | 66,930 | 67,564 | 67,752 | 67,869 | 67,997 | 68,156 | 68,309 |
| South | 85,456 | 100,235 | 114,563 | 118,393 | 119,658 | 121,038 | 122,401 | 123,598 | 124,754 |
| West | 52,837 | 63,199 | 71,947 | 74,193 | 74,961 | 75,788 | 76,614 | 77,320 | 77,994 |
| Alabama | 4,040 | 4,447 | 4,780 | 4,830 | 4,842 | 4,853 | 4,865 | 4,875 | 4,888 |
| Alaska | 550 | 627 | 710 | 737 | 736 | 738 | 742 | 740 | 737 |
| Arizona | 3,665 | 5,130 | 6,392 | 6,635 | 6,734 | 6,834 | 6,945 | 7,049 | 7,172 |
| Arkansas | 2,351 | 2,673 | 2,916 | 2,960 | 2,968 | 2,978 | 2,990 | 3,003 | 3,014 |
| California | 29,811 | 33,872 | 37,255 | 38,281 | 38,625 | 38,953 | 39,209 | 39,399 | 39,557 |
| Colorado | 3,294 | 4,302 | 5,029 | 5,270 | 5,351 | 5,452 | 5,541 | 5,616 | 5,696 |
| Connecticut | 3,287 | 3,406 | 3,574 | 3,595 | 3,595 | 3,588 | 3,579 | 3,574 | 3,573 |
| Delaware | 666 | 784 | 898 | 924 | 933 | 941 | 949 | 957 | 967 |
| District of Columbia | 607 | 572 | 602 | 650 | 663 | 675 | 687 | 696 | 702 |
| Florida | 12,938 | 15,983 | 18,805 | 19,563 | 19,860 | 20,224 | 20,630 | 20,977 | 21,299 |
| Georgia | 6,478 | 8,187 | 9,689 | 9,973 | 10,069 | 10,181 | 10,305 | 10,413 | 10,519 |
| Hawaii | 1,108 | 1,211 | 1,360 | 1,408 | 1,415 | 1,422 | 1,428 | 1,424 | 1,420 |
| Idaho | 1,007 | 1,294 | 1,568 | 1,612 | 1,631 | 1,652 | 1,683 | 1,719 | 1,754 |
| Illinois | 11,431 | 12,420 | 12,832 | 12,898 | 12,889 | 12,864 | 12,827 | 12,786 | 12,741 |
| Indiana | 5,544 | 6,081 | 6,484 | 6,568 | 6,594 | 6,608 | 6,633 | 6,660 | 6,692 |
| Iowa | 2,777 | 2,927 | 3,047 | 3,093 | 3,110 | 3,121 | 3,132 | 3,144 | 3,156 |
| Kansas | 2,478 | 2,689 | 2,853 | 2,894 | 2,901 | 2,910 | 2,911 | 2,911 | 2,912 |
| Kentucky | 3,687 | 4,042 | 4,339 | 4,405 | 4,414 | 4,426 | 4,438 | 4,454 | 4,468 |
| Louisiana | 4,222 | 4,469 | 4,533 | 4,625 | 4,644 | 4,665 | 4,678 | 4,671 | 4,660 |
| Maine | 1,228 | 1,275 | 1,328 | 1,328 | 1,331 | 1,328 | 1,331 | 1,335 | 1,338 |
| Maryland | 4,781 | 5,297 | 5,774 | 5,924 | 5,958 | 5,987 | 6,005 | 6,025 | 6,043 |
| Massachusetts | 6,016 | 6,349 | 6,548 | 6,714 | 6,764 | 6,796 | 6,826 | 6,863 | 6,902 |
| Michigan | 9,295 | 9,939 | 9,884 | 9,913 | 9,931 | 9,933 | 9,952 | 9,976 | 9,996 |
| Minnesota | 4,376 | 4,920 | 5,304 | 5,414 | 5,452 | 5,483 | 5,523 | 5,568 | 5,611 |
| Mississippi | 2,575 | 2,845 | 2,968 | 2,989 | 2,991 | 2,989 | 2,988 | 2,990 | 2,987 |
| Missouri | 5,117 | 5,597 | 5,989 | 6,041 | 6,056 | 6,072 | 6,087 | 6,100 | 6,126 |
| Montana | 799 | 902 | 989 | 1,014 | 1,022 | 1,031 | 1,041 | 1,053 | 1,062 |
| Nebraska | 1,578 | 1,711 | 1,826 | 1,865 | 1,880 | 1,892 | 1,906 | 1,918 | 1,929 |
| Nevada | 1,202 | 1,998 | 2,701 | 2,777 | 2,819 | 2,869 | 2,920 | 2,972 | 3,034 |
| New Hampshire | 1,109 | 1,236 | 1,316 | 1,326 | 1,333 | 1,336 | 1,342 | 1,350 | 1,356 |
| New Jersey | 7,748 | 8,415 | 8,792 | 8,858 | 8,867 | 8,871 | 8,875 | 8,889 | 8,909 |
| New Mexico | 1,515 | 1,819 | 2,059 | 2,093 | 2,090 | 2,090 | 2,093 | 2,093 | 2,095 |
| New York | 17,991 | 18,977 | 19,378 | 19,628 | 19,656 | 19,661 | 19,642 | 19,591 | 19,542 |
| North Carolina | 6,632 | 8,046 | 9,536 | 9,844 | 9,934 | 10,033 | 10,157 | 10,271 | 10,384 |
| North Dakota | 639 | 642 | 673 | 722 | 737 | 754 | 754 | 755 | 760 |
| Ohio | 10,847 | 11,353 | 11,537 | 11,577 | 11,603 | 11,618 | 11,635 | 11,664 | 11,689 |
| Oklahoma | 3,146 | 3,450 | 3,752 | 3,853 | 3,878 | 3,910 | 3,927 | 3,933 | 3,943 |
| Oregon | 2,842 | 3,422 | 3,831 | 3,923 | 3,964 | 4,017 | 4,091 | 4,147 | 4,191 |
| Pennsylvania | 11,883 | 12,281 | 12,703 | 12,777 | 12,789 | 12,786 | 12,784 | 12,790 | 12,807 |
| Rhode Island | 1,003 | 1,048 | 1,053 | 1,055 | 1,056 | 1,056 | 1,057 | 1,056 | 1,057 |
| South Carolina | 3,486 | 4,012 | 4,625 | 4,764 | 4,824 | 4,892 | 4,958 | 5,021 | 5,084 |
| South Dakota | 696 | 755 | 814 | 842 | 849 | 854 | 863 | 873 | 882 |
| Tennessee | 4,877 | 5,689 | 6,346 | 6,493 | 6,541 | 6,591 | 6,645 | 6,709 | 6,770 |
| Texas | 16,986 | 20,851 | 25,146 | 26,489 | 26,977 | 27,487 | 27,937 | 28,323 | 28,702 |
| Utah | 1,723 | 2,233 | 2,764 | 2,898 | 2,937 | 2,982 | 3,043 | 3,103 | 3,161 |
| Vermont | 563 | 609 | 626 | 626 | 625 | 625 | 624 | 625 | 626 |
| Virginia | 6,189 | 7,079 | 8,001 | 8,253 | 8,312 | 8,363 | 8,411 | 8,465 | 8,518 |
| Washington | 4,867 | 5,894 | 6,725 | 6,963 | 7,052 | 7,164 | 7,295 | 7,425 | 7,536 |
| West Virginia | 1,793 | 1,808 | 1,853 | 1,854 | 1,849 | 1,842 | 1,831 | 1,817 | 1,806 |
| Wisconsin | 4,892 | 5,364 | 5,687 | 5,737 | 5,752 | 5,761 | 5,773 | 5,792 | 5,814 |
| Wyoming | 454 | 494 | 564 | 582 | 583 | 586 | 584 | 579 | 578 |

[1] The April 1, 1990 census counts include corrections processed through August 1997, results of special censuses and test censuses, and do not include adjustments for census coverage errors. [2] The April 1, 2000 population estimates base reflects changes to the Census 2000 population from the Count Question Resolution program, legal boundary updates, and other geographic program revisions. [3] The April 1, 2010 population estimates base reflects changes to the Census 2010 population from the Count Question Resolution program and geographic program revisions.

Source: U.S. Census Bureau, 1990 Census of Population and Housing, Population and Housing Unit Counts (CPH-2); Current Population Reports, P25-1106; "Table CO-EST2001-12-00 - Time Series of Intercensal State Population Estimates: April 1, 1990 to April 1, 2000," April 2002, <http://www2.census.gov/programs-surveys/popest/tables/1990-2000/intercensal/st-co/co-est2001-12-00.pdf>; "Table 1. Intercensal Estimates of the Resident Population for the United States, Regions, States, and Puerto Rico: April 1, 2000 to July 1, 2010 (ST-EST00INT-01)," September 2011, <http://www.census.gov/data/tables/time-series/demo/popest/intercensal-2000-2010-state.html>; and "Table 1. Annual Estimates of the Resident Population for the United States, Regions, States, and Puerto Rico: April 1, 2010 to July 1, 2018 (NST-EST2018-01)," December 2018, <https://www.census.gov/data/tables/time-series/demo/popest/2010s-national-total.html>.

# Table 15. State Population—Rank, Percent Change, and Population Density: 1990 to 2018

[As of April 1, except 2018 as of July 1. Insofar as possible, population shown for all years is that of present area of state. For land area by State, see Table 399. Minus sign (-) indicates decrease. See Appendix III]

| State | Rank | | | | Percent change | | | Population per square mile of land area [1] | | |
|---|---|---|---|---|---|---|---|---|---|---|
| | 1990 | 2000 | 2010 | 2018 | 1990 to 2000 | 2000 to 2010 | 2010 to 2018 [2] | 2000 | 2010 | 2018 |
| United States......... | (X) | (X) | (X) | (X) | 13.1 | 9.7 | 6.0 | 79.7 | 87.4 | 92.6 |
| Alabama............... | 22 | 23 | 23 | 24 | 10.1 | 7.5 | 2.3 | 87.8 | 94.4 | 96.5 |
| Alaska................. | 49 | 48 | 47 | 48 | 14.0 | 13.3 | 3.8 | 1.1 | 1.2 | 1.3 |
| Arizona............... | 24 | 20 | 16 | 14 | 40.0 | 24.6 | 12.2 | 45.2 | 56.3 | 63.1 |
| Arkansas.............. | 33 | 33 | 32 | 33 | 13.7 | 9.1 | 3.4 | 51.4 | 56.0 | 57.9 |
| California............. | 1 | 1 | 1 | 1 | 13.8 | 10.0 | 6.2 | 217.4 | 239.1 | 253.9 |
| Colorado.............. | 26 | 24 | 22 | 21 | 30.6 | 16.9 | 13.2 | 41.5 | 48.5 | 55.0 |
| Connecticut........... | 27 | 29 | 29 | 29 | 3.6 | 4.9 | 0.0 | 703.3 | 738.1 | 737.8 |
| Delaware.............. | 46 | 45 | 45 | 45 | 17.6 | 14.6 | 7.7 | 402.1 | 460.8 | 496.4 |
| District of Columbia.... | (X) | (X) | (X) | (X) | -5.7 | 5.2 | 16.7 | 9,370.6 | 9,856.2 | 11,506.2 |
| Florida............... | 4 | 4 | 4 | 3 | 23.5 | 17.6 | 13.3 | 298.0 | 350.6 | 397.2 |
| Georgia............... | 11 | 10 | 9 | 8 | 26.4 | 18.3 | 8.6 | 142.3 | 168.4 | 182.9 |
| Hawaii................ | 41 | 42 | 40 | 40 | 9.3 | 12.3 | 4.4 | 188.6 | 211.8 | 221.2 |
| Idaho................. | 42 | 39 | 39 | 39 | 28.5 | 21.1 | 11.9 | 15.7 | 19.0 | 21.2 |
| Illinois............... | 6 | 5 | 5 | 6 | 8.6 | 3.3 | -0.7 | 223.7 | 231.1 | 229.5 |
| Indiana............... | 14 | 14 | 15 | 17 | 9.7 | 6.6 | 3.2 | 169.7 | 181.0 | 186.8 |
| Iowa.................. | 30 | 30 | 30 | 31 | 5.4 | 4.1 | 3.6 | 52.4 | 54.5 | 56.5 |
| Kansas................ | 32 | 32 | 33 | 35 | 8.5 | 6.1 | 2.0 | 32.9 | 34.9 | 35.6 |
| Kentucky.............. | 23 | 25 | 26 | 26 | 9.6 | 7.4 | 3.0 | 102.4 | 109.9 | 113.2 |
| Louisiana............. | 21 | 22 | 25 | 25 | 5.9 | 1.4 | 2.8 | 103.4 | 104.9 | 107.9 |
| Maine................. | 38 | 40 | 41 | 42 | 3.8 | 4.2 | 0.8 | 41.3 | 43.1 | 43.4 |
| Maryland.............. | 19 | 19 | 19 | 19 | 10.8 | 9.0 | 4.7 | 545.6 | 594.8 | 622.5 |
| Massachusetts......... | 13 | 13 | 14 | 15 | 5.5 | 3.1 | 5.4 | 814.0 | 839.4 | 884.9 |
| Michigan.............. | 8 | 8 | 8 | 10 | 6.9 | -0.6 | 1.1 | 175.8 | 174.8 | 176.8 |
| Minnesota............. | 20 | 21 | 21 | 22 | 12.4 | 7.8 | 5.8 | 61.8 | 66.6 | 70.5 |
| Mississippi........... | 31 | 31 | 31 | 34 | 10.5 | 4.3 | 0.6 | 60.6 | 63.2 | 63.6 |
| Missouri.............. | 15 | 17 | 18 | 18 | 9.3 | 7.0 | 2.3 | 81.4 | 87.1 | 89.1 |
| Montana............... | 44 | 44 | 44 | 43 | 12.9 | 9.7 | 7.4 | 6.2 | 6.8 | 7.3 |
| Nebraska.............. | 36 | 38 | 38 | 37 | 8.4 | 6.7 | 5.6 | 22.3 | 23.8 | 25.1 |
| Nevada................ | 39 | 35 | 35 | 32 | 66.3 | 35.1 | 12.4 | 18.2 | 24.6 | 27.6 |
| New Hampshire........ | 40 | 41 | 42 | 41 | 11.4 | 6.5 | 3.0 | 138.0 | 147.0 | 151.5 |
| New Jersey............ | 9 | 9 | 11 | 11 | 8.9 | 4.5 | 1.3 | 1,144.2 | 1,195.5 | 1,211.3 |
| New Mexico............ | 37 | 36 | 36 | 36 | 20.1 | 13.2 | 1.8 | 15.0 | 17.0 | 17.3 |
| New York.............. | 2 | 3 | 3 | 4 | 5.5 | 2.1 | 0.8 | 402.7 | 411.2 | 414.7 |
| North Carolina......... | 10 | 11 | 10 | 9 | 21.4 | 18.5 | 8.9 | 165.6 | 196.1 | 213.6 |
| North Dakota.......... | 47 | 47 | 48 | 47 | 0.5 | 4.7 | 13.0 | 9.3 | 9.7 | 11.0 |
| Ohio.................. | 7 | 7 | 7 | 7 | 4.7 | 1.6 | 1.3 | 277.8 | 282.3 | 286.1 |
| Oklahoma.............. | 28 | 27 | 28 | 28 | 9.7 | 8.7 | 5.1 | 50.3 | 54.7 | 57.5 |
| Oregon................ | 29 | 28 | 27 | 27 | 20.4 | 12.0 | 9.4 | 35.6 | 39.9 | 43.7 |
| Pennsylvania.......... | 5 | 6 | 6 | 5 | 3.4 | 3.4 | 0.8 | 274.5 | 283.9 | 286.2 |
| Rhode Island.......... | 43 | 43 | 43 | 44 | 4.5 | 0.4 | 0.4 | 1,014.0 | 1,018.1 | 1,022.7 |
| South Carolina........ | 25 | 26 | 24 | 23 | 15.1 | 15.3 | 9.9 | 133.5 | 153.9 | 169.1 |
| South Dakota.......... | 45 | 46 | 46 | 46 | 8.5 | 7.9 | 8.4 | 10.0 | 10.7 | 11.6 |
| Tennessee............. | 17 | 16 | 17 | 16 | 16.7 | 11.5 | 6.7 | 138.0 | 153.9 | 164.2 |
| Texas................. | 3 | 2 | 2 | 2 | 22.8 | 20.6 | 14.1 | 79.8 | 96.3 | 109.9 |
| Utah.................. | 35 | 34 | 34 | 30 | 29.6 | 23.8 | 14.4 | 27.2 | 33.6 | 38.5 |
| Vermont............... | 48 | 49 | 49 | 49 | 8.2 | 2.8 | 0.1 | 66.1 | 67.9 | 68.0 |
| Virginia.............. | 12 | 12 | 12 | 12 | 14.4 | 13.0 | 6.5 | 179.2 | 202.6 | 215.7 |
| Washington............ | 18 | 15 | 13 | 13 | 21.1 | 14.1 | 12.1 | 88.7 | 101.2 | 113.4 |
| West Virginia......... | 34 | 37 | 37 | 38 | 0.8 | 2.5 | -2.5 | 75.2 | 77.1 | 75.1 |
| Wisconsin............. | 16 | 18 | 20 | 20 | 9.6 | 6.0 | 2.2 | 99.0 | 105.0 | 107.3 |
| Wyoming............... | 50 | 50 | 50 | 50 | 8.9 | 14.1 | 2.5 | 5.1 | 5.8 | 6.0 |

X Not applicable. [1] Persons per square mile were calculated on the basis of land area data from the 2010 Census. [2] Based on 2010 population estimates base that reflects changes to the Census 2010 population from the Count Question Resolution program and geographic program revisions.

Source: U.S. Census Bureau, *2000 Census of Population and Housing, PHC-3-1, United States Summary*, 2004, <http://www.census.gov/prod/cen2000/phc3-us-pt1.pdf>; *2010 Census Briefs, Population Distribution and Change: 2000 to 2010,* March 2011, <http://www.census.gov/prod/cen2010/briefs/c2010br-01.pdf>; and "Table 1. Annual Estimates of the Resident Population for the United States, Regions, States, and Puerto Rico: April 1, 2010 to July 1, 2018 (NST-EST2018-01)," December 2018, <https://www.census.gov/data/tables/time-series/demo/popest/2010s-national-total.html>.

# Table 16. State and Region Resident Population—Components of Change: 2010 to 2018

[Covers period April 1, 2010 to July 1, 2018. Minus sign (-) indicates net decrease or net outflow]

| State and region | Numeric population change [1] | Births | Deaths | Natural increase (births minus deaths) | Net migration Total | Net migration International [2] | Net migration Domestic |
|---|---|---|---|---|---|---|---|
| United States........... | 18,409,329 | 32,514,580 | 21,799,621 | 10,714,959 | 7,694,370 | 7,694,370 | (X) |
| Northeast................. | 792,649 | 5,204,239 | 3,970,020 | 1,234,219 | -425,095 | 1,786,346 | -2,211,441 |
| Midwest.................. | 1,379,001 | 6,835,841 | 5,002,259 | 1,833,582 | -441,750 | 1,065,306 | -1,507,056 |
| South.................... | 10,190,903 | 12,520,210 | 8,481,816 | 4,038,394 | 6,117,386 | 3,082,344 | 3,035,042 |
| West..................... | 6,046,776 | 7,954,290 | 4,345,526 | 3,608,764 | 2,443,829 | 1,760,374 | 683,455 |
| Alabama.................. | 107,733 | 484,329 | 418,734 | 65,595 | 42,748 | 37,551 | 5,197 |
| Alaska................... | 27,189 | 92,762 | 34,995 | 57,767 | -31,287 | 17,792 | -49,079 |
| Arizona.................. | 779,358 | 703,872 | 434,572 | 269,300 | 508,013 | 145,998 | 362,015 |
| Arkansas................. | 97,797 | 314,960 | 251,951 | 63,009 | 34,163 | 25,253 | 8,910 |
| California............... | 2,302,522 | 4,078,895 | 2,094,459 | 1,984,436 | 333,168 | 1,043,561 | -710,393 |
| Colorado................. | 666,248 | 543,471 | 289,139 | 254,332 | 406,752 | 84,970 | 321,782 |
| Connecticut.............. | -1,482 | 298,938 | 247,536 | 51,402 | -52,931 | 122,999 | -175,930 |
| Delaware................. | 69,237 | 90,864 | 69,108 | 21,756 | 47,568 | 14,957 | 32,611 |
| District of Columbia..... | 100,689 | 78,391 | 40,740 | 37,651 | 61,805 | 32,265 | 29,540 |
| Florida.................. | 2,494,745 | 1,801,326 | 1,549,217 | 252,109 | 2,232,735 | 1,072,348 | 1,160,387 |
| Georgia.................. | 830,766 | 1,074,297 | 634,603 | 439,694 | 387,595 | 182,190 | 205,405 |
| Hawaii................... | 60,184 | 152,292 | 90,763 | 61,529 | -549 | 55,050 | -55,599 |
| Idaho.................... | 186,551 | 186,921 | 103,264 | 83,657 | 102,127 | 16,562 | 85,565 |
| Illinois................. | -90,492 | 1,294,578 | 866,111 | 428,467 | -519,943 | 241,894 | -761,837 |
| Indiana.................. | 207,817 | 685,293 | 500,513 | 184,780 | 25,243 | 80,287 | -55,044 |
| Iowa..................... | 109,273 | 320,992 | 237,810 | 83,182 | 26,463 | 48,288 | -21,825 |
| Kansas................... | 58,379 | 320,372 | 210,809 | 109,563 | -50,988 | 45,473 | -96,461 |
| Kentucky................. | 129,069 | 456,319 | 369,344 | 86,975 | 42,993 | 54,633 | -11,640 |
| Louisiana................ | 126,493 | 516,732 | 357,057 | 159,675 | -34,167 | 41,559 | -75,726 |
| Maine.................... | 10,035 | 104,761 | 112,173 | -7,412 | 18,302 | 10,343 | 7,959 |
| Maryland................. | 268,920 | 600,546 | 384,372 | 216,174 | 55,763 | 192,345 | -136,582 |
| Massachusetts............ | 354,359 | 592,466 | 458,279 | 134,187 | 224,482 | 351,069 | -126,587 |
| Michigan................. | 111,798 | 933,558 | 767,504 | 166,054 | -53,152 | 189,665 | -242,817 |
| Minnesota................ | 307,254 | 570,171 | 341,882 | 228,289 | 81,671 | 107,830 | -26,159 |
| Mississippi.............. | 18,412 | 316,072 | 251,454 | 64,618 | -46,825 | 18,614 | -65,439 |
| Missouri................. | 137,500 | 617,794 | 478,044 | 139,750 | -331 | 59,677 | -60,008 |
| Montana.................. | 72,896 | 100,933 | 78,277 | 22,656 | 49,992 | 6,640 | 43,352 |
| Nebraska................. | 102,963 | 216,048 | 130,333 | 85,715 | 17,767 | 33,765 | -15,998 |
| Nevada................... | 333,713 | 294,505 | 183,602 | 110,903 | 221,704 | 30,103 | 191,601 |
| New Hampshire............ | 39,994 | 102,554 | 93,479 | 9,075 | 31,684 | 24,869 | 6,815 |
| New Jersey............... | 116,558 | 852,207 | 595,714 | 256,493 | -140,088 | 302,522 | -442,610 |
| New Mexico............... | 36,248 | 213,795 | 142,845 | 70,950 | -34,628 | 27,423 | -62,051 |
| New York................. | 164,085 | 1,954,011 | 1,264,995 | 689,016 | -523,216 | 674,384 | -1,197,600 |
| North Carolina........... | 847,884 | 990,630 | 708,132 | 282,498 | 560,003 | 157,614 | 402,389 |
| North Dakota............. | 87,501 | 87,442 | 50,698 | 36,744 | 49,192 | 13,264 | 35,928 |
| Ohio..................... | 152,685 | 1,138,227 | 946,276 | 191,951 | -35,269 | 169,396 | -204,665 |
| Oklahoma................. | 191,496 | 433,393 | 318,855 | 114,538 | 76,774 | 52,615 | 24,159 |
| Oregon................... | 359,638 | 374,486 | 283,146 | 91,340 | 267,949 | 61,237 | 206,712 |
| Pennsylvania............. | 104,187 | 1,160,725 | 1,071,084 | 89,641 | 22,862 | 259,739 | -236,877 |
| Rhode Island............. | 4,358 | 89,601 | 80,297 | 9,304 | -1,624 | 31,873 | -36,497 |
| South Carolina........... | 458,746 | 471,964 | 375,950 | 96,014 | 359,822 | 45,047 | 314,775 |
| South Dakota............. | 68,037 | 99,830 | 61,308 | 38,522 | 29,312 | 16,801 | 12,511 |
| Tennessee................ | 423,724 | 662,136 | 529,573 | 132,563 | 290,164 | 70,779 | 219,385 |
| Texas.................... | 3,555,731 | 3,221,263 | 1,511,232 | 1,710,031 | 1,832,775 | 813,341 | 1,019,434 |
| Utah..................... | 397,214 | 420,885 | 136,102 | 284,783 | 113,137 | 46,555 | 66,582 |
| Vermont.................. | 555 | 48,976 | 46,463 | 2,513 | -1,566 | 8,548 | -10,114 |
| Virginia................. | 516,630 | 843,184 | 528,521 | 314,663 | 200,978 | 263,741 | -62,763 |
| Washington............... | 811,051 | 729,978 | 435,888 | 294,090 | 516,914 | 221,434 | 295,480 |
| West Virginia............ | -47,169 | 163,804 | 182,973 | -19,169 | -27,508 | 7,492 | -35,000 |
| Wisconsin................ | 126,286 | 551,536 | 410,971 | 140,565 | -11,715 | 58,966 | -70,681 |
| Wyoming.................. | 13,964 | 61,495 | 38,474 | 23,021 | -9,463 | 3,049 | -12,512 |

X Not applicable. [1] Total population change includes a residual. This residual represents the change in population that cannot be attributed to any specific demographic component. [2] Net international migration includes the international migration of both native and foreign-born populations. Specifically, it includes: (a) the net international migration of the foreign born, (b) the net migration between the United States and Puerto Rico, (c) the net migration of natives to and from the United States, and (d) the net movement of the Armed Forces population between the United States and overseas.

Source: U.S. Census Bureau, Population Division, "Cumulative Estimates of the Components of Resident Population Change for the United States, Regions, States, and Puerto Rico: April 1, 2010 to July 1, 2018 (NST-EST2018-04)," December 2018, <https://www.census.gov/data/tables/time-series/demo/popest/2010s-national-total.html>.

# Table 17. Resident Population by Age and State: 2018

[In thousands (327,167 represents 327,167,000), unless otherwise noted. As of July 1]

| State | Total | Under 5 years | 5 to 14 years | 15 to 24 years | 25 to 34 years | 35 to 44 years | 45 to 54 years | 55 to 64 years | 65 to 74 years | 75 to 84 years | 85 years and over | Median age (years) | Percent 65 years old and over |
|---|---|---|---|---|---|---|---|---|---|---|---|---|---|
| United States | 327,167 | 19,810 | 41,075 | 42,971 | 45,698 | 41,278 | 41,632 | 42,273 | 30,492 | 15,394 | 6,545 | 38.2 | 16.0 |
| Alabama | 4,888 | 293 | 608 | 641 | 644 | 592 | 627 | 655 | 488 | 249 | 90 | 39.2 | 16.9 |
| Alaska | 737 | 53 | 102 | 99 | 119 | 95 | 88 | 95 | 59 | 22 | 7 | 34.6 | 11.8 |
| Arizona | 7,172 | 436 | 928 | 966 | 986 | 880 | 851 | 866 | 726 | 390 | 142 | 37.9 | 17.5 |
| Arkansas | 3,014 | 190 | 394 | 399 | 397 | 369 | 369 | 384 | 296 | 157 | 59 | 38.3 | 17.0 |
| California | 39,557 | 2,441 | 5,037 | 5,257 | 6,044 | 5,256 | 5,072 | 4,781 | 3,285 | 1,640 | 744 | 36.8 | 14.3 |
| Colorado | 5,696 | 337 | 713 | 742 | 894 | 780 | 710 | 711 | 501 | 219 | 88 | 36.9 | 14.2 |
| Connecticut | 3,573 | 183 | 414 | 485 | 445 | 423 | 495 | 512 | 344 | 180 | 92 | 41.0 | 17.2 |
| Delaware | 967 | 55 | 114 | 119 | 129 | 111 | 122 | 136 | 108 | 53 | 20 | 40.7 | 18.7 |
| District of Columbia | 702 | 46 | 66 | 90 | 164 | 106 | 75 | 70 | 49 | 24 | 12 | 34.0 | 12.1 |
| Florida | 21,299 | 1,143 | 2,364 | 2,476 | 2,788 | 2,569 | 2,746 | 2,855 | 2,398 | 1,389 | 571 | 42.2 | 20.5 |
| Georgia | 10,519 | 657 | 1,414 | 1,445 | 1,473 | 1,373 | 1,411 | 1,286 | 895 | 418 | 147 | 36.9 | 13.9 |
| Hawaii | 1,420 | 88 | 169 | 168 | 203 | 181 | 171 | 181 | 149 | 71 | 41 | 39.2 | 18.4 |
| Idaho | 1,754 | 116 | 254 | 239 | 231 | 220 | 200 | 215 | 168 | 81 | 29 | 36.6 | 15.9 |
| Illinois | 12,741 | 761 | 1,597 | 1,676 | 1,770 | 1,640 | 1,640 | 1,665 | 1,142 | 584 | 267 | 38.3 | 15.6 |
| Indiana | 6,692 | 419 | 879 | 927 | 877 | 822 | 840 | 873 | 616 | 309 | 131 | 37.9 | 15.8 |
| Iowa | 3,156 | 198 | 410 | 442 | 398 | 380 | 371 | 418 | 301 | 160 | 79 | 38.2 | 17.1 |
| Kansas | 2,912 | 189 | 398 | 413 | 383 | 356 | 336 | 373 | 263 | 134 | 66 | 36.9 | 15.9 |
| Kentucky | 4,468 | 275 | 563 | 589 | 585 | 552 | 577 | 597 | 435 | 215 | 81 | 38.9 | 16.4 |
| Louisiana | 4,660 | 307 | 609 | 605 | 667 | 584 | 563 | 606 | 428 | 209 | 81 | 37.2 | 15.4 |
| Maine | 1,338 | 64 | 141 | 152 | 160 | 152 | 180 | 212 | 163 | 79 | 33 | 44.9 | 20.6 |
| Maryland | 6,043 | 365 | 749 | 758 | 835 | 774 | 819 | 813 | 545 | 267 | 118 | 38.8 | 15.4 |
| Massachusetts | 6,902 | 360 | 759 | 949 | 993 | 841 | 922 | 939 | 654 | 325 | 160 | 39.4 | 16.5 |
| Michigan | 9,996 | 572 | 1,206 | 1,348 | 1,297 | 1,163 | 1,290 | 1,403 | 1,005 | 498 | 214 | 39.8 | 17.2 |
| Minnesota | 5,611 | 355 | 731 | 718 | 761 | 710 | 691 | 754 | 510 | 258 | 122 | 38.1 | 15.9 |
| Mississippi | 2,987 | 185 | 400 | 413 | 394 | 365 | 369 | 386 | 281 | 142 | 52 | 37.7 | 15.9 |
| Missouri | 6,126 | 373 | 770 | 801 | 824 | 745 | 752 | 830 | 593 | 310 | 132 | 38.7 | 16.9 |
| Montana | 1,062 | 63 | 129 | 137 | 137 | 126 | 120 | 151 | 120 | 57 | 23 | 39.9 | 18.7 |
| Nebraska | 1,929 | 133 | 266 | 269 | 256 | 239 | 220 | 243 | 173 | 88 | 43 | 36.6 | 15.7 |
| Nevada | 3,034 | 186 | 389 | 363 | 445 | 403 | 395 | 377 | 293 | 140 | 43 | 38.1 | 15.7 |
| New Hampshire | 1,356 | 64 | 145 | 175 | 169 | 155 | 190 | 213 | 147 | 68 | 30 | 43.0 | 18.1 |
| New Jersey | 8,909 | 519 | 1,092 | 1,109 | 1,156 | 1,139 | 1,236 | 1,219 | 810 | 426 | 202 | 40.0 | 16.1 |
| New Mexico | 2,095 | 124 | 275 | 281 | 284 | 251 | 241 | 274 | 218 | 107 | 41 | 38.1 | 17.5 |
| New York | 19,542 | 1,140 | 2,237 | 2,491 | 2,879 | 2,432 | 2,555 | 2,595 | 1,809 | 948 | 456 | 39.0 | 16.4 |
| North Carolina | 10,384 | 610 | 1,292 | 1,382 | 1,393 | 1,296 | 1,378 | 1,343 | 1,010 | 493 | 186 | 38.9 | 16.3 |
| North Dakota | 760 | 55 | 98 | 111 | 115 | 90 | 80 | 95 | 64 | 34 | 19 | 35.2 | 15.3 |
| Ohio | 11,689 | 695 | 1,446 | 1,521 | 1,545 | 1,391 | 1,485 | 1,612 | 1,150 | 588 | 256 | 39.4 | 17.1 |
| Oklahoma | 3,943 | 260 | 538 | 538 | 543 | 490 | 460 | 493 | 359 | 188 | 73 | 36.7 | 15.7 |
| Oregon | 4,191 | 234 | 492 | 513 | 596 | 560 | 513 | 544 | 448 | 206 | 84 | 39.4 | 17.6 |
| Pennsylvania | 12,807 | 703 | 1,481 | 1,625 | 1,701 | 1,499 | 1,653 | 1,810 | 1,311 | 691 | 334 | 40.8 | 18.2 |
| Rhode Island | 1,057 | 54 | 114 | 148 | 146 | 124 | 139 | 149 | 103 | 52 | 28 | 40.1 | 17.2 |
| South Carolina | 5,084 | 292 | 626 | 656 | 674 | 611 | 646 | 678 | 550 | 261 | 89 | 39.6 | 17.7 |
| South Dakota | 882 | 62 | 122 | 117 | 116 | 104 | 97 | 117 | 85 | 41 | 21 | 37.1 | 16.6 |
| Tennessee | 6,770 | 407 | 842 | 871 | 931 | 840 | 883 | 886 | 662 | 328 | 120 | 38.8 | 16.4 |
| Texas | 28,702 | 2,024 | 4,139 | 4,031 | 4,236 | 3,882 | 3,553 | 3,234 | 2,167 | 1,035 | 400 | 34.8 | 12.6 |
| Utah | 3,161 | 253 | 526 | 510 | 465 | 435 | 322 | 300 | 210 | 103 | 38 | 31.0 | 11.1 |
| Vermont | 626 | 30 | 65 | 88 | 74 | 71 | 81 | 96 | 73 | 34 | 14 | 42.8 | 19.4 |
| Virginia | 8,518 | 511 | 1,043 | 1,121 | 1,190 | 1,105 | 1,125 | 1,107 | 779 | 384 | 152 | 38.4 | 15.4 |
| Washington | 7,536 | 463 | 930 | 928 | 1,153 | 1,003 | 934 | 961 | 709 | 322 | 133 | 37.7 | 15.4 |
| West Virginia | 1,806 | 95 | 205 | 220 | 215 | 217 | 234 | 258 | 213 | 107 | 40 | 42.7 | 19.9 |
| Wisconsin | 5,814 | 334 | 719 | 774 | 737 | 705 | 738 | 821 | 572 | 285 | 129 | 39.6 | 17.0 |
| Wyoming | 578 | 36 | 77 | 74 | 78 | 73 | 65 | 80 | 58 | 27 | 11 | 38.0 | 16.5 |

Source: U.S. Census Bureau, "Annual Estimates of the Resident Population for Selected Age Groups by Sex for the United States, States, Counties, and Puerto Rico Commonwealth and Municipios: April 1, 2010 to July 1, 2018," <http://factfinder.census.gov>, accessed June 2019.

# Table 18. Age Dependency Ratios by State: 2000 to 2018

[As of April, except 2018 as of July]

| State | Age dependency ratio [1] | | | Child dependency ratio [2] | | | Old-age dependency ratio [3] | | |
|---|---|---|---|---|---|---|---|---|---|
| | 2000 | 2010 | 2018 | 2000 | 2010 | 2018 | 2000 | 2010 | 2018 |
| **United States.........** | **61.6** | **58.9** | **62.5** | **41.5** | **38.2** | **36.5** | **20.1** | **20.7** | **26.0** |
| Alabama................. | 62.1 | 59.9 | 64.5 | 40.9 | 37.9 | 36.7 | 21.1 | 22.0 | 27.8 |
| Alaska.................. | 56.5 | 51.8 | 58.0 | 47.6 | 40.0 | 39.4 | 8.9 | 11.7 | 18.6 |
| Arizona................. | 65.7 | 64.7 | 67.9 | 44.2 | 42.0 | 38.5 | 21.6 | 22.7 | 29.5 |
| Arkansas............... | 65.1 | 63.4 | 67.5 | 42.0 | 39.9 | 39.1 | 23.1 | 23.5 | 28.5 |
| California.............. | 61.1 | 57.1 | 58.9 | 44.0 | 39.2 | 36.1 | 17.1 | 17.9 | 22.8 |
| Colorado............... | 54.5 | 54.6 | 57.2 | 39.5 | 37.7 | 34.9 | 14.9 | 16.9 | 22.3 |
| Connecticut............ | 62.7 | 58.8 | 60.8 | 40.2 | 36.3 | 33.1 | 22.5 | 22.5 | 27.7 |
| Delaware............... | 60.8 | 59.5 | 66.0 | 39.9 | 36.6 | 35.0 | 20.9 | 23.0 | 31.1 |
| District of Columbia.... | 47.8 | 39.3 | 43.5 | 29.7 | 23.3 | 26.0 | 18.1 | 15.9 | 17.4 |
| Florida................. | 67.7 | 62.9 | 67.6 | 38.3 | 34.7 | 33.3 | 29.5 | 28.2 | 34.3 |
| Georgia................ | 56.5 | 57.2 | 60.5 | 41.5 | 40.4 | 38.2 | 15.0 | 16.7 | 22.3 |
| Hawaii................. | 60.4 | 57.9 | 65.9 | 39.2 | 35.3 | 35.4 | 21.3 | 22.7 | 30.5 |
| Idaho.................. | 66.1 | 66.1 | 70.5 | 47.4 | 45.5 | 43.4 | 18.7 | 20.6 | 27.0 |
| Illinois................. | 61.8 | 58.6 | 61.5 | 42.3 | 38.7 | 36.2 | 19.5 | 19.9 | 25.3 |
| Indiana................ | 62.0 | 60.7 | 64.5 | 41.9 | 39.9 | 38.5 | 20.1 | 20.9 | 25.9 |
| Iowa................... | 66.6 | 63.3 | 67.4 | 41.8 | 39.0 | 38.8 | 24.8 | 24.3 | 28.6 |
| Kansas................. | 66.0 | 63.0 | 67.0 | 44.0 | 41.5 | 40.5 | 22.0 | 21.5 | 26.5 |
| Kentucky............... | 59.0 | 58.5 | 63.7 | 39.1 | 37.4 | 37.0 | 19.9 | 21.1 | 26.8 |
| Louisiana.............. | 63.6 | 58.6 | 63.8 | 44.6 | 39.1 | 38.5 | 18.9 | 19.5 | 25.2 |
| Maine.................. | 61.3 | 57.6 | 64.8 | 38.1 | 32.6 | 30.8 | 23.2 | 25.0 | 34.0 |
| Maryland............... | 58.5 | 55.5 | 60.2 | 40.6 | 36.4 | 35.5 | 17.9 | 19.1 | 24.7 |
| Massachusetts......... | 59.2 | 54.9 | 57.0 | 37.6 | 33.6 | 31.1 | 21.6 | 21.4 | 25.9 |
| Michigan............... | 62.3 | 60.0 | 63.5 | 42.4 | 37.9 | 35.4 | 19.9 | 22.0 | 28.1 |
| Minnesota.............. | 61.9 | 59.0 | 64.1 | 42.4 | 38.5 | 38.1 | 19.6 | 20.5 | 26.0 |
| Mississippi............. | 64.8 | 62.0 | 65.4 | 44.9 | 41.2 | 39.1 | 19.9 | 20.8 | 26.3 |
| Missouri............... | 64.0 | 60.8 | 64.9 | 41.8 | 38.3 | 37.1 | 22.1 | 22.5 | 27.8 |
| Montana............... | 63.7 | 59.8 | 67.6 | 41.7 | 36.1 | 36.2 | 21.9 | 23.7 | 31.4 |
| Nebraska.............. | 66.3 | 63.0 | 67.9 | 43.8 | 41.0 | 41.5 | 22.6 | 22.0 | 26.4 |
| Nevada................ | 57.6 | 57.8 | 62.3 | 40.4 | 38.9 | 36.9 | 17.3 | 19.0 | 25.5 |
| New Hampshire........ | 58.8 | 54.7 | 59.1 | 39.8 | 33.8 | 30.3 | 19.0 | 20.9 | 28.8 |
| New Jersey............ | 61.4 | 58.7 | 61.5 | 40.0 | 37.3 | 35.4 | 21.4 | 21.4 | 26.1 |
| New Mexico............ | 65.6 | 62.4 | 68.0 | 46.3 | 40.9 | 38.7 | 19.3 | 21.5 | 29.4 |
| New York.............. | 60.3 | 55.8 | 59.4 | 39.6 | 34.8 | 33.2 | 20.7 | 21.1 | 26.2 |
| North Carolina......... | 57.3 | 58.4 | 62.4 | 38.4 | 37.9 | 36.0 | 19.0 | 20.5 | 26.4 |
| North Dakota........... | 66.0 | 58.2 | 63.5 | 41.6 | 35.2 | 38.5 | 24.4 | 22.9 | 25.1 |
| Ohio................... | 63.2 | 60.6 | 64.6 | 41.5 | 38.0 | 36.5 | 21.7 | 22.6 | 28.1 |
| Oklahoma.............. | 64.1 | 62.1 | 66.6 | 42.4 | 40.2 | 40.4 | 21.7 | 21.9 | 26.2 |
| Oregon................ | 60.1 | 57.6 | 62.5 | 39.6 | 35.6 | 33.9 | 20.5 | 21.9 | 28.6 |
| Pennsylvania........... | 65.1 | 59.8 | 63.7 | 39.3 | 35.1 | 33.9 | 25.8 | 24.6 | 29.9 |
| Rhode Island.......... | 61.8 | 55.5 | 57.8 | 38.2 | 33.1 | 30.6 | 23.5 | 22.4 | 27.2 |
| South Carolina......... | 59.4 | 58.8 | 65.2 | 40.1 | 37.1 | 35.9 | 19.3 | 21.7 | 29.2 |
| South Dakota.......... | 70.0 | 64.5 | 70.4 | 45.6 | 41.0 | 42.0 | 24.4 | 23.6 | 28.4 |
| Tennessee............. | 58.6 | 58.8 | 63.0 | 39.0 | 37.4 | 36.3 | 19.6 | 21.4 | 26.7 |
| Texas.................. | 61.7 | 60.4 | 62.1 | 45.7 | 43.8 | 41.8 | 16.1 | 16.6 | 20.4 |
| Utah................... | 68.6 | 68.2 | 68.3 | 54.3 | 53.0 | 49.6 | 14.4 | 15.2 | 18.7 |
| Vermont................ | 58.6 | 54.3 | 61.0 | 38.4 | 31.9 | 29.8 | 20.2 | 22.5 | 31.1 |
| Virginia................ | 55.6 | 54.7 | 59.7 | 38.2 | 35.9 | 35.1 | 17.4 | 18.9 | 24.7 |
| Washington............ | 58.5 | 55.8 | 60.1 | 40.7 | 36.6 | 35.3 | 17.8 | 19.2 | 24.7 |
| West Virginia.......... | 60.2 | 58.6 | 66.9 | 35.6 | 33.2 | 33.7 | 24.5 | 25.5 | 33.3 |
| Wisconsin............. | 62.9 | 59.3 | 63.7 | 41.6 | 37.5 | 35.9 | 21.3 | 21.8 | 27.7 |
| Wyoming.............. | 60.7 | 57.4 | 66.2 | 41.9 | 37.8 | 38.8 | 18.8 | 19.6 | 27.4 |

[1] The age dependency ratio is derived by dividing the sum of populations age under 18 and age 65 and over by the population age 18-64, and multiplying by 100. [2] The child dependency ratio is derived by dividing the population under age 18 by the population age 18-64, and multiplying by 100. [3] The old-age dependency ratio is derived by dividing the population age 65 and over by the population age 18-64, and multiplying by 100.

Source: U.S. Census Bureau, Census 2010 Briefs, "Age and Sex Composition: 2010," May 2011; and "Annual Estimates of the Resident Population for Selected Age Groups by Sex for the United States, States, Counties, and Puerto Rico Commonwealth and Municipios: April 1, 2010 to July 1, 2018," <http://factfinder.census.gov>, accessed June 2019.

# Table 19. Resident Population by Hispanic Origin and State: 2018

[In thousands, except as indicated (327,167 represents 327,167,000). As of July 1. Hispanic origin is considered an ethnicity, not a race. Persons of Hispanic origin may be of any race]

| State | Number (1,000) | | | | Percent | | |
|---|---|---|---|---|---|---|---|
| | Total population | Hispanic or Latino | Total Non-Hispanic | Non-Hispanic White alone | Hispanic or Latino | Total Non-Hispanic | Non-Hispanic White alone |
| **United States**......... | **327,167** | **59,872** | **267,296** | **197,546** | **18.3** | **81.7** | **60.4** |
| Alabama............... | 4,888 | 217 | 4,671 | 3,197 | 4.4 | 95.6 | 65.4 |
| Alaska................. | 737 | 53 | 684 | 444 | 7.2 | 92.8 | 60.3 |
| Arizona............... | 7,172 | 2,266 | 4,905 | 3,903 | 31.6 | 68.4 | 54.4 |
| Arkansas............. | 3,014 | 233 | 2,781 | 2,177 | 7.7 | 92.3 | 72.2 |
| California............. | 39,557 | 15,540 | 24,017 | 14,569 | 39.3 | 60.7 | 36.8 |
| Colorado............. | 5,696 | 1,235 | 4,460 | 3,868 | 21.7 | 78.3 | 67.9 |
| Connecticut.......... | 3,573 | 590 | 2,983 | 2,376 | 16.5 | 83.5 | 66.5 |
| Delaware............. | 967 | 92 | 875 | 599 | 9.5 | 90.5 | 61.9 |
| District of Columbia.... | 702 | 79 | 623 | 260 | 11.3 | 88.7 | 37.1 |
| Florida................ | 21,299 | 5,562 | 15,737 | 11,399 | 26.1 | 73.9 | 53.5 |
| Georgia.............. | 10,519 | 1,027 | 9,493 | 5,511 | 9.8 | 90.2 | 52.4 |
| Hawaii................ | 1,420 | 151 | 1,269 | 309 | 10.7 | 89.3 | 21.8 |
| Idaho................. | 1,754 | 223 | 1,531 | 1,434 | 12.7 | 87.3 | 81.7 |
| Illinois................ | 12,741 | 2,214 | 10,527 | 7,773 | 17.4 | 82.6 | 61.0 |
| Indiana............... | 6,692 | 475 | 6,217 | 5,277 | 7.1 | 92.9 | 78.9 |
| Iowa.................. | 3,156 | 194 | 2,962 | 2,691 | 6.2 | 93.8 | 85.3 |
| Kansas............... | 2,912 | 351 | 2,560 | 2,203 | 12.1 | 87.9 | 75.7 |
| Kentucky............. | 4,468 | 172 | 4,296 | 3,766 | 3.8 | 96.2 | 84.3 |
| Louisiana............ | 4,660 | 244 | 4,416 | 2,729 | 5.2 | 94.8 | 58.6 |
| Maine................ | 1,338 | 23 | 1,316 | 1,247 | 1.7 | 98.3 | 93.1 |
| Maryland............. | 6,043 | 628 | 5,414 | 3,051 | 10.4 | 89.6 | 50.5 |
| Massachusetts........ | 6,902 | 847 | 6,055 | 4,928 | 12.3 | 87.7 | 71.4 |
| Michigan............. | 9,996 | 519 | 9,477 | 7,485 | 5.2 | 94.8 | 74.9 |
| Minnesota............ | 5,611 | 309 | 5,302 | 4,459 | 5.5 | 94.5 | 79.5 |
| Mississippi........... | 2,987 | 100 | 2,886 | 1,686 | 3.4 | 96.6 | 56.5 |
| Missouri.............. | 6,126 | 263 | 5,863 | 4,858 | 4.3 | 95.7 | 79.3 |
| Montana.............. | 1,062 | 43 | 1,020 | 913 | 4.0 | 96.0 | 85.9 |
| Nebraska............. | 1,929 | 216 | 1,713 | 1,516 | 11.2 | 88.8 | 78.6 |
| Nevada............... | 3,034 | 881 | 2,153 | 1,476 | 29.0 | 71.0 | 48.7 |
| New Hampshire........ | 1,356 | 53 | 1,304 | 1,220 | 3.9 | 96.1 | 90.0 |
| New Jersey........... | 8,909 | 1,839 | 7,069 | 4,893 | 20.6 | 79.4 | 54.9 |
| New Mexico........... | 2,095 | 1,029 | 1,066 | 778 | 49.1 | 50.9 | 37.1 |
| New York............. | 19,542 | 3,754 | 15,788 | 10,831 | 19.2 | 80.8 | 55.4 |
| North Carolina......... | 10,384 | 997 | 9,386 | 6,526 | 9.6 | 90.4 | 62.8 |
| North Dakota........... | 760 | 30 | 731 | 638 | 3.9 | 96.1 | 84.0 |
| Ohio.................. | 11,689 | 461 | 11,229 | 9,196 | 3.9 | 96.1 | 78.7 |
| Oklahoma............. | 3,943 | 429 | 3,514 | 2,576 | 10.9 | 89.1 | 65.3 |
| Oregon............... | 4,191 | 556 | 3,634 | 3,155 | 13.3 | 86.7 | 75.3 |
| Pennsylvania.......... | 12,807 | 976 | 11,831 | 9,742 | 7.6 | 92.4 | 76.1 |
| Rhode Island......... | 1,057 | 168 | 889 | 761 | 15.9 | 84.1 | 72.0 |
| South Carolina........ | 5,084 | 296 | 4,788 | 3,239 | 5.8 | 94.2 | 63.7 |
| South Dakota......... | 882 | 36 | 846 | 718 | 4.1 | 95.9 | 81.4 |
| Tennessee............ | 6,770 | 381 | 6,389 | 4,990 | 5.6 | 94.4 | 73.7 |
| Texas................ | 28,702 | 11,369 | 17,333 | 11,913 | 39.6 | 60.4 | 41.5 |
| Utah................. | 3,161 | 450 | 2,711 | 2,466 | 14.2 | 85.8 | 78.0 |
| Vermont.............. | 626 | 13 | 614 | 580 | 2.0 | 98.0 | 92.5 |
| Virginia.............. | 8,518 | 821 | 7,697 | 5,235 | 9.6 | 90.4 | 61.5 |
| Washington............ | 7,536 | 970 | 6,565 | 5,125 | 12.9 | 87.1 | 68.0 |
| West Virginia.......... | 1,806 | 30 | 1,776 | 1,662 | 1.7 | 98.3 | 92.1 |
| Wisconsin............. | 5,814 | 404 | 5,410 | 4,713 | 6.9 | 93.1 | 81.1 |
| Wyoming.............. | 578 | 58 | 520 | 484 | 10.1 | 89.9 | 83.8 |

Source: U.S. Census Bureau, "Annual Estimates of the Resident Population by Sex, Race, and Hispanic Origin for the United States, States, and Counties: April 1, 2010 to July 1, 2018," <http://factfinder.census.gov>, accessed June 2019.

# Table 20. Resident Population by Race and State: 2018

[In thousands, except as indicated (327,167 represents 327,167,000). As of July 1]

| State | Total population | Number (1,000) White[1] | Black[1] | American Indian[1,2] | Asian[1] | Native Hawaiian[1,3] | Two or more races | Percent distribution White[1] | Black[1] | American Indian[1,2] | Asian[1] | Native Hawaiian[1,3] | Two or more races |
|---|---|---|---|---|---|---|---|---|---|---|---|---|---|
| U.S. | 327,167 | 250,139 | 43,804 | 4,148 | 19,331 | 799 | 8,946 | 76.5 | 13.4 | 1.3 | 5.9 | 0.2 | 2.7 |
| AL | 4,888 | 3,380 | 1,311 | 34 | 73 | 5 | 84 | 69.1 | 26.8 | 0.7 | 1.5 | 0.1 | 1.7 |
| AK | 737 | 482 | 28 | 114 | 49 | 10 | 55 | 65.3 | 3.8 | 15.4 | 6.6 | 1.4 | 7.4 |
| AZ | 7,172 | 5,938 | 364 | 380 | 264 | 20 | 206 | 82.8 | 5.1 | 5.3 | 3.7 | 0.3 | 2.9 |
| AR | 3,014 | 2,385 | 472 | 30 | 50 | 11 | 65 | 79.1 | 15.7 | 1.0 | 1.7 | 0.4 | 2.2 |
| CA | 39,557 | 28,532 | 2,556 | 651 | 6,064 | 200 | 1,555 | 72.1 | 6.5 | 1.6 | 15.3 | 0.5 | 3.9 |
| CO | 5,696 | 4,959 | 260 | 91 | 198 | 11 | 177 | 87.1 | 4.6 | 1.6 | 3.5 | 0.2 | 3.1 |
| CT | 3,573 | 2,859 | 429 | 20 | 174 | 4 | 87 | 80.0 | 12.0 | 0.6 | 4.9 | 0.1 | 2.4 |
| DE | 967 | 672 | 222 | 6 | 40 | 1 | 26 | 69.5 | 23.0 | 0.7 | 4.1 | 0.1 | 2.7 |
| DC | 702 | 320 | 326 | 4 | 31 | – | 20 | 45.6 | 46.4 | 0.6 | 4.4 | 0.1 | 2.8 |
| FL | 21,299 | 16,472 | 3,600 | 107 | 632 | 24 | 464 | 77.3 | 16.9 | 0.5 | 3.0 | 0.1 | 2.2 |
| GA | 10,519 | 6,361 | 3,411 | 55 | 453 | 12 | 227 | 60.5 | 32.4 | 0.5 | 4.3 | 0.1 | 2.2 |
| HI | 1,420 | 364 | 31 | 6 | 535 | 145 | 341 | 25.6 | 2.2 | 0.4 | 37.6 | 10.2 | 24.0 |
| ID | 1,754 | 1,632 | 16 | 30 | 28 | 4 | 44 | 93.0 | 0.9 | 1.7 | 1.6 | 0.2 | 2.5 |
| IL | 12,741 | 9,792 | 1,860 | 76 | 749 | 8 | 256 | 76.9 | 14.6 | 0.6 | 5.9 | 0.1 | 2.0 |
| IN | 6,692 | 5,694 | 659 | 28 | 165 | 5 | 141 | 85.1 | 9.8 | 0.4 | 2.5 | 0.1 | 2.1 |
| IA | 3,156 | 2,864 | 125 | 17 | 86 | 4 | 61 | 90.7 | 4.0 | 0.5 | 2.7 | 0.1 | 1.9 |
| KS | 2,912 | 2,515 | 179 | 35 | 91 | 4 | 88 | 86.4 | 6.1 | 1.2 | 3.1 | 0.1 | 3.0 |
| KY | 4,468 | 3,914 | 376 | 13 | 73 | 4 | 88 | 87.6 | 8.4 | 0.3 | 1.6 | 0.1 | 2.0 |
| LA | 4,660 | 2,930 | 1,526 | 37 | 84 | 3 | 80 | 62.9 | 32.7 | 0.8 | 1.8 | 0.1 | 1.7 |
| ME | 1,338 | 1,266 | 22 | 10 | 17 | (Z) | 24 | 94.6 | 1.6 | 0.7 | 1.2 | (Z) | 1.8 |
| MD | 6,043 | 3,552 | 1,868 | 36 | 406 | 7 | 174 | 58.8 | 30.9 | 0.6 | 6.7 | 0.1 | 2.9 |
| MA | 6,902 | 5,577 | 617 | 34 | 493 | 7 | 174 | 80.8 | 8.9 | 0.5 | 7.1 | 0.1 | 2.5 |
| MI | 9,996 | 7,924 | 1,408 | 73 | 337 | 4 | 249 | 79.3 | 14.1 | 0.7 | 3.4 | (Z) | 2.5 |
| MN | 5,611 | 4,718 | 380 | 77 | 289 | 4 | 143 | 84.1 | 6.8 | 1.4 | 5.1 | 0.1 | 2.5 |
| MS | 2,987 | 1,766 | 1,129 | 18 | 32 | 2 | 39 | 59.1 | 37.8 | 0.6 | 1.1 | 0.1 | 1.3 |
| MO | 6,126 | 5,083 | 725 | 35 | 131 | 10 | 144 | 83.0 | 11.8 | 0.6 | 2.1 | 0.2 | 2.3 |
| MT | 1,062 | 945 | 6 | 71 | 10 | 1 | 30 | 89.0 | 0.6 | 6.6 | 0.9 | 0.1 | 2.8 |
| NE | 1,929 | 1,703 | 99 | 29 | 52 | 2 | 44 | 88.3 | 5.1 | 1.5 | 2.7 | 0.1 | 2.3 |
| NV | 3,034 | 2,254 | 306 | 51 | 264 | 24 | 136 | 74.3 | 10.1 | 1.7 | 8.7 | 0.8 | 4.5 |
| NH | 1,356 | 1,264 | 23 | 4 | 40 | 1 | 24 | 93.2 | 1.7 | 0.3 | 3.0 | (Z) | 1.8 |
| NJ | 8,909 | 6,416 | 1,338 | 55 | 889 | 10 | 200 | 72.0 | 15.0 | 0.6 | 10.0 | 0.1 | 2.3 |
| NM | 2,095 | 1,719 | 54 | 228 | 37 | 3 | 54 | 82.0 | 2.6 | 10.9 | 1.8 | 0.2 | 2.6 |
| NY | 19,542 | 13,620 | 3,448 | 190 | 1,750 | 27 | 507 | 69.7 | 17.6 | 1.0 | 9.0 | 0.1 | 2.6 |
| NC | 10,384 | 7,334 | 2,307 | 163 | 329 | 13 | 237 | 70.6 | 22.2 | 1.6 | 3.2 | 0.1 | 2.3 |
| ND | 760 | 662 | 26 | 42 | 13 | 1 | 17 | 87.0 | 3.4 | 5.5 | 1.8 | 0.2 | 2.2 |
| OH | 11,689 | 9,572 | 1,518 | 34 | 287 | 7 | 272 | 81.9 | 13.0 | 0.3 | 2.5 | 0.1 | 2.3 |
| OK | 3,943 | 2,924 | 307 | 367 | 92 | 8 | 245 | 74.2 | 7.8 | 9.3 | 2.3 | 0.2 | 6.2 |
| OR | 4,191 | 3,636 | 93 | 76 | 202 | 19 | 164 | 86.8 | 2.2 | 1.8 | 4.8 | 0.5 | 3.9 |
| PA | 12,807 | 10,476 | 1,531 | 50 | 474 | 10 | 266 | 81.8 | 12.0 | 0.4 | 3.7 | 0.1 | 2.1 |
| RI | 1,057 | 887 | 88 | 11 | 38 | 2 | 30 | 83.9 | 8.4 | 1.1 | 3.6 | 0.2 | 2.8 |
| SC | 5,084 | 3,483 | 1,380 | 28 | 90 | 5 | 98 | 68.5 | 27.1 | 0.5 | 1.8 | 0.1 | 1.9 |
| SD | 882 | 745 | 21 | 79 | 15 | 1 | 21 | 84.4 | 2.4 | 9.0 | 1.7 | 0.1 | 2.4 |
| TN | 6,770 | 5,315 | 1,156 | 32 | 129 | 6 | 132 | 78.5 | 17.1 | 0.5 | 1.9 | 0.1 | 2.0 |
| TX | 28,702 | 22,625 | 3,674 | 291 | 1,486 | 42 | 584 | 78.8 | 12.8 | 1.0 | 5.2 | 0.1 | 2.0 |
| UT | 3,161 | 2,866 | 46 | 49 | 85 | 33 | 82 | 90.7 | 1.4 | 1.5 | 2.7 | 1.1 | 2.6 |
| VT | 626 | 590 | 9 | 2 | 13 | (Z) | 12 | 94.2 | 1.4 | 0.4 | 2.0 | (Z) | 2.0 |
| VA | 8,518 | 5,919 | 1,691 | 46 | 589 | 10 | 262 | 69.5 | 19.9 | 0.5 | 6.9 | 0.1 | 3.1 |
| WA | 7,536 | 5,945 | 323 | 144 | 703 | 59 | 361 | 78.9 | 4.3 | 1.9 | 9.3 | 0.8 | 4.8 |
| WV | 1,806 | 1,688 | 65 | 5 | 15 | 1 | 32 | 93.5 | 3.6 | 0.3 | 0.8 | (Z) | 1.8 |
| WI | 5,814 | 5,064 | 389 | 68 | 176 | 3 | 114 | 87.1 | 6.7 | 1.2 | 3.0 | 0.1 | 2.0 |
| WY | 578 | 535 | 8 | 16 | 6 | 1 | 13 | 92.6 | 1.3 | 2.7 | 1.1 | 0.1 | 2.2 |

Z Less than 500 or 0.05 percent. [1] Data shown for each race alone. [2] Includes Alaska Natives. [3] Includes Other Pacific Islanders.

Source: U.S. Census Bureau, "Annual Estimates of the Resident Population by Sex, Race, and Hispanic Origin for the United States, States, and Counties: April 1, 2010 to July 1, 2018," <http://factfinder.census.gov>, accessed July 2019.

# Table 21. Large Metropolitan Statistical Areas—Population: 2000 to 2018

[In thousands, except as indicated (695 represents 695,000). As of April 1, except 2018 as of July 1. Covers metropolitan statistical areas with population of 250,000 and over in 2018, as delineated by the U.S. Office of Management and Budget as of August 2017. All geographic boundaries for 2010 to 2018 population estimates are defined as of January 1, 2018. For definitions and components of all metropolitan and micropolitan areas, see Appendix II. Minus sign (-) indicates decrease]

| Metropolitan statistical area | 2000 | 2010, esti-mates base [1] | 2018 | Change 2000–2010 [2] Number | Change 2000–2010 [2] Percent | Change 2010–2018 Number | Change 2010–2018 Percent | Rank, 2018 |
|---|---|---|---|---|---|---|---|---|
| Akron, OH | 695 | 703 | 705 | 8 | 1.2 | 2 | 0.2 | 82 |
| Albany-Schenectady-Troy, NY | 826 | 871 | 883 | 45 | 5.4 | 12 | 1.4 | 64 |
| Albuquerque, NM | 730 | 887 | 916 | 157 | 21.6 | 29 | 3.3 | 60 |
| Allentown-Bethlehem-Easton, PA-NJ | 740 | 821 | 843 | 81 | 10.9 | 22 | 2.6 | 69 |
| Amarillo, TX | 229 | 252 | 266 | 23 | 10.2 | 14 | 5.6 | 183 |
| Anchorage, AK | 320 | 381 | 399 | 61 | 19.2 | 18 | 4.8 | 134 |
| Ann Arbor, MI | 323 | 345 | 371 | 22 | 6.8 | 26 | 7.5 | 144 |
| Asheville, NC | 369 | 425 | 460 | 56 | 15.1 | 35 | 8.2 | 117 |
| Atlanta-Sandy Springs-Roswell, GA | 4,263 | 5,287 | 5,950 | 1,023 | 24.0 | 663 | 12.5 | 9 |
| Atlantic City-Hammonton, NJ | 253 | 275 | 265 | 22 | 8.7 | -9 | -3.3 | 185 |
| Augusta-Richmond County, GA-SC | 508 | 565 | 604 | 57 | 11.2 | 39 | 7.0 | 92 |
| Austin-Round Rock, TX | 1,250 | 1,716 | 2,168 | 467 | 37.3 | 452 | 26.3 | 30 |
| Bakersfield, CA | 662 | 840 | 897 | 178 | 26.9 | 57 | 6.8 | 62 |
| Baltimore-Columbia-Towson, MD | 2,553 | 2,711 | 2,803 | 157 | 6.2 | 92 | 3.4 | 21 |
| Baton Rouge, LA | 706 | 803 | 831 | 97 | 13.7 | 29 | 3.6 | 71 |
| Beaumont-Port Arthur, TX | 400 | 403 | 410 | 3 | 0.8 | 6 | 1.6 | 132 |
| Birmingham-Hoover, AL | 1,052 | 1,128 | 1,152 | 76 | 7.2 | 24 | 2.1 | 49 |
| Boise City, ID | 465 | 617 | 730 | 152 | 32.6 | 114 | 18.5 | 80 |
| Boston-Cambridge-Newton, MA-NH | 4,391 | 4,553 | 4,875 | 161 | 3.7 | 323 | 7.1 | 10 |
| Boulder, CO [3] | 270 | 295 | 326 | 25 | 9.2 | 32 | 10.7 | 155 |
| Bremerton-Silverdale, WA | 232 | 251 | 270 | 19 | 8.3 | 19 | 7.4 | 180 |
| Bridgeport-Stamford-Norwalk, CT | 883 | 917 | 944 | 34 | 3.9 | 27 | 2.9 | 58 |
| Brownsville-Harlingen, TX | 335 | 406 | 424 | 71 | 21.2 | 18 | 4.4 | 127 |
| Buffalo-Cheektowaga-Niagara Falls, NY | 1,170 | 1,136 | 1,130 | -35 | -3.0 | -5 | -0.5 | 50 |
| Canton-Massillon, OH | 407 | 404 | 399 | -3 | -0.6 | -6 | -1.4 | 135 |
| Cape Coral-Fort Myers, FL | 441 | 619 | 755 | 178 | 40.3 | 136 | 22.0 | 76 |
| Cedar Rapids, IA | 237 | 258 | 272 | 21 | 8.7 | 14 | 5.6 | 177 |
| Charleston-North Charleston, SC | 549 | 665 | 788 | 116 | 21.1 | 123 | 18.5 | 74 |
| Charlotte-Concord-Gastonia, NC-SC | 1,717 | 2,217 | 2,569 | 500 | 29.1 | 352 | 15.9 | 23 |
| Chattanooga, TN-GA | 477 | 528 | 561 | 52 | 10.8 | 33 | 6.2 | 99 |
| Chicago-Naperville-Elgin, IL-IN-WI | 9,098 | 9,462 | 9,499 | 363 | 4.0 | 37 | 0.4 | 3 |
| Cincinnati, OH-KY-IN | 1,995 | 2,115 | 2,190 | 120 | 6.0 | 76 | 3.6 | 29 |
| Clarksville, TN-KY | 220 | 261 | 292 | 41 | 18.7 | 32 | 12.1 | 166 |
| Cleveland-Elyria, OH | 2,148 | 2,077 | 2,057 | -71 | -3.3 | -20 | -1.0 | 33 |
| College Station-Bryan, TX | 185 | 229 | 262 | 44 | 23.7 | 34 | 14.8 | 187 |
| Colorado Springs, CO | 537 | 646 | 739 | 108 | 20.1 | 93 | 14.5 | 79 |
| Columbia, SC | 647 | 767 | 833 | 120 | 18.6 | 65 | 8.5 | 70 |
| Columbus, GA-AL | 282 | 296 | 305 | 13 | 4.6 | 10 | 3.4 | 163 |
| Columbus, OH | 1,675 | 1,902 | 2,107 | 227 | 13.5 | 205 | 10.8 | 32 |
| Corpus Christi, TX | 403 | 428 | 453 | 25 | 6.2 | 25 | 5.8 | 118 |
| Crestview-Fort Walton Beach-Destin, FL | 211 | 236 | 279 | 25 | 11.7 | 43 | 18.1 | 173 |
| Dallas-Fort Worth-Arlington, TX | 5,204 | 6,426 | 7,540 | 1,222 | 23.5 | 1,113 | 17.3 | 4 |
| Davenport-Moline-Rock Island, IA-IL | 376 | 380 | 381 | 4 | 1.0 | 2 | 0.5 | 140 |
| Dayton, OH | 806 | 799 | 807 | -7 | -0.8 | 7 | 0.9 | 73 |
| Deltona-Daytona Beach-Ormond Beach, FL | 493 | 590 | 660 | 97 | 19.7 | 69 | 11.7 | 86 |
| Denver-Aurora-Lakewood, CO [3] | 2,179 | 2,544 | 2,932 | 364 | 16.7 | 389 | 15.3 | 19 |
| Des Moines-West Des Moines, IA | 481 | 570 | 655 | 88 | 18.3 | 86 | 15.1 | 87 |
| Detroit-Warren-Dearborn, MI | 4,453 | 4,296 | 4,326 | -156 | -3.5 | 30 | 0.7 | 14 |
| Duluth, MN-WI | 275 | 280 | 279 | 4 | 1.6 | -1 | -0.3 | 172 |
| Durham-Chapel Hill, NC | 426 | 507 | 575 | 78 | 18.3 | 69 | 13.6 | 96 |
| El Paso, TX | 683 | 804 | 846 | 121 | 17.7 | 41 | 5.2 | 68 |
| Erie, PA | 281 | 281 | 272 | (-Z) | -0.1 | -9 | -3.0 | 178 |
| Eugene, OR | 323 | 352 | 380 | 29 | 8.9 | 28 | 7.9 | 141 |
| Evansville, IN-KY | 296 | 312 | 315 | 15 | 5.2 | 3 | 1.0 | 159 |
| Fayetteville, NC | 337 | 366 | 387 | 30 | 8.8 | 21 | 5.7 | 138 |
| Fayetteville-Springdale-Rogers, AR-MO | 347 | 463 | 549 | 116 | 33.5 | 86 | 18.6 | 102 |
| Flint, MI | 436 | 426 | 407 | -10 | -2.4 | -19 | -4.4 | 133 |
| Fort Collins, CO | 251 | 300 | 351 | 48 | 19.1 | 51 | 17.0 | 150 |
| Fort Smith, AR-OK | 255 | 281 | 282 | 25 | 9.8 | 2 | 0.6 | 171 |
| Fort Wayne, IN | 390 | 416 | 438 | 26 | 6.7 | 21 | 5.1 | 123 |
| Fresno, CA | 799 | 930 | 994 | 131 | 16.4 | 64 | 6.9 | 54 |
| Gainesville, FL | 232 | 264 | 288 | 32 | 13.7 | 24 | 9.1 | 168 |
| Grand Rapids-Wyoming, MI | 931 | 989 | 1,069 | 58 | 6.3 | 80 | 8.1 | 52 |
| Greeley, CO [3] | 181 | 253 | 314 | 72 | 39.7 | 61 | 24.3 | 160 |
| Green Bay, WI | 283 | 306 | 322 | 24 | 8.4 | 15 | 5.0 | 157 |
| Greensboro-High Point, NC | 643 | 724 | 768 | 80 | 12.5 | 44 | 6.1 | 75 |
| Greenville-Anderson-Mauldin, SC | 726 | 824 | 907 | 98 | 13.6 | 83 | 10.0 | 61 |
| Gulfport-Biloxi-Pascagoula, MS | 364 | 371 | 397 | 7 | 1.8 | 26 | 7.1 | 136 |
| Hagerstown-Martinsburg, MD-WV | 208 | 252 | 268 | 44 | 21.1 | 16 | 6.5 | 181 |
| Harrisburg-Carlisle, PA | 509 | 549 | 575 | 40 | 7.9 | 25 | 4.6 | 97 |
| Hartford-West Hartford-East Hartford, CT | 1,149 | 1,212 | 1,206 | 64 | 5.6 | -6 | -0.5 | 48 |
| Hickory-Lenoir-Morganton, NC | 342 | 366 | 368 | 24 | 6.9 | 3 | 0.7 | 146 |
| Houston-The Woodlands-Sugar Land, TX | 4,693 | 5,920 | 6,997 | 1,227 | 26.1 | 1,077 | 18.2 | 5 |
| Huntington-Ashland, WV-KY-OH | 362 | 365 | 353 | 3 | 0.7 | -12 | -3.3 | 149 |
| Huntsville, AL | 342 | 418 | 463 | 75 | 22.0 | 45 | 10.8 | 116 |

See footnotes at end of table.

| Metropolitan statistical area | 2000 | 2010, estimates base [1] | 2018 | Change | | | | Rank, 2018 |
|---|---|---|---|---|---|---|---|---|
| | | | | 2000–2010 [2] | | 2010–2018 | | |
| | | | | Number | Percent | Number | Percent | |
| Indianapolis-Carmel-Anderson, IN | 1,658 | 1,888 | 2,049 | 229 | 13.8 | 161 | 8.5 | 34 |
| Jackson, MS | 525 | 568 | 580 | 42 | 8.0 | 13 | 2.2 | 95 |
| Jacksonville, FL | 1,123 | 1,346 | 1,535 | 223 | 19.8 | 189 | 14.1 | 40 |
| Kalamazoo-Portage, MI | 315 | 327 | 340 | 12 | 3.7 | 14 | 4.2 | 152 |
| Kansas City, MO-KS | 1,811 | 2,009 | 2,144 | 198 | 10.9 | 134 | 6.7 | 31 |
| Kennewick-Richland, WA | 192 | 253 | 296 | 62 | 32.1 | 43 | 16.9 | 164 |
| Killeen-Temple, TX | 331 | 405 | 452 | 75 | 22.6 | 46 | 11.4 | 119 |
| Kingsport-Bristol-Bristol, TN-VA | 298 | 310 | 307 | 11 | 3.7 | -3 | -0.9 | 162 |
| Knoxville, TN | 748 | 838 | 883 | 89 | 11.9 | 46 | 5.4 | 63 |
| Lafayette, LA | 425 | 467 | 489 | 42 | 9.8 | 23 | 4.8 | 109 |
| Lakeland-Winter Haven, FL | 484 | 602 | 708 | 118 | 24.4 | 106 | 17.6 | 81 |
| Lancaster, PA | 471 | 519 | 544 | 49 | 10.4 | 24 | 4.6 | 103 |
| Lansing-East Lansing, MI | 448 | 464 | 482 | 16 | 3.6 | 18 | 3.9 | 111 |
| Laredo, TX | 193 | 250 | 276 | 57 | 29.6 | 26 | 10.2 | 174 |
| Las Vegas-Henderson-Paradise, NV | 1,376 | 1,951 | 2,232 | 576 | 41.8 | 280 | 14.4 | 28 |
| Lexington-Fayette, KY | 408 | 472 | 517 | 64 | 15.6 | 45 | 9.4 | 106 |
| Lincoln, NE | 267 | 302 | 335 | 35 | 13.3 | 32 | 10.7 | 154 |
| Little Rock-North Little Rock-Conway, AR | 611 | 700 | 741 | 89 | 14.6 | 41 | 5.9 | 78 |
| Los Angeles-Long Beach-Anaheim, CA | 12,366 | 12,829 | 13,291 | 463 | 3.7 | 463 | 3.6 | 2 |
| Louisville/Jefferson County, KY-IN | 1,121 | 1,236 | 1,297 | 115 | 10.2 | 62 | 5.0 | 45 |
| Lubbock, TX | 256 | 291 | 319 | 35 | 13.5 | 28 | 9.7 | 158 |
| Lynchburg, VA | 229 | 253 | 263 | 24 | 10.5 | 11 | 4.2 | 186 |
| Madison, WI | 535 | 605 | 660 | 70 | 13.1 | 55 | 9.1 | 85 |
| Manchester-Nashua, NH | 381 | 401 | 415 | 20 | 5.2 | 15 | 3.6 | 129 |
| McAllen-Edinburg-Mission, TX | 569 | 775 | 866 | 205 | 36.1 | 91 | 11.8 | 65 |
| Memphis, TN-MS-AR | 1,213 | 1,325 | 1,351 | 112 | 9.2 | 26 | 1.9 | 43 |
| Merced, CA | 211 | 256 | 275 | 45 | 21.5 | 19 | 7.4 | 175 |
| Miami-Fort Lauderdale-West Palm Beach, FL | 5,008 | 5,566 | 6,199 | 557 | 11.1 | 632 | 11.4 | 7 |
| Milwaukee-Waukesha-West Allis, WI | 1,501 | 1,556 | 1,576 | 55 | 3.7 | 20 | 1.3 | 39 |
| Minneapolis-St. Paul-Bloomington, MN-WI | 3,032 | 3,349 | 3,629 | 317 | 10.5 | 280 | 8.4 | 16 |
| Mobile, AL | 400 | 413 | 414 | 13 | 3.3 | 1 | 0.1 | 130 |
| Modesto, CA | 447 | 514 | 550 | 67 | 15.1 | 35 | 6.9 | 101 |
| Montgomery, AL | 347 | 375 | 373 | 28 | 8.1 | -1 | -0.4 | 143 |
| Myrtle Beach-Conway-North Myrtle Beach, SC-NC | 270 | 377 | 481 | 107 | 39.6 | 104 | 27.7 | 112 |
| Naples-Immokalee-Marco Island, FL | 251 | 322 | 378 | 70 | 27.9 | 57 | 17.7 | 142 |
| Nashville-Davidson-Murfreesboro-Franklin, TN | 1,381 | 1,671 | 1,931 | 290 | 21.0 | 260 | 15.6 | 36 |
| New Haven-Milford, CT | 824 | 862 | 858 | 38 | 4.7 | -5 | -0.6 | 66 |
| New Orleans-Metairie, LA | 1,338 | 1,190 | 1,270 | -148 | -11.1 | 81 | 6.8 | 46 |
| New York-Newark-Jersey City, NY-NJ-PA | 18,945 | 19,567 | 19,979 | 623 | 3.3 | 413 | 2.1 | 1 |
| North Port-Sarasota-Bradenton, FL | 590 | 702 | 822 | 112 | 19.0 | 119 | 17.0 | 72 |
| Norwich-New London, CT | 259 | 274 | 267 | 15 | 5.8 | -7 | -2.7 | 182 |
| Ocala, FL | 259 | 331 | 360 | 72 | 28.0 | 29 | 8.7 | 148 |
| Ogden-Clearfield, UT | 485 | 597 | 675 | 112 | 23.0 | 78 | 13.0 | 83 |
| Oklahoma City, OK | 1,095 | 1,253 | 1,396 | 158 | 14.4 | 143 | 11.4 | 41 |
| Olympia-Tumwater, WA | 207 | 252 | 286 | 45 | 21.7 | 34 | 13.5 | 169 |
| Omaha-Council Bluffs, NE-IA | 767 | 865 | 942 | 98 | 12.8 | 77 | 8.9 | 59 |
| Orlando-Kissimmee-Sanford, FL | 1,645 | 2,134 | 2,573 | 490 | 29.8 | 439 | 20.5 | 22 |
| Oxnard-Thousand Oaks-Ventura, CA | 753 | 823 | 851 | 70 | 9.3 | 28 | 3.3 | 67 |
| Palm Bay-Melbourne-Titusville, FL | 476 | 543 | 597 | 67 | 14.1 | 53 | 9.8 | 94 |
| Pensacola-Ferry Pass-Brent, FL | 412 | 449 | 495 | 37 | 8.9 | 46 | 10.2 | 108 |
| Peoria, IL | 367 | 379 | 368 | 12 | 3.3 | -11 | -2.9 | 147 |
| Philadelphia-Camden-Wilmington, PA-NJ-DE-MD | 5,687 | 5,966 | 6,096 | 278 | 4.9 | 131 | 2.2 | 8 |
| Phoenix-Mesa-Scottsdale, AZ | 3,252 | 4,193 | 4,858 | 941 | 28.9 | 665 | 15.9 | 11 |
| Pittsburgh, PA | 2,431 | 2,356 | 2,325 | -75 | -3.1 | -32 | -1.3 | 27 |
| Port St. Lucie, FL | 319 | 424 | 482 | 105 | 32.8 | 58 | 13.7 | 110 |
| Portland-South Portland, ME | 488 | 514 | 535 | 27 | 5.4 | 21 | 4.1 | 105 |
| Portland-Vancouver-Hillsboro, OR-WA | 1,928 | 2,226 | 2,479 | 298 | 15.5 | 253 | 11.4 | 25 |
| Providence-Warwick, RI-MA | 1,583 | 1,601 | 1,621 | 18 | 1.1 | 20 | 1.3 | 38 |
| Provo-Orem, UT | 377 | 527 | 634 | 150 | 39.8 | 107 | 20.3 | 90 |
| Raleigh, NC | 797 | 1,130 | 1,363 | 333 | 41.8 | 232 | 20.5 | 42 |
| Reading, PA | 374 | 412 | 420 | 38 | 10.1 | 9 | 2.1 | 128 |
| Reno, NV | 343 | 425 | 470 | 83 | 24.1 | 44 | 10.4 | 113 |
| Richmond, VA | 1,056 | 1,208 | 1,306 | 152 | 14.4 | 98 | 8.1 | 44 |
| Riverside-San Bernardino-Ontario, CA | 3,255 | 4,225 | 4,622 | 970 | 29.8 | 397 | 9.4 | 13 |
| Roanoke, VA | 288 | 309 | 314 | 20 | 7.1 | 6 | 1.8 | 161 |
| Rochester, NY | 1,062 | 1,080 | 1,071 | 17 | 1.6 | -9 | -0.8 | 51 |
| Rockford, IL | 320 | 349 | 338 | 29 | 9.1 | -12 | -3.4 | 153 |
| Sacramento-Roseville-Arden-Arcade, CA | 1,797 | 2,149 | 2,345 | 352 | 19.6 | 196 | 9.1 | 26 |
| Salem, OR | 347 | 391 | 432 | 44 | 12.5 | 41 | 10.6 | 126 |
| Salinas, CA | 402 | 415 | 436 | 13 | 3.3 | 21 | 4.9 | 125 |
| Salisbury, MD-DE | 313 | 374 | 410 | 61 | 19.6 | 36 | 9.7 | 131 |
| Salt Lake City, UT | 939 | 1,088 | 1,223 | 149 | 15.8 | 135 | 12.4 | 47 |
| San Antonio-New Braunfels, TX | 1,712 | 2,143 | 2,518 | 431 | 25.2 | 376 | 17.5 | 24 |
| San Diego-Carlsbad, CA | 2,814 | 3,095 | 3,343 | 281 | 10.0 | 248 | 8.0 | 17 |
| San Francisco-Oakland-Hayward, CA | 4,124 | 4,336 | 4,729 | 212 | 5.1 | 394 | 9.1 | 12 |
| San Jose-Sunnyvale-Santa Clara, CA | 1,736 | 1,837 | 1,999 | 101 | 5.8 | 162 | 8.8 | 35 |
| San Luis Obispo-Paso Robles-Arroyo Grande, CA | 247 | 270 | 284 | 23 | 9.3 | 14 | 5.3 | 170 |
| Santa Cruz-Watsonville, CA | 256 | 262 | 274 | 7 | 2.7 | 12 | 4.5 | 176 |

See footnotes at end of table.

| Metropolitan statistical area | 2000 | 2010, estimates base [1] | 2018 | Change 2000–2010 [2] Number | Change 2000–2010 [2] Percent | Change 2010–2018 Number | Change 2010–2018 Percent | Rank, 2018 |
|---|---|---|---|---|---|---|---|---|
| Santa Maria-Santa Barbara, CA | 399 | 424 | 447 | 25 | 6.1 | 23 | 5.3 | 122 |
| Santa Rosa, CA | 459 | 484 | 500 | 25 | 5.5 | 16 | 3.3 | 107 |
| Savannah, GA | 293 | 348 | 389 | 55 | 18.6 | 42 | 12.1 | 137 |
| Scranton-Wilkes-Barre-Hazleton, PA | 561 | 564 | 555 | 3 | 0.5 | -8 | -1.4 | 100 |
| Seattle-Tacoma-Bellevue, WA | 3,044 | 3,440 | 3,939 | 396 | 13.0 | 500 | 14.5 | 15 |
| Shreveport-Bossier City, LA | 418 | 440 | 436 | 22 | 5.3 | -3 | -0.8 | 124 |
| Sioux Falls, SD | 187 | 228 | 266 | 41 | 22.0 | 37 | 16.4 | 184 |
| South Bend-Mishawaka, IN-MI | 317 | 319 | 322 | 3 | 0.8 | 3 | 1.0 | 156 |
| Spartanburg, SC | 284 | 313 | 341 | 30 | 10.4 | 28 | 8.9 | 151 |
| Spokane-Spokane Valley, WA | 470 | 528 | 573 | 58 | 12.4 | 46 | 8.7 | 98 |
| Springfield, MA | 608 | 622 | 632 | 13 | 2.2 | 10 | 1.6 | 91 |
| Springfield, MO | 368 | 437 | 467 | 68 | 18.6 | 30 | 6.9 | 114 |
| St. Louis, MO-IL [4] | 2,675 | 2,788 | 2,805 | 112 | 4.2 | 18 | 0.6 | 20 |
| Stockton-Lodi, CA | 564 | 685 | 753 | 122 | 21.6 | 67 | 9.8 | 77 |
| Syracuse, NY | 650 | 663 | 651 | 12 | 1.9 | -12 | -1.8 | 88 |
| Tallahassee, FL | 320 | 369 | 385 | 47 | 14.7 | 16 | 4.4 | 139 |
| Tampa-St. Petersburg-Clearwater, FL | 2,396 | 2,783 | 3,143 | 387 | 16.2 | 359 | 12.9 | 18 |
| Toledo, OH | 618 | 610 | 603 | -8 | -1.3 | -7 | -1.2 | 93 |
| Trenton, NJ | 351 | 368 | 370 | 16 | 4.5 | 2 | 0.6 | 145 |
| Tucson, AZ | 844 | 980 | 1,039 | 137 | 16.2 | 59 | 6.0 | 53 |
| Tulsa, OK | 860 | 938 | 994 | 78 | 9.1 | 56 | 6.0 | 55 |
| Urban Honolulu, HI | 876 | 953 | 980 | 77 | 8.8 | 27 | 2.8 | 56 |
| Utica-Rome, NY | 300 | 299 | 291 | (-Z) | -0.2 | -8 | -2.6 | 167 |
| Vallejo-Fairfield, CA | 395 | 413 | 447 | 19 | 4.8 | 33 | 8.1 | 121 |
| Virginia Beach-Norfolk-Newport News, VA-NC | 1,580 | 1,677 | 1,729 | 97 | 6.1 | 52 | 3.1 | 37 |
| Visalia-Porterville, CA | 368 | 442 | 466 | 74 | 20.2 | 24 | 5.4 | 115 |
| Waco, TX | 232 | 253 | 272 | 21 | 8.9 | 19 | 7.6 | 179 |
| Washington-Arlington-Alexandria, DC-VA-MD-WV | 4,837 | 5,636 | 6,250 | 799 | 16.5 | 614 | 10.9 | 6 |
| Wichita, KS | 580 | 631 | 645 | 51 | 8.8 | 14 | 2.2 | 89 |
| Wilmington, NC | 201 | 255 | 294 | 53 | 26.6 | 40 | 15.5 | 165 |
| Winston-Salem, NC | 569 | 641 | 671 | 71 | 12.5 | 31 | 4.8 | 84 |
| Worcester, MA-CT | 860 | 917 | 948 | 57 | 6.6 | 31 | 3.4 | 57 |
| Yakima, WA | 223 | 243 | 251 | 21 | 9.3 | 8 | 3.4 | 188 |
| York-Hanover, PA | 382 | 435 | 448 | 53 | 13.9 | 13 | 3.0 | 120 |
| Youngstown-Warren-Boardman, OH-PA | 603 | 566 | 539 | -37 | -6.2 | -27 | -4.7 | 104 |

Z Less than 500 or .05 percent. [1] The April 1, 2010 population estimates base reflects changes to the Census 2010 population from the Count Question Resolution program and geographic program revisions. [2] Based on census data. [3] Broomfield County, CO, was formed from parts of Adams, Boulder, Jefferson, and Weld Counties, CO, on November 15, 2001, and is coextensive with Broomfield city. For purposes of defining and presenting data for metropolitan statistical areas, Broomfield city is treated as if it were a county at the time of the 2000 census. [4] The portion of Sullivan city in Crawford County, Missouri, is legally part of the St. Louis, MO-IL MSA. Data shown here do not include this area.

Source: U.S. Census Bureau, "CPH-T-5. Population Change for Metropolitan and Micropolitan Statistical Areas in the United States and Puerto Rico (February 2013 Delineations): 2000 to 2010," March 2013, <http://www.census.gov/population/www/cen2010/cph-t/cph-t-5.html>; and Metropolitan and Micropolitan Statistical Areas Population Totals: 2010-2018, "Annual Estimates of the Resident Population: April 1, 2010 to July 1, 2018" and "Cumulative Estimates of Resident Population Change and Rankings: April 1, 2010 to July 1, 2018," April 2019, <https://www.census.gov/programs-surveys/popest/data/tables.html>; accessed April 2019.

# Table 22. The 50 Largest Metropolitan Statistical Areas in 2018—Components of Population Change: 2010 to 2018

[Covers period April 1, 2010 to July 1, 2018. Covers metropolitan statistical areas as delineated by the U.S. Office of Management and Budget as of August 2017. For definitions and components of all metropolitan and micropolitan areas, see Appendix II. Minus sign (-) indicates decrease or outmigration]

| Metropolitan statistical area | Number | | | | | | | Percent change |
|---|---|---|---|---|---|---|---|---|
| | Total change [1] | Natural increase | | | Net migration | | | |
| | | Total | Births | Deaths | Total | International | Domestic migration | |
| Atlanta-Sandy Springs-Roswell, GA............. | 663,201 | 310,444 | 600,415 | 289,971 | 351,958 | 138,098 | 213,860 | 11.1 |
| Austin-Round Rock, TX............................ | 451,995 | 136,139 | 214,624 | 78,485 | 310,931 | 59,368 | 251,563 | 20.8 |
| Baltimore-Columbia-Towson, MD............... | 92,187 | 79,414 | 277,512 | 198,098 | 14,554 | 61,402 | -46,848 | 3.3 |
| Birmingham-Hoover, AL........................... | 23,743 | 22,943 | 119,160 | 96,217 | 1,466 | 8,081 | -6,615 | 2.1 |
| Boston-Cambridge-Newton, MA-NH............ | 322,792 | 129,112 | 424,813 | 295,701 | 197,049 | 274,852 | -77,803 | 6.6 |
| Buffalo-Cheektowaga-Niagara Falls, NY....... | -5,462 | 156 | 99,888 | 99,732 | -4,873 | 22,783 | -27,656 | -0.5 |
| Charlotte-Concord-Gastonia, NC-SC........... | 352,216 | 100,545 | 248,073 | 147,528 | 250,067 | 45,794 | 204,273 | 13.7 |
| Chicago-Naperville-Elgin, IL-IN-WI............. | 37,177 | 402,723 | 978,809 | 576,086 | -365,909 | 198,688 | -564,597 | 0.4 |
| Cincinnati, OH-KY-IN............................... | 75,550 | 65,861 | 222,609 | 156,748 | 10,873 | 31,557 | -20,684 | 3.4 |
| Cleveland-Elyria, OH.............................. | -20,269 | 14,921 | 190,463 | 175,542 | -34,535 | 37,196 | -71,731 | -1.0 |
| Columbus, OH....................................... | 204,534 | 98,662 | 224,140 | 125,478 | 106,381 | 56,711 | 49,670 | 9.7 |
| Dallas-Fort Worth-Arlington, TX................. | 1,113,489 | 469,719 | 815,184 | 345,465 | 641,751 | 230,158 | 411,593 | 14.8 |
| Denver-Aurora-Lakewood, CO.................. | 388,813 | 148,308 | 287,545 | 139,237 | 237,154 | 54,479 | 182,675 | 13.3 |
| Detroit-Warren-Dearborn, MI.................... | 30,152 | 77,683 | 413,334 | 335,651 | -47,656 | 108,183 | -155,839 | 0.7 |
| Hartford-West Hartford-East Hartford, CT...... | -6,153 | 12,444 | 98,709 | 86,265 | -18,697 | 42,410 | -61,107 | -0.5 |
| Houston-The Woodlands-Sugar Land, TX...... | 1,076,897 | 490,271 | 798,397 | 308,126 | 584,110 | 322,120 | 261,990 | 15.4 |
| Indianapolis-Carmel-Anderson, IN.............. | 160,618 | 88,588 | 219,513 | 130,925 | 72,585 | 34,315 | 38,270 | 7.8 |
| Jacksonville, FL..................................... | 189,110 | 48,295 | 148,758 | 100,463 | 140,382 | 33,622 | 106,760 | 12.3 |
| Kansas City, MO-KS............................... | 134,310 | 89,529 | 227,214 | 137,685 | 45,997 | 24,059 | 21,938 | 6.3 |
| Las Vegas-Henderson-Paradise, NV............ | 280,376 | 96,269 | 221,151 | 124,882 | 183,271 | 29,132 | 154,139 | 12.6 |
| Los Angeles-Long Beach-Anaheim, CA........ | 462,540 | 693,915 | 1,357,648 | 663,733 | -226,757 | 392,900 | -619,657 | 3.5 |
| Louisville/Jefferson County, KY-IN.............. | 61,610 | 29,926 | 129,976 | 100,050 | 32,465 | 21,354 | 11,111 | 4.7 |
| Memphis, TN-MS-AR............................... | 25,791 | 58,652 | 153,471 | 94,819 | -32,900 | 11,636 | -44,536 | 1.9 |
| Miami-Fort Lauderdale-West Palm Beach, FL.. | 632,488 | 160,074 | 558,369 | 398,295 | 472,395 | 592,814 | -120,419 | 10.2 |
| Milwaukee-Waukesha-West Allis, WI........... | 20,159 | 54,367 | 163,878 | 109,511 | -33,585 | 25,675 | -59,260 | 1.3 |
| Minneapolis-St. Paul-Bloomington, MN-WI..... | 280,328 | 190,045 | 376,747 | 186,702 | 92,289 | 84,429 | 7,860 | 7.7 |
| Nashville-Davidson-Murfreesboro-Franklin, TN.. | 260,085 | 79,542 | 194,457 | 114,915 | 178,958 | 35,766 | 143,192 | 13.5 |
| New Orleans-Metairie, LA........................ | 80,510 | 40,522 | 130,891 | 90,369 | 38,789 | 19,529 | 19,260 | 6.3 |
| New York-Newark-Jersey City, NY-NJ-PA...... | 412,950 | 861,724 | 2,051,037 | 1,189,313 | -448,336 | 826,989 | -1,275,325 | 2.1 |
| Oklahoma City, OK................................. | 143,455 | 61,651 | 155,700 | 94,049 | 81,389 | 24,199 | 57,190 | 10.3 |
| Orlando-Kissimmee-Sanford, FL................. | 438,560 | 93,437 | 229,739 | 136,302 | 344,022 | 171,087 | 172,935 | 17.0 |
| Philadelphia-Camden-Wilmington, PA-NJ-DE-MD.. | 130,667 | 143,134 | 589,193 | 446,059 | -8,994 | 151,225 | -160,219 | 2.1 |
| Phoenix-Mesa-Scottsdale, AZ.................... | 664,835 | 227,794 | 485,384 | 257,590 | 435,114 | 108,521 | 326,593 | 13.7 |
| Pittsburgh, PA....................................... | -31,559 | -29,823 | 195,598 | 225,421 | 169 | 29,286 | -29,117 | -1.4 |
| Portland-Vancouver-Hillsboro, OR-WA......... | 252,814 | 90,272 | 228,316 | 138,044 | 162,056 | 49,599 | 112,457 | 10.2 |
| Providence-Warwick, RI-MA..................... | 20,126 | 13,170 | 136,514 | 123,344 | 7,768.0 | 42,967 | -35,199 | 1.2 |
| Raleigh, NC.......................................... | 232,052 | 70,793 | 128,634 | 57,841 | 159,756 | 32,068 | 127,688 | 17.0 |
| Richmond, VA........................................ | 98,083 | 37,299 | 122,833 | 85,534 | 60,899 | 27,235 | 33,664 | 7.5 |
| Riverside-San Bernardino-Ontario, CA......... | 397,395 | 265,101 | 503,697 | 238,596 | 133,831 | 34,970 | 98,861 | 8.6 |
| Sacramento-Roseville-Arden-Arcade, CA...... | 196,059 | 87,639 | 225,512 | 137,873 | 109,665 | 49,929 | 59,736 | 8.4 |
| Salt Lake City, UT.................................. | 134,732 | 99,912 | 154,505 | 54,593 | 35,552 | 30,333 | 5,219 | 11.0 |
| San Antonio-New Braunfels, TX.................. | 375,515 | 134,147 | 268,933 | 134,786 | 239,501 | 47,750 | 191,751 | 14.9 |
| San Diego-Carlsbad, CA.......................... | 248,015 | 186,724 | 358,797 | 172,073 | 64,089 | 110,685 | -46,596 | 7.4 |
| San Francisco-Oakland-Hayward, CA.......... | 393,897 | 180,995 | 427,815 | 246,820 | 213,751 | 218,854 | -5,103 | 8.3 |
| San Jose-Sunnyvale-Santa Clara, CA.......... | 162,170 | 114,532 | 199,013 | 84,481 | 48,707 | 145,265 | -96,558 | 8.1 |
| Seattle-Tacoma-Bellevue, WA................... | 499,558 | 183,697 | 381,978 | 198,281 | 315,825 | 183,524 | 132,301 | 12.7 |
| St. Louis, MO-IL [2]................................ | 17,713 | 64,965 | 278,468 | 213,503 | -46,493 | 30,875 | -77,368 | 0.6 |
| Tampa-St. Petersburg-Clearwater, FL.......... | 359,201 | 13,169 | 261,857 | 248,688 | 344,163 | 102,668 | 241,495 | 11.4 |
| Virginia Beach-Norfolk-Newport News, VA-NC.. | 51,910 | 72,524 | 184,903 | 112,379 | -20,469 | 36,774 | -57,243 | 3.0 |
| Washington-Arlington-Alexandria, DC-VA-MD-WV.. | 613,587 | 386,172 | 665,561 | 279,389 | 225,170 | 322,356 | -97,186 | 9.8 |

[1] Total population change includes residual. This residual represents the change in population that cannot be attributed to any specific demographic component of change. [2] The portion of Sullivan city in Crawford County, Missouri, is legally part of the St. Louis, MO-IL MSA. Data shown here do not include this area.

Source: U.S. Census Bureau, Metropolitan and Micropolitan Statistical Areas Population Totals: 2010-2018, "Estimates of the Components of Resident Population Change: April 1, 2010 to July 1, 2018," <https://www.census.gov/data/tables/time-series/demo/popest/2010s-total-metro-and-micro-statistical-areas.html>, accessed April 2019.

# Table 23. Population by Core Based Statistical Area (CBSA) Status and State: 2018

[327,167 represents 327,167,000. As of July 1. Covers core based statistical areas (metropolitan and micropolitan statistical areas) as delineated by the U.S. Office of Management and Budget as of August 2017. For definitions and components of all metropolitan and micropolitan statistical areas, see Appendix II. Minus sign (-) indicates decrease]

| State | Total population, 2018 (1,000) | Inside Core-Based Statistical Area (metropolitan or micropolitan statistical area), 2018 | | | | Outside CBSA, 2018 | | Percent change, 2010–2018 | | |
| | | Total | | Metro-politan (1,000) | Micro-politan (1,000) | Number (1,000) | Percent | Metro-politan | Micro-politan | Outside CBSAs |
| | | Number (1,000) | Percent | | | | | | | |
|---|---|---|---|---|---|---|---|---|---|---|
| United States.......... | 327,167 | 308,866 | 94.4 | 281,238 | 27,628 | 18,301 | 5.6 | 7.1 | 0.4 | -1.7 |
| Alabama............... | 4,888 | 4,450 | 91.1 | 3,749 | 701 | 437 | 8.9 | 3.9 | -1.2 | -5.2 |
| Alaska................ | 737 | 544 | 73.8 | 498 | 46 | 193 | 26.2 | 4.1 | 2.8 | 3.3 |
| Arizona............... | 7,172 | 7,069 | 98.6 | 6,820 | 249 | 102 | 1.4 | 12.8 | 1.3 | 1.9 |
| Arkansas.............. | 3,014 | 2,480 | 82.3 | 1,884 | 596 | 534 | 17.7 | 7.5 | -2.0 | -3.9 |
| California............. | 39,557 | 39,285 | 99.3 | 38,720 | 565 | 272 | 0.7 | 6.3 | -0.5 | -1.7 |
| Colorado.............. | 5,696 | 5,382 | 94.5 | 4,983 | 399 | 313 | 5.5 | 14.8 | 4.7 | 2.4 |
| Connecticut........... | 3,573 | 3,573 | 100.0 | 3,392 | 181 | – | – | 0.2 | -4.6 | (X) |
| Delaware.............. | 967 | 967 | 100.0 | 967 | – | – | – | 7.7 | (X) | (X) |
| District of Columbia.... | 702 | 702 | 100.0 | 702 | – | – | – | 16.7 | (X) | (X) |
| Florida................ | 21,299 | 20,951 | 98.4 | 20,583 | 368 | 349 | 1.6 | 13.7 | 3.0 | -0.5 |
| Georgia............... | 10,519 | 9,727 | 92.5 | 8,725 | 1,002 | 792 | 7.5 | 10.2 | 1.8 | 0.3 |
| Hawaii................ | 1,420 | 1,420 | 100.0 | 1,147 | 273 | – | – | 3.5 | 8.3 | (X) |
| Idaho................. | 1,754 | 1,612 | 91.9 | 1,292 | 320 | 142 | 8.1 | 15.1 | 4.8 | 1.8 |
| Illinois............... | 12,741 | 12,147 | 95.3 | 11,286 | 861 | 594 | 4.7 | -0.1 | -4.9 | -4.8 |
| Indiana............... | 6,692 | 6,235 | 93.2 | 5,232 | 1,003 | 457 | 6.8 | 4.5 | -1.0 | -2.0 |
| Iowa.................. | 3,156 | 2,433 | 77.1 | 1,889 | 544 | 723 | 22.9 | 8.2 | -1.6 | -3.3 |
| Kansas................ | 2,912 | 2,529 | 86.8 | 1,992 | 536 | 383 | 13.2 | 5.0 | -2.9 | -5.2 |
| Kentucky.............. | 4,468 | 3,526 | 78.9 | 2,638 | 888 | 942 | 21.1 | 5.6 | 2.4 | -3.1 |
| Louisiana............. | 4,660 | 4,338 | 93.1 | 3,910 | 428 | 322 | 6.9 | 4.0 | -2.8 | -3.9 |
| Maine................. | 1,338 | 916 | 68.5 | 794 | 122 | 422 | 31.5 | 2.4 | -0.1 | -1.9 |
| Maryland.............. | 6,043 | 5,961 | 98.6 | 5,892 | 69 | 82 | 1.4 | 4.8 | -2.0 | -1.9 |
| Massachusetts......... | 6,902 | 6,891 | 99.8 | 6,803 | 88 | 11 | 0.2 | 5.5 | 11.4 |
| Michigan.............. | 9,996 | 9,333 | 93.4 | 8,197 | 1,136 | 663 | 6.6 | 1.6 | (-Z) | -2.5 |
| Minnesota............. | 5,611 | 5,099 | 90.9 | 4,368 | 732 | 512 | 9.1 | 7.5 | 1.3 | -1.7 |
| Mississippi............ | 2,987 | 2,350 | 78.7 | 1,391 | 959 | 637 | 21.3 | 4.8 | -2.3 | -3.3 |
| Missouri.............. | 6,126 | 5,300 | 86.5 | 4,586 | 714 | 826 | 13.5 | 3.6 | -0.1 | -2.2 |
| Montana.............. | 1,062 | 702 | 66.1 | 372 | 330 | 360 | 33.9 | 6.5 | 13.9 | 2.9 |
| Nebraska.............. | 1,929 | 1,593 | 82.6 | 1,265 | 328 | 336 | 17.4 | 9.7 | 0.5 | -3.0 |
| Nevada............... | 3,034 | 3,002 | 98.9 | 2,757 | 245 | 32 | 1.1 | 13.4 | 4.3 | -3.6 |
| New Hampshire........ | 1,356 | 1,308 | 96.4 | 855 | 453 | 49 | 3.6 | 4.3 | 0.8 | 2.0 |
| New Jersey............ | 8,909 | 8,909 | 100.0 | 8,909 | – | – | – | 1.3 | (X) | (X) |
| New Mexico............ | 2,095 | 2,024 | 96.6 | 1,409 | 616 | 71 | 3.4 | 2.8 | 0.8 | -8.7 |
| New York.............. | 19,542 | 19,155 | 98.0 | 18,175 | 979 | 388 | 2.0 | 1.2 | -3.6 | -4.5 |
| North Carolina......... | 10,384 | 9,753 | 93.9 | 8,168 | 1,585 | 630 | 6.1 | 11.3 | 2.0 | -2.3 |
| North Dakota.......... | 760 | 564 | 74.3 | 385 | 179 | 196 | 25.7 | 16.2 | 16.9 | 4.3 |
| Ohio.................. | 11,689 | 11,242 | 96.2 | 9,337 | 1,905 | 448 | 3.8 | 2.1 | -1.6 | -2.1 |
| Oklahoma............. | 3,943 | 3,405 | 86.3 | 2,669 | 736 | 539 | 13.7 | 7.9 | 0.9 | -1.7 |
| Oregon............... | 4,191 | 4,089 | 97.6 | 3,515 | 574 | 101 | 2.4 | 10.6 | 3.4 | 3.5 |
| Pennsylvania.......... | 12,807 | 12,434 | 97.1 | 11,353 | 1,080 | 373 | 2.9 | 1.4 | -3.7 | -3.7 |
| Rhode Island.......... | 1,057 | 1,057 | 100.0 | 1,057 | – | – | – | 0.4 | (X) | (X) |
| South Carolina........ | 5,084 | 4,785 | 94.1 | 4,340 | 445 | 300 | 5.9 | 12.4 | 0.2 | -6.3 |
| South Dakota.......... | 882 | 663 | 75.2 | 430 | 233 | 219 | 24.8 | 14.0 | 5.2 | 1.8 |
| Tennessee............. | 6,770 | 6,138 | 90.7 | 5,254 | 883 | 632 | 9.3 | 8.1 | 3.4 | -0.1 |
| Texas................. | 28,702 | 27,305 | 95.1 | 25,629 | 1,677 | 1,396 | 4.9 | 15.8 | 2.4 | 2.1 |
| Utah.................. | 3,161 | 3,014 | 95.3 | 2,830 | 184 | 147 | 4.7 | 14.9 | 14.8 | 4.3 |
| Vermont............... | 626 | 464 | 74.1 | 221 | 243 | 162 | 25.9 | 4.6 | -2.9 | -1.2 |
| Virginia............... | 8,518 | 7,743 | 90.9 | 7,480 | 263 | 775 | 9.1 | 8.0 | -6.4 | -2.1 |
| Washington............ | 7,536 | 7,375 | 97.9 | 6,781 | 594 | 160 | 2.1 | 12.6 | 7.6 | 5.1 |
| West Virginia.......... | 1,806 | 1,413 | 78.3 | 1,117 | 296 | 393 | 21.7 | -1.4 | -3.3 | -5.2 |
| Wisconsin............. | 5,814 | 5,091 | 87.6 | 4,312 | 779 | 723 | 12.4 | 3.2 | -0.1 | -0.8 |
| Wyoming.............. | 578 | 419 | 72.5 | 178 | 241 | 159 | 27.5 | 6.4 | 1.3 | 0.1 |

– Represents zero. Z less than .05. X Not applicable.

Source: U.S. Census Bureau, Metropolitan and Micropolitan Statistical Areas Population Totals: 2010-2018, "Datasets, CBSA-EST2018-alldata," <https://www.census.gov/data/datasets/time-series/demo/popest/2010s-total-metro-and-micro-statistical-areas.html>, accessed April 2019.

# Table 24. Population of Incorporated Places With 175,000 or More Inhabitants in 2018: 1990 to 2018

[In thousands, except as indicated (223 represents 223,000). Census years as of April 1; all other years, as of July 1. Data for the 2010 estimates base and July estimates are based on the 2010 Census and reflect changes to the April 1, 2010 population due to the Count Question Resolution program and geographic program revisions. All geographic boundaries for the 2018 population estimates series are defined as of January 1, 2018. For 1990 and 2000, the counts relate to places as defined on January 1, 2010. Minus sign (-) indicates decrease. See Appendix III]

| City | Number (1,000) | | | | | Percent change | | | Rank, 2018 |
|------|------|------|------------------------|------|------|----------------|----------------|----------------|------|
| | 1990 | 2000 | 2010, estimates base | 2017 | 2018 | 1990 to 2000 [1] | 2000 to 2010 [1] | 2010 to 2018 | |
| Akron, Ohio | 223 | 217 | 199 | 198 | 198 | -2.7 | -8.3 | -0.6 | 120 |
| Albuquerque, New Mexico | 385 | 449 | 546 | 560 | 560 | 16.6 | 21.7 | 2.6 | 32 |
| Amarillo, Texas | 158 | 174 | 191 | 200 | 200 | 10.2 | 9.8 | 4.9 | 116 |
| Anaheim, California | 267 | 328 | 336 | 351 | 352 | 23.0 | 2.5 | 4.6 | 55 |
| Anchorage, Alaska | 226 | 260 | 292 | 294 | 292 | 15.0 | 12.1 | -0.1 | 68 |
| Arlington, Texas | 262 | 333 | 365 | 397 | 398 | 27.2 | 9.8 | 9.0 | 48 |
| Atlanta, Georgia | 394 | 416 | 427 | 492 | 498 | 5.7 | 0.8 | 16.7 | 37 |
| Augusta-Richmond County, Georgia [2] | 186 | 200 | 196 | 197 | 197 | 7.3 | -2.0 | 0.6 | 123 |
| Aurora, Colorado | 222 | 276 | 325 | 367 | 374 | 24.6 | 17.6 | 15.2 | 54 |
| Aurora, Illinois | 100 | 143 | 198 | 201 | 200 | 43.6 | 38.4 | 0.9 | 118 |
| Austin, Texas | 466 | 657 | 802 | 952 | 964 | 41.0 | 20.4 | 20.2 | 11 |
| Bakersfield, California | 175 | 247 | 348 | 379 | 384 | 41.2 | 40.6 | 10.1 | 53 |
| Baltimore, Maryland | 736 | 651 | 621 | 610 | 602 | -11.5 | -4.6 | -3.0 | 30 |
| Baton Rouge, Louisiana | 223 | 228 | 229 | 224 | 222 | 2.2 | 0.7 | -3.4 | 99 |
| Birmingham, Alabama | 265 | 243 | 212 | 211 | 210 | -8.5 | -12.6 | -1.0 | 107 |
| Boise City, Idaho | 126 | 186 | 209 | 228 | 229 | 48.0 | 10.7 | 9.3 | 97 |
| Boston, Massachusetts | 575 | 589 | 618 | 688 | 695 | 2.5 | 4.8 | 12.4 | 21 |
| Brownsville, Texas | 114 | 140 | 175 | 183 | 183 | 22.6 | 25.3 | 4.9 | 137 |
| Buffalo, New York | 328 | 293 | 261 | 256 | 256 | -10.8 | -10.7 | -1.9 | 83 |
| Cape Coral, Florida | 75 | 102 | 154 | 183 | 189 | 36.1 | 50.9 | 22.7 | 132 |
| Chandler, Arizona | 90 | 177 | 236 | 254 | 257 | 96.5 | 33.7 | 8.9 | 82 |
| Charlotte, North Carolina | 428 | 541 | 736 | 859 | 872 | 26.4 | 35.2 | 18.6 | 16 |
| Chattanooga, Tennessee | 153 | 156 | 170 | 179 | 181 | 1.5 | 7.8 | 6.0 | 142 |
| Chesapeake, Virginia | 152 | 199 | 222 | 240 | 243 | 31.1 | 11.6 | 9.1 | 92 |
| Chicago, Illinois | 2,783 | 2,896 | 2,696 | 2,713 | 2,706 | 4.1 | -6.9 | 0.4 | 3 |
| Chula Vista, California | 135 | 174 | 244 | 269 | 272 | 28.4 | 40.5 | 11.4 | 76 |
| Cincinnati, Ohio | 364 | 331 | 297 | 302 | 303 | -9.0 | -10.4 | 1.9 | 65 |
| Cleveland, Ohio | 506 | 478 | 397 | 385 | 384 | -5.5 | -17.1 | -3.2 | 52 |
| Colorado Springs, Colorado | 280 | 361 | 417 | 465 | 473 | 28.7 | 15.4 | 13.2 | 39 |
| Columbus, Georgia | 179 | 186 | 191 | 194 | 194 | 3.9 | 2.2 | 1.9 | 126 |
| Columbus, Ohio | 633 | 711 | 789 | 882 | 893 | 12.4 | 10.6 | 13.1 | 14 |
| Corpus Christi, Texas | 258 | 277 | 305 | 325 | 327 | 7.4 | 10.0 | 7.0 | 59 |
| Dallas, Texas | 1,008 | 1,189 | 1,198 | 1,343 | 1,345 | 18.0 | 0.8 | 12.3 | 9 |
| Denver, Colorado | 468 | 555 | 600 | 705 | 716 | 18.6 | 8.2 | 19.5 | 19 |
| Des Moines, Iowa | 193 | 199 | 204 | 217 | 217 | 2.8 | 2.4 | 6.2 | 101 |
| Detroit, Michigan | 1,028 | 951 | 714 | 674 | 673 | -7.5 | -25.0 | -5.8 | 23 |
| Durham, North Carolina | 137 | 187 | 230 | 270 | 274 | 36.9 | 22.1 | 19.3 | 75 |
| El Paso, Texas | 515 | 564 | 648 | 683 | 683 | 9.4 | 15.2 | 5.3 | 22 |
| Fayetteville, North Carolina | 76 | 121 | 201 | 209 | 209 | 59.5 | 65.7 | 4.4 | 109 |
| Fontana, California | 88 | 129 | 196 | 211 | 214 | 47.3 | 52.1 | 8.8 | 105 |
| Fort Lauderdale, Florida | 149 | 152 | 166 | 180 | 183 | 2.1 | 8.6 | 10.2 | 139 |
| Fort Wayne, Indiana | 173 | 206 | 254 | 265 | 268 | 18.9 | 23.3 | 5.5 | 77 |
| Fort Worth, Texas | 448 | 535 | 745 | 875 | 895 | 19.5 | 38.6 | 20.2 | 13 |
| Fremont, California | 173 | 203 | 214 | 234 | 238 | 17.3 | 5.2 | 11.1 | 96 |
| Fresno, California | 354 | 428 | 497 | 526 | 530 | 20.8 | 15.7 | 6.6 | 34 |
| Frisco, Texas | 6 | 34 | 117 | 177 | 188 | 449.3 | 247.0 | 60.6 | 134 |
| Garland, Texas | 181 | 216 | 227 | 239 | 243 | 19.4 | 5.1 | 6.9 | 93 |
| Gilbert, Arizona | 29 | 110 | 208 | 242 | 248 | 276.7 | 90.0 | 19.1 | 88 |
| Glendale, Arizona | 148 | 219 | 226 | 248 | 251 | 48.0 | 3.6 | 10.9 | 87 |
| Glendale, California | 180 | 195 | 192 | 202 | 201 | 8.3 | -1.7 | 5.0 | 112 |
| Grand Prairie, Texas | 100 | 127 | 175 | 194 | 195 | 27.9 | 37.6 | 10.9 | 125 |
| Grand Rapids, Michigan | 189 | 198 | 188 | 199 | 200 | 4.6 | -4.9 | 6.5 | 115 |
| Greensboro, North Carolina | 184 | 224 | 269 | 292 | 295 | 21.8 | 20.4 | 9.6 | 67 |
| Henderson, Nevada | 65 | 175 | 257 | 300 | 310 | 170.0 | 47.0 | 20.7 | 62 |
| Hialeah, Florida | 188 | 226 | 225 | 239 | 239 | 20.4 | -0.8 | 6.3 | 95 |
| Houston, Texas | 1,631 | 1,954 | 2,094 | 2,317 | 2,326 | 19.8 | 7.5 | 11.1 | 4 |
| Huntington Beach, California | 182 | 190 | 191 | 201 | 201 | 4.4 | 0.2 | 5.0 | 113 |
| Huntsville, Alabama | 160 | 158 | 180 | 195 | 197 | -1.0 | 13.8 | 9.4 | 122 |
| Indianapolis, Indiana [2] | 731 | 792 | 820 | 862 | 867 | 8.3 | 3.6 | 5.7 | 17 |
| Irvine, California | 110 | 143 | 212 | 276 | 283 | 29.7 | 48.4 | 33.3 | 72 |
| Irving, Texas | 155 | 192 | 216 | 241 | 242 | 23.6 | 12.9 | 12.0 | 94 |
| Jacksonville, Florida | 635 | 736 | 822 | 892 | 904 | 15.8 | 11.7 | 10.0 | 12 |
| Jersey City, New Jersey | 229 | 240 | 248 | 263 | 266 | 5.0 | 3.1 | 7.2 | 78 |
| Kansas City, Missouri | 435 | 442 | 460 | 488 | 492 | 1.5 | 4.1 | 7.0 | 38 |
| Knoxville, Tennessee | 165 | 174 | 178 | 187 | 188 | 5.4 | 2.9 | 5.2 | 135 |
| Laredo, Texas | 123 | 177 | 236 | 260 | 262 | 43.7 | 33.7 | 11.0 | 80 |
| Las Vegas, Nevada | 258 | 478 | 585 | 636 | 645 | 85.3 | 22.0 | 10.3 | 28 |
| Lexington-Fayette, Kentucky | 225 | 261 | 296 | 322 | 324 | 15.6 | 13.5 | 9.4 | 60 |
| Lincoln, Nebraska | 192 | 226 | 259 | 285 | 287 | 17.5 | 14.5 | 11.1 | 70 |
| Little Rock, Arkansas | 176 | 183 | 193 | 198 | 198 | 4.2 | 5.7 | 2.3 | 121 |
| Long Beach, California | 429 | 462 | 462 | 467 | 467 | 7.5 | 0.2 | 1.1 | 43 |
| Los Angeles, California | 3,486 | 3,695 | 3,793 | 3,982 | 3,990 | 6.0 | 2.6 | 5.2 | 2 |
| Louisville/Jefferson County, Kentucky [2] | [3] 270 | [3] 256 | 595 | 620 | 620 | [3] -4.9 | (X) | 4.2 | 29 |
| Lubbock, Texas | 186 | 200 | 230 | 254 | 256 | 7.2 | 15.0 | 11.4 | 84 |
| Madison, Wisconsin | 191 | 208 | 233 | 255 | 258 | 9.1 | 12.1 | 10.7 | 81 |
| McKinney, Texas | 21 | 54 | 131 | 182 | 192 | 155.5 | 141.2 | 46.1 | 130 |

See footnotes at end of table.

# Table 24. Population of Incorporated Places With 175,000 or More Inhabitants in 2018: 1990 to 2018-Continued.

See headnote on page 29.

| City | Number (1,000) | | | | | Percent change | | | Rank, 2018 |
|---|---|---|---|---|---|---|---|---|---|
| | 1990 | 2000 | 2010, estimates base | 2017 | 2018 | 1990 to 2000 [1] | 2000 to 2010 [1] | 2010 to 2018 | |
| Memphis, Tennessee................ | 610 | 650 | 652 | 652 | 651 | 6.5 | -0.5 | -0.2 | 26 |
| Mesa, Arizona.................... | 288 | 396 | 440 | 500 | 509 | 37.6 | 10.8 | 15.7 | 35 |
| Miami, Florida.................... | 359 | 362 | 400 | 462 | 471 | 1.1 | 10.2 | 17.9 | 40 |
| Milwaukee, Wisconsin............. | 628 | 597 | 595 | 594 | 592 | -5.0 | -0.4 | -0.4 | 31 |
| Minneapolis, Minnesota............ | 368 | 383 | 383 | 421 | 425 | 3.9 | 0.0 | 11.2 | 46 |
| Mobile, Alabama.................. | 196 | 199 | 195 | 191 | 190 | 1.4 | -1.9 | -2.6 | 131 |
| Modesto, California............... | 165 | 189 | 203 | 213 | 215 | 14.6 | 6.5 | 5.9 | 104 |
| Montgomery, Alabama............. | 188 | 202 | 206 | 200 | 198 | 7.5 | 2.1 | -3.5 | 119 |
| Moreno Valley, California.......... | 119 | 142 | 193 | 207 | 209 | 19.9 | 35.8 | 8.1 | 110 |
| Nashville-Davidson, Tennessee [2].... | 488 | 570 | 603 | 665 | 669 | 16.7 | 5.5 | 10.9 | 24 |
| New Orleans, Louisiana............ | 497 | 485 | 344 | 392 | 391 | -2.5 | -29.1 | 13.7 | 50 |
| New York, New York............... | 7,323 | 8,008 | 8,175 | 8,438 | 8,399 | 9.4 | 2.1 | 2.7 | 1 |
| Newark, New Jersey.............. | 275 | 274 | 277 | 281 | 282 | -0.6 | 1.3 | 1.8 | 73 |
| Newport News, Virginia............ | 171 | 180 | 181 | 179 | 179 | 5.1 | 0.3 | -1.3 | 144 |
| Norfolk, Virginia.................. | 261 | 234 | 243 | 245 | 244 | -10.3 | 3.6 | 0.5 | 91 |
| North Las Vegas, Nevada.......... | 48 | 115 | 217 | 241 | 246 | 141.4 | 87.9 | 13.5 | 90 |
| Oakland, California................ | 372 | 399 | 391 | 424 | 429 | 7.3 | -2.2 | 9.8 | 45 |
| Oceanside, California.............. | 128 | 161 | 167 | 176 | 176 | 25.7 | 3.8 | 5.2 | 147 |
| Oklahoma City, Oklahoma.......... | 445 | 506 | 580 | 643 | 649 | 13.8 | 14.6 | 11.9 | 27 |
| Omaha, Nebraska................. | 336 | 390 | 450 | 467 | 468 | 16.2 | 4.9 | 4.0 | 42 |
| Ontario, California................ | 133 | 158 | 164 | 175 | 181 | 18.6 | 3.7 | 10.5 | 141 |
| Orlando, Florida.................. | 165 | 186 | 239 | 281 | 286 | 12.9 | 28.2 | 19.6 | 71 |
| Overland Park, Kansas............ | 112 | 149 | 173 | 191 | 193 | 33.4 | 16.3 | 11.1 | 128 |
| Oxnard, California................ | 143 | 170 | 198 | 209 | 210 | 19.5 | 16.2 | 6.0 | 108 |
| Philadelphia, Pennsylvania......... | 1,586 | 1,518 | 1,526 | 1,580 | 1,584 | -4.3 | 0.6 | 3.8 | 6 |
| Phoenix, Arizona................. | 983 | 1,321 | 1,447 | 1,635 | 1,660 | 34.3 | 9.4 | 14.7 | 5 |
| Pittsburgh, Pennsylvania........... | 370 | 335 | 305 | 302 | 301 | -9.5 | -8.6 | -1.4 | 66 |
| Plano, Texas..................... | 128 | 222 | 260 | 287 | 288 | 73.6 | 17.0 | 10.9 | 69 |
| Port St. Lucie, Florida............. | 56 | 89 | 164 | 189 | 195 | 59.2 | 85.4 | 18.9 | 124 |
| Portland, Oregon................. | 439 | 529 | 584 | 649 | 653 | 20.6 | 10.3 | 11.9 | 25 |
| Providence, Rhode Island.......... | 161 | 174 | 178 | 180 | 179 | 8.0 | 2.5 | 0.8 | 143 |
| Raleigh, North Carolina............ | 212 | 276 | 404 | 466 | 469 | 30.2 | 46.3 | 16.1 | 41 |
| Rancho Cucamonga, California...... | 101 | 128 | 165 | 177 | 178 | 26.0 | 29.4 | 7.5 | 145 |
| Reno, Nevada.................... | 134 | 180 | 225 | 247 | 251 | 34.8 | 24.8 | 11.4 | 86 |
| Richmond, Virginia................ | 203 | 198 | 204 | 227 | 229 | -2.5 | 3.2 | 12.0 | 98 |
| Riverside, California............... | 227 | 255 | 304 | 327 | 330 | 12.6 | 19.1 | 8.6 | 58 |
| Rochester, New York.............. | 230 | 220 | 211 | 206 | 206 | -4.6 | -4.2 | -2.1 | 111 |
| Sacramento, California............. | 369 | 407 | 466 | 501 | 509 | 10.2 | 14.6 | 9.0 | 36 |
| Salt Lake City, Utah.............. | 160 | 182 | 186 | 201 | 201 | 13.6 | 2.6 | 7.6 | 114 |
| San Antonio, Texas............... | 935 | 1,145 | 1,327 | 1,511 | 1,532 | 22.4 | 16.0 | 15.5 | 7 |
| San Bernardino, California......... | 165 | 185 | 210 | 216 | 216 | 12.6 | 13.2 | 3.0 | 103 |
| San Diego, California.............. | 1,111 | 1,223 | 1,302 | 1,414 | 1,426 | 10.2 | 6.9 | 9.5 | 8 |
| San Francisco, California........... | 724 | 777 | 805 | 879 | 883 | 7.3 | 3.7 | 9.7 | 15 |
| San Jose, California............... | 782 | 895 | 952 | 1,032 | 1,030 | 14.4 | 5.7 | 8.2 | 10 |
| Santa Ana, California.............. | 294 | 338 | 325 | 333 | 333 | 15.0 | -4.0 | 2.4 | 57 |
| Santa Clarita, California........... | 111 | 151 | 204 | 210 | 210 | 36.5 | 16.7 | 2.9 | 106 |
| Santa Rosa, California............. | 113 | 148 | 175 | 182 | 178 | 30.3 | 13.7 | 1.4 | 146 |
| Scottsdale, Arizona............... | 130 | 203 | 217 | 252 | 255 | 55.8 | 7.2 | 17.4 | 85 |
| Seattle, Washington............... | 516 | 563 | 609 | 730 | 745 | 9.1 | 8.0 | 22.4 | 18 |
| Shreveport, Louisiana............. | 199 | 200 | 200 | 192 | 189 | 0.8 | -0.4 | -5.7 | 133 |
| Sioux Falls, South Dakota.......... | 101 | 124 | 154 | 178 | 182 | 22.9 | 24.1 | 18.1 | 140 |
| Spokane, Washington.............. | 177 | 196 | 209 | 217 | 219 | 10.4 | 6.8 | 4.6 | 100 |
| St. Louis, Missouri................ | 397 | 348 | 319 | 308 | 303 | -12.2 | -8.3 | -5.1 | 64 |
| St. Paul, Minnesota............... | 272 | 287 | 285 | 305 | 308 | 5.5 | -0.7 | 7.9 | 63 |
| St. Petersburg, Florida............ | 240 | 248 | 245 | 263 | 265 | 3.3 | -1.4 | 8.1 | 79 |
| Stockton, California............... | 211 | 244 | 292 | 309 | 311 | 15.6 | 19.7 | 6.7 | 61 |
| Tacoma, Washington.............. | 177 | 194 | 198 | 213 | 216 | 9.6 | 2.5 | 9.1 | 102 |
| Tallahassee, Florida............... | 125 | 151 | 181 | 192 | 194 | 20.7 | 20.4 | 6.8 | 127 |
| Tampa, Florida................... | 280 | 303 | 336 | 387 | 393 | 8.4 | 10.6 | 16.9 | 49 |
| Tempe, Arizona.................. | 142 | 159 | 162 | 186 | 192 | 11.7 | 2.0 | 18.9 | 129 |
| Toledo, Ohio..................... | 333 | 314 | 287 | 277 | 275 | -5.8 | -8.4 | -4.3 | 74 |
| Tucson, Arizona.................. | 405 | 487 | 527 | 542 | 546 | 20.1 | 6.9 | 3.7 | 33 |
| Tulsa, Oklahoma................. | 367 | 393 | 392 | 402 | 401 | 7.0 | -0.3 | 2.2 | 47 |
| Urban Honolulu CDP, Hawaii [4]....... | (NA) | (NA) | 338 | 350 | 347 | (NA) | (NA) | 2.9 | 56 |
| Vancouver, Washington............ | 46 | 144 | 167 | 180 | 183 | 209.5 | 12.7 | 9.5 | 138 |
| Virginia Beach, Virginia............ | 393 | 425 | 438 | 450 | 450 | 8.2 | 3.0 | 2.8 | 44 |
| Washington, District of Columbia..... | 607 | 572 | 602 | 696 | 702 | -5.7 | 5.2 | 16.7 | 20 |
| Wichita, Kansas.................. | 304 | 344 | 382 | 390 | 389 | 13.2 | 11.1 | 1.8 | 51 |
| Winston-Salem, North Carolina....... | 143 | 186 | 230 | 244 | 246 | 29.5 | 23.6 | 7.3 | 89 |
| Worcester, Massachusetts.......... | 170 | 173 | 181 | 185 | 186 | 1.7 | 4.9 | 2.7 | 136 |
| Yonkers, New York................ | 188 | 196 | 196 | 200 | 200 | 4.3 | -0.1 | 1.9 | 117 |

NA Not available. X Not applicable. [1] Based on census data. [2] Represents the portion of a consolidated city that is not within one or more separately incorporated places. [3] Data are for the incorporated place of Louisville city before consolidation of the city and county governments. [4] CDP=Census Designated Place.

Source: U.S. Census Bureau, 1990, 2000 and 2010 census data: *Census of Population and Housing, 2010, CPH-2. Population and Housing Unit Counts*; and beginning 2010, City and Town Population Totals Tables: 2010-2018, "Annual Estimates of the Resident Population for Incorporated Places Over 50,000, Ranked by July 1, 2018 Population: April 1, 2010 to July 1, 2018," May 2019, <https://www.census.gov/ programs-surveys/popest/data/tables.html>, accessed June 2019.

## Table 25. Incorporated Places by Population Size: 1990 to 2018

[153.1 represents 153,100,000. See Appendix III]

| Population size | Number of incorporated places | | | | Population (mil.) | | | | Percent of total | | | |
|---|---|---|---|---|---|---|---|---|---|---|---|---|
| | 1990 | 2000 | 2010 | 2018 | 1990 | 2000 | 2010 | 2018 | 1990 | 2000 | 2010 | 2018 |
| **Total**........... | **19,262** | **19,452** | **19,540** | **19,495** | **153.1** | **173.5** | **192.0** | **206.1** | **100.0** | **100.0** | **100.0** | **100.0** |
| 1,000,000 or more......... | 8 | 9 | 9 | 10 | 20.0 | 22.9 | 23.6 | 26.0 | 13.1 | 13.2 | 12.3 | 12.6 |
| 500,000 to 999,999........ | 15 | 20 | 24 | 26 | 10.1 | 12.9 | 16.1 | 18.2 | 6.6 | 7.4 | 8.4 | 8.8 |
| 250,000 to 499,999........ | 41 | 37 | 40 | 51 | 14.2 | 13.3 | 14.0 | 17.3 | 9.3 | 7.7 | 7.3 | 8.4 |
| 100,000 to 249,999........ | 131 | 172 | 200 | 223 | 19.1 | 25.5 | 30.2 | 33.0 | 12.5 | 14.7 | 15.7 | 16.0 |
| 50,000 to 99,999.......... | 309 | 363 | 432 | 465 | 21.2 | 24.9 | 30.1 | 32.6 | 13.8 | 14.4 | 15.7 | 15.8 |
| 25,000 to 49,999.......... | 567 | 644 | 723 | 735 | 20.0 | 22.6 | 25.2 | 25.7 | 13.1 | 13.0 | 13.1 | 12.4 |
| 10,000 to 24,999.......... | 1,290 | 1,435 | 1,542 | 1,574 | 20.3 | 22.6 | 24.2 | 24.8 | 13.3 | 13.0 | 12.6 | 12.1 |
| Under 10,000.............. | 16,901 | 16,772 | 16,570 | 16,411 | 28.2 | 28.7 | 28.7 | 28.5 | 18.4 | 16.5 | 14.9 | 13.8 |

Source: U.S. Census Bureau, *1990 Census of Population and Housing, Population and Housing Unit Counts (CPH-2-1)*; *Census 2000 PHC-3, Population and Housing Unit Counts*; *2010 Census Redistricting Data (Public Law 94-171) Summary File*; and City and Town Population Totals Tables: 2010-2018, Incorporated Places and Minor Civil Divisions Datasets, "SUB-EST2018: Subcounty Resident Population Estimates: April 1, 2010 to July 1, 2018," May 2019, <https://www2.census.gov/programs-surveys/popest/datasets/2010-2018/cities/totals/>.

## Table 26. Urban and Rural Population by State: 2000 and 2010

[222,361 represents 222,361,000. As of April 1. Resident population. Based on current urban definitions, see text, this section]

| State | 2000 | | 2010 | | | State | 2000 | | 2010 | | |
|---|---|---|---|---|---|---|---|---|---|---|---|
| | Urban (1,000) | Rural (1,000) | Urban Number (1,000) | Urban Percent | Rural (1,000) | | Urban (1,000) | Rural (1,000) | Urban Number (1,000) | Urban Percent | Rural (1,000) |
| **U.S.......** | **222,361** | **59,061** | **249,253** | **80.7** | **59,492** | MO......... | 3,883 | 1,712 | 4,218 | 70.4 | 1,771 |
| AL......... | 2,466 | 1,981 | 2,822 | 59.0 | 1,958 | MT......... | 488 | 414 | 553 | 55.9 | 436 |
| AK......... | 411 | 216 | 469 | 66.0 | 241 | NE......... | 1,194 | 518 | 1,336 | 73.1 | 491 |
| AZ......... | 4,524 | 607 | 5,741 | 89.8 | 651 | NV......... | 1,829 | 170 | 2,544 | 94.2 | 157 |
| AR......... | 1,404 | 1,269 | 1,638 | 56.2 | 1,278 | NH......... | 732 | 503 | 794 | 60.3 | 523 |
| CA......... | 31,990 | 1,882 | 35,374 | 95.0 | 1,880 | NJ......... | 7,939 | 475 | 8,324 | 94.7 | 468 |
| CO......... | 3,633 | 668 | 4,333 | 86.2 | 696 | NM......... | 1,364 | 456 | 1,594 | 77.4 | 465 |
| CT......... | 2,988 | 418 | 3,145 | 88.0 | 429 | NY......... | 16,603 | 2,374 | 17,028 | 87.9 | 2,350 |
| DE......... | 628 | 156 | 748 | 83.3 | 150 | NC......... | 4,849 | 3,200 | 6,302 | 66.1 | 3,234 |
| DC......... | 572 | 0 | 602 | 100.0 | 0 | ND......... | 359 | 283 | 403 | 59.9 | 270 |
| FL......... | 14,270 | 1,712 | 17,140 | 91.2 | 1,661 | OH......... | 8,782 | 2,571 | 8,990 | 77.9 | 2,547 |
| GA......... | 5,864 | 2,322 | 7,272 | 75.1 | 2,416 | OK......... | 2,255 | 1,196 | 2,485 | 66.2 | 1,266 |
| HI......... | 1,108 | 103 | 1,250 | 91.9 | 110 | OR......... | 2,694 | 727 | 3,104 | 81.0 | 727 |
| ID......... | 859 | 434 | 1,106 | 70.6 | 461 | PA......... | 9,464 | 2,817 | 9,991 | 78.7 | 2,711 |
| IL......... | 10,910 | 1,510 | 11,354 | 88.5 | 1,477 | RI......... | 953 | 95 | 955 | 90.7 | 98 |
| IN......... | 4,304 | 1,776 | 4,697 | 72.4 | 1,787 | SC......... | 2,427 | 1,585 | 3,068 | 66.3 | 1,558 |
| IA......... | 1,787 | 1,139 | 1,950 | 64.0 | 1,096 | SD......... | 391 | 363 | 461 | 56.7 | 353 |
| KS......... | 1,921 | 768 | 2,117 | 74.2 | 736 | TN......... | 3,620 | 2,069 | 4,213 | 66.4 | 2,133 |
| KY......... | 2,254 | 1,788 | 2,533 | 58.4 | 1,806 | TX......... | 17,204 | 3,648 | 21,298 | 84.7 | 3,848 |
| LA......... | 3,246 | 1,223 | 3,318 | 73.2 | 1,216 | UT......... | 1,970 | 263 | 2,504 | 90.6 | 260 |
| ME......... | 513 | 762 | 514 | 38.7 | 815 | VT......... | 232 | 376 | 243 | 38.9 | 382 |
| MD......... | 4,559 | 738 | 5,034 | 87.2 | 739 | VA......... | 5,170 | 1,909 | 6,037 | 75.5 | 1,964 |
| MA......... | 5,801 | 548 | 6,022 | 92.0 | 526 | WA......... | 4,831 | 1,063 | 5,652 | 84.1 | 1,073 |
| MI......... | 7,419 | 2,519 | 7,370 | 74.6 | 2,514 | WV......... | 833 | 976 | 903 | 48.7 | 950 |
| MN......... | 3,490 | 1,429 | 3,886 | 73.3 | 1,418 | WI......... | 3,664 | 1,700 | 3,990 | 70.2 | 1,697 |
| MS......... | 1,387 | 1,457 | 1,464 | 49.4 | 1,503 | WY......... | 321 | 172 | 365 | 64.8 | 199 |

Source: U.S. Census Bureau, 2000 Census of Population and Housing, *Population and Housing Unit Counts PHC-3*; 2010 Census of Population and Housing, *Population and Housing Unit Counts, CPH-2-1, United States Summary*; and "Percent Urban and Rural in 2010 by State," <https://www.census.gov/geo/reference/ua/urban-rural-2010.html>, accessed March 2013.

## Table 27. Population in Coastal Counties: 1990 to 2018

[3,537 represents 3,537,000. Data for 1990 to 2010 as of April 1; beginning 2015, data as of July 1. Data for 1990 and 2000 are based on 675 counties in areas as defined by U.S. National Oceanic and Atmospheric Administration, 1992. Beginning 2010, data cover 678 counties and equivalent areas in a coastal watershed; see headnote, Table 28. See Appendix III]

| Year | Total | Counties in coastal regions | | | | | Balance of United States |
|---|---|---|---|---|---|---|---|
| | | Total | Atlantic | Gulf of Mexico | Great Lakes | Pacific | |
| Land area, 2010 (1,000 sq. mi.)...... | 3,537 | 888 | 147 | 116 | 115 | 510 | 2,649 |
| POPULATION | | | | | | | |
| 1990 (millions)....................... | 248.7 | 133.4 | 59.0 | 15.2 | 25.9 | 33.2 | 115.3 |
| 2000 (millions)....................... | 281.4 | 148.3 | 65.2 | 18.0 | 27.3 | 37.8 | 133.1 |
| 2010 (millions)....................... | 308.7 | 159.7 | 70.2 | 20.9 | 27.2 | 41.4 | 149.0 |
| 2015 (millions)....................... | 320.7 | 166.0 | 72.8 | 22.4 | 27.3 | 43.5 | 154.7 |
| 2016 (millions)....................... | 323.1 | 167.1 | 73.2 | 22.7 | 27.2 | 43.9 | 156.0 |
| 2017 (millions)....................... | 325.1 | 167.9 | 73.5 | 23.0 | 27.2 | 44.2 | 157.2 |
| 2018 (millions)....................... | 327.2 | 168.7 | 73.9 | 23.2 | 27.2 | 44.4 | 158.5 |
| 1990 (percent)....................... | 100.0 | 53.6 | 23.7 | 6.1 | 10.4 | 13.3 | 46.4 |
| 2000 (percent)....................... | 100.0 | 53.0 | 23.0 | 6.0 | 10.0 | 13.0 | 47.0 |
| 2010 (percent)....................... | 100.0 | 51.7 | 22.7 | 6.8 | 8.8 | 13.4 | 48.3 |
| 2015 (percent)....................... | 100.0 | 51.8 | 22.7 | 7.0 | 8.5 | 13.6 | 48.2 |
| 2016 (percent)....................... | 100.0 | 51.7 | 22.7 | 7.0 | 8.4 | 13.6 | 48.3 |
| 2017 (percent)....................... | 100.0 | 51.6 | 22.6 | 7.1 | 8.4 | 13.6 | 48.4 |
| 2018 (percent)....................... | 100.0 | 51.6 | 22.6 | 7.1 | 8.3 | 13.6 | 48.4 |

Source: U.S. Census Bureau, *1990 Census of Population and Housing (CPH1)*; "Annual Estimates of the Resident Population for Counties: April 1, 2000 to July 1, 2009," March 2011, <https://www2.census.gov/programs-surveys/popest/datasets/2000-2009/counties/totals/>; and "PEPANNRES: Annual Estimates of the Resident Population: April 1, 2010 to July 1, 2018," <http://factfinder.census.gov>, accessed September 2019.

# Table 28. States With Coastal Watershed Counties—Population and Housing Units, Establishments, and Employees by Coastal Region and State: 2010 to 2018

[308,758 represents 308,758,000. Data for 2010 as of April 1 and reflect population estimates base. Data for 2018 are as of July 1. Beginning in 2010, data cover 678 counties and equivalent areas in a coastal watershed. A county is considered a coastal watershed county if one of the following criteria is met: (1) at a minimum, 15 percent of the county's total land area is located within a coastal watershed or (2) a portion of, or an entire county accounts for at least 15 percent of a coastal watershed. The 15 percent rule was selected as an appropriate level for capturing counties with a significant impact on coastal and ocean resources. See Appendix III. Minus sign (-) indicates decrease]

| Coastal region and state | Number of counties | Population 2010 (1,000) | Population 2018 Number (1,000) | Population 2018 Percent of state total | Population Percent change, 2010–2018 | Population Per square mile, 2018 [1] | Housing units Number 2010 (1,000) | Housing units Number 2018 (1,000) | Housing units Percent change, 2010–2018 | Housing units Per square mile, 2018 [1] | Private nonfarm Establishments, 2016 (1,000) | Private nonfarm Employees, 2016 (1,000) |
|---|---|---|---|---|---|---|---|---|---|---|---|---|
| **United States, total** | **3,142** | **308,758** | **327,167** | (X) | **6.0** | **92** | **131,705** | **138,537** | **5.2** | **39** | **7,730** | **121,595** |
| Interior U.S. | 2,464 | 149,009 | 158,470 | (X) | 6.3 | 60 | 64,631 | 68,420 | 5.9 | 26 | 3,585 | (NA) |
| **Coastal counties, total** | **678** | **159,749** | **168,698** | (X) | **5.6** | **190** | **67,075** | **70,117** | **4.5** | **79** | **4,146** | **(NA)** |
| **Atlantic** | **286** | **70,242** | **73,881** | (X) | **5.2** | **501** | **29,916** | **31,160** | **4.2** | **211** | **1,920** | **29,264** |
| Maine | 14 | 1,239 | 1,254 | 94 | 1.3 | 62 | 667 | 691 | 3.6 | 34 | 39 | 483 |
| New Hampshire | 6 | 1,073 | 1,115 | 82 | 3.9 | 265 | 485 | 505 | 4.1 | 120 | 31 | 465 |
| Massachusetts | 12 | 6,318 | 6,670 | 97 | 5.6 | 1,015 | 2,712 | 2,817 | 3.9 | 429 | 172 | 3,118 |
| Rhode Island | 5 | 1,053 | 1,057 | 100 | 0.4 | 1,023 | 463 | 469 | 1.2 | 454 | 28 | 430 |
| Connecticut | 8 | 3,574 | 3,573 | 100 | 0.0 | 738 | 1,488 | 1,521 | 2.2 | 314 | 89 | 1,506 |
| New York | 18 | 13,952 | 14,214 | 73 | 1.9 | 1,840 | 5,601 | 5,791 | 3.4 | 749 | 422 | 5,999 |
| New Jersey | 20 | 8,683 | 8,803 | 99 | 1.4 | 1,258 | 3,509 | 3,583 | 2.1 | 512 | 229 | 3,472 |
| Pennsylvania | 12 | 6,108 | 6,294 | 49 | 3.0 | 917 | 2,512 | 2,584 | 2.9 | 376 | 146 | 2,663 |
| Delaware | 3 | 898 | 967 | 100 | 7.7 | 496 | 406 | 439 | 8.1 | 225 | 25 | 392 |
| Maryland | 20 | 5,288 | 5,536 | 92 | 4.7 | 736 | 2,176 | 2,246 | 3.2 | 299 | 126 | 2,054 |
| District of Columbia | 1 | 602 | 702 | 100 | 16.7 | 11,516 | 297 | 320 | 7.7 | 5,238 | 23 | 527 |
| Virginia | 61 | 5,426 | 5,821 | 68 | 7.3 | 420 | 2,216 | 2,334 | 5.3 | 168 | 138 | 2,271 |
| North Carolina | 38 | 2,254 | 2,342 | 23 | 3.9 | 118 | 1,078 | 1,153 | 7.0 | 58 | 47 | 639 |
| South Carolina | 22 | 1,932 | 2,165 | 43 | 12.1 | 142 | 953 | 1,045 | 9.6 | 69 | 48 | 664 |
| Georgia | 25 | 945 | 1,007 | 10 | 6.5 | 85 | 414 | 438 | 5.9 | 37 | 20 | 291 |
| Florida | 21 | 10,896 | 12,360 | 58 | 13.4 | 664 | 4,940 | 5,225 | 5.8 | 280 | 339 | 4,288 |
| **Gulf of Mexico** | **144** | **20,888** | **23,211** | (X) | **11.1** | **201** | **9,294** | **10,069** | **8.3** | **87** | **494** | **7,597** |
| Florida | 41 | 7,535 | 8,542 | 40 | 13.4 | 265 | 3,887 | 4,153 | 6.8 | 129 | 198 | 2,511 |
| Georgia | 3 | 98 | 96 | 1 | -1.9 | 60 | 43 | 44 | 2.0 | 28 | 2 | 27 |
| Alabama | 8 | 765 | 793 | 16 | 3.7 | 91 | 363 | 383 | 5.5 | 44 | 17 | 254 |
| Mississippi | 12 | 629 | 658 | 22 | 4.7 | 97 | 280 | 300 | 7.1 | 44 | 12 | 186 |
| Louisiana | 39 | 3,574 | 3,717 | 80 | 4.0 | 142 | 1,543 | 1,632 | 5.8 | 62 | 85 | 1,365 |
| Texas | 41 | 8,288 | 9,405 | 33 | 13.5 | 235 | 3,178 | 3,557 | 11.9 | 89 | 181 | 3,253 |
| **Great Lakes** | **158** | **27,191** | **27,218** | (X) | **0.1** | **236** | **12,128** | **12,332** | **1.7** | **107** | **637** | **11,182** |
| New York | 21 | 3,635 | 3,579 | 18 | -1.5 | 167 | 1,647 | 1,688 | 2.5 | 79 | 83 | 1,389 |
| Pennsylvania | 1 | 281 | 272 | 2 | -3.0 | 341 | 119 | 122 | 2.1 | 152 | 6 | 114 |
| Ohio | 24 | 4,326 | 4,272 | 37 | -1.2 | 406 | 1,967 | 1,982 | 0.7 | 188 | 100 | 1,813 |
| Michigan | 74 | 8,797 | 8,918 | 89 | 1.4 | 175 | 4,050 | 4,125 | 1.9 | 81 | 199 | 3,339 |
| Indiana | 9 | 1,433 | 1,441 | 22 | 0.6 | 354 | 607 | 623 | 2.8 | 153 | 31 | 580 |
| Illinois | 2 | 5,898 | 5,881 | 46 | -0.3 | 4,234 | 2,441 | 2,465 | 1.0 | 1,775 | 153 | 2,725 |
| Wisconsin | 23 | 2,569 | 2,602 | 45 | 1.3 | 169 | 1,165 | 1,191 | 2.3 | 77 | 59 | 1,120 |
| Minnesota | 4 | 252 | 252 | 4 | 0.0 | 24 | 132 | 135 | 2.3 | 13 | 7 | 101 |
| **Pacific** | **90** | **41,429** | **44,387** | (X) | **7.1** | **87** | **15,737** | **16,556** | **5.2** | **32** | **1,094** | **(NA)** |
| Washington | 19 | 5,229 | 5,908 | 78 | 13.0 | 240 | 2,264 | 2,475 | 9.3 | 100 | 150 | 2,173 |
| Oregon | 12 | 1,982 | 2,153 | 51 | 8.6 | 103 | 895 | 954 | 6.5 | 45 | 62 | 849 |
| California | 29 | 32,259 | 34,282 | 87 | 6.3 | 441 | 11,803 | 12,317 | 4.4 | 158 | 832 | 12,684 |
| Alaska | 25 | 598 | 624 | 85 | 4.3 | 2 | 255 | 264 | 3.4 | 1 | 18 | 233 |
| Hawaii | 5 | 1,360 | 1,420 | 100 | 4.4 | 221 | 520 | 546 | 5.1 | 85 | 32 | (NA) |

NA Not available. X Not applicable. [1] Calculated on the basis of land area data from the 2010 census. [2] Covers establishments with payroll. Excludes most government employees, railroad employees, and self-employed persons. Employees are for the week including March 12.

Source: U.S. Census Bureau, "PEPANNRES: Annual Estimates of the Resident Population: April 1, 2010 to July 1, 2018"; "PEPANNHU: Annual Estimates of Housing Units for the United States, Regions, Divisions, States, and Counties: April 1, 2010 to July 1, 2018"; and "2016 County Business Patterns"; <http://factfinder.census.gov>, accessed September 2019.

# Table 29. Geographic Mobility Status of the Population by Selected Characteristics: 1980 to 2018

[221,641 represents 221,641,000. As of March. For persons 1 year old and over, unless otherwise noted. Based on comparison of place of residence in year shown vs. previous year. Excludes members of the Armed Forces except those living off post or with their families on post. 2011 data based on population controls from Census 2000. 2018 data based on population controls from Census 2010. Based on Current Population Survey, Annual Social and Economic Supplement. See text, this section and Appendix III. For composition of regions, see map, inside front cover]

| Mobility period and characteristic | Total persons (1,000) | Percent distribution by geographic mobility | | | | | | Movers from abroad |
|---|---|---|---|---|---|---|---|---|
| | | Non–movers | Movers (different house in United States) | | | | | |
| | | | Total | Same county | Different county | | | |
| | | | | | Total | Same state | Different state | |
| 1980 to 1981 | 221,641 | 82.8 | 16.6 | 10.4 | 6.2 | 3.4 | 2.8 | 0.6 |
| 1990 to 1991 | 244,884 | 83.0 | 16.4 | 10.3 | 6.1 | 3.2 | 2.9 | 0.6 |
| 2000 to 2001 | 275,611 | 85.8 | 13.5 | 8.0 | 5.6 | 2.7 | 2.8 | 0.6 |
| 2010 to 2011 | 302,005 | 88.4 | 11.3 | 7.7 | 3.5 | 2.0 | 1.6 | 0.4 |
| **2017 to 2018, total** | **319,319** | **89.9** | **9.8** | **6.2** | **3.5** | **2.0** | **1.5** | **0.4** |
| By age: | | | | | | | | |
| 1 to 4 years old | 16,092 | 84.7 | 14.8 | 9.9 | 4.9 | 2.8 | 2.1 | 0.5 |
| 5 to 9 years old | 20,243 | 87.9 | 11.7 | 7.7 | 4.0 | 2.4 | 1.6 | 0.4 |
| 10 to 14 years old | 20,812 | 90.8 | 8.9 | 6.1 | 2.8 | 1.5 | 1.3 | 0.3 |
| 15 to 19 years old | 20,907 | 90.2 | 9.5 | 6.3 | 3.2 | 1.8 | 1.4 | 0.3 |
| 20 to 24 years old | 21,434 | 79.7 | 19.6 | 12.1 | 7.5 | 4.2 | 3.3 | 0.7 |
| 25 to 29 years old | 23,160 | 79.8 | 19.2 | 12.3 | 6.9 | 4.0 | 2.9 | 0.9 |
| 30 to 44 years old | 62,355 | 88.1 | 11.4 | 7.3 | 4.1 | 2.3 | 1.8 | 0.5 |
| 45 to 64 years old | 83,237 | 93.7 | 6.1 | 3.7 | 2.5 | 1.5 | 1.0 | 0.2 |
| 65 to 74 years old | 30,366 | 96.2 | 3.7 | 2.1 | 1.6 | 0.9 | 0.7 | 0.1 |
| 75 to 84 years old | 14,559 | 97.0 | 3.0 | 1.9 | 1.1 | 0.5 | 0.6 | – |
| 85 years old and over | 6,154 | 96.7 | 3.2 | 2.0 | 1.2 | 0.6 | 0.6 | 0.1 |
| By region: | | | | | | | | |
| Northeast | 55,495 | 92.3 | 7.3 | 4.6 | 2.6 | 1.7 | 0.9 | 0.4 |
| Midwest | 66,611 | 89.6 | 10.2 | 6.3 | 3.9 | 2.5 | 1.3 | 0.2 |
| South | 121,014 | 89.2 | 10.4 | 6.4 | 4.0 | 2.2 | 1.8 | 0.4 |
| West | 76,200 | 89.3 | 10.3 | 7.0 | 3.3 | 1.6 | 1.6 | 0.4 |
| By housing tenure: | | | | | | | | |
| Owner occupied units | 212,827 | 94.9 | 5.0 | 3.1 | 1.9 | 1.1 | 0.7 | 0.1 |
| Renter occupied units | 106,493 | 79.9 | 19.3 | 12.4 | 6.9 | 3.8 | 3.1 | 0.8 |
| **Persons 16 years old and over** | **258,052** | **90.3** | **9.4** | **5.9** | **3.5** | **2.0** | **1.5** | **0.4** |
| Civilian labor force | 161,626 | 89.0 | 10.7 | 6.8 | 3.9 | 2.3 | 1.6 | 0.3 |
| Employed | 154,815 | 89.2 | 10.5 | 6.8 | 3.7 | 2.2 | 1.5 | 0.3 |
| Unemployed | 6,811 | 83.6 | 15.9 | 8.6 | 7.3 | 3.2 | 4.1 | 0.5 |
| Armed Forces | 955 | 76.6 | 21.4 | 8.8 | 12.6 | 4.6 | 8.0 | 2.0 |
| Not in labor force | 95,471 | 92.6 | 7.0 | 4.2 | 2.8 | 1.5 | 1.2 | 0.4 |
| By occupation: | | | | | | | | |
| Employed civilians, 16 years old and over | 154,815 | 89.2 | 10.5 | 6.8 | 3.7 | 2.2 | 1.5 | 0.3 |
| Management, business, and financial | 25,818 | 90.3 | 9.4 | 5.9 | 3.4 | 2.1 | 1.3 | 0.4 |
| Professional | 37,108 | 88.4 | 11.2 | 6.9 | 4.3 | 2.6 | 1.9 | 0.4 |
| Service | 26,447 | 87.8 | 11.7 | 7.9 | 3.8 | 2.4 | 1.4 | 0.5 |
| Sales | 15,507 | 89.7 | 10.2 | 6.7 | 3.5 | 2.2 | 1.3 | 0.1 |
| Office and administrative support | 17,612 | 89.5 | 10.3 | 6.7 | 3.5 | 2.2 | 1.3 | 0.2 |
| Farming, fishing, and forestry | 1,082 | 91.6 | 8.0 | 5.3 | 2.8 | 1.9 | 0.8 | 0.5 |
| Construction and extraction | 7,935 | 90.2 | 9.5 | 6.0 | 3.5 | 2.1 | 1.4 | 0.3 |
| Installation, maintenance, and repair | 4,818 | 90.0 | 9.9 | 6.2 | 3.7 | 1.9 | 1.8 | 0.1 |
| Production | 8,615 | 90.5 | 9.3 | 6.4 | 2.9 | 1.8 | 1.2 | 0.1 |
| Transportation and material moving | 9,872 | 89.1 | 10.8 | 7.0 | 3.8 | 2.2 | 1.5 | 0.2 |

– Represents or rounds to zero.

Source: U.S. Census Bureau, "Geographical Mobility: 2017 to 2018," November 2018, and earlier releases, <https://www.census.gov/topics/population/migration.html>.

# Table 30. Movers by Type of Move and Reason for Moving: 2018

[32,352 represents 32,352,000. As of March. For persons 1 year old and over. Based on comparison of place of residence in 2018 vs. 2017. Excludes members of the Armed Forces except those living off post or with their families on post. Based on Current Population Survey, Annual Social and Economic Supplement. See text, this section and Appendix III]

| Reason for move | All movers | Intra-county | Inter-county | From abroad | Reason for move | All movers | Intra-county | Inter-county | From abroad |
|---|---|---|---|---|---|---|---|---|---|
| **Total (1,000)** | **32,352** | **19,852** | **11,334** | **1,165** | **Housing–related reasons** | **41.5** | **51.2** | **27.7** | **10.0** |
| PERCENT DISTRIBUTION | | | | | Wanted to own home/not rent | 7.3 | 9.4 | 4.0 | 1.8 |
| Total | 100.0 | 100.0 | 100.0 | 100.0 | New/better house/apartment | 16.4 | 20.5 | 10.5 | 3.1 |
| **Family–related reasons** | **28.1** | **28.4** | **27.9** | **25.9** | Better neighborhood/less crime | 2.6 | 3.2 | 1.8 | 0.8 |
| Change in marital status | 4.4 | 4.6 | 4.2 | 4.5 | Cheaper housing | 7.9 | 9.0 | 6.7 | 0.8 |
| To establish own household | 12.6 | 15.3 | 8.4 | 6.4 | Foreclosure/eviction | 0.7 | 0.8 | 0.4 | – |
| Other family reasons [1] | 11.1 | 8.4 | 15.3 | 14.9 | Other housing | 6.7 | 8.2 | 4.3 | 3.4 |
| **Work–related reasons** | **19.7** | **11.7** | **32.0** | **35.7** | **Other reasons** | **10.7** | **8.7** | **12.5** | **28.5** |
| New job/job transfer | 10.3 | 3.8 | 20.3 | 24.3 | Attend/leave college | 2.8 | 1.6 | 3.8 | 13.6 |
| To look for work/lost job | 1.5 | 1.0 | 2.4 | 2.2 | Change of climate | 0.7 | 0.2 | 1.4 | 0.9 |
| Closer to work/easier commute | 5.6 | 5.6 | 5.9 | 2.7 | Health reasons | 1.8 | 1.9 | 1.7 | 1.1 |
| Retired | 1.1 | 0.8 | 1.6 | 0.5 | Natural disaster | 0.5 | 0.6 | 0.2 | 2.2 |
| Other job–related reason [1] | 1.1 | 0.5 | 1.7 | 5.8 | Other reason [1] | 5.0 | 4.5 | 5.2 | 10.7 |

– Represents or rounds to zero. [1] Beginning in 2016, respondents who selected "other family," "other job-related," "other housing," and "other reason" were asked to provide their specific reason for move. These responses could potentially be coded to more specific reasons. Prior to 2016, only respondents who selected "other reason" were asked to specify a reason.

Source: U.S. Census Bureau, "Geographical Mobility: 2017 to 2018," November 2018, <https://www.census.gov/topics/population/migration.html>.

# Table 31. Geographic Mobility Status of Resident Population by State: 2017

[In percent, except as indicated (321,994 represents 321,994,000). Based on comparison of place of residence in 2017 vs. 2016. The American Community Survey universe includes the household population and the population living in institutions, college dormitories, and other group quarters. Based on a sample and subject to sampling variability. See text, this section and Appendix III]

| State | Population 1 year old and over (1,000) | Same house in 2016 | Different house in United States in 2016 | | Different county | | | Abroad in 2016 |
| | | | Total | Same county | Total | Same state | Different state | |
|---|---|---|---|---|---|---|---|---|
| United States | 321,994 | 85.7 | 14.3 | 8.1 | 5.6 | 3.3 | 2.3 | 0.7 |
| Alabama | 4,819 | 86.3 | 13.7 | 8.0 | 5.4 | 3.1 | 2.3 | 0.3 |
| Alaska | 731 | 81.5 | 18.5 | 11.1 | 6.4 | 2.3 | 4.1 | 0.9 |
| Arizona | 6,935 | 82.4 | 17.6 | 11.3 | 5.6 | 1.9 | 3.8 | 0.7 |
| Arkansas | 2,968 | 84.5 | 15.5 | 8.6 | 6.6 | 3.9 | 2.7 | 0.3 |
| California | 39,086 | 87.0 | 13.0 | 8.1 | 4.1 | 2.8 | 1.3 | 0.8 |
| Colorado | 5,542 | 82.0 | 18.0 | 8.2 | 9.1 | 5.0 | 4.1 | 0.6 |
| Connecticut | 3,556 | 88.2 | 11.8 | 6.8 | 4.3 | 1.9 | 2.3 | 0.7 |
| Delaware | 952 | 87.2 | 12.8 | 7.2 | 5.1 | 1.1 | 4.0 | 0.4 |
| District of Columbia | 685 | 80.9 | 19.1 | 9.3 | 8.2 | 0.0 | 8.2 | 1.5 |
| Florida | 20,772 | 84.5 | 15.5 | 8.4 | 5.9 | 3.2 | 2.7 | 1.2 |
| Georgia | 10,299 | 85.1 | 14.9 | 7.0 | 7.4 | 4.7 | 2.7 | 0.6 |
| Hawaii | 1,411 | 87.3 | 12.7 | 7.7 | 3.8 | 0.5 | 3.3 | 1.2 |
| Idaho | 1,694 | 83.0 | 17.0 | 9.2 | 7.4 | 3.2 | 4.2 | 0.4 |
| Illinois | 12,659 | 87.1 | 12.9 | 8.1 | 4.2 | 2.6 | 1.5 | 0.6 |
| Indiana | 6,592 | 85.5 | 14.5 | 8.3 | 5.9 | 3.7 | 2.2 | 0.4 |
| Iowa | 3,107 | 85.4 | 14.6 | 8.1 | 6.1 | 3.6 | 2.5 | 0.4 |
| Kansas | 2,877 | 83.9 | 16.1 | 9.0 | 6.7 | 3.7 | 3.0 | 0.4 |
| Kentucky | 4,404 | 84.5 | 15.5 | 8.9 | 6.3 | 3.9 | 2.4 | 0.4 |
| Louisiana | 4,630 | 87.1 | 12.9 | 7.5 | 5.1 | 3.5 | 1.6 | 0.3 |
| Maine | 1,323 | 86.2 | 13.8 | 7.5 | 6.0 | 3.4 | 2.6 | 0.3 |
| Maryland | 5,988 | 86.3 | 13.7 | 7.4 | 5.5 | 2.8 | 2.8 | 0.8 |
| Massachusetts | 6,790 | 86.7 | 13.3 | 7.0 | 5.1 | 2.9 | 2.2 | 1.1 |
| Michigan | 9,851 | 85.8 | 14.2 | 8.3 | 5.4 | 3.9 | 1.5 | 0.5 |
| Minnesota | 5,511 | 85.8 | 14.2 | 7.3 | 6.5 | 4.4 | 2.1 | 0.4 |
| Mississippi | 2,947 | 86.6 | 13.4 | 6.8 | 6.3 | 3.8 | 2.5 | 0.2 |
| Missouri | 6,040 | 84.6 | 15.4 | 8.1 | 6.9 | 4.2 | 2.7 | 0.4 |
| Montana | 1,039 | 85.0 | 15.0 | 8.1 | 6.6 | 3.1 | 3.4 | 0.4 |
| Nebraska | 1,894 | 83.8 | 16.2 | 9.2 | 6.4 | 3.6 | 2.8 | 0.6 |
| Nevada | 2,963 | 82.0 | 18.0 | 12.1 | 5.3 | 0.9 | 4.5 | 0.6 |
| New Hampshire | 1,331 | 85.2 | 14.8 | 7.6 | 6.7 | 2.7 | 4.0 | 0.5 |
| New Jersey | 8,910 | 89.4 | 10.6 | 5.5 | 4.2 | 2.5 | 1.7 | 0.9 |
| New Mexico | 2,063 | 87.3 | 12.7 | 7.1 | 5.0 | 2.3 | 2.8 | 0.5 |
| New York | 19,639 | 89.4 | 10.6 | 6.0 | 3.9 | 2.5 | 1.5 | 0.7 |
| North Carolina | 10,159 | 85.1 | 14.9 | 7.7 | 6.6 | 3.5 | 3.1 | 0.6 |
| North Dakota | 745 | 81.8 | 18.2 | 8.6 | 8.9 | 3.9 | 5.0 | 0.8 |
| Ohio | 11,520 | 85.3 | 14.7 | 9.1 | 5.3 | 3.5 | 1.7 | 0.4 |
| Oklahoma | 3,876 | 83.0 | 17.0 | 9.7 | 6.9 | 4.3 | 2.6 | 0.4 |
| Oregon | 4,102 | 83.0 | 17.0 | 9.3 | 7.1 | 3.4 | 3.6 | 0.6 |
| Pennsylvania | 12,675 | 87.4 | 12.6 | 7.4 | 4.8 | 2.8 | 2.0 | 0.5 |
| Rhode Island | 1,049 | 88.0 | 12.0 | 6.4 | 5.1 | 1.6 | 3.5 | 0.6 |
| South Carolina | 4,966 | 85.5 | 14.5 | 7.4 | 6.6 | 3.3 | 3.4 | 0.4 |
| South Dakota | 857 | 84.5 | 15.5 | 7.2 | 7.5 | 4.4 | 3.0 | 0.8 |
| Tennessee | 6,642 | 85.5 | 14.5 | 8.1 | 6.0 | 3.1 | 2.9 | 0.4 |
| Texas | 27,925 | 84.3 | 15.7 | 9.1 | 5.8 | 3.9 | 1.9 | 0.8 |
| Utah | 3,056 | 82.9 | 17.1 | 9.6 | 6.7 | 3.5 | 3.3 | 0.8 |
| Vermont | 619 | 86.6 | 13.4 | 7.0 | 5.9 | 2.3 | 3.5 | 0.5 |
| Virginia | 8,373 | 84.7 | 15.3 | 6.6 | 7.9 | 4.9 | 3.0 | 0.9 |
| Washington | 7,319 | 82.2 | 17.8 | 10.0 | 7.0 | 3.4 | 3.6 | 0.9 |
| West Virginia | 1,798 | 88.4 | 11.6 | 6.6 | 4.8 | 2.6 | 2.2 | 0.2 |
| Wisconsin | 5,732 | 85.6 | 14.4 | 8.5 | 5.4 | 3.5 | 2.0 | 0.4 |
| Wyoming | 573 | 83.9 | 16.1 | 10.0 | 5.6 | 2.4 | 3.2 | 0.4 |

Source: U.S. Census Bureau, 2017 American Community Survey, B07003, "Geographical Mobility in the Past Year by Sex for Current Residence in the United States," <http://factfinder.census.gov/>, accessed November 2018.

# Table 32. Geographic Mobility Status of Households by Household Income: 2018

[127,602 represents 127,602,000. As of March. Covers householders 15 years old and over. Based on comparison of place of residence in 2018 vs. 2017. Excludes members of the Armed Forces except those living off post or with their families on post. Based on Current Population Survey, Annual Social and Economic Supplement. See text, this section and Appendix III]

| Household income in 2017 | Percent distribution | | | | | | | |
| | Total (1,000) | Non-movers | Movers (different house in United States) | | Different county | | | Movers from abroad |
| | | | Total | Same county | Total | Same state | Different state | |
|---|---|---|---|---|---|---|---|---|
| Householders, 15 years and over | 127,602 | 90.1 | 9.6 | 6.1 | 3.5 | 2.0 | 1.5 | 0.3 |
| Under $5,000 or loss | 4,218 | 84.6 | 13.6 | 9.0 | 4.6 | 2.6 | 2.0 | 1.8 |
| $5,000 to $9,999 | 3,497 | 86.4 | 13.1 | 8.9 | 4.2 | 2.9 | 1.3 | 0.5 |
| $10,000 to $14,999 | 5,876 | 90.6 | 9.1 | 5.9 | 3.2 | 1.9 | 1.3 | 0.3 |
| $15,000 to $24,999 | 12,218 | 88.9 | 10.9 | 7.5 | 3.3 | 1.7 | 1.6 | 0.3 |
| $25,000 to $34,999 | 11,773 | 88.7 | 10.9 | 6.9 | 4.0 | 2.0 | 2.0 | 0.3 |
| $35,000 to $49,999 | 15,728 | 89.0 | 10.8 | 6.9 | 3.9 | 2.3 | 1.7 | 0.2 |
| $50,000 to $69,999 | 17,209 | 89.9 | 10.0 | 6.3 | 3.6 | 2.3 | 1.3 | 0.2 |
| $70,000 to $84,999 | 11,207 | 90.3 | 9.4 | 5.7 | 3.7 | 2.2 | 1.6 | 0.2 |
| $85,000 to $99,999 | 8,555 | 91.1 | 8.7 | 5.3 | 3.4 | 1.8 | 1.6 | 0.2 |
| $100,000 and over | 37,321 | 92.2 | 7.5 | 4.5 | 3.0 | 1.7 | 1.3 | 0.3 |

Source: U.S. Census Bureau, "Geographical Mobility: 2017 to 2018," November 2018, and earlier data releases, <https://www.census.gov/topics/population/migration/data/tables.html>, accessed June 2019.

# Table 33. Persons 65 Years Old and Over—Characteristics by Sex: 2000 to 2018

[In percent except as noted (32.6 represents 32,600,000). As of March, except as noted. Covers civilian noninstitutional population. Excludes members of Armed Forces except those living off post or with their families on post. Data for 2000 data based on 1990 Census population controls; data for 2010 based on 2000 Census population controls; and data for 2015 and 2018 based on 2010 Census population controls. Beginning 2005, data based on an expanded sample of households. Based on Current Population Survey. See text, this section]

| Characteristic | Total | | | | Male | | | | Female | | | |
|---|---|---|---|---|---|---|---|---|---|---|---|---|
| | 2000 | 2010 | 2015 | 2018 | 2000 | 2010 | 2015 | 2018 | 2000 | 2010 | 2015 | 2018 |
| **Total (million)** | **32.6** | **38.6** | **46.0** | **51.0** | **13.9** | **16.8** | **20.4** | **23.0** | **18.7** | **21.8** | **25.5** | **28.0** |
| PERCENT DISTRIBUTION | | | | | | | | | | | | |
| Marital status: | | | | | | | | | | | | |
| Never married | 3.9 | 4.3 | 4.8 | 5.6 | 4.2 | 4.1 | 4.9 | 5.8 | 3.6 | 4.5 | 4.8 | 5.5 |
| Married | 57.2 | 57.6 | 58.6 | 59.4 | 75.2 | 74.5 | 72.4 | 72.4 | 43.8 | 44.5 | 47.6 | 48.7 |
| Spouse present | 54.6 | 55.2 | 56.2 | 56.8 | 72.6 | 71.7 | 70.0 | 69.6 | 41.3 | 42.4 | 45.2 | 46.4 |
| Spouse absent [1] | 2.6 | 2.4 | 2.4 | 2.6 | 2.6 | 2.8 | 2.4 | 2.9 | 2.5 | 2.1 | 2.4 | 2.3 |
| Widowed | 32.1 | 28.1 | 24.4 | 22.5 | 14.4 | 12.7 | 11.9 | 11.2 | 45.3 | 39.9 | 34.3 | 31.8 |
| Divorced | 6.7 | 10.0 | 12.2 | 12.5 | 6.1 | 8.7 | 10.8 | 10.6 | 7.2 | 11.1 | 13.3 | 14.0 |
| Educational attainment: | | | | | | | | | | | | |
| Less than 9th grade | 16.7 | 10.2 | 7.5 | 6.2 | 17.8 | 10.2 | 7.5 | 5.9 | 15.9 | 10.1 | 7.4 | 6.5 |
| Completed 9th to 12th grade, but no high school diploma | 13.8 | 10.3 | 8.2 | 7.3 | 12.7 | 9.7 | 7.0 | 7.0 | 14.7 | 10.8 | 9.2 | 7.6 |
| High school graduate | 35.9 | 36.4 | 34.6 | 32.5 | 30.4 | 32.0 | 30.8 | 29.1 | 39.9 | 39.8 | 37.6 | 35.3 |
| Some college or associate's degree | 18.0 | 20.6 | 23.1 | 24.7 | 17.8 | 19.7 | 22.8 | 23.9 | 18.2 | 21.2 | 23.3 | 25.3 |
| Bachelor's or advanced degree | 15.6 | 22.5 | 26.7 | 29.3 | 21.4 | 28.4 | 31.8 | 34.2 | 11.4 | 18.0 | 22.5 | 25.3 |
| Labor force status: [2] | | | | | | | | | | | | |
| Employed | 12.4 | 16.2 | 18.2 | 18.9 | 16.9 | 20.5 | 22.5 | 23.3 | 9.1 | 12.9 | 14.7 | 15.4 |
| Unemployed | 0.4 | 1.2 | 0.7 | 0.6 | 0.6 | 1.6 | 0.9 | 0.8 | 0.3 | 0.9 | 0.6 | 0.5 |
| Not in labor force | 87.2 | 82.6 | 81.1 | 80.4 | 82.5 | 77.9 | 76.6 | 76.0 | 90.6 | 86.2 | 84.7 | 84.1 |
| Percent below poverty level [3] | 9.7 | 8.9 | 10.0 | 9.2 | 6.9 | 6.6 | 7.4 | 7.5 | 11.8 | 10.7 | 12.1 | 10.5 |

[1] Includes separated. [2] Annual averages of monthly figures. Source: U.S. Bureau of Labor Statistics, "Labor Force Statistics from the Current Population Survey," <https://www.bls.gov/cps/tables.htm>. [3] Poverty status based on income in preceding year.

Source: Except as noted, U.S. Census Bureau, Current Population Reports, P20-546, and earlier reports; series P-23, No. 59; series P-60, No. 226; "The Older Population in the United States: March 2002 Detailed Tables (PPL-167)," May 2003; and "Educational Attainment," <https://www.census.gov/topics/education/educational-attainment.html>, "Families and Living Arrangements," <https://www.census.gov/topics/families/families-and-households.html>, and "Poverty," <https://www.census.gov/data/tables/time-series/demo/income-poverty/cps-pov.html>, accessed February 2019.

# Table 34. Persons 65 Years Old and Over by Living Arrangement: 2010 to 2017

[In thousands (40,434 represents 40,434,000), except as indicated. Based on the American Community Survey (ACS). Based on a sample and subject to sampling variability; see text, this section and Appendix III]

| Relationship by household type | 2010 | | 2015 | | 2016 | | 2017 | |
|---|---|---|---|---|---|---|---|---|
| | Number | Percent distribution | Number | Percent distribution | Number | Percent distribution | Number | Percent distribution |
| **Total** | **40,434** | **100.0** | **47,732** | **100.0** | **49,215** | **100.0** | **50,816** | **100.0** |
| In households | 38,869 | 96.1 | 46,232 | 96.9 | 47,690 | 96.9 | 49,274 | 97.0 |
| In family households | 26,809 | 66.3 | 32,232 | 67.5 | 33,281 | 67.6 | 34,560 | 68.0 |
| Householder | 13,379 | 33.1 | 15,801 | 33.1 | 16,301 | 33.1 | 16,869 | 33.2 |
| Spouse | 9,563 | 23.7 | 11,707 | 24.5 | 12,098 | 24.6 | 12,660 | 24.9 |
| Parent | 2,208 | 5.5 | 2,637 | 5.5 | 2,646 | 5.4 | 2,755 | 5.4 |
| Parent-in-law | 661 | 1.6 | 766 | 1.6 | 795 | 1.6 | 806 | 1.6 |
| Other relatives | 807 | 2.0 | 1,030 | 2.2 | 1,133 | 2.3 | 1,154 | 2.3 |
| Nonrelatives | 191 | 0.5 | 291 | 0.6 | 309 | 0.6 | 315 | 0.6 |
| In nonfamily households | 12,060 | 29.8 | 14,000 | 29.3 | 14,409 | 29.3 | 14,713 | 29.0 |
| Householder | 11,495 | 28.4 | 13,199 | 27.7 | 13,562 | 27.6 | 13,823 | 27.2 |
| Male | 3,417 | 8.5 | 4,244 | 8.9 | 4,430 | 9.0 | 4,570 | 9.0 |
| Living alone | 3,124 | 7.7 | 3,851 | 8.1 | 4,008 | 8.1 | 4,125 | 8.1 |
| Female | 8,078 | 20.0 | 8,955 | 18.8 | 9,133 | 18.6 | 9,253 | 18.2 |
| Living alone | 7,784 | 19.3 | 8,563 | 17.9 | 8,724 | 17.7 | 8,817 | 17.4 |
| Nonrelatives | 565 | 1.4 | 801 | 1.7 | 847 | 1.7 | 890 | 1.8 |
| In group quarters | 1,565 | 3.9 | 1,500 | 3.1 | 1,525 | 3.1 | 1,542 | 3.0 |

Source: U.S. Census Bureau, American Community Survey, B09020, "Relationship by Household Type (Including Living Alone) for the Population 65 Years and Over," <http://factfinder.census.gov>, accessed November 2018.

# Table 35. Persons 65 Years Old and Over with a Disability by Type and Sex: 2017

[In thousands (17,141 represents 17,141,000). Based on data from the American Community Survey (ACS). Disability data limited to civilian noninstitutionalized population. Based on a sample and subject to sampling variability; see text in this section, and Appendix III]

| Type of disability | Number | | | | | Percent | | | | |
|---|---|---|---|---|---|---|---|---|---|---|
| | Total age 65 and over | Males | | Females | | Total age 65 and over | Males | | Females | |
| | | Age 65 to 74 | Age 75 and over | Age 65 to 74 | Age 75 and over | | Age 65 to 74 | Age 75 and over | Age 65 to 74 | Age 75 and over |
| **Persons with any disability** | **17,141** | **3,652** | **3,928** | **3,703** | **5,858** | **34.6** | **26.6** | **47.1** | **23.6** | **49.8** |
| With a hearing difficulty | 7,150 | 1,795 | 2,265 | 889 | 2,200 | 14.4 | 13.1 | 27.1 | 5.7 | 18.7 |
| With a vision difficulty | 3,118 | 583 | 700 | 665 | 1,170 | 6.3 | 4.3 | 8.4 | 4.2 | 9.9 |
| With a cognitive difficulty | 4,278 | 750 | 975 | 814 | 1,739 | 8.6 | 5.5 | 11.7 | 5.2 | 14.8 |
| With an ambulatory difficulty | 10,864 | 1,879 | 2,245 | 2,580 | 4,160 | 21.9 | 13.7 | 26.9 | 16.4 | 35.4 |
| With a self-care difficulty | 3,883 | 554 | 889 | 679 | 1,761 | 7.8 | 4.0 | 10.7 | 4.3 | 15.0 |
| With an independent living difficulty | 7,021 | 892 | 1,504 | 1,307 | 3,319 | 14.2 | 6.5 | 18.0 | 8.3 | 28.2 |

Source: U.S. Census Bureau, 2017 American Community Survey, Tables B18101, B18102, B18103, B18104, B18105, B18106, and B18107, <http://factfinder.census.gov>, accessed November 2018.

# Table 36. Selected Characteristics of Racial Groups and Hispanic or Latino Population: 2017

[In thousands (221,250 represents 221,250,000), except as indicated. The American Community Survey universe includes the household population and the population living in institutions, college dormitories, and other group quarters. Based on a sample and subject to sampling variability; see text, this section and Appendix III]

| Characteristic | Total population | White alone | Black or African American alone | American Indian, Alaska Native alone | Asian alone | Native Hawaiian and Other Pacific Islander alone | Some other race alone | Two or more races | Hispanic or Latino origin [1] | White alone, not Hispanic or Latino |
|---|---|---|---|---|---|---|---|---|---|---|
| **EDUCATIONAL ATTAINMENT** | | | | | | | | | | |
| **Persons 25 years old and over, total** | 221,250 | 165,626 | 26,473 | 1,702 | 12,886 | 382 | 9,679 | 4,502 | 33,474 | 143,648 |
| Less than 9th grade | 11,267 | 6,706 | 1,036 | 124 | 998 | 20 | 2,182 | 201 | 6,090 | 3,013 |
| 9th to 12th grade, no diploma | 15,315 | 9,955 | 2,706 | 213 | 684 | 27 | 1,427 | 303 | 4,388 | 7,208 |
| High school graduate (includes equivalency) | 60,032 | 45,196 | 8,387 | 528 | 1,932 | 135 | 2,827 | 1,026 | 9,412 | 39,085 |
| Some college, no degree | 45,110 | 33,969 | 6,433 | 432 | 1,486 | 97 | 1,582 | 1,111 | 6,028 | 29,946 |
| Associate's degree | 18,761 | 14,507 | 2,255 | 155 | 847 | 34 | 527 | 436 | 2,196 | 12,999 |
| Bachelor's degree | 43,585 | 34,215 | 3,532 | 170 | 3,895 | 49 | 813 | 911 | 3,684 | 31,581 |
| Graduate degree | 27,181 | 21,079 | 2,125 | 80 | 3,044 | 18 | 322 | 514 | 1,677 | 19,816 |
| **OCCUPATION** | | | | | | | | | | |
| **Employed civilian population, 16 years old and over, total** | 155,058 | 114,537 | 18,137 | 1,066 | 9,317 | 288 | 7,889 | 3,823 | 26,614 | 97,312 |
| Management, business, science, and arts occupations | 59,160 | 45,892 | 5,359 | 291 | 4,852 | 71 | 1,340 | 1,355 | 5,841 | 41,770 |
| Management, business, and financial occupations | 24,009 | 19,175 | 1,977 | 120 | 1,625 | 31 | 572 | 510 | 2,465 | 17,423 |
| Computer, engineering, and science occupations | 8,926 | 6,421 | 600 | 32 | 1,475 | 10 | 161 | 227 | 731 | 5,899 |
| Education, legal, community service, arts, and media occupations | 16,853 | 13,309 | 1,741 | 95 | 844 | 20 | 427 | 417 | 1,840 | 12,029 |
| Healthcare practitioners and technical occupations | 9,372 | 6,988 | 1,041 | 44 | 907 | 10 | 181 | 201 | 805 | 6,419 |
| Service occupations | 27,736 | 18,336 | 4,473 | 269 | 1,565 | 70 | 2,197 | 826 | 6,650 | 14,274 |
| Sales and office occupations | 35,541 | 26,512 | 4,420 | 230 | 1,768 | 74 | 1,592 | 945 | 5,776 | 22,697 |
| Natural resources, construction, and maintenance occupations | 13,743 | 10,786 | 911 | 127 | 269 | 27 | 1,346 | 277 | 4,108 | 8,173 |
| Farming, fishing, and forestry occupations | 1,049 | 784 | 33 | 14 | 16 | 2 | 180 | 21 | 529 | 453 |
| Construction and extraction occupations | 7,988 | 6,222 | 502 | 79 | 115 | 15 | 898 | 155 | 2,693 | 4,520 |
| Installation, maintenance, and repair occupations | 4,706 | 3,780 | 376 | 35 | 138 | 9 | 267 | 100 | 886 | 3,201 |
| Production, transportation, and material moving occupations | 18,878 | 13,011 | 2,974 | 150 | 862 | 46 | 1,415 | 421 | 4,239 | 10,397 |
| Production occupations | 8,877 | 6,245 | 1,173 | 69 | 517 | 20 | 674 | 180 | 1,990 | 5,020 |
| Transportation occupations | 5,846 | 4,071 | 1,029 | 46 | 207 | 11 | 352 | 130 | 1,127 | 3,355 |
| Material moving occupations | 4,155 | 2,695 | 773 | 34 | 138 | 15 | 389 | 111 | 1,122 | 2,022 |
| **FAMILY INCOME IN THE PAST 12 MONTHS** | | | | | | | | | | |
| **Total families** | 78,631 | 59,791 | 8,939 | 591 | 4,243 | 124 | 3,397 | 1,547 | 12,022 | 51,794 |
| Less than $10,000 | 3,019 | 1,774 | 768 | 53 | 133 | 6 | 197 | 87 | 670 | 1,344 |
| $10,000 to $19,999 | 4,318 | 2,717 | 911 | 60 | 187 | 7 | 320 | 115 | 1,076 | 2,023 |
| $20,000 to $29,999 | 5,731 | 3,842 | 1,036 | 66 | 237 | 13 | 409 | 129 | 1,379 | 2,940 |
| $30,000 to $39,999 | 6,333 | 4,502 | 949 | 65 | 248 | 10 | 424 | 136 | 1,373 | 3,618 |
| $40,000 to $49,999 | 6,209 | 4,565 | 839 | 54 | 246 | 12 | 376 | 117 | 1,220 | 3,777 |
| $50,000 to $59,999 | 5,945 | 4,517 | 714 | 47 | 238 | 10 | 306 | 112 | 1,047 | 3,832 |
| $60,000 to $74,999 | 8,289 | 6,415 | 903 | 62 | 359 | 14 | 383 | 154 | 1,312 | 5,553 |
| $75,000 to $99,999 | 11,255 | 8,960 | 1,060 | 70 | 535 | 17 | 402 | 211 | 1,491 | 7,950 |
| $100,000 to $124,999 | 8,508 | 6,895 | 672 | 46 | 484 | 13 | 244 | 156 | 953 | 6,236 |
| $125,000 to $149,999 | 5,596 | 4,572 | 405 | 26 | 349 | 8 | 135 | 100 | 542 | 4,196 |
| $150,000 to $199,999 | 6,321 | 5,163 | 392 | 23 | 506 | 8 | 119 | 110 | 536 | 4,778 |
| $200,000 or more | 7,106 | 5,867 | 291 | 20 | 720 | 6 | 81 | 122 | 425 | 5,547 |
| Median family income in the past 12 months (in dollars) [2] | 73,891 | 78,941 | 49,549 | 49,634 | 96,495 | 63,886 | 49,096 | 67,240 | 52,183 | 82,851 |
| **POVERTY STATUS IN THE PAST 12 MONTHS [3]** | | | | | | | | | | |
| Persons below poverty level | 42,584 | 25,668 | 9,122 | 671 | 1,976 | 108 | 3,297 | 1,741 | 11,174 | 18,604 |
| Families below poverty level | 7,501 | 4,477 | 1,715 | 123 | 331 | 19 | 624 | 213 | 2,059 | 3,156 |
| **HOUSING TENURE** | | | | | | | | | | |
| **Total householders** | 120,063 | 91,620 | 14,800 | 883 | 5,740 | 160 | 4,383 | 2,477 | 15,833 | 81,072 |
| Owner-occupied | 76,684 | 63,631 | 6,126 | 480 | 3,422 | 66 | 1,749 | 1,210 | 7,472 | 58,261 |
| Renter-occupied | 43,379 | 27,990 | 8,674 | 402 | 2,318 | 94 | 2,634 | 1,267 | 8,361 | 22,810 |

[1] Persons of Hispanic origin may be of any race. [2] For definition of median, see Guide to Tabular Presentation. [3] For explanation of poverty level, see text, Section 13.

Source: U.S. Census Bureau, 2017 American Community Survey, Tables B15002, B17001, B17010, B19101, B19113, B24010, and B25003, <http://factfinder.census.gov/>, accessed December 2018.

# Table 37. Social and Economic Characteristics of the Hispanic Population: 2018

[59,227 represents 59,227,000, except as noted. As of March, except labor force status is annual average. Excludes members of the Armed Forces except those living off post or with their families on post. Based on Current Population Survey, Annual Social and Economic Supplement; see text, this section and Appendix III]

| Characteristic | Number (1,000) | | | | | | Percent distribution | | | | | |
|---|---|---|---|---|---|---|---|---|---|---|---|---|
| | His-panic total [1] | Mexi-can | Puerto Rican | Cuban | Central Ameri-can [2] | South Ameri-can | His-panic total [1] | Mexi-can | Puerto Rican | Cuban | Central Ameri-can [2] | South Ameri-can |
| **Total persons** | **59,227** | **36,974** | **5,452** | **2,372** | **5,221** | **3,960** | **100.0** | **100.0** | **100.0** | **100.0** | **100.0** | **100.0** |
| Under 5 years old | 5,194 | 3,452 | 459 | 139 | 400 | 325 | 8.8 | 9.3 | 8.4 | 5.9 | 7.7 | 8.2 |
| 5 to 14 years old | 10,540 | 6,968 | 887 | 318 | 887 | 579 | 17.8 | 18.9 | 16.2 | 13.4 | 17.0 | 14.6 |
| 15 to 44 years old | 27,370 | 17,201 | 2,471 | 957 | 2,714 | 1,800 | 46.2 | 46.6 | 45.3 | 40.3 | 52.0 | 45.4 |
| 45 to 64 years old | 11,801 | 7,000 | 1,110 | 602 | 1,003 | 898 | 20.0 | 18.9 | 20.4 | 25.4 | 19.2 | 22.7 |
| 65 years old and over | 4,321 | 2,352 | 525 | 359 | 217 | 359 | 7.3 | 6.4 | 9.6 | 15.1 | 4.2 | 9.1 |
| **EDUCATIONAL ATTAINMENT** | | | | | | | | | | | | |
| **Persons 25 years old and over** | **33,877** | **20,245** | **3,227** | **1,609** | **3,125** | **2,519** | **100.0** | **100.0** | **100.0** | **100.0** | **100.0** | **100.0** |
| Less than high school graduate | 9,626 | 6,732 | 559 | 204 | 1,302 | 231 | 28.4 | 33.2 | 17.3 | 12.7 | 41.7 | 9.2 |
| High school graduate | 10,412 | 6,403 | 1,044 | 548 | 810 | 669 | 30.7 | 31.6 | 32.4 | 34.0 | 25.9 | 26.5 |
| Some college or associate degree | 7,626 | 4,341 | 882 | 389 | 590 | 606 | 22.5 | 21.4 | 27.3 | 24.2 | 18.9 | 24.1 |
| Bachelor's degree or more | 6,213 | 2,769 | 742 | 468 | 423 | 1,013 | 18.3 | 13.7 | 23.0 | 29.1 | 13.5 | 40.2 |
| **NATIVITY AND CITIZENSHIP STATUS** | | | | | | | | | | | | |
| **Total** | **59,227** | **36,974** | **5,452** | **2,372** | **5,221** | **3,960** | **100.0** | **100.0** | **100.0** | **100.0** | **100.0** | **100.0** |
| Native | 38,795 | 25,237 | 5,413 | 985 | 2,195 | 1,544 | 65.5 | 68.3 | 99.3 | 41.5 | 42.0 | 39.0 |
| Foreign born | 20,432 | 11,737 | 39 | 1,387 | 3,026 | 2,416 | 34.5 | 31.7 | 0.7 | 58.5 | 58.0 | 61.0 |
| Naturalized citizen | 7,566 | 3,784 | 21 | 705 | 933 | 1,161 | 12.8 | 10.2 | 0.4 | 29.7 | 17.9 | 29.3 |
| Not a citizen | 12,866 | 7,953 | 18 | 683 | 2,093 | 1,255 | 21.7 | 21.5 | 0.3 | 28.8 | 40.1 | 31.7 |
| **LABOR FORCE STATUS [3]** | | | | | | | | | | | | |
| **Civilians 16 years old and over** | **42,734** | **26,031** | **3,938** | **1,905** | **(NA)** | **(NA)** | **100.0** | **100.0** | **100.0** | **100.0** | **(NA)** | **(NA)** |
| Civilian labor force | 28,336 | 17,312 | 2,408 | 1,181 | (NA) | (NA) | 66.3 | 66.5 | 61.1 | 62.0 | (NA) | (NA) |
| Employed | 27,012 | 16,497 | 2,272 | 1,139 | (NA) | (NA) | 63.2 | 63.4 | 57.7 | 59.8 | (NA) | (NA) |
| Unemployed | 1,323 | 815 | 136 | 41 | (NA) | (NA) | 3.1 | 3.1 | 3.5 | 2.2 | (NA) | (NA) |
| Not in labor force | 14,398 | 8,718 | 1,529 | 725 | (NA) | (NA) | 33.7 | 33.5 | 38.8 | 38.1 | (NA) | (NA) |
| **HOUSEHOLDS [4]** | | | | | | | | | | | | |
| **Total** | **17,318** | **10,040** | **1,914** | **851** | **1,470** | **1,286** | **100.0** | **100.0** | **100.0** | **100.0** | **100.0** | **100.0** |
| Family households | 13,192 | 7,975 | 1,286 | 559 | 1,174 | 957 | 76.2 | 79.4 | 67.2 | 65.7 | 79.8 | 74.4 |
| Married-couple families | 8,362 | 5,174 | 699 | 364 | 697 | 669 | 48.3 | 51.5 | 36.5 | 42.7 | 47.4 | 52.0 |
| Male householder, no spouse present | 1,497 | 918 | 135 | 56 | 167 | 89 | 8.6 | 9.1 | 7.1 | 6.6 | 11.4 | 6.9 |
| Female householder, no spouse present [5] | 3,333 | 1,883 | 452 | 140 | 309 | 198 | 19.2 | 18.8 | 23.6 | 16.4 | 21.0 | 15.4 |
| Nonfamily households | 4,125 | 2,065 | 628 | 292 | 297 | 330 | 23.8 | 20.6 | 32.8 | 34.3 | 20.2 | 25.6 |
| Male householder | 2,176 | 1,186 | 301 | 137 | 162 | 157 | 12.6 | 11.8 | 15.8 | 16.1 | 11.0 | 12.2 |
| Female householder | 1,950 | 879 | 327 | 155 | 135 | 172 | 11.3 | 8.8 | 17.1 | 18.2 | 9.2 | 13.4 |
| **MONEY INCOME IN 2017** | | | | | | | | | | | | |
| **Total families** | **13,192** | **7,975** | **1,286** | **559** | **1,174** | **957** | **100.0** | **100.0** | **100.0** | **100.0** | **100.0** | **100.0** |
| Under $5,000 | 351 | 213 | 55 | 16 | 24 | 19 | 2.7 | 2.7 | 4.3 | 2.9 | 2.0 | 2.0 |
| $5,000 to $9,999 | 240 | 145 | 35 | 3 | 21 | 17 | 1.8 | 1.8 | 2.7 | 0.5 | 1.8 | 1.7 |
| $10,000 to $14,999 | 418 | 250 | 55 | 14 | 47 | 17 | 3.2 | 3.1 | 4.3 | 2.5 | 4.0 | 1.8 |
| $15,000 to $19,999 | 584 | 355 | 59 | 34 | 45 | 30 | 4.4 | 4.4 | 4.6 | 6.1 | 3.8 | 1.8 |
| $20,000 to $24,999 | 711 | 430 | 80 | 19 | 62 | 37 | 5.4 | 5.4 | 6.2 | 3.3 | 5.3 | 3.1 |
| $25,000 to $34,999 | 1,491 | 915 | 135 | 67 | 156 | 95 | 11.3 | 11.5 | 10.5 | 12.0 | 13.3 | 3.8 |
| $35,000 to $49,999 | 2,024 | 1,257 | 183 | 64 | 212 | 139 | 15.3 | 15.8 | 14.2 | 11.5 | 18.1 | 10.0 |
| $50,000 to $74,999 | 2,588 | 1,636 | 243 | 108 | 203 | 160 | 19.6 | 20.5 | 18.9 | 19.3 | 17.3 | 14.5 |
| $75,000 to $99,999 | 1,812 | 1,120 | 148 | 74 | 175 | 146 | 13.7 | 14.0 | 11.5 | 13.2 | 14.9 | 16.7 |
| $100,000 and over | 2,973 | 1,653 | 292 | 160 | 230 | 297 | 22.5 | 20.7 | 22.7 | 28.7 | 19.6 | 15.3 |
| **POVERTY STATUS IN 2017** | | | | | | | | | | | | |
| **Total persons [6]** | **59,053** | **36,887** | **5,415** | **2,372** | **5,191** | **3,954** | **100.0** | **100.0** | **100.0** | **100.0** | **100.0** | **100.0** |
| Below poverty level | 10,790 | 6,844 | 1,126 | 365 | 998 | 493 | 18.3 | 18.6 | 20.8 | 15.4 | 19.2 | 12.5 |
| At or above poverty level | 48,263 | 30,043 | 4,289 | 2,008 | 4,193 | 3,461 | 81.7 | 81.4 | 79.2 | 84.6 | 80.8 | 87.5 |

NA Not available. [1] Includes other Hispanic groups not shown separately. [2] Central American totals exclude Mexican and Cuban. [3] Source: U.S. Bureau of Labor Statistics, "Labor Force Statistics from the Current Population Survey," <https://www.bls.gov/cps/tables.htm> [4] Shown by the Hispanic origin of the householder. [5] Nonfamily households include a single householder living alone or sharing a home with unrelated persons. [6] Persons for whom poverty level determined. Excludes unrelated individuals under 15 years old.

Source: U.S. Census Bureau, "The Hispanic Population in the United States: 2018," <https://www.census.gov/data/tables/2018/demo/hispanic-origin/2018-cps.html>, accessed August 2019.

# Table 38. Native and Foreign-Born Population by State: 2017

[281,193 represents 281,193,000. The term foreign-born refers to anyone who is not a U.S. citizen at birth. This includes naturalized U.S. citizens, legal permanent residents (immigrants), temporary migrants (such as foreign students), humanitarian migrants (such as refugees), and persons illegally present in the United States. The American Community Survey universe includes the household population and the population living in institutions, college dormitories, and other group quarters. Based on a sample and subject to sampling variability; see text, this section and Appendix III]

| State | Native population (1,000) | Foreign-born population | | | State | Native population (1,000) | Foreign-born population | | |
|---|---|---|---|---|---|---|---|---|---|
| | | Number (1,000) | Percent of total population | Percent entered 2010 or later | | | Number (1,000) | Percent of total population | Percent entered 2010 or later |
| U.S......... | 281,193 | 44,526 | 13.7 | 21.3 | MO.......... | 5,856 | 257 | 4.2 | 27.5 |
| AL........... | 4,706 | 169 | 3.5 | 23.2 | MT.......... | 1,027 | 23 | 2.2 | (NA) |
| AK.......... | 682 | 58 | 7.9 | 25.6 | NE.......... | 1,777 | 143 | 7.5 | 25.8 |
| AZ.......... | 6,091 | 925 | 13.2 | 18.8 | NV.......... | 2,402 | 596 | 19.9 | 15.2 |
| AR.......... | 2,864 | 140 | 4.7 | 23.4 | NH.......... | 1,260 | 83 | 6.2 | 28.8 |
| CA.......... | 28,883 | 10,653 | 26.9 | 15.4 | NJ........... | 6,951 | 2,055 | 22.8 | 21.6 |
| CO.......... | 5,056 | 551 | 9.8 | 21.3 | NM.......... | 1,893 | 196 | 9.4 | 17.9 |
| CT.......... | 3,058 | 530 | 14.8 | 20.8 | NY.......... | 15,309 | 4,540 | 22.9 | 19.9 |
| DE.......... | 863 | 98 | 10.2 | 25.6 | NC.......... | 9,444 | 829 | 8.1 | 23.4 |
| DC.......... | 592 | 102 | 14.7 | 35.4 | ND.......... | 724 | 31 | 4.1 | (NA) |
| FL........... | 16,605 | 4,379 | 20.9 | 23.6 | OH.......... | 11,130 | 528 | 4.5 | 32.9 |
| GA.......... | 9,363 | 1,066 | 10.2 | 22.9 | OK.......... | 3,707 | 224 | 5.7 | 26.8 |
| HI........... | 1,162 | 266 | 18.6 | 19.7 | OR.......... | 3,734 | 409 | 9.9 | 21.1 |
| ID........... | 1,616 | 101 | 5.9 | 22.9 | PA.......... | 11,912 | 894 | 7.0 | 26.2 |
| IL........... | 10,970 | 1,832 | 14.3 | 17.9 | RI........... | 913 | 147 | 13.9 | 24.9 |
| IN........... | 6,316 | 351 | 5.3 | 32.2 | SC.......... | 4,780 | 244 | 4.9 | 23.6 |
| IA........... | 2,979 | 167 | 5.3 | 32.5 | SD.......... | 840 | 29 | 3.4 | (NA) |
| KS.......... | 2,713 | 201 | 6.9 | 24.7 | TN.......... | 6,368 | 348 | 5.2 | 28.5 |
| KY.......... | 4,285 | 169 | 3.8 | 36.3 | TX.......... | 23,450 | 4,854 | 17.1 | 22.9 |
| LA.......... | 4,493 | 191 | 4.1 | 29.2 | UT.......... | 2,833 | 269 | 8.7 | 24.3 |
| ME.......... | 1,290 | 45 | 3.4 | 27.6 | VT.......... | 596 | 28 | 4.5 | (NA) |
| MD.......... | 5,124 | 928 | 15.3 | 23.4 | VA.......... | 7,408 | 1,062 | 12.5 | 24.5 |
| MA.......... | 5,703 | 1,156 | 16.9 | 28.2 | WA.......... | 6,346 | 1,060 | 14.3 | 24.5 |
| MI........... | 9,259 | 704 | 7.1 | 30.1 | WV.......... | 1,786 | 30 | 1.6 | 24.7 |
| MN.......... | 5,090 | 486 | 8.7 | 27.5 | WI........... | 5,507 | 288 | 5.0 | 23.6 |
| MS.......... | 2,918 | 66 | 2.2 | 31.1 | WY.......... | 559 | 21 | 3.5 | (NA) |

NA Not available.

Source: U.S. Census Bureau, 2017 American Community Survey, B05002, "Place of Birth by Nativity and Citizenship Status"; and B05007, "Place of Birth by Year of Entry by Citizenship Status for the Foreign-Born Population"; <http://factfinder.census.gov>, accessed November 2018.

# Table 39. Nativity and Place of Birth of Resident Population—25 Largest Cities: 2017

[The American Community Survey universe includes the household population and the population living in institutions, college dormitories, and other group quarters. Based on a sample and subject to sampling variability; see text, this section and Appendix III. See headnote, Table 38]

| City | Native population | | | Foreign born | | | |
|---|---|---|---|---|---|---|---|
| | | | | Total | | Entered 2010 or later | |
| | Total population | Total | Born in United States | Born outside United States | Number | Percent of total population | Number | Percent of foreign-born population |
| Austin, TX........................ | 950,714 | 772,870 | 753,518 | 19,352 | 177,844 | 18.7 | 59,064 | 33.2 |
| Boston, MA...................... | 683,015 | 483,085 | 453,930 | 29,155 | 199,930 | 29.3 | 62,868 | 31.4 |
| Charlotte, NC................... | 859,052 | 711,978 | 700,499 | 11,479 | 147,074 | 17.1 | 50,793 | 34.5 |
| Chicago, IL....................... | 2,716,462 | 2,152,774 | 2,102,379 | 50,395 | 563,688 | 20.8 | 107,442 | 19.1 |
| Columbus, OH.................. | 881,901 | 776,075 | 764,553 | 11,522 | 105,826 | 12.0 | 44,316 | 41.9 |
| Dallas, TX........................ | 1,341,103 | 1,007,444 | 991,845 | 15,599 | 333,659 | 24.9 | 87,368 | 26.2 |
| Denver, CO...................... | 704,621 | 599,020 | 588,058 | 10,962 | 105,601 | 15.0 | 23,129 | 21.9 |
| Detroit, MI....................... | 673,103 | 631,729 | 626,121 | 5,608 | 41,374 | 6.1 | 10,264 | 24.8 |
| El Paso, TX...................... | 683,583 | 515,320 | 500,819 | 14,501 | 168,263 | 24.6 | 23,320 | 13.9 |
| Fort Worth, TX.................. | 876,060 | 718,449 | 708,912 | 9,537 | 157,611 | 18.0 | 39,323 | 24.9 |
| Houston, TX..................... | 2,313,230 | 1,640,261 | 1,609,800 | 30,461 | 672,969 | 29.1 | 199,488 | 29.6 |
| Indianapolis, IN [1]............. | 857,386 | 767,921 | 759,100 | 8,821 | 89,465 | 10.4 | 34,038 | 38.0 |
| Jacksonville, FL................ | 892,064 | 784,330 | 761,624 | 22,706 | 107,734 | 12.1 | 28,978 | 26.9 |
| Los Angeles, CA............... | 3,999,742 | 2,525,438 | 2,471,668 | 53,770 | 1,474,304 | 36.9 | 211,676 | 14.4 |
| Memphis, TN.................... | 652,231 | 608,230 | 605,879 | 2,351 | 44,001 | 6.7 | 12,121 | 27.5 |
| Nashville–Davidson, TN [1]........ | 665,967 | 579,696 | 570,838 | 8,858 | 86,271 | 13.0 | 26,063 | 30.2 |
| New York, NY................... | 8,622,698 | 5,427,758 | 5,109,456 | 318,302 | 3,194,940 | 37.1 | 645,937 | 20.2 |
| Philadelphia, PA............... | 1,580,863 | 1,362,033 | 1,310,463 | 51,570 | 218,830 | 13.8 | 59,151 | 27.0 |
| Phoenix, AZ..................... | 1,626,085 | 1,312,599 | 1,290,548 | 22,051 | 313,486 | 19.3 | 54,692 | 17.4 |
| San Antonio, TX............... | 1,511,913 | 1,299,804 | 1,267,488 | 32,316 | 212,109 | 14.0 | 45,716 | 21.6 |
| San Diego, CA.................. | 1,419,488 | 1,051,467 | 1,018,779 | 32,688 | 368,021 | 25.9 | 68,913 | 18.7 |
| San Francisco, CA............ | 884,363 | 569,897 | 550,378 | 19,519 | 314,466 | 35.6 | 62,306 | 19.8 |
| San Jose, CA.................... | 1,035,353 | 618,205 | 603,301 | 14,904 | 417,148 | 40.3 | 85,235 | 20.4 |
| Seattle, WA...................... | 724,764 | 592,201 | 579,936 | 12,265 | 132,563 | 18.3 | 42,461 | 32.0 |
| Washington, DC................ | 693,972 | 592,112 | 576,978 | 15,134 | 101,860 | 14.7 | 36,071 | 35.4 |

[1] Represents the portion of a consolidated city that is not within one or more separately incorporated places.

Source: U.S. Census Bureau, 2017 American Community Survey, C05002, "Place of Birth by Nativity"; and C05005, "Period of Entry by Nativity and Citizenship Status in the United States"; <http://factfinder.census.gov>, accessed December 2018.

# Table 40. Native and Foreign-Born Populations by Selected Characteristics: 2018

[In thousands (323,156 represents 323,156,000). As of March. The foreign-born population includes anyone who is not a U.S. citizen at birth. This includes legal permanent residents (immigrants), temporary migrants (such as foreign students), humanitarian migrants (such as refugees), and persons illegally present in the United States. Based on Current Population Survey, Annual Social and Economic Supplement, which includes the civilian noninstitutional population plus Armed Forces living in housing units on or off post with at least one other civilian adult; see text, this section, and Appendix III]

| Characteristic | Total population | Native population | Foreign-born population | | | |
|---|---|---|---|---|---|---|
| | | | Total | Natural-ized citizen | Not a U.S. citizen | Year of entry: 2000 or later |
| **Total** | **323,156** | **277,748** | **45,408** | **21,854** | **23,554** | **22,552** |
| Under 5 years old | 19,929 | 19,581 | 348 | 60 | 287 | 348 |
| 5 to 9 years old | 20,243 | 19,548 | 694 | 127 | 567 | 694 |
| 10 to 14 years old | 20,812 | 19,961 | 850 | 256 | 594 | 850 |
| 15 to 19 years old | 20,908 | 19,544 | 1,364 | 420 | 943 | 1,302 |
| 20 to 24 years old | 21,434 | 19,110 | 2,324 | 671 | 1,653 | 1,895 |
| 25 to 29 years old | 23,160 | 19,533 | 3,627 | 1,099 | 2,527 | 2,853 |
| 30 to 34 years old | 21,695 | 17,204 | 4,490 | 1,429 | 3,062 | 3,469 |
| 35 to 39 years old | 21,269 | 16,305 | 4,964 | 1,920 | 3,043 | 3,103 |
| 40 to 44 years old | 19,391 | 14,635 | 4,756 | 2,118 | 2,638 | 2,338 |
| 45 to 49 years old | 20,638 | 16,043 | 4,595 | 2,337 | 2,258 | 1,712 |
| 50 to 54 years old | 20,899 | 16,819 | 4,080 | 2,304 | 1,775 | 1,191 |
| 55 to 59 years old | 21,622 | 18,108 | 3,515 | 2,228 | 1,286 | 892 |
| 60 to 64 years old | 20,078 | 16,938 | 3,140 | 2,058 | 1,082 | 716 |
| 65 to 69 years old | 17,007 | 14,640 | 2,367 | 1,666 | 702 | 433 |
| 70 to 74 years old | 13,359 | 11,698 | 1,661 | 1,217 | 445 | 281 |
| 75 to 79 years old | 8,912 | 7,804 | 1,108 | 802 | 307 | 242 |
| 80 to 84 years old | 5,647 | 4,859 | 788 | 602 | 186 | 134 |
| 85 years and over | 6,154 | 5,416 | 738 | 540 | 198 | 99 |
| Median age (years) | 38 | 36 | 44 | 51 | 39 | 35 |
| MARITAL STATUS | | | | | | |
| **Persons 15 years old and over** | **262,172** | **218,657** | **43,516** | **21,410** | **22,105** | **20,660** |
| Married | 131,436 | 104,197 | 27,239 | 14,020 | 13,219 | 12,095 |
| Widowed | 15,125 | 13,093 | 2,033 | 1,389 | 644 | 519 |
| Divorced | 25,909 | 22,788 | 3,121 | 1,993 | 1,128 | 999 |
| Separated | 5,105 | 3,951 | 1,154 | 466 | 688 | 511 |
| Never married | 84,596 | 74,628 | 9,969 | 3,542 | 6,426 | 6,536 |
| EDUCATIONAL ATTAINMENT | | | | | | |
| **Persons 25 years old and over** | **219,830** | **180,002** | **39,828** | **20,319** | **19,509** | **17,463** |
| Not high school graduate | 22,411 | 12,896 | 9,515 | 3,246 | 6,268 | 3,897 |
| High school graduate | 62,685 | 52,465 | 10,220 | 5,180 | 5,040 | 4,245 |
| Some college or associate's degree | 57,810 | 51,258 | 6,552 | 4,089 | 2,463 | 2,551 |
| Bachelor's degree | 48,235 | 40,393 | 7,843 | 4,631 | 3,212 | 3,915 |
| Advanced degree | 28,689 | 22,990 | 5,699 | 3,173 | 2,526 | 2,855 |
| EMPLOYMENT STATUS | | | | | | |
| **Persons 16 years old and over** | **161,626** | **133,282** | **28,344** | **13,750** | **14,594** | **13,753** |
| Employed | 154,815 | 127,499 | 27,316 | 13,300 | 14,016 | 13,232 |
| Unemployed | 6,811 | 5,783 | 1,029 | 451 | 578 | 520 |
| EARNINGS IN 2017 [1] | | | | | | |
| **Persons 15 years old and over with earnings** | **115,672** | **94,732** | **20,939** | **10,603** | **10,336** | **9,751** |
| $1 to $14,999 or loss | 4,046 | 3,106 | 939 | 324 | 615 | 486 |
| $15,000 to $29,999 | 21,297 | 16,128 | 5,169 | 1,894 | 3,275 | 2,741 |
| $30,000 to $39,999 | 18,243 | 14,671 | 3,572 | 1,709 | 1,864 | 1,670 |
| $40,000 to $49,999 | 15,520 | 13,000 | 2,520 | 1,417 | 1,103 | 993 |
| $50,000 to $74,999 | 25,879 | 22,227 | 3,652 | 2,163 | 1,489 | 1,624 |
| $75,000 to $99,999 | 12,646 | 10,741 | 1,905 | 1,145 | 760 | 856 |
| $100,000 and over | 18,040 | 14,858 | 3,182 | 1,952 | 1,230 | 1,382 |
| Median earnings (dollars) | 48,500 | 50,212 | 41,560 | 49,357 | 36,032 | 39,763 |
| HOUSEHOLD SIZE [2] | | | | | | |
| **Total households** | **127,586** | **107,653** | **19,933** | **10,877** | **9,056** | **8,433** |
| One person | 35,740 | 31,921 | 3,819 | 2,333 | 1,485 | 1,326 |
| Two people | 44,038 | 38,912 | 5,126 | 3,095 | 2,031 | 1,993 |
| Three people | 19,333 | 15,630 | 3,703 | 1,924 | 1,778 | 1,747 |
| Four people | 16,468 | 12,644 | 3,824 | 1,871 | 1,953 | 1,840 |
| Five or more people | 12,007 | 8,547 | 3,461 | 1,653 | 1,808 | 1,528 |
| INCOME IN 2017 [2] | | | | | | |
| **Total family households** | **83,088** | **68,073** | **15,015** | **8,177** | **6,838** | **6,413** |
| $1 to $14,999 or loss | 4,650 | 3,594 | 1,056 | 432 | 624 | 578 |
| $15,000 to $29,999 | 8,163 | 6,218 | 1,945 | 865 | 1,080 | 926 |
| $30,000 to $39,999 | 6,752 | 5,374 | 1,378 | 630 | 748 | 650 |
| $40,000 to $49,999 | 6,228 | 4,869 | 1,359 | 612 | 747 | 622 |
| $50,000 to $74,999 | 14,101 | 11,482 | 2,619 | 1,410 | 1,209 | 1,046 |
| $75,000 to $99,999 | 12,145 | 10,150 | 1,995 | 1,119 | 876 | 828 |
| $100,000 and over | 31,049 | 26,386 | 4,663 | 3,109 | 1,554 | 1,764 |
| Median income (dollars) | 77,713 | 80,486 | 66,219 | 77,561 | 53,014 | 59,357 |
| POVERTY STATUS IN 2017 [3] | | | | | | |
| Persons below poverty level | 39,698 | 33,095 | 6,603 | 2,213 | 4,390 | 4,060 |
| Persons at or above poverty level | 282,851 | 244,063 | 38,788 | 19,638 | 19,150 | 18,474 |
| HOUSEHOLD TENURE [2] | | | | | | |
| **Total households** | **127,586** | **107,654** | **19,933** | **10,877** | **9,056** | **8,433** |
| Owner occupied unit | 82,105 | 71,898 | 10,207 | 6,883 | 3,324 | 2,945 |
| Renter occupied unit [4] | 45,482 | 35,755 | 9,727 | 3,994 | 5,732 | 5,488 |

[1] Covers only year-round full-time workers. [2] Based on citizenship of householder. [3] Persons for whom poverty status is determined. Excludes unrelated individuals under 15 years old. [4] Includes occupiers who paid no cash rent.

Source: U.S. Census Bureau, "Foreign Born CPS Data Tables," <https://www.census.gov/topics/population/foreign-born/data/tables.html>, accessed August 2019.

# Table 41. Foreign-Born Population—Selected Characteristics by Region of Origin: 2018

[In thousands (45,408 represents 45,408,000). As of March. The term foreign-born refers to anyone who is not a U.S. citizen at birth. This includes naturalized U.S. citizens, legal permanent residents (immigrants), temporary migrants (such as foreign students), humanitarian migrants (such as refugees), and persons illegally present in the United States. Based on Current Population Survey, Annual Social and Economic Supplement; see text, this section and Appendix III]

| Characteristic | Total foreign-born | Asia | Europe | Latin America Total | Mexico | Other Latin America | Other areas [1] |
|---|---|---|---|---|---|---|---|
| **Total** | **45,408** | **14,128** | **4,597** | **23,198** | **11,948** | **11,250** | **3,485** |
| 0 to 4 years old | 348 | 151 | 29 | 124 | 34 | 90 | 44 |
| 5 to 9 years old | 694 | 232 | 81 | 295 | 78 | 217 | 87 |
| 10 to 14 years old | 850 | 316 | 59 | 385 | 110 | 275 | 91 |
| 15 to 19 years old | 1,364 | 425 | 108 | 710 | 336 | 374 | 120 |
| 20 to 24 years old | 2,324 | 744 | 210 | 1,187 | 550 | 637 | 183 |
| 25 to 29 years old | 3,627 | 1,186 | 310 | 1,786 | 896 | 890 | 344 |
| 30 to 34 years old | 4,490 | 1,378 | 359 | 2,377 | 1,318 | 1,060 | 376 |
| 35 to 39 years old | 4,964 | 1,445 | 388 | 2,769 | 1,489 | 1,280 | 361 |
| 40 to 44 years old | 4,756 | 1,377 | 365 | 2,671 | 1,548 | 1,123 | 343 |
| 45 to 49 years old | 4,595 | 1,339 | 369 | 2,550 | 1,484 | 1,066 | 337 |
| 50 to 54 years old | 4,080 | 1,176 | 324 | 2,307 | 1,265 | 1,042 | 273 |
| 55 to 59 years old | 3,515 | 1,062 | 396 | 1,759 | 902 | 857 | 298 |
| 60 to 64 years old | 3,140 | 1,078 | 313 | 1,520 | 715 | 805 | 229 |
| 65 to 69 years old | 2,367 | 837 | 353 | 1,039 | 487 | 552 | 138 |
| 70 to 74 years old | 1,661 | 558 | 296 | 681 | 292 | 389 | 127 |
| 75 to 79 years old | 1,108 | 340 | 242 | 478 | 206 | 271 | 47 |
| 80 to 84 years old | 788 | 263 | 181 | 310 | 144 | 166 | 34 |
| 85 years old and over | 738 | 221 | 213 | 252 | 95 | 156 | 52 |
| Median age (years) [2] | 44.3 | 44.3 | 50.3 | 43.7 | 43.8 | 43.6 | 42.0 |
| EDUCATIONAL ATTAINMENT | | | | | | | |
| **Persons 25 years old and over** | **39,828** | **12,260** | **4,111** | **20,497** | **10,840** | **9,657** | **2,960** |
| Not high school graduate | 9,515 | 1,250 | 260 | 7,735 | 5,354 | 2,381 | 269 |
| High school graduate/some college or associate's degree | 16,772 | 4,160 | 1,820 | 9,459 | 4,497 | 4,962 | 1,334 |
| Bachelor's degree | 7,843 | 3,683 | 1,012 | 2,308 | 773 | 1,535 | 840 |
| Advanced degree | 5,699 | 3,167 | 1,019 | 996 | 217 | 779 | 516 |
| INCOME IN 2017 | | | | | | | |
| **Total family households** | **15,015** | **4,508** | **1,466** | **7,850** | **4,188** | **3,662** | **1,191** |
| $1 to $14,999 or loss | 1,056 | 284 | 70 | 624 | 343 | 281 | 78 |
| $15,000 to $29,999 | 1,945 | 421 | 106 | 1,301 | 746 | 555 | 118 |
| $30,000 to $39,999 | 1,378 | 224 | 86 | 965 | 519 | 447 | 103 |
| $40,000 to $49,999 | 1,359 | 330 | 83 | 842 | 500 | 342 | 104 |
| $50,000 to $74,999 | 2,619 | 632 | 191 | 1,564 | 928 | 637 | 232 |
| $75,000 to $99,999 | 1,995 | 587 | 217 | 1,036 | 534 | 502 | 155 |
| $100,000 and over | 4,663 | 2,031 | 713 | 1,518 | 619 | 899 | 401 |
| Median income (dollars) [2] | 66,219 | 88,137 | 95,525 | 51,909 | 49,671 | 57,492 | 70,056 |
| POVERTY STATUS IN 2017 [3] | | | | | | | |
| Persons below poverty level | 6,603 | 1,744 | 480 | 3,938 | 2,131 | 1,807 | 441 |
| Persons at or above poverty level | 38,788 | 12,383 | 4,117 | 19,243 | 9,813 | 9,430 | 3,045 |

[1] Africa, Oceania, Northern America, and born at sea. [2] For definition of median, see Guide to Tabular Presentation. [3] Persons for whom poverty status is determined. Excludes unrelated individuals under age 15.

Source: U.S. Census Bureau, Foreign Born Data Tables, "Foreign Born CPS Data Tables," <https://www.census.gov/topics/population/foreign-born/data/tables.html>, accessed August 2019.

# Table 42. Foreign-Born Population by Citizenship Status and Place of Birth: 2017

[The term foreign-born refers to anyone who is not a U.S. citizen at birth. This includes naturalized U.S. citizens, legal permanent residents (immigrants), temporary migrants (such as foreign students), humanitarian migrants (such as refugees), and persons illegally present in the United States. The American Community Survey universe includes the household population and the population living in institutions, college dormitories, and other group quarters. Based on a sample and subject to sampling variability; see text, this section and Appendix III]

| Region and country | Foreign-born population, total | Naturalized citizens | Not a U.S. citizen Number | Percent of foreign-born |
|---|---|---|---|---|
| **Total [1]** | **44,525,855** | **21,948,732** | **22,577,123** | **50.7** |
| Latin America | 22,425,056 | 8,993,400 | 13,431,656 | 59.9 |
| Caribbean [2] | 4,414,943 | 2,620,368 | 1,794,575 | 40.6 |
| Cuba | 1,311,803 | (NA) | (NA) | (NA) |
| Central America [2] | 14,796,926 | 4,670,903 | 10,126,023 | 68.4 |
| Mexico | 11,269,913 | 3,454,984 | 7,814,929 | 69.3 |
| Other Central America [2] | 3,527,013 | 1,215,919 | 2,311,094 | 65.5 |
| El Salvador | 1,401,832 | (NA) | (NA) | (NA) |
| South America | 3,213,187 | 1,702,129 | 1,511,058 | 47.0 |
| Asia [2] | 13,907,844 | 8,088,584 | 5,819,260 | 41.8 |
| China, excluding Hong Kong and Taiwan | 2,216,810 | (NA) | (NA) | (NA) |
| India | 2,610,537 | (NA) | (NA) | (NA) |
| Korea | 1,063,074 | (NA) | (NA) | (NA) |
| Philippines | 2,008,080 | (NA) | (NA) | (NA) |
| Vietnam | 1,342,568 | (NA) | (NA) | (NA) |
| Europe | 4,818,662 | 3,129,192 | 1,689,470 | 35.1 |
| Africa | 2,293,028 | 1,246,961 | 1,046,067 | 45.6 |
| North America | 816,903 | 388,150 | 428,753 | 52.5 |
| Oceania | 263,965 | 102,445 | 161,520 | 61.2 |

NA Not available. [1] Includes persons born at sea. [2] Includes other countries not shown separately.

Source: U.S. Census Bureau, 2017 American Community Survey, B05002, "Place of Birth by Nativity and Citizenship Status"; B05006, "Place of Birth for the Foreign-Born Population in the United States"; and B05007, "Place of Birth by Year of Entry by Citizenship Status for the Foreign-Born Population"; <http://factfinder.census.gov/>, accessed December 2018.

## Table 43. American Indian Reservations and Alaska Native Village Statistical Areas With Largest American Indian and Alaska Native Populations: 2010

[As of April. Rankings of the American Indian reservations and Alaska Native village statistical areas are based on the American Indian and Alaska Native alone-or-in-combination population]

| Area | Total population | American Indian and Alaska Native | | | Not American Indian and Alaska Native alone or in combination [1] |
|---|---|---|---|---|---|
| | | Alone or in combination [1] | Alone | In combination [1] | |
| AMERICAN INDIAN RESERVATION | | | | | |
| Navajo Nation Reservation and Off-Reservation Trust Land, AZ–NM–UT.......... | 173,667 | 169,321 | 166,824 | 2,497 | 4,346 |
| Pine Ridge Reservation, SD–NE.......... | 18,834 | 16,906 | 16,580 | 326 | 1,928 |
| Fort Apache Reservation, AZ.......... | 13,409 | 13,014 | 12,870 | 144 | 395 |
| Gila River Indian Reservation, AZ.......... | 11,712 | 11,251 | 10,845 | 406 | 461 |
| Osage Reservation, OK.......... | 47,472 | 9,920 | 6,858 | 3,062 | 37,552 |
| San Carlos Reservation, AZ.......... | 10,068 | 9,901 | 9,835 | 66 | 167 |
| Rosebud Indian Reservation and Off-Reservation Trust Land, SD.......... | 10,869 | 9,809 | 9,617 | 192 | 1,060 |
| Tohono O'odham Nation Reservation and Off-Reservation Trust Land, AZ.......... | 10,201 | 9,278 | 9,139 | 139 | 923 |
| Blackfeet Indian Reservation and Off-Reservation Trust Land, MT.......... | 10,405 | 9,149 | 8,944 | 205 | 1,256 |
| Flathead Reservation, MT.......... | 28,359 | 9,138 | 7,042 | 2,096 | 19,221 |
| ALASKA NATIVE VILLAGE STATISTICAL AREA | | | | | |
| Knik Alaska Native village statistical area.......... | 65,768 | 6,582 | 3,529 | 3,053 | 59,186 |
| Bethel Alaska Native village statistical area.......... | 6,080 | 4,334 | 3,953 | 381 | 1,746 |
| Kenaitze Alaska Native village statistical area.......... | 32,902 | 3,417 | 2,001 | 1,416 | 29,485 |
| Barrow Alaska Native village statistical area.......... | 4,212 | 2,889 | 2,577 | 312 | 1,323 |
| Ketchikan Alaska Native village statistical area.......... | 12,742 | 2,605 | 1,692 | 913 | 10,137 |
| Kotzebue Alaska Native village statistical area.......... | 3,201 | 2,585 | 2,355 | 230 | 616 |
| Nome Alaska Native village statistical area.......... | 3,681 | 2,396 | 1,994 | 402 | 1,285 |
| Chickaloon Alaska Native village statistical area.......... | 23,087 | 2,373 | 1,369 | 1,004 | 20,714 |
| Dillingham Alaska Native village statistical area.......... | 2,378 | 1,583 | 1,333 | 250 | 795 |
| Sitka Alaska Native village statistical area.......... | 4,480 | 1,240 | 855 | 385 | 3,240 |

[1] In combination with one or more other race groups.

Source: U.S. Census Bureau, 2010 Census Briefs, *The American Indian and Alaska Native Population: 2010*, January 2012. See also <https://www.census.gov/about/partners/cic/resources/data-links/aian.html>.

## Table 44. American Indian and Alaska Native Population by Selected Tribal Groupings: 2010

[As of April. Data shown for American Indian and Alaska Native tribes alone or in combination of tribes or races]

| Tribal grouping | American Indian and Alaska Native tribal grouping alone or in any combination [1] | Tribal grouping | American Indian and Alaska Native tribal grouping alone or in any combination [1] |
|---|---|---|---|
| **Total [2]**.......... | **5,220,579** | Navajo.......... | 332,129 |
| AMERICAN INDIAN TRIBES | | Osage.......... | 18,576 |
| Apache.......... | 111,810 | Ottawa.......... | 13,033 |
| Arapaho.......... | 10,861 | Paiute.......... | 13,767 |
| Blackfeet.......... | 105,304 | Pima.......... | 26,655 |
| Canadian and French American Indian..... | 14,822 | Potawatomi.......... | 33,771 |
| Central American Indian.......... | 27,844 | Pueblo.......... | 62,540 |
| Cherokee.......... | 819,105 | Puget Sound Salish.......... | 20,260 |
| Cheyenne.......... | 19,051 | Seminole.......... | 31,971 |
| Chickasaw.......... | 52,278 | Shoshone.......... | 13,002 |
| Chippewa.......... | 170,742 | Sioux.......... | 170,110 |
| Choctaw.......... | 195,764 | South American Indian.......... | 47,233 |
| Colville.......... | 10,549 | Spanish American Indian.......... | 19,951 |
| Comanche.......... | 23,330 | Tohono O'odham.......... | 23,478 |
| Cree.......... | 7,983 | Ute.......... | 11,491 |
| Creek.......... | 88,332 | Yakama.......... | 11,527 |
| Crow.......... | 15,203 | Yaqui.......... | 32,595 |
| Delaware.......... | 18,264 | Yuman.......... | 10,089 |
| Hopi.......... | 18,327 | ALASKA NATIVE TRIBES | |
| Houma.......... | 10,768 | Alaskan Athabascan.......... | 22,484 |
| Iroquois.......... | 81,002 | Aleut.......... | 19,282 |
| Kiowa.......... | 13,787 | Inupiat.......... | 33,360 |
| Lumbee.......... | 73,691 | Tlingit-Haida.......... | 26,080 |
| Menominee.......... | 11,133 | Tsimshian.......... | 3,755 |
| Mexican American Indian.......... | 175,494 | Yup'ik.......... | 33,889 |

[1] The numbers by American Indian and Alaska Native tribal grouping do not add to the total American Indian and Alaska Native population. This is because the American Indian and Alaska Native tribal groupings are tallies of the number of American Indian and Alaska Native responses rather than the number of American Indian or Alaska Native respondents. Respondents reporting several American Indian or Alaska Native groups are counted several times. [2] Includes other tribal groupings not shown separately.

Source: U.S. Census Bureau, 2010 Census Briefs, *The American Indian and Alaska Native Population: 2010*, January 2012. See also <https://www.census.gov/about/partners/cic/resources/data-links/aian.html>.

# Table 45. Refugee Arrivals and Individuals Granted Asylum by Country of Nationality: 2009 to 2017

[For year ending September 30. Data shown provide information on the number of persons admitted to the U.S. as refugees or granted asylum in the United States in the year shown. In cases with no country of nationality, the applicant's last country of residence is assigned. For definitions of refugee and asylee, see text, this section. The refugee data were derived from data on refugee admissions that are maintained in the Worldwide Refugee Admissions Processing System (WRAPS) of the Bureau of Population, Refugees, and Migration (PRM) of the U.S. Department of State. The asylee data were derived from data on applications for asylum maintained in the Refugee, Asylum, and Parole System (RAPS) of the U.S. Citizenship and Immigration Services (USCIS) of the U.S. Department of Homeland Security and obtained from the Executive Office for Immigration Review (EOIR) of the U.S. Department of Justice]

| Country of nationality | 2009 | 2010 | 2011 | 2012 | 2013 | 2014 | 2015 | 2016 | 2017 |
|---|---|---|---|---|---|---|---|---|---|
| **REFUGEE ARRIVALS** | | | | | | | | | |
| **Total** | 74,602 | 73,293 | 56,384 | 58,179 | 69,909 | 69,975 | 69,920 | 84,988 | 53,691 |
| Congo, Democratic Republic | 1,135 | 3,174 | 977 | 1,863 | 2,563 | 4,540 | 7,876 | 16,370 | 9,377 |
| Iraq | 18,838 | 18,016 | 9,388 | 12,163 | 19,488 | 19,769 | 12,676 | 9,880 | 6,886 |
| Syria | 25 | 25 | 29 | 31 | 36 | 105 | 1,682 | 12,587 | 6,557 |
| Somalia | 4,189 | 4,884 | 3,161 | 4,911 | 7,608 | 9,000 | 8,858 | 9,020 | 6,130 |
| Burma | 18,202 | 16,693 | 16,972 | 14,160 | 16,299 | 14,598 | 18,386 | 12,347 | 5,078 |
| Ukraine | 601 | 449 | 428 | 372 | 227 | 490 | 1,451 | 2,543 | 4,264 |
| Bhutan | 13,452 | 12,363 | 14,999 | 15,070 | 9,134 | 8,434 | 5,775 | 5,817 | 3,550 |
| Iran | 5,381 | 3,543 | 2,032 | 1,758 | 2,578 | 2,846 | 3,109 | 3,750 | 2,577 |
| Eritrea | 1,571 | 2,570 | 2,032 | 1,346 | 1,824 | 1,488 | 1,596 | 1,949 | 1,917 |
| Afghanistan | 349 | 515 | 428 | 481 | 661 | 753 | 910 | 2,737 | 1,311 |
| El Salvador | 0 | 0 | 0 | 0 | 0 | 0 | 0 | 364 | 1,124 |
| Sudan | 683 | 558 | 334 | 1,077 | 2,160 | 1,315 | 1,578 | 1,458 | 980 |
| Ethiopia | 321 | 668 | 560 | 620 | 765 | 728 | 626 | 1,131 | 766 |
| Burundi | 762 | 530 | 110 | 186 | 193 | 68 | 1,186 | 694 | 291 |
| Cuba | 4,800 | 4,818 | 2,920 | 1,948 | 4,205 | 4,062 | 1,527 | 354 | 177 |
| Vietnam | 1,486 | 873 | 79 | 41 | 69 | 67 | 22 | 52 | 21 |
| All other countries [1] | 2,807 | 3,614 | 1,935 | 2,152 | 2,099 | 1,712 | 2,662 | 3,935 | 2,685 |
| **ASYLEES** | | | | | | | | | |
| **Total** | 22,303 | 19,771 | 23,569 | 27,948 | 24,996 | 23,369 | 26,011 | 20,340 | 26,568 |
| China, People's Republic | 6,168 | 6,315 | 8,176 | 9,670 | 8,556 | 7,895 | 6,190 | 4,483 | 5,581 |
| El Salvador | 323 | 281 | 234 | 291 | 252 | 365 | 2,164 | 2,148 | 3,469 |
| Guatemala | 507 | 423 | 434 | 505 | 381 | 486 | 2,071 | 1,921 | 2,963 |
| Honduras | 86 | 106 | 117 | 211 | 200 | 243 | 1,407 | 1,482 | 2,048 |
| Egypt | 482 | 511 | 1,003 | 2,848 | 3,362 | 2,822 | 1,651 | 828 | 1,162 |
| Mexico | 255 | 170 | 264 | 420 | 357 | 589 | 861 | 914 | 1,046 |
| Syria | 26 | 23 | 52 | 355 | 794 | 912 | 965 | 719 | 763 |
| India | 411 | 308 | 307 | 344 | 405 | 483 | 476 | 475 | 687 |
| Eritrea | 436 | 355 | 620 | 456 | 320 | 315 | 383 | 405 | 587 |
| Venezuela | 586 | 610 | 1,057 | 1,060 | 677 | 410 | 499 | 345 | 553 |
| Iraq | 910 | 391 | 361 | 406 | 464 | 615 | 750 | 613 | 512 |
| Ethiopia | 1,110 | 1,044 | 1,010 | 1,072 | 878 | 829 | 868 | 485 | 445 |
| Haiti | 1,006 | 773 | 861 | 666 | 498 | 527 | 410 | 136 | 146 |
| Colombia | 1,006 | 546 | 500 | 432 | 245 | 309 | 299 | 98 | 113 |
| All other countries [1] | 8,991 | 7,915 | 8,573 | 9,212 | 7,607 | 6,569 | 7,017 | 5,288 | 6,493 |

[1] Includes unknown.

Source: U.S. Department of Homeland Security, Office of Immigration Statistics, *Annual Flow Report, Refugees and Asylees: 2017*, March 2019; and "2017 Yearbook of Immigration Statistics," <https://www.dhs.gov/immigration-statistics/yearbook>, accessed April 2019.

# Table 46. Immigrant Orphans Adopted by U.S. Citizens by Sex, Age, Region, and Country of Birth: 2017

[For year ending September 30]

| Region and country of birth | Total | Sex | | Age | | |
|---|---|---|---|---|---|---|
| | | Male | Female | Under 1 year old | 1 to 4 years old | 5 years old and over |
| **Total** [1] | 4,701 | 2,358 | 2,343 | 135 | 2,538 | 2,028 |
| REGION | | | | | | |
| Africa | 764 | 396 | 368 | 35 | 380 | 349 |
| Asia | 2,783 | 1,400 | 1,383 | 70 | 1,873 | 840 |
| Europe | 530 | 254 | 276 | 4 | 133 | 393 |
| North America | 371 | 172 | 199 | 5 | 100 | 266 |
| Oceania | 21 | 11 | 10 | 9 | 8 | 4 |
| South America | 232 | 125 | 107 | 12 | 44 | 176 |
| COUNTRY [2] | | | | | | |
| China | 1,934 | 964 | 970 | 19 | 1,287 | 628 |
| Ethiopia | 295 | 165 | 130 | (D) | 187 | (D) |
| Korea, South | 278 | 214 | 64 | – | 278 | – |
| India | 222 | 46 | 176 | 8 | 170 | 44 |
| Haiti | 212 | 101 | 111 | – | 76 | 136 |
| Ukraine | 204 | 100 | 104 | (D) | (D) | 177 |

– Represents zero. D Data withheld to limit disclosure. [1] Includes countries not shown separately. [2] Data ranked for countries with 200 or more immigrant orphans.

Source: U.S. Department of Homeland Security, Office of Immigration Statistics, "2017 Yearbook of Immigration Statistics," <https://www.dhs.gov/immigration-statistics/yearbook>, accessed January 2019.

## Table 47. Immigrants Obtaining Legal Permanent Resident Status: 1901 to 2017

[8,795 represents 8,795,000. For fiscal years ending in year shown; see text, Section 8. Rates based on Census Bureau estimates as of July 1 for resident population through 1929 and for total population thereafter (excluding Alaska and Hawaii prior to 1959)]

| Period/year | Number (1,000) | Rate [1] | Period/year | Number (1,000) | Rate [1] | Period/year | Number (1,000) | Rate [1] |
|---|---|---|---|---|---|---|---|---|
| 1901 to 1910..... | 8,795 | 10.4 | 2001 to 2010..... | 10,501 | 3.5 | 2008........... | 1,107 | 3.6 |
| 1911 to 1920..... | 5,736 | 5.7 | 2011 to 2017..... | 7,462 | 3.3 | 2009........... | 1,131 | 3.7 |
| 1921 to 1930..... | 4,107 | 3.5 | 1990............. | 1,536 | 6.1 | 2010........... | 1,043 | 3.4 |
| 1931 to 1940..... | 528 | 0.4 | 1995............. | 720 | 2.7 | 2011........... | 1,062 | 3.4 |
| 1941 to 1950..... | 1,035 | 0.7 | 2000............. | 841 | 3.0 | 2012........... | 1,032 | 3.3 |
| 1951 to 1960..... | 2,515 | 1.5 | 2003............. | 704 | 2.4 | 2013........... | 991 | 3.1 |
| 1961 to 1970..... | 3,322 | 1.7 | 2004............. | 958 | 3.3 | 2014........... | 1,017 | 3.2 |
| 1971 to 1980..... | 4,399 | 2.0 | 2005............. | 1,122 | 3.8 | 2015........... | 1,051 | 3.3 |
| 1981 to 1990..... | 7,256 | 3.0 | 2006............. | 1,266 | 4.2 | 2016........... | 1,184 | 3.7 |
| 1991 to 2000..... | 9,081 | 3.4 | 2007............. | 1,052 | 3.5 | 2017........... | 1,127 | 3.5 |

[1] Annual rate per 1,000 U.S. population. Rate computed by dividing sum of annual immigration totals by sum of annual U.S. population totals for same number of years.

Source: U.S. Department of Homeland Security, Office of Immigration Statistics, "2017 Yearbook of Immigration Statistics," <https://www.dhs.gov/immigration-statistics/yearbook>, accessed January 2019.

## Table 48. Petitions for Naturalization Filed, Persons Naturalized, and Petitions Denied: 1910 to 2017

[For years ending September 30. Naturalizations refer to immigrants aged 18 and over who become citizens of the United States]

| Year | Petitions filed | Persons naturalized | | | | Petitions denied |
|---|---|---|---|---|---|---|
| | | Total | Civilian | Military | Not reported | |
| 1920........... | 218,732 | 177,683 | 125,711 | 51,972 | – | 15,586 |
| 1930........... | 113,151 | 169,377 | 167,637 | 1,740 | – | 9,068 |
| 1940........... | 278,028 | 235,260 | 232,500 | 2,760 | – | 6,549 |
| 1950........... | 66,038 | 66,346 | 64,279 | 2,067 | – | 2,276 |
| 1960........... | 127,543 | 119,442 | 117,848 | 1,594 | – | 2,277 |
| 1970........... | 114,760 | 110,399 | 99,783 | 10,616 | – | 1,979 |
| 1980........... | 192,230 | 156,627 | 152,073 | 4,554 | – | 4,370 |
| 1990........... | 233,843 | 267,586 | 245,410 | 1,618 | 20,558 | 6,516 |
| 1995........... | 959,963 | 485,720 | 472,518 | 3,855 | 9,347 | 46,067 |
| 2000........... | 460,916 | 886,026 | 812,579 | 836 | 72,611 | 399,670 |
| 2005........... | 602,972 | 604,280 | 589,269 | 4,614 | 10,397 | 108,247 |
| 2006........... | 730,642 | 702,589 | 684,484 | 6,259 | 11,846 | 120,722 |
| 2007........... | 1,382,993 | 660,477 | 648,005 | 3,808 | 8,664 | 89,683 |
| 2008........... | 525,786 | 1,046,539 | 1,032,281 | 4,342 | 9,916 | 121,283 |
| 2009........... | 570,442 | 743,715 | 726,043 | 7,100 | 10,572 | 109,832 |
| 2010........... | 710,544 | 619,913 | 604,410 | 9,122 | 6,381 | 56,994 |
| 2011........... | 756,008 | 694,193 | 677,385 | 8,373 | 8,435 | 57,065 |
| 2012........... | 899,162 | 757,434 | 745,932 | 7,257 | 4,245 | 65,874 |
| 2013........... | 772,623 | 779,929 | 769,073 | 6,652 | 4,204 | 83,112 |
| 2014........... | 773,824 | 653,416 | 642,431 | 7,468 | 3,517 | 66,767 |
| 2015........... | 783,062 | 730,259 | 720,045 | 7,234 | 2,380 | 75,810 |
| 2016........... | 972,151 | 753,060 | 742,090 | 8,885 | 2,085 | 86,033 |
| 2017........... | 986,851 | 707,265 | 695,718 | 6,883 | 4,664 | 83,176 |

– Represents zero.

Source: U.S. Department of Homeland Security, Office of Immigration Statistics, "2017 Yearbook of Immigration Statistics," <https://www.dhs.gov/immigration-statistics/yearbook>, accessed January 2019.

## Table 49. Estimated Unauthorized Immigrants (Illegal Aliens) by Selected Country of Birth and State: 2000 to 2015

[In thousands (8,460 represents 8,460,000). As of January. The unauthorized resident immigrant population is defined as all foreign-born non-citizens who are not legal U.S. residents; most entered the U.S. without inspection or were admitted temporarily and stayed past the date they were required to leave. Unauthorized immigrants applying for adjustment to legal permanent resident status under the Immigration and Nationality Act are unauthorized until they have been granted lawful permanent residence, though they may have been authorized to work. These estimates were calculated using a "residual method," whereby estimates of the legally resident foreign-born population were subtracted from the total foreign-born population. All of these component populations were resident in the United States on January 1 and entered during the period from 1980 to the year prior to the year shown. Persons who entered the U.S. prior to 1980 were assumed to be legally resident. Estimates of the legally resident foreign-born population were based primarily on administrative data of the Department of Homeland Security, while estimates of the total foreign-born population were obtained from the American Community Survey of the U.S. Census Bureau]

| Country of birth | 2000 | 2010 [1] | 2015 | State of residence | 2000 | 2010 [1] | 2015 |
|---|---|---|---|---|---|---|---|
| **Total**.................. | **8,460** | **11,590** | **11,960** | **Total**.................. | **8,460** | **11,590** | **11,960** |
| Mexico....................... | 4,680 | 6,830 | 6,580 | California....................... | 2,510 | 2,910 | 2,880 |
| El Salvador.................... | 430 | 670 | 750 | Texas.......................... | 1,090 | 1,780 | 1,940 |
| Guatemala..................... | 290 | 520 | 620 | Florida......................... | 800 | 730 | 810 |
| India.......................... | 120 | 270 | 470 | New York....................... | 540 | 690 | 590 |
| Honduras...................... | 160 | 380 | 440 | Illinois......................... | 440 | 550 | 450 |
| Philippines.................... | 200 | 290 | 370 | New Jersey..................... | 350 | 440 | 440 |
| China......................... | 190 | 300 | 320 | Georgia........................ | 220 | 430 | 390 |
| Korea......................... | 180 | 220 | 230 | North Carolina................. | 260 | 390 | 390 |
| Vietnam....................... | 160 | 190 | 170 | Arizona........................ | 330 | 350 | 380 |
| Ecuador....................... | (NA) | 210 | 150 | Virginia........................ | 160 | 220 | 310 |
| Other countries............... | 1,940 | 1,720 | 1,870 | Other states................... | 1,760 | 3,080 | 3,390 |

NA Not available. [1] Revised to be consistent with estimates derived from the 2010 Census.

Source: U.S. Department of Homeland Security, Office of Immigration Statistics, *Illegal Alien Population Residing in the United States, January 2015*, December 2018. See also <https://www.dhs.gov/immigration-statistics>.

# Table 50. Immigrants Obtaining Legal Permanent Resident Status by Class of Admission: 2000 to 2017

[For years ending September 30. For definition of immigrants, see text, this section]

| Class of admission | 2000 | 2005 | 2010 | 2015 | 2016 | 2017 |
|---|---|---|---|---|---|---|
| Total | 841,002 | 1,122,257 | 1,042,625 | 1,051,031 | 1,183,505 | 1,127,167 |
| New arrivals | 407,279 | 383,955 | 476,049 | 508,716 | 618,078 | 578,081 |
| Adjustments | 433,723 | 738,302 | 566,576 | 542,315 | 565,427 | 549,086 |
| Family-sponsored preferences | 235,092 | 212,970 | 214,589 | 213,910 | 238,087 | 232,238 |
| Unmarried sons/daughters of U.S. citizens and their children | 27,635 | 24,729 | 26,998 | 24,533 | 22,072 | 26,219 |
| Spouses, children, and unmarried sons/daughters of alien residents | 124,540 | 100,139 | 92,088 | 104,892 | 121,267 | 113,500 |
| Married sons/daughters of U.S. citizens [1] | 22,804 | 22,953 | 32,817 | 24,271 | 27,392 | 23,260 |
| Brothers or sisters of U.S. citizens age 21 and older [1] | 60,113 | 65,149 | 62,686 | 60,214 | 67,356 | 69,259 |
| Immediate relatives of U.S. citizens | 346,350 | 436,115 | 476,414 | 465,068 | 566,706 | 516,508 |
| Spouses | 196,405 | 259,144 | 271,909 | 265,367 | 304,358 | 292,909 |
| Children [2] | 82,638 | 94,858 | 88,297 | 66,740 | 88,494 | 74,989 |
| Parents | 67,307 | 82,113 | 116,208 | 132,961 | 173,854 | 148,610 |
| Employment-based preferences | 106,642 | 246,865 | 148,343 | 144,047 | 137,893 | 137,855 |
| Priority workers [1] | 27,566 | 64,731 | 41,055 | 41,688 | 42,862 | 41,060 |
| Professionals with advanced degrees or aliens of exceptional ability [1] | 20,255 | 42,597 | 53,946 | 44,344 | 38,858 | 39,331 |
| Skilled workers, professionals, unskilled workers [1] | 49,589 | 129,070 | 39,762 | 37,243 | 35,933 | 38,083 |
| Special immigrants [1] | 9,014 | 10,121 | 11,100 | 10,584 | 10,377 | 9,504 |
| Employment creation (investors) [1] | 218 | 346 | 2,480 | 10,188 | 9,863 | 9,877 |
| Diversity (lottery) [3] | 50,920 | 46,234 | 49,763 | 47,934 | 49,865 | 51,592 |
| Refugees | 56,091 | 112,676 | 92,741 | 118,431 | 120,216 | 120,356 |
| Asylees | 6,837 | 30,286 | 43,550 | 33,564 | 37,209 | 25,647 |
| Parolees | 3,162 | 7,715 | 1,592 | 23 | 15 | 26 |
| Children born abroad to alien residents | (NA) | 571 | 716 | 403 | 92 | 75 |
| Nicaraguan Adjustment and Central American Relief Act | 20,364 | 1,155 | 248 | 49 | 34 | (NA) |
| Haitian Refugee Immigration Fairness Act (HRIFA) | 435 | 2,820 | 386 | 9 | 15 | (NA) |
| Certain Iraqis and Afghans employed by U.S. Government [1] | (NA) | (NA) | 2,575 | 7,048 | 12,151 | 19,191 |
| Victims of human trafficking | (NA) | (NA) | 511 | 970 | 1,069 | 1,317 |
| Victims of crimes and their spouses and children | (NA) | (NA) | 2,165 | 14,138 | 16,184 | 18,065 |
| Cancellation of removal | 12,154 | 20,785 | 8,180 | 4,713 | 3,453 | 3,539 |
| Other | 2,955 | 4,065 | 852 | 724 | 516 | 758 |

NA Not available. [1] Includes spouses and children. [2] Includes orphans. [3] The Diversity Visa Program is a lottery available to nationals of countries with fewer than 50,000 persons granted legal permanent residency status during the preceding 5 years in the employment-based and family-sponsored preferences and immediate relative classes of admission. Includes categories of immigrants admitted under three laws intended to diversify immigration: P.L. 99-603, P.L. 100-658, and P.L. 101-649.

Source: U.S. Department of Homeland Security, Office of Immigration Statistics, "2017 Yearbook of Immigration Statistics," <https://www.dhs.gov/immigration-statistics/yearbook>, accessed January 2019.

# Table 51. Immigrants Obtaining Legal Permanent Resident Status by Selected Country of Birth and Selected Characteristics: 2017

[For year ending September 30]

| Age, marital status, occupation, class of admission | All countries [1] | Mexico | China | Cuba | India | Dominican Republic | Philippines | Vietnam | El Salvador |
|---|---|---|---|---|---|---|---|---|---|
| Total | 1,127,167 | 170,581 | 71,565 | 65,028 | 60,394 | 58,520 | 49,147 | 38,231 | 25,109 |
| AGE | | | | | | | | | |
| Under 18 years old | 212,364 | 21,763 | 10,390 | 8,233 | 7,286 | 18,159 | 10,103 | 6,714 | 5,293 |
| 18 to 24 years old | 133,495 | 22,249 | 5,423 | 6,448 | 5,034 | 8,072 | 5,584 | 5,573 | 4,338 |
| 25 to 34 years old | 278,821 | 43,499 | 18,034 | 18,307 | 13,501 | 10,280 | 9,454 | 7,590 | 5,030 |
| 35 to 44 years old | 209,343 | 37,881 | 12,722 | 12,872 | 15,195 | 8,579 | 9,093 | 4,878 | 4,724 |
| 45 to 54 years old | 142,128 | 28,218 | 11,162 | 10,957 | 7,411 | 7,054 | 6,280 | 6,265 | 2,845 |
| 55 to 64 years old | 89,456 | 10,601 | 7,785 | 4,403 | 6,282 | 4,038 | 5,185 | 5,300 | 1,556 |
| 65 years old and over | 61,560 | 6,370 | 6,049 | 3,808 | 5,685 | 2,338 | 3,448 | 1,911 | 1,323 |
| MARITAL STATUS | | | | | | | | | |
| Married | 656,878 | 117,898 | 48,850 | 26,822 | 44,148 | 24,113 | 27,289 | 22,962 | 11,902 |
| Single | 405,916 | 44,048 | 18,590 | 30,056 | 12,981 | 31,493 | 19,215 | 12,680 | 11,626 |
| Other | 58,187 | 7,075 | 3,982 | 7,849 | 3,056 | 2,753 | 2,437 | 2,264 | 1,060 |
| Unknown | 6,186 | 1,560 | 143 | 301 | 209 | 161 | 206 | 325 | 521 |
| OCCUPATION [2] | | | | | | | | | |
| Management, professional, and related | 114,218 | 6,976 | 12,000 | 2,200 | 13,268 | 849 | 5,940 | 1,927 | 796 |
| Service | 28,021 | 6,657 | 3,154 | 2,698 | 362 | 484 | 842 | 440 | 842 |
| Sales and office | 41,284 | 4,920 | 5,914 | 1,075 | 2,176 | 755 | 1,553 | 4,103 | 487 |
| Farming, fishing, and forestry | 12,594 | 4,041 | 1,591 | 98 | 1,660 | 168 | 354 | 1,566 | 402 |
| Construction, extraction, maintenance and repair | 12,867 | 6,189 | (D) | 1,523 | 45 | 221 | 83 | 194 | (D) |
| Production, transportation, and material moving | 42,745 | 19,414 | 1,814 | 5,781 | 314 | 2,486 | 210 | 828 | 934 |
| MAJOR CLASS OF ADMISSION | | | | | | | | | |
| Immediate relatives of U.S. citizens | 516,508 | 114,431 | 27,683 | 4,752 | 20,549 | 27,844 | 25,684 | 17,515 | 13,063 |
| Family-sponsored preferences | 232,238 | 34,413 | 15,773 | 4,743 | 14,962 | 30,147 | 13,495 | 19,218 | 7,764 |
| Employment-based preferences | 137,855 | 5,493 | 19,221 | 12 | 23,569 | 314 | 9,341 | 1,364 | 1,349 |
| Diversity programs | 51,592 | 6 | 19 | 396 | 40 | 3 | 5 | 4 | (D) |
| Refugees and asylees | 146,003 | 1,056 | 8,700 | 55,117 | 795 | 105 | 22 | 73 | (D) |
| Other | 42,971 | 15,182 | 169 | 8 | 479 | 107 | 600 | 57 | 1,614 |

D Data withheld to avoid disclosure. [1] Includes other countries not shown separately. [2] Those in the military and without an occupation and unknown occupation are not shown.

Source: U.S. Department of Homeland Security, Office of Immigration Statistics, "Profiles on Lawful Permanent Residents: 2017," <https://www.dhs.gov/profiles-lawful-permanent-residents-2017-country#>, accessed January 2019.

## Table 52. Immigrants Obtaining Legal Permanent Resident Status by Country of Birth: 1991 to 2017

[In thousands (9,080.5 represents 9,080,500). For years ending September 30. Persons by country prior to 1996 are unrevised]

| Region and country of birth | 1991-2000 | 2001-2010 | 2011-2016 | 2017 |
|---|---|---|---|---|
| **All countries [1]** | **9,080.5** | **10,501.1** | **7,377.9** | **1,127.2** |
| **Europe [1]** | **1,226.0** | **1,263.9** | **603.5** | **84.3** |
| Albania | 26.2 | 50.5 | 29.1 | 5.7 |
| France | 27.4 | 39.6 | 29.9 | 4.8 |
| Germany | 67.6 | 77.7 | 41.2 | 4.7 |
| Italy | 22.5 | 26.5 | 21.6 | 3.7 |
| Poland | 169.5 | 116.8 | 43.8 | 4.8 |
| Romania | 57.5 | 53.6 | 25.6 | 3.0 |
| Russia | 2 127.8 | 139.7 | 61.6 | 8.9 |
| Spain | 13.7 | 15.8 | 17.6 | 3.0 |
| Ukraine | 2 141.0 | 149.3 | 58.8 | 10.1 |
| United Kingdom | 135.6 | 153.5 | 86.9 | 10.9 |
| **Asia [1]** | **2,973.2** | **3,784.6** | **3,015.9** | **424.7** |
| Afghanistan | 17.4 | 24.3 | 38.8 | 19.5 |
| Armenia | 2 26.6 | 29.9 | 20.8 | 3.4 |
| Bangladesh | 66.0 | 106.7 | 105.3 | 14.7 |
| Bhutan | – | 7.0 | 53.2 | 2.9 |
| Burma | 11.0 | 45.0 | 96.4 | 12.9 |
| Cambodia | 18.5 | 35.6 | 18.4 | 4.1 |
| China | 424.4 | 662.7 | 543.9 | 71.6 |
| India | 383.0 | 662.5 | 479.8 | 60.4 |
| Iran | 112.5 | 125.9 | 92.8 | 13.8 |
| Iraq | 40.7 | 65.0 | 130.1 | 14.2 |
| Israel | 31.9 | 46.6 | 28.4 | 3.8 |
| Japan | 61.4 | 76.1 | 40.6 | 4.6 |
| Jordan [3] | 39.7 | 38.7 | 31.2 | 5.3 |
| Korea, South [4] | 171.1 | 221.5 | 148.4 | 19.2 |
| Malaysia | 14.8 | 20.5 | 17.8 | 4.1 |
| Nepal | 3.6 | 33.1 | 79.8 | 11.6 |
| Pakistan | 124.5 | 157.0 | 117.8 | 17.4 |
| Philippines | 505.3 | 587.2 | 386.7 | 49.1 |
| Syria | 26.1 | 25.9 | 23.9 | 5.9 |
| Taiwan | 106.3 | 87.9 | 38.3 | 4.9 |
| Thailand | 48.4 | 68.3 | 57.1 | 6.3 |
| Turkey | 26.3 | 41.1 | 29.7 | 4.8 |
| Uzbekistan | 2 22.9 | 36.0 | 32.5 | 4.1 |
| Vietnam | 420.8 | 306.1 | 222.8 | 38.2 |
| Yemen | 16.3 | 24.6 | 32.8 | 6.0 |
| **Africa [1]** | **382.5** | **860.4** | **720.5** | **118.8** |
| Cameroon | 5.8 | 23.2 | 29.9 | 4.7 |
| Congo, Dem. Rep. of the | 2.5 | 7.9 | 27.2 | 8.7 |
| Egypt | 46.7 | 73.1 | 71.6 | 9.8 |
| Ethiopia | 49.3 | 109.7 | 92.6 | 14.6 |
| Ghana | 35.6 | 65.3 | 57.2 | 8.5 |
| Kenya | 14.0 | 59.7 | 46.1 | 7.0 |
| Liberia | 16.0 | 45.2 | 27.7 | 4.2 |
| Morocco | 20.0 | 44.4 | 28.3 | 4.2 |
| Nigeria | 67.2 | 111.2 | 91.4 | 13.5 |
| Somalia | 20.1 | 64.2 | 36.9 | 7.4 |
| South Africa | 22.6 | 32.9 | 19.4 | 2.9 |
| Sudan | 12.6 | 32.9 | 18.6 | 3.5 |
| **Oceania [1]** | **47.9** | **58.1** | **36.4** | **5.1** |
| **North America [1]** | **3,910.1** | **3,605.1** | **2,431.7** | **413.7** |
| Canada | 137.2 | 168.2 | 89.3 | 11.5 |
| Cuba | 178.7 | 318.4 | 302.7 | 65.0 |
| Dominican Republic | 340.8 | 329.1 | 339.2 | 58.5 |
| El Salvador | 217.3 | 252.8 | 134.2 | 25.1 |
| Guatemala | 103.0 | 160.7 | 77.1 | 13.2 |
| Haiti | 181.7 | 213.8 | 143.7 | 21.8 |
| Honduras | 66.7 | 65.4 | 59.1 | 11.4 |
| Jamaica | 173.4 | 180.7 | 139.6 | 21.9 |
| Mexico | 2,250.5 | 1,693.2 | 1,031.2 | 170.6 |
| Nicaragua | 94.6 | 60.9 | 22.8 | 3.1 |
| Trinidad and Tobago | 63.2 | 61.8 | 31.1 | 3.1 |
| **South America [1]** | **539.3** | **906.0** | **559.3** | **79.1** |
| Argentina | 24.3 | 50.5 | 29.3 | 3.5 |
| Brazil | 52.2 | 123.8 | 82.2 | 15.0 |
| Colombia | 130.8 | 251.3 | 141.2 | 18.0 |
| Ecuador | 76.3 | 112.5 | 74.4 | 10.6 |
| Guyana | 73.8 | 76.2 | 42.5 | 5.5 |
| Peru | 105.6 | 145.7 | 85.2 | 10.1 |
| Venezuela | 29.9 | 84.4 | 65.9 | 11.8 |

– Represents or rounds to zero. [1] Includes other countries not shown separately. [2] Covers years 1992–2000. [3] Prior to 2003, includes Palestine; beginning in 2003, Palestine included in Unknown. [4] Prior to 2009, includes a small number of cases from North Korea.

Source: U.S. Department of Homeland Security, Office of Immigration Statistics, "2017 Yearbook of Immigration Statistics," <https://www.dhs.gov/immigration-statistics/yearbook>, accessed January 2019.

## Table 53. Refugees and Asylees Obtaining Legal Permanent Resident Status by Country of Birth: 1991 to 2017

[For years ending September 30]

| Country of birth | 1991-2000 | 2001-2010 | 2011-2016 | 2017 |
|---|---|---|---|---|
| **Total [1]** | **1,016,820** | **1,325,365** | **882,366** | **146,003** |
| **Europe [1]** | **425,047** | **296,794** | **24,406** | **4,103** |
| Belarus | 2 21,592 | 9,310 | 1,683 | 145 |
| Moldova | 2 10,150 | 10,813 | 2,694 | 286 |
| Russia | 2 54,488 | 32,819 | 4,330 | 603 |
| Soviet Union [3] | 117,783 | 6,794 | 2,234 | 196 |
| Spain | 438 | 610 | 1,939 | 450 |
| Ukraine | 2 96,974 | 57,186 | 4,430 | 1,656 |
| **Asia** | **350,702** | **389,469** | **431,926** | **52,003** |
| Afghanistan | 9,711 | 13,533 | 3,429 | 1,013 |
| Armenia | 1,794 | 12,408 | 2,448 | 171 |
| Bhutan | (D) | 6,762 | 46,898 | 2,873 |
| Burma | 721 | 32,904 | 74,605 | 11,243 |
| China | 7,577 | 111,632 | 94,308 | 8,700 |
| India | 2,538 | 24,010 | 5,789 | 795 |
| Indonesia | 201 | 7,618 | 1,783 | 137 |
| Iran | 24,251 | 45,515 | 20,685 | 3,656 |
| Iraq | 22,488 | 40,789 | 89,910 | 9,536 |
| Jordan | 331 | 1,013 | 2,292 | 333 |
| Malaysia | 383 | 1,125 | 6,901 | 2,693 |
| Nepal | 32 | 6,000 | 32,409 | 3,287 |
| Pakistan | 1,649 | 8,339 | 4,314 | 763 |
| Sri Lanka | 353 | 1,852 | 1,921 | 146 |
| Syria | 2,119 | 2,223 | 4,227 | 2,390 |
| Thailand | 22,716 | 22,405 | 21,550 | 2,304 |
| Uzbekistan | 2 17,991 | 14,047 | 2,216 | 157 |
| Vietnam | 206,530 | 36,990 | 2,955 | 73 |
| **Africa** | **51,469** | **242,839** | **144,494** | **26,615** |
| Burundi | 148 | 3,387 | 1,867 | 902 |
| Cameroon | 299 | 7,564 | 6,370 | 432 |
| Congo, Dem. Rep. of the | 922 | 5,643 | 11,454 | 4,872 |
| Congo, Republic of the | 25 | 5,243 | 2,494 | 466 |
| Cote d' Ivoire | 119 | 4,404 | 2,245 | 193 |
| Egypt | 419 | 7,987 | 14,483 | 1,298 |
| Eritrea | 608 | 4,534 | 8,222 | 1,298 |
| Ethiopia [4] | 17,829 | 31,900 | 23,276 | 3,247 |
| Gambia, The | 53 | 1,221 | 1,464 | 192 |
| Guinea | 50 | 4,467 | 3,660 | 192 |
| Kenya | 1,438 | 15,351 | 9,105 | 1,637 |
| Liberia | 3,836 | 28,808 | 5,072 | 287 |
| Rwanda | 389 | 2,939 | 2,840 | 1,024 |
| Somalia | 16,737 | 59,069 | 24,647 | 5,344 |
| Sudan | 5,174 | 23,580 | 7,500 | 1,200 |
| Tanzania | 16 | 3,503 | 2,366 | 825 |
| Uganda | 439 | 2,482 | 2,410 | 910 |
| Zimbabwe | 32 | 1,563 | 1,392 | 133 |
| **Oceania** | **291** | **1,453** | **268** | **36** |
| **North America** | **183,251** | **326,846** | **259,220** | **60,617** |
| Cuba | 142,571 | 276,331 | 232,807 | 55,117 |
| El Salvador | 4,072 | 4,061 | 2,947 | (D) |
| Guatemala | 2,029 | 7,399 | 4,750 | 1,513 |
| Haiti | 9,354 | 29,824 | 10,265 | 454 |
| Honduras | 1,047 | 1,684 | 1,684 | 737 |
| Mexico | 415 | 2,780 | 4,096 | 1,056 |
| **South America** | **5,840** | **65,912** | **21,423** | **2,582** |
| Colombia | 1,129 | 40,321 | 7,172 | 821 |
| Peru | 2,500 | 7,258 | 1,686 | 115 |
| Venezuela | 1,390 | 10,726 | 7,678 | 1,001 |

D Data withheld to avoid disclosure. [1] Includes other countries and unknown not shown separately. [2] Covers years 1992-2000. [3] Data are for unknown republics only. [4] Prior to 1993, data include Eritrea.

Source: U.S. Department of Homeland Security, Office of Immigration Statistics, "2017 Yearbook of Immigration Statistics," <https://www.dhs.gov/immigration-statistics/yearbook>, accessed January 2019.

# Table 54. Population by Selected Ancestry Group and Region: 2017

[In thousands (325,719 represents 325,719,000), except percent. Covers single and multiple ancestries. Ancestry refers to a person's ethnic origin or descent, "roots," or heritage; or the place of birth of the person, the person's parents, or ancestors before their arrival in the United States. The American Community Survey universe includes the household population and the population living in institutions, college dormitories, and other group quarters. Based on a sample and subject to sampling variability; see text, this section, and Appendix III]

| Ancestry group | Total, (1,000) | Northeast | Midwest | South | West | Ancestry group | Total, (1,000) | Northeast | Midwest | South | West |
|---|---|---|---|---|---|---|---|---|---|---|---|
| **Total population [1]** | **325,719** | **17** | **21** | **38** | **24** | Irish | 31,479 | 26 | 24 | 31 | 18 |
| Afghan | 121 | 12 | 5 | 34 | 49 | Israeli | 139 | 36 | 9 | 23 | 33 |
| Albanian | 205 | 54 | 24 | 15 | 7 | Italian | 16,651 | 42 | 17 | 24 | 17 |
| American | 20,025 | 13 | 18 | 56 | 13 | Lithuanian | 631 | 37 | 27 | 20 | 15 |
| Arab [1] | 2,005 | 23 | 25 | 29 | 23 | Northern European | 430 | 13 | 17 | 26 | 45 |
| Egyptian | 260 | 35 | 12 | 29 | 24 | Norwegian | 4,296 | 6 | 49 | 13 | 32 |
| Iraqi | 158 | 12 | 34 | 29 | 24 | Pennsylvania German | 326 | 59 | 26 | 10 | 6 |
| Lebanese | 489 | 23 | 28 | 29 | 20 | Polish | 9,012 | 31 | 37 | 19 | 13 |
| Moroccan | 119 | 31 | 13 | 39 | 17 | Portuguese | 1,372 | 44 | 4 | 16 | 37 |
| Palestinian | 131 | 16 | 29 | 30 | 26 | Romanian | 478 | 22 | 26 | 24 | 28 |
| Syrian | 177 | 31 | 20 | 28 | 21 | Russian | 2,608 | 34 | 17 | 22 | 27 |
| Arab | 275 | 17 | 32 | 26 | 25 | Scandinavian | 951 | 8 | 29 | 23 | 39 |
| Armenian | 486 | 20 | 8 | 9 | 63 | Scotch-Irish | 3,008 | 12 | 17 | 51 | 20 |
| Australian | 115 | 18 | 16 | 24 | 43 | Scottish | 5,399 | 16 | 20 | 38 | 26 |
| Austrian | 695 | 26 | 26 | 25 | 23 | Serbian | 188 | 19 | 39 | 21 | 21 |
| Belgian | 359 | 11 | 52 | 19 | 18 | Slavic | 124 | 26 | 26 | 23 | 25 |
| Brazilian | 484 | 40 | 7 | 38 | 15 | Slovak | 671 | 42 | 33 | 16 | 9 |
| British | 1,891 | 13 | 17 | 40 | 30 | Slovene | 181 | 14 | 53 | 16 | 17 |
| Cajun | 125 | 3 | 4 | 85 | 8 | Sub-Saharan African [1] | 3,894 | 20 | 18 | 46 | 15 |
| Canadian | 676 | 24 | 17 | 29 | 30 | Ethiopian | 312 | 7 | 20 | 46 | 28 |
| Croatian | 408 | 23 | 37 | 16 | 24 | Ghanaian | 134 | 36 | 13 | 39 | 11 |
| Czech | 1,379 | 10 | 45 | 28 | 17 | Nigerian | 426 | 26 | 16 | 49 | 10 |
| Czechoslovakian | 321 | 21 | 31 | 26 | 22 | Somali | 174 | 5 | 59 | 18 | 19 |
| Danish | 1,284 | 9 | 31 | 15 | 46 | African | 2,133 | 16 | 17 | 52 | 15 |
| Dutch | 3,906 | 15 | 37 | 25 | 23 | Swedish | 3,683 | 13 | 38 | 17 | 31 |
| Eastern European | 913 | 34 | 16 | 27 | 22 | Swiss | 916 | 16 | 33 | 21 | 30 |
| English | 23,075 | 17 | 21 | 37 | 26 | Turkish | 223 | 35 | 13 | 31 | 21 |
| European | 5,322 | 11 | 20 | 35 | 34 | Ukrainian | 1,007 | 36 | 18 | 20 | 25 |
| Finnish | 639 | 12 | 46 | 14 | 28 | Welsh | 1,801 | 19 | 22 | 32 | 27 |
| French (except Basque) | 7,674 | 23 | 23 | 34 | 20 | West Indian [1,2] | 3,023 | 43 | 4 | 48 | 5 |
| French Canadian | 2,110 | 41 | 19 | 26 | 14 | Haitian | 1,065 | 37 | 3 | 59 | 2 |
| German | 43,094 | 16 | 39 | 26 | 19 | Jamaican | 1,124 | 45 | 5 | 45 | 5 |
| Greek | 1,246 | 32 | 22 | 26 | 21 | Trinidadian and Tobagonian | 226 | 56 | 3 | 36 | 4 |
| Guyanese | 246 | 73 | 2 | 22 | 2 | West Indian | 295 | 55 | 4 | 35 | 6 |
| Hungarian | 1,374 | 30 | 32 | 22 | 17 | Yugoslavian | 257 | 19 | 33 | 23 | 25 |
| Iranian | 477 | 11 | 7 | 28 | 55 | | | | | | |

[1] Includes other groups, not shown separately. [2] Excludes Hispanic-origin groups.

Source: U.S. Census Bureau, 2017 American Community Survey, B04006, "People Reporting Ancestry," <http://factfinder.census.gov/>, accessed November 2018.

# Table 55. Language Spoken at Home and English Speaking Ability: 2017

[305,924 represents 305,924,000. See headnote, Table 54]

| Language | Number of speakers of language at home (1,000) | Percent who speak English less than "very well" | Language | Number of speakers of language at home (1,000) | Percent who speak English less than "very well" |
|---|---|---|---|---|---|
| **Total population 5 years old and over** | **305,924** | **(X)** | Bengali | 351 | 40.2 |
| | | | Nepali, Marathi, or other Indic | 433 | 35.3 |
| Speak only English | 239,332 | (X) | Other Indo-European | 573 | 29.3 |
| Spanish | 41,018 | 40.1 | Telugu | 415 | 19.4 |
| French (including Cajun) | 1,202 | 20.9 | Tamil | 287 | 15.9 |
| Haitian | 887 | 38.9 | Malayalam, Kannada, or other Dravidian | 246 | 21.5 |
| Italian | 567 | 25.7 | Chinese (including Mandarin, Cantonese) | 3,462 | 54.6 |
| Portuguese | 795 | 36.3 | Japanese | 467 | 39.9 |
| German | 918 | 14.6 | Korean | 1,095 | 51.8 |
| Yiddish, Pennsylvania Dutch [1] | 506 | 28.0 | Hmong | 234 | 39.3 |
| Greek | 268 | 24.5 | Vietnamese | 1,499 | 58.3 |
| Russian | 936 | 42.8 | Khmer | 207 | 52.5 |
| Polish | 520 | 37.1 | Thai, Lao, or other Tai-Kadai | 315 | 49.2 |
| Serbo-Croatian | 250 | 31.7 | Tagalog (including Filipino) | 1,746 | 30.7 |
| Ukrainian or other Slavic languages | 331 | 35.5 | Ilocano, Samoan, Hawaiian [2] | 459 | 36.9 |
| Armenian | 248 | 43.2 | Arabic | 1,228 | 37.2 |
| Persian (including Farsi, Dari) | 420 | 38.1 | Hebrew | 226 | 14.0 |
| Gujarati | 434 | 34.0 | Amharic, Somali, or other Afro-Asiatic | 526 | 43.7 |
| Hindi | 863 | 19.1 | Yoruba, Twi, Igbo [3] | 541 | 22.1 |
| Urdu | 507 | 27.9 | Swahili and other African [4] | 268 | 34.2 |
| Punjabi | 311 | 41.0 | Navajo | 169 | 18.7 |

X Not applicable. [1] Includes other West Germanic. [2] Includes other Austronesian. [3] Includes other West African. [4] Other languages of Central, Eastern, and Southern Africa.

Source: U.S. Census Bureau, 2017 American Community Survey, B16001, "Language Spoken at Home by Ability to Speak English for the Population 5 Years and Over," <http://factfinder.census.gov/>, accessed December 2018.

# Table 56. Language Spoken at Home by State: 2017

[In thousands (305,924 represents 305,924,000), except percent. The American Community Survey universe includes the household population and the population living in institutions, college dormitories, and other group quarters. Based on a sample and subject to sampling variability; see text, this section, and Appendix III]

| State | Population 5 years old and over (1,000) | English only (1,000) | Language other than English — Number (1,000) | Language other than English — Percent of population 5 years and over | State | Population 5 years old and over (1,000) | English only (1,000) | Language other than English — Number (1,000) | Language other than English — Percent of population 5 years and over |
|---|---|---|---|---|---|---|---|---|---|
| U.S........ | 305,924 | 239,332 | 66,592 | 21.8 | MO......... | 5,740 | 5,383 | 357 | 6.2 |
| AL........... | 4,586 | 4,351 | 234 | 5.1 | MT......... | 989 | 947 | 42 | 4.3 |
| AK.......... | 687 | 577 | 109 | 15.9 | NE......... | 1,788 | 1,576 | 213 | 11.9 |
| AZ.......... | 6,581 | 4,778 | 1,803 | 27.4 | NV......... | 2,814 | 1,939 | 875 | 31.1 |
| AR.......... | 2,818 | 2,608 | 210 | 7.5 | NH......... | 1,279 | 1,177 | 102 | 8.0 |
| CA.......... | 37,076 | 20,597 | 16,480 | 44.4 | NJ......... | 8,485 | 5,786 | 2,700 | 31.8 |
| CO.......... | 5,275 | 4,384 | 891 | 16.9 | NM......... | 1,962 | 1,315 | 647 | 33.0 |
| CT.......... | 3,406 | 2,642 | 764 | 22.4 | NY......... | 18,692 | 12,923 | 5,769 | 30.9 |
| DE.......... | 907 | 781 | 126 | 13.9 | NC......... | 9,672 | 8,535 | 1,138 | 11.8 |
| DC.......... | 649 | 535 | 114 | 17.6 | ND......... | 703 | 661 | 42 | 5.9 |
| FL.......... | 19,855 | 13,967 | 5,888 | 29.7 | OH......... | 10,963 | 10,170 | 794 | 7.2 |
| GA.......... | 9,774 | 8,398 | 1,376 | 14.1 | OK......... | 3,668 | 3,295 | 374 | 10.2 |
| HI.......... | 1,338 | 993 | 345 | 25.8 | OR......... | 3,911 | 3,311 | 599 | 15.3 |
| ID.......... | 1,601 | 1,430 | 170 | 10.6 | PA......... | 12,101 | 10,704 | 1,396 | 11.5 |
| IL.......... | 12,035 | 9,209 | 2,825 | 23.5 | RI......... | 1,005 | 775 | 230 | 22.9 |
| IN.......... | 6,247 | 5,695 | 553 | 8.8 | SC......... | 4,735 | 4,395 | 340 | 7.2 |
| IA.......... | 2,947 | 2,709 | 238 | 8.1 | SD......... | 809 | 758 | 52 | 6.4 |
| KS.......... | 2,720 | 2,396 | 324 | 11.9 | TN......... | 6,311 | 5,860 | 451 | 7.1 |
| KY.......... | 4,178 | 3,942 | 236 | 5.6 | TX......... | 26,284 | 16,937 | 9,348 | 35.6 |
| LA.......... | 4,378 | 4,024 | 354 | 8.1 | UT......... | 2,849 | 2,403 | 446 | 15.6 |
| ME.......... | 1,272 | 1,197 | 74 | 5.8 | VT......... | 594 | 560 | 33 | 5.6 |
| MD.......... | 5,689 | 4,605 | 1,084 | 19.1 | VA......... | 7,968 | 6,655 | 1,313 | 16.5 |
| MA.......... | 6,499 | 4,937 | 1,562 | 24.0 | WA......... | 6,951 | 5,590 | 1,360 | 19.6 |
| MI.......... | 9,390 | 8,460 | 930 | 9.9 | WV......... | 1,718 | 1,676 | 42 | 2.4 |
| MN.......... | 5,223 | 4,600 | 623 | 11.9 | WI......... | 5,461 | 4,993 | 469 | 8.6 |
| MS.......... | 2,802 | 2,698 | 103 | 3.7 | WY......... | 541 | 497 | 44 | 8.2 |

Source: U.S. Census Bureau, 2017 American Community Survey, C16005, "Nativity by Language Spoken at Home by Ability to Speak English for the Population 5 Years and Over," <http://factfinder.census.gov/>, accessed December 2018.

# Table 57. Language Spoken at Home—25 Largest Cities: 2017

[In thousands (890 represents 890,000), except percent. Data shown for population aged 5 and over. The American Community Survey universe includes the household population and the population living in institutions, college dormitories, and other group quarters. Based on a sample and subject to sampling variability; see text, this section, and Appendix III]

| City | Population 5 years old and over (1,000) | English only (1,000) | Language other than English, total[1] — Number (1,000) | Language other than English, total[1] — Percent | Speak English less than "very well" (1,000) | Spanish (1,000) | Other Indo-European languages (1,000)[?] | Asian and Pacific Island languages (1,000)[2] |
|---|---|---|---|---|---|---|---|---|
| Austin, TX...................... | 890 | 603 | 288 | 32.3 | 104 | 208 | 31 | 36 |
| Boston, MA.................... | 650 | 400 | 250 | 38.5 | 121 | 111 | 75 | 49 |
| Charlotte, NC................. | 803 | 627 | 176 | 21.9 | 88 | 96 | 37 | 31 |
| Chicago, IL.................... | 2,544 | 1,625 | 919 | 36.1 | 382 | 611 | 166 | 99 |
| Columbus, OH................ | 818 | 693 | 126 | 15.4 | 49 | 37 | 35 | 21 |
| Dallas, TX..................... | 1,239 | 691 | 548 | 44.2 | 270 | 470 | 26 | 28 |
| Denver, CO.................... | 661 | 495 | 167 | 25.2 | 62 | 124 | 16 | 16 |
| Detroit, MI..................... | 623 | 557 | 66 | 10.6 | 28 | 36 | 12 | 3 |
| El Paso, TX.................... | 634 | 198 | 435 | 68.7 | 208 | 422 | 6 | 5 |
| Fort Worth, TX................ | 807 | 538 | 269 | 33.3 | 125 | 221 | 15 | 24 |
| Houston, TX................... | 2,126 | 1,093 | 1,033 | 48.6 | 495 | 832 | 72 | 86 |
| Indianapolis, IN [3].......... | 794 | 675 | 119 | 14.9 | 56 | 68 | 16 | 19 |
| Jacksonville, FL.............. | 831 | 705 | 127 | 15.2 | 46 | 56 | 35 | 27 |
| Los Angeles, CA............. | 3,770 | 1,545 | 2,225 | 59.0 | 963 | 1,603 | 251 | 321 |
| Nashville–Davidson, TN [3].... | 621 | 511 | 110 | 17.8 | 65 | 55 | 17 | 15 |
| New York, NY................. | 8,070 | 4,127 | 3,943 | 48.9 | 1,852 | 1,958 | 1,007 | 748 |
| Philadelphia, PA............. | 1,475 | 1,130 | 345 | 23.4 | 153 | 158 | 84 | 75 |
| Phoenix, AZ................... | 1,506 | 941 | 565 | 37.5 | 206 | 468 | 38 | 35 |
| Portland, OR.................. | 612 | 489 | 123 | 20.1 | 48 | 48 | 25 | 40 |
| San Antonio, TX.............. | 1,406 | 816 | 591 | 42.0 | 169 | 536 | 24 | 22 |
| San Diego, CA................ | 1,335 | 793 | 542 | 40.6 | 187 | 305 | 63 | 155 |
| San Francisco, CA........... | 845 | 470 | 374 | 44.3 | 165 | 97 | 48 | 221 |
| San Jose, CA................. | 971 | 413 | 558 | 57.5 | 241 | 225 | 75 | 245 |
| Seattle, WA................... | 688 | 546 | 143 | 20.8 | 59 | 27 | 26 | 72 |
| Washington, DC.............. | 649 | 535 | 114 | 17.6 | 41 | 61 | 27 | 12 |

[1] Includes other language groups, not shown separately. [2] Beginning 2016, data is not comparable with prior years due to change in language classifications; see <https://www.census.gov/content/dam/Census/programs-surveys/acs/tech-doc/user-notes/2016_Language_User_Note.pdf> for more information. [3] Represents the portion of a consolidated city that is not within one or more separately incorporated places.

Source: U.S. Census Bureau, 2017 American Community Survey, C16005, "Nativity by Language Spoken at Home by Ability to Speak English for the Population 5 Years and Over," <http://factfinder.census.gov/>, accessed February 2019.

# Table 58. Marital Status of the Population by Sex, Race, and Hispanic Origin: 2000 to 2018

[In millions, except percent (213.8 represents 213,800,000). As of March. Data are shown for persons aged 15 years and over. Excludes members of Armed Forces except those living off post or with their families on post. Beginning 2005 based on an expanded sample of households. Data for 2010 based on population controls from Census 2000. 2015 and 2018 data based on population controls from Census 2010. Based on Current Population Survey; see text, this section and Appendix III]

| Marital status, race and Hispanic origin | Total | | | | Male | | | | Female | | | |
|---|---|---|---|---|---|---|---|---|---|---|---|---|
| | 2000 | 2010 | 2015 | 2018 | 2000 | 2010 | 2015 | 2018 | 2000 | 2010 | 2015 | 2018 |
| **Total [1]** | **213.8** | **242.0** | **255.0** | **262.1** | **103.1** | **117.7** | **123.6** | **127.2** | **110.7** | **124.4** | **131.4** | **134.8** |
| Never married | 60.0 | 74.2 | 81.0 | 84.6 | 32.3 | 40.2 | 43.1 | 44.8 | 27.8 | 34.0 | 38.0 | 39.8 |
| Married [2] | 120.2 | 129.7 | 133.6 | 136.5 | 59.7 | 64.5 | 66.3 | 68.0 | 60.5 | 65.2 | 67.2 | 68.5 |
| Widowed | 13.7 | 14.3 | 14.6 | 15.1 | 2.6 | 3.0 | 3.3 | 3.4 | 11.1 | 11.4 | 11.3 | 11.7 |
| Divorced | 19.9 | 23.7 | 25.8 | 25.9 | 8.6 | 10.0 | 11.0 | 11.1 | 11.3 | 13.8 | 14.9 | 14.8 |
| Percent of total | 100.0 | 100.0 | 100.0 | 100.0 | 100.0 | 100.0 | 100.0 | 100.0 | 100.0 | 100.0 | 100.0 | 100.0 |
| Never married | 28.1 | 30.7 | 31.8 | 32.3 | 31.3 | 34.2 | 34.8 | 35.2 | 25.1 | 27.4 | 28.9 | 29.5 |
| Married [2] | 56.2 | 53.6 | 52.4 | 52.1 | 57.9 | 54.8 | 53.7 | 53.4 | 54.7 | 52.4 | 51.2 | 50.8 |
| Widowed | 6.4 | 5.9 | 5.7 | 5.8 | 2.5 | 2.5 | 2.6 | 2.7 | 10.0 | 9.1 | 8.6 | 8.7 |
| Divorced | 9.3 | 9.8 | 10.1 | 9.9 | 8.3 | 8.5 | 8.9 | 8.7 | 10.2 | 11.1 | 11.3 | 11.0 |
| **White, total [3]** | **177.6** | **195.5** | **200.1** | **203.7** | **86.4** | **96.2** | **98.1** | **100.0** | **91.1** | **99.3** | **102.1** | **103.6** |
| Never married | 45.3 | 54.7 | 57.3 | 59.1 | 25.1 | 30.6 | 31.4 | 32.2 | 20.2 | 24.1 | 25.9 | 26.9 |
| Married [2] | 104.2 | 109.6 | 110.1 | 111.6 | 51.9 | 54.7 | 55.0 | 56.0 | 52.3 | 54.8 | 55.1 | 55.6 |
| Widowed | 11.5 | 11.8 | 11.9 | 12.1 | 2.2 | 2.5 | 2.7 | 2.8 | 9.3 | 9.3 | 9.3 | 9.4 |
| Divorced | 16.5 | 19.4 | 20.8 | 20.8 | 7.2 | 8.3 | 9.0 | 9.1 | 9.3 | 11.1 | 11.8 | 11.7 |
| Percent of total | 100.0 | 100.0 | 100.0 | 100.0 | 100.0 | 100.0 | 100.0 | 100.0 | 100.0 | 100.0 | 100.0 | 100.0 |
| Never married | 25.5 | 28.0 | 28.6 | 29.0 | 29.1 | 31.8 | 32.0 | 32.2 | 22.1 | 24.3 | 25.4 | 26.0 |
| Married [2] | 58.7 | 56.1 | 55.0 | 54.8 | 60.0 | 56.9 | 56.1 | 55.9 | 57.4 | 55.2 | 54.0 | 53.7 |
| Widowed | 6.5 | 6.0 | 6.0 | 6.0 | 2.5 | 2.6 | 2.7 | 2.8 | 10.2 | 9.3 | 9.1 | 9.0 |
| Divorced | 9.3 | 9.9 | 10.4 | 10.2 | 8.4 | 8.7 | 9.2 | 9.1 | 10.2 | 11.2 | 11.6 | 11.3 |
| **Black, total [3]** | **25.9** | **29.4** | **32.0** | **33.4** | **11.7** | **13.3** | **14.6** | **15.3** | **14.2** | **16.0** | **17.4** | **18.1** |
| Never married | 11.3 | 13.7 | 15.5 | 16.3 | 5.2 | 6.5 | 7.3 | 7.7 | 6.0 | 7.2 | 8.2 | 8.6 |
| Married [2] | 10.1 | 10.6 | 11.1 | 11.6 | 5.0 | 5.2 | 5.5 | 5.8 | 5.1 | 5.4 | 5.6 | 5.8 |
| Widowed | 1.7 | 1.8 | 1.8 | 1.9 | 0.3 | 0.4 | 0.4 | 0.4 | 1.4 | 1.5 | 1.4 | 1.5 |
| Divorced | 2.8 | 3.2 | 3.6 | 3.5 | 1.1 | 1.2 | 1.4 | 1.4 | 1.7 | 2.0 | 2.2 | 2.2 |
| Percent of total | 100.0 | 100.0 | 100.0 | 100.0 | 100.0 | 100.0 | 100.0 | 100.0 | 100.0 | 100.0 | 100.0 | 100.0 |
| Never married | 43.5 | 46.8 | 48.5 | 48.9 | 44.9 | 48.8 | 49.9 | 50.3 | 42.4 | 45.2 | 47.4 | 47.8 |
| Married [2] | 39.2 | 36.1 | 34.7 | 34.7 | 42.8 | 39.4 | 37.8 | 37.9 | 36.2 | 33.4 | 32.0 | 32.0 |
| Widowed | 6.6 | 6.2 | 5.7 | 5.7 | 2.8 | 2.7 | 2.9 | 2.7 | 9.6 | 9.1 | 8.0 | 8.3 |
| Divorced | 10.7 | 10.9 | 11.2 | 10.6 | 9.5 | 9.1 | 9.4 | 9.1 | 11.8 | 12.4 | 12.6 | 11.9 |
| **Asian, total [3]** | **8.4** | **11.2** | **14.6** | **16.2** | **4.0** | **5.3** | **6.9** | **7.7** | **4.4** | **5.9** | **7.7** | **8.5** |
| Never married | 2.8 | 3.2 | 4.5 | 5.0 | 1.5 | 1.7 | 2.4 | 2.7 | 1.3 | 1.4 | 2.1 | 2.2 |
| Married [2] | 4.9 | 7.0 | 9.0 | 9.9 | 2.3 | 3.3 | 4.2 | 4.7 | 2.6 | 3.7 | 4.8 | 5.3 |
| Widowed | 0.3 | 0.5 | 0.6 | 0.7 | 0.0 | 0.1 | 0.1 | 0.1 | 0.3 | 0.5 | 0.5 | 0.6 |
| Divorced | 0.4 | 0.5 | 0.7 | 0.7 | 0.1 | 0.2 | 0.2 | 0.2 | 0.2 | 0.3 | 0.4 | 0.5 |
| Percent of total | 100.0 | 100.0 | 100.0 | 100.0 | 100.0 | 100.0 | 100.0 | 100.0 | 100.0 | 100.0 | 100.0 | 100.0 |
| Never married | 33.1 | 28.3 | 30.4 | 30.6 | 37.7 | 32.8 | 34.8 | 35.5 | 28.8 | 24.2 | 26.6 | 26.1 |
| Married [2] | 58.6 | 62.8 | 61.2 | 61.1 | 57.8 | 62.6 | 60.7 | 60.5 | 59.4 | 62.9 | 61.6 | 61.7 |
| Widowed | 4.0 | 4.7 | 3.9 | 4.1 | 1.2 | 1.3 | 1.5 | 1.4 | 6.6 | 7.7 | 6.1 | 6.6 |
| Divorced | 4.3 | 4.3 | 4.5 | 4.2 | 3.2 | 3.3 | 3.0 | 2.6 | 5.3 | 5.2 | 5.7 | 5.6 |
| **Hispanic, total [4]** | **22.8** | **34.3** | **40.4** | **43.5** | **11.3** | **17.7** | **20.2** | **21.7** | **11.5** | **16.6** | **20.2** | **21.8** |
| Never married | 7.5 | 13.3 | 16.1 | 17.8 | 4.2 | 7.7 | 8.8 | 9.8 | 3.3 | 5.6 | 7.3 | 8.0 |
| Married [2] | 12.7 | 17.2 | 19.8 | 21.0 | 6.2 | 8.6 | 9.7 | 10.2 | 6.5 | 8.6 | 10.1 | 10.8 |
| Widowed | 0.9 | 1.2 | 1.3 | 1.4 | 0.2 | 0.3 | 0.3 | 0.3 | 0.7 | 0.9 | 1.0 | 1.1 |
| Divorced | 1.6 | 2.6 | 3.1 | 3.3 | 0.7 | 1.1 | 1.3 | 1.4 | 1.0 | 1.5 | 1.8 | 1.9 |
| Percent of total | 100.0 | 100.0 | 100.0 | 100.0 | 100.0 | 100.0 | 100.0 | 100.0 | 100.0 | 100.0 | 100.0 | 100.0 |
| Never married | 33.1 | 38.7 | 39.9 | 41.0 | 37.5 | 43.4 | 43.7 | 45.2 | 28.9 | 33.7 | 36.1 | 36.8 |
| Married [2] | 55.9 | 50.1 | 49.1 | 48.3 | 55.1 | 48.7 | 48.1 | 47.1 | 56.6 | 51.7 | 50.1 | 49.6 |
| Widowed | 3.9 | 3.5 | 3.2 | 3.2 | 1.5 | 1.7 | 1.5 | 1.5 | 6.2 | 5.4 | 5.0 | 4.9 |
| Divorced | 7.1 | 7.7 | 7.8 | 7.5 | 5.9 | 6.2 | 6.6 | 6.3 | 8.3 | 9.2 | 8.9 | 8.7 |

[1] Includes persons of other races not shown separately. [2] Includes persons who are married with spouse present, married with spouse absent, and separated. [3] Beginning 2003, data represent persons who selected this race group only and exclude persons reporting more than one race. Prior to 2003, the CPS only allowed respondents to report one race group. See also comments on race in the text for this section. [4] Hispanic persons may be of any race.

Source: U.S. Census Bureau, Families and Living Arrangements, Historical Marital Status Tables, "Table MS-1. Marital Status of the Population 15 Years Old and Over, by Sex, Race and Hispanic Origin: 1950 to Present," <https://census.gov/data/tables/time-series/demo/families/marital.html>, accessed December 2018.

# Table 59. Marital Status of the Population by Sex and Age: 2018

[127,233 represents 127,233,000. As of March. Data are shown for population aged 15 and older. Excludes members of Armed Forces except those living off post or with their families on post. Population controls based on Census 2010. Based on Current Population Survey, see text, this section, and Appendix III]

| Sex and age | Number of persons (1,000) | | | | | Percent distribution | | | | |
|---|---|---|---|---|---|---|---|---|---|---|
| | Total | Never married | Married [1] | Widowed | Divorced | Total | Never married | Married [1] | Widowed | Divorced |
| **MALE** | | | | | | | | | | |
| **Total** | **127,233** | **44,792** | **67,976** | **3,405** | **11,060** | **100.0** | **35.2** | **53.4** | **2.7** | **8.7** |
| 15 to 17 years old | 6,582 | 6,462 | 105 | 7 | 8 | 100.0 | 98.2 | 1.6 | 0.1 | 0.1 |
| 18 years old and over | 120,651 | 38,330 | 67,871 | 3,398 | 11,051 | 100.0 | 31.8 | 56.3 | 2.8 | 9.2 |
| 18 to 19 years old | 4,034 | 3,950 | 79 | 2 | 4 | 100.0 | 97.9 | 2.0 | 0.1 | 0.1 |
| 20 to 24 years old | 10,803 | 9,743 | 1,006 | 3 | 52 | 100.0 | 90.2 | 9.3 | 0.0 | 0.5 |
| 25 to 29 years old | 11,669 | 8,212 | 3,200 | 12 | 245 | 100.0 | 70.4 | 27.5 | 0.1 | 2.1 |
| 30 to 34 years old | 10,808 | 4,725 | 5,514 | 25 | 544 | 100.0 | 43.7 | 51.0 | 0.2 | 5.0 |
| 35 to 39 years old | 10,561 | 2,969 | 6,838 | 28 | 726 | 100.0 | 28.1 | 64.8 | 0.3 | 6.9 |
| 40 to 44 years old | 9,503 | 1,915 | 6,567 | 32 | 990 | 100.0 | 20.1 | 69.0 | 0.3 | 10.4 |
| 45 to 49 years old | 10,122 | 1,659 | 7,012 | 109 | 1,342 | 100.0 | 16.4 | 69.2 | 1.1 | 13.3 |
| 50 to 54 years old | 10,209 | 1,619 | 6,879 | 132 | 1,579 | 100.0 | 15.9 | 67.4 | 1.3 | 15.5 |
| 55 to 64 years old | 19,893 | 2,211 | 14,080 | 482 | 3,120 | 100.0 | 11.1 | 70.8 | 2.4 | 15.7 |
| 65 to 74 years old | 14,339 | 935 | 10,791 | 862 | 1,751 | 100.0 | 6.5 | 75.3 | 6.0 | 12.2 |
| 75 to 84 years old | 6,447 | 294 | 4,583 | 965 | 606 | 100.0 | 4.6 | 71.1 | 15.0 | 9.4 |
| 85 years old and over | 2,262 | 100 | 1,323 | 747 | 91 | 100.0 | 4.4 | 58.5 | 33.0 | 4.0 |
| **FEMALE** | | | | | | | | | | |
| **Total** | **134,825** | **39,770** | **68,530** | **11,691** | **14,833** | **100.0** | **29.5** | **50.9** | **8.7** | **11.0** |
| 15 to 17 years old | 6,397 | 6,293 | 75 | 13 | 16 | 100.0 | 98.4 | 1.2 | 0.2 | 0.2 |
| 18 years old and over | 128,428 | 33,477 | 68,456 | 11,678 | 14,818 | 100.0 | 26.1 | 53.3 | 9.1 | 11.5 |
| 18 to 19 years old | 3,894 | 3,750 | 123 | 7 | 15 | 100.0 | 96.3 | 3.2 | 0.2 | 0.4 |
| 20 to 24 years old | 10,616 | 9,007 | 1,486 | 24 | 100 | 100.0 | 84.8 | 14.0 | 0.2 | 0.9 |
| 25 to 29 years old | 11,481 | 6,653 | 4,464 | 21 | 342 | 100.0 | 58.0 | 38.9 | 0.2 | 3.0 |
| 30 to 34 years old | 10,874 | 3,595 | 6,597 | 45 | 637 | 100.0 | 33.1 | 60.0 | 0.4 | 5.9 |
| 35 to 39 years old | 10,698 | 2,493 | 6,999 | 165 | 1,040 | 100.0 | 23.3 | 65.5 | 1.5 | 9.7 |
| 40 to 44 years old | 9,886 | 1,589 | 6,861 | 169 | 1,268 | 100.0 | 16.1 | 69.4 | 1.7 | 12.8 |
| 45 to 49 years old | 10,514 | 1,367 | 7,190 | 270 | 1,687 | 100.0 | 13.0 | 68.4 | 2.6 | 16.0 |
| 50 to 54 years old | 10,680 | 1,266 | 7,074 | 452 | 1,889 | 100.0 | 11.9 | 66.3 | 4.2 | 17.7 |
| 55 to 64 years old | 21,794 | 2,222 | 14,029 | 1,612 | 3,931 | 100.0 | 10.2 | 64.4 | 7.4 | 18.0 |
| 65 to 74 years old | 16,018 | 1,037 | 9,428 | 2,970 | 2,584 | 100.0 | 6.5 | 58.9 | 18.5 | 16.1 |
| 75 to 84 years old | 8,104 | 344 | 3,478 | 3,224 | 1,058 | 100.0 | 4.2 | 42.8 | 39.8 | 13.1 |
| 85 years old and over | 3,869 | 155 | 728 | 2,718 | 268 | 100.0 | 4.0 | 18.8 | 70.2 | 6.9 |

[1] Includes persons who are married with spouse present, married with spouse absent, and separated.

Source: U.S. Census Bureau, America's Families and Living Arrangements, Adult (A table series), "Table A1. Marital Status of People 15 Years and Over, by Age, Sex, and Personal Earnings: 2018," <https://www.census.gov/data/tables/2018/demo/families/cps-2018.html>, accessed December 2018.

# Table 60. Living Arrangements of Persons 18 Years Old and Over by Age and Sex: 2018

[In thousands (249,079 represents 249,079,000), except percent. As of March. Excludes members of Armed Forces except those living off post or with their families on post. Population controls based on Census 2010 and an expanded sample of households. Based on Current Population Survey (CPS); see text, this section, and Appendix III]

| Living arrangement | Total | 18 to 24 years old | 25 to 34 years old | 35 to 64 years old | 65 to 74 years old | 75 years old and over |
|---|---|---|---|---|---|---|
| **NUMBER (1,000)** | | | | | | |
| **Total** | **249,079** | **29,348** | **44,832** | **123,860** | **30,357** | **20,682** |
| Male | 120,651 | 14,838 | 22,477 | 60,288 | 14,339 | 8,709 |
| Female | 128,428 | 14,510 | 22,355 | 63,572 | 16,018 | 11,973 |
| **PERCENT DISTRIBUTION** | | | | | | |
| **Male, total** | **100.0** | **100.0** | **100.0** | **100.0** | **100.0** | **100.0** |
| Alone | (NA) | 5.0 | 11.8 | 13.0 | 18.5 | 24.2 |
| With spouse [1] | (NA) | 5.6 | 35.6 | 64.4 | 72.2 | 65.3 |
| Child of householder [2] | (NA) | 56.9 | 19.6 | 4.8 | – | – |
| Living with partner | (NA) | 7.7 | 14.8 | 7.4 | 3.4 | 2.0 |
| Other relatives | (NA) | 13.5 | 9.4 | 7.2 | 4.6 | 7.0 |
| Nonrelatives | (NA) | 11.3 | 8.8 | 3.1 | 1.4 | 1.5 |
| **Female, total** | **100.0** | **100.0** | **100.0** | **100.0** | **100.0** | **100.0** |
| Alone | (NA) | 5.4 | 8.7 | 11.8 | 26.2 | 44.3 |
| With spouse [1] | (NA) | 9.1 | 45.1 | 61.9 | 56.1 | 33.3 |
| Child of householder [2] | (NA) | 51.1 | 11.8 | 2.7 | – | – |
| Living with partner | (NA) | 11.2 | 14.8 | 6.3 | 2.5 | 1.4 |
| Other relatives | (NA) | 14.2 | 14.3 | 15.6 | 13.9 | 20.0 |
| Nonrelatives | (NA) | 8.9 | 5.2 | 1.7 | 1.2 | 1.0 |

– Represents or rounds to zero. NA Not available. [1] Includes only adults who are married, spouse present in the household. This living arrangement supersedes the others shown in the table. For example people living with their parents and a spouse are counted as living with a spouse, not as a child of the householder. [2] Children of the householder are not living with a spouse or unmarried partner, and are residing in the household of a parent. In CPS, unmarried college students living in dormitories are counted as living in the parental home.

Source: U.S. Census Bureau, America's Families and Living Arrangements, Historical Living Arrangements of Adults, "Table AD-3. Living Arrangements of Adults 18 and Over, 1967 to Present," <https://www.census.gov/data/tables/time-series/demo/families/adults.html>, accessed December 2018.

## Table 61. Households, Families, Subfamilies, and Married Couples: 1990 to 2018

[In thousands (93,347 represents 93,347,000), except as indicated. As of March. Excludes members of the Armed Services except those living off post or with their families on post. Beginning 2001, based on an expanded sample of households. Population controls for 2010 based on Census 2000; beginning 2012, population controls based on Census 2010. Based on Current Population Survey (CPS), see text, this section and Appendix III. Minus sign (-) indicates decrease]

| Type of unit | 1990 | 2000 | 2010 | 2015 | 2017 | 2018 | Percent change 1990 to 2000 | Percent change 2000 to 2010 | Percent change 2010 to 2018 |
|---|---|---|---|---|---|---|---|---|---|
| **Households** | **93,347** | **104,705** | **117,538** | **124,587** | **126,224** | **127,586** | **12.2** | **12.3** | **8.5** |
| Persons per household | 2.63 | 2.62 | 2.59 | 2.54 | 2.54 | 2.53 | (X) | (X) | (X) |
| White [1] | 80,163 | 87,671 | 95,489 | 98,679 | 99,400 | 100,065 | 9.4 | 8.9 | 4.8 |
| Black [1] | 10,486 | 12,849 | 14,730 | 16,437 | 16,733 | 16,997 | 22.5 | 14.6 | 15.4 |
| Asian [1] | (NA) | (NA) | 4,687 | 6,040 | 6,392 | 6,735 | (NA) | (NA) | 43.7 |
| Hispanic [2] | 5,933 | 9,319 | 13,298 | 16,239 | 16,915 | 17,318 | 57.1 | 42.7 | 30.2 |
| Family households | 66,090 | 72,025 | 78,833 | 81,716 | 82,827 | 83,088 | 9.0 | 9.5 | 5.4 |
| Married couple | 52,317 | 55,311 | 58,410 | 60,010 | 60,804 | 61,241 | 5.7 | 5.6 | 4.8 |
| Male householder [3] | 2,884 | 4,028 | 5,580 | 6,162 | 6,452 | 6,424 | 39.7 | 38.5 | 15.1 |
| Female householder [3] | 10,890 | 12,687 | 14,843 | 15,544 | 15,572 | 15,423 | 16.5 | 17.0 | 3.9 |
| Nonfamily households | 27,257 | 32,680 | 38,705 | 42,871 | 43,396 | 44,498 | 19.9 | 18.4 | 15.0 |
| Male householder | 11,606 | 14,641 | 18,263 | 20,143 | 20,539 | 21,017 | 26.2 | 24.7 | 15.1 |
| Female householder | 15,651 | 18,039 | 20,442 | 22,728 | 22,858 | 23,481 | 15.3 | 13.3 | 14.9 |
| One person | 22,999 | 26,724 | 31,399 | 34,866 | 35,252 | 35,740 | 16.2 | 17.5 | 13.8 |
| **Families** | **66,090** | **72,025** | **78,833** | **81,716** | **82,827** | **83,088** | **9.0** | **9.5** | **5.4** |
| Persons per family | 3.17 | 3.17 | 3.16 | 3.14 | 3.14 | 3.14 | (X) | (X) | (X) |
| With own children under age 18 | 32,289 | 34,605 | 35,218 | 34,979 | 34,292 | 34,452 | 7.2 | 1.8 | -2.2 |
| Without own children under age 18 | 33,801 | 37,420 | 43,615 | 46,737 | 48,535 | 48,635 | 10.7 | 16.6 | 11.5 |
| Married couple | 52,317 | 55,311 | 58,410 | 60,010 | 60,804 | 61,241 | 5.7 | 5.6 | 4.8 |
| With own children under age 18 | 24,537 | 25,248 | 24,575 | 24,040 | 23,651 | 23,812 | 2.9 | -2.7 | -3.1 |
| Without own children under age 18 | 27,780 | 30,062 | 33,835 | 35,970 | 37,153 | 37,430 | 8.2 | 12.6 | 10.6 |
| Male householder [3] | 2,884 | 4,028 | 5,580 | 6,162 | 6,452 | 6,424 | 39.7 | 38.5 | 15.1 |
| With own children under age 18 | 1,153 | 1,786 | 2,224 | 2,388 | 2,395 | 2,484 | 54.9 | 24.5 | 11.7 |
| Without own children under age 18 | 1,731 | 2,242 | 3,356 | 3,774 | 4,057 | 3,939 | 29.5 | 49.7 | 17.4 |
| Female householder [3] | 10,890 | 12,687 | 14,843 | 15,544 | 15,572 | 15,423 | 16.5 | 17.0 | 3.9 |
| With own children under age 18 | 6,599 | 7,571 | 8,419 | 8,551 | 8,246 | 8,156 | 14.7 | 11.2 | -3.1 |
| Without own children under age 18 | 4,290 | 5,116 | 6,424 | 6,993 | 7,326 | 7,267 | 19.3 | 25.6 | 13.1 |
| **Unrelated subfamilies [4]** | **534** | **571** | **484** | **566** | **456** | **396** | **6.9** | **-15.2** | **-18.2** |
| Married couple | 68 | 37 | 93 | 76 | 91 | 94 | (B) | (B) | 1.1 |
| Male reference persons [3] | 45 | 57 | 44 | 63 | 67 | 52 | (B) | (B) | (B) |
| Female reference persons [3] | 421 | 477 | 347 | 428 | 299 | 250 | 13.3 | -27.3 | -28.0 |
| **Related subfamilies [4]** | **2,403** | **2,984** | **4,300** | **4,508** | **4,831** | **4,619** | **24.2** | **44.1** | **7.4** |
| Married couple | 871 | 1,149 | 1,881 | 2,144 | 2,430 | 2,404 | 31.9 | 63.7 | 27.8 |
| Father-child [3] | 153 | 201 | 313 | 308 | 533 | 430 | 31.4 | 55.7 | 37.4 |
| Mother-child [3] | 1,378 | 1,634 | 2,106 | 2,056 | 1,868 | 1,785 | 18.6 | 28.9 | -15.2 |
| **Married couples** | **53,256** | **56,497** | **60,384** | **62,230** | **63,325** | **63,739** | **6.1** | **6.9** | **5.6** |
| With own household | 52,317 | 55,311 | 58,410 | 60,010 | 60,804 | 61,241 | 5.7 | 5.6 | 4.8 |
| Without own household | 939 | 1,186 | 1,974 | 2,220 | 2,522 | 2,498 | 26.3 | 66.4 | 26.5 |
| Percent without | 1.8 | 2.1 | 3.2 | 3.6 | 4.0 | 3.9 | (X) | (X) | (X) |

B Base less than 75,000. NA Not available. X Not applicable. [1] Beginning with the 2003 CPS, respondents could choose more than one race. Beginning in 2003, data represent persons who selected this race group only and exclude persons reporting more than one race. The CPS in prior years only allowed respondents to report one race group. See also comments on race in text for this section. [2] Persons of Hispanic origin may be of any race. [3] No spouse present. [4] A subfamily is a married couple or parent/child group that does not maintain its own household. A subfamily may be related to the householder, or unrelated to the householder.

Source: U.S. Census Bureau, America's Families and Living Arrangements, Tables F1, FG1, FG7, and H1, and Historical Households Tables, Table HH-6, <https://www.census.gov/topics/families/families-and-households/data/tables.html>, accessed December 2018, and earlier releases.

## Table 62. Interracially Married Couples by Race and Hispanic Origin of Spouses: 1980 to 2018

[In thousands (49,714 represents 49,714,000), except percent. As of March. Persons 15 years old and over. Persons of Hispanic origin may be of any race. Population controls for 2010 based on Census 2000; beginning 2012, based on Census 2010. Based on Current Population Survey; see headnote, Table 61 and Appendix III]

| Race and origin of spouses | 1980 | 1990 | 2000 | 2010 | 2015 | 2016 | 2017 | 2018 |
|---|---|---|---|---|---|---|---|---|
| **Married couples, total [1]** | **49,714** | **53,256** | **56,497** | **60,384** | **62,230** | **62,628** | **63,325** | **63,739** |
| Interracial married couples, percent | 1.3 | 1.8 | 2.6 | 4.1 | 4.8 | 4.9 | 5.0 | 5.1 |
| **Interracial married couples, total** | **651** | **964** | **1,464** | **2,478** | **3,010** | **3,076** | **3,158** | **3,237** |
| White [2] and Black [2] | 167 | 211 | 363 | 558 | 562 | 594 | 695 | 665 |
| Black husband and White wife | 122 | 150 | 268 | 390 | 383 | 417 | 490 | 411 |
| White husband and Black wife | 45 | 61 | 95 | 168 | 179 | 177 | 205 | 254 |
| White [2] and other race [3] | 450 | 720 | 1,051 | 1,723 | 2,171 | 2,218 | 2,179 | 2,240 |
| Black [2] and other race [3] | 34 | 33 | 50 | 132 | 187 | 186 | 213 | 250 |
| Other [4] | (NA) | (NA) | (NA) | 65 | 90 | 78 | 71 | 82 |
| HISPANIC ORIGIN | | | | | | | | |
| Hispanic and Hispanic | 1,906 | 3,085 | 4,739 | 6,166 | 7,176 | 7,481 | 7,624 | 7,662 |
| Hispanic and other origin (not Hispanic) | 891 | 1,193 | 1,743 | 2,289 | 2,830 | 2,849 | 3,154 | 3,300 |
| All other couples (not of Hispanic origin) | 46,917 | 48,979 | 50,015 | 51,928 | 52,224 | 52,297 | 52,546 | 52,778 |

NA Not available. [1] Includes other married couples not shown separately. [2] See footnote 1, Table 61. [3] "Other race," is any race other than White or Black, such as Asian; and, beginning 2003, includes other single race alone or any combination of races. [4] One spouse is Asian only and the other spouse is any other race or combination of races.

Source: U.S. Census Bureau, America's Families and Living Arrangements, Historical Marital Status Tables, "Table MS-3. Interracial Married Couples: 1980 to 2002"; and Family groups (FG table series), "Table FG3. Married Couple Family Groups, By Presence Of Own Children Under 18, And Age, Earnings, Education, And Race And Hispanic Origin Of Both Spouses," <https://www.census.gov/topics/families/families-and-households/data/tables.html>; accessed December 2018, and earlier releases.

## Table 63. Households and Persons Per Household by Type of Household: 2000 to 2018

[104,705 represents 104,705,000. As of March. See headnote, Table 61]

| Type of household | Households | | | | | | Persons per household | | |
|---|---|---|---|---|---|---|---|---|---|
| | Number (1,000) | | | Percent distribution | | | | | |
| | 2000 | 2010 | 2018 | 2000 | 2010 | 2018 | 2000 | 2010 | 2018 |
| **Total households**............................ | **104,705** | **117,538** | **127,586** | **100.0** | **100.0** | **100.0** | **2.62** | **2.59** | **2.53** |
| Family households................................. | 72,025 | 78,833 | 83,088 | 68.8 | 67.1 | 65.1 | 3.24 | 3.24 | 3.21 |
| Married couple family.......................... | 55,311 | 58,410 | 61,241 | 52.8 | 49.7 | 48.0 | 3.26 | 3.24 | 3.19 |
| Male householder, no spouse present........ | 4,028 | 5,580 | 6,424 | 3.8 | 4.7 | 5.0 | 3.16 | 3.24 | 3.23 |
| Female householder, no spouse present..... | 12,687 | 14,843 | 15,423 | 12.1 | 12.6 | 12.1 | 3.17 | 3.23 | 3.29 |
| Nonfamily households............................ | 32,680 | 38,705 | 44,498 | 31.2 | 32.9 | 34.9 | 1.25 | 1.26 | 1.26 |
| Living alone.................................. | 26,724 | 31,399 | 35,740 | 25.5 | 26.7 | 28.0 | 1.00 | 1.00 | 1.00 |
| Male householder.............................. | 14,641 | 18,263 | 21,017 | 14.0 | 15.5 | 16.5 | 1.34 | 1.35 | 1.33 |
| Living alone.................................. | 11,181 | 13,971 | 16,016 | 10.7 | 11.9 | 12.6 | 1.00 | 1.00 | 1.00 |
| Female householder............................ | 18,039 | 20,442 | 23,481 | 17.2 | 17.4 | 18.4 | 1.17 | 1.18 | 1.20 |
| Living alone.................................. | 15,543 | 17,428 | 19,724 | 14.8 | 14.8 | 15.5 | 1.00 | 1.00 | 1.00 |

Source: U.S. Census Bureau, Current Population Reports, P20-537, 2001, and earlier reports; and America's Families and Living Arrangements, "Table AVG1" and "Table H1," <https://www.census.gov/data/tables/2018/demo/families/cps-2018.html>, accessed December 2018, and earlier releases.

## Table 64. Households by Age of Householder and Size of Household: 1990 to 2018

[In millions (93.3 represents 93,300,000). As of March. Based on Current Population Survey; see headnote, Table 61]

| Age of householder and size of household | 1990 | 2000 | 2005 | 2010 | 2013 | 2014 | 2015 | 2016 | 2017 | 2018 |
|---|---|---|---|---|---|---|---|---|---|---|
| **Total.....................** | **93.3** | **104.7** | **113.3** | **117.5** | **122.5** | **123.2** | **124.6** | **125.8** | **126.2** | **127.6** |
| 15 to 24 years old......... | 5.1 | 5.9 | 6.7 | 6.2 | 6.3 | 6.4 | 6.4 | 6.4 | 6.2 | 6.2 |
| 25 to 29 years old......... | 9.4 | 8.5 | 9.2 | 9.4 | 9.3 | 9.3 | 9.4 | 9.5 | 9.5 | 9.5 |
| 30 to 34 years old......... | 11.0 | 10.1 | 10.1 | 9.8 | 10.8 | 10.7 | 10.7 | 10.6 | 10.6 | 10.7 |
| 35 to 44 years old......... | 20.6 | 24.0 | 23.2 | 21.5 | 21.3 | 21.1 | 21.1 | 21.2 | 21.5 | 21.6 |
| 45 to 54 years old......... | 14.5 | 20.9 | 23.4 | 24.9 | 24.1 | 23.7 | 23.6 | 23.3 | 22.8 | 22.5 |
| 55 to 64 years old......... | 12.5 | 13.6 | 17.5 | 20.4 | 22.8 | 23.2 | 23.5 | 23.9 | 23.8 | 24.0 |
| 65 to 74 years old......... | 11.7 | 11.3 | 11.5 | 13.2 | 15.3 | 16.0 | 16.9 | 17.6 | 18.2 | 19.0 |
| 75 years old and over..... | 8.4 | 10.4 | 11.6 | 12.1 | 12.6 | 12.8 | 13.1 | 13.4 | 13.6 | 14.0 |
| One person.................. | 23.0 | 26.7 | 30.1 | 31.4 | 33.6 | 34.2 | 34.9 | 35.4 | 35.3 | 35.7 |
| Male....................... | 9.0 | 11.2 | 12.8 | 14.0 | 15.0 | 15.2 | 15.5 | 15.8 | 15.8 | 16.0 |
| Female..................... | 14.0 | 15.5 | 17.3 | 17.4 | 18.6 | 19.0 | 19.4 | 19.6 | 19.5 | 19.7 |
| Two persons............... | 30.1 | 34.7 | 37.4 | 39.5 | 41.5 | 41.6 | 41.9 | 42.8 | 43.5 | 44.0 |
| Three persons............. | 16.1 | 17.2 | 18.3 | 18.6 | 19.3 | 19.4 | 19.3 | 19.4 | 19.5 | 19.3 |
| Four persons.............. | 14.5 | 15.3 | 16.4 | 16.1 | 16.4 | 16.2 | 16.5 | 16.3 | 16.2 | 16.5 |
| Five persons.............. | 6.2 | 7.0 | 7.2 | 7.4 | 7.4 | 7.5 | 7.5 | 7.5 | 7.3 | 7.4 |
| Six persons............... | 2.1 | 2.4 | 2.5 | 2.8 | 2.7 | 2.8 | 2.8 | 2.8 | 2.8 | 2.9 |
| Seven persons or more... | 1.3 | 1.4 | 1.4 | 1.7 | 1.6 | 1.6 | 1.7 | 1.6 | 1.6 | 1.7 |

Source: U.S. Census Bureau, Current Population Reports, P20-537, and earlier reports; and America's Families and Living Arrangements, Households (H table series), <https://www.census.gov/data/tables/2018/demo/families/cps-2018.html>, accessed December 2018.

## Table 65. Family Households With Own Children Under 18 Years of Age by Type of Family, 2000 to 2018, and by Age of Householder, 2018

[34,605 represents 34,605,000. As of March. See headnote, Table 66]

| Age of householder | Family households with children | | Married couple households with children | | Male householder with children [1] | | Female householder with children [1] | |
|---|---|---|---|---|---|---|---|---|
| | Number (1,000) | Percent of all family households | Number (1,000) | Percent of all married couple households | Number (1,000) | Percent of all male house-holder families [1] | Number (1,000) | Percent of all female house-holder families [1] |
| 2000, total................. | 34,605 | 48 | 25,248 | 46 | 1,786 | 44 | 7,571 | 60 |
| 2010, total................. | 35,218 | 45 | 24,575 | 42 | 2,224 | 40 | 8,419 | 57 |
| 2015, total................. | 34,979 | 43 | 24,040 | 40 | 2,388 | 39 | 8,551 | 55 |
| **2018, total................** | **34,452** | **41** | **23,812** | **39** | **2,484** | **39** | **8,156** | **53** |
| 15 to 24 years old....... | 1,209 | 40 | 429 | 48 | 130 | 15 | 650 | 52 |
| 25 to 34 years old....... | 8,999 | 70 | 5,683 | 68 | 723 | 50 | 2,593 | 85 |
| 35 to 44 years old....... | 13,670 | 80 | 9,817 | 80 | 899 | 70 | 2,954 | 85 |
| 45 to 54 years old....... | 8,259 | 50 | 6,129 | 49 | 548 | 45 | 1,581 | 52 |
| 55 to 64 years old....... | 1,877 | 12 | 1,447 | 11 | 166 | 19 | 264 | 12 |
| 65 years old and over... | 439 | 2 | 307 | 2 | 19 | 3 | 113 | 5 |

[1] No spouse present.

Source: U.S. Census Bureau, Current Population Reports, P20-537, 2001; and America's Families and Living Arrangements, Family households (F table series), "Table F1. Family Households, by Type, Age of Own Children, Age of Family Members, and Age of Householder," <https://www.census.gov/data/tables/2018/demo/families/cps-2018.html>, accessed December 2018, and earlier releases.

# Table 66. Family Groups With Children Under 18 Years of Age by Race and Hispanic Origin: 2000 to 2018

[In thousands (37,496 represents 37,496,000). As of March. Family groups are family households, related subfamilies, and unrelated subfamilies; each married couple or parent/child group is counted separately, even if they reside in the same household. Excludes members of Armed Forces except those living off post or with their families on post. Beginning 2005, based on an expanded sample of households. Data for 2010 based on Census 2000 population controls. Data for 2015 and 2018 based on Census 2010 population controls. Based on Current Population Survey, Annual Social and Economic Supplement, see text, this section and Appendix III]

| Race and Hispanic origin of householder or reference person | Number (1,000) | | | | Percent distribution | | | |
|---|---|---|---|---|---|---|---|---|
| | 2000 | 2010 | 2015 | 2018 | 2000 | 2010 | 2015 | 2018 |
| **All races, total [1]** | **37,496** | **39,947** | **39,934** | **38,912** | **100** | **100** | **100** | **100** |
| Two-parent family groups [2] | 25,771 | 27,082 | 26,862 | 26,384 | 69 | 68 | 67 | 68 |
| One-parent family groups | 11,725 | 11,686 | 11,780 | 11,322 | 31 | 29 | 29 | 29 |
| Maintained by mother | 9,681 | 9,924 | 9,891 | 9,232 | 26 | 25 | 25 | 24 |
| Maintained by father | 2,044 | 1,762 | 1,889 | 2,090 | 5 | 4 | 5 | 5 |
| Grandparent householder with grandchild(ren) under 18 | (NA) | 1,179 | 1,292 | 1,206 | (NA) | 3 | 3 | 3 |
| **White, total [3]** | **30,079** | **30,933** | **30,131** | **28,997** | **100** | **100** | **100** | **100** |
| Two-parent family groups [2] | 22,241 | 22,457 | 21,664 | 21,008 | 74 | 73 | 72 | 72 |
| One-parent family groups | 7,838 | 7,729 | 7,639 | 7,218 | 26 | 25 | 25 | 25 |
| Maintained by mother | 6,216 | 6,396 | 6,177 | 5,639 | 21 | 21 | 21 | 19 |
| Maintained by father | 1,622 | 1,333 | 1,462 | 1,579 | 5 | 4 | 5 | 5 |
| Grandparent householder with grandchild(ren) under 18 | (NA) | 747 | 828 | 771 | (NA) | 2 | 3 | 3 |
| **Black, total [3]** | **5,530** | **5,903** | **5,837** | **5,720** | **100** | **100** | **100** | **100** |
| Two-parent family groups [2] | 2,135 | 2,275 | 2,209 | 2,183 | 39 | 39 | 38 | 38 |
| One-parent family groups | 3,396 | 3,280 | 3,262 | 3,212 | 61 | 56 | 56 | 56 |
| Maintained by mother | 3,060 | 2,977 | 2,971 | 2,855 | 55 | 50 | 51 | 50 |
| Maintained by father | 335 | 303 | 291 | 357 | 6 | 5 | 5 | 6 |
| Grandparent householder with grandchild(ren) under 18 | (NA) | 348 | 366 | 325 | (NA) | 6 | 6 | 6 |
| **Asian, total [3]** | **1,469** | **2,025** | **2,443** | **2,659** | **100** | **100** | **100** | **100** |
| Two-parent family groups [2] | 1,184 | 1,694 | 2,071 | 2,290 | 81 | 84 | 85 | 86 |
| One-parent family groups | 285 | 292 | 340 | 323 | 19 | 14 | 14 | 12 |
| Maintained by mother | 236 | 235 | 291 | 262 | 16 | 12 | 12 | 10 |
| Maintained by father | 49 | 57 | 49 | 61 | 3 | 3 | 2 | 2 |
| Grandparent householder with grandchild(ren) under 18 | (NA) | 39 | 32 | 46 | (NA) | 2 | 1 | 2 |
| **Hispanic, total [4]** | **5,503** | **7,572** | **8,345** | **8,476** | **100** | **100** | **100** | **100** |
| Two-parent family groups [2] | 3,625 | 4,856 | 5,407 | 5,552 | 66 | 64 | 65 | 66 |
| One-parent family groups | 1,877 | 2,499 | 2,688 | 2,681 | 34 | 33 | 32 | 32 |
| Maintained by mother | 1,565 | 2,186 | 2,338 | 2,257 | 28 | 29 | 28 | 27 |
| Maintained by father | 313 | 313 | 350 | 424 | 6 | 4 | 4 | 5 |
| Grandparent householder with grandchild(ren) under 18 | (NA) | 217 | 250 | 243 | (NA) | 3 | 3 | 3 |
| **Non-Hispanic White, total [3]** | **24,847** | **23,911** | **22,657** | **21,477** | **100** | **100** | **100** | **100** |
| Two-parent family groups [2] | 18,750 | 17,911 | 16,738 | 15,987 | 75 | 75 | 74 | 74 |
| One-parent family groups | 6,096 | 5,457 | 5,317 | 4,929 | 25 | 23 | 23 | 23 |
| Maintained by mother | 4,766 | 4,404 | 4,171 | 3,712 | 19 | 18 | 18 | 17 |
| Maintained by father | 1,331 | 1,053 | 1,146 | 1,217 | 5 | 4 | 5 | 6 |
| Grandparent householder with grandchild(ren) under 18 | (NA) | 543 | 602 | 561 | (NA) | 2 | 3 | 3 |

NA Not available. [1] Includes other race/ethnicities, not shown separately. [2] Beginning 2007, includes children living both with married and unmarried parents. [3] Beginning with the 2003 Current Population Survey (CPS), respondents could choose more than one race. Beginning 2003, data represent persons who selected this race group only and exclude persons reporting more than one race. The CPS prior to 2003 allowed respondents to report only one race group. See also comments on race in the text for this section. [4] Hispanic persons may be of any race.

Source: U.S. Census Bureau, Families and Living Arrangements, Current Population Reports, P20-537, 2001; and America's Families and Living Arrangements, Family groups (FG table series), "Table FG10. Family Groups: 2018," <https://www.census.gov/topics/families/families-and-households/data/tables.html>, accessed December 2018, and earlier releases.

# Table 67. Parents and Children in Stay-At-Home Parent Family Groups: 1995 to 2018

[In thousands (22,973 represents 22,973,000), except percent. Family groups with children include those families that maintain their own household (family households with own children); those that live in the home of a relative (related subfamilies); and those that live in the home of a nonrelative (unrelated subfamilies). Stay-at-home family groups are married-couple family groups with children under age 15 where one parent is in the labor force all of the previous year and the other parent is out of the labor force for the entire year with the reason 'taking care of home and family.' Only married couples with children under age 15 are included. Based on Current Population Survey; see Appendix III]

| Year | Married-couple family groups with children under 15 years old | | | | | Children under 15 years old in married-couple family groups | | | | |
|---|---|---|---|---|---|---|---|---|---|---|
| | Number | | | Percent | | Number | | | Percent | |
| | Total | With stay-at-home mothers | With stay-at-home fathers | With stay-at-home mothers | With stay-at-home fathers | Total | With stay-at-home mothers | With stay-at-home fathers | With stay-at-home mothers | With stay-at-home fathers |
| 1995 | 22,973 | 4,440 | 64 | 19.3 | 0.3 | 41,008 | 9,106 | 125 | 22.2 | 0.3 |
| 2000 | 22,953 | 4,785 | 93 | 20.8 | 0.4 | 41,860 | 10,087 | 180 | 24.1 | 0.4 |
| 2005 | 23,305 | 5,584 | 142 | 24.0 | 0.6 | 41,111 | 11,224 | 247 | 27.3 | 0.6 |
| 2010 | 22,138 | 5,020 | 154 | 22.7 | 0.7 | 41,026 | 10,833 | 287 | 26.4 | 0.7 |
| 2012 | 21,334 | 5,091 | 189 | 23.9 | 0.9 | 39,222 | 10,675 | 369 | 27.2 | 0.9 |
| 2013 | 21,547 | 5,215 | 214 | 24.2 | 1.0 | 39,448 | 10,818 | 434 | 27.4 | 1.1 |
| 2014 | 21,549 | 5,203 | 211 | 24.1 | 1.0 | 39,424 | 10,791 | 420 | 27.4 | 1.1 |
| 2015 | 21,586 | 5,210 | 199 | 24.1 | 0.9 | 39,621 | 10,758 | 368 | 27.2 | 0.9 |
| 2016 | 21,531 | 5,031 | 209 | 23.4 | 1.0 | 39,693 | 10,360 | 392 | 26.1 | 1.0 |
| 2017 | 21,330 | 4,965 | 267 | 23.3 | 1.3 | 39,659 | 10,427 | 503 | 26.3 | 1.3 |
| 2018 | 21,361 | 5,061 | 190 | 23.7 | 0.9 | 39,813 | 10,574 | 336 | 26.6 | 0.8 |

Source: U.S. Census Bureau, America's Families and Living Arrangements, Historical Families Tables, "Table SHP-1. Parents and Children in Stay-At-Home Parent Family Groups: 1994 to Present," <https://www.census.gov/topics/families/families-and-households/data/tables.html>, accessed December 2018.

# Table 68. Children Under 18 Years of Age by Presence of Parents: 2000 to 2018

[72,012 represents 72,012,000. As of March. Excludes persons under 18 years old who maintained households or family groups and their spouses. Based on Current Population Survey; see headnote, Table 66]

| Race, Hispanic origin, and year | Number (1,000) | Both parents [1] | Percent living with— | | | | | | Father only | Neither parent |
|---|---|---|---|---|---|---|---|---|---|---|
| | | | Mother only | | | | | | | |
| | | | Total | Divorced | Married, spouse absent [2] | Never married | Widowed | | | |
| **ALL RACES** [3] | | | | | | | | | | |
| 2000............................ | 72,012 | 69.1 | 22.4 | 7.9 | 4.5 | 9.2 | 1.0 | | 4.2 | 4.2 |
| 2005............................ | 73,494 | 67.3 | 23.4 | 7.9 | 4.6 | 10.1 | 0.8 | | 4.8 | 4.5 |
| 2010............................ | 74,718 | 69.4 | 23.1 | 7.1 | 5.1 | 10.1 | 0.8 | | 3.4 | 4.1 |
| 2015............................ | 73,623 | 69.2 | 23.1 | 6.6 | 4.4 | 11.3 | 0.8 | | 3.7 | 3.9 |
| 2018............................ | 73,741 | 69.1 | 22.2 | 6.2 | 4.2 | 10.9 | 0.9 | | 4.4 | 4.3 |
| **WHITE** [4] | | | | | | | | | | |
| 2000............................ | 56,455 | 75.3 | 17.3 | (NA) | (NA) | (NA) | (NA) | | 4.3 | 3.1 |
| 2005............................ | 56,234 | 73.5 | 18.4 | 7.9 | 4.0 | 5.8 | 0.7 | | 4.7 | 3.4 |
| 2010............................ | 56,416 | 74.9 | 18.3 | 6.9 | 4.5 | 6.1 | 0.8 | | 3.5 | 3.4 |
| 2015............................ | 53,621 | 74.9 | 18.2 | 6.6 | 4.0 | 6.7 | 0.8 | | 3.7 | 3.2 |
| 2018............................ | 53,291 | 74.6 | 17.4 | 6.4 | 3.8 | 6.4 | 0.8 | | 4.4 | 3.6 |
| **BLACK** [4] | | | | | | | | | | |
| 2000............................ | 11,412 | 37.6 | 49.0 | (NA) | (NA) | (NA) | (NA) | | 4.2 | 9.2 |
| 2005............................ | 11,293 | 35.0 | 50.2 | 8.7 | 8.1 | 32.0 | 1.3 | | 5.0 | 9.8 |
| 2010............................ | 11,272 | 39.2 | 49.7 | 8.6 | 8.4 | 31.5 | 1.2 | | 3.6 | 7.5 |
| 2015............................ | 11,091 | 38.7 | 49.4 | 7.6 | 6.7 | 33.9 | 1.1 | | 4.2 | 7.7 |
| 2018............................ | 11,044 | 39.7 | 48.1 | 7.0 | 5.7 | 33.9 | 1.4 | | 5.0 | 7.1 |
| **ASIAN** [4] | | | | | | | | | | |
| 2005............................ | 2,843 | 83.6 | 10.2 | 4.0 | 2.3 | 2.7 | 1.3 | | 3.6 | 2.5 |
| 2010............................ | 3,300 | 85.5 | 10.1 | 3.8 | 3.7 | 2.1 | 0.6 | | 2.2 | 2.1 |
| 2015............................ | 3,736 | 85.7 | 10.6 | 2.8 | 3.4 | 3.9 | 0.5 | | 2.0 | 1.7 |
| 2018............................ | 4,004 | 86.8 | 8.5 | 2.7 | 2.9 | 2.1 | 0.8 | | 2.2 | 2.4 |
| **HISPANIC** [5] | | | | | | | | | | |
| 2000............................ | 11,613 | 65.1 | 25.1 | (NA) | (NA) | (NA) | (NA) | | 4.4 | 5.4 |
| 2005............................ | 14,241 | 64.7 | 25.4 | 6.1 | 7.1 | 11.4 | 0.8 | | 4.8 | 5.2 |
| 2010............................ | 16,941 | 67.0 | 26.3 | 5.8 | 8.1 | 11.7 | 0.7 | | 2.7 | 4.0 |
| 2015............................ | 17,981 | 67.0 | 25.9 | 5.3 | 7.1 | 13.0 | 0.6 | | 3.0 | 4.1 |
| 2018............................ | 18,665 | 67.0 | 24.9 | 5.6 | 6.0 | 12.7 | 0.5 | | 4.0 | 4.2 |
| **NON-HISPANIC WHITE** [4] | | | | | | | | | | |
| 2005............................ | 43,106 | 75.9 | 16.4 | 8.5 | 3.1 | 4.2 | 0.7 | | 4.8 | 2.9 |
| 2010............................ | 41,089 | 77.5 | 15.5 | 7.5 | 3.1 | 4.2 | 0.8 | | 3.8 | 3.1 |
| 2015............................ | 38,084 | 77.5 | 15.5 | 7.2 | 2.7 | 4.7 | 0.8 | | 4.1 | 2.9 |
| 2018............................ | 37,244 | 77.2 | 14.7 | 6.8 | 2.7 | 4.3 | 1.0 | | 4.7 | 3.4 |

NA Not available. [1] Beginning in 2007, includes children living both with married and unmarried parents. [2] Includes separated. [3] Includes other races and non-Hispanic groups, not shown separately. [4] Beginning with the 2003 Current Population Survey (CPS), respondents could choose more than one race. Data represents persons who selected this race group only and exclude persons reporting more than one race. Prior to 2003, the CPS allowed respondents to report only one race group. See also comments on race in the text for this section. [5] Hispanic persons may be of any race.

Source: U.S. Census Bureau, America's Families and Living Arrangements, Children (C table series), "Table C3. Living Arrangements of Children Under 18 Years and Marital Status of Parents, by Age, Sex, Race, and Hispanic Origin and Selected Characteristics of the Child for All Children: 2018," <https://www.census.gov/data/tables/2018/demo/families/cps-2018.html>, accessed December 2018, and earlier releases.

# Table 69. Grandparents Living With Grandchildren by Race, Hispanic Origin, and Sex: 2017

[In thousands (7,245 represents 7,245,000), except percent. Covers both grandparents living in own home with grandchildren present and grandparents living in grandchildren's home. The American Community Survey universe includes the household population and the population living in institutions, college dormitories, and other group quarters. Based on a sample and subject to sampling variability; see Appendix III]

| Race, Hispanic origin, and sex | Grandparents living with own grandchildren, total | Grandparents responsible for grandchildren | | |
|---|---|---|---|---|
| | | Total | 30 to 59 years old | 60 years old and over |
| **Grandparents living with own grandchildren under 18 years old (1,000)**............ | **7,245** | **2,417** | **1,337** | **1,080** |
| PERCENT DISTRIBUTION | | | | |
| Total.......................................... | 100.0 | 100.0 | 100.0 | 100.0 |
| One race..................................... | 98.0 | 98.1 | 97.8 | 98.4 |
| White alone................................ | 62.8 | 66.6 | 66.2 | 67.2 |
| Black or African American alone........... | 16.0 | 19.5 | 20.3 | 18.5 |
| American Indian and Alaska Native alone.............. | 1.6 | 2.4 | 2.4 | 2.3 |
| Asian alone................................ | 9.1 | 3.9 | 2.2 | 6.0 |
| Native Hawaiian and Other Pacific Islander alone...... | 0.3 | 0.3 | 0.3 | 0.3 |
| Some other race alone...................... | 8.2 | 5.4 | 6.6 | 4.0 |
| Two or more races.......................... | 2.0 | 1.9 | 2.2 | 1.6 |
| Hispanic origin [1]......................... | 26.2 | 19.6 | 22.6 | 15.9 |
| White alone, not Hispanic.................. | 46.0 | 53.5 | 51.3 | 56.1 |
| Male........................................ | 36.3 | 36.4 | 32.7 | 41.0 |
| Female...................................... | 63.7 | 63.6 | 67.3 | 59.0 |

[1] Persons of Hispanic origin may be of any race.

Source: U.S. Census Bureau, 2017 American Community Survey, S1002, "Grandparents," <http://factfinder.census.gov/>, accessed November 2018.

# Table 70. Group Quarters Population by Type of Group Quarter and Selected Resident Characteristics: 2017

[In percent, except as indicated. The American Community Survey universe includes the household population and the population living in institutions, college dormitories, and other group quarters. Based on a sample and subject to sampling variability]

| Characteristic | Total group quarters population [1] | Institutionalized group quarters population | | | Noninstitutionalized group quarters population | |
|---|---|---|---|---|---|---|
| | | Total [1] | Adult correctional facilities | Nursing facilities/ skilled nursing facilities | Total [1] | College/ university housing |
| **Total population**....... | **8,087,237** | **3,895,419** | **2,176,356** | **1,497,488** | **4,191,818** | **2,702,374** |
| PERCENT DISTRIBUTION | | | | | | |
| Male........ | 60.6 | 68.9 | 90.9 | 36.4 | 53.0 | 45.3 |
| Female....... | 39.4 | 31.1 | 9.1 | 63.6 | 47.0 | 54.7 |
| Under 15 years old........ | 0.9 | 1.1 | (X) | (X) | 0.7 | (X) |
| 15 to 17 years old........ | 1.7 | 2.5 | 0.2 | (X) | 1.0 | 1.0 |
| 18 to 24 years old........ | 41.3 | 8.2 | 13.1 | 0.2 | 72.1 | 96.8 |
| 25 to 34 years old........ | 12.7 | 18.7 | 32.6 | 0.6 | 7.0 | 1.9 |
| 35 to 44 years old........ | 9.6 | 15.3 | 26.0 | 1.2 | 4.3 | 0.2 |
| 45 to 54 years old........ | 7.9 | 11.3 | 17.2 | 3.7 | 4.7 | 0.1 |
| 55 to 64 years old........ | 6.9 | 9.2 | 8.4 | 11.0 | 4.8 | – |
| 65 to 74 years old........ | 5.4 | 8.7 | 2.1 | 19.2 | 2.4 | – |
| 75 to 84 years old........ | 5.6 | 10.0 | 0.4 | 25.3 | 1.5 | (X) |
| 85 years old and over........ | 8.0 | 15.0 | 0.1 | 38.8 | 1.5 | (X) |
| Median age (years)........ | 29.4 | 48.5 | 36.3 | 81.0 | 20.5 | 19.6 |
| One race........ | 100.0 | 100.0 | 100.0 | 100.0 | 100.0 | 100.0 |
| White........ | 67.6 | 63.7 | 52.5 | 80.8 | 71.3 | 73.6 |
| Black........ | 23.1 | 29.1 | 38.2 | 15.4 | 17.4 | 14.3 |
| American Indian and Alaska Native........ | 1.1 | 1.5 | 2.1 | 0.6 | 0.8 | 0.4 |
| Asian........ | 4.5 | 1.2 | 0.9 | 1.6 | 7.5 | 9.6 |
| Native Hawaiian/Pacific Islander........ | 0.2 | 0.2 | 0.3 | 0.1 | 0.3 | 0.2 |
| Some other race........ | 3.5 | 4.2 | 6.0 | 1.5 | 2.7 | 1.9 |
| Hispanic origin [2]........ | 13.5 | 14.7 | 20.6 | 5.4 | 12.3 | 10.4 |
| Not Hispanic........ | 86.5 | 85.3 | 79.4 | 94.6 | 87.7 | 89.6 |
| White alone, not Hispanic........ | 56.7 | 52.8 | 37.9 | 76.3 | 60.3 | 63.1 |

– Represents or rounds to zero. X Not applicable. [1] Includes other types of group quarters, not shown separately. [2] Persons of Hispanic origin may be of any race.

Source: U.S. Census Bureau, 2017 American Community Survey, S2601A, "Characteristics of the Group Quarters Population"; and S2602, "Characteristics of the Group Quarters Population by Group Quarters Type (3 Types)"; <http://factfinder.census.gov/>, accessed December 2018.

# Table 71. Population in Group Quarters by State: 2000 to 2018

[In thousands (7,780 represents 7,780,000). 2000 and 2010, as of April. 2017 and 2018, as of July. All persons not living in housing units are classified as living in group quarters. These individuals may be institutionalized, e.g., under care or custody in juvenile facilities, jails, correctional centers, hospitals, or nursing homes; or they may be residents in noninstitutional group quarters such as college dormitories, group homes, or military barracks]

| State | 2000 [1] | 2010 [2] | 2017 | 2018 | State | 2000 [1] | 2010 [2] | 2017 | 2018 |
|---|---|---|---|---|---|---|---|---|---|
| **United States........** | **7,780** | **7,999** | **8,087** | **8,092** | Missouri............ | 164 | 174 | 175 | 174 |
| Alabama............ | 115 | 116 | 117 | 117 | Montana............ | 25 | 29 | 29 | 29 |
| Alaska............ | 19 | 26 | 27 | 27 | Nebraska............ | 51 | 51 | 52 | 51 |
| Arizona............ | 110 | 140 | 155 | 159 | Nevada............ | 34 | 36 | 38 | 38 |
| Arkansas............ | 74 | 79 | 84 | 84 | New Hampshire.... | 36 | 40 | 43 | 43 |
| California............ | 820 | 820 | 820 | 826 | New Jersey......... | 195 | 187 | 183 | 182 |
| Colorado............ | 103 | 116 | 121 | 121 | New Mexico........ | 36 | 43 | 43 | 43 |
| Connecticut............ | 108 | 118 | 113 | 113 | New York............ | 581 | 586 | 573 | 573 |
| Delaware............ | 25 | 24 | 25 | 25 | North Carolina...... | 254 | 257 | 276 | 275 |
| District of Columbia.... | 36 | 40 | 40 | 40 | North Dakota....... | 24 | 25 | 25 | 25 |
| Florida............ | 389 | 425 | 432 | 430 | Ohio............ | 299 | 306 | 318 | 316 |
| Georgia............ | 234 | 254 | 259 | 265 | Oklahoma.......... | 112 | 112 | 110 | 110 |
| Hawaii............ | 36 | 43 | 44 | 44 | Oregon............ | 77 | 87 | 88 | 88 |
| Idaho............ | 31 | 29 | 30 | 30 | Pennsylvania....... | 433 | 427 | 422 | 422 |
| Illinois............ | 322 | 302 | 297 | 297 | Rhode Island....... | 39 | 43 | 42 | 41 |
| Indiana............ | 178 | 187 | 187 | 188 | South Carolina..... | 135 | 139 | 137 | 136 |
| Iowa............ | 104 | 99 | 99 | 99 | South Dakota...... | 28 | 34 | 34 | 34 |
| Kansas............ | 82 | 79 | 80 | 80 | Tennessee......... | 148 | 154 | 157 | 157 |
| Kentucky............ | 115 | 126 | 132 | 132 | Texas............ | 561 | 582 | 601 | 600 |
| Louisiana............ | 136 | 128 | 130 | 129 | Utah............ | 40 | 46 | 48 | 48 |
| Maine............ | 35 | 36 | 36 | 36 | Vermont............ | 21 | 25 | 25 | 26 |
| Maryland............ | 134 | 139 | 140 | 140 | Virginia............ | 231 | 240 | 243 | 245 |
| Massachusetts........ | 221 | 239 | 249 | 248 | Washington........ | 136 | 139 | 143 | 143 |
| Michigan............ | 250 | 230 | 230 | 226 | West Virginia....... | 43 | 49 | 48 | 48 |
| Minnesota............ | 136 | 135 | 132 | 131 | Wisconsin.......... | 156 | 151 | 145 | 145 |
| Mississippi............ | 95 | 93 | 98 | 98 | Wyoming............ | 14 | 14 | 14 | 14 |

[1] The April 1, 2000, population estimates base reflects changes to the Census 2000 population from the Count Question Resolution program and geographic program revisions. [2] The April 1, 2010 population estimates base reflects changes to the Census 2010 population from the Count Question Resolution program and geographic program revisions.

Source: U.S. Census Bureau, "Annual Resident Population Estimates, Estimated Components of Resident Population Change, and Rates of the Components of Resident Population Change for States and Counties: April 1, 2000 to July 1, 2009"; and "Population, population change and estimated components of population change: April 1, 2010 to July 1, 2018 (CO-EST2018-alldata)," <https://www.census.gov/data/tables/time-series/demo/popest/2010s-counties-total.html>, accessed June 2019.

# Table 72. Opposite-Sex and Same-Sex Couple Households by Selected Characteristics: 2017

[In percent, except as indicated (57,292 represents 57,292,000). The American Community Survey universe includes the household population and the population living in institutions, college dormitories, and other group quarters. Based on a sample and subject to sampling variability. See text, this section and Appendix III]

| Characteristic | Married opposite-sex couples | Unmarried opposite-sex couples | Married and unmarried same-sex couples | | | Married same-sex couples |
| --- | --- | --- | --- | --- | --- | --- |
| | | | Total | Male-male couples | Female-female couples | |
| **Total households (1,000)**.......................... | **57,292** | **6,986** | **935** | **451** | **484** | **555** |
| Age of householder: | | | | | | |
| 15 to 24 years old........................... | 1.1 | 11.1 | 4.3 | 3.3 | 5.4 | 2.0 |
| 25 to 34 years old........................... | 12.9 | 35.0 | 19.5 | 17.8 | 21.1 | 15.3 |
| 35 to 44 years old........................... | 19.7 | 21.0 | 20.0 | 19.3 | 20.7 | 20.0 |
| 45 to 54 years old........................... | 21.3 | 15.5 | 21.2 | 23.0 | 19.6 | 22.1 |
| 55 to 64 years old........................... | 21.4 | 10.6 | 19.3 | 20.2 | 18.4 | 21.4 |
| 65 years old and over........................ | 23.6 | 6.7 | 15.6 | 16.5 | 14.9 | 19.2 |
| Average age of householder (years)............... | 52.4 | 39.6 | 48.0 | 48.9 | 47.1 | 50.7 |
| Average age of spouse/partner (years)............... | 51.7 | 38.8 | 46.4 | 46.6 | 46.1 | 49.3 |
| Race of householder: | | | | | | |
| White........................................ | 81.0 | 76.6 | 82.5 | 84.7 | 80.5 | 84.1 |
| Black or African American.................... | 7.0 | 10.9 | 7.4 | 5.4 | 9.3 | 6.4 |
| American Indian or Alaska Native.................... | 0.6 | 1.1 | 0.7 | 0.6 | 0.9 | 0.7 |
| Asian........................................ | 6.0 | 2.6 | 3.2 | 3.6 | 2.8 | 3.5 |
| Native Hawaiian or Pacific Islander................. | 0.1 | 0.2 | 0.2 | 0.1 | 0.2 | 0.1 |
| Some other race............................. | 3.5 | 5.6 | 2.9 | 2.5 | 3.1 | 2.5 |
| Two or more races........................... | 1.7 | 3.0 | 3.1 | 3.0 | 3.2 | 2.6 |
| Percent of couples interracial.................. | 7.4 | 14.3 | 16.0 | 18.3 | 13.9 | 13.8 |
| Hispanic origin of householder: | | | | | | |
| Hispanic [1]................................... | 13.1 | 18.3 | 12.8 | 12.7 | 12.8 | 11.8 |
| White alone, not Hispanic.................... | 72.0 | 65.0 | 73.8 | 75.6 | 72.1 | 75.8 |
| Children in the household: | | | | | | |
| Children in the household [2]................... | 38.9 | 38.2 | 16.4 | 8.5 | 23.8 | 18.8 |
| Own children in the household................. | 38.8 | 35.6 | 15.6 | 8.3 | 22.4 | 18.7 |
| Household Income: | | | | | | |
| Less than $35,000........................... | 12.6 | 20.9 | 13.0 | 10.4 | 15.4 | 12.0 |
| $35,000 to $49,999.......................... | 10.3 | 14.6 | 9.3 | 7.7 | 10.7 | 7.9 |
| $50,000 to $74,999.......................... | 18.0 | 22.2 | 17.1 | 15.1 | 18.9 | 15.7 |
| $75,000 to $99,999.......................... | 15.9 | 15.9 | 15.0 | 14.3 | 15.7 | 14.9 |
| $100,000 or more............................ | 43.3 | 26.4 | 45.7 | 52.4 | 39.3 | 49.5 |
| Median household income (dollars).................. | 88,683 | 65,594 | 92,225 | 104,130 | 82,063 | 98,889 |
| Housing tenure: | | | | | | |
| Owner occupied.............................. | 79.8 | 44.3 | 66.2 | 68.2 | 64.3 | 73.6 |
| Renter occupied............................. | 20.2 | 55.7 | 33.8 | 31.8 | 35.7 | 26.4 |

[1] Persons of Hispanic origin may be of any race. [2] Includes biological children, stepchildren, adopted children, and nonrelatives of the householder under 18 years old.

Source: U.S. Census Bureau, 2017 American Community Survey, "Characteristics of Same-Sex Couple Households: 2005 to Present," <https://www.census.gov/topics/families/same-sex-couples/data/tables.html>, accessed February 2019.

# Table 73. Opposite Sex Unmarried Couples by Presence of Biological Children: 2018

[In thousands (8,522 represents 8,522,000), except percent. As of March. Excludes members of Armed Forces except those living off post or with their families on post. All opposite-sex unmarried couples are included, regardless of householder status. Unmarried couples of the opposite sex with children under 18 years old are included in the estimates if either partner had at least one never-married biological child living with them. Population controls based on Census 2010. Based on Current Population Survey; see text, this section and Appendix III]

| Sex and age of partner | Unmarried couples, total | Without children under 18 years old | With children under 18 years old | |
| --- | --- | --- | --- | --- |
| | | | Number | Percent of total |
| **Total**.............................................. | **8,522** | **5,494** | **3,028** | **35.5** |
| Age of male partner: | | | | |
| 15 to 24 years old............................ | 1,101 | 777 | 324 | 29.4 |
| 25 to 29 years old............................ | 1,724 | 1,117 | 607 | 35.2 |
| 30 to 34 years old............................ | 1,315 | 674 | 642 | 48.8 |
| 35 to 39 years old............................ | 955 | 394 | 562 | 58.8 |
| 40 to 44 years old............................ | 754 | 350 | 404 | 53.6 |
| 45 to 49 years old............................ | 633 | 360 | 273 | 43.1 |
| 50 to 54 years old............................ | 595 | 459 | 136 | 22.9 |
| 55 to 64 years old............................ | 853 | 786 | 68 | 8.0 |
| 65 years old and over........................ | 590 | 577 | 13 | 2.2 |
| Age of female partner: | | | | |
| 15 to 24 years old............................ | 1,570 | 1,070 | 500 | 31.8 |
| 25 to 29 years old............................ | 1,844 | 1,151 | 693 | 37.6 |
| 30 to 34 years old............................ | 1,250 | 611 | 639 | 51.1 |
| 35 to 39 years old............................ | 885 | 313 | 571 | 64.5 |
| 40 to 44 years old............................ | 635 | 286 | 349 | 55.0 |
| 45 to 49 years old............................ | 576 | 386 | 191 | 33.2 |
| 50 to 54 years old............................ | 471 | 420 | 51 | 10.8 |
| 55 to 64 years old............................ | 838 | 819 | 19 | 2.3 |
| 65 years old and over........................ | 452 | 436 | 16 | 3.5 |

Source: U.S. Census Bureau, America's Families and Living Arrangements, Unmarried couples (UC table series), "Table UC3. Opposite Sex Unmarried Couples by Presence of Biological Children under 18, and Age, Earnings, Education, and Race send Hispanic Origin of Both Partners," <https://www.census.gov/data/tables/2018/demo/families/cps-2018.html>, accessed December 2018.

# Table 74. Opposite and Same-Sex Unmarried-Partner Households by Region: 2017

[120,063 represents 120,063,000. The American Community Survey universe includes the household population and the population living in institutions, college dormitories, and other group quarters. For composition of regions, see map inside front cover. Based on a sample and subject to sampling variability; see text, this section and Appendix III]

| Item | Total (1,000s) | | | | | Percent distribution | | | | |
|---|---|---|---|---|---|---|---|---|---|---|
| | Total | North-east | Midwest | South | West | Total | North-east | Midwest | South | West |
| **Total households............** | **120,063** | **21,229** | **26,662** | **45,210** | **26,962** | **100.0** | **100.0** | **100.0** | **100.0** | **100.0** |
| Unmarried-partner households.... | 7,365 | 1,327 | 1,730 | 2,501 | 1,807 | 6.1 | 6.3 | 6.5 | 5.5 | 6.7 |
| Male householder and male partner............................. | 189 | 34 | 34 | 68 | 54 | 0.2 | 0.2 | 0.1 | 0.1 | 0.2 |
| Male householder and female partner............................. | 3,571 | 631 | 854 | 1,219 | 867 | 3.0 | 3.0 | 3.2 | 2.7 | 3.2 |
| Female householder and female partner............................. | 191 | 34 | 40 | 69 | 47 | 0.2 | 0.2 | 0.2 | 0.2 | 0.2 |
| Female householder and male partner............................. | 3,415 | 628 | 802 | 1,145 | 840 | 2.8 | 3.0 | 3.0 | 2.5 | 3.1 |
| All other households............... | 112,698 | 19,902 | 24,932 | 42,709 | 25,154 | 93.9 | 93.7 | 93.5 | 94.5 | 93.3 |

Source: U.S. Census Bureau, 2017 American Community Survey, B11009, "Unmarried-Partner Households by Sex of Partner," <http://factfinder.census.gov/>, accessed December 2018.

# Table 75. Young Adults Living in Parental Home by Sex and Age: 1990 to 2018

[In thousands (12,450 represents 12,450,000), except percent. As of March. Excludes members of Armed Forces except those living off post or with their families on post. Unmarried college students living in dormitories are counted as living in the home of their parent(s). Beginning 2005, based on an expanded sample of households. Population controls for 2005 to 2010 based on Census 2000; beginning 2011, population controls based on Census 2010. Based on Current Population Survey; see text, this section and Appendix III]

| Year | Male young adults | | | Female young adults | | |
|---|---|---|---|---|---|---|
| | | Child of householder living at home | | | Child of householder living at home | |
| | Total | Number | Percent of total | Total | Number | Percent of total |
| **18 TO 24 YEARS OLD** | | | | | | |
| 1990........................ | 12,450 | 7,232 | 58.1 | 12,860 | 6,135 | 47.7 |
| 1995........................ | 12,545 | 7,328 | 58.4 | 12,613 | 5,896 | 46.7 |
| 2000........................ | 13,291 | 7,593 | 57.1 | 13,242 | 6,232 | 47.1 |
| 2005........................ | 14,060 | 7,448 | 53.0 | 13,933 | 6,413 | 46.0 |
| 2010........................ | 14,824 | 8,501 | 57.3 | 14,469 | 7,123 | 49.2 |
| 2014........................ | 15,280 | 8,892 | 58.2 | 14,852 | 7,645 | 51.5 |
| 2015........................ | 15,123 | 8,808 | 58.2 | 14,893 | 7,714 | 51.8 |
| 2016........................ | 15,023 | 8,875 | 59.1 | 14,646 | 7,664 | 52.3 |
| 2017........................ | 14,777 | 8,518 | 57.6 | 14,488 | 7,518 | 51.9 |
| 2018........................ | 14,837 | 8,573 | 57.8 | 14,510 | 7,534 | 51.9 |
| **25 TO 34 YEARS OLD** | | | | | | |
| 1990........................ | 21,462 | 3,213 | 15.0 | 21,779 | 1,774 | 8.1 |
| 1995........................ | 20,589 | 3,166 | 15.4 | 20,800 | 1,759 | 8.5 |
| 2000........................ | 18,563 | 2,387 | 12.9 | 19,222 | 1,602 | 8.3 |
| 2005........................ | 19,656 | 2,660 | 13.5 | 19,632 | 1,597 | 8.1 |
| 2010........................ | 20,685 | 3,387 | 16.4 | 20,383 | 2,133 | 10.5 |
| 2014........................ | 21,186 | 3,755 | 17.7 | 21,219 | 2,478 | 11.7 |
| 2015........................ | 21,417 | 3,896 | 18.2 | 21,574 | 2,613 | 12.1 |
| 2016........................ | 21,839 | 4,284 | 19.6 | 21,912 | 2,736 | 12.5 |
| 2017........................ | 22,105 | 4,333 | 19.6 | 22,123 | 2,775 | 12.5 |
| 2018........................ | 22,477 | 4,669 | 20.8 | 22,355 | 2,868 | 12.8 |

Source: U.S. Census Bureau, America's Families and Living Arrangements, Historical Living Arrangements of Adults, "Table AD-1. Young Adults, 18-34 Years Old, Living At Home: 1960 to Present," <https://www.census.gov/data/tables/time-series/demo/families/adults.html>, accessed December 2018.

# Table 76. Children of Householders by Age and Whether Biological, Adopted, and Stepchildren: 2010

[88,820 represents 88,820,000. As of April. Includes children of the householder regardless of marital status and excludes persons under age 18 who are not children of the householder. Includes Puerto Rico. Based on 2010 Census of Population; see Appendix III]

| Type of relationship | | Under 18 years old | | | | | 18 years old and over | | |
|---|---|---|---|---|---|---|---|---|---|
| | Total | Total | Under 6 years old | 6 to 11 years old | 12 to 14 years old | 15 to 17 years old | Total | 18 to 24 years old | 25 years old and over |
| **NUMBER (1,000)** | | | | | | | | | |
| **Total children of householders..** | **88,820** | **64,778** | **20,277** | **21,903** | **11,188** | **11,410** | **24,042** | **13,649** | **10,393** |
| Adopted children........................ | 2,072 | 1,527 | 351 | 569 | 304 | 303 | 545 | 325 | 220 |
| Stepchildren.............................. | 4,166 | 2,785 | 284 | 978 | 718 | 806 | 1,381 | 889 | 492 |
| Biological children..................... | 82,582 | 60,467 | 19,643 | 20,356 | 10,166 | 10,301 | 22,115 | 12,435 | 9,681 |
| **PERCENT DISTRIBUTION** | | | | | | | | | |
| Total children of householders..... | 100.0 | 100.0 | 100.0 | 100.0 | 100.0 | 100.0 | 100.0 | 100.0 | 100.0 |
| Adopted children........................ | 2.3 | 2.4 | 1.7 | 2.6 | 2.7 | 2.7 | 2.3 | 2.4 | 2.1 |
| Stepchildren.............................. | 4.7 | 4.3 | 1.4 | 4.5 | 6.4 | 7.1 | 5.7 | 6.5 | 4.7 |
| Biological children..................... | 93.0 | 93.3 | 96.9 | 92.9 | 90.9 | 90.3 | 92.0 | 91.1 | 93.1 |

Source: U.S. Census Bureau, *Adopted Children and Stepchildren: 2010*, Current Population Reports, P20-572, April 2014. See also <https://www.census.gov/content/census/en/library/publications/2014/demo/p20-572.html>.

# Table 77. Children in Households by Relationship to Householder: 2010 to 2017

[In thousands (73,904 represents 73,904,000). Data shown for population under age 18 in households, excluding householders, spouses, and unmarried partners. Based on a sample and subject to sampling variability; see text this section and Appendix III]

| Type of relationship | 2010 | 2011 | 2012 | 2013 | 2014 | 2015 | 2016 | 2017 |
|---|---|---|---|---|---|---|---|---|
| **NUMBER** | | | | | | | | |
| **Total children in households**............. | **73,904** | **73,650** | **73,462** | **73,336** | **73,325** | **73,386** | **73,399** | **73,403** |
| Own child........................... | 65,472 | 65,214 | 64,953 | 64,595 | 64,426 | 64,445 | 64,392 | 64,367 |
| Biological child.......................... | 61,540 | 61,392 | 61,139 | 60,766 | 60,628 | 60,632 | 60,564 | 60,518 |
| Adopted child............................ | 1,582 | 1,546 | 1,520 | 1,496 | 1,447 | 1,423 | 1,428 | 1,439 |
| Stepchild................................ | 2,351 | 2,276 | 2,293 | 2,332 | 2,351 | 2,391 | 2,400 | 2,410 |
| Grandchild................................. | 5,397 | 5,499 | 5,603 | 5,712 | 5,830 | 5,887 | 5,964 | 5,957 |
| Other relatives........................... | 1,826 | 1,768 | 1,732 | 1,738 | 1,792 | 1,793 | 1,762 | 1,803 |
| Foster child or other unrelated child....... | 1,209 | 1,168 | 1,175 | 1,292 | 1,277 | 1,261 | 1,280 | 1,276 |
| **PERCENT DISTRIBUTION** | | | | | | | | |
| Total children in households................. | 100.0 | 100.0 | 100.0 | 100.0 | 100.0 | 100.0 | 100.0 | 100.0 |
| Own child........................... | 88.6 | 88.5 | 88.4 | 88.1 | 87.9 | 87.8 | 87.7 | 87.7 |
| Biological child.......................... | 83.3 | 83.4 | 83.2 | 82.9 | 82.7 | 82.6 | 82.5 | 82.4 |
| Adopted child............................ | 2.1 | 2.1 | 2.1 | 2.0 | 2.0 | 1.9 | 1.9 | 2.0 |
| Stepchild................................ | 3.2 | 3.1 | 3.1 | 3.2 | 3.2 | 3.3 | 3.3 | 3.3 |
| Grandchild................................. | 7.3 | 7.5 | 7.6 | 7.8 | 8.0 | 8.0 | 8.1 | 8.1 |
| Other relatives........................... | 2.5 | 2.4 | 2.4 | 2.4 | 2.4 | 2.4 | 2.4 | 2.5 |
| Foster child or other unrelated child....... | 1.6 | 1.6 | 1.6 | 1.8 | 1.7 | 1.7 | 1.7 | 1.7 |

Source: U.S. Census Bureau, American Community Survey, B09018, "Relationship to Householder for Children Under 18 in Households," <https://factfinder.census.gov>, accessed December 2018.

# Table 78. Living Arrangements of Young Adults by Selected Characteristics: 2015

[In thousands (15,795 represents 15,795,000), except as noted. Based on the American Community Survey; see Appendix III]

| Characteristics | Young adults aged 18 to 24 | | | | Young adults aged 25 to 34 | | | |
|---|---|---|---|---|---|---|---|---|
| | Living in parents' home [1] | | Living independ-ently [2] | Living with room-mates [3] | Living in parents' home [1] | | Living independ-ently [2] | Living with room-mates [3] |
| | Number | Percent | | | Number | Percent | | |
| **Total**................................. | **15,795** | **100.0** | **4,458** | **7,757** | **8,382** | **100.0** | **24,362** | **10,118** |
| By sex: | | | | | | | | |
| Female................................. | 7,317 | 46.3 | 2,587 | 3,851 | 3,679 | 43.9 | 12,662 | 5,252 |
| Male.................................... | 8,479 | 53.7 | 1,871 | 3,907 | 4,702 | 56.1 | 11,700 | 4,866 |
| By race/ethnicity: | | | | | | | | |
| White alone, non-Hispanic............ | 8,148 | 51.6 | 2,852 | 4,054 | 4,192 | 50.0 | 15,525 | 4,702 |
| Black alone, non-Hispanic............ | 2,350 | 14.9 | 463 | 1,203 | 1,428 | 17.0 | 2,168 | 1,837 |
| Asian alone, non-Hispanic............ | 769 | 4.9 | 137 | 534 | 571 | 6.8 | 1,554 | 750 |
| Other race, non-Hispanic.............. | 665 | 4.2 | 179 | 338 | 326 | 3.9 | 746 | 365 |
| Hispanic [4]............................. | 3,864 | 24.5 | 828 | 1,628 | 1,864 | 22.2 | 4,369 | 2,464 |
| Has a disability [5]...................... | 1,044 | 6.6 | 224 | 413 | 904 | 10.8 | 1,019 | 630 |
| Work status: | | | | | | | | |
| Employed.............................. | 9,033 | 57.2 | 3,399 | 4,981 | 5,778 | 68.9 | 19,869 | 7,863 |
| Worked full-time, year-round........ | 2,813 | 17.8 | 2,109 | 2,174 | 3,651 | 43.6 | 15,557 | 5,617 |
| Mean hours worked per week....... | 29.9 | (X) | 38.3 | 33.3 | 37.1 | (X) | 41.6 | 39.5 |
| Unemployed........................... | 1,594 | 10.1 | 247 | 643 | 851 | 10.2 | 830 | 682 |
| Not in labor force...................... | 5,168 | 32.7 | 812 | 2,133 | 1,752 | 20.9 | 3,662 | 1,573 |
| Educational attainment: | | | | | | | | |
| High school diploma or less........... | 7,850 | 49.7 | 1,681 | 3,209 | 3,474 | 41.4 | 6,834 | 4,044 |
| Associate's degree or some college | 6,632 | 42.0 | 1,930 | 3,544 | 2,840 | 33.9 | 7,563 | 3,211 |
| Bachelor's degree or higher.......... | 1,312 | 8.3 | 848 | 1,004 | 2,068 | 24.7 | 9,965 | 2,864 |
| Enrolled in school...................... | 8,463 | 53.6 | 1,198 | 3,586 | 1,276 | 15.2 | 2,564 | 1,425 |
| Personal income: [6] | | | | | | | | |
| $0 to $29,999........................... | 14,973 | 94.8 | 3,416 | 6,917 | 6,247 | 74.6 | 10,998 | 6,402 |
| $30,000 to $59,999..................... | 736 | 4.7 | 885 | 715 | 1,730 | 20.7 | 8,292 | 2,706 |
| $60,000 to $99,999..................... | 71 | 0.4 | 135 | 101 | 336 | 4.0 | 3,653 | 806 |
| $100,000 or more...................... | 13 | 0.1 | 22 | 23 | 65 | 0.8 | 1,408 | 201 |
| Housing type: | | | | | | | | |
| Single-family home.................... | 12,512 | 79.2 | 1,628 | 3,975 | 6,687 | 79.8 | 14,531 | 5,478 |
| Apartment or multifamily building..... | 2,421 | 15.3 | 2,507 | 3,391 | 1,233 | 14.7 | 8,610 | 4,136 |
| Other housing type..................... | 863 | 5.5 | 324 | 391 | 462 | 5.5 | 1,222 | 504 |
| Lived at same address a year ago.... | 14,127 | 89.4 | 2,158 | 4,506 | 7,341 | 87.6 | 18,005 | 7,178 |
| Tenure: | | | | | | | | |
| Own home............................. | 10,831 | 68.6 | 802 | 2,459 | 6,230 | 74.3 | 10,918 | 3,439 |
| Rent home............................. | 4,965 | 31.4 | 3,656 | 5,298 | 2,152 | 25.7 | 13,444 | 6,679 |

X Not applicable. [1] Child of the householder, regardless of the young adult's marital status. [2] The young adult lives alone, or is the householder living with a spouse or unmarried partner, or is the spouse or unmarried partner of the householder. [3] Living with other relatives or nonrelatives. [4] Persons of Hispanic origin may be of any race. [5] "Has a disability" means the young adult reported having at least one of the following six types of disabilities: hearing, vision, cognitive, ambulatory, self-care, or independent living difficulty. [6] Excludes young adults with incomes less than $0.

Source: U.S. Census Bureau, *The Changing Economics and Demographics of Young Adulthood: 1975-2016*, Current Population Reports, P20-579, April 2017. See also <https://www.census.gov/topics/families.html>.

# Table 79. Self-Described Religious Identification of Adult Population: 1990, 2001, and 2008

[In thousands (175,440 represents 175,440,000). The methodology of the American Religious Identification Survey (ARIS) 2008 replicated that used in previous surveys. The three surveys are based on random-digit-dialing telephone surveys of residential households in the continental U.S. (48 states): 54,461 interviews in 2008; 50,281 in 2001; and 113,723 in 1990. Respondents were asked to describe themselves in terms of religion with an open-ended question. Interviewers did not prompt or offer a suggested list of potential answers. Moreover, the self-description of respondents was not based on whether established religious bodies, institutions, churches, mosques or synagogues considered them to be members. Instead, the surveys sought to determine whether the respondents regarded themselves as adherents of a religious community. Subjective rather than objective standards of religious identification were tapped by the surveys]

| Religious group | 1990 | 2001 | 2008 |
|---|---|---|---|
| Adult population, total [1] | 175,440 | 207,983 | 228,182 |
| Christian, total [2] | 151,225 | 159,514 | 173,402 |
| Catholic | 46,004 | 50,873 | 57,199 |
| Baptist | 33,964 | 33,820 | 36,148 |
| Methodist | 14,174 | 14,039 | 11,366 |
| Lutheran | 9,110 | 9,580 | 8,674 |
| Presbyterian | 4,985 | 5,596 | 4,723 |
| Episcopalian/Anglican | 3,043 | 3,451 | 2,405 |
| Orthodox (Eastern) | 502 | 645 | 824 |
| United Church of Christ | 438 | 1,378 | 736 |
| Disciples of Christ | 144 | 492 | 263 |
| Reformed/Dutch Reform | 161 | 289 | 206 |
| Quaker | 67 | 217 | 130 |
| Christian unspecified | 8,073 | 14,190 | 16,834 |
| Nondenominational Christian [3] | 194 | 2,489 | 8,032 |
| Protestant unspecified | 17,214 | 4,647 | 5,187 |
| Evangelical/Born Again [3] | 546 | 1,088 | 2,154 |
| Independent Christian Church | 25 | 71 | 86 |
| Pentecostal unspecified | 3,116 | 4,407 | 5,416 |
| Assemblies of God | 617 | 1,105 | 810 |
| Church of God | 590 | 943 | 663 |
| Holiness/Holy | 610 | 569 | 352 |
| Church of the Nazarene | 549 | 544 | 358 |
| Foursquare Gospel | 28 | 70 | 116 |
| Churches of Christ | 1,769 | 2,593 | 1,921 |
| Jehovah's Witness | 1,381 | 1,331 | 1,914 |
| Apostolic/New Apostolic | 117 | 254 | 970 |
| Seventh-day Adventist | 668 | 724 | 938 |
| Mennonite | 235 | 346 | 438 |
| Christian Reform | 40 | 79 | 381 |
| Christian Science | 214 | 194 | 339 |
| Church of the Brethren | 206 | 358 | 231 |
| Mormon/Latter-day Saints [4] | 2,487 | 2,697 | 3,158 |
| Other Christian [4] | 105 | 254 | 206 |
| **Other religions, total [2]** | **5,853** | **7,740** | **8,796** |
| Jewish | 3,137 | 2,837 | 2,680 |
| Buddhist | 404 | 1,082 | 1,189 |
| Hindu | 227 | 766 | 582 |
| Sikh | 13 | 57 | 78 |
| Muslim | 527 | 1,104 | 1,349 |
| Unitarian/Universalist | 502 | 629 | 586 |
| Spiritualist | (NA) | 116 | 426 |
| Wiccan | 8 | 134 | 342 |
| Pagan | (NA) | 140 | 340 |
| Native American | 47 | 103 | 186 |
| Other unclassified [4] | 991 | 774 | 1,030 |
| **No religion specified, total [2]** | **14,331** | **29,481** | **34,169** |
| Agnostic | [5] 1,186 | 991 | 1,985 |
| Atheist | (5) | 902 | 1,621 |
| Humanist | 29 | 49 | 90 |
| No Religion | 13,116 | 27,486 | 30,427 |
| Other No Religion [4] | (NA) | 57 | 45 |
| **Refused to reply to question** | **4,031** | **11,246** | **11,815** |

NA Not available. [1] Refers to the total number of adults in all fifty states. All other figures are based on projections from surveys conducted in the continental United States (48 states). [2] Includes other groups, not shown separately. [3] Because of the subjective nature of replies to open-ended questions, these categories are the most unstable as they do not refer to clearly identifiable denominations as much as underlying feelings about religion. Thus they may be the most subject to fluctuation over time. [4] Estimates for subpopulations smaller than 75,000 adults are aggregated to minimize sampling errors. [5] Atheist included in Agnostic.

Source: 1990 data, Barry A. Kosmin and Seymour P. Lachman, "One Nation Under God: Religion in Contemporary American Society, 1993;" 2001 data, Barry A. Kosmin and Ariela Keysar, *Religion in A Free Market: Religious and Non-Religious Americans, Who, What, Why, Where*, 2006; and 2008 data, Barry A. Kosmin & Ariela Keysar, *American Religious Identification Survey (ARIS 2008) Summary Report*, 2009, Institute for the Study of Secularism in Society and Culture, Trinity College, Hartford, CT <http://www.trincoll.edu/Academics/centers/ISSSC/Pages/ARIS-Data-Archive.aspx> and <www.AmericanReligionSurvey-ARIS.org> ©.

# Table 80. Religious Adherents and Jewish Population—States: 2010 to 2011

[137,450 represents 137,450,000. Adherents were defined as "all members, including full members, their children and others who regularly attend services." The Jewish population includes Jews who define themselves as Jewish by religion as well as those who define themselves as Jewish in cultural or ethnic terms. Data on Jewish population are based on both scientific studies and informant estimates provided by local Jewish communities]

| State | Number (1,000) | | | Percent of population [3] | | |
|---|---|---|---|---|---|---|
| | Christian adherents, [1] 2010 | Other religious adherents, [2] 2010 | Jewish population, 2011 | Christian adherents, [1] 2010 | Other religious adherents, [2] 2010 | Jewish population, 2011 |
| **United States** | **137,450** | **10,890** | **6,588** | **44.5** | **3.5** | **2.1** |
| Alabama | 2,948 | 52 | 9 | 61.7 | 1.1 | 0.2 |
| Alaska | 200 | 40 | 6 | 28.1 | 5.7 | 0.9 |
| Arizona | 1,894 | 466 | 106 | 29.6 | 7.3 | 1.7 |
| Arkansas | 1,573 | 40 | 2 | 53.9 | 1.4 | 0.1 |
| California | 15,021 | 1,530 | 1,220 | 40.3 | 4.1 | 3.3 |
| Colorado | 1,684 | 199 | 91 | 33.5 | 4.0 | 1.8 |
| Connecticut | 1,735 | 48 | 116 | 48.6 | 1.3 | 3.2 |
| Delaware | 349 | 22 | 15 | 38.9 | 2.5 | 1.7 |
| District of Columbia | 298 | 16 | 28 | 49.6 | 2.7 | 4.7 |
| Florida | 6,829 | 400 | 639 | 36.3 | 2.1 | 3.4 |
| Georgia | 4,702 | 186 | 128 | 48.5 | 1.9 | 1.3 |
| Hawaii | 421 | 140 | 7 | 31.0 | 10.3 | 0.5 |
| Idaho | 384 | 417 | 2 | 24.5 | 26.6 | 0.1 |
| Illinois | 6,529 | 486 | 298 | 50.9 | 3.8 | 2.3 |
| Indiana | 2,793 | 69 | 17 | 43.1 | 1.1 | 0.3 |
| Iowa | 1,592 | 46 | 6 | 52.3 | 1.5 | 0.2 |
| Kansas | 1,375 | 61 | 18 | 48.2 | 2.1 | 0.6 |
| Kentucky | 2,182 | 49 | 11 | 50.3 | 1.1 | 0.3 |
| Louisiana | 2,688 | 50 | 11 | 59.3 | 1.1 | 0.2 |
| Maine | 345 | 19 | 14 | 26.0 | 1.4 | 1.0 |
| Maryland | 2,214 | 118 | 238 | 38.3 | 2.0 | 4.1 |
| Massachusetts | 3,546 | 122 | 278 | 54.2 | 1.9 | 4.2 |
| Michigan | 3,910 | 211 | 82 | 39.6 | 2.1 | 0.8 |
| Minnesota | 2,894 | 69 | 46 | 54.6 | 1.3 | 0.9 |
| Mississippi | 1,709 | 33 | 2 | 57.6 | 1.1 | 0.1 |
| Missouri | 2,806 | 123 | 59 | 46.9 | 2.0 | 1.0 |
| Montana | 326 | 50 | 1 | 33.0 | 5.0 | 0.1 |
| Nebraska | 974 | 38 | 6 | 53.3 | 2.1 | 0.3 |
| Nevada | 725 | 196 | 74 | 26.8 | 7.3 | 2.8 |
| New Hampshire | 444 | 14 | 10 | 33.7 | 1.1 | 0.8 |
| New Jersey | 4,321 | 272 | 504 | 49.1 | 3.1 | 5.7 |
| New Mexico | 940 | 87 | 12 | 45.6 | 4.2 | 0.6 |
| New York | 8,529 | 611 | 1,635 | 44.0 | 3.2 | 8.4 |
| North Carolina | 4,372 | 140 | 31 | 45.9 | 1.5 | 0.3 |
| North Dakota | 443 | 8 | (Z) | 65.9 | 1.2 | 0.1 |
| Ohio | 4,861 | 146 | 148 | 42.1 | 1.3 | 1.3 |
| Oklahoma | 2,148 | 75 | 5 | 57.3 | 2.0 | 0.1 |
| Oregon | 998 | 187 | 41 | 26.1 | 4.9 | 1.1 |
| Pennsylvania | 6,530 | 206 | 295 | 51.4 | 1.6 | 2.3 |
| Rhode Island | 558 | 10 | 19 | 53.1 | 0.9 | 1.8 |
| South Carolina | 2,337 | 70 | 13 | 50.5 | 1.5 | 0.3 |
| South Dakota | 464 | 13 | (Z) | 57.0 | 1.6 | (Z) |
| Tennessee | 3,425 | 82 | 20 | 54.0 | 1.3 | 0.3 |
| Texas | 13,062 | 872 | 140 | 51.9 | 3.5 | 0.6 |
| Utah | 256 | 1,929 | 6 | 9.3 | 69.8 | 0.2 |
| Vermont | 199 | 9 | 5 | 31.8 | 1.4 | 0.9 |
| Virginia | 3,206 | 351 | 97 | 40.1 | 4.4 | 1.2 |
| Washington | 1,945 | 364 | 46 | 28.9 | 5.4 | 0.7 |
| West Virginia | 635 | 22 | 2 | 34.3 | 1.2 | 0.1 |
| Wisconsin | 2,973 | 62 | 28 | 52.3 | 1.1 | 0.5 |
| Wyoming | 158 | 65 | 1 | 28.0 | 11.5 | 0.2 |

Z Fewer than 500 or less than 0.05 percent. [1] Comprises evangelical Protestants, Black Protestants, mainline Protestants, Orthodox and Catholic groups. [2] Includes counts of Jain, Shinto, Sikh, Tao, National Spiritualist Association, Church of Jesus Christ of Latter Day Saints, Unitarian Universalist, Jehovah's Witnesses, Church of Christ Scientist, Bahá'í, three Buddhist groupings, four Hindu groupings, Muslims, and Zoroastrians. Excludes four Judaism groups. [3] Based on U.S. Census Bureau data for resident population enumerated as of April 1, 2010 and estimated as of July 2012.

Source: Religious adherents: Clifford Grammich, Kirk Hadaway, Richard Houseal, Dale E. Jones, Alexei Krindatch, Richie Stanley, and Richard H. Taylor, *2010 U.S. Religion Census: Religious Congregations & Membership Study* ©, 2012, Association of Statisticians of American Religious Bodies. See also <http://www.asarb.org>. Jewish population: Ira M. Sheskin and Arnold Dashefsky, University of Miami and University of Connecticut, *Jewish Population of the United States, 2011*, published by the Mandell L. Berman North American Jewish Data Bank in cooperation with the Association for the Social Scientific Study of Jewry and the Jewish Federations of North America, see also <http://www.jewishdatabank.org>

## Table 81. Religious Adherents by Metropolitan Area Status and Religious Groups: 2010

[Groups shown have 500,000 adherents or more. Adherents were defined as all members, including full members, their children and the estimated number of other participants who are not considered members. Based on a study of 236 religious bodies sponsored by the Association of Statisticians of American Religious Bodies. Participants included 217 Christian denominations, associations, or communions (including Latter-day Saints, Messianic Jews, and Unitarian/Universalist groups); counts of Jain, Shinto, Sikh, Tao, and National Spiritualist Association congregations, and counts of congregations and individuals for Bahá'í, three Buddhist groupings, four Hindu groupings, four Jewish groupings, Muslims, and Zoroastrians. For definition of metropolitan and micropolitan areas, see Appendix II]

| Religious group | Total adherents (1,000) | Percent | | |
|---|---|---|---|---|
| | | In metropolitan area | In micropolitan area | Outside metro/micro area |
| U.S. population, total.......................... | 308,746 | 83.7 | 10.0 | 6.3 |
| **Total adherents**.................................. | **150,686** | **83.5** | **10.0** | **6.5** |
| Catholic........................................ | 58,929 | 90.5 | 6.2 | 3.3 |
| Southern Baptist Convention.................. | 19,897 | 69.3 | 17.2 | 13.5 |
| Non-denominational Christian Churches........ | 12,241 | 88.7 | 7.8 | 3.5 |
| United Methodist Church....................... | 9,948 | 73.6 | 15.3 | 11.1 |
| Church of Jesus Christ of Latter-day Saints..... | 6,145 | 82.8 | 11.6 | 5.6 |
| Evangelical Lutheran Church in America........ | 4,181 | 70.4 | 16.0 | 13.6 |
| Assemblies of God.............................. | 2,945 | 82.7 | 11.0 | 6.3 |
| Muslim, estimate............................... | 2,600 | 97.4 | 2.0 | 0.6 |
| Presbyterian Church (U.S.A.)................... | 2,452 | 82.5 | 11.4 | 6.1 |
| Lutheran Church—Missouri Synod............... | 2,271 | 72.7 | 13.7 | 13.6 |
| Episcopal...................................... | 1,952 | 88.2 | 8.1 | 3.7 |
| National Baptist Convention, USA, Inc.......... | 1,881 | 90.3 | 7.0 | 2.7 |
| Churches of Christ............................. | 1,584 | 69.8 | 17.1 | 13.1 |
| American Baptist Churches in the USA.......... | 1,561 | 83.8 | 9.8 | 6.4 |
| Christian Churches and Churches of Christ..... | 1,453 | 72.6 | 15.9 | 11.5 |
| United Church of Christ........................ | 1,284 | 79.3 | 13.5 | 7.2 |
| Seventh-day Adventist Church.................. | 1,195 | 87.7 | 8.2 | 4.1 |
| Church of God (Cleveland, Tennessee).......... | 1,110 | 72.2 | 17.5 | 10.3 |
| African Methodist Episcopal Church............ | 1,010 | 77.7 | 12.3 | 10.0 |
| Orthodox Judaism.............................. | 947 | 99.6 | 0.0 | 0.4 |
| Church of the Nazarene........................ | 894 | 76.2 | 15.6 | 8.2 |
| Christian Church (Disciples of Christ)........... | 786 | 70.3 | 17.7 | 12.0 |
| Reform Judaism................................ | 766 | 98.3 | 1.3 | 0.4 |
| Mahayana Buddhism........................... | 733 | 92.8 | 6.8 | 0.4 |
| Church of God in Christ........................ | 624 | 87.8 | 7.3 | 4.9 |
| Conservative Judaism.......................... | 502 | 99.5 | 0.4 | 0.1 |

Source: Clifford Grammich, Kirk Hadaway, Richard Houseal, Dale E. Jones, Alexei Krindatch, Richie Stanley, and Richard H. Taylor. *2010 U.S. Religion Census: Religious Congregations & Membership Study*, 2012 ©. Association of Statisticians of American Religious Bodies.

## Table 82. Religious Bodies—Selected Data: 1988 to 2010

[Includes the self-reported membership of religious bodies with 750,000 or more as reported to the Yearbook of American and Canadian Churches. Groups may be excluded if they do not supply information. The data are not standardized so comparisons between groups are difficult. The definition of "church member" is determined by the religious body]

| Religious body | Year reported | Churches reported | Membership |
|---|---|---|---|
| African Methodist Episcopal Church...................................... | 2009 | 4,100 | 2,500,000 |
| African Methodist Episcopal Zion Church................................ | 2010 | (NA) | 1,400,000 |
| American Baptist Churches in the USA................................. | 2010 | 5,366 | 1,308,054 |
| Assemblies of God...................................................... | 2010 | 12,457 | 3,030,944 |
| Catholic Church......................................................... | 2010 | 18,199 | 68,202,492 |
| Christian Churches and Churches of Christ............................. | 1988 | 5,579 | 1,071,616 |
| Christian Methodist Episcopal Church.................................. | 2006 | 3,500 | 850,000 |
| Church of God in Christ................................................. | 1991 | 15,300 | 5,499,875 |
| Church of God (Cleveland, Tennessee)................................. | 2010 | 6,481 | 1,074,047 |
| Church of Jesus Christ of Latter-day Saints............................ | 2010 | 13,601 | 6,157,238 |
| Churches of Christ...................................................... | 2006 | 13,000 | 1,639,495 |
| Episcopal Church....................................................... | 2010 | 6,794 | 1,951,907 |
| Evangelical Lutheran Church in America............................... | 2010 | 9,995 | 4,274,855 |
| Greek Orthodox Archdiocese of America.............................. | 2006 | 560 | 1,500,000 |
| Jehovah's Witnesses................................................... | 2010 | 13,021 | 1,184,249 |
| Lutheran Church—Missouri Synod...................................... | 2010 | 6,158 | 2,278,586 |
| National Baptist Convention of America Inc............................ | 2000 | (NA) | 3,500,000 |
| National Baptist Convention, U.S.A., Inc............................... | 2010 | 10,358 | 5,197,512 |
| National Missionary Baptist Convention of America.................... | 1992 | (NA) | 2,500,000 |
| Pentecostal Assemblies of the World, Inc.............................. | 2010 | 2,550 | 1,800,000 |
| Presbyterian Church (U.S.A.)........................................... | 2010 | 10,560 | 2,675,873 |
| Progressive National Baptist Convention, Inc.......................... | 2009 | 1,500 | 1,010,000 |
| Seventh-day Adventist Church.......................................... | 2010 | 4,916 | 1,060,386 |
| Southern Baptist Convention........................................... | 2010 | 45,727 | 16,136,044 |
| United Church of Christ................................................. | 2010 | 5,227 | 1,058,423 |
| United Methodist Church................................................ | 2009 | 33,583 | 7,679,850 |

NA Not available.

Source: National Council of Churches of Christ in the USA, *2012 Yearbook of American and Canadian Churches* ©. See also <http://nationalcouncilofchurches.us/>.

# Section 2
# Births, Deaths, Marriages, and Divorces

This section presents vital statistics data on births, mortality, marriages, and divorces, as well as factors that help explain fertility, such as use of contraception, sexual activity, and prevalence of abortions and fetal deaths. Vital statistics are collected and disseminated for the nation through the National Vital Statistics System by the National Center for Health Statistics (NCHS) and published annually in *Vital Statistics of the United States, National Vital Statistics Reports (NVSR),* and other selected publications. Reports are also issued by various state bureaus participating in the National Vital Statistics System. Factors influencing fertility are collected in NCHS's National Survey of Family Growth and the U.S. Census Bureau's American Community Survey and Current Population Reports (published in *Fertility of American Women*).

Additionally, data on births, deaths, and other public health topics can be accessed via the Center for Disease Control's WONDER Online databases at <https://wonder.cdc.gov/>. Data on abortions are published by the Guttmacher Institute in selected issues of *Perspectives on Sexual and Reproductive Health.*

**Registration of vital events**—The registration of births, deaths, fetal deaths, and other vital events in the United States is primarily a state and local function. There are 57 vital registration jurisdictions in the United States: the 50 states, five territories (Puerto Rico, etc.), District of Columbia, and New York City. Each of the 57 jurisdictions has a direct statistical reporting relationship with NCHS. Vital events occurring to U.S. residents outside the United States are not included in the data.

**Births and deaths**—The live-birth, death, and fetal-death statistics prepared by NCHS are based on vital records filed in the registration offices of all states, New York City, and the District of Columbia. The annual collection of death statistics on a national basis began in 1900 with a national death-registration area of ten states and the District of Columbia; a similar annual collection of birth statistics for a national birth-registration area began in 1915, also with ten reporting states and the District of Columbia. Since 1933, the birth- and death-registration areas have comprised the entire United States, including Alaska (beginning 1959) and Hawaii (beginning 1960). National statistics on fetal deaths were first compiled for 1918 and annually since 1922. Prior to 1951, birth statistics came from a complete count of records received in the Public Health Service (now received in NCHS). From 1951 through 1971, they were based on a 50-percent sample of all registered births (except for a complete count in 1955 and a 20- to 50-percent sample in 1967). Since 1972, they have been based on a complete count for states participating in the Vital Statistics Cooperative Program (VSCP) (for details, see the technical appendix in *U.S. Vital Statistics System: Major Activities and Developments, 1950-95*) and on a 50-percent sample of all other areas. Beginning in 1986, all reporting areas participated in the VSCP. Mortality data have been based on a complete count of records for each area (except for a 50-percent sample in 1972). Beginning in 1970, births to and deaths of nonresident aliens of the United States and

U.S. citizens outside the United States have been excluded from the data. Fetal deaths and deaths among Armed Forces abroad are excluded. Data based on samples are subject to sampling error; for details, see annual issues of *National Vital Statistics Reports.*

Mortality statistics by cause of death are compiled in accordance with World Health Organization regulations according to the *International Classification of Diseases* (ICD). The ICD is revised approximately every 10 years. The tenth revision of the ICD was employed beginning in 1999. Deaths for prior years were classified according to the revision of the ICD in use at the time. Each revision of the ICD introduces a number of discontinuities in mortality statistics; for a discussion of those between the ninth and tenth revisions of the ICD, see *Deaths: Final Data for 2017, National Vital Statistics Report,* Vol. 68, No. 9. Information on tests of statistical significance, differences between death rates, and standard errors can also be found in the aforementioned report.

Some of the tables present age-adjusted death rates in addition to crude death rates. Age-adjusted death rates shown in this section were prepared using the direct method, in which age-specific death rates for a population of interest are applied to a standard population distributed by age. Age adjustment eliminates the differences in observed rates between points in time or among compared population groups that result from age differences in population composition.

**Fertility and life expectancy**—The total fertility rate, defined as the number of births that 1,000 women would have in their lifetime if at each year of age they experienced the birth rates occurring in the specified year, is compiled and published by NCHS. See *Births: Final Data for 2017, National Vital Statistics Reports,* Vol. 67, No. 8. Data on life expectancy, the average remaining lifetime in years for persons who attain a given age, are also computed and published by NCHS. See *Deaths: Final Data for 2017, National Vital Statistics Reports,* Vol. 68, No. 9 and <https://www.cdc.gov/nchs/nvss/deaths.htm> for details.

**Marriage and divorce**—In 1957 and 1958 respectively, the National Office of Vital Statistics established marriage- and divorce-registration areas consisting of an increasing number of States over time. Procedures for estimating the number of marriages and divorces in the registration States are discussed in *Vital Statistics of the United States, Vol. III—Marriage and Divorce.* Total counts of events for registration and nonregistration states are gathered by collecting already summarized data on marriages and divorces reported by state offices of vital statistics and by county offices of registration. The collection and publication of detailed marriage and divorce statistics was suspended beginning in January 1996. For additional information, visit the National Center for Health Statistics online at <https://www.cdc.gov/nchs/nvss/marriage-divorce.htm>.

With the suspension of detailed data collection by the NCHS, data on marriage and divorce can be found in the Census Bureau's American Community Survey data tables. See <https://www.census.gov/programs-surveys/acs/> for information and data access.

**Vital statistics rates**—Except as noted, vital statistics rates computed by NCHS are based on decennial census population figures as of April 1 for 1960, 1970, 1980, 1990, 2000, and 2010; and on midyear population figures for other years, as estimated by the Census Bureau (see text, Section 1).

**Race**—Data by race for births, deaths, marriages, and divorces from NCHS are based on information contained in the certificates of registration. The Census Bureau's Current Population Survey obtains information on race by asking respondents to classify their race as (1) White, (2) Black, (3) American Indian or Alaska Native, (4) Native Hawaiian or Other Pacific Islander, or (5) Asian. Beginning with the 1989 data year, NCHS has tabulated birth data primarily by race of the mother. In 1988 and prior years, births were tabulated by race of the child, which was determined from the race of the parents as entered on the birth certificate. Trend data by race shown in this section are by race of mother beginning with the 1980 data. Hispanic origin of the mother is reported and tabulated independently of race. Thus, persons of Hispanic origin may be of any race. The majority of women of Hispanic origin are reported as White.

Race categorizations found in the *National Vital Statistics Reports* are variously shown according to either 1977 or 1997 Office of Management and Budget (OMB) standards. States reporting multiple-race data according to new 1997 OMB standards has varied widely. In some cases, to provide a comparison of data by race between the 1977 and 1997 OMB standards, the responses of those reporting more than one race were "bridged" to a single race. See headnotes of individual tables and respective source reports for additional information.

**Statistical reliability**—For a discussion of statistical collection, estimation, and sampling procedures and measures of reliability applicable to data from NCHS and the Census Bureau, see Appendix III.

# Table 83. Live Births, Deaths, Marriages, and Divorces: 1960 to 2017

[4,258 represents 4,258,000. Beginning 1970, excludes births to and deaths of nonresidents of the United States. See Appendix III]

| Year | Number (1,000) | | | | | Rate per 1,000 population | | | | |
|---|---|---|---|---|---|---|---|---|---|---|
| | | Deaths | | Mar- | Divorces[3] | | Deaths | | Mar- | Divorces[3] |
| | Births | Total | Infant[1] | riages[2] | | Births | Total | Infant[1] | riages[2] | |
| 1960 | 4,258 | 1,712 | 111 | 1,523 | 393 | 23.7 | 9.5 | 26.0 | 8.5 | 2.2 |
| 1965 | 3,760 | 1,828 | 93 | 1,800 | 479 | 19.4 | 9.4 | 24.7 | 9.3 | 2.5 |
| 1970 | 3,731 | 1,921 | 75 | 2,159 | 708 | 18.4 | 9.5 | 20.0 | 10.6 | 3.5 |
| 1971 | 3,556 | 1,928 | 68 | 2,190 | 773 | 17.2 | 9.3 | 19.1 | 10.6 | 3.7 |
| 1972 | 3,258 | 1,964 | 60 | 2,282 | 845 | 15.6 | 9.4 | 18.5 | 10.9 | 4.0 |
| 1973 | 3,137 | 1,973 | 56 | 2,284 | 915 | 14.8 | 9.3 | 17.7 | 10.8 | 4.3 |
| 1974 | 3,160 | 1,934 | 53 | 2,230 | 977 | 14.8 | 9.1 | 16.7 | 10.5 | 4.6 |
| 1975 | 3,144 | 1,893 | 51 | 2,153 | 1,036 | 14.6 | 8.8 | 16.1 | 10.0 | 4.8 |
| 1976 | 3,168 | 1,909 | 48 | 2,155 | 1,083 | 14.6 | 8.8 | 15.2 | 9.9 | 5.0 |
| 1977 | 3,327 | 1,900 | 47 | 2,178 | 1,091 | 15.1 | 8.6 | 14.1 | 9.9 | 5.0 |
| 1978 | 3,333 | 1,928 | 46 | 2,282 | 1,130 | 15.0 | 8.7 | 13.8 | 10.3 | 5.1 |
| 1979 | 3,494 | 1,914 | 46 | 2,331 | 1,181 | 15.6 | 8.5 | 13.1 | 10.4 | 5.3 |
| 1980 | 3,612 | 1,990 | 46 | 2,390 | 1,189 | 15.9 | 8.8 | 12.6 | 10.6 | 5.2 |
| 1981 | 3,629 | 1,978 | 43 | 2,422 | 1,213 | 15.8 | 8.6 | 11.9 | 10.6 | 5.3 |
| 1982 | 3,681 | 1,975 | 42 | 2,456 | 1,170 | 15.9 | 8.5 | 11.5 | 10.6 | 5.1 |
| 1983 | 3,639 | 2,019 | 41 | 2,446 | 1,158 | 15.6 | 8.6 | 11.2 | 10.5 | 5.0 |
| 1984 | 3,669 | 2,039 | 40 | 2,477 | 1,169 | 15.6 | 8.6 | 10.8 | 10.5 | 5.0 |
| 1985 | 3,761 | 2,086 | 40 | 2,413 | 1,190 | 15.8 | 8.8 | 10.6 | 10.1 | 5.0 |
| 1986 | 3,757 | 2,105 | 39 | 2,407 | 1,178 | 15.6 | 8.8 | 10.4 | 10.0 | 4.9 |
| 1987 | 3,809 | 2,123 | 38 | 2,403 | 1,166 | 15.7 | 8.8 | 10.1 | 9.9 | 4.8 |
| 1988 | 3,910 | 2,168 | 39 | 2,396 | 1,167 | 16.0 | 8.9 | 10.0 | 9.8 | 4.8 |
| 1989 | 4,041 | 2,150 | 40 | 2,403 | 1,157 | 16.4 | 8.7 | 9.8 | 9.7 | 4.7 |
| 1990 | 4,158 | 2,148 | 38 | 2,443 | 1,182 | 16.7 | 8.6 | 9.2 | 9.8 | 4.7 |
| 1991 | 4,111 | 2,170 | 37 | 2,371 | 1,187 | 16.2 | 8.6 | 8.9 | 9.4 | 4.7 |
| 1992 | 4,065 | 2,176 | 35 | 2,362 | 1,215 | 15.8 | 8.5 | 8.5 | 9.3 | 4.8 |
| 1993 | 4,000 | 2,269 | 33 | 2,334 | 1,187 | 15.4 | 8.7 | 8.4 | 9.0 | 4.6 |
| 1994 | 3,953 | 2,279 | 31 | 2,362 | 1,191 | 15.0 | 8.7 | 8.0 | 9.1 | 4.6 |
| 1995 | 3,900 | 2,312 | 30 | 2,336 | 1,169 | 14.6 | 8.7 | 7.6 | 8.9 | 4.4 |
| 1996 | 3,891 | 2,315 | 28 | 2,344 | 1,150 | 14.4 | 8.6 | 7.3 | 8.8 | 4.3 |
| 1997 | 3,881 | 2,314 | 28 | 2,384 | 1,163 | 14.2 | 8.5 | 7.2 | 8.9 | 4.3 |
| 1998 | 3,942 | 2,337 | 28 | 2,244 | [4] 1,135 | 14.3 | 8.5 | 7.2 | 8.4 | [4] 4.2 |
| 1999 | 3,959 | 2,391 | 28 | 2,358 | (NA) | 14.2 | 8.6 | 7.1 | 8.6 | [4] 4.1 |
| 2000 | 4,059 | 2,403 | 28 | 2,315 | [5] 944 | 14.4 | 8.5 | 6.9 | 8.2 | [5] 4.0 |
| 2001 | 4,026 | 2,416 | 28 | 2,326 | [5] 940 | 14.1 | 8.5 | 6.9 | 8.2 | [5] 4.0 |
| 2002 | 4,022 | 2,443 | 28 | 2,290 | [6] 955 | 14.0 | 8.5 | 7.0 | 8.0 | [6] 3.9 |
| 2003 | 4,090 | 2,448 | 28 | 2,245 | [7] 927 | 14.1 | 8.4 | 6.9 | 7.7 | [7] 3.8 |
| 2004 | 4,112 | 2,398 | 28 | 2,279 | [8] 879 | 14.0 | 8.2 | 6.8 | 7.8 | [8] 3.7 |
| 2005 | 4,138 | 2,448 | 28 | 2,249 | [9] 847 | 14.0 | 8.3 | 6.9 | 7.6 | [9] 3.6 |
| 2006 | 4,266 | 2,426 | 29 | [10] 2,193 | [9] 872 | 14.3 | 8.1 | 6.7 | [10] 7.5 | [9] 3.7 |
| 2007 | 4,316 | 2,424 | 29 | 2,197 | [9] 856 | 14.3 | 8.0 | 6.8 | 7.3 | [9] 3.6 |
| 2008 | 4,248 | 2,472 | 28 | 2,157 | [9] 844 | 14.0 | 8.1 | 6.6 | 7.1 | [9] 3.5 |
| 2009 | 4,131 | 2,437 | 26 | 2,080 | [9] 840 | 13.5 | 7.9 | 6.4 | 6.8 | [9] 3.5 |
| 2010 | 3,999 | 2,468 | 25 | 2,096 | [9] 872 | 13.0 | 8.0 | 6.2 | 6.8 | [9] 3.6 |
| 2011 | 3,954 | 2,515 | 24 | 2,118 | [9] 877 | 12.7 | 8.1 | 6.1 | 6.8 | [9] 3.6 |
| 2012 | 3,953 | 2,543 | 24 | 2,131 | [9] 851 | 12.6 | 8.1 | 6.0 | 6.8 | [9] 3.4 |
| 2013 | 3,932 | 2,597 | 23 | [11] 2,081 | [12] 832 | 12.4 | 8.2 | 6.0 | [11] 6.8 | [12] 3.3 |
| 2014 | 3,988 | 2,626 | 23 | [11] 2,140 | [12] 814 | 12.5 | 8.2 | 5.8 | [11] 6.9 | [12] 3.2 |
| 2015 | 3,978 | 2,713 | 23 | 2,222 | [12] 801 | 12.4 | 8.4 | 5.9 | 6.9 | [12] 3.1 |
| 2016 | 3,946 | 2,744 | 23 | 2,251 | [13] 776 | 12.2 | 8.5 | 5.9 | 7.0 | [13] 3.0 |
| 2017 | 3,856 | 2,814 | 22 | 2,236 | [14] 787 | 11.8 | 8.6 | 5.8 | 6.9 | [14] 2.9 |

NA Not available. [1] Infant mortality rate; infants under 1 year, excluding fetal deaths. [2] Marriages and marriage rates are by place of occurrence. Beginning 1991, data are provisional. Includes estimates for some States through 1965 and for 1976-1977, and marriage licenses for some states for all years except 1973 and 1975. Beginning 1978, includes nonlicensed marriages in California. [3] Divorces and divorce rates are by place of occurrence. Includes reported annulments and some estimated state figures for all years. Beginning 1991, data are provisional. [4] Excludes data for California, Colorado, Indiana, and Louisiana. [5] Excludes data for California, Indiana, Louisiana, and Oklahoma. [6] Excludes data for California, Indiana, New York City, and Oklahoma. [7] Excludes data for California, Hawaii, Indiana, and Oklahoma. [8] Excludes data for California, Georgia, Hawaii, Indiana, and Louisiana. [9] Excludes data for California, Georgia, Hawaii, Indiana, Louisiana, and Minnesota. [10] Excludes data for Louisiana. [11] Excludes data for Georgia. [12] Excludes data for California, Georgia, Hawaii, Indiana, and Minnesota. [13] Excludes data for California, Georgia, Hawaii, Indiana, Minnesota, and New Mexico. [14] Excludes data for California, Hawaii, Indiana, Minnesota, and New Mexico.

Source: U.S. National Center for Health Statistics, *Births: Final Data for 2017*, Vol. 67, No. 8, November 2018; *Deaths: Final Data for 2017*, Vol. 68, No. 9, June 2019; and "National Marriage and Divorce Rate Trends," <https://www.cdc.gov/nchs/nvss/marriage-divorce.htm>, accessed August 2019.

# Table 84. Births, Birth Rates, and Fertility Rates by Sex and Mother's Race and Age: 1980 to 2017

[Births in thousands (3,612 represents 3,612,000). Beginning 2016, all States and the District of Columbia reported race data according to 1997 OMB standards. To maintain comparability of 2016 data with earlier data, data for mothers reporting multiple-race were bridged to single-race categories; see Technical Notes in source for details. For population bases used to derive these data, see text this section, and Appendix III]

| Item | 1980 | 1990 | 2000 | 2005 | 2010 | 2012 | 2013 | 2014 | 2015 | 2016 | 2017 |
|---|---|---|---|---|---|---|---|---|---|---|---|
| **Live births** [1] | **3,612** | **4,158** | **4,059** | **4,138** | **3,999** | **3,953** | **3,932** | **3,988** | **3,978** | **3,946** | **3,856** |
| Male | 1,853 | 2,129 | 2,077 | 2,119 | 2,047 | 2,021 | 2,013 | 2,041 | 2,036 | 2,018 | 1,973 |
| Female | 1,760 | 2,029 | 1,982 | 2,019 | 1,952 | 1,931 | 1,919 | 1,947 | 1,942 | 1,928 | 1,883 |
| Males per 100 females (sex ratio) | 105 | 105 | 105 | 105 | 105 | 105 | 105 | 105 | 105 | 105 | 105 |
| *Race/ethnicity of mother:* | | | | | | | | | | | |
| Non-Hispanic | (NA) | (NA) | (NA) | (NA) | (NA) | (NA) | (NA) | (NA) | (NA) | 2,991 | 2,924 |
| White alone | (NA) | (NA) | (NA) | (NA) | (NA) | (NA) | (NA) | (NA) | (NA) | 2,056 | 1,992 |
| Black or African American alone | (NA) | (NA) | (NA) | (NA) | (NA) | (NA) | (NA) | (NA) | (NA) | 559 | 561 |
| American Indian or Alaska Native alone | (NA) | (NA) | (NA) | (NA) | (NA) | (NA) | (NA) | (NA) | (NA) | 31 | 30 |
| Asian alone | (NA) | (NA) | (NA) | (NA) | (NA) | (NA) | (NA) | (NA) | (NA) | 254 | 249 |
| Native Hawaiian or Other Pacific Islander alone | (NA) | (NA) | (NA) | (NA) | (NA) | (NA) | (NA) | (NA) | (NA) | 9 | 9 |
| Hispanic | (NA) | 595 | 816 | 986 | 945 | 908 | 901 | 914 | 924 | 918 | 899 |
| *Bridged race estimates:* [2] | | | | | | | | | | | |
| White | 2,936 | 3,290 | 3,194 | 3,229 | 3,069 | 3,000 | 2,986 | 3,020 | 3,013 | 2,946 | 2,858 |
| Black | 568 | 684 | 623 | 633 | 636 | 634 | 635 | 641 | 640 | 654 | 658 |
| American Indian or Alaska Native | 29 | 39 | 42 | 45 | 47 | 46 | 46 | 45 | 44 | 44 | 42 |
| Asian or Pacific Islander | 74 | 142 | 201 | 231 | 247 | 273 | 266 | 283 | 281 | 302 | 298 |
| *Age of mother:* | | | | | | | | | | | |
| Under 20 years old | 562 | 533 | 478 | 421 | 372 | 309 | 276 | 252 | 232 | 212 | 196 |
| 20 to 24 years old | 1,226 | 1,094 | 1,018 | 1,040 | 952 | 917 | 897 | 883 | 851 | 804 | 765 |
| 25 to 29 years old | 1,108 | 1,277 | 1,088 | 1,132 | 1,134 | 1,124 | 1,121 | 1,145 | 1,152 | 1,149 | 1,124 |
| 30 to 34 years old | 550 | 886 | 929 | 951 | 962 | 1,013 | 1,037 | 1,081 | 1,095 | 1,111 | 1,092 |
| 35 to 39 years old | 141 | 318 | 452 | 483 | 465 | 472 | 484 | 509 | 528 | 547 | 555 |
| 40 to 44 years old | (NA) | (NA) | 90 | 105 | 107 | 110 | 109 | 110 | 112 | 113 | 115 |
| 45 to 54 years old | (NA) | (NA) | 4 | 6 | 8 | 8 | 8 | 8 | 9 | 9 | 9 |
| Mean age of mother at first birth (years) | 22.7 | 24.2 | 24.9 | 25.2 | 25.4 | 25.8 | 26.0 | 26.3 | 26.4 | 26.6 | 26.8 |
| **Birth rate per 1,000 population** | **15.9** | **16.7** | **14.4** | **14.0** | **13.0** | **12.6** | **12.4** | **12.5** | **12.4** | **12.2** | **11.8** |
| *Race/ethnicity of mother:* | | | | | | | | | | | |
| Non-Hispanic | (NA) | (NA) | (NA) | (NA) | (NA) | (NA) | (NA) | (NA) | (NA) | 11.3 | 11.0 |
| White alone | (NA) | (NA) | (NA) | (NA) | (NA) | (NA) | (NA) | (NA) | (NA) | 10.5 | 10.2 |
| Black or African American alone | (NA) | (NA) | (NA) | (NA) | (NA) | (NA) | (NA) | (NA) | (NA) | 14.0 | 13.9 |
| American Indian or Alaska Native alone | (NA) | (NA) | (NA) | (NA) | (NA) | (NA) | (NA) | (NA) | (NA) | 13.3 | 12.6 |
| Asian alone | (NA) | (NA) | (NA) | (NA) | (NA) | (NA) | (NA) | (NA) | (NA) | 14.6 | 13.8 |
| Native Hawaiian or Other Pacific Islander alone | (NA) | (NA) | (NA) | (NA) | (NA) | (NA) | (NA) | (NA) | (NA) | 16.8 | 16.7 |
| Hispanic | 23.5 | 26.7 | 23.1 | 22.9 | 18.7 | 17.1 | 16.7 | 16.5 | 16.3 | 16.0 | 15.3 |
| *Bridged race estimates:* [2] | | | | | | | | | | | |
| White | 15.1 | 15.8 | 13.9 | 13.6 | 12.5 | 12.1 | 12.0 | 12.0 | 12.0 | 11.7 | 11.3 |
| Black | 21.3 | 22.4 | 17.0 | 16.1 | 15.1 | 14.7 | 14.5 | 14.5 | 14.3 | 14.4 | 14.3 |
| American Indian or Alaska Native | 20.7 | 18.9 | 14.0 | 12.6 | 11.0 | 10.5 | 10.3 | 9.9 | 9.7 | 9.4 | 8.9 |
| Asian or Pacific Islander | 19.9 | 19.0 | 17.1 | 15.9 | 14.5 | 15.1 | 14.3 | 14.6 | 14.0 | 14.8 | 14.0 |
| *Age of mother:* | | | | | | | | | | | |
| 10 to 14 years old | 1.1 | 1.4 | 0.9 | 0.6 | 0.4 | 0.4 | 0.3 | 0.3 | 0.2 | 0.2 | 0.2 |
| 15 to 19 years old | 53.0 | 59.9 | 47.7 | 39.7 | 34.2 | 29.4 | 26.5 | 24.2 | 22.3 | 20.3 | 18.8 |
| 20 to 24 years old | 115.1 | 116.5 | 109.7 | 101.8 | 90.0 | 83.1 | 80.7 | 79.0 | 76.8 | 73.8 | 71.0 |
| 25 to 29 years old | 112.9 | 120.2 | 113.5 | 116.5 | 108.3 | 106.5 | 105.5 | 105.8 | 104.3 | 102.1 | 98.0 |
| 30 to 34 years old | 61.9 | 80.8 | 91.2 | 96.7 | 96.5 | 97.3 | 98.0 | 100.8 | 101.5 | 102.7 | 100.3 |
| 35 to 39 years old | 19.8 | 31.7 | 39.7 | 46.4 | 45.9 | 48.3 | 49.3 | 51.0 | 51.8 | 52.7 | 52.3 |
| 40 to 44 years old | 3.9 | 5.5 | 8.0 | 9.1 | 10.2 | 10.4 | 10.4 | 10.6 | 11.0 | 11.4 | 11.6 |
| 45 to 54 years old [3] | 0.2 | 0.2 | 0.5 | 0.6 | 0.7 | 0.7 | 0.8 | 0.8 | 0.8 | 0.9 | 0.9 |
| **Fertility rate per 1,000 women** [4] | **68.4** | **70.9** | **65.9** | **66.7** | **64.1** | **63.0** | **62.5** | **62.9** | **62.5** | **62.0** | **60.3** |
| *Race/ethnicity of mother:* | | | | | | | | | | | |
| Non-Hispanic | (NA) | (NA) | (NA) | (NA) | (NA) | (NA) | (NA) | (NA) | (NA) | 59.1 | 57.7 |
| White alone | (NA) | (NA) | (NA) | (NA) | (NA) | (NA) | (NA) | (NA) | (NA) | 58.8 | 57.2 |
| Black or African American alone | (NA) | (NA) | (NA) | (NA) | (NA) | (NA) | (NA) | (NA) | (NA) | 63.3 | 63.1 |
| American Indian or Alaska Native alone | (NA) | (NA) | (NA) | (NA) | (NA) | (NA) | (NA) | (NA) | (NA) | 62.7 | 59.5 |
| Asian alone | (NA) | (NA) | (NA) | (NA) | (NA) | (NA) | (NA) | (NA) | (NA) | 61.1 | 58.0 |
| Native Hawaiian or Other Pacific Islander alone | (NA) | (NA) | (NA) | (NA) | (NA) | (NA) | (NA) | (NA) | (NA) | 72.9 | 72.8 |
| Hispanic | 95.4 | 107.7 | 95.9 | 96.4 | 80.2 | 74.4 | 72.9 | 72.1 | 71.7 | 70.6 | 67.6 |
| *Bridged race estimates:* [2] | | | | | | | | | | | |
| White | 65.6 | 68.3 | 65.3 | 66.8 | 64.4 | 63.0 | 62.7 | 63.2 | 63.1 | 61.8 | 59.8 |
| Black | 84.7 | 86.8 | 70.0 | 68.5 | 66.3 | 65.1 | 64.7 | 64.6 | 64.0 | 65.1 | 64.9 |
| American Indian or Alaska Native | 82.7 | 76.2 | 58.7 | 53.6 | 48.6 | 47.0 | 46.4 | 44.8 | 43.9 | 42.8 | 40.8 |
| Asian or Pacific Islander | 73.2 | 69.6 | 65.8 | 63.0 | 59.2 | 62.2 | 59.2 | 60.7 | 58.5 | 62.1 | 59.3 |

NA Not available. [1] Includes other races not shown separately. [2] Bridged race categories consistent with 1977 Office of Management and Budget standards. [3] Birth rates computed by relating births to women age 45 and over (includes mothers up to age 64) to women age 45-49. [4] Number of live births per 1,000 women, 15 to 44 years old in specified group.

Source: U.S. National Center for Health Statistics, National Vital Statistics Reports, *Births: Final Data for 2017*, Vol. 67, No. 8, November 2018, and earlier reports; and CDC WONDER Online Database, "Natality for 2007-2017," <https://wonder.cdc.gov/natality.html>, accessed April 2019.

# Table 85. Births—Number and Rate by Race/Ethnicity and State and Island Area: 2017

[For registered births by place of residence. Excludes births to nonresidents of the United States. Based on race and Hispanic origin of mother. Race categories are consistent with 1997 Office of Management and Budget standards; see Technical Notes in source. Race alone is defined as only one race reported on the birth certificate. See Appendix III]

| State and Island Area | All races [1] | White alone [2] | Black alone [2] | American Indian or Alaska Native alone [2] | Asian alone [2] | Native Hawaiian or Other Pacific Islander alone [2] | Hispanic [3] | Birth rate [4] | Fertility rate [5] |
|---|---|---|---|---|---|---|---|---|---|
| **United States [6]** | **3,855,500** | **1,992,461** | **560,715** | **29,957** | **249,250** | **9,426** | **898,764** | **11.8** | **60.3** |
| Alabama | 58,941 | 34,377 | 17,963 | 131 | 950 | 44 | 4,546 | 12.1 | 62.0 |
| Alaska | 10,445 | 5,259 | 329 | 1,903 | 686 | 308 | 799 | 14.1 | 71.5 |
| Arizona | 81,872 | 33,694 | 4,241 | 4,256 | 2,987 | 217 | 34,377 | 11.7 | 60.8 |
| Arkansas | 37,520 | 24,089 | 7,082 | 239 | 783 | 470 | 4,048 | 12.5 | 65.0 |
| California | 471,658 | 127,822 | 23,441 | 1,411 | 72,049 | 1,809 | 220,122 | 11.9 | 58.2 |
| Colorado | 64,382 | 37,516 | 3,110 | 421 | 2,611 | 145 | 18,125 | 11.5 | 56.6 |
| Connecticut | 35,221 | 18,842 | 4,301 | 28 | 2,475 | 7 | 8,833 | 9.8 | 52.3 |
| Delaware | 10,855 | 5,309 | 2,818 | 20 | 646 | 3 | 1,748 | 11.3 | 60.2 |
| District of Columbia | 9,560 | 3,042 | 4,573 | 9 | 396 | 2 | 1,336 | 13.8 | 51.3 |
| Florida | 223,630 | 96,280 | 49,428 | 270 | 7,015 | 159 | 67,049 | 10.7 | 58.4 |
| Georgia | 129,243 | 56,985 | 44,447 | 113 | 6,039 | 110 | 17,954 | 12.4 | 60.2 |
| Hawaii | 17,517 | 3,407 | 406 | 39 | 4,653 | 1,684 | 2,672 | 12.3 | 65.9 |
| Idaho | 22,181 | 17,151 | 243 | 289 | 366 | 48 | 3,598 | 12.9 | 67.4 |
| Illinois | 149,390 | 78,925 | 25,685 | 90 | 9,650 | 43 | 31,428 | 11.7 | 59.0 |
| Indiana | 82,170 | 60,515 | 9,971 | 70 | 2,535 | 54 | 7,669 | 12.3 | 63.4 |
| Iowa | 38,430 | 30,010 | 2,657 | 183 | 1,321 | 128 | 3,527 | 12.2 | 64.9 |
| Kansas | 36,519 | 25,594 | 2,548 | 171 | 1,255 | 77 | 5,963 | 12.5 | 65.4 |
| Kentucky | 54,752 | 44,280 | 5,006 | 49 | 1,173 | 68 | 3,162 | 12.3 | 64.5 |
| Louisiana | 61,018 | 31,509 | 22,469 | 295 | 1,169 | 23 | 4,778 | 13.0 | 65.2 |
| Maine | 12,298 | 10,958 | 545 | 85 | 219 | 3 | 229 | 9.2 | 53.1 |
| Maryland | 71,641 | 29,809 | 22,327 | 87 | 5,276 | 40 | 12,223 | 11.8 | 60.0 |
| Massachusetts | 70,702 | 40,773 | 6,953 | 63 | 6,067 | 23 | 13,609 | 10.3 | 51.2 |
| Michigan | 111,426 | 75,578 | 20,849 | 396 | 4,468 | 30 | 7,339 | 11.2 | 59.4 |
| Minnesota | 68,595 | 47,088 | 8,163 | 1,042 | 5,323 | 56 | 5,023 | 12.3 | 64.3 |
| Mississippi | 37,357 | 18,620 | 16,087 | 213 | 502 | 12 | 1,650 | 12.5 | 63.1 |
| Missouri | 73,034 | 53,800 | 10,495 | 167 | 1,773 | 183 | 4,156 | 11.9 | 62.3 |
| Montana | 11,799 | 9,372 | 64 | 1,231 | 121 | 18 | 585 | 11.2 | 62.1 |
| Nebraska | 25,821 | 17,827 | 1,688 | 372 | 861 | 27 | 4,382 | 13.4 | 69.8 |
| Nevada | 35,756 | 13,171 | 4,471 | 305 | 2,685 | 322 | 13,176 | 11.9 | 60.7 |
| New Hampshire | 12,116 | 10,524 | 234 | 21 | 479 | 5 | 673 | 9.0 | 50.2 |
| New Jersey | 101,250 | 45,825 | 13,684 | 46 | 11,691 | 26 | 27,354 | 11.2 | 59.0 |
| New Mexico | 23,767 | 6,522 | 387 | 2,677 | 420 | 17 | 13,362 | 11.4 | 60.1 |
| New York | 229,737 | 111,690 | 34,062 | 331 | 25,429 | 51 | 53,112 | 11.6 | 57.4 |
| North Carolina | 120,125 | 64,278 | 27,886 | 1,466 | 5,006 | 131 | 18,464 | 11.7 | 59.6 |
| North Dakota | 10,737 | 7,931 | 608 | 817 | 286 | 10 | 587 | 14.2 | 73.4 |
| Ohio | 136,832 | 98,762 | 22,431 | 116 | 4,380 | 61 | 7,468 | 11.7 | 62.1 |
| Oklahoma | 50,214 | 28,976 | 4,085 | 4,614 | 1,328 | 232 | 7,441 | 12.8 | 65.3 |
| Oregon | 43,631 | 29,232 | 994 | 429 | 2,376 | 300 | 8,275 | 10.5 | 53.8 |
| Pennsylvania | 137,745 | 92,297 | 18,400 | 92 | 6,401 | 43 | 15,840 | 10.8 | 57.8 |
| Rhode Island | 10,638 | 6,142 | 776 | 44 | 542 | 7 | 2,760 | 10.0 | 50.9 |
| South Carolina | 57,029 | 32,283 | 16,851 | 138 | 1,125 | 45 | 5,221 | 11.4 | 59.1 |
| South Dakota | 12,134 | 8,620 | 398 | 1,807 | 248 | 9 | 624 | 14.0 | 76.4 |
| Tennessee | 81,016 | 53,721 | 16,050 | 90 | 1,905 | 60 | 7,684 | 12.1 | 61.7 |
| Texas | 382,050 | 127,533 | 48,242 | 664 | 20,385 | 510 | 180,216 | 13.5 | 64.9 |
| Utah | 48,585 | 36,492 | 569 | 445 | 1,233 | 469 | 7,832 | 15.7 | 72.0 |
| Vermont | 5,655 | 5,134 | 115 | 14 | 159 | 2 | 123 | 9.1 | 49.7 |
| Virginia | 100,391 | 55,540 | 21,101 | 155 | 7,670 | 125 | 13,999 | 11.9 | 59.7 |
| Washington | 87,562 | 50,679 | 3,944 | 1,112 | 8,836 | 1,164 | 15,973 | 11.8 | 59.8 |
| West Virginia | 18,675 | 16,943 | 629 | 15 | 201 | 11 | 390 | 10.3 | 58.0 |
| Wisconsin | 64,975 | 46,309 | 6,864 | 715 | 3,017 | 30 | 6,368 | 11.2 | 60.0 |
| Wyoming | 6,903 | 5,426 | 45 | 201 | 79 | 5 | 892 | 11.9 | 64.1 |
| Puerto Rico | 24,310 | 596 | 65 | – | 25 | 1 | 23,582 | 7.3 | 37.0 |
| Virgin Islands | (NA) | (NA) | (NA) | (NA) | (NA) | (NA) | (NA) | (NA) | (NA) |
| Guam | 3,297 | 193 | 31 | 8 | 796 | 2,102 | 27 | 19.7 | 99.3 |
| American Samoa | 977 | (NA) | (NA) | (NA) | (NA) | (NA) | (NA) | 19.0 | 87.6 |
| Northern Marianas | 363 | 2 | 1 | – | 53 | 289 | – | 6.9 | 39.6 |

– Represents zero. NA Not available. [1] Includes persons of other racial/ethnic groups, not shown separately. [2] Non-Hispanic. [3] Persons of Hispanic origin may be of any race. [4] Per 1,000 estimated population. [5] Number of births per 1,000 women aged 15 to 44 years. [6] Does not include data for the Island Areas.

Source: U.S. National Center for Health Statistics, National Vital Statistics Reports, *Births: Final Data for 2017*, Vol. 67, No. 8, November 2018. See also <https://www.cdc.gov/nchs/nvss/births.htm>.

## Table 86. Births, Twin Births, and Triplet and Higher-order Births by Race and Hispanic Origin of Mother: 2010 to 2017

[Represents registered births. Excludes births to nonresidents of the United States. Data are based on Hispanic origin and race of mother. Persons of Hispanic origin may be of any race. Race categories are consistent with 1997 Office of Management and Budget standards; see source for details. See also Appendix III]

| Year and race and Hispanic origin | Number | | | Rate | | |
|---|---|---|---|---|---|---|
| | Total births | Twin births | Triplet and higher-order births | Multiple births, total [1] | Twin births [2] | Triplet and higher-order births [3] |
| All races and origins: [4] | | | | | | |
| 2010.................... | 3,999,386 | 132,562 | 5,503 | 34.5 | 33.1 | 137.6 |
| 2011.................... | 3,953,590 | 131,269 | 5,417 | 34.6 | 33.2 | 137.0 |
| 2012.................... | 3,952,841 | 131,024 | 4,919 | 34.4 | 33.1 | 124.4 |
| 2013.................... | 3,932,181 | 132,324 | 4,700 | 34.8 | 33.7 | 119.5 |
| 2014.................... | 3,988,076 | 135,336 | 4,526 | 35.1 | 33.9 | 113.5 |
| 2015.................... | 3,978,497 | 133,155 | 4,123 | 34.5 | 33.5 | 103.6 |
| 2016.................... | 3,945,875 | 131,723 | 4,003 | 34.4 | 33.4 | 101.4 |
| 2017.................... | 3,855,500 | 128,310 | 3,917 | 34.3 | 33.3 | 101.6 |
| White alone, non-Hispanic | | | | | | |
| 2016.................... | 2,056,332 | 73,425 | 2,502 | 36.9 | 35.7 | 121.7 |
| 2017.................... | 1,992,461 | 70,704 | 2,324 | 36.7 | 35.5 | 116.6 |
| Black alone, non-Hispanic | | | | | | |
| 2016.................... | 558,622 | 22,267 | 628 | 41.0 | 39.9 | 112.4 |
| 2017.................... | 560,715 | 22,982 | 671 | 42.2 | 41.0 | 119.7 |
| Hispanic [5] | | | | | | |
| 2016.................... | 918,447 | 22,625 | 538 | 25.2 | 24.6 | 58.6 |
| 2017.................... | 898,764 | 22,041 | 614 | 25.2 | 24.5 | 68.3 |

[1] Number of live births in all multiple deliveries per 1,000 live births. [2] Number of births in twin deliveries per 1,000 live births. [3] Number of births in greater than twin deliveries per 100,000 live births. [4] Includes other races not shown separately. [5] Persons of Hispanic origin may be of any race.

Source: U.S. National Center for Health Statistics, National Vital Statistics Reports, *Births: Final Data for 2017*, Vol. 67, No. 8, November 2018. See also <https://www.cdc.gov/nchs/nvss/births.htm>.

## Table 87. Births by Method of Delivery and Race and Hispanic Origin: 2010 to 2017

[In thousands (3,999 represents 3,999,000), except rate. Race categories are consistent with 1997 Office of Management and Budget standards. Persons of Hispanic origin may be of any race. See Appendix III]

| Method of delivery | 2010 | 2012 | 2013 | 2014 | 2015 | 2016 | 2017 | | | |
|---|---|---|---|---|---|---|---|---|---|---|
| | | | | | | | Total [1] | White alone, non-Hispanic | Black alone, non-Hispanic | Hispanic |
| **Births, total**................. | **3,999** | **3,953** | **3,932** | **3,988** | **3,978** | **3,946** | **3,856** | **1,992** | **561** | **899** |
| Vaginal.................. | 2,681 | 2,651 | 2,643 | 2,700 | 2,704 | 2,685 | 2,621 | 1,376 | 358 | 613 |
| Cesarean.................. | 1,309 | 1,296 | 1,284 | 1,285 | 1,273 | 1,259 | 1,232 | 616 | 202 | 285 |
| Not stated.................. | 9 | 6 | 5 | 4 | 2 | 2 | 2 | 1 | (Z) | (Z) |
| Cesarean delivery rate [2]...... | 32.8 | 32.8 | 32.7 | 32.2 | 32.0 | 31.9 | 32.0 | 30.9 | 36.0 | 31.8 |
| Rate of vaginal birth after previous Cesarean [3].......... | (NA) | (NA) | (NA) | (NA) | (NA) | 12.4 | 12.8 | 13.0 | 12.8 | 12.0 |

Z Represents less than 500. NA Not available. [1] Includes other races, not shown separately. [2] Percent of all live births by cesarean delivery. [3] Number of births to women having a vaginal delivery per 100 births to women with a previous cesarean delivery.

Source: U.S. National Center for Health Statistics, National Vital Statistics Reports, *Births: Final Data for 2017*, Vol. 67, No. 8, November 2018, and earlier reports. See also <https://www.cdc.gov/nchs/nvss/births.htm>.

## Table 88. Births Delivered by Physicians, Midwives, and Other Attendants by Place of Delivery: 2017

| Place of delivery | Total births [1] | Physician | | | Midwife | | | Other |
|---|---|---|---|---|---|---|---|---|
| | | Total | Doctor of medicine | Doctor of osteopathy | Total | Certified nurse midwife | Other midwife | |
| **Total**.................. | **3,855,500** | **3,438,416** | **3,142,479** | **295,937** | **381,894** | **351,968** | **29,926** | **32,401** |
| In hospital [2]......................... | 3,793,272 | 3,435,769 | 3,140,158 | 295,611 | 335,932 | 331,141 | 4,791 | 20,002 |
| Not in hospital..................... | 62,047 | 2,598 | 2,274 | 324 | 45,937 | 20,809 | 25,128 | 12,344 |
| Freestanding birthing center.... | 19,878 | 530 | 396 | 134 | 18,468 | 11,203 | 7,265 | 778 |
| Clinic or doctor's office........... | 553 | 134 | 121 | 13 | 381 | 302 | 79 | 30 |
| Residence..................... | 38,343 | 1,385 | 1,261 | 124 | 26,223 | 9,139 | 17,084 | 9,889 |
| Other.................. | 3,273 | 549 | 496 | 53 | 865 | 165 | 700 | 1,647 |
| Not specified..................... | 181 | 49 | 47 | 2 | 25 | 18 | 7 | 55 |

[1] Includes those unspecified, not shown separately. [2] Includes births occurring en route to or upon arrival at hospital.

Source: U.S. National Center for Health Statistics, National Vital Statistics Reports, *Births: Final Data for 2017, Supplemental Tables*, Vol. 67, No. 8, November 2018. See also <https://www.cdc.gov/nchs/nvss/births.htm>.

# Table 89. Total Fertility Rate by Race and Hispanic Origin: 2010 to 2017

[Based on race of mother. Excludes births to nonresidents of United States. The total fertility rate estimates the number of births that a hypothetical cohort of 1,000 women would have if they experienced throughout their childbearing years the same age-specific birth rates observed in a given year. The rate can be expressed as the average number of children that would be born per woman. A total fertility rate of 2,100 represents "replacement level" fertility for the total population under current mortality conditions (assuming no net immigration). Race categories are consistent with the 1997 Office of Management and Budget standards. See Appendix III]

| Race and Hispanic origin | 2010 | 2011 | 2012 | 2013 | 2014 | 2015 | 2016 | 2017 |
|---|---|---|---|---|---|---|---|---|
| **Total** | **1,931** | **1,895** | **1,881** | **1,858** | **1,863** | **1,844** | **1,821** | **1,766** |
| Non-Hispanic: | | | | | | | | |
| White alone | (NA) | (NA) | (NA) | (NA) | (NA) | (NA) | 1,719 | 1,667 |
| Black alone | (NA) | (NA) | (NA) | (NA) | (NA) | (NA) | 1,833 | 1,825 |
| American Indian or Alaska Native alone | (NA) | (NA) | (NA) | (NA) | (NA) | (NA) | 1,795 | 1,702 |
| Asian alone | (NA) | (NA) | (NA) | (NA) | (NA) | (NA) | 1,691 | 1,597 |
| Native Hawaiian or other Pacific Islander alone | (NA) | (NA) | (NA) | (NA) | (NA) | (NA) | 2,077 | 2,086 |
| Hispanic [1] | 2,350 | 2,240 | 2,190 | 2,149 | 2,131 | 2,124 | 2,093 | 2,007 |

NA Not available. [1] Persons of Hispanic origin may be of any race.

Source: U.S. National Center for Health Statistics, National Vital Statistics Reports, *Births: Final Data for 2017, Supplemental Tables*, Vol. 67, No. 8, November 2018. See also <https://www.cdc.gov/nchs/nvss/births.htm>.

# Table 90. Teenagers—Births and Birth Rates by Age, Race, and Hispanic Origin: 2010 to 2017

[Birth rates per 1,000 women in specified group. Based on race and Hispanic origin of mother. Race categories are consistent with the 1997 Office of Management and Budget (OMB) standards. See source for details]

| Item | Number of births | | | Birth rate | | |
|---|---|---|---|---|---|---|
| | 2010 | 2016 | 2017 | 2010 | 2016 | 2017 |
| **All races, 15 to 19 years** [1] | **367,678** | **209,809** | **194,377** | **34.2** | **20.3** | **18.8** |
| 15 to 17 years | 109,173 | 54,741 | 48,547 | 17.3 | 8.8 | 7.9 |
| 18 to 19 years | 258,505 | 155,068 | 145,830 | 58.2 | 37.5 | 35.1 |
| Non-Hispanic: | | | | | | |
| White alone | (NA) | 78,133 | 71,854 | (NA) | 14.3 | 13.2 |
| Black alone | (NA) | 42,836 | 40,016 | (NA) | 29.3 | 27.5 |
| American Indian or Alaska Native alone | (NA) | 3,107 | 2,878 | (NA) | 35.1 | 32.9 |
| Asian alone | (NA) | 1,949 | 1,723 | (NA) | 3.9 | 3.3 |
| Native Hawaiian or other Pacific Islander alone | (NA) | 556 | 491 | (NA) | 28.6 | 25.5 |
| Hispanic [2] | (NA) | 74,822 | 69,354 | (NA) | 31.9 | 28.9 |

NA Not available. [1] Includes other racial/ethnic groups, not shown separately. [2] Persons of Hispanic origin may be of any race.

Source: U.S. National Center for Health Statistics, National Vital Statistics Reports, *Births: Final Data for 2017*, Vol. 67, No. 8, November 2018. See also <https://www.cdc.gov/nchs/nvss/births.htm>.

# Table 91. Births to Unmarried Women by Age, Race, and Hispanic Origin of Mother: 2017

[Data are based on Hispanic origin and race of mother. Race categories are consistent with 1997 Office of Management and Budget standards; see source for details. See also Appendix III]

| Race/ethnicity of mother | | Age of mother | | | | | | |
|---|---|---|---|---|---|---|---|---|
| | Total | Under 15 years old | 15 to 19 years old | 20 to 24 years old | 25 to 29 years old | 30 to 34 years old | 35 to 39 years old | 40 years and over |
| **NUMBER** | | | | | | | | |
| **Total** | **1,533,901** | **1,906** | **173,368** | **502,932** | **440,644** | **257,944** | **125,382** | **31,725** |
| Non-Hispanic: | | | | | | | | |
| White alone | 566,264 | 397 | 61,298 | 190,569 | 164,480 | 94,469 | 43,985 | 11,066 |
| Black alone | 388,979 | 612 | 39,012 | 130,703 | 119,288 | 64,017 | 28,970 | 6,377 |
| American Indian or Alaska Native alone | 20,734 | 37 | 2,720 | 6,783 | 6,066 | 3,386 | 1,433 | 309 |
| Asian alone | 29,287 | 13 | 1,159 | 5,561 | 8,853 | 7,624 | 4,567 | 1,510 |
| Native Hawaiian or other Pacific Islander alone | 4,576 | 2 | 429 | 1,526 | 1,309 | 830 | 405 | 75 |
| Hispanic [1] | 468,528 | 765 | 61,266 | 148,174 | 125,696 | 79,322 | 42,007 | 11,298 |
| **PERCENT** | | | | | | | | |
| **Total** | **39.8** | **99.4** | **89.2** | **65.8** | **39.2** | **23.6** | **22.6** | **25.6** |
| Non-Hispanic: | | | | | | | | |
| White alone | 28.4 | 99.5 | 85.3 | 55.6 | 27.7 | 15.1 | 14.8 | 18.9 |
| Black alone | 69.4 | 99.8 | 97.5 | 88.3 | 71.1 | 52.2 | 44.5 | 38.6 |
| American Indian or Alaska Native alone | 69.2 | 97.4 | 94.5 | 79.2 | 66.1 | 56.9 | 52.0 | 51.2 |
| Asian alone | 11.8 | (S) | 67.3 | 33.4 | 14.1 | 7.8 | 8.1 | 11.2 |
| Native Hawaiian or other Pacific Islander alone | 48.5 | (S) | 87.4 | 63.5 | 46.1 | 36.8 | 34.3 | 29.4 |
| Hispanic [1] | 52.1 | 98.8 | 88.3 | 67.6 | 49.3 | 38.3 | 36.1 | 36.9 |

S Figure does not meet standards of reliability. [1] Persons of Hispanic origin may be of any race.

Source: U.S. National Center for Health Statistics, National Vital Statistics Reports, *Births: Final Data for 2017*, Vol. 67, No. 8, November 2018. See also <https://www.cdc.gov/nchs/nvss/births.htm>.

## Table 92. Percent of Births to Teenage Mothers, Unmarried Women, and Births with Low Birth Weight by State: 2010 and 2017

[In percent. By place of residence. Excludes nonresidents of the United States]

| State | Births to teenage mothers [1] | | Births to unmarried women | | Births with low birth weight [2] | | State | Births to teenage mothers [1] | | Births to unmarried women | | Births with low birth weight [2] | |
|---|---|---|---|---|---|---|---|---|---|---|---|---|---|
| | 2010 | 2017 | 2010 | 2017 | 2010 | 2017 | | 2010 | 2017 | 2010 | 2017 | 2010 | 2017 |
| U.S. | **9.2** | **5.0** | **40.8** | **39.8** | **8.1** | **8.3** | MO | 10.0 | 5.9 | 40.2 | 39.9 | 8.2 | 8.7 |
| AL | 12.2 | 7.2 | 41.9 | 47.1 | 10.3 | 10.3 | MT | 9.4 | 5.5 | 36.4 | 35.9 | 7.5 | 8.0 |
| AK | 8.3 | 4.7 | 37.6 | 35.3 | 5.7 | 6.2 | NE | 7.6 | 4.5 | 33.6 | 33.2 | 7.1 | 7.5 |
| AZ | 10.7 | 6.1 | 44.9 | 44.8 | 7.1 | 7.5 | NV | 9.5 | 5.3 | 44.3 | 48.4 | 8.3 | 9.1 |
| AR | 13.6 | 8.5 | 45.3 | 45.5 | 8.8 | 9.3 | NH | 5.6 | 2.9 | 33.2 | 32.6 | 6.9 | 6.9 |
| CA | 8.5 | 4.0 | 40.5 | 37.5 | 6.8 | 6.9 | NJ | 5.4 | 2.8 | 35.4 | 33.9 | 8.2 | 7.9 |
| CO | 8.2 | 4.3 | 23.9 | 22.5 | 8.8 | 9.1 | NM | 13.9 | 8.0 | 52.3 | 51.7 | 8.7 | 9.5 |
| CT | 6.0 | 3.0 | 37.4 | 36.6 | 8.0 | 8.1 | NY | 6.2 | 3.3 | 41.7 | 38.0 | 8.2 | 8.1 |
| DE | 8.6 | 5.1 | 47.4 | 47.6 | 8.9 | 9.0 | NC | 10.1 | 5.7 | 42.0 | 40.9 | 9.1 | 9.4 |
| DC | 10.4 | 4.3 | 54.8 | 47.8 | 10.2 | 10.5 | ND | 7.2 | 3.4 | 32.7 | 31.5 | 6.7 | 6.7 |
| FL | 8.9 | 4.8 | 47.5 | 47.0 | 8.7 | 8.8 | OH | 9.9 | 5.7 | 43.8 | 43.2 | 8.6 | 8.7 |
| GA | 10.7 | 6.0 | 45.8 | 44.9 | 9.7 | 9.9 | OK | 12.2 | 7.6 | 41.8 | 42.0 | 8.4 | 8.1 |
| HI | 7.1 | 4.1 | 37.8 | 38.6 | 8.3 | 8.5 | OR | 7.7 | 4.1 | 35.7 | 36.2 | 6.3 | 6.8 |
| ID | 8.0 | 5.0 | 26.5 | 28.1 | 6.8 | 7.0 | PA | 8.3 | 4.3 | 41.5 | 41.0 | 8.3 | 8.4 |
| IL | 9.0 | 4.8 | 40.5 | 39.8 | 8.3 | 8.5 | RI | 8.0 | 3.9 | 45.0 | 43.9 | 7.7 | 7.5 |
| IN | 10.3 | 6.2 | 43.0 | 42.8 | 8.0 | 8.3 | SC | 11.7 | 6.0 | 47.6 | 46.1 | 9.9 | 9.7 |
| IA | 7.8 | 4.4 | 34.2 | 35.4 | 7.0 | 6.6 | SD | 8.3 | 5.1 | 37.6 | 37.2 | 6.8 | 6.9 |
| KS | 9.5 | 5.6 | 37.8 | 35.7 | 7.1 | 7.4 | TN | 11.6 | 6.8 | 44.1 | 43.6 | 9.0 | 9.2 |
| KY | 12.0 | 7.4 | 41.2 | 41.6 | 9.0 | 8.8 | TX | 12.4 | 7.1 | 42.4 | 41.0 | 8.4 | 8.4 |
| LA | 12.3 | 7.0 | 53.3 | 52.7 | 10.7 | 10.7 | UT | 5.8 | 3.7 | 19.2 | 18.5 | 7.0 | 7.2 |
| ME | 7.1 | 4.1 | 41.2 | 39.0 | 6.3 | 7.1 | VT | 6.4 | 3.6 | 39.2 | 40.1 | 6.1 | 6.7 |
| MD | 7.3 | 3.7 | 41.9 | 39.6 | 8.8 | 8.9 | VA | 7.2 | 4.0 | 35.5 | 34.6 | 8.2 | 8.4 |
| MA | 5.4 | 2.6 | 34.7 | 33.0 | 7.7 | 7.5 | WA | 6.9 | 3.6 | 33.0 | 31.6 | 6.3 | 6.6 |
| MI | 9.5 | 4.8 | 41.8 | 41.1 | 8.4 | 8.8 | WV | 12.7 | 7.6 | 43.9 | 45.6 | 9.2 | 9.5 |
| MN | 5.9 | 3.1 | 33.2 | 32.0 | 6.4 | 6.7 | WI | 7.4 | 3.9 | 36.7 | 37.7 | 7.0 | 7.7 |
| MS | 15.2 | 8.4 | 54.8 | 53.5 | 12.1 | 11.6 | WY | 9.6 | 6.1 | 34.0 | 33.5 | 9.0 | 8.7 |

[1] Defined as teenage mothers aged 15-19. [2] Less than 2,500 grams (5 pounds, 8 ounces).

Source: U.S. National Center for Health Statistics, National Vital Statistics Reports, *Births: Final Data for 2017, Supplemental Tables*, Vol. 67, No. 8, November 2018, and earlier reports; and CDC WONDER Online Database, "Natality for 2007-2017," <https://wonder.cdc.gov/natality.html>, accessed January 2019.

## Table 93. Rate of Pregnancy Risk Factors, Labor and Delivery Characteristics, and Birth Defects by Age of Mother: 2017

[Rates are number of live births with specified risk factor, procedure, or characteristic per 1,000 live births in specified group, except as noted; birth defects are per 100,000 live births. In 2017, total number of births to residents of areas reporting risk factors, procedure, or defects was 3,855,500]

| Factor/characteristic | Births with factor reported (number) | Rates by age | | | | | | |
|---|---|---|---|---|---|---|---|---|
| | | All ages | Under 20 years | 20 to 24 years | 25 to 29 years | 30 to 34 years | 35 to 39 years | 40 to 54 years |
| RISK FACTORS IN CURRENT PREGNANCY | | | | | | | | |
| Diabetes: | | | | | | | | |
| Prepregnancy (diagnosis prior to pregnancy) | 35,336 | 9.2 | 4.2 | 5.7 | 7.5 | 10.0 | 14.8 | 21.4 |
| Gestational (diagnosis in current pregnancy) | 244,716 | 63.5 | 21.2 | 34.7 | 53.5 | 74.5 | 101.4 | 133.5 |
| Hypertension: | | | | | | | | |
| Prepregnancy (chronic) | 73,032 | 19.0 | 7.2 | 11.2 | 15.4 | 20.7 | 31.1 | 47.6 |
| Gestational (pregnancy-induced, preeclampsia) | 248,282 | 64.5 | 70.1 | 64.3 | 62.0 | 61.8 | 68.2 | 84.6 |
| Eclampsia [1] | 10,644 | 2.9 | 3.7 | 3.0 | 2.7 | 2.6 | 3.0 | 4.1 |
| Previous preterm birth | 126,500 | 32.8 | 8.0 | 24.8 | 33.1 | 35.8 | 42.8 | 48.4 |
| Pregnancy resulted from infertility treatment | 72,120 | 18.7 | 0.2 | 2.1 | 9.3 | 23.5 | 41.3 | 92.1 |
| Mother had previous cesarean delivery [2] | 595,213 | 224.5 | 103.7 | 167.5 | 210.0 | 239.7 | 271.6 | 288.4 |
| LABOR AND DELIVERY CHARACTERISTICS | | | | | | | | |
| Induction of labor | 992,068 | 257.5 | 294.2 | 278.4 | 261.1 | 242.6 | 238.0 | 255.5 |
| Breech presentation (rate per 100 live births) | 151,273 | 3.9 | 2.5 | 2.9 | 3.6 | 4.4 | 5.1 | 6.5 |
| BIRTH DEFECTS (CONGENITAL ANOMALIES) | | | | | | | | |
| Anencephaly | 432 | 11.2 | 14.8 | 11.3 | 11.9 | 10.0 | 11.2 | 9.7 |
| Meningomyelocele or spina bifida | 595 | 15.5 | 18.9 | 15.8 | 14.6 | 14.9 | 15.5 | 19.4 |
| Cyanotic congenital heart disease | 2,126 | 55.2 | 48.0 | 52.4 | 52.8 | 54.6 | 60.5 | 87.9 |
| Gastroschisis | 925 | 24.0 | 87.7 | 51.2 | 21.0 | 8.0 | 6.1 | 4.0 |
| Cleft lip with or without cleft palate | 1,990 | 51.7 | 52.5 | 56.6 | 54.6 | 45.3 | 49.8 | 58.1 |
| Down syndrome | 2,039 | 53.0 | 31.1 | 25.1 | 27.4 | 39.9 | 108.1 | 358.2 |

[1] Excludes data for South Carolina and Tennessee. [2] Excludes women who have not had a previous pregnancy and from whom total birth order is unknown.

Source: U.S. National Center for Health Statistics, National Vital Statistics Reports, *Births: Final Data for 2017, Supplemental Tables*, Vol. 67, No. 8, November 2018. See also <https://www.cdc.gov/nchs/nvss/births.htm>.

# Table 94. Percent of Premature Births by Whether Early or Late Preterm and by Age, Race, and Hispanic Origin of Mother: 2017

[Preterm/premature births are those with less than 37 completed weeks of gestation based on obstetric estimates. Based on race and Hispanic origin of mother. Race categories are consistent with 1997 Office of Management and Budget standards. See source for details]

| Characteristic | Total births (number) | Total under 37 weeks | Percent preterm | | | |
|---|---|---|---|---|---|---|
| | | | Early preterm | | | Late preterm |
| | | | Under 28 weeks | 28 to 31 weeks | 32 to 33 weeks | 34 to 36 weeks |
| **Total** [1]............................. | **3,855,500** | **9.9** | **0.7** | **0.9** | **1.2** | **7.2** |
| Age of mother: | | | | | | |
| Under 15 years.......................... | 1,917 | 13.2 | 2.0 | 1.2 | 1.8 | 8.2 |
| 15 to 19 years.......................... | 194,377 | 10.3 | 0.9 | 1.0 | 1.2 | 7.1 |
| 20 to 24 years.......................... | 764,780 | 9.6 | 0.7 | 0.9 | 1.1 | 6.9 |
| 25 to 29 years.......................... | 1,123,577 | 9.3 | 0.6 | 0.9 | 1.1 | 6.7 |
| 30 to 34 years.......................... | 1,091,917 | 9.6 | 0.6 | 0.9 | 1.2 | 7.0 |
| 35 to 39 years.......................... | 554,796 | 11.3 | 0.7 | 1.1 | 1.4 | 8.1 |
| 40 to 44 years.......................... | 114,813 | 14.0 | 0.8 | 1.4 | 1.8 | 10.0 |
| 45 to 54 years.......................... | 9,323 | 22.2 | 1.2 | 2.6 | 3.5 | 14.9 |
| Race and Hispanic origin of mother: | | | | | | |
| White alone, non-Hispanic................. | 1,992,461 | 9.1 | 0.5 | 0.8 | 1.1 | 6.8 |
| Black alone, non-Hispanic................. | 560,715 | 13.9 | 1.5 | 1.6 | 1.7 | 9.1 |
| Hispanic [2]............................. | 898,764 | 9.6 | 0.6 | 0.9 | 1.1 | 7.1 |

[1] Total includes those with gestational age not stated; and races other than White and Black, not shown separately. [2] Persons of Hispanic origin may be of any race.

Source: U.S. National Center for Health Statistics, *Births, Final Data for 2017*, Vol. 67, No. 8, November 2018. See also <https://www.cdc.gov/nchs/nvss/births.htm>.

# Table 95. Women Who Had a Birth in the Past 12 Months by Selected Characteristics: 2017

[For women aged 15 to 50 years old. Based on the 2017 American Community Survey (ACS). The ACS sample includes the household population and the population living in institutions, dormitories, and other group quarters. Based on a sample and subject to sampling variability. See Appendix III for details]

| Characteristic | Total women (number) | Women who had a child in the past 12 months | | | |
|---|---|---|---|---|---|
| | | Number | Percent distribution | Rate per 1,000 women | Percent unmarried |
| **Total, aged 15 to 50 years**...................... | **76,791,565** | **3,997,394** | **(X)** | **52** | **33.7** |
| Age: | | | | | |
| 15 to 19 years............................ | 10,493,304 | 126,099 | 3.2 | 12 | 85.8 |
| 20 to 34 years............................ | 32,891,322 | 2,904,603 | 72.7 | 88 | 36.1 |
| 35 to 50 years............................ | 33,406,939 | 966,692 | 24.2 | 29 | 19.9 |
| Race/ethnicity: | | | | | |
| One race................................. | 74,279,325 | 3,874,709 | 96.9 | 52 | 33.4 |
| White.................................... | 52,850,357 | 2,709,612 | 67.8 | 51 | 27.9 |
| Black or African American................ | 10,835,268 | 592,963 | 14.8 | 55 | 62.7 |
| American Indian and Alaska Native......... | 677,431 | 41,786 | 1.0 | 62 | 61.1 |
| Asian.................................... | 5,217,662 | 269,849 | 6.8 | 52 | 10.5 |
| Native Hawaiian and Other Pacific Islander.... | 164,998 | 9,126 | 0.2 | 55 | 33.5 |
| Some other race.......................... | 4,533,609 | 251,373 | 6.3 | 55 | 43.4 |
| Two or more races........................ | 2,512,240 | 122,685 | 3.1 | 49 | 45.2 |
| Hispanic origin: | | | | | |
| Hispanic or Latino origin (of any race)......... | 15,472,583 | 878,666 | 22.0 | 57 | 40.8 |
| White alone, not Hispanic or Latino........ | 42,860,604 | 2,136,880 | 53.5 | 50 | 24.9 |
| Nativity: | | | | | |
| Native................................... | 63,729,486 | 3,199,281 | 80.0 | 50 | 36.8 |
| Foreign born [1]......................... | 13,062,079 | 798,113 | 20.0 | 61 | 21.3 |
| Education: | | | | | |
| Less than high school graduate........... | 12,771,839 | 464,989 | 11.6 | 36 | 52.1 |
| High school graduate (includes equivalency)...... | 16,155,823 | 937,373 | 23.4 | 58 | 50.4 |
| Some college or associate's degree....... | 24,386,124 | 1,234,003 | 30.9 | 51 | 39.7 |
| Bachelor's degree........................ | 15,362,890 | 841,544 | 21.1 | 55 | 12.8 |
| Graduate or professional degree.......... | 8,114,889 | 519,485 | 13.0 | 64 | 7.1 |
| Poverty status in past 12 months: | | | | | |
| Women 15 to 50 years old with poverty status determined...... | 75,028,851 | 3,984,932 | (X) | 53 | 33.6 |
| Below 100 percent of poverty level....... | 11,797,384 | 894,924 | 22.5 | 76 | 66.2 |
| 100 to 199 percent of poverty level....... | 13,407,433 | 825,721 | 20.7 | 62 | 40.3 |
| 200 percent or more above poverty level...... | 49,824,034 | 2,264,287 | 56.8 | 45 | 18.2 |
| Labor force status: | | | | | |
| In labor force [2]........................ | 54,220,770 | 2,533,860 | 63.5 | 47 | 34.9 |
| Public assistance income in past 12 months: | | | | | |
| Received public assistance income........ | 1,505,636 | 179,327 | 4.5 | 119 | 68.2 |
| Did not receive public assistance income...... | 75,285,929 | 3,818,067 | 95.5 | 51 | 32.1 |

X Not applicable. [1] Excludes persons born outside of the United States to a parent who is a U.S. citizen. [2] Data are shown for women aged 16 to 50 years old.

Source: U.S. Census Bureau, 2017 American Community Survey, S1301, "Fertility," <http://factfinder.census.gov>, accessed December 2018.

# Table 96. Women by Number of Children Ever Born by Age, Marital Status, and Race/Ethnicity: 2018

[76,414 represents 76,414,000. As of June. Data shown are for women aged 15 to 50. Based on the Current Population Survey; for more information, see <http://www.census.gov/cps/methodology>]

| Age and marital status | Total women (1,000) | Percent distribution by number of children ever born | | | | | | |
|---|---|---|---|---|---|---|---|---|
| | | None | One | Two | Three | Four | Five and six | Seven or more |
| Total women: [1] | 76,414 | 44.2 | 16.8 | 21.7 | 10.7 | 4.3 | 1.9 | 0.4 |
| By age: | | | | | | | | |
| 15 to 19 years old | 10,294 | 96.9 | 2.1 | 0.8 | 0.1 | – | 0.1 | – |
| 20 to 24 years old | 10,607 | 78.6 | 14.0 | 6.0 | 1.0 | 0.3 | 0.2 | – |
| 25 to 29 years old | 11,476 | 54.2 | 20.4 | 16.2 | 6.5 | 2.1 | 0.5 | 0.1 |
| 30 to 34 years old | 10,889 | 33.6 | 22.3 | 24.6 | 12.8 | 4.4 | 1.9 | 0.3 |
| 35 to 39 years old | 10,727 | 20.0 | 19.2 | 32.6 | 17.4 | 7.3 | 3.2 | 0.4 |
| 40 to 44 years old | 9,896 | 15.0 | 18.7 | 34.6 | 18.6 | 8.7 | 3.8 | 0.7 |
| 45 to 50 years old | 12,524 | 15.4 | 19.8 | 35.4 | 17.3 | 7.4 | 3.6 | 1.2 |
| By marital status: | | | | | | | | |
| Women ever married | 41,451 | 17.5 | 21.6 | 33.8 | 16.6 | 6.8 | 3.0 | 0.6 |
| Women never married | 34,963 | 75.8 | 11.1 | 7.5 | 3.6 | 1.4 | 0.6 | 0.1 |
| By race and Hispanic origin: | | | | | | | | |
| White alone | 56,229 | 44.4 | 16.1 | 22.1 | 11.1 | 4.2 | 1.8 | 0.4 |
| White alone, non-Hispanic | 42,373 | 45.7 | 16.1 | 22.8 | 10.1 | 3.5 | 1.5 | 0.4 |
| Black alone | 11,258 | 40.8 | 19.8 | 20.1 | 10.4 | 5.6 | 2.8 | 0.5 |
| Asian alone | 5,519 | 45.5 | 18.1 | 25.0 | 7.7 | 2.4 | 1.0 | 0.4 |
| Hispanic [2] | 15,674 | 40.2 | 16.7 | 19.9 | 13.7 | 6.3 | 2.7 | 0.5 |

– Represents or rounds to zero. [1] Includes women of other races, not shown separately. [2] Persons of Hispanic origin may be of any race.

Source: U.S. Census Bureau, "Fertility of Women in the United States: 2018," <https://www.census.gov/topics/health/fertility/data/tables.html>, accessed June 2019.

# Table 97. Women's Relationship Status and Age at First Birth by Current Age and Race/Ethnicity: 2018

[In percent, except as noted (42,670 represents 42,670,000). As of June. Data are from the Current Population Survey; for more information, see <https://www.census.gov/programs-surveys/cps.html>.

| Current age and race/ethnicity | Total mothers, 1,000 | Married at first birth | | | Not married at first birth | | | | | |
|---|---|---|---|---|---|---|---|---|---|---|
| | | | | | Living with unmarried partner | | | Neither married nor living with unmarried partner | | |
| | | Under age 20 at first birth | Age 20 to 25 at first birth | Over age 25 at first birth | Under age 20 at first birth | Age 20 to 25 at first birth | Over age 25 at first birth | Under age 20 at first birth | Age 20 to 25 at first birth | Over age 25 at first birth |
| TOTAL | | | | | | | | | | |
| 15 to 50 years old | 42,670 | 5.9 | 21.9 | 34.7 | 6.7 | 9.9 | 4.6 | 6.4 | 7.3 | 2.5 |
| 15 to 19 years old | 321 | 6.7 | (X) | (X) | 52.3 | (X) | (X) | 41.0 | (X) | (X) |
| 20 to 24 years old | 2,274 | 10.4 | 15.4 | (X) | 18.1 | 22.0 | (X) | 16.4 | 17.6 | (X) |
| 25 to 29 years old | 5,258 | 6.6 | 22.1 | 10.9 | 12.7 | 19.5 | 3.3 | 9.8 | 12.7 | 2.4 |
| 30 to 34 years old | 7,230 | 6.7 | 20.5 | 32.0 | 7.8 | 12.1 | 5.9 | 5.7 | 6.7 | 2.6 |
| 35 to 39 years old | 8,583 | 6.0 | 21.6 | 38.3 | 5.6 | 8.9 | 5.6 | 6.1 | 5.4 | 2.5 |
| 40 to 44 years old | 8,411 | 5.6 | 21.8 | 43.3 | 4.9 | 6.3 | 4.9 | 5.7 | 4.9 | 2.7 |
| 45 to 50 years old | 10,593 | 4.1 | 25.1 | 47.0 | 1.6 | 5.2 | 4.5 | 3.0 | 6.5 | 3.0 |
| WHITE ALONE | | | | | | | | | | |
| 15 to 50 years old | 31,275 | 6.3 | 24.3 | 37.4 | 6.4 | 9.4 | 4.3 | 4.9 | 5.3 | 1.8 |
| 15 to 19 years old | 252 | 8.2 | (X) | (X) | 51.9 | (X) | (X) | 39.9 | (X) | (X) |
| 20 to 24 years old | 1,533 | 12.3 | 19.0 | (X) | 20.0 | 20.7 | (X) | 12.6 | 15.5 | (X) |
| 25 to 29 years old | 3,644 | 8.2 | 26.1 | 12.3 | 12.3 | 18.9 | 2.7 | 7.7 | 9.8 | 2.0 |
| 30 to 34 years old | 5,269 | 7.3 | 23.2 | 33.0 | 7.8 | 11.9 | 5.5 | 4.8 | 4.6 | 1.9 |
| 35 to 39 years old | 6,315 | 5.7 | 23.0 | 41.4 | 5.3 | 8.4 | 5.6 | 4.7 | 3.9 | 2.1 |
| 40 to 44 years old | 6,237 | 6.1 | 24.1 | 45.5 | 4.3 | 6.5 | 4.3 | 3.8 | 3.5 | 1.8 |
| 45 to 50 years old | 8,025 | 4.2 | 27.0 | 50.3 | 1.5 | 4.6 | 4.1 | 2.1 | 4.5 | 1.8 |
| BLACK ALONE | | | | | | | | | | |
| 15 to 50 years old | 6,666 | 4.4 | 11.5 | 14.4 | 9.3 | 13.7 | 7.1 | 15.3 | 18.4 | 6.0 |
| 15 to 19 years old | 42 | – | (X) | (X) | 45.1 | (X) | (X) | 54.9 | (X) | (X) |
| 20 to 24 years old | 492 | 4.1 | 3.6 | (X) | 12.4 | 21.9 | (X) | 30.9 | 27.1 | (X) |
| 25 to 29 years old | 1,078 | 2.2 | 7.7 | 3.1 | 16.3 | 21.2 | 5.2 | 17.8 | 23.1 | 3.5 |
| 30 to 34 years old | 1,146 | 3.7 | 8.8 | 15.6 | 9.3 | 16.5 | 9.0 | 12.5 | 18.6 | 6.1 |
| 35 to 39 years old | 1,286 | 6.5 | 13.3 | 15.1 | 8.9 | 13.7 | 7.3 | 14.8 | 14.3 | 6.1 |
| 40 to 44 years old | 1,181 | 5.2 | 12.1 | 19.2 | 8.8 | 7.7 | 10.6 | 16.2 | 13.2 | 7.0 |
| 45 to 50 years old | 1,439 | 4.2 | 17.4 | 22.5 | 2.5 | 8.3 | 6.7 | 8.9 | 20.2 | 9.3 |
| HISPANIC [1] | | | | | | | | | | |
| 15 to 50 years old | 9,376 | 9.8 | 25.5 | 21.4 | 10.2 | 11.9 | 5.4 | 6.9 | 6.7 | 2.2 |
| 15 to 19 years old | 83 | 3.9 | (X) | (X) | 64.7 | (X) | (X) | 31.4 | (X) | (X) |
| 20 to 24 years old | 663 | 12.7 | 13.2 | (X) | 25.4 | 16.1 | (X) | 17.5 | 15.2 | (X) |
| 25 to 29 years old | 1,329 | 11.0 | 21.1 | 5.9 | 15.2 | 18.9 | 3.7 | 11.5 | 11.0 | 1.8 |
| 30 to 34 years old | 1,660 | 11.7 | 21.5 | 17.8 | 13.8 | 15.6 | 5.6 | 6.9 | 5.1 | 2.0 |
| 35 to 39 years old | 1,803 | 10.3 | 25.3 | 22.7 | 8.1 | 11.1 | 6.9 | 7.8 | 5.1 | 2.9 |
| 40 to 44 years old | 1,794 | 9.0 | 28.9 | 29.9 | 6.3 | 10.0 | 6.0 | 4.3 | 3.8 | 1.9 |
| 45 to 50 years old | 2,044 | 7.0 | 33.9 | 33.6 | 2.2 | 5.9 | 6.5 | 1.2 | 6.6 | 3.3 |

– Represents or rounds to zero. X Not applicable. [1] Persons of Hispanic origin may be of any race.

Source: U.S. Census Bureau, "Fertility of Women in the United States: 2018," <https://www.census.gov/topics/health/fertility/data/tables.html>, accessed June 2019.

## Table 98. Women Who Had a Birth in the Past Year Who Are in the Labor Force by Educational Attainment: 2010 to 2017

[In thousands (2,562 represents 2,562,000), except percent. For women aged 16 to 50 years old. Based on the American Community Survey (ACS). The ACS universe includes the household population and population living in institutions, college dormitories, and other group quarters. Based on a sample and subject to sampling variability, see Appendix III]

| Year | Number of women who had a birth in the past year who are in the labor force | | | | | Percent of women who had a birth in the past year who are in the labor force | | | | |
|---|---|---|---|---|---|---|---|---|---|---|
| | Total | Less than high school diploma | High school diploma or GED | Some college | Bachelor's degree or higher | Total | Less than high school diploma | High school diploma or GED | Some college | Bachelor's degree or higher |
| 2010........ | 2,562 | 278 | 589 | 859 | 836 | 61.6 | 39.7 | 57.9 | 66.4 | 72.7 |
| 2013........ | 2,418 | 221 | 513 | 805 | 879 | 61.7 | 38.8 | 56.4 | 64.4 | 73.8 |
| 2014........ | 2,436 | 203 | 508 | 815 | 909 | 61.8 | 38.2 | 55.4 | 64.9 | 73.7 |
| 2015........ | 2,447 | 196 | 508 | 816 | 927 | 62.4 | 38.2 | 56.0 | 65.1 | 74.2 |
| 2016........ | 2,493 | 194 | 526 | 804 | 970 | 63.3 | 39.6 | 57.2 | 65.3 | 74.7 |
| 2017........ | 2,534 | 182 | 532 | 794 | 1,027 | 63.5 | 39.6 | 56.7 | 64.3 | 75.4 |

Source: U.S. Census Bureau, "Fertility: Historical Time Series Tables," <https://www.census.gov/topics/health/fertility/data/tables.html>, accessed June 2019.

## Table 99. Women With Births in the Past 12 Months by Citizenship Status, Educational Attainment, and Poverty Status by State: 2017

[In percent, except for total. For women 15 to 50 years old. Based on 2017 American Community Survey (ACS). See headnote, Table 98]

| State | Total (number) | Citizenship status | | Educational attainment | | | | | Below poverty [3] |
|---|---|---|---|---|---|---|---|---|---|
| | | Native born | Foreign born [1] | Less than high school graduate | High school graduate [2] | Some college or associate's degree | Bachelor's degree | Graduate or professional degree | |
| **United States......** | **3,997,394** | **80.0** | **20.0** | **11.6** | **23.4** | **30.9** | **21.1** | **13.0** | **22.5** |
| Alabama............... | 59,028 | 95.3 | 4.7 | 14.2 | 28.0 | 30.8 | 18.9 | 8.1 | 30.3 |
| Alaska................ | 9,961 | 78.7 | 21.3 | 8.7 | 27.0 | 40.4 | 17.5 | 6.4 | 18.3 |
| Arizona............... | 88,721 | 76.2 | 23.8 | 14.2 | 24.6 | 32.1 | 19.7 | 9.4 | 22.6 |
| Arkansas.............. | 41,016 | 89.6 | 10.4 | 11.5 | 31.1 | 31.8 | 15.5 | 10.0 | 30.6 |
| California............. | 468,957 | 65.5 | 34.5 | 14.3 | 23.0 | 30.0 | 20.6 | 12.1 | 20.8 |
| Colorado.............. | 70,949 | 85.3 | 14.7 | 8.7 | 22.1 | 28.8 | 24.9 | 15.5 | 18.2 |
| Connecticut........... | 33,995 | 78.4 | 21.6 | 11.3 | 20.9 | 23.8 | 23.3 | 20.7 | 15.5 |
| Delaware.............. | 9,580 | 76.5 | 23.5 | 18.4 | 26.5 | 29.9 | 14.3 | 10.9 | 25.8 |
| District of Columbia... | 9,007 | 80.0 | 20.0 | 12.9 | 21.1 | 12.0 | 19.3 | 34.7 | 26.8 |
| Florida................ | 231,116 | 72.8 | 27.2 | 11.4 | 26.3 | 32.6 | 19.8 | 9.9 | 24.8 |
| Georgia............... | 141,334 | 83.7 | 16.3 | 11.7 | 26.7 | 31.2 | 20.2 | 10.2 | 27.0 |
| Hawaii................ | 19,672 | 81.2 | 18.8 | 6.3 | 24.5 | 42.8 | 17.1 | 9.2 | 14.4 |
| Idaho................. | 24,723 | 90.3 | 9.7 | 8.2 | 28.2 | 37.2 | 20.0 | 6.4 | 27.1 |
| Illinois................ | 153,400 | 79.5 | 20.5 | 10.2 | 20.8 | 29.5 | 23.2 | 16.2 | 22.4 |
| Indiana............... | 77,269 | 90.2 | 9.8 | 12.6 | 26.3 | 31.2 | 21.4 | 8.5 | 22.5 |
| Iowa.................. | 41,142 | 86.2 | 13.8 | 11.5 | 20.0 | 33.3 | 21.4 | 12.9 | 21.9 |
| Kansas................ | 38,940 | 89.4 | 10.6 | 9.2 | 17.6 | 36.4 | 25.2 | 11.6 | 17.5 |
| Kentucky.............. | 53,444 | 92.0 | 8.0 | 10.3 | 25.1 | 35.9 | 16.1 | 12.4 | 29.0 |
| Louisiana............. | 58,623 | 92.4 | 7.6 | 14.8 | 25.0 | 32.2 | 20.2 | 7.8 | 31.0 |
| Maine................. | 14,945 | 96.0 | 4.0 | 5.5 | 19.5 | 33.0 | 25.3 | 16.7 | 22.0 |
| Maryland.............. | 74,868 | 76.2 | 23.8 | 10.8 | 18.1 | 25.9 | 23.8 | 21.3 | 16.3 |
| Massachusetts........ | 76,690 | 73.6 | 26.4 | 6.7 | 20.4 | 23.6 | 26.8 | 22.5 | 17.1 |
| Michigan.............. | 117,528 | 86.9 | 13.1 | 12.5 | 22.2 | 33.2 | 19.8 | 12.2 | 26.2 |
| Minnesota............ | 70,957 | 81.6 | 18.4 | 10.1 | 15.0 | 30.2 | 29.1 | 15.7 | 13.7 |
| Mississippi........... | 38,333 | 96.1 | 3.9 | 13.2 | 20.4 | 44.8 | 14.3 | 7.3 | 28.4 |
| Missouri.............. | 80,273 | 92.5 | 7.5 | 8.3 | 24.5 | 35.9 | 20.2 | 11.0 | 22.0 |
| Montana.............. | 13,055 | 96.4 | 3.6 | 11.9 | 24.8 | 38.0 | 17.4 | 7.9 | 19.2 |
| Nebraska............. | 29,620 | 84.5 | 15.5 | 12.9 | 21.0 | 30.2 | 22.8 | 13.1 | 20.1 |
| Nevada............... | 37,802 | 73.2 | 26.8 | 19.5 | 28.6 | 31.6 | 13.7 | 6.5 | 25.0 |
| New Hampshire....... | 13,862 | 88.6 | 11.4 | 6.9 | 22.8 | 26.4 | 23.9 | 20.1 | 14.5 |
| New Jersey............ | 98,578 | 64.6 | 35.4 | 6.7 | 20.4 | 24.1 | 26.8 | 22.0 | 14.1 |
| New Mexico........... | 28,338 | 90.0 | 10.0 | 15.2 | 26.1 | 37.6 | 10.5 | 10.6 | 30.9 |
| New York.............. | 219,214 | 67.9 | 32.1 | 11.4 | 21.4 | 25.2 | 22.8 | 19.3 | 21.9 |
| North Carolina........ | 127,760 | 85.5 | 14.5 | 12.1 | 19.5 | 32.6 | 22.2 | 13.5 | 26.5 |
| North Dakota......... | 10,777 | 95.3 | 4.7 | 10.7 | 15.6 | 29.4 | 34.6 | 9.7 | 12.3 |
| Ohio.................. | 151,068 | 91.3 | 8.7 | 10.8 | 26.5 | 30.0 | 18.7 | 14.0 | 26.2 |
| Oklahoma............. | 59,955 | 90.3 | 9.7 | 12.4 | 28.5 | 32.9 | 19.3 | 6.9 | 25.9 |
| Oregon............... | 48,087 | 84.1 | 15.9 | 11.8 | 23.0 | 37.4 | 15.7 | 12.2 | 25.7 |
| Pennsylvania.......... | 143,272 | 88.4 | 11.6 | 9.9 | 25.8 | 26.2 | 20.8 | 17.4 | 18.6 |
| Rhode Island.......... | 11,713 | 82.5 | 17.5 | 13.2 | 19.8 | 20.6 | 28.3 | 18.0 | 18.4 |
| South Carolina........ | 66,875 | 92.4 | 7.6 | 12.1 | 28.5 | 31.0 | 17.4 | 11.0 | 25.8 |
| South Dakota......... | 12,915 | 93.9 | 6.1 | 12.3 | 20.1 | 41.8 | 16.6 | 9.3 | 20.6 |
| Tennessee............ | 76,574 | 88.5 | 11.5 | 10.7 | 26.8 | 34.6 | 17.8 | 10.2 | 25.1 |
| Texas................. | 395,121 | 75.7 | 24.3 | 14.3 | 24.2 | 31.9 | 19.3 | 10.3 | 23.6 |
| Utah.................. | 51,456 | 88.4 | 11.6 | 8.1 | 20.5 | 33.9 | 29.1 | 8.4 | 13.7 |
| Vermont.............. | 5,096 | 93.7 | 6.3 | 3.2 | 24.6 | 33.7 | 25.4 | 13.1 | 15.2 |
| Virginia............... | 100,976 | 78.7 | 21.3 | 7.6 | 19.9 | 29.1 | 25.4 | 18.1 | 17.7 |
| Washington........... | 97,643 | 75.2 | 24.8 | 12.0 | 19.8 | 32.2 | 22.3 | 13.8 | 18.6 |
| West Virginia......... | 18,881 | 97.2 | 2.8 | 11.7 | 31.9 | 34.4 | 12.4 | 9.6 | 36.6 |
| Wisconsin............. | 67,283 | 89.4 | 10.6 | 7.4 | 24.6 | 31.3 | 26.1 | 10.7 | 21.1 |
| Wyoming.............. | 7,002 | 93.6 | 6.4 | 2.7 | 33.3 | 36.8 | 20.6 | 6.6 | 19.4 |

[1] Foreign born excludes people born outside the U.S. to a parent who is a U.S. citizen. [2] Includes equivalency. [3] The population universe used when determining poverty status excludes people institutionalized, in military group quarters, and in college dormitories, and unrelated individuals under 15 years old.

Source: U.S. Census Bureau, 2017 American Community Survey, Tables B13008, B13010, and B13014, <http://factfinder.census.gov>, accessed December 2018.

## Table 100. Women Who Had a Birth in the Past 12 Months by Household Income and Marital Status: 2017

[In thousands (3,412.3 represents 3,412,300), except percent. Data shown for women aged 15 to 50 years old; does not include women living in group quarters. Based on the American Community Survey (ACS). Based on a sample and subject to sampling variability]

| Annual household income | Total women | Women with a birth in the past 12 months | | | Percent of total women | Percent of women with a birth in the past 12 months | | |
|---|---|---|---|---|---|---|---|---|
| | | Total | Married [1] | Unmarried [2] | | Total | Married [1] | Unmarried [2] |
| Under $10,000............... | 3,412.3 | 226.7 | 60.2 | 166.5 | 4.6 | 5.7 | 2.3 | 11.9 |
| $10,000–$14,999............ | 1,912.2 | 113.9 | 35.0 | 78.9 | 2.6 | 2.9 | 1.4 | 5.6 |
| $15,000–$24,999............ | 4,861.7 | 299.4 | 120.3 | 179.2 | 6.5 | 7.5 | 4.7 | 12.8 |
| $25,000–$34,999............ | 5,530.4 | 334.3 | 166.5 | 167.8 | 7.4 | 8.4 | 6.5 | 12.0 |
| $35,000–$49,999............ | 8,520.1 | 494.1 | 286.0 | 208.1 | 11.4 | 12.4 | 11.1 | 14.8 |
| $50,000–$74,999............ | 13,210.4 | 705.1 | 470.1 | 235.0 | 17.7 | 17.8 | 18.3 | 16.8 |
| $75,000–$99,999............ | 10,813.8 | 559.0 | 411.1 | 147.9 | 14.5 | 14.1 | 16.0 | 10.5 |
| $100,000–$149,999.......... | 13,829.4 | 670.6 | 533.8 | 136.8 | 18.5 | 16.9 | 20.8 | 9.8 |
| $150,000–$199,999.......... | 6,262.7 | 283.3 | 236.6 | 46.7 | 8.4 | 7.1 | 9.2 | 3.3 |
| $200,000 or more............. | 6,454.4 | 283.5 | 248.1 | 35.4 | 8.6 | 7.1 | 9.7 | 2.5 |

[1] Includes women who are married, spouse present. [2] Includes women who are widowed, divorced, separated, and never married.

Source: U.S. Census Bureau, "Fertility of Women in the United States: 2018," <https://www.census.gov/topics/health/fertility/data/tables.html>, accessed June 2019.

## Table 101. Sexually Active High School Students and Birth Control Use by Sex, Race/Ethnicity, and Grade: 2017

[In percent. For public and private school students in grades 9 to 12. Current sexual activity defined as having had sexual intercourse with at least one person during the 3 months before the survey. Based on the Youth Risk Behavior Survey; see source for details]

| Item | Total | Race/ethnicity | | | Grade level | | | |
|---|---|---|---|---|---|---|---|---|
| | | White [1] | Black [1] | Hispanic | 9th | 10th | 11th | 12th |
| TOTAL | | | | | | | | |
| Ever had sexual intercourse................ | 39.5 | 38.6 | 45.8 | 41.1 | 20.4 | 36.2 | 47.3 | 57.3 |
| Currently sexually active.................... | 28.7 | 28.8 | 31.3 | 29.2 | 12.9 | 24.9 | 35.3 | 44.3 |
| Condom use [2]................ | 53.8 | 54.1 | 52.1 | 54.9 | 54.5 | 57.8 | 56.3 | 49.9 |
| Birth control use [3]................. | 29.4 | 37.4 | 22.5 | 16.8 | 14.3 | 24.1 | 30.4 | 36.9 |
| No pregnancy prevention method [2]....... | 13.8 | 10.0 | 17.8 | 19.0 | 20.1 | 15.0 | 11.5 | 12.3 |
| MALE | | | | | | | | |
| Ever had sexual intercourse................ | 41.4 | 38.5 | 52.7 | 44.1 | 23.3 | 38.0 | 48.8 | 58.9 |
| Currently sexually active.................... | 28.6 | 27.6 | 34.6 | 30.0 | 14.1 | 25.3 | 34.7 | 43.5 |
| Condom use [2]................ | 61.3 | 61.9 | 57.9 | 62.4 | 61.1 | 63.2 | 63.1 | 59.1 |
| Birth control use [3]................. | 23.9 | 30.3 | 21.1 | 13.4 | 10.1 | 19.6 | 27.8 | 28.5 |
| No pregnancy prevention method [2]....... | 10.5 | 7.7 | 10.8 | 16.1 | 13.8 | 12.6 | 7.0 | 10.7 |
| FEMALE | | | | | | | | |
| Ever had sexual intercourse................ | 37.7 | 38.7 | 39.4 | 37.9 | 17.2 | 34.4 | 45.8 | 55.8 |
| Currently sexually active.................... | 28.8 | 30.0 | 28.4 | 28.2 | 11.7 | 24.6 | 35.8 | 45.1 |
| Condom use [2]................ | 46.9 | 47.0 | 45.8 | 47.1 | 46.8 | 52.4 | 50.0 | 41.3 |
| Birth control use [3]................. | 34.6 | 43.9 | 23.7 | 20.4 | 19.2 | 28.5 | 32.8 | 44.7 |
| No pregnancy prevention method [2]....... | 16.7 | 11.8 | 25.5 | 22.0 | 27.6 | 17.2 | 15.4 | 13.7 |

[1] Non-Hispanic. [2] During last sexual intercourse. [3] Includes use of birth control pills, an IUD or implant, or a shot, patch, or birth control ring.

Source: U.S. Centers for Disease Control and Prevention, *Morbidity and Mortality Weekly Report, Surveillance Summaries*, 67:8, June 15, 2018, "Youth Risk Behavior Surveillance—United States, 2017." See also <http://www.cdc.gov/healthyyouth/data/yrbs/index.htm>.

## Table 102. Adults Reporting Sexual Contact with Opposite- and Same-Sex Partners by Sex, Age, and Race/Ethnicity: 2011 to 2013

[In percent, except as indicated (55,271 represents 55,271,000). Data shown for persons aged 18 to 44 years old who have ever had specified types of sexual contact. Based on the 2011-2013 National Survey of Family Growth. See Appendix III]

| Sex and selected characteristics | Number (1,000) | Percent reporting type of sexual contact [1] | | | | |
|---|---|---|---|---|---|---|
| | | Opposite-sex sexual contact [2] | Vaginal intercourse with opposite-sex partner | Oral sex with opposite-sex partner | Anal sex with opposite-sex partner | Same-sex sexual contact [3] |
| **Women [1]**................................. | **55,271** | **95.3** | **94.2** | **86.2** | **35.9** | **17.4** |
| By age: | | | | | | |
| 18 to 24 years old.................... | 14,269 | 85.6 | 81.7 | 77.3 | 28.4 | 19.4 |
| 25 to 44 years old.................... | 41,002 | 98.7 | 98.5 | 89.3 | 38.5 | 16.7 |
| By race/ethnicity: | | | | | | |
| White alone, non-Hispanic................. | 31,880 | 95.4 | 93.9 | 91.9 | 40.5 | 19.6 |
| Black alone, non-Hispanic................. | 7,581 | 96.3 | 95.6 | 82.7 | 27.5 | 19.4 |
| Hispanic.................................... | 10,811 | 95.8 | 95.5 | 77.7 | 32.3 | 11.2 |
| **Men [1]**................................... | **54,685** | **93.5** | **92.0** | **87.4** | **42.3** | **6.2** |
| By age: | | | | | | |
| 18 to 24 years old.................... | 14,718 | 83.5 | 79.9 | 77.6 | 29.3 | 6.6 |
| 25 to 44 years old.................... | 39,967 | 97.2 | 96.5 | 91.0 | 47.0 | 6.0 |
| By race/ethnicity: | | | | | | |
| White alone, non-Hispanic................. | 31,423 | 93.7 | 92.0 | 91.0 | 44.1 | 6.9 |
| Black alone, non-Hispanic................. | 6,304 | 96.3 | 95.4 | 90.4 | 35.4 | 5.3 |
| Hispanic.................................... | 11,292 | 93.3 | 92.4 | 78.6 | 40.4 | 6.2 |

[1] Includes other race/ethnicities not shown separately. [2] Includes vaginal, oral, or anal sex. [3] For women, any sexual contact with same-sex (female) partners includes oral sex or any sexual experience. For men, includes oral or anal sex with male partners.

Source: U.S. National Center for Health Statistics, National Health Statistics Reports, *Sexual Behavior, Sexual Attraction, and Sexual Orientation Among Adults Aged 18-44 in the United States: Data From the 2011-2013 National Survey of Family Growth*, No. 88, January 2016. See also <http://www.cdc.gov/nchs/nsfg/>.

# Table 103. Sexual Attraction and Orientation by Sex, Age, and Race/Ethnicity: 2011 to 2013

[In percent, except as indicated (55,271 represents 55,271,000). Data shown for persons aged 18 to 44 years old. Based on the 2011-2013 National Survey of Family Growth. See Appendix III]

| Sex and sexual attraction and orientation | Total [1] | Age | | | | Race/ethnicity | | |
|---|---|---|---|---|---|---|---|---|
| | | 18 to 24 years old | 25 to 44 years old | | | White, Non-His-panic | Black, Non-His-panic | His-panic |
| | | | Total | 25 to 34 years old | 35 to 44 years old | | | |
| **Women (1,000)** | **55,271** | **14,269** | **41,002** | **20,790** | **20,212** | **31,880** | **7,581** | **10,811** |
| **Percent distribution** | | | | | | | | |
| *Sexual attraction:* | | | | | | | | |
| Total | 100.0 | 100.0 | 100.0 | 100.0 | 100.0 | 100.0 | 100.0 | 100.0 |
| Only opposite sex | 81.0 | 75.9 | 82.8 | 79.1 | 86.6 | 79.6 | 84.2 | 84.7 |
| Mostly opposite sex | 12.9 | 14.4 | 12.4 | 15.4 | 9.2 | 15.2 | 9.1 | 9.3 |
| Equally to both | 3.2 | 5.3 | 2.5 | 3.3 | 1.7 | 2.9 | 3.7 | 3.5 |
| Mostly same sex | 0.8 | 1.7 | 0.5 | 0.3 | 0.7 | 0.8 | 0.6 | 1.1 |
| Only same sex | 0.8 | 1.0 | 0.8 | 0.9 | 0.6 | 0.9 | 0.8 | 0.8 |
| Not sure | 1.2 | 1.6 | 1.1 | 0.9 | 1.3 | 0.7 | 1.7 | 0.5 |
| *Sexual orientation:* | | | | | | | | |
| Total | 100.0 | 100.0 | 100.0 | 100.0 | 100.0 | 100.0 | 100.0 | 100.0 |
| Heterosexual or straight | 92.3 | 89.5 | 93.3 | 92.5 | 94.2 | 93.1 | 93.1 | 92.6 |
| Homosexual, gay, or lesbian | 1.3 | 1.8 | 1.1 | 1.2 | 0.9 | 1.3 | 1.1 | 1.2 |
| Bisexual | 5.5 | 7.8 | 4.7 | 5.4 | 4.0 | 5.4 | 4.9 | 4.2 |
| Not reported [2] | 0.9 | 0.9 | 0.9 | 1.0 | 0.9 | 0.2 | 0.9 | 1.9 |
| **Men (1,000)** | **54,685** | **14,718** | **39,967** | **20,453** | **19,514** | **31,423** | **6,304** | **11,292** |
| **Percent distribution** | | | | | | | | |
| *Sexual attraction:* | | | | | | | | |
| Total | 100.0 | 100.0 | 100.0 | 100.0 | 100.0 | 100.0 | 100.0 | 100.0 |
| Only opposite sex | 92.1 | 88.6 | 93.4 | 92.7 | 94.1 | 92.5 | 93.5 | 91.5 |
| Mostly opposite sex | 4.1 | 5.9 | 3.4 | 3.4 | 3.5 | 3.9 | 2.8 | 3.9 |
| Equally to both | 0.9 | 1.0 | 0.7 | 0.9 | 0.6 | 0.9 | 0.4 | 1.1 |
| Mostly same sex | 0.8 | 0.7 | 0.8 | 1.2 | 0.3 | 0.6 | 1.1 | 0.8 |
| Only same sex | 1.5 | 2.5 | 1.2 | 1.0 | 1.4 | 1.7 | 0.9 | 1.8 |
| Not sure | 0.7 | 1.3 | 0.5 | 0.8 | (S) | 0.3 | 1.3 | 0.8 |
| *Sexual orientation:* | | | | | | | | |
| Total | 100.0 | 100.0 | 100.0 | 100.0 | 100.0 | 100.0 | 100.0 | 100.0 |
| Heterosexual or straight | 95.1 | 94.0 | 95.4 | 95.4 | 95.5 | 95.4 | 96.5 | 93.2 |
| Homosexual, gay, or lesbian | 1.9 | 2.6 | 1.7 | 1.6 | 1.7 | 2.0 | 1.5 | 2.1 |
| Bisexual | 2.0 | 2.5 | 1.8 | 2.2 | 1.3 | 2.2 | 1.6 | 2.0 |
| Not reported [2] | 1.0 | 0.9 | 1.1 | 0.8 | 1.4 | 0.4 | 0.4 | 2.7 |

S Figure does not meet publication standards. [1] Includes other race/ethnicities not shown separately. [2] Includes "don't know" and "refused."

Source: U.S. National Center for Health Statistics, National Health Statistics Reports, *Sexual Behavior, Sexual Attraction, and Sexual Orientation Among Adults Aged 18-44 in the United States: Data From the 2011-2013 National Survey of Family Growth*, No. 88, January 2016. See also <http://www.cdc.gov/nchs/nsfg/>.

# Table 104. Contraceptive Use Among Women by Race/Ethnicity, Age, and Method: 1995 to 2015

[In percent. Covers women who are sexually active. Based on National Survey of Family Growth interviews of women of childbearing age. Survey collects up to four methods of contraception used in the month of interview; percents may not add to total because more than one method could have been used in month of interview]

| Year and race/ethnicity | By age [1,2] | | | | | By method | | | | | |
|---|---|---|---|---|---|---|---|---|---|---|---|
| | 15 to 44 years, total | 15 to 19 years | 20 to 24 years | 25 to 34 years | 35 to 44 years | Female steril-ization | Inject-able | Pill [3] | Intra-uterine device | Con-dom | With-drawal |
| Total women: [4] | | | | | | | | | | | |
| 1995 | 92.5 | 80.2 | 91.7 | 94.0 | 93.9 | 27.8 | 3.0 | 27.0 | 0.8 | 23.4 | 6.1 |
| 2002 | 89.3 | 82.0 | 87.9 | 90.2 | 90.7 | 27.0 | 5.5 | 31.0 | 2.1 | 23.8 | 8.8 |
| 2006 to 2010 | 89.0 | 82.0 | 87.0 | 89.8 | 90.6 | 26.6 | 3.9 | 28.4 | 5.6 | 23.1 | 10.1 |
| 2011 to 2015 | 89.7 | 84.9 | 89.1 | 89.9 | 90.9 | 23.2 | 4.2 | 26.6 | 11.5 | 22.2 | 14.0 |
| White alone, non-Hispanic: | | | | | | | | | | | |
| 1995 | 93.0 | 81.7 | 93.0 | 93.9 | 94.2 | 24.5 | 2.4 | 28.7 | 0.7 | 22.5 | 6.4 |
| 2002 | 90.9 | 84.4 | 90.9 | 91.5 | 91.7 | 23.9 | 4.3 | 34.9 | 1.7 | 21.7 | 9.5 |
| 2006 to 2010 | 90.5 | 85.7 | 89.1 | 91.6 | 91.2 | 23.6 | 2.5 | 33.1 | 5.6 | 20.8 | 10.3 |
| 2011 to 2015 | 91.2 | 89.4 | 90.0 | 91.3 | 92.2 | 20.7 | 2.8 | 30.9 | 11.4 | 20.9 | 13.8 |
| Black alone, non-Hispanic: | | | | | | | | | | | |
| 1995 | 90.0 | 80.0 | 91.3 | 91.6 | 90.9 | 39.9 | 5.4 | 23.7 | (S) | 24.9 | 3.3 |
| 2002 | 84.7 | 82.2 | 74.8 | 88.9 | 86.0 | 39.2 | 9.4 | 23.1 | (S) | 29.6 | 4.8 |
| 2006 to 2010 | 82.8 | 77.3 | 79.4 | 82.1 | 86.3 | 37.3 | 8.9 | 18.7 | 5.0 | 29.9 | 7.1 |
| 2011 to 2015 | 86.5 | 78.5 | 85.4 | 89.0 | 86.6 | 30.9 | 10.0 | 19.5 | 8.8 | 25.6 | 12.4 |
| Hispanic or Latina: [5] | | | | | | | | | | | |
| 1995 | 91.4 | 75.5 | 82.5 | 95.4 | 95.2 | 36.6 | 4.7 | 23.0 | (S) | 21.2 | 5.7 |
| 2002 | 88.4 | 76.4 | 87.5 | 87.4 | 92.3 | 33.8 | 7.8 | 22.0 | 5.3 | 24.1 | 6.3 |
| 2006 to 2010 | 89.6 | 75.5 | 87.0 | 89.7 | 93.4 | 31.7 | 6.0 | 20.2 | 6.8 | 22.2 | 10.4 |
| 2011 to 2015 | 87.1 | 72.0 | 87.5 | 87.1 | 90.4 | 28.2 | 5.0 | 18.3 | 14.3 | 21.3 | 13.9 |

S Figure does not meet standards of reliability or precision. [1] Includes women using contraception in the month of interview, or not using contraception in the month of interview but who had sexual intercourse in the 3 months prior to interview. [2] Any contraceptive use. Includes methods not shown separately. [3] For 2011-2015, includes the oral contraceptive pill only. Prior to 2011, also includes the emergency contraception/morning-after pill. [4] Includes women of other or multiple races, not shown separately. [5] Persons of Hispanic origin may be of any race.

Source: U.S. National Center for Health Statistics, *Health, United States, 2017,* September 2018. See also <https://www.cdc.gov/nchs/>.

## Table 105. Abortions—Number and Rate by Race: 1990 to 2010

[In thousands (58,700 represents 58,700,000), except rate. Data for 2000-09 have been revised based on Census Bureau intercensal population estimates, as of October 2012]

| Year | All races | | | White | | | Black | | | Other | | |
|---|---|---|---|---|---|---|---|---|---|---|---|---|
| | Women aged 15 to 44 | Abortions | | Women aged 15 to 44 | Abortions | | Women aged 15 to 44 | Abortions | | Women aged 15 to 44 | Abortions | |
| | | Number (1,000) | Rate per 1,000 women [1] | | Number (1,000) | Rate per 1,000 women [1] | | Number (1,000) | Rate per 1,000 women [1] | | Number (1,000) | Rate per 1,000 women [1] |
| 1990 [2] | 58,700 | 1,609 | 27.4 | 48,224 | 1,039 | 21.5 | 7,905 | 505 | 63.9 | 2,571 | 65 | 25.1 |
| 1991 | 59,305 | 1,557 | 26.2 | 48,560 | 982 | 20.2 | 8,053 | 507 | 62.9 | 2,692 | 68 | 26.2 |
| 1992 | 59,417 | 1,529 | 25.7 | 48,435 | 943 | 19.5 | 8,170 | 517 | 63.3 | 2,812 | 69 | 24.4 |
| 1993 [2] | 59,712 | 1,495 | 25.0 | 48,497 | 908 | 18.7 | 8,282 | 517 | 62.4 | 2,933 | 70 | 23.9 |
| 1994 [2] | 60,020 | 1,423 | 23.7 | 48,592 | 856 | 17.6 | 8,390 | 492 | 58.6 | 3,039 | 76 | 23.7 |
| 1995 | 60,368 | 1,359 | 22.5 | 48,719 | 817 | 16.8 | 8,496 | 462 | 54.4 | 3,153 | 80 | 25.3 |
| 1996 | 60,704 | 1,360 | 22.4 | 48,837 | 797 | 16.3 | 8,592 | 483 | 56.2 | 3,275 | 81 | 24.6 |
| 1997 [2] | 61,041 | 1,335 | 21.9 | 48,942 | 777 | 15.9 | 8,694 | 479 | 55.1 | 3,405 | 79 | 23.1 |
| 1998 [2] | 61,326 | 1,319 | 21.5 | 49,012 | 762 | 15.5 | 8,785 | 476 | 54.2 | 3,528 | 81 | 23.1 |
| 1999 | 61,475 | 1,315 | 21.4 | 48,974 | 743 | 15.2 | 8,851 | 485 | 54.8 | 3,650 | 87 | 24.0 |
| 2000 | 61,642 | 1,313 | 21.3 | 48,939 | 733 | 15.0 | 8,911 | 488 | 54.8 | 3,792 | 92 | 24.3 |
| 2001 [2] | 61,795 | 1,291 | 20.9 | 48,877 | 717 | 14.7 | 8,977 | 476 | 53.0 | 3,941 | 99 | 25.1 |
| 2002 [2] | 61,856 | 1,269 | 20.5 | 48,735 | 706 | 14.5 | 9,034 | 468 | 51.8 | 4,088 | 96 | 23.4 |
| 2003 [2] | 61,888 | 1,250 | 20.2 | 48,570 | 695 | 14.3 | 9,092 | 458 | 50.4 | 4,227 | 97 | 23.0 |
| 2004 | 61,969 | 1,222 | 19.7 | 48,438 | 674 | 13.9 | 9,168 | 453 | 49.4 | 4,364 | 95 | 21.8 |
| 2005 | 62,071 | 1,206 | 19.4 | 48,321 | 662 | 13.7 | 9,246 | 452 | 48.9 | 4,504 | 92 | 20.5 |
| 2006 [2] | 62,190 | 1,242 | 20.0 | 48,205 | 681 | 14.1 | 9,335 | 464 | 49.7 | 4,649 | 97 | 20.8 |
| 2007 | 62,292 | 1,210 | 19.4 | 48,082 | 668 | 13.9 | 9,421 | 448 | 47.6 | 4,789 | 93 | 19.5 |
| 2008 | 62,360 | 1,212 | 19.4 | 47,943 | 664 | 13.8 | 9,499 | 458 | 48.2 | 4,918 | 90 | 18.4 |
| 2009 [2] | 62,373 | 1,152 | 18.5 | 47,771 | 621 | 13.0 | 9,562 | 445 | 46.6 | 5,040 | 86 | 17.0 |
| 2010 | 62,414 | 1,103 | 17.7 | 47,644 | 591 | 12.4 | 9,613 | 427 | 44.4 | 5,157 | 85 | 16.6 |

[1] Aged 15–44. [2] Total numbers of abortions in 1990, 1993, 1994, 1997, 1998, 2001-2003, 2006, and 2009 have been estimated by interpolation.

Source: R.K. Jones and K. Kooistra, "Abortion Incidence and Access to Services in the United States, 2008," *Perspectives on Sexual and Reproductive Health*, 43.1 (2011) ©; R.K. Jones and J. Jerman, "Abortion Incidence and Service Availability in the United States, 2011," *Perspectives on Sexual and Reproductive Health*, 46.1 (2014) ©; and unpublished data from the Guttmacher Institute ©. See also <http://www.guttmacher.org/>.

## Table 106. Abortions by Selected Characteristics: 1990 to 2010

[1,609 represents 1,609,000. Number of abortions from surveys conducted by source; characteristics from the U.S. Centers for Disease Control's (CDC) annual abortion surveillance summaries, with adjustments for changes in states reporting data to the Centers for Disease Control each year. Data for 2000 have been revised based on Census Bureau intercensal population estimates, as of October 2012]

| Characteristic | Number (1,000) | | | Percent distribution | | | Abortion rate per 1,000 women | | |
|---|---|---|---|---|---|---|---|---|---|
| | 1990 | 2000 | 2010 | 1990 | 2000 | 2010 | 1990 | 2000 | 2010 |
| **Total abortions** | **1,609** | **1,313** | **1,103** | **100.0** | **100.0** | **100.0** | **27.4** | **21.3** | **17.7** |
| Age of woman: | | | | | | | | | |
| Less than 15 years [1] | 13 | 9 | 5 | 0.8 | 0.7 | 0.5 | 7.9 | 4.3 | 2.5 |
| 15 to 19 years | 351 | 235 | 157 | 21.8 | 17.9 | 14.3 | 40.6 | 23.9 | 14.7 |
| 20 to 24 years | 532 | 430 | 362 | 33.1 | 32.7 | 32.9 | 56.7 | 45.9 | 34.1 |
| 25 to 29 years | 360 | 303 | 272 | 22.4 | 23.0 | 24.7 | 34.0 | 31.7 | 26.0 |
| 30 to 34 years | 216 | 190 | 172 | 13.4 | 14.5 | 15.6 | 19.7 | 18.6 | 17.1 |
| 35 to 39 years | 108 | 110 | 97 | 6.7 | 8.4 | 8.8 | 10.7 | 9.7 | 9.6 |
| 40 years and over [2] | 29 | 37 | 37 | 1.8 | 2.8 | 3.3 | 3.2 | 3.2 | 3.3 |
| Race/ethnicity of woman: | | | | | | | | | |
| White | 1,039 | 733 | 591 | 64.6 | 55.8 | 53.6 | 21.5 | 15.0 | 12.4 |
| Black | 505 | 488 | 427 | 31.4 | 37.2 | 38.7 | 63.9 | 54.8 | 44.4 |
| Other | 65 | 92 | 85 | 4.0 | 7.0 | 7.7 | 25.1 | 24.3 | 16.6 |
| Hispanic | 195 | 261 | 239 | 12.1 | 19.8 | 21.7 | 35.1 | 30.3 | 20.2 |
| Non-Hispanic White | 852 | 479 | 366 | 52.9 | 36.5 | 33.2 | 19.7 | 11.7 | 9.5 |
| Marital status of woman: [3] | | | | | | | | | |
| Married | 341 | 246 | 164 | 21.0 | 19.0 | 14.8 | 10.6 | 7.9 | 5.8 |
| Unmarried | 1,268 | 1,067 | 939 | 79.0 | 81.0 | 85.2 | 47.7 | 35.0 | 27.4 |
| Number of prior live births: | | | | | | | | | |
| None | 780 | 533 | 448 | 49.0 | 41.0 | 40.6 | 32.0 | 20.2 | 15.2 |
| One | 396 | 361 | 296 | 25.0 | 28.0 | 26.8 | 36.9 | 32.5 | 28.0 |
| Two | 280 | 260 | 208 | 17.0 | 20.0 | 18.9 | 20.5 | 18.9 | 16.3 |
| Three | 102 | 104 | 95 | 6.0 | 8.0 | 8.6 | 15.6 | 14.9 | 14.5 |
| Four or more | 50 | 56 | 56 | 3.0 | 4.0 | 5.1 | 14.7 | 16.4 | 17.4 |
| Number of prior induced abortions: | | | | | | | | | |
| None | 891 | 699 | 585 | 55.0 | 53.0 | 53.0 | (NA) | (NA) | (NA) |
| One | 443 | 355 | 288 | 28.0 | 27.0 | 26.2 | (NA) | (NA) | (NA) |
| Two or more | 275 | 259 | 229 | 17.0 | 20.0 | 20.8 | (NA) | (NA) | (NA) |
| Weeks of gestation: | | | | | | | | | |
| Less than 9 weeks | 825 | 749 | 696 | 51.3 | 57.1 | 63.1 | (NA) | (NA) | (NA) |
| 9 to 10 weeks | 416 | 269 | 182 | 25.8 | 20.5 | 16.5 | (NA) | (NA) | (NA) |
| 11 to 12 weeks | 195 | 138 | 102 | 12.1 | 10.5 | 9.2 | (NA) | (NA) | (NA) |
| 13 weeks or more | 173 | 156 | 129 | 10.8 | 11.9 | 11.2 | (NA) | (NA) | (NA) |

NA Not available. [1] Denominator of rate is women aged 14. [2] Denominator of rate is women aged 40–44. [3] Separated women are included with married.

Source: R.K. Jones and K. Kooistra, "Abortion Incidence and Access to Services in the United States, 2008," *Perspectives on Sexual and Reproductive Health*, 43.1 (2011) ©; R.K. Jones and J. Jerman, "Abortion Incidence and Service Availability in the United States, 2011," *Perspectives on Sexual and Reproductive Health*, 46.1 (2014) ©; and unpublished data from the Guttmacher Institute ©. See also <http://www.guttmacher.org/>.

## Table 107. Abortions—Number and Rate by State of Occurrence: 2000 to 2010

[Number of abortions by state of occurrence from surveys of hospitals, clinics, and physicians identified as providers of abortion services conducted by the Guttmacher Institute. The Guttmacher Institute reallocates abortions to the woman's state of residence for survey years. Abortion rates are computed per 1,000 women 15 to 44 years of age. Estimates for 2000-08 have been revised based on Census Bureau intercensal population estimates, as of October 2012]

| State | Number 2000 | Number 2005 | Number 2010 | Rate[1] 2000 | Rate[1] 2005 | Rate[1] 2010 | State | Number 2000 | Number 2005 | Number 2010 | Rate[1] 2000 | Rate[1] 2005 | Rate[1] 2010 |
|---|---|---|---|---|---|---|---|---|---|---|---|---|---|
| U.S..... | 1,312,990 | 1,206,200 | 1,102,670 | 21.3 | 19.4 | 17.7 | MO...... | 7,920 | 8,400 | 6,160 | 6.6 | 7.0 | 5.2 |
| AL....... | 13,830 | 11,340 | 10,280 | 14.3 | 11.9 | 10.7 | MT....... | 2,510 | 2,150 | 2,220 | 13.5 | 11.9 | 12.4 |
| AK....... | 1,660 | 1,880 | 1,930 | 11.8 | 13.3 | 13.4 | NE....... | 4,250 | 3,220 | 2,490 | 11.6 | 9.0 | 7.0 |
| AZ....... | 17,940 | 19,480 | 15,180 | 16.5 | 16.3 | 12.0 | NV....... | 13,740 | 13,530 | 11,850 | 32.1 | 26.8 | 21.6 |
| AR....... | 5,540 | 4,710 | 4,680 | 9.8 | 8.3 | 8.2 | NH....... | 3,010 | 3,170 | 3,040 | 11.2 | 11.9 | 12.2 |
| CA...... | 236,060 | 208,430 | 191,550 | 31.1 | 26.8 | 24.3 | NJ....... | 65,780 | 61,150 | 48,840 | 36.2 | 34.2 | 28.1 |
| CO...... | 15,530 | 16,120 | 15,060 | 15.9 | 16.3 | 14.7 | NM...... | 5,760 | 6,220 | 5,630 | 14.7 | 15.7 | 14.1 |
| CT...... | 15,240 | 16,780 | 15,430 | 21.1 | 23.6 | 22.3 | NY...... | 164,630 | 155,960 | 142,790 | 39.1 | 37.9 | 35.3 |
| DE...... | 5,440 | 5,150 | 6,570 | 31.3 | 28.9 | 36.6 | NC...... | 37,610 | 34,500 | 32,700 | 21.1 | 18.7 | 16.8 |
| DC...... | 9,800 | 7,230 | 4,660 | 68.2 | 50.2 | 28.6 | ND...... | 1,340 | 1,230 | 1,290 | 9.9 | 9.5 | 10.0 |
| FL....... | 103,050 | 92,300 | 86,180 | 31.9 | 26.2 | 24.2 | OH...... | 40,230 | 35,060 | 30,220 | 16.5 | 15.0 | 13.5 |
| GA...... | 32,140 | 33,180 | 35,590 | 16.9 | 16.7 | 17.1 | OK...... | 7,390 | 6,950 | 6,290 | 10.1 | 9.6 | 8.5 |
| HI....... | 5,630 | 5,350 | 5,520 | 22.2 | 20.7 | 21.0 | OR...... | 17,010 | 13,200 | 11,010 | 23.5 | 18.1 | 14.6 |
| ID....... | 1,950 | 1,810 | 1,740 | 7.0 | 6.2 | 5.7 | PA...... | 36,570 | 34,150 | 38,650 | 14.3 | 13.7 | 15.8 |
| IL....... | 63,690 | 50,970 | 44,400 | 23.2 | 19.1 | 16.9 | RI........ | 5,600 | 5,290 | 4,290 | 24.1 | 23.2 | 20.0 |
| IN....... | 12,490 | 11,150 | 10,400 | 9.4 | 8.6 | 8.1 | SC....... | 8,210 | 7,080 | 6,730 | 9.3 | 7.9 | 7.2 |
| IA....... | 5,970 | 6,370 | 6,000 | 9.8 | 10.8 | 10.4 | SD...... | 870 | 790 | 740 | 5.5 | 5.1 | 4.8 |
| KS...... | 12,270 | 10,410 | 7,240 | 21.4 | 18.6 | 13.0 | TN...... | 19,010 | 18,140 | 17,850 | 15.2 | 14.5 | 14.0 |
| KY...... | 4,700 | 3,870 | 4,040 | 5.3 | 4.5 | 4.7 | TX...... | 89,160 | 85,760 | 79,390 | 18.7 | 17.2 | 14.9 |
| LA...... | 13,100 | 11,400 | 12,710 | 13.0 | 11.6 | 13.7 | UT...... | 3,510 | 3,630 | 3,540 | 6.6 | 6.5 | 5.9 |
| ME...... | 2,650 | 2,770 | 2,490 | 9.9 | 10.7 | 10.3 | VT....... | 1,660 | 1,490 | 1,370 | 12.7 | 11.9 | 11.6 |
| MD...... | 34,560 | 37,590 | 34,310 | 29.0 | 31.1 | 28.7 | VA...... | 28,780 | 26,520 | 27,660 | 18.1 | 16.2 | 16.7 |
| MA...... | 30,410 | 27,270 | 24,360 | 21.4 | 19.8 | 18.0 | WA...... | 26,200 | 23,260 | 22,240 | 20.2 | 17.7 | 16.4 |
| MI....... | 46,470 | 40,600 | 30,770 | 21.6 | 19.7 | 16.1 | WV...... | 2,540 | 2,360 | 2,540 | 6.8 | 6.7 | 7.4 |
| MN...... | 14,610 | 13,910 | 11,570 | 13.5 | 13.0 | 11.1 | WI....... | 11,130 | 9,800 | 8,080 | 9.6 | 8.6 | 7.4 |
| MS...... | 3,780 | 3,090 | 2,300 | 6.0 | 5.0 | 3.8 | WY...... | 100 | 70 | 90 | 1.0 | 0.7 | 0.8 |

[1] Rate per 1,000 women, 15 to 44 years old on July 1 of specified year.

Source: R.K. Jones et al., "Abortion in the United States: Incidence and Access to Services, 2005," *Perspectives on Sexual and Reproductive Health*, 40.1 (2008) ©; R.K. Jones and K. Kooistra, "Abortion Incidence and Access to Services in the United States, 2008," *Perspectives on Sexual and Reproductive Health*, 43.1 (2011) ©; R.K. Jones and J. Jerman, "Abortion Incidence and Service Availability in the United States, 2011," *Perspectives on Sexual and Reproductive Health*, 46.1 (2014) ©; and unpublished data from the Guttmacher Institute ©. See also <http://www.guttmacher.org/>.

## Table 108. Percent of Babies Breastfed by Selected Characteristics of Mother: 1986 to 2013

[In percent. Annual averages for 3-year period shown. Based on the National Survey of Family Growth. Data are from household interviews with a sample of women aged 15-44 years old]

| Mother's characteristics | 1986-1988 | 1989-1991 | 1992-1994 | 1995-1998 | 1999-2001 | 2002-2004 | 2005-2007 | 2008-2010 | 2011-2013 |
|---|---|---|---|---|---|---|---|---|---|
| **PERCENT OF BABIES EVER BREASTFED 3 MONTHS OR MORE** | | | | | | | | | |
| **Total**........................ | **34.6** | **31.8** | **33.6** | **45.8** | **48.4** | **50.6** | **46.6** | **50.2** | **56.6** |
| Age at baby's birth: | | | | | | | | | |
| Under 20 years.............. | 18.5 | (S) | (S) | 30.0 | 30.0 | 37.6 | 26.6 | 35.5 | 38.4 |
| 20-24 years................. | 26.1 | 24.1 | 25.1 | 36.6 | 41.8 | 38.0 | 38.6 | 37.6 | 43.8 |
| 25-29 years................. | 36.9 | 32.3 | 35.6 | 46.3 | 43.7 | 50.2 | 49.0 | 54.8 | 58.3 |
| 30-44 years................. | 50.1 | 46.8 | 46.7 | 57.5 | 62.4 | 63.9 | 56.3 | 59.6 | 65.6 |
| Race and Hispanic origin: [1] | | | | | | | | | |
| Not Hispanic or Latina | | | | | | | | | |
| White alone................ | 37.7 | 35.2 | 36.6 | 47.8 | 49.7 | 54.5 | 49.5 | 48.4 | 57.8 |
| Black or African American alone.......... | 11.6 | 11.5 | 13.3 | 29.6 | 33.7 | 29.2 | 26.3 | 35.7 | 37.0 |
| Hispanic or Latina.............. | 38.2 | 33.9 | 35.0 | 49.7 | 54.3 | 55.9 | 49.4 | 55.6 | 58.8 |
| Education: [2] | | | | | | | | | |
| No high school diploma or GED............. | 21.8 | 17.6 | 25.2 | 33.9 | 37.0 | 39.9 | 41.3 | 42.8 | 50.8 |
| High school diploma or GED................ | 28.2 | 28.0 | 27.4 | 36.9 | 43.1 | 41.9 | 36.8 | 44.4 | 45.1 |
| Some college, no bachelor's degree........ | 38.7 | 33.1 | 38.7 | 49.6 | 52.8 | 43.2 | 48.7 | 46.7 | 52.3 |
| Bachelor's degree or higher................ | 55.0 | 56.1 | 59.3 | 64.5 | 64.1 | 75.9 | 65.8 | 63.7 | 73.9 |
| Region: | | | | | | | | | |
| Northeast.................... | 29.9 | 37.2 | 36.4 | 48.2 | 48.8 | 59.9 | 51.5 | 46.9 | 57.7 |
| Midwest..................... | 30.3 | 31.5 | 30.1 | 42.0 | 42.8 | 46.8 | 41.6 | 42.1 | 50.8 |
| South....................... | 27.7 | 20.1 | 26.2 | 38.9 | 44.4 | 42.7 | 40.5 | 45.6 | 51.8 |
| West........................ | 52.4 | 42.9 | 45.3 | 58.2 | 59.2 | 62.6 | 57.8 | 66.0 | 68.5 |

S Figure does not meet publication standards. [1] Starting with 1995 data, race-specific estimates are tabulated according to 1997 Revisions to the Standards for the Classification of Federal Data on Race and Ethnicity and are not strictly comparable with estimates for earlier years. Starting with 1995 data, race-specific estimates are for persons who reported only one racial group. Prior to data year 1995, data were tabulated according to the 1977 Standards. Estimates for single-race categories prior to 1995 included persons who reported one race or, if they reported more than one race, identified one race as best representing their race. [2] Educational attainment is presented only for women age 22 to 44 years old, as of day of interview.

Source: U.S. National Center for Health Statistics, *Health, United States, 2017*, September 2018. See also <http://www.cdc.gov/nchs/hus.htm>.

# Table 109. Assisted Reproductive Technology (ART) Procedures and Outcomes: 2000 to 2017

[Covers ART procedures with the intent to transfer at least one embryo; excludes freezing/banking cycles. In 1996, Centers for Disease Control (CDC) initiated data collection regarding Assisted Reproductive Technology (ART) procedures performed in the United States, as mandated by the Fertility Clinic Success Rate and Certification Act. ARTs include those infertility treatments in which both eggs and sperm are handled in the laboratory for the purpose of establishing a pregnancy (i.e., in vitro fertilization and related procedures)]

| Year | Procedures started [1] | Number of pregnancies [2] | Live birth deliveries [3] | Live born infants |
|---|---|---|---|---|
| 2000 | 99,629 | 30,557 | 25,228 | 35,025 |
| 2005 | 134,260 | 47,651 | 38,910 | 52,041 |
| 2010 | 147,260 | 57,773 | 47,090 | 61,564 |
| 2014 | 173,198 | 68,988 | 57,323 | 70,354 |
| 2015 | 186,157 | 72,870 | 60,778 | 72,913 |
| 2016 | 197,737 | 80,971 | 65,969 | 76,897 |
| 2017 | 196,850 | (NA) | 68,908 | 78,052 |

NA Not available. [1] Excludes procedures for which new treatments were being evaluated. [2] Beginning in 2012, excludes pregnancies from procedures performed in U.S. territories other than Puerto Rico; and, beginning in 2013, excludes pregnancies resulting from oocyte thaw procedures. [3] A live birth delivery is defined as the delivery of one or more live born infants.

Source: U.S. Centers for Disease Control and Prevention, *2016 Assisted Reproductive Technology, National Summary Report*, October 2018; *Assisted Reproductive Technology Surveillance - United States, 2016*, MMWR Surveillance Summaries, Vol. 68, No. 4, April 2019 and earlier reports; and "Assisted Reproductive Technology," <http://www.cdc.gov/art/artdata/index.html>, accessed August 2019.

# Table 110. Life Expectancy at Birth, 1940 to 2017, and Projected, 2020 to 2060

[In years. Beginning 2001, life table data are based on revised life table methodology. Race and Hispanic-origin categories are consistent with 1977 Office of Management and Budget (OMB) standards. From 2003-2017, the number of states reporting multiple-race data according to new 1997 OMB standards varied widely. To provide a comparison of data by race between the 1977 and 1997 OMB standards, those reporting more than one race were "bridged" to single-race categories. For more information, see Technical notes, source]

| Year | Total [1] | | | White, non-Hispanic | | | Black, non-Hispanic | | | Hispanic [2] | | |
|---|---|---|---|---|---|---|---|---|---|---|---|---|
| | Total | Male | Female | Total | Male | Female | Total | Male | Female | Total | Male | Female |
| 1940 | 62.9 | 60.8 | 65.2 | (NA) | (NA) | (NA) | (NA) | (NA) | (NA) | (NA) | (NA) | (NA) |
| 1950 | 68.2 | 65.6 | 71.1 | (NA) | (NA) | (NA) | (NA) | (NA) | (NA) | (NA) | (NA) | (NA) |
| 1960 | 69.7 | 66.6 | 73.1 | (NA) | (NA) | (NA) | (NA) | (NA) | (NA) | (NA) | (NA) | (NA) |
| 1970 | 70.8 | 67.1 | 74.7 | (NA) | (NA) | (NA) | (NA) | (NA) | (NA) | (NA) | (NA) | (NA) |
| 1980 | 73.7 | 70.0 | 77.4 | (NA) | (NA) | (NA) | (NA) | (NA) | (NA) | (NA) | (NA) | (NA) |
| 1990 | 75.4 | 71.8 | 78.8 | (NA) | (NA) | (NA) | (NA) | (NA) | (NA) | (NA) | (NA) | (NA) |
| 2000 | 76.8 | 74.1 | 79.3 | (NA) | (NA) | (NA) | (NA) | (NA) | (NA) | (NA) | (NA) | (NA) |
| 2010 [3] | 78.7 | 76.2 | 81.0 | 78.8 | 76.4 | 81.1 | 74.7 | 71.5 | 77.7 | 81.7 | 78.8 | 84.3 |
| 2017 [3] | 78.6 | 76.1 | 81.1 | 78.5 | 76.1 | 81.0 | 74.9 | 71.5 | 78.1 | 81.8 | 79.1 | 84.3 |
| Projections: [4] | | | | | | | | | | | | |
| 2020 | 80.2 | 78.0 | 82.4 | 80.6 | 78.4 | 82.7 | (NA) | (NA) | (NA) | 82.1 | 79.9 | 84.2 |
| 2030 | 81.7 | 79.6 | 83.7 | 82.1 | 80.2 | 84.0 | (NA) | (NA) | (NA) | 82.6 | 80.6 | 84.5 |
| 2040 | 83.0 | 81.2 | 84.8 | 83.5 | 81.7 | 85.2 | (NA) | (NA) | (NA) | 83.5 | 81.7 | 85.2 |
| 2050 | 84.4 | 82.7 | 86.0 | 84.8 | 83.2 | 86.4 | (NA) | (NA) | (NA) | 84.8 | 83.2 | 86.4 |
| 2060 | 85.6 | 84.0 | 87.1 | 86.0 | 84.5 | 87.4 | (NA) | (NA) | (NA) | 86.0 | 84.5 | 87.4 |

NA Not available. [1] Includes races and origins not shown separately. [2] Based on death rates adjusted for misclassification; see Technical notes, source. [3] Life expectancies by Hispanic origin were revised using updated adjustment factors to correct for race and Hispanic-origin misclassification. [4] Based on mortality assumptions; for details, see source: U.S. Census Bureau, 2014 National Population Projections, "Table 17: Projected Life Expectancy at Birth by Sex, Race, and Hispanic Origin for the United States: 2015 to 2060 (NP2014-T17)," December 2014.

Source: Except as noted. U.S. National Center for Health Statistics, National Vital Statistics Reports (NVSR), *Deaths: Final Data for 2017*, Vol. 68, No. 9, June 2019. See also <https://www.cdc.gov/nchs/nvss/deaths.htm>.

# Table 111. Life Expectancy by Sex, Age, and Race and Hispanic Origin: 2017

[Average number of years of life remaining. Excludes deaths of nonresidents of the United States. Race categories are consistent with 1977 Office of Management and Budget (OMB) standards; see source for details]

| Age | Total [1] | | | White, Non-Hispanic [2] | | | Black, Non-Hispanic [2] | | | Hispanic [3] | | |
|---|---|---|---|---|---|---|---|---|---|---|---|---|
| | Total | Male | Female | Total | Male | Female | Total | Male | Female | Total | Male | Female |
| 0 | 78.6 | 76.1 | 81.1 | 78.5 | 76.1 | 81.0 | 74.9 | 71.5 | 78.1 | 81.8 | 79.1 | 84.3 |
| 1 | 78.1 | 75.6 | 80.5 | 77.9 | 75.5 | 80.3 | 74.7 | 71.4 | 77.9 | 81.2 | 78.5 | 83.7 |
| 5 | 74.1 | 71.7 | 76.6 | 74.0 | 71.6 | 76.4 | 70.8 | 67.5 | 74.0 | 77.3 | 74.6 | 79.8 |
| 10 | 69.2 | 66.7 | 71.6 | 69.0 | 66.6 | 71.4 | 65.9 | 62.5 | 69.0 | 72.3 | 69.6 | 74.8 |
| 15 | 64.2 | 61.8 | 66.7 | 64.0 | 61.7 | 66.4 | 61.0 | 57.6 | 64.1 | 67.4 | 64.7 | 69.8 |
| 20 | 59.4 | 57.0 | 61.8 | 59.2 | 56.9 | 61.5 | 56.2 | 53.0 | 59.2 | 62.5 | 59.9 | 64.9 |
| 25 | 54.7 | 52.4 | 56.9 | 54.5 | 52.2 | 56.7 | 51.6 | 48.5 | 54.4 | 57.7 | 55.2 | 60.1 |
| 30 | 50.0 | 47.8 | 52.1 | 49.8 | 47.7 | 51.9 | 47.0 | 44.1 | 49.6 | 53.0 | 50.5 | 55.2 |
| 35 | 45.3 | 43.2 | 47.3 | 45.2 | 43.2 | 47.2 | 42.5 | 39.7 | 44.9 | 48.2 | 45.8 | 50.3 |
| 40 | 40.7 | 38.7 | 42.6 | 40.6 | 38.6 | 42.5 | 38.0 | 35.3 | 40.3 | 43.5 | 41.2 | 45.5 |
| 45 | 36.1 | 34.2 | 37.9 | 36.0 | 34.2 | 37.8 | 33.6 | 31.0 | 35.8 | 38.8 | 36.6 | 40.7 |
| 50 | 31.6 | 29.8 | 33.4 | 31.6 | 29.8 | 33.3 | 29.3 | 26.9 | 31.4 | 34.2 | 32.1 | 36.0 |
| 55 | 27.4 | 25.6 | 28.9 | 27.3 | 25.6 | 28.8 | 25.2 | 23.0 | 27.2 | 29.8 | 27.7 | 31.4 |
| 60 | 23.3 | 21.7 | 24.7 | 23.2 | 21.7 | 24.6 | 21.5 | 19.4 | 23.3 | 25.5 | 23.6 | 27.0 |
| 65 | 19.4 | 18.0 | 20.6 | 19.3 | 18.0 | 20.5 | 18.1 | 16.2 | 19.5 | 21.4 | 19.7 | 22.7 |
| 70 | 15.7 | 14.5 | 16.7 | 15.6 | 14.5 | 16.6 | 14.9 | 13.3 | 16.0 | 17.5 | 16.0 | 18.6 |
| 75 | 12.3 | 11.3 | 13.0 | 12.2 | 11.2 | 12.9 | 11.9 | 10.6 | 12.7 | 13.8 | 12.6 | 14.7 |
| 80 | 9.2 | 8.4 | 9.8 | 9.1 | 8.3 | 9.7 | 9.2 | 8.1 | 9.8 | 10.5 | 9.4 | 11.1 |
| 85 | 6.6 | 5.9 | 7.0 | 6.5 | 5.9 | 6.9 | 6.9 | 6.1 | 7.3 | 7.6 | 6.7 | 8.0 |
| 90 | 4.5 | 4.1 | 4.8 | 4.5 | 4.0 | 4.7 | 5.0 | 4.5 | 5.2 | 5.3 | 4.6 | 5.5 |
| 95 | 3.1 | 2.8 | 3.2 | 3.0 | 2.7 | 3.2 | 3.6 | 3.3 | 3.7 | 3.6 | 3.2 | 3.7 |
| 100 | 2.2 | 2.0 | 2.2 | 2.1 | 1.9 | 2.2 | 2.7 | 2.5 | 2.7 | 2.6 | 2.2 | 2.6 |

[1] Includes other races and origins not shown separately. [2] Multiple-race data reported according to 1997 OMB standards were bridged to the single-race categories of 1977 OMB standards; see source for details. [3] Life expectancies by Hispanic origin are based on death rates adjusted for misclassification; see Technical Notes, source.

Source: U.S. National Center for Health Statistics, National Vital Statistics Reports (NVSR), *Deaths, Final Data for 2017*, Vol. 68, No. 9, June 2019. See also <https://www.cdc.gov/nchs/nvss/deaths.htm>.

# Table 112. Selected Life Table Values—Life Expectancy and Percent Surviving by Age: 1959 to 2015

[Decennial life tables are based on population data from a decennial census and reported deaths of the 3-year period surrounding the census year; the census year is the middle year. The annual tables are based on deaths in a single year, and except for census years, on postcensal population estimates. Beginning in 1970, data exclude deaths of nonresidents of the United States. See Technical Notes, source]

| Age and sex | All races | | | | | | White | | | | | | Black | | | | | |
|---|---|---|---|---|---|---|---|---|---|---|---|---|---|---|---|---|---|---|
| | 1959-1961 | 1969-1971 | 1979-1981 | 1989-1991 | 1999-2001 | 2015 | 1959-1961 | 1969-1971 | 1979-1981 | 1989-1991 | 1999-2001 | 2015 | 1959-1961 | 1969-1971 | 1979-1981 | 1989-1991 | 1999-2001 | 2015 |
| **LIFE EXPECTANCY IN YEARS** | | | | | | | | | | | | | | | | | | |
| **Male by age:** | | | | | | | | | | | | | | | | | | |
| At birth | 66.8 | 67.0 | 70.1 | 71.8 | 74.1 | 76.3 | 67.6 | 67.9 | 70.8 | 72.7 | 74.8 | 76.6 | 61.5 | 60.0 | 64.1 | 64.5 | 68.2 | 72.2 |
| Age 20 | 49.8 | 49.5 | 51.9 | 53.3 | 55.2 | 57.2 | 50.3 | 50.2 | 52.5 | 54.0 | 55.7 | 57.3 | 45.8 | 43.5 | 46.5 | 46.7 | 49.9 | 53.7 |
| Age 30 | 40.6 | 40.5 | 42.8 | 44.1 | 45.9 | 47.9 | 41.0 | 41.1 | 43.3 | 44.7 | 46.3 | 48.0 | 37.1 | 35.4 | 37.8 | 38.1 | 41.0 | 44.7 |
| Age 40 | 31.4 | 31.5 | 33.6 | 35.1 | 36.6 | 38.7 | 31.7 | 31.9 | 34.0 | 35.6 | 37.0 | 38.8 | 28.7 | 27.6 | 29.5 | 30.1 | 32.2 | 35.8 |
| Age 50 | 23.0 | 23.1 | 25.0 | 26.4 | 27.8 | 29.8 | 23.2 | 23.3 | 25.3 | 26.7 | 28.1 | 29.9 | 21.3 | 20.7 | 22.0 | 22.5 | 24.1 | 27.1 |
| Age 60 | 15.9 | 16.0 | 17.5 | 18.5 | 19.7 | 21.7 | 16.0 | 16.1 | 17.6 | 18.7 | 19.9 | 21.7 | 15.3 | 14.9 | 15.9 | 16.0 | 17.2 | 19.6 |
| Age 65 | 13.0 | 13.0 | 14.2 | 15.1 | 16.1 | 18.0 | 13.0 | 13.0 | 14.3 | 15.2 | 16.2 | 18.0 | 12.8 | 12.5 | 13.3 | 13.3 | 14.1 | 16.4 |
| Age 70 | 10.3 | 10.4 | 11.4 | 12.1 | 12.8 | 14.5 | 10.3 | 10.4 | 11.4 | 12.1 | 12.9 | 14.4 | 10.8 | 10.4 | 10.9 | 10.9 | 11.4 | 13.3 |
| Age 80 | 6.0 | 6.3 | 6.8 | 7.1 | 7.4 | 8.3 | 5.9 | 6.2 | 6.8 | 7.1 | 7.4 | 8.3 | 6.9 | 7.4 | 7.0 | 7.0 | 7.1 | 8.2 |
| Age 90 | 3.2 | 3.6 | 3.9 | 3.9 | 4.0 | 4.1 | 3.2 | 3.5 | 3.8 | 3.9 | 3.9 | 4.0 | 3.4 | 4.7 | 4.5 | 4.2 | 4.2 | 4.5 |
| **Female by age:** | | | | | | | | | | | | | | | | | | |
| At birth | 73.2 | 74.6 | 77.6 | 78.8 | 79.5 | 81.1 | 74.2 | 75.5 | 78.2 | 79.5 | 80.0 | 81.3 | 66.5 | 68.3 | 72.9 | 73.7 | 75.2 | 78.5 |
| Age 20 | 55.6 | 56.6 | 59.0 | 59.9 | 60.3 | 61.8 | 56.3 | 57.2 | 59.4 | 60.4 | 60.7 | 61.9 | 50.1 | 51.2 | 54.9 | 55.5 | 56.5 | 59.6 |
| Age 30 | 46.0 | 47.0 | 49.3 | 50.2 | 50.6 | 52.1 | 46.6 | 47.6 | 49.8 | 50.7 | 51.0 | 52.2 | 40.8 | 42.0 | 45.4 | 46.0 | 47.0 | 49.9 |
| Age 40 | 36.6 | 37.6 | 39.8 | 40.7 | 41.0 | 42.6 | 37.1 | 38.1 | 40.2 | 41.0 | 41.3 | 42.6 | 32.2 | 33.3 | 36.3 | 37.0 | 37.7 | 40.5 |
| Age 50 | 27.7 | 28.8 | 30.7 | 31.4 | 31.8 | 33.3 | 28.1 | 29.1 | 31.0 | 31.7 | 32.0 | 33.3 | 24.3 | 25.5 | 27.8 | 28.4 | 29.1 | 31.6 |
| Age 60 | 19.5 | 20.6 | 22.3 | 22.9 | 23.1 | 24.6 | 19.7 | 20.8 | 22.5 | 23.1 | 23.3 | 24.6 | 17.8 | 18.7 | 20.4 | 20.7 | 21.2 | 23.4 |
| Age 65 | 15.8 | 16.8 | 18.4 | 19.0 | 19.1 | 20.5 | 15.9 | 16.9 | 18.6 | 19.1 | 19.2 | 20.5 | 15.1 | 15.7 | 17.1 | 17.4 | 17.7 | 19.6 |
| Age 70 | 12.4 | 13.4 | 14.8 | 15.4 | 15.4 | 16.6 | 12.4 | 13.4 | 14.9 | 15.5 | 15.5 | 16.5 | 12.5 | 13.0 | 14.1 | 14.3 | 14.4 | 16.0 |
| Age 80 | 6.7 | 7.7 | 8.7 | 9.1 | 9.1 | 9.7 | 6.7 | 7.6 | 8.7 | 9.1 | 9.0 | 9.7 | 7.7 | 8.9 | 9.0 | 9.1 | 9.0 | 9.8 |
| Age 90 | 3.3 | 4.1 | 4.7 | 4.7 | 4.7 | 4.8 | 3.2 | 4.1 | 4.6 | 4.7 | 4.7 | 4.7 | 3.5 | 5.4 | 5.5 | 5.2 | 5.2 | 5.2 |
| **PERCENT SURVIVING OUT OF 100,000 BORN ALIVE** | | | | | | | | | | | | | | | | | | |
| **Male by age:** | | | | | | | | | | | | | | | | | | |
| At birth | 100.0 | 100.0 | 100.0 | 100.0 | 100.0 | 100.0 | 100.0 | 100.0 | 100.0 | 100.0 | 100.0 | 100.0 | 100.0 | 100.0 | 100.0 | 100.0 | 100.0 | 100.0 |
| Age 20 | 95.5 | 96.1 | 97.3 | 97.9 | 98.4 | 98.8 | 95.9 | 96.5 | 97.5 | 98.1 | 98.6 | 98.9 | 93.1 | 94.1 | 96.1 | 96.3 | 97.3 | 97.9 |
| Age 30 | 93.8 | 94.1 | 95.4 | 96.2 | 97.1 | 97.4 | 94.4 | 94.7 | 95.8 | 96.7 | 97.4 | 97.6 | 90.3 | 89.6 | 93.1 | 93.1 | 94.9 | 95.9 |
| Age 40 | 91.6 | 91.5 | 93.3 | 93.8 | 95.4 | 95.6 | 92.4 | 92.6 | 94.0 | 94.6 | 95.9 | 95.9 | 85.7 | 83.4 | 88.5 | 87.9 | 91.9 | 93.3 |
| Age 50 | 86.2 | 86.1 | 89.0 | 89.9 | 91.8 | 92.7 | 87.4 | 87.7 | 90.1 | 91.1 | 92.6 | 93.0 | 77.2 | 73.3 | 80.1 | 80.0 | 85.7 | 89.3 |
| Age 60 | 73.9 | 74.0 | 79.0 | 81.4 | 84.6 | 85.8 | 75.5 | 76.0 | 79.9 | 83.2 | 85.8 | 86.3 | 61.7 | 57.5 | 65.0 | 66.3 | 73.6 | 80.2 |
| Age 65 | 64.2 | 64.3 | 70.6 | 74.0 | 78.2 | 80.3 | 65.8 | 66.3 | 72.4 | 76.0 | 79.7 | 80.9 | 51.4 | 47.5 | 55.1 | 56.8 | 65.0 | 72.5 |
| Age 70 | 52.2 | 52.3 | 59.7 | 64.1 | 69.5 | 73.3 | 53.8 | 54.1 | 61.4 | 66.2 | 71.0 | 74.0 | 39.9 | 36.9 | 44.2 | 45.7 | 54.3 | 63.5 |
| Age 80 | 25.3 | 24.9 | 31.8 | 36.7 | 42.8 | 51.2 | 26.0 | 25.9 | 32.8 | 38.2 | 44.1 | 51.7 | 20.0 | 16.6 | 22.0 | 22.5 | 28.5 | 39.8 |
| Age 90 | 4.6 | 5.1 | 7.7 | 9.9 | 12.5 | 18.5 | 4.6 | 5.1 | 7.9 | 10.2 | 12.8 | 18.6 | 5.2 | 4.7 | 5.7 | 6.0 | 7.6 | 13.7 |
| **Female by age:** | | | | | | | | | | | | | | | | | | |
| At birth | 100.0 | 100.0 | 100.0 | 100.0 | 100.0 | 100.0 | 100.0 | 100.0 | 100.0 | 100.0 | 100.0 | 100.0 | 100.0 | 100.0 | 100.0 | 100.0 | 100.0 | 100.0 |
| Age 20 | 96.8 | 97.3 | 98.2 | 98.6 | 98.9 | 99.1 | 97.1 | 97.6 | 98.4 | 98.8 | 99.0 | 99.2 | 94.7 | 95.7 | 97.2 | 97.6 | 98.1 | 98.5 |
| Age 30 | 96.0 | 96.5 | 97.6 | 98.0 | 98.4 | 98.6 | 96.5 | 96.9 | 97.8 | 98.3 | 98.6 | 98.7 | 93.1 | 94.1 | 96.2 | 96.5 | 97.3 | 97.9 |
| Age 40 | 94.6 | 95.1 | 96.5 | 97.0 | 97.5 | 97.6 | 95.3 | 95.8 | 96.9 | 97.5 | 97.8 | 97.8 | 89.7 | 90.8 | 94.1 | 94.4 | 95.6 | 96.6 |
| Age 50 | 91.3 | 91.9 | 94.1 | 94.9 | 95.4 | 95.7 | 92.5 | 92.9 | 94.7 | 95.6 | 96.0 | 95.9 | 83.0 | 84.2 | 89.6 | 90.3 | 91.7 | 93.8 |
| Age 60 | 84.4 | 85.1 | 88.4 | 89.7 | 90.8 | 91.3 | 86.3 | 86.7 | 89.5 | 90.8 | 91.5 | 91.6 | 69.9 | 72.8 | 80.3 | 81.9 | 84.0 | 87.6 |
| Age 65 | 78.5 | 79.7 | 83.5 | 85.1 | 86.4 | 87.8 | 80.7 | 81.6 | 84.8 | 86.3 | 87.4 | 88.2 | 60.8 | 64.7 | 73.3 | 75.0 | 77.9 | 82.7 |
| Age 70 | 70.1 | 72.0 | 76.7 | 78.5 | 80.2 | 82.8 | 72.5 | 74.1 | 78.1 | 80.0 | 81.4 | 83.3 | 51.3 | 54.9 | 64.7 | 66.3 | 69.8 | 76.5 |
| Age 80 | 43.1 | 46.4 | 54.4 | 57.0 | 58.5 | 64.4 | 44.7 | 48.2 | 55.8 | 58.5 | 59.7 | 64.8 | 30.3 | 31.8 | 41.7 | 43.6 | 46.5 | 56.5 |
| Age 90 | 10.1 | 14.2 | 20.6 | 23.7 | 23.9 | 29.8 | 10.2 | 14.4 | 21.0 | 24.3 | 24.5 | 29.7 | 9.7 | 12.2 | 16.3 | 17.5 | 18.3 | 25.6 |

Source: U.S. National Center for Health Statistics, National Vital Statistics Reports (NVSR), *United States Life Tables, 2015*, Vol. 67, No. 7, November 2018. See also <http://www.cdc.gov/nchs/products/life_tables.htm>.

# Table 113. Life Expectancy at Birth by Sex, Race, and State: 1989 to 2001

[Average number of years of life remaining. Excludes deaths of nonresidents of the United States. Decennial life tables are based on population data from a decennial census and reported deaths of the 3-year period surrounding the census year; the census year is the middle year. The annual tables are based on deaths in a single year, and except for census years, on postcensal population estimates]

| State | Total, 1989–1991 | 1999-2001 | | | | | | |
|---|---|---|---|---|---|---|---|---|
| | | Total | Male | | | Female | | |
| | | | Total | White | Black | Total | White | Black |
| **United States** | **75.37** | **76.83** | **74.10** | **74.74** | **68.08** | **79.45** | **79.97** | **75.12** |
| Alabama | 73.64 | 74.80 | 71.32 | 72.85 | 66.42 | 78.34 | 79.14 | 74.94 |
| Alaska | 74.83 | 76.63 | 74.18 | 75.45 | (B) | 79.41 | 80.10 | (B) |
| Arizona | 76.10 | 78.15 | 75.25 | 75.51 | 70.95 | 81.16 | 81.64 | 77.70 |
| Arkansas | 74.33 | 75.43 | 72.05 | 73.17 | 67.30 | 78.99 | 79.59 | 73.58 |
| California | 75.86 | 78.80 | 76.02 | 76.11 | 69.97 | 81.63 | 81.36 | 76.67 |
| Colorado | 76.96 | 78.72 | 76.29 | 76.23 | 71.71 | 81.16 | 81.31 | 76.59 |
| Connecticut | 76.91 | 78.90 | 76.13 | 76.73 | 71.73 | 81.63 | 81.92 | 77.71 |
| Delaware | 74.76 | 77.04 | 74.24 | 75.05 | 70.27 | 79.78 | 80.55 | 75.21 |
| District of Columbia | 67.99 | 73.09 | 68.57 | 78.94 | 64.59 | 77.59 | 84.31 | 74.46 |
| Florida | 75.84 | 78.10 | 74.97 | 75.64 | 68.98 | 81.40 | 82.14 | 75.53 |
| Georgia | 73.61 | 75.27 | 72.28 | 73.88 | 68.29 | 78.22 | 79.53 | 76.16 |
| Hawaii | 78.21 | 80.23 | 77.17 | 78.40 | (B) | 83.65 | 83.31 | (B) |
| Idaho | 76.88 | 78.29 | 76.18 | 76.46 | (B) | 80.50 | 80.53 | (B) |
| Illinois | 74.90 | 77.06 | 73.91 | 75.33 | 66.81 | 80.26 | 80.78 | 74.20 |
| Indiana | 75.39 | 76.47 | 73.55 | 74.24 | 67.47 | 79.45 | 79.69 | 76.55 |
| Iowa | 77.29 | 78.76 | 76.11 | 76.19 | 70.81 | 81.39 | 81.35 | 75.16 |
| Kansas | 76.76 | 77.78 | 74.84 | 75.46 | 68.47 | 80.88 | 81.00 | 75.02 |
| Kentucky | 74.37 | 75.20 | 72.25 | 72.73 | 69.01 | 78.20 | 78.42 | 74.46 |
| Louisiana | 73.05 | 74.28 | 71.12 | 73.47 | 66.45 | 77.44 | 79.41 | 75.30 |
| Maine | 76.35 | 77.46 | 75.23 | 75.59 | (B) | 79.63 | 80.88 | (B) |
| Maryland | 74.79 | 76.36 | 73.55 | 75.58 | 68.41 | 79.08 | 80.66 | 75.78 |
| Massachusetts | 76.72 | 78.76 | 75.79 | 76.35 | 73.14 | 81.68 | 81.63 | 79.33 |
| Michigan | 75.04 | 76.90 | 73.98 | 75.26 | 67.38 | 79.83 | 80.59 | 75.95 |
| Minnesota | 77.76 | 79.26 | 76.74 | 77.03 | 71.59 | 81.80 | 82.61 | 76.60 |
| Mississippi | 73.03 | 73.88 | 70.30 | 72.25 | 66.72 | 77.62 | 79.13 | 73.68 |
| Missouri | 75.25 | 76.52 | 73.59 | 74.29 | 67.22 | 79.46 | 79.93 | 74.50 |
| Montana | 76.23 | 77.74 | 75.18 | 75.07 | (B) | 80.56 | 81.24 | (B) |
| Nebraska | 76.92 | 78.37 | 76.00 | 76.17 | 69.15 | 80.78 | 81.14 | 74.67 |
| Nevada | 74.18 | 76.05 | 73.34 | 73.49 | 70.56 | 79.24 | 78.97 | 74.75 |
| New Hampshire | 76.72 | 78.79 | 76.24 | 76.46 | (B) | 81.40 | 81.30 | (B) |
| New Jersey | 75.42 | 77.58 | 74.77 | 75.82 | 68.85 | 80.32 | 81.32 | 75.54 |
| New Mexico | 75.74 | 77.26 | 74.52 | 75.19 | 71.63 | 80.06 | 80.69 | 74.37 |
| New York | 74.68 | 78.20 | 75.13 | 75.78 | 70.13 | 81.16 | 81.49 | 77.84 |
| North Carolina | 74.48 | 76.27 | 73.05 | 74.27 | 66.33 | 79.56 | 80.34 | 76.68 |
| North Dakota | 77.62 | 79.06 | 75.96 | 76.65 | (B) | 82.61 | 82.67 | (B) |
| Ohio | 75.32 | 76.49 | 73.94 | 74.58 | 68.60 | 78.95 | 80.01 | 74.91 |
| Oklahoma | 75.10 | 75.61 | 72.75 | 73.00 | 68.97 | 78.59 | 78.75 | 74.34 |
| Oregon | 76.44 | 78.09 | 75.82 | 75.72 | 70.67 | 80.37 | 80.20 | 78.24 |
| Pennsylvania | 75.38 | 77.02 | 74.09 | 75.03 | 67.26 | 79.90 | 80.65 | 75.34 |
| Rhode Island | 76.54 | 78.65 | 75.83 | 76.06 | 72.18 | 81.42 | 81.60 | 77.39 |
| South Carolina | 73.51 | 75.04 | 71.68 | 73.76 | 67.34 | 78.49 | 79.77 | 75.41 |
| South Dakota | 76.91 | 78.34 | 75.19 | 76.35 | (B) | 81.79 | 82.61 | (B) |
| Tennessee | 74.32 | 75.29 | 71.98 | 73.31 | 66.86 | 78.66 | 79.28 | 74.16 |
| Texas | 75.14 | 77.04 | 74.12 | 74.74 | 69.18 | 80.05 | 80.35 | 74.76 |
| Utah | 77.70 | 78.89 | 76.84 | 76.95 | (B) | 80.95 | 80.93 | (B) |
| Vermont | 76.54 | 78.24 | 76.18 | 76.30 | (B) | 80.29 | 80.90 | (B) |
| Virginia | 75.22 | 76.95 | 74.48 | 75.62 | 69.37 | 79.34 | 80.69 | 76.20 |
| Washington | 76.82 | 78.64 | 76.18 | 76.10 | 71.90 | 81.14 | 80.98 | 77.11 |
| West Virginia | 74.26 | 75.28 | 72.75 | 72.75 | 69.87 | 77.84 | 78.36 | 72.65 |
| Wisconsin | 76.87 | 78.56 | 75.61 | 76.12 | 68.41 | 81.64 | 81.87 | 74.34 |
| Wyoming | 76.21 | 76.64 | 74.83 | 75.33 | (B) | 78.55 | 80.41 | (B) |

B Base figure too small to meet statistical standards for reliability.

Source: U.S. National Center for Health Statistics, National Vital Statistics Reports (NVSR), *U.S. Decennial Life Tables for 1999-2001: State Life Tables*, Vol. 60, No. 9, September 2012, and earlier reports. See also <http://www.cdc.gov/nchs/products/life_tables.htm>.

# Table 114. Deaths and Death Rates by Sex, Race, and Hispanic Origin: 1970 to 2017

[Deaths in thousands (1,921 represents 1,921,000). Rates are per 100,000 population for specified groups. Excludes deaths of nonresidents of the United States and fetal deaths. Rates are based on population enumerated as of April 1 for census years and estimated as of July 1 for all other years. Data for Hispanic origin and specified races other than White and Black should be interpreted with caution because of inconsistent reporting of race and Hispanic origin on death certificates and censuses and surveys]

| Sex and race | 1970 | 1980 | 1990 | 2000 | 2010 | 2012 | 2013 | 2014 | 2015 | 2016 | 2017 |
|---|---|---|---|---|---|---|---|---|---|---|---|
| **Deaths** [1]............ | **1,921** | **1,990** | **2,148** | **2,403** | **2,468** | **2,543** | **2,597** | **2,626** | **2,713** | **2,744** | **2,814** |
| Male [1]............ | 1,078 | 1,075 | 1,113 | 1,178 | 1,232 | 1,274 | 1,306 | 1,328 | 1,373 | 1,400 | 1,439 |
| Female [1]............ | 843 | 915 | 1,035 | 1,226 | 1,236 | 1,270 | 1,291 | 1,298 | 1,339 | 1,344 | 1,374 |
| White, non-Hispanic [2]............ | (NA) | (NA) | (NA) | 1,960 | 1,970 | 2,017 | 2,053 | 2,067 | 2,124 | 2,133 | 2,180 |
| Male............ | (NA) | (NA) | (NA) | 945 | 972 | 999 | 1,021 | 1,035 | 1,064 | 1,077 | 1,103 |
| Female............ | (NA) | (NA) | (NA) | 1,015 | 998 | 1,018 | 1,032 | 1,032 | 1,060 | 1,056 | 1,077 |
| Black, non-Hispanic [2]............ | (NA) | (NA) | (NA) | 283 | 283 | 291 | 299 | 304 | 315 | 327 | 336 |
| Male............ | (NA) | (NA) | (NA) | 143 | 144 | 148 | 153 | 155 | 162 | 169 | 174 |
| Female............ | (NA) | (NA) | (NA) | 139 | 140 | 143 | 147 | 149 | 153 | 158 | 161 |
| American Indian or Alaska Native, non-Hispanic [2]............ | (NA) | (NA) | (NA) | 11 | 15 | 16 | 16 | 17 | 18 | 19 | 19 |
| Male............ | (NA) | (NA) | (NA) | 6 | 8 | 9 | 9 | 9 | 10 | 10 | 11 |
| Female............ | (NA) | (NA) | (NA) | 5 | 7 | 7 | 7 | 8 | 8 | 8 | 9 |
| Asian or Pacific Islander, non-Hispanic [2]............ | (NA) | (NA) | (NA) | 34 | 50 | 55 | 59 | 60 | 65 | 68 | 73 |
| Male............ | (NA) | (NA) | (NA) | 19 | 26 | 28 | 30 | 31 | 33 | 35 | 37 |
| Female............ | (NA) | (NA) | (NA) | 16 | 24 | 27 | 28 | 29 | 32 | 33 | 35 |
| Hispanic origin [3]............ | (NA) | (NA) | (NA) | 107 | 144 | 156 | 163 | 169 | 179 | 188 | 197 |
| Male............ | (NA) | (NA) | (NA) | 60 | 80 | 85 | 89 | 92 | 98 | 104 | 109 |
| Female............ | (NA) | (NA) | (NA) | 47 | 65 | 71 | 74 | 77 | 81 | 85 | 89 |
| **Death rates** [1]............ | **945.3** | **878.3** | **863.8** | **854.0** | **799.5** | **810.2** | **821.5** | **823.7** | **844.0** | **849.3** | **863.8** |
| Male [1]............ | 1,090.3 | 976.9 | 918.4 | 853.0 | 812.0 | 824.5 | 839.1 | 846.4 | 868.0 | 880.2 | 897.2 |
| Female [1]............ | 807.8 | 785.3 | 812.0 | 855.0 | 787.4 | 796.4 | 804.4 | 801.7 | 820.7 | 819.3 | 831.4 |
| White, non-Hispanic [2]............ | (NA) | (NA) | (NA) | 993.2 | 984.3 | 1,004.9 | 1,021.6 | 1,028.1 | 1,055.3 | 1,059.7 | 1,083.2 |
| Male............ | (NA) | (NA) | (NA) | 978.5 | 987.5 | 1,011.2 | 1,032.1 | 1,045.4 | 1,072.5 | 1,085.6 | 1,111.4 |
| Female............ | (NA) | (NA) | (NA) | 1,007.3 | 981.2 | 998.8 | 1,011.5 | 1,011.3 | 1,038.5 | 1,034.6 | 1,055.8 |
| Black, non-Hispanic [2]............ | (NA) | (NA) | (NA) | 805.5 | 718.7 | 720.9 | 733.4 | 735.4 | 754.6 | 775.5 | 787.5 |
| Male............ | (NA) | (NA) | (NA) | 859.5 | 764.5 | 768.5 | 782.5 | 783.3 | 809.4 | 836.2 | 854.2 |
| Female............ | (NA) | (NA) | (NA) | 756.7 | 676.9 | 677.3 | 688.4 | 691.4 | 704.3 | 719.7 | 726.1 |
| American Indian or Alaska Native, non-Hispanic [2]............ | (NA) | (NA) | (NA) | 470.3 | 577.8 | 599.3 | 613.7 | 642.5 | 670.7 | 685.9 | 703.4 |
| Male............ | (NA) | (NA) | (NA) | 517.0 | 640.1 | 668.7 | 681.4 | 713.4 | 747.4 | 772.8 | 784.4 |
| Female............ | (NA) | (NA) | (NA) | 425.0 | 517.7 | 532.5 | 548.3 | 574.2 | 596.7 | 602.2 | 625.5 |
| Asian or Pacific Islander, non-Hispanic [2]............ | (NA) | (NA) | (NA) | 301.4 | 310.0 | 322.0 | 331.8 | 327.7 | 341.5 | 350.3 | 359.8 |
| Male............ | (NA) | (NA) | (NA) | 338.3 | 336.7 | 344.1 | 359.2 | 352.7 | 364.9 | 374.9 | 386.2 |
| Female............ | (NA) | (NA) | (NA) | 266.5 | 285.6 | 301.7 | 306.7 | 305.0 | 320.1 | 327.8 | 335.6 |
| Hispanic origin [3]............ | (NA) | (NA) | (NA) | 303.8 | 286.2 | 295.0 | 301.9 | 305.8 | 317.1 | 327.6 | 334.6 |
| Male............ | (NA) | (NA) | (NA) | 331.3 | 310.8 | 316.5 | 323.7 | 330.1 | 343.2 | 356.8 | 364.6 |
| Female............ | (NA) | (NA) | (NA) | 274.6 | 260.9 | 272.7 | 279.4 | 281.0 | 290.4 | 297.7 | 304.0 |
| **Age-adjusted death rates** [1,4]...... | **1,222.6** | **1,039.1** | **938.7** | **869.0** | **747.0** | **732.8** | **731.9** | **724.6** | **733.1** | **728.8** | **731.9** |
| Male [1]............ | 1,542.1 | 1,348.1 | 1,202.8 | 1,053.8 | 887.1 | 865.1 | 863.6 | 855.1 | 863.2 | 861.0 | 864.5 |
| Female [1]............ | 971.4 | 817.9 | 750.9 | 731.4 | 634.9 | 624.7 | 623.5 | 616.7 | 624.2 | 617.5 | 619.7 |
| White, non-Hispanic [2]............ | (NA) | (NA) | (NA) | 855.5 | 755.0 | 745.8 | 747.1 | 742.8 | 753.2 | 749.0 | 755.0 |
| Male............ | (NA) | (NA) | (NA) | 1,035.4 | 892.5 | 876.2 | 876.8 | 872.3 | 881.3 | 879.5 | 885.1 |
| Female............ | (NA) | (NA) | (NA) | 721.5 | 643.3 | 637.6 | 638.4 | 633.8 | 644.1 | 637.2 | 642.8 |
| Black, non-Hispanic [2]............ | (NA) | (NA) | (NA) | 1,137.0 | 920.4 | 887.1 | 885.2 | 870.7 | 876.1 | 882.8 | 881.0 |
| Male............ | (NA) | (NA) | (NA) | 1,422.0 | 1,131.7 | 1,086.4 | 1,083.3 | 1,060.3 | 1,070.1 | 1,081.2 | 1,083.3 |
| Female............ | (NA) | (NA) | (NA) | 941.2 | 770.8 | 742.1 | 740.6 | 731.2 | 731.0 | 734.1 | 728.0 |
| American Indian or Alaska Native, non-Hispanic [2]............ | (NA) | (NA) | (NA) | 800.5 | 818.8 | 787.8 | 787.5 | 796.9 | 805.7 | 800.3 | 800.2 |
| Male............ | (NA) | (NA) | (NA) | 955.6 | 965.8 | 929.9 | 930.6 | 935.0 | 950.2 | 954.0 | 943.9 |
| Female............ | (NA) | (NA) | (NA) | 679.1 | 696.8 | 666.3 | 666.4 | 677.4 | 679.5 | 668.0 | 674.0 |
| Asian or Pacific Islander, non-Hispanic [2]............ | (NA) | (NA) | (NA) | 507.0 | 425.6 | 409.6 | 407.5 | 390.5 | 396.2 | 394.4 | 395.3 |
| Male............ | (NA) | (NA) | (NA) | 624.9 | 513.0 | 486.3 | 490.2 | 464.2 | 468.9 | 466.6 | 470.1 |
| Female............ | (NA) | (NA) | (NA) | 417.3 | 360.6 | 351.4 | 344.8 | 333.3 | 339.6 | 337.4 | 336.4 |
| Hispanic origin [3]............ | (NA) | (NA) | (NA) | 665.7 | 558.6 | 539.1 | 535.4 | 523.3 | 525.3 | 525.8 | 524.7 |
| Male............ | (NA) | (NA) | (NA) | 818.1 | 677.7 | 643.9 | 639.8 | 626.8 | 628.9 | 631.8 | 631.8 |
| Female............ | (NA) | (NA) | (NA) | 546.0 | 463.4 | 452.5 | 448.6 | 437.5 | 438.3 | 436.4 | 434.2 |

NA Not available. [1] Includes other races not shown separately. [2] Multiple-race data reported according to 1997 OMB standards were bridged to single-race categories of 1977 OMB standards; see Technical Notes in source for details. [3] Persons of Hispanic origin may be of any race. [4] Age-adjusted death rates are better indicators than crude death rates for showing changes in the risk of death over time when the age distribution of the population is changing, and for comparing the mortality of population subgroups that have different age compositions. All age-adjusted death rates are standardized to the year 2000 population.

Source: U.S. National Center for Health Statistics, National Vital Statistics Reports (NVSR), *Deaths: Final Data for 2017*, Vol. 68, No. 9, June 2019. See also <http://www.cdc.gov/nchs/nvss/deaths.htm>.

# Table 115. Death Rates by Age, Sex, and Race: 1960 to 2017

[Rates per 100,000 population]

| Characteristic | All ages [1] | Under 1 year | 1 to 4 years | 5 to 14 years | 15 to 24 years | 25 to 34 years | 35 to 44 years | 45 to 54 years | 55 to 64 years | 65 to 74 years | 75 to 84 years | 85 years and over |
|---|---|---|---|---|---|---|---|---|---|---|---|---|
| **MALE** | | | | | | | | | | | | |
| **Total:** | | | | | | | | | | | | |
| 1960 | 1,105 | 3,059 | 120 | 56 | 152 | 188 | 373 | 992 | 2,310 | 4,914 | 10,178 | 21,186 |
| 1970 | 1,090 | 2,410 | 93 | 51 | 189 | 215 | 403 | 959 | 2,283 | 4,874 | 10,010 | 17,822 |
| 1980 | 977 | 1,429 | 73 | 37 | 172 | 196 | 299 | 767 | 1,815 | 4,105 | 8,817 | 18,801 |
| 1990 | 918 | 1,083 | 52 | 29 | 147 | 204 | 310 | 610 | 1,553 | 3,492 | 7,889 | 18,057 |
| 2000 | 853 | 807 | 36 | 21 | 115 | 139 | 255 | 543 | 1,231 | 2,980 | 6,973 | 17,501 |
| 2010 | 812 | 680 | 30 | 15 | 98 | 142 | 213 | 506 | 1,076 | 2,275 | 5,694 | 15,414 |
| 2017 | 897 | 619 | 27 | 16 | 106 | 183 | 249 | 497 | 1,112 | 2,190 | 5,254 | 14,689 |
| **White:** | | | | | | | | | | | | |
| 1990 | 931 | 896 | 46 | 26 | 131 | 176 | 268 | 549 | 1,467 | 3,398 | 7,845 | 18,268 |
| 2000 | 888 | 668 | 33 | 20 | 106 | 124 | 234 | 497 | 1,163 | 2,906 | 6,933 | 17,716 |
| 2010 | 866 | 584 | 27 | 14 | 92 | 136 | 207 | 492 | 1,033 | 2,232 | 5,704 | 15,640 |
| 2015 | 933 | 542 | 25 | 14 | 92 | 157 | 221 | 487 | 1,071 | 2,160 | 5,427 | 15,203 |
| 2016 | 944 | 537 | 25 | 14 | 100 | 176 | 239 | 489 | 1,078 | 2,150 | 5,306 | 14,942 |
| 2017 | 963 | 515 | 25 | 14 | 99 | 181 | 245 | 487 | 1,079 | 2,153 | 5,304 | 15,150 |
| **Black:** | | | | | | | | | | | | |
| 1990 | 1,008 | 2,112 | 86 | 41 | 252 | 431 | 700 | 1,261 | 2,618 | 4,946 | 9,130 | 16,955 |
| 2000 | 834 | 1,568 | 55 | 28 | 181 | 261 | 453 | 1,018 | 2,080 | 4,254 | 8,486 | 16,791 |
| 2010 | 725 | 1,207 | 43 | 20 | 143 | 217 | 308 | 716 | 1,662 | 3,206 | 6,722 | 14,715 |
| 2015 | 765 | 1,150 | 46 | 21 | 151 | 229 | 326 | 678 | 1,613 | 3,042 | 6,205 | 13,066 |
| 2016 | 790 | 1,134 | 43 | 21 | 164 | 249 | 350 | 688 | 1,623 | 3,081 | 6,134 | 13,029 |
| 2017 | 805 | 1,150 | 40 | 23 | 161 | 253 | 361 | 694 | 1,628 | 3,099 | 6,095 | 12,851 |
| **Asian or Pacific Islander: [2]** | | | | | | | | | | | | |
| 1990 | 334 | 605 | 45 | 21 | 76 | 80 | 131 | 287 | 789 | 2,041 | 5,009 | 12,446 |
| 2000 | 333 | 529 | 23 | 13 | 55 | 55 | 105 | 250 | 642 | 1,661 | 4,328 | 12,125 |
| 2010 | 327 | 434 | 19 | 8 | 43 | 53 | 84 | 214 | 519 | 1,226 | 3,439 | 10,825 |
| 2015 | 355 | 438 | 15 | 10 | 49 | 56 | 85 | 205 | 508 | 1,131 | 3,092 | 9,406 |
| 2016 | 364 | 449 | 16 | 10 | 52 | 58 | 99 | 211 | 522 | 1,134 | 3,019 | 9,075 |
| 2017 | 375 | 451 | 19 | 9 | 49 | 60 | 92 | 217 | 504 | 1,148 | 3,076 | 9,190 |
| **American Indian or Alaska Native: [2]** | | | | | | | | | | | | |
| 1990 | 476 | 1,057 | 77 | 33 | 220 | 256 | 365 | 620 | 1,211 | 2,462 | 5,389 | 11,244 |
| 2000 | 416 | 700 | 45 | 20 | 136 | 179 | 295 | 520 | 1,090 | 2,478 | 5,351 | 10,726 |
| 2010 | 398 | 543 | 34 | 18 | 116 | 156 | 258 | 496 | 951 | 1,971 | 4,452 | 10,268 |
| 2015 | 455 | 486 | 35 | 15 | 101 | 191 | 281 | 544 | 994 | 1,841 | 4,171 | 8,277 |
| 2016 | 471 | 524 | 29 | 15 | 115 | 215 | 285 | 525 | 1,013 | 1,871 | 4,016 | 8,251 |
| 2017 | 478 | 479 | 24 | 16 | 114 | 217 | 297 | 535 | 982 | 1,811 | 4,075 | 7,733 |
| **FEMALE** | | | | | | | | | | | | |
| **Total:** | | | | | | | | | | | | |
| 1960 | 809 | 2,321 | 98 | 37 | 61 | 107 | 229 | 527 | 1,196 | 2,872 | 7,633 | 19,008 |
| 1970 | 808 | 1,864 | 75 | 32 | 68 | 102 | 231 | 517 | 1,099 | 2,580 | 6,678 | 15,518 |
| 1980 | 785 | 1,142 | 55 | 24 | 58 | 76 | 159 | 413 | 934 | 2,145 | 5,440 | 14,747 |
| 1990 | 812 | 856 | 41 | 19 | 49 | 74 | 138 | 343 | 879 | 1,991 | 4,883 | 14,274 |
| 2000 | 855 | 663 | 29 | 15 | 43 | 64 | 143 | 313 | 772 | 1,921 | 4,815 | 14,719 |
| 2010 | 787 | 564 | 23 | 11 | 36 | 64 | 129 | 311 | 644 | 1,528 | 4,138 | 13,219 |
| 2017 | 831 | 513 | 21 | 11 | 40 | 81 | 141 | 309 | 675 | 1,440 | 3,869 | 12,967 |
| **White:** | | | | | | | | | | | | |
| 1990 | 847 | 690 | 36 | 18 | 46 | 62 | 117 | 309 | 823 | 1,924 | 4,839 | 14,401 |
| 2000 | 912 | 551 | 26 | 14 | 41 | 55 | 126 | 281 | 731 | 1,868 | 4,785 | 14,891 |
| 2010 | 857 | 488 | 22 | 11 | 36 | 61 | 123 | 295 | 618 | 1,505 | 4,165 | 13,419 |
| 2015 | 899 | 455 | 20 | 11 | 38 | 72 | 132 | 307 | 640 | 1,444 | 4,028 | 13,443 |
| 2016 | 895 | 444 | 21 | 11 | 39 | 79 | 138 | 306 | 648 | 1,429 | 3,921 | 13,146 |
| 2017 | 910 | 426 | 19 | 11 | 40 | 82 | 139 | 301 | 654 | 1,434 | 3,923 | 13,385 |
| **Black:** | | | | | | | | | | | | |
| 1990 | 748 | 1,736 | 68 | 28 | 69 | 160 | 299 | 639 | 1,453 | 2,866 | 5,688 | 13,310 |
| 2000 | 733 | 1,280 | 45 | 20 | 58 | 122 | 272 | 588 | 1,227 | 2,690 | 5,697 | 13,941 |
| 2010 | 643 | 994 | 33 | 15 | 43 | 93 | 199 | 481 | 972 | 2,021 | 4,581 | 12,590 |
| 2015 | 666 | 970 | 32 | 15 | 46 | 93 | 192 | 447 | 970 | 1,864 | 4,310 | 11,741 |
| 2016 | 680 | 986 | 34 | 16 | 52 | 100 | 198 | 456 | 981 | 1,885 | 4,296 | 11,472 |
| 2017 | 685 | 946 | 35 | 16 | 48 | 101 | 200 | 438 | 981 | 1,868 | 4,262 | 11,401 |
| **Asian or Pacific Islander: [2]** | | | | | | | | | | | | |
| 1990 | 234 | 518 | 32 | 13 | 29 | 38 | 70 | 183 | 483 | 1,089 | 3,128 | 10,254 |
| 2000 | 262 | 434 | 20 | 12 | 22 | 28 | 66 | 156 | 391 | 996 | 2,882 | 9,052 |
| 2010 | 277 | 342 | 16 | 8 | 17 | 27 | 49 | 128 | 299 | 789 | 2,446 | 8,590 |
| 2015 | 311 | 358 | 15 | 7 | 19 | 26 | 51 | 128 | 288 | 705 | 2,264 | 8,142 |
| 2016 | 318 | 361 | 17 | 9 | 21 | 27 | 53 | 126 | 304 | 699 | 2,193 | 8,071 |
| 2017 | 326 | 390 | 11 | 8 | 22 | 27 | 50 | 129 | 290 | 689 | 2,197 | 8,125 |
| **American Indian or Alaska Native: [2]** | | | | | | | | | | | | |
| 1990 | 330 | 689 | 38 | 26 | 69 | 102 | 156 | 381 | 806 | 1,679 | 3,073 | 8,201 |
| 2000 | 346 | 492 | 40 | 18 | 59 | 85 | 172 | 285 | 772 | 1,900 | 3,850 | 9,118 |
| 2010 | 332 | 366 | 24 | 11 | 44 | 86 | 147 | 326 | 624 | 1,482 | 3,392 | 9,278 |
| 2015 | 376 | 431 | 27 | 14 | 47 | 105 | 171 | 354 | 622 | 1,360 | 3,193 | 7,637 |
| 2016 | 380 | 369 | 32 | 12 | 54 | 118 | 180 | 353 | 615 | 1,274 | 3,198 | 7,181 |
| 2017 | 392 | 400 | 28 | 13 | 48 | 126 | 188 | 350 | 639 | 1,263 | 3,146 | 7,132 |

[1] Figures for age not stated are included in "All ages" but not distributed among age groups. [2] The death rates for specified races other than White and Black should be interpreted with caution because of inconsistencies between reporting race on death certificates and censuses and surveys.

Source: U.S. National Center for Health Statistics, *Health, United States, 2017*, September 2018; and CDC WONDER Online Database, "Multiple Cause of Death, 1999-2017," <https://wonder.cdc.gov/>, accessed June 2019. See also <https://www.cdc.gov/nchs/nvss/deaths.htm>.

# Table 116. Deaths and Death Rates by Age, Sex, Race, and Hispanic Origin: 2017

[Rates per 100,000 population in specified group; see Technical Notes. Race and Hispanic-origin categories are consistent with 1977 Office of Management and Budget (OMB) standards. Multiple-race data reported according to 1997 OMB standards were bridged to single-race categories of 1977 OMB standards. Data for specified race or Hispanic-origin groups other than non-Hispanic White and non-Hispanic Black should be interpreted with caution because of inconsistencies in reporting these items on death certificates and surveys; see Technical Notes, source]

| Age | Total[1] Total | Total[1] Male | Total[1] Female | White, non-Hispanic Total | White, non-Hispanic Male | White, non-Hispanic Female | Black, non-Hispanic Total | Black, non-Hispanic Male | Black, non-Hispanic Female | American Indian or Alaska Native, non-Hispanic Total | Am. Indian Male | Am. Indian Female | Asian or Pacific Islander, non-Hispanic Total | Asian Male | Asian Female | Hispanic[2] Total | Hispanic Male | Hispanic Female |
|---|---|---|---|---|---|---|---|---|---|---|---|---|---|---|---|---|---|---|
| **DEATHS** | | | | | | | | | | | | | | | | | | |
| All ages | 2,813,503 | 1,439,111 | 1,374,392 | 2,179,857 | 1,102,838 | 1,077,019 | 335,667 | 174,403 | 161,264 | 19,198 | 10,502 | 8,696 | 72,598 | 37,236 | 35,362 | 197,249 | 108,579 | 88,670 |
| Under 1 year | 22,335 | 12,468 | 9,867 | 9,359 | 5,281 | 4,078 | 6,730 | 3,760 | 2,970 | 284 | 151 | 133 | 957 | 528 | 429 | 4,808 | 2,635 | 2,173 |
| 1 to 4 years | 3,880 | 2,232 | 1,648 | 1,858 | 1,107 | 751 | 985 | 535 | 450 | 72 | 33 | 39 | 148 | 96 | 52 | 805 | 455 | 350 |
| 5 to 9 years | 2,354 | 1,299 | 1,055 | 1,115 | 623 | 492 | 573 | 319 | 254 | 38 | 19 | 19 | 100 | 52 | 48 | 521 | 282 | 239 |
| 10 to 14 years | 3,217 | 1,970 | 1,247 | 1,667 | 1,005 | 662 | 723 | 465 | 258 | 64 | 36 | 28 | 108 | 62 | 46 | 644 | 395 | 249 |
| 15 to 19 years | 10,886 | 7,849 | 3,037 | 5,592 | 3,894 | 1,693 | 2,560 | 2,019 | 541 | 208 | 148 | 60 | 325 | 222 | 103 | 2,175 | 1,547 | 628 |
| 20 to 24 years | 21,139 | 15,654 | 5,485 | 11,615 | 8,391 | 3,224 | 4,804 | 3,692 | 1,112 | 354 | 244 | 110 | 635 | 445 | 190 | 3,679 | 2,840 | 839 |
| 25 to 29 years | 28,276 | 20,385 | 7,891 | 16,736 | 11,865 | 4,871 | 6,066 | 4,454 | 1,612 | 547 | 348 | 199 | 680 | 477 | 203 | 4,166 | 3,181 | 985 |
| 30 to 34 years | 31,939 | 21,764 | 10,175 | 20,028 | 13,495 | 6,533 | 6,018 | 4,098 | 1,920 | 647 | 431 | 216 | 820 | 536 | 284 | 4,326 | 3,128 | 1,198 |
| 35 to 39 years | 36,901 | 24,105 | 12,796 | 22,872 | 14,806 | 8,066 | 7,251 | 4,663 | 2,538 | 680 | 441 | 239 | 944 | 584 | 360 | 5,014 | 3,516 | 1,498 |
| 40 to 44 years | 42,895 | 26,687 | 16,208 | 26,524 | 16,468 | 10,056 | 8,475 | 5,058 | 3,417 | 729 | 430 | 299 | 1,283 | 790 | 493 | 5,724 | 3,842 | 1,882 |
| 45 to 49 years | 65,698 | 40,223 | 25,475 | 42,453 | 25,965 | 16,488 | 12,288 | 7,229 | 5,059 | 948 | 592 | 356 | 2,007 | 1,181 | 826 | 7,738 | 5,072 | 2,666 |
| 50 to 54 years | 104,444 | 63,581 | 40,863 | 70,312 | 42,816 | 27,496 | 18,938 | 10,952 | 7,986 | 1,338 | 775 | 563 | 2,678 | 1,613 | 1,065 | 10,671 | 7,073 | 3,598 |
| 55 to 59 years | 162,098 | 98,387 | 63,711 | 114,084 | 69,506 | 44,578 | 28,790 | 16,723 | 12,067 | 1,686 | 1,000 | 686 | 3,611 | 2,133 | 1,478 | 13,056 | 8,392 | 4,664 |
| 60 to 64 years | 209,908 | 126,948 | 82,960 | 150,915 | 91,792 | 59,123 | 35,708 | 20,829 | 14,879 | 1,857 | 1,068 | 789 | 4,891 | 2,898 | 1,993 | 15,477 | 9,582 | 5,895 |
| 65 to 69 years | 248,087 | 145,258 | 102,829 | 184,996 | 108,920 | 76,076 | 37,568 | 21,346 | 16,222 | 1,889 | 1,087 | 802 | 6,260 | 3,600 | 2,660 | 16,280 | 9,533 | 6,747 |
| 70 to 74 years | 283,523 | 158,673 | 124,850 | 223,431 | 125,660 | 97,771 | 33,453 | 18,050 | 15,403 | 1,855 | 997 | 858 | 6,633 | 3,752 | 2,881 | 17,088 | 9,499 | 7,589 |
| 75 to 79 years | 307,498 | 163,505 | 143,993 | 245,250 | 131,567 | 113,683 | 32,828 | 16,251 | 16,577 | 1,798 | 933 | 865 | 8,035 | 4,393 | 3,642 | 18,699 | 9,834 | 8,865 |
| 80 to 84 years | 350,261 | 173,166 | 177,095 | 284,866 | 142,527 | 142,339 | 32,248 | 14,488 | 17,760 | 1,731 | 829 | 902 | 9,495 | 4,705 | 4,790 | 21,131 | 10,177 | 10,954 |
| 85 years and over | 878,035 | 334,866 | 543,169 | 746,124 | 287,103 | 459,021 | 59,645 | 19,462 | 40,183 | 2,473 | 940 | 1,533 | 22,988 | 9,169 | 13,819 | 45,236 | 17,588 | 27,648 |
| **DEATH RATES** | | | | | | | | | | | | | | | | | | |
| All ages | 863.8 | 897.2 | 831.4 | 1,083.2 | 1,111.4 | 1,055.8 | 787.5 | 854.2 | 726.1 | 703.4 | 784.4 | 625.5 | 359.8 | 386.2 | 335.6 | 334.6 | 364.6 | 304.0 |
| Under 1 year | 567.0 | 618.7 | 512.8 | 458.5 | 505.2 | 409.5 | 1,110.6 | 1,215.4 | 1,001.3 | 723.8 | 755.9 | 690.6 | 431.2 | 464.0 | 396.7 | 466.4 | 500.3 | 431.0 |
| 1 to 4 years | 24.3 | 27.3 | 21.1 | 22.4 | 26.1 | 18.6 | 40.1 | 42.9 | 37.3 | 45.3 | 40.8 | 50.0 | 15.6 | 19.6 | 11.3 | 19.4 | 21.5 | 17.2 |
| 5 to 9 years | 11.6 | 12.5 | 10.6 | 10.6 | 11.5 | 9.6 | 18.5 | 20.2 | 16.6 | 18.6 | 18.6 | (S) | 8.4 | 8.6 | 8.3 | 9.9 | 10.5 | 9.3 |
| 10 to 14 years | 15.5 | 18.6 | 12.3 | 15.0 | 17.7 | 12.2 | 23.4 | 29.7 | 17.0 | 31.1 | 34.7 | (S) | 8.9 | 10.1 | 7.6 | 12.5 | 15.0 | 9.8 |
| 15 to 19 years | 51.5 | 72.7 | 29.4 | 48.2 | 65.5 | 30.1 | 80.0 | 124.2 | 34.4 | 99.5 | 139.8 | 27.5 | 26.5 | 35.9 | 16.9 | 44.4 | 61.8 | 26.2 |
| 20 to 24 years | 95.6 | 137.9 | 50.9 | 95.1 | 133.6 | 54.3 | 140.8 | 213.0 | 66.3 | 163.3 | 221.7 | 58.2 | 44.2 | 61.2 | 26.8 | 76.1 | 113.7 | 35.9 |
| 25 to 29 years | 121.0 | 171.3 | 68.8 | 127.9 | 178.2 | 75.8 | 171.4 | 252.3 | 90.9 | 245.7 | 307.8 | 103.0 | 39.2 | 55.8 | 23.1 | 86.9 | 126.7 | 43.2 |
| 30 to 34 years | 145.4 | 196.3 | 93.5 | 159.3 | 212.4 | 105.0 | 203.9 | 286.3 | 126.3 | 343.2 | 459.6 | 181.7 | 47.4 | 64.5 | 31.6 | 95.5 | 131.5 | 55.7 |
| 35 to 39 years | 173.8 | 227.1 | 120.5 | 187.5 | 241.1 | 133.2 | 257.9 | 349.0 | 175.4 | 394.3 | 518.1 | 227.9 | 57.8 | 76.3 | 41.5 | 113.5 | 153.7 | 70.3 |
| 40 to 44 years | 218.4 | 273.6 | 163.9 | 233.9 | 289.1 | 178.2 | 332.4 | 422.2 | 252.3 | 465.5 | 561.2 | 373.8 | 83.2 | 109.4 | 60.1 | 141.2 | 186.5 | 94.4 |
| 45 to 49 years | 313.2 | 387.3 | 240.6 | 326.7 | 399.0 | 254.1 | 461.4 | 578.4 | 357.9 | 584.1 | 748.4 | 427.9 | 137.6 | 173.3 | 106.4 | 209.4 | 271.5 | 146.0 |
| 50 to 54 years | 488.0 | 604.4 | 375.5 | 499.8 | 613.5 | 387.8 | 703.6 | 869.7 | 557.6 | 784.4 | 945.4 | 635.5 | 210.9 | 272.4 | 157.1 | 333.4 | 439.8 | 225.9 |
| 55 to 59 years | 736.5 | 919.5 | 563.4 | 741.6 | 919.5 | 569.7 | 1,088.2 | 1,365.8 | 849.1 | 969.7 | 1,219.9 | 746.4 | 313.1 | 402.2 | 237.2 | 492.5 | 643.2 | 346.5 |
| 60 to 64 years | 1,050.2 | 1,328.3 | 795.4 | 1,040.5 | 1,305.4 | 791.3 | 1,583.5 | 2,051.5 | 1,200.3 | 1,251.2 | 1,549.5 | 992.5 | 475.1 | 625.4 | 352.0 | 754.5 | 979.9 | 549.2 |
| 65 to 69 years | 1,473.5 | 1,831.8 | 1,154.5 | 1,463.6 | 1,799.6 | 1,154.9 | 2,168.8 | 2,831.9 | 1,657.9 | 1,649.4 | 2,037.6 | 1,310.8 | 736.9 | 957.5 | 561.7 | 1,085.1 | 1,372.9 | 837.1 |
| 70 to 74 years | 2,206.9 | 2,668.0 | 1,809.5 | 2,240.1 | 2,675.8 | 1,852.4 | 2,899.5 | 3,717.9 | 2,305.0 | 2,355.3 | 2,739.0 | 2,025.5 | 1,122.0 | 1,426.1 | 878.2 | 1,628.5 | 2,037.5 | 1,301.5 |
| 75 to 79 years | 3,871.7 | 4,193.7 | 2,973.6 | 3,603.5 | 4,259.2 | 3,058.6 | 4,258.0 | 5,298.3 | 3,570.7 | 3,598.9 | 4,166.7 | 3,137.7 | 1,962.4 | 2,418.3 | 1,598.9 | 2,652.3 | 3,288.8 | 2,183.5 |
| 80 to 84 years | 5,871.7 | 6,901.6 | 5,123.9 | 6,078.8 | 7,102.6 | 5,312.1 | 6,363.6 | 7,821.4 | 5,523.7 | 5,805.8 | 6,639.4 | 5,205.1 | 3,529.8 | 4,126.1 | 3,091.0 | 4,462.8 | 5,338.6 | 3,872.5 |
| 85 years and over | 13,573.6 | 14,689.2 | 12,966.5 | 14,336.0 | 15,521.8 | 13,682.1 | 12,101.9 | 13,164.9 | 11,646.4 | 9,157.2 | 9,649.9 | 8,879.2 | 8,567.8 | 9,252.7 | 8,166.7 | 9,504.4 | 10,147.1 | 9,136.3 |

S Does not meet standards of reliability. [1] Includes deaths for origin not stated. [2] Persons of Hispanic origin may be of any race.

Source: U.S. National Center for Health Statistics, National Vital Statistics Reports (NVSR), Deaths: Final Data for 2017, Vol. 68. No. 9, June 2019. See also <http://www.cdc.gov/nchs/nvss/deaths.htm>.

# Table 117. Deaths and Death Rates by State: 1990 to 2017

[2,148 represents 2,148,000. By state of residence. Excludes deaths of nonresidents of the United States. Caution should be used in comparing death rates by state; rates are affected by the population composition of the area. See also Appendix III]

| State | Number of deaths (1,000) | | | | | | Death rate per 1,000 population [1] | | | | | | Age-adjusted rate, 2017 [1,2] |
|---|---|---|---|---|---|---|---|---|---|---|---|---|---|
| | 1990 | 2000 | 2010 | 2015 | 2016 | 2017 | 1990 | 2000 | 2010 | 2015 | 2016 | 2017 | |
| **United States**......... | **2,148** | **2,403** | **2,468** | **2,713** | **2,744** | **2,814** | **8.6** | **8.5** | **8.0** | **8.4** | **8.5** | **8.6** | **7.3** |
| Alabama............... | 39 | 45 | 48 | 52 | 52 | 53 | 9.7 | 10.1 | 10.1 | 10.7 | 10.8 | 10.9 | 9.2 |
| Alaska................. | 2 | 3 | 4 | 4 | 4 | 4 | 4.0 | 4.6 | 5.2 | 5.8 | 6.1 | 6.0 | 7.1 |
| Arizona............... | 29 | 41 | 47 | 54 | 57 | 58 | 7.9 | 7.9 | 7.3 | 8.0 | 8.2 | 8.2 | 6.8 |
| Arkansas............. | 25 | 28 | 29 | 32 | 32 | 33 | 10.5 | 10.6 | 9.9 | 10.6 | 10.6 | 10.8 | 9.0 |
| California............. | 214 | 230 | 234 | 259 | 262 | 268 | 7.2 | 6.8 | 6.3 | 6.6 | 6.7 | 6.8 | 6.2 |
| Colorado............. | 22 | 27 | 31 | 36 | 38 | 38 | 6.6 | 6.3 | 6.3 | 6.7 | 6.8 | 6.8 | 6.6 |
| Connecticut.......... | 28 | 30 | 29 | 31 | 31 | 31 | 8.4 | 8.8 | 8.0 | 8.5 | 8.5 | 8.7 | 6.5 |
| Delaware............. | 6 | 7 | 8 | 9 | 9 | 9 | 8.7 | 8.8 | 8.6 | 9.1 | 9.3 | 9.5 | 7.5 |
| District of Columbia.... | 7 | 6 | 5 | 5 | 5 | 5 | 12.0 | 10.5 | 7.8 | 7.2 | 7.4 | 7.2 | 7.3 |
| Florida................. | 134 | 164 | 174 | 192 | 197 | 204 | 10.4 | 10.3 | 9.2 | 9.5 | 9.6 | 9.7 | 6.7 |
| Georgia............... | 52 | 64 | 71 | 80 | 81 | 83 | 8.0 | 7.8 | 7.4 | 7.8 | 7.9 | 8.0 | 7.9 |
| Hawaii................. | 7 | 8 | 10 | 11 | 11 | 11 | 6.1 | 6.8 | 7.1 | 7.7 | 7.6 | 8.0 | 5.8 |
| Idaho.................. | 7 | 10 | 11 | 13 | 13 | 14 | 7.4 | 7.4 | 7.3 | 7.9 | 7.9 | 8.2 | 7.4 |
| Illinois................. | 103 | 107 | 100 | 107 | 107 | 110 | 9.0 | 8.6 | 7.8 | 8.3 | 8.4 | 8.6 | 7.2 |
| Indiana................ | 50 | 55 | 57 | 63 | 63 | 66 | 8.9 | 9.1 | 8.8 | 9.5 | 9.6 | 9.8 | 8.5 |
| Iowa................... | 27 | 28 | 28 | 30 | 30 | 31 | 9.7 | 9.6 | 9.1 | 9.5 | 9.4 | 9.7 | 7.4 |
| Kansas................ | 22 | 25 | 25 | 27 | 26 | 27 | 9.0 | 9.2 | 8.6 | 9.2 | 9.0 | 9.3 | 7.7 |
| Kentucky.............. | 35 | 40 | 42 | 47 | 48 | 48 | 9.5 | 9.8 | 9.7 | 10.5 | 10.8 | 10.8 | 9.3 |
| Louisiana............. | 38 | 41 | 41 | 44 | 44 | 46 | 8.9 | 9.2 | 9.0 | 9.4 | 9.5 | 9.8 | 8.8 |
| Maine.................. | 11 | 12 | 13 | 14 | 14 | 15 | 9.0 | 9.7 | 9.6 | 10.9 | 10.7 | 11.0 | 7.7 |
| Maryland.............. | 38 | 44 | 43 | 47 | 49 | 50 | 8.0 | 8.3 | 7.5 | 7.9 | 8.1 | 8.2 | 7.2 |
| Massachusetts........ | 53 | 57 | 53 | 58 | 57 | 59 | 8.8 | 8.9 | 8.0 | 8.5 | 8.4 | 8.6 | 6.8 |
| Michigan.............. | 79 | 87 | 88 | 95 | 96 | 98 | 8.5 | 8.7 | 8.9 | 9.6 | 9.7 | 9.8 | 7.8 |
| Minnesota............ | 35 | 38 | 39 | 43 | 43 | 44 | 7.9 | 7.7 | 7.3 | 7.8 | 7.8 | 8.0 | 6.6 |
| Mississippi........... | 25 | 29 | 29 | 32 | 32 | 32 | 9.8 | 10.1 | 9.8 | 10.6 | 10.6 | 10.8 | 9.5 |
| Missouri.............. | 50 | 55 | 55 | 60 | 60 | 62 | 9.8 | 9.8 | 9.2 | 9.8 | 9.8 | 10.1 | 8.2 |
| Montana.............. | 7 | 8 | 9 | 10 | 10 | 10 | 8.6 | 9.0 | 8.9 | 9.6 | 9.5 | 9.7 | 7.6 |
| Nebraska............. | 15 | 15 | 15 | 17 | 16 | 17 | 9.4 | 8.8 | 8.3 | 8.8 | 8.5 | 8.8 | 7.3 |
| Nevada............... | 9 | 15 | 20 | 23 | 24 | 25 | 7.8 | 7.6 | 7.3 | 7.9 | 8.1 | 8.2 | 7.7 |
| New Hampshire........ | 8 | 10 | 10 | 12 | 12 | 13 | 7.7 | 7.8 | 7.7 | 9.0 | 9.1 | 9.3 | 7.2 |
| New Jersey........... | 70 | 75 | 69 | 72 | 73 | 75 | 9.1 | 8.9 | 7.9 | 8.1 | 8.2 | 8.3 | 6.7 |
| New Mexico........... | 11 | 13 | 16 | 18 | 18 | 19 | 7.0 | 7.4 | 7.7 | 8.5 | 8.8 | 8.9 | 7.5 |
| New York............. | 169 | 158 | 146 | 154 | 154 | 155 | 9.4 | 8.3 | 7.6 | 7.8 | 7.8 | 7.8 | 6.2 |
| North Carolina........ | 57 | 72 | 79 | 89 | 90 | 93 | 8.6 | 8.9 | 8.3 | 8.9 | 8.9 | 9.1 | 7.9 |
| North Dakota.......... | 6 | 6 | 6 | 6 | 6 | 6 | 8.9 | 9.1 | 8.8 | 8.2 | 8.2 | 8.5 | 6.9 |
| Ohio................... | 99 | 108 | 109 | 118 | 120 | 124 | 9.1 | 9.5 | 9.4 | 10.2 | 10.3 | 10.6 | 8.5 |
| Oklahoma............. | 30 | 35 | 37 | 39 | 39 | 40 | 9.7 | 10.2 | 9.7 | 10.1 | 10.0 | 10.3 | 9.0 |
| Oregon................ | 25 | 30 | 32 | 36 | 36 | 37 | 8.8 | 8.6 | 8.3 | 8.9 | 8.7 | 8.8 | 7.2 |
| Pennsylvania......... | 122 | 131 | 125 | 133 | 133 | 136 | 10.3 | 10.7 | 9.8 | 10.4 | 10.4 | 10.6 | 7.8 |
| Rhode Island.......... | 10 | 10 | 10 | 10 | 10 | 10 | 9.5 | 9.6 | 9.1 | 9.6 | 9.2 | 9.6 | 7.1 |
| South Carolina........ | 30 | 37 | 42 | 47 | 48 | 49 | 8.5 | 9.2 | 9.0 | 9.6 | 9.7 | 9.8 | 8.3 |
| South Dakota......... | 6 | 7 | 7 | 8 | 8 | 8 | 9.1 | 9.3 | 8.7 | 9.0 | 9.1 | 9.2 | 7.4 |
| Tennessee............ | 46 | 55 | 60 | 67 | 68 | 70 | 9.5 | 9.7 | 9.4 | 10.1 | 10.2 | 10.4 | 9.0 |
| Texas................. | 125 | 150 | 167 | 190 | 192 | 198 | 7.4 | 7.2 | 6.6 | 6.9 | 6.9 | 7.0 | 7.4 |
| Utah................... | 9 | 12 | 15 | 17 | 18 | 18 | 5.3 | 5.5 | 5.3 | 5.8 | 5.9 | 5.8 | 7.0 |
| Vermont............... | 5 | 5 | 5 | 6 | 6 | 6 | 8.2 | 8.4 | 8.6 | 9.5 | 9.5 | 9.6 | 7.1 |
| Virginia................ | 48 | 56 | 59 | 66 | 66 | 69 | 7.8 | 8.0 | 7.4 | 7.8 | 7.9 | 8.1 | 7.2 |
| Washington........... | 37 | 44 | 48 | 55 | 55 | 57 | 7.6 | 7.5 | 7.2 | 7.6 | 7.5 | 7.7 | 6.9 |
| West Virginia.......... | 19 | 21 | 21 | 23 | 23 | 23 | 10.8 | 11.7 | 11.5 | 12.3 | 12.4 | 12.8 | 9.6 |
| Wisconsin............. | 43 | 46 | 47 | 51 | 52 | 53 | 8.7 | 8.7 | 8.3 | 8.9 | 9.0 | 9.1 | 7.2 |
| Wyoming.............. | 3 | 4 | 4 | 5 | 5 | 5 | 7.1 | 7.9 | 7.9 | 8.2 | 8.1 | 8.2 | 7.1 |

[1] Rates based on enumerated resident population as of April 1 for 1990, 2000, and 2010; estimated resident population as of July 1 for all other years. [2] Age-adjusted death rates are better indicators than crude death rates for showing changes in the risk of death over time when the age distribution of the population is changing, and for comparing the mortality of population subgroups that have different age compositions. See text this section.

Source: U.S. National Center for Health Statistics, CDC WONDER Online Database, "Multiple Cause of Death, 1999-2017," <http://wonder.cdc.gov/>; and National Vital Statistics Reports (NVSR), *Deaths: Final Data for 2017*, Vol. 68, No. 9, June 2019 and earlier reports. See also <http://www.cdc.gov/nchs/nvss/deaths.htm>.

# Table 118. Fetal and Infant Deaths: 1990 to 2017

[The term "fetal death," defined on an all inclusive basis to end confusion arising from the use of such terms as stillbirth, spontaneous abortion, and miscarriage, has been adopted by the National Center for Health Statistics (NCHS) as the nationally recommended standard. Fetal deaths do not include induced terminations of pregnancy. In 2014, the NCHS transitioned to the use of the obstetric estimate of gestational age (OE) rather than the last normal menses (LMP) estimate, introducing a discontinuity in perinatal measures for earlier years]

| Year | Fetal deaths [1] | | | Infant deaths | | Fetal mortality rate [2,6] | | | Perinatal mortality rate [6] | |
|---|---|---|---|---|---|---|---|---|---|---|
| | Total [1] | 20 to 27 weeks [3] | 28 weeks or more [3] | Less than 7 days | Less than 28 days | Total [1] | 20 to 27 weeks [3] | 28 weeks or more [3] | Definition I [4] | Definition II [5] |
| 1990..... | 31,386 | 13,427 | 17,959 | 19,439 | 23,591 | 7.5 | 3.2 | 4.3 | 9.0 | 13.1 |
| 1995..... | 27,294 | 13,043 | 14,251 | 15,483 | 19,186 | 7.0 | 3.3 | 3.6 | 7.6 | 11.8 |
| 2000..... | 27,003 | 13,497 | 13,506 | 14,893 | 18,733 | 6.6 | 3.3 | 3.3 | 7.0 | 11.2 |
| 2005..... | 25,894 | 13,326 | 12,568 | 15,013 | 18,782 | 6.2 | 3.2 | 3.0 | 6.6 | 10.7 |
| 2006..... | 25,972 | 13,269 | 12,703 | 15,148 | 19,041 | 6.1 | 3.1 | 3.0 | 6.5 | 10.5 |
| 2007..... | 26,593 | 13,822 | 12,771 | 15,139 | 19,094 | 6.1 | 3.2 | 3.0 | 6.4 | 10.5 |
| 2008..... | 26,335 | 13,347 | 12,988 | 14,648 | 18,238 | 6.2 | 3.1 | 3.0 | 6.5 | 10.4 |
| 2009..... | 24,872 | 12,813 | 12,059 | 13,768 | 17,261 | 6.0 | 3.1 | 2.9 | 6.2 | 10.1 |
| 2010..... | 24,258 | 12,388 | 11,870 | 12,900 | 16,193 | 6.0 | 3.1 | 3.0 | 6.2 | 10.1 |
| 2011..... | 24,289 | 12,432 | 11,857 | 12,960 | 16,065 | 6.1 | 3.1 | 3.0 | 6.3 | 10.1 |
| 2012..... | 24,073 | 12,334 | 11,739 | 12,911 | 15,887 | 6.1 | 3.1 | 3.0 | 6.2 | 10.1 |
| 2013..... | 23,595 | 11,874 | 11,721 | 12,900 | 15,893 | 6.0 | 3.0 | 3.0 | 6.2 | 10.0 |
| 2014..... | 23,980 | (NA) | (NA) | 12,772 | 15,737 | 6.0 | (NA) | 2.8 | 6.0 | (NA) |
| 2015..... | 23,776 | (NA) | (NA) | 12,578 | 15,671 | 5.9 | (NA) | 2.9 | 6.0 | (NA) |
| 2016..... | 23,880 | (NA) | (NA) | 12,353 | 15,302 | (NA) | (NA) | 2.9 | 6.0 | (NA) |
| 2017..... | 22,827 | (NA) | (NA) | 11,971 | 14,844 | (NA) | (NA) | (NA) | (NA) | (NA) |

NA Not available. [1] Fetal deaths with stated or presumed gestation of 20 weeks or more. [2] Rate per 1,000 live births and fetal deaths in specified age group. [3] Not stated gestational age proportionally distributed. [4] Infant deaths of less than 7 days and fetal deaths with stated or presumed period of gestation of 28 weeks or more, per 1,000 live births and fetal deaths. [5] Infant deaths of less than 28 days and fetal deaths with stated or presumed period of gestation of 20 weeks or more per 1,000 live births and fetal deaths. [6] Prior to 2014, based on LMP (last normal menses) measure of gestational age. Beginning 2014, based on the OE (obstetric measure) of gestational age.

Source: U.S. National Center for Health Statistics, National Vital Statistics Reports (NVSR), *Fetal and Perinatal Mortality, United States, 2013*, Vol. 64. No. 8, July 2015; *Lack of change in Perinatal Mortality in the United States, 2014-2016*, NCHS Data Brief, August 2018; *Health, United States, 2017*, September 2018; and CDC WONDER Online Database, "Linked Birth / Infant Death Records, 2007-2017," and "Fetal Deaths, 2005-2017," <https://wonder.cdc.gov/>, accessed August 2019.

# Table 119. Fetal, Infant, Neonatal, and Maternal Mortality Rates by Race: 1980 to 2016

[Deaths per 1,000 live births, except as noted. Data based on death certificates, fetal death records, and birth certificates. Excludes deaths of nonresidents of the United States. See also Appendix III]

| Race and year | Infant [1] | Neonatal [1] | | Post-neonatal [1] | Fetal mortality rate [2] | Late fetal mortality rate [3] | Perinatal mortality rate [4] | Maternal mortality rate [5] |
|---|---|---|---|---|---|---|---|---|
| | | Under 28 days | Under 7 days | | | | | |
| **ALL RACES** | | | | | | | | |
| 1980.............. | 12.6 | 8.5 | 7.1 | 4.1 | 9.1 | 6.2 | 13.2 | 9.2 |
| 1990.............. | 9.2 | 5.8 | 4.8 | 3.4 | 7.5 | 4.3 | 9.0 | 8.2 |
| 1995.............. | 7.6 | 4.9 | 4.0 | 2.7 | 7.0 | 3.6 | 7.6 | 7.1 |
| 2000.............. | 6.9 | 4.6 | 3.7 | 2.3 | 6.6 | 3.3 | 7.0 | 9.8 |
| 2005.............. | 6.9 | 4.5 | 3.6 | 2.3 | 6.2 | 3.0 | 6.6 | [6] 15.1 |
| 2010.............. | 6.1 | 4.0 | 3.2 | 2.1 | 6.0 | 3.0 | 6.2 | (NA) |
| 2015.............. | 5.9 | 3.9 | 3.2 | 2.0 | 5.9 | 2.8 | 6.0 | (NA) |
| 2016.............. | 5.9 | 3.9 | 3.1 | 2.0 | (NA) | (NA) | (NA) | (NA) |
| **WHITE [7]** | | | | | | | | |
| 1980.............. | 10.9 | 7.4 | 6.1 | 3.5 | 8.1 | 5.7 | 11.8 | 6.7 |
| 1990.............. | 7.6 | 4.8 | 3.9 | 2.8 | 6.4 | 3.8 | 7.7 | 5.4 |
| 1995.............. | 6.3 | 4.1 | 3.3 | 2.2 | 5.9 | 3.3 | 6.5 | 4.2 |
| 2000.............. | 5.7 | 3.8 | 3.0 | 1.9 | 5.6 | 2.9 | 5.9 | 7.5 |
| 2005.............. | 5.7 | 3.8 | 3.0 | 1.9 | 5.3 | 2.7 | 5.7 | [6] 11.1 |
| 2010.............. | 5.2 | 3.5 | 2.7 | 1.7 | (NA) | (NA) | (NA) | (NA) |
| 2015.............. | 4.9 | 3.3 | 2.7 | 1.6 | (NA) | (NA) | (NA) | (NA) |
| 2016.............. | 4.9 | 3.3 | 2.6 | 1.7 | (NA) | (NA) | (NA) | (NA) |
| **BLACK [7]** | | | | | | | | |
| 1980.............. | 22.2 | 14.6 | 12.3 | 7.6 | 14.7 | 9.1 | 21.3 | 22.4 |
| 1990.............. | 18.0 | 11.6 | 9.7 | 6.4 | 13.3 | 6.7 | 16.4 | 22.4 |
| 1995.............. | 15.1 | 9.8 | 8.2 | 5.3 | 12.7 | 5.7 | 13.8 | 22.1 |
| 2000.............. | 14.1 | 9.4 | 7.6 | 4.7 | 12.4 | 5.4 | 13.0 | 22.0 |
| 2005.............. | 13.7 | 9.1 | 7.3 | 4.7 | 11.4 | 4.9 | 12.1 | [6] 36.5 |
| 2010.............. | 11.6 | 7.5 | 6.0 | 4.1 | (NA) | (NA) | (NA) | (NA) |
| 2015.............. | 11.4 | 7.4 | 6.0 | 4.0 | (NA) | (NA) | (NA) | (NA) |
| 2016.............. | 11.1 | 7.2 | 5.8 | 3.9 | (NA) | (NA) | (NA) | (NA) |

NA Not available. [1] Infant (under 1 year of age), neonatal (under 28 days), early neonatal (under 7 days), and postneonatal (28 days–11 months). [2] Number of fetal deaths of 20 weeks or more gestation per 1,000 live births plus fetal deaths. [3] Number of fetal deaths of 28 weeks or more gestation (late fetal deaths) per 1,000 live births plus late fetal deaths. [4] Number of late fetal deaths plus infant deaths within 7 days of birth per 1,000 live births plus late fetal deaths. [5] Per 100,000 live births from deliveries and complications of pregnancy, childbirth, and the puerperium. Beginning 2000, deaths are classified according to the tenth revision of the International Classification of Diseases; earlier years classified according to the revision in use at the time; see text, this section. [6] Increase partially reflects the use of a separate item on the death certificate on pregnancy status by an increasing number of states. [7] Infant deaths are tabulated by race of decedent; fetal deaths and live births are tabulated by race of mother.

Source: U.S. National Center for Health Statistics, *Fetal and Perinatal Mortality, United States, 2013*, Vol. 64, No. 8, July 2015; and *Health, United States, 2017*, September 2018. See also <http://www.cdc.gov/nchs/hus.htm>.

# Table 120. Infant Deaths and Mortality Rates by Race, Hispanic Origin, and State and Island Area: 2017

[Rates are for infant (under 1 year old) deaths per 1,000 live births in specified group. Infant deaths are based on race or Hispanic origin of decedent; live births are based on race or Hispanic origin of mother. Race and Hispanic-origin categories are consistent with 1977 Office of Management and Budget (OMB) standards. Multiple-race data reported according to 1997 OMB standards were bridged to the single-race categories of 1977 OMB standards. See Technical Notes in source for more detail]

| State and Island Area | Total [1] | | White, non-Hispanic | | Black, non-Hispanic | | Hispanic | |
|---|---|---|---|---|---|---|---|---|
| | Number | Rate | Number | Rate | Number | Rate | Number | Rate |
| United States [2] | 22,335 | 5.8 | 9,359 | 4.6 | 6,730 | 11.5 | 4,808 | 5.4 |
| Alabama | 434 | 7.4 | 196 | 5.6 | 205 | 11.2 | 22 | 4.8 |
| Alaska | 59 | 5.7 | 25 | 4.4 | 4 | (B) | 2 | (B) |
| Arizona | 469 | 5.7 | 145 | 4.2 | 54 | 11.3 | 205 | 6.0 |
| Arkansas | 307 | 8.2 | 176 | 7.2 | 94 | 12.9 | 24 | 5.9 |
| California | 1,973 | 4.2 | 436 | 3.3 | 222 | 8.4 | 1,089 | 5.0 |
| Colorado | 291 | 4.5 | 149 | 3.9 | 31 | 8.7 | 96 | 5.3 |
| Connecticut | 160 | 4.5 | 63 | 3.3 | 47 | 10.3 | 41 | 4.6 |
| Delaware | 72 | 6.6 | 19 | (B) | 38 | 12.8 | 12 | (B) |
| District of Columbia | 77 | 8.1 | 13 | (B) | 57 | 12.2 | 7 | (B) |
| Florida | 1,358 | 6.1 | 453 | 4.6 | 515 | 10.2 | 353 | 5.3 |
| Georgia | 932 | 7.2 | 286 | 4.9 | 525 | 11.5 | 92 | 5.1 |
| Hawaii | 92 | 5.3 | 16 | (B) | 12 | (B) | 21 | 7.9 |
| Idaho | 102 | 4.6 | 77 | 4.4 | 1 | (B) | 19 | (B) |
| Illinois | 912 | 6.1 | 347 | 4.4 | 352 | 13.3 | 168 | 5.4 |
| Indiana | 600 | 7.3 | 361 | 5.9 | 163 | 15.3 | 58 | 7.6 |
| Iowa | 203 | 5.3 | 145 | 4.8 | 31 | 10.6 | 22 | 6.2 |
| Kansas | 221 | 6.1 | 130 | 5.0 | 34 | 11.8 | 43 | 7.2 |
| Kentucky | 355 | 6.5 | 275 | 6.2 | 54 | 10.1 | 20 | 6.3 |
| Louisiana | 431 | 7.1 | 146 | 4.6 | 252 | 11.1 | 28 | 5.9 |
| Maine | 70 | 5.7 | 64 | 5.8 | 4 | (B) | 2 | (B) |
| Maryland | 460 | 6.4 | 121 | 4.0 | 257 | 11.1 | 57 | 4.7 |
| Massachusetts | 262 | 3.7 | 121 | 2.9 | 50 | 6.8 | 71 | 5.2 |
| Michigan | 755 | 6.8 | 354 | 4.6 | 306 | 14.0 | 57 | 7.8 |
| Minnesota | 328 | 4.8 | 171 | 3.6 | 81 | 9.4 | 25 | 5.0 |
| Mississippi | 322 | 8.6 | 118 | 6.3 | 188 | 11.6 | 6 | (B) |
| Missouri | 456 | 6.2 | 284 | 5.2 | 146 | 13.0 | 18 | (B) |
| Montana | 64 | 5.4 | 42 | 4.4 | – | (B) | 4 | (B) |
| Nebraska | 144 | 5.6 | 94 | 5.2 | 20 | 10.4 | 20 | 4.6 |
| Nevada | 208 | 5.8 | 68 | 4.9 | 52 | 10.4 | 71 | 5.4 |
| New Hampshire | 51 | 4.2 | 41 | 3.9 | 3 | (B) | 4 | (B) |
| New Jersey | 453 | 4.5 | 139 | 3.0 | 155 | 11.0 | 124 | 4.5 |
| New Mexico | 140 | 5.9 | 33 | 5.0 | 4 | (B) | 81 | 6.1 |
| New York | 1,047 | 4.6 | 381 | 3.4 | 304 | 8.6 | 230 | 4.3 |
| North Carolina | 847 | 7.1 | 329 | 5.0 | 360 | 12.4 | 106 | 5.7 |
| North Dakota | 46 | 4.3 | 27 | 3.3 | 8 | (B) | 1 | (B) |
| Ohio | 983 | 7.2 | 527 | 5.3 | 383 | 15.9 | 54 | 7.2 |
| Oklahoma | 387 | 7.7 | 183 | 5.9 | 69 | 14.3 | 63 | 8.5 |
| Oregon | 236 | 5.4 | 138 | 4.6 | 18 | (B) | 58 | 7.0 |
| Pennsylvania | 841 | 6.1 | 435 | 4.6 | 268 | 13.5 | 100 | 6.3 |
| Rhode Island | 66 | 6.2 | 35 | 5.6 | 15 | (B) | 13 | (B) |
| South Carolina | 371 | 6.5 | 164 | 5.0 | 176 | 10.1 | 26 | 5.0 |
| South Dakota | 94 | 7.8 | 64 | 7.2 | 8 | (B) | 3 | (B) |
| Tennessee | 597 | 7.4 | 325 | 6.0 | 211 | 12.7 | 50 | 6.5 |
| Texas | 2,237 | 5.9 | 634 | 4.9 | 529 | 10.7 | 989 | 5.5 |
| Utah | 285 | 5.9 | 206 | 5.6 | 8 | (B) | 52 | 6.6 |
| Vermont | 27 | 4.8 | 22 | 4.3 | 4 | (B) | – | (B) |
| Virginia | 592 | 5.9 | 254 | 4.5 | 219 | 10.1 | 71 | 5.1 |
| Washington | 341 | 3.9 | 182 | 3.5 | 50 | 10.2 | 75 | 4.7 |
| West Virginia | 131 | 7.0 | 114 | 6.6 | 15 | (B) | 2 | (B) |
| Wisconsin | 414 | 6.4 | 205 | 4.4 | 128 | 17.3 | 49 | 7.7 |
| Wyoming | 32 | 4.6 | 26 | 4.7 | – | (B) | 4 | (B) |
| Puerto Rico | 163 | 6.7 | – | (B) | – | (B) | 163 | 6.9 |
| Virgin Islands | 10 | (B) | – | (B) | 4 | (B) | 2 | (B) |
| Guam | 24 | 7.3 | – | (B) | – | (B) | 2 | (B) |
| American Samoa | 12 | (B) | – | (B) | – | (B) | – | (B) |
| Northern Marianas | 8 | (B) | 1 | (B) | – | (B) | – | (B) |

– Represents zero. B Base figure too small to meet statistical standards for reliability. [1] Includes other races, not shown separately. [2] Excludes data for Puerto Rico, Virgin Islands, Guam, American Samoa, and Northern Mariana Islands.

Source: U.S. National Center for Health Statistics, National Vital Statistics Reports (NVSR), *Deaths: Final Data for 2017*, Vol. 68, No. 9, June 2019 and earlier reports. See also <http://www.cdc.gov/nchs/nvss/deaths.htm>.

# Table 121. Age-Adjusted Death Rates by Major Cause: 1960 to 2017

[Age-adjusted rates per 100,000 population. Age-adjusted death rates were prepared using the direct method, in which age specific death rates for a population of interest are applied to a standard population distributed by age. Age adjustment eliminates the differences in observed rates between points in time or among compared population groups that result from age differences in population composition. Beginning 1999, deaths classified according to tenth revision of International Classification of Diseases; for earlier years, causes of death were classified according to the revisions then in use. Changes in classification of causes of death due to these revisions may result in discontinuities in cause-of-death trends. See Appendix III]

| Year | Diseases of the heart | Malignant neo-plasms (cancer) | Accidents [1] | Chronic lower res-piratory diseases | Cerebro-vascular diseases | Alz-heimer's disease | Dia-betes mellitus | Influenza and pneu-monia | Inten-tional self-harm (suicide) | Nephritis, nephrotic syndrome and nephrosis |
|---|---|---|---|---|---|---|---|---|---|---|
| 1960...... | 559.0 | 193.9 | 63.1 | 12.5 | 177.9 | (NA) | 22.5 | 53.7 | 12.5 | 10.6 |
| 1970...... | 492.7 | 198.6 | 62.2 | 21.3 | 147.7 | (NA) | 24.3 | 41.7 | 13.1 | 5.5 |
| 1980...... | 412.1 | 207.9 | 46.4 | 28.3 | 96.4 | (NA) | 18.1 | 31.4 | 12.2 | 9.1 |
| 1990...... | 321.8 | 216.0 | 36.3 | 37.2 | 65.3 | 6.3 | 20.7 | 36.8 | 12.5 | 9.3 |
| 1995...... | 293.4 | 209.9 | 34.4 | 40.1 | 63.1 | 8.4 | 23.2 | 33.4 | 11.8 | 9.5 |
| 1996...... | 285.7 | 206.7 | 34.5 | 40.6 | 62.5 | 8.5 | 23.8 | 32.9 | 11.5 | 9.6 |
| 1997...... | 277.7 | 203.4 | 34.2 | 41.1 | 61.1 | 8.7 | 23.7 | 33.3 | 11.2 | 9.8 |
| 1998...... | 267.4 | 202.1 | 35.6 | 43.8 | 62.8 | 8.6 | 24.2 | 24.2 | 11.1 | 9.8 |
| 1999...... | 266.5 | 200.8 | 35.3 | 45.4 | 61.6 | 16.5 | 25.0 | 23.5 | 10.5 | 13.0 |
| 2000...... | 257.6 | 199.6 | 34.9 | 44.2 | 60.9 | 18.1 | 25.0 | 23.7 | 10.4 | 13.5 |
| 2001...... | 249.5 | 196.5 | 35.7 | 43.9 | 58.4 | 19.3 | 25.4 | 22.2 | 10.7 | 14.1 |
| 2002...... | 244.6 | 194.3 | 37.1 | 43.9 | 57.2 | 20.8 | 25.6 | 23.2 | 10.9 | 14.4 |
| 2003...... | 236.3 | 190.9 | 37.6 | 43.7 | 54.6 | 22.1 | 25.5 | 22.6 | 10.8 | 14.7 |
| 2004...... | 221.6 | 186.8 | 38.1 | 41.6 | 51.2 | 22.6 | 24.7 | 20.4 | 11.0 | 14.5 |
| 2005...... | 216.8 | 185.1 | 39.5 | 43.9 | 48.0 | 24.0 | 24.9 | 21.0 | 10.9 | 14.7 |
| 2006...... | 205.5 | 181.8 | 40.2 | 41.0 | 44.8 | 23.7 | 23.6 | 18.4 | 11.0 | 14.8 |
| 2007...... | 196.1 | 179.3 | 40.4 | 41.4 | 43.5 | 23.8 | 22.8 | 16.8 | 11.3 | 14.9 |
| 2008...... | 192.1 | 176.4 | 39.2 | 44.7 | 42.1 | 25.8 | 22.0 | 17.6 | 11.6 | 15.1 |
| 2009...... | 182.8 | 173.5 | 37.5 | 42.7 | 39.6 | 24.2 | 21.0 | 16.5 | 11.8 | 15.1 |
| 2010...... | 179.1 | 172.8 | 38.0 | 42.2 | 39.1 | 25.1 | 20.8 | 15.1 | 12.1 | 15.3 |
| 2011...... | 173.7 | 169.0 | 39.1 | 42.5 | 37.9 | 24.7 | 21.6 | 15.7 | 12.3 | 13.4 |
| 2012...... | 170.5 | 166.5 | 39.1 | 41.5 | 36.9 | 23.8 | 21.2 | 14.4 | 12.6 | 13.1 |
| 2013...... | 169.8 | 163.2 | 39.4 | 42.1 | 36.2 | 23.5 | 21.2 | 15.9 | 12.6 | 13.2 |
| 2014...... | 167.0 | 161.2 | 40.5 | 40.5 | 36.5 | 25.4 | 20.9 | 15.1 | 13.0 | 13.2 |
| 2015...... | 168.5 | 158.5 | 43.2 | 41.6 | 37.6 | 29.4 | 21.3 | 15.2 | 13.3 | 13.4 |
| 2016...... | 165.5 | 155.8 | 47.4 | 40.6 | 37.3 | 30.3 | 21.0 | 13.5 | 13.5 | 13.1 |
| 2017...... | 165.0 | 152.5 | 49.4 | 40.9 | 37.6 | 31.0 | 21.5 | 14.3 | 14.0 | 13.0 |

NA Not available. [1] Unintentional injuries.

Source: U.S. National Center for Health Statistics, National Vital Statistics Reports (NVSR), *Deaths: Final Data for 2017*, Vol. 68, No. 9, June 2019 and earlier reports. See also <http://www.cdc.gov/nchs/nvss/deaths.htm>.

# Table 122. Deaths by Leading Cause, Race, and Hispanic Origin: 2017

[Rank based on number of deaths. Race and Hispanic origin are reported separately on death certificates. Persons of Hispanic origin may be of any race. Data for Hispanic persons are not tabulated by race; data for non-Hispanic persons are tabulated by race. Data for racial and ethnic groups other than non-Hispanic White and non-Hispanic Black should be interpreted with caution because of misreporting of Hispanic origin and race on the death certificate. Cause of death based on International Classification of Diseases, Tenth Revision (ICD-10). See Appendix III]

| Cause of death | Non-Hispanic White Rank | Non-Hispanic White Deaths | Non-Hispanic Black Rank | Non-Hispanic Black Deaths | Non-Hispanic American Indian or Alaska Native Rank | Non-Hispanic American Indian or Alaska Native Deaths | Non-Hispanic Asian or Pacific Islander Rank | Non-Hispanic Asian or Pacific Islander Deaths | Hispanic Rank | Hispanic Deaths |
|---|---|---|---|---|---|---|---|---|---|---|
| All causes...................... | (X) | 2,179,857 | (X) | 335,667 | (X) | 19,198 | (X) | 72,598 | (X) | 197,249 |
| Diseases of heart.................. | 1 | 508,485 | 1 | 78,161 | 1 | 3,472 | 2 | 15,490 | 2 | 39,402 |
| Malignant neoplasms (cancer).... | 2 | 465,679 | 2 | 69,872 | 2 | 3,257 | 1 | 18,257 | 1 | 40,550 |
| Chronic lower respiratory diseases.............. | 3 | 139,833 | 6 | 11,217 | 6 | 939 | 8 | 2,063 | 8 | 5,599 |
| Accidents (unintended injuries).............. | 4 | 127,029 | 3 | 19,869 | 3 | 2,229 | 4 | 3,256 | 3 | 16,757 |
| Cerebrovascular diseases......... | 5 | 110,038 | 4 | 19,088 | 7 | 737 | 3 | 5,430 | 4 | 10,775 |
| Alzheimer's disease............... | 6 | 101,876 | 9 | 8,991 | 10 | 376 | 6 | 2,583 | 6 | 7,383 |
| Diabetes mellitus.................. | 7 | 55,116 | 5 | 14,798 | 4 | 1,114 | 5 | 3,047 | 5 | 9,216 |
| Influenza and pneumonia.......... | 8 | 43,397 | 12 | 5,556 | 9 | 391 | 7 | 2,286 | 11 | 3,851 |
| Intentional self-harm (suicide)..... | 9 | 38,106 | 16 | 2,940 | 8 | 602 | 11 | 1,414 | 9 | 3,933 |
| Nephritis, nephrotic syndrome and nephrosis......... | 10 | 35,191 | 8 | 9,542 | 11 | 333 | 9 | 1,534 | 10 | 3,928 |
| Chronic liver disease and cirrhosis...................... | 11 | 30,223 | 14 | 3,290 | 5 | 1,047 | 14 | 725 | 7 | 6,286 |
| Septicemia....................... | 12 | 30,198 | 10 | 6,568 | 12 | 295 | 12 | 879 | 13 | 2,869 |
| Essential hypertension and hypertensive renal disease...... | 14 | 24,465 | 11 | 6,273 | 14 | 190 | 10 | 1,472 | 14 | 2,799 |
| Assault (homicide)................. | 20 | 5,747 | 7 | 9,908 | 13 | 266 | 18 | 347 | 12 | 3,186 |

X Not applicable.

Source: U.S. National Center for Health Statistics, National Vital Statistics Reports (NVSR), *Deaths: Leading Causes for 2017*, Vol. 68, No. 6, June 2019. See also <http://www.cdc.gov/nchs/nvss/deaths.htm>.

# Table 123. Deaths and Death Rates by Selected Causes: 2016 and 2017

[Rates per 100,000 population. Figures are weighted data rounded to the nearest individual, so categories may not add to total or subtotal. Excludes deaths of nonresidents of the United States. Deaths classified according to the International Classification of Diseases, Tenth Revision (ICD-10). See also Appendix III]

| Cause of death | 2016 | | | 2017 | | |
|---|---|---|---|---|---|---|
| | Number | Rate | Age-adjusted rate [1] | Number | Rate | Age-adjusted rate [1] |
| **All causes [2]** | **2,744,248** | **849.3** | **728.8** | **2,813,503** | **863.8** | **731.9** |
| Major cardiovascular diseases [2] | 835,947 | 258.7 | 218.2 | 854,390 | 262.3 | 218.1 |
| Diseases of heart | 635,260 | 196.6 | 165.5 | 647,457 | 198.8 | 165.0 |
| Acute rheumatic fever and chronic rheumatic heart disease | 3,553 | 1.1 | 0.9 | 3,320 | 1.0 | 0.9 |
| Hypertensive heart disease | 43,734 | 13.5 | 11.4 | 47,523 | 14.6 | 12.2 |
| Hypertensive heart and renal disease | 5,755 | 1.8 | 1.5 | 7,259 | 2.2 | 1.9 |
| Ischemic heart disease | 363,452 | 112.5 | 94.3 | 365,914 | 112.3 | 92.9 |
| Acute myocardial infarction | 111,777 | 34.6 | 29.1 | 110,346 | 33.9 | 28.1 |
| Other heart diseases | 218,766 | 67.7 | 57.3 | 223,441 | 68.6 | 57.3 |
| Heart failure | 78,356 | 24.2 | 20.3 | 80,480 | 24.7 | 20.4 |
| Essential (primary) hypertension and hypertensive renal disease | 33,246 | 10.3 | 8.6 | 35,316 | 10.8 | 9.0 |
| Cerebrovascular diseases | 142,142 | 44.0 | 37.3 | 146,383 | 44.9 | 37.6 |
| Atherosclerosis | 5,727 | 1.8 | 1.5 | 5,547 | 1.7 | 1.4 |
| Malignant neoplasms (cancer) [2] | 598,038 | 185.1 | 155.8 | 599,108 | 183.9 | 152.5 |
| Malignant neoplasms of lip, oral cavity, and pharynx | 10,170 | 3.1 | 2.6 | 10,126 | 3.1 | 2.5 |
| Malignant neoplasms of esophagus | 15,459 | 4.8 | 3.9 | 15,321 | 4.7 | 3.8 |
| Malignant neoplasms of stomach | 11,433 | 3.5 | 3.0 | 11,158 | 3.4 | 2.9 |
| Malignant neoplasms of colon, rectum and anus | 53,145 | 16.4 | 13.9 | 53,447 | 16.4 | 13.7 |
| Malignant neoplasms of liver and intrahepatic bile ducts | 26,569 | 8.2 | 6.7 | 27,106 | 8.3 | 6.7 |
| Malignant neoplasms of pancreas | 42,757 | 13.2 | 11.1 | 44,012 | 13.5 | 11.1 |
| Malignant neoplasms of trachea, bronchus and lung | 148,945 | 46.1 | 38.4 | 145,932 | 44.8 | 36.6 |
| Malignant melanoma of skin | 8,188 | 2.5 | 2.2 | 8,056 | 2.5 | 2.1 |
| Malignant neoplasm of breast | 41,952 | 13.0 | 11.1 | 42,510 | 13.1 | 11.0 |
| Malignant neoplasm of ovary | 14,223 | 4.4 | 3.7 | 14,193 | 4.4 | 3.6 |
| Malignant neoplasm of prostate | 30,370 | 9.4 | 7.9 | 30,488 | 9.4 | 7.8 |
| Malignant neoplasms of kidney and renal pelvis | 13,842 | 4.3 | 3.6 | 13,960 | 4.3 | 3.5 |
| Malignant neoplasms of bladder | 16,646 | 5.2 | 4.4 | 16,657 | 5.1 | 4.3 |
| Malignant neoplasms of meninges, brain and other parts of central nervous system | 16,834 | 5.2 | 4.5 | 16,804 | 5.2 | 4.4 |
| Malignant neoplasms of lymphoid, hematopoietic and related tissue [2] | 57,234 | 17.7 | 15.2 | 57,737 | 17.7 | 15.0 |
| Non-Hodgkin's lymphoma | 20,269 | 6.3 | 5.4 | 20,460 | 6.3 | 5.3 |
| Leukemia | 23,130 | 7.2 | 6.2 | 23,359 | 7.2 | 6.1 |
| Accidents (unintentional injuries) | 161,374 | 49.9 | 47.4 | 169,936 | 52.2 | 49.4 |
| Transport accidents [2] | 43,048 | 13.3 | 12.9 | 43,024 | 13.2 | 12.8 |
| Motor vehicle accidents | 40,327 | 12.5 | 12.1 | 40,231 | 12.4 | 12.0 |
| Nontransport accidents [2] | 118,326 | 36.6 | 34.5 | 126,912 | 39.0 | 36.6 |
| Falls | 34,673 | 10.7 | 9.1 | 36,338 | 11.2 | 9.4 |
| Accidental discharge of firearms | 495 | 0.2 | 0.2 | 486 | 0.1 | 0.2 |
| Accidental drowning and submersion | 3,786 | 1.2 | 1.2 | 3,709 | 1.1 | 1.1 |
| Accidental exposure to smoke, fire and flames | 2,730 | 0.8 | 0.8 | 2,812 | 0.9 | 0.8 |
| Accidental poisoning and exposure to noxious substances | 58,335 | 18.1 | 18.2 | 64,795 | 19.9 | 20.1 |
| Chronic lower respiratory diseases [2] | 154,596 | 47.8 | 40.6 | 160,201 | 49.2 | 40.9 |
| Bronchitis, chronic and unspecified | 518 | 0.2 | 0.1 | 502 | 0.2 | 0.1 |
| Emphysema | 6,977 | 2.2 | 1.8 | 7,085 | 2.2 | 1.8 |
| Asthma | 3,518 | 1.1 | 1.0 | 3,564 | 1.1 | 1.0 |
| Pneumonitis due to solids and liquids | 19,715 | 6.1 | 5.2 | 20,108 | 6.2 | 5.1 |
| Influenza and pneumonia [2] | 51,537 | 15.9 | 13.5 | 55,672 | 17.1 | 14.3 |
| Influenza | 2,905 | 0.9 | 0.8 | 6,515 | 2.0 | 1.7 |
| Pneumonia | 48,632 | 15.1 | 12.8 | 49,157 | 15.1 | 12.6 |
| Septicemia (blood poisoning) | 40,613 | 12.6 | 10.7 | 40,922 | 12.6 | 10.6 |
| Viral hepatitis | 6,421 | 2.0 | 1.6 | 5,611 | 1.7 | 1.4 |
| Human immunodeficiency virus (HIV) disease | 6,160 | 1.9 | 1.8 | 5,698 | 1.7 | 1.6 |
| Anemias | 5,349 | 1.7 | 1.4 | 5,382 | 1.7 | 1.4 |
| Diabetes mellitus | 80,058 | 24.8 | 21.0 | 83,564 | 25.7 | 21.5 |
| Nutritional deficiencies | 6,329 | 2.0 | 1.6 | 7,846 | 2.4 | 2.0 |
| Malnutrition | 6,127 | 1.9 | 1.6 | 7,592 | 2.3 | 1.9 |
| Parkinson's disease | 29,697 | 9.2 | 8.0 | 31,963 | 9.8 | 8.4 |
| Alzheimer's disease | 116,103 | 35.9 | 30.3 | 121,404 | 37.3 | 31.0 |
| Chronic liver disease and cirrhosis | 40,545 | 12.5 | 10.7 | 41,743 | 12.8 | 10.9 |
| Alcoholic liver disease | 21,815 | 6.8 | 5.9 | 22,246 | 6.8 | 5.9 |
| Nephritis, nephrotic syndrome, and nephrosis [2] | 50,046 | 15.5 | 13.1 | 50,633 | 15.5 | 13.0 |
| Renal failure | 49,179 | 15.2 | 12.9 | 49,709 | 15.3 | 12.8 |
| Intentional self-harm (suicide) | 44,965 | 13.9 | 13.5 | 47,173 | 14.5 | 14.0 |
| Intentional self-harm (suicide) by discharge of firearms | 22,938 | 7.1 | 6.8 | 23,854 | 7.3 | 6.9 |
| Assault (homicide) | 19,362 | 6.0 | 6.2 | 19,510 | 6.0 | 6.2 |
| Assault (homicide) by discharge of firearms | 14,415 | 4.5 | 4.6 | 14,542 | 4.5 | 4.6 |
| Events of undetermined intent | 5,723 | 1.8 | 1.7 | 5,799 | 1.8 | 1.8 |
| Complications of medical and surgical care | 3,203 | 1.0 | 0.9 | 4,459 | 1.4 | 1.2 |
| Enterocolitis due to Clostridium difficile [3] | 6,768 | 2.1 | 1.8 | 6,118 | 1.9 | 1.6 |
| Drug-induced deaths [3] | 67,265 | 20.8 | 20.8 | 73,990 | 22.7 | 22.8 |
| Alcohol-induced deaths [3] | 34,865 | 10.8 | 9.5 | 35,823 | 11.0 | 9.6 |
| Injury by firearms [3] | 38,658 | 12.0 | 11.8 | 39,773 | 12.2 | 12.0 |

[1] See text, this section. [2] Includes other causes, not shown separately. [3] Also included in selected other categories.

Source: U.S. National Center for Health Statistics, National Vital Statistics Reports, *Deaths: Final Data for 2017*, Vol. 68, No. 9, June 2019 and earlier reports; and CDC WONDER Online database, "Multiple Cause of Death, 1999-2017," <https://wonder.cdc.gov/>, accessed June 2019. See also <http://www.cdc.gov/nchs/nvss/deaths.htm>.

# Table 124. Deaths by Age and Selected Cause: 2017

[Deaths are classified according to the International Classification of Diseases, Tenth Revision (ICD-10). See Appendix III]

| Cause of death | All ages [1] | Under 1 year | 1 to 4 years | 5 to 14 years | 15 to 24 years | 25 to 34 years | 35 to 44 years | 45 to 54 years | 55 to 64 years | 65 to 74 years | 75 to 84 years | 85 years and over |
|---|---|---|---|---|---|---|---|---|---|---|---|---|
| **All causes** [2] | 2,813,503 | 22,335 | 3,880 | 5,571 | 32,025 | 60,215 | 79,796 | 170,142 | 372,006 | 531,610 | 657,759 | 878,035 |
| Septicemia | 40,922 | 147 | 48 | 57 | 123 | 392 | 854 | 2,441 | 5,838 | 9,164 | 10,648 | 11,210 |
| Human immunodeficiency virus (HIV) disease | 5,698 | – | – | – | 69 | 513 | 831 | 1,609 | 1,737 | 685 | 220 | 34 |
| Malignant neoplasms (cancer) [2] | 599,108 | 57 | 325 | 855 | 1,374 | 3,616 | 10,900 | 39,266 | 114,810 | 168,458 | 155,917 | 103,521 |
| Malignant neoplasm of esophagus | 15,321 | – | – | – | 12 | 35 | 206 | 1,137 | 3,821 | 4,948 | 3,443 | 1,719 |
| Malignant neoplasms of colon, rectum, and anus | 53,447 | – | – | 1 | 40 | 342 | 1,453 | 4,976 | 10,398 | 13,011 | 12,447 | 10,779 |
| Malignant neoplasms of liver and intrahepatic bile ducts | 27,106 | – | 14 | 21 | 21 | 110 | 338 | 1,847 | 7,754 | 8,580 | 5,657 | 2,762 |
| Malignant neoplasms of pancreas | 44,012 | – | – | 1 | 3 | 56 | 470 | 2,556 | 8,633 | 13,692 | 11,839 | 6,761 |
| Malignant neoplasms of trachea, bronchus, and lung | 145,932 | – | – | 6 | 17 | 112 | 843 | 6,989 | 29,505 | 47,654 | 41,701 | 19,099 |
| Malignant neoplasm of breast | 42,510 | – | – | – | 13 | 385 | 1,873 | 4,978 | 9,024 | 10,272 | 8,472 | 7,493 |
| Malignant neoplasm of ovary | 14,193 | – | – | 1 | 20 | 82 | 290 | 1,215 | 3,113 | 4,077 | 3,488 | 1,907 |
| Malignant neoplasm of prostate | 30,488 | – | – | 1 | 1 | 1 | 8 | 399 | 2,743 | 7,280 | 10,143 | 9,910 |
| Malignant neoplasms of kidney and renal pelvis | 13,960 | 3 | 16 | 19 | 26 | 58 | 247 | 980 | 2,743 | 4,000 | 3,538 | 2,329 |
| Malignant neoplasm of bladder | 16,657 | – | – | 2 | – | 12 | 78 | 430 | 1,848 | 3,733 | 5,207 | 5,347 |
| Malignant neoplasms of meninges, brain and other parts of central nervous system | 16,804 | 13 | 73 | 336 | 232 | 421 | 803 | 1,846 | 4,040 | 4,603 | 3,126 | 1,311 |
| Malignant neoplasms of lymphoid, hematopoietic and related tissue [2] | 57,737 | 20 | 114 | 216 | 409 | 597 | 1,018 | 2,707 | 7,553 | 14,440 | 17,761 | 12,901 |
| Non-Hodgkins lymphoma | 20,460 | 1 | 4 | 29 | 69 | 167 | 332 | 947 | 2,678 | 5,069 | 6,356 | 4,807 |
| Leukemia | 23,359 | 19 | 110 | 186 | 310 | 367 | 541 | 1,115 | 2,839 | 5,481 | 7,036 | 5,355 |
| Diabetes mellitus | 83,564 | 1 | 6 | 34 | 248 | 823 | 2,118 | 6,409 | 14,904 | 21,344 | 20,703 | 16,973 |
| Parkinson's disease | 31,963 | – | – | – | 1 | 4 | 7 | 60 | 714 | 4,661 | 13,172 | 13,344 |
| Alzheimer's disease | 121,404 | – | – | – | – | – | 11 | 95 | 1,189 | 7,281 | 32,309 | 80,517 |
| Major cardiovascular diseases [2] | 854,390 | 421 | 195 | 288 | 1,126 | 4,596 | 13,179 | 40,643 | 99,610 | 150,078 | 204,614 | 339,597 |
| Diseases of heart [2] | 647,457 | 304 | 127 | 179 | 913 | 3,681 | 10,401 | 32,658 | 80,102 | 116,633 | 151,249 | 251,170 |
| Hypertensive heart disease | 47,523 | – | – | – | 73 | 521 | 1,631 | 4,289 | 8,096 | 7,882 | 8,280 | 16,745 |
| Ischemic heart diseases | 365,914 | 21 | 6 | 14 | 109 | 939 | 4,611 | 18,697 | 49,967 | 73,182 | 88,352 | 129,992 |
| Acute myocardial infarction | 110,346 | 8 | 2 | 5 | 55 | 342 | 1,783 | 7,032 | 17,741 | 25,063 | 26,738 | 31,572 |
| Heart failure | 80,480 | 22 | 7 | 13 | 35 | 156 | 468 | 1,448 | 3,991 | 9,889 | 19,459 | 44,334 |
| Essential (primary) hypertension and hypertensive renal disease | 35,316 | 1 | 1 | 1 | 10 | 119 | 514 | 1,642 | 4,647 | 5,856 | 8,211 | 14,969 |
| Cerebrovascular diseases | 146,383 | 100 | 66 | 97 | 155 | 593 | 1,811 | 5,198 | 12,708 | 22,690 | 38,697 | 64,266 |
| Influenza and pneumonia | 55,672 | 157 | 104 | 113 | 190 | 405 | 782 | 2,013 | 5,045 | 8,784 | 13,802 | 24,276 |
| Influenza | 6,515 | 12 | 34 | 65 | 49 | 48 | 116 | 250 | 605 | 925 | 1,466 | 2,945 |
| Pneumonia | 49,157 | 145 | 70 | 48 | 141 | 357 | 666 | 1,763 | 4,440 | 7,859 | 12,336 | 21,331 |
| Chronic lower respiratory diseases [2] | 160,201 | 14 | 31 | 134 | 188 | 332 | 713 | 3,975 | 18,667 | 39,704 | 51,116 | 45,319 |
| Emphysema | 7,085 | – | – | – | – | 7 | 33 | 222 | 1,009 | 1,938 | 2,232 | 1,642 |
| Pneumonitis due to solids and liquids | 20,108 | 6 | 6 | 12 | 42 | 96 | 162 | 585 | 1,610 | 2,992 | 5,236 | 9,361 |
| Chronic liver disease and cirrhosis [2] | 41,743 | 2 | 1 | 2 | 23 | 918 | 3,000 | 8,312 | 13,737 | 9,400 | 4,610 | 1,736 |
| Alcoholic liver disease | 22,246 | – | – | – | 14 | 753 | 2,266 | 5,786 | 8,126 | 3,976 | 1,097 | 227 |
| Nephritis, nephrotic syndrome, and nephrosis [2] | 50,633 | 79 | 7 | 10 | 52 | 255 | 692 | 2,197 | 5,671 | 10,302 | 14,093 | 17,275 |
| Renal failure | 49,709 | 73 | 5 | 7 | 49 | 241 | 662 | 2,156 | 5,592 | 10,111 | 13,852 | 16,961 |
| Congenital malformations, deformations and chromosomal abnormalities | 9,902 | 4,580 | 424 | 379 | 355 | 437 | 419 | 735 | 1,228 | 650 | 367 | 327 |
| Accidents (unintentional injuries) [2] | 169,936 | 1,317 | 1,267 | 1,578 | 13,441 | 25,569 | 22,828 | 24,461 | 23,408 | 15,038 | 16,661 | 24,252 |
| Transport accidents | 43,024 | 91 | 469 | 928 | 7,128 | 7,394 | 5,715 | 6,157 | 6,395 | 4,221 | 3,006 | 1,519 |
| Motor vehicle accidents | 40,231 | 91 | 453 | 855 | 6,864 | 7,024 | 5,324 | 5,660 | 5,828 | 3,823 | 2,836 | 1,473 |
| Nontransport accidents | 126,912 | 1,226 | 798 | 650 | 6,313 | 18,275 | 17,113 | 18,304 | 17,013 | 10,817 | 13,655 | 22,733 |
| Falls | 36,338 | 13 | 12 | 30 | 212 | 351 | 522 | 1,248 | 2,760 | 4,752 | 9,218 | 17,220 |
| Accidental poisoning and exposure to noxious substances | 64,795 | 9 | 29 | 45 | 5,030 | 16,478 | 15,032 | 14,707 | 10,581 | 2,241 | 406 | 224 |
| Intentional self-harm (suicide) | 47,173 | – | – | 522 | 6,252 | 7,948 | 7,335 | 8,561 | 7,982 | 4,620 | 2,648 | 1,300 |
| Assault (homicide) | 19,510 | 302 | 303 | 332 | 4,905 | 5,488 | 3,351 | 2,275 | 1,552 | 633 | 252 | 116 |
| Assault (homicide) by discharge of firearms | 14,542 | 12 | 44 | 204 | 4,391 | 4,594 | 2,561 | 1,447 | 824 | 322 | 109 | 34 |
| Enterocolitis due to clostridium difficile | 6,118 | 2 | – | 4 | 7 | 20 | 48 | 178 | 529 | 1,192 | 1,834 | 2,304 |

– Represents zero. [1] Includes persons with age not stated, not shown separately. [2] Includes other causes, not shown separately.

Source: U.S. National Center for Health Statistics, National Vital Statistics Reports (NVSR), *Deaths: Final Data for 2017*, Vol. 68, No. 9, June 2019; and CDC WONDER Online Database, "Multiple Cause of Death, 1999–2017," <https://wonder.cdc.gov/>, accessed June 2019. See also <http://www.cdc.gov/nchs/nvss/deaths.htm>.

# Table 125. Deaths and Death Rates by Leading Cause and Age: 2017

[Rates per 100,000 population in specified group. Data are based on the International Classification of Diseases, Tenth Revision (ICD-10)]

| Age and cause of death | Number | Rate |
|---|---|---|
| **ALL AGES [1]** | | |
| All causes | 2,813,503 | 863.8 |
| Diseases of heart | 647,457 | 198.8 |
| Malignant neoplasms (cancer) | 599,108 | 183.9 |
| Accidents (unintentional injuries) | 169,936 | 52.2 |
| Chronic lower respiratory diseases | 160,201 | 49.2 |
| Cerebrovascular diseases | 146,383 | 44.9 |
| Alzheimer's disease | 121,404 | 37.3 |
| Diabetes mellitus | 83,564 | 25.7 |
| Influenza and pneumonia | 55,672 | 17.1 |
| Nephritis, nephrotic syndrome and nephrosis | 50,633 | 15.5 |
| Intentional self-harm (suicide) | 47,173 | 14.5 |
| **1 TO 4 YEARS** | | |
| All causes | 3,880 | 24.3 |
| Accidents (unintentional injuries) | 1,267 | 7.9 |
| Congenital malformations [2] | 424 | 2.7 |
| Malignant neoplasms (cancer) | 325 | 2.0 |
| Assault (homicide) | 303 | 1.9 |
| Diseases of heart | 127 | 0.8 |
| Influenza and pneumonia | 104 | 0.7 |
| Cerebrovascular diseases | 66 | 0.4 |
| Septicemia | 48 | 0.3 |
| In situ and benign neoplasms and neoplasms of uncertain or unknown behavior | 44 | 0.3 |
| Conditions originating in the perinatal period | 42 | 0.3 |
| **5 TO 9 YEARS** | | |
| All causes | 2,354 | 11.6 |
| Accidents (unintentional injuries) | 718 | 3.5 |
| Malignant neoplasms (cancer) | 418 | 2.1 |
| Congenital malformations [2] | 188 | 0.9 |
| Assault (homicide) | 154 | 0.8 |
| Diseases of heart | 75 | 0.4 |
| Influenza and pneumonia | 62 | 0.3 |
| Chronic lower respiratory diseases | 59 | 0.3 |
| Cerebrovascular diseases | 41 | 0.2 |
| Septicemia | 33 | 0.2 |
| In situ and benign neoplasms and neoplasms of uncertain or unknown behavior | 31 | 0.2 |
| **10 TO 14 YEARS** | | |
| All causes | 3,217 | 15.5 |
| Accidents (unintentional injuries) | 860 | 4.1 |
| Intentional self-harm (suicide) | 517 | 2.5 |
| Malignant neoplasms (cancer) | 437 | 2.1 |
| Congenital malformations [2] | 191 | 0.9 |
| Assault (homicide) | 178 | 0.9 |
| Diseases of heart | 104 | 0.5 |
| Chronic lower respiratory diseases | 75 | 0.4 |
| Cerebrovascular diseases | 56 | 0.3 |
| Influenza and pneumonia | 51 | 0.2 |
| In situ and benign neoplasms and neoplasms of uncertain or unknown behavior | 31 | 0.1 |
| **15 TO 19 YEARS** | | |
| All causes | 10,886 | 51.5 |
| Accidents (unintentional injuries) | 3,948 | 18.7 |
| Intentional self-harm (suicide) | 2,491 | 11.8 |
| Assault (homicide) | 1,835 | 8.7 |
| Malignant neoplasms (cancer) | 560 | 2.7 |
| Diseases of heart | 307 | 1.5 |
| Congenital malformations [2] | 168 | 0.8 |
| Diabetes mellitus | 76 | 0.4 |
| Influenza and pneumonia | 69 | 0.3 |
| Cerebrovascular diseases | 66 | 0.3 |
| Chronic lower respiratory diseases | 65 | 0.3 |
| **20 TO 24 YEARS** | | |
| All causes | 21,139 | 95.6 |
| Accidents (unintentional injuries) | 9,493 | 42.9 |
| Intentional self-harm (suicide) | 3,761 | 17.0 |
| Assault (homicide) | 3,070 | 13.9 |
| Malignant neoplasms (cancer) | 814 | 3.7 |
| Diseases of heart | 606 | 2.7 |
| Congenital malformations [2] | 187 | 0.8 |
| Diabetes mellitus | 172 | 0.8 |
| Pregnancy, childbirth and the puerperium | 140 | 0.6 |
| Chronic lower respiratory diseases | 123 | 0.6 |
| Influenza and pneumonia | 121 | 0.5 |
| **25 TO 34 YEARS** | | |
| All causes | 60,215 | 132.8 |
| Accidents (unintentional injuries) | 25,669 | 56.6 |
| Intentional self-harm (suicide) | 7,948 | 17.5 |
| Assault (homicide) | 5,488 | 12.1 |
| Diseases of heart | 3,681 | 8.1 |
| **25 TO 34 YEARS (continued)** | | |
| Malignant neoplasms (cancer) | 3,616 | 8.0 |
| Chronic liver disease and cirrhosis | 918 | 2.0 |
| Diabetes mellitus | 823 | 1.8 |
| Cerebrovascular diseases | 593 | 1.3 |
| Human immunodeficiency virus (HIV) | 513 | 1.1 |
| Pregnancy, childbirth and the puerperium | 512 | 1.1 |
| **35 TO 44 YEARS** | | |
| All causes | 79,796 | 195.2 |
| Accidents (unintentional injuries) | 22,828 | 55.8 |
| Malignant neoplasms (cancer) | 10,900 | 26.7 |
| Diseases of heart | 10,401 | 25.4 |
| Intentional self-harm (suicide) | 7,335 | 17.9 |
| Assault (homicide) | 3,351 | 8.2 |
| Chronic liver disease and cirrhosis | 3,000 | 7.3 |
| Diabetes mellitus | 2,118 | 5.2 |
| Cerebrovascular diseases | 1,811 | 4.4 |
| Septicemia | 854 | 2.1 |
| Human immunodeficiency virus (HIV) | 831 | 2.0 |
| **45 TO 54 YEARS** | | |
| All causes | 170,142 | 401.5 |
| Malignant neoplasms (cancer) | 39,266 | 92.7 |
| Diseases of heart | 32,658 | 77.1 |
| Accidents (unintentional injuries) | 24,461 | 57.7 |
| Intentional self-harm (suicide) | 8,561 | 20.2 |
| Chronic liver disease and cirrhosis | 8,312 | 19.6 |
| Diabetes mellitus | 6,409 | 15.1 |
| Cerebrovascular diseases | 5,198 | 12.3 |
| Chronic lower respiratory diseases | 3,975 | 9.4 |
| Septicemia | 2,441 | 5.8 |
| Assault (homicide) | 2,275 | 5.4 |
| **55 TO 64 YEARS** | | |
| All causes | 372,006 | 885.8 |
| Malignant neoplasms (cancer) | 114,810 | 273.4 |
| Diseases of heart | 80,102 | 190.7 |
| Accidents (unintentional injuries) | 23,408 | 55.7 |
| Chronic lower respiratory diseases | 18,667 | 44.4 |
| Diabetes mellitus | 14,904 | 35.5 |
| Chronic liver disease and cirrhosis | 13,737 | 32.7 |
| Cerebrovascular diseases | 12,708 | 30.3 |
| Intentional self-harm (suicide) | 7,982 | 19.0 |
| Septicemia | 5,838 | 13.9 |
| Nephritis, nephrotic syndrome and nephrosis | 5,671 | 13.5 |
| **65 to 74 YEARS** | | |
| All causes | 531,610 | 1,790.9 |
| Malignant neoplasms (cancer) | 168,458 | 567.5 |
| Diseases of heart | 116,633 | 392.9 |
| Chronic lower respiratory diseases | 39,704 | 133.8 |
| Cerebrovascular diseases | 22,690 | 76.4 |
| Diabetes mellitus | 21,344 | 71.9 |
| Accidents (unintentional injuries) | 15,038 | 50.7 |
| Nephritis, nephrotic syndrome and nephrosis | 10,302 | 34.7 |
| Chronic liver disease and cirrhosis | 9,400 | 31.7 |
| Septicemia | 9,164 | 30.9 |
| Influenza and pneumonia | 8,784 | 29.6 |
| **75 TO 84 YEARS** | | |
| All causes | 657,759 | 4,472.6 |
| Malignant neoplasms (cancer) | 155,917 | 1,060.2 |
| Diseases of heart | 151,249 | 1,028.4 |
| Chronic lower respiratory diseases | 51,116 | 347.6 |
| Cerebrovascular diseases | 38,697 | 263.1 |
| Alzheimer's disease | 32,309 | 219.7 |
| Diabetes mellitus | 20,703 | 140.8 |
| Accidents (unintentional injuries) | 16,661 | 113.3 |
| Nephritis, nephrotic syndrome and nephrosis | 14,093 | 95.8 |
| Influenza and pneumonia | 13,802 | 93.8 |
| Parkinson's disease | 13,172 | 89.6 |
| **85 YEARS AND OVER** | | |
| All causes | 878,035 | 13,573.6 |
| Diseases of heart | 251,170 | 3,882.9 |
| Malignant neoplasms (cancer) | 103,521 | 1,600.3 |
| Alzheimer's disease | 80,517 | 1,244.7 |
| Cerebrovascular diseases | 64,266 | 993.5 |
| Chronic lower respiratory diseases | 45,319 | 700.6 |
| Influenza and pneumonia | 24,276 | 375.3 |
| Accidents (unintentional injuries) | 24,252 | 374.9 |
| Nephritis, nephrotic syndrome and nephrosis | 17,275 | 267.1 |
| Diabetes mellitus | 16,973 | 262.4 |
| Essential hypertension and hypertensive renal disease | 14,969 | 231.4 |

[1] Includes deaths under 1 year of age. [2] Congenital malformations, deformations and chromosomal abnormalities.

Source: U.S. National Center for Health Statistics, *Deaths: Leading Causes for 2017*, Vol. 68 No. 6, June 2019. See also <http://www.cdc.gov/nchs/nvss/deaths.htm>.

# Table 126. Age-Adjusted Death Rates for Major Causes of Death by State: 2017

[Age-adjusted rates per 100,000 resident population as of July 1. Excludes nonresidents of the United States. Causes of death classified according to the International Classification of Diseases, Tenth Revision (ICD-10)]

| State | All causes of death | Diseases of heart | Malignant neoplasms (cancer) | Accidents Total | Motor vehicle accidents | Chronic lower respiratory disease | Cerebro-vascular diseases | Alz-heimer's disease | Diabetes mellitus | Influenza and pneumonia | Intentional self-harm (suicide) |
|---|---|---|---|---|---|---|---|---|---|---|---|
| U.S............ | 731.9 | 165.0 | 152.5 | 49.4 | 12.0 | 40.9 | 37.6 | 31.0 | 21.5 | 14.3 | 14.0 |
| AL.............. | 917.7 | 223.2 | 170.0 | 53.8 | 20.9 | 57.8 | 50.0 | 45.2 | 19.8 | 20.2 | 16.6 |
| AK.............. | 708.8 | 135.0 | 139.2 | 63.7 | 14.2 | 35.9 | 35.1 | 22.1 | 19.3 | 11.7 | 27.0 |
| AZ.............. | 678.5 | 141.9 | 135.8 | 56.2 | 14.2 | 42.7 | 30.8 | 35.1 | 23.7 | 10.1 | 18.2 |
| AR.............. | 900.1 | 223.8 | 173.6 | 51.8 | 18.9 | 66.7 | 43.8 | 39.4 | 32.4 | 19.8 | 20.8 |
| CA.............. | 618.7 | 142.9 | 136.7 | 33.1 | 10.3 | 32.2 | 37.6 | 37.1 | 22.1 | 14.6 | 10.5 |
| CO.............. | 663.4 | 122.7 | 130.9 | 53.6 | 11.8 | 45.6 | 35.8 | 34.2 | 17.2 | 10.1 | 20.3 |
| CT.............. | 651.2 | 141.6 | 139.5 | 53.2 | 7.8 | 30.4 | 27.8 | 20.4 | 14.5 | 13.1 | 10.5 |
| DE.............. | 749.6 | 158.4 | 160.4 | 61.9 | 12.9 | 40.7 | 46.2 | 30.5 | 19.1 | 14.9 | 11.6 |
| DC.............. | 725.4 | 189.8 | 152.8 | 61.0 | 4.7 | 19.6 | 35.9 | 17.6 | 20.1 | 11.4 | 6.6 |
| FL.............. | 672.1 | 145.8 | 145.9 | 56.1 | 14.8 | 39.0 | 38.9 | 20.7 | 20.2 | 9.6 | 14.0 |
| GA.............. | 793.7 | 175.8 | 154.9 | 45.2 | 14.6 | 46.2 | 43.5 | 46.0 | 21.5 | 13.8 | 13.6 |
| HI.............. | 584.9 | 129.8 | 128.6 | 35.7 | 7.2 | 19.0 | 37.5 | 19.7 | 15.9 | 29.6 | 15.2 |
| ID.............. | 741.8 | 162.4 | 153.2 | 49.8 | 15.5 | 47.2 | 38.5 | 36.6 | 20.3 | 13.7 | 23.2 |
| IL.............. | 724.2 | 163.3 | 157.9 | 44.4 | 9.3 | 37.6 | 38.9 | 25.6 | 19.2 | 15.6 | 11.2 |
| IN.............. | 848.6 | 183.2 | 170.0 | 58.7 | 13.5 | 55.2 | 40.2 | 35.3 | 26.6 | 13.8 | 16.3 |
| IA.............. | 737.0 | 167.4 | 158.0 | 42.7 | 12.0 | 46.5 | 32.8 | 35.3 | 22.8 | 13.2 | 15.0 |
| KS.............. | 771.2 | 157.9 | 157.2 | 49.4 | 15.6 | 51.7 | 37.7 | 24.3 | 25.2 | 15.0 | 19.1 |
| KY.............. | 929.9 | 195.9 | 185.7 | 72.9 | 18.3 | 64.5 | 39.4 | 35.0 | 27.7 | 18.1 | 16.9 |
| LA.............. | 881.1 | 214.4 | 174.9 | 58.8 | 17.6 | 46.6 | 47.4 | 43.7 | 23.9 | 15.1 | 15.2 |
| ME.............. | 771.6 | 143.5 | 170.8 | 68.0 | 13.7 | 48.7 | 37.5 | 30.4 | 19.7 | 15.2 | 18.9 |
| MD.............. | 718.1 | 164.5 | 151.5 | 36.9 | 9.2 | 29.9 | 40.2 | 17.1 | 20.3 | 14.0 | 9.8 |
| MA.............. | 677.1 | 134.6 | 149.3 | 51.5 | 5.7 | 32.4 | 26.5 | 19.9 | 15.1 | 15.9 | 9.5 |
| MI.............. | 783.5 | 196.1 | 161.3 | 53.0 | 10.2 | 44.3 | 39.3 | 34.5 | 22.1 | 14.2 | 14.1 |
| MN.............. | 656.4 | 119.1 | 146.8 | 44.6 | 7.8 | 36.3 | 32.6 | 34.9 | 19.3 | 9.9 | 13.8 |
| MS.............. | 951.3 | 231.6 | 183.1 | 56.3 | 25.7 | 58.3 | 51.1 | 49.5 | 33.3 | 23.0 | 15.0 |
| MO.............. | 820.1 | 191.1 | 167.2 | 58.8 | 16.0 | 50.7 | 41.0 | 32.3 | 21.0 | 16.7 | 18.5 |
| MT.............. | 757.5 | 155.0 | 152.6 | 50.2 | 17.0 | 53.5 | 35.6 | 20.9 | 21.6 | 13.3 | 28.9 |
| NE.............. | 726.0 | 149.3 | 152.6 | 38.5 | 13.3 | 52.6 | 31.5 | 28.5 | 25.0 | 16.1 | 14.7 |
| NV.............. | 765.5 | 199.3 | 155.3 | 47.8 | 11.2 | 50.0 | 35.9 | 27.3 | 18.3 | 19.6 | 20.3 |
| NH.............. | 717.2 | 149.7 | 153.5 | 62.9 | 7.3 | 43.0 | 28.9 | 24.8 | 19.2 | 13.1 | 18.9 |
| NJ.............. | 667.5 | 162.3 | 144.6 | 47.3 | 6.7 | 28.6 | 30.2 | 23.6 | 16.9 | 11.7 | 8.3 |
| NM.............. | 754.7 | 151.4 | 138.3 | 68.2 | 19.3 | 44.2 | 34.7 | 22.7 | 26.5 | 13.6 | 23.3 |
| NY.............. | 623.6 | 171.2 | 141.2 | 35.5 | 5.5 | 28.9 | 24.6 | 13.2 | 16.8 | 17.7 | 8.1 |
| NC.............. | 785.6 | 156.5 | 157.1 | 56.3 | 14.4 | 45.3 | 43.0 | 37.3 | 23.6 | 17.5 | 14.3 |
| ND.............. | 692.7 | 137.8 | 142.6 | 41.3 | 15.4 | 38.3 | 35.4 | 36.5 | 21.8 | 15.3 | 20.1 |
| OH.............. | 849.7 | 186.2 | 171.2 | 75.1 | 11.1 | 48.5 | 42.8 | 33.6 | 25.2 | 14.9 | 14.8 |
| OK.............. | 902.4 | 237.2 | 177.3 | 62.5 | 18.1 | 65.8 | 43.3 | 39.3 | 30.6 | 13.9 | 19.1 |
| OR.............. | 717.2 | 134.0 | 154.2 | 44.7 | 11.7 | 39.7 | 39.9 | 36.0 | 23.9 | 11.1 | 19.0 |
| PA.............. | 777.3 | 176.0 | 161.0 | 70.2 | 9.5 | 37.1 | 36.5 | 21.7 | 21.0 | 14.6 | 15.0 |
| RI.............. | 713.4 | 155.7 | 154.2 | 60.0 | 9.4 | 36.2 | 29.4 | 27.3 | 18.0 | 13.9 | 11.8 |
| SC.............. | 828.0 | 172.0 | 162.7 | 60.2 | 20.8 | 47.9 | 44.9 | 44.9 | 24.5 | 12.3 | 16.3 |
| SD.............. | 736.6 | 150.1 | 156.9 | 56.1 | 18.9 | 45.3 | 36.7 | 36.9 | 24.9 | 19.0 | 22.5 |
| TN.............. | 897.1 | 202.2 | 173.4 | 63.0 | 15.7 | 57.4 | 45.0 | 46.7 | 24.0 | 21.3 | 16.8 |
| TX.............. | 735.7 | 169.2 | 146.5 | 38.8 | 13.8 | 40.5 | 41.3 | 38.5 | 21.2 | 11.2 | 13.4 |
| UT.............. | 700.1 | 150.2 | 120.3 | 44.2 | 9.9 | 32.1 | 36.2 | 42.1 | 22.9 | 13.3 | 22.7 |
| VT.............. | 714.9 | 152.5 | 164.5 | 56.9 | 12.3 | 43.0 | 28.8 | 42.9 | 19.2 | 9.7 | 18.3 |
| VA.............. | 719.4 | 154.5 | 152.6 | 44.0 | 10.1 | 34.9 | 37.5 | 27.6 | 20.1 | 13.1 | 13.4 |
| WA.............. | 688.6 | 138.8 | 148.4 | 44.0 | 8.8 | 38.0 | 36.9 | 46.0 | 21.6 | 12.6 | 16.9 |
| WV.............. | 957.1 | 192.0 | 179.4 | 100.3 | 18.2 | 64.3 | 41.8 | 30.6 | 34.0 | 18.2 | 21.1 |
| WI.............. | 722.0 | 157.6 | 153.2 | 58.3 | 10.9 | 38.3 | 33.5 | 31.6 | 19.4 | 12.9 | 15.4 |
| WY.............. | 714.5 | 148.9 | 136.1 | 56.9 | 19.1 | 53.8 | 28.4 | 32.7 | 18.1 | 17.5 | 26.9 |

Source: U.S. National Center for Health Statistics, National Vital Statistics Reports (NVSR), *Deaths: Final Data for 2017*, Vol. 68, No. 9, June 2019; and CDC WONDER Online database, "Multiple Cause of Death, 1999-2017," <https://wonder.cdc.gov/>, accessed June 2019. See also <http://www.cdc.gov/nchs/nvss/deaths.htm>.

# Table 127. Death Rates For Heart Disease by Selected Characteristics: 1980 to 2017

[Rates per 100,000 population. Excludes deaths of nonresidents of the United States. Beginning 1999, deaths classified according to the International Classification of Diseases, Tenth Revision (ICD-10); for earlier years, causes of death were classified according to the revisions then in use. Changes in classification of causes of death due to these revisions may result in discontinuities in cause-of-death trends. See Appendix III]

| Characteristics | 1980 | 1990 | 2000 | 2005 | 2010 | 2014 | 2015 | 2016 | 2017 |
|---|---|---|---|---|---|---|---|---|---|
| **All ages, age-adjusted** [1] | **412.1** | **321.8** | **257.6** | **216.8** | **179.1** | **167.0** | **168.5** | **165.5** | **165.0** |
| **All ages, crude rate** | **336.0** | **289.5** | **252.6** | **220.7** | **193.6** | **192.7** | **197.2** | **196.6** | **198.8** |
| Under 1 year | 22.8 | 20.1 | 13.0 | 8.9 | 8.3 | 8.0 | 7.3 | 7.4 | 7.7 |
| 1 to 4 years | 2.6 | 1.9 | 1.2 | 0.9 | 1.0 | 0.9 | 0.9 | 0.7 | 0.8 |
| 5 to 14 years | 0.9 | 0.9 | 0.7 | 0.6 | 0.5 | 0.5 | 0.5 | 0.5 | 0.4 |
| 15 to 24 years | 2.9 | 2.5 | 2.6 | 2.6 | 2.4 | 2.2 | 2.3 | 2.2 | 2.1 |
| 25 to 34 years | 8.3 | 7.6 | 7.4 | 8.3 | 7.8 | 7.7 | 8.0 | 7.7 | 8.1 |
| 35 to 44 years | 44.6 | 31.4 | 29.2 | 29.2 | 25.8 | 25.6 | 25.6 | 25.9 | 25.4 |
| 45 to 54 years | 180.2 | 120.5 | 94.2 | 89.7 | 81.6 | 80.1 | 79.3 | 79.5 | 77.1 |
| 55 to 64 years | 494.1 | 367.3 | 261.2 | 212.8 | 186.6 | 185.8 | 188.1 | 189.6 | 190.7 |
| 65 to 74 years | 1,218.6 | 894.3 | 665.6 | 512.3 | 409.2 | 385.2 | 389.5 | 392.5 | 392.9 |
| 75 to 84 years | 2,993.1 | 2,295.7 | 1,780.3 | 1,458.5 | 1,172.0 | 1,070.2 | 1,071.6 | 1,037.1 | 1,028.4 |
| 85 years and over | 7,777.1 | 6,739.9 | 5,926.1 | 5,188.3 | 4,285.2 | 3,920.9 | 3,986.5 | 3,873.4 | 3,882.9 |
| MALE | | | | | | | | | |
| **All ages, age-adjusted** [1] | **538.9** | **412.4** | **320.0** | **268.2** | **225.1** | **210.9** | **211.8** | **209.1** | **209.0** |
| White | 539.6 | 409.2 | 316.7 | 264.8 | 222.9 | 210.0 | 211.2 | 208.4 | 208.3 |
| Black | 561.4 | 485.4 | 392.5 | 338.8 | 280.6 | 259.5 | 258.6 | 258.1 | 257.5 |
| American Indian, Alaska Native | 320.5 | 264.1 | 222.2 | 191.7 | 158.7 | 149.7 | 148.0 | 147.7 | 148.0 |
| Asian, Pacific Islander | 286.9 | 220.7 | 185.5 | 149.4 | 127.2 | 109.1 | 109.7 | 106.6 | 108.0 |
| Hispanic origin [2] | (NA) | 270.0 | 238.2 | 210.5 | 165.1 | 145.7 | 146.4 | 144.6 | 143.9 |
| Non-Hispanic, White [2] | (NA) | 413.6 | 319.9 | 267.9 | 226.9 | 215.2 | 216.3 | 213.9 | 214.0 |
| **All ages, crude rate** | **368.6** | **297.6** | **249.8** | **222.3** | **202.5** | **207.1** | **211.7** | **213.3** | **216.9** |
| Under 1 year | 25.5 | 21.9 | 13.3 | 9.6 | 9.8 | 8.6 | 7.5 | 7.2 | 7.8 |
| 1 to 4 years | 2.8 | 1.9 | 1.4 | 1.0 | 1.1 | 0.9 | 1.0 | 0.8 | 0.8 |
| 5 to 14 years | 1.0 | 0.9 | 0.8 | 0.6 | 0.5 | 0.5 | 0.5 | 0.5 | 0.5 |
| 15 to 24 years | 3.7 | 3.1 | 3.2 | 3.5 | 3.2 | 2.7 | 3.0 | 2.8 | 2.8 |
| 25 to 34 years | 11.4 | 10.3 | 9.6 | 11.2 | 10.7 | 10.3 | 10.3 | 10.2 | 10.7 |
| 35 to 44 years | 68.7 | 48.1 | 41.4 | 41.3 | 36.0 | 34.8 | 35.1 | 35.5 | 34.7 |
| 45 to 54 years | 282.6 | 183.0 | 140.2 | 131.6 | 117.8 | 113.5 | 112.1 | 112.5 | 109.1 |
| 55 to 64 years | 746.8 | 537.3 | 371.7 | 303.9 | 269.5 | 268.1 | 269.4 | 271.3 | 273.2 |
| 65 to 74 years | 1,728.0 | 1,250.0 | 898.3 | 680.1 | 553.0 | 525.7 | 529.7 | 536.4 | 538.5 |
| 75 to 84 years | 3,834.3 | 2,968.2 | 2,248.1 | 1,815.1 | 1,475.7 | 1,354.8 | 1,354.4 | 1,312.0 | 1,306.8 |
| 85 years and over | 8,752.7 | 7,418.4 | 6,430.0 | 5,713.2 | 4,833.6 | 4,453.4 | 4,495.1 | 4,403.5 | 4,421.1 |
| FEMALE | | | | | | | | | |
| **All ages, age-adjusted** [1] | **320.8** | **257.0** | **210.9** | **177.5** | **143.3** | **131.8** | **133.6** | **130.4** | **129.6** |
| White | 315.9 | 250.9 | 205.6 | 173.2 | 140.4 | 130.0 | 132.4 | 128.7 | 128.4 |
| Black | 378.6 | 327.5 | 277.6 | 234.5 | 185.3 | 167.7 | 165.7 | 166.4 | 161.9 |
| American Indian, Alaska Native | 175.4 | 153.1 | 143.6 | 129.3 | 103.5 | 94.0 | 94.0 | 89.1 | 89.3 |
| Asian, Pacific Islander | 132.3 | 149.2 | 115.7 | 97.5 | 81.2 | 68.2 | 68.5 | 68.4 | 67.6 |
| Hispanic origin [2] | (NA) | 177.2 | 163.7 | 139.9 | 107.8 | 92.4 | 93.0 | 92.6 | 90.1 |
| Non-Hispanic, White [2] | (NA) | 252.6 | 206.8 | 174.8 | 142.5 | 133.0 | 135.6 | 131.7 | 131.9 |
| **All ages, crude rate** | **305.1** | **281.8** | **255.3** | **219.0** | **184.9** | **178.6** | **183.1** | **180.4** | **181.2** |
| Under 1 year | 20.0 | 18.3 | 12.5 | 8.2 | 6.8 | 7.4 | 7.2 | 7.6 | 7.6 |
| 1 to 4 years | 2.5 | 1.9 | 1.0 | 0.9 | 0.9 | 0.9 | 0.9 | 0.7 | 0.8 |
| 5 to 14 years | 0.9 | 0.8 | 0.5 | 0.6 | 0.4 | 0.4 | 0.5 | 0.4 | 0.4 |
| 15 to 24 years | 2.1 | 1.8 | 2.1 | 1.7 | 1.5 | 1.6 | 1.5 | 1.5 | 1.4 |
| 25 to 34 years | 5.3 | 5.0 | 5.2 | 5.3 | 4.9 | 5.0 | 5.6 | 5.2 | 5.5 |
| 35 to 44 years | 21.4 | 15.1 | 17.2 | 17.2 | 15.6 | 16.4 | 16.2 | 16.4 | 16.2 |
| 45 to 54 years | 84.5 | 61.0 | 49.8 | 49.1 | 46.5 | 47.5 | 47.4 | 47.4 | 45.9 |
| 55 to 64 years | 272.1 | 215.7 | 159.3 | 128.0 | 109.3 | 109.3 | 112.3 | 113.5 | 113.9 |
| 65 to 74 years | 828.6 | 616.8 | 474.0 | 369.5 | 284.2 | 261.7 | 266.2 | 266.0 | 265.1 |
| 75 to 84 years | 2,497.0 | 1,893.8 | 1,475.1 | 1,213.8 | 952.7 | 854.8 | 855.9 | 826.4 | 813.5 |
| 85 years and over | 7,350.5 | 6,478.1 | 5,720.9 | 4,955.1 | 4,020.3 | 3,643.8 | 3,717.6 | 3,589.7 | 3,589.9 |

NA Not available. [1] Age-adjusted death rates were prepared using the direct method, in which age-specific death rates for a population of interest are applied to a standard population distributed by age. Age adjustment eliminates the differences in observed rates between points in time or among compared population groups that result from age differences in population composition. [2] Persons of Hispanic origin may be of any race. Prior to 1997, excludes data from states lacking a Hispanic-origin item on their death certificates. See text, this section.

Source: U.S. National Center for Health Statistics, *Health, United States, 2017*, September 2018; and CDC WONDER Online database, "Multiple Cause of Death, 1999-2017," <https://wonder.cdc.gov/>, accessed April 2019. See also <http://www.cdc.gov/nchs/hus.htm>.

## Table 128. Death Rates For Cerebrovascular Diseases (Stroke) by Sex and Age: 1990 to 2017

[Rates per 100,000 population. Excludes deaths of nonresidents of the United States. Beginning 1999, deaths classified according to the International Classification of Diseases, Tenth Revision (ICD-10); for earlier years, causes of death were classified according to the revisions then in use. Changes in classification of causes of death due to these revisions may result in discontinuities in cause-of-death trends. For explanation of age adjustment, see text, this section]

| Characteristics | Total | | | | Male | | | | Female | | | |
|---|---|---|---|---|---|---|---|---|---|---|---|---|
| | 1990 | 2000 | 2010 | 2017 | 1990 | 2000 | 2010 | 2017 | 1990 | 2000 | 2010 | 2017 |
| All ages, age-adjusted [1] | 65.3 | 60.9 | 39.1 | 37.6 | 68.5 | 62.4 | 39.3 | 38.0 | 62.6 | 59.1 | 38.3 | 36.6 |
| All ages, crude rate | 57.8 | 59.6 | 41.9 | 44.9 | 46.7 | 46.9 | 34.5 | 38.4 | 68.4 | 71.8 | 49.1 | 51.3 |
| Under 1 year | 3.8 | 3.3 | 3.3 | 2.5 | 4.4 | 3.8 | 3.2 | 2.9 | 3.1 | 2.7 | 3.4 | 2.2 |
| 1 to 4 years | 0.3 | 0.3 | 0.3 | 0.4 | 0.3 | (B) | 0.3 | 0.5 | 0.3 | 0.4 | 0.3 | 0.3 |
| 5 to 14 years | 0.2 | 0.2 | 0.2 | 0.2 | 0.2 | 0.2 | 0.3 | 0.3 | 0.2 | 0.2 | 0.2 | 0.2 |
| 15 to 24 years | 0.6 | 0.5 | 0.4 | 0.4 | 0.7 | 0.5 | 0.5 | 0.4 | 0.6 | 0.5 | 0.4 | 0.3 |
| 25 to 34 years | 2.2 | 1.5 | 1.3 | 1.3 | 2.1 | 1.5 | 1.3 | 1.5 | 2.2 | 1.5 | 1.2 | 1.1 |
| 35 to 44 years | 6.4 | 5.8 | 4.6 | 4.4 | 6.8 | 5.8 | 5.0 | 5.1 | 6.1 | 5.7 | 4.2 | 3.8 |
| 45 to 54 years | 18.7 | 16.0 | 13.1 | 12.3 | 20.5 | 17.5 | 14.9 | 14.4 | 17.0 | 14.5 | 11.4 | 10.2 |
| 55 to 64 years | 47.9 | 41.0 | 29.3 | 30.3 | 54.3 | 47.2 | 34.7 | 36.2 | 42.2 | 35.3 | 24.3 | 24.7 |
| 65 to 74 years | 144.2 | 128.6 | 81.7 | 76.4 | 166.6 | 145.0 | 92.0 | 86.7 | 126.7 | 115.1 | 72.8 | 67.4 |
| 75 to 84 years | 498.0 | 461.3 | 288.3 | 263.1 | 551.1 | 490.8 | 295.2 | 273.5 | 466.2 | 442.1 | 283.4 | 255.1 |
| 85 years and over | 1,628.9 | 1,589.2 | 993.8 | 993.5 | 1,528.5 | 1,484.3 | 892.0 | 883.3 | 1,667.6 | 1,632.0 | 1,043.0 | 1,053.4 |

B Figure too small to meet statistical standards for reliability. [1] See footnote 1, Table 127.

Source: U.S. National Center for Health Statistics, *Health, United States, 2017*, September 2018; and CDC WONDER Online database, "Multiple Cause of Death, 1999-2017," <https://wonder.cdc.gov/>, accessed April 2019. See also <http://www.cdc.gov/nchs/hus.htm>.

## Table 129. Death Rates For All and Selected Types of Malignant Neoplasms (Cancer) by Age: 1990 to 2017

[Rates per 100,000 population. Excludes deaths of nonresidents of the United States. Beginning 1999, deaths classified according to the International Classification of Diseases, Tenth Revision (ICD-10); for earlier years, causes of death were classified according to the revisions then in use. Changes in classification of causes of death due to these revisions may result in discontinuities in cause-of-death trends. For explanation of age adjustment, see text, this section. See Appendix III]

| Characteristic | 1990 | 2000 | 2005 | 2010 | 2014 | 2015 | 2016 | 2017 |
|---|---|---|---|---|---|---|---|---|
| All ages, age-adjusted [1] | 216.0 | 199.6 | 185.1 | 172.8 | 161.2 | 158.5 | 155.8 | 152.5 |
| All ages, crude rate | 203.2 | 196.5 | 189.3 | 186.2 | 185.6 | 185.4 | 185.1 | 183.9 |
| Under 1 year | 2.3 | 2.4 | 1.9 | 1.6 | 1.3 | 1.3 | 1.7 | 1.4 |
| 1 to 4 years | 3.5 | 2.7 | 2.4 | 2.1 | 2.0 | 2.2 | 2.4 | 2.0 |
| 5 to 14 years | 3.1 | 2.5 | 2.5 | 2.2 | 2.1 | 2.1 | 2.1 | 2.1 |
| 15 to 24 years | 4.9 | 4.4 | 4.0 | 3.7 | 3.6 | 3.4 | 3.3 | 3.2 |
| 25 to 34 years | 12.6 | 9.8 | 9.2 | 8.8 | 8.3 | 8.4 | 8.5 | 8.0 |
| 35 to 44 years | 43.3 | 36.6 | 33.5 | 28.8 | 27.8 | 26.9 | 26.9 | 26.7 |
| 45 to 54 years | 158.9 | 127.5 | 118.6 | 111.6 | 103.2 | 99.7 | 96.5 | 92.7 |
| 55 to 64 years | 449.6 | 366.7 | 323.9 | 300.1 | 287.6 | 284.1 | 280.6 | 273.4 |
| 65 to 74 years | 872.3 | 816.3 | 733.2 | 666.1 | 603.1 | 594.3 | 578.3 | 567.5 |
| 75 to 84 years | 1,348.5 | 1,335.6 | 1,272.8 | 1,202.2 | 1,125.9 | 1,100.8 | 1,081.7 | 1,060.2 |
| 85 years old and over | 1,752.9 | 1,819.4 | 1,778.2 | 1,729.5 | 1,632.9 | 1,628.6 | 1,620.3 | 1,600.3 |
| **DEATH RATES FOR MALIGNANT NEOPLASM OF BREASTS FOR FEMALES** | | | | | | | | |
| All ages, age-adjusted [1] | 33.3 | 26.8 | 24.2 | 22.1 | 20.6 | 20.3 | 20.1 | 19.9 |
| All ages, crude rate | 34.0 | 29.2 | 27.4 | 26.1 | 25.5 | 25.4 | 25.3 | 25.4 |
| Under 25 years | (B) | (B) | (B) | (B) | (B) | (B) | (B) | (B) |
| 25 to 34 years | 2.9 | 2.3 | 1.8 | 1.6 | 1.6 | 1.8 | 2.0 | 1.7 |
| 35 to 44 years | 17.8 | 12.4 | 11.4 | 9.8 | 9.7 | 9.0 | 9.4 | 9.1 |
| 45 to 54 years | 45.4 | 33.0 | 28.7 | 25.7 | 23.8 | 23.7 | 23.5 | 23.0 |
| 55 to 64 years | 78.6 | 59.3 | 54.0 | 47.7 | 43.3 | 43.3 | 41.3 | 41.0 |
| 65 to 74 years | 111.7 | 88.3 | 78.5 | 73.9 | 67.5 | 66.7 | 64.9 | 64.0 |
| 75 to 84 years | 146.3 | 128.9 | 119.6 | 109.1 | 104.2 | 101.7 | 102.6 | 100.8 |
| 85 years old and over | 196.8 | 205.7 | 191.2 | 185.8 | 174.0 | 173.3 | 169.6 | 177.3 |
| **DEATH RATES FOR MALIGNANT NEOPLASM OF TRACHEA, BRONCHUS, AND LUNG** | | | | | | | | |
| All ages, age-adjusted [1] | 59.3 | 56.1 | 52.7 | 47.6 | 42.1 | 40.5 | 38.4 | 36.6 |
| All ages, crude rate | 56.8 | 55.3 | 53.9 | 51.3 | 48.8 | 47.9 | 46.1 | 44.8 |
| Under 25 years | (Z) | (Z) | (Z) | (Z) | (Z) | (Z) | (Z) | (Z) |
| 25 to 34 years | 0.7 | 0.5 | 0.3 | 0.4 | 0.3 | 0.3 | 0.3 | 0.2 |
| 35 to 44 years | 6.8 | 6.1 | 5.3 | 3.3 | 2.7 | 2.5 | 2.2 | 2.1 |
| 45 to 54 years | 46.8 | 31.6 | 29.7 | 26.9 | 22.4 | 20.5 | 18.6 | 16.5 |
| 55 to 64 years | 160.6 | 122.4 | 102.4 | 85.4 | 78.5 | 76.8 | 73.2 | 70.3 |
| 65 to 74 years | 288.4 | 284.2 | 256.3 | 223.9 | 189.4 | 181.0 | 167.9 | 160.5 |
| 75 to 84 years | 333.3 | 370.8 | 375.0 | 357.2 | 321.2 | 306.4 | 295.4 | 283.6 |
| 85 years old and over | 242.5 | 302.1 | 328.2 | 332.4 | 311.7 | 316.1 | 305.2 | 295.3 |

B Base figure too small to meet statistical standards for reliability of a derived figure. Z Less than 0.05. [1] Age-adjusted death rates were prepared using the direct method, in which age specific death rates for a population of interest are applied to a standard population distributed by age. Age adjustment eliminates the differences in observed rates between points in time or among compared population groups that result from age differences in population composition.

Source: U.S. National Center for Health Statistics, *Health, United States, 2017*, September 2018; and CDC Wonder Online database, "Multiple Cause of Death, 1999-2017," <https://wonder.cdc.gov/>, accessed April 2019. See also <http://www.cdc.gov/nchs/hus.htm>.

# Table 130. Death Rates For Suicide by Selected Characteristics: 1990 to 2017

[Rates per 100,000 population. Excludes deaths of nonresidents of the United States. Beginning 1999, deaths classified according to the International Classification of Diseases, Tenth Revision (ICD-10). See Appendix III]

| Characteristic | 1990 | 2000 | 2005 | 2010 | 2013 | 2014 | 2015 | 2016 | 2017 |
|---|---|---|---|---|---|---|---|---|---|
| **All ages, age-adjusted** [1] | **12.5** | **10.4** | **10.9** | **12.1** | **12.6** | **13.0** | **13.3** | **13.5** | **14.0** |
| **All ages, crude rate** | **12.4** | **10.4** | **11.0** | **12.4** | **13.0** | **13.4** | **13.7** | **13.9** | **14.5** |
| 5 to 14 years | 0.8 | 0.7 | 0.7 | 0.7 | 1.0 | 1.0 | 1.0 | 1.1 | 1.3 |
| 15 to 24 years | 13.2 | 10.2 | 9.9 | 10.5 | 11.1 | 11.6 | 12.5 | 13.2 | 14.5 |
| 25 to 34 years | 15.2 | 12.0 | 12.7 | 14.0 | 14.8 | 15.1 | 15.7 | 16.5 | 17.5 |
| 35 to 44 years | 15.3 | 14.5 | 15.1 | 16.0 | 16.2 | 16.6 | 17.1 | 17.4 | 17.9 |
| 45 to 54 years | 14.8 | 14.4 | 16.5 | 19.6 | 19.7 | 20.2 | 20.3 | 19.7 | 20.2 |
| 55 to 64 years | 16.0 | 12.1 | 13.7 | 17.5 | 18.1 | 18.8 | 18.9 | 18.7 | 19.0 |
| 65 to 74 years | 17.9 | 12.5 | 12.4 | 13.7 | 15.0 | 15.6 | 15.2 | 15.4 | 15.6 |
| 75 to 84 years | 24.9 | 17.6 | 16.8 | 15.7 | 17.1 | 17.5 | 17.9 | 18.2 | 18.0 |
| 85 years and over | 22.2 | 19.6 | 18.3 | 17.6 | 18.6 | 19.3 | 19.4 | 19.0 | 20.1 |
| AGE-ADJUSTED RATES [1] | | | | | | | | | |
| **Male** | **21.5** | **17.7** | **18.1** | **19.8** | **20.3** | **20.7** | **21.1** | **21.4** | **22.4** |
| White | 22.8 | 19.1 | 19.8 | 22.0 | 22.6 | 23.3 | 23.6 | 23.9 | 25.1 |
| Black | 12.8 | 10.0 | 9.2 | 9.1 | 9.3 | 9.5 | 9.6 | 10.2 | 11.0 |
| American Indian, Alaska Native | 20.1 | 16.0 | 17.3 | 15.5 | 18.1 | 16.4 | 18.8 | 20.7 | 20.4 |
| Asian, Pacific Islander | 9.6 | 8.6 | 7.3 | 9.5 | 9.1 | 8.9 | 9.1 | 10.1 | 9.7 |
| Hispanic [2] | 13.7 | 10.3 | 9.6 | 9.9 | 9.3 | 10.3 | 9.9 | 10.9 | 11.2 |
| Non-Hispanic, White [2] | 23.5 | 20.2 | 21.4 | 24.2 | 25.3 | 25.9 | 26.6 | 26.6 | 28.2 |
| **Female** | **4.8** | **4.0** | **4.4** | **5.0** | **5.5** | **5.8** | **6.0** | **6.0** | **6.1** |
| White | 5.2 | 4.3 | 4.9 | 5.6 | 6.3 | 6.6 | 6.9 | 6.9 | 6.9 |
| Black | 2.4 | 1.8 | 1.8 | 1.8 | 2.0 | 2.1 | 2.0 | 2.4 | 2.7 |
| American Indian, Alaska Native | 3.6 | 3.8 | 4.2 | 6.1 | 5.3 | 5.5 | 6.5 | 6.4 | 6.6 |
| Asian, Pacific Islander | 4.1 | 2.8 | 3.2 | 3.4 | 3.0 | 3.4 | 4.0 | 3.6 | 3.8 |
| Hispanic [2] | 2.3 | 1.7 | 1.8 | 2.1 | 2.3 | 2.5 | 2.6 | 2.6 | 2.6 |
| Non-Hispanic, White [2] | 5.4 | 4.7 | 5.3 | 6.2 | 7.1 | 7.5 | 7.8 | 7.9 | 7.9 |

[1] Age-adjusted death rates were prepared using the direct method, in which age-specific death rates for a population of interest are applied to a standard population distributed by age. Age adjustment eliminates the differences in observed rates between points in time or among compared population groups that result from age differences in population composition. [2] Persons of Hispanic origin may be of any race. Excludes data from states lacking a Hispanic-origin item on their death certificates.

Source: U.S. National Center for Health Statistics, *Health, United States, 2017*, September 2018; and CDC WONDER Online database, "Multiple Cause of Death, 1999-2017," <https://wonder.cdc.gov/>, accessed April 2019. See also <http://www.cdc.gov/nchs/hus.htm>.

# Table 131. Suicide Deaths by Age, Sex, and Method: 2017

[It is generally accepted that children under 5 years of age cannot commit suicide. Deaths based on the International Classification of Diseases, Tenth Revision (ICD-10)]

| Method | Total | 5-14 years | 15-24 years | 25-34 years | 35-44 years | 45-54 years | 55-64 years | 65-74 years | 75-84 years | 85+ years |
|---|---|---|---|---|---|---|---|---|---|---|
| **Total** [1] | **47,173** | **522** | **6,252** | **7,948** | **7,335** | **8,561** | **7,982** | **4,620** | **2,648** | **1,300** |
| MEN | | | | | | | | | | |
| **Total** [1] | **36,782** | **352** | **5,027** | **6,348** | **5,596** | **6,331** | **6,040** | **3,638** | **2,293** | **1,154** |
| Knife or other sharp object | 681 | 1 | 31 | 90 | 101 | 168 | 164 | 82 | 28 | 16 |
| Drowning | 298 | 1 | 45 | 55 | 43 | 59 | 43 | 23 | 18 | 11 |
| Jumping from a high place [2] | 807 | 2 | 154 | 160 | 120 | 128 | 140 | 62 | 23 | 18 |
| Fire/flame | 125 | 0 | 18 | 19 | 18 | 22 | 26 | 14 | 4 | 4 |
| Firearm | 20,615 | 156 | 2,638 | 2,962 | 2,590 | 3,203 | 3,574 | 2,660 | 1,901 | 930 |
| Poisoning | 3,295 | 7 | 255 | 463 | 579 | 773 | 698 | 319 | 128 | 73 |
| Hanging, suffocation, strangulation | 10,175 | 183 | 1,729 | 2,418 | 1,998 | 1,836 | 1,303 | 438 | 175 | 94 |
| WOMEN | | | | | | | | | | |
| **Total** [1] | **10,391** | **170** | **1,225** | **1,600** | **1,739** | **2,230** | **1,942** | **982** | **355** | **146** |
| Knife or other sharp object | 165 | 0 | 1 | 20 | 26 | 37 | 35 | 28 | 14 | 4 |
| Drowning | 181 | 0 | 12 | 22 | 25 | 39 | 42 | 27 | 7 | 6 |
| Jumping from a high place [2] | 317 | 2 | 37 | 45 | 45 | 69 | 66 | 35 | 11 | 7 |
| Fire/flame | 71 | 0 | 4 | 3 | 15 | 16 | 24 | 8 | 1 | 0 |
| Firearm | 3,239 | 30 | 321 | 496 | 508 | 734 | 645 | 329 | 139 | 37 |
| Poisoning | 3,259 | 32 | 208 | 325 | 510 | 831 | 761 | 405 | 124 | 62 |
| Hanging, suffocation, strangulation | 2,900 | 101 | 592 | 645 | 564 | 458 | 328 | 134 | 52 | 26 |

[1] Includes other methods not shown separately and deaths with age not stated. [2] Includes other fall.

Source: U.S. National Center for Health Statistics, CDC WONDER Online database, "Multiple Cause of Death, 1999-2017," <https://wonder.cdc.gov/>, accessed April 2019.

# Table 132. Firearm Deaths and Death Rates by Sex and Race/Ethnicity: 2010 to 2017

[Rates are age-adjusted, per 100,000 population, and based on populations enumerated as of April 1 for census years and as of July 1 for all other years. Deaths are those attributable to injury by firearms. Race and Hispanic-origin categories are consistent with 1977 Office of Management and Budget (OMB) standards. From 2003-2017, the number of states reporting multiple-race data according to new 1997 OMB standards varied widely. To provide a comparison of data by race between the 1977 and 1997 OMB standards, those reporting more than one race were "bridged" to single-race categories; see Technical notes, source]

| Sex and race/ethnicity | Number of deaths | | | | | Age-adjusted rates | | | | |
|---|---|---|---|---|---|---|---|---|---|---|
| | 2010 | 2014 | 2015 | 2016 | 2017 | 2010 | 2014 | 2015 | 2016 | 2017 |
| Total [1] | 31,672 | 33,594 | 36,252 | 38,658 | 39,773 | 10.1 | 10.3 | 11.1 | 11.8 | 12.0 |
| Male | 27,356 | 28,715 | 31,032 | 32,994 | 34,062 | 17.9 | 18.0 | 19.4 | 20.5 | 20.9 |
| Female | 4,316 | 4,879 | 5,220 | 5,664 | 5,711 | 2.7 | 3.0 | 3.2 | 3.4 | 3.4 |
| Non-Hispanic: | | | | | | | | | | |
| White | 20,513 | 22,141 | 23,026 | 23,857 | 24,690 | 9.5 | 10.1 | 10.6 | 11.0 | 11.4 |
| Male | 17,350 | 18,515 | 19,208 | 19,893 | 20,686 | 16.6 | 17.3 | 18.0 | 18.7 | 19.3 |
| Female | 3,163 | 3,626 | 3,818 | 3,964 | 4,004 | 3.0 | 3.4 | 3.6 | 3.8 | 3.8 |
| Black | 7,330 | 7,601 | 8,904 | 9,973 | 10,117 | 17.8 | 17.8 | 20.7 | 23.0 | 23.2 |
| Male | 6,607 | 6,873 | 8,068 | 8,906 | 9,107 | 33.4 | 33.3 | 38.6 | 42.2 | 42.8 |
| Female | 723 | 728 | 836 | 1,067 | 1,010 | 3.4 | 3.4 | 3.8 | 4.8 | 4.5 |
| American Indian or Alaska Native | 293 | 311 | 353 | 390 | 394 | 11.2 | 12.0 | 13.3 | 14.4 | 14.4 |
| Male | 246 | 261 | 301 | 323 | 333 | 18.7 | 20.6 | 23.0 | 24.4 | 24.9 |
| Female | 47 | 50 | 52 | 67 | 61 | 3.9 | 3.9 | 4.0 | 4.9 | 4.3 |
| Asian or Pacific Islander | 383 | 418 | 504 | 584 | 588 | 2.2 | 2.2 | 2.5 | 2.9 | 2.8 |
| Male | 329 | 340 | 426 | 480 | 479 | 4.1 | 3.7 | 4.4 | 4.9 | 4.7 |
| Female | 54 | 78 | 78 | 104 | 109 | 0.6 | 0.8 | 0.8 | 1.0 | 1.0 |
| Hispanic [2] | 3,008 | 3,010 | 3,332 | 3,771 | 3,884 | 5.9 | 5.4 | 5.8 | 6.4 | 6.5 |
| Male | 2,694 | 2,630 | 2,912 | 3,316 | 3,369 | 10.5 | 9.4 | 10.1 | 11.2 | 11.1 |
| Female | 314 | 380 | 420 | 455 | 515 | 1.3 | 1.4 | 1.5 | 1.6 | 1.8 |

[1] Includes deaths for other races and those not stated, not shown separately. [2] Persons of Hispanic origin may be of any race.

Source: U.S. National Center for Health Statistics, *Deaths: Final Data for 2017, Supplemental Tables*, Vol. 68, No. 9, June 2019. See also <http://www.cdc.gov/nchs/nvss/deaths.htm>

# Table 133. Drug Overdose/Poisoning Deaths and Those Involving Opioid Analgesics and Heroin: 1999 to 2017

[Rates are age-adjusted and per 100,000 population. Deaths are classified according to the International Classification of Diseases, Tenth Revision (ICD-10)]

| Year | Total [1] | | Opioid analgesics | | Heroin | |
|---|---|---|---|---|---|---|
| | Number | Rate | Number | Rate | Number | Rate |
| 1999 | 16,849 | 6.1 | 4,030 | 1.4 | 1,960 | 0.7 |
| 2000 | 17,415 | 6.2 | 4,400 | 1.5 | 1,842 | 0.7 |
| 2001 | 19,394 | 6.8 | 5,528 | 1.9 | 1,779 | 0.6 |
| 2002 | 23,518 | 8.2 | 7,456 | 2.6 | 2,089 | 0.7 |
| 2003 | 25,785 | 8.9 | 8,517 | 2.9 | 2,080 | 0.7 |
| 2004 | 27,424 | 9.4 | 9,857 | 3.4 | 1,878 | 0.6 |
| 2005 | 29,813 | 10.1 | 10,928 | 3.7 | 2,009 | 0.7 |
| 2006 | 34,425 | 11.5 | 13,723 | 4.6 | 2,088 | 0.7 |
| 2007 | 36,010 | 11.9 | 14,408 | 4.8 | 2,399 | 0.8 |
| 2008 | 36,450 | 11.9 | 14,800 | 4.8 | 3,041 | 1.0 |
| 2009 | 37,004 | 11.9 | 15,597 | 5.0 | 3,278 | 1.1 |
| 2010 | 38,329 | 12.3 | 16,651 | 5.4 | 3,036 | 1.0 |
| 2011 | 41,340 | 13.2 | 16,917 | 5.4 | 4,397 | 1.4 |
| 2012 | 41,502 | 13.1 | 16,007 | 5.1 | 5,925 | 1.9 |
| 2013 | 43,982 | 13.8 | 16,235 | 5.1 | 8,257 | 2.7 |
| 2014 | 47,055 | 14.7 | 18,893 | 5.9 | 10,574 | 3.4 |
| 2015 | 52,404 | 16.3 | 22,598 | 7.0 | 12,989 | 4.1 |
| 2016 | 63,632 | 19.8 | 32,445 | 10.2 | 15,469 | 4.9 |
| 2017 | 70,237 | 21.7 | 40,051 | 12.5 | 15,482 | 4.9 |

[1] Includes deaths due to other drug types not shown separately.

Source: U.S. National Center for Health Statistics, CDC WONDER Online database, "Multiple Cause of Death, 1999-2017," <https://wonder.cdc.gov/>, accessed April 2019.

# Table 134. Drug Overdose Death Rates by Sex, Age, and Race/Ethnicity: 2000 to 2016

[Rates per 100,000 resident population. Drug overdose deaths include those resulting from accidental or intentional overdose of a drug, being given the wrong drug, taking the wrong drug in error, taking a drug inadvertently, or other misuses of drugs. These deaths are from all manners and intents, including unintentional, suicide, homicide, legal intervention, operations of war, and undetermined intent. Deaths classified according to the International Classification of Diseases, Tenth Revision (ICD-10). See Appendix III]

| Characteristic | 2000 | 2005 | 2010 | 2011 | 2012 | 2013 | 2014 | 2015 | 2016 |
|---|---|---|---|---|---|---|---|---|---|
| ALL PERSONS | | | | | | | | | |
| All ages, age-adjusted [1] | 6.2 | 10.1 | 12.3 | 13.2 | 13.1 | 13.8 | 14.7 | 16.3 | 19.8 |
| All ages, crude | 6.2 | 10.1 | 12.4 | 13.3 | 13.2 | 13.9 | 14.8 | 16.3 | 19.7 |
| Under 15 years old | 0.1 | 0.2 | 0.2 | 0.2 | 0.2 | 0.2 | 0.2 | 0.2 | 0.2 |
| 15 to 24 years old | 3.7 | 6.9 | 8.2 | 8.6 | 8.0 | 8.3 | 8.6 | 9.7 | 12.4 |
| 25 to 34 years old | 7.9 | 13.6 | 18.4 | 20.2 | 20.1 | 20.9 | 23.1 | 26.9 | 34.6 |
| 35 to 44 years old | 14.3 | 19.6 | 20.8 | 22.5 | 22.1 | 23.0 | 25.0 | 28.3 | 35.0 |
| 45 to 54 years old | 11.6 | 21.1 | 25.1 | 26.7 | 26.9 | 27.5 | 28.2 | 30.0 | 34.5 |
| 55 to 64 years old | 4.2 | 9.0 | 15.0 | 15.9 | 16.6 | 19.2 | 20.3 | 21.8 | 25.6 |
| 65 to 74 years old | 2.0 | 3.2 | 4.7 | 5.4 | 5.8 | 6.4 | 6.9 | 7.2 | 8.2 |
| 75 to 84 years old | 2.4 | 3.1 | 3.4 | 3.4 | 3.4 | 3.6 | 3.6 | 3.6 | 3.4 |
| 85 years old and over | 4.4 | 4.1 | 4.7 | 4.2 | 4.3 | 4.3 | 4.1 | 4.4 | 4.0 |
| AGE-ADJUSTED RATES [1] | | | | | | | | | |
| MALE | | | | | | | | | |
| Total | 8.3 | 12.8 | 15.0 | 16.1 | 16.1 | 17.0 | 18.3 | 20.8 | 26.2 |
| White | 8.4 | 13.6 | 16.8 | 18.1 | 18.1 | 19.0 | 20.4 | 23.2 | 28.8 |
| Black | 10.8 | 12.8 | 10.1 | 11.0 | 11.3 | 12.9 | 13.8 | 16.8 | 24.0 |
| American Indian, Alaska Native | 6.1 | 10.8 | 11.8 | 12.9 | 12.8 | 12.9 | 15.9 | 16.0 | 17.7 |
| Asian or Pacific Islander | 1.4 | 2.2 | 2.5 | 3.2 | 3.1 | 3.2 | 3.3 | 4.1 | 4.7 |
| Hispanic [2] | 7.1 | 8.4 | 7.6 | 8.1 | 8.5 | 9.2 | 9.3 | 10.9 | 13.9 |
| Non-Hispanic, White | 8.6 | 14.7 | 19.0 | 20.5 | 20.4 | 21.4 | 23.2 | 26.2 | 32.7 |
| Non-Hispanic, Black | 10.9 | 13.0 | 10.5 | 11.3 | 11.6 | 13.3 | 14.2 | 17.3 | 24.7 |
| FEMALE | | | | | | | | | |
| Total | 4.1 | 7.3 | 9.6 | 10.2 | 10.2 | 10.6 | 11.1 | 11.8 | 13.4 |
| White | 4.3 | 8.0 | 10.9 | 11.7 | 11.6 | 12.1 | 12.7 | 13.6 | 15.2 |
| Black | 4.1 | 6.0 | 5.7 | 5.9 | 6.0 | 6.3 | 7.0 | 7.5 | 10.0 |
| American Indian, Alaska Native | 3.7 | 8.6 | 9.7 | 10.7 | 12.2 | 11.6 | 11.2 | 11.3 | 13.1 |
| Asian or Pacific Islander | 0.8 | 1.3 | 1.5 | 1.6 | 1.4 | 1.5 | 1.7 | 1.5 | 1.8 |
| Hispanic [2] | 2.0 | 3.0 | 3.6 | 4.0 | 4.0 | 4.1 | 4.1 | 4.4 | 5.0 |
| Non-Hispanic, White | 4.5 | 8.8 | 12.5 | 13.3 | 13.2 | 13.8 | 14.6 | 15.8 | 17.7 |
| Non-Hispanic, Black | 4.2 | 6.2 | 5.9 | 6.2 | 6.2 | 6.5 | 7.3 | 7.7 | 10.4 |

[1] Age-adjusted rates are calculated using the year 2000 standard population and were prepared using the direct method, in which age specific death rates for a population of interest are applied to a standard population distributed by age. Age adjustment eliminates the differences in observed rates between points in time or among compared population groups that result from age differences in population composition. [2] Persons of Hispanic origin may be of any race.

Source: U.S. National Center for Health Statistics, *Health, United States, 2017*, September 2018. See also <http://www.cdc.gov/nchs/hus.htm>.

# Table 135. Drug Overdose Deaths and Age-adjusted Death Rates Involving Opioids, Benzodiazepines, and Stimulants by Drug: 2011 to 2016

[Age-adjusted rates per 100,000 population. Deaths may involve other drugs in addition to the referent drug and those involving more than one drug are counted in both totals. Deaths classified according to the International Classification of Diseases, Tenth Revision (ICD-10). See Appendix III]

| Drug | Deaths | | | | | | Age-adjusted death rates | | | | | |
|---|---|---|---|---|---|---|---|---|---|---|---|---|
| | 2011 | 2012 | 2013 | 2014 | 2015 | 2016 | 2011 | 2012 | 2013 | 2014 | 2015 | 2016 |
| Total | 41,340 | 41,502 | 43,982 | 47,055 | 52,404 | 63,632 | 13.2 | 13.1 | 13.8 | 14.7 | 16.3 | 19.8 |
| OPIOIDS | | | | | | | | | | | | |
| Fentanyl | 1,662 | 1,615 | 1,919 | 4,223 | 8,251 | 18,335 | 0.5 | 0.5 | 0.6 | 1.3 | 2.6 | 5.9 |
| Heroin | 4,571 | 6,155 | 8,418 | 10,882 | 13,318 | 15,961 | 1.5 | 2.0 | 2.7 | 3.5 | 4.3 | 5.1 |
| Hydrocodone | 3,206 | 3,037 | 3,113 | 3,299 | 3,051 | 3,199 | 1.0 | 1.0 | 1.0 | 1.0 | 0.9 | 1.0 |
| Methadone | 4,545 | 4,087 | 3,700 | 3,498 | 3,376 | 3,493 | 1.4 | 1.3 | 1.2 | 1.1 | 1.1 | 1.1 |
| Morphine | 3,290 | 3,513 | 3,772 | 4,024 | 4,226 | 5,014 | 1.0 | 1.1 | 1.2 | 1.2 | 1.3 | 1.5 |
| Oxycodone | 5,587 | 5,178 | 4,967 | 5,431 | 5,792 | 6,199 | 1.8 | 1.7 | 1.6 | 1.7 | 1.8 | 1.9 |
| BENZODIAZEPINES | | | | | | | | | | | | |
| Alprazolam | 4,066 | 3,803 | 3,724 | 4,237 | 4,801 | 6,209 | 1.3 | 1.2 | 1.2 | 1.3 | 1.5 | 2.0 |
| Diazepam | 1,698 | 1,577 | 1,618 | 1,748 | 1,796 | 2,022 | 0.5 | 0.5 | 0.5 | 0.5 | 0.5 | 0.6 |
| STIMULANTS | | | | | | | | | | | | |
| Cocaine | 5,070 | 4,780 | 5,319 | 5,892 | 7,324 | 11,316 | 1.6 | 1.5 | 1.7 | 1.8 | 2.3 | 3.6 |
| Methamphetamine | 1,887 | 2,267 | 3,194 | 3,747 | 5,092 | 6,762 | 0.6 | 0.7 | 1.0 | 1.2 | 1.6 | 2.1 |

Source: National Center for Health Statistics, National Vital Statistics Reports, "Drugs Most Frequently Involved in Drug Overdose Deaths: United States, 2011-2016," Vol. 67, No. 9, December 2018. See also <https://www.cdc.gov/nchs/products/nvsr.htm>.

# Table 136. People Who Got Married and Divorced in the Past 12 Months by State: 2017

[For 12-month period prior to interview date, which occurred for each month in calendar year. For example, a person interviewed in January 2017 could report they got married between January 2016 and January 2017. Data shown for persons 15 years old and over. Vital event is counted in state in which respondent lived at the time of survey. Based on 2017 American Community Survey (ACS). The ACS universe includes the household population and the group quarters population. Based on a sample and subject to sampling variability. See Appendix III]

| State | People who got married in the past 12 months | | | | People who got divorced in the past 12 months | | | |
| --- | --- | --- | --- | --- | --- | --- | --- | --- |
| | Males | Marriage rate per 1,000 men | Females | Marriage rate per 1,000 women | Males | Divorce rate per 1,000 men | Females | Divorce rate per 1,000 women |
| United States............ | 2,348,243 | 18.2 | 2,319,672 | 17.1 | 974,618 | 7.5 | 1,075,500 | 7.9 |
| Alabama................. | 30,238 | 15.9 | 31,366 | 15.1 | 18,304 | 9.7 | 22,690 | 10.9 |
| Alaska.................. | 7,702 | 25.1 | 6,985 | 25.3 | 2,780 | 9.1 | 2,142 | 7.7 |
| Arizona................. | 45,466 | 16.3 | 44,791 | 15.6 | 25,544 | 9.1 | 24,076 | 8.4 |
| Arkansas................ | 26,482 | 22.5 | 26,713 | 21.6 | 13,388 | 11.4 | 16,520 | 13.3 |
| California............... | 273,105 | 17.3 | 262,779 | 16.2 | 97,315 | 6.2 | 112,111 | 6.9 |
| Colorado................ | 50,942 | 22.3 | 50,143 | 22.0 | 18,616 | 8.2 | 23,185 | 10.2 |
| Connecticut.............. | 23,512 | 16.3 | 20,367 | 13.2 | 10,618 | 7.4 | 10,775 | 7.0 |
| Delaware................ | 7,635 | 20.1 | 7,530 | 18.2 | 2,035 | 5.4 | 4,730 | 11.4 |
| District of Columbia...... | 6,586 | 24.0 | 6,337 | 20.4 | 1,411 | 5.1 | 1,079 | 3.5 |
| Florida................. | 148,429 | 17.5 | 141,699 | 15.7 | 67,752 | 8.0 | 74,210 | 8.2 |
| Georgia................. | 76,816 | 19.2 | 74,997 | 17.3 | 37,756 | 9.4 | 39,539 | 9.1 |
| Hawaii.................. | 11,323 | 19.4 | 10,229 | 17.5 | 2,958 | 5.1 | 2,994 | 5.1 |
| Idaho................... | 14,999 | 22.3 | 15,472 | 22.9 | 6,352 | 9.4 | 7,785 | 11.5 |
| Illinois................. | 83,333 | 16.4 | 84,816 | 15.9 | 29,832 | 5.9 | 33,270 | 6.2 |
| Indiana................. | 49,777 | 19.0 | 54,127 | 19.7 | 23,863 | 9.1 | 24,510 | 8.9 |
| Iowa................... | 22,748 | 18.2 | 22,644 | 17.6 | 8,527 | 6.8 | 10,044 | 7.8 |
| Kansas.................. | 23,789 | 20.7 | 24,283 | 20.8 | 9,455 | 8.2 | 8,811 | 7.5 |
| Kentucky................ | 39,309 | 22.3 | 39,326 | 21.2 | 16,881 | 9.6 | 21,685 | 11.7 |
| Louisiana............... | 28,745 | 15.8 | 27,538 | 14.2 | 14,448 | 8.0 | 15,549 | 8.0 |
| Maine.................. | 7,440 | 13.6 | 7,837 | 13.5 | 4,740 | 8.6 | 5,860 | 10.1 |
| Maryland................ | 44,791 | 18.9 | 44,612 | 17.4 | 15,598 | 6.6 | 21,358 | 8.3 |
| Massachusetts........... | 46,746 | 16.9 | 46,167 | 15.5 | 15,987 | 5.8 | 23,792 | 8.0 |
| Michigan................ | 67,680 | 16.9 | 67,503 | 16.1 | 29,947 | 7.5 | 31,821 | 7.6 |
| Minnesota............... | 34,662 | 15.6 | 35,016 | 15.4 | 14,646 | 6.6 | 16,317 | 7.2 |
| Mississippi.............. | 18,864 | 16.5 | 20,401 | 16.3 | 8,595 | 7.5 | 10,132 | 8.1 |
| Missouri................ | 47,241 | 19.6 | 47,112 | 18.5 | 23,241 | 9.6 | 21,080 | 8.3 |
| Montana................ | 6,933 | 16.2 | 7,540 | 17.5 | 3,501 | 8.2 | 2,794 | 6.5 |
| Nebraska................ | 13,326 | 17.7 | 12,469 | 16.2 | 5,630 | 7.5 | 6,454 | 8.4 |
| Nevada................. | 24,773 | 20.4 | 22,659 | 18.6 | 9,382 | 7.7 | 11,640 | 9.6 |
| New Hampshire........... | 9,908 | 17.8 | 9,055 | 15.7 | 3,865 | 6.9 | 5,488 | 9.5 |
| New Jersey.............. | 52,350 | 14.7 | 52,582 | 13.8 | 22,944 | 6.4 | 23,708 | 6.2 |
| New Mexico.............. | 11,256 | 13.6 | 12,962 | 15.2 | 7,709 | 9.3 | 6,774 | 7.9 |
| New York................ | 133,485 | 16.9 | 130,312 | 15.3 | 41,808 | 5.3 | 50,703 | 5.9 |
| North Carolina........... | 73,501 | 18.3 | 74,922 | 17.2 | 31,567 | 7.8 | 36,660 | 8.4 |
| North Dakota............ | 6,746 | 21.6 | 6,774 | 23.0 | 2,371 | 7.6 | 2,595 | 8.8 |
| Ohio................... | 83,849 | 18.2 | 84,776 | 17.3 | 32,434 | 7.0 | 37,475 | 7.6 |
| Oklahoma............... | 31,396 | 20.4 | 32,077 | 20.1 | 16,251 | 10.6 | 16,843 | 10.6 |
| Oregon................. | 30,763 | 18.3 | 30,671 | 17.7 | 13,937 | 8.3 | 13,949 | 8.0 |
| Pennsylvania............ | 85,287 | 16.6 | 85,831 | 15.7 | 34,528 | 6.7 | 37,563 | 6.9 |
| Rhode Island............ | 6,121 | 14.4 | 5,075 | 10.9 | 2,294 | 5.4 | 3,321 | 7.2 |
| South Carolina........... | 32,506 | 16.5 | 34,628 | 16.2 | 16,013 | 8.1 | 18,612 | 8.7 |
| South Dakota............ | 6,577 | 18.9 | 6,175 | 18.0 | 3,847 | 11.1 | 2,670 | 7.8 |
| Tennessee.............. | 53,954 | 20.5 | 55,517 | 19.6 | 24,776 | 9.4 | 28,847 | 10.2 |
| Texas.................. | 229,661 | 21.0 | 224,915 | 20.0 | 88,612 | 8.1 | 92,008 | 8.2 |
| Utah................... | 32,506 | 27.9 | 31,711 | 27.3 | 11,275 | 9.7 | 10,544 | 9.1 |
| Vermont................ | 3,981 | 15.4 | 4,008 | 14.9 | 1,364 | 5.3 | 1,945 | 7.2 |
| Virginia................ | 65,344 | 19.4 | 63,509 | 17.9 | 27,878 | 8.3 | 28,481 | 8.0 |
| Washington.............. | 58,637 | 19.6 | 54,377 | 17.9 | 24,541 | 8.2 | 25,563 | 8.4 |
| West Virginia............ | 12,306 | 16.7 | 12,127 | 15.8 | 8,397 | 11.4 | 6,888 | 9.0 |
| Wisconsin............... | 39,469 | 16.9 | 38,717 | 16.1 | 16,879 | 7.2 | 16,100 | 6.7 |
| Wyoming................ | 5,248 | 22.3 | 5,493 | 24.2 | 2,226 | 9.4 | 1,810 | 8.0 |

Source: U.S. Census Bureau, 2017 American Community Survey, B12501, "Marriage in the Last Year by Sex by Marital Status for the Population 15 Years and Over," and B12503, "Divorces in the Last Year by Sex by Marital Status for the Population 15 Years and Over"; <http://factfinder.census.gov>, accessed December 2018.

# Table 137. Marriage and Divorce Rates by State: 1990 to 2017

[Rate per 1,000 population residing in area. Population enumerated as of April 1 for 1990, 2000, and 2010; estimated as of July 1 for all other years. Rates are based on provisional counts by state of occurrence. See Appendix III]

| State | Marriage rates | | | | | | Divorce rates [1] | | | | | |
|---|---|---|---|---|---|---|---|---|---|---|---|---|
| | 1990 | 2000 | 2005 | 2010 | 2015 | 2017 | 1990 | 2000 | 2005 | 2010 | 2015 | 2017 |
| **United States** [2] | **9.8** | **8.2** | **7.6** | **6.8** | **6.9** | **6.9** | **4.7** | **4.0** | **3.6** | **3.6** | **3.1** | **2.9** |
| Alabama | 10.6 | 10.1 | 9.2 | 8.2 | 7.4 | 7.0 | 6.1 | 5.5 | 4.9 | 4.4 | 3.9 | 3.7 |
| Alaska | 10.2 | 8.9 | 8.2 | 8.0 | 7.4 | 6.9 | 5.5 | 3.9 | 4.3 | 4.7 | 4.1 | 3.6 |
| Arizona | 10.0 | 7.5 | 6.6 | 5.9 | 5.9 | 5.8 | 6.9 | 4.6 | 4.2 | 3.5 | 3.6 | 3.5 |
| Arkansas | 15.3 | 15.4 | 12.9 | 10.8 | 10.0 | 9.5 | 6.9 | 6.4 | 6.0 | 5.7 | 4.8 | 3.7 |
| California [3] | 7.9 | 5.8 | 6.4 | 5.8 | 6.2 | 6.3 | 4.3 | (NA) | (NA) | (NA) | (NA) | (NA) |
| Colorado | 9.8 | 8.3 | 7.6 | 6.9 | 6.8 | 7.3 | 5.5 | 4.7 | 4.4 | 4.3 | 3.7 | 3.2 |
| Connecticut | 7.9 | 5.7 | 5.8 | 5.6 | 5.3 | 5.6 | 3.2 | 3.3 | 3.0 | 2.9 | 3.1 | 2.9 |
| Delaware | 8.4 | 6.5 | 5.9 | 5.2 | 5.7 | 5.5 | 4.4 | 3.9 | 3.8 | 3.5 | 3.1 | 3.0 |
| District of Columbia | 8.2 | 4.9 | 4.1 | 7.6 | 8.2 | 8.2 | 4.5 | 3.2 | 2.0 | 2.8 | 2.8 | 2.5 |
| Florida | 10.9 | 8.9 | 8.9 | 7.3 | 8.2 | 7.8 | 6.3 | 5.1 | 4.6 | 4.4 | 4.0 | 3.6 |
| Georgia | 10.3 | 6.8 | 7.0 | 7.3 | 6.2 | 6.9 | 5.5 | 3.3 | (NA) | (NA) | (NA) | 3.5 |
| Hawaii | 16.4 | 20.6 | 22.6 | 17.6 | 15.9 | 15.3 | 4.6 | 3.9 | (NA) | (NA) | (NA) | (NA) |
| Idaho | 13.9 | 10.8 | 10.5 | 8.8 | 8.2 | 7.8 | 6.5 | 5.5 | 5.0 | 5.2 | 4.1 | 3.9 |
| Illinois | 8.8 | 6.9 | 5.9 | 5.7 | 5.9 | 6.0 | 3.8 | 3.2 | 2.6 | 2.6 | 2.2 | 1.9 |
| Indiana | 9.6 | 7.9 | 6.9 | 6.3 | 6.9 | 6.9 | (NA) | (NA) | (NA) | (NA) | (NA) | (NA) |
| Iowa | 9.0 | 6.9 | 6.9 | 6.9 | 6.3 | 6.2 | 3.9 | 3.3 | 2.7 | 2.4 | 1.2 | 2.0 |
| Kansas | 9.2 | 8.3 | 6.8 | 6.4 | 5.9 | 6.0 | 5.0 | 3.6 | 3.1 | 3.7 | 2.8 | 2.4 |
| Kentucky | 13.5 | 9.8 | 8.7 | 7.4 | 7.2 | 7.2 | 5.8 | 5.1 | 4.6 | 4.5 | 3.7 | 3.7 |
| Louisiana | 9.6 | 9.1 | 8.0 | 6.9 | 6.8 | 5.6 | (NA) | (NA) | (NA) | (NA) | 2.8 | 1.9 |
| Maine | 9.7 | 8.8 | 8.2 | 7.1 | 7.6 | 7.6 | 4.3 | 5.0 | 4.1 | 4.2 | 3.4 | 3.2 |
| Maryland | 9.7 | 7.5 | 6.9 | 5.7 | 6.2 | 6.3 | 3.4 | 3.3 | 3.1 | 2.8 | 2.6 | 2.5 |
| Massachusetts | 7.9 | 5.8 | 6.2 | 5.6 | 5.5 | 5.7 | 2.8 | 2.5 | 2.2 | 2.5 | 2.6 | 2.2 |
| Michigan | 8.2 | 6.7 | 6.1 | 5.5 | 6.0 | 5.9 | 4.3 | 3.9 | 3.4 | 3.5 | 3.0 | 2.8 |
| Minnesota | 7.7 | 6.8 | 6.0 | 5.3 | 5.6 | 5.6 | 3.5 | 3.2 | (NA) | (NA) | (NA) | (NA) |
| Mississippi | 9.4 | 6.9 | 5.8 | 4.9 | 7.0 | 6.7 | 5.5 | 5.0 | 4.4 | 4.3 | 3.4 | 2.9 |
| Missouri | 9.6 | 7.8 | 7.0 | 6.5 | 6.2 | 6.6 | 5.1 | 4.5 | 3.6 | 3.9 | 3.2 | 3.1 |
| Montana | 8.6 | 7.3 | 7.4 | 7.4 | 8.0 | 8.0 | 5.1 | 4.2 | 4.5 | 3.9 | 3.4 | 3.1 |
| Nebraska | 8.0 | 7.6 | 7.0 | 6.6 | 6.4 | 6.3 | 4.0 | 3.7 | 3.3 | 3.6 | 3.2 | 3.0 |
| Nevada | 99.0 | 72.2 | 57.4 | 38.3 | 31.0 | 28.6 | 11.4 | 9.9 | 7.4 | 5.9 | 4.6 | 4.5 |
| New Hampshire | 9.5 | 9.4 | 7.3 | 7.3 | 6.9 | 7.0 | 4.7 | 4.8 | 3.9 | 3.8 | 3.3 | 3.1 |
| New Jersey | 7.6 | 6.0 | 5.7 | 5.1 | 5.6 | 5.5 | 3.0 | 3.0 | 2.9 | 3.0 | 2.8 | 2.6 |
| New Mexico | 8.8 | 8.0 | 6.6 | 7.7 | 6.2 | 5.9 | 4.9 | 5.1 | 4.6 | 4.0 | 3.3 | (NA) |
| New York | 8.6 | 7.1 | 6.8 | 6.5 | 7.1 | 7.3 | 3.2 | 3.0 | 2.9 | 2.9 | 2.7 | 2.7 |
| North Carolina | 7.8 | 8.2 | 7.3 | 6.6 | 7.0 | 6.8 | 5.1 | 4.5 | 4.1 | 3.8 | 3.1 | 3.1 |
| North Dakota | 7.5 | 7.2 | 6.8 | 6.5 | 6.2 | 5.8 | 3.6 | 3.4 | 2.9 | 3.1 | 2.8 | 2.5 |
| Ohio | 9.0 | 7.8 | 6.5 | 5.8 | 5.9 | 5.8 | 4.7 | 4.2 | 3.5 | 3.4 | 3.1 | 2.9 |
| Oklahoma | 10.6 | (NA) | 7.3 | 7.2 | 7.4 | 6.8 | 7.7 | (NA) | 5.6 | 5.2 | 4.4 | 4.1 |
| Oregon | 8.9 | 7.6 | 7.3 | 6.5 | 6.9 | 6.7 | 5.5 | 4.8 | 4.2 | 4.0 | 3.4 | 3.4 |
| Pennsylvania | 7.1 | 6.0 | 5.8 | 5.3 | 5.7 | 5.7 | 3.3 | 3.1 | 2.3 | 2.7 | 2.6 | 2.6 |
| Rhode Island | 8.1 | 7.6 | 7.0 | 5.8 | 6.4 | 6.8 | 3.7 | 2.9 | 3.0 | 3.2 | 3.0 | 2.9 |
| South Carolina | 15.9 | 10.6 | 8.3 | 7.4 | 7.5 | 7.0 | 4.5 | 3.8 | 2.9 | 3.1 | 2.8 | 2.6 |
| South Dakota | 11.1 | 9.4 | 8.4 | 7.3 | 7.2 | 6.7 | 3.7 | 3.5 | 2.8 | 3.4 | 2.6 | 2.7 |
| Tennessee | 13.9 | 15.5 | 10.9 | 8.8 | 8.5 | 8.2 | 6.5 | 5.9 | 4.6 | 4.2 | 3.7 | 3.5 |
| Texas | 10.5 | 9.4 | 7.8 | 7.1 | 7.2 | 7.1 | 5.5 | 4.0 | 3.3 | 3.3 | 2.6 | 2.2 |
| Utah | 11.2 | 10.8 | 9.8 | 8.5 | 8.1 | 8.7 | 5.1 | 4.3 | 4.1 | 3.7 | 3.6 | 3.4 |
| Vermont | 10.9 | 10.0 | 8.9 | 9.3 | 8.1 | 7.9 | 4.5 | 4.1 | 3.6 | 3.8 | 3.1 | 2.9 |
| Virginia | 11.4 | 8.8 | 8.2 | 6.8 | 7.0 | 6.8 | 4.4 | 4.3 | 4.0 | 3.8 | 3.3 | 3.0 |
| Washington | 9.5 | 6.9 | 6.5 | 6.0 | 6.2 | 6.2 | 5.9 | 4.6 | 4.3 | 4.2 | 3.4 | 3.4 |
| West Virginia | 7.2 | 8.7 | 7.4 | 6.7 | 6.6 | 6.3 | 5.3 | 5.1 | 5.1 | 5.1 | 4.0 | 3.5 |
| Wisconsin | 7.9 | 6.7 | 6.1 | 5.3 | 5.6 | 5.6 | 3.6 | 3.2 | 2.9 | 3.0 | 2.6 | 2.4 |
| Wyoming | 10.7 | 10.0 | 9.3 | 7.6 | 7.3 | 7.1 | 6.6 | 5.8 | 5.2 | 5.1 | 4.1 | 4.0 |

NA Not available. [1] Includes annulments. Includes divorce petitions filed or legal separations for some counties or States. [2] Beginning 2000, rates based solely on the combined counts and populations for reporting states and the District of Columbia. [3] Marriage data includes nonlicensed marriages registered.

Source: U.S. National Center for Health Statistics, National Vital Statistics System, "Marriages and Divorces, Detailed State Tables," <https://www.cdc.gov/nchs/nvss/marriage-divorce.htm>, accessed December 2018.

## Table 138. People Who Got Married or Divorced in the Past 12 Months by Selected Characteristics: 2017

[In units, as indicated (264,697 represents 264,697,000). For 12-month period prior to interview date, which occurred for each month in calendar year. For example, a person interviewed in January 2017 could report they got married between January 2016 and January 2017. Persons 15 years and over. Based on 2017 American Community Survey (ACS). The ACS universe includes the household population and the group quarters population. Based on a sample and subject to sampling variability. See Appendix III]

| Characteristic | Total population | Married in the past 12 months | | Divorced in the past 12 months | |
|---|---|---|---|---|---|
| | | Males | Females | Males | Females |
| **Population 15 years old and over (1,000)**.......... | **264,697** | **2,348** | **2,320** | **975** | **1,076** |
| AGE | | | | | |
| Median age............................................. | 45.7 | 32.4 | 30.4 | 45.2 | 43.7 |
| EDUCATIONAL ATTAINMENT | | | | | |
| Population 18 years and over (1,000)................... | 252,070 | 2,324 | 2,291 | 972 | 1,073 |
| Bachelor's degree or higher (percent)............... | 29.4 | 32.9 | 39.1 | 24.6 | 29.0 |
| LABOR FORCE PARTICIPATION | | | | | |
| Population 16 years and over (1,000)................... | 260,564 | 2,336 | 2,305 | 975 | 1,076 |
| In labor force (percent)............................... | 63.2 | 88.6 | 77.9 | 79.2 | 78.5 |
| Not in labor force (percent).......................... | 36.8 | 11.4 | 22.1 | 20.8 | 21.5 |
| POVERTY STATUS IN PAST 12 MONTHS | | | | | |
| Population for whom poverty status is determined (1,000).......... | 257,790 | 2,310 | 2,312 | 943 | 1,069 |
| Below poverty (percent)............................. | 12.1 | 7.0 | 8.4 | 11.2 | 20.0 |
| PRESENCE OF OWN CHILD UNDER 18 YEARS | | | | | |
| Population in households (1,000)...................... | 256,681 | 2,305 | 2,308 | 938 | 1,067 |
| With an own child under 18 years (percent)......... | 23.5 | 30.4 | 32.9 | 18.2 | 38.0 |
| HOUSING TENURE | | | | | |
| Population 15 years and over in occupied housing units (1,000)... | 256,681 | 2,305 | 2,308 | 938 | 1,067 |
| Owner-occupied housing units (percent)............. | 67.2 | 51.5 | 51.5 | 54.9 | 51.7 |
| Renter-occupied housing units (percent)............ | 32.8 | 48.5 | 48.5 | 45.1 | 48.3 |

Source: U.S. Census Bureau, 2017 American Community Survey, S1251, "Characteristics of People with a Marital Event in the Last 12 Months," <http://factfinder.census.gov>, accessed December 2018.

## Table 139. Marital Status of Population and Number of Times Married by Sex and Median Duration of Marriage: 2010 to 2017

[248,056 represents 248,056,000. Data shown are for the population age 15 years and over. Based on the American Community Survey (ACS). The ACS universe includes the household population and the group quarters population. Based on a sample and subject to sampling variability. See Appendix III]

| Characteristic | 2010 | 2011 | 2012 | 2013 | 2014 | 2015 | 2016 | 2017 |
|---|---|---|---|---|---|---|---|---|
| NUMBER (1,000) | | | | | | | | |
| **Population aged 15 years and over**...... | **248,056** | **250,393** | **252,745** | **255,017** | **257,771** | **260,415** | **262,140** | **264,697** |
| Male........................................... | 120,743 | 121,988 | 123,175 | 124,380 | 125,665 | 127,013 | 127,864 | 129,186 |
| Never married.............................. | 42,741 | 43,675 | 44,292 | 45,175 | 45,865 | 46,677 | 47,195 | 47,654 |
| Ever married................................ | 78,001 | 78,313 | 78,883 | 79,205 | 79,800 | 80,336 | 80,669 | 81,532 |
| Once....................................... | 58,734 | 58,865 | 59,349 | 59,667 | 60,106 | 60,648 | 60,898 | 61,580 |
| Two times................................. | 15,183 | 15,332 | 15,382 | 15,284 | 15,406 | 15,381 | 15,438 | 15,592 |
| Three or more times...................... | 4,085 | 4,116 | 4,152 | 4,253 | 4,287 | 4,307 | 4,333 | 4,359 |
| Female........................................ | 127,313 | 128,405 | 129,571 | 130,637 | 132,106 | 133,402 | 134,277 | 135,511 |
| Never married.............................. | 36,899 | 37,709 | 38,367 | 39,145 | 39,944 | 40,667 | 41,143 | 41,442 |
| Ever married................................ | 90,414 | 90,696 | 91,203 | 91,492 | 92,162 | 92,734 | 93,134 | 94,070 |
| Once....................................... | 68,330 | 68,426 | 68,939 | 69,185 | 69,723 | 70,088 | 70,419 | 71,248 |
| Two times................................. | 17,449 | 17,665 | 17,620 | 17,533 | 17,642 | 17,776 | 17,838 | 17,945 |
| Three or more times...................... | 4,636 | 4,605 | 4,644 | 4,774 | 4,796 | 4,871 | 4,876 | 4,876 |
| PERCENT DISTRIBUTION | | | | | | | | |
| Male: | | | | | | | | |
| Never married.............................. | 35.4 | 35.8 | 36.0 | 36.3 | 36.5 | 36.7 | 36.9 | 36.9 |
| Ever married................................ | 64.6 | 64.2 | 64.0 | 63.7 | 63.5 | 63.3 | 63.1 | 63.1 |
| Once....................................... | 48.6 | 48.3 | 48.2 | 48.0 | 47.8 | 47.7 | 47.6 | 47.7 |
| Two times................................. | 12.6 | 12.6 | 12.5 | 12.3 | 12.3 | 12.1 | 12.1 | 12.1 |
| Three or more times...................... | 3.4 | 3.4 | 3.4 | 3.4 | 3.4 | 3.4 | 3.4 | 3.4 |
| Female: | | | | | | | | |
| Never married.............................. | 29.0 | 29.4 | 29.6 | 30.0 | 30.2 | 30.5 | 30.6 | 30.6 |
| Ever married................................ | 71.0 | 70.6 | 70.4 | 70.0 | 69.8 | 69.5 | 69.4 | 69.4 |
| Once....................................... | 53.7 | 53.3 | 53.2 | 53.0 | 52.8 | 52.5 | 52.4 | 52.6 |
| Two times................................. | 13.7 | 13.8 | 13.6 | 13.4 | 13.4 | 13.3 | 13.3 | 13.2 |
| Three or more times...................... | 3.6 | 3.6 | 3.6 | 3.7 | 3.6 | 3.7 | 3.6 | 3.6 |
| Median duration of marriage (years) [1]........ | 19.0 | 19.2 | 19.3 | 19.5 | 19.5 | 19.6 | 19.7 | 19.7 |

[1] Data shown for current marriage.

Source: U.S. Census Bureau, American Community Survey, B12504, "Median Duration of Current Marriage in Years By Sex By Marital Status for the Married Population 15 years and Over," and B12505, "Number of Times Married by Sex By Marital Status for the Population 15 Years and Over"; <http://factfinder.census.gov>, accessed December 2018.

# Section 3
# Health and Nutrition

This section presents statistics on numerous indicators of the nation's health care system, the health care industry and its institutions, and the health of its population. Data in this section cover national and personal health expenditures, health insurance coverage, Medicare and Medicaid, medical personnel, hospitals, nursing homes and other health care facilities, injuries, diseases, disability status, substance use (including alcohol, tobacco, and illicit drug use), exercise, and food consumption. This section also includes data on selected health conditions and indicators among children.

Data on national health expenditures, medical costs, and insurance coverage are compiled by the U.S. Centers for Medicare & Medicaid Services (CMS) and appear on the CMS website at <http://www.cms.gov/NationalHealthExpendData/>. In the past, Medicare and Medicaid data came from the annual *Medicare and Medicaid Statistical Supplement,* but this report was discontinued after the 2013 release, and has been replaced with "CMS Program Statistics." Internet users can use the online CMS Program Statistics tool to obtain data on Medicare enrollment, utilization, and expenditures, and also data on Medicare-certified institutional and noninstitutional health care providers. Another key source of information on Medicare is the annual report to Congress from the Boards of Trustees for Medicare. The Trustees' report covers the financial operations and actuarial status of Medicare. Medicaid data had been available from CMS's Medicaid Statistical Information System (MSIS), but this system is no longer being updated, and a new system is currently in development, and known as the Transformed MSIS (T-MSIS). CMS is working to transition all states into the T-MSIS. Selected data on Medicaid and the Children's Health Insurance Program (CHIP) continue to be available from other sources, including the U.S. National Center for Health Statistics (NCHS), and the Medicaid and CHIP Payment and Access Commission, a nonpartisan legislative branch agency that provides analysis to the states, Congress, and the Secretary of the Department of Health and Human Services.

Summary statistics showing recent trends in health care and health indicators of the population, and discussions of selected health issues are published annually by the NCHS in *Health, United States.* Statistics on health insurance are collected by surveys conducted by the Census Bureau. The NCHS also collects health insurance data and other detailed data on the population's health status annually in its National Health Interview Survey, the results of which are released in brief reports under the Early Release Program, and in online summary tables. After issuing reports covering the 2012 NHIS, the NCHS discontinued issuing NHIS data in *Vital and Health Statistics* Series 10 reports. NCHS also operates other programs to track various health indicators such as food and nutrition, exercise, body weight, and incidence of high blood cholesterol and blood pressure (hypertension).

Statistics on hospitals are published annually by the Health Forum, LLC, an affiliate of the American Hospital Association (AHA), in *AHA Hospital Statistics.* As a proxy for actual food consumption, the U.S. Dept of Agriculture's Economic Research Service provides data on food availability online at <https://www.ers.usda.gov/data-products/food-availability-per-capita-data-system/>. Data on nutrient availability are no longer updated; data through 2010 are archived and available at the website for food availability.

**National health expenditures**—CMS compiles estimates of national health expenditures (NHE) to measure spending for health care in the United States. The NHE accounts are structured to show spending by type of expenditure: hospital care, physician and clinical care, dental care, and other professional care; home health care; retail sales of prescription drugs; other medical nondurable goods; nursing home care and other personal health expenditures; other health expenditures such as public health activities, administration, and the net cost of private health insurance; and medical sector investment, which is the sum of noncommercial medical research and capital formation in medical sector structures and equipment. The NHE also shows spending by source of funding (e.g., private health insurance, Medicare, Medicaid, out-of-pocket payments, and other third party payers and programs).

Data used to estimate health expenditures come from numerous public and private sources. The expenditure type estimates rely upon statistics produced by such groups as the AHA, the Census Bureau, and the U.S. Department of Health and Human Services (HHS). Funding source estimates are constructed using administrative and statistical records from the Medicare and Medicaid programs, the U.S. Department of Defense and Veterans Affairs medical programs, the Social Security Administration, the Census Bureau, state and local governments, other HHS agencies, and other nongovernment sources.

The Health Care Satellite Account (HCSA), developed by the Bureau of Economic Analysis, is a tool that measures health care spending as the cost to treat specific diseases and medical conditions (such as cancer, or diseases of the circulatory system), as opposed to spending on specific types of health care services (physician services, or prescription drugs). The HCSA can help answer questions regarding whether changes in medical expenditures are due to changes in costs of treatments or changes in number of persons receiving care, which medical conditions account for larger portions of spending, and which medical conditions experience the greatest changes in treatment costs. The BEA presents two versions of the HCSA. One version, the "MEPS Account," uses data from the Medical Expenditure Panel Survey; the other version, the "Blended Account," combines data from multiple sources, including large claims databases that cover millions of health insurance enrollees and billions of claims. The table in this section presents data from the Blended Account. See <https://www.bea.gov/data/special-topics/health-care> for detailed information about how the Health Care Satellite Account is constructed.

**Medicare, Medicaid, and Children's Health Insurance Program (CHIP)**—The Original Medicare program has two components. Hospital Insurance (HI), also known as Medicare Part A, helps pay for in-patient hospital stays, care in a skilled nursing facility, hospice care, and some home health care. Supplementary Medical Insurance (SMI) consists of Medicare Part B and Part D. Part B coverage is optional, and helps pay for physician and outpatient hospital care services, durable medical equipment, and preventive services. Part D provides subsidized access to drug insurance coverage on a voluntary basis for all beneficiaries, and premium and cost-sharing subsidies for low-income enrollees. Participants in Parts B and D pay monthly premiums. In addition to covering persons age 65 and older, Medicare covers persons under age 65 with a disability and who have been receiving for the past 24 months disability benefits from Social Security or the Railroad Retirement Board; persons of any age with ALS (Amyotrophic Lateral Sclerosis, also known as Lou Gehrig's disease); and persons of any age with end-stage renal disease. Medicare's HI and SMI have separate trust funds, sources of revenue, and categories of expenditures.

Medicare also has an alternative option to Original Medicare coverage, the Medicare Advantage Plan (also known as Part C). Medicare Advantage plans are offered by private companies and organizations, are required to provide at least services covered by Medicare Parts A and B (except hospice services), and are financed from both Medicare's Hospital Insurance (HI) trust fund and the Part B account within the Supplementary Medical Insurance (SMI) trust fund in proportion to the relative weights of Part A and Part B benefits to the total benefits paid by the Medicare program.

Medicaid is a health insurance program for certain low-income people, families and children, pregnant women, the elderly, and people with disabilities. There are special rules for those who live in nursing homes and for disabled children living at home. Medicaid is funded and administered through a federal-state partnership. Although there are broad federal requirements for Medicaid, states have a wide degree of flexibility to design their programs.

The Children's Health Insurance Program Reauthorization Act of 2009 (CHIPRA or Public Law 111-3) reauthorized CHIP, which was originally signed into law in 1997. The program went into effect on April 1, 2009. CHIP replaced the State Children's Health Insurance Program (SCHIP). It preserves coverage for the millions of children who rely on CHIP, and provides the resources for states to reach millions of additional children who would otherwise be without health insurance coverage. CHIP is a federal-state partnership, similar to Medicaid, that expands health insurance to children whose families earn too much money to be eligible for Medicaid, but not enough money to purchase private health insurance. CHIPRA also gives states the option to provide prenatal, delivery, and postpartum care to low-income pregnant women without health insurance. Under CHIP, states can operate their programs as an expansion of Medicaid, a program entirely separate from Medicaid, or a combination of both approaches. Most states have either expanded Medicaid or run a combination of both types of programs. Only two states, Connecticut and Washington, run separate programs without Medicaid expansions.

**Health care resources and utilization**—Hospital statistics based on data from AHA's yearly survey are published annually in *AHA Hospital Statistics* and cover all hospitals accepted for registration by the Association. To be accepted for registration, hospitals

may provide proof of accreditation by the Joint Commission on Accreditation of Healthcare Organizations or certification under Title 18 of the Social Security Act; or meet certain requirements relating to number of beds, construction, equipment, medical and nursing staff, patient care and services, clinical records, and other factors. Beginning with fiscal year 2017, the AHA no longer uses its own methodology to classify hospitals as registered for inclusion in its database, and now uses the following definition: an institution is a hospital if it is licensed as a general or specialty hospital by the appropriate state agency and accredited by one of the following organizations: The Joint Commission, Healthcare Facilities Accreditation Program (HFAP), DNV Health Accreditation, Center for Improvement in Healthcare Quality Accreditation, or Medicare certified as a provider of acute services under Title 18 of the Social Security Act.

Ambulatory care data, including emergency room visits, are presented here from the National Hospital Ambulatory Medical Care Survey (NHAMCS). Data on physicians generally come from the professional organizations that collect data on medical school graduates and physicians. Statistics on patient visits to health care providers come from the National Health Interview Survey and the National Ambulatory Medical Care Survey.

**Disability and illness, mental health, and substance use**—General health statistics, including morbidity, disability, injuries, preventive care, and findings from physiological testing are collected by NCHS in its National Health Interview Survey and its National Health and Nutrition Examination Surveys. The Centers for Disease Control and Prevention in Atlanta, Georgia is responsible for collecting and publishing data on nationally notifiable diseases. Data are collected from State health departments and territories under the National Notifiable Diseases Surveillance System (NNDSS), which is operated by the CDC in collaboration with the Council of State and Territorial Epidemiologists. The list of diseases is revised annually. The Substance Abuse and Mental Health Services Administration, an agency within HHS, studies and provides data regarding mental health disorders and treatment (including mental health treatment facilities and clients), and substance use (including tobacco, alcohol, and prescription and illicit drugs).

**Statistical reliability**—For discussion of statistical collection, estimation, and sampling procedures and measures of reliability applicable to data from NCHS and CMS, see Appendix III.

# Table 140. National Health Expenditures by Type of Service—Summary: 1960 to 2017

[In billions of dollars (27.2 represents $27,200,000,000). Excludes Puerto Rico and Island Areas. For definitions, methodology, and related information, see <https://www.cms.gov/NationalHealthExpendData/Downloads/DSM-17.pdf>]

| Year | Total expenditures [1] | Health consumption expenditures, total [2] | Personal health care expenditures | | | | | | | | | |
|---|---|---|---|---|---|---|---|---|---|---|---|---|
| | | | Total [3] | Hospital care | Physician and clinical services | Dental services | Other professional services [4] | Home health care [5] | Nursing care facilities [6] | Prescription drugs | Durable medical equipment [7] | Nondurable medical equipment [8] |
| 1960..... | 27.2 | 24.7 | 23.3 | 9.0 | 5.6 | 2.0 | 0.4 | 0.1 | 0.8 | 2.7 | 0.7 | 1.6 |
| 1961..... | 29.1 | 26.3 | 24.8 | 9.8 | 5.8 | 2.1 | 0.4 | 0.1 | 0.8 | 2.7 | 0.8 | 1.8 |
| 1962..... | 31.8 | 28.4 | 26.7 | 10.4 | 6.3 | 2.2 | 0.4 | 0.1 | 0.9 | 3.0 | 0.9 | 1.9 |
| 1963..... | 34.6 | 30.9 | 29.1 | 11.5 | 7.1 | 2.4 | 0.5 | 0.1 | 1.0 | 3.2 | 0.9 | 1.9 |
| 1964..... | 38.4 | 34.1 | 32.0 | 12.5 | 8.1 | 2.6 | 0.5 | 0.1 | 1.2 | 3.3 | 1.0 | 2.1 |
| 1965..... | 41.9 | 37.2 | 34.7 | 13.5 | 8.6 | 2.8 | 0.5 | 0.1 | 1.4 | 3.7 | 1.1 | 2.2 |
| 1966..... | 46.1 | 41.2 | 38.4 | 15.3 | 9.3 | 3.0 | 0.6 | 0.1 | 1.7 | 4.0 | 1.2 | 2.4 |
| 1967..... | 51.6 | 46.5 | 43.5 | 17.8 | 10.4 | 3.4 | 0.6 | 0.2 | 2.2 | 4.2 | 1.1 | 2.5 |
| 1968..... | 58.4 | 52.7 | 49.1 | 20.5 | 11.3 | 3.7 | 0.6 | 0.2 | 2.9 | 4.7 | 1.3 | 2.7 |
| 1969..... | 65.9 | 59.1 | 55.5 | 23.4 | 12.7 | 4.2 | 0.7 | 0.3 | 3.4 | 5.1 | 1.5 | 3.0 |
| 1970..... | 74.6 | 67.0 | 63.1 | 27.2 | 14.3 | 4.7 | 0.7 | 0.2 | 4.0 | 5.5 | 1.7 | 3.3 |
| 1971..... | 82.7 | 74.3 | 69.4 | 30.2 | 15.9 | 5.2 | 0.8 | 0.2 | 4.6 | 5.9 | 1.8 | 3.5 |
| 1972..... | 92.7 | 83.4 | 77.2 | 33.8 | 17.7 | 5.6 | 0.9 | 0.2 | 5.2 | 6.3 | 2.0 | 3.7 |
| 1973..... | 102.8 | 93.1 | 86.2 | 37.9 | 19.6 | 6.4 | 1.0 | 0.3 | 6.0 | 6.8 | 2.2 | 4.0 |
| 1974..... | 116.5 | 105.9 | 98.8 | 44.1 | 22.2 | 7.1 | 1.2 | 0.4 | 6.9 | 7.4 | 2.5 | 4.5 |
| 1975..... | 133.3 | 121.1 | 113.2 | 51.2 | 25.3 | 8.0 | 1.3 | 0.6 | 8.0 | 8.1 | 2.8 | 4.9 |
| 1976..... | 152.7 | 139.3 | 129.3 | 59.4 | 28.7 | 9.0 | 1.6 | 0.9 | 9.1 | 8.7 | 3.0 | 5.4 |
| 1977..... | 173.9 | 159.9 | 146.7 | 67.0 | 33.1 | 10.1 | 2.1 | 1.1 | 10.3 | 9.2 | 3.2 | 6.1 |
| 1978..... | 195.3 | 180.0 | 164.2 | 75.6 | 35.8 | 11.0 | 2.4 | 1.6 | 11.8 | 9.9 | 3.4 | 7.1 |
| 1979..... | 221.5 | 204.6 | 187.1 | 86.2 | 41.2 | 12.0 | 2.8 | 1.9 | 13.3 | 10.7 | 3.8 | 8.5 |
| 1980..... | 255.3 | 235.5 | 217.0 | 100.5 | 47.7 | 13.3 | 3.5 | 2.4 | 15.3 | 12.0 | 4.1 | 9.8 |
| 1981..... | 296.2 | 273.4 | 251.8 | 117.5 | 55.6 | 15.7 | 4.3 | 2.9 | 17.3 | 13.4 | 4.3 | 11.3 |
| 1982..... | 334.0 | 308.0 | 283.1 | 133.6 | 61.6 | 17.0 | 4.9 | 3.5 | 19.5 | 15.0 | 4.6 | 12.6 |
| 1983..... | 367.8 | 339.5 | 311.7 | 144.7 | 68.6 | 18.3 | 5.7 | 4.2 | 21.7 | 17.3 | 5.3 | 13.8 |
| 1984..... | 405.0 | 375.1 | 341.6 | 154.4 | 77.4 | 19.9 | 7.3 | 5.1 | 23.7 | 19.6 | 6.1 | 15.0 |
| 1985..... | 442.9 | 412.8 | 376.4 | 164.6 | 90.9 | 21.7 | 8.1 | 5.6 | 26.2 | 21.8 | 7.1 | 16.0 |
| 1986..... | 474.7 | 443.7 | 408.8 | 175.6 | 100.7 | 23.2 | 9.3 | 6.4 | 28.6 | 24.3 | 8.1 | 17.1 |
| 1987..... | 516.5 | 482.3 | 447.7 | 189.5 | 112.8 | 25.3 | 11.3 | 6.6 | 30.6 | 26.9 | 9.5 | 18.3 |
| 1988..... | 579.3 | 540.5 | 498.5 | 206.5 | 128.4 | 27.4 | 13.7 | 8.4 | 34.2 | 30.6 | 11.1 | 19.4 |
| 1989..... | 644.8 | 602.3 | 550.4 | 226.0 | 142.9 | 29.4 | 14.5 | 10.2 | 38.6 | 34.8 | 11.9 | 20.8 |
| 1990..... | 721.4 | 674.1 | 615.3 | 250.4 | 158.4 | 31.6 | 17.3 | 12.5 | 44.7 | 40.3 | 13.8 | 22.4 |
| 1991..... | 788.1 | 737.7 | 675.9 | 275.8 | 175.8 | 33.4 | 18.6 | 15.1 | 49.2 | 44.4 | 13.1 | 23.2 |
| 1992..... | 854.1 | 798.7 | 731.5 | 298.5 | 190.2 | 37.1 | 20.9 | 18.7 | 52.8 | 47.0 | 13.5 | 23.2 |
| 1993..... | 916.6 | 857.7 | 778.7 | 315.7 | 201.4 | 39.0 | 23.0 | 22.7 | 55.8 | 49.6 | 14.1 | 23.7 |
| 1994..... | 967.2 | 905.7 | 820.2 | 328.4 | 210.5 | 41.6 | 24.0 | 27.3 | 58.4 | 53.0 | 15.3 | 24.3 |
| 1995..... | 1,021.6 | 958.2 | 869.6 | 339.3 | 220.3 | 44.6 | 26.7 | 32.3 | 64.2 | 59.8 | 15.9 | 25.1 |
| 1996..... | 1,074.4 | 1,009.6 | 917.5 | 350.8 | 228.4 | 46.9 | 28.9 | 35.7 | 60.2 | 60.1 | 17.4 | 26.0 |
| 1997..... | 1,135.2 | 1,064.8 | 969.2 | 363.4 | 238.9 | 50.3 | 31.3 | 36.9 | 74.1 | 77.6 | 19.2 | 27.6 |
| 1998..... | 1,201.5 | 1,126.3 | 1,025.6 | 374.9 | 256.5 | 53.6 | 33.4 | 34.1 | 79.1 | 88.5 | 21.4 | 28.6 |
| 1999..... | 1,277.7 | 1,197.0 | 1,085.7 | 393.6 | 269.5 | 57.3 | 34.6 | 32.8 | 80.6 | 104.6 | 23.0 | 30.6 |
| 2000..... | 1,369.2 | 1,285.9 | 1,161.5 | 415.5 | 288.2 | 62.1 | 36.6 | 32.3 | 85.0 | 121.0 | 25.2 | 31.6 |
| 2001..... | 1,486.2 | 1,398.8 | 1,261.4 | 449.4 | 312.7 | 67.7 | 40.3 | 34.3 | 90.8 | 139.0 | 25.1 | 32.3 |
| 2002..... | 1,628.7 | 1,531.9 | 1,367.1 | 486.5 | 337.7 | 73.6 | 43.3 | 36.5 | 94.5 | 157.9 | 27.1 | 33.3 |
| 2003..... | 1,767.6 | 1,663.9 | 1,477.2 | 525.9 | 364.3 | 76.3 | 46.5 | 40.2 | 100.1 | 176.7 | 28.5 | 36.2 |
| 2004..... | 1,895.8 | 1,784.1 | 1,587.5 | 565.3 | 389.4 | 82.2 | 50.2 | 44.6 | 105.1 | 192.8 | 30.4 | 38.1 |
| 2005..... | 2,023.8 | 1,904.1 | 1,695.7 | 608.6 | 413.0 | 87.2 | 52.8 | 49.3 | 111.4 | 205.2 | 32.4 | 40.8 |
| 2006..... | 2,156.3 | 2,031.1 | 1,804.3 | 651.2 | 434.7 | 91.8 | 55.3 | 52.1 | 115.9 | 224.1 | 34.4 | 43.7 |
| 2007..... | 2,295.4 | 2,157.0 | 1,918.4 | 691.9 | 457.5 | 97.7 | 60.1 | 57.5 | 124.9 | 235.7 | 37.1 | 47.8 |
| 2008..... | 2,399.3 | 2,251.3 | 2,010.7 | 725.6 | 481.9 | 102.7 | 64.5 | 62.3 | 130.5 | 241.5 | 37.7 | 49.5 |
| 2009..... | 2,495.6 | 2,356.6 | 2,114.6 | 779.6 | 497.7 | 103.1 | 67.0 | 67.7 | 135.2 | 252.7 | 37.8 | 50.4 |
| 2010..... | 2,598.6 | 2,455.9 | 2,196.1 | 822.3 | 512.6 | 105.9 | 69.9 | 71.6 | 140.5 | 253.1 | 39.9 | 51.3 |
| 2011..... | 2,690.7 | 2,541.3 | 2,274.1 | 851.9 | 535.9 | 108.0 | 72.8 | 74.6 | 145.4 | 258.8 | 42.3 | 52.9 |
| 2012..... | 2,798.0 | 2,644.9 | 2,367.4 | 902.5 | 557.1 | 109.7 | 76.4 | 78.3 | 147.4 | 259.2 | 43.7 | 53.9 |
| 2013..... | 2,881.8 | 2,728.6 | 2,438.0 | 937.6 | 569.6 | 111.1 | 78.7 | 81.4 | 149.0 | 265.2 | 45.1 | 56.0 |
| 2014..... | 3,030.9 | 2,881.1 | 2,561.5 | 978.2 | 595.7 | 113.8 | 83.0 | 84.8 | 152.4 | 297.9 | 46.7 | 57.5 |
| 2015..... | 3,205.9 | 3,051.5 | 2,717.8 | 1,034.5 | 631.2 | 118.9 | 87.8 | 89.2 | 158.1 | 324.5 | 48.6 | 60.2 |
| 2016..... | 3,361.1 | 3,202.9 | 2,851.9 | 1,092.8 | 666.5 | 125.1 | 92.4 | 93.1 | 163.0 | 332.0 | 51.0 | 62.7 |
| 2017..... | 3,492.1 | 3,324.5 | 2,961.0 | 1,142.6 | 694.3 | 129.1 | 96.6 | 97.0 | 166.3 | 333.4 | 54.4 | 64.1 |

[1] Includes Health Consumption Expenditures plus, not shown here, expenditures for noncommercial medical research, and medical structures and equipment. [2] Includes Personal Health Expenditures plus, not shown, expenditures for government administration, net cost of health insurance, and government public health activities. [3] Includes items shown here, and also other health, residential, and personal services. [4] Includes health practitioners other than physicians and dentists, such as, but not limited to, chiropractors, optometrists, physical, occupational, and speech therapists, podiatrists, and private-duty nurses. [5] Services delivered by freestanding home health care facilities only. [6] Care provided in nursing care facilities (NAICS 6231), continuing care retirement communities (623311), state and local government nursing facilities, and nursing facilities operated by the Department of Veterans Affairs. [7] Retail sales of items such as contact lenses, eyeglasses and other ophthalmic products, surgical and orthopedic products, medical equipment rental, oxygen, and hearing aids. Durable products generally last over 3 years. [8] Non-prescription drugs and sundry medical items.

Source: U.S. Centers for Medicare and Medicaid Services, Office of the Actuary, National Health Statistics Group, "National Health Expenditure Data, Historical," <http://cms.gov/nationalhealthexpenddata>, accessed January 2019.

# Table 141. National Health Expenditures by Source of Funds: 1990 to 2017

[In billions of dollars (721.4 represents $721,400,000,000), except percent. Excludes Puerto Rico and Island Areas. For definitions and related information, see <https://www.cms.gov/NationalHealthExpendData/Downloads/DSM-17.pdf>]

| Source of funds | 1990 | 2000 | 2005 | 2010 | 2014 | 2015 | 2016 | 2017 |
|---|---|---|---|---|---|---|---|---|
| **National health expenditure, total** | **721.4** | **1,369.2** | **2,023.8** | **2,598.6** | **3,030.9** | **3,205.9** | **3,361.1** | **3,492.1** |
| Annual percent change [1] | 11.9 | 7.2 | 6.8 | 4.1 | 5.2 | 5.8 | 4.8 | 3.9 |
| Percent of gross domestic product | 12.1 | 13.4 | 15.5 | 17.3 | 17.3 | 17.6 | 18.0 | 17.9 |
| Consumer out of pocket | 137.9 | 198.9 | 263.8 | 299.8 | 330.9 | 340.9 | 356.1 | 365.5 |
| Health insurance | 439.1 | 919.0 | 1,414.2 | 1,877.1 | 2,229.7 | 2,382.4 | 2,504.5 | 2,604.2 |
| Private health insurance | 233.9 | 458.0 | 701.2 | 864.3 | 1,000.7 | 1,069.8 | 1,136.4 | 1,183.9 |
| Medicare | 110.2 | 224.8 | 339.8 | 519.8 | 618.6 | 649.0 | 677.1 | 705.9 |
| Medicaid (Title XIX) | 73.7 | 200.4 | 309.4 | 397.4 | 497.8 | 542.6 | 565.6 | 581.9 |
| CHIP (Title XIX and Title XXI) | (X) | 3.0 | 7.6 | 11.5 | 13.2 | 14.7 | 16.8 | 18.2 |
| Department of Defense | 10.4 | 13.7 | 26.5 | 38.3 | 41.5 | 41.6 | 41.1 | 42.3 |
| Department of Veterans Affairs | 10.9 | 19.1 | 29.8 | 45.7 | 57.9 | 64.7 | 67.4 | 72.1 |
| Other third party payers and programs | 77.1 | 124.9 | 168.9 | 203.4 | 239.0 | 244.9 | 256.8 | 265.8 |
| Worksite health care | 2.2 | 3.5 | 4.3 | 4.7 | 5.7 | 6.2 | 6.6 | 6.9 |
| Other private revenues [2] | 29.2 | 57.2 | 70.7 | 99.1 | 119.7 | 122.9 | 133.0 | 142.0 |
| Indian health services | 1.0 | 1.9 | 2.4 | 3.5 | 3.7 | 3.7 | 3.9 | 4.0 |
| Workers' compensation | 17.5 | 26.5 | 41.5 | 36.5 | 47.3 | 48.1 | 48.6 | 47.4 |
| General assistance | 5.0 | 3.9 | 6.2 | 7.1 | 6.9 | 6.8 | 6.2 | 5.9 |
| Maternal and Child health | 1.7 | 3.2 | 3.4 | 3.9 | 3.8 | 3.8 | 3.7 | 3.8 |
| Vocational rehabilitation | 0.3 | 0.4 | 0.5 | 0.6 | 0.5 | 0.5 | 0.5 | 0.5 |
| Other federal programs [3] | 1.6 | 4.5 | 6.4 | 7.7 | 12.2 | 12.6 | 12.4 | 12.0 |
| Substance Abuse and Mental Health Services Administration | 1.4 | 2.6 | 3.2 | 3.4 | 3.5 | 3.5 | 3.8 | 4.2 |
| Other state and local programs [4] | 15.9 | 18.7 | 26.9 | 32.6 | 31.0 | 32.0 | 33.1 | 33.8 |
| School health | 1.3 | 2.5 | 3.4 | 4.3 | 4.6 | 4.8 | 5.0 | 5.3 |
| Public health activity [5] | 20.0 | 43.1 | 57.3 | 75.7 | 81.4 | 83.3 | 85.6 | 88.9 |
| **Investment** | **47.3** | **83.3** | **119.7** | **142.7** | **149.9** | **154.4** | **158.2** | **167.6** |
| Research [6] | 12.7 | 25.5 | 40.3 | 49.1 | 46.0 | 46.5 | 47.6 | 50.7 |
| Structures & equipment [7] | 34.6 | 57.8 | 79.4 | 93.5 | 103.8 | 107.9 | 110.6 | 116.9 |

X Not applicable. [1] Average percent change from prior year. [2] Most common source is philanthropy; support can come from individuals or through philanthropic fund-raising organizations, and also from foundations or corporations. [3] Includes federal general hospital/medical, and pre-existing conditions insurance plans. [4] Includes temporary disability insurance, and state and local subsidies to providers. [5] Governments provide health services such as epidemiological surveillance, inoculations, immunization/vaccination services, disease prevention programs, and public health laboratories. In the National Health Expenditure Accounts, spending for these activities is reported in government public health activity. [6] Non-profit or government entities. Excludes R&D expenditures by drug and medical supply and equipment manufacturers. [7] Structures are defined as the value of new construction by the medical sector. Equipment includes the value of new capital equipment (including software). Includes establishments that provide health care, and excludes retail establishments that sell non-durable or durable medical goods. Excludes maintenance and repairs.

Source: U.S. Centers for Medicare and Medicaid Services, Office of the Actuary, National Health Statistics Group, "National Health Expenditure Data, Historical," <http://cms.gov/nationalhealthexpenddata>, accessed January 2019.

# Table 142. National Health Expenditure Projections by Source of Funds and Type of Expenditure: 2018 to 2026

[In billions of dollars (3,675.3 represents $3,675,300,000,000). For calendar years. Projections are based on the 2016 version of the National Health Expenditures (NHE) released in December 2017; projections as of February 2018. Methodology available at <https://www.cms.gov/NationalHealthExpendData/Downloads/ProjectionsMethodology.pdf>. Excludes Puerto Rico and Island Areas]

| Funding source and expenditure type | 2018 | 2019 | 2020 | 2021 | 2022 | 2023 | 2024 | 2025 | 2026 |
|---|---|---|---|---|---|---|---|---|---|
| **Total** | **3,675.3** | **3,867.6** | **4,090.9** | **4,322.0** | **4,561.8** | **4,818.5** | **5,090.9** | **5,369.8** | **5,696.2** |
| **SOURCE OF FUNDS** | | | | | | | | | |
| Consumer out-of-pocket | 379.8 | 398.3 | 417.3 | 436.7 | 459.2 | 482.0 | 506.0 | 530.7 | 555.3 |
| Health insurance | 2,755.2 | 2,898.9 | 3,075.6 | 3,258.3 | 3,446.3 | 3,649.4 | 3,866.0 | 4,086.2 | 4,351.9 |
| Private health insurance [1] | 1,244.1 | 1,286.0 | 1,348.8 | 1,410.9 | 1,472.9 | 1,544.4 | 1,619.8 | 1,697.7 | 1,776.0 |
| Medicare | 748.1 | 807.6 | 873.1 | 942.6 | 1,015.7 | 1,092.5 | 1,175.9 | 1,253.0 | 1,366.0 |
| Medicaid | 622.0 | 656.3 | 696.4 | 738.4 | 782.4 | 828.3 | 877.0 | 932.8 | 996.2 |
| Other health insurance programs [2] | 141.1 | 149.1 | 157.3 | 166.4 | 175.3 | 184.2 | 193.3 | 202.8 | 213.8 |
| Other third party payers and programs | 540.3 | 570.4 | 598.1 | 627.0 | 656.3 | 687.1 | 718.9 | 752.8 | 789.0 |
| **TYPE OF EXPENDITURE** | | | | | | | | | |
| Health consumption expenditures [3] | 3,504.3 | 3,687.8 | 3,901.7 | 4,122.6 | 4,351.7 | 4,597.2 | 4,858.0 | 5,124.3 | 5,437.1 |
| Personal health care | 3,112.7 | 3,284.0 | 3,466.3 | 3,664.1 | 3,868.9 | 4,087.7 | 4,320.2 | 4,557.1 | 4,836.3 |
| Hospital care | 1,189.9 | 1,256.0 | 1,326.4 | 1,401.7 | 1,478.3 | 1,559.8 | 1,645.3 | 1,735.5 | 1,848.2 |
| Physician and clinical services | 733.9 | 774.7 | 814.2 | 857.3 | 900.7 | 948.2 | 999.9 | 1,050.9 | 1,110.2 |
| Dental services | 134.4 | 140.4 | 147.0 | 153.7 | 161.2 | 168.7 | 176.5 | 184.3 | 192.0 |
| Other professional services [4] | 101.6 | 107.7 | 113.7 | 120.0 | 126.4 | 133.2 | 140.7 | 147.3 | 155.6 |
| Home health care [5] | 102.8 | 109.7 | 117.1 | 125.0 | 133.3 | 142.1 | 151.3 | 160.9 | 172.6 |
| Nursing care facilities and continuing care retirement communities [6] | 174.6 | 182.7 | 191.9 | 201.6 | 211.9 | 223.0 | 234.8 | 246.8 | 261.0 |
| Prescription drugs | 360.2 | 380.5 | 404.4 | 432.2 | 462.5 | 495.1 | 530.1 | 565.2 | 604.8 |
| Durable medical equipment | 55.7 | 58.8 | 62.4 | 66.4 | 70.7 | 75.1 | 79.7 | 84.1 | 89.1 |
| Nondurable medical products | 68.0 | 71.3 | 74.9 | 78.8 | 83.1 | 87.6 | 92.4 | 97.1 | 101.7 |
| Other health, residential, and personal care [7] | 191.6 | 202.2 | 214.4 | 227.4 | 240.8 | 254.8 | 269.5 | 284.9 | 301.1 |
| Government public health activity [8] | 87.1 | 89.6 | 92.1 | 94.7 | 97.5 | 100.5 | 103.5 | 106.8 | 110.9 |
| Research [9] | 52.9 | 55.4 | 58.1 | 61.0 | 64.0 | 67.2 | 70.4 | 74.2 | 78.4 |
| Structures & equipment [10] | 118.2 | 124.4 | 131.2 | 138.4 | 146.1 | 154.1 | 162.5 | 171.3 | 180.7 |

[1] Includes employer sponsored insurance and other private insurance, which also includes marketplace plans. [2] Children's Health Insurance Program (Titles XIX and XXI), Department of Defense, and Department of Veterans' Affairs. [3] See footnote 2, Table 140. [4] See footnote 4, Table 140. [5] See footnote 5, Table 140. [6] See footnote 6, Table 140. [7] See footnote 4, Table 143. [8] See footnote 5, Table 141. [9] See footnote 6, Table 141. [10] See footnote 7, Table 141.

Source: U.S. Centers for Medicare and Medicaid Services, Office of the Actuary, National Health Statistics Group, "National Health Expenditure Data, Projected," <http://cms.gov/nationalhealthexpenddata>, accessed January 2019.

## Table 143. Health Consumption Expenditures—Per Capita Spending by Type of Expenditure: 2000 to 2017

[In dollars, except percent. Based on U.S. Census Bureau estimates of total U.S. resident population. Health consumption expenditures include all personal health care spending, government administration and the net cost of private health insurance, and public health activities. Excludes investment in research, structures, and equipment. Excludes Puerto Rico and Island Areas]

| Type of expenditure | 2000 | 2005 | 2010 | 2012 | 2013 | 2014 | 2015 | 2016 | 2017 |
|---|---|---|---|---|---|---|---|---|---|
| **Total** [1] | **4,560** | **6,448** | **7,950** | **8,438** | **8,644** | **9,057** | **9,524** | **9,920** | **10,224** |
| Annual percent change [2] | (NA) | 5.7 | 3.4 | 3.3 | 2.4 | 4.8 | 5.2 | 4.2 | 3.1 |
| Hospital care | 1,474 | 2,061 | 2,662 | 2,879 | 2,970 | 3,075 | 3,229 | 3,385 | 3,514 |
| Physician and clinical services | 1,022 | 1,399 | 1,659 | 1,777 | 1,804 | 1,873 | 1,970 | 2,064 | 2,135 |
| Dental services | 220 | 295 | 343 | 350 | 352 | 358 | 371 | 387 | 397 |
| Other professional services [3] | 130 | 179 | 226 | 244 | 249 | 261 | 274 | 286 | 297 |
| Other health, residential, and personal care [4] | 227 | 322 | 418 | 444 | 457 | 476 | 514 | 537 | 563 |
| Home health care | 115 | 167 | 232 | 250 | 258 | 266 | 278 | 288 | 298 |
| Nursing care facilities and continuing care retirement communities | 302 | 377 | 455 | 470 | 472 | 479 | 493 | 505 | 511 |
| Prescription drugs | 429 | 695 | 819 | 827 | 840 | 937 | 1,013 | 1,028 | 1,025 |
| Durable medical equipment [5] | 89 | 110 | 129 | 139 | 143 | 147 | 152 | 158 | 167 |
| Other nondurable medical products [6] | 112 | 138 | 166 | 172 | 177 | 181 | 188 | 194 | 197 |
| Public health activities [7] | 153 | 194 | 245 | 246 | 250 | 256 | 260 | 265 | 273 |

NA Not available. [1] Includes other items, not shown separately. [2] Average annual growth from previous year. [3] See footnote 4, Table 140. [4] Includes expenditures for residential care facilities (NAICS 623210 and 623220), ambulance providers (NAICS 621910), medical care delivered in non-traditional settings (such as community centers, senior citizens centers, schools, and military field stations), and expenditures for Home and Community Waiver programs under Medicaid. [5] See footnote 7, Table 140. [6] See footnote 8, Table 140. [7] See footnote 5, Table 141.

Source: U.S. Centers for Medicare and Medicaid Services, Office of the Actuary, National Health Statistics Group, "National Health Expenditure Data, Historical," <https://cms.gov/nationalhealthexpenddata>, accessed January 2019.

## Table 144. Health Consumption Expenditures by Type of Expenditure and Source of Funds: 2017

[In billions of dollars (3,324.5 represents $3,324,500,000,000). Excludes Puerto Rico and Island Areas. Excludes investment in research, structures, and equipment]

| Type of expenditure | Total | Out-of-pocket | Health insurance Total | Private health insurance | Medicare | Medicaid | Other health insurance programs [1] | Other third party payers and programs [2] |
|---|---|---|---|---|---|---|---|---|
| **Total** | **3,324.5** | **365.5** | **2,604.2** | **1,183.9** | **705.9** | **581.9** | **132.6** | **265.8** |
| Personal health care [3] | 2,961.0 | 365.5 | 2,347.3 | 1,039.8 | 660.0 | 521.3 | 126.1 | 248.3 |
| Hospital care | 1,142.6 | 33.9 | 1,001.8 | 455.3 | 282.9 | 193.9 | 69.6 | 106.9 |
| Physician and clinical services | 694.3 | 60.1 | 567.6 | 300.9 | 159.0 | 75.3 | 32.3 | 66.7 |
| Dental services | 129.1 | 53.0 | 75.6 | 58.2 | 0.9 | 12.5 | 4.0 | 0.5 |
| Other health, residential, and personal care [4] | 183.1 | 6.5 | 127.0 | 13.6 | 5.0 | 105.9 | 2.5 | 49.6 |
| Home health care | 97.0 | 9.0 | 85.4 | 10.8 | 38.8 | 35.0 | 0.7 | 2.7 |
| Nursing care facilities and continuing care retirement communities | 166.3 | 44.3 | 109.8 | 16.6 | 37.7 | 50.2 | 5.4 | 12.1 |
| Prescription drugs | 333.4 | 46.7 | 285.0 | 140.1 | 100.9 | 33.0 | 11.0 | 1.8 |
| Durable medical equipment | 54.4 | 26.0 | 27.6 | 11.4 | 8.1 | 7.9 | 0.2 | 0.9 |
| Government administration [5] | 45.0 | (X) | 41.8 | (X) | 9.7 | 27.0 | 5.1 | 3.1 |
| Net cost of health insurance [5] | 229.5 | (X) | 215.1 | 144.1 | 36.1 | 33.6 | 1.4 | 14.4 |
| Public health activities [6] | 88.9 | (X) | (X) | (X) | (X) | (X) | (X) | (X) |

X Not applicable. [1] Includes Children's Health Insurance Program (CHIP) Titles XIX and XXI, Department of Defense, and Department of Veterans Affairs. [2] Includes worksite health care, other private revenues, Indian Health Service, workers' compensation, general assistance, maternal and child health, vocational rehabilitation, other federal programs, Substance Abuse and Mental Health Services Administration, other state and local programs, and school health. [3] Comprises all medical goods and services that are rendered to treat or prevent a specific disease or condition in a specific person. Includes expenditures for other items, not shown separately. [4] See footnote 4, Table 143. [5] See source for definitions. [6] See footnote 5, Table 141.

Source: U.S. Centers for Medicare and Medicaid Services, Office of the Actuary, National Health Statistics Group, "National Health Expenditure Data, Historical," <https://cms.gov/nationalhealthexpenddata>, accessed January 2019.

## Table 145. Personal Health Care Expenditures by Source of Funds: 2000 to 2017

[In billions of dollars (1,161.5 represents $1,161,500,000,000). Excludes Puerto Rico and Island Areas]

| Source of funds | 2000 | 2005 | 2010 | 2012 | 2013 | 2014 | 2015 | 2016 | 2017 |
|---|---|---|---|---|---|---|---|---|---|
| **Personal health care expenditures** | **1,161.5** | **1,695.7** | **2,196.1** | **2,367.4** | **2,438.0** | **2,561.5** | **2,717.8** | **2,851.9** | **2,961.0** |
| Out-of-pocket | 198.9 | 263.8 | 299.8 | 318.8 | 325.9 | 330.9 | 340.9 | 356.1 | 365.5 |
| Health insurance | 843.8 | 1,278.8 | 1,701.0 | 1,835.9 | 1,892.5 | 2,009.7 | 2,150.9 | 2,257.8 | 2,347.3 |
| Private health insurance | 405.6 | 604.4 | 755.9 | 816.4 | 831.3 | 875.3 | 944.2 | 1,004.3 | 1,039.8 |
| Medicare | 216.3 | 326.3 | 489.1 | 533.8 | 554.6 | 580.5 | 607.3 | 630.3 | 660.0 |
| Medicaid | 186.9 | 287.6 | 365.8 | 388.4 | 405.9 | 446.6 | 484.1 | 504.2 | 521.3 |
| Other health insurance [1] | 34.9 | 60.5 | 90.3 | 97.3 | 100.8 | 107.3 | 115.2 | 119.1 | 126.1 |
| Other third party payers and programs [2] | 118.9 | 153.1 | 195.3 | 212.7 | 219.5 | 220.9 | 226.0 | 238.0 | 248.3 |

[1] Includes Children's Health Insurance Program (Titles XIX and XXI), Department of Defense, and Department of Veterans Affairs. [2] See footnote 2, Table 144.

Source: U.S. Centers for Medicare and Medicaid Services, Office of the Actuary, National Health Statistics Group, "National Health Expenditure Data, Historical," <https://cms.gov/nationalhealthexpenddata>, accessed January 2019.

## Table 146. National Health Expenditures by Sponsor: 2000 to 2017

[In billions of dollars (1,369.2 represents $1,369,200,000,000). Excludes Puerto Rico and Island Areas. Type of sponsor is defined as the entity that is ultimately responsible for financing the health care bill. These sponsors pay health insurance premiums and out-of-pocket costs, or finance health care through dedicated taxes and/or general revenues. See source for sponsor inclusion and exclusion details]

| Type of sponsor | 2000 | 2005 | 2010 | 2013 | 2014 | 2015 | 2016 | 2017 |
|---|---|---|---|---|---|---|---|---|
| Total | 1,369.2 | 2,023.8 | 2,598.6 | 2,881.8 | 3,030.9 | 3,205.9 | 3,361.1 | 3,492.1 |
| Business, households and other private revenues | 882.8 | 1,225.4 | 1,445.6 | 1,620.6 | 1,668.8 | 1,746.9 | 1,836.7 | 1,914.1 |
| Private business [1] | 335.3 | 469.5 | 519.0 | 580.4 | 607.9 | 634.5 | 669.1 | 696.5 |
| Household [2] | 443.3 | 618.8 | 751.6 | 833.0 | 855.8 | 899.7 | 942.8 | 978.6 |
| Other private revenues | 104.2 | 137.1 | 175.0 | 207.2 | 205.0 | 212.7 | 224.7 | 239.0 |
| Governments | 486.4 | 798.5 | 1,153.0 | 1,261.2 | 1,362.2 | 1,459.0 | 1,524.4 | 1,577.9 |
| Federal government [3] | 260.8 | 450.6 | 731.2 | 752.7 | 835.0 | 907.9 | 952.4 | 982.4 |
| State and local government [4] | 225.6 | 347.9 | 421.8 | 508.5 | 527.2 | 551.1 | 572.0 | 595.5 |

[1] Includes employer contributions to employer-sponsored health insurance premiums, employer Medicare Hospital Insurance (HI) Trust Fund payroll taxes, workers' compensation, temporary disability insurance, and worksite health care. [2] Includes employee contributions to employer-sponsored health insurance premiums, directly purchased health insurance, the medical portion of property and casualty insurance premiums, employee and self-employment payroll taxes and premiums paid to the Medicare HI Trust Fund, premiums paid to the Medicare Supplementary Medical Insurance (SMI) Trust Fund, premiums paid for the Pre-existing Condition Insurance Program (PCIP) for 2010-2014, and out-of-pocket health spending. [3] Includes employer contributions to employer-sponsored health insurance premiums, employer Medicare HI payroll taxes, federal general revenue and Medicare net Trust Fund expenditures, federal Medicaid expenditures, the federal portion of Medicaid buy-ins for the Medicare premiums of people eligible for both Medicaid and Medicare (dual eligibles), Medicare Retiree Drug Subsidy (RDS) payments to private business and state and local government employer plans beginning in 2006, Marketplace tax credits and subsidies, and other federal health programs. [4] Includes employer contributions to employer-sponsored health insurance premiums, employer Medicare HI payroll taxes, state and local Medicaid expenditures, the state and local portion of Medicaid buy-ins for the Medicare premiums of people eligible for both Medicaid and Medicare (dual eligibles), and other programs.

Source: U.S. Centers for Medicare and Medicaid Services, Office of the Actuary, National Health Statistics Group, "National Health Expenditure Data, Historical," <https://cms.gov/nationalhealthexpenddata>, accessed January 2019.

## Table 147. Hospital Care, Physician and Clinical Services, Nursing Care Facilities and Continuing Care Retirement Communities, and Prescription Drug Expenditures by Source of Funds: 2000 to 2017

[In billions of dollars (415.5 represents $415,500,000,000). Excludes Puerto Rico and Island Areas]

| Source of payment | 2000 | 2005 | 2010 | 2013 | 2014 | 2015 | 2016 | 2017 |
|---|---|---|---|---|---|---|---|---|
| Hospital care, total | 415.5 | 608.6 | 822.3 | 937.6 | 978.2 | 1,034.5 | 1,092.8 | 1,142.6 |
| Out-of-pocket | 13.4 | 19.7 | 27.8 | 33.8 | 32.8 | 31.2 | 32.1 | 33.9 |
| Health insurance | 358.2 | 531.6 | 714.0 | 808.1 | 849.5 | 908.9 | 961.9 | 1,001.8 |
| Private health insurance | 141.0 | 215.9 | 300.6 | 349.4 | 366.2 | 400.4 | 433.7 | 455.3 |
| Medicare | 123.4 | 176.4 | 220.3 | 245.7 | 252.7 | 260.7 | 272.6 | 282.9 |
| Medicaid | 70.9 | 103.8 | 141.8 | 156.1 | 169.8 | 183.9 | 189.4 | 193.9 |
| CHIP [1] | 0.9 | 2.7 | 3.2 | 3.5 | 3.4 | 3.7 | 4.4 | 4.7 |
| Dept. of Defense | 7.6 | 12.0 | 16.5 | 16.5 | 16.7 | 15.8 | 16.2 | 16.5 |
| Veterans Affairs | 14.3 | 20.8 | 31.7 | 36.9 | 40.7 | 44.5 | 45.8 | 48.4 |
| Other third party payers and programs [2] | 43.9 | 57.3 | 80.5 | 95.8 | 95.8 | 94.4 | 98.7 | 106.9 |
| Physician and clinical services, total | 288.2 | 413.0 | 512.6 | 569.6 | 595.7 | 631.2 | 666.5 | 694.3 |
| Out-of-pocket | 31.9 | 41.7 | 48.7 | 53.4 | 54.4 | 56.4 | 58.9 | 60.1 |
| Health insurance | 220.1 | 325.6 | 411.1 | 457.7 | 484.0 | 513.2 | 540.5 | 567.6 |
| Private health insurance | 135.4 | 197.9 | 231.1 | 249.7 | 257.1 | 271.4 | 288.8 | 300.9 |
| Medicare | 58.7 | 85.6 | 115.8 | 132.1 | 137.9 | 144.4 | 149.3 | 159.0 |
| Medicaid | 19.3 | 30.1 | 43.3 | 51.5 | 63.4 | 69.1 | 72.2 | 75.3 |
| CHIP [1] | 0.7 | 1.7 | 3.1 | 3.5 | 3.2 | 3.5 | 3.9 | 4.3 |
| Dept. of Defense | 4.7 | 7.9 | 12.1 | 13.7 | 14.4 | 14.8 | 15.4 | 16.1 |
| Veterans Affairs | 1.3 | 2.5 | 5.8 | 7.2 | 7.9 | 9.9 | 10.9 | 12.0 |
| Other third party payers and programs [2] | 36.1 | 45.7 | 52.7 | 58.4 | 57.3 | 61.5 | 67.1 | 66.7 |
| Nursing care facilities and continuing care retirement communities, total | 85.0 | 111.4 | 140.5 | 149.0 | 152.4 | 158.1 | 163.0 | 166.3 |
| Out-of-pocket | 27.1 | 32.5 | 37.5 | 39.4 | 39.6 | 41.5 | 44.0 | 44.3 |
| Health insurance | 52.0 | 71.8 | 93.4 | 99.0 | 101.6 | 105.5 | 107.4 | 109.8 |
| Private health insurance | 7.5 | 7.1 | 10.7 | 11.7 | 12.2 | 14.0 | 15.4 | 16.6 |
| Medicare | 10.8 | 20.5 | 32.3 | 34.7 | 35.6 | 37.1 | 37.2 | 37.7 |
| Medicaid | 31.9 | 41.3 | 46.3 | 48.1 | 49.1 | 49.4 | 49.8 | 50.2 |
| Veterans Affairs | 1.9 | 2.8 | 4.0 | 4.5 | 4.7 | 5.0 | 5.0 | 5.4 |
| Other third party payers and programs [2] | 5.9 | 7.1 | 9.6 | 10.7 | 11.2 | 11.1 | 11.6 | 12.1 |
| Prescription drugs, total | 121.0 | 205.2 | 253.1 | 265.2 | 297.9 | 324.5 | 332.0 | 333.4 |
| Out-of-pocket | 33.6 | 51.3 | 45.2 | 43.6 | 44.8 | 45.5 | 46.7 | 46.7 |
| Health insurance | 85.1 | 150.0 | 204.5 | 219.2 | 251.1 | 277.0 | 283.5 | 285.0 |
| Private health insurance | 61.1 | 102.1 | 116.1 | 113.9 | 128.8 | 142.9 | 144.6 | 140.1 |
| Medicare | 2.1 | 3.9 | 58.9 | 74.0 | 84.8 | 92.4 | 96.6 | 100.9 |
| Medicaid | 19.8 | 36.5 | 20.4 | 22.1 | 27.3 | 30.5 | 32.0 | 33.0 |
| CHIP [1] | 0.3 | 1.1 | 1.4 | 1.5 | 1.4 | 1.6 | 1.8 | 2.0 |
| Dept. of Defense | 0.7 | 3.6 | 4.7 | 4.9 | 5.8 | 6.3 | 4.9 | 5.1 |
| Veterans Affairs | 1.1 | 2.7 | 3.0 | 2.8 | 3.0 | 3.3 | 3.6 | 3.9 |
| Other third party payers and programs [2] | 2.3 | 3.9 | 3.4 | 2.4 | 2.0 | 1.9 | 1.8 | 1.8 |

[1] Children's Health Insurance Program (Titles XIX and XXI), signed into law in 1997. [2] Includes worksite health care, other private revenues, Indian Health Service, workers' compensation, general assistance, maternal and child health, vocational rehabilitation, other federal programs, Substance Abuse and Mental Health Services Administration, other state and local programs, and school health.

Source: U.S. Centers for Medicare and Medicaid Services, Office of the Actuary, National Health Statistics Group, "National Health Expenditure Data, Historical," <https://cms.gov/nationalhealthexpenddata>, accessed January 2019.

# Table 148. Medical Care Consumer Price Indexes: 1990 to 2018

[Indexes with base of 1982-1984=100. Indexes are annual averages of monthly data based on components of consumer price index for all urban consumers; for explanation, see text, Section 14 and Appendix III]

| Year | Medical care, total | Medical care services | | | | Medical care commodities | | Annual percent change [3] | | |
|---|---|---|---|---|---|---|---|---|---|---|
| | | Total [1] | Professional services | | | Hospital and related services | Total [2] | Pre-scription drugs | Medical care, total | Medical care services | Medical care com-modities |
| | | | Total [1] | Physi-cians | Dental | | | | | | |
| 1990........ | 162.8 | 162.7 | 156.1 | 160.8 | 155.8 | 178.0 | 163.4 | 181.7 | 9.0 | 9.3 | 8.4 |
| 1995........ | 220.5 | 224.2 | 201.0 | 208.8 | 206.8 | 257.8 | 204.5 | 235.0 | 4.5 | 5.1 | 1.9 |
| 2000........ | 260.8 | 266.0 | 237.7 | 244.7 | 258.5 | 317.3 | 238.1 | 285.4 | 4.1 | 4.3 | 3.2 |
| 2005........ | 323.2 | 336.7 | 281.7 | 287.5 | 324.0 | 439.9 | 276.0 | 349.0 | 4.2 | 4.8 | 2.5 |
| 2010........ | 388.4 | 411.2 | 328.2 | 331.3 | 398.8 | 607.7 | 314.7 | 407.8 | 3.4 | 3.5 | 3.1 |
| 2011........ | 400.3 | 423.8 | 335.7 | 340.3 | 408.0 | 641.5 | 324.1 | 425.0 | 3.0 | 3.1 | 3.0 |
| 2012........ | 414.9 | 440.3 | 342.0 | 347.3 | 417.5 | 672.1 | 333.6 | 440.1 | 3.7 | 3.9 | 2.9 |
| 2013........ | 425.1 | 454.0 | 349.5 | 354.2 | 431.8 | 701.3 | 335.1 | 442.6 | 2.5 | 3.1 | 0.4 |
| 2014........ | 435.3 | 464.8 | 355.2 | 359.1 | 441.0 | 733.8 | 343.4 | 458.3 | 2.4 | 2.4 | 2.5 |
| 2015........ | 446.8 | 476.2 | 361.5 | 366.1 | 452.2 | 761.9 | 354.6 | 479.3 | 2.6 | 2.4 | 3.3 |
| 2016........ | 463.7 | 494.8 | 371.5 | 378.1 | 465.0 | 795.1 | 366.8 | 502.5 | 3.8 | 3.9 | 3.4 |
| 2017........ | 475.3 | 506.8 | 375.1 | 380.1 | 472.6 | 831.7 | 377.0 | 519.6 | 2.5 | 2.4 | 2.8 |
| 2018........ | 484.7 | 517.8 | 378.4 | 380.5 | 485.5 | 866.9 | 381.4 | 528.0 | 2.0 | 2.2 | 1.2 |

[1] Includes other services not shown separately. [2] Includes other commodities not shown separately. [3] Percent change from the immediate prior year.

Source: U.S. Bureau of Labor Statistics, Consumer Price Index Databases, <https://www.bls.gov/cpi/data.htm>, accessed January 2019.

# Table 149. Average Annual Expenditures Per Consumer Unit for Health Care: 2017

[In dollars, except percent. Expenditures are direct out-of-pocket expenditures. Consumers units may be all members in a housing unit (families), a person living alone or sharing a household with others and financially independent, or 2 or more unrelated persons living together who share expenses. See also text for Section 13, and source. For composition of regions, see map, inside front cover]

| Consumer characteristic | Health care, total | | Health Insur-ance | Medical services | Drugs and medical sup-plies [1] | Percent distribution | | |
|---|---|---|---|---|---|---|---|---|
| | Amount | Percent of total expendi-tures | | | | Health insur-ance | Medical services | Drugs and medical sup-plies [1] |
| **Total**........................ | **4,928** | **8.2** | **3,414** | **872** | **642** | **69.3** | **17.7** | **13.0** |
| Age of reference person: | | | | | | | | |
| Under 25 years old........................ | 1,547 | 4.6 | 1,009 | 387 | 150 | 65.2 | 25.0 | 9.7 |
| 25 to 34 years old........................ | 3,163 | 5.7 | 2,261 | 588 | 315 | 71.5 | 18.6 | 10.0 |
| 35 to 44 years old........................ | 4,348 | 6.3 | 3,005 | 832 | 511 | 69.1 | 19.1 | 11.8 |
| 45 to 54 years old........................ | 4,967 | 6.7 | 3,429 | 928 | 610 | 69.0 | 18.7 | 12.3 |
| 55 to 64 years old........................ | 5,777 | 8.9 | 3,815 | 1,196 | 765 | 66.0 | 20.7 | 13.2 |
| 65 years old and older........................ | 6,620 | 13.4 | 4,712 | 911 | 997 | 71.2 | 13.8 | 15.1 |
| Race of reference person: | | | | | | | | |
| White and other [2]........................ | 5,244 | 8.5 | 3,575 | 960 | 709 | 68.2 | 18.3 | 13.5 |
| Asian........................ | 4,658 | 6.4 | 3,482 | 782 | 395 | 74.8 | 16.8 | 8.5 |
| Black........................ | 3,079 | 7.1 | 2,402 | 364 | 314 | 78.0 | 11.8 | 10.2 |
| Origin of reference person: | | | | | | | | |
| Hispanic........................ | 2,946 | 6.0 | 2,148 | 479 | 320 | 72.9 | 16.3 | 10.9 |
| Non-Hispanic........................ | 5,239 | 8.5 | 3,613 | 934 | 692 | 69.0 | 17.8 | 13.2 |
| Region of residence: | | | | | | | | |
| Northeast........................ | 5,126 | 8.0 | 3,582 | 884 | 660 | 69.9 | 17.2 | 12.9 |
| Midwest........................ | 5,262 | 9.2 | 3,607 | 961 | 694 | 68.5 | 18.3 | 13.2 |
| South........................ | 4,669 | 8.5 | 3,299 | 742 | 628 | 70.7 | 15.9 | 13.5 |
| West........................ | 4,892 | 7.1 | 3,291 | 1,000 | 601 | 67.3 | 20.4 | 12.3 |
| Size of consumer unit: | | | | | | | | |
| One person........................ | 2,967 | 8.2 | 2,051 | 479 | 437 | 69.1 | 16.1 | 14.7 |
| Two or more persons........................ | 5,720 | 8.2 | 3,964 | 1,030 | 725 | 69.3 | 18.0 | 12.7 |
| Two persons........................ | 6,218 | 9.6 | 4,277 | 1,077 | 865 | 68.8 | 17.3 | 13.9 |
| Three persons........................ | 5,529 | 7.8 | 3,921 | 966 | 642 | 70.9 | 17.5 | 11.6 |
| Four persons........................ | 5,558 | 6.9 | 3,871 | 1,102 | 586 | 69.6 | 19.8 | 10.5 |
| Five persons or more........................ | 4,467 | 6.1 | 3,052 | 874 | 541 | 68.3 | 19.6 | 12.1 |
| Income before taxes, by quintile: | | | | | | | | |
| Lowest 20 percent........................ | 2,492 | 9.6 | 1,761 | 335 | 396 | 70.7 | 13.4 | 15.9 |
| Second 20 percent........................ | 3,889 | 9.9 | 2,775 | 525 | 588 | 71.4 | 13.5 | 15.1 |
| Third 20 percent........................ | 4,642 | 9.2 | 3,236 | 771 | 634 | 69.7 | 16.6 | 13.7 |
| Fourth 20 percent........................ | 5,764 | 8.5 | 3,967 | 1,119 | 678 | 68.8 | 19.4 | 11.8 |
| Highest 20 percent........................ | 7,857 | 6.7 | 5,335 | 1,610 | 912 | 67.9 | 20.5 | 11.6 |
| Education: | | | | | | | | |
| Less than a high school graduate............ | 2,601 | 8.7 | 1,777 | 415 | 408 | 68.3 | 16.0 | 15.7 |
| High school graduate........................ | 3,553 | 9.4 | 2,510 | 549 | 495 | 70.6 | 15.5 | 13.9 |
| High school graduate with some college.... | 4,031 | 8.3 | 2,839 | 651 | 540 | 70.4 | 16.1 | 13.4 |
| Associate's degree........................ | 4,781 | 8.7 | 3,391 | 795 | 595 | 70.9 | 16.6 | 12.4 |
| Bachelor's degree........................ | 5,757 | 8.0 | 3,964 | 1,098 | 695 | 68.9 | 19.1 | 12.1 |
| Master's, professional, or doctoral degree... | 7,290 | 7.6 | 4,943 | 1,388 | 959 | 67.8 | 19.0 | 13.2 |

[1] Includes prescription and nonprescription drugs. [2] Other races includes Native Hawaiian or other Pacific Islander, American Indian or Alaska Native, and approximately 1 percent reporting more than one race.

Source: U.S. Bureau of Labor Statistics, "Consumer Expenditure Survey, Annual Calendar Year Tables, 2017," <http://www.bls.gov/cex/tables.htm>, accessed December 2018.

# Table 150. Medical Expenditures by Health Condition in Current and Chained (2009) Dollars and Per Capita: 2000 to 2015

[In billions of dollars (1,109.59 represents $1,109,590,000,000), except as noted. Health conditions are classified according to the International Classification of Diseases, 9th revision (ICD-9). Based on Bureau of Economic Analysis' Health Care Satellite Account, Blended Account. The Blended Account blends data from multiple sources, including large claims databases. The BEA also has available health expenditure data based on the Medical Expenditure Panel Survey. See source for details]

| Health expense item | Current dollars (billions) | | | Chained (2009) billion dollars | | | Per capita (dollars) | | |
|---|---|---|---|---|---|---|---|---|---|
| | 2000 | 2010 | 2015 | 2000 | 2010 | 2015 | 2000 | 2010 | 2015 |
| **Total health** | **1,109.59** | **2,080.44** | **2,595.53** | **1,616.19** | **2,006.89** | **2,226.15** | **3,932.45** | **6,725.24** | **8,088.37** |
| Health services | 1,052.23 | 1,979.19 | 2,471.32 | 1,554.03 | 1,905.19 | 2,102.99 | 3,729.16 | 6,397.94 | 7,701.30 |
| Medical services by disease | 900.75 | 1,722.41 | 2,180.62 | 1,333.63 | 1,654.18 | 1,845.01 | 3,192.31 | 5,567.87 | 6,795.40 |
| Infectious and parasitic diseases | 20.31 | 55.40 | 89.73 | 34.64 | 48.92 | 52.95 | 71.98 | 179.09 | 279.62 |
| Neoplasms | 60.18 | 110.18 | 135.84 | 75.08 | 102.77 | 128.53 | 213.28 | 356.17 | 423.31 |
| Endocrine, nutritional, and metabolic diseases and immunity disorders | 54.58 | 126.63 | 168.66 | 80.00 | 118.54 | 135.57 | 193.43 | 409.34 | 525.59 |
| Mental illness | 41.20 | 78.08 | 109.60 | 50.85 | 82.17 | 103.90 | 146.02 | 252.40 | 341.54 |
| Diseases of the nervous system and sense organs | 60.05 | 117.66 | 159.53 | 100.63 | 104.93 | 135.53 | 212.82 | 380.35 | 497.14 |
| Diseases of the circulatory system | 153.72 | 234.98 | 259.15 | 160.22 | 234.63 | 258.48 | 544.79 | 759.60 | 807.58 |
| Diseases of the respiratory system | 92.06 | 147.43 | 176.48 | 150.56 | 136.20 | 133.23 | 326.27 | 476.58 | 549.96 |
| Diseases of the digestive system | 58.47 | 97.48 | 118.20 | 107.68 | 100.03 | 92.68 | 207.22 | 315.11 | 368.34 |
| Diseases of the genitourinary system | 58.36 | 110.46 | 129.49 | 87.30 | 109.41 | 107.70 | 206.83 | 357.07 | 403.53 |
| Complications of pregnancy, childbirth, and the puerperium | 25.73 | 40.23 | 50.53 | 43.52 | 39.05 | 40.40 | 91.19 | 130.05 | 157.47 |
| Diseases of the skin and subcutaneous organs | 21.12 | 39.47 | 52.07 | 43.13 | 44.59 | 46.09 | 74.85 | 127.59 | 162.26 |
| Diseases of the musculoskeletal system and connective tissue | 77.35 | 171.89 | 219.80 | 111.37 | 164.77 | 176.17 | 274.13 | 555.65 | 684.96 |
| Injury and poisoning | 65.12 | 110.66 | 133.36 | 102.11 | 100.79 | 109.13 | 230.79 | 357.72 | 415.59 |
| Symptoms, signs, and ill-defined conditions | 80.14 | 210.42 | 289.88 | 137.35 | 202.17 | 253.32 | 284.02 | 680.20 | 903.34 |
| Other diseases | 32.35 | 71.44 | 88.46 | 64.61 | 67.27 | 79.81 | 114.65 | 230.94 | 275.17 |
| Diseases of blood and blood-forming organs | 8.71 | 21.41 | 25.49 | 24.28 | 17.37 | 14.97 | 30.87 | 69.21 | 79.43 |
| Congenital anomalies | 4.59 | 7.45 | 8.55 | 5.10 | 5.64 | 8.68 | 16.27 | 24.08 | 26.64 |
| Conditions originating in perinatal period | 4.87 | 6.86 | 6.81 | 7.20 | 7.46 | 15.98 | 17.26 | 22.18 | 21.22 |
| Residual codes, unclassified, all E codes [1] | 14.18 | 35.73 | 47.45 | 29.45 | 37.36 | 45.21 | 50.25 | 115.50 | 147.87 |
| Medical services by provider | 151.48 | 256.78 | 290.70 | 220.78 | 251.04 | 257.87 | 536.80 | 830.07 | 905.90 |
| Dental services | 63.57 | 104.48 | 118.03 | 95.42 | 101.69 | 101.41 | 225.30 | 337.74 | 367.81 |
| Nursing homes | 87.91 | 152.29 | 172.67 | 125.35 | 149.35 | 156.50 | 311.56 | 492.29 | 538.09 |
| Proprietary and government nursing homes | 56.85 | 100.22 | 118.23 | 81.06 | 98.28 | 107.15 | 201.48 | 323.97 | 368.44 |
| Nonprofit nursing homes services to households | 31.06 | 52.07 | 54.44 | 44.29 | 51.08 | 49.35 | 110.08 | 168.32 | 169.65 |
| Medical products, appliances and equipment | 57.36 | 101.26 | 124.21 | 63.43 | 101.83 | 124.34 | 203.29 | 327.33 | 387.07 |
| Pharmaceutical and other medical products | 25.19 | 45.64 | 56.55 | 27.40 | 45.86 | 57.94 | 89.27 | 147.54 | 176.22 |
| Pharmaceutical products (excludes prescription drugs) [2] | 23.24 | 41.66 | 51.44 | 25.35 | 41.79 | 52.75 | 82.36 | 134.67 | 160.30 |
| Nonprescription drugs | 23.24 | 41.66 | 51.44 | 25.35 | 41.79 | 52.75 | 82.36 | 134.67 | 160.30 |
| Other medical products | 1.95 | 3.99 | 5.12 | 2.06 | 4.07 | 5.19 | 6.91 | 12.90 | 15.96 |
| Therapeutic appliances and equipment | 32.17 | 55.61 | 67.66 | 36.05 | 55.97 | 66.45 | 114.01 | 179.77 | 210.85 |
| Corrective eyeglasses and contact lenses | 19.91 | 29.71 | 34.78 | 23.34 | 29.51 | 33.18 | 70.56 | 96.04 | 108.38 |
| Therapeutic medical equipment | 12.26 | 25.91 | 32.88 | 12.95 | 26.46 | 33.36 | 43.45 | 83.76 | 102.46 |

[1] E codes cover external causes of injury or poisoning. [2] Excludes prescription drugs; prescription drug expenses have been allocated by health condition.

Source: U.S. Bureau of Economic Analysis, Health Care Satellite Account, "Blended Account, 2000-2015," <http://www.bea.gov/national/health_care_satellite_account.htm>, accessed January 2019.

# Table 151. Medicare Enrollment by State: 2017 and 2018

[In thousands (58,457.2 represents 58,457,200). Covers Medicare beneficiaries enrolled in either Hospital Insurance and/or Supplementary Medical Insurance. Enrollment counts are determined by using a person-year methodology; for each calendar year, total person-year counts are determined by summing the total number of months that each beneficiary is enrolled during the year and dividing by 12 (see source for more information). Numbers may not add to totals because of rounding]

| State | 2017 | | | 2018 | | |
|---|---|---|---|---|---|---|
| | Total Medicare | Original Medicare [1] | Medicare Advantage [2] | Total Medicare | Original Medicare [1] | Medicare Advantage [2] |
| **Total** | **58,457.2** | **38,667.8** | **19,789.4** | **59,924.4** | **38,599.7** | **21,324.7** |
| **United States [3]** | **57,223.8** | **38,001.8** | **19,222.0** | **58,678.1** | **37,930.7** | **20,747.4** |
| Alabama | 1,007.4 | 640.5 | 366.9 | 1,026.6 | 623.6 | 403.0 |
| Alaska | 91.9 | 90.5 | 1.3 | 96.1 | 94.6 | 1.5 |
| Arizona | 1,226.7 | 753.9 | 472.7 | 1,270.0 | 773.8 | 496.2 |
| Arkansas | 616.2 | 480.2 | 136.0 | 627.1 | 475.7 | 151.4 |
| California | 5,965.5 | 3,473.4 | 2,492.1 | 6,115.2 | 3,502.7 | 2,612.4 |
| Colorado | 847.7 | 530.1 | 317.6 | 880.1 | 547.2 | 332.9 |
| Connecticut | 654.7 | 469.8 | 184.9 | 667.0 | 420.5 | 246.5 |
| Delaware | 193.6 | 171.2 | 22.4 | 200.9 | 173.0 | 27.9 |
| District of Columbia | 91.1 | 76.6 | 14.5 | 92.4 | 75.8 | 16.5 |
| Florida | 4,295.2 | 2,468.0 | 1,827.2 | 4,408.7 | 2,455.5 | 1,953.2 |
| Georgia | 1,624.1 | 1,051.5 | 572.6 | 1,674.2 | 1,044.9 | 629.3 |
| Hawaii | 259.4 | 142.3 | 117.1 | 266.6 | 145.1 | 121.5 |
| Idaho | 306.4 | 210.4 | 96.0 | 320.0 | 216.7 | 103.4 |
| Illinois | 2,149.6 | 1,632.4 | 517.3 | 2,191.5 | 1,633.2 | 558.3 |
| Indiana | 1,204.9 | 883.8 | 321.1 | 1,232.3 | 869.2 | 363.1 |
| Iowa | 598.2 | 490.2 | 108.0 | 611.9 | 490.4 | 121.5 |
| Kansas | 509.9 | 429.8 | 80.1 | 522.8 | 433.9 | 88.9 |
| Kentucky | 896.0 | 637.6 | 258.3 | 911.6 | 630.9 | 280.7 |
| Louisiana | 828.7 | 551.5 | 277.2 | 848.2 | 546.8 | 301.4 |
| Maine | 322.2 | 231.1 | 91.0 | 331.0 | 226.2 | 104.8 |
| Maryland | 984.0 | 872.7 | 111.3 | 1,010.3 | 886.7 | 123.6 |
| Massachusetts | 1,275.6 | 985.0 | 290.6 | 1,303.2 | 991.9 | 311.4 |
| Michigan | 1,981.5 | 1,260.7 | 720.8 | 2,022.5 | 1,212.2 | 810.3 |
| Minnesota | 967.3 | 412.9 | 554.4 | 995.2 | 417.2 | 577.9 |
| Mississippi | 580.0 | 481.2 | 98.8 | 590.6 | 479.7 | 110.9 |
| Missouri | 1,183.0 | 804.8 | 378.2 | 1,203.8 | 795.2 | 408.7 |
| Montana | 215.5 | 171.0 | 44.5 | 222.9 | 181.6 | 41.3 |
| Nebraska | 329.5 | 286.4 | 43.0 | 337.7 | 288.0 | 49.7 |
| Nevada | 492.3 | 319.2 | 173.1 | 511.1 | 325.9 | 185.2 |
| New Hampshire | 281.0 | 250.6 | 30.4 | 289.9 | 251.7 | 38.2 |
| New Jersey | 1,553.3 | 1,214.4 | 338.9 | 1,582.7 | 1,212.1 | 370.6 |
| New Mexico | 396.9 | 262.9 | 134.0 | 409.3 | 267.4 | 141.9 |
| New York | 3,482.2 | 2,126.6 | 1,355.6 | 3,553.4 | 2,114.4 | 1,439.0 |
| North Carolina | 1,877.4 | 1,275.2 | 602.2 | 1,929.7 | 1,263.0 | 666.7 |
| North Dakota | 124.1 | 101.5 | 22.6 | 127.6 | 104.2 | 23.3 |
| Ohio | 2,249.1 | 1,372.6 | 876.4 | 2,292.7 | 1,339.3 | 953.4 |
| Oklahoma | 700.3 | 578.3 | 128.0 | 721.7 | 581.3 | 140.4 |
| Oregon | 807.6 | 447.5 | 360.1 | 836.1 | 458.4 | 377.7 |
| Pennsylvania | 2,629.8 | 1,552.5 | 1,077.2 | 2,680.7 | 1,565.7 | 1,115.1 |
| Rhode Island | 211.7 | 120.9 | 90.8 | 216.2 | 120.5 | 95.6 |
| South Carolina | 1,006.4 | 745.5 | 260.9 | 1,039.5 | 752.2 | 287.2 |
| South Dakota | 165.4 | 130.7 | 34.7 | 170.8 | 135.3 | 35.6 |
| Tennessee | 1,294.9 | 820.0 | 474.9 | 1,323.9 | 816.8 | 507.1 |
| Texas | 3,883.6 | 2,522.4 | 1,361.2 | 4,014.8 | 2,477.0 | 1,537.8 |
| Utah | 371.9 | 240.6 | 131.4 | 385.8 | 245.8 | 139.9 |
| Vermont | 139.2 | 126.5 | 12.7 | 143.4 | 128.5 | 14.9 |
| Virginia | 1,427.7 | 1,149.6 | 278.1 | 1,468.7 | 1,175.2 | 293.5 |
| Washington | 1,277.4 | 885.0 | 392.4 | 1,319.1 | 893.9 | 425.3 |
| West Virginia | 427.9 | 304.1 | 123.8 | 433.5 | 298.3 | 135.2 |
| Wisconsin | 1,110.3 | 667.6 | 442.7 | 1,141.3 | 669.9 | 471.4 |
| Wyoming | 101.9 | 97.9 | 4.0 | 106.0 | 101.8 | 4.3 |
| Guam | 16.2 | 16.1 | 0.1 | 16.7 | 16.7 | 0.1 |
| Puerto Rico | 734.1 | 171.9 | 562.2 | 740.8 | 167.7 | 573.1 |
| U.S. Virgin Islands | 19.7 | 19.4 | 0.3 | 19.6 | 19.3 | 0.4 |
| Foreign and other outlying areas | 447.2 | 444.3 | 2.9 | 461.6 | 458.2 | 3.4 |

[1] Original Medicare consists of Part A (Hospital Insurance) and Part B (Supplementary Medical Insurance). Enrollment in Original Medicare includes beneficiaries enrolled in either Part A and/or Part B. [2] Medicare Advantage and other health plans are also known as Medicare Part C. Medicare Part C includes both Part A and Part B coverage. Medicare Advantage and other health plan enrollees are Medicare beneficiaries who are enrolled in health plans offered by private companies approved by Medicare. [3] U.S. total excludes territories, possessions, foreign countries or outlying areas, and unknown.

Source: U.S. Centers for Medicare and Medicaid Services, CMS Program Statistics, "Medicare Enrollment Dashboard," <https://www.cms.gov/Research-Statistics-Data-and-Systems/Statistics-Trends-and-Reports/CMSProgramStatistics/index.html>, accessed April 2019.

## Table 152. Medicare Enrollment by Type: 2011 to 2017

[In thousands (48,893 represents 48,893,000), except as noted. Based on person-year methodology; see source for details. Medicare Advantage is an alternative to traditional Medicare. Medicare Advantage plans are offered by private companies and organizations, are required to provide at least services covered by Medicare Parts A and B (except hospice services), and are financed from both Medicare's Hospital Insurance (HI) trust fund and the Part B account within the Supplementary Medical Insurance (SMI) trust fund in proportion to the relative weights of Part A and Part B benefits to the total benefits paid by the Medicare program. Numbers and percentages may not add to totals because of rounding]

| Enrollment by type | 2011 | 2012 | 2013 | 2014 | 2015 | 2016 | 2017 |
|---|---|---|---|---|---|---|---|
| **Total Medicare enrollment** [1] | **48,893** | **50,769** | **52,426** | **54,013** | **55,496** | **56,981** | **58,457** |
| Aged | 40,686 | 42,313 | 43,761 | 45,217 | 46,631 | 48,143 | 49,678 |
| Disabled [2] | 8,207 | 8,456 | 8,664 | 8,796 | 8,865 | 8,838 | 8,779 |
| Part A, Hospital insurance | 48,541 | 50,428 | 52,087 | 53,675 | 55,153 | 56,639 | 58,115 |
| Aged | 40,334 | 41,973 | 43,423 | 44,879 | 46,289 | 47,802 | 49,338 |
| Disabled [2] | 8,206 | 8,455 | 8,664 | 8,796 | 8,865 | 8,837 | 8,778 |
| Part B, Medical insurance | 44,937 | 46,493 | 47,959 | 49,412 | 50,758 | 52,086 | 53,350 |
| Aged | 37,629 | 38,937 | 40,175 | 41,475 | 42,741 | 44,074 | 45,394 |
| Disabled [2] | 7,308 | 7,556 | 7,784 | 7,937 | 8,017 | 8,012 | 7,956 |
| **Original Medicare enrollment** [1] | **36,539** | **37,214** | **37,613** | **37,790** | **38,025** | **38,610** | **38,668** |
| Percent of total | 74.7 | 73.3 | 71.8 | 70.0 | 68.5 | 67.8 | 66.2 |
| Aged | 29,813 | 30,440 | 30,847 | 31,110 | 31,479 | 32,204 | 32,471 |
| Disabled [2] | 6,726 | 6,773 | 6,766 | 6,681 | 6,547 | 6,406 | 6,197 |
| Part A, Hospital insurance | 36,199 | 36,895 | 37,298 | 37,477 | 37,708 | 38,288 | 38,348 |
| Aged | 29,474 | 30,122 | 30,533 | 30,796 | 31,162 | 31,883 | 32,152 |
| Disabled [2] | 6,726 | 6,773 | 6,765 | 6,680 | 6,546 | 6,406 | 6,196 |
| Part B, Medical insurance | 32,584 | 32,939 | 33,147 | 33,190 | 33,287 | 33,715 | 33,562 |
| Aged | 26,756 | 27,065 | 27,261 | 27,368 | 27,589 | 28,136 | 28,188 |
| Disabled [2] | 5,828 | 5,874 | 5,886 | 5,822 | 5,698 | 5,580 | 5,374 |
| **Medicare Advantage enrollment** [1] | **12,353** | **13,555** | **14,813** | **16,223** | **17,471** | **18,371** | **19,789** |
| Percent of total | 25.3 | 26.7 | 28.3 | 30.0 | 31.5 | 32.2 | 33.9 |
| Part A, Hospital insurance | 12,341 | 13,533 | 14,789 | 16,198 | 17,445 | 18,351 | 19,768 |
| Aged | 10,861 | 11,851 | 12,891 | 14,082 | 15,127 | 15,919 | 17,186 |
| Disabled [2] | 1,480 | 1,682 | 1,898 | 2,116 | 2,319 | 2,432 | 2,582 |
| Part B, Medical insurance | 12,353 | 13,555 | 14,812 | 16,222 | 17,471 | 18,370 | 19,788 |
| Aged | 10,873 | 11,872 | 12,914 | 14,107 | 15,152 | 15,939 | 17,206 |
| Disabled [2] | 1,480 | 1,682 | 1,898 | 2,116 | 2,318 | 2,432 | 2,582 |

[1] Enrollment in Medicare Part A and/or Part B. [2] Persons enrolled due to end stage renal disease-only are included in the disabled enrollee counts.

Source: U.S. Centers for Medicare & Medicaid Services, "CMS Program Statistics," <https://www.cms.gov/Research-Statistics-Data-and-Systems/Statistics-Trends-and-Reports/CMSProgramStatistics/index.html>, accessed April 2019.

## Table 153. Medicare Utilization—Persons Utilizing Medicare, Program Payments, and Cost Sharing: 2012 to 2017

[37,214 represents 37,214,000. Covers all Original Medicare (also known as "fee-for-service"), which consists of Part A (Hospital Insurance), and Part B (Medical Insurance). Persons utilizing Medicare do not include beneficiaries who received services but for whom no program payments were reported. Amounts do not sum to totals because beneficiaries may have used more than one type of service during a year, and for payments and costs, due to rounding]

| Item | 2012 | 2013 | 2014 | 2015 | 2016 | 2017 |
|---|---|---|---|---|---|---|
| ORIGINAL MEDICARE ENROLLEES (1,000) | | | | | | |
| **Part A and/or Part B** | **37,214** | **37,613** | **37,790** | **38,025** | **38,610** | **38,668** |
| Part A | 36,895 | 37,298 | 37,477 | 37,708 | 38,288 | 38,348 |
| Part B | 32,939 | 33,147 | 33,190 | 33,287 | 33,715 | 33,562 |
| UTILIZATION (1,000) | | | | | | |
| **Medicare Part A and/or Part B** | **33,732** | **34,064** | **34,277** | **34,398** | **34,827** | **34,790** |
| Part A | 7,885 | 7,750 | 7,603 | 7,656 | 7,680 | 7,719 |
| Inpatient hospital services | 6,978 | 6,797 | 6,628 | 6,630 | 6,619 | 6,609 |
| Skilled nursing facility services | 1,845 | 1,843 | 1,832 | 1,845 | 1,803 | 1,764 |
| Hospice services [1] | 1,277 | 1,319 | 1,333 | 1,395 | 1,441 | 1,505 |
| Home health agency services | 1,698 | 1,699 | 1,653 | 1,671 | 1,642 | 1,610 |
| Part B | 33,218 | 33,532 | 33,734 | 33,824 | 34,241 | 34,170 |
| Physician and other medical services | 32,843 | 33,104 | 33,264 | 33,311 | 33,713 | 33,609 |
| Outpatient services | 24,586 | 24,846 | 25,010 | 25,283 | 25,711 | 25,715 |
| Home health agency services | 1,902 | 1,921 | 1,931 | 1,954 | 1,982 | 1,953 |
| PAYMENTS AND COSTS (mil. dol.) | | | | | | |
| **Medicare Part A and/or Part B** | **344,393** | **345,657** | **350,424** | **360,096** | **368,728** | **376,979** |
| Part A | 178,342 | 179,085 | 179,056 | 182,146 | 185,493 | 188,093 |
| Inpatient hospital services | 128,786 | 129,024 | 128,719 | 130,168 | 133,380 | 135,274 |
| Skilled nursing facility services | 27,696 | 28,218 | 28,637 | 29,152 | 28,409 | 28,064 |
| Hospice services [1] | 15,099 | 15,092 | 15,071 | 15,892 | 16,847 | 17,922 |
| Home health agency services | 6,761 | 6,750 | 6,628 | 6,934 | 6,857 | 6,833 |
| Part B | 166,051 | 166,572 | 171,368 | 177,950 | 183,235 | 188,886 |
| Physician and other medical services | 99,866 | 98,331 | 99,090 | 102,235 | 103,806 | 105,610 |
| Outpatient services | 54,926 | 57,066 | 61,169 | 64,445 | 68,169 | 72,278 |
| Home health agency services | 11,258 | 11,175 | 11,108 | 11,270 | 11,260 | 10,998 |
| BENEFICIARY COST SHARING (mil. dol.) [2] | | | | | | |
| **Medicare Part A and/or Part B** | **57,898** | **58,691** | **60,006** | **61,391** | **63,045** | **64,488** |
| Part A | 15,752 | 15,826 | 15,923 | 16,302 | 16,210 | 16,171 |
| Part B | 42,146 | 42,865 | 44,083 | 45,089 | 46,835 | 48,317 |

[1] The total Medicare Part A enrollee counts are based on enrollees in Original Medicare and Medicare Advantage/Other Health Plans (also known as Part C), combined, because once a beneficiary enrolled in a Medicare Advantage/Other Health Plan elects the hospice benefit, his or her Medicare benefits revert to fee-for-service. [2] Includes costs for copayments, coinsurance, deductibles, and out-of-pocket payments for balanced billing (the difference between Medicare allowed charges and physicians' submitted charges). Excludes monthly premium for Part B coverage, Part D coverage, voluntary hospital insurance coverage, and supplemental insurance.

Source: U.S. Centers for Medicare and Medicaid Services, "CMS Program Statistics," <https://www.cms.gov/Research-Statistics-Data-and-Systems/Statistics-Trends-and-Reports/CMSProgramStatistics/index.html>, accessed April 2019.

# Table 154. Medicare and Medicaid Dual Enrollment by Type of Eligibility: 2012 to 2017

[In thousands (9,329.6 represents 9,329,600). Covers Medicare beneficiaries who have low incomes and limited resources who also receive Medicaid program benefits. Services that are covered by Medicare are paid for by the Medicare program first before any payments are made by Medicaid. Based on person-year methodology; see source for details. See headnote, Table 152. Numbers may not sum to totals due to rounding]

| Year | Total Medicare-Medicaid dual enrollment | Type of eligibility | | | | | | | |
|---|---|---|---|---|---|---|---|---|---|
| | | Full benefit enrollment | | | | Partial benefit enrollment | | | |
| | | Total | Qualified Medicare beneficiary plus [1] | Specified low-income Medicare beneficiary plus [2] | Other full-benefit enrollees with Medicaid | Total | Qualified Medicare beneficiary [1] | Specified low-income Medicare beneficiary [2] | Qualified disabled & working individuals [3] |
| **Total Medicare:** | | | | | | | | | |
| 2012................... | 9,329.6 | 6,769.1 | 4,958.0 | 242.6 | 1,568.5 | 2,560.5 | 1,184.0 | 879.7 | 496.7 |
| 2013................... | 9,586.4 | 6,902.3 | 5,080.4 | 245.2 | 1,576.7 | 2,684.1 | 1,255.4 | 911.1 | 517.5 |
| 2014................... | 9,913.8 | 7,131.2 | 5,188.1 | 251.1 | 1,691.9 | 2,782.6 | 1,329.1 | 922.7 | 530.7 |
| 2015................... | 10,192.6 | 7,317.9 | 5,302.7 | 256.9 | 1,758.3 | 2,874.7 | 1,383.0 | 940.6 | 551.0 |
| 2016................... | 10,415.7 | 7,464.6 | 5,394.7 | 263.1 | 1,806.8 | 2,951.1 | 1,447.9 | 961.8 | 541.4 |
| 2017................... | 10,632.6 | 7,602.3 | 5,491.3 | 270.5 | 1,840.6 | 3,030.3 | 1,520.4 | 976.8 | 533.0 |
| **Original Medicare:** | | | | | | | | | |
| 2012................... | 7,260.4 | 5,546.9 | 4,033.0 | 202.1 | 1,311.8 | 1,713.5 | 862.9 | 557.0 | 293.6 |
| 2013................... | 7,219.8 | 5,494.4 | 4,002.0 | 200.5 | 1,292.0 | 1,725.4 | 875.1 | 555.1 | 295.1 |
| 2014................... | 7,178.2 | 5,453.4 | 3,911.9 | 200.3 | 1,341.2 | 1,724.8 | 890.1 | 541.3 | 293.4 |
| 2015................... | 7,025.4 | 5,312.3 | 3,777.7 | 196.6 | 1,338.0 | 1,713.1 | 889.6 | 529.7 | 293.9 |
| 2016................... | 6,994.9 | 5,296.6 | 3,753.8 | 196.6 | 1,346.2 | 1,698.3 | 900.5 | 520.2 | 277.6 |
| 2017................... | 6,889.5 | 5,222.5 | 3,689.1 | 195.4 | 1,338.0 | 1,667.0 | 898.4 | 506.4 | 262.3 |
| **Medicare Advantage:** | | | | | | | | | |
| 2012................... | 2,069.2 | 1,222.2 | 925.0 | 40.5 | 256.7 | 847.0 | 321.1 | 322.7 | 203.2 |
| 2013................... | 2,366.6 | 1,407.9 | 1,078.5 | 44.7 | 284.7 | 958.7 | 380.3 | 356.0 | 222.4 |
| 2014................... | 2,735.6 | 1,677.8 | 1,276.2 | 50.9 | 350.8 | 1,057.8 | 439.0 | 381.4 | 237.3 |
| 2015................... | 3,167.2 | 2,005.6 | 1,524.9 | 60.3 | 420.3 | 1,161.5 | 493.4 | 411.0 | 257.2 |
| 2016................... | 3,420.8 | 2,168.0 | 1,640.8 | 66.5 | 460.6 | 1,252.8 | 547.5 | 441.6 | 263.8 |
| 2017................... | 3,743.0 | 2,379.8 | 1,802.2 | 75.1 | 502.6 | 1,363.2 | 622.0 | 470.5 | 270.7 |

[1] A qualified Medicare beneficiary (QMB) has Medicare Part A, income less than or equal to 100 percent of the Federal poverty level, and resources below twice the value allowed under supplemental security income (SSI). For those who qualify, the Medicaid program pays Medicare Part A premiums (if applicable), Part B premiums, and Medicare deductibles and coinsurance amounts for Medicare covered services depending on the Medicaid state plan. An individual qualifying for full Medicaid benefits is sometimes referred to as "QMB plus." [2] A specified low-income Medicare beneficiary (SLMB) has Medicare Part A, income above 100 percent but less than 120 percent of the Federal poverty level, and resources below twice the value allowed under SSI. For those who qualify, the Medicaid program pays only the Medicare Part B premium. An individual who qualifies for full Medicaid benefits is sometimes referred to as "SLMB plus". [3] Data are combined for qualified disabled and working individuals (QDWIs) and qualifying individuals; total counts for QDWIs are less than 100. For QDWIs, Medicaid pays Medicare Part A premiums for certain disabled individuals who lost Medicare coverage because they returned to work. These individuals have incomes below 200 percent of the Federal Poverty Level, resources not more than twice the value allowed under SSI, and are not otherwise eligible for Medicaid. Qualifying individuals are entitled to Medicare Part A, have income of at least 120% but less than 135% of the Federal Poverty Level, resources that do not exceed twice the limit for SSI eligibility, and are not otherwise eligible for Medicaid. Medicaid pays their Medicare Part B premiums only. There is an annual cap on the amount of money available, which may limit the number of individuals in the group.

Source: U.S. Centers for Medicare and Medicaid Services, "CMS Program Statistics," <https://www.cms.gov/Research-Statistics-Data-and-Systems/Statistics-Trends-and-Reports/CMSProgramStatistics/index.html>, accessed April 2019.

# Table 155. Medicare Hospital Insurance and Supplementary Medical Insurance—Average Costs per Beneficiary: 1978 to 2019

[In dollars. See headnote, Table 156]

| Year | Total | Hospital Insurance | SMI Part B | SMI Part D | Year | Total | Hospital Insurance | SMI Part B | SMI Part D |
|---|---|---|---|---|---|---|---|---|---|
| 1978........ | 1,010 | 697 | 314 | (X) | 1999........ | 5,561 | 3,306 | 2,255 | (X) |
| 1979........ | 1,147 | 786 | 361 | (X) | 2000........ | 5,879 | 3,383 | 2,496 | (X) |
| 1980........ | 1,352 | 929 | 423 | (X) | 2001........ | 6,416 | 3,656 | 2,760 | (X) |
| 1981........ | 1,583 | 1,093 | 490 | (X) | 2002........ | 6,813 | 3,839 | 2,975 | (X) |
| 1982........ | 1,819 | 1,249 | 570 | (X) | 2003........ | 7,144 | 3,922 | 3,221 | (X) |
| 1983........ | 2,025 | 1,367 | 658 | (X) | 2004........ | 7,722 | 4,162 | 3,561 | (X) |
| 1984........ | 2,236 | 1,512 | 724 | (X) | 2005........ | 8,278 | 4,439 | 3,839 | (X) |
| 1985........ | 2,373 | 1,579 | 795 | (X) | 2006........ | 10,179 | 4,601 | 4,116 | 1,461 |
| 1986........ | 2,504 | 1,596 | 907 | (X) | 2007........ | 10,703 | 4,759 | 4,313 | 1,630 |
| 1987........ | 2,661 | 1,636 | 1,024 | (X) | 2008........ | 11,232 | 4,996 | 4,574 | 1,662 |
| 1988........ | 2,781 | 1,646 | 1,135 | (X) | 2009........ | 11,701 | 5,174 | 4,798 | 1,730 |
| 1989........ | 3,097 | 1,860 | 1,237 | (X) | 2010........ | 11,908 | 5,193 | 4,907 | 1,808 |
| 1990........ | 3,334 | 1,979 | 1,355 | (X) | 2011........ | 12,170 | 5,275 | 5,037 | 1,858 |
| 1991........ | 3,569 | 2,125 | 1,443 | (X) | 2012........ | 12,207 | 5,194 | 5,174 | 1,839 |
| 1992........ | 3,941 | 2,411 | 1,530 | (X) | 2013........ | 12,200 | 5,152 | 5,174 | 1,874 |
| 1993........ | 4,259 | 2,648 | 1,611 | (X) | 2014........ | 12,458 | 5,034 | 5,393 | 2,031 |
| 1994........ | 4,678 | 2,948 | 1,730 | (X) | 2015........ | 12,741 | 5,047 | 5,542 | 2,152 |
| 1995........ | 5,061 | 3,194 | 1,867 | (X) | 2016........ | 12,935 | 5,109 | 5,670 | 2,155 |
| 1996........ | 5,378 | 3,424 | 1,954 | (X) | 2017........ | 13,162 | 5,168 | 5,874 | 2,120 |
| 1997........ | 5,649 | 3,616 | 2,033 | (X) | 2018........ | 13,665 | 5,241 | 6,253 | 2,171 |
| 1998........ | 5,602 | 3,468 | 2,134 | (X) | 2019 (P)..... | 14,162 | 5,425 | 6,600 | 2,137 |

X Not applicable. P Projected.

Source: U.S. Centers for Medicare and Medicaid Services, Trustees Report & Trust Funds, "2019 Expanded and Supplementary Tables and Figures," <https://www.cms.gov/Research-Statistics-Data-and-Systems/Statistics-Trends-and-Reports/ReportsTrustFunds/index.html>, accessed April 2019.

# Table 156. Medicare Insurance Trust Funds: 1990 to 2018

[In billions of dollars (126.3 represents $126,300,000,000), on cash basis, for calendar years. The Medicare program has two components: Medicare Part A Hospital Insurance (HI); and Supplementary Medical Insurance (SMI), consisting of Part B Medical Insurance, and Part D Prescription Drug Coverage. See text, this section, for details]

| Type of trust fund | 1990 | 2000 | 2005 | 2010 | 2014 | 2015 | 2016 | 2017 | 2018 |
|---|---|---|---|---|---|---|---|---|---|
| **TOTAL MEDICARE** | | | | | | | | | |
| Total income [1] | 126.3 | 257.1 | 357.5 | 486.1 | 599.3 | 644.4 | 710.2 | 705.1 | 755.7 |
| Total expenditures | 111.0 | 221.8 | 336.4 | 522.9 | 613.3 | 647.6 | 678.7 | 710.2 | 740.6 |
| Net change in assets | 15.3 | 35.3 | 21.0 | -36.8 | -14.1 | -3.2 | 31.5 | -5.1 | 15.1 |
| Assets, end of year | 114.4 | 221.5 | 309.8 | 344.0 | 266.4 | 263.2 | 294.7 | 289.6 | 304.7 |
| **HOSPITAL INSURANCE, PART A** | | | | | | | | | |
| Net contribution income [2] | 71.9 | 155.5 | 183.3 | 199.5 | 249.6 | 265.3 | 280.6 | 289.9 | 296.8 |
| Interest and other income [3,4] | 8.5 | 11.7 | 16.1 | 16.1 | 11.7 | 10.1 | 10.1 | 9.4 | 9.8 |
| Benefit payments [4,5] | 66.2 | 128.5 | 180.0 | 244.5 | 264.9 | 273.4 | 280.5 | 293.4 | 303.0 |
| Trust fund balance, end of year | 98.9 | 177.5 | 285.8 | 271.9 | 197.3 | 193.8 | 199.1 | 202.0 | 200.4 |
| **SMI, PART B** | | | | | | | | | |
| Premiums from enrollees [1] | 11.3 | 20.6 | 37.5 | 52.0 | 65.6 | 69.4 | 72.1 | 81.5 | 93.3 |
| Government contributions [6] | 33.0 | 65.9 | 118.1 | 153.5 | 188.5 | 203.9 | 235.6 | 217.3 | 253.2 |
| Interest and other income [3,4] | 1.6 | 3.5 | 1.4 | 3.3 | 5.7 | 5.7 | 5.5 | 6.8 | 7.1 |
| Benefit payments [1,4,5] | 42.5 | 88.9 | 149.2 | 209.7 | 261.9 | 275.8 | 289.5 | 308.6 | 333.0 |
| Trust fund balance, end of year | 15.5 | 44.0 | 24.0 | 71.4 | 68.1 | 68.2 | 88.0 | 79.9 | 96.3 |
| **SMI, PART D** | | | | | | | | | |
| Premiums from enrollees [7] | (X) | (X) | – | 6.5 | 11.4 | 12.8 | 13.8 | 15.5 | 15.8 |
| Government contributions [8] | (X) | (X) | 1.1 | 51.1 | 58.1 | 68.4 | 82.4 | 73.2 | 67.8 |
| Interest and other income | (X) | (X) | – | (Z) | (Z) | (Z) | (Z) | 0.1 | 0.1 |
| Benefit payments [9] | (X) | (X) | 1.1 | 61.7 | 77.7 | 89.5 | 99.5 | 100.1 | 94.7 |
| Trust fund balance, end of year | (X) | (X) | – | 0.7 | 1.1 | 1.3 | 7.6 | 7.8 | 8.0 |

– Represents zero. X Not applicable. Z Less than $50 million. [1] Includes adjustments for benefit checks issued at the end of the year instead of the following January; see source for details on this and other adjustments. [2] Includes income from payroll taxes, taxation of benefits, railroad retirement account transfers, reimbursement for uninsured persons, premiums from voluntary enrollees, and payments for military wage credits. [3] Includes recoveries of amounts reimbursed from the trust fund, receipts from fraud and abuse control program, and other miscellaneous income. [4] Values after 2005 include additional premiums for Medicare Advantage (MA) plans that are deducted from beneficiaries' Social Security checks; see source for details. [5] Includes monies transferred to the SMI trust fund in 1998-2003 for home health agency costs. In 2008 benefit payments were $224 million and include a transfer of $8.5 million to the general fund of the Treasury for HI hospice costs that were misallocated to, and paid from, the Part B account of the SMI trust fund from May 2005 to September 2007. (The general fund, in turn, transferred $8.5 million to the Part B account.) [6] Matching payments from the general fund, plus certain interest-adjustment items. See also footnote 1. [7] Premiums include both amounts withheld from Social Security benefit checks (and other certain Federal benefit payments) and amounts paid directly to Part D plans. [8] Includes, net of transfers from States, all government transfers required to fund benefit payments, administrative expenses, and State expenses for making low-income eligibility determinations. [9] Includes payments to plans, subsidies to employer-sponsored retiree prescription drug plans, payments to States for making low-income eligibility determinations, Part D drug premiums collected from beneficiaries and transferred to Medicare Advantage plans and private drug plans, and premium amounts paid directly by enrollees to plans. Includes amounts for transitional assistance benefits in 2004-2007.

Source: U.S. Centers for Medicare and Medicaid Services, Trustees Report & Trust Funds, "2019 Expanded and Supplementary Tables and Figures," <https://www.cms.gov/Research-Statistics-Data-and-Systems/Statistics-Trends-and-Reports/ReportsTrustFunds/index.html>, accessed April 2019.

# Table 157. Medicaid Enrollment by Race/Ethnicity, Age, and Poverty Status: 2017

[In thousands, except percent (62,032 represents 62,032,000). Based on the Current Population Survey, Annual Social and Economic Supplement (CPS ASEC). Represents number of persons who were enrolled at any time in year shown. Covers persons for whom poverty status was determined, and excludes unrelated individuals under age 15. Persons did not have to receive medical care paid for by Medicaid in order to be counted. For explanation of poverty level, see text, Section 13]

| Poverty status | Total [1] | White alone [2] | Black alone [2] | Asian alone [2] | His-panic [3] | Under age 18 | Age 18 to 24 | Age 25 to 44 | Age 45 to 64 | Age 65 and over |
|---|---|---|---|---|---|---|---|---|---|---|
| **Persons covered, total** | **62,032** | **42,195** | **12,451** | **3,498** | **18,046** | **27,844** | **6,416** | **12,978** | **11,142** | **3,652** |
| Below poverty level | 19,932 | 12,662 | 5,087 | 851 | 6,055 | 9,615 | 1,789 | 3,880 | 3,475 | 1,173 |
| Above poverty level | 42,100 | 29,533 | 7,364 | 2,646 | 11,991 | 18,229 | 4,627 | 9,097 | 7,667 | 2,479 |
| Percent of population covered by Medicaid: | | | | | | | | | | |
| **All persons** | **19.2** | **17.1** | **29.3** | **18.0** | **30.6** | **38.0** | **21.9** | **15.2** | **13.4** | **7.1** |
| Persons in poverty | 50.2 | 47.9 | 56.6 | 43.6 | 56.1 | 75.1 | 37.8 | 40.8 | 43.6 | 25.1 |
| Persons not in poverty | 14.9 | 13.4 | 22.0 | 15.1 | 24.8 | 30.1 | 18.8 | 12.0 | 10.2 | 5.3 |

[1] Includes other races, not shown separately. [2] Refers to people who reported specified race and did not report any other race category. [3] Persons of Hispanic origin may be of any race.

Source: U.S. Census Bureau, 2018 Current Population Survey Annual Social and Economic Supplement, CPS Table Creator, <https://www.census.gov/cps/data/cpstablecreator.html>, accessed November 2018. See also *Health Insurance Coverage in the United States: 2017,* Current Population Reports, P60-P264, <https://www.census.gov/topics/health/health-insurance.html>.

# Table 158. Medicaid Benefit Spending by Source of Funds and Per Enrollee by State and Island Area: 2017

[In units as indicated (572,243.9 represents $572,243,900,000). Data exclude spending for program administration and Medicaid-expansion Children's Health Insurance Program enrollees. Data are based on analysis of administrative data submitted to the Centers for Medicare & Medicaid Services (CMS) via CMS-64 records, as of July 2018 for expenditures and as of September 2018 for enrollment]

| State and Island Area | Medicaid benefit spending (million dollars) | | | Medicaid full year enrollees (1,000) [1] | Total spending per enrollee (dollars) |
|---|---|---|---|---|---|
| | Total | Federal funds | State funds | | |
| Total [2] | 572,243.9 | 352,470.2 | 219,773.7 | 75,807.9 | 7,548.6 |
| U.S. total [3] | 569,730.2 | 350,809.9 | 218,920.3 | 74,433.8 | 7,654.2 |
| Alabama | 5,562.2 | 3,919.8 | 1,642.4 | 1,021.7 | 5,444.1 |
| Alaska | 1,961.6 | 1,370.8 | 590.8 | 184.4 | 10,637.5 |
| Arizona | 11,823.7 | 8,974.4 | 2,849.3 | 1,943.1 | 6,084.8 |
| Arkansas | 6,363.9 | 4,943.0 | 1,421.0 | 945.9 | 6,728.0 |
| California | 82,384.2 | 48,600.8 | 33,783.3 | 12,182.4 | 6,762.5 |
| Colorado | 7,805.3 | 4,507.9 | 3,297.4 | 1,353.4 | 5,766.9 |
| Connecticut | 7,401.3 | 4,294.4 | 3,106.9 | 894.1 | 8,277.6 |
| Delaware | 2,133.8 | 1,313.4 | 820.4 | 206.7 | 10,321.0 |
| District of Columbia | 2,783.2 | 2,058.4 | 724.8 | 255.0 | 10,916.5 |
| Florida | 23,169.2 | 14,186.1 | 8,983.1 | 4,029.3 | 5,750.2 |
| Georgia | 10,106.0 | 6,881.7 | 3,224.3 | 1,853.1 | 5,453.5 |
| Hawaii | 2,338.4 | 1,528.2 | 810.2 | 331.0 | 7,064.3 |
| Idaho | 1,822.3 | 1,303.1 | 519.2 | 319.1 | 5,710.2 |
| Illinois | 15,054.1 | 9,343.5 | 5,710.6 | 2,889.9 | 5,209.2 |
| Indiana | 11,106.2 | 8,016.8 | 3,089.4 | 1,339.8 | 8,289.5 |
| Iowa | 4,065.9 | 2,548.3 | 1,517.6 | 596.2 | 6,819.7 |
| Kansas | 3,214.4 | 1,809.8 | 1,404.6 | 383.6 | 8,380.2 |
| Kentucky | 9,527.3 | 7,400.8 | 2,126.4 | 1,332.5 | 7,149.8 |
| Louisiana | 10,913.5 | 7,711.1 | 3,202.4 | 1,630.7 | 6,692.5 |
| Maine | 2,565.1 | 1,653.9 | 911.2 | 259.8 | 9,871.9 |
| Maryland | 11,161.4 | 6,775.3 | 4,386.1 | 1,201.7 | 9,288.3 |
| Massachusetts | 17,120.9 | 9,354.6 | 7,766.3 | 1,818.4 | 9,415.2 |
| Michigan | 16,711.2 | 12,125.9 | 4,585.3 | 2,115.9 | 7,898.0 |
| Minnesota | 11,352.0 | 6,492.6 | 4,859.4 | 1,130.6 | 10,040.7 |
| Mississippi | 5,462.3 | 4,081.4 | 1,380.9 | 712.0 | 7,672.1 |
| Missouri | 10,095.8 | 6,397.3 | 3,698.5 | 983.5 | 10,265.5 |
| Montana | 1,772.4 | 1,419.4 | 353.1 | 233.0 | 7,606.0 |
| Nebraska | 2,041.5 | 1,059.8 | 981.7 | 240.3 | 8,494.3 |
| Nevada | 3,530.3 | 2,646.4 | 883.9 | 601.2 | 5,872.2 |
| New Hampshire | 2,055.5 | 1,224.2 | 831.3 | 197.7 | 10,395.8 |
| New Jersey | 14,743.9 | 8,866.9 | 5,877.0 | 1,708.3 | 8,630.5 |
| New Mexico | 4,804.5 | 3,712.8 | 1,091.7 | 891.7 | 5,387.7 |
| New York [4] | 76,398.1 | 37,264.1 | 39,134.0 | 6,094.0 | 12,536.6 |
| North Carolina | 13,336.8 | 8,937.2 | 4,399.6 | 2,100.6 | 6,349.1 |
| North Dakota | 1,216.2 | 747.4 | 468.8 | 92.5 | 13,142.6 |
| Ohio | 23,055.8 | 15,889.3 | 7,166.5 | 3,075.8 | 7,495.9 |
| Oklahoma | 4,630.0 | 2,854.3 | 1,775.7 | 675.7 | 6,852.4 |
| Oregon | 8,312.7 | 6,199.2 | 2,113.5 | 996.9 | 8,338.5 |
| Pennsylvania | 28,081.2 | 17,112.3 | 10,968.8 | 2,817.6 | 9,966.3 |
| Rhode Island | 2,623.1 | 1,554.1 | 1,069.0 | 303.3 | 8,648.7 |
| South Carolina | 5,964.0 | 4,255.0 | 1,708.9 | 1,257.9 | 4,741.2 |
| South Dakota | 851.2 | 501.0 | 350.1 | 107.2 | 7,942.0 |
| Tennessee | 9,088.3 | 5,914.7 | 3,173.6 | 1,641.2 | 5,537.5 |
| Texas | 35,644.9 | 20,111.5 | 15,533.4 | 4,332.3 | 8,227.7 |
| Utah | 2,451.6 | 1,717.5 | 734.1 | 306.2 | 8,007.9 |
| Vermont | 1,600.2 | 942.8 | 657.4 | 184.8 | 8,660.7 |
| Virginia | 8,987.6 | 4,503.5 | 4,484.1 | 1,019.8 | 8,813.6 |
| Washington | 11,892.8 | 7,573.1 | 4,319.8 | 1,832.8 | 6,488.8 |
| West Virginia | 4,000.8 | 3,165.2 | 835.6 | 558.5 | 7,163.7 |
| Wisconsin | 8,049.9 | 4,741.2 | 3,308.7 | 1,188.7 | 6,771.7 |
| Wyoming | 591.6 | 303.7 | 287.9 | 61.7 | 9,583.5 |
| American Samoa | 33.2 | 18.5 | 14.7 | 41.2 | 806.0 |
| Guam | 79.3 | 51.2 | 28.2 | 35.8 | 2,215.8 |
| Northern Mariana Islands | 29.9 | 16.6 | 13.2 | 15.5 | 1,931.7 |
| Puerto Rico | 2,317.7 | 1,540.0 | 777.6 | 1,256.7 | 1,844.3 |
| Virgin Islands | 53.6 | 34.0 | 19.6 | 24.9 | 2,149.0 |

[1] Full year equivalent enrollment; may also be referred to as average monthly enrollment. [2] Total includes 50 states, DC, and Island Areas. [3] Includes 50 states and DC. [4] New York's CMS-64 quarterly enrollment data is missing the last two quarters of FY2017. The count displayed here is the average monthly enrollment based on the first two quarters of enrollment for FY2017.

Source: Medicaid and CHIP Payment and Access Commission, "MACStats," <https://www.macpac.gov/macstats/>, accessed August 2019.

# Table 159. Children's Health Insurance Program (CHIP) by State—Expenditures, 2017, and Enrollment, 2017 and 2018

[17,283.0 represents $17,283,000,000. For fiscal year. Expenditure data reported as of June 2018. Enrollment data reported as of May 2019, and subject to revision. Components may not add to total due to rounding. CHIP is a federal-state program that provides health benefits coverage to children without health insurance and living in families whose incomes are too high to qualify for Medicaid. States may create CHIP programs as an expansion of Medicaid, a program separate from Medicaid, or a combination of both approaches. Based on analysis of CHIP data from the Centers for Medicare & Medicaid Services; see source for details]

| State | Expenditures, 2017 (million dollars) | | | Children enrolled (number) | |
|---|---|---|---|---|---|
| | Total | Federal | State | 2017 | 2018 |
| **United States**.................... | **17,283.0** | **16,074.5** | **1,208.5** | **9,462,794** | **9,632,367** |
| Alabama [1,2]................... | 332.3 | 335.8 | -3.5 | 220,980 | 222,072 |
| Alaska.............................. | 32.6 | 28.6 | 4.0 | 18,704 | 19,747 |
| Arizona [1]......................... | 215.0 | 215.0 | -(Z) | 115,400 | 127,063 |
| Arkansas [1,3]................... | 158.0 | 158.0 | -(Z) | 143,618 | 98,127 |
| California [4]...................... | 3,890.4 | 3,213.5 | 676.9 | 2,028,716 | 1,976,284 |
| Colorado.......................... | 262.4 | 232.3 | 30.1 | 176,426 | 182,199 |
| Connecticut...................... | 42.2 | 95.6 | -53.4 | 28,889 | 28,900 |
| Delaware.......................... | 38.3 | 34.8 | 3.5 | 13,890 | 13,958 |
| District of Columbia.......... | 36.5 | 36.5 | – | 11,771 | 16,125 |
| Florida............................. | 715.4 | 684.5 | 30.9 | 465,631 | 496,080 |
| Georgia [1,5]..................... | 406.2 | 406.4 | -0.2 | 237,011 | 262,135 |
| Hawaii.............................. | 67.2 | 61.5 | 5.7 | 27,589 | 29,375 |
| Idaho [1]........................... | 76.2 | 76.1 | 0.1 | 36,658 | 39,657 |
| Illinois............................. | 262.7 | 237.3 | 25.4 | 324,282 | 296,186 |
| Indiana............................ | 217.5 | 217.0 | 0.4 | 126,317 | 135,308 |
| Iowa................................ | 134.7 | 124.9 | 9.8 | 91,866 | 99,314 |
| Kansas............................ | 111.7 | 103.0 | 8.7 | 64,601 | 63,850 |
| Kentucky [1]...................... | 212.9 | 212.9 | (Z) | 96,379 | 103,244 |
| Louisiana......................... | 368.8 | 355.7 | 13.1 | 158,298 | 172,934 |
| Maine.............................. | 34.9 | 34.2 | 0.7 | 23,318 | 25,219 |
| Maryland.......................... | 316.7 | 278.7 | 38.0 | 141,836 | 151,179 |
| Massachusetts.................. | 768.7 | 677.3 | 91.4 | 220,128 | 227,819 |
| Michigan [6]...................... | 255.9 | 251.7 | 4.1 | 79,737 | 81,391 |
| Minnesota [1]..................... | 13.7 | 115.2 | -101.5 | 4,051 | 4,043 |
| Mississippi....................... | 262.1 | 262.1 | – | 90,904 | 88,491 |
| Missouri [7]....................... | 225.2 | 219.2 | 6.0 | 93,800 | 109,169 |
| Montana.......................... | 101.1 | 100.0 | 1.1 | 32,121 | 31,284 |
| Nebraska......................... | 83.1 | 75.5 | 7.6 | 56,197 | 59,608 |
| Nevada............................ | 69.2 | 68.0 | 1.2 | 80,342 | 71,994 |
| New Hampshire................. | 34.5 | 43.5 | -9.0 | 17,823 | 17,781 |
| New Jersey....................... | 529.9 | 466.5 | 63.4 | 239,813 | 254,284 |
| New Mexico [1]................... | 107.2 | 107.3 | -0.1 | 13,709 | 13,224 |
| New York.......................... | 1,445.7 | 1,272.2 | 173.5 | 762,685 | 768,259 |
| North Carolina.................. | 461.3 | 460.5 | 0.8 | 273,850 | 296,759 |
| North Dakota.................... | 27.2 | 24.2 | 3.1 | 7,883 | 8,689 |
| Ohio................................ | 570.1 | 542.9 | 27.2 | 250,195 | 260,890 |
| Oklahoma......................... | 236.4 | 224.5 | 11.9 | 201,006 | 206,350 |
| Oregon............................ | 295.2 | 289.4 | 5.8 | 177,590 | 189,618 |
| Pennsylvania.................... | 682.0 | 608.7 | 73.3 | 363,323 | 369,172 |
| Rhode Island.................... | 36.0 | 45.3 | -9.3 | 27,433 | 35,920 |
| South Carolina.................. | 166.5 | 166.5 | – | 87,624 | 111,051 |
| South Dakota.................... | 31.7 | 29.0 | 2.7 | 20,308 | 20,129 |
| Tennessee........................ | 211.7 | 208.4 | 3.3 | 103,293 | 107,140 |
| Texas............................... | 1,812.0 | 1,672.9 | 139.1 | 1,137,899 | 1,136,587 |
| Utah [1]............................. | 138.3 | 138.4 | -0.2 | 62,140 | 60,423 |
| Vermont........................... | 12.1 | 27.8 | -15.7 | 5,841 | 4,942 |
| Virginia............................ | 333.6 | 293.0 | 40.6 | 202,974 | 207,725 |
| Washington....................... | 154.2 | 242.5 | -88.3 | 74,051 | 87,732 |
| West Virginia [8]................. | 64.8 | 64.8 | – | 37,464 | 39,419 |
| Wisconsin........................ | 207.7 | 223.1 | -15.4 | 179,342 | 196,416 |
| Wyoming.......................... | 13.3 | 11.7 | 1.6 | 7,088 | 7,102 |

– Represents zero. Z Less than $50,000. NA Not available. [1] State reports negative state CHIP spending for benefits or state program administration due to federal CHIP spending exceeding total CHIP spending. Federal CHIP spending exceeds total CHIP spending due to negative prior period adjustments and the 23 percent increase in the enhanced federal medical assistance percentage (E-FMAP) that went into effect in FY 2016. Because these prior period adjustments apply to periods before the 23 percent increase to the E-FMAP, these negative adjustments decrease total spending to a greater extent than federal spending. [2] The Alabama FY2017 enrollment totals are artificially high, as reports contain duplicate enrollees. [3] Due to system challenges and data limitations, the Arkansas FY2017 enrollment totals contain duplicates and are artificially high. [4] Due to reporting system updates, California's CHIP enrollment totals for FY2017 and FY2018 are estimates. [5] For Georgia, some Title XIX Medicaid children may be reported with the Title XXI CHIP children, and vice versa. [6] Michigan Title XXI funded Medicaid enrollees are included in Medicaid enrollment counts, rather than in CHIP for FY2017. [7] The Missouri FY2017 CHIP enrollment total is artificially low due to the inadvertent exclusion of certain CHIP members from reporting. [8] West Virginia CHIP annual numbers are artificially low in FY2017 due to de-duplication of data and other data quality improvement efforts.

Source: Medicaid and CHIP Payment and Access Commission, "MACStats: Program Enrollment and Spending, CHIP," <https://www.macpac.gov/macstats/>; and U.S. Centers for Medicare & Medicaid Services, CHIP Reports & Evaluations, "Annual Enrollment Reports," <https://www.medicaid.gov/chip/reports-and-evaluations/index.html>; accessed July 2019.

# Table 160. Medicaid and Children's Health Insurance Program—Beneficiaries and Payments by Basis of Eligibility and Service Category: 2000 to 2013

[In units, as indicated (42.8 represents 42,800,000). For years ending September 30. Beneficiaries include those who were enrolled or received services through Medicaid or the Children's Health Insurance Program (CHIP). Beginning 2011, also includes separate CHIP beneficiaries. Also beginning 2011, a new tabular methodology was used. Therefore, estimates may not be comparable to earlier data and caution should be used with trend analysis. Beneficiaries receiving more than one type of service appear in multiple categories; percents may not sum to 100 percent]

| Basis of eligibility and type of service | 2000 | 2005 | 2008 | 2009 | 2010 | 2011 | 2012 | 2013 |
|---|---|---|---|---|---|---|---|---|
| **Total beneficiaries (millions)** | **42.8** | **57.7** | **58.8** | **62.6** | **65.7** | **71.4** | **71.6** | **73.7** |
| **Total payments (billion dollars)** | **168.3** | **274.9** | **296.8** | **326.0** | **339.0** | **368.6** | **363.9** | **375.3** |
| Payments per beneficiary (dollars) | 3,936 | 4,768 | 5,051 | 5,209 | 5,160 | 5,159 | 5,082 | 5,094 |
| **PERCENT OF BENEFICIARIES** | | | | | | | | |
| By basis of eligibility: | | | | | | | | |
| Age 65 and over | 8.7 | 7.6 | 7.1 | 6.7 | 6.5 | 5.7 | 5.7 | 5.6 |
| Blind and disabled | 16.1 | 14.2 | 14.8 | 14.4 | 14.3 | 13.1 | 13.2 | 13.0 |
| Adults in families with dependent children [1] | 20.5 | 21.8 | 22.0 | 23.1 | 23.7 | 18.9 | 19.5 | 19.0 |
| Children under age 21 [2] | 46.1 | 47.2 | 47.8 | 47.7 | 48.3 | 40.5 | 40.6 | 40.4 |
| Other Title XIX [3] | 8.6 | 9.1 | 8.4 | 8.1 | 7.2 | 9.6 | 8.7 | 9.8 |
| Separate CHIP [4] | (NA) | (NA) | (NA) | (NA) | (NA) | 12.2 | 12.3 | 12.1 |
| By service category: | | | | | | | | |
| Inpatient hospital | 11.5 | 9.5 | 8.9 | 8.7 | 6.9 | 11.4 | 11.8 | 12.5 |
| Mental health facility | 0.2 | 0.2 | 0.2 | 0.2 | 0.2 | 0.2 | 0.2 | 0.2 |
| Intermediate care facility for individuals with intellectual disabilities | 0.3 | 0.2 | 0.2 | 0.2 | 0.2 | 0.1 | 0.1 | 0.1 |
| Nursing facility | 4.0 | 3.0 | 2.7 | 2.6 | 2.4 | 2.5 | 2.3 | 2.3 |
| Physician | 44.7 | 42.0 | 36.9 | 36.9 | 36.9 | 62.6 | 64.4 | 65.5 |
| Dental | 13.8 | 16.2 | 16.7 | 17.8 | 19.1 | 26.6 | 27.4 | 28.3 |
| Other practitioner | 11.1 | 10.2 | 8.8 | 8.8 | 9.2 | 13.6 | 14.2 | 14.3 |
| Outpatient hospital | 30.9 | 28.2 | 25.2 | 26.4 | 24.2 | 38.8 | 39.5 | 40.1 |
| Clinic | 17.9 | 20.7 | 20.2 | 20.6 | 20.7 | 24.4 | 23.6 | 23.9 |
| Laboratory and radiological | 26.6 | 27.7 | 26.6 | 26.2 | 25.8 | 41.6 | 42.0 | 42.5 |
| Home health | 2.3 | 2.1 | 1.9 | 1.7 | 1.7 | 2.4 | 2.5 | 2.4 |
| Prescribed drugs | 48.0 | 49.2 | 41.8 | 42.6 | 44.7 | 56.8 | 57.2 | 57.5 |
| Capitated care | 49.7 | 58.1 | 64.9 | 66.6 | 70.8 | 93.6 | 86.9 | 88.4 |
| Primary care case management | 13.0 | 15.1 | 14.9 | 13.1 | 13.3 | 13.3 | 13.6 | 11.4 |
| Personal support | 10.6 | 11.8 | 10.8 | 10.7 | 11.0 | 1.7 | 1.7 | 1.6 |
| Other care | 21.4 | 21.9 | 21.3 | 20.6 | 19.9 | 47.6 | 47.9 | 49.3 |
| **PAYMENTS PER BENEFICIARY (dollars) [5]** | | | | | | | | |
| By basis of eligibility: | | | | | | | | |
| Age 65 and over | 11,929 | 14,427 | 14,742 | 15,337 | 15,286 | 15,073 | 14,862 | 15,194 |
| Blind and disabled | 10,559 | 14,531 | 14,843 | 15,670 | 15,695 | 16,104 | 15,825 | 16,115 |
| Adults in families with dependent children [1] | 2,030 | 2,583 | 2,912 | 3,144 | 3,095 | 3,443 | 3,460 | 3,503 |
| Children under age 21 [2] | 1,358 | 1,732 | 2,035 | 2,145 | 2,122 | 2,300 | 2,281 | 2,315 |
| Other Title XIX [3] | 1,778 | 2,380 | 2,407 | 2,104 | 2,219 | 2,402 | 2,030 | 1,803 |
| Separate CHIP [4] | (NA) | (NA) | (NA) | (NA) | (NA) | 3,125 | 2,979 | 3,083 |
| By service category: | | | | | | | | |
| Inpatient hospital | 4,919 | 6,411 | 7,083 | 7,070 | 7,347 | 4,858 | 4,437 | 3,885 |
| Mental health facility | 17,800 | 19,252 | 21,975 | 21,404 | 20,782 | 14,557 | 13,221 | 12,691 |
| Intermediate care facility for individuals with intellectual disabilities | 79,330 | 107,028 | 123,053 | 127,837 | 125,851 | 129,806 | 119,903 | 120,995 |
| Nursing facility | 20,220 | 26,185 | 29,533 | 29,551 | 31,617 | 26,995 | 28,060 | 27,808 |
| Physician | 356 | 465 | 485 | 496 | 492 | 271 | 238 | 219 |
| Dental | 238 | 326 | 389 | 423 | 432 | 301 | 245 | 181 |
| Other practitioner | 139 | 200 | 171 | 171 | 190 | 186 | 183 | 173 |
| Outpatient hospital | 533 | 617 | 736 | 735 | 803 | 470 | 454 | 424 |
| Clinic | 805 | 749 | 772 | 792 | 791 | 712 | 680 | 709 |
| Laboratory and radiological | 113 | 183 | 188 | 198 | 205 | 119 | 102 | 91 |
| Home health | 3,135 | 4,487 | 5,789 | 6,628 | 6,375 | 4,286 | 3,565 | 3,581 |
| Prescribed drugs | 975 | 1,509 | 957 | 951 | 926 | 719 | 540 | 432 |
| Capitated care | 1,148 | 1,386 | 1,786 | 1,991 | 1,983 | 1,627 | 1,964 | 2,178 |
| Primary care case management | 30 | 27 | 32 | 41 | 49 | 45 | 47 | 50 |
| Personal support | 2,543 | 3,035 | 3,852 | 3,903 | 3,593 | 9,959 | 9,619 | 9,588 |
| Other care | 1,600 | 2,228 | 2,856 | 3,015 | 3,289 | 1,724 | 1,653 | 1,554 |

NA Not available. [1] Includes adults in the Temporary Assistance for Needy Families (TANF) program. Beginning 2001, also includes women in the Breast and Cervical Cancer Prevention and Treatment Program, and unemployed adults. [2] Includes children (including those in the foster care system) in the TANF program. [3] Includes participants in the Supplemental Security Income program, and other people deemed medically needy in participating states. Excludes foster care children. Includes unknown eligibility. Prior to 2001, includes unemployed adults. [4] Children's Health Insurance Program (CHIP) provides federal funds for states to provide health care coverage to eligible low-income, uninsured children who do not qualify for Medicaid. Some states use CHIP funds to expand Medicaid. For 2012 data, all states except Colorado and Idaho had separate CHIP beneficiaries. [5] Medicaid payment data for 2010 and earlier excluded disproportionate share hospital (DSH) payments and DSH mental health facility payments.

Source: U.S. National Center for Health Statistics, *Health, United States, 2017,* September 2018. See also <https://www.cdc.gov/nchs/hus/index.htm>.

## Table 161. Medicaid Managed Care Enrollment by State and Other Areas: 2000 to 2017

[In thousands except as noted (33,690 represents 33,690,000). Through 2011, for year ending June 30; beginning with 2013, as of July 1. Medicaid managed care provides Medicaid health benefits and additional services through contracted arrangements between state Medicaid agencies and managed care entities. The unduplicated Medicaid enrollment figures include dual Medicare-Medicaid enrollees. The unduplicated managed care enrollment figures include enrollees in any Medicaid managed care program, including comprehensive managed care organizations (MCOs), limited benefit MCOs, and primary care case management programs]

| State and other areas | Total enroll-ment | Managed care enrollment Number | Percent of total | State and other areas | Total enroll-ment | Managed care enrollment Number | Percent of total | State and other areas | Total enroll-ment | Managed care enrollment Number | Percent of total |
|---|---|---|---|---|---|---|---|---|---|---|---|
| 2000 | 33,690 | 18,786 | 55.8 | GA | 1,813 | 1,257 | 69.3 | NM | 899 | 696 | 77.4 |
| 2010 | 54,612 | 39,020 | 71.5 | HI | 365 | 361 | 98.9 | NY | 6,105 | 4,711 | 77.2 |
| 2011 | 57,107 | 42,385 | 74.2 | ID | 299 | 293 | 97.8 | NC | 2,111 | 1,608 | 76.2 |
| 2012 | (NA) | (NA) | (NA) | IL | 3,193 | 1,913 | 59.9 | ND | 93 | 50 | 53.7 |
| 2013 | 62,507 | 45,923 | 73.5 | IN | 1,475 | 1,138 | 77.1 | OH | 3,083 | 2,551 | 82.7 |
| 2014 | 72,050 | 55,459 | 77.0 | IA | 624 | 557 | 89.3 | OK | 808 | 653 | 80.8 |
| 2015 | 77,847 | 62,373 | 80.1 | KS | 417 | 399 | 95.7 | OR | 1,067 | 860 | 80.5 |
| 2016 | 80,185 | 65,006 | 81.1 | KY | 1,403 | 1,308 | 93.2 | PA | 2,836 | 2,562 | 90.4 |
| **2017 Total [1]** | **80,243** | **65,797** | **82.0** | LA | 1,626 | 1,493 | 91.8 | RI | 338 | 309 | 91.5 |
| U.S. | 78,841 | 64,395 | 81.7 | ME | 273 | 239 | 87.4 | SC | 1,217 | 1,217 | 100.0 |
| AL | 1,038 | 637 | 61.4 | MD | 1,326 | 1,161 | 87.6 | SD | 125 | 93 | 74.9 |
| AK [2] | 156 | – | – | MA | 1,875 | 1,248 | 66.5 | TN | 1,523 | 1,410 | 92.6 |
| AZ | 1,917 | 1,618 | 84.4 | MI | 4,669 | 4,655 | 99.7 | TX | 4,038 | 3,903 | 96.7 |
| AR | 994 | 522 | 52.6 | MN | 1,107 | 846 | 76.4 | UT | 284 | 283 | 99.4 |
| CA | 13,515 | 10,806 | 80.0 | MS | 709 | 487 | 68.7 | VT | 184 | 97 | 52.6 |
| CO [3] | 1,381 | 1,327 | 96.1 | MO | 984 | 975 | 99.1 | VA | 1,084 | 724 | 66.8 |
| CT [2] | 861 | – | – | MT | 230 | 175 | 76.0 | WA | 1,825 | 1,825 | 100.0 |
| DE | 223 | 208 | 93.4 | NE | 248 | 247 | 99.5 | WV | 521 | 425 | 81.5 |
| DC | 266 | 197 | 74.1 | NV | 654 | 579 | 88.5 | WI | 1,198 | 799 | 66.7 |
| FL | 3,916 | 3,280 | 83.8 | NH | 204 | 134 | 65.4 | WY | 62 | (Z) | 0.6 |
| | | | | NJ | 1,679 | 1,560 | 92.9 | PR [4] | 1,402 | 1,402 | 100.0 |

– Represents zero. NA Not available. Z Less than 500. [1] Includes enrollment for Puerto Rico. [2] Alaska and Connecticut did not provide total Medicaid enrollment as of July 1, 2017. This figure is from the September-December 2016 enrollment data collected through the Medicaid Budget and Expenditure System, updated December 2017. See <https://data.medicaid.gov/Enrollment/2016-4Q-Medicaid-MBES-Enrollment/capi-ym43>. [3] Colorado reported plan level enrollment as 30 for plans that had less than 30 beneficiaries. [4] Puerto Rico expanded Medicaid to 372,142 low-income, childless adults under an authority other than Affordable Care Act, Section VIII.

Source: U.S. Centers for Medicare and Medicaid Services, "Medicaid Managed Care Enrollment Report: 2017 Medicaid Managed Care Enrollment Summary," <https://www.medicaid.gov/medicaid/managed-care/enrollment/index.html>, June 2019, and earlier releases and reports.


## Table 162. Medicare Hospital Insurance and Supplemental Medical Insurance Expenditures, Total and as a Percent of GDP: 1990 to 2038

[In millions of dollars (5,963,145 represents $5,963,145,000,000), except percent. Incurred amounts relate to expenditures for services performed in a given year, even if payment for those expenditures occurs in a later year. The Medicare program has two components: Medicare Part A Hospital Insurance (HI); and Supplementary Medical Insurance (SMI), consisting of Part B Medical Insurance, and Part D Prescription Drug Coverage. See text in this section for details]

| Year | GDP | Medicare expenditures Total | HI Part A | SMI Part B | SMI Part D | Medicare expenditures as percent of GDP Total | HI Part A | SMI Part B | SMI Part D |
|---|---|---|---|---|---|---|---|---|---|
| **ACTUAL** | | | | | | | | | |
| 1990 | 5,963,145 | 110,903 | 66,785 | 44,118 | (X) | 1.86 | 1.12 | 0.74 | (X) |
| 2000 | 10,252,346 | 225,983 | 132,803 | 93,180 | (X) | 2.20 | 1.30 | 0.91 | (X) |
| 2005 | 13,036,637 | 342,106 | 187,456 | 153,553 | 1,098 | 2.62 | 1.44 | 1.18 | 0.01 |
| 2010 | 14,992,052 | 524,160 | 245,985 | 215,318 | 62,857 | 3.50 | 1.64 | 1.44 | 0.42 |
| 2011 | 15,542,582 | 548,718 | 256,079 | 226,260 | 66,379 | 3.53 | 1.65 | 1.46 | 0.43 |
| 2012 | 16,197,007 | 571,850 | 262,511 | 240,454 | 68,885 | 3.53 | 1.62 | 1.48 | 0.43 |
| 2013 | 16,784,851 | 590,174 | 268,796 | 248,085 | 73,294 | 3.52 | 1.60 | 1.48 | 0.44 |
| 2014 | 17,521,747 | 619,428 | 270,704 | 266,472 | 82,253 | 3.54 | 1.54 | 1.52 | 0.47 |
| 2015 | 18,219,297 | 650,079 | 278,816 | 281,312 | 89,951 | 3.57 | 1.53 | 1.54 | 0.49 |
| 2016 | 18,707,189 | 678,380 | 289,845 | 295,389 | 93,147 | 3.63 | 1.55 | 1.58 | 0.50 |
| 2017 | 19,485,394 | 708,411 | 300,620 | 313,498 | 94,293 | 3.64 | 1.54 | 1.61 | 0.48 |
| 2018 | 20,501,574 | 752,858 | 312,260 | 341,278 | 99,320 | 3.67 | 1.52 | 1.66 | 0.48 |
| **PROJECTED [1]** | | | | | | | | | |
| 2019 | 21,485,262 | 800,550 | 330,961 | 368,769 | 100,820 | 3.73 | 1.54 | 1.72 | 0.47 |
| 2020 | 22,523,023 | 858,012 | 353,004 | 397,411 | 107,597 | 3.81 | 1.57 | 1.76 | 0.48 |
| 2021 | 23,558,235 | 928,051 | 377,406 | 432,022 | 118,623 | 3.94 | 1.60 | 1.83 | 0.50 |
| 2022 | 24,615,823 | 1,003,757 | 405,212 | 468,546 | 130,000 | 4.08 | 1.65 | 1.90 | 0.53 |
| 2023 | 25,735,040 | 1,083,290 | 434,374 | 507,823 | 141,092 | 4.21 | 1.69 | 1.97 | 0.55 |
| 2028 | 31,972,113 | 1,591,078 | 612,449 | 778,078 | 200,551 | 4.98 | 1.92 | 2.43 | 0.63 |
| 2033 | 39,500,850 | 2,182,929 | 817,121 | 1,092,752 | 273,057 | 5.53 | 2.07 | 2.77 | 0.69 |
| 2038 | 48,689,254 | 2,859,934 | 1,056,687 | 1,444,848 | 358,399 | 5.87 | 2.17 | 2.97 | 0.74 |

X Not applicable. [1] Projections are a projected baseline, and are based on current law; that is, they assume that laws on the books will be implemented and adhered to with respect to scheduled taxes, premium revenues, and payments to providers and health plans. The one exception is that the projections disregard payment reductions that would result from the projected depletion of the Medicare Hospital Insurance trust fund (Part A), thus allowing the size of deficits to become apparent. To date, Congress has not allowed the assets of the Medicare Hospital Insurance trust fund to become depleted.

Source: U.S. Centers for Medicare and Medicaid Services, Trustees Report & Trust Funds, "2019 Expanded and Supplementary Tables and Figures," <https://www.cms.gov/Research-Statistics-Data-and-Systems/Statistics-Trends-and-Reports/ReportsTrustFunds/index.html>, accessed April 2019.

# Table 163. Health Insurance Coverage Status by Selected Characteristics: 2017

[323,156 represents 323,156,000. Data for coverage during all or part of 2017; people not covered had no health insurance for the entire year. Based on the Current Population Survey, Annual Social and Economic Supplement (CPS ASEC); see text, Section 1, and Appendix III. The CPS ASEC defines private health insurance as a plan provided through an employer or a union, or coverage purchased directly by an individual from an insurance company or through an exchange. Government health insurance includes Medicare, Medicaid, the Children's Health Insurance Program (CHIP), individual state health plans, TRICARE, CHAMPVA (Civilian Health and Medical Program of the Department of Veterans Affairs), and care provided by the Department of Veterans Affairs and the military. People covered only through the Indian Health Service are considered uninsured]

| Characteristic | Number (1,000) | | | | | | | Percent | | | |
| | Total persons | Not covered by health insur- ance | Covered by private or government health insurance | | | | | Not covered by health insur- ance | Covered by private or government health insurance | | |
| | | | Total [1] | Private | | Government | | | Total [1] | Private | Medic- aid |
| | | | | Total | Employer based | Medic- aid | Medi- are | | | | |
| Total............... | 323,156 | 28,543 | 294,613 | 217,007 | 181,036 | 62,492 | 55,623 | 8.8 | 91.2 | 67.2 | 19.3 |
| Age: | | | | | | | | | | | |
| Under 18 years...... | 73,963 | 3,930 | 70,033 | 46,570 | 41,803 | 28,304 | 325 | 5.3 | 94.7 | 63.0 | 38.3 |
| 18 to 24 years....... | 29,363 | 3,782 | 25,580 | 20,534 | 17,732 | 6,416 | 219 | 12.9 | 87.1 | 69.9 | 21.9 |
| 25 to 34 years....... | 44,854 | 6,981 | 37,873 | 31,365 | 27,723 | 7,132 | 532 | 15.6 | 84.4 | 69.9 | 15.9 |
| 35 to 44 years....... | 40,659 | 5,407 | 35,253 | 29,912 | 26,853 | 5,846 | 919 | 13.3 | 86.7 | 73.6 | 14.4 |
| 45 to 54 years....... | 41,537 | 4,252 | 37,285 | 31,792 | 27,995 | 5,193 | 1,977 | 10.2 | 89.8 | 76.5 | 12.5 |
| 55 to 64 years....... | 41,700 | 3,513 | 38,187 | 30,708 | 25,498 | 5,949 | 4,067 | 8.4 | 91.6 | 73.6 | 14.3 |
| 65 years and over... | 51,080 | 678 | 50,402 | 26,125 | 13,434 | 3,652 | 47,584 | 1.3 | 98.7 | 51.1 | 7.1 |
| Sex: | | | | | | | | | | | |
| Male................. | 158,426 | 15,186 | 143,240 | 107,323 | 90,310 | 29,335 | 24,979 | 9.6 | 90.4 | 67.7 | 18.5 |
| Female.............. | 164,730 | 13,358 | 151,372 | 109,684 | 90,727 | 33,156 | 30,644 | 8.1 | 91.9 | 66.6 | 20.1 |
| Race: | | | | | | | | | | | |
| White alone [2]........ | 247,695 | 21,075 | 226,621 | 170,913 | 141,460 | 42,506 | 46,236 | 8.5 | 91.5 | 69.0 | 17.2 |
| Black alone [2]........ | 42,564 | 4,512 | 38,052 | 24,041 | 20,675 | 12,528 | 5,977 | 10.6 | 89.4 | 56.5 | 29.4 |
| Asian alone [2]....... | 19,484 | 1,413 | 18,071 | 14,068 | 11,795 | 3,505 | 2,282 | 7.3 | 92.7 | 72.2 | 18.0 |
| Hispanic origin [3]...... | 59,227 | 9,508 | 49,719 | 31,672 | 26,844 | 18,171 | 4,852 | 16.1 | 83.9 | 53.5 | 30.7 |
| Household income: | | | | | | | | | | | |
| Less than $25,000... | 46,682 | 6,482 | 40,199 | 14,071 | 7,525 | 19,385 | 14,801 | 13.9 | 86.1 | 30.1 | 41.5 |
| $25,000–$49,999... | 62,187 | 7,618 | 54,569 | 31,800 | 22,996 | 17,606 | 15,151 | 12.3 | 87.7 | 51.1 | 28.3 |
| $50,000–$74,999... | 53,710 | 5,570 | 48,141 | 35,844 | 29,513 | 10,125 | 8,764 | 10.4 | 89.6 | 66.7 | 18.9 |
| $75,000 or more..... | 160,577 | 8,873 | 151,703 | 135,292 | 121,002 | 15,376 | 16,907 | 5.5 | 94.5 | 84.3 | 9.6 |
| Persons below poverty.............. | 39,698 | 6,748 | 32,950 | 11,185 | 6,917 | 19,932 | 6,234 | 17.0 | 83.0 | 28.2 | 50.2 |

[1] Includes other private and government insurance, not shown separately. Persons with coverage counted only once in total, even if covered by more than one type of policy. [2] Refers to people who reported specified race and no other race category. [3] Persons of Hispanic origin may be of any race.

Source: U.S. Census Bureau, *Health Insurance Coverage in the United States: 2017*, Current Population Reports, P60-264, September 2018; and "Current Population Survey Tables for Health Insurance Coverage: HI-01. Health Insurance Coverage Status and Type of Coverage by Selected Characteristics" and "HI-03. Health Insurance Coverage Status and Type of Coverage by Selected Characteristics for Poor People Below Poverty in the Poverty Universe," <https://www.census.gov/topics/health/health-insurance/data/tables.html>, accessed November 2018.

# Table 164. Persons With and Without Health Insurance Coverage by State: 2017

[292,756 represents 292,756,000. Data are from the American Community Survey (ACS), and measures population without health insurance coverage at the time of the interview. See source for more information]

| State | Total persons covered (1,000) | Total persons not covered | | Children not covered [1] | | State | Total persons covered (1,000) | Total persons not covered | | Children not covered [1] | |
| | | Number (1,000) | Percent of total | Number (1,000) | Percent of total | | | Number (1,000) | Percent of total | Number (1,000) | Percent of total |
| U.S......... | 292,756 | 28,019 | 8.7 | 3,925 | 5.0 | MO.......... | 5,452 | 548 | 9.1 | 75 | 5.1 |
| AL.......... | 4,345 | 449 | 9.4 | 36 | 3.1 | MT.......... | 949 | 88 | 8.5 | 14 | 5.8 |
| AK.......... | 618 | 98 | 13.7 | 19 | 9.6 | NE.......... | 1,735 | 157 | 8.3 | 26 | 5.1 |
| AZ.......... | 6,213 | 695 | 10.1 | 133 | 7.7 | NV.......... | 2,630 | 333 | 11.2 | 58 | 8.0 |
| AR.......... | 2,718 | 232 | 7.9 | 33 | 4.4 | NH.......... | 1,248 | 77 | 5.8 | 6 | 2.3 |
| CA.......... | 36,250 | 2,797 | 7.2 | 301 | 3.1 | NJ.......... | 8,214 | 688 | 7.7 | 78 | 3.7 |
| CO.......... | 5,100 | 414 | 7.5 | 57 | 4.3 | NM.......... | 1,867 | 187 | 9.1 | 26 | 5.1 |
| CT.......... | 3,343 | 194 | 5.5 | 24 | 3.1 | NY.......... | 18,495 | 1,113 | 5.7 | 118 | 2.7 |
| DE.......... | 896 | 51 | 5.4 | 8 | 3.5 | NC.......... | 8,995 | 1,076 | 10.7 | 119 | 4.8 |
| DC.......... | 658 | 26 | 3.8 | 2 | 1.2 | ND.......... | 683 | 56 | 7.5 | 14 | 7.5 |
| FL.......... | 18,003 | 2,676 | 12.9 | 325 | 7.3 | OH.......... | 10,799 | 686 | 6.0 | 125 | 4.5 |
| GA.......... | 8,866 | 1,375 | 13.4 | 200 | 7.5 | OK.......... | 3,306 | 545 | 14.2 | 82 | 8.1 |
| HI.......... | 1,320 | 53 | 3.8 | 7 | 2.2 | OR.......... | 3,822 | 281 | 6.8 | 33 | 3.6 |
| ID.......... | 1,523 | 172 | 10.1 | 22 | 4.6 | PA.......... | 11,910 | 692 | 5.5 | 125 | 4.4 |
| IL.......... | 11,761 | 859 | 6.8 | 89 | 2.9 | RI.......... | 996 | 48 | 4.6 | 5 | 2.1 |
| IN.......... | 6,032 | 536 | 8.2 | 106 | 6.3 | SC.......... | 4,387 | 542 | 11.0 | 60 | 5.1 |
| IA.......... | 2,956 | 146 | 4.7 | 24 | 3.1 | SD.......... | 774 | 77 | 9.1 | 14 | 6.2 |
| KS.......... | 2,606 | 249 | 8.7 | 39 | 5.2 | TN.......... | 5,983 | 629 | 9.5 | 71 | 4.4 |
| KY.......... | 4,136 | 235 | 5.4 | 41 | 3.8 | TX.......... | 23,020 | 4,817 | 17.3 | 835 | 10.7 |
| LA.......... | 4,198 | 383 | 8.4 | 36 | 3.1 | UT.......... | 2,795 | 282 | 9.2 | 71 | 7.3 |
| ME.......... | 1,215 | 107 | 8.1 | 13 | 4.9 | VT.......... | 589 | 28 | 4.6 | 2 | 1.6 |
| MD.......... | 5,592 | 366 | 6.1 | 54 | 3.8 | VA.......... | 7,528 | 729 | 8.8 | 101 | 5.1 |
| MA.......... | 6,596 | 190 | 2.8 | 22 | 1.5 | WA.......... | 6,854 | 446 | 6.1 | 46 | 2.6 |
| MI.......... | 9,344 | 510 | 5.2 | 69 | 3.0 | WV.......... | 1,678 | 109 | 6.1 | 11 | 2.6 |
| MN.......... | 5,277 | 243 | 4.4 | 47 | 3.4 | WI.......... | 5,415 | 309 | 5.4 | 53 | 3.9 |
| MS.......... | 2,569 | 352 | 12.0 | 37 | 4.8 | WY.......... | 499 | 70 | 12.3 | 14 | 9.5 |

[1] Children under age 19, who are eligible for health insurance coverage under Medicaid and the Children's Health Insurance Program.

Source: U.S. Census Bureau, 2017 American Community Survey, S2701 "Selected Characteristics of Health Insurance Coverage in the United States," <http://factfinder.census.gov>, accessed November 2018.

## Table 165. Health Insurance Coverage—Public, Private, and Exchange-Based Coverage by Selected Characteristics: 2010 to 2018

[In percent, except as noted (10.2 represents 10,200,000). Covers persons age 18 to 64, except as noted. Based on the National Health Interview Survey. Data are estimates that have been released prior to final data editing and final weighting; see source for details. Data are based on a sample of the civilian noninstitutionalized population and are subject to sampling error]

| Year and characteristics | No insurance [1] | Private health insurance [2] | Public health plan [3] | Exchange-based private health insurance [4] | |
|---|---|---|---|---|---|
| | | | | Total (millions) | Percent |
| **Total age 64 and under:** | | | | | |
| 2010 | 18.2 | 61.2 | 22.0 | (NA) | (NA) |
| 2015 | 10.5 | 65.6 | 25.3 | 10.2 | 3.8 |
| 2017 | 10.7 | 65.4 | 25.3 | 9.9 | 3.7 |
| 2018 | 11.1 | 65.1 | 25.5 | 10.0 | 3.7 |
| **Age 17 and under:** | | | | | |
| 2010 | 7.8 | 53.8 | 39.8 | (NA) | (NA) |
| 2015 | 4.5 | 54.7 | 42.2 | 1.4 | 2.0 |
| 2017 | 5.0 | 55.0 | 41.3 | 1.4 | 1.9 |
| 2018 | 5.2 | 54.7 | 41.8 | 1.7 | 2.3 |
| **Age 18 to 64:** | | | | | |
| 2010 | 22.3 | 64.1 | 15.0 | (NA) | (NA) |
| 2015 | 12.8 | 69.7 | 18.9 | 8.8 | 4.5 |
| 2017 | 12.8 | 69.3 | 19.3 | 8.5 | 4.3 |
| 2018 | 13.3 | 68.9 | 19.4 | 8.4 | 4.2 |
| **Male:** | | | | | |
| 2010 | 25.3 | 63.4 | 12.5 | (NA) | (NA) |
| 2015 | 14.9 | 69.9 | 16.6 | 4.0 | 4.1 |
| 2017 | 14.5 | 69.7 | 17.3 | 3.9 | 4.0 |
| 2018 | 15.0 | 69.4 | 17.3 | 3.9 | 4.0 |
| **Female:** | | | | | |
| 2010 | 19.3 | 64.7 | 17.4 | (NA) | (NA) |
| 2015 | 10.8 | 69.6 | 21.2 | 4.8 | 4.8 |
| 2017 | 11.2 | 68.8 | 21.3 | 4.6 | 4.6 |
| 2018 | 11.6 | 68.5 | 21.5 | 4.4 | 4.4 |
| **White only, non-Hispanic:** | | | | | |
| 2010 | 16.4 | 72.2 | 12.8 | (NA) | (NA) |
| 2015 | 8.7 | 77.3 | 15.7 | 5.2 | 4.3 |
| 2017 | 8.5 | 77.2 | 15.8 | 5.1 | 4.3 |
| 2018 | 9.0 | 76.7 | 16.2 | 4.7 | 3.9 |
| **Black only, non-Hispanic:** | | | | | |
| 2010 | 27.2 | 49.3 | 25.3 | (NA) | (NA) |
| 2015 | 14.4 | 57.8 | 29.7 | 1.0 | 4.0 |
| 2017 | 14.1 | 57.0 | 30.3 | 0.8 | 3.4 |
| 2018 | 15.2 | 57.9 | 29.0 | 1.0 | 3.9 |
| **Hispanic or Latino:** [5] | | | | | |
| 2010 | 43.2 | 41.1 | 16.3 | (NA) | (NA) |
| 2015 | 27.7 | 50.0 | 23.0 | 1.7 | 5.1 |
| 2017 | 27.2 | 50.2 | 23.7 | 1.5 | 4.3 |
| 2018 | 26.7 | 50.8 | 23.3 | 1.7 | 4.7 |
| **Poor:** [6] | | | | | |
| 2010 | 42.2 | 19.6 | 38.8 | (NA) | (NA) |
| 2015 | 25.2 | 24.3 | 51.7 | 0.9 | 3.8 |
| 2017 | 24.4 | 26.5 | 50.2 | 0.7 | 2.8 |
| 2018 | 27.4 | 21.4 | 52.7 | 0.6 | 2.7 |
| **Near poor:** [6] | | | | | |
| 2010 | 43.0 | 34.7 | 23.7 | (NA) | (NA) |
| 2015 | 24.1 | 43.8 | 34.2 | 2.7 | 7.9 |
| 2017 | 23.8 | 40.5 | 37.6 | 2.5 | 7.6 |
| 2018 | 25.1 | 39.3 | 37.8 | 2.3 | 7.2 |
| **Not poor:** [6] | | | | | |
| 2010 | 12.6 | 80.8 | 8.1 | (NA) | (NA) |
| 2015 | 7.6 | 84.7 | 9.1 | 5.1 | 3.8 |
| 2017 | 8.2 | 83.3 | 9.9 | 5.3 | 3.8 |
| 2018 | 8.3 | 83.1 | 10.1 | 5.6 | 3.8 |

NA Not available. [1] Also includes persons who had only Indian Health Service coverage or only a private plan that paid for one type of service, such as accidents or dental care. [2] Includes plans obtained through an employer, purchased directly, purchased through local or community programs, or purchased through the Health Insurance Marketplace or a state-based exchange. Excludes plans that pay for only one type of service, such as accidents or dental care. A small number of persons covered by both public and private plans are included in both categories. [3] Includes Medicaid, Children's Health Insurance Program (CHIP), state-sponsored or other government-sponsored health plan, Medicare, and military plans. A small number of persons covered by both public and private plans are included in both categories. [4] Covers persons who purchased a private health insurance plan through the Health Insurance Marketplace or state-based exchanges that were established under the Affordable Care Act of 2010 (P.L. 111-148, P.L. 111-152). These persons are also included under "private health insurance." [5] Persons of Hispanic or Latino origin may be of any race or combination of races. [6] Based on family income and family size, using the U.S. Census Bureau's poverty thresholds. "Poor" persons have incomes below the poverty threshold; "Near poor" persons have incomes of 100% to less than 200% of the poverty threshold; and "Not poor" persons have incomes of 200% of the poverty threshold or greater. Excludes persons with unknown poverty status.

Source: U.S. National Center for Health Statistics, "Early Release Reports and Tabulations on Special Topics," *Health Insurance Coverage: Early Release of Quarterly Estimates from the National Health Interview Survey, January 2010-December 2018*, May 2019. See also <https://www.cdc.gov/nchs/nhis/releases.htm>.

# Table 166. Health Insurance Coverage Status and Plan Type: 1970 to 2018

[142.3 represents 142,300,000. Based on the National Health Interview Survey. Covers persons under age 65. Persons may report more than one type of health insurance coverage]

| Year | Private insurance, any [1] | Private, employer based | Private, other [2] | Medicaid | Medicare | Other public | No health insurance [3] |
|---|---|---|---|---|---|---|---|
| **NUMBER (mil.)** | | | | | | | |
| 1970................ | 142.3 | 124.1 | 18.0 | (NA) | (NA) | (NA) | (NA) |
| 1976................ | 148.9 | 129.4 | 19.5 | 9.3 | 0.5 | 4.9 | 26.6 |
| 1980................ | 154.1 | 138.5 | 15.6 | 13.8 | 2.7 | 3.9 | 23.3 |
| 1982................ | 157.5 | 141.8 | 16.0 | 12.2 | 2.5 | 7.5 | 28.0 |
| 1984................ | 156.7 | 139.4 | 17.7 | 13.9 | 2.3 | 7.3 | 29.7 |
| 1986................ | 157.5 | 141.7 | 15.7 | 13.9 | 2.4 | 7.6 | 29.8 |
| 1989................ | 160.4 | 144.6 | 15.8 | 13.4 | 2.5 | 6.9 | 31.3 |
| 1990................ | 162.7 | 146.3 | 16.3 | 15.4 | 3.0 | 6.1 | 33.4 |
| 1991................ | 160.5 | 143.7 | 16.8 | 15.4 | 2.8 | 6.5 | 37.2 |
| 1992................ | 160.8 | 137.1 | 23.7 | 18.6 | 3.0 | 6.4 | 35.8 |
| 1993................ | 158.9 | 143.2 | 15.8 | 21.6 | 3.2 | 6.4 | 37.1 |
| 1994................ | 158.8 | 145.9 | 12.9 | 23.9 | 3.0 | 6.1 | 38.8 |
| 1995................ | 159.8 | 146.2 | 13.5 | 25.6 | 3.1 | 6.4 | 40.6 |
| 1996................ | 164.4 | 151.3 | 13.1 | 26.6 | 3.7 | 5.9 | 37.7 |
| 1997................ | 165.5 | 151.4 | 14.2 | 25.8 | 3.7 | 6.0 | 38.9 |
| 1998................ | 165.8 | 155.9 | 9.8 | 22.9 | 3.8 | 6.4 | 41.0 |
| 1999................ | 170.8 | 159.8 | 10.8 | 21.1 | 4.1 | 6.3 | 39.2 |
| 2000................ | 174.2 | 163.4 | 10.5 | 21.9 | 4.1 | 5.2 | 38.5 |
| 2001................ | 173.0 | 162.5 | 10.1 | 22.9 | 4.0 | 5.4 | 40.5 |
| 2002................ | 174.1 | 163.8 | 10.0 | 25.2 | 4.3 | 5.1 | 39.2 |
| 2003................ | 173.6 | 162.1 | 10.1 | 30.9 | 4.5 | 6.1 | 41.6 |
| 2004................ | 174.5 | 162.3 | 11.6 | 31.6 | 4.5 | 6.1 | 41.6 |
| 2005................ | 174.7 | 162.9 | 11.1 | 33.2 | 4.5 | 6.4 | 42.1 |
| 2006................ | 171.2 | 158.8 | 11.8 | 36.2 | 5.4 | 6.5 | 43.9 |
| 2007................ | 174.1 | 160.7 | 12.7 | 36.2 | 5.4 | 7.0 | 43.3 |
| 2008................ | 171.9 | 158.6 | 12.6 | 38.4 | 5.9 | 7.0 | 44.1 |
| 2009................ | 166.7 | 152.8 | 13.1 | 42.4 | 6.2 | 7.7 | 46.2 |
| 2010................ | 163.9 | 150.2 | 12.7 | 44.8 | 6.0 | 8.1 | 48.3 |
| 2011................ | 164.5 | 150.1 | 12.7 | 47.4 | 6.4 | 7.9 | 45.8 |
| 2012................ | 164.9 | 151.8 | 11.8 | 48.1 | 6.5 | 8.1 | 45.2 |
| 2013................ | 165.3 | 151.5 | 12.5 | 48.5 | 7.1 | 8.1 | 44.6 |
| 2014................ | 170.7 | 151.3 | 17.2 | 52.6 | 6.7 | 8.4 | 35.7 |
| 2015................ | 176.6 | 154.7 | 20.8 | 55.4 | 7.0 | 8.1 | 28.7 |
| 2016................ | 177.7 | 155.5 | 21.2 | 57.0 | 7.5 | 7.6 | 27.9 |
| 2017................ | 177.7 | 157.5 | 19.2 | 54.6 | 7.3 | 8.5 | 28.9 |
| 2018................ | 177.5 | 157.8 | 18.9 | 54.7 | 7.8 | 10.2 | 30.0 |
| **PERCENT** | | | | | | | |
| 1970................ | 78.7 | 68.6 | 10.0 | (NA) | (NA) | (NA) | (NA) |
| 1976................ | 78.9 | 68.5 | 10.3 | 4.9 | 0.2 | 2.6 | 14.1 |
| 1980................ | 79.4 | 71.4 | 8.0 | 7.1 | 1.4 | 2.0 | 12.0 |
| 1982................ | 78.1 | 70.3 | 7.9 | 6.1 | 1.2 | 3.7 | 13.9 |
| 1984................ | 76.9 | 68.4 | 8.7 | 6.8 | 1.1 | 3.6 | 14.6 |
| 1986................ | 76.7 | 69.1 | 7.7 | 6.8 | 1.2 | 3.7 | 14.5 |
| 1989................ | 76.8 | 69.3 | 7.6 | 6.4 | 1.2 | 3.3 | 15.0 |
| 1990................ | 75.9 | 68.3 | 7.6 | 7.2 | 1.4 | 2.9 | 15.6 |
| 1991................ | 74.2 | 66.4 | 7.8 | 7.1 | 1.3 | 3.0 | 17.2 |
| 1992................ | 73.6 | 62.8 | 10.8 | 8.5 | 1.4 | 2.9 | 16.4 |
| 1993................ | 72.0 | 64.9 | 7.1 | 9.8 | 1.4 | 2.9 | 16.8 |
| 1994................ | 69.9 | 64.0 | 5.9 | 11.2 | 1.4 | 2.8 | 17.8 |
| 1995................ | 71.3 | 65.6 | 5.7 | 11.5 | 1.6 | 2.6 | 16.3 |
| 1996................ | 71.2 | 65.1 | 6.1 | 11.1 | 1.6 | 2.6 | 16.7 |
| 1997................ | 70.7 | 66.4 | 4.2 | 9.7 | 1.6 | 2.7 | 17.5 |
| 1998................ | 72.1 | 67.5 | 4.6 | 8.9 | 1.7 | 2.7 | 16.6 |
| 1999................ | 72.8 | 68.3 | 4.4 | 9.1 | 1.7 | 2.2 | 16.1 |
| 2000................ | 71.7 | 67.3 | 4.2 | 9.5 | 1.7 | 2.2 | 16.8 |
| 2001................ | 71.5 | 67.2 | 4.1 | 10.4 | 1.8 | 2.1 | 16.1 |
| 2002................ | 69.7 | 65.6 | 3.9 | 11.8 | 1.7 | 2.3 | 16.5 |
| 2003................ | 68.9 | 64.4 | 4.0 | 12.3 | 1.8 | 2.4 | 16.5 |
| 2004................ | 68.8 | 64.0 | 4.6 | 12.5 | 1.8 | 2.4 | 16.4 |
| 2005................ | 68.2 | 63.6 | 4.4 | 12.9 | 1.8 | 2.5 | 16.4 |
| 2006................ | 66.3 | 61.5 | 4.6 | 14.0 | 2.1 | 2.5 | 17.0 |
| 2007................ | 66.8 | 61.6 | 4.9 | 13.9 | 2.1 | 2.7 | 16.6 |
| 2008................ | 65.6 | 60.5 | 4.8 | 14.7 | 2.3 | 2.7 | 16.8 |
| 2009................ | 63.3 | 58.0 | 5.0 | 16.1 | 2.3 | 2.9 | 17.5 |
| 2010................ | 61.7 | 56.6 | 4.8 | 16.9 | 2.3 | 3.1 | 18.2 |
| 2011................ | 61.8 | 56.4 | 4.8 | 17.8 | 2.4 | 3.0 | 17.2 |
| 2012................ | 61.8 | 56.9 | 4.4 | 18.0 | 2.4 | 3.0 | 16.9 |
| 2013................ | 61.8 | 56.6 | 4.7 | 18.1 | 2.6 | 3.0 | 16.7 |
| 2014................ | 63.7 | 56.4 | 6.4 | 19.6 | 2.5 | 3.1 | 13.3 |
| 2015................ | 65.5 | 57.4 | 7.7 | 20.6 | 2.6 | 3.0 | 10.6 |
| 2016................ | 65.7 | 57.4 | 7.8 | 21.1 | 2.8 | 2.8 | 10.3 |
| 2017................ | 65.7 | 58.2 | 7.1 | 20.2 | 2.7 | 3.1 | 10.7 |
| 2018................ | 65.3 | 58.1 | 6.9 | 20.2 | 2.9 | 3.7 | 11.0 |

NA Not available. [1] Private health insurance coverage obtained through an employer, purchased directly, or obtained through any other means. Beginning in 2014, also includes plans purchased through the Health Insurance Marketplace or a state-based exchange under the Affordable Care Act of 2010. Excludes plans that cover only one type of service such as accidents or dental care. [2] Private insurance that is directly purchased as well as plans obtained through school or other means. Beginning in 2014, also includes plans purchased through the Health Insurance Marketplace or a state-based exchange. [3] Includes persons who did not have any private or government-sponsored health plan, or military-related coverage. Also includes persons with only Indian Health Service coverage or a private plan that covers only one type of service.

Source: U.S. National Center for Health Statistics, "Long-term Trends in Health Insurance: Estimates from the National Health Interview Survey, United States, 1968-2018," <https://www.cdc.gov/nchs/health_policy/coverage_and_access.htm>, accessed July 2019.

# Table 167. People Without Health Insurance for the Entire Year by Age, Sex, Race/Ethnicity, and Family Type: 2016 and 2017

[In thousands, except as noted (320,372 represents 320,372,000). Based on the Current Population Survey, Annual Social and Economic Supplement (CPS ASEC); see text, Section 1 and Appendix III]

| Characteristic | 2016 | | | 2017 | | |
|---|---|---|---|---|---|---|
| | | Uninsured persons | | | Uninsured persons | |
| | Total persons | Number | Percent of total persons | Total persons | Number | Percent of total persons |
| Total [1] | 320,372 | 28,052 | 8.8 | 323,156 | 28,543 | 8.8 |
| Under 18 years | 74,047 | 3,924 | 5.3 | 73,963 | 3,930 | 5.3 |
| 18 to 24 years | 29,404 | 3,508 | 11.9 | 29,363 | 3,782 | 12.9 |
| 25 to 34 years | 44,250 | 6,906 | 15.6 | 44,854 | 6,981 | 15.6 |
| 35 to 44 years | 40,046 | 5,252 | 13.1 | 40,659 | 5,407 | 13.3 |
| 45 to 54 years | 42,026 | 4,343 | 10.3 | 41,537 | 4,252 | 10.2 |
| 55 to 64 years | 41,325 | 3,521 | 8.5 | 41,700 | 3,513 | 8.4 |
| 65 years and over | 49,274 | 598 | 1.2 | 51,080 | 678 | 1.3 |
| Male | 156,939 | 15,143 | 9.6 | 158,426 | 15,186 | 9.6 |
| Female | 163,433 | 12,909 | 7.9 | 164,730 | 13,358 | 8.1 |
| White alone [2] | 246,310 | 20,813 | 8.4 | 247,695 | 21,075 | 8.5 |
| Black alone [2] | 42,040 | 4,428 | 10.5 | 42,564 | 4,512 | 10.6 |
| Asian alone [2] | 18,897 | 1,442 | 7.6 | 19,484 | 1,413 | 7.3 |
| Hispanic [3] | 57,670 | 9,237 | 16.0 | 59,227 | 9,508 | 16.1 |
| In families | 259,863 | 21,208 | 8.2 | 260,709 | 21,542 | 8.3 |
| In married-couple families | 192,838 | 12,715 | 6.6 | 194,037 | 13,121 | 6.8 |
| In families with male householders, no spouse present | 18,782 | 2,894 | 15.4 | 18,674 | 2,794 | 15.0 |
| In families with female householders, no spouse present | 48,243 | 5,599 | 11.6 | 47,999 | 5,627 | 11.7 |

[1] Includes other races not shown separately. [2] Refers to people who reported specified race and did not report any other race category. [3] Persons of Hispanic origin may be of any race.

Source: U.S. Census Bureau, *Health Insurance Coverage in the United States: 2017*, Current Population Reports, P60-264, September 2018, and earlier reports; and "Current Population Survey Tables for Health Insurance Coverage: HI-01, Health Insurance Coverage Status and Type of Coverage by Selected Characteristics," <https://www.census.gov/topics/health/health-insurance/data/tables.html>, accessed November 2018.

# Table 168. Worker Participation in Employer-Sponsored Health Insurance and Benefit Programs, and Participant Contributions: 2018

[Based on the March 2018 National Compensation Survey; survey drew responses from approximately 6,588 private industry establishments of all sizes, representing about 118 million workers. Excludes federal government workers, the military, agricultural workers, private household workers, and the self-employed. For more information, see Appendix III, and the Bureau of Labor Statistics (BLS) Handbook of Methods, National Compensation Measures, at <https://www.bls.gov/opub/hom/ncs/home.htm>]

| Characteristic | Percent of workers participating— | | | | Single coverage medical plans | | Family coverage medical plans | |
|---|---|---|---|---|---|---|---|---|
| | Medical care | Dental care | Vision care | Outpatient prescription drug coverage | Percent of employees required to contribute to premiums | Average monthly contribution [1] (dol.) | Percent of employees required to contribute to premiums | Average monthly contribution [1] (dol.) |
| Total | 50 | 33 | 19 | 49 | 86 | 135.80 | 93 | 564.99 |
| Management, professional, and related | 66 | 49 | 29 | 65 | 87 | 131.79 | 94 | 554.19 |
| Management, business, and financial | 72 | 51 | 30 | 70 | 90 | 133.20 | 96 | 528.77 |
| Professional and related | 63 | 47 | 28 | 63 | 85 | 130.83 | 93 | 570.82 |
| Service | 26 | 16 | 10 | 25 | 87 | 134.76 | 93 | 633.12 |
| Sales and office | 45 | 29 | 16 | 45 | 89 | 137.09 | 96 | 572.77 |
| Sales and related | 35 | 20 | 11 | 34 | 93 | 134.11 | 97 | 565.17 |
| Office and administrative support | 53 | 36 | 19 | 52 | 88 | 138.49 | 96 | 576.22 |
| Natural resources, construction, and maintenance | 57 | 32 | 21 | 56 | 79 | 144.12 | 86 | 588.35 |
| Production, transportation, and material moving | 56 | 36 | 21 | 55 | 85 | 138.44 | 89 | 521.87 |
| Production | 61 | 37 | 21 | 60 | 86 | 134.92 | 89 | 494.96 |
| Transportation, and material moving | 51 | 35 | 21 | 50 | 85 | 142.44 | 89 | 551.55 |
| Full-time [2] | 63 | 42 | 24 | 62 | 87 | 135.45 | 93 | 559.60 |
| Part-time [2] | 11 | 7 | 5 | 11 | 84 | 141.63 | 88 | 656.19 |
| Union [3] | 77 | 62 | 45 | 76 | 64 | 126.54 | 68 | 432.49 |
| Nonunion | 47 | 30 | 17 | 46 | 90 | 136.84 | 97 | 579.54 |
| Average hourly wage percentile: [4] | | | | | | | | |
| Lowest 25 percent | 20 | 11 | 6 | 20 | 91 | 142.19 | 95 | 648.43 |
| Lowest 10 percent | 12 | 6 | 5 | 12 | 86 | 151.78 | 95 | 612.51 |
| Second 25 percent | 51 | 31 | 17 | 50 | 88 | 137.73 | 95 | 582.77 |
| Third 25 percent | 64 | 42 | 24 | 63 | 85 | 137.58 | 92 | 573.10 |
| Highest 25 percent | 72 | 55 | 33 | 71 | 84 | 130.14 | 91 | 512.34 |
| Highest 10 percent | 74 | 58 | 34 | 73 | 85 | 126.82 | 92 | 488.27 |

[1] The average is for all workers with medical care benefits, and cover plans that have a flat monthly cost. [2] Employees are classified as working either a full-time or part-time schedule based on the definition used by each establishment. [3] Union workers are those whose wages are determined through collective bargaining. [4] Tenth percentile, $10.00; 25th, $12.75; 50th (median), $18.78; 75th, $30.08; and 90th, $46.73. See "Technical Note" in source, <https://www.bls.gov/ncs/ebs/benefits/2018/tech_note.htm>.

Source: U.S. Bureau of Labor Statistics, Annual Bulletin on Benefit Coverage, *National Compensation Survey: Employee Benefits in the United States, March 2018*, Bulletin 2789, September 2018. See also <https://www.bls.gov/ncs/ebs/benefits/2018/home.htm>.

# Table 169. Employer-Sponsored Health Insurance Enrollment by Type of Plan and Employer Size: 2015

[In millions (177.5 represents 177,500,000). Based on the Current Population Survey, Annual and Social Economic Supplement, and Agency for Healthcare Research and Quality's Medical Expenditure Panel Surveys. For persons and their dependents covered by health insurance sponsored by a current or former employer. Abbreviations: HMO = health maintenance organization; PPO = preferred provider organization; POS = point-of-service plan; and HDED = high deductible health plan (including but not limited to IRS-qualified high deductible health plans)]

| Employer sector and size | Total | | | | | Self-insured plans [1] | | | | | Fully insured plans [2] | | | | |
|---|---|---|---|---|---|---|---|---|---|---|---|---|---|---|---|
| | Total | HMO | PPO | POS | HDED | Total | HMO | PPO | POS | HDED | Total | HMO | PPO | POS | HDED |
| **TOTAL** | | | | | | | | | | | | | | | |
| Total...... | 177.5 | 25.1 | 101.1 | 15.8 | 35.5 | 101.2 | 8.1 | 64.5 | 4.9 | 23.8 | 76.3 | 17.0 | 36.6 | 11.0 | 11.7 |
| Less than 50 employees.......... | 27.9 | 4.1 | 11.8 | 5.6 | 6.3 | 4.0 | (Z) | 2.6 | 0.5 | 1.0 | 23.9 | 4.1 | 9.3 | 5.2 | 5.3 |
| 50 to 99 employees....... | 11.7 | 1.5 | 5.3 | 2.1 | 2.7 | 2.5 | (Z) | 1.6 | 0.2 | 0.6 | 9.2 | 1.5 | 3.6 | 1.9 | 2.1 |
| 100 to 499 employees.... | 23.7 | 2.8 | 14.6 | 2.4 | 4.0 | 10.4 | 0.4 | 7.7 | 0.6 | 1.7 | 13.4 | 2.4 | 7.0 | 1.8 | 2.2 |
| 500 to 999 employees.... | 12.9 | 1.4 | 8.3 | 1.1 | 2.1 | 6.5 | 0.3 | 4.9 | 0.3 | 1.0 | 6.4 | 1.2 | 3.4 | 0.8 | 1.1 |
| 1,000 or more employees.......... | 101.3 | 15.2 | 61.1 | 4.6 | 20.5 | 77.9 | 7.4 | 47.7 | 3.4 | 19.5 | 23.4 | 7.8 | 13.4 | 1.2 | 1.0 |
| **PRIVATE SECTOR [3]** | | | | | | | | | | | | | | | |
| Total...... | 134.7 | 16.7 | 74.9 | 13.8 | 29.4 | 84.4 | 6.7 | 53.7 | 4.4 | 19.6 | 50.3 | 10.0 | 21.2 | 9.4 | 9.7 |
| Less than 50 employees.......... | 26.6 | 3.9 | 11.2 | 5.5 | 6.0 | 3.9 | (Z) | 2.5 | 0.4 | 1.0 | 22.7 | 3.9 | 8.8 | 5.0 | 5.0 |
| 50 to 99 employees....... | 10.7 | 1.4 | 4.8 | 2.0 | 2.5 | 2.3 | (Z) | 1.5 | 0.2 | 0.6 | 8.4 | 1.4 | 3.3 | 1.8 | 1.9 |
| 100 to 499 employees.... | 20.1 | 2.2 | 12.5 | 2.0 | 3.4 | 9.5 | 0.4 | 7.0 | 0.5 | 1.5 | 10.6 | 1.8 | 5.4 | 1.5 | 1.9 |
| 500 to 999 employees.... | 10.0 | 1.1 | 6.5 | 0.8 | 1.5 | 5.6 | 0.2 | 4.4 | 0.3 | 0.8 | 4.4 | 0.8 | 2.2 | 0.6 | 0.8 |
| 1,000 or more employees.......... | 67.3 | 8.1 | 39.9 | 3.4 | 16.0 | 63.1 | 6.1 | 38.4 | 3.0 | 15.7 | 4.2 | 2.0 | 1.5 | 0.5 | 0.2 |

Z Less than 50,000 persons. [1] Self-insured plans are those in which the employer directly assumes some or all medical claim and administrative costs. [2] Fully insured plans are those in which the employer contracts with another organization to assume financial responsibility for the enrollees' medical claims and administrative costs. [3] Private sector includes self-employed.

Source: U.S. Department of Labor, Employee Benefits Security Administration, *Health Insurance Coverage Bulletin: Abstract of Auxiliary Data for the March 2016 Annual Social and Economic Supplement to the Current Population Survey*, July 2017. See also <https://www.dol.gov/agencies/ebsa/researchers/data/auxiliary-data>.

# Table 170. Health Insurance Enrollment in High Deductible Health Plans (HDHP) and Health Savings Accounts: 2010 to 2018

[In percent. Covers persons under age 65 with private health insurance coverage. For 2018, an HDHP is a private health plan with an annual deductible of at least $1,350 for self-only coverage or $2,700 for family coverage. For 2015 to 2017, these amounts were $1,300 for self-only coverage and $2,600 for family coverage. The deductible is adjusted annually for inflation. For deductibles for earlier years, see Technical Notes in source. Components of HDHP may not sum due to rounding. The measures of HDHP enrollment, consumer driven health plan (CDHP) enrollment, and being in a family with a flexible spending account (FSA) for medical expenses are not mutually exclusive; a person may be counted in more than one measure. Based on the National Health Interview Survey. Data are based on a sample of the civilian noninstitutionalized population and are subject to sampling error]

| Year | HDHP enrollment | | | | | In a family with a flexible spending account [5] |
|---|---|---|---|---|---|---|
| | Total | HDHP without health savings account [1] | CDHP [2] | By source | | |
| | | | | Employment based [3] | Directly purchased [4] | |
| 2010.......... | 25.3 | 17.6 | 7.7 | 23.3 | 48.0 | 20.4 |
| 2011.......... | 29.0 | 19.9 | 9.2 | 26.9 | 52.4 | 21.4 |
| 2012.......... | 31.1 | 20.3 | 10.8 | 29.2 | 54.7 | 21.6 |
| 2013.......... | 33.9 | 22.2 | 11.7 | 32.0 | 56.4 | 21.6 |
| 2014.......... | 36.9 | 23.6 | 13.3 | 36.2 | 54.1 | 21.2 |
| 2015.......... | 36.7 | 23.4 | 13.3 | 36.6 | 50.9 | 21.7 |
| 2016.......... | 39.4 | 23.9 | 15.5 | 39.6 | 51.9 | 22.1 |
| 2017.......... | 43.7 | 25.5 | 18.2 | 44.1 | 55.3 | 23.6 |
| 2018 (P)....... | 45.8 | 25.4 | 20.4 | 46.6 | 52.2 | 23.9 |

P Preliminary. [1] Health savings accounts are tax-favored accounts available only to persons with an HDHP to pay for current and future medical expenses. Funds contributed are not subject to federal income tax at the time of deposit and may be used to cover qualified medical expenses without federal tax liability. HSA funds are rolled over annually and accumulate year to year. [2] A consumer driven health plan is an HDHP coupled with a health savings account. [3] Private insurance originally obtained through a current or former employer, union, or professional association. [4] Private insurance originally obtained through direct purchase or other means not related to employment. [5] A flexible spending account allows employees to set aside pretax dollars to cover out-of-pocket medical expenses. FSAs are typically available to persons who do not have an HDHP and thus are not eligible for an HSA. Any money not used during the year is lost to the employee.

Source: U.S. National Center for Health Statistics, *Health Insurance Coverage: Early Release of Estimates From the National Health Interview Survey, 2018*, May 2019. See also <https://www.cdc.gov/nchs/nhis/releases.htm>.

# Table 171. Revenue for Health Care Industries: 2015 to 2017

[In millions of dollars (2,304,000 represents $2,340,000,000,000). For all employer firms, and taxable employer firms. Estimates have been adjusted to the results of the 2012 Economic Census. Based on the Service Annual Survey and administrative data; see Appendix III]

| Kind of business | NAICS code [1] | Total, all firms [2] | | | Taxable employer firms | | |
|---|---|---|---|---|---|---|---|
| | | 2015 | 2016 | 2017 | 2015 | 2016 | 2017 |
| **Health care and social assistance** [3] | **62** | **2,304,000** | **2,429,233** | **2,541,261** | **1,138,936** | **1,197,012** | **1,244,999** |
| **Ambulatory health care services** [3] | **621** | **912,343** | **960,336** | **1,000,235** | **824,835** | **868,027** | **902,818** |
| Offices of physicians (except mental health specialists) | 621111 | 442,965 | 466,035 | 484,891 | 442,965 | 466,035 | 484,891 |
| Offices of physicians, mental health specialists | 621112 | 5,295 | 5,599 | 5,971 | 5,295 | 5,599 | 5,971 |
| Offices of dentists | 6212 | 113,855 | 119,857 | 123,839 | 113,855 | 119,857 | 123,839 |
| Offices of chiropractors | 62131 | 12,334 | 12,711 | 13,206 | 12,334 | 12,711 | 13,206 |
| Offices of optometrists | 62132 | 13,912 | 14,682 | 15,214 | 13,912 | 14,682 | 15,214 |
| Offices of mental health practitioners, (except physicians) | 62133 | 9,092 | 10,257 | 11,211 | 9,092 | 10,257 | 11,211 |
| Offices of PT/OT/speech therapists and audiologists [4] | 62134 | 28,365 | 29,892 | 30,729 | 28,365 | 29,892 | 30,729 |
| Offices of podiatrists | 621391 | 4,410 | 4,442 | 4,572 | 4,410 | 4,442 | 4,572 |
| Outpatient care centers | 6214 | 118,042 | 127,296 | 134,933 | 61,843 | 67,560 | 70,887 |
| Family planning centers | 62141 | 2,417 | 2,630 | 2,843 | 1,065 | 1,230 | 1,284 |
| Outpatient mental health and substance abuse centers | 62142 | 18,089 | 19,946 | 21,389 | 5,705 | 6,931 | 7,478 |
| HMO medical centers [5] | 621491 | 8,080 | 8,704 | 9,758 | (S) | 982 | 1,064 |
| Kidney dialysis centers | 621492 | 20,947 | 22,709 | 23,926 | 19,452 | 21,206 | 22,353 |
| Freestanding ambulatory surgical and emergency centers | 621493 | 23,843 | (S) | 27,729 | 21,092 | (S) | 24,782 |
| All other outpatient care centers | 621498 | 44,666 | 46,927 | 49,288 | 13,780 | 13,703 | 13,926 |
| Medical and diagnostic laboratories | 6215 | 47,975 | 48,898 | 51,178 | 47,975 | 48,898 | 51,178 |
| Home health care services | 6216 | 74,447 | 77,741 | 80,021 | 55,730 | 58,471 | 60,339 |
| Ambulance services | 62191 | 14,932 | 14,855 | 15,284 | 11,779 | 11,526 | 11,885 |
| Blood and organ banks | 621991 | 9,994 | 10,479 | 10,972 | (S) | (S) | 2,625 |
| **Hospitals** | **622** | **1,003,499** | **1,061,923** | **1,114,639** | **123,916** | **127,242** | **131,097** |
| General medical and surgical hospitals, government | 622118 | 174,697 | 185,730 | 200,442 | (X) | (X) | (X) |
| General medical and surgical hospitals, private | 622119 | 760,060 | 804,343 | 838,941 | 101,190 | 103,403 | 106,191 |
| Psychiatric and substance abuse hospitals, government | 622218 | 13,077 | 13,252 | 13,365 | (X) | (X) | (X) |
| Psychiatric and substance abuse hospitals, private | 622219 | 10,724 | 11,487 | 12,464 | 6,215 | 6,681 | 7,258 |
| Specialty hospitals, government | 622318 | 7,309 | 7,586 | 8,178 | (X) | (X) | (X) |
| Specialty hospitals, private | 622319 | 37,632 | 39,525 | 41,249 | 16,511 | 17,158 | 17,648 |
| **Nursing and residential care facilities** [3] | **623** | **223,345** | **232,727** | **239,323** | **143,163** | **150,237** | **154,997** |
| Nursing care facilities (skilled nursing facilities) | 6231 | 117,714 | 122,252 | 123,392 | 94,406 | 98,548 | 100,065 |
| Residential intellectual/developmental disability facilities | 62321 | 24,142 | 25,168 | 26,743 | 6,952 | 7,316 | 8,022 |
| Residential mental health and substance abuse facilities | 62322 | 14,297 | 15,087 | 16,195 | 6,099 | 6,668 | 7,310 |
| Continuing care retirement communities | 623311 | 30,373 | 31,640 | 32,953 | 10,477 | 11,203 | 12,026 |
| Assisted living facilities for the elderly | 623312 | 28,115 | 29,520 | 30,674 | 23,808 | 25,032 | 26,101 |

X Not applicable. S Figure does not meet publication standards. [1] 2012 North American Industry Classification System (NAICS); see text, Section 15. [2] Includes taxable and tax-exempt employer firms. [3] Includes other kinds of business, not shown separately. See Table 602, for data on NAICS 624 Social assistance industries. [4] Offices of physical, occupational, and speech therapists, and audiologists. [5] HMO is health maintenance organization.

Source: U.S. Census Bureau, Service Annual Survey, "Service Annual Survey Latest Data (NAICS-basis): 2017," <https://www.census.gov/programs-surveys/sas/data/tables.html>, accessed November 2018.

# Table 172. Revenue for Selected Health Care Industries by Source: 2017

[In millions of dollars (490,862 represents $490,862,000,000). For all employer firms regardless of tax status. Estimates are adjusted to the results of the 2012 Economic Census, and are shown by industry classification based on the 2012 North American Industry Classification System (NAICS). Based on Service Annual Survey and administrative data; see Appendix III]

| Source of revenue | Offices of physicians (NAICS 6211) | Offices of dentists (NAICS 6212) | Outpatient care centers (NAICS 6214) | Home health care services (NAICS 6216) | Hospitals (NAICS 622) | Nursing and residential care facilities (NAICS 623) [1] |
|---|---|---|---|---|---|---|
| **Revenue, total** | **490,862** | **123,839** | **134,933** | **80,021** | **1,114,639** | **239,323** |
| Medicare [2] | 78,833 | (S) | 19,094 | 34,351 | 264,186 | 37,508 |
| Medicaid (fee for service only) | 17,847 | 6,489 | 15,544 | 14,047 | 87,107 | 74,001 |
| Workers' compensation | 4,613 | (S) | 1,965 | 489 | 6,862 | (S) |
| All other government programs | 8,268 | 1,600 | 8,778 | 3,419 | 32,142 | 16,638 |
| Revenue from health care providers for patient care | 33,632 | 3,181 | 3,151 | 1,582 | 8,158 | (NA) |
| Private health insurance [3] | 202,742 | 52,089 | 47,203 | 15,845 | 545,957 | 26,226 |
| Property, auto, and casualty insurance | 2,344 | (S) | 357 | (S) | 3,487 | 252 |
| Patient out-of-pocket from patients and their families | 36,358 | 47,741 | 6,215 | 4,051 | 30,800 | 45,179 |
| All other sources of revenue for patient care | 71,241 | 10,931 | 13,145 | 4,043 | 49,815 | 16,911 |
| Contributions, gifts, and grants received | (NA) | (NA) | 7,794 | 503 | 13,657 | 4,938 |
| Investment and property income | (NA) | (NA) | (S) | 164 | 17,339 | 1,688 |
| Revenue from health care providers for non-patient care [4] | 16,159 | (S) | 4,265 | (S) | 8,804 | (NA) |
| All other non-patient care revenue | 15,850 | 217 | 5,881 | 750 | 46,161 | 12,137 |

NA Not available. S Figure does not meet publication standards. [1] Total revenue for NAICS 623 also includes $3,097 million in revenue from social security benefits—direct payments of social security on behalf of patients. [2] Fee for service, Medicare Part A hospital insurance, Part B medical insurance, and Part D prescription drug coverage. [3] Includes Medicare Part C (Medicare Advantage plans providing coverage from private insurance companies), and Medicaid managed care plans. [4] Includes revenue from medical administration and other administrative services, incentive payments, management fees, medical director fees, etc.

Source: U.S. Census Bureau, Service Annual Survey, "Service Annual Survey Latest Data (NAICS-basis): 2017," <https://www.census.gov/programs-surveys/sas/data/tables.html>, accessed December 2018.

## Table 173. Employment in the Health Service Industries: 2000 to 2018

[In thousands (12,861 represents 12,861,000). Covers persons on establishment payrolls who worked or received pay for any part of the pay period that includes the 12th day of the month. Excludes proprietors, the unincorporated self-employed, unpaid volunteer or family employees, farm employees, domestic employees, and military personnel. Based on the 2017 North American Industry Classification System (NAICS); see text, Section 15]

| Industry | 2017 NAICS code | 2000 | 2005 | 2010 | 2014 | 2015 | 2016 | 2017 | 2018 |
|---|---|---|---|---|---|---|---|---|---|
| **Health care and social assistance** [1] | **62** | **12,861** | **14,840** | **16,820** | **18,022** | **18,557** | **19,069** | **19,520** | **19,939** |
| **Health care** | **621,2,3** | **10,858** | **12,314** | **13,777** | **14,677** | **15,042** | **15,414** | **15,717** | **16,006** |
| Ambulatory health care services [1] | 621 | 4,320 | 5,114 | 5,975 | 6,632 | 6,856 | 7,080 | 7,297 | 7,499 |
| Offices of physicians | 6211 | 1,801 | 2,049 | 2,264 | 2,411 | 2,471 | 2,527 | 2,581 | 2,621 |
| Office of physicians, except mental health | 621111 | 1,764 | 2,006 | 2,218 | 2,361 | 2,420 | 2,473 | 2,527 | 2,564 |
| Office of mental health physicians | 621112 | 37 | 43 | 46 | 50 | 51 | 53 | 55 | 57 |
| Offices of dentists | 6212 | 688 | 774 | 828 | 887 | 905 | 923 | 936 | 956 |
| Offices of other health practitioners | 6213 | 438 | 549 | 671 | 780 | 813 | 855 | 889 | 930 |
| Outpatient care centers | 6214 | 425 | 517 | 649 | 764 | 806 | 853 | 897 | 934 |
| Medical and diagnostic laboratories | 6215 | 102 | 198 | 228 | 249 | 260 | 266 | 269 | 278 |
| Home health care services | 6216 | 633 | 821 | 1,085 | 1,262 | 1,315 | 1,365 | 1,420 | 1,473 |
| Hospitals | 622 | 3,954 | 4,345 | 4,679 | 4,787 | 4,896 | 5,015 | 5,072 | 5,145 |
| General medical and surgical hospitals | 6221 | 3,745 | 4,096 | 4,357 | 4,433 | 4,498 | 4,608 | 4,669 | 4,724 |
| Psychiatric and substance abuse hospitals | 6222 | 86 | 93 | 109 | 126 | 138 | 142 | 140 | 152 |
| Other hospitals | 6223 | 123 | 156 | 213 | 228 | 260 | 265 | 263 | 268 |
| Nursing and residential care facilities [1] | 623 | 2,583 | 2,855 | 3,124 | 3,258 | 3,291 | 3,318 | 3,348 | 3,362 |
| Nursing care facilities | 6231 | 1,514 | 1,577 | 1,657 | 1,650 | 1,648 | 1,642 | 1,627 | 1,609 |

[1] Includes other industries, not shown separately.

Source: U.S. Bureau of Labor Statistics, Current Employment Statistics, "Employment, Hours, and Earnings—National," <https://stats.bls.gov/ces/data.htm>, accessed May 2019.

## Table 174. Physicians by Sex, Osteopathic Physicians, and International Medical Graduates by Specialty: 2017

[Covers federal and nonfederal physicians working 20 or more hours per week in specialties in which there are over 2,500 active physicians. Active physicians include those working in direct patient care, administration, medical teaching, research, or other non-patient care activities. Physicians selected their specialties on the American Medical Association's Census of Physicians]

| Specialty | Total [1] | By sex | | | By type | | International medical graduates [2] |
|---|---|---|---|---|---|---|---|
| | | Male | Female | Percent female | Patient care physicians | Osteopathic physicians | |
| **Total** | **892,856** | **577,962** | **313,808** | **35.2** | **782,585** | **69,581** | **218,540** |
| Allergy & immunology | 4,774 | 2,939 | 1,833 | 38.4 | 4,132 | 166 | 1,093 |
| Anatomic/clinical pathology | 12,839 | 7,983 | 4,847 | 37.8 | 9,130 | 322 | 3,932 |
| Anesthesiology | 41,762 | 31,094 | 10,624 | 25.5 | 38,960 | 2,752 | 9,017 |
| Cardiovascular disease | 22,211 | 19,054 | 3,138 | 14.1 | 20,303 | 861 | 6,738 |
| Child & adolescent psychiatry | 9,204 | 4,350 | 4,849 | 52.7 | 8,181 | 507 | 2,794 |
| Critical care medicine | 11,559 | 8,529 | 3,013 | 26.1 | 9,932 | 617 | 4,741 |
| Dermatology | 12,051 | 6,151 | 5,889 | 48.9 | 11,338 | 691 | 591 |
| Emergency medicine | 42,348 | 30,657 | 11,658 | 27.6 | 38,964 | 4,789 | 2,765 |
| Endocrinology [3] | 7,495 | 3,815 | 3,668 | 49.0 | 6,045 | 216 | 2,969 |
| Family medicine/general practice | 113,514 | 68,004 | 45,342 | 40.0 | 104,937 | 18,762 | 25,860 |
| Gastroenterology | 14,747 | 12,135 | 2,593 | 17.6 | 13,488 | 594 | 4,270 |
| General surgery | 25,042 | 19,865 | 5,157 | 20.6 | 21,644 | 1,111 | 4,904 |
| Geriatric medicine | 5,598 | 2,653 | 2,939 | 52.6 | 4,733 | 308 | 2,844 |
| Hematology & oncology | 15,410 | 10,268 | 5,122 | 33.3 | 12,926 | 463 | 5,614 |
| Infectious disease | 9,136 | 5,369 | 3,753 | 41.1 | 7,012 | 310 | 3,136 |
| Internal medicine | 115,557 | 71,577 | 43,770 | 37.9 | 101,953 | 6,386 | 45,274 |
| Internal medicine/pediatrics | 5,122 | 2,416 | 2,704 | 52.8 | 4,581 | 275 | 551 |
| Interventional cardiology | 3,847 | 3,546 | 294 | 7.7 | 3,475 | 159 | 1,724 |
| Neonatal-perinatal medicine | 5,530 | 2,700 | 2,826 | 51.1 | 4,657 | 224 | 2,131 |
| Nephrology | 10,798 | 7,728 | 3,057 | 28.3 | 9,462 | 459 | 5,293 |
| Neurological surgery | 5,531 | 5,065 | 463 | 8.4 | 5,053 | 108 | 681 |
| Neurology | 13,717 | 9,674 | 4,029 | 29.4 | 11,674 | 703 | 4,289 |
| Neuroradiology | 3,682 | 2,958 | 718 | 19.5 | 3,160 | 162 | 532 |
| Obstetrics & gynecology | 41,656 | 17,879 | 23,740 | 57.0 | 38,850 | 2,813 | 5,943 |
| Ophthalmology | 18,817 | 14,041 | 4,767 | 25.3 | 17,488 | 462 | 1,327 |
| Orthopedic surgery | 19,001 | 17,981 | 1,016 | 5.3 | 18,069 | 1,053 | 988 |
| Otolaryngology | 9,526 | 7,890 | 1,630 | 17.1 | 8,932 | 385 | 603 |
| Pain medicine & management | 5,345 | 4,350 | 982 | 18.4 | 5,003 | 529 | 1,482 |
| Pediatric cardiology | 2,733 | 1,750 | 979 | 35.9 | 2,242 | 62 | 715 |
| Pediatric hematology/oncology | 2,794 | 1,302 | 1,489 | 53.4 | 2,041 | 79 | 711 |
| Pediatrics | 58,435 | 21,437 | 36,945 | 63.3 | 52,824 | 2,720 | 14,577 |
| Physical medicine & rehabilitation | 9,343 | 6,032 | 3,284 | 35.3 | 8,532 | 1,330 | 2,239 |
| Plastic surgery | 7,142 | 5,995 | 1,144 | 16.0 | 6,813 | 119 | 724 |
| Preventive medicine | 6,613 | 4,374 | 2,235 | 33.8 | 4,123 | 573 | 824 |
| Psychiatry | 38,205 | 23,244 | 14,941 | 39.1 | 33,364 | 1,705 | 11,615 |
| Pulmonary disease | 5,265 | 4,644 | 620 | 11.8 | 4,640 | 204 | 1,576 |
| Radiation oncology | 5,029 | 3,661 | 1,365 | 27.2 | 4,628 | 88 | 597 |
| Radiology & diagnostic radiology | 27,719 | 20,601 | 7,101 | 25.6 | 24,682 | 1,035 | 3,127 |
| Rheumatology | 5,881 | 3,246 | 2,622 | 44.7 | 5,029 | 315 | 1,973 |
| Sports medicine (orthopedic surgery) | 2,612 | 2,440 | 172 | 6.6 | 2,457 | 176 | 108 |
| Thoracic surgery | 4,411 | 4,102 | 309 | 7.0 | 4,052 | 98 | 875 |
| Urology | 9,921 | 9,051 | 866 | 8.7 | 9,374 | 251 | 1,087 |
| Vascular & interventional radiology | 3,416 | 3,090 | 325 | 9.5 | 3,011 | 112 | 457 |
| Vascular surgery | 3,688 | 3,204 | 482 | 13.1 | 3,384 | 149 | 642 |

[1] Includes active physicians with unknown sex and type of medical degree. [2] All physicians, including U.S. citizens, who completed their medical education in a school outside the U.S., Puerto Rico, and Canada. [3] Includes diabetes and metabolism specialties.

Source: Association of American Medical Colleges, *2018 Physician Specialty Data Report* ©. See also <https://www.aamc.org/data/workforce/>.

# Table 175. Physicians, Doctors of Osteopathy, and Female Physicians by State: 2016

[As of year end. Rates per 100,000 resident population, based on U.S. Census Bureau estimates as of July 1 of year shown. Covers active federal and nonfederal physicians who work at least 20 hours per week]

| State | Active physicians [1] | | | Active physicians in patient care | | | | | |
| | Total (number) | Female | | Total [3] | | Osteopathic physicians | | Primary care physicians [4] | |
| | | Number | Percent [2] | Number | Rate | Number | Rate | Number | Rate |
|---|---|---|---|---|---|---|---|---|---|
| U.S. [5] | 877,616 | 303,306 | 34.6 | 765,115 | 236.8 | 60,528 | 18.7 | 266,421 | 82.5 |
| AL. | 10,329 | 2,808 | 27.2 | 9,398 | 193.2 | 505 | 10.4 | 3,440 | 70.7 |
| AK. | 1,961 | 730 | 37.3 | 1,806 | 243.4 | 213 | 28.7 | 752 | 101.4 |
| AZ. | 16,345 | 5,141 | 31.5 | 15,007 | 216.5 | 1,800 | 26.0 | 5,009 | 72.3 |
| AR. | 6,088 | 1,640 | 27.0 | 5,518 | 184.7 | 275 | 9.2 | 2,220 | 74.3 |
| CA. | 105,907 | 38,524 | 36.4 | 92,614 | 236.0 | 4,447 | 11.3 | 33,289 | 84.8 |
| CO. | 15,422 | 5,764 | 37.4 | 14,033 | 253.3 | 1,324 | 23.9 | 4,820 | 87.0 |
| CT. | 12,341 | 4,554 | 36.9 | 10,579 | 295.8 | 433 | 12.1 | 3,353 | 93.8 |
| DE. | 2,592 | 971 | 37.5 | 2,306 | 242.2 | 280 | 29.4 | 821 | 86.2 |
| DC. | 5,901 | 2,760 | 46.8 | 4,263 | 625.8 | 88 | 12.9 | 1,229 | 180.4 |
| FL. | 53,685 | 15,757 | 29.4 | 48,666 | 236.1 | 4,385 | 21.3 | 16,486 | 80.0 |
| GA. | 23,215 | 7,910 | 34.1 | 20,583 | 199.6 | 951 | 9.2 | 7,381 | 71.6 |
| HI. | 4,350 | 1,463 | 33.7 | 3,772 | 264.0 | 195 | 13.7 | 1,457 | 102.0 |
| ID. | 3,241 | 812 | 25.1 | 3,058 | 181.7 | 412 | 24.5 | 1,151 | 68.4 |
| IL. | 35,927 | 13,543 | 37.7 | 30,503 | 238.3 | 2,148 | 16.8 | 11,232 | 87.7 |
| IN. | 15,025 | 4,590 | 30.6 | 13,780 | 207.7 | 986 | 14.9 | 4,923 | 74.2 |
| IA. | 6,627 | 2,051 | 31.0 | 5,860 | 186.9 | 1,166 | 37.2 | 2,390 | 76.2 |
| KS. | 6,380 | 2,047 | 32.1 | 5,770 | 198.5 | 683 | 23.5 | 2,249 | 77.4 |
| KY. | 10,158 | 3,083 | 30.4 | 9,391 | 211.7 | 596 | 13.4 | 3,257 | 73.4 |
| LA. | 11,737 | 3,568 | 30.4 | 10,451 | 223.2 | 187 | 4.0 | 3,466 | 74.0 |
| ME. | 4,320 | 1,533 | 35.5 | 3,986 | 299.4 | 698 | 52.4 | 1,609 | 120.8 |
| MD. | 22,731 | 9,013 | 39.7 | 17,850 | 296.7 | 634 | 10.5 | 5,757 | 95.7 |
| MA. | 30,213 | 12,455 | 41.3 | 23,933 | 351.3 | 734 | 10.8 | 7,814 | 114.7 |
| MI. | 28,206 | 9,535 | 33.9 | 24,462 | 246.4 | 4,515 | 45.5 | 8,708 | 87.7 |
| MN. | 16,105 | 5,817 | 36.1 | 14,122 | 255.8 | 653 | 11.8 | 5,301 | 96.0 |
| MS. | 5,562 | 1,444 | 26.0 | 5,075 | 169.8 | 328 | 11.0 | 1,785 | 59.7 |
| MO. | 16,268 | 5,372 | 33.0 | 14,085 | 231.2 | 1,915 | 31.4 | 4,826 | 79.2 |
| MT. | 2,401 | 705 | 29.4 | 2,272 | 217.9 | 196 | 18.8 | 857 | 82.2 |
| NE. | 4,426 | 1,380 | 31.2 | 3,971 | 208.2 | 188 | 9.9 | 1,525 | 80.0 |
| NV. | 5,884 | 1,640 | 27.9 | 5,250 | 178.6 | 531 | 18.1 | 1,846 | 62.8 |
| NH. | 4,113 | 1,436 | 34.9 | 3,742 | 280.3 | 347 | 26.0 | 1,315 | 98.5 |
| NJ. | 26,378 | 9,444 | 35.9 | 23,389 | 261.5 | 2,611 | 29.2 | 7,690 | 86.0 |
| NM. | 5,023 | 1,878 | 37.4 | 4,396 | 211.2 | 270 | 13.0 | 1,712 | 82.3 |
| NY. | 72,095 | 27,279 | 37.9 | 59,201 | 299.8 | 3,227 | 16.3 | 18,612 | 94.3 |
| NC. | 25,295 | 8,645 | 34.2 | 22,155 | 218.3 | 1,134 | 11.2 | 7,813 | 77.0 |
| ND. | 1,759 | 518 | 29.5 | 1,606 | 211.9 | 88 | 11.6 | 594 | 78.4 |
| OH. | 33,621 | 11,345 | 33.8 | 28,616 | 246.4 | 3,708 | 31.9 | 9,725 | 83.7 |
| OK. | 8,057 | 2,332 | 29.0 | 7,432 | 189.4 | 1,609 | 41.0 | 2,755 | 70.2 |
| OR. | 12,050 | 4,577 | 38.0 | 10,763 | 262.9 | 813 | 19.9 | 4,050 | 98.9 |
| PA. | 39,863 | 13,596 | 34.1 | 34,035 | 266.2 | 5,087 | 39.8 | 11,202 | 87.6 |
| RI. | 3,770 | 1,501 | 39.8 | 3,255 | 308.1 | 221 | 20.9 | 1,091 | 103.3 |
| SC. | 11,269 | 3,406 | 30.3 | 10,129 | 204.2 | 592 | 11.9 | 3,603 | 72.6 |
| SD. | 2,038 | 627 | 30.8 | 1,878 | 217.0 | 148 | 17.1 | 724 | 83.7 |
| TN. | 16,627 | 4,867 | 29.3 | 14,817 | 222.8 | 704 | 10.6 | 5,182 | 77.9 |
| TX. | 61,132 | 20,712 | 33.9 | 53,962 | 193.7 | 4,007 | 14.4 | 18,225 | 65.4 |
| UT. | 6,389 | 1,521 | 23.8 | 5,881 | 192.7 | 492 | 16.1 | 1,859 | 60.9 |
| VT. | 2,233 | 897 | 40.2 | 1,957 | 313.3 | 72 | 11.5 | 764 | 122.3 |
| VA. | 22,072 | 8,099 | 36.7 | 19,417 | 230.8 | 1,071 | 12.7 | 6,957 | 82.7 |
| WA. | 19,623 | 7,303 | 37.3 | 17,280 | 237.1 | 1,091 | 15.0 | 6,489 | 89.0 |
| WV. | 4,671 | 1,349 | 28.9 | 4,094 | 223.6 | 694 | 37.9 | 1,634 | 89.2 |
| WI. | 15,026 | 5,068 | 33.7 | 13,636 | 236.0 | 950 | 16.4 | 5,041 | 87.2 |
| WY. | 1,165 | 296 | 25.4 | 1,110 | 189.6 | 126 | 21.5 | 431 | 73.6 |
| PR. | 9,874 | 3,665 | 37.2 | 8,060 | 236.3 | 1 | – | 3,502 | 102.7 |

– Represents zero. [1] Active physicians work in direct patient care, administration, medical teaching, research, or other nonpatient care activities. [2] Excludes physicians whose sex was not reported. [3] Includes physicians with Doctor of Medicine degrees, and unknown degree type. [4] Primary care physicians include physicians in the following specialties: adolescent medicine (pediatrics), family medicine, general practice, geriatric medicine (family practice and internal medicine), internal medicine, and pediatrics. [5] U.S. totals exclude Puerto Rico (PR).

Source: Association of American Medical Colleges, *2017 State Physician Workforce Data Report*, November 2017 ©. See also <https://www.aamc.org/data/workforce/>.

# Table 176. Registered Nurses, Nurse Practitioners, and Licensed Practical and Vocational Nurses by State: 2018

[Covers nurses working in the health care and social assistance industry (North American Industry Classification System code 62), as of May. Rates per 100,000 resident population; based on U.S. Census Bureau estimates as of July 1 for year shown]

| State | Registered nurses (RNs) Total | Registered nurses (RNs) Rate [2] | Nurse practitioners Total | Nurse practitioners Rate [2] | Licensed practical and vocational nurses (LPNs, VPNs) Total | Licensed practical and vocational nurses (LPNs, VPNs) Rate [2] |
|---|---|---|---|---|---|---|
| **United States [1]** | **2,585,930** | **790.4** | **164,570** | **50.3** | **608,010** | **185.8** |
| Alabama | 43,670 | 893.4 | 3,240 | 66.3 | 10,420 | 213.2 |
| Alaska | 4,830 | 655.0 | 400 | 54.2 | 340 | 46.1 |
| Arizona | 47,700 | 665.1 | 3,220 | 44.9 | 5,080 | 70.8 |
| Arkansas | 21,870 | 725.7 | 1,800 | 59.7 | 10,860 | 360.3 |
| California | 264,130 | 667.7 | 12,280 | 31.0 | 55,150 | 139.4 |
| Colorado | 45,900 | 805.9 | 2,750 | 48.3 | 4,760 | 83.6 |
| Connecticut | 26,520 | 742.3 | 2,060 | 57.7 | 7,530 | 210.8 |
| Delaware | 10,620 | 1,098.0 | 710 | 73.4 | 2,160 | 223.3 |
| District of Columbia | 9,440 | 1,343.9 | 740 | 105.3 | 1,610 | 229.2 |
| Florida | 159,180 | 747.3 | 10,070 | 47.3 | 43,710 | 205.2 |
| Georgia | 67,730 | 643.9 | 5,850 | 55.6 | 18,530 | 176.1 |
| Hawaii | 9,480 | 667.4 | 390 | 27.5 | 960 | 67.6 |
| Idaho | 12,250 | 698.3 | 630 | 35.9 | 2,220 | 126.6 |
| Illinois | 114,020 | 894.9 | 5,120 | 40.2 | 18,130 | 142.3 |
| Indiana | 62,170 | 929.0 | 4,670 | 69.8 | 14,420 | 215.5 |
| Iowa | 29,800 | 944.2 | 1,620 | 51.3 | 5,430 | 172.0 |
| Kansas | 24,510 | 841.8 | 2,020 | 69.4 | 6,860 | 235.6 |
| Kentucky | 41,190 | 921.8 | 3,060 | 68.5 | 8,740 | 195.6 |
| Louisiana | 37,740 | 809.9 | 2,580 | 55.4 | 17,790 | 381.8 |
| Maine | 12,730 | 951.1 | 1,210 | 90.4 | 1,030 | 77.0 |
| Maryland | 46,290 | 766.0 | 3,410 | 56.4 | 9,060 | 149.9 |
| Massachusetts | 70,340 | 1,019.1 | 5,830 | 84.5 | 14,000 | 202.8 |
| Michigan | 89,040 | 890.8 | 4,360 | 43.6 | 13,190 | 132.0 |
| Minnesota | 62,410 | 1,112.2 | 3,450 | 61.5 | 14,220 | 253.4 |
| Mississippi | 26,570 | 889.7 | 2,600 | 87.1 | 8,420 | 281.9 |
| Missouri | 63,120 | 1,030.3 | 3,870 | 63.2 | 12,730 | 207.8 |
| Montana | 8,750 | 823.7 | 600 | 56.5 | 1,890 | 177.9 |
| Nebraska | 19,660 | 1,019.0 | 940 | 48.7 | 4,760 | 246.7 |
| Nevada | 20,050 | 660.8 | 670 | 22.1 | 2,170 | 71.5 |
| New Hampshire | 12,030 | 886.9 | 1,090 | 80.4 | 1,650 | 121.6 |
| New Jersey | 67,280 | 755.2 | 5,640 | 63.3 | 14,710 | 165.1 |
| New Mexico | 13,910 | 663.8 | 950 | 45.3 | 1,900 | 90.7 |
| New York | 154,200 | 789.1 | 12,220 | 62.5 | 39,720 | 203.3 |
| North Carolina | 88,890 | 856.1 | 4,330 | 41.7 | 15,660 | 150.8 |
| North Dakota | 7,580 | 997.3 | 440 | 57.9 | 2,240 | 294.7 |
| Ohio | 110,380 | 944.3 | 7,080 | 60.6 | 36,200 | 309.7 |
| Oklahoma | 25,380 | 643.7 | 1,290 | 32.7 | 9,640 | 244.5 |
| Oregon | 28,790 | 687.0 | 1,800 | 43.0 | 3,030 | 72.3 |
| Pennsylvania | 131,900 | 1,029.9 | 6,840 | 53.4 | 33,610 | 262.4 |
| Rhode Island | 10,770 | 1,018.6 | 640 | 60.5 | 970 | 91.7 |
| South Carolina | 37,070 | 729.1 | 1,820 | 35.8 | 8,470 | 166.6 |
| South Dakota | 11,000 | 1,246.8 | 530 | 60.1 | 1,610 | 182.5 |
| Tennessee | 53,860 | 795.6 | 6,150 | 90.8 | 20,880 | 308.4 |
| Texas | 182,430 | 635.6 | 10,400 | 36.2 | 62,350 | 217.2 |
| Utah | 19,390 | 613.4 | 1,230 | 38.9 | 1,860 | 58.8 |
| Vermont | 5,410 | 863.8 | 470 | 75.0 | 1,160 | 185.2 |
| Virginia | 53,610 | 629.4 | 4,330 | 50.8 | 18,140 | 213.0 |
| Washington | 48,050 | 637.6 | 3,130 | 41.5 | 6,090 | 80.8 |
| West Virginia | 17,600 | 974.6 | 1,040 | 57.6 | 5,170 | 286.3 |
| Wisconsin | 50,710 | 872.3 | 2,740 | 47.1 | 6,300 | 108.4 |
| Wyoming | 3,980 | 688.9 | 260 | 45.0 | 480 | 83.1 |
| Puerto Rico | 14,730 | 461.0 | 540 | 16.9 | 2,670 | 83.6 |

[1] U.S. total excludes Puerto Rico. [2] Rates are calculated using data from the U.S. Census Bureau, "Annual Estimates of the Resident Population: April 1, 2010 to July 1, 2018," <https://www.census.gov/data/tables/time-series/demo/popest/2010s-state-total.html>, accessed May 2019.

Source: U.S. Bureau of Labor Statistics, Occupational Employment Statistics, "OES Data: Research Estimates by State and Industry," <https://www.bls.gov/oes/home.htm>, accessed May 2019.

# Table 177. Physician Use of Electronic Medical or Health Record System by Physician Specialty: 2015 and 2017

[In percent. Data are from the National Electronic Health Records Survey of nonfederal office-based patient care physicians; survey excludes anesthesiologists, radiologists, and pathologists. Using any electronic health record/electronic medical record system was defined by physicians answering "yes" to use of an electronic health record system at the reporting location. Having a certified system was defined by physicians answering "yes" to having a current system that "meet meaningful use criteria defined by the Department of Health and Human Services." For more information on certified systems and meaningful use (renamed "promoting interoperability") criteria, see <https://www.cms.gov/ehrincentiveprograms>]

| | 2015 | | 2017 | |
|---|---|---|---|---|
| Physician specialty | Any electronic medical/health record system | Certified system | Any electronic medical/health record system | Certified system |
| **All physicians** | **86.9** | **77.9** | **85.9** | **79.7** |
| Primary care | 89.6 | 80.9 | 88.5 | 83.5 |
| Non-primary care | 84.4 | 75.1 | 83.6 | 76.0 |
| Surgical | 84.5 | 77.0 | 84.2 | 77.3 |
| Medical | 84.4 | 74.0 | 83.1 | 75.1 |
| BY SPECIALTY | | | | |
| Cardiovascular disease | 95.6 | 83.2 | (S) | (S) |
| Dermatology | 70.2 | 62.3 | 80.0 | 79.5 |
| General surgery | 93.8 | 77.6 | 95.8 | 94.2 |
| General/family practice | 92.7 | 84.0 | 86.1 | 81.5 |
| Internal medicine | 88.2 | 81.4 | 84.9 | 81.6 |
| Neurology | 94.5 | 89.9 | (S) | (S) |
| Obstetrics/gynecology | 89.2 | 80.6 | 95.7 | 90.7 |
| Ophthalmology | 72.7 | 70.0 | (S) | (S) |
| Orthopedic surgery | 93.2 | 86.6 | 96.7 | (S) |
| Otolaryngology | 89.4 | 82.7 | 94.6 | (S) |
| Pediatrics | 87.4 | 76.3 | 92.1 | 84.9 |
| Psychiatry | 61.3 | 40.8 | (S) | (S) |
| Urology | 94.0 | 92.6 | 88.7 | 86.7 |
| Other | 86.4 | 78.6 | 89.3 | 81.1 |

S Estimate does not meet standards of reliability.

Source: U.S. National Center for Health Statistics, Ambulatory Health Care Data, NAMCS and NHAMCS Web Tables, "NEHRS Specialty and Overall Physicians Electronic Health Record Adoption Summary Tables," <https://www.cdc.gov/nchs/ahcd/web_tables.htm>, accessed March 2019.

# Table 178. Medical Record Confidentiality Breaches Reported—Incidents and Persons Affected by Type and Location of Breach: 2015 to 2018

[113,308 represents 113,308,000. Data for breaches by date of submission to the Secretary of Health and Human Services (HHS), affecting 500 or more individuals. As required by section 13402(e)(4) of the Health Information Technology for Economic and Clinical Health (HITECH) Act, the Secretary of HHS must post a list of breaches of unsecured protected health information affecting 500 or more individuals. The Privacy Rule of the Health Insurance Portability and Accountability Act of 1996 (HIPAA) provides federal protections for individually identifiable health information held by covered entities and their business associates. Covered entities include health care providers, health plans, and health care clearinghouses]

| | 2015 | | 2016 | | 2017 | | 2018 | |
|---|---|---|---|---|---|---|---|---|
| Item | Incidents (number) | Individuals affected (1,000) | Incidents (number) | Individuals affected (1,000) | Incidents (number) | Individuals affected (1,000) | Incidents (number) | Individuals affected (1,000) |
| **Total** | **270** | **113,308** | **329** | **16,659** | **360** | **5,140** | **372** | **13,949** |
| TYPE OF BREACH | | | | | | | | |
| Hacking/information technology incident | 56 | 111,812 | 114 | 13,428 | 149 | 3,478 | 162 | 9,395 |
| Improper disposal | 6 | 82 | 7 | 126 | 11 | 31 | 10 | 342 |
| Loss | 24 | 52 | 16 | 558 | 16 | 39 | 13 | 30 |
| Theft | 81 | 738 | 62 | 904 | 56 | 348 | 42 | 697 |
| Unauthorized access/disclosure | 103 | 623 | 130 | 1,643 | 128 | 1,244 | 145 | 3,484 |
| LOCATION OF INFORMATION BREACHED [1] | | | | | | | | |
| Desktop computer | 27 | 303 | 27 | 139 | 31 | 661 | 36 | 551 |
| Electronic medical record | 19 | 3,964 | 30 | 433 | 32 | 167 | 22 | 167 |
| E-mail | 37 | 584 | 47 | 998 | 86 | 673 | 113 | 3,652 |
| Laptop computer | 38 | 392 | 26 | 813 | 21 | 110 | 19 | 76 |
| Network server | 42 | 107,295 | 85 | 13,180 | 89 | 2,495 | 62 | 6,381 |
| Other portable electronic device | 17 | 221 | 14 | 24 | 20 | 821 | 15 | 43 |
| Paper/films | 69 | 247 | 74 | 898 | 60 | 135 | 77 | 1,199 |
| Other [2] | 21 | 303 | 26 | 174 | 21 | 77 | 28 | 1,880 |

[1] Locations of information breached can include a combination of other locations within the categories specified. For example, incidents involving desktop computers can also involve breaches of information via laptop computer, network server, email, and other locations. Incidents are categorized according to the first type as given in the source. [2] Other locations of information breaches can include incidents involving mailings (postal and electronic), computer hard drives, computer disks, the internet/websites, and other miscellaneous materials or locations. Also includes unknown locations of breaches.

Source: U.S. Department of Health and Human Services, Office for Civil Rights, HIPAA for Professionals—Breach Notification Rule, "Breaches Affecting 500 or More Individuals," <http://www.hhs.gov/hipaa/for-professionals/breach-notification/index.html>, accessed May 2019.

## Table 179. Long-Term Care Facilities, Staff, and Clients by Provider Type and Selected Characteristics: 2016

[Data for 2016 except as noted. Based on the National Study of Long-Term Care Providers. Long-term care services assist the needs of frail older people and other adults with limited capacity for self-care due to chronic illness, injury, disability, or other health-related conditions]

| Item | Facilities by provider type | | | | |
|---|---|---|---|---|---|
| | Adult day services center | Home health agency | Hospice | Nursing home | Residential care community |
| **Number of providers**......... | **4,600** | **12,200** | **4,300** | **15,600** | **28,900** |
| Number of beds or licensed maximum capacity [1]............ | 298,400 | (X) | (X) | 1,660,400 | 996,100 |
| Average capacity [1]......... | 66 | (X) | (X) | 106 | 35 |
| Average number of people served [2]............ | 42 | 401 | 353 | 86 | 28 |
| Provider ownership type (percent): | | | | | |
| For profit......... | 44.7 | 80.6 | 63.0 | 69.3 | 81.0 |
| Not for profit......... | 50.8 | 14.8 | 22.8 | 23.5 | 17.7 |
| Government and other......... | 4.6 | 4.6 | 14.1 | 7.2 | 1.3 |
| Services provided (percent): | | | | | |
| Social work......... | 52.1 | 82.5 | 100.0 | 88.5 | 51.1 |
| Mental health or counseling......... | 33.8 | (NA) | 97.0 | 87.6 | 55.0 |
| Therapy [3]......... | 46.7 | 96.3 | 98.2 | 99.5 | 71.4 |
| Skilled nursing or nursing......... | 64.5 | 100.0 | 100.0 | 100.0 | 66.1 |
| Pharmacy or pharmacist......... | 30.0 | 4.9 | (NA) | 97.2 | 83.6 |
| Hospice......... | 20.8 | 5.7 | (X) | 80.7 | 67.7 |
| **Total nursing and social work employee FTEs [4]**......... | **19,900** | **145,000** | **85,600** | **945,700** | **298,800** |
| Percent of total nursing employee FTEs: | | | | | |
| Registered nurse......... | 20.6 | 53.0 | 48.0 | 11.9 | 6.1 |
| Licensed practical nurse or licensed vocational nurse......... | 11.3 | 19.5 | 8.8 | 22.4 | 9.9 |
| Aide......... | 56.8 | 25.1 | 31.8 | 63.9 | 83.3 |
| **Clients [2]**......... | **286,300** | **4,455,700** | **1,426,000** | **1,347,600** | **811,500** |
| By age (percent): | | | | | |
| Under 65......... | 37.4 | 18.1 | 5.5 | 16.5 | 6.6 |
| 65 and over......... | 62.5 | 81.9 | 94.6 | 83.5 | 93.4 |
| 65 to 74......... | 20.3 | 26.8 | 17.5 | 18.2 | 11.0 |
| 75 to 84......... | 25.9 | 29.9 | 29.3 | 26.7 | 30.3 |
| 85 and over......... | 16.3 | 25.2 | 47.8 | 38.6 | 52.1 |
| By sex (percent): | | | | | |
| Men......... | 41.8 | 39.1 | 41.3 | 35.4 | 29.4 |
| Women......... | 58.2 | 60.9 | 58.7 | 64.6 | 70.6 |
| Selected conditions (percent): | | | | | |
| Diagnosed with Alzheimer's or other dementia......... | 30.9 | 32.3 | 44.5 | 47.8 | 41.9 |
| Diagnosed with depression......... | 28.2 | 39.4 | 23.4 | 46.3 | 30.9 |

NA Not available. X Not applicable. [1] For adult day services, capacity is based on licensed maximum capacity. For nursing homes and residential care communities, capacity is based on number of licensed or certified beds. [2] For adult day services, nursing homes, and residential care communities, data are daily average or totals for 2016. For home health agencies, data are annual average or total discharges in 2015. For hospices, data are annual average or total patients served in 2015. [3] Physical, occupational, or speech therapy. [4] FTE is full-time equivalent.

Source: U.S. Centers for Disease Control and Prevention, National Center for Health Statistics, *Long-Term Care Providers and Services Users in the United States: Data From the National Study of Long-Term Care Providers, 2015-2016*, Series 3, No. 43, February 2019. See also <http://www.cdc.gov/nchs/nsltcp.htm>.

## Table 180. Mental Health Treatment Facilities, Clients, and Beds by Service Setting and Facility Type: 2016

[Covers facilities in the 50 states, the District of Columbia, American Samoa, Guam, Puerto Rico, and the U.S. Virgin Islands. Excludes: (1) Department of Defense (DoD) military treatment facilities, (2) individual private practitioners or small group practices not licensed as a mental health clinic or center, and (3) jails or prisons. Based on the National Mental Health Services Survey; the 2016 survey had a 91.1 percent response rate]

| Facility type | 24-hour hospital inpatient care | | | 24-hour residential care | | | Outpatient, day treatment, or partial hospitalization | |
|---|---|---|---|---|---|---|---|---|
| | Facilities | Clients [1] | Beds [1] | Facilities | Clients [1] | Beds [1] | Facilities | Clients [2] |
| **Total**......... | **2,011** | **105,860** | **106,486** | **2,090** | **65,324** | **67,560** | **9,716** | **4,161,697** |
| Psychiatric hospitals......... | 678 | 60,116 | 63,986 | 132 | 7,989 | 9,198 | 324 | 120,830 |
| Public......... | 203 | 30,385 | 32,995 | 30 | 3,782 | 4,483 | 43 | 33,807 |
| Private......... | 475 | 29,731 | 30,991 | 102 | 4,207 | 4,715 | 281 | 87,023 |
| General hospitals [3]......... | 1,142 | 33,507 | 35,395 | 39 | 1,017 | 1,321 | 491 | 152,947 |
| Residential treatment centers for children.. | 11 | 2,757 | 651 | 669 | 23,043 | 25,173 | 128 | 19,459 |
| Residential treatment centers for adults.... | 9 | 332 | 523 | 912 | 17,408 | 17,257 | 105 | 18,923 |
| Other types of residential facilities......... | 4 | 946 | 395 | 48 | 2,047 | 2,033 | 16 | 2,486 |
| Veterans Administration medical centers... | 92 | 3,041 | 2,673 | 71 | 3,734 | 4,275 | 405 | 394,814 |
| Community mental health centers......... | 30 | 831 | 921 | 31 | 1,622 | 1,445 | 2,626 | 1,322,543 |
| Partial hospitalization or day treatment facilities......... | 2 | 58 | 64 | 0 | 28 | 25 | 419 | 49,359 |
| Outpatient mental health facilities......... | 16 | 1,455 | 672 | 18 | 899 | 1,021 | 4,804 | 1,924,047 |
| Multi-setting mental health facilities [4]....... | 27 | 2,817 | 1,206 | 170 | 7,537 | 5,812 | 398 | 156,289 |

[1] On April 29, 2016. [2] For the month of April 2016, and enrolled on April 29, 2016. [3] Nonfederal general hospitals with separate psychiatric units. [4] Facilities providing mental health services in two or more service settings (residential and outpatient and/or day treatment/partial hospitalization) and not classified as psychiatric hospital, general hospital, medical center, or residential treatment center.

Source: U.S. Substance Abuse and Mental Health Services Administration, *National Mental Health Services Survey (N-MHSS): 2016, Data on Mental Health Treatment Facilities*, October 2017. See also <https://www.samhsa.gov/data/data-we-collect/nmhss-national-mental-health-services-survey>.

# Table 181. Mental Health Treatment Facilities by Type: 2017

[Covers facilities in the 50 states, District of Columbia, American Samoa, Guam, Puerto Rico, and the U.S. Virgin Islands. Excludes: (1) Department of Defense (DoD) military treatment facilities, (2) individual private practitioners or small group practices not licensed as a mental health clinic or center, and (3) jails or prisons. Based on the National Mental Health Services Survey]

| Characteristic | Total [1] | Psychiatric hospitals | General hospitals [2] | RTCs, total [3] | Veterans Affairs medical centers | Community centers [4] | PHP/day treatment facilities [5] | Outpatient facilities [6] | Multi-setting facilities [7] |
|---|---|---|---|---|---|---|---|---|---|
| **Total (number)**........................ | **11,582** | **668** | **1,076** | **1,548** | **357** | **2,538** | **391** | **4,612** | **388** |
| Percent.............................. | 100.0 | 5.8 | 9.3 | 13.4 | 3.1 | 21.9 | 3.4 | 39.8 | 3.4 |
| SERVICE SETTING [8] | | | | | | | | | |
| 24-hour hospital inpatient............. | 1,885 | 659 | 1,066 | 18 | 82 | 33 | – | 10 | 16 |
| 24-hour residential...................... | 2,004 | 135 | 35 | 1,521 | 70 | 34 | 1 | 19 | 188 |
| Less than 24-hour day treatment or partial hospitalization................ | 1,802 | 246 | 251 | 110 | 48 | 310 | 373 | 256 | 207 |
| Less than 24-hour outpatient......... | 8,853 | 237 | 410 | 180 | 357 | 2,514 | 195 | 4,598 | 358 |
| FACILITY CONTROL | | | | | | | | | |
| Private for-profit........................ | 2,054 | 294 | 196 | 333 | 3 | 147 | 107 | 891 | 82 |
| Private non-profit....................... | 7,390 | 167 | 770 | 1,110 | 1 | 1,862 | 241 | 2,959 | 277 |
| Public [9]................................ | 2,138 | 207 | 110 | 105 | 353 | 529 | 43 | 762 | 29 |
| AGE OF PATIENTS ACCEPTED [8] | | | | | | | | | |
| All ages................................. | 4,966 | 169 | 144 | 14 | 1 | 1,803 | 19 | 2,639 | 175 |
| Children age 12 and younger........ | 6,738 | 232 | 189 | 438 | 1 | 2,037 | 143 | 3,444 | 252 |
| Children age 13 to 17.................. | 7,355 | 325 | 263 | 650 | 1 | 2,072 | 178 | 3,583 | 281 |
| Young adults age 18 to 25............ | 10,046 | 568 | 852 | 896 | 354 | 2,441 | 274 | 4,289 | 368 |
| Adults age 26 to 64.................... | 9,627 | 595 | 946 | 879 | 357 | 2,325 | 243 | 3,955 | 323 |
| Senior adults age 65 and older...... | 9,255 | 585 | 996 | 782 | 357 | 2,275 | 230 | 3,733 | 293 |

– Represents zero. [1] Total includes other types of hospitals or facilities, not shown separately. [2] Nonfederal general hospitals with separate psychiatric units. [3] RTC is residential treatment center. [4] Community mental health centers provide outpatient services, 24-hour emergency care, day treatment or partial hospitalization or psychosocial rehabilitation services, or patient screening for admission to state facilities. [5] PHP (partial hospitalization program) and day treatment facilities provide services to ambulatory patients in 3/more hour sessions. [6] Outpatient mental health facilities provide services to ambulatory clients, usually in under 3 hours per visit. [7] Mental health services are provided in two or more service settings (residential, and outpatient and/or PHP/day treatment), not classified as psychiatric or general hospitals, medical centers, or RTCs. [8] Sums to more than the total because a facility could offer mental health treatment in more than one service setting and to more than one age group. [9] Includes facilities operated by state mental health and other agencies, local/county/municipal governments, tribal governments, Indian Health Service, and Department of Veterans Affairs.

Source: U.S. Substance Abuse and Mental Health Services Administration, *National Mental Health Services Survey (N-MHSS): 2017, Data on Mental Health Treatment Facilities*, August 2018. See also <https://www.samhsa.gov/data/>.

# Table 182. Mental Health Care Client Characteristics by Treatment Setting: 2016

[Covers facilities in the 50 states, the District of Columbia, American Samoa, Guam, Puerto Rico, and the U.S. Virgin Islands. Data are reported for patients receiving inpatient or residential services on April 29, 2016, and for clients who were receiving outpatient services at least once during April 2016 and were enrolled in treatment on April 29, 2016. Based on the National Mental Health Services Survey; the 2016 survey had 91.1 response rate]

| Client characteristic | 24-hour hospital inpatient treatment | | 24-hour residential treatment | | Outpatient, day treatment, or partial hospitalization [1] | |
|---|---|---|---|---|---|---|
| | Number | Percent | Number | Percent | Number | Percent |
| **Total clients**.......................... | **105,860** | **100.0** | **65,324** | **100.0** | **4,161,697** | **100.0** |
| SEX | | | | | | |
| Male................................... | 61,788 | 58.4 | 39,618 | 60.6 | 2,140,844 | 51.4 |
| Female................................ | 44,072 | 41.6 | 25,706 | 39.4 | 2,020,854 | 48.6 |
| AGE | | | | | | |
| 17 years old and under................ | 17,012 | 16.1 | 29,577 | 45.3 | 1,137,086 | 27.3 |
| 18 to 64 years old..................... | 72,420 | 68.4 | 32,329 | 49.5 | 2,502,501 | 60.1 |
| 65 years old and over................. | 16,428 | 15.5 | 3,418 | 5.2 | 522,112 | 12.5 |
| RACE | | | | | | |
| American Indian or Alaska Native.... | 472 | 0.4 | 853 | 1.3 | 34,854 | 0.8 |
| Asian.................................. | 1,277 | 1.2 | 707 | 1.1 | 45,581 | 1.1 |
| Black or African American............ | 15,794 | 14.9 | 11,239 | 17.2 | 518,933 | 12.5 |
| Native Hawaiian or Other Pacific Islander........ | 385 | 0.4 | 263 | 0.4 | 13,843 | 0.3 |
| White.................................. | 32,414 | 30.6 | 24,160 | 37.0 | 1,444,031 | 34.7 |
| Two or more races.................... | 1,516 | 1.4 | 2,111 | 3.2 | 206,234 | 5.0 |
| Unknown or not collected............. | 54,002 | 51.0 | 25,991 | 39.8 | 1,898,221 | 45.6 |
| HISPANIC ORIGIN [2] | | | | | | |
| Hispanic or Latino..................... | 6,453 | 6.1 | 5,336 | 8.2 | 461,802 | 11.1 |
| Not Hispanic or Latino................. | 47,799 | 45.2 | 36,508 | 55.9 | 1,985,270 | 47.7 |
| Unknown or not collected............. | 51,608 | 48.8 | 23,480 | 35.9 | 1,714,625 | 41.2 |
| LEGAL STATUS [3] | | | | | | |
| Voluntary.............................. | 49,505 | 46.8 | 46,283 | 70.9 | 3,844,989 | 92.4 |
| Involuntary, non-forensic.............. | 40,688 | 38.4 | 13,679 | 20.9 | 120,457 | 2.9 |
| Involuntary, forensic.................. | 15,668 | 14.8 | 5,362 | 8.2 | 196,251 | 4.7 |

[1] Less than 24-hour care provided to ambulatory patients. Outpatient care typically involves care for less than 3 hours per visit. Day treatment and partial hospitalization programs typically involve care lasting more than 3 hours per visit, on a regular schedule. [2] Persons of Hispanic origin may be of any race. [3] Clients may voluntarily admit themselves to receive mental health treatment, or be admitted involuntarily with a forensic (criminal) or non-forensic (noncriminal) status.

Source: U.S. Substance Abuse and Mental Health Services Administration, *National Mental Health Services Survey (N-MHSS): 2016, Data on Mental Health Treatment Facilities*, October 2017. See also <https://www.samhsa.gov/data/data-we-collect/nmhss-national-mental-health-services-survey>.

# Table 183. Opioid Treatment and Medication-Assisted Therapy—Facilities and Clients: 2017

[As of the end of March. Based on the National Survey of Substance Abuse Treatment Services, a census of all known public and private facilities that provide substance abuse treatment in the United States and associated jurisdictions. Medication-assisted opioid therapy includes the use of methadone or buprenorphine for the treatment of opioid addiction or dependence, and the use of naltrexone for preventing a relapse in opioid addiction. Methadone is available only at opioid treatment programs (OTPs) certified by the Substance Abuse and Mental Health Services Administration (SAMHSA). Physicians or other authorized medical practitioners who receive Drug Addiction Treatment Act of 2000 (DATA 2000) specific training and a waiver may prescribe buprenorphine. All physicians or approved medical personnel can prescribe naltrexone. Selected missing data for responding facilities were imputed. Data for 2017 are based on responses from 13,585 eligible facilities]

| Facilities and clients by type of therapy | Total | Private non-profit | Private for-profit | Local, county, or community govern-ment | State govern-ment | Federal govern-ment [1] | Tribal govern-ment |
|---|---|---|---|---|---|---|---|
| Clients receiving medication assisted opioid therapy, total | 518,155 | 173,590 | 309,405 | 12,820 | 10,070 | 9,923 | 2,347 |
| Methadone [2] | 382,867 | 126,797 | 234,844 | 9,948 | 8,232 | 1,888 | 1,158 |
| Buprenorphine [3] | 112,223 | 35,037 | 66,265 | 2,441 | 1,537 | 5,912 | 1,031 |
| Injectable naltrexone [3, 4] | 23,065 | 11,756 | 8,296 | 431 | 301 | 2,123 | 158 |
| Facilities offering detoxification from opioids | 2,430 | 1,051 | 1,157 | 86 | 38 | 93 | 5 |
| Facilities providing medication-assisted therapy, total [5] | 5,143 | 2,438 | 2,118 | 210 | 119 | 195 | 63 |
| Buprenorphine | 3,900 | 1,850 | 1,621 | 147 | 84 | 166 | 32 |
| Injectable naltrexone [4] | 3,197 | 1,624 | 1,140 | 144 | 77 | 171 | 41 |
| Opioid treatment program (OTP) [6] | 1,317 | 427 | 793 | 38 | 27 | 26 | 6 |
| Outpatient treatment | 1,218 | 372 | 759 | 34 | 21 | 26 | 6 |
| Regular | 929 | 297 | 563 | 25 | 15 | 24 | 5 |
| Intensive | 334 | 157 | 138 | 10 | 6 | 20 | 3 |
| Day treatment or partial hospitalization | 67 | 33 | 23 | 2 | 2 | 7 | 0 |
| Detoxification | 620 | 169 | 413 | 12 | 6 | 19 | 1 |
| Methadone/buprenorphine maintenance or injectable naltrexone treatment | 1,190 | 363 | 740 | 34 | 21 | 26 | 6 |
| Residential, non-hospital | 106 | 52 | 36 | 3 | 3 | 12 | 0 |
| Hospital inpatient | 95 | 45 | 34 | 4 | 5 | 7 | 0 |

[1] Includes Department of Veteran's Affairs, Department of Defense, Indian Health Service, and other, not shown separately. [2] These clients are in facilities SAMHSA certified to use methadone. [3] Includes clients in SAMHSA certified facilities and other facilities providing opioid medication-assisted therapy. Does not include clients of independent physicians. [4] Extended release injectable naltrexone (Vivitrol®). [5] Total includes all facilities providing any type of medication-assisted opioid therapy. [6] Facilities that have opioid treatment programs certified by SAMHSA. Methadone is only available at these facilities.

Source: U.S. Substance Abuse and Mental Health Services Administration, *National Survey of Substance Abuse Treatment Services (N-SSATS): 2017, Data on Substance Abuse Treatment Facilities*, July 2018. See also <https://www.samhsa.gov/data/data-we-collect/nssats-national-survey-substance-abuse-treatment-services>.

# Table 184. Community Health Centers, Patients, and Medical Personnel: 2017

[Patient and patient visit data in thousands (27,174 represents 27,174,000). Community health centers are community-based and patient-directed organizations that provide primary health care services to underserved populations with limited access to health care. Populations served include low-income persons, the uninsured, those with limited English proficiency, migratory and seasonal agricultural workers and their families, people experiencing homelessness, and residents of public housing. Most health centers receive Health Center Program federal grant funding. Some health centers that meet all Health Center Program requirements do not receive Federal award funding; these are called health center program look-alikes]

| Item | Health Center Program grantees | Health Center Program look-alikes | Item | Health Center Program grantees | Health Center Program look-alikes |
|---|---|---|---|---|---|
| **Health centers, total (number)** | **1,373** | **56** | Insurance source: | | |
| PATIENTS (1,000s) | | | None/uninsured | 6,217 | 106 |
| **Total patients** | **27,174** | **722** | Regular Medicaid (Title XIX) | 13,169 | 422 |
| Male | 11,487 | 297 | CHIP Medicaid [2] | 172 | 19 |
| Female | 15,688 | 425 | Dual eligible (Medicare and Medicaid) | 1,039 | 35 |
| | | | Medicare [3] | 2,555 | 72 |
| Age 17 and under | 8,395 | 227 | Other public insurance [4] | 273 | 5 |
| Age 18 to 64 | 16,417 | 428 | Private insurance | 4,788 | 99 |
| Age 65 and older | 2,362 | 68 | PERSONNEL (FTEs) [5] | | |
| | | | Total physicians [6] | 12,894 | 422 |
| Non-Hispanic, total [1] | 16,891 | 379 | Family, general practice, and internist | 8,341 | 262 |
| White | 9,604 | 163 | Obstetrician/gynecologists | 1,266 | 42 |
| Black/African American | 5,026 | 136 | Pediatricians | 2,832 | 99 |
| American Indian/Alaska native | 251 | 2 | Nurse practitioners | 8,852 | 172 |
| Asian | 942 | 51 | Physician assistants | 3,077 | 100 |
| Native Hawaiian/Other Pacific Islander | 208 | 3 | Certified nurse midwives | 692 | 17 |
| Multiracial | 329 | 4 | | | |
| Hispanic | 9,401 | 276 | PATIENT VISITS (1,000s) | | |
| Unreported race and ethnicity | 883 | 67 | By type of practitioner seen: | | |
| | | | Total physicians [6] | 38,959 | 1,348 |
| Income as percent of poverty level: | | | Family, general practice, and internist | 24,702 | 852 |
| 100% and under | 13,484 | 371 | Obstetrician/gynecologists | 3,586 | 141 |
| 101 to 150% | 2,986 | 86 | Pediatricians | 9,040 | 301 |
| 151 to 200% | 1,367 | 25 | Nurse practitioners | 22,366 | 438 |
| Over 200% | 1,662 | 32 | Physician assistants | 8,677 | 248 |
| Unknown | 7,676 | 208 | Certified nurse midwives | 1,510 | 33 |

[1] Includes unknown/unreported race, not shown separately. [2] CHIP, Children's Health Insurance Program. [3] Includes dual eligible and other Title XVIII beneficiaries. [4] CHIP and non-CHIP. [5] FTE, full-time equivalent. [6] Includes data for other specialty physicians, not shown separately.

Source: U.S. Health Resources & Services Administration, Bureau of Primary Health Care, "Health Center Program Data," <https://bphc.hrsa.gov/datareporting/index.html>, accessed April 2019.

# Table 185. Health Care Sources Used Most Often—Percent Distribution of Persons Age 18 and Over by Selected Characteristics: 2017

[In percent, except as noted (246,657 represents 246,657,000). Data are age-adjusted, unless otherwise noted. Based on a survey question that asked, "Is there a place that you usually go to when you are sick or need advice about your health?" If there was at least one such place, a follow-up question was asked: "What kind of place [is it/do you go to most often]—a clinic, a doctor's office, an emergency room, or some other place?" From the National Health Interview Survey, a sample survey of the civilian noninstitutionalized population; see Appendix III]

| Characteristic | Adults age 18 and over, number (1,000) | Without a usual place for health care | With a usual place for health care | Usual place of health care | | | |
|---|---|---|---|---|---|---|---|
| | | | | Physician office or Health Maintenance Organization (HMO) | Clinic or health center | Hospital emergency room or outpatient department | Other place |
| Total [1] | 246,657 | 13.9 | 86.1 | 72.0 | 24.5 | 2.4 | 1.2 |
| SEX | | | | | | | |
| Male | 118,990 | 17.5 | 82.5 | 70.6 | 25.6 | 2.6 | 1.2 |
| Female | 127,667 | 10.3 | 89.7 | 73.1 | 23.5 | 2.1 | 1.1 |
| AGE [2] | | | | | | | |
| 18 to 44 years | 113,636 | 19.9 | 80.1 | 67.0 | 29.0 | 2.6 | 1.4 |
| 45 to 64 years | 83,494 | 9.2 | 90.8 | 75.7 | 20.8 | 2.5 | 0.9 |
| 65 to 74 years | 29,454 | 3.8 | 96.2 | 79.3 | 18.3 | 1.8 | 0.6 |
| 75 years and over | 20,073 | 2.5 | 97.5 | 82.6 | 15.5 | 1.1 | 0.8 |
| RACE | | | | | | | |
| Single race [3] | 241,760 | 13.7 | 86.3 | 72.0 | 24.5 | 2.3 | 1.1 |
| White | 192,033 | 14.0 | 86.0 | 72.9 | 24.3 | 1.7 | 1.1 |
| Black or African American | 30,560 | 12.3 | 87.7 | 69.5 | 23.8 | 5.2 | 1.5 |
| American Indian or Alaska Native | 2,944 | 12.8 | 87.2 | 37.9 | 54.9 | (NA) | 0.2 |
| Asian | 15,675 | 13.3 | 86.7 | 74.4 | 21.8 | 2.6 | 1.2 |
| Native Hawaiian or Other Pacific Islander | 548 | 22.8 | 77.2 | (B) | (B) | (NA) | (B) |
| Two or more races [4] | 4,897 | 18.9 | 81.1 | 67.8 | 26.2 | 4.2 | 1.8 |
| Black or African American, white | 1,183 | 24.1 | 75.9 | 76.6 | 16.9 | (NA) | (B) |
| American Indian or Alaska Native, white | 1,863 | 18.2 | 81.8 | 54.8 | 39.3 | (NA) | (B) |
| HISPANIC ORIGIN AND RACE [5] | | | | | | | |
| Hispanic or Latino | 39,416 | 19.8 | 80.2 | 60.5 | 35.7 | 3.0 | 0.8 |
| Mexican or Mexican American | 23,657 | 20.0 | 80.0 | 55.2 | 41.6 | 2.3 | 1.0 |
| Not Hispanic or Latino | 207,242 | 12.5 | 87.5 | 74.1 | 22.4 | 2.3 | 1.2 |
| White, single race | 157,443 | 12.3 | 87.7 | 75.5 | 21.8 | 1.5 | 1.1 |
| Black or African American, single race | 29,127 | 12.3 | 87.7 | 70.2 | 23.1 | 5.2 | 1.5 |
| EDUCATION [6] | | | | | | | |
| Less than high school diploma | 24,473 | 20.5 | 79.5 | 56.8 | 38.4 | 4.5 | 0.3 |
| High school diploma or GED [7] | 51,376 | 15.6 | 84.4 | 68.7 | 27.2 | 3.3 | 0.8 |
| Some college | 61,418 | 11.7 | 88.3 | 71.3 | 24.7 | 2.7 | 1.3 |
| Bachelor's degree or higher | 78,981 | 9.4 | 90.6 | 80.9 | 16.6 | 1.2 | 1.3 |
| FAMILY INCOME | | | | | | | |
| Less than $35,000 | 62,681 | 18.6 | 81.4 | 59.4 | 34.3 | 5.1 | 1.2 |
| $35,000 to $49,999 | 24,774 | 17.0 | 83.0 | 65.8 | 30.2 | 2.8 | 1.3 |
| $50,000 to $74,999 | 38,018 | 15.2 | 84.8 | 73.0 | 23.9 | 1.6 | 1.5 |
| $75,000 to $99,999 | 28,310 | 11.7 | 88.3 | 76.1 | 21.4 | 1.9 | 0.7 |
| $100,000 or more | 67,166 | 8.4 | 91.6 | 81.6 | 16.2 | 1.1 | 1.1 |
| HEALTH INSURANCE COVERAGE [8] | | | | | | | |
| Under age 65: | | | | | | | |
| Private | 136,430 | 11.7 | 88.3 | 76.3 | 21.1 | 1.3 | 1.3 |
| Medicaid | 25,831 | 11.9 | 88.1 | 60.1 | 35.3 | 3.7 | 0.9 |
| Other | 9,334 | 9.0 | 91.0 | 57.5 | 35.9 | 5.8 | 0.7 |
| Uninsured | 24,357 | 45.4 | 54.6 | 38.5 | 49.7 | 9.8 | 1.9 |
| Age 65 and over: | | | | | | | |
| Private | 20,155 | 2.6 | 97.4 | 82.7 | 15.8 | 0.9 | 0.6 |
| Medicare and Medicaid | 3,643 | 3.1 | 96.9 | 73.2 | 23.6 | 2.5 | 0.7 |
| Medicare Advantage | 13,349 | 2.2 | 97.8 | 86.0 | 12.9 | 0.7 | 0.3 |
| Medicare only | 8,457 | 4.9 | 95.1 | 80.2 | 17.3 | 1.8 | 0.8 |
| Other | 3,578 | 2.9 | 97.1 | 62.3 | 29.8 | 5.6 | 2.3 |
| Uninsured | 261 | (B) | (B) | (B) | (B) | (NA) | (B) |

B Estimate is considered unreliable. NA Not available. [1] Includes other races not shown separately, and persons with unknown education, family income, and health insurance characteristics. [2] Estimates for age groups are not age adjusted. [3] Persons who indicated only a single race group. [4] Persons who indicated more than one race group. [5] Persons of Hispanic or Latino origin may be of any race or combination of races. [6] Shown only for adults age 25 and over. [7] GED is General Educational Development high school equivalency diploma. [8] Based on a hierarchy of mutually exclusive categories. Persons with more than one type of health insurance were assigned to the first appropriate category in the hierarchy. "Uninsured" includes adults who had no coverage, had only Indian Health Service coverage, or had only a private plan that paid for one type of service such as accidents or dental care.

Source: U.S. National Center for Health Statistics, 2017 National Health Interview Survey, "Tables of Summary Health Statistics," <https://www.cdc.gov/nchs/nhis/SHS.htm>, accessed January 2019.

## Table 186. Health Care Visits—Percent Distribution by Selected Patient Characteristics: 2010 and 2016

[Covers visits to hospital emergency departments, home health care visits, and visits to doctor's offices, clinics, or some other place during a 12-month period. Excludes dental visits. Based on the National Health Interview Survey. See source, and Appendix III]

| Characteristic | None 2010 | None 2016 | 1–3 visits 2010 | 1–3 visits 2016 | 4–9 visits 2010 | 4–9 visits 2016 | 10 or more visits 2010 | 10 or more visits 2016 |
|---|---|---|---|---|---|---|---|---|
| **All persons [1,2]** | **15.6** | **14.6** | **45.4** | **49.5** | **25.8** | **23.2** | **13.2** | **12.7** |
| *SEX [2]* | | | | | | | | |
| Male | 20.4 | 18.6 | 46.4 | 50.1 | 22.7 | 21.1 | 10.5 | 10.3 |
| Female | 10.9 | 10.6 | 44.4 | 49.1 | 28.8 | 25.2 | 15.9 | 15.1 |
| *AGE* | | | | | | | | |
| Under 18 years | 8.1 | 8.3 | 55.6 | 60.4 | 28.2 | 24.2 | 8.2 | 7.0 |
| Under 6 years | 3.7 | 4.9 | 48.9 | 52.5 | 36.8 | 34.6 | 10.6 | 7.9 |
| 6 to 17 years | 10.4 | 10.0 | 59.1 | 64.3 | 23.6 | 19.1 | 6.9 | 6.6 |
| 18 to 44 years | 24.2 | 22.0 | 43.9 | 48.6 | 20.6 | 17.9 | 11.3 | 11.5 |
| 45 to 64 years | 14.8 | 12.8 | 42.8 | 45.6 | 26.1 | 25.1 | 16.4 | 16.5 |
| 65 years and over | 5.3 | 6.4 | 33.8 | 37.2 | 36.7 | 35.0 | 24.2 | 21.4 |
| 75 years and over | 4.1 | 5.8 | 31.0 | 33.6 | 38.0 | 35.7 | 27.0 | 25.0 |
| *RACE [2,3]* | | | | | | | | |
| White | 15.3 | 14.3 | 44.9 | 48.9 | 26.1 | 23.6 | 13.7 | 13.1 |
| Black or African American | 15.7 | 14.6 | 47.2 | 51.3 | 24.7 | 22.4 | 12.4 | 11.7 |
| American Indian or Alaska Native | 19.4 | 19.0 | 40.3 | 41.2 | 28.1 | 22.2 | 12.2 | 17.7 |
| Asian | 20.4 | 16.6 | 49.9 | 56.0 | 22.1 | 19.2 | 7.6 | 8.2 |
| Native Hawaiian or Other Pacific Islander only | (B) | 19.9 | (B) | 62.0 | (B) | 11.6 | (B) | (B) |
| Two or more races | 13.9 | 14.5 | 42.3 | 45.2 | 25.2 | 23.6 | 18.6 | 16.6 |
| *HISPANIC ORIGIN AND RACE [2,3,4]* | | | | | | | | |
| Hispanic or Latino | 23.5 | 19.4 | 43.2 | 48.0 | 22.6 | 21.2 | 10.7 | 11.4 |
| Mexican | 25.2 | 20.9 | 43.3 | 50.1 | 21.4 | 18.2 | 10.1 | 10.8 |
| Not Hispanic or Latino | 14.0 | 13.4 | 45.8 | 49.8 | 26.5 | 23.8 | 13.7 | 13.1 |
| White, non-Hispanic | 13.2 | 12.7 | 45.3 | 48.9 | 27.1 | 24.6 | 14.4 | 13.8 |
| Black, non-Hispanic | 15.6 | 14.6 | 47.3 | 51.4 | 24.9 | 22.4 | 12.2 | 11.6 |
| *HEALTH INSURANCE STATUS [5,6]* | | | | | | | | |
| Insured | 12.3 | 12.8 | 48.5 | 52.6 | 26.1 | 22.4 | 13.1 | 12.2 |
| Private | 12.4 | 12.9 | 51.0 | 55.4 | 25.5 | 21.7 | 11.1 | 10.0 |
| Medicaid | 10.9 | 12.5 | 38.2 | 43.5 | 28.0 | 23.7 | 23.0 | 20.3 |
| Uninsured | 37.2 | 40.4 | 42.2 | 41.8 | 15.2 | 12.2 | 5.4 | 5.6 |
| Insured continuously 12 months prior to interview | 12.1 | 12.5 | 48.6 | 52.8 | 26.2 | 22.5 | 13.0 | 12.2 |
| Uninsured for any period up to 12 months prior to interview | 18.5 | 24.2 | 47.8 | 47.2 | 22.0 | 18.0 | 11.6 | 10.5 |
| Uninsured more than 12 months prior to interview | 43.8 | 49.9 | 39.7 | 38.0 | 12.6 | 9.1 | 3.9 | 3.0 |

B Base figure too small to meet standards for reliability of a derived figure. [1] Includes other categories not shown separately. [2] Age adjusted to the year 2000 standard population. [3] Race groups include persons of Hispanic and non-Hispanic origin. Race-specific estimates are for persons reporting one race only. [4] Persons of Hispanic or Latino origin may be of any race. [5] For persons under age 65, at time of interview. Estimates are age-adjusted to the year 2000 standard population. [6] Health insurance categories are mutually exclusive. Persons who reported both Medicaid and private coverage are classified as having private coverage. Medicaid coverage includes State-sponsored health plans and the Children's Health Insurance Program (CHIP). The insured category also includes military plans, other government-sponsored health plans, and Medicare, not shown separately. Persons not covered by private insurance, Medicaid, CHIP, state-sponsored or other government-sponsored health plans, Medicare, or military plans are considered to have no health insurance coverage. Persons with only Indian Health Service coverage are considered to have no health insurance coverage.

Source: U.S. National Center for Health Statistics, *Health, United States, 2017*, September 2018. See also <http://www.cdc.gov/nchs/hus.htm>.

## Table 187. Physician Office Visits by Leading Reason for Visit by Patient Sex: 2016

[883,725 represents 883,725,000. Based on the 2016 National Ambulatory Medical Care Survey (NAMCS). NAMCS is an annual nationally representative sample survey of visits to nonfederal office-based patient care physicians, excluding anesthesiologists, radiologists, and pathologists. The sampling frame for the 2016 NAMCS was composed of all physicians contained in the master files maintained by the American Medical Association and the American Osteopathic Association. Data are subject to sampling and nonsampling errors]

| Leading reason for visit | Number of visits (1,000) | Percent distribution Male [1] | Percent distribution Female [2] | Leading reason for visit | Number of visits (1,000) | Percent distribution Male [1] | Percent distribution Female [2] |
|---|---|---|---|---|---|---|---|
| **All visits [3]** | **883,725** | **100.0** | **100.0** | Hypertension | 11,406 | 1.3 | 1.3 |
| Progress visit [4] | 127,535 | 14.7 | 14.2 | Knee symptoms | 10,581 | 1.4 | 1.0 |
| General medical examination | 72,132 | 10.1 | 6.7 | Preoperative visit | 10,129 | 1.3 | 1.1 |
| Prenatal examination, routine | 22,477 | (X) | 4.4 | Symptoms referable to throat | 10,056 | 0.9 | 1.3 |
| Postoperative visit | 18,636 | 2.2 | 2.0 | For test results | 9,786 | 1.1 | 1.1 |
| Medication | 17,283 | 2.6 | 1.5 | Vision dysfunctions | 9,666 | 1.0 | 1.1 |
| Cough | 16,417 | 2.2 | 1.6 | Fever | 8,836 | 1.5 | 0.7 |
| Well-baby examination | 15,865 | 1.8 | 1.8 | Other special examination | 8,739 | 1.2 | 0.8 |
| Medical counseling [4] | 13,485 | 1.4 | 1.6 | Diabetes mellitus | 8,512 | 1.1 | 0.9 |
| Skin rash | 13,374 | 1.7 | 1.4 | Earache or ear infection | 8,507 | 1.0 | 0.9 |
| Gynecological examination | 11,743 | (X) | 2.3 | All other reasons | 458,559 | 51.4 | 52.3 |

X Not applicable. [1] Based on 371,533,000 visits made by males. [2] Based on 512,192,000 visits made by females. [3] Numbers may not sum to totals due to rounding. [4] Not otherwise specified.

Source: U.S. National Center for Health Statistics, *National Ambulatory Medical Care Survey: 2016 State and National Summary Tables*, May 2019. See also <https://www.cdc.gov/nchs/ahcd/web_tables.htm>.

# Table 188. Emergency Room Visits by Wait Time and Total Time Spent: 2014 to 2016

[141,420 represents 141,420,000. Based on the National Hospital Ambulatory Medical Care Survey (NHAMCS), an annual nationally representative sample survey of visits to hospital emergency departments and outpatient departments, and hospital-based and freestanding ambulatory surgical centers]

| Visit characteristic | Number of visits (1,000) | | | Percent distribution of visits | | |
|---|---|---|---|---|---|---|
| | 2014 | 2015 | 2016 | 2014 | 2015 | 2016 |
| **Total visits** [1] | **141,420** | **136,943** | **145,591** | **100.0** | **100.0** | **100.0** |
| WAIT TIME TO SEE MEDICAL PROFESSIONAL [2] | | | | | | |
| Fewer than 15 minutes | 45,573 | 48,540 | 56,822 | 32.2 | 35.4 | 39.0 |
| 15 to 59 minutes | 50,544 | 43,925 | 45,974 | 35.7 | 32.1 | 31.6 |
| 1 hour, but less than 2 hours | 14,876 | 13,228 | 14,567 | 10.5 | 9.7 | 10.0 |
| 2 hours, but less than 3 hours | 3,890 | 3,894 | 4,715 | 2.8 | 2.8 | 3.2 |
| 3 hours, but less than 4 hours | 1,449 | 1,496 | 1,742 | 1.0 | 1.1 | 1.2 |
| 4 hours, but less than 6 hours | 963 | 1,028 | 1,345 | 0.7 | 0.8 | 0.9 |
| 6 hours or more | 662 | 870 | 750 | 0.5 | 0.6 | 0.5 |
| TIME SPENT IN EMERGENCY DEPARTMENT | | | | | | |
| Less than 1 hour | 15,681 | 15,361 | 17,588 | 11.1 | 11.2 | 12.1 |
| 1 hour, but less than 2 hours | 34,146 | 30,987 | 32,816 | 24.1 | 22.6 | 22.5 |
| 2 hours, but less than 4 hours | 46,994 | 45,699 | 49,128 | 33.2 | 33.4 | 33.8 |
| 4 hours, but less than 6 hours | 19,228 | 19,462 | 21,940 | 13.6 | 14.2 | 15.1 |
| 6 hours, but less than 10 hours | 8,845 | 9,410 | 11,315 | 6.3 | 6.9 | 7.8 |
| 10 hours, but less than 14 hours | 1,906 | 2,093 | 2,293 | 1.3 | 1.5 | 1.6 |
| 14 hours, but less than 24 hours | 1,715 | 1,902 | 2,246 | 1.2 | 1.4 | 1.5 |
| 24 hours or more | 1,360 | 1,093 | 1,546 | 1.0 | 0.8 | 1.1 |

[1] Totals include nonresponse and nonapplicable categories. [2] Medical professional may be a medical doctor, doctor of osteopathy, physician assistant, or nurse practitioner.

Source: U.S. National Center for Health Statistics, *National Hospital Ambulatory Medical Care Survey: 2016 Emergency Department Summary Tables*, March 2019, and earlier reports. See also <https://www.cdc.gov/nchs/ahcd/index.htm>.

# Table 189. Ambulatory Care Visits to Physician Offices and Emergency Departments by Patient and Other Characteristics: 2016

[883,725 represents 883,725,000. Based on the annual National Ambulatory Medical Care Survey and National Hospital Ambulatory Medical Care Survey, and subject to sampling error; see source for details]

| Characteristic | Physician office visits | | Emergency department visits | |
|---|---|---|---|---|
| | Number (1,000) | Per 100 persons [1] | Number (1,000) | Per 100 persons [1] |
| **Total** | **883,725** | **277.9** | **145,591** | **45.8** |
| PATIENT AGE | | | | |
| Under 15 years old | 156,860 | 257.4 | 27,436 | 45.0 |
| 15 to 24 years old | 65,077 | 153.0 | 20,674 | 48.6 |
| 25 to 44 years old | 170,734 | 205.4 | 40,014 | 48.1 |
| 45 to 64 years old | 252,037 | 301.9 | 34,359 | 41.2 |
| 65 years and over | 239,016 | 498.5 | 23,108 | 48.2 |
| 65 to 74 years old | 132,148 | 465.2 | 10,985 | 38.7 |
| 75 years old and over | 106,868 | 546.8 | 12,123 | 62.0 |
| PATIENT SEX | | | | |
| Male | 371,533 | 239.0 | 65,996 | 42.5 |
| Female | 512,192 | 315.0 | 79,595 | 49.0 |
| PATIENT RACE/ETHNICITY [2] | | | | |
| White | 740,740 | 302.3 | 106,602 | 43.5 |
| Black or African American | 93,410 | 224.3 | 33,476 | 80.4 |
| Other | 49,575 | 158.1 | 5,513 | 17.6 |
| Hispanic or Latino | 146,703 | 258.2 | 22,936 | 40.4 |
| EXPECTED PAYMENT SOURCE [3] | | | | |
| Private insurance | 526,607 | (X) | 46,332 | (X) |
| Medicare | 217,966 | (X) | 25,916 | (X) |
| Medicaid/CHIP/state-based program [4] | 137,745 | (X) | 54,949 | (X) |
| No insurance: [5] | 28,325 | (X) | 12,287 | (X) |
| Self pay | 27,148 | (X) | 11,483 | (X) |
| No charge/charity | [6] 1,177 | (X) | [6] 1,047 | (X) |
| Worker's compensation | [6] 6,311 | (X) | 1,581 | (X) |

X Not applicable. [1] Rates are based on Census Bureau July 1, 2016 estimates of the civilian noninstitutional population. [2] Race groups White, Black or African American, and Other include persons of Hispanic origin. Persons of Hispanic origin may be of any race. See source for information on missing and imputed data. [3] Estimates include all expected sources of payment. Other and unknown not shown separately. [4] Children's Health Insurance Program (CHIP). [5] "No insurance" is having only "self-pay" or "no charge/charity" as payment sources. [6] Figure does not meet standards of reliability or precision.

Source: U.S. National Center for Health Statistics, Ambulatory Health Care Data, "NAMCS and NHAMCS Web Tables: 2016," <https://www.cdc.gov/nchs/ahcd/web_tables.htm>, accessed May 2019.

## Table 190. Medicare-Certified Hospitals, Institutions, and Physicians by Provider Type: 2010 to 2016

[Inpatient hospitals and other institutional providers are active and Medicare-certified in the reporting year. Physician provider counts originate from Medicare fee-for-service Part B claims, and reflect services provided by participating and non-participating physicians]

| Providers by type | 2010 | 2011 | 2012 | 2013 | 2014 | 2015 | 2016 |
|---|---|---|---|---|---|---|---|
| **INPATIENT HOSPITALS** | | | | | | | |
| **Total hospitals [1]**............ | **6,169** | **6,172** | **6,170** | **6,164** | **6,142** | **6,140** | **6,146** |
| Beds (1,000)........... | 927,535 | 925,951 | 931,458 | 934,874 | 931,057 | 931,951 | 933,209 |
| Beds per 1,000 enrollees [2]........ | 19.6 | 19.1 | 18.5 | 17.9 | 17.3 | 16.9 | 16.5 |
| Short stay........ | 3,566 | 3,549 | 3,521 | 3,506 | 3,466 | 3,436 | 3,419 |
| Psychiatric units........ | 1,180 | 1,156 | 1,135 | 1,128 | 1,114 | 1,118 | 1,113 |
| Rehabilitation units........ | 938 | 927 | 918 | 914 | 915 | 908 | 911 |
| Swing bed hospitals........ | 510 | 522 | 515 | 513 | 502 | 488 | 474 |
| Psychiatric........ | 511 | 509 | 527 | 541 | 551 | 560 | 570 |
| Rehabilitation........ | 235 | 235 | 241 | 245 | 255 | 266 | 277 |
| Children's........ | 77 | 93 | 97 | 98 | 98 | 100 | 99 |
| Long term care........ | 438 | 437 | 437 | 430 | 423 | 426 | 420 |
| Critical access........ | 1,325 | 1,331 | 1,331 | 1,329 | 1,334 | 1,336 | 1,343 |
| **SELECTED INSTITUTIONAL PROVIDERS** | | | | | | | |
| Skilled nursing facilities........ | 15,084 | 15,132 | 15,143 | 15,156 | 15,179 | 15,236 | 15,274 |
| Beds (1,000)........ | 1,572,511 | 1,581,549 | 1,586,378 | 1,588,797 | 1,594,927 | 1,600,752 | 1,607,056 |
| Beds per 1,000 enrollees [2]........ | 33.2 | 32.6 | 31.5 | 30.5 | 29.7 | 29.0 | 28.4 |
| Home health agencies........ | 10,914 | 11,930 | 12,253 | 12,459 | 12,268 | 12,149 | 11,956 |
| Hospices........ | 3,509 | 3,630 | 3,782 | 3,941 | 4,140 | 4,302 | 4,473 |
| Independent and clinical labs........ | 224,684 | 229,611 | 235,408 | 244,427 | 250,247 | 252,044 | 254,133 |
| Outpatient physical therapy/speech pathology.... | 2,536 | 2,351 | 2,248 | 2,172 | 2,102 | 2,130 | 2,080 |
| End stage renal disease........ | 5,631 | 5,766 | 5,916 | 6,145 | 6,374 | 6,558 | 6,843 |
| Rural health clinics........ | 3,845 | 3,940 | 4,001 | 4,026 | 4,062 | 4,104 | 4,153 |
| Ambulatory surgical centers........ | 5,316 | 5,335 | 5,349 | 5,368 | 5,444 | 5,470 | 5,529 |
| Community mental health centers........ | 644 | 606 | 545 | 524 | (NA) | (NA) | (NA) |
| Federally qualified health centers........ | 4,308 | 5,082 | 5,534 | 5,882 | 6,451 | 7,022 | 7,723 |
| **PHYSICIAN PROVIDERS** | | | | | | | |
| **All physician specialties [1,3]**........ | **595,783** | **614,024** | **627,448** | **639,225** | **648,375** | **656,195** | **665,771** |
| Primary care........ | 212,849 | 216,573 | 218,408 | 221,351 | 225,387 | 227,370 | 228,907 |
| Family practice........ | 84,982 | 86,903 | 88,419 | 89,917 | 91,570 | 92,830 | 93,893 |
| General practice........ | 13,401 | 12,235 | 11,324 | 10,724 | 10,470 | 9,985 | 9,492 |
| Internal medicine........ | 106,343 | 108,310 | 109,368 | 111,075 | 113,207 | 114,420 | 115,335 |
| Pediatric medicine........ | 8,123 | 9,125 | 9,297 | 9,635 | 10,140 | 10,135 | 10,187 |
| Surgical specialties........ | 108,093 | 109,169 | 109,603 | 110,485 | 111,213 | 111,272 | 111,439 |
| Radiology........ | 36,656 | 37,004 | 37,311 | 37,622 | 37,955 | 38,156 | 38,736 |
| Obstetrics/gynecology........ | 32,881 | 33,673 | 34,192 | 34,607 | 34,914 | 34,890 | 35,092 |
| Psychiatry........ | 27,550 | 27,887 | 28,092 | 28,162 | 28,258 | 28,139 | 28,150 |

NA Not available. [1] Includes other provider types not shown separately. [2] Beds per 1,000 enrollees based on Medicare Part A enrollee counts. [3] Physicians may be counted in more than one specialty.

Source: U.S. Centers for Medicare & Medicaid Services, "CMS Program Statistics," <https://www.cms.gov/Research-Statistics-Data-and-Systems/Statistics-Trends-and-Reports/CMSProgramStatistics/index.html>, accessed January 2019.

## Table 191. Nursing Homes, Beds, Residents, and Occupancy Rate by State: 2016

[Based on a census of certified nursing facilities. Annual numbers of nursing homes, beds, and residents are based on the Centers for Medicare & Medicaid Services' reporting cycle. Starting with 2013 data, a new editing rule was used for number of beds. For the U.S., the number of beds decreased by less than 1%. For most states, this caused little or no change in the data. The change in the number of beds also caused a change in some occupancy rates. Because of the methodology change, interpret trends with caution]

| State | Nursing homes | Beds | Residents | Occupancy rate [1] | State | Nursing homes | Beds | Residents | Occupancy rate [1] |
|---|---|---|---|---|---|---|---|---|---|
| **U.S.........** | **15,647** | **1,690,304** | **1,346,941** | **79.7** | MO......... | 513 | 55,120 | 38,279 | 69.4 |
| AL......... | 229 | 26,702 | 22,554 | 84.5 | MT......... | 78 | 6,614 | 4,385 | 66.3 |
| AK......... | 18 | 693 | 591 | 85.3 | NE......... | 214 | 15,750 | 11,718 | 74.4 |
| AZ......... | 147 | 16,535 | 11,480 | 69.4 | NV......... | 58 | 6,649 | 4,967 | 74.7 |
| AR......... | 229 | 24,649 | 17,707 | 71.8 | NH......... | 75 | 7,471 | 6,655 | 89.1 |
| CA......... | 1,205 | 118,666 | 101,744 | 85.7 | NJ......... | 366 | 52,784 | 44,598 | 84.5 |
| CO......... | 221 | 20,904 | 16,267 | 77.8 | NM......... | 75 | 7,198 | 5,713 | 79.4 |
| CT......... | 225 | 27,252 | 23,224 | 85.2 | NY......... | 624 | 115,542 | 104,187 | 90.2 |
| DE......... | 45 | 4,807 | 4,206 | 87.5 | NC......... | 425 | 45,537 | 36,654 | 80.5 |
| DC......... | 19 | 2,766 | 2,494 | 90.2 | ND......... | 81 | 6,169 | 5,562 | 90.2 |
| FL......... | 690 | 83,823 | 73,183 | 87.3 | OH......... | 963 | 90,547 | 74,844 | 82.7 |
| GA......... | 358 | 39,905 | 33,324 | 83.5 | OK......... | 304 | 28,517 | 18,729 | 65.7 |
| HI......... | 46 | 4,385 | 3,564 | 81.3 | OR......... | 137 | 11,419 | 7,462 | 65.3 |
| ID......... | 78 | 5,858 | 3,892 | 66.4 | PA......... | 701 | 88,263 | 78,042 | 88.4 |
| IL......... | 742 | 94,923 | 68,188 | 71.8 | RI......... | 84 | 8,720 | 7,829 | 89.8 |
| IN......... | 546 | 61,604 | 38,884 | 63.1 | SC......... | 189 | 19,948 | 16,932 | 84.9 |
| IA......... | 440 | 31,624 | 24,106 | 76.2 | SD......... | 110 | 6,867 | 6,234 | 90.8 |
| KS......... | 340 | 25,685 | 17,810 | 69.3 | TN......... | 320 | 36,902 | 27,486 | 74.5 |
| KY......... | 291 | 27,119 | 23,442 | 86.4 | TX......... | 1,216 | 137,028 | 92,737 | 67.7 |
| LA......... | 279 | 34,642 | 26,300 | 75.9 | UT......... | 98 | 8,479 | 5,443 | 64.2 |
| ME......... | 103 | 6,918 | 6,142 | 88.8 | VT......... | 37 | 3,174 | 2,603 | 82.0 |
| MD......... | 228 | 28,090 | 24,534 | 87.3 | VA......... | 288 | 32,783 | 27,713 | 84.5 |
| MA......... | 412 | 47,779 | 40,065 | 83.9 | WA......... | 221 | 21,109 | 16,652 | 78.9 |
| MI......... | 446 | 47,285 | 38,847 | 82.2 | WV......... | 126 | 10,866 | 9,446 | 86.9 |
| MN......... | 378 | 29,816 | 25,279 | 84.8 | WI......... | 386 | 33,079 | 25,766 | 77.9 |
| MS......... | 205 | 18,389 | 16,100 | 87.6 | WY......... | 38 | 2,950 | 2,378 | 80.6 |

[1] Percentage of beds occupied (number of nursing home residents per 100 nursing home beds).

Source: U.S. National Center for Health Statistics, *Health, United States, 2017*, September 2018. See also <https://www.cdc.gov/nchs/hus/index.htm>.

## Table 192. Hospital Emergency Department Visits by Leading Reason for Visit by Patient Age and Sex: 2016

[145,591 represents 145,591,000. Based on the annual National Hospital Ambulatory Medical Care Survey and subject to sampling error; see source for details]

| Principal reason for visit | Visits (1,000) | Percent of visits | Principal reason for visit | Visits (1,000) | Percent of visits |
|---|---|---|---|---|---|
| **Total, all ages** | **145,591** | **100.0** | **Patients age 15 to 64 years [2]** | **95,048** | **100.0** |
| | | | Female | 53,909 | 56.7 |
| Stomach & abdominal pain, cramps, spasms | 12,525 | 8.6 | Stomach & abdominal pain, cramps, spasms | 6,614 | 7.0 |
| Chest pain and related symptoms [1] | 7,565 | 5.2 | Chest pain and related symptoms [1] | 3,192 | 3.4 |
| Fever | 5,494 | 3.8 | Headache, pain in head | 2,169 | 2.3 |
| Cough | 5,146 | 3.5 | Pain [1] | 1,759 | 1.9 |
| Headache, pain in head | 4,104 | 2.8 | Back symptoms | 1,614 | 1.7 |
| Back symptoms | 3,691 | 2.5 | Male | 41,139 | 43.3 |
| Pain [1] | 3,513 | 2.4 | Stomach & abdominal pain, cramps, spasms | 3,116 | 3.3 |
| Shortness of breath | 3,444 | 2.4 | Chest pain and related symptoms [1] | 2,495 | 2.6 |
| Accident | 3,216 | 2.2 | Back symptoms | 1,453 | 1.5 |
| Vomiting | 2,769 | 1.9 | Pain [1] | 1,302 | 1.4 |
| All other reasons | 94,124 | 64.6 | Headache, pain in head | 1,136 | 1.2 |
| **Patients under age 15 years [2]** | **27,436** | **100.0** | **Patients age 65 years and over [2]** | **23,108** | **100.0** |
| Female | 12,810 | 46.7 | Female | 12,876 | 55.7 |
| Fever | 2,212 | 8.1 | Stomach & abdominal pain, cramps, spasms | 1,083 | 4.7 |
| Cough | 1,102 | 4.0 | Accident | 845 | 3.7 |
| Stomach & abdominal pain, cramps, spasms | 603 | 2.2 | Chest pain and related symptoms [1] | 776 | 3.4 |
| Vomiting | 596 | 2.2 | Shortness of breath | 661 | 2.9 |
| Skin rash | 511 | 1.9 | Vertigo—dizziness | 496 | 2.1 |
| Male | 14,625 | 53.3 | Male | 10,232 | 44.3 |
| Fever | 2,114 | 7.7 | Chest pain and related symptoms [1] | 877 | 3.8 |
| Cough | 1,348 | 4.9 | Stomach & abdominal pain, cramps, spasms | 675 | 2.9 |
| Vomiting | 651 | 2.4 | Shortness of breath | 639 | 2.8 |
| Skin rash | 614 | 2.2 | Accident | 461 | 2.0 |
| Earache or ear infection | 506 | 1.8 | General weakness | 421 | 1.8 |

[1] Not referable to body systems or specific body system. [2] Totals for each age group and sex include all other reasons not shown separately, including unknown and blank responses.

Source: U.S. National Center for Health Statistics, *National Hospital Ambulatory Medical Care Survey, 2016 Emergency Department Summary Tables*, March 2019. See also <https://www.cdc.gov/nchs/ahcd/index.htm>.

## Table 193. Hospital Overnight Stays by Selected Characteristics: 2017

[Numbers in thousands (320,182 represents 320,182,000). Covers overnight hospitals stays in the past 12 months. Hospital stays due to childbirth for both the mother and the child are included. Excludes overnight stays in hospital emergency rooms or departments. Based on the National Health Interview Survey, a sample survey of the civilian noninstitutionalized population; see Appendix III]

| Selected characteristic | Total persons | Percent distribution by number of overnight hospital stays [1] | | | |
|---|---|---|---|---|---|
| | | None | One | Two | Three or more |
| **Total [2]** | **320,182** | **92.8** | **5.4** | **1.0** | **0.7** |
| SEX | | | | | |
| Male | 156,508 | 94.0 | 4.5 | 0.9 | 0.7 |
| Female | 163,674 | 91.7 | 6.4 | 1.1 | 0.8 |
| AGE | | | | | |
| Under 12 years old | 48,697 | 93.9 | 5.3 | 0.4 | 0.3 |
| 12 to 17 years old | 24,832 | 98.3 | 1.3 | 0.3 | 0.1 |
| 18 to 44 years old | 113,635 | 94.2 | 4.7 | 0.6 | 0.5 |
| 45 to 64 years old | 83,511 | 92.1 | 5.5 | 1.4 | 1.0 |
| 65 years old and over | 49,509 | 84.7 | 10.7 | 2.7 | 1.9 |
| RACE AND ETHNICITY | | | | | |
| Single race [3] | 311,780 | 92.9 | 5.4 | 1.0 | 0.7 |
| White | 245,791 | 92.8 | 5.6 | 1.0 | 0.6 |
| Black or African American | 41,464 | 92.2 | 5.3 | 1.4 | 1.2 |
| American Indian or Alaska Native | 4,014 | 90.6 | 6.8 | 1.1 | 1.5 |
| Asian | 19,723 | 95.6 | 3.4 | 0.4 | 0.5 |
| Native Hawaiian or Other Pacific Islander | 788 | [6] 92.0 | (B) | 0.3 | 0.9 |
| Two or more races [3] | 8,403 | 91.0 | 6.4 | 1.3 | 1.3 |
| Hispanic or Latino [4] | 57,905 | 93.4 | 4.7 | 1.0 | 0.9 |
| Not Hispanic or Latino | 262,277 | 92.7 | 5.6 | 1.0 | 0.7 |
| HEALTH INSURANCE COVERAGE [5] | | | | | |
| Private | 175,732 | 94.8 | 4.3 | 0.5 | 0.3 |
| Medicaid or other public insurance | 52,393 | 89.7 | 7.1 | 1.7 | 1.6 |
| Other coverage | 10,946 | 92.0 | 5.3 | 1.6 | 1.1 |
| Uninsured | 28,591 | 95.3 | 3.5 | 0.6 | 0.5 |

B Figure considered unreliable. [1] May not sum to total due to rounding. Estimates are age-adjusted using the projected 2000 U.S. population. Estimates for age groups are not age-adjusted. [2] Includes other races not shown separately and persons with unknown health insurance coverage. [3] Includes persons of Hispanic and Latino origin. [4] Persons of Hispanic or Latino origin may be of any race. [5] For persons under age 65. Based on a hierarchy of mutually exclusive categories. Persons with more than one type of insurance were assigned to the first appropriate category in the hierarchy. "Uninsured" includes persons who had no coverage, had only Indian Health Service coverage, or had only a private plan with one type of service such as accidents or dental care. [6] Data considered unreliable.

Source: U.S. National Center for Health Statistics, 2017 National Health Interview Survey, "Tables of Summary Statistics," <https//:www.cdc.gov/nchs/nhis/SHS.htm>, accessed July 2019.

# Table 194. Hospitals—Summary Characteristics: 2000 to 2017

[In units indicated (984 represents 984,000). Covers hospitals accepted for registration by the American Hospital Association; see text, this section. Short-term hospitals have an average patient stay of less than 30 days; long-term, an average stay of longer duration]

| Item | 2000 | 2005 | 2010 | 2012 | 2013 | 2014 | 2015 | 2016 | 2017 [8] |
|---|---|---|---|---|---|---|---|---|---|
| **NUMBER** | | | | | | | | | |
| All hospitals............... | 5,810 | 5,756 | 5,754 | 5,723 | 5,686 | 5,627 | 5,564 | 5,534 | 6,210 |
| With 100 beds or more.............. | 3,102 | 2,942 | 2,832 | 2,772 | 2,740 | 2,709 | 2,682 | 2,659 | 2,763 |
| Nonfederal [1]................... | 5,565 | 5,530 | 5,541 | 5,512 | 5,473 | 5,414 | 5,352 | 5,325 | 6,002 |
| Community hospitals [2]........... | 4,915 | 4,936 | 4,985 | 4,999 | 4,974 | 4,926 | 4,862 | 4,840 | 5,262 |
| Nongovernmental nonprofit.......... | 3,003 | 2,958 | 2,904 | 2,894 | 2,904 | 2,870 | 2,845 | 2,849 | 2,968 |
| For profit................ | 749 | 868 | 1,013 | 1,068 | 1,060 | 1,053 | 1,034 | 1,035 | 1,322 |
| State and local government.......... | 1,163 | 1,110 | 1,068 | 1,037 | 1,010 | 1,003 | 983 | 956 | 972 |
| Long term general and special.......... | 131 | 115 | 109 | 88 | 80 | 74 | 77 | 76 | 106 |
| Psychiatric................ | 496 | 456 | 435 | 413 | 406 | 403 | 401 | 397 | 620 |
| Tuberculosis................ | 4 | 3 | 2 | 1 | 1 | 1 | 2 | 2 | 2 |
| Federal................... | 245 | 226 | 213 | 211 | 213 | 213 | 212 | 209 | 208 |
| **BEDS (1,000) [3]** | | | | | | | | | |
| All hospitals............... | 984 | 947 | 942 | 921 | 915 | 902 | 898 | 895 | 931 |
| Rate per 1,000 population [4]......... | 3.5 | 3.2 | 3.0 | 2.9 | 2.9 | 2.8 | 2.8 | 2.8 | 2.9 |
| Beds per hospital............... | 169 | 165 | 164 | 161 | 161 | 160 | 160 | 162 | 150 |
| Nonfederal [1]............... | 931 | 901 | 897 | 882 | 876 | 863 | 859 | 857 | 893 |
| Community hospitals [2]........... | 824 | 802 | 805 | 801 | 796 | 787 | 782 | 780 | 799 |
| Rate per 1,000 population [4]......... | 2.9 | 2.7 | 2.6 | 2.6 | 2.5 | 2.5 | 2.4 | 2.4 | 2.5 |
| Nongovernmental nonprofit.......... | 583 | 561 | 556 | 545 | 544 | 535 | 531 | 533 | 545 |
| For profit................ | 110 | 114 | 125 | 135 | 135 | 136 | 135 | 134 | 142 |
| State and local government.......... | 131 | 128 | 125 | 120 | 117 | 116 | 117 | 113 | 111 |
| Long term general and special......... | 18 | 15 | 15 | 11 | 10 | 8 | 8 | 8 | 11 |
| Psychiatric................. | 87 | 82 | 76 | 70 | 69 | 68 | 68 | 68 | 82 |
| Federal.................. | 53 | 46 | 45 | 39 | 39 | 39 | 39 | 38 | 38 |
| **AVERAGE DAILY CENSUS (1,000) [5]** | | | | | | | | | |
| All hospitals................ | 650 | 656 | 627 | 600 | 592 | 584 | 588 | 589 | 614 |
| Community hospitals [2]......... | 526 | 540 | 520 | 507 | 500 | 494 | 497 | 499 | 510 |
| Nongovernmental nonprofit.......... | 382 | 388 | 368 | 354 | 351 | 344 | 346 | 349 | 357 |
| For profit................ | 61 | 68 | 71 | 77 | 76 | 77 | 77 | 78 | 81 |
| State and local government.......... | 83 | 85 | 80 | 77 | 74 | 73 | 74 | 72 | 72 |
| **EXPENSES (bil. dol.) [6]** | | | | | | | | | |
| All hospitals................ | 395.4 | 570.5 | 750.6 | 829.7 | 859.4 | 892.7 | 936.5 | 991.5 | 1,061.0 |
| Nonfederal [1]................ | 371.5 | 533.7 | 698.2 | 775.4 | 801.5 | 828.4 | 872.0 | 923.0 | 993.0 |
| Community hospitals [2]............. | 356.6 | 515.7 | 678.0 | 756.9 | 782.0 | 808.9 | 851.5 | 902.9 | 966.0 |
| Nongovernmental nonprofit.......... | 267.1 | 386.0 | 510.7 | 564.0 | 585.5 | 602.6 | 636.0 | 677.0 | 721.0 |
| For profit................ | 35.0 | 51.8 | 67.2 | 79.1 | 81.6 | 85.4 | 88.8 | 94.0 | 105.0 |
| State and local government.......... | 54.5 | 77.9 | 100.1 | 113.8 | 115.0 | 120.9 | 126.7 | 132.1 | 140.0 |
| Long term general and special........ | 2.8 | 3.6 | 4.2 | 2.8 | 3.0 | 3.0 | 3.2 | 2.9 | 3.9 |
| Psychiatric................. | 11.9 | 13.9 | 15.8 | 15.4 | 16.1 | 16.3 | 16.8 | 17.2 | 22.5 |
| Federal.................. | 23.9 | 36.8 | 52.4 | 54.3 | 57.9 | 64.3 | 64.5 | 68.1 | 67.6 |
| **PERSONNEL (1,000) [7]** | | | | | | | | | |
| All hospitals................ | 4,454 | 4,790 | 5,184 | 5,258 | 5,342 | 5,314 | 5,397 | 5,562 | 5,841 |
| Nonfederal [1]................ | 4,157 | 4,479 | 4,825 | 4,927 | 4,984 | 4,945 | 5,056 | 5,184 | 5,459 |
| Community hospitals [2]........... | 3,911 | 4,260 | 4,600 | 4,731 | 4,786 | 4,755 | 4,859 | 4,992 | 5,216 |
| Nongovernmental nonprofit.......... | 2,919 | 3,154 | 3,388 | 3,477 | 3,500 | 3,494 | 3,562 | 3,681 | 3,841 |
| For profit................ | 378 | 421 | 474 | 515 | 553 | 522 | 534 | 551 | 591 |
| State and local government.......... | 614 | 681 | 738 | 739 | 734 | 739 | 762 | 759 | 783 |
| Long term general and special........ | 41 | 38 | 39 | 26 | 25 | 22 | 23 | 21 | 28 |
| Psychiatric................. | 200 | 182 | 182 | 169 | 171 | 167 | 172 | 169 | 212 |
| Federal.................. | 297 | 311 | 359 | 331 | 358 | 369 | 341 | 379 | 382 |
| **OUTPATIENT VISITS (mil.)** | | | | | | | | | |
| Total................... | 592.7 | 673.7 | 750.4 | 778.0 | 787.4 | 802.7 | 832.3 | 863.7 | 880.4 |
| Emergency visits................ | 106.9 | 118.9 | 131.5 | 137.3 | 137.5 | 140.2 | 145.3 | 146.7 | 150.2 |

[1] Includes hospital units of institutions; and tuberculosis hospitals, not shown separately. [2] Short-term (average stay less than 30 days) general and special (e.g., obstetrics and gynecology, rehabilitation, etc. except psychiatric, tuberculosis, alcoholism, and chemical dependency). Excludes hospital units of institutions. [3] Number of beds at end of reporting period. [4] See footnote 2, Table 195. [5] The average number of people served on an inpatient basis on a single day during the reporting period. [6] Excludes new construction. [7] Includes full-time equivalents of part-time personnel. [8] Beginning with the 2019 edition of *AHA Hospital Statistics* presenting data from the 2017 annual survey, the AHA no longer employs its own methodology to classify hospitals as registered. As a result of the application of a new, broader hospital definition, the number of hospitals in 2017 increased significantly.

Source: Health Forum LLC, an affiliate of the American Hospital Association, Chicago, IL, *AHA Hospital Statistics 2019 Edition* ©, and previous editions. See also <http://www.ahadata.com/>.

# Table 195. Hospital Utilization Rates by Type of Hospital: 1990 to 2017

[In units, as indicated (21.9 represents 21,900,000)]

| Type of hospital | 1990 | 2000 | 2005 | 2010 | 2014 | 2015 | 2016 | 2017 [4] |
|---|---|---|---|---|---|---|---|---|
| **Community hospitals: [1]** | | | | | | | | |
| Admissions per 1,000 population [2]............... | 125 | 117 | 119 | 114 | 104 | 104 | 103 | 105 |
| Admissions per bed............... | 34 | 40 | 44 | 44 | 42 | 43 | 43 | 43 |
| Average length of stay (days) [3]................... | 7.2 | 5.8 | 5.6 | 5.4 | 5.5 | 5.5 | 5.5 | 5.5 |
| Outpatient visits per admission............... | 9.7 | 15.8 | 16.6 | 18.5 | 21.0 | 21.7 | 21.6 | 22.3 |
| Outpatient visits per 1,000 population [2].......... | 1,207 | 1,852 | 1,976 | 2,108 | 2,174 | 2,247 | 2,312 | 2,352 |
| Surgical operations (million)............... | 21.9 | 26.1 | 27.5 | 27.3 | 26.4 | 26.5 | 27.2 | 28.2 |
| Number per admission............... | 0.7 | 0.8 | 0.8 | 0.8 | 0.8 | 0.8 | 0.8 | 0.8 |
| **Nonfederal psychiatric:** | | | | | | | | |
| Admissions per 1,000 population [2]............... | 2.9 | 2.4 | 2.5 | 2.5 | 2.5 | 2.6 | 2.5 | 3.7 |
| Days in hospital per 1,000 population [2].......... | 190 | 93 | 89 | 77 | 65 | 67 | 65 | 77 |

[1] See headnote, Table 196. [2] Based on Census Bureau estimated resident population as of July 1. Data for 1990, 2000, and 2010 based on enumerated resident population as of April 1. [3] Number of inpatient days divided by number of admissions. [4] See footnote 8, Table 194.

Source: Health Forum LLC, an affiliate of the American Hospital Association, Chicago, IL, *AHA Hospital Statistics 2019 Edition* ©, and previous editions. See also <http://www.ahadata.com/>.

# Table 196. Community Hospital Summary Data by State: 2010 and 2017

[In units indicated (804.9 represents 804,900). Community hospitals are defined as all nonfederal, short-term general, and other special hospitals. Other special hospitals include obstetrics and gynecology; eye, ear, nose, and throat; rehabilitation; orthopedic; and other individually described specialty services. Community hospitals include academic medical centers or other teaching hospitals if they are nonfederal short-term hospitals. Excluded are hospitals not accessible by the general public, such as prison hospitals or college infirmaries]

| State | Number of hospitals 2010 | Number of hospitals 2017[2] | Beds (1,000) 2010 | Beds (1,000) 2017[2] | Patients admitted (1,000) 2010 | Patients admitted (1,000) 2017[2] | Average daily census[1] (1,000) 2010 | Average daily census[1] (1,000) 2017[2] | Outpatient visits (mil.) 2010 | Outpatient visits (mil.) 2017[2] | Average cost per day (dol.) 2010 | Average cost per day (dol.) 2017[2] |
|---|---|---|---|---|---|---|---|---|---|---|---|---|
| United States | 4,985 | 5,262 | 804.9 | 799.0 | 35,149 | 34,306 | 519.5 | 510.1 | 651.4 | 766.1 | 1,910 | 2,424 |
| Alabama | 105 | 102 | 15.1 | 15.2 | 642 | 629 | 9.2 | 9.9 | 8.8 | 9.3 | 1,372 | 1,549 |
| Alaska | 22 | 21 | 1.5 | 1.6 | 57 | 52 | 0.9 | 1.0 | 1.8 | 2.2 | 2,020 | 2,817 |
| Arizona | 73 | 83 | 13.4 | 13.9 | 712 | 651 | 8.7 | 8.4 | 8.1 | 8.6 | 2,173 | 2,638 |
| Arkansas | 85 | 88 | 9.5 | 9.7 | 370 | 363 | 5.2 | 5.1 | 5.0 | 6.1 | 1,477 | 1,787 |
| California | 343 | 362 | 70.4 | 73.2 | 3,424 | 3,452 | 47.8 | 48.6 | 51.7 | 57.2 | 2,566 | 3,437 |
| Colorado | 80 | 89 | 10.2 | 10.8 | 449 | 445 | 6.1 | 6.1 | 8.3 | 9.4 | 2,190 | 2,911 |
| Connecticut | 34 | 32 | 8.1 | 7.1 | 407 | 371 | 6.3 | 5.5 | 8.3 | 9.3 | 2,154 | 2,671 |
| Delaware | 7 | 8 | 2.2 | 2.1 | 102 | 103 | 1.6 | 1.5 | 1.8 | 2.1 | 2,227 | 3,045 |
| District of Columbia | 11 | 11 | 3.5 | 3.5 | 132 | 128 | 2.5 | 2.6 | 2.3 | 2.6 | 2,434 | 2,893 |
| Florida | 210 | 220 | 53.3 | 55.1 | 2,452 | 2,570 | 33.4 | 35.7 | 24.2 | 26.3 | 1,837 | 2,100 |
| Georgia | 154 | 147 | 25.5 | 25.2 | 961 | 1,004 | 16.8 | 17.4 | 14.3 | 19.4 | 1,338 | 1,777 |
| Hawaii | 26 | 23 | 3.1 | 2.6 | 111 | 111 | 2.3 | 1.9 | 2.2 | 2.7 | 1,755 | 2,405 |
| Idaho | 41 | 46 | 3.4 | 3.5 | 131 | 143 | 1.7 | 2.0 | 3.2 | 5.8 | 1,748 | 3,085 |
| Illinois | 189 | 189 | 33.3 | 32.0 | 1,543 | 1,364 | 20.7 | 18.9 | 32.6 | 37.6 | 1,983 | 2,515 |
| Indiana | 125 | 132 | 17.8 | 17.8 | 718 | 715 | 10.3 | 10.1 | 18.7 | 20.9 | 1,964 | 2,501 |
| Iowa | 118 | 117 | 10.1 | 9.4 | 342 | 316 | 5.7 | 5.3 | 11.0 | 11.6 | 1,288 | 1,529 |
| Kansas | 130 | 144 | 10.0 | 9.9 | 305 | 316 | 5.4 | 5.2 | 6.7 | 8.3 | 1,304 | 1,773 |
| Kentucky | 106 | 109 | 14.2 | 14.1 | 609 | 560 | 8.6 | 8.5 | 10.4 | 14.4 | 1,546 | 1,942 |
| Louisiana | 126 | 163 | 15.4 | 15.6 | 625 | 583 | 9.2 | 9.0 | 12.4 | 13.0 | 1,561 | 1,953 |
| Maine | 37 | 34 | 3.6 | 3.4 | 146 | 133 | 2.2 | 2.4 | 6.0 | 6.3 | 2,077 | 2,383 |
| Maryland | 47 | 51 | 11.7 | 11.6 | 708 | 582 | 8.7 | 8.2 | 8.4 | 9.3 | 2,383 | 2,751 |
| Massachusetts | 79 | 75 | 15.7 | 15.7 | 823 | 781 | 11.4 | 11.3 | 21.8 | 22.9 | 2,419 | 3,018 |
| Michigan | 156 | 145 | 25.6 | 25.0 | 1,208 | 1,148 | 17.0 | 15.8 | 30.3 | 38.2 | 1,959 | 2,319 |
| Minnesota | 133 | 129 | 15.3 | 14.0 | 592 | 558 | 9.9 | 9.1 | 11.1 | 13.8 | 1,731 | 2,334 |
| Mississippi | 96 | 100 | 12.9 | 12.3 | 403 | 378 | 7.0 | 6.8 | 4.6 | 6.7 | 1,154 | 1,352 |
| Missouri | 122 | 126 | 18.7 | 18.9 | 821 | 773 | 11.5 | 11.3 | 19.8 | 24.9 | 1,981 | 2,294 |
| Montana | 48 | 55 | 3.7 | 3.6 | 97 | 99 | 2.3 | 2.1 | 3.5 | 4.4 | 1,190 | 1,066 |
| Nebraska | 88 | 94 | 7.2 | 7.0 | 209 | 205 | 4.0 | 3.9 | 4.6 | 5.6 | 1,516 | 1,909 |
| Nevada | 36 | 44 | 5.2 | 6.5 | 241 | 287 | 3.6 | 4.4 | 2.7 | 3.3 | 1,885 | 1,971 |
| New Hampshire | 28 | 28 | 2.9 | 2.8 | 120 | 126 | 1.7 | 1.8 | 4.8 | 5.4 | 2,164 | 2,574 |
| New Jersey | 73 | 82 | 21.1 | 21.2 | 1,067 | 1,077 | 14.9 | 13.9 | 16.0 | 15.4 | 2,179 | 2,671 |
| New Mexico | 36 | 41 | 4.0 | 3.9 | 186 | 180 | 2.3 | 2.5 | 4.6 | 6.4 | 2,058 | 2,618 |
| New York | 185 | 168 | 59.5 | 51.8 | 2,510 | 2,273 | 47.2 | 41.0 | 53.7 | 57.6 | 1,883 | 2,718 |
| North Carolina | 117 | 114 | 23.0 | 21.8 | 1,038 | 1,019 | 16.0 | 15.2 | 18.3 | 23.6 | 1,633 | 2,126 |
| North Dakota | 41 | 40 | 3.3 | 3.2 | 94 | 89 | 2.0 | 1.9 | 3.1 | 2.3 | 1,342 | 1,814 |
| Ohio | 183 | 198 | 34.3 | 33.6 | 1,517 | 1,452 | 20.8 | 19.9 | 35.8 | 44.2 | 2,138 | 2,741 |
| Oklahoma | 113 | 129 | 11.2 | 11.5 | 429 | 420 | 6.4 | 6.2 | 5.7 | 7.8 | 1,499 | 1,921 |
| Oregon | 58 | 61 | 6.4 | 6.9 | 321 | 348 | 3.8 | 4.3 | 9.2 | 12.0 | 2,818 | 3,578 |
| Pennsylvania | 196 | 201 | 39.9 | 37.2 | 1,810 | 1,603 | 26.8 | 23.8 | 38.6 | 41.5 | 1,906 | 2,397 |
| Rhode Island | 11 | 11 | 2.5 | 2.2 | 123 | 116 | 1.7 | 1.5 | 2.7 | 2.1 | 2,325 | 2,730 |
| South Carolina | 67 | 70 | 12.5 | 12.4 | 523 | 526 | 8.2 | 7.7 | 6.4 | 9.4 | 1,788 | 2,094 |
| South Dakota | 53 | 57 | 4.1 | 4.2 | 101 | 107 | 2.6 | 2.6 | 2.0 | 2.8 | 1,113 | 1,507 |
| Tennessee | 134 | 122 | 20.8 | 20.1 | 833 | 842 | 12.5 | 12.5 | 11.4 | 13.7 | 1,462 | 1,987 |
| Texas | 426 | 528 | 61.4 | 66.8 | 2,580 | 2,774 | 36.5 | 40.0 | 38.3 | 45.2 | 1,943 | 2,523 |
| Utah | 44 | 53 | 5.1 | 5.7 | 224 | 241 | 2.7 | 3.1 | 5.5 | 9.0 | 2,233 | 3,037 |
| Vermont | 14 | 14 | 1.3 | 1.3 | 49 | 49 | 0.8 | 0.8 | 3.4 | 3.1 | 1,656 | 2,385 |
| Virginia | 89 | 95 | 17.7 | 17.8 | 777 | 797 | 11.8 | 12.4 | 13.8 | 18.2 | 1,736 | 2,035 |
| Washington | 86 | 92 | 11.5 | 12.6 | 589 | 612 | 7.2 | 8.3 | 11.8 | 15.2 | 2,810 | 3,470 |
| West Virginia | 56 | 56 | 7.3 | 7.0 | 278 | 257 | 4.4 | 4.2 | 6.7 | 8.1 | 1,323 | 1,782 |
| Wisconsin | 124 | 134 | 13.5 | 12.3 | 589 | 534 | 8.1 | 7.3 | 14.6 | 19.7 | 1,953 | 2,501 |
| Wyoming | 24 | 29 | 2.0 | 2.0 | 50 | 43 | 1.1 | 1.1 | 1.0 | 1.3 | 1,103 | 1,538 |

[1] The average number of people served on an inpatient basis on a single day during the reporting period. [2] Beginning with the 2019 edition of *AHA Hospital Statistics* presenting data from the 2017 annual survey, the AHA no longer employs its own methodology to classify hospitals as registered. As a result of the application of a new, broader hospital definition, the number of hospitals in 2017 increased significantly.

Source: Health Forum LLC, an affiliate of the American Hospital Association, Chicago, IL, *AHA Hospital Statistics 2019 Edition ©*, and previous editions. See also <http://www.ahadata.com/>.

# Table 197. Average Cost to Community Hospitals Per Patient: 1990 to 2017

[In dollars, except percent. Covers non-federal short-term general or specialty hospitals (excluding psychiatric or tuberculosis hospitals and hospital units of institutions). Total cost per patient based on total hospital expenses (payroll, employee benefits, professional fees, supplies, etc.). Data have been adjusted for outpatient visits]

| Type of expense and hospital | 1990 | 2000 | 2005 | 2010 | 2012 | 2013 | 2014 | 2015 | 2016 | 2017[2] |
|---|---|---|---|---|---|---|---|---|---|---|
| **Average cost per day, total** | 687 | 1,149 | 1,522 | 1,910 | 2,090 | 2,157 | 2,212 | 2,271 | 2,338 | 2,424 |
| Annual percent change [1] | 7.8 | 4.2 | 5.0 | 3.1 | 6.6 | 3.2 | 2.5 | 2.7 | 2.9 | 3.7 |
| Nongovernmental nonprofit | 692 | 1,182 | 1,585 | 2,025 | 2,214 | 2,289 | 2,346 | 2,413 | 2,488 | 2,574 |
| For profit | 752 | 1,057 | 1,412 | 1,629 | 1,747 | 1,791 | 1,798 | 1,831 | 1,889 | 1,996 |
| State and local government | 635 | 1,064 | 1,329 | 1,625 | 1,831 | 1,878 | 1,974 | 2,013 | 2,013 | 2,129 |
| **Average cost per stay, total** | 4,947 | 6,649 | 8,793 | 10,313 | 11,221 | 11,651 | 12,015 | 12,359 | 12,777 | 13,126 |
| Nongovernmental nonprofit | 5,001 | 6,717 | 8,670 | 10,652 | 11,563 | 12,000 | 12,385 | 12,755 | 13,182 | 13,504 |
| For profit | 4,727 | 5,642 | 7,351 | 8,336 | 8,861 | 9,296 | 9,414 | 9,510 | 9,698 | 10,273 |
| State and local government | 4,838 | 7,106 | 8,793 | 10,283 | 11,668 | 12,028 | 12,601 | 13,070 | 13,720 | 14,015 |

[1] Change from immediate prior year. [2] Beginning with the 2019 edition of *AHA Hospital Statistics* presenting data from the 2017 annual survey, the AHA no longer employs its own methodology to classify hospitals as registered. As a result of the application of a new, broader hospital definition, the number of hospitals in 2017 increased significantly.

Source: Health Forum LLC, an affiliate of the American Hospital Association, Chicago, IL, *AHA Hospital Statistics 2019 Edition ©*, and previous editions. See also <http://www.ahadata.com/>.

## Table 198. Cosmetic Plastic Surgical and Nonsurgical Procedures: 2017 and 2018

[Data are projected to reflect nationwide statistics. Data cover procedures performed only by plastic surgeons who are certified by the American Board of Plastic Surgery. Previous surveys included procedures performed by physicians from specialties other than plastic surgery. For more information, see March 2018 press release, <https://www.surgery.org/media/news-releases/the-american-society-for-aesthetic-plastic-surgery-reports-that-modern-cosmetic-procedures-are-on-the-rise>]

| Procedure | 2017, Total | 2018 Total | 2018 Women | 2018 Men |
|---|---|---|---|---|
| **Total surgical procedures** | **1,540,129** | **1,533,640** | **1,425,495** | **108,144** |
| Breast augmentation | 333,392 | 329,914 | 329,914 | (X) |
| Breast implant removal | 45,024 | 49,834 | 49,834 | (X) |
| Breast lift | 142,710 | 158,964 | 158,964 | (X) |
| Breast reduction, female | 71,422 | 84,599 | 84,599 | (X) |
| Brow lift | 22,713 | 21,868 | 19,555 | 2,313 |
| Buttock augmentation | 23,115 | 26,774 | 26,551 | 223 |
| Buttock lift | 4,690 | 5,257 | 4,994 | 263 |
| Chin augmentation | 5,963 | 7,149 | 6,308 | 841 |
| Ear surgery | 10,519 | 10,724 | 6,518 | 4,205 |
| Eyelid surgery | 145,390 | 115,508 | 97,916 | 17,593 |
| Facelift | 82,410 | 73,174 | 68,828 | 4,346 |
| Fat transfer: breast | 21,708 | 23,340 | 23,200 | 140 |
| Fat transfer: face | 54,739 | 39,461 | 37,428 | 2,033 |
| Labiaplasty (excluding vaginal rejuvenation) | 10,787 | 12,756 | 12,756 | (X) |
| Liposuction | 304,850 | 289,261 | 257,020 | 32,241 |
| Lower body lift | 6,499 | 6,098 | 4,696 | 1,402 |
| Male breast reduction (treats gynecomastia) | 20,167 | 24,672 | (X) | 24,672 |
| Neck lift | 28,542 | 27,475 | 22,639 | 4,836 |
| Nose surgery | 38,659 | 41,213 | 34,484 | 6,729 |
| Thigh lift | 7,839 | 9,743 | 9,322 | 421 |
| Tummy tuck | 140,834 | 157,492 | 152,446 | 5,046 |
| Upper arm lift | 18,157 | 18,364 | 17,523 | 841 |
| **Total nonsurgical procedures** | **3,036,440** | **3,315,888** | **3,062,254** | **253,633** |
| Total injectables | 2,344,330 | 2,671,130 | 2,465,161 | 205,969 |
|   Botulinum toxin [1] | 1,548,236 | 1,801,033 | 1,638,940 | 162,093 |
|   Calcium hydroxylapatite [2] | 42,143 | 31,821 | 29,017 | 2,804 |
|   Hyaluronic acid [3] | 722,394 | 810,240 | 770,149 | 40,091 |
|   Poly-L-Latic acid [4] | 31,557 | 28,036 | 27,055 | 981 |
| Total facial rejuvenation | 323,409 | 341,619 | 331,386 | 10,233 |
|   Chemical peel | 118,523 | 129,596 | 127,494 | 2,103 |
|   Full field ablative (laser skin resurfacing) | 31,892 | 37,849 | 36,587 | 1,262 |
|   Micro-ablative resurfacing (fractional resurfacing) | 59,764 | 38,550 | 37,568 | 981 |
|   Photorejuvenation (IPL, intense pulsed light) | 113,230 | 135,624 | 129,737 | 5,888 |
| Total other nonsurgical procedures | 368,701 | 303,139 | 265,708 | 37,431 |
|   Hair removal (laser or pulsed light) | 178,488 | 118,592 | 103,593 | 14,999 |
|   Nonsurgical fat reduction [5] | 180,833 | 174,244 | 151,885 | 22,359 |
|   Sclerotherapy | 9,380 | 10,303 | 10,230 | 73 |

X Not applicable. [1] Includes Botox, Dysport, and Xeomin. [2] Radiesse. [3] Includes Juvederm Ultra, Ultra Plus, Voluma, Perlane, Restylane, and Belotero. [4] Sculptra. [5] Includes CoolSculpting, Vaser Shape, and Liposonix.

Source: The American Society for Aesthetic Plastic Surgery, *2018 Cosmetic Surgery National Data Bank Statistics* ©. See also <https://www.surgery.org/media/statistics>.

## Table 199. Cancer Survival Rates by Race and Type/Body Site and Year of Diagnosis: 1996 to 2015

[For invasive cancer, unless otherwise noted. For top 15 cancers ranked by incidence rates per 100,000 persons for 2012-2016 period. Based on follow-up of patients into 2016. The 5-year relative survival rate represents the proportion of patients alive 5 years after their cancer diagnosis, compared to similar persons among the general population without cancer. Based on information collected as part of the National Cancer Institute's Surveillance, Epidemiology and End Results (SEER) program, a collection of population-based registries in 9 areas]

| Cancer type | 5-year relative survival rates by year of diagnosis (percent) White 1996 to 1998 | White 1999 to 2001 | White 2002 to 2004 | White 2005 to 2008 | White 2009 to 2015 | Black 1996 to 1998 | Black 1999 to 2001 | Black 2002 to 2004 | Black 2005 to 2008 | Black 2009 to 2015 |
|---|---|---|---|---|---|---|---|---|---|---|
| **All types [1]** | **64.4** | **67.2** | **68.4** | **69.8** | **70.3** | **55.4** | **58.1** | **59.7** | **62.0** | **63.6** |
| Female breast | 89.4 | 90.8 | 91.4 | 92.1 | 92.4 | 76.2 | 79.0 | 77.9 | 80.3 | 83.4 |
| Lung and bronchus | 14.8 | 15.5 | 16.5 | 18.5 | 20.7 | 12.3 | 12.7 | 13.3 | 14.7 | 19.3 |
| Prostate | 97.9 | 99.7 | 99.8 | 99.8 | 99.0 | 95.0 | 97.4 | 97.9 | 98.2 | 96.5 |
| Colon and rectum | 63.0 | 66.6 | 66.8 | 67.6 | 66.9 | 54.0 | 54.4 | 56.6 | 58.8 | 59.5 |
| Melanoma of skin | 90.9 | 92.2 | 93.2 | 93.4 | 94.1 | [4] 73.9 | [4] 73.9 | [4] 72.0 | [4] 72.6 | [4] 69.8 |
| Urinary bladder [2] | 79.8 | 81.0 | 80.8 | 80.2 | 79.1 | 62.9 | 67.7 | 61.4 | 65.0 | 64.9 |
| Non-Hodgkin's lymphoma [3] | 59.5 | 65.0 | 71.0 | 72.8 | 75.7 | 54.7 | 55.8 | 63.6 | 62.5 | 69.5 |
| Kidney and renal pelvis | 62.1 | 64.9 | 69.3 | 74.5 | 75.3 | 66.9 | 64.1 | 65.5 | 74.7 | 77.1 |
| Thyroid | 95.9 | 96.8 | 97.4 | 98.2 | 98.8 | 95.1 | 92.1 | 95.9 | 96.6 | 96.9 |
| Corpus and uterus | 85.2 | 85.9 | 85.3 | 85.7 | 85.6 | 61.7 | 61.4 | 60.4 | 65.1 | 64.2 |
| Leukemia [3] | 49.8 | 52.0 | 59.1 | 63.3 | 66.8 | 38.6 | 43.7 | 54.0 | 56.0 | 59.6 |
| Pancreas | 4.1 | 5.0 | 5.7 | 7.5 | 9.8 | 3.4 | 5.6 | 4.5 | 6.3 | 8.9 |
| Oral cavity and pharynx | 59.9 | 62.2 | 65.7 | 67.4 | 70.3 | 36.4 | 44.6 | 48.2 | 43.0 | 50.9 |
| Liver & intrahepatic bile duct | 8.4 | 10.3 | 14.1 | 16.9 | 18.8 | 4.6 | 7.6 | 9.6 | 12.7 | 15.8 |
| Stomach | 20.4 | 22.3 | 26.1 | 28.7 | 31.2 | 22.6 | 23.1 | 29.2 | 28.6 | 32.7 |

[1] Includes other sites, not shown separately. [2] Invasive and in situ. [3] All types combined. [4] Standard error is 5 to 10 percent.

Source: U.S. National Institutes of Health, National Cancer Institute, Surveillance Epidemiology and End Results Program, "SEER Cancer Statistics Review (CSR), 1975-2016," <https://seer.cancer.gov/csr/1975_2016/>, accessed April 2019.

# Table 200. Top 15 Cancers Among Men and Women by Race/Ethnicity: 2012 to 2016

[Rates per 100,000 population, age-adjusted to the 2000 U.S. standard population. Cancer incidence measures the number of newly diagnosed cancers occurring during a year. Data are for 2012 to 2016 period, based on cancer registries in 21 areas monitored by the Surveillance, Epidemiology, and End Results (SEER) Program, covering 34 percent of the U.S. population. See source for more information]

| Cancer by site, and sex | All race/ethnicities Rank | Rate | White Rank | Rate | Black Rank | Rate | Hispanic [1] Rank | Rate |
|---|---|---|---|---|---|---|---|---|
| **TOTAL** | | | | | | | | |
| **All Sites** | (X) | **442.0** | (X) | **451.7** | (X) | **442.9** | (X) | **345.8** |
| Breast | 1 | 68.4 | 1 | 69.2 | 2 | 70.9 | 1 | 52.3 |
| Lung and bronchus | 2 | 54.9 | 2 | 56.7 | 3 | 56.2 | 4 | 29.1 |
| Prostate [2] | 3 | 50.0 | 3 | 47.0 | 1 | 74.9 | 2 | 41.3 |
| Colon and rectum | 4 | 38.6 | 4 | 38.1 | 4 | 44.6 | 3 | 33.7 |
| Melanoma of the skin | 5 | 22.2 | 5 | 26.6 | (X) | (X) | (X) | (X) |
| Urinary bladder | 6 | 20.1 | 6 | 22.2 | 10 | 11.8 | 11 | 11.1 |
| Non-Hodgkin lymphoma | 7 | 19.6 | 7 | 20.6 | 8 | 14.7 | 5 | 17.9 |
| Kidney and renal pelvis | 8 | 16.1 | 8 | 16.6 | 5 | 17.4 | 6 | 15.7 |
| Thyroid | 9 | 15.8 | 9 | 16.5 | 14 | 9.6 | 7 | 13.9 |
| Corpus and uterus, NOS [2,6] | 10 | 14.6 | 11 | 14.8 | 6 | 15.6 | 9 | 12.8 |
| Leukemia | 11 | 14.1 | 10 | 14.9 | 11 | 10.9 | 12 | 10.8 |
| Pancreas | 12 | 12.9 | 12 | 13.0 | 7 | 15.2 | 10 | 11.3 |
| Oral cavity and pharynx | 13 | 11.3 | 13 | 11.9 | 15 | 8.6 | 14 | 6.9 |
| Liver and IBD [3] | 14 | 8.8 | 14 | 8.0 | 12 | 10.8 | 8 | 13.6 |
| Stomach | 15 | 7.4 | (X) | (X) | 13 | 10.3 | 13 | 10.4 |
| Brain and ONS [4] | (X) | (X) | 15 | 7.0 | (X) | (X) | (X) | (X) |
| Myeloma | (X) | (X) | (X) | (X) | 9 | 13.7 | 15 | 6.7 |
| **MEN** | | | | | | | | |
| **All Sites** | (X) | **481.0** | (X) | **486.0** | (X) | **520.8** | (X) | **370.4** |
| Prostate | 1 | 109.5 | 1 | 101.9 | 1 | 176.7 | 1 | 93.4 |
| Lung and bronchus | 2 | 63.0 | 2 | 63.5 | 2 | 73.5 | 3 | 35.2 |
| Colon and rectum | 3 | 44.2 | 3 | 43.4 | 3 | 52.4 | 2 | 40.0 |
| Urinary bladder | 4 | 35.2 | 4 | 38.5 | 5 | 19.7 | 7 | 19.5 |
| Melanoma of the skin | 5 | 28.8 | 5 | 33.9 | (X) | (X) | (X) | (X) |
| Non-Hodgkin lymphoma | 6 | 23.9 | 6 | 25.0 | 7 | 17.7 | 5 | 20.7 |
| Kidney and renal pelvis | 7 | 22.1 | 7 | 22.8 | 4 | 24.3 | 4 | 20.8 |
| Leukemia | 8 | 18.1 | 8 | 19.1 | 11 | 13.9 | 8 | 13.0 |
| Oral cavity and pharynx | 9 | 17.0 | 9 | 17.9 | 12 | 13.4 | 11 | 10.1 |
| Pancreas | 10 | 14.6 | 10 | 14.8 | 8 | 16.7 | 10 | 12.0 |
| Liver and IBD [3] | 11 | 13.6 | 11 | 12.2 | 6 | 17.8 | 6 | 20.3 |
| Stomach | 12 | 10.0 | 12 | 8.9 | 10 | 14.1 | 9 | 13.0 |
| Myeloma | 13 | 8.7 | 15 | 8.1 | 9 | 16.3 | 12 | 8.2 |
| Thyroid | 14 | 8.0 | 13 | 8.6 | (X) | (X) | 14 | 5.7 |
| Brain and ONS [4] | 15 | 7.5 | 14 | 8.3 | 15 | 4.7 | 13 | 5.8 |
| Larynx | (X) | (X) | (X) | (X) | 13 | 7.6 | (X) | (X) |
| Esophagus | (X) | (X) | (X) | (X) | 14 | 6.4 | (X) | (X) |
| Testis | (X) | (X) | (X) | (X) | (X) | (X) | 15 | 5.2 |
| **WOMEN** | | | | | | | | |
| **All Sites** | (X) | **417.1** | (X) | **430.9** | (X) | **391.3** | (X) | **334.9** |
| Breast | 1 | 127.5 | 1 | 130.5 | 1 | 124.0 | 1 | 97.2 |
| Lung and bronchus | 2 | 48.9 | 2 | 51.8 | 2 | 44.6 | 3 | 24.8 |
| Colon and rectum | 3 | 33.9 | 3 | 33.6 | 3 | 39.1 | 2 | 28.8 |
| Corpus and uterus, NOS [6] | 4 | 27.5 | 4 | 28.1 | 4 | 27.4 | 4 | 24.1 |
| Thyroid | 5 | 23.3 | 5 | 24.5 | 5 | 14.3 | 5 | 21.9 |
| Melanoma of the skin | 6 | 17.5 | 6 | 21.3 | (X) | (X) | (X) | (X) |
| Non-Hodgkin lymphoma | 7 | 16.2 | 7 | 17.0 | 7 | 12.4 | 6 | 15.7 |
| Pancreas | 8 | 11.5 | 10 | 11.4 | 6 | 14.0 | 8 | 10.7 |
| Ovary [5] | 9 | 11.4 | 8 | 11.9 | 10 | 9.2 | 9 | 10.3 |
| Kidney and renal pelvis | 10 | 10.9 | 11 | 11.3 | 8 | 12.1 | 7 | 11.6 |
| Leukemia | 11 | 10.9 | 9 | 11.5 | 11 | 8.9 | 11 | 9.1 |
| Urinary bladder | 12 | 8.7 | 12 | 9.5 | 14 | 6.6 | 15 | 5.1 |
| Cervix uteri | 13 | 7.3 | 13 | 7.2 | 12 | 8.7 | 10 | 9.3 |
| Oral cavity and pharynx | 14 | 6.4 | 14 | 6.6 | (X) | (X) | (X) | (X) |
| Myeloma | 15 | 5.6 | (X) | (X) | 9 | 11.9 | 14 | 5.5 |
| Brain and ONS [4] | (X) | (X) | 15 | 6.0 | (X) | (X) | (X) | (X) |
| Stomach | (X) | (X) | (X) | (X) | 13 | 7.7 | 12 | 8.5 |
| Liver and IBD [3] | (X) | (X) | (X) | (X) | 15 | 5.4 | 13 | 7.9 |

X Not applicable. [1] Persons of Hispanic origin may be of any race. [2] Rates for sex-specific cancer sites are calculated using the population for both sexes combined. [3] IBD, intrahepatic bile duct. [4] ONS, other nervous system. [5] Ovary excludes borderline cases or histologies 8442, 8451, 8462, 8472, and 8473. [6] NOS, not otherwise specified.

Source: National Institutes of Health, National Cancer Institute, Surveillance, Epidemiology, and End Results Program, "SEER Cancer Statistics Review, 1975-2016," <https://seer.cancer.gov/csr/1975_2016/>, accessed April 2019.

# Table 201. Selected Notifiable Diseases—Cases Reported: 1990 to 2017

[In thousands only where indicated (690.2 represents 690,200). Interpret figures with caution. Although reporting of some of these diseases is incomplete, the figures are of value in indicating trends of disease incidence. Includes cases imported from outside the U.S.]

| Disease | 1990 | 2000 | 2005 | 2010 | 2013 | 2014 | 2015 | 2016 | 2017 |
|---|---|---|---|---|---|---|---|---|---|
| AIDS/HIV [2] | 41,595 | 40,758 | 41,120 | 35,741 | 34,969 | 35,606 | 33,817 | 34,775 | 33,938 |
| Babesiosis | ([1]) | ([1]) | ([1]) | ([1]) | 1,796 | 1,760 | 2,100 | 1,910 | 2,368 |
| Botulism [3] | 92 | 138 | 135 | 112 | 152 | 161 | 195 | 201 | 177 |
| Campylobacteriosis | ([1]) | ([1]) | ([1]) | ([1]) | ([1]) | ([1]) | 54,556 | 60,120 | 67,537 |
| Chikungunya virus | ([1]) | ([1]) | ([1]) | ([1]) | ([1]) | ([1]) | 896 | 247 | 156 |
| Coccidioidomycosis | ([1]) | 2,867 | 6,542 | ([1]) | 9,438 | 8,232 | 11,072 | 11,829 | 14,364 |
| Cryptosporidiosis | ([1]) | 3,128 | 5,659 | 8,944 | 9,056 | 8,682 | 9,735 | 13,453 | 11,414 |
| Dengue virus infections [4] | ([1]) | ([1]) | ([1]) | 700 | 843 | 680 | 951 | 953 | 437 |
| Giardiasis | ([1]) | ([1]) | 19,733 | 19,811 | 15,106 | 14,554 | 14,485 | 16,310 | 15,193 |
| Haemophilus influenza | ([1]) | 1,398 | 2,304 | 3,151 | 3,792 | 3,541 | 4,138 | 4,895 | 5,548 |
| Hepatitis virus, acute: A | 31,441 | 13,397 | 4,488 | 1,670 | 1,781 | 1,239 | 1,390 | 2,007 | 3,365 |
| Hepatitis virus, acute: B | 21,102 | 8,036 | 5,119 | 3,374 | 3,050 | 2,791 | 3,370 | 3,218 | 3,409 |
| Hepatitis virus, acute: C | 2,553 | 3,197 | 652 | 849 | 2,138 | 2,204 | 2,447 | 2,942 | 4,225 |
| Invasive pneumococcal disease [5] | (X) | (X) | (X) | 16,569 | 17,193 | 15,356 | 16,163 | 17,626 | 19,780 |
| Legionellosis | 1,370 | 1,127 | 2,301 | 3,346 | 4,954 | 5,166 | 6,079 | 6,141 | 7,458 |
| Listeriosis | ([1]) | 755 | 896 | 821 | 735 | 769 | 768 | 786 | 887 |
| Lyme disease | ([1]) | 17,730 | 23,305 | 30,158 | 36,307 | 33,461 | 38,069 | 36,429 | 42,743 |
| Malaria | 1,292 | 1,560 | 1,494 | 1,773 | 1,594 | 1,653 | 1,390 | 1,955 | 2,056 |
| Measles | 27,786 | 86 | 66 | 63 | 187 | 667 | 188 | 85 | 120 |
| Meningococcal infections | 2,451 | 2,256 | 1,245 | 833 | 556 | 433 | 372 | 375 | 353 |
| Mumps | 5,292 | 338 | 314 | 2,612 | 584 | 1,223 | 1,329 | 6,369 | 6,109 |
| Pertussis (whooping cough) | 4,570 | 7,867 | 25,616 | 27,550 | 28,639 | 32,971 | 20,762 | 17,972 | 18,975 |
| Rabies, animal | 4,826 | 6,934 | 5,915 | 4,331 | 4,248 | 5,988 | 5,491 | 4,609 | 4,423 |
| Rubella [6] | 1,125 | 176 | 11 | 5 | 9 | 6 | 5 | 1 | 7 |
| Salmonellosis [7] | 48,603 | 39,574 | 45,322 | 54,424 | 50,634 | 51,455 | 55,108 | 53,850 | 54,285 |
| Shiga toxin-producing E. coli (STEC) | ([1]) | ([1]) | ([1]) | 5,476 | 6,663 | 6,179 | 7,059 | 8,169 | 8,672 |
| Shigellosis [8] | 27,077 | 22,922 | 16,168 | 14,786 | 12,729 | 20,745 | 23,590 | 21,097 | 14,912 |
| Spotted fever rickettsiosis (including Rocky Mountain spotted fever) | ([1]) | 495 | 1,936 | 1,985 | 3,359 | 3,757 | 4,198 | 4,269 | 6,248 |
| Streptococcal toxic-shock syndrome | ([1]) | 83 | 129 | 142 | 224 | 259 | 335 | 283 | 372 |
| Tetanus | 64 | 35 | 27 | 26 | 26 | 25 | 29 | 34 | 33 |
| Toxic-shock syndrome | 322 | 135 | 90 | 82 | 71 | 59 | 64 | 40 | 30 |
| Tuberculosis [9] | 25,701 | 16,377 | 14,097 | 11,182 | 9,582 | 9,421 | 9,557 | 9,272 | 9,105 |
| Typhoid fever | 552 | 377 | 324 | 467 | 338 | 349 | 367 | 376 | 419 |
| Varicella (chickenpox) morbidity [10] | 173,099 | 27,382 | 32,242 | 15,427 | 11,359 | 10,172 | 9,789 | 8,953 | 8,775 |
| West Nile virus, neuroinvasive [4] | ([1]) | ([1]) | 1,309 | 629 | 1,267 | 1,347 | 1,455 | 1,308 | 1,425 |
| West Nile virus, nonneuroinvasive [4] | ([1]) | ([1]) | 1,691 | 392 | 1,202 | 858 | 720 | 841 | 672 |
| Zika virus disease and infections [11] | ([1]) | ([1]) | ([1]) | ([1]) | ([1]) | ([1]) | ([1]) | 6,118 | 1,177 |
| Sexually transmitted diseases: | | | | | | | | | |
| Chlamydia (1,000) | ([1]) | 702.1 | 976.4 | 1,307.9 | 1,401.9 | 1,441.8 | 1,526.7 | 1,598.4 | 1,708.6 |
| Gonorrhea (1,000) | 690.2 | 359.0 | 339.6 | 309.3 | 333.0 | 350.1 | 395.2 | 468.5 | 555.6 |
| Syphilis (1,000) | 134.3 | 31.6 | 33.3 | 45.8 | 56.5 | 63.5 | 74.7 | 88.0 | 101.6 |

X Not applicable. [1] Disease was not notifiable. [2] Acquired immunodeficiency syndrome/Human immunodeficiency virus. Cases reported to the Division of HIV/AIDS Prevention, National Center for HIV/AIDS, Viral Hepatitis, STD, and TB Prevention. In 2008, CDC published a revised HIV case definition which combined definitions for HIV infection and AIDS into a single case definition for HIV infection that includes AIDS. [3] Includes foodborne, infant, wound, and unspecified cases. [4] Totals reported to the Division of Vector-Borne Diseases (DVBD), National Center for Emerging and Zoonotic Infectious Diseases (NCEZID) (ArboNET Surveillance). [5] Data for 2010, 2011, and 2015 reported as Streptococcus pneumoniae invasive disease. [6] German measles. Excludes congenital syndrome. [7] Excludes typhoid fever. [8] Bacillary dysentery. [9] Totals reported to the Division of Tuberculosis Elimination, NCHHSTP. [10] Varicella (chickenpox) was removed from the nationally notifiable disease list in 1981; it became notifiable again in 2003. [11] Includes Zika virus diseases and infections, congenital and noncongenital.

Source: U.S. Centers for Disease Control and Prevention, National Notifiable Diseases Surveillance System, "Summary of Notifiable Infectious Diseases and Conditions—United States, 2015," *Morbidity and Mortality Weekly Report*, 64:53, August 11, 2017, and earlier reports, and "Annual Tables of Infectious Diseases and Conditions (2016 to present): Annual data for 2017," <https://wwwn.cdc.gov/nndss/infectious-tables.html>, accessed February 2019.

# Table 202. HIV Diagnoses and Chlamydia and Lyme Disease Cases Reported by State: 2017

| State | HIV diagnoses [1] | Chlamydia [1] | Lyme disease | State | HIV diagnoses [1] | Chlamydia [1] | Lyme disease | State | HIV diagnoses [1] | Chlamydia [1] | Lyme disease |
|---|---|---|---|---|---|---|---|---|---|---|---|
| U.S. | 33,938 | 1,708,569 | 42,743 | IA | 121 | 13,893 | 255 | NC | 1,284 | 62,876 | 295 |
| | | | | KS | 115 | 13,554 | 40 | ND | 32 | 3,278 | 56 |
| | | | | KY | 279 | 19,320 | 20 | OH | 934 | 61,389 | 270 |
| AL | 493 | 29,935 | 41 | LA | 1,105 | 34,756 | 12 | OK | 218 | 21,752 | 1 |
| AK | 28 | 5,934 | 10 | ME | 25 | 4,555 | 1,850 | OR | 189 | 18,634 | 84 |
| AZ | 740 | 39,598 | 28 | MD | 878 | 33,416 | 1,891 | PA | 996 | 56,447 | 11,900 |
| AR | 276 | 17,320 | 6 | MA | 516 | 29,315 | 410 | RI | 75 | 5,282 | 1,132 |
| CA | 3,562 | 218,785 | 145 | MI | 748 | 50,595 | 291 | SC | 696 | 32,235 | 21 |
| CO | 407 | 26,995 | 4 | MN | 247 | 23,539 | 2,318 | SD | 16 | 4,437 | 12 |
| CT | 232 | 17,750 | 2,051 | MS | 415 | 21,149 | 1 | TN | 588 | 35,087 | 47 |
| DE | 99 | 5,392 | 608 | MO | 481 | 32,683 | 12 | TX | 3,560 | 151,533 | 58 |
| DC | 261 | 9,107 | 84 | MT | 31 | 4,560 | 12 | UT | 109 | 10,135 | 25 |
| FL | 4,913 | 100,018 | 210 | NE | 86 | 8,595 | 14 | VT | 18 | 1,858 | 1,092 |
| GA | 2,294 | 65,104 | 8 | NV | 437 | 16,260 | 17 | VA | 835 | 42,374 | 1,657 |
| HI | 76 | 6,850 | ([2]) | NH | 34 | 4,412 | 1,381 | WA | 429 | 32,231 | 37 |
| ID | 43 | 6,200 | 20 | NJ | 874 | 35,239 | 5,092 | WV | 73 | 4,140 | 648 |
| IL | 799 | 75,518 | 273 | NM | 78 | 13,560 | 3 | WI | 244 | 27,740 | 3,000 |
| IN | 476 | 34,278 | 142 | NY | 2,463 | 116,814 | 5,155 | WY | 10 | 2,142 | 4 |

[1] Total diagnoses reported to the National Center for HIV/AIDS, Viral Hepatitis, STD, and TB Prevention. [2] Not reportable.

Source: U.S. Centers for Disease Control and Prevention, National Notifiable Diseases Surveillance System, "Annual Tables of Infectious Diseases and Conditions (2016 to present): Annual data for 2017," <https://www.cdc.gov/nndss/infectious-tables.html>, accessed March 2019.

## Table 203. Estimated Number of Persons with Stage 3 HIV Infection (AIDS) by Year of Diagnosis, Sex and Transmission Category: 2012 to 2017

[Data reported to the CDC as of June 30, 2018. HIV infection is classified as stage 3 (AIDS) when the immune system of a person infected with human immunodeficiency virus becomes severely compromised (measured by CD4 lymphocyte count or percentages) and/or the person becomes ill with an AIDS-defining opportunistic illness. Data cover the 50 states, the District of Columbia, and 6 U.S. dependent areas (American Samoa, Guam, Northern Mariana Islands, Puerto Rico, Republic of Palau, and the U.S. Virgin Islands). As of April 2008, all jurisdictions had implemented confidential name-based HIV infection reporting. Beginning with the 2015 *HIV Surveillance Report,* data are presented without statistical adjustments for delays in reporting cases to the CDC. Data may not be representative of all persons with HIV. As of December 2017, completeness of HIV infection reporting is estimated to be at least 85% in all but 1 jurisdiction. See source for more information]

| Transmission category and sex | 2012 | 2013 | 2014 | 2015 | 2016 | 2017 (P) | Cumulative through 2017 [1] |
|---|---|---|---|---|---|---|---|
| **Total, all ages [2]** | **25,279** | **24,146** | **19,769** | **19,203** | **18,832** | **17,803** | **1,281,787** |
| **Males age 13 and over, total** | **18,985** | **18,305** | **14,846** | **14,559** | **14,401** | **13,462** | **1,007,969** |
| Male-to-male sexual contact | 13,255 | 13,078 | 10,498 | 10,472 | 10,387 | 9,781 | 612,861 |
| Injection drug use | 1,599 | 1,394 | 1,214 | 1,054 | 969 | 968 | 198,078 |
| Male-to-male sexual contact and injection drug use | 1,237 | 1,052 | 806 | 846 | 817 | 766 | 91,982 |
| Heterosexual contact [3] | 2,785 | 2,653 | 2,252 | 2,095 | 2,150 | 1,877 | 93,163 |
| Other [4] | 109 | 128 | 76 | 92 | 78 | 70 | 11,886 |
| **Females age 13 and over, total** | **6,282** | **5,832** | **4,853** | **4,605** | **4,391** | **4,308** | **263,816** |
| Injection drug use | 1,196 | 1,044 | 861 | 795 | 752 | 740 | 94,269 |
| Heterosexual contact [3] | 4,979 | 4,650 | 3,896 | 3,729 | 3,528 | 3,478 | 163,271 |
| Other [4] | 107 | 139 | 96 | 81 | 111 | 90 | 6,276 |

P Preliminary. [1] From the beginning of the epidemic through 2017. [2] Because column totals for estimated numbers were calculated independently of the values for the subpopulations, the values in each column may not sum to the column total. [3] Heterosexual contact with a person known to have, or to be at high risk for, HIV infection. [4] Includes hemophilia, blood transfusion, perinatal exposure, and risk factor not reported or not identified.

Source: U.S. Centers for Disease Control and Prevention, *HIV Surveillance Report: Diagnoses of HIV Infection in the United States and Dependent Areas, 2017,* Vol. 29, November 2018. See also <https://www.cdc.gov/hiv/library/reports/hiv-surveillance.html>.

## Table 204. Estimated Number of Persons Living with HIV Infection Ever Classified as Stage 3 (AIDS) Diagnosis by Selected Characteristics: 2012 to 2016

[See headnote, Table 203]

| Characteristic and transmission category | 2012 | 2013 | 2014 | 2015 | 2016 |
|---|---|---|---|---|---|
| **Total persons [1]** | **505,274** | **516,064** | **522,346** | **528,441** | **534,805** |
| *AGE AS OF END OF YEAR* | | | | | |
| Less than 13 years [2] | 328 | 284 | 304 | 279 | 290 |
| 13 and 14 years | 198 | 158 | 133 | 130 | 104 |
| 15 to 19 years | 1,998 | 1,735 | 1,334 | 994 | 847 |
| 20 to 24 years | 8,351 | 8,343 | 7,602 | 6,827 | 6,046 |
| 25 to 34 years | 45,247 | 46,013 | 45,862 | 45,754 | 45,814 |
| 35 to 44 years | 109,894 | 104,530 | 98,943 | 93,412 | 89,691 |
| 45 to 54 years | 199,028 | 199,630 | 197,457 | 193,601 | 187,139 |
| 55 to 64 years | 109,203 | 119,482 | 129,547 | 139,894 | 150,565 |
| 65 years and over | 31,027 | 35,889 | 41,164 | 47,550 | 54,309 |
| *RACE/ETHNICITY* | | | | | |
| American Indian/Alaska Native | 1,317 | 1,349 | 1,388 | 1,428 | 1,489 |
| Asian [3] | 5,256 | 5,544 | 5,814 | 6,093 | 6,363 |
| Black/African American | 202,715 | 207,891 | 210,994 | 214,027 | 217,236 |
| Hispanic/Latino [4] | 119,236 | 122,150 | 124,018 | 125,988 | 128,134 |
| Native Hawaiian/Other Pacific Islander | 380 | 392 | 404 | 424 | 433 |
| White | 152,068 | 154,023 | 154,879 | 155,651 | 156,344 |
| Multiple races | 24,260 | 24,674 | 24,808 | 24,789 | 24,765 |
| *TRANSMISSION CATEGORY [5]* | | | | | |
| Males age 13 and over, total | 384,656 | 393,018 | 397,833 | 402,487 | 407,482 |
| Male-to-male sexual contact | 246,086 | 253,890 | 259,045 | 264,176 | 269,461 |
| Injection drug use | 54,018 | 53,327 | 52,420 | 51,485 | 50,640 |
| Male-to-male sexual contact and injection drug use | 35,528 | 35,425 | 35,067 | 34,718 | 34,424 |
| Heterosexual contact [6] | 44,544 | 45,830 | 46,733 | 47,518 | 48,354 |
| Other [7] | 4,480 | 4,546 | 4,567 | 4,589 | 4,603 |
| Females age 13 and over, total | 120,290 | 122,762 | 124,209 | 125,675 | 127,033 |
| Injection drug use | 32,326 | 32,087 | 31,722 | 31,398 | 31,058 |
| Heterosexual contact [6] | 84,259 | 86,861 | 88,603 | 90,341 | 91,980 |
| Other [7] | 3,705 | 3,814 | 3,884 | 3,935 | 3,995 |
| Children under age 13 at end of year [2] | 328 | 284 | 304 | 279 | 290 |
| Perinatal | 305 | 261 | 271 | 244 | 251 |
| Other [7] | 23 | 23 | 33 | 35 | 39 |

[1] Because column totals were calculated independently of the values for the subpopulations, the values in each column may not sum to the column total. [2] The criteria for HIV Stage 3 (AIDS) classification among pediatric cases were expanded in 2014; see Technical Notes in source. [3] Includes Asian/Pacific Islander legacy cases. See Technical Notes in source. [4] Hispanics/Latinos may be of any race. [5] Data are statistically adjusted to account for missing transmission category information. [6] Heterosexual contact with a person known to have, or to be at high risk for, HIV infection. [7] Includes hemophilia, blood transfusion, perinatal for persons age 13 and over, and risk factor not reported or not identified.

Source: U.S. Centers for Disease Control and Prevention, *HIV Surveillance Report: Diagnoses of HIV Infection in the United States and Dependent Areas, 2017,* Vol. 29, November 2018. See also <https://www.cdc.gov/hiv/library/reports/hiv-surveillance.html>.

## Table 205. Organ Transplants: 2000 to 2018

[As of year end. Based on Organ Procurement and Transplantation Network data; data are from work supported in part by Health Resources and Services Administration contract 234-2005-37011C]

| Procedure | Number of procedures | | | | | Number of people waiting | | | | |
|---|---|---|---|---|---|---|---|---|---|---|
| | 2000 | 2005 | 2010 | 2017 | 2018 | 2000 | 2005 | 2010 | 2017 | 2018 |
| Transplant: [1] | | | | | | | | | | |
| Kidney............. | 13,631 | 16,485 | 16,900 | 19,849 | 21,167 | 50,426 | 68,429 | 93,486 | 103,801 | 103,099 |
| Liver............... | 5,001 | 6,444 | 6,291 | 8,082 | 8,250 | 17,132 | 17,831 | 16,857 | 14,337 | 13,767 |
| Pancreas........... | 439 | 542 | 349 | 213 | 191 | 1,032 | 1,706 | 1,431 | 922 | 883 |
| Kidney-pancreas...... | 915 | 903 | 828 | 789 | 836 | 2,553 | 2,571 | 2,293 | 1,752 | 1,683 |
| Heart.............. | 2,199 | 2,125 | 2,332 | 3,244 | 3,408 | 4,164 | 3,004 | 3,202 | 3,966 | 3,846 |
| Lung............... | 959 | 1,406 | 1,769 | 2,449 | 2,530 | 3,679 | 3,192 | 1,824 | 1,398 | 1,455 |
| Heart-lung.......... | 48 | 35 | 42 | 29 | 32 | 209 | 143 | 70 | 43 | 48 |
| Intestine........... | 82 | 178 | 151 | 109 | 104 | 151 | 205 | 265 | 259 | 246 |
| Multi-organ......... | 222 | 522 | 560 | 1,035 | 1,017 | (NA) | (NA) | (NA) | (NA) | (NA) |

NA Not available. [1] Kidney-pancreas and heart-lung transplants are each counted as one procedure. All other multiorgan transplants are included in the multi-organ row.

Source: U.S. Department of Health and Human Services, Health Resources and Services Administration, Organ Procurement and Transplantation Network (OPTN), <https://optn.transplant.hrsa.gov/data/view-data-reports/>, accessed June 2019; and unpublished data, based on OPTN data as of May 31, 2019.

## Table 206. Disability Prevalence Among Adults Age 18 and Over by Type of Disability: 2014

[Numbers in thousands (240,054 represents 240,054,000). Covers civilian household population, and excludes persons living in institutions (including correctional facilities, nursing homes, and long-term care hospitals) and military barracks. Based on data from the Social Security Administration Supplement to the 2014 panel of the Survey of Income and Program Participation]

| Type of disability | Adults age 18 and over | | Adults age 18 to 64 | | Adults age 65 and over | |
|---|---|---|---|---|---|---|
| | Number | Percent | Number | Percent | Number | Percent |
| Total persons.................... | 240,054 | 100.0 | 194,788 | 100.0 | 45,266 | 100.0 |
| **Persons with any disability**................ | **72,732** | **30.3** | **46,238** | **23.7** | **26,494** | **58.5** |
| Nonsevere................ | 24,804 | 10.3 | 17,121 | 8.8 | 7,684 | 17.0 |
| Severe [1]................ | 47,928 | 20.0 | 29,117 | 14.9 | 18,810 | 41.6 |
| Person needs assistance with ADLs or IADLs [2,3].............. | 24,229 | 10.1 | 15,372 | 7.9 | 8,856 | 19.6 |
| Serious difficulty seeing............. | 12,316 | 5.1 | 8,044 | 4.1 | 4,272 | 9.4 |
| Blind..................... | 1,561 | 0.7 | 1,051 | 0.5 | 510 | 1.1 |
| Serious difficulty hearing............ | 17,063 | 7.1 | 7,972 | 4.1 | 9,091 | 20.1 |
| Deaf..................... | 3,442 | 1.4 | 1,700 | 0.9 | 1,742 | 3.8 |
| Use of hearing aid............ | 8,195 | 3.4 | 2,165 | 1.1 | 6,030 | 13.3 |
| Difficulty with speech............ | 4,937 | 2.1 | 3,337 | 1.7 | 1,601 | 3.5 |
| Difficulty walking a quarter of a mile............ | 32,251 | 13.4 | 17,530 | 9.0 | 14,721 | 32.5 |
| Difficulty climbing a flight of stairs............ | 29,032 | 12.1 | 16,268 | 8.4 | 12,764 | 28.2 |
| Used a wheelchair............ | 5,473 | 2.3 | 2,721 | 1.4 | 2,752 | 6.1 |
| Used a cane/crutches/walker for 6 months or longer............ | 15,372 | 6.4 | 6,940 | 3.6 | 8,432 | 18.6 |
| Difficulty with physical tasks or movement [4]............ | 29,729 | 12.4 | 17,921 | 9.2 | 11,809 | 26.1 |
| Difficulty with activities of daily living (ADLs) (self-care)............ | 17,701 | 7.4 | 10,705 | 5.5 | 6,996 | 15.5 |
| Need assistance with at least one activity of daily living............ | 9,621 | 4.0 | 5,851 | 3.0 | 3,770 | 8.3 |
| Difficulty getting around............ | 4,621 | 1.9 | 2,718 | 1.4 | 1,903 | 4.2 |
| Difficulty getting into bed............ | 11,467 | 4.8 | 7,341 | 3.8 | 4,126 | 9.1 |
| Difficulty bathing............ | 10,334 | 4.3 | 6,060 | 3.1 | 4,274 | 9.4 |
| Difficulty dressing............ | 7,668 | 3.2 | 4,773 | 2.5 | 2,894 | 6.4 |
| Difficulty eating............ | 2,546 | 1.1 | 1,755 | 0.9 | 791 | 1.7 |
| Difficulty toileting............ | 4,240 | 1.8 | 2,631 | 1.4 | 1,609 | 3.6 |
| Difficulties with IADLs [3]............ | 27,499 | 11.5 | 17,173 | 8.8 | 10,326 | 22.8 |
| Need assistance with at least one IADL [3]............ | 23,084 | 9.6 | 14,605 | 7.5 | 8,479 | 18.7 |
| Mental disability............ | 30,057 | 12.5 | 23,217 | 11.9 | 6,840 | 15.1 |
| Learning disability............ | 8,462 | 3.5 | 7,221 | 3.7 | 1,242 | 2.7 |
| Alzheimer's, senility, or dementia............ | 7,903 | 3.3 | 4,790 | 2.5 | 3,113 | 6.9 |
| Intellectual disability............ | 2,807 | 1.2 | 2,450 | 1.3 | 357 | 0.8 |
| Developmental disability............ | 1,458 | 0.6 | 1,350 | 0.7 | 108 | 0.2 |
| Other mental/emotional condition............ | 10,318 | 4.3 | 8,496 | 4.4 | 1,822 | 4.0 |
| With one or more mental health symptoms or difficulties [5]............ | 16,121 | 6.7 | 12,762 | 6.6 | 3,360 | 7.4 |

[1] Severe disability is indicated by the person's use of a wheelchair, cane, crutches, or walker; being blind or deaf; need for assistance with any of the activities of daily living; and presence of a mental disability (cognitive, developmental, or emotional) that interferes with everyday activities. See source for more information. [2] Activities of daily living (ADL) include getting around inside the home, getting in or out of bed or a chair, bathing, dressing, eating, and toileting. [3] Instrumental activities of daily living (IADL) include going out, managing money, preparing meals, housework, taking medication, and using the telephone. [4] Physical tasks or movement include lifting ten pounds, grasping, pushing/pulling, standing, sitting, crouching, and reaching. [5] Includes being depressed or anxious, trouble getting along with other people, trouble concentrating, and trouble coping with stress.

Source: U.S. Census Bureau, *Americans with Disabilities: 2014*, Current Population Reports P70-152, November 2018. See also <https://www.census.gov/topics/health/disability.html>.

# Table 207. Population With a Disability by Age Group and State: 2010 and 2017

[In thousands (36,355 represents 36,355,000). Disability data limited to civilian noninstitutionalized population. Covers children under age 5 with a hearing or vision difficulty. Covers children age 5 to 14 with a hearing, vision, cognitive, ambulatory, or self-care difficulty. For people age 15 and older, also covers independent living difficulty. American Community Survey (ACS) disability data should not be compared with disability estimates from Census 2000, and more detailed measures of disability from sources such as the National Health Interview Survey and the Survey of Income and Program Participation. Based on a sample and subject to sampling variability; see Appendix III]

| State | 2010 | | | | 2017 | | | |
|---|---|---|---|---|---|---|---|---|
| | Total [1] | 5 to 17 years | 18 to 64 years | 65 years and over | Total [1] | 5 to 17 years | 18 to 64 years | 65 years and over |
| United States......... | 36,355 | 2,799 | 19,048 | 14,352 | 40,679 | 2,948 | 20,444 | 17,141 |
| Alabama............... | 760 | 54 | 423 | 281 | 789 | 47 | 418 | 322 |
| Alaska................. | 75 | 6 | 48 | 20 | 90 | 5 | 53 | 32 |
| Arizona................ | 706 | 52 | 364 | 287 | 900 | 61 | 428 | 407 |
| Arkansas.............. | 468 | 37 | 255 | 173 | 531 | 42 | 285 | 202 |
| California.............. | 3,640 | 263 | 1,818 | 1,539 | 4,151 | 279 | 1,981 | 1,875 |
| Colorado.............. | 499 | 38 | 273 | 185 | 604 | 44 | 311 | 245 |
| Connecticut........... | 368 | 28 | 179 | 159 | 392 | 29 | 189 | 172 |
| Delaware.............. | 108 | 8 | 60 | 39 | 108 | 6 | 53 | 49 |
| District of Columbia..... | 66 | 6 | 37 | 23 | 91 | 5 | 54 | 32 |
| Florida................. | 2,367 | 148 | 1,115 | 1,096 | 2,811 | 181 | 1,258 | 1,365 |
| Georgia............... | 1,113 | 96 | 615 | 397 | 1,251 | 94 | 661 | 491 |
| Hawaii................. | 141 | 11 | 66 | 63 | 149 | 7 | 59 | 81 |
| Idaho.................. | 196 | 17 | 103 | 74 | 240 | 21 | 126 | 92 |
| Illinois................. | 1,291 | 101 | 640 | 544 | 1,404 | 88 | 691 | 620 |
| Indiana................ | 800 | 66 | 435 | 295 | 915 | 80 | 478 | 355 |
| Iowa................... | 337 | 25 | 172 | 138 | 349 | 26 | 170 | 151 |
| Kansas................ | 341 | 26 | 178 | 136 | 374 | 26 | 192 | 154 |
| Kentucky.............. | 711 | 51 | 423 | 233 | 765 | 54 | 430 | 278 |
| Louisiana............. | 672 | 58 | 378 | 232 | 680 | 55 | 362 | 261 |
| Maine.................. | 198 | 15 | 104 | 78 | 219 | 16 | 112 | 90 |
| Maryland.............. | 581 | 48 | 298 | 231 | 660 | 50 | 335 | 274 |
| Massachusetts......... | 699 | 57 | 354 | 285 | 804 | 54 | 397 | 349 |
| Michigan.............. | 1,325 | 109 | 715 | 496 | 1,390 | 99 | 727 | 559 |
| Minnesota............ | 523 | 45 | 266 | 209 | 616 | 50 | 305 | 259 |
| Mississippi............ | 473 | 36 | 267 | 168 | 492 | 33 | 265 | 192 |
| Missouri............... | 814 | 60 | 440 | 311 | 894 | 66 | 464 | 362 |
| Montana............... | 125 | 8 | 64 | 52 | 142 | 9 | 70 | 63 |
| Nebraska.............. | 206 | 16 | 104 | 85 | 228 | 17 | 112 | 97 |
| Nevada................ | 283 | 19 | 152 | 110 | 363 | 22 | 184 | 156 |
| New Hampshire........ | 146 | 14 | 77 | 54 | 172 | 13 | 84 | 74 |
| New Jersey............ | 845 | 69 | 398 | 375 | 914 | 67 | 429 | 415 |
| New Mexico........... | 269 | 16 | 140 | 112 | 322 | 19 | 169 | 132 |
| New York............. | 2,020 | 142 | 1,012 | 858 | 2,266 | 165 | 1,100 | 993 |
| North Carolina........ | 1,235 | 95 | 673 | 460 | 1,343 | 92 | 690 | 559 |
| North Dakota.......... | 69 | 4 | 32 | 32 | 76 | 6 | 37 | 32 |
| Ohio................... | 1,506 | 128 | 804 | 569 | 1,613 | 128 | 840 | 640 |
| Oklahoma............. | 577 | 39 | 323 | 212 | 635 | 48 | 340 | 245 |
| Oregon................ | 525 | 37 | 287 | 198 | 573 | 37 | 288 | 245 |
| Pennsylvania.......... | 1,638 | 132 | 824 | 677 | 1,775 | 136 | 881 | 751 |
| Rhode Island.......... | 140 | 12 | 75 | 53 | 141 | 10 | 76 | 54 |
| South Carolina........ | 629 | 37 | 352 | 237 | 728 | 51 | 377 | 297 |
| South Dakota......... | 90 | 6 | 43 | 40 | 99 | 6 | 50 | 43 |
| Tennessee............. | 947 | 66 | 530 | 348 | 1,019 | 74 | 538 | 404 |
| Texas................. | 2,864 | 273 | 1,549 | 1,029 | 3,173 | 276 | 1,623 | 1,258 |
| Utah................... | 234 | 22 | 124 | 85 | 297 | 35 | 151 | 109 |
| Vermont............... | 82 | 7 | 45 | 30 | 89 | 5 | 47 | 36 |
| Virginia................ | 845 | 59 | 447 | 336 | 979 | 69 | 501 | 406 |
| Washington............ | 792 | 56 | 425 | 307 | 942 | 64 | 481 | 393 |
| West Virginia.......... | 345 | 21 | 197 | 126 | 361 | 21 | 189 | 151 |
| Wisconsin............. | 606 | 51 | 306 | 246 | 678 | 50 | 339 | 286 |
| Wyoming.............. | 66 | 5 | 36 | 25 | 82 | 6 | 42 | 34 |

[1] Total population with a disability includes population under age 5, not shown separately.

Source: U.S. Census Bureau, 2010 and 2017 American Community Survey, S1810, "Disability Characteristics," <http://factfinder.census.gov>, accessed December 2018.

# Table 208. Use of Complementary and Alternative Health Practices Among Adults Age 18 and Over, in the Past 12 Months by Type of Therapy: 2007 and 2012

[3,141 represents 3,141,000. Percentages are age-adjusted. Based on the National Health Interview Survey of civilian noninstitutional population. The denominators for percent calculations exclude persons with unknown complementary health approach use. Estimates are age-adjusted using the projected 2000 U.S. population as the standard population, using age groups 18-24, 25-44, 45-64 and 65/over]

| Therapy | 2007 | | 2012 | |
|---|---|---|---|---|
| | Number (1,000) | Percent | Number (1,000) | Percent |
| Acupuncture | 3,141 | 1.4 | 3,484 | 1.5 |
| Ayurveda | 214 | 0.1 | 241 | 0.1 |
| Biofeedback | 362 | 0.2 | 281 | 0.1 |
| Chiropractic or osteopathic manipulation | 18,740 | 8.6 | 19,369 | 8.4 |
| Deep-breathing exercises [1] | 27,794 | 12.7 | 24,218 | 10.9 |
| Energy healing therapy | 1,216 | 0.5 | 1,077 | 0.5 |
| Guided imagery | 4,866 | 2.2 | 3,846 | 1.7 |
| Homeopathic treatment [2] | 3,909 | 1.8 | 5,046 | 2.2 |
| Hypnosis | 561 | 0.2 | 347 | 0.1 |
| Massage therapy | 18,068 | 8.3 | 15,411 | 6.9 |
| Meditation [3] | 20,541 | 9.4 | 17,948 | 8.0 |
| Naturopathy | 729 | 0.3 | 957 | 0.4 |
| Nonvitamin, nonmineral dietary supplements [4] | 38,797 | 17.7 | 40,579 | 17.7 |
| Progressive relaxation | 6,454 | 2.9 | 4,766 | 2.1 |
| Special diets [5] | 6,040 | 2.8 | 6,853 | 3.0 |
| Yoga, tai chi, and qi gong | 14,436 | 6.7 | 22,281 | 10.1 |

[1] In 2012, deep-breathing exercises included deep-breathing exercises as part of hypnosis, biofeedback, Mantra meditation, mindfulness meditation, spiritual meditation, guided imagery, progressive relaxation, yoga, tai chi, or qi gong. In 2007, the use of deep-breathing exercises was asked broadly and not if used as part of other complementary health approaches. [2] No distinction was made between persons who sought treatment from a homeopathic practitioner and those who self-medicated. [3] In 2012, meditation included Mantra, mindfulness, and spiritual meditation; and meditation used as part of other practices. In 2007, the use of meditation was asked broadly and not if practiced as part of other complementary health approaches. [4] While questions were asked about nonvitamin, nonmineral dietary supplements in 2007 and 2012, the data should be interpreted with caution due to question order and the specific nonvitamin, nonmineral dietary supplements covered. [5] Respondents used one or more named special diets for 2 weeks or more in the past 12 months. Special diets included vegetarian (including vegan), macrobiotic, Atkins, Pritikin, and Ornish diets.

Source: U.S. National Center for Health Statistics, *Trends in the Use of Complementary Health Approaches Among Adults: United States, 2002–2012,* National Health Statistics Reports, Number 79, February 10, 2015. See also <https://nccih.nih.gov/research/statistics/NHIS> or <http://www.cdc.gov/nchs/products/nhsr.htm>.

# Table 209. Respiratory Diseases Among Persons Age 18 and Over by Selected Characteristics: 2017

[In thousands (246,657 represents 246,657,000). Respondents were asked in two separate questions if they had ever been told by a doctor or other health professional that they had emphysema or asthma. Respondents who had been told they had asthma were asked if they still had asthma. Respondents were asked in separate questions if they had been told by a doctor or other health professional in the past 12 months that they had hay fever, sinusitis, or chronic bronchitis. Based on the National Health Interview Survey, a sample survey of the civilian noninstitutionalized population; see Appendix III]

| Selected characteristic | Total persons | Selected respiratory conditions [1] | | | | | |
|---|---|---|---|---|---|---|---|
| | | Emphysema | Asthma | | Hay fever | Sinusitis | Chronic bronchitis |
| | | | Ever | Still | | | |
| **Total [2]** | **246,657** | **3,418** | **33,090** | **19,009** | **19,883** | **30,837** | **8,568** |
| SEX | | | | | | | |
| Male | 118,990 | 1,703 | 14,036 | 6,466 | 8,428 | 10,817 | 2,556 |
| Female | 127,667 | 1,714 | 19,054 | 12,544 | 11,455 | 20,020 | 6,011 |
| AGE | | | | | | | |
| 18 to 44 years | 113,636 | 130 | 16,771 | 8,518 | 6,048 | 9,875 | 2,272 |
| 45 to 64 years | 83,494 | 1,442 | 10,817 | 7,044 | 9,204 | 13,176 | 3,782 |
| 65 to 74 years | 29,454 | 922 | 3,493 | 2,211 | 3,016 | 4,810 | 1,504 |
| 75 years and over | 20,073 | 923 | 2,009 | 1,236 | 1,614 | 2,977 | 1,009 |
| RACE | | | | | | | |
| Single race [3] | 241,760 | 3,308 | 32,204 | 18,592 | 19,351 | 30,217 | 8,406 |
| White | 192,033 | 2,957 | 26,171 | 14,865 | 16,589 | 25,510 | 6,818 |
| Black or African American | 30,560 | 230 | 4,353 | 2,749 | 1,490 | 3,295 | 1,149 |
| American Indian or Alaska Native | 2,944 | 16 | 300 | 225 | 139 | 271 | 85 |
| Asian | 15,675 | 90 | 1,318 | 706 | 1,112 | 1,133 | 323 |
| Native Hawaiian or other Pacific Islander | 548 | (B) | (B) | (B) | (B) | (B) | (B) |
| Two or more races [4] | 4,897 | 110 | 886 | 417 | 532 | 620 | 162 |
| HISPANIC ORIGIN AND RACE [5] | | | | | | | |
| Hispanic or Latino | 39,416 | 242 | 4,663 | 2,276 | 1,995 | 3,035 | 829 |
| Mexican or Mexican American | 23,657 | 86 | 2,578 | 1,069 | 1,316 | 1,790 | 564 |
| Not Hispanic or Latino | 207,242 | 3,175 | 28,427 | 16,733 | 17,888 | 27,802 | 7,739 |
| White | 157,443 | 2,714 | 21,851 | 12,800 | 14,848 | 22,807 | 6,119 |
| Black or African American | 29,127 | 230 | 4,239 | 2,679 | 1,426 | 3,252 | 1,130 |

B Figure considered unreliable. [1] A person may be represented in more than one column. [2] Total includes other races not shown separately. [3] Refers to persons who indicated only a single race group, including those of Hispanic and Latino origin. [4] Refers to all persons who indicated more than one race group. [5] Persons of Hispanic or Latino origin may be of any race or combination of races.

Source: U.S. National Center for Health Statistics, 2017 National Health Interview Survey, "Tables of Summary Statistics," <https://www.cdc.gov/nchs/nhis/SHS.htm>, accessed January 2019.

## Table 210. Selected Diseases and Conditions Among Persons Age 18 and Over by Selected Characteristics: 2017

[In thousands (246,657 represents 246,657,000). Persons with selected diseases and conditions may be represented in more than one column. Based on the National Health Interview Survey, a sample survey of the civilian noninstitutionalized population; see Appendix III]

| Selected characteristic | Total persons | Persons with selected diseases and conditions | | | | | |
|---|---|---|---|---|---|---|---|
| | | Diabe-tes [1] | Ulcers [1] | Kidney dis-ease [2] | Liver dis-ease [2] | Arthritis diag-nosis [3] | Chronic joint symp-toms [3] |
| **Total [4]** | **246,657** | **23,048** | **15,257** | **5,117** | **4,497** | **58,515** | **74,248** |
| SEX | | | | | | | |
| Male | 118,990 | 12,242 | 6,457 | 2,474 | 2,261 | 23,499 | 32,220 |
| Female | 127,667 | 10,807 | 8,800 | 2,642 | 2,236 | 35,015 | 42,028 |
| AGE | | | | | | | |
| 18 to 44 years | 113,636 | 3,014 | 4,296 | 654 | 1,247 | 7,924 | 19,122 |
| 45 to 64 years | 83,494 | 10,598 | 6,041 | 1,697 | 2,258 | 25,244 | 31,681 |
| 65 to 74 years | 29,454 | 5,619 | 2,749 | 1,395 | 704 | 14,236 | 13,602 |
| 75 years and over | 20,073 | 3,817 | 2,171 | 1,371 | 288 | 11,111 | 9,842 |
| RACE | | | | | | | |
| Single race [5] | 241,760 | 22,615 | 14,885 | 5,050 | 4,363 | 57,451 | 72,609 |
| White | 192,033 | 17,455 | 12,421 | 4,125 | 3,553 | 48,222 | 60,910 |
| Black or African American | 30,560 | 3,341 | 1,680 | 682 | 406 | 6,634 | 7,999 |
| American Indian or Alaska Native | 2,944 | 424 | 97 | 73 | 122 | 622 | 596 |
| Asian | 15,675 | 1,329 | 663 | 144 | 273 | 1,917 | 2,911 |
| Native Hawaiian or other Pacific Islander | 548 | (B) | (B) | (B) | (B) | (B) | (B) |
| Two or more races [6] | 4,897 | 434 | 373 | 66 | 134 | 1,064 | 1,639 |
| HISPANIC ORIGIN [7] | | | | | | | |
| Hispanic or Latino | 39,416 | 4,087 | 1,586 | 846 | 912 | 5,314 | 7,725 |
| Not Hispanic or Latino | 207,242 | 18,961 | 13,671 | 4,270 | 3,585 | 53,201 | 66,523 |

B Estimate is considered unreliable. [1] Respondents who had ever been told by a health professional that they had an ulcer or diabetes (excludes borderline and pregnancy-related diabetes). [2] Respondents who had been told in the last 12 months by a health professional that they had weak or failing kidneys or any kind of liver condition. Excludes kidney stones, bladder infections, or incontinence. [3] Respondents with an arthritis diagnosis had ever been told by a health professional that they had some form of arthritis, rheumatoid arthritis, gout, lupus or fibromyalgia. Respondents with joint symptoms (excluding back and neck) that began more than 3 months prior to interview were classified as having chronic joint symptoms. [4] Total includes other races not shown separately. [5] Refers to persons who indicated only a single race group, including Hispanic or Latino origin. [6] Refers to all persons who indicated more than one race group. [7] Persons of Hispanic or Latino origin may be of any race or combination of races.

Source: U.S. National Center for Health Statistics, 2017 National Health Interview Survey, "Tables of Summary Health Statistics," <https://www.cdc.gov/nchs/nhis/SHS.htm>, accessed January 2019.

## Table 211. Circulatory Diseases Among Persons Age 18 and Over by Selected Characteristics: 2017

[In thousands (246,657 represents 246,657,000). In separate questions, respondents were asked if they had ever been told by a doctor or other health professional that they have: hypertension (or high blood pressure), coronary heart disease, angina (or angina pectoris), heart attack (or myocardial infarction), any other heart condition or disease not already mentioned, or a stroke. A person may be represented in more than one column. Based on the National Health Interview Survey, a sample survey of the civilian noninstitutionalized population; see Appendix III]

| Characteristic | Total adults | Selected circulatory diseases | | | |
|---|---|---|---|---|---|
| | | Heart disease | | Hyper-tension [3] | Stroke |
| | | All types [1] | Coronary [2] | | |
| **Total [4]** | **246,657** | **28,214** | **15,184** | **66,257** | **7,758** |
| SEX | | | | | |
| Male | 118,990 | 14,855 | 9,125 | 33,057 | 4,161 |
| Female | 127,667 | 13,360 | 6,059 | 33,200 | 3,596 |
| AGE | | | | | |
| 18 to 44 years | 113,636 | 4,536 | 981 | 9,522 | 732 |
| 45 to 64 years | 83,494 | 9,908 | 5,347 | 29,003 | 2,739 |
| 65 to 74 years | 29,454 | 6,782 | 4,118 | 15,767 | 1,890 |
| 75 years and over | 20,073 | 6,988 | 4,738 | 11,965 | 2,398 |
| RACE | | | | | |
| Single race [5] | 241,760 | 27,664 | 14,918 | 65,045 | 7,616 |
| White | 192,033 | 23,662 | 12,448 | 51,062 | 6,003 |
| Black or African American | 30,560 | 2,886 | 1,763 | 9,731 | 1,274 |
| American Indian or Alaska Native | 2,944 | 197 | 69 | 829 | 83 |
| Asian | 15,675 | 904 | 637 | 3,309 | 245 |
| Native Hawaiian or Other Pacific Islander | 548 | (B) | (B) | 115 | (B) |
| Two or more races [6] | 4,897 | 551 | 266 | 1,212 | 142 |
| HISPANIC ORIGIN [7] | | | | | |
| Hispanic or Latino | 39,416 | 2,349 | 1,426 | 6,940 | 884 |
| Not Hispanic or Latino | 207,242 | 25,866 | 13,759 | 59,317 | 6,873 |

B Estimate is considered unreliable. [1] Heart disease includes coronary heart disease, angina pectoris, heart attack, or any other heart condition or disease. [2] Coronary heart disease includes coronary heart disease, angina pectoris, or heart attack. [3] Persons told on two or more different visits that they have hypertension, or high blood pressure, are classified as hypertensive. [4] Includes other races not shown separately. [5] Refers to persons who indicated only a single race group, including Hispanic or Latino origin. [6] Refers to all persons who indicated more than one race group. [7] Persons of Hispanic or Latino origin may be of any race or combination of races.

Source: U.S. National Center for Health Statistics, 2017 National Health Interview Survey, "Tables of Summary Health Statistics," <https://www.cdc.gov/nchs/nhis/SHS.htm>, accessed January 2019.

## Table 212. Migraine Headaches and Pain in the Neck, Lower Back, Face or Jaw Among Persons Age 18 and Over by Selected Characteristics: 2017

[In thousands (246,657 represents 246,657,000). Based on the National Health Interview Survey, a sample survey of the civilian noninstitutionalized population. See Appendix III]

| Selected characteristic | Total persons | Migraine and pain [1] | | | |
|---|---|---|---|---|---|
| | | Migraine or severe headache [2] | Pain in neck [2] | Pain in lower back [2] | Pain in face or jaw [2] |
| **Total [3]**............................... | **246,657** | **37,039** | **37,729** | **70,576** | **10,732** |
| SEX | | | | | |
| Male.......................... | 118,990 | 11,892 | 14,973 | 31,241 | 3,288 |
| Female........................ | 127,667 | 25,148 | 22,755 | 39,335 | 7,445 |
| AGE | | | | | |
| 18 to 44 years.................... | 113,636 | 21,178 | 13,902 | 27,036 | 5,028 |
| 45 to 64 years.................... | 83,494 | 12,613 | 16,040 | 27,206 | 4,068 |
| 65 to 74 years.................... | 29,454 | 2,149 | 4,665 | 9,615 | 910 |
| 75 years and over................. | 20,073 | 1,100 | 3,121 | 6,719 | 726 |
| RACE | | | | | |
| Single race [4]..................... | 241,760 | 36,097 | 36,874 | 68,914 | 10,476 |
| White.......................... | 192,033 | 29,332 | 30,815 | 56,762 | 8,842 |
| Black or African American......... | 30,560 | 4,600 | 3,658 | 8,031 | 991 |
| American Indian or Alaska Native... | 2,944 | 439 | 450 | 935 | 121 |
| Asian......................... | 15,675 | 1,604 | 1,887 | 3,018 | 450 |
| Native Hawaiian or Other Pacific Islander........... | 548 | (B) | (B) | (B) | (B) |
| Two or more races [5].............. | 4,897 | 942 | 855 | 1,661 | 257 |
| HISPANIC ORIGIN AND RACE [6] | | | | | |
| Hispanic or Latino................ | 39,416 | 5,741 | 4,996 | 9,733 | 1,509 |
| Mexican or Mexican American...... | 23,657 | 3,131 | 2,743 | 5,381 | 1,001 |
| Not Hispanic or Latino............. | 207,242 | 31,298 | 32,733 | 60,843 | 9,224 |
| White, single race............... | 157,443 | 24,304 | 26,465 | 48,438 | 7,486 |
| Black or African American, single race........... | 29,127 | 4,272 | 3,487 | 7,620 | 938 |

B Figure is considered unreliable. [1] A person may be represented in more than one column. [2] Respondents were asked, in separate questions, "During the past 3 months, did you have a severe headache or migraine [or neck pain; or low back pain; or facial ache or pain in the jaw muscles or the joint in front of the ear]?" Respondents were instructed to report pain that had lasted a whole day or more and, conversely, not to report fleeting or minor aches or pains. [3] Total includes other races not shown separately. [4] Refers to persons who indicated only a single race group. [5] Refers to all persons who indicated more than one race group. [6] Persons of Hispanic or Latino origin may be of any race or combination of races.

Source: U.S. National Center for Health Statistics, 2017 National Health Interview Survey, "Tables of Summary Health Statistics," <https://www.cdc.gov/nchs/nhis/SHS.htm>, accessed January 2019.

## Table 213. Nonfatal Injury and Poisoning Episodes by Cause, Sex, and Age: 2017

[Data are from the National Electronic Injury Surveillance System–All Injury Program, which collects data on nonfatal injuries and poisonings treated in participating hospital emergency departments]

| Cause of injury | Total | | Male | Female | Under age 1 | Age 1 to 14 | Age 15 to 24 | Age 25 to 64 | Age 65 and over |
|---|---|---|---|---|---|---|---|---|---|
| | Number | Percent | | | | | | | |
| **Total [1]**.................... | **30,320,552** | **100.0** | **16,364,388** | **13,955,255** | **217,137** | **4,817,068** | **4,771,839** | **15,754,190** | **4,752,299** |
| UNINTENTIONAL | | | | | | | | | |
| Fall............................ | 8,591,683 | 28.3 | 3,883,980 | 4,707,559 | 120,007 | 1,680,680 | 671,408 | 3,148,095 | 2,970,720 |
| Struck by or against [2].......... | 3,685,012 | 12.2 | 2,188,954 | 1,495,940 | 23,356 | 1,029,585 | 755,114 | 1,563,777 | 312,954 |
| Overexertion................... | 2,569,850 | 8.5 | 1,287,366 | 1,282,484 | 3,433 | 346,573 | 493,072 | 1,498,955 | 227,817 |
| Motor vehicle occupant......... | 2,500,353 | 8.2 | 1,127,221 | 1,373,086 | 2,115 | 145,751 | 595,092 | 1,541,136 | 215,666 |
| Cut/pierce/stab................. | 1,823,358 | 6.0 | 1,168,384 | 654,950 | 3,844 | 248,158 | 345,982 | 1,062,533 | 162,819 |
| Poisoning..................... | 1,755,044 | 5.8 | 1,142,744 | 612,133 | 3,459 | 59,490 | 246,611 | 1,305,819 | 137,849 |
| Bite or sting exlc. dog bites [3]... | 1,142,130 | 3.8 | 543,059 | 599,041 | 13,505 | 304,532 | 147,861 | 560,018 | 116,191 |
| Foreign object [4]............... | 557,650 | 1.8 | 327,837 | 229,708 | 8,618 | 193,612 | 57,236 | 238,230 | 59,954 |
| Fire/burn/smoke inhalation..... | 388,402 | 1.3 | 199,228 | 189,174 | 7,567 | 75,287 | 64,066 | 213,429 | 28,054 |
| Dog bite....................... | 349,962 | 1.2 | 177,993 | 171,969 | 3,125 | 93,401 | 53,229 | 167,339 | 32,746 |
| VIOLENCE RELATED [5] | | | | | | | | | |
| Assault (all)................... | 1,718,208 | 5.7 | 1,019,515 | 698,692 | 3,950 | 117,097 | 449,803 | 1,105,860 | 39,246 |

[1] Total includes injuries from various other causes not shown separately and for injuries with unknown age of victim. [2] Injury from being struck, hit, or crushed by, or hitting against, another person, object or force; excludes vehicles and machinery. [3] Include bites and stings from another person or any insect, animal, or plant; excludes dogs. [4] Injury resulting from the entrance of a foreign object into or through the eye or other natural body opening; excludes objects blocking an airway or causing suffocation. [5] Violence also includes legal intervention and self harm, not shown separately.

Source: U.S. Centers for Disease Control and Prevention, National Center for Injury Prevention and Control, "WISQARS (Web-based Injury Statistics Query and Reporting System)," <https://www.cdc.gov/injury/wisqars/index.html>, accessed April 2019.

# Table 214. Injuries Associated With Selected Consumer Products: 2017

[Estimates are based on a national probability sample of hospitals in the U.S. and its territories. Patient information is collected from each participating hospital for every emergency visit involving an injury associated with consumer products. From this sample, the total number of product-related injuries treated in hospital emergency rooms nationwide is estimated. A person's injury may be represented in up to two product groups]

| Product type | Number | Product type | Number |
|---|---|---|---|
| **Items for infants/children:** | | **Housewares:** | |
| All nursery equipment........................... | 98,396 | Cans, other containers........................ | 304,718 |
| Baby strollers.................................... | 15,396 | Drinking glasses............................... | 58,946 |
| High chairs....................................... | 12,101 | Knives (not elsewhere classified)........... | 329,184 |
| Playground equipment (excluding swings)............. | 242,359 | Soaps, detergents............................ | 61,416 |
| Swings or swings sets.......................... | 48,552 | Tableware and accessories................... | 95,276 |
| Toys.............................................. | 251,366 | **Tools & garden equipment:** | |
| **Sports & recreational equipment:** | | Chain saws..................................... | 30,872 |
| All terrain vehicles, mopeds, minibikes, etc............. | 214,761 | Hand garden tools............................. | 55,903 |
| Baseball, softball............................... | 187,447 | Lawn mowers................................... | 89,608 |
| Basketball....................................... | 500,085 | Power home tools (excluding saws).......... | 32,819 |
| Bicycles & accessories......................... | 457,266 | Power home workshop saws................... | 80,955 |
| Exercise, exercise equipment.................. | 526,350 | Workshop manual tools........................ | 138,854 |
| Football.......................................... | 341,150 | **Household appliances:** | |
| Lacrosse, rugby, misc. ball games............. | 73,829 | Cooking ranges, ovens, etc................... | 57,082 |
| Skateboards..................................... | 98,486 | Heating stoves, space heaters................ | 25,086 |
| Skating (excluding in-line)...................... | 67,132 | Refrigerators, freezers........................ | 55,537 |
| Soccer........................................... | 218,926 | Small kitchen appliances...................... | 59,921 |
| Swimming, pools, equipment................... | 199,246 | **Home furnishings & fixtures:** | |
| Trampolines...................................... | 145,207 | Bathroom structures & fixtures................ | 552,500 |
| **Home entertainment equipment:** | | Beds, mattresses, pillows..................... | 898,485 |
| Computers (equipment and electronic games)......... | 28,828 | Carpets, rugs.................................. | 202,806 |
| Television sets & stands........................ | 51,260 | Chairs, sofas, sofa beds...................... | 669,992 |
| **Personal use items:** | | Desks, cabinets, shelves, racks.............. | 304,169 |
| Grooming devices............................... | 49,974 | Glass doors, windows, panels................. | 139,313 |
| Mobility carts, electric [1]..................... | 20,199 | Ladders, stools................................ | 268,695 |
| Razors, shavers, razor blades................. | 51,652 | Tables [2]...................................... | 355,821 |

[1] Motorized vehicles, not elsewhere classified (three or more wheels). [2] Excludes baby-changing tables, billiard or pool tables, and television tables or stands.

Source: Consumer Product Safety Commission, National Electronic Injury Surveillance System (NEISS), *2017 NEISS Data Highlights: Overview—All Products;* and "NEISS Estimates Query Builder," <https://www.cpsc.gov/cgibin/NEISSQuery/home.aspx>, accessed March 2019. See also <https://www.cpsc.gov/Research--Statistics/NEISS-Injury-Data/>.

# Table 215. Food Security Status of Households and Households with Children: 2005 to 2017

[114,437 represents 114,437,000. Food security status of households is measured through a series of questions about experiences and behaviors known to characterize households that are having difficulty meeting basic food needs. All questions refer to the previous 12 months and include a qualifying phrase reminding respondents to report only conditions resulting from inadequate financial resources; survey excludes voluntary fasting and dieting to lose weight. *Food-secure* households report 0-2 food-insecure conditions. *Food-insecure* households report 3 or more conditions. Low and very low food security differ in the extent and character of the adjustments the household makes to its eating patterns and food intake. Households classified as having *low food security* report multiple indications of food access problems, but typically report few, if any, indications of reduced food intake. Households classified as having *very low food security* report multiple indications of reduced food intake and disrupted eating patterns due to inadequate resources for food. Prior to 2006, households with very low food security were described as "food insecure with hunger." The omission of homeless persons biases the statistics downward. Data are from the Food Security Supplement to the Current Population Survey (CPS); for details about the CPS, see text, Section 1 and Appendix III]

| Household status | Number (1,000) | | | | | Percent distribution | | | | |
|---|---|---|---|---|---|---|---|---|---|---|
| | 2005 | 2010 | 2015 | 2016 | 2017 | 2005 | 2010 | 2015 | 2016 | 2017 |
| **Households, total [1]**.................... | **114,437** | **118,756** | **125,164** | **126,401** | **127,272** | **100.0** | **100.0** | **100.0** | **100.0** | **100.0** |
| Food-secure............................... | 101,851 | 101,527 | 109,315 | 110,850 | 112,254 | 89.0 | 85.5 | 87.3 | 87.7 | 88.2 |
| Food-insecure............................. | 12,586 | 17,229 | 15,849 | 15,551 | 15,018 | 11.0 | 14.5 | 12.7 | 12.3 | 11.8 |
| With low food security................... | 8,158 | 10,872 | 9,540 | 9,413 | 9,261 | 7.1 | 9.1 | 7.7 | 7.4 | 7.3 |
| With very low food security............. | 4,428 | 6,357 | 6,309 | 6,138 | 5,757 | 3.9 | 5.4 | 5.0 | 4.9 | 4.5 |
| **Adult members [2]**..................... | **217,897** | **229,129** | **242,706** | **245,200** | **246,517** | **100.0** | **100.0** | **100.0** | **100.0** | **100.0** |
| In food-secure households.............. | 195,172 | 196,505 | 213,586 | 216,934 | 219,013 | 89.6 | 85.8 | 88.0 | 88.5 | 88.8 |
| In food-insecure households........... | 22,725 | 32,624 | 29,120 | 28,266 | 27,504 | 10.4 | 14.2 | 12.0 | 11.5 | 11.2 |
| With low food security.................. | 15,146 | 21,357 | 18,235 | 17,498 | 17,796 | 7.0 | 9.3 | 7.5 | 7.1 | 7.2 |
| With very low food security............. | 7,579 | 11,267 | 10,885 | 10,768 | 9,708 | 3.5 | 4.9 | 4.5 | 4.4 | 3.9 |
| **Child members [2, 3]**.................. | **73,604** | **74,905** | **73,455** | **73,829** | **73,901** | **100.0** | **100.0** | **100.0** | **100.0** | **100.0** |
| In food-secure households.............. | 61,201 | 58,697 | 60,337 | 60,891 | 61,361 | 83.1 | 78.4 | 82.1 | 82.5 | 83.0 |
| In food-insecure households........... | 12,403 | 16,208 | 13,118 | 12,938 | 12,540 | 16.9 | 21.6 | 17.9 | 17.5 | 17.0 |
| With very low food security among children...................... | 606 | 976 | 541 | 703 | 540 | 0.8 | 1.3 | 0.7 | 1.0 | 0.7 |

[1] Total excludes households for which food security status is unknown. [2] The food security survey measures food security status at the household level. Not all individuals and children residing in food-insecure households were directly affected by the households' food insecurity. Similarly, not all individuals and children in households classified as having very low food security were subject to the reductions in food intake and disruptions in eating patterns that characterize this condition. Young children, in particular, are often protected from effects of the households' food insecurity. [3] Percents among only households with children.

Source: U.S. Department of Agriculture, Economic Research Service, *Household Food Security in the United States in 2017*, Economic Research Report Number 256, September 2018. See also <https://www.ers.usda.gov/topics/food-nutrition-assistance/food-security-in-the-us.aspx>.

# Table 216. Mammography Use Among Women Age 40 and Over by Patient Characteristics: 2000 to 2015

[Percent of women having a mammogram within the past 2 years. Covers civilian noninstitutional population. Based on National Health Interview Survey; see Appendix III]

| Characteristic | 2000 | 2003 | 2005 | 2008 | 2010 | 2013 | 2015 |
|---|---|---|---|---|---|---|---|
| **Women age 40 and over, total** [1] | **70.4** | **69.7** | **66.8** | **67.6** | **67.1** | **66.8** | **65.3** |
| AGE | | | | | | | |
| 40 to 49 years | 64.3 | 64.4 | 63.5 | 61.5 | 62.3 | 59.6 | 58.3 |
| 50 to 64 years | 78.7 | 76.2 | 71.8 | 74.2 | 72.6 | 71.4 | 71.3 |
| 65 years and over | 67.9 | 67.7 | 63.8 | 65.5 | 64.4 | 66.9 | 63.3 |
| RACE AND ETHNICITY | | | | | | | |
| White, non-Hispanic | 72.2 | 70.5 | 68.3 | 68.7 | 67.8 | 67.6 | 65.8 |
| Black, non-Hispanic | 67.9 | 70.5 | 65.2 | 68.3 | 67.4 | 67.2 | 69.7 |
| Hispanic origin [2] | 61.2 | 65.0 | 58.8 | 61.2 | 64.2 | 61.4 | 60.9 |
| HEALTH INSURANCE STATUS [3] | | | | | | | |
| Insured | 76.0 | 75.1 | 72.5 | 73.4 | 74.1 | 72.1 | 69.7 |
| Private insurance | 77.1 | 76.3 | 74.5 | 74.2 | 75.6 | 73.4 | 72.2 |
| Medicaid | 61.7 | 63.5 | 55.6 | 64.2 | 64.4 | 63.5 | 57.7 |
| Uninsured | 40.7 | 41.5 | 38.1 | 39.7 | 36.0 | 37.3 | 30.0 |
| EDUCATION | | | | | | | |
| No high school diploma nor GED [4] | 57.7 | 58.1 | 52.8 | 53.8 | 53.0 | 53.6 | 51.7 |
| High school diploma or GED | 69.7 | 67.8 | 64.9 | 65.2 | 64.4 | 63.4 | 60.1 |
| Some college or more | 76.2 | 75.1 | 72.7 | 73.4 | 72.1 | 71.6 | 70.5 |
| POVERTY STATUS [5] | | | | | | | |
| Below 100% poverty | 54.8 | 55.4 | 48.5 | 51.4 | 51.4 | 49.9 | 52.2 |
| 100% to 199% poverty | 58.1 | 60.8 | 55.3 | 55.8 | 53.8 | 56.7 | 54.9 |
| 200% to 399% poverty | 68.8 | 69.9 | 67.2 | 64.4 | 66.2 | 66.0 | 63.4 |
| 400% and over poverty | 81.5 | 77.7 | 76.6 | 79.0 | 78.1 | 77.2 | 74.7 |

[1] Includes other races not shown separately and unknown education level and poverty status. [2] Persons of Hispanic origin may be of any race or combination of races. [3] Health insurance status at time of interview, only for women age 40 to 64. Health insurance categories are mutually exclusive. Persons who reported both Medicaid and private coverage are classified as having private coverage. Persons with only Indian Health Service coverage are considered to have no health insurance coverage. [4] GED is General Educational Development high school equivalency diploma. [5] Poverty as percent of Federal poverty level based on family income and family size and composition using U.S. Census Bureau poverty thresholds.

Source: U.S. National Center for Health Statistics, *Health, United States, 2017*, September 2018. See also <http://www.cdc.gov/nchs/hus.htm>.

# Table 217. Current Cigarette Smoking Among Adults: 2000 to 2016

[In percent. A current smoker is a person who has smoked at least 100 cigarettes and who now smokes every day or some days. Excludes unknown smoking status. Race groups White and Black include persons of Hispanic and non-Hispanic origin. For definition of age adjustment, see text, Section 2. Based on National Health Interview Survey; for details, see Appendix III]

| Sex, age, and race | 2000 | 2005 | 2010 | 2016 | Sex, age, and race | 2000 | 2005 | 2010 | 2016 |
|---|---|---|---|---|---|---|---|---|---|
| **Total smokers, age-adjusted** [1] | **23.1** | **20.8** | **19.3** | **15.7** | Black, total | 26.2 | 26.5 | 24.3 | 20.0 |
| Male | 25.2 | 23.4 | 21.2 | 17.7 | 18 to 24 years | 20.9 | 21.6 | 18.8 | 10.6 |
| Female | 21.1 | 18.3 | 17.5 | 13.7 | 25 to 34 years | 23.2 | 29.8 | 25.7 | 23.2 |
| | | | | | 35 to 44 years | 30.7 | 23.3 | 22.6 | 23.3 |
| White male | 25.4 | 23.3 | 21.4 | 17.5 | 45 to 64 years | 32.2 | 32.4 | 31.8 | 21.1 |
| Black male | 25.7 | 25.9 | 23.3 | 20.3 | 65 years and over | 14.2 | 16.8 | 10.0 | 19.1 |
| | | | | | **Female, total** | **20.9** | **18.1** | **17.3** | **13.5** |
| White female | 22.0 | 19.1 | 18.3 | 14.4 | 18 to 24 years | 24.9 | 20.7 | 17.4 | 11.5 |
| Black female | 20.7 | 17.1 | 16.6 | 13.2 | 25 to 34 years | 22.3 | 21.5 | 20.6 | 13.9 |
| | | | | | 35 to 44 years | 26.2 | 21.3 | 19.0 | 15.4 |
| | | | | | 45 to 64 years | 21.7 | 18.8 | 19.1 | 16.8 |
| **Total smokers** [2] | **23.2** | **20.9** | **19.3** | **15.5** | 65 years and over | 9.3 | 8.3 | 9.3 | 7.7 |
| **Male, total** | **25.6** | **23.9** | **21.5** | **17.5** | White, total | 21.4 | 18.7 | 17.9 | 14.0 |
| 18 to 24 years | 28.1 | 28.0 | 22.8 | 14.7 | 18 to 24 years | 28.5 | 22.6 | 18.4 | 12.5 |
| 25 to 34 years | 28.9 | 27.7 | 26.1 | 20.7 | 25 to 34 years | 24.9 | 23.1 | 22.0 | 14.2 |
| 35 to 44 years | 30.2 | 26.0 | 22.5 | 20.6 | 35 to 44 years | 26.6 | 22.2 | 20.5 | 16.7 |
| 45 to 64 years | 26.4 | 25.2 | 23.2 | 19.3 | 45 to 64 years | 21.4 | 18.9 | 19.5 | 17.4 |
| 65 years and over | 10.2 | 8.9 | 9.7 | 10.1 | 65 years and over | 9.1 | 8.4 | 9.4 | 7.6 |
| White, total | 25.7 | 23.6 | 21.4 | 17.2 | Black, total | 20.8 | 17.3 | 17.0 | 13.2 |
| 18 to 24 years | 30.4 | 29.7 | 23.8 | 15.5 | 18 to 24 years | 14.2 | 14.2 | 14.2 | 7.6 |
| 25 to 34 years | 29.7 | 27.7 | 26.6 | 20.9 | 25 to 34 years | 15.5 | 16.9 | 19.3 | 14.5 |
| 35 to 44 years | 30.6 | 26.3 | 23.1 | 20.6 | 35 to 44 years | 30.2 | 19.0 | 17.2 | 15.5 |
| 45 to 64 years | 25.8 | 24.5 | 22.5 | 18.8 | 45 to 64 years | 25.6 | 21.0 | 19.8 | 15.6 |
| 65 years and over | 9.8 | 7.9 | 9.6 | 9.1 | 65 years and over | 10.2 | 10.0 | 9.4 | 8.7 |

[1] Data are age-adjusted to the year 2000 standard population using five age groups: 18–24 years, 25–34 years, 35–44 years, 45–64 years, 65 years and over. [2] Crude, not age-adjusted.

Source: U.S. National Center for Health Statistics, *Health, United States, 2017*, September 2018. See also <http://www.cdc.gov/nchs/hus.htm>.

## Table 218. Current Cigarette Smoking by Sex and State: 2017

[In percent. Current cigarette smoking is defined as persons age 18 and older who reported having smoked 100 or more cigarettes during their lifetime and who currently smoke every day or some days. Based on the Behavioral Risk Factor Surveillance System (BRFSS), a telephone survey of health behaviors of the civilian, noninstitutionalized U.S. population, age 18 and over. New methods, including surveying cellular telephone-only households, and a new weighting method, were implemented for the 2011 BRFSS and prior data cannot accurately be compared to current survey results; for details, see source]

| State | Total | Male | Female | State | Total | Male | Female | State | Total | Male | Female |
|---|---|---|---|---|---|---|---|---|---|---|---|
| U.S.[1] | 17.1 | (NA) | (NA) | KY | 24.6 | 26.9 | 22.4 | OH | 21.1 | 22.4 | 19.9 |
| AL | 20.9 | 23.4 | 18.7 | LA | 23.1 | 25.4 | 21.0 | OK | 20.1 | 21.2 | 19.2 |
| AK | 21.0 | 24.2 | 17.1 | ME | 17.3 | 20.5 | 14.3 | OR | 16.1 | 18.1 | 14.2 |
| AZ | 15.6 | 18.3 | 12.9 | MD | 13.8 | 16.0 | 11.9 | PA | 18.7 | 20.8 | 16.9 |
| AR | 22.3 | 22.8 | 21.6 | MA | 13.7 | 14.8 | 12.6 | RI | 14.9 | 17.2 | 12.9 |
| CA | 11.3 | 14.9 | 7.8 | MI | 19.3 | 21.8 | 16.9 | SC | 18.8 | 21.8 | 16.0 |
| CO | 14.6 | 16.6 | 12.6 | MN | 14.5 | 16.3 | 12.8 | SD | 19.3 | 22.1 | 16.5 |
| CT | 12.7 | 14.1 | 11.5 | MS | 22.2 | 22.2 | 22.1 | TN | 22.6 | 24.3 | 21.1 |
| DE | 17.0 | 17.9 | 16.2 | MO | 20.8 | 21.6 | 20.0 | TX | 15.7 | 17.8 | 13.6 |
| DC | 14.3 | 17.8 | 11.3 | MT | 17.2 | 17.5 | 16.8 | UT | 8.9 | 11.0 | 6.8 |
| FL | 16.1 | 18.8 | 13.5 | NE | 15.4 | 16.4 | 14.5 | VT | 15.8 | 17.0 | 14.7 |
| GA | 17.5 | 20.9 | 14.3 | NV | 17.6 | 19.4 | 15.8 | VA | 16.4 | 18.4 | 14.4 |
| HI | 12.8 | 16.1 | 9.4 | NH | 15.7 | 16.8 | 14.5 | WA | 13.5 | 14.8 | 12.2 |
| ID | 14.3 | 15.7 | 13.1 | NJ | 13.7 | 16.1 | 11.5 | WV | 26.0 | 25.1 | 26.9 |
| IL | 15.5 | 17.3 | 13.8 | NM | 17.5 | 20.6 | 14.5 | WI | 16.0 | 17.1 | 15.0 |
| IN | 21.8 | 23.5 | 20.2 | NY | 14.1 | 17.5 | 10.9 | WY | 18.7 | 19.0 | 18.4 |
| IA | 17.1 | 18.5 | 15.8 | NC | 17.2 | 19.2 | 15.4 | GU[2] | 26.4 | 30.0 | 22.5 |
| KS | 17.4 | 18.3 | 16.4 | ND | 18.3 | 19.4 | 17.1 | PR[2] | 11.3 | 16.9 | 6.4 |

NA Not available. [1] Represents median value among the states and DC. For definition of median, see Guide to Tabular Presentation. [2] GU is Guam. PR is Puerto Rico.

Source: U.S. Centers for Disease Control and Prevention, Tobacco Use Data Portal: Tobacco Use, "Behavioral Risk Factor Data: Tobacco Use (2011 to present)," <https://chronicdata.cdc.gov/browse?category=Survey+Data>, accessed February 2019.

## Table 219. Substance Abuse Treatment Facilities and Clients: 2010 to 2017

[As of the end of March. Based on the National Survey of Substance Abuse Treatment Services, a census of all known public and private facilities that provide substance abuse treatment in the United States and associated jurisdictions. Selected missing data for responding facilities were imputed. Beginning 2013, the full survey on facilities and clients is administered in odd-numbered years; an alternate survey collecting facility data, and occasionally a limited amount of client data, is administered in even-numbered years]

| Facility characteristic | Number of facilities | | | Number of clients | | |
|---|---|---|---|---|---|---|
| | 2010 | 2015 | 2017 | 2010 | 2015 | 2017 |
| **Total** | **13,339** | **13,873** | **13,585** | **1,175,462** | **1,305,647** | **1,356,015** |
| FACILITY OPERATIONAL STRUCTURE | | | | | | |
| Private non-profit | 7,683 | 7,577 | 7,163 | 625,321 | 670,593 | 658,896 |
| Private for-profit | 3,985 | 4,659 | 4,931 | 372,525 | 475,531 | 550,992 |
| Local, county, or community government | 751 | 702 | 640 | 70,963 | 67,060 | 66,577 |
| State government | 380 | 350 | 304 | 47,203 | 30,675 | 28,529 |
| Federal government | 348 | 321 | 289 | 47,676 | 46,721 | 34,435 |
| Dept. of Veterans Affairs | 218 | 203 | 183 | 39,157 | 39,501 | 29,619 |
| Dept. of Defense | 91 | 80 | 74 | 7,035 | 5,774 | 3,618 |
| Indian Health Service | 36 | 31 | 27 | 1,431 | 1,218 | 1,103 |
| Other | 3 | 7 | 5 | 53 | 228 | 95 |
| Tribal government | 192 | 264 | 258 | 11,774 | 15,067 | 16,586 |
| TYPE OF CARE OFFERED/RECEIVED [1] | | | | | | |
| Outpatient | 10,753 | 11,336 | 11,184 | 1,056,532 | 1,161,456 | 1,238,654 |
| Regular | 9,914 | 10,582 | 10,437 | 593,077 | 604,819 | 599,290 |
| Intensive | 5,990 | 6,261 | 6,241 | 138,188 | 128,536 | 133,850 |
| Detoxification | 1,227 | 1,350 | 1,366 | 13,216 | 14,457 | 11,839 |
| Day treatment/partial hospitalization | 1,678 | 1,747 | 1,805 | 22,458 | 23,138 | 23,310 |
| Medication-assisted treatment [2] | 1,137 | 2,673 | 3,395 | 289,593 | 390,506 | 470,365 |
| Residential (non-hospital) | 3,452 | 3,383 | 3,125 | 103,692 | 119,900 | 99,881 |
| Detoxification | 893 | 887 | 908 | 7,549 | 13,748 | 10,938 |
| Short-term treatment (30 days or fewer) | 1,691 | 1,740 | 1,738 | 26,014 | 36,651 | 32,156 |
| Long-term treatment (more than 30 days) | 2,801 | 2,769 | 2,513 | 70,129 | 69,501 | 56,787 |
| Hospital inpatient | 748 | 724 | 715 | 15,238 | 24,291 | 17,480 |
| Detoxification | 666 | 639 | 655 | 6,476 | 12,394 | 7,551 |
| Treatment | 548 | 527 | 532 | 8,762 | 11,897 | 9,929 |
| TREATMENT FOR SUBSTANCE ABUSE PROBLEM | | | | | | |
| Both alcohol and drug | (NA) | 11,915 | 11,555 | 498,671 | 520,866 | 500,948 |
| Drug abuse only | (NA) | 10,692 | 10,571 | 459,069 | 531,963 | 642,713 |
| Alcohol abuse only | (NA) | 10,121 | 9,759 | 215,101 | 200,187 | 211,460 |
| Both substance abuse and mental health disorders | (NA) | 11,752 | 11,496 | 479,699 | 614,789 | 683,810 |

NA Not available. [1] Number of facilities can sum to more than the total because a facility could provide more than 1 type of care. [2] Methadone/buprenorphine maintenance or injectable naltrexone treatment.

Source: U.S. Substance Abuse and Mental Health Services Administration, *National Survey of Substance Abuse Treatment Services (N-SSATS): 2017, Data on Substance Abuse Treatment Facilities,* July 2018, and earlier reports. See also <https://www.samhsa.gov/data/data-we-collect/nssats-national-survey-substance-abuse-treatment-services>.

# Table 220. Drug Use by Type of Drug and Age Group: 2010 to 2017

[In percent. Data comes from the National Survey on Drug Use and Health (NSDUH). Based on a representative sample of the U.S. population age 12 and older, including persons living in households, in noninstitutional group quarters such as dormitories and homeless shelters, and civilians on military bases. Estimates are based on computer-assisted interviews of approximately 68,000 respondents. Please note that the NSDUH was redesigned in 2015, and therefore data from previous surveys for several survey items are not comparable to data from the 2015 NSDUH and subsequent surveys; see source for more information. Subject to sampling variability]

| Age and type of drug | Lifetime (ever) use | | | Past year use | | | Past month use | | |
|---|---|---|---|---|---|---|---|---|---|
| | 2010 | 2016 | 2017 | 2010 | 2016 | 2017 | 2010 | 2016 | 2017 |
| **12 YEARS OLD AND OVER** | | | | | | | | | |
| Any illicit drug [1] | (NA) | 48.5 | 49.5 | (NA) | 18.0 | 19.0 | (NA) | 10.6 | 11.2 |
| Marijuana | 42.0 | 44.0 | 45.2 | 11.6 | 13.9 | 15.0 | 6.9 | 8.9 | 9.6 |
| Cocaine | 14.7 | 14.4 | 14.9 | 1.8 | 1.9 | 2.2 | 0.6 | 0.7 | 0.8 |
| Crack | 3.6 | 3.3 | 3.5 | 0.3 | 0.3 | 0.3 | 0.1 | 0.2 | 0.2 |
| Heroin | 1.6 | 1.8 | 1.9 | 0.2 | 0.4 | 0.3 | 0.1 | 0.2 | 0.2 |
| Hallucinogens | (NA) | 15.4 | 15.5 | (NA) | 1.8 | 1.9 | (NA) | 0.5 | 0.5 |
| LSD | 9.2 | 9.6 | 9.6 | 0.3 | 0.7 | 0.8 | 0.1 | 0.1 | 0.2 |
| PCP | 2.5 | 2.4 | 2.2 | 0.0 | 0.0 | 0.0 | 0.0 | 0.0 | 0.0 |
| Ecstasy | (NA) | 6.9 | 7.0 | (NA) | 0.9 | 0.9 | (NA) | 0.2 | 0.2 |
| Inhalants | (NA) | 9.1 | 9.3 | (NA) | 0.6 | 0.6 | (NA) | 0.2 | 0.2 |
| Methamphetamine [2] | (NA) | 5.4 | 5.4 | (NA) | 0.5 | 0.6 | (NA) | 0.2 | 0.3 |
| Tobacco products [3] | 68.8 | 62.9 | 62.7 | (NA) | 28.5 | 27.5 | 27.5 | 23.5 | 22.4 |
| Cigarettes | 64.2 | 57.4 | 57.1 | (NA) | 22.7 | 21.5 | 23.0 | 19.1 | 17.9 |
| Smokeless tobacco | (NA) | 16.1 | 16.1 | (NA) | 4.4 | 4.3 | (NA) | 3.3 | 3.2 |
| Cigars | 35.0 | 31.7 | 31.7 | (NA) | 8.5 | 8.6 | 5.2 | 4.6 | 4.6 |
| Pipe tobacco | 13.6 | 12.3 | 12.2 | (NA) | (NA) | (NA) | 0.8 | 0.8 | 0.9 |
| Alcohol | 82.5 | 80.2 | 80.9 | (NA) | 64.8 | 65.7 | 51.8 | 50.7 | 51.7 |
| "Binge" alcohol use [4] | (NA) | (NA) | (NA) | (NA) | (NA) | (NA) | (NA) | 24.2 | 24.5 |
| **12 TO 17 YEARS OLD** | | | | | | | | | |
| Any illicit drug [1] | (NA) | 23.0 | 23.9 | (NA) | 15.8 | 16.3 | (NA) | 7.9 | 7.9 |
| Marijuana | 17.1 | 14.8 | 15.3 | 14.0 | 12.0 | 12.4 | 7.4 | 6.5 | 6.5 |
| Cocaine | 1.5 | 0.9 | 0.7 | 1.0 | 0.5 | 0.5 | 0.2 | 0.1 | 0.1 |
| Hallucinogens | (NA) | 2.7 | 2.8 | (NA) | 1.8 | 2.1 | (NA) | 0.5 | 0.6 |
| Inhalants | (NA) | 8.3 | 8.6 | (NA) | 2.2 | 2.3 | (NA) | 0.6 | 0.6 |
| Methamphetamine [2] | (NA) | 0.3 | 0.3 | (NA) | 0.1 | 0.2 | (NA) | 0.0 | 0.1 |
| Tobacco products [3] | 25.1 | 15.3 | 14.9 | (NA) | 10.5 | 9.7 | 10.7 | 5.3 | 4.9 |
| Cigarettes | 20.5 | 11.6 | 10.8 | (NA) | 7.2 | 6.3 | 8.4 | 3.4 | 3.2 |
| Smokeless tobacco | (NA) | 4.7 | 5.0 | (NA) | 3.0 | 3.0 | (NA) | 1.4 | 1.3 |
| Cigars | 11.1 | 6.1 | 6.4 | (NA) | 4.4 | 4.6 | 3.2 | 1.8 | 1.9 |
| Alcohol | 35.4 | 27.0 | 27.1 | (NA) | 21.6 | 21.9 | 13.6 | 9.2 | 9.9 |
| "Binge" alcohol use [4] | (NA) | (NA) | (NA) | (NA) | (NA) | (NA) | (NA) | 4.9 | 5.3 |
| **18 TO 25 YEARS OLD** | | | | | | | | | |
| Any illicit drug [1] | (NA) | 56.3 | 57.0 | (NA) | 37.7 | 39.4 | (NA) | 23.2 | 24.2 |
| Marijuana | 51.4 | 51.8 | 52.7 | 30.0 | 33.0 | 34.9 | 18.5 | 20.8 | 22.1 |
| Cocaine | 13.4 | 11.3 | 12.0 | 4.7 | 5.6 | 6.2 | 1.5 | 1.6 | 1.9 |
| Crack | 2.6 | 1.1 | 1.3 | 0.5 | 0.3 | 0.3 | 0.2 | 0.0 | 0.1 |
| Heroin | 1.8 | 1.6 | 1.8 | 0.6 | 0.7 | 0.6 | 0.3 | 0.3 | 0.3 |
| Hallucinogens | (NA) | 17.2 | 17.1 | (NA) | 6.9 | 7.0 | (NA) | 1.9 | 1.7 |
| Inhalants | (NA) | 0.8 | 9.5 | (NA) | 1.4 | 1.6 | (NA) | 0.4 | 0.5 |
| Methamphetamine [2] | (NA) | 2.4 | 3.0 | (NA) | 0.8 | 1.1 | (NA) | 0.2 | 0.4 |
| Tobacco products [3] | 68.8 | 59.3 | 57.9 | (NA) | 40.5 | 39.8 | 40.9 | 30.0 | 29.1 |
| Cigarettes | 62.3 | 50.5 | 49.5 | (NA) | 31.7 | 31.0 | 34.3 | 23.5 | 22.3 |
| Smokeless tobacco | (NA) | 18.2 | 18.0 | (NA) | 8.0 | 7.7 | (NA) | 5.2 | 4.8 |
| Cigars | 41.1 | 34.9 | 33.4 | (NA) | 18.0 | 17.9 | 11.3 | 8.8 | 9.1 |
| Alcohol | 85.7 | 81.3 | 81.1 | (NA) | 74.4 | 74.0 | 61.4 | 57.1 | 56.3 |
| "Binge" alcohol use [4] | (NA) | (NA) | (NA) | (NA) | (NA) | (NA) | (NA) | 38.4 | 36.9 |
| **26 YEARS OLD AND OVER** | | | | | | | | | |
| Any illicit drug [1] | (NA) | 50.2 | 51.3 | (NA) | 15.0 | 16.1 | (NA) | 8.9 | 9.5 |
| Marijuana | 43.5 | 46.2 | 47.5 | 8.0 | 11.0 | 12.2 | 4.8 | 7.2 | 7.9 |
| Cocaine | 16.6 | 16.6 | 17.0 | 1.4 | 1.4 | 1.7 | 0.5 | 0.6 | 0.7 |
| Crack | 4.2 | 4.0 | 4.3 | 0.4 | 0.4 | 0.4 | 0.2 | 0.2 | 0.2 |
| Heroin | 1.8 | 2.1 | 2.2 | 0.2 | 0.3 | 0.3 | 0.1 | 0.2 | 0.2 |
| Hallucinogens | (NA) | 16.6 | 16.7 | (NA) | 1.0 | 1.0 | (NA) | 0.3 | 0.3 |
| Inhalants | (NA) | 9.0 | 9.3 | (NA) | 0.3 | 0.3 | (NA) | 0.2 | 0.1 |
| Methamphetamine [2] | (NA) | 6.5 | 6.4 | (NA) | 0.5 | 0.6 | (NA) | 0.3 | 0.3 |
| Tobacco products [3] | 74.2 | 69.1 | 69.0 | (NA) | 28.6 | 27.6 | 27.2 | 24.6 | 23.4 |
| Cigarettes | 70.0 | 64.0 | 63.8 | (NA) | 23.1 | 21.7 | 22.8 | 20.2 | 18.9 |
| Smokeless tobacco | (NA) | 17.1 | 17.1 | (NA) | 4.0 | 3.9 | (NA) | 3.1 | 3.1 |
| Cigars | 36.9 | 34.2 | 34.4 | (NA) | 7.4 | 7.6 | 4.4 | 4.2 | 4.2 |
| Alcohol | 87.8 | 86.4 | 87.1 | (NA) | 68.4 | 69.5 | 54.9 | 54.6 | 55.8 |
| "Binge" alcohol use [4] | (NA) | (NA) | (NA) | (NA) | (NA) | (NA) | (NA) | 24.2 | 24.7 |

NA Not available. [1] Illicit drugs include marijuana, cocaine (including crack), heroin, hallucinogens, inhalants, methamphetamine, and the misuse of prescription psychotherapeutic drugs. Prior to 2015, methamphetamine was included with prescription psychotherapeutic drugs. [2] Beginning with 2015, methamphetamine is included with illicit drugs. [3] Includes other products not shown separately. Tobacco product use in the past year excludes past year pipe tobacco use, but includes past month pipe tobacco use. [4] Binge alcohol use is defined as drinking five or more drinks (for males) or four or more drinks (for females) on the same occasion (i.e., at the same time or within a couple of hours of each other) on at least 1 day in the past 30 days. In 2015, the definition for females changed from five to four drinks.

Source: U.S. Substance Abuse and Mental Health Services Administration, *Results from the 2017 National Survey on Drug Use and Health: Detailed Tables,* September 2018, and earlier reports. See also <https://www.samhsa.gov/data/data-we-collect/nsduh-national-survey-drug-use-and-health>.

# Table 221. Drug, Alcohol, and Cigarette Estimated Users by State: 2016 to 2017

[29,519 represents 29,519,000. Table presents annual averages for a 2-year period. Data are based on the National Survey on Drug Use and Health (NSDUH). Covers persons age 12 years and over who indicated use of a substance within the past month (during the 30 days prior to the interview). Based on a representative sample of the U.S. population, including persons living in households, noninstitutional group quarters such as dormitories and homeless shelters, and civilians living on military bases. Data were collected in 2016 and 2017 from 135,974 persons. State estimates have been developed using small area estimation procedure in which State-level data are combined with county and census block group/tract-level data from the State. For methodology information, see "2016-2017 NSDUH: Guide to State Tables and Summary of Small Area Estimation Methodology " at <https://www.samhsa.gov/data/nsduh/state-reports-NSDUH-2017>]

| State | Estimated current users (1,000) | | | | | Current users as percent of population | | | | |
|---|---|---|---|---|---|---|---|---|---|---|
| | Illicit drug use [1] | Mari-juana | Any illicit drug other than mari-juana [2] | Binge alcohol use [3] | Cigarette use | Illicit drug use [1] | Mari-juana | Any illicit drug other than mari-juana [2] | Binge alcohol use [3] | Cigarette use |
| United States........... | 29,519 | 24,988 | 9,139 | 65,982 | 50,013 | 10.9 | 9.2 | 3.4 | 24.4 | 18.5 |
| Northeast................. | 5,536 | 4,713 | 1,633 | 12,679 | 8,408 | 11.5 | 9.8 | 3.4 | 26.4 | 17.5 |
| Midwest.................... | 5,868 | 4,984 | 1,864 | 15,030 | 11,726 | 10.3 | 8.8 | 3.3 | 26.4 | 20.6 |
| South...................... | 9,325 | 7,617 | 3,234 | 23,240 | 20,158 | 9.2 | 7.5 | 3.2 | 22.8 | 19.8 |
| West........................ | 8,790 | 7,675 | 2,408 | 15,034 | 9,720 | 13.7 | 12.0 | 3.8 | 23.5 | 15.2 |
| Alabama.................. | 353 | 259 | 140 | 871 | 955 | 8.7 | 6.4 | 3.4 | 21.4 | 23.5 |
| Alaska..................... | 98 | 93 | 21 | 142 | 115 | 16.8 | 15.8 | 3.5 | 24.2 | 19.7 |
| Arizona................... | 624 | 485 | 200 | 1,337 | 979 | 10.8 | 8.4 | 3.5 | 23.1 | 16.9 |
| Arkansas................ | 260 | 203 | 90 | 482 | 610 | 10.5 | 8.2 | 3.7 | 19.5 | 24.6 |
| California................. | 4,309 | 3,723 | 1,256 | 7,726 | 4,383 | 13.1 | 11.3 | 3.8 | 23.5 | 13.3 |
| Colorado................. | 829 | 764 | 183 | 1,253 | 735 | 17.8 | 16.4 | 3.9 | 27.0 | 15.8 |
| Connecticut............ | 377 | 324 | 114 | 866 | 516 | 12.3 | 10.6 | 3.7 | 28.3 | 16.8 |
| Delaware................ | 95 | 80 | 28 | 182 | 148 | 11.7 | 9.9 | 3.4 | 22.5 | 18.4 |
| District of Columbia...... | 117 | 101 | 31 | 217 | 110 | 19.9 | 17.2 | 5.4 | 37.0 | 18.7 |
| Florida.................... | 1,836 | 1,532 | 563 | 4,370 | 2,956 | 10.4 | 8.6 | 3.2 | 24.7 | 16.7 |
| Georgia.................. | 711 | 574 | 262 | 1,757 | 1,611 | 8.3 | 6.7 | 3.1 | 20.6 | 18.9 |
| Hawaii.................... | 111 | 95 | 31 | 237 | 158 | 9.6 | 8.2 | 2.7 | 20.4 | 13.6 |
| Idaho...................... | 125 | 106 | 42 | 302 | 253 | 9.0 | 7.6 | 3.0 | 21.7 | 18.2 |
| Illinois.................... | 1,076 | 944 | 342 | 2,949 | 1,948 | 10.0 | 8.8 | 3.2 | 27.5 | 18.2 |
| Indiana................... | 621 | 513 | 208 | 1,273 | 1,180 | 11.2 | 9.3 | 3.8 | 23.1 | 21.4 |
| Iowa....................... | 212 | 174 | 79 | 775 | 548 | 8.1 | 6.6 | 3.0 | 29.7 | 21.0 |
| Kansas................... | 197 | 157 | 69 | 620 | 467 | 8.3 | 6.6 | 2.9 | 26.1 | 19.7 |
| Kentucky................ | 336 | 287 | 109 | 805 | 984 | 9.1 | 7.8 | 3.0 | 21.8 | 26.7 |
| Louisiana............... | 356 | 291 | 133 | 1,024 | 917 | 9.3 | 7.6 | 3.5 | 26.7 | 23.9 |
| Maine..................... | 189 | 183 | 34 | 272 | 233 | 16.3 | 15.8 | 3.0 | 23.5 | 20.2 |
| Maryland................ | 599 | 539 | 169 | 1,199 | 792 | 11.9 | 10.7 | 3.4 | 23.8 | 15.7 |
| Massachusetts....... | 940 | 786 | 250 | 1,851 | 973 | 16.0 | 13.4 | 4.3 | 31.5 | 16.6 |
| Michigan................ | 1,129 | 979 | 310 | 2,120 | 1,823 | 13.4 | 11.6 | 3.7 | 25.2 | 21.6 |
| Minnesota.............. | 422 | 357 | 147 | 1,219 | 845 | 9.1 | 7.7 | 3.2 | 26.3 | 18.3 |
| Mississippi............. | 227 | 170 | 82 | 505 | 601 | 9.3 | 7.0 | 3.3 | 20.6 | 24.5 |
| Missouri................. | 526 | 428 | 169 | 1,282 | 1,084 | 10.4 | 8.4 | 3.3 | 25.2 | 21.3 |
| Montana................. | 126 | 114 | 31 | 257 | 180 | 14.3 | 13.0 | 3.6 | 29.3 | 20.5 |
| Nebraska................ | 141 | 121 | 45 | 454 | 326 | 9.0 | 7.7 | 2.9 | 29.0 | 20.8 |
| Nevada.................. | 332 | 292 | 96 | 585 | 484 | 13.4 | 11.8 | 3.9 | 23.6 | 19.5 |
| New Hampshire......... | 165 | 149 | 42 | 331 | 205 | 14.3 | 12.9 | 3.7 | 28.6 | 17.7 |
| New Jersey............. | 641 | 542 | 208 | 1,836 | 1,264 | 8.5 | 7.1 | 2.7 | 24.2 | 16.7 |
| New Mexico............ | 233 | 206 | 64 | 421 | 346 | 13.5 | 12.0 | 3.7 | 24.4 | 20.1 |
| New York................ | 1,858 | 1,592 | 555 | 4,201 | 2,715 | 11.1 | 9.5 | 3.3 | 25.0 | 16.2 |
| North Carolina.......... | 828 | 673 | 278 | 1,728 | 1,705 | 9.8 | 7.9 | 3.3 | 20.4 | 20.1 |
| North Dakota........... | 47 | 40 | 18 | 192 | 125 | 7.7 | 6.4 | 3.0 | 31.2 | 20.2 |
| Ohio....................... | 990 | 837 | 309 | 2,425 | 2,234 | 10.1 | 8.6 | 3.2 | 24.8 | 22.9 |
| Oklahoma............... | 270 | 221 | 103 | 707 | 734 | 8.4 | 6.9 | 3.2 | 22.1 | 22.9 |
| Oregon................... | 732 | 673 | 159 | 874 | 654 | 20.9 | 19.2 | 4.6 | 25.0 | 18.7 |
| Pennsylvania.......... | 1,102 | 893 | 364 | 2,909 | 2,230 | 10.2 | 8.2 | 3.4 | 26.8 | 20.5 |
| Rhode Island.......... | 159 | 143 | 39 | 264 | 160 | 17.5 | 15.7 | 4.3 | 29.1 | 17.7 |
| South Carolina........... | 348 | 277 | 155 | 978 | 910 | 8.4 | 6.7 | 3.7 | 23.5 | 21.9 |
| South Dakota............ | 60 | 50 | 22 | 217 | 159 | 8.6 | 7.1 | 3.2 | 30.8 | 22.6 |
| Tennessee.............. | 538 | 447 | 194 | 1,140 | 1,307 | 9.6 | 8.0 | 3.5 | 20.4 | 23.4 |
| Texas..................... | 1,736 | 1,357 | 639 | 5,302 | 4,163 | 7.6 | 6.0 | 2.8 | 23.3 | 18.3 |
| Utah....................... | 196 | 152 | 75 | 394 | 324 | 8.0 | 6.3 | 3.1 | 16.2 | 13.3 |
| Vermont.................. | 105 | 101 | 26 | 148 | 112 | 19.4 | 18.6 | 4.7 | 27.3 | 20.5 |
| Virginia................... | 575 | 486 | 211 | 1,641 | 1,190 | 8.2 | 7.0 | 3.0 | 23.5 | 17.0 |
| Washington............ | 1,034 | 938 | 236 | 1,392 | 1,012 | 16.9 | 15.3 | 3.9 | 22.7 | 16.5 |
| West Virginia........... | 140 | 118 | 46 | 334 | 464 | 9.0 | 7.6 | 2.9 | 21.5 | 29.9 |
| Wisconsin............... | 445 | 385 | 146 | 1,503 | 987 | 9.1 | 7.9 | 3.0 | 30.8 | 20.2 |
| Wyoming................. | 41 | 34 | 14 | 114 | 96 | 8.6 | 7.1 | 2.9 | 23.8 | 20.0 |

[1] "Illicit drug use" includes the misuse of prescription psychotherapeutics or the use of marijuana, cocaine (including crack), heroin, hallucinogens, inhalants, or methamphetamine. Misuse of prescription psychotherapeutics is defined as use in any way not directed by a doctor, including use without a prescription of one's own; use in greater amounts, more often, or longer than told; or use in any other way not directed by a doctor. Prescription psychotherapeutics do not include over-the-counter drugs. [2] "Illicit drug use other than marijuana" includes the misuse of prescription psychotherapeutics or the use of cocaine (including crack), heroin, hallucinogens, inhalants, or methamphetamine. [3] "Binge alcohol use" is defined as drinking 5/more drinks (for males) or 4/more drinks (for females) on the same occasion (i.e., at the same time or within a couple of hours of each other) on at least 1 day in the past 30 days. In 2015, the definition for females changed from five to four drinks.

Source: U.S. Substance Abuse and Mental Health Services Administration, National Survey on Drug Use and Health, "State Reports," <https://www.samhsa.gov/data/data-we-collect/nsduh-national-survey-drug-use-and-health>, accessed February 2019.

## Table 222. Prescription Psychotherapeutic Drug Use and Misuse by Drug Type and User Characteristics: 2017

[In percent. Data are from the National Survey on Drug Use and Health, and cover persons age 12 and older. Misuse of prescription drugs is defined as use in any way not directed by a physician, including use without a prescription of one's own medication; use in greater amounts, more often, or longer than instructed to take a drug; or use in any other way not directed by a physician. Excludes over-the-counter drugs. See also headnote, Table 220]

| User characteristics | Any use in past year | | | | | Misuse in past year | | | | |
|---|---|---|---|---|---|---|---|---|---|---|
| | Any drug | Pain relievers | Tranquil-izers | Stimu-lants | Seda-tives | Any drug | Pain relievers | Tranquil-izers | Stimu-lants | Seda-tives |
| **Total** | **42.2** | **33.4** | **14.0** | **6.8** | **6.2** | **6.6** | **4.1** | **2.2** | **2.1** | **0.5** |
| SEX | | | | | | | | | | |
| Male | 38.5 | 30.9 | 10.4 | 7.0 | 5.0 | 7.2 | 4.6 | 2.3 | 2.6 | 0.5 |
| Female | 45.6 | 35.7 | 17.5 | 6.7 | 7.2 | 6.1 | 3.6 | 2.1 | 1.7 | 0.5 |
| AGE | | | | | | | | | | |
| 12 to 17 years | 23.7 | 17.4 | 4.6 | 7.2 | 2.3 | 4.9 | 3.1 | 1.8 | 1.8 | 0.3 |
| 18 years and over | 44.0 | 35.0 | 15.0 | 6.8 | 6.5 | 6.8 | 4.2 | 2.2 | 2.2 | 0.5 |
| 18 to 25 years | 41.1 | 29.9 | 11.9 | 14.7 | 3.4 | 14.4 | 7.2 | 5.5 | 7.4 | 0.6 |
| 26 years and over | 44.5 | 35.8 | 15.5 | 5.5 | 7.1 | 5.6 | 3.7 | 1.7 | 1.3 | 0.5 |
| RACE AND ETHNICITY | | | | | | | | | | |
| Not Hispanic | 43.8 | 34.6 | 14.9 | 7.2 | 6.6 | 6.8 | 4.1 | 2.3 | 2.2 | 0.5 |
| White | 46.6 | 35.8 | 17.3 | 8.1 | 7.4 | 7.5 | 4.4 | 2.6 | 2.6 | 0.6 |
| Black or African American | 38.5 | 34.5 | 8.4 | 3.6 | 4.5 | 4.5 | 3.5 | 1.2 | 0.8 | 0.2 |
| American Indian or Alaska Native | 46.3 | 41.0 | 12.6 | 9.2 | 9.1 | 7.0 | 5.7 | 1.5 | 1.7 | 0.3 |
| Native Hawaiian or Other Pacific Islander | 46.4 | 43.0 | 6.9 | 5.1 | 4.2 | 3.4 | 2.2 | 1.6 | 1.4 | (S) |
| Asian | 23.2 | 18.9 | 4.1 | 3.2 | 1.9 | 3.1 | 1.8 | 0.7 | 1.1 | 0.1 |
| Two or more races | 45.6 | 36.4 | 13.7 | 8.9 | 6.5 | 7.9 | 4.9 | 2.6 | 2.0 | 0.5 |
| Hispanic or Latino | 34.0 | 27.5 | 9.5 | 5.2 | 3.9 | 6.1 | 4.0 | 1.8 | 1.7 | 0.4 |
| REGION | | | | | | | | | | |
| Northeast | 39.1 | 28.9 | 13.5 | 6.3 | 5.7 | 6.4 | 3.6 | 2.3 | 2.4 | 0.4 |
| Midwest | 43.0 | 34.3 | 14.5 | 7.5 | 5.4 | 7.1 | 4.2 | 2.4 | 2.8 | 0.4 |
| South | 43.9 | 35.1 | 14.9 | 7.4 | 6.8 | 6.4 | 4.0 | 2.2 | 1.9 | 0.5 |
| West | 41.0 | 33.2 | 12.6 | 5.9 | 6.1 | 6.8 | 4.4 | 1.9 | 1.8 | 0.6 |
| METRO STATUS | | | | | | | | | | |
| Large metro [1] | 40.3 | 31.5 | 13.0 | 6.8 | 5.7 | 6.7 | 3.9 | 2.2 | 2.3 | 0.5 |
| Small metro [2] | 44.9 | 35.6 | 15.7 | 7.2 | 7.0 | 6.8 | 4.3 | 2.2 | 2.2 | 0.5 |
| Nonmetro | 44.1 | 36.1 | 14.5 | 6.1 | 6.2 | 5.9 | 4.0 | 2.0 | 1.7 | 0.5 |

S Figure does not meet standards of reliability or precision. [1] Over 1 million population. [2] Less than 1 million population.

Source: U.S. Substance Abuse and Mental Health Services Administration, *Results From the 2017 National Survey on Drug Use and Health: Detailed Tables*, September 2018. See also <https://www.samhsa.gov/data/population-data-nsduh>.

## Table 223. Prescription Drug Use in Past 30 Days by Sex, Race/Ethnicity, and Age: 1988 to 2014

[Data shown as percent of population using prescription drugs in past 30 days. Based on the National Health and Nutrition Examination Survey, covering a sample of the civilian noninstitutionalized population]

| Sex, race/ethnicity, and age | Use of 1 or more prescription drugs | | | Use of 3 or more prescription drugs | | | Use of 5 or more prescription drugs | | |
|---|---|---|---|---|---|---|---|---|---|
| | 1988-1994 | 2007-2010 | 2011-2014 | 1988-1994 | 2007-2010 | 2011-2014 | 1988-1994 | 2007-2010 | 2011-2014 |
| **Both sexes, age adjusted [1,2]** | **39.1** | **47.5** | **46.9** | **11.8** | **20.8** | **21.5** | **4.0** | **10.1** | **10.9** |
| Male | 32.7 | 42.8 | 42.6 | 9.4 | 19.1 | 19.7 | 2.9 | 9.2 | 9.7 |
| Female | 45.0 | 52.0 | 51.2 | 13.9 | 22.5 | 23.2 | 4.9 | 11.0 | 12.0 |
| White alone [3] | 41.1 | 52.8 | 51.9 | 12.4 | 22.4 | 23.1 | 4.2 | 10.7 | 11.5 |
| Male | 34.2 | 47.5 | 46.8 | 9.9 | 20.6 | 21.0 | 3.1 | 9.8 | 10.2 |
| Female | 47.6 | 57.9 | 57.0 | 14.6 | 24.3 | 25.1 | 5.1 | 11.6 | 12.8 |
| Black or African American alone [3] | 36.9 | 42.3 | 44.2 | 12.6 | 20.7 | 22.5 | 3.8 | 10.8 | 12.1 |
| Male | 31.1 | 36.7 | 38.3 | 10.2 | 17.7 | 19.4 | 2.9 | 9.1 | 10.1 |
| Female | 41.4 | 46.8 | 49.0 | 14.3 | 22.9 | 24.9 | 4.5 | 12.0 | 13.7 |
| Asian alone [3] | (NA) | (NA) | 34.3 | (NA) | (NA) | 14.3 | (NA) | (NA) | 6.2 |
| Male | (NA) | (NA) | 31.9 | (NA) | (NA) | 14.1 | (NA) | (NA) | 6.2 |
| Female | (NA) | (NA) | 36.3 | (NA) | (NA) | 14.6 | (NA) | (NA) | 6.1 |
| Hispanic or Latino [4] | (NA) | 35.2 | 35.7 | (NA) | 15.7 | 16.0 | (NA) | 8.4 | 8.4 |
| Male | (NA) | 31.7 | 32.1 | (NA) | 14.0 | 15.0 | (NA) | 7.3 | 7.9 |
| Female | (NA) | 38.8 | 39.2 | (NA) | 17.4 | 17.1 | (NA) | 9.5 | 8.8 |
| **Both sexes, crude** | **37.8** | **48.5** | **48.9** | **11.0** | **21.7** | **23.1** | **3.6** | **10.6** | **11.9** |
| Male | 30.6 | 43.0 | 43.7 | 8.3 | 19.0 | 20.4 | 2.5 | 9.1 | 10.0 |
| Under 18 years | 20.4 | 24.5 | 21.1 | 2.6 | 4.4 | 4.3 | (B) | 0.8 | 0.9 |
| 18 to 44 years | 21.5 | 29.5 | 28.8 | 3.6 | 7.1 | 7.5 | [5] 0.8 | 2.1 | 3.0 |
| 45 to 64 years | 47.2 | 61.3 | 65.6 | 15.1 | 30.4 | 33.0 | 4.8 | 14.4 | 15.7 |
| 65 years and over | 67.2 | 88.8 | 88.7 | 31.3 | 66.8 | 65.2 | 11.3 | 39.5 | 38.4 |
| Female | 44.6 | 53.8 | 53.9 | 13.6 | 24.2 | 25.8 | 4.7 | 12.1 | 13.6 |
| Under 18 years | 20.6 | 23.5 | 22.0 | 2.3 | 3.1 | 3.5 | (B) | [5] 0.7 | (B) |
| 18 to 44 years | 40.7 | 47.6 | 45.3 | 7.6 | 12.2 | 12.6 | 1.7 | 4.0 | 4.8 |
| 45 to 64 years | 62.0 | 70.8 | 72.1 | 24.7 | 38.1 | 39.4 | 9.7 | 19.1 | 20.7 |
| 65 years and over | 78.3 | 90.4 | 92.1 | 38.2 | 66.4 | 68.1 | 15.6 | 39.8 | 42.6 |

NA Not available. B Estimate has a relative standard error greater than 30%. [1] Estimates are age-adjusted to the year 2000 standard population using four age groups: under 18 years, 18-44 years, 45-64 years, and 65 years and over. [2] Includes persons of other race/ethnicities, not shown separately. [3] Not Hispanic or Latino. [4] Persons of Hispanic or Latino origin may be of any race. [5] Estimate has a relative standard error (RSE) of 20% to 30% and is considered unreliable.

Source: U.S. National Center for Health Statistics, *Health, United States, 2017*, September 2018. See also <http://www.cdc.gov/nchs/hus.htm>.

# Table 224. Height of Population Age 20 and Over by Sex, Age, and Race/Ethnicity: 2011 to 2014

[In inches. Data are for the 2011-2014 period. Based on National Health and Nutrition Examination Survey (NHANES), a sample of the civilian noninstitutional population. Data are collected through household interviews and health examinations. Height was measured without shoes. Survey oversampled persons age 80 and over, Hispanic persons, and non-Hispanic Black and Asian persons; see source for more information]

| Age and race/ethnicity | Males, height in inches | | | | | | Females, height in inches | | | | | |
|---|---|---|---|---|---|---|---|---|---|---|---|---|
| | Mean | Percentile | | | | | Mean | Percentile | | | | |
| | | 10th | 25th | 50th | 75th | 90th | | 10th | 25th | 50th | 75th | 90th |
| **Total:** [1] | | | | | | | | | | | | |
| 20 years and over...... | 69.2 | 65.4 | 67.2 | 69.1 | 71.2 | 73.0 | 63.7 | 60.1 | 61.7 | 63.7 | 65.5 | 67.2 |
| 20-29 years............. | 69.4 | 65.7 | 67.4 | 69.4 | 71.4 | 73.4 | 64.1 | 60.8 | 62.3 | 64.1 | 65.8 | 67.4 |
| 30-39 years............. | 69.5 | 65.8 | 67.5 | 69.5 | 71.5 | 73.5 | 64.3 | 60.5 | 62.3 | 64.4 | 66.4 | 67.9 |
| 40-49 years............. | 69.4 | 65.7 | 67.3 | 69.3 | 71.2 | 73.1 | 64.1 | 60.5 | 62.2 | 64.2 | 65.9 | 67.6 |
| 50-59 years............. | 69.3 | 65.7 | 67.2 | 69.1 | 71.4 | 73.0 | 63.7 | 60.2 | 61.8 | 63.9 | 65.3 | 67.1 |
| 60-69 years............. | 69.0 | 65.2 | 67.1 | 69.1 | 71.2 | 72.5 | 63.2 | 60.1 | 61.5 | 63.2 | 64.9 | 66.5 |
| 70-79 years............. | 68.1 | 64.7 | 66.3 | 67.9 | 69.8 | 71.7 | 62.7 | 59.2 | 60.8 | 63.0 | 64.5 | 66.1 |
| 80 years and over...... | 67.6 | 64.2 | 65.9 | 67.7 | 69.4 | 71.0 | 61.3 | 57.7 | 59.6 | 61.3 | 63.1 | 64.3 |
| **White, non-Hispanic:** | | | | | | | | | | | | |
| 20 years and over...... | 69.7 | 66.2 | 67.7 | 69.6 | 71.5 | 73.3 | 64.1 | 60.6 | 62.3 | 64.1 | 65.8 | 67.5 |
| 20-39 years............. | 70.1 | 66.6 | 68.2 | 70.2 | 72.1 | 73.8 | 64.9 | 61.7 | 63.2 | 64.9 | 66.6 | 68.2 |
| 40-59 years............. | 69.9 | 66.5 | 68.1 | 69.9 | 71.7 | 73.3 | 64.4 | 61.1 | 62.8 | 64.4 | 66.0 | 67.8 |
| 60 years and over...... | 69.0 | 65.3 | 67.0 | 69.0 | 70.9 | 72.4 | 63.0 | 59.7 | 61.1 | 63.0 | 64.7 | 66.3 |
| **Black, non-Hispanic:** | | | | | | | | | | | | |
| 20 years and over...... | 69.5 | 66.0 | 67.4 | 69.3 | 71.4 | 73.3 | 64.2 | 60.7 | 62.5 | 64.2 | 65.9 | 67.4 |
| 20-39 years............. | 69.8 | 66.3 | 67.6 | 69.7 | 71.9 | 73.6 | 64.4 | 60.9 | 62.9 | 64.4 | 66.0 | 67.5 |
| 40-59 years............. | 69.5 | 66.1 | 67.6 | 69.3 | 71.4 | 72.8 | 64.5 | 61.1 | 62.9 | 64.6 | 66.1 | 67.7 |
| 60 years and over...... | 68.5 | 65.2 | 66.7 | 68.4 | 70.3 | 72.4 | 63.1 | 59.6 | 61.4 | 63.2 | 64.9 | 66.4 |
| **Hispanic:** | | | | | | | | | | | | |
| 20 years and over...... | 67.4 | 63.8 | 65.5 | 67.3 | 69.3 | 71.1 | 62.0 | 58.7 | 60.3 | 61.9 | 63.7 | 65.3 |
| 20-39 years............. | 67.9 | 64.4 | 65.9 | 67.8 | 69.8 | 71.5 | 62.6 | 59.2 | 60.8 | 62.6 | 64.2 | 65.5 |
| 40-59 years............. | 67.2 | 63.6 | 65.3 | 67.2 | 69.1 | 70.9 | 61.9 | 58.7 | 60.1 | 61.6 | 63.5 | 65.4 |
| 60 years and over...... | 66.0 | 62.6 | 64.1 | 65.9 | 67.6 | 69.4 | 60.6 | 57.5 | 59.1 | 60.6 | 62.1 | 63.6 |

[1] Total includes persons of other race/ethnicities not shown separately.

Source: U.S. Centers for Disease Control and Prevention, National Health and Nutrition Examination Survey, *Anthropometric Reference Data For Children and Adults: United States, 2011-2014*, Series 3, No. 39, August 2016. See also <http://www.cdc.gov/nchs/nhanes.htm>.

# Table 225. Weight of Population Age 20 and Over by Age, Sex, and Race/Ethnicity: 2011 to 2014

[In pounds. Data are for 2011-2014 period. Based on National Health and Nutrition Examination Survey (NHANES). Pregnant females are excluded from the tabulations on weight. See headnote, Table 224]

| Age and race/ethnicity | Males, weight in pounds | | | | | | Females, weight in pounds | | | | | |
|---|---|---|---|---|---|---|---|---|---|---|---|---|
| | Mean | Percentile | | | | | Mean | Percentile | | | | |
| | | 10th | 25th | 50th | 75th | 90th | | 10th | 25th | 50th | 75th | 90th |
| **Total:** [1] | | | | | | | | | | | | |
| 20 years and over....... | 195.7 | 146.2 | 165.1 | 189.3 | 218.8 | 249.9 | 168.5 | 119.8 | 136.0 | 159.1 | 191.1 | 229.3 |
| 20–29 years............. | 186.8 | 137.6 | 152.9 | 177.8 | 208.5 | 247.2 | 161.8 | 113.9 | 128.8 | 149.8 | 184.6 | 228.7 |
| 30–39 years............. | 198.8 | 150.2 | 168.1 | 190.8 | 221.2 | 259.6 | 172.9 | 124.0 | 137.7 | 160.5 | 195.9 | 237.7 |
| 40–49 years............. | 201.7 | 156.3 | 171.7 | 196.4 | 222.5 | 249.0 | 173.1 | 124.8 | 138.8 | 164.0 | 196.8 | 237.2 |
| 50–59 years............. | 199.5 | 152.0 | 170.2 | 195.9 | 222.3 | 250.4 | 174.4 | 124.9 | 141.0 | 167.4 | 197.2 | 239.4 |
| 60–69 years............. | 199.7 | 147.0 | 168.0 | 195.3 | 223.1 | 255.3 | 168.8 | 122.5 | 140.3 | 164.4 | 191.2 | 224.8 |
| 70–79 years............. | 189.3 | 146.2 | 166.6 | 183.6 | 212.0 | 236.3 | 165.8 | 120.2 | 138.6 | 158.5 | 188.5 | 216.5 |
| 80 years and over....... | 174.6 | 132.6 | 154.2 | 171.1 | 194.5 | 216.1 | 141.9 | 103.8 | 121.7 | 141.0 | 160.6 | 180.4 |
| **White, non-Hispanic:** | | | | | | | | | | | | |
| 20 years and over....... | 198.8 | 151.6 | 169.1 | 192.9 | 221.4 | 250.5 | 168.4 | 122.2 | 137.4 | 158.7 | 190.3 | 226.5 |
| 20–39 years............. | 193.8 | 144.9 | 161.7 | 183.5 | 218.5 | 255.0 | 167.9 | 119.8 | 134.0 | 155.9 | 189.0 | 230.8 |
| 40–59 years............. | 204.6 | 161.2 | 175.7 | 199.3 | 225.5 | 250.4 | 173.4 | 127.0 | 140.9 | 166.1 | 195.4 | 237.5 |
| 60 years and over....... | 196.5 | 149.0 | 168.9 | 190.2 | 219.3 | 249.2 | 162.9 | 117.0 | 136.2 | 157.0 | 183.4 | 215.3 |
| **Black, non-Hispanic:** | | | | | | | | | | | | |
| 20 years and over....... | 199.3 | 141.4 | 161.4 | 191.6 | 227.2 | 264.4 | 190.2 | 131.6 | 154.0 | 183.1 | 217.8 | 256.8 |
| 20–39 years............. | 197.7 | 138.6 | 157.9 | 189.0 | 228.0 | 264.2 | 190.0 | 129.6 | 151.0 | 183.1 | 219.0 | 263.3 |
| 40–59 years............. | 204.8 | 147.0 | 169.8 | 196.6 | 231.4 | 270.3 | 196.5 | 140.0 | 159.2 | 187.3 | 223.5 | 259.6 |
| 60 years and over....... | 191.4 | 141.2 | 158.8 | 185.5 | 214.4 | 251.9 | 179.9 | 126.0 | 147.2 | 174.7 | 208.9 | 235.1 |
| **Hispanic:** | | | | | | | | | | | | |
| 20 years and over....... | 189.9 | 143.1 | 161.6 | 184.7 | 209.1 | 240.0 | 164.7 | 121.3 | 135.5 | 157.4 | 186.2 | 219.2 |
| 20–39 years............. | 192.2 | 142.3 | 160.7 | 186.0 | 214.1 | 243.9 | 163.5 | 120.7 | 134.8 | 152.9 | 182.5 | 220.7 |
| 40–59 years............. | 190.1 | 147.2 | 166.0 | 186.8 | 207.2 | 232.2 | 169.1 | 122.7 | 138.6 | 163.6 | 191.8 | 221.7 |
| 60 years and over....... | 179.3 | 140.1 | 153.3 | 175.4 | 198.3 | 226.5 | 158.3 | 114.4 | 132.5 | 154.0 | 179.9 | 204.8 |

[1] Total includes persons of other race/ethnicities not shown separately.

Source: U.S. Centers for Disease Control and Prevention, National Health and Nutrition Examination Survey, *Anthropometric Reference Data For Children and Adults: United States, 2011-2014*, Series 3, No. 39, August 2016. See also <http://www.cdc.gov/nchs/nhanes.htm>.

## Table 226. Body Mass Index of Population Age 20 and Over by Age, Sex, and Race/Ethnicity: 2011 to 2014

[Data are for 2011-2014 period. Body Mass Index (BMI) is a measure that adjusts body weight for height, and is calculated as weight in kilograms divided by the square of height in meters. For both men and women, BMI weight categories are: under 18.5 underweight, 18.5-24.9 normal, 25.0-29.9 overweight, and 30.0 and over obese. Data are based on National Health and Nutrition Examination Survey (NHANES), a sample of the civilian noninstitutional population. Data are collected through household interviews and health examinations. Excludes pregnant women. Survey oversampled persons age 80 and over, Hispanic persons, and non-Hispanic Black and Asian persons; see source for more information]

| Age and race/ethnicity | Males, BMI | | | | | | Females, BMI | | | | | |
| | Mean | Percentile | | | | | Mean | Percentile | | | | |
| | | 10th | 25th | 50th | 75th | 90th | | 10th | 25th | 50th | 75th | 90th |
|---|---|---|---|---|---|---|---|---|---|---|---|---|
| Total: [1] | | | | | | | | | | | | |
| 20 years and over...... | 28.7 | 22.2 | 24.6 | 27.7 | 31.6 | 36.1 | 29.2 | 21.0 | 23.6 | 27.7 | 33.2 | 39.3 |
| 20–29 years............ | 27.2 | 20.5 | 22.5 | 25.5 | 30.5 | 35.1 | 27.6 | 19.8 | 21.9 | 25.6 | 31.8 | 38.9 |
| 30–39 years............ | 28.9 | 22.4 | 24.8 | 27.5 | 31.9 | 36.5 | 29.4 | 21.1 | 23.3 | 27.6 | 33.1 | 40.0 |
| 40–49 years............ | 29.4 | 23.4 | 25.7 | 28.5 | 31.9 | 36.5 | 29.6 | 21.5 | 23.7 | 28.1 | 33.4 | 39.6 |
| 50–59 years............ | 29.1 | 22.7 | 25.4 | 28.3 | 32.0 | 35.2 | 30.2 | 21.5 | 24.5 | 28.6 | 34.4 | 40.7 |
| 60–69 years............ | 29.4 | 22.7 | 25.3 | 28.0 | 32.4 | 36.9 | 29.7 | 21.7 | 24.5 | 28.9 | 33.4 | 38.7 |
| 70–79 years............ | 28.6 | 23.2 | 25.4 | 27.8 | 30.9 | 34.9 | 29.6 | 22.1 | 24.6 | 28.3 | 33.4 | 39.1 |
| 80 years and over...... | 26.7 | 21.5 | 24.1 | 26.3 | 29.0 | 32.3 | 26.6 | 20.4 | 23.3 | 26.1 | 29.7 | 32.8 |
| White, non-Hispanic: | | | | | | | | | | | | |
| 20 years and over...... | 28.7 | 22.3 | 24.8 | 27.7 | 31.6 | 36.0 | 28.8 | 20.9 | 23.4 | 27.3 | 32.6 | 38.8 |
| 20–39 years............ | 27.7 | 21.1 | 23.2 | 26.4 | 30.6 | 35.9 | 28.0 | 20.4 | 22.3 | 25.9 | 31.8 | 38.9 |
| 40–59 years............ | 29.4 | 23.2 | 25.7 | 28.5 | 32.2 | 36.0 | 29.4 | 21.4 | 23.6 | 27.9 | 33.4 | 40.1 |
| 60 years and over...... | 29.0 | 22.8 | 25.3 | 27.9 | 31.6 | 36.0 | 28.9 | 21.4 | 24.2 | 27.9 | 32.4 | 37.5 |
| Black, non-Hispanic: | | | | | | | | | | | | |
| 20 years and over...... | 28.9 | 21.1 | 24.0 | 27.9 | 32.2 | 37.7 | 32.5 | 22.8 | 26.6 | 31.3 | 36.8 | 43.5 |
| 20–39 years............ | 28.4 | 20.5 | 23.3 | 26.4 | 32.5 | 37.2 | 32.1 | 21.8 | 25.9 | 31.0 | 36.9 | 43.4 |
| 40–59 years............ | 29.7 | 21.9 | 25.1 | 28.7 | 32.4 | 39.2 | 33.3 | 23.5 | 27.1 | 31.9 | 37.2 | 44.8 |
| 60 years and over...... | 28.6 | 22.1 | 24.2 | 27.7 | 31.6 | 36.5 | 31.7 | 22.8 | 26.2 | 30.9 | 35.8 | 41.3 |
| Hispanic: | | | | | | | | | | | | |
| 20 years and over...... | 29.3 | 22.9 | 25.5 | 28.6 | 32.0 | 36.4 | 30.0 | 22.1 | 25.1 | 28.9 | 33.9 | 38.8 |
| 20–39 years............ | 29.3 | 22.1 | 24.9 | 28.6 | 32.4 | 37.3 | 29.3 | 21.7 | 24.4 | 27.9 | 32.9 | 38.6 |
| 40–59 years............ | 29.5 | 23.8 | 26.4 | 28.8 | 31.7 | 35.3 | 31.0 | 22.7 | 26.1 | 30.2 | 34.9 | 39.5 |
| 60 years and over...... | 28.8 | 23.7 | 25.5 | 27.9 | 31.6 | 34.5 | 30.3 | 22.4 | 25.9 | 29.5 | 34.3 | 38.4 |

[1] Total includes persons of other race/ethnicities not shown separately.

Source: U.S. Centers for Disease Control and Prevention, National Health and Nutrition Examination Survey, *Anthropometric Reference Data For Children and Adults: United States, 2011-2014*, Series 3, No. 39, August 2016. See also <http://www.cdc.gov/nchs/nhanes.htm>.

## Table 227. Leisure-Time Aerobic and Muscle-Strengthening Activity Among Adults Age 18 and Over by Selected Characteristics: 2017

[In percent. Percents are age-adjusted and allow for comparisons to results from earlier surveys and within demographic groups. Covers persons age 18 and over. Based on the National Health Interview Survey (NHIS), a sample survey of the civilian noninstitutionalized population. Measures of physical activity reflect the federal "2008 Physical Activity Guidelines for Americans"; see <https://health.gov/PAGuidelines/>. The guidelines include an aerobic component; the full physical activity guidelines include muscle-strengthening and aerobic activities. NHIS questions ask about frequency and duration of light-to moderate-intensity and vigorous-intensity leisure-time physical activities, and frequency of leisure-time muscle strengthening activities. Questions are phrased in terms of current behavior and lack a specific reference period. For definition of age adjustment, see text, Section 2]

| Characteristic | Inactive/insufficiently active [1] | Sufficiently active [2] | Met muscle strength-ening and aerobic guide-lines [3] | Characteristic | Inactive/insufficiently active [1] | Sufficiently active [2] | Met muscle strength-ening and aerobic guide-lines [3] |
|---|---|---|---|---|---|---|---|
| **Total**.................... | **46.0** | **54.0** | **24.4** | Asian........................ | 48.7 | 51.3 | 22.3 |
| SEX | | | | Native Hawaiian/ Pacific Islander............... | (NA) | (B) | (B) |
| Male......................... | 41.4 | 58.6 | 28.9 | Two or more races.............. | 42.6 | 57.4 | 24.8 |
| Female...................... | 50.3 | 49.7 | 20.1 | HISPANIC ORIGIN AND RACE | | | |
| AGE [4] | | | | Hispanic or Latino [5]............ | 55.1 | 44.9 | 18.9 |
| 18 to 44 years................. | 39.5 | 60.5 | 30.3 | Not Hispanic or Latino........... | 44.2 | 55.8 | 25.5 |
| 45 to 64 years................. | 48.5 | 51.5 | 20.7 | White, non-Hispanic............ | 41.6 | 58.5 | 26.8 |
| 65 to 74 years................. | 54.6 | 45.4 | 15.7 | Black, non-Hispanic............ | 55.8 | 44.2 | 21.0 |
| 75 years and over.............. | 70.2 | 29.8 | 8.7 | | | | |
| RACE | | | | EDUCATION [6] | | | |
| Single race.................. | 46.1 | 53.9 | 24.4 | | | | |
| White....................... | 44.3 | 55.7 | 25.1 | Less than high school diploma... | 67.1 | 32.9 | 9.0 |
| Black or African American.... | 56.0 | 44.0 | 20.7 | High school diploma or GED [7]... | 56.9 | 43.0 | 15.2 |
| American Indian/ | | | | Some college................. | 48.2 | 51.8 | 21.8 |
| Alaska Native............... | 45.7 | 54.2 | 23.8 | Bachelor's degree or higher...... | 34.1 | 65.8 | 32.6 |

NA Not available. B Base figure too small to meet statistical standards for reliability of a derived figure. [1] "Inactive" is having no leisure-time aerobic activity that lasted at least 10 minutes. "Insufficiently active" is having aerobic activity for 10 minutes or more but less than 150 minutes per week. [2] "Sufficiently active," which meets the aerobic component of the 2008 federal physical activity guidelines, is participating in moderate-intensity leisure-time physical activity 150 minutes or more per week, or in vigorous-intensity leisure-time physical activity 75 minutes or more per week, or an equivalent combination. [3] Persons who are sufficiently active, and who engage in muscle strengthening activities at least 2 times a week. [4] Age data are not age-adjusted. [5] Persons of Hispanic or Latino origin may be of any race. [6] For persons age 25 and over. [7] General educational development high school equivalency diploma.

Source: U.S. National Center for Health Statistics, 2017 National Health Interview Survey, "Tables of Summary Health Statistics," <http://www.cdc.gov/nchs/nhis/SHS.htm>, accessed January 2019.

# Table 228. Overweight and Obesity Prevalence Among Adults Age 20 and Over by Sex, Age, and Race/Ethnicity: 1988 to 2016

[Shown as percent of population age 20 and over. Weight status is determined by body mass index (BMI), which is calculated as weight in kilograms divided by the square of height in meters. Excludes pregnant women. Data are based on the National Health and Nutrition Examination Survey (NHANES); measurements of height and weight of a sample of the civilian noninstitutionalized population were taken without shoes. Percents do not sum to 100 because data for persons with BMI under 18.5 are not shown, and percent of persons with obesity are included with the overweight]

| Characteristics | Normal weight [1] | | | Overweight or obese [2] | | | Obese [3] | | |
|---|---|---|---|---|---|---|---|---|---|
| | 1988 to 1994 | 2001 to 2004 | 2013 to 2016 | 1988 to 1994 | 2001 to 2004 | 2013 to 2016 | 1988 to 1994 | 2001 to 2004 | 2013 to 2016 |
| **Total, age-adjusted [4]** | **41.6** | **32.3** | **27.7** | **56.0** | **66.0** | **70.9** | **22.9** | **31.4** | **38.8** |
| Male | 37.9 | 28.3 | 24.2 | 60.9 | 70.5 | 74.6 | 20.2 | 29.5 | 36.8 |
| Female | 45.0 | 36.1 | 31.0 | 51.4 | 61.6 | 67.4 | 25.5 | 33.2 | 40.7 |
| **Total, crude** | **42.6** | **32.2** | **27.4** | **54.9** | **66.1** | **71.1** | **22.3** | **31.5** | **38.9** |
| Male | 39.4 | 28.4 | 24.4 | 59.4 | 70.4 | 74.3 | 19.5 | 29.5 | 36.6 |
| Female | 45.7 | 35.8 | 30.3 | 50.7 | 61.9 | 68.1 | 25.0 | 33.3 | 41.0 |
| White, non-Hispanic | 43.6 | 33.2 | 27.8 | 53.8 | 65.1 | 70.9 | 21.3 | 30.9 | 37.9 |
| Male | 38.2 | 27.4 | 23.2 | 60.6 | 71.6 | 75.6 | 19.8 | 30.5 | 36.9 |
| Female | 48.8 | 38.8 | 32.1 | 47.4 | 58.7 | 66.3 | 22.7 | 31.2 | 38.8 |
| Black or African American, non-Hispanic | 35.9 | 24.8 | 22.8 | 61.8 | 73.3 | 75.7 | 29.5 | 41.9 | 47.6 |
| Male | 41.5 | 31.5 | 29.2 | 56.7 | 66.3 | 69.8 | 20.7 | 30.7 | 37.5 |
| Female | 31.2 | 19.3 | 17.6 | 66.0 | 79.1 | 80.5 | 36.7 | 51.1 | 56.1 |
| Asian, non-Hispanic | (NA) | (NA) | 53.7 | (NA) | (NA) | 42.6 | (NA) | (NA) | 12.7 |
| Male | (NA) | (NA) | 47.4 | (NA) | (NA) | 49.5 | (NA) | (NA) | 11.7 |
| Female | (NA) | (NA) | 59.2 | (NA) | (NA) | 36.5 | (NA) | (NA) | 13.6 |
| Hispanic [5] | (NA) | (NA) | 19.6 | (NA) | (NA) | 79.6 | (NA) | (NA) | 44.8 |
| Male | (NA) | (NA) | 18.0 | (NA) | (NA) | 81.3 | (NA) | (NA) | 41.2 |
| Female | (NA) | (NA) | 21.3 | (NA) | (NA) | 77.8 | (NA) | (NA) | 48.4 |
| Male by age: | | | | | | | | | |
| 20 to 34 years | 51.1 | 38.3 | 34.6 | 47.5 | 59.0 | 63.0 | 14.1 | 23.2 | 30.7 |
| 35 to 44 years | 33.4 | 26.5 | 19.3 | 65.5 | 72.9 | 80.6 | 21.3 | 33.8 | 43.1 |
| 45 to 54 years | 33.6 | 21.2 | 18.5 | 66.1 | 78.5 | 80.8 | 23.2 | 31.8 | 38.0 |
| 55 to 64 years | 28.6 | 22.2 | 22.3 | 70.5 | 77.3 | 76.7 | 27.2 | 36.0 | 39.3 |
| 65 to 74 years | 30.1 | 23.1 | 19.3 | 68.5 | 76.1 | 79.0 | 24.1 | 32.1 | 40.2 |
| 75 years and over | 40.9 | 32.1 | 24.3 | 56.5 | 66.8 | 74.9 | 13.2 | 19.9 | 28.0 |
| Female by age: | | | | | | | | | |
| 20 to 34 years | 57.9 | 44.2 | 37.5 | 37.0 | 51.6 | 59.6 | 18.5 | 28.6 | 34.8 |
| 35 to 44 years | 47.1 | 38.3 | 31.3 | 49.6 | 60.1 | 67.7 | 25.5 | 33.3 | 43.4 |
| 45 to 54 years | 37.2 | 31.0 | 29.3 | 60.3 | 67.4 | 69.5 | 32.4 | 38.0 | 42.9 |
| 55 to 64 years | 31.5 | 29.2 | 23.8 | 66.3 | 69.9 | 74.5 | 33.7 | 39.0 | 48.2 |
| 65 to 74 years | 37.0 | 27.0 | 23.9 | 60.3 | 71.5 | 75.6 | 26.9 | 37.9 | 43.5 |
| 75 years and over | 43.0 | 34.6 | 31.0 | 52.3 | 63.7 | 67.4 | 19.2 | 23.2 | 32.7 |

NA Not available. [1] Normal weight status is a BMI of 18.5 to 24.9. [2] Overweight or obese is a BMI of 25.0 or more. [3] Obese is a BMI of 30.0 or more. [4] Estimates are age-adjusted to the year 2000 standard population using five age groups: 20–34 years, 35–44 years, 45–54 years, 55–64 years, and 65 years and over. [5] Persons of Hispanic origin may be of any race.

Source: U.S. National Center for Health Statistics, *Health, United States, 2017,* September 2018. See also <http://www.cdc.gov/nchs/hus/>.

# Table 229. Dental Care Visit in the Past Year—Percent of Population by Age and Selected Characteristics: 2000 to 2016

[In percent. Covers civilian noninstitutionalized population who had a dental care visit in the past year. Based on National Health Interview Survey; see Appendix III]

| Characteristic | Age 2 years and over | | | Age 2 to 17 years | | | Age 18 to 64 years | | | Age 65 years and over | | |
|---|---|---|---|---|---|---|---|---|---|---|---|---|
| | 2000 | 2010 | 2016 | 2000 | 2010 | 2016 | 2000 | 2010 | 2016 | 2000 | 2010 | 2016 |
| **Total [1]** | **66.2** | **64.7** | **68.7** | **74.1** | **78.9** | **84.6** | **65.1** | **61.1** | **64.4** | **56.6** | **57.7** | **64.3** |
| Sex: | | | | | | | | | | | | |
| Male | 63.5 | 61.7 | 66.3 | 73.7 | 78.3 | 84.3 | 60.7 | 56.8 | 60.9 | 56.1 | 56.2 | 62.1 |
| Female | 68.8 | 67.5 | 71.0 | 74.6 | 79.6 | 84.9 | 69.4 | 65.4 | 67.8 | 56.9 | 58.9 | 66.2 |
| Race ethnicity: [2] | | | | | | | | | | | | |
| White alone | 67.9 | 65.6 | 69.5 | 75.8 | 79.2 | 84.3 | 67.2 | 62.4 | 65.6 | 58.4 | 59.3 | 66.4 |
| Black or African American alone | 59.5 | 58.8 | 64.7 | 70.0 | 79.0 | 86.6 | 57.1 | 53.1 | 59.1 | 38.2 | 40.6 | 48.4 |
| American Indian/Alaska Native alone | 58.6 | 57.4 | 58.3 | 71.3 | 73.2 | 85.8 | 55.0 | 49.8 | 49.8 | (B) | 72.2 | (B) |
| Asian alone | 67.1 | 66.5 | 69.0 | 72.8 | 74.8 | 84.0 | 65.6 | 64.6 | 66.2 | 60.6 | 61.9 | 60.4 |
| Two or more races | 65.1 | 65.2 | 69.1 | 71.4 | 77.9 | 83.5 | 60.5 | 54.7 | 59.1 | 57.4 | 48.1 | 59.2 |
| Hispanic [3] | 52.3 | 56.5 | 63.4 | 60.6 | 74.8 | 83.7 | 48.6 | 48.5 | 55.3 | 44.5 | 42.1 | 51.8 |
| Percent of poverty level: [4] | | | | | | | | | | | | |
| Below 100% | 50.4 | 50.6 | 57.2 | 62.4 | 73.2 | 80.8 | 46.8 | 41.0 | 49.0 | 33.3 | 32.8 | 37.4 |
| 100% to 199% | 52.2 | 51.6 | 54.9 | 66.1 | 73.4 | 81.3 | 48.4 | 44.1 | 46.4 | 43.0 | 43.8 | 42.8 |
| 200% to 399% | 65.6 | 63.5 | 66.4 | 75.5 | 79.0 | 84.2 | 62.2 | 59.6 | 60.9 | 62.8 | 57.9 | 63.6 |
| 400% or more | 79.5 | 79.3 | 81.2 | 85.9 | 88.0 | 90.0 | 78.5 | 77.5 | 79.1 | 73.8 | 77.2 | 81.8 |

B Base figure too small to meet statistical standards of reliability of a derived figure. Data have a relative standard error greater than 30%. [1] Includes persons of other race and ethnic groups, not shown separately. [2] Race groups include persons of Hispanic and non-Hispanic origin. [3] Persons of Hispanic origin may be of any race. [4] Poverty level is based on family income and family size and composition using Census Bureau poverty thresholds.

Source: U.S. National Center for Health Statistics, *Health, United States, 2017,* September 2018. See also <http://www.cdc.gov/nchs/hus/>.

# Table 230. Sleep—Percent Distribution of Adults Age 18 and Over by Hours of Sleep by Selected Characteristics: 2011 to 2014

[235,845 represents 235,845,000. Data are annualized over 2011-2014 (4-year) period. Estimates are age-adjusted using the projected 2000 U.S. population as the standard population and using three age groups: 18–44 years, 45–64 years, and 65 years and over. All estimates are based on data from the Sample Adult files, which are derived from the Sample Adult component of the National Health Interview Survey. Survey respondents where asked, "On average, how many hours of sleep do you get in a 24 hour period?" Response options were 1-24 hours]

| Characteristic | Adults age 18 and over (1,000) | Hours of sleep (percent distribution) | | |
|---|---|---|---|---|
| | | 6 or less | 7 to 8 | 9 or more |
| Total [1] | 235,845 | 29.7 | 61.6 | 8.7 |
| SEX | | | | |
| Male | 113,760 | 29.6 | 62.4 | 8.0 |
| Female | 122,085 | 29.8 | 60.9 | 9.3 |
| AGE [2] | | | | |
| 18 to 24 years old | 30,153 | 22.9 | 63.6 | 13.4 |
| 25 to 44 years old | 81,276 | 31.8 | 62.4 | 5.8 |
| 45 to 64 years old | 81,945 | 33.8 | 60.1 | 6.2 |
| 65 to 74 years old | 24,278 | 25.1 | 63.6 | 11.3 |
| 75 years old and over | 18,194 | 22.0 | 57.1 | 20.9 |
| RACE | | | | |
| Single race [3] | 232,068 | 29.6 | 61.7 | 8.6 |
| White | 188,610 | 28.3 | 63.0 | 8.7 |
| Black or African American | 28,367 | 37.8 | 52.6 | 9.7 |
| American Indian or Alaska Native | 1,954 | 35.0 | 55.3 | 9.6 |
| Asian | 12,745 | 29.6 | 64.4 | 6.0 |
| Native Hawaiian or Other Pacific Islander | 393 | 47.5 | 44.3 | 8.2 |
| Two or more races [4] | 3,776 | 37.7 | 53.0 | 9.2 |
| Black or African American, white | 753 | 40.5 | 54.3 | 5.2 |
| American Indian or Alaska Native, white | 1,557 | 40.5 | 48.7 | 10.8 |
| HISPANIC ORIGIN AND RACE [5] | | | | |
| Hispanic or Latino | 34,996 | 28.8 | 62.2 | 8.9 |
| Mexican or Mexican American | 21,611 | 26.8 | 63.5 | 9.7 |
| Not Hispanic or Latino | 200,849 | 30.1 | 61.4 | 8.6 |
| White, single race | 156,720 | 28.5 | 62.9 | 8.6 |
| Black or African American, single race | 27,201 | 38.0 | 52.4 | 9.6 |
| EDUCATION [6] | | | | |
| Less than high school graduate | 27,998 | 30.9 | 57.6 | 11.4 |
| GED diploma [7] | 6,018 | 37.3 | 53.2 | 9.5 |
| High school graduate | 46,650 | 32.1 | 59.1 | 8.8 |
| Some college, no degree | 35,745 | 35.2 | 57.3 | 7.5 |
| Associate of arts degree | 23,771 | 33.3 | 59.2 | 7.5 |
| Bachelor of arts, science degree | 40,524 | 27.0 | 67.3 | 5.7 |
| Masters, doctorate, medical degree | 23,877 | 24.5 | 70.3 | 5.3 |
| POVERTY STATUS [8] | | | | |
| Below poverty level | 32,666 | 33.6 | 55.0 | 11.4 |
| 100% to less than 200% poverty level | 45,025 | 32.2 | 57.2 | 10.6 |
| 200% to less than 400% poverty level | 70,656 | 30.4 | 60.9 | 8.7 |
| 400% or more of poverty level | 87,498 | 26.8 | 66.6 | 6.5 |
| MARITAL STATUS | | | | |
| Never married | 52,245 | 28.9 | 60.5 | 10.6 |
| Married | 124,885 | 29.0 | 64.0 | 7.1 |
| Cohabiting | 17,226 | 32.4 | 58.6 | 9.0 |
| Divorced or separated | 26,937 | 38.5 | 54.0 | 7.6 |
| Widowed | 14,165 | 38.4 | 54.0 | 7.7 |

[1] Includes persons of other races and unknown race and ethnicity, unknown education, unknown poverty status, and unknown marital status. [2] Estimates for age groups are not age adjusted. [3] Refers to persons who indicated only a single race group, including those of Hispanic or Latino origin. [4] Refers to all persons who indicated more than one race group, including those of Hispanic or Latino origin. [5] Persons of Hispanic or Latino origin may be of any race or combination of races. [6] Shown only for adults age 25 and over. Estimates are age adjusted to the projected 2000 U.S. population as the standard population using three age groups: 25–44, 45–64, and 65 and over. [7] General Educational Development high school equivalency diploma. [8] Based on family income and family size using the U.S. Census Bureau poverty thresholds for 2010, 2011, 2012, and 2013.

Source: U.S. National Center for Health Statistics, National Health Interview Survey, "Tables of Summary Health Statistics," <http://www.cdc.gov/nchs/nhis/SHS.htm>, accessed February 2017.

# Table 231. Depression and Receipt of Mental Health Treatment in the Past Year Among Adults Age 18 and Over by Selected Characteristics: 2016 and 2017

[In thousands (16,225 represents 16,225,000), except percent. Based on the National Survey on Drug Use and Health. Covers adults who had a major depressive episode as defined in the 5th edition of the *Diagnostic and Statistical Manual of Mental Disorders* (DSM-5), which specifies a period of at least 2 weeks when a person experienced a depressed mood or loss of interest or pleasure in daily activities and had a majority of specified depression symptoms. Treatment is defined as seeing or talking to a professional or using prescription medication for depression in the past year; respondents with unknown treatment data were excluded]

| Characteristic | Had major depressive episode (MDE) | | | | Those with an MDE who received treatment for depression | | | |
| --- | --- | --- | --- | --- | --- | --- | --- | --- |
| | 2016 | | 2017 | | 2016 | | 2017 | |
| | Number (1,000) | Percent of population | Number (1,000) | Percent of population | Number (1,000) | Percent | Number (1,000) | Percent |
| Total | 16,225 | 6.7 | 17,297 | 7.1 | 10,574 | 65.3 | 11,548 | 66.8 |
| **AGE** | | | | | | | | |
| 18 to 25 years old | 3,705 | 10.9 | 4,416 | 13.1 | 1,631 | 44.1 | 2,238 | 50.7 |
| 26 to 49 years old | 7,236 | 7.4 | 7,635 | 7.7 | 4,871 | 67.4 | 5,128 | 67.3 |
| 50 years old and older | 5,284 | 4.8 | 5,245 | 4.7 | 4,072 | 77.3 | 4,182 | 79.7 |
| **SEX AND AGE** | | | | | | | | |
| Male | 5,639 | 4.8 | 6,266 | 5.3 | 3,174 | 56.6 | 3,650 | 58.3 |
| 18 to 25 years old | 1,357 | 7.9 | 1,618 | 9.5 | 507 | 37.3 | 701 | 43.3 |
| 26 to 49 years old | 2,620 | 5.4 | 2,744 | 5.6 | 1,534 | 58.7 | 1,500 | 54.7 |
| 50 years old and older | 1,662 | 3.2 | 1,904 | 3.7 | 1,134 | 69.0 | 1,449 | 76.1 |
| Female | 10,586 | 8.5 | 11,031 | 8.7 | 7,400 | 69.9 | 7,898 | 71.7 |
| 18 to 25 years old | 2,349 | 13.8 | 2,799 | 16.6 | 1,124 | 47.9 | 1,537 | 55.0 |
| 26 to 49 years old | 4,616 | 9.3 | 4,891 | 9.7 | 3,338 | 72.3 | 3,628 | 74.4 |
| 50 years old and older | 3,622 | 6.2 | 3,341 | 5.6 | 2,938 | 81.1 | 2,733 | 81.8 |
| **RACE AND HISPANIC ORIGIN** | | | | | | | | |
| Not Hispanic or Latino | 14,088 | 6.9 | 15,188 | 7.4 | 9,448 | 67.2 | 10,370 | 68.4 |
| White | 11,551 | 7.4 | 12,398 | 7.9 | 8,037 | 69.7 | 8,737 | 70.5 |
| Black or African American | 1,409 | 5.0 | 1,579 | 5.4 | 855 | 60.8 | 994 | 63.1 |
| American Indian or Alaska Native | 120 | 8.7 | 102 | 8.0 | (B) | (B) | (B) | (B) |
| Native Hawaiian or other Pacific Islander | 79 | 7.3 | 45 | 4.7 | (B) | (B) | (B) | (B) |
| Asian | 511 | 3.9 | 600 | 4.4 | (B) | (B) | 251 | 41.9 |
| Two or more races | 419 | 10.5 | 465 | 11.3 | 244 | 58.4 | 296 | 64.8 |
| Hispanic or Latino | 2,137 | 5.6 | 2,109 | 5.4 | 1,126 | 52.7 | 1,178 | 55.9 |

B Low precision; does not meet statistical standards for reliability of a derived figure.

Source: U.S. Substance Abuse and Mental Health Services Administration, *Results from the 2017 National Survey on Drug Use and Health: Detailed Tables,* September 2018. See also <https://www.samhsa.gov/data/data-we-collect/nsduh-national-survey-drug-use-and-health>.

# Table 232. Children With Allergies by Type and Selected Characteristics: 2017

[In percent, except as indicated (73,529 represents 73,529,000). Covers incidence of allergies in the past 12 months among children under age 18. A child may have multiple types of allergies. Based on household interviews of a sample of the civilian noninstitutionalized population, regarding the sample child, not all children in the family. Percent data are age-adjusted, except as indicated. Unknowns for the columns were not included in the denominators when calculating percentages]

| Selected characteristic | Total (1,000) | Hay fever | Respiratory allergies | Food allergies | Skin allergies |
| --- | --- | --- | --- | --- | --- |
| Total [1] | 73,529 | 7.6 | 10.8 | 6.5 | 13.5 |
| **SEX** | | | | | |
| Male | 37,520 | 8.0 | 12.7 | 7.0 | 12.9 |
| Female | 36,009 | 7.3 | 8.9 | 5.9 | 14.1 |
| **AGE [2]** | | | | | |
| 4 years and under | 19,694 | 3.4 | 6.8 | 6.6 | 15.1 |
| 5 to 11 years | 28,875 | 7.9 | 11.7 | 6.8 | 13.9 |
| 12 to 17 years | 24,960 | 10.8 | 13.1 | 6.0 | 11.8 |
| **RACE** | | | | | |
| Single race [3] | 69,897 | 7.6 | 10.6 | 6.3 | 13.3 |
| White | 53,672 | 8.2 | 11.2 | 6.3 | 12.5 |
| Black or African American | 10,796 | 5.3 | 10.5 | 6.6 | 17.5 |
| American Indian or Alaska Native | 1,063 | (B) | (B) | (B) | (B) |
| Asian | 4,189 | 6.2 | 4.2 | 5.9 | 12.8 |
| Native Hawaiian or Other Pacific Islander | 177 | (B) | (B) | (B) | (B) |
| Two or more races [3] | 3,632 | 9.4 | 15.2 | 9.1 | 18.1 |
| **HISPANIC ORIGIN AND RACE [4]** | | | | | |
| Hispanic or Latino | 18,490 | 4.8 | 7.8 | 4.4 | 10.7 |
| Not Hispanic or Latino | 55,039 | 8.6 | 11.9 | 7.2 | 14.4 |
| White only | 37,781 | 9.5 | 12.6 | 7.2 | 13.7 |
| Black or African American only | 9,761 | 5.7 | 10.9 | 7.2 | 17.7 |

B Estimate is considered unreliable. [1] Total includes children of other races not shown separately, and children with unknown health status. [2] Estimates for age groups are not age-adjusted. [3] Includes children of Hispanic or Latino origin. [4] Children of Hispanic or Latino origin may be of any race or combination of races.

Source: U.S. National Center for Health Statistics, 2017 National Health Interview Survey, "Tables of Summary Health Statistics," <https://www.cdc.gov/nchs/nhis/shs.htm>, accessed January 2019.

## Table 233. Learning Disability and Attention Deficit Hyperactivity Disorder Among Children Age 3 to 17 Years by Selected Characteristics: 2017

[In thousands (62,076 represents 62,076,000), except percent. Learning disability is based on the question, "Has a representative from a school or a health professional ever told you that (child's name) had a learning disability?" Attention deficit hyperactivity disorder is based on the question, "Has a doctor or other health professional ever told you that (child's name) had attention deficit hyperactivity disorder or attention deficit disorder?" Based on household interviews of a sample of the civilian noninstitutionalized population regarding the sample child, not all children in the family]

| Selected characteristic | Total | Ever told child had— | | | |
| | | Learning disability | | Attention deficit hyperactivity disorder | |
| | | Number [1] | Percent [2] | Number [1] | Percent [2] |
|---|---|---|---|---|---|
| **Total [3]**..... | **62,076** | **5,040** | **8.1** | **5,833** | **9.4** |
| SEX | | | | | |
| Male..... | 31,662 | 3,104 | 9.8 | 4,079 | 12.9 |
| Female..... | 30,413 | 1,935 | 6.4 | 1,753 | 5.8 |
| AGE [4] | | | | | |
| 3 to 4 years..... | 8,240 | 285 | 3.5 | 77 | 0.9 |
| 5 to 11 years..... | 28,875 | 2,210 | 7.7 | 2,485 | 8.6 |
| 12 to 17 years..... | 24,960 | 2,545 | 10.2 | 3,270 | 13.1 |
| RACE | | | | | |
| Single race [5]..... | 59,157 | 4,843 | 8.2 | 5,457 | 9.3 |
| White..... | 45,356 | 3,719 | 8.2 | 4,362 | 9.6 |
| Black or African American..... | 9,119 | 898 | 9.9 | 929 | 10.2 |
| American Indian or Alaska Native..... | 806 | 79 | (B) | (B) | (B) |
| Asian..... | 3,733 | 139 | 3.7 | 84 | 2.2 |
| Native Hawaiian or other Pacific Islander..... | 142 | (B) | (B) | (B) | (B) |
| Two or more races [6]..... | 2,919 | 197 | 6.7 | 376 | 12.7 |
| Black or African American and White..... | 1,339 | (B) | (B) | 233 | 17.2 |
| American Indian or Alaska Native and White..... | 483 | (B) | (B) | (B) | (B) |
| HISPANIC ORIGIN AND RACE [7] | | | | | |
| Hispanic or Latino..... | 15,343 | 1,360 | 8.9 | 1,093 | 7.2 |
| Mexican or Mexican American..... | 10,003 | 820 | 8.2 | 652 | 6.6 |
| Not Hispanic or Latino..... | 46,733 | 3,679 | 7.9 | 4,740 | 10.1 |
| White, single race..... | 32,117 | 2,582 | 8.0 | 3,457 | 10.7 |
| Black or African American, single race..... | 8,272 | 796 | 9.7 | 822 | 10.0 |
| CURRENT HEALTH STATUS | | | | | |
| Excellent or very good..... | 52,400 | 3,246 | 6.2 | 4,449 | 8.6 |
| Good..... | 8,555 | 1,475 | 17.2 | 1,181 | 13.6 |
| Fair or poor..... | 1,116 | 319 | 31.2 | 203 | 19.3 |

B Estimate is considered unreliable. [1] Unknowns for the columns are not included in the frequencies, but they are included in the "Total" column. [2] Unknowns for the column variables are not included in the denominators when calculating percentages. Percents are age-adjusted to the projected 2000 U.S. standard population using age groups 3-4 years, 5-11 years, and 12-17 years, except for data shown by age group. [3] Includes other races not shown separately, and children with unknown health status. [4] Estimates for age groups are not age adjusted. [5] Refers to children of only a single race group, including those of Hispanic or Latino origin. [6] Refers to children of more than once race group, including those of Hispanic or Latino origin. [7] Persons of Hispanic or Latino origin may be of any race.

Source: U.S. National Center for Health Statistics, 2017 National Health Interview Survey, "Tables of Summary Health Statistics," <https://www.cdc.gov/nchs/nhis/shs.htm>, accessed January 2019.

## Table 234. Autism and Other Developmental Disability Prevalence Among Children Age 3 to 17: 2014 to 2016

[As percent of all children age 3 to 17. Covers the 3-year period 2014 to 2016. Based on the National Health Interview Survey that asked the parent or guardian whether their child had been diagnosed with a developmental delay. Excludes conditions such as attention-deficit/ hyperactivity disorder (ADHD), and learning disabilities. The NHIS is a nationally representative survey of the noninstitutionalized population. The Sample Child component of the NHIS collects information about one randomly selected child per family]

| Characteristic | Any developmental disability [1] | Autism spectrum disorder [2] | Intellectual disability [3] | Other developmental delay [4] |
|---|---|---|---|---|
| **Total**..... | **6.27** | **2.47** | **1.19** | **3.89** |
| By sex: | | | | |
| Male..... | 8.15 | 3.63 | 1.48 | 4.77 |
| Female..... | 4.29 | 1.25 | 0.90 | 2.98 |
| By age: | | | | |
| 3 to 7 years..... | 6.18 | 2.23 | 0.73 | 4.37 |
| 8 to 12 years..... | 6.87 | 2.88 | 1.45 | 4.24 |
| 13 to 17 years..... | 5.76 | 2.30 | 1.40 | 3.08 |
| By race/ethnicity: | | | | |
| White, non-Hispanic..... | 7.04 | 2.76 | 1.10 | 4.43 |
| Black, non-Hispanic..... | 6.20 | 2.49 | 1.53 | 3.67 |
| Other, non-Hispanic..... | 6.16 | 2.48 | 0.86 | 3.62 |
| Hispanic [5]..... | 4.69 | 1.82 | 1.33 | 2.98 |

[1] A composite measure of children with a diagnosis of autism spectrum disorder, intellectual disability, or any other developmental delay. [2] Based on positive responses to the question, "Has a doctor or health professional ever told you that [sample child] had Autism, Asperger's disorder, pervasive developmental disorder, or autism spectrum disorder?" [3] Based on positive responses to the question, "Has a doctor or health professional ever told you that [sample child] had an intellectual disability, also known as mental retardation?" [4] Based on positive responses to the question, "Has a doctor or health professional ever told you that [sample child] had any other developmental delay?" [5] Persons of Hispanic origin may be of any race.

Source: U.S. National Center for Health Statistics, *Estimated Prevalence of Children With Diagnosed Developmental Disabilities in the United States, 2014–2016*, Data Brief No. 291, November 2017. See also <https://www.cdc.gov/nchs/nhis/nhis_products.htm>.

# Table 235. Children Under Age 18 Receiving Special Education or Early Intervention Services: 2016 and 2017

[In thousands (73,564 represents 73,564,000), except percent. Percents are age-adjusted. Receiving special education or early intervention services is based on the question, "Do any of these family members (under 18 years of age) receive special education or early intervention services?" Based on household interviews of a sample of the civilian noninstitutionalized population, and about all children in the family]

| Selected characteristic | 2016 | | | 2017 | | |
| --- | --- | --- | --- | --- | --- | --- |
| | | Children receiving special education or early intervention services | | | Children receiving special education or early intervention services | |
| | Total | Number [1] | Percent [2] | Total | Number [1] | Percent [2] |
| Total [3]......................... | **73,564** | **6,042** | **8.2** | **73,528** | **6,259** | **8.5** |
| *SEX* | | | | | | |
| Male................................ | 37,542 | 3,996 | 10.7 | 37,520 | 4,114 | 11.0 |
| Female.............................. | 36,022 | 2,046 | 5.7 | 36,009 | 2,145 | 6 |
| *AGE [4]* | | | | | | |
| 4 years and under................... | 19,880 | 808 | 4.1 | 19,852 | 992 | 5.0 |
| 5 to 11 years....................... | 28,776 | 2,800 | 9.8 | 28,844 | 2,882 | 10.0 |
| 12 to 17 years...................... | 24,909 | 2,434 | 9.8 | 24,832 | 2,385 | 9.6 |
| *RACE* | | | | | | |
| Single race [5]..................... | 69,872 | 5,743 | 8.2 | 70,076 | 5,884 | 8.4 |
| White............................ | 54,115 | 4,540 | 8.4 | 53,696 | 4,684 | 8.7 |
| Black or African American........ | 10,686 | 969 | 9.1 | 10,920 | 974 | 8.9 |
| American Indian or Alaska Native... | 1,005 | 72 | 7.3 | 1,078 | 88 | 8.0 |
| Asian............................ | 3,863 | 138 | 3.5 | 4,170 | 124 | 2.9 |
| Native Hawaiian or other Pacific Islander......................... | 204 | (B) | (B) | 212 | (B) | (B) |
| Two or more races [6].............. | 3,692 | 299 | 8.7 | 3,453 | 375 | 11.3 |
| *HISPANIC ORIGIN AND RACE [7]* | | | | | | |
| Hispanic or Latino.................. | 18,310 | 1,405 | 7.7 | 18,490 | 1,383 | 7.5 |
| Mexican or Mexican American...... | 11,707 | 787 | 6.8 | 11,922 | 865 | 7.3 |
| Not Hispanic or Latino.............. | 55,254 | 4,637 | 8.4 | 55,038 | 4,877 | 8.9 |
| White, single race............... | 37,934 | 3,284 | 8.7 | 37,805 | 3,558 | 9.4 |
| Black or African American, single race. .. | 9,902 | 879 | 8.9 | 9,883 | 855 | 8.6 |

B Estimate is considered unreliable. [1] Unknowns for the columns are not included in the frequencies, but they are included in the "Total" column. [2] Unknowns for the column variables are not included in the denominators when calculating percentages. Percents are age-adjusted to the 2000 projected U.S. standard population using the age groups shown; data by age group are not age-adjusted. [3] Includes other races not shown separately. [4] Estimates for the age groups are not age-adjusted. [5] Refers to persons who indicated only a single race group, including those of Hispanic or Latino origin. [6] Refers to all persons who indicated more than one race group, including those of Hispanic or Latino origin. [7] Persons of Hispanic or Latino origin may be of any race.

Source: U.S. National Center for Health Statistics, 2016 and 2017 National Health Interview Surveys, "Tables of Summary Health Statistics," <https://www.cdc.gov/nchs/nhis/shs.htm>, accessed January 2019.

# Table 236. Children and Youth With Disabilities Receiving Special Education and Related Services by Type of Disability: 2000 to 2017

[In thousands (5,773.9 represents 5,773,900). As of Fall. For children and youth age 6 to 21 receiving special education and related services under the Individuals with Disabilities Education Act (IDEA) Part B. Includes outlying areas]

| Disability | 2000 | 2005 | 2010 | 2013 | 2014 | 2015 | 2016 | 2017 |
| --- | --- | --- | --- | --- | --- | --- | --- | --- |
| Total........................ | **5,773.9** | **6,109.6** | **5,834.9** | **5,847.6** | **5,944.2** | **6,050.7** | **6,048.9** | **6,130.6** |
| Autism............................ | 79.6 | 193.6 | 370.6 | 479.0 | 513.7 | 550.4 | 578.8 | 616.2 |
| Deaf-blindness.................... | 1.3 | 1.6 | 1.3 | 1.3 | 1.2 | 1.3 | 1.3 | 1.3 |
| Developmental delay [1]........... | 28.6 | 79.1 | 109.4 | 133.8 | 141.9 | 149.3 | 154.0 | 159.5 |
| Emotional disturbance............. | 474.3 | 472.4 | 388.2 | 352.3 | 347.8 | 346.5 | 335.3 | 335.0 |
| Hearing impairment............... | 70.8 | 72.4 | 69.9 | 68.2 | 67.9 | 67.4 | 65.5 | 64.8 |
| Intellectual disability............... | 613.4 | 545.5 | 445.8 | 417.6 | 415.3 | 418.5 | 416.2 | 418.4 |
| Multiple disabilities............... | 122.9 | 133.9 | 123.8 | 125.6 | 125.5 | 125.2 | 125.9 | 122.4 |
| Orthopedic impairment............ | 73.0 | 63.1 | 55.8 | 50.3 | 46.3 | 41.2 | 36.3 | 34.9 |
| Other health impairment.......... | 294.0 | 561.0 | 706.1 | 809.9 | 857.5 | 907.2 | 934.0 | 970.0 |
| Specific learning disability........ | 2,881.6 | 2,780.2 | 2,420.0 | 2,311.1 | 2,328.5 | 2,348.9 | 2,337.0 | 2,339.9 |
| Speech or language impairment..... | 1,093.4 | 1,157.2 | 1,093.7 | 1,047.7 | 1,047.6 | 1,044.3 | 1,014.8 | 1,018.5 |
| Traumatic brain injury............. | 14.9 | 23.5 | 24.7 | 25.3 | 25.4 | 25.5 | 25.2 | 25.3 |
| Visual impairment................. | 26.0 | 26.0 | 25.7 | 25.5 | 25.6 | 24.9 | 24.7 | 24.4 |

[1] States had the option of reporting children ages 3 to 9 under developmental delay beginning 1997.

Source: U.S. Department of Education, Office of Special Education Programs, "IDEA Section 618 Data Products: State Level Data Files," <https://www2.ed.gov/programs/osepidea/618-data/index.html>, accessed January 2019.

# Table 237. Immunization of Children Age 19 to 35 Months by Vaccine Type and State: 2017

[In percent. Covers civilian noninstitutionalized children age 19 months to 35 months; born January 2014 to May 2016. Based on estimates from the National Immunization Survey (NIS). The NIS consists of a household survey, and a survey of health care providers of the children to verify and/or complete vaccination information. Abbreviations: DTaP = diphtheria and tetanus toxoids, and acellular pertussis vaccine; MMR = measles, mumps, and rubella vaccine; HepB = hepatitis B vaccine; HepA = hepatitis A vaccine; Hib = Haemophilus influenzae type b vaccine; PCV = pneumococcal conjugate vaccine]

| State | DTaP, ≥3 doses | DTaP, ≥4 doses | Polio, ≥3 doses | MMR, ≥1 dose | Hib, primary series[1] | Hib, full series[1] | HepB, ≥3 doses | HepB, birth dose[2] | Varicella, ≥1 dose | PCV, ≥3 doses | PCV, ≥4 doses | HepA, ≥2 doses | Rotavirus[3] | Combined series[4] |
|---|---|---|---|---|---|---|---|---|---|---|---|---|---|---|
| U.S.[5] | 94.0 | 83.2 | 92.7 | 91.5 | 92.8 | 80.7 | 91.4 | 73.6 | 91.0 | 91.9 | 82.4 | 59.7 | 73.2 | 70.4 |
| AL | 95.5 | 81.4 | 94.2 | 92.3 | 95.4 | 79.7 | 92.1 | 77.6 | 92.0 | 95.5 | 82.0 | 61.1 | 74.2 | 71.2 |
| AK | 92.8 | 75.1 | 90.3 | 89.3 | 93.2 | 82.4 | 91.9 | 70.8 | 85.6 | 92.6 | 79.5 | 53.6 | 72.4 | 69.5 |
| AZ | 95.4 | 82.2 | 94.3 | 91.7 | 93.5 | 78.7 | 91.6 | 80.0 | 92.4 | 92.5 | 79.1 | 62.9 | 70.6 | 66.5 |
| AR | 92.2 | 80.0 | 91.5 | 92.6 | 89.8 | 79.7 | 92.1 | 80.2 | 91.2 | 88.9 | 79.2 | 58.9 | 70.7 | 69.4 |
| CA | 94.6 | 83.9 | 91.9 | 92.9 | 93.5 | 80.5 | 90.9 | 66.1 | 92.6 | 90.1 | 81.0 | 65.0 | 64.7 | 68.6 |
| CO | 92.0 | 79.9 | 90.9 | 87.2 | 89.6 | 78.6 | 88.2 | 73.9 | 87.6 | 90.0 | 79.6 | 57.0 | 73.7 | 71.0 |
| CT | 96.5 | 86.8 | 94.0 | 94.6 | 96.6 | 85.4 | 93.2 | 78.5 | 95.4 | 93.6 | 87.7 | 73.0 | 84.0 | 75.3 |
| DE | 96.0 | 88.9 | 95.4 | 92.9 | 95.2 | 90.7 | 89.4 | 72.9 | 92.1 | 96.0 | 92.0 | 69.6 | 84.3 | 77.1 |
| DC | 92.9 | 85.3 | 91.3 | 94.1 | 93.4 | 79.7 | 90.3 | 69.8 | 93.5 | 90.5 | 85.2 | 72.9 | 77.3 | 74.0 |
| FL | 92.5 | 85.3 | 92.4 | 91.9 | 90.8 | 81.7 | 90.4 | 66.0 | 93.2 | 90.1 | 83.8 | 53.6 | 69.1 | 76.2 |
| GA | 95.2 | 80.1 | 92.8 | 90.7 | 90.7 | 76.7 | 93.3 | 74.6 | 92.4 | 92.9 | 79.4 | 64.3 | 71.2 | 65.6 |
| HI | 91.5 | 82.3 | 90.3 | 90.5 | 90.3 | 77.9 | 89.0 | 76.3 | 90.0 | 88.0 | 80.2 | 56.2 | 73.2 | 69.8 |
| ID | 92.6 | 82.3 | 90.8 | 92.2 | 92.0 | 83.8 | 90.7 | 75.6 | 90.1 | 91.8 | 82.4 | 66.0 | 78.5 | 69.2 |
| IL | 96.1 | 84.4 | 95.6 | 91.9 | 95.4 | 84.6 | 92.9 | 73.4 | 92.4 | 94.8 | 84.1 | 60.0 | 75.4 | 75.4 |
| IN | 93.2 | 82.1 | 91.1 | 87.0 | 90.6 | 74.6 | 90.1 | 78.0 | 86.4 | 90.4 | 79.4 | 63.9 | 77.6 | 66.3 |
| IA | 96.1 | 83.9 | 95.7 | 91.5 | 94.9 | 80.4 | 95.2 | 82.3 | 90.1 | 95.1 | 86.2 | 64.4 | 76.4 | 72.8 |
| KS | 93.6 | 78.5 | 93.3 | 89.8 | 94.3 | 82.7 | 91.5 | 72.6 | 87.1 | 92.5 | 83.0 | 63.2 | 75.5 | 69.5 |
| KY | 97.0 | 84.6 | 96.0 | 92.7 | 96.7 | 81.1 | 93.7 | 84.1 | 92.3 | 95.3 | 84.9 | 58.6 | 80.4 | 71.0 |
| LA | 94.6 | 80.7 | 93.4 | 91.3 | 94.9 | 83.6 | 96.4 | 78.6 | 89.8 | 93.7 | 80.7 | 53.2 | 72.4 | 70.0 |
| ME | 94.7 | 90.3 | 92.7 | 93.7 | 92.4 | 83.5 | 88.9 | 63.1 | 91.6 | 89.6 | 82.4 | 61.0 | 75.6 | 72.7 |
| MD | 93.3 | 82.4 | 90.9 | 92.4 | 91.5 | 80.7 | 89.2 | 76.0 | 90.2 | 92.8 | 80.8 | 59.3 | 74.6 | 75.2 |
| MA | 96.8 | 92.6 | 96.1 | 98.3 | 94.7 | 89.4 | 92.9 | 75.0 | 97.6 | 96.8 | 92.0 | 56.9 | 80.1 | 82.1 |
| MI | 97.4 | 81.3 | 96.4 | 92.2 | 95.0 | 80.0 | 93.7 | 81.2 | 93.9 | 93.6 | 82.6 | 61.4 | 76.0 | 69.9 |
| MN | 96.9 | 83.3 | 96.2 | 94.3 | 97.0 | 76.6 | 92.4 | 72.1 | 93.1 | 92.9 | 80.5 | 56.1 | 70.9 | 66.1 |
| MS | 96.0 | 82.9 | 94.1 | 91.8 | 95.1 | 78.9 | 93.7 | 71.0 | 92.4 | 95.4 | 83.8 | 49.8 | 75.6 | 68.7 |
| MO | 90.4 | 77.0 | 89.3 | 85.8 | 90.2 | 80.4 | 89.0 | 80.4 | 85.9 | 89.4 | 79.0 | 43.9 | 74.7 | 71.2 |
| MT | 94.3 | 80.1 | 92.7 | 92.3 | 93.8 | 86.0 | 92.4 | 72.7 | 90.3 | 94.0 | 84.1 | 52.8 | 73.2 | 66.2 |
| NE | 95.4 | 86.4 | 94.8 | 93.7 | 94.8 | 85.1 | 93.7 | 83.1 | 93.4 | 94.0 | 86.1 | 68.3 | 78.7 | 77.9 |
| NV | 93.7 | 82.0 | 94.1 | 92.4 | 93.1 | 81.8 | 95.6 | 80.6 | 93.8 | 93.3 | 81.4 | 66.4 | 66.0 | 71.3 |
| NH | 97.9 | 89.8 | 97.9 | 94.1 | 97.2 | 87.5 | 93.9 | 67.2 | 92.1 | 97.3 | 88.8 | 64.9 | 84.5 | 78.9 |
| NJ | 95.0 | 82.8 | 92.5 | 89.0 | 92.6 | 82.0 | 91.2 | 60.0 | 90.8 | 92.0 | 84.1 | 49.5 | 70.2 | 69.3 |
| NM | 94.0 | 88.1 | 93.4 | 89.3 | 94.0 | 83.2 | 92.4 | 71.7 | 86.4 | 93.6 | 81.6 | 67.3 | 76.4 | 71.9 |
| NY | 94.9 | 83.3 | 93.3 | 92.5 | 93.2 | 79.0 | 91.9 | 71.3 | 91.4 | 91.5 | 80.4 | 56.2 | 74.3 | 67.5 |
| NC | 92.8 | 86.7 | 91.1 | 92.2 | 92.2 | 79.5 | 88.8 | 77.7 | 91.0 | 92.8 | 04.0 | 56.1 | 79.1 | 70.9 |
| ND | 96.9 | 86.1 | 96.2 | 95.7 | 94.0 | 89.8 | 97.7 | 84.0 | 95.0 | 95.4 | 88.1 | 73.3 | 83.1 | 78.8 |
| OH | 89.5 | 81.1 | 88.2 | 88.3 | 88.8 | 76.7 | 89.5 | 76.5 | 85.2 | 88.9 | 78.8 | 51.0 | 67.2 | 66.4 |
| OK | 93.0 | 78.5 | 92.7 | 91.7 | 93.0 | 77.8 | 89.8 | 78.8 | 91.5 | 89.6 | 70.7 | 62.7 | 67.3 | 67.3 |
| OR | 88.1 | 79.7 | 86.4 | 90.3 | 87.0 | 80.3 | 89.0 | 76.4 | 88.9 | 87.0 | 77.6 | 59.3 | 74.1 | 70.3 |
| PA | 92.9 | 83.1 | 92.0 | 91.7 | 91.0 | 78.5 | 93.3 | 78.9 | 88.4 | 91.0 | 83.0 | 57.8 | 74.4 | 70.4 |
| RI | 97.7 | 89.2 | 97.3 | 95.3 | 96.3 | 84.1 | 96.9 | 75.7 | 94.6 | 94.8 | 89.2 | 69.0 | 85.1 | 74.4 |
| SC | 94.2 | 81.4 | 92.8 | 88.0 | 93.8 | 75.4 | 94.3 | 72.4 | 90.3 | 91.3 | 80.5 | 58.3 | 67.2 | 66.0 |
| SD | 90.5 | 81.8 | 90.3 | 89.9 | 91.4 | 79.8 | 90.4 | 80.2 | 89.9 | 89.7 | 83.1 | 62.3 | 75.9 | 74.7 |
| TN | 94.2 | 88.5 | 93.9 | 92.3 | 92.9 | 86.6 | 95.0 | 73.9 | 93.1 | 93.3 | 87.0 | 67.2 | 75.6 | 79.3 |
| TX | 94.0 | 81.2 | 93.1 | 90.3 | 92.7 | 80.9 | 90.1 | 76.3 | 89.1 | 92.5 | 83.0 | 62.7 | 76.0 | 67.8 |
| UT | 90.8 | 80.6 | 90.3 | 88.7 | 91.0 | 79.3 | 90.5 | 78.2 | 86.9 | 90.1 | 81.1 | 59.6 | 77.0 | 67.9 |
| VT | 95.0 | 85.5 | 93.9 | 93.7 | 93.4 | 83.8 | 92.3 | 52.4 | 88.6 | 94.2 | 89.6 | 58.1 | 75.8 | 74.0 |
| VA | 98.0 | 92.8 | 96.9 | 97.6 | 97.1 | 87.6 | 92.9 | 71.0 | 97.2 | 95.1 | 90.9 | 58.4 | 81.2 | 77.1 |
| WA | 89.8 | 81.0 | 88.7 | 88.5 | 89.8 | 78.8 | 88.3 | 67.4 | 89.2 | 89.1 | 81.3 | 60.8 | 73.6 | 69.9 |
| WV | 93.8 | 85.3 | 92.7 | 89.9 | 92.7 | 82.4 | 90.5 | 69.7 | 92.3 | 93.3 | 85.9 | 70.3 | 77.4 | 74.7 |
| WI | 91.4 | 81.1 | 89.7 | 89.9 | 92.4 | 81.9 | 90.3 | 80.9 | 87.1 | 89.9 | 80.6 | 56.6 | 79.1 | 69.2 |
| WY | 93.4 | 77.6 | 92.9 | 89.1 | 92.0 | 81.1 | 92.1 | 65.8 | 89.2 | 91.9 | 84.3 | 46.4 | 78.2 | 72.0 |
| GU | 87.1 | 67.1 | 82.0 | 82.5 | 82.4 | 62.6 | 84.7 | 91.6 | 76.3 | 82.8 | 64.6 | 50.2 | 51.8 | 49.1 |

[1] Hib primary series: receipt of ≥2 or ≥3 doses, depending on product type received. Full series: receipt of ≥3 or ≥4 doses, depending on product type received (primary series and booster dose). [2] HepB administered from birth through age 3 days. [3] ≥2 or ≥3 doses of Rotavirus vaccine, depending on product type received. [4] The combined 7 vaccine series (4:3:1:3*:3:1:4) includes ≥4 doses of DTaP, ≥3 doses of poliovirus vaccine, ≥1 dose of measles-containing vaccine, full series of Hib vaccine (≥3 or ≥4 doses, depending on product type), ≥3 doses of HepB, ≥1 dose of varicella vaccine, and ≥4 doses of PCV. [5] U.S. total does not include U.S. territories.

Source: U.S. Centers for Disease Control and Prevention, Immunization Managers, "ChildVaxView," <https://www.cdc.gov/vaccines/imz-managers/coverage/childvaxview/index.html>, accessed March 2019.

## Table 238. Child Immunization Rates by Vaccine, Race/Ethnicity, and Poverty Status: 2010 and 2017

[In percent. Covers civilian noninstitutionalized children age 19 months to 35 months. Based on estimates from the National Immunization Survey (NIS). The survey also contacts the health care providers of the children to verify and/or complete vaccination information. Results are based on race/ethnic status of the child as reported by parent or guardian. DTaP = diphtheria, tetanus toxoids, and acellular pertussis vaccine; MMR = measles, mumps, and rubella vaccine; Hib = Haemophilus influenzae type b vaccine; HepB = hepatitis B vaccine; PCV = pneumococcal conjugate vaccine; HepA = hepatitis A vaccine]

| Vaccination | 2010, total | 2017 [1] Total | White [2] | Black [2] | His-panic [3] | American Indian/ Alaska Native only [2] | Asian [2] | At or above poverty | Below poverty |
|---|---|---|---|---|---|---|---|---|---|
| DTaP, ≥3 doses | 95.0 | 94.0 | 93.9 | 92.2 | 94.7 | 89.8 | 97.6 | 94.7 | 92.4 |
| DTaP, ≥4 doses | 84.4 | 83.2 | 83.0 | 79.7 | 84.7 | 74.4 | 89.1 | 85.2 | 78.5 |
| Poliovirus, ≥3 doses | 93.3 | 92.7 | 92.3 | 91.5 | 93.2 | 89.7 | 96.7 | 93.3 | 91.4 |
| MMR, ≥1 dose | 91.5 | 91.5 | 91.2 | 89.5 | 92.2 | 89.5 | 95.1 | 92.7 | 88.7 |
| Hib, Primary series [4] | 92.2 | 92.8 | 92.9 | 91.2 | 93.3 | 87.9 | 95.2 | 93.8 | 90.4 |
| Hib, Full series [4] | 66.8 | 80.7 | 81.0 | 77.4 | 81.0 | 77.1 | 87.3 | 83.2 | 75.2 |
| HepB, ≥ 3 doses | 91.8 | 91.4 | 91.1 | 91.8 | 91.3 | 88.1 | 94.7 | 92.1 | 89.8 |
| HepB, 1 dose within 3 days of birth | 64.1 | 73.6 | 71.3 | 75.6 | 76.2 | 83.6 | 76.7 | 73.1 | 74.6 |
| Varicella (chickenpox), ≥1 dose [5] | 90.4 | 91.0 | 90.3 | 89.3 | 91.8 | 88.1 | 95.7 | 92.0 | 88.9 |
| PCV, ≥3 doses | 92.6 | 91.9 | 92.2 | 91.2 | 92.0 | 85.6 | 89.9 | 93.1 | 89.5 |
| HepA, ≥1 dose | 78.3 | 86.0 | 84.3 | 85.4 | 87.9 | 89.5 | 91.1 | 87.4 | 84.0 |
| HepA, ≥2 doses | 49.7 | 59.7 | 58.3 | 54.0 | 63.5 | (⁸) | 68.9 | 61.4 | 56.0 |
| Rotavirus [6] | 59.2 | 73.2 | 76.6 | 65.7 | 71.1 | (⁸) | 73.0 | 77.9 | 64.4 |
| Combined series [7] | 56.6 | 70.4 | 71.5 | 66.5 | 70.4 | 65.9 | 72.4 | 73.8 | 62.8 |

[1] 2017 NIS covers children born January 2014 to May 2016. [2] Non-Hispanic. [3] Children of Hispanic origin may be of any race. [4] Hib primary series: receipt of ≥2 or ≥3 doses, depending on product type received. Full series: receipt of ≥3 or ≥4 doses, depending on product type received (primary series and booster dose). [5] Includes children who may have been vaccinated with measles, mumps, rubella, and varicella vaccine. [6] Rotavirus vaccine includes ≥2 or ≥3 doses, depending on the product type received (≥2 doses for Rotarix [RV1] or ≥3 doses for RotaTeq [RV5]). [7] The combined 7 vaccine series (4:3:1:3*:3:1:4) includes ≥4 doses of DTaP, ≥3 doses of poliovirus vaccine, ≥1 dose of measles-containing vaccine, full series of Hib vaccine (≥3 or ≥4 doses, depending on product type), ≥3 doses of HepB, ≥1 dose of varicella vaccine, and ≥4 doses of PCV. [8] Estimate not available because the 95% confidence interval (CI) ≥20.

Source: U.S. Centers for Disease Control and Prevention, Immunization Managers, "ChildVaxView," <https://www.cdc.gov/vaccines/imz-managers/coverage/childvaxview/index.html>, accessed March 2019; and Hill, Holly A. et al, "Vaccination Coverage Among Children Aged 19-35 Months—United States, 2017," *Morbidity and Mortality Weekly Report,* 67:40 (2018), <https://www.cdc.gov/vaccines/imz-managers/coverage/childvaxview/pubs-presentations.html>.

## Table 239. Asthma Incidence Among Children Under Age 18 by Selected Characteristics: 2017

[In thousands (73,529 represents 73,529,000), except percent. Based on the National Health Interview Survey, a sample survey of the civilian noninstitutionalized population; see Appendix III. Survey responses cover the sample child selected for the survey, not all children in the family]

| Characteristic | Total (1,000) | Ever told had asthma Number (1,000) [1] | Percent [2] | Still have asthma Number (1,000) [1] | Percent [2] |
|---|---|---|---|---|---|
| **Total [3]** | **73,529** | **9,562** | **13.0** | **6,182** | **8.4** |
| *SEX* | | | | | |
| Male | 37,520 | 5,661 | 15.1 | 3,569 | 9.5 |
| Female | 36,009 | 3,902 | 10.8 | 2,613 | 7.3 |
| *AGE [4]* | | | | | |
| 4 years and under | 19,694 | 1,101 | 5.6 | 869 | 4.4 |
| 5 to 11 years | 28,875 | 3,802 | 13.2 | 2,548 | 8.8 |
| 12 to 17 years | 24,960 | 4,659 | 18.7 | 2,765 | 11.1 |
| *RACE* | | | | | |
| Single race [5] | 69,897 | 8,916 | 12.7 | 5,717 | 8.2 |
| White | 53,672 | 6,488 | 12.1 | 4,073 | 7.6 |
| Black or African American | 10,796 | 1,863 | 17.2 | 1,379 | 12.8 |
| American Indian or Alaska Native | 1,063 | 133 | 12.9 | (B) | (B) |
| Asian | 4,189 | 402 | 9.3 | 159 | 3.6 |
| Native Hawaiian or Other Pacific Islander | 177 | (B) | (B) | (B) | (B) |
| Two or more races [6] | 3,632 | 646 | 18.1 | 465 | 13.0 |
| *HISPANIC ORIGIN AND RACE [7]* | | | | | |
| Hispanic or Latino | 18,490 | 2,272 | 12.4 | 1,416 | 7.8 |
| Mexican or Mexican American | 12,090 | 1,205 | 10.2 | 753 | 6.4 |
| Not Hispanic or Latino | 55,039 | 7,291 | 13.1 | 4,765 | 8.6 |
| White, single race | 37,781 | 4,627 | 12.1 | 2,918 | 7.7 |
| Black or African American, single race | 9,761 | 1,676 | 17.1 | 1,231 | 12.6 |

B Estimate is considered unreliable. [1] Unknowns for the columns are not included in the frequencies, but they are included in the "Total" column. [2] Unknowns for the column variables are not included in the denominators when calculating percentages. Percents are age-adjusted to the projected 2000 U.S. standard population using the age groups shown. [3] Includes other races, not shown separately. [4] Estimates for the age groups are not age-adjusted. [5] Refers to persons who indicated only a single race group, including those of Hispanic or Latino origin. [6] Refers to all persons who indicated more than one race group, including those of Hispanic or Latino origin. [7] Persons of Hispanic or Latino origin may be of any race or combination of races.

Source: U.S. National Center for Health Statistics, 2017 National Health Interview Survey, "Tables of Summary Health Statistics," <https://www.cdc.gov/nchs/nhis/shs.htm>, accessed January 2019.

# Table 240. Child Obesity by Age, Sex, and Race/Ethnicity: 1976 to 2016

[In percent. For children age 6 to 17. Data are from U.S. National Center for Health Statistics, National Health and Nutrition Examination Surveys, a program of studies that combines interviews and physical examinations to assess the health and nutritional status of adults and children. Children classified as obese have a body mass index (BMI) at or above the 95th percentile]

| Selected characteristic | 1976 to 1980 | 1988 to 1994 | 1999 to 2002 | 2003 to 2006 | 2009 to 2012 | 2013 to 2016 |
|---|---|---|---|---|---|---|
| **Total** [1] | **5.7** | **11.2** | **16.0** | **17.3** | **19.5** | **19.3** |
| RACE AND HISPANIC ORIGIN | | | | | | |
| White, non-Hispanic | 4.9 | 10.5 | 13.2 | 15.5 | 17.0 | 15.5 |
| Black, non-Hispanic | 8.2 | 14.0 | 20.7 | 21.5 | 22.7 | 23.5 |
| Asian, non-Hispanic | (NA) | (NA) | (NA) | (NA) | 9.7 | 11.0 |
| Hispanic origin [2,3] | (NA) | (NA) | (NA) | (NA) | 25.1 | 25.5 |
| Mexican-American [2,3] | (NA) | 15.4 | 23.0 | 22.7 | 26.6 | 26.4 |
| SEX AND AGE | | | | | | |
| Male | 5.5 | 11.8 | 17.2 | 18.1 | 18.4 | 19.8 |
| Female | 5.8 | 10.6 | 14.7 | 16.3 | 20.6 | 18.8 |
| Ages 6 to 11 | 6.5 | 11.3 | 15.8 | 17.0 | 17.7 | 17.9 |
| Male | 6.7 | 11.6 | 16.9 | 18.0 | 16.4 | 19.6 |
| Female | 6.4 | 11.0 | 14.7 | 15.8 | 19.1 | 16.1 |
| Ages 12 to 17 | 4.9 | 11.1 | 16.1 | 17.5 | 21.1 | 20.7 |
| Male | 4.5 | 12.0 | 17.5 | 18.2 | 20.3 | 20.0 |
| Female | 5.4 | 10.2 | 14.7 | 16.8 | 21.9 | 21.4 |

NA Not available. [1] Includes other races not shown separately. [2] Persons of Hispanic and Mexican origin may be of any race. [3] From 1976 to 2006, the survey sample was designed to provide estimates specifically for persons of Mexican origin. Beginning in 2007, the survey allows for reporting of both total Hispanics and Mexican Americans.

Source: Federal Interagency Forum on Child and Family Statistics, "America's Children: Key National Indicators of Well-Being, 2018," <http://www.childstats.gov/index.asp>, accessed December 2018.

# Table 241. High School Students Engaged in Physical Activity by Sex: 2017

[In percent. For students in grades 9 to 12. Based on the Youth Risk Behavior Survey, a school-based survey and subject to sampling error; for details, see source]

| Characteristic | Physically active for 60+ min. on 5 of last 7 days [1] | Physically active for 60+ min. on all 7 days [2] | No physical activity for 60+ min. on any day [3] | Attended physical education class Total [4] | Attended daily [5] | Played on at least one sports team [6] | Used computers 3 or more hours/ day [7] | Watched TV 3 or more hours/ day [8] |
|---|---|---|---|---|---|---|---|---|
| **All students** | **46.5** | **26.1** | **15.4** | **51.7** | **29.9** | **54.3** | **43.0** | **20.7** |
| **Male** | **56.9** | **35.3** | **11.0** | **55.9** | **34.7** | **59.7** | **43.0** | **20.8** |
| Grade 9 | 63.1 | 39.7 | 8.1 | 73.5 | 45.5 | 63.9 | 45.7 | 21.1 |
| Grade 10 | 56.4 | 36.7 | 10.7 | 60.0 | 36.7 | 59.2 | 43.6 | 20.6 |
| Grade 11 | 56.3 | 34.5 | 12.3 | 44.9 | 28.3 | 59.5 | 41.1 | 21.0 |
| Grade 12 | 51.2 | 29.8 | 13.5 | 42.0 | 26.5 | 55.9 | 40.8 | 20.5 |
| **Female** | **36.8** | **17.5** | **19.5** | **47.6** | **25.3** | **49.3** | **43.1** | **20.6** |
| Grade 9 | 45.3 | 22.0 | 12.9 | 70.8 | 39.2 | 56.4 | 44.0 | 20.7 |
| Grade 10 | 34.2 | 15.2 | 19.1 | 51.0 | 24.2 | 49.2 | 46.5 | 22.7 |
| Grade 11 | 34.6 | 15.9 | 23.0 | 33.4 | 20.3 | 47.0 | 43.4 | 10.0 |
| Grade 12 | 32.2 | 16.4 | 23.7 | 32.2 | 15.9 | 43.8 | 37.5 | 18.6 |

[1] Participated in any physical activity that increased their heart rate and made them breathe hard some of the time for at least 60 minutes/day for 5 or more days during the 7 days before the survey. [2] Participated in any physical activity that increased their heart rate and made them breathe hard some of the time for at least 60 minutes/day on all 7 days before the survey. [3] Did not participate in 60 or more minutes in any physical activity that increased their heart rate and made them breathe hard some of the time for at least 1 day during the 7 days before the survey. [4] On one or more days in an average week when they were in school. [5] Five days in an average week when they were in school. [6] Run by their school or community groups during the past 12 months. [7] Includes playing video games, using social media, and using mobile devices and computers for non-school activities on a school day. [8] On a school day.

Source: U.S. Centers for Disease Control and Prevention, *Morbidity and Mortality Weekly Report, Surveillance Summaries,* 67:8, June 15, 2018, "Youth Risk Behavior Surveillance—United States, 2017." See also <http://www.cdc.gov/healthyyouth/data/yrbs/index.htm>.

# Table 242. High School Student Use of Tobacco and Nicotine Products by Sex and Race/Ethnicity: 2018

[In percent, except as noted (4,040 represents 4,040,000). Data represent current use of tobacco and nicotine products, defined as use within the past 30 days. Data are based on the National Youth Tobacco Survey, administered to students in middle school (grades 6-8) and high school (grades 9-12). Only high school data are shown here]

| Tobacco and nicotine products | Total Number (1,000) [1] | Total Percent | Sex Male | Sex Female | White, non-Hispanic | Black, non-Hispanic | Other race, non-Hispanic | Hispanic [2] |
|---|---|---|---|---|---|---|---|---|
| **Use of any tobacco product** [3] | **4,040** | **27.1** | **29.1** | **24.9** | **32.4** | **17.4** | **18.4** | **21.7** |
| Electronic cigarettes (vaping) [4] | 3,050 | 20.8 | 22.6 | 18.8 | 26.8 | 7.5 | 14.5 | 14.8 |
| Cigarettes | 1,180 | 8.1 | 8.8 | 7.3 | 9.9 | 3.2 | 4.4 | 7.2 |
| Cigars | 1,100 | 7.6 | 9.0 | 6.0 | 7.8 | 9.2 | 3.4 | 7.3 |
| Smokeless tobacco [5] | 870 | 5.9 | 8.4 | 3.3 | 7.6 | 2.2 | 3.0 | 4.2 |
| Hookah [6] | 590 | 4.1 | 4.0 | 4.1 | 3.3 | 3.7 | 4.1 | 6.0 |
| Pipe tobacco | 160 | 1.1 | 1.4 | 0.8 | 1.1 | (B) | (B) | 1.4 |
| Two or more tobacco products | 1,680 | 11.3 | 13.1 | 9.3 | 13.6 | 5.5 | 6.3 | 9.9 |

B Statistically unreliable. Sample size less than 50 or relative standard error greater than 0.3. [1] Estimates are rounded down to nearest 10,000. [2] Persons of Hispanic origin may be of any race. [3] Includes use of bidis (small imported cigarettes wrapped in a leaf), not shown separately. [4] Electronic cigarettes (e-cigarettes) are battery-powered devices that vaporize a nicotine-based liquid for the user to inhale. [5] Includes chewing tobacco, snuff, dip, snus, and dissolvable tobacco. [6] Water pipes used to smoke tobacco, which is often flavored.

Source: U.S. Centers for Disease Control and Prevention, Gentzke, Andrea S. et al., "*Vital Signs:* Tobacco Product Use Among Middle and High School Students—United States, 2011–2018," *Morbidity and Mortality Weekly Report,* 68:6, February 15, 2019, early release. See also <http://www.cdc.gov/tobacco/data_statistics/by_topic/youth_data/index.htm>.

## Table 243. Depression and Receipt of Mental Health Treatment in the Past Year Among Youth Age 12 to 17 by Selected Characteristics: 2005 to 2017

[In percent. Data are from Substance Abuse and Mental Health Services Administration, National Survey on Drug Use and Health. Covers youth age 12 to 17 who had a major depressive episode (MDE) as defined in the 5th edition of the *Diagnostic and Statistical Manual of Mental Disorders* (DSM-5), which specifies a period of at least 2 weeks when a person experienced a depressed mood or loss of interest or pleasure in daily activities and had a majority of specified depression symptoms. Treatment is defined as seeing or talking to a medical doctor or other professional, or using prescription medication in the past year for depression. Respondents with unknown incidence of major depressive episode and unknown treatment data were excluded]

| Characteristic | Youth with major depressive episode (MDE) | | | | Youth with an MDE receiving treatment for depression | | | |
|---|---|---|---|---|---|---|---|---|
| | 2005 | 2010 | 2016 | 2017 | 2005 | 2010 | 2016 | 2017 |
| **Total [1]** | **8.8** | **8.0** | **12.8** | **13.3** | **37.8** | **37.8** | **40.9** | **41.5** |
| AGE | | | | | | | | |
| 12 to 13 years old | 5.2 | 4.3 | 7.3 | 6.9 | 32.9 | 32.5 | 35.3 | 37.6 |
| 14 to 15 years old | 9.5 | 9.0 | 13.3 | 14.5 | 41.1 | 38.4 | 41.3 | 37.9 |
| 16 to 17 years old | 11.5 | 10.6 | 17.2 | 17.7 | 37.1 | 39.3 | 42.6 | 45.8 |
| SEX | | | | | | | | |
| Male | 4.5 | 4.4 | 6.4 | 6.8 | 34.1 | 32.0 | 33.5 | 32.5 |
| Female | 13.3 | 11.9 | 19.4 | 20.0 | 39.0 | 40.1 | 43.4 | 44.8 |
| RACE ETHNICITY | | | | | | | | |
| White, non-Hispanic | 9.1 | 8.6 | 13.8 | 14.0 | 39.3 | 41.1 | 45.1 | 47.5 |
| Black, non-Hispanic | 7.6 | 6.8 | 9.1 | 9.5 | 39.3 | 23.0 | 34.5 | 35.1 |
| American Indian or Alaska Native | 6.1 | 7.4 | 11.5 | 16.3 | (NA) | (NA) | (NA) | (NA) |
| Asian | 6.0 | 5.5 | 11.9 | 11.3 | (NA) | (NA) | (NA) | (NA) |
| Two or more races | 10.5 | 9.4 | 13.8 | 16.9 | (NA) | (NA) | (NA) | (NA) |
| Hispanic [2] | 9.1 | 7.8 | 12.7 | 13.8 | 31.8 | 38.4 | 34.1 | 32.7 |
| POVERTY STATUS [3] | | | | | | | | |
| Below 100% poverty | 8.1 | 7.2 | 12.1 | 11.8 | 37.3 | 33.8 | 36.1 | 37.1 |
| 100-199% poverty | 9.6 | 9.0 | 13.2 | 14.2 | 32.1 | 39.1 | 42.6 | 40.2 |
| 200% poverty and above | 8.7 | 7.9 | 12.9 | 13.5 | 40.1 | 38.4 | 41.8 | 43.5 |

NA Not available. [1] Total includes persons of other races, not shown separately. [2] Persons of Hispanic origin may be of any race. [3] Estimates are based on a definition of poverty level that incorporates information on family income, size, and composition and is calculated as a percentage of the U.S. Census Bureau's poverty thresholds.

Source: Substance Abuse and Mental Health Services Administration, *Results From the 2017 National Survey on Drug Use and Health: Detailed Tables,* September 2018; see also <https://www.samhsa.gov/data/population-data-nsduh>. Prior to 2016, Federal Interagency Forum on Child and Family Statistics, "America's Children: Key National Indicators of Well-Being, 2017," <http://www.childstats.gov/>, accessed July 2017, and previous editions.

## Table 244. Foodborne Disease Outbreaks and Illnesses by Etiology, Food Category, and Location of Food Preparation: 2016

[Data reported as of February 7, 2018. Foodborne disease outbreaks are a nationally notifiable condition. An outbreak involves 2 or more cases of a similar illness resulting from consuming a common food. Public health agencies in all 50 States, D.C., and the U.S. territories voluntarily submit reports of foodborne disease outbreaks that their agencies investigate. Excludes outbreaks on cruise ships that dock in U.S. and international ports and those in which food was eaten outside the U.S. Not all outbreaks are identified, investigated, or reported. Data are subject to change. See source for other limitations]

| Item | Out-breaks | Ill-nesses | Hospital-izations | Item | Out-breaks | Ill-nesses |
|---|---|---|---|---|---|---|
| **Total** | **839** | **14,259** | **875** | **By food category:** | | |
| **By etiology (cause): [1]** | | | | Aquatic animals | 55 | 737 |
| Bacterial [2] | 286 | 5,481 | 641 | Land animals [2] | 76 | 1,662 |
| Salmonella | 135 | 3,081 | 456 | Dairy | 19 | 252 |
| Clostridium perfringens | 30 | 756 | 8 | Eggs | 6 | 161 |
| Escherichia coli (E. coli) [3] | 27 | 386 | 103 | Beef | 11 | 340 |
| Campylobacter | 25 | 187 | 18 | Pork | 18 | 438 |
| Bacillus cereus | 19 | 641 | 0 | Chicken | 17 | 356 |
| Staphylococcus aureus enterotoxin | 14 | 237 | 21 | Plant products | 45 | 1,339 |
| Chemical and toxin | 27 | 150 | 3 | Other [4] | 670 | 10,730 |
| Parasitic | 6 | 57 | 1 | **By location of food preparation:** | | |
| Giardia | 1 | 25 | 0 | Restaurant | 459 | 5,353 |
| Cyclospora | 1 | 15 | 0 | Catering or banquet facility | 102 | 3,116 |
| Viral [2] | 326 | 6,406 | 202 | Private home | 76 | 895 |
| Norovirus | 322 | 5,934 | 61 | Institutional location | 21 | 1,377 |
| Hepatitis A | 3 | 457 | 141 | Grocery store | 15 | 239 |
| Other [4] | 194 | 2,165 | 28 | Hospital or nursing home | 16 | 412 |

[1] Includes both confirmed and suspected etiologies. [2] Includes other categories not shown separately. [3] Also includes E. coli that produce shiga toxins, known as Shiga toxin-producing E. coli (STEC). These bacteria are also called verocytotoxic-producing E. coli and enterohemorrhagic E. coli. [4] Other includes incidents that involved multiple categories and unknown or not reported categories.

Source: U.S. Centers for Disease Control and Prevention, *Surveillance for Foodborne Disease Outbreaks, United States, 2016: Annual Report,* 2018. See also <https://www.cdc.gov/foodsafety/fdoss/index.html>.

# Table 245. Fruit and Vegetable Availability for Consumption Per Capita by Commodity: 1980 to 2016

[In pounds, farm weight. Available supply of fresh fruits and vegetables at the farm level or early stage of processing for domestic consumption after subtracting measurable uses, such as farm inputs (feed and seed), exports, ending stocks, and industrial uses. Food availability is a proxy for actual food consumption. Based on Census Bureau estimated resident population plus Armed Forces overseas for most commodities]

| Commodity | 1980 | 1990 | 2000 | 2005 | 2010 | 2013 | 2014 | 2015 | 2016 |
|---|---|---|---|---|---|---|---|---|---|
| **Fruits and vegetables, total [1]** | **604.6** | **662.1** | **712.5** | **684.7** | **652.3** | **636.8** | **637.1** | **633.3** | **640.9** |
| **Fruits, total** | **266.2** | **270.8** | **288.2** | **270.8** | **256.0** | **254.5** | **250.1** | **252.7** | **255.8** |
| Fresh fruits | 106.6 | 117.1 | 128.8 | 125.3 | 128.6 | 136.3 | 136.3 | 136.1 | 141.6 |
| Noncitrus [2] | 80.5 | 95.6 | 105.3 | 103.7 | 107.0 | 112.3 | 113.0 | 113.4 | 117.6 |
| Apples | 19.4 | 19.8 | 17.6 | 16.8 | 15.4 | 17.5 | 18.7 | 17.5 | 18.7 |
| Avocados | 2.1 | 1.4 | 2.2 | 3.5 | 4.0 | 6.2 | 7.0 | 7.2 | 7.1 |
| Bananas | 20.8 | 24.3 | 28.4 | 25.2 | 25.6 | 28.1 | 28.0 | 28.0 | 27.5 |
| Blueberries | 0.2 | 0.1 | 0.3 | 0.4 | 1.1 | 1.4 | 1.5 | 1.6 | 1.8 |
| Cantaloupes | 5.8 | 9.2 | 11.1 | 9.6 | 8.5 | 8.3 | 6.6 | 6.8 | 7.1 |
| Cherries | 0.7 | 0.4 | 0.6 | 0.9 | 1.3 | 1.0 | 1.2 | 1.1 | 1.2 |
| Grapes | 4.0 | 7.9 | 7.5 | 8.7 | 8.0 | 7.8 | 7.7 | 7.9 | 8.1 |
| Honeydew melons | 1.4 | 2.1 | 2.3 | 1.9 | 1.7 | 1.6 | 1.7 | 1.7 | 1.6 |
| Mangoes | 0.2 | 0.5 | 1.8 | 1.9 | 2.2 | 2.9 | 2.5 | 2.6 | 3.0 |
| Papayas | 0.2 | 0.2 | 0.7 | 0.9 | 1.2 | 1.1 | 1.1 | 1.3 | 1.4 |
| Peaches and nectarines | 7.1 | 5.5 | 5.3 | 4.8 | 4.7 | 3.0 | 3.3 | 3.0 | 2.9 |
| Pears | 2.6 | 3.3 | 3.4 | 2.9 | 2.9 | 2.9 | 2.9 | 2.7 | 2.8 |
| Pineapples | 1.5 | 2.0 | 3.2 | 4.9 | 5.7 | 6.7 | 7.2 | 7.0 | 7.3 |
| Plums | 1.5 | 1.5 | 1.2 | 1.1 | 0.8 | 0.5 | 0.6 | 0.6 | 0.8 |
| Strawberries | 2.0 | 3.2 | 4.9 | 5.8 | 7.2 | 8.0 | 8.0 | 7.7 | 8.0 |
| Watermelons | 10.7 | 13.3 | 13.8 | 13.5 | 15.7 | 14.5 | 13.9 | 14.9 | 16.6 |
| Fresh citrus | 26.1 | 21.5 | 23.5 | 21.6 | 21.6 | 23.9 | 23.2 | 22.7 | 24.0 |
| Oranges and temples | 14.3 | 12.4 | 11.7 | 11.4 | 9.7 | 10.4 | 9.4 | 8.7 | 9.2 |
| Tangerines and tangelos | 2.2 | 1.3 | 2.9 | 2.5 | 3.8 | 4.5 | 5.0 | 5.2 | 5.3 |
| Grapefruit | 7.3 | 4.6 | 5.1 | 2.6 | 2.8 | 2.6 | 2.4 | 2.2 | 1.9 |
| Lemons | 1.9 | 2.6 | 2.4 | 2.9 | 2.8 | 3.5 | 3.4 | 3.6 | 4.1 |
| Limes | 0.4 | 0.7 | 1.4 | 2.1 | 2.6 | 3.0 | 3.1 | 3.0 | 3.5 |
| Processed fruit | 159.7 | 153.6 | 159.4 | 145.5 | 127.4 | 118.2 | 113.9 | 116.7 | 114.2 |
| Canned fruit [3] | 24.6 | 21.1 | 17.6 | 16.7 | 15.0 | 15.1 | 13.7 | 14.4 | 13.7 |
| Fruit juice [4] | 119.7 | 115.8 | 126.5 | 112.9 | 97.2 | 87.5 | 84.1 | 85.4 | 84.8 |
| Frozen fruit [5] | 3.3 | 4.3 | 4.5 | 5.2 | 5.1 | 4.8 | 5.6 | 5.6 | 5.1 |
| Dried fruit [6] | 11.3 | 12.2 | 10.5 | 10.1 | 9.4 | 10.0 | 9.7 | 10.4 | 9.9 |
| **Vegetables, total** | **338.4** | **391.4** | **424.3** | **413.9** | **396.3** | **382.3** | **387.0** | **380.6** | **385.1** |
| Fresh vegetables [7] | 151.8 | 176.4 | 200.7 | 196.4 | 190.3 | 184.5 | 186.3 | 186.3 | 188.1 |
| Asparagus | 0.3 | 0.6 | 1.0 | 1.1 | 1.4 | 1.4 | 1.7 | 1.5 | 1.5 |
| Bell peppers (all uses) | 2.9 | 5.9 | 8.2 | 9.2 | 10.3 | 10.0 | 10.7 | 10.7 | 11.0 |
| Broccoli | 1.4 | 3.4 | 5.9 | 5.3 | 6.0 | 6.9 | 6.6 | 7.4 | 7.4 |
| Cabbage | 8.0 | 8.3 | 8.9 | 7.8 | 7.5 | 6.9 | 6.7 | 6.3 | 5.9 |
| Carrots | 6.2 | 8.3 | 9.2 | 8.7 | 7.8 | 8.0 | 8.5 | 8.8 | 7.8 |
| Cauliflower | 1.1 | 2.2 | 1.7 | 1.8 | 1.3 | 1.3 | 1.3 | 1.6 | 1.6 |
| Celery (all uses) | 7.4 | 7.2 | 6.3 | 5.9 | 6.1 | 5.5 | 5.5 | 5.4 | 5.0 |
| Corn, sweet | 6.5 | 6.7 | 9.0 | 8.7 | 9.2 | 8.0 | 7.0 | 8.8 | 7.2 |
| Cucumbers | 3.9 | 4.7 | 6.4 | 6.2 | 6.7 | 7.3 | 7.4 | 7.6 | 8.2 |
| Garlic (all uses) | 0.9 | 1.4 | 2.2 | 2.4 | 2.3 | 2.3 | 2.2 | 2.4 | 2.9 |
| Kale | (NA) | (NA) | 0.4 | 0.4 | 0.5 | 0.6 | 0.5 | 0.6 | 0.5 |
| Lettuce, head | 25.6 | 27.7 | 23.5 | 20.9 | 15.9 | 14.1 | 14.5 | 13.6 | 14.2 |
| Lettuce, Romaine and leaf | (NA) | 3.8 | 8.4 | 9.7 | 12.0 | 11.4 | 10.8 | 11.0 | 12.7 |
| Mushrooms | 1.2 | 2.0 | 2.6 | 2.6 | 2.6 | 2.7 | 2.9 | 3.0 | 3.0 |
| Onions | 11.4 | 15.1 | 18.9 | 20.9 | 19.6 | 18.5 | 18.4 | 18.9 | 19.0 |
| Potatoes | 51.1 | 46.7 | 47.1 | 41.3 | 36.8 | 34.5 | 33.6 | 34.1 | 33.6 |
| Pumpkin (all uses) | (NA) | 4.4 | 4.6 | 4.8 | 4.4 | 4.7 | 5.3 | 3.1 | 4.8 |
| Snap beans | 1.3 | 1.1 | 2.0 | 1.8 | 1.9 | 1.6 | 1.5 | 1.6 | 1.7 |
| Spinach | 0.4 | 0.8 | 1.4 | 2.3 | 1.7 | 1.6 | 1.7 | 1.7 | 1.8 |
| Squash (all uses) | 2.3 | 3.5 | 4.4 | 4.4 | 4.3 | 4.4 | 4.6 | 4.6 | 5.1 |
| Sweet potatoes (all uses) | 4.4 | 4.4 | 4.2 | 4.5 | 6.3 | 6.3 | 7.5 | 7.6 | 7.2 |
| Tomatoes | 12.8 | 15.5 | 19.0 | 20.2 | 20.6 | 20.2 | 20.6 | 20.5 | 20.4 |
| Processed vegetables | 186.7 | 214.9 | 223.6 | 217.5 | 206.0 | 197.8 | 200.7 | 194.3 | 197.0 |
| Canned vegetables [8] | 102.5 | 110.3 | 103.2 | 104.8 | 99.1 | 91.8 | 93.5 | 82.2 | 88.6 |
| Frozen vegetables [9] | 51.6 | 66.7 | 79.7 | 76.4 | 71.0 | 67.1 | 66.8 | 70.1 | 68.0 |
| Dehydrated vegetables [10] | 10.5 | 14.9 | 17.3 | 13.9 | 12.5 | 13.9 | 13.5 | 12.9 | 13.8 |
| Chips, potato | 16.5 | 16.3 | 15.6 | 16.0 | 15.0 | 17.8 | 19.9 | 19.5 | 16.6 |
| Legumes [11] | 5.6 | 6.8 | 7.9 | 6.3 | 8.3 | 7.2 | 6.9 | 9.5 | 10.0 |

NA Not available. [1] Excludes wine grapes. [2] Includes other fruits not shown separately. [3] Canned fruit include apples, apricots, cherries, olives, peaches, pears, pineapples, plums, and prunes. [4] Fruit juice includes apple, cranberry, grape, grapefruit, lemon, lime, orange, pineapple, and prune juice. [5] Frozen fruit include apples, apricots, blackberries, blueberries, boysenberries, cherries, loganberries, peaches, plums, prunes, raspberries, strawberries, and other miscellaneous fruit and berries. [6] Dried fruit include apples, apricots, dates, figs, peaches, pears, prunes, and raisins. [7] Includes other vegetables not shown separately. [8] Canned vegetables include asparagus, lima beans, snap beans, beets, cabbage, carrots, sweet corn, cucumbers, mushrooms, green peas, chile peppers, potatoes, spinach, tomatoes, and other miscellaneous vegetables. [9] Frozen vegetables include asparagus, lima beans, snap beans, broccoli, carrots, cauliflower, sweet corn, green peas, potatoes, spinach and other miscellaneous vegetables. [10] Onions and potatoes. [11] Dry peas, beans, and lentils.

Source: U.S. Department of Agriculture, Economic Research Service, "Food Availability (Per Capita) Data System," <https://www.ers.usda.gov/data-products/food-availability-per-capita-data-system/>, accessed January 2019.

# Table 246. Food Availability for Consumption Per Capita by Major Food Commodity: 1980 to 2016

[In pounds, retail weight, except as indicated. Available supply for domestic consumption after subtracting measurable uses, such as farm inputs (feed and seed), exports, ending stocks, and industrial uses. Food availability is a proxy for actual food consumption. Based on Census Bureau estimated resident population plus Armed Forces overseas for most commodities. For commodities not shipped overseas in substantial amounts, such as fluid milk and cream, the resident population is used]

| Commodity | Unit | 1980 | 1990 | 2000 | 2005 | 2010 | 2015 | 2016 |
|---|---|---|---|---|---|---|---|---|
| Red meat, total (boneless, trimmed weight) [1] | Pounds | 126.4 | 112.2 | 113.7 | 110.2 | 102.0 | 98.6 | 100.4 |
| Beef | Pounds | 72.1 | 63.9 | 64.5 | 62.5 | 56.7 | 51.4 | 52.9 |
| Veal | Pounds | 1.3 | 0.9 | 0.5 | 0.4 | 0.3 | 0.2 | 0.2 |
| Pork | Pounds | 52.1 | 46.4 | 47.8 | 46.5 | 44.4 | 46.3 | 46.6 |
| Lamb | Pounds | 1.0 | 1.0 | 0.8 | 0.8 | 0.7 | 0.7 | 0.8 |
| Poultry (boneless, trimmed weight) | Pounds | 40.8 | 56.3 | 67.9 | 73.7 | 70.9 | 75.1 | 76.3 |
| Chicken | Pounds | 32.7 | 42.5 | 54.2 | 60.5 | 58.0 | 62.6 | 63.1 |
| Turkey | Pounds | 8.1 | 13.8 | 13.7 | 13.2 | 12.9 | 12.6 | 13.1 |
| Fish and shellfish (boneless, trimmed weight) | Pounds | 12.4 | 14.9 | 15.2 | 16.2 | 15.8 | 15.5 | 14.9 |
| Eggs | Number | 271.1 | 234.1 | 251.2 | 256.0 | 247.5 | 255.6 | 271.8 |
| Shell | Number | 236.2 | 186.2 | 178.0 | 176.9 | 172.1 | 179.6 | 189.4 |
| Processed | Number | 34.9 | 47.9 | 73.2 | 79.1 | 75.5 | 76.0 | 82.4 |
| Dairy products, total [2] | Pounds | 543.1 | 568.0 | 591.1 | 604.3 | 604.5 | 629.8 | 645.9 |
| Fluid milk products [3] | Gallons | 27.9 | 26.1 | 23.6 | 22.6 | 22.1 | 19.7 | 19.4 |
| Beverage milks | Gallons | 27.6 | 25.7 | 22.8 | 21.4 | 20.6 | 18.0 | 17.8 |
| Plain whole milk | Gallons | 16.5 | 10.2 | 7.8 | 6.8 | 5.5 | 5.3 | 5.6 |
| Plain reduced-fat milk (2%) | Gallons | 6.3 | 9.1 | 7.2 | 7.0 | 7.2 | 6.1 | 6.0 |
| Plain reduced-fat milk (1%) | Gallons | 1.8 | 2.3 | 2.6 | 2.5 | 2.8 | 2.8 | 2.6 |
| Plain skim milk | Gallons | 1.3 | 2.6 | 3.4 | 3.2 | 3.2 | 2.0 | 1.8 |
| Flavored whole milk | Gallons | 0.6 | 0.3 | 0.4 | 0.3 | 0.2 | 0.2 | 0.2 |
| Flavored milk, low-fat and skim | Gallons | 0.6 | 0.8 | 1.1 | 1.4 | 1.5 | 1.4 | 1.4 |
| Buttermilk | Gallons | 0.5 | 0.4 | 0.3 | 0.2 | 0.2 | 0.2 | 0.2 |
| Yogurt (excl. frozen) | 1/2 pints | 4.6 | 7.2 | 12.0 | 19.1 | 24.9 | 26.6 | 25.4 |
| Fluid cream products [4] | 1/2 pints | 10.5 | 14.3 | 18.6 | 22.4 | (NA) | (NA) | (NA) |
| Cream [5] | 1/2 pints | 6.3 | 8.7 | 11.6 | 14.9 | (NA) | (NA) | (NA) |
| Sour cream | 1/2 pints | 3.4 | 4.7 | 6.1 | 6.6 | 7.5 | 7.8 | 8.0 |
| Condensed and evaporated milks | Pounds | 7.0 | 7.9 | 5.8 | 6.1 | 7.2 | 7.7 | 7.4 |
| Whole milk | Pounds | 3.8 | 3.1 | 2.0 | 2.4 | 2.0 | 2.2 | 2.0 |
| Skim milk | Pounds | 3.3 | 4.8 | 3.8 | 3.7 | 5.2 | 5.5 | 5.4 |
| Butter (product weight) | Pounds | 4.5 | 4.3 | 4.5 | 4.5 | 4.9 | 5.6 | 5.7 |
| Cheese [6] | Pounds | 17.5 | 24.6 | 29.5 | 31.3 | 32.7 | 35.1 | 36.3 |
| American [7] | Pounds | 9.6 | 11.1 | 12.7 | 12.6 | 13.3 | 14.0 | 14.3 |
| Cheddar | Pounds | 6.8 | 9.1 | 9.9 | 10.2 | 10.1 | 10.2 | 10.4 |
| Italian [7] | Pounds | 4.4 | 8.9 | 11.4 | 12.7 | 13.5 | 14.5 | 15.2 |
| Mozzarella | Pounds | 3.0 | 6.9 | 9.1 | 9.9 | 10.6 | 11.3 | 11.7 |
| Other [7] | Pounds | 3.5 | 4.6 | 5.4 | 6.0 | 5.9 | 6.6 | 6.8 |
| Swiss | Pounds | 1.3 | 1.3 | 1.0 | 1.2 | 1.2 | 1.1 | 1.1 |
| Cream and Neufchatel | Pounds | 1.0 | 1.7 | 2.4 | 2.4 | 2.3 | 2.5 | 2.6 |
| Cottage cheese, total | Pounds | 4.4 | 3.3 | 2.6 | 2.6 | 2.3 | 2.1 | 2.2 |
| Low-fat | Pounds | 0.8 | 1.2 | 1.3 | 1.4 | 1.3 | 1.1 | 1.1 |
| Frozen dairy products [8] | Pounds | 26.0 | 28.4 | 27.5 | 25.2 | 23.9 | 23.2 | 23.0 |
| Ice cream | Pounds | 17.1 | 15.4 | 16.1 | 15.1 | 14.0 | 12.9 | 13.1 |
| Low-fat ice cream | Pounds | 6.1 | 6.6 | 6.6 | 6.0 | 6.5 | 6.5 | 6.4 |
| Sherbet | Pounds | 1.2 | 1.2 | 1.1 | 1.1 | 1.0 | 0.8 | 0.8 |
| Frozen yogurt | Pounds | (NA) | 2.8 | 2.0 | 1.3 | 1.0 | 1.4 | 1.2 |
| Flour and cereal products [9] | Pounds | 146.4 | 181.1 | 199.5 | 190.9 | 194.2 | 172.9 | 171.8 |
| Wheat flour | Pounds | 116.9 | 135.6 | 146.3 | 134.4 | 134.8 | 133.0 | 131.7 |
| Rice, milled | Pounds | 11.0 | 16.2 | 19.2 | 19.4 | 20.4 | (NA) | (NA) |
| Corn products | Pounds | 12.9 | 21.4 | 28.4 | 31.4 | 33.1 | 34.0 | 34.2 |
| Oat products | Pounds | 3.9 | 6.5 | 4.4 | 4.6 | 4.7 | 4.6 | 4.6 |
| Caloric sweeteners, total [10] | Pounds | 120.2 | 132.3 | 151.2 | 143.5 | 133.7 | 131.6 | 130.6 |
| Sugar, refined cane and beet | Pounds | 83.6 | 64.4 | 65.5 | 63.0 | 65.9 | 69.1 | 69.6 |
| Corn sweeteners [11] | Pounds | 35.3 | 66.8 | 83.9 | 78.9 | 66.0 | 60.3 | 59.1 |
| High-fructose corn syrup | Pounds | 19.0 | 49.6 | 64.8 | 60.3 | 50.5 | 45.1 | 44.0 |
| Honey | Pounds | 0.8 | 0.7 | 1.1 | 1.1 | 1.0 | 1.3 | 1.3 |
| Other: | | | | | | | | |
| Cocoa, bean equivalent | Pounds | 3.4 | 5.4 | 5.9 | 6.5 | 5.5 | 5.3 | (NA) |
| Coffee, green bean equivalent | Pounds | 10.3 | 10.3 | 10.3 | 9.5 | 9.2 | 10.2 | (NA) |
| Tea, dry leaf equivalent | Pounds | 0.8 | 0.7 | 0.8 | 0.8 | 1.0 | 0.9 | (NA) |
| Peanuts, total | Pounds | 5.1 | 6.1 | 5.9 | 6.7 | 7.0 | 7.4 | 7.2 |
| Tree nuts, total | Pounds | 1.8 | 2.5 | 2.6 | 2.7 | 3.9 | 4.1 | 4.8 |

NA Not available. [1] Excludes edible offal. [2] Milk-equivalent. Includes fluid milk and cream, butter, cheese, frozen and dry dairy products, and evaporated and condensed milk. [3] Fluid milk figures are aggregates of commercial sales and milk produced and consumed on farms. [4] Includes eggnog, not shown separately. [5] Heavy cream, light cream, and half-and-half. [6] Excludes full-skim American, cottage, pot, and baker's cheese. [7] Includes other cheeses, not shown separately. [8] Includes mellorine until 1995, and other nonstandardized frozen dairy products. [9] Includes rye flour and barley products, not shown separately. Excludes wheat not ground into flour. [10] Dry weight. Includes edible syrups (maple, molasses, etc.), not shown separately. [11] Includes glucose and dextrose, not shown separately.

Source: U.S. Department of Agriculture, Economic Research Service, "Food Availability (Per Capita) Data System," <https://www.ers.usda.gov/data-products/food-availability-per-capita-data-system/>, accessed January 2019.

# Section 4
# Education

This section presents data primarily concerning formal education as a whole, at various levels, and for public and private schools. Data shown relate to the school-age population and school enrollment, educational attainment, education personnel, and financial aspects of education. In addition, data are shown for charter schools, homeschooling, post-secondary education, security measures used in schools, and academic libraries. The chief sources are the decennial census of population and the Current Population Survey (CPS), both conducted by the U.S. Census Bureau (see text, Section 1, Population); annual, biennial, and other periodic surveys conducted by the National Center for Education Statistics (NCES), a part of the U.S. Department of Education; and surveys conducted by the National Education Association.

The censuses of population have included data on school enrollment since 1840 and on educational attainment since 1940. The CPS has reported on school enrollment annually and on educational attainment periodically since 1947.

The NCES is continuing the pattern of statistical studies and surveys conducted by the U.S. Office of Education since 1870. The annual *Digest of Education Statistics*, found at <http://nces.ed.gov/programs/digest/>, provides summary data on pupils, staff, finances, including government expenditures, and organization at the elementary, secondary, and higher education levels. It is also a primary source for detailed information on federal funds for education, projections of enrollment, graduates, and teachers. The *Condition of Education*, issued annually and found at <http://nces.ed.gov/programs/coe/>, presents a summary of information on education of particular interest to policymakers. NCES also conducts special studies periodically.

The census of governments, conducted by the Census Bureau every 5 years (for the years ending in "2" and "7"), provides data on school district finances and state and local government expenditures for education. Reports published by the Bureau of Labor Statistics contain data relating civilian labor force experience to educational attainment (see also Tables 618, 647, and 654 in Section 12, Labor Force, Employment, and Earnings).

**Types and sources of data**—The statistics in this section are of two general types. One type, exemplified by data from the Census Bureau, is based on direct interviews with individuals to obtain information about their own and their family members' education. Data of this type relate to school enrollment and level of education attained, classified by age, sex, and other characteristics of the population. The school enrollment statistics reflect attendance or enrollment in any regular school within a given period; educational attainment statistics reflect the highest grade completed by an individual, or beginning 1992, the highest diploma or degree received.

Beginning in 2012, CPS estimates reflect population controls based on Census 2010. From 2000–2011, the CPS used Census 2000 population controls. From 1994 to 2000, the CPS used 1990 census population controls plus adjustment for undercount. Also beginning 1994, the survey is conducted through computer-assisted technology rather than by paper forms. For years 1981 through 1993, 1980 census population controls were used; 1971 through 1980, 1970 census population controls had been used. These changes had little impact on summary measures (e.g., medians) and proportional measures (e.g., enrollment rates); however, use of the controls may have significant impact on absolute numbers.

The second type of data, generally exemplified by data from the NCES and the National Education Association, is based on reports from administrators of educational institutions and of state and local agencies having jurisdiction over education. Data of this type relate to enrollment, attendance, staff, and finances for the nation, individual states, and local areas.

Unlike the NCES, the Census Bureau does not regularly include specialized vocational, trade, business, or correspondence schools in its surveys. The NCES includes nursery schools and kindergartens that are part of regular grade schools in their enrollment figures. The Census Bureau includes all nursery schools and kindergartens. At the higher education level, the statistics of both agencies are concerned with institutions granting degrees or offering work acceptable for degree-credit, such as junior colleges.

**School attendance**—All states require that children attend school. While state laws vary as to the ages and circumstances of compulsory attendance, generally they require that formal schooling begin by age 6 and continue to age 16.

**Schools**—The NCES defines a school as "a division of the school system consisting of students composing one or more grade groups or other identifiable groups, organized as one unit with one or more teachers to give instruction of a defined type, and housed in a school plant of one or more buildings. More than one school may be housed in one school plant, as is the case when the elementary and secondary programs are housed in the same school plant."

*Regular* schools are those which advance a person toward a diploma or degree. They include public and private nursery schools, kindergartens, graded schools, colleges, universities, and professional schools.

*Public* schools are schools controlled and supported by local, state, or federal governmental agencies.

*Private* schools are those controlled and supported mainly by religious organizations or by private persons or organizations.

The Census Bureau defines *elementary* schools as including grades 1 through 8; *high* schools as including grades 9 through 12; and *colleges* as including junior or community colleges, regular 4-year colleges, and universities and graduate or professional schools. Statistics reported by the NCES and the National Education Association by type of organization, such as elementary level and secondary level, may not be strictly comparable with those from the Census Bureau because the grades included at the two levels vary, depending on the level assigned to the middle or junior high school by the local school systems.

**School year**—Except as otherwise indicated in the tables, data refer to the school year which, for elementary and secondary schools, generally begins in August or September of the preceding year and ends in June of the year stated. For the most part, statistics concerning school finances are for a 12-month period, usually July 1 to June 30. Enrollment data generally refer to a specific point in time, such as Fall, as indicated in the tables.

**Statistical reliability**—For a discussion of statistical collection, estimation, and sampling procedures and measures of statistical reliability applicable to the Census Bureau and the NCES data, see Appendix III.

# Table 247. Federal Funds for Education and Related Programs: 2010 to 2017

[In millions of dollars (170,531.5 represents $170,531,500,000), except percent. For fiscal years ending in September. Figures represent on-budget funds (appropriations or outlays). Excludes federal support for medical education benefits under Medicare in the U.S. Department of Health and Human Services]

| Level, agency, and program | 2010 | 2016 | 2017 |
|---|---|---|---|
| **Total, all programs** | **170,531.5** | **188,713.5** | **228,394.2** |
| Percent of federal budget outlays | 4.9 | 4.9 | 5.7 |
| **Elementary/secondary education programs** | **75,187.1** | **82,087.3** | **81,833.2** |
| Department of Education [1] | 39,646.5 | 38,648.9 | 37,568.3 |
| Education for the disadvantaged | 15,864.7 | 15,963.0 | 16,143.8 |
| Impact aid program [2] | 1,276.2 | 1,305.6 | 1,328.6 |
| School improvement programs | 6,999.9 | 5,851.3 | 4,408.6 |
| Indian education | 127.3 | 143.9 | 164.9 |
| Special education | 12,587.0 | 12,930.8 | 13,064.4 |
| Vocational and adult education | 2,016.4 | 1,716.8 | 1,720.7 |
| Department of Agriculture [1] | 18,336.1 | 23,342.5 | 23,947.4 |
| Child nutrition programs | 16,891.0 | 22,158.0 | 22,782.0 |
| Agricultural Marketing Service—commodities [3] | 1,053.0 | 805.0 | 842.0 |
| Department of Defense [1] | 1,981.3 | 2,073.1 | 2,111.0 |
| Junior Reserve Officers Training Corps (JROTC) | 359.7 | 365.0 | 368.4 |
| Overseas dependents schools | 1,186.6 | 1,135.8 | 1,155.6 |
| Domestic schools [4] | 435.1 | 572.3 | 587.0 |
| Department of Health and Human Services | 7,234.0 | 9,168.1 | 9,150.7 |
| Head Start | 7,234.0 | 9,168.1 | 9,150.7 |
| Department of Homeland Security [1] | 0.5 | 0.3 | 0.4 |
| Department of the Interior [1] | 781.1 | 880.1 | 879.9 |
| Mineral Leasing Act and other funds [5] | 73.0 | 54.1 | 55.5 |
| Indian Education | 707.1 | 826.0 | 824.4 |
| Department of Justice | 137.5 | 141.2 | 137.2 |
| Department of Labor | 4,845.7 | 5,024.6 | 5,018.4 |
| Job Corps | 1,017.2 | 1,689.2 | 1,685.9 |
| Department of Veterans Affairs | 760.5 | 1,332.2 | 1,522.5 |
| Vocational rehab for disabled veterans | 760.5 | 1,314.7 | 1,504.9 |
| Other agencies and programs [1] | 1,325.6 | 1,390.5 | 1,382.3 |
| Social Security student benefits | 1,313.0 | 1,377.5 | 1,362.7 |
| **Higher education programs** [1] | **49,118.9** | **62,537.3** | **101,021.6** |
| Department of Education [1] | 35,518.2 | 44,128.9 | 82,309.5 |
| Student financial assistance | 24,596.6 | 30,130.2 | 31,199.1 |
| Direct loan program [6] | 3,481.9 | 9,878.1 | 37,028.3 |
| Federal Family Education Loans [6] | 4,274.4 | 1,446.8 | 11,155.8 |
| Department of Agriculture | 80.7 | 84.7 | 84.5 |
| Department of Defense | 2,550.7 | 2,329.4 | 2,334.1 |
| Tuition assistance for military personnel | 669.9 | 571.6 | 540.1 |
| Service academies [5] | 402.6 | 230.8 | 234.9 |
| Senior ROTC | 885.5 | 870.8 | 850.9 |
| Professional development education | 592.6 | 656.1 | 708.2 |
| Department of Health and Human Services [1] | 1,292.6 | 1,466.4 | 1,492.4 |
| Health professions training programs | 406.0 | 541.9 | 538.7 |
| National Health Service Corps scholarships | 41.0 | 44.0 | 33.7 |
| National Institutes of Health training grants [7] | 775.2 | 804.0 | 843.0 |
| Department of Homeland Security | 45.8 | 39.4 | 15.8 |
| Department of the Interior | 143.0 | 78.6 | 78.8 |
| Shared revenues, Mineral Leasing Act and other receipts—estimated education share [5] | 16.3 | 14.0 | 14.3 |
| Indian programs | 126.8 | 64.6 | 64.5 |
| Department of State | 657.7 | 599.2 | 589.8 |
| Department of Transportation | 90.0 | 116.1 | 118.4 |
| Department of Veterans Affairs [1] | 8,034.5 | 12,628.2 | 12,900.9 |
| Post-Vietnam veterans | 1.5 | 0.2 | 0.2 |
| All-volunteer-force educational assistance | 1,854.9 | 501.9 | 455.0 |
| Other agencies and programs [1] | 669.2 | 1,006.2 | 1,041.6 |
| National Endowment for the Humanities | 47.9 | 46.0 | 25.3 |
| National Science Foundation | 618.8 | 935.2 | 994.8 |
| **Other education programs** [1] | **9,232.2** | **9,634.1** | **9,680.7** |
| Department of Education [1] | 5,062.7 | 5,475.4 | 5,503.3 |
| Administration | 1,531.2 | 2,150.1 | 2,176.6 |
| Rehabilitative services and disability research | 3,506.9 | 3,299.0 | 3,301.1 |
| Department of Agriculture | 565.4 | 533.7 | 532.8 |
| Department of Health and Human Services | 339.7 | 394.7 | 394.7 |
| Department of Homeland Security | 341.1 | 244.5 | 244.0 |
| Department of Justice | 33.6 | 31.9 | 30.1 |
| Department of State | 143.5 | 265.2 | 264.5 |
| Other agencies and programs [1] | 2,746.2 | 2,688.8 | 2,711.2 |
| Agency for International Development | 542.7 | 605.4 | 639.1 |
| Library of Congress | 510.9 | 469.5 | 500.9 |
| National Endowment for the Arts | 2.9 | 3.9 | 4.0 |
| National Endowment for the Humanities | 94.6 | 75.7 | 74.4 |
| **Research programs at universities and related institutions** [1,8] | **36,993.3** | **34,454.8** | **35,858.7** |
| Department of Agriculture | 737.2 | 866.7 | 880.8 |
| Department of Defense | 3,154.3 | 2,977.1 | 2,871.2 |
| Department of Energy | 3,402.6 | 3,890.8 | 4,271.9 |
| Department of Health and Human Services | 21,796.2 | 17,807.8 | 18,206.1 |
| National Aeronautics and Space Administration | 1,585.5 | 2,667.4 | 2,947.7 |
| National Science Foundation | 4,914.7 | 4,936.5 | 5,265.5 |

[1] Includes other programs and agencies, not shown separately. [2] Includes funds used to support school districts with concentrations of children who reside on Indian lands, military bases, low-rent housing properties, and other federal properties, or who have parents in the uniformed services or employed on eligible federal properties. [3] Purchased under Section 32 of the Agricultural Adjustment Act of 1935 (Public Law 74-320) for use in child nutrition programs. [4] The DoD Domestic Dependent Elementary and Secondary Schools (DDESS) program supports students in military communities in the United States, Guam, and Puerto Rico. [5] Data for 2013 through 2017 are estimated. [6] The Education Department reestimated the subsidy costs of the Direct Loan Program and Federal Family Education Loan (FFEL) Program. In 2017, the majority of the net upward reestimates of $28.4 billion for the Direct Loan Program and $10.79 billion for the FFEL program reflect changes in collection and technical assumptions. The Direct Loan Program reestimate reflects an increase in loan discharges for student borrowers harmed by institutional misconduct, and the FFEL Program reflects reestimates for the Ensuring Continued Access to Student Loans Act (ECASLA) of 2008. The Federal Family Education Loan (FFEL) Program eliminated the authorization to originate new FFEL loans after June 30, 2010; all new loans are originated through the Direct Loan Program. [7] Includes alcohol, drug abuse, and mental health training programs. [8] Data for 2016 and 2017 are estimated.

Source: U.S. National Center for Education Statistics, *Digest of Education Statistics 2017*, January 2019. See also <http://www.nces.ed.gov/programs/digest/>.

# Table 248. School Expenditures by Level of Instruction in Current and Constant (2017 to 2018) Dollars: 1980 to 2018

[In millions of dollars (160,075 represents $160,075,000,000). For school years ending in year shown. Data shown reflect historical revisions. Total expenditures for public elementary and secondary schools include current expenditures, interest on school debt, and capital outlay. Based on survey of state education agencies; see source for details]

| Year | Current dollars | | | Constant 2017-2018 dollars [1] | | | |
|---|---|---|---|---|---|---|---|
| | Total | Elementary and secondary schools | Colleges and universities [2] | Total | Elementary and secondary schools | | Colleges and universities [2] |
| | | | | | Total | Public | |
| 1980 | 160,075 | 103,162 | 56,914 | 511,623 | 329,719 | 306,707 | 181,904 |
| 1990 | 365,825 | 231,170 | 134,656 | 714,871 | 451,736 | 415,780 | 263,135 |
| 2000 | 649,322 | 412,538 | 236,784 | 951,692 | 604,644 | 559,648 | 347,047 |
| 2001 | 705,017 | 444,811 | 260,206 | 999,092 | 630,350 | 582,168 | 368,742 |
| 2002 | 752,780 | 472,064 | 280,715 | 1,048,219 | 657,333 | 606,229 | 390,886 |
| 2003 | 795,691 | 492,807 | 302,884 | 1,084,146 | 671,460 | 619,820 | 412,686 |
| 2004 | 830,293 | 513,542 | 316,751 | 1,107,072 | 684,731 | 632,331 | 422,340 |
| 2005 | 875,988 | 540,969 | 335,019 | 1,133,878 | 700,230 | 646,641 | 433,648 |
| 2006 | 925,249 | 571,669 | 353,580 | 1,153,706 | 712,822 | 658,706 | 440,884 |
| 2007 | 984,048 | 608,495 | 375,553 | 1,196,092 | 739,614 | 683,337 | 456,478 |
| 2008 | 1,054,901 | 646,414 | 408,487 | 1,236,400 | 757,631 | 700,083 | 478,769 |
| 2009 | 1,089,683 | 658,926 | 430,757 | 1,259,579 | 761,661 | 705,484 | 497,918 |
| 2010 | 1,100,897 | 654,418 | 446,479 | 1,260,346 | 749,202 | 694,936 | 511,145 |
| 2011 | 1,124,352 | 652,356 | 471,997 | 1,261,861 | 732,139 | 678,269 | 529,722 |
| 2012 | 1,136,876 | 648,794 | 488,083 | 1,239,596 | 707,414 | 656,385 | 532,182 |
| 2013 | 1,153,874 | 655,013 | 498,861 | 1,237,535 | 702,505 | 650,810 | 535,030 |
| 2014 | 1,192,886 | 675,818 | 517,067 | 1,259,697 | 713,670 | 660,024 | 546,027 |
| 2015 | 1,241,626 | 706,135 | 535,491 | 1,301,688 | 740,294 | 682,633 | 561,394 |
| 2016 | 1,296,307 | 736,841 | 559,466 | 1,350,000 | 767,000 | 706,000 | 583,000 |
| 2017 [3] | 1,343,000 | 759,000 | 584,000 | 1,373,000 | 776,000 | 715,000 | 597,000 |
| 2018 [4] | 1,397,000 | 789,000 | 608,000 | 1,397,000 | 789,000 | 726,000 | 608,000 |

[1] Constant dollars based on the Consumer Price Index, prepared by the Bureau of Labor Statistics, U.S. Department of Labor, adjusted to a school-year basis. [2] Postsecondary data through 1996 are for institutions of higher education; thereafter, data are for degree-granting institutions. See source for details. [3] Data for elementary and secondary education are estimated; data for degree-granting institutions are actual. [4] Estimated.

Source: U.S. National Center for Education Statistics, *Digest of Education Statistics*, "Advance Release of Selected 2018 Digest Tables," <http://www.nces.ed.gov/programs/digest/>, accessed June 2019.

# Table 249. School Enrollment: 1990 to 2028

[In thousands (60,683 represents 60,683,000). As of Fall]

| Year | All levels | | | Pre-kindergarten through grade 8 | | Grades 9 through 12 | | College [3] | |
|---|---|---|---|---|---|---|---|---|---|
| | Total | Public | Private | Public | Private [1,2] | Public | Private [1] | Public | Private |
| 1990 | 60,683 | 52,061 | 8,622 | 29,876 | 4,512 | 11,341 | 1,136 | 10,845 | 2,974 |
| 1995 | 65,020 | 55,933 | 9,087 | 32,338 | 4,756 | 12,502 | 1,163 | 11,092 | 3,169 |
| 2000 | 68,685 | 58,956 | 9,729 | 33,686 | 4,906 | 13,517 | 1,264 | 11,753 | 3,560 |
| 2001 | 69,920 | 59,905 | 10,014 | 33,936 | 5,023 | 13,736 | 1,296 | 12,233 | 3,695 |
| 2002 | 71,015 | 60,935 | 10,080 | 34,114 | 4,915 | 14,069 | 1,306 | 12,752 | 3,860 |
| 2003 | 71,551 | 61,399 | 10,152 | 34,201 | 4,788 | 14,339 | 1,311 | 12,859 | 4,053 |
| 2004 | 72,154 | 61,776 | 10,379 | 34,178 | 4,756 | 14,618 | 1,331 | 12,980 | 4,292 |
| 2005 | 72,674 | 62,135 | 10,539 | 34,204 | 4,724 | 14,909 | 1,349 | 13,022 | 4,466 |
| 2006 | 73,061 | 62,491 | 10,570 | 34,235 | 4,631 | 15,081 | 1,360 | 13,175 | 4,579 |
| 2007 | 73,459 | 62,791 | 10,667 | 34,204 | 4,546 | 15,086 | 1,364 | 13,501 | 4,757 |
| 2008 | 74,055 | 63,236 | 10,818 | 34,286 | 4,365 | 14,980 | 1,342 | 13,971 | 5,111 |
| 2009 | 75,163 | 64,172 | 10,991 | 34,409 | 4,179 | 14,952 | 1,309 | 14,811 | 5,503 |
| 2010 | 75,886 | 64,626 | 11,260 | 34,625 | 4,084 | 14,860 | 1,299 | 15,142 | 5,877 |
| 2011 | 75,800 | 64,638 | 11,162 | 34,773 | 3,977 | 14,749 | 1,291 | 15,116 | 5,894 |
| 2012 | 75,748 | 64,656 | 11,092 | 35,018 | 4,031 | 14,753 | 1,302 | 14,885 | 5,760 |
| 2013 | 75,817 | 64,791 | 11,026 | 35,251 | 4,084 | 14,794 | 1,312 | 14,747 | 5,630 |
| 2014 | 76,097 | 64,967 | 11,130 | 35,370 | 4,202 | 14,943 | 1,373 | 14,655 | 5,554 |
| 2015 | 76,177 | 65,011 | 11,166 | 35,388 | 4,304 | 15,050 | 1,446 | 14,573 | 5,415 |
| 2016 | 76,238 | 65,201 | 11,037 | 35,477 | 4,301 | 15,138 | 1,474 | 14,586 | 5,261 |
| 2017, projections [4] | 76,242 | 65,255 | 10,987 | 35,473 | 4,300 | 15,222 | 1,481 | 14,560 | 5,205 |
| 2018, projections | 76,346 | 65,336 | 11,010 | 35,465 | 4,297 | 15,264 | 1,492 | 14,608 | 5,220 |
| 2019, projections | 76,476 | 65,435 | 11,041 | 35,457 | 4,308 | 15,313 | 1,494 | 14,665 | 5,239 |
| 2020, projections | 76,606 | 65,542 | 11,064 | 35,384 | 4,316 | 15,473 | 1,505 | 14,685 | 5,243 |
| 2021, projections | 76,675 | 65,600 | 11,075 | 35,231 | 4,310 | 15,661 | 1,517 | 14,708 | 5,248 |
| 2022, projections | 76,856 | 65,748 | 11,108 | 35,189 | 4,337 | 15,823 | 1,515 | 14,736 | 5,255 |
| 2023, projections | 77,013 | 65,872 | 11,141 | 35,235 | 4,356 | 15,863 | 1,520 | 14,774 | 5,266 |
| 2024, projections | 77,126 | 65,949 | 11,177 | 35,376 | 4,374 | 15,748 | 1,521 | 14,824 | 5,283 |
| 2025, projections | 77,206 | 65,995 | 11,211 | 35,519 | 4,392 | 15,601 | 1,518 | 14,876 | 5,301 |
| 2026, projections | 77,308 | 66,059 | 11,248 | 35,703 | 4,413 | 15,420 | 1,514 | 14,936 | 5,321 |
| 2027, projections | 77,471 | 66,193 | 11,277 | 35,894 | 4,434 | 15,334 | 1,514 | 14,965 | 5,329 |
| 2028, projections | 77,693 | 66,394 | 11,299 | 36,073 | 4,454 | 15,346 | 1,515 | 14,975 | 5,330 |

[1] Since the biennial Private School Universe Survey (PSS) is collected in the fall of odd numbered years, data for even numbered years are estimated based on data from the PSS. [2] Includes private nursery and pre-kindergarten enrollment in schools that offer kindergarten or higher grades. [3] Data beginning 1996 based on new classification system. See footnote 1, Table 289. [4] Pre-K through 12 are projections; college data are actual.

Source: U.S. National Center for Education Statistics, *Digest of Education Statistics*, "Advance Release of Selected 2018 Digest Tables," <http://www.nces.ed.gov/programs/digest/>, accessed June 2019.

# Table 250. School Enrollment, Faculty, Graduates, and Finances—Projections: 2018 to 2024

[In units as indicated (56,618 represents 56,618,000). As of the fall for the academic years indicated below, except as noted. Data for higher education are for degree-granting institutions that grant associate's or higher degrees and participate in Title IV federal financial aid programs]

| Item | Unit | 2018 | 2019 | 2020 | 2021 | 2022 | 2023 | 2024 |
|---|---|---|---|---|---|---|---|---|
| **ELEMENTARY AND SECONDARY SCHOOLS** | | | | | | | | |
| **School enrollment, total** | **1,000** | **56,618** | **56,753** | **56,961** | **57,175** | **57,371** | **57,572** | **57,733** |
| Pre-kindergarten through grade 8 | 1,000 | 39,961 | 40,057 | 40,111 | 40,116 | 40,165 | 40,343 | 40,534 |
| Grades 9 through 12 | 1,000 | 16,658 | 16,696 | 16,850 | 17,059 | 17,206 | 17,228 | 17,200 |
| Public | 1,000 | 50,701 | 50,803 | 50,971 | 51,146 | 51,317 | 51,488 | 51,619 |
| Pre-kindergarten through grade 8 | 1,000 | 35,606 | 35,683 | 35,717 | 35,711 | 35,745 | 35,902 | 36,071 |
| Grades 9 through 12 | 1,000 | 15,095 | 15,120 | 15,254 | 15,435 | 15,572 | 15,585 | 15,549 |
| Private | 1,000 | 5,917 | 5,951 | 5,989 | 6,029 | 6,054 | 6,084 | 6,114 |
| Pre-kindergarten through grade 8 | 1,000 | 4,355 | 4,374 | 4,394 | 4,405 | 4,420 | 4,441 | 4,463 |
| Grades 9 through 12 | 1,000 | 1,563 | 1,576 | 1,596 | 1,624 | 1,634 | 1,643 | 1,651 |
| **Classroom teachers, total FTE [1]** | **1,000** | **3,644** | **3,675** | **3,704** | **3,737** | **3,768** | **3,798** | **3,829** |
| Public | 1,000 | 3,161 | 3,188 | 3,213 | 3,242 | 3,268 | 3,294 | 3,320 |
| Private | 1,000 | 483 | 487 | 491 | 495 | 500 | 504 | 509 |
| **High school graduates, total [2]** | **1,000** | **3,643** | **3,597** | **3,613** | **3,640** | **3,644** | **3,706** | **3,768** |
| Public | 1,000 | 3,285 | 3,252 | 3,271 | 3,291 | 3,305 | 3,366 | 3,425 |
| Private | 1,000 | 358 | 345 | 342 | 350 | 339 | 339 | 343 |
| **Public schools: [2]** | | | | | | | | |
| Constant (2016-2017) dollars: [3] | | | | | | | | |
| Current school expenditure | Bil. dol. | 630 | 640 | 650 | 661 | 670 | 678 | 685 |
| Per pupil in fall enrollment | Dollar | 12,430 | 12,600 | 12,760 | 12,930 | 13,050 | 13,170 | 13,280 |
| **HIGHER EDUCATION** | | | | | | | | |
| **Enrollment, total** | **1,000** | **19,924** | **20,014** | **20,047** | **20,085** | **20,129** | **20,186** | **20,259** |
| Full-time | 1,000 | 12,128 | 12,166 | 12,164 | 12,166 | 12,178 | 12,197 | 12,230 |
| Males | 1,000 | 5,482 | 5,499 | 5,496 | 5,495 | 5,499 | 5,507 | 5,523 |
| Females | 1,000 | 6,646 | 6,667 | 6,668 | 6,671 | 6,679 | 6,690 | 6,707 |
| Part-time | 1,000 | 7,796 | 7,847 | 7,883 | 7,919 | 7,952 | 7,989 | 8,029 |
| Males | 1,000 | 3,193 | 3,214 | 3,230 | 3,244 | 3,257 | 3,272 | 3,287 |
| Females | 1,000 | 4,603 | 4,633 | 4,654 | 4,675 | 4,695 | 4,717 | 4,743 |
| Public | 1,000 | 14,797 | 14,865 | 14,888 | 14,914 | 14,946 | 14,989 | 15,044 |
| Four-year institutions | 1,000 | 8,416 | 8,451 | 8,466 | 8,481 | 8,497 | 8,519 | 8,548 |
| Two-year institutions | 1,000 | 6,381 | 6,413 | 6,423 | 6,433 | 6,448 | 6,470 | 6,496 |
| Private | 1,000 | 5,126 | 5,149 | 5,159 | 5,171 | 5,183 | 5,198 | 5,215 |
| Four-year institutions | 1,000 | 4,844 | 4,865 | 4,876 | 4,887 | 4,899 | 4,913 | 4,929 |
| Two-year institutions | 1,000 | 283 | 204 | 284 | 283 | 284 | 285 | 286 |
| Undergraduate | 1,000 | 16,998 | 17,069 | 17,088 | 17,109 | 17,136 | 17,179 | 17,242 |
| Postbaccalaureate | 1,000 | 2,926 | 2,945 | 2,960 | 2,975 | 2,993 | 3,008 | 3,017 |
| Full-time equivalent | 1,000 | 14,953 | 15,011 | 15,022 | 15,037 | 15,060 | 15,094 | 15,141 |
| Public | 1,000 | 10,689 | 10,730 | 10,737 | 10,746 | 10,762 | 10,786 | 10,821 |
| 2-year | 1,000 | 3,715 | 3,732 | 3,732 | 3,734 | 3,743 | 3,754 | 3,768 |
| 4-year | 1,000 | 6,974 | 6,998 | 7,004 | 7,011 | 7,019 | 7,032 | 7,053 |
| Private | 1,000 | 4,264 | 4,280 | 4,285 | 4,291 | 4,298 | 4,307 | 4,319 |
| 2-year | 1,000 | 261 | 262 | 262 | 262 | 262 | 263 | 264 |
| 4 year | 1,000 | 4,003 | 4,018 | 4,023 | 4,029 | 4,036 | 4,044 | 4,056 |
| **Degrees conferred, total [2]** | **1,000** | **3,878** | **3,898** | **3,905** | **3,916** | **3,925** | **3,937** | **3,951** |
| Associate's | 1,000 | 1,034 | 1,040 | 1,041 | 1,043 | 1,045 | 1,049 | 1,053 |
| Bachelor's | 1,000 | 1,882 | 1,889 | 1,891 | 1,893 | 1,895 | 1,898 | 1,905 |
| Master's | 1,000 | 780 | 786 | 789 | 794 | 798 | 802 | 805 |
| Doctoral [4] | 1,000 | 182 | 183 | 184 | 186 | 187 | 188 | 188 |

[1] Full-time equivalent. [2] For the academic year beginning in year shown. [3] Based on the Consumer Price Index (CPI) for all urban consumers, U.S. Bureau of Labor Statistics. CPI adjusted to a school year basis by NCES. [4] Doctoral degrees include Ph.D., Ed.D., and comparable degrees at the doctoral level. Includes most degrees formerly classified as first-professional, such as M.D., D.D.S., and law degrees.

Source: U.S. National Center for Education Statistics, *Projections of Education Statistics to 2027*, February 2019. See also <https://nces.ed.gov/surveys/annualreports/>.

# Table 251. School Enrollment by Control and Level: 1980 to 2019

[In thousands (58,305 represents 58,305,000). As of Fall. Data below college level are for regular day schools and exclude subcollegiate departments of colleges, federal schools, and home-schooled children. Based on survey of state education agencies; see source for details. For more projections, see Table 249 and Table 250]

| Control of school and level | 1980 | 1990 | 2000 | 2005 | 2010 | 2015 | 2016 | 2017, proj. | 2018, proj. | 2019, proj. |
|---|---|---|---|---|---|---|---|---|---|---|
| **Total** | **58,305** | **60,683** | **68,685** | **72,674** | **75,886** | **[5] 76,177** | **[5] 76,238** | **76,242** | **76,346** | **76,476** |
| Public | 50,335 | 52,061 | 58,956 | 62,135 | 64,626 | [5] 65,011 | [5] 65,201 | 65,255 | 65,336 | 65,435 |
| Private | 7,971 | 8,622 | 9,729 | 10,539 | 11,260 | 11,166 | 11,037 | 10,987 | 11,010 | 11,041 |
| Pre-kindergarten through 8 | 31,639 | 34,388 | 38,592 | 38,928 | 38,708 | [5] 39,692 | [5] 39,779 | 39,773 | 39,761 | 39,766 |
| Public | 27,647 | 29,876 | 33,686 | 34,204 | 34,625 | [5] 35,388 | [5] 35,477 | 35,473 | 35,465 | 35,457 |
| Private [1] | 3,992 | [4] 4,512 | [4] 4,906 | 4,724 | [4] 4,084 | 4,304 | [6] 4,301 | 4,300 | 4,297 | 4,308 |
| Grades 9 through 12 | 14,570 | 12,476 | 14,781 | 16,258 | 16,159 | 16,496 | 16,612 | 16,703 | 16,756 | 16,806 |
| Public | 13,231 | 11,341 | 13,517 | 14,909 | 14,860 | 15,050 | 15,138 | 15,222 | 15,264 | 15,313 |
| Private [1] | 1,339 | [4] 1,136 | [4] 1,264 | 1,349 | [4] 1,299 | 1,446 | [6] 1,474 | 1,481 | 1,492 | 1,494 |
| College [2, 3] | 12,097 | 13,819 | 15,312 | 17,487 | 21,019 | 19,988 | 19,847 | 19,766 | 19,828 | 19,904 |
| Public | 9,457 | 10,845 | 11,753 | 13,022 | 15,142 | 14,573 | 14,586 | 14,560 | 14,608 | 14,665 |
| Private | 2,640 | 2,974 | 3,560 | 4,466 | 5,877 | 5,415 | 5,261 | 5,205 | 5,220 | 5,239 |
| Not-for-profit | 2,528 | 2,760 | 3,109 | 3,455 | 3,854 | 4,066 | 4,079 | 4,106 | (NA) | (NA) |
| For profit | 112 | 214 | 450 | 1,011 | 2,023 | 1,349 | 1,182 | 1,099 | (NA) | (NA) |

NA Not available. [1] Beginning in fall 1985, data include estimates for an expanded universe of private schools; avoid direct comparisons with data for earlier years. [2] Beginning 2000, reflects new classification system. See both headnote and footnote 1, Table 289. [3] Data for 2017 are actual. [4] Estimated. [5] Data for public school prekindergarten enrollment includes imputations for California and Oregon for 2015, and imputations for California for 2016. [6] Private school data projected for 2016.

Source: U.S. National Center for Education Statistics, *Digest of Education Statistics*, "Advance Release of Selected 2018 Digest Tables," <http://www.nces.ed.gov/programs/digest/>, accessed June 2019.

## Table 252. School Enrollment by Age: 1970 to 2017

[Enrollment in thousands (60,357 represents 60,357,000); rate as percent of total population in each age group. As of October. Covers civilian noninstitutional population enrolled in nursery school and above. Based on Current Population Survey; see text, Section 1 and Appendix III]

| Age | 1970 | 1980 | 1990 | 1995 | 2000 | 2005 | 2010 | 2015 | 2016 | 2017 |
|---|---|---|---|---|---|---|---|---|---|---|
| **ENROLLMENT (1,000)** | | | | | | | | | | |
| **Total, 3 to 34 years old** | **60,357** | **57,348** | **60,588** | **66,939** | **69,560** | **72,768** | **75,148** | **77,066** | **74,672** | **73,883** |
| 3 and 4 years old | 1,461 | 2,280 | 3,292 | 4,042 | 4,097 | 4,383 | 4,706 | 4,203 | 4,289 | 4,319 |
| 5 and 6 years old | 7,000 | 5,853 | 7,207 | 7,901 | 7,648 | 7,486 | 7,955 | 7,507 | 7,507 | 7,516 |
| 7 to 13 years old | 28,943 | 23,751 | 25,016 | 27,003 | 28,296 | 27,936 | 27,984 | 28,250 | 28,381 | 28,152 |
| 14 and 15 years old | 7,869 | 7,282 | 6,555 | 7,651 | 7,885 | 8,375 | 7,736 | 8,207 | 8,107 | 8,082 |
| 16 and 17 years old | 6,927 | 7,129 | 6,098 | 6,997 | 7,341 | 8,472 | 7,963 | 7,923 | 7,879 | 7,933 |
| 18 and 19 years old | 3,322 | 3,788 | 4,044 | 4,274 | 4,926 | 5,109 | 5,904 | 5,591 | 5,741 | 5,606 |
| 20 and 21 years old | 1,949 | 2,515 | 2,852 | 3,025 | 3,314 | 4,069 | 4,552 | 4,641 | 4,597 | 4,570 |
| 22 to 24 years old | 1,410 | 1,931 | 2,231 | 2,545 | 2,731 | 3,254 | 3,602 | 3,793 | 3,841 | 3,696 |
| 25 to 29 years old | 1,011 | 1,714 | 2,013 | 2,216 | 2,030 | 2,340 | 3,088 | 2,880 | 2,966 | 2,758 |
| 30 to 34 years old | 466 | 1,105 | 1,281 | 1,284 | 1,292 | 1,344 | 1,658 | 1,398 | 1,364 | 1,251 |
| 35 years old and over | (NA) | 1,290 | 2,439 | 2,830 | 2,653 | 3,013 | 3,372 | 2,674 | 2,561 | 2,526 |
| **ENROLLMENT RATE** | | | | | | | | | | |
| **Total, 3 to 34 years old** | **56.4** | **49.7** | **50.2** | **53.7** | **55.9** | **56.5** | **56.5** | **55.2** | **55.2** | **54.6** |
| 3 and 4 years old | 20.5 | 36.7 | 44.4 | 48.7 | 52.1 | 53.6 | 53.2 | 52.7 | 53.8 | 53.8 |
| 5 and 6 years old | 89.5 | 95.7 | 96.5 | 96.0 | 95.6 | 95.4 | 94.5 | 94.2 | 93.3 | 93.5 |
| 7 to 13 years old | 99.2 | 99.3 | 99.6 | 98.9 | 98.2 | 98.6 | 98.0 | 97.7 | 98.2 | 97.5 |
| 14 and 15 years old | 98.1 | 98.2 | 99.0 | 98.9 | 98.7 | 98.0 | 98.1 | 98.0 | 98.0 | 98.2 |
| 16 and 17 years old | 90.0 | 89.0 | 92.5 | 93.6 | 92.8 | 95.1 | 96.1 | 93.7 | 93.0 | 92.9 |
| 18 and 19 years old | 47.7 | 46.4 | 57.3 | 59.4 | 61.2 | 67.6 | 69.2 | 68.5 | 69.5 | 68.2 |
| 20 and 21 years old | 31.9 | 31.0 | 39.7 | 44.9 | 44.1 | 48.7 | 52.4 | 53.3 | 55.5 | 55.0 |
| 22 to 24 years old | 14.9 | 16.3 | 21.0 | 23.2 | 24.6 | 27.3 | 28.9 | 28.8 | 28.8 | 28.4 |
| 25 to 29 years old | 7.5 | 9.3 | 9.7 | 11.6 | 11.4 | 11.9 | 14.6 | 13.2 | 13.2 | 12.1 |
| 30 to 34 years old | 4.2 | 6.5 | 5.8 | 6.0 | 6.7 | 6.9 | 8.3 | 6.6 | 6.4 | 5.9 |
| 35 years old and over | (NA) | 1.6 | 2.1 | 2.2 | 1.9 | 2.0 | 2.1 | 1.6 | 1.5 | 1.5 |

NA Not available.

Source: U.S. Census Bureau, Current Population Reports, P-20, and earlier reports; and "School Enrollment," <https://www.census.gov/topics/education/school-enrollment/data/tables.All.html>, accessed December 2018.

## Table 253. School Enrollment by Race, Hispanic Origin, and Age: 2000 to 2017

[Enrollment in thousands (54,257 represents 54,257,000); rate as percent of total population in each age group. As of October. See headnote, Table 252]

| Age | White [1] | | | Black [1] | | | Hispanic [2] | | |
|---|---|---|---|---|---|---|---|---|---|
| | 2000 | 2010 | 2017 | 2000 | 2010 | 2017 | 2000 | 2010 | 2017 |
| **ENROLLMENT (1,000)** | | | | | | | | | |
| **Total, 3 to 34 years old** | **54,257** | **56,776** | **53,353** | **11,115** | **11,272** | **11,066** | **9,928** | **15,235** | **17,539** |
| 3 and 4 years old | 3,091 | 3,439 | 3,052 | 725 | 776 | 718 | 518 | 1,025 | 1,015 |
| 5 and 6 years old | 5,959 | 5,956 | 5,400 | 1,219 | 1,207 | 1,088 | 1,390 | 1,961 | 1,960 |
| 7 to 13 years old | 22,061 | 21,201 | 20,327 | 4,675 | 4,108 | 4,280 | 4,373 | 6,241 | 7,211 |
| 14 and 15 years old | 6,176 | 5,907 | 5,954 | 1,260 | 1,157 | 1,167 | 1,093 | 1,555 | 1,896 |
| 16 and 17 years old | 5,845 | 6,059 | 5,758 | 1,106 | 1,245 | 1,148 | 959 | 1,448 | 1,774 |
| 18 and 19 years old | 3,924 | 4,566 | 4,174 | 716 | 837 | 835 | 617 | 1,171 | 1,321 |
| 20 and 21 years old | 2,688 | 3,432 | 3,292 | 416 | 678 | 607 | 311 | 582 | 837 |
| 22 to 24 years old | 2,101 | 2,720 | 2,585 | 393 | 514 | 533 | 309 | 559 | 744 |
| 25 to 29 years old | 1,473 | 2,289 | 1,915 | 353 | 462 | 468 | 198 | 462 | 571 |
| 30 to 34 years old | 939 | 1,207 | 896 | 252 | 288 | 222 | 160 | 231 | 210 |
| 35 years old and over | 2,087 | 2,462 | 1,795 | 387 | 697 | 543 | 235 | 435 | 434 |
| **ENROLLMENT RATE** | | | | | | | | | |
| **Total, 3 to 34 years old** | **55.1** | **55.8** | **53.9** | **59.0** | **58.4** | **55.1** | **51.3** | **55.1** | **56.4** |
| 3 and 4 years old | 50.2 | 52.1 | 53.4 | 52.1 | 56.2 | 57.7 | 35.9 | 44.2 | 47.9 |
| 5 and 6 years old | 95.3 | 94.2 | 93.5 | 94.2 | 94.4 | 91.5 | 94.3 | 94.3 | 95.0 |
| 7 to 13 years old | 98.2 | 97.9 | 97.3 | 97.9 | 98.0 | 98.0 | 97.5 | 97.8 | 97.2 |
| 14 and 15 years old | 98.4 | 98.1 | 98.4 | 98.0 | 98.5 | 96.6 | 96.2 | 97.9 | 98.4 |
| 16 and 17 years old | 92.8 | 96.2 | 93.1 | 96.2 | 95.5 | 90.7 | 87.0 | 96.0 | 92.7 |
| 18 and 19 years old | 61.3 | 70.0 | 67.8 | 70.0 | 62.7 | 67.0 | 49.5 | 66.2 | 67.2 |
| 20 and 21 years old | 44.9 | 51.6 | 54.7 | 51.6 | 50.2 | 47.5 | 26.1 | 37.0 | 46.0 |
| 22 to 24 years old | 23.7 | 28.1 | 26.9 | 28.1 | 29.0 | 27.5 | 18.2 | 23.8 | 25.9 |
| 25 to 29 years old | 10.4 | 13.9 | 11.5 | 13.9 | 16.0 | 13.5 | 7.4 | 11.4 | 12.3 |
| 30 to 34 years old | 6.0 | 7.8 | 5.6 | 7.8 | 10.9 | 7.7 | 5.6 | 5.7 | 4.8 |
| 35 years old and over | 1.8 | 1.9 | 1.3 | 2.6 | 4.0 | 2.7 | 2.0 | 2.3 | 1.8 |

[1] Beginning 2003, represents persons who selected this race group only. See footnote 4, Table 256. [2] Persons of Hispanic origin may be of any race.

Source: U.S. Census Bureau, Current Population Reports, P-20, and earlier reports; and "School Enrollment," <https://www.census.gov/topics/education/school-enrollment/data/tables.All.html>, accessed December 2018.

# Table 254. Enrollment in Public and Private Schools: 1970 to 2017

[In millions (52.2 represents 52,200,000), except percent. As of October. For civilian noninstitutional population. Prior to 1995, total enrolled does not include the population age 35 and over. For enrollment of population age 35 and over, see Table 252. Based on Current Population Survey]

| Year | Public | | | | | | Private | | | | | |
|---|---|---|---|---|---|---|---|---|---|---|---|---|
| | Total | Nursery | Kinder-garten | Elemen-tary | High school | College | Total | Nursery | Kinder-garten | Elemen-tary | High school | College |
| 1970.......... | 52.2 | 0.3 | 2.6 | 30.0 | 13.5 | 5.7 | 8.1 | 0.8 | 0.5 | 3.9 | 1.2 | 1.7 |
| 1980.......... | (NA) | 0.6 | 2.7 | 24.4 | (NA) | (NA) | (NA) | 1.4 | 0.5 | 3.1 | (NA) | (NA) |
| 1985.......... | 49.0 | 0.9 | 3.2 | 23.8 | 12.8 | 8.4 | 9.0 | 1.6 | 0.6 | 3.1 | 1.2 | 2.5 |
| 1990 [1]....... | 51.8 | 1.2 | 3.3 | 26.6 | 11.8 | 8.9 | 8.7 | 2.2 | 0.6 | 2.7 | 0.9 | 2.4 |
| 2000.......... | 61.2 | 2.2 | 3.2 | 29.4 | 14.4 | 12.0 | 11.0 | 2.2 | 0.7 | 3.5 | 1.3 | 3.3 |
| 2001.......... | 62.4 | 2.2 | 3.1 | 29.8 | 14.8 | 12.4 | 10.8 | 2.1 | 0.6 | 3.4 | 1.2 | 3.5 |
| 2002.......... | 62.8 | 2.2 | 3.0 | 29.7 | 15.1 | 12.8 | 11.3 | 2.2 | 0.6 | 3.5 | 1.3 | 3.7 |
| 2003.......... | 63.8 | 2.6 | 3.1 | 29.2 | 15.8 | 13.1 | 11.1 | 2.4 | 0.6 | 3.4 | 1.3 | 3.5 |
| 2004.......... | 64.2 | 2.5 | 3.4 | 29.2 | 15.5 | 13.7 | 11.2 | 2.3 | 0.6 | 3.4 | 1.3 | 3.7 |
| 2005.......... | 64.3 | 2.5 | 3.3 | 29.1 | 15.9 | 13.4 | 11.5 | 2.1 | 0.6 | 3.4 | 1.4 | 4.0 |
| 2006.......... | 64.1 | 2.5 | 3.6 | 29.0 | 15.6 | 13.5 | 11.1 | 2.2 | 0.5 | 3.1 | 1.5 | 3.8 |
| 2007.......... | 65.2 | 2.6 | 3.7 | 29.1 | 15.8 | 14.1 | 10.8 | 2.1 | 0.5 | 3.1 | 1.3 | 3.9 |
| 2008.......... | 65.5 | 2.6 | 3.6 | 29.2 | 15.4 | 14.7 | 10.8 | 2.0 | 0.5 | 3.2 | 1.3 | 3.9 |
| 2009.......... | 66.9 | 2.7 | 3.8 | 29.4 | 15.3 | 15.7 | 10.4 | 2.0 | 0.4 | 2.9 | 1.2 | 4.0 |
| 2010.......... | 67.9 | 2.8 | 3.8 | 29.8 | 15.3 | 16.2 | 10.6 | 2.1 | 0.4 | 2.8 | 1.2 | 4.1 |
| 2011.......... | 68.2 | 2.9 | 3.7 | 30.0 | 15.4 | 16.1 | 10.9 | 2.0 | 0.5 | 2.9 | 1.2 | 4.3 |
| 2012.......... | 67.8 | 2.7 | 3.7 | 29.9 | 15.7 | 15.8 | 10.7 | 1.9 | 0.5 | 2.8 | 1.3 | 4.2 |
| 2013.......... | 67.4 | 2.6 | 3.7 | 30.2 | 15.5 | 15.5 | 10.3 | 2.1 | 0.4 | 2.7 | 1.1 | 4.0 |
| 2014.......... | 66.8 | 2.7 | 3.6 | 29.8 | 15.4 | 15.3 | 10.4 | 2.0 | 0.5 | 2.8 | 1.3 | 3.9 |
| 2015.......... | 67.0 | 2.6 | 3.6 | 30.2 | 15.4 | 15.2 | 10.1 | 1.9 | 0.4 | 2.7 | 1.2 | 3.9 |
| 2016.......... | 66.7 | 2.8 | 3.7 | 30.0 | 15.3 | 15.0 | 10.5 | 1.9 | 0.4 | 2.6 | 1.3 | 4.2 |
| 2017.......... | 66.5 | 2.8 | 3.5 | 29.9 | 15.5 | 14.8 | 9.9 | 1.9 | 0.4 | 2.7 | 1.3 | 3.6 |
| Percent White: | | | | | | | | | | | | |
| 1970.......... | 84.5 | 59.5 | 84.4 | 83.1 | 85.6 | 90.7 | 93.4 | 91.1 | 88.2 | 94.1 | 96.1 | 92.8 |
| 1980.......... | (NA) | 68.2 | 80.7 | 80.9 | (NA) | (NA) | (NA) | 89.0 | 87.0 | 90.7 | (NA) | (NA) |
| 1990.......... | 79.6 | 71.7 | 78.3 | 78.9 | 79.3 | 83.4 | 87.5 | 89.6 | 83.2 | 88.2 | 89.4 | 85.1 |
| 2000.......... | 77.0 | 69.4 | 77.3 | 76.7 | 78.0 | 78.0 | 83.5 | 84.8 | 82.7 | 85.9 | 84.6 | 79.8 |
| 2005 [2]....... | 75.7 | 71.3 | 78.0 | 75.2 | 76.0 | 76.7 | 81.4 | 83.6 | 79.0 | 83.0 | 83.6 | 78.4 |
| 2010 [2]....... | 74.9 | 71.8 | 72.9 | 75.0 | 75.1 | 75.4 | 78.9 | 81.0 | 79.4 | 80.9 | 84.5 | 74.7 |
| 2013 [2]....... | 72.8 | 68.0 | 69.5 | 73.2 | 72.9 | 73.3 | 75.9 | 76.6 | 81.2 | 79.5 | 78.3 | 72.4 |
| 2014 [2]....... | 72.7 | 67.4 | 70.7 | 72.7 | 73.6 | 73.3 | 74.6 | 77.0 | 68.2 | 78.4 | 76.0 | 70.8 |
| 2015 [2]....... | 72.3 | 68.1 | 72.2 | 72.2 | 72.9 | 72.7 | 75.5 | 75.5 | 79.4 | 78.7 | 79.4 | 71.9 |
| 2016 [2]....... | 72.2 | 70.7 | 70.6 | 72.7 | 71.9 | 72.4 | 74.3 | 75.3 | 77.2 | 74.1 | 78.7 | 72.3 |
| 2017 [2]....... | 71.6 | 67.8 | 72.8 | 71.6 | 72.7 | 71.1 | 75.8 | 75.5 | 80.1 | 76.3 | 75.3 | 75.2 |

NA Not available. [1] Beginning 1990, based on a revised edit and tabulation package. [2] Beginning in 2003, represents persons who selected this race group only. See footnote 4, Table 256.

Source: U.S. Census Bureau, Current Population Reports, P-20, and earlier reports; and "School Enrollment," <https://www.census.gov/topics/education/school-enrollment/data/tables.All.html>, accessed December 2018.

# Table 255. School Enrollment by Sex and Level: 1970 to 2017

[In millions (60.4 represents 60,400,000). As of October. For the civilian noninstitutional population. Prior to 1980, data cover persons age 3 to 34; beginning 1980, age 3 and over. Elementary includes kindergarten and grades 1–8; high school, grades 9–12; and college, 2-year and 4-year colleges, universities, and graduate and professional schools. Data for college represent degree-credit enrollment. See headnote, Table 252]

| Year | All levels [1] | | | Elementary | | | High school | | | College | | |
|---|---|---|---|---|---|---|---|---|---|---|---|---|
| | Total | Male | Female | Total | Male | Female | Total | Male | Female | Total | Male | Female |
| 1970.......... | 60.4 | 31.4 | 28.9 | 37.1 | 19.0 | 18.1 | 14.7 | 7.4 | 7.3 | 7.4 | 4.4 | 3.0 |
| 1980.......... | 58.6 | 29.6 | 29.1 | 30.6 | 15.8 | 14.9 | 14.6 | 7.3 | 7.3 | 11.4 | 5.4 | 6.0 |
| 1990 [2]....... | 63.0 | 31.5 | 31.5 | 33.2 | 17.1 | 16.0 | 12.8 | 6.5 | 6.4 | 13.6 | 6.2 | 7.4 |
| 1998.......... | 72.1 | 36.0 | 36.1 | 36.4 | 18.7 | 17.7 | 15.6 | 7.9 | 7.6 | 15.5 | 6.9 | 8.6 |
| 1999.......... | 72.4 | 36.3 | 36.1 | 36.7 | 18.8 | 17.9 | 15.9 | 8.2 | 7.7 | 15.2 | 7.0 | 8.2 |
| 2000.......... | 72.2 | 35.8 | 36.4 | 36.7 | 18.9 | 17.9 | 15.8 | 8.1 | 7.7 | 15.3 | 6.7 | 8.6 |
| 2001.......... | 73.1 | 36.3 | 36.9 | 36.9 | 19.0 | 17.9 | 16.1 | 8.2 | 7.8 | 15.9 | 6.9 | 9.0 |
| 2002.......... | 74.0 | 36.8 | 37.3 | 36.7 | 18.9 | 17.8 | 16.4 | 8.3 | 8.0 | 16.5 | 7.2 | 9.3 |
| 2003.......... | 74.9 | 37.3 | 37.6 | 36.3 | 18.7 | 17.6 | 17.1 | 8.6 | 8.4 | 16.6 | 7.3 | 9.3 |
| 2004.......... | 75.5 | 37.4 | 38.0 | 36.5 | 19.0 | 17.6 | 16.8 | 8.4 | 8.4 | 17.4 | 7.6 | 9.8 |
| 2005.......... | 75.8 | 37.4 | 38.4 | 36.4 | 18.6 | 17.7 | 17.4 | 8.9 | 8.5 | 17.5 | 7.5 | 9.9 |
| 2006.......... | 75.2 | 37.2 | 38.0 | 36.1 | 18.5 | 17.6 | 17.1 | 8.8 | 8.4 | 17.2 | 7.5 | 9.7 |
| 2007.......... | 76.0 | 37.6 | 38.4 | 36.3 | 18.6 | 17.7 | 17.1 | 8.8 | 8.3 | 18.0 | 7.8 | 10.1 |
| 2008.......... | 76.4 | 37.8 | 38.6 | 36.4 | 18.7 | 17.7 | 16.7 | 8.5 | 8.2 | 18.6 | 8.3 | 10.3 |
| 2009.......... | 77.3 | 38.0 | 39.3 | 36.4 | 18.6 | 17.7 | 16.4 | 8.4 | 8.1 | 19.8 | 8.6 | 11.1 |
| 2010.......... | 78.5 | 38.7 | 39.8 | 36.8 | 18.8 | 18.1 | 16.6 | 8.5 | 8.1 | 20.3 | 9.0 | 11.3 |
| 2011.......... | 79.0 | 39.2 | 39.8 | 37.1 | 19.0 | 18.1 | 16.6 | 8.6 | 8.1 | 20.4 | 9.1 | 11.3 |
| 2012.......... | 78.4 | 38.5 | 39.9 | 36.8 | 19.0 | 17.9 | 17.0 | 8.6 | 8.5 | 19.9 | 8.6 | 11.3 |
| 2013.......... | 77.8 | 38.3 | 39.5 | 37.0 | 19.0 | 18.0 | 16.6 | 8.4 | 8.2 | 19.5 | 8.5 | 10.9 |
| 2014.......... | 77.2 | 38.2 | 39.0 | 36.7 | 18.8 | 17.9 | 16.7 | 8.4 | 8.2 | 19.2 | 8.6 | 10.5 |
| 2015.......... | 77.1 | 38.2 | 38.9 | 36.9 | 18.9 | 18.0 | 16.5 | 8.4 | 8.1 | 19.1 | 8.5 | 10.6 |
| 2016.......... | 77.2 | 38.4 | 38.9 | 36.6 | 18.7 | 17.9 | 16.7 | 8.5 | 8.1 | 19.2 | 8.6 | 10.6 |
| 2017.......... | 76.4 | 37.8 | 38.6 | 36.5 | 18.7 | 17.8 | 16.8 | 8.6 | 8.3 | 18.4 | 8.1 | 10.3 |

[1] Includes nursery schools, not shown separately. [2] For data beginning 1990, based on a revised edit and tabulation package.

Source: U.S. Census Bureau, Current Population Reports, P-20, and earlier reports; and "School Enrollment," <https://www.census.gov/topics/education/school-enrollment/data/tables.All.html>, accessed December 2018.

## Table 256. Educational Attainment by Race and Hispanic Origin: 1970 to 2018

[In percent. For persons 25 years old and over. 1970 and 1980 data as of April 1 and based on sample data from the censuses of population. Other years as of March and based on the Current Population Survey; see text, Section 1 and Appendix III. See Table 257 for data by sex]

| Year | High school graduate or more [1] | | | | | College graduate or more [2] | | | | |
|------|--------|---------|---------|---------------------------|------------|--------|---------|---------|---------------------------|------------|
| | Total [3] | White [4] | Black [4] | Asian and Pacific Islander [4,5] | His-panic [6] | Total [3] | White [4] | Black [4] | Asian and Pacific Islander [4,5] | His-panic [6] |
| 1970 | 52.3 | 54.5 | 31.4 | 62.2 | 32.1 | 10.7 | 11.3 | 4.4 | 20.4 | 4.5 |
| 1975 | 62.5 | 64.5 | 42.5 | (NA) | 37.9 | 13.9 | 14.5 | 6.4 | (NA) | 6.3 |
| 1980 | 66.5 | 68.8 | 51.2 | 74.8 | 44.0 | 16.2 | 17.1 | 8.4 | 32.9 | 7.6 |
| 1985 | 73.9 | 75.5 | 59.8 | (NA) | 47.9 | 19.4 | 20.0 | 11.1 | (NA) | 8.5 |
| 1990 | 77.6 | 79.1 | 66.2 | 80.4 | 50.8 | 21.3 | 22.0 | 11.3 | 39.9 | 9.2 |
| 1995 | 81.7 | 83.0 | 73.8 | (NA) | 53.4 | 23.0 | 24.0 | 13.2 | (NA) | 9.3 |
| 2000 | 84.1 | 84.9 | 78.5 | 85.7 | 57.0 | 25.6 | 26.1 | 16.5 | 43.9 | 10.6 |
| 2003 | 84.6 | 85.1 | 80.0 | 87.6 | 57.0 | 27.2 | 27.6 | 17.3 | 49.8 | 11.4 |
| 2004 | 85.2 | 85.8 | 80.6 | 86.8 | 58.4 | 27.7 | 28.2 | 17.6 | 49.4 | 12.1 |
| 2005 | 85.2 | 85.8 | 81.1 | 87.6 | 58.5 | 27.7 | 28.1 | 17.6 | 50.2 | 12.0 |
| 2006 | 85.5 | 86.1 | 80.7 | 87.4 | 59.3 | 28.0 | 28.4 | 18.5 | 49.7 | 12.4 |
| 2007 | 85.7 | 86.2 | 82.3 | 87.8 | 60.3 | 28.7 | 29.1 | 18.5 | 52.1 | 12.7 |
| 2008 | 86.6 | 87.1 | 83.0 | 88.7 | 62.3 | 29.4 | 29.8 | 19.6 | 52.6 | 13.3 |
| 2009 | 86.7 | 87.1 | 84.1 | 88.2 | 61.9 | 29.5 | 29.9 | 19.3 | 52.3 | 13.2 |
| 2010 | 87.1 | 87.6 | 84.2 | 88.9 | 62.9 | 29.9 | 30.3 | 19.8 | 52.4 | 13.9 |
| 2011 | 87.6 | 88.1 | 84.5 | 88.6 | 64.3 | 30.4 | 31.0 | 19.9 | 50.3 | 14.1 |
| 2012 | 87.6 | 88.1 | 85.0 | 88.9 | 65.0 | 30.9 | 31.3 | 21.2 | 51.0 | 14.5 |
| 2013 | 88.2 | 88.6 | 85.1 | 90.1 | 66.2 | 31.7 | 32.0 | 21.8 | 53.2 | 15.1 |
| 2014 | 88.3 | 88.8 | 85.8 | 89.5 | 66.5 | 32.0 | 32.3 | 22.2 | 52.3 | 15.2 |
| 2015 | 88.4 | 88.8 | 87.0 | 89.1 | 66.7 | 32.5 | 32.8 | 22.5 | 53.9 | 15.5 |
| 2016 | 89.1 | 89.5 | 87.1 | 90.3 | 68.5 | 33.4 | 33.7 | 23.3 | 55.9 | 16.4 |
| 2017 | 89.6 | 90.1 | 87.3 | 90.9 | 70.5 | 34.2 | 34.5 | 23.9 | 54.8 | 17.2 |
| 2018 | 89.8 | 90.2 | 87.9 | 90.5 | 71.6 | 35.0 | 35.2 | 25.2 | 56.5 | 18.3 |

NA Not available. [1] Through 1991, completed 4 years of high school or more. [2] Through 1991, completed 4 years of college or more. [3] Includes other races not shown separately. [4] The 2003 Current Population Survey (CPS) allowed respondents to choose more than one race. Beginning 2003, data represent persons who selected this race group only and exclude persons reporting more than one race. Before 2003, the CPS permitted respondents to report only one race group. See also comments on race in the text for Section 1, Population. [5] Starting in 2003, data are for Asians only; excludes Pacific Islanders. [6] Persons of Hispanic origin may be of any race.

Source: U.S. Census Bureau, U.S. Census of Population,1960, 1970, and 1980, Summary File 3; Current Population Reports, P20-550, and earlier reports; and "Educational Attainment in the United States: Historical Tables," <https://www.census.gov/topics/education/educational-attainment.html>, accessed February 2019.

## Table 257. Educational Attainment by Race, Hispanic Origin, and Sex: 1970 to 2018

[In percent. See Table 256 for headnote and totals for both sexes]

| Year | All races [1] | | White [2] | | Black [2] | | Asian and Pacific Islander [2,5] | | Hispanic [3] | |
|------|------|--------|------|--------|------|--------|------|--------|------|--------|
| | Male | Female | Male | Female | Male | Female | Male | Female | Male | Female |
| HIGH SCHOOL GRADUATE OR MORE [4] | | | | | | | | | | |
| 1970 | 51.9 | 52.8 | 54.0 | 55.0 | 30.1 | 32.5 | 61.3 | 63.1 | 37.9 | 34.2 |
| 1980 | 67.3 | 65.8 | 69.6 | 68.1 | 50.8 | 51.5 | 78.8 | 71.4 | 45.4 | 42.7 |
| 1990 | 77.7 | 77.5 | 79.1 | 79.0 | 65.8 | 66.5 | 84.0 | 77.2 | 50.3 | 51.3 |
| 2000 | 84.2 | 84.0 | 84.8 | 85.0 | 78.7 | 78.3 | 88.2 | 83.4 | 56.6 | 57.5 |
| 2010 | 86.6 | 87.6 | 86.9 | 88.2 | 83.6 | 84.6 | 91.2 | 87.0 | 61.4 | 64.4 |
| 2012 | 87.3 | 88.0 | 87.6 | 88.5 | 84.3 | 85.5 | 90.4 | 87.6 | 64.0 | 66.0 |
| 2013 | 87.6 | 88.6 | 88.0 | 89.2 | 84.1 | 86.0 | 91.5 | 89.0 | 64.6 | 67.9 |
| 2014 | 87.7 | 88.9 | 88.0 | 89.6 | 85.3 | 86.2 | 91.9 | 87.4 | 65.1 | 67.9 |
| 2015 | 88.0 | 88.8 | 88.3 | 89.3 | 86.4 | 87.6 | 91.0 | 87.4 | 65.5 | 67.8 |
| 2016 | 88.5 | 89.6 | 88.8 | 90.1 | 86.4 | 87.7 | 91.9 | 89.0 | 67.2 | 69.7 |
| 2017 | 89.1 | 90.0 | 89.5 | 90.6 | 86.5 | 87.9 | 92.6 | 89.4 | 69.5 | 71.6 |
| 2018 | 89.4 | 90.2 | 89.6 | 90.8 | 87.7 | 88.1 | 92.7 | 88.6 | 70.7 | 72.5 |
| COLLEGE GRADUATE OR MORE [4] | | | | | | | | | | |
| 1970 | 13.5 | 8.1 | 14.4 | 8.4 | 4.2 | 4.6 | 23.5 | 17.3 | 7.8 | 4.3 |
| 1980 | 20.1 | 12.8 | 21.3 | 13.3 | 8.4 | 8.3 | 39.8 | 27.0 | 9.4 | 6.0 |
| 1990 | 24.4 | 18.4 | 25.3 | 19.0 | 11.9 | 10.8 | 44.9 | 35.4 | 9.8 | 8.7 |
| 2000 | 27.8 | 23.6 | 28.5 | 23.9 | 16.3 | 16.7 | 47.6 | 40.7 | 10.7 | 10.6 |
| 2010 | 30.3 | 29.6 | 30.8 | 29.9 | 17.7 | 21.4 | 55.6 | 49.5 | 12.9 | 14.9 |
| 2012 | 31.4 | 30.6 | 31.9 | 30.8 | 19.2 | 22.9 | 53.7 | 48.8 | 13.3 | 15.8 |
| 2013 | 32.0 | 31.4 | 32.4 | 31.6 | 19.8 | 23.3 | 56.1 | 50.8 | 13.9 | 16.2 |
| 2014 | 31.9 | 32.0 | 32.3 | 32.3 | 20.4 | 23.7 | 54.7 | 50.3 | 14.2 | 16.1 |
| 2015 | 32.3 | 32.7 | 32.6 | 32.9 | 20.6 | 24.0 | 56.8 | 51.5 | 14.3 | 16.6 |
| 2016 | 33.2 | 33.7 | 33.4 | 34.0 | 21.7 | 24.6 | 58.8 | 53.4 | 15.4 | 17.4 |
| 2017 | 33.7 | 34.6 | 34.0 | 35.0 | 22.1 | 25.4 | 56.6 | 53.2 | 15.8 | 18.6 |
| 2018 | 34.6 | 35.3 | 34.9 | 35.5 | 23.2 | 26.9 | 59.3 | 54.0 | 16.6 | 20.1 |

[1] Includes other races not shown separately. [2] Beginning 2003, for persons who selected this race group only. See footnote 4, Table 256. [3] Persons of Hispanic origin may be of any race. [4] Through 1990, completed 4 years of high school or more and 4 years of college or more. [5] Starting in 2003, data are for Asians only; excludes Pacific Islanders.

Source: U.S. Census Bureau, U.S. Census of Population, 1960, 1970, and 1980, Summary File 3; Current Population Reports, P20-550, and earlier reports; and "Educational Attainment: CPS Historical Time Series Tables," <https://www.census.gov/topics/education/educational-attainment.html>, accessed February 2019.

# Table 258. Educational Attainment by Selected Characteristics: 2018

[219,830 represents 219,830,000. For persons 25 years old and over. As of March. Based on the Current Population Survey; see text, Section 1 and Appendix III]

| Characteristic | Population (1,000) | Percent of population— | | | | | |
|---|---|---|---|---|---|---|---|
| | | Not a high school graduate | High school graduate | Some college, but no degree | Associate's degree [1] | Bachelor's degree | Advanced degree |
| **Total persons** | **219,830** | **10.2** | **28.5** | **16.1** | **10.2** | **21.9** | **13.1** |
| Age: | | | | | | | |
| 25 to 34 years old | 44,855 | 7.6 | 25.5 | 17.5 | 10.4 | 27.6 | 11.4 |
| 35 to 44 years old | 40,660 | 9.6 | 24.4 | 15.1 | 10.6 | 24.7 | 15.7 |
| 45 to 54 years old | 41,537 | 9.8 | 28.3 | 15.2 | 11.0 | 22.0 | 13.7 |
| 55 to 64 years old | 41,700 | 9.9 | 31.0 | 16.4 | 10.9 | 19.8 | 11.9 |
| 65 to 74 years old | 30,366 | 10.8 | 29.7 | 16.7 | 9.5 | 18.8 | 14.5 |
| 75 years old or over | 20,713 | 17.6 | 36.7 | 15.6 | 6.7 | 13.1 | 10.3 |
| Sex: | | | | | | | |
| Male | 105,862 | 10.6 | 29.6 | 16.0 | 9.2 | 21.8 | 12.8 |
| Female | 113,969 | 9.8 | 27.5 | 16.2 | 11.1 | 22.1 | 13.2 |
| Race: | | | | | | | |
| White [2] | 172,685 | 9.8 | 28.6 | 16.0 | 10.4 | 22.3 | 13.0 |
| Black [2] | 27,047 | 12.1 | 32.7 | 19.7 | 10.3 | 16.3 | 8.9 |
| Asian [2] | 13,677 | 9.5 | 19.0 | 8.4 | 6.6 | 31.4 | 25.1 |
| Hispanic origin: | | | | | | | |
| Hispanic | 33,877 | 28.4 | 30.7 | 14.5 | 8.1 | 13.0 | 5.3 |
| Non-Hispanic white | 142,420 | 5.7 | 28.1 | 16.4 | 10.9 | 24.2 | 14.6 |
| Marital status: | | | | | | | |
| Never married | 45,386 | 10.5 | 29.5 | 17.9 | 9.0 | 23.0 | 10.1 |
| Married, spouse present | 125,323 | 8.7 | 26.3 | 14.8 | 10.4 | 24.1 | 15.7 |
| Married, spouse absent [3] | 3,569 | 15.6 | 29.3 | 14.2 | 8.2 | 19.2 | 13.6 |
| Separated | 4,769 | 19.1 | 33.5 | 18.6 | 9.2 | 13.8 | 5.8 |
| Widowed | 15,069 | 18.7 | 37.8 | 15.5 | 8.8 | 11.7 | 7.5 |
| Divorced | 25,715 | 9.5 | 30.8 | 19.7 | 12.2 | 17.7 | 10.0 |
| Civilian labor force status: | | | | | | | |
| Employed | 135,851 | 7.0 | 25.1 | 15.5 | 11.1 | 25.7 | 15.5 |
| Unemployed | 4,941 | 13.6 | 33.4 | 19.2 | 8.8 | 17.4 | 7.6 |
| Not in the labor force | 79,039 | 15.6 | 34.0 | 16.9 | 8.6 | 15.7 | 9.1 |

[1] Includes vocational degrees. [2] For persons who selected this race group only. See footnote 4, Table 256. [3] Excludes those separated.

Source: U.S. Census Bureau, "Educational Attainment in the United States: 2018," <https://www.census.gov/topics/education/educational-attainment.html>, accessed February 2019.

# Table 259. Mean Earnings by Highest Level of Education or Degree and Selected Characteristics: 2017

[In dollars. Persons as of March 2018. For persons 18 years old and over with earnings. Based on Current Population Survey, Annual Social and Economic Supplement; see text, Section 1 and Appendix III. For definition of mean, see Guide to Tabular Presentation]

| Characteristic | Mean earnings, total [1] | Mean earnings by highest level of education or degree (dollars) | | | | | | | |
|---|---|---|---|---|---|---|---|---|---|
| | | Ninth to twelfth grade, non-graduate | High school graduate only | Some college, no degree | Associate's | Bachelor's | Master's | Professional | Doctorate |
| **All persons [2]** | **53,536** | **26,469** | **38,145** | **38,695** | **46,381** | **67,763** | **87,674** | **138,378** | **118,903** |
| Age: | | | | | | | | | |
| 25 to 34 years old | 46,965 | 27,782 | 33,605 | 35,979 | 40,165 | 57,152 | 75,896 | 89,122 | 90,109 |
| 35 to 44 years old | 62,125 | 30,755 | 43,920 | 47,091 | 52,754 | 74,390 | 91,879 | 140,316 | 125,779 |
| 45 to 54 years old | 63,945 | 32,479 | 43,875 | 52,979 | 53,563 | 80,447 | 94,163 | 159,783 | 132,249 |
| 55 to 64 years old | 63,099 | 32,597 | 46,354 | 51,299 | 50,177 | 78,463 | 99,108 | 163,496 | 131,565 |
| 65 years old and over | 51,673 | 28,130 | 31,736 | 43,337 | 41,886 | 57,599 | 69,749 | 132,755 | 112,622 |
| Sex: | | | | | | | | | |
| Male | 62,662 | 31,549 | 44,466 | 46,780 | 56,286 | 81,607 | 107,270 | 158,712 | 136,630 |
| Female | 43,240 | 18,597 | 29,158 | 29,988 | 37,841 | 53,804 | 71,262 | 111,145 | 94,894 |
| White [3] | 54,838 | 26,872 | 39,781 | 40,143 | 47,389 | 69,284 | 88,154 | 139,255 | 119,267 |
| Male | 64,266 | 31,952 | 46,284 | 49,100 | 57,363 | 83,478 | 109,729 | 158,414 | 138,667 |
| Female | 43,749 | 18,082 | 30,089 | 29,981 | 38,443 | 54,436 | 70,561 | 110,943 | 92,331 |
| Black [3] | 41,570 | 23,205 | 31,889 | 34,697 | 41,059 | 53,938 | 72,345 | 112,352 | 92,518 |
| Male | 46,085 | 27,102 | 36,451 | 38,114 | 49,167 | 61,434 | 84,133 | (B) | 108,217 |
| Female | 37,585 | 19,248 | 26,507 | 31,794 | 35,617 | 48,158 | 65,284 | 91,521 | 81,020 |
| Asian [3] | 67,599 | 29,904 | 35,164 | 33,329 | 46,512 | 71,845 | 98,639 | 148,733 | 128,948 |
| Male | 79,440 | 34,908 | 41,576 | 39,746 | 56,434 | 86,369 | 109,563 | 175,197 | 140,973 |
| Female | 54,045 | 24,396 | 27,099 | 25,820 | 38,096 | 57,009 | 83,812 | 120,672 | 109,515 |
| Hispanic [4] | 38,816 | 27,717 | 34,472 | 33,925 | 44,656 | 54,190 | 75,813 | 113,495 | 99,477 |
| Male | 43,300 | 32,718 | 38,865 | 40,217 | 51,337 | 62,469 | 85,042 | 144,826 | 100,677 |
| Female | 32,961 | 18,629 | 27,743 | 26,949 | 38,916 | 46,237 | 69,089 | 75,255 | (B) |

B Base figure too small to meet statistical standards for reliability of a derived figure. [1] Includes those with less than ninth grade education, not shown separately. [2] Includes other races not shown separately. [3] For persons who selected this race group only. See footnote 4, Table 256. [4] Persons of Hispanic origin may be of any race.

Source: U.S. Census Bureau, *Income and Poverty in the United States: 2017*, Current Population Reports, P60-263, September 2018; and "Current Population Survey Tables for Personal Income: Table PINC-04," <https://www.census.gov/data/tables/time-series/demo/income-poverty/cps-pinc/pinc-04.html>, accessed November 2018.

# Table 260. Educational Attainment by State: 2000 to 2017

[In percent. 2000 as of April; 2010 and 2017 represents annual averages for calendar year. For persons 25 years old and over. Based on the 2000 Census of Population, and the American Community Survey, which includes the household population and the population living in institutions, college dormitories, and other group quarters. See text, Section 1 and Appendix III. For margin of error data, see source]

| State | 2000 | | | 2010 | | | 2017 | | |
|---|---|---|---|---|---|---|---|---|---|
| | High school graduate or more | Bachelor's degree or more | Advanced degree or more | High school graduate or more | Bachelor's degree or more | Advanced degree or more | High school graduate or more | Bachelor's degree or more | Advanced degree or more |
| **United States**............. | **80.4** | **24.4** | **8.9** | **85.6** | **28.2** | **10.4** | **88.0** | **32.0** | **12.3** |
| Alabama......... | 75.3 | 19.0 | 6.9 | 82.1 | 21.9 | 8.0 | 86.5 | 25.5 | 9.6 |
| Alaska........... | 88.3 | 24.7 | 8.6 | 91.0 | 27.9 | 9.4 | 91.7 | 28.8 | 10.8 |
| Arizona.......... | 81.0 | 23.5 | 8.4 | 85.6 | 25.9 | 9.2 | 87.2 | 29.4 | 11.0 |
| Arkansas........ | 75.3 | 16.7 | 5.7 | 82.9 | 19.5 | 6.3 | 86.7 | 23.4 | 8.4 |
| California....... | 76.8 | 26.6 | 9.5 | 80.7 | 30.1 | 11.0 | 83.3 | 33.6 | 12.6 |
| Colorado......... | 86.9 | 32.7 | 11.1 | 89.7 | 36.4 | 13.0 | 91.6 | 41.2 | 15.2 |
| Connecticut...... | 84.0 | 31.4 | 13.3 | 88.6 | 35.5 | 15.3 | 90.4 | 38.7 | 17.3 |
| Delaware......... | 82.6 | 25.0 | 9.4 | 87.7 | 27.8 | 11.3 | 90.6 | 31.5 | 13.5 |
| District of Columbia......... | 77.8 | 39.1 | 21.0 | 87.4 | 50.1 | 26.9 | 90.2 | 57.3 | 33.4 |
| Florida.......... | 79.9 | 22.3 | 8.1 | 85.5 | 25.8 | 9.2 | 88.4 | 29.7 | 10.8 |
| Georgia.......... | 78.6 | 24.3 | 8.3 | 84.3 | 27.3 | 9.8 | 87.0 | 30.9 | 11.9 |
| Hawaii........... | 84.6 | 26.2 | 8.4 | 89.9 | 29.5 | 9.6 | 92.3 | 32.9 | 11.2 |
| Idaho............ | 84.7 | 21.7 | 6.8 | 88.3 | 24.4 | 7.7 | 90.8 | 26.8 | 8.5 |
| Illinois......... | 81.4 | 26.1 | 9.5 | 86.9 | 30.8 | 11.5 | 89.1 | 34.4 | 13.4 |
| Indiana.......... | 82.1 | 19.4 | 7.2 | 87.0 | 22.7 | 8.1 | 88.6 | 26.8 | 9.8 |
| Iowa............. | 86.1 | 21.2 | 6.5 | 90.6 | 24.9 | 7.9 | 92.1 | 28.9 | 9.5 |
| Kansas........... | 86.0 | 25.8 | 8.7 | 89.2 | 29.8 | 10.5 | 91.0 | 33.7 | 12.6 |
| Kentucky......... | 74.1 | 17.1 | 6.9 | 81.9 | 20.5 | 8.1 | 86.3 | 24.0 | 9.9 |
| Louisiana........ | 74.8 | 18.7 | 6.5 | 81.9 | 21.4 | 7.0 | 85.1 | 23.8 | 8.3 |
| Maine............ | 85.4 | 22.9 | 7.9 | 90.3 | 26.8 | 9.5 | 92.3 | 32.1 | 12.1 |
| Maryland......... | 83.8 | 31.4 | 13.4 | 88.1 | 36.1 | 16.4 | 89.9 | 39.7 | 18.3 |
| Massachusetts.... | 84.8 | 33.2 | 13.7 | 89.1 | 39.0 | 16.7 | 90.8 | 43.4 | 19.5 |
| Michigan......... | 83.4 | 21.8 | 8.1 | 88.7 | 25.2 | 9.6 | 90.9 | 29.1 | 11.5 |
| Minnesota........ | 87.9 | 27.4 | 8.3 | 91.8 | 31.8 | 10.3 | 93.1 | 36.1 | 12.5 |
| Mississippi...... | 72.9 | 16.9 | 5.8 | 81.0 | 19.5 | 7.1 | 84.4 | 21.9 | 8.3 |
| Missouri......... | 81.3 | 21.6 | 7.6 | 86.9 | 25.6 | 9.5 | 89.7 | 29.1 | 11.1 |
| Montana.......... | 87.2 | 24.4 | 7.2 | 91.7 | 28.8 | 9.0 | 93.0 | 32.3 | 10.6 |
| Nebraska......... | 86.6 | 23.7 | 7.3 | 90.4 | 28.6 | 9.0 | 91.3 | 31.7 | 10.8 |
| Nevada........... | 80.7 | 18.2 | 6.1 | 84.7 | 21.7 | 7.4 | 86.8 | 24.9 | 8.4 |
| New Hampshire.... | 87.4 | 28.7 | 10.0 | 91.5 | 32.8 | 12.4 | 93.1 | 36.9 | 14.3 |
| New Jersey....... | 82.1 | 29.8 | 11.0 | 88.0 | 35.4 | 13.3 | 89.9 | 39.7 | 15.6 |
| New Mexico....... | 78.9 | 23.5 | 9.8 | 83.3 | 25.0 | 10.8 | 86.1 | 27.1 | 11.8 |
| New York......... | 79.1 | 27.4 | 11.8 | 84.9 | 32.5 | 14.0 | 86.6 | 36.0 | 15.8 |
| North Carolina... | 78.1 | 22.5 | 7.2 | 84.7 | 26.5 | 8.7 | 87.8 | 31.3 | 11.2 |
| North Dakota..... | 83.9 | 22.0 | 5.5 | 90.3 | 27.6 | 7.9 | 92.9 | 30.7 | 9.0 |
| Ohio............. | 83.0 | 21.1 | 7.4 | 88.1 | 24.6 | 8.9 | 90.3 | 28.0 | 10.6 |
| Oklahoma......... | 80.6 | 20.3 | 6.8 | 86.2 | 22.9 | 7.5 | 88.1 | 25.5 | 8.6 |
| Oregon........... | 85.1 | 25.1 | 8.7 | 88.8 | 28.8 | 10.5 | 91.0 | 33.7 | 12.7 |
| Pennsylvania..... | 81.9 | 22.4 | 8.4 | 88.4 | 27.1 | 10.4 | 90.6 | 31.4 | 12.5 |
| Rhode Island..... | 78.0 | 25.6 | 9.7 | 83.5 | 30.2 | 12.2 | 88.3 | 33.5 | 13.1 |
| South Carolina... | 76.3 | 20.4 | 6.9 | 84.1 | 24.5 | 8.8 | 87.4 | 28.0 | 10.4 |
| South Dakota..... | 84.6 | 21.5 | 6.0 | 89.6 | 26.3 | 7.7 | 91.7 | 28.1 | 9.0 |
| Tennessee........ | 75.9 | 19.6 | 6.8 | 83.6 | 23.1 | 8.5 | 87.8 | 27.3 | 10.1 |
| Texas............ | 75.7 | 23.2 | 7.6 | 80.7 | 25.9 | 8.6 | 83.6 | 29.6 | 10.3 |
| Utah............. | 87.7 | 26.1 | 8.3 | 90.6 | 29.3 | 9.4 | 92.1 | 34.6 | 11.8 |
| Vermont.......... | 86.4 | 29.4 | 11.1 | 91.0 | 33.6 | 13.3 | 92.6 | 38.3 | 15.8 |
| Virginia......... | 81.5 | 29.5 | 11.6 | 86.5 | 34.2 | 14.2 | 89.7 | 38.7 | 16.7 |
| Washington....... | 87.1 | 27.7 | 9.3 | 89.8 | 31.1 | 11.1 | 91.3 | 35.5 | 13.3 |
| West Virginia.... | 75.2 | 14.8 | 5.9 | 83.2 | 17.5 | 6.6 | 87.1 | 20.2 | 8.0 |
| Wisconsin........ | 85.1 | 22.4 | 7.2 | 90.1 | 24.1 | 9.0 | 92.4 | 30.4 | 10.6 |
| Wyoming.......... | 87.9 | 21.9 | 7.0 | 92.3 | 22.3 | 8.4 | 92.9 | 27.6 | 10.3 |

Source: U.S. Census Bureau, 2000 Census of Population, P37, "Sex by Educational Attainment for the Population 25 Years and Over"; and American Community Survey, GCT1501, "Percent of People 25 Years and Over Who Have Completed High School (Includes Equivalency)," GCT1502, "Percent of People 25 Years and Over Who Have Completed a Bachelor's Degree," and GCT1503, "Percent of People 25 Years and Over Who Have Completed an Advanced Degree," <http://factfinder.census.gov>, accessed November 2018.

## Table 261. Children Who Speak a Language Other Than English at Home by Region: 2017

[In thousands (12,132 represents 12,132,000), except percent. For children 5 to 17 years old. For more on languages spoken at home, see Table 56 and Table 57. Based on the American Community Survey; see text Section 1, and Appendix III. For composition of regions, see map inside front cover]

| Characteristic | U.S. | Northeast | Midwest | South | West |
|---|---|---|---|---|---|
| **Children who speak another language at home** | **12,132** | **2,021** | **1,481** | **4,307** | **4,323** |
| Percent of children 5 to 17 years old | 22.5 | 23.5 | 13.0 | 20.7 | 33.2 |
| Speak Spanish | 8,675 | 1,115 | 860 | 3,390 | 3,311 |
| Speak English "very well" | 7,032 | 904 | 710 | 2,637 | 2,781 |
| Speak English less than "very well" | 1,643 | 210 | 150 | 752 | 530 |
| Speak other Indo-European languages | 1,546 | 515 | 281 | 434 | 316 |
| Speak English "very well" | 1,259 | 403 | 218 | 368 | 270 |
| Speak English less than "very well" | 287 | 111 | 64 | 66 | 46 |
| Speak Asian and Pacific Island languages | 1,294 | 260 | 178 | 315 | 542 |
| Speak English "very well" | 976 | 190 | 130 | 244 | 412 |
| Speak English less than "very well" | 318 | 69 | 48 | 72 | 129 |
| Speak other languages | 617 | 132 | 162 | 168 | 154 |
| Speak English "very well" | 485 | 110 | 120 | 129 | 126 |
| Speak English less than "very well" | 132 | 22 | 42 | 39 | 28 |
| Have difficulty speaking English [1] | 2,379 | 413 | 303 | 929 | 733 |
| Language spoken at home in linguistically isolated households [2] | 2,644 | 486 | 308 | 1,020 | 830 |
| Speak only English | 197 | 46 | 25 | 71 | 55 |
| Speak Spanish | 1,812 | 262 | 162 | 788 | 601 |
| Speak other Indo-European languages | 209 | 82 | 39 | 51 | 37 |
| Speak Asian and Pacific Island languages | 304 | 74 | 41 | 74 | 115 |
| Speak other languages | 122 | 22 | 42 | 37 | 22 |

[1] Children age 5 to 17 who speak English less than "very well." [2] A household in which no person age 14 or over speaks English at least "very well."

Source: U.S. Census Bureau, 2017 American Community Survey, B16003, "Age by Language Spoken at Home for the Population 5 Years and Over" and B16004, "Age by Language Spoken at Home by Ability to Speak English for the Population 5 Years and Over," <http://factfinder.census.gov>, accessed November 2018.

## Table 262. Preprimary School Enrollment—Summary: 1970 to 2017

[10,949 represents 10,949,000. As of October. Civilian noninstitutional population. Includes public and private preschool (or nursery school) and kindergarten programs. Excludes 5-year-olds enrolled in elementary school. Based on Current Population Survey. See text, Section 1 and Appendix III]

| Item | 1970 | 1980 | 1990 | 2000 | 2005 | 2010 | 2015 | 2016 | 2017 |
|---|---|---|---|---|---|---|---|---|---|
| **NUMBER OF CHILDREN (1,000)** | | | | | | | | | |
| **Population, 3 to 5 years old** | **10,949** | **9,284** | **11,207** | **11,858** | **12,134** | **12,949** | **11,958** | **12,032** | **12,001** |
| **Total enrolled** [1] | **4,104** | **4,878** | **6,659** | **7,592** | **7,801** | **8,493** | **7,683** | **7,777** | **7,717** |
| Preschool (or nursery school) | 1,094 | 1,981 | 3,378 | 4,326 | 4,529 | 4,797 | 4,475 | 4,701 | 4,620 |
| Public | 332 | 628 | 1,202 | 2,146 | 2,409 | 2,749 | 2,561 | 2,764 | 2,738 |
| Private | 762 | 1,353 | 2,177 | 2,180 | 2,120 | 2,048 | 1,014 | 1,937 | 1,882 |
| Kindergarten | 3,010 | 2,807 | 3,281 | 3,266 | 3,272 | 3,449 | 3,207 | 3,075 | 3,097 |
| Public | 2,498 | 2,438 | 2,767 | 2,701 | 2,804 | 3,079 | 2,864 | 2,822 | 2,763 |
| Private | 511 | 459 | 513 | 565 | 468 | 369 | 342 | 253 | 334 |
| White [2] | 3,443 | 3,994 | 5,389 | 5,861 | 6,025 | 6,160 | 5,515 | 5,579 | 5,527 |
| Black [2] | 586 | 725 | 964 | 1,265 | 1,148 | 1,301 | 1,193 | 1,133 | 1,151 |
| Hispanic [3] | (NA) | 370 | 642 | 1,155 | 1,494 | 1,874 | 1,810 | 1,907 | 1,919 |
| 3 years old | 454 | 857 | 1,205 | 1,540 | 1,715 | 1,718 | 1,513 | 1,656 | 1,641 |
| 4 years old | 1,007 | 1,423 | 2,086 | 2,556 | 2,668 | 2,988 | 2,691 | 2,633 | 2,678 |
| 5 years old | 2,643 | 2,598 | 3,367 | 3,496 | 3,418 | 3,787 | 3,479 | 3,488 | 3,398 |
| **PERCENT ENROLLED** | | | | | | | | | |
| **Total enrolled** [1] | **37.5** | **52.5** | **59.4** | **64.0** | **64.3** | **63.7** | **64.2** | **64.6** | **64.3** |
| White [2] | 37.8 | 52.7 | 59.7 | 63.2 | 65.1 | 63.4 | 63.9 | 65.0 | 64.4 |
| Black [2] | 34.9 | 51.8 | 57.8 | 68.5 | 62.0 | 64.1 | 65.3 | 62.4 | 63.7 |
| Hispanic [3] | (NA) | 43.3 | 49.0 | 52.6 | 56.1 | 56.0 | 58.7 | 61.9 | 60.9 |
| 3 years old | 12.9 | 27.3 | 32.6 | 39.2 | 41.3 | 38.2 | 38.4 | 41.6 | 40.2 |
| 4 years old | 27.8 | 46.3 | 56.0 | 64.9 | 66.2 | 68.6 | 66.7 | 65.9 | 67.9 |
| 5 years old | 69.3 | 84.7 | 88.8 | 87.6 | 86.4 | 88.1 | 87.3 | 85.9 | 90.0 |

NA Not available. [1] Includes races not shown separately. [2] Beginning 2003, for persons who selected this race group only. See footnote 4, Table 256. [3] Persons of Hispanic origin may be of any race. The method of identifying Hispanic children was changed in 1980 from allocation based on status of mother to status reported for each child. The number of Hispanic children using the new method is larger.

Source: U.S. Census Bureau, Current Population Reports, P-20, and unpublished data; and "School Enrollment," <https://www.census.gov/topics/education/school-enrollment.html>, accessed December 2018.

# Table 263. Public Elementary and Secondary School Finances by Enrollment-Size Group: 2017

[In units, as indicated. 694,111 represents $694,111,000,000). School fiscal year ending in 2017. Enrollment as of Fall 2016. Data are based on the Annual Government Finance Survey. For details, see source. See also Appendix III]

| Item | All school systems | School systems with enrollment of— | | | | | | |
|---|---|---|---|---|---|---|---|---|
| | | 50,000 or more | 25,000 to 49,999 | 15,000 to 24,999 | 7,500 to 14,999 | 5,000 to 7,499 | 3,000 to 4,999 | Under 3,000 |
| **TOTAL (Millions of dollars)** | | | | | | | | |
| **General revenue** | **694,111** | **153,064** | **84,587** | **66,238** | **98,745** | **60,824** | **78,950** | **151,704** |
| From federal sources | 55,292 | 13,762 | 7,254 | 5,381 | 7,089 | 4,196 | 5,173 | 12,437 |
| Through state [1] | 51,055 | 12,889 | 6,826 | 5,089 | 6,656 | 3,822 | 4,819 | 10,955 |
| Child nutrition programs | 16,137 | 4,206 | 2,303 | 1,762 | 2,252 | 1,245 | 1,543 | 2,826 |
| Direct | 4,237 | 873 | 428 | 292 | 433 | 374 | 355 | 1,482 |
| From state sources [1] | 327,082 | 64,783 | 42,403 | 34,979 | 49,615 | 27,581 | 35,554 | 72,168 |
| General formula assistance | 223,747 | 42,766 | 31,047 | 25,479 | 35,207 | 18,597 | 23,297 | 47,355 |
| Compensatory programs | 5,170 | 1,463 | 726 | 569 | 758 | 332 | 494 | 827 |
| Special education | 20,639 | 5,772 | 2,224 | 1,650 | 2,356 | 1,536 | 2,416 | 4,685 |
| From local sources | 311,737 | 74,518 | 34,929 | 25,879 | 42,041 | 29,047 | 38,223 | 67,100 |
| Taxes [1] | 212,633 | 38,198 | 24,220 | 19,182 | 31,085 | 21,692 | 28,531 | 49,725 |
| Property taxes | 203,125 | 36,193 | 22,308 | 18,209 | 29,751 | 21,034 | 27,472 | 48,158 |
| Contributions from parent government | 57,983 | 28,855 | 5,510 | 2,758 | 5,251 | 3,898 | 5,255 | 6,456 |
| From other local governments | 8,954 | 702 | 1,305 | 958 | 1,349 | 795 | 974 | 2,872 |
| Current charges [1] | 14,937 | 2,497 | 1,735 | 1,358 | 2,109 | 1,327 | 1,723 | 4,189 |
| School lunch | 5,591 | 811 | 619 | 556 | 901 | 562 | 739 | 1,405 |
| Other | 17,231 | 4,267 | 2,159 | 1,623 | 2,248 | 1,335 | 1,741 | 3,857 |
| **General expenditure** | **694,235** | **155,321** | **84,878** | **66,023** | **98,985** | **60,785** | **77,714** | **150,528** |
| Current spending [2] | 610,301 | 134,888 | 74,046 | 57,738 | 86,489 | 53,479 | 69,337 | 134,324 |
| By function: | | | | | | | | |
| Instruction | 370,486 | 86,535 | 44,315 | 34,395 | 52,453 | 32,548 | 42,147 | 78,092 |
| Support services | 208,731 | 41,640 | 25,663 | 20,169 | 29,503 | 18,368 | 23,939 | 49,449 |
| Other current spending [2] | 31,084 | 6,712 | 4,067 | 3,174 | 4,532 | 2,563 | 3,251 | 6,783 |
| By object: | | | | | | | | |
| Total salaries and wages | 343,013 | 75,094 | 43,199 | 33,586 | 49,426 | 30,015 | 38,617 | 73,076 |
| Total employee benefits | 144,531 | 30,417 | 16,510 | 13,367 | 21,121 | 13,269 | 17,321 | 32,526 |
| Capital outlay | 62,785 | 14,834 | 8,107 | 6,230 | 9,462 | 5,569 | 6,327 | 12,255 |
| Interest on debt | 17,990 | 4,251 | 2,607 | 1,966 | 2,693 | 1,528 | 1,868 | 3,076 |
| Payments to other governments | 3,159 | 1,349 | 117 | 89 | 340 | 208 | 182 | 872 |
| Debt outstanding | 452,120 | 106,004 | 58,974 | 51,686 | 68,077 | 38,705 | 47,804 | 80,870 |
| Long-term | 442,922 | 103,220 | 57,994 | 51,151 | 67,095 | 37,921 | 46,801 | 78,739 |
| Short-term | 9,198 | 2,783 | 980 | 536 | 982 | 784 | 1,002 | 2,131 |
| Long-term debt issued | 72,625 | 16,634 | 8,778 | 8,545 | 11,234 | 6,120 | 8,019 | 13,296 |
| Long-term debt retired | 53,742 | 13,058 | 6,054 | 5,027 | 7,720 | 4,789 | 5,966 | 11,129 |
| Fall enrollment (1,000s) | 48,631 | 10,736 | 6,649 | 5,146 | 7,326 | 4,157 | 5,274 | 9,345 |
| **PER PUPIL (Dollars)** | | | | | | | | |
| General revenue | 14,273 | 14,257 | 12,722 | 12,872 | 13,479 | 14,632 | 14,971 | 16,234 |
| From federal sources | 1,137 | 1,282 | 1,091 | 1,046 | 968 | 1,009 | 981 | 1,331 |
| From state sources [1] | 6,726 | 6,034 | 6,377 | 6,797 | 6,773 | 6,635 | 6,742 | 7,723 |
| General formula assistance | 4,601 | 3,984 | 4,669 | 4,951 | 4,806 | 4,474 | 4,418 | 5,068 |
| Special education | 424 | 538 | 335 | 321 | 322 | 369 | 458 | 501 |
| From local sources | 6,410 | 6,941 | 5,253 | 5,029 | 5,739 | 6,988 | 7,248 | 7,180 |
| Taxes [1] | 4,372 | 3,558 | 3,643 | 3,728 | 4,243 | 5,218 | 5,410 | 5,321 |
| Property taxes | 4,177 | 3,371 | 3,355 | 3,539 | 4,061 | 5,060 | 5,209 | 5,153 |
| Contributions from parent government | 1,192 | 2,688 | 829 | 536 | 717 | 938 | 996 | 691 |
| Current charges [1] | 307 | 233 | 261 | 264 | 288 | 319 | 327 | 448 |
| School lunch | 115 | 75 | 93 | 108 | 123 | 135 | 140 | 150 |
| General expenditure [1] | 13,927 | 13,980 | 12,456 | 12,586 | 13,225 | 14,258 | 14,386 | 15,792 |
| Current spending [2] | 12,201 | 12,077 | 10,827 | 10,976 | 11,520 | 12,501 | 12,797 | 14,058 |
| By function: | | | | | | | | |
| Instruction | 7,406 | 7,691 | 6,492 | 6,570 | 7,013 | 7,600 | 7,776 | 8,200 |
| Support services | 4,292 | 3,879 | 3,860 | 3,919 | 4,027 | 4,419 | 4,540 | 5,292 |
| By object: | | | | | | | | |
| Total salaries and wages | 7,053 | 6,995 | 6,497 | 6,527 | 6,747 | 7,221 | 7,323 | 7,820 |
| Total employee benefits | 2,972 | 2,833 | 2,483 | 2,598 | 2,883 | 3,192 | 3,284 | 3,481 |
| Capital outlay | 1,291 | 1,382 | 1,219 | 1,211 | 1,292 | 1,340 | 1,200 | 1,311 |
| Interest on debt | 370 | 396 | 392 | 382 | 368 | 368 | 354 | 329 |
| Debt outstanding | 9,297 | 9,874 | 8,870 | 10,044 | 9,293 | 9,311 | 9,065 | 8,654 |
| Long-term | 9,108 | 9,615 | 8,722 | 9,940 | 9,159 | 9,122 | 8,875 | 8,426 |

[1] Includes other sources not shown separately. [2] Expenditures for adult education, community services, and other non-elementary/secondary programs are included in total "Current spending" and "Other current spending" but excluded under pupil amounts.

Source: U.S. Census Bureau, "Annual Survey of School System Finances Tables: 2017 Public Elementary-Secondary Education Finance Data," May 2019, <https://www.census.gov/programs-surveys/school-finances/data/tables.html>.

# Table 264. Public Elementary and Secondary School Estimated Finances by State: 2017

[In millions of dollars (694,111 represents $694,111,000,000), except as noted. For the school fiscal year. Includes finances of charter schools whose charters are held directly by a government or government agency; excludes charters schools whose charters are held by nongovernmental entities]

| State | Revenue receipts | | | | Expenditures | | | | |
|---|---|---|---|---|---|---|---|---|---|
| | | Source | | | | Per capita [2] (dol.) | Current expenditures | | |
| | | | | | | | Total current spending [3] | Average per pupil [4] | |
| | Total | Federal | State | Local | Total [1] | | | Amount [5] (dol.) | Rank |
| Total............... | 694,111 | 55,292 | 327,082 | 311,737 | 694,235 | 2,149 | 610,301 | 12,201 | (X) |
| Alabama............. | 7,910 | 811 | 4,351 | 2,748 | 8,021 | 1,649 | 7,209 | 9,511 | 41 |
| Alaska.............. | 2,504 | 350 | 1,601 | 554 | 2,587 | 3,489 | 2,376 | 17,838 | 6 |
| Arizona............. | 8,601 | 1,178 | 3,446 | 3,977 | 8,387 | 1,207 | 7,631 | 8,003 | 48 |
| Arkansas............ | 5,462 | 597 | 4,138 | 727 | 5,461 | 1,826 | 4,807 | 9,967 | 37 |
| California.......... | 89,109 | 7,890 | 51,047 | 30,173 | 86,828 | 2,214 | 76,532 | 12,143 | 21 |
| Colorado............ | 10,384 | 698 | 4,479 | 5,207 | 10,418 | 1,880 | 8,774 | 9,809 | 40 |
| Connecticut......... | 11,074 | 475 | 4,210 | 6,390 | 10,487 | 2,930 | 9,925 | 19,322 | 3 |
| Delaware............ | 2,207 | 138 | 1,306 | 762 | 2,071 | 2,182 | 1,921 | 15,302 | 13 |
| District of Columbia.......... | 1,521 | 168 | (X) | 1,353 | 1,563 | 2,276 | 1,147 | 21,974 | 2 |
| Florida............. | 28,996 | 3,202 | 11,347 | 14,448 | 28,900 | 1,401 | 25,995 | 9,075 | 45 |
| Georgia............. | 20,374 | 1,846 | 9,212 | 9,315 | 20,123 | 1,953 | 17,952 | 10,205 | 34 |
| Hawaii.............. | 2,844 | 252 | 2,534 | 58 | 2,779 | 1,946 | 2,617 | 14,322 | 15 |
| Idaho............... | 2,396 | 236 | 1,558 | 602 | 2,260 | 1,343 | 2,093 | 7,486 | 50 |
| Illinois............ | 35,271 | 2,309 | 14,471 | 18,490 | 34,250 | 2,670 | 31,366 | 15,337 | 12 |
| Indiana............. | 12,684 | 932 | 7,940 | 3,812 | 11,608 | 1,750 | 10,164 | 10,045 | 36 |
| Iowa................ | 6,898 | 478 | 3,732 | 2,688 | 6,800 | 2,171 | 5,875 | 11,461 | 27 |
| Kansas.............. | 6,280 | 537 | 4,016 | 1,727 | 6,520 | 2,239 | 5,424 | 10,961 | 31 |
| Kentucky............ | 7,918 | 911 | 4,330 | 2,676 | 7,950 | 1,791 | 6,986 | 10,121 | 35 |
| Louisiana........... | 8,407 | 1,046 | 3,484 | 3,877 | 8,143 | 1,741 | 7,364 | 11,199 | 30 |
| Maine............... | 2,768 | 184 | 1,061 | 1,523 | 2,740 | 2,058 | 2,547 | 13,690 | 17 |
| Maryland............ | 14,913 | 852 | 6,500 | 7,562 | 14,423 | 2,402 | 13,179 | 14,848 | 14 |
| Massachusetts....... | 18,039 | 773 | 6,988 | 10,279 | 17,377 | 2,546 | 16,106 | 16,197 | 8 |
| Michigan............ | 18,757 | 1,522 | 10,997 | 6,237 | 18,088 | 1,818 | 16,086 | 11,907 | 24 |
| Minnesota........... | 12,440 | 653 | 8,077 | 3,709 | 13,474 | 2,439 | 10,863 | 12,647 | 18 |
| Mississippi......... | 4,751 | 671 | 2,413 | 1,666 | 4,675 | 1,565 | 4,242 | 8,771 | 47 |
| Missouri............ | 11,086 | 926 | 4,676 | 5,484 | 10,709 | 1,759 | 9,634 | 10,589 | 33 |
| Montana............. | 1,814 | 217 | 851 | 746 | 1,886 | 1,812 | 1,675 | 11,443 | 28 |
| Nebraska............ | 4,432 | 341 | 1,451 | 2,639 | 4,800 | 2,518 | 4,013 | 12,579 | 20 |
| Nevada.............. | 4,670 | 426 | 2,953 | 1,291 | 4,781 | 1,637 | 4,153 | 9,320 | 43 |
| New Hampshire....... | 3,125 | 169 | 1,004 | 1,952 | 3,017 | 2,248 | 2,828 | 15,683 | 11 |
| New Jersey.......... | 29,395 | 1,205 | 12,038 | 16,152 | 29,114 | 3,281 | 27,454 | 18,920 | 4 |
| New Mexico.......... | 3,798 | 548 | 2,521 | 728 | 3,778 | 1,805 | 3,159 | 9,881 | 39 |
| New York............ | 70,032 | 3,683 | 28,600 | 37,748 | 70,376 | 3,583 | 63,617 | 23,091 | 1 |
| North Carolina...... | 13,976 | 1,563 | 8,596 | 3,816 | 14,856 | 1,463 | 13,288 | 9,072 | 46 |
| North Dakota........ | 1,773 | 163 | 1,028 | 582 | 1,846 | 2,447 | 1,521 | 13,760 | 16 |
| Ohio................ | 23,573 | 1,678 | 9,505 | 12,390 | 24,225 | 2,082 | 21,406 | 12,645 | 19 |
| Oklahoma............ | 6,166 | 686 | 2,871 | 2,609 | 6,020 | 1,533 | 5,342 | 7,940 | 49 |
| Oregon.............. | 7,655 | 558 | 4,019 | 3,078 | 7,935 | 1,940 | 6,755 | 11,264 | 29 |
| Pennsylvania........ | 31,179 | 2,003 | 12,058 | 17,118 | 30,954 | 2,421 | 27,505 | 15,798 | 10 |
| Rhode Island........ | 2,442 | 177 | 990 | 1,275 | 2,475 | 2,342 | 2,307 | 15,943 | 9 |
| South Carolina...... | 9,727 | 854 | 4,624 | 4,248 | 9,634 | 1,943 | 8,051 | 10,590 | 32 |
| South Dakota........ | 1,568 | 200 | 535 | 834 | 1,559 | 1,806 | 1,373 | 9,939 | 38 |
| Tennessee........... | 10,066 | 1,158 | 4,625 | 4,283 | 10,334 | 1,555 | 9,272 | 9,184 | 44 |
| Texas............... | 58,891 | 5,966 | 20,995 | 31,930 | 62,986 | 2,255 | 48,025 | 9,375 | 42 |
| Utah................ | 5,161 | 423 | 2,675 | 2,063 | 5,230 | 1,719 | 4,279 | 7,179 | 51 |
| Vermont............. | 1,805 | 110 | 1,630 | 65 | 1,759 | 2,820 | 1,693 | 18,290 | 5 |
| Virginia............ | 16,529 | 1,132 | 6,566 | 8,832 | 17,014 | 2,023 | 15,374 | 11,886 | 25 |
| Washington.......... | 15,646 | 1,068 | 9,823 | 4,756 | 16,079 | 2,204 | 13,247 | 11,989 | 22 |
| West Virginia....... | 3,476 | 404 | 1,872 | 1,200 | 3,413 | 1,864 | 3,199 | 11,554 | 26 |
| Wisconsin........... | 11,686 | 803 | 6,197 | 4,686 | 11,613 | 2,012 | 10,390 | 11,968 | 23 |
| Wyoming............. | 1,930 | 118 | 1,142 | 671 | 1,911 | 3,271 | 1,558 | 16,537 | 7 |

X Not applicable. [1] Includes interest on school debt and payments to state and local governments, not shown separately. [2] Based on U.S. Census Bureau estimated resident population, as of July 1, 2016. [3] Includes expenditures for adult education, community services, and other nonelementary-secondary programs. [4] Based on Fall 2016 enrollment, National Center for Education Statistics, Common Core of Data. [5] Per pupil amounts exclude expenditures for payments to other school systems, adult education, community services, and other nonelementary-secondary programs.

Source: U.S. Census Bureau, Annual Survey of School System Finances, "2017 Public Elementary-Secondary Education Finance Data," May 2019, <https://www.census.gov/programs-surveys/school-finances/data/tables.html>.

# Table 265. Public Elementary and Secondary Schools—Summary: 1990 to 2019

[In units as indicated (44,949 represents 44,949,000). For school year ending in year shown, except as indicated. Data are estimates]

| Item | Unit | 1990 | 2000 | 2010 | 2016 | 2017 | 2018 | 2019 |
|---|---|---|---|---|---|---|---|---|
| **School districts, total**.............. | **Number** | **15,552** | **15,403** | **16,340** | **16,649** | **16,919** | **16,909** | **16,921** |
| ENROLLMENT | | | | | | | | |
| Population 5-17 years old [1]............. | 1,000 | 44,949 | 53,119 | 53,980 | 53,727 | 53,691 | 53,589 | (NA) |
| Percent of resident population................. | Percent | 18.2 | 18.9 | 17.5 | 16.6 | 16.5 | 16.4 | (NA) |
| **Fall enrollment [2]**................. | **1,000** | **40,527** | **46,577** | **49,104** | **49,981** | **49,966** | **50,014** | **50,092** |
| Percent of population 5-17 years old......... | Percent | 90.2 | 87.7 | 91.0 | 93.0 | 93.1 | 93.3 | (NA) |
| Elementary [3]................ | 1,000 | 26,253 | 29,243 | (NA) | (NA) | (NA) | (NA) | (NA) |
| Secondary [4]................. | 1,000 | 14,274 | 17,334 | (NA) | (NA) | (NA) | (NA) | (NA) |
| Average daily attendance................. | 1,000 | 37,573 | 43,313 | 45,835 | 47,096 | 47,181 | 47,149 | 47,383 |
| High school graduates................. | 1,000 | 2,327 | 2,544 | 3,088 | 3,249 | 3,282 | 3,309 | 3,339 |
| INSTRUCTIONAL STAFF | | | | | | | | |
| **Total [5]**................. | **1,000** | **2,685** | **3,273** | **3,644** | **3,700** | **3,732** | **3,762** | **3,780** |
| Classroom teachers................. | 1,000 | 2,362 | 2,891 | 3,182 | 3,113 | 3,143 | 3,159 | 3,168 |
| Average salaries: | | | | | | | | |
| Instructional staff................. | Dollar | 32,638 | 43,837 | 56,995 | 60,551 | 61,733 | 62,760 | 64,143 |
| Classroom teachers................. | Dollar | 31,367 | 41,807 | 55,370 | 58,316 | 59,539 | 60,477 | 61,730 |
| REVENUES | | | | | | | | |
| **Revenue receipts**................. | **Mil. dol.** | **208,656** | **369,754** | **586,995** | **673,067** | **689,008** | **709,585** | **729,537** |
| Federal................. | Mil. dol. | 13,184 | 26,346 | 75,592 | 54,179 | 54,572 | 53,176 | 53,044 |
| State................. | Mil. dol. | 100,787 | 183,986 | 258,396 | 317,103 | 323,630 | 334,232 | 345,014 |
| Local................. | Mil. dol. | 94,685 | 159,421 | 253,006 | 301,784 | 310,806 | 322,177 | 331,479 |
| Percent of total: | | | | | | | | |
| Federal................. | Percent | 6.3 | 7.1 | 12.9 | 8.0 | 7.9 | 7.5 | 7.3 |
| State................. | Percent | 48.3 | 49.8 | 44.0 | 47.1 | 47.0 | 47.1 | 47.3 |
| Local/other................. | Percent | 45.4 | 43.1 | 43.1 | 44.8 | 45.1 | 45.4 | 45.4 |
| EXPENDITURES | | | | | | | | |
| **Total**................. | **Mil. dol.** | **209,698** | **374,782** | **615,210** | **686,578** | **712,796** | **733,657** | **753,180** |
| Current expenditures (day schools)............. | Mil. dol. | 186,583 | 320,954 | 526,146 | 591,838 | 611,094 | 630,277 | 647,176 |
| Other current expenditures [6]................. | Mil. dol. | 3,341 | 6,618 | 10,621 | 12,732 | 12,783 | 12,820 | 12,988 |
| Capital outlay................. | Mil. dol. | 16,012 | 37,552 | 53,052 | 51,287 | 57,067 | 57,607 | 58,678 |
| Interest on school debt................. | Mil. dol. | 3,762 | 9,659 | 25,391 | 30,721 | 31,852 | 32,953 | 34,339 |
| Current expenditures per pupil enrolled........... | Dollar | 4,604 | 6,891 | 10,715 | 11,841 | 12,230 | 12,602 | 12,920 |

NA Not available. [1] Estimated resident population as of July 1 of the previous year, except 1990, 2000, and 2010 population enumerated as of April 1. Estimates reflect revisions based on the 2010 Census of Population. [2] Fall enrollment of the previous year. [3] Kindergarten through grades not higher than 8. [4] Starting from grade 7, 8, or 9, through grade 12. [5] Full-time equivalent. [6] Current expenses for summer schools, adult education, post-high school vocational education, personnel retraining, etc., when operated by local school districts and not part of regular public elementary and secondary day-school program.

Source: National Education Association, Washington, DC. Data from *Rankings of the States 2018 and Estimates of School Statistics 2019*, used with permission of the National Education Association © 2019. All rights reserved.

# Table 266. Public Elementary and Secondary School Enrollment by Grade: 1980 to 2016

[In thousands (40,877 represents 40,877,000). As of Fall of year shown. Covers the 50 states and DC. Based on survey of state education agencies; see source for details]

| Grade | 1980 | 1990 | 1995 | 2000 | 2005 | 2010 | 2012 | 2013 | 2014 | 2015 | 2016 |
|---|---|---|---|---|---|---|---|---|---|---|---|
| **Pupils enrolled [1]**......... | **40,877** | **41,217** | **44,840** | **47,204** | **49,113** | **49,484** | **49,771** | **50,045** | **50,313** | **50,438** | **50,615** |
| Pre-kindergarten to 8 [1]....... | 27,647 | 29,878 | 32,341 | 33,688 | 34,205 | 34,625 | 35,018 | 35,251 | 35,370 | 35,388 | 35,477 |
| Pre-K and kindergarten.... | 2,689 | 3,610 | 4,173 | 4,158 | 4,656 | 4,961 | 5,138 | 5,162 | 5,142 | 5,115 | 5,125 |
| First................. | 2,894 | 3,499 | 3,671 | 3,636 | 3,691 | 3,754 | 3,824 | 3,885 | 3,863 | 3,768 | 3,694 |
| Second................. | 2,800 | 3,327 | 3,507 | 3,634 | 3,606 | 3,701 | 3,729 | 3,791 | 3,857 | 3,842 | 3,761 |
| Third................. | 2,893 | 3,297 | 3,445 | 3,676 | 3,586 | 3,686 | 3,719 | 3,738 | 3,806 | 3,869 | 3,874 |
| Fourth................. | 3,107 | 3,248 | 3,431 | 3,711 | 3,578 | 3,711 | 3,690 | 3,708 | 3,719 | 3,793 | 3,858 |
| Fifth................. | 3,130 | 3,197 | 3,438 | 3,707 | 3,633 | 3,718 | 3,673 | 3,697 | 3,719 | 3,733 | 3,814 |
| Sixth................. | 3,038 | 3,110 | 3,395 | 3,663 | 3,670 | 3,682 | 3,723 | 3,684 | 3,710 | 3,731 | 3,754 |
| Seventh................. | 3,085 | 3,067 | 3,422 | 3,629 | 3,777 | 3,676 | 3,746 | 3,748 | 3,710 | 3,732 | 3,761 |
| Eighth................. | 3,086 | 2,979 | 3,356 | 3,538 | 3,802 | 3,659 | 3,699 | 3,753 | 3,757 | 3,719 | 3,749 |
| Grades 9 to 12 [1]............. | 13,231 | 11,338 | 12,500 | 13,515 | 14,909 | 14,860 | 14,753 | 14,794 | 14,943 | 15,050 | 15,138 |
| Ninth................. | 3,377 | 3,169 | 3,704 | 3,963 | 4,287 | 4,008 | 3,975 | 3,980 | 4,033 | 4,019 | 3,986 |
| Tenth................. | 3,368 | 2,896 | 3,237 | 3,491 | 3,866 | 3,800 | 3,730 | 3,761 | 3,794 | 3,846 | 3,860 |
| Eleventh................. | 3,195 | 2,612 | 2,826 | 3,083 | 3,455 | 3,538 | 3,528 | 3,526 | 3,568 | 3,598 | 3,669 |
| Twelfth................. | 2,925 | 2,381 | 2,487 | 2,803 | 3,180 | 3,472 | 3,477 | 3,476 | 3,496 | 3,537 | 3,571 |

[1] Includes unclassified students, not shown separately.

Source: U.S. National Center for Education Statistics, *Digest of Education Statistics*, "Advance Release of Selected 2018 Digest Tables," <http://www.nces.ed.gov/programs/digest/>, accessed May 2019.

# Table 267. Selected Statistics for the Largest Public School Districts: 2015

[For the 50 largest districts by enrollment size. For school year ending in 2015. Data from the Common Core Data Program; see source for details. School district boundaries are not necessarily the same as city or county boundaries]

| School district | City | County | Number of students [1] | Number of full-time equivalent (FTE) teachers [2] | Number of schools [3] | Total expenditures per pupil |
|---|---|---|---|---|---|---|
| New York City Public Schools, NY.................. | New York | (X) | 995,192 | 67,482 | 1,636 | 27,611 |
| Los Angeles Unified School District, CA.............. | Los Angeles | Los Angeles | 646,683 | 27,669 | 999 | 14,176 |
| City of Chicago School District, IL................... | Chicago | Cook | 392,558 | 22,559 | 594 | 15,924 |
| Miami-Dade County Public School District, FL...... | Miami | Miami-Dade | 356,964 | 20,837 | 527 | 10,153 |
| Clark County School District, NV.................... | Las Vegas | Clark | 324,093 | 15,423 | 367 | 8,964 |
| Broward County School District, FL................. | Fort Lauderdale | Broward | 266,265 | 15,211 | 355 | 9,619 |
| Houston Independent School District, TX............ | Houston | Harris | 215,225 | 11,422 | 283 | 10,544 |
| Hillsborough County School District, FL............. | Tampa | Hillsborough | 207,469 | 16,788 | 310 | 10,438 |
| Orange County Public Schools, FL.................. | Orlando | Orange | 191,648 | 12,069 | 250 | 10,771 |
| Palm Beach County School District, FL............. | West Palm Beach | Palm Beach | 186,605 | 12,683 | 274 | 10,451 |
| Fairfax County Public Schools, VA.................. | Falls Church | Fairfax | 185,541 | 14,283 | 222 | 15,160 |
| Hawaii Department of Education, HI................. | Honolulu | Honolulu | 182,384 | (NA) | 289 | 13,823 |
| Gwinnett County School District, GA................ | Suwanee | Gwinnett | 173,246 | 10,744 | 132 | 10,443 |
| Dallas Independent School District, TX.............. | Dallas | Dallas | 160,253 | 10,595 | 234 | 11,142 |
| Wake County Schools, NC........................... | Raleigh | Wake | 155,820 | 9,940 | 171 | 9,803 |
| Montgomery County Public Schools, MD........... | Rockville | Montgomery | 154,434 | 10,309 | 207 | 17,192 |
| Charlotte-Mecklenburg Schools, NC................. | Charlotte | Mecklenburg | 145,636 | 8,647 | 165 | 10,198 |
| Philadelphia City School District, PA................ | Philadelphia | Philadelphia | 134,241 | 7,611 | 218 | 19,716 |
| San Diego City Unified School District, CA.......... | San Diego | San Diego | 129,779 | 5,544 | 225 | 13,540 |
| Duval County School District, FL.................... | Jacksonville | Duval | 128,685 | 7,653 | 209 | 9,455 |
| Prince George's County Public Schools, MD........ | Upper Marlboro | Prince George's | 127,576 | 8,691 | 211 | 16,356 |
| Shelby County School District, TN.................. | Memphis | Shelby | 115,810 | 6,644 | 241 | 11,050 |
| Cypress-Fairbanks Independent School District, TX.................................................. | Houston | Harris | 113,023 | 6,727 | 85 | 10,294 |
| Cobb County School District, GA.................... | Marietta | Cobb | 111,751 | 7,204 | 111 | 10,503 |
| Baltimore County Public Schools, MD............... | Towson | Baltimore | 109,830 | 7,262 | 173 | 15,173 |
| Pinellas County School District, FL.................. | Largo | Pinellas | 103,774 | 6,837 | 174 | 10,225 |
| Northside Independent School District, TX........... | San Antonio | Bexar | 103,606 | 6,715 | 115 | 10,676 |
| DeKalb County School District, GA.................. | Decatur | DeKalb | 101,103 | 6,491 | 134 | 10,399 |
| Jefferson County School District, KY................ | Louisville | Jefferson | 100,602 | 6,073 | 173 | 12,905 |
| Polk County School District, FL..................... | Bartow | Polk | 99,723 | 6,342 | 161 | 9,384 |
| Fulton County, GA................................... | Atlanta | Fulton | 95,460 | 6,392 | 103 | 12,846 |
| Albuquerque Public Schools, NM.................... | Albuquerque | Bernalillo | 93,001 | 6,193 | 161 | 11,221 |
| Lee County School District, FL...................... | Fort Myers | Lee | 89,364 | 5,555 | 124 | 9,805 |
| Denver School District, CO.......................... | Denver | Denver | 88,839 | 5,857 | 189 | 15,110 |
| Prince William County Public Schools, VA.......... | Manassas | Prince William | 86,641 | 5,476 | 90 | 12,635 |
| Jefferson County Public School District, CO......... | Golden | Jefferson | 86,581 | 4,724 | 165 | 10,165 |
| Fort Worth Independent School District, TX......... | Fort Worth | Tarrant | 85,975 | 5,457 | 144 | 10,212 |
| Baltimore City Public Schools, MD.................. | Baltimore | Baltimore City | 84,976 | 5,234 | 182 | 16,699 |
| Austin Independent School District, TX.............. | Austin | Travis | 84,564 | 5,823 | 129 | 13,703 |
| Nashville Davidson County Schools, TN............. | Nashville | Davidson | 84,069 | 5,641 | 158 | 12,225 |
| Long Beach Unified School District, CA............. | Long Beach | Los Angeles | 79,709 | 2,983 | 86 | 12,636 |
| Anne Arundel County Public Schools, MD........... | Annapolis | Anne Arundel | 79,518 | 5,392 | 122 | 15,683 |
| Milwaukee School District, WI...................... | Milwaukee | Milwaukee | 77,316 | (NA) | 158 | 15,292 |
| Greenville County School District, SC................ | Greenville | Greenville | 75,508 | 4,523 | 96 | 10,077 |
| Alpine School District, UT........................... | American Fork | Utah | 75,161 | (NA) | 83 | 7,299 |
| Fresno Unified School District, CA.................. | Fresno | Fresno | 73,543 | 3,114 | 107 | 11,810 |
| Loudoun County Public Schools, VA................. | Ashburn | Loudoun | 73,418 | 4,736 | 89 | 14,768 |
| Guilford County Schools, NC....................... | Greensboro | Guilford | 73,416 | 4,726 | 126 | 10,426 |
| Brevard County School District, FL.................. | Viera | Brevard | 72,285 | 4,776 | 122 | 9,032 |
| Fort Bend Independent School District, TX.......... | Sugar Land | Fort Bend | 72,152 | 4,418 | 73 | 9,564 |

NA Not available. [1] Number of students receiving educational services from the school district. [2] Full-time equivalent is the amount of time required to perform an assignment stated as a proportion of a full-time position. [3] Totals for number of schools may differ from published estimates since they exclude closed, inactive, and future schools.

Source: U.S. Department of Education, National Center for Education Statistics, "Elementary/Secondary Information System," <http://nces.ed.gov/ccd/elsi/>, accessed May 2019.

# Table 268. Public Elementary and Secondary School Enrollment by State: 1990 to 2016

[In thousands (29,876 represents 29,876,000). As of Fall. Includes unclassified/ungraded students. Based on survey of state education agencies; see source for details]

| State | Pre-kindergarten through grade 8 | | | | | Grades 9 through 12 | | | | |
|---|---|---|---|---|---|---|---|---|---|---|
| | 1990 | 2000 | 2005 | 2010 | 2016 | 1990 | 2000 | 2005 | 2010 | 2016 |
| United States............. | 29,876 | 33,686 | 34,204 | 34,625 | 35,477 | 11,341 | 13,517 | 14,909 | 14,860 | 15,138 |
| Alabama....................... | 527 | 539 | 529 | 534 | 522 | 195 | 201 | 212 | 222 | 223 |
| Alaska........................ | 85 | 94 | 91 | 92 | 94 | 29 | 39 | 42 | 40 | 39 |
| Arizona....................... | 479 | 641 | 740 | 752 | 784 | 161 | 237 | 355 | 320 | 339 |
| Arkansas..................... | 314 | 318 | 336 | 346 | 350 | 123 | 132 | 138 | 136 | 143 |
| California.................... | 3,614 | 4,407 | 4,466 | 4,294 | 4,368 | 1,337 | 1,734 | 1,972 | 1,996 | 1,942 |
| Colorado..................... | 420 | 517 | 550 | 601 | 640 | 154 | 208 | 230 | 242 | 266 |
| Connecticut.................. | 347 | 406 | 400 | 387 | 369 | 122 | 156 | 175 | 173 | 166 |
| Delaware..................... | 73 | 81 | 85 | 90 | 96 | 27 | 34 | 36 | 39 | 41 |
| District of Columbia........... | 61 | 54 | 56 | 54 | 67 | 19 | 15 | 21 | 18 | 19 |
| Florida........................ | 1,370 | 1,760 | 1,873 | 1,858 | 1,969 | 492 | 675 | 802 | 785 | 848 |
| Georgia....................... | 849 | 1,060 | 1,145 | 1,202 | 1,246 | 303 | 385 | 453 | 475 | 519 |
| Hawaii........................ | 123 | 132 | 127 | 128 | 131 | 49 | 52 | 55 | 52 | 50 |
| Idaho......................... | 160 | 170 | 183 | 194 | 209 | 61 | 75 | 79 | 82 | 89 |
| Illinois........................ | 1,310 | 1,474 | 1,480 | 1,455 | 1,409 | 512 | 575 | 631 | 637 | 618 |
| Indiana....................... | 676 | 703 | 724 | 729 | 726 | 279 | 286 | 311 | 318 | 324 |
| Iowa.......................... | 345 | 334 | 326 | 348 | 363 | 139 | 161 | 157 | 148 | 147 |
| Kansas....................... | 320 | 323 | 321 | 343 | 351 | 117 | 147 | 147 | 141 | 143 |
| Kentucky..................... | 459 | 471 | 487 | 480 | 485 | 177 | 194 | 192 | 193 | 199 |
| Louisiana..................... | 586 | 547 | 482 | 512 | 516 | 199 | 197 | 172 | 184 | 200 |
| Maine......................... | 155 | 146 | 133 | 129 | 125 | 60 | 61 | 62 | 60 | 56 |
| Maryland...................... | 527 | 609 | 589 | 588 | 630 | 188 | 244 | 271 | 264 | 256 |
| Massachusetts................ | 604 | 703 | 675 | 666 | 669 | 230 | 273 | 297 | 289 | 295 |
| Michigan...................... | 1,145 | 1,222 | 1,191 | 1,076 | 1,047 | 440 | 498 | 551 | 511 | 481 |
| Minnesota.................... | 546 | 578 | 558 | 570 | 607 | 211 | 277 | 281 | 268 | 268 |
| Mississippi................... | 372 | 364 | 358 | 351 | 345 | 131 | 134 | 137 | 140 | 138 |
| Missouri...................... | 588 | 645 | 635 | 643 | 647 | 228 | 268 | 283 | 276 | 268 |
| Montana...................... | 111 | 105 | 98 | 98 | 104 | 42 | 50 | 48 | 43 | 42 |
| Nebraska..................... | 198 | 195 | 195 | 210 | 226 | 76 | 91 | 92 | 88 | 93 |
| Nevada....................... | 150 | 251 | 296 | 307 | 334 | 51 | 90 | 116 | 130 | 140 |
| New Hampshire............... | 126 | 147 | 139 | 132 | 124 | 46 | 61 | 67 | 63 | 57 |
| New Jersey................... | 783 | 968 | 971 | 981 | 991 | 306 | 346 | 425 | 421 | 420 |
| New Mexico................... | 208 | 225 | 230 | 239 | 236 | 94 | 95 | 97 | 99 | 100 |
| New York..................... | 1,827 | 2,029 | 1,909 | 1,869 | 1,887 | 771 | 853 | 907 | 866 | 843 |
| North Carolina................ | 783 | 945 | 1,003 | 1,058 | 1,080 | 304 | 348 | 413 | 432 | 470 |
| North Dakota................. | 85 | 72 | 66 | 66 | 79 | 33 | 37 | 33 | 30 | 30 |
| Ohio.......................... | 1,258 | 1,294 | 1,261 | 1,223 | 1,190 | 514 | 541 | 578 | 531 | 520 |
| Oklahoma..................... | 425 | 445 | 457 | 483 | 504 | 154 | 178 | 178 | 176 | 190 |
| Oregon....................... | 340 | 379 | 380 | 393 | 426 | 132 | 167 | 173 | 178 | 181 |
| Pennsylvania................. | 1,172 | 1,258 | 1,228 | 1,210 | 1,184 | 496 | 556 | 603 | 584 | 544 |
| Rhode Island................. | 102 | 114 | 104 | 98 | 99 | 37 | 44 | 50 | 46 | 43 |
| South Carolina................ | 452 | 493 | 498 | 516 | 548 | 170 | 184 | 204 | 210 | 223 |
| South Dakota................. | 95 | 88 | 84 | 88 | 99 | 34 | 41 | 38 | 38 | 38 |
| Tennessee.................... | 598 | 668 | 677 | 702 | 708 | 226 | 241 | 277 | 286 | 294 |
| Texas......................... | 2,511 | 2,943 | 3,268 | 3,587 | 3,836 | 872 | 1,117 | 1,257 | 1,349 | 1,525 |
| Utah.......................... | 325 | 333 | 358 | 425 | 471 | 122 | 148 | 151 | 161 | 189 |
| Vermont...................... | 71 | 70 | 65 | 68 | 63 | 25 | 32 | 32 | 29 | 26 |
| Virginia....................... | 728 | 816 | 841 | 871 | 898 | 270 | 329 | 372 | 380 | 389 |
| Washington................... | 613 | 694 | 699 | 714 | 762 | 227 | 310 | 333 | 330 | 339 |
| West Virginia................. | 224 | 201 | 197 | 201 | 194 | 98 | 85 | 84 | 81 | 79 |
| Wisconsin.................... | 565 | 595 | 584 | 598 | 602 | 232 | 285 | 291 | 274 | 263 |
| Wyoming..................... | 71 | 60 | 57 | 63 | 67 | 27 | 30 | 27 | 26 | 27 |

Source: U.S. National Center for Education Statistics, *Digest of Education Statistics*, "Advance Release of Selected 2018 Digest Tables," and earlier releases, <http://www.nces.ed.gov/programs/digest/>, accessed May 2019.

# Table 269. Parent Participation in School-Related Activities by Selected School, Student, and Family Characteristics: 2016

[In percent, except as noted (51,162 represents 51,162,000). For school year ending in year shown. Covers parents with children in kindergarten through grade 12. Homeschooled students are excluded]

| Characteristic | Number of students in grades K through 12 (1,000) | Attended a general school or PTO/PTA meeting [1] | Attended regularly scheduled parent-teacher conference | Attended a school or class event | Volunteered or served on school committee | Participated in school fundraising |
|---|---|---|---|---|---|---|
| **Total** | **51,162** | **89** | **78** | **79** | **43** | **59** |
| School type: [2] | | | | | | |
| Public, assigned | 38,730 | 88 | 76 | 78 | 39 | 57 |
| Public, chosen | 7,282 | 90 | 79 | 78 | 46 | 58 |
| Private, religious | 3,686 | 92 | 85 | 92 | 73 | 80 |
| Private, nonreligious | 1,043 | 97 | 92 | 90 | 67 | 71 |
| Student's sex: | | | | | | |
| Male | 26,495 | 87 | 79 | 77 | 42 | 58 |
| Female | 24,667 | 90 | 77 | 82 | 45 | 61 |
| Student's race/ethnicity: | | | | | | |
| White, non-Hispanic | 25,703 | 91 | 79 | 86 | 49 | 69 |
| Black, non-Hispanic | 7,139 | 87 | 79 | 72 | 34 | 48 |
| Hispanic [3] | 12,281 | 87 | 75 | 71 | 36 | 48 |
| Asian or Pacific Islander, non-Hispanic | 3,199 | 80 | 76 | 71 | 42 | 51 |
| Other, non-Hispanic [4] | 2,840 | 91 | 79 | 83 | 49 | 60 |
| Student's grade level: | | | | | | |
| K–2nd grade | 13,090 | 91 | 92 | 85 | 56 | 67 |
| 3rd–5th grade | 12,040 | 92 | 90 | 84 | 51 | 65 |
| 6th–8th grade | 11,602 | 90 | 73 | 76 | 35 | 55 |
| 9th–12th grade | 14,430 | 82 | 58 | 73 | 32 | 51 |
| Parents' highest education level: | | | | | | |
| Less than high school | 5,530 | 76 | 70 | 54 | 25 | 29 |
| High school graduate or equivalent | 9,986 | 82 | 73 | 69 | 27 | 49 |
| Vocational/technical or some college | 13,174 | 90 | 76 | 80 | 39 | 60 |
| Bachelor's degree | 13,789 | 93 | 82 | 87 | 54 | 70 |
| Graduate or professional school | 8,683 | 95 | 84 | 93 | 65 | 73 |
| Parents' language at home: | | | | | | |
| Both/only parent(s) speak(s) English | 43,115 | 90 | 79 | 82 | 46 | 64 |
| One of two parents speaks English | 1,882 | 86 | 74 | 71 | 38 | 47 |
| No parent speaks English | 6,165 | 81 | 68 | 62 | 25 | 33 |

[1] Parent Teacher Organization (PTO) or Parent Teacher Association (PTA) meeting. [2] School type classifies the school currently attended as either public or private. Public schools are further classified according to whether the school was chosen or assigned. Private schools are classified as being religious or nonreligious. [3] Persons of Hispanic origin may be of any race. [4] Includes children who were multiracial and not of Hispanic ethnicity, were American Indian or Alaska Native, or were not Hispanic, White, Black, Asian, or Pacific Islander.

Source: U.S. Department of Education, National Center for Education Statistics, *Parent and Family Involvement in Education, from the National Household Education Surveys Program of 2016*, September 2017. See also <http://nces.ed.gov/nhes/>.

# Table 270. School Enrollment Below Postsecondary—Summary by Sex, Race, and Hispanic Origin: 2017

[In thousands (58,011 represents 58,011,000), except percent. As of October. Covers civilian noninstitutional population enrolled in nursery school through high school. Based on Current Population Survey, see text, Section 1 and Appendix III]

| Characteristic | Total | | | Race and Hispanic origin | | | | |
|---|---|---|---|---|---|---|---|---|
| | | | | White [2] | | | | |
| | Number [1] | Male | Female | Total | Non-Hispanic | Black [2] | Asian [2] | Hispanic [3] |
| **All students** | **58,011** | **29,667** | **28,343** | **41,924** | **29,593** | **8,797** | **3,055** | **14,399** |
| Nursery | 4,676 | 2,377 | 2,300 | 3,315 | 2,461 | 754 | 253 | 1,007 |
| Full day | 2,619 | (NA) | (NA) | 1,694 | 1,291 | 565 | 140 | 508 |
| Part day | 2,057 | (NA) | (NA) | 1,620 | 1,170 | 189 | 113 | 500 |
| Public schools | 2,782 | (NA) | (NA) | 1,885 | 1,211 | 576 | 123 | 751 |
| Full day | 1,510 | (NA) | (NA) | 897 | 600 | 428 | 56 | 352 |
| Part day | 1,272 | (NA) | (NA) | 988 | 612 | 147 | 67 | 398 |
| Private schools | 1,894 | (NA) | (NA) | 1,430 | 1,250 | 178 | 130 | 257 |
| Full day | 1,109 | (NA) | (NA) | 797 | 692 | 137 | 84 | 155 |
| Part day | 785 | (NA) | (NA) | 633 | 559 | 42 | 46 | 101 |
| Kindergarten | 3,964 | 2,027 | 1,937 | 2,918 | 1,955 | 507 | 239 | 1,116 |
| Elementary | 32,530 | 16,710 | 15,820 | 23,411 | 16,272 | 5,048 | 1,632 | 8,340 |
| High school | 16,841 | 8,554 | 8,287 | 12,281 | 8,905 | 2,488 | 931 | 3,936 |
| Population 18 to 24 years old | 29,538 | 14,833 | 14,705 | 21,789 | 15,945 | 4,458 | 1,754 | 6,653 |
| Percent dropouts [4] | 6.0 | 6.9 | 5.1 | 6.2 | 4.7 | 6.1 | 1.6 | 10.6 |
| Percent high school graduates | 87.5 | 85.6 | 89.3 | 87.5 | 89.4 | 85.4 | 94.5 | 82.0 |
| Percent enrolled in college | 40.4 | 36.8 | 44.0 | 39.9 | 41.0 | 35.8 | 62.8 | 36.2 |

NA Not available. [1] Includes other races not shown separately. [2] For persons who selected this race group only. See footnote 4, Table 256. [3] Persons of Hispanic origin may be of any race. [4] For persons not in regular school and who have not completed the 12th grade nor received a general equivalency degree.

Source: U.S. Census Bureau, "School Enrollment in the United States: October 2017 - Detailed Tables," <https://www.census.gov/topics/education/school-enrollment/data/tables.All.html>, accessed December 2018.

# Table 271. Elementary and Secondary Schools—Teachers, Enrollment, and Pupil-Teacher Ratio: 1970 to 2017

[In thousands (2,292 represents 2,292,000), except ratios. As of Fall. Data are for full-time equivalent teachers. Based on surveys of state education agencies and private schools; see source for details]

| Year | Teachers | | | Enrollment | | | Pupil-teacher ratio | | |
|---|---|---|---|---|---|---|---|---|---|
| | Total | Public | Private [1] | Total | Public | Private [1] | Total | Public | Private [1] |
| 1970 | 2,292 | 2,059 | 233 | 51,257 | 45,894 | 5,363 | 22.4 | 22.3 | 23.0 |
| 1980 | 2,485 | 2,184 | 301 | 46,208 | 40,877 | 5,331 | 18.6 | 18.7 | 17.7 |
| 1990 | 2,759 | 2,398 | 361 | 46,864 | 41,217 | 5,648 | 17.0 | 17.2 | 15.6 |
| 2000 | 3,366 | 2,941 | 424 | 53,373 | 47,204 | 6,169 | 15.9 | 16.0 | 14.5 |
| 2002 | 3,476 | 3,034 | 442 | 54,403 | 48,183 | 6,220 | 15.7 | 15.9 | 14.1 |
| 2003 | 3,490 | 3,049 | 441 | 54,639 | 48,540 | 6,099 | 15.7 | 15.9 | 13.8 |
| 2004 | 3,536 | 3,091 | 445 | 54,882 | 48,795 | 6,087 | 15.5 | 15.8 | 13.7 |
| 2005 | 3,593 | 3,143 | 450 | 55,187 | 49,113 | 6,073 | 15.4 | 15.6 | 13.5 |
| 2006 | 3,622 | 3,166 | 456 | 55,307 | 49,316 | 5,991 | 15.3 | 15.6 | 13.2 |
| 2007 | 3,656 | 3,200 | 456 | 55,201 | 49,291 | 5,910 | 15.1 | 15.4 | 13.0 |
| 2008 | 3,670 | 3,222 | 448 | 54,973 | 49,266 | 5,707 | 15.0 | 15.3 | 12.8 |
| 2009 | 3,647 | 3,210 | 437 | 54,849 | 49,361 | 5,488 | 15.0 | 15.4 | 12.5 |
| 2010 | 3,512 | 3,099 | 413 | 54,867 | 49,484 | 5,382 | 15.6 | 16.0 | 13.0 |
| 2011 | 3,508 | 3,103 | 405 | 54,790 | 49,522 | 5,268 | 15.6 | 16.0 | 13.0 |
| 2012 | 3,517 | 3,109 | 408 | 55,104 | 49,771 | 5,333 | 15.7 | 16.0 | 13.1 |
| 2013 | 3,555 | 3,114 | 441 | 55,440 | 50,045 | 5,396 | 15.6 | 16.1 | 12.2 |
| 2014 | 3,594 | 3,132 | 461 | 55,888 | 50,313 | 5,575 | 15.6 | 16.1 | 12.1 |
| 2015 | 3,633 | 3,151 | 482 | 56,189 | 50,438 | 5,751 | 15.5 | 16.0 | 11.9 |
| 2016 | 3,655 | 3,169 | 485 | 56,391 | 50,615 | 5,776 | 15.4 | 16.0 | 11.9 |
| 2017, projected | 3,641 | 3,156 | 485 | 56,477 | 50,695 | 5,781 | 15.5 | 16.1 | 11.9 |

[1] Private school data are estimated based on the Private School Universe Survey, biennially 1990-2014.

Source: U.S. National Center for Education Statistics, *Digest of Education Statistics*, "Advance Release of Selected 2018 Digest Tables," <http://www.nces.ed.gov/programs/digest/>, accessed August 2019.

# Table 272. Private Schools—Number, Students, and Teachers by School Characteristics: 2018

[In thousands where indicated (4,898 represents 4,898,000). For school year ending in year shown. Based on the Private School Survey, conducted every 2 years; see source for details. For composition of regions, see map inside front cover]

| Characteristic | Schools (number) | Students (1,000) | Teachers (1,000) [1] | Average enrollment by school level | | | | Student to teacher ratio by school level | | | |
|---|---|---|---|---|---|---|---|---|---|---|---|
| | | | | Total | Ele-mentary | Sec-ondary | Com-bined | Total | Ele-mentary | Sec-ondary | Com-bined |
| **Total** | **32,461** | **4,898** | **482** | **150.9** | **108.0** | **284.2** | **201.5** | **10.2** | **10.8** | **11.0** | **9.2** |
| School type: | | | | | | | | | | | |
| Catholic | 7,047 | 1,962 | 153 | 278.4 | 218.6 | 509.7 | 397.8 | 12.8 | 13.3 | 12.6 | 10.9 |
| Parochial | 2,422 | 582 | 43 | 240.1 | 222.7 | 427.9 | 432.6 | 13.4 | 13.7 | 12.9 | 11.5 |
| Diocesan | 3,477 | 960 | 73 | 276.2 | 222.2 | 522.8 | 304.3 | 13.1 | 13.5 | 12.7 | 10.6 |
| Private | 1,148 | 420 | 36 | 365.7 | 176.3 | 509.2 | 439.6 | 11.6 | 10.5 | 12.6 | 10.8 |
| Other religious | 14,501 | 1,858 | 183 | 128.1 | 79.5 | 147.5 | 193.9 | 10.2 | 10.5 | 9.3 | 10.1 |
| Conservative Christian | 3,782 | 599 | 57 | 158.2 | 104.1 | 144.0 | 181.9 | 10.5 | 10.4 | 11.5 | 10.5 |
| Affiliated | 2,982 | 558 | 57 | 187.1 | 123.5 | 180.0 | 293.2 | 9.7 | 9.7 | 8.6 | 9.9 |
| Unaffiliated | 7,737 | 701 | 68 | 90.7 | 60.4 | 124.7 | 160.2 | 10.3 | 11.1 | 9.4 | 9.7 |
| Nonsectarian | 10,913 | 1,079 | 147 | 98.8 | 52.6 | 123.0 | 184.6 | 7.4 | 6.9 | 7.4 | 7.6 |
| Regular | 4,250 | 706 | 87 | 166.1 | 76.7 | 195.1 | 334.9 | 8.1 | 7.9 | 7.5 | 8.3 |
| Special emphasis | 4,889 | 262 | 39 | 53.6 | 37.1 | 87.6 | 121.7 | 6.8 | 6.1 | 8.3 | 7.6 |
| Special education | 1,774 | 111 | 21 | 62.6 | 45.5 | 39.7 | 70.7 | 5.3 | 4.7 | 5.2 | 5.4 |
| Program emphasis: | | | | | | | | | | | |
| Regular | 22,088 | 4,346 | 403 | 196.7 | 148.3 | 341.2 | 242.3 | 10.8 | 11.8 | 11.3 | 9.7 |
| Montessori | 3,053 | 120 | 19 | 39.5 | 32.9 | (B) | 92.9 | 6.2 | 5.5 | 7.3 | 9.5 |
| Special program emphasis | 1,042 | 165 | 20 | 158.0 | 106.5 | 177.1 | 214.3 | 8.4 | 7.8 | 8.5 | 8.8 |
| Special education | 1,979 | 122 | 23 | 61.5 | 46.1 | 40.8 | 68.6 | 5.4 | 4.7 | 5.3 | 5.5 |
| Vocational/technical | 22 | 3 | (Z) | 131.1 | (B) | (B) | (B) | 9.9 | (B) | (B) | (B) |
| Alternative | 2,245 | 107 | 13 | 47.6 | 28.6 | 82.7 | 98.6 | 8.5 | 8.5 | 10.2 | 7.8 |
| Early childhood | 2,031 | 36 | 5 | 17.7 | 17.3 | (X) | [2] 25.8 | 7.2 | 7.1 | (X) | [2] 8.3 |
| Enrollment size: | | | | | | | | | | | |
| Less than 50 | 13,969 | 299 | 50 | 21.4 | 19.8 | 23.5 | 25.8 | 5.9 | 6.5 | 4.5 | 5.2 |
| 50 to 149 | 8,172 | 750 | 91 | 91.8 | 93.1 | 94.8 | 88.7 | 8.2 | 9.1 | 7.2 | 7.2 |
| 150 to 299 | 5,727 | 1,206 | 111 | 210.5 | 207.6 | 220.2 | 214.3 | 10.9 | 12.1 | 9.6 | 9.2 |
| 300 to 499 | 2,594 | 996 | 88 | 383.9 | 383.7 | 388.4 | 382.1 | 11.4 | 12.7 | 10.9 | 9.8 |
| 500 to 749 | 1,154 | 699 | 62 | 606.0 | 591.3 | 608.4 | 612.0 | 11.2 | 14.3 | 11.9 | 9.9 |
| 750 or more | 845 | 949 | 80 | 1,122.3 | 1,053.9 | 1,058.3 | 1,167.7 | 11.9 | 14.1 | 13.7 | 10.9 |
| Region: | | | | | | | | | | | |
| Northeast | 7,007 | 1,076 | 117 | 153.6 | 103.8 | 279.1 | 215.5 | 9.2 | 10.5 | 9.9 | 7.8 |
| Midwest | 7,937 | 1,195 | 103 | 150.6 | 117.7 | 338.3 | 196.8 | 11.6 | 12.0 | 11.7 | 10.7 |
| South | 11,156 | 1,706 | 175 | 152.9 | 102.5 | 253.1 | 201.3 | 9.7 | 10.0 | 11.0 | 9.3 |
| West | 6,360 | 920 | 87 | 144.7 | 106.9 | 276.1 | 191.7 | 10.6 | 10.8 | 11.9 | 9.7 |
| Urban/rural status: | | | | | | | | | | | |
| City | 10,531 | 2,153 | 207 | 204.4 | 141.8 | 350.6 | 289.8 | 10.4 | 10.9 | 12.0 | 9.4 |
| Suburban | 12,152 | 1,906 | 185 | 156.9 | 115.2 | 318.5 | 208.4 | 10.3 | 10.9 | 11.1 | 9.3 |
| Town | 2,754 | 312 | 31 | 113.3 | 95.7 | 168.6 | 133.5 | 9.9 | 11.0 | 8.6 | 9.2 |
| Rural | 7,024 | 527 | 59 | 75.0 | 44.0 | 124.7 | 114.6 | 9.0 | 10.2 | 7.9 | 8.6 |

X Not applicable. Z Less than 500. B Base figure too small to meet statistical standards. [1] Full-time equivalents. [2] Interpret data with caution.

Source: U.S. National Center for Education Statistics, Private School Universe Survey, "Data Tables," <http://nces.ed.gov/surveys/pss/>, accessed August 2019.

## Table 273. Public Elementary and Secondary Schools by Type and Size of School: 2017

[Enrollment in thousands (50,275 represents 50,275,000), except for average enrollment. For school year ending in 2017. Data reported by schools, rather than school districts. Based on the Common Core of Data Survey; see source for details]

| Enrollment size of school | Number of schools | | | | | Enrollment [1] | | | | |
|---|---|---|---|---|---|---|---|---|---|---|
| | Total | Elemen- tary [2] | Second- ary [3] | Com- bined [4] | Other [5] | Total | Elemen- tary [2] | Second- ary [3] | Com- bined [4] | Other [5] |
| **Total**..................... | **98,158** | **66,837** | **23,814** | **6,783** | **724** | **50,275** | **32,133** | **15,798** | **2,336** | **8** |
| PERCENT | | | | | | | | | | |
| Total........................ | 100.0 | 100.0 | 100.0 | 100.0 | 100.0 | 100.0 | 100.0 | 100.0 | 100.0 | 100.0 |
| Under 100 students........ | 10.0 | 5.2 | 17.2 | 33.7 | 81.7 | 0.9 | 0.5 | 1.1 | 3.6 | 48.1 |
| 100 to 199 students....... | 8.9 | 7.6 | 11.1 | 15.2 | 14.8 | 2.5 | 2.4 | 2.3 | 5.9 | 28.5 |
| 200 to 299 students...... | 11.0 | 11.6 | 9.2 | 10.4 | 1.7 | 5.2 | 6.1 | 3.2 | 7.0 | 5.4 |
| 300 to 399 students....... | 13.7 | 16.1 | 8.0 | 8.8 | 0.9 | 9.1 | 11.7 | 4.0 | 8.3 | 4.0 |
| 400 to 499 students....... | 14.1 | 17.1 | 7.1 | 7.5 | – | 12.0 | 15.9 | 4.5 | 9.1 | – |
| 500 to 599 students........ | 11.6 | 14.1 | 5.9 | 5.3 | – | 12.0 | 16.0 | 4.6 | 7.9 | – |
| 600 to 699 students....... | 8.6 | 10.4 | 4.7 | 4.2 | – | 10.6 | 13.9 | 4.3 | 7.4 | – |
| 700 to 799 students....... | 6.0 | 7.0 | 4.0 | 3.4 | – | 8.5 | 10.8 | 4.2 | 6.9 | – |
| 800 to 999 students....... | 6.7 | 7.0 | 6.8 | 4.0 | – | 11.3 | 12.7 | 8.6 | 9.7 | – |
| 1,000 to 1,499 students. .. | 5.5 | 3.7 | 11.3 | 4.7 | 0.9 | 12.5 | 8.8 | 19.7 | 15.0 | 14.0 |
| 1,500 to 1,999 students. .. | 2.0 | 0.3 | 7.4 | 1.4 | – | 6.6 | 1.0 | 18.0 | 6.4 | – |
| 2,000 to 2,999 students. .. | 1.5 | – | 6.0 | 0.8 | – | 6.7 | 0.2 | 20.1 | 4.9 | – |
| 3,000 or more students. .. | 0.3 | – | 1.1 | 0.5 | – | 2.1 | – | 5.4 | 7.9 | – |
| Average enrollment [1].... | (X) | (X) | (X) | (X) | (X) | 528 | 483 | 708 | 371 | 70 |

– Represents or rounds to zero. X Not applicable. [1] Excludes data for schools not reporting enrollment. [2] Includes schools beginning with grade 6 or below and with no grade higher than 8. [3] Includes schools with no grade lower than 7. [4] Includes schools beginning with grade 6 or below and ending with grade 9 or above. [5] Includes special education, alternative, and other schools not classified by grade span.

Source: U.S. National Center for Education Statistics, *Digest of Education Statistics*, "Advance Release of Selected 2018 Digest Tables," <http://www.nces.ed.gov/programs/digest/>, accessed May 2019.

## Table 274. Public Elementary and Secondary Schools—Number and Average Salary of Classroom Teachers: 1990 to 2017, and by State, 2018

[2,361.6 represents 2,361,600. Estimates for school year ending in June of year shown]

| Year and state | Teachers [1] (1,000) | Average salary (dollars) | Year and state | Teachers [1] (1,000) | Average salary (dollars) | Year and state | Teachers [1] (1,000) | Average salary (dollars) |
|---|---|---|---|---|---|---|---|---|
| 1990......... | 2,361.6 | 31,367 | HI............. | 11.2 | 57,866 | NM............ | 21.1 | 47,152 |
| 2000......... | 2,891.1 | 41,807 | ID............. | 16.5 | 49,225 | NY............ | 214.3 | 84,227 |
| 2005......... | 3,072.5 | 47,516 | IL............. | 127.2 | 65,721 | NC............ | 94.1 | 51,231 |
| 2010......... | 3,182.2 | 55,370 | IN............. | 61.5 | 50,614 | ND............ | 8.6 | 52,850 |
| 2015......... | 3,132.0 | 57,626 | IA............. | 37.3 | 57,018 | OH............ | 115.0 | 58,000 |
| 2016......... | 3,112.6 | 58,316 | KS............. | 34.8 | 49,754 | OK............ | 41.3 | 46,300 |
| 2017......... | 3,142.6 | 59,539 | KY............. | 40.3 | 52,952 | OR............ | 29.7 | 63,061 |
| **2018** | | | LA............. | 47.6 | 50,359 | PA............ | 119.4 | 67,535 |
| **U.S. total. ..** | **3,159.0** | **60,477** | ME............. | 14.7 | 53,815 | RI............ | 10.7 | 66,758 |
| AL............ | 46.4 | 50,568 | MD............. | 60.7 | 69,627 | SC............ | 50.9 | 50,182 |
| AK............ | 8.0 | 69,682 | MA............. | 73.4 | 80,357 | SD............ | 9.7 | 47,631 |
| AZ............ | 48.7 | 48,723 | MI............. | 83.8 | 61,911 | TN............ | 66.1 | 50,900 |
| AR............ | 31.7 | 50,544 | MN............. | 53.7 | 57,782 | TX............ | 356.9 | 53,334 |
| CA............ | 274.5 | 80,680 | MS............. | 31.3 | 44,926 | UT............ | 29.2 | 49,655 |
| CO............ | 56.0 | 52,701 | MO............. | 75.4 | 49,304 | VT............ | 8.1 | 60,556 |
| CT............ | 41.8 | 74,517 | MT............. | 10.5 | 52,776 | VA............ | 102.1 | 51,994 |
| DE............ | 9.4 | 61,795 | NE............. | 24.9 | 54,213 | WA............ | 61.1 | 55,693 |
| DC............ | 6.9 | 76,486 | NV............. | 21.4 | 54,280 | WV............ | 18.9 | 45,642 |
| FL............ | 143.5 | 48,168 | NH............. | 14.8 | 57,833 | WI............ | 55.5 | 51,469 |
| GA............ | 115.4 | 56,329 | NJ............. | 115.9 | 69,917 | WY............ | 7.2 | 58,352 |

[1] Full-time equivalent.

Source: National Education Association, Washington, DC. Data from *Rankings of the States 2018 and Estimates of School Statistics 2019*, used with permission of the National Education Association © 2019. All rights reserved.

# Table 275. Homeschooled Students by Selected Characteristics: 2007 to 2016

[1,520 represents 1,520,000. As of Spring. For students age 5 to 17 with a grade equivalent of K–12. Homeschoolers are students whose parents reported them to be schooled at home instead of a public or private school. Excludes students who were enrolled in school for more than 25 hours a week or were homeschooled due to a temporary illness. Based on the Parent and Family Involvement in Education Survey of the National Household Education Surveys Program; see source and Appendix III for details]

| Characteristic | 2007 | | 2012 [1] | | 2016 | |
|---|---|---|---|---|---|---|
| | Home-schooled (1,000) | Percent home-schooled | Home-schooled (1,000) | Percent home-schooled | Home-schooled (1,000) | Percent home-schooled |
| Total................................ | **1,520** | **3.0** | **1,773** | **3.4** | **1,690** | **3.3** |
| Grade equivalent: [2] | | | | | | |
| Kindergarten to grade 5............... | 717 | 3.0 | 833 | 3.2 | 767 | 3.0 |
| Kindergarten....................... | (S) | (S) | 212 | 4.0 | 181 | 3.5 |
| Grades 1 to 3...................... | 406 | 3.4 | 353 | 2.9 | 300 | 2.4 |
| Grades 4 to 5...................... | 197 | 2.5 | 268 | 3.2 | 287 | 3.4 |
| Grades 6 to 8......................... | 371 | 3.0 | 424 | 3.5 | 398 | 3.3 |
| Grades 9 to 12........................ | 422 | 2.8 | 516 | 3.8 | 525 | 3.8 |
| Sex: | | | | | | |
| Male................................. | 639 | 2.4 | 875 | 3.3 | 807 | 3.0 |
| Female............................... | 881 | 3.5 | 898 | 3.6 | 882 | 3.5 |
| Race/ethnicity: [3] | | | | | | |
| White, non-Hispanic................... | 1,171 | 3.9 | 1,205 | 4.5 | 998 | 3.8 |
| Black, non-Hispanic.................. | [6] 61 | [6] 0.8 | 140 | 2.0 | 132 | 1.9 |
| Hispanic [4]........................... | 147 | 1.5 | 265 | 2.3 | 444 | 3.5 |
| Asian/Pacific Islander................ | (S) | (S) | [6] 73 | [6] 2.8 | 44 | 1.4 |
| Other [5]............................. | 111 | 4.8 | 82 | 3.2 | 69 | 2.7 |
| Number of children in the household: | | | | | | |
| One child............................. | 197 | 2.3 | 418 | 3.4 | 338 | 2.7 |
| Two children.......................... | 414 | 2.0 | 493 | 2.5 | 475 | 2.3 |
| Three or more children................ | 909 | 4.1 | 862 | 4.5 | 877 | 4.7 |
| Number of parents in the household: | | | | | | |
| Two parents.......................... | 1,357 | 3.6 | 1,354 | 3.8 | 1,358 | 3.7 |
| One parent........................... | 118 | 1.0 | 342 | 2.5 | 293 | 2.3 |
| Nonparental guardians................ | (S) | (S) | [6] 77 | [6] 4.0 | 38 | 2.0 |
| Parents' participation in the labor force: | | | | | | |
| Two parents—both in labor force........ | 518 | 2.0 | 588 | 2.5 | 427 | 1.7 |
| Two parents—one in labor force......... | 808 | 7.5 | 719 | 6.2 | 935 | 7.2 |
| One parent in labor force.............. | 127 | 1.3 | 247 | 2.2 | 189 | 1.8 |
| No parent in labor force............... | (S) | (S) | 130 | 4.8 | 139 | 4.0 |
| Household income: | | | | | | |
| $20,000 or less........................ | 186 | 2.2 | 219 | 2.9 | 184 | 2.9 |
| $20,001 to 50,000...................... | 420 | 3.1 | 528 | 3.8 | 483 | 3.7 |
| $50,001 to 75,000...................... | 414 | 4.0 | 370 | 3.9 | 435 | 4.8 |
| $75,001 to 100,000..................... | 264 | 3.8 | 288 | 4.2 | 268 | 3.8 |
| $100,000 or more....................... | 236 | 2.0 | 367 | 2.7 | 319 | 1.9 |
| Parents' highest educational attainment: | | | | | | |
| High school diploma or less............ | 208 | 1.5 | 560 | 3.4 | 510 | 3.3 |
| Vocational/technical degree or some college........... | 559 | 3.8 | 525 | 3.4 | 418 | 3.1 |
| Bachelor's degree..................... | 444 | 3.9 | 434 | 3.7 | 501 | 3.6 |
| Graduate/professional school.......... | 309 | 2.9 | 255 | 3.3 | 260 | 3.0 |

S Figure does not meet publication standards. [1] The NCES uses a statistical adjustment for estimates of total homeschoolers in 2012; therefore, data will not add to total. All other estimates about homeschoolers do not use a statistical adjustment. [2] Excludes those ungraded. [3] Includes other race/ethnicities not shown separately. [4] Persons of Hispanic origin may be of any race. [5] Includes two or more races and race/ethnicity not reported. [6] Interpret data with caution.

Source: U.S. National Center for Education Statistics, *Digest of Education Statistics,* "Advance Release of Selected 2017 Digest Tables," and earlier releases, <http://www.nces.ed.gov/programs/digest/>, accessed August 2018.

# Table 276. Public School Teachers, Base Salary, and Additional Income by Selected Characteristics: 2016

[3,556 represents 3,556,000. Salary and income shown in current dollars. For school year ending in 2016. Data shown for regular full-time teachers only; excludes other staff even when they have full-time teaching duties. Based on the 2015-16 National Teacher and Principal Survey and subject to sampling error; for details, see <https://nces.ed.gov/surveys/ntps/>]

| Characteristic | Number of full-time teachers (1,000) | Base teacher salary (dollars) | Total income from school and nonschool sources [1,2] (dollars) | Teachers with additional income | | | | | |
| | | | | Job outside the school system during the school year | | Supplemental school system contract during summer [3] | | Employed in a non-school job during the summer | |
| | | | | Percent of teachers | Average income (dollars) | Percent of teachers | Average income (dollars) | Percent of teachers | Average income (dollars) |
|---|---|---|---|---|---|---|---|---|---|
| Total........................... | 3,556 | 55,120 | 59,050 | 17.9 | 5,140 | 19.8 | 2,700 | 15.9 | 4,060 |
| **Sex:** | | | | | | | | | |
| Male........................... | 852 | 56,920 | 63,740 | 26.1 | 6,500 | 23.2 | 3,240 | 24.2 | 4,910 |
| Female....................... | 2,704 | 54,560 | 57,560 | 15.3 | 4,420 | 18.7 | 2,490 | 13.3 | 3,570 |
| **Race/ethnicity:** | | | | | | | | | |
| White.......................... | 2,835 | 55,120 | 59,080 | 18.7 | 5,010 | 18.7 | 2,640 | 17.1 | 4,030 |
| Black.......................... | 243 | 52,420 | 56,680 | 16.8 | 6,120 | 25.2 | 2,960 | 12.5 | 4,660 |
| Hispanic..................... | 322 | 56,240 | 59,750 | 12.3 | 5,500 | 23.8 | 2,830 | 9.1 | 3,970 |
| Asian.......................... | 79 | 61,350 | 64,430 | 11.8 | 6,010 | 23.6 | 3,140 | 11.2 | 4,820 |
| Pacific Islander............... | 8 | 59,900 | 64,190 | 26.0 | (S) | 18.5 | (S) | 16.3 | (S) |
| American Indian or Alaska Native................. | 16 | 48,600 | 52,830 | 17.5 | (S) | 23.8 | 2,520 | 12.3 | (S) |
| Two or more races........... | 51 | 52,750 | 56,760 | 20.3 | 6,050 | 18.0 | 2,260 | 17.2 | 3,160 |
| **Age:** | | | | | | | | | |
| Less than 30 years old....... | 541 | 42,850 | 46,420 | 19.6 | 3,760 | 22.3 | 2,370 | 26.0 | 3,140 |
| 30 to 39 years old........... | 1,022 | 52,110 | 55,890 | 18.1 | 4,860 | 20.6 | 2,670 | 15.7 | 3,990 |
| 40 to 49 years old........... | 977 | 58,030 | 61,770 | 18.0 | 5,520 | 19.0 | 2,670 | 14.3 | 4,200 |
| 50 or more years old......... | 1,015 | 61,890 | 66,330 | 16.7 | 5,930 | 18.2 | 2,990 | 12.3 | 5,030 |
| **Years of full-time teaching experience:** | | | | | | | | | |
| 1 year or less................. | 176 | 41,620 | 45,930 | 18.1 | 5,140 | 18.1 | 2,490 | 31.9 | 5,410 |
| 2 to 4 years.................... | 515 | 43,590 | 47,090 | 18.2 | 4,660 | 21.8 | 2,280 | 20.1 | 3,630 |
| 5 to 9 years.................... | 673 | 48,110 | 51,760 | 18.9 | 4,410 | 22.9 | 2,670 | 16.6 | 3,440 |
| 10 to 14 years................. | 691 | 55,460 | 59,100 | 18.2 | 5,180 | 19.4 | 2,810 | 14.2 | 3,580 |
| 15 to 19 years................. | 602 | 61,170 | 64,920 | 17.0 | 5,720 | 18.3 | 2,810 | 13.3 | 4,480 |
| 20 to 24 years................. | 401 | 64,460 | 68,340 | 17.1 | 5,840 | 17.5 | 2,890 | 13.0 | 4,430 |
| 25 to 29 years................. | 262 | 65,490 | 69,740 | 17.8 | 5,220 | 17.7 | 2,930 | 13.4 | 4,210 |
| 30 or more years.............. | 234 | 66,760 | 73,020 | 17.1 | 5,770 | 18.3 | 2,870 | 12.6 | 4,940 |
| **Highest degree held:** | | | | | | | | | |
| Less than bachelors'.......... | 87 | 51,800 | 57,030 | 19.0 | 6,030 | 18.6 | 3,820 | 19.6 | 5,890 |
| Bachelor's..................... | 1,465 | 47,770 | 51,240 | 16.6 | 4,670 | 18.9 | 2,470 | 17.4 | 3,670 |
| Master's....................... | 1,669 | 60,140 | 64,260 | 18.5 | 5,420 | 20.1 | 2,780 | 14.8 | 4,230 |
| Education specialist........... | 289 | 62,790 | 67,020 | 19.2 | 4,770 | 22.3 | 2,760 | 13.6 | 4,450 |
| Doctorate...................... | 45 | 65,700 | 72,610 | 27.8 | 8,090 | 18.8 | 4,430 | 17.9 | 5,170 |
| **Instructional level:** [4] | | | | | | | | | |
| Elementary.................... | 1,734 | 54,020 | 56,730 | 14.5 | 4,640 | 18.4 | 2,480 | 13.7 | 3,600 |
| Secondary..................... | 1,821 | 56,180 | 61,250 | 21.2 | 5,470 | 21.0 | 2,880 | 18.0 | 4,400 |
| **School locale:** | | | | | | | | | |
| City............................. | (S) | (S) | (S) | (S) | (S) | (S) | (S) | (S) | (S) |
| Suburban...................... | 1,399 | 59,790 | 63,540 | 17.8 | 4,940 | 18.4 | 2,590 | 15.4 | 3,920 |
| Town........................... | 388 | 48,010 | 52,140 | 18.5 | 5,020 | 21.2 | 2,610 | 18.1 | 3,800 |
| Rural........................... | 666 | 47,790 | 51,790 | 18.7 | 5,060 | 17.8 | 2,540 | 18.1 | 4,350 |

S Figure does not meet publication standards. [1] Includes retirement pension funds paid during the school year. [2] Includes types of income not shown separately. [3] Includes teaching summer sessions and other non-teaching jobs at any school. [4] Teachers were classified as elementary or secondary on the basis of the grades they taught, rather than on the level of the school in which they taught. In general, elementary teachers include those teaching pre-kindergarten through grade 5 and those teaching multiple grades, with a preponderance of grades taught being kindergarten through grade 6. In general, secondary teachers include those teaching grades 7 through 12 and those teaching multiple grades, with a preponderance of grades taught being grades 7 through 12 and usually no grade taught being lower than grade 5.

Source: U.S. National Center for Education Statistics, *Digest of Education Statistics*, "Advance Release of Selected 2017 Digest Tables," <http://www.nces.ed.gov/programs/digest/>, accessed March 2018.

# Table 277. Education and Teaching Experience of Public Elementary and Secondary School Teachers by Selected Characteristics: 2016

[3,827 represents 3,827,000. For school year ending in 2016. Excludes prekindergarten teachers. Data are based on a head count of full-time and part-time teachers. Based on the National Teacher and Principal Survey (NTPS); see source for details]

| Characteristic | Number of teachers (1,000s) | Percent of teachers by highest degree earned | | | | | Percent of teachers by years of teaching experience [1] | | | |
|---|---|---|---|---|---|---|---|---|---|---|
| | | Less than bachelor's | Bach-elor's | Master's | Education specialist [2] | Doctor's | Less than 3 | 3 to 9 | 10 to 20 | Over 20 |
| Total............ | 3,827 | 2.4 | 40.5 | 47.3 | 8.4 | 1.3 | 9.9 | 28.3 | 39.3 | 22.5 |
| Sex: | | | | | | | | | | |
| Male.................. | 897 | 4.1 | 40.9 | 46.1 | 6.8 | 2.1 | 10.1 | 28.7 | 38.2 | 23.0 |
| Female................. | 2,930 | 1.9 | 40.4 | 47.7 | 9.0 | 1.0 | 9.9 | 28.2 | 39.6 | 22.3 |
| Race/ethnicity: [3] | | | | | | | | | | |
| White................. | 3,067 | 2.5 | 39.7 | 48.5 | 8.1 | 1.2 | 9.2 | 27.6 | 39.3 | 23.9 |
| Black................. | 256 | (S) | 45.1 | 42.8 | [6] 9.6 | (S) | 14.2 | 27.5 | 41.3 | 17.0 |
| Asian................. | 86 | [6] 1.5 | 35.4 | 50.4 | 11.5 | [6] 1.2 | 10.7 | 35.3 | 37.9 | 16.1 |
| Pacific Islander.............. | 9 | 2.2 | 36.9 | 44.5 | 14.0 | 2.4 | 12.4 | 29.9 | 38.6 | 19.2 |
| American Indian/Alaska Native................. | 17 | [6] 7.3 | 43.5 | 40.5 | [6] 7.9 | (S) | 11.0 | 26.7 | 36.7 | 25.7 |
| Two or more races........... | 54 | [6] 2.5 | 42.4 | 46.2 | 6.9 | [6] 2.1 | 16.8 | 30.5 | 36.4 | 16.3 |
| Hispanic..................... | 338 | 2.0 | 50.8 | 39.1 | 6.9 | 1.2 | 13.1 | 31.7 | 40.4 | 14.7 |
| Age: | | | | | | | | | | |
| Under age 30................ | 574 | 2.5 | 66.5 | 28.2 | 2.6 | [6] 0.2 | 39.7 | 60.3 | (S) | (S) |
| Age 30 to 39................. | 1,090 | 1.8 | 37.9 | 52.2 | 7.3 | 0.7 | 7.3 | 43.4 | 49.3 | (S) |
| Age 40 to 49................. | 1,050 | 2.7 | 35.0 | 51.3 | 9.7 | 1.3 | 4.4 | 15.8 | 57.7 | 22.1 |
| Age 50 to 59................. | 823 | 2.7 | 35.6 | 49.4 | 10.5 | 1.9 | 2.7 | 9.5 | 34.4 | 53.3 |
| Age 60 and over............. | 290 | 3.0 | 32.7 | 46.7 | 13.8 | 3.8 | 1.4 | 6.7 | 26.5 | 65.3 |
| Level of instruction: [4] | | | | | | | | | | |
| Elementary.................. | 1,908 | 1.7 | 43.3 | 45.7 | 8.5 | 0.8 | 10.1 | 28.3 | 39.3 | 22.3 |
| General..................... | 1,166 | 1.7 | 45.7 | 44.6 | 7.3 | 0.6 | 10.1 | 28.3 | 40.0 | 21.6 |
| Arts/music.................. | 108 | [6] 1.4 | 46.6 | 45.8 | 4.2 | 2.0 | 9.3 | 25.7 | 37.8 | 27.2 |
| English..................... | 138 | 1.5 | 37.4 | 46.1 | 13.9 | [6] 1.1 | 8.4 | 25.8 | 37.9 | 27.8 |
| ESL/bilingual [5]............. | 53 | (S) | 35.6 | 49.1 | 13.8 | (S) | (S) | 29.2 | 40.2 | 19.3 |
| Health/physical education................. | 70 | 2.4 | 52.2 | 40.8 | 4.3 | (S) | 9.6 | 21.6 | 39.5 | 29.3 |
| Mathematics................. | 42 | (S) | 46.4 | 41.9 | 9.7 | (S) | 10.0 | 27.7 | 39.8 | 22.5 |
| Science..................... | 25 | [6] 2.5 | 49.5 | 39.0 | 8.7 | (S) | (S) | 26.1 | 39.7 | 23.2 |
| Special education........... | 247 | 1.3 | 35.5 | 50.3 | 12.5 | [6] 0.4 | 11.6 | 33.4 | 36.6 | 18.5 |
| Other elementary........... | 59 | 2.7 | 28.2 | 56.0 | 11.2 | [6] 1.9 | 9.8 | 26.6 | 41.2 | 22.5 |
| Secondary................... | 1,920 | 3.2 | 37.7 | 48.9 | 8.3 | 1.8 | 9.7 | 28.3 | 39.3 | 22.7 |
| Arts/music.................. | 150 | 2.3 | 45.4 | 44.9 | 5.7 | 1.6 | 9.3 | 29.0 | 34.7 | 26.9 |
| English..................... | 339 | 1.5 | 37.9 | 50.0 | 8.7 | 1.8 | 9.7 | 29.6 | 41.2 | 19.4 |
| ESL/bilingual [5]............. | 25 | (S) | 29.7 | 49.3 | 18.8 | (S) | 13.4 | 28.7 | 35.3 | 22.6 |
| Foreign language........... | 95 | 1.9 | 32.5 | 55.3 | 7.2 | 3.1 | 9.4 | 27.4 | 39.1 | 24.0 |
| Health/physical education................. | 108 | 3.4 | 46.5 | 43.1 | 6.2 | [6] 0.8 | 6.5 | 25.1 | 39.9 | 28.5 |
| Mathematics................. | 281 | 2.1 | 38.8 | 50.6 | 7.1 | 1.4 | 9.6 | 27.8 | 39.3 | 23.3 |
| Science..................... | 232 | 2.6 | 34.3 | 53.5 | 6.6 | 2.9 | 10.7 | 29.4 | 38.7 | 21.2 |
| Social studies............... | 232 | 2.1 | 38.1 | 50.2 | 7.6 | 2.0 | 8.2 | 27.5 | 42.6 | 21.7 |
| Special education........... | 207 | 1.9 | 30.4 | 51.8 | 14.1 | 1.8 | 10.1 | 30.0 | 37.9 | 22.1 |
| Vocational/technical........ | 172 | 13.1 | 39.7 | 37.6 | 8.1 | 1.4 | 11.6 | 25.7 | 38.5 | 24.2 |
| Other secondary........... | 80 | 4.8 | 38.4 | 46.4 | 9.8 | (S) | 10.9 | 28.3 | 38.5 | 22.4 |

S Figure does not meet publication standards. [1] Includes full- and part-time teaching experience. [2] Education specialist degrees or certificates are generally awarded for 1 year of work beyond the master's degree level. Includes certificate of advanced graduate studies. [3] Data for race categories exclude persons of Hispanic origin. [4] Teachers were classified as elementary or secondary on the basis of the grades they taught, rather than on the level of the school in which they taught. Elementary teachers generally include those teaching prekindergarten through grade 5 and those teaching multiple grades, with a preponderance of grades taught being kindergarten through grade 6. Secondary teachers generally include those teaching any of grades 7 through 12 and those teaching multiple grades, with a preponderance of grades taught being grades 7 through 12. [5] ESL is English as a second language. [6] Interpret data with caution. The coefficient of variation (CV) for this estimate is between 30 and 50 percent.

Source: U.S. National Center for Education Statistics, *Digest of Education Statistics*, "Advance Release of Selected 2018 Digest Tables," <http://www.nces.ed.gov/programs/digest/>, accessed July 2019.

## Table 278. Counselors, Psychologists, and Social Workers in Public Schools by Selected Characteristics: 2015 to 2016

[114 represents 114,000. Data are for academic year indicated. Detail may not sum to totals because of rounding and because some data are not shown. Based on the National Teacher and Principal Survey, "Public School Data File"]

| Characteristic | Schools with at least one full- or part-time counselor | | | Schools with at least one full- or part-time psychologist | | | Schools with at least one full- or part-time social worker | | |
|---|---|---|---|---|---|---|---|---|---|
| | Percent of schools | Number of FTE counselors (1,000)[1] | Number of students per FTE counselor[1] | Percent of schools | Number of FTE psychologists (1,000)[1] | Number of students per FTE psychologists[1] | Percent of schools | Number of FTE social workers (1,000)[1] | Number of students per FTE social worker[1] |
| Total..................... | 80.7 | 114 | 380 | 66.5 | 44 | 820 | 41.5 | 33 | 700 |
| School classifcation: | | | | | | | | | |
| Traditional public......... | 82.3 | 108 | 380 | 68.1 | 42 | 820 | 42.2 | 31 | 720 |
| Charter school........... | 62.0 | 6 | 360 | 47.0 | 2 | 750 | 33.2 | 2 | 480 |
| Community type: | | | | | | | | | |
| City........................ | 80.1 | 34 | 380 | 70.5 | 13 | 840 | 50.9 | 12 | 680 |
| Suburban................. | 79.8 | 43 | 390 | 79.6 | 18 | 900 | 48.4 | 13 | 800 |
| Town...................... | 82.4 | 14 | 370 | 55.7 | 5 | 710 | 33.7 | 3 | 590 |
| Rural...................... | 81.6 | 24 | 340 | 52.3 | 8 | 670 | 27.5 | 5 | 600 |
| School level:[2] | | | | | | | | | |
| Primary................... | 75.3 | 39 | 480 | 71.7 | 25 | 720 | 42.3 | 17 | 610 |
| Middle.................... | 91.9 | 22 | 370 | 71.7 | 7 | 880 | 46.6 | 6 | 760 |
| High....................... | 90.6 | 45 | 310 | 59.1 | 9 | 1,120 | 42.8 | 8 | 990 |
| Combined................ | 73.7 | 9 | 290 | 42.5 | 3 | 500 | 25.3 | 2 | 320 |
| Student enrollment: | | | | | | | | | |
| Less than 100........... | 49.4 | 3 | 60 | 42.0 | 2 | 80 | 24.5 | 2 | 50 |
| 100 to 199............... | 70.2 | 5 | 170 | 46.1 | 2 | 240 | 27.5 | 2 | 180 |
| 200 to 499 students..... | 80.2 | 30 | 340 | 64.1 | 15 | 540 | 40.4 | 11 | 450 |
| 500 to 749 students..... | 83.6 | 26 | 450 | 73.5 | 12 | 830 | 44.8 | 9 | 720 |
| 750 to 999 students..... | 90.9 | 17 | 430 | 77.7 | 6 | 1,100 | 46.7 | 4 | 860 |
| 1,000 students or more.................. | 96.7 | 34 | 380 | 81.5 | 7 | 1,530 | 56.1 | 5 | 1,480 |

[1] Full-time equivalent. [2] Primary schools are those with at least one grade lower than 5 and no grade higher than 8, middle schools have no grade lower than 5 and no grade higher than 8, high schools have no grade lower than 7 and at least one grade higher than 8, and all other schools are classified as combined.

Source: U.S. National Center for Education Statistics, *Mental Health Staff in Public Schools, by School Racial and Ethnic Composition,* Supplemental Tables, <https://nces.ed.gov/pubsearch/pubsinfo.asp?pubid=2019020>, accessed January 2019.

## Table 279. English as a Second Language (ESL)—Public High School Learners, Programs, and Services by District Characteristics: 2016

[In percent, except where noted. For school year ending in year shown. Programs and services only shown for districts with English learners at the high school level. Based on a survey conducted using the Fast Response Survey System]

| District characteristics | Number of high school English learners | Percent of districts with high school English learners | Districts with English learners with programs and services | | | | | |
|---|---|---|---|---|---|---|---|---|
| | | | Bilingual instruction for English learners only in content classes | English as a Second Language (ESL) | | Instructional support by a paraprofessional who— | | Sheltered English/ content instruction[2] |
| | | | | Instruction in scheduled class periods | Push-in or pull-out instruction[1] | Does not speak student's native language | Speaks student's native language | |
| All public school districts.... | 774,500 | 62 | 8 | 68 | 61 | 33 | 31 | 47 |
| District enrollment size: | | | | | | | | |
| Less than 1,000................ | 8,200 | 29 | [3] 8 | 44 | 58 | 32 | 25 | 34 |
| 1,000 to 2,499................. | 34,900 | 69 | 6 | 59 | 60 | 30 | 27 | 38 |
| 2,500 to 9,999................. | 150,700 | 95 | 8 | 77 | 64 | 32 | 31 | 52 |
| 10,000 or more................ | 580,800 | 100 | 13 | 93 | 62 | 46 | 55 | 76 |
| Community type: | | | | | | | | |
| City......................... | 354,400 | 100 | 14 | 89 | 64 | 47 | 55 | 81 |
| Suburban.................... | 319,200 | 90 | 9 | 84 | 62 | 35 | 30 | 53 |
| Town........................ | 58,100 | 74 | 7 | 64 | 61 | 27 | 33 | 50 |
| Rural........................ | 42,800 | 42 | 5 | 50 | 61 | 32 | 26 | 32 |
| Region: | | | | | | | | |
| Northeast................... | 115,400 | 67 | 8 | 82 | 71 | 25 | 16 | 46 |
| Southeast................... | 127,000 | 77 | 5 | 59 | 67 | 25 | 24 | 46 |
| Central...................... | 116,000 | 47 | 9 | 58 | 63 | 41 | 35 | 34 |
| West........................ | 416,100 | 71 | 8 | 71 | 51 | 36 | 43 | 62 |

[1] During push-in instruction the ESL instructor works with students within an ongoing content class; during pull-out instruction students move out of an ongoing class for an ESL session. [2] Regular grade-level instruction in core content areas is provided in English through instructional strategies that make the academic content accessible to English learner students while also assisting them to acquire academic English. [3] Interpret data with caution.

Source: U.S. National Center for Education Statistics, *Programs and Services for High School English Learners in Public School Districts: 2015-16,* September 2016. See also <https://nces.ed.gov/pubsearch/pubsinfo.asp?pubid=2016150>.

# Table 280. Public Charter and Traditional Schools by Selected Characteristics: 2010 and 2016

[49,178 represents 49,178,000. As of Fall. A public charter school is a public school that, in accordance with an enabling state statute, has been granted a charter exempting it from selected state and local rules and regulations]

| Characteristic | 2010 | | | 2016 | | |
|---|---|---|---|---|---|---|
| | Total | Traditional | Public charter | Total | Traditional | Public charter |
| **Enrollment (1,000)** | **49,178** | **47,391** | **1,787** | **50,275** | **47,264** | **3,010** |
| PERCENT DISTRIBUTION OF STUDENTS | | | | | | |
| Race/ethnicity | 100.0 | 100.0 | 100.0 | 100.0 | 100.0 | 100.0 |
| White, non-Hispanic | 52.5 | 53.1 | 36.2 | 48.2 | 49.2 | 32.2 |
| Black, non-Hispanic | 16.0 | 15.5 | 28.9 | 15.3 | 14.6 | 26.5 |
| Hispanic | 23.1 | 22.9 | 27.3 | 26.4 | 26.0 | 32.6 |
| Asian/Pacific Islander | 5.0 | 5.0 | 3.7 | 5.5 | 5.5 | 4.4 |
| American Indian/Alaska Native | 1.1 | 1.1 | 0.9 | 1.0 | 1.0 | 0.7 |
| Two or more races | 2.4 | 2.3 | 2.9 | 3.6 | 3.6 | 3.6 |
| Number of teachers (1,000) | 3,002 | 2,911 | 91 | 3,096 | 2,943 | 154 |
| Pupil/teacher ratio | 16.4 | 16.4 | 18.0 | 16.2 | 16.1 | 17.8 |
| **Total number of schools** | **98,817** | **93,543** | **5,274** | **98,158** | **91,147** | **7,011** |
| PERCENT DISTRIBUTION OF SCHOOLS | | | | | | |
| School level | 100.0 | 100.0 | 100.0 | 100.0 | 100.0 | 100.0 |
| Elementary [1] | 67.9 | 68.7 | 54.3 | 68.1 | 69.0 | 56.1 |
| Secondary [2] | 24.8 | 24.8 | 25.9 | 24.3 | 24.4 | 23.1 |
| Combined [3] | 6.2 | 5.5 | 19.5 | 6.9 | 5.8 | 20.7 |
| Other | 1.1 | 1.1 | 0.2 | 0.7 | 0.8 | 0.1 |
| Size of enrollment | 100.0 | 100.0 | 100.0 | 100.0 | 100.0 | 100.0 |
| Less than 300 students | 30.9 | 29.3 | 59.0 | 30.0 | 28.7 | 46.8 |
| 300 to 499 students | 27.8 | 28.1 | 22.3 | 27.8 | 28.0 | 25.4 |
| 500 to 999 students | 32.3 | 33.4 | 14.8 | 32.8 | 33.7 | 21.6 |
| 1,000 students or more | 9.0 | 9.3 | 3.9 | 9.3 | 9.6 | 6.2 |
| Region | 100.0 | 100.0 | 100.0 | 100.0 | 100.0 | 100.0 |
| Northeast | 15.5 | 15.9 | 9.5 | 15.5 | 15.9 | 10.1 |
| Midwest | 26.4 | 26.6 | 23.1 | 25.8 | 26.2 | 20.5 |
| South | 34.7 | 35.0 | 29.5 | 34.8 | 35.0 | 32.9 |
| West | 23.4 | 22.5 | 37.9 | 23.9 | 22.9 | 36.6 |

[1] Includes schools beginning with grade 6 or below and no grade higher than 8. [2] Includes schools with no grade lower than 7. [3] Includes schools beginning with grade 6 or below and ending with grade 9 or above.

Source: U.S. National Center for Education Statistics, *Digest of Education Statistics,* "Advance Release of Selected 2018 Digest Tables," <http://www.nces.ed.gov/programs/digest/>, accessed May 2019.

# Table 281. Public Charter Schools and Enrollment by State: 2016

[3,010.3 represents 3,101,300. As of Fall]

| State | Number of charter schools | Number of students (1,000) | Charter schools as a percent of public schools | Charter school enrollment as a percent of public school enrollment | State | Number of charter schools | Number of students (1,000) | Charter schools as a percent of public schools | Charter school enrollment as a percent of public school enrollment |
|---|---|---|---|---|---|---|---|---|---|
| **United States** | **7,011** | **3,010.3** | **7.1** | **6.0** | Missouri | 72 | 22.8 | 3.0 | 2.5 |
| Alabama | 1 | (NA) | 0.1 | (NA) | Montana | – | – | – | – |
| Alaska | 28 | 6.7 | 5.5 | 5.0 | Nebraska | – | – | – | – |
| Arizona | 550 | 185.6 | 23.8 | 16.6 | Nevada | 49 | 40.1 | 7.5 | 8.5 |
| Arkansas | 75 | 27.9 | 6.9 | 5.7 | New Hampshire | 31 | 3.4 | 6.3 | 1.9 |
| California | 1,248 | 602.8 | 12.1 | 9.7 | New Jersey | 88 | 46.3 | 3.4 | 3.4 |
| Colorado | 238 | 114.7 | 12.6 | 12.7 | New Mexico | 99 | 25.1 | 11.4 | 7.6 |
| Connecticut | 24 | 9.6 | 1.9 | 1.8 | New York | 267 | 128.8 | 5.6 | 4.8 |
| Delaware | 27 | 14.7 | 11.8 | 10.8 | North Carolina | 167 | 92.3 | 6.4 | 6.0 |
| Dist. of Columbia | 110 | 37.2 | 49.3 | 43.7 | North Dakota | – | – | – | – |
| Florida | 655 | 283.6 | 15.7 | 10.1 | Ohio | 362 | 116.3 | 10.1 | 6.8 |
| Georgia | 84 | 66.9 | 3.7 | 3.8 | Oklahoma | 48 | 24.2 | 2.7 | 3.5 |
| Hawaii | 34 | 10.7 | 11.7 | 5.9 | Oregon | 124 | 32.3 | 10.0 | 5.7 |
| Idaho | 57 | 20.6 | 7.7 | 6.9 | Pennsylvania | 179 | 133.0 | 6.0 | 7.8 |
| Illinois | 63 | 65.2 | 1.5 | 3.2 | Rhode Island | 30 | 8.1 | 9.5 | 5.8 |
| Indiana | 93 | 43.1 | 4.8 | 4.1 | South Carolina | 70 | 32.3 | 5.6 | 4.2 |
| Iowa | 3 | 0.4 | 0.2 | 0.1 | South Dakota | – | – | – | – |
| Kansas | 10 | 3.2 | 0.8 | 0.6 | Tennessee | 104 | 35.0 | 5.9 | 3.5 |
| Kentucky | – | – | – | – | Texas | 753 | 310.8 | 8.5 | 5.8 |
| Louisiana | 151 | 79.0 | 10.8 | 11.0 | Utah | 124 | 71.4 | 12.0 | 10.8 |
| Maine | 9 | 2.0 | 1.5 | 1.1 | Vermont | – | – | – | – |
| Maryland | 49 | 22.4 | 3.4 | 2.5 | Virginia | 8 | 1.2 | 0.4 | 0.1 |
| Massachusetts | 78 | 42.6 | 4.2 | 4.5 | Washington | 8 | 1.7 | 0.3 | 0.2 |
| Michigan | 376 | 147.1 | 10.9 | 10.0 | West Virginia | – | – | – | – |
| Minnesota | 220 | 54.2 | 8.8 | 6.2 | Wisconsin | 237 | 44.2 | 10.5 | 5.1 |
| Mississippi | 3 | 0.5 | 0.3 | 0.1 | Wyoming | 5 | 0.5 | 1.3 | 0.5 |

NA Not available. – Represents or rounds to zero.

Source: U.S. National Center for Education Statistics, *Digest of Education Statistics,* "Advance Release of Selected 2018 Digest Tables," <http://www.nces.ed.gov/programs/digest/>, accessed May 2019.

## Table 282. Career and Technology Education (CTE) Programs in Public School Districts by District Characteristics: 2017

[In percent. For school year ending in year shown]

| | Districts offering CTE programs to high school students [1] | Entities providing CTE Programs [2] | | | CTE program offerings [2] | | | |
|---|---|---|---|---|---|---|---|---|
| | | Area CTE center or group/ consortium of school districts | District individually | 2-year community or technical college | Student-run enterprises or services | Mentoring by local employers | On-the-job training, etc. [3] | Apprentice-ships or preapprenticeship programs |
| All public school districts.......... | 98 | 54 | 77 | 46 | 55 | 65 | 77 | 31 |
| District enrollment size: | | | | | | | | |
| Less than 1,000............ | 98 | 54 | 75 | 41 | 38 | 52 | 61 | 23 |
| 1,000 to 2,499.............. | 98 | 61 | 72 | 44 | 57 | 64 | 83 | 32 |
| 2,500 to 9,999.............. | 99 | 53 | 79 | 50 | 70 | 78 | 89 | 39 |
| 10,000 or more.............. | 100 | 38 | 95 | 61 | 86 | 86 | 96 | 42 |
| Community type: | | | | | | | | |
| City........................ | 99 | 35 | 92 | 55 | 72 | 87 | 95 | 35 |
| Suburban................... | 97 | 66 | 69 | 44 | 74 | 77 | 90 | 38 |
| Town....................... | 100 | 52 | 80 | 49 | 59 | 67 | 79 | 33 |
| Rural...................... | 98 | 53 | 78 | 43 | 43 | 55 | 68 | 26 |
| Region: | | | | | | | | |
| Northeast.................. | 97 | 78 | 50 | 24 | 75 | 75 | 92 | 33 |
| Southeast.................. | 100 | 34 | 94 | 63 | 50 | 66 | 84 | 39 |
| Central.................... | 98 | 62 | 76 | 49 | 56 | 66 | 75 | 36 |
| West...................... | 99 | 37 | 89 | 46 | 42 | 55 | 66 | 17 |

[1] Respondents were asked to include all CTE programs that the district offered to high school students, including programs provided by the district or by other entities (such as an area/regional CTE center, a consortium of districts, or a community or technical college). [2] Based on the 98 percent of public school districts that offer CTE programs to students at the high school level. [3] Includes on-the-job training, internships, practicums, clinical experiences, or cooperative education (co-op).

Source: U.S. National Center for Education Statistics, *Career and Technical Education Programs in Public School Districts: 2016–17,* April 2018. See also <https://nces.ed.gov/pubsearch/pubsinfo.asp?pubid=2018028>.

## Table 283. ACT Program Scores and Characteristics of College-Bound Students: 1990 to 2018

[For academic year ending in year shown. Except as indicated, test scores and characteristics of college-bound students. Data based on all ACT tested seniors graduating in year shown. Beginning 1990, not comparable with previous years because a new version of the ACT was introduced]

| Type of test and characteristic | Unit | 1990 | 1995 | 2000 | 2010 | 2013 | 2014 | 2015 | 2016 | 2017 | 2018 |
|---|---|---|---|---|---|---|---|---|---|---|---|
| **TEST SCORES** [1] | | | | | | | | | | | |
| **Composite.............** | **Point** | **20.6** | **20.8** | **21.0** | **21.0** | **20.9** | **21.0** | **21.0** | **20.8** | **21.0** | **20.8** |
| Male ..................... | Point | 21.0 | 21.0 | 21.2 | 21.2 | 20.9 | 21.1 | 21.1 | 20.9 | 21.0 | 20.8 |
| Female................... | Point | 20.3 | 20.7 | 20.9 | 20.9 | 20.9 | 20.9 | 21.0 | 20.9 | 21.1 | 20.9 |
| English................... | Point | 20.5 | 20.2 | 20.5 | 20.5 | 20.2 | 20.3 | 20.4 | 20.1 | 20.3 | 20.2 |
| Male..................... | Point | 20.1 | 19.8 | 20.0 | 20.1 | 19.8 | 20.0 | 20.0 | 19.8 | 19.9 | 19.7 |
| Female................... | Point | 20.9 | 20.6 | 20.9 | 20.8 | 20.6 | 20.7 | 20.8 | 20.6 | 20.8 | 20.7 |
| Math..................... | Point | 19.9 | 20.2 | 20.7 | 21.0 | 20.9 | 20.9 | 20.8 | 20.6 | 20.7 | 20.5 |
| Male..................... | Point | 20.7 | 20.9 | 21.4 | 21.6 | 21.4 | 21.1 | 21.3 | 21.0 | 21.2 | 20.9 |
| Female................... | Point | 19.3 | 19.7 | 20.2 | 20.5 | 20.5 | 20.5 | 20.4 | 20.3 | 20.4 | 20.2 |
| Reading [2]............... | Point | (NA) | 21.3 | 21.4 | 21.3 | 21.1 | 21.3 | 21.4 | 21.3 | 21.4 | 21.3 |
| Male..................... | Point | (NA) | 21.1 | 21.2 | 21.1 | 20.9 | 21.1 | 21.2 | 21.0 | 21.2 | 21.0 |
| Female................... | Point | (NA) | 21.4 | 21.5 | 21.4 | 21.4 | 21.5 | 21.6 | 21.6 | 21.8 | 21.7 |
| Science reasoning [3].............. | Point | (NA) | 21.0 | 21.0 | 20.9 | 20.7 | 20.8 | 20.9 | 20.8 | 21.0 | 20.7 |
| Male..................... | Point | (NA) | 21.6 | 21.6 | 21.4 | 21.2 | 21.2 | 21.3 | 21.1 | 21.3 | 20.9 |
| Female................... | Point | (NA) | 20.5 | 20.6 | 20.5 | 20.4 | 20.5 | 20.6 | 20.6 | 20.8 | 20.6 |
| **PARTICIPANTS** [4] | | | | | | | | | | | |
| **Total** [5]..................... | **1,000** | 817 | 945 | 1,065 | 1,569 | 1,799 | 1,846 | 1,924 | 2,090 | 2,030 | 1,915 |
| Male...................... | Percent | 46 | 44 | 43 | 45 | 46 | 46 | 47 | 46 | 46 | 47 |
| White..................... | Percent | 73 | 69 | 72 | 62 | 58 | 56 | 55 | 54 | 52 | 52 |
| Black..................... | Percent | 9 | 9 | 10 | 14 | 13 | 13 | 13 | 13 | 13 | 13 |
| Obtaining composite scores of: [6] | | | | | | | | | | | |
| 27 or above................ | Percent | 12 | 13 | 14 | 16 | 16 | 17 | 18 | 14 | 15 | 15 |
| 18 or below................ | Percent | 35 | 34 | 32 | 35 | 36 | 36 | 37 | 39 | 38 | 40 |

NA Not available. [1] Minimum score, 1; maximum score, 36. [2] Prior to 1990, social studies; data not comparable with previous years. [3] Prior to 1990, natural sciences; data not comparable with previous years. [4] Data by race are for those responding to the race question. [5] 817 represents 817,000. [6] Prior to 1990, 26 or above and 15 or below.

Source: ACT, Inc., Iowa City, IA. Most recent score reported in the *The ACT® Profile Report - National*, annual ©. Reproduced with permission.

# Table 284. Proficiency Levels on Selected NAEP Tests for Students in Public Schools by State: 2017

[Represents percent of public school students scoring at or above basic and proficient levels. Basic denotes partial mastery of the knowledge and skills that are fundamental for proficient work at a given grade level. Proficient represents solid academic performance. Students reaching this level demonstrated competency over challenging subject matter. For more detail, see <http://nationsreportcard.gov/>. Based on the National Assessment of Educational Progress (NAEP) tests which are administered to a representative sample of students in public schools, private schools, and Department of Defense schools]

| State | Grade 4 Math | | Grade 8 Math | | Grade 4 Reading | | Grade 8 Reading | |
|---|---|---|---|---|---|---|---|---|
| | At or above Basic | At or above Proficient | At or above Basic | At or above Proficient | At or above Basic | At or above Proficient | At or above Basic | At or above Proficient |
| **U.S. average** | **79** | **40** | **69** | **33** | **67** | **35** | **75** | **35** |
| Alabama | 73 | 31 | 55 | 21 | 63 | 31 | 67 | 28 |
| Alaska | 71 | 32 | 66 | 29 | 56 | 28 | 70 | 26 |
| Arizona | 73 | 34 | 71 | 34 | 61 | 30 | 75 | 30 |
| Arkansas | 75 | 33 | 62 | 25 | 63 | 31 | 71 | 29 |
| California | 71 | 31 | 62 | 29 | 61 | 31 | 72 | 32 |
| Colorado | 80 | 42 | 74 | 38 | 71 | 40 | 79 | 41 |
| Connecticut | 79 | 40 | 72 | 36 | 74 | 43 | 80 | 44 |
| Delaware | 77 | 36 | 66 | 28 | 67 | 36 | 72 | 33 |
| District of Columbia | 69 | 32 | 51 | 21 | 56 | 29 | 55 | 20 |
| Florida | 88 | 48 | 66 | 29 | 75 | 41 | 77 | 35 |
| Georgia | 77 | 35 | 68 | 31 | 66 | 35 | 76 | 35 |
| Hawaii | 79 | 38 | 66 | 27 | 62 | 32 | 72 | 30 |
| Idaho | 81 | 40 | 74 | 35 | 70 | 38 | 81 | 39 |
| Illinois | 76 | 39 | 68 | 32 | 66 | 35 | 77 | 36 |
| Indiana | 86 | 48 | 75 | 38 | 73 | 41 | 82 | 41 |
| Iowa | 83 | 46 | 76 | 37 | 69 | 36 | 80 | 37 |
| Kansas | 82 | 42 | 74 | 35 | 70 | 37 | 78 | 37 |
| Kentucky | 80 | 40 | 65 | 29 | 70 | 38 | 75 | 34 |
| Louisiana | 71 | 27 | 54 | 19 | 56 | 26 | 67 | 25 |
| Maine | 81 | 40 | 72 | 36 | 67 | 36 | 79 | 39 |
| Maryland | 78 | 42 | 66 | 33 | 69 | 40 | 74 | 38 |
| Massachusetts | 87 | 53 | 81 | 50 | 80 | 51 | 85 | 49 |
| Michigan | 75 | 36 | 67 | 31 | 64 | 32 | 76 | 34 |
| Minnesota | 86 | 53 | 80 | 46 | 71 | 39 | 79 | 39 |
| Mississippi | 77 | 31 | 59 | 22 | 60 | 27 | 66 | 25 |
| Missouri | 79 | 40 | 70 | 30 | 69 | 37 | 77 | 35 |
| Montana | 83 | 41 | 76 | 37 | 70 | 38 | 79 | 35 |
| Nebraska | 85 | 49 | 76 | 41 | 72 | 38 | 79 | 38 |
| Nevada | 73 | 31 | 62 | 27 | 61 | 31 | 71 | 28 |
| New Hampshire | 85 | 48 | 81 | 45 | 75 | 43 | 84 | 45 |
| New Jersey | 87 | 50 | 76 | 44 | 78 | 49 | 82 | 47 |
| New Mexico | 69 | 27 | 57 | 20 | 54 | 25 | 66 | 24 |
| New York | 76 | 35 | 68 | 34 | 68 | 36 | 73 | 34 |
| North Carolina | 81 | 42 | 68 | 35 | 69 | 39 | 74 | 33 |
| North Dakota | 85 | 46 | 78 | 40 | 70 | 34 | 77 | 33 |
| Ohio | 81 | 41 | 74 | 40 | 71 | 39 | 77 | 39 |
| Oklahoma | 80 | 35 | 64 | 24 | 63 | 29 | 74 | 28 |
| Oregon | 73 | 33 | 70 | 34 | 63 | 33 | 76 | 36 |
| Pennsylvania | 80 | 44 | 73 | 38 | 71 | 40 | 78 | 40 |
| Rhode Island | 79 | 39 | 66 | 30 | 69 | 39 | 75 | 37 |
| South Carolina | 75 | 32 | 62 | 26 | 59 | 29 | 71 | 30 |
| South Dakota | 83 | 43 | 76 | 38 | 69 | 36 | 80 | 36 |
| Tennessee | 77 | 36 | 68 | 30 | 64 | 33 | 73 | 31 |
| Texas | 82 | 41 | 70 | 33 | 60 | 29 | 71 | 28 |
| Utah | 81 | 45 | 75 | 39 | 72 | 41 | 79 | 38 |
| Vermont | 81 | 42 | 76 | 39 | 73 | 43 | 82 | 45 |
| Virginia | 87 | 50 | 77 | 40 | 74 | 43 | 77 | 37 |
| Washington | 80 | 42 | 75 | 41 | 68 | 39 | 80 | 42 |
| West Virginia | 78 | 35 | 62 | 24 | 64 | 32 | 70 | 28 |
| Wisconsin | 79 | 42 | 76 | 39 | 66 | 35 | 79 | 39 |
| Wyoming | 89 | 51 | 79 | 38 | 74 | 41 | 80 | 38 |

Source: U.S. National Center for Education Statistics, "National Assessment of Educational Progress (NAEP), 2017 Mathematics and Reading Assessments," <http://nces.ed.gov/nationsreportcard/naepdata/dataset.aspx>, accessed April 2018.

# Table 285. Public High School Graduates by State: 1980 to 2018

[In thousands (2,747.7 represents 2,747,700). For school year ending in year shown. Data include regular diploma recipients, but exclude students receiving a certificate of attendance and persons receiving high school equivalency certificates]

| State | 1980 | 1990 | 2000 | 2010 | 2015 (P) | 2016 (P) | 2017 (P) | 2018 (P) |
|---|---|---|---|---|---|---|---|---|
| **United States**............... | **2,747.7** | **¹ 2,320.3** | **2,553.8** | **3,128.0** | **3,187.0** | **3,224.1** | **3,255.3** | **3,319.8** |
| Alabama........................ | 45.2 | 40.5 | 37.8 | 43.2 | 45.4 | 46.1 | 47.6 | 48.3 |
| Alaska.......................... | 5.2 | 5.4 | 6.6 | 8.2 | 7.9 | 7.8 | 7.9 | 8.1 |
| Arizona......................... | 28.6 | 32.1 | 38.3 | 61.1 | 67.2 | 67.1 | 68.8 | 69.6 |
| Arkansas....................... | 29.1 | 26.5 | 27.3 | 28.3 | 30.4 | 30.3 | 30.8 | 31.0 |
| California....................... | 249.2 | 236.3 | 309.9 | 405.0 | 422.8 | 419.2 | 411.7 | 420.5 |
| Colorado........................ | 36.8 | 33.0 | 38.9 | 49.3 | 51.5 | 53.3 | 54.1 | 56.1 |
| Connecticut.................... | 37.7 | 27.9 | 31.6 | 34.5 | 37.2 | 37.4 | 37.9 | 37.1 |
| Delaware....................... | 7.6 | 5.6 | 6.1 | 8.1 | 8.4 | 8.5 | 8.7 | 8.9 |
| District of Columbia ²......... | 5.0 | 3.6 | 2.7 | 3.6 | 4.0 | 4.5 | 4.4 | 4.2 |
| Florida.......................... | 87.3 | 88.9 | 106.7 | 156.1 | 163.7 | 166.5 | 170.8 | 176.2 |
| Georgia......................... | 61.6 | 56.6 | 62.6 | 91.6 | 97.4 | 100.1 | 102.1 | 105.9 |
| Hawaii.......................... | 11.5 | 10.3 | 10.4 | 11.0 | 10.8 | 10.9 | 10.7 | 11.1 |
| Idaho........................... | 13.2 | 12.0 | 16.2 | 17.8 | 18.1 | 18.2 | 19.1 | 19.3 |
| Illinois.......................... | 135.6 | 108.1 | 111.8 | 139.0 | 140.5 | 140.9 | 141.3 | 143.5 |
| Indiana......................... | 73.1 | 60.0 | 57.0 | 64.6 | 66.8 | 66.7 | 69.0 | 69.6 |
| Iowa............................ | 43.4 | 31.8 | 33.9 | 34.5 | 32.5 | 32.7 | 32.9 | 33.4 |
| Kansas.......................... | 30.9 | 25.4 | 29.1 | 31.6 | 31.9 | 32.8 | 32.9 | 33.5 |
| Kentucky........................ | 41.2 | 38.0 | 36.8 | 42.7 | 42.5 | 43.3 | 43.3 | 44.3 |
| Louisiana....................... | 46.3 | 36.1 | 38.4 | 36.6 | 37.7 | 38.8 | 39.4 | 42.0 |
| Maine........................... | 15.4 | 13.8 | 12.2 | 14.1 | 12.6 | 12.8 | 12.6 | 12.5 |
| Maryland........................ | 54.3 | 41.6 | 47.8 | 59.1 | 57.7 | 57.5 | 57.3 | 59.0 |
| Massachusetts................. | 73.8 | 55.9 | 53.0 | 64.5 | 65.8 | 68.6 | 68.6 | 69.3 |
| Michigan........................ | 124.3 | 93.8 | 97.7 | 110.7 | 102.0 | 100.8 | 101.6 | 102.4 |
| Minnesota...................... | 64.9 | 49.1 | 57.4 | 59.7 | 56.8 | 56.6 | 57.3 | 58.4 |
| Mississippi..................... | 27.6 | 25.2 | 24.2 | 25.5 | 26.3 | 26.8 | 26.9 | 28.1 |
| Missouri........................ | 62.3 | 49.0 | 52.8 | 64.0 | 60.6 | 61.6 | 60.9 | 61.7 |
| Montana........................ | 12.1 | 9.4 | 10.9 | 10.1 | 9.4 | 9.3 | 9.4 | 9.2 |
| Nebraska....................... | 22.4 | 17.7 | 20.1 | 19.4 | 20.7 | 21.1 | 21.1 | 22.0 |
| Nevada.......................... | 8.5 | 9.5 | 14.6 | 21.0 | 23.0 | 23.2 | 23.8 | 24.2 |
| New Hampshire................. | 11.7 | 10.8 | 11.8 | 15.0 | 13.5 | 13.6 | 13.2 | 13.2 |
| New Jersey..................... | 94.6 | 69.8 | 74.4 | 96.2 | 95.3 | 97.1 | 98.0 | 98.3 |
| New Mexico..................... | 18.4 | 14.9 | 18.0 | 18.6 | 19.5 | 19.5 | 19.8 | 20.2 |
| New York........................ | 204.1 | 143.3 | 141.7 | 183.8 | 179.1 | 178.3 | 181.8 | 185.6 |
| North Carolina.................. | 70.9 | 64.8 | 62.1 | 88.7 | 97.0 | 99.0 | 101.7 | 105.3 |
| North Dakota................... | 9.9 | 7.7 | 8.6 | 7.2 | 7.0 | 7.0 | 6.9 | 6.6 |
| Ohio............................ | 144.2 | 114.5 | 111.7 | 123.4 | 120.9 | 125.1 | 126.6 | 122.4 |
| Oklahoma....................... | 39.3 | 35.6 | 37.6 | 38.5 | 38.4 | 39.7 | 40.2 | 41.2 |
| Oregon.......................... | 29.9 | 25.5 | 30.2 | 34.7 | 34.8 | 35.7 | 34.7 | 35.4 |
| Pennsylvania................... | 146.5 | 110.5 | 114.0 | 131.2 | 123.6 | 121.8 | 124.0 | 123.2 |
| Rhode Island.................... | 10.9 | 7.8 | 8.5 | 9.9 | 9.9 | 10.1 | 9.4 | 9.7 |
| South Carolina................. | 38.7 | 32.5 | 31.6 | 40.4 | 42.7 | 43.8 | 45.1 | 46.6 |
| South Dakota................... | 10.7 | 7.7 | 9.3 | 8.2 | 8.1 | 8.1 | 8.2 | 8.3 |
| Tennessee...................... | 49.8 | 46.1 | 41.6 | 62.4 | 62.0 | 63.5 | 63.7 | 66.3 |
| Texas........................... | 171.4 | 172.5 | 212.9 | 280.9 | 309.3 | 318.7 | 327.7 | 340.0 |
| Utah............................ | 20.0 | 21.2 | 32.5 | 31.5 | 34.1 | 35.4 | 36.6 | 37.7 |
| Vermont......................... | 6.7 | 6.1 | 6.7 | 7.2 | 6.2 | 6.1 | 6.0 | 5.9 |
| Virginia......................... | 66.6 | 60.6 | 65.6 | 81.5 | 82.7 | 84.6 | 84.7 | 87.5 |
| Washington..................... | 50.4 | 45.9 | 57.6 | 66.0 | 68.2 | 69.8 | 70.8 | 72.5 |
| West Virginia................... | 23.4 | 21.9 | 19.4 | 17.7 | 17.5 | 17.6 | 17.4 | 17.5 |
| Wisconsin....................... | 69.3 | 52.0 | 58.5 | 64.7 | 60.5 | 60.7 | 60.7 | 61.6 |
| Wyoming........................ | 6.1 | 5.8 | 6.5 | 5.7 | 5.6 | 5.7 | 5.7 | 5.7 |

P Projected. ¹ U.S. total includes estimates for nonreporting states. ² Beginning in 1985-86, graduates from adult programs are excluded.

Source: U.S. National Center for Education Statistics, *Digest of Education Statistics*, "Advance Release of Selected 2018 Digest Tables," and earlier releases, <http://www.nces.ed.gov/programs/digest/>, accessed August 2019.

## Table 286. High School Dropouts by Race and Hispanic Origin: 1980 to 2017

[In percent. As of October. Dropouts are persons 18 to 24 years old who have not completed high school and are not enrolled, regardless of when they dropped out]

| Item | 1980 | 1985 | 1990 [1] | 1995 | 2000 | 2005 | 2010 | 2014 | 2015 | 2016 | 2017 |
|---|---|---|---|---|---|---|---|---|---|---|---|
| Total [2] | 15.6 | 13.9 | 14.4 | 13.9 | 12.4 | 11.3 | 8.7 | 6.9 | 6.4 | 6.4 | 6.0 |
| White [3] | 14.4 | 13.5 | 14.1 | 13.6 | 12.2 | 11.3 | 8.5 | 7.1 | 6.4 | 6.3 | 6.2 |
| Male | 15.7 | 14.7 | 15.4 | 14.3 | 13.5 | 13.2 | 9.7 | 7.6 | 7.0 | 7.4 | 7.1 |
| Female | 13.2 | 12.3 | 12.8 | 13.0 | 10.9 | 9.4 | 7.3 | 6.6 | 5.8 | 5.2 | 5.4 |
| Black [3] | 23.5 | 17.6 | 16.4 | 14.4 | 15.3 | 12.9 | 10.1 | 7.3 | 7.5 | 6.9 | 6.1 |
| Male | 26.0 | 18.8 | 18.6 | 14.2 | 17.4 | 14.8 | 12.1 | 7.2 | 7.3 | 9.2 | 7.5 |
| Female | 21.5 | 16.6 | 14.5 | 14.6 | 13.5 | 11.2 | 8.2 | 7.4 | 7.7 | 4.8 | 4.7 |
| Hispanic [4] | 40.3 | 31.5 | 37.7 | 34.7 | 32.3 | 27.3 | 18.5 | 11.8 | 10.4 | 9.9 | 10.6 |
| Male | 42.6 | 35.8 | 40.3 | 34.2 | 36.8 | 32.1 | 21.3 | 12.8 | 11.1 | 12.0 | 12.8 |
| Female | 38.1 | 27.0 | 35.0 | 35.4 | 27.3 | 21.8 | 15.4 | 10.9 | 9.6 | 7.8 | 8.3 |

[1] Beginning 1990, reflects new editing procedures for cases with missing data on school enrollment. [2] Includes other races, not shown separately. [3] Beginning 2003, for persons who selected this race group only. See footnote 4, Table 256. [4] Persons of Hispanic origin may be of any race.

Source: U.S. Census Bureau, Current Population Reports, P-20, and earlier reports; and "School Enrollment," <https://www.census.gov/topics/education/school-enrollment/data/tables.All.html>, accessed December 2018.

## Table 287. High School Dropouts by Age, Race, and Hispanic Origin: 1980 to 2017

[5,212 represents 5,212,000. As of October. For persons 14 to 24 years old. Dropouts are persons not in regular school and who have not completed the 12th grade nor received a general equivalency degree. Based on Current Population Survey; see text, Section 1 and Appendix III]

| Age and race | Number of dropouts (1,000) | | | | | Percent of population | | | | |
|---|---|---|---|---|---|---|---|---|---|---|
| | 1980 | 1990 | 2000 | 2010 | 2017 | 1980 | 1990 | 2000 | 2010 | 2017 |
| Total dropouts [1,2] | 5,212 | 3,854 | 3,883 | 2,952 | 2,344 | 12.0 | 10.1 | 9.1 | 6.4 | 5.1 |
| 16 to 17 years | 709 | 418 | 460 | 227 | 426 | 8.8 | 6.3 | 5.8 | 2.7 | 5.0 |
| 18 to 21 years | 2,578 | 1,921 | 2,005 | 1,445 | 1,025 | 15.8 | 13.4 | 12.9 | 8.4 | 6.2 |
| 22 to 24 years | 1,798 | 1,458 | 1,310 | 1,144 | 747 | 15.2 | 13.8 | 11.8 | 9.2 | 5.7 |
| White [2,3] | 4,169 | 3,127 | 3,065 | 2,232 | 1,756 | 11.3 | 10.1 | 9.1 | 6.3 | 5.2 |
| 16 to 17 years | 619 | 334 | 366 | 181 | 301 | 9.2 | 6.4 | 5.8 | 2.9 | 4.9 |
| 18 to 21 years | 2,032 | 1,516 | 1,558 | 1,048 | 785 | 14.7 | 13.1 | 12.6 | 8.0 | 6.4 |
| 22 to 24 years | 1,416 | 1,235 | 1,040 | 893 | 573 | 14.0 | 14.0 | 11.7 | 9.2 | 6.0 |
| Black [2,3] | 934 | 611 | 705 | 498 | 385 | 16.0 | 10.9 | 10.9 | 7.2 | 5.6 |
| 16 to 17 years | 80 | 73 | 84 | 30 | 74 | 6.9 | 6.9 | 7.0 | 2.3 | 5.9 |
| 18 to 21 years | 486 | 345 | 383 | 283 | 146 | 23.0 | 16.0 | 16.0 | 10.5 | 5.8 |
| 22 to 24 years | 346 | 185 | 232 | 167 | 124 | 24.0 | 13.5 | 14.3 | 9.4 | 6.4 |
| Hispanic [2,4] | 919 | 1,122 | 1,499 | 1,122 | 841 | 29.5 | 26.8 | 23.5 | 12.8 | 8.0 |
| 16 to 17 years | 92 | 89 | 121 | 40 | 107 | 16.6 | 12.9 | 11.0 | 2.7 | 5.6 |
| 18 to 21 years | 470 | 502 | 733 | 506 | 366 | 40.3 | 32.9 | 30.0 | 15.2 | 9.7 |
| 22 to 24 years | 323 | 523 | 602 | 543 | 337 | 40.6 | 42.8 | 35.5 | 23.2 | 11.8 |

[1] Includes other racial/ethnic groups not shown separately. [2] Includes persons age 14 to 15, not shown separately. [3] Beginning 2003, for persons who selected this race only. See footnote 4, Table 256. [4] Persons of Hispanic origin may be of any race.

Source: U.S. Census Bureau, Current Population Reports, series PPL and P-20; and "School Enrollment," <https://www.census.gov/topics/education/school-enrollment/data/tables.All.html>, accessed December 2018.

## Table 288. School Enrollment Status by Race, Hispanic Origin, and Sex: 2010 and 2017

[17,210 represents 17,210,000. As of October. For persons 18 to 21 years old. For the civilian noninstitutional population. Based on the Current Population Survey; see text, Section 1 and Appendix III]

| Characteristic | Total persons 18 to 21 years old (1,000) | | Percent distribution | | | | | | | |
|---|---|---|---|---|---|---|---|---|---|---|
| | | | Enrolled in high school | | High school graduates | | | | Not high school graduates and not enrolled in high school | |
| | | | | | Total | | In college | | | |
| | 2010 | 2017 | 2010 | 2017 | 2010 | 2017 | 2010 | 2017 | 2010 | 2017 |
| Total [1] | 17,210 | 16,533 | 9.9 | 11.2 | 81.5 | 82.5 | 50.6 | 50.3 | 8.4 | 6.2 |
| White | 13,176 | 12,174 | 9.7 | 10.7 | 82.2 | 82.8 | 50.8 | 50.6 | 8.0 | 6.4 |
| Black | 2,538 | 2,523 | 13.9 | 14.6 | 73.0 | 79.5 | 41.5 | 42.4 | 13.0 | 5.8 |
| Hispanic [2] | 3,339 | 3,784 | 13.5 | 12.1 | 71.3 | 78.2 | 38.9 | 44.9 | 15.2 | 9.7 |
| Male [1] | 8,824 | 8,355 | 11.0 | 12.7 | 79.8 | 79.6 | 46.7 | 45.1 | 9.0 | 7.6 |
| White | 6,867 | 6,170 | 10.8 | 12.6 | 80.4 | 79.5 | 46.6 | 45.4 | 8.7 | 7.8 |
| Black | 1,277 | 1,263 | 15.5 | 14.1 | 69.1 | 78.3 | 36.2 | 38.4 | 15.4 | 7.4 |
| Hispanic [2] | 1,744 | 1,850 | 14.0 | 13.5 | 70.0 | 73.6 | 35.7 | 39.1 | 15.8 | 12.8 |
| Female [1] | 8,386 | 8,179 | 8.8 | 9.7 | 83.2 | 85.5 | 54.8 | 55.5 | 7.8 | 4.8 |
| White | 6,308 | 6,004 | 8.4 | 8.7 | 84.1 | 86.3 | 55.5 | 56.0 | 7.2 | 5.0 |
| Black | 1,261 | 1,261 | 12.3 | 15.1 | 76.9 | 80.6 | 46.9 | 46.5 | 10.5 | 4.2 |
| Hispanic [2] | 1,595 | 1,935 | 12.9 | 10.6 | 72.7 | 82.6 | 42.4 | 50.4 | 14.4 | 6.7 |

[1] Includes other races not shown separately. [2] Persons of Hispanic origin may be of any race.

Source: U.S. Census Bureau, Current Population Reports, P-20, and earlier reports; and "School Enrollment," <https://www.census.gov/topics/education/school-enrollment/data/tables.All.html>, accessed December 2018.

# Table 289. Higher Education—Institutions and Enrollment: 1990 to 2017

[817 represents 817,000. As of Fall. Covers universities, colleges, professional schools, and junior and teachers' colleges, both publicly and privately controlled, regular session. Includes estimates for institutions not reporting. Data for 1990 cover institutions of higher education; beginning 2000, data cover degree-granting institutions. Degree-granting institutions grant associate's or higher degrees and participate in Title IV federal financial aid programs. The degree-granting classification includes more 2-year colleges and excludes a few higher education institutions that did not grant degrees. Data are based on the Integrated Postsecondary Education Data System. See also Appendix III]

| Item | Unit | 1990 | 2000 | 2005 | 2010 | 2015 | 2016 | 2017 |
|---|---|---|---|---|---|---|---|---|
| **ALL INSTITUTIONS** | | | | | | | | |
| **Number of institutions** [1] | **Number** | **3,559** | **4,182** | **4,276** | **4,599** | **4,583** | **4,360** | **4,313** |
| 4-year | Number | 2,141 | 2,450 | 2,582 | 2,870 | 3,004 | 2,832 | 2,828 |
| 2-year | Number | 1,418 | 1,732 | 1,694 | 1,729 | 1,579 | 1,528 | 1,485 |
| **Instructional staff— lecturer or above** [2] | **1,000** | **817** | **(NA)** | **1,290** | **(NA)** | **1,552** | **1,546** | **1,544** |
| Percent full-time | Percent | 61 | (NA) | 52 | (NA) | 52 | 53 | 53 |
| **Total enrollment** [3] | **1,000** | **13,819** | **15,312** | **17,487** | **21,019** | **19,988** | **19,847** | **19,766** |
| Male | 1,000 | 6,284 | 6,722 | 7,456 | 9,046 | 8,724 | 8,638 | 8,568 |
| Female | 1,000 | 7,535 | 8,591 | 10,032 | 11,974 | 11,264 | 11,208 | 11,198 |
| 4-year institutions | 1,000 | 8,579 | 9,364 | 10,999 | 13,336 | 13,489 | 13,754 | 13,824 |
| 2-year institutions | 1,000 | 5,240 | 5,948 | 6,488 | 7,684 | 6,499 | 6,092 | 5,942 |
| Full-time | 1,000 | 7,821 | 9,010 | 10,797 | 13,087 | 12,288 | 12,125 | 12,077 |
| Part-time | 1,000 | 5,998 | 6,303 | 6,690 | 7,932 | 7,701 | 7,722 | 7,688 |
| Public | 1,000 | 10,845 | 11,753 | 13,022 | 15,142 | 14,573 | 14,586 | 14,560 |
| Private | 1,000 | 2,974 | 3,560 | 4,466 | 5,877 | 5,415 | 5,261 | 5,205 |
| Not-for-profit | 1,000 | 2,760 | 3,109 | 3,455 | 3,854 | 4,066 | 4,079 | 4,106 |
| For profit | 1,000 | 214 | 450 | 1,011 | 2,023 | 1,349 | 1,182 | 1,099 |
| Undergraduate | 1,000 | 11,959 | 13,155 | 14,964 | 18,082 | 17,047 | 16,875 | 16,760 |
| Men | 1,000 | 5,380 | 5,778 | 6,409 | 7,836 | 7,502 | 7,417 | 7,347 |
| Women | 1,000 | 6,579 | 7,377 | 8,555 | 10,246 | 9,544 | 9,458 | 9,413 |
| Full-time | 1,000 | 6,976 | 7,923 | 9,446 | 11,457 | 10,603 | 10,430 | 10,371 |
| Part-time | 1,000 | 4,983 | 5,232 | 5,518 | 6,625 | 6,444 | 6,445 | 6,390 |
| First-time freshmen [4] | 1,000 | 2,257 | 2,428 | 2,657 | 3,157 | 2,883 | 2,883 | 2,880 |
| Postbaccalaureate | 1,000 | 1,860 | 2,157 | 2,524 | 2,937 | 2,942 | 2,972 | 3,005 |
| Men | 1,000 | 904 | 944 | 1,047 | 1,209 | 1,222 | 1,222 | 1,220 |
| Women | 1,000 | 955 | 1,213 | 1,476 | 1,728 | 1,720 | 1,751 | 1,785 |
| **2-YEAR INSTITUTIONS** | | | | | | | | |
| Number of institutions [1] | Number | 1,418 | 1,732 | 1,694 | 1,729 | 1,579 | 1,528 | 1,485 |
| Public | Number | 972 | 1,076 | 1,053 | 978 | 910 | 886 | 876 |
| Private | Number | 446 | 656 | 641 | 751 | 669 | 642 | 609 |
| Instructional staff— lecturer or above [2] | 1,000 | (NA) | (NA) | 373 | (NA) | 372 | 349 | 337 |
| Enrollment [3] | 1,000 | 5,240 | 5,948 | 6,488 | 7,684 | 6,499 | 6,092 | 5,942 |
| Public | 1,000 | 4,996 | 5,697 | 6,184 | 7,218 | 6,224 | 5,843 | 5,707 |
| Private | 1,000 | 244 | 251 | 304 | 466 | 275 | 250 | 235 |
| Male | 1,000 | 2,233 | 2,559 | 2,680 | 3,266 | 2,818 | 2,637 | 2,563 |
| Female | 1,000 | 3,007 | 3,390 | 3,808 | 4,418 | 3,681 | 3,455 | 3,379 |
| **4-YEAR INSTITUTIONS** | | | | | | | | |
| Number of institutions [1] | Number | 2,141 | 2,450 | 2,582 | 2,870 | 3,004 | 2,832 | 2,828 |
| Public | Number | 595 | 622 | 640 | 678 | 710 | 737 | 750 |
| Private | Number | 1,546 | 1,828 | 1,942 | 2,192 | 2,294 | 2,095 | 2,078 |
| Instructional staff— lecturer or above [2] | 1,000 | (NA) | (NA) | 917 | (NA) | 1,181 | 1,197 | 1,207 |
| Enrollment [3] | 1,000 | 8,579 | 9,364 | 10,999 | 13,336 | 13,489 | 13,754 | 13,824 |
| Public | 1,000 | 5,848 | 6,055 | 6,838 | 7,924 | 8,349 | 8,743 | 8,853 |
| Private | 1,000 | 2,730 | 3,308 | 4,162 | 5,412 | 5,140 | 5,012 | 4,970 |
| Male | 1,000 | 4,051 | 4,163 | 4,776 | 5,780 | 5,906 | 6,001 | 6,005 |
| Female | 1,000 | 4,527 | 5,201 | 6,224 | 7,556 | 7,583 | 7,753 | 7,819 |

NA Not available. [1] Number of institutions includes count of branch campuses. Includes schools accredited by the National Association of Trade and Technical Schools. [2] Beginning in 2007, includes institutions with fewer than 15 full-time employees; prior to 2007, these institutions did not report staff. [3] Branch campuses counted according to actual status, e.g., 2-year branch in 2-year category. May include unclassified students taking courses for credit but not towards a degree. [4] Students seeking certificates or degrees.

Source: U.S. National Center for Education Statistics, *Digest of Education Statistics*, "Advance Release of Selected 2018 Digest Tables," and earlier releases, <http://nces.ed.gov/Programs/digest/>, accessed June 2019.

# Table 290. Degree-Granting Higher Education Institutions—Number and Enrollment by State and Selected Characteristics: 2017

[19,766 represents 19,766,000. Number of institutions beginning in academic year. Opening Fall enrollment of resident and extension students attending full-time or part-time. Based on data from the Integrated Postsecondary Education Data System (IPEDS)]

| State | Num-ber of institu-tions [1] | Enrollment (1,000) | | | | | | | Minority | | | Non-resi-dent alien |
|---|---|---|---|---|---|---|---|---|---|---|---|---|
| | | Total | Male | Female | Public | Private | Full-time | White [2] | Total [3] | Black [2] | His-panic | |
| **United States** | **4,313** | **19,766** | **8,568** | **11,198** | **14,560** | **5,205** | **12,077** | **10,511** | **8,254** | **2,546** | **3,541** | **1,001** |
| Alabama | 72 | 307 | 131 | 175 | 254 | 53 | 211 | 190 | 108 | 81 | 11 | 9 |
| Alaska | 8 | 27 | 11 | 16 | 26 | 1 | 12 | 16 | 10 | 1 | 2 | 1 |
| Arizona | 78 | 592 | 236 | 355 | 367 | 225 | 339 | 289 | 283 | 75 | 147 | 20 |
| Arkansas | 53 | 164 | 68 | 96 | 147 | 17 | 104 | 112 | 46 | 26 | 10 | 6 |
| California | 441 | 2,714 | 1,221 | 1,493 | 2,247 | 467 | 1,494 | 762 | 1,804 | 171 | 1,086 | 148 |
| Colorado | 79 | 360 | 160 | 200 | 279 | 81 | 205 | 225 | 123 | 27 | 63 | 12 |
| Connecticut | 43 | 198 | 84 | 114 | 116 | 81 | 129 | 113 | 73 | 25 | 30 | 11 |
| Delaware | 8 | 60 | 24 | 36 | 42 | 18 | 37 | 33 | 22 | 13 | 5 | 5 |
| District of Columbia | 19 | 96 | 38 | 58 | 5 | 91 | 64 | 42 | 43 | 24 | 9 | 11 |
| Florida | 201 | 1,071 | 448 | 624 | 798 | 273 | 615 | 468 | 557 | 190 | 289 | 46 |
| Georgia | 123 | 538 | 220 | 318 | 429 | 110 | 339 | 259 | 256 | 168 | 41 | 23 |
| Hawaii | 20 | 64 | 26 | 38 | 52 | 12 | 37 | 11 | 49 | 1 | 7 | 4 |
| Idaho | 17 | 132 | 57 | 75 | 76 | 56 | 60 | 98 | 22 | 1 | 12 | 11 |
| Illinois | 171 | 757 | 325 | 432 | 478 | 279 | 437 | 403 | 312 | 96 | 140 | 43 |
| Indiana | 80 | 399 | 179 | 220 | 302 | 97 | 264 | 284 | 90 | 38 | 25 | 25 |
| Iowa | 62 | 261 | 115 | 146 | 170 | 91 | 153 | 189 | 59 | 23 | 20 | 13 |
| Kansas | 69 | 214 | 98 | 116 | 180 | 34 | 124 | 144 | 57 | 19 | 21 | 13 |
| Kentucky | 67 | 258 | 110 | 148 | 202 | 56 | 156 | 203 | 45 | 22 | 10 | 11 |
| Louisiana | 60 | 242 | 96 | 146 | 211 | 31 | 161 | 132 | 102 | 75 | 13 | 7 |
| Maine | 31 | 72 | 29 | 43 | 47 | 25 | 44 | 60 | 10 | 3 | 2 | 2 |
| Maryland | 56 | 364 | 162 | 203 | 304 | 61 | 189 | 164 | 179 | 101 | 33 | 22 |
| Massachusetts | 116 | 504 | 219 | 285 | 213 | 290 | 354 | 285 | 158 | 44 | 56 | 60 |
| Michigan | 94 | 558 | 253 | 305 | 479 | 79 | 334 | 388 | 140 | 66 | 29 | 31 |
| Minnesota | 95 | 413 | 160 | 253 | 249 | 164 | 220 | 273 | 124 | 61 | 22 | 16 |
| Mississippi | 38 | 172 | 68 | 103 | 152 | 19 | 129 | 95 | 73 | 63 | 4 | 3 |
| Missouri | 115 | 383 | 164 | 219 | 236 | 148 | 236 | 273 | 93 | 46 | 20 | 18 |
| Montana | 23 | 51 | 23 | 27 | 46 | 5 | 35 | 40 | 9 | (Z) | 2 | 1 |
| Nebraska | 41 | 136 | 60 | 76 | 101 | 35 | 87 | 100 | 31 | 7 | 14 | 6 |
| Nevada | 24 | 118 | 50 | 68 | 108 | 10 | 63 | 51 | 64 | 9 | 33 | 2 |
| New Hampshire | 25 | 149 | 58 | 91 | 40 | 109 | 68 | 107 | 39 | 18 | 12 | 3 |
| New Jersey | 75 | 419 | 191 | 228 | 335 | 84 | 275 | 199 | 199 | 59 | 89 | 22 |
| New Mexico | 42 | 129 | 54 | 75 | 125 | 4 | 64 | 42 | 84 | 4 | 62 | 3 |
| New York | 301 | 1,260 | 551 | 710 | 697 | 563 | 896 | 598 | 554 | 171 | 224 | 108 |
| North Carolina | 144 | 564 | 234 | 330 | 455 | 109 | 359 | 327 | 218 | 127 | 45 | 20 |
| North Dakota | 20 | 54 | 26 | 27 | 48 | 6 | 37 | 43 | 8 | 2 | 2 | 3 |
| Ohio | 185 | 650 | 287 | 363 | 497 | 152 | 413 | 474 | 144 | 74 | 27 | 32 |
| Oklahoma | 59 | 202 | 88 | 114 | 174 | 28 | 131 | 116 | 76 | 17 | 18 | 10 |
| Oregon | 57 | 230 | 103 | 127 | 192 | 38 | 143 | 148 | 69 | 7 | 30 | 12 |
| Pennsylvania | 239 | 717 | 315 | 402 | 401 | 316 | 523 | 473 | 197 | 80 | 52 | 47 |
| Rhode Island | 13 | 83 | 35 | 47 | 41 | 42 | 62 | 54 | 24 | 6 | 11 | 5 |
| South Carolina | 73 | 246 | 101 | 145 | 201 | 46 | 171 | 155 | 86 | 61 | 12 | 5 |
| South Dakota | 23 | 54 | 24 | 29 | 45 | 9 | 33 | 43 | 8 | 2 | 2 | 2 |
| Tennessee | 100 | 323 | 136 | 188 | 223 | 100 | 231 | 219 | 95 | 60 | 15 | 9 |
| Texas | 261 | 1,631 | 706 | 924 | 1,448 | 182 | 853 | 593 | 968 | 204 | 612 | 70 |
| Utah | 32 | 332 | 147 | 185 | 180 | 152 | 243 | 250 | 75 | 15 | 34 | 7 |
| Vermont | 23 | 44 | 20 | 24 | 25 | 19 | 32 | 35 | 7 | 2 | 2 | 2 |
| Virginia | 122 | 554 | 240 | 314 | 389 | 165 | 341 | 315 | 219 | 109 | 48 | 20 |
| Washington | 80 | 368 | 164 | 204 | 318 | 50 | 254 | 212 | 133 | 17 | 48 | 24 |
| West Virginia | 44 | 143 | 72 | 71 | 84 | 59 | 74 | 107 | 31 | 14 | 9 | 4 |
| Wisconsin | 76 | 341 | 151 | 190 | 280 | 61 | 209 | 261 | 67 | 18 | 23 | 12 |
| Wyoming | 10 | 33 | 16 | 17 | 33 | (Z) | 18 | 27 | 5 | (Z) | 3 | 1 |
| U.S. military [4] | 5 | 15 | 11 | 4 | 15 | (X) | 15 | 10 | 5 | 1 | 2 | (Z) |

X Not applicable. Z Fewer than 500. [1] Branch campuses counted as separate institutions. [2] Non-Hispanic. [3] Includes other races not shown separately. [4] Service academies.

Source: U.S. National Center for Education Statistics, *Digest of Education Statistics*, "Advance Release of Selected 2018 Digest Tables," <http://www.nces.ed.gov/programs/digest/>, accessed May 2019.

# Table 291. College Enrollment of Recent High School Completers: 1970 to 2017

[2,758 represents 2,758,000. For persons 16 to 24 years old who graduated from high school in the preceding 12 months. Includes persons receiving GEDs. Based on sample surveys and subject to sampling error; data not comparable with that in other tables]

| Year | Number of high school completers (1,000) | | | | | | Percent enrolled in college [5] | | | | | |
|---|---|---|---|---|---|---|---|---|---|---|---|---|
| | Total [1] | Male | Female | White [2] | Black [2,3] | His-panic [3,4] | Total [1] | Male | Female | White [2] | Black [2,3] | His-panic [3,4] |
| 1970 | 2,758 | 1,343 | 1,415 | 2,461 | (NA) | (NA) | 51.7 | 55.2 | 48.5 | 52.0 | (NA) | (NA) |
| 1975 | 3,185 | 1,513 | 1,672 | 2,701 | 302 | 132 | 50.7 | 52.6 | 49.0 | 51.1 | 41.7 | 58.0 |
| 1980 | 3,088 | 1,498 | 1,589 | 2,554 | 350 | 130 | 49.3 | 46.7 | 51.8 | 49.8 | 42.7 | 52.3 |
| 1985 | 2,668 | 1,287 | 1,381 | 2,104 | 332 | 141 | 57.7 | 58.6 | 56.8 | 60.1 | 42.2 | 51.0 |
| 1990 | 2,362 | 1,173 | 1,189 | 1,819 | 331 | 121 | 60.1 | 58.0 | 62.2 | 63.0 | 46.8 | 42.7 |
| 1991 | 2,276 | 1,140 | 1,136 | 1,727 | 310 | 154 | 62.5 | 57.9 | 67.1 | 65.4 | 46.4 | 57.2 |
| 1992 | 2,397 | 1,216 | 1,180 | 1,724 | 354 | 198 | 61.9 | 60.0 | 63.8 | 64.3 | 48.2 | 55.0 |
| 1993 | 2,342 | 1,120 | 1,223 | 1,719 | 304 | 201 | 62.6 | 59.9 | 65.2 | 62.9 | 55.6 | 62.2 |
| 1994 | 2,517 | 1,244 | 1,273 | 1,915 | 316 | 178 | 61.9 | 60.6 | 63.2 | 64.5 | 50.8 | 49.1 |
| 1995 | 2,599 | 1,238 | 1,361 | 1,861 | 349 | 288 | 61.9 | 62.6 | 61.3 | 64.3 | 51.2 | 53.7 |
| 1996 | 2,660 | 1,297 | 1,363 | 1,875 | 406 | 227 | 65.0 | 60.1 | 69.7 | 67.4 | 56.0 | 50.8 |
| 1997 | 2,769 | 1,354 | 1,415 | 1,909 | 384 | 336 | 67.0 | 63.6 | 70.3 | 68.2 | 58.5 | 65.6 |
| 1998 | 2,810 | 1,452 | 1,358 | 1,980 | 386 | 314 | 65.6 | 62.4 | 69.1 | 68.5 | 61.9 | 47.4 |
| 1999 | 2,897 | 1,474 | 1,423 | 1,978 | 436 | 329 | 62.9 | 61.4 | 64.4 | 66.3 | 58.9 | 42.3 |
| 2000 | 2,756 | 1,251 | 1,505 | 1,938 | 393 | 300 | 63.3 | 59.9 | 66.2 | 65.7 | 54.9 | 52.9 |
| 2001 | 2,549 | 1,277 | 1,273 | 1,834 | 381 | 241 | 61.8 | 60.1 | 63.5 | 64.3 | 55.0 | 51.7 |
| 2002 | 2,796 | 1,412 | 1,384 | 1,903 | 382 | 344 | 65.2 | 62.1 | 68.4 | 69.1 | 59.4 | 53.6 |
| 2003 | 2,677 | 1,306 | 1,372 | 1,832 | 327 | 314 | 63.9 | 61.2 | 66.5 | 66.2 | 57.5 | 58.6 |
| 2004 | 2,752 | 1,327 | 1,425 | 1,854 | 398 | 286 | 66.7 | 61.4 | 71.5 | 68.8 | 62.5 | 61.8 |
| 2005 | 2,675 | 1,262 | 1,414 | 1,799 | 345 | 390 | 68.6 | 66.5 | 70.4 | 73.2 | 55.7 | 54.0 |
| 2006 | 2,692 | 1,328 | 1,363 | 1,805 | 318 | 382 | 66.0 | 65.8 | 66.1 | 68.5 | 55.5 | 57.9 |
| 2007 | 2,955 | 1,511 | 1,444 | 2,043 | 416 | 355 | 67.2 | 66.1 | 68.3 | 69.5 | 55.7 | 64.0 |
| 2008 | 3,151 | 1,640 | 1,511 | 2,091 | 416 | 458 | 68.6 | 65.9 | 71.6 | 71.7 | 55.7 | 63.9 |
| 2009 | 2,937 | 1,407 | 1,531 | 1,863 | 415 | 459 | 70.1 | 66.0 | 73.8 | 71.3 | 69.5 | 59.3 |
| 2010 | 3,160 | 1,679 | 1,482 | 1,937 | 461 | 507 | 68.1 | 62.8 | 74.0 | 70.5 | 62.0 | 59.7 |
| 2011 | 3,079 | 1,611 | 1,468 | 1,747 | 464 | 623 | 68.2 | 64.7 | 72.2 | 68.3 | 67.1 | 66.6 |
| 2012 | 3,203 | 1,622 | 1,581 | (NA) | (NA) | (NA) | 66.2 | 61.3 | 71.3 | 65.7 | 56.4 | 70.3 |
| 2013 | 2,977 | 1,524 | 1,453 | (NA) | (NA) | (NA) | 65.9 | 63.5 | 68.4 | 68.8 | 56.7 | 59.8 |
| 2014 | 2,868 | 1,423 | 1,445 | (NA) | (NA) | (NA) | 68.4 | 64.0 | 72.6 | 67.7 | 70.2 | 65.2 |
| 2015 | 2,965 | 1,448 | 1,516 | (NA) | (NA) | (NA) | 69.2 | 65.8 | 72.5 | 71.3 | 55.6 | 68.9 |
| 2016 | 3,137 | 1,517 | 1,620 | (NA) | (NA) | (NA) | 69.8 | 67.5 | 71.9 | 69.7 | 57.3 | 72.0 |
| 2017 | 2,870 | 1,345 | 1,525 | (NA) | (NA) | (NA) | 66.7 | 61.1 | 71.7 | 69.1 | 59.4 | 61.0 |

NA Not available. [1] Includes persons of other racial/ethnic groups, not shown separately. [2] Beginning 2003, for persons of this race group only. See footnote 4, Table 256. [3] Due to small sample size, data are subject to relatively large sampling errors. [4] Persons of Hispanic origin may be of any race. [5] As of October.

Source: U.S. National Center for Education Statistics, *Digest of Education Statistics*, "Advance Release of Selected 2018 Digest Tables," <http://www.nces.ed.gov/programs/digest/>, accessed January 2019.

# Table 292. College Enrollment by Sex and Attendance Status: 2000 to 2017

[In thousands (15,312 represents 15,312,000). As of Fall. Includes enrollment at branch campuses, some additional (primarily 2-year) colleges, and excludes a few institutions that did not award degrees. Includes enrollment at institutions that were eligible to participate in Title IV federal financial aid programs. Includes unclassified students (students taking courses for credit, but are not candidates for degrees)]

| Sex and age | 2000 | | 2010 | | 2015 | | 2016 | | 2017 | |
|---|---|---|---|---|---|---|---|---|---|---|
| | Total | Part-time | Total | Part-time | Total | Part-time | Total | Part-time | Total | Part-time |
| **Total** | **15,312** | **6,303** | **21,019** | **7,932** | **19,988** | **7,701** | **19,847** | **7,722** | **19,766** | **7,688** |
| **Male** | **6,722** | **2,611** | **9,046** | **3,207** | **8,724** | **3,165** | **8,638** | **3,166** | **8,568** | **3,143** |
| 14 to 17 years old | 58 | 7 | 94 | 23 | 94 | 13 | 83 | 12 | 74 | 11 |
| 18 to 19 years old | 1,464 | 212 | 1,820 | 245 | 1,684 | 270 | 1,688 | 272 | 1,666 | 239 |
| 20 to 21 years old | 1,411 | 255 | 1,948 | 362 | 1,954 | 408 | 1,945 | 393 | 1,914 | 379 |
| 22 to 24 years old | 1,222 | 388 | 1,723 | 508 | 1,746 | 538 | 1,739 | 566 | 1,731 | 571 |
| 25 to 29 years old | 908 | 498 | 1,410 | 695 | 1,382 | 673 | 1,366 | 677 | 1,358 | 674 |
| 30 to 34 years old | 581 | 395 | 731 | 430 | 655 | 405 | 670 | 417 | 660 | 409 |
| 35 years old and over | 1,077 | 855 | 1,320 | 944 | 1,208 | 859 | 1,148 | 829 | 1,164 | 859 |
| **Female** | **8,591** | **3,692** | **11,974** | **4,725** | **11,264** | **4,535** | **11,208** | **4,556** | **11,198** | **4,545** |
| 14 to 17 years old | 73 | 3 | 108 | 9 | 120 | 19 | 131 | 16 | 147 | 22 |
| 18 to 19 years old | 1,794 | 223 | 2,237 | 316 | 2,049 | 275 | 2,050 | 305 | 2,082 | 303 |
| 20 to 21 years old | 1,593 | 298 | 2,155 | 377 | 2,194 | 450 | 2,259 | 446 | 2,252 | 437 |
| 22 to 24 years old | 1,378 | 497 | 2,036 | 666 | 2,038 | 679 | 1,997 | 668 | 2,019 | 679 |
| 25 to 29 years old | 1,136 | 660 | 1,844 | 953 | 1,783 | 973 | 1,826 | 1,037 | 1,831 | 1,043 |
| 30 to 34 years old | 752 | 520 | 1,074 | 630 | 945 | 595 | 919 | 589 | 900 | 593 |
| 35 years old and over | 1,865 | 1,491 | 2,520 | 1,774 | 2,136 | 1,544 | 2,026 | 1,493 | 1,967 | 1,467 |

Source: U.S. National Center for Education Statistics, *Digest of Education Statistics*, "Advance Release of Selected 2018 Digest Tables," <https://nces.ed.gov/programs/digest/>, accessed August 2019.

# Table 293. College Enrollment by Selected Characteristics: 1990 to 2017

[In thousands (13,818.6 represents 13,818,600). As of Fall. Nonresident alien students are not distributed among racial/ethnic groups. Beginning in 2000, data reflect a new classification of institutions; this includes some additional, primarily 2-year, colleges and excludes a few institutions that did not award degrees. Includes institutions that were eligible to participate in Title IV federal financial aid programs and schools accredited by the National Association of Trade and Technical Schools. Based on data from the Integrated Postsecondary Education Data System (IPEDS)]

| Characteristic | 1990 | 2000 | 2005 | 2010 | 2015 | 2016 | 2017 |
|---|---|---|---|---|---|---|---|
| **Total** | **13,818.6** | **15,312.3** | **17,487.5** | **21,019.4** | **19,988.2** | **19,846.9** | **19,765.6** |
| Male | 6,283.9 | 6,721.8 | 7,455.9 | 9,045.8 | 8,723.8 | 8,638.4 | 8,567.6 |
| Female | 7,534.7 | 8,590.5 | 10,031.6 | 11,973.7 | 11,264.4 | 11,208.5 | 11,198.0 |
| Public | 10,844.7 | 11,752.8 | 13,021.8 | 15,142.2 | 14,572.8 | 14,585.8 | 14,560.2 |
| Private | 2,973.9 | 3,559.5 | 4,465.6 | 5,877.3 | 5,415.4 | 5,261.1 | 5,205.4 |
| 2-year | 5,240.1 | 5,948.4 | 6,488.1 | 7,683.6 | 6,499.5 | 6,092.4 | 5,942.0 |
| 4-year | 8,578.6 | 9,363.9 | 10,999.4 | 13,335.8 | 13,488.7 | 13,754.5 | 13,823.6 |
| Undergraduate | 11,959.2 | 13,155.4 | 14,964.0 | 18,082.4 | 17,046.7 | 16,874.6 | 16,760.3 |
| Postbaccalaureate | 1,859.6 | 2,156.9 | 2,523.5 | 2,937.0 | 2,941.5 | 2,972.3 | 3,005.3 |
| **White** [1] | **10,722.5** | **10,462.1** | **11,495.4** | **12,720.8** | **10,939.2** | **10,716.6** | **10,510.8** |
| Male | 4,861.0 | 4,634.6 | 5,007.2 | 5,605.8 | 4,848.5 | 4,736.1 | 4,629.2 |
| Female | 5,861.5 | 5,827.5 | 6,488.2 | 7,115.0 | 6,090.7 | 5,980.5 | 5,881.6 |
| Public | 8,385.4 | 7,963.4 | 8,518.2 | 9,182.1 | 7,910.7 | 7,787.3 | 7,641.2 |
| Private | 2,337.0 | 2,498.7 | 2,977.3 | 3,538.7 | 3,028.5 | 2,929.3 | 2,869.5 |
| 2-year | 3,954.3 | 3,804.1 | 3,998.6 | 4,321.3 | 3,225.8 | 3,001.6 | 2,873.2 |
| 4-year | 6,768.1 | 6,658.0 | 7,496.9 | 8,399.5 | 7,713.4 | 7,715.0 | 7,637.6 |
| Undergraduate | 9,272.6 | 8,983.5 | 9,828.6 | 10,895.9 | 9,303.8 | 9,085.6 | 8,876.9 |
| Postbaccalaureate | 1,449.9 | 1,478.6 | 1,666.8 | 1,824.9 | 1,635.4 | 1,631.0 | 1,633.9 |
| **Black** [1] | **1,247.0** | **1,730.3** | **2,214.6** | **3,039.0** | **2,681.0** | **2,589.4** | **2,545.9** |
| Male | 484.7 | 635.3 | 774.1 | 1,089.0 | 998.9 | 959.5 | 940.9 |
| Female | 762.3 | 1,095.0 | 1,440.4 | 1,949.9 | 1,682.1 | 1,630.0 | 1,605.0 |
| Public | 976.4 | 1,319.2 | 1,580.4 | 1,988.8 | 1,775.1 | 1,739.6 | 1,722.8 |
| Private | 270.6 | 411.1 | 634.2 | 1,050.2 | 906.0 | 849.8 | 823.1 |
| 2-year | 524.3 | 734.9 | 901.1 | 1,198.9 | 940.5 | 865.5 | 842.7 |
| 4-year | 722.8 | 995.4 | 1,313.4 | 1,840.0 | 1,740.5 | 1,724.0 | 1,703.2 |
| Undergraduate | 1,147.2 | 1,548.9 | 1,955.4 | 2,677.1 | 2,316.5 | 2,226.4 | 2,180.5 |
| Postbaccalaureate | 99.8 | 181.4 | 259.2 | 361.9 | 364.5 | 363.0 | 365.4 |
| **Hispanic** | **782.4** | **1,461.8** | **1,882.0** | **2,748.8** | **3,297.7** | **3,428.0** | **3,540.6** |
| Male | 353.9 | 627.1 | 774.6 | 1,157.6 | 1,389.2 | 1,439.3 | 1,477.4 |
| Female | 428.5 | 834.7 | 1,107.3 | 1,591.2 | 1,908.5 | 1,988.7 | 2,063.2 |
| Public | 671.4 | 1,229.3 | 1,525.6 | 2,163.8 | 2,694.5 | 2,819.5 | 2,923.7 |
| Private | 111.0 | 232.5 | 356.4 | 585.0 | 603.2 | 608.5 | 616.8 |
| 2-year | 424.2 | 843.9 | 981.5 | 1,393.0 | 1,555.6 | 1,495.4 | 1,506.0 |
| 4-year | 358.2 | 617.9 | 900.5 | 1,355.9 | 1,742.1 | 1,932.5 | 2,034.6 |
| Undergraduate | 724.6 | 1,351.0 | 1,733.6 | 2,551.0 | 3,055.0 | 3,168.3 | 3,265.6 |
| Postbaccalaureate | 57.9 | 110.8 | 148.4 | 197.8 | 242.7 | 259.6 | 275.0 |
| **Asian/Pacific Islander** [1] | **572.4** | **978.2** | **1,134.4** | **1,281.6** | **1,284.3** | **1,306.7** | **1,329.7** |
| Male | 294.9 | 465.9 | 522.0 | 600.6 | 602.9 | 610.1 | 618.5 |
| Female | 277.5 | 512.3 | 612.4 | 681.0 | 681.5 | 696.6 | 711.2 |
| Public | 461.0 | 770.5 | 881.9 | 968.7 | 970.1 | 990.5 | 1,008.7 |
| Private | 111.5 | 207.7 | 252.4 | 312.8 | 314.2 | 316.2 | 321.0 |
| 2-year | 215.2 | 401.9 | 434.4 | 463.1 | 401.9 | 377.1 | 370.1 |
| 4-year | 357.2 | 576.3 | 700.0 | 818.5 | 882.5 | 929.6 | 959.6 |
| Undergraduate | 500.5 | 845.5 | 971.4 | 1,087.3 | 1,084.0 | 1,100.3 | 1,114.9 |
| Postbaccalaureate | 72.0 | 132.7 | 163.0 | 194.3 | 200.3 | 206.3 | 214.8 |
| **American Indian/Alaska Native** [1] | **102.8** | **151.2** | **176.3** | **196.2** | **146.1** | **142.3** | **137.6** |
| Male | 43.1 | 61.4 | 68.4 | 78.7 | 58.2 | 56.3 | 53.9 |
| Female | 59.7 | 89.7 | 107.9 | 117.5 | 88.0 | 86.0 | 83.8 |
| Public | 90.4 | 127.3 | 143.0 | 150.8 | 113.7 | 110.7 | 107.9 |
| Private | 12.4 | 23.9 | 33.3 | 45.5 | 32.5 | 31.7 | 29.7 |
| 2-year | 54.9 | 74.7 | 80.7 | 87.2 | 62.8 | 58.7 | 55.8 |
| 4-year | 47.9 | 76.5 | 95.6 | 109.0 | 83.4 | 83.6 | 81.8 |
| Undergraduate | 95.5 | 138.5 | 160.4 | 179.1 | 132.2 | 128.6 | 124.0 |
| Postbaccalaureate | 7.3 | 12.6 | 15.9 | 17.1 | 13.9 | 13.7 | 13.6 |
| **Nonresident alien** | **391.5** | **528.7** | **584.8** | **707.7** | **982.3** | **998.1** | **1,000.7** |
| Male | 246.3 | 297.3 | 309.5 | 379.6 | 548.6 | 555.6 | 551.8 |
| Female | 145.2 | 231.4 | 275.3 | 328.0 | 433.7 | 442.5 | 448.9 |
| Public | 260.0 | 343.1 | 372.8 | 453.0 | 626.8 | 633.5 | 624.9 |
| Private | 131.4 | 185.6 | 212.0 | 254.7 | 355.5 | 364.6 | 375.8 |
| 2-year | 67.1 | 89.0 | 91.8 | 99.3 | 104.2 | 94.1 | 89.1 |
| 4-year | 324.3 | 439.7 | 493.1 | 608.3 | 878.1 | 904.0 | 911.6 |
| Undergraduate | 218.7 | 288.0 | 314.7 | 398.4 | 565.1 | 570.2 | 575.0 |
| Postbaccalaureate | 172.7 | 240.7 | 270.1 | 309.3 | 417.2 | 428.0 | 425.7 |

[1] Non-Hispanic.

Source: U.S. National Center for Education Statistics, *Digest of Education Statistics*, "Advance Release of Selected 2018 Digest Tables," and earlier releases, <http://nces.ed.gov/programs/digest/>, accessed May 2019.

# Table 294. College Enrollment by Sex, Age, and Race/Ethnicity: 1980 to 2017

[In thousands (11,387 represents 11,387,000). As of October for the civilian noninstitutional population, 14 years old and over. Based on the Current Population Survey; see text, Section 1 and Appendix III]

| Characteristic | 1980 | 1990 [1] | 1995 | 2000 | 2005 | 2010 | 2013 | 2014 | 2015 | 2016 | 2017 |
|---|---|---|---|---|---|---|---|---|---|---|---|
| **Total** [2]............................ | **11,387** | **13,621** | **14,715** | **15,314** | **17,472** | **20,275** | **19,467** | **19,175** | **19,101** | **19,196** | **18,398** |
| Male [3]....................... | 5,430 | 6,192 | 6,703 | 6,682 | 7,539 | 9,007 | 8,536 | 8,629 | 8,484 | 8,644 | 8,112 |
| 18 to 24 years................ | 3,604 | 3,922 | 4,089 | 4,342 | 4,972 | 5,698 | 5,629 | 5,677 | 5,694 | 5,800 | 5,459 |
| 25 to 34 years................ | 1,325 | 1,412 | 1,561 | 1,361 | 1,486 | 2,055 | 1,775 | 1,792 | 1,803 | 1,838 | 1,714 |
| 35 years old and over.......... | 405 | 772 | 985 | 918 | 1,019 | 1,161 | 984 | 1,036 | 878 | 927 | 854 |
| Female [3]..................... | 5,957 | 7,429 | 8,013 | 8,631 | 9,933 | 11,268 | 10,931 | 10,546 | 10,617 | 10,551 | 10,287 |
| 18 to 24 years................ | 3,625 | 4,042 | 4,452 | 5,109 | 5,859 | 6,515 | 6,572 | 6,455 | 6,460 | 6,520 | 6,477 |
| 25 to 34 years................ | 1,378 | 1,749 | 1,788 | 1,846 | 2,115 | 2,569 | 2,291 | 2,197 | 2,372 | 2,380 | 2,167 |
| 35 years old and over.......... | 802 | 1,546 | 1,684 | 1,589 | 1,838 | 2,049 | 1,907 | 1,784 | 1,672 | 1,491 | 1,492 |
| White [3, 4]................... | 9,925 | 11,488 | 12,021 | 11,999 | 13,467 | 15,258 | 14,240 | 13,953 | 13,859 | 13,901 | 13,224 |
| 18 to 24 years................ | 6,334 | 6,635 | 7,011 | 7,566 | 8,499 | 9,324 | 9,050 | 9,077 | 8,969 | 9,106 | 8,690 |
| 25 to 34 years................ | 2,328 | 2,698 | 2,686 | 2,339 | 2,647 | 3,414 | 2,849 | 2,830 | 2,966 | 2,966 | 2,706 |
| 35 years old and over.......... | 1,051 | 2,023 | 2,208 | 1,978 | 2,206 | 2,365 | 2,107 | 1,899 | 1,776 | 1,664 | 1,672 |
| Male.......................... | 4,804 | 5,235 | 5,535 | 5,311 | 5,844 | 6,883 | 6,241 | 6,398 | 6,253 | 6,222 | 5,864 |
| Female........................ | 5,121 | 6,253 | 6,486 | 6,689 | 7,624 | 8,375 | 7,999 | 7,555 | 7,607 | 7,678 | 7,360 |
| Black [3, 4]................... | 1,163 | 1,393 | 1,772 | 2,164 | 2,297 | 3,083 | 2,857 | 2,934 | 2,826 | 2,885 | 2,812 |
| 18 to 24 years................ | 688 | 894 | 988 | 1,216 | 1,229 | 1,692 | 1,599 | 1,529 | 1,637 | 1,644 | 1,595 |
| 25 to 34 years................ | 289 | 258 | 426 | 567 | 520 | 715 | 686 | 656 | 627 | 652 | 674 |
| 35 years old and over.......... | 156 | 207 | 334 | 361 | 448 | 642 | 540 | 695 | 537 | 559 | 509 |
| Male.......................... | 476 | 587 | 710 | 815 | 864 | 1,185 | 1,116 | 1,132 | 1,147 | 1,217 | 1,175 |
| Female........................ | 686 | 807 | 1,062 | 1,349 | 1,435 | 1,898 | 1,740 | 1,802 | 1,679 | 1,669 | 1,637 |
| Asian [3, 4].................. | (NA) | (NA) | (NA) | (NA) | 1,184 | 1,322 | 1,576 | 1,543 | 1,616 | 1,585 | 1,581 |
| 18 to 24 years................ | (NA) | (NA) | (NA) | (NA) | 696 | 811 | 1,001 | 1,022 | 1,026 | 1,003 | 1,101 |
| 25 to 34 years................ | (NA) | (NA) | (NA) | (NA) | 341 | 354 | 372 | 353 | 426 | 436 | 352 |
| 35 years old and over.......... | (NA) | (NA) | (NA) | (NA) | 130 | 125 | 173 | 148 | 143 | 127 | 95 |
| Male.......................... | (NA) | (NA) | (NA) | (NA) | 605 | 647 | 789 | 797 | 752 | 835 | 750 |
| Female........................ | (NA) | (NA) | (NA) | (NA) | 579 | 676 | 787 | 746 | 864 | 749 | 831 |
| Hispanic origin [3, 5]......... | 443 | 748 | 1,207 | 1,426 | 1,942 | 2,879 | 3,219 | 3,295 | 3,374 | 3,661 | 3,574 |
| 18 to 24 years................ | 315 | 435 | 745 | 899 | 1,216 | 1,814 | 2,192 | 2,282 | 2,369 | 2,564 | 2,410 |
| 25 to 34 years................ | 118 | 168 | 250 | 309 | 438 | 652 | 639 | 630 | 648 | 682 | 717 |
| 35 years old and over.......... | (NA) | 130 | 193 | 195 | 257 | 372 | 345 | 332 | 315 | 326 | 368 |
| Male.......................... | 222 | 364 | 568 | 619 | 804 | 1,302 | 1,438 | 1,441 | 1,484 | 1,582 | 1,529 |
| Female........................ | 221 | 384 | 639 | 807 | 1,139 | 1,576 | 1,781 | 1,855 | 1,890 | 2,079 | 2,045 |

NA Not available. [1] Beginning 1990, based on a revised edit and tabulation package. [2] Includes other races not shown separately. [3] Includes persons 14 to 17 years old not shown separately. [4] Beginning 2003, for persons who selected this race group only. See footnote 4, Table 256. [5] Persons of Hispanic origin may be of any race.

Source: U.S. Census Bureau, Current Population Reports, P-20, and earlier reports; and "School Enrollment," <https://www.census.gov/topics/education/school-enrollment/data/tables.All.html>, accessed December 2018.

# Table 295. College Enrollment by Type of College, Sex, and Selected Characteristics: 2017

[In thousands (18,398 represents 18,398,000). As of October. Covers civilian noninstitutional population 15 years old and over enrolled in colleges and graduate schools. Based on Current Population Survey. See text, Section 1 and Appendix III]

| Characteristic | Total | | | | Male | | Female | |
|---|---|---|---|---|---|---|---|---|
| | Total enrolled | Two-year college | Four-year college | Graduate school | Total enrolled [1] | Four-year college | Total enrolled [1] | Four-year college |
| **Total enrollment** [2]............... | **18,398** | **4,272** | **10,318** | **3,809** | **8,112** | **4,594** | **10,287** | **5,724** |
| Age: | | | | | | | | |
| 15 to 19 years old................. | 4,179 | 1,292 | 2,833 | 53 | 1,831 | 1,140 | 2,348 | 1,693 |
| 20 to 24 years old................. | 7,994 | 1,600 | 5,277 | 1,117 | 3,713 | 2,449 | 4,280 | 2,828 |
| 25 to 34 years old................. | 3,880 | 887 | 1,407 | 1,586 | 1,714 | 698 | 2,166 | 708 |
| 35 years old and over.............. | 2,346 | 491 | 801 | 1,053 | 853 | 307 | 1,492 | 494 |
| Race/ethnicity: | | | | | | | | |
| White [3].......................... | 13,224 | 3,015 | 7,430 | 2,779 | 5,864 | 3,320 | 7,360 | 4,110 |
| White non-Hispanic [3]............. | 10,055 | 2,020 | 5,705 | 2,329 | 4,518 | 2,611 | 5,537 | 3,095 |
| Black [3].......................... | 2,812 | 795 | 1,519 | 498 | 1,175 | 622 | 1,637 | 897 |
| Asian [3].......................... | 1,581 | 226 | 903 | 451 | 750 | 454 | 831 | 450 |
| Hispanic [4]....................... | 3,574 | 1,107 | 1,947 | 519 | 1,529 | 811 | 2,045 | 1,137 |
| Control of school: | | | | | | | | |
| Public............................. | 14,806 | 3,979 | 8,257 | 2,570 | 6,699 | 3,744 | 8,107 | 4,513 |
| Private............................ | 3,592 | 293 | 2,060 | 1,238 | 1,412 | 850 | 2,180 | 1,211 |
| Employment status: | | | | | | | | |
| Employed full-time................. | 4,751 | 1,087 | 1,909 | 1,754 | 2,090 | 892 | 2,660 | 1,017 |
| Employed part-time................. | 5,322 | 1,482 | 3,009 | 831 | 2,199 | 1,259 | 3,123 | 1,750 |
| Not employed....................... | 8,326 | 1,702 | 5,400 | 1,224 | 3,822 | 2,442 | 4,503 | 2,958 |
| Enrollment status: | | | | | | | | |
| Full time students................. | 13,606 | 2,688 | 8,646 | 2,271 | 6,203 | 3,892 | 7,403 | 4,753 |
| 15 to 19 years old................. | 3,821 | 1,039 | 2,729 | 53 | 1,685 | 1,103 | 2,136 | 1,625 |
| 20 to 24 years old................. | 6,716 | 1,122 | 4,671 | 922 | 3,167 | 2,203 | 3,549 | 2,468 |
| 25 to 34 years old................. | 2,214 | 405 | 864 | 946 | 1,035 | 434 | 1,178 | 429 |
| 35 years old and over.............. | 856 | 123 | 382 | 351 | 316 | 152 | 540 | 230 |
| Part time students................. | 4,792 | 1,583 | 1,672 | 1,538 | 1,908 | 701 | 2,884 | 972 |
| 15 to 19 years old................. | 358 | 253 | 105 | – | 146 | 36 | 212 | 68 |
| 20 to 24 years old................. | 1,278 | 477 | 605 | 195 | 547 | 246 | 731 | 359 |
| 25 to 34 years old................. | 1,667 | 484 | 543 | 641 | 679 | 263 | 988 | 279 |
| 35 years old and over.............. | 1,490 | 369 | 419 | 703 | 537 | 155 | 953 | 264 |

– Represents or rounds to zero. [1] Includes enrollment in two-year colleges and graduate school, not shown separately. [2] Includes other races not shown separately. [3] For persons who selected this race group only. [4] Persons of Hispanic origin may be of any race.

Source: U.S. Census Bureau, "School Enrollment," <https://www.census.gov/topics/education/school-enrollment/data/tables.All.html>, accessed December 2018.

## Table 296. Foreign (Nonimmigrant) Student Enrollment in U.S. Colleges and Universities by World Region and Selected Country of Origin: 1980 to 2018

[In thousands (286 represents 286,000). For Fall of the previous year]

| Region of origin | 1980 | 1990 | 1995 | 2000 | 2005 | 2009 | 2010 | 2011 | 2012 | 2013 | 2014 | 2015 | 2016 | 2017 | 2018 |
|---|---|---|---|---|---|---|---|---|---|---|---|---|---|---|---|
| **All regions** | **286** | **387** | **453** | **515** | **565** | **672** | **691** | **723** | **764** | **820** | **886** | **975** | **1044** | **1,079** | **1,095** |
| Africa [1] | 36 | 25 | 21 | 30 | 36 | 37 | 37 | 37 | 35 | 36 | 37 | 40 | 43 | 45 | 47 |
| Nigeria | 16 | 4 | 2 | 4 | 6 | 6 | 7 | 7 | 7 | 7 | 8 | 9 | 11 | 12 | 13 |
| Asia [1,2,3] | 165 | 245 | 292 | 315 | 356 | 444 | 469 | 504 | 547 | 597 | 655 | 724 | 790 | 827 | 842 |
| China | 1 | 33 | 39 | 54 | 63 | 98 | 128 | 158 | 194 | 236 | 274 | 304 | 329 | 351 | 363 |
| Taiwan | 18 | 31 | 36 | 29 | 26 | 28 | 27 | 25 | 23 | 22 | 21 | 21 | 21 | 22 | 22 |
| Hong Kong | 10 | 11 | 13 | 8 | 7 | 8 | 8 | 8 | 8 | 8 | 8 | 8 | 8 | 8 | 7 |
| India | 9 | 26 | 34 | 42 | 80 | 103 | 105 | 104 | 100 | 97 | 103 | 133 | 166 | 186 | 196 |
| Indonesia | 2 | 9 | 12 | 11 | 8 | 8 | 7 | 7 | 7 | 8 | 8 | 8 | 9 | 9 | 9 |
| Iran | 51 | 7 | 3 | 2 | 2 | 4 | 5 | 6 | 7 | 9 | 10 | 11 | 12 | 13 | 13 |
| Japan | 12 | 30 | 45 | 47 | 42 | 29 | 25 | 21 | 20 | 20 | 19 | 19 | 19 | 19 | 19 |
| Malaysia | 4 | 14 | 14 | 9 | 6 | 6 | 6 | 7 | 7 | 7 | 7 | 7 | 8 | 8 | 8 |
| Saudi Arabia | 10 | 4 | 4 | 5 | 3 | 13 | 16 | 23 | 34 | 45 | 54 | 60 | 61 | 53 | 44 |
| South Korea | 5 | 22 | 34 | 41 | 53 | 75 | 72 | 73 | 73 | 71 | 68 | 64 | 61 | 59 | 55 |
| Thailand | 7 | 7 | 11 | 11 | 9 | 9 | 9 | 8 | 8 | 7 | 7 | 7 | 7 | 7 | 7 |
| Europe [4] | 23 | 46 | 65 | 78 | 72 | 88 | 85 | 84 | 85 | 86 | 87 | 91 | 92 | 93 | 93 |
| Latin America [1,5] | 42 | 48 | 47 | 62 | 68 | 68 | 66 | 64 | 64 | 67 | 72 | 86 | 85 | 80 | 80 |
| Mexico | 6 | 7 | 9 | 11 | 13 | 15 | 13 | 14 | 14 | 14 | 15 | 17 | 17 | 17 | 15 |
| Venezuela | 10 | 3 | 4 | 5 | 5 | 5 | 5 | 5 | 6 | 6 | 7 | 8 | 8 | 9 | 8 |
| North America [6] | 16 | 19 | 23 | 24 | 29 | 30 | 29 | 28 | 27 | 27 | 28 | 27 | 27 | 27 | 26 |
| Canada | 15 | 18 | 23 | 24 | 28 | 30 | 28 | 28 | 27 | 27 | 28 | 27 | 27 | 27 | 26 |
| Oceania | 4 | 4 | 4 | 5 | 4 | 5 | 5 | 6 | 6 | 6 | 6 | 6 | 7 | 7 | 7 |

[1] Includes countries not shown separately. [2] Includes the Middle East. [3] Beginning 2006, excludes Cyprus and Turkey. [4] Beginning 2006, includes Cyprus and Turkey. [5] Includes Mexico, Central America, Caribbean, and South America. Prior to 2011, excludes Bermuda. [6] Prior to 2011, includes Bermuda.

Source: Institute of International Education, New York, NY, *Open Doors Report on International Educational Exchange* ©, annual (2018). See also <https://www.iie.org/opendoors>.

## Table 297. Higher Education Enrollment in Languages Other Than English: 1970 to 2016

[1,153.2 represents 1,153,200. As of Fall. For credit enrollment]

| Enrollment | 1970 | 1980 | 1986 | 1990 | 1995 | 2006 | 2009 | 2013 | 2016 |
|---|---|---|---|---|---|---|---|---|---|
| **Registrations [1] (1,000)** | **1,153.2** | **924.3** | **1,003.2** | **1,185.5** | **1,138.8** | **1,575.8** | **1,673.6** | **1,561.1** | **1,417.9** |
| By selected language (1,000): | | | | | | | | | |
| Spanish | 386.6 | 379.0 | 411.4 | 534.1 | 606.3 | 822.1 | 861.0 | 789.9 | 712.2 |
| French | 358.5 | 248.3 | 275.1 | 273.1 | 205.4 | 206.0 | 215.2 | 197.7 | 175.7 |
| American Sign Language | (NA) | (NA) | (NA) | 1.6 | 4.3 | 79.7 | 92.1 | 109.6 | 107.1 |
| German | 201.8 | 127.0 | 120.9 | 133.6 | 96.3 | 94.1 | 95.6 | 86.8 | 80.6 |
| Japanese | 6.6 | 11.5 | 23.5 | 45.8 | 44.7 | 65.4 | 72.4 | 66.8 | 68.8 |
| Italian | 34.2 | 34.8 | 40.9 | 49.8 | 43.8 | 78.2 | 80.3 | 71.0 | 56.7 |
| Chinese | 6.1 | 11.4 | 16.9 | 19.4 | 26.5 | 51.4 | 59.9 | 61.1 | 53.1 |
| Arabic | 1.3 | 3.5 | 3.4 | 3.7 | 4.4 | 24.0 | 35.2 | 33.5 | 31.6 |
| Latin | 28.4 | 25.0 | 25.0 | 28.2 | 25.9 | 32.2 | 32.4 | 27.2 | 24.9 |
| Russian | 36.4 | 24.0 | 33.9 | 44.5 | 24.7 | 24.8 | 26.7 | 22.0 | 20.4 |
| Korean | 0.1 | 0.4 | 0.9 | 2.4 | 3.3 | 7.1 | 8.4 | 12.3 | 13.9 |
| Ancient Greek | 16.5 | 22.1 | 17.8 | 16.4 | 16.3 | 22.8 | 21.5 | 17.0 | 13.3 |
| Hebrew | 16.6 | 19.3 | 15.7 | 13.0 | 13.1 | 23.8 | 22.1 | 19.3 | 15.1 |
| Portuguese | 5.1 | 4.9 | 5.1 | 6.1 | 6.5 | 10.3 | 11.3 | 12.4 | 9.8 |
| Index (1965=100) | 111.5 | 89.3 | 97.0 | 114.6 | 110.1 | 152.3 | 161.8 | 150.9 | 137.0 |

NA Not available. [1] Includes other languages, not shown separately.

Source: Modern Language Association, Dennis Looney and Natalia Lusin. *Enrollments in Languages Other Than English in United States Institutions of Higher Education, Summer 2016 and Fall 2016: Preliminary Report*, February 2018 ©. For 1970 to 2009, consult Association of Departments of Foreign Languages (ADFL) Bulletins. For 2002 to 2016 reports, go to: <https://www.mla.org/Resources/Research/Surveys-Reports-and-Other-Documents/Teaching-Enrollments-and-Programs/Enrollments-in-Languages-Other-Than-English-in-United-States-Institutions-of-Higher-Education>.

## Table 298. Active Duty Military Personnel and Veterans Enrolled in Higher Education: 2008 and 2012

[20,510.7 represents 20,510,700. For school year ending in year shown. Based on the National Postsecondary Student-Aid Study]

| Characteristic | Undergraduate | | | | Graduate | | | |
|---|---|---|---|---|---|---|---|---|
| | 2008 | | 2012 | | 2008 | | 2012 | |
| | Number (1,000) | Percent | Number (1,000) | Percent | Number (1,000) | Percent | Number (1,000) | Percent |
| **Total students** | **20,510.7** | **100.0** | **23,055.4** | **100.0** | **3,476.1** | **100.0** | **3,682.2** | **100.0** |
| **Total military students** | **913.8** | **4.5** | **1,132.9** | **4.9** | **146.5** | **4.2** | **159.7** | **4.3** |
| Veterans | 688.0 | 3.4 | 855.9 | 3.7 | 106.7 | 3.1 | 109.7 | 3.0 |
| Military service members | 225.8 | 1.1 | 277.0 | 1.1 | 39.8 | 1.1 | 50.0 | 1.3 |
| Active duty | 150.4 | 0.7 | 170.8 | 0.7 | 31.4 | 0.9 | 26.3 | 0.7 |
| Reserves | 75.4 | 0.4 | 74.3 | 0.3 | 8.4 | 0.2 | 18.2 | 0.5 |
| National Guard [1] | (NA) | (NA) | 31.9 | 0.1 | (NA) | (NA) | 5.5 | 0.1 |
| Nonmilitary students | 19,596.8 | 95.5 | 21,922.6 | 95.1 | 3,329.5 | 95.8 | 3,522.4 | 95.7 |

NA Not available. [1] Information on National Guard status was not collected in 2008; students were only considered military students if they were veterans or military service members on active duty or in the reserves.

Source: U.S. National Center for Education Statistics, *After the Post-9/11 GI Bill: A Profile of Military Service Members and Veterans Enrolled in Undergraduate and Graduate Education*, August 2016. See also <https://nces.ed.gov/pubsearch/pubsinfo.asp?pubid=2016435>.

# Table 299. College Students Reporting Disability Status by Selected Characteristic: 2015 to 2016

[19,308 represents 19,308,000. Students with disabilities are those who reported having deafness or serious difficulty hearing; blindness or serious difficulty seeing; serious difficulty concentrating, remembering, or making decisions because of a physical, mental, or emotional condition; or serious difficulty walking or climbing stairs. For 2015-16, the question about difficulty concentrating, remembering, or making decisions was expanded to include examples of relevant conditions. Specifically, students were instructed to "consider conditions including, but not limited to, a serious learning disability, depression, ADD, or ADHD." Therefore, data for 2015-16 cannot be compared to estimates of the percentages in earlier years. Based on the 2015-2016 National Postsecondary Student-Aid Study; see source for details. See also Appendix III]

| Student characteristic | Undergraduate | | | Graduate and first-professional | | |
|---|---|---|---|---|---|---|
| | All students | Disabled students | Nondisabled students | All students | Disabled students | Nondisabled students |
| Total students (1,000)............................... | 19,308 | 3,755 | 15,554 | 3,547 | 423 | 3,124 |
| PERCENT DISTRIBUTION | | | | | | |
| Total........................................ | 100.0 | 19.4 | 80.6 | 100.0 | 11.9 | 88.1 |
| Age: | | | | | | |
| 15 to 23 years old............................ | 100.0 | 17.6 | 82.4 | 100.0 | 8.1 | 91.9 |
| 24 to 29 years old............................ | 100.0 | 21.6 | 78.4 | 100.0 | 11.3 | 88.7 |
| 30 years or older............................. | 100.0 | 22.6 | 77.4 | 100.0 | 13.5 | 86.5 |
| Sex: | | | | | | |
| Male........................................ | 100.0 | 19.2 | 80.8 | 100.0 | 9.9 | 90.1 |
| Female...................................... | 100.0 | 19.6 | 80.4 | 100.0 | 13.3 | 86.7 |
| Race/ethnicity of student: | | | | | | |
| White non-Hispanic.......................... | 100.0 | 20.8 | 79.2 | 100.0 | 13.0 | 87.0 |
| Black non-Hispanic.......................... | 100.0 | 17.2 | 82.8 | 100.0 | 10.3 | 89.7 |
| Hispanic.................................... | 100.0 | 18.3 | 81.7 | 100.0 | 14.3 | 85.7 |
| Asian...................................... | 100.0 | 15.2 | 84.8 | 100.0 | 6.2 | 93.8 |
| Pacific Islander............................. | 100.0 | 23.6 | 76.4 | 100.0 | [1] 14.9 | 85.1 |
| American Indian/Alaska Native.............. | 100.0 | 27.8 | 72.2 | 100.0 | [1] 11.8 | 88.2 |
| Two or more races.......................... | 100.0 | 22.1 | 77.9 | 100.0 | 19.7 | 80.3 |
| Attendance status: | | | | | | |
| Full-time, full-year.......................... | 100.0 | 17.3 | 82.7 | 100.0 | 12.0 | 88.0 |
| Part-time or part-year....................... | 100.0 | 20.8 | 79.2 | 100.0 | 11.9 | 88.1 |
| Student housing status: | | | | | | |
| On-campus................................. | 100.0 | 15.8 | 84.2 | (NA) | (NA) | (NA) |
| Off-campus................................. | 100.0 | 20.6 | 79.4 | (NA) | (NA) | (NA) |
| With parents or relatives.................... | 100.0 | 19.5 | 80.5 | (NA) | (NA) | (NA) |
| Attended more than one institution.......... | 100.0 | 18.7 | 81.3 | (NA) | (NA) | (NA) |
| Dependency status: | | | | | | |
| Dependent................................. | 100.0 | 17.2 | 82.8 | (NA) | (NA) | (NA) |
| Independent, unmarried.................... | 100.0 | 23.9 | 76.1 | 100.0 | 11.5 | 88.5 |
| Independent, married....................... | 100.0 | 20.5 | 79.5 | 100.0 | 10.3 | 89.7 |
| Independent with dependents............... | 100.0 | 20.3 | 79.7 | 100.0 | 13.4 | 86.6 |

NA Not available. [1] Interpret data with caution.

Source: U.S. National Center for Education Statistics, *2017 Digest of Education Statistics*, January 2019. See also <http://www.nces.ed.gov/programs/digest/>.

# Table 300. College Freshmen—Summary Characteristics: 1980 to 2017

[In percent. As of Fall for first-time full-time freshmen in 4-year colleges and universities. Based on sample survey and subject to sampling error; see source]

| Characteristic | 1980 | 1990 | 2000 | 2005 | 2010 | 2014 | 2015 | 2016 | 2017 |
|---|---|---|---|---|---|---|---|---|---|
| Sex: | | | | | | | | | |
| Male........................................ | 48.8 | 46.9 | 45.2 | 45.0 | 44.3 | 43.4 | 43.8 | 42.2 | 44.8 |
| Female...................................... | 51.2 | 53.1 | 54.8 | 55.0 | 55.7 | 56.6 | 56.2 | 57.8 | 55.2 |
| Applied to more than three colleges..................... | 31.5 | 42.9 | 50.5 | 55.4 | 64.1 | 72.5 | 71.9 | 71.3 | 71.0 |
| Average grade in high school: | | | | | | | | | |
| A- to A+.................................... | 26.6 | 29.4 | 42.9 | 46.6 | 48.4 | 53.1 | 58.7 | 55.1 | 57.4 |
| B- to B+.................................... | 58.2 | 57.0 | 50.5 | 48.0 | 47.5 | 43.9 | 38.5 | 42.3 | 39.6 |
| C to C+..................................... | 14.9 | 13.4 | 6.5 | 5.4 | 4.1 | 2.9 | 2.8 | 2.6 | 3.1 |
| D........................................... | 0.2 | 0.2 | 0.1 | 0.1 | 0.1 | – | – | – | – |
| Political orientation: | | | | | | | | | |
| Liberal...................................... | 21.0 | 24.6 | 24.8 | 27.1 | 27.3 | 28.8 | 29.6 | 31.3 | 32.2 |
| Middle of the road.......................... | 57.0 | 51.7 | 51.9 | 45.0 | 46.4 | 47.2 | 44.9 | 42.3 | 41.4 |
| Conservative............................... | 19.0 | 20.6 | 18.9 | 22.6 | 21.7 | 19.4 | 19.8 | 20.2 | 20.4 |
| Probable field of study: | | | | | | | | | |
| Biological sciences......................... | 4.5 | 4.9 | 6.6 | 7.6 | 10.8 | 13.8 | 14.9 | 15.7 | 15.5 |
| Business.................................... | 21.2 | 21.1 | 16.7 | 17.4 | 13.7 | 14.6 | 13.4 | 13.8 | 13.8 |
| Education................................... | 8.4 | 10.3 | 11.0 | 9.9 | 7.2 | 5.0 | 4.2 | 4.6 | 4.4 |
| Engineering................................. | 11.2 | 9.7 | 8.7 | 8.3 | 10.3 | 11.7 | 13.1 | 10.7 | 11.5 |
| Physical science............................ | 3.2 | 2.8 | 2.6 | 3.1 | 2.7 | 2.5 | 2.7 | 2.7 | 2.7 |
| Social science.............................. | 8.2 | 11.0 | 10.0 | 10.7 | 8.9 | 10.2 | 10.8 | 10.7 | 11 |
| Communications [1]......................... | 2.4 | 2.9 | 2.7 | 2.0 | 1.8 | 2.2 | 1.9 | 2.1 | 1.6 |
| Computer science........................... | 2.6 | 1.7 | 3.7 | 1.1 | 1.0 | 3.5 | 3.8 | 3.7 | 4.2 |
| Personal objectives—very important or essential: | | | | | | | | | |
| Being very well off financially............... | 62.5 | 72.3 | 73.4 | 74.5 | 77.4 | 82.4 | 81.9 | 82.3 | 82.5 |
| Developing a meaningful philosophy of life........... | 62.5 | 45.9 | 42.4 | 45.0 | 46.9 | 44.6 | 46.5 | 46.8 | 48.1 |
| Keeping up to date with political affairs............... | 45.2 | 46.6 | 28.1 | 36.4 | 33.2 | 35.0 | 40.4 | 46.0 | 48.1 |

– Represents or rounds to zero. [1] Beginning in 2012, the communications field includes journalism majors.

Source: The Higher Education Research Institute, University of California, Los Angeles, CA, *The American Freshman: National Norms Fall 2017* ©, 2019, and earlier editions. See also <https://heri.ucla.edu/publications-tfs/>.

## Table 301. Residence and Migration of College Freshmen by State: 2016

[As of Fall. Includes first-time postsecondary students who had graduated from high school in the previous 12 months and were enrolled at public and private nonprofit 4-year degree-granting institutions that participated in Title IV federal financial aid programs. Excludes respondents for whom state residence and/or migration are unknown. Also excludes U.S. Service Academies (Air Force Academy, Coast Guard Academy, Merchant Marine Academy, Military Academy, and Naval Academy). Based on data from the Integrated Postsecondary Education Data System (IPEDS). See source for more information]

| State | Total freshmen enrollment in institutions located in the state | Ratio of in-state students to freshmen enrollment | Ratio of in-state students to residents enrolled in any state [1] | State | Total freshmen enrollment in institutions located in the state | Ratio of in-state students to freshmen enrollment | Ratio of in-state students to residents enrolled in any state [1] |
|---|---|---|---|---|---|---|---|
| U.S. | 1,603,177 | 0.71 | 0.74 | MO | 29,328 | 0.67 | 0.73 |
| AL | 28,063 | 0.58 | 0.83 | MT | 6,204 | 0.56 | 0.78 |
| AK | 2,115 | 0.91 | 0.62 | NE | 11,896 | 0.69 | 0.79 |
| AZ | 27,211 | 0.57 | 0.79 | NV | 10,798 | 0.83 | 0.75 |
| AR | 17,491 | 0.68 | 0.86 | NH | 8,439 | 0.33 | 0.39 |
| CA | 152,141 | 0.85 | 0.78 | NJ | 29,875 | 0.86 | 0.45 |
| CO | 27,047 | 0.69 | 0.69 | NM | 7,121 | 0.78 | 0.75 |
| CT | 19,303 | 0.53 | 0.42 | NY | 110,379 | 0.69 | 0.73 |
| DE | 7,942 | 0.56 | 0.68 | NC | 48,778 | 0.74 | 0.82 |
| DC | 7,926 | 0.06 | 0.20 | ND | 6,404 | 0.48 | 0.78 |
| FL | 109,554 | 0.86 | 0.87 | OH | 69,451 | 0.75 | 0.82 |
| GA | 56,697 | 0.81 | 0.80 | OK | 19,635 | 0.68 | 0.86 |
| HI | 3,895 | 0.64 | 0.44 | OR | 15,744 | 0.54 | 0.68 |
| ID | 8,894 | 0.51 | 0.69 | PA | 83,708 | 0.62 | 0.76 |
| IL | 46,601 | 0.73 | 0.52 | RI | 11,707 | 0.25 | 0.54 |
| IN | 46,240 | 0.67 | 0.85 | SC | 24,791 | 0.63 | 0.83 |
| IA | 20,979 | 0.52 | 0.80 | SD | 6,088 | 0.55 | 0.73 |
| KS | 15,275 | 0.66 | 0.76 | TN | 30,353 | 0.72 | 0.76 |
| KY | 23,774 | 0.72 | 0.84 | TX | 108,133 | 0.91 | 0.82 |
| LA | 24,935 | 0.80 | 0.87 | UT | 19,331 | 0.66 | 0.90 |
| ME | 7,659 | 0.50 | 0.60 | VT | 6,483 | 0.24 | 0.46 |
| MD | 18,287 | 0.65 | 0.45 | VA | 43,571 | 0.69 | 0.74 |
| MA | 50,916 | 0.49 | 0.57 | WA | 30,723 | 0.77 | 0.74 |
| MI | 52,957 | 0.82 | 0.85 | WV | 12,270 | 0.61 | 0.89 |
| MN | 25,326 | 0.70 | 0.58 | WI | 36,162 | 0.71 | 0.77 |
| MS | 13,124 | 0.54 | 0.83 | WY | 1,453 | 0.51 | 0.51 |

[1] Students residing in a particular state when admitted to an institution anywhere, either in their home state or another state.

Source: U.S. National Center for Education Statistics, *Digest of Education Statistics*, "Advance Release of Selected 2017 Digest Tables," <http://www.nces.ed.gov/programs/digest/>, accessed May 2018.

## Table 302. Average Total Price of Attendance of Undergraduate Education: 2016

[In dollars. For school year ending in 2016. Excludes students attending more than one institution. Price of attendance includes tuition and fees, books and supplies, room and board, transportation, and personal and other expenses allowed for federal cost of attendance budgets. Based on the 2015–2016 National Postsecondary Student-Aid Study; see source for details. Includes Puerto Rico. See also Appendix III]

| Student characteristic | All institutions [1] | Public 2-year | Public 4-year Non-doctorate granting | Public 4-year Doctorate granting | Private nonprofit 4-year Non-doctorate granting | Private nonprofit 4-year Doctorate granting | Private for-profit |
|---|---|---|---|---|---|---|---|
| Total | 18,288 | 9,400 | 14,806 | 23,238 | 31,343 | 39,225 | 20,963 |
| Age: [2] | | | | | | | |
| 18 years or younger | 23,318 | 10,870 | 17,812 | 26,127 | 42,967 | 51,969 | 23,058 |
| 19 to 23 years | 21,799 | 9,712 | 16,104 | 24,748 | 38,557 | 47,102 | 22,073 |
| 24 to 29 years | 13,313 | 9,112 | 12,961 | 18,441 | 20,061 | 24,912 | 21,333 |
| 30 to 39 years | 11,959 | 8,958 | 12,609 | 17,351 | 15,725 | 17,906 | 20,326 |
| 40 years or older | 10,632 | 8,283 | 11,210 | 16,023 | 14,395 | 16,174 | 18,674 |
| Sex: | | | | | | | |
| Male | 18,286 | 9,121 | 14,820 | 23,150 | 31,825 | 40,930 | 21,701 |
| Female | 18,289 | 9,626 | 14,795 | 23,317 | 30,985 | 37,963 | 20,561 |
| Race: | | | | | | | |
| One race: | | | | | | | |
| White | 19,129 | 9,162 | 15,308 | 23,104 | 33,192 | 39,217 | 20,769 |
| Black or African American | 16,714 | 9,667 | 14,951 | 22,611 | 25,514 | 32,691 | 20,110 |
| Hispanic or Latino [3] | 15,363 | 9,298 | 13,527 | 21,709 | 26,368 | 36,105 | 21,168 |
| Asian | 23,053 | 10,530 | 14,768 | 27,497 | 41,178 | 50,871 | 26,028 |
| American Indian/Alaska Native | 13,666 | 9,594 | 14,686 | 19,702 | 20,831 | (S) | 21,495 |
| Native Hawaiian or other Pacific Islander | 14,473 | 11,084 | 12,090 | 21,204 | (S) | (S) | 23,161 |
| More than one race | 19,522 | 9,938 | 15,767 | 23,965 | 33,818 | 44,272 | 22,175 |
| Attendance pattern: | | | | | | | |
| Full-time, full-year | 30,392 | 16,138 | 22,243 | 28,180 | 43,004 | 51,320 | 32,574 |
| Full-time, part-year | 12,719 | 8,145 | 11,543 | 15,063 | 18,949 | 22,914 | 17,346 |
| Part-time, full-year | 15,529 | 12,349 | 14,559 | 20,732 | 21,545 | 29,291 | 23,784 |
| Part-time, part-year | 6,250 | 4,959 | 6,685 | 10,145 | 9,780 | 10,027 | 12,451 |

S Data do not meet publication standards. [1] Includes public less-than-2-year and private nonprofit less-than-4-year. [2] As of December 31, 2015. [3] Persons of Hispanic origin may be of any race.

Source: U.S. Department of Education, National Center for Education Statistics, National Postsecondary Student Aid Study (NPSAS), "Datalab," <http://nces.ed.gov/datalab/>, accessed May 2018.

# Table 303. Institutions of Higher Education—Average Charges: 1985 to 2018

[In current dollars. Estimated. For the entire academic year ending in year shown. Figures are average charges per full-time equivalent student. Room and board are based on full-time students]

| Academic control and year | Tuition and required fees [1] | | | Board rates [2] | | | Dormitory room charges | | |
|---|---|---|---|---|---|---|---|---|---|
| | All institutions | 2-yr. institutions | 4-yr. institutions | All institutions | 2-yr. institutions | 4-yr. institutions | All institutions | 2-yr. institutions | 4-yr. institutions |
| **Public:** | | | | | | | | | |
| 1985. | 971 | 584 | 1,228 | 1,241 | 1,302 | 1,237 | 1,196 | 921 | 1,217 |
| 1990. | 1,356 | 756 | 1,780 | 1,635 | 1,581 | 1,638 | 1,513 | 962 | 1,557 |
| 1995. | 2,057 | 1,192 | 2,681 | 1,949 | 1,712 | 1,967 | 1,959 | 1,232 | 2,023 |
| 2000. | 2,504 | 1,348 | 3,349 | 2,364 | 1,834 | 2,406 | 2,440 | 1,549 | 2,519 |
| 2005. | 3,629 | 1,849 | 5,027 | 2,931 | 2,353 | 2,981 | 3,304 | 2,174 | 3,418 |
| 2010. | 4,763 | 2,283 | 6,717 | 3,655 | 2,571 | 3,755 | 4,401 | 2,854 | 4,564 |
| 2011. | 5,075 | 2,441 | 7,132 | 3,845 | 2,683 | 3,956 | 4,646 | 2,955 | 4,832 |
| 2012. | 5,563 | 2,651 | 7,713 | 3,946 | 2,866 | 4,042 | 4,849 | 3,100 | 5,031 |
| 2013. | 5,899 | 2,792 | 8,070 | 4,061 | 2,888 | 4,163 | 5,062 | 3,247 | 5,241 |
| 2014. | 6,120 | 2,881 | 8,312 | 4,205 | 2,955 | 4,308 | 5,304 | 3,448 | 5,479 |
| 2015. | 6,370 | 2,955 | 8,543 | 4,313 | 3,072 | 4,412 | 5,504 | 3,559 | 5,677 |
| 2016. | 6,612 | 3,038 | 8,778 | 4,469 | 3,118 | 4,576 | 5,686 | 3,759 | 5,850 |
| 2017. | 6,818 | 3,156 | 8,804 | 4,562 | 3,111 | 4,666 | 5,859 | 3,823 | 6,018 |
| 2018. | 7,054 | 3,243 | 9,037 | 4,683 | 3,204 | 4,786 | 6,060 | 3,834 | 6,227 |
| **Private:** | | | | | | | | | |
| 1985. | 5,315 | 3,485 | 5,556 | 1,462 | 1,294 | 1,469 | 1,426 | 1,424 | 1,426 |
| 1990. | 8,147 | 5,196 | 8,396 | 1,948 | 1,811 | 1,953 | 1,923 | 1,663 | 1,935 |
| 1995. | 11,111 | 6,914 | 11,481 | 2,509 | 2,023 | 2,520 | 2,587 | 2,233 | 2,601 |
| 2000. | 14,100 | 8,225 | 14,616 | 2,877 | 2,753 | 2,879 | 3,236 | 3,067 | 3,242 |
| 2005. | 18,154 | 12,122 | 18,604 | 3,485 | 3,700 | 3,483 | 4,178 | 4,475 | 4,173 |
| 2010. | 21,764 | 14,862 | 22,269 | 4,329 | 4,390 | 4,329 | 5,248 | 5,211 | 5,248 |
| 2011. | 22,042 | 13,687 | 22,677 | 4,430 | 4,475 | 4,430 | 5,403 | 4,939 | 5,410 |
| 2012. | 22,850 | 13,961 | 23,464 | 4,586 | 4,475 | 4,586 | 5,622 | 5,169 | 5,627 |
| 2013. | 23,943 | 14,149 | 24,523 | 4,709 | 3,977 | 4,712 | 5,831 | 5,228 | 5,837 |
| 2014. | 25,110 | 14,170 | 25,707 | 4,864 | 4,211 | 4,866 | 6,021 | 5,489 | 6,026 |
| 2015. | 26,182 | 14,261 | 26,739 | 5,019 | 4,560 | 5,021 | 6,221 | 5,506 | 6,228 |
| 2016. | 27,436 | 14,528 | 27,942 | 5,123 | 4,181 | 5,128 | 6,457 | 5,666 | 6,464 |
| 2017. | 28,945 | 14,589 | 29,476 | 5,268 | 4,350 | 5,273 | 6,710 | 5,949 | 6,717 |
| 2018. | 30,282 | 14,894 | 30,731 | 5,437 | 4,645 | 5,441 | 6,961 | 6,057 | 6,967 |

[1] For public institutions, data are for in-state students. [2] Beginning 1990, rates reflect 20 meals per week, rather than meals served 7 days a week.

Source: U.S. National Center for Education Statistics, *Digest of Education Statistics*, "Advance Release of Selected 2018 Digest Tables," <http://www.nces.ed.gov/programs/digest/>, accessed March 2019.

# Table 304. Average Out-of-Pocket Net Price of Attendance for Undergraduates: 2016

[In dollars. For school year ending in 2016. Excludes students attending more than one institution. Net price of attendance is the price that students pay to receive postsecondary education after taking financial aid into account. Based on net tuition and net price for all students. Based on the 2015–2016 National Postsecondary Student Aid Study; see source for details. Includes Puerto Rico. See also Appendix III]

| Student characteristic | | Type of institution | | | | | |
|---|---|---|---|---|---|---|---|
| | All institutions [1] | Public 2-year | Public 4-year | | Private nonprofit 4-year | | Private for-profit |
| | | | Non-doctorate granting | Doctorate granting | Non-doctorate granting | Doctorate granting | |
| **Total** | **9,842** | **6,695** | **8,630** | **11,995** | **12,744** | **17,442** | **10,487** |
| **Age:** [2] | | | | | | | |
| 18 years or younger | 11,641 | 7,670 | 9,514 | 12,942 | 15,920 | 21,535 | 10,164 |
| 19 to 23 years | 11,517 | 7,137 | 9,102 | 13,153 | 15,320 | 20,940 | 11,623 |
| 24 to 29 years | 7,549 | 6,263 | 8,177 | 8,684 | 9,312 | 11,265 | 10,432 |
| 30 to 39 years | 6,903 | 6,103 | 7,752 | 8,191 | 6,947 | 8,549 | 9,742 |
| 40 years or older | 6,615 | 5,939 | 7,209 | 7,884 | 7,217 | 8,352 | 9,674 |
| **Sex:** | | | | | | | |
| Male | 10,147 | 6,656 | 8,664 | 12,438 | 12,765 | 19,575 | 10,098 |
| Female | 9,594 | 6,726 | 8,604 | 11,595 | 12,729 | 15,863 | 10,699 |
| **Race:** | | | | | | | |
| One race: | | | | | | | |
| White | 10,337 | 6,586 | 8,967 | 12,476 | 13,729 | 17,620 | 10,219 |
| Black or African American | 7,173 | 6,176 | 7,791 | 7,834 | 8,121 | 8,988 | 9,645 |
| Hispanic or Latino [3] | 8,581 | 6,845 | 8,191 | 10,454 | 10,506 | 14,891 | 11,025 |
| Asian | 15,136 | 8,419 | 10,162 | 17,902 | 23,191 | 30,116 | 15,668 |
| American Indian/Alaska Native | 6,958 | 5,933 | 6,251 | 10,375 | [4] 9,889 | (S) | 10,276 |
| Native Hawaiian or other Pacific Islander | 7,830 | 6,843 | 7,151 | 11,871 | (S) | (S) | 10,600 |
| More than one race | 9,684 | 6,398 | 8,125 | 11,007 | 12,407 | 20,539 | 10,160 |
| **Attendance pattern:** | | | | | | | |
| Full-time, full-year | 14,730 | 10,382 | 11,510 | 14,383 | 16,660 | 22,089 | 16,730 |
| Full-time, part-year | 6,974 | 5,572 | 6,929 | 7,166 | 8,253 | 12,191 | 8,987 |
| Part-time, full-year | 9,821 | 9,011 | 9,462 | 11,431 | 10,326 | 13,576 | 10,929 |
| Part-time, part-year | 4,370 | 3,893 | 4,817 | 5,787 | 5,028 | 5,593 | 5,705 |

S Data do not meet publication standards. [1] Includes public less-than-2-year and private nonprofit less-than-4-year. [2] As of December 31, 2015. [3] Persons of Hispanic origin may be of any race. [4] Interpret data with caution. Estimate is unstable because the standard error represents more than 30 percent of the estimate.

Source: U.S. Department of Education, National Center for Education Statistics, National Postsecondary Student Aid Study (NPSAS), "Datalab," <http://nces.ed.gov/datalab/>, accessed May 2018.

# Table 305. Average Cost of Attendance for Undergraduate Education by Control of Institution and Type of Cost: 2016 and 2018

[In constant 2017-2018 dollars, except percent change. Data are preliminary. For school year ending in year shown. Data shown are for full-time, first-time degree/certificate-seeking undergraduates at Title IV institutions. Amounts are institutional averages as reported by the institution, not average amounts paid by students. Based on data from the Integrated Postsecondary Education Data System (IPEDS)]

| Item | 4-year | | | 2-year | | | Less than 2-year | | |
|---|---|---|---|---|---|---|---|---|---|
| | 2016 | 2018 | Percent change | 2016 | 2018 | Percent change | 2016 | 2018 | Percent change |
| Tuition and required fees: | | | | | | | | | |
| Public: | | | | | | | | | |
| In-district [1] | 8,115 | 8,309 | 2.4 | 3,494 | 3,600 | 3.0 | 7,263 | 7,437 | 2.4 |
| In-state | 8,138 | 8,336 | 2.4 | 4,122 | 4,235 | 2.7 | 7,263 | 7,437 | 2.4 |
| Out-of-state | 18,304 | 18,674 | 2.0 | 8,015 | 8,186 | 2.1 | 8,322 | 8,578 | 3.1 |
| Private nonprofit [2] | 27,063 | 27,963 | 3.3 | 14,394 | 14,572 | 1.2 | 14,639 | 14,667 | 0.2 |
| Private for-profit [2] | 16,449 | 16,200 | -1.5 | 15,010 | 14,749 | -1.7 | 16,669 | 17,106 | 2.6 |
| Books and supplies: | | | | | | | | | |
| Public | 1,321 | 1,284 | -2.8 | 1,456 | 1,447 | -0.6 | 1,060 | 1,123 | 5.9 |
| Private nonprofit | 1,225 | 1,192 | -2.7 | 1,423 | 1,380 | -3.0 | 1,607 | 1,683 | 4.7 |
| Private for-profit | 1,414 | 1,293 | -8.5 | 1,659 | 1,489 | -10.3 | 1,141 | 1,055 | -7.5 |
| Room and board: | | | | | | | | | |
| Public: | | | | | | | | | |
| On campus | 9,850 | 10,096 | 2.5 | 6,530 | 6,700 | 2.6 | 4,316 | 6,036 | 39.8 |
| Off campus (not with family) | 9,788 | 9,857 | 0.7 | 8,270 | 8,409 | 1.7 | 8,236 | 8,265 | 0.3 |
| Private nonprofit: | | | | | | | | | |
| On campus | 10,149 | 10,391 | 2.4 | 8,783 | 9,110 | 3.7 | (X) | (X) | (X) |
| Off campus (not with family) | 9,709 | 9,940 | 2.4 | 9,693 | 9,657 | -0.4 | 7,437 | 7,289 | -2.0 |
| Private for-profit: | | | | | | | | | |
| On campus | 10,168 | 10,550 | 3.8 | 9,312 | 9,241 | -0.8 | (X) | (X) | (X) |
| Off campus (not with family) | 8,503 | 8,373 | -1.5 | 8,647 | 8,428 | -2.5 | 9,974 | 9,843 | -1.3 |
| Other expenses: [3] | | | | | | | | | |
| Public: | | | | | | | | | |
| On campus | 3,407 | 3,360 | -1.4 | 3,314 | 3,288 | -0.8 | 1,275 | 1,200 | -5.9 |
| Off campus (not with family) | 3,890 | 3,804 | -2.2 | 4,074 | 4,001 | -1.8 | 4,499 | 4,071 | -9.5 |
| Off campus (with family) | 4,090 | 3,957 | -3.3 | 4,072 | 4,030 | -1.0 | 4,322 | 3,810 | -11.8 |
| Private nonprofit: | | | | | | | | | |
| On campus | 2,927 | 2,887 | -1.3 | 3,513 | 3,405 | -3.1 | (X) | (X) | (X) |
| Off campus (not with family) | 3,662 | 3,597 | -1.8 | 4,540 | 4,846 | 6.7 | 2,689 | 3,021 | 12.4 |
| Off campus (with family) | 3,887 | 3,811 | -1.9 | 4,579 | 4,659 | 1.7 | 1,821 | 2,193 | 20.5 |
| Private for-profit: | | | | | | | | | |
| On campus | 4,148 | 4,494 | 8.3 | 2,875 | 3,654 | 27.1 | (X) | (X) | (X) |
| Off campus (not with family) | 4,551 | 4,371 | -4.0 | 5,243 | 5,243 | – | 5,190 | 4,606 | -11.2 |
| Off campus (with family) | 4,338 | 3,993 | -8.0 | 4,609 | 4,523 | -1.9 | 4,126 | 4,394 | 6.5 |

X Not applicable. – Rounds to zero. [1] For public institutions, "in-district" refers to the charges paid by a student who lives in the locality surrounding the institution, such as county. [2] For private institutions that reported varying tuitions by residency, out-of-state tuition and required fees were used in the averages displayed in this table. [3] Other expenses refers to the amount of money needed by a student to cover expenses such as laundry, transportation, and entertainment.

Source: U.S. National Center for Education Statistics, *Postsecondary Institutions and Cost of Attendance in 2017–18; Degrees and Other Awards Conferred, 2016–17; and 12-Month Enrollment, 2016–17,* November 2018.

# Table 306. Bachelor's Degree Recipients with Loans and Amount Borrowed in Constant (2009) Dollars by Selected Characteristics: 2001 to 2017

[For first-time Bachelor's degree recipients 1 year after they complete their degrees. Estimates cover students who were enrolled in Title IV eligible postsecondary institutions in the 50 states, D.C., and Puerto Rico. Based on Baccalaureate and Beyond Longitudinal Studies]

| Characteristic | Percent with loans | | | Average cumulative amount borrowed for undergraduate education (2009 dollars) | | |
|---|---|---|---|---|---|---|
| | 2001 [2] | 2009 | 2017 | 2001 [2] | 2009 | 2017 |
| **Total loans** | **63.5** | **65.6** | **67.4** | **21,800** | **24,700** | **30,500** |
| Sex: | | | | | | |
| Male | 62.5 | 62.9 | 63.7 | 21,300 | 23,900 | 29,800 |
| Female | 64.3 | 67.6 | 70.3 | 22,100 | 25,200 | 31,000 |
| Race/ethnicity: [1] | | | | | | |
| White | 62.2 | 64.6 | 66.8 | 21,700 | 24,500 | 30,500 |
| Black | 78.8 | 80.3 | 85.9 | 25,200 | 28,700 | 36,900 |
| Hispanic | 66.7 | 67.0 | 69.7 | 19,900 | 22,800 | 26,900 |
| Asian | 55.5 | 53.4 | 45.4 | 19,100 | 21,000 | 24,600 |
| Other | 62.8 | 68.8 | 70.4 | 21,500 | 25,600 | 30,300 |
| Age at receipt of bachelor's degree: | | | | | | |
| 18 to 23 | 60.0 | 61.0 | 62.4 | 20,800 | 23,700 | 27,400 |
| 24 to 29 | 71.3 | 76.8 | 73.4 | 23,100 | 24,900 | 33,100 |
| 30 and older | 65.7 | 72.5 | 82.0 | 23,000 | 28,300 | 37,700 |
| Institution type: | | | | | | |
| 2-year or less: | | | | | | |
| Public 2-year | 67.8 | 67.5 | 71.1 | 21,500 | 24,500 | 30,600 |
| Other 2-year or less | 64.6 | 85.0 | 85.6 | 24,500 | 31,600 | 38,300 |
| 4-year: | | | | | | |
| Public | 59.5 | 62.1 | 64.1 | 20,100 | 21,900 | 28,600 |
| Private nonprofit | 69.0 | 69.4 | 66.4 | 24,100 | 27,900 | 31,200 |
| For-profit | 77.3 | 87.7 | 84.1 | 27,400 | 36,000 | 42,700 |

[1] Asian includes Pacific Islander and Native Hawaiian and other includes American Indian, Alaska Native, and graduates of two or more races or a race not listed. Excludes persons of Hispanic origin, unless specified. [2] Includes loans from family and friends.

Source: National Center for Education Statistics, *Trends in Debt for Bachelor's Degree Recipients a Year After Graduation: 1994, 2001, and 2009,* December 2012; and *Baccalaureate and Beyond (B&B:16/17): A First Look at the Employment and Educational Experiences of College Graduates, 1 Year Later,* June 2019. See also <https://nces.ed.gov/surveys/b&b/>.

# Table 307. SAT Scores and Characteristics of College-Bound Seniors: 2017

[Data reflect 2017 high school graduates who took the new SAT during high school. If a student took the SAT more than once, the most recent score and self-reported SAT questionnaire responses are summarized. Maximum total score is 1600. Data not comparable with prior years due to the new SAT test that was introduced in 2017]

| Characteristic | Test takers | | Mean score | | | Percent with benchmarks met | | | |
|---|---|---|---|---|---|---|---|---|---|
| | Number | Percent | Total | ERW [1] | Math | Both | ERW [1] | Math | None |
| **Total**............................. | **1,715,481** | **100** | **1,060** | **533** | **527** | **46** | **70** | **49** | **27** |
| Took essay [2]..................... | 1,202,640 | 70 | 1,082 | 544 | 538 | 51 | 74 | 53 | 24 |
| Race/ethnicity: | | | | | | | | | |
| White........................ | 760,362 | 44 | 1,118 | 565 | 553 | 59 | 83 | 61 | 15 |
| Black........................ | 225,860 | 13 | 941 | 479 | 462 | 20 | 49 | 22 | 50 |
| Hispanic/Latino............... | 408,067 | 24 | 990 | 500 | 489 | 31 | 58 | 33 | 39 |
| Asian........................ | 158,031 | 9 | 1,181 | 569 | 612 | 70 | 81 | 76 | 12 |
| American Indian/Alaska Native......... | 7,782 | (Z) | 963 | 486 | 477 | 27 | 53 | 29 | 45 |
| Native Hawaiian/Other Pacific Islander....................... | 4,131 | (Z) | 986 | 498 | 488 | 32 | 57 | 34 | 40 |
| Two or more races.................. | 57,049 | 3 | 1,103 | 560 | 544 | 54 | 80 | 56 | 18 |
| Sex: | | | | | | | | | |
| Male........................ | 809,462 | 47 | 1,070 | 532 | 538 | 50 | 69 | 53 | 27 |
| Female....................... | 906,019 | 53 | 1,050 | 534 | 516 | 43 | 71 | 44 | 27 |
| High school grade point average: | | | | | | | | | |
| A+ (97-100)..................... | 104,731 | 6 | 1,254 | 626 | 628 | 84 | 93 | 85 | 5 |
| A (93-96)...................... | 300,326 | 18 | 1,187 | 595 | 592 | 74 | 90 | 75 | 8 |
| A- (90-92)..................... | 296,589 | 17 | 1,122 | 564 | 558 | 61 | 85 | 64 | 13 |
| B (80-89)...................... | 710,579 | 41 | 1,005 | 508 | 497 | 33 | 64 | 36 | 33 |
| C (70-79)...................... | 171,096 | 10 | 899 | 456 | 444 | 13 | 37 | 15 | 60 |
| D, E, or F (below 70)............. | 10,815 | 1 | 850 | 429 | 421 | 8 | 25 | 10 | 72 |
| First language learned: | | | | | | | | | |
| English only.................. | 1,138,783 | 66 | 1,074 | 545 | 530 | 49 | 75 | 51 | 23 |
| English and another language........... | 319,299 | 19 | 1,034 | 516 | 518 | 40 | 63 | 43 | 33 |
| Another language.............. | 203,124 | 12 | 1,049 | 513 | 537 | 44 | 61 | 50 | 32 |
| Highest level of parental education: | | | | | | | | | |
| No High school diploma............ | 137,437 | 8 | 944 | 472 | 472 | 22 | 46 | 26 | 50 |
| High school diploma.............. | 482,194 | 28 | 1,003 | 507 | 497 | 33 | 62 | 36 | 35 |
| Associate degree............... | 134,451 | 8 | 1,036 | 525 | 511 | 40 | 71 | 43 | 27 |
| Bachelor's degree............... | 473,103 | 28 | 1,118 | 562 | 556 | 59 | 83 | 62 | 15 |
| Graduate degree................ | 339,743 | 20 | 1,177 | 591 | 586 | 69 | 88 | 71 | 10 |

Z Represents less than .05%. [1] Evidence-based reading and writing. [2] Reflects test takers who completed the SAT essay at any point, not necessarily on the most recent test administration date.

Source: The College Board, *2017 SAT Suite of Assessments Annual Report*, © 2018. Reproduced with permission. See also <http://www.collegeboard.org>.

# Table 308. Federal Student Financial Assistance: 1995 to 2016

[5,472 represents $5,472,000,000. For award years July 1 of year shown to the following June 30. Funds utilized exclude operating costs, and so forth, and represent funds given to students]

| Type of assistance | 1995 | 2000 | 2005 | 2010 | 2014 | 2015 | 2016 |
|---|---|---|---|---|---|---|---|
| **FUNDS UTILIZED (mil. dol.)** | | | | | | | |
| Federal Pell Grants............................... | 5,472 | 7,956 | 12,693 | 35,677 | 30,626 | 28,559 | 26,894 |
| TEACH Grants [1]............... | (X) | (X) | (X) | 121 | (NA) | (NA) | (NA) |
| Federal Supplemental Educational Opportunity Grant...... | 764 | 908 | 1,084 | 1,013 | 983 | 993 | 987 |
| Federal Work-Study............... | 764 | 939 | 1,050 | 1,198 | 1,100 | 1,096 | 1,086 |
| Federal Perkins Loan............... | 1,020 | 1,144 | 1,594 | 857 | 1,160 | 1,045 | 886 |
| Federal Direct Student Loan (FDSL)....... | 8,296 | 10,348 | 12,930 | 84,704 | (NA) | (NA) | (NA) |
| **NUMBER OF AWARDS (1,000)** | | | | | | | |
| Federal Pell Grants............... | 3,612 | 3,899 | 5,168 | 9,308 | 8,316 | 7,660 | 7,195 |
| TEACH Grants [1]............... | (X) | (X) | (X) | 39 | (NA) | (NA) | (NA) |
| Federal Supplemental Educational Opportunity Grant...... | 1,083 | 1,174 | 1,419 | 1,633 | 1,619 | 1,530 | 1,484 |
| Federal Work-Study............... | 702 | 713 | 711 | 718 | 651 | 635 | 617 |
| Federal Perkins Loan............... | 688 | 639 | 728 | 461 | 528 | 422 | 356 |
| Federal Direct Student Loan (FDSL)....... | 2,339 | 2,739 | 2,971 | 16,647 | (NA) | (NA) | (NA) |
| **AVERAGE AWARD (dol. )** | | | | | | | |
| Federal Pell Grants............... | 1,515 | 2,040 | 2,456 | 3,833 | 3,683 | 3,728 | 3,738 |
| TEACH Grants [1]............... | (X) | (X) | (X) | 3,137 | (NA) | (NA) | (NA) |
| Federal Supplemental Educational Opportunity Grant...... | 706 | 773 | 764 | 620 | 607 | 649 | 665 |
| Federal Work-Study............... | 1,087 | 1,318 | 1,478 | 1,668 | 1,689 | 1,726 | 1,759 |
| Federal Perkins Loan............... | 1,497 | 1,790 | 2,190 | 1,860 | 2,198 | 2,479 | 2,491 |
| Federal Direct Student Loan (FDSL)....... | 3,547 | 3,778 | 4,352 | 5,088 | (NA) | (NA) | (NA) |

X Not applicable. NA Not available. [1] Teacher Education Assistance for College and Higher Education (TEACH) Grant Program.

Source: U.S. Department of Education, Office of Postsecondary Education, "OPE Program Data," <https://www2.ed.gov/finaid/prof/resources/data/ope.html>, accessed August 2019.

# Table 309. Voluntary Financial Support of Higher Education: 1990 to 2018

[9,800 represents $9,800,000,000. For school years ending in years shown. Voluntary support, as defined in Gift Reporting Standards, excludes income from endowment and other invested funds as well as all support received from federal, state, and local governments and their agencies and contract research]

| Item | Unit | 1990 | 2000 | 2005 | 2010 | 2015 | 2016 | 2017 | 2018 |
|---|---|---|---|---|---|---|---|---|---|
| **Estimated support, total** | Mil. dol. | **9,800** | **23,200** | **25,600** | **28,000** | **40,300** | **41,000** | **43,600** | **46,730** |
| SOURCES OF SUPPORT | | | | | | | | | |
| Individuals, total | Mil. dol. | 4,770 | 12,220 | 12,100 | 12,020 | 18,850 | 17,450 | 19,230 | 20,721 |
| Alumni | Mil. dol. | 2,540 | 6,800 | 7,100 | 7,100 | 10,850 | 9,930 | 11,370 | 12,154 |
| Nonalumni individuals | Mil. dol. | 2,230 | 5,420 | 5,000 | 4,920 | 8,000 | 7,520 | 7,860 | 8,567 |
| Organizations, total | Mil. dol. | 5,030 | 10,980 | 13,500 | 15,675 | 21,450 | 23,550 | 24,370 | 26,008 |
| Corporations | Mil. dol. | 2,170 | 4,150 | 4,400 | 4,730 | 5,750 | 6,600 | 6,600 | 6,732 |
| Foundations | Mil. dol. | 1,920 | 5,080 | 7,000 | 8,400 | 11,600 | 12,450 | 13,130 | 14,010 |
| Other organizations | Mil. dol. | 940 | 1,750 | 2,100 | 2,545 | 4,100 | 4,500 | 4,640 | 5,266 |
| PURPOSES OF SUPPORT | | | | | | | | | |
| Current operations, total | Mil. dol. | 5,440 | 11,270 | 14,200 | 17,000 | 24,650 | 25,150 | 25,800 | 27,400 |
| Capital purposes | Mil. dol. | 4,360 | 11,930 | 11,400 | 11,000 | 15,650 | 15,850 | 17,800 | 19,330 |
| Support for institutions reporting support only: | | | | | | | | | |
| Institutions reporting support | Number | 1,056 | 945 | 997 | 996 | 983 | 950 | 933 | 929 |
| Total support reported | Mil. dol. | 8,214 | 19,419 | 20,953 | 23,487 | 35,082 | 33,604 | 35,301 | 37,221 |
| Private 4-year institutions | Mil. dol. | 5,072 | 11,047 | 11,011 | 12,189 | 17,944 | 17,378 | 18,590 | 17,726 |
| Public 4-year institutions | Mil. dol. | 3,056 | 8,254 | 9,780 | 11,114 | 14,876 | 16,039 | 16,421 | 19,251 |
| 2-year colleges | Mil. dol. | 85 | 117 | 163 | 185 | 192 | 187 | 290 | 244 |

Source: Council for Advancement and Support of Education, Washington, DC, *Voluntary Support of Education* ©, annual. See also <http://www.case.org/>.

# Table 310. Undergraduate Students Who Received a Pell Grant by Selected Characteristics: 2004 to 2016

[In units as indicated. For school year ending in year shown. Data shown for students enrolled in Title IV eligible postsecondary institutions in the 50 States, the District of Columbia, and Puerto Rico. Based on the National Postsecondary Student-Aid Study; see source for details]

| Institutional and student characteristics | 2004 | | 2008 | | 2012 [1] | | 2016 | |
|---|---|---|---|---|---|---|---|---|
| | Percent | Average amount (dollars) | Percent | Average amount (dollars) | Percent | Average amount (dollars) | Percent | Average amount (dollars) |
| **Total** | **27.2** | **2,400** | **27.8** | **2,500** | **41.3** | **3,400** | **39.1** | **3,700** |
| AGE | | | | | | | | |
| 23 or younger | 25.5 | 2,600 | 25.6 | 2,700 | 37.8 | 3,600 | (NA) | (NA) |
| 18 or younger | (NA) | (NA) | (NA) | (NA) | (NA) | (NA) | 39.7 | 4,100 |
| 19 to 23 | (NA) | (NA) | (NA) | (NA) | (NA) | (NA) | 36.2 | 4,000 |
| 24 to 29 | 36.6 | 2,400 | 36.1 | 2,400 | 48.9 | 3,200 | 47.3 | 3,500 |
| 30 or older | 24.8 | 2,300 | 26.9 | 2,300 | 43.5 | 3,200 | (NA) | (NA) |
| 30 to 39 | (NA) | (NA) | (NA) | (NA) | (NA) | (NA) | 42.7 | 3,400 |
| 40 or older | (NA) | (NA) | (NA) | (NA) | (NA) | (NA) | 33.2 | 3,300 |
| SEX | | | | | | | | |
| Male | 22.3 | 2,500 | 21.9 | 2,600 | 36.5 | 3,400 | 34.0 | 3,700 |
| Female | 30.8 | 2,400 | 32.2 | 2,500 | 44.8 | 3,400 | 43.1 | 3,700 |
| RACE/ETHNICITY | | | | | | | | |
| White | 20.7 | 2,300 | 20.9 | 2,400 | 33.5 | 3,300 | 31.5 | 3,600 |
| Black | 47.9 | 2,500 | 46.0 | 2,600 | 61.9 | 3,400 | 57.7 | 3,700 |
| Hispanic | 37.5 | 2,600 | 39.8 | 2,700 | 50.0 | 3,500 | 46.9 | 3,900 |
| Asian/Pacific Islander | 21.9 | 2,800 | 23.3 | 2,800 | 33.8 | 3,800 | (NA) | (NA) |
| Asian | (NA) | (NA) | (NA) | (NA) | (NA) | (NA) | 30.9 | 4,200 |
| Pacific Islander | (NA) | (NA) | (NA) | (NA) | (NA) | (NA) | 35.6 | 4,100 |
| American Indian | 31.9 | 2,400 | 36.0 | 2,500 | 54.0 | 3,400 | 51.1 | 3,500 |
| Other or two or more races | 29.8 | 2,500 | 31.1 | 2,600 | 45.2 | 3,500 | 42.2 | 3,800 |
| ATTENDANCE STATUS | | | | | | | | |
| Full-time, full-year | 32.2 | 3,100 | 33.6 | 3,300 | 47.1 | 4,400 | 44.7 | 4,700 |
| Part-time, full-year | (NA) | (NA) | (NA) | (NA) | (NA) | (NA) | 44.0 | 3,500 |
| Part-time or part-year | 23.8 | 1,900 | 24.4 | 1,900 | 37.6 | 2,600 | (NA) | (NA) |
| TYPE OF INSTITUTION | | | | | | | | |
| Public 4-year | 26.4 | 2,600 | 26.2 | 2,800 | 38.0 | 3,800 | 38.2 | 4,100 |
| Private nonprofit 4-year | 27.9 | 2,600 | 26.8 | 2,900 | 35.8 | 3,700 | 36.4 | 4,000 |
| Public 2-year | 22.3 | 2,200 | 21.1 | 2,300 | 37.7 | 3,000 | 33.5 | 3,300 |
| EMPLOYMENT STATUS [2] | | | | | | | | |
| Not employed | 28.8 | 2,600 | 31.0 | 2,700 | 44.7 | 3,500 | 41.7 | 3,900 |
| Employed part-time | 28.1 | 2,500 | 29.2 | 2,600 | 41.4 | 3,500 | 38.3 | 3,800 |
| Employed full-time | 24.5 | 2,300 | 23.4 | 2,200 | 36.2 | 3,000 | 36.4 | 3,300 |

NA Not available. [1] 2012 excludes Puerto Rico. [2] Work-study, assistantships, and traineeships. Full-time work is defined as 35 or more hours per week, and part-time less than 35 hours.

Source: U.S. Department of Education, National Center for Education Statistics, *Trends in Pell Grant Receipt and the Characteristics of Pell Grant Recipients: Selected Years, 1999–2000 to 2011–12*, September 2015; and *Student Financing of Undergraduate Education in 2015-16: Financial Aid by Types and Source*, March 2019. See also <http://nces.ed.gov/surveys/npsas/>.

## Table 311. Undergraduate Student Receipt of Financial Aid by Source and Type of Institution Attended: 2016

[In percent. For school year ending in 2016. Covers students enrolled in Title IV eligible postsecondary institutions in the 50 states, DC, and Puerto Rico. Based on the National Postsecondary Student-Aid Study; see source for details]

| Type of institution | Total [1] | Source of aid | | | | |
|---|---|---|---|---|---|---|
| | | Federal [2] | Non-federal [3] | State [4] | Institu-tional [5] | Employer [6] |
| **Total**........................... | **72.3** | **54.5** | **48.8** | **22.4** | **24.6** | **6.3** |
| Institution attended: | | | | | | |
| Public 2-year................................. | 57.5 | 38.9 | 35.1 | 23.0 | 6.6 | 5.3 |
| Public 4-year................................. | 77.1 | 58.9 | 57.1 | 27.6 | 30.4 | 6.3 |
| Private nonprofit 4-year................. | 86.3 | 63.3 | 71.0 | 18.1 | 57.2 | 9.9 |
| Private for-profit 2-year or more.............. | 87.0 | 76.3 | 43.8 | 10.6 | 28.5 | 6.7 |
| Private for-profit less-than-2-year............ | 82.9 | 77.4 | 24.8 | 6.7 | 9.3 | 1.8 |

[1] Excludes aid from parents, friends, or relatives, and federal tax credits for education. Includes Direct PLUS Loans to parents and aid from Veterans' benefits and job training grants. [2] Includes federal grants, loans, work-study awards, and federal loans including Direct PLUS loans. Includes aid from programs in Title IV of the Higher Education Act, and aid from other federal sources such as Public Health Service Loans, Bureau of Indian Affairs Grants, and District of Columbia Tuition Assistance Grants. Excludes federal veterans' benefits and education tax credits and tax deduction benefits. [3] Includes grants from states, institutions, and private organizations, and loans from private sources. [4] Includes all grants and scholarships, loans, and work-study provided by state governments, including vocational rehabilitation and job training grants funded by the federal Workforce Investment Opportunity Act (WIA). [5] Includes all institution need- and merit-based grants, scholarships, tuition waivers, loans, and work-study assistance. [6] Excludes tuition waivers to students holding assistantships.

Source: U.S. Department of Education, National Center for Education Statistics, *Trends in Undergraduate Nonfederal Grant and Scholarship Aid by Demographic and Enrollment Characteristics, Selected Years: 2003–04 to 2015–16,* August 2019. See also <http://nces.ed.gov/surveys /npsas/>.

## Table 312. Financial Aid for Graduate Students by Degree Type and Source of Aid: 2016

[For school year ending in 2016. Based on the National Postsecondary Student-Aid Study; see source for details. Excludes Puerto Rico]

| Degree type | Percent receiving aid by source | | | | Average aid received (dollars) | Tuition and fees (dollars) | Price of atten-dance [4] (dollars) | Out-of-pocket net price [5] (dollars) |
|---|---|---|---|---|---|---|---|---|
| | Total [1] | Federal [2] | Institu-tional [3] | Em-ployer | | | | |
| **Total**........................... | **72.5** | **42.6** | **30.5** | **12.8** | **22,200** | **15,100** | **29,400** | **13,400** |
| Master's degree program: | | | | | | | | |
| Business administration (M.B.A.)..................... | 71.0 | 35.0 | 24.0 | 21.9 | 18,700 | 14,700 | 27,600 | 14,600 |
| Education (any master's)................ | 66.9 | 44.4 | 20.9 | 13.3 | 14,100 | 8,400 | 19,300 | 9,900 |
| M.A. (except in education)................ | 71.1 | 43.4 | 29.1 | 9.9 | 16,900 | 11,200 | 24,100 | 12,300 |
| M.S. (except in education)................ | 68.7 | 35.4 | 28.5 | 13.4 | 17,100 | 12,200 | 25,300 | 13,800 |
| Other master's [6]........................ | 74.4 | 47.2 | 27.4 | 14.4 | 19,500 | 14,000 | 27,900 | 13,600 |
| Control of institution: | | | | | | | | |
| Public........................ | 66.2 | 34.3 | 26.5 | 14.0 | 16,000 | 9,600 | 22,000 | 11,500 |
| Private nonprofit........................ | 72.9 | 43.3 | 25.5 | 15.4 | 19,300 | 15,400 | 29,200 | 15,300 |
| For-profit........................ | 74.7 | 52.9 | 24.5 | 14.6 | 14,900 | 9,400 | 19,500 | 8,700 |
| Doctor's degree program - research/scholarship: | | | | | | | | |
| Ph.D. (except in education)................ | 84.8 | 23.4 | 66.5 | 6.9 | 20,000 | 19,000 | 36,900 | 13,200 |
| Education (any doctorate)................ | 73.6 | 44.0 | 33.4 | 16.3 | 16,200 | 9,500 | 22,300 | 10,800 |
| Other doctorate........................ | 77.1 | 42.1 | 34.4 | 11.7 | 20,700 | 15,000 | 29,300 | 13,200 |
| Control of institution: | | | | | | | | |
| Public........................ | 80.4 | 18.0 | 64.3 | 8.4 | 21,500 | 12,800 | 28,900 | 11,800 |
| Private nonprofit........................ | 82.8 | 27.2 | 59.3 | 9.9 | 33,700 | 25,000 | 44,800 | 16,900 |
| For-profit........................ | 79.9 | 70.1 | 17.6 | 11.5 | 16,500 | 10,800 | 20,500 | 7,300 |
| Doctor's degree program - professional practice: | | | | | | | | |
| Medicine (M.D. or D.O.)................ | 83.7 | 73.8 | 40.9 | (S) | 53,100 | 37,400 | 65,700 | 21,300 |
| Other health science [7]................ | 86.0 | 75.7 | 34.5 | (S) | 50,600 | 36,100 | 59,700 | 15,900 |
| Law (LL.B. or J.D.)................ | 89.7 | 71.1 | 57.8 | [8] 1.6 | 45,700 | 35,700 | 58,300 | 18,400 |
| Control of institution: | | | | | | | | |
| Public........................ | 83.0 | 70.3 | 47.0 | 2.7 | 41,000 | 28,800 | 51,300 | 17,400 |
| Private nonprofit........................ | 85.6 | 69.1 | 43.8 | [8] 4.1 | 53,100 | 40,400 | 65,600 | 20,200 |
| For-profit........................ | 91.8 | 82.3 | 37.5 | [8] 9.9 | 43,300 | 30,300 | 49,700 | 10,300 |

S Figure does not meet publication standards. [1] Financial aid includes all types of financial aid from any source except parents, friends, or relatives. Types of aid such as employer aid, veterans benefits, and job-training grants are included, but federal tax credits for education are not included. [2] Consists of federal loans, federal grants, and federal work-study. Does not include military benefits. [3] Includes all institution need- and merit-based grants, scholarships, tuition waivers, graduate assistantships, loans, and work-study assistance funded by the institution attended. [4] Price of attendance is the total budget (attendance intensity-adjusted) at the institution for students who attended only one institution during the academic year. The budget includes tuition, fees, housing, meals, books, supplies, transportation, and personal expenses. Institutions typically use this value as a student's budget for the purpose of awarding federal financial aid. [5] Out-of-pocket net price is the total price of attendance minus all financial aid received, including Direct PLUS Loans. The total price of attendance includes tuition and fees, room and board, books and supplies, transportation, and personal or miscellaneous expenses. Federal education tax benefits are not included in the calculation. Averages include students who received no aid. [6] Includes M.S.W. (Master of Social Work), M.P.A. (Master of Public Administration), and M.F.A. (Master of Fine Arts). [7] Includes chiropractic (D.C. or D.C.M.), dentistry (D.D.S. or D.M.D.), optometry (O.D.), pharmacy (D.Pharm.), podiatry (Pod.D. or D.P.M.), and veterinary medicine (D.V.M.). [8] Underlying data has a standard error between 30-50%.

Source: U.S. Department of Education, National Center for Education Statistics, *Profile and Financial Aid Estimates of Graduate Students: 2015–16,* January 2019. See also <http://nces.ed.gov/surveys/npsas/>.

# Table 313. State and Local Financial Support for Higher Education by State: 2018

[10,929.4 represents 10,929,400. For fiscal year ending in 2018. Educational appropriations include State and local appropriations for general operating expenses of public postsecondary education. Includes state-funded financial aid to students attending in-state public institutions. Excludes appropriations for independent institutions, financial aid for students attending independent institutions, research, hospitals, and medical education]

| State | FTE enroll- ment [2] (1,000) | Educational appropri- ations (million dollars) | Educational appropri- ations per FTE enrollment (dollars) | State | FTE enroll- ment [2] (1,000) | Educational appropri- ations (million dollars) | Educational appropri- ations per FTE enrollment (dollars) |
|---|---|---|---|---|---|---|---|
| Total U.S. [1]... | 10,929.4 | 85,828.2 | 7,853 | MO............ | 186.9 | 1,300.2 | 6,958 |
| AL............... | 202.2 | 1,372.5 | 6,788 | MT............ | 37.4 | 236.2 | 6,321 |
| AK............... | 17.5 | 265.4 | 15,151 | NE............ | 76.8 | 744.8 | 9,699 |
| AZ............... | 290.8 | 1,461.4 | 5,025 | NV............ | 70.5 | 570.2 | 8,094 |
| AR............... | 114.7 | 902.7 | 7,873 | NH............ | 37.6 | 105.6 | 2,806 |
| CA............... | 1,557.0 | 13,316.3 | 8,553 | NJ............ | 264.4 | 1,676.3 | 6,339 |
| CO............... | 183.9 | 771.9 | 4,198 | NM............ | 83.7 | 905.8 | 10,816 |
| CT............... | 86.0 | 698.6 | 8,123 | NY............ | 545.1 | 4,740.8 | 8,697 |
| DE. [3]............ | 36.1 | 174.6 | 4,841 | NC............ | 392.1 | 4,089.6 | 10,429 |
| DC [3]............ | 2.9 | 32.5 | 11,092 | ND............ | 35.0 | 289.2 | 8,273 |
| FL............... | 602.7 | 4,284.4 | 7,109 | OH............ | 387.1 | 2,462.4 | 6,361 |
| GA............... | 350.4 | 3,212.2 | 9,166 | OK............ | 131.1 | 839.8 | 6,407 |
| HI............... | 36.0 | 452.5 | 12,560 | OR............ | 142.7 | 890.2 | 6,237 |
| ID............... | 53.6 | 528.0 | 9,857 | PA............ | 344.7 | 1,480.8 | 4,296 |
| IL............... | 311.1 | 4,543.6 | 14,605 | RI............ | 30.3 | 183.7 | 6,061 |
| IN............... | 220.7 | 1,497.2 | 6,785 | SC............ | 164.4 | 995.1 | 6,053 |
| IA............... | 125.3 | 751.0 | 5,992 | SD............ | 32.9 | 209.8 | 6,378 |
| KS............... | 125.0 | 860.3 | 6,885 | TN............ | 185.0 | 1,623.0 | 8,774 |
| KY............... | 144.7 | 1,087.6 | 7,514 | TX............ | 1,052.9 | 8,114.6 | 7,707 |
| LA............... | 161.7 | 950.0 | 5,876 | UT............ | 125.6 | 910.2 | 7,250 |
| ME............... | 33.9 | 263.1 | 7,750 | VT............ | 20.7 | 58.9 | 2,846 |
| MD............... | 231.8 | 1,721.2 | 7,426 | VA............ | 303.3 | 1,643.9 | 5,420 |
| MA............... | 163.7 | 1,236.7 | 7,556 | WA............ | 237.3 | 1,653.0 | 6,966 |
| MI............... | 372.2 | 2,520.6 | 6,773 | WV............ | 68.7 | 324.7 | 4,723 |
| MN............... | 187.7 | 1,456.2 | 7,758 | WI............ | 211.6 | 1,361.7 | 6,435 |
| MS............... | 130.3 | 867.0 | 6,655 | WY............ | 22.7 | 408.6 | 18,001 |

[1] The U.S. total does not include data from the District of Columbia. [2] Full-time equivalent. Includes degree enrollment and enrollment in public postsecondary programs resulting in a certificate or other formal recognition. Includes summer sessions. Excludes medical education enrollments. [3] Adjustment factors to arrive at constant dollar figures include Cost of Living Index (COLI), Enrollment Mix Index (EMI), and Higher Education Cost Adjustment (HECA). The Cost of Living Index (COLI) is not a measure of inflation over time. The District of Columbia is not adjusted for COLI or EMI.

Source: State Higher Education Executive Officers, Boulder, CO, *State Higher Education Finance: FY2018* ©, 2019. See also <http://www.sheeo.org>.

# Table 314. Higher Education Price Indexes: 2010 to 2018 ©

[1983=100. For years ending June 30. The Higher Education Price Index (HEPI), calculated for the July-June academic fiscal year, reflects prices paid by colleges and universities for the following eight cost factors: faculty salaries, administrative salaries, clerical and service employees, fringe benefits, miscellaneous services, supplies and materials, and utilities. Minus sign (-) indicates decrease]

| Item and year | Total | Personnel compensation | | | | | Contracted services, supplies, and equipment | | |
|---|---|---|---|---|---|---|---|---|---|
| | | Faculty salaries [1] | Admin- istrative salaries | Clerical salaries | Service employ- ees salaries | Fringe benefits [1] | Miscel- laneous services | Supplies and materials | Utilities |
| INDEXES | | | | | | | | | |
| 2010..................... | 281.8 | 280.6 | 337.6 | 255.2 | 230.0 | 402.8 | 255.8 | 179.3 | 193.6 |
| 2011..................... | 288.4 | 284.5 | 343.2 | 260.2 | 233.2 | 417.6 | 260.3 | 193.9 | 201.5 |
| 2012..................... | 293.2 | 289.6 | 352.3 | 264.8 | 235.7 | 425.3 | 264.6 | 203.9 | 191.7 |
| 2013..................... | 297.8 | 294.6 | 362.4 | 269.8 | 239.4 | 437.5 | 269.4 | 180.0 | 195.6 |
| 2014..................... | 306.7 | 301.0 | 366.4 | 274.8 | 242.0 | 458.3 | 274.2 | 200.2 | 211.4 |
| 2015..................... | 313.3 | 307.7 | 381.9 | 280.4 | 248.4 | 484.0 | 279.8 | 190.6 | 183.5 |
| 2016..................... | 319.0 | 316.0 | 393.3 | 289.1 | 253.3 | 503.9 | 285.7 | 179.5 | 146.5 |
| 2017..................... | 329.5 | 323.5 | 405.2 | 297.3 | 262.7 | 524.7 | 290.7 | 178.6 | 167.8 |
| 2018..................... | 338.6 | 333.9 | 414.1 | 305.9 | 271.6 | 536.7 | 297.8 | 183.7 | 170.7 |
| ANNUAL PERCENT CHANGE [2] | | | | | | | | | |
| 2010..................... | 0.9 | 1.2 | 2.0 | 1.4 | 1.4 | 2.1 | 1.1 | -1.3 | -9.5 |
| 2011..................... | 2.3 | 1.4 | 1.7 | 2.0 | 1.4 | 3.7 | 1.8 | 8.2 | 4.1 |
| 2012..................... | 1.7 | 1.8 | 2.7 | 1.7 | 1.1 | 1.8 | 1.7 | 5.2 | -4.9 |
| 2013..................... | 1.6 | 1.7 | 2.9 | 1.9 | 1.6 | 2.9 | 1.8 | -11.7 | 2.1 |
| 2014..................... | 3.0 | 2.2 | 1.1 | 1.9 | 1.1 | 4.8 | 1.8 | 11.2 | 8.1 |
| 2015..................... | 2.1 | 2.2 | 4.2 | 2.1 | 2.6 | 5.6 | 2.1 | -4.8 | -13.2 |
| 2016..................... | 1.8 | 2.7 | 3.0 | 3.1 | 2.0 | 4.1 | 2.1 | -5.8 | -20.2 |
| 2017..................... | 3.3 | 2.4 | 3.0 | 2.8 | 3.7 | 4.1 | 1.7 | -0.5 | 14.5 |
| 2018..................... | 2.8 | 3.2 | 2.2 | 2.9 | 3.4 | 2.3 | 2.4 | 2.8 | 1.7 |

[1] Data are derived from faculty compensation data published by the American Association of University Professors (AAUP), which in FY2016 began using a new methodology; data based on the new methodology are not comparable with prior year data. [2] Percent change from the immediate prior year.

Source: The Commonfund Institute, Wilton, CT ©. See also <http://www.commonfund.org>.

# Table 315. Average Salaries for College Faculty Members: 2017 to 2019

[In thousands of dollars (79.1 represents $79,100). For academic year ending in year shown. Figures are for 9 months teaching for full-time faculty members in 2-year and 4-year institutions]

| Type of control and academic rank | 2017 | 2018 | 2019 | Type of control and academic rank | 2017 | 2018 | 2019 |
|---|---|---|---|---|---|---|---|
| **Public: All ranks** | **79.1** | **85.1** | **93.4** | **Private:** [1] **All ranks** | **83.6** | **104.5** | **121.2** |
| Professor | 103.0 | 125.8 | 128.2 | Professor | 105.3 | 167.5 | 172.0 |
| Associate professor | 80.2 | 89.4 | 91.2 | Associate professor | 81.2 | 102.9 | 106.0 |
| Assistant professor | 69.7 | 77.4 | 78.9 | Assistant professor | 70.4 | 89.8 | 91.7 |
| Instructor | 54.3 | 60.2 | 61.0 | Instructor | 57.6 | 74.6 | 77.1 |

[1] Excludes religiously-affiliated colleges and universities.

Source: American Association of University Professors, Washington, DC, *AAUP Annual Report on the Economic Status of the Profession* © 2019. See also <http://www.aaup.org/>.

# Table 316. Employees in Higher Education Institutions by Employment Status, Sex, and Occupation: 2017

[In thousands (3,914.5 represents 3,914,500). As of Fall. Covers institutions that grant associate's or higher degrees and that participate in Title IV federal financial aid programs. Includes institutions with fewer than 15 full-time employees. Detail may not sum to totals because of rounding. Based on Integrated Postsecondary Education Data System data]

| Primary occupation | Full-time and part-time | | | | Full-time | | Part-time | |
|---|---|---|---|---|---|---|---|---|
| | | | Female | | | | | |
| | Total | Male | Total | Percent | Male | Female | Male | Female |
| **All institutions** | **3,914.5** | **1,773.7** | **2,140.9** | **54.7** | **1,129.4** | **1,396.2** | **644.2** | **744.7** |
| Faculty | 1,543.6 | 777.8 | 765.7 | 49.6 | 440.8 | 380.3 | 337.0 | 385.4 |
| Instruction | 1,425.1 | 712.1 | 712.9 | 50.0 | 385.9 | 338.2 | 326.2 | 374.8 |
| Research | 89.4 | 51.7 | 37.8 | 42.2 | 44.3 | 31.4 | 7.4 | 6.4 |
| Public service | 29.1 | 14.0 | 15.0 | 51.8 | 10.6 | 10.8 | 3.4 | 4.2 |
| Graduate assistants [1] | 377.2 | 196.1 | 181.1 | 48.0 | (X) | (X) | 196.1 | 181.1 |
| Librarians, curators, and archivists | 41.5 | 12.4 | 29.1 | 70.2 | 10.8 | 24.7 | 1.6 | 4.4 |
| Student and academic affairs, and other education services | 181.7 | 58.6 | 123.2 | 67.8 | 36.3 | 86.8 | 22.3 | 36.4 |
| Management | 260.0 | 113.6 | 146.4 | 56.3 | 110.9 | 142.3 | 2.7 | 4.2 |
| Business and financial operations | 214.5 | 58.1 | 156.4 | 72.9 | 54.5 | 146.5 | 3.6 | 9.9 |
| Computer, engineering, and science | 235.7 | 142.7 | 93.0 | 39.5 | 134.0 | 82.3 | 8.7 | 10.7 |
| Community, social service, legal, arts, design, entertainment, sports, and media | 184.7 | 82.4 | 102.2 | 55.4 | 65.7 | 84.2 | 16.7 | 18.0 |
| Healthcare practitioners and technicians | 109.9 | 33.0 | 76.9 | 70.0 | 27.8 | 62.9 | 5.2 | 14.0 |
| Service occupations | 241.4 | 139.9 | 101.3 | 42.0 | 117.5 | 82.5 | 22.4 | 18.9 |
| Sales and related occupations | 13.2 | 4.6 | 8.6 | 65.2 | 4.0 | 6.8 | 0.6 | 1.8 |
| Office and administrative support | 418.5 | 71.1 | 347.5 | 83.0 | 49.7 | 289.6 | 21.4 | 57.8 |
| Natural resources, construction, and maintenance | 74.0 | 68.0 | 6.0 | 8.1 | 64.9 | 4.8 | 3.1 | 1.2 |
| Production, transportation, and material moving | 19.0 | 15.5 | 3.5 | 18.2 | 12.8 | 2.5 | 2.8 | 1.0 |

X Not applicable. [1] By definition, all graduate assistants are part time.

Source: U.S. National Center for Education Statistics, *Digest of Education Statistics*, "Advance Release of Selected 2018 Digest Tables," and earlier releases, <http://nces.ed.gov/programs/digest/>, accessed March 2019.

# Table 317. Faculty in Institutions of Higher Education: 1980 to 2017

[In thousands (686 represents 686,000), except percent. As of Fall. Beginning in 1997, data reflect a new classification of institutions; this classification includes some additional, primarily 2-year, colleges and excludes a few institutions that did not award degrees. Includes institutions that were eligible to participate in Title IV federal financial aid programs. Includes schools accredited by the National Association of Trade and Technical Schools. Based on complete census taken every other year; see source]

| Year | Total | Employment status | | Control | | Level | | Percent | | |
|---|---|---|---|---|---|---|---|---|---|---|
| | | Full-time | Part-time | Public | Private | 4-year | 2-year or less | Part-time | Public | 2-year or less |
| 1980 [1] | 686 | 450 | 236 | 495 | 191 | 494 | 192 | 34 | 72 | 28 |
| 1985 [1] | 715 | 459 | 256 | 503 | 212 | 504 | 211 | 36 | 70 | 30 |
| 1991 [2] | 826 | 536 | 291 | 581 | 245 | 591 | 235 | 35 | 70 | 28 |
| 1995 | 932 | 551 | 381 | 657 | 275 | 647 | 285 | 41 | 70 | 31 |
| 2001 | 1,113 | 618 | 495 | 771 | 342 | 764 | 349 | 44 | 69 | 31 |
| 2003 | 1,174 | 630 | 544 | 792 | 382 | 814 | 359 | 46 | 67 | 31 |
| 2005 | 1,290 | 676 | 615 | 841 | 449 | 917 | 373 | 48 | 65 | 29 |
| 2007 [3] | 1,372 | 704 | 668 | 877 | 495 | 992 | 379 | 49 | 64 | 28 |
| 2009 [3] | 1,439 | 729 | 710 | 914 | 525 | 1,038 | 401 | 49 | 63 | 28 |
| 2011 [3] | 1,524 | 762 | 762 | 954 | 570 | 1,116 | 409 | 50 | 63 | 27 |
| 2013 [3] | 1,545 | 791 | 754 | 969 | 577 | 1,152 | 394 | 49 | 63 | 25 |
| 2015 [3] | 1,552 | 807 | 745 | 971 | 581 | 1,181 | 372 | 48 | 63 | 24 |
| 2016 [3] | 1,546 | 814 | 732 | 974 | 572 | 1,197 | 349 | 47 | 63 | 23 |
| 2017 [3] | 1,544 | 821 | 722 | 971 | 572 | 1,207 | 337 | 47 | 63 | 22 |

[1] Estimated on the basis of enrollment. [2] Data beginning 1991 not comparable to prior years. [3] Beginning in 2007, data include institutions with fewer than 15 full-time employees; these institutions did not report staff data prior to 2007.

Source: U.S. National Center for Education Statistics, *Digest of Education Statistics*, "Advance Release of Selected 2018 Digest Tables," <http://www.nces.ed.gov/programs/digest/>, accessed March 2019.

## Table 318. Starting Salaries for New College Graduates by Degree and Field of Study: 2016 to 2018

[In dollars. Data are actual starting base salaries. Data reported by representative colleges throughout the United States]

| Field of study | Bachelors | | | Masters [1] | | | Doctorate | | |
|---|---|---|---|---|---|---|---|---|---|
| | 2016 | 2017 | 2018 | 2016 | 2017 | 2018 | 2016 | 2017 | 2018 |
| Accounting | 53,539 | 52,343 | 51,783 | 57,429 | 54,086 | 54,307 | (NA) | [3] 161,520 | (NA) |
| Business administration/ management [2] | 50,962 | 51,851 | 52,149 | 81,757 | 78,980 | 74,949 | [3] 106,032 | [3] 115,750 | 118,326 |
| Marketing | 44,858 | 45,842 | 45,539 | 67,903 | 72,732 | 56,921 | (NA) | (NA) | (NA) |
| Engineering: | | | | | | | | | |
| Civil | 57,091 | 57,495 | 57,965 | 62,636 | 62,172 | 66,012 | 66,684 | [3] 71,477 | 67,097 |
| Chemical | 68,239 | 66,490 | 67,913 | 65,074 | 74,517 | 71,970 | 87,879 | 89,710 | 87,292 |
| Computer | 74,439 | 76,070 | 76,881 | 81,905 | 102,171 | 99,805 | [3] 105,447 | [3] 105,412 | 105,009 |
| Electrical | 70,950 | 72,930 | 72,619 | 91,693 | 93,543 | 86,398 | 104,212 | 118,871 | 105,975 |
| Mechanical | 64,241 | 63,070 | 64,829 | 74,321 | 78,886 | 79,659 | 84,768 | 88,135 | 84,889 |
| Nuclear [4] | [3] 60,121 | [3] 59,122 | [3] 68,741 | [3] 86,594 | [3] 78,100 | [3] 63,800 | [3] 96,720 | [3] 107,769 | [3] 89,389 |
| Petroleum | 78,541 | 73,084 | 78,801 | [3] 97,985 | (NA) | [3] 82,411 | [3] 110,000 | (NA) | (NA) |
| Chemistry | 43,622 | 42,355 | 42,403 | [3] 54,775 | 58,220 | [3] 68,191 | 74,243 | 68,089 | 69,098 |
| Mathematics | 59,759 | 59,846 | 59,681 | 53,466 | 56,861 | 50,195 | 69,551 | 74,091 | 65,979 |
| Physics | 56,178 | 52,313 | 57,082 | [3] 55,100 | 71,069 | [3] 65,499 | 71,319 | 72,768 | 67,643 |
| Humanities | 42,902 | 42,763 | 48,961 | 72,271 | 58,033 | 56,017 | [3] 72,795 | 63,746 | 69,774 |
| Social sciences [5] | 46,749 | 46,707 | 46,797 | 53,760 | 57,849 | 57,418 | 74,456 | 84,889 | 84,980 |
| Computer science | 78,199 | 78,803 | 77,564 | 76,934 | 95,603 | 96,852 | 118,457 | 114,373 | 125,168 |

NA Not available. [1] Candidates with 1 year or less of full-time nonmilitary employment. [2] For master's degree, starting salaries are after nontechnical undergraduate degree. [3] Fewer than 50 salaries reported. [4] Includes engineering physics. [5] Excludes economics.

Source: National Association of Colleges and Employers, Bethlehem, PA ©. Reprinted with permission from Fall 2010-2014, Spring 2015-2018, and Summer 2019 Salary Surveys. All rights reserved.

## Table 319. Degrees Earned by Level and Sex: 1960 to 2017

[In thousands (477 represents 477,000), except percent. Based on data from the Integrated Postsecondary Education Data System (IPEDS)]

| Year ending | All degrees | | Associate's | | Bachelor's | | Master's | | Doctoral [1] | |
|---|---|---|---|---|---|---|---|---|---|---|
| | Total | Percent male | Male | Female | Male | Female | Male | Female | Male | Female |
| 1960 | 477 | 65.8 | (NA) | (NA) | [2] 254 | [2] 138 | 51 | 24 | 9 | 1 |
| 1970 | 1,271 | 59.2 | 117 | 89 | 451 | 341 | 131 | 83 | 54 | 6 |
| 1975 | 1,666 | 56.0 | 191 | 169 | 505 | 418 | 166 | 131 | 71 | 14 |
| 1980 | 1,732 | 51.1 | 184 | 217 | 474 | 456 | 157 | 148 | 70 | 26 |
| 1985 | 1,828 | 49.3 | 203 | 252 | 483 | 497 | 149 | 144 | 66 | 35 |
| 1986 | 1,830 | 49.0 | 196 | 250 | 486 | 502 | 149 | 146 | 65 | 35 |
| 1987 | 1,823 | 48.4 | 191 | 245 | 481 | 510 | 147 | 149 | 63 | 36 |
| 1988 | 1,835 | 48.0 | 190 | 245 | 477 | 518 | 150 | 156 | 63 | 36 |
| 1989 | 1,873 | 47.3 | 186 | 250 | 483 | 535 | 154 | 163 | 63 | 38 |
| 1990 | 1,940 | 46.6 | 191 | 264 | 492 | 560 | 158 | 172 | 64 | 40 |
| 1991 | 2,025 | 45.8 | 199 | 283 | 504 | 590 | 161 | 182 | 64 | 41 |
| 1992 | 2,108 | 45.6 | 207 | 297 | 521 | 616 | 166 | 192 | 67 | 43 |
| 1993 | 2,167 | 45.5 | 212 | 303 | 533 | 632 | 173 | 202 | 67 | 45 |
| 1994 | 2,206 | 45.1 | 215 | 315 | 532 | 637 | 181 | 212 | 67 | 46 |
| 1995 | 2,218 | 44.9 | 218 | 321 | 526 | 634 | 183 | 221 | 67 | 47 |
| 1996 | 2,248 | 44.2 | 220 | 336 | 522 | 642 | 183 | 229 | 67 | 48 |
| 1997 | 2,288 | 43.6 | 224 | 347 | 521 | 652 | 185 | 240 | 68 | 50 |
| 1998 | 2,298 | 43.2 | 218 | 341 | 520 | 664 | 189 | 247 | 67 | 52 |
| 1999 | 2,330 | 42.7 | 221 | 344 | 520 | 682 | 190 | 256 | 65 | 51 |
| 2000 | 2,385 | 42.6 | 225 | 340 | 530 | 708 | 196 | 267 | 65 | 54 |
| 2001 | 2,416 | 42.4 | 232 | 347 | 532 | 712 | 198 | 276 | 64 | 55 |
| 2002 | 2,494 | 42.2 | 238 | 357 | 550 | 742 | 203 | 285 | 63 | 57 |
| 2003 | 2,623 | 42.1 | 253 | 381 | 573 | 776 | 215 | 304 | 63 | 59 |
| 2004 | 2,755 | 41.8 | 260 | 405 | 595 | 804 | 233 | 331 | 64 | 62 |
| 2005 | 2,850 | 41.6 | 268 | 429 | 613 | 826 | 237 | 343 | 67 | 67 |
| 2006 | 2,936 | 41.3 | 270 | 443 | 631 | 855 | 242 | 358 | 69 | 69 |
| 2007 | 3,008 | 41.2 | 275 | 453 | 650 | 875 | 242 | 368 | 71 | 73 |
| 2008 | 3,094 | 41.2 | 283 | 467 | 668 | 896 | 250 | 381 | 73 | 76 |
| 2009 | 3,205 | 41.3 | 298 | 489 | 685 | 916 | 264 | 399 | 76 | 79 |
| 2010 | 3,351 | 41.2 | 323 | 526 | 707 | 943 | 275 | 418 | 77 | 82 |
| 2011 | 3,554 | 41.3 | 361 | 582 | 734 | 982 | 292 | 439 | 80 | 84 |
| 2012 | 3,740 | 41.3 | 393 | 628 | 766 | 1,026 | 302 | 453 | 83 | 88 |
| 2013 | 3,775 | 41.4 | 389 | 618 | 787 | 1,053 | 302 | 450 | 85 | 90 |
| 2014 | 3,807 | 41.5 | 391 | 614 | 802 | 1,068 | 303 | 452 | 86 | 92 |
| 2015 | 3,847 | 41.6 | 397 | 618 | 813 | 1,082 | 307 | 452 | 85 | 94 |
| 2016 | 3,893 | 41.6 | 392 | 616 | 822 | 1,099 | 321 | 465 | 84 | 94 |
| 2017 | 3,948 | 41.6 | 394 | 611 | 836 | 1,120 | 327 | 478 | 85 | 97 |

NA Not available. [1] Includes Ph.D., Ed.D., and comparable degrees at the doctoral level. Includes most degrees formerly classified as first-professional, such as M.D., D.D.S., and law degrees. [2] Includes some degrees classified as master's or doctor's degrees in later years.

Source: U.S. National Center for Education Statistics, *Digest of Education Statistics*, "Advance Release of Selected 2018 Digest Tables," <https://nces.ed.gov/programs/digest/index.asp>, accessed January 2019.

# Table 320. Degrees Earned by Level and Race/Ethnicity: 1990 to 2017

[For school year ending in year shown. Based on Integrated Postsecondary Education Data System surveys; see Appendix III]

| Level of degree and race/ethnicity | Total | | | | | Percent distribution | | |
|---|---|---|---|---|---|---|---|---|
| | 1990 | 2000 [1] | 2010 | 2016 | 2017 | 2000 [1] | 2010 | 2017 |
| **Associate's degrees, total**............ | **455,102** | **564,933** | **848,856** | **1,008,228** | **1,005,649** | **100.0** | **100.0** | **100.0** |
| White, non-Hispanic................... | 376,816 | 408,822 | 552,376 | 566,622 | 551,033 | 72.4 | 65.1 | 54.8 |
| Black, non-Hispanic................... | 34,326 | 60,208 | 113,867 | 134,012 | 129,874 | 10.7 | 13.4 | 12.9 |
| Hispanic................................. | 21,504 | 51,563 | 112,403 | 196,044 | 209,138 | 9.1 | 13.2 | 20.8 |
| Asian or Pacific Islander.............. | 13,066 | 27,778 | 44,026 | 53,753 | 55,801 | 4.9 | 5.2 | 5.5 |
| American Indian/Alaska Native....... | 3,430 | 6,474 | 10,101 | 9,490 | 9,268 | 1.2 | 1.2 | 0.9 |
| Two or more races..................... | (NA) | (NA) | (NA) | 28,933 | 29,630 | (NA) | (NA) | 2.9 |
| Nonresident alien...................... | 5,960 | 10,088 | 16,083 | 19,374 | 20,905 | 1.8 | 1.9 | 2.1 |
| **Bachelor's degrees, total**............ | **1,051,344** | **1,237,875** | **1,649,919** | **1,920,750** | **1,956,032** | **100.0** | **100.0** | **100.0** |
| White, non-Hispanic................... | 887,151 | 929,102 | 1,167,322 | 1,197,323 | 1,196,007 | 75.1 | 70.8 | 61.1 |
| Black, non-Hispanic................... | 61,046 | 108,018 | 164,789 | 194,408 | 196,300 | 8.7 | 10.0 | 10.0 |
| Hispanic................................. | 32,829 | 75,063 | 140,426 | 235,190 | 252,166 | 6.1 | 8.5 | 12.9 |
| Asian or Pacific Islander.............. | 39,230 | 77,909 | 117,391 | 138,257 | 144,078 | 6.3 | 7.1 | 7.4 |
| American Indian/Alaska Native....... | 4,390 | 8,717 | 12,405 | 9,735 | 9,582 | 0.7 | 0.8 | 0.5 |
| Two or more races..................... | (NA) | (NA) | (NA) | 61,584 | 66,526 | (NA) | (NA) | 3.4 |
| Nonresident alien...................... | 26,698 | 39,066 | 47,586 | 84,253 | 91,373 | 3.2 | 2.9 | 4.7 |
| **Master's degrees, total** [2]............ | **(NA)** | **463,185** | **693,313** | **785,757** | **804,684** | **100.0** | **100.0** | **100.0** |
| White, non-Hispanic................... | (NA) | 324,990 | 445,158 | 431,885 | 433,625 | 70.2 | 64.2 | 53.9 |
| Black, non-Hispanic................... | (NA) | 36,606 | 76,472 | 88,786 | 89,577 | 7.9 | 11.0 | 11.1 |
| Hispanic................................. | (NA) | 19,379 | 43,603 | 63,060 | 67,166 | 4.2 | 6.3 | 8.3 |
| Asian or Pacific Islander.............. | (NA) | 23,523 | 42,520 | 45,921 | 47,841 | 5.1 | 6.1 | 5.9 |
| American Indian/Alaska Native....... | (NA) | 2,263 | 3,965 | 3,538 | 3,396 | 0.5 | 0.6 | 0.4 |
| Two or more races..................... | (NA) | (NA) | (NA) | 16,589 | 17,668 | (NA) | (NA) | 2.2 |
| Nonresident alien...................... | (NA) | 56,424 | 81,595 | 135,978 | 145,411 | 12.2 | 11.8 | 18.1 |
| **Doctoral degrees, total** [2, 3]........ | **(NA)** | **118,736** | **158,590** | **178,134** | **181,352** | **100.0** | **100.0** | **100.0** |
| White, non-Hispanic................... | (NA) | 82,984 | 104,419 | 107,235 | 107,445 | 69.9 | 65.8 | 59.2 |
| Black, non-Hispanic................... | (NA) | 7,078 | 10,413 | 13,377 | 14,067 | 6.0 | 6.6 | 7.8 |
| Hispanic................................. | (NA) | 5,042 | 8,085 | 11,781 | 12,493 | 4.2 | 5.1 | 6.9 |
| Asian or Pacific Islander.............. | (NA) | 10,682 | 16,560 | 19,614 | 20,344 | 9.0 | 10.4 | 11.2 |
| American Indian/Alaska Native....... | (NA) | 708 | 952 | 811 | 746 | 0.6 | 0.6 | 0.4 |
| Two or more races..................... | (NA) | (NA) | (NA) | 3,782 | 4,166 | (NA) | (NA) | 2.3 |
| Nonresident alien...................... | (NA) | 12,242 | 18,161 | 21,534 | 22,091 | 10.3 | 11.5 | 12.2 |
| **First-professional degrees, total**.... | **70,988** | **80,057** | **94,103** | **95,140** | **94,760** | **100.0** | **100.0** | **100.0** |
| White, non-Hispanic................... | 60,487 | 59,637 | 66,172 | 60,826 | 59,667 | 74.5 | 70.3 | 63.0 |
| Black, non-Hispanic................... | 3,409 | 5,555 | 6,850 | 7,275 | 7,253 | 6.9 | 7.3 | 7.7 |
| Hispanic................................. | 2,425 | 3,865 | 5,430 | 7,115 | 7,426 | 4.8 | 5.8 | 7.8 |
| Asian or Pacific Islander.............. | 3,362 | 8,584 | 12,691 | 14,338 | 14,618 | 10.7 | 13.5 | 15.4 |
| American Indian/Alaska Native....... | 257 | 564 | 665 | 482 | 407 | 0.7 | 0.7 | 0.4 |
| Two or more races..................... | (NA) | (NA) | (NA) | 2,372 | 2,466 | (NA) | (NA) | 2.6 |
| Nonresident alien...................... | 1,048 | 1,852 | 2,295 | 2,732 | 2,923 | 2.3 | 2.4 | 3.1 |

NA Not available. [1] Beginning 2000, data reflect the new classification of institutions. See headnote, Table 289. [2] Data prior to 2009 have been revised. Revisions for 1990 not available. [3] Includes Ph.D., Ed.D., and comparable degrees at the doctoral level, as well as M.D., D.D.S., and law degrees that were formerly classified as first-professional degrees.

Source: U.S. National Center for Education Statistics, *Digest of Education Statistics*, "Advance Release of Selected 2018 Digest Tables," <http://www.nces.ed.gov/programs/digest/>, accessed May 2019.

# Table 321. Bachelor's Degrees Earned by Field: 1980 to 2017

[For school year ending in year shown. The new Classification of Instructional Programs was introduced in 2009-2010. Data for previous years has been reclassified where necessary to conform to the new classifications. Based on data from the Integrated Postsecondary Education Data System (IPEDS)]

| Field of study | 1980 | 1990 | 2000 | 2010 | 2016 | 2017 |
|---|---|---|---|---|---|---|
| **Total** [1]........................................ | **929,417** | **1,051,344** | **1,237,875** | **1,649,919** | **1,920,750** | **1,956,032** |
| Agriculture and natural resources.......... | 22,802 | 12,900 | 24,238 | 26,343 | 36,995 | 37,719 |
| Architecture and related services........... | 9,132 | 9,364 | 8,462 | 10,051 | 8,825 | 8,573 |
| Area, ethnic, cultural, and gender studies.. | 2,840 | 4,447 | 6,212 | 8,620 | 7,840 | 7,720 |
| Biological and biomedical sciences......... | 46,190 | 37,204 | 63,005 | 86,391 | 113,794 | 116,759 |
| Business....................................... | 186,264 | 248,568 | 256,070 | 358,119 | 371,690 | 381,353 |
| Communication, journalism, and related programs [2]... | 28,616 | 51,572 | 57,058 | 86,062 | 97,375 | 98,393 |
| Computer and information sciences........ | 11,154 | 27,347 | 37,788 | 39,593 | 64,402 | 71,420 |
| Education...................................... | 118,038 | 105,112 | 108,034 | 101,287 | 87,221 | 85,118 |
| Engineering and engineering technologies.. | 69,387 | 82,480 | 73,419 | 88,735 | 123,948 | 133,761 |
| English language and literature/letters..... | 32,187 | 46,803 | 50,106 | 53,229 | 42,797 | 41,317 |
| Family and consumer sciences/human sciences.. | 18,411 | 13,514 | 16,321 | 21,832 | 25,389 | 25,077 |
| Foreign languages, literatures, and linguistics.. | 12,480 | 13,133 | 15,886 | 21,507 | 18,436 | 17,642 |
| Health professions and related clinical sciences.. | 63,848 | 58,983 | 80,863 | 129,623 | 228,907 | 238,014 |
| Homeland security, law enforcement, and firefighting.. | 15,015 | 15,354 | 24,877 | 43,613 | 61,159 | 59,581 |
| Legal professions and studies.............. | 683 | 1,632 | 1,969 | 3,886 | 4,243 | 4,272 |
| Liberal arts and sciences, general studies, and humanities.. | 23,196 | 27,985 | 36,104 | 46,963 | 43,669 | 43,841 |
| Mathematics and statistics................. | 11,378 | 14,276 | 11,418 | 16,029 | 22,778 | 24,073 |
| Multi/interdisciplinary studies.............. | 11,457 | 16,557 | 28,561 | 37,717 | 48,833 | 49,658 |
| Parks, recreation, leisure, and fitness studies.. | 5,753 | 4,582 | 17,571 | 33,332 | 50,912 | 53,264 |
| Philosophy and religious studies........... | 7,069 | 7,034 | 8,535 | 12,503 | 10,155 | 9,712 |
| Physical sciences and science technologies.. | 23,407 | 16,056 | 18,331 | 23,381 | 30,483 | 31,268 |
| Psychology.................................... | 42,093 | 53,952 | 74,194 | 97,215 | 117,447 | 116,861 |
| Public administration and social services.. | 16,644 | 13,908 | 20,185 | 25,421 | 34,433 | 35,464 |
| Social sciences and history................. | 103,662 | 118,083 | 127,101 | 172,782 | 161,211 | 159,099 |
| Theology and religious vocations.......... | 6,170 | 5,185 | 6,789 | 8,719 | 9,804 | 9,491 |
| Transportation and materials moving....... | 213 | 2,387 | 3,395 | 4,998 | 4,531 | 4,710 |
| Visual and performing arts.................. | 40,892 | 39,934 | 58,791 | 91,798 | 92,979 | 91,262 |

[1] Includes other fields of study, not shown separately. [2] Includes communications technologies.

Source: U.S. National Center for Education Statistics, *Digest of Education Statistics*, "Advance Release of Selected 2018 Digest Tables," <https://nces.ed.gov/programs/digest/index.asp>, accessed January 2019.

# Table 322. Associate's Degrees by Field of Study and Sex: 2010 to 2017

[For school year ending in year shown. Covers associate's degrees conferred by degree-granting institutions. Based on Integrated Postsecondary Education Data System (IPEDS) survey; see Appendix III]

| Field of study | 2010 | 2013 | 2014 | 2015 | 2016 | 2017 Total | 2017 Male | 2017 Female |
|---|---|---|---|---|---|---|---|---|
| **Total** [1] | **848,856** | **1,007,427** | **1,005,155** | **1,014,341** | **1,008,228** | **1,005,649** | **394,159** | **611,490** |
| Agriculture and natural resources, total | 5,852 | 6,826 | 7,057 | 7,693 | 7,858 | 8,207 | 5,039 | 3,168 |
| Architecture and related services | 553 | 468 | 425 | 491 | 478 | 503 | 332 | 171 |
| Area, ethnic, cultural, gender, and group studies | 199 | 271 | 363 | 382 | 419 | 420 | 181 | 239 |
| Biological and biomedical sciences | 2,664 | 4,185 | 4,557 | 4,883 | 5,266 | 5,550 | 1,749 | 3,801 |
| Business [1] | 133,265 | 134,114 | 129,957 | 132,374 | 128,259 | 122,234 | 48,404 | 73,830 |
| Business, management, marketing, and support services [1] | 116,798 | 114,842 | 113,056 | 113,681 | 110,036 | 108,353 | 43,299 | 65,054 |
| Accounting and related services | 17,925 | 18,061 | 17,400 | 16,080 | 14,790 | 13,751 | 4,027 | 9,724 |
| Business administration, management, and operations | 46,086 | 49,816 | 50,121 | 52,668 | 52,758 | 53,927 | 24,416 | 29,511 |
| Personal and culinary services | 16,467 | 19,272 | 16,901 | 18,693 | 18,223 | 13,881 | 5,105 | 8,776 |
| Communication, journalism, and related programs | 2,841 | 4,299 | 4,970 | 6,034 | 6,759 | 7,377 | 3,202 | 4,175 |
| Communications technologies | 4,418 | 5,028 | 4,713 | 4,628 | 4,569 | 4,305 | 2,840 | 1,465 |
| Computer and information sciences and support services | 32,351 | 38,954 | 37,646 | 36,420 | 30,571 | 31,162 | 24,816 | 6,346 |
| Construction trades | 4,684 | 5,038 | 4,837 | 4,643 | 4,699 | 5,308 | 4,956 | 352 |
| Education | 17,346 | 18,744 | 17,605 | 17,178 | 17,032 | 16,593 | 1,882 | 14,711 |
| Engineering | 2,508 | 3,732 | 4,306 | 4,875 | 5,278 | 5,915 | 4,995 | 920 |
| Engineering technologies and engineering-related fields | 31,883 | 33,752 | 31,792 | 31,958 | 27,243 | 27,024 | 23,278 | 3,746 |
| English language and literature/letters | 1,658 | 2,089 | 2,082 | 2,324 | 2,551 | 2,870 | 953 | 1,917 |
| Family and consumer sciences | 9,515 | 8,996 | 8,669 | 8,750 | 8,930 | 8,881 | 360 | 8,521 |
| Foreign languages, literatures, and linguistics | 1,683 | 2,131 | 2,284 | 2,102 | 2,208 | 2,363 | 597 | 1,766 |
| Health professions and related programs | 177,321 | 214,040 | 208,885 | 200,018 | 191,442 | 186,299 | 29,779 | 156,520 |
| Dental assisting | 7,063 | 7,823 | 7,988 | 7,762 | 7,584 | 7,397 | 399 | 6,998 |
| Emergency medical technician (EMT paramedic) | 2,413 | 3,520 | 3,521 | 3,456 | 3,380 | 3,452 | 2,318 | 1,134 |
| Clinical/medical lab science | 2,621 | 3,387 | 3,517 | 3,143 | 3,186 | 3,062 | 769 | 2,293 |
| Medical and other health assisting | 29,776 | 41,921 | 39,126 | 36,813 | 34,749 | 32,285 | 4,826 | 27,459 |
| Nursing and patient care assistant | 1 | 35 | 38 | 50 | 52 | 56 | 2 | 54 |
| Practical nursing | 1,973 | 2,361 | 2,230 | 1,858 | 1,404 | 1,420 | 125 | 1,295 |
| Nursing, R.N. and other | 81,281 | 86,380 | 86,435 | 82,953 | 78,577 | 77,073 | 10,895 | 66,178 |
| Health sciences, other | 52,193 | 68,613 | 66,030 | 63,983 | 62,510 | 61,554 | 10,445 | 51,109 |
| Homeland security, law enforcement, and firefighting | 37,154 | 48,460 | 45,771 | 43,041 | 39,930 | 37,361 | 21,010 | 16,351 |
| Legal professions and studies | 9,999 | 11,862 | 10,502 | 9,095 | 8,017 | 6,900 | 1,034 | 5,866 |
| Liberal arts and sciences, general studies, and humanities | 284,954 | 344,171 | 353,946 | 367,852 | 381,202 | 386,658 | 147,523 | 239,135 |
| Library science | 112 | 181 | 194 | 170 | 146 | 158 | 20 | 138 |
| Mathematics and statistics | 1,051 | 1,801 | 2,148 | 2,697 | 3,027 | 3,454 | 2,370 | 1,084 |
| Mechanic and repair technologies/technicians | 16,326 | 20,487 | 20,100 | 19,984 | 20,543 | 20,827 | 19,401 | 1,426 |
| Military technologies and applied sciences | 668 | 1,002 | 1,084 | 1,229 | 1,047 | 1,093 | 879 | 214 |
| Multi/interdisciplinary studies | 17,279 | 27,407 | 28,167 | 29,139 | 30,482 | 30,780 | 12,873 | 17,907 |
| Parks, recreation, leisure, and fitness studies | 2,006 | 3,455 | 4,383 | 4,669 | 4,771 | 5,037 | 2,955 | 2,082 |
| Philosophy and religious studies | 256 | 326 | 435 | 697 | 814 | 1,002 | 574 | 428 |
| Physical sciences and science technologies | 4,141 | 6,376 | 6,916 | 7,568 | 8,484 | 9,223 | 5,457 | 3,766 |
| Precision production | 2,794 | 3,345 | 3,903 | 4,382 | 4,794 | 5,272 | 4,905 | 367 |
| Psychology | 6,582 | 6,122 | 7,604 | 8,780 | 10,603 | 11,286 | 2,673 | 8,613 |
| Public administration and social service professions | 4,522 | 8,788 | 8,914 | 8,436 | 7,988 | 7,591 | 1,052 | 6,539 |
| Social sciences and history | 10,649 | 15,668 | 16,554 | 17,916 | 20,056 | 21,392 | 7,981 | 13,411 |
| Theology and religious vocations | 613 | 881 | 944 | 1,135 | 1,089 | 1,619 | 992 | 627 |
| Transportation and materials moving | 1,444 | 2,119 | 2,102 | 1,810 | 1,497 | 1,547 | 1,338 | 209 |
| Visual and performing arts | 19,565 | 22,309 | 21,340 | 20,988 | 20,176 | 19,438 | 7,759 | 11,679 |

[1] Includes other fields of study, not shown separately.

Source: U.S. National Center for Education Statistics, *Digest of Education Statistics*, "Advance Release of Selected 2018 Digest Tables," <https://nces.ed.gov/programs/digest/index.asp>, accessed January 2019.

## Table 323. Education Certificates Awarded by Field of Study and Sex: 2016

[For school year ending in 2016. Covers certificates below the associate's degree level based on postsecondary curriculums of less than 4 years in degree- and nondegree-granting institutions of higher education. Based on Integrated Postsecondary Education Data System (IPEDS) survey; see Appendix III]

| Field of study | Less than 1-year awards | | | 1- to less than 4-year awards | | |
|---|---|---|---|---|---|---|
| | Total | Male | Female | Total | Male | Female |
| **Total**........................................ | **485,034** | **226,021** | **259,013** | **454,209** | **170,647** | **283,562** |
| Agriculture and natural resources, total............................ | 4,137 | 2,597 | 1,540 | 2,359 | 1,498 | 861 |
| Agriculture, agriculture operations, and related sciences.......... | 3,312 | 2,047 | 1,265 | 2,208 | 1,396 | 812 |
| Natural resources and conservation................................ | 825 | 550 | 275 | 151 | 102 | 49 |
| Architecture and related services.................................... | 231 | 141 | 90 | 106 | 73 | 33 |
| Area, ethnic, cultural, gender, and group studies.................. | 487 | 136 | 351 | 127 | 23 | 104 |
| Biological and biomedical sciences.................................. | 913 | 260 | 653 | 224 | 59 | 165 |
| Business, management, marketing, and support services........... | 60,367 | 21,930 | 38,437 | 22,065 | 6,231 | 15,834 |
| Accounting and related services.................................. | 10,623 | 3,141 | 7,482 | 5,347 | 1,267 | 4,080 |
| Business/commerce, general....................................... | 3,246 | 1,447 | 1,799 | 1,683 | 865 | 818 |
| Business administration, management, and operations............. | 17,025 | 7,029 | 9,996 | 3,969 | 1,371 | 2,598 |
| Management information systems and services................... | 645 | 428 | 217 | 143 | 84 | 59 |
| Business operations support and assistant services.............. | 9,258 | 2,305 | 6,953 | 5,967 | 822 | 5,145 |
| Business and management, other.................................. | 19,570 | 7,580 | 11,990 | 4,956 | 1,822 | 3,134 |
| Communication, journalism, and related programs.................. | 2,545 | 1,262 | 1,283 | 1,472 | 851 | 621 |
| Communications technologies........................................ | 2,522 | 1,515 | 1,007 | 3,164 | 2,394 | 770 |
| Computer and information sciences and support services.......... | 27,081 | 19,606 | 7,475 | 9,057 | 6,975 | 2,082 |
| Construction trades.................................................. | 12,569 | 11,811 | 758 | 12,575 | 12,018 | 557 |
| Education............................................................ | 6,638 | 686 | 5,952 | 3,756 | 427 | 3,329 |
| Engineering......................................................... | 792 | 683 | 109 | 314 | 261 | 53 |
| Engineering technologies and engineering-related fields............ | 21,073 | 18,052 | 3,021 | 13,728 | 12,258 | 1,470 |
| English language and literature/letters............................. | 1,943 | 700 | 1,243 | 545 | 227 | 318 |
| Family and consumer sciences...................................... | 15,634 | 1,202 | 14,432 | 3,574 | 151 | 3,423 |
| Foreign languages, literatures, and linguistics..................... | 1,385 | 294 | 1,091 | 651 | 126 | 525 |
| Health professions and related programs............................ | 151,038 | 29,594 | 121,444 | 164,627 | 21,867 | 142,760 |
| Dental assisting.................................................... | 6,874 | 581 | 6,293 | 13,433 | 1,005 | 12,428 |
| Emergency medical technician (EMT paramedic)................... | 17,040 | 10,943 | 6,097 | 5,339 | 3,888 | 1,451 |
| Clinical/medical lab science....................................... | 10,276 | 1,411 | 8,865 | 1,899 | 476 | 1,423 |
| Medical assisting................................................... | 10,943 | 924 | 10,019 | 49,453 | 4,192 | 45,261 |
| Pharmacy assisting................................................ | 3,880 | 848 | 3,032 | 6,003 | 1,219 | 4,784 |
| Other allied health assisting...................................... | 6,339 | 1,998 | 4,341 | 2,699 | 311 | 2,388 |
| Nursing and patient care assistant................................ | 40,932 | 5,158 | 35,774 | 1,345 | 158 | 1,187 |
| Practical nursing................................................... | 4,342 | 546 | 3,796 | 42,664 | 4,324 | 38,340 |
| Nursing, R.N. and other........................................... | 1,471 | 156 | 1,315 | 3,126 | 435 | 2,691 |
| Health sciences, other............................................. | 48,941 | 7,029 | 41,912 | 38,666 | 5,859 | 32,807 |
| Homeland security, law enforcement, and firefighting.............. | 29,501 | 21,453 | 8,048 | 7,882 | 5,096 | 2,786 |
| Criminal justice and corrections................................... | 21,813 | 14,705 | 7,108 | 6,549 | 3,945 | 2,604 |
| Fire control and safety............................................. | 6,807 | 6,184 | 623 | 1,153 | 1,039 | 114 |
| Homeland security and related protective services, other.......... | 881 | 564 | 317 | 180 | 112 | 68 |
| Legal professions and studies....................................... | 2,012 | 379 | 1,633 | 2,809 | 452 | 2,357 |
| Library science...................................................... | 168 | 30 | 138 | 51 | 5 | 46 |
| Mathematics and statistics.......................................... | 156 | 128 | 28 | 32 | 21 | 11 |
| Mechanic and repair technologies/technicians...................... | 35,411 | 33,258 | 2,153 | 46,991 | 44,927 | 2,064 |
| Military technologies and applied sciences.......................... | 13 | 11 | 2 | 10 | 8 | 2 |
| Multi/interdisciplinary studies....................................... | 1,897 | 704 | 1,193 | 1,238 | 645 | 593 |
| Parks, recreation, leisure, and fitness studies..................... | 1,901 | 942 | 959 | 707 | 418 | 289 |
| Personal and culinary services...................................... | 38,020 | 5,167 | 32,853 | 75,849 | 11,180 | 64,669 |
| Philosophy and religious studies.................................... | 58 | 26 | 32 | 34 | 18 | 16 |
| Physical sciences and science technologies......................... | 1,600 | 808 | 792 | 1,072 | 722 | 350 |
| Physical sciences.................................................. | 192 | 125 | 67 | 25 | 18 | 7 |
| Science technologies/technicians.................................. | 1,408 | 683 | 725 | 1,047 | 704 | 343 |
| Precision production.................................................. | 27,735 | 25,976 | 1,759 | 18,228 | 17,211 | 1,017 |
| Psychology........................................................... | 65 | 9 | 56 | 67 | 16 | 51 |
| Public administration and social service professions................ | 1,888 | 454 | 1,434 | 832 | 129 | 703 |
| Social sciences and history.......................................... | 1,154 | 658 | 496 | 320 | 171 | 149 |
| Social sciences..................................................... | 1,135 | 650 | 485 | 310 | 164 | 146 |
| History.............................................................. | 19 | 8 | 11 | 10 | 7 | 3 |
| Theology and religious vocations.................................... | 291 | 139 | 152 | 876 | 345 | 531 |
| Transportation and materials moving................................ | 23,543 | 21,262 | 2,281 | 1,003 | 957 | 46 |
| Visual and performing arts.......................................... | 6,495 | 2,774 | 3,721 | 4,637 | 2,057 | 2,580 |
| Fine and studio arts............................................... | 919 | 307 | 612 | 256 | 73 | 183 |
| Music and dance.................................................. | 260 | 172 | 88 | 459 | 286 | 173 |
| Visual and performing arts, other................................. | 5,316 | 2,295 | 3,021 | 3,922 | 1,698 | 2,224 |

Source: U.S. National Center for Education Statistics, *2017 Digest of Education Statistics*, December 2018. See also <http://www.nces.ed.gov/programs/digest/>.

## Table 324. Master's and Doctoral Degrees Earned by Field: 1971 to 2017

[For school years ending in years shown. The new Classification of Instructional Programs was introduced in 2009-2010. Data for previous years has been reclassified where necessary to conform to the new classifications. Based on data from the Integrated Postsecondary Education Data System (IPEDS)]

| Field of study | 1971 | 1981 | 1991 | 2001 | 2011 | 2017 |
|---|---|---|---|---|---|---|
| **MASTER'S DEGREES** | | | | | | |
| **Total** [1] | **235,564** | **302,637** | **342,863** | **473,502** | **730,922** | **804,684** |
| Agriculture and natural resources | 2,457 | 4,003 | 3,295 | 4,272 | 5,766 | 6,844 |
| Architecture and related services | 1,705 | 3,153 | 3,490 | 4,302 | 7,788 | 7,911 |
| Area, ethnic, cultural, gender, and group studies | 1,032 | 802 | 1,233 | 1,555 | 1,913 | 1,717 |
| Biological and biomedical sciences | 5,625 | 5,766 | 4,834 | 7,017 | 11,324 | 16,284 |
| Business | 26,490 | 57,888 | 78,255 | 115,602 | 187,178 | 187,404 |
| Communication, journalism, and related programs | 1,770 | 2,896 | 4,123 | 5,218 | 8,302 | 10,128 |
| Communications technologies | 86 | 209 | 204 | 427 | 502 | 539 |
| Computer and information sciences | 1,588 | 4,218 | 9,324 | 16,911 | 19,516 | 46,555 |
| Education | 87,666 | 96,713 | 87,352 | 127,829 | 185,127 | 145,680 |
| Engineering | 16,813 | 16,893 | 24,454 | 25,174 | 38,664 | 52,841 |
| Engineering technologies | 134 | 323 | 996 | 2,013 | 4,515 | 7,403 |
| English language and literature/letters | 10,441 | 5,742 | 6,784 | 6,763 | 9,475 | 8,247 |
| Family and consumer sciences/human sciences | 1,452 | 2,570 | 1,541 | 1,838 | 2,918 | 3,295 |
| Foreign languages, literatures, and linguistics | 5,480 | 2,934 | 3,049 | 3,035 | 3,727 | 3,274 |
| Health professions and related programs | 5,330 | 16,176 | 21,354 | 43,623 | 75,571 | 119,273 |
| Homeland security, law enforcement, and firefighting | 194 | 1,538 | 1,108 | 2,514 | 7,433 | 10,210 |
| Legal professions and studies | 955 | 1,832 | 2,057 | 3,829 | 6,475 | 8,674 |
| Liberal arts and sciences, general studies, and humanities | 885 | 2,375 | 2,213 | 3,193 | 3,997 | 2,485 |
| Library science | 7,001 | 4,859 | 4,763 | 4,727 | 7,729 | 4,843 |
| Mathematics and statistics | 5,191 | 2,567 | 3,549 | 3,209 | 5,866 | 9,086 |
| Parks, recreation, leisure, and fitness studies | 218 | 643 | 483 | 2,354 | 6,546 | 8,655 |
| Philosophy and religious studies | 1,326 | 1,231 | 1,471 | 1,386 | 1,839 | 1,705 |
| Physical sciences and science technologies | 6,336 | 5,246 | 5,281 | 5,134 | 6,386 | 7,143 |
| Psychology | 5,717 | 10,223 | 11,349 | 16,539 | 25,062 | 27,542 |
| Public administration and social services | 7,785 | 17,803 | 17,905 | 25,268 | 38,614 | 45,393 |
| Social sciences and history | 16,539 | 11,945 | 12,233 | 13,791 | 21,085 | 20,015 |
| Theology and religious vocations | 7,747 | 11,061 | 10,498 | 9,876 | 13,170 | 13,654 |
| Transportation and materials moving | – | – | 406 | 756 | 1,390 | 839 |
| Visual and performing arts | 6,675 | 8,629 | 8,657 | 11,404 | 16,277 | 17,523 |
| **DOCTORAL DEGREES** | | | | | | |
| **Total** [1] | **64,998** | **98,016** | **105,547** | **119,585** | **163,827** | **181,352** |
| Agriculture and natural resources | 1,086 | 1,067 | 1,185 | 1,127 | 1,246 | 1,561 |
| Architecture and related services | 36 | 93 | 135 | 153 | 205 | 291 |
| Area, ethnic, cultural, gender, and group studies | 143 | 161 | 159 | 216 | 278 | 349 |
| Biological and biomedical sciences | 3,603 | 3,640 | 4,152 | 5,225 | 7,693 | 8,087 |
| Business | 774 | 808 | 1,185 | 1,180 | 2,286 | 3,329 |
| Communication, journalism, and related programs | 145 | 171 | 259 | 368 | 577 | 615 |
| Computer and information sciences | 128 | 252 | 676 | 768 | 1,588 | 1,982 |
| Education | 6,041 | 7,279 | 6,189 | 6,284 | 9,642 | 12,687 |
| Engineering | 3,687 | 2,598 | 5,316 | 5,485 | 8,369 | 10,371 |
| English language and literature/letters | 1,554 | 1,040 | 1,056 | 1,330 | 1,344 | 1,347 |
| Foreign languages, literatures, and linguistics | 1,084 | 931 | 871 | 1,078 | 1,158 | 1,168 |
| Health professions and related programs | 15,988 | 29,595 | 29,842 | 39,019 | 60,221 | 77,693 |
| Legal professions and studies | 17,441 | 36,391 | 38,035 | 38,190 | 44,853 | 35,123 |
| Mathematics and statistics | 1,199 | 728 | 978 | 997 | 1,586 | 1,925 |
| Philosophy and religious studies | 555 | 411 | 464 | 600 | 804 | 741 |
| Physical sciences and science technologies | 4,324 | 3,105 | 4,248 | 3,968 | 5,295 | 6,027 |
| Psychology | 2,144 | 3,576 | 3,932 | 5,091 | 5,851 | 6,702 |
| Public administration and social services | 174 | 362 | 430 | 574 | 851 | 1,116 |
| Social sciences and history | 3,660 | 3,122 | 3,012 | 3,930 | 4,390 | 4,706 |
| Theology and religious vocations | 312 | 1,273 | 1,076 | 1,461 | 2,374 | 1,791 |
| Visual and performing arts | 621 | 654 | 838 | 1,167 | 1,646 | 1,774 |

– Represents zero. [1] Includes other fields of study, not shown separately.

Source: U.S. National Center for Education Statistics, *Digest of Education Statistics*, "Advance Release of Selected 2018 Digest Tables," <http://www.nces.ed.gov/programs/digest/>, accessed January 2019.

## Table 325. First Professional Degrees Earned in Selected Professions: 1970 to 2017

[First professional degrees include degrees which require at least 6 years of college work for completion (including at least 2 years of preprofessional training). Based on Integrated Postsecondary Education Data System surveys; see Appendix III]

| Type of degree and sex of recipient | 1970 | 1980 | 1990 | 1995 | 2000 | 2005 | 2010 | 2015 | 2016 | 2017 |
|---|---|---|---|---|---|---|---|---|---|---|
| Medicine (M.D.): | | | | | | | | | | |
| Institutions conferring degrees | 86 | 112 | 124 | 119 | 118 | 120 | 120 | 127 | 128 | 131 |
| Degrees conferred, total | 8,314 | 14,902 | 15,075 | 15,537 | 15,286 | 15,461 | 16,356 | 18,302 | 18,409 | 18,698 |
| Percent to women | 8.4 | 23.4 | 34.2 | 38.8 | 42.7 | 47.3 | 48.2 | 47.8 | 46.5 | 47.4 |
| Dentistry (D.D.S. or D.M.D.): | | | | | | | | | | |
| Institutions conferring degrees | 48 | 58 | 57 | 53 | 54 | 53 | 55 | 60 | 61 | 63 |
| Degrees conferred, total | 3,718 | 5,258 | 4,100 | 3,897 | 4,250 | 4,454 | 5,062 | 5,816 | 5,951 | 6,388 |
| Percent to women | 0.9 | 13.3 | 30.9 | 36.4 | 40.1 | 43.8 | 45.8 | 47.9 | 49.1 | 47.9 |
| Law (LL.B. or J.D.): | | | | | | | | | | |
| Institutions conferring degrees | 145 | 179 | 182 | 183 | 190 | 198 | 205 | 212 | 214 | 214 |
| Degrees conferred, total | 14,916 | 35,647 | 36,485 | 39,349 | 38,152 | 43,423 | 44,346 | 40,024 | 36,798 | 34,894 |
| Percent to women | 5.4 | 30.2 | 42.2 | 42.6 | 45.9 | 48.7 | 47.3 | 48.0 | 48.5 | 49.6 |
| Theological (B.D., M.Div., M.H.L.): | | | | | | | | | | |
| Institutions conferring degrees | (NA) | (NA) | (NA) | 192 | 198 | (NA) | (NA) | (NA) | (NA) | (NA) |
| Degrees conferred, total | 5,298 | 7,115 | 5,851 | 5,978 | 6,129 | 5,533 | 5,825 | 6,300 | 5,950 | 5,801 |
| Percent to women | 2.3 | 13.8 | 24.8 | 25.7 | 29.2 | 35.6 | (NA) | 31.4 | 32.4 | 31.8 |

NA Not available.

Source: U.S. National Center for Education Statistics, *Digest of Education Statistics*, "Advance Release of Selected 2018 Digest Tables," <http://www.nces.ed.gov/programs/digest/>, accessed May 2019.

## Table 326. Graduate and Undergraduate Students Taking Online Classes and Degree Programs by Selected Characteristics: 2016

[In thousands (19,308 represents 19,308,000), except percent. For school year ending in 2016]

| Student characteristics | Undergraduate students | | | | Graduate students | | | |
|---|---|---|---|---|---|---|---|---|
| | Number of students | | Percent of students taking— | | Number of students | | Percent of students taking— | |
| | Total enroll-ment | Students taking any online classes | Any online classes | Entire degree program is online [1] | Total enroll-ment | Students taking any online classes | Any online classes | Entire degree program is online [1] |
| **Total**........................ | **19,308** | **8,319** | **43.1** | **10.8** | **3,547** | **1,617** | **45.6** | **27.3** |
| Sex: | | | | | | | | |
| Male........................ | 8,406 | 3,340 | 39.7 | 9.2 | 1,446 | 591 | 40.8 | 24.6 |
| Female...................... | 10,903 | 4,979 | 45.7 | 12.1 | 2,101 | 1,026 | 48.9 | 29.3 |
| Race/ethnicity: | | | | | | | | |
| White........................ | 10,276 | 4,671 | 45.5 | 11.1 | 2,105 | 942 | 44.8 | 26.0 |
| Black........................ | 3,006 | 1,278 | 42.5 | 14.9 | 504 | 315 | 62.5 | 45.3 |
| Hispanic.................... | 3,723 | 1,431 | 38.4 | 7.7 | 326 | 161 | 49.5 | 31.2 |
| Asian....................... | 1,399 | 544 | 38.9 | 7.8 | 500 | 138 | 27.5 | 10.8 |
| Pacific Islander........... | 83 | 35 | 42.2 | 12.0 | 8 | 5 | 64.1 | [2] 33.4 |
| American Indian or | | | | | | | | |
| Alaska Native.......... | 160 | 76 | 47.5 | 12.2 | 17 | 8 | 43.9 | 33.1 |
| Two or more races....... | 661 | 283 | 42.8 | 10.4 | 88 | 49 | 55.6 | 33.8 |
| Age: | | | | | | | | |
| 15 to 23 years old....... | 11,368 | 4,157 | 36.6 | 3.5 | 466 | 130 | 27.9 | 8.0 |
| 24 to 29 years old....... | 3,536 | 1,793 | 50.7 | 17.5 | 1,387 | 525 | 37.8 | 16.8 |
| 30 years old and over.... | 4,404 | 2,369 | 53.8 | 24.9 | 1,695 | 962 | 56.8 | 41.6 |
| Attendance status: | | | | | | | | |
| Exclusively full-time...... | 7,239 | 2,789 | 38.5 | 6.0 | 1,279 | 408 | 31.9 | 15.2 |
| Exclusively part-time..... | 5,059 | 2,398 | 47.4 | 14.7 | 850 | 453 | 53.3 | 36.7 |
| Mixed full-time and | | | | | | | | |
| part-time................. | 7,010 | 3,131 | 44.7 | 13.2 | 1,418 | 756 | 53.3 | 33.1 |
| Field of study: | | | | | | | | |
| Business/management.... | 2,973 | 1,525 | 51.3 | 17.0 | 592 | 320 | 54.1 | 36.7 |
| Education................... | 841 | 384 | 45.7 | 9.7 | 605 | 352 | 58.2 | 34.3 |
| Engineering................ | 1,140 | 380 | 33.3 | 5.1 | (NA) | (NA) | (NA) | (NA) |
| Health...................... | 3,438 | 1,547 | 45.0 | 13.3 | 694 | 325 | 46.8 | 26.6 |
| Humanities................. | 3,083 | 1,274 | 41.3 | 7.8 | 281 | 99 | 35.3 | 18.2 |
| Law......................... | (NA) | (NA) | (NA) | (NA) | 132 | 21 | 15.9 | 8.0 |
| Social/behavioral | | | | | | | | |
| sciences................. | 1,323 | 556 | 42.0 | 9.1 | 245 | 112 | 45.7 | 29.0 |
| Vocational/technical...... | 594 | 188 | 31.7 | 6.0 | (NA) | (NA) | (NA) | (NA) |

NA Not available. [1] Excludes students not in a degree or certificate program. [2] Interpret data with caution. The coefficient of variation (CV) for this estimate is between 30 and 50 percent.

Source: U.S. National Center for Education Statistics, *Digest of Education Statistics*, "Advance Release of Selected 2018 Digest Tables," <http://www.nces.ed.gov/programs/digest/>, accessed May 2019.

## Table 327. College and University Libraries by Selected Characteristics: 2009 to 2014

[As of Fall of year shown. In units as indicated (176,736 represents 176,736,000). Data shown for degree-granting postsecondary institution libraries. FTE is full-time equivalent. Based on data from the Integrated Postsecondary Education Data System (IPEDS)]

| Collections, staff, and operating expenditures | Unit | 2009 | 2011 | 2014 | | | |
|---|---|---|---|---|---|---|---|
| | | | | Total | Public | Private non-profit | Private for-profit |
| Number of libraries........................ | Number | 3,689 | 3,793 | 4,266 | 1,581 | 1,652 | 1,033 |
| Percent of institutions with libraries........ | Percent | 82.1 | 80.6 | 92.2 | 97.5 | 98.8 | 77.4 |
| Circulation transactions.................... | 1,000 | 176,736 | 154,409 | 939,702 | 456,462 | 226,604 | 256,636 |
| Physical transaction.................... | 1,000 | (NA) | (NA) | 82,583 | 48,955 | 32,160 | 1,468 |
| Electronic transaction.................. | 1,000 | (NA) | (NA) | 857,119 | 407,507 | 194,444 | 255,168 |
| Circulation transactions per FTE student..... | Number | 11 | 10 | 62 | 43 | 67 | 205 |
| ENROLLMENT | | | | | | | |
| Total enrollment........................... | 1,000 | 20,428 | 20,994 | 20,207 | 14,655 | 3,996 | 1,556 |
| Full-time-equivalent (FTE) enrollment....... | 1,000 | 15,496 | 15,886 | 15,262 | 10,625 | 3,388 | 1,249 |
| COLLECTIONS | | | | | | | |
| Total number of physical and electronic materials........ | 1,000 | (NA) | (NA) | 2,154,718 | 1,198,015 | 766,348 | 190,354 |
| Number of books......................... | 1,000 | (NA) | (NA) | 1,732,362 | 936,396 | 648,676 | 147,290 |
| Number of media......................... | 1,000 | (NA) | (NA) | 417,457 | 260,924 | 116,271 | 40,263 |
| Number of databases..................... | 1,000 | (NA) | (NA) | 4,899 | 696 | 1,402 | 2,801 |
| LIBRARY STAFF (FTE) | | | | | | | |
| Total staff in regular positions [1]............. | Number | 66,562 | 65,242 | (NA) | (NA) | (NA) | (NA) |
| Librarians and professional staff.......... | Number | 34,147 | 34,423 | (NA) | (NA) | (NA) | (NA) |
| Other paid staff.......................... | Number | 32,415 | 30,819 | (NA) | (NA) | (NA) | (NA) |
| Student assistants....................... | Number | 22,382 | 20,509 | (NA) | (NA) | (NA) | (NA) |
| OPERATING EXPENDITURES (CURRENT DOLLARS) | | | | | | | |
| Total operating expenditures [2,3]............ | Mil. dol. | 6,829 | 7,008 | 8,029 | 4,721 | 3,219 | 89 |
| Salaries and wages [4]..................... | Mil. dol. | 3,402 | 3,444 | 3,453 | 2,126 | 1,291 | 37 |
| Fringe benefits........................... | Mil. dol. | (NA) | (NA) | 756 | 460 | 291 | 4 |
| Computer hardware/software............. | Mil. dol. | 143 | 144 | (NA) | (NA) | (NA) | (NA) |
| Information resources.................... | Mil. dol. | 2,680 | 2,790 | 3,040 | 1,737 | 1,264 | 39 |
| Operating expenditures per FTE student..... | Dollars | 441 | 441 | 526 | 444 | 950 | 71 |

NA Not available. [1] Excludes student assistants. [2] Excludes capital outlay. Expenditure data are reported only by degree-granting institutions with total expenditures over $100,000. [3] Includes other expenditures not shown separately. [4] Includes student hourly wages.

Source: U.S. National Center for Education Statistics, *Digest of Education Statistics*, "Advance Release of Selected 2017 Digest Tables," and earlier releases, <http://www.nces.ed.gov/programs/digest/>, accessed March 2018.

# Table 328. College Campus Crime—Incidents and Rates by Type of Crime and Institution: 2001 to 2016

[For school year ending in year shown. Data are from Department of Education's Campus Safety and Security Reporting System. Data are for degree-granting institutions, which are institutions that grant associate's or higher degrees and participate in Title IV federal financial aid programs. Some institutions that report data as mandated by the Clery Act, specifically, non-degree-granting institutions and institutions outside of the 50 states and the District of Columbia, are excluded from this table. Crimes, arrests, and referrals include incidents involving students, staff, and on-campus guests. Excludes off-campus crimes and arrests even if they involve college students or staff]

| Control and level of institution and type of crime | Total, in residence halls and other locations | | | | | | 2016 | | |
|---|---|---|---|---|---|---|---|---|---|
| | | | | | | | | In residence | At other |
| | 2001 | 2006 | 2010 | 2013 | 2014 | 2015 | Total | halls | locations |
| **NUMBER OF INCIDENTS** | | | | | | | | | |
| **Selected crimes against persons and property** | **41,596** | **44,492** | **32,097** | **27,236** | **26,818** | **27,638** | **28,406** | **14,606** | **13,800** |
| Murder [1] | 17 | 8 | 15 | 23 | 11 | 28 | 15 | 3 | 12 |
| Negligent manslaughter [2] | 2 | – | 1 | – | 2 | 2 | 2 | – | 2 |
| Sex offenses, forcible [3] | 2,201 | 2,670 | 2,927 | 4,977 | 6,751 | 8,031 | 8,906 | 6,588 | 2,318 |
| Sex offenses, nonforcible [4] | 461 | 43 | 33 | 45 | 53 | 63 | 60 | 27 | 33 |
| Robbery | 1,663 | 1,547 | 1,392 | 1,317 | 1,041 | 1,048 | 1,106 | 208 | 898 |
| Aggravated assault | 2,947 | 2,817 | 2,221 | 2,044 | 2,048 | 2,265 | 2,205 | 726 | 1,479 |
| Burglary | 26,904 | 31,260 | 21,335 | 15,232 | 13,419 | 12,386 | 12,015 | 6,716 | 5,299 |
| Motor vehicle theft | 6,221 | 5,231 | 3,441 | 2,971 | 2,890 | 3,236 | 3,499 | 9 | 3,490 |
| Arson | 1,180 | 916 | 732 | 627 | 603 | 579 | 598 | 329 | 269 |
| **Arrests [5]** | **40,348** | **50,187** | **51,519** | **46,975** | **44,531** | **40,348** | **39,049** | **19,321** | **19,728** |
| Illegal weapons possession | 1,073 | 1,316 | 1,112 | 1,018 | 990 | 1,186 | 1,211 | 311 | 900 |
| Drug law violations | 11,854 | 13,952 | 18,589 | 19,799 | 19,172 | 19,466 | 19,266 | 9,421 | 9,845 |
| Liquor law violations | 27,421 | 34,919 | 31,818 | 26,158 | 24,369 | 19,696 | 18,572 | 9,589 | 8,983 |
| **Referrals for disciplinary action [5]** | **155,201** | **218,040** | **230,269** | **244,985** | **253,315** | **242,185** | **231,568** | **212,497** | **19,071** |
| Illegal weapons possession | 1,277 | 1,871 | 1,314 | 1,410 | 1,425 | 1,434 | 1,426 | 971 | 455 |
| Drug law violations | 23,900 | 27,251 | 42,022 | 53,439 | 56,575 | 56,125 | 56,481 | 48,888 | 7,593 |
| Liquor law violations | 130,024 | 188,918 | 186,933 | 190,136 | 195,315 | 184,626 | 173,661 | 162,638 | 11,023 |
| **INCIDENTS PER 10,000 FTE STUDENTS [6, 7]** | | | | | | | | | |
| **Selected crimes against persons and property** | **35.6** | **33.4** | **20.9** | **18.5** | **18.1** | **18.7** | **19.2** | **24.8** | **5.9** |
| By type of crime: | | | | | | | | | |
| Murder [1] | (Z) | (Z) | (Z) | (Z) | (Z) | (Z) | (Z) | (Z) | (Z) |
| Negligent manslaughter [2] | (Z) | (Z) | (Z) | (Z) | (Z) | (Z) | (Z) | (Z) | (Z) |
| Sex offenses, forcible [3] | 1.9 | 2.0 | 1.9 | 3.4 | 4.5 | 5.4 | 6.0 | 8.2 | 0.8 |
| Sex offenses, nonforcible [4] | 0.4 | (Z) | (Z) | (Z) | (Z) | (Z) | (Z) | (Z) | (Z) |
| Robbery | 1.4 | 1.2 | 0.9 | 0.9 | 0.7 | 0.7 | 0.7 | 0.9 | 0.4 |
| Aggravated assault | 2.5 | 2.1 | 1.4 | 1.4 | 1.4 | 1.5 | 1.5 | 1.8 | 0.8 |
| Burglary | 23.0 | 23.4 | 13.9 | 10.3 | 9.0 | 8.4 | 8.1 | 10.7 | 2.1 |
| Motor vehicle theft | 5.3 | 3.9 | 2.2 | 2.0 | 1.9 | 2.2 | 2.4 | 2.7 | 1.6 |
| Arson | 1.0 | 0.7 | 0.5 | 0.4 | 0.4 | 0.4 | 0.4 | 0.5 | 0.1 |
| By type of institution: | | | | | | | | | |
| Public 4-year | 36.2 | 35.5 | 23.4 | 19.6 | 19.5 | 19.6 | 19.7 | 21.3 | 6.4 |
| Nonprofit 4-year | 57.4 | 57.7 | 35.2 | 31.2 | 30.2 | 31.2 | 32.7 | 35.2 | 7.8 |
| For-profit 4-year | 19.1 | 9.6 | 6.5 | 8.6 | 5.8 | 4.6 | 4.4 | 13.4 | 1.9 |
| Public 2-year | 19.9 | 15.4 | 10.2 | 7.9 | 7.7 | 8.4 | 7.9 | 14.3 | 6.2 |
| Nonprofit 2-year | 64.0 | 81.9 | 48.4 | 27.0 | 27.4 | 16.2 | 21.7 | 48.9 | 12.6 |
| For profit-2-year | 25.4 | 18.2 | 8.2 | 7.1 | 6.1 | 6.3 | 6.5 | 14.2 | 6.1 |
| **Arrests [5]** | **34.6** | **37.6** | **33.5** | **31.8** | **30.0** | **27.3** | **26.4** | **36.2** | **3.4** |
| Illegal weapons possession | 0.9 | 1.0 | 0.7 | 0.7 | 0.7 | 0.8 | 0.8 | 0.9 | 0.5 |
| Drug law violations | 10.2 | 10.5 | 12.1 | 13.4 | 12.9 | 13.2 | 13.0 | 17.6 | 2.3 |
| Liquor law violations | 23.5 | 26.2 | 20.7 | 17.7 | 16.4 | 13.3 | 12.6 | 17.6 | 0.6 |
| By type of institution: | | | | | | | | | |
| Public 4-year | 60.1 | 68.7 | 63.5 | 56.7 | 53.1 | 47.2 | 44.0 | 48.7 | 4.2 |
| Nonprofit 4-year | 24.5 | 21.0 | 17.2 | 17.1 | 14.9 | 13.7 | 13.3 | 14.4 | 1.7 |
| For-profit 4-year | 0.4 | 0.8 | 1.9 | 1.2 | 1.5 | 1.6 | 1.7 | 6.6 | 0.3 |
| Public 2-year | 7.8 | 10.9 | 8.8 | 7.9 | 8.4 | 7.9 | 8.1 | 23.7 | 4.0 |
| Nonprofit 2-year | 27.9 | 22.0 | 19.8 | 27.0 | 16.7 | 11.3 | 18.6 | 42.4 | 10.7 |
| For profit-2-year | 8.8 | 1.8 | 1.1 | 2.6 | 2.7 | 1.4 | 1.9 | 8.1 | 1.5 |
| **Referrals for disciplinary action [5]** | **132.9** | **163.4** | **149.7** | **166.1** | **170.7** | **163.7** | **156.5** | **221.4** | **3.5** |
| Illegal weapons possession | 1.1 | 1.4 | 0.9 | 1.0 | 1.0 | 1.0 | 1.0 | 1.3 | 0.3 |
| Drug law violations | 20.5 | 20.4 | 27.3 | 36.2 | 38.1 | 37.9 | 38.2 | 53.7 | 1.5 |
| Liquor law violations | 111.3 | 141.6 | 121.5 | 128.9 | 131.6 | 124.8 | 117.4 | 166.5 | 1.6 |
| By type of institution: | | | | | | | | | |
| Public 4-year | 153.1 | 184.6 | 175.5 | 189.4 | 196.7 | 183.8 | 167.9 | 187.2 | 1.8 |
| Nonprofit 4-year | 275.5 | 353.9 | 329.7 | 331.5 | 332.3 | 314.4 | 302.8 | 331.1 | 20.0 |
| For-profit 4-year | 12.0 | 7.6 | 8.8 | 19.4 | 12.2 | 12.8 | 13.1 | 58.9 | 0.3 |
| Public 2-year | 10.3 | 16.1 | 18.6 | 17.6 | 19.5 | 20.3 | 20.6 | 86.7 | 2.8 |
| Nonprofit 2-year | 160.9 | 176.0 | 152.2 | 130.9 | 191.5 | 144.1 | 102.4 | 405.6 | 1.3 |
| For profit-2-year | 15.4 | 13.9 | 3.8 | 8.8 | 11.3 | 9.1 | 5.7 | 91.4 | 0.6 |

– Represents zero. Z Data rounds to less than .05. [1] Excludes suicides, fetal deaths, traffic fatalities, accidental deaths, and justifiable homicide (such as the killing of a felon by a law enforcement officer in the line of duty). [2] Defined as the killing of another person through gross negligence (excludes traffic fatalities). [3] Any sexual act directed against another person forcibly and/or against that person's will. [4] Includes only statutory rape or incest. [5] If an individual is both arrested and referred to college officials for disciplinary action for a single offense, only the arrest is counted. [6] FTE is full-time equivalent. Although crimes, arrests, and referrals include incidents involving students, staff, and campus guests, they are expressed as a ratio to FTE students because comprehensive FTE counts of all these groups are not available. [7] Data on incidents per 10,000 FTE students are shown for institutions with and without residence halls.

Source: U.S. National Center for Education Statistics, *Digest of Education Statistics*, "Advance Release of Selected 2018 Digest Tables," <http://nces.ed.gov/programs/digest/index.asp>, accessed January 2019.

# Table 329. Public Schools Reporting Incidents of Crime by Incident Type and Selected School Characteristics: 2016

[For school year ending in 2016. Includes incidents that happen in school buildings, on school grounds, on school buses, and at places that hold school-sponsored events or activities. Based on sample; see source for details]

| School characteristic | Total number of schools | Number of incidents | | Percent of schools with— | | Rate per 1,000 students | |
|---|---|---|---|---|---|---|---|
| | | Violent incidents [1] | Serious violent incidents [2] | Violent incidents [1] | Serious violent incidents [2] | Violent incidents [1] | Serious violent incidents [2] |
| **All public schools** | **83,600** | **864,900** | **40,800** | **68.9** | **15.5** | **17.5** | **0.8** |
| Level: [3] | | | | | | | |
| Primary | 49,100 | 355,500 | 12,800 | 57.2 | 9.2 | 14.7 | 0.5 |
| Middle | 15,600 | 263,000 | 12,500 | 88.0 | 22.9 | 27.1 | 1.3 |
| High school | 12,800 | 207,900 | 13,200 | 89.8 | 30.5 | 16.2 | 1.0 |
| Combined | 6,200 | 38,500 | [4] 2,300 | 71.1 | 15.9 | 14.8 | [4] 0.9 |
| Enrollment size: | | | | | | | |
| Less than 300 | 18,200 | 66,400 | [4] 3,300 | 52.6 | 7.3 | 15.7 | [4] 0.8 |
| 300 to 499 | 25,000 | 177,000 | 8,700 | 63.0 | 12.7 | 17.3 | 0.8 |
| 500 to 999 | 31,700 | 399,100 | 15,700 | 76.0 | 17.1 | 18.2 | 0.7 |
| 1,000 or more | 8,700 | 222,300 | 13,200 | 94.5 | 34.6 | 17.2 | 1.0 |
| Percent minority enrollment: | | | | | | | |
| Less than 5 percent | 5,300 | 28,800 | [4] 1,300 | 58.0 | 11.0 | 14.9 | [4] 0.7 |
| 5 to 20 percent | 21,300 | 147,000 | 6,400 | 68.4 | 14.7 | 13.6 | 0.6 |
| 20 to 50 percent | 21,900 | 199,800 | 9,700 | 66.8 | 14.5 | 14.8 | 0.7 |
| 50 percent or more | 35,100 | 489,300 | 23,300 | 72.3 | 17.3 | 21.2 | 1.0 |

[1] Violent incidents Include rape, sexual battery other than rape, physical attack or fight with or without a weapon, threat of physical attack with or without a weapon, and robbery with or without a weapon. [2] Serious violent incidents include rape, sexual battery other than rape, physical attack or fight with a weapon, threat of physical attack with a weapon, and robbery with or without a weapon. [3] Primary schools are defined as schools in which the lowest grade is not higher than grade 3 and the highest grade is not higher than grade 8. Middle schools are defined as schools in which the lowest grade is not lower than grade 4 and the highest grade is not higher than grade 9. High schools are defined as schools in which the lowest grade is not lower than grade 9 and the highest grade is not higher than grade 12. Combined schools include all other combinations of grades, including K–12 schools. [4] Interpret data with caution.

Source: U.S. National Center for Education Statistics, *Digest of Education Statistics*, "Advance Release of Selected 2018 Digest Tables," <http://nces.ed.gov/programs/digest/index.asp>, accessed May 2019; and *Indicators of School Crime and Safety*, annual. See also <http://nces.ed.gov/surveys/ssocs/>.


# Table 330. Disciplinary Problems Reported at Public Schools by Selected School Characteristics: 2016

[In percent. For school year ending in 2016. "At school" includes activities that happen in school buildings, on school grounds, on school buses, and at places that hold school-sponsored events or activities. Based on the School Survey on Crime and Safety (SSOCS). Respondents to the survey had the option of either completing the survey on paper and mailing it back, or completing the survey online. Based on sample; see source for details]

| School characteristic | Happens at least once a week | | | | | | Happens at all |
|---|---|---|---|---|---|---|---|
| | Student racial tensions | Student bullying | Student sexual harassment of other students [1] | Student verbal abuse of teachers | Wide-spread disorder in classrooms | Student acts of disrespect for teachers | Gang activities [2] |
| **All public schools** | **1.7** | **11.9** | **1.0** | **4.8** | **2.3** | **10.3** | **10.4** |
| Level: [3] | | | | | | | |
| Primary | [4] 1.2 | 8.1 | (S) | 3.6 | [4] 1.6 | 8.8 | 2.7 |
| Middle | 3.2 | 21.8 | 2.1 | 8.2 | 4.9 | 15.9 | 19.4 |
| High school | 2.3 | 14.7 | 2.5 | 7.6 | 2.6 | 12.1 | 30.6 |
| Combined | (S) | 11.0 | (S) | (S) | (S) | [4] 4.3 | [4] 7.2 |
| Enrollment size: | | | | | | | |
| Less than 300 | (S) | 6.4 | (S) | [4] 3.6 | (S) | 6.4 | 6.0 |
| 300 to 499 | (S) | 9.6 | [4] 0.7 | 3.4 | 1.3 | 9.1 | 6.5 |
| 500 to 999 | 2.3 | 14.0 | 1.4 | 6.0 | 3.8 | 12.4 | 9.3 |
| 1,000 or more | 2.6 | 22.1 | [4] 2.4 | 7.0 | 3.8 | 14.4 | 35.0 |
| Percent minority enrollment: | | | | | | | |
| Less than 5 percent | (S) | 15.6 | (S) | (S) | (S) | (S) | (S) |
| 5 to 20 percent | [4] 1.0 | 10.8 | [4] 1.4 | [4] 2.1 | [4] 0.8 | 6.5 | 1.9 |
| 20 to 50 percent | [4] 1.4 | 11.0 | 0.9 | 3.6 | 1.1 | 9.9 | 7.7 |
| 50 percent or more | 2.6 | 12.5 | 1.0 | 7.9 | 4.3 | 13.7 | 18.6 |

S Figure does not meet publication standards. [1] Sexual harassment was defined as conduct that is unwelcome, sexual in nature, and denies or limits a student's ability to participate in or benefit from a school's education program. The conduct can be carried out by school employees, other students, and non-employee third parties. Both male and female students can be victims of sexual harassment, and the harasser and the victim can be of the same sex. The conduct can be verbal, nonverbal, or physical. [2] Gang includes an "ongoing loosely organized association of three or more persons, whether formal or informal, that has a common name, signs, symbols or colors, whose members engage, either individually or collectively, in violent or other forms of illegal behavior." [3] Primary schools are defined as schools in which the lowest grade is not higher than grade 3 and the highest grade is not higher than grade 8. Middle schools are defined as schools in which the lowest grade level is not lower than grade 4 and the highest grade is not higher than grade 9. High schools are defined as schools in which the lowest grade is not lower than grade 9 and the highest grade is not higher than grade 12. Combined schools include all other combinations of grades, including K–12 schools. [4] Interpret data with caution.

Source: U.S. National Center for Education Statistics, *Digest of Education Statistics*, "Advance Release of Selected 2018 Digest Tables," <http://nces.ed.gov/programs/digest/index.asp>, accessed May 2019; and *Indicators of School Crime and Safety*, annual. See also <http://nces.ed.gov/surveys/ssocs/>.

# Table 331. Students Who Reported Being Threatened or Injured With a Weapon on School Property by Selected Student Characteristics: 2003 to 2017

[In percent. Based on the Centers for Disease Control and Prevention's Youth Risk Behavior Surveillance System, which surveys students in public and private schools, in grades 9 to 12. Data are for previous 12 months. "On school property" was not defined for survey respondents. "Weapon" was defined as a gun, knife, or club for survey respondents]

| Characteristic | 2003 | 2005 | 2007 | 2009 | 2011 | 2013 | 2015 | 2017 |
|---|---|---|---|---|---|---|---|---|
| **Total** | **9.2** | **7.9** | **7.8** | **7.7** | **7.4** | **6.9** | **6.0** | **6.0** |
| Sex: | | | | | | | | |
| Male | 11.6 | 9.7 | 10.2 | 9.6 | 9.5 | 7.7 | 7.0 | 7.8 |
| Female | 6.5 | 6.1 | 5.4 | 5.5 | 5.2 | 6.1 | 4.6 | 4.1 |
| Race/ethnicity: [1] | | | | | | | | |
| White | 7.8 | 7.2 | 6.9 | 6.4 | 6.1 | 5.8 | 4.9 | 5.0 |
| Black | 10.9 | 8.1 | 9.7 | 9.4 | 8.9 | 8.4 | 7.9 | 7.8 |
| Hispanic | 9.4 | 9.8 | 8.7 | 9.1 | 9.2 | 8.5 | 6.6 | 6.1 |
| Asian | 11.5 | 4.6 | [2] 7.6 | 5.5 | 7.0 | 5.3 | [2] 3.6 | 4.3 |
| American Indian/Alaska Native | 22.1 | 9.8 | 5.9 | 16.5 | 8.2 | 18.5 | [2] 8.2 | [2] 7.0 |
| Pacific Islander/Native Hawaiian | 16.3 | [2] 14.5 | [2] 8.1 | 12.5 | 11.3 | [2] 8.7 | [2] 20.5 | 13.7 |
| More than one race | 18.7 | 10.7 | 13.3 | 9.2 | 9.9 | 7.7 | 8.0 | 8.0 |
| Grade: | | | | | | | | |
| 9th | 12.1 | 10.5 | 9.2 | 8.7 | 8.3 | 8.5 | 7.2 | 7.2 |
| 10th | 9.2 | 8.8 | 8.4 | 8.4 | 7.7 | 7.0 | 6.2 | 6.2 |
| 11th | 7.3 | 5.5 | 6.8 | 7.9 | 7.3 | 6.8 | 5.5 | 5.5 |
| 12th | 6.3 | 5.8 | 6.3 | 5.2 | 5.9 | 4.9 | 4.4 | 4.4 |
| Sexual orientation: [3] | | | | | | | | |
| Heterosexual | (NA) | (NA) | (NA) | (NA) | (NA) | (NA) | 5.1 | 5.4 |
| Gay, lesbian, or bisexual | (NA) | (NA) | (NA) | (NA) | (NA) | (NA) | 10.0 | 9.4 |
| Not sure | (NA) | (NA) | (NA) | (NA) | (NA) | (NA) | 12.6 | 11.1 |

NA Not available. [1] Race categories exclude persons of Hispanic ethnicity. [2] Interpret data with caution. [3] Students were asked which sexual orientation, "heterosexual (straight)," "gay or lesbian," "bisexual," or "not sure," which best described them.

Source: U.S. National Center for Education Statistics, *Digest of Education Statistics*, "Advance Release of Selected 2018 Digest Tables," <https://nces.ed.gov/programs/digest/index.asp>, accessed January 2019; and *Indicators of School Crime and Safety*, annual. See also <https://nces.ed.gov/surveys/ssocs/>.

# Table 332. Public Schools Using Selected Safety and Security Measures by Type: 2000 to 2016

[In percent. For school year ending in year shown. Based on the School Survey on Crime and Safety and subject to sampling error; see source for details]

| Measure | 2000 | 2006 | 2008 | 2010 | 2014 [1] | 2016 |
|---|---|---|---|---|---|---|
| Controlled access during school hours: | | | | | | |
| Buildings (locked or monitored doors) | 74.6 | 84.9 | 89.5 | 91.7 | 93.3 | 94.1 |
| Grounds (locked or monitored gates) | 33.7 | 41.1 | 42.6 | 46.0 | 42.7 | 49.9 |
| Visitors required to sign or check in | 96.6 | 97.6 | 98.7 | 99.3 | 98.6 | 93.5 |
| Classrooms equipped with locks so that doors can be locked from the inside | (NA) | (NA) | (NA) | (NA) | (NA) | 66.7 |
| Campus closed for most students during lunch | 64.6 | 66.1 | 65.0 | 66.9 | 92.6 | (NA) |
| Student dress, IDs, and school supplies: | | | | | | |
| Required students to wear uniforms | 11.8 | 13.8 | 17.5 | 18.9 | 20.4 | 21.5 |
| Enforced a strict dress code | 47.4 | 55.3 | 54.8 | 56.9 | 58.5 | 53.1 |
| Required students to wear badges or picture IDs | 3.9 | 6.2 | 7.6 | 6.9 | 8.9 | 7.0 |
| Required faculty and staff to wear badges or picture IDs | 25.4 | 47.9 | 58.3 | 62.9 | 68.0 | 67.9 |
| Required clear book bags or banned book bags on school grounds | 5.9 | 6.4 | 6.0 | 5.5 | 6.3 | 3.9 |
| Provided school lockers to students | 46.5 | 50.5 | 48.9 | 52.1 | 49.9 | 50.4 |
| Drug testing: | | | | | | |
| Athletes | (NA) | 5.0 | 6.4 | 6.0 | 6.6 | 7.2 |
| Students in non-athletic extracurricular activities | (NA) | 3.4 | 4.5 | 4.6 | 4.3 | 6.0 |
| Any other students | (NA) | 3.0 | 3.0 | 3.0 | 3.5 | (NA) |
| Metal detectors, dogs, and sweeps: | | | | | | |
| Random metal detector checks on students | 7.2 | 4.9 | 5.3 | 5.2 | 4.2 | 4.5 |
| Students required to pass through metal detectors daily | 0.9 | 1.1 | 1.3 | 1.4 | 2.0 | 1.8 |
| Random dog sniffs to check for drugs | 20.6 | 23.0 | 21.5 | 22.9 | 24.1 | 24.6 |
| Random sweeps for contraband [2] | 11.8 | 13.1 | 11.4 | 12.1 | 11.4 | 11.9 |
| Communications systems and technology: | | | | | | |
| Provided telephones in most classrooms | 44.6 | 66.9 | 71.6 | 74.0 | 78.7 | 79.3 |
| Provided electronic notification system for school wide emergencies | (NA) | (NA) | 43.2 | 63.1 | 81.6 | 73.0 |
| Provided structured anonymous threat reporting system [3] | (NA) | (NA) | 31.2 | 35.9 | 46.5 | 43.9 |
| Had silent alarms directly connected to law enforcement | (NA) | (NA) | (NA) | (NA) | (NA) | 27.1 |
| Used security cameras to monitor the school | 19.4 | 42.8 | 55.0 | 61.1 | 75.1 | 80.6 |
| Provided two-way radios to any staff | (NA) | 70.9 | 73.1 | 73.3 | 74.2 | 73.3 |
| Limited access to social networking sites from school computers | (NA) | (NA) | (NA) | 93.4 | 91.9 | 89.1 |
| Prohibited use of cell phones and text messaging devices | (NA) | (NA) | (NA) | 90.9 | 75.9 | 65.8 |

NA Not available. [1] Data for 2013-14 were collected using the Fast Response Survey System. The 2013-14 survey was designed to allow comparisons with School Survey on Crime and Safety (SSOCS) data. However, respondents to the 2013-14 survey could choose either to complete the survey by mail or online, whereas respondents to SSOCS did not have the online option. The 2013-14 survey also relied on a smaller sample. These differences may have impacted 2013-14 results. [2] Does not include random dog sniffs. [3] For example, a system for reporting threats through online submission, telephone hotline, or written submission via drop box.

Source: U.S. National Center for Education Statistics, *Digest of Education Statistics*, "Advance Release of Selected 2018 Digest Tables," <http://nces.ed.gov/programs/digest/index.asp>, accessed May 2019; and *Indicators of School Crime and Safety*, annual. See also <http://nces.ed.gov/surveys/ssocs/>.

# Table 333. Students Who Reported Being Bullied at School or Cyber-Bullied by Student Characteristics: 2017

[In percent. For school year ending in 2017. For students aged 12 through 18. "At school" includes the school building, on school property, on a school bus, or going to and from school. Based on the Bureau of Justice Statistics' School Crime Supplement to the National Crime Victimization Survey. For more information, see Appendix A of source]

| Characteristic | Bullied at school | | | | | | |
| --- | --- | --- | --- | --- | --- | --- | --- |
| | Total bullying at school [1] | Made fun of, called names, or insulted | Subject of rumors | Threatened with harm | Purposefully excluded | Pushed, shoved, tripped, or spit on | Online or by text |
| **Total** | **20.2** | **13.0** | **13.4** | **3.9** | **5.2** | **5.3** | **15.3** |
| Sex: | | | | | | | |
| Male | 16.7 | 10.3 | 9.3 | 4.2 | 3.5 | 6.1 | 6.8 |
| Female | 23.8 | 15.8 | 17.5 | 3.6 | 6.9 | 4.4 | 21.4 |
| Race/ethnicity: [2] | | | | | | | |
| White | 22.8 | 15.0 | 15.2 | 4.2 | 6.7 | 5.4 | 17.4 |
| Black | 22.9 | 16.0 | 14.5 | 5.4 | 3.9 | 6.5 | 12.1 |
| Hispanic | 15.7 | 8.9 | 10.6 | 2.6 | 3.3 | 4.6 | 12.8 |
| Asian | 7.3 | 5.3 | 4.7 | (S) | (S) | [3] 1.7 | [3] (S) |
| Two or more races | 23.2 | 12.9 | 15.7 | 7.6 | 7.5 | 6.9 | [3] 11.0 |
| Grade: | | | | | | | |
| 6th | 29.5 | 23.1 | 17.1 | 8.5 | 8.4 | 10.5 | [3] 6.7 |
| 7th | 24.4 | 17.7 | 14.2 | 4.9 | 7.6 | 8.2 | 13.1 |
| 8th | 25.3 | 16.3 | 16.0 | 4.4 | 5.7 | 6.9 | 12.5 |
| 9th | 19.3 | 12.5 | 12.3 | 3.7 | 4.3 | 5.4 | 19.7 |
| 10th | 18.9 | 9.4 | 16.1 | 3.6 | 4.4 | 3.7 | 22.0 |
| 11th | 14.7 | 9.5 | 9.6 | 2.5 | 3.2 | 3.3 | 22.3 |
| 12th | 12.2 | 6.0 | 9.1 | [3] 1.3 | 3.5 | [3] 0.7 | 11.5 |

S Reporting standards not met. [1] In the total for students bullied at school, students who reported more than one type of bullying were counted only once. [2] Race categories exclude persons of Hispanic ethnicity. [3] Interpret data with caution.

Source: U.S. National Center for Education Statistics, *Digest of Education Statistics,* "Advance Release of Selected 2018 Digest Tables," <http://nces.ed.gov/programs/digest/>, accessed May 2019; and *Indicators of School Crime and Safety,* annual. See also <http://nces.ed.gov/surveys/ssocs/>.

# Table 334. Cyberbullying Among Students in Grades 9 to 12 by Student Characteristics: 2011 to 2017

[In percent. Covers students in grades 9 to 12 who reported being electronically bullied during the previous 12 months. Data are based on the U.S. Centers for Disease Control and Prevention's Youth Risk Behavior Surveillance System. Electronic bullying, or cyberbullying, for 2011-2015 includes "being bullied through e-mail, chat rooms, Instant messaging, websites, or texting," and for 2017 "being bullied through texting, Instagram, Facebook, or other social media"]

| Student characteristic | 2011 | 2013 | 2015 | 2017 |
| --- | --- | --- | --- | --- |
| **Total** | **16.2** | **14.8** | **15.5** | **14.9** |
| Sex: | | | | |
| Male | 10.8 | 8.5 | 9.7 | 9.9 |
| Female | 22.1 | 21.0 | 21.7 | 19.7 |
| Race/ethnicity. [1] | | | | |
| White | 18.6 | 16.9 | 18.4 | 17.3 |
| Black | 8.9 | 8.7 | 8.6 | 10.9 |
| Asian | 14.4 | 12.9 | 13.9 | 10.0 |
| Pacific Islander | 19.6 | 15.7 | [2] 11.8 | 15.0 |
| American Indian/Alaska Native | 16.2 | 18.0 | 18.7 | 13.2 |
| Two or more races | 21.0 | 18.9 | 20.4 | 16.0 |
| Hispanic ethnicity | 13.6 | 12.8 | 12.4 | 12.3 |
| Sexual orientation: | | | | |
| Heterosexual | (NA) | (NA) | 14.2 | 13.3 |
| Gay, lesbian, or bisexual | (NA) | (NA) | 28.0 | 27.1 |
| Not sure | (NA) | (NA) | 22.5 | 22.0 |
| Grade: | | | | |
| 9th | 15.5 | 16.1 | 16.5 | 16.7 |
| 10th | 18.1 | 14.5 | 16.6 | 14.8 |
| 11th | 16.0 | 14.9 | 14.7 | 14.2 |
| 12th | 15.0 | 13.5 | 14.3 | 13.5 |

NA Not available. [1] Race categories exclude persons of Hispanic ethnicity. [2] Interpret data with caution. The coefficient of variation (CV) for this estimate is between 30 and 50 percent.

Source: U.S. National Center for Education Statistics, *Digest of Education Statistics,* "Advance Release of Selected 2018 Tables," <https://nces.ed.gov/programs/digest/>, accessed May 2019. See also *Indicators of School Crime and Safety: 2018,* <https://nces.ed.gov/surveys/ssocs/>.

# Table 335. Violent Deaths, Homicides, and Suicides Occurring at Schools, Total and for Youth Aged 5 to 18: 1993 to 2016

[For school year ending in year shown. A school-associated violent death is defined as a homicide, suicide, or legal intervention (involving a law enforcement officer) in which the fatal injury occurred on the campus of a functioning elementary or secondary school in the United States, including while the victim was on the way to or from regular sessions at school or while the victim was attending or traveling to or from an official school-sponsored event. Victims include students, staff members, and others who are not students. Data from school year 2000 onward are subject to change until interviews with school and law enforcement officials have been completed. The details learned during interviews can occasionally change the classification of a case. Based on data from U.S. Centers for Disease Control and Prevention, and Federal Bureau of Investigation and Bureau of Justice Statistics]

| Year | School-associated violent deaths | | | | Homicides of youth aged 5 to 18 | | Suicides of youth aged 5 to 18 | |
|------|---------|-----------|------------|---------------------------|-------|-----------|----------|-----------|
| | Total [1] | Homicides | Suicides [2] | Legal inter-ventions | Total | At school | Total [2] | At school |
| 1993 | 57 | 47 | 10 | 0 | 3,003 | 34 | 1,657 | 6 |
| 1994 | 48 | 38 | 10 | 0 | 3,253 | 29 | 1,779 | 7 |
| 1995 | 48 | 39 | 8 | 0 | 3,001 | 28 | 1,704 | 7 |
| 1996 | 53 | 46 | 6 | 1 | 2,791 | 32 | 1,691 | 6 |
| 1997 | 48 | 45 | 2 | 1 | 2,430 | 28 | 1,584 | 1 |
| 1998 | 57 | 47 | 9 | 1 | 2,231 | 34 | 1,681 | 6 |
| 1999 | 47 | 38 | 6 | 2 | 1,923 | 33 | 1,480 | 4 |
| 2000 | 37 | 26 | 11 | 0 | 1,694 | 14 | 1,420 | 8 |
| 2001 | 34 | 26 | 7 | 1 | 1,636 | 14 | 1,451 | 6 |
| 2002 | 36 | 27 | 8 | 1 | 1,593 | 16 | 1,343 | 5 |
| 2003 | 36 | 25 | 11 | 0 | 1,658 | 18 | 1,264 | 10 |
| 2004 | 45 | 37 | 7 | 1 | 1,620 | 23 | 1,411 | 5 |
| 2005 | 52 | 40 | 10 | 2 | 1,720 | 22 | 1,484 | 8 |
| 2006 | 44 | 37 | 6 | 1 | 1,859 | 21 | 1,311 | 3 |
| 2007 | 63 | 48 | 13 | 2 | 1,906 | 32 | 1,243 | 9 |
| 2008 | 48 | 39 | 7 | 2 | 1,858 | 21 | 1,256 | 5 |
| 2009 | 44 | 29 | 15 | 0 | 1,720 | 18 | 1,425 | 7 |
| 2010 | 35 | 27 | 5 | 3 | 1,551 | 19 | 1,441 | 2 |
| 2011 | 32 | 26 | 6 | 0 | 1,436 | 11 | 1,559 | 3 |
| 2012 | 45 | 26 | 14 | 5 | 1,360 | 15 | 1,541 | 5 |
| 2013 | 53 | 41 | 11 | 1 | 1,310 | 31 | 1,608 | 6 |
| 2014 | 48 | 26 | 20 | 1 | 1,160 | 12 | 1,638 | 8 |
| 2015 | 47 | 28 | 17 | 2 | 1,273 | 20 | 1,882 | 9 |
| 2016 | 38 | 30 | 7 | 1 | 1,478 | 18 | 1,941 | 3 |

[1] Total includes unintentional firearm-related deaths, not shown separately. [2] Excludes self-inflicted deaths among children age 5 to 9. The number of self-inflicted deaths among children age 5 to 9 was generally less than 7 per year during the period covered by this table.

Source: U.S. National Center for Education Statistics, *Digest of Education Statistics*, "Advance Release of Selected 2018 Digest Tables," <http://nces.ed.gov/programs/digest/>, accessed May 2019; and *Indicators of School Crime and Safety,* annual. See also <http://nces.ed.gov/surveys/ssocs/>.

# Law Enforcement, Courts, and Prisons

This section presents data on crimes committed, victims of crimes, arrests, and data related to criminal violations and the criminal justice system. The major sources of these data are the Bureau of Justice Statistics (BJS), the Federal Bureau of Investigation (FBI), and the Administrative Office of the U.S. Courts. BJS issues many reports—see our Guide to Sources for a complete listing. The Federal Bureau of Investigation's major annual reports are *Crime in the United States, Law Enforcement Officers Killed and Assaulted*, and *Hate Crimes*, which present data on reported crimes as gathered from state and local law enforcement agencies.

**Legal jurisdiction and law enforcement**—Law enforcement is, for the most part, a function of state and local officers and agencies. The U.S. Constitution reserves general police powers to the states. By act of Congress, federal offenses include only offenses against the U.S. government and against or by its employees while engaged in their official duties, and offenses which involve the crossing of state lines or an interference with interstate commerce. Excluding the military, there are 52 separate criminal law Jurisdictions in the United States: one in each of the 50 states, one in the District of Columbia, and the federal jurisdiction. Each of these has its own criminal law and procedure and its own law enforcement agencies. While the systems of law enforcement are quite similar among the states, there are often substantial differences in the penalties for like offenses.

Law enforcement can be divided into three parts: Investigation of crimes and arrests of persons suspected of committing them; prosecution of those charged with crime; and the punishment or treatment of persons convicted of crime.

**Crime**—The U.S. Department of Justice administers two statistical programs to measure the magnitude, nature, and impact of crime in the nation: the Uniform Crime Reporting (UCR) Program and the National Crime Victimization Survey (NCVS). Each of these programs produces valuable information about aspects of the nation's crime problem. Because the UCR and NCVS programs are conducted for different purposes, use different methods, and focus on somewhat different aspects of crime, the information they produce together provides a more comprehensive panorama of the nation's crime problem than either could produce alone.

**Uniform Crime Reports (UCR)**—The FBI's UCR Program, which began in 1929, collects information on the following crimes reported to law enforcement authorities: Part 1 offenses, for which detailed data is reported—murder and nonnegligent manslaughter, rape, robbery, aggravated assault, burglary, larceny-theft, motor vehicle theft, and arson; and Part 2 offenses, 20 additional crime categories for which law enforcement agencies report only arrest data. UCR definitions of criminal offenses (including those listed) can be found at <https://ucr.fbi.gov/crime-in-the-u.s/2017/crime-in-the-u.s.-2017/topic-pages/offense-definitions>.

Beginning in 2013, the UCR program implemented a revised definition of rape. Not all state and local agencies have been able to effect the change in their records management systems and some agencies currently can report the offense based on only the legacy definition. Therefore, rape data collected under both definitions are used in the *Crime in the United States* report. In 2016, the FBI Director approved the recommendation to discontinue the reporting of rape data using the UCR legacy definition beginning in 2017. However, to maintain the availability of 20-year trend data, national estimates for rape under the legacy definition are provided along with estimates under the revised definition for 2017.

The UCR Program compiles data from monthly law enforcement reports or individual crime incident records transmitted directly to the FBI or to centralized state agencies that then report to the FBI. The Program thoroughly examines each report it receives for reasonableness, accuracy, and deviations that may indicate errors. Large variations in crime levels may indicate modified records procedures, incomplete reporting, or changes in a jurisdiction's boundaries. To identify any unusual fluctuations in an agency's crime counts, the Program compares monthly reports to previous submissions of the agency and with those for similar agencies.

The UCR Program presents crime counts for the nation as a whole, as well as for regions, states, counties, cities, towns, tribal law enforcement, and colleges and universities. This permits studies among neighboring Jurisdictions and among those with similar populations and other common characteristics.

The UCR Program annually publishes its findings online in a preliminary release in the spring of the following calendar year, followed by a detailed report, *Crime in the United States*, issued in the fall. In addition to crime counts and trends, this report includes data on crimes cleared, persons arrested (age, sex, and race), law enforcement personnel (including the number of sworn officers killed or assaulted), and the characteristics of homicides (including age, sex, and race of victims and offenders; victim-offender relationships; weapons used; and circumstances surrounding the homicides). Other periodic reports are also available from the UCR Program.

**National Crime Victimization Survey (NCVS)**—A second perspective on crime is provided by this survey of the Bureau of Justice Statistics (BJS). The NCVS is an annual data collection (interviews of persons aged 12 or older), conducted by the U.S. Census Bureau for the BJS. As an ongoing survey of households, the NCVS measures crimes of violence and property both reported and not reported to police. It produces national rates and levels of personal and property victimization. No attempt is made to validate the information against police records or any other source.

The NCVS measures rape/sexual assault, robbery, assault, pocket-picking, purse snatching, burglary, and motor vehicle theft. Murder and kidnaping are not covered. The so-called victimless crimes, such as drunkenness, drug abuse, and prostitution, also are excluded, as are crimes for which it is difficult to identify knowledgeable respondents or to locate data records.

Crimes of which the victim may not be aware also cannot be measured effectively. Buying stolen property may fall into this category, as may some instances of embezzlement. Attempted crimes of many types probably are under-recorded for this reason. Events in which the victim has shown a willingness to participate in illegal activity also are excluded.

In any encounter involving a personal crime, more than one criminal act can be committed against an individual. For example, a rape may be associated with a robbery, or a household property offense, such as a burglary, can escalate into something more serious in the event of a personal confrontation. Each criminal incident has been counted only once, by the most serious act that took place during the incident, and ranked in accordance with the seriousness classification system used by the FBI. The order of seriousness for crimes against persons is as follows: rape, robbery, assault, and larceny. Personal crimes take precedence over household offenses.

A *victimization*, the basic measure of the occurrence of crime, is a specific criminal act as it affects a single victim. The number of victimizations is determined by the number of victims of such acts. Victimization counts serve as key elements in computing rates of victimization. For crimes against persons, the rates are based on the total number of individuals aged 12 and over or on a portion of that population sharing a particular characteristic or set of traits. As general indicators of the danger of having been victimized during the reference period, the rates are not sufficiently refined to represent true measures of risk for specific individuals or households.

An *incident* is a specific criminal act involving one or more victims; therefore the number of incidents of personal crimes is lower than that of victimizations.

**Courts**—Statistics on criminal offenses and the outcome of prosecutions are incomplete for the country as a whole, although data are available for many states individually.

State courts handle the majority of civil and criminal litigation in the country. Only when the U.S. Constitution and acts of Congress specifically confer jurisdiction upon the federal courts may civil or criminal litigation be heard and decided by them. Generally, the federal courts have jurisdiction over the following types of cases: suits or proceedings by or against the United States; civil actions between private parties arising under the Constitution, laws, or treaties of the United States; civil actions between private litigants who are citizens of different states; civil cases

involving admiralty, maritime, or private jurisdiction; and all matters in bankruptcy.

There are several types of courts with varying degrees of legal jurisdiction. These jurisdictions include original, appellate, general, and limited or special. A court of original jurisdiction is one having the authority initially to try a case and pass judgment on the law and the facts; a court of appellate jurisdiction is one with the legal authority to review cases and hear appeals; a court of general jurisdiction is a trial court of unlimited original jurisdiction in civil and/or criminal cases, also called a "major trial court"; a court of limited or special jurisdiction is a trial court with legal authority over only a particular class of cases, such as probate, juvenile, or traffic cases.

The 94 federal courts of original jurisdiction are known as the U.S. district courts. One or more of these courts is established in every state and one each in the District of Columbia, Puerto Rico, the Virgin Islands, the Northern Mariana Islands, and Guam. Appeals from the district courts are taken to intermediate appellate courts of which there are 13, known as U.S. courts of appeals and the United States Court of Appeals for the Federal Circuit. The Supreme Court of the United States is the final and highest appellate court in the federal system of courts.

**Juvenile offenders**—For statistical purposes, the FBI and most states classify as juvenile offenders persons under the age of 18 years who have committed a crime or crimes.

Delinquency cases are all cases of youths referred to a juvenile court for violation of a law or ordinance or for seriously "antisocial" conduct. Several types of facilities are available for those adjudicated delinquents, ranging from short-term physically unrestricted to long-term very restrictive supervision.

**Prisoners and jail inmates**—BJS started to collect annual data in 1979 on prisoners in federal and state prisons and reformatories. Adults convicted of criminal activity may be given a prison or jail sentence. A *prison* is a confinement facility having custodial authority over adults sentenced to confinement of more than 1 year. A *jail* is a facility, usually operated by a local law enforcement agency, holding persons detained pending adjudication and/or persons committed after adjudication for 1 year or less.

Data on inmates in local jails were collected by the BJS for the first time in 1970. Jail censuses are taken periodically. For details, see <https://www.bjs.gov/index.cfm?ty=tp&tid=12#data_collections>.

**Statistical reliability**—For discussion of statistical collection, estimation and sampling procedures, and measures of statistical reliability pertaining to the National Crime Victimization Survey and Uniform Crime Reporting Program, see Appendix III.

# Table 336. Crimes and Crime Rates by Type of Offense: 1980 to 2017

[13,408 represents 13,408,000. Data include offenses reported to law enforcement, and offense estimations for nonreporting and partially reporting agencies within each state. Rates are based on Census Bureau estimated resident population as of July 1, except 1980, 1990, 2000, and 2010, which are enumerated as of April 1. See source for details]

| Item and year | All crimes | Violent crime | | | | | | Property crimes | | | |
|---|---|---|---|---|---|---|---|---|---|---|---|
| | | Total | Murder [1] | Rape [2] | Rape legacy def. [2] | Robbery | Aggra-vated assault | Total | Burglary | Larceny/ theft | Motor vehicle theft |
| **NUMBER OF OFFENSES (1,000)** | | | | | | | | | | | |
| 1980.................... | 13,408 | 1,345 | 23.0 | (NA) | 83.0 | 566 | 673 | 12,064 | 3,795 | 7,137 | 1,132 |
| 1990.................... | 14,476 | 1,820 | 23.4 | (NA) | 102.6 | 639 | 1,055 | 12,655 | 3,074 | 7,946 | 1,636 |
| 1995.................... | 13,863 | 1,799 | 21.6 | (NA) | 97.5 | 581 | 1,099 | 12,064 | 2,594 | 7,998 | 1,472 |
| 2000.................... | 11,608 | 1,425 | 15.6 | (NA) | 90.2 | 408 | 912 | 10,183 | 2,051 | 6,972 | 1,160 |
| 2001 [3]................ | 11,877 | 1,439 | 16.0 | (NA) | 90.9 | 424 | 909 | 10,437 | 2,117 | 7,092 | 1,228 |
| 2002.................... | 11,879 | 1,424 | 16.2 | (NA) | 95.2 | 421 | 891 | 10,455 | 2,151 | 7,057 | 1,247 |
| 2003.................... | 11,827 | 1,384 | 16.5 | (NA) | 93.9 | 414 | 859 | 10,443 | 2,155 | 7,027 | 1,261 |
| 2004.................... | 11,679 | 1,360 | 16.1 | (NA) | 95.1 | 401 | 847 | 10,319 | 2,144 | 6,937 | 1,238 |
| 2005.................... | 11,565 | 1,391 | 16.7 | (NA) | 94.3 | 417 | 862 | 10,175 | 2,155 | 6,783 | 1,236 |
| 2006.................... | 11,455 | 1,435 | 17.3 | (NA) | 94.5 | 449 | 874 | 10,020 | 2,195 | 6,626 | 1,198 |
| 2007.................... | 11,305 | 1,423 | 17.1 | (NA) | 92.2 | 447 | 866 | 9,882 | 2,190 | 6,592 | 1,100 |
| 2008.................... | 11,169 | 1,394 | 16.5 | (NA) | 90.8 | 444 | 844 | 9,774 | 2,229 | 6,586 | 959 |
| 2009.................... | 10,663 | 1,326 | 15.4 | (NA) | 89.2 | 409 | 813 | 9,337 | 2,203 | 6,338 | 796 |
| 2010.................... | 10,364 | 1,251 | 14.7 | (NA) | 85.6 | 369 | 782 | 9,113 | 2,168 | 6,205 | 740 |
| 2011.................... | 10,259 | 1,206 | 14.7 | (NA) | 84.2 | 355 | 752 | 9,053 | 2,185 | 6,151 | 717 |
| 2012.................... | 10,219 | 1,217 | 14.9 | (NA) | 85.1 | 355 | 762 | 9,002 | 2,110 | 6,169 | 723 |
| 2013.................... | 9,820 | 1,168 | 14.3 | 113.7 | 82.1 | 345 | 727 | 8,652 | 1,932 | 6,019 | 700 |
| 2014.................... | 9,362 | 1,153 | 14.2 | 118.0 | 84.9 | 323 | 731 | 8,209 | 1,713 | 5,809 | 687 |
| 2015.................... | 9,223 | 1,199 | 15.9 | 126.1 | 91.3 | 328 | 764 | 8,024 | 1,588 | 5,723 | 713 |
| 2016.................... | 9,179 | 1,250 | 17.4 | 132.4 | 97.0 | 333 | 803 | 7,929 | 1,516 | 5,645 | 767 |
| 2017.................... | 8,941 | 1,247 | 17.3 | 135.8 | 99.9 | 319 | 811 | 7,694 | 1,402 | 5,519 | 773 |
| **RATE PER 100,000 POPULATION** | | | | | | | | | | | |
| 1980.................... | 5,950 | 597 | 10.2 | (NA) | 36.8 | 251 | 299 | 5,353 | 1,684 | 3,167 | 502 |
| 1990.................... | 5,803 | 730 | 9.4 | (NA) | 41.1 | 256 | 423 | 5,073 | 1,232 | 3,185 | 656 |
| 1995.................... | 5,276 | 685 | 8.2 | (NA) | 37.1 | 221 | 418 | 4,591 | 987 | 3,043 | 560 |
| 2000.................... | 4,125 | 507 | 5.5 | (NA) | 32.0 | 145 | 324 | 3,618 | 729 | 2,477 | 412 |
| 2001 [3]................ | 4,163 | 505 | 5.6 | (NA) | 31.8 | 149 | 319 | 3,658 | 742 | 2,486 | 431 |
| 2002.................... | 4,125 | 494 | 5.6 | (NA) | 33.1 | 146 | 310 | 3,631 | 747 | 2,451 | 433 |
| 2003.................... | 4,067 | 476 | 5.7 | (NA) | 32.3 | 143 | 295 | 3,591 | 741 | 2,417 | 434 |
| 2004.................... | 3,977 | 463 | 5.5 | (NA) | 32.4 | 137 | 289 | 3,514 | 730 | 2,362 | 422 |
| 2005.................... | 3,901 | 469 | 5.6 | (NA) | 31.8 | 141 | 291 | 3,432 | 727 | 2,288 | 417 |
| 2006.................... | 3,826 | 479 | 5.8 | (NA) | 31.6 | 150 | 292 | 3,347 | 733 | 2,213 | 400 |
| 2007.................... | 3,748 | 472 | 5.7 | (NA) | 30.6 | 148 | 287 | 3,276 | 726 | 2,185 | 365 |
| 2008.................... | 3,673 | 459 | 5.4 | (NA) | 29.8 | 146 | 278 | 3,215 | 733 | 2,166 | 315 |
| 2009.................... | 3,473 | 432 | 5.0 | (NA) | 29.1 | 133 | 265 | 3,041 | 718 | 2,065 | 259 |
| 2010.................... | 3,350 | 405 | 4.8 | (NA) | 27.7 | 119 | 253 | 2,946 | 701 | 2,006 | 239 |
| 2011.................... | 3,292 | 387 | 4.7 | (NA) | 27.0 | 114 | 242 | 2,905 | 701 | 1,974 | 230 |
| 2012.................... | 3,256 | 388 | 4.7 | (NA) | 27.1 | 113 | 243 | 2,868 | 672 | 1,965 | 230 |
| 2013.................... | 3,103 | 369 | 4.5 | 35.9 | 25.9 | 109 | 230 | 2,734 | 611 | 1,902 | 221 |
| 2014.................... | 2,936 | 362 | 4.4 | 37.0 | 26.6 | 101 | 229 | 2,574 | 537 | 1,822 | 215 |
| 2015.................... | 2,874 | 374 | 4.9 | 39.3 | 28.4 | 102 | 238 | 2,501 | 495 | 1,784 | 222 |
| 2016.................... | 2,838 | 387 | 5.4 | 40.9 | 30.0 | 103 | 248 | 2,452 | 469 | 1,745 | 237 |
| 2017.................... | 2,745 | 383 | 5.3 | 41.7 | 30.7 | 98 | 249 | 2,362 | 430 | 1,694 | 237 |

NA Not available. [1] Includes nonnegligent manslaughter. [2] Beginning 2013, the FBI introduced a revised definition of rape. For more information, see <https://ucr.fbi.gov/crime-in-the-u.s/2017/crime-in-the-u.s.-2017/topic-pages/rape>. [3] The murder and non-negligent homicides that occurred as a result of the events of September 11, 2001, were not included in this table.

Source: U.S. Department of Justice, Federal Bureau of Investigation, "Crime in the United States 2017," <https://ucr.fbi.gov/>, accessed November 2018.

# Table 337. Crimes and Crime Rates by Offense Type and Geographic Area: 2017

[In thousands (981.6 represents 981,600), except rate. Rate per 100,000 population. For area definitions, see <https://ucr.fbi.gov/crime-in-the-u.s/2017/crime-in-the-u.s.-2017/topic-pages/area-definitions>. See headnote, Table 336]

| Type of crime | Cities | | Metropolitan counties [1] | | Nonmetropolitan counties [1] | | Suburban areas [2] | |
|---|---|---|---|---|---|---|---|---|
| | Total | Rate | Total | Rate | Total | Rate | Total | Rate |
| Violent crime.............. | 981.6 | 469.6 | 191.5 | 262.9 | 48.7 | 206.7 | 335.1 | 252.9 |
| Murder [3]................. | 13.0 | 6.2 | 2.6 | 3.6 | 0.8 | 3.5 | 4.2 | 3.2 |
| Rape [4].................... | 94.0 | 46.2 | 22.8 | 32.5 | 8.8 | 39.2 | 41.2 | 32.1 |
| Robbery.................... | 272.0 | 130.2 | 34.3 | 47.1 | 2.6 | 11.0 | 65.5 | 49.4 |
| Aggravated assault.... | 602.5 | 288.3 | 131.8 | 180.9 | 36.5 | 154.9 | 224.2 | 169.1 |
| Property crime.......... | 5,792.8 | 2,771.5 | 1,189.8 | 1,633.0 | 283.0 | 1,201.8 | 2,435.0 | 1,837.3 |
| Burglary................... | 972.5 | 465.3 | 251.1 | 344.6 | 87.1 | 369.8 | 437.1 | 329.8 |
| Larceny-theft............ | 4,224.9 | 2,021.3 | 818.0 | 1,122.6 | 169.9 | 721.6 | 1,788.9 | 1,349.8 |
| Motor vehicle theft..... | 595.4 | 284.9 | 120.8 | 165.8 | 26.0 | 110.4 | 209.0 | 157.7 |

[1] Includes state police agencies that report aggregately for the entire state. [2] Suburban areas include law enforcement agencies in cities with less than 50,000 inhabitants and county law enforcement agencies within a Metropolitan Statistical Area. Excludes all metropolitan agencies associated with a principal city. Agencies associated with suburban areas also appear in other groups within this table. [3] Includes nonnegligent manslaughter. [4] Estimated using the revised FBI Uniform Crime Reporting (UCR) definition of rape. For more information, see <https://ucr.fbi.gov/crime-in-the-u.s/2017/crime-in-the-u.s.-2017/topic-pages/rape>.

Source: U.S. Department of Justice, Federal Bureau of Investigation, "Crime in the United States 2017," <https://ucr.fbi.gov/>, accessed November 2018.

# Table 338. Crime Rates by State, 2016 and 2017, and by Type, 2017

[For year ending December 31. Rates per 100,000 population. Offenses reported to law enforcement. Based on Census Bureau estimated resident population as of July 1]

| State | Violent crime | | | | | | Property crime | | | | |
|---|---|---|---|---|---|---|---|---|---|---|---|
| | 2016, total | 2017 | | | | | 2016, total | 2017 | | | |
| | | Total | Murder | Rape [1] | Robbery | Aggravated assault | | Total | Burglary | Larceny/ theft | Motor vehicle theft |
| United States............. | 397.5 | 394.0 | 5.3 | 41.7 | 98.0 | 248.9 | 2,451.6 | 2,362.2 | 430.4 | 1,694.4 | 237.4 |
| Alabama................... | 532.4 | 524.2 | 8.3 | 41.6 | 86.5 | 387.8 | 2,947.4 | 2,957.3 | 645.7 | 2,048.1 | 263.4 |
| Alaska.................... | 804.6 | 829.0 | 8.4 | 116.7 | 128.5 | 575.4 | 3,354.7 | 3,542.1 | 563.8 | 2,402.7 | 575.6 |
| Arizona................... | 471.0 | 508.0 | 5.9 | 51.0 | 106.0 | 345.0 | 3,000.8 | 2,914.9 | 536.3 | 2,107.0 | 271.6 |
| Arkansas.................. | 554.3 | 554.9 | 8.6 | 68.3 | 64.4 | 413.6 | 3,282.6 | 3,078.6 | 727.7 | 2,109.5 | 241.4 |
| California................. | 444.8 | 449.3 | 4.6 | 37.2 | 143.2 | 264.2 | 2,550.0 | 2,496.7 | 446.9 | 1,623.9 | 425.9 |
| Colorado.................. | 344.1 | 368.1 | 3.9 | 68.8 | 68.4 | 226.9 | 2,751.2 | 2,701.6 | 406.9 | 1,904.9 | 389.9 |
| Connecticut............... | 227.7 | 228.0 | 2.8 | 23.3 | 78.4 | 123.4 | 1,808.3 | 1,769.9 | 247.8 | 1,318.5 | 203.7 |
| Delaware.................. | 510.0 | 453.4 | 5.6 | 34.7 | 112.5 | 300.5 | 2,767.9 | 2,440.6 | 412.7 | 1,885.6 | 142.3 |
| District of Columbia [2]...... | 1,203.5 | 1,004.9 | 16.7 | 64.0 | 378.0 | 546.3 | 4,731.2 | 4,283.9 | 260.7 | 3,650.4 | 372.8 |
| Florida.................... | 429.4 | 408.0 | 5.0 | 37.8 | 88.6 | 276.5 | 2,681.0 | 2,512.4 | 423.4 | 1,884.5 | 204.5 |
| Georgia................... | 390.4 | 357.2 | 6.7 | 26.1 | 96.3 | 228.1 | 2,979.6 | 2,860.2 | 530.9 | 2,077.4 | 251.8 |
| Hawaii.................... | 241.6 | 250.6 | 2.7 | 39.7 | 75.4 | 132.7 | 2,964.5 | 2,829.5 | 388.7 | 2,071.7 | 369.1 |
| Idaho..................... | 230.7 | 226.4 | 1.9 | 41.2 | 11.4 | 172.0 | 1,747.4 | 1,635.4 | 329.4 | 1,181.1 | 125.0 |
| Illinois................... | 436.7 | 438.8 | 7.8 | 43.4 | 137.2 | 250.4 | 2,051.0 | 2,011.4 | 339.5 | 1,508.8 | 163.1 |
| Indiana................... | 399.7 | 399.0 | 6.0 | 39.4 | 99.0 | 254.6 | 2,539.3 | 2,416.9 | 452.1 | 1,733.8 | 231.0 |
| Iowa...................... | 292.9 | 293.4 | 3.3 | 39.2 | 39.8 | 211.0 | 2,104.5 | 2,125.3 | 479.3 | 1,468.6 | 177.4 |
| Kansas................... | 401.2 | 413.0 | 5.5 | 55.9 | 61.3 | 290.3 | 2,830.1 | 2,800.9 | 478.2 | 2,053.3 | 269.3 |
| Kentucky.................. | 235.6 | 225.8 | 5.9 | 37.3 | 66.4 | 116.2 | 2,202.7 | 2,129.1 | 453.4 | 1,445.7 | 230.0 |
| Louisiana................. | 565.0 | 557.0 | 12.4 | 39.9 | 114.4 | 390.3 | 3,297.2 | 3,366.8 | 731.5 | 2,401.3 | 234.0 |
| Maine..................... | 124.0 | 121.0 | 1.7 | 35.4 | 18.6 | 65.3 | 1,646.9 | 1,507.1 | 249.6 | 1,198.1 | 59.4 |
| Maryland.................. | 481.7 | 500.2 | 9.0 | 27.9 | 185.1 | 278.2 | 2,319.0 | 2,222.3 | 388.4 | 1,609.7 | 224.2 |
| Massachusetts............. | 380.7 | 358.0 | 2.5 | 32.0 | 71.0 | 252.5 | 1,559.7 | 1,437.0 | 249.1 | 1,078.0 | 109.9 |
| Michigan.................. | 460.9 | 450.0 | 5.7 | 70.6 | 65.1 | 308.5 | 1,915.2 | 1,800.0 | 357.8 | 1,245.7 | 196.5 |
| Minnesota................. | 241.9 | 238.3 | 2.0 | 42.8 | 64.9 | 128.6 | 2,130.7 | 2,191.5 | 336.9 | 1,675.7 | 178.9 |
| Mississippi............... | 281.7 | 285.7 | 8.2 | 36.6 | 69.4 | 171.5 | 2,764.1 | 2,733.9 | 828.1 | 1,750.6 | 155.2 |
| Missouri.................. | 520.8 | 530.3 | 9.8 | 44.6 | 103.9 | 372.0 | 2,801.8 | 2,833.9 | 492.0 | 2,016.0 | 325.9 |
| Montana.................. | 374.1 | 377.1 | 3.9 | 58.4 | 28.1 | 286.7 | 2,710.8 | 2,591.6 | 344.1 | 2,000.8 | 246.7 |
| Nebraska................. | 296.8 | 305.9 | 2.2 | 62.0 | 50.4 | 191.2 | 2,264.5 | 2,274.0 | 337.1 | 1,666.0 | 271.0 |
| Nevada................... | 677.9 | 555.9 | 9.1 | 63.0 | 161.5 | 322.3 | 2,583.0 | 2,612.4 | 668.7 | 1,516.4 | 427.3 |
| New Hampshire............ | 199.8 | 198.7 | 1.0 | 49.4 | 31.2 | 117.1 | 1,522.3 | 1,381.8 | 191.7 | 1,122.0 | 68.1 |
| New Jersey............... | 243.5 | 228.8 | 3.6 | 16.7 | 87.7 | 120.8 | 1,537.2 | 1,555.5 | 265.3 | 1,155.1 | 135.1 |
| New Mexico............... | 699.4 | 783.5 | 7.1 | 60.3 | 178.3 | 537.8 | 3,928.7 | 3,941.7 | 858.1 | 2,519.9 | 563.8 |
| New York................. | 374.6 | 356.7 | 2.8 | 31.9 | 101.3 | 220.8 | 1,538.7 | 1,514.2 | 176.3 | 1,270.3 | 67.6 |
| North Carolina [3]........... | 371.8 | 363.7 | 5.8 | 26.4 | 91.0 | 240.5 | 2,734.8 | 2,545.3 | 630.6 | 1,760.9 | 153.8 |
| North Dakota............. | 252.1 | 281.3 | 1.3 | 52.8 | 24.2 | 202.9 | 2,309.7 | 2,197.8 | 389.5 | 1,573.6 | 234.7 |
| Ohio...................... | 307.7 | 297.5 | 6.1 | 50.3 | 99.5 | 141.6 | 2,589.3 | 2,419.1 | 502.4 | 1,743.0 | 173.7 |
| Oklahoma................. | 455.3 | 456.2 | 6.2 | 54.5 | 76.3 | 319.3 | 3,009.5 | 2,876.4 | 727.8 | 1,836.9 | 311.7 |
| Oregon................... | 268.8 | 281.8 | 2.5 | 48.3 | 58.7 | 172.3 | 2,978.9 | 2,986.5 | 427.4 | 2,145.3 | 413.7 |
| Pennsylvania.............. | 315.9 | 313.3 | 5.8 | 32.8 | 92.1 | 182.6 | 1,739.2 | 1,649.4 | 250.3 | 1,297.7 | 101.4 |
| Rhode Island............. | 239.1 | 232.2 | 1.9 | 42.0 | 44.7 | 143.5 | 1,788.1 | 1,751.6 | 303.6 | 1,308.1 | 140.0 |
| South Carolina............ | 506.8 | 506.2 | 7.8 | 49.8 | 77.0 | 371.5 | 3,256.9 | 3,195.9 | 623.1 | 2,289.1 | 283.8 |
| South Dakota............. | 422.0 | 433.6 | 2.9 | 68.4 | 27.4 | 335.0 | 1,997.2 | 1,876.2 | 311.3 | 1,405.9 | 159.0 |
| Tennessee................ | 638.5 | 651.5 | 7.8 | 43.7 | 117.1 | 482.9 | 2,875.4 | 2,940.6 | 576.5 | 2,088.3 | 275.8 |
| Texas.................... | 433.8 | 438.9 | 5.0 | 51.1 | 114.0 | 268.8 | 2,759.0 | 2,562.6 | 473.7 | 1,848.5 | 240.4 |
| Utah..................... | 243.3 | 238.9 | 2.4 | 54.7 | 47.3 | 134.5 | 2,974.8 | 2,780.2 | 381.0 | 2,092.1 | 307.2 |
| Vermont.................. | 136.5 | 165.8 | 2.2 | 35.0 | 14.8 | 113.8 | 1,556.9 | 1,436.7 | 297.3 | 1,108.3 | 31.1 |
| Virginia.................. | 219.8 | 208.2 | 5.3 | 33.8 | 51.1 | 117.9 | 1,869.3 | 1,792.9 | 218.0 | 1,454.7 | 120.1 |
| Washington............... | 303.5 | 304.5 | 3.1 | 44.0 | 72.8 | 184.6 | 3,502.2 | 3,173.6 | 590.4 | 2,194.4 | 388.8 |
| West Virginia............. | 362.7 | 350.7 | 4.7 | 43.8 | 28.9 | 273.4 | 2,038.8 | 1,852.0 | 420.1 | 1,266.6 | 165.3 |
| Wisconsin................. | 306.9 | 319.9 | 3.2 | 36.9 | 75.0 | 204.8 | 1,938.6 | 1,808.3 | 303.7 | 1,341.3 | 163.4 |
| Wyoming.................. | 244.7 | 237.5 | 2.6 | 45.4 | 13.1 | 176.4 | 1,959.3 | 1,830.4 | 275.0 | 1,421.0 | 134.5 |
| Puerto Rico............... | 224.4 | 232.6 | 20.3 | 6.3 | 91.5 | 114.4 | 1,033.3 | 934.2 | 238.2 | 588.3 | 107.7 |

[1] Estimated using the revised FBI Uniform Crime Reporting (UCR) definition of rape. Data are not comparable with those found in previous versions of this table. For more information, see <https://ucr.fbi.gov/crime-in-the-u.s/2017/crime-in-the-u.s.-2017/topic-pages/rape>. [2] Includes offenses reported by the Metro Transit Police and the District of Columbia Fire and Emergency Medical Services: Arson Investigation Unit. [3] Submitted rape data according to the legacy UCR definition of rape.

Source: U.S. Department of Justice, Federal Bureau of Investigation, "Crime in the United States 2017," <https://ucr.fbi.gov/>, accessed November 2018.

# Table 339. Crime Rates by Type—Selected Large Cities: 2017

[For year ending December 31. Rates per 100,000 population. Offenses reported to law enforcement]

| Cities ranked by population size, 2017 | Violent crime | | | | | Property crime | | | |
|---|---|---|---|---|---|---|---|---|---|
| | Total | Murder | Rape [1] | Robbery | Aggra-vated assault | Total | Burglary | Larceny/ theft | Motor vehicle theft |
| New York, NY.................... | 538.9 | 3.4 | 27.6 | 162.4 | 345.5 | 1,448.6 | 128.9 | 1,253.2 | 66.6 |
| Los Angeles, CA............... | 761.3 | 7.0 | 61.3 | 269.9 | 423.2 | 2,535.9 | 416.0 | 1,641.0 | 479.0 |
| Chicago, IL...................... | 1,098.9 | 24.1 | 65.1 | 439.3 | 570.4 | 3,263.8 | 477.1 | 2,358.8 | 427.8 |
| Houston, TX..................... | 1,095.2 | 11.5 | 58.4 | 418.0 | 607.3 | 4,128.4 | 731.7 | 2,900.8 | 495.9 |
| Phoenix, AZ..................... | 760.9 | 9.5 | 69.5 | 200.3 | 481.6 | 3,670.7 | 778.6 | 2,426.7 | 465.5 |
| Las Vegas, NV.................. | 618.9 | 12.6 | 79.6 | 211.2 | 315.5 | 2,943.4 | 805.2 | 1,635.2 | 503.1 |
| Philadelphia, PA................ | 947.6 | 20.1 | 75.0 | 382.5 | 470.0 | 3,063.5 | 418.3 | 2,297.2 | 348.0 |
| San Antonio, TX................ | 707.5 | 8.2 | 83.5 | 151.1 | 464.7 | 4,844.8 | 770.8 | 3,622.6 | 451.4 |
| San Diego, CA.................. | 366.6 | 2.5 | 39.3 | 99.0 | 225.9 | 1,843.0 | 268.0 | 1,214.4 | 360.6 |
| Dallas, TX....................... | 774.6 | 12.5 | 62.1 | 327.0 | 373.1 | 3,185.1 | 737.7 | 1,856.3 | 591.2 |
| San Jose, CA................... | 403.7 | 3.1 | 55.0 | 132.6 | 212.9 | 2,440.7 | 378.4 | 1,284.7 | 777.6 |
| Honolulu, HI..................... | 246.4 | 3.2 | 28.8 | 91.7 | 122.7 | 2,774.4 | 336.3 | 2,073.9 | 364.1 |
| Austin, TX....................... | 414.8 | 2.6 | 85.8 | 101.5 | 224.9 | 3,189.6 | 450.6 | 2,525.0 | 213.9 |
| Charlotte-Mecklenburg, NC [2]... | (NA) | 9.4 | (NA) | 220.5 | 433.5 | 3,815.2 | 701.5 | 2,827.0 | 286.7 |
| Jacksonville, FL................. | 631.3 | 12.2 | 60.1 | 153.8 | 405.2 | 3,526.7 | 631.1 | 2,568.6 | 326.9 |
| San Francisco, CA............. | 715.0 | 6.4 | 41.6 | 365.4 | 301.6 | 6,168.0 | 560.0 | 5,059.5 | 548.5 |
| Fort Worth, TX.................. | 560.2 | 8.0 | 65.2 | 147.3 | 339.7 | 3,215.3 | 586.0 | 2,319.4 | 309.9 |
| Columbus, OH.................. | 513.4 | 16.3 | 105.4 | 225.1 | 166.7 | 3,944.9 | 815.3 | 2,650.9 | 478.8 |
| Indianapolis, IN................. | 1,334.0 | 17.9 | 76.7 | 400.2 | 839.1 | 4,411.9 | 1,027.2 | 2,821.5 | 563.2 |
| Seattle, WA..................... | 632.7 | 3.7 | 36.9 | 210.0 | 382.1 | 5,258.6 | 1,082.0 | 3,673.5 | 503.2 |
| Denver, CO...................... | 675.6 | 8.3 | 98.9 | 174.4 | 394.0 | 3,667.1 | 612.9 | 2,267.3 | 786.8 |
| Washington, DC................ | 948.7 | 16.7 | 63.8 | 338.8 | 529.4 | 4,156.2 | 260.5 | 3,529.0 | 366.7 |
| El Paso, TX...................... | 378.8 | 2.8 | 53.9 | 58.1 | 264.1 | 1,818.9 | 188.3 | 1,514.4 | 116.2 |
| Louisville Metro, KY........... | 647.0 | 15.9 | 25.6 | 193.8 | 411.8 | 4,122.2 | 821.6 | 2,736.0 | 564.6 |
| Boston, MA...................... | 669.2 | 8.3 | 42.5 | 205.6 | 412.8 | 2,089.0 | 308.8 | 1,603.7 | 176.5 |
| Nashville, TN.................... | 1,138.2 | 16.3 | 72.9 | 303.1 | 745.8 | 3,818.0 | 631.3 | 2,806.6 | 380.0 |
| Detroit, MI....................... | 2,056.7 | 39.8 | 103.9 | 393.4 | 1,519.5 | 4,540.6 | 1,231.1 | 2,093.8 | 1,215.7 |
| Memphis, TN.................... | 2,003.3 | 27.7 | 90.4 | 529.6 | 1,355.6 | 6,297.8 | 1,460.2 | 4,224.5 | 613.1 |
| Portland, OR.................... | 515.7 | 3.7 | 67.4 | 160.9 | 283.6 | 5,677.0 | 729.1 | 3,824.6 | 1,123.3 |
| Oklahoma City, OK............ | 787.3 | 12.5 | 73.1 | 172.8 | 529.0 | 3,752.5 | 941.8 | 2,378.8 | 431.9 |
| Baltimore, MD.................. | 2,027.0 | 55.8 | 62.3 | 958.7 | 950.2 | 4,928.1 | 1,311.3 | 2,773.6 | 843.3 |
| Milwaukee, WI.................. | 1,597.4 | 19.8 | 72.9 | 490.4 | 1,014.2 | 3,792.0 | 927.1 | 1,940.3 | 924.6 |
| Albuquerque, NM.............. | 1,369.1 | 12.5 | 84.3 | 521.9 | 750.5 | 7,365.8 | 1,246.2 | 4,750.8 | 1,368.8 |
| Tucson, AZ...................... | 801.8 | 8.6 | 93.6 | 268.8 | 430.8 | 5,251.7 | 831.1 | 3,968.5 | 452.2 |
| Fresno, CA...................... | 565.0 | 10.6 | 33.1 | 182.0 | 339.3 | 3,841.4 | 693.2 | 2,618.3 | 529.9 |
| Sacramento, CA................ | 675.6 | 7.8 | 19.8 | 220.0 | 428.0 | 2,936.6 | 577.6 | 1,815.4 | 543.6 |
| Mesa, AZ........................ | 415.8 | 4.7 | 51.2 | 92.2 | 267.7 | 2,172.0 | 381.5 | 1,610.9 | 179.6 |
| Kansas City, MO............... | 1,724.3 | 30.9 | 91.8 | 383.1 | 1,218.5 | 4,543.8 | 960.5 | 2,670.4 | 912.9 |
| Atlanta, GA...................... | 935.7 | 16.4 | 58.6 | 293.6 | 567.2 | 4,776.4 | 704.3 | 3,387.2 | 685.0 |
| Colorado Springs, CO......... | 524.1 | 6.1 | 103.4 | 101.9 | 312.7 | 3,216.8 | 530.3 | 2,235.1 | 451.4 |
| Long Beach, CA................ | 657.8 | 4.7 | 43.1 | 262.4 | 347.7 | 2,672.5 | 586.6 | 1,507.0 | 578.9 |
| Miami, FL........................ | 720.9 | 11.2 | 22.7 | 211.2 | 475.8 | 4,014.2 | 527.0 | 3,090.9 | 396.3 |
| Virginia Beach, VA............. | 137.6 | 3.1 | 22.4 | 59.9 | 52.2 | 1,934.6 | 166.0 | 1,667.6 | 101.0 |
| Omaha, NE...................... | 647.3 | 6.9 | 91.2 | 139.1 | 410.1 | 3,880.2 | 464.6 | 2,636.7 | 778.8 |
| Oakland, CA..................... | 1,299.3 | 16.2 | 94.1 | 629.8 | 559.2 | 5,982.8 | 617.1 | 4,072.6 | 1,293.2 |
| Minneapolis, MN............... | 1,101.3 | 10.0 | 122.7 | 434.2 | 534.4 | 4,641.4 | 897.9 | 3,173.5 | 570.0 |
| Tulsa, OK........................ | 1,040.8 | 17.3 | 104.5 | 238.1 | 681.0 | 5,455.6 | 1,370.7 | 3,224.3 | 854.6 |
| New Orleans, LA............... | 1,121.4 | 39.5 | 144.7 | 329.1 | 608.1 | 4,243.8 | 560.8 | 3,046.2 | 636.8 |
| Arlington, TX.................... | 516.9 | 4.8 | 63.9 | 145.0 | 303.2 | 3,197.7 | 453.2 | 2,402.3 | 342.2 |
| Wichita, KS...................... | 1,022.3 | 8.9 | 97.7 | 153.2 | 762.5 | 5,535.6 | 839.0 | 4,063.1 | 633.6 |
| Cleveland, OH.................. | 1,556.8 | 27.8 | 129.0 | 699.9 | 700.1 | 4,916.0 | 1,518.9 | 2,516.1 | 881.0 |
| Tampa, FL....................... | 464.4 | 10.1 | 31.5 | 105.6 | 317.2 | 1,743.7 | 321.3 | 1,274.8 | 147.5 |
| Bakersfield, CA................. | 479.3 | 10.8 | 24.1 | 197.6 | 246.9 | 4,068.4 | 962.1 | 2,377.8 | 728.6 |
| Aurora, CO...................... | 608.4 | 8.2 | 86.7 | 184.5 | 329.1 | 3,003.7 | 454.1 | 1,954.8 | 594.8 |
| Anaheim, CA.................... | 354.6 | 2.8 | 32.5 | 135.8 | 183.4 | 2,630.4 | 382.3 | 1,809.0 | 439.2 |
| Santa Ana, CA.................. | 488.5 | 6.3 | 56.0 | 180.2 | 246.1 | 2,090.3 | 276.7 | 1,223.7 | 589.8 |
| Corpus Christi, TX............. | 702.5 | 6.4 | 70.5 | 142.7 | 482.9 | 3,565.3 | 677.9 | 2,665.4 | 222.0 |
| Riverside, CA................... | 508.8 | 3.7 | 50.6 | 165.8 | 288.7 | 3,058.3 | 510.0 | 2,020.9 | 527.4 |
| Lexington, KY................... | 350.9 | 9.0 | 62.0 | 169.7 | 110.1 | 3,782.1 | 647.5 | 2,739.7 | 394.9 |
| St. Louis, MO................... | 2,082.3 | 66.1 | 93.1 | 626.5 | 1,296.6 | 6,041.2 | 1,011.3 | 4,155.5 | 874.4 |
| Stockton, CA.................... | 1,414.6 | 17.8 | 49.7 | 390.2 | 956.8 | 3,627.3 | 691.3 | 2,274.2 | 661.9 |
| St. Paul, MN.................... | 650.8 | 7.2 | 70.8 | 227.3 | 345.6 | 3,565.4 | 741.5 | 2,144.5 | 679.5 |
| Pittsburgh, PA.................. | 656.4 | 18.0 | 29.4 | 262.1 | 346.8 | 3,114.4 | 526.3 | 2,365.9 | 222.3 |
| Henderson, NV.................. | 185.1 | 3.3 | 28.7 | 80.2 | 72.8 | 1,833.0 | 363.9 | 1,255.0 | 214.2 |
| Cincinnati, OH.................. | 947.1 | 23.4 | 97.6 | 399.8 | 426.3 | 5,049.9 | 1,152.7 | 3,400.7 | 496.5 |
| Anchorage, AK.................. | 1,203.3 | 9.1 | 132.0 | 262.7 | 799.5 | 5,415.8 | 748.2 | 3,619.7 | 1,048.0 |
| Plano, TX........................ | 149.8 | 5.2 | 27.9 | 41.0 | 75.8 | 1,733.7 | 250.7 | 1,366.3 | 116.7 |
| Greensboro, NC [2]............. | (NA) | 15.9 | (NA) | 228.9 | 480.6 | 3,562.1 | 710.9 | 2,559.5 | 291.7 |
| Orlando, FL...................... | 744.1 | 8.1 | 64.4 | 213.0 | 458.5 | 5,454.6 | 840.9 | 4,125.3 | 488.4 |
| Newark, NJ...................... | 896.5 | 27.1 | 40.9 | 377.2 | 451.2 | 2,395.0 | 423.7 | 1,128.1 | 843.2 |
| Toledo, OH...................... | (NA) | 12.6 | (NA) | 281.5 | 661.8 | 4,003.7 | 1,119.7 | 2,615.2 | 268.8 |
| Irvine, CA........................ | 61.2 | 0.7 | 16.7 | 19.9 | 23.9 | 1,316.5 | 227.1 | 1,019.1 | 70.3 |
| Chula Vista, CA................ | 298.0 | 0.7 | 22.9 | 112.1 | 162.3 | 1,432.3 | 236.1 | 915.5 | 280.7 |
| Durham, NC [2].................. | (NA) | 8.5 | (NA) | 316.6 | 467.1 | 3,826.3 | 867.4 | 2,675.7 | 283.2 |
| Jersey City, NJ................. | 509.5 | 7.8 | 45.9 | 199.3 | 256.4 | 1,807.0 | 417.7 | 1,206.0 | 183.3 |

NA Not available. [1] Beginning in 2013, the FBI has revised the definition of rape as used in Uniform Crime Reporting (UCR) Program. For more information, see <https://ucr.fbi.gov/crime-in-the-u.s/2017/crime-in-the-u.s.-2017/topic-pages/rape>. [2] This agency/state submits rape data classified according to the legacy UCR definition; therefore the rape offense and violent crime total, which rape is a part of, is not included in this table. See the data declaration for further explanation.

Source: U.S. Department of Justice, Federal Bureau of Investigation, "Crime in the United States 2017," <https://ucr.fbi.gov/>, accessed December 2018.

# Table 340. Homicide Trends: 1990 to 2016

[Based on Federal Bureau of Investigation's Uniform Crime Reports Supplementary Homicide Reports. Homicide includes murder and nonnegligent manslaughter, which is the willful killing of one human being by another. Excludes deaths caused by negligence, suicide, or accident; justifiable homicides; and attempts to murder. Justifiable homicides based on the reports of law enforcement agencies are analyzed separately. Deaths from the terrorist attacks of September 11, 2001 are not included. Data based on criminal homicides handled by state and local law enforcement, and as determined solely by police investigation, and not by the determination of a court, medical examiner, coroner, jury, or other non-law enforcement body. Excludes homicides handled by Federal law enforcement]

| Year | Number of victims | | | | | | | Rate [1] | | | | | | |
| | Total [2] | Male | Female | White | Black | American Indian/ Alaskan Native | Asian [3] | Total [2] | Male | Female | White | Black | American Indian/ Alaska Native | Asian [3] |
|---|---|---|---|---|---|---|---|---|---|---|---|---|---|---|
| 1990... | 23,438 | 18,303 | 5,115 | 11,278 | 11,487 | 150 | 250 | 9.4 | 15.0 | 4.0 | 5.4 | 37.5 | 7.3 | 3.3 |
| 1991... | 24,703 | 19,273 | 5,395 | 11,662 | 12,227 | 152 | 457 | 9.8 | 15.6 | 4.2 | 5.5 | 39.1 | 7.1 | 5.7 |
| 1992... | 23,760 | 18,513 | 5,217 | 11,229 | 11,777 | 158 | 415 | 9.3 | 14.8 | 4.0 | 5.2 | 36.8 | 7.2 | 4.9 |
| 1993... | 24,526 | 18,934 | 5,550 | 11,276 | 12,433 | 141 | 460 | 9.4 | 14.9 | 4.2 | 5.2 | 38.1 | 6.2 | 5.2 |
| 1994... | 23,326 | 18,291 | 5,007 | 10,772 | 11,854 | 133 | 393 | 8.9 | 14.2 | 3.7 | 4.9 | 35.6 | 5.6 | 4.3 |
| 1995... | 21,606 | 16,549 | 5,021 | 10,374 | 10,442 | 160 | 421 | 8.1 | 12.7 | 3.7 | 4.7 | 30.9 | 6.6 | 4.4 |
| 1996... | 19,645 | 15,149 | 4,468 | 9,480 | 9,473 | 134 | 377 | 7.3 | 11.5 | 3.2 | 4.3 | 27.5 | 5.3 | 3.8 |
| 1997... | 18,208 | 14,055 | 4,124 | 8,619 | 8,841 | 149 | 375 | 6.7 | 10.5 | 3.0 | 3.8 | 25.3 | 5.7 | 3.6 |
| 1998... | 16,974 | 12,756 | 4,140 | 8,391 | 7,933 | 141 | 252 | 6.2 | 9.4 | 2.9 | 3.7 | 22.3 | 5.2 | 2.3 |
| 1999... | 15,522 | 11,704 | 3,800 | 7,777 | 7,139 | 160 | 298 | 5.6 | 8.6 | 2.7 | 3.4 | 19.7 | 5.7 | 2.6 |
| 2000... | 15,586 | 11,818 | 3,733 | 7,560 | 7,425 | 119 | 280 | 5.5 | 8.6 | 2.6 | 3.3 | 20.3 | 4.0 | 2.4 |
| 2001... | 16,037 | 12,232 | 3,775 | 7,884 | 7,522 | 105 | 319 | 5.6 | 8.7 | 2.6 | 3.4 | 20.2 | 3.4 | 2.6 |
| 2002... | 16,229 | 12,429 | 3,770 | 7,796 | 7,770 | 130 | 308 | 5.6 | 8.8 | 2.6 | 3.3 | 20.6 | 4.1 | 2.4 |
| 2003... | 16,528 | 12,792 | 3,707 | 7,944 | 7,883 | 117 | 351 | 5.7 | 9.0 | 2.5 | 3.4 | 20.6 | 3.5 | 2.6 |
| 2004... | 16,148 | 12,553 | 3,555 | 7,939 | 7,570 | 134 | 282 | 5.5 | 8.7 | 2.4 | 3.4 | 19.5 | 3.9 | 2.0 |
| 2005... | 16,740 | 13,149 | 3,565 | 8,045 | 8,016 | 131 | 312 | 5.7 | 9.1 | 2.4 | 3.4 | 20.4 | 3.7 | 2.2 |
| 2006... | 17,309 | 13,605 | 3,661 | 8,063 | 8,548 | 123 | 343 | 5.8 | 9.3 | 2.4 | 3.4 | 21.5 | 3.3 | 2.3 |
| 2007... | 17,128 | 13,411 | 3,678 | 8,017 | 8,450 | 104 | 302 | 5.7 | 9.1 | 2.4 | 3.3 | 20.9 | 2.7 | 1.9 |
| 2008... | 16,465 | 12,844 | 3,573 | 7,953 | 7,860 | 124 | 250 | 5.4 | 8.6 | 2.3 | 3.3 | 19.2 | 3.1 | 1.6 |
| 2009... | 15,399 | 11,846 | 3,535 | 7,450 | 7,374 | 119 | 290 | 5.0 | 7.9 | 2.3 | 3.1 | 17.7 | 2.9 | 1.8 |
| 2010... | 14,722 | 11,371 | 3,328 | 6,851 | 7,322 | 117 | 260 | 4.8 | 7.5 | 2.1 | 2.8 | 17.4 | 2.7 | 1.5 |
| 2011... | 14,661 | 11,354 | 3,281 | 6,786 | 7,277 | 111 | 284 | 4.7 | 7.4 | 2.1 | 2.8 | 17.1 | 2.6 | 1.6 |
| 2012... | 14,856 | 11,534 | 3,302 | 6,812 | 7,502 | 101 | 285 | 4.7 | 7.5 | 2.1 | 2.7 | 17.4 | 2.3 | 1.6 |
| 2013... | 14,319 | 11,116 | 3,178 | 6,519 | 7,268 | 104 | 257 | 4.5 | 7.1 | 2.0 | 2.6 | 16.6 | 2.3 | 1.4 |
| 2014... | 14,164 | 10,940 | 3,187 | 6,427 | 7,187 | 121 | 251 | 4.4 | 7.0 | 2.0 | 2.6 | 16.2 | 2.7 | 1.3 |
| 2015... | 15,883 | 12,499 | 3,354 | 6,938 | 8,293 | 183 | 253 | 4.9 | 7.9 | 2.1 | 2.8 | 18.5 | 4.0 | 1.3 |
| 2016... | 17,250 | 13,520 | 3,684 | 7,556 | 8,999 | 167 | 295 | 5.3 | 8.5 | 2.3 | 3.0 | 19.9 | 3.6 | 1.4 |

[1] Rate is per 100,000 inhabitants. [2] Includes unknown sex, race, or ethnicity. [3] Includes Native Hawaiian and Pacific Islanders.

Source: U.S. Department of Justice, Office of Justice Programs, "Easy Access to the FBI's Supplementary Homicide Reports (EZASHR)," <http://www.ojjdp.gov/ojstatbb/ezashr/>; and U.S. Centers for Disease Control and Prevention, WONDER Online Database, "Multiple Cause of Death, 1999-2016," <http://wonder.cdc.gov/>; accessed September 2018.

# Table 341. Homicide Victims by Race and Sex: 1990 to 2017

[Excludes deaths to nonresidents of United States. Effective with data for 1999, causes of death are classified by the International Classification of Diseases, Tenth Revision (ICD-10), replacing the Ninth Revision (ICD-9) used for 1979–1998 data. In ICD-9, the category Homicide also includes death as a result of legal intervention. ICD-10 differentiates between homicides due to assault and deaths due to legal intervention. Some caution should be used in comparing data. See text, Section 2]

| Year | Homicide victims | | | | | Homicide rate [2] | | | | |
| | Total [1] | White | | Black | | Total [1] | White | | Black | |
| | | Male | Female | Male | Female | | Male | Female | Male | Female |
|---|---|---|---|---|---|---|---|---|---|---|
| 1990... | 24,932 | 9,147 | 3,006 | 9,981 | 2,163 | 10.0 | 9.0 | 2.8 | 69.2 | 13.5 |
| 1991... | 26,513 | 9,581 | 3,201 | 10,628 | 2,330 | 10.5 | 9.3 | 3.0 | 72.0 | 14.2 |
| 1992... | 25,488 | 9,456 | 3,012 | 10,131 | 2,187 | 10.0 | 9.1 | 2.8 | 67.5 | 13.1 |
| 1993... | 26,009 | 9,054 | 3,232 | 10,640 | 2,297 | 10.1 | 8.6 | 3.0 | 69.7 | 13.6 |
| 1994... | 24,926 | 9,055 | 2,921 | 10,083 | 2,124 | 9.6 | 8.5 | 2.6 | 65.1 | 12.4 |
| 1995... | 22,895 | 8,336 | 3,028 | 8,847 | 1,936 | 8.7 | 7.8 | 2.7 | 56.3 | 11.1 |
| 1996... | 20,971 | 7,570 | 2,747 | 8,183 | 1,800 | 7.9 | 7.0 | 2.5 | 51.5 | 10.2 |
| 1997... | 19,846 | 7,343 | 2,570 | 7,601 | 1,652 | 7.4 | 6.7 | 2.3 | 47.1 | 9.3 |
| 1998... | 18,272 | 6,707 | 2,534 | 6,873 | 1,547 | 6.8 | 6.1 | 2.2 | 42.1 | 8.6 |
| 1999... | 16,889 | 6,162 | 2,466 | 6,214 | 1,434 | 6.1 | 5.5 | 2.1 | 36.1 | 7.6 |
| 2000... | 16,765 | 5,925 | 2,414 | 6,482 | 1,385 | 6.0 | 5.2 | 2.1 | 37.2 | 7.2 |
| 2001... | 20,308 | 8,254 | 3,074 | 6,780 | 1,446 | 7.1 | 7.2 | 2.6 | 38.2 | 7.4 |
| 2002... | 17,638 | 6,282 | 2,403 | 6,896 | 1,391 | 6.1 | 5.4 | 2.0 | 38.4 | 7.0 |
| 2003... | 17,732 | 6,337 | 2,372 | 7,083 | 1,309 | 6.1 | 5.5 | 2.0 | 38.9 | 6.5 |
| 2004... | 17,357 | 6,302 | 2,341 | 6,839 | 1,296 | 5.9 | 5.4 | 2.0 | 37.0 | 6.4 |
| 2005... | 18,124 | 6,457 | 2,313 | 7,412 | 1,257 | 6.1 | 5.5 | 1.9 | 39.6 | 6.1 |
| 2006... | 18,573 | 6,514 | 2,346 | 7,677 | 1,355 | 6.2 | 5.5 | 1.9 | 40.4 | 6.5 |
| 2007... | 18,361 | 6,541 | 2,373 | 7,584 | 1,286 | 6.1 | 5.5 | 1.9 | 39.3 | 6.1 |
| 2008... | 17,826 | 6,556 | 2,337 | 7,148 | 1,187 | 5.9 | 5.5 | 1.9 | 36.5 | 5.5 |
| 2009... | 16,799 | 5,983 | 2,340 | 6,715 | 1,159 | 5.5 | 4.9 | 1.9 | 33.8 | 5.3 |
| 2010... | 16,259 | 5,648 | 2,215 | 6,704 | 1,114 | 5.3 | 4.7 | 1.8 | 33.4 | 5.1 |
| 2011... | 16,238 | 5,569 | 2,199 | 6,739 | 1,119 | 5.2 | 4.6 | 1.8 | 33.0 | 5.0 |
| 2012... | 16,688 | 5,639 | 2,197 | 7,129 | 1,112 | 5.3 | 4.6 | 1.8 | 34.5 | 4.9 |
| 2013... | 16,121 | 5,393 | 2,130 | 6,937 | 1,122 | 5.1 | 4.4 | 1.7 | 33.1 | 4.9 |
| 2014... | 15,872 | 5,304 | 2,093 | 6,823 | 1,080 | 5.0 | 4.3 | 1.7 | 32.1 | 4.7 |
| 2015... | 17,793 | 5,798 | 2,209 | 8,021 | 1,152 | 5.5 | 4.6 | 1.7 | 37.3 | 4.9 |
| 2016... | 19,362 | 6,325 | 2,343 | 8,650 | 1,345 | 6.0 | 5.1 | 1.8 | 39.8 | 5.7 |
| 2017... | 19,510 | 6,274 | 2,496 | 8,776 | 1,297 | 6.0 | 5.0 | 1.9 | 39.8 | 5.4 |

[1] Includes other races not shown separately. [2] Rates per 100,000 resident population in specified group. Based on enumerated population figures as of April 1 for 1990, 2000, and 2010; estimated resident population as of July 1 for other years.

Source: U.S. National Center for Health Statistics, through 2014, National Vital Statistics Reports (NVSR), *Deaths: Final Data for 2014*, Vol. 65, No. 4, June 2016 and earlier reports; thereafter, CDC WONDER Online Database, "Multiple Cause of Death, 1999-2017," <http://wonder.cdc.gov/>.

# Table 342. Criminal Victimizations and Victimization Rates: 2010 to 2017

[20,348 represents 20,348,000. A victimization refers to a single victim or household that experienced a criminal incident. Includes victimizations reported and not reported to the police. Criminal incidents or crimes are distinguished from victimizations in that one criminal incident may have multiple victims or victimizations. Based on the National Crime Victimization Survey (NCVS). See source for more information]

| Type of crime | Number of victimizations (1,000) | | | | Victimization rates [1] | | | |
|---|---|---|---|---|---|---|---|---|
| | 2010 | 2015 | 2016 | 2017 | 2010 | 2015 | 2016 | 2017 |
| Total | 20,348 | 19,618 | 21,169 | 18,953 | (X) | (X) | (X) | (X) |
| Violent victimization [2] | 4,936 | 5,007 | 5,354 | 5,613 | 19.3 | 18.6 | 19.7 | 20.6 |
| Not injured | 3,646 | 3,703 | 4,133 | 4,364 | 14.2 | 13.7 | 15.2 | 16.0 |
| Injured | 1,290 | 1,303 | 1,221 | 1,248 | 5.0 | 4.8 | 4.5 | 4.6 |
| Serious violent victimization [3] | 1,695 | 1,827 | 1,798 | 2,001 | 6.6 | 6.8 | 6.6 | 7.3 |
| Rape/sexual assault | 269 | 432 | 298 | 394 | 1.0 | 1.6 | 1.1 | 1.4 |
| Robbery | 569 | 579 | 459 | 614 | 2.2 | 2.1 | 1.7 | 2.3 |
| Not injured | 370 | 370 | 293 | 410 | 1.4 | 1.4 | 1.1 | 1.5 |
| Injured | 198 | 209 | 166 | 203 | 0.8 | 0.8 | 0.6 | 0.7 |
| Aggravated assault | 858 | 817 | 1,041 | 993 | 3.4 | 3.0 | 3.8 | 3.6 |
| Not injured | 538 | 526 | 723 | 669 | 2.1 | 1.9 | 2.7 | 2.5 |
| Injured | 320 | 291 | 318 | 325 | 1.2 | 1.1 | 1.2 | 1.2 |
| Simple assault | 3,241 | 3,179 | 3,556 | 3,612 | 12.7 | 11.8 | 13.1 | 13.3 |
| Not injured | 2,619 | 2,534 | 3,004 | 3,007 | 10.2 | 9.4 | 11.0 | 11.0 |
| Injured | 622 | 645 | 552 | 605 | 2.4 | 2.4 | 2.0 | 2.2 |
| Personal theft/larceny [4] | 138 | 89 | 92 | 101 | 0.5 | 0.3 | 0.3 | 0.4 |
| Property crimes | 15,412 | 14,611 | 15,815 | 13,340 | 125.4 | 110.7 | 118.6 | 108.4 |
| Household burglary | 3,176 | 2,905 | 3,160 | 2,538 | 25.8 | 22.0 | 23.7 | 20.6 |
| Motor vehicle theft | 607 | 564 | 618 | 517 | 4.9 | 4.3 | 4.6 | 4.2 |
| Theft [5] | 11,628 | 11,142 | 12,037 | 10,285 | 94.6 | 84.4 | 90.3 | 83.6 |

X Not applicable. [1] Per 1,000 persons age 12 or older for violent victimization and personal theft/larceny; per 1,000 households for property crime. [2] Excludes homicide because the NCVS is based on interviews with victims and therefore cannot measure murder. [3] Includes rape, sexual assault, personal robbery, and aggravated assault, attempted and completed crimes. [4] Includes pocket picking, completed purse snatching, and attempted purse snatching. [5] The taking or attempted unlawful taking of property or cash without personal contact with the victim. Incidents involving theft of property from within a household are classified as theft if the offender has a legal right to be in the house (such as a maid, delivery person, or guest).

Source: U.S. Department of Justice, Bureau of Justice Statistics, "NCVS Victimization Analysis Tool," <http://www.bjs.gov/index.cfm?ty=nvat>, accessed April 2019.

# Table 343. Victimization Rates by Type of Crime and Characteristics of the Victim: 2017

[Rate per 1,000 persons age 12 years or older. Based on the National Crime Victimization Survey. See text, this section and Appendix III]

| Victim characteristics | Violent victimization | | | | | | Personal theft [1] |
|---|---|---|---|---|---|---|---|
| | Total | Serious violent victim- ization | Rape/ sexual assault | Robbery | Aggravated assault | Simple assault | |
| Total | 20.6 | 7.3 | 1.4 | 2.3 | 3.6 | 13.3 | 0.4 |
| Male | 20.4 | 7.0 | 0.2 | 2.6 | 4.1 | 13.4 | 0.4 |
| Female | 20.8 | 7.7 | 2.6 | 1.9 | 3.2 | 13.1 | 0.4 |
| 12 to 14 years old | 37.4 | 11.2 | [3] 1.3 | 3.1 | 6.7 | 26.2 | [3] (Z) |
| 15 to 17 years old | 29.5 | 9.6 | [3] 1.3 | [3] 3.2 | 5.1 | 20.0 | [3] (Z) |
| 18 to 20 years old | 38.7 | 23.4 | 8.6 | 4.9 | 9.9 | 15.3 | [3] 0.9 |
| 21 to 24 years old | 31.7 | 14.5 | 2.4 | 5.2 | 6.9 | 17.2 | [3] 0.5 |
| 25 to 34 years old | 26.3 | 8.5 | 1.3 | 2.6 | 4.6 | 17.8 | 0.5 |
| 35 to 49 years old | 20.1 | 7.4 | 2.0 | 1.8 | 3.6 | 12.8 | [3] 0.3 |
| 50 to 64 years old | 16.3 | 4.4 | 0.4 | 2.0 | 2.1 | 11.9 | [3] 0.3 |
| 65 years old and over | 6.5 | 1.8 | [3] 0.3 | 0.6 | 0.9 | 4.7 | 0.4 |
| White | 20.5 | 7.2 | 1.4 | 2.2 | 3.7 | 13.2 | 0.3 |
| Black | 21.5 | 8.0 | 1.9 | 2.7 | 3.4 | 13.5 | [3] 0.6 |
| Other [2] | 20.5 | 7.4 | 1.6 | 2.0 | 3.8 | 13.1 | [3] 0.4 |
| White, non-Hispanic | 20.8 | 6.8 | 1.3 | 2.0 | 3.6 | 13.9 | 0.3 |
| Black, non-Hispanic | 21.8 | 7.9 | 1.9 | 2.5 | 3.5 | 13.9 | [3] 0.5 |
| Hispanic | 20.7 | 9.5 | 1.8 | 3.6 | 4.1 | 11.2 | [3] 0.4 |
| Household income: | | | | | | | |
| Less than $7,500 | 67.4 | 33.1 | 6.1 | 11.8 | 15.2 | 34.3 | [3] 0.8 |
| $7,500 to $14,999 | 34.0 | 13.3 | 2.0 | 7.9 | 3.5 | 20.7 | [3] 0.7 |
| $15,000 to $24,999 | 31.2 | 11.2 | 1.4 | 3.2 | 6.6 | 20.1 | [3] 0.3 |
| $25,000 to $34,999 | 29.0 | 10.7 | 2.2 | 2.5 | 5.9 | 18.3 | [3] 0.3 |
| $35,000 to $49,999 | 20.9 | 8.0 | 1.5 | 2.6 | 3.9 | 12.9 | [3] 0.3 |
| $50,000 to $74,999 | 22.2 | 6.7 | 1.2 | 1.7 | 3.8 | 15.5 | [3] 0.3 |
| $75,000 or more | [3] (Z) | [3] (Z) | [3] (Z) | [3] (Z) | [3] (Z) | [3] (Z) | [3] (Z) |
| Unknown | 12.0 | 4.1 | 1.0 | 0.9 | 2.2 | 7.9 | 0.3 |

Z Rounds to less than .05 victimizations per 1,000. [1] Includes pocket picking and purse snatching. [2] Includes American Indians and Alaska Natives, Asians, Native Hawaiians, other Pacific Islanders, and persons of two or more races. [3] Based on 10 or fewer sample cases or the coefficient of variation is greater than 50%.

Source: U.S. Department of Justice, Bureau of Justice Statistics, "NCVS Victimization Analysis Tool," <http://www.bjs.gov/index.cfm?ty=nvat>, accessed May 2019.

# Table 344. Criminal Victimizations by Age of Victim and Selected Characteristics: 2003 to 2013

[In percent, unless otherwise noted. Covers period 2003 to 2013. Data are for violent victimizations that are nonfatal. Based on the National Crime Victimization Survey. For details, see source <http://www.bjs.gov/index.cfm?ty=dcdetail&iid=245>]

| Item | Age 12–24 years old | Age 25–49 years old | Age 50–64 years old | Age Aged 65 years or older |
|---|---|---|---|---|
| VIOLENT VICTIMIZATIONS | | | | |
| **Average annual (number)** | 2,709,260 | 2,899,310 | 834,510 | 136,720 |
| Rate per 1,000 households | 49.9 | 27.6 | 15.2 | 3.6 |
| By type of weapon: | | | | |
| Total | 100.0 | 100.0 | 100.0 | 100.0 |
| No weapon used | 72.6 | 70.2 | 69.9 | 69.3 |
| Weapon used | 21.5 | 22.4 | 21.0 | 19.5 |
| Firearm | 6.2 | 7.7 | 7.0 | 7.6 |
| Knife | 6.4 | 5.9 | 5.6 | 4.3 |
| Other | 7.2 | 7.1 | 6.9 | 6.2 |
| Type unknown | 1.6 | 1.7 | 1.5 | [5] 1.4 |
| Don't know | 5.9 | 7.5 | 9.0 | 11.1 |
| By victim-offender relationship: | | | | |
| Total | 100.0 | 100.0 | 100.0 | 100.0 |
| Known to victim | 57.2 | 50.6 | 52.1 | 48.8 |
| Domestic | 16.4 | 26.0 | 19.9 | 14.3 |
| Intimate partner [1] | 9.9 | 20.4 | 9.6 | 6.1 |
| Immediate family | 4.2 | 3.5 | 7.3 | 4.6 |
| Other relative | 2.2 | 2.1 | 3.0 | 3.6 |
| Well-known/casual acquaintance | 40.8 | 24.6 | 32.3 | 34.5 |
| Stranger | 34.0 | 41.2 | 39.8 | 43.4 |
| Unknown [2] | 8.8 | 8.1 | 8.1 | 7.8 |
| By location of crime: | | | | |
| Total | 100.0 | 100.0 | 100.0 | 100.0 |
| At or near victim's home | 25.4 | 41.1 | 43.5 | 59.3 |
| At or near friend, neighbor, or relative's home | 11.3 | 5.9 | 5.5 | 6.0 |
| Other location [3] | 63.3 | 53.1 | 51.0 | 34.7 |
| Type of crime by whether reported to police: | | | | |
| Violent crime | 38.0 | 53.5 | 50.5 | 56.2 |
| Serious violent crime | 48.0 | 63.9 | 58.2 | 64.3 |
| Rape/sexual assault | 30.9 | 43.5 | 25.4 | [1] 28.0 |
| Robbery | 52.8 | 64.8 | 61.2 | 76.1 |
| Aggravated assault | 50.0 | 68.2 | 63.1 | 64.3 |
| Simple assault | 32.9 | 48.5 | 47.0 | 51.8 |
| PROPERTY VICTIMIZATIONS [4] | | | | |
| **Average annual (number)** | 2,031,930 | 9,924,460 | 4,307,210 | 1,796,740 |
| Rate per 1,000 households | 262.0 | 177.1 | 134.6 | 72.3 |
| Type of crime by whether reported to police: | | | | |
| Property crime | 36.9 | 38.2 | 36.6 | 38.3 |
| Household burglary | 52.3 | 56.2 | 51.7 | 50.1 |
| Motor vehicle theft | 78.6 | 82.8 | 79.0 | 83.5 |
| Theft | 29.3 | 31.1 | 30.3 | 31.9 |

[1] Includes current or former spouses, boyfriends, and girlfriends. [2] Includes unknown victim–offender relationships and unknown number of offenders. [3] Includes commercial places, parking lots or garages, schools, open areas, public transportation, and other locations. [4] Data by age of householder. [5] Interpret with caution.

Source: U.S. Department of Justice, Bureau of Justice Statistics, *Crimes Against the Elderly, 2003–2013*, NCJ 248339, November 2014. See also <http://www.bjs.gov/index.cfm?ty=pbse&sid=21>.

# Table 345. Rape and Sexual Assault Rates Among College-Age Females: 1998 to 2013

[Estimated victimization rates per 1,000 females, based on 3-year rolling averages centered on the most recent year. Data from the National Crime Victimization Survey]

| Year | Students 18 to 24 years old [1] | Nonstudents 18 to 24 years old [2] | Not college-age females [3] | Year | Students 18 to 24 years old [1] | Nonstudents 18 to 24 years old [2] | Not college-age females [3] |
|---|---|---|---|---|---|---|---|
| 1998 | 7.8 | 8.9 | 3.1 | 2006 | 5.4 | 5.5 | 1.7 |
| 1999 | 6.0 | 11.2 | 3.5 | 2007 | 5.5 | 5.4 | 1.7 |
| 2000 | 7.1 | 12.2 | 2.8 | 2008 | 5.2 | 6.7 | 1.9 |
| 2001 | 8.8 | 11.2 | 3.0 | 2009 | 3.7 | 8.3 | 1.6 |
| 2002 | 8.9 | 10.0 | 2.2 | 2010 | [4] 4.1 | 8.4 | 1.6 |
| 2003 | 7.6 | 8.8 | 2.2 | 2011 | 4.6 | 7.1 | 1.4 |
| 2004 | 6.5 | 7.0 | 1.8 | 2012 | 5.9 | 4.1 | 1.3 |
| 2005 | 4.7 | 5.6 | 1.6 | 2013 | 4.4 | 4.3 | 1.4 |

[1] Includes female victims age 18 to 24 enrolled part time or full time in a post-secondary institution (i.e., college or university, trade school, or vocational school). [2] Includes female victims age 18 to 24 not enrolled in a post-secondary institution. [3] Includes females age 12 to 17 and age 25 or older. [4] Interpret with caution, subject to sampling error.

Source: U.S. Bureau of Justice Statistics, *Rape and Sexual Assault Victimization Among College-Age Females, 1995–2013*, NCJ 248471, December 2014. See also <http://www.bjs.gov/index.cfm?ty=tp&tid=317>.

## Table 346. Violent Crime Between Intimate Partners by Sex of Victims: 1993 to 2017

[Intimate partners are defined as current and former spouses, boyfriends, and girlfriends. Based on the National Crime Victimization Survey (NCVS); see text this section, and source]

| Year | Female victims | | | | Male victims | | | |
|------|---|---|---|---|---|---|---|---|
| | | Rate per 1,000 [1] | | | | Rate per 1,000 [1] | | |
| | Total intimate partner violence | Overall intimate partner violence | Serious violence [3] | Simple assault [4] | Total intimate partner violence | Overall intimate partner violence | Serious violence [3] | Simple assault [4] |
| 1993.............. | 1,689,687 | 15.5 | 5.7 | 9.9 | 347,924 | 3.4 | 1.5 | 1.9 |
| 1994.............. | 1,843,713 | 16.8 | 6.1 | 10.7 | 258,990 | 2.5 | 0.7 | 1.8 |
| 1995.............. | 1,727,462 | 15.5 | 3.7 | 11.8 | 285,907 | 2.8 | 1.0 | 1.8 |
| 1996.............. | 1,626,516 | 14.5 | 4.7 | 9.8 | 194,647 | 1.9 | 0.8 | 1.1 |
| 1997.............. | 1,661,683 | 14.7 | 4.8 | 9.8 | 176,651 | 1.7 | 0.5 | 1.2 |
| 1998.............. | 1,336,585 | 11.7 | 3.6 | 8.0 | 228,793 | 2.1 | 0.6 | 1.5 |
| 1999.............. | 1,164,554 | 10.0 | 3.5 | 6.5 | 230,230 | 2.1 | 0.5 | 1.6 |
| 2000.............. | 783,762 | 6.7 | 1.9 | 4.8 | 116,152 | 1.1 | [5] 0.2 | 0.9 |
| 2001.............. | 981,671 | 8.3 | 2.9 | 5.4 | 108,740 | 1.0 | 0.5 | 0.5 |
| 2002.............. | 797,805 | 6.7 | 2.0 | 4.7 | 131,956 | 1.2 | [5] 0.5 | 0.7 |
| 2003.............. | 906,628 | 7.4 | 3.6 | 3.8 | 133,657 | 1.2 | 0.5 | 0.7 |
| 2004.............. | 816,139 | 6.6 | 2.3 | 4.3 | 215,582 | 1.8 | 0.5 | 1.4 |
| 2005.............. | 621,041 | 4.9 | 1.6 | 3.4 | 194,966 | 1.6 | [5] 0.9 | 0.7 |
| 2006 [2]........... | 1,063,775 | 8.4 | 3.2 | 5.2 | 241,475 | 2.0 | 1.1 | 0.9 |
| 2007.............. | 780,979 | 6.1 | 2.1 | 4.0 | 124,831 | 1.0 | [5] 0.4 | 0.7 |
| 2008.............. | 914,422 | 7.1 | 2.5 | 4.6 | 188,970 | 1.5 | 0.7 | 0.9 |
| 2009.............. | 914,529 | 7.0 | 1.6 | 5.4 | 125,121 | 1.0 | 0.3 | 0.7 |
| 2010.............. | 636,770 | 4.9 | 1.7 | 3.2 | 136,663 | 1.1 | 0.4 | 0.7 |
| 2011.............. | 604,645 | 4.6 | 1.6 | 3.0 | 246,127 | 2.0 | [5] 0.4 | 1.6 |
| 2012.............. | 682,417 | 5.1 | 1.7 | 3.4 | 128,378 | 1.0 | 0.4 | 0.6 |
| 2013.............. | 619,357 | 4.6 | 2.1 | 2.5 | 129,438 | 1.0 | 0.6 | 0.4 |
| 2014.............. | 500,920 | 3.7 | 1.4 | 2.2 | 133,692 | 1.0 | 0.6 | 0.5 |
| 2015.............. | 741,645 | 5.4 | 2.2 | 3.1 | 64,403 | 0.5 | [5] 0.2 | 0.3 |
| 2016 [6]........... | 513,494 | 3.7 | 1.6 | 2.0 | 83,705 | 0.6 | 0.3 | 0.4 |
| 2017.............. | 602,902 | 4.3 | 1.7 | 2.6 | 63,407 | 0.5 | 0.2 | 0.2 |

[1] Rates are per 1,000 persons age 12 and older. [2] Due to methodological changes, use caution when comparing 2006 National Crime Victimization Survey criminal victimization estimates to other years. See Criminal Victimization, 2007, NCJ 224390. [3] Rape or sexual assault, robbery, and aggravated assault. [4] Attack or attempted attack without a weapon that results in no injury, minor injury, or an undetermined injury requiring less than two days of hospitalization. [5] Interpret data with caution. [6] Due to methodological changes in the 2016 NCVS, use caution when comparing 2016 criminal victimization estimates to other years. See Criminal Victimization, 2016 (BJS Web, NCJ 251150, December, 2017) for more information.

Source: U.S. Department of Justice, Bureau of Justice Statistics, "NCVS Victimization Analysis Tool," <https://www.bjs.gov/index.cfm?ty=nvat>, accessed February 2019.

## Table 347. Nonfatal Firearm and Nonfirearm Violence by Victim-Offender Relationship and Location of Crime: 2007 to 2011

[Data are for victimizations. Covers period from 2007 to 2011. Detail may not sum to total due to rounding. Data from National Crime Victimization Survey]

| Characteristic | Total nonfatal violence | | Firearm violence | | Nonfirearm violence | |
|---|---|---|---|---|---|---|
| | Number | Percent [1] | Number | Percent [1] | Number | Percent [1] |
| **RELATIONSHIP TO VICTIM** | | | | | | |
| **Total**........ | **29,611,300** | **(X)** | **2,218,500** | **7.5** | **27,392,800** | **92.5** |
| Nonstranger.................... | 15,715,900 | (X) | 738,000 | 4.7 | 14,977,900 | 95.3 |
| Intimate [2].................... | 4,673,600 | (X) | 195,700 | 4.2 | 4,477,900 | 95.8 |
| Other relative.................. | 2,157,700 | (X) | 158,100 | 7.3 | 1,999,500 | 92.7 |
| Friend/acquaintance............ | 8,884,600 | (X) | 384,100 | 4.3 | 8,500,500 | 95.7 |
| Stranger....................... | 10,983,100 | (X) | 1,177,900 | 10.7 | 9,805,200 | 89.3 |
| Unknown [3].................... | 2,912,300 | (X) | 302,600 | 10.4 | 2,609,600 | 89.6 |
| **LOCATION** | | | | | | |
| **Total**........ | **29,618,300** | **100.0** | **2,218,500** | **100.0** | **27,399,800** | **100.0** |
| Victim's home or lodging......... | 6,491,400 | 21.9 | 427,600 | 19.3 | 6,063,800 | 22.1 |
| Near victim's home.............. | 4,804,700 | 16.2 | 504,500 | 22.7 | 4,300,200 | 15.7 |
| In, at, or near a friend, neighbor, or relative's home...... | 2,175,900 | 7.3 | 132,600 | 6.0 | 2,043,300 | 7.5 |
| Commercial place................ | 2,878,600 | 9.7 | 195,400 | 8.8 | 2,683,200 | 9.8 |
| Parking lot or garage............ | 1,688,400 | 5.7 | 340,600 | 15.4 | 1,347,900 | 4.9 |
| School [4]...................... | 3,931,100 | 13.3 | [5] 12,600 | [5] 0.6 | 3,918,500 | 14.3 |
| Open area, on street, or public transportation............. | 4,636,900 | 15.7 | 508,400 | 22.9 | 4,128,500 | 15.1 |
| Other location................. | 3,011,200 | 10.2 | 96,800 | 4.4 | 2,914,400 | 10.6 |

X Not applicable. [1] Percent of total violence is shown for data by relationship to victim. Percent distribution of specified type of violence is shown for data by location. [2] Includes current or former spouses, boyfriends, or girlfriends. [3] Includes relationships unknown and number of offenders unknown. [4] Includes inside a school building or on school property. [5] Interpret with caution. Estimate based on 10 or fewer sample cases, or coefficient of variation is greater than 50%.

Source: Department of Justice, Bureau of Justice Statistics, *Firearm Violence, 1993-2011*, NCJ 241730, May 2013. See also <http://www.bjs.gov/index.cfm?ty=pbdetail&iid=4616>.

## Table 348. Hate Crimes—Number of Incidents, Offenses, Victims, and Known Offenders by Bias Motivation: 2000 to 2017

[2,040 law enforcement agencies submitted data on hate crimes. 16,149 law enforcement agencies covering over 306 million people participated in the Hate Crime Statistics Program in 2017. Hate crime offenses cover incidents motivated by race, ethnicity/national origin, religion, sexual orientation, gender identity, and disability. See source and Appendix III]

| Bias motivation | Incidents reported | Offenses | Victims [1] | Known offenders [2] |
|---|---|---|---|---|
| 2000............................ | 8,213 | 9,619 | 10,117 | 7,690 |
| 2010............................ | 6,628 | 7,699 | 8,208 | 6,008 |
| **2017, total [3]**............... | **7,175** | **8,437** | **8,828** | **6,370** |
| **Race/ethnicity/ancestry, total**...... | **4,131** | **4,832** | **5,060** | **3,747** |
| Anti-White...................... | 741 | 844 | 864 | 758 |
| Anti-Black or African American...... | 2,013 | 2,358 | 2,458 | 1,742 |
| Anti-American Indian/Alaska native... | 251 | 281 | 321 | 228 |
| Anti-Asian....................... | 131 | 152 | 165 | 108 |
| Anti-Native Hawaiian or Other Pacific Islander.......... | 16 | 17 | 18 | 10 |
| Anti-multiple races, group......... | 180 | 215 | 229 | 100 |
| Anti-Arab........................ | 102 | 128 | 131 | 100 |
| Anti-Hispanic or Latino........... | 427 | 525 | 552 | 491 |
| Anti-Other race/ethnicity/ancestry... | 270 | 312 | 322 | 210 |
| **Religion, total [3]**.............. | **1,564** | **1,679** | **1,749** | **1,009** |
| Anti-Jewish...................... | 938 | 976 | 1,017 | 523 |
| Anti-Catholic.................... | 73 | 75 | 76 | 59 |
| Anti-Protestant.................. | 40 | 40 | 40 | 15 |
| Anti-Islamic..................... | 273 | 314 | 325 | 231 |
| Anti-other religion.............. | 76 | 82 | 86 | 56 |
| Anti-multiple religions group..... | 47 | 54 | 57 | 35 |
| Anti-Eastern Orthodox (Russian, Greek, Other)........... | 23 | 23 | 27 | 14 |
| **Sexual orientation, total**........ | **1,130** | **1,303** | **1,338** | **1,250** |
| Anti-gay (male homosexual)........ | 679 | 758 | 774 | 778 |
| Anti-lesbian (female homosexual)... | 126 | 159 | 164 | 129 |
| Anti-lesbian, gay, bisexual, or transgender.......... | 268 | 321 | 333 | 282 |
| Anti-heterosexual................ | 32 | 37 | 37 | 28 |
| Anti-bisexual.................... | 25 | 28 | 30 | 33 |
| **Disability, total**................ | **116** | **128** | **160** | **124** |
| Anti-physical.................... | 32 | 35 | 37 | 31 |
| Anti-mental...................... | 84 | 93 | 123 | 93 |
| **Gender identity**.................. | **119** | **131** | **132** | **137** |
| Anti-transgender................. | 106 | 118 | 119 | 127 |
| Anti-gender non-conforming....... | 13 | 13 | 13 | 10 |
| **Multiple bias [4]**................ | **69** | **311** | **335** | **63** |

[1] "Victim" may refer to a person, business, institution, or a society as a whole. [2] "Known offender" does not imply that the identity of the suspect is known, but only that an attribute of the suspect has been identified which distinguishes him/her from an unknown offender. [3] Includes motivation types not shown separately. [4] Incident in which one or more offense types are motivated by two or more biases.

Source: U.S. Department of Justice, Federal Bureau of Investigation, "Hate Crime Statistics 2017," <https://www.fbi.gov/services/cjis/ucr>, accessed April 2019.

## Table 349. Hate Crimes by Bias Motivation and Location of Incident: 2017

[See headnote, Table 348]

| Location | Total incidents | Bias motivation | | | | | | Multiple-bias incidents [1] |
|---|---|---|---|---|---|---|---|---|
| | | Race/ ethnicity/ ancestry | Religion | Sexual orientation | Disability | Gender | Gender identity | |
| **Total [2]**..................... | **7,175** | **4,131** | **1,564** | **1,130** | **116** | **46** | **119** | **69** |
| Air/bus/train terminal............. | 118 | 84 | 13 | 15 | 1 | – | 4 | 1 |
| Bank/savings and loan.............. | 25 | 16 | 5 | 2 | 2 | – | – | – |
| Bar/nightclub...................... | 99 | 52 | 5 | 37 | 2 | – | 2 | 1 |
| Church/synagogue/temple/mosque... | 292 | 44 | 234 | 12 | – | – | 1 | 1 |
| Commercial office building......... | 139 | 90 | 32 | 9 | 2 | 1 | 3 | 2 |
| Community center................... | 22 | 7 | 14 | 1 | – | – | – | – |
| Construction site................. | 25 | 19 | 3 | 2 | 1 | – | – | – |
| Convenience store................. | 105 | 71 | 13 | 14 | 3 | 1 | 1 | 2 |
| Department/discount store.......... | 91 | 63 | 13 | 8 | 3 | 1 | 1 | 2 |
| Drug store/doctor's office/hospital.... | 75 | 49 | 15 | 8 | – | 1 | 1 | 1 |
| Field/woods....................... | 50 | 29 | 13 | 4 | 1 | – | 2 | 1 |
| Government/public building.......... | 117 | 78 | 19 | 17 | 2 | 1 | – | – |
| Grocery/supermarket................ | 75 | 57 | 11 | 4 | 1 | – | 2 | – |
| Highway/road/alley/street/sidewalk... | 1,218 | 778 | 139 | 241 | 16 | 5 | 29 | 10 |
| Hotel/motel/etc................... | 63 | 41 | 11 | 9 | 1 | 1 | – | – |
| Jail/prison/penitentiary/corrections facility........................ | 59 | 42 | 3 | 13 | 1 | – | 1 | 6 |
| Park/playground................... | 128 | 67 | 33 | 20 | 1 | – | 1 | 6 |
| Parking/drop lot/garage............ | 419 | 271 | 62 | 66 | 7 | 2 | 4 | 7 |
| Residence/home.................... | 1,971 | 1,133 | 360 | 366 | 46 | 24 | 22 | 20 |
| Restaurant........................ | 192 | 126 | 20 | 38 | 3 | 1 | 3 | 1 |
| School/college [3]................ | 199 | 85 | 87 | 22 | 3 | – | 2 | – |
| School—college/university......... | 214 | 129 | 45 | 29 | 1 | 1 | 6 | 3 |
| School—elementary/secondary....... | 340 | 207 | 67 | 42 | 7 | 2 | 9 | 6 |
| Service/gas station............... | 73 | 58 | 8 | 4 | 2 | 1 | – | – |
| Other/unknown..................... | 1,066 | 535 | 339 | 147 | 10 | 4 | 26 | 5 |

– Represents zero. [1] See footnote 4, Table 348. [2] Includes locations not shown separately. [3] The location designation school/college has been retained for agencies that have not updated their records to include the new location designations of school, which allow for more specificity in reporting.

Source: U.S. Department of Justice, Federal Bureau of Investigation, "Hate Crime Statistics 2017," <https://www.fbi.gov/services/cjis/ucr>, accessed April 2019.

# Table 350. Property Crime by Selected Household Characteristics: 2017

[123,086 represents 123,086,000. For crimes against households (burglary, theft, and motor vehicle theft), each household affected by a crime is counted as a single victimization. Based on National Crime Victimization Survey (NCVS); see text, this section and Appendix III]

| Characteristic | Number of house-holds (1,000) | Property crimes | | | | | | | |
|---|---|---|---|---|---|---|---|---|---|
| | | Number of victimizations (1,000) | | | | Victimization rate per 1,000 households | | | |
| | | Total | Burglary | Motor vehicle theft | Theft | Total | Burglary | Motor vehicle theft | Theft |
| **Total**.................. | **123,086** | **13,340** | **2,538** | **517** | **10,285** | **108.4** | **20.6** | **4.2** | **83.6** |
| Race: | | | | | | | | | |
| White.................. | 97,258 | 10,404 | 1,921 | 370 | 8,113 | 107.0 | 19.7 | 3.8 | 83.4 |
| Black.................. | 16,192 | 1,719 | 410 | 91 | 1,218 | 106.1 | 25.3 | 5.6 | 75.2 |
| Other [1].................. | 9,635 | 1,218 | 208 | 56 | 954 | 126.4 | 21.6 | 5.8 | 99.0 |
| Ethnicity: | | | | | | | | | |
| Hispanic.............. | 16,728 | 2,190 | 393 | 116 | 1,680 | 130.9 | 23.5 | 6.9 | 100.4 |
| Non-Hispanic.......... | 106,358 | 11,151 | 2,145 | 401 | 8,605 | 104.8 | 20.2 | 3.8 | 80.9 |
| Household income: | | | | | | | | | |
| Less than $7,500...... | 4,508 | 772 | 187 | 26 | 559 | 171.3 | 41.5 | 5.8 | 124.0 |
| $7,500 to $14,999..... | 6,703 | 1,134 | 294 | 38 | 802 | 169.1 | 43.8 | 5.7 | 119.6 |
| $15,000 to $24,999.... | 9,131 | 1,200 | 261 | 46 | 893 | 131.4 | 28.6 | 5.0 | 97.8 |
| $25,000 to $34,999.... | 10,081 | 1,253 | 258 | 62 | 933 | 124.3 | 25.6 | 6.1 | 92.5 |
| $35,000 to $49,999.... | 13,863 | 1,779 | 380 | 51 | 1,348 | 128.3 | 27.4 | 3.7 | 97.2 |
| $50,000 to $74,999.... | 15,874 | 1,760 | 294 | 67 | 1,399 | 110.9 | 18.5 | 4.2 | 88.1 |
| $75,000 or more....... | 29,020 | (NA) | (NA) | (NA) | (NA) | (NA) | (NA) | (NA) | (NA) |
| Unknown.............. | 33,905 | 2,547 | 531 | 120 | 1,896 | 75.1 | 15.7 | 3.5 | 55.9 |
| Number of persons in household: | | | | | | | | | |
| 1...................... | 40,173 | 3,542 | 904 | 123 | 2,516 | 88.2 | 22.5 | 3.0 | 62.6 |
| 2 or 3................. | 59,896 | 6,291 | 1,131 | 245 | 4,915 | 105.0 | 18.9 | 4.1 | 82.1 |
| 4 or 5................. | 19,696 | 2,795 | 414 | 119 | 2,263 | 141.9 | 21.0 | 6.0 | 114.9 |
| 6 or more.............. | 3,321 | 712 | 89 | 30 | 592 | 214.3 | 26.9 | 9.1 | 178.4 |

NA Not available. [1] Includes American Indians and Alaska Natives, Asians, Native Hawaiians and other Pacific Islanders, and persons of two or more races.

Source: U.S. Department of Justice, Bureau of Justice Statistics, "NCVS Victimization Analysis Tool," <http://www.bjs.gov/index.cfm?ty=nvat>, accessed June 2019.

# Table 351. Robbery and Property Crimes by Type, Location, and Average Value Lost: 2010 to 2017

[300.3 represents 300,300. Data are from the FBI's Unified Crime Reporting (UCR) Program]

| Characteristic of offense | Number of offenses (1,000) | | | | Average value lost (dol.) | | | |
|---|---|---|---|---|---|---|---|---|
| | 2010 | 2015 | 2016 | 2017 | 2010 | 2015 | 2016 | 2017 |
| **Robbery, total**..................... | **300.3** | **284.8** | **280.4** | **280.5** | **1,239** | **1,190** | **1,400** | **1,373** |
| Location of crime: | | | | | | | | |
| Street or highway........................ | 129.6 | 113.5 | 109.0 | 104.3 | 908 | 1,023 | 1,191 | 1,202 |
| Commercial house........................ | 39.7 | 41.0 | 42.8 | 43.4 | 1,858 | 1,416 | 1,689 | 1,284 |
| Gas or service station................... | 7.0 | 7.7 | 8.2 | 8.4 | 939 | 938 | 970 | 1,087 |
| Convenience store........................ | 15.7 | 16.2 | 17.4 | 18.4 | 782 | 623 | 732 | 957 |
| Residence............................... | 51.9 | 47.0 | 46.4 | 44.9 | 1,491 | 1,545 | 1,758 | 1,732 |
| Bank.................................... | 6.5 | 4.9 | 5.0 | 4.8 | 4,410 | 3,884 | 3,531 | 3,483 |
| Miscellaneous........................... | 49.9 | 54.5 | 51.6 | 56.4 | 1,115 | 1,023 | 1,367 | 1,474 |
| **Burglary, total**..................... | **1,898.0** | **1,395.9** | **1,354.9** | **1,251.0** | **2,119** | **2,316** | **2,361** | **2,416** |
| Location and time of burglary: | | | | | | | | |
| Residence (dwelling):.................... | 1,402.2 | 999.4 | 942.2 | 841.3 | 2,137 | 2,296 | 2,273 | 2,368 |
| Night.................................. | 389.9 | 289.1 | 278.6 | 255.5 | 1,868 | 1,904 | 1,913 | 1,995 |
| Day.................................... | 722.2 | 522.9 | 486.0 | 424.9 | 2,158 | 2,316 | 2,258 | 2,383 |
| Unknown................................ | 290.1 | 187.5 | 177.6 | 160.9 | 2,445 | 2,844 | 2,879 | 2,924 |
| Nonresidence (store, office, etc.):...... | 495.7 | 396.5 | 412.7 | 409.7 | 2,070 | 2,366 | 2,562 | 2,514 |
| Night.................................. | 204.6 | 166.3 | 178.5 | 179.9 | 1,765 | 2,154 | 2,585 | 2,337 |
| Day.................................... | 168.9 | 140.0 | 142.6 | 140.9 | 2,010 | 2,244 | 2,182 | 2,211 |
| Unknown................................ | 122.2 | 90.2 | 91.6 | 88.9 | 2,662 | 2,946 | 3,109 | 3,353 |
| **Larceny-theft, total** [1]............. | **5,391.6** | **5,014.3** | **4,971.9** | **4,917.3** | **988** | **929** | **999** | **1,007** |
| Type of larceny: | | | | | | | | |
| Pocket-picking........................... | 21.1 | 27.3 | 24.4 | 27.7 | 526 | 652 | 646 | 648 |
| Purse-snatching......................... | 24.5 | 20.3 | 20.0 | 19.6 | 400 | 563 | 475 | 564 |
| Shoplifting............................. | 925.1 | 1,118.4 | 1,038.6 | 1,021.2 | 174 | 262 | 250 | 260 |
| From motor vehicles (except accessories)...... | 1,423.9 | 1,203.5 | 1,301.4 | 1,318.0 | 704 | 782 | 869 | 879 |
| Motor vehicle accessories................ | 477.8 | 350.0 | 366.0 | 363.0 | 681 | 573 | 541 | 505 |
| Bicycles................................ | 179.6 | 180.1 | 162.5 | 155.9 | 351 | 444 | 483 | 477 |
| From buildings.......................... | 607.9 | 582.1 | 533.6 | 523.2 | 1,406 | 1,394 | 1,449 | 1,381 |
| From coin-operated machines.............. | 17.6 | 11.4 | 10.9 | 10.7 | 365 | 497 | 607 | 538 |
| All others.............................. | 1,714.0 | 1,521.2 | 1,514.6 | 1,477.9 | 1,654 | 1,512 | 1,649 | 1,700 |
| Larceny-theft by value: | | | | | | | | |
| Over $200............................... | 2,443.1 | 2,289.5 | 2,256.3 | 2,256.3 | 2,089 | 1,969 | 2,140 | 2,137 |
| $50 to $200............................. | 1,235.1 | 1,119.7 | 1,075.7 | 1,043.2 | 111 | 106 | 108 | 105 |
| Under $50............................... | 1,713.3 | 1,605.1 | 1,640.0 | 1,617.7 | 17 | 20 | 14 | 13 |
| **Motor vehicle theft, total**.......... | **641.9** | **638.0** | **700.1** | **705.3** | **6,152** | **7,001** | **7,680** | **7,708** |

[1] Excludes motor vehicles.

Source: U.S. Department of Justice, Federal Bureau of Investigation, "Crime in the United States 2017," and earlier releases, <https://ucr.fbi.gov/>, accessed November 2018.

# Table 352. Fraud and Identity Theft—Consumer Complaints by State: 2018

[Rate per 100,000 population. As of December 31. Rates based on U.S. Census Bureau's 2018 population estimates. The Consumer Sentinel Network is a secure online database of consumer complaints available only to law enforcement. Based on unverified complaints reported by consumers. Excludes complaints from state-specific data contributors]

| State | Fraud and other complaints | | Identity theft victims | | State | Fraud and other complaints | | Identity theft victims | |
|---|---|---|---|---|---|---|---|---|---|
| | Number | Rate | Number | Rate | | Number | Rate | Number | Rate |
| U.S. | 2,143,141 | 655 | 415,579 | 127 | MO | 40,165 | 657 | 5,222 | 85 |
| AL | 33,539 | 688 | 5,241 | 108 | MT | 5,943 | 566 | 799 | 76 |
| AK | 3,531 | 477 | 507 | 69 | NE | 8,416 | 438 | 1,281 | 67 |
| AZ | 51,816 | 739 | 8,853 | 126 | NV | 26,088 | 870 | 5,816 | 194 |
| AR | 15,692 | 522 | 2,197 | 73 | NH | 7,642 | 569 | 1,565 | 117 |
| CA | 250,509 | 634 | 73,668 | 186 | NJ | 56,438 | 627 | 11,273 | 125 |
| CO | 37,686 | 672 | 6,151 | 110 | NM | 13,573 | 650 | 2,000 | 96 |
| CT | 21,022 | 586 | 3,864 | 108 | NY | 117,567 | 592 | 24,248 | 122 |
| DE | 7,743 | 805 | 1,517 | 158 | NC | 66,486 | 647 | 11,481 | 112 |
| DC | 8,182 | 1,179 | 1,156 | 167 | ND | 2,549 | 337 | 474 | 63 |
| FL | 210,174 | 1,002 | 37,797 | 180 | OH | 73,212 | 628 | 10,268 | 88 |
| GA | 93,249 | 894 | 23,871 | 229 | OK | 19,347 | 492 | 3,109 | 79 |
| HI | 6,516 | 456 | 1,021 | 72 | OR | 25,120 | 606 | 4,179 | 101 |
| ID | 9,560 | 557 | 1,368 | 80 | PA | 77,714 | 607 | 13,725 | 107 |
| IL | 73,000 | 570 | 16,296 | 127 | RI | 6,210 | 586 | 990 | 93 |
| IN | 35,366 | 530 | 4,918 | 74 | SC | 36,062 | 718 | 6,339 | 126 |
| IA | 13,329 | 424 | 1,654 | 53 | SD | 3,074 | 353 | 486 | 56 |
| KS | 15,999 | 549 | 2,142 | 74 | TN | 53,014 | 789 | 6,808 | 101 |
| KY | 23,707 | 532 | 2,522 | 57 | TX | 204,531 | 723 | 45,030 | 159 |
| LA | 27,236 | 581 | 5,202 | 111 | UT | 15,356 | 495 | 2,915 | 94 |
| ME | 6,340 | 475 | 744 | 56 | VT | 2,690 | 431 | 316 | 51 |
| MD | 45,298 | 748 | 8,747 | 145 | VA | 56,135 | 663 | 8,196 | 97 |
| MA | 35,869 | 523 | 6,387 | 93 | WA | 43,113 | 582 | 7,380 | 100 |
| MI | 71,339 | 716 | 13,952 | 140 | WV | 10,134 | 558 | 1,051 | 58 |
| MN | 28,471 | 511 | 4,070 | 73 | WI | 28,952 | 500 | 3,731 | 64 |
| MS | 15,790 | 529 | 2,894 | 97 | WY | 2,647 | 457 | 338 | 58 |

Source: U.S. Federal Trade Commission, *Consumer Sentinel Network Data Book 2018,* February 2019. See also <https://www.ftc.gov/enforcement/consumer-sentinel-network/reports>.

# Table 353. Victims of Identity Theft by Type of Account and Selected Victim Characteristics: 2016

[25,952.4 represents 25,952,400. Data shown are for persons age 16 or older who experienced at least one identity theft incident during the past 12 months. Estimates are based on the most recent identity theft incident. Includes successful and attempted identity theft, regardless of whether the victim experienced a loss. Details do not sum to totals because persons could experience more than one type of identity theft. Based on the National Crime Victimization Survey's Identity Theft Supplement]

| Characteristic | Any identity theft | | Misuse of existing credit card | | Misuse of existing bank account | | New account or personal information [1] | |
|---|---|---|---|---|---|---|---|---|
| | Number of victims | Percent of all persons | Number of victims | Percent of persons with credit card | Number of victims | Percent of persons with bank account | Number of victims | Percent of all persons |
| Total | 25,952.4 | 10.2 | 13,422.8 | 7.5 | 11,950.1 | 5.4 | 2,610.0 | 1.0 |
| By sex: | | | | | | | | |
| Male | 12,496.4 | 10.1 | 6,816.4 | 7.9 | 5,432.2 | 5.0 | 1,215.4 | 1.0 |
| Female | 13,456.0 | 10.3 | 6,606.4 | 7.1 | 6,517.9 | 5.7 | 1,394.6 | 1.1 |
| By race/Hispanic origin: | | | | | | | | |
| White [3] | 19,425.2 | 11.8 | 10,661.5 | 8.4 | 8,476.0 | 5.6 | 1,639.7 | 1.0 |
| Black [3] | 2,314.8 | 7.4 | 756.1 | 4.5 | 1,424.0 | 5.9 | 398.9 | 1.3 |
| Hispanic/Latino | 2,538.3 | 6.3 | 1,026.2 | 4.5 | 1,427.5 | 4.7 | 354.6 | 0.9 |
| Other race [3,4] | 1,307.9 | 8.4 | 839.2 | 7.0 | 393.3 | 2.9 | 162.3 | 1.0 |
| Two or more races [3] | 366.2 | 12.0 | 139.7 | 8.1 | 229.3 | 8.8 | 54.5 | 1.8 |
| By age: | | | | | | | | |
| 16 to 17 years old | 81.4 | 1.0 | [2] 13.7 | [2] 2.5 | 50.5 | 1.6 | [2] 2.0 | [2] (Z) |
| 18 to 24 years old | 1,997.5 | 6.6 | 537.8 | 4.1 | 1,379.7 | 5.7 | 192.4 | 0.6 |
| 25 to 34 years old | 4,781.7 | 10.8 | 2,030.1 | 6.5 | 2,521.0 | 6.6 | 463.3 | 1.1 |
| 35 to 49 years old | 7,541.2 | 12.4 | 3,809.5 | 8.3 | 3,592.6 | 6.6 | 781.0 | 1.3 |
| 50 to 64 years old | 7,480.0 | 11.8 | 4,235.0 | 8.4 | 3,115.9 | 5.4 | 800.3 | 1.3 |
| 65 years or older | 4,070.6 | 8.5 | 2,796.7 | 7.3 | 1,290.5 | 2.9 | 371.0 | 0.8 |
| By household income: | | | | | | | | |
| $24,999 or less | 3,273.3 | 6.2 | 1,053.6 | 4.2 | 1,831.2 | 4.6 | 548.0 | 1.0 |
| $25,000-$49,999 | 5,315.6 | 8.0 | 2,349.0 | 5.4 | 2,800.4 | 4.9 | 588.6 | 0.9 |
| $50,000-$74,999 | 4,623.3 | 10.2 | 2,212.9 | 6.4 | 2,285.7 | 5.6 | 374.7 | 0.8 |
| $75,000 or more | 12,740.3 | 14.1 | 7,807.3 | 10.2 | 5,032.9 | 6.0 | 1,098.7 | 1.2 |

Z Less than 1 or less than 0.05%. [1] Includes the misuse of personal information to open a new account or to commit other fraud. [2] Interpret with caution; estimates are based on 10 or fewer sample cases or coefficient of variation is greater than 50%. [3] Excludes persons of Hispanic or Latino origin. [4] Includes persons identifying as American Indian, Alaska Native, Asian, Hawaiian, or other Pacific Islander.

Source: U.S. Department of Justice, Bureau of Justice Statistics, *Victims of Identity Theft, 2016*, NCJ 251147, January 2019. See also <https://www.bjs.gov/index.cfm?ty=pbse&sid=60>.

## Table 354. Firearm Violence, Homicides and Nonfatal Victimizations: 1995 to 2011

[Detail may not sum to total due to rounding. Data are primarily from the Bureau of Justice Statistics' National Crime Victimization Survey and Centers for Disease Control and Prevention's Injury Statistics Query and Reporting System]

| Year | Fatal and nonfatal firearm violence | | | | Percent | | Rate of nonfatal firearm victimization [3] |
|------|-------|-------------------|-----------------------------------|------------------------------|----------------------------------------|---------------------------------------|---|
| | Total | Firearm homicides | Nonfatal firearm victimizations [1] | Nonfatal firearm incidents [2] | All violence involving firearms | All firearm violence that was homicide | |
| 1995....... | 1,208,800 | 15,551 | 1,193,200 | 1,028,900 | 7.9 | 1.3 | 5.5 |
| 2000....... | 621,000 | 10,801 | 610,200 | 483,700 | 7.3 | 1.7 | 2.7 |
| 2005....... | 515,900 | 12,352 | 503,500 | 446,400 | 7.4 | 2.4 | 2.1 |
| 2006....... | 627,200 | 12,791 | 614,400 | 552,000 | 7.4 | 2.0 | 2.5 |
| 2007....... | 567,400 | 12,632 | 554,800 | 448,400 | 8.3 | 2.2 | 2.2 |
| 2008....... | 383,500 | 12,179 | 371,300 | 331,600 | 6.0 | 3.2 | 1.5 |
| 2009....... | 421,600 | 11,493 | 410,100 | 383,400 | 7.4 | 2.7 | 1.6 |
| 2010....... | 426,100 | 11,078 | 415,000 | 378,800 | 8.6 | 2.6 | 1.6 |
| 2011 [4]..... | 478,400 | 11,101 | 467,300 | 414,600 | 8.2 | 2.3 | 1.8 |

[1] A victimization refers to a single victim that experienced a criminal incident. [2] An incident is a specific criminal act involving one or more victims or victimizations. [3] Per 1,000 persons age 12 or older. [4] Preliminary homicide estimates from Centers for Disease Control, *Deaths: Preliminary Data for 2011*, NVSR Vol. 61, No. 6.

Source: Department of Justice, Bureau of Justice Statistics, *Firearm Violence, 1993-2011*, NCJ 241730, May 2013. See also <http://www.bjs.gov/index.cfm?ty=pbdetail&iid=4616>

## Table 355. Active Shooter Incidents and Casualties: 2000 to 2018

[The Federal Bureau of Investigation (FBI) defines active shooters as "one or more individuals actively engaged in killing or attempting to kill people in a populated area." This definition encompasses shootings that happen in schools, workplaces, and other public spaces. A shooting can be categorized as an active shooter incident even if no one is killed or wounded. Excluded from this report are gang- and drug-related shootings and gun-related incidents that appeared not to have put other people in peril (e.g., the accidental discharge of a firearm in a bar)]

| Year and location | Active shooter incidents | Casualties | | |
|-------------------|--------------------------|-------|-------|--------|
| | | Total | Fatal | Injury |
| 2000................................................... | 1 | 7 | 7 | 0 |
| 2001................................................... | 6 | 43 | 12 | 31 |
| 2002................................................... | 4 | 29 | 11 | 18 |
| 2003................................................... | 11 | 51 | 29 | 22 |
| 2004................................................... | 4 | 20 | 14 | 6 |
| 2005................................................... | 9 | 51 | 24 | 27 |
| 2006................................................... | 10 | 46 | 23 | 23 |
| 2007................................................... | 14 | 126 | 69 | 57 |
| 2008................................................... | 8 | 63 | 29 | 34 |
| 2009................................................... | 19 | 143 | 65 | 78 |
| 2010................................................... | 26 | 86 | 37 | 49 |
| 2011................................................... | 10 | 84 | 32 | 52 |
| 2012................................................... | 21 | 208 | 90 | 118 |
| 2013................................................... | 17 | 86 | 44 | 42 |
| 2014................................................... | 20 | 97 | 36 | 61 |
| 2015................................................... | 20 | 134 | 56 | 78 |
| 2016................................................... | 20 | 214 | 83 | 129 |
| 2017................................................... | 30 | 729 | 138 | 591 |
| 2018................................................... | 27 | 213 | 85 | 128 |
| BY LOCATION 2000-2018 | | | | |
| Place of commerce................................... | 121 | (NA) | (NA) | (NA) |
| Education facility..................................... | 57 | (NA) | (NA) | (NA) |
| Open space........................................... | 37 | (NA) | (NA) | (NA) |
| Government........................................... | 26 | (NA) | (NA) | (NA) |
| Residence............................................. | 12 | (NA) | (NA) | (NA) |
| Place of worship..................................... | 11 | (NA) | (NA) | (NA) |
| Health care facility.................................. | 12 | (NA) | (NA) | (NA) |
| Other location........................................ | 1 | (NA) | (NA) | (NA) |

NA Not available.

Source: U.S. Department of Justice, Federal Bureau of Investigation, Office of Partner Engagement, "Active Shooter Resources," <https://www.fbi.gov/about/partnerships/office-of-partner-engagement/active-shooter-resources#FBI-Resources>, accessed August 2019.

## Table 356. Background Checks for Firearm Transfers: 2005 to 2015

[In thousands (8,324 represents 8,324,000), except as noted. The Brady Handgun Violence Prevention Act (Brady Act) P.L. 103–159, 1993 requires a background check on an applicant for a firearm purchase from a dealer who is a Federal Firearms Licensee. The period beginning November 30, 1998 is the effective date for the Brady Act. The National Instant Criminal Background Check System (NICS) began operations in 1998. Checks on handgun and long gun transfers are conducted by the FBI, and by state and local agencies. Totals combine Firearm Inquiry Statistics (FIST) estimates for state and local agencies with transactions and denials reported by the FBI]

| Inquiries and rejections | 2005 | 2006 | 2007 | 2008 | 2009 | 2010 | 2011 | 2012 | 2013 | 2014 | 2015 |
|--------------------------|------|------|------|------|------|------|------|------|------|------|------|
| Applications received................ | 8,324 | 8,772 | 8,836 | 10,131 | 11,071 | 10,643 | 12,135 | 15,718 | 17,602 | 14,993 | 16,610 |
| Applications denied.................. | 132 | 135 | 136 | 147 | 150 | 153 | 160 | 192 | 193 | 193 | 226 |
| *Denied (percent)*................ | *1.6* | *1.6* | *1.6* | *1.5* | *1.4* | *1.5* | *1.3* | *1.2* | *1.1* | *1.3* | *1.4* |
| Selected reasons for rejection: [1] | | | | | | | | | | | |
| Felony indictment/conviction...... | (NA) | (NA) | (NA) | 77 | 67 | 62 | (NA) | 82 | (NA) | 82 | 100 |
| Other................................... | (NA) | (NA) | (NA) | 70 | 83 | 91 | (NA) | 110 | (NA) | 111 | 126 |
| Felony denials per 1,000 applications............. | (NA) | (NA) | (NA) | 7.2 | 6.2 | 6.0 | (NA) | 5.2 | (NA) | 5.5 | 6.0 |

NA Not available. [1] Beginning in 2008, the FBI instituted a new classification system; therefore, data prior to 2008 aren't comparable to previously published estimates.

Source: U.S. Department of Justice, Bureau of Justice Statistics, *Background Checks for Firearm Transfers, 2015 Statistical Tables*, NCJ 250978, November 2017. See also <https://www.bjs.gov/index.cfm?ty=pbse&sid=13>.

# Table 357. Denials of Firearm Transfer Applications by Reason and Agency Type: 2013 to 2015

[In percent. Reasons for denials are based on The Brady Handgun Violence Prevention Act, pursuant to 18 U.S.C. 922 and state laws. Denial occurs when an applicant is prohibited from receiving a firearm or a permit that can be used to receive a firearm because a disqualifying factor was found during a background check. Application for firearm transfer is information submitted by a person to a state or local checking agency to purchase a firearm or obtain a permit that can be used for a purchase. Information may be submitted directly to a checking agency or forwarded by a prospective seller. Totals were based on federal and state agencies that reported counts on reasons for denial. Reasons for denial for local agencies were estimated]

| Reason for denial | 2013 [1] | | 2014 | | | 2015 | | |
|---|---|---|---|---|---|---|---|---|
| | FBI | State | FBI | State | Local | FBI | State | Local |
| Felony indictment/conviction.................... | 48.5 | 30.6 | 47.7 | 31.0 | 18.8 | 48.1 | 30.2 | 19.5 |
| Felony indictment/information.................. | 5.6 | 3.5 | 5.5 | 8.7 | 2.7 | 5.3 | 1.6 | 3.1 |
| Felony conviction................................ | 42.9 | 27.1 | 42.2 | 22.3 | 16.1 | 42.8 | 28.6 | 16.4 |
| Felony arrest with no disposition.................. | (X) | 7.7 | (X) | 4.4 | 2.5 | (X) | 11.9 | 3.2 |
| Fugitive................................ | 18.2 | 12.9 | 19.1 | 10.8 | 3.2 | 18.7 | 7.0 | 3.9 |
| Domestic violence.................... | 9.2 | 11.8 | 9.7 | 11.0 | 19.7 | 10.1 | 11.9 | 18.4 |
| Misdemeanor conviction............... | 6.1 | 6.3 | 6.8 | 6.1 | 15.0 | 7.3 | 6.8 | 14.4 |
| Protection/restraining order................ | 3.1 | 5.5 | 2.9 | 4.9 | 4.7 | 2.8 | 5.1 | 4.0 |
| Drug user/addict.................... | 10.4 | 3.7 | 10.4 | 5.3 | 4.6 | 9.6 | 5.2 | 5.0 |
| Mental health commitment/adjudication.......... | 3.3 | 3.5 | 3.9 | 5.3 | 6.9 | 4.4 | 8.0 | 6.0 |
| Illegal/unlawful alien.................... | 1.3 | 2.4 | 1.6 | 2.7 | 1.2 | 2.0 | 2.2 | 0.6 |
| State law prohibition.................... | 8.8 | 23.9 | 7.3 | 25.7 | 19.9 | 6.8 | 20.1 | 25.0 |
| Local law prohibition.................... | (X) | (NA) | (X) | (NA) | 2.3 | (X) | (NA) | 2.8 |
| Other prohibitions [2].................... | 0.3 | 3.5 | 0.2 | 4.0 | 21.0 | 0.2 | 3.5 | 15.7 |

NA Not available. X Not applicable. [1] Data not available for local law prohibition; see source. [2] Includes juveniles, persons dishonorably discharged from the Armed Services, persons who have renounced their U.S. citizenship, and other unspecified persons.

Source: U.S. Department of Justice, Bureau of Justice Statistics, *Background Checks For Firearm Transfers, 2015 - Statistical Tables*, NCJ 250978, November 2017, and earlier reports. See also <https://www.bjs.gov/index.cfm?ty=pbse&sid=13>.

# Table 358. Employment by State and Local Law Enforcement Agencies by Type of Agency and Employee: 2008

[As of September 30. Based on census of all state and local law enforcement agencies operating nationwide, conducted every 4 years]

| Type of agency | Number of agencies | Full-time employees (number) | | | Part-time employees (number) | | |
|---|---|---|---|---|---|---|---|
| | | Total | Sworn | Civilian | Total | Sworn | Civilian |
| Total [1]............................ | 17,985 | 1,133,905 | 765,237 | 368,668 | 100,340 | 44,062 | 56,278 |
| Local police............................ | 12,501 | 593,003 | 461,054 | 131,949 | 58,129 | 27,810 | 30,319 |
| Sheriffs' offices.................... | 3,063 | 353,461 | 182,979 | 170,482 | 26,052 | 11,334 | 14,718 |
| Primary State.................... | 50 | 93,148 | 60,772 | 32,376 | 947 | 54 | 893 |
| Special jurisdiction................. | 1,733 | 90,262 | 56,968 | 33,294 | 14,681 | 4,451 | 10,230 |
| Constable/marshal................. | 638 | 4,031 | 3,464 | 567 | 531 | 413 | 118 |

[1] Excludes agencies with less than one full-time officer or the equivalent in part-time officers.

Source: U.S. Bureau of Justice Statistics, *Census of State and Local Law Enforcement Agencies, 2008*. See also <https://www.bjs.gov/index.cfm?ty=pbse&sid=73>.

# Table 359. State and Local Government Criminal Justice Expenditures Per Capita by State: 2016

[In dollars. Based on Census Bureau's Annual Survey of State and Local Government Finances]

| State | Total justice system | Police protec-tion | Judicial and legal | Correc-tions | State | Total justice system | Police protec-tion | Judicial and legal | Correc-tions |
|---|---|---|---|---|---|---|---|---|---|
| Total.................... | 723 | 338 | 143 | 241 | Missouri.................. | 536 | 286 | 92 | 158 |
| Alabama................ | 480 | 257 | 74 | 148 | Montana................ | 729 | 279 | 203 | 247 |
| Alaska................... | 1,298 | 499 | 343 | 456 | Nebraska................ | 600 | 241 | 97 | 262 |
| Arizona................. | 710 | 326 | 142 | 243 | Nevada................. | 812 | 406 | 163 | 244 |
| Arkansas............... | 504 | 231 | 74 | 199 | New Hampshire......... | 546 | 293 | 105 | 148 |
| California............... | 1,064 | 448 | 221 | 395 | New Jersey............ | 791 | 388 | 173 | 230 |
| Colorado............... | 711 | 338 | 136 | 237 | New Mexico............ | 825 | 335 | 157 | 333 |
| Connecticut............ | 768 | 346 | 231 | 191 | New York............ | 1,049 | 505 | 212 | 332 |
| Delaware.............. | 911 | 367 | 219 | 325 | North Carolina.......... | 577 | 322 | 75 | 180 |
| District of Columbia..... | 1,268 | 864 | 193 | 211 | North Dakota.......... | 675 | 276 | 167 | 232 |
| Florida................. | 701 | 380 | 115 | 206 | Ohio.................... | 656 | 334 | 150 | 172 |
| Georgia................ | 568 | 264 | 118 | 186 | Oklahoma.............. | 558 | 271 | 96 | 192 |
| Hawaii................. | 680 | 321 | 206 | 152 | Oregon................ | 808 | 322 | 190 | 297 |
| Idaho.................. | 594 | 272 | 119 | 204 | Pennsylvania.......... | 714 | 291 | 149 | 274 |
| Illinois................. | 672 | 407 | 121 | 144 | Rhode Island.......... | 761 | 412 | 139 | 210 |
| Indiana................ | 450 | 189 | 86 | 175 | South Carolina......... | 465 | 241 | 72 | 152 |
| Iowa................... | 505 | 249 | 114 | 142 | South Dakota.......... | 547 | 233 | 106 | 208 |
| Kansas................ | 565 | 274 | 113 | 177 | Tennessee............. | 571 | 279 | 115 | 177 |
| Kentucky.............. | 506 | 160 | 142 | 204 | Texas................. | 592 | 273 | 108 | 212 |
| Louisiana.............. | 742 | 345 | 153 | 243 | Utah.................. | 504 | 215 | 115 | 173 |
| Maine................. | 504 | 222 | 84 | 198 | Vermont............... | 651 | 302 | 129 | 220 |
| Maryland.............. | 913 | 441 | 155 | 316 | Virginia................ | 706 | 278 | 123 | 304 |
| Massachusetts......... | 690 | 367 | 159 | 164 | Washington............ | 660 | 268 | 156 | 237 |
| Michigan.............. | 620 | 252 | 115 | 253 | West Virginia.......... | 556 | 211 | 152 | 193 |
| Minnesota............. | 664 | 348 | 132 | 183 | Wisconsin.............. | 709 | 325 | 115 | 269 |
| Mississippi............. | 507 | 248 | 92 | 167 | Wyoming............... | 997 | 414 | 216 | 367 |

Source: U.S. Census Bureau, "2016 State and Local Government Finance Historical Datasets and Tables," <https://www.census.gov/programs-surveys/gov-finances.html>, accessed August 2019; and "Annual Estimates of the Resident Population for the United States, Regions, States, and Puerto Rico: April 1, 2010 to July 1, 2018 (NST-EST2018-01)," December 2018, <https://www.census.gov/programs-surveys/popest/data/tables.html>.

# Table 360. Equal Employment Opportunity Commission (EEOC) Charges Filed by Type and Litigation: 2010 to 2018

[Number, except as noted (85.1 represents $85,100,000). For fiscal years ending in year shown. The EEOC enforces federal laws making it illegal to discriminate against a job applicant or employee for charges listed below. Most employers with at least 15 employees, labor unions, and employment agencies are covered by EEOC laws. If the EEOC does not resolve charges through conciliation or other informal methods, the Commission may pursue litigation against private sector employers, employment agencies, labor unions and, in cases alleging age discrimination or equal pay violations, against state and local governments. The number for total charges reflects the number of individual charge filings. Charge data do not sum to total because individuals often file charges claiming multiple types of discrimination. See <https://www.eeoc.gov/> for more information]

| Charges and litigation | 2010 | 2012 | 2013 | 2014 | 2015 | 2016 | 2017 | 2018 |
|---|---|---|---|---|---|---|---|---|
| **CHARGES FILED** | | | | | | | | |
| **Total charges filed with EEOC**......... | **99,922** | **99,412** | **93,727** | **88,778** | **89,385** | **91,503** | **84,254** | **76,418** |
| Race............................ | 35,890 | 33,512 | 33,068 | 31,073 | 31,027 | 32,309 | 28,528 | 24,600 |
| Sex............................. | 29,029 | 30,356 | 27,687 | 26,027 | 26,396 | 26,934 | 25,605 | 24,655 |
| National origin................. | 11,304 | 10,883 | 10,642 | 9,579 | 9,438 | 9,840 | 8,299 | 7,106 |
| Religion........................ | 3,790 | 3,811 | 3,721 | 3,549 | 3,502 | 3,825 | 3,436 | 2,859 |
| Color........................... | 2,780 | 2,662 | 3,146 | 2,756 | 2,833 | 3,102 | 3,240 | 3,166 |
| Retaliation, all statutes........ | 36,258 | 37,836 | 38,539 | 37,955 | 39,757 | 42,018 | 41,097 | 39,469 |
| Retaliation, Title VII only [1]... | 30,948 | 31,208 | 31,478 | 30,771 | 31,893 | 33,082 | 32,023 | 30,556 |
| Age............................. | 23,264 | 22,857 | 21,396 | 20,588 | 20,144 | 20,857 | 18,376 | 16,911 |
| Disability (ADA) [2]............. | 25,165 | 26,379 | 25,957 | 25,369 | 26,968 | 28,073 | 26,838 | 24,605 |
| Equal Pay Act................... | 1,044 | 1,082 | 1,019 | 938 | 973 | 1,075 | 996 | 1,066 |
| GINA [3]........................ | 201 | 280 | 333 | 333 | 257 | 238 | 206 | 220 |
| **LITIGATION [4]** | | | | | | | | |
| Suits filed...................... | 271 | 155 | 148 | 167 | 174 | 114 | 201 | 217 |
| Resolutions..................... | 315 | 283 | 222 | 144 | 171 | 171 | 125 | 156 |
| Monetary benefits (mil. dol.).... | 85.1 | 44.2 | 38.6 | 22.5 | 65.3 | 52.2 | 42.4 | 53.6 |

[1] Title VII of the Civil Rights Act of 1964. [2] Americans with Disabilities Act. [3] Genetic Information Non-Discrimination Act. [4] Suits filed and resolved in federal district courts.

Source: U.S. Equal Employment Opportunity Commission, "Enforcement and Litigation Statistics," <https://www.eeoc.gov/eeoc/statistics/enforcement/index.cfm>, accessed April 2019.

# Table 361. Asset Forfeiture Fund—Net Deposits by State: 2016 to 2018

[In thousands of dollars (1,921,274 represents $1,921,274,000). For fiscal years ending September 30. Transactions to or from the Department of Justice's (DOJ) Asset Forfeiture Fund (AFF). Seizure and forfeiture of assets that represent the proceeds of or were used to facilitate federal crimes. These figures represent official accounting transactions. They do not reflect total forfeiture activity for any jurisdiction. See source for more details. Minus sign indicates refunds]

| State or territory | 2016 | 2017 | 2018 | State or territory | 2016 | 2017 | 2018 |
|---|---|---|---|---|---|---|---|
| **Total**.................. | **1,921,274** | **1,643,290** | **1,379,047** | Montana................... | 422 | 811 | – |
| | | | | Nebraska................. | 2,277 | 2,757 | 3,951 |
| Investment income [1]...... | 34,336 | 56,912 | 103,184 | Nevada.................... | 6,264 | 2,866 | 2,513 |
| Alabama.................... | 1,254 | 2,583 | 12,256 | New Hampshire........... | 1,604 | 1,113 | 820 |
| Alaska..................... | 584 | 1,181 | 1,260 | New Jersey................ | 30,059 | 21,031 | 21,700 |
| Arizona.................... | 7,562 | 4,038 | 8,933 | New Mexico............... | 5,494 | 6,244 | 2,829 |
| Arkansas................... | 14,959 | 4,500 | 5,266 | New York.................. | 1,187,090 | 306,497 | 157,328 |
| California.................. | 117,545 | 395,190 | 437,560 | North Carolina............ | 16,242 | 22,727 | 30,925 |
| Colorado................... | 9,001 | 9,393 | 7,019 | North Dakota.............. | 674 | 8 | 7 |
| Connecticut................ | 5,321 | 4,899 | 6,617 | Ohio...................... | 19,135 | 17,943 | 42,594 |
| Delaware................... | – | – | – | Oklahoma................. | 8,204 | 2,429 | 4,258 |
| District of Columbia....... | 35,353 | 163,079 | 2,477 | Oregon................... | 3,935 | 2,721 | 4,472 |
| Florida.................... | 74,196 | 95,600 | 121,747 | Pennsylvania............. | 13,552 | 15,367 | 25,868 |
| Georgia................... | 17,933 | 165,468 | 13,929 | Rhode Island............. | 3,262 | 502 | – |
| Hawaii.................... | 608 | 1,772 | 810 | South Carolina........... | 5,738 | 2,623 | 4,088 |
| Idaho..................... | 1,185 | 1,982 | 49 | South Dakota............. | 68 | 17 | 58 |
| Illinois................... | 47,495 | 41,586 | 25,201 | Tennessee................ | 13,012 | 4,255 | 12,747 |
| Indiana................... | 12,957 | 4,875 | 7,064 | Texas..................... | 97,832 | 60,618 | 86,881 |
| Iowa...................... | 643 | 1,177 | 954 | Utah...................... | 1,985 | 2,535 | 2,501 |
| Kansas.................... | 3,412 | 2,668 | 9,313 | Vermont.................. | 1,568 | 401 | 473 |
| Kentucky.................. | 14,605 | 4,612 | 9,046 | Virginia.................. | 10,213 | 12,752 | 22,170 |
| Louisiana................. | 6,401 | 6,392 | 5,591 | Washington............... | 6,853 | 4,888 | 36,107 |
| Maine..................... | 240 | 216 | 6 | West Virginia............. | 3,413 | 2,447 | 1,717 |
| Maryland.................. | 10,694 | 14,277 | 56,038 | Wisconsin................ | 2,308 | 3,052 | 3,785 |
| Massachusetts............. | 12,784 | 110,510 | 19,922 | Wyoming................. | 195 | 1,012 | 425 |
| Michigan.................. | 31,268 | 17,858 | 19,530 | Guam..................... | 819 | 1,615 | 353 |
| Minnesota................. | 3,600 | 6,103 | 13,209 | Puerto Rico............... | 5,078 | 5,688 | 7,624 |
| Mississippi............... | 6,446 | 7,489 | 6,336 | Virgin Islands............ | 652 | 1,112 | 491 |
| Missouri.................. | 13,509 | 24,647 | 27,419 | Other [2]................. | -10,563 | -11,751 | -18,373 |

– Represents or rounds to zero. [1] Idle funds invested in U.S. Treasury Securities. [2] Comprised of transactions made to the AFF where a district has not been identified, where Federal reimbursements were made for services rendered, or summary estimates for financial reporting purposes where details by state were not available.

Source: U.S. Department of Justice, Asset Forfeiture Program, "Annual Reports to Congress," <https://www.justice.gov/afp>, accessed September 2019.

# Table 362. Arrests by Type of Offense, Sex, and Age: 2017

[8,247.6 represents 8,247,600. For year ending December 31. Based on Uniform Crime Reporting Program. Arrests reported by 12,606 agencies with a total population of 253,634,894 as estimated by the FBI. Some persons may be arrested more than once during a year; therefore, in some cases, the data in this table could represent multiple arrests of the same person]

| Offense charged | Total | | | Male | | | Female | | |
|---|---|---|---|---|---|---|---|---|---|
| | Total | Under 18 years old | 18 years and over | Total | Under 18 years old | 18 years and over | Total | Under 18 years old | 18 years and over |
| Total......... | 8,247.6 | 634.5 | 7,613.1 | 6,016.7 | 450.4 | 5,566.4 | 2,230.9 | 184.2 | 2,046.7 |
| Violent crime......... | 407.5 | 41.2 | 366.3 | 323.8 | 33.6 | 290.2 | 83.7 | 7.6 | 76.1 |
| Murder and nonnegligent manslaughter... | 9.6 | 0.7 | 8.9 | 8.4 | 0.7 | 7.7 | 1.2 | 0.1 | 1.1 |
| Rape [1]......... | 18.3 | 3.0 | 15.3 | 17.8 | 2.9 | 14.9 | 0.5 | 0.1 | 0.4 |
| Robbery......... | 74.3 | 15.3 | 59.1 | 63.5 | 13.7 | 49.8 | 10.9 | 1.6 | 9.3 |
| Aggravated assault......... | 305.3 | 22.2 | 283.1 | 234.1 | 16.3 | 217.8 | 71.2 | 5.9 | 65.3 |
| Property crime......... | 985.8 | 132.5 | 853.3 | 632.8 | 92.1 | 540.7 | 353.0 | 40.4 | 312.6 |
| Burglary......... | 156.5 | 24.2 | 132.2 | 127.0 | 21.4 | 105.6 | 29.5 | 2.8 | 26.6 |
| Larceny-theft......... | 750.8 | 93.7 | 657.0 | 444.5 | 58.8 | 385.8 | 306.2 | 34.9 | 271.3 |
| Motor vehicle theft......... | 71.5 | 12.8 | 58.7 | 55.5 | 10.4 | 45.1 | 15.9 | 2.4 | 13.6 |
| Arson......... | 7.2 | 1.8 | 5.4 | 5.7 | 1.5 | 4.2 | 1.4 | 0.3 | 1.2 |
| Other assaults......... | 833.4 | 96.5 | 736.9 | 594.1 | 60.4 | 533.7 | 239.3 | 36.1 | 203.2 |
| Forgery and counterfeiting......... | 43.5 | 1.0 | 42.6 | 28.5 | 0.7 | 27.8 | 15.0 | 0.2 | 14.8 |
| Fraud......... | 96.9 | 3.7 | 93.2 | 60.6 | 2.5 | 58.1 | 36.3 | 1.2 | 35.1 |
| Embezzlement......... | 12.5 | 0.5 | 12.0 | 6.4 | 0.3 | 6.1 | 6.2 | 0.2 | 5.9 |
| Stolen property—buying, receiving, possessing......... | 77.5 | 8.2 | 69.2 | 60.4 | 6.9 | 53.5 | 17.0 | 1.3 | 15.7 |
| Vandalism......... | 148.0 | 28.8 | 119.1 | 114.7 | 23.7 | 91.0 | 33.3 | 5.2 | 28.1 |
| Weapons—carrying, possessing, etc......... | 129.2 | 14.4 | 114.8 | 117.2 | 12.9 | 104.3 | 12.1 | 1.5 | 10.6 |
| Prostitution and commercialized vice...... | 28.5 | 0.2 | 28.3 | 11.1 | 0.1 | 11.0 | 17.4 | 0.1 | 17.2 |
| Sex offenses except rape & prostitution.... | 37.9 | 6.6 | 31.2 | 35.0 | 5.9 | 29.1 | 2.8 | 0.8 | 2.1 |
| Drug abuse violations......... | 1,275.8 | 74.1 | 1,201.7 | 966.1 | 56.4 | 909.7 | 309.7 | 17.6 | 292.0 |
| Gambling......... | 2.5 | 0.2 | 2.3 | 2.0 | 0.2 | 1.8 | 0.5 | (Z) | 0.5 |
| Offenses against family and children...... | 72.2 | 2.9 | 69.3 | 50.7 | 1.8 | 48.8 | 21.6 | 1.1 | 20.5 |
| Driving under the influence......... | 764.6 | 4.7 | 759.9 | 569.1 | 3.5 | 565.6 | 195.4 | 1.2 | 194.3 |
| Liquor laws......... | 161.3 | 26.1 | 135.2 | 111.9 | 15.4 | 96.6 | 49.3 | 10.7 | 38.6 |
| Drunkenness......... | 289.6 | 3.4 | 286.2 | 229.8 | 2.4 | 227.4 | 59.8 | 1.0 | 58.8 |
| Disorderly conduct......... | 277.0 | 49.0 | 227.9 | 195.0 | 31.2 | 163.8 | 82.0 | 17.8 | 64.2 |
| Vagrancy......... | 18.5 | 0.6 | 18.0 | 14.1 | 0.5 | 13.6 | 4.5 | 0.1 | 4.3 |
| All other offenses (except traffic)......... | 2,560.9 | 116.0 | 2,444.9 | 1,876.3 | 83.2 | 1,793.1 | 684.6 | 32.8 | 651.8 |
| Suspicion......... | 0.7 | 0.1 | 0.6 | 0.5 | 0.1 | 0.5 | 0.2 | (Z) | 0.2 |
| Curfew and loitering law violations......... | 23.7 | 23.7 | (X) | 16.6 | 16.6 | (X) | 7.1 | 7.1 | (X) |

X Not applicable. Z Less than 50. [1] The rape figures in this table are an aggregate total of the data submitted using both the revised and legacy Uniform Crime Reporting definitions. For more information, see <https://ucr.fbi.gov/crime-in-the-u.s/2017/crime-in-the-u.s.-2017/topic-pages/rape>.

Source: U.S. Department of Justice, Federal Bureau of Investigation, "Crime in the United States 2017," and earlier releases, <https://ucr.fbi.gov/>, accessed November 2018.

# Table 363. Arrests by Offense and Race/Ethnicity: 2017

[Arrests reported by 12,599 agencies with an estimate total population of 253,405,839. See headnote, Table 362]

| Offense charged | Total | White | Black | Hispanic or Latino [1] | American Indian/ Alaska Native | Asian | Native Hawaiian/ other Pacific Islander |
|---|---|---|---|---|---|---|---|
| Total......... | 8,162,849 | 5,626,140 | 2,221,697 | 1,190,671 | 196,908 | 97,049 | 21,055 |
| Violent crime......... | 404,236 | 236,590 | 151,744 | 79,078 | 8,640 | 5,979 | 1,283 |
| Murder and nonnegligent manslaughter...... | 9,468 | 4,188 | 5,025 | 1,462 | 108 | 127 | 20 |
| Rape [2]......... | 18,063 | 12,187 | 5,182 | 3,787 | 322 | 307 | 65 |
| Robbery......... | 73,764 | 32,128 | 40,024 | 12,722 | 679 | 664 | 269 |
| Aggravated assault......... | 302,941 | 188,087 | 101,513 | 61,107 | 7,531 | 4,881 | 929 |
| Property crime......... | 973,219 | 657,574 | 285,080 | 119,392 | 16,630 | 11,576 | 2,359 |
| Burglary......... | 154,970 | 104,671 | 46,227 | 24,873 | 1,968 | 1,710 | 394 |
| Larceny-theft......... | 740,546 | 501,231 | 215,650 | 78,921 | 13,242 | 8,770 | 1,653 |
| Motor vehicle theft......... | 70,617 | 46,621 | 21,415 | 14,525 | 1,308 | 980 | 293 |
| Arson......... | 7,086 | 5,051 | 1,788 | 1,073 | 112 | 116 | 19 |
| Other assaults......... | 822,671 | 534,188 | 258,542 | 118,922 | 17,062 | 10,371 | 2,508 |
| Forgery and counterfeiting......... | 43,203 | 28,130 | 13,980 | 5,333 | 386 | 619 | 88 |
| Fraud......... | 95,997 | 63,908 | 29,556 | 8,836 | 1,256 | 1,174 | 103 |
| Embezzlement......... | 12,437 | 7,441 | 4,683 | 1,248 | 96 | 190 | 27 |
| Stolen property—buying, receiving, possessing......... | 76,477 | 48,607 | 25,585 | 11,351 | 1,034 | 940 | 311 |
| Vandalism......... | 145,934 | 99,818 | 40,861 | 21,549 | 3,265 | 1,681 | 309 |
| Weapons—carrying, possessing, etc......... | 128,009 | 68,787 | 56,143 | 23,125 | 1,357 | 1,400 | 322 |
| Prostitution and commercialized vice......... | 28,229 | 15,812 | 10,605 | 5,093 | 116 | 1,610 | 86 |
| Sex offenses except rape & prostitution........ | 37,518 | 26,615 | 9,355 | 7,632 | 691 | 741 | 116 |
| Drug abuse violations......... | 1,262,660 | 889,030 | 342,513 | 201,858 | 15,038 | 13,691 | 2,388 |
| Gambling......... | 2,493 | 955 | 1,294 | 382 | 20 | 183 | 41 |
| Offenses against the family and children....... | 71,656 | 46,926 | 20,106 | 6,674 | 4,067 | 534 | 23 |
| Driving under the influence......... | 755,726 | 617,443 | 105,585 | 140,918 | 15,950 | 14,294 | 2,454 |
| Liquor laws......... | 157,285 | 122,929 | 22,095 | 15,704 | 9,705 | 2,347 | 209 |
| Drunkenness......... | 287,985 | 212,908 | 41,073 | 57,521 | 30,632 | 2,931 | 441 |
| Disorderly conduct......... | 273,664 | 172,098 | 87,094 | 24,687 | 11,832 | 2,232 | 408 |
| Vagrancy......... | 18,453 | 12,609 | 5,148 | 2,195 | 473 | 209 | 14 |
| All other offenses (except traffic)......... | 2,540,842 | 1,750,366 | 700,984 | 335,002 | 57,979 | 24,046 | 7,467 |
| Suspicion......... | 669 | 250 | 148 | 44 | 258 | 7 | 6 |
| Curfew and loitering law violations......... | 23,486 | 13,156 | 9,523 | 4,127 | 421 | 294 | 92 |

[1] Persons of Hispanic origin may be of any race. [2] See footnote 1, Table 362.

Source: U.S. Department of Justice, Federal Bureau of Investigation, "Crime in the United States 2017," <https://ucr.fbi.gov/>, accessed November 2018.

# Table 364. Law Enforcement Officers Killed and Assaulted: 1990 to 2017

[The statistics presented in this table are based on information collected by the staff of the FBI's Law Enforcement Officers Killed and Assaulted Program from law enforcement agencies throughout the U.S. and U.S. Territories. It contains statistics on line-of-duty felonious deaths, accidental deaths, and assaults of duly sworn local, state, tribal, and federal law enforcement officers]

| Item | 1990 | 2000 | 2010 | 2011 | 2012 | 2013 | 2014 | 2015 | 2016 | 2017 |
|---|---|---|---|---|---|---|---|---|---|---|
| **OFFICERS KILLED** | | | | | | | | | | |
| **Total killed** | **132** | **134** | **127** | **125** | **97** | **76** | **96** | **86** | **118** | **93** |
| By region and area: | | | | | | | | | | |
| Northeast | 13 | 13 | 11 | 18 | 15 | 7 | 16 | 9 | 9 | 8 |
| Midwest | 20 | 32 | 24 | 28 | 9 | 8 | 12 | 11 | 25 | 20 |
| South | 68 | 67 | 61 | 56 | 50 | 46 | 36 | 48 | 54 | 51 |
| West | 23 | 19 | 28 | 20 | 17 | 15 | 27 | 14 | 26 | 12 |
| Puerto Rico | 8 | 3 | 3 | 3 | 5 | – | 5 | 4 | 4 | 2 |
| Island Areas | – | – | – | – | 1 | – | – | – | – | – |
| **Total feloniously killed** | **65** | **51** | **55** | **72** | **49** | **27** | **51** | **41** | **66** | **46** |
| By type of weapon: | | | | | | | | | | |
| Firearms | 56 | 47 | 54 | 63 | 44 | 26 | 46 | 38 | 62 | 42 |
| Handgun | 47 | 33 | 38 | 49 | 34 | 18 | 33 | 29 | 37 | 32 |
| Rifle | 8 | 10 | 15 | 7 | 7 | 5 | 10 | 7 | 23 | 9 |
| Shotgun | 1 | 4 | 1 | 6 | 3 | 3 | 3 | 1 | 1 | 1 |
| Multiple firearms [1] | (NA) | (NA) | (NA) | 1 | – | – | – | – | 1 | – |
| Firearm type not reported | – | – | – | – | – | – | – | 1 | – | – |
| Knife/cutting instrument [2] | 3 | 1 | – | 1 | 1 | – | – | – | – | 1 |
| Knife [2] | (NA) | (NA) | (NA) | 1 | 1 | – | – | – | – | 1 |
| Other cutting instrument [2] | (NA) | (NA) | (NA) | – | – | – | – | – | – | – |
| Personal weapons [3] | 2 | – | – | 2 | 2 | – | 1 | – | – | – |
| Vehicle | 1 | 3 | 1 | 6 | 2 | 1 | 4 | 3 | 4 | 3 |
| Other | 3 | – | – | – | – | – | – | – | – | – |
| **Total accidentally killed** | **67** | **83** | **72** | **53** | **48** | **49** | **45** | **45** | **52** | **47** |
| **OFFICERS ASSAULTED** | | | | | | | | | | |
| Population covered (1,000) [4] | 197,426 | 204,599 | 248,727 | 254,535 | 250,151 | 256,689 | 246,681 | 251,555 | 269,401 | 269,608 |
| Number of— | | | | | | | | | | |
| Reporting agencies | 9,343 | 8,940 | 11,826 | 12,031 | 11,794 | 11,958 | 11,235 | 12,102 | 12,293 | 12,198 |
| Officers employed | 410,131 | 452,531 | 557,884 | 539,282 | 525,217 | 551,893 | 543,331 | 547,398 | 593,097 | 596,604 |
| **Total assaulted** | **72,091** | **58,398** | **56,491** | **55,631** | **53,867** | **50,802** | **48,988** | **50,991** | **58,011** | **60,211** |
| By type of weapon: | | | | | | | | | | |
| Firearm | 3,651 | 1,749 | 1,925 | 2,240 | 2,276 | 2,299 | 1,976 | 2,050 | 2,388 | 2,677 |
| Knife/cutting instrument | 1,647 | 1,015 | 918 | 1,003 | 909 | 901 | 966 | 921 | 1,107 | 1,083 |
| Other dangerous weapon | 7,423 | 8,132 | 7,413 | 7,856 | 7,435 | 7,042 | 6,976 | 7,705 | 9,201 | 10,209 |
| Personal weapons [1] | 59,370 | 47,502 | 46,235 | 44,532 | 43,247 | 40,560 | 39,070 | 40,315 | 45,315 | 46,242 |

– Represents zero. NA Not available. [1] Beginning in 2011, a new option was added: "Multiple firearms used by offender(s), unable to determine which caused fatal injury." [2] Prior to 2011, the type of weapon categories "Knife" and "Other cutting instrument" were combined. [3] Includes hands, fists, feet, etc. [4] Represents the number of persons covered by reporting agencies.

Source: U.S. Department of Justice, Federal Bureau of Investigation, "Law Enforcement Officers Killed and Assaulted, 2017," and previous reports, <https://ucr.fbi.gov/>, accessed November 2018.

# Table 365. Presidential Pardons and Commutations: 1961 to 2019

[For fiscal years shown. Not shown are petitions pending at the beginning of the fiscal year, or in the case of a change of administration, the number of cases pending at the time of the new President's inauguration]

| Period | President | Petitions received | Petitions granted [1] | | | Petitions denied or closed without Presidential Action |
|---|---|---|---|---|---|---|
| | | | Pardon | Commutation | Remission | |
| **1961 to 2019** | **Total** | **79,668** | **4,485** | **2,244** | **17** | **59,619** |
| 1961 to 1964 | John F. Kennedy | 1,749 | 472 | 100 | 3 | 831 |
| 1964 to 1969 | Lyndon B. Johnson | 4,537 | 960 | 226 | 1 | 2,830 |
| 1969 to 1975 | Richard M. Nixon | 2,591 | 863 | 60 | 3 | 2,614 |
| 1975 to 1977 | Gerald R. Ford | 1,527 | 382 | 22 | 5 | 900 |
| 1977 to 1981 | Jimmy Carter | 2,627 | 534 | 29 | 3 | 2,056 |
| 1981 to 1989 | Ronald W. Reagan | 3,404 | 393 | 13 | – | 2,804 |
| 1989 to 1993 | George H.W. Bush | 1,466 | 74 | 3 | – | 1,621 |
| 1993 to 2001 | William J. Clinton | 7,489 | 396 | 61 | 2 | 4,554 |
| 2001 to 2009 | George W. Bush | 11,074 | 189 | 11 | – | 11,914 |
| 2009 to 2017 | Barack Obama | 36,544 | 212 | 1,715 | – | 25,217 |
| 2017 to 2019 [2] | Donald J. Trump | 6,660 | 10 | 4 | – | 4,278 |

– Represents zero. [1] Petitions granted are taken from a count of clemency warrants maintained by the Office of the Pardon Attorney. Cases in which multiple forms of relief were granted are counted in only one category. Cases in which clemency was granted to a person who did not file an application with the Office of the Pardon Attorney are counted as "petitions granted" but have not been counted as "petitions pending" or "petitions received" since at least FY1990. Excludes individual members of a class of persons granted pardons by proclamation. [2] As of July 11, 2019.

Source: U.S. Department of Justice, Office of the Pardon Attorney, "Clemency Statistics," <https://www.justice.gov/pardon/clemency-statistics>, accessed August 2019.

## Table 366. Forensic Services Requests and Backlog by Type of Request: 2014

[Numbers are rounded to the nearest hundred. Census of 409 laboratories, with a 88% return rate. Totals exclude requests outsourced to other laboratories. Request is classified as backlogged if it has been submitted to a crime lab, but has not yet been examined and reported to the submitting agency within 30 days. Estimates based on imputations for labs that did not report backlog data, see source for details]

| Type of request | Received | | Completed | | Backlogged requests | |
|---|---|---|---|---|---|---|
| | Number | Percent | Number | Percent | Number | Percent |
| **All requests** | **3,783,000** | **100** | **3,646,000** | **100** | **570,100** | **100** |
| Controlled substances | 1,265,000 | 33 | 1,197,000 | 33 | 213,700 | 37 |
| Crime scene | 171,000 | 5 | 170,000 | 5 | (X) | (X) |
| Digital evidence | 25,000 | 1 | 24,000 | 1 | 7,800 | 1 |
| Firearms/toolmarks | 154,000 | 4 | 142,000 | 4 | 51,100 | 9 |
| Forensic biology: | | | | | | |
|   Casework [1] | 333,000 | 9 | 296,000 | 8 | 107,800 | 19 |
|   Convicted offender/arrestee samples [1] | 908,000 | 24 | 904,000 | 25 | 64,800 | 11 |
| Impressions | 7,000 | (Z) | 7,000 | (Z) | 2,400 | (Z) |
| Latent prints | 295,000 | 8 | 301,000 | 8 | 69,400 | 12 |
| Questioned documents | 9,000 | (Z) | 9,000 | (Z) | 800 | (Z) |
| Toxicology | 566,000 | 15 | 554,000 | 15 | 40,000 | 7 |
| Trace evidence | 49,000 | 1 | 41,000 | 1 | 12,200 | 2 |

X Not applicable. Z Less than 0.5%. [1] Includes biology screening and DNA analysis.

Source: U.S. Bureau of Justice Statistics, *Publicly Funded Forensic Crime Laboratories: Resources and Services, 2014*, NCJ 250151, November 2016. See also <https://www.bjs.gov/index.cfm?ty=dcdetail&iid=244>.

## Table 367. Freedom of Information Act (FOIA) Requests Received, Processed, Granted and Denied by Federal Department and Selected Agency: 2018

[For year ending September 30. Freedom of Information Act (FOIA) provides the public the right to request access to records from any executive federal agency. Agencies are required to disclose any information requested under the FOIA unless it falls under one of nine exemptions; see <https://www.foia.gov/faq.html#exemptions> for full listing. Each agency is required to file an annual report with the Department of Justice detailing their administration of the FOIA. Data are compiled from those reports]

| Department or agency | Requests pending from prior year | Requests received | Requests processed | Requests pending at year end | Disposition | | |
|---|---|---|---|---|---|---|---|
| | | | | | Requests granted in full | Requests granted in part | Full denials [2] |
| **Total [1]** | **158,987** | **863,729** | **830,060** | **192,656** | **222,989** | **322,520** | **284,551** |
| Department of Agriculture | 5,559 | 36,547 | 35,482 | 6,624 | 29,350 | 3,494 | 2,638 |
| Department of Commerce | 629 | 2,269 | 1,976 | 922 | 474 | 392 | 1,110 |
| Department of Defense | 14,194 | 57,032 | 54,323 | 16,903 | 18,571 | 15,801 | 19,951 |
| Department of Education | 848 | 3,041 | 2,858 | 1,031 | 400 | 1,647 | 811 |
| Department of Energy | 483 | 2,073 | 1,893 | 663 | 531 | 359 | 1,003 |
| Department of Health and Human Services | 6,097 | 35,445 | 33,876 | 7,666 | 13,062 | 4,068 | 16,746 |
| Department of Homeland Security | 62,968 | 395,751 | 374,945 | 83,774 | 25,696 | 226,015 | 123,234 |
| Department of Housing and Urban Development | 916 | 2,383 | 2,245 | 1,054 | 430 | 440 | 1,375 |
| Department of Interior | 2,306 | 8,402 | 7,001 | 3,707 | 2,265 | 1,979 | 2,757 |
| Department of Justice | 19,725 | 96,875 | 91,383 | 25,217 | 41,661 | 10,086 | 39,636 |
| Department of Labor | 1,483 | 14,696 | 14,679 | 1,500 | 1,461 | 6,258 | 6,960 |
| Department of State | 13,772 | 8,448 | 10,928 | 11,292 | 1,364 | 3,808 | 5,756 |
| Department of the Treasury | 1,728 | 12,535 | 12,098 | 2,165 | 3,776 | 2,981 | 5,341 |
| Department of Transportation | 5,459 | 15,049 | 16,082 | 4,426 | 8,383 | 3,326 | 4,373 |
| Department of Veterans Affairs | 4,368 | 24,555 | 22,851 | 6,072 | 4,203 | 10,142 | 8,506 |
| Board of Governors of the Federal Reserve System | 49 | 610 | 626 | 33 | 333 | 60 | 233 |
| Central Intelligence Agency | 1,949 | 2,726 | 2,345 | 2,330 | 129 | 348 | 1,868 |
| Consumer Financial Protection Bureau | 23 | 788 | 642 | 169 | 119 | 260 | 263 |
| Court Services and Offender Supervision Agency | 93 | 437 | 517 | 13 | 13 | 421 | 83 |
| Environmental Protection Agency | 2,808 | 11,364 | 10,442 | 3,730 | 4,778 | 1,022 | 4,642 |
| Equal Employment Opportunity Commission | 3,719 | 19,065 | 19,134 | 3,650 | 525 | 13,306 | 5,303 |
| Federal Communications Commission | 87 | 820 | 848 | 59 | 122 | 367 | 359 |
| Federal Deposit Insurance Corporation | 22 | 423 | 431 | 14 | 67 | 66 | 298 |
| Federal Trade Commission | 57 | 1,441 | 1,459 | 39 | 451 | 532 | 476 |
| General Services Administration | 296 | 1,324 | 1,239 | 381 | 238 | 584 | 417 |
| Merit Systems Protection Board | 78 | 173 | 200 | 51 | 59 | 58 | 83 |
| National Aeronautics and Space Administration | 91 | 853 | 880 | 64 | 158 | 182 | 540 |
| National Archives and Records Administration | 3,286 | 52,850 | 53,101 | 3,035 | 36,163 | 4,038 | 12,900 |
| National Labor Relations Board | 405 | 1,305 | 1,547 | 163 | 287 | 802 | 458 |
| National Science Foundation | 278 | 329 | 349 | 258 | 26 | 219 | 104 |
| National Transportation Safety Board | 927 | 521 | 549 | 899 | 53 | 68 | 428 |
| Nuclear Regulatory Commission | 85 | 643 | 496 | 232 | 118 | 115 | 263 |
| Office of Government and Ethics | 141 | 126 | 206 | 61 | 27 | 99 | 80 |
| Office of Management and Budget | 279 | 547 | 301 | 525 | 34 | 101 | 166 |
| Office of Personnel Management | 213 | 10,668 | 10,575 | 306 | 7,683 | 2,370 | 522 |
| Office of Special Counsel | 222 | 189 | 282 | 129 | 15 | 88 | 179 |
| Office of the Director of National Intelligence | 402 | 498 | 349 | 551 | 43 | 171 | 135 |
| Pension Benefit Guaranty Corporation | 69 | 1,618 | 1,598 | 89 | 799 | 449 | 350 |
| Securities and Exchange Commission | 559 | 14,229 | 14,248 | 540 | 5,819 | 858 | 7,571 |
| Small Business Administration | 24 | 1,089 | 1,061 | 52 | 543 | 197 | 321 |
| Social Security Administration | 728 | 16,427 | 16,631 | 524 | 11,029 | 3,083 | 2,519 |
| Tennessee Valley Authority | 16 | 222 | 212 | 26 | 51 | 122 | 39 |
| U.S. Agency for International Development | 342 | 280 | 337 | 285 | 44 | 148 | 145 |
| U.S. Consumer Product Safety Commission | 259 | 554 | 440 | 373 | 115 | 173 | 152 |
| U.S. Postal Service | 160 | 3,150 | 3,116 | 194 | 472 | 568 | 2,076 |

[1] Includes other agencies not shown below. [2] Denials due to FOIA exemptions and other nonexemption reasons including no records available, incorrect agency, duplicate, and not reasonably descriptive.

Source: U.S. Department of Justice, Office of Information Policy, "Annual FOIA Reports – FY 2018," <https://www.justice.gov/oip/annual-foia-reports-fy-2018>, accessed June 2019. See also <https://www.foia.gov/>.

## Table 368. Suspects Arrested by Drug Enforcement Administration by Type of Drug and Arrestee Characteristics: 2014

[For fiscal year ending in year shown. Data are from Drug Enforcement Administration's (DEA) Defendant Statistical System]

| Arrestee characteristic | Total arrested | Percent arrested | Drug type | | | | | |
|---|---|---|---|---|---|---|---|---|
| | | | Cocaine powder | Crack cocaine | Marijuana | Metham-phetamine | Opiates | Other or non drug [2] |
| **Total [1]** | **29,549** | **100.0** | **5,582** | **1,782** | **5,082** | **7,005** | **4,852** | **5,245** |
| *SEX* | | | | | | | | |
| Male | 23,968 | 81.3 | 4,871 | 1,521 | 4,380 | 5,394 | 3,960 | 3,842 |
| Female | 5,521 | 18.7 | 695 | 260 | 695 | 1,595 | 882 | 1,393 |
| *RACE* | | | | | | | | |
| White | 20,280 | 70.1 | 3,448 | 362 | 3,668 | 6,170 | 3,121 | 3,511 |
| Black/African American | 7,799 | 27.0 | 1,947 | 1,394 | 1,080 | 408 | 1,563 | 1,406 |
| American Indian/Alaska Native | 166 | 0.6 | 16 | 1 | 34 | 63 | 14 | 38 |
| Asian/Pacific Islander | 667 | 2.3 | 31 | 7 | 217 | 210 | 23 | 179 |
| *HISPANIC ORIGIN* | | | | | | | | |
| Hispanic/Latino | 12,085 | 42.2 | 3,082 | 215 | 2,313 | 3,268 | 2,109 | 1,098 |
| Non-Hispanic/Latino | 16,549 | 57.8 | 2,309 | 1,501 | 2,639 | 3,572 | 2,582 | 3,946 |
| *AGE* | | | | | | | | |
| 18 years old and under | 374 | 1.3 | 33 | 13 | 128 | 72 | 77 | 51 |
| 19 to 20 years old | 1,157 | 3.9 | 143 | 69 | 314 | 247 | 206 | 178 |
| 21 to 30 years old | 10,431 | 35.3 | 1,675 | 710 | 2,024 | 2,336 | 1,938 | 1,747 |
| 31 to 40 years old | 9,726 | 32.9 | 2,102 | 597 | 1,467 | 2,441 | 1,515 | 1,604 |
| 41 years old and older | 7,861 | 26.6 | 1,629 | 393 | 1,149 | 1,909 | 1,116 | 1,665 |

[1] Details may not sum to the total number of arrestees due to missing data. [2] Includes pharmaceutical controlled substances, equipment used to manufacture controlled substances, and drug use paraphernalia.

Source: U.S. Department of Justice, Bureau of Justice Statistics, *Federal Justice Statistics 2014 - Statistical Tables*, NCJ 250183, March 2017. See also <https://www.bjs.gov/index.cfm?ty=pbse&sid=62>.

## Table 369. Missing Person Reports by Selected Characteristics: 2016 to 2018

[Data shown are missing person records entered into the National Crime Information Center's (NCIC) Missing Person File during the year shown and does not include records removed (canceled, cleared, and located). The NCIC contained 85,459 active missing person records remaining in the database as of December 31, 2018; this figure includes entries from earlier years. For more information, see source]

| Characteristic | 2016 | | | 2017 | | | 2018 | | |
|---|---|---|---|---|---|---|---|---|---|
| | All ages | Under age 18 | Age 18 and older | All ages | Under age 18 | Age 18 and older | All ages | Under age 18 | Age 18 and older |
| **Total missing person entries** | **647,435** | **465,676** | **181,759** | **651,226** | **464,324** | **186,902** | **612,846** | **424,066** | **188,780** |
| By type: | | | | | | | | | |
| Juvenile (under age 21) [1] | 447,444 | 443,053 | 4,391 | 445,345 | 441,165 | 4,180 | 405,046 | 401,218 | 3,828 |
| Endangered [2] | 45,654 | 9,046 | 36,608 | 45,967 | 9,518 | 36,449 | 45,673 | 9,482 | 36,191 |
| Involuntary [3] | 17,505 | 5,176 | 12,329 | 17,127 | 5,271 | 11,856 | 14,934 | 4,925 | 10,009 |
| Disability [4] | 32,991 | 4,649 | 28,342 | 33,896 | 4,978 | 28,918 | 33,014 | 4,770 | 28,244 |
| Catastrophe [5] | 309 | 121 | 188 | 327 | 85 | 242 | 379 | 88 | 291 |
| Other (over age 21) | 103,532 | 3,631 | 99,901 | 108,564 | 3,307 | 105,257 | 113,800 | 3,583 | 110,217 |
| By sex: | | | | | | | | | |
| Female | 322,263 | 247,846 | 74,417 | 322,865 | 246,108 | 76,757 | 302,218 | 225,640 | 76,578 |
| Male | 325,129 | 217,798 | 107,331 | 328,270 | 218,143 | 110,127 | 310,517 | 198,327 | 112,190 |
| Unknown | 43 | 32 | 11 | 91 | 73 | 18 | 111 | 99 | 12 |
| By race/ethnicity: | | | | | | | | | |
| White [6] | 384,478 | 264,443 | 120,035 | 387,104 | 264,253 | 122,851 | 362,988 | 239,662 | 123,326 |
| Black | 218,818 | 170,899 | 47,919 | 219,484 | 169,426 | 50,058 | 207,394 | 155,966 | 51,428 |
| Asian | 12,903 | 7,336 | 5,567 | 13,177 | 7,479 | 5,698 | 12,994 | 7,060 | 5,934 |
| American Indian | 10,574 | 8,181 | 2,393 | 10,642 | 8,177 | 2,465 | 9,914 | 7,497 | 2,417 |
| Unknown | 20,662 | 14,817 | 5,845 | 20,819 | 14,989 | 5,830 | 19,556 | 13,881 | 5,675 |

[1] A person under the age of 21 who is missing and does not meet any of the entry criteria set forth in the other categories. [2] Indicating that physical safety may be in danger. [3] Disappearance may not have been voluntary, i.e. abduction or kidnapping. [4] Proven physical/mental disability or senile and subjecting themselves or others to personal and immediate danger. [5] Person missing after a catastrophe. [6] Includes Hispanic ethnicity or origin.

Source: U.S. Department of Justice, Federal Bureau of Investigation, "2018 NCIC Missing Person and Unidentified Person Statistics," and earlier releases, <https://www.fbi.gov/services/cjis/ncic>, accessed April 2019.

## Table 370. Federal Prosecutions of Public Corruption by Prosecution Status: 2000 to 2017

[As of December 31. Prosecution of persons who have corrupted public office in violation of Federal Criminal Statutes]

| Type of official | 2000 | | | 2010 | | | 2016 | | | 2017 | | |
|---|---|---|---|---|---|---|---|---|---|---|---|---|
| | Charged | Con-victed | Await-ing trial | Charged | Con-victed | Await-ing trial | Charged | Con-victed | Await-ing trial | Charged | Con-victed | Await-ing trial |
| **Total** | **1,000** | **938** | **327** | **1,184** | **1,036** | **554** | **982** | **886** | **569** | **863** | **837** | **521** |
| Federal officials | 441 | 422 | 92 | 422 | 397 | 103 | 354 | 326 | 170 | 383 | 334 | 169 |
| State officials | 92 | 91 | 37 | 168 | 108 | 105 | 139 | 125 | 74 | 63 | 68 | 53 |
| Local officials | 211 | 183 | 89 | 296 | 280 | 146 | 234 | 213 | 148 | 223 | 208 | 150 |
| Others involved [1] | 256 | 242 | 109 | 298 | 251 | 200 | 255 | 222 | 177 | 194 | 227 | 149 |

[1] Includes individuals who are neither public officials nor employees, but were involved with public officials or employees in violating the law.

Source: U.S. Department of Justice, Criminal Division, *Report to Congress on the Activities and Operations of the Public Integrity Section for 2017*, and earlier reports. See also <http://www.justice.gov/criminal/pin/>.

## Table 371. U.S. Supreme Court—Cases on Docket, Disposed of, and Remaining: 2000 to 2017

[Statutory term of court begins first Monday in October. Often the Court grants or denies cases after the Court recesses but before the next statutory term]

| Action | 2000 | 2005 | 2010 | 2012 | 2013 | 2014 | 2015 | 2016 | 2017 |
|---|---|---|---|---|---|---|---|---|---|
| **NUMBER OF CASES ON DOCKET** | | | | | | | | | |
| Total | **8,965** | **9,608** | **9,066** | **8,806** | **8,580** | **8,066** | **7,535** | **7,334** | **7,390** |
| Original | 9 | 8 | 4 | 3 | 5 | 6 | 8 | 7 | 8 |
| Paid | 2,305 | 2,025 | 1,895 | 1,806 | 1,869 | 1,845 | 1,839 | 1,850 | 2,062 |
| In Forma Pauperis | 6,651 | 7,575 | 7,167 | 6,997 | 6,706 | 6,215 | 5,688 | 5,477 | 5,320 |
| **CASES DISPOSED OF** | | | | | | | | | |
| Total | **7,762** | **8,240** | **7,827** | **7,647** | **7,547** | **7,006** | **6,506** | **6,258** | **6,192** |
| Original | 2 | 4 | 2 | 0 | 0 | 1 | 1 | 1 | 1 |
| Paid | 2,024 | 1,703 | 1,580 | 1,544 | 1,568 | 1,552 | 1,539 | 1,505 | 1,728 |
| In Forma Pauperis | 5,736 | 6,533 | 6,245 | 6,103 | 5,979 | 5,453 | 4,966 | 4,752 | 4,463 |
| **NUMBER REMAINING ON DOCKET** | | | | | | | | | |
| Total | **1,203** | **1,368** | **1,239** | **1,159** | **1,033** | **1,060** | **1,029** | **1,076** | **1,198** |
| Original | 7 | 4 | 2 | 3 | 5 | 5 | 7 | 6 | 7 |
| Paid | 281 | 322 | 315 | 262 | 301 | 293 | 300 | 345 | 334 |
| In Forma Pauperis | 915 | 1,042 | 922 | 894 | 727 | 762 | 722 | 725 | 857 |
| Cases argued during term | 86 | 90 | 86 | 77 | 79 | 75 | 82 | 71 | 69 |
| Number disposed of by full opinions | 83 | 82 | 83 | 76 | 77 | 75 | 70 | 68 | 63 |
| Number disposed of by per curiam opinions | 4 | 5 | 3 | 1 | 2 | 0 | 12 | 1 | 6 |
| Number set for re-argument next term | 0 | 3 | 0 | 0 | 0 | 1 | 0 | 2 | 0 |
| Total cases granted plenary review | 99 | 78 | 90 | 93 | 76 | 71 | 81 | 75 | 78 |
| Cases reviewed and decided without oral argument | 127 | 105 | 84 | 88 | 72 | 109 | 145 | 66 | 103 |
| Total cases available for argument at start of next term | 49 | 31 | 43 | 45 | 40 | 33 | 31 | 32 | 38 |

Source: Administrative Office of the U.S. Courts, "Judicial Business of the United States Courts, Table A-1–Supreme Court of the United States Judicial Business," September 2018, and earlier reports, <http://www.uscourts.gov/data-table-topics/us-supreme-court>. See also <http://www.supremecourt.gov/orders/journal.aspx>.

## Table 372. Federal Judiciary Caseloads: 2000 to 2018

[For 12-month periods ending June 30]

| Judicial caseload | 2000 | 2010 | 2014 | 2015 | 2016 | 2017 | 2018 |
|---|---|---|---|---|---|---|---|
| **U.S. Courts of Appeals:** [1] | | | | | | | |
| Cases filed | 54,642 | 56,097 | 55,260 | 53,032 | 60,099 | 52,028 | 49,220 |
| Cases terminated | 56,509 | 59,343 | 55,803 | 53,934 | 56,244 | 56,709 | 50,804 |
| Cases pending | 40,815 | 46,816 | 41,945 | 40,913 | 44,739 | 40,040 | 38,456 |
| **U.S. District Courts Civil:** | | | | | | | |
| Cases filed | 263,049 | 289,630 | 298,713 | 280,037 | 290,430 | 271,721 | 281,202 |
| Cases terminated | 260,277 | 295,908 | 260,352 | 273,562 | 258,894 | 299,002 | 248,093 |
| Cases pending | 247,973 | 285,071 | 334,261 | 340,401 | 371,756 | 364,117 | 397,226 |
| **U.S. District Courts Criminal (includes transfers):** | | | | | | | |
| Cases filed | 62,523 | 78,213 | 64,027 | 60,866 | 61,021 | 58,121 | 67,257 |
| Defendants filed | 84,147 | 100,031 | 84,017 | 79,154 | 79,968 | 75,235 | 84,828 |
| Cases terminated | 57,543 | 77,633 | 67,115 | 61,299 | 60,521 | 57,610 | 61,287 |
| Cases pending | 46,796 | 80,506 | 73,829 | 72,094 | 72,041 | 72,454 | 78,869 |
| **U.S. Bankruptcy Courts:** | | | | | | | |
| Cases filed | 1,276,922 | 1,572,597 | 1,000,083 | 879,736 | 819,159 | 796,037 | 775,578 |
| Cases terminated | 1,271,300 | 1,441,419 | 1,124,534 | 1,024,504 | 931,085 | 869,448 | 825,364 |
| Cases pending | 1,396,916 | 1,659,399 | 1,461,132 | 1,316,672 | 1,194,843 | 1,100,309 | 1,050,518 |
| **Post-conviction supervision:** | | | | | | | |
| Persons under supervision | 99,577 | 126,642 | 132,597 | 133,428 | 137,882 | 135,947 | 131,036 |
| **Pretrial services:** | | | | | | | |
| Total cases activated | 86,067 | 110,666 | 103,640 | 95,538 | 93,220 | 87,517 | 97,144 |
| Pretrial services cases activated | 84,107 | 109,711 | 102,949 | 94,757 | 92,599 | 86,974 | 96,718 |
| Pretrial diversion cases activated | 1,960 | 955 | 691 | 781 | 621 | 543 | 426 |
| Total released on supervision | 31,607 | 29,748 | 26,197 | 24,429 | 24,027 | 22,960 | 22,474 |
| Pretrial supervision | 31,927 | 28,440 | 25,183 | 23,368 | 23,141 | 22,190 | 22,843 |
| Diversion supervision | 2,166 | 1,308 | 1,014 | 1,061 | 886 | 770 | 631 |

[1] Excludes the U.S. Court of Appeals for the Federal Circuit.

Source: Administrative Office of the United States Courts, "Statistical Tables for the Federal Judiciary," <http://www.uscourts.gov/statistics-reports/analysis-reports/statistical-tables-federal-judiciary>, accessed March 2019.

# Table 373. U.S. District Courts—Civil Cases Filed by Basis of Jurisdiction and Nature of Suit: 2010 to 2018

[For 12-month periods ending June 30]

| Type of case | Cases filed | | | | | | |
|---|---|---|---|---|---|---|---|
| | 2010 | 2013 | 2014 | 2015 | 2016 | 2017 | 2018 |
| **Total cases filed [1]** | **285,215** | **283,087** | **298,713** | **280,037** | **290,430** | **271,721** | **281,202** |
| BASIS OF JURISDICTION | | | | | | | |
| U.S. cases: | | | | | | | |
| U.S. plaintiff | 8,427 | 7,863 | 6,833 | 6,182 | 5,007 | 5,014 | 4,705 |
| U.S. defendant | 34,306 | 39,778 | 39,926 | 35,651 | 52,943 | 41,677 | 38,235 |
| Private cases: | | | | | | | |
| Federal question | 137,776 | 146,086 | 149,380 | 151,330 | 149,294 | 149,577 | 149,243 |
| Diversity of citizenship | 104,703 | 89,359 | 102,568 | 86,865 | 83,170 | 75,449 | 89,018 |
| Local jurisdiction | 3 | 1 | 6 | 9 | 16 | 4 | 1 |
| NATURE OF SUIT | | | | | | | |
| Contract actions [1] | 31,461 | 28,591 | 28,631 | 26,506 | 24,796 | 23,678 | 26,100 |
| Insurance | 9,236 | 10,285 | 11,728 | 9,923 | 8,894 | 8,774 | 10,374 |
| Recovery of overpayments [2] | 3,079 | 2,499 | 2,357 | 2,307 | 1,670 | 1,515 | 1,114 |
| Real property actions [1] | 6,809 | 11,530 | 8,454 | 8,963 | 9,147 | 8,202 | 7,018 |
| Foreclosure | 3,836 | 6,832 | 4,401 | 4,043 | 4,882 | 4,070 | 3,176 |
| Tort actions | 87,256 | 67,172 | 81,024 | 69,875 | 62,646 | 57,007 | 68,776 |
| Personal injury | 82,057 | 62,715 | 77,443 | 62,318 | 56,452 | 53,030 | 64,545 |
| Personal injury product liability | 66,958 | 48,754 | 63,245 | 41,607 | 41,019 | 35,340 | 47,335 |
| Other personal injury [1] | 15,099 | 13,961 | 14,198 | 20,711 | 15,433 | 17,690 | 17,210 |
| Medical malpractice | 1,120 | 1,034 | 976 | 1,097 | 1,344 | 1,243 | 1,169 |
| Personal property damage | 5,199 | 4,457 | 3,581 | 7,557 | 6,194 | 3,977 | 4,231 |
| Actions under statutes [1] | 159,683 | 175,794 | 180,604 | 174,693 | 193,841 | 182,834 | 179,308 |
| Bankruptcy suits | 2,615 | 2,708 | 2,708 | 2,688 | 2,492 | 2,141 | 2,132 |
| Civil rights [1] | 34,427 | 35,965 | 34,829 | 37,015 | 37,477 | 39,056 | 40,617 |
| Employment | 14,343 | 13,832 | 12,035 | 12,258 | 11,583 | 12,198 | 12,387 |
| Environmental matters | 826 | 1,253 | 749 | 578 | 1,784 | 1,160 | 1,965 |
| Prisoner petitions | 52,450 | 55,369 | 62,402 | 52,844 | 70,863 | 61,031 | 53,626 |
| Forfeiture and penalty | 2,297 | 2,238 | 1,959 | 1,620 | 1,138 | 1,110 | 1,205 |
| Labor laws | 18,878 | 17,977 | 18,702 | 19,047 | 19,235 | 17,887 | 17,816 |
| Immigration | 1,262 | 1,044 | 1,134 | 1,244 | 1,552 | 1,907 | 1,696 |
| Protected property rights [3] | 8,519 | 13,232 | 13,195 | 14,145 | 12,415 | 11,060 | 11,845 |
| Securities commodities and exchanges | 1,442 | 1,187 | 1,000 | 1,012 | 1,069 | 1,353 | 1,527 |
| Social security laws | 13,725 | 19,121 | 19,530 | 19,102 | 18,407 | 18,953 | 19,115 |
| Tax suits | 1,171 | 1,103 | 969 | 1,005 | 973 | 993 | 948 |
| Freedom of information | 315 | 367 | 432 | 481 | 516 | 602 | 859 |
| **Cases terminated** | **295,909** | **257,057** | **260,352** | **273,562** | **258,894** | **299,002** | **248,093** |
| **Cases pending** | **285,071** | **295,780** | **334,261** | **340,401** | **371,756** | **364,117** | **397,226** |

[1] Includes other types not shown separately. [2] Includes enforcement of judgments in student loan cases, and overpayments of veterans' benefits. [3] Includes copyright, patent, and trademark rights.

Source: Administrative Office of the United States Courts, "Statistical Tables for the Federal Judiciary," <http://www.uscourts.gov/statistics-reports/analysis-reports/statistical-tables-federal-judiciary>, accessed March 2019.

# Table 374. U.S. Courts of Appeals—Nature of Suit or Offense in Cases Arising from the U.S. District Courts: 2010 to 2018

[For 12-month periods ending June 30. Excludes data for the U.S. Court of Appeals for the Federal Circuit. Includes appeals reopened, remanded, and reinstated (after being terminated due to procedural defaults) as well as original appeals]

| Nature of suit and offense | 2010 | 2013 | 2014 | 2015 | 2016 | 2017 | 2018 |
|---|---|---|---|---|---|---|---|
| **Total cases** | **43,880** | **42,227** | **41,618** | **40,234** | **39,506** | **38,594** | **37,487** |
| Criminal cases | 12,863 | 11,975 | 11,340 | 10,902 | 11,945 | 10,216 | 9,614 |
| Civil cases | 31,017 | 30,252 | 30,278 | 29,332 | 27,561 | 28,378 | 27,873 |
| U.S cases | 7,772 | 7,513 | 7,668 | 7,471 | 6,586 | 7,609 | 7,660 |
| U.S. plaintiff | 435 | 345 | 292 | 353 | 321 | 305 | 261 |
| U.S. defendant | 7,337 | 7,168 | 7,376 | 7,118 | 6,265 | 7,304 | 7,399 |
| Private cases | 23,245 | 22,739 | 22,610 | 21,861 | 20,975 | 20,769 | 20,213 |
| Federal question | 20,599 | 19,647 | 19,012 | 18,821 | 18,005 | 17,918 | 17,423 |
| Diversity of citizenship | 2,646 | 3,092 | 3,598 | 3,040 | 2,969 | 2,851 | 2,790 |
| General local jurisdiction | – | – | – | – | 1 | – | – |
| Criminal cases | 12,863 | 11,975 | 11,340 | 10,902 | 11,945 | 10,216 | 9,614 |
| Violent offenses | 621 | 550 | 563 | 483 | 477 | 570 | 512 |
| Property offenses | 1,624 | 1,620 | 1,606 | 1,420 | 1,403 | 1,271 | 1,212 |
| Drug offenses | 5,066 | 4,547 | 3,766 | 3,843 | 4,844 | 3,578 | 3,207 |
| Firearms and explosives offenses | 1,927 | 1,653 | 1,620 | 1,560 | 1,806 | 1,860 | 1,888 |
| Sex offenses | 651 | 732 | 733 | 786 | 736 | 769 | 762 |
| Justice system offenses | 142 | 151 | 138 | 169 | 129 | 147 | 134 |
| Immigration offenses | 1,787 | 1,551 | 1,473 | 1,491 | 1,342 | 957 | 897 |
| General offenses | 411 | 338 | 348 | 289 | 261 | 253 | 235 |
| Other [1] | 634 | 833 | 1,093 | 861 | 947 | 811 | 767 |

– Represents or rounds to zero. [1] Other includes regulatory, traffic, and unclassified offenses.

Source: Administrative Office of the United States Courts, "Statistical Tables for the Federal Judiciary," <http://www.uscourts.gov/statistics-reports/analysis-reports/statistical-tables-federal-judiciary>, accessed March 2019.

# Table 375. Total Incoming Caseloads in State Trial Courts by Case Category: 2017

[States reporting incomplete data or data not conforming to reporting guidelines are not shown. Represents new filings, plus reopened and reactivated cases when provided, as reported to the Court Statistics Project. Since state court caseload statistics should only be viewed in the context of each state's court structure, comparisons of the data reported here should not be made without additional information. See source for state court structures and characteristics]

| State | Total | Civil [1] | Domestic relations [2] | Criminal [3] | Juvenile [4] | Traffic/other violations [5] |
|---|---|---|---|---|---|---|
| Alabama | 823,840 | 173,358 | 77,066 | 254,489 | 41,391 | 277,536 |
| Alaska | 122,329 | 23,208 | 11,613 | 26,480 | 3,179 | 57,849 |
| California | 6,114,740 | 892,989 | 375,041 | 1,211,479 | 81,831 | 3,553,400 |
| Colorado | 871,344 | 280,202 | 43,879 | 268,738 | 14,753 | 263,772 |
| Connecticut | 683,667 | 198,426 | 49,010 | 107,191 | 21,631 | 307,409 |
| Delaware | 410,322 | 62,850 | 35,267 | 88,507 | 4,978 | 218,720 |
| District of Columbia | 97,783 | 53,996 | 13,187 | 28,639 | 1,961 | ([6]) |
| Florida | 3,286,397 | 788,221 | 232,645 | 709,903 | 49,797 | 1,505,831 |
| Hawaii | 517,800 | 35,597 | 13,329 | 74,909 | 7,883 | 386,082 |
| Indiana | 1,357,490 | 383,036 | 95,065 | 302,074 | 58,679 | 518,636 |
| Iowa | 733,178 | 128,598 | 34,209 | 122,756 | 12,128 | 435,487 |
| Kansas | 715,294 | 141,889 | 33,679 | 46,906 | 13,923 | 478,897 |
| Kentucky | 901,500 | 227,309 | 66,840 | 341,346 | 38,971 | 227,034 |
| Louisiana | 1,355,054 | 194,257 | 59,695 | 262,222 | 35,615 | 803,265 |
| Maine | 185,518 | 29,041 | 15,747 | 45,304 | 2,232 | 93,194 |
| Maryland | 1,977,504 | 1,025,925 | 115,440 | 300,440 | 14,788 | 520,911 |
| Massachusetts | 674,411 | 284,911 | 76,473 | 187,765 | 18,188 | 107,074 |
| Michigan | 3,339,462 | 634,411 | 114,095 | 897,979 | 34,416 | 1,658,561 |
| Minnesota | 1,290,382 | 171,527 | 53,910 | 184,980 | 30,858 | 849,107 |
| Missouri | 2,057,828 | 268,742 | 115,182 | 216,613 | 11,619 | 1,445,672 |
| Montana | 297,948 | 48,008 | 15,435 | 66,021 | 3,893 | 164,591 |
| Nebraska | 480,509 | 116,006 | 31,615 | 154,728 | 23,201 | 154,959 |
| Nevada | 899,474 | 176,722 | 57,988 | 191,462 | 12,316 | 460,986 |
| New Hampshire | 137,616 | 43,720 | 14,490 | 41,404 | 4,814 | 33,188 |
| New Jersey | 7,263,806 | 798,252 | 235,919 | 739,611 | 37,468 | 5,452,556 |
| New York | 3,280,319 | 1,445,298 | 558,927 | 533,109 | 61,527 | 681,458 |
| Ohio | 3,293,228 | 559,511 | 208,776 | 788,287 | 102,832 | 1,633,822 |
| Pennsylvania | 3,593,713 | 476,964 | 327,188 | 494,324 | 39,439 | 2,255,798 |
| Rhode Island | 173,406 | 49,431 | 9,590 | 30,209 | 6,028 | 78,148 |
| Texas | 11,786,697 | 1,664,723 | 388,675 | 2,598,655 | 48,532 | 7,086,112 |
| Utah | 666,273 | 112,448 | 23,642 | 127,100 | 23,969 | 379,114 |
| Vermont | 142,716 | 15,375 | 13,924 | 14,823 | 2,074 | 96,520 |

[1] Includes tort, contract, real property, small claims, probate/estate, mental health, and civil appeals cases. [2] Includes divorce/dissolution, paternity, custody, support, visitation, adoption, and civil protection/restraining order cases. [3] Includes felony, misdemeanor, and appeals from limited jurisdiction courts. [4] Includes delinquency, dependency, and status offense petitions. [5] Includes non-criminal traffic violations (infractions), parking violations, and ordinance violations. [6] Data are not applicable because the reporting unit does not have jurisdiction over the case type or case category.

Source: National Center for State Courts, Court Statistics Project, DataViewer, "Statewide Incoming Caseloads," <http://www.courtstatistics.org>, accessed July 2019 ©.

# Table 376. U.S. District Courts—National Petit and Grand Juror Service: 2010 to 2018

[For years ending September 30. Includes data on jury selection days only. Data on juror service after the selection day are not included]

| Juror service | 2010 | 2012 | 2013 | 2014 | 2015 | 2016 | 2017 | 2018 |
|---|---|---|---|---|---|---|---|---|
| **PETIT JUROR SERVICE** | | | | | | | | |
| Jurors present for jury selection or orientation | 262,376 | 237,411 | 237,251 | 218,203 | 195,206 | 194,211 | 184,019 | 189,504 |
| Percent selected | 22.7 | 23.1 | 22.2 | 22.4 | 22.6 | 22.5 | 22.8 | 22.0 |
| Percent challenged | 38.5 | 39.5 | 40.3 | 40.1 | 40.6 | 39.5 | 39.8 | 40.5 |
| Percent not selected or challenged | 38.7 | 37.3 | 37.5 | 37.4 | 36.8 | 38.0 | 37.5 | 37.5 |
| Voir Dire [1] | 24.9 | 24.7 | 23.5 | 24.3 | 23.7 | 25.2 | 25.0 | 24.0 |
| Non-Voir Dire [2] | 13.9 | 12.7 | 14.0 | 13.1 | 13.1 | 12.8 | 12.4 | 13.4 |
| Total juries selected | 5,332 | 4,899 | 4,656 | 4,278 | 4,149 | 3,887 | 3,708 | 3,660 |
| **GRAND JUROR SERVICE** | | | | | | | | |
| Juries serving | 784 | 783 | 778 | 763 | 749 | 743 | 755 | 755 |
| Sessions convened | 9,277 | 8,923 | 8,531 | 8,230 | 8,087 | 8,249 | 8,124 | 8,258 |
| Jurors in session | 186,020 | 179,076 | 171,038 | 164,856 | 161,493 | 164,733 | 161,759 | 163,859 |
| Average per session | 20.1 | 20.1 | 20.0 | 20.0 | 20.0 | 20.0 | 19.9 | 19.8 |
| Hours in session | 44,845 | 41,477 | 39,565 | 36,719 | 36,098 | 36,621 | 35,823 | 36,458 |
| Average hours per session | 4.8 | 4.6 | 4.6 | 4.5 | 4.5 | 4.4 | 4.4 | 4.4 |
| Proceedings filed by indictment: | | | | | | | | |
| Cases | 49,654 | (NA) | (NA) | (NA) | (NA) | (NA) | (NA) | (NA) |
| Defendants | 70,433 | 66,670 | 64,015 | 55,890 | 56,164 | 55,227 | 55,818 | 63,877 |
| Average defendants indicted per session | 7.6 | 7.5 | 7.5 | 6.8 | 6.9 | 6.7 | 6.9 | 7.7 |

NA Not available. [1] Jurors who completed pre-screening questionnaires or were in the courtroom during the conducting of voir dire. [2] Other jurors not selected or challenged who were not called to the courtroom or otherwise did not participate in the actual voir dire.

Source: Administrative Office of the United States Courts, "Judicial Business of the United States Courts 2018," <http://www.uscourts.gov/Statistics/JudicialBusiness.aspx>, accessed April 2019.

## Table 377. Problem-Solving Courts—Point of Case Entry and Case Outcomes by Type of Court: 2012

[In percent, except number of courts. Problem-solving courts generally allow participants to agree to follow court guidelines in order to avoid prosecution, incarceration, or other typical criminal justice outcomes. The concept has also been extended to civil and family court. Multiple responses to survey questions were allowed, so detail may sum to more than 100 percent. See source for methodology]

| Item | All courts | Drug | Mental health | Family | Youth specialty | Hybrid DWI/ drug [1] | DWI | Domestic violence | Veter-ans | Tribal well-ness | Other |
|---|---|---|---|---|---|---|---|---|---|---|---|
| **Total problem-solving courts**....... | **3,052** | **1,330** | **337** | **261** | **244** | **217** | **183** | **170** | **133** | **31** | **146** |
| POINT OF ENTRY INTO PROBLEM-SOLVING COURTS | | | | | | | | | | | |
| Pre-plea or at case filing............... | 35.5 | 27.1 | 44.1 | 43.3 | 49.5 | 24.0 | 14.7 | 72.8 | 46.3 | 29.2 | 49.2 |
| Post-plea.............................. | 65.1 | 73.9 | 73.1 | 16.1 | 54.3 | 85.4 | 68.4 | 39.1 | 81.0 | 83.3 | 45.8 |
| Post-sentence or post-release [2]....... | 35.7 | 44.5 | 41.1 | 12.1 | 11.7 | 40.1 | 41.2 | 14.6 | 27.3 | 54.2 | 36.7 |
| Judicial order............................ | 8.5 | 2.1 | 3.7 | 60.7 | 3.2 | 1.6 | 2.3 | 15.9 | 2.5 | 16.7 | 7.5 |
| Other [3] | 2.4 | 0.9 | 0.7 | 10.7 | 6.4 | 0.5 | 1.1 | 2.0 | 3.3 | – | 4.2 |
| BENEFITS OF SUCCESSFUL PROGRAM COMPLETION | | | | | | | | | | | |
| Case dismissed....................... | 61.3 | 65.2 | 74.1 | 45.5 | 75.5 | 56.6 | 13.5 | 49.3 | 80.0 | 78.3 | 58.7 |
| Sentence suspended.................... | 39.5 | 42.6 | 48.6 | 10.3 | 11.7 | 54.4 | 49.7 | 41.3 | 55.0 | 65.2 | 33.0 |
| Record expunged...................... | 22.4 | 26.8 | 22.1 | 3.6 | 36.7 | 24.2 | 4.3 | 21.7 | 22.5 | 21.7 | 12.8 |
| Expedited settlement.................... | 11.1 | 7.6 | 12.1 | 33.5 | 4.3 | 13.7 | 7.4 | 13.0 | 11.7 | 4.3 | 11.0 |
| Other [4] | 34.0 | 28.8 | 28.3 | 57.6 | 18.6 | 36.8 | 49.7 | 44.9 | 35.8 | 8.7 | 45.9 |

– Represents zero. [1] DWI is driving while intoxicated. Handles alcohol- or drug-dependent offenders also charged with a driving offense. [2] Includes entry after violation or revocation of parole. [3] Includes acceptance on a case-by-case basis, post-referral from outside agency, entry after child adjudicated dependent, and entry after admitting to impaired ability to care for child. [4] Includes benefits such as case closure, charge reduction, and successful completion of probation.

Source: U.S. Department of Justice, Bureau of Justice Statistics, *Census of Problem-Solving Courts, 2012*, NCJ 249803, September 2016. See also <https://www.bjs.gov/index.cfm?ty=pbdetail&iid=5744>.

## Table 378. U.S. Sentencing Commission Summary—Cases Reviewed by Disposition and Primary Offense: 2018

[In numbers, except as noted. For fiscal year ending in year shown. Covers federal felony and Class A misdemeanor cases reported to the U.S. Sentencing Commission by federal courts as required under the Sentencing Reform Act. See source for details]

| Characteristic | Total [1] | Immigra-tion | Drug traffick-ing | Firearms | Fraud, theft, embezzle-ment | Robbery | Child porn-ography | Money launder-ing | All other |
|---|---|---|---|---|---|---|---|---|---|
| **Total sentenced**..................... | **69,425** | **23,883** | **18,747** | **7,512** | **6,620** | **1,720** | **1,416** | **1,297** | **8,230** |
| CASES INVOLVING PRISON | | | | | | | | | |
| **Total receiving prison**.................. | **63,065** | **22,619** | **18,052** | **7,133** | **4,848** | **1,701** | **1,403** | **1,132** | **6,177** |
| Prison only........................... | 60,976 | 22,390 | 17,366 | 6,865 | 4,472 | 1,631 | 1,371 | 1,082 | 5,799 |
| Prison term ordered: | | | | | | | | | |
| Up to 12 months..................... | 19,809 | 15,121 | 1,119 | 408 | 1,238 | 36 | 23 | 153 | 1,711 |
| 13 to 60 months..................... | 25,850 | 7,089 | 7,809 | 4,401 | 2,693 | 487 | 403 | 628 | 2,440 |
| 61 to 120 months..................... | 9,436 | 176 | 5,200 | 1,637 | 427 | 579 | 564 | 225 | 549 |
| Over 120 months..................... | 5,881 | 5 | 3,158 | 419 | 114 | 529 | 381 | 176 | 1,099 |
| Prison and alternatives [2].............. | 2,089 | 229 | 686 | 268 | 376 | 70 | 32 | 50 | 378 |
| Mean sentence (in months) [3]........ | 44 | 10 | 76 | 53 | 23 | 106 | 104 | 59 | 54 |
| Median sentence (in months) [3]........ | 20 | 6 | 60 | 41 | 12 | 88 | 87 | 35 | 12 |
| CASES INVOLVING PROBATION | | | | | | | | | |
| **Total receiving probation**............... | **5,838** | **1,263** | **691** | **376** | **1,683** | **19** | **13** | **164** | **1,629** |
| Probation only........................ | 4,444 | 1,113 | 446 | 250 | 1,214 | 12 | 8 | 111 | 1,290 |
| Probation and confinement............. | 1,394 | 150 | 245 | 126 | 469 | 7 | 5 | 53 | 339 |
| CASES INVOLVING FINES AND RESTITUTION | | | | | | | | | |
| Total receiving fines and restitution....... | [4] 12,390 | 275 | 1,259 | 644 | 5,022 | 1,184 | 505 | 427 | 3,074 |
| Median amount (in dollars)................ | 11,434 | 1,000 | 1,500 | 2,000 | 82,234 | 5,388 | 6,000 | 313,314 | (NA) |
| Fine only.............................. | 522 | 1 | 4 | 3 | 89 | – | – | 1 | 424 |

NA Not available. – Represents zero. [1] Details may not sum to total due to rounding. [2] Includes cases receiving prison with additional conditions of a term of community confinement, home detention, or intermittent confinement. [3] Life sentences are included in these calculations as 470 months. [4] 1,575 cases are excluded due to missing information.

Source: U.S. Sentencing Commission, "2018 Sourcebook of Federal Sentencing Statistics," <https://www.ussc.gov/research/sourcebook-2018>, accessed June 2019.

## Table 379. Mandatory Minimum Sentencing Summary: 2015 to 2018

[For fiscal year ending in year shown for cases reported to the U.S. Sentencing Commission (USSC). Relief from mandatory minimum sentencing may be provided through a safety valve provision and/or by providing the government with substantial assistance; see source]

| Item | 2015 | 2016 | 2017 | 2018 |
|---|---|---|---|---|
| Cases reported to USSC (number)........................................ | 71,003 | 67,742 | 66,873 | 69,425 |
| Cases involving a mandatory minimum penalty (number)........................... | 14,138 | 13,604 | 13,577 | 16,228 |
| Percent subject to mandatory minimum penalties........................... | 22.2 | 21.9 | 21.8 | 24.7 |
| Percent receiving relief.................................................. | 39.2 | 38.7 | 37.3 | 40.6 |
| Percent not receiving relief.............................................. | 60.8 | 61.3 | 62.7 | 59.4 |
| Percent remaining subject to mandatory minimum at sentencing.................. | 13.5 | 13.4 | 13.7 | 14.2 |
| Offenders convicted of an offence carrying a mandatory minimum sentence by race/ethnicity (percent distribution): | | | | |
| White........................................................... | 27.2 | 27.2 | 26.9 | 27.3 |
| Black........................................................... | 28.9 | 29.7 | 29.5 | 27.4 |
| Hispanic........................................................ | 41.5 | 40.4 | 41.0 | 42.7 |
| Other.......................................................... | 2.4 | 2.7 | 2.6 | 2.6 |

Source: U.S. Sentencing Commission, *Quick Facts: Mandatory Minimum Penalties*, August 2019 and earlier reports. See also <https://www.ussc.gov/research/quick-facts>.

## Table 380. Delinquency Cases Disposed by Juvenile Courts by Type of Offense: 1990 to 2016

[In thousands (1,325 represents 1,325,000), except rate. A delinquency offense is an act committed by a juvenile for which an adult could be prosecuted in a criminal court. Disposition of a case involves taking a definite action such as waiving the case to criminal court, dismissing the case, placing the youth on probation, placing the youth in a facility for delinquents, or actions such as fines, restitution, and community service. Data are developed and maintained by the National Center for Juvenile Justice]

| Type of offense | 1990 | 1995 | 2000 | 2005 | 2008 | 2009 | 2010 | 2011 | 2012 | 2013 | 2014 | 2015 | 2016 |
|---|---|---|---|---|---|---|---|---|---|---|---|---|---|
| **All delinquency offenses..** | **1,325** | **1,826** | **1,720** | **1,679** | **1,597** | **1,465** | **1,344** | **1,224** | **1,120** | **1,020** | **948** | **889** | **851** |
| Case rate [1] | 51.7 | 63.6 | 55.9 | 52.3 | 50.3 | 46.4 | 42.6 | 39.0 | 35.8 | 32.6 | 30.1 | 28.2 | 26.9 |
| Person offenses [2] | 258 | 414 | 402 | 437 | 397 | 362 | 342 | 316 | 289 | 267 | 254 | 248 | 245 |
| Criminal homicide | 2 | 3 | 1 | 1 | 1 | 1 | 1 | 1 | 1 | 1 | 1 | 1 | 1 |
| Rape | 6 | 9 | 10 | 11 | 10 | 9 | 9 | 8 | 9 | 8 | 8 | 8 | 8 |
| Robbery | 27 | 42 | 23 | 27 | 33 | 30 | 27 | 24 | 21 | 21 | 20 | 20 | 20 |
| Aggravated assault | 44 | 62 | 48 | 48 | 43 | 38 | 35 | 31 | 28 | 25 | 25 | 26 | 26 |
| Simple assault | 136 | 234 | 260 | 282 | 252 | 231 | 223 | 210 | 191 | 176 | 167 | 163 | 159 |
| Property offenses [2] | 776 | 921 | 712 | 616 | 608 | 561 | 497 | 445 | 402 | 354 | 327 | 303 | 284 |
| Burglary | 145 | 149 | 118 | 102 | 105 | 96 | 86 | 79 | 72 | 62 | 57 | 55 | 55 |
| Larceny-theft | 347 | 442 | 334 | 278 | 281 | 274 | 244 | 218 | 200 | 177 | 163 | 145 | 127 |
| Motor vehicle theft | 65 | 52 | 36 | 32 | 23 | 19 | 16 | 13 | 12 | 11 | 12 | 13 | 16 |
| Arson | 6 | 10 | 8 | 7 | 7 | 6 | 5 | 5 | 4 | 4 | 4 | 3 | 3 |
| Drug law violations | 68 | 164 | 187 | 184 | 175 | 164 | 161 | 153 | 145 | 135 | 125 | 112 | 107 |
| Public order offenses [2] | 224 | 327 | 420 | 442 | 416 | 378 | 344 | 311 | 285 | 265 | 242 | 226 | 215 |
| Obstruction of justice | 89 | 135 | 216 | 203 | 195 | 184 | 167 | 152 | 140 | 130 | 123 | 114 | 109 |
| Disorderly conduct | 55 | 90 | 104 | 131 | 123 | 108 | 99 | 89 | 81 | 74 | 65 | 59 | 56 |
| Weapons offenses | 30 | 46 | 34 | 42 | 38 | 32 | 29 | 26 | 23 | 23 | 20 | 19 | 18 |
| Liquor law violations | 14 | 12 | 17 | 15 | 17 | 15 | 14 | 10 | 9 | 7 | 6 | 6 | 5 |
| Nonviolent sex offenses | 10 | 8 | 14 | 13 | 12 | 12 | 12 | 11 | 11 | 10 | 11 | 11 | 11 |

[1] Number of cases disposed per 1,000 juveniles (ages 10 to upper age of juvenile court jurisdiction). The upper age of juvenile court jurisdiction is defined by statute in each state. [2] Total includes other offenses not shown.

Source: U.S. Department of Justice, Office of Juvenile Justice and Delinquency Prevention, "Delinquency Case Rates by Offense, Sex, and Race (1985-2016)," <https://www.ojjdp.gov/ojstatbb/court/data.html>; and "Easy Access to Juvenile Court Statistics, Detailed Offenses," <https://ojjdp.gov/ojstatbb/ezajcs/>; accessed February 2019.

## Table 381. Delinquency Cases Disposed by Juvenile Courts by Type of Offense, Sex, and Race: 2005 to 2016

[See headnote, Table 380. Data are developed and maintained by the National Center for Juvenile Justice]

| Sex, race, and offense | Number of cases disposed | | | | Case rate [1] | | | |
|---|---|---|---|---|---|---|---|---|
| | 2005 | 2010 | 2015 | 2016 | 2005 | 2010 | 2015 | 2016 |
| **Male, total** | **1,217,205** | **966,505** | **642,128** | **614,911** | **73.9** | **59.9** | **39.9** | **38.1** |
| Person | 305,657 | 236,372 | 171,832 | 169,423 | 18.6 | 14.6 | 10.7 | 10.5 |
| Property | 446,129 | 349,051 | 220,928 | 208,761 | 27.1 | 21.6 | 13.7 | 12.9 |
| Drugs | 147,833 | 131,836 | 87,095 | 82,265 | 9.0 | 8.2 | 5.4 | 5.1 |
| Public order | 317,585 | 249,246 | 162,274 | 154,463 | 19.3 | 15.4 | 10.1 | 9.6 |
| **Female, total** | **461,435** | **377,024** | **246,758** | **235,634** | **29.5** | **24.5** | **16.0** | **15.2** |
| Person | 130,886 | 105,273 | 76,282 | 75,430 | 8.4 | 6.9 | 4.9 | 4.9 |
| Property | 170,110 | 147,563 | 82,124 | 74,866 | 10.9 | 9.6 | 5.3 | 4.8 |
| Drugs | 36,050 | 29,008 | 24,881 | 25,133 | 2.3 | 1.9 | 1.6 | 1.6 |
| Public order | 124,388 | 95,180 | 63,471 | 60,204 | 8.0 | 6.2 | 4.1 | 3.9 |
| **White, total [2]** | **809,797** | **607,593** | **387,064** | **370,192** | **41.8** | **33.8** | **22.3** | **21.5** |
| Person | 192,807 | 143,356 | 101,166 | 99,025 | 10.0 | 8.0 | 5.8 | 5.7 |
| Property | 324,730 | 235,824 | 132,274 | 122,946 | 16.8 | 13.1 | 7.6 | 7.1 |
| Drugs | 104,353 | 89,267 | 62,129 | 60,290 | 5.4 | 5.0 | 3.6 | 3.5 |
| Public order | 187,906 | 139,147 | 91,494 | 87,931 | 9.7 | 7.7 | 5.3 | 5.1 |
| **Black, total [2]** | **558,872** | **450,413** | **313,981** | **302,077** | **110.9** | **94.2** | **67.6** | **65.1** |
| Person | 176,108 | 137,636 | 99,148 | 97,775 | 34.9 | 28.8 | 21.3 | 21.1 |
| Property | 179,898 | 157,091 | 110,851 | 105,392 | 35.7 | 32.9 | 23.9 | 22.7 |
| Drugs | 43,854 | 32,904 | 20,937 | 19,833 | 8.7 | 6.9 | 4.5 | 4.3 |
| Public order | 159,012 | 122,781 | 83,044 | 79,077 | 31.5 | 25.7 | 17.9 | 17.0 |
| **Hispanic, total** | **263,130** | **248,238** | **163,802** | **154,593** | **45.6** | **37.6** | **22.8** | **21.1** |
| Person | 57,305 | 52,625 | 42,151 | 42,163 | 9.9 | 8.0 | 5.9 | 5.8 |
| Property | 91,787 | 88,200 | 50,877 | 46,379 | 15.9 | 13.4 | 7.1 | 6.3 |
| Drugs | 30,976 | 34,127 | 25,175 | 23,786 | 5.4 | 5.2 | 3.5 | 3.3 |
| Public order | 83,061 | 73,287 | 45,598 | 42,265 | 14.4 | 11.1 | 6.4 | 5.8 |
| **American Indian, total [3]** | **24,109** | **19,808** | **14,372** | **14,570** | **45.1** | **34.3** | **24.7** | **24.9** |
| Person | 5,503 | 4,583 | 3,439 | 3,618 | 10.3 | 7.9 | 5.9 | 6.2 |
| Property | 9,789 | 7,643 | 5,336 | 5,541 | 18.3 | 13.2 | 9.2 | 9.5 |
| Drugs | 2,785 | 2,617 | 2,300 | 2,264 | 5.2 | 4.5 | 4.0 | 3.9 |
| Public order | 6,032 | 4,964 | 3,297 | 3,147 | 11.3 | 8.6 | 5.7 | 5.4 |
| **Asian/Native Hawaiian/Pacific Islander, total [2]** | **22,732** | **17,477** | **9,668** | **9,113** | **16.2** | **11.2** | **5.5** | **5.0** |
| Person | 4,820 | 3,445 | 2,209 | 2,273 | 3.4 | 2.2 | 1.3 | 1.3 |
| Property | 10,035 | 7,856 | 3,712 | 3,369 | 7.2 | 5.0 | 2.1 | 1.9 |
| Drugs | 1,915 | 1,929 | 1,434 | 1,225 | 1.4 | 1.2 | 0.8 | 0.7 |
| Public order | 5,962 | 4,247 | 2,312 | 2,246 | 4.3 | 2.7 | 1.3 | 1.2 |

[1] Cases per 1,000 juveniles (ages 10 to upper age of juvenile court jurisdiction). The upper age of juvenile court jurisdiction is defined by statute in each state. [2] Non-Hispanic. [3] Data did not always allow for identification of Hispanic ethnicity for cases involving American Indian youth. The American Indian group includes an unknown proportion of Hispanic youth.

Source: U.S. Department of Justice, Office of Juvenile Justice and Delinquency Prevention, "Delinquency Case Rates by Offense, Sex, and Race (1985-2016)," <http://www.ojjdp.gov/ojstatbb/court/data.html>; and "Easy Access to Juvenile Court Statistics, Analyze Delinquency Cases," <http://ojjdp.gov/ojstatbb/ezajcs/>; accessed February 2019.

# Table 382. Child Victims of Abuse and Neglect—Total and First-Time Victims by State: 2016 and 2017

[For fiscal years ending in year shown. Data are unique counts, which count a child once, regardless of the number of reports concerning that child. Based on available State submissions to National Child Abuse and Neglect Data System (NCANDS) of alleged child abuse and neglect. States reporting 95 percent or more first-time victims are excluded due to potential issues with data quality. NCANDS collects case level data on children who received child protective services response in the form of an investigative or alternative response. Each state has its own definition of child abuse and neglect based on standards set by federal law. Child abuse is defined as any recent act or failure to act on the part of a parent or caretaker which results in death, serious physical or emotional harm, sexual abuse or exploitation; or an act or failure to act which presents an imminent risk or serious harm. See source for details]

| State | 2016 | | | | 2017 | | | |
|---|---|---|---|---|---|---|---|---|
| | | | First-time victims | | | | First-time victims | |
| | Total child population | Victims | Number | Rate per 1,000 children | Total child population | Victims | Number | Rate per 1,000 children |
| Total............... | 74,352,938 | 671,716 | 469,372 | 6.5 | 74,312,174 | 673,830 | 460,703 | 6.7 |
| Alabama................ | 1,098,851 | 10,157 | 8,414 | 7.7 | 1,095,473 | 10,847 | 8,930 | 8.2 |
| Alaska.................. | 186,324 | 3,142 | 2,158 | 11.6 | 184,928 | 2,783 | 1,884 | 10.2 |
| Arizona................. | 1,628,054 | 10,841 | 8,669 | 5.3 | 1,633,490 | 9,909 | 7,780 | 4.8 |
| Arkansas............... | 705,243 | 9,707 | 7,958 | 11.3 | 705,540 | 9,334 | 7,790 | 11.0 |
| California.............. | 9,089,743 | 68,663 | 57,950 | 6.4 | 9,060,136 | 65,342 | 55,585 | 6.1 |
| Colorado............... | 1,259,553 | 11,226 | 8,366 | 6.6 | 1,261,833 | 11,578 | 8,549 | 6.8 |
| Connecticut........... | 752,076 | 7,903 | 5,664 | 7.5 | 743,826 | 8,442 | 6,013 | 8.1 |
| Delaware.............. | 204,439 | 1,572 | 1,276 | 6.2 | 204,484 | 1,542 | 1,255 | 6.1 |
| District of Columbia..... | 120,911 | 1,366 | 989 | 8.2 | 124,492 | 1,639 | 1,202 | 9.7 |
| Florida................. | 4,163,893 | 41,894 | 19,629 | 4.7 | 4,201,983 | 40,103 | 18,773 | 4.5 |
| Georgia................ | 2,510,284 | 21,635 | 17,052 | 6.8 | 2,514,698 | 10,487 | 7,507 | 3.0 |
| Hawaii................. | 307,133 | 1,491 | 1,249 | 4.1 | 305,744 | 1,280 | 1,105 | 3.6 |
| Idaho.................. | 437,641 | 1,847 | 1,546 | 3.5 | 443,792 | 1,832 | 1,536 | 3.5 |
| Illinois................. | 2,928,924 | 29,059 | 20,504 | 7.0 | 2,897,185 | 28,751 | 19,802 | 6.8 |
| Indiana................ | 1,575,055 | 28,430 | 20,817 | 13.2 | 1,573,409 | 29,198 | 21,064 | 13.4 |
| Iowa................... | 730,383 | 8,555 | 6,079 | 8.3 | 731,947 | 10,643 | 7,633 | 10.4 |
| Kansas................ | 715,479 | 2,403 | 2,185 | 3.1 | 712,538 | 4,153 | 3,782 | 5.3 |
| Kentucky.............. | 1,011,521 | 20,010 | 13,726 | 13.6 | 1,010,539 | 22,410 | 15,230 | 15.1 |
| Louisiana............. | 1,114,593 | 11,289 | 8,702 | 7.8 | 1,108,403 | 10,356 | 7,920 | 7.1 |
| Maine................. | 254,211 | 3,446 | 2,303 | 9.1 | 252,634 | 3,475 | 2,346 | 9.3 |
| Maryland.............. | 1,348,377 | 6,993 | 5,174 | 3.8 | 1,347,506 | 7,578 | 5,565 | 4.1 |
| Massachusetts........ | 1,376,019 | 32,093 | 17,760 | 12.9 | 1,369,955 | 25,092 | 13,589 | 9.9 |
| Michigan.............. | 2,189,505 | 37,293 | 17,325 | 7.9 | 2,176,049 | 38,064 | 17,212 | 7.9 |
| Minnesota............ | 1,290,638 | 7,941 | 6,807 | 5.3 | 1,298,657 | 8,709 | 7,310 | 5.6 |
| Mississippi........... | 720,685 | 10,179 | 8,996 | 12.5 | 713,567 | 10,429 | 9,315 | 13.1 |
| Missouri.............. | 1,386,363 | 5,481 | 4,696 | 3.4 | 1,382,971 | 4,585 | 3,972 | 2.9 |
| Montana.............. | 227,377 | 3,116 | 2,554 | 11.2 | 228,889 | 3,534 | 2,926 | 12.8 |
| Nebraska............. | 473,569 | 2,783 | 2,013 | 4.3 | 475,733 | 3,246 | 2,421 | 5.1 |
| Nevada............... | 677,630 | 4,885 | 3,119 | 4.6 | 685,463 | 4,859 | 3,085 | 4.5 |
| New Hampshire........ | 260,665 | 905 | 761 | 2.9 | 258,773 | 1,148 | 977 | 3.8 |
| New Jersey............ | 1,987,515 | 8,264 | 6,560 | 3.3 | 1,979,018 | 6,698 | 5,198 | 2.6 |
| New Mexico........... | 493,051 | 7,526 | 5,425 | 11.0 | 488,090 | 8,577 | 6,191 | 12.7 |
| New York.............. | 4,181,345 | 65,123 | 39,498 | 9.4 | 4,154,497 | 71,226 | 43,061 | 10.4 |
| North Carolina......... | 2,295,504 | 7,134 | 5,054 | 2.2 | 2,302,346 | 7,392 | 5,955 | 2.6 |
| North Dakota.......... | 175,056 | 1,805 | 1,364 | 7.8 | 175,772 | 1,981 | 1,432 | 8.1 |
| Ohio.................. | 2,614,072 | 23,635 | 17,015 | 6.5 | 2,605,235 | 24,897 | 18,050 | 6.9 |
| Oklahoma............. | 961,246 | 14,308 | 11,176 | 11.6 | 959,285 | 14,457 | 11,254 | 11.7 |
| Oregon............... | 869,426 | 11,851 | 7,757 | 8.9 | 873,619 | 11,070 | 6,739 | 7.7 |
| Pennsylvania.......... | 2,673,992 | 4,355 | 4,133 | 1.5 | 2,664,515 | 4,625 | (NA) | (NA) |
| Rhode Island.......... | 208,770 | 2,955 | 2,059 | 9.9 | 207,332 | 3,095 | 2,168 | 10.5 |
| South Carolina........ | 1,098,070 | 17,331 | 13,183 | 12.0 | 1,104,674 | 17,071 | 12,974 | 11.7 |
| South Dakota.......... | 213,115 | 1,246 | 1,008 | 4.7 | 214,856 | 1,339 | 1,045 | 4.9 |
| Tennessee............. | 1,502,805 | 9,665 | 4,701 | 3.1 | 1,507,502 | 8,983 | 4,284 | 2.8 |
| Texas................. | 7,305,001 | 57,374 | 45,999 | 6.3 | 7,366,039 | 61,506 | 49,535 | 6.7 |
| Utah.................. | 919,428 | 9,614 | 6,866 | 7.5 | 926,699 | 9,947 | 7,227 | 7.8 |
| Vermont.............. | 118,142 | 822 | 710 | 6.0 | 116,825 | 878 | 751 | 6.4 |
| Virginia............... | 1,868,225 | 5,941 | (NA) | (NA) | 1,869,176 | 6,277 | (NA) | (NA) |
| Washington........... | 1,628,413 | 4,725 | 2,290 | 1.4 | 1,645,816 | 4,386 | 2,054 | 1.2 |
| West Virginia.......... | 374,322 | 5,938 | 5,192 | 13.9 | 369,718 | 6,496 | 5,743 | 15.5 |
| Wisconsin............. | 1,287,543 | 4,822 | 4,129 | 3.2 | 1,282,644 | 4,902 | 4,185 | 3.3 |
| Wyoming.............. | 138,632 | 977 | 812 | 5.9 | 136,483 | 950 | 799 | 5.9 |

NA Not available.

Source: U.S. Department of Health and Human Services, Administration for Children and Families, Statistics and Research, *Child Maltreatment 2017*, January 2019. See also <http://www.acf.hhs.gov/programs/cb/research-data-technology/statistics-research/child-maltreatment>.

## Table 383. Child Abuse and Neglect Victims by Type of Maltreatment and Age and Sex of Victim: 2010 to 2017

[For fiscal years ending in year shown. Data are unique counts, which count a child once, regardless of the number of reports concerning that child. Based on available State submissions to National Child Abuse and Neglect Data System (NCANDS) of alleged child abuse and neglect. NCANDS collects case level data on children who received child protective services response in the form of an investigative or alternative response. Each state has its own definition of child abuse and neglect based on standards set by federal law. Child abuse is defined as any recent act or failure to act on the part of a parent or caretaker which results in death, serious physical or emotional harm, sexual abuse or exploitation; or an act or failure to act which presents an imminent risk or serious harm]

| Item | 2010 | 2012 | 2013 | 2014 | 2015 | 2016 | 2017 |
|---|---|---|---|---|---|---|---|
| Victims, total [1] | 688,251 | 678,810 | 678,932 | 702,208 | 683,487 | 671,622 | 673,830 |
| TYPES OF MALTREATMENT [2,3] | | | | | | | |
| Neglect | 499,691 | 531,241 | 539,576 | 526,744 | 514,500 | 502,615 | 504,545 |
| Physical abuse | 118,502 | 124,544 | 122,159 | 119,517 | 117,772 | 122,067 | 123,065 |
| Sexual abuse | 62,057 | 62,936 | 60,956 | 58,105 | 57,286 | 57,329 | 58,114 |
| Psychological or emotional | 53,426 | 57,880 | 59,236 | 42,290 | 42,549 | 37,859 | 38,635 |
| Medical neglect | 15,711 | 15,705 | 15,450 | 15,645 | 15,169 | 14,028 | 15,160 |
| Other and unknown | 68,590 | 73,172 | 68,266 | 48,256 | 47,514 | 46,394 | 47,747 |
| SEX OF VICTIM | | | | | | | |
| Male | 333,864 | 330,620 | 330,914 | 343,684 | 332,464 | 326,707 | 327,373 |
| Female | 352,174 | 345,823 | 345,633 | 355,928 | 348,087 | 342,203 | 343,949 |
| Unknown | 2,213 | 2,367 | 2,385 | 2,596 | 2,936 | 2,712 | 2,508 |
| AGE OF VICTIM | | | | | | | |
| 1 year and younger | 136,910 | 134,024 | 139,360 | 146,300 | 144,354 | 145,976 | 147,300 |
| 2 to 5 years old | 180,271 | 182,845 | 179,949 | 180,654 | 172,337 | 166,930 | 166,392 |
| 6 to 9 years old | 145,354 | 145,190 | 147,888 | 156,232 | 153,019 | 149,514 | 146,435 |
| 10 to 13 years old | 119,555 | 118,021 | 115,125 | 119,253 | 115,153 | 113,788 | 116,980 |
| 14 to 17 years old | 103,764 | 95,734 | 93,459 | 96,428 | 95,134 | 92,921 | 93,955 |
| 18 years old and over [4] | 490 | (NA) | (NA) | (NA) | (NA) | (NA) | (NA) |
| Unknown [5] | 979 | 2,996 | 3,151 | 3,341 | 3,490 | 2,493 | 2,768 |

NA Not available. [1] Total victims is the sum for states contributing data to the Child File. The number of states not contributing data varies by year. [2] This is a count of the number of distinct victims of the specified types of maltreatment. A child may be a victim of more than one type of maltreatment, so the sum of types is greater than the count of victims. [3] Not all states use this taxonomy, nor do states define the categories in the same way. [4] Beginning in 2011, data included in unknown. [5] Includes unborn, unknown age, and beginning 2011, victims age 18–21.

Source: U.S. Department of Health and Human Services, Administration for Children and Families, Statistics and Research, *Child Maltreatment 2017*, January 2019, and earlier editions, and unpublished data. See also <http://www.acf.hhs.gov/programs/cb/research-data-technology/statistics-research/child-maltreatment>.

## Table 384. Prisoners Under Jurisdiction of Federal or State Correctional Authorities—Summary by State: 2000 to 2017

[For years ending December 31. Jurisdiction refers to the legal authority over a prisoner, regardless of where held. Occasionally, states do not submit data in a given year and estimates will be imputed; see source for details]

| State | 2000 | 2010 | 2015 | 2016 | 2017 | State | 2000 | 2010 | 2015 | 2016 | 2017 |
|---|---|---|---|---|---|---|---|---|---|---|---|
| U.S. | 1,394,231 | 1,613,803 | 1,526,603 | 1,508,129 | 1,489,363 | MS. | 20,241 | 21,067 | 18,911 | 19,192 | 19,103 |
| Federal [1] | 145,416 | 209,771 | 196,455 | 189,192 | 183,058 | MO. | 27,543 | 30,623 | 32,330 | 32,461 | 32,601 |
| State | 1,248,815 | 1,404,032 | 1,330,148 | 1,318,937 | 1,306,305 | MT. | 3,105 | 3,716 | 3,685 | 3,814 | 3,698 |
| AL [2] | 26,406 | 31,764 | 30,810 | 28,883 | 27,608 | NE. | 3,895 | 4,587 | 5,372 | 5,302 | 5,313 |
| AK [3] | 4,173 | 5,391 | 5,338 | 4,434 | 4,399 | NV. | 10,063 | 12,653 | 13,071 | 13,757 | 13,671 |
| AZ [4] | 26,510 | 40,209 | 42,719 | 42,320 | 42,030 | NH. | 2,257 | 2,761 | 2,897 | 2,818 | 2,750 |
| AR. | 11,915 | 16,204 | 17,707 | 17,537 | 18,010 | NJ. | 29,784 | 25,007 | 20,489 | 19,786 | 19,585 |
| CA. | 163,001 | 165,062 | 129,593 | 130,084 | 131,039 | NM. | 5,342 | 6,763 | 7,104 | 7,055 | 7,276 |
| CO. | 16,833 | 22,815 | 20,041 | 19,981 | 19,946 | NY. | 70,199 | 56,656 | 51,727 | 50,716 | 49,461 |
| CT [3] | 18,355 | 19,321 | 15,816 | 14,957 | 14,040 | NC. | 31,266 | 40,382 | 36,617 | 35,697 | 36,394 |
| DE [3,4] | 6,921 | 6,615 | 6,654 | 6,585 | 6,443 | ND. | 1,076 | 1,487 | 1,795 | 1,791 | 1,723 |
| DC [5] | 10,352 | (NA) | (NA) | (NA) | (NA) | OH. | 45,833 | 51,712 | 52,233 | 52,175 | 51,478 |
| FL. | 71,319 | 104,306 | 101,424 | 99,974 | 98,504 | OK [7] | 23,181 | 26,252 | 28,547 | 29,916 | 28,143 |
| GA. | 44,232 | 56,432 | 52,193 | 53,627 | 53,667 | OR. | 10,580 | 14,876 | 15,245 | 15,166 | 15,218 |
| HI [3,6] | 5,053 | 5,912 | 5,879 | 5,602 | 5,630 | PA. | 36,847 | 51,264 | 49,858 | 49,244 | 48,333 |
| ID. | 5,535 | 7,431 | 8,052 | 8,252 | 8,579 | RI [3,6] | 3,286 | 3,357 | 3,248 | 3,103 | 2,861 |
| IL. | 45,281 | 48,418 | 46,240 | 43,657 | 41,471 | SC. | 21,778 | 23,578 | 20,929 | 20,858 | 19,906 |
| IN. | 20,125 | 28,028 | 27,355 | 25,546 | 26,024 | SD. | 2,616 | 3,434 | 3,564 | 3,831 | 3,970 |
| IA. | 7,955 | 9,455 | 8,849 | 9,031 | 9,024 | TN. | 22,166 | 27,451 | 28,172 | 28,203 | 28,980 |
| KS. | 8,344 | 9,051 | 9,857 | 9,920 | 9,971 | TX. | 166,719 | 173,649 | 163,909 | 163,703 | 162,523 |
| KY. | 14,919 | 20,544 | 21,701 | 23,022 | 23,543 | UT. | 5,637 | 6,807 | 6,495 | 6,175 | 6,443 |
| LA. | 35,207 | 39,445 | 36,377 | 35,682 | 33,739 | VT [3] | 1,697 | 2,079 | 1,750 | 1,735 | 1,546 |
| ME. | 1,679 | 2,154 | 2,279 | 2,404 | 2,404 | VA. | 30,168 | 37,638 | 38,403 | 37,813 | 37,158 |
| MD. | 23,538 | 22,645 | 20,764 | 19,994 | 19,367 | WA. | 14,915 | 18,235 | 18,284 | 19,104 | 19,656 |
| MA. | 10,722 | 11,313 | 9,922 | 9,403 | 9,133 | WV. | 3,856 | 6,681 | 7,118 | 7,162 | 7,092 |
| MI. | 47,718 | 44,165 | 42,628 | 41,122 | 39,666 | WI. | 20,754 | 22,729 | 22,975 | 23,377 | 23,945 |
| MN. | 6,238 | 9,796 | 10,798 | 10,592 | 10,708 | WY. | 1,680 | 2,112 | 2,424 | 2,374 | 2,473 |

NA Not available. [1] Includes inmates held in nonsecure privately operated community corrections facilities and juveniles held in contract facilities. [2] Data from 2017 include offenders with Class D felonies and parole revocations and should not be compared to 2016 data. [3] Data include both total jail and prison population. Prisons and jails form one integrated system. [4] Numbers are for custody rather than jurisdiction counts. [5] As of December 31, 2001, sentenced felons from the District of Columbia are the responsibility of the Federal Bureau of Prisons. [6] Counts include dual jurisdiction cases where the inmate is currently housed in another jurisdiction's facilities. [7] 2016 and 2017 counts includes persons who were waiting in county jails to be moved to state prison.

Source: U.S. Department of Justice, Bureau of Justice Statistics, *Prisoners in 2017*, NCJ 252156, April 2019; and "Corrections Statistical Analysis Tool," <https://www.bjs.gov/index.cfm?ty=nps>, accessed January 2018.

# Table 385. Jail Inmates by Sex, Race, and Hispanic Origin: 2010 to 2017

[Based on the number of inmates on the last weekday of June, except as noted. Data adjusted for nonresponse and rounded to the nearest 100. See source for methodology. Does not include offenders supervised outside of jail facilities. Based on the Annual Survey of Jails]

| Characteristic | 2010 | 2011 | 2012 | 2013 | 2014 | 2015 [1] | 2016 [1] | 2017 |
|---|---|---|---|---|---|---|---|---|
| **Total inmates** | **748,700** | **735,600** | **744,500** | **731,200** | **744,600** | **727,400** | **740,700** | **745,200** |
| Incarceration rate per 100,000 U.S. residents | 242 | 236 | 237 | 231 | 233 | 226 | 229 | 229 |
| Adults | 741,200 | 729,700 | 739,100 | 726,600 | 740,400 | 723,800 | 736,800 | 741,600 |
| Male | 649,300 | 636,900 | 640,900 | 624,700 | 631,600 | 620,300 | 629,700 | 628,200 |
| Female | 91,900 | 92,800 | 98,100 | 101,900 | 108,800 | 103,500 | 107,100 | 113,400 |
| Juveniles [2] | 7,600 | 5,900 | 5,400 | 4,600 | 4,200 | 3,600 | 3,900 | 3,600 |
| Held as adult [3] | 5,600 | 4,600 | 4,600 | 3,500 | 3,700 | 3,200 | 3,200 | 3,200 |
| Held as juvenile | 1,900 | 1,400 | 900 | 1,100 | 500 | 400 | 700 | 300 |
| White, non-Hispanic | 331,600 | 329,400 | 341,100 | 344,900 | 352,800 | 351,600 | 356,100 | 370,100 |
| Black, non-Hispanic | 283,200 | 276,400 | 274,600 | 261,500 | 263,800 | 255,200 | 254,600 | 250,100 |
| Hispanic/Latino [4] | 118,100 | 113,900 | 112,700 | 107,900 | 110,600 | 103,900 | 112,700 | 108,400 |
| American Indian or Alaska Native non-Hispanic | 9,900 | 9,400 | 9,300 | 10,200 | 10,400 | 9,000 | 9,000 | 8,800 |
| Asian or Pacific Islander | 4,400 | 4,800 | 4,700 | 4,500 | 5,400 | 5,200 | 5,200 | 4,800 |
| Other [5] | 1,500 | 1,600 | 2,200 | 2,200 | 1,700 | 2,500 | 2,900 | 2,900 |
| Rated capacity [6] | 857,900 | 870,400 | 877,400 | 872,900 | 890,500 | 901,400 | 915,400 | 915,100 |

[1] In 2015 and 2016, the Annual Survey of Jails collected demographic data on the inmate population at year-end instead of midyear. Jails typically hold fewer inmates at year-end than at midyear. The inmate populations were adjusted for seasonal variation and represent estimated midyear counts, see source for Methodology. [2] Juveniles age 17 or younger at midyear. [3] Includes juveniles who were tried or awaiting trial as adults. [4] Persons of Hispanic origin may be of any race. [5] Includes Native Hawaiians, Other Pacific Islanders, and persons of two or more races. [6] Maximum number of beds or inmates assigned by a rating official to a facility, excluding separate temporary holding areas.

Source: U.S. Department of Justice, Bureau of Justice Statistics, *Jail Inmates 2017*, NCJ 251774, April 2019. See also <https://www.bjs.gov/index.cfm?ty=pbse&sid=38>.

# Table 386. Prisoners Under Federal or State Jurisdiction by Sex: 1980 to 2017

[As of December 31. Represents prisoners sentenced to more than one year under jurisdiction of federal or state authorities rather than those in the custody of such authorities. Federal prisoners includes inmates held in nonsecure privately operated community corrections facilities and juveniles held in contract facilities. From the National Prisoner Statistics Program. See source for methodology]

| Year | Total [1] | Rate [2] | Federal | State | Male | Female | White [3,4] | Black [3,4] | Hispanic [3] |
|---|---|---|---|---|---|---|---|---|---|
| 1980 | 315,974 | 139 | 20,611 | 295,363 | 303,643 | 12,331 | (NA) | (NA) | (NA) |
| 1981 | 353,673 | 154 | 22,169 | 331,504 | 339,375 | 14,298 | (NA) | (NA) | (NA) |
| 1982 | 395,516 | 171 | 23,652 | 371,864 | 379,075 | 16,441 | (NA) | (NA) | (NA) |
| 1983 | 419,346 | 179 | 26,331 | 393,015 | 401,870 | 17,476 | (NA) | (NA) | (NA) |
| 1984 | 443,398 | 188 | 27,602 | 415,796 | 424,193 | 19,205 | (NA) | (NA) | (NA) |
| 1985 | 480,568 | 202 | 32,695 | 447,873 | 459,223 | 21,345 | (NA) | (NA) | (NA) |
| 1986 | 522,084 | 217 | 36,531 | 485,553 | 497,540 | 24,544 | (NA) | (NA) | (NA) |
| 1987 | 560,812 | 231 | 39,523 | 521,289 | 533,990 | 26,822 | (NA) | (NA) | (NA) |
| 1988 | 603,732 | 247 | 42,738 | 560,994 | 573,587 | 30,145 | (NA) | (NA) | (NA) |
| 1989 | 680,907 | 276 | 47,168 | 633,739 | 643,643 | 37,264 | (NA) | (NA) | (NA) |
| 1990 | 739,980 | 297 | 50,403 | 689,577 | 699,416 | 40,564 | (NA) | (NA) | (NA) |
| 1991 | 789,610 | 313 | 56,696 | 732,914 | 745,808 | 43,802 | (NA) | (NA) | (NA) |
| 1992 | 846,277 | 332 | 66,706 | 700,571 | 799,776 | 46,501 | (NA) | (NA) | (NA) |
| 1993 | 932,074 | 359 | 74,399 | 857,675 | 878,037 | 54,037 | (NA) | (NA) | (NA) |
| 1994 | 1,016,691 | 389 | 79,795 | 936,896 | 956,566 | 60,125 | (NA) | (NA) | (NA) |
| 1995 | 1,085,022 | 411 | 83,663 | 1,001,359 | 1,021,059 | 63,963 | (NA) | (NA) | (NA) |
| 1996 | 1,137,722 | 427 | 88,815 | 1,048,907 | 1,068,123 | 69,599 | (NA) | (NA) | (NA) |
| 1997 | 1,195,498 | 445 | 94,987 | 1,100,511 | 1,121,663 | 73,835 | (NA) | (NA) | (NA) |
| 1998 | 1,245,402 | 461 | 103,682 | 1,141,720 | 1,167,802 | 77,600 | (NA) | (NA) | (NA) |
| 1999 | 1,304,074 | 476 | 114,275 | 1,189,799 | 1,221,611 | 82,463 | (NA) | (NA) | (NA) |
| 2000 | 1,334,174 | [7] 470 | 125,044 | 1,209,130 | 1,249,130 | 85,044 | (NA) | (NA) | (NA) |
| 2001 | 1,345,217 | 470 | 136,509 | 1,208,708 | 1,260,033 | 85,184 | (NA) | (NA) | (NA) |
| 2002 | 1,380,516 | 477 | 143,040 | 1,237,476 | 1,291,450 | 89,066 | (NA) | (NA) | (NA) |
| 2003 | 1,408,361 | 483 | 151,919 | 1,256,442 | 1,315,790 | 92,571 | (NA) | (NA) | (NA) |
| 2004 | 1,433,728 | 487 | 159,137 | 1,274,591 | 1,337,730 | 95,998 | (NA) | (NA) | (NA) |
| 2005 | 1,462,866 | 492 | 166,173 | 1,296,693 | 1,364,178 | 98,688 | (NA) | (NA) | (NA) |
| 2006 | 1,504,598 | 501 | 173,533 | 1,331,065 | 1,401,261 | 103,337 | 507,100 | 590,300 | 313,600 |
| 2007 | 1,532,851 | 506 | 179,204 | 1,353,647 | 1,427,088 | 105,763 | 499,800 | 592,900 | 330,400 |
| 2008 | 1,547,742 | 506 | 182,333 | 1,365,409 | 1,441,384 | 106,358 | 499,900 | 592,800 | 329,800 |
| 2009 | 1,553,574 | 504 | 187,886 | 1,365,688 | 1,448,239 | 105,335 | 490,000 | 584,800 | 341,200 |
| 2010 | 1,552,669 | 500 | 190,641 | 1,362,028 | 1,447,766 | 104,903 | 484,400 | 572,700 | 345,800 |
| 2011 | 1,538,847 | 492 | 197,050 | 1,341,797 | 1,435,141 | 103,706 | 474,300 | 557,100 | 347,800 |
| 2012 | 1,512,430 | 479 | 196,574 | 1,315,856 | 1,411,076 | 101,354 | 466,600 | 537,800 | 340,300 |
| 2013 | 1,520,403 | 479 | 195,098 | 1,325,305 | 1,416,102 | 104,301 | 463,900 | 529,900 | 341,200 |
| 2014 | 1,507,781 | 471 | 191,374 | 1,316,407 | 1,401,685 | 106,096 | 461,500 | 518,700 | 338,900 |
| 2015 | 1,476,847 | 459 | 178,688 | 1,298,159 | 1,371,879 | 104,968 | 450,200 | 499,400 | 333,200 |
| 2016 [5] | 1,459,948 | 450 | 171,482 | 1,288,466 | 1,354,109 | 105,839 | 440,200 | 487,300 | 339,600 |
| 2017 [6] | 1,439,808 | 440 | 166,203 | 1,273,605 | 1,334,775 | 105,033 | 436,500 | 475,900 | 336,500 |

NA Not available. [1] Includes prisoners under the legal authority of state or federal correctional officials. [2] Rate per 100,000 estimated population. Based on U.S. Census Bureau estimated resident population. [3] Rounded to the nearest 100. [4] Excludes persons of Hispanic or Latino origin and persons of two or more races. [5] Total and state estimates include imputed counts for North Dakota, which did not submit data. [6] Total and state estimates include imputed counts for New Mexico and North Dakota, which did not submit 2017 NPS data. [7] Decrease in incarceration rate from 1999 to 2000 due to use of new Census numbers.

Source: U.S. Department of Justice, Bureau of Justice Statistics, *Prisoners in 2017*, NCJ 252156, April 2019, and earlier reports. See also <https://www.bjs.gov/index.cfm?ty=pbse&sid=40>.

## Table 387. Prisoners Executed Under Civil Authority by State: 1977 to 2017

[Alaska, Connecticut, District of Columbia, Hawaii, Illinois, Iowa, Maine, Maryland, Massachusetts, Michigan, Minnesota, New Jersey, North Dakota, Rhode Island, Vermont, West Virginia, and Wisconsin are jurisdictions without a death penalty. New Mexico abolished the death penalty for offenses committed after July 1, 2009. As of December 31, 2016, two males in New Mexico were under previously imposed death sentences. In Delaware, capital cases are no longer pursued due to a 2016 court ruling; however, one prisoner remained under a previously imposed death sentence]

| State | 1977 to 2017 | 2000 | 2010 | 2015 | 2016 | 2017 | State | 1977 to 2017 | 2000 | 2010 | 2015 | 2016 | 2017 |
|---|---|---|---|---|---|---|---|---|---|---|---|---|---|
| United States [1] | 1,465 | 85 | 46 | 28 | 20 | 23 | Missouri | 88 | 5 | – | 6 | 1 | 1 |
|  |  |  |  |  |  |  | Montana | 3 | – | – | – | – | – |
| Alabama | 61 | 4 | 5 | – | 2 | 3 | Nebraska | 3 | – | – | – | – | – |
| Arizona | 37 | 3 | 1 | – | – | – | Nevada | 12 | – | – | – | – | – |
| Arkansas | 31 | 2 | – | – | – | 4 | New Mexico | 1 | – | – | – | – | – |
| California | 13 | 1 | – | – | – | – | North Carolina | 43 | 1 | – | – | – | – |
| Colorado | 1 | – | – | – | – | – | Ohio | 55 | – | 8 | – | – | 2 |
| Connecticut | 1 | – | – | – | – | – | Oklahoma | 112 | 11 | 3 | 1 | – | – |
| Delaware | 16 | 1 | – | – | – | – | Oregon | 2 | – | – | – | – | – |
| Florida | 95 | 6 | 1 | 2 | 1 | 3 | Pennsylvania | 3 | – | – | – | – | – |
| Georgia | 70 | – | 2 | 5 | 9 | 1 | South Carolina | 43 | 1 | – | – | – | – |
| Idaho | 3 | – | – | – | – | – | South Dakota | 3 | – | – | – | – | – |
| Illinois | 12 | – | – | – | – | – | Tennessee | 6 | 1 | – | – | – | – |
| Indiana | 20 | – | – | – | – | – | Texas | 545 | 40 | 17 | 13 | 7 | 7 |
| Kentucky | 3 | – | – | – | – | – | Utah | 7 | – | 1 | – | – | – |
| Louisiana | 28 | 1 | 1 | – | – | – | Virginia | 113 | 8 | 3 | 1 | – | 2 |
| Maryland | 5 | – | – | – | – | – | Washington | 5 | – | 1 | – | – | – |
| Mississippi | 21 | – | 3 | – | – | – | Wyoming | 1 | – | – | – | – | – |

– Represents zero. [1] Includes persons executed within the Federal system.

Source: Through 1978, U.S. Law Enforcement Assistance Administration; thereafter, U.S. Department of Justice, Bureau of Justice Statistics, *Capital Punishment, 2017: Selected Findings*, NCJ 253060, July 2019, and earlier reports. See also <https://www.bjs.gov/index.cfm?ty=pbse&sid=1>.

## Table 388. Prisoners Executed Under Civil Authority by Sex and Race: 1930 to 2017

[Excludes executions by military authorities. See source for more information]

| Period or year | Total [1] | Male | Female | White [2] | Black [2] | Hispanic | Period or year | Total [1] | Male | Female | White [2] | Black [2] | Hispanic |
|---|---|---|---|---|---|---|---|---|---|---|---|---|---|
| 1930 to 1939 | 1,667 | 1,656 | 11 | 827 | 816 | (NA) | 1995 | 56 | 56 | – | 31 | 22 | 2 |
| 1940 to 1949 | 1,284 | 1,272 | 12 | 490 | 781 | (NA) | 1996 | 45 | 45 | – | 29 | 14 | 2 |
| 1950 to 1959 | 717 | 709 | 8 | 336 | 376 | (NA) | 1997 | 74 | 74 | – | 41 | 26 | 5 |
| 1960 to 1967 | 191 | 190 | 1 | 98 | 93 | (NA) | 1998 | 68 | 66 | 2 | 40 | 18 | 8 |
| 1968 to 1976 [3] | – | – | – | – | – | – | 1999 | 98 | 98 | – | 53 | 33 | 9 |
| 1977 | 1 | 1 | – | 1 | – | – | 2000 | 85 | 83 | 2 | 43 | 35 | 6 |
| 1978 | – | – | – | – | – | – | 2001 | 66 | 63 | 3 | 45 | 17 | 3 |
| 1979 | 2 | 2 | – | 2 | – | – | 2002 | 71 | 69 | 2 | 47 | 18 | 6 |
| 1980 | – | – | – | – | – | – | 2003 | 65 | 65 | – | 41 | 20 | 3 |
| 1981 | 1 | 1 | – | 1 | – | – | 2004 | 59 | 59 | – | 36 | 19 | 3 |
| 1982 | 2 | 2 | – | 1 | 1 | – | 2005 | 60 | 59 | 1 | 38 | 19 | 3 |
| 1983 | 5 | 5 | – | 4 | 1 | – | 2006 | 53 | 53 | – | 25 | 20 | 8 |
| 1984 | 21 | 20 | 1 | 13 | 8 | – | 2007 | 42 | 42 | – | 22 | 14 | 6 |
| 1985 | 18 | 18 | – | 9 | 7 | 2 | 2008 | 37 | 37 | – | 17 | 17 | 3 |
| 1986 | 18 | 18 | – | 9 | 7 | 2 | 2009 | 52 | 52 | – | 24 | 21 | 7 |
| 1987 | 25 | 25 | – | 11 | 11 | 3 | 2010 | 46 | 45 | 1 | 28 | 13 | 5 |
| 1988 | 11 | 11 | – | 6 | 5 | – | 2011 | 43 | 43 | – | 22 | 16 | 5 |
| 1989 | 16 | 16 | – | 6 | 8 | 2 | 2012 | 43 | 43 | – | 25 | 11 | 7 |
| 1990 | 23 | 23 | – | 16 | 7 | – | 2013 | 39 | 38 | 1 | 23 | 13 | 3 |
| 1991 | 14 | 14 | – | 6 | 7 | 1 | 2014 | 35 | 33 | 2 | (NA) | (NA) | (NA) |
| 1992 | 31 | 31 | – | 17 | 11 | 2 | 2015 | 28 | (NA) | (NA) | (NA) | (NA) | (NA) |
| 1993 | 38 | 38 | – | 19 | 14 | 4 | 2016 | 20 | (NA) | (NA) | 16 | 2 | 2 |
| 1994 | 31 | 31 | – | 19 | 11 | 1 | 2017 | 23 | (NA) | (NA) | 13 | 8 | 2 |

– Represents zero. NA Not available. [1] Includes American Indians, Alaska Natives, Asians, Native Hawaiians, and other Pacific Islanders, not shown separately. [2] Excludes persons of Hispanic or Latino origin. In 2017, two of the white prisoners executed in Texas were of Hispanic or Latino origin. [3] In 1972, the U.S. Supreme Court invalidated capital punishment statutes in several states, effecting a moratorium on executions. Executions resumed in 1977 when the Supreme Court found revisions to several state statutes had effectively addressed the issues previously held as unconstitutional.

Source: Through 1978, U.S. Law Enforcement Assistance Administration; thereafter, U.S. Department of Justice, Bureau of Justice Statistics, *Capital Punishment, 2017: Selected Findings*, NCJ 253060, July 2019. See also <https://www.bjs.gov/index.cfm?ty=pbse&sid=1>.

## Table 389. Prisoners Under Death Sentence by Race: 1980 to 2017

[As of December 31. Excludes prisoners under sentence of death who remained within local correctional systems pending exhaustion of appellate process or who had not been committed to prison. Data from the National Prisoner Statistics Program]

| Year | Total | White | Black | Other | Year | Total | White | Black | Other |
|------|-------|-------|-------|-------|------|-------|-------|-------|-------|
| 1980 | 692 | 424 | 264 | 4 | 1999 | 3,540 | 1,960 | 1,515 | 65 |
| 1981 | 860 | 499 | 353 | 8 | 2000 | 3,601 | 1,989 | 1,541 | 71 |
| 1982 | 1,066 | 613 | 441 | 12 | 2001 | 3,577 | 1,968 | 1,538 | 71 |
| 1983 | 1,209 | 692 | 505 | 12 | 2002 | 3,562 | 1,939 | 1,551 | 72 |
| 1984 | 1,420 | 806 | 598 | 16 | 2003 | 3,377 | 1,882 | 1,417 | 78 |
| 1985 | 1,575 | 896 | 664 | 15 | 2004 | 3,320 | 1,856 | 1,390 | 74 |
| 1986 | 1,800 | 1,013 | 762 | 25 | 2005 | 3,245 | 1,802 | 1,366 | 77 |
| 1987 | 1,967 | 1,128 | 813 | 26 | 2006 | 3,233 | 1,806 | 1,353 | 74 |
| 1988 | 2,117 | 1,235 | 848 | 34 | 2007 | 3,215 | 1,806 | 1,338 | 71 |
| 1989 | 2,243 | 1,308 | 898 | 37 | 2008 | 3,210 | 1,795 | 1,343 | 72 |
| 1990 | 2,346 | 1,368 | 940 | 38 | 2009 | 3,173 | 1,779 | 1,318 | 76 |
| 1991 | 2,465 | 1,449 | 979 | 37 | 2010 | 3,139 | 1,743 | 1,309 | 87 |
| 1992 | 2,580 | 1,511 | 1,031 | 38 | 2011 | 3,065 | 1,721 | 1,274 | 70 |
| 1993 | 2,727 | 1,575 | 1,111 | 41 | 2012 | 3,011 | 1,684 | 1,258 | 69 |
| 1994 | 2,905 | 1,653 | 1,203 | 49 | 2013 | 2,983 | 1,670 | 1,251 | 62 |
| 1995 | 3,064 | 1,732 | 1,284 | 48 | 2014 | 2,942 | 1,647 | 1,233 | 62 |
| 1996 | 3,242 | 1,833 | 1,358 | 51 | 2015 | 2,872 | 1,606 | 1,202 | 64 |
| 1997 | 3,328 | 1,864 | 1,408 | 56 | 2016 | 2,797 | 1,553 | 1,179 | 65 |
| 1998 | 3,465 | 1,917 | 1,489 | 59 | 2017 | 2,703 | 1,508 | 1,129 | 66 |

Source: U.S. Department of Justice, Bureau of Justice Statistics, *Capital Punishment, 2017: Selected Findings*, NCJ 253060, July 2019, and earlier reports. See also <http://www.bjs.gov/index.cfm?ty=pbse&sid=1>.

## Table 390. Prisoners—Firearm Possession and Use During Offense That Led to Imprisonment by Type of Controlling Offense: 2016

[Controlling offense for sentenced prisoners and those awaiting sentencing with one offense is that one offense. For sentenced prisoners with multiple offenses and sentences, the controlling offense is the one with the longest sentence. For sentenced prisoners with multiple offenses and one sentence and those awaiting sentencing with multiple offenses, the controlling offense is the most serious offense. Data are from the Survey of Prison Inmates]

| Controlling offense | State prisoners | | | Federal prisoners | | |
|---------------------|-----------------|--|--|-------------------|--|--|
| | | Percent who— | | | Percent who— | |
| | Number [1] | Possessed a firearm [1] | Used a firearm [2] | Number [1] | Possessed a firearm [1] | Used a firearm [2] |
| **Total** | **1,211,200** | **20.9** | **13.9** | **170,400** | **20.0** | **5.0** |
| Violent | 667,300 | 29.1 | 23.0 | 20,900 | 36.2 | 25.3 |
| Homicide [3] | 191,400 | 43.6 | 37.2 | 3,800 | 35.9 | 28.4 |
| Rape/sexual assault | 144,800 | 2.0 | 0.8 | 2,400 | (B) | (B) |
| Robbery | 149,600 | 43.3 | 31.5 | 10,700 | 46.3 | 32.1 |
| Assault | 149,400 | 25.0 | 20.6 | 2,900 | 29.0 | 18.1 |
| Other violent [4] | 32,200 | 17.0 | 12.6 | 1,200 | 34.1 | (B) |
| Property | 186,100 | [9] 4.9 | [9] 2.0 | 12,000 | [9] 2.6 | (B) |
| Burglary | 88,100 | 6.7 | 3.2 | 300 | (B) | (B) |
| Other property [5] | 98,000 | 3.3 | 1.0 | 11,800 | 2.4 | (B) |
| Drug | 180,800 | [9] 8.4 | [9] 0.8 | 80,500 | [9] 12.3 | [9] 0.6 |
| Trafficking [6] | 130,500 | 9.4 | 0.9 | 72,300 | 12.9 | 0.7 |
| Possession | 45,900 | 6.1 | (B) | 3,500 | (B) | (B) |
| Other/unspecified drug | 4,300 | (B) | (B) | 4,700 | (B) | (B) |
| Public order | 158,300 | [9] 21.5 | [9] 5.6 | 52,900 | 30.2 | [9] 5.3 |
| Weapons [7] | 43,800 | 67.2 | 15.7 | 22,200 | 66.9 | 11.3 |
| Other public order [8] | 114,400 | 4.0 | 1.7 | 30,700 | 3.6 | (B) |
| Other | 3,900 | (B) | (B) | 1,800 | (B) | (B) |
| Unknown | 14,900 | [9] 4.3 | (B) | 2,200 | (B) | (B) |

B Not calculated. Too few cases to provide a reliable estimate, or coefficient of variation is greater than 50%. [1] Data are estimates. Excludes prisoners who were missing responses on firearm possession; includes prisoners who were missing responses on firearm use. [2] Excludes prisoners who were missing responses on firearm use. [3] Includes murder and negligent and non-negligent manslaughter. [4] Includes kidnapping, blackmail, extortion, hit-and-run driving with bodily injury, child abuse, and criminal endangerment. [5] Includes larceny, theft, motor vehicle theft, arson, fraud, stolen property, destruction of property, vandalism, hit-and-run driving with no bodily injury, criminal tampering, trespassing, entering without breaking, and possession of burglary tools. [6] Includes possession with intent to distribute. [7] Includes being armed while committing a crime; possession of ammunition, concealed weapons, firearms and explosive devices; selling or trafficking weapons; and other weapons offenses. [8] Includes commercialized vice, immigration crimes, DUI, violations of probation/parole, and other public-order offenses. [9] Difference with comparison group (total violent offenders) is significant at the 95% confidence level across main categories, and no testing was done on subcategories (e.g., homicide).

Source: U.S. Department of Justice, Bureau of Justice Statistics, *Source and Use of Firearms Involved in Crimes: Survey of Prison Inmates, 2016*, NCJ 251776, January 2019. See also <https://www.bjs.gov/index.cfm?ty=pbdetail&iid=6486>.

## Table 391. Rate of Adults Under Community Supervision, Probation, and Parole: 2000 to 2016

[From Annual Survey of Probation and Parole. Probation is a court-ordered period of correctional supervision in the community, generally as an alternative to incarceration. Probation can be a combined sentence of incarceration followed by a period of community supervision. Parole is a period of conditional supervised release in the community following a prison term. Including parolees released through discretionary or mandatory supervised release from prison, those released through other types of post-custody conditional supervision, and those sentenced to a term of supervised release]

| Year | Rate per 100,000 population | | | U.S. residents on— | | |
|------|----------------------------|----------|--------|--------------------|-----------|--------|
|      | Community supervision [1,2] | Probation | Parole | Community supervision [1] | Probation | Parole |
| 2000 | 2,162 | 1,818 | 344 | 1 in 46 | 1 in 53 | 1 in 285 |
| 2010 | 2,067 | 1,715 | 356 | 1 in 48 | 1 in 58 | 1 in 281 |
| 2013 | 1,946 | 1,603 | 348 | 1 in 51 | 1 in 62 | 1 in 287 |
| 2014 | 1,911 | 1,568 | 348 | 1 in 52 | 1 in 64 | 1 in 288 |
| 2015 | 1,872 | 1,526 | 350 | 1 in 53 | 1 in 66 | 1 in 285 |
| 2016 | 1,811 | 1,467 | 349 | 1 in 55 | 1 in 68 | 1 in 287 |

[1] Adults on probation, parole or other post-prison supervision. [2] Beginning 2008, detail does not sum to total because the community supervision rate was adjusted to exclude parolees who were also on probation.

Source: U.S. Department of Justice, Bureau of Justice Statistics, *Probation and Parole in the United States, 2016*, NCJ 251148, April 2018, and earlier reports. See also <https://www.bjs.gov/index.cfm?ty=pbse&sid=42>.

## Table 392. Adults Under Community Supervision, Probation, and Parole by State: 2016

[As of December 31, 2016, unless otherwise noted. Counts are rounded to nearest hundred. Rates are per 100,000, computed using the estimated U.S. adult resident population in each jurisdiction on January 1, 2017. Counts may not be actual as reporting agencies may provide estimates on some or all detailed data; see source for details. From Annual Survey of Probation and Parole]

| Area | Community supervision [1] | | Probation | | Parole | |
|------|---------|-----------------|---------|-----------------|---------|-----------------|
|      | Number | Rate per 100,000 | Number | Rate per 100,000 | Number | Rate per 100,000 |
| United States, total | 4,537,100 | 1,810 | 3,673,120 | 1,466 | 874,777 | 349 |
| Federal | 131,700 | 53 | 17,284 | 7 | 114,385 | 46 |
| States | 4,405,400 | 1,758 | 3,655,836 | 1,459 | 760,392 | 303 |
| Alabama | 60,700 | 1,609 | 52,177 | 1,382 | 8,562 | 227 |
| Alaska | 8,400 | 1,520 | 6,621 | 1,193 | 1,812 | 326 |
| Arizona | 84,800 | 1,587 | 77,373 | 1,447 | 7,500 | 140 |
| Arkansas [3] | 51,500 | 2,246 | 30,881 | 1,347 | 23,792 | 1,038 |
| California [3] | 333,300 | 1,100 | 239,735 | 791 | [2] 93,598 | 309 |
| Colorado [3] | 90,900 | 2,106 | 80,740 | 1,870 | 10,186 | 236 |
| Connecticut | 44,700 | 1,580 | 41,311 | 1,461 | 3,379 | 119 |
| Delaware | 15,800 | 2,101 | 15,395 | 2,049 | 387 | 52 |
| District of Columbia | 9,600 | 1,709 | 5,838 | 1,034 | 4,025 | 713 |
| Florida [3] | 218,600 | 1,315 | 214,066 | 1,288 | 4,566 | 27 |
| Georgia [3] | (NA) | (NA) | (NA) | (NA) | 22,386 | 285 |
| Hawaii | 21,900 | 1,949 | 20,516 | 1,828 | 1,367 | 122 |
| Idaho | 37,500 | 2,980 | 32,409 | 2,578 | 5,054 | 402 |
| Illinois | 143,400 | 1,451 | 113,989 | 1,154 | 29,428 | 298 |
| Indiana | 116,700 | 2,300 | 108,302 | 2,135 | 8,385 | 165 |
| Iowa | 35,100 | 1,456 | 29,254 | 1,213 | 6,051 | 251 |
| Kansas | 21,500 | 978 | 16,654 | 758 | 4,830 | 220 |
| Kentucky | 63,800 | 1,858 | 48,457 | 1,411 | 15,383 | 448 |
| Louisiana | 71,000 | 1,985 | 40,174 | 1,124 | 30,907 | 864 |
| Maine | 6,800 | 634 | 6,817 | 632 | 21 | 2 |
| Maryland | 82,800 | 1,770 | 72,529 | 1,550 | 10,305 | 220 |
| Massachusetts | 63,600 | 1,167 | 61,789 | 1,133 | 1,851 | 34 |
| Michigan [3] | (NA) | (NA) | (NA) | (NA) | (NA) | 216 |
| Minnesota | 103,900 | 2,447 | 96,852 | 2,280 | 7,075 | 167 |
| Mississippi [3] | 37,700 | 1,660 | 29,067 | 1,280 | 8,645 | 381 |
| Missouri | 61,600 | 1,305 | 43,799 | 928 | 17,792 | 377 |
| Montana | 10,200 | 1,247 | 9,132 | 1,115 | 1,074 | 131 |
| Nebraska | 14,600 | 1,013 | 13,489 | 937 | 1,088 | 76 |
| Nevada | 19,000 | 831 | 13,724 | 601 | 5,261 | 230 |
| New Hampshire | 6,400 | 592 | 3,939 | 366 | 2,436 | 226 |
| New York | 142,400 | 913 | 97,928 | 628 | 44,426 | 285 |
| North Carolina | 95,200 | 1,205 | 82,466 | 1,044 | 12,726 | 161 |
| North Dakota | 7,100 | 1,228 | 6,341 | 1,090 | 804 | 138 |
| Ohio [3] | 256,400 | 2,842 | 236,754 | 2,624 | 19,634 | 218 |
| Oklahoma | 35,500 | 1,193 | 33,562 | 1,129 | 1,895 | 64 |
| Oregon | 61,400 | 1,887 | 36,658 | 1,127 | 24,711 | 760 |
| Pennsylvania | 291,600 | 2,880 | 180,492 | 1,783 | 111,087 | 1,097 |
| South Dakota | 9,300 | 1,420 | 6,610 | 1,009 | 2,687 | 410 |
| Tennessee | 74,700 | 1,443 | 62,609 | 1,209 | 12,092 | 234 |
| Texas | 482,900 | 2,328 | 374,285 | 1,805 | 111,287 | 537 |
| Utah | 15,900 | 740 | 12,229 | 568 | 3,707 | 172 |
| Vermont | 5,800 | 1,153 | 4,904 | 969 | 935 | 185 |
| Virginia | 62,500 | 952 | 60,821 | 927 | 1,650 | 25 |
| Washington [3] | 100,600 | 1,763 | 89,317 | 1,565 | 11,322 | 198 |
| West Virginia | 10,100 | 692 | 6,523 | 448 | 3,550 | 244 |
| Wisconsin [3] | 64,900 | 1,442 | 44,489 | 988 | 20,401 | 453 |
| Wyoming | 5,500 | 1,235 | 4,666 | 1,046 | 842 | 189 |

NA Not available. [1] December 31, 2016 population excludes 10,822 offenders under community supervision who were on both probation and parole. [2] In California, includes post-release community supervision and mandatory supervision parolees. [3] Includes estimates for nonreporting agencies; see source for explanatory notes.

Source: U.S. Department of Justice, Bureau of Justice Statistics, *Probation and Parole in the United States, 2016*, NCJ 251148, April 2018. See also <https://www.bjs.gov/index.cfm?ty=pbse&sid=42>.

# Table 393. Prisoner Recidivism by Selected Characteristics: 2005 to 2010

[In percent. Prisoners released on community supervision in 2005 who were arrested for a new crime/returned to prison 2005 through 2010. See source for details]

| Characteristic | Federal prisoners | | State prisoners | |
|---|---|---|---|---|
| | Arrested | Returned to prison [1] | Arrested [2] | Returned to prison [1, 3] |
| **Total, released prisoners** | **47.2** | **31.6** | **76.5** | **59.4** |
| SEX | | | | |
| Male | 49.6 | 33.4 | 77.5 | 56.4 |
| Female | 35.4 | 22.1 | 68.1 | 44.9 |
| RACE/HISPANIC ORIGIN | | | | |
| White alone, non-Hispanic | 39.7 | 26.2 | 73.1 | 53.2 |
| Black alone, non-Hispanic | 55.1 | 35.7 | 80.6 | 55.6 |
| Hispanic/Latino | 48.3 | 33.1 | 75.7 | 57.8 |
| Other [4] | 48.5 | 38.5 | 74.2 | 58.8 |
| AGE AT RELEASE | | | | |
| 24 years old and under | 64.7 | 45.8 | 84.2 | 62.2 |
| 25 to 29 years old | 59.3 | 40.7 | 80.6 | 57.3 |
| 30 to 34 years old | 52.9 | 34.7 | 77.0 | 54.8 |
| 35 to 39 years old | 48.6 | 31.9 | 78.1 | 56.0 |
| 40 to 44 years old | 44.5 | 29.4 | 74.2 | 55.0 |
| 45 to 49 years old | 37.7 | 24.7 | 69.0 | 48.8 |
| 50 years old and over | 23.5 | 14.7 | 58.8 | 41.9 |
| MOST SERIOUS COMMITMENT OFFENSE | | | | |
| Violent [5] | 58.1 | 44.3 | 73.8 | 51.0 |
| Property | 39.5 | 26.1 | 82.2 | 62.5 |
| Drug | 44.0 | 27.1 | 76.7 | 53.2 |
| Other public order [6] | 57.0 | 40.2 | 73.0 | 54.2 |
| Sex offense [7] | 36.7 | 33.9 | 61.0 | 45.4 |
| NUMBER OF PRIOR ARRESTS [8] | | | | |
| 1-2 | 27.0 | 16.3 | 52.4 | 31.1 |
| 3-4 | 46.4 | 29.6 | 67.3 | 44.3 |
| 5-9 | 59.9 | 40.8 | 75.6 | 53.8 |
| 10 or more | 72.2 | 52.4 | 86.3 | 65.8 |

[1] Includes returns to a federal or state prison. [2] Based on prisoners released conditionally in 30 states. [3] Based on prisoners released conditionally in 23 states that provided the necessary prison admission data. [4] Includes American Indian, Alaska Native, Asian, Native Hawaiian, Other Pacific Islander, and persons of two or more races. [5] Excludes rape and sexual assault. [6] Excludes sex offenses. [7] Includes rape, sexual assault, and sexual abuse; possession, distribution, and production of child pornography; and transportation for illegal sexual purposes. [8] Number of times prisoner arrested before release in 2005, including the arrest that led to the 2005 release.

Source: U.S. Department of Justice, Bureau of Justice Statistics, *Recidivism of Offenders Placed on Federal Community Supervision in 2005: Patterns from 2005 to 2010*, NCJ 249743, June 2016. See also <http://www.bjs.gov/index.cfm?ty=pbdetail&iid=5642>.

# Table 394. Fires—Number and Loss by Type and Property Use: 2014 to 2017

[Number of fires in thousands (1,298 represents 1,298,000); property loss in millions of dollars (11,605 represents $11,605,000,000). Based on annual sample survey of fire departments. No adjustments were made for unreported fires and losses]

| Type and property use | Number (1,000) | | | | Direct property loss (mil. dol.) [1] | | | |
|---|---|---|---|---|---|---|---|---|
| | 2014 | 2015 | 2016 | 2017 | 2014 | 2015 [7] | 2016 [8] | 2017 [9] |
| **Fires, total** | **1,298** | **1,346** | **1,342** | **1,320** | **11,605** | **14,298** | **10,628** | **23,000** |
| Structure | 494 | 502 | 476 | 499 | 9,846 | 10,280 | 7,898 | 10,700 |
| Outside of structure [2] | 65 | 76 | 88 | 74 | 141 | 151 | 333 | 137 |
| Brush and rubbish | 448 | 460 | 471 | 458 | – | – | – | – |
| Vehicle [3] | 194 | 205 | 204 | 198 | 1,522 | 1,816 | 1,356 | 2,044 |
| Other | 98 | 104 | 104 | 91 | 96 | 101 | 130 | 136 |
| Structure fires by property use: | | | | | | | | |
| Public assembly | 14 | 17 | 14 | 15 | 429 | 323 | 308 | 285 |
| Educational | 5 | 5 | 4 | 6 | 59 | 40 | 34 | 51 |
| Institutional | 7 | 7 | 6 | 7 | 40 | 51 | 37 | 40 |
| Stores and offices | 18 | 17 | 16 | 18 | 708 | 635 | 436 | 763 |
| Residential | 387 | 388 | 372 | 379 | 6,992 | 7,210 | 5,804 | 7,900 |
| 1-2 family homes [4] | 274 | 271 | 257 | 263 | 5,844 | 5,799 | 4,943 | 6,141 |
| Apartments | 94 | 95 | 95 | 95 | 982 | 1,161 | 711 | 1,600 |
| Other residential [5] | 19 | 23 | 20 | 23 | 166 | 250 | 150 | 162 |
| Storage | 28 | 31 | 27 | 28 | 781 | 1,032 | 665 | 834 |
| Industry, utility, defense [6] | 10 | 9 | 9 | 9 | 626 | 924 | 419 | 503 |
| Special structures | 27 | 29 | 29 | 39 | 211 | 65 | 195 | 331 |

– Represents zero. [1] Direct property damage figures do not include indirect losses (such as business interruption and temporary shelter costs) and adjustments for inflation. [2] Includes outside storage, crops, timber, etc. [3] Includes highway and other vehicles (trains, boats, ships, aircraft, and farm and construction vehicles). [4] Includes manufactured homes. [5] Includes hotels and motels, college dormitories, boarding houses, etc. [6] Data underreported as some incidents were handled by private fire brigades or fixed suppression systems which do not report. [7] Includes $1,950 million, total property loss for the Valley and Butte Wildfires in California. Loss by specific property type was not available for these fires. [8] Includes $911 million, total property loss estimate for the Gatlinburg, Tennessee Wildfires. Loss by specific property type was not available for these fires. [9] Includes $10 billion estimated property loss for Northern California Wildfires.

Source: National Fire Protection Association, Quincy, MA, *Fire Loss in the United States During 2017* ©, October 2018, and earlier reports. See also <http://www.nfpa.org/News-and-Research>.

## Table 395. The U.S. Fire Service: Departments, Personnel, and Responses by Type: 1990 to 2017

[In thousands (1,025.7 represents 1,025,700), except where noted. A fire department is a public or private organization that provides fire prevention, fire suppression, and associated emergency and non-emergency services to a jurisdiction such as a county, municipality, or organized fire district]

| Items | 1990 | 2000 | 2005 | 2010 | 2013 | 2014 | 2015 | 2016 | 2017 |
|---|---|---|---|---|---|---|---|---|---|
| **FIRE DEPARTMENTS (NUMBER)** | | | | | | | | | |
| **Total departments** | **30,391** | **30,339** | **30,300** | **30,125** | **30,052** | **29,980** | **29,727** | **29,710** | **29,819** |
| All career | 1,949 | 2,178 | 2,087 | 2,495 | 2,477 | 2,440 | 2,651 | 2,775 | 2,785 |
| Mostly career | 1,338 | 1,667 | 1,766 | 1,860 | 1,971 | 2,045 | 1,893 | 2,048 | 2,316 |
| Mostly volunteer | 4,000 | 4,523 | 4,902 | 5,290 | 5,797 | 5,580 | 5,421 | 5,451 | 5,405 |
| All volunteer | 23,104 | 21,971 | 21,575 | 20,480 | 19,807 | 19,915 | 19,762 | 19,436 | 19,313 |
| By whether Emergency Medical Service (EMS) provided: | | | | | | | | | |
| Provide EMS service only | (NA) | (NA) | 12,900 | 13,440 | 13,400 | 13,665 | 13,500 | (NA) | 13,631 |
| Provide EMS service and advance life support | (NA) | (NA) | 4,260 | 4,515 | 5,050 | 4,635 | 4,617 | (NA) | 4,629 |
| No EMS service | (NA) | (NA) | 13,170 | 12,170 | 11,600 | 11,680 | 11,610 | (NA) | 11,559 |
| **FIRE DEPARTMENT PERSONNEL (1,000)** | | | | | | | | | |
| **Total personnel** | **1,025.7** | **1,064.2** | **1,136.7** | **1,103.3** | **1,140.8** | **1,134.4** | **1,160.5** | **1,090.1** | **1,056.2** |
| Career [1] | 253.0 | 286.8 | 313.3 | 335.2 | 354.6 | 346.2 | 345.6 | 361.1 | 373.6 |
| Volunteer [2] | 772.7 | 777.4 | 823.7 | 768.2 | 786.2 | 788.3 | 814.9 | 729.0 | 682.6 |
| **RESPONSES BY TYPE (1,000)** | | | | | | | | | |
| **Total responses** | **13,708** | **20,520** | **23,252** | **28,205** | **31,645** | **31,645** | **33,636** | **35,320** | **34,684** |
| Fires | 2,019 | 1,708 | 1,602 | 1,332 | 1,240 | 1,298 | 1,346 | 1,342 | 1,320 |
| Medical aid | 7,650 | 12,251 | 14,375 | 18,522 | 21,372 | 20,178 | 21,500 | 22,751 | 22,341 |
| False alarms | 1,476 | 2,127 | 2,134 | 2,187 | 2,343 | 2,488 | 2,567 | 2,622 | 2,547 |
| Malicious mischievous | 442 | 300 | 241 | 163 | 165 | 162 | 166 | 173 | 141 |
| System malfunctions | 593 | 884 | 746 | 709 | 757 | 820 | 828 | 837 | 752 |
| Unintentional calls | 318 | 714 | 838 | 992 | 1,080 | 1,166 | 1,200 | 1,226 | 1,286 |
| Other [3] | 124 | 230 | 310 | 324 | 341 | 342 | 374 | 387 | 369 |
| Mutual aid/assistance | 487 | 864 | 1,091 | 1,190 | 1,298 | 1,447 | 1,493 | 1,515 | 1,353 |
| Hazardous material | 210 | 319 | 375 | 402 | 367 | 405 | 442 | 425 | 424 |
| Other hazardous [4] | 423 | 544 | 667 | 660 | 678 | 615 | 643 | 685 | 693 |
| All other [5] | 1,443 | 2,708 | 3,009 | 3,913 | 4,347 | 5,214 | 5,646 | 5,981 | 6,006 |

NA Not available. [1] Includes full-time uniform firefighters regardless of assignment (i.e., suppression, administrative, prevention/inspection, etc.). Does not include firefighters who work for the state or federal government or in private fire brigades. [2] Volunteer firefighters include any active part-time (call or volunteer) firefighters. [3] Bomb scares, etc. [4] Arcing wires, bomb removal, power line down, biological hazard, etc. [5] Smoke scares, lock-outs, animal rescue, unauthorized burning, severe weather, etc.

Source: National Fire Protection Association, Quincy, MA, *U.S. Fire Department Profile 2017* ©, and *Fire Loss in the United States During 2017* ©, and earlier reports. See also <http://www.nfpa.org/News-and-Research>.

## Table 396. Fire Losses—Total and Per Capita: 1980 to 2016

[5,579 represents $5,579,000,000. Includes allowances for Fair Access to Insurance Requirements Plan and uninsured losses]

| Year | Property loss total, (mil. dol.) | Per capita [1] (dol.) | Year | Property loss total, (mil. dol.) | Per capita [1] (dol.) | Year | Property loss total, (mil. dol.) | Per capita [1] (dol.) |
|---|---|---|---|---|---|---|---|---|
| 1980 | 5,579 | 24.56 | 1993 | 11,331 | 43.96 | 2005 | 20,427 | 69.12 |
| 1982 | 5,894 | 25.61 | 1994 | 12,778 | 49.08 | 2006 | 20,340 | 68.17 |
| 1983 | 6,320 | 27.20 | 1995 | 11,887 | 45.23 | 2007 | 24,399 | 81.00 |
| 1984 | 7,602 | 32.35 | 1996 | 12,544 | 47.29 | 2008 | 24,734 | 81.34 |
| 1985 | 7,753 | 32.70 | 1997 | 12,940 | 48.32 | 2009 | 22,911 | 74.68 |
| 1986 | 8,488 | 35.21 | 1998 | 11,510 | 45.59 | 2010 | 20,486 | 66.22 |
| 1987 | 8,504 | 34.96 | 1999 | 12,428 | 45.58 | 2011 | 19,511 | 62.60 |
| 1988 | 9,626 | 39.11 | 2000 | 13,457 | 47.69 | 2012 | 23,977 | 76.36 |
| 1989 | 9,514 | 38.33 | 2001 [2] | 17,118 | 60.07 | 2013 | 19,054 | 60.26 |
| 1990 | 9,495 | 38.07 | 2002 | 17,586 | 61.14 | 2014 | 21,801 | 68.44 |
| 1991 | 11,302 | 44.82 | 2003 | 21,129 | 72.83 | 2015 | 19,759 | 61.57 |
| 1992 | 13,588 | 53.28 | 2004 | 17,344 | 59.23 | 2016 | 19,293 | 59.71 |

[1] Based on enumerated population as of April 1 for Census years and estimated resident population as of July 1 for all other years. [2] Does not include insured fire losses related to terrorism.

Source: Insurance Information Institute, New York, NY. *The Insurance Fact Book, 2018* ©, and previous reports. See also <http://www.iii.org>.

## Table 397. Fires and Property Loss for Incendiary and Suspicious Fires and Civilian Fire Deaths and Injuries by Selected Property Type: 2010 to 2017

[In thousands (482 represents 482,000), except as indicated. Based on sample survey of fire departments]

| Characteristic | 2010 | 2011 | 2012 | 2013 | 2014 | 2015 | 2016 | 2017 |
|---|---|---|---|---|---|---|---|---|
| NUMBER (1,000) | | | | | | | | |
| Structure fires, total.................. | 482 | 485 | 481 | 488 | 494 | 502 | 476 | 499 |
| Structure fires that were intentionally set............ | 28 | 27 | 26 | 23 | 19 | 23 | 20 | 23 |
| PROPERTY LOSS (mil. dol.) [1] | | | | | | | | |
| Structure fires, total.................. | 9,716 | 9,693 | 9,776 | 9,526 | 9,846 | 10,280 | 7,898 | 10,700 |
| Structure fires that were intentionally set............ | 585 | 601 | 581 | 577 | 613 | 460 | 473 | 582 |
| CIVILIAN FIRE DEATHS | | | | | | | | |
| Deaths, total [2]................. | 3,120 | 3,005 | 2,855 | 3,240 | 3,275 | 3,280 | 3,390 | 3,400 |
| Residential property................... | 2,665 | 2,550 | 2,405 | 2,785 | 2,795 | 2,605 | 2,800 | 2,710 |
| One- and two-family dwellings................. | 2,200 | 2,105 | 2,000 | 2,430 | 2,345 | 2,155 | 2,410 | 2,290 |
| Apartments....................... | 440 | 415 | 380 | 325 | 400 | 405 | 325 | 340 |
| Vehicles [3]............................ | 310 | 300 | 325 | 320 | 345 | 500 | 355 | 430 |
| CIVILIAN FIRE INJURIES | | | | | | | | |
| Injuries, total [2]................. | 17,720 | 17,500 | 16,500 | 15,925 | 15,775 | 15,700 | 14,650 | 14,670 |
| Residential property................... | 13,800 | 14,360 | 13,175 | 12,575 | 12,175 | 11,575 | 11,125 | 10,910 |
| One- and two-family dwellings................. | 9,400 | 9,485 | 8,825 | 8,300 | 8,025 | 8,050 | 7,375 | 7,470 |
| Apartments....................... | 3,950 | 4,425 | 4,050 | 3,900 | 3,800 | 3,025 | 3,375 | 3,130 |
| Vehicles [3]............................ | 1,590 | 1,190 | 975 | 1,050 | 1,450 | 1,875 | 1,225 | 1,610 |

[1] Direct property loss only. [2] Includes deaths or injuries from other types of fires, not shown separately. [3] Includes highway vehicles, and trains, boats, ships, farm vehicles, and construction vehicles.

Source: National Fire Protection Association, Quincy, MA, *Fire Loss in the United States During 2017* ©, October 2018, and earlier reports. See also <http://www.nfpa.org/News-and-Research>.

## Table 398. Firefighter On-Duty Fatalities and Injuries: 2009 to 2017

[Number, unless otherwise noted. On-duty refers to involvement in operations at the scene of an emergency, whether it is a fire or nonfire incident; responding to or returning from an incident; performing other officially assigned duties including training; and being on call]

| Item | 2009 | 2010 | 2011 | 2012 | 2013 | 2014 | 2015 | 2016 | 2017 |
|---|---|---|---|---|---|---|---|---|---|
| Total fatalities [1]..................... | 96 | 90 | 87 | 85 | 109 | 96 | 90 | 91 | 87 |
| Fatalities per 100,000 fires (rate)...... | 2.97 | 2.33 | 2.52 | 2.33 | 4.84 | 2.39 | 2.45 | 2.01 | (NA) |
| Emergency duty deaths (percent)..... | 63 | 55 | 54 | 56 | 73 | 46 | 49 | 40 | 46 |
| By incident characteristic: | | | | | | | | | |
| Wildland related fatalities............. | 17 | 12 | 10 | 16 | 31 | 11 | 12 | 15 | 10 |
| Incidents with multiple fatalities...... | 6 | 4 | 3 | 4 | 4 | 2 | 3 | 3 | 1 |
| Training fatalities..................... | 10 | 12 | 8 | 8 | 7 | 9 | 7 | 9 | 12 |
| Cause of fatal injury: | | | | | | | | | |
| Stress/overexertion [2].................. | 52 | 56 | 54 | 48 | 39 | 63 | 60 | 43 | 52 |
| Vehicle collision..................... | 16 | 11 | 5 | 18 | 9 | 9 | 5 | 19 | 10 |
| Total nonfatal injuries [3]............ | 78,150 | 71,875 | 70,090 | 69,400 | 65,880 | 63,350 | 68,085 | 62,085 | 58,835 |
| Fireground injuries................... | 32,205 | 32,675 | 30,505 | 31,490 | 29,760 | 27,015 | 29,130 | 24,325 | 24,105 |
| Injuries at nonfire emergencies....... | 15,455 | 13,355 | 14,905 | 12,760 | 12,535 | 14,595 | 14,320 | 12,780 | 12,240 |
| Nature of injury: | | | | | | | | | |
| Burns (fire or chemical)............... | 2,965 | 2,585 | 2,385 | 2,220 | 1,975 | 1,810 | 2,020 | 1,900 | 1,310 |
| Smoke or gas inhalation............... | 2,340 | 1,500 | 1,760 | 1,685 | 1,895 | 1,980 | 1,645 | 2,355 | 2,135 |
| Other respiratory distress............ | 915 | 940 | 1,060 | 910 | 915 | 855 | 1,060 | 800 | 850 |
| Burns and smoke inhalation........... | 565 | 635 | 695 | 320 | 195 | 585 | 535 | 880 | 1,525 |
| Wound, cut, bleeding, bruise......... | 11,685 | 11,110 | 10,210 | 9,905 | 10,530 | 9,705 | 10,205 | 9,450 | 9,470 |
| Dislocation, fracture.................... | 1,950 | 1,820 | 1,885 | 1,695 | 1,900 | 1,995 | 1,685 | 1,850 | 1,330 |
| Heart attack or stroke................. | 1,140 | 810 | 860 | 780 | 620 | 905 | 920 | 575 | 550 |
| Strain, sprain, muscular pain......... | 42,585 | 40,385 | 39,960 | 39,535 | 37,565 | 35,015 | 37,945 | 32,650 | 30,970 |
| Thermal stress (frostbite, heat exhaustion)............................. | 2,530 | 3,195 | 2,945 | 2,465 | 2,080 | 2,245 | 2,860 | 2,475 | 2,095 |
| Other.................................. | 11,475 | 8,895 | 8,660 | 9,885 | 8,205 | 8,255 | 9,210 | 9,150 | 8,600 |
| Fire department vehicle collisions..... | 15,100 | 14,200 | 14,850 | 14,300 | 12,350 | 14,910 | 16,600 | 15,425 | 15,430 |
| Injuries................................ | 820 | 775 | 970 | 725 | 730 | 550 | 1,150 | 700 | 1,005 |
| Personal vehicle collisions............. | 870 | 1,000 | 790 | 750 | 830 | 620 | 700 | 850 | 795 |
| Injuries................................ | 100 | 75 | 190 | 70 | 185 | 90 | 50 | 175 | 75 |

NA Not available. [1] Includes causes not shown, such as struck by object, caught/trapped, structural collapse, fall, violence, lost/disoriented, and unknown. [2] Stress/overexertion include all firefighter deaths that are cardiac or cerebrovascular in nature such as heart attacks, strokes, and other events such as extreme climatic thermal exposure (heat exhaustion). [3] Includes other types of nonfatal injuries not shown separately.

Source: Fatalities: U.S. Department of Homeland Security, Federal Emergency Management Agency, *U.S. Fire Administration, Firefighter Fatalities in the United States in 2017*, September 2018, and earlier reports. See also <https://apps.usfa.fema.gov/firefighter-fatalities/>. Nonfatal Injuries: National Fire Protection Association, *United States Firefighter Injuries 2017* ©, November 2018, and earlier reports. See also <https://www.nfpa.org/News-and-Research>.

# Geography and Environment

This section presents a variety of information on the physical environment of the United States, starting with basic area measurement data and ending with climatic data for selected weather stations around the country. The subjects covered between those points are mostly concerned with environmental trends but include related subjects such as land use, water consumption, air pollutant emissions, toxic releases, oil spills, hazardous waste sites, municipal waste and recycling, threatened and endangered wildlife, and the environmental industry.

The information in this section is selected from a wide range of federal agencies that compile the data for various administrative or regulatory purposes, such as the Environmental Protection Agency (EPA), U.S. Geological Survey (USGS), National Oceanic and Atmospheric Administration (NOAA), and the Natural Resources Conservation Service (NRCS).

**Area**—2018 area measurements are the latest available. These measurements were calculated by computer based on the information contained in a single, consistent geographic database, the Topologically Integrated Geographic Encoding & Referencing system (TIGER®) database, a national geographic and cartographic database prepared by the Census Bureau. The 2018 area measurements may be found in Table 399.

**Geography**—The USGS conducts investigations, surveys, and research in the fields of geography, geology, topography, geographic information systems, mineralogy, hydrology, and geothermal energy resources as well as natural hazards. The USGS provides United States cartographic data through the Earth Sciences Information Center and water resources data through the *Water Resources of the United States* at <https://water.usgs.gov/>. In a joint project with the U.S. Census Bureau, during the 1980s, the USGS provided the basic information on geographic features for input into the TIGER® database. Since then, using a variety of sources, the Census Bureau has updated these features and their related attributes (names, descriptions, etc.) and inserted current information on the boundaries, names, and codes of legal and statistical geographic entities. The 2018 measures of land and water area, including their classifications, reflect base feature updates made in the Master Address File (MAF)/TIGER® database through May 2018. The boundaries of the states and equivalent areas are as of January 1, 2018. Maps prepared by the Census Bureau using the TIGER® database show the names and boundaries of entities and are available on a current basis.

An inventory of the nation's land resources by type of use/cover was conducted by the NRCS every 5 years from 1977 through 1997. Since 2000, data have been gathered annually, though major releases of these data continue to be reported at 5-year intervals. The most recent survey results, which were published for the year 2015, covered all nonfederal land for the contiguous 48 states. Details available at <https://www.nrcs.usda.gov/wps/portal/nrcs/main/national/technical/nra/nri/ >.

**Environment**—The principal federal agency responsible for pollution abatement and control activities is the EPA. It is responsible for establishing and monitoring national air quality standards, water quality activities, solid and hazardous waste disposal, and control of toxic substances. Many of these series now appear in the "Envirofacts" portion of the EPA website at <https://www3.epa.gov/enviro/>.

The Clean Air Act, which was last amended in 1990, requires the EPA to set National Ambient Air Quality Standards (NAAQS) (40 CFR part 50) for pollutants considered harmful to public health and the environment. The Clean Air Act established two types of national air quality standards. *Primary standards* set limits to protect public health, including the health of "sensitive" populations such as asthmatics, children, and the elderly. *Secondary standards* set limits to protect public welfare, including protection against decreased visibility and damage to animals, crops vegetation, and buildings. See <https://www.epa.gov/criteria-air-pollutants/naaqs-table> for more information. The EPA Office of Air Quality Planning and Standards (OAQPS) has set National Ambient Air Quality Standards for six principal pollutants, which are called "criteria" pollutants. These pollutants are: carbon monoxide, lead, nitrogen dioxide, particulate matter, ozone, and sulfur dioxide. NAAQS are periodically reviewed and revised to include any additional or new health or welfare data. Table 413 gives some of the health-related standards for the six air pollutants having NAAQS. Data gathered from state networks are periodically submitted to EPA's National Aerometric Information Retrieval System (AIRS) for summarization in annual reports on the nationwide status and trends in air quality. For details, see "Air Trends" on the EPA website at <http://www.epa.gov/airtrends/>.

The Toxics Release Inventory (TRI), a database published by the EPA, is a valuable source of information on approximately 595 chemicals that are being used, manufactured, treated, transported, or released into the environment. Sections 313 of the Emergency Planning and Community Right-to-Know Act (EPCRA) and 6607 of the Pollution Prevention Act (PPA) mandate that a publicly-accessible toxic chemical database be developed and maintained by the EPA. The TRI database contains information concerning waste management activities and the release of toxic chemicals by facilities that manufacture, process, or otherwise use said materials. Data on the release of these chemicals are collected from about 21,000 facilities that have the equivalent of 10 or more full time employees and meet the established thresholds for manufacturing, processing, or "other use" of listed chemicals. Facilities must report their releases and other waste management quantities. Since 1994 federal facilities have been required to report their data regardless of industry classification. More current information on this program can be found at <https://www.epa.gov/toxics-release-inventory-tri-program>.

**Climate**—NOAA, through the National Weather Service and the National Environmental Satellite, Data, and Information Service, is responsible for collecting climate data. NOAA maintains about 8,000 weather stations, of which a portion produce precipitation measurement records, some take hourly readings of a series of weather elements, and the remainder record data once a day. These data are reported monthly in *Storm Data*, and published monthly and annually in the *Local Climatological Data* (published by location for major cities). Data can be found in tables 433–437.

# Table 399. Land and Water Area of States and Other Entities: 2018

[One square mile = 2.59 square kilometers. The area measurements were derived from the Census Bureau's Master Address File/Topologically Integrated Geographic Encoding and Referencing (MAF/TIGER®) database. The boundaries of the states and equivalent areas are as of January 1, 2018. The land and water areas, including their classifications, reflect base feature updates made in the MAF/TIGER® database through May 2018. For more details, see <http://www.census.gov/geo/maps-data/data/tiger-line.html>]

| State and other areas [2] | Total area Sq. mi. | Total area Sq. km. | Land area [1] Sq. mi. | Land area [1] Sq. km. | Water area [1] Total Sq. mi. | Water area [1] Total Sq. km. | Inland (sq. mi.) | Coastal (sq. mi.) | Great Lakes (sq. mi.) | Territorial (sq. mi.) |
|---|---|---|---|---|---|---|---|---|---|---|
| **Total [3]** | **3,806,358** | **9,858,422** | **3,536,641** | **9,159,859** | **269,717** | **698,563** | **85,076** | **42,390** | **60,093** | **82,157** |
| **United States [4]** | **3,797,173** | **9,834,633** | **3,532,614** | **9,149,429** | **264,559** | **685,204** | **84,961** | **42,355** | **60,093** | **77,150** |
| Alabama | 52,420 | 135,767 | 50,647 | 131,174 | 1,773 | 4,593 | 1,057 | 517 | – | 200 |
| Alaska | 665,764 | 1,724,321 | 570,640 | 1,478,840 | 94,781 | 245,482 | 18,983 | 26,139 | – | 49,658 |
| Arizona | 113,987 | 295,226 | 113,591 | 294,199 | 397 | 1,027 | 397 | – | – | – |
| Arkansas | 53,179 | 137,732 | 52,035 | 134,769 | 1,144 | 2,963 | 1,144 | – | – | – |
| California | 163,695 | 423,968 | 155,794 | 403,504 | 7,901 | 20,464 | 2,818 | 245 | – | 4,838 |
| Colorado | 104,095 | 269,605 | 103,639 | 268,423 | 456 | 1,182 | 456 | – | – | – |
| Connecticut | 5,544 | 14,358 | 4,843 | 12,542 | 701 | 1,816 | 171 | 530 | – | – |
| Delaware | 2,489 | 6,446 | 1,948 | 5,046 | 541 | 1,400 | 92 | 355 | – | 94 |
| District of Columbia | 68 | 177 | 61 | 158 | 7 | 19 | 7 | – | – | – |
| Florida | 65,757 | 170,310 | 53,649 | 138,949 | 12,109 | 31,361 | 5,002 | 1,349 | – | 5,757 |
| Georgia | 59,423 | 153,905 | 57,715 | 149,482 | 1,708 | 4,423 | 1,211 | 47 | – | 450 |
| Hawaii | 10,970 | 28,412 | 6,422 | 16,634 | 4,547 | 11,778 | 42 | 9 | – | 4,496 |
| Idaho | 83,569 | 216,442 | 82,645 | 214,050 | 923 | 2,392 | 923 | – | – | – |
| Illinois | 57,914 | 149,995 | 55,514 | 143,781 | 2,400 | 6,215 | 826 | – | 1,574 | – |
| Indiana | 36,420 | 94,327 | 35,826 | 92,789 | 594 | 1,538 | 361 | – | 232 | – |
| Iowa | 56,273 | 145,745 | 55,854 | 144,661 | 419 | 1,084 | 419 | – | – | – |
| Kansas | 82,278 | 213,099 | 81,759 | 211,755 | 519 | 1,344 | 519 | – | – | – |
| Kentucky | 40,407 | 104,655 | 39,490 | 102,279 | 917 | 2,375 | 917 | – | – | – |
| Louisiana | 52,375 | 135,651 | 43,204 | 111,898 | 9,171 | 23,754 | 4,562 | 2,876 | – | 1,733 |
| Maine | 35,380 | 91,634 | 30,845 | 79,887 | 4,535 | 11,747 | 2,312 | 591 | – | 1,633 |
| Maryland | 12,406 | 32,131 | 9,711 | 25,151 | 2,695 | 6,980 | 765 | 1,820 | – | 111 |
| Massachusetts | 10,554 | 27,335 | 7,801 | 20,205 | 2,753 | 7,130 | 483 | 1,176 | – | 1,093 |
| Michigan | 96,713 | 250,487 | 56,603 | 146,601 | 40,111 | 103,886 | 1,937 | – | 38,174 | – |
| Minnesota | 86,940 | 225,174 | 79,625 | 206,229 | 7,315 | 18,945 | 4,769 | – | 2,546 | – |
| Mississippi | 48,441 | 125,460 | 46,924 | 121,534 | 1,516 | 3,927 | 768 | 620 | – | 129 |
| Missouri | 69,707 | 180,540 | 68,746 | 178,051 | 961 | 2,489 | 961 | – | – | – |
| Montana | 147,040 | 380,832 | 145,546 | 376,963 | 1,494 | 3,869 | 1,494 | – | – | – |
| Nebraska | 77,347 | 200,328 | 76,818 | 198,957 | 530 | 1,372 | 530 | – | – | – |
| Nevada | 110,571 | 286,377 | 109,780 | 284,330 | 790 | 2,047 | 790 | – | – | – |
| New Hampshire | 9,350 | 24,216 | 8,953 | 23,189 | 396 | 1,027 | 328 | – | – | 69 |
| New Jersey | 8,723 | 22,593 | 7,354 | 19,048 | 1,369 | 3,545 | 437 | 427 | – | 505 |
| New Mexico | 121,593 | 314,925 | 121,312 | 314,196 | 281 | 729 | 281 | – | – | – |
| New York | 54,555 | 141,296 | 47,123 | 122,049 | 7,431 | 19,247 | 1,992 | 976 | 3,986 | 478 |
| North Carolina | 53,819 | 139,390 | 48,619 | 125,924 | 5,199 | 13,466 | 4,050 | – | – | 1,149 |
| North Dakota | 70,699 | 183,111 | 68,999 | 178,708 | 1,700 | 4,403 | 1,700 | – | – | – |
| Ohio | 44,826 | 116,098 | 40,861 | 105,829 | 3,965 | 10,269 | 474 | – | 3,491 | – |
| Oklahoma | 69,899 | 181,038 | 68,596 | 177,663 | 1,303 | 3,375 | 1,303 | – | – | – |
| Oregon | 98,379 | 254,799 | 95,988 | 248,607 | 2,391 | 6,192 | 1,068 | 72 | – | 1,251 |
| Pennsylvania | 46,054 | 119,279 | 44,743 | 115,884 | 1,311 | 3,395 | 562 | – | 748 | – |
| Rhode Island | 1,545 | 4,001 | 1,034 | 2,678 | 511 | 1,324 | 182 | 64 | – | 266 |
| South Carolina | 32,023 | 82,940 | 30,064 | 77,865 | 1,960 | 5,075 | 1,061 | 109 | – | 790 |
| South Dakota | 77,116 | 199,730 | 75,810 | 196,347 | 1,306 | 3,383 | 1,306 | – | – | – |
| Tennessee | 42,144 | 109,153 | 41,237 | 106,803 | 907 | 2,350 | 907 | – | – | – |
| Texas | 268,596 | 695,659 | 261,257 | 676,653 | 7,338 | 19,006 | 5,590 | 401 | – | 1,347 |
| Utah | 84,898 | 219,885 | 82,196 | 212,886 | 2,702 | 6,999 | 2,702 | – | – | – |
| Vermont | 9,616 | 24,905 | 9,218 | 23,874 | 398 | 1,030 | 398 | – | – | – |
| Virginia | 42,775 | 110,786 | 39,482 | 102,258 | 3,293 | 8,529 | 1,289 | 1,565 | – | 438 |
| Washington | 71,302 | 184,672 | 66,453 | 172,113 | 4,849 | 12,559 | 1,715 | 2,467 | – | 668 |
| West Virginia | 24,230 | 62,756 | 24,041 | 62,266 | 189 | 489 | 189 | – | – | – |
| Wisconsin | 65,496 | 169,635 | 54,166 | 140,290 | 11,330 | 29,345 | 1,989 | – | 9,341 | – |
| Wyoming | 97,810 | 253,326 | 97,089 | 251,459 | 721 | 1,868 | 721 | – | – | – |
| Puerto Rico | 5,325 | 13,791 | 3,424 | 8,869 | 1,901 | 4,922 | 76 | 13 | – | 1,812 |
| Island Areas: | 3,860 | 9,998 | 603 | 1,562 | 3,257 | 8,436 | 39 | 22 | – | 3,196 |
| American Samoa | 581 | 1,505 | 76 | 198 | 505 | 1,307 | 8 | – | – | 497 |
| Guam | 571 | 1,478 | 210 | 544 | 361 | 934 | 8 | 1 | – | 352 |
| Northern Mariana Islands | 1,976 | 5,117 | 182 | 472 | 1,793 | 4,644 | 6 | 5 | – | 1,782 |
| U.S. Virgin Islands | 733 | 1,898 | 134 | 348 | 599 | 1,550 | 17 | 16 | – | 565 |

– Represents or rounds to zero. [1] Water area calculations in this table include only perennial water. All other water (intermittent, glacier, and marsh/swamp) is included in this table as part of land area calculations. [2] This table does not include area calculations for the U.S. Minor Outlying Islands. [3] Includes all 50 states, the District of Columbia, Puerto Rico, and the Island Areas. [4] Includes all 50 states and the District of Columbia.

Source: U.S. Census Bureau, unpublished data from the MAF/TIGER® database. See <https://www.census.gov/geo/maps-data/data/tiger.html>.

# Table 400. Great Lakes Profile

[The Great Lakes contain the largest supply of freshwater in the world, holding about 21% of the world's total freshwater and about 84% of the United States' total freshwater. The Lakes are a series of five interconnecting large lakes, one small lake, four connecting channels, and the St. Lawrence Seaway. Combined, the lakes cover an area of over 94,000 square miles (245,000 square kilometers) and contain over 5,400 cubic miles (23,000 cubic kilometers) of water]

| Characteristics | Unit | Lake Superior | Lake Michigan | Lake Huron | Lake Erie | Lake Ontario |
|---|---|---|---|---|---|---|
| Length | Miles | 350 | 307 | 206 | 241 | 193 |
| Breadth | Miles | 160 | 118 | 183 | 57 | 53 |
| Depth: | | | | | | |
| Average | Feet | 489 | 279 | 195 | 62 | 283 |
| Maximum | Feet | 1,333 | 923 | 750 | 210 | 802 |
| Volume | Cubic miles | 2,935 | 1,180 | 849 | 116 | 393 |
| Water surface area [1] | Square miles | 31,700 | 22,300 | 23,000 | 9,910 | 7,340 |
| Surface area in U.S. | Square miles | 20,598 | 22,300 | 9,111 | 4,977 | 3,560 |
| Retention/replacement time [2] | Years | 173 | 62 | 21 | 3 | 6 |

[1] Includes surface area in both U.S. and Canada. [2] The amount of time it takes for lakes to get rid of pollutants.

Source: Department of Commerce, National Oceanic and Atmospheric Administration, Great Lakes Environmental Research Laboratory, "About Our Great Lakes, Lake by Lake Profiles,"<https://www.glerl.noaa.gov/education/ourlakes/>, accessed April 2019.

# Table 401. Great Lakes Length of Shoreline in Separate Basin

[In statute miles]

| Shorelines | Total | Canada | U.S. | MI | MN | WI | IL | IN | OH | PA | NY |
|---|---|---|---|---|---|---|---|---|---|---|---|
| **Total** | **10,368** | **5,127** | **5,241** | **3,288** | **189** | **820** | **63** | **45** | **312** | **51** | **473** |
| Lake Superior | 2,980 | 1,549 | 1,431 | 917 | 189 | 325 | – | – | – | – | – |
| St. Marys River | 297 | 206 | 91 | 91 | – | – | – | – | – | – | – |
| Lake Michigan | 1,661 | – | 1,661 | 1,058 | – | 495 | 63 | 45 | – | – | – |
| Lake Huron | 3,350 | 2,416 | 934 | 934 | – | – | – | – | – | – | – |
| St. Clair River | 128 | 47 | 81 | 81 | – | – | – | – | – | – | – |
| Lake St. Clair | 160 | 71 | 89 | 89 | – | – | – | – | – | – | – |
| Detroit River | 107 | 43 | 64 | 64 | – | – | – | – | – | – | – |
| Lake Erie | 860 | 366 | 494 | 54 | – | – | – | – | 312 | 51 | 77 |
| Niagara River | 99 | 34 | 65 | – | – | – | – | – | – | – | 65 |
| Lake Ontario | 726 | 395 | 331 | – | – | – | – | – | – | – | 331 |

– Represents zero.

Source: State of Michigan, Department of Environment Quality, "Great Lakes, Shorelines of the Great Lakes," and U.S. Lake Survey, File no. 3-3284 corrected to 1952, <https://www.michigan.gov/ogl>.

# Table 402. Largest Lakes in the United States

[The list of lakes include manmade lakes and those that are only partially within the United States]

| Lake | Location | Area in sq. mi. | Lake | Location | Area in sq. mi. |
|---|---|---|---|---|---|
| Lake Superior | MI-MN-WI-Ontario | 31,700 | Lake Pontchartrain | Louisiana | 631 |
| Lake Huron | MI-Ontario | 23,000 | Lake Sakakawea [1] | North Dakota | 520 |
| Lake Michigan | IL-IN-MI-WI | 22,300 | Lake Champlain | NY-VT-Quebec | 490 |
| Lake Erie | MI-NY-OH-PA-Ontario | 9,910 | Becharof Lake | Alaska | 453 |
| Lake Ontario | NY-Ontario | 7,340 | Lake St. Clair | MI-Ontario | 430 |
| Great Salt Lake | Utah | 2,117 | Red Lake | Minnesota | 427 |
| Lake of the Woods | MN-Manitoba-Ontario | 1,485 | Selawik Lake | Alaska | 404 |
| Iliamna Lake | Alaska | 1,014 | Fort Peck Lake [1] | Montana | 393 |
| Lake Oahe [1] | ND-SD | 685 | Salton Sea | California | 347 |
| Lake Okeechobee | Florida | 662 | Rainy Lake | MN-Ontario | 345 |

[1] Manmade lakes.

Source: U.S. Geological Survey, 2003, and National Oceanic and Atmospheric Administration, "Great Lakes, 2002" and The National Atlas of the United States of America, *Lakes*, <http://nationalmap.gov/small_scale/#ten>.

# Table 403. Coastline Counties Most Frequently Hit by Hurricanes: 1960 to 2008

[Hurricane is a type of tropical cyclone, an intense tropical weather system of strong thunderstorms with a well-defined surface circulation and maximum sustained winds of 74 miles per hour or higher. See <https://coast.noaa.gov/digitalcoast/> for more info]

| County and State | Coastline region | Number of hurricanes | Percent change in population | | Percent change in housing units | |
|---|---|---|---|---|---|---|
| | | | 1960 to 2008 | 2000 to 2008 | 1960 to 2008 | 2000 to 2008 |
| Monroe County, FL | Gulf of Mexico | 15 | 50.8 | -9.2 | 221.8 | 4.3 |
| Lafourche Parish, LA | Gulf of Mexico | 14 | 67.2 | 2.9 | 151.5 | 8.9 |
| Carteret County, NC | Atlantic | 14 | 104.3 | 6.4 | 366.4 | 12.4 |
| Dare County, NC | Atlantic | 13 | 465.9 | 12.1 | 709.6 | 22.8 |
| Hyde County, NC | Atlantic | 13 | -10.1 | -11.1 | 83.7 | 5.8 |
| Jefferson Parish, LA | Gulf of Mexico | 12 | 108.9 | -4.2 | 201.4 | -3.5 |
| Palm Beach County, FL | Atlantic | 12 | 454.7 | 11.9 | 616.9 | 15.2 |
| Miami-Dade County, FL | Atlantic | 11 | 156.5 | 6.4 | 180.6 | 14.9 |
| St. Bernard Parish, LA | Gulf of Mexico | 11 | 17.2 | -43.9 | -2.6 | -67.9 |
| Cameron Parish, LA | Gulf of Mexico | 11 | 4.8 | -27.6 | 87.7 | -8.1 |
| Terrebonne Parish, LA | Gulf of Mexico | 11 | 78.7 | 3.9 | 179.4 | 11.0 |

Source: U.S. National Oceanic and Atmospheric Administration (NOAA), Coastal Services Center, Historical Hurricane Tracks: 1851 to 2008; U.S. Census Bureau, Current Population Reports, P25-1139, Population Estimates and Projections, "Coastline Population Trends in the United States: 1960 to 2008," May 2010. See also <https://www.census.gov/topics/preparedness/about/coastal-areas.html>.

## Table 404. U.S.–Canada and U.S.–Mexico Border Lengths

[In statute miles. Each statute mile equals one mile. For 2016, there were over 49 million personal vehicle passengers entering the United States from Canada, and over 140 million personal vehicle passengers entering the United States from Mexico]

| State | Length of international border | State | Length of international border |
|---|---|---|---|
| **United States–Canada total** | **5,525** | Ohio | 146 |
| Alaska | 1,538 | Pennsylvania | 42 |
| Idaho | 45 | Vermont | 90 |
| Maine | 611 | Washington | 427 |
| Michigan | 721 | | |
| Minnesota | 547 | **United States–Mexico total** | **1,933** |
| Montana | 545 | Arizona | 373 |
| New Hampshire | 58 | California | 140 |
| New York | 445 | New Mexico | 180 |
| North Dakota | 310 | Texas | 1,241 |

Source: U.S.–Canada lengths: International Boundary Commission, 2003; U.S. Mexico lengths: U.S. Geological Survey; and The National Atlas of the United States, 1976, "Borders," <https://www.usgs.gov/core-science-systems/national-geospatial-program>.

## Table 405. Coastline and Shoreline of the United States by State

[In statute miles. Each statute mile equals one mile. The term coastline is used to describe the general outline of the seacoast. For the table below, United States coastline measurements were made from small-scale maps, and the coastline was generalized. The coastlines of large sounds and bays were included. Measurements were made in 1948. Shoreline is the term used to describe a more detailed measure of the seacoast. The tidal shoreline figures in the table below were obtained in 1939-1940 from the largest-scale charts and maps then available. Shoreline of the outer coast, offshore islands, sounds, and bays was included, as well as the tidal portion of rivers and creeks. Only States with coastline or shoreline are included in the following table]

| State | General coastline | Tidal shoreline | State | General coastline | Tidal shoreline |
|---|---|---|---|---|---|
| **United States** | **12,383** | **88,633** | Mississippi | 44 | 359 |
| Alabama | 53 | 607 | New Hampshire | 13 | 131 |
| Alaska | 6,640 | 33,904 | New Jersey | 130 | 1,792 |
| California | 840 | 3,427 | New York | 127 | 1,850 |
| Connecticut | – | 618 | North Carolina | 301 | 3,375 |
| Delaware | 28 | 381 | Oregon | 296 | 1,410 |
| Florida | 1,350 | 8,426 | Pennsylvania | – | 89 |
| Georgia | 100 | 2,344 | Rhode Island | 40 | 384 |
| Hawaii | 750 | 1,052 | South Carolina | 187 | 2,876 |
| Louisiana | 397 | 7,721 | Texas | 367 | 3,359 |
| Maine | 228 | 3,478 | Virginia | 112 | 3,315 |
| Maryland | 31 | 3,190 | Washington | 157 | 3,026 |
| Massachusetts | 192 | 1,519 | | | |

– Represents zero.

Source: National Oceanic Atmospheric Administration, 1975 and The National Atlas of the United States, "Coastline and Shoreline," <http://nationalmap.gov/small_scale/>. See also <http://shoreline.noaa.gov/>.

## Table 406. Flows of Largest U.S. Rivers—Length, Discharge, and Drainage Area

[A flow of 1,000 cubic ft. per second is equal to 646 million gallons per day, 724,000 acre-feet per year, or 28.3 cubic meters per second. One acre-foot is the volume of water that would cover 1 acre to a depth of 1 foot]

| River | Location of mouth | Source stream (name and location) | Length (miles) [1] | Average discharge at mouth (1,000 cubic feet per second) | Drainage area (1,000 sq. miles) |
|---|---|---|---|---|---|
| Missouri | Missouri | Red Rock Creek, MT | [2] 2,540 | 76.2 | [3] 529 |
| Mississippi | Louisiana | Mississippi River, MN | 2,340 | [4] 593 | [3,5] 1,150 |
| Yukon | Alaska | McNeil River, Canada | 1,980 | 225 | [3] 328 |
| St. Lawrence | Canada | North River, MN | 1,900 | 348 | [3] 396 |
| Rio Grande | Mexico-Texas | Rio Grande, CO | 1,900 | ([6]) | 336 |
| Arkansas | Arkansas | East Fork Arkansas River, CO | 1,460 | 41 | 161 |
| Colorado | Mexico | Colorado River, CO | 1,450 | ([6]) | 246 |
| Atchafalaya [7] | Louisiana | Tierra Blanca Creek, NM | 1,420 | 58 | 95 |
| Ohio | Illinois-Kentucky | Allegheny River, PA | 1,310 | 281 | 203 |
| Red [7] | Louisiana | Tierra Blanca Creek, NM | 1,290 | 56 | 93 |
| Brazos | Texas | Blackwater Draw, NM | 1,280 | ([6]) | 46 |
| Columbia | Oregon-Washington | Columbia River, Canada | 1,240 | 265 | [3] 258 |
| Snake | Washington | Snake River, WY | 1,040 | 56.9 | 108 |
| Platte | Nebraska | Grizzly Creek, CO | 990 | ([6]) | 85 |
| Pecos | Texas | Pecos River, NM | 926 | ([6]) | 44 |
| Canadian | Oklahoma | Canadian River, CO | 906 | ([6]) | 47 |
| Tennessee | Kentucky | Courthouse Creek, NC | 886 | 68 | 41 |

[1] From source to mouth. [2] The length from the source of the Missouri River to the Mississippi River and thence to the Gulf of Mexico is about 3,710 miles. [3] Drainage area includes both the United States and Canada. [4] Includes about 167,000 cubic feet per second diverted from the Mississippi into the Atchafalaya River but excludes the flow of the Red River. [5] Excludes the drainage areas of the Red and Atchafalaya Rivers. [6] Less than 15,000 cubic feet per second. [7] In east-central Louisiana, the Red River flows into the Atchafalaya River, a distributary of the Mississippi River. Data on average discharge, length, and drainage area include the Red River, but exclude all water diverted into the Atchafalaya from the Mississippi River.

Source: U.S. Geological Survey, *Largest Rivers in the United States*, September 2005, <http://pubs.usgs.gov/of/1987/ofr87-242/>.

# Table 407. Extreme and Mean Elevations by State and Other Areas

[One foot = .305 meter. There are 2,130 square miles of the United States below sea level (Death Valley is the lowest point). There are 20,230 square miles above 10,000 feet (Mount McKinley is the highest point in the United States). Minus sign (-) indicates below sea level]

| State and other areas | Highest point Name | Highest point Elevation Feet | Highest point Elevation Meters | Lowest point Name | Lowest point Elevation Feet | Lowest point Elevation Meters | Approximate mean elevation Feet | Approximate mean elevation Meters |
|---|---|---|---|---|---|---|---|---|
| U.S...... | **Mount McKinley (AK)** | **20,310** | **6,190** | **Death Valley (CA)** | **-282** | **-86** | **2,500** | **763** |
| AL......... | Cheaha Mountain | 2,407 | 734 | Gulf of Mexico | ([1]) | ([1]) | 500 | 153 |
| AK......... | Mount McKinley | 20,310 | 6,190 | Pacific Ocean | ([1]) | ([1]) | 1,900 | 580 |
| AZ......... | Humphreys Peak | 12,633 | 3,853 | Colorado River | 70 | 21 | 4,100 | 1,251 |
| AR......... | Magazine Mountain | 2,753 | 840 | Ouachita River | 55 | 17 | 650 | 198 |
| CA......... | Mount Whitney | 14,494 | 4,419 | Death Valley | -282 | -86 | 2,900 | 885 |
| CO......... | Mount Elbert | 14,433 | 4,402 | Arikaree River | 3,315 | 1,011 | 6,800 | 2,074 |
| CT......... | Mount Frissell on south slope | 2,380 | 726 | Long Island Sound | ([1]) | ([1]) | 500 | 153 |
| DE......... | Ebright Road [2] | 448 | 137 | Atlantic Ocean | ([1]) | ([1]) | 60 | 18 |
| DC......... | Tenleytown at Reno Reservoir | 410 | 125 | Potomac River | 1 | (Z) | 150 | 46 |
| FL......... | Britton Hill | 345 | 105 | Atlantic Ocean | ([1]) | ([1]) | 100 | 31 |
| GA......... | Brasstown Bald | 4,784 | 1,459 | Atlantic Ocean | ([1]) | ([1]) | 600 | 183 |
| HI......... | Pu'u Wekiu, Mauna Kea | 13,796 | 4,208 | Pacific Ocean | ([1]) | ([1]) | 3,030 | 924 |
| ID......... | Borah Peak | 12,662 | 3,862 | Snake River | 710 | 217 | 5,000 | 1,525 |
| IL......... | Charles Mound | 1,235 | 377 | Mississippi River | 279 | 85 | 600 | 183 |
| IN......... | Hoosier Hill | 1,257 | 383 | Ohio River | 320 | 98 | 700 | 214 |
| IA......... | Hawkeye Point | 1,670 | 509 | Mississippi River | 480 | 146 | 1,100 | 336 |
| KS......... | Mount Sunflower | 4,039 | 1,232 | Verdigris River | 679 | 207 | 2,000 | 610 |
| KY......... | Black Mountain | 4,145 | 1,264 | Mississippi River | 257 | 78 | 750 | 229 |
| LA......... | Driskill Mountain | 535 | 163 | New Orleans | -8 | -2 | 100 | 31 |
| ME......... | Mount Katahdin | 5,268 | 1,607 | Atlantic Ocean | ([1]) | ([1]) | 600 | 183 |
| MD......... | Hoye Crest | 3,360 | 1,025 | Atlantic Ocean | ([1]) | ([1]) | 350 | 107 |
| MA......... | Mount Greylock | 3,491 | 1,065 | Atlantic Ocean | ([1]) | ([1]) | 500 | 153 |
| MI......... | Mount Arvon | 1,979 | 604 | Lake Erie | 571 | 174 | 900 | 275 |
| MN......... | Eagle Mountain | 2,301 | 702 | Lake Superior | 601 | 183 | 1,200 | 366 |
| MS......... | Woodall Mountain | 806 | 246 | Gulf of Mexico | ([1]) | ([1]) | 300 | 92 |
| MO......... | Taum Sauk Mountain | 1,772 | 540 | St. Francis River | 230 | 70 | 800 | 244 |
| MT......... | Granite Peak | 12,799 | 3,904 | Kootenai River | 1,800 | 549 | 3,400 | 1,037 |
| NE......... | Panorama Point | 5,424 | 1,654 | Missouri River | 840 | 256 | 2,600 | 793 |
| NV......... | Boundary Peak | 13,140 | 4,007 | Colorado River | 479 | 146 | 5,500 | 1,678 |
| NH......... | Mount Washington | 6,288 | 1,918 | Atlantic Ocean | ([1]) | ([1]) | 1,000 | 305 |
| NJ......... | High Point | 1,803 | 550 | Atlantic Ocean | ([1]) | ([1]) | 250 | 76 |
| NM......... | Wheeler Peak | 13,161 | 4,014 | Red Bluff Reservoir | 2,842 | 867 | 5,700 | 1,739 |
| NY......... | Mount Marcy | 5,344 | 1,630 | Atlantic Ocean | ([1]) | ([1]) | 1,000 | 305 |
| NC......... | Mount Mitchell | 6,684 | 2,039 | Atlantic Ocean | ([1]) | ([1]) | 700 | 214 |
| ND......... | White Butte | 3,506 | 1,069 | Red River of the North | 750 | 229 | 1,900 | 580 |
| OH......... | Campbell Hill | 1,550 | 473 | Ohio River | 455 | 139 | 850 | 259 |
| OK......... | Black Mesa | 4,973 | 1,517 | Little River | 289 | 88 | 1,300 | 397 |
| OR......... | Mount Hood | 11,239 | 3,428 | Pacific Ocean | ([1]) | ([1]) | 3,300 | 1,007 |
| PA......... | Mount Davis | 3,213 | 980 | Delaware River | ([1]) | ([1]) | 1,100 | 336 |
| RI......... | Jerimoth Hill | 812 | 248 | Atlantic Ocean | ([1]) | ([1]) | 200 | 61 |
| SC......... | Sassafras Mountain | 3,560 | 1,086 | Atlantic Ocean | ([1]) | ([1]) | 350 | 107 |
| SD......... | Harney Peak | 7,242 | 2,209 | Big Stone Lake | 966 | 295 | 2,200 | 671 |
| TN......... | Clingmans Dome | 6,643 | 2,026 | Mississippi River | 178 | 54 | 900 | 275 |
| TX......... | Guadalupe Peak | 8,749 | 2,668 | Gulf of Mexico | ([1]) | ([1]) | 1,700 | 519 |
| UT......... | Kings Peak | 13,528 | 4,126 | Beaverdam Wash | 2,000 | 610 | 6,100 | 1,861 |
| VT......... | Mount Mansfield | 4,393 | 1,340 | Lake Champlain | 95 | 29 | 1,000 | 305 |
| VA......... | Mount Rogers | 5,729 | 1,747 | Atlantic Ocean | ([1]) | ([1]) | 950 | 290 |
| WA......... | Mount Rainier | 14,411 | 4,395 | Pacific Ocean | ([1]) | ([1]) | 1,700 | 519 |
| WV......... | Spruce Knob | 4,863 | 1,483 | Potomac River | 240 | 73 | 1,500 | 458 |
| WI......... | Timms Hill | 1,951 | 595 | Lake Michigan | 579 | 177 | 1,050 | 320 |
| WY......... | Gannett Peak | 13,804 | 4,210 | Belle Fourche River | 3,099 | 945 | 6,700 | 2,044 |
| Other areas: |  |  |  |  |  |  |  |  |
| Puerto Rico...... | Cerro de Punta | 4,390 | 1,339 | Atlantic Ocean | ([1]) | ([1]) | 1,800 | 549 |
| American Samoa.... | Lata Mountain | 3,160 | 964 | Pacific Ocean | ([1]) | ([1]) | 1,300 | 397 |
| Guam....... | Mount Lamlam | 1,332 | 406 | Pacific Ocean | ([1]) | ([1]) | 330 | 101 |
| U.S. Virgin Islands.... | Crown Mountain | 1,556 | 475 | Atlantic Ocean | ([1]) | ([1]) | 750 | 229 |

Z Less than .5 meter. [1] Sea level. [2] At DE–PA state line.

Source: For highest and lowest points, see U.S. Geological Survey, "Elevations and Distances in the United States," <https://www.usgs.gov/products/publications/official-usgs-publications>, released April 2005. For mean elevations, see *Elevations and Distances in the United States*, 1983 edition.

# Table 408. Acres of Land Cover by Type and Use: 1997 to 2015

[In millions of acres (1,944 represents 1,944,000,000), except percent. Excludes Alaska and District of Columbia. For inventory-specific glossary of key terms, see <http://www.nrcs.usda.gov/wps/portal/nrcs/main/national/technical/nra/nri/>]

| Year | Total surface area [1] | Nonfederal rural land | | | | | | | Devel- oped land | Water areas | Federal land |
| | | Rural land total | Crop- land | CRP land [2] | Pasture- land | Range- land | Forest land | Other rural land | | | |
|---|---|---|---|---|---|---|---|---|---|---|---|
| **Land** | | | | | | | | | | | |
| 1997.................. | 1,944 | 1,395 | 376 | 33 | 120 | 408 | 414 | 43 | 96 | 51 | 403 |
| 2002.................. | 1,944 | 1,384 | 368 | 31 | 119 | 408 | 415 | 43 | 105 | 51 | 404 |
| 2007.................. | 1,944 | 1,377 | 359 | 33 | 120 | 407 | 414 | 44 | 111 | 52 | 405 |
| 2012.................. | 1,944 | 1,373 | 362 | 24 | 122 | 405 | 415 | 45 | 114 | 52 | 405 |
| 2015.................. | 1,944 | 1,372 | 367 | 18 | 122 | 404 | 416 | 45 | 115 | 52 | 405 |
| **Percent of total land** | | | | | | | | | | | |
| 1997.................. | 100.0 | 71.7 | 19.4 | 1.7 | 6.2 | 21.0 | 21.3 | 2.2 | 4.9 | 2.6 | 20.7 |
| 2002.................. | 100.0 | 71.2 | 18.9 | 1.6 | 6.1 | 21.0 | 21.3 | 2.2 | 5.4 | 2.6 | 20.8 |
| 2007.................. | 100.0 | 70.8 | 18.5 | 1.7 | 6.2 | 20.9 | 21.3 | 2.3 | 5.7 | 2.7 | 20.8 |
| 2012.................. | 100.0 | 70.6 | 18.6 | 1.2 | 6.3 | 20.8 | 21.3 | 2.3 | 5.8 | 2.7 | 20.8 |
| 2015.................. | 100.0 | 70.6 | 18.9 | 0.9 | 6.3 | 20.8 | 21.4 | 2.3 | 5.9 | 2.7 | 20.8 |

[1] Includes Puerto Rico and Virgin Islands. [2] Conservation Reserve Program (CRP) land. CRP is a federal program established under the Food Security Act of 1985 to assist private landowners to convert highly erodible cropland to vegetative cover for 10 years.

Source: U.S. Department of Agriculture, Natural Resources Conservation Service, *Summary Report: 2015 National Resources Inventory*, September 2018. See also <http://www.nrcs.usda.gov/technical/NRI/>.

# Table 409. Wetlands on Nonfederal Land and Water Areas by Land Cover Type and Farm Production Region: 2015

[In thousands of acres (110,639 represents 110,639,000). Covers both palustrine (nontidal) and estuarine (tidal) wetlands; see source]

| Farm production region [1] | Total | Crop- land [3] | Forest land | Range- land | Other rural land | Developed land | Water area |
|---|---|---|---|---|---|---|---|
| **Wetlands, total [2]**........... | **110,639** | **17,262** | **65,848** | **7,816** | **14,648** | **1,476** | **3,588** |
| Southeast..................... | 22,725 | 897 | 16,737 | 945 | 3,164 | 380 | 603 |
| Lake states.................... | 22,170 | 3,110 | 14,980 | – | 3,714 | 164 | 202 |
| Delta states................... | 17,405 | 2,881 | 11,277 | 152 | 2,501 | 179 | 416 |
| Northeast..................... | 13,513 | 1,101 | 10,466 | – | 1,481 | 233 | 232 |
| Northern plains................ | 7,873 | 3,226 | 226 | 2,822 | 1,141 | 80 | 379 |
| Appalachian................... | 7,437 | 381 | 6,087 | – | 544 | 117 | 309 |
| Southern plains................ | 5,660 | 1,021 | 2,622 | 833 | 389 | 164 | 630 |
| Mountain...................... | 5,020 | 1,692 | 250 | 2,343 | 601 | 15 | 119 |
| Corn belt...................... | 4,720 | 1,350 | 2,406 | – | 389 | 104 | 471 |
| Pacific........................ | 3,982 | 1,582 | 733 | 719 | 694 | 40 | 214 |

– Represents zero. [1] Ten regions established by USDA, Economic Research Service, that group states according to differences in soils, slope of land, climate, distance to market, and storage and marketing facilities. [2] Total includes Hawaii and Caribbean territories, which are not included in the regions. [3] Cultivated and non-cultivated. Includes pastureland and Conservation Reserve Program (CRP) lands.

Source: U.S. Department of Agriculture, Natural Resources Conservation Service, *Summary Report: 2015 National Resources Inventory*, September 2018. See also <http://www.nrcs.usda.gov/technical/NRI/>.

# Table 410. Acres of Federal and Non-Federal Land Cover by Type and State: 2015

[In thousands of acres (1,944,143 represents 1,944,143,000), except percent. Excludes Alaska and District of Columbia]

| State | Total surface area [1] | Selected nonfederal rural land, percent of total | | | State | Total surface area [1] | Selected nonfederal rural land, percent of total | | |
| | | Crop- land | Range- land | Forest land | | | Crop- land | Range- land | Forest land |
|---|---|---|---|---|---|---|---|---|---|
| **United States [2]**.... | **1,944,143** | **18.9** | **20.8** | **21.4** | Montana........... | 94,110 | 16.4 | 39.2 | 6.2 |
| Alabama.............. | 33,424 | 6.8 | 0.2 | 65.5 | Nebraska.......... | 49,510 | 40.7 | 46.1 | 1.7 |
| Arizona.............. | 72,964 | 1.2 | 45.7 | 5.7 | Nevada............ | 70,763 | 0.8 | 12.4 | 0.5 |
| Arkansas............. | 34,037 | 21.0 | 0.1 | 44.3 | New Hampshire... | 5,941 | 1.9 | – | 63.7 |
| California............ | 101,510 | 9.2 | 18.7 | 13.9 | New Jersey........ | 5,216 | 9.2 | – | 31.1 |
| Colorado............. | 66,625 | 12.1 | 36.8 | 5.3 | New Mexico....... | 77,823 | 1.8 | 52.7 | 7.2 |
| Connecticut......... | 3,195 | 5.2 | – | 49.9 | New York.......... | 31,409 | 15.9 | – | 56.0 |
| Delaware............ | 1,534 | 26.0 | – | 22.6 | North Carolina.... | 33,709 | 15.1 | – | 46.5 |
| Florida............... | 37,534 | 7.5 | 6.6 | 35.2 | North Dakota...... | 45,251 | 55.8 | 23.6 | 1.0 |
| Georgia.............. | 37,741 | 11.7 | – | 57.8 | Ohio.............. | 26,445 | 42.2 | – | 27.1 |
| Hawaii............... | 4,123 | 2.1 | 27.1 | 36.1 | Oklahoma......... | 44,738 | 19.5 | 30.2 | 17.9 |
| Idaho................ | 53,488 | 10.1 | 12.7 | 7.5 | Oregon........... | 62,161 | 5.8 | 14.4 | 19.9 |
| Illinois............... | 36,059 | 66.4 | – | 11.3 | Pennsylvania..... | 28,995 | 17.0 | – | 54.2 |
| Indiana.............. | 23,158 | 57.5 | – | 16.9 | Rhode Island...... | 813 | 2.1 | – | 44.1 |
| Iowa................ | 36,017 | 72.3 | – | 6.6 | South Carolina.... | 19,939 | 10.7 | – | 56.4 |
| Kansas.............. | 52,661 | 49.8 | 29.8 | 3.4 | South Dakota..... | 49,358 | 36.5 | 44.9 | 1.1 |
| Kentucky............ | 25,863 | 21.9 | – | 41.8 | Tennessee....... | 26,974 | 16.9 | – | 44.3 |
| Louisiana............ | 31,377 | 15.7 | 0.6 | 41.6 | Texas............. | 171,052 | 13.8 | 54.0 | 8.7 |
| Maine............... | 20,966 | 1.8 | – | 83.5 | Utah.............. | 54,339 | 2.9 | 19.8 | 4.1 |
| Maryland............ | 7,870 | 18.1 | – | 29.4 | Vermont.......... | 6,154 | 8.5 | – | 65.9 |
| Massachusetts..... | 5,339 | 4.1 | – | 47.7 | Virginia........... | 27,087 | 10.4 | – | 48.9 |
| Michigan............ | 37,349 | 21.4 | – | 44.6 | Washington....... | 44,035 | 13.8 | 13.6 | 28.0 |
| Minnesota........... | 54,010 | 39.5 | – | 30.4 | West Virginia...... | 15,508 | 4.2 | – | 67.8 |
| Mississippi.......... | 30,527 | 15.6 | – | 56.8 | Wisconsin......... | 35,920 | 28.8 | – | 41.2 |
| Missouri............. | 44,614 | 33.2 | 0.1 | 28.3 | Wyoming.......... | 62,603 | 3.4 | 43.3 | 1.7 |

– Represents or rounds to zero. [1] Total surface area includes both Federal and non-Federal land. [2] Includes Puerto Rico and U.S. Virgin Islands, not shown separately.

Source: U.S. Department of Agriculture, Natural Resources Conservation Service, *Summary Report, 2015 National Resources Inventory*, September 2018. See also <http://www.nrcs.usda.gov/technical/NRI/>.

## Table 411. U.S. Wetland Resources and Deepwater Habitats by Type: 2004 and 2009

[In thousands of acres (153,121.4 represents 153,121,400). Wetlands and deepwater habitats are defined separately because the term wetland does not include permanent water bodies. Deepwater habitats are permanently flooded land lying below the deepwater boundary of wetlands. Deepwater habitats include environments where surface water is permanent and often deep, so that water, rather than air, is the principal medium within which the dominant organisms live, whether or not they are attached to the substrate. As in wetlands, the dominant plants are hydrophytes; however, the substrates are considered nonsoil because the water is too deep to support emergent vegetation. In general terms, wetlands are lands where saturation with water is the dominant factor determining the nature of soil development and the types of plant and animal communities living in the soil and on its surface. The single feature that most wetlands share is soil or substrate that is at least periodically saturated with or covered by water. Wetlands are lands transitional between terrestrial and aquatic systems where the water table is usually at or near the surface or the land is covered by shallow water. For more information on wetlands, see the "Classification of Wetlands and Deepwater Habitats of the United States" at <https://www.fws.gov/wetlands/documents/classwet/index.html>]

| Wetland or deepwater category | Estimated area, 2004 | Estimated area, 2009 | Change, 2004 to 2009 |
|---|---|---|---|
| **All wetlands and deepwater habitats, total** | **153,121.4** | **153,206.4** | **85.0** |
| All deepwater habitats, total | 42,999.4 | 43,146.6 | 147.2 |
| Lacustrine [1] | 16,786.0 | 16,859.6 | 73.6 |
| Riverine [2] | 7,517.9 | 7,510.5 | -7.4 |
| Estuarine Subtidal [3] | 18,695.4 | 18,776.5 | 81.1 |
| All wetlands, total | 110,122.1 | 110,059.8 | -62.3 |
| Intertidal wetlands [4] | 5,869.3 | 5,785.2 | -84.1 |
| Marine intertidal | 219.2 | 227.8 | 8.5 |
| Estuarine intertidal nonvegetated | 999.4 | 1,017.7 | 18.3 |
| Estuarine intertidal vegetated | 4,650.7 | 4,539.7 | -110.9 |
| Freshwater wetlands | 104,252.7 | 104,274.6 | 21.9 |
| Freshwater nonvegetated | 6,502.1 | 6,709.3 | 207.2 |
| Freshwater vegetated | 97,750.6 | 97,565.3 | -185.3 |
| Freshwater emergent [5] | 27,162.7 | 27,430.5 | 267.8 |
| Freshwater forested [6] | 52,256.5 | 51,623.3 | -633.1 |
| Freshwater shrub [7] | 18,331.4 | 18,511.5 | 180.1 |

[1] The lacustrine system includes deepwater habitats with all of the following characteristics: (1) situated in a topographic depression or a dammed river channel; (2) lacking trees, shrubs, persistent emergents, emergent mosses or lichens with greater than 30 percent coverage; and (3) total area exceeds 20 acres (8 hectares). [2] The riverine system includes deepwater habitats contained within a channel, with the exception of habitats with water containing ocean derived salts in excess of 0.5 parts per thousand. [3] The estuarine system consists of deepwater tidal habitats and adjacent tidal wetlands that are usually semi-enclosed by land but have open, partly obstructed, or sporadic access to the open ocean, and in which ocean water is at least occasionally diluted by freshwater runoff from the land. Subtidal is where the substrate is continuously submerged by marine or estuarine waters. [4] Intertidal is where the substrate is exposed and flooded by tides. Intertidal includes the splash zone of coastal waters. [5] Emergent wetlands are characterized by erect, rooted, herbaceous hydrophytes, excluding mosses and lichens. This vegetation is present for most of the growing season in most years. These wetlands are usually dominated by perennial plants. [6] Forested wetlands are characterized by woody vegetation that is 20 feet tall or taller. [7] Shrub wetlands include areas dominated by woody vegetation less than 20 feet tall. The species include true shrubs, young trees, and trees or shrubs that are small or stunted because of environmental conditions.

Source: U.S. Fish and Wildlife Service, *Status and Trends of Wetlands in the Conterminous United States, 2004 to 2009*, September 2011. See also <http://www.fws.gov/wetlands/Status-And-Trends-2009/index.html>.

## Table 412. U.S. Water Withdrawals Per Day by End Use: 1950 to 2015

[In billions of gallons of water per day (180 represents 180,000,000,000). Includes the District of Columbia, Puerto Rico and U.S. Virgin Islands, as noted. Withdrawal signifies water physically withdrawn from a source. Includes fresh and saline water; excludes water used for hydroelectric power. For information on changes in data collection and presentation methods, see source report]

| Year | Total with-drawals | Public supply | Rural domestic and livestock - Self supplied domestic | Rural domestic and livestock - Live-stock | Irri-gation | Thermo-electric power | Other - Self supplied industrial | Other - Mining | Other - Com-mercial | Other - Aqua-culture |
|---|---|---|---|---|---|---|---|---|---|---|
| 1950 [1] | 180 | 14 | 2.1 | 1.5 | 89 | 40 | 37.0 | (5) | (5) | (5) |
| 1955 [2] | 240 | 17 | 2.1 | 1.5 | 110 | 72 | 39.0 | (5) | (5) | (5) |
| 1960 [3] | 270 | 21 | 2.0 | 1.6 | 110 | 100 | 38.0 | (5) | (5) | (5) |
| 1965 [4] | 310 | 24 | 2.3 | 1.7 | 120 | 130 | 46.0 | (5) | (5) | (5) |
| 1970 [4] | 370 | 27 | 2.6 | 1.9 | 130 | 170 | 47.0 | (5) | (5) | (5) |
| 1975 [3] | 420 | 29 | 2.8 | 2.1 | 140 | 200 | 45.0 | (5) | (5) | (5) |
| 1980 [3] | 430 | 33 | 3.4 | 2.2 | 150 | 210 | 45.0 | (5) | (5) | (5) |
| 1985 [3] | 397 | 37 | 3.3 | 2.2 | 135 | 187 | 25.8 | 3.4 | 1.2 | 2.2 |
| 1990 [3] | 404 | 39 | 3.4 | 2.3 | 134 | 194 | 22.4 | 4.9 | 2.4 | 2.2 |
| 1995 [3] | 398 | 40 | 3.4 | 2.3 | 130 | 190 | 21.6 | 3.6 | 2.9 | 3.3 |
| 2000 [3] | 413 | 43 | 3.6 | 2.4 | 139 | 195 | 19.5 | 4.1 | (NA) | 5.8 |
| 2005 [3] | 410 | 44 | 3.7 | 2.2 | 127 | 201 | 18.1 | 3.8 | (NA) | 8.8 |
| 2010 [3] | 354 | 42 | 3.5 | 2.0 | 116 | 162 | 16.2 | 4.0 | (NA) | 9.0 |
| 2015 [3] | 322 | 39 | 3.3 | 2.0 | 118 | 133 | 14.8 | 4.0 | (NA) | 7.6 |

NA Not available. [1] Population covered: 48 states, District of Columbia (D.C.), and Hawaii. [2] Population covered: 48 states and D.C. [3] Population covered: 50 states, D.C., Puerto Rico, and the Virgin Islands. [4] Population covered: 50 states, D.C., and Puerto Rico. [5] Included in "self-supplied industrial."

Source: U.S. Geological Survey, *Estimated Use of Water in the United States in 2015*, circular 1441, 2018. See also <https://pubs.er.usgs.gov/publication/cir1441>.

## Table 413. National Ambient Air Pollutant Concentrations by Type of Pollutant: 2010 to 2017

[Data represent composite averages across monitoring stations meeting minimum data completeness requirements for the trend period. Carbon monoxide is based on the second-highest, nonoverlapping, 8-hour average; ozone, the fourth-highest maximum 8-hour value; particulates (PM-10) on the second highest daily 24-hour average; fine particulates (PM2.5) annual average on the weighted annual mean of daily 24-hour averages; and lead on the maximum rolling three-month average. Based on data from the Air Quality System. $\mu g/m^3$ = micrograms of pollutant per cubic meter of air; ppm = parts per million; ppb = parts per billion]

| Pollutant | Unit | Monitoring stations, number | Air quality standard [1] | 2010 | 2011 | 2012 | 2013 | 2014 | 2015 | 2016 | 2017 |
|---|---|---|---|---|---|---|---|---|---|---|---|
| Carbon monoxide............. | ppm | 234 | [2] 9 | 1.4 | 1.4 | 1.3 | 1.3 | 1.2 | 1.2 | 1.2 | 1.2 |
| Ozone......................... | ppm | 1,181 | [3] 0.070 | 0.071 | 0.072 | 0.073 | 0.066 | 0.066 | 0.067 | 0.067 | 0.067 |
| Sulfur dioxide................. | ppb | 317 | [4] 75 | 44 | 39 | 35 | 30 | 29 | 24 | 19 | 15 |
| Particulates (PM-10)......... | $\mu g/m^3$ | 613 | [5] 150 | 77.3 | 85.6 | 84.5 | 76.3 | 73.1 | 70.0 | 67.9 | 77.7 |
| Fine particulates (PM2.5) annual average............. | $\mu g/m^3$ | 684 | [6] 12 | 9.7 | 9.6 | 9.0 | 8.8 | 8.6 | 8.4 | 7.6 | 8.0 |
| Nitrogen dioxide.............. | ppb | 247 | [7] 100 | 42 | 41 | 39 | 39 | 39 | 37 | 35 | 36 |
| Lead............................ | $\mu g/m^3$ | 133 | [8] 0.15 | 0.14 | 0.15 | 0.13 | 0.08 | 0.05 | 0.03 | 0.03 | 0.03 |

[1] Refers to the primary National Ambient Air Quality Standard. [2] Based on 8-hour standard of 9 ppm. [3] Based on 8-hour standard of 0.070 ppm. On December 28, 2015, EPA revised the level of the primary and secondary 8-hour ozone standards to 0.070 ppm. [4] Based on a 1-hour daily maximum concentration of 75 ppb. [5] Based on 24-hour (daily) standard of 150 $\mu g/m^3$. The particulates (PM-10) standard replaced the previous standard for total suspended particulates in 1987. In 2006, EPA revoked the annual PM-10 standard. [6] Based on annual standard of 12 $\mu g/m^3$. The PM-2.5 national monitoring network was deployed in 1999. [7] Based on a 1-hour daily maximum concentration of 100 ppb. [8] Based on 3-month rolling average of 0.15 $\mu g/m^3$.

Source: U.S. Environmental Protection Agency, "Air Trends," <https://www.epa.gov/air-trends>, accessed November 2018.

## Table 414. Selected Air Pollutant Emissions: 1990 to 2018

[In thousands of tons (4,320 represents 4,320,000). For documentation regarding the data, see <https://www.epa.gov/air-emissions-inventories/national-emissions-inventory-nei>]

| Year | Ammonia | Carbon monoxide | Nitrogen oxide | PM-10 [1] | PM-2.5 [1] | Sulfur dioxide | VOCs [2] |
|---|---|---|---|---|---|---|---|
| 1990.............. | 4,320 | 154,188 | 25,527 | 27,753 | 7,560 | 23,077 | 24,108 |
| 2000.............. | 4,907 | 114,467 | 22,598 | 23,747 | 7,288 | 16,347 | 17,512 |
| 2005.............. | 3,932 | 88,546 | 20,355 | 21,302 | 5,592 | 14,546 | 17,753 |
| 2010.............. | 4,271 | 73,771 | 14,846 | 20,823 | 5,964 | 7,732 | 17,835 |
| 2011.............. | 4,032 | 73,762 | 14,519 | 20,723 | 6,100 | 6,479 | 18,154 |
| 2012.............. | 3,823 | 71,758 | 13,879 | 19,970 | 5,940 | 5,079 | 17,872 |
| 2013.............. | 3,813 | 69,755 | 13,239 | 19,217 | 5,780 | 4,873 | 17,590 |
| 2014.............. | 3,571 | 65,537 | 12,589 | 18,183 | 5,381 | 4,674 | 16,883 |
| 2015.............. | 3,568 | 64,462 | 11,843 | 18,166 | 5,363 | 3,685 | 16,701 |
| 2016.............. | 3,565 | 61,846 | 11,304 | 18,153 | 5,348 | 2,960 | 16,429 |
| 2017.............. | 3,562 | 60,000 | 10,771 | 18,138 | 5,331 | 2,809 | 16,202 |
| 2018.............. | 3,559 | 58,155 | 10,327 | 18,123 | 5,315 | 2,735 | 15,975 |

[1] PM = Particular Matter; PM-10 is equal to or less than ten microns in diameter; PM-2.5 to or less than 2.5 microns effective diameter. [2] Volatile organic compounds.

Source: U.S. Environmental Protection Agency, "National Emissions Inventory (NEI) Air Pollutant Emissions Trends Data, 1970-2018," <https://www.epa.gov/air-emissions-inventories/air-pollutant-emissions-trends-data>, accessed August 2019.

## Table 415. Selected Air Pollutant Emissions by Pollutant and Source: 2018

[In thousands of tons (3,559 represents 3,559,000). See headnote, Table 414]

| Source | Ammonia | Carbon monoxide | Nitrogen oxide | PM-10 [1] | PM-2.5 [1] | Sulfur dioxide | VOCs [2] |
|---|---|---|---|---|---|---|---|
| **Total emissions**..................... | **3,559** | **58,155** | **10,327** | **18,123** | **5,315** | **2,735** | **15,975** |
| Fuel combustion, stationary sources................. | 108 | 4,065 | 2,798 | 867 | 749 | 1,956 | 519 |
| Electric utilities........................... | 26 | 731 | 1,114 | 234 | 182 | 1,306 | 38 |
| Industrial................................... | 15 | 926 | 1,143 | 286 | 224 | 534 | 110 |
| Other fuel combustion................. | 67 | 2,408 | 541 | 348 | 343 | 116 | 372 |
| Industrial and other processes...................... | 83 | 4,001 | 1,282 | 1,112 | 603 | 534 | 7,557 |
| Chemical and allied product manufacturing........ | 22 | 129 | 47 | 19 | 14 | 123 | 77 |
| Metals processing......................... | 1 | 610 | 70 | 58 | 44 | 105 | 29 |
| Petroleum and related industries.................... | 2 | 702 | 717 | 33 | 29 | 104 | 3,145 |
| Other........................................ | 22 | 584 | 330 | 677 | 265 | 167 | 346 |
| Solvent utilization........................ | 1 | 2 | 1 | 4 | 4 | – | 3,052 |
| Storage and transport.................... | 5 | 8 | 6 | 43 | 17 | 3 | 675 |
| Waste disposal and recycling........................ | 30 | 1,967 | 110 | 277 | 230 | 32 | 233 |
| Highway vehicles.......................... | 96 | 17,045 | 3,300 | 247 | 100 | 27 | 1,609 |
| Off highway [3]............................ | 3 | 13,271 | 2,653 | 184 | 173 | 69 | 1,622 |
| Miscellaneous [4]......................... | 3,268 | 19,773 | 294 | 15,713 | 3,689 | 150 | 4,669 |

– Rounds to zero. [1] See footnote 1, Table 414. [2] Volatile organic compounds. [3] Includes emissions from farm tractors and other farm machinery, construction equipment, industrial machinery, recreational marine vessels, and small general utility engines such as lawn mowers. [4] Includes emissions from forest fires and other kinds of burning, various agricultural activities, fugitive dust from paved and unpaved roads, other construction and mining activities, and natural sources.

Source: U.S. Environmental Protection Agency, "National Emissions Inventory (NEI) Air Pollutant Emissions Trends Data, 1970-2018," <https://www.epa.gov/air-emissions-inventories/air-pollutant-emissions-trends-data>, accessed September 2019.

# Table 416. Greenhouse Gas Emissions by Type and Source: 1990 to 2017

[In millions of metric tons of carbon dioxide equivalent (MMT CO2 Eq.). 6,371.0 represents 6,371,000,000. MMT CO2 Eq. weights each gas by its global warming potential (GWP) value. GWP is a quantified measure of the globally averaged relative radiative forcing impacts of a particular greenhouse gas. The reference gas used is CO2; therefore, GWP-weighted emissions are measured in MMT CO2 Eq. See source for details]

| Type and/or source | 1990 | 2013 | 2014 | 2015 | 2016 | 2017 |
|---|---|---|---|---|---|---|
| **Total emissions** | **6,371.0** | **6,710.2** | **6,760.0** | **6,623.8** | **6,492.3** | **6,456.7** |
| BY SOURCE | | | | | | |
| Energy | 5,339.8 | 5,695.0 | 5,736.4 | 5,584.7 | 5,465.3 | 5,424.8 |
| Industrial processes and product use [1] | 342.1 | 353.1 | 365.2 | 360.8 | 354.6 | 358.9 |
| Sulfur hexafluoride (SF6) | 28.8 | 6.3 | 6.3 | 5.8 | 6.3 | 6.1 |
| Hydrofluorocarbons (HFCs) | 46.6 | 146.1 | 150.7 | 153.8 | 155.0 | 158.3 |
| Perfluorocarbons (PFCs) | 24.3 | 5.9 | 5.6 | 5.1 | 4.4 | 4.1 |
| Agriculture | 490.2 | 526.3 | 522.8 | 543.8 | 541.2 | 542.1 |
| Land use, land-use change, and forestry | 7.8 | 17.5 | 17.7 | 28.3 | 15.5 | 15.5 |
| Waste | 198.9 | 135.8 | 135.6 | 134.5 | 131.1 | 131.0 |
| *Net CO2 flux from land use, land use change, and forestry* | *-807.0* | *-713.5* | *-670.0* | *-711.1* | *-722.6* | *-714.1* |
| Net emissions (sources and sinks) [2] | 5,564.0 | 5,996.8 | 6,090.0 | 5,912.7 | 5,769.7 | 5,742.6 |
| BY TYPE AND SOURCE | | | | | | |
| **Carbon dioxide (CO2), total** | **5,121.2** | **5,522.9** | **5,572.1** | **5,423.0** | **5,306.7** | **5,270.7** |
| Energy | 4,905.3 | 5,341.5 | 5,384.8 | 5,241.5 | 5,134.1 | 5,095.6 |
| Fossil fuel combustion | 4,738.8 | 5,157.4 | 5,199.3 | 5,047.1 | 4,961.9 | 4,912.0 |
| Electricity | 1,820.0 | 2,038.3 | 2,037.1 | 1,900.6 | 1,808.9 | 1,732.0 |
| Transportation | 1,469.1 | 1,682.7 | 1,721.6 | 1,734.0 | 1,779.0 | 1,800.6 |
| Industrial | 857.5 | 840.0 | 819.6 | 807.9 | 807.6 | 810.7 |
| Residential | 338.2 | 329.3 | 346.8 | 317.8 | 292.9 | 294.5 |
| Commercial | 226.5 | 224.6 | 232.9 | 245.5 | 232.1 | 232.9 |
| Biomass (wood) [3] | 215.2 | 227.3 | 233.8 | 224.7 | 216.3 | 221.4 |
| Industrial processes and product use | 208.8 | 173.1 | 179.2 | 173.0 | 164.5 | 166.9 |
| Agriculture | 7.1 | 8.4 | 8.1 | 8.5 | 8.1 | 8.2 |
| *Land use, land-use change, and forestry (sink)* | *-814.8* | *-731.0* | *-687.8* | *-739.4* | *-738.1* | *-729.6* |
| **Methane (CH4), total** | **779.8** | **663.0** | **662.1** | **661.4** | **654.9** | **656.3** |
| Energy | 366.9 | 298.4 | 298.1 | 293.5 | 283.0 | 283.3 |
| Industrial processes and product use | 0.3 | 0.1 | 0.2 | 0.2 | 0.3 | 0.3 |
| Agriculture | 217.4 | 235.3 | 234.9 | 239.9 | 247.3 | 248.7 |
| Land use, land-use change, and forestry | 5.0 | 9.9 | 10.1 | 16.5 | 8.8 | 8.8 |
| Waste management | 195.2 | 129.3 | 128.9 | 127.8 | 124.3 | 124.1 |
| **Nitrous oxide (N2O), total** | **370.3** | **365.4** | **362.7** | **374.1** | **364.5** | **360.5** |
| Energy | 67.6 | 55.2 | 53.5 | 49.7 | 48.3 | 45.9 |
| Industrial processes and product use | 33.3 | 21.0 | 22.8 | 22.3 | 23.6 | 22.6 |
| Agriculture | 265.7 | 282.7 | 279.7 | 295.4 | 285.8 | 285.2 |
| Land use, land-use change, and forestry | 2.8 | 7.6 | 7.7 | 11.8 | 6.7 | 6.7 |
| Waste management | 3.7 | 6.5 | 6.6 | 6.7 | 6.8 | 6.9 |

[1] Total includes items not shown separately. [2] The net CO2 flux total includes both emissions and sequestration, and constitutes a sink in the United States. Sinks are only included in net emissions total. [3] Emissions from wood biomass and ethanol consumption are not included specifically in summing energy sector totals. Net carbon fluxes from changes in biogenic carbon reservoirs are accounted for in the estimates for land use, land-use change, and forestry.

Source: U.S. Environmental Protection Agency, *Inventory of U.S. Greenhouse Gas Emissions and Sinks, 1990-2017*, April 2019. See also <https://www.epa.gov/ghgemissions/inventory-us-greenhouse-gas-emissions-and-sinks>.

# Table 417. Carbon Dioxide Emissions from Fossil Fuel Combustion by Fuel Type and Sector: 1990 to 2017

[In millions of metric tons of carbon dioxide equivalent (MMT CO2 Eq.); 4,738.8 represents 4,738,800,000. See source for details on methodology]

| Fuel and sector | 1990 | 2000 | 2010 | 2013 | 2014 | 2015 | 2016 | 2017 |
|---|---|---|---|---|---|---|---|---|
| **Total** [1] | **4,738.8** | **5,590.2** | **5,358.5** | **5,157.4** | **5,199.3** | **5,047.1** | **4,961.9** | **4,912.0** |
| **Coal** | **1,717.3** | **2,064.4** | **1,927.5** | **1,654.1** | **1,652.4** | **1,424.7** | **1,307.5** | **1,267.5** |
| Residential | 3.0 | 1.1 | – | – | – | – | – | – |
| Commercial | 12.0 | 8.8 | 6.6 | 3.9 | 3.8 | 3.0 | 2.3 | 2.0 |
| Industrial | 155.2 | 127.3 | 90.2 | 76.0 | 76.0 | 66.3 | 59.2 | 54.4 |
| Electricity generation | 1,546.5 | 1,926.4 | 1,827.2 | 1,571.3 | 1,568.6 | 1,351.4 | 1,242.0 | 1,207.1 |
| **Natural gas** | **999.7** | **1,219.7** | **1,273.9** | **1,391.9** | **1,420.0** | **1,460.2** | **1,471.8** | **1,450.3** |
| Residential | 237.8 | 270.8 | 258.9 | 266.4 | 277.7 | 252.7 | 238.4 | 241.5 |
| Commercial | 142.0 | 172.5 | 168.0 | 179.2 | 189.2 | 175.4 | 170.5 | 173.2 |
| Industrial | 408.5 | 459.2 | 407.9 | 452.1 | 467.1 | 464.4 | 474.8 | 484.7 |
| Transportation | 36.0 | 35.7 | 38.2 | 47.0 | 40.2 | 39.4 | 40.1 | 42.3 |
| Electricity generation | 175.4 | 280.8 | 399.5 | 444.2 | 442.9 | 525.2 | 545.0 | 505.6 |
| **Petroleum** | **2,021.2** | **2,305.6** | **2,156.6** | **2,111.0** | **2,126.5** | **2,161.8** | **2,182.1** | **2,193.7** |
| Residential | 97.4 | 99.0 | 76.0 | 63.0 | 69.2 | 65.1 | 54.5 | 53.0 |
| Commercial | 72.6 | 55.0 | 50.3 | 41.5 | 39.9 | 67.1 | 59.3 | 57.7 |
| Industrial | 293.7 | 285.6 | 302.2 | 311.9 | 276.5 | 277.1 | 273.6 | 271.5 |
| Transportation | 1,433.1 | 1,743.7 | 1,659.2 | 1,635.6 | 1,681.3 | 1,694.6 | 1,739.0 | 1,758.3 |
| Electricity generation | 97.5 | 88.4 | 31.4 | 22.4 | 25.3 | 23.7 | 21.4 | 18.9 |

– Represents zero. [1] Includes data for geothermal energy-related carbon dioxide emissions and U.S. territories, not shown separately.

Source: U.S. Environmental Protection Agency, *Inventory of U.S. Greenhouse Gas Emissions and Sinks, 1990-2017*, April 2019. See also <https://www.epa.gov/ghgemissions/inventory-us-greenhouse-gas-emissions-and-sinks>.

## Table 418. Municipal Solid Waste Generation, Materials Recovery, Recycling, Combustion With Energy Recovery, and Discards: 1980 to 2015

[In millions of tons (151.6 represents 151,600,000), except as indicated. Covers post-consumer residential, commercial, and institutional solid wastes which comprise the major portion of typical municipal collections. Excludes mining, agricultural and industrial processing, demolition and construction wastes, sewage sludge, junked autos and obsolete equipment wastes. Based on material-flows estimating procedure and wet weight as generated]

| Item and material | 1980 | 1990 | 2000 | 2005 | 2010 | 2014 | 2015 |
|---|---|---|---|---|---|---|---|
| **Waste generated** | **151.6** | **208.3** | **243.5** | **253.7** | **251.1** | **259.0** | **262.4** |
| Per person per day (lb.) | 3.7 | 4.6 | 4.7 | 4.7 | 4.5 | 4.5 | 4.5 |
| **Total materials recovery** | **14.5** | **33.2** | **69.5** | **79.8** | **85.4** | **89.6** | **91.2** |
| Per person per day (lb.) | 0.4 | 0.7 | 1.4 | 1.5 | 1.5 | 1.5 | 1.6 |
| Recovery for recycling | 14.5 | 29.0 | 53.0 | 59.2 | 65.3 | 66.6 | 67.8 |
| Per person per day (lb.) | 0.4 | 0.6 | 1.0 | 1.1 | 1.2 | 1.1 | 1.2 |
| Recovery for composting [1] | (Z) | 4.2 | 16.5 | 20.6 | 20.2 | 23.0 | 23.4 |
| Per person per day (lb.) | (Z) | 0.1 | 0.3 | 0.4 | 0.4 | 0.4 | 0.4 |
| Combustion with energy recovery | 2.8 | 29.8 | 33.7 | 31.7 | 29.3 | 33.2 | 33.6 |
| Per person per day (lb.) | 0.1 | 0.7 | 0.7 | 0.6 | 0.5 | 0.6 | 0.6 |
| Discards to landfill, other disposal | 134.4 | 145.3 | 140.3 | 142.3 | 136.3 | 136.2 | 137.7 |
| Per person per day (lb.) | 3.2 | 3.2 | 2.7 | 2.6 | 2.4 | 2.3 | 2.4 |
| **PERCENT DISTRIBUTION OF GENERATION** | | | | | | | |
| **Percent of total generation** | **71.8** | **70.3** | **73.4** | **72.9** | **70.9** | **70.2** | **70.1** |
| Paper and paperboard | 36.4 | 34.9 | 36.0 | 33.4 | 28.4 | 26.5 | 25.9 |
| Glass | 10.0 | 6.3 | 5.2 | 4.9 | 4.6 | 4.4 | 4.4 |
| Metals | 10.2 | 7.9 | 7.8 | 8.0 | 8.9 | 9.1 | 9.1 |
| Plastics | 4.5 | 8.2 | 10.5 | 11.6 | 12.5 | 12.9 | 13.1 |
| Rubber and leather | 2.8 | 2.8 | 2.7 | 2.9 | 3.1 | 3.2 | 3.2 |
| Textiles | 1.7 | 2.8 | 3.9 | 4.5 | 5.3 | 5.9 | 6.1 |
| Wood | 4.6 | 5.9 | 5.6 | 5.8 | 6.3 | 6.2 | 6.2 |
| Other | 1.7 | 1.5 | 1.6 | 1.7 | 1.9 | 2.0 | 2.1 |
| **Total other waste** | **28.2** | **29.7** | **26.6** | **27.1** | **29.1** | **29.8** | **29.9** |
| Food waste | 8.6 | 11.5 | 12.6 | 13.0 | 14.2 | 14.9 | 15.1 |
| Yard trimmings | 18.1 | 16.8 | 12.5 | 12.6 | 13.3 | 13.3 | 13.3 |
| Miscellaneous inorganic wastes | 1.5 | 1.4 | 1.4 | 1.5 | 1.5 | 1.5 | 1.5 |

Z Less than 5,000 tons or 0.05 percent. [1] Composting of yard trimmings, food scraps, and other municipal solid waste organic material. Does not include backyard composting.

Source: U.S. Environmental Protection Agency, *Advancing Sustainable Materials Management: 2015 Tables and Figures*, July 2018. See also <https://www.epa.gov/smm>.

## Table 419. Generation and Recovery of Selected Materials in Municipal Solid Waste: 1980 to 2015

[In millions of tons (151.6 represents 151,600,000), except as indicated. Covers post-consumer residential, commercial, and institutional solid wastes which comprise the major portion of typical municipal collections. Excludes mining, agricultural and industrial processing, demolition and construction wastes, sewage sludge, and junked autos and obsolete equipment wastes. Based on material-flows estimating procedure and wet weight as generated. Material recovered includes material recycled and composted]

| Item and material | 1980 | 1990 | 2000 | 2005 | 2010 | 2014 | 2015 |
|---|---|---|---|---|---|---|---|
| **Waste generated, total [1]** | **151.6** | **208.3** | **243.5** | **253.7** | **251.1** | **259.0** | **262.4** |
| Paper and paperboard | 55.2 | 72.7 | 87.7 | 84.8 | 71.3 | 68.6 | 68.1 |
| Glass | 15.1 | 13.1 | 12.8 | 12.5 | 11.5 | 11.5 | 11.5 |
| Ferrous metals | 12.6 | 12.6 | 14.2 | 15.2 | 16.9 | 17.9 | 18.2 |
| Aluminum | 1.7 | 2.8 | 3.2 | 3.3 | 3.5 | 3.5 | 3.6 |
| Other nonferrous metals | 1.2 | 1.1 | 1.6 | 1.9 | 2.0 | 2.2 | 2.2 |
| Plastics | 6.8 | 17.1 | 25.6 | 29.4 | 31.4 | 33.4 | 34.5 |
| Food waste | 13.0 | 23.9 | 30.7 | 32.9 | 35.7 | 38.7 | 39.7 |
| Yard trimmings | 27.5 | 35.0 | 30.5 | 32.1 | 33.4 | 34.5 | 34.7 |
| **Materials recovered, total [1]** | **14.5** | **33.2** | **69.5** | **79.8** | **85.4** | **89.6** | **91.2** |
| Paper and paperboard | 11.7 | 20.2 | 37.6 | 42.0 | 44.6 | 44.4 | 45.3 |
| Glass | 0.8 | 2.6 | 2.9 | 2.6 | 3.1 | 3.0 | 3.0 |
| Ferrous metals | 0.4 | 2.2 | 4.7 | 5.0 | 5.8 | 6.0 | 6.1 |
| Aluminum | 0.3 | 1.0 | 0.9 | 0.7 | 0.7 | 0.7 | 0.7 |
| Other nonferrous metals | 0.5 | 0.7 | 1.1 | 1.3 | 1.4 | 1.6 | 1.5 |
| Plastics | (Z) | 0.4 | 1.5 | 1.8 | 2.5 | 3.2 | 3.1 |
| Food waste [2] | (Z) | (Z) | 0.7 | 0.7 | 1.0 | 1.9 | 2.1 |
| Yard trimmings | (Z) | 4.2 | 15.8 | 19.9 | 19.2 | 21.1 | 21.3 |
| **Percent of generation recovered, total [1]** | **9.6** | **16.0** | **28.5** | **31.4** | **34.0** | **34.6** | **34.7** |
| Paper and paperboard | 21.3 | 27.8 | 42.8 | 49.5 | 62.5 | 64.7 | 66.6 |
| Glass | 5.0 | 20.1 | 22.6 | 20.7 | 27.2 | 26.0 | 26.4 |
| Ferrous metals | 2.9 | 17.6 | 33.1 | 33.0 | 34.3 | 33.4 | 33.4 |
| Aluminum | 17.9 | 35.9 | 27.0 | 20.7 | 19.4 | 20.1 | 18.6 |
| Other nonferrous metals | 46.6 | 66.4 | 66.3 | 68.8 | 71.3 | 69.5 | 67.6 |
| Plastics | 0.3 | 2.2 | 5.8 | 6.1 | 8.0 | 9.6 | 9.1 |
| Food waste [2] | (Z) | (Z) | 2.2 | 2.1 | 2.7 | 5.0 | 5.3 |
| Yard trimmings | (Z) | 12.0 | 51.7 | 61.9 | 57.5 | 61.1 | 61.3 |

Z Less than 5,000 tons or 0.05 percent. [1] Includes other types of materials not shown separately. [2] Includes collection of other municipal solid waste organic materials for composting.

Source: U.S. Environmental Protection Agency, *Advancing Sustainable Materials Management: 2015 Tables and Figures*, July 2018. See also <https://www.epa.gov/smm>.

## Table 420. Municipal Solid Waste—Generation, Recycling, and Landfill Disposal by Selected Type of Product: 2015

[68,040 represents 68,040,000. See headnote, Table 419]

| Type of product | Generation (1,000 tons) | Recycling — Volume recycled (1,000 tons) | Recycling — Percent of generation | Landfill disposal (1,000 tons) |
|---|---|---|---|---|
| **Paper and paperboard products** [1] | **68,040** | **45,320** | **66.6** | **18,270** |
| Nondurable goods | 28,120 | 14,120 | 50.2 | 11,260 |
| Newspapers/mechanical papers | 6,730 | 4,790 | 71.2 | 1,560 |
| Other paper nondurable goods | 21,390 | 9,330 | 43.6 | 9,700 |
| Containers and packaging | 39,920 | 31,200 | 78.2 | 7,010 |
| Corrugated boxes | 31,330 | 28,930 | 92.3 | 1,930 |
| Other paper and paperboard packaging | 8,590 | 2,270 | 26.4 | 5,080 |
| **Glass products** [1] | **11,470** | **3,030** | **26.4** | **6,970** |
| Containers and packaging | 9,120 | 3,030 | 33.2 | 4,890 |
| Beer and soft drink bottles | 5,320 | 2,230 | 41.9 | 2,480 |
| Wine and liquor bottles | 1,810 | 500 | 27.6 | 1,050 |
| Other bottles and jars | 1,990 | 300 | 15.1 | 1,360 |
| **Metal products** [1] | **24,000** | **8,230** | **34.3** | **13,070** |
| Metals in durable goods | 19,720 | 5,940 | 30.1 | 11,480 |
| Ferrous | 15,950 | 4,440 | 27.8 | 9,490 |
| Aluminum | 1,550 | (NA) | (NA) | 1,330 |
| Other nonferrous | 700 | (Z) | (Z) | 640 |
| Metals in containers and packaging | 4,060 | 2,290 | 56.4 | 1,410 |
| **Plastics** [1] | **34,500** | **3,140** | **9.1** | **26,010** |
| Plastics in durable goods | 12,500 | 830 | 6.6 | 10,180 |
| Plastics in nondurable goods | 7,320 | 160 | 2.2 | 5,760 |
| Plastics in containers and packaging | 14,680 | 2,150 | 14.6 | 10,070 |
| **Rubber and leather** [1] | **8,480** | **1,510** | **17.8** | **4,480** |
| Durable goods | 7,350 | 1,510 | 20.5 | 3,570 |
| Rubber in tires | 3,750 | 1,510 | 40.3 | 460 |
| Other durables | 3,600 | (Z) | (Z) | 3,110 |
| Nondurable goods | 1,130 | (Z) | (Z) | 910 |
| Clothing and footwear | 860 | (Z) | (Z) | 690 |
| Other nondurables | 270 | (Z) | (Z) | 220 |

NA Not available. Z Less than 5,000 tons or .05 percent. [1] Includes products not shown separately.

Source: U.S. Environmental Protection Agency, *Advancing Sustainable Materials Management: 2015 Tables and Figures,* July 2018. See also <https://www.epa.gov/smm>.

## Table 421. Environmental Industry—Revenues and Employment by Industry Segment: 2000 to 2018

[210.1 represents $210,100,000,000. Covers approximately 30,000 private and public companies engaged in revenue-generating environmental activities]

| Industry segment | Revenue (billion dollars) | | | | Employment | | | |
|---|---|---|---|---|---|---|---|---|
| | 2000 | 2010 | 2017 | 2018 | 2000 | 2010 | 2017 | 2018 |
| **Industry total** | **210.1** | **303.3** | **382.8** | **394.5** | **1,264,600** | **1,595,400** | **1,723,400** | **1,721,100** |
| SERVICES | | | | | | | | |
| Analytical services [1] | 1.8 | 1.9 | 2.0 | 2.1 | 17,900 | 17,000 | 16,300 | 16,400 |
| Wastewater treatment works [2] | 28.7 | 45.5 | 61.2 | 63.1 | 118,800 | 170,100 | 197,700 | 198,500 |
| Solid waste management [3] | 39.4 | 53.4 | 62.9 | 64.6 | 221,400 | 278,000 | 293,000 | 289,800 |
| Hazardous waste management [4] | 8.8 | 10.0 | 10.9 | 11.0 | 48,300 | 48,500 | 48,000 | 47,700 |
| Remediation/industrial services | 9.9 | 12.4 | 14.0 | 14.2 | 98,400 | 105,000 | 99,000 | 97,400 |
| Consulting and engineering | 17.4 | 26.8 | 31.3 | 32.7 | 170,400 | 240,400 | 230,800 | 230,600 |
| EQUIPMENT | | | | | | | | |
| Water equipment and chemicals | 19.8 | 26.9 | 31.8 | 32.8 | 130,500 | 160,100 | 167,900 | 167,900 |
| Instrument manufacturing | 3.8 | 5.4 | 7.5 | 7.9 | 30,200 | 37,100 | 46,500 | 48,300 |
| Air pollution control equipment [5] | 19.0 | 14.9 | 17.4 | 17.3 | 129,600 | 96,400 | 98,800 | 95,900 |
| Waste management equipment [6] | 11.1 | 12.7 | 15.6 | 15.8 | 84,300 | 86,600 | 95,500 | 95,400 |
| RESOURCES | | | | | | | | |
| Water utilities [7] | 29.9 | 43.5 | 59.2 | 61.8 | 130,000 | 172,100 | 211,700 | 214,600 |
| Resource recovery [8] | 16.0 | 28.5 | 26.1 | 23.0 | 61,900 | 102,600 | 83,100 | 72,800 |
| Clean energy systems and power [9] | 4.4 | 21.4 | 42.9 | 48.5 | 22,900 | 81,500 | 135,100 | 145,800 |

[1] Covers environmental laboratory testing and services. [2] Mostly revenues collected by municipal entities for sewage or wastewater plants. [3] Covers public & private sector collection, transportation, transfer stations, disposal, landfill ownership and management for solid waste and recyclables. [4] Transportation and disposal of hazardous, medical, and nuclear waste. [5] Includes stationary and mobile sources. [6] Equipment for handling, storing or transporting solid, liquid or hazardous waste. Includes recycling/remediation equipment. [7] Revenues generated from the sale of water, majority in public sector. [8] Revenues generated from the sale of recovered metals, paper, plastic, etc. [9] Revenues generated from the sale of equipment and systems and electricity.

Source: Environmental Business International, Inc., San Diego, CA, publisher of *Environmental Business Journal;* © 2019 EBI Inc. See also <http://www.ebionline.org>.

## Table 422. Toxic Chemical Releases and Transfers by Media: 2011 to 2017

[In millions of pounds (4,117.2 represents 4,117,200,000), except as indicated. Based on reports filed to the Toxic Release Inventory (TRI) Program, as required by Section 313 of the Emergency Planning and Community Right-to-Know Act (EPCRA). The Pollution Prevention Act (PPA) of 1990 mandates collection of data on toxic chemicals that are treated on-site, recycled, and combusted for energy recovery. Owners and operators of facilities within specific North American Industry Classification System industries that have 10 or more full-time employees, and that manufacture, process, or otherwise use any listed toxic chemical in quantities greater than the established threshold in the course of a calendar year are covered and required to report. For trend analysis, a 2011 core list of must-be-reported chemicals is used. Includes carcinogens; persistent, bioaccumulative, toxic (PBT) chemicals; and dioxin and dioxin-like compounds. Does not include off-site disposal or other releases transferred to other TRI program facilities that reported the amounts as on-site disposal or other releases]

| Media | 2011 | 2012 | 2013 | 2014 | 2015 | 2016 | 2017 |
|---|---|---|---|---|---|---|---|
| **Total facilities reporting (number)** | **21,921** | **22,090** | **22,275** | **22,336** | **22,273** | **21,956** | **21,698** |
| **Total on- and off-site disposal or other releases** | **4,117.2** | **3,621.7** | **4,127.1** | **3,939.3** | **3,383.6** | **3,447.4** | **3,839.8** |
| On-site releases | 3,701.1 | 3,205.3 | 3,694.5 | 3,511.2 | 2,940.3 | 3,078.8 | 3,484.0 |
| Air emissions [1] | 808.0 | 753.0 | 747.1 | 736.1 | 670.1 | 593.4 | 581.9 |
| Surface water discharges | 222.9 | 218.4 | 213.8 | 218.7 | 199.0 | 192.4 | 190.9 |
| Underground injection class I | 197.8 | 204.0 | 200.3 | 202.0 | 209.2 | 198.4 | 198.6 |
| Underground injection class II-V | 0.2 | 0.2 | 2.1 | 0.9 | 0.8 | 0.6 | 0.5 |
| RCRA subtitle C landfills [2] | 69.4 | 94.3 | 68.3 | 58.1 | 78.4 | 90.7 | 83.6 |
| Other landfills | 273.6 | 269.9 | 297.6 | 298.1 | 290.4 | 279.3 | 306.1 |
| Land treatment/application farming | 15.0 | 16.0 | 14.0 | 13.3 | 14.1 | 12.2 | 14.5 |
| Surface impoundments | 884.8 | 724.3 | 738.7 | 757.1 | 792.2 | 839.6 | 909.1 |
| Other land disposal | 1,229.5 | 925.3 | 1,412.6 | 1,227.0 | 686.1 | 872.3 | 1,198.9 |
| Off-site releases | 416.1 | 416.4 | 432.5 | 428.1 | 443.2 | 368.6 | 355.8 |
| **Total transfers offsite for further waste management** | **3,724.1** | **3,919.7** | **3,620.2** | **3,679.5** | **3,622.8** | **3,569.3** | **3,669.6** |
| Transfers to recycling | 2,370.4 | 2,485.7 | 2,199.2 | 2,238.1 | 2,173.3 | 2,194.0 | 2,322.8 |
| Transfers to energy recovery | 354.7 | 388.3 | 407.8 | 422.4 | 412.9 | 424.8 | 403.6 |
| Transfers to treatment | 308.3 | 346.3 | 301.6 | 309.9 | 311.8 | 301.7 | 282.8 |
| Transfers to POTWs (non metals) [3] | 242.0 | 248.5 | 239.2 | 242.1 | 242.2 | 244.2 | 259.2 |
| Transfers to POTWs (metal and metal compounds) [3] | 0.8 | 0.9 | 0.7 | 0.7 | 0.6 | 0.7 | 0.7 |
| Other off-site transfers | 0.2 | 0.1 | – | – | – | 0.1 | – |
| Transfers off-site for disposal or other releases | 447.8 | 449.9 | 471.7 | 466.4 | 482.0 | 403.8 | 400.5 |
| **Total production-related waste managed** | **22,713.4** | **22,513.3** | **25,409.6** | **28,688.2** | **27,684.4** | **27,613.9** | **28,287.8** |
| Recycled on-site | 6,295.0 | 6,640.2 | 8,796.1 | 11,822.6 | 11,477.4 | 11,661.9 | 11,884.2 |
| Recycled off-site | 2,367.0 | 2,181.5 | 2,198.7 | 2,236.3 | 2,172.5 | 2,190.9 | 2,321.0 |
| Energy recovery on-site | 2,110.7 | 2,146.6 | 2,195.1 | 2,560.0 | 2,455.3 | 2,426.0 | 2,433.9 |
| Energy recovery off-site | 354.9 | 387.4 | 407.4 | 421.3 | 412.0 | 422.7 | 402.0 |
| Treated on-site | 6,899.7 | 6,923.5 | 7,307.8 | 7,129.2 | 7,205.8 | 6,891.8 | 6,829.6 |
| Treated off-site | 523.9 | 570.0 | 518.7 | 524.6 | 523.4 | 511.5 | 508.4 |
| Quantity disposed or otherwise release of on- and off-site | 4,162.2 | 3,664.1 | 3,985.9 | 3,994.2 | 3,438.1 | 3,509.2 | 3,908.6 |
| Non-production-related waste managed | 14.6 | 14.3 | 203.8 | 14.0 | 17.2 | 14.1 | 13.5 |

– Represents or rounds zero. [1] Air emissions include both fugitive and point source. [2] RCRA=Resource Conservation and Recovery Act. [3] POTW (Publicly Owned Treatment Work) is a wastewater treatment facility that is owned by a state or municipality.

Source: U.S. Environmental Protection Agency, Toxic Release Inventory (TRI) Program, "TRI Explorer, 2017 data set (released April 2019)," <https://iaspub.epa.gov/triexplorer/tri_release.chemical>, accessed September 2019.

## Table 423. Industrial Pollution—Toxic Chemical Releases by Industry: 2017

[In millions of pounds (3,849.2 represents 3,849,200,000). Based on 21,508 facilities. See headnote, Table 422]

| Industry | NAICS [1] code | Total on- and off-site releases | On-site releases Total [2] | On-site releases Air emissions | On-site releases Other surface impoundments | Off-site releases/ transfers to disposal [3] |
|---|---|---|---|---|---|---|
| **Total [4]** | **(X)** | **3,849.2** | **3,469.4** | **580.2** | **903.8** | **379.8** |
| Coal mining | 2121 | 5.5 | 5.5 | (Z) | 0.2 | (Z) |
| Metal mining | 2122 | 1,954.3 | 1,949.5 | 2.0 | 797.1 | 4.8 |
| Electric utilities | 2211 | 340.3 | 290.7 | 82.3 | 39.0 | 49.6 |
| Food/beverages/tobacco | 311/312 | 129.6 | 122.6 | 42.6 | 0.2 | 6.9 |
| Textiles | 313/314 | 3.3 | 2.8 | 1.2 | (Z) | 0.4 |
| Apparel | 315 | (Z) | (Z) | (Z) | – | (Z) |
| Leather | 316 | 1.7 | 0.2 | 0.2 | – | 1.5 |
| Wood products | 321 | 9.7 | 9.4 | 9.2 | (Z) | 0.3 |
| Paper | 322 | 151.2 | 146.3 | 111.9 | 2.0 | 4.9 |
| Printing and publishing | 323/51 | 4.1 | 3.6 | 3.6 | – | 0.5 |
| Petroleum | 324 | 73.1 | 68.4 | 36.8 | (Z) | 4.7 |
| Chemicals | 325 | 483.5 | 423.3 | 148.5 | 23.1 | 60.1 |
| Plastics and rubber | 326 | 35.7 | 31.1 | 30.9 | (Z) | 4.6 |
| Stone/clay/glass | 327 | 28.0 | 23.8 | 19.7 | 0.1 | 4.2 |
| Primary metals | 331 | 315.3 | 182.9 | 31.0 | 40.6 | 132.5 |
| Fabricated metals | 332 | 37.7 | 18.8 | 17.3 | (Z) | 18.9 |
| Machinery | 333 | 4.6 | 2.0 | 2.0 | (Z) | 2.5 |
| Computers/electronic products | 334 | 3.9 | 2.2 | 1.0 | (Z) | 1.7 |
| Electrical equipment | 335 | 3.9 | 1.4 | 1.4 | (Z) | 2.5 |
| Transportation equipment | 336 | 32.7 | 26.6 | 26.3 | 0.1 | 6.1 |
| Furniture | 337 | 4.6 | 4.4 | 4.4 | – | 0.2 |
| Miscellaneous manufacturing | 339 | 2.4 | 1.4 | 1.4 | – | 1.0 |
| Chemical wholesalers | 4246 | 1.1 | 0.9 | 0.8 | – | 0.3 |
| Petroleum bulk terminals | 4247 | 1.6 | 1.5 | 1.5 | (Z) | 0.1 |
| Hazardous waste | 562 | 179.4 | 116.5 | 0.5 | (Z) | 62.9 |
| No codes [4] | (X) | 41.9 | 33.5 | 3.7 | 1.4 | 8.5 |

– Represents zero. X Not applicable. Z less than 50,000 lbs. [1] North American Industry Classification System, see text, Section 12. [2] Includes other on-site releases, not shown separately. [3] Includes off-site disposal to underground injection for Class I wells, Class II to V wells, other surface impoundments, land releases, and other releases, not shown separately. [4] Includes industries with no specific industry identified, and uses a double counting algorithm.

Source: U.S. Environmental Protection Agency, Toxic Release Inventory (TRI) Program, "TRI Explorer, 2017 data set (released April 2019)," <https://iaspub.epa.gov/triexplorer/tri_release.chemical>, accessed September 2019.

# Table 424. Pollution—Toxic Chemical Releases by State and Outlying Area: 2017

[In millions of pounds (3,849.2 represents 3,849,200,000). Based on reports filed as required by Section 313 of the EPCRA. See headnote, Table 422]

| State and outlying area | Total on- and off-site releases | On-site releases or other disposal | | | Off-site releases/ trans- fers to disposal | State and outlying area | Total on- and off-site releases | On-site releases or other disposal | | | Off-site releases/ trans- fers to disposal |
|---|---|---|---|---|---|---|---|---|---|---|---|
| | | Total [2] | Total air emis- sions | Other surface im- pound- ments | | | | Total [2] | Total air emis- sions | Other surface im- pound- ments | |
| Total [1] | 3,849.2 | 3,469.4 | 580.2 | 903.8 | 379.8 | MO | 55.4 | 51.4 | 8.1 | 29.8 | 4.0 |
| U.S. total | 3,847.2 | 3,467.6 | 578.7 | 903.8 | 379.5 | MT | 39.4 | 38.7 | 2.0 | 21.5 | 0.7 |
| AL | 75.0 | 60.0 | 25.0 | 3.5 | 15.0 | NE | 16.4 | 13.6 | 5.4 | (Z) | 2.7 |
| AK | 1,174.1 | 1,173.6 | 0.3 | 374.7 | 0.5 | NV | 397.7 | 392.8 | 0.7 | 254.5 | 4.9 |
| AZ | 77.6 | 76.3 | 2.3 | 23.3 | 1.2 | NH | 0.3 | 0.1 | 0.1 | – | 0.2 |
| AR | 30.6 | 27.6 | 14.0 | 0.1 | 3.0 | NJ | 10.6 | 5.5 | 1.7 | – | 5.1 |
| CA | 26.2 | 19.5 | 7.1 | 0.1 | 6.6 | NM | 11.3 | 8.5 | 0.9 | 1.0 | 2.8 |
| CO | 31.7 | 26.9 | 2.3 | 4.1 | 4.9 | NY | 12.7 | 10.0 | 4.5 | (Z) | 2.7 |
| CT | 1.7 | 0.8 | 0.7 | – | 1.0 | NC | 48.9 | 36.1 | 19.4 | 2.4 | 12.8 |
| DE | 4.9 | 4.6 | 0.7 | – | 0.3 | ND | 32.0 | 25.7 | 8.9 | 2.7 | 6.3 |
| DC | (Z) | (Z) | (Z) | (Z) | (Z) | OH | 111.4 | 89.0 | 35.8 | 4.9 | 22.4 |
| FL | 58.2 | 54.5 | 18.3 | 0.1 | 3.8 | OK | 29.8 | 27.3 | 16.7 | 0.5 | 2.5 |
| GA | 45.8 | 42.9 | 29.4 | 2.8 | 2.9 | OR | 17.6 | 16.8 | 5.7 | (Z) | 0.8 |
| HI | 3.1 | 2.8 | 2.0 | (Z) | 0.2 | PA | 51.5 | 33.6 | 14.2 | (Z) | 17.8 |
| ID | 35.8 | 35.4 | 5.0 | 6.8 | 0.4 | RI | 0.4 | 0.2 | 0.2 | – | 0.2 |
| IL | 108.4 | 64.2 | 24.7 | 2.3 | 44.3 | SC | 32.3 | 26.1 | 19.0 | 0.4 | 6.2 |
| IN | 125.8 | 78.7 | 25.2 | 0.9 | 47.1 | SD | 6.4 | 6.1 | 1.2 | (Z) | 0.3 |
| IA | 34.1 | 27.2 | 16.9 | 0.4 | 7.0 | TN | 81.2 | 68.6 | 23.9 | 15.6 | 12.7 |
| KS | 17.0 | 14.9 | 9.1 | 0.7 | 2.1 | TX | 199.4 | 180.0 | 50.8 | 2.2 | 19.4 |
| KY | 49.1 | 39.4 | 20.5 | 1.9 | 9.8 | UT | 304.1 | 302.5 | 12.1 | 95.8 | 1.5 |
| LA | 142.5 | 131.3 | 54.2 | 2.4 | 11.2 | VT | 0.4 | 0.2 | (Z) | – | 0.2 |
| ME | 11.3 | 9.3 | 2.7 | – | 2.0 | VA | 33.9 | 30.2 | 15.9 | 0.5 | 3.7 |
| MD | 4.8 | 3.4 | 3.1 | (Z) | 1.3 | WA | 31.1 | 25.7 | 6.4 | 11.5 | 5.4 |
| MA | 4.4 | 1.3 | 1.2 | – | 3.1 | WV | 30.1 | 22.7 | 12.2 | 1.2 | 7.4 |
| MI | 92.6 | 47.9 | 11.6 | 9.1 | 44.7 | WI | 30.0 | 16.4 | 8.8 | (Z) | 13.6 |
| MN | 22.8 | 18.2 | 8.3 | 7.4 | 4.6 | WY | 20.1 | 17.8 | 2.1 | 3.3 | 2.3 |
| MS | 65.2 | 61.3 | 17.2 | 15.1 | 3.9 | PR | 1.5 | 1.3 | 1.2 | – | 0.2 |

– Represents zero. Z Less than 50,000 lbs. [1] Total includes all states, Puerto Rico, and other outlying areas not shown separately. [2] Includes other types of release, not shown separately.

Source: U.S. Environmental Protection Agency, Toxic Release Inventory (TRI) Program, "TRI Explorer, 2017 data set (released April 2019)," <https://iaspub.epa.gov/triexplorer/tri_release.chemical>, accessed September 2019.

# Table 425. Hazardous Waste Sites on the Superfund National Priority List by State and Outlying Area: 2018

[As of August 2019. Includes both proposed and final sites listed on the National Priorities List for the Superfund program as authorized by the Comprehensive Environmental Response, Compensation, and Liability Act (CERCLA) of 1980 and the Superfund Amendments and Reauthorization Act (SARA) of 1986. For information on CERCLA and SARA, see <https://www.epa.gov/superfund/superfund-cercla-overview> and <https://www.epa.gov/superfund/superfund-amendments-and-reauthorization-act-sara>]

| State and outlying area | Total sites | Rank | Per- cent distri- bution | Federal | Non- fed- eral | State and outlying area | Total sites | Rank | Per- cent distri- bution | Federal | Non- fed- eral |
|---|---|---|---|---|---|---|---|---|---|---|---|
| Total [1] | 1,391 | (X) | (X) | 160 | 1,231 | Missouri | 34 | 14 | 2.5 | 3 | 31 |
| United States | 1,369 | (X) | (X) | 158 | 1,211 | Montana | 18 | 22 | 1.3 | – | 18 |
| Alabama | 14 | 30 | 1.0 | 3 | 11 | Nebraska | 17 | 24 | 1.2 | 1 | 16 |
| Alaska | 6 | 45 | 0.4 | 5 | 1 | Nevada | 2 | 47 | 0.1 | – | 2 |
| Arizona | 9 | 41 | 0.7 | 2 | 7 | New Hampshire | 21 | 19 | 1.5 | 1 | 20 |
| Arkansas | 9 | 41 | 0.7 | – | 9 | New Jersey | 115 | 1 | 8.4 | 6 | 109 |
| California | 101 | 2 | 7.4 | 24 | 77 | New Mexico | 16 | 26 | 1.2 | 1 | 15 |
| Colorado | 21 | 19 | 1.5 | 3 | 18 | New York | 88 | 4 | 6.4 | 4 | 84 |
| Connecticut | 14 | 30 | 1.0 | 1 | 13 | North Carolina | 38 | 12 | 2.8 | 2 | 36 |
| Delaware | 16 | 26 | 1.2 | 1 | 15 | North Dakota | – | 51 | – | – | – |
| Dist. of Columbia | 1 | 50 | 0.1 | 1 | – | Ohio | 44 | 10 | 3.2 | 4 | 40 |
| Florida | 54 | 7 | 3.9 | 6 | 48 | Oklahoma | 9 | 41 | 0.7 | 1 | 8 |
| Georgia | 17 | 24 | 1.2 | 2 | 15 | Oregon | 14 | 30 | 1.0 | 2 | 12 |
| Hawaii | 3 | 46 | 0.2 | 2 | 1 | Pennsylvania | 94 | 3 | 6.9 | 6 | 88 |
| Idaho | 9 | 41 | 0.7 | 2 | 7 | Rhode Island | 12 | 36 | 0.9 | 2 | 10 |
| Illinois | 50 | 8 | 3.7 | 5 | 45 | South Carolina | 26 | 17 | 1.9 | 2 | 24 |
| Indiana | 42 | 11 | 3.1 | – | 42 | South Dakota | 2 | 47 | 0.1 | 1 | 1 |
| Iowa | 13 | 33 | 0.9 | 1 | 12 | Tennessee | 18 | 22 | 1.3 | 3 | 15 |
| Kansas | 13 | 33 | 0.9 | 1 | 12 | Texas | 56 | 6 | 4.1 | 4 | 52 |
| Kentucky | 13 | 33 | 0.9 | 1 | 12 | Utah | 16 | 26 | 1.2 | 5 | 11 |
| Louisiana | 16 | 26 | 1.2 | 1 | 15 | Vermont | 12 | 36 | 0.9 | – | 12 |
| Maine | 12 | 36 | 0.9 | 3 | 9 | Virginia | 31 | 16 | 2.3 | 11 | 20 |
| Maryland | 21 | 19 | 1.5 | 10 | 11 | Washington | 48 | 9 | 3.5 | 13 | 35 |
| Massachusetts | 32 | 15 | 2.3 | 6 | 26 | West Virginia | 10 | 39 | 0.7 | 2 | 8 |
| Michigan | 68 | 5 | 5.0 | 1 | 67 | Wisconsin | 37 | 13 | 2.7 | – | 37 |
| Minnesota | 25 | 18 | 1.8 | 2 | 23 | Wyoming | 2 | 47 | 0.1 | 1 | 1 |
| Mississippi | 10 | 39 | 0.7 | – | 10 | Puerto Rico | 19 | (X) | (X) | 1 | 18 |

– Represents zero. X Not applicable. [1] Total includes areas not shown separately.

Source: U.S. Environmental Protection Agency, "Superfund National Priorities List," <http://www.epa.gov/superfund>, accessed August 2019.

## Table 426. Hazardous Waste Generated, Shipped, and Received by State and Other Areas: 2017

[In thousands of tons (35,155.7 represents 33,151,700). Covers hazardous waste regulated under the Resource Conservation and Recovery Act (RCRA) of 1976 as amended. See source for data exclusions]

| State and other area | Hazardous waste quantity | | | State and other area | Hazardous waste quantity | | |
|---|---|---|---|---|---|---|---|
| | Generated | Shipped | Received | | Generated | Shipped | Received |
| **Total.**.................... | **35,155.7** | **6,493.8** | **6,354.5** | Montana....................... | 36.8 | 36.8 | – |
| **United States**.............. | **35,133.8** | **6,474.3** | **6,354.1** | Nebraska....................... | 29.7 | 43.0 | 56.5 |
| Alabama....................... | 706.3 | 204.7 | 448.0 | Nevada.......................... | 21.9 | 27.2 | 95.2 |
| Alaska......................... | 2.2 | 2.1 | 0.2 | New Hampshire............... | 4.9 | 4.9 | – |
| Arizona........................ | 190.9 | 33.6 | 9.3 | New Jersey.................... | 243.3 | 239.9 | 145.6 |
| Arkansas...................... | 334.9 | 243.9 | 275.0 | New Mexico................... | 4.3 | 6.1 | 2.3 |
| California...................... | 345.4 | 659.3 | 198.1 | New York....................... | 157.1 | 141.6 | 56.3 |
| Colorado....................... | 28.9 | 35.7 | 29.1 | North Carolina................ | 80.2 | 93.7 | 22.2 |
| Connecticut................... | 47.5 | 47.5 | 19.0 | North Dakota.................. | 421.8 | 2.1 | 0.1 |
| Delaware...................... | 11.1 | 11.0 | 0.1 | Ohio............................. | 1,580.6 | 547.3 | 638.8 |
| District of Columbia.......... | 0.8 | 0.8 | – | Oklahoma...................... | 103.0 | 79.1 | 181.7 |
| Florida......................... | 141.1 | 47.2 | 13.7 | Oregon......................... | 52.5 | 46.7 | 67.2 |
| Georgia........................ | 86.3 | 61.4 | 0.5 | Pennsylvania.................. | 308.2 | 257.6 | 380.3 |
| Hawaii......................... | 499.2 | 0.7 | (Z) | Rhode Island.................. | 8.0 | 15.3 | 8.0 |
| Idaho.......................... | 10.6 | 8.8 | 24.0 | South Carolina................ | 164.5 | 192.3 | 337.3 |
| Illinois......................... | 676.5 | 228.4 | 262.8 | South Dakota.................. | 2.0 | 2.1 | 0.1 |
| Indiana........................ | 951.8 | 444.2 | 576.5 | Tennessee..................... | 162.3 | 91.7 | 97.7 |
| Iowa........................... | 56.4 | 55.8 | 0.2 | Texas........................... | 17,761.3 | 704.0 | 625.7 |
| Kansas........................ | 1,210.6 | 92.5 | 122.6 | Utah............................ | 34.4 | 76.6 | 169.9 |
| Kentucky...................... | 111.8 | 160.0 | 78.5 | Vermont........................ | 2.1 | 3.4 | 148.4 |
| Louisiana...................... | 5,015.9 | 444.3 | 339.0 | Virginia......................... | 61.1 | 61.4 | 0.4 |
| Maine.......................... | 2.1 | 2.2 | 0.6 | Washington.................... | 107.0 | 72.5 | 24.6 |
| Maryland....................... | 42.8 | 43.3 | 34.5 | West Virginia.................. | 65.3 | 50.6 | 12.9 |
| Massachusetts............... | 31.8 | 38.9 | 10.7 | Wisconsin...................... | 215.0 | 231.7 | 100.7 |
| Michigan....................... | 368.8 | 349.0 | 481.9 | Wyoming....................... | 4.7 | 4.7 | – |
| Minnesota..................... | 84.7 | 52.2 | 27.3 | Guam........................... | 0.2 | 0.2 | 0.1 |
| Mississippi.................... | 2,259.1 | 101.1 | 23.8 | Puerto Rico.................... | 19.1 | 16.7 | 0.3 |
| Missouri....................... | 284.5 | 73.7 | 206.9 | Virgin Islands................. | 2.6 | 2.6 | – |

– Represents zero. Z Less than 50.

Source: U.S. Environmental Protection Agency, Office of Resource Conservation and Recovery, RCRAInfo Web, "Biennial Report," <https://rcrainfo.epa.gov/rcrainfoweb/>, accessed March 2019.

## Table 427. Oil Spills in U.S. Water—Number and Volume: 2000 to 2017

[Based on reported discharges of oil and petroleum based products into U.S. navigable waters, including territorial waters (extending 3 to 12 miles from the coastline), tributaries, the contiguous zone, onto shoreline, or into other waters that threaten the marine environment. Data from the U.S. Coast Guard; see also *Polluting Incidents In and Around U.S. Waters, A Spill/Release Compendium: 1969–2011*]

| Spill source | Number of spills | | | | | Spill volume (gallons) | | | | |
|---|---|---|---|---|---|---|---|---|---|---|
| | 2000 | 2010 | 2015 | 2016 | 2017 | 2000 | 2010 | 2015 | 2016 | 2017 |
| **Total**..................... | **8,354** | **3,008** | **2,873** | **2,663** | **2,472** | **1,431,370** | **207,712,793** | **301,482** | **301,723** | **241,204** |
| **Vessel sources, total**.......... | **5,560** | **1,508** | **1,545** | **1,500** | **1,390** | **1,033,643** | **894,934** | **296,520** | **238,651** | **214,153** |
| Tankship.................. | 111 | 23 | 75 | 73 | 10 | 608,176 | 421,583 | 147,087 | 32,165 | 100 |
| Tank barge................ | 229 | 73 | 24 | 17 | 50 | 133,540 | 965 | 1,147 | 87,416 | 84,319 |
| Other vessels [1]........... | 5,220 | 1,412 | 1,446 | 1,410 | 1,330 | 291,927 | 472,386 | 148,286 | 119,070 | 129,734 |
| **Nonvessel sources, total**..... | **1,645** | **1,008** | **931** | **943** | **887** | **373,761** | **206,809,141** | **63,027** | **59,318** | **22,184** |
| Offshore pipelines......... | 4 | 34 | 26 | 22 | 16 | 17 | 4,627 | 474 | 9,139 | 83 |
| Onshore pipelines......... | 21 | – | – | – | – | 17,004 | – | – | – | – |
| Other [2]................... | 1,620 | 974 | 905 | 921 | 871 | 356,740 | 206,804,514 | 62,553 | 50,179 | 22,101 |
| **Unknown source**.............. | **1,149** | **492** | **397** | **220** | **195** | **23,966** | **8,718** | **1,935** | **3,754** | **4,868** |

– Represents zero. [1] Commercial vessels, fishing boats, freight barges, freight ships, industrial vessels, oil recovery vessels, passenger vessels, unclassified public vessels, recreational boats, research vessels, school ships, tow and tug boats, mobile offshore drilling units, offshore supply vessels, publicly owned tank and freight ships, and vessels not fitting any particular class (unclassified). [2] Deepwater ports, designated waterfront facilities, nonmarine land facilities, fixed offshore and inshore platforms, mobile facility, municipal facility, aircraft, land vehicles, railroad equipment, bridges, factories, fleeting areas, industrial facilities, intakes, locks, marinas, MARPOL reception facilities, nonvessel common carrier facilities, outfalls, sewers, drains, permanently moored facilities, shipyards, and ship repair facilities.

Source: U.S. Bureau of Transportation Statistics, "National Transportation Statistics," <https://www.bts.gov/topics/national-transportation-statistics>, accessed November 2018.

## Table 428. Petroleum and Hazardous Waste Underground Storage Tanks, Releases, and Corrective Actions: 2010 to 2018

[For year ending September 30. EPA collects data from states and territories regarding Underground Storage Tank (UST) systems storing either petroleum or certain hazardous substances. Approximately 1,200 substances (excluding radionuclides) are identified as hazardous under the Comprehensive Environmental Response, Compensation, and Liability Act (CERCLA). See <https://www.epa.gov/ust>.]

| Year | Active tanks | Closed tanks | Confirmed releases | | Cleanups initiated [1] | Cleanups completed | | Cleanups remaining |
|---|---|---|---|---|---|---|---|---|
| | | | Current year actions | Cumulative | | Current year actions | Cumulative | |
| 2010.......... | 597,333 | 1,748,204 | 6,328 | 494,997 | 470,460 | 11,591 | 401,874 | 93,123 |
| 2014.......... | 570,731 | 1,816,695 | 6,847 | 521,271 | 498,173 | 10,393 | 447,323 | 73,948 |
| 2015.......... | 565,956 | 1,823,543 | 6,830 | 528,521 | 505,468 | 9,869 | 456,660 | 71,861 |
| 2016.......... | 560,872 | 1,840,070 | 5,582 | 532,420 | 510,426 | 8,977 | 461,441 | 70,979 |
| 2017.......... | 555,079 | 1,856,451 | 5,678 | 538,193 | 516,882 | 8,775 | 469,898 | 68,295 |
| 2018.......... | 550,379 | 1,871,148 | 5,654 | 543,812 | 522,801 | 8,128 | 478,366 | 65,446 |

[1] Cleanups initiated Hare cumulative. Even as a cleanup progresses and is completed, it is still counted in the cleanups initiated category.

Source: Environmental Protection Agency, "Underground Storage Tanks (USTs), UST Performance Measures," <https://www.epa.gov/ust/ust-performance-measures>, accessed February 2019.

## Table 429. Tornadoes, Floods, Tropical Storms, and Lightning: 2000 to 2018

[424 represents $424,000,000]

| Weather type | 2000 | 2005 | 2010 | 2012 | 2013 | 2014 | 2015 | 2016 | 2017 | 2018 |
|---|---|---|---|---|---|---|---|---|---|---|
| Tornadoes: [1] | | | | | | | | | | |
| Number | 1,072 | 1,262 | 1,282 | 938 | 906 | 886 | 1,177 | 976 | 1,429 | 1,124 |
| Lives lost | 41 | 38 | 45 | 70 | 55 | 47 | 36 | 18 | 35 | 10 |
| Injuries | 882 | 537 | 699 | 822 | 756 | 641 | 924 | 325 | 516 | 199 |
| Property loss (mil. dol.) | 424 | 422 | 1,107 | 1,649 | 3,642 | 622 | 317 | 181 | 632 | 670 |
| Floods and flash floods: | | | | | | | | | | |
| Lives lost | 38 | 43 | 103 | 29 | 82 | 40 | 187 | 126 | 116 | 80 |
| Injuries | 47 | 38 | 310 | 25 | 33 | 20 | 50 | 31 | 19 | 21 |
| Property loss (mil. dol.) | 1,255 | 1,538 | 3,927 | 494 | 2,173 | 2,626 | 2,277 | 10,708 | 60,576 | 1,188 |
| North Atlantic tropical cyclones and hurricanes: [2] | 15 | 27 | 21 | 19 | 15 | 9 | 12 | 16 | 18 | 15 |
| Hurricanes | 8 | 15 | 12 | 10 | 2 | 6 | 4 | 7 | 10 | 8 |
| Lives lost | – | 1,016 | – | 4 | 1 | – | 14 | 11 | 43 | 7 |
| Property loss (mil. dol.) | 8 | 93,064 | 15 | 172 | 10 | 3 | 41 | 3,054 | 22,383 | 12,145 |
| Lightning: | | | | | | | | | | |
| Deaths | 51 | 38 | 29 | 28 | 23 | 26 | 27 | 38 | 16 | 20 |
| Injuries | 364 | 309 | 182 | 139 | 145 | 154 | 130 | 120 | 86 | 82 |

– Represents zero. [1] Source: U.S. National Weather Service, <http://www.spc.noaa.gov/climo/online/monthly/newm.html>. A violent, rotating column of air descending from a cumulonimbus cloud in the form of a tubular- or funnel-shaped cloud, usually characterized by movements along a narrow path and wind speeds from 100 to over 300 miles per hour. Also known as a "twister" or "waterspout." [2] Tropical cyclones include depressions, storms and hurricanes. Fatalities are assumed to be caused by wind-driven debris or structural failure due to winds. For data on individual hurricanes, see National Hurricane Center (NHC) at <http://www.nhc.noaa.gov/>.

Source: Except as noted, U.S. National Oceanic and Atmospheric Administration (NOAA), National Weather Service (NWS), Office of Climate, Water, and Weather Services, "Natural Hazard Statistics," <http://www.nws.noaa.gov/om/hazstats.shtml>, accessed August 2019.

## Table 430. Number of Earthquakes in the United States: 2000 to 2012

[For information by region, see <https://earthquake.usgs.gov/earthquakes/byregion>]

| Magnitude (Richter seismic scale) | 2000 | 2004 | 2005 | 2006 | 2007 | 2008 | 2009 | 2010 | 2011 | 2012 | Top earthquake states | 1974–2003 [1] |
|---|---|---|---|---|---|---|---|---|---|---|---|---|
| Total | 2,342 | 3,550 | 3,685 | 2,783 | 2,791 | 3,618 | 4,262 | 8,496 | 5,237 | 3,365 | Total | 21,080 |
| 8.0 to 9.9 | – | – | – | – | – | – | – | – | – | – | AK | [2] 12,053 |
| 7.0 to 7.9 | – | – | 1 | – | 1 | – | – | 1 | 1 | – | CA | 4,895 |
| 6.0 to 6.9 | 6 | 2 | 4 | 7 | 9 | 9 | 4 | 8 | 3 | 4 | HI | 1,533 |
| 5.0 to 5.9 | 63 | 25 | 47 | 51 | 72 | 85 | 58 | 89 | 51 | 25 | NV | 778 |
| 4.0 to 4.9 | 281 | 284 | 345 | 346 | 366 | 432 | 288 | 631 | 347 | 250 | WA | 424 |
| 3.0 to 3.9 | 917 | 1,362 | 1,475 | 1,213 | 1,137 | 1,486 | 1,492 | 3,584 | 1,838 | 1,096 | ID | 404 |
| 2.0 to 2.9 | 660 | 1,336 | 1,738 | 1,145 | 1,173 | 1,573 | 2,379 | 4,132 | 2,941 | 1,951 | WY | 217 |
| 1.0 to 1.9 | – | 1 | 2 | 7 | 11 | 13 | 26 | 39 | 47 | 34 | MT | 186 |
| 0.1 to 0.9 | – | – | – | 1 | – | – | 1 | – | 1 | – | UT | 139 |
| No magnitude | 415 | 540 | 73 | 13 | 22 | 20 | 14 | 12 | 8 | 5 | OR | 73 |

– Represents zero. [1] The total number represents earthquakes of a magnitude range of 3.5 and greater. [2] The number of earthquakes is underreported. Events in the magnitude range of 3.5 to 4.0 in the Aleutian Islands are not recorded on enough seismograph stations to be located.

Source: U.S. Geological Survey, *Earthquake Facts and Statistics*, <http://earthquake.usgs.gov/earthquakes>, accessed August 2016.

## Table 431. Wildland Fires, Number, and Acres: 1970 to 2018

[Acres in thousands (3,278.6 represents 3,278,600). As of December 31. Wildland fire is any nonstructural fire that occurs in the wildland. Wildland fires include those that are unplanned and unwanted, and include unauthorized human-caused fires, and escaped prescribed fire projects)]

| Year | Total [1] Fires | Total [1] Acres (1,000) | Year | Total [1] Fires | Total [1] Acres (1,000) | State | Top states ranked by wildland acres burned in 2018 [1] Fires | Top states ranked by wildland acres burned in 2018 [1] Acres (1,000) |
|---|---|---|---|---|---|---|---|---|
| 1970 | 121,736 | 3,278.6 | 2007 | 85,705 | 9,328.0 | Total | 58,083 | 8,767.5 |
| 1975 | 134,872 | 1,791.3 | 2008 | 78,949 | 5,292.5 | CA | 8,054 | 1,823.2 |
| 1980 | 234,892 | 5,260.8 | 2009 | 78,792 | 5,921.8 | NV | 649 | 1,002.0 |
| 1985 | 82,591 | 2,896.1 | 2010 | 71,971 | 3,422.7 | OR | 2,019 | 897.3 |
| 1990 | 66,481 | 4,621.6 | 2011 | 74,126 | 8,711.4 | OK | 1,707 | 745.1 |
| 1995 | 82,234 | 1,840.5 | 2012 | 67,774 | 9,326.2 | ID | 1,132 | 604.5 |
| 2000 | 92,250 | 7,393.5 | 2013 | 47,579 | 4,319.5 | TX | 10,541 | 569.8 |
| 2003 | 63,629 | 3,960.8 | 2014 | 63,612 | 3,595.6 | CO | 1,328 | 475.8 |
| 2004 [2] | 65,461 | 8,097.9 | 2015 | 68,151 | 10,125.1 | UT | 1,333 | 439.0 |
| 2005 | 66,753 | 8,689.4 | 2016 | 67,743 | 5,510.0 | WA | 1,743 | 438.8 |
| 2006 | 96,385 | 9,873.7 | 2017 | 71,499 | 10,026.1 | AK | 367 | 410.7 |

[1] Data are for wildland fires only. Data do not include prescribed fires. [2] 2004 fires and acres do not include state lands for North Carolina.

Source: National Interagency Coordination Center, *Wildland Fire Summary and Statistics Annual Report, 2018*, and earlier reports. See also <http://www.predictiveservices.nifc.gov/intelligence/intelligence.htm>.

# Table 432. Major U.S. Weather and Climate Disasters: 2018

[24.2 represents $24,200,000,000. Cost in CPI-adjusted dollars. Covers only weather and climate related disasters costing $1 billion or more. See source for more information]

| Event | Description | Time period | Estimated cost (bil. dol.) | Deaths (number) |
|---|---|---|---|---|
| Western Wildfires, California Firestorm | In 2018, California experienced its costliest, deadliest, and largest wildfires to date, with records back to 1933. The Camp Fire was the costliest and deadliest wildfire - destroying more than 18,500 buildings. California also endured its largest wildfire on record - the Medincino Complex Fire - burning over 450,000 acres. Additionally, California was impacted by other destructive wildfires: the Carr Fire in Northern California and the Woolsey Fire in Southern California. The total 2018 wildfire costs in California (with minor costs in other Western states) approach $24 billion - a new U.S. record. In total, over 8.7 million acres has burned across the U.S. during 2018, which is well above the 10-year average (2009-2018) of 6.8 million acres. The last 2 years of U.S. wildfire damage has been unprecedented in damage, with losses exceeding $40 billion. | June 1 to Dec. 31, 2018 | 24.2 | 106 |
| Southwest/ Southern Plains Drought | Drought conditions were present across numerous Southwestern and Plains states (TX, OK, KS, MO, CO, NM, AZ, UT). The most extreme drought conditions continue to persist across the Four Corners region of the Southwest. The agriculture sector has been impacted across the affected states including damage to field crops from lack of rainfall. Ranchers have also been forced to sell-off livestock early in some regions due to high feeding costs. | June 1 to Dec. 30, 2018 | 3.0 | – |
| Hurricane Michael | A category 5 hurricane made landfall at Mexico Beach, Florida with devastating winds of 160 mph and storm surge in excess of 15 feet. Mexico Beach was nearly destroyed, while Panama City suffered extensive damage. Florida's Tyndall Air Force Base suffered a direct strike from Michael's most intense eye wall winds causing billions of dollars in damage. Michael's intense winds also reached well inland causing billions of dollars in damage to agriculture and forestry, as high winds hit during harvest season for numerous crops across several states. | October, 10-11, 2018 | 25.2 | 49 |
| Hurricane Florence | Hurricane Florence was a large and very slow moving hurricane that produced extreme rainfall across eastern North Carolina (up to 35.93") and South Carolina (up to 23.81"). Florence made landfall as a category 1, at Wrightsville Beach, NC with damaging storm surge up to 10 feet and wind gusts reported over 100 mph. However, the majority of the damage caused by Florence was due to the rainfall inland, which caused many rivers to surpass previous record flood heights. U.S. Marine base Camp Lejeune in North Carolina suffered extensive damage that will cost billions of dollars to repair. | September 13-16, 2018 | 24.2 | 53 |
| Rockies and Plains Hail Storms | Severe hail impacts from baseball to softball size impacted several states including Colorado, Nebraska and Wyoming. The most costly impacts occurred in numerous locations of eastern Colorado. | August 6-7, 2018 | 1.0 | – |
| Central and Eastern Tornadoes and Severe Weather | At least 41 tornadoes and high wind damage from thunderstorms impact numerous Central and Eastern states (MO, IA, IL, IN, KS, KY, AL, AR, GA, TN, NC, SC, VA, MD, PA) over a multi-day event. The tornado damage was most severe across Iowa. | July 19-22, 2018 | 1.6 | – |
| Colorado Hail Storm | Severe hail storms cause golf ball to baseball-sized hail and widespread damage in many areas from northern Denver to Boulder and Fort Collins. Many homes, businesses and vehicles were impacted. Utah also experienced moderate hail damage. | June 18-19, 2018 | 2.2 | – |
| Texas Hail Storm | Large-hail impacts highly-populated area of the Dallas-Ft. Worth metroplex. Golf ball to baseball-sized hail damaged many homes, vehicles and businesses. | June 6, 2018 | 1.3 | – |
| Central and Eastern Severe Weather | Severe storm damage across many Central states including TX, KS, CO, OK, MO, IL, IN, IA and OH. This was followed by a derecho event across MD, NJ, NY, PA, VA, WV, MA and CT that caused widespread high wind damage. Additionally, a dozen tornadoes reported across PA, NY and CT caused further damage. | May 13-15, 2018 | 1.4 | 5 |
| Central and Northeastern Severe Weather | Numerous central states (KS, NE, OK, TX, NM, MO, IA, IL, IN, OH, WI) were impacted by large hail and tornadoes. Northeastern states (NY, PA and VT) were impacted by high wind damage from severe storms. | May 1-4, 2018 | 1.4 | – |
| Southern and Eastern Tornadoes and Severe Weather | Tornadoes and severe storms with large hail cause widespread damage across many Southern and Eastern states (AR, FL, GA, LA, MD, MI, MS, MO, NJ, NY, NC, PA, SC, TX, VA) over a multi-day period. There were over 70 confirmed tornadoes largely clustered in Louisiana, Mississippi, North Carolina and Virginia. This same system also caused winter storm impacts of high wind and ice accumulation in northeastern states. | April 13-15, 2018 | 1.3 | 3 |
| Southeastern Tornadoes and Severe Weather | A potent severe storm system caused over 20 tornadoes across Alabama and also widespread hail damage from Texas to Florida. Most notably this system produced an EF-3 tornado that caused extensive damage in Jacksonville, Alabama and across the campus of Jacksonville State University. | March 18-21, 2018 | 1.5 | – |
| Northeast Winter Storm | Powerful Nor'easter impacted many northeastern states including MD, MA, NH, NJ, NY, PA, CT, DE, RA and VA. Widespread damage resulted from high winds, heavy snow and heavy coastal erosion. | March 1-3, 2018 | 2.2 | 9 |
| Central and Eastern Winter Storm | A Nor'easter caused damage across many Northeastern states including MA, NJ, NY, CT, ME, NH, PA, MD, RI, SC, TN, VA, NC and GA. | January 3-5, 2018 | 1.1 | 22 |

– Represents zero.

Source: U.S. National Oceanic and Atmospheric Administration, National Centers for Environmental Information, "Billion-Dollar Weather and Climate Disasters, 1980-2018," <http://www.ncdc.noaa.gov/billions/events>, accessed June 2019.

# Table 433. Highest and Lowest Temperatures by State Through 2016

[Data have been evaluated by the National Oceanic and Atmospheric Administration National Climatic Data Center, and/or by the State Climate Extremes Committee and determined to be valid. The data may come from sources other than official NOAA-supervised weather stations, but are archived, officially recognized observations]

| State | Highest temperatures | | | Lowest temperatures | | |
|---|---|---|---|---|---|---|
| | Station | Temperature (°F) | Date | Station | Temperature (°F) | Date |
| **U.S.**......... | **Greenland Ranch, CA** | **134** | **July 10, 1913** | **Prospect Creek Camp, AK** | **-80** | **Jan. 23, 1971** |
| AL............ | Centerville | 112 | Sep. 5, 1925 | New Market | -27 | Jan. 30, 1966 |
| AK............ | Fort Yukon | 100 | June 27, 1915 | Prospect Creek Camp | -80 | Jan. 23, 1971 |
| AZ............ | Lake Havasu City | 128 | June 29, 1994 | Hawley Lake | -40 | Jan. 7, 1971 |
| AR............ | Ozark | 120 | Aug. 10, 1936 | Gravette | -29 | Feb. 13, 1905 |
| CA............ | Greenland Ranch | 134 | July 10, 1913 | Boca | -45 | Jan. 20, 1937 |
| CO........... | Sedgwick | 114 | [1] July 11, 1954 | Maybell | -61 | Feb. 1, 1985 |
| CT............ | Danbury | 106 | [1] July 15, 1995 | Coventry | -32 | [1] Jan. 22, 1961 |
| DE............ | Millsboro | 110 | July 21, 1930 | Millsboro | -17 | Jan. 17, 1893 |
| FL............. | Monticello | 109 | June 29, 1931 | Tallahassee | -2 | Feb. 13, 1899 |
| GA........... | Greenville 2 NNW | 112 | [1] Aug. 20, 1983 | CCC Camp F-16 | -17 | Jan. 27, 1940 |
| HI............. | Pahala | 100 | Apr. 27, 1931 | Mauna Kea Obs. 111.2 | 12 | May 17, 1979 |
| ID............. | Orofino | 118 | July 28, 1934 | Island Park Dam | -60 | Jan. 18, 1943 |
| IL.............. | East St. Louis | 117 | July 14, 1954 | Congerville | -36 | Jan. 5, 1999 |
| IN............. | Collegeville | 116 | July 14, 1936 | New Whiteland | -36 | Jan. 19, 1994 |
| IA............. | Keokuk | 118 | July 20, 1934 | Elkader | -47 | [1] Feb. 3, 1996 |
| KS........... | Alton | 121 | July 24, 1936 | Lebanon | -40 | Feb. 13, 1905 |
| KY........... | Greensburg | 114 | July 28, 1930 | Shelbyville | -37 | Jan. 19, 1994 |
| LA............ | Plain Dealing | 114 | Aug. 10, 1936 | Minden | -16 | Feb. 13, 1899 |
| ME............ | North Bridgton | 105 | [1] July 10, 1911 | Big Black River | -48 | Jan. 16, 2009 |
| MD........... | Cumberland & Frederick | 109 | [1] July 10, 1936 | Oakland | -40 | Jan. 13, 1912 |
| MA........... | New Bedford & Chester | 107 | [1] Aug. 2, 1975 | Chester | -35 | [1] Jan. 12, 1981 |
| MI............ | Mio Hydro Plant & Stanwood | 112 | July 13, 1936 | Vanderbilt | -51 | Feb. 9, 1934 |
| MN........... | Beardsley | 115 | July 29, 1917 | Tower | -60 | Feb. 2, 1996 |
| MS........... | Holly Springs | 115 | July 29, 1930 | Corinth | -19 | Jan. 30, 1966 |
| MO........... | Warsaw & Union | 118 | [1] July 14, 1954 | Warsaw | -40 | Feb. 13, 1905 |
| MT........... | Medicine Lake | 117 | [1] July 5, 1937 | Rogers Pass | -70 | Jan. 20, 1954 |
| NE........... | Minden | 118 | [1] July 24, 1936 | Oshkosh | -47 | [1] Dec. 22, 1989 |
| NV........... | Laughlin | 125 | June 29, 1994 | San Jacinto | -50 | Jan. 8, 1937 |
| NH........... | Nashua | 106 | July 4, 1911 | Mt. Washington | -47 | Jan. 22, 1885 |
| NJ............ | Runyon | 110 | July 10, 1936 | River Vale | -34 | Jan. 5, 1904 |
| NM........... | Waste Isolation Pilot Plant | 122 | June 27, 1994 | Gavilan | -50 | Feb. 1, 1951 |
| NY........... | Troy | 108 | July 22, 1926 | Old Forge | -52 | Feb. 18, 1979 |
| NC........... | Fayetteville | 110 | Aug. 21, 1983 | Mt. Mitchell | -34 | Jan. 21, 1985 |
| ND........... | Steele | 121 | July 6, 1936 | Parshall | -60 | Feb. 15, 1936 |
| OH........... | Gallipolis (near) | 113 | July 21, 1934 | Milligan | -39 | Feb. 10, 1899 |
| OK........... | Altus Irig Res | 120 | [1] Aug. 12, 1936 | Nowata | -31 | Feb. 10, 2011 |
| OR........... | Pendleton. | 119 | [1] Aug. 10, 1898 | Seneca | -54 | [1] Feb. 10, 1933 |
| PA............ | Phoenixville | 111 | July 10, 1936 | Smethport | -42 | Jan. 5, 1904 |
| RI............. | Providence | 104 | Aug. 2, 1975 | Wood River Junction | -25 | Jan. 11, 1942 |
| SC............ | Columbis Univ. of SC | 113 | June 29, 2012 | Caesars Head | -19 | Jan. 21, 1985 |
| SD........... | Fort Pierre | 120 | [1] July 15, 2006 | McIntosh | -58 | Feb. 17, 1936 |
| TN............ | Perryville | 113 | Aug. 9, 1930 | Mountain City | -32 | Dec. 30, 1917 |
| TX............ | Monahans | 120 | [1] June 28, 1994 | Seminole | -23 | Feb. 8, 1933 |
| UT............ | Saint George | 117 | July 5, 1985 | East Portal | -69 | Jan. 5, 1913 |
| VT............ | Vernon | 107 | July 7, 1912 | Bloomfield | -50 | Dec. 30, 1933 |
| VA............ | Balcony Falls | 110 | [1] July 15, 1954 | Mtn. Lake Bio. Stn. | -30 | Jan. 22, 1985 |
| WA........... | Ice Harbor Dam | 118 | [1] Aug. 5, 1961 | Mazama & Winthrop | -48 | [1] Dec. 30, 1968 |
| WV........... | Martinsburg | 112 | [1] July 10, 1936 | Lewisburg | -37 | Dec. 30, 1917 |
| WI............ | Wisconsin Dells | 114 | July 13, 1936 | Couderay | -55 | [1] Feb. 4, 1996 |
| WY........... | Diversion Dam | 115 | [1] July 15, 1988 | Riverside R.S. | -66 | Feb. 9, 1933 |

[1] Also on earlier dates at the same or other places.

Source: U.S. National Oceanic and Atmospheric Administration, National Climatic Data Center, State Climate Extremes Committee, "Maximum and Minimum Temperature Records," <http://www.ncdc.noaa.gov/extremes/scec/records>, accessed July 2017.

# Table 434. Highest Temperature of Record—Selected Cities

[In degrees Fahrenheit. Airport data, except as noted. Data for each city are shown for varying periods of record; see source for date ranges for each location]

| State | Station | Jan. | Feb. | Mar. | Apr. | May | June | July | Aug. | Sept. | Oct. | Nov. | Dec. | Annual [1] |
|---|---|---|---|---|---|---|---|---|---|---|---|---|---|---|
| AL..... | Mobile | 84 | 84 | 89 | 94 | 100 | 103 | 104 | 105 | 99 | 93 | 88 | 81 | 105 |
| AK..... | Juneau | 60 | 57 | 61 | 74 | 80 | 86 | 90 | 84 | 78 | 63 | 56 | 54 | 90 |
| AZ..... | Phoenix | 88 | 92 | 100 | 105 | 113 | 122 | 121 | 117 | 118 | 107 | 96 | 88 | 122 |
| AK..... | Little Rock | 83 | 85 | 91 | 95 | 98 | 107 | 112 | 114 | 106 | 98 | 86 | 81 | 114 |
| CA.... | Los Angeles | 95 | 95 | 98 | 106 | 102 | 112 | 108 | 105 | 113 | 108 | 100 | 92 | 113 |
| CA. ... | Sacramento | 76 | 78 | 88 | 95 | 105 | 115 | 114 | 110 | 109 | 104 | 87 | 73 | 115 |
| CA.... | San Diego | 88 | 90 | 93 | 98 | 97 | 101 | 99 | 98 | 111 | 107 | 100 | 88 | 111 |
| CA.... | San Francisco | 79 | 81 | 87 | 94 | 93 | 103 | 95 | 98 | 106 | 102 | 86 | 76 | 106 |
| CO.... | Denver | 74 | 83 | 84 | 90 | 96 | 104 | 104 | 102 | 98 | 89 | 81 | 75 | 104 |
| CT..... | Hartford | 72 | 77 | 89 | 96 | 99 | 101 | 103 | 102 | 101 | 91 | 83 | 76 | 103 |
| DE. ... | Wilmington | 75 | 78 | 86 | 94 | 96 | 100 | 103 | 101 | 100 | 91 | 85 | 75 | 103 |
| DC. ... | Washington | 79 | 82 | 89 | 95 | 99 | 104 | 105 | 105 | 101 | 94 | 86 | 79 | 105 |
| FL..... | Jacksonville | 85 | 88 | 91 | 95 | 102 | 103 | 105 | 102 | 100 | 96 | 89 | 85 | 105 |
| FL..... | Miami | 88 | 89 | 93 | 96 | 98 | 98 | 98 | 98 | 97 | 95 | 91 | 89 | 98 |
| GA.... | Atlanta | 79 | 80 | 89 | 93 | 97 | 106 | 105 | 104 | 99 | 95 | 84 | 79 | 106 |
| HI..... | Honolulu | 88 | 88 | 89 | 91 | 93 | 92 | 94 | 93 | 95 | 94 | 93 | 89 | 95 |
| ID..... | Boise | 63 | 71 | 81 | 92 | 99 | 110 | 111 | 110 | 102 | 94 | 78 | 65 | 111 |
| IL...... | Chicago | 65 | 72 | 88 | 91 | 97 | 104 | 104 | 101 | 99 | 91 | 78 | 71 | 104 |
| IL...... | Peoria | 70 | 74 | 86 | 92 | 97 | 105 | 104 | 103 | 100 | 93 | 81 | 71 | 105 |
| IN..... | Indianapolis | 71 | 77 | 85 | 89 | 95 | 104 | 105 | 102 | 100 | 91 | 81 | 74 | 105 |
| IA...... | Des Moines | 67 | 75 | 91 | 93 | 99 | 103 | 106 | 108 | 101 | 95 | 81 | 69 | 108 |
| KS..... | Wichita | 75 | 87 | 89 | 96 | 102 | 110 | 113 | 111 | 108 | 97 | 86 | 83 | 113 |
| KY..... | Louisville | 77 | 82 | 86 | 91 | 95 | 105 | 106 | 105 | 104 | 93 | 85 | 76 | 106 |
| LA..... | New Orleans | 83 | 85 | 89 | 92 | 97 | 101 | 101 | 102 | 101 | 94 | 88 | 85 | 102 |
| ME.... | Portland | 67 | 68 | 88 | 92 | 94 | 98 | 100 | 103 | 95 | 88 | 74 | 71 | 103 |
| MD.... | Baltimore | 75 | 79 | 89 | 94 | 100 | 103 | 106 | 105 | 100 | 99 | 86 | 77 | 106 |
| MA.... | Boston | 72 | 73 | 89 | 94 | 96 | 100 | 103 | 102 | 100 | 90 | 83 | 76 | 103 |
| MI..... | Detroit | 64 | 70 | 86 | 89 | 95 | 104 | 102 | 100 | 98 | 91 | 78 | 69 | 104 |
| MI..... | Sault Ste. Marie | 47 | 49 | 83 | 85 | 89 | 93 | 97 | 98 | 95 | 81 | 74 | 62 | 98 |
| MN.... | Duluth | 48 | 55 | 75 | 88 | 92 | 94 | 97 | 95 | 95 | 86 | 71 | 55 | 97 |
| MN.... | Minneapolis-St. Paul | 58 | 63 | 83 | 95 | 100 | 103 | 105 | 102 | 98 | 90 | 77 | 68 | 105 |
| MS.... | Jackson | 83 | 86 | 89 | 94 | 99 | 105 | 106 | 107 | 104 | 96 | 88 | 84 | 107 |
| MO.... | Kansas City | 74 | 79 | 87 | 93 | 95 | 105 | 107 | 109 | 106 | 95 | 82 | 74 | 109 |
| MO.... | St. Louis | 77 | 85 | 89 | 93 | 98 | 108 | 115 | 107 | 104 | 94 | 85 | 76 | 115 |
| MT.... | Great Falls | 67 | 70 | 78 | 89 | 93 | 101 | 105 | 106 | 98 | 91 | 76 | 69 | 106 |
| NE.... | Omaha | 69 | 78 | 91 | 97 | 101 | 105 | 110 | 107 | 103 | 95 | 83 | 69 | 110 |
| NV.... | Reno | 71 | 75 | 83 | 90 | 97 | 104 | 108 | 105 | 101 | 93 | 77 | 71 | 108 |
| NH.... | Concord | 69 | 74 | 89 | 95 | 97 | 98 | 102 | 101 | 98 | 90 | 80 | 73 | 102 |
| NJ..... | Atlantic City | 78 | 76 | 87 | 94 | 99 | 106 | 105 | 103 | 99 | 90 | 81 | 77 | 106 |
| NM.... | Albuquerque | 69 | 76 | 85 | 89 | 98 | 107 | 105 | 101 | 100 | 91 | 77 | 72 | 107 |
| NY.... | Albany | 71 | 74 | 89 | 93 | 94 | 99 | 100 | 99 | 100 | 91 | 82 | 72 | 100 |
| NY.... | Buffalo | 72 | 71 | 82 | 94 | 91 | 96 | 97 | 99 | 98 | 87 | 80 | 74 | 99 |
| NY.... | New York City Central Park | 72 | 78 | 86 | 96 | 99 | 101 | 106 | 104 | 102 | 94 | 84 | 75 | 106 |
| NC.... | Charlotte | 79 | 82 | 90 | 93 | 100 | 104 | 104 | 104 | 104 | 98 | 85 | 80 | 104 |
| NC.... | Raleigh | 80 | 84 | 92 | 95 | 97 | 105 | 105 | 105 | 104 | 98 | 88 | 81 | 105 |
| ND.... | Bismarck | 63 | 73 | 81 | 93 | 96 | 111 | 112 | 107 | 105 | 95 | 79 | 65 | 112 |
| OH.... | Cincinnati | 74 | 79 | 84 | 89 | 93 | 102 | 104 | 102 | 102 | 91 | 82 | 75 | 104 |
| OH.... | Cleveland | 73 | 77 | 83 | 88 | 93 | 104 | 103 | 102 | 101 | 90 | 82 | 77 | 104 |
| OH.... | Columbus | 74 | 78 | 85 | 89 | 93 | 101 | 104 | 101 | 100 | 91 | 80 | 76 | 104 |
| OK.... | Oklahoma City | 80 | 92 | 93 | 100 | 104 | 105 | 110 | 113 | 108 | 96 | 87 | 86 | 113 |
| OR.... | Portland | 66 | 71 | 80 | 90 | 100 | 102 | 107 | 107 | 105 | 92 | 73 | 65 | 107 |
| PA..... | Philadelphia | 74 | 77 | 86 | 95 | 97 | 100 | 104 | 101 | 100 | 89 | 84 | 73 | 104 |
| PA..... | Pittsburgh | 75 | 78 | 83 | 89 | 91 | 98 | 103 | 100 | 97 | 89 | 82 | 74 | 103 |
| RI..... | Providence | 69 | 72 | 85 | 98 | 96 | 97 | 102 | 104 | 100 | 88 | 81 | 77 | 104 |
| SC.... | Columbia | 84 | 84 | 91 | 94 | 101 | 109 | 107 | 107 | 101 | 101 | 90 | 83 | 109 |
| SD.... | Sioux Falls | 66 | 70 | 88 | 94 | 104 | 110 | 110 | 109 | 104 | 94 | 81 | 63 | 110 |
| TN.... | Memphis | 79 | 81 | 86 | 94 | 99 | 104 | 108 | 107 | 103 | 95 | 86 | 81 | 108 |
| TN..... | Nashville | 78 | 84 | 87 | 91 | 95 | 109 | 107 | 106 | 105 | 94 | 88 | 79 | 109 |
| TX..... | Dallas | 88 | 95 | 97 | 100 | 103 | 112 | 112 | 111 | 110 | 100 | 92 | 89 | 112 |
| TX..... | El Paso | 80 | 85 | 93 | 98 | 105 | 114 | 112 | 108 | 104 | 96 | 87 | 80 | 114 |
| TX..... | Houston | 84 | 91 | 91 | 95 | 99 | 107 | 104 | 109 | 109 | 96 | 89 | 85 | 109 |
| UT..... | Salt Lake City | 63 | 69 | 80 | 89 | 99 | 105 | 107 | 106 | 100 | 89 | 75 | 69 | 107 |
| VT..... | Burlington | 66 | 72 | 84 | 91 | 93 | 100 | 100 | 101 | 98 | 85 | 75 | 68 | 101 |
| VA..... | Norfolk | 80 | 82 | 88 | 97 | 100 | 101 | 105 | 104 | 99 | 95 | 86 | 82 | 105 |
| VA..... | Richmond | 81 | 82 | 91 | 96 | 100 | 104 | 105 | 104 | 103 | 99 | 86 | 81 | 105 |
| WA.... | Seattle | 64 | 70 | 78 | 89 | 93 | 96 | 103 | 99 | 98 | 89 | 74 | 66 | 103 |
| WA.... | Spokane | 62 | 63 | 72 | 90 | 97 | 105 | 108 | 108 | 98 | 87 | 70 | 60 | 108 |
| WV.... | Charleston | 79 | 81 | 89 | 94 | 94 | 103 | 104 | 104 | 102 | 93 | 85 | 80 | 104 |
| WI..... | Milwaukee | 63 | 71 | 84 | 91 | 95 | 101 | 103 | 103 | 98 | 89 | 77 | 68 | 103 |
| WY.... | Cheyenne | 70 | 71 | 76 | 83 | 91 | 100 | 100 | 98 | 95 | 84 | 75 | 69 | 100 |
| PR. ... | San Juan | 92 | 96 | 96 | 97 | 96 | 97 | 95 | 97 | 97 | 98 | 96 | 94 | 98 |

[1] Represents the highest observed temperature in any month.

Source: U.S. National Oceanic and Atmospheric Administration, *Comparative Climatic Data for the United States Through 2018*. See also <https://www.ncdc.noaa.gov/ghcn/comparative-climatic-data>.

# Table 435. Lowest Temperature of Record—Selected Cities

[In degrees Fahrenheit. Airport data, except as noted. Data for each city are shown for varying periods of record; see source for date ranges for each location]

| State | Station | Jan. | Feb. | Mar. | Apr. | May | June | July | Aug. | Sept. | Oct. | Nov. | Dec. | Annual [1] |
|-------|---------|------|------|------|------|-----|------|------|------|-------|------|------|------|--------|
| AL...... | Mobile | 3 | 11 | 21 | 32 | 43 | 49 | 62 | 59 | 42 | 30 | 22 | 8 | 3 |
| AK...... | Juneau | -22 | -22 | -15 | 6 | 25 | 31 | 36 | 27 | 23 | 11 | -5 | -21 | -22 |
| AZ...... | Phoenix | 17 | 22 | 25 | 34 | 40 | 50 | 61 | 60 | 47 | 34 | 25 | 22 | 17 |
| AR...... | Little Rock | -4 | -5 | 11 | 28 | 38 | 46 | 54 | 52 | 37 | 28 | 17 | -1 | -5 |
| CA...... | Los Angeles | 28 | 29 | 35 | 39 | 43 | 49 | 53 | 51 | 50 | 41 | 38 | 30 | 28 |
| CA.... | Sacramento | 20 | 23 | 26 | 31 | 34 | 41 | 48 | 48 | 42 | 35 | 26 | 18 | 18 |
| CA.... | San Diego | 29 | 36 | 39 | 41 | 48 | 50 | 55 | 57 | 51 | 43 | 38 | 34 | 29 |
| CA.... | San Francisco | 30 | 31 | 35 | 40 | 43 | 47 | 47 | 48 | 48 | 43 | 39 | 27 | 27 |
| CO.... | Denver | -25 | -25 | -10 | -2 | 22 | 30 | 43 | 41 | 17 | 3 | -10 | -25 | -25 |
| CT...... | Hartford | -26 | -21 | -8 | 9 | 28 | 37 | 44 | 36 | 27 | 17 | 1 | -14 | -26 |
| DE..... | Wilmington | -14 | -6 | 2 | 18 | 30 | 41 | 48 | 43 | 36 | 24 | 14 | -7 | -14 |
| DC..... | Washington Nat'l (VA) | -5 | 4 | 14 | 24 | 34 | 47 | 54 | 49 | 39 | 29 | 16 | 3 | -5 |
| FL...... | Jacksonville | 7 | 19 | 23 | 31 | 45 | 47 | 61 | 63 | 48 | 33 | 21 | 11 | 7 |
| FL...... | Miami | 30 | 35 | 32 | 42 | 55 | 60 | 69 | 68 | 68 | 53 | 39 | 30 | 30 |
| GA...... | Atlanta | -8 | 5 | 10 | 26 | 37 | 46 | 53 | 55 | 36 | 28 | 3 | 0 | -8 |
| HI...... | Honolulu | 52 | 53 | 55 | 56 | 60 | 65 | 66 | 65 | 66 | 61 | 57 | 54 | 52 |
| ID...... | Boise | -17 | -15 | 6 | 19 | 22 | 31 | 35 | 34 | 23 | 11 | -3 | -25 | -25 |
| IL...... | Chicago | -27 | -19 | -8 | 7 | 24 | 36 | 40 | 41 | 28 | 17 | 1 | -25 | -27 |
| IL...... | Peoria | -25 | -19 | -10 | 14 | 25 | 39 | 47 | 41 | 29 | 19 | -2 | -23 | -25 |
| IN...... | Indianapolis | -27 | -21 | -7 | 18 | 28 | 37 | 48 | 41 | 32 | 20 | -2 | -23 | -27 |
| IA...... | Des Moines | -24 | -26 | -22 | 9 | 28 | 41 | 47 | 40 | 28 | 14 | -4 | -22 | -26 |
| KS...... | Wichita | -12 | -21 | -2 | 15 | 31 | 43 | 51 | 48 | 31 | 18 | 1 | -16 | -21 |
| KY...... | Louisville | -22 | -19 | -1 | 22 | 31 | 42 | 50 | 46 | 33 | 23 | -1 | -15 | -22 |
| LA...... | New Orleans | 14 | 16 | 25 | 32 | 41 | 50 | 60 | 60 | 42 | 35 | 24 | 11 | 11 |
| ME...... | Portland | -26 | -39 | -21 | 8 | 23 | 33 | 40 | 33 | 23 | 15 | 3 | -21 | -39 |
| MD..... | Baltimore | -7 | -3 | 4 | 20 | 32 | 40 | 50 | 45 | 35 | 25 | 13 | 0 | -7 |
| MA..... | Boston | -12 | -14 | 1 | 16 | 34 | 41 | 50 | 46 | 37 | 25 | 12 | -11 | -14 |
| MI...... | Detroit | -21 | -15 | -4 | 10 | 25 | 36 | 41 | 38 | 29 | 17 | 9 | -10 | -21 |
| MI...... | Sault Ste. Marie | -36 | -37 | -28 | -2 | 18 | 26 | 36 | 29 | 25 | 16 | -10 | -31 | -37 |
| MN..... | Duluth | -39 | -39 | -29 | -5 | 17 | 27 | 35 | 32 | 23 | 8 | -23 | -34 | -39 |
| MN..... | Minneapolis-St. Paul | -34 | -32 | -32 | 2 | 18 | 34 | 43 | 39 | 26 | 13 | -17 | -29 | -34 |
| MS..... | Jackson | 2 | 10 | 15 | 27 | 36 | 47 | 51 | 54 | 35 | 26 | 17 | 4 | 2 |
| MO..... | Kansas City | -17 | -19 | -10 | 12 | 30 | 42 | 51 | 43 | 31 | 17 | 1 | -23 | -23 |
| MO..... | St. Louis | -18 | -12 | -5 | 22 | 31 | 43 | 51 | 47 | 32 | 22 | 1 | -16 | -18 |
| MT..... | Great Falls | -37 | -35 | -29 | -8 | 12 | 31 | 36 | 30 | 16 | -11 | -25 | -43 | -43 |
| NE..... | Omaha | -23 | -21 | -16 | 5 | 27 | 38 | 44 | 43 | 25 | 13 | -9 | -23 | -23 |
| NV..... | Reno | -16 | -16 | 0 | 13 | 18 | 25 | 33 | 24 | 20 | 8 | 1 | -16 | -16 |
| NH..... | Concord | -33 | -37 | -16 | 4 | 21 | 26 | 33 | 29 | 20 | 10 | -5 | -22 | -37 |
| NJ...... | Atlantic City | -10 | -11 | 2 | 12 | 25 | 37 | 42 | 40 | 32 | 20 | 10 | -2 | -11 |
| NM..... | Albuquerque | -17 | -7 | 8 | 18 | 28 | 40 | 52 | 50 | 35 | 21 | -7 | -7 | -17 |
| NY..... | Albany | -28 | -22 | -21 | 10 | 26 | 35 | 40 | 34 | 24 | 16 | -11 | -22 | -28 |
| NY..... | Buffalo | -16 | -20 | -7 | 12 | 26 | 35 | 43 | 38 | 31 | 20 | 7 | -10 | -20 |
| NY..... | Central Park | -6 | -15 | 3 | 12 | 32 | 44 | 52 | 50 | 39 | 28 | 5 | -13 | -15 |
| NC..... | Charlotte | -5 | 5 | 4 | 21 | 32 | 45 | 53 | 50 | 39 | 24 | 11 | 2 | -5 |
| NC..... | Raleigh | -9 | 0 | 11 | 23 | 29 | 38 | 48 | 46 | 37 | 19 | 11 | 4 | -9 |
| ND..... | Bismarck | -44 | -43 | -31 | -12 | 15 | 30 | 35 | 33 | 11 | -10 | -30 | -43 | -44 |
| OH..... | Cincinnati | -25 | -15 | -11 | 15 | 27 | 39 | 47 | 43 | 31 | 16 | 0 | -20 | -25 |
| OH..... | Cleveland | -20 | -17 | -5 | 10 | 25 | 31 | 41 | 38 | 32 | 19 | 3 | -15 | -20 |
| OH..... | Columbus | -22 | -13 | -6 | 14 | 25 | 35 | 43 | 39 | 31 | 17 | -4 | -17 | -22 |
| OK..... | Oklahoma City | -4 | -5 | 1 | 20 | 32 | 47 | 53 | 50 | 36 | 16 | 11 | -8 | -8 |
| OR..... | Portland | -2 | -3 | 19 | 29 | 29 | 39 | 43 | 44 | 34 | 26 | 13 | 6 | -3 |
| PA...... | Philadelphia | -7 | -4 | 7 | 19 | 28 | 44 | 51 | 44 | 35 | 25 | 15 | 1 | -7 |
| PA...... | Pittsburgh | -22 | -12 | -5 | 14 | 26 | 34 | 42 | 39 | 31 | 16 | -1 | -12 | -22 |
| RI...... | Providence | -13 | -9 | 1 | 14 | 29 | 41 | 48 | 40 | 32 | 20 | 6 | -10 | -13 |
| SC..... | Columbia | -1 | 5 | 4 | 26 | 34 | 44 | 54 | 53 | 40 | 23 | 12 | 4 | -1 |
| SD..... | Sioux Falls | -36 | -31 | -23 | 4 | 17 | 33 | 38 | 34 | 22 | 9 | -17 | -28 | -36 |
| TN..... | Memphis | -4 | -11 | 12 | 28 | 36 | 48 | 52 | 48 | 36 | 25 | 9 | -13 | -13 |
| TN..... | Nashville | -17 | -13 | 2 | 23 | 34 | 42 | 54 | 49 | 36 | 26 | -1 | -10 | -17 |
| TX...... | Dallas | 0 | 7 | 11 | 31 | 39 | 53 | 60 | 56 | 36 | 27 | 17 | 1 | 0 |
| TX...... | El Paso | -8 | 1 | 14 | 21 | 31 | 46 | 57 | 56 | 41 | 25 | 1 | 5 | -8 |
| TX...... | Houston | 12 | 20 | 22 | 31 | 42 | 52 | 62 | 60 | 48 | 29 | 19 | 7 | 7 |
| UT...... | Salt Lake City | -22 | -14 | 2 | 15 | 25 | 35 | 40 | 37 | 27 | 16 | -14 | -15 | -22 |
| VT...... | Burlington | -30 | -30 | -20 | 2 | 24 | 33 | 39 | 35 | 25 | 15 | -2 | -26 | -30 |
| VA...... | Norfolk | -3 | 8 | 18 | 28 | 36 | 45 | 54 | 49 | 45 | 27 | 20 | 7 | -3 |
| VA...... | Richmond | -12 | -8 | 10 | 23 | 31 | 40 | 51 | 47 | 35 | 21 | 14 | 1 | -12 |
| WA..... | Seattle | 0 | 1 | 11 | 29 | 28 | 38 | 43 | 44 | 35 | 28 | 6 | 6 | 0 |
| WA..... | Spokane | -24 | -24 | -10 | 14 | 24 | 33 | 37 | 35 | 22 | 7 | -21 | -25 | -25 |
| WV..... | Charleston | -16 | -12 | 0 | 19 | 26 | 33 | 46 | 41 | 34 | 17 | 6 | -12 | -16 |
| WI...... | Milwaukee | -26 | -26 | -10 | 12 | 21 | 33 | 40 | 44 | 28 | 18 | -5 | -20 | -26 |
| WY..... | Cheyenne | -30 | -34 | -21 | -8 | 9 | 25 | 33 | 36 | 8 | -1 | -21 | -28 | -34 |
| PR..... | San Juan | 61 | 62 | 60 | 64 | 66 | 69 | 69 | 70 | 69 | 67 | 66 | 63 | 60 |

[1] Represents the lowest observed temperature in any month.

Source: U.S. National Oceanic and Atmospheric Administration, *Comparative Climatic Data for the United States Through 2018*. See also <https://www.ncdc.noaa.gov/ghcn/comparative-climatic-data>.

# Table 436. Average Snow, Hail, Ice Pellets, and Sleet—Selected Cities

[Average in inches. Data for each city are shown for varying periods of record; see source for date ranges for each location. T denotes trace. Stations may show snowfall (hail) during the warm months]

| State | Station | Jan. | Feb. | Mar. | Apr. | May | June | July | Aug. | Sept. | Oct. | Nov. | Dec. | Annual |
|---|---|---|---|---|---|---|---|---|---|---|---|---|---|---|
| AL..... | Mobile | 0.1 | 0.1 | 0.1 | – | – | – | – | – | – | – | – | 0.1 | 0.4 |
| AK..... | Juneau | 25.3 | 18.1 | 13.9 | 2.5 | – | – | – | – | – | 1.0 | 12.5 | 21.0 | 94.3 |
| AZ..... | Phoenix | – | – | – | – | – | – | – | – | – | – | – | – | – |
| AR..... | Little Rock | 2.0 | 1.5 | 0.5 | – | – | – | – | – | – | – | 0.1 | 0.6 | 4.7 |
| CA..... | Los Angeles | – | – | – | – | – | – | – | – | – | – | – | – | – |
| CA..... | Sacramento | – | – | – | – | – | – | – | – | – | – | – | – | – |
| CA..... | San Diego | – | – | – | – | – | – | – | – | – | – | – | – | – |
| CA..... | San Francisco | – | – | – | – | – | – | – | – | – | – | – | – | – |
| CO.... | Denver | 7.4 | 7.5 | 11.8 | 7.9 | 1.6 | – | – | – | 1.3 | 3.9 | 8.0 | 7.6 | 57.0 |
| CT..... | Hartford | 13.2 | 12.9 | 9.0 | 1.3 | – | – | – | – | – | 0.3 | 1.8 | 9.8 | 48.3 |
| DE..... | Wilmington | 6.6 | 6.8 | 3.2 | 0.2 | – | – | – | – | – | – | 0.7 | 3.3 | 20.8 |
| DC..... | Washington Nat'l (VA) | 5.3 | 5.4 | 2.2 | – | – | – | – | – | – | – | 0.6 | 2.7 | 16.2 |
| FL..... | Jacksonville | – | – | – | – | – | – | – | – | – | – | – | – | – |
| FL..... | Miami | – | – | – | – | – | – | – | – | – | – | – | – | – |
| GA.... | Atlanta | 0.9 | 0.5 | 0.4 | – | – | – | – | – | – | – | – | 0.2 | 2.0 |
| HI...... | Honolulu | – | – | – | – | – | – | – | – | – | – | – | – | – |
| ID..... | Boise | 6.3 | 3.4 | 1.6 | 0.5 | 0.1 | – | – | – | – | 0.1 | 2.1 | 5.9 | 20.0 |
| IL..... | Chicago | 11.2 | 9.2 | 6.3 | 1.4 | – | – | – | – | – | 0.3 | 1.9 | 8.4 | 38.7 |
| IL..... | Peoria | 6.8 | 6.0 | 3.9 | 0.7 | T | – | – | – | – | – | 1.8 | 6.1 | 25.3 |
| IN..... | Indianapolis | 7.9 | 6.2 | 3.6 | 0.4 | – | – | – | – | – | 0.2 | 1.4 | 5.8 | 25.5 |
| IA..... | Des Moines | 8.3 | 8.3 | 5.7 | 1.7 | 0.1 | – | – | – | – | 0.3 | 2.7 | 7.2 | 34.3 |
| KS..... | Wichita | 3.8 | 4.1 | 2.4 | 0.3 | – | – | – | – | – | – | 1.1 | 3.3 | 15.0 |
| KY..... | Louisville | 5.1 | 4.4 | 2.9 | 0.1 | – | – | – | – | – | 0.1 | 0.8 | 2.3 | 15.7 |
| LA..... | New Orleans | – | – | – | – | – | – | – | – | – | – | – | 0.1 | 0.1 |
| MF..... | Portland | 19.2 | 17.6 | 13.0 | 2.8 | 0.1 | – | – | – | – | 0.2 | 2.9 | 14.5 | 70.3 |
| MD.... | Baltimore | 5.9 | 6.8 | 3.4 | – | – | – | – | – | – | – | 0.6 | 3.1 | 19.8 |
| MA.... | Boston | 13.2 | 12.6 | 8.0 | 1.2 | – | – | – | – | – | – | 1.1 | 7.9 | 44.0 |
| MI..... | Detroit | 11.9 | 10.7 | 6.7 | 1.6 | – | – | – | – | – | 0.1 | 2.4 | 9.8 | 43.2 |
| MI..... | Sault Ste. Marie | 30.1 | 19.8 | 14.2 | 6.3 | 0.4 | – | – | – | 0.1 | 2.0 | 15.4 | 30.4 | 118.7 |
| MN.... | Duluth | 17.2 | 12.7 | 14.0 | 7.7 | 0.6 | – | – | – | – | 0.1 | 1.8 | 11.9 | 17.0 | 83.0 |
| MN.... | Minneapolis-St. Paul | 10.3 | 8.4 | 10.1 | 3.0 | 0.1 | – | – | – | – | 0.5 | 6.8 | 10.1 | 49.3 |
| MS.... | Jackson | 0.4 | 0.3 | 0.1 | – | – | – | – | – | – | – | – | 0.2 | 1.0 |
| MO.... | Kansas City | 5.1 | 5.5 | 2.2 | 0.6 | – | – | – | – | – | 0.2 | 1.2 | 4.2 | 19.0 |
| MO.... | St. Louis | 5.4 | 4.4 | 3.7 | 0.3 | – | – | – | – | – | – | 1.2 | 3.6 | 18.6 |
| MT.... | Great Falls | 9.6 | 8.8 | 10.4 | 8.0 | 1.8 | 0.3 | – | 0.1 | 1.1 | 3.4 | 7.7 | 9.3 | 60.5 |
| NE..... | Omaha | 6.9 | 6.8 | 5.5 | 0.8 | 0.1 | – | – | – | – | 0.3 | 2.4 | 5.8 | 28.6 |
| NV..... | Reno | 5.4 | 4.9 | 3.8 | 1.0 | 0.6 | – | – | – | – | 0.3 | 1.9 | 4.6 | 22.5 |
| NH.... | Concord | 17.9 | 15.6 | 11.8 | 2.4 | 0.1 | – | – | – | – | 0.4 | 3.4 | 13.7 | 65.3 |
| NJ..... | Atlantic City | 6.0 | 6.3 | 2.3 | 0.4 | – | – | – | – | – | – | 0.3 | 2.9 | 18.2 |
| NM.... | Albuquerque | 2.1 | 1.9 | 1.5 | 0.5 | – | – | – | – | – | 0.1 | 1.0 | 2.5 | 9.6 |
| NY..... | Albany | 16.3 | 13.9 | 11.4 | 2.4 | 0.1 | – | – | – | – | 0.2 | 3.8 | 13.6 | 61.7 |
| NY..... | Buffalo | 24.6 | 18.2 | 12.4 | 2.9 | 0.2 | – | – | – | – | 0.5 | 10.0 | 23.1 | 91.9 |
| NY..... | New York Central Park | 7.9 | 8.9 | 4.9 | 0.8 | – | – | – | – | – | – | 0.8 | 5.4 | 28.7 |
| NC..... | Charlotte | 2.0 | 1.0 | 0.9 | T | – | – | – | – | – | – | 0.1 | 0.5 | 5.1 |
| NC..... | Raleigh | 2.5 | 2.3 | 1.0 | – | – | – | – | – | – | – | 0.1 | 0.8 | 6.7 |
| ND.... | Bismarck | 8.3 | 7.2 | 8.5 | 4.0 | 0.7 | – | – | – | 0.1 | 1.4 | 6.7 | 8.5 | 45.4 |
| OH.... | Cincinnati | 7.3 | 6.0 | 4.1 | 0.5 | – | – | – | – | – | 0.2 | 1.6 | 4.1 | 23.8 |
| OH.... | Cleveland | 14.7 | 13.1 | 10.5 | 2.5 | – | – | – | – | – | 0.4 | 4.9 | 11.9 | 58.0 |
| OH.... | Columbus | 8.9 | 6.7 | 4.4 | 0.8 | – | – | – | – | – | 0.1 | 1.9 | 5.5 | 28.3 |
| OK.... | Oklahoma City | 2.6 | 2.3 | 1.2 | – | – | – | – | – | – | T | 0.6 | 1.9 | 8.6 |
| OR.... | Portland | 3.0 | 1.3 | 0.4 | – | – | – | – | – | – | – | 0.4 | 1.3 | 6.4 |
| PA..... | Philadelphia | 7.1 | 7.4 | 3.7 | 0.3 | – | – | – | – | – | – | 0.5 | 3.6 | 22.6 |
| PA..... | Pittsburgh | 12.1 | 10.1 | 8.0 | 1.5 | 0.1 | – | – | – | – | 0.3 | 3.5 | 8.2 | 43.8 |
| RI...... | Providence | 10.4 | 10.2 | 6.8 | 0.7 | 0.1 | – | – | – | – | 0.1 | 1.0 | 7.0 | 36.3 |
| SC..... | Columbia | 0.6 | 0.7 | 0.2 | – | – | – | – | – | – | – | – | 0.2 | 1.7 |
| SD..... | Sioux Falls | 7.0 | 8.4 | 8.7 | 3.2 | 0.1 | – | – | – | – | 0.7 | 5.1 | 7.8 | 41.0 |
| TN..... | Memphis | 1.9 | 1.2 | 0.6 | – | – | – | – | – | – | – | 0.1 | 0.5 | 4.3 |
| TN..... | Nashville | 3.6 | 2.6 | 1.2 | – | – | – | – | – | – | – | 0.4 | 1.1 | 8.9 |
| TX..... | Dallas | 0.9 | 0.7 | 0.2 | – | – | – | – | – | – | – | 0.1 | 0.2 | 2.1 |
| TX..... | El Paso | 1.2 | 0.7 | 0.3 | 0.3 | – | – | – | – | – | – | 0.9 | 1.6 | 5.0 |
| TX..... | Houston | 0.1 | 0.1 | – | – | – | – | – | – | – | – | – | 0.1 | 0.3 |
| UT..... | Salt Lake City | 13.1 | 10.1 | 8.9 | 4.9 | 0.6 | – | – | – | 0.1 | 1.3 | 6.6 | 13.0 | 58.6 |
| VT..... | Burlington | 19.5 | 17.4 | 14.1 | 3.9 | 0.1 | – | – | – | T | 0.3 | 6.4 | 18.7 | 80.4 |
| VA..... | Norfolk | 3.1 | 2.7 | 0.9 | – | – | – | – | – | – | – | – | 1.0 | 7.7 |
| VA..... | Richmond | 5.0 | 3.9 | 2.1 | 0.1 | – | – | – | – | – | – | 0.3 | 1.9 | 13.3 |
| WA.... | Seattle | 4.5 | 1.7 | 1.2 | 0.1 | – | – | – | – | – | – | 0.8 | 2.4 | 10.7 |
| WA.... | Spokane | 13.0 | 7.6 | 3.6 | 0.6 | 0.1 | – | – | – | – | 0.2 | 5.6 | 11.8 | 42.5 |
| WV.... | Charleston | 10.7 | 8.7 | 5.2 | 0.8 | – | – | – | – | – | 0.3 | 2.0 | 5.0 | 32.7 |
| WI..... | Milwaukee | 13.7 | 10.6 | 8.2 | 1.8 | 0.1 | – | – | – | – | 0.2 | 2.9 | 10.4 | 47.9 |
| WY.... | Cheyenne | 6.0 | 7.4 | 11.0 | 10.4 | 3.3 | 0.2 | – | – | 0.7 | 4.2 | 7.1 | 7.1 | 57.4 |
| PR..... | San Juan | – | – | – | – | – | – | – | – | – | – | – | – | – |

– Represents zero.

Source: U.S. National Oceanic and Atmospheric Administration, *Comparative Climatic Data for the United States Through 2018*. See also <https://www.ncdc.noaa.gov/ghcn/comparative-climatic-data>.

# Table 437. Cloudiness, Average Wind Speed, and Average Relative Humidity—Selected Cities

[Airport data, except as noted. Data shown for varying periods of record; see source for date ranges for each location. M = morning. A = afternoon]

| State | Station | Cloudiness-average percent of days annually [1] | Average wind speed (miles per hour, m.p.h.) | | | Average relative humidity (percent) | | | | | |
|---|---|---|---|---|---|---|---|---|---|---|---|
| | | | Annual | Jan-uary | July | Annual | | Jan. | | July | |
| | | | | | | M | A | M | A | M | A |
| AL........ | Mobile | 72.1 | 7.5 | 8.6 | 5.7 | 87 | 57 | 83 | 60 | 90 | 61 |
| AK........ | Juneau | 87.9 | 7.4 | 7.3 | 6.6 | 84 | 74 | 84 | 80 | 84 | 72 |
| AZ........ | Phoenix | 42.5 | 6.1 | 5.0 | 7.3 | 46 | 23 | 60 | 33 | 42 | 21 |
| AR........ | Little Rock | 67.7 | 7.0 | 7.7 | 6.0 | 84 | 57 | 80 | 61 | 87 | 56 |
| CA........ | Los Angeles | 49.0 | 1.9 | 1.4 | 2.2 | 58 | 54 | 52 | 49 | 65 | 59 |
| CA........ | Sacramento | 48.5 | 6.3 | 5.0 | 7.6 | 78 | 45 | 87 | 69 | 71 | 29 |
| CA........ | San Diego | 60.0 | 6.4 | 5.2 | 7.0 | 74 | 63 | 69 | 58 | 80 | 67 |
| CA........ | San Francisco | 56.2 | 10.5 | 6.8 | 13.1 | 87 | 69 | 87 | 66 | 91 | 71 |
| CO........ | Denver | 68.5 | 8.0 | 7.8 | 7.9 | 50 | 43 | 53 | 54 | 46 | 35 |
| CT........ | Hartford | 77.5 | 7.8 | 8.3 | 6.7 | 76 | 53 | 73 | 57 | 78 | 51 |
| DE........ | Wilmington | 73.4 | 8.5 | 9.2 | 7.4 | 78 | 55 | 75 | 59 | 78 | 54 |
| DC........ | Washington Nat'l (VA) | 74.0 | 8.9 | 9.5 | 8.1 | 74 | 53 | 71 | 55 | 76 | 53 |
| FL........ | Jacksonville | 74.2 | 6.7 | 7.0 | 5.9 | 88 | 56 | 87 | 57 | 89 | 59 |
| FL........ | Miami | 79.5 | 8.4 | 8.6 | 7.3 | 82 | 61 | 84 | 59 | 81 | 63 |
| GA........ | Atlanta | 70.1 | 8.3 | 9.3 | 7.1 | 81 | 55 | 79 | 58 | 86 | 58 |
| HI........ | Honolulu | 75.3 | 10.3 | 8.4 | 11.9 | 74 | 56 | 79 | 61 | 70 | 53 |
| ID........ | Boise | 67.1 | 7.6 | 6.5 | 7.5 | 64 | 42 | 79 | 70 | 49 | 20 |
| IL........ | Chicago | 77.0 | 9.9 | 11.2 | 8.2 | 80 | 60 | 78 | 68 | 81 | 55 |
| IL........ | Peoria | 73.7 | 8.3 | 9.5 | 6.4 | 83 | 61 | 80 | 70 | 86 | 58 |
| IN........ | Indianapolis | 76.2 | 9.5 | 10.9 | 7.6 | 82 | 60 | 81 | 70 | 83 | 58 |
| IA........ | Des Moines | 71.5 | 9.8 | 10.6 | 8.3 | 81 | 60 | 78 | 68 | 84 | 58 |
| KS........ | Wichita | 64.9 | 11.5 | 11.1 | 10.8 | 80 | 55 | 79 | 61 | 80 | 50 |
| KY........ | Louisville | 74.8 | 7.8 | 9.0 | 6.6 | 79 | 56 | 78 | 64 | 81 | 56 |
| LA........ | New Orleans | 72.3 | 8.0 | 9.1 | 5.9 | 87 | 62 | 84 | 65 | 90 | 65 |
| ME........ | Portland | 72.3 | 7.9 | 8.2 | 6.9 | 78 | 59 | 75 | 59 | 79 | 60 |
| MD........ | Baltimore | 71.2 | 7.2 | 7.9 | 6.3 | 77 | 53 | 73 | 56 | 78 | 52 |
| MA........ | Boston | 73.2 | 11.5 | 12.6 | 10.2 | 72 | 57 | 69 | 58 | 72 | 56 |
| MI........ | Detroit | 79.5 | 9.4 | 11.1 | 7.9 | 80 | 59 | 80 | 69 | 80 | 53 |
| MI........ | Sault Ste. Marie | 81.9 | 7.7 | 7.9 | 6.7 | 84 | 65 | 80 | 73 | 87 | 61 |
| MN........ | Duluth | 79.2 | 10.0 | 10.6 | 8.5 | 82 | 63 | 78 | 70 | 86 | 60 |
| MN........ | Minneapolis-St. Paul | 74.0 | 9.7 | 9.6 | 8.7 | 79 | 59 | 77 | 68 | 81 | 54 |
| MS........ | Jackson | 69.6 | 6.1 | 7.2 | 4.6 | 90 | 57 | 85 | 62 | 93 | 58 |
| MO........ | Kansas City | 67.1 | 10.4 | 11.0 | 8.9 | 81 | 60 | 78 | 64 | 85 | 59 |
| MO........ | St. Louis | 72.6 | 9.0 | 10.1 | 7.6 | 81 | 58 | 79 | 65 | 82 | 55 |
| MT........ | Great Falls | 78.4 | 11.4 | 13.9 | 9.1 | 63 | 46 | 65 | 61 | 60 | 30 |
| NE........ | Omaha | 69.6 | 10.0 | 10.2 | 8.5 | 81 | 59 | 79 | 66 | 85 | 57 |
| NV........ | Reno | 56.7 | 6.4 | 4.5 | 7.2 | 63 | 31 | 75 | 51 | 54 | 18 |
| NH........ | Concord | 75.3 | 6.0 | 6.6 | 5.1 | 80 | 53 | 76 | 58 | 81 | 51 |
| NJ........ | Atlantic City | 74.2 | 8.7 | 9.5 | 7.4 | 80 | 56 | 77 | 58 | 81 | 57 |
| NM........ | Albuquerque | 54.2 | 8.2 | 7.3 | 8.2 | 53 | 29 | 62 | 40 | 54 | 28 |
| NY........ | Albany | 81.1 | 7.9 | 8.7 | 6.6 | 79 | 57 | 77 | 63 | 79 | 54 |
| NY........ | Buffalo | 85.2 | 10.3 | 12.5 | 9.0 | 79 | 62 | 79 | 72 | 78 | 55 |
| NY........ | Central Park | 71.0 | 6.2 | 7.6 | 4.8 | 70 | 54 | 67 | 56 | 73 | 54 |
| NC........ | Charlotte | 70.4 | 6.4 | 6.6 | 5.7 | 81 | 52 | 78 | 54 | 84 | 55 |
| NC........ | Raleigh | 69.9 | 6.5 | 6.9 | 6.1 | 83 | 53 | 79 | 53 | 86 | 56 |
| ND........ | Bismarck | 74.5 | 9.4 | 9.2 | 8.6 | 81 | 58 | 77 | 71 | 85 | 49 |
| OH........ | Cincinnati | 77.8 | 8.3 | 9.7 | 6.6 | 81 | 59 | 80 | 68 | 84 | 57 |
| OH........ | Cleveland | 81.9 | 9.6 | 11.4 | 7.8 | 79 | 61 | 79 | 70 | 80 | 56 |
| OH........ | Columbus | 80.3 | 7.6 | 9.1 | 6.1 | 80 | 58 | 78 | 68 | 82 | 55 |
| OK........ | Oklahoma City | 61.9 | 11.3 | 11.6 | 9.9 | 80 | 55 | 78 | 59 | 82 | 51 |
| OR........ | Portland | 81.1 | 7.4 | 9.2 | 7.1 | 82 | 59 | 84 | 76 | 77 | 44 |
| PA........ | Philadelphia | 74.5 | 9.3 | 9.9 | 8.3 | 76 | 54 | 73 | 58 | 77 | 52 |
| PA........ | Pittsburgh | 83.8 | 7.8 | 9.2 | 6.3 | 79 | 57 | 77 | 66 | 82 | 54 |
| RI........ | Providence | 73.2 | 9.2 | 9.7 | 8.5 | 75 | 55 | 71 | 57 | 76 | 56 |
| SC........ | Columbia | 68.5 | 6.1 | 6.6 | 5.7 | 84 | 50 | 82 | 52 | 86 | 52 |
| SD........ | Sioux Falls | 71.2 | 10.2 | 10.3 | 9.1 | 82 | 60 | 77 | 69 | 85 | 55 |
| TN........ | Memphis | 67.7 | 8.1 | 9.0 | 6.9 | 80 | 56 | 77 | 62 | 84 | 57 |
| TN........ | Nashville | 71.8 | 7.1 | 8.1 | 5.9 | 84 | 56 | 80 | 64 | 87 | 56 |
| TX........ | Dallas | 63.0 | 9.5 | 8.9 | 8.9 | 78 | 54 | 76 | 58 | 77 | 49 |
| TX........ | El Paso | 47.1 | 8.1 | 7.4 | 7.7 | 50 | 27 | 58 | 34 | 56 | 29 |
| TX........ | Houston | 75.3 | 7.5 | 7.9 | 6.1 | 89 | 59 | 85 | 62 | 93 | 57 |
| UT........ | Salt Lake City | 65.8 | 8.4 | 6.5 | 9.1 | 63 | 43 | 78 | 70 | 47 | 21 |
| VT........ | Burlington | 84.1 | 8.3 | 9.2 | 7.1 | 76 | 58 | 74 | 64 | 77 | 53 |
| VA........ | Norfolk | 71.2 | 9.6 | 10.0 | 8.5 | 78 | 57 | 74 | 58 | 80 | 59 |
| VA........ | Richmond | 72.9 | 7.7 | 8.3 | 6.9 | 81 | 53 | 78 | 55 | 83 | 55 |
| WA........ | Seattle | 80.5 | 7.9 | 8.4 | 7.4 | 82 | 63 | 83 | 76 | 79 | 48 |
| WA........ | Spokane | 76.4 | 8.7 | 8.1 | 8.6 | 74 | 52 | 86 | 80 | 59 | 26 |
| WV........ | Charleston | 82.2 | 4.6 | 5.7 | 3.5 | 83 | 56 | 78 | 62 | 89 | 58 |
| WI........ | Milwaukee | 75.3 | 10.1 | 11.0 | 8.9 | 79 | 63 | 76 | 68 | 81 | 60 |
| WY........ | Cheyenne | 71.2 | 12.3 | 14.4 | 9.9 | 61 | 45 | 55 | 51 | 63 | 38 |
| PR........ | San Juan | 80.0 | 7.9 | 7.7 | 9.5 | 78 | 66 | 81 | 65 | 78 | 67 |

[1] Percent of days that are either partly cloudy or cloudy.

Source: U.S. National Oceanic and Atmospheric Administration, *Comparative Climatic Data For the United States Through 2018*. See also <https://www.ncdc.noaa.gov/ghcn/comparative-climatic-data>.

## Table 438. Drought Conditions—Area and Population Impacted by Level of Drought: 2018

[In percent. For continental United States. Data shown for the last week of each month, as of Tuesday. Drought classifications are measured in four intensity levels—D0: Abnormally dry, D1: Moderate drought, D2: Severe drought, D3: Extreme drought, and D4: Exceptional drought. Data are categorical statistics showing percent of the area or population that is in a certain drought category. See source for details, <http://droughtmonitor.unl.edu/AboutUSDM.aspx>. The U.S. Drought Monitor is jointly produced by the National Drought Mitigation Center at the University of Nebraska-Lincoln, the United States Department of Agriculture, and the National Oceanic and Atmospheric Administration]

| Week | Area (percent of continental U.S. square miles) | | | | | | Population (percent of continental U.S. population) | | | | | |
|---|---|---|---|---|---|---|---|---|---|---|---|---|
| | None | D0 | D1 | D2 | D3 | D4 | None | D0 | D1 | D2 | D3 | D4 |
| 1/30/2018.... | 32.90 | 28.68 | 21.21 | 15.49 | 1.72 | – | 44.83 | 26.36 | 17.22 | 11.10 | 0.49 | – |
| 2/27/2018.... | 45.34 | 23.36 | 16.99 | 11.09 | 3.22 | – | 61.24 | 20.00 | 9.75 | 8.43 | 0.58 | – |
| 3/27/2018.... | 50.80 | 18.44 | 14.41 | 9.10 | 6.71 | 0.55 | 64.71 | 15.48 | 10.71 | 7.16 | 1.90 | 0.04 |
| 4/24/2018.... | 57.51 | 13.50 | 12.64 | 7.85 | 6.53 | 1.97 | 70.26 | 10.99 | 9.01 | 7.69 | 1.87 | 0.19 |
| 5/29/2018.... | 57.44 | 16.13 | 9.50 | 7.68 | 7.15 | 2.09 | 74.76 | 9.58 | 4.82 | 7.72 | 2.77 | 0.35 |
| 6/26/2018.... | 51.31 | 19.90 | 12.86 | 7.65 | 6.44 | 1.84 | 63.48 | 16.13 | 9.21 | 8.15 | 2.70 | 0.33 |
| 7/31/2018.... | 45.58 | 20.29 | 14.72 | 10.90 | 6.90 | 1.61 | 58.48 | 17.12 | 9.16 | 11.13 | 3.78 | 0.33 |
| 8/28/2018.... | 44.11 | 21.47 | 15.04 | 11.88 | 5.95 | 1.55 | 58.60 | 17.34 | 9.47 | 12.13 | 2.10 | 0.37 |
| 9/25/2018.... | 51.36 | 19.10 | 12.08 | 9.97 | 5.76 | 1.73 | 69.77 | 11.62 | 5.94 | 10.12 | 2.25 | 0.30 |
| 10/30/2018... | 63.41 | 14.59 | 9.44 | 7.90 | 3.31 | 1.35 | 74.10 | 11.66 | 5.53 | 7.89 | 0.65 | 0.17 |
| 11/27/2018... | 65.97 | 11.17 | 11.45 | 7.14 | 2.96 | 1.32 | 73.93 | 8.03 | 10.10 | 6.88 | 0.89 | 0.16 |
| 12/25/2018... | 66.00 | 11.50 | 11.52 | 7.63 | 2.20 | 1.15 | 75.01 | 7.83 | 9.80 | 6.61 | 0.59 | 0.15 |

– Represents zero.

Source: National Drought Mitigation Center, "United States Drought Monitor," <http://droughtmonitor.unl.edu/>, accessed January 2019.

## Table 439. Top 20 Significant Flood Event Losses Covered by the National Flood Insurance Program, as of January 30, 2019

[In nominal dollars. Covers period beginning in 1978. A significant event is one with 1,500 or more paid losses, or occasionally one added for other reasons]

| Event | Date | Number of paid losses | Amount paid ($) | Average paid loss ($) |
|---|---|---|---|---|
| Hurricane Katrina.......................... | Aug. 2005 | 166,790 | 16,257,744,061 | 97,474 |
| Hurricane Harvey.......................... | Sept. 2017 | 76,257 | 8,908,547,689 | 116,823 |
| Superstorm Sandy.......................... | Oct. 2012 | 132,360 | 8,804,242,152 | 66,517 |
| Hurricane Ike.......................... | Sept. 2008 | 46,701 | 2,702,388,727 | 57,866 |
| Louisiana severe storms and flooding............. | Aug. 2016 | 26,976 | 2,468,493,541 | 91,507 |
| Hurricane Ivan.......................... | Sept. 2004 | 28,154 | 1,607,512,533 | 57,097 |
| Hurricane Irene.......................... | Aug. 2011 | 44,314 | 1,345,775,273 | 30,369 |
| Tropical Storm Allison.......................... | June 2001 | 30,671 | 1,105,003,344 | 36,028 |
| Hurricane Irma.......................... | Sept. 2017 | 21,920 | 1,054,248,877 | 48,095 |
| Hurricane Matthew.......................... | Oct. 2016 | 16,586 | 654,394,214 | 39,455 |
| Hurricane Florence.......................... | Sept. 2018 | 13,754 | 648,333,990 | 47,138 |
| Louisiana flood.......................... | May 1995 | 31,343 | 585,071,593 | 18,667 |
| Hurricane Isaac.......................... | Aug. 2012 | 12,084 | 561,527,299 | 46,469 |
| Hurricane Isabel.......................... | Sept. 2003 | 19,938 | 500,270,118 | 25,091 |
| Texas torrential rain.......................... | Apr. 2016 | 7,437 | 471,517,374 | 63,402 |
| Texas flooding.......................... | May 2015 | 6,774 | 468,799,696 | 69,206 |
| Hurricane Rita.......................... | Sept. 2005 | 9,354 | 466,223,897 | 49,842 |
| Tropical Storm Lee.......................... | Sept. 2011 | 9,905 | 462,459,225 | 46,689 |
| Hurricane Floyd.......................... | Sept. 1999 | 20,439 | 462,326,389 | 22,620 |
| Hurricane Opal.......................... | Oct. 1995 | 10,343 | 405,527,543 | 39,208 |

Source: U.S. Department of Homeland Security, Federal Emergency Management Agency, National Flood Insurance Program Statistics, "Significant Flood Events [since 1978], as of January 31, 2019," <http://www.fema.gov/significant-flood-events>, accessed September 2019.

## Table 440. Threatened and Endangered Wildlife and Plant Species: 2019

[As of May 2019. Endangered species: one in danger of becoming extinct throughout all or a significant part of its natural range. Threatened species: one likely to become endangered in the foreseeable future]

| Item | Total [1] | Mammals | Birds | Reptiles | Amphibians | Fishes | Snails | Clams | Crustaceans | Insects | Arachnids | Plants |
|---|---|---|---|---|---|---|---|---|---|---|---|---|
| Total listings.......... | 2,349 | 377 | 339 | 141 | 45 | 195 | 53 | 93 | 28 | 89 | 17 | 947 |
| **Endangered species, total**............... | 1,870 | 326 | 298 | 88 | 29 | 115 | 41 | 78 | 24 | 78 | 17 | 773 |
| United States [2].......... | 1,275 | 66 | 80 | 17 | 21 | 93 | 40 | 76 | 24 | 74 | 12 | 772 |
| Foreign.................. | 595 | 260 | 218 | 71 | 8 | 22 | 1 | 2 | – | 4 | 5 | 1 |
| **Threatened species, total**............... | 479 | 51 | 41 | 53 | 16 | 80 | 12 | 15 | 4 | 11 | – | 174 |
| United States [2].......... | 388 | 28 | 21 | 29 | 15 | 74 | 12 | 15 | 4 | 11 | – | 172 |
| Foreign.................. | 91 | 23 | 20 | 24 | 1 | 6 | – | – | – | – | – | 2 |

– Represents zero. [1] Includes other categories not shown separately. Twenty-two animal species (14 in the U.S. and 8 Foreign) are counted more than once, primarily because these animals have distinct population segments (each with its own individual listing status). [2] United States listings include those populations in which the U.S. shares jurisdiction with another nation.

Source: U.S. Fish and Wildlife Service, Environmental Conservation Online System, Threatened & Endangered Species, "Listed Species Summary," <http://ecos.fws.gov/ecp/>, accessed May 2019.

# Elections

This section relates primarily to presidential, congressional, and gubernatorial elections. Also presented are summary tables on congressional legislation; state legislatures; minority and female officeholders; population of voting age; voter participation; and campaign finances.

Official statistics on federal elections, collected by the Clerk of the House, are published biennially in *Statistics of the Presidential and Congressional Election* and *Statistics of the Congressional Election*. Federal elections data also appear in the *Congressional Directory* and in official state documents. Data on reported registration and voting for social and economic groups are obtained by the U.S. Census Bureau as part of the Current Population Survey (CPS) and are published in *Current Population Reports*, Series P20 (see text, Section 1).

Almost all federal, state, and local governmental units in the United States conduct elections for political offices and other purposes. The conduct of elections is regulated by state laws or, in some cities and counties, by local charter. An exception is that the U.S. Constitution prescribes the basis of representation in Congress and the manner of electing the president and grants to Congress the right to regulate the times, places, and manner of electing federal officers. Amendments to the Constitution have prescribed national criteria for voting eligibility. The 15th Amendment, adopted in 1870, gave all male citizens the right to vote regardless of race, color, or previous condition of servitude. The 19th Amendment, adopted in 1920, further extended the right to vote to all citizens regardless of sex. The payment of poll taxes as a prerequisite to voting in federal elections was banned by the 24th Amendment in 1964. In 1971, as a result of the 26th Amendment, eligibility to vote in national elections was extended to all citizens, 18 years old and over.

**Presidential election**—The Constitution specifies how the president and vice president are selected. Each state elects, by popular vote, a group of electors equal in number to its total of members of Congress. The 23rd Amendment, adopted in 1961, grants the District of Columbia three presidential electors, a number equal to that of the least populous state. Subsequent to the election, the electors meet in their respective states to vote for president and vice president. Usually, each elector votes for the candidate receiving the most popular votes in his or her state. A majority vote of all electors is necessary to elect the president and vice president. If no candidate receives a majority, the House of Representatives, with each state having one vote, is empowered to elect the president and vice president, again, with a majority of votes required.

The 22nd Amendment to the Constitution, adopted in 1951, limits presidential tenure to two elective terms of 4 years each or to one elective term for any person who, upon succession to the presidency, has held the office or acted as President for more than 2 years.

**Congressional election**—The Constitution provides that representatives be apportioned among the states according to their population, that a census of population be taken every 10 years as a basis for apportionment, and that each state have at least one representative. At the time of each apportionment, Congress decides what the total number of representatives will be. Since 1912, the total has been 435, except during 1960 to 1962 when it increased to 437, adding one representative each for Alaska and Hawaii. The total reverted to 435 after reapportionment following the 1960 census. Members are elected for 2-year terms, all terms covering the same period. The District of Columbia, American Samoa, Guam, and the Virgin Islands each elect one nonvoting delegate, and Puerto Rico elects a nonvoting resident commissioner.

The Senate is composed of 100 members, two from each state, who are elected to serve for a term of 6 years. One-third of the Senate is elected every 2 years. Senators were originally chosen by the state legislatures. The 17th Amendment to the Constitution, adopted in 1913, prescribed that senators be elected by popular vote.

**Voter eligibility and participation**—The Census Bureau publishes estimates of the population of voting age and the percent casting votes in each state for presidential and congressional election years. These voting-age estimates include a number of persons who meet the age requirement but are not eligible to vote, (e.g. aliens and some institutionalized persons). In addition, since 1964, voter participation and voter characteristics data have been collected during November of election years as part of the CPS. Survey data on voting age population estimates includes non-citizens but excludes members of the Armed Forces and institutionalized populations. Data on percent casting votes excludes institutionalized populations, members of the Armed forces and citizens residing outside the U.S. casting absentee ballots.

**Statistical reliability**—For a discussion of statistical collection and estimation, sampling procedures, and measures of statistical reliability applicable to Census Bureau data, see Appendix III.

# Table 441. Participation in Elections for President and U.S. Representatives: 1934 to 2018

[77,997 represents 77,997,000. As of November, except as noted. Estimated resident population 21 years old and over, 1934 to 1970, except as noted, and 18 years old and over thereafter. Includes Armed Forces stationed in the U.S. Prior to 1958, excludes Alaska and prior to 1960, excludes Hawaii. District of Columbia is included in votes cast for President beginning 1964]

| Year | Resident population (includes aliens) of voting age [1] (1,000) | Votes cast | | | |
|---|---|---|---|---|---|
| | | For President (1,000) | Percent of voting-age population | For U.S. Representatives (1,000) | Percent of voting-age population |
| 1934 | 77,997 | (X) | (X) | 32,804 | 42.1 |
| 1936 | 80,174 | 45,647 | 56.9 | (NA) | (NA) |
| 1938 | 82,354 | (X) | (X) | (NA) | (NA) |
| 1940 | 84,728 | 49,815 | 58.8 | (NA) | (NA) |
| 1942 | 86,465 | (X) | (X) | 28,074 | 32.5 |
| 1944 | 85,654 | 48,026 | 56.1 | 45,110 | 52.7 |
| 1946 | 92,659 | (X) | (X) | 34,410 | 37.1 |
| 1948 | 95,573 | 48,834 | 51.1 | 46,220 | 48.4 |
| 1950 | 98,134 | (X) | (X) | 40,430 | 41.2 |
| 1952 | 99,929 | 61,552 | 61.6 | 57,571 | 57.6 |
| 1954 | 102,075 | (X) | (X) | 42,583 | 41.7 |
| 1956 | 104,515 | 62,027 | 59.3 | 58,886 | 56.3 |
| 1958 | 106,447 | (X) | (X) | 45,719 | 43.0 |
| 1960 | 109,672 | 68,836 | 62.8 | 64,124 | 58.5 |
| 1962 | 112,952 | (X) | (X) | 51,242 | 45.4 |
| 1964 | 114,090 | 70,098 | 61.4 | 65,879 | 57.7 |
| 1966 | 116,638 | (X) | (X) | 52,902 | 45.4 |
| 1968 | 120,285 | 73,027 | 60.7 | 66,109 | 55.0 |
| 1970 | 124,498 | (X) | (X) | 54,259 | 43.6 |
| 1972 | 140,777 | 77,625 | 55.1 | 71,188 | 50.6 |
| 1974 | 146,338 | (X) | (X) | 52,313 | 35.7 |
| 1976 | 152,308 | 81,603 | 53.6 | 74,259 | 48.8 |
| 1978 | 158,369 | (X) | (X) | 54,584 | 34.5 |
| 1980 | 163,945 | 86,497 | 52.8 | 77,874 | 47.5 |
| 1982 | 169,643 | (X) | (X) | 63,881 | 37.7 |
| 1984 | 173,995 | 92,655 | 53.3 | 82,422 | 47.4 |
| 1986 | 177,922 | (X) | (X) | 59,758 | 33.6 |
| 1988 | 181,956 | 91,587 | 50.3 | 81,682 | 44.9 |
| 1990 | 185,812 | (X) | (X) | 62,355 | 33.6 |
| 1992 | 189,493 | 104,600 | 55.2 | 97,198 | 51.3 |
| 1994 | 193,010 | (X) | (X) | 70,494 | 36.5 |
| 1996 | 196,789 | 96,390 | 49.0 | 90,233 | 45.9 |
| 1998 | 201,270 | (X) | (X) | 66,605 | 33.1 |
| 2000 | [2] 209,130 | 105,594 | 50.5 | 98,800 | 47.2 |
| 2002 | [2] 214,689 | (X) | (X) | 74,707 | 34.8 |
| 2004 | [2] 219,508 | 122,349 | 55.7 | 113,192 | 51.6 |
| 2006 | [2] 224,622 | (X) | (X) | 80,976 | 36.0 |
| 2008 | [2] 229,989 | 131,407 | 57.1 | 122,586 | 53.3 |
| 2010 | [2] 234,576 | (X) | (X) | 86,785 | 37.0 |
| 2012 | [2] 240,177 | 129,140 | 53.8 | 122,346 | 50.9 |
| 2014 | [2] 244,821 | (X) | (X) | 78,813 | 32.2 |
| 2016 | [2] 249,422 | 136,787 | 54.8 | 129,833 | 52.1 |
| 2018 | [2] 253,768 | (X) | (X) | 114,017 | 44.9 |

X Not applicable. NA Not available. [1] Population 18 and over in Georgia, 1944-70, and in Kentucky, 1956–70; and 20 and over in Alaska and Hawaii, 1960–70. Source: Through 1990, U.S. Census Bureau, "Table 4. Participation in Elections for President and U.S. Representatives: 1930 to 1992," May 1994, <http://www.census.gov/population/socdemo/voting/p25-1117/tab03-04.pdf>. For 1992–1998, "Estimates and Projections of the Voting-Age Population, 1992 to 2000, and Percent Casting Votes for President, by State: November 1992 and 1996," July 2000, <http://www.census.gov/population/socdemo/voting/proj00/tab03.txt>. For 2000-2009, "Annual Estimates of the Resident Population for Selected Age Groups by Sex for the United States, States, Counties, and Puerto Rico Commonwealth and Municipios: April 1, 2000 to July 1, 2009," <https://www.census.gov/topics/population.html>, accessed June 2015. Starting 2010, "Annual estimates of the resident population by single year of age and sex for the United States: April 1, 2010 to July 1, 2018," <https://www.census.gov/programs-surveys/popest.html>, accessed July 2019. [2] 2000 and 2010, as of April 1, population estimates base. All other years as of July 1.

Source: Except as noted, U.S. House of Representatives, Office of the Clerk, *Statistics of the Presidential and Congressional Election*, February 2019, and earlier reports. See also <http://clerk.house.gov/member_info/election.aspx>.

# Table 442. Voters by Whether Voting on Election Day or Utilizing Alternative Early Voting: 1996 to 2016

[Percent distribution of persons voting. As of November. Data are from November Voting and Registration Supplements to the Current Population Survey (see text, Section 1, and Appendix III)]

| Election Year | Total | On election day [1] | Alternative early voting methods | | |
|---|---|---|---|---|---|
| | | | Total | Before election day [1] | By mail |
| 1996 [2] | 100.0 | 89.5 | 10.5 | 2.7 | 7.8 |
| 1998 | 100.0 | 89.2 | 10.8 | 2.4 | 8.4 |
| 2000 [2] | 100.0 | 86.0 | 14.0 | 3.8 | 10.2 |
| 2002 | 100.0 | 85.9 | 14.1 | 3.4 | 10.7 |
| 2004 [2] | 100.0 | 79.3 | 20.7 | 7.8 | 12.9 |
| 2006 | 100.0 | 80.4 | 19.6 | 5.8 | 13.7 |
| 2008 [2] | 100.0 | 69.3 | 30.7 | 14.3 | 16.4 |
| 2010 | 100.0 | 73.5 | 26.5 | 8.4 | 18.1 |
| 2012 [2] | 100.0 | 67.2 | 32.8 | 14.3 | 18.5 |
| 2014 | 100.0 | 68.9 | 31.2 | 10.3 | 20.9 |
| 2016 [2] | 100.0 | 59.9 | 40.1 | 19.1 | 21.0 |

[1] Voted in person. [2] Presidential election year.

Source: U.S. Census Bureau, *Characteristics of Voters in the Presidential Election of 2016*, September 2018. See also <https://www.census.gov/library/publications/2018/demo/p20-582.html>.

# Table 443. Resident Population of Voting-Age, Total Votes Cast, and Percent Casting Votes—States: 2016 to 2018

[249,422 represents 249,422,000. Votes cast as of November. Estimated population, 18 years old and over. Includes Armed Forces stationed in each state, aliens, and institutional population]

| State | Voting-age population (1,000) [1] | | Total votes cast (1,000) | | | Percent casting votes for– | | |
|---|---|---|---|---|---|---|---|---|
| | | | Presidential electors | U.S. Representatives | | Presidential electors | U.S. Representatives | |
| | 2016 | 2018 | 2016 | 2016 | 2018 | 2016 | 2016 | 2018 |
| **U.S.** | **249,422** | **253,768** | **136,787** | **129,833** | **114,017** | **54.8** | **52.1** | **44.9** |
| AL | 3,765 | 3,798 | 2,123 | 1,890 | 1,660 | 56.4 | 50.2 | 43.7 |
| AK | 555 | 554 | 319 | 308 | 282 | 57.4 | 55.6 | 51.0 |
| AZ | 5,309 | 5,529 | 2,573 | 2,412 | 2,341 | 48.5 | 45.4 | 42.3 |
| AR | 2,284 | 2,311 | 1,131 | 1,069 | 889 | 49.5 | 46.8 | 38.5 |
| CA | 30,122 | 30,567 | 14,182 | 13,414 | 12,185 | 47.1 | 44.5 | 39.9 |
| CO | 4,278 | 4,430 | 2,780 | 2,701 | 2,514 | 65.0 | 63.1 | 56.7 |
| CT | 2,827 | 2,837 | 1,645 | 1,575 | 1,380 | 58.2 | 55.7 | 48.6 |
| DE | 746 | 764 | 442 | 421 | 354 | 59.2 | 56.4 | 46.3 |
| DC | 565 | 575 | 313 | (X) | (X) | 55.3 | (X) | (X) |
| FL | 16,471 | 17,070 | 9,420 | 8,837 | 7,021 | 57.2 | 53.7 | 41.1 |
| GA | 7,797 | 8,014 | 4,115 | 3,773 | 3,802 | 52.8 | 48.4 | 47.4 |
| HI | 1,121 | 1,117 | 438 | 438 | 399 | 39.1 | 39.1 | 35.7 |
| ID | 1,245 | 1,307 | 690 | 682 | 596 | 55.5 | 54.8 | 45.6 |
| IL | 9,897 | 9,884 | 5,536 | 5,242 | 4,540 | 55.9 | 53.0 | 45.9 |
| IN | 5,058 | 5,124 | 2,735 | 2,658 | 2,256 | 54.1 | 52.6 | 44.0 |
| IA | 2,401 | 2,425 | 1,566 | 1,516 | 1,316 | 65.2 | 63.1 | 54.3 |
| KS | 2,194 | 2,206 | 1,184 | 1,174 | 1,050 | 54.0 | 53.5 | 47.6 |
| KY | 3,426 | 3,460 | 1,924 | 1,765 | 1,570 | 56.2 | 51.5 | 45.4 |
| LA | 3,564 | 3,564 | 2,029 | 1,749 | 1,461 | 56.9 | 49.1 | 41.0 |
| ME | 1,077 | 1,088 | 772 | 772 | 631 | 71.7 | 71.7 | 58.0 |
| MD | 4,659 | 4,703 | 2,781 | 2,708 | 2,286 | 59.7 | 58.1 | 48.6 |
| MA | 5,448 | 5,535 | 3,379 | 3,379 | 2,753 | 62.0 | 62.0 | 49.7 |
| MI | 7,757 | 7,831 | 4,799 | 4,671 | 4,155 | 61.9 | 60.2 | 53.1 |
| MN | 4,232 | 4,309 | 2,945 | 2,860 | 2,577 | 69.6 | 67.6 | 59.8 |
| MS | 2,267 | 2,280 | 1,209 | 1,182 | 939 | 53.3 | 52.1 | 41.2 |
| MO | 4,701 | 4,750 | 2,809 | 2,750 | 2,418 | 59.7 | 58.5 | 50.9 |
| MT | 813 | 833 | 495 | 508 | 504 | 60.8 | 62.5 | 60.6 |
| NE | 1,432 | 1,452 | 844 | 788 | 697 | 58.9 | 55.0 | 48.0 |
| NV | 2,245 | 2,345 | 1,125 | 1,078 | 961 | 50.1 | 48.0 | 41.0 |
| NH | 1,080 | 1,098 | 744 | 716 | 571 | 68.9 | 66.4 | 52.0 |
| NJ | 6,904 | 6,955 | 3,874 | 3,463 | 3,099 | 56.1 | 50.2 | 44.6 |
| NM | 1,598 | 1,613 | 798 | 780 | 693 | 50.0 | 48.8 | 43.0 |
| NY | 15,493 | 15,474 | 7,802 | 7,800 | 6,251 | 50.4 | 50.3 | 40.4 |
| NC | 7,863 | 8,083 | 4,742 | 4,598 | 3,381 | 60.3 | 58.5 | 41.8 |
| ND | 579 | 581 | 344 | 338 | 322 | 59.5 | 58.5 | 55.3 |
| OH | 9,017 | 9,096 | 5,496 | 5,218 | 4,406 | 61.0 | 57.9 | 48.4 |
| OK | 2,964 | 2,987 | 1,453 | 1,133 | 1,179 | 49.0 | 38.2 | 39.5 |
| OR | 3,221 | 3,317 | 2,001 | 1,912 | 1,848 | 62.1 | 59.4 | 55.7 |
| PA | 10,109 | 10,158 | 6,115 | 5,744 | 4,930 | 60.5 | 56.8 | 48.5 |
| RI | 848 | 852 | 464 | 432 | 373 | 54.7 | 50.9 | 43.8 |
| SC | 3,860 | 3,978 | 2,103 | 2,012 | 1,709 | 54.5 | 52.1 | 43.0 |
| SD | 649 | 665 | 370 | 370 | 336 | 57.0 | 57.0 | 50.5 |
| TN | 5,142 | 5,264 | 2,508 | 2,391 | 2,160 | 48.8 | 46.5 | 41.0 |
| TX | 20,621 | 21,304 | 8,969 | 8,529 | 8,203 | 43.5 | 41.4 | 38.5 |
| UT | 2,122 | 2,229 | 1,131 | 1,114 | 1,053 | 53.3 | 52.5 | 47.2 |
| VT | 505 | 510 | 320 | 320 | 278 | 63.4 | 63.4 | 54.5 |
| VA | 6,542 | 6,648 | 3,983 | 3,782 | 3,313 | 60.9 | 57.8 | 49.8 |
| WA | 5,662 | 5,872 | 3,317 | 3,141 | 3,022 | 58.6 | 55.5 | 51.5 |
| WV | 1,457 | 1,442 | 713 | 686 | 578 | 49.0 | 47.1 | 40.1 |
| WI | 4,485 | 4,537 | 2,976 | 2,774 | 2,572 | 66.4 | 61.8 | 56.7 |
| WY | 446 | 443 | 259 | 259 | 205 | 58.1 | 58.1 | 46.3 |

X Not applicable. [1] As of July 1. Source: U.S. Census Bureau, "Annual Estimates of the Resident Population for Selected Age Groups by Sex for the United States, States, Counties, and Puerto Rico Commonwealth and Municipios: April 1, 2010 to July 1, 2018," <http://factfinder.census.gov>, accessed July 2019.

Source: Except as noted, U.S. House of Representatives, Office of the Clerk, *Statistics of the Presidential and Congressional Election*, November 2018, and earlier reports. See also <http://history.house.gov/Institution/Election-Statistics/Election-Statistics/>.

# Table 444. Voting-Age Population—Reported Registration and Voting by Selected Characteristics: 2006 to 2018

[220.6 represents 220,600,000. As of November. Covers civilian noninstitutional population 18 years old and over. Includes aliens. Figures are based on Current Population Survey (see text, Section 1 and Appendix III) and differ from those in Table 441 based on population estimates and official vote counts]

| Characteristic | Voting-age population (mil.) | | | | | | | Percent reporting they registered | | | | | | | Percent reporting they voted | | | | | | |
| | | | | | | | | Presidential election years | | | | Congressional election years | | | Presidential election years | | | | Congressional election years | | |
| | 2006 | 2008 | 2010 | 2012 | 2014 | 2016 | 2018 | 2004 | 2008 | 2012 | 2016 | 2010 | 2014 | 2018 | 2004 | 2008 | 2012 | 2016 | 2010 | 2014 | 2018 |
|---|---|---|---|---|---|---|---|---|---|---|---|---|---|---|---|---|---|---|---|---|---|
| **Total [1]** | **220.6** | **225.5** | **229.7** | **235.2** | **239.9** | **245.5** | **249.7** | **65.9** | **64.9** | **65.1** | **64.2** | **59.8** | **59.3** | **61.3** | **58.3** | **58.2** | **56.5** | **56.0** | **41.8** | **38.5** | **49.0** |
| **AGE** | | | | | | | | | | | | | | | | | | | | | |
| 18 to 20 years old | 11.6 | 11.7 | 12.2 | 12.3 | 11.9 | 11.7 | 12.0 | 50.7 | 49.3 | 44.2 | 46.7 | 34.4 | 32.6 | 40.8 | 41.0 | 41.0 | 35.1 | 36.4 | 16.4 | 14.1 | 27.2 |
| 21 to 24 years old | 16.2 | 16.6 | 16.7 | 17.6 | 17.8 | 13.2 | 17.0 | 52.1 | 56.2 | 53.1 | 71.4 | 47.2 | 43.6 | 49.1 | 42.5 | 46.6 | 40.0 | 55.2 | 22.0 | 17.1 | 32.1 |
| 25 to 34 years old | 39.4 | 40.2 | 41.2 | 41.1 | 42.3 | 43.8 | 44.8 | 55.6 | 56.5 | 57.0 | 56.4 | 49.8 | 49.4 | 52.1 | 46.9 | 48.5 | 46.1 | 46.4 | 26.9 | 24.2 | 37.0 |
| 35 to 44 years old | 42.6 | 41.5 | 39.9 | 39.6 | 39.6 | 39.9 | 40.8 | 64.2 | 61.4 | 61.7 | 60.0 | 57.3 | 56.3 | 57.3 | 56.6 | 55.2 | 52.9 | 51.8 | 37.7 | 32.8 | 44.2 |
| 45 to 64 years old | 75.0 | 78.1 | 80.7 | 82.1 | 82.8 | 83.8 | 83.3 | 72.7 | 70.4 | 70.4 | 68.5 | 66.3 | 65.4 | 66.1 | 66.6 | 65.0 | 63.4 | 61.7 | 51.1 | 46.0 | 55.0 |
| 65 years old and over | 35.8 | 37.5 | 39.0 | 42.5 | 45.6 | 48.7 | 51.9 | 76.9 | 75.0 | 76.9 | 75.3 | 72.5 | 73.0 | 73.3 | 68.9 | 68.1 | 69.7 | 68.4 | 58.9 | 57.5 | 63.8 |
| **SEX** | | | | | | | | | | | | | | | | | | | | | |
| Male | 106.5 | 109.0 | 111.1 | 113.2 | 115.6 | 118.5 | 120.6 | 64.0 | 62.6 | 63.1 | 62.3 | 57.9 | 57.2 | 59.5 | 56.3 | 55.7 | 54.4 | 53.8 | 40.9 | 37.2 | 47.2 |
| Female | 114.1 | 116.5 | 118.6 | 122.0 | 124.2 | 127.0 | 129.2 | 67.6 | 67.0 | 67.0 | 66.0 | 61.5 | 61.2 | 63.0 | 60.1 | 60.4 | 58.5 | 58.1 | 42.7 | 39.6 | 50.6 |
| **RACE/ETHNICITY** | | | | | | | | | | | | | | | | | | | | | |
| White [2] | 179.9 | 183.2 | 185.8 | 187.1 | 189.3 | 192.1 | 194.1 | 67.9 | 66.6 | 66.7 | 66.3 | 61.6 | 61.3 | 63.7 | 60.3 | 59.6 | 57.6 | 58.2 | 43.4 | 40.3 | 51.1 |
| Black [2] | 25.7 | 26.5 | 27.4 | 28.7 | 29.7 | 30.6 | 31.6 | 64.4 | 65.5 | 68.5 | 65.3 | 58.8 | 59.7 | 60.2 | 56.3 | 60.8 | 62.0 | 55.9 | 40.7 | 37.3 | 48.0 |
| Asian [2,3] | 9.9 | 10.5 | 11.0 | 12.5 | 13.5 | 14.9 | 15.7 | 34.9 | 37.3 | 37.2 | 38.9 | 34.1 | 34.4 | 37.7 | 29.8 | 32.1 | 37.3 | 33.9 | 21.3 | 19.1 | 28.9 |
| Hispanic [4] | 29.0 | 30.9 | 32.5 | 35.2 | 36.8 | 39.0 | 41.0 | 34.3 | 37.6 | 38.9 | 39.2 | 33.8 | 34.9 | 37.9 | 28.0 | 31.6 | 31.8 | 32.5 | 20.5 | 18.4 | 28.5 |
| **REGION [5]** | | | | | | | | | | | | | | | | | | | | | |
| Northeast | 41.2 | 41.5 | 42.3 | 42.9 | 43.5 | 43.9 | 44.2 | 65.3 | 63.7 | 65.2 | 64.0 | 59.7 | 58.3 | 60.7 | 58.6 | 57.4 | 56.6 | 56.2 | 41.6 | 36.3 | 48.4 |
| Midwest | 49.1 | 49.4 | 50.1 | 50.6 | 51.0 | 51.6 | 51.8 | 72.8 | 70.6 | 71.4 | 70.2 | 65.0 | 65.0 | 67.5 | 65.0 | 63.4 | 62.3 | 61.4 | 45.1 | 42.3 | 53.5 |
| South | 80.0 | 82.4 | 84.2 | 87.1 | 89.2 | 92.0 | 94.5 | 65.5 | 65.5 | 65.3 | 64.0 | 59.4 | 60.0 | 60.8 | 56.4 | 57.7 | 55.7 | 54.9 | 39.3 | 38.4 | 47.3 |
| West | 50.4 | 52.2 | 53.2 | 54.6 | 56.1 | 58.0 | 59.3 | 60.1 | 59.4 | 58.9 | 59.3 | 55.5 | 53.7 | 57.0 | 54.4 | 54.6 | 52.3 | 52.9 | 42.7 | 36.8 | 48.0 |
| **EDUCATIONAL ATTAINMENT** | | | | | | | | | | | | | | | | | | | | | |
| 8 years or less | 12.1 | 11.1 | 11.1 | 10.5 | 9.9 | 9.8 | 8.9 | 32.5 | 30.1 | 28.7 | 24.5 | 27.0 | 24.5 | 22.9 | 23.6 | 23.4 | 21.6 | 18.3 | 15.8 | 13.2 | 14.4 |
| High school: Less than high school graduate | 20.2 | 19.1 | 18.8 | 18.7 | 18.6 | 17.7 | 16.7 | 45.8 | 43.2 | 42.6 | 39.0 | 37.8 | 37.5 | 36.6 | 34.6 | 33.7 | 32.2 | 29.3 | 20.8 | 18.2 | 23.2 |
| High school graduate or GED [6] | 70.0 | 70.4 | 71.0 | 70.6 | 70.6 | 71.3 | 71.6 | 61.5 | 59.5 | 59.0 | 57.5 | 54.0 | 53.5 | 53.1 | 52.4 | 50.9 | 48.7 | 47.4 | 35.2 | 31.5 | 38.8 |
| College: Some college or Associate's degree | 60.2 | 63.8 | 65.3 | 67.7 | 68.8 | 69.9 | 69.5 | 73.7 | 72.0 | 71.2 | 69.8 | 65.5 | 64.0 | 67.0 | 66.1 | 65.0 | 61.5 | 60.5 | 44.4 | 40.0 | 52.2 |
| Bachelor's or advanced degree | 58.2 | 61.1 | 63.5 | 67.8 | 72.0 | 76.8 | 83.1 | 78.1 | 76.8 | 77.2 | 76.2 | 72.5 | 70.8 | 72.7 | 74.2 | 73.3 | 71.7 | 71.0 | 57.1 | 52.5 | 63.9 |
| **EMPLOYMENT STATUS** | | | | | | | | | | | | | | | | | | | | | |
| Employed | 143.8 | 143.2 | 138.3 | 142.6 | 146.2 | 150.9 | 156.0 | 67.1 | 66.4 | 67.1 | 65.9 | 61.5 | 60.4 | 62.4 | 60.0 | 60.1 | 58.6 | 57.8 | 42.5 | 38.2 | 49.6 |
| Unemployed | 6.2 | 9.5 | 13.9 | 11.1 | 8.4 | 6.9 | 5.5 | 56.3 | 57.2 | 56.9 | 57.0 | 52.3 | 50.7 | 56.5 | 46.4 | 48.8 | 46.1 | 44.8 | 31.6 | 26.9 | 40.2 |
| Not in labor force | 70.5 | 72.8 | 77.5 | 81.6 | 85.2 | 87.8 | 88.2 | 64.4 | 62.9 | 62.8 | 61.8 | 58.0 | 58.2 | 59.6 | 56.2 | 55.5 | 54.3 | 53.8 | 42.3 | 40.1 | 48.4 |

[1] Includes other races, not shown separately. [2] Beginning with the 2003 Current Population Survey (CPS), respondents could choose more than one race. As of 2004, data represent persons who selected this race group only and exclude persons reporting more than one race. The CPS in prior years allowed respondents to report only one race group. See also comment on race in the text for Section 1. [3] Prior to 2004, this category was "Asian and Pacific Islanders," therefore rates are not comparable with prior years. [4] Persons of Hispanic origin may be of any race. [5] For composition of regions, see map, inside cover. [6] The General Educational Development (GED) Test measures how well a non-high school graduate has mastered the skills and general knowledge that are acquired in a 4-year high school education. Successfully passing the exam is a credential generally considered to be equivalent to a high school diploma.

Source: U.S. Census Bureau, "Voting and Registration in the Election of November 2018 – Detailed Tables," <https://www.census.gov/topics/public-sector/voting.html>, accessed April 2019, and earlier releases.

# Table 445. Persons Reporting Voter Registration and Whether Voted by State: 2018

[249,748 represents 249,748,000. As of November. See headnote, Table 444]

| State | Voting-age population (1,000) | Percent of voting-age population Registered | Percent of voting-age population Voted | State | Voting-age population (1,000) | Percent of voting-age population Registered | Percent of voting-age population Voted |
|---|---|---|---|---|---|---|---|
| **United States........** | **249,748** | **61.3** | **49.0** | Missouri.................. | 4,676 | 70.6 | 53.7 |
| Alabama................. | 3,753 | 66.4 | 48.8 | Montana................. | 822 | 70.4 | 63.0 |
| Alaska................... | 523 | 64.4 | 50.2 | Nebraska............... | 1,428 | 61.9 | 47.3 |
| Arizona.................. | 5,361 | 60.8 | 52.2 | Nevada................. | 2,324 | 55.0 | 43.3 |
| Arkansas................ | 2,261 | 55.8 | 40.6 | New Hampshire......... | 1,080 | 67.2 | 53.3 |
| California................ | 30,243 | 51.9 | 43.8 | New Jersey............. | 7,009 | 61.3 | 48.3 |
| Colorado................ | 4,353 | 60.8 | 53.8 | New Mexico............. | 1,576 | 58.1 | 45.3 |
| Connecticut............. | 2,834 | 60.9 | 48.3 | New York................ | 15,478 | 55.3 | 43.8 |
| Delaware................ | 756 | 62.4 | 48.8 | North Carolina.......... | 7,911 | 65.2 | 49.3 |
| District of Columbia..... | 567 | 70.0 | 55.2 | North Dakota........... | 560 | 70.9 | 59.8 |
| Florida.................. | 16,845 | 56.0 | 47.0 | Ohio.................... | 8,873 | 68.3 | 51.1 |
| Georgia................. | 7,850 | 61.7 | 52.0 | Oklahoma.............. | 2,868 | 62.0 | 47.1 |
| Hawaii.................. | 1,057 | 49.5 | 40.4 | Oregon................. | 3,293 | 69.1 | 58.2 |
| Idaho................... | 1,299 | 57.2 | 45.2 | Pennsylvania........... | 9,928 | 65.2 | 52.1 |
| Illinois.................. | 9,732 | 62.4 | 48.7 | Rhode Island........... | 828 | 64.2 | 48.7 |
| Indiana................. | 5,006 | 62.5 | 47.2 | South Carolina......... | 3,914 | 62.1 | 46.9 |
| Iowa.................... | 2,376 | 69.8 | 56.2 | South Dakota.......... | 648 | 66.2 | 51.0 |
| Kansas................. | 2,149 | 67.4 | 53.6 | Tennessee............. | 5,202 | 61.2 | 47.8 |
| Kentucky............... | 3,370 | 70.9 | 51.8 | Texas.................. | 21,064 | 55.2 | 42.2 |
| Louisiana............... | 3,458 | 65.4 | 47.9 | Utah................... | 2,247 | 64.2 | 54.0 |
| Maine................... | 1,074 | 77.1 | 64.5 | Vermont................ | 503 | 68.1 | 54.2 |
| Maryland................ | 4,666 | 66.3 | 49.7 | Virginia................. | 6,386 | 65.1 | 52.0 |
| Massachusetts......... | 5,460 | 61.3 | 50.0 | Washington............. | 5,775 | 66.7 | 56.0 |
| Michigan................ | 7,657 | 71.2 | 57.7 | West Virginia........... | 1,406 | 63.4 | 43.4 |
| Minnesota.............. | 4,238 | 70.8 | 59.5 | Wisconsin.............. | 4,436 | 70.5 | 62.6 |
| Mississippi.............. | 2,194 | 72.9 | 53.8 | Wyoming............... | 430 | 62.4 | 51.2 |

Source: U.S. Census Bureau, "Voting and Registration in the Election of November 2018 - Detailed Tables," <https://www.census.gov/data/tables/time-series/demo/voting-and-registration/p20-583.html>, accessed April 2019.

# Table 446. Reported Voting and Registration Among Native and Naturalized Citizens by Race and Hispanic Origin: 2018

[In thousands, except percent, (228,832 represents 228,832,000). Data shown for population aged 18 years and over. As of November]

| Nativity status, race, and Hispanic origin | Total citizen population (1,000) | Reported registered Number (1,000) | Reported registered Percent | Not registered Number (1,000) | Not registered Percent | Reported voted Number (1,000) | Reported voted Percent | Did not vote Number (1,000) | Did not vote Percent |
|---|---|---|---|---|---|---|---|---|---|
| **TOTAL** | | | | | | | | | |
| All races [1]............... | 228,832 | 153,066 | 66.9 | 33,791 | 14.8 | 122,281 | 53.4 | 66,109 | 28.9 |
| White alone [2]........... | 180,522 | 123,727 | 68.5 | 25,850 | 14.3 | 99,255 | 55.0 | 51,597 | 28.6 |
| White alone, non-Hispanic......... | 154,982 | 110,054 | 71.0 | 19,640 | 12.7 | 89,075 | 57.5 | 41,671 | 26.9 |
| Black alone [2]........... | 29,758 | 19,023 | 63.9 | 4,041 | 13.6 | 15,194 | 51.1 | 7,928 | 26.6 |
| Asian alone [2]........... | 11,128 | 5,898 | 53.0 | 2,245 | 20.2 | 4,519 | 40.6 | 3,764 | 33.8 |
| Hispanic [3]............. | 28,955 | 15,558 | 53.7 | 6,994 | 24.2 | 11,695 | 40.4 | 11,091 | 38.3 |
| **NATIVE CITIZEN** | | | | | | | | | |
| All races [1]............... | 207,022 | 140,377 | 67.8 | 28,947 | 14.0 | 112,303 | 54.2 | 58,321 | 28.2 |
| White alone [2]........... | 168,406 | 116,762 | 69.3 | 23,200 | 13.8 | 93,680 | 55.6 | 47,453 | 28.2 |
| White alone, non-Hispanic......... | 149,884 | 106,939 | 71.3 | 18,759 | 12.5 | 86,591 | 57.8 | 40,122 | 26.8 |
| Black alone [2]........... | 26,974 | 17,234 | 63.9 | 3,551 | 13.2 | 13,742 | 50.9 | 7,076 | 26.2 |
| Asian alone [2]........... | 4,795 | 2,278 | 47.5 | 700 | 14.6 | 1,798 | 37.5 | 1,222 | 25.5 |
| Hispanic [3]............. | 21,193 | 11,298 | 53.3 | 5,053 | 23.8 | 8,261 | 39.0 | 8,258 | 39.0 |
| White alone or in combination [4]..... | 172,046 | 119,099 | 69.2 | 23,856 | 13.9 | 95,450 | 55.5 | 48,710 | 28.3 |
| Black alone or in combination [4]..... | 28,544 | 18,170 | 63.7 | 3,836 | 13.4 | 14,392 | 50.4 | 7,675 | 26.9 |
| Asian alone or in combination [4]..... | 5,791 | 2,945 | 50.9 | 860 | 14.9 | 2,344 | 40.5 | 1,514 | 26.1 |
| **NATURALIZED CITIZEN** | | | | | | | | | |
| All races [1]............... | 21,810 | 12,689 | 58.2 | 4,844 | 22.2 | 9,978 | 45.7 | 7,787 | 35.7 |
| White alone [2]........... | 12,116 | 6,965 | 57.5 | 2,650 | 21.9 | 5,575 | 46.0 | 4,144 | 34.2 |
| White alone, non-Hispanic......... | 5,098 | 3,115 | 61.1 | 881 | 17.3 | 2,485 | 48.7 | 1,549 | 30.4 |
| Black alone [2]........... | 2,785 | 1,789 | 64.2 | 490 | 17.6 | 1,453 | 52.2 | 852 | 30.6 |
| Asian alone [2]........... | 6,333 | 3,620 | 57.2 | 1,546 | 24.4 | 2,721 | 43.0 | 2,542 | 40.1 |
| Hispanic [3]............. | 7,763 | 4,260 | 54.9 | 1,941 | 25.0 | 3,433 | 44.2 | 2,833 | 36.5 |
| White alone or in combination [4]..... | 12,348 | 7,094 | 57.5 | 2,710 | 21.9 | 5,666 | 45.9 | 4,248 | 34.4 |
| Black alone or in combination [4]..... | 2,878 | 1,845 | 64.1 | 517 | 18.0 | 1,495 | 52.0 | 899 | 31.2 |
| Asian alone or in combination [4]..... | 6,379 | 3,650 | 57.2 | 1,553 | 24.3 | 2,736 | 42.9 | 2,564 | 40.2 |

[1] Includes other races, not shown separately. [2] Beginning with the 2003 Current Population Survey (CPS), respondents could choose more than one race. Data shown represent persons who selected this race group only and exclude persons reporting more than one race. [3] Persons of Hispanic origin may be of any race. [4] In combination with one or more races.

Source: U.S. Census Bureau, "Voting and Registration in the Election of November 2018 - Detailed Tables," <https://www.census.gov/data/tables/time-series/demo/voting-and-registration/p20-583.html>, accessed April 2019.

# Table 447. Vote Cast for President by Major Political Party: 1948 to 2016

[In thousands (48,834 represents 48,834,000), except percent and electoral vote. Prior to 1960, excludes Alaska and Hawaii; prior to 1964, excludes DC. Vote cast for major party candidates includes the votes of minor parties cast for those candidates]

| Year | Candidates for President | | Vote cast for President | | | | | | |
| | Democratic | Republican | Total popular vote [1] (1,000) | Democratic | | | Republican | | |
| | | | | Popular vote | | Electoral vote | Popular vote | | Electoral vote |
| | | | | Number (1,000) | Percent | | Number (1,000) | Percent | |
|---|---|---|---|---|---|---|---|---|---|
| 1948.......... | Truman | Dewey | 48,834 | 24,106 | 49.4 | 303 | 21,969 | 45.0 | 189 |
| 1952.......... | Stevenson | Eisenhower | 61,552 | 27,315 | 44.4 | 89 | 33,779 | 54.9 | 442 |
| 1956.......... | Stevenson | Eisenhower | 62,027 | 26,739 | 43.1 | 73 | 35,581 | 57.4 | 457 |
| 1960.......... | Kennedy | Nixon | 68,836 | 34,227 | 49.7 | 303 | 34,108 | 49.5 | 219 |
| 1964.......... | Johnson | Goldwater | 70,098 | 42,825 | 61.1 | 486 | 27,147 | 38.7 | 52 |
| 1968.......... | Humphrey | Nixon | 73,027 | 30,989 | 42.4 | 191 | 31,710 | 43.4 | 301 |
| 1972.......... | McGovern | Nixon | 77,625 | 28,902 | 37.2 | 17 | 46,740 | 60.2 | 520 |
| 1976.......... | Carter | Ford | 81,603 | 40,826 | 50.0 | 297 | 39,148 | 48.0 | 240 |
| 1980.......... | Carter | Reagan | 86,497 | 35,481 | 41.0 | 49 | 43,643 | 50.5 | 489 |
| 1984.......... | Mondale | Reagan | 92,655 | 37,450 | 40.4 | 13 | 54,167 | 58.5 | 525 |
| 1988.......... | Dukakis | Bush | 91,587 | 41,717 | 45.5 | 111 | 48,643 | 53.1 | 426 |
| 1992.......... | Clinton | Bush | 104,600 | 44,858 | 42.9 | 370 | 38,799 | 37.1 | 168 |
| 1996.......... | Clinton | Dole | 96,390 | 47,402 | 49.2 | 379 | 39,198 | 40.7 | 159 |
| 2000.......... | Gore | Bush | 105,594 | 50,996 | 48.3 | 266 | 50,465 | 47.8 | 271 |
| 2004.......... | Kerry | Bush | 122,349 | 58,895 | 48.1 | 251 | 61,873 | 50.6 | 286 |
| 2008.......... | Obama | McCain | 131,407 | 69,498 | 52.9 | 365 | 59,948 | 45.6 | 173 |
| 2012.......... | Obama | Romney | 129,140 | 65,752 | 50.9 | 332 | 60,670 | 47.0 | 206 |
| 2016.......... | Clinton | Trump | 136,787 | 65,677 | 48.0 | 227 | 62,692 | 45.8 | 304 |

[1] Include votes for minor party candidates, independents, unpledged electors, and scattered write-in votes.

Source: U.S. House of Representatives, Office of the Clerk, *Statistics of the Presidential and Congressional Election*, February 2017, and earlier reports. See also <http://clerk.house.gov/member_info/election.aspx>.

# Table 448. Vote Cast for Leading Minority Party Candidates for President: 1948 to 2016

[In thousands (1,169 represents 1,169,000). See headnote, Table 447. Data do not include write-ins, scatterings, or votes for candidates who ran on party tickets not shown, unless otherwise noted]

| Year | Candidate | Party | Popular vote (1,000) | Candidate | Party | Popular vote (1,000) |
|---|---|---|---|---|---|---|
| 1948.......... | Strom Thurmond | States' Rights | 1,169 | Henry Wallace | Progressive | 1,156 |
| 1952.......... | Vincent Hallinan | Progressive | 135 | Stuart Hamblen | Prohibition | 73 |
| 1956 [1]........ | T. Coleman Andrews | States' Rights | 91 | Eric Hass | Socialist Labor | 41 |
| 1960.......... | Eric Hass | Socialist Labor | 46 | Rutherford Decker | Prohibition | 46 |
| 1964.......... | Eric Hass | Socialist Labor | 43 | Clifton DeBerry | Socialist Workers | 22 |
| 1968.......... | George Wallace | American Independent | 9,446 | Henning Blomen | Socialist Labor | 52 |
| 1972 [1]........ | John Schmitz | American | 993 | Benjamin Spock | People's | 9 |
| 1976.......... | Eugene McCarthy | Independent | 680 | Roger McBride | Libertarian | 172 |
| 1980.......... | John Anderson | Independent | 5,251 | Ed Clark | Libertarian | 920 |
| 1984.......... | David Bergland | Libertarian | 227 | Lyndon H. LaRouche | Independent | 79 |
| 1988.......... | Ron Paul | Libertarian | 410 | Lenora B. Fulani | New Alliance | 129 |
| 1992.......... | H. Ross Perot | Independent | 19,722 | Andre Marrou | Libertarian | 281 |
| 1996.......... | H. Ross Perot | Reform | 7,137 | Ralph Nader | Green | 527 |
| 2000.......... | Ralph Nader | Green | 2,530 | Pat Buchanan | Reform | 324 |
| 2004.......... | Michael Badnarik | Libertarian | 369 | Ralph Nader | Independent | 156 |
| 2008.......... | Ralph Nader | Independent | 739 | Bob Barr | Libertarian | 515 |
| 2012.......... | Gary Johnson | Libertarian | 1,216 | Jill Stein | Green | 401 |
| 2016.......... | Gary Johnson | Libertarian | 4,081 | Jill Stein | Green | 1,351 |

[1] Data include write-ins, scatterings, and/or votes for candidates who ran on party tickets not shown.

Source: U.S. House of Representatives, Office of the Clerk, *Statistics of the Presidential and Congressional Election*, February 2017, and earlier reports. See also <http://clerk.house.gov/member_info/election.aspx>.

# Table 449. Electoral Vote Cast for President by Major Political Party—States: 1976 to 2016

[D = Democratic, R = Republican. For composition of regions, see map, inside front cover]

| State | 1976 [1] | 1980 | 1984 | 1988 [2] | 1992 | 1996 | 2000 [3] | 2004 [4] | 2008 [5] | 2012 | 2016 [6] |
|---|---|---|---|---|---|---|---|---|---|---|---|
| **Democratic** | **297** | **49** | **13** | **111** | **370** | **379** | **266** | **251** | **365** | **332** | **227** |
| **Republican** | **240** | **489** | **525** | **426** | **168** | **159** | **271** | **286** | **173** | **206** | **304** |
| **Northeast:** | | | | | | | | | | | |
| Democratic | 86 | 4 | – | 53 | 106 | 106 | 102 | 101 | 101 | 96 | 75 |
| Republican | 36 | 118 | 113 | 60 | – | – | 4 | – | – | – | 21 |
| **Midwest:** | | | | | | | | | | | |
| Democratic | 58 | 10 | 10 | 29 | 100 | 100 | 68 | 57 | 97 | 80 | 30 |
| Republican | 87 | 135 | 127 | 108 | 29 | 29 | 61 | 66 | 27 | 38 | 88 |
| **South:** | | | | | | | | | | | |
| Democratic | 149 | 31 | 3 | 8 | 68 | 80 | 15 | 16 | 71 | 58 | 29 |
| Republican | 20 | 138 | 174 | 168 | 116 | 104 | 168 | 173 | 118 | 138 | 165 |
| **West:** | | | | | | | | | | | |
| Democratic | 4 | 4 | – | 21 | 96 | 93 | 81 | 77 | 96 | 98 | 93 |
| Republican | 97 | 98 | 111 | 90 | 23 | 26 | 38 | 47 | 28 | 30 | 30 |
| Alabama | D-9 | R-9 | R-9 | R-9 | R-9 | R-9 | R-9 | R-9 | R-9 | R-9 | R-9 |
| Alaska | R-3 | R-3 | R-3 | R-3 | R-3 | R-3 | R-3 | R-3 | R-3 | R-3 | R-3 |
| Arizona | R-6 | R-6 | R-7 | R-7 | R-8 | D-8 | R-8 | R-10 | R-10 | R-11 | R-11 |
| Arkansas | D-6 | R-6 | R-6 | R-6 | D-6 | D-6 | R-6 | R-6 | R-6 | R-6 | R-6 |
| California | R-45 | R-45 | R-47 | R-47 | D-54 | D-54 | D-54 | D-55 | D-55 | D-55 | D-55 |
| Colorado | R-7 | R-7 | R-8 | R-8 | D-8 | R-8 | R-8 | R-9 | D-9 | D-9 | D-9 |
| Connecticut | R-8 | R-8 | R-8 | R-8 | D-8 | D-8 | D-8 | D-7 | D-7 | D-7 | D-7 |
| Delaware | D-3 | R-3 | R-3 | R-3 | D-3 | D-3 | D-3 | D-3 | D-3 | D-3 | D-3 |
| District of Columbia | D-3 | D-3 | D-3 | D-3 | D-3 | D-3 | D-2 | D-3 | D-3 | D-3 | D-3 |
| Florida | D-17 | R-17 | R-21 | R-21 | R-25 | D-25 | R-25 | R-27 | D-27 | D-29 | R-29 |
| Georgia | D-12 | D-12 | R-12 | R-12 | D-13 | R-13 | R-13 | R-15 | R-15 | R-16 | R-16 |
| Hawaii | D-4 | D-4 | R-4 | D-4 | D-4 | D-4 | D-4 | D-4 | D-4 | D-4 | D-3 |
| Idaho | R-4 | R-4 | R-4 | R-4 | R-4 | R-4 | R-4 | R-4 | R-4 | R-4 | R-4 |
| Illinois | R-26 | R-26 | R-24 | R-24 | D-22 | D-22 | D-22 | D-21 | D-21 | D-20 | D-20 |
| Indiana | R-13 | R-13 | R-12 | R-12 | R-12 | R-12 | R-12 | R-11 | D-11 | R-11 | R-11 |
| Iowa | R-8 | R-8 | R-8 | D-8 | D-7 | D-7 | D-7 | R-7 | D-7 | D-6 | R-6 |
| Kansas | R-7 | R-7 | R-7 | R-7 | R-6 | R-6 | R-6 | R-6 | R-6 | R-6 | R-6 |
| Kentucky | D-9 | R-9 | R-9 | R-9 | D-8 | D-8 | R-8 | R-8 | R-8 | R-8 | R-8 |
| Louisiana | D-10 | R-10 | R-10 | R-10 | D-9 | D-9 | R-9 | R-9 | R-9 | R-8 | R-8 |
| Maine | R-4 | R-4 | R-4 | R-4 | D-4 | D-4 | D-4 | D-4 | D-4 | D-4 | D-3 |
| Maryland | D-10 | D-10 | R-10 | R-10 | D-10 | D-10 | D-10 | D-10 | D-10 | D-10 | D-10 |
| Massachusetts | D-14 | R-14 | R-13 | D-13 | D-12 | D-12 | D-12 | D-12 | D-12 | D-11 | D-11 |
| Michigan | R-21 | R-21 | R-20 | R-20 | D-18 | D-18 | D-18 | D-17 | D-17 | D-16 | R-16 |
| Minnesota | D-10 | D-10 | D-10 | D-10 | D-10 | D-10 | D-10 | D-9 | D-10 | D-10 | D-10 |
| Mississippi | D-7 | R-7 | R-7 | R-7 | R-7 | R-7 | R-7 | R-6 | R-6 | R-6 | R-6 |
| Missouri | D-12 | R-12 | R-11 | R-11 | D-11 | D-11 | R-11 | R-11 | R-11 | R-10 | R-10 |
| Montana | R-4 | R-4 | R-4 | R-4 | D-3 | R-3 | R-3 | R-3 | R-3 | R-3 | R-3 |
| Nebraska | R-5 | R-5 | R-5 | R-5 | R-5 | R-5 | R-5 | R-5 | R-4 | R-5 | R-5 |
| Nevada | R-3 | R-3 | R-4 | R-4 | D-4 | D-4 | R-4 | R-5 | D-5 | D-6 | D-6 |
| New Hampshire | R-4 | R-4 | R-4 | R-4 | D-4 | D-4 | R-4 | D-4 | D-4 | D-4 | D-4 |
| New Jersey | R-17 | R-17 | R-16 | R-16 | D-15 | D-15 | D-15 | D-15 | D-15 | D-14 | D-14 |
| New Mexico | R-4 | R-4 | R-5 | R-5 | D-5 | D-5 | D-5 | R-5 | D-5 | D-5 | D-5 |
| New York | D-41 | R-41 | R-36 | D-36 | D-33 | D-33 | D-33 | D-31 | D-31 | D-29 | D-29 |
| North Carolina | D-13 | R-13 | R-13 | R-13 | R-14 | R-14 | R-14 | R-15 | D-15 | R-15 | R-15 |
| North Dakota | R-3 | R-3 | R-3 | R-3 | R-3 | R-3 | R-3 | R-3 | R-3 | R-3 | R-3 |
| Ohio | D-25 | R-25 | R-23 | R-23 | D-21 | D-21 | R-21 | R-20 | D-20 | D-18 | R-18 |
| Oklahoma | R-8 | R-8 | R-8 | R-8 | R-8 | R-8 | R-8 | R-7 | R-7 | R-7 | R-7 |
| Oregon | R-6 | R-6 | R-7 | D-7 | D-7 | D-7 | D-7 | D-7 | D-7 | D-7 | D-7 |
| Pennsylvania | D-27 | R-27 | R-25 | R-25 | D-23 | D-23 | D-23 | D-21 | D-21 | D-20 | R-20 |
| Rhode Island | D-4 | D-4 | R-4 | D-4 | D-4 | D-4 | D-4 | D-4 | D-4 | D-4 | D-4 |
| South Carolina | D-8 | R-8 | R-8 | R-8 | R-8 | R-8 | R-8 | R-8 | R-8 | R-9 | R-9 |
| South Dakota | R-4 | R-4 | R-3 | R-3 | R-3 | R-3 | R-3 | R-3 | R-3 | R-3 | R-3 |
| Tennessee | D-10 | R-10 | R-11 | R-11 | D-11 | D-11 | R-11 | R-11 | R-11 | R-11 | R-11 |
| Texas | D-26 | R-26 | R-29 | R-29 | R-32 | R-32 | R-32 | R-34 | R-34 | R-38 | R-36 |
| Utah | R-4 | R-4 | R-5 | R-5 | R-5 | R-5 | R-5 | R-5 | R-5 | R-6 | R-6 |
| Vermont | R-3 | R-3 | R-3 | R-3 | D-3 | D-3 | D-3 | D-3 | D-3 | D-3 | D-3 |
| Virginia | R-12 | R-12 | R-12 | R-12 | R-13 | R-13 | R-13 | R-13 | D-13 | D-13 | D-13 |
| Washington | R-8 | R-9 | R-10 | D-10 | D-11 | D-11 | D-11 | D-11 | D-11 | D-12 | D-8 |
| West Virginia | D-6 | D-6 | R-6 | D-5 | D-5 | D-5 | R-5 | R-5 | R-5 | R-5 | R-5 |
| Wisconsin | D-11 | R-11 | R-11 | D-11 | D-11 | D-11 | D-11 | D-10 | D-10 | D-10 | R-10 |
| Wyoming | R-3 | R-3 | R-3 | R-3 | R-3 | R-3 | R-3 | R-3 | R-3 | R-3 | R-3 |

– Represents zero. [1] Excludes one electoral vote cast for Ronald Reagan in Washington. [2] Excludes one electoral vote cast for Lloyd Bentsen for President in West Virginia. [3] Excludes one electoral vote left blank by a Democratic elector in the District of Columbia. [4] Excludes one electoral vote cast for Democratic vice presidential nominee John Edwards in Minnesota. [5] Excludes one electoral vote for Barack Obama in Nebraska. [6] Excludes one electoral vote cast for Bernie Sanders in Hawaii, one electoral vote cast for Donald J. Trump in Maine, one electoral vote each cast for John Kasich and Ron Paul in Texas, and three electoral votes for Colin Powell and one electoral vote for Faith Spotted Eagle in Washington.

Source: U.S. House of Representatives, Office of the Clerk, *Statistics of the Presidential and Congressional Election*, February 2017, and earlier reports. See also <http://clerk.house.gov/member_info/election.aspx>.

# Table 450. Popular Vote Cast for President by Political Party—States: 2012 and 2016

[In thousands (129,140 represents 129,140,000), except percent]

| State | 2012 | | | Percent of total vote | | 2016 | | | Percent of total vote | |
|---|---|---|---|---|---|---|---|---|---|---|
| | Total [1] | Demo-cratic party | Republi-can party | Demo-cratic party | Republi-can party | Total [1] | Demo-cratic party | Republi-can party | Demo-cratic party | Republi-can party |
| **United States.........** | **129,140** | **65,752** | **60,670** | **50.9** | **47.0** | **136,787** | **65,677** | **62,692** | **48.0** | **45.8** |
| Alabama................. | 2,074 | 796 | 1,256 | 38.4 | 60.5 | 2,123 | 730 | 1,318 | 34.4 | 62.1 |
| Alaska................... | 300 | 123 | 165 | 40.8 | 54.8 | 319 | 116 | 163 | 36.6 | 51.3 |
| Arizona.................. | 2,299 | 1,025 | 1,234 | 44.6 | 53.7 | 2,573 | 1,161 | 1,252 | 45.1 | 48.7 |
| Arkansas................ | 1,069 | 394 | 648 | 36.9 | 60.6 | 1,131 | 380 | 685 | 33.7 | 60.6 |
| California............... | 13,039 | 7,854 | 4,840 | 60.2 | 37.1 | 14,182 | 8,754 | 4,484 | 61.7 | 31.6 |
| Colorado................ | 2,570 | 1,323 | 1,185 | 51.5 | 46.1 | 2,780 | 1,339 | 1,202 | 48.2 | 43.3 |
| Connecticut............. | 1,558 | 905 | 635 | 58.1 | 40.7 | 1,645 | 898 | 673 | 54.6 | 40.9 |
| Delaware................ | 414 | 243 | 165 | 58.6 | 40.0 | 442 | 236 | 185 | 53.4 | 41.9 |
| District of Columbia..... | 294 | 267 | 21 | 90.9 | 7.3 | 313 | 283 | 13 | 90.5 | 4.1 |
| Florida.................. | 8,474 | 4,238 | 4,163 | 50.0 | 49.1 | 9,420 | 4,505 | 4,618 | 47.8 | 49.0 |
| Georgia................. | 3,898 | 1,774 | 2,079 | 45.5 | 53.3 | 4,115 | 1,878 | 2,089 | 45.6 | 50.8 |
| Hawaii.................. | 437 | 307 | 121 | 70.1 | 27.7 | 438 | 267 | 129 | 61.0 | 29.4 |
| Idaho................... | 652 | 213 | 421 | 32.6 | 64.5 | 690 | 190 | 409 | 27.5 | 59.3 |
| Illinois.................. | 5,242 | 3,020 | 2,135 | 57.6 | 40.7 | 5,536 | 3,091 | 2,146 | 55.8 | 38.8 |
| Indiana................. | 2,625 | 1,153 | 1,421 | 43.9 | 54.1 | 2,735 | 1,033 | 1,557 | 37.8 | 56.9 |
| Iowa.................... | 1,582 | 823 | 731 | 52.0 | 46.2 | 1,566 | 654 | 801 | 41.8 | 51.2 |
| Kansas................. | 1,160 | 441 | 693 | 38.0 | 59.7 | 1,184 | 427 | 671 | 36.1 | 56.7 |
| Kentucky............... | 1,797 | 679 | 1,087 | 37.8 | 60.5 | 1,924 | 629 | 1,203 | 32.7 | 62.5 |
| Louisiana............... | 1,994 | 809 | 1,152 | 40.6 | 57.8 | 2,029 | 780 | 1,179 | 38.4 | 58.1 |
| Maine................... | 725 | 401 | 292 | 55.4 | 40.3 | 772 | 358 | 336 | 46.3 | 43.5 |
| Maryland................ | 2,707 | 1,678 | 972 | 62.0 | 35.9 | 2,781 | 1,678 | 943 | 60.3 | 33.9 |
| Massachusetts.......... | 3,184 | 1,921 | 1,188 | 60.3 | 37.3 | 3,379 | 1,995 | 1,091 | 59.1 | 32.3 |
| Michigan................ | 4,731 | 2,565 | 2,115 | 54.2 | 44.7 | 4,799 | 2,269 | 2,280 | 47.3 | 47.5 |
| Minnesota............... | 2,937 | 1,546 | 1,320 | 52.7 | 45.0 | 2,945 | 1,368 | 1,323 | 46.4 | 44.9 |
| Mississippi.............. | 1,286 | 563 | 711 | 43.8 | 55.3 | 1,209 | 485 | 701 | 40.1 | 57.9 |
| Missouri................ | 2,757 | 1,224 | 1,482 | 44.4 | 53.8 | 2,809 | 1,071 | 1,595 | 38.1 | 56.8 |
| Montana................ | 484 | 202 | 268 | 41.7 | 55.4 | 495 | 178 | 279 | 35.9 | 56.5 |
| Nebraska............... | 794 | 302 | 475 | 38.0 | 59.8 | 844 | 284 | 496 | 33.7 | 58.7 |
| Nevada................. | 1,015 | 531 | 464 | 52.4 | 45.7 | 1,125 | 539 | 512 | 47.9 | 45.5 |
| New Hampshire.......... | 711 | 370 | 330 | 52.0 | 46.4 | 744 | 349 | 346 | 46.8 | 46.5 |
| New Jersey............. | 3,638 | 2,123 | 1,478 | 58.3 | 40.6 | 3,874 | 2,148 | 1,602 | 55.5 | 41.4 |
| New Mexico............. | 784 | 415 | 336 | 53.0 | 42.8 | 798 | 385 | 320 | 48.3 | 40.0 |
| New York............... | 7,117 | 4,324 | 2,223 | 60.8 | 31.2 | 7,802 | 4,380 | 2,527 | 56.1 | 32.4 |
| North Carolina.......... | 4,505 | 2,178 | 2,270 | 48.4 | 50.4 | 4,742 | 2,189 | 2,363 | 46.2 | 49.8 |
| North Dakota............ | 323 | 125 | 188 | 38.7 | 58.3 | 344 | 94 | 217 | 27.2 | 63.0 |
| Ohio.................... | 5,581 | 2,828 | 2,661 | 50.7 | 47.7 | 5,496 | 2,394 | 2,841 | 43.6 | 51.7 |
| Oklahoma............... | 1,335 | 444 | 891 | 33.2 | 66.8 | 1,453 | 420 | 949 | 28.9 | 65.3 |
| Oregon.................. | 1,789 | 970 | 754 | 54.2 | 42.1 | 2,001 | 1,002 | 782 | 50.1 | 39.1 |
| Pennsylvania............ | 5,742 | 2,990 | 2,680 | 52.1 | 46.7 | 6,115 | 2,926 | 2,971 | 47.9 | 48.6 |
| Rhode Island............ | 446 | 280 | 157 | 62.7 | 35.2 | 464 | 253 | 181 | 54.4 | 38.9 |
| South Carolina.......... | 1,964 | 866 | 1,072 | 44.1 | 54.6 | 2,103 | 855 | 1,155 | 40.7 | 54.9 |
| South Dakota........... | 364 | 145 | 211 | 39.9 | 57.9 | 370 | 117 | 228 | 31.7 | 61.5 |
| Tennessee.............. | 2,459 | 961 | 1,462 | 39.1 | 59.5 | 2,508 | 871 | 1,523 | 34.7 | 60.7 |
| Texas................... | 7,994 | 3,308 | 4,570 | 41.4 | 57.2 | 8,969 | 3,878 | 4,685 | 43.2 | 52.2 |
| Utah.................... | 1,017 | 252 | 741 | 24.7 | 72.8 | 1,131 | 311 | 515 | 27.5 | 45.5 |
| Vermont................. | 299 | 199 | 93 | 66.6 | 31.0 | 320 | 179 | 95 | 55.7 | 29.8 |
| Virginia................. | 3,854 | 1,972 | 1,823 | 51.2 | 47.3 | 3,983 | 1,981 | 1,769 | 49.8 | 44.4 |
| Washington.............. | 3,126 | 1,755 | 1,291 | 56.2 | 41.3 | 3,317 | 1,743 | 1,222 | 52.5 | 36.8 |
| West Virginia............ | 670 | 238 | 418 | 35.5 | 62.3 | 713 | 189 | 489 | 26.5 | 68.6 |
| Wisconsin............... | 3,071 | 1,621 | 1,411 | 52.8 | 45.9 | 2,976 | 1,383 | 1,405 | 46.5 | 47.2 |
| Wyoming................ | 251 | 69 | 171 | 27.6 | 68.2 | 259 | 56 | 174 | 21.6 | 67.4 |

[1] Includes other parties.

Source: U.S. House of Representatives, Office of the Clerk, *Statistics of the Presidential and Congressional Election*, February 2017, and earlier reports. See also <http://clerk.house.gov/member_info/election.aspx>.

## Table 451. Vote Cast for U.S. Senators, 2016 and 2018, and Incumbent Senators, 2019—States

[2,087 represents 2,087,000. D = Democrat, R = Republican, I = Independent]

| State | 2016 Total[2] (1,000) | 2016 Percent for leading party | 2018 Total[2] (1,000) | 2018 Percent for leading party | Incumbent senators and year term expires[1] Name, party, and year | Incumbent senators and year term expires[1] Name, party, and year |
|---|---|---|---|---|---|---|
| Alabama | 2,087 | R-64.0 | (X) | (X) | Doug Jones[3] (D) 2021 | Richard C. Shelby (R) 2023 |
| Alaska | 311 | R-44.4 | (X) | (X) | Lisa Murkowski (R) 2023 | Dan Sullivan (R) 2021 |
| Arizona | 2,531 | R-53.7 | 2,384 | D-50.0 | Kyrsten Sinema (D) 2025 | Martha McSally[4] (R) 2023 |
| Arkansas | 1,108 | R-59.8 | (X) | (X) | John Boozman (R) 2023 | Tom Cotton (R) 2021 |
| California | 12,244 | [5] D-100.0 | 11,113 | [5] D-100.0 | Kamala D. Harris (D) 2023 | Dianne Feinstein (D) 2025 |
| Colorado | 2,743 | D-50.0 | (X) | (X) | Cory Gardner (R) 2021 | Michael F. Bennet (D) 2023 |
| Connecticut | 1,596 | D-57.7 | 1,387 | D-56.8 | Richard Blumenthal (D) 2023 | Christopher Murphy (D) 2025 |
| Delaware | (X) | (X) | 363 | D-60.0 | Christopher Coons (D) 2021 | Thomas R. Carper (D) 2025 |
| Florida | 9,302 | R-52.0 | 8,190 | R-50.1 | Marco Rubio (R) 2023 | Rick Scott (R) 2025 |
| Georgia | 3,899 | R-54.8 | (X) | (X) | David A. Perdue (R) 2021 | Johnny Isakson (R) 2023 |
| Hawaii | 438 | D-70.1 | 399 | D-69.3 | Brian Schatz (D) 2023 | Mazie Hirono (D) 2025 |
| Idaho | 679 | R-66.1 | (X) | (X) | James E. Risch (R) 2021 | Mike Crapo (R) 2023 |
| Illinois | 5,492 | D-54.9 | (X) | (X) | Richard J. Durbin (D) 2021 | Tammy Duckworth (D) 2023 |
| Indiana | 2,733 | R-52.1 | 2,283 | R-50.7 | Todd C. Young (R) 2023 | Mike Braun (R) 2025 |
| Iowa | 1,541 | R-60.1 | (X) | (X) | Chuck Grassley (R) 2023 | Joni Ernst (R) 2021 |
| Kansas | 1,178 | R-62.2 | (X) | (X) | Jerry Moran (R) 2023 | Pat Roberts (R) 2021 |
| Kentucky | 1,903 | R-57.3 | (X) | (X) | Rand Paul (R) 2023 | Mitch McConnell (R) 2021 |
| Louisiana[6] | 820 | R-58.8 | (X) | (X) | Bill Cassidy (R) 2021 | John Kennedy (R) 2023 |
| Maine | (X) | (X) | 646 | I-53.3 | Susan M. Collins (R) 2021 | Angus King (I) 2025 |
| Maryland | 2,726 | D-60.9 | 2,300 | D-64.9 | Chris Van Hollen (D) 2023 | Benjamin L. Cardin (D) 2025 |
| Massachusetts | (X) | (X) | 2,753 | D-59.3 | Elizabeth Warren (D) 2025 | Ed Markey (D) 2021 |
| Michigan | (X) | (X) | 4,237 | D-52.3 | Gary C. Peters (D) 2021 | Debbie Stabenow (D) 2025 |
| Minnesota | (X) | (X) | 2,597 | D-60.3 | Tina Smith[7] (D) 2021 | Amy Klobuchar (D) 2025 |
| Mississippi | (X) | (X) | 936 | R-58.5 | Cindy Hyde-Smith[8] (R) 2021 | Roger F. Wicker (R) 2025 |
| Missouri | 2,803 | R-49.2 | 2,442 | R-51.4 | Roy Blunt (R) 2023 | Josh Hawley (R) 2025 |
| Montana | (X) | (X) | 504 | D-50.3 | Steve Daines (R) 2021 | John Tester (D) 2025 |
| Nebraska | (X) | (X) | 699 | R-57.7 | Ben Sasse (R) 2021 | Deb Fischer (R) 2025 |
| Nevada | 1,108 | D-47.1 | 972 | D-50.4 | Jacky Rosen (D) 2025 | Catherine Cortez Masto (D) 2023 |
| New Hampshire | 739 | D-48.0 | (X) | (X) | Maggie Hassan (D) 2023 | Jeanne Shaheen (D) 2021 |
| New Jersey | (X) | (X) | 3,169 | D-54.0 | Robert Menendez (D) 2025 | Cory A. Booker (D) 2021 |
| New Mexico | (X) | (X) | 697 | D-54.1 | Martin Heinrich (D) 2025 | Tom Udall (D) 2021 |
| New York | 7,801 | D-61.3 | 6,251 | D-60.1 | Kirsten E. Gillibrand (D) 2025 | Charles E. Schumer (D) 2023 |
| North Carolina | 4,691 | R-51.1 | (X) | (X) | Richard Burr (R) 2023 | Thom Tillis (R) 2021 |
| North Dakota | 343 | R-78.5 | 326 | R-55.1 | Kevin Cramer (R) 2025 | John Hoeven (R) 2023 |
| Ohio | 5,374 | R-58.0 | 4,411 | D-53.4 | Sherrod Brown (D) 2025 | Rob Portman (R) 2023 |
| Oklahoma | 1,448 | R-67.7 | (X) | (X) | James Lankford (R) 2023 | James M. Inhofe (R) 2021 |
| Oregon | 1,952 | D-56.6 | (X) | (X) | Jeff Merkley (D) 2021 | Ron Wyden (D) 2023 |
| Pennsylvania | 6,052 | R-48.8 | 5,009 | D-55.7 | Robert P. Casey Jr. (D) 2025 | Patrick J. Toomey (R) 2023 |
| Rhode Island | (X) | (X) | 377 | D-61.4 | Sheldon Whitehouse (D) 2025 | Jack Reed (D) 2021 |
| South Carolina | 2,050 | R-60.6 | (X) | (X) | Tim Scott (R) 2023 | Lindsey Graham (R) 2021 |
| South Dakota | 370 | R-71.8 | (X) | (X) | Mike Rounds (R) 2021 | John Thune (R) 2023 |
| Tennessee | (X) | (X) | 2,244 | R-54.7 | Lamar Alexander (R) 2021 | Marsha Blackburn (R) 2025 |
| Texas | (X) | (X) | 8,372 | R-50.9 | John Cornyn (R) 2021 | Ted Cruz (R) 2025 |
| Utah | 1,116 | R-68.1 | 1,063 | R-62.6 | Mike Lee (R) 2023 | Mitt Romney (R) 2025 |
| Vermont | 320 | D-60.0 | 278 | I-70.6 | Bernard Sanders (I) 2025 | Patrick J. Leahy (D) 2023 |
| Virginia | (X) | (X) | 3,351 | D-57.0 | Tim Kaine (D) 2025 | Mark R. Warner (D) 2021 |
| Washington | 3,243 | D-59.0 | 3,086 | D-58.4 | Maria Cantwell (D) 2025 | Patty Murray (D) 2023 |
| West Virginia | (X) | (X) | 586 | D-49.6 | Joe Manchin III (D) 2025 | Shelley Moore Capito (R) 2021 |
| Wisconsin | 2,949 | R-50.2 | 2,661 | D-55.4 | Ronald H. Johnson (R) 2023 | Tammy Baldwin (D) 2025 |
| Wyoming | (X) | (X) | 205 | R-66.4 | Michael B. Enzi (R) 2021 | John Barrasso (R) 2025 |

X Not applicable. [1] As of March 14, 2019; see <http://www.senate.gov/pagelayout/reference/three_column_table/Senators.htm>. [2] Includes vote cast for minor parties. [3] Elected in a special election on December 12, 2017 to fill the vacancy caused by the resignation of Jeff Sessions. [4] Appointed December 18, 2018 to fill the vacancy caused by the resignation of Jon Kyl. [5] Two Democrats ran for Senate; no Republican challenger. [6] Louisiana holds an open-primary election with candidates from all parties running on the same ballot. Any candidate who receives a majority is elected. No candidate received a majority in the 2016 open-primary and a runoff election was held on Dec. 10, 2016. Data shown are runoff election totals. [7] Appointed December 13, 2017 to fill the vacancy caused by the resignation of Al Franken, and elected in a special election on November 6, 2018 to serve the remainder of the term. [8] Elected in a runoff election on November 27, 2018 to fill the vacancy caused by the resignation of Thad Cochran.

Source: U.S. House of Representatives, Office of the Clerk, *Statistics of the Congressional Election of November 6, 2018*, February 2019, and earlier reports; and ProQuest research. See also <http://clerk.house.gov/member_info/election.aspx>.

# Table 452. Vote Cast for U.S. House of Representatives by Major Political Party—States: 2014 to 2018

[In thousands (78,813 represents 78,813,000), except percent. R = Republican, D = Democrat, and I = Independent. In each state, totals represent the sum of votes cast in each Congressional District or votes cast for Representative-at-Large in states where only one member is elected. In all years there are numerous districts within the state where either the Republican or Democratic party had no candidate. In some states the Republican and Democratic vote includes votes cast for the party candidate by endorsing parties]

| State | 2014 | | | | 2016 | | | | 2018 | | | |
|---|---|---|---|---|---|---|---|---|---|---|---|---|
| | Total [1] | Demo-cratic | Republi-can | Percent for leading party | Total [1] | Demo-cratic | Republi-can | Percent for leading party | Total [1] | Demo-cratic | Republi-can | Percent for leading party |
| U.S. | 78,813 | 35,369 | 39,927 | R-50.7 | 129,833 | 61,417 | 62,772 | R-48.3 | 114,017 | 60,320 | 50,467 | D-52.9 |
| AL. | 1,081 | 332 | 705 | R-65.2 | 1,890 | 622 | 1,222 | R-64.7 | 1,660 | 679 | 976 | R-58.8 |
| AK. | 280 | 115 | 143 | R-51.0 | 308 | 111 | 155 | R-50.3 | 282 | 131 | 150 | R-53.1 |
| AZ. | 1,468 | 578 | 817 | R-55.7 | 2,412 | 1,035 | 1,264 | R-52.4 | 2,341 | 1,179 | 1,139 | D-50.4 |
| AR. | 831 | 255 | 510 | R-61.4 | 1,069 | 111 | 760 | R-71.2 | 889 | 313 | 556 | R-62.6 |
| CA. | 7,132 | 4,068 | 2,951 | D-57.0 | 13,414 | 8,624 | 4,682 | D-64.3 | 12,185 | 8,010 | 3,973 | D-65.7 |
| CO. | 2,001 | 936 | 1,000 | R-50.0 | 2,701 | 1,264 | 1,289 | R-47.7 | 2,514 | 1,343 | 1,080 | D-53.4 |
| CT. | 1,068 | 596 | 410 | D-55.8 | 1,575 | 917 | 558 | D-58.2 | 1,380 | 809 | 512 | D-58.6 |
| DE. | 232 | 137 | 85 | D-59.3 | 421 | 234 | 172 | D-55.5 | 354 | 227 | 125 | D-64.3 |
| FL [2] | 4,999 | 2,131 | 2,713 | R-54.3 | 8,837 | 3,985 | 4,734 | R-53.6 | 7,021 | 3,307 | 3,675 | R-52.3 |
| GA. | 2,306 | 956 | 1,349 | R-58.5 | 3,773 | 1,498 | 2,272 | R-60.2 | 3,802 | 1,814 | 1,987 | R-52.3 |
| HI. | 370 | 235 | 120 | D-63.7 | 438 | 316 | 86 | D-72.3 | 399 | 288 | 87 | D-72.2 |
| ID. | 435 | 160 | 275 | R-63.2 | 682 | 209 | 448 | R-65.7 | 596 | 207 | 368 | R-61.8 |
| IL. | 3,568 | 1,823 | 1,722 | D-51.1 | 5,242 | 2,811 | 2,397 | D-53.6 | 4,540 | 2,758 | 1,754 | D-60.7 |
| IN. | 1,342 | 502 | 789 | R-58.8 | 2,658 | 1,053 | 1,443 | R-54.3 | 2,256 | 1,000 | 1,248 | R-55.3 |
| IA. | 1,120 | 509 | 596 | R-53.2 | 1,516 | 674 | 813 | R-53.7 | 1,316 | 665 | 612 | D-50.5 |
| KS. | 862 | 312 | 541 | R-62.7 | 1,174 | 318 | 694 | R-59.1 | 1,050 | 464 | 563 | R-53.6 |
| KY. | 1,398 | 508 | 887 | R-63.5 | 1,765 | 517 | 1,248 | R-70.7 | 1,570 | 613 | 935 | R-59.6 |
| LA [2] | 1,569 | 406 | 1,031 | R-65.7 | 1,749 | 530 | 1,178 | R-67.3 | 1,461 | 553 | 836 | R-57.2 |
| ME. | 617 | 305 | 228 | D-49.5 | 772 | 387 | 357 | D-50.1 | 631 | 344 | 250 | D-54.4 |
| MD. | 1,703 | 978 | 704 | D-57.4 | 2,708 | 1,636 | 962 | D-60.4 | 2,286 | 1,493 | 738 | D-65.3 |
| MA. | 2,187 | 1,475 | 309 | D-67.5 | 3,379 | 2,345 | 451 | D-69.4 | 2,753 | 1,944 | 498 | D-70.6 |
| MI. | 3,089 | 1,519 | 1,467 | D-49.2 | 4,671 | 2,194 | 2,243 | R-48.0 | 4,155 | 2,175 | 1,853 | D-52.4 |
| MN. | 1,964 | 986 | 914 | D-50.2 | 2,860 | 1,435 | 1,335 | D-50.2 | 2,577 | 1,421 | 1,126 | D-55.1 |
| MS. | 626 | 230 | 329 | R-52.6 | 1,182 | 450 | 681 | R-57.6 | 939 | 399 | 471 | R-50.2 |
| MO. | 1,426 | 514 | 838 | R-58.8 | 2,750 | 1,041 | 1,601 | R-58.2 | 2,418 | 1,028 | 1,331 | R-55.0 |
| MT. | 368 | 149 | 204 | R-55.4 | 508 | 206 | 285 | R-56.2 | 504 | 233 | 257 | R-50.9 |
| NE. | 536 | 185 | 341 | R-63.6 | 788 | 221 | 558 | R-70.7 | 697 | 264 | 432 | R-62.0 |
| NV. | 543 | 210 | 305 | R-56.1 | 1,078 | 508 | 498 | D-47.1 | 961 | 491 | 440 | D-51.1 |
| NH. | 481 | 247 | 232 | D-51.5 | 716 | 336 | 316 | D-47.0 | 571 | 311 | 249 | D-54.5 |
| NJ. | 1,821 | 914 | 877 | D-50.2 | 3,463 | 1,822 | 1,542 | D-52.6 | 3,099 | 1,857 | 1,199 | D-59.9 |
| NM. | 512 | 271 | 241 | D-53.0 | 780 | 437 | 343 | D-56.0 | 693 | 404 | 265 | D-58.3 |
| NY. | 3,935 | 1,788 | 1,257 | D-45.4 | 7,800 | 4,202 | 2,141 | D-53.9 | 6,251 | 3,761 | 1,640 | D-60.2 |
| NC. | 2,808 | 1,234 | 1,555 | R-55.4 | 4,598 | 2,143 | 2,447 | R-53.2 | 3,381 | 1,633 | 1,707 | R-50.5 |
| ND. | 249 | 96 | 138 | R-55.5 | 338 | 80 | 234 | R-69.1 | 322 | 114 | 194 | R-60.2 |
| OH. | 3,000 | 1,180 | 1,771 | R-59.0 | 5,218 | 2,155 | 2,996 | R-57.4 | 4,406 | 2,083 | 2,291 | R-52.0 |
| OK [2] | 653 | 174 | 458 | R-70.0 | 1,133 | 305 | 782 | R-69.0 | 1,179 | 428 | 731 | R-62.0 |
| OR. | 1,451 | 778 | 583 | D-53.6 | 1,912 | 1,027 | 731 | D-53.7 | 1,848 | 1,061 | 703 | D-57.4 |
| PA. | 3,324 | 1,468 | 1,833 | R-55.2 | 5,744 | 2,625 | 3,097 | R-53.9 | 4,930 | 2,713 | 2,206 | D-55.0 |
| RI. | 316 | 193 | 123 | D-61.0 | 432 | 264 | 141 | D-61.1 | 373 | 243 | 130 | D-65.0 |
| SC. | 1,156 | 377 | 734 | R-63.5 | 2,012 | 768 | 1,177 | R-58.5 | 1,709 | 758 | 927 | R-54.3 |
| SD. | 276 | 92 | 184 | R-66.5 | 370 | 133 | 237 | R-64.1 | 336 | 121 | 203 | R-60.3 |
| TN. | 1,371 | 448 | 849 | R-61.9 | 2,391 | 814 | 1,494 | R-62.5 | 2,160 | 846 | 1,280 | R-59.2 |
| TX. | 4,453 | 1,474 | 2,685 | R-60.3 | 8,529 | 3,161 | 4,878 | R-57.2 | 8,203 | 3,853 | 4,135 | R-50.4 |
| UT. | 566 | 183 | 351 | R-62.0 | 1,114 | 356 | 711 | R-63.8 | 1,053 | 374 | 617 | R-58.7 |
| VT. | 192 | 123 | 59 | D-64.4 | 320 | 264 | (X) | D-82.5 | 278 | 189 | 71 | D-67.8 |
| VA. | 2,135 | 846 | 1,144 | R-53.6 | 3,782 | 1,859 | 1,843 | D-49.2 | 3,313 | 1,867 | 1,409 | D-56.4 |
| WA. | 2,030 | 1,048 | 982 | D-51.6 | 3,141 | 1,736 | 1,405 | D-55.3 | 3,022 | 1,889 | 900 | D-62.5 |
| WV. | 439 | 182 | 243 | R-55.3 | 686 | 224 | 445 | R-64.8 | 578 | 235 | 337 | R-58.3 |
| WI. | 2,356 | 1,103 | 1,233 | R-52.4 | 2,774 | 1,380 | 1,270 | D-49.8 | 2,572 | 1,367 | 1,173 | D-53.2 |
| WY. | 171 | 38 | 113 | R-66.0 | 259 | 75 | 156 | R-60.3 | 205 | 60 | 128 | R-62.3 |

X Not applicable. [1] Includes votes cast for minor parties. [2] State law does not require tabulation of votes for unopposed candidates.

Source: U.S. House of Representatives, Office of the Clerk, *Statistics of the Congressional Election of November 6, 2018*, February 2019, and earlier reports. See also <http://clerk.house.gov/member_info/election.aspx>.

# Table 453. Vote Cast for U.S. House of Representatives by Major Political Party—Congressional Districts: 2018

[As of February 2019. Does not include special elections or votes received from endorsing parties. If multiple candidates from the same party ran in the general election, only the candidate with the leading number of votes is shown]

| State and district | Democrat Name | Percent of total | Republican Name | Percent of total |
|---|---|---|---|---|
| AL...... | (X) | (X) | (X) | (X) |
| 1st.... | Kennedy Jr. | 36.8 | Byrne | 63.2 |
| 2d..... | Isner | 38.4 | Roby | 61.4 |
| 3d..... | Hagan | 36.2 | Rogers | 63.7 |
| 4th.... | Auman | 20.1 | Aderholt | 79.8 |
| 5th.... | Joffrion | 38.9 | Brooks | 61.0 |
| 6th.... | Kline | 30.8 | Palmer | 69.2 |
| 7th.... | Sewell | 97.8 | ([1]) | ([1]) |
| AK..... | Galvin | 46.5 | Young | 53.1 |
| AZ..... | (X) | (X) | (X) | (X) |
| 1st.... | O'Halleran | 53.8 | Rogers | 46.1 |
| 2d..... | Kirkpatrick | 54.7 | Marquez Peterson | 45.2 |
| 3d..... | Grijalva | 63.9 | Pierson | 36.1 |
| 4th.... | Brill | 30.5 | Gosar | 68.2 |
| 5th.... | Greene | 40.6 | Biggs | 59.4 |
| 6th.... | Malik | 44.8 | Schweikert | 55.2 |
| 7th.... | Gallego | 85.6 | ([1]) | ([1]) |
| 8th.... | Tipirneni | 44.5 | Lesko | 55.5 |
| 9th.... | Stanton | 61.1 | Ferrara | 38.9 |
| AR..... | (X) | (X) | (X) | (X) |
| 1st.... | Desai | 28.8 | Crawford | 68.9 |
| 2d..... | Tucker | 45.8 | Hill | 52.1 |
| 3d..... | Mahony | 32.6 | Womack | 64.8 |
| 4th.... | Shamel | 31.2 | Westerman | 66.7 |
| CA..... | (X) | (X) | (X) | (X) |
| 1st.... | Denney | 45.1 | LaMalfa | 54.9 |
| 2d..... | Huffman | 77.0 | Mensing | 23.0 |
| 3d..... | Garamendi | 58.1 | Schaupp | 41.9 |
| 4th.... | Morse | 45.9 | McClintock | 54.1 |
| 5th.... | Thompson | 78.9 | ([1]) | ([1]) |
| 6th.... | Matsui | 80.4 | ([1]) | ([1]) |
| 7th.... | Bera | 55.0 | Grant | 45.0 |
| 8th.... | ([1]) | ([1]) | Cook | 60.0 |
| 9th.... | McNerney | 56.5 | Livengood | 43.5 |
| 10th... | Harder | 52.3 | Denham | 47.7 |
| 11th... | DeSaulnier | 74.1 | Fitzgerald | 25.9 |
| 12th... | Pelosi | 86.8 | Remmer | 13.2 |
| 13th... | Lee | 88.4 | ([1]) | ([1]) |
| 14th... | Speier | 79.2 | Osmeña | 20.8 |
| 15th... | Swalwell | 73.0 | Peters Jr. | 27.0 |
| 16th... | Costa | 57.5 | Heng | 42.5 |
| 17th... | Khanna | 75.3 | Cohen | 24.7 |
| 18th... | Eshoo | 74.5 | Russell | 25.5 |
| 19th... | Lofgren | 73.8 | Aguilera | 26.2 |
| 20th... | Panetta | 81.4 | ([1]) | ([1]) |
| 21st... | Cox | 50.4 | Valadao | 49.6 |
| 22d... | Janz | 47.3 | Nunes | 52.7 |
| 23d... | Matta | 36.3 | McCarthy | 63.7 |
| 24th... | Carbajal | 58.6 | Fareed | 41.4 |
| 25th... | Hill | 54.4 | Knight | 45.6 |
| 26th... | Brownley | 61.9 | Sabato Jr. | 38.1 |
| 27th... | Chu | 79.2 | ([1]) | ([1]) |
| 28th... | Schiff | 78.4 | Nalbandian | 21.6 |
| 29th... | Cárdenas | 80.6 | Bernal | 19.4 |
| 30th... | Sherman | 73.4 | Reed | 26.6 |
| 31st... | Aguilar | 58.7 | Flynn | 41.3 |
| 32d... | Napolitano | 68.8 | Scott | 31.2 |
| 33d... | Lieu | 70.0 | Wright | 30.0 |
| 34th... | Gomez | 72.5 | ([1]) | ([1]) |
| 35th... | Torres | 69.4 | Valiente | 30.6 |
| 36th... | Ruiz | 59.0 | Pelzer | 41.0 |
| 37th... | Bass | 89.1 | Bassilian | 10.9 |
| 38th... | Sánchez | 68.9 | Downing | 31.1 |
| 39th... | Cisneros | 51.6 | Kim | 48.4 |
| 40th... | Roybal-Allard | 77.3 | ([1]) | ([1]) |
| 41st... | Takano | 65.1 | Smith | 34.9 |
| 42d... | Peacock | 43.5 | Calvert | 56.5 |
| 43d... | Waters | 77.7 | Navarro | 22.3 |
| 44th... | Barragán | 68.3 | ([1]) | ([1]) |
| 45th... | Porter | 52.1 | Walters | 47.9 |
| 46th... | Correa | 69.1 | Lambert | 30.9 |
| 47th... | Lowenthal | 64.9 | Briscoe | 35.1 |
| 48th... | Rouda | 53.6 | Rohrabacher | 46.4 |
| 49th... | Levin | 56.4 | Harkey | 43.6 |
| 50th... | Campa-Najjar | 48.3 | Hunter | 51.7 |
| 51st... | Vargas | 71.2 | Hidalgo Jr. | 28.8 |
| 52d... | Peterson | 63.8 | Qudrat | 36.2 |
| 53d... | Davis | 69.1 | Murtaugh | 30.9 |
| CO..... | (X) | (X) | (X) | (X) |
| 1st.... | DeGette | 73.8 | Stockham | 23.0 |
| 2d..... | Neguse | 60.3 | Yu | 33.6 |
| 3d..... | Bush | 43.6 | Tipton | 51.5 |
| 4th.... | McCormick | 39.4 | Buck | 60.6 |
| 5th.... | Spaulding | 39.3 | Lamborn | 57.0 |
| 6th.... | Crow | 54.1 | Coffman | 42.9 |
| 7th.... | Perlmutter | 60.4 | Barrington | 35.4 |
| CT...... | (X) | (X) | (X) | (X) |
| 1st.... | Larson | 60.6 | Nye | 35.0 |
| 2d..... | Courtney | 58.0 | Postemski Jr. | 35.4 |
| 3d..... | DeLauro | 60.4 | Cadena | 35.4 |
| 4th.... | Himes | 61.2 | Arora | 37.4 |
| 5th.... | Hayes | 52.8 | Santos | 42.5 |
| DE..... | Rochester | 64.3 | Walker | 35.4 |
| DC..... | (X) | (X) | (X) | (X) |
| FL..... | (X) | (X) | (X) | (X) |
| 1st.... | Zimmerman | 32.9 | Gaetz | 67.1 |
| 2d..... | Rackleff | 32.6 | Dunn | 67.4 |
| 3d..... | Hinson | 42.4 | Yoho | 57.6 |
| 4th.... | Selmont | 32.4 | Rutherford | 65.2 |
| 5th.... | Lawson Jr. | 66.8 | Fuller | 33.2 |
| 6th.... | Soderberg | 43.7 | Waltz | 56.3 |
| 7th.... | Murphy | 57.7 | Miller | 42.3 |
| 8th.... | Patel | 39.5 | Posey | 60.5 |
| 9th.... | Soto | 58.0 | Liebnitzky | 42.0 |
| 10th... | Demings | ([2]) | ([1]) | ([1]) |
| 11th... | Cottrell | 34.8 | Webster | 65.1 |
| 12th... | Hunter | 39.7 | Bilirakis | 58.1 |
| 13th... | Crist | 57.6 | Buck | 42.4 |
| 14th... | Castor | ([2]) | ([1]) | ([1]) |
| 15th... | Carlson | 47.0 | Spano | 53.0 |
| 16th... | Shapiro | 45.4 | Buchanan | 54.6 |
| 17th... | Ellison | 37.7 | Steube | 62.3 |
| 18th... | Baer | 45.7 | Mast | 54.3 |
| 19th... | Holden | 37.7 | Rooney | 62.3 |
| 20th... | Hastings | 99.9 | ([1]) | ([1]) |
| 21st... | Frankel | ([2]) | ([1]) | ([1]) |
| 22d... | Deutch | 62.0 | Kimaz | 38.0 |
| 23d... | Wasserman Schultz | 58.5 | Kaufman | 36.0 |
| 24th... | Wilson | ([2]) | ([1]) | ([1]) |
| 25th... | Flores | 39.5 | Diaz-Balart | 60.5 |
| 26th... | Mucarsel-Powell | 50.9 | Curbelo | 49.1 |
| 27th... | Shalala | 51.8 | Salazar | 45.8 |
| GA..... | (X) | (X) | (X) | (X) |
| 1st.... | Ring | 42.3 | Carter | 57.7 |
| 2d..... | Bishop Jr. | 59.6 | West Jr. | 40.4 |
| 3d | Enderlin | 34.5 | Ferguson IV | 65.5 |
| 4th.... | Johnson Jr. | 78.8 | Profit | 21.2 |
| 5th.... | Lewis | 100.0 | ([1]) | ([1]) |
| 6th.... | McBath | 50.5 | Handel | 49.5 |
| 7th.... | Bourdeaux | 49.9 | Woodall | 50.1 |
| 8th.... | ([1]) | ([1]) | Scott | 99.7 |
| 9th.... | McCall | 20.5 | Collins | 79.5 |
| 10th... | Johnson-Green | 37.1 | Hice | 62.9 |
| 11th... | Broady Jr. | 38.2 | Loudermilk | 61.8 |
| 12th... | Johnson | 40.5 | Allen | 59.5 |
| 13th... | Scott | 76.2 | Callahan | 23.8 |
| 14th... | Foster | 23.5 | Graves | 76.5 |
| HI...... | (X) | (X) | (X) | (X) |
| 1st.... | Case | 70.3 | Cavasso | 22.2 |
| 2d..... | Gabbard | 74.0 | Evans | 21.7 |
| ID...... | (X) | (X) | (X) | (X) |
| 1st.... | McNeil | 30.8 | Fulcher | 62.8 |
| 2d..... | Swisher | 39.3 | Simpson | 60.7 |
| IL...... | (X) | (X) | (X) | (X) |
| 1st.... | Rush | 73.5 | Tillman II | 19.8 |
| 2d..... | Kelly | 81.1 | Merkle | 18.9 |
| 3d.... | Lipinski | 73.0 | Jones | 25.9 |
| 4th.... | Garcia | 86.6 | Lorch | 13.4 |
| 5th.... | Quigley | 76.7 | Hanson | 23.3 |
| 6th.... | Casten | 53.6 | Roskam | 46.4 |
| 7th.... | Davis | 87.6 | Cameron | 12.4 |
| 8th.... | Krishnamoorthi | 66.0 | Diganvker | 34.0 |
| 9th.... | Schawkowsky | 73.5 | Elleson | 26.5 |
| 10th... | Schneider | 65.6 | Bennett | 34.4 |
| 11th... | Foster | 63.8 | Stella | 36.2 |
| 12th... | Kelly | 45.4 | Bost | 51.6 |
| 13th... | Londrigan | 49.6 | Davis | 50.4 |
| 14th... | Underwood | 52.5 | Hultgren | 47.5 |
| 15th... | Gaither | 29.1 | Shimkus | 70.9 |
| 16th... | Dady | 40.9 | Kinzinger | 59.1 |
| 17th... | Bustos | 62.1 | Fawell | 37.9 |
| 18th... | Rodriguez | 32.8 | LaHood | 67.2 |

See footnotes at end of table.

# Table 453. Vote Cast for U.S. House of Representatives by Major Political Party—Congressional Districts: 2018-Continued.

See headnote on page 285.

| State and district | Democrat Name | Democrat Percent of total | Republican Name | Republican Percent of total |
|---|---|---|---|---|
| **IN......** | (X) | (X) | (X) | (X) |
| 1st.... | Visclosky | 65.1 | Leyva | 34.9 |
| 2d.... | Hall | 45.2 | Walorski | 54.8 |
| 3d.... | Tritch | 35.3 | Banks | 64.7 |
| 4th.... | Beck | 35.9 | Baird | 64.1 |
| 5th.... | Thornton | 43.2 | Brooks | 56.8 |
| 6th.... | Lake | 32.9 | Pence | 63.8 |
| 7th.... | Carson | 64.9 | Harmon | 35.1 |
| 8th.... | Tanoos | 35.6 | Bucshon | 64.4 |
| 9th.... | Watson | 43.5 | Hollingsworth | 56.5 |
| **IA.....** | (X) | (X) | (X) | (X) |
| 1st.... | Finkenauer | 51.0 | Blum | 45.9 |
| 2d.... | Loebsack | 54.8 | Peters | 42.6 |
| 3d.... | Axne | 49.3 | Young | 47.1 |
| 4th.... | Scholten | 47.0 | King | 50.4 |
| **KS....** | (X) | (X) | (X) | (X) |
| 1st.... | LaPolice | 31.9 | Marshall | 68.1 |
| 2d.... | Davis | 46.8 | Watkins | 47.6 |
| 3d.... | Davids | 53.6 | Yoder | 43.9 |
| 4th.... | Thompson | 40.6 | Estes | 59.4 |
| **KY....** | (X) | (X) | (X) | (X) |
| 1st.... | Walker | 31.4 | Comer | 68.6 |
| 2d.... | Linderman | 31.1 | Guthrie | 66.7 |
| 3d.... | Yarmuth | 62.1 | Glisson | 36.6 |
| 4th.... | Hall | 34.6 | Massie | 62.2 |
| 5th.... | Stepp | 21.0 | Rogers | 78.9 |
| 6th.... | McGrath | 47.8 | Barr | 51.0 |
| **LA....** | (X) | (X) | (X) | (X) |
| 1st.... | Savoie | 16.4 | Scalise | 71.5 |
| 2d.... | Richmond | 80.6 | ([1]) | ([1]) |
| 3d.... | Methvin | 17.8 | Higgins | 55.7 |
| 4th.... | Trundle | 33.6 | Johnson | 64.2 |
| 5th.... | Fleenor | 30.0 | Abraham | 66.5 |
| 6th.... | Dewitt | 20.5 | Graves | 69.5 |
| **ME.....** | (X) | (X) | (X) | (X) |
| 1st.... | Pingree | 57.5 | Holbrook | 31.8 |
| 2d.... | Golden | 50.6 | Poliquin | 49.4 |
| **MD.....** | (X) | (X) | (X) | (X) |
| 1st.... | Colvin | 38.1 | Harris | 60.0 |
| 2d.... | Ruppersberger | 66.0 | Matory | 30.7 |
| 3d.... | Sarbanes | 69.1 | Anthony | 28.3 |
| 4th.... | Brown | 78.1 | McDermott | 19.9 |
| 5th.... | Hoyer | 70.3 | Devine III | 27.1 |
| 6th.... | Trone | 59.0 | Hoeber | 38.0 |
| 7th.... | Cummings | 76.4 | Davis | 21.3 |
| 8th.... | Raskin | 68.2 | Walsh | 30.2 |
| **MA....** | (X) | (X) | (X) | (X) |
| 1st.... | Neal | 77.0 | ([1]) | ([1]) |
| 2d.... | McGovern | 65.3 | Lovvorn | 31.9 |
| 3d.... | Trahan | 60.4 | Green | 32.6 |
| 4th.... | Kennedy III | 76.1 | ([1]) | ([1]) |
| 5th.... | Clark | 73.0 | Hugo | 23.1 |
| 6th.... | Moulton | 63.3 | Schneider | 30.5 |
| 7th.... | Pressley | 86.8 | ([1]) | ([1]) |
| 8th.... | Lynch | 79.2 | ([1]) | ([1]) |
| 9th.... | Keating | 58.0 | Tedeschi | 39.7 |
| **MI......** | (X) | (X) | (X) | (X) |
| 1st.... | Morgan | 43.7 | Bergman | 56.3 |
| 2d.... | Davidson | 43.0 | Huizenga | 55.3 |
| 3d.... | Albro | 43.2 | Amash | 54.4 |
| 4th.... | Hilliard | 37.4 | Moolenaar | 62.6 |
| 5th.... | Kildee | 59.5 | Wines | 35.9 |
| 6th.... | Longjohn | 45.7 | Upton | 50.2 |
| 7th.... | Driskell | 46.2 | Walberg | 53.8 |
| 8th.... | Slotkin | 50.6 | Bishop | 46.8 |
| 9th.... | Levin | 59.7 | Stearns | 36.8 |
| 10th.... | Bizon | 35.0 | Mitchell | 60.3 |
| 11th.... | Stevens | 51.8 | Epstein | 45.2 |
| 12th.... | Dingell | 68.1 | Jones | 28.9 |
| 13th.... | Tlaib | 84.2 | ([1]) | ([1]) |
| 14th.... | Lawrence | 80.9 | Herschfus | 17.3 |
| **MN.....** | (X) | (X) | (X) | (X) |
| 1st.... | Feehan | 49.7 | Hagedorn | 50.1 |
| 2d.... | Craig | 52.7 | Lewis | 47.1 |
| 3d.... | Phillips | 55.6 | Paulsen | 44.2 |
| 4th.... | McCollum | 66.0 | Ryan | 29.7 |
| 5th.... | Omar | 78.0 | Zielinski | 21.7 |
| 6th.... | Todd | 38.7 | Emmer | 61.1 |
| 7th.... | Peterson | 52.1 | Hughes | 47.8 |
| 8th.... | Radinovich | 45.2 | Stauber | 50.7 |
| **MS.....** | (X) | (X) | (X) | (X) |
| 1st.... | Wadkins | 32.4 | Kelly | 66.9 |
| 2d.... | Thompson | 71.8 | ([1]) | ([1]) |
| 3d.... | Evans | 36.7 | Guest | 62.3 |
| 4th.... | Anderson | 30.7 | Palazzo | 68.2 |
| **MO.....** | (X) | (X) | (X) | (X) |
| 1st.... | Clay | 80.1 | Vroman | 16.7 |
| 2d.... | VanOstran | 47.2 | Wagner | 51.2 |
| 3d.... | Geppert | 32.8 | Luetkemeyer | 65.1 |
| 4th.... | Hoagenson | 32.7 | Hartzler | 64.8 |
| 5th.... | Cleaver | 61.7 | Turk | 35.6 |
| 6th.... | Martin | 32.0 | Graves | 65.4 |
| 7th.... | Schoolcraft | 30.1 | Long | 66.2 |
| 8th.... | Ellis | 25.0 | Smith | 73.4 |
| **MT.....** | Williams | 46.2 | Gianforte | 50.9 |
| **NE.....** | (X) | (X) | (X) | (X) |
| 1st.... | McClure | 39.6 | Fortenberry | 60.4 |
| 2d.... | Eastman | 49.0 | Bacon | 51.0 |
| 3d.... | Theobald | 23.3 | Smith | 76.7 |
| **NV.....** | (X) | (X) | (X) | (X) |
| 1st.... | Titus | 66.2 | Bentley | 30.9 |
| 2d.... | Koble | 41.8 | Amodei | 58.2 |
| 3d.... | Lee | 51.9 | Tarkanian | 42.8 |
| 4th.... | Horsford | 51.9 | Hardy | 43.7 |
| **NH.....** | (X) | (X) | (X) | (X) |
| 1st.... | Pappas | 53.6 | Edwards | 45.0 |
| 2d.... | Kuster | 55.5 | Negron | 42.2 |
| **NJ......** | (X) | (X) | (X) | (X) |
| 1st.... | Norcross | 64.4 | Dilks | 33.3 |
| 2d.... | Van Drew | 52.9 | Grossman | 45.2 |
| 3d.... | Kim | 50.0 | MacArthur | 48.7 |
| 4th.... | Welle | 43.1 | Smith | 55.4 |
| 5th.... | Gottheimer | 56.2 | McCann Jr. | 42.5 |
| 6th.... | Pallone Jr. | 63.6 | Pezzullo | 36.4 |
| 7th.... | Malinowski | 51.7 | Lance | 46.7 |
| 8th.... | Sires | 78.1 | Muniz | 18.7 |
| 9th.... | Pascrell Jr. | 70.3 | Fisher | 28.9 |
| 10th.... | Payne Jr. | 87.6 | Khan | 10.1 |
| 11th.... | Sherrill | 56.8 | Webber | 42.1 |
| 12th.... | Coleman | 68.7 | Kipnis | 31.3 |
| **NM.....** | (X) | (X) | (X) | (X) |
| 1st.... | Haaland | 59.1 | Arnold-Jones | 36.3 |
| 2d.... | Small | 50.9 | Herrell | 49.1 |
| 3d.... | Luján | 63.4 | McFall | 31.2 |
| **NY......** | (X) | (X) | (X) | (X) |
| 1st.... | Gershon | 45.3 | Zeldin | 44.3 |
| 2d.... | Shirley | 44.2 | King | 45.8 |
| 3d.... | Suozzi | 54.9 | DeBono | 36.1 |
| 4th.... | Rice | 58.7 | Benno | 33.8 |
| 5th.... | Meeks | 86.1 | ([1]) | ([1]) |
| 6th.... | Meng | 69.7 | ([1]) | ([1]) |
| 7th.... | Velázquez | 81.4 | ([1]) | ([1]) |
| 8th.... | Jeffries | 83.4 | ([1]) | ([1]) |
| 9th.... | Clarke | 80.5 | Gayot | 9.0 |
| 10th... | Nadler | 75.0 | Levin | 15.6 |
| 11th.... | Rose | 49.6 | Donovan Jr. | 41.2 |
| 12th.... | Maloney | 80.3 | Rabin | 11.9 |
| 13th... | Espaillat | 86.9 | Butler | 4.8 |
| 14th.... | Ocasio-Cortez | 75.4 | Pappas | 13.1 |
| 15th.... | Serrano | 91.1 | Gonzalez | 3.4 |
| 16th.... | Engel | 76.4 | ([1]) | ([1]) |
| 17th.... | Lowey | 62.2 | ([1]) | ([1]) |
| 18th.... | Maloney | 48.4 | O'Donnell | 36.9 |
| 19th.... | Delgado | 46.2 | Faso | 38.3 |
| 20th.... | Tonko | 58.2 | Vitollo | 32.1 |
| 21st.... | Cobb | 39.1 | Stefanik | 48.7 |
| 22d... | Brindisi | 45.5 | Tenney | 43.2 |
| 23d... | Mitrano | 41.0 | Reed | 46.7 |
| 24th.... | Balter | 43.7 | Katko | 42.8 |
| 25th.... | Morelle | 53.7 | Maxwell | 33.1 |
| 26th.... | Higgins | 64.8 | Zeno | 25.4 |
| 27th.... | McMurray | 43.7 | Collins | 39.1 |
| **NC......** | (X) | (X) | (X) | (X) |
| 1st.... | Butterfield | 69.8 | Allison | 30.2 |
| 2d..... | Coleman | 45.8 | Holding | 51.3 |
| 3d..... | ([1]) | ([1]) | Jones | 100.0 |
| 4th.... | Price | 72.4 | Von Loor | 24.0 |
| 5th.... | Adams | 43.0 | Foxx | 57.0 |
| 6th.... | Watts | 43.5 | Walker | 56.5 |
| 7th.... | Horton | 42.8 | Rouzer | 55.5 |
| 8th.... | McNeill | 44.7 | Hudson | 55.3 |
| 9th.... | ([3]) | ([3]) | ([3]) | ([3]) |
| 10th... | Brown | 40.7 | McHenry | 59.3 |
| 11th.... | Price | 38.7 | Meadows | 59.2 |
| 12th.... | Adams | 73.1 | Wright | 26.9 |
| 13th... | Manning | 45.5 | Budd | 51.5 |

See footnotes at end of table.

See headnote on page 285.

| State and district | Democrat Name | Percent of total | Republican Name | Percent of total | State and district | Democrat Name | Percent of total | Republican Name | Percent of total |
|---|---|---|---|---|---|---|---|---|---|
| ND..... | Schneider | 35.6 | Armstrong | 60.2 | 5th.... | Wood | 37.5 | Gooden | 62.3 |
| OH..... | (X) | (X) | (X) | (X) | 6th.... | Sanchez | 45.4 | Wright | 53.1 |
| 1st.... | Pureval | 46.9 | Chabot | 51.3 | 7th.... | Fletcher | 52.5 | Culberson | 47.5 |
| 2d..... | Schiller | 41.2 | Wenstrup | 57.6 | 8th.... | David | 24.9 | Brady | 73.4 |
| 3d..... | Beatty | 73.6 | Burgess | 26.4 | 9th.... | Green | 89.1 | (1) | (1) |
| 4th.... | Garrett | 34.7 | Jordan | 65.3 | 10th... | Siegel | 46.8 | McCaul | 51.1 |
| 5th.... | Galbraith | 35.1 | Latta | 62.3 | 11th... | Leeder | 18.4 | Conaway | 80.1 |
| 6th.... | Roberts | 30.7 | Johnson | 69.3 | 12th... | Adia | 33.9 | Granger | 64.3 |
| 7th.... | Harbaugh | 41.3 | Gibbs | 58.7 | 13th... | Sagan | 16.9 | Thornberry | 81.5 |
| 8th.... | Enoch | 33.4 | Davidson | 66.6 | 14th... | Bell | 39.3 | Weber Sr. | 59.2 |
| 9th.... | Kaptur | 67.8 | Kraus | 32.2 | 15th... | Gonzalez | 59.7 | Westley | 38.8 |
| 10th... | Gasper | 42.2 | Turner | 55.9 | 16th... | Escobar | 68.5 | Seeberger | 27.0 |
| 11th... | Fudge | 82.2 | Goldstein | 17.7 | 17th... | Kennedy | 41.3 | Flores | 56.8 |
| 12th... | O'Connor | 47.2 | Balderson | 51.4 | 18th... | Lee | 75.2 | Pate | 20.8 |
| 13th... | Ryan | 61.0 | DePizzo | 39.0 | 19th... | Levario | 24.8 | Arrington | 75.2 |
| 14th... | Rader | 44.8 | Joyce | 55.2 | 20th... | Castro | 80.9 | (1) | (1) |
| 15th... | Neal | 39.7 | Stivers | 58.3 | 21st... | Kopser | 47.6 | Roy | 50.2 |
| 16th... | Palmer | 43.3 | Gonzalez | 56.7 | 22d.... | Kulkarni | 46.5 | Olson | 51.4 |
| OK..... | (X) | (X) | (X) | (X) | 23d.... | Ortiz Jones | 48.7 | Hurd | 49.2 |
| 1st.... | Gilpin | 40.7 | Hern | 59.3 | 24th... | McDowell | 47.5 | Marchant | 50.6 |
| 2d..... | Nichols | 30.1 | Mullin | 65.0 | 25th... | Oliver | 44.8 | Williams | 53.5 |
| 3d..... | Robbins | 26.1 | Lucas | 73.9 | 26th... | Fagan | 39.0 | Burgess | 59.4 |
| 4th.... | Brannon | 33.0 | Cole | 63.1 | 27th... | Holguin | 36.6 | Cloud | 60.3 |
| 5th.... | Horn | 50.7 | Russell | 49.3 | 28th... | Cuellar | 84.4 | (1) | (1) |
| OR..... | (X) | (X) | (X) | (X) | 29th... | Garcia | 75.1 | Aronoff | 23.9 |
| 1st.... | Bonamici | 63.6 | Verbeek | 32.1 | 30th... | Johnson | 91.1 | (1) | (1) |
| 2d..... | McLeod-Skinner | 39.4 | Walden | 56.3 | 31st... | Hegar | 47.7 | Carter | 50.6 |
| 3d..... | Blumenauer | 72.6 | Harrison | 19.8 | 32d.... | Allred | 52.3 | Sessions | 45.8 |
| 4th.... | DeFazio | 56.0 | Robinson | 40.9 | 33d.... | Veasey | 76.2 | Billups | 21.9 |
| 5th.... | Schrader | 55.0 | Callahan | 41.8 | 34th... | Vela | 60.0 | Gonzalez | 40.0 |
| PA..... | (X) | (X) | (X) | (X) | 35th... | Doggett | 71.3 | Smalling | 26.0 |
| 1st.... | Wallace | 48.7 | Fitzpatrick | 51.3 | 36th... | Steele | 27.4 | Babin | 72.6 |
| 2d..... | Boyle | 79.0 | Torres | 21.0 | UT...... | (X) | (X) | (X) | (X) |
| 3d..... | Evans | 93.4 | Leib | 6.6 | 1st.... | Castillo | 24.9 | Bishop | 61.6 |
| 4th.... | Dean | 63.5 | David | 36.5 | 2d..... | Ghorbani | 38.9 | Stewart | 56.1 |
| 5th.... | Scanlon | 65.2 | Kim | 34.8 | 3d..... | Singer | 27.3 | Curtis | 67.5 |
| 6th.... | Houlahan | 58.9 | McCauley | 41.1 | 4th.... | McAdams | 50.1 | Love | 49.9 |
| 7th.... | Wild | 53.5 | Nothstein | 43.5 | VT...... | Welch | 67.8 | Tynio | 25.4 |
| 8th.... | Cartwright | 54.6 | Chrin | 45.4 | VA...... | (X) | (X) | (X) | (X) |
| 9th.... | Wolff | 40.3 | Meuser | 59.7 | 1st.... | Williams | 44.7 | Wittman | 55.2 |
| 10th... | Scott | 48.7 | Perry | 51.3 | 2d..... | Luria | 51.1 | Taylor | 48.8 |
| 11th... | King | 41.0 | Smucker | 59.0 | 3d..... | Scott | 91.2 | (1) | (1) |
| 12th... | Friedenberg | 34.0 | Marino | 66.0 | 4th.... | McEachin | 62.6 | McAdams | 35.9 |
| 13th... | Ottaway | 29.5 | Joyce | 70.5 | 5th.... | Cockburn | 46.6 | Riggleman III | 53.2 |
| 14th... | Boerio | 42.1 | Reschenthaler | 57.9 | 6th.... | Lewis | 40.2 | Cline | 59.7 |
| 15th... | Boser | 32.2 | Thompson | 67.8 | 7th.... | Spanberger | 50.3 | Brat | 48.4 |
| 16th... | DiNicola | 47.3 | Kelly | 51.6 | 8th.... | Beyer Jr. | 76.1 | Oh | 23.7 |
| 17th... | Lamb | 56.3 | Rothfus | 43.7 | 9th.... | Flaccavento | 34.8 | Griffith | 65.2 |
| 18th... | Doyle | 100.0 | (1) | (1) | 10th... | Wexton | 56.1 | Comstock | 43.7 |
| RI...... | (X) | (X) | (X) | (X) | 11th... | Connolly | 71.1 | Dove Jr. | 26.9 |
| 1st.... | Cicilline | 66.7 | Donovan | 33.1 | WA..... | (X) | (X) | (X) | (X) |
| 2d..... | Langevin | 63.5 | Caiozzo | 36.3 | 1st.... | DelBene | 59.3 | Beeler | 40.7 |
| SC...... | (X) | (X) | (X) | (X) | 2d..... | Larsen | 71.3 | (1) | (1) |
| 1st.... | Cunningham | 50.6 | Arrington | 49.2 | 3d..... | Long | 47.3 | Beutler | 52.7 |
| 2d..... | Carrigan | 42.5 | Wilson | 56.3 | 4th.... | Brown | 37.2 | Newhouse | 62.8 |
| 3d..... | Geren | 31.0 | Duncan | 67.8 | 5th.... | Brown | 45.2 | McMorris Rodgers | 54.8 |
| 4th.... | Brown | 36.6 | Timmons | 59.6 | 6th.... | Kilmer | 63.9 | Dightman | 36.1 |
| 5th.... | Parnell | 41.5 | Norman | 57.0 | 7th.... | Jayapal | 83.6 | Keller | 16.4 |
| 6th.... | Clyburn | 70.1 | Gressman | 28.2 | 8th.... | Schrier | 52.4 | Rossi | 47.6 |
| 7th.... | Williams | 40.3 | Rice | 59.6 | 9th.... | Smith | 67.9 | (1) | (1) |
| SD..... | Bjorkman | 36.0 | Johnson | 60.3 | 10th... | Heck | 61.5 | Brumbles | 38.5 |
| TN...... | (X) | (X) | (X) | (X) | WV..... | (X) | (X) | (X) | (X) |
| 1st.... | Olsen | 21.0 | Roe | 77.1 | 1st.... | Fershee | 35.4 | McKinley | 64.6 |
| 2d..... | Hoyos | 33.1 | Burchett | 65.9 | 2d..... | Sergent | 43.0 | Mooney | 54.0 |
| 3d..... | Mitchell | 34.5 | Fleischmann | 63.7 | 3d..... | Ojeda II | 43.6 | Miller | 56.4 |
| 4th.... | Phillips | 33.6 | DesJarlais | 63.4 | WI...... | (X) | (X) | (X) | (X) |
| 5th.... | Cooper | 67.8 | Ball | 32.2 | 1st.... | Bryce | 42.3 | Steil | 54.6 |
| 6th.... | Barlow | 28.3 | Rose | 69.5 | 2d..... | Pocan | 97.4 | (1) | (1) |
| 7th.... | Kanew | 32.1 | Green | 66.9 | 3d..... | Kind | 59.6 | Toft | 40.3 |
| 8th.... | Pearson | 30.1 | Kustoff | 67.7 | 4th.... | Moore | 74.3 | Rogers | 21.2 |
| 9th.... | Cohen | 80.0 | Bergman | 19.2 | 5th.... | Palzewicz | 38.0 | Sensenbrenner Jr. | 61.9 |
| TX...... | (X) | (X) | (X) | (X) | 6th.... | Kohl | 44.5 | Grothman | 55.5 |
| 1st.... | McKellar | 26.3 | Gohmert | 72.3 | 7th.... | Engebretson | 38.5 | Duffy | 60.1 |
| 2d..... | Litton | 45.6 | Crenshaw | 52.8 | 8th.... | Liegeois | 36.3 | Gallagher | 63.7 |
| 3d..... | Burch | 44.3 | Taylor | 54.3 | WY..... | Hunter | 29.2 | Cheney | 62.3 |
| 4th.... | Krantz | 23.0 | Ratcliffe | 75.7 | | | | | |

X Not applicable. [1] No candidate. [2] According to Florida law, the names of those with no opposition are not printed on the ballot. [3] On February 21, 2019, the North Carolina State Board of Elections ordered a new election in this Congressional District.

Source: U.S. House of Representatives, Office of the Clerk, *Statistics of the Congressional Election of November 6, 2018* February 2019, and earlier reports. See also <http://clerk.house.gov/member_info/election.aspx>.

# Table 454. Apportionment of Membership in House of Representatives by State: 1800 to 2010

[Total membership includes Representatives assigned to newly admitted States after the apportionment acts. Population figures used for apportionment purposes are those determined for States by each decennial census. No reapportionment based on 1920 population census. For method of calculating apportionment and a short history of apportionment, see House Report 91-1314, 91st Congress, 2d session, The Decennial Population Census and Congressional Apportionment]

| State | \multicolumn{21}{c}{Membership based on Census of—} | | | | | | | | | | | | | | | | | | | | |
|---|---|---|---|---|---|---|---|---|---|---|---|---|---|---|---|---|---|---|---|---|---|
| | 1800 | 1820 | 1830 | 1840 | 1850 | 1860 | 1870 | 1880 | 1890 | 1900 | 1910 | 1920 | 1930 | 1940 | 1950 | 1960 | 1970 | 1980 | 1990 | 2000 | 2010 |
| U.S. | 142 | 213 | 242 | 232 | 237 | 243 | 293 | 332 | 357 | 391 | 435 | 435 | 435 | 435 | 437 | 435 | 435 | 435 | 435 | 435 | 435 |
| AL | (X) | 3 | 5 | 7 | 7 | 6 | 8 | 8 | 9 | 9 | 10 | 10 | 9 | 9 | 9 | 8 | 7 | 7 | 7 | 7 | 7 |
| AK | (X) | (X) | (X) | (X) | (X) | (X) | (X) | (X) | (X) | (X) | (X) | (X) | (X) | (X) | 1[1] | 1 | 1 | 1 | 1 | 1 | 1 |
| AZ | (X) | (X) | (X) | (X) | (X) | (X) | (X) | (X) | (X) | (X) | 1[2] | 1 | 1 | 2 | 2 | 3 | 4 | 5 | 6 | 8 | 9 |
| AR | (X) | (X) | (X) | 1 | 2 | 3 | 4 | 5 | 6 | 7 | 7 | 7 | 7 | 7 | 6 | 4 | 4 | 4 | 4 | 4 | 4 |
| CA | (X) | (X) | (X) | (X) | 2[1] | 3 | 4 | 6 | 7 | 8 | 11 | 11 | 20 | 23 | 30 | 38 | 43 | 45 | 52 | 53 | 53 |
| CO | (X) | (X) | (X) | (X) | (X) | (X) | (X) | 1 | 2 | 3 | 4 | 4 | 4 | 4 | 4 | 4 | 5 | 6 | 6 | 7 | 7 |
| CT | 7 | 6 | 6 | 4 | 4 | 4 | 4 | 4 | 4 | 5 | 5 | 5 | 6 | 6 | 6 | 6 | 6 | 6 | 6 | 5 | 5 |
| DE | 1 | 1 | 1 | 1 | 1 | 1 | 1 | 1 | 1 | 1 | 1 | 1 | 1 | 1 | 1 | 1 | 1 | 1 | 1 | 1 | 1 |
| FL | (X) | (X) | (X) | (X) | 1 | 1 | 2 | 2 | 2 | 3 | 4 | 4 | 5 | 6 | 8 | 12 | 15 | 19 | 23 | 25 | 27 |
| GA | 4 | 7 | 9 | 8 | 8 | 7 | 9 | 10 | 11 | 11 | 12 | 12 | 10 | 10 | 10 | 10 | 10 | 10 | 11 | 13 | 14 |
| HI | (X) | (X) | (X) | (X) | (X) | (X) | (X) | (X) | (X) | (X) | (X) | (X) | (X) | (X) | 1[1] | 2 | 2 | 2 | 2 | 2 | 2 |
| ID | (X) | (X) | (X) | (X) | (X) | (X) | (X) | (X) | 1 | 1 | 2 | 2 | 2 | 2 | 2 | 2 | 2 | 2 | 2 | 2 | 2 |
| IL | (X) | 1 | 3 | 7 | 9 | 14 | 19 | 20 | 22 | 25 | 27 | 27 | 27 | 26 | 25 | 24 | 24 | 22 | 20 | 19 | 18 |
| IN | (X) | 3 | 7 | 10 | 11 | 11 | 13 | 13 | 13 | 13 | 13 | 13 | 12 | 11 | 11 | 11 | 11 | 10 | 10 | 9 | 9 |
| IA | (X) | (X) | (X) | (X) | 2 | 6 | 9 | 11 | 11 | 11 | 11 | 11 | 9 | 8 | 8 | 7 | 6 | 6 | 5 | 5 | 4 |
| KS | (X) | (X) | (X) | (X) | (X) | (X) | 3 | 7 | 8 | 8 | 8 | 8 | 7 | 6 | 6 | 5 | 5 | 5 | 4 | 4 | 4 |
| KY | 6 | 12 | 13 | 10 | 10 | 9 | 10 | 11 | 11 | 11 | 11 | 11 | 9 | 9 | 8 | 7 | 7 | 7 | 6 | 6 | 6 |
| LA | (X) | 3 | 3 | 4 | 4 | 5 | 6 | 6 | 6 | 7 | 8 | 8 | 8 | 8 | 8 | 8 | 8 | 8 | 7 | 7 | 6 |
| ME | (X) | 7 | 8 | 7 | 6 | 5 | 5 | 4 | 4 | 4 | 4 | 4 | 3 | 3 | 3 | 2 | 2 | 2 | 2 | 2 | 2 |
| MD | 8 | 9 | 8 | 6 | 6 | 5 | 6 | 6 | 6 | 6 | 6 | 6 | 6 | 6 | 7 | 8 | 8 | 8 | 8 | 8 | 8 |
| MA | 17 | 13 | 12 | 10 | 11 | 10 | 11 | 12 | 13 | 14 | 16 | 16 | 15 | 14 | 14 | 12 | 12 | 11 | 10 | 10 | 9 |
| MI | (X) | (X) | (X) | 3 | 4 | 6 | 9 | 11 | 12 | 12 | 13 | 13 | 17 | 17 | 18 | 19 | 19 | 18 | 16 | 15 | 14 |
| MN | (X) | (X) | (X) | (X) | (X) | 2 | 3 | 5 | 7 | 9 | 10 | 10 | 9 | 9 | 9 | 8 | 8 | 8 | 8 | 8 | 8 |
| MS | (X) | 1 | 2 | 4 | 5 | 5 | 6 | 7 | 7 | 8 | 8 | 8 | 7 | 7 | 6 | 5 | 5 | 5 | 5 | 4 | 4 |
| MO | (X) | 1 | 2 | 5 | 7 | 9 | 13 | 14 | 15 | 16 | 16 | 16 | 13 | 13 | 11 | 10 | 10 | 9 | 9 | 9 | 8 |
| MT | (X) | (X) | (X) | (X) | (X) | (X) | (X) | (X) | 1 | 1 | 2 | 2 | 2 | 2 | 2 | 2 | 2 | 2 | 1 | 1 | 1 |
| NE | (X) | (X) | (X) | (X) | (X) | (X) | 1 | 3 | 6 | 6 | 6 | 6 | 5 | 4 | 4 | 3 | 3 | 3 | 3 | 3 | 3 |
| NV | (X) | (X) | (X) | (X) | (X) | (X) | 1 | 1 | 1 | 1 | 1 | 1 | 1 | 1 | 1 | 1 | 1 | 2 | 2 | 3 | 4 |
| NH | 5 | 6 | 5 | 4 | 3 | 3 | 3 | 2 | 2 | 2 | 2 | 2 | 2 | 2 | 2 | 2 | 2 | 2 | 2 | 2 | 2 |
| NJ | 6 | 6 | 6 | 5 | 5 | 5 | 7 | 7 | 8 | 10 | 12 | 12 | 14 | 14 | 14 | 15 | 15 | 14 | 13 | 13 | 12 |
| NM | (X) | (X) | (X) | (X) | (X) | (X) | (X) | (X) | (X) | (X) | 1[2] | 1 | 1 | 2 | 2 | 2 | 2 | 3 | 3 | 3 | 3 |
| NY | 17 | 34 | 40 | 34 | 33 | 31 | 33 | 34 | 34 | 37 | 43 | 43 | 45 | 45 | 43 | 41 | 39 | 34 | 31 | 29 | 27 |
| NC | 12 | 13 | 13 | 9 | 8 | 7 | 8 | 9 | 9 | 10 | 10 | 10 | 11 | 12 | 12 | 11 | 11 | 11 | 12 | 13 | 13 |
| ND | (X) | (X) | (X) | (X) | (X) | (X) | (X) | (X) | 1 | 2 | 3 | 3 | 2 | 2 | 2 | 2 | 1 | 1 | 1 | 1 | 1 |
| OH | (X) | 14 | 19 | 21 | 21 | 19 | 20 | 21 | 21 | 21 | 22 | 22 | 24 | 23 | 23 | 24 | 23 | 21 | 19 | 18 | 16 |
| OK | (X) | (X) | (X) | (X) | (X) | (X) | (X) | (X) | (X) | 5[1] | 8 | 8 | 9 | 8 | 6 | 6 | 6 | 6 | 6 | 5 | 5 |
| OR | (X) | (X) | (X) | (X) | (X) | 1 | 1 | 1 | 2 | 2 | 3 | 3 | 3 | 4 | 4 | 4 | 4 | 5 | 5 | 5 | 5 |
| PA | 18 | 26 | 28 | 24 | 25 | 24 | 27 | 28 | 30 | 32 | 36 | 36 | 34 | 33 | 30 | 27 | 25 | 23 | 21 | 19 | 18 |
| RI | 2 | 2 | 2 | 2 | 2 | 2 | 2 | 2 | 2 | 2 | 3 | 3 | 2 | 2 | 2 | 2 | 2 | 2 | 2 | 2 | 2 |
| SC | 8 | 9 | 9 | 7 | 6 | 4 | 5 | 7 | 7 | 7 | 7 | 7 | 6 | 6 | 6 | 6 | 6 | 6 | 6 | 6 | 7 |
| SD | (X) | (X) | (X) | (X) | (X) | (X) | (X) | (X) | 2 | 2 | 3 | 3 | 2 | 2 | 2 | 2 | 2 | 1 | 1 | 1 | 1 |
| TN | 3 | 9 | 13 | 11 | 10 | 8 | 10 | 10 | 10 | 10 | 10 | 10 | 9 | 10 | 9 | 9 | 8 | 9 | 9 | 9 | 9 |
| TX | (X) | (X) | (X) | (X) | 2 | 4 | 6 | 11 | 13 | 16 | 18 | 18 | 21 | 21 | 22 | 23 | 24 | 27 | 30 | 32 | 36 |
| UT | (X) | (X) | (X) | (X) | (X) | (X) | (X) | (X) | (X) | 1 | 2 | 2 | 2 | 2 | 2 | 2 | 2 | 3 | 3 | 3 | 4 |
| VA | 22 | 22 | 21 | 15 | 13 | 11 | 9 | 10 | 10 | 10 | 10 | 10 | 9 | 9 | 10 | 10 | 10 | 10 | 11 | 11 | 11 |
| VT | 4 | 5 | 5 | 4 | 3 | 3 | 3 | 2 | 2 | 2 | 2 | 2 | 1 | 1 | 1 | 1 | 1 | 1 | 1 | 1 | 1 |
| WA | (X) | (X) | (X) | (X) | (X) | (X) | (X) | (X) | 2 | 3 | 5 | 5 | 6 | 6 | 7 | 7 | 7 | 8 | 9 | 9 | 10 |
| WV | (X) | (X) | (X) | (X) | (X) | (X) | 3 | 4 | 4 | 5 | 6 | 6 | 6 | 6 | 6 | 5 | 4 | 4 | 3 | 3 | 3 |
| WI | (X) | (X) | (X) | (X) | 3 | 6 | 8 | 9 | 10 | 11 | 11 | 11 | 10 | 10 | 10 | 10 | 9 | 9 | 9 | 8 | 8 |
| WY | (X) | (X) | (X) | (X) | (X) | (X) | (X) | (X) | 1 | 1 | 1 | 1 | 1 | 1 | 1 | 1 | 1 | 1 | 1 | 1 | 1 |

X Not applicable. [1] Assigned after apportionment. [2] Included in apportionment in anticipation of statehood.

Source: U.S. Census Bureau, Congressional Apportionment, Census 2010, <https://www.census.gov/topics/public-sector/congressional-apportionment.html>.

## Table 455. Composition of Congress by Political Party Affiliation—States: 2013 to 2019

[Figures are for the beginning of the first session, except as noted. Dem. = Democratic; Rep. = Republican]

| State | Representatives | | | | | | | | Senators | | | | | | | |
|---|---|---|---|---|---|---|---|---|---|---|---|---|---|---|---|---|
| | 113th Cong.,[1] 2013 | | 114th Cong.,[2] 2015 | | 115th Cong., 2017 | | 116th Cong.,[3] 2019 | | 113th Cong.,[4] 2013 | | 114th Cong.,[4] 2015 | | 115th Cong.,[4] 2017 | | 116th Cong.,[4] 2019 | |
| | Dem. | Rep. | Dem. | Rep. | Dem. | Rep. | Dem. | Rep. | Dem. | Rep. | Dem. | Rep. | Dem. | Rep. | Dem. | Rep. |
| U.S....... | 201 | 232 | 188 | 245 | 194 | 241 | 235 | 197 | 53 | 45 | 44 | 54 | 46 | 52 | 47 | 53 |
| AL......... | 1 | 6 | 1 | 6 | 1 | 6 | 1 | 6 | – | 2 | – | 2 | – | 2 | 1 | 1 |
| AK......... | – | 1 | – | 1 | – | 1 | – | 1 | 1 | 1 | – | 2 | – | 2 | – | 2 |
| AZ......... | 5 | 4 | 4 | 5 | 4 | 5 | 5 | 4 | – | 2 | – | 2 | – | 2 | 1 | 1 |
| AR......... | – | 4 | – | 4 | – | 4 | – | 4 | 1 | 1 | – | 2 | – | 2 | – | 2 |
| CA......... | 38 | 15 | 39 | 14 | 39 | 14 | 46 | 7 | 2 | – | 2 | – | 2 | – | 2 | – |
| CO......... | 3 | 4 | 3 | 4 | 3 | 4 | 4 | 3 | 2 | – | 1 | 1 | 1 | 1 | 1 | 1 |
| CT......... | 5 | – | 5 | – | 5 | – | 5 | – | 2 | – | 2 | – | 2 | – | 2 | – |
| DE......... | 1 | – | 1 | – | 1 | – | 1 | – | 2 | – | 2 | – | 2 | – | 2 | – |
| FL......... | 10 | 17 | 10 | 17 | 11 | 16 | 13 | 14 | 1 | 1 | 1 | 1 | 1 | 1 | – | 2 |
| GA......... | 5 | 9 | 4 | 10 | 4 | 10 | 5 | 9 | – | 2 | – | 2 | – | 2 | – | 2 |
| HI......... | 2 | – | 2 | – | 2 | – | 2 | – | 2 | – | 2 | – | 2 | – | 2 | – |
| ID......... | – | 2 | – | 2 | – | 2 | – | 2 | – | 2 | – | 2 | – | 2 | – | 2 |
| IL......... | 12 | 6 | 10 | 8 | 11 | 7 | 13 | 5 | 1 | 1 | 1 | 1 | 2 | – | 2 | – |
| IN......... | 2 | 7 | 2 | 7 | 2 | 7 | 2 | 7 | 1 | 1 | 1 | 1 | 1 | 1 | – | 2 |
| IA......... | 2 | 2 | 1 | 3 | 1 | 3 | 3 | 1 | 1 | 1 | – | 2 | – | 2 | – | 2 |
| KS......... | – | 4 | – | 4 | – | 4 | 1 | 3 | – | 2 | – | 2 | – | 2 | – | 2 |
| KY......... | 1 | 5 | 1 | 5 | 1 | 5 | 1 | 5 | – | 2 | – | 2 | – | 2 | – | 2 |
| LA......... | 1 | 5 | 1 | 5 | 1 | 5 | 1 | 5 | 1 | 1 | – | 2 | – | 2 | – | 2 |
| ME......... | 2 | – | 1 | 1 | 1 | 1 | 2 | – | – | 1 | – | 1 | – | 1 | – | 1 |
| MD......... | 7 | 1 | 7 | 1 | 7 | 1 | 7 | 1 | 2 | – | 2 | – | 2 | – | 2 | – |
| MA......... | 9 | – | 9 | – | 9 | – | 9 | – | 2 | – | 2 | – | 2 | – | 2 | – |
| MI......... | 5 | 9 | 5 | 9 | 5 | 9 | 7 | 7 | 2 | – | 2 | – | 2 | – | 2 | – |
| MN......... | 5 | 3 | 5 | 3 | 5 | 3 | 5 | 3 | 2 | – | 2 | – | 2 | – | 2 | – |
| MS......... | 1 | 3 | 1 | 2 | 1 | 3 | 1 | 3 | – | 2 | – | 2 | – | 2 | – | 2 |
| MO......... | 2 | 5 | 2 | 6 | 2 | 6 | 2 | 6 | 1 | 1 | 1 | 1 | 1 | 1 | – | 2 |
| MT......... | – | 1 | 1 | 1 | – | 1 | – | 1 | 2 | – | 1 | 1 | 1 | 1 | 1 | 1 |
| NE......... | – | 3 | 1 | 2 | – | 3 | – | 3 | – | 2 | – | 2 | – | 2 | – | 2 |
| NV......... | 2 | 2 | 1 | 3 | 3 | 1 | 3 | 1 | 1 | 1 | 1 | 1 | 1 | 1 | 2 | – |
| NH......... | 2 | – | 1 | 1 | 2 | – | 2 | – | 1 | 1 | 1 | 1 | 2 | – | 2 | – |
| NJ......... | 6 | 6 | 6 | 6 | 7 | 5 | 11 | 1 | 2 | – | 2 | – | 2 | – | 2 | – |
| NM......... | 2 | 1 | 2 | 1 | 2 | 1 | 3 | – | 2 | – | 2 | – | 2 | – | 2 | – |
| NY......... | 21 | 6 | 18 | 8 | 18 | 9 | 21 | 6 | 2 | – | 2 | – | 2 | – | 2 | – |
| NC......... | 4 | 9 | 3 | 10 | 3 | 10 | 3 | 8 | 1 | 1 | – | 2 | – | 2 | – | 2 |
| ND......... | – | 1 | – | 1 | – | 1 | – | 1 | 1 | 1 | 1 | 1 | 1 | 1 | – | 2 |
| OH......... | 4 | 12 | 4 | 12 | 4 | 12 | 4 | 12 | 1 | 1 | 1 | 1 | 1 | 1 | 1 | 1 |
| OK......... | – | 5 | – | 5 | – | 5 | 1 | 4 | – | 2 | – | 2 | – | 2 | – | 2 |
| OR......... | 4 | 1 | 4 | 1 | 4 | 1 | 4 | 1 | 2 | – | 2 | – | 2 | – | 2 | – |
| PA......... | 5 | 13 | 5 | 13 | 5 | 13 | 9 | 8 | 1 | 1 | 1 | 1 | 1 | 1 | 1 | 1 |
| RI......... | 2 | – | 2 | – | 2 | – | 2 | – | 2 | – | 2 | – | 2 | – | 2 | – |
| SC......... | 1 | 5 | 1 | 6 | 1 | 6 | 2 | 5 | – | 2 | – | 2 | – | 2 | – | 2 |
| SD......... | – | 1 | – | 1 | – | 1 | – | 1 | 1 | 1 | – | 2 | – | 2 | – | 2 |
| TN......... | 2 | 7 | 2 | 7 | 2 | 7 | 2 | 7 | – | 2 | – | 2 | – | 2 | – | 2 |
| TX......... | 12 | 24 | 11 | 25 | 11 | 25 | 13 | 23 | – | 2 | – | 2 | – | 2 | – | 2 |
| UT......... | 1 | 3 | – | 4 | – | 4 | 1 | 3 | – | 2 | – | 2 | – | 2 | – | 2 |
| VT......... | 1 | – | 1 | – | 1 | – | 1 | – | 1 | – | 1 | – | 1 | – | 1 | – |
| VA......... | 3 | 8 | 3 | 8 | 4 | 7 | 7 | 4 | 2 | – | 2 | – | 2 | – | 2 | – |
| WA......... | 6 | 4 | 6 | 4 | 6 | 4 | 7 | 3 | 2 | – | 2 | – | 2 | – | 2 | – |
| WV......... | 1 | 2 | – | 3 | – | 3 | – | 3 | 2 | – | 1 | 1 | 1 | 1 | 1 | 1 |
| WI......... | 3 | 5 | 3 | 5 | 3 | 5 | 3 | 5 | 1 | 1 | 1 | 1 | 1 | 1 | 1 | 1 |
| WY......... | – | 1 | – | 1 | – | 1 | – | 1 | – | 2 | – | 2 | – | 2 | – | 2 |

– Represents zero. [1] Two vacancies—one in Missouri due to the resignation of Jo Ann Emerson, January 22, 2013, and one in South Carolina due to the resignation of Tim Scott, January 2, 2013. [2] Two vacancies—one in Mississippi due to the death of Alan Nunnelee, February 6, 2015, and one in New York due to the resignation of Michael G. Grimm, January 5, 2015. [3] Three vacancies—one in Pennsylvania due the resignation of Tom Marino on January 23, 2019; and two in North Carolina, one due to the death of Walter Jones on February 10, 2019, and one due to North Carolina's State Board of Elections and Ethics Reform's refusal to certify the results of the NC-09 election due to irregularities involving absentee ballots. [4] Vermont and Maine had one Independent senator each.

Source: U.S. House of Representatives, Office of the Clerk, *Official List of Members*, February 2019, and earlier editions. See also <http://clerk.house.gov/member_info/>.

# Table 456. Members of Congress—Seniority of Senators and Representatives: 1963 to 2019

[Represents the makeup of Congress on the 1st day of the session]

| Congress | Senators | | | | | Representatives | | | | |
|---|---|---|---|---|---|---|---|---|---|---|
| | Number by length of service | | | | Mean years of service | Number by terms served | | | | Mean terms of service |
| | 6 years or less [1] | 7-12 years | 13-18 years | 19 or more years | | 1-3 terms | 4-6 terms | 7-9 terms | 10+ terms | |
| 88th (1963) | 42 (12) | 26 | 18 | 14 | 9.9 | 182 | 106 | 78 | 68 | 5.5 |
| 89th (1965) | 29 (8) | 36 | 16 | 19 | 11.1 | 198 | 97 | 73 | 67 | 5.1 |
| 90th (1967) | 28 (7) | 34 | 19 | 19 | 11.6 | 183 | 108 | 69 | 73 | 5.3 |
| 91st (1969) | 32 (14) | 32 | 17 | 19 | 11.2 | 171 | 126 | 65 | 73 | 5.6 |
| 92nd (1971) | 25 (10) | 24 | 29 | 22 | 11.5 | 162 | 122 | 68 | 83 | 5.8 |
| 93rd (1973) | 40 (13) | 20 | 20 | 20 | 11.2 | 162 | 128 | 66 | 76 | 5.5 |
| 94th (1975) | [2] 36 (12) | 22 | 23 | 19 | 11.5 | 196 | 100 | 78 | 61 | 5.2 |
| 95th (1977) | 42 (17) | 25 | 13 | 20 | 10.6 | 219 | 87 | 70 | 59 | 4.9 |
| 96th (1979) | 48 (20) | 24 | 10 | 18 | 9.6 | 219 | 95 | 65 | 54 | 4.8 |
| 97th (1981) | 55 (18) | 20 | 10 | 15 | 8.5 | 209 | 121 | 56 | 49 | 4.7 |
| 98th (1983) | 43 (5) | 28 | 16 | 13 | 9.6 | 210 | 125 | 45 | 54 | 4.7 |
| 99th (1985) | 32 (7) | 38 | 18 | 12 | 10.1 | 184 | 138 | 58 | 54 | 5.1 |
| 100th (1987) | 26 (13) | 44 | 16 | 14 | 9.6 | 163 | 143 | 64 | 65 | 5.5 |
| 101st (1989) | 31 (10) | 26 | 29 | 14 | 9.8 | 120 | 167 | 86 | 60 | 5.8 |
| 102nd (1991) | 30 (5) | 23 | 28 | 19 | 11.1 | 133 | 137 | 91 | 74 | 6.1 |
| 103rd (1993) | 30 (13) | 17 | 32 | 21 | 11.3 | 192 | 109 | 69 | 65 | 5.2 |
| 104th (1995) | 29 (11) | 26 | 20 | 25 | 12.3 | 220 | 78 | 78 | 59 | 4.9 |
| 105th (1997) | 40 (15) | 24 | 13 | 23 | 11.2 | 243 | 71 | 65 | 56 | 4.8 |
| 106th (1999) | 35 (8) | 24 | 16 | 25 | 11.2 | 185 | 127 | 58 | 65 | 4.8 |
| 107th (2001) | 37 (11) | 21 | 19 | 23 | 11.5 | 149 | 155 | 54 | 76 | 5.6 |
| 108th (2003) | 30 (10) | 29 | 16 | 25 | 12.7 | 149 | 158 | 60 | 68 | 5.5 |
| 109th (2005) | 29 (9) | 27 | 15 | 29 | 12.5 | 137 | 128 | 97 | 72 | 5.9 |
| 110th (2007) | 29 (10) | 26 | 14 | 31 | 13.1 | 149 | 116 | 99 | 71 | 6.0 |
| 111th (2009) | [3] 32 (11) | 19 | 20 | 29 | 14.0 | 147 | 102 | 106 | 79 | 6.2 |
| 112th (2011) | 42 (13) | 17 | 14 | 27 | 12.3 | 170 | 97 | 69 | 97 | 6.0 |
| 113th (2013) | 43 (13) | 23 | 15 | 19 | 10.2 | 196 | 91 | 72 | 74 | 5.7 |
| 114th (2015) | 45 (13) | 24 | 11 | 20 | 9.4 | 205 | 91 | 51 | 88 | 5.5 |
| 115th (2017) | 36 (7) | 34 | 11 | 19 | 10.2 | 177 | 118 | 55 | 85 | 5.8 |
| 116th (2019) | 32 (9) | 33 | 17 | 18 | 10.1 | 184 | 121 | 56 | 73 | 5.4 |

[1] Numbers in parentheses are number of freshman senators. Senators who are currently in their first full term are listed under "6 years or less." [2] Total includes John Durkin (D-NH). After a contested election in 1974, the Senate declared the seat vacant as of August 8, 1975. Durkin was then elected by special election, September 16, 1975, to fill the vacancy. [3] Total includes Al Franken (D-MN), who was declared elected after a challenge in court to the vote count by his Republican challenger on June 30, 2009; and Roland Burris (D-IL) who was appointed to fill the seat vacated by Barack Obama on December 31, 2008. Total also includes Joe Biden (D-DE), who resigned his seat on January 15, 2009, but was present on the first day of the session.

Source: The Brookings Institution, "Vital Statistics on Congress" ©, March 2019, <https://www.brookings.edu/multi-chapter-report/vital-statistics-on-congress/>.

# Table 457. Women, Black, Asian, and Hispanic Members of Congress by Party Affiliation: 1999 to 2019

[As of beginning of first session of each Congress. Data do not include delegates or commissioners]

| Characteristic | Congress | | | | | | | | | | |
|---|---|---|---|---|---|---|---|---|---|---|---|
| | 106th (1999) | 107th (2001) | 108th (2003) | 109th (2005) | 110th (2007) | 111th (2009) [1] | 112th (2011) | 113th (2013) [2] | 114th (2015) | 115th (2017) | 116th (2019) |
| **Women, total** | 65 | 72 | 73 | 79 | 87 | 91 | 93 | 96 | 104 | 104 | 127 |
| Representatives | 56 | 59 | 59 | 65 | 71 | 74 | 76 | 76 | 84 | 83 | 102 |
| Democrat | 40 | 41 | 38 | 42 | 50 | 57 | 52 | 56 | 62 | 62 | 89 |
| Republican | 16 | 18 | 21 | 23 | 21 | 17 | 24 | 20 | 22 | 21 | 13 |
| Senators | 9 | 13 | 14 | 14 | 16 | 17 | 17 | 20 | 20 | 21 | 25 |
| Democrat | 6 | 10 | 9 | 9 | 11 | 13 | 12 | 16 | 14 | 16 | 17 |
| Republican | 3 | 3 | 5 | 5 | 5 | 4 | 5 | 4 | 6 | 5 | 8 |
| **Black, total** | 37 | 36 | 37 | 41 | 41 | 39 | 42 | 42 | 46 | 50 | 56 |
| Representatives | 37 | 36 | 37 | 40 | 40 | 39 | 42 | 41 | 44 | 47 | 53 |
| Democrat | 36 | 35 | 37 | 40 | 40 | 39 | 40 | 41 | 42 | 45 | 52 |
| Republican | 1 | 1 | 0 | 0 | 0 | 0 | 2 | 0 | 2 | 2 | 1 |
| Senators | 0 | 0 | 0 | 1 | 1 | 0 | 0 | 1 | 2 | 3 | 3 |
| Democrat | 0 | 0 | 0 | 1 | 1 | 0 | 0 | 0 | 1 | 2 | 2 |
| Republican | 0 | 0 | 0 | 0 | 0 | 0 | 0 | 1 | 1 | 1 | 1 |
| **Asian, total** | 6 | 7 | 6 | 7 | 8 | 7 | 10 | 11 | 12 | 15 | 15 |
| Representatives | 4 | 5 | 4 | 5 | 6 | 5 | 8 | 10 | 11 | 12 | 12 |
| Democrat | 4 | 5 | 4 | 4 | 5 | 4 | 7 | 10 | 11 | 12 | 12 |
| Republican | 0 | 0 | 0 | 1 | 1 | 1 | 1 | 0 | 0 | 0 | 0 |
| Senators | 2 | 2 | 2 | 2 | 2 | 2 | 2 | 1 | 1 | 3 | 3 |
| Democrat | 2 | 2 | 2 | 2 | 2 | 2 | 2 | 1 | 1 | 3 | 3 |
| Republican | 0 | 0 | 0 | 0 | 0 | 0 | 0 | 0 | 0 | 0 | 0 |
| **Hispanic, total** | 19 | 19 | 22 | 25 | 26 | 26 | 29 | 31 | 35 | 42 | 43 |
| Representatives | 19 | 19 | 22 | 23 | 23 | 24 | 27 | 28 | 32 | 38 | 39 |
| Democrat | 16 | 16 | 18 | 19 | 20 | 21 | 19 | 23 | 23 | 28 | 32 |
| Republican | 3 | 3 | 4 | 4 | 3 | 3 | 8 | 5 | 9 | 10 | 7 |
| Senators | 0 | 0 | 0 | 2 | 3 | 2 | 2 | 3 | 3 | 4 | 4 |
| Democrat | 0 | 0 | 0 | 1 | 2 | 1 | 1 | 1 | 1 | 2 | 2 |
| Republican | 0 | 0 | 0 | 1 | 1 | 1 | 1 | 2 | 2 | 2 | 2 |

[1] Roland Burris was not seated on the first day of the 111th session. [2] Tim Scott, who was appointed on December 17th to replace outgoing Senator Jim DeMint, is included in the Senate totals.

Source: The Brookings Institution, "Vital Statistics on Congress" ©, March 2019, <https://www.brookings.edu/multi-chapter-report/vital-statistics-on-congress/>.

## Table 458. Composition of Congress by Political Party: 1977 to 2019

[D = Democratic, R = Republican. As of beginning of first session of each Congress. Data reflect immediate result of elections. Vacancies and third party candidates are noted]

| Year | Party and president | Congress | House Majority party | House Minority party | House Other | Senate Majority party | Senate Minority party | Senate Other |
|------|---------------------|----------|----------------------|----------------------|-------------|-----------------------|-----------------------|--------------|
| 1977 [1] | D (Carter) | 95th | D-292 | R-143 | – | D-61 | R-38 | 1 |
| 1979 [1] | D (Carter) | 96th | D-277 | R-158 | – | D-58 | R-41 | 1 |
| 1981 [2] | R (Reagan) | 97th | D-242 | R-192 | 1 | R-53 | D-46 | 1 |
| 1983 | R (Reagan) | 98th | D-269 | R-166 | – | R-54 | D-46 | – |
| 1985 | R (Reagan) | 99th | D-253 | R-182 | – | R-53 | D-47 | – |
| 1987 | R (Reagan) | 100th | D-258 | R-177 | – | D-55 | R-45 | – |
| 1989 | R (Bush) | 101st | D-260 | R-175 | – | D-55 | R-45 | – |
| 1991 [3] | R (Bush) | 102nd | D-267 | R-167 | 1 | D-56 | R-44 | – |
| 1993 [3] | D (Clinton) | 103rd | D-258 | R-176 | 1 | D-57 | R-43 | – |
| 1995 [3] | D (Clinton) | 104th | R-230 | D-204 | 1 | R-52 | D-48 | – |
| 1997 [4] | D (Clinton) | 105th | R-226 | D-207 | 2 | R-55 | D-45 | – |
| 1999 [3] | D (Clinton) | 106th | R-223 | D-211 | 1 | R-55 | D-45 | – |
| 2001 [4] | R (Bush) | 107th | R-221 | D-212 | 2 | D-50 | R-50 | – |
| 2003 [2, 5] | R (Bush) | 108th | R-229 | D-204 | 1 | R-51 | D-48 | 1 |
| 2005 [2] | R (Bush) | 109th | R-232 | D-202 | 1 | R-55 | D-44 | 1 |
| 2007 [6] | R (Bush) | 110th | D-233 | R-202 | – | D-49 | R-49 | 2 |
| 2009 [5, 6, 7] | D (Obama) | 111th | D-256 | R-178 | – | D-55 | R-41 | 2 |
| 2011 [6] | D (Obama) | 112th | R-242 | D-193 | – | D-51 | R-47 | 2 |
| 2013 [5, 6] | D (Obama) | 113th | R-234 | D-200 | – | D-53 | R-45 | 2 |
| 2015 [6] | D (Obama) | 114th | R-247 | D-188 | – | R-54 | D-44 | 2 |
| 2017 [6] | R (Trump) | 115th | R-241 | D-194 | – | R-52 | D-46 | 2 |
| 2019 [6, 8] | R (Trump) | 116th | D-235 | R-197 | – | R-53 | D-47 | 2 |

– Represents zero. [1] Senate had one Independent. [2] House and Senate each had one Independent. [3] House had one Independent-Socialist. [4] House had one Independent-Socialist and one Independent. [5] House had one vacancy. [6] Senate had two Independents. [7] Senate had two vacancies. [8] House had three vacancies.

Source: U.S. House of Representatives, Office of the Clerk, *Official List of Members*, February 2019, and earlier editions. See also <http://clerk.house.gov/member_info/>.

## Table 459. U.S. Congress—Measures Introduced and Enacted and Time in Session: 2001 to 2018

[Excludes simple and concurrent resolutions]

| Item | 107th Cong., 2001–02 | 108th Cong., 2003–04 | 109th Cong., 2005–06 | 110th Cong., 2007–08 | 111th Cong., 2009–10 | 112th Cong., 2011-12 | 113th Cong., 2013-14 | 114th Cong., 2015-16 | 115th Cong., 2017-18 |
|------|------|------|------|------|------|------|------|------|------|
| Measures introduced | 9,130 | 8,625 | 10,703 | 11,228 | 10,778 | 10,612 | 9,097 | 10,223 | 13,558 |
| Bills | 8,953 | 8,468 | 10,560 | 11,081 | 10,629 | 10,439 | 8,919 | 10,074 | 11,201 |
| Joint resolutions | 177 | 157 | 143 | 147 | 149 | 173 | 178 | 149 | 215 |
| Measures enacted | 337 | 504 | 590 | 460 | 385 | 239 | 296 | 329 | 339 |
| Public [1] | 331 | 498 | 589 | 460 | 383 | 238 | 296 | 329 | 338 |
| Private [2] | 6 | 6 | 1 | 0 | 2 | 1 | 0 | 0 | 1 |
| **HOUSE OF REPRESENTATIVES** | | | | | | | | | |
| Number of days | 265 | 243 | 241 | 283 | 286 | 327 | 295 | 288 | 366 |
| Number of hours | 1,694 | 1,894 | 1,917 | 2,138 | 2,126 | 1,718 | 1,471 | 1,438 | 1,515 |
| Number of hours per day | 6.4 | 7.8 | 8.0 | 7.6 | 7.4 | 5.3 | 5.0 | 5.0 | 4.1 |
| **SENATE** | | | | | | | | | |
| Number of days | 322 | 300 | 297 | 374 | 349 | 323 | 292 | 333 | 386 |
| Number of hours | 2,279 | 2,486 | 2,250 | 2,364 | 2,495 | 2,032 | 2,003 | 1,855 | 2,181 |
| Number of hours per day | 7.1 | 8.3 | 7.6 | 6.3 | 7.1 | 6.3 | 6.9 | 5.6 | 5.7 |

[1] Laws on public matters that apply to all persons. [2] Laws designed to provide legal relief to specified persons or entities adversely affected by laws of general applicability.

Source: U.S. Congress, *Résumé of Congressional Activity*, Jan 2019, and earlier reports. See also <https://www.senate.gov/legislative/ResumesofCongressionalActivity1947present.htm>.

## Table 460. Congressional Bills Vetoed: 1961 to 2019

| Period | President | Total vetoes | Regular vetoes | Pocket vetoes | Vetoes sustained | Bills passed over veto |
|--------|-----------|--------------|----------------|---------------|------------------|------------------------|
| 1961 to 1963 | John F. Kennedy | 21 | 12 | 9 | 21 | 0 |
| 1963 to 1969 | Lyndon B. Johnson | 30 | 16 | 14 | 30 | 0 |
| 1969 to 1974 | Richard M. Nixon | 43 | 26 | 17 | 36 | 7 |
| 1974 to 1977 | Gerald R. Ford | 66 | 48 | 18 | 54 | 12 |
| 1977 to 1981 | Jimmy Carter | 31 | 13 | 18 | 29 | 2 |
| 1981 to 1989 | Ronald W. Reagan | 78 | 39 | 39 | 69 | 9 |
| 1989 to 1993 | George Bush | 44 | 29 | 15 | 43 | 1 |
| 1993 to 2001 | William J. Clinton | 37 | 36 | 1 | 35 | 2 |
| 2001 to 2009 | George W. Bush | 12 | 12 | 0 | 8 | 4 |
| 2009 to 2017 | Barack Obama | 12 | 12 | 0 | 11 | 1 |
| 2017 to 2019 [1] | Donald J. Trump | 5 | 5 | 0 | 5 | 0 |

[1] For the period January 20, 2017 through August 6, 2019.

Source: Congressional Research Service, *Regular Vetoes and Pocket Vetoes: In Brief,* July 2019; and U.S. Senate, "Summary of Bills Vetoed," <https://www.senate.gov/reference/reference_index_subjects/Vetoes_vrd.htm>, and "Vetoes by President Donald J. Trump," <https://www.senate.gov/legislative/vetoes/TrumpDJ.htm>, accessed August 2019.

# Table 461. Number of Governors by Political Party Affiliation: 1975 to 2019

[Reflects figures after inaugurations for each year. State governors only]

| Year | Demo-cratic | Republi-can | Inde-pendent/other | Year | Demo-cratic | Republi-can | Inde-pendent/other | Year | Demo-cratic | Republi-can | Inde-pendent/other |
|------|------|------|------|------|------|------|------|------|------|------|------|
| 1975........ | 36 | 13 | 1 | 2005........ | 22 | 28 | – | 2014........ | 21 | 29 | – |
| 1980........ | 31 | 19 | – | 2009........ | 28 | 22 | – | 2015........ | 18 | 31 | 1 |
| 1985........ | 34 | 16 | – | 2010........ | 26 | 24 | – | 2016........ | 18 | 31 | 1 |
| 1990........ | 29 | 21 | – | 2011........ | 20 | 29 | 1 | 2017........ | 16 | 33 | 1 |
| 1995........ | 19 | 30 | 1 | 2012........ | 20 | 29 | 1 | 2018........ | 16 | 33 | 1 |
| 2000........ | 18 | 30 | 2 | 2013........ | 20 | 30 | – | 2019........ | 23 | 27 | – |

– Represents zero.

Source: ProQuest research.

# Table 462. Vote Cast for and Governor Elected by State: 2014 to 2017

[D = Democratic, R = Republican, I = Independent]

| State | Current governor [1] | Year of election | Total vote [2] | Republican | Democratic | Percent leading party |
|-------|-------|-------|-------|-------|-------|-------|
| Alabama............ | Kay Ivey [3] | 2014 | 1,180,413 | 750,231 | 427,787 | R-63.6 |
| Alaska.............. | Bill Walker | 2014 | 279,958 | 128,435 | 8,985 | I-48.4 |
| Arizona............. | Doug Ducey | 2014 | 1,506,416 | 805,062 | 626,921 | R-53.4 |
| Arkansas........... | Asa Hutchinson | 2014 | 848,952 | 470,429 | 352,115 | R-55.4 |
| California........... | Edmund Gerald "Jerry" Brown | 2014 | 7,317,581 | 2,929,213 | 4,388,368 | D-60.0 |
| Colorado........... | John Hickenlooper | 2014 | 2,041,574 | 938,195 | 1,006,433 | D-49.3 |
| Connecticut........ | Dan Malloy | 2014 | 1,092,773 | 526,295 | 554,314 | D-50.7 |
| Delaware........... | John Carney Jr. | 2016 | 425,784 | 166,852 | 248,404 | D-58.3 |
| Florida............. | Rick Scott | 2014 | 5,951,561 | 2,865,343 | 2,801,198 | R-48.1 |
| Georgia............ | Nathan Deal | 2014 | 2,550,648 | 1,345,237 | 1,144,794 | R-52.7 |
| Hawaii............. | David Ige | 2014 | 366,210 | 135,775 | 181,106 | D-49.5 |
| Idaho.............. | C.L. "Butch" Otter | 2014 | 442,268 | 235,378 | 169,595 | R-53.2 |
| Illinois............. | Bruce Rauner | 2014 | 3,637,690 | 1,833,627 | 1,681,343 | R-50.4 |
| Indiana............ | Eric Holcomb | 2016 | 2,719,968 | 1,397,396 | 1,235,503 | R-51.4 |
| Iowa............... | Kim Reynolds [4] | 2014 | 1,129,034 | 666,023 | 420,778 | R-59.0 |
| Kansas............. | Jeff Colyer [5] | 2014 | 869,502 | 433,196 | 401,100 | R-49.8 |
| Kentucky........... | Matt Bevin | 2015 | 973,692 | 511,374 | 426,620 | R-52.5 |
| Louisiana.......... | John Bel Edwards | 2015 | 1,152,864 | 505,940 | 646,924 | D-56.1 |
| Maine.............. | Paul LePage | 2014 | 611,227 | 294,519 | 265,114 | R-48.2 |
| Maryland........... | Larry Hogan | 2014 | 1,728,975 | 884,400 | 818,890 | R-51.2 |
| Massachusetts..... | Charlie Baker | 2014 | 2,158,326 | 1,044,573 | 1,004,408 | R-48.4 |
| Michigan........... | Rick Snyder | 2014 | 3,156,531 | 1,607,399 | 1,479,057 | R-50.9 |
| Minnesota.......... | Mark Dayton | 2014 | 1,975,406 | 879,257 | 989,113 | D-50.1 |
| Mississippi......... | Phil Bryant | 2015 | 718,185 | 476,697 | 231,643 | R-66.4 |
| Missouri............ | Mark Parson [6] | 2016 | 2,777,854 | 1,424,730 | 1,261,110 | R-51.3 |
| Montana............ | Steve Bullock | 2016 | 509,360 | 236,115 | 255,933 | D-50.2 |
| Nebraska........... | Pete Ricketts | 2014 | 539,657 | 308,751 | 211,905 | R-57.2 |
| Nevada............. | Brian Sandoval | 2014 | 547,349 | 386,340 | 130,722 | R-70.6 |
| New Hampshire.... | Chris Sununu | 2016 | 724,863 | 354,040 | 337,589 | R-48.8 |
| New Jersey......... | Phil Murphy | 2017 | 2,147,415 | 899,583 | 1,203,110 | D-56.0 |
| New Mexico........ | Susana Martinez | 2014 | 512,805 | 293,443 | 219,362 | R-57.2 |
| New York........... | Andrew Cuomo | 2014 | 3,819,427 | 1,536,879 | 2,069,480 | D-54.2 |
| North Carolina...... | Roy Cooper | 2016 | 4,711,014 | 2,298,880 | 2,309,157 | D-49.0 |
| North Dakota....... | Doug Burgum | 2016 | 339,601 | 259,863 | 65,855 | R-76.5 |
| Ohio............... | John Kasich | 2014 | 3,055,913 | 1,944,848 | 1,009,359 | R-63.6 |
| Oklahoma.......... | Mary Fallin | 2014 | 824,831 | 460,298 | 338,239 | R-55.8 |
| Oregon............. | Kate Brown | 2016 | 1,561,819 | 684,321 | 796,006 | D-51.0 |
| Pennsylvania....... | Tom Wolf | 2014 | 3,495,866 | 1,575,511 | 1,920,355 | D-54.9 |
| Rhode Island....... | Gina Raimondo | 2014 | 324,055 | 117,428 | 131,899 | D-40.7 |
| South Carolina..... | Henry McMaster [7] | 2014 | 1,246,303 | 696,645 | 516,166 | R-55.9 |
| South Dakota....... | Dennis Daugaard | 2014 | 277,403 | 195,477 | 70,549 | R-70.5 |
| Tennessee.......... | Bill Haslam | 2014 | 1,353,728 | 951,796 | 309,237 | R-70.3 |
| Texas.............. | Greg Abbot | 2014 | 4,718,268 | 2,796,547 | 1,835,596 | R-59.3 |
| Utah............... | Gary Hebert | 2016 | 1,124,913 | 750,828 | 322,462 | R-66.7 |
| Vermont............ | Phil Scott | 2016 | 314,982 | 166,817 | 139,253 | R-53.0 |
| Virginia............ | Ralph Northam | 2017 | 2,614,282 | 1,175,731 | 1,409,175 | D-53.9 |
| Washington......... | Jay Inslee | 2016 | 3,236,866 | 1,476,346 | 1,760,520 | D-54.4 |
| West Virginia....... | Jim Justice [8] | 2016 | 713,858 | 301,987 | 350,408 | D-49.1 |
| Wisconsin.......... | Scott Walker | 2014 | 2,410,314 | 1,259,706 | 1,122,913 | R-52.3 |
| Wyoming........... | Matt Mead | 2014 | 167,877 | 99,700 | 45,752 | R-59.4 |

[1] As of August 2018. [2] Includes minor party and scattered votes. [3] Lt. Gov. Kay Ivey was sworn in as governor on April 10, 2017 after Gov. Robert Bentley resigned to avoid being impeached. [4] Lt. Gov. Kim Reynolds was sworn in as governor on May 24, 2017 when Gov. Terry Branstad accepted the U.S. Ambassadorship to China. [5] Lt. Gov. Colyer was sworn in as governor on Jan. 31, 2018 following Gov. Sam Brownback's appointment as U.S. ambassador-at-large for international religious freedom. [6] Lt. Gov. Mark Parson was sworn in as governor in June 2018 after Eric Greitens resigned. [7] Lt. Gov. Henry McMaster was sworn in on January 24, 2017 after Gov. Nikki Haley resigned to become the United States Ambassador to the United Nations. [8] In August 2017, Gov. Jim Justice switched from the Democratic party to the Republican party.

Source: The Council of State Governments, Lexington, KY, *The Book of the States 2018*, and earlier reports ©. See also <http://www.csg.org/>.

# Table 463. Political Party Control of State Legislatures by Party: 1990 to 2019

[As of beginning of year. Nebraska has a nonpartisan legislature]

| Year | Legislatures under— Democratic control | Split control or tie | Republican control | Year | Legislatures under— Democratic control | Split control or tie | Republican control | Year | Legislatures under— Democratic control | Split control or tie | Republican control |
|---|---|---|---|---|---|---|---|---|---|---|---|
| 1990...... | 29 | 11 | 9 | 2006...... | 19 | 10 | 20 | 2013...... | 19 | 4 | 26 |
| 1995...... | 18 | 12 | 19 | 2007...... | 22 | 12 | 15 | 2014...... | 19 | 3 | 27 |
| 2000...... | 16 | 15 | 18 | 2008...... | 23 | 14 | 12 | 2015...... | 11 | 8 | 30 |
| 2002...... | 17 | 15 | 17 | 2009...... | 27 | 8 | 14 | 2016...... | 11 | 8 | 30 |
| 2003...... | 16 | 12 | 21 | 2010...... | 27 | 8 | 14 | 2017...... | 14 | 3 | 32 |
| 2004...... | 17 | 11 | 21 | 2011...... | 15 | 8 | 26 | 2018...... | 13 | 4 | 32 |
| 2005...... | 19 | 10 | 20 | 2012...... | 15 | 8 | 26 | 2019...... | 18 | 1 | 30 |

Source: National Conference of State Legislatures, Denver, CO, *State Legislatures* ©. See also <ncsl.org>.

# Table 464. Composition of State Legislatures by Political Party Affiliation: 2017 and 2018

[Data as of January. Figures reflect immediate results of elections, including holdover members in state houses which do not have all of their members running for reelection. Dem. = Democrat, Rep. = Republican, Vac. = Vacancies. In general, Lower House refers to body consisting of state representatives and Upper House of state senators]

| State | Lower House 2017 Dem. | Rep. | Other | Vac. | 2018 Dem. | Rep. | Other | Vac. | Upper House 2017 Dem. | Rep. | Other | Vac. | 2018 Dem. | Rep. | Other | Vac. |
|---|---|---|---|---|---|---|---|---|---|---|---|---|---|---|---|---|
| **U.S.......** | **2,331** | **3,045** | **27** | **14** | **2,339** | **3,002** | **32** | **37** | **795** | **1,122** | **3** | **4** | **791** | **1,112** | **6** | **15** |
| AL [1]......... | 31 | 72 | – | 2 | 32 | 70 | – | 3 | 8 | 26 | 1 | – | 7 | 26 | 1 | 1 |
| AK [2]......... | 17 | 21 | 2 | – | 17 | 21 | 2 | – | 6 | 14 | – | – | 6 | 14 | – | – |
| AZ [3]......... | 25 | 35 | – | – | 25 | 35 | – | – | 13 | 17 | – | – | 13 | 17 | – | – |
| AR [2]......... | 24 | 76 | – | – | 24 | 75 | – | 1 | 9 | 26 | – | – | 9 | 23 | – | 3 |
| CA [2]......... | 55 | 25 | – | – | 52 | 25 | – | 3 | 27 | 13 | – | – | 27 | 13 | – | – |
| CO [2]......... | 37 | 28 | – | – | 36 | 29 | – | – | 17 | 18 | – | – | 16 | 18 | 1 | – |
| CT [3]......... | 79 | 72 | – | 1 | 80 | 71 | – | – | 18 | 18 | – | – | 18 | 18 | – | – |
| DE [2]......... | 25 | 16 | – | – | 25 | 16 | – | – | 10 | 10 | – | 1 | 11 | 10 | – | – |
| FL [2]......... | 41 | 79 | – | – | 40 | 75 | – | 5 | 15 | 25 | – | – | 16 | 23 | – | 1 |
| GA [3]......... | 62 | 118 | – | 1 | 64 | 116 | – | – | 18 | 38 | – | – | 19 | 37 | – | – |
| HI [2]......... | 45 | 5 | 1 | – | 46 | 5 | – | – | 25 | – | – | – | 25 | – | – | – |
| ID [3]......... | 11 | 59 | – | – | 11 | 59 | – | – | 6 | 29 | – | – | 6 | 29 | – | – |
| IL [4]......... | 71 | 47 | – | – | 67 | 51 | – | – | 39 | 20 | – | – | 37 | 22 | – | – |
| IN [2]......... | 30 | 70 | – | – | 30 | 70 | – | – | 9 | 41 | – | – | 9 | 41 | – | – |
| IA [2]......... | 41 | 59 | – | – | 41 | 59 | – | – | 20 | 29 | 1 | – | 20 | 29 | 1 | – |
| KS [2]......... | 40 | 85 | – | – | 40 | 85 | – | – | 9 | 31 | – | – | 9 | 31 | – | – |
| KY [2]......... | 36 | 64 | – | 4 | 37 | 63 | – | – | 11 | 27 | – | – | 11 | 27 | – | – |
| LA [1]......... | 41 | 60 | 3 | 1 | 41 | 61 | 3 | – | 13 | 25 | – | 1 | 14 | 25 | – | – |
| ME [3]......... | 77 | 72 | 2 | – | 74 | 70 | 7 | – | 17 | 18 | – | – | 17 | 18 | – | – |
| MD [1]......... | 91 | 50 | – | – | 91 | 50 | – | – | 33 | 14 | – | – | 32 | 14 | – | 1 |
| MA [3]......... | 125 | 35 | – | – | 121 | 34 | 2 | 3 | 34 | 6 | – | – | 32 | 7 | – | 1 |
| MI [2]......... | 47 | 63 | – | – | 46 | 63 | – | 1 | 11 | 27 | – | – | 11 | 27 | – | – |
| MN [2]......... | 57 | 77 | – | – | 57 | 77 | – | – | 33 | 34 | – | – | 33 | 34 | – | – |
| MS [1]......... | 48 | 74 | – | – | 48 | 73 | – | 1 | 20 | 32 | – | – | 19 | 33 | – | – |
| MO [2]......... | 46 | 117 | – | – | 47 | 115 | – | 1 | 9 | 25 | – | – | 9 | 24 | – | 1 |
| MT [2]......... | 41 | 59 | – | – | 41 | 59 | – | – | 18 | 32 | – | – | 18 | 32 | – | – |
| NE [5]......... | ([5]) | ([5]) | ([5]) | ([5]) | ([5]) | ([5]) | ([5]) | ([5]) | ([5]) | ([5]) | ([5]) | ([5]) | ([5]) | ([5]) | ([5]) | ([5]) |
| NV [2]......... | 27 | 15 | – | – | 27 | 14 | – | 1 | 11 | 9 | 1 | – | 10 | 8 | 1 | 2 |
| NH [3]......... | 172 | 222 | 2 | 4 | 175 | 218 | 3 | 4 | 9 | 14 | – | – | 10 | 14 | – | – |
| NJ [2]......... | 52 | 28 | – | – | 54 | 26 | – | – | 24 | 16 | – | – | 25 | 15 | – | – |
| NM [2]......... | 38 | 32 | – | – | 38 | 32 | – | – | 26 | 16 | – | – | 26 | 16 | – | – |
| NY [3]......... | 106 | 43 | 1 | – | 103 | 37 | 1 | 9 | 32 | 31 | – | – | 30 | 31 | – | 2 |
| NC [3]......... | 46 | 74 | – | – | 45 | 75 | – | – | 15 | 35 | – | – | 15 | 35 | – | – |
| ND [1]......... | 13 | 81 | – | – | 13 | 81 | – | – | 9 | 38 | – | – | 9 | 38 | – | – |
| OH [2]......... | 33 | 66 | – | – | 33 | 66 | – | – | 9 | 24 | – | – | 9 | 24 | – | – |
| OK [2]......... | 26 | 75 | – | – | 28 | 72 | – | 1 | 6 | 42 | – | 1 | 8 | 40 | – | 1 |
| OR [2]......... | 35 | 25 | – | – | 35 | 25 | – | – | 17 | 13 | – | – | 17 | 13 | – | – |
| PA [2]......... | 82 | 121 | – | – | 81 | 120 | – | 1 | 16 | 34 | – | – | 16 | 34 | – | – |
| RI [3]......... | 64 | 10 | 1 | – | 64 | 11 | – | – | 33 | 5 | – | 1 | 33 | 4 | – | 1 |
| SC [2]......... | 44 | 80 | – | – | 44 | 79 | – | 1 | 18 | 28 | – | – | 18 | 28 | – | – |
| SD [3]......... | 10 | 60 | – | – | 10 | 60 | – | – | 6 | 29 | – | – | 6 | 29 | – | – |
| TN [2]......... | 25 | 73 | – | 1 | 25 | 74 | – | – | 5 | 28 | – | – | 5 | 28 | – | – |
| TX [2]......... | 55 | 95 | – | – | 56 | 93 | – | 1 | 11 | 20 | – | – | 11 | 20 | – | – |
| UT [2]......... | 13 | 62 | – | – | 13 | 62 | – | – | 5 | 24 | – | – | 5 | 24 | – | – |
| VT [3]......... | 83 | 53 | 14 | – | 83 | 53 | 14 | – | 23 | 7 | – | – | 21 | 7 | 2 | – |
| VA [2]......... | 34 | 66 | – | – | 49 | 51 | – | – | 19 | 21 | – | – | 19 | 21 | – | – |
| WA [2]......... | 50 | 48 | – | – | 50 | 48 | – | – | 25 | 24 | – | – | 26 | 23 | – | – |
| WV [2]......... | 36 | 63 | 1 | – | 36 | 64 | – | – | 12 | 22 | – | – | 12 | 22 | – | – |
| WI [2]......... | 35 | 64 | – | – | 35 | 63 | – | 1 | 13 | 20 | – | – | 13 | 19 | – | 1 |
| WY [2]......... | 9 | 51 | – | – | 9 | 51 | – | – | 3 | 27 | – | – | 3 | 27 | – | – |

– Represents zero. [1] Members of both houses serve 4-year terms. [2] Upper House members serve 4-year terms and Lower House members serve 2-year terms. [3] Members of both houses serve 2-year terms. [4] Illinois– 4- and 2-year term depending on district. [5] Nebraska– 4-year term and only state to have a nonpartisan unicameral legislature. For 2017 and 2018, Nebraska legislature has 49 members.

Source: The Council of State Governments, Lexington, KY, *The Book of the States 2018*, and earlier reports ©. See also <http://www.csg.org/>.

# Table 465. Women Holding State Public Offices by Office and State: 2019

[As of August]

| State | Total | Statewide elective executive office[1] | State legislature Total | Percent | State | Total | Statewide elective executive office[1] | State legislature Total | Percent |
|---|---|---|---|---|---|---|---|---|---|
| U.S. | 2,223 | 91 | 2,132 | 29 | MO. | 48 | 1 | 47 | 24 |
|  |  |  |  |  | MT. | 46 | 1 | 45 | 30 |
| AL. | 24 | 2 | 22 | 16 | NE. | 14 | – | 14 | 29 |
| AK. | 23 | – | 23 | 38 | NV. | 36 | 3 | 33 | 52 |
| AZ. | 40 | 5 | 35 | 39 | NH. | 145 | – | 145 | 34 |
| AR. | 34 | 2 | 32 | 24 | NJ. | 38 | 1 | 37 | 31 |
| CA. | 40 | 3 | 37 | 31 | NM. | 43 | 3 | 40 | 36 |
| CO. | 49 | 2 | 47 | 47 | NY. | 71 | 2 | 69 | 32 |
| CT. | 64 | 2 | 62 | 33 | NC. | 46 | 3 | 43 | 25 |
| DE. | 19 | 4 | 15 | 24 | ND. | 33 | 3 | 30 | 21 |
| FL. | 51 | 3 | 48 | 30 | OH. | 35 | – | 35 | 27 |
| GA. | 73 | 1 | 72 | 31 | OK. | 36 | 4 | 32 | 21 |
| HI. | 24 | – | 24 | 32 | OR. | 42 | 4 | 38 | 42 |
| ID. | 36 | 3 | 33 | 31 | PA. | 67 | – | 67 | 26 |
| IL. | 66 | 2 | 64 | 36 | RI. | 45 | 2 | 43 | 38 |
| IN. | 41 | 5 | 36 | 24 | SC. | 29 | 2 | 27 | 16 |
| IA. | 45 | 1 | 44 | 29 | SD. | 27 | 2 | 25 | 24 |
| KS. | 48 | 2 | 46 | 28 | TN. | 20 | – | 20 | 15 |
| KY. | 34 | 3 | 31 | 22 | TX. | 44 | 1 | 43 | 24 |
| LA. | 22 | – | 22 | 15 | UT. | 25 | – | 25 | 24 |
| ME. | 72 | 1 | 71 | 38 | VT. | 73 | 1 | 72 | 40 |
| MD. | 73 | – | 73 | 39 | VA. | 37 | – | 37 | 26 |
| MA. | 61 | 4 | 57 | 29 | WA. | 64 | 3 | 61 | 41 |
| MI. | 56 | 3 | 53 | 36 | WV. | 19 | – | 19 | 14 |
| MN. | 66 | 2 | 64 | 32 | WI. | 38 | 2 | 36 | 27 |
| MS. | 25 | 1 | 24 | 14 | WY. | 16 | 2 | 14 | 16 |

– Represents zero. [1] Excludes women elected to the judiciary, women appointed to state cabinet-level positions, women elected to executive posts by the legislature, and elected members of university Boards of Trustees or Boards of Education.

Source: Center for American Women and Politics, Eagleton Institute of Politics, Rutgers University, New Brunswick, NJ, "Women in Elective Office," <http://www.cawp.rutgers.edu/> ©, accessed August 2019.

# Table 466. Hispanic Public Elected Officials by Office, 2010 to 2018, and by State, 2018

[As of January or November of year shown. For states not shown, no Hispanic public officials had been identified]

| State | Total[1] | State executives and legislators[2] | County and municipal officials | Judicial and law enforcement | Education and school boards | State | Total[1] | State executives and legislators[2] | County and municipal officials | Judicial and law enforcement | Education and school boards |
|---|---|---|---|---|---|---|---|---|---|---|---|
| 2010. | 5,763 | 275 | 2,270 | 874 | 2,072 | MD. | 17 | 6 | 9 | 0 | 2 |
| 2012. | 5,954 | 292 | 2,293 | 881 | 2,225 | MA. | 55 | 8 | 28 | 1 | 18 |
| 2013. | 6,042 | 320 | 2,285 | 878 | 2,287 | MI. | 23 | 6 | 7 | 4 | 6 |
| 2014. | 6,115 | 334 | 2,313 | 878 | 2,322 | MN. | 18 | 5 | 3 | 8 | 2 |
| 2015. | 6,124 | 349 | 2,334 | 860 | 2,342 | MO. | 1 | 1 | 0 | 0 | 0 |
| 2016. | 6,176 | 347 | 2,388 | 859 | 2,344 | MT. | 0 | 0 | 0 | 0 | 0 |
| 2017. | 6,600 | 377 | 2,638 | 879 | 2,473 | NE. | 4 | 1 | 0 | 0 | 3 |
|  |  |  |  |  |  | NV. | 28 | 12 | 7 | 5 | 4 |
| 2018. | 6,749 | 378 | 2,733 | 890 | 2,496 | NH. | 4 | 2 | 1 | 1 | 0 |
| AK. | 1 | 0 | 1 | 0 | 0 | NJ. | 175 | 12 | 94 | 1 | 68 |
| AZ. | 387 | 25 | 141 | 45 | 171 | NM. | 685 | 50 | 326 | 123 | 144 |
| AR. | 1 | 0 | 0 | 0 | 1 | NY. | 176 | 23 | 66 | 51 | 36 |
| CA. | 1,508 | 43 | 489 | 85 | 766 | NC. | 3 | 0 | 1 | 1 | 1 |
| CO. | 162 | 12 | 87 | 17 | 39 | OH. | 27 | 3 | 16 | 3 | 5 |
| CT. | 78 | 14 | 44 | 0 | 20 | OK. | 3 | 3 | 0 | 0 | 0 |
| DE. | 3 | 3 | 0 | 0 | 0 | OR. | 43 | 4 | 7 | 9 | 20 |
| FL. | 213 | 29 | 112 | 63 | 7 | PA. | 24 | 2 | 11 | 4 | 7 |
| GA. | 14 | 4 | 6 | 2 | 2 | RI. | 22 | 8 | 10 | 0 | 4 |
| HI. | 4 | 4 | 0 | 0 | 0 | TN. | 6 | 1 | 4 | 1 | 0 |
| ID. | 7 | 1 | 5 | 1 | 0 | TX. | 2,753 | 50 | 1,092 | 445 | 1,105 |
| IL. | 123 | 16 | 76 | 8 | 16 | UT. | 8 | 5 | 3 | 0 | 0 |
| IN. | 28 | 2 | 14 | 3 | 9 | VT. | 4 | 1 | 1 | 1 | 1 |
| IA. | 21 | 0 | 10 | 0 | 11 | VA. | 13 | 4 | 6 | 0 | 3 |
| KS. | 8 | 4 | 4 | 0 | 0 | WA. | 61 | 6 | 41 | 0 | 14 |
| KY. | 1 | 1 | 0 | 0 | 0 | WI. | 5 | 4 | 0 | 1 | 0 |
| LA. | 4 | 0 | 1 | 2 | 1 | WV. | 13 | 2 | 3 | 5 | 3 |
| ME. | 5 | 0 | 2 | 0 | 3 | WY. | 10 | 1 | 5 | 0 | 4 |

[1] Includes special district officials, not shown separately. [2] Includes U.S. Senators and Representatives, not shown separately.

Source: National Association of Latino Elected and Appointed Officials (NALEO) Educational Fund, Washington, DC, *National Directory of Latino Elected Officials* ©, and earlier reports. See also <http://www.naleo.org/>.

## Table 467. Political Action Committees—Financial Activity Summary by Committee Type: 2013 to 2018

[In millions of dollars (2,368.6 represents $2,368,600,000). Covers financial activity during 2-year calendar period indicated]

| Committee type | Receipts | | | Disbursements [1] | | | Contributions to candidates | | |
|---|---|---|---|---|---|---|---|---|---|
| | 2013 to 2014 | 2015 to 2016 | 2017 to 2018 | 2013 to 2014 | 2015 to 2016 | 2017 to 2018 | 2013 to 2014 | 2015 to 2016 | 2017 to 2018 |
| Total | **2,368.6** | **4,046.3** | **4,674.2** | **2,304.8** | **3,973.3** | **4,554.1** | **435.9** | **444.0** | **465.6** |
| Corporate | 384.8 | 405.5 | 417.2 | 370.7 | 385.7 | 404.8 | 178.1 | 182.8 | 178.1 |
| Labor | 305.7 | 342.4 | 365.8 | 289.2 | 331.5 | 342.2 | 50.6 | 46.7 | 53.8 |
| Trade | 146.3 | 159.9 | 174.3 | 140.4 | 148.2 | 164.1 | 79.2 | 82.8 | 87.3 |
| Membership | 156.4 | 159.8 | 100.4 | 150.1 | 152.0 | 97.6 | 40.1 | 40.3 | 33.0 |
| Cooperative | 7.7 | 8.0 | 9.1 | 7.0 | 7.0 | 8.4 | 4.9 | 4.7 | 5.1 |
| Corporation without stock | 19.7 | 15.7 | 14.3 | 19.4 | 14.5 | 14.4 | 7.0 | 7.5 | 7.4 |
| Nonconnected | 1,347.9 | 2,954.9 | 3,593.0 | 1,327.9 | 2,934.3 | 3,522.5 | 76.0 | 79.2 | 100.8 |

[1] Comprises contributions to candidates, independent expenditures, and other disbursements.

Source: U.S. Federal Election Commission, Campaign Finance Statistics, "Public Action Committee (PAC) Data Summary Tables," <http://www.fec.gov/press/campaign_finance_statistics.shtml>, accessed March 2019.

## Table 468. Congressional Campaign Finances—Receipts and Disbursements: 2009 to 2018

[In millions of dollars (1,103.2 represents $1,103,200,000). Covers all campaign finance activity during 2-year calendar period indicated for primary, general, run-off, and special elections. Data have been adjusted to eliminate transfers between all committees within a campaign. For further information on legal limits of contributions, see Federal Election Campaign Act of 1971, as amended]

| Item | House of Representatives | | | | | Senate | | | | |
|---|---|---|---|---|---|---|---|---|---|---|
| | 2009 to 2010 | 2011 to 2012 | 2013 to 2014 | 2015 to 2016 | 2017 to 2018 | 2009 to 2010 | 2011 to 2012 | 2013 to 2014 | 2015 to 2016 | 2017 to 2018 |
| Total receipts [1] | **1,103.2** | **1,136.5** | **1,033.9** | **1,049.8** | **1,740.8** | **757.2** | **742.3** | **635.4** | **594.5** | **1,033.3** |
| Individual contributions | 640.6 | 637.0 | 557.0 | 546.4 | 1,063.0 | 468.0 | 466.1 | 439.4 | 424.2 | 691.4 |
| Other committees | 326.2 | 351.0 | 341.9 | 354.5 | 406.1 | 87.6 | 80.9 | 98.4 | 92.8 | 84.8 |
| Candidate contributions & loans | 109.6 | 108.2 | 96.4 | 107.0 | 165.5 | 149.6 | 167.3 | 51.2 | 31.6 | 188.4 |
| Democrats | 510.3 | 486.8 | 446.4 | 476.4 | 1,034.5 | 314.7 | 307.9 | 299.6 | 313.4 | 571.5 |
| Incumbents | 393.0 | 249.1 | 286.1 | 249.9 | 299.3 | 139.5 | 172.1 | 204.1 | 67.0 | 399.2 |
| Challengers | 64.4 | 174.8 | 82.9 | 126.7 | 446.7 | 38.8 | 71.4 | 41.3 | 176.2 | 119.5 |
| Open seats [2] | 52.9 | 62.9 | 77.3 | 99.7 | 288.6 | 136.5 | 64.4 | 54.1 | 70.1 | 52.8 |
| Republicans | 587.5 | 632.7 | 583.7 | 559.4 | 693.1 | 427.4 | 416.1 | 327.9 | 278.8 | 430.8 |
| Incumbents | 231.7 | 436.2 | 355.5 | 406.7 | 494.5 | 109.5 | 77.8 | 90.2 | 201.3 | 80.4 |
| Challengers | 266.0 | 125.7 | 119.7 | 51.5 | 61.6 | 148.9 | 143.1 | 144.1 | 29.1 | 295.0 |
| Open seats [2] | 89.8 | 70.7 | 108.5 | 101.2 | 137.0 | 169.1 | 195.3 | 93.5 | 48.5 | 55.5 |
| Others | 5.4 | 17.0 | 3.9 | 14.0 | 13.1 | 15.0 | 18.3 | 8.0 | 2.3 | 30.9 |
| Incumbents | 1.7 | 2.2 | 0.1 | 4.4 | 0.9 | – | 6.3 | – | – | 15.6 |
| Challengers | 3.2 | 13.5 | 1.3 | 5.0 | 8.0 | 0.5 | 8.7 | 6.4 | 2.1 | 15.2 |
| Open seats [2] | 0.5 | 1.3 | 2.5 | 4.6 | 4.2 | 14.5 | 3.3 | 1.5 | 0.2 | 0.2 |
| Total disbursements | **1,096.3** | **1,099.3** | **960.8** | **971.7** | **1,698.9** | **737.3** | **747.9** | **654.2** | **625.3** | **1,019.5** |
| Democrats | 534.7 | 479.1 | 422.5 | 425.1 | 983.5 | 319.3 | 315.7 | 311.5 | 316.0 | 557.8 |
| Republicans | 556.6 | 604.3 | 534.5 | 533.5 | 703.0 | 403.2 | 417.7 | 334.8 | 306.8 | 436.4 |
| Others | 5.1 | 15.9 | 3.9 | 13.1 | 12.4 | 14.9 | 14.5 | 8.0 | 2.5 | 25.3 |

– Represents or rounds to zero. [1] Includes other types of receipts, not shown separately. [2] Elections in which an incumbent did not seek reelection.

Source: U.S. Federal Election Commission, Campaign Finance Statistics, "Congressional Candidate Data Summary Tables," <http://www.fec.gov/press/campaign_finance_statistics.shtml>, accessed March 2019.

## Table 469. Contributions to Congressional Campaigns by Political Action Committees (PAC) by Type of Committee: 2015 to 2018

[In millions of dollars (351.5 represents $351,500,000). Covers amounts given to candidates in primary, general, run-off, and special elections during the 2-year calendar period indicated]

| Type of committee | Total [1] | Democrats | Republicans | Incumbents | Challengers | Open seats [2] |
|---|---|---|---|---|---|---|
| HOUSE OF REPRESENTATIVES | | | | | | |
| 2015–2016 | 351.5 | 145.1 | 203.6 | 313.8 | 17.7 | 20.0 |
| **2017–2018, total [3]** | **383.9** | **167.7** | **215.1** | **328.9** | **24.5** | **30.5** |
| Corporate | 148.2 | 52.3 | 95.6 | 142.4 | 0.8 | 5.0 |
| Trade association [4] | 101.4 | 37.5 | 63.7 | 92.6 | 2.4 | 6.4 |
| Labor | 47.2 | 39.8 | 7.3 | 33.3 | 7.5 | 6.4 |
| Nonconnected [5] | 76.0 | 33.6 | 41.9 | 50.1 | 13.7 | 12.2 |
| Cooperative | 4.5 | 1.9 | 2.6 | 4.2 | 0.1 | 0.3 |
| Corporation without stock | 6.5 | 2.6 | 4.0 | 6.3 | 0.1 | 0.2 |
| SENATE | | | | | | |
| 2015–2016 | 89.8 | 29.4 | 60.4 | 68.4 | 9.4 | 12.0 |
| **2017–2018, total [3]** | **81.5** | **47.8** | **32.4** | **60.5** | **12.1** | **8.9** |
| Corporate | 29.8 | 16.6 | 12.8 | 23.8 | 3.2 | 2.8 |
| Trade association [4] | 18.8 | 10.1 | 8.4 | 13.9 | 2.9 | 2.0 |
| Labor | 6.6 | 5.9 | 0.5 | 5.3 | 0.6 | 0.7 |
| Nonconnected [5] | 24.8 | 14.3 | 10.2 | 16.2 | 5.2 | 3.3 |
| Cooperative | 0.6 | 0.4 | 0.2 | 0.5 | 0.1 | (Z) |
| Corporation without stock | 0.9 | 0.6 | 0.3 | 0.7 | 0.1 | 0.1 |

Z represents less than $50,000. [1] Includes other parties, not shown separately. [2] Elections in which an incumbent did not seek reelection. [3] Includes other types of political action committees, not shown separately. [4] Includes membership organizations and health organizations. [5] Represents "ideological" groups as well as other issue groups not necessarily ideological in nature.

Source: U.S. Federal Election Commission, Campaign Finance Statistics, "Political Action Committees (PAC) Data Summary Tables," <http://www.fec.gov/press/campaign_finance_statistics.shtml>, accessed March 2019.

# Section 8
# State and Local Government Finances and Employment

This section presents data on revenues, expenditures, debt, and employment of state and local governments. Nationwide statistics relating to state and local governments, their numbers, finances, and employment are compiled primarily by the U.S. Census Bureau through a program of censuses and surveys. Every fifth year (for years ending in "2" and "7"), the Census Bureau conducts a census of governments involving collection of data for all governmental units in the United States. In addition, the Census Bureau conducts annual surveys which cover all the state governments and a sample of local governments.

Annually, the Census Bureau releases information on financial data for the federal government, nationwide totals for state and local governments, and state-local data by states. Also released annually is a series on state, city, county, and school finances and on state and local public employment. There is also a series of quarterly data releases covering tax revenue and finances of major public employee retirement systems.

Basic information for Census Bureau statistics on governments is obtained by mail canvass from state and local officials; however, financial data for each state government and for many of the large local governments are compiled from their official records and reports by Census Bureau personnel. In over two-thirds of the states, all or part of local government financial data are obtained through central collection arrangements with state governments. Financial data on the federal government are primarily based on the *Budget of the United States Government* published by the Office of Management and Budget.

**Governmental units**—The governmental structure of the United States includes, in addition to the federal government and the states, thousands of local governments—counties, municipalities, townships, school districts, and many "special districts." In 2017, 90,075 local governments were identified by the census of governments (see table 470 and table 471). As defined by the census, governmental units include all agencies or bodies having an organized existence, governmental character, and substantial autonomy. While most of these governments can impose taxes, many of the special districts—such as independent public housing authorities and numerous local irrigation, power, and other types of districts—are financed from rentals, charges for services, benefit assessments, grants from other governments, and other non-tax sources. The count of governments excludes semi-autonomous agencies through which states, cities, and counties sometimes provide for certain functions—for example, "dependent" school systems, state institutions of higher education, and certain other "authorities" and special agencies which are under the administrative or fiscal control of an established governmental unit.

**Finances**—The financial statistics relate to government fiscal years ending June 30 or at some date within the 12 previous months. The following governments are exceptions and are included as though they were part of the June 30 group: the state governments of Alabama and Michigan, and the city government of The District of Columbia, with fiscal years ending September 30; the state government of Texas ending August 31; and New York State ending its fiscal year on March 31. The federal government ended the fiscal year June 30 until 1976 when its fiscal year, by an act of Congress, was revised to extend from Oct. 1 to Sept. 30. A 3-month quarter (July 1 to Sept. 30, 1976) bridged the transition.

Nationwide government finance statistics have been classified and presented in terms of uniform concepts and categories, rather than according to the highly diverse terminology, organization, and fund structure utilized by individual governments.

Statistics on governmental finances distinguish among general government, utilities, liquor stores, and insurance trusts. *General government* comprises all activities except utilities, liquor stores, and insurance trusts. *Utilities* include government water supply, electric light and power, gas supply, and transit systems. *Liquor stores* and *dispensaries* are operated by 17 states and by local governments in 4 states. *Insurance trusts* relate to employee retirement, unemployment compensation, and other social insurance systems administered by the federal, state, and local governments.

Data for cities or counties relate only to municipal or county and their dependent agencies and do not include amounts for other local governments in the same geographic location. Therefore, expenditure figures for "education" do not include spending by the separate school districts which administer public schools within most municipal or county areas. Variations in the assignment of governmental responsibility for public assistance, health, hospitals, public housing, and other functions to a lesser degree also have an important effect upon reported amounts of city or county expenditure, revenue, and debt.

**Employment and payrolls**—These data are based mainly on mail canvassing of state and local governments. Payroll includes all salaries, wages, and individual fee payments for the month specified. Employment relates to all persons on governmental payrolls during a pay period of the month covered, including paid officials, temporary help, and (unless otherwise specified) part-time as well as full-time personnel. Effective with the 1997 Census of Governments, the reference period for measuring government employment was changed from October of the calendar year to March of the calendar year. As a result, there was no annual survey of government employment covering the October 1996 period. The prior reference month of October was used from 1958 to 1995. Figures shown for individual governments cover major dependent agencies such as institutions of higher education, as well as the basic central departments and agencies of the government.

**Statistical reliability**—For a discussion of statistical collection and estimation, sampling procedures, and measures of statistical reliability applicable to Census Bureau data, see Appendix III.

## Table 470. Number of Governmental Units by Type: 1972 to 2017

| Type of government | 1972 | 1977 | 1982 | 1987 | 1992 | 1997 | 2002 | 2007 | 2012 | 2017 |
|---|---|---|---|---|---|---|---|---|---|---|
| Total units | 78,269 | 79,913 | 81,831 | 83,237 | 85,006 | 87,504 | 87,576 | 89,527 | 90,107 | 90,126 |
| U.S. government | 1 | 1 | 1 | 1 | 1 | 1 | 1 | 1 | 1 | 1 |
| State governments | 50 | 50 | 50 | 50 | 50 | 50 | 50 | 50 | 50 | 50 |
| Local governments | 78,218 | 79,862 | 81,780 | 83,186 | 84,955 | 87,453 | 87,525 | 89,476 | 90,056 | 90,075 |
| County | 3,044 | 3,042 | 3,041 | 3,042 | 3,043 | 3,043 | 3,034 | 3,033 | 3,031 | 3,031 |
| Municipal | 18,517 | 18,862 | 19,076 | 19,200 | 19,279 | 19,372 | 19,429 | 19,492 | 19,519 | 19,495 |
| Township and town | 16,991 | 16,822 | 16,734 | 16,691 | 16,656 | 16,629 | 16,504 | 16,519 | 16,360 | 16,253 |
| School district | 15,781 | 15,174 | 14,851 | 14,721 | 14,422 | 13,726 | 13,506 | 13,051 | 12,880 | 12,754 |
| Special district | 23,885 | 25,962 | 28,078 | 29,532 | 31,555 | 34,683 | 35,052 | 37,381 | 38,266 | 38,542 |

Source: U.S. Census Bureau, Census of Governments, "2017 Census of Governments Organization Tables," <https://www.census.gov/programs-surveys/cog.html>, accessed May 2019.

## Table 471. Number of Local Governments by Type—States: 2017

[Governments in existence in January. Excludes a few counties and numerous townships and incorporated places existing as areas for which statistics can be presented as to population and other subjects, but lacking any separate organized county, township, or municipal government. See Appendix III]

| State | All governmental units [1] | County | Municipal | Township [1] | School district | Special district Total [2] | Special district Natural resources | Special district Fire protection | Special district Housing [3] |
|---|---|---|---|---|---|---|---|---|---|
| United States | 90,075 | 3,031 | 19,495 | 16,253 | 12,754 | 38,542 | 7,253 | 5,975 | 3,344 |
| Alabama | 1,195 | 67 | 461 | – | 137 | 530 | 68 | 13 | 147 |
| Alaska | 179 | 15 | 149 | – | – | 15 | – | – | 14 |
| Arizona | 658 | 15 | 91 | – | 242 | 310 | 84 | 151 | – |
| Arkansas | 1,541 | 75 | 501 | – | 235 | 730 | 258 | 73 | 117 |
| California | 4,444 | 57 | 482 | – | 1,011 | 2,894 | 484 | 357 | 64 |
| Colorado | 3,141 | 62 | 271 | – | 180 | 2,628 | 168 | 261 | 91 |
| Connecticut | 625 | – | 30 | 149 | 17 | 429 | 1 | 65 | 113 |
| Delaware | 334 | 3 | 57 | – | 19 | 255 | 233 | – | 4 |
| District of Columbia | 2 | – | 1 | – | – | 1 | – | – | – |
| Florida | 1,712 | 66 | 412 | – | 95 | 1,139 | 119 | 54 | 92 |
| Georgia | 1,380 | 152 | 537 | – | 180 | 511 | 37 | – | 191 |
| Hawaii | 21 | 3 | 1 | – | – | 17 | 16 | – | – |
| Idaho | 1,170 | 44 | 200 | – | 118 | 808 | 177 | 156 | 11 |
| Illinois | 6,918 | 102 | 1,297 | 1,429 | 886 | 3,204 | 1,014 | 838 | 113 |
| Indiana | 2,638 | 91 | 567 | 1,004 | 289 | 687 | 142 | 2 | 64 |
| Iowa | 1,941 | 99 | 943 | – | 348 | 551 | 238 | 60 | 27 |
| Kansas | 3,792 | 103 | 625 | 1,265 | 306 | 1,493 | 256 | 1 | 177 |
| Kentucky | 1,322 | 118 | 417 | – | 173 | 614 | 126 | 151 | 19 |
| Louisiana | 516 | 60 | 304 | – | 69 | 83 | 8 | 2 | – |
| Maine | 834 | 16 | 23 | 465 | 98 | 232 | 17 | – | 30 |
| Maryland | 344 | 23 | 157 | – | – | 164 | 128 | – | 20 |
| Massachusetts | 858 | 5 | 53 | 298 | 85 | 417 | 17 | 11 | 250 |
| Michigan | 2,863 | 83 | 533 | 1,240 | 571 | 436 | 77 | 24 | – |
| Minnesota | 3,643 | 87 | 853 | 1,780 | 333 | 590 | 144 | 9 | 153 |
| Mississippi | 969 | 82 | 298 | – | 157 | 432 | 233 | 30 | 52 |
| Missouri | 3,768 | 114 | 944 | 283 | 530 | 1,897 | 323 | 401 | 135 |
| Montana | 1,226 | 54 | 129 | – | 313 | 730 | 132 | 214 | 13 |
| Nebraska | 2,538 | 93 | 529 | 366 | 269 | 1,281 | 87 | 413 | 163 |
| Nevada | 189 | 16 | 19 | – | 17 | 137 | 34 | 15 | 3 |
| New Hampshire | 541 | 10 | 13 | 221 | 168 | 129 | 11 | 14 | 21 |
| New Jersey | 1,338 | 21 | 324 | 241 | 519 | 233 | 15 | 183 | – |
| New Mexico | 1013 | 33 | 105 | – | 96 | 779 | 561 | – | – |
| New York | 3,450 | 57 | 601 | 929 | 678 | 1,185 | 1 | 885 | – |
| North Carolina | 970 | 100 | 552 | – | – | 318 | 136 | – | 93 |
| North Dakota | 2,664 | 53 | 357 | 1,308 | 179 | 767 | 74 | 275 | 38 |
| Ohio | 3,897 | 88 | 931 | 1,308 | 666 | 904 | 103 | 116 | 81 |
| Oklahoma | 1,830 | 77 | 590 | – | 542 | 621 | 104 | 27 | 128 |
| Oregon | 1,510 | 36 | 240 | – | 230 | 1,004 | 186 | 265 | 19 |
| Pennsylvania | 4,830 | 66 | 1,013 | 1,546 | 514 | 1,691 | 5 | – | 90 |
| Rhode Island | 129 | – | 8 | 31 | 4 | 86 | 5 | 31 | 26 |
| South Carolina | 671 | 46 | 270 | – | 81 | 274 | 45 | 64 | 42 |
| South Dakota | 1,916 | 66 | 311 | 902 | 150 | 487 | 105 | 80 | 1 |
| Tennessee | 906 | 92 | 345 | – | 14 | 455 | 105 | 1 | 93 |
| Texas | 5,343 | 254 | 1,218 | – | 1,073 | 2,798 | 435 | 267 | 384 |
| Utah | 619 | 29 | 250 | – | 41 | 299 | 79 | 12 | 19 |
| Vermont | 729 | 14 | 42 | 237 | 277 | 159 | 14 | 16 | 8 |
| Virginia | 517 | 95 | 228 | – | 1 | 193 | 47 | – | – |
| Washington | 1,900 | 39 | 281 | – | 295 | 1,285 | 181 | 368 | 43 |
| West Virginia | 651 | 55 | 232 | – | 55 | 309 | 14 | – | 35 |
| Wisconsin | 3,096 | 72 | 601 | 1,251 | 438 | 734 | 272 | 1 | 160 |
| Wyoming | 794 | 23 | 99 | – | 55 | 617 | 134 | 69 | – |

– Represents zero. [1] Includes town governments in the six New England States and in Minnesota, New York, and Wisconsin. [2] Includes other special districts not shown separately. [3] Includes community development.

Source: U.S. Census Bureau, Census of Governments, "2017 Census of Governments Organization Tables," <https://www.census.gov/programs-surveys/cog.html>, accessed May 2019.

## Table 472. State and Local Government Current Receipts and Expenditures in the National Income and Product Accounts: 1990 to 2018

[In billions of dollars (730.1 represents $730,100,000,000). For explanation of national income, see text, Section 13. Minus sign (-) indicates net loss]

| Item | 1990 | 2000 | 2005 | 2010 | 2014 | 2015 | 2016 | 2017 | 2018 |
|---|---|---|---|---|---|---|---|---|---|
| **Current receipts** | **730.1** | **1,304.1** | **1,718.5** | **1,994.4** | **2,259.4** | **2,368.6** | **2,421.9** | **2,484.2** | **2,588.4** |
| Current tax receipts | 519.1 | 893.2 | 1,173.2 | 1,306.4 | 1,543.5 | 1,592.8 | 1,628.5 | 1,689.9 | 1,764.9 |
| Personal current taxes | 122.6 | 236.7 | 275.2 | 294.1 | 382.3 | 406.9 | 408.6 | 421.2 | 436.1 |
| Income taxes | 109.6 | 217.4 | 249.1 | 265.8 | 350.3 | 374.3 | 375.1 | 386.7 | 400.1 |
| Other | 13.0 | 19.4 | 26.2 | 28.3 | 32.0 | 32.7 | 33.5 | 34.5 | 36.1 |
| Taxes on production and imports | 374.1 | 621.3 | 843.0 | 966.3 | 1,104.6 | 1,129.5 | 1,166.1 | 1,215.7 | 1,268.6 |
| Sales taxes | 125.6 | 221.4 | 272.8 | 295.1 | 361.8 | 372.3 | 380.9 | 395.7 | 414.2 |
| Excise taxes | 58.7 | 95.5 | 127.4 | 154.8 | 174.9 | 180.5 | 185.3 | 190.7 | 196.4 |
| Property taxes | 161.5 | 254.7 | 351.2 | 438.6 | 474.8 | 487.8 | 508.4 | 532.2 | 553.0 |
| Other | 28.2 | 49.8 | 91.7 | 77.8 | 93.0 | 89.0 | 91.5 | 97.1 | 105.0 |
| Taxes on corporate income | 22.5 | 35.2 | 54.9 | 46.1 | 56.6 | 56.3 | 53.9 | 52.9 | 60.2 |
| Contributions for government social insurance | 10.0 | 10.8 | 24.6 | 17.8 | 18.7 | 19.2 | 20.0 | 20.6 | 21.7 |
| Income receipts on assets | 68.5 | 94.2 | 89.6 | 83.5 | 84.8 | 85.2 | 85.0 | 86.0 | 87.3 |
| Interest receipts | 64.1 | 86.6 | 77.3 | 69.0 | 67.1 | 68.3 | 68.2 | 68.8 | 69.8 |
| Dividends | 0.2 | 1.4 | 2.5 | 3.0 | 5.1 | 5.2 | 5.5 | 5.9 | 6.0 |
| Rents and royalties | 4.2 | 6.3 | 9.8 | 11.4 | 12.7 | 11.7 | 11.2 | 11.3 | 11.4 |
| Current transfer receipts | 126.4 | 299.7 | 436.6 | 604.4 | 616.2 | 673.7 | 689.0 | 690.7 | 718.3 |
| Federal grants-in-aid | 104.4 | 233.1 | 343.5 | 505.2 | 495.1 | 533.4 | 557.1 | 559.3 | 578.1 |
| From business (net) | 7.1 | 28.6 | 36.5 | 40.3 | 45.9 | 65.0 | 55.1 | 51.5 | 54.5 |
| From persons | 14.9 | 38.0 | 56.5 | 58.8 | 70.0 | 74.9 | 76.8 | 80.0 | 84.3 |
| Current surplus of government enterprises | 6.1 | 6.1 | -5.5 | -17.7 | -3.9 | -2.2 | -0.6 | -2.9 | -3.7 |
| **Current expenditures** | **766.3** | **1,344.8** | **1,821.3** | **2,301.8** | **2,496.1** | **2,592.2** | **2,667.8** | **2,743.3** | **2,830.3** |
| Consumption expenditures | 544.0 | 961.7 | 1,237.3 | 1,509.5 | 1,614.9 | 1,656.9 | 1,691.9 | 1,744.5 | 1,811.2 |
| Government social benefit payments to persons | 127.7 | 271.4 | 406.5 | 523.9 | 617.7 | 665.6 | 693.3 | 712.3 | 739.1 |
| Interest payments | 94.3 | 111.1 | 177.1 | 266.9 | 263.1 | 269.2 | 281.9 | 286.0 | 279.4 |
| Subsidies | 0.4 | 0.5 | 0.4 | 1.6 | 0.5 | 0.5 | 0.5 | 0.6 | 0.6 |
| **Net state and local government saving** | **-36.2** | **-40.6** | **-102.8** | **-307.5** | **-236.7** | **-223.6** | **-245.8** | **-259.1** | **-241.8** |
| Social insurance funds | 2.0 | 2.0 | 7.2 | 0.9 | 2.9 | 3.4 | 3.8 | 4.0 | 4.5 |
| Other | -38.2 | -42.6 | -110.0 | -308.4 | -239.7 | -227.0 | -249.7 | -263.1 | -246.3 |

Source: U.S. Bureau of Economic Analysis, National Income and Product Accounts Tables, "Table 3.3. State and Local Government Current Receipts and Expenditures," <http://www.bea.gov/itable/>, accessed April 2019.

## Table 473. Federal Grants-in-Aid to State and Local Governments: 1990 to 2019

[135,325 represents $135,325,000,000, except as indicated. For fiscal year ending September 30. Minus sign (-) indicates decrease]

| | Current dollars | | | | | | | Constant (2012) dollars | |
|---|---|---|---|---|---|---|---|---|---|
| | | | Grants to individuals | | Grants as percent of— | | | | |
| Year | Total grants (mil. dol.) | Annual percent change [1] | Total (mil. dol.) | Percent of total grants | State & local government expenditures from own sources [2] | Federal outlays | Gross domestic product | Total grants (bil. dol.) | Annual percent change [1] |
| 1990 | 135,325 | 11.0 | 77,431 | 57.2 | 25.2 | 10.8 | 2.3 | 238.9 | 5.9 |
| 1995 | 224,991 | 6.8 | 145,652 | 64.7 | 31.5 | 14.8 | 3.0 | 338.7 | 3.9 |
| 2000 | 285,874 | 6.7 | 186,534 | 65.3 | 27.4 | 16.0 | 2.8 | 389.1 | 3.8 |
| 2001 | 318,542 | 11.4 | 208,008 | 65.3 | 28.4 | 17.1 | 3.0 | 422.5 | 8.6 |
| 2002 | 352,895 | 10.8 | 231,854 | 65.7 | 29.5 | 17.5 | 3.3 | 460.9 | 9.1 |
| 2003 | 388,542 | 10.1 | 251,235 | 64.7 | 30.5 | 18.0 | 3.4 | 496.7 | 7.8 |
| 2004 | 407,512 | 4.9 | 267,046 | 65.5 | 30.9 | 17.8 | 3.4 | 506.2 | 1.9 |
| 2005 | 428,018 | 5.0 | 278,764 | 65.1 | 30.8 | 17.3 | 3.3 | 511.6 | 1.1 |
| 2006 | 434,099 | 1.4 | 277,559 | 63.9 | 29.7 | 16.3 | 3.2 | 500.1 | -2.2 |
| 2007 | 443,797 | 2.2 | 289,460 | 65.2 | 28.4 | 16.3 | 3.1 | 494.2 | -1.2 |
| 2008 | 461,317 | 3.9 | 306,123 | 66.4 | 27.4 | 15.5 | 3.1 | 493.7 | -0.1 |
| 2009 | 537,991 | 16.6 | 362,031 | 67.3 | 33.1 | 15.3 | 3.7 | 573.0 | 16.1 |
| 2010 | 608,390 | 13.1 | 391,427 | 64.3 | 37.5 | 17.6 | 4.1 | 637.6 | 11.3 |
| 2011 | 606,770 | -0.3 | 392,713 | 64.7 | (NA) | 16.8 | 3.9 | 620.9 | -2.6 |
| 2012 | 544,573 | -10.3 | 364,095 | 66.9 | (NA) | 15.4 | 3.4 | 544.6 | -12.3 |
| 2013 | 546,178 | 0.3 | 379,008 | 69.4 | (NA) | 15.8 | 3.3 | 536.4 | -1.5 |
| 2014 | 576,978 | 5.6 | 412,466 | 71.5 | (NA) | 16.5 | 3.3 | 556.8 | 3.8 |
| 2015 | 624,357 | 8.2 | 463,392 | 74.2 | (NA) | 16.9 | 3.5 | 599.3 | 7.6 |
| 2016 | 660,833 | 5.8 | 495,711 | 75.0 | (NA) | 17.2 | 3.6 | 630.3 | 5.2 |
| 2017 | 674,712 | 2.1 | 507,976 | 75.3 | (NA) | 16.9 | 3.5 | 632.2 | 0.3 |
| 2018 | 696,507 | 3.2 | 525,813 | 75.5 | (NA) | 17.0 | 3.4 | 635.1 | 0.5 |
| 2019, estimate | 749,554 | 7.6 | 564,299 | 75.3 | (NA) | 16.5 | 3.5 | 667.3 | 5.1 |

NA Not available. [1] Average annual percent change from previous year. [2] Expenditures from own sources as defined in the national income and product accounts.

Source: U.S. Office of Management and Budget, *Budget of the U.S. Government, Fiscal Year 2020: Historical Tables*, March 2019. See also <http://www.whitehouse.gov/omb/budget>.

# Table 474. Federal Outlays for Grants to State and Local Governments—Selected Agencies and Programs: 1990 to 2020

[In millions of dollars (135,325 represents $135,325,000,000)). For fiscal year ending September 30. Includes trust funds]

| Agency and program | 1990 | 1995 | 2000 | 2005 | 2010 | 2015 | 2016 | 2017 | 2018 | 2019 est. | 2020 est. |
|---|---|---|---|---|---|---|---|---|---|---|---|
| **Total outlays for grants** | **135,325** | **224,991** | **285,874** | **428,018** | **608,390** | **624,357** | **660,833** | **674,712** | **696,507** | **749,554** | **750,722** |
| Energy | 461 | 492 | 433 | 636 | 2,656 | 577 | 764 | 774 | 771 | 805 | 842 |
| Natural resources and environment | 3,745 | 3,985 | 4,595 | 5,858 | 9,132 | 7,043 | 6,702 | 6,155 | 6,394 | 6,168 | 6,134 |
| Environmental Protection Agency [1] | 2,874 | 2,912 | 3,490 | 3,734 | 6,883 | 4,570 | 4,270 | 3,750 | 3,862 | 3,086 | 3,224 |
| Agriculture | 1,118 | 780 | 724 | 933 | 843 | 707 | 806 | 763 | 815 | 934 | 888 |
| Transportation | 19,174 | 25,787 | 32,222 | 43,370 | 60,981 | 60,835 | 63,876 | 64,795 | 64,836 | 67,211 | 68,600 |
| Grants for airports [1] | 1,220 | 1,859 | 1,624 | 3,530 | 3,156 | 2,988 | 2,963 | 3,129 | 3,036 | 3,987 | 4,137 |
| Federal-aid highways [2] | 13,854 | 18,945 | 24,711 | 30,915 | 30,385 | 41,205 | 43,035 | 43,236 | 43,939 | 43,939 | 44,678 |
| Urban mass transportation [1] | 3,728 | 4,353 | 5,262 | 8,114 | 12,939 | 11,784 | 12,271 | 12,124 | 12,608 | 13,342 | 14,097 |
| Community and regional development | 4,965 | 7,230 | 8,665 | 20,167 | 18,908 | 14,357 | 15,298 | 14,797 | 19,089 | 21,917 | 26,442 |
| Rural Community Advancement Program | 139 | 333 | 479 | 814 | – | – | – | – | – | – | – |
| Community Development Fund | 2,818 | 4,333 | 4,955 | 4,985 | 7,043 | 6,548 | 6,013 | 5,616 | 5,889 | 6,818 | 9,434 |
| Homeland Security | 1,184 | 1,772 | 2,439 | 13,541 | 8,483 | 5,924 | 7,951 | 7,758 | 12,038 | 13,240 | 14,278 |
| State and local programs | – | – | – | 2,116 | 3,337 | 2,918 | 2,683 | 2,119 | 1,704 | 1,142 | 231 |
| Firefighter assistance grants | – | – | – | 1,185 | – | – | – | – | – | – | – |
| Operations and support, FEMA | 11 | 79 | 192 | 132 | – | – | – | – | – | – | – |
| Natural predisaster mitigation grants | – | – | 13 | 39 | – | – | – | – | – | – | – |
| Disaster relief fund | 1,173 | 1,693 | 2,234 | 10,069 | 5,141 | 2,919 | 5,155 | 5,348 | 9,715 | 10,239 | 11,341 |
| Education, training, employment, social services | 21,780 | 30,881 | 36,672 | 57,247 | 97,586 | 60,527 | 60,867 | 61,553 | 60,591 | 67,500 | 63,617 |
| Education for the disadvantaged [3] | 4,437 | 6,785 | 8,511 | 14,539 | 19,515 | 15,199 | 15,570 | 16,186 | 15,277 | 17,447 | 16,422 |
| School improvement programs | 1,080 | 1,288 | 2,394 | 6,569 | 5,184 | 4,138 | 4,224 | 4,295 | 4,060 | 4,846 | 5,082 |
| Special education | 1,485 | 2,938 | 4,696 | 10,661 | 17,075 | 12,077 | 12,357 | 12,479 | 12,753 | 13,233 | 13,195 |
| Social Services block grant | 2,749 | 2,797 | 1,827 | 1,822 | 2,035 | 1,832 | 1,780 | 1,661 | 1,587 | 1,619 | 487 |
| Children and family services programs | 2,618 | 4,463 | 5,843 | 8,490 | 10,473 | 9,608 | 10,026 | 10,232 | 10,651 | 10,859 | 11,161 |
| Training and employment services | 3,042 | 3,620 | 2,957 | 3,372 | 4,592 | 2,639 | 2,673 | 2,783 | 2,724 | 2,878 | 2,834 |
| Health | 43,890 | 93,587 | 124,843 | 197,848 | 290,168 | 368,026 | 396,666 | 406,946 | 421,117 | 453,862 | 452,820 |
| Substance abuse and mental health services [4] | 1,241 | 2,444 | 1,931 | 3,203 | 2,846 | 2,671 | 2,927 | 2,903 | 3,258 | 4,167 | 4,922 |
| Grants to states for Medicaid [4] | 41,103 | 89,070 | 117,921 | 181,720 | 272,771 | 349,762 | 368,280 | 374,682 | 389,157 | 418,681 | 418,151 |
| State children's health insurance fund [4] | – | – | 1,220 | 5,129 | 7,887 | 9,233 | 14,305 | 16,224 | 17,282 | 18,434 | 16,882 |
| Income security | 36,935 | 58,366 | 68,653 | 90,885 | 115,156 | 101,082 | 104,769 | 107,400 | 110,649 | 114,169 | 110,130 |
| Supplemental Nutrition Assistance Program (SNAP) (formerly Food Stamp Program) [4] | 2,130 | 2,740 | 3,508 | 4,385 | 5,739 | 5,100 | 6,406 | 6,954 | 7,485 | 7,347 | 6,978 |
| Child nutrition programs [4] | 4,871 | 7,387 | 9,060 | 11,726 | 16,259 | 20,999 | 21,952 | 22,445 | 22,803 | 23,854 | 24,837 |
| Temporary Assistance for Needy Families (TANF) [4] | – | – | 15,464 | 17,357 | 17,513 | 15,940 | 15,620 | 15,972 | 16,414 | 16,533 | 15,140 |
| Veterans benefits and services [4] | 134 | 253 | 434 | 552 | 836 | 1,821 | 1,829 | 1,992 | 2,061 | 2,292 | 2,581 |
| Administration of justice | 574 | 1,222 | 5,263 | 4,784 | 5,086 | 3,664 | 3,536 | 3,973 | 4,195 | 7,303 | 7,033 |

– Represents zero. [1] Grants include trust funds. [2] Trust funds. [3] Formerly Accelerating Achievement and Ensuring Equity. [4] Includes grants for payments to individuals.

Source: U.S. Office of Management and Budget, *Budget of the U.S. Government, Fiscal Year 2020: Historical Tables*, March 2019. See also <http://www.whitehouse.gov/omb/budget>.

# Table 475. State and Local Governments—Summary of Finances: 1990 to 2016

[In millions of dollars (1,032,115 represents $1,032,115,000,000). For fiscal year ending in year shown; see text, this section. Local government amounts are estimates subject to sampling variation; see Appendix III and source]

| Item | 1990 | 2000 | 2005 | 2010 | 2015 | 2016 |
|---|---|---|---|---|---|---|
| **Revenue** [1] | **1,032,115** | **1,942,328** | **2,528,546** | **3,180,023** | **3,414,009** | **3,401,788** |
| From federal government | 136,802 | 291,950 | 438,558 | 623,801 | 657,573 | 690,198 |
| Public welfare | 59,961 | 148,549 | (NA) | (NA) | (NA) | (NA) |
| Highways | 14,368 | 24,414 | (NA) | (NA) | (NA) | (NA) |
| Education | 23,233 | 45,873 | (NA) | (NA) | (NA) | (NA) |
| Health and hospitals | 5,904 | 15,611 | (NA) | (NA) | (NA) | (NA) |
| Housing and community development | 9,655 | 17,690 | (NA) | (NA) | (NA) | (NA) |
| Other and unallocable | 23,683 | 39,812 | (NA) | (NA) | (NA) | (NA) |
| From state and local sources | 895,313 | 1,650,379 | 2,089,988 | 2,556,222 | 2,756,436 | 2,711,589 |
| General, net intergovernmental | 712,700 | 1,249,373 | 1,587,476 | 1,887,045 | 2,258,045 | 2,317,902 |
| Taxes | 501,619 | 872,351 | 1,098,513 | 1,278,847 | 1,564,201 | 1,599,449 |
| Property | 155,613 | 249,178 | 335,779 | 443,947 | 484,437 | 503,239 |
| Sales and gross receipts | 177,885 | 309,290 | 384,266 | 435,571 | 544,995 | 558,847 |
| Individual income | 105,640 | 211,661 | 242,273 | 261,510 | 367,917 | 376,297 |
| Corporation net income | 23,566 | 36,059 | 43,256 | 44,108 | 57,235 | 54,259 |
| Other | 38,915 | 66,164 | 92,939 | 93,710 | 109,617 | 106,807 |
| Charges and miscellaneous | 211,081 | 377,022 | 488,963 | 608,198 | 693,844 | 718,453 |
| Utility and liquor stores | 58,642 | 89,546 | 119,608 | 154,758 | 175,149 | 173,594 |
| Water supply system | 17,674 | 30,515 | 37,378 | 49,327 | 61,113 | 61,845 |
| Electric power system | 29,268 | 42,436 | 59,157 | 76,492 | 81,147 | 79,006 |
| Gas supply system | 3,043 | 3,954 | 6,937 | 8,219 | 7,438 | 6,544 |
| Transit system | 5,216 | 8,049 | 10,146 | 13,003 | 16,329 | 16,689 |
| Liquor stores | 3,441 | 4,592 | 5,990 | 7,716 | 9,124 | 9,511 |
| Insurance trust revenue [2] | 123,970 | 311,460 | 382,904 | 514,420 | 323,242 | 220,094 |
| Employee retirement | 94,268 | 273,881 | 316,576 | 416,536 | 247,486 | 149,692 |
| Unemployment compensation | 18,441 | 23,366 | 35,367 | 75,191 | 52,451 | 46,500 |
| **Direct expenditure** | **972,695** | **1,742,914** | **2,363,696** | **3,110,833** | **3,397,912** | **3,506,658** |
| **By function:** | | | | | | |
| Direct general expenditure [2] | 831,573 | 1,502,768 | 2,007,490 | 2,537,892 | 2,839,723 | 2,936,902 |
| Education [2] | 288,148 | 521,612 | 688,314 | 860,118 | 935,750 | 965,307 |
| Elementary and secondary | 202,009 | 365,181 | 473,843 | 573,641 | 609,587 | 625,151 |
| Higher education | 73,418 | 134,352 | 182,003 | 243,515 | 274,131 | 287,810 |
| Highways | 61,057 | 101,336 | 126,350 | 155,912 | 167,850 | 174,941 |
| Public welfare | 107,287 | 233,350 | 360,730 | 456,200 | 614,592 | 637,641 |
| Health | 24,223 | 51,366 | 66,637 | 81,383 | 93,041 | 96,626 |
| Hospitals | 50,412 | 75,976 | 103,555 | 145,902 | 170,363 | 183,116 |
| Police protection | 30,577 | 56,798 | 74,131 | 95,772 | 105,186 | 109,175 |
| Fire protection | 13,186 | 23,102 | 30,830 | 41,335 | 45,869 | 47,761 |
| Natural resources | 12,330 | 20,235 | 23,519 | 28,433 | 28,778 | 30,797 |
| Parks and recreation | 14,326 | 25,038 | 31,925 | 40,247 | 39,583 | 41,946 |
| Housing and community development | 15,479 | 26,590 | 40,014 | 53,923 | 49,928 | 50,145 |
| Sanitation and sewerage | 28,453 | 45,261 | 57,940 | 75,620 | 75,696 | 80,223 |
| Financial administration | 16,217 | 29,300 | 36,695 | 40,241 | 41,928 | 43,010 |
| Interest on general debt [3] | 49,739 | 69,814 | 81,122 | 105,715 | 105,306 | 104,626 |
| Utility and liquor stores [3] | 77,801 | 114,916 | 160,470 | 213,914 | 233,094 | 231,780 |
| Water supply system | 22,101 | 35,789 | 45,695 | 60,655 | 67,864 | 69,809 |
| Electric power system | 30,997 | 39,719 | 58,612 | 78,478 | 78,980 | 75,452 |
| Gas supply system | 2,989 | 3,724 | 7,075 | 8,273 | 7,398 | 6,917 |
| Transit system | 18,788 | 31,883 | 44,203 | 60,149 | 71,462 | 71,919 |
| Liquor stores | 2,926 | 3,801 | 4,885 | 6,359 | 7,390 | 7,683 |
| Insurance trust expenditure [2] | 63,321 | 125,230 | 195,735 | 359,027 | 325,095 | 337,976 |
| Employee retirement | 38,355 | 95,679 | 145,796 | 204,803 | 275,406 | 289,447 |
| Unemployment compensation | 16,499 | 18,648 | 29,849 | 135,367 | 33,352 | 32,533 |
| **By character and object:** | | | | | | |
| Current operation | 700,131 | 1,288,746 | 1,760,283 | 2,228,794 | 2,562,411 | 2,639,487 |
| Capital outlay | 123,102 | 217,063 | 278,063 | 355,437 | 332,517 | 350,901 |
| Construction | 89,144 | 161,694 | 218,691 | 284,213 | 268,196 | 282,117 |
| Equipment, land, and existing structures | 33,958 | 55,369 | 59,372 | 71,224 | 64,321 | 68,784 |
| Assistance and subsidies | 27,227 | 31,375 | 37,755 | 47,636 | 56,119 | 57,609 |
| Interest on debt (general and utility) | 58,914 | 80,499 | 91,859 | 119,939 | 121,770 | 120,685 |
| Insurance benefits and repayments | 63,321 | 125,230 | 195,735 | 359,027 | 325,095 | 337,976 |
| Expenditure for salaries and wages [4] | 340,654 | 548,796 | 694,583 | 844,650 | 900,861 | 927,896 |
| **Debt outstanding, year end** | **858,006** | **1,451,815** | **2,085,026** | **2,844,190** | **2,974,109** | **3,002,720** |
| Long-term | 838,700 | 1,427,524 | 2,054,268 | 2,799,101 | 2,937,682 | 2,965,101 |
| Short-term | 19,306 | 24,291 | 30,758 | 45,088 | 36,427 | 37,618 |
| Long-term debt: | | | | | | |
| Issued | 108,468 | 184,831 | 323,739 | 398,962 | 365,600 | 387,277 |
| Retired | 64,831 | 121,897 | 224,639 | 275,810 | 367,314 | 370,028 |

NA Not available. [1] Aggregates exclude duplicative transactions between state and local governments; see source. [2] Includes amounts not shown separately. [3] Interest on utility debt included in "utility and liquor stores expenditure." For total interest on debt, see "Interest on debt (general and utility)." [4] Included in items above.

Source: U.S. Census Bureau, Federal, State, and Local Governments, Government Finance Statistics, "Annual Surveys of State and Local Government Finances," <https://www.census.gov/programs-surveys/gov-finances.html>, accessed December 2018.

# Table 476. State and Local Governments—Revenue and Expenditures by Function: 2010 and 2016

[In millions of dollars (3,180,023 represents $3,180,023,000,000). For fiscal year ending in year shown; see text, this section. Local government amounts are estimates subject to sampling variation; see Appendix III and source]

| Item | 2010 Total | 2010 State | 2010 Local | 2016 Total | 2016 State | 2016 Local |
|---|---|---|---|---|---|---|
| **Revenue** [1] | **3,180,023** | **2,039,927** | **1,635,634** | **3,401,788** | **2,136,454** | **1,802,160** |
| Intergovernmental revenue [1] | 623,801 | 575,372 | 543,967 | 690,198 | 637,168 | 589,857 |
| Total revenue from own sources [1] | 2,556,222 | 1,464,555 | 1,091,667 | 2,711,589 | 1,514,946 | 1,733,471 |
| General revenue from own sources | 1,887,045 | 991,835 | 895,210 | 2,317,902 | 1,272,154 | 1,045,748 |
| Taxes [2] | 1,278,847 | 705,929 | 572,917 | 1,599,449 | 922,856 | 676,593 |
| Property | 443,947 | 14,454 | 429,494 | 503,239 | 15,945 | 487,293 |
| Individual income | 261,510 | 236,987 | 24,524 | 376,297 | 343,621 | 32,677 |
| Corporation income | 44,108 | 38,006 | 6,102 | 54,259 | 46,202 | 8,057 |
| Sales and gross receipts | 435,571 | 344,522 | 91,048 | 558,847 | 441,124 | 117,722 |
| General sales | 288,499 | 224,314 | 64,185 | 376,911 | 291,473 | 85,439 |
| Selective sales [2] | 147,072 | 120,208 | 26,864 | 181,935 | 149,652 | 32,284 |
| Motor fuel | 37,922 | 36,632 | 1,291 | 45,126 | 43,732 | 1,394 |
| Alcoholic beverages | 6,021 | 5,511 | 511 | 7,256 | 6,614 | 642 |
| Tobacco products | 17,303 | 16,858 | 444 | 18,447 | 17,981 | 465 |
| Public utilities | 28,487 | 14,653 | 13,834 | 27,628 | 13,070 | 14,559 |
| Motor vehicle and operators' licenses | 22,459 | 20,861 | 1,598 | 27,502 | 25,566 | 1,935 |
| Charges and miscellaneous [2] | 608,198 | 285,906 | 322,293 | 718,453 | 349,298 | 369,154 |
| Current charges [2] | 411,200 | 169,855 | 241,345 | 498,040 | 208,904 | 289,136 |
| Education [2] | 121,138 | 94,530 | 26,608 | 128,361 | 104,719 | 23,642 |
| School lunch sales | 6,600 | 34 | 6,567 | 5,612 | 49 | 5,563 |
| Higher education | 105,515 | 93,081 | 12,434 | 112,656 | 103,678 | 8,978 |
| Hospitals | 113,339 | 42,938 | 70,401 | 151,292 | 63,764 | 87,528 |
| Highways | 12,001 | 6,885 | 5,116 | 18,717 | 10,471 | 8,246 |
| Airports | 18,067 | 1,327 | 16,740 | 22,647 | 1,614 | 21,033 |
| Sea and inland port facilities | 3,881 | 1,038 | 2,843 | 5,145 | 1,504 | 3,641 |
| Natural resources | 4,633 | 2,788 | 1,845 | 4,691 | 2,884 | 1,807 |
| Parks and recreation | 9,329 | 1,516 | 7,813 | 10,991 | 1,802 | 9,189 |
| Housing and community development | 5,789 | 622 | 5,167 | 6,793 | 708 | 6,085 |
| Sewerage | 43,472 | 612 | 42,860 | 55,810 | 988 | 54,822 |
| Solid waste management | 15,738 | 420 | 15,317 | 17,616 | 348 | 17,269 |
| Interest earnings | 59,828 | 34,523 | 25,305 | 47,818 | 33,646 | 14,172 |
| Special assessments | 7,001 | 165 | 6,836 | 8,813 | 64 | 8,750 |
| Sale of property | 2,829 | 692 | 2,137 | 4,261 | 1,226 | 3,035 |
| Utility and liquor store revenue | 154,758 | 21,617 | 133,141 | 173,594 | 21,912 | 151,682 |
| Insurance trust revenue | 514,420 | 451,103 | 63,316 | 220,094 | 205,221 | 14,873 |
| **Expenditures** [1] | **3,115,172** | **1,943,523** | **1,666,796** | **3,510,046** | **2,225,107** | **1,830,588** |
| Intergovernmental expenditure [1] | 4,339 | 485,557 | 13,929 | 3,388 | 532,699 | 16,338 |
| Direct expenditure [1] | 3,110,833 | 1,457,965 | 1,652,867 | 3,506,658 | 1,692,408 | 1,814,250 |
| General expenditure [2] | 2,537,892 | 1,108,137 | 1,429,755 | 2,936,902 | 1,373,167 | 1,563,735 |
| Education [1] | 860,118 | 253,758 | 606,360 | 965,307 | 304,301 | 661,006 |
| Elementary and secondary education | 573,641 | 7,832 | 565,809 | 625,151 | 6,635 | 618,516 |
| Higher education | 243,515 | 202,964 | 40,551 | 287,810 | 245,320 | 42,490 |
| Public welfare | 456,200 | 403,572 | 52,627 | 637,641 | 581,912 | 55,729 |
| Hospitals | 145,902 | 58,752 | 87,150 | 183,116 | 79,102 | 104,014 |
| Health | 81,383 | 39,971 | 41,412 | 96,626 | 44,165 | 52,461 |
| Highways | 155,912 | 93,127 | 62,786 | 174,941 | 104,849 | 70,092 |
| Police protection | 95,772 | 12,376 | 83,395 | 109,175 | 15,003 | 94,172 |
| Fire protection | 41,335 | – | 41,335 | 47,761 | – | 47,761 |
| Corrections | 73,100 | 46,095 | 27,005 | 78,025 | 49,040 | 28,985 |
| Natural resources | 28,433 | 19,336 | 9,097 | 30,797 | 21,508 | 9,289 |
| Parks and recreation | 40,247 | 4,912 | 35,335 | 41,946 | 5,539 | 36,407 |
| Housing and community development | 53,923 | 11,487 | 42,437 | 50,145 | 8,676 | 41,469 |
| Sewerage | 51,991 | 1,118 | 50,873 | 55,627 | 1,246 | 54,381 |
| Solid waste management | 23,629 | 2,281 | 21,348 | 24,596 | 1,348 | 23,248 |
| Governmental administration | 126,719 | 52,147 | 74,572 | 135,114 | 55,361 | 79,753 |
| Interest on general debt | 105,715 | 45,260 | 60,455 | 104,626 | 44,624 | 60,002 |
| Utility | 207,555 | 23,864 | 183,691 | 224,097 | 27,246 | 196,851 |
| Liquor store expenditure | 6,359 | 5,244 | 1,115 | 7,683 | 6,447 | 1,236 |
| Insurance trust expenditure | 359,027 | 320,721 | 38,306 | 337,976 | 285,548 | 52,428 |
| By character and object: | | | | | | |
| Current operation | 2,228,794 | 934,322 | 1,294,473 | 2,639,487 | 1,184,406 | 1,455,081 |
| Capital outlay | 355,437 | 118,011 | 237,426 | 350,901 | 128,606 | 222,295 |
| Construction | 284,213 | 100,962 | 183,251 | 282,117 | 108,288 | 173,829 |
| Equipment, land, and existing structures | 71,224 | 17,048 | 54,175 | 68,784 | 20,318 | 48,466 |
| Assistance and subsidies | 47,636 | 37,562 | 10,074 | 57,609 | 46,723 | 10,886 |
| Interest on debt (general and utility) | 119,939 | 47,351 | 72,588 | 120,685 | 47,126 | 73,559 |
| Insurance benefits and repayments | 359,027 | 320,721 | 38,306 | 337,976 | 285,548 | 52,428 |
| Expenditure for salaries and wages [3] | 844,650 | 244,952 | 599,698 | 927,896 | 265,784 | 662,112 |

– Represents or rounds to zero. [1] Aggregates exclude duplicative transactions between levels of government; see source. [2] Includes other items, not shown separately. [3] Included in items shown above.

Source: U.S. Census Bureau, Federal, State, and Local Governments, Government Finance Statistics, "Annual Surveys of State and Local Government Finances," <https://www.census.gov/programs-surveys/gov-finances.html>, accessed December 2018.

# Table 477. State and Local Governments—Capital Outlays: 1990 to 2016

[In millions of dollars (123,102 represents $123,102,000,000), except percent. For fiscal year ending in year shown; see text, this section. Local government amounts are subject to sampling variation; see Appendix III and source]

| Level and function | 1990 | 2000 | 2005 | 2010 | 2012 | 2013 | 2014 | 2015 | 2016 |
|---|---|---|---|---|---|---|---|---|---|
| **State & local governments: Total.** . . . | **123,102** | **217,063** | **278,063** | **355,437** | **332,177** | **319,505** | **319,649** | **332,517** | **350,901** |
| Percent of direct expenditure. . . . . . . . . . | 12.7 | 12.5 | 11.8 | 11.4 | 10.5 | 10.1 | 9.8 | 9.8 | 10.0 |
| By function: | | | | | | | | | |
| Education [1]. . . . . . . . . . . . . . . . . . . . . . . . . | 25,997 | 60,968 | 77,780 | 93,562 | 84,649 | 80,448 | 79,630 | 84,703 | 93,043 |
| Elementary and secondary. . . . . . . . . . . . | 18,057 | 45,150 | 54,563 | 60,240 | 51,201 | 47,903 | 48,681 | 53,047 | 58,213 |
| Higher education. . . . . . . . . . . . . . . . . . . . | 7,441 | 15,257 | 22,735 | 31,644 | 32,659 | 31,720 | 30,111 | 30,815 | 34,210 |
| Highways. . . . . . . . . . . . . . . . . . . . . . . . . . . . | 33,867 | 56,439 | 70,689 | 89,895 | 90,828 | 87,852 | 86,952 | 92,098 | 96,795 |
| Health and hospitals [2]. . . . . . . . . . . . . . . . | 3,848 | 5,502 | 6,100 | 8,553 | 9,496 | 9,320 | 9,951 | 8,649 | 8,952 |
| Natural resources. . . . . . . . . . . . . . . . . . . . | 2,545 | 4,347 | 4,541 | 5,214 | 5,453 | 4,915 | 4,374 | 4,911 | 6,050 |
| Parks and recreation. . . . . . . . . . . . . . . . . . | 3,877 | 6,916 | 8,136 | 10,711 | 8,296 | 7,902 | 7,697 | 8,163 | 9,281 |
| Sewerage. . . . . . . . . . . . . . . . . . . . . . . . . . . | 8,356 | 10,093 | 14,081 | 21,915 | 20,654 | 18,436 | 18,177 | 17,876 | 20,145 |
| Utilities. . . . . . . . . . . . . . . . . . . . . . . . . . . . . | 16,601 | 24,847 | 34,790 | 49,258 | 46,126 | 48,585 | 49,129 | 52,543 | 51,502 |
| **State governments: Total.** . . . . . . . . . . . . | **45,524** | **76,233** | **95,155** | **118,011** | **119,668** | **114,840** | **116,646** | **123,940** | **128,606** |
| Percent of direct expenditure. . . . . . . . . . | 11.5 | 10.1 | 8.9 | 8.1 | 8.0 | 7.6 | 7.5 | 7.6 | 7.6 |
| By function: | | | | | | | | | |
| Education [1]. . . . . . . . . . . . . . . . . . . . . . . . . | 7,253 | 14,077 | 20,585 | 28,643 | 28,651 | 28,620 | 27,418 | 28,671 | 31,227 |
| Elementary and secondary. . . . . . . . . . . . | 388 | 521 | 447 | 1,066 | 600 | 658 | 728 | 904 | 927 |
| Higher education. . . . . . . . . . . . . . . . . . . . | 6,366 | 12,995 | 19,656 | 25,899 | 27,262 | 27,137 | 25,852 | 26,927 | 29,679 |
| Highways. . . . . . . . . . . . . . . . . . . . . . . . . . . . | 24,850 | 41,651 | 52,607 | 64,755 | 67,342 | 63,249 | 63,482 | 67,097 | 70,277 |
| Health and hospitals [2]. . . . . . . . . . . . . . . . | 1,531 | 2,228 | 2,363 | 2,654 | 3,298 | 3,062 | 3,381 | 3,448 | 3,625 |
| Natural resources. . . . . . . . . . . . . . . . . . . . | 1,593 | 2,758 | 2,667 | 2,337 | 2,303 | 2,266 | 2,080 | 2,832 | 3,764 |
| Parks and recreation. . . . . . . . . . . . . . . . . . | 601 | 1,044 | 915 | 910 | 732 | 754 | 710 | 888 | 928 |
| Sewerage. . . . . . . . . . . . . . . . . . . . . . . . . . . | 333 | 403 | 486 | 488 | 188 | 134 | 123 | 58 | 95 |
| Utilities. . . . . . . . . . . . . . . . . . . . . . . . . . . . . | 2,605 | 4,232 | 4,319 | 5,318 | 4,700 | 6,082 | 7,038 | 8,843 | 7,441 |
| **Local governments: Total.** . . . . . . . . . . . . . | **77,578** | **140,830** | **182,908** | **237,426** | **212,509** | **204,665** | **203,003** | **208,577** | **222,295** |
| Percent of direct expenditure. . . . . . . . . . | 13.5 | 14.3 | 14.1 | 14.4 | 12.9 | 12.3 | 11.9 | 11.8 | 12.3 |
| By function: | | | | | | | | | |
| Education [1]. . . . . . . . . . . . . . . . . . . . . . . . . | 18,744 | 46,890 | 57,195 | 64,919 | 55,998 | 51,829 | 52,213 | 56,031 | 61,817 |
| Elementary and secondary. . . . . . . . . . . . | 17,669 | 44,629 | 54,116 | 59,174 | 50,601 | 47,246 | 47,954 | 52,143 | 57,286 |
| Higher education. . . . . . . . . . . . . . . . . . . . | 1,076 | 2,261 | 3,079 | 5,745 | 5,397 | 4,583 | 4,259 | 3,888 | 4,531 |
| Highways. . . . . . . . . . . . . . . . . . . . . . . . . . . . | 9,017 | 14,789 | 18,083 | 25,140 | 23,486 | 24,603 | 23,469 | 25,001 | 26,518 |
| Health and hospitals [2]. . . . . . . . . . . . . . . . | 2,316 | 3,274 | 3,737 | 5,899 | 6,198 | 6,258 | 6,570 | 5,201 | 5,327 |
| Natural resources. . . . . . . . . . . . . . . . . . . . | 952 | 1,589 | 1,873 | 2,878 | 3,151 | 2,650 | 2,293 | 2,079 | 2,287 |
| Parks and recreation. . . . . . . . . . . . . . . . . . | 3,276 | 5,872 | 7,221 | 9,802 | 7,564 | 7,148 | 6,986 | 7,275 | 8,354 |
| Sewerage. . . . . . . . . . . . . . . . . . . . . . . . . . . | 8,023 | 9,690 | 13,595 | 21,426 | 20,467 | 18,302 | 18,054 | 17,818 | 20,049 |
| Utilities. . . . . . . . . . . . . . . . . . . . . . . . . . . . . | 13,996 | 20,615 | 30,471 | 43,940 | 41,426 | 42,503 | 42,091 | 43,701 | 44,062 |

[1] Includes other education, not shown separately. [2] After 2003, includes only hospital outlays.

Source: U.S. Census Bureau, Federal, State, and Local Governments, Government Finance Statistics, "Annual Surveys of State and Local Government Finances," <https://www.census.gov/programs-surveys/gov-finances.html>, accessed December 2018.

# Table 478. State and Local Governments—Expenditures for Public Works: 2000 to 2016

[In millions of dollars (230,569 represents $230,569,000,000), except percent. Represents direct expenditures excluding intergovernmental grants]

| Item | Total | Highways | Air trans-portation | Sea and inland port facilities | Sewerage | Solid waste manage-ment | Water supply | Mass transit |
|---|---|---|---|---|---|---|---|---|
| 2000, total. . . . . . . . . . . . . . . . . . . . . . . . . . . | 230,569 | 101,336 | 13,160 | 3,141 | 28,052 | 17,208 | 35,789 | 31,883 |
| State. . . . . . . . . . . . . . . . . . . . . . . . . . . . . | 74,974 | 61,942 | 1,106 | 863 | 955 | 2,347 | 354 | 7,407 |
| Local. . . . . . . . . . . . . . . . . . . . . . . . . . . . . | 155,595 | 39,394 | 12,054 | 2,277 | 27,098 | 14,861 | 35,435 | 24,476 |
| Capital expenditures (percent). . . . . | 42 | 56 | 51 | 52 | 36 | 9 | 30 | 31 |
| 2010, total. . . . . . . . . . . . . . . . . . . . . . . . . . . | 381,808 | 155,912 | 24,209 | 5,263 | 51,991 | 23,629 | 60,655 | 60,149 |
| State. . . . . . . . . . . . . . . . . . . . . . . . . . . . . | 111,280 | 93,127 | 1,724 | 1,245 | 1,118 | 2,281 | 378 | 11,407 |
| Local. . . . . . . . . . . . . . . . . . . . . . . . . . . . . | 270,529 | 62,786 | 22,485 | 4,019 | 50,873 | 21,348 | 60,277 | 48,742 |
| Capital expenditures (percent). . . . . | (NA) | 58 | (NA) | (NA) | 42 | 9 | (NA) | (NA) |
| 2012, total. . . . . . . . . . . . . . . . . . . . . . . . . . . | 385,817 | 160,299 | 20,859 | 5,262 | 51,780 | 24,311 | 61,600 | 61,706 |
| State. . . . . . . . . . . . . . . . . . . . . . . . . . . . . | 117,525 | 97,509 | 1,892 | 1,579 | 773 | 2,451 | 420 | 12,902 |
| Local. . . . . . . . . . . . . . . . . . . . . . . . . . . . . | 268,292 | 62,790 | 18,968 | 3,684 | 51,007 | 21,860 | 61,179 | 48,804 |
| Capital expenditures (percent). . . . . | (NA) | 57 | (NA) | (NA) | 40 | 8 | (NA) | (NA) |
| 2013, total. . . . . . . . . . . . . . . . . . . . . . . . . . . | 386,062 | 157,627 | 21,435 | 5,337 | 50,105 | 24,158 | 63,660 | 63,740 |
| State. . . . . . . . . . . . . . . . . . . . . . . . . . . . . | 114,478 | 94,016 | 1,848 | 1,568 | 721 | 2,386 | 371 | 13,569 |
| Local. . . . . . . . . . . . . . . . . . . . . . . . . . . . . | 271,584 | 63,612 | 19,587 | 3,769 | 49,384 | 21,772 | 63,289 | 50,171 |
| Capital expenditures (percent). . . . . | (NA) | 56 | (NA) | (NA) | 37 | 8 | (NA) | (NA) |
| 2014, total. . . . . . . . . . . . . . . . . . . . . . . . . . . | 397,624 | 161,954 | 21,830 | 6,279 | 51,349 | 23,038 | 65,473 | 67,701 |
| State. . . . . . . . . . . . . . . . . . . . . . . . . . . . . | 118,308 | 96,330 | 1,980 | 1,654 | 909 | 1,053 | 398 | 15,984 |
| Local. . . . . . . . . . . . . . . . . . . . . . . . . . . . . | 279,317 | 65,623 | 19,850 | 4,626 | 50,440 | 21,985 | 65,075 | 51,717 |
| Capital expenditures (percent). . . . . | (NA) | 54 | (NA) | (NA) | 35 | 8 | (NA) | (NA) |
| 2015, total. . . . . . . . . . . . . . . . . . . . . . . . . . . | 411,718 | 167,850 | 22,490 | 6,355 | 51,937 | 23,759 | 67,864 | 71,462 |
| State. . . . . . . . . . . . . . . . . . . . . . . . . . . . . | 124,595 | 99,716 | 2,238 | 1,756 | 1,024 | 1,129 | 358 | 18,375 |
| Local. . . . . . . . . . . . . . . . . . . . . . . . . . . . . | 287,123 | 68,134 | 20,252 | 4,599 | 50,914 | 22,630 | 67,507 | 53,087 |
| Capital expenditures (percent). . . . . | (NA) | 55 | (NA) | (NA) | 34 | 9 | (NA) | (NA) |
| 2016, total. . . . . . . . . . . . . . . . . . . . . . . . . . . | 426,608 | 174,941 | 23,749 | 5,966 | 55,627 | 24,596 | 69,809 | 71,919 |
| State. . . . . . . . . . . . . . . . . . . . . . . . . . . . . | 129,416 | 104,849 | 2,101 | 1,802 | 1,246 | 1,348 | 497 | 17,572 |
| Local. . . . . . . . . . . . . . . . . . . . . . . . . . . . . | 297,192 | 70,092 | 21,648 | 4,164 | 54,381 | 23,248 | 69,312 | 54,347 |
| Capital expenditures (percent). . . . . | (NA) | 55 | (NA) | (NA) | 36 | 9 | (NA) | (NA) |

NA Not available.

Source: U.S. Census Bureau, Federal, State, and Local Governments, Government Finance Statistics, "Annual Surveys of State and Local Government Finances," <https://www.census.gov/programs-surveys/gov-finances.html>, accessed December 2018, and unpublished data.

## Table 479. State and Local Governments—Indebtedness: 1990 to 2016

[In billions of dollars (858.0 represents $858,000,000,000). For fiscal year ending in year shown; see text, this section. Local government amounts are estimates subject to sampling variation; see Appendix III and source]

| Item | Debt outstanding | | | | | | Long-term | | |
|---|---|---|---|---|---|---|---|---|---|
| | | Cash and security holdings | Long-term | | | Short-term | Net long-term [1] | Debt issued | Debt retired |
| | Total | | Total | Public debt for private purposes | All other | | | | |
| 1990: Total....... | 858.0 | 1,490.8 | 838.7 | 294.1 | 544.6 | 19.3 | 474.4 | 108.5 | 64.8 |
| State........... | 318.3 | 963.3 | 315.5 | 154.4 | 161.1 | 2.8 | 125.5 | 43.5 | 22.9 |
| Local........... | 539.8 | 527.5 | 523.2 | 139.7 | 383.5 | 16.5 | 348.9 | 65.0 | 42.0 |
| 1995: Total....... | 1,115.4 | 2,058.5 | 1,088.3 | 300.6 | 787.7 | 27.0 | 697.3 | 129.3 | 95.1 |
| State........... | 427.2 | 1,393.9 | 421.1 | 176.8 | 244.4 | 6.1 | 205.3 | 52.6 | 37.5 |
| Local........... | 688.1 | 664.6 | 667.2 | 123.9 | 543.3 | 20.9 | 491.9 | 76.8 | 57.6 |
| 2000: Total....... | 1,451.8 | 3,503.7 | 1,427.5 | 372.6 | 1,054.9 | 24.3 | 959.6 | 184.8 | 121.9 |
| State........... | 547.9 | 2,518.9 | 541.5 | 227.3 | 314.2 | 6.4 | 266.9 | 75.0 | 44.4 |
| Local........... | 903.9 | 984.8 | 886.0 | 145.3 | 740.7 | 17.9 | 692.7 | 109.8 | 77.5 |
| 2005: Total....... | 2,085.0 | 4,439.2 | 2,054.3 | 483.3 | 1,571.0 | 30.8 | (NA) | 323.7 | 224.6 |
| State........... | 810.9 | 3,153.8 | 805.3 | 297.4 | 507.9 | 5.6 | (NA) | 131.6 | 93.6 |
| Local........... | 1,274.2 | 1,285.4 | 1,249.0 | 185.9 | 1,063.0 | 25.2 | (NA) | 192.2 | 131.1 |
| 2009: Total....... | 2,713.2 | 4,537.4 | 2,676.3 | 627.8 | 2,048.6 | 36.9 | (NA) | 371.3 | 256.5 |
| State........... | 1,048.7 | 3,082.5 | 1,041.3 | 395.1 | 646.2 | 7.3 | (NA) | 154.2 | 109.0 |
| Local........... | 1,664.6 | 1,454.9 | 1,635.0 | 232.7 | 1,402.3 | 29.6 | (NA) | 217.1 | 147.6 |
| 2010: Total....... | 2,844.2 | 4,826.0 | 2,799.1 | 625.9 | 2,173.2 | 45.1 | (NA) | 399.0 | 275.8 |
| State........... | 1,115.5 | 3,323.0 | 1,100.8 | 397.1 | 703.6 | 14.7 | (NA) | 183.7 | 125.1 |
| Local........... | 1,728.7 | 1,503.0 | 1,698.3 | 228.8 | 1,469.6 | 30.4 | (NA) | 215.2 | 150.7 |
| 2011: Total....... | 2,923.1 | 5,265.1 | 2,888.4 | 616.1 | 2,272.3 | 34.7 | (NA) | 364.6 | 275.1 |
| State........... | 1,139.7 | 3,681.4 | 1,134.2 | 389.1 | 745.1 | 5.4 | (NA) | 138.1 | 112.4 |
| Local........... | 1,783.5 | 1,583.7 | 1,754.2 | 227.0 | 1,527.2 | 29.3 | (NA) | 226.5 | 162.7 |
| 2012: Total....... | 2,949.8 | 5,291.9 | 2,906.0 | 597.3 | 2,308.7 | 43.8 | (NA) | 339.6 | 335.7 |
| State........... | 1,148.9 | 3,694.1 | 1,133.5 | 375.6 | 757.8 | 15.5 | (NA) | 136.2 | 140.9 |
| Local........... | 1,800.8 | 1,597.7 | 1,772.5 | 221.7 | 1,550.8 | 28.3 | (NA) | 203.4 | 194.7 |
| 2013: Total....... | 2,962.2 | 5,606.1 | 2,929.4 | 585.1 | 2,344.3 | 32.8 | (NA) | 373.3 | 357.7 |
| State........... | 1,138.0 | 3,923.0 | 1,132.3 | 354.3 | 778.0 | 5.7 | (NA) | 147.5 | 149.1 |
| Local........... | 1,824.2 | 1,683.1 | 1,797.1 | 230.8 | 1,566.3 | 27.1 | (NA) | 225.8 | 208.6 |
| 2014: Total....... | 2,970.2 | 6,055.2 | 2,934.3 | 560.8 | 2,373.5 | 35.9 | (NA) | 307.7 | 309.2 |
| State........... | 1,148.4 | 4,301.2 | 1,139.7 | 340.4 | 799.3 | 8.7 | (NA) | 128.9 | 125.7 |
| Local........... | 1,821.8 | 1,754.0 | 1,794.6 | 220.4 | 1,574.2 | 27.2 | (NA) | 178.8 | 183.5 |
| 2015: Total....... | 2,974.1 | 6,207.0 | 2,937.7 | 549.7 | 2,388.0 | 36.4 | (NA) | 365.6 | 367.3 |
| State........... | 1,150.1 | 4,356.1 | 1,141.6 | 340.0 | 801.5 | 8.6 | (NA) | 140.8 | 141.3 |
| Local........... | 1,824.0 | 1,851.0 | 1,796.1 | 209.6 | 1,586.5 | 27.9 | (NA) | 224.8 | 226.0 |
| 2016: Total....... | 3,002.7 | 6,229.9 | 2,965.1 | 536.4 | 2,428.7 | 37.6 | (NA) | 387.3 | 370.0 |
| State........... | 1,160.5 | 4,342.0 | 1,151.5 | 338.3 | 813.2 | 9.0 | (NA) | 144.0 | 134.5 |
| Local........... | 1,842.2 | 1,888.0 | 1,813.6 | 198.1 | 1,615.4 | 28.6 | (NA) | 243.3 | 235.5 |

NA Not available. [1] Net long-term debt outstanding is the amount of long-term debt held by a government for which no funds have been set aside for its repayment.

Source: U.S. Census Bureau, Federal, State, and Local Governments, Government Finance Statistics, "Annual Surveys of State and Local Government Finances," <https://www.census.gov/programs-surveys/gov-finances.html>, accessed December 2018.

## Table 480. New Security Issues—State and Local Governments: 1990 to 2018

[In billions of dollars (122.9 represents $122,900,000,000)]

| Type of issue, issuer, or use | 1990 | 1995 | 2000 | 2005 | 2010 | 2014 | 2015 | 2016 | 2017 | 2018 |
|---|---|---|---|---|---|---|---|---|---|---|
| **All issues, new and refunding** [1]....... | **122.9** | **145.7** | **180.4** | **409.6** | **460.8** | **318.5** | **399.6** | **431.0** | **425.6** | **351.2** |
| By type of issue: | | | | | | | | | | |
| General obligation......................... | 39.5 | 57.0 | 64.5 | 145.8 | 137.5 | 126.4 | 161.1 | 161.4 | 152.4 | 107.6 |
| Revenue................................ | 83.3 | 88.7 | 115.9 | 263.8 | 323.2 | 192.1 | 238.7 | 269.9 | 273.3 | 243.6 |
| By type of issuer: | | | | | | | | | | |
| State.................................. | 15.0 | 14.7 | 19.9 | 31.6 | 55.2 | (NA) | (NA) | (NA) | (NA) | (NA) |
| Special district or statutory authority [2].... | 75.9 | 93.5 | 121.2 | 298.6 | 294.9 | (NA) | (NA) | (NA) | (NA) | (NA) |
| Municipality, county, or township......... | 32.0 | 37.5 | 39.3 | 79.4 | 86.6 | (NA) | (NA) | (NA) | (NA) | (NA) |
| **Issues for new capital**.................. | **97.9** | **102.4** | **154.3** | **223.8** | **278.5** | **140.8** | **169.5** | **168.4** | **197.5** | **230.9** |
| By use of proceeds: | | | | | | | | | | |
| Education................................. | 17.1 | 24.0 | 38.7 | 71.0 | 60.4 | 36.2 | 46.5 | 50.4 | 57.6 | 59.1 |
| Transportation............................ | 11.8 | 11.9 | 19.7 | 25.4 | 32.3 | 16.0 | 13.9 | 19.6 | 20.2 | 25.7 |
| Utilities and conservation.................. | 10.0 | 9.6 | 11.9 | 9.9 | 22.3 | 5.0 | 8.5 | 3.9 | 7.4 | 10.9 |
| Industrial aid............................. | 6.6 | 6.6 | 7.1 | 18.6 | 35.7 | 12.6 | 14.7 | 14.1 | 17.7 | 32.6 |
| Other purposes........................... | 31.7 | 30.8 | 47.3 | 60.6 | 92.4 | 54.5 | 56.0 | 56.7 | 60.5 | 64.0 |

NA Not available. [1] Par amounts of long-term issues based on date of sale. [2] Includes school districts.

Source: Board of Governors of the Federal Reserve System, Business Finance, "New Security Issues, State and Local Governments," <https://www.federalreserve.gov/data.htm>, accessed June 2019.

[In millions of dollars (1,942,328 represents $1,942,328,000,000). For fiscal year ending in year shown; see text, this section. These data cannot be used to compute the deficit or surplus for any single government, as these are estimates for all state and local governments within a state area. For further information, see the 2006 Government Finance and Employment Classification Manual at <http://www.census.gov/govs/classification/>]

| State | Revenue | | | | Expenditures | | | |
|---|---|---|---|---|---|---|---|---|
| | 2000 | 2005 | 2010 | 2016 | 2000 | 2005 | 2010 | 2016 |
| United States............ | 1,942,328 | 2,528,546 | 3,180,023 | 3,401,788 | 1,746,943 | 2,368,316 | 3,115,172 | 3,510,046 |
| Alabama................... | 25,726 | 33,377 | 42,189 | 45,929 | 25,319 | 31,752 | 42,255 | 45,186 |
| Alaska.................... | 10,525 | 11,404 | 15,643 | 11,643 | 8,628 | 10,027 | 14,450 | 15,851 |
| Arizona................... | 27,778 | 41,057 | 54,099 | 59,013 | 27,293 | 39,458 | 53,432 | 59,021 |
| Arkansas.................. | 13,833 | 18,866 | 24,539 | 26,742 | 12,245 | 16,682 | 22,798 | 27,291 |
| California................. | 270,380 | 381,059 | 453,354 | 515,690 | 236,645 | 342,546 | 432,363 | 533,937 |
| Colorado.................. | 29,603 | 38,915 | 49,260 | 55,244 | 26,173 | 35,063 | 48,630 | 57,155 |
| Connecticut............... | 25,828 | 30,490 | 39,427 | 41,963 | 24,011 | 29,631 | 39,311 | 45,650 |
| Delaware.................. | 6,224 | 7,637 | 9,831 | 10,197 | 5,153 | 7,595 | 9,745 | 11,414 |
| District of Columbia....... | 6,383 | 10,046 | 11,644 | 14,626 | 6,527 | 8,947 | 13,682 | 16,585 |
| Florida.................... | 92,402 | 135,491 | 166,817 | 162,751 | 84,301 | 130,860 | 163,536 | 167,229 |
| Georgia................... | 49,310 | 60,297 | 76,370 | 78,433 | 43,517 | 60,730 | 78,158 | 82,188 |
| Hawaii.................... | 8,488 | 11,000 | 14,666 | 17,379 | 8,254 | 10,534 | 14,340 | 16,218 |
| Idaho..................... | 7,590 | 10,004 | 12,490 | 13,108 | 6,404 | 8,915 | 12,054 | 12,506 |
| Illinois................... | 80,695 | 99,670 | 126,384 | 129,388 | 74,727 | 97,723 | 129,518 | 139,837 |
| Indiana................... | 32,716 | 44,302 | 54,803 | 58,977 | 31,250 | 42,164 | 53,247 | 57,922 |
| Iowa...................... | 17,220 | 23,204 | 31,055 | 35,363 | 17,275 | 21,486 | 29,537 | 34,916 |
| Kansas.................... | 16,235 | 19,990 | 26,330 | 27,700 | 14,419 | 18,948 | 26,536 | 28,765 |
| Kentucky.................. | 25,200 | 28,069 | 37,560 | 40,310 | 21,473 | 27,308 | 38,595 | 45,455 |
| Louisiana................. | 27,109 | 35,858 | 47,078 | 43,113 | 25,018 | 32,578 | 48,755 | 47,493 |
| Maine..................... | 8,554 | 11,383 | 12,557 | 12,762 | 7,652 | 10,207 | 12,286 | 12,964 |
| Maryland.................. | 33,949 | 45,076 | 57,493 | 64,103 | 30,598 | 41,373 | 57,485 | 66,183 |
| Massachusetts............. | 46,103 | 62,019 | 76,100 | 85,844 | 44,362 | 57,862 | 76,679 | 89,446 |
| Michigan.................. | 70,112 | 81,138 | 93,819 | 98,858 | 61,506 | 76,063 | 90,935 | 96,650 |
| Minnesota................. | 38,785 | 45,465 | 57,410 | 63,721 | 35,424 | 42,936 | 55,975 | 65,611 |
| Mississippi............... | 16,672 | 21,113 | 28,690 | 29,312 | 15,379 | 20,041 | 27,216 | 29,930 |
| Missouri.................. | 31,635 | 41,340 | 51,592 | 52,506 | 27,953 | 37,186 | 50,040 | 53,642 |
| Montana................... | 5,643 | 7,438 | 9,784 | 9,432 | 4,983 | 6,412 | 9,296 | 10,008 |
| Nebraska.................. | 11,650 | 15,905 | 20,121 | 22,805 | 10,831 | 14,332 | 19,315 | 23,072 |
| Nevada.................... | 11,885 | 18,953 | 22,830 | 26,272 | 11,230 | 17,405 | 23,856 | 24,541 |
| New Hampshire............. | 6,948 | 8,911 | 11,581 | 12,646 | 6,222 | 8,679 | 11,439 | 12,587 |
| New Jersey................ | 62,331 | 79,126 | 99,751 | 103,774 | 54,590 | 78,522 | 102,667 | 109,768 |
| New Mexico................ | 13,073 | 16,656 | 21,998 | 23,395 | 11,195 | 15,427 | 22,372 | 23,591 |
| New York.................. | 188,907 | 234,689 | 313,781 | 328,342 | 171,858 | 226,867 | 295,467 | 327,196 |
| North Carolina............ | 50,542 | 64,813 | 86,699 | 90,340 | 46,135 | 60,080 | 79,955 | 88,963 |
| North Dakota.............. | 4,495 | 5,239 | 7,890 | 9,926 | 4,041 | 4,794 | 6,746 | 10,793 |
| Ohio...................... | 80,074 | 102,498 | 123,289 | 117,495 | 68,418 | 91,972 | 113,844 | 125,583 |
| Oklahoma.................. | 18,760 | 24,552 | 32,939 | 32,833 | 15,962 | 22,044 | 31,338 | 34,528 |
| Oregon.................... | 28,644 | 32,406 | 41,031 | 47,156 | 24,086 | 29,084 | 39,506 | 49,655 |
| Pennsylvania.............. | 80,546 | 103,692 | 124,379 | 134,885 | 75,624 | 101,484 | 130,085 | 143,550 |
| Rhode Island.............. | 7,427 | 9,731 | 11,726 | 11,706 | 6,432 | 9,220 | 11,303 | 12,166 |
| South Carolina............ | 23,467 | 33,278 | 42,509 | 45,742 | 23,436 | 33,012 | 42,800 | 47,534 |
| South Dakota.............. | 4,277 | 5,857 | 6,941 | 7,395 | 3,760 | 4,973 | 6,845 | 7,968 |
| Tennessee................. | 33,625 | 44,888 | 54,297 | 56,988 | 32,010 | 42,800 | 53,554 | 57,782 |
| Texas..................... | 120,666 | 162,806 | 209,930 | 246,151 | 109,634 | 151,960 | 218,807 | 252,399 |
| Utah...................... | 14,954 | 19,183 | 24,149 | 27,366 | 13,044 | 17,247 | 24,552 | 27,330 |
| Vermont................... | 4,019 | 5,393 | 7,016 | 7,728 | 3,766 | 5,172 | 6,781 | 7,775 |
| Virginia.................. | 44,175 | 56,658 | 71,093 | 78,736 | 38,092 | 51,529 | 67,673 | 80,177 |
| Washington................ | 46,372 | 57,510 | 71,623 | 85,067 | 41,794 | 55,800 | 75,167 | 86,882 |
| West Virginia............. | 10,760 | 14,587 | 16,993 | 17,311 | 9,990 | 12,110 | 15,685 | 18,055 |
| Wisconsin................. | 43,003 | 48,235 | 66,291 | 54,428 | 34,559 | 43,146 | 55,839 | 59,030 |
| Wyoming................... | 7,030 | 7,269 | 10,176 | 9,102 | 3,743 | 5,619 | 8,720 | 10,068 |

Source: U.S. Census Bureau, Federal, State, and Local Governments, Government Finance Statistics, "Annual Surveys of State and Local Government Finances," <https://www.census.gov/programs-surveys/gov-finances.html>, accessed December 2018.

# Table 482. State and Local Governments—Revenue by State: 2016

[In millions of dollars (3,401,788 represents $3,401,788,000,000). For fiscal year ending in year shown; see text, this section]

| State | Total revenue | General revenue Total | Intergovernmental from federal government Total | General revenue from own sources | Select taxes Total | Property | Sales and gross receipt | Individual income | Corporation income | Current charges and miscellaneous revenue Total | Current charges Total[1] | Education | Hospitals | Sewerage | Miscellaneous revenue Total[1] | Interest earnings | Special assessments | Utility and liquor stores | Insurance trust revenue |
|---|---|---|---|---|---|---|---|---|---|---|---|---|---|---|---|---|---|---|---|
| U.S. | 3,401,788 | 3,008,100 | 690,198 | 2,317,902 | 1,599,449 | 503,239 | 558,847 | 376,297 | 54,259 | 718,453 | 498,040 | 128,361 | 151,292 | 55,810 | 220,413 | 47,818 | 8,813 | 173,594 | 220,094 |
| AL | 45,929 | 38,020 | 10,410 | 27,610 | 15,570 | 2,650 | 7,648 | 3,612 | 377 | 12,040 | 9,966 | 2,908 | 5,488 | 540 | 2,074 | 310 | 29 | 3,306 | 4,603 |
| AK | 11,643 | 10,803 | 3,129 | 7,675 | 2,827 | 1,518 | 598 | (NA) | 212 | 4,848 | 1,640 | 230 | 393 | 115 | 3,208 | 745 | 9 | 418 | 421 |
| AZ | 59,013 | 50,410 | 15,017 | 35,393 | 24,744 | 7,335 | 11,917 | 3,968 | 571 | 10,649 | 6,939 | 2,931 | 816 | 916 | 3,710 | 980 | 52 | 4,908 | 3,695 |
| AR | 26,742 | 24,653 | 7,674 | 16,979 | 11,826 | 2,127 | 5,921 | 2,781 | 450 | 5,152 | 3,627 | 1,070 | 1,457 | 298 | 1,525 | 299 | 25 | 982 | 1,107 |
| CA | 515,690 | 445,416 | 103,472 | 341,944 | 238,805 | 61,266 | 72,186 | 80,753 | 9,902 | 103,139 | 78,954 | 10,214 | 25,489 | 7,606 | 24,185 | 4,723 | 1,674 | 27,688 | 42,585 |
| CO | 55,244 | 48,562 | 9,506 | 39,056 | 25,558 | 7,880 | 9,231 | 6,486 | 626 | 13,498 | 9,277 | 3,335 | 2,025 | 894 | 4,221 | 1,095 | 313 | 2,716 | 3,966 |
| CT | 41,963 | 39,031 | 7,872 | 31,159 | 25,905 | 10,501 | 6,150 | 7,557 | 719 | 5,254 | 3,228 | 1,462 | 411 | 446 | 2,026 | 690 | 36 | 817 | 2,115 |
| DE | 10,197 | 9,590 | 2,240 | 7,350 | 4,532 | 820 | 555 | 1,170 | 324 | 2,818 | 1,608 | 830 | 6 | 165 | 1,211 | 113 | 26 | 488 | 119 |
| DC | 14,626 | 13,610 | 4,484 | 9,126 | 7,419 | 2,419 | 1,784 | 1,908 | 556 | 1,708 | 797 | 38 | 147 | 300 | 911 | 61 | (Z) | 1,034 | -18 |
| FL | 162,751 | 147,847 | 30,736 | 117,111 | 71,847 | 26,098 | 36,448 | (NA) | 2,272 | 45,264 | 30,216 | 4,666 | 7,906 | 3,432 | 15,048 | 1,746 | 2,863 | 9,565 | 5,340 |
| GA | 78,433 | 69,908 | 15,655 | 54,252 | 37,744 | 11,958 | 13,233 | 10,440 | 981 | 16,509 | 12,282 | 3,036 | 4,068 | 1,561 | 4,227 | 614 | 45 | 4,826 | 3,699 |
| HI | 17,379 | 16,440 | 3,327 | 13,113 | 9,239 | 1,629 | 4,766 | 2,116 | 108 | 3,874 | 2,510 | 450 | 650 | 488 | 1,363 | 90 | 34 | 441 | 498 |
| ID | 13,108 | 11,612 | 2,853 | 8,759 | 5,903 | 1,586 | 2,162 | 1,521 | 189 | 2,856 | 2,155 | 517 | 556 | 250 | 701 | 149 | 27 | 400 | 1,096 |
| IL | 129,388 | 116,554 | 23,075 | 93,479 | 72,575 | 27,211 | 24,128 | 13,807 | 3,367 | 20,904 | 13,616 | 4,389 | 1,802 | 1,541 | 7,288 | 1,838 | 405 | 5,160 | 7,674 |
| IN | 58,977 | 53,795 | 13,506 | 40,290 | 25,690 | 6,418 | 10,826 | 6,539 | 1,034 | 14,600 | 10,954 | 3,743 | 4,381 | 1,719 | 3,646 | 1,126 | 17 | 2,710 | 2,471 |
| IA | 35,363 | 31,580 | 7,132 | 24,448 | 15,291 | 4,954 | 5,173 | 3,656 | 377 | 9,157 | 7,135 | 1,992 | 3,549 | 596 | 2,022 | 247 | 21 | 1,432 | 2,351 |
| KS | 27,700 | 24,984 | 4,059 | 20,925 | 13,069 | 4,331 | 5,541 | 2,234 | 392 | 7,856 | 5,801 | 1,487 | 2,897 | 437 | 2,055 | 343 | 122 | 1,539 | 1,177 |
| KY | 40,310 | 36,766 | 12,105 | 24,661 | 16,958 | 3,438 | 6,288 | 5,640 | 789 | 7,703 | 5,913 | 1,675 | 2,348 | 645 | 1,789 | 544 | 11 | 1,805 | 1,740 |
| LA | 43,113 | 39,164 | 11,229 | 27,935 | 18,219 | 4,155 | 9,963 | 2,866 | 172 | 9,716 | 5,999 | 1,593 | 2,316 | 451 | 3,717 | 691 | 12 | 1,232 | 2,717 |
| ME | 12,762 | 11,953 | 2,972 | 8,980 | 6,953 | 2,825 | 2,088 | 1,552 | 137 | 2,027 | 1,423 | 363 | 133 | 174 | 605 | 168 | 7 | 308 | 502 |
| MD | 64,103 | 59,792 | 13,124 | 46,668 | 36,310 | 9,319 | 9,765 | 13,711 | 1,129 | 10,358 | 7,144 | 2,611 | 184 | 1,288 | 3,214 | 561 | 52 | 1,356 | 2,955 |
| MA | 85,844 | 76,489 | 17,254 | 59,235 | 44,142 | 16,085 | 9,084 | 14,430 | 2,334 | 15,093 | 8,470 | 3,052 | 313 | 1,724 | 6,624 | 1,623 | 12 | 3,861 | 5,494 |
| MI | 98,858 | 85,799 | 22,389 | 63,410 | 40,549 | 14,039 | 13,515 | 9,798 | 898 | 22,861 | 16,594 | 5,973 | 4,311 | 1,959 | 6,267 | 1,427 | 211 | 3,742 | 9,317 |
| MN | 63,721 | 58,045 | 11,844 | 46,202 | 33,650 | 8,659 | 10,484 | 10,733 | 1,516 | 12,551 | 8,267 | 2,493 | 2,020 | 1,136 | 4,284 | 975 | 433 | 2,667 | 3,009 |
| MS | 29,312 | 26,521 | 8,682 | 17,839 | 10,785 | 2,950 | 4,893 | 1,800 | 463 | 7,053 | 5,897 | 1,336 | 3,600 | 274 | 1,157 | 148 | 8 | 1,203 | 1,589 |
| MO | 52,506 | 45,680 | 11,496 | 34,183 | 22,430 | 5,917 | 8,532 | 6,414 | 404 | 11,754 | 7,832 | 2,625 | 2,646 | 1,013 | 3,922 | 975 | 97 | 2,630 | 4,196 |
| MT | 9,432 | 8,439 | 2,658 | 5,781 | 3,972 | 1,576 | 572 | 1,181 | 119 | 1,810 | 1,125 | 494 | 90 | 119 | 685 | 299 | 76 | 235 | 758 |
| NE | 22,805 | 17,441 | 3,449 | 13,991 | 9,705 | 3,642 | 2,845 | 2,245 | 308 | 4,287 | 3,109 | 1,006 | 815 | 280 | 1,178 | 262 | 45 | 4,532 | 832 |
| NV | 26,272 | 22,139 | 4,930 | 17,210 | 12,571 | 2,923 | 7,866 | (NA) | (NA) | 4,638 | 3,238 | 558 | 703 | 495 | 1,401 | 191 | 98 | 1,277 | 2,855 |
| NH | 12,646 | 11,194 | 2,343 | 8,850 | 6,432 | 4,159 | 986 | 88 | 700 | 2,419 | 1,410 | 663 | 7 | 134 | 1,009 | 369 | 3 | 791 | 662 |
| NJ | 103,774 | 96,701 | 18,314 | 78,387 | 60,238 | 28,079 | 13,369 | 13,356 | 2,229 | 18,149 | 11,403 | 4,028 | 1,256 | 1,745 | 6,746 | 1,313 | 2 | 2,244 | 4,828 |
| NM | 23,395 | 20,754 | 7,213 | 13,541 | 8,114 | 1,602 | 4,016 | 1,410 | 114 | 5,427 | 2,599 | 695 | 1,100 | 200 | 2,828 | 716 | 28 | 624 | 2,017 |
| NY | 328,342 | 294,565 | 62,535 | 232,030 | 177,667 | 55,176 | 43,427 | 58,103 | 10,614 | 54,362 | 31,073 | 4,340 | 9,727 | 2,913 | 23,289 | 6,579 | 130 | 15,840 | 17,937 |

See footnotes at end of table.

**Table 482. State and Local Governments—Revenue by State: 2016**-Continued.
See headnote on page 306.

| State | Total revenue | Intergovernmental from federal government Total | General revenue from own sources | Select taxes Total [1] | Property | Sales and gross receipt | Individual income | Corporation income | Total | Current charges Total [1] | Education | Hospitals | Sewerage | Miscellaneous revenue Total [1] | Interest earnings | Special assessments | Utility and liquor stores | Insurance trust revenue |
|---|---|---|---|---|---|---|---|---|---|---|---|---|---|---|---|---|---|---|
| NC... | 90,340 | 18,918 | 62,051 | 39,805 | 9,906 | 14,394 | 12,043 | 1,067 | 22,246 | 17,408 | 3,950 | 9,318 | 1,392 | 4,838 | 807 | 15 | 5,247 | 4,125 |
| ND... | 9,926 | 1,839 | 7,217 | 5,009 | 979 | 1,787 | 351 | 103 | 2,207 | 1,261 | 501 | 5 | 66 | 947 | 401 | 131 | 255 | 615 |
| OH... | 117,495 | 25,817 | 77,756 | 51,993 | 14,690 | 20,846 | 13,323 | 298 | 25,763 | 17,536 | 6,196 | 4,930 | 2,401 | 8,226 | 1,437 | 229 | 4,238 | 9,684 |
| OK... | 32,833 | 7,525 | 22,082 | 13,558 | 2,741 | 6,005 | 2,997 | 328 | 8,523 | 5,423 | 2,326 | 1,287 | 416 | 3,100 | 417 | 34 | 1,855 | 1,371 |
| OR... | 47,156 | 10,865 | 30,035 | 18,420 | 5,902 | 2,073 | 7,690 | 691 | 11,615 | 8,222 | 2,167 | 2,309 | 1,131 | 3,393 | 665 | 84 | 2,153 | 4,103 |
| PA... | 134,885 | 28,866 | 90,845 | 64,678 | 18,891 | 20,641 | 16,916 | 2,916 | 26,167 | 19,087 | 6,876 | 3,770 | 2,836 | 7,080 | 1,436 | 93 | 4,964 | 10,210 |
| RI... | 11,796 | 2,645 | 8,110 | 5,882 | 2,554 | 1,694 | 1,236 | 144 | 2,228 | 1,236 | 489 | 5 | 226 | 992 | 364 | 4 | 240 | 802 |
| SC... | 45,742 | 8,185 | 31,695 | 17,038 | 5,773 | 5,436 | 3,869 | 440 | 14,658 | 11,501 | 2,533 | 6,779 | 683 | 3,157 | 534 | 56 | 3,672 | 2,190 |
| SD... | 7,395 | 1,647 | 5,072 | 3,393 | 1,201 | 1,845 | (NA) | 33 | 1,679 | 970 | 423 | 85 | 101 | 709 | 232 | 18 | 388 | 289 |
| TN... | 56,988 | 11,920 | 33,560 | 22,090 | 5,560 | 12,465 | 324 | 1,539 | 11,470 | 8,149 | 2,117 | 2,888 | 973 | 3,321 | 446 | 114 | 8,934 | 2,574 |
| TX... | 246,151 | 45,162 | 166,065 | 112,181 | 49,167 | 56,197 | (NA) | (NA) | 53,884 | 36,322 | 9,920 | 12,088 | 3,847 | 17,562 | 4,923 | 397 | 13,802 | 21,121 |
| UT... | 27,366 | 4,663 | 18,947 | 11,398 | 3,102 | 4,123 | 3,375 | 333 | 7,549 | 5,769 | 1,884 | 2,072 | 398 | 1,780 | 394 | 52 | 2,396 | 1,360 |
| VT... | 7,728 | 2,209 | 4,902 | 3,680 | 1,616 | 1,054 | 730 | 98 | 1,222 | 838 | 569 | (NA) | 75 | 384 | 111 | 6 | 306 | 311 |
| VA... | 78,736 | 11,503 | 58,894 | 38,373 | 13,001 | 9,720 | 12,258 | 753 | 20,521 | 14,893 | 4,558 | 4,733 | 1,620 | 5,628 | 1,067 | 57 | 2,677 | 5,662 |
| WA... | 85,067 | 15,047 | 55,976 | 36,771 | 10,458 | 22,667 | (NA) | (NA) | 19,205 | 14,631 | 3,257 | 4,081 | 2,493 | 4,574 | 960 | 456 | 6,805 | 7,239 |
| WV... | 17,311 | 4,938 | 11,305 | 7,162 | 1,674 | 2,684 | 1,846 | 145 | 4,143 | 2,701 | 918 | 395 | 285 | 1,442 | 232 | 45 | 335 | 733 |
| WI... | 54,428 | 9,681 | 39,859 | 27,535 | 9,377 | 8,222 | 7,487 | 987 | 12,324 | 8,209 | 2,683 | 1,798 | 937 | 4,115 | 861 | 84 | 2,198 | 2,689 |
| WY... | 9,102 | 2,085 | 5,957 | 3,243 | 1,400 | 1,034 | (NA) | (NA) | 2,714 | 1,686 | 188 | 1,138 | 76 | 1,028 | 524 | 16 | 350 | 710 |

NA Not available or not comparable. Z Less than 50,000. [1] Includes items not shown separately.

Source: U.S. Census Bureau, Federal, State, and Local Governments, Government: Finance Statistics, "Annual Surveys of State and Local Government Finances," <https://www.census.gov/programs-surveys/gov-finances.html>, accessed December 2018.

# Table 483. State and Local Governments—Expenditures and Debt by State: 2016

[In millions of dollars (3,510,046 represents $3,510,046,000,000). For fiscal year ending in year shown; see text, this section]

| State | Total expendi-tures | General expenditures Total [1] | Direct general expenditures Total [1] | Educa-tion | Public welfare | Health | Hospi-tals | High-ways | Police protec-tion | Correc-tions | Natural resour-ces | Parks and recre-ation | Housing and community devel-opment | Sewer-age | Solid waste | Govern-mental adminis-tration | Inter-est on general debt | Utility and liquor store expend-itures | Insur-ance trust expend-itures | Total debt out-standing |
|---|---|---|---|---|---|---|---|---|---|---|---|---|---|---|---|---|---|---|---|---|
| U.S... | 3,510,046 | 2,940,290 | 2,936,902 | 965,307 | 637,641 | 96,626 | 183,116 | 174,941 | 109,175 | 78,025 | 30,797 | 41,946 | 50,145 | 55,627 | 24,596 | 135,114 | 104,626 | 231,780 | 337,976 | 3,002,720 |
| AL.... | 45,186 | 38,111 | 38,111 | 13,461 | 7,158 | 823 | 5,930 | 2,420 | 1,251 | 722 | 234 | 389 | 501 | 387 | 280 | 1,545 | 976 | 3,299 | 3,776 | 28,868 |
| AK.... | 15,851 | 13,718 | 13,718 | 3,541 | 2,234 | 288 | 462 | 1,583 | 371 | 338 | 427 | 117 | 379 | 97 | 158 | 994 | 283 | 770 | 1,363 | 9,284 |
| AZ.... | 59,021 | 48,772 | 48,772 | 14,511 | 14,021 | 2,851 | 999 | 2,458 | 2,262 | 1,685 | 496 | 659 | 448 | 726 | 424 | 2,397 | 1,591 | 5,538 | 4,711 | 48,795 |
| AR.... | 27,291 | 24,303 | 24,302 | 8,418 | 6,996 | 359 | 1,213 | 1,734 | 691 | 597 | 351 | 274 | 186 | 319 | 223 | 1,088 | 479 | 991 | 1,998 | 15,887 |
| CA.... | 533,937 | 429,889 | 427,077 | 122,580 | 98,459 | 20,199 | 26,922 | 17,145 | 17,570 | 15,468 | 7,685 | 6,448 | 8,163 | 8,737 | 3,181 | 20,976 | 16,763 | 42,067 | 61,982 | 433,826 |
| CO.... | 57,155 | 46,979 | 46,974 | 16,075 | 8,502 | 860 | 2,354 | 2,882 | 1,873 | 1,313 | 524 | 1,213 | 892 | 956 | 145 | 2,715 | 2,119 | 4,267 | 5,909 | 52,924 |
| CT.... | 45,650 | 38,425 | 38,425 | 13,563 | 7,517 | 968 | 1,396 | 2,051 | 1,237 | 684 | 245 | 289 | 970 | 642 | 299 | 2,156 | 1,882 | 1,728 | 5,497 | 48,339 |
| DE.... | 11,414 | 10,092 | 10,092 | 3,662 | 2,447 | 478 | 46 | 758 | 348 | 308 | 99 | 88 | 148 | 178 | 68 | 662 | 269 | 540 | 782 | 7,588 |
| DC.... | 16,585 | 12,762 | 12,762 | 2,757 | 3,785 | 456 | 270 | 355 | 593 | 145 | 68 | 328 | 679 | 593 | 118 | 699 | 562 | 3,314 | 509 | 14,521 |
| FL.... | 167,229 | 144,861 | 144,861 | 41,519 | 26,728 | 4,933 | 8,700 | 9,696 | 7,848 | 4,249 | 3,025 | 2,981 | 2,273 | 3,502 | 2,538 | 6,988 | 4,036 | 10,942 | 11,427 | 139,084 |
| GA.... | 82,188 | 68,697 | 68,697 | 26,726 | 11,743 | 2,247 | 4,803 | 4,135 | 2,719 | 1,920 | 458 | 1,118 | 1,235 | 1,192 | 654 | 3,690 | 1,422 | 6,056 | 7,436 | 57,938 |
| HI.... | 16,218 | 13,628 | 13,627 | 3,386 | 2,855 | 544 | 626 | 772 | 459 | 217 | 180 | 306 | 247 | 409 | 227 | 856 | 321 | 1,205 | 1,385 | 15,383 |
| ID.... | 12,506 | 11,039 | 11,039 | 3,363 | 2,456 | 256 | 707 | 842 | 457 | 343 | 286 | 152 | 147 | 216 | 163 | 712 | 240 | 371 | 1,096 | 5,973 |
| IL.... | 139,837 | 111,438 | 111,434 | 37,733 | 20,181 | 2,533 | 3,804 | 9,564 | 5,216 | 1,852 | 662 | 2,631 | 1,969 | 2,131 | 594 | 5,315 | 6,705 | 8,515 | 19,884 | 151,666 |
| IN.... | 57,922 | 52,077 | 52,074 | 17,589 | 12,712 | 784 | 5,289 | 2,710 | 1,255 | 1,159 | 377 | 561 | 878 | 992 | 291 | 2,001 | 1,888 | 2,883 | 2,962 | 50,845 |
| IA.... | 34,916 | 30,894 | 30,894 | 10,996 | 6,463 | 442 | 3,564 | 2,582 | 779 | 444 | 408 | 330 | 165 | 509 | 285 | 1,136 | 613 | 1,498 | 2,525 | 18,524 |
| KS.... | 28,765 | 25,174 | 25,174 | 9,388 | 4,183 | 409 | 2,927 | 1,970 | 799 | 516 | 272 | 331 | 294 | 363 | 166 | 1,109 | 745 | 1,590 | 1,999 | 29,231 |
| KY.... | 45,455 | 38,879 | 38,879 | 12,550 | 11,209 | 837 | 2,429 | 2,767 | 712 | 904 | 433 | 346 | 452 | 678 | 226 | 1,699 | 1,402 | 2,107 | 4,469 | 38,830 |
| LA.... | 47,493 | 41,343 | 41,343 | 13,043 | 8,700 | 724 | 3,098 | 2,394 | 1,614 | 1,138 | 1,029 | 738 | 754 | 778 | 352 | 2,169 | 1,524 | 1,500 | 4,650 | 37,080 |
| ME.... | 12,964 | 11,761 | 11,761 | 3,465 | 3,379 | 257 | 183 | 1,019 | 295 | 264 | 205 | 96 | 284 | 191 | 117 | 606 | 284 | 205 | 997 | 7,811 |
| MD.... | 66,183 | 57,354 | 57,354 | 18,747 | 12,088 | 1,861 | 601 | 3,401 | 2,649 | 1,899 | 519 | 1,177 | 1,450 | 1,340 | 1,003 | 2,921 | 2,021 | 2,960 | 5,869 | 52,894 |
| MA.... | 89,446 | 74,870 | 74,669 | 22,376 | 19,971 | 1,994 | 1,418 | 3,804 | 2,502 | 1,119 | 339 | 493 | 2,761 | 1,227 | 417 | 2,986 | 3,405 | 6,050 | 8,526 | 95,002 |
| MI.... | 96,650 | 82,822 | 82,814 | 29,997 | 16,876 | 4,373 | 4,628 | 3,833 | 2,509 | 2,521 | 425 | 998 | 1,138 | 2,354 | 498 | 3,156 | 3,169 | 4,253 | 9,575 | 72,507 |
| MN.... | 65,611 | 56,957 | 56,957 | 18,292 | 15,640 | 1,170 | 2,130 | 4,996 | 1,922 | 1,013 | 876 | 1,112 | 1,021 | 958 | 358 | 2,527 | 1,611 | 3,164 | 5,491 | 51,208 |
| MS.... | 29,930 | 26,105 | 26,105 | 8,322 | 6,254 | 410 | 3,905 | 1,660 | 742 | 498 | 245 | 216 | 274 | 377 | 193 | 1,021 | 482 | 1,179 | 2,646 | 14,010 |
| MO.... | 53,642 | 45,526 | 45,483 | 15,078 | 8,928 | 2,180 | 3,839 | 2,392 | 1,744 | 960 | 358 | 742 | 638 | 1,167 | 170 | 1,689 | 1,592 | 2,795 | 5,321 | 45,884 |
| MT.... | 10,008 | 8,775 | 8,775 | 2,894 | 1,759 | 357 | 165 | 864 | 290 | 258 | 262 | 94 | 83 | 152 | 81 | 665 | 173 | 287 | 946 | 5,270 |
| NE.... | 23,072 | 17,470 | 17,426 | 7,279 | 2,712 | 571 | 825 | 1,590 | 459 | 500 | 285 | 237 | 217 | 325 | 109 | 686 | 320 | 4,488 | 1,114 | 15,281 |
| NV.... | 24,541 | 20,506 | 20,500 | 6,133 | 4,229 | 377 | 946 | 1,430 | 1,184 | 712 | 257 | 593 | 293 | 600 | 29 | 1,188 | 779 | 1,457 | 2,579 | 29,104 |
| NH.... | 12,587 | 11,127 | 11,127 | 4,131 | 2,551 | 173 | 55 | 715 | 394 | 198 | 72 | 97 | 213 | 164 | 137 | 577 | 435 | 678 | 782 | 10,436 |
| NJ.... | 109,768 | 92,463 | 92,450 | 36,108 | 17,716 | 1,699 | 2,535 | 4,677 | 3,445 | 2,043 | 414 | 792 | 1,366 | 1,581 | 988 | 3,512 | 3,330 | 4,158 | 13,147 | 100,133 |
| NM.... | 23,591 | 20,521 | 20,521 | 6,647 | 5,723 | 539 | 1,366 | 981 | 701 | 696 | 295 | 321 | 145 | 204 | 231 | 1,126 | 496 | 761 | 2,309 | 15,313 |
| NY.... | 327,196 | 264,290 | 264,290 | 78,425 | 65,608 | 6,746 | 16,528 | 11,754 | 9,922 | 6,524 | 576 | 3,048 | 5,901 | 3,407 | 2,847 | 9,940 | 11,882 | 28,997 | 33,909 | 356,519 |

See footnotes at end of table.

# Table 483. State and Local Governments—Expenditures and Debt by State: 2016-Continued.

See headnote on page 308.

| State | Total expendi-tures | General expenditures Total¹ | Direct general expenditures Total¹ | Educa-tion | Public welfare | Health | Hospi-tals | High-ways | Police protec-tion | Correc-tions | Natural resour-ces | Parks and recre-ation | Hous-ing and com-munity devel-opment | Sewer-age | Solid waste | Govern-mental adminis-tration | Inter-est on general debt | Utility and liquor store expend-itures | Insur-ance trust expend-itures | Total debt out-standing |
|---|---|---|---|---|---|---|---|---|---|---|---|---|---|---|---|---|---|---|---|---|
| NC.... | 88,963 | 77,211 | 77,211 | 25,448 | 13,386 | 4,689 | 10,249 | 4,263 | 3,271 | 1,823 | 638 | 1,089 | 1,466 | 1,043 | 784 | 3,271 | 1,825 | 5,783 | 5,969 | 47,240 |
| ND.... | 10,793 | 9,577 | 9,577 | 3,187 | 1,627 | 308 | 27 | 1,814 | 208 | 175 | 182 | 249 | 93 | 131 | 71 | 387 | 175 | 438 | 779 | 6,783 |
| OH.... | 125,583 | 103,622 | 103,579 | 34,482 | 26,164 | 4,377 | 5,261 | 5,995 | 3,882 | 2,007 | 476 | 1,388 | 2,135 | 2,175 | 493 | 5,362 | 2,786 | 4,597 | 17,364 | 85,225 |
| OK.... | 34,528 | 29,191 | 29,145 | 10,629 | 6,563 | 1,090 | 1,153 | 2,566 | 1,064 | 752 | 143 | 495 | 445 | 338 | 218 | 1,413 | 562 | 2,393 | 2,944 | 18,719 |
| OR.... | 49,655 | 41,373 | 41,373 | 12,591 | 10,439 | 1,437 | 2,633 | 2,091 | 1,316 | 1,216 | 699 | 652 | 650 | 888 | 146 | 2,425 | 1,281 | 2,704 | 5,577 | 33,906 |
| PA. ... | 143,550 | 122,300 | 122,172 | 41,365 | 30,314 | 5,263 | 4,381 | 10,421 | 3,717 | 3,516 | 719 | 1,035 | 1,839 | 2,316 | 869 | 6,241 | 4,353 | 6,377 | 14,873 | 121,869 |
| RI. ... | 12,166 | 10,221 | 10,202 | 3,409 | 2,621 | 203 | 67 | 424 | 425 | 222 | 68 | 97 | 279 | 184 | 104 | 550 | 541 | 411 | 1,535 | 11,731 |
| SC.... | 47,534 | 40,888 | 40,888 | 14,353 | 7,360 | 1,317 | 6,583 | 1,980 | 1,194 | 755 | 244 | 602 | 494 | 533 | 359 | 1,613 | 985 | 3,206 | 3,440 | 43,614 |
| SD.... | 7,968 | 6,991 | 6,991 | 2,456 | 1,060 | 218 | 101 | 1,048 | 201 | 180 | 166 | 161 | 101 | 108 | 49 | 400 | 186 | 392 | 585 | 5,768 |
| TN.... | 57,782 | 45,000 | 44,998 | 13,977 | 11,532 | 974 | 3,650 | 2,260 | 1,855 | 1,176 | 363 | 595 | 805 | 882 | 379 | 2,264 | 1,174 | 9,377 | 3,406 | 42,713 |
| TX. ... | 252,399 | 215,062 | 215,062 | 83,062 | 36,946 | 5,269 | 17,827 | 14,039 | 7,616 | 5,921 | 1,585 | 2,496 | 1,987 | 4,148 | 1,425 | 8,019 | 9,230 | 17,318 | 20,020 | 279,310 |
| UT.... | 27,330 | 23,290 | 23,289 | 9,752 | 3,564 | 587 | 1,878 | 1,140 | 656 | 527 | 252 | 479 | 338 | 273 | 149 | 1,222 | 433 | 2,240 | 1,801 | 18,430 |
| VT.... | 7,775 | 7,031 | 7,031 | 2,678 | 1,772 | 398 | 20 | 623 | 188 | 137 | 103 | 60 | 150 | 86 | 37 | 285 | 134 | 343 | 401 | 3,630 |
| VA.... | 80,177 | 70,887 | 70,887 | 25,100 | 12,100 | 2,287 | 5,087 | 4,678 | 2,338 | 2,561 | 262 | 1,082 | 978 | 1,686 | 601 | 3,576 | 2,360 | 3,263 | 6,026 | 66,084 |
| WA.... | 86,882 | 70,600 | 70,596 | 23,786 | 12,853 | 2,422 | 5,606 | 4,186 | 1,954 | 1,728 | 1,301 | 1,153 | 1,356 | 1,943 | 765 | 2,975 | 2,712 | 9,007 | 7,275 | 85,085 |
| WV.... | 18,055 | 15,916 | 15,916 | 5,359 | 4,436 | 289 | 479 | 1,243 | 387 | 354 | 222 | 174 | 139 | 318 | 77 | 933 | 382 | 414 | 1,726 | 10,703 |
| WI.... | 59,030 | 50,719 | 50,719 | 17,796 | 12,277 | 1,491 | 2,249 | 3,520 | 1,849 | 1,554 | 648 | 678 | 313 | 1,043 | 384 | 2,029 | 1,652 | 2,447 | 5,864 | 44,037 |
| WY. ... | 10,068 | 8,784 | 8,777 | 3,119 | 843 | 303 | 1,204 | 715 | 242 | 215 | 336 | 145 | 15 | 79 | 113 | 643 | 58 | 457 | 827 | 1,914 |

¹ Includes items not shown separately.

Source: U.S. Census Bureau, Federal, State, and Local Governments, Government: Finance Statistics, "Annual Surveys of State and Local Government Finances," <https://www.census.gov/programs-surveys/gov-finances.html>, accessed December 2018.

# Table 484. Estimated State and Local Taxes Paid by a Family of Three for Largest City in Selected States: 2017

[Data based on average family of three (two wage earners and one school age child) owning their own home and living in a city where taxes apply. Comprises state and local sales, income, auto, and real estate taxes. For definition of median, see Guide to Tabular Presentation]

| City | Total taxes paid by gross family income level (dollars) | | | | | Total taxes paid as percent of income | | | | |
|------|-----------|-----------|-----------|------------|------------|-----------|-----------|-----------|------------|------------|
| | $25,000 | $50,000 | $75,000 | $100,000 | $150,000 | $25,000 | $50,000 | $75,000 | $100,000 | $150,000 |
| Albuquerque, NM...... | 1,714 | 4,030 | 6,706 | 9,174 | 14,006 | 6.9 | 8.1 | 8.9 | 9.2 | 9.3 |
| Atlanta, GA............... | 3,599 | 5,282 | 7,674 | 10,500 | 15,754 | 14.4 | 10.6 | 10.2 | 10.5 | 10.5 |
| Baltimore, MD.......... | 2,264 | 6,793 | 10,520 | 14,111 | 21,614 | 9.1 | 13.6 | 14.0 | 14.1 | 14.4 |
| Boston, MA............. | 3,347 | 5,041 | 7,705 | 10,291 | 15,791 | 13.4 | 10.1 | 10.3 | 10.3 | 10.5 |
| Charlotte, NC.......... | 2,912 | 4,378 | 7,088 | 9,623 | 14,492 | 11.6 | 8.8 | 9.5 | 9.6 | 9.7 |
| Chicago, IL.............. | 3,566 | 5,447 | 8,553 | 11,488 | 16,590 | 14.3 | 10.9 | 11.4 | 11.5 | 11.1 |
| Columbus, OH.......... | 2,896 | 5,388 | 8,210 | 10,980 | 16,666 | 11.6 | 10.8 | 10.9 | 11.0 | 11.1 |
| Denver, CO.............. | 2,492 | 3,627 | 5,902 | 8,083 | 12,599 | 10.0 | 7.3 | 7.9 | 8.1 | 8.4 |
| Detroit, MI............... | 3,104 | 6,678 | 10,172 | 13,584 | 20,165 | 12.4 | 13.4 | 13.6 | 13.6 | 13.4 |
| Honolulu, HI............. | 4,088 | 3,651 | 7,338 | 8,205 | 12,539 | 16.4 | 7.3 | 9.8 | 8.2 | 8.4 |
| Houston, TX............. | 2,497 | 3,224 | 4,668 | 6,141 | 8,754 | 10.0 | 6.4 | 6.2 | 6.1 | 5.8 |
| Indianapolis, IN......... | 3,351 | 4,781 | 7,482 | 10,151 | 15,308 | 13.4 | 9.6 | 10.0 | 10.2 | 10.2 |
| Jacksonville, FL........ | 2,388 | 2,729 | 4,453 | 6,129 | 9,013 | 9.6 | 5.5 | 5.9 | 6.1 | 6.0 |
| Kansas City, MO......... | 3,337 | 5,561 | 8,837 | 11,525 | 17,489 | 13.3 | 11.1 | 11.8 | 11.5 | 11.7 |
| Las Vegas, NV........... | 2,655 | 3,466 | 5,071 | 6,534 | 9,515 | 10.6 | 6.9 | 6.8 | 6.5 | 6.3 |
| Los Angeles, CA........ | 3,478 | 4,864 | 7,893 | 11,068 | 18,071 | 13.9 | 9.7 | 10.5 | 11.1 | 12.0 |
| Louisville, KY.......... | 3,207 | 5,704 | 8,507 | 11,357 | 16,927 | 12.8 | 11.4 | 11.3 | 11.4 | 11.3 |
| Milwaukee, WI.......... | 2,024 | 5,287 | 9,184 | 12,170 | 18,800 | 8.1 | 10.6 | 12.2 | 12.2 | 12.5 |
| Minneapolis, MN....... | 1,478 | 3,833 | 6,690 | 9,391 | 14,739 | 5.9 | 7.7 | 8.9 | 9.4 | 9.8 |
| Nashville, TN........... | 3,063 | 3,054 | 4,156 | 5,324 | 7,232 | 12.3 | 6.1 | 5.5 | 5.3 | 4.8 |
| New Orleans, LA....... | 3,258 | 4,145 | 6,529 | 8,950 | 13,652 | 13.0 | 8.3 | 8.7 | 9.0 | 9.1 |
| New York, NY........... | 3,060 | 4,908 | 8,657 | 12,100 | 19,411 | 12.2 | 9.8 | 11.5 | 12.1 | 12.9 |
| Oklahoma City, OK..... | 2,482 | 4,200 | 6,435 | 8,771 | 12,863 | 9.9 | 8.4 | 8.6 | 8.8 | 8.6 |
| Philadelphia, PA....... | 4,516 | 6,178 | 9,320 | 12,401 | 18,033 | 18.1 | 12.4 | 12.4 | 12.4 | 12.0 |
| Phoenix, AZ............. | 2,739 | 4,421 | 6,518 | 8,735 | 13,415 | 11.0 | 8.8 | 8.7 | 8.7 | 8.9 |
| Portland, OR............ | 2,528 | 4,766 | 8,185 | 11,472 | 17,863 | 10.1 | 9.5 | 10.9 | 11.5 | 11.9 |
| Seattle, WA............. | 3,875 | 3,628 | 5,230 | 6,715 | 9,425 | 15.5 | 7.3 | 7.0 | 6.7 | 6.3 |
| Virginia Beach, VA..... | 2,899 | 4,670 | 7,054 | 9,028 | 13,751 | 11.6 | 9.3 | 9.4 | 9.0 | 9.2 |
| Washington, DC........ | 2,792 | 3,892 | 6,483 | 8,652 | 13,748 | 11.2 | 7.8 | 8.6 | 8.7 | 9.2 |
| Wichita, KS.............. | 2,276 | 4,187 | 6,823 | 9,255 | 14,201 | 9.1 | 8.4 | 9.1 | 9.3 | 9.5 |
| **Average** [1]............ | **2,659** | **4,533** | **7,199** | **9,642** | **14,774** | **10.6** | **9.1** | **9.6** | **9.6** | **9.8** |
| **Median** [1]............ | **2,631** | **4,378** | **7,075** | **9,391** | **14,496** | **10.5** | **8.8** | **9.4** | **9.4** | **9.7** |

[1] Based on selected cities and District of Columbia. For complete list of cities, see Table 485.

Source: Government of the District of Columbia, Office of the Chief Financial Officer, *Tax Rates and Tax Burdens in the District of Columbia – A Nationwide Comparison 2017*, March 2019, and earlier reports. See also <http://cfo.dc.gov/>.

# Table 485. Residential Property Tax Rates for Largest City in Each State: 2017

[The real property tax is a function of housing values, real estate tax rates, assessment levels, and homeowner exemptions and credits. Effective rate is the amount each jurisdiction considers based upon assessment level used. Assessment level is ratio of assessed value to assumed market value. Nominal rates represent the "announced" rates levied by the jurisdiction]

| City | Effective tax rate per $100 | | Assessment level (percent) | Nominal rate per $100 | City | Effective tax rate per $100 | | Assessment level (percent) | Nominal rate per $100 |
|------|------|------|------|------|------|------|------|------|------|
| | Rank | Rate | | | | Rank | Rate | | |
| Bridgeport, CT.......... | 1 | 3.43 | 63.0 | 5.44 | Wichita, KS............... | 28 | 1.35 | 11.5 | 11.73 |
| Detroit, MI.............. | 2 | 3.41 | 50.0 | 6.81 | Phoenix, AZ............. | 29 | 1.34 | 10.0 | 13.36 |
| Newark, NJ.............. | 3 | 3.03 | 85.1 | 3.56 | Minneapolis, MN......... | 30 | 1.28 | 94.2 | 1.36 |
| Indianapolis, IN......... | 4 | 2.75 | 100.0 | 2.75 | Portland, OR............. | 31 | 1.26 | 54.2 | 2.32 |
| Milwaukee, WI.......... | 5 | 2.73 | 100.0 | 2.73 | Louisville, KY........... | 32 | 1.25 | 100.0 | 1.25 |
| Des Moines, IA......... | 6 | 2.64 | 55.6 | 4.75 | Oklahoma City, OK....... | 33 | 1.25 | 11.0 | 11.34 |
| Houston, TX............. | 7 | 2.53 | 100.0 | 2.53 | Charleston, SC......... | 34 | 1.15 | 4.0 | 28.86 |
| Baltimore, MD........... | 8 | 2.36 | 100.0 | 2.36 | Las Vegas, NV........... | 35 | 1.15 | 35.0 | 3.28 |
| Chicago, IL.............. | 9 | 2.15 | [1] 29.6 | 7.27 | Los Angeles, CA......... | 36 | 1.14 | 100.0 | 1.14 |
| Manchester, NH......... | 10 | 2.10 | 90.2 | 2.33 | Fargo, ND................. | 37 | 1.12 | 3.9 | 28.55 |
| Omaha, NE.............. | 11 | 2.09 | 93.0 | 2.25 | Boston, MA............... | 38 | 1.05 | 100.0 | 1.05 |
| Columbus, Oh.......... | 12 | 2.05 | 30.0 | 6.83 | Charlotte, NC........... | 39 | 1.04 | 80.0 | 1.29 |
| Burlington, VT.......... | 13 | 2.04 | 79.0 | 2.59 | Billings, MT.............. | 40 | 0.95 | 1.4 | 70.55 |
| Portland, ME............ | 14 | 2.04 | 94.0 | 2.17 | Cheyenne, WY........... | 41 | 0.95 | 9.5 | 10.02 |
| Jackson, MS............. | 15 | 1.89 | 10.0 | 18.94 | Virginia Beach, VA....... | 42 | 0.89 | 90.0 | 0.99 |
| Jacksonville, FL......... | 16 | 1.82 | 100.0 | 1.82 | Seattle, WA.............. | 43 | 0.88 | 92.8 | 0.95 |
| Atlanta, GA............. | 17 | 1.73 | 40.0 | 4.32 | Charleston, WV......... | 44 | 0.85 | 60.0 | 1.42 |
| Providence, RI.......... | 18 | 1.69 | 90.0 | 1.88 | Washington, DC......... | 45 | 0.85 | 100.0 | 0.85 |
| New Orleans, LA....... | 19 | 1.65 | 10.0 | 16.50 | Nashville, TN............ | 46 | 0.82 | 25.0 | 3.27 |
| Albuquerque, NM...... | 20 | 1.62 | 33.3 | 4.87 | New York City, NY....... | 47 | 0.82 | 4.1 | 19.92 |
| Wilmington, DE......... | 21 | 1.60 | 30.1 | 5.32 | Salt Lake City, UT....... | 48 | 0.78 | 55.0 | 1.42 |
| Anchorage, AK.......... | 22 | 1.57 | 100.0 | 1.57 | Birmingham, AL......... | 49 | 0.73 | 10.0 | 7.25 |
| Boise, ID................ | 23 | 1.53 | 95.2 | 1.61 | Denver, CO.............. | 50 | 0.58 | 7.2 | 8.03 |
| Sioux Falls, SD......... | 24 | 1.51 | 85.0 | 1.78 | Honolulu, HI............. | 51 | 0.35 | 100.0 | 0.35 |
| Kansas City, MO........ | 25 | 1.47 | 19.0 | 7.73 | | | | | |
| Little Rock, AR.......... | 26 | 1.40 | 20.0 | 7.00 | **Unweighted average...** | **(X)** | **1.57** | **58.1** | **7.05** |
| Philadelphia, PA........ | 27 | 1.40 | 100.0 | 1.40 | **Median................** | **(X)** | **1.40** | **60.0** | **2.75** |

X Not applicable. [1] The state equalizer of 2.8 percent was applied to the assessment level of 10 percent to reflect the equalizer's impact on the final rate.

Source: Government of the District of Columbia, Office of the Chief Financial Officer, *Tax Rates and Tax Burdens in the District of Columbia—A Nationwide Comparison 2017*, March 2019. See also <https://cfo.dc.gov/>.

## Table 486. Gross Revenue From Parimutuel and Amusement Taxes and Lotteries by State: 2015 to 2017

[In millions of dollars (74,455.6 represents $74,445,600,000). For fiscal years; see text, this section]

| State | 2015, total gross revenue | 2016, total gross revenue | 2017 Total gross revenue | 2017 Amusement taxes [1] | 2017 Parimutuel taxes [2] | 2017 Lottery revenue Total [3] | 2017 Apportionment of funds Prizes | 2017 Administration | 2017 Proceeds available from ticket sales |
|---|---|---|---|---|---|---|---|---|---|
| **United States** | **74,455.6** | **80,491.7** | **80,290.5** | **7,866.3** | **118.4** | **72,305.8** | **46,817.5** | **3,278.2** | **23,020.0** |
| Alabama | 1.5 | 1.2 | 1.2 | – | 1.2 | (X) | (X) | (X) | (X) |
| Alaska | 9.1 | 10.3 | 10.7 | 10.7 | (X) | (X) | (X) | (X) | (X) |
| Arizona | 699.2 | 815.8 | 815.9 | 4.0 | 0.1 | 811.8 | 557.4 | 43.5 | 160.8 |
| Arkansas | 435.7 | 488.5 | 486.7 | 60.4 | 2.5 | 423.8 | 306.4 | 34.4 | 83.0 |
| California | 5,538.9 | 6,290.1 | 6,248.2 | (X) | 14.7 | 6,233.5 | 3,963.5 | 359.1 | 1,911.9 |
| Colorado | 608.9 | 667.5 | 632.5 | 117.2 | 0.6 | 514.6 | 341.5 | 41.0 | 133.1 |
| Connecticut | 1,393.9 | 1,473.2 | 1,451.1 | 297.0 | 5.8 | 1,148.3 | 756.3 | 55.8 | 336.2 |
| Delaware | 400.7 | 400.7 | 460.2 | (X) | 0.1 | 460.1 | 135.0 | 85.7 | 239.5 |
| Florida | 5,483.2 | 5,941.3 | 6,034.4 | 207.1 | 7.8 | 5,819.4 | 3,996.6 | 168.2 | 1,654.6 |
| Georgia | 3,674.0 | 4,028.4 | 4,016.4 | (X) | (X) | 4,016.4 | 2,737.5 | 175.3 | 1,103.5 |
| Hawaii | – | – | – | (X) | (X) | (X) | (X) | (X) | (X) |
| Idaho | 197.3 | 195.7 | 222.1 | (X) | 0.6 | 221.5 | 160.3 | 12.3 | 48.9 |
| Illinois | 3,591.0 | 3,649.5 | 3,685.5 | 835.4 | 6.1 | 2,844.0 | 1,820.1 | 297.9 | 726.0 |
| Indiana | 1,591.3 | 1,732.2 | 1,730.3 | 596.9 | 1.9 | 1,131.5 | 774.4 | 71.0 | 286.2 |
| Iowa | 616.7 | 668.6 | 655.9 | 300.2 | 3.5 | 352.2 | 215.6 | 55.5 | 81.1 |
| Kansas | 231.6 | 256.3 | 243.0 | 0.3 | (X) | 242.7 | 149.7 | 25.7 | 67.3 |
| Kentucky | 834.2 | 926.5 | 932.1 | 0.2 | 6.6 | 925.3 | 628.8 | 46.6 | 249.9 |
| Louisiana | 1,145.3 | 1,185.8 | 1,132.4 | 698.3 | 4.7 | 429.5 | 242.9 | 29.9 | 156.6 |
| Maine | 289.6 | 291.0 | 304.2 | 54.4 | 1.5 | 248.3 | 171.8 | 14.2 | 62.3 |
| Maryland | 2,331.4 | 2,559.9 | 2,776.7 | 847.5 | 1.2 | 1,928.1 | 1,349.9 | 52.7 | 524.5 |
| Massachusetts | 5,011.3 | 5,302.1 | 5,153.6 | 65.7 | 0.9 | 5,086.9 | 3,669.7 | 96.5 | 1,320.8 |
| Michigan | 2,640.4 | 2,935.2 | 3,135.5 | 113.0 | 3.5 | 3,019.0 | 2,044.1 | 93.5 | 881.3 |
| Minnesota | 563.6 | 570.9 | 578.8 | 63.9 | 0.9 | 514.0 | 351.7 | 25.0 | 137.3 |
| Mississippi | 131.3 | 133.8 | 132.9 | 132.9 | (X) | (X) | (X) | (X) | (X) |
| Missouri | 1,473.4 | 1,660.1 | 1,631.0 | 366.8 | (X) | 1,264.2 | 932.1 | 58.9 | 273.2 |
| Montana | 115.3 | 115.9 | 123.1 | 59.8 | – | 63.2 | 33.7 | 9.6 | 19.9 |
| Nebraska | 156.2 | 174.0 | 168.6 | 5.8 | 0.2 | 162.7 | 101.9 | 19.4 | 41.4 |
| Nevada | 952.6 | 930.0 | 919.6 | 919.6 | – | (X) | (X) | (X) | (X) |
| New Hampshire | 282.5 | 291.6 | 288.2 | 0.5 | 0.6 | 287.0 | 191.8 | 19.1 | 76.1 |
| New Jersey | 3,037.2 | 3,313.3 | 3,223.7 | 218.7 | (X) | 3,005.0 | 1,972.5 | 73.6 | 958.9 |
| New Mexico | 210.0 | 228.6 | 204.8 | 78.0 | 0.8 | 126.0 | 67.2 | 19.6 | 39.3 |
| New York | 7,893.9 | 8,365.0 | 8,349.5 | 2.9 | 16.4 | 8,330.2 | 4,639.1 | 398.9 | 3,292.3 |
| North Carolina | 1,836.3 | 2,217.2 | 2,258.6 | – | (X) | 2,258.6 | 1,542.6 | 95.9 | 789.0 |
| North Dakota | 30.8 | 38.9 | 31.3 | 3.2 | 1.7 | 26.4 | 14.3 | 4.9 | 7.1 |
| Ohio | 2,988.6 | 3,145.9 | 3,083.4 | 262.0 | 5.5 | 2,816.0 | 1,910.0 | 80.3 | 825.6 |
| Oklahoma | 193.6 | 211.7 | 173.4 | 20.8 | 1.1 | 151.5 | 73.3 | 23.5 | 54.7 |
| Oregon | 904.0 | 957.2 | 1,488.4 | (X) | 1.9 | 1,486.4 | 217.2 | 95.4 | 1,173.9 |
| Pennsylvania | 4,964.9 | 5,271.8 | 5,138.2 | 1,406.4 | 10.4 | 3,721.4 | 2,588.3 | 81.8 | 1,051.3 |
| Rhode Island | 543.8 | 543.3 | 531.9 | (X) | 1.1 | 530.8 | 157.0 | 10.8 | 363.0 |
| South Carolina | 1,339.6 | 1,524.1 | 1,559.1 | 38.8 | (X) | 1,520.3 | 1,086.2 | 39.2 | 394.9 |
| South Dakota | 157.3 | 165.7 | 161.8 | 8.9 | 0.3 | 152.6 | 28.7 | 8.3 | 115.6 |
| Tennessee | 1,379.0 | 1,520.6 | 1,360.9 | (X) | (X) | 1,360.9 | 948.3 | 29.3 | 383.2 |
| Texas | 4,319.2 | 4,830.9 | 4,837.2 | 29.7 | 6.3 | 4,801.2 | 3,257.4 | 200.6 | 1,619.5 |
| Utah | – | – | – | (X) | (X) | (X) | (X) | (X) | (X) |
| Vermont | 104.9 | 116.5 | 114.9 | (X) | (X) | 114.9 | 79.6 | 9.8 | 25.5 |
| Virginia | 1,740.1 | 1,894.3 | 1,878.0 | 0.1 | (X) | 1,877.9 | 1,214.3 | 103.7 | 559.9 |
| Washington | 660.3 | 660.7 | 675.1 | (X) | 1.8 | 673.3 | 499.3 | 43.6 | 130.4 |
| West Virginia | 1,160.3 | 1,133.4 | 651.7 | 39.0 | 2.6 | 610.1 | 512.0 | 22.0 | 490.0 |
| Wisconsin | 574.9 | 627.4 | 569.2 | 0.2 | 0.1 | 568.9 | 363.0 | 42.8 | 163.1 |
| Wyoming | 16.8 | 29.0 | 28.5 | (X) | 3.2 | 25.3 | 14.5 | 3.4 | 7.4 |

– Represents or rounds to zero. X Not applicable. [1] Represents nonlicense taxes. [2] Represents legalized gambling taxes. [3] Excludes commissions.

Source: U.S. Census Bureau, "Annual Survey of State Government Finances," and "Annual Survey of State Government Tax Collections," <https://www.census.gov/govs/>, accessed April 2019.

## Table 487. Lottery Sales—Type of Game and Proceeds: 1990 to 2018

[In millions of dollars (20,137 represents $20,137,000,000). For fiscal years]

| Game | 1990 | 2000 | 2005 | 2010 | 2015 | 2016 | 2017 | 2018 |
|---|---|---|---|---|---|---|---|---|
| **Total ticket sales** | **20,137** | **37,201** | **47,425** | **54,200** | **66,715** | **73,058** | **73,519** | **77,351** |
| Instant [1] | 5,204 | 15,387 | 26,006 | 30,665 | 41,653 | 44,775 | 46,495 | 48,921 |
| Three-digit [2] | 4,572 | 5,780 | 5,858 | 5,861 | 5,925 | 6,098 | 5,566 | 6,119 |
| Four-digit [2] | 1,302 | 2,273 | 2,869 | 3,419 | 3,865 | 4,025 | 4,601 | 4,175 |
| Lotto [3] | 8,563 | 9,339 | 9,828 | 10,894 | 10,820 | 13,188 | 11,178 | 12,158 |
| Other [4] | 497 | 4,423 | 2,864 | 3,362 | 4,452 | 4,972 | 5,678 | 5,979 |
| State proceeds (net income) [5] | 7,703 | 11,871 | 15,792 | 17,957 | 21,154 | 22,829 | 22,563 | 23,695 |

[1] Player scratches a latex section on ticket which reveals instantly whether ticket is a winner. [2] Players choose and bet on three or four digits, depending on game, with various payoffs for different straight order or mixed combination bets. [3] Players typically select six digits out of a large field of numbers. Varying prizes are offered for matching three through six numbers drawn by lottery. [4] Includes break-open tickets, spiel, keno, video lottery, etc. [5] Sales minus prizes and expenses equal net government income.

Source: TLF Publications, Inc. © 2019. All Rights Reserved.

# Table 488. State Financial Resources, Expenditures, and Balances: 2017 and 2018

[In millions of dollars (1,942,288 represents $1,942,288,000,000). For fiscal year ending in year shown; see text, this section. General funds exclude special funds earmarked for particular purposes, such as highway trust funds and federal funds; they support most on-going broad-based state services, and are available for appropriation to support any governmental activity. Minus sign (-) indicates deficit]

| State | Expenditures by fund source | | | | State general fund | | | | | |
| | Total, 2017 actual | 2018 estimated | | | Resources [2,3] | | Expenditures [3] | | Balance [4] | |
| | | Total [1] | General fund | Federal fund | 2017 | 2018 (P) | 2017 | 2018 (P) | 2017 | 2018 (P) |
|---|---|---|---|---|---|---|---|---|---|---|
| United States...... | 1,942,288 | 2,032,369 | 822,655 | 634,802 | 845,073 | 895,857 | 808,396 | 838,236 | 33,818 | 43,238 |
| Alabama.............. | 26,645 | 26,636 | 8,138 | 10,159 | 8,432 | 8,796 | 8,166 | 8,393 | 150 | 403 |
| Alaska................ | 9,744 | 11,055 | 4,535 | 3,985 | 2,099 | 3,082 | 4,498 | 4,489 | -3,162 | -2,227 |
| Arizona.............. | 42,026 | 43,343 | 9,821 | 15,615 | 9,787 | 10,261 | 9,636 | 9,812 | 151 | 450 |
| Arkansas............ | 25,136 | 25,391 | 5,372 | 8,168 | 5,349 | 5,495 | 5,349 | 5,495 | – | – |
| California............ | 261,217 | 288,630 | 127,045 | 98,107 | 124,354 | 135,527 | 119,292 | 127,045 | 5,702 | 8,482 |
| Colorado............ | 36,530 | 36,955 | 11,293 | 9,627 | 10,833 | 12,436 | 10,425 | 11,184 | 614 | 1,274 |
| Connecticut......... | 31,719 | 32,762 | 18,600 | 6,253 | 17,703 | 18,199 | 17,727 | 18,685 | -23 | -483 |
| Delaware............ | 10,675 | 10,855 | 4,118 | 2,492 | 4,581 | 4,868 | 4,106 | 4,118 | 475 | 750 |
| Florida............... | 76,381 | 84,953 | 31,508 | 28,706 | 31,836 | 33,434 | 30,322 | 31,989 | 1,515 | 1,445 |
| Georgia.............. | 49,649 | 51,296 | 23,903 | 13,956 | 25,660 | 26,935 | 23,188 | 24,207 | 2,472 | 2,729 |
| Hawaii................ | 14,666 | 15,199 | 7,804 | 2,628 | 8,379 | 8,554 | 7,486 | 7,804 | 894 | 750 |
| Idaho................. | 7,471 | 7,931 | 3,465 | 2,683 | 3,526 | 3,845 | 3,262 | 3,466 | 101 | 239 |
| Illinois............... | 68,003 | 70,935 | 35,065 | 18,689 | 31,471 | 42,819 | 31,011 | 35,100 | 1,368 | 125 |
| Indiana.............. | 31,928 | 33,698 | 15,923 | 13,578 | 16,273 | 16,289 | 15,455 | 15,736 | 303 | 366 |
| Iowa.................. | 22,687 | 22,687 | 7,258 | 6,389 | 7,258 | 7,384 | 7,258 | 7,224 | – | 127 |
| Kansas.............. | 15,573 | 16,335 | 6,692 | 3,818 | 6,385 | 7,407 | 6,277 | 6,645 | 109 | 763 |
| Kentucky............ | 32,802 | 34,068 | 11,237 | 12,441 | 11,486 | 11,527 | 11,169 | 11,330 | 116 | 29 |
| Louisiana............ | 28,422 | 32,444 | 9,635 | 13,894 | 9,297 | 9,759 | 9,149 | 9,759 | 123 | – |
| Maine................ | 8,248 | 8,410 | 3,416 | 2,697 | 3,526 | 3,595 | 3,346 | 3,515 | 57 | 75 |
| Maryland............ | 43,322 | 45,169 | 17,131 | 13,053 | 17,317 | 17,662 | 17,289 | 17,287 | 259 | 585 |
| Massachusetts...... | 55,544 | 57,995 | 28,896 | 13,347 | 43,267 | 46,491 | 41,202 | 43,077 | 1,448 | 2,280 |
| Michigan............ | 54,385 | 55,508 | 10,231 | 22,499 | 10,507 | 10,611 | 9,809 | 10,185 | 623 | 101 |
| Minnesota........... | 37,468 | 41,420 | 22,695 | 11,891 | 24,436 | 25,200 | 21,103 | 22,695 | 3,333 | 2,505 |
| Mississippi.......... | 20,374 | 21,570 | 5,560 | 9,184 | 5,661 | 5,638 | 5,656 | 5,633 | 4 | 5 |
| Missouri............. | 25,550 | 26,038 | 9,263 | 8,360 | 9,324 | 9,762 | 9,156 | 9,267 | 168 | 495 |
| Montana............. | 6,957 | 6,952 | 2,242 | 2,863 | 2,396 | 2,455 | 2,365 | 2,287 | 48 | 186 |
| Nebraska............ | 11,867 | 12,141 | 4,350 | 3,101 | 4,577 | 4,803 | 4,329 | 4,350 | 248 | 454 |
| Nevada.............. | 13,914 | 13,954 | 4,003 | 4,448 | 4,490 | 4,517 | 3,990 | 3,981 | 434 | 486 |
| New Hampshire...... | 5,933 | 6,122 | 1,526 | 2,289 | 1,592 | 1,599 | 1,511 | 1,503 | – | 80 |
| New Jersey.......... | 59,281 | 61,396 | 35,324 | 15,937 | 35,203 | 36,431 | 34,416 | 35,658 | 787 | 772 |
| New Mexico......... | 19,586 | 19,379 | 6,140 | 8,083 | 6,687 | 7,370 | 6,130 | 6,201 | 505 | 1,112 |
| New York............ | 157,015 | 163,744 | 69,724 | 56,808 | 75,829 | 79,169 | 68,080 | 69,724 | 7,749 | 9,445 |
| North Carolina....... | 48,166 | 49,831 | 22,746 | 15,296 | 23,295 | 24,037 | 22,085 | 22,746 | 472 | 995 |
| North Dakota........ | 6,792 | 6,036 | 2,103 | 1,472 | 2,669 | 2,414 | 2,503 | 2,160 | 65 | 253 |
| Ohio.................. | 68,223 | 69,637 | 31,681 | 15,113 | 35,371 | 33,028 | 34,814 | 31,807 | 557 | 1,221 |
| Oklahoma........... | 23,262 | 22,669 | 5,854 | 7,522 | 5,820 | 6,416 | 5,737 | 6,034 | 84 | – |
| Oregon.............. | 40,040 | 40,609 | 10,180 | 10,476 | 10,094 | 11,315 | 9,093 | 9,764 | 1,000 | 1,552 |
| Pennsylvania........ | 80,324 | 82,271 | 31,997 | 29,768 | 30,402 | 31,993 | 31,942 | 31,948 | -1,539 | 22 |
| Rhode Island........ | 8,850 | 9,575 | 3,832 | 3,231 | 3,744 | 3,861 | 3,673 | 3,806 | 62 | 46 |
| South Carolina...... | 24,553 | 25,060 | 8,040 | 8,592 | 8,853 | 9,221 | 7,646 | 7,895 | 1,076 | 1,187 |
| South Dakota........ | 4,227 | 4,462 | 1,591 | 1,406 | 1,570 | 1,616 | 1,548 | 1,591 | 8 | 17 |
| Tennessee........... | 32,840 | 36,182 | 15,820 | 13,627 | 15,582 | 15,806 | 13,238 | 14,485 | 1,647 | 530 |
| Texas................ | 111,090 | 112,263 | 56,049 | 36,714 | 56,035 | 58,922 | 53,683 | 56,050 | 883 | 131 |
| Utah................. | 14,223 | 16,074 | 6,574 | 4,398 | 6,487 | 7,094 | 6,411 | 6,739 | 76 | 355 |
| Vermont............. | 5,557 | 5,675 | 1,587 | 1,926 | 1,574 | 1,641 | 1,540 | 1,564 | – | – |
| Virginia.............. | 50,302 | 52,076 | 20,884 | 10,163 | 20,898 | 20,662 | 20,115 | 20,450 | 783 | 212 |
| Washington.......... | 44,684 | 45,781 | 20,535 | 12,293 | 20,440 | 22,402 | 19,339 | 20,455 | 1,101 | 1,947 |
| West Virginia........ | 17,019 | 16,574 | 3,275 | 4,557 | 4,660 | 4,648 | 4,248 | 4,232 | 398 | 378 |
| Wisconsin........... | 46,992 | 48,199 | 16,464 | 11,575 | 16,528 | 17,332 | 17,099 | 17,139 | 579 | 589 |
| Wyoming............. | 4,426 | 4,424 | 1,530 | 925 | 1,530 | 1,530 | 1,530 | 1,530 | – | – |

P Preliminary. – Represents zero. [1] Includes bonds and other state funds, not shown separately. [2] Includes funds budgeted, adjustments, and balances from previous year. [3] May or may not include budget stabilization fund transfers, depending on state accounting practices. [4] Resources less expenditures, minus adjustments.

Source: National Association of State Budget Officers, Washington, DC, *2018 State Expenditure Report: Fiscal Years 2016-2018* ©, 2018; and *Fiscal Survey of the States, Fall 2018* ©, 2018. See also <http://www.nasbo.org>.

# Table 489. State Governments—Summary of Finances: 2000 to 2017

[In millions of dollars (1,260,829 represents $1,260,829,000,000). For fiscal year ending in year shown; see text, this section]

| Item | 2000 | 2005 | 2010 | 2011 | 2012 | 2013 | 2014 | 2015 | 2016 | 2017 |
|---|---|---|---|---|---|---|---|---|---|---|
| Total revenue | 1,260,829 | 1,642,468 | 2,039,927 | 2,266,850 | 1,905,807 | 2,196,211 | 2,365,154 | 2,202,563 | 2,136,635 | 2,549,878 |
| General revenue | 984,783 | 1,286,899 | 1,567,207 | 1,658,378 | 1,629,268 | 1,688,574 | 1,742,916 | 1,853,525 | 1,909,322 | 1,975,243 |
| Intergovernmental revenue | 274,382 | 407,792 | 575,372 | 595,029 | 533,655 | 526,670 | 550,722 | 604,628 | 637,168 | 655,916 |
| Total taxes | 539,655 | 650,612 | 705,929 | 762,379 | 798,587 | 850,842 | 870,437 | 911,720 | 922,856 | 942,959 |
| General sales and gross receipts taxes | 174,461 | 212,921 | 224,314 | 237,814 | 245,239 | 261,709 | 273,899 | 286,383 | 291,473 | 299,680 |
| Selective sales and gross receipts taxes | 77,685 | 99,663 | 120,208 | 131,662 | 133,895 | 139,650 | 141,007 | 144,955 | 149,652 | 151,253 |
| License taxes | 32,598 | 42,584 | 50,429 | 51,701 | 54,474 | 51,030 | 51,318 | 52,032 | 51,984 | 55,003 |
| Individual income taxes | 194,573 | 221,597 | 236,987 | 259,613 | 280,614 | 309,881 | 311,562 | 336,173 | 343,621 | 350,914 |
| Corporation net income taxes | 32,522 | 38,691 | 38,006 | 41,230 | 41,724 | 44,871 | 46,492 | 48,685 | 46,202 | 44,644 |
| All other taxes | 27,815 | 35,155 | 35,985 | 40,308 | 42,642 | 43,700 | 46,159 | 43,491 | 39,925 | 41,465 |
| Current charges | 86,467 | 123,129 | 169,855 | 181,092 | 174,234 | 183,412 | 191,021 | 198,583 | 208,904 | 229,236 |
| Miscellaneous general revenue | 84,279 | 105,367 | 116,051 | 119,878 | 122,792 | 127,650 | 130,736 | 138,595 | 140,394 | 146,373 |
| Utility revenue | 4,513 | 14,628 | 15,122 | 14,991 | 13,626 | 13,575 | 14,311 | 14,715 | 13,824 | 13,605 |
| Liquor stores revenue | 3,895 | 5,118 | 6,495 | 6,739 | 7,114 | 6,868 | 7,179 | 7,732 | 8,089 | 8,199 |
| Insurance trust revenue [1] | 267,639 | 335,822 | 451,103 | 586,742 | 255,798 | 487,195 | 600,748 | 326,591 | 205,401 | 553,731 |
| Total expenditure | 1,084,097 | 1,472,542 | 1,943,523 | 2,005,948 | 1,981,198 | 2,005,863 | 2,048,937 | 2,192,190 | 2,224,960 | 2,316,081 |
| Intergovernmental expenditure | 327,070 | 405,925 | 485,557 | 496,832 | 481,883 | 489,445 | 498,710 | 515,048 | 532,699 | 546,689 |
| Direct expenditure | 757,027 | 1,066,617 | 1,457,965 | 1,509,116 | 1,499,315 | 1,516,418 | 1,550,227 | 1,677,142 | 1,692,261 | 1,768,912 |
| Current operations | 523,114 | 738,886 | 934,322 | 984,181 | 986,063 | 1,019,820 | 1,063,610 | 1,144,426 | 1,184,406 | 1,248,592 |
| Capital outlay | 76,233 | 95,155 | 118,011 | 115,571 | 119,668 | 114,816 | 116,583 | 123,940 | 128,606 | 131,472 |
| Insurance benefits and repayments | 105,456 | 168,200 | 320,721 | 320,564 | 303,670 | 291,069 | 278,190 | 316,274 | 285,400 | 293,783 |
| Assistance and subsidies | 22,136 | 28,403 | 37,562 | 39,762 | 40,078 | 42,175 | 43,934 | 45,176 | 46,723 | 47,978 |
| Interest on debt | 30,089 | 35,974 | 47,351 | 49,038 | 49,835 | 48,538 | 47,911 | 47,326 | 47,126 | 46,433 |
| Exhibit: salaries and wages | 154,504 | 194,907 | 244,352 | 252,453 | 251,329 | 245,673 | 253,443 | 258,821 | 265,784 | 275,139 |
| General expenditure | 964,723 | 1,278,434 | 1,593,694 | 1,654,429 | 1,648,196 | 1,685,103 | 1,738,757 | 1,840,905 | 1,905,866 | 1,982,934 |
| Intergovernmental general expenditure | 327,070 | 405,925 | 485,557 | 496,832 | 481,883 | 489,445 | 498,710 | 515,048 | 532,699 | 546,689 |
| Direct general expenditure | 637,653 | 872,508 | 1,108,137 | 1,157,596 | 1,166,312 | 1,195,658 | 1,240,047 | 1,325,857 | 1,373,167 | 1,438,236 |
| General expenditure, by function: | | | | | | | | | | |
| Education | 346,465 | 454,348 | 571,147 | 592,863 | 588,340 | 599,080 | 613,748 | 637,316 | 664,418 | 686,655 |
| Public welfare | 238,890 | 368,765 | 462,431 | 494,829 | 489,162 | 519,127 | 544,711 | 612,554 | 638,962 | 676,248 |
| Hospitals | 32,578 | 43,623 | 64,509 | 65,986 | 69,266 | 67,433 | 71,712 | 73,917 | 80,924 | 88,771 |
| Health | 42,066 | 48,634 | 58,245 | 60,035 | 61,356 | 63,253 | 64,207 | 62,745 | 63,694 | 61,728 |
| Highways | 74,415 | 92,816 | 111,170 | 109,398 | 115,297 | 112,174 | 117,322 | 120,136 | 124,525 | 129,305 |
| Police protection | 9,788 | 11,395 | 13,828 | 14,249 | 14,276 | 15,107 | 15,669 | 16,108 | 16,480 | 17,081 |
| Correction | 35,129 | 40,562 | 48,550 | 49,167 | 48,440 | 48,605 | 50,219 | 51,728 | 51,836 | 51,314 |
| Natural resources | 15,967 | 18,822 | 21,515 | 21,990 | 22,051 | 21,344 | 21,391 | 22,484 | 24,072 | 23,965 |
| Parks and recreation | 4,676 | 5,334 | 5,720 | 5,761 | 5,721 | 5,658 | 5,765 | 6,168 | 6,517 | 6,549 |
| Governmental administration | 35,527 | 46,464 | 53,976 | 53,224 | 52,627 | 52,992 | 54,789 | 55,696 | 57,615 | 61,506 |
| Interest on general debt | 29,187 | 34,242 | 45,260 | 46,653 | 47,274 | 46,148 | 45,479 | 44,835 | 44,624 | 43,946 |
| Other and unallocable | 100,034 | 113,427 | 137,344 | 140,275 | 134,386 | 134,180 | 133,744 | 137,217 | 132,199 | 137,549 |
| Utility expenditure | 10,723 | 21,827 | 23,864 | 25,549 | 23,724 | 24,522 | 26,284 | 28,827 | 27,246 | 29,492 |
| Liquor store expenditure [1] | 3,195 | 4,082 | 5,244 | 5,407 | 5,608 | 5,169 | 5,705 | 6,184 | 6,447 | 6,718 |
| Insurance trust expenditure [1] | 105,456 | 168,200 | 320,721 | 320,564 | 303,670 | 291,069 | 278,190 | 316,274 | 285,400 | 293,783 |
| Debt outstanding, long term and short term [2] | 547,876 | 810,852 | 1,115,463 | 1,139,664 | 1,148,934 | 1,137,965 | 1,148,393 | 1,150,140 | 1,160,489 | 1,153,936 |
| Cash and security holdings | 2,518,936 | 3,153,795 | 3,323,047 | 3,672,783 | 3,667,671 | 3,828,644 | 4,180,757 | 4,746,496 | 4,159,814 | 4,477,542 |

[1] Within insurance trust revenue, net earnings of state-administered pension systems is a calculated statistic, and thus can be positive or negative. Net earnings is the sum of earnings on investments plus gains on investments minus losses on investments. [2] As of fiscal year 2005 the Census Bureau no longer collects government debt information by the character of long-term debt. For further information see the 2006 Government Finance and Employment Classification Manual at <http://www.census.gov/govs/pubs/>.

Source: U.S. Census Bureau, "Annual Survey of State Government Finances," <https://www.census.gov/programs-surveys/state.html>, accessed April 2019.

# Table 490. State Governments—Revenue by State: 2016

[In millions of dollars (2,136,454 represents $2,136,454,000,000). For fiscal year ending in year shown. See text, this section. Includes local shares of state imposed taxes]

| State | Total revenue [1,2] | General revenue | | | | | | | Utilities and liquor store revenue | Insurance trust revenue |
|---|---|---|---|---|---|---|---|---|---|---|
| | | Total | Intergovernmental revenue | | General revenue from own sources | | | | | |
| | | | Total [1] | From federal government | Total | Total taxes | Current charges | Miscellaneous general revenue | | |
| United States...... | 2,136,454 | 1,909,322 | 637,168 | 621,509 | 1,272,154 | 922,856 | 208,904 | 140,394 | 21,912 | 205,221 |
| Alabama.............. | 30,172 | 25,289 | 9,522 | 9,391 | 15,767 | 9,920 | 4,705 | 1,142 | 325 | 4,558 |
| Alaska............... | 8,060 | 7,629 | 2,853 | 2,846 | 4,775 | 1,042 | 701 | 3,033 | 19 | 413 |
| Arizona.............. | 38,241 | 34,583 | 14,540 | 14,232 | 20,042 | 14,676 | 2,880 | 2,486 | 29 | 3,629 |
| Arkansas............. | 21,432 | 20,346 | 7,432 | 7,387 | 12,915 | 9,453 | 2,455 | 1,007 | (NA) | 1,086 |
| California............. | 322,332 | 282,908 | 94,336 | 91,205 | 188,572 | 155,231 | 23,164 | 10,176 | 775 | 38,649 |
| Colorado............. | 31,420 | 27,555 | 8,704 | 8,440 | 18,851 | 12,795 | 3,862 | 2,194 | (NA) | 3,866 |
| Connecticut.......... | 28,131 | 26,172 | 7,321 | 7,303 | 18,851 | 15,245 | 2,039 | 1,567 | 35 | 1,925 |
| Delaware............. | 8,084 | 7,963 | 2,231 | 2,163 | 5,732 | 3,522 | 1,201 | 1,009 | 21 | 100 |
| Florida.............. | 85,094 | 80,261 | 27,390 | 27,071 | 52,871 | 37,640 | 8,234 | 6,997 | 25 | 4,808 |
| Georgia.............. | 45,860 | 42,280 | 14,572 | 14,517 | 27,708 | 21,455 | 3,680 | 2,573 | 6 | 3,575 |
| Hawaii............... | 13,418 | 12,919 | 2,943 | 2,936 | 9,976 | 6,919 | 1,799 | 1,258 | (Z) | 498 |
| Idaho............... | 9,402 | 8,151 | 2,722 | 2,697 | 5,429 | 4,206 | 771 | 452 | 155 | 1,096 |
| Illinois.............. | 75,492 | 68,847 | 20,265 | 19,825 | 48,582 | 38,907 | 5,234 | 4,442 | (NA) | 6,645 |
| Indiana.............. | 38,688 | 36,260 | 13,042 | 12,972 | 23,218 | 17,588 | 3,618 | 2,012 | (NA) | 2,428 |
| Iowa................ | 23,715 | 21,074 | 6,646 | 6,620 | 14,429 | 9,559 | 3,503 | 1,367 | 291 | 2,350 |
| Kansas.............. | 17,609 | 16,460 | 3,828 | 3,790 | 12,631 | 8,059 | 3,453 | 1,120 | (NA) | 1,149 |
| Kentucky............ | 29,917 | 28,198 | 11,564 | 11,526 | 16,635 | 11,779 | 3,685 | 1,171 | (NA) | 1,719 |
| Louisiana............ | 26,819 | 24,110 | 10,362 | 10,291 | 13,748 | 9,310 | 1,950 | 2,489 | 13 | 2,696 |
| Maine............... | 8,987 | 8,310 | 2,894 | 2,834 | 5,417 | 4,130 | 823 | 463 | 175 | 502 |
| Maryland............ | 42,026 | 39,160 | 12,290 | 11,911 | 26,869 | 20,894 | 3,665 | 2,310 | 156 | 2,710 |
| Massachusetts....... | 60,353 | 54,701 | 16,401 | 15,813 | 38,300 | 27,277 | 5,337 | 5,686 | 878 | 4,774 |
| Michigan............ | 71,180 | 61,246 | 20,908 | 20,726 | 40,338 | 27,437 | 8,688 | 4,213 | 1,022 | 8,912 |
| Minnesota........... | 44,248 | 41,213 | 11,321 | 11,008 | 29,892 | 25,189 | 2,636 | 2,067 | 104 | 2,930 |
| Mississippi.......... | 20,881 | 18,954 | 8,299 | 8,210 | 10,655 | 7,660 | 2,297 | 698 | 338 | 1,589 |
| Missouri............. | 33,012 | 28,850 | 10,988 | 10,751 | 17,863 | 12,245 | 3,046 | 2,572 | (NA) | 4,162 |
| Montana............. | 6,863 | 6,011 | 2,446 | 2,440 | 3,566 | 2,628 | 490 | 447 | 94 | 758 |
| Nebraska............ | 10,882 | 10,130 | 3,162 | 3,089 | 6,968 | 5,117 | 1,175 | 676 | (NA) | 752 |
| Nevada.............. | 16,809 | 13,904 | 4,558 | 4,358 | 9,346 | 8,025 | 775 | 546 | 49 | 2,855 |
| New Hampshire...... | 8,329 | 6,997 | 2,609 | 2,231 | 4,388 | 2,642 | 923 | 822 | 671 | 661 |
| New Jersey.......... | 66,895 | 60,953 | 17,976 | 17,303 | 42,977 | 31,547 | 6,547 | 4,883 | 1,119 | 4,823 |
| New Mexico.......... | 18,553 | 16,537 | 7,030 | 6,816 | 9,507 | 5,462 | 1,628 | 2,416 | (NA) | 2,017 |
| New York............ | 185,620 | 164,399 | 56,823 | 55,734 | 107,576 | 81,354 | 9,800 | 16,422 | 8,081 | 13,140 |
| North Carolina....... | 55,217 | 51,110 | 15,909 | 15,705 | 35,202 | 26,202 | 5,817 | 3,183 | (Z) | 4,106 |
| North Dakota........ | 7,303 | 6,699 | 1,641 | 1,592 | 5,058 | 3,709 | 825 | 523 | (Z) | 604 |
| Ohio................ | 78,250 | 67,466 | 24,258 | 23,650 | 43,209 | 28,695 | 9,075 | 5,439 | 1,154 | 9,629 |
| Oklahoma............ | 22,858 | 20,921 | 7,246 | 7,102 | 13,674 | 8,491 | 2,835 | 2,348 | 615 | 1,323 |
| Oregon.............. | 32,764 | 28,109 | 10,027 | 10,006 | 18,081 | 11,043 | 4,644 | 2,394 | 568 | 4,087 |
| Pennsylvania........ | 90,792 | 79,738 | 26,240 | 26,031 | 53,498 | 37,395 | 11,411 | 4,693 | 1,938 | 9,116 |
| Rhode Island........ | 8,201 | 7,430 | 2,518 | 2,465 | 4,912 | 3,266 | 798 | 848 | 23 | 749 |
| South Carolina....... | 28,938 | 24,905 | 8,272 | 7,693 | 16,633 | 9,556 | 4,961 | 2,116 | 1,865 | 2,168 |
| South Dakota........ | 4,535 | 4,251 | 1,475 | 1,443 | 2,775 | 1,748 | 438 | 590 | (NA) | 284 |
| Tennessee........... | 31,426 | 28,984 | 11,239 | 11,179 | 17,746 | 13,386 | 2,234 | 2,125 | (NA) | 2,441 |
| Texas............... | 143,832 | 122,795 | 43,751 | 41,175 | 79,044 | 52,133 | 15,102 | 11,809 | (NA) | 21,037 |
| Utah................ | 18,162 | 16,441 | 4,234 | 4,225 | 12,207 | 7,083 | 4,008 | 1,116 | 361 | 1,360 |
| Vermont............. | 6,488 | 6,121 | 2,139 | 2,137 | 3,982 | 3,086 | 601 | 295 | 62 | 305 |
| Virginia............. | 51,656 | 45,426 | 10,228 | 9,582 | 35,198 | 21,220 | 9,732 | 4,246 | 737 | 5,494 |
| Washington.......... | 51,095 | 43,977 | 13,705 | 13,289 | 30,272 | 22,280 | 5,260 | 2,732 | (Z) | 7,117 |
| West Virginia........ | 13,645 | 12,845 | 4,846 | 4,761 | 7,999 | 5,128 | 1,678 | 1,194 | 95 | 705 |
| Wisconsin........... | 36,853 | 34,643 | 9,318 | 9,098 | 25,325 | 17,608 | 4,517 | 3,200 | (NA) | 2,211 |
| Wyoming............. | 5,914 | 5,090 | 2,143 | 1,938 | 2,947 | 1,914 | 202 | 832 | 114 | 710 |

NA Not available or not comparable. Z Less than $500,000. [1] Includes amounts for categories not shown separately. [2] Duplicate intergovernmental transactions are excluded.

Source: U.S. Census Bureau, Federal, State, and Local Governments, Government Finance Statistics, "Annual Surveys of State and Local Government Finances," <http://www.census.gov/govs/local/>, accessed December 2018.

# Table 491. State Government Tax Collections by State: 2018

[In millions of dollars (1,031,001 represents $1,031,001,000,000)]

| State | All taxes | Total property taxes | Selective sales and gross receipts — Total[1] | Total general sales and gross receipts — Total | Selective sales tax — Total[1] | Alcoholic beverage sales | Insurance premiums | Motor fuels sales | Public utilities | Tobacco products | License taxes — Total[1] | Corporation | Motor vehicle | Occupancy and business n.e.c.[2] | Income taxes — Total | Individual income | Corporation net income | Other taxes — Total[1] | Death and gift | Severance |
|---|---|---|---|---|---|---|---|---|---|---|---|---|---|---|---|---|---|---|---|---|
| U.S. | 1,031,001 | 20,079 | 482,393 | 317,423 | 164,970 | 6,795 | 22,457 | 48,263 | 12,550 | 19,502 | 57,375 | 6,031 | 27,901 | 14,834 | 440,292 | 392,070 | 48,223 | 30,862 | 5,072 | 12,625 |
| AL | 11,056 | 406 | 5,535 | 2,787 | 2,748 | 215 | 377 | 649 | 748 | 180 | 522 | 153 | 220 | 76 | 4,490 | 3,913 | 578 | 102 | (X) | 56 |
| AK | 1,642 | 122 | 253 | (X) | 253 | 39 | 62 | 47 | 5 | 56 | 140 | (X) | 35 | 52 | 196 | (X) | 196 | 931 | (X) | 931 |
| AZ | 16,294 | 1,047 | 9,709 | 7,688 | 2,021 | 76 | 550 | 869 | 22 | 313 | 495 | 14 | 230 | 173 | 4,918 | 4,545 | 373 | 125 | (X) | 25 |
| AR | 9,843 | 1,213 | 4,835 | 3,498 | 1,337 | 58 | 223 | 493 | (X) | 227 | 410 | 30 | 165 | 149 | 3,257 | 2,866 | 391 | 129 | – | 55 |
| CA | 175,017 | 2,837 | 53,846 | 36,189 | 17,657 | 377 | 2,569 | 6,352 | 688 | 2,428 | 10,505 | 80 | 4,635 | 4,536 | 107,641 | 95,152 | 12,488 | 188 | 1 | 109 |
| CO | 14,802 | (X) | 5,712 | 3,212 | 2,500 | 47 | 262 | 676 | (X) | 194 | 817 | 21 | 597 | 57 | 8,170 | 7,510 | 660 | 103 | (X) | 103 |
| CT | 19,081 | (X) | 7,700 | 4,531 | 3,169 | 63 | 209 | 487 | 261 | 377 | 476 | 31 | 238 | 141 | 10,511 | 9,733 | 778 | 394 | 224 | (X) |
| DE | 4,220 | (X) | 586 | (X) | 586 | 27 | 110 | 132 | 53 | 123 | 1,575 | 1,378 | 59 | 117 | 1,907 | 1,652 | 255 | 152 | 4 | (X) |
| DC | 7,959 | 2,622 | 1,930 | 1,493 | 437 | 7 | 115 | 26 | 179 | 28 | 199 | 36 | 40 | 58 | 2,642 | 2,067 | 575 | 567 | 36 | (X) |
| FL | 45,961 | (X) | 38,457 | 29,563 | 8,894 | 293 | 1,085 | 2,800 | 2,388 | 1,172 | 2,123 | 264 | 1,450 | 172 | 2,427 | (X) | 2,427 | 2,954 | 2 | 36 |
| GA | 23,603 | 928 | 9,133 | 5,938 | 3,195 | 196 | 505 | 1,802 | (X) | 225 | 719 | 60 | 395 | 81 | 12,648 | 11,644 | 1,004 | 174 | – | (X) |
| HI | 7,714 | (X) | 4,732 | 3,529 | 1,203 | 51 | 166 | 88 | 118 | 120 | 276 | 2 | 192 | 54 | 2,577 | 2,430 | 147 | 130 | 29 | (X) |
| ID | 4,848 | (X) | 2,396 | 1,791 | 605 | 10 | 97 | 362 | 3 | 51 | 367 | 3 | 195 | 47 | 2,077 | 1,836 | 241 | 8 | (X) | 5 |
| IL | 39,857 | 60 | 18,700 | 11,337 | 7,363 | 296 | 456 | 1,368 | 1,440 | 764 | 2,751 | 343 | 1,619 | 553 | 17,884 | 15,297 | 2,587 | 462 | 382 | (X) |
| IN | 19,398 | 13 | 12,120 | 7,795 | 4,324 | 52 | 236 | 1,420 | 202 | 419 | 749 | 9 | 321 | 52 | 6,515 | 5,816 | 699 | 1 | – | 1 |
| IA | 10,088 | 2 | 4,687 | 3,280 | 1,407 | 22 | 114 | 672 | 39 | 212 | 955 | 35 | 564 | 146 | 4,340 | 3,897 | 443 | 105 | 83 | (X) |
| KS | 9,547 | 715 | 4,495 | 3,304 | 1,191 | 142 | 408 | 461 | – | 130 | 433 | 28 | 223 | 98 | 3,852 | 3,414 | 438 | 52 | – | 52 |
| KY | 12,060 | 661 | 5,714 | 3,601 | 2,114 | 146 | 165 | 703 | 61 | 229 | 500 | 116 | 212 | 112 | 5,010 | 4,499 | 511 | 175 | 48 | 123 |
| LA | 11,358 | 60 | 6,865 | 4,253 | 2,612 | 76 | 871 | 632 | 9 | 164 | 393 | 148 | 79 | 106 | 3,604 | 3,246 | 358 | 435 | (X) | 435 |
| ME | 4,411 | 39 | 2,250 | 1,529 | 721 | 20 | 100 | 250 | 22 | 133 | 281 | 11 | 113 | 113 | 1,791 | 1,605 | 186 | 49 | 14 | (X) |
| MD | 22,427 | 809 | 9,567 | 4,716 | 4,851 | 32 | 542 | 1,084 | 145 | 373 | 851 | 119 | 501 | 180 | 10,541 | 9,508 | 1,033 | 659 | 214 | (X) |
| MA | 29,655 | 7 | 9,022 | 6,490 | 2,532 | 86 | 406 | 769 | (X) | 594 | 1,155 | 26 | 445 | 302 | 18,689 | 16,280 | 2,409 | 781 | 473 | (X) |
| MI | 30,508 | 2,161 | 14,693 | 9,854 | 4,839 | 157 | 396 | 1,446 | 42 | 1,003 | 1,948 | 26 | 1,323 | 217 | 11,334 | 10,239 | 1,095 | 372 | – | 31 |
| MN | 26,697 | 819 | 10,615 | 5,830 | 4,785 | 92 | 520 | 937 | – | 593 | 1,476 | 9 | 801 | 484 | 13,239 | 11,882 | 1,357 | 549 | 215 | 50 |
| MS | 7,891 | 30 | 5,031 | 3,558 | 1,473 | 41 | 339 | 436 | 1 | 140 | 492 | 138 | 158 | 82 | 2,290 | 1,853 | 437 | 47 | – | 47 |
| MO | 13,028 | 33 | 5,539 | 3,686 | 1,853 | 39 | 464 | 718 | (X) | 97 | 599 | 2 | 297 | 143 | 6,844 | 6,510 | 334 | 12 | – | – |
| MT | 2,945 | 295 | 632 | (X) | 632 | 34 | 111 | 254 | 42 | 81 | 352 | 5 | 155 | 113 | 1,477 | 1,301 | 176 | 190 | – | 186 |
| NE | 5,393 | – | 2,502 | 1,900 | 602 | 31 | 63 | 374 | 45 | 57 | 196 | 16 | 114 | 36 | 2,674 | 2,361 | 314 | 20 | – | 3 |
| NV | 9,157 | 317 | 7,329 | 5,096 | 2,234 | 45 | 396 | 343 | 46 | 177 | 661 | 79 | 198 | 257 | (X) | (X) | (X) | 849 | (X) | 156 |
| NH | 2,921 | 409 | 1,026 | (X) | 1,026 | 13 | 112 | 183 | 49 | 213 | 436 | 67 | 82 | 216 | 896 | 106 | 790 | 155 | (X) | (X) |
| NJ | 35,365 | 5 | 15,425 | 10,459 | 4,965 | 142 | 591 | 459 | 679 | 660 | 1,542 | 248 | 658 | 486 | 17,273 | 15,038 | 2,236 | 1,120 | 606 | (X) |
| NM | 5,672 | 84 | 2,886 | 2,073 | 813 | 45 | 169 | 230 | 32 | 94 | 317 | 32 | 201 | 45 | 1,344 | 1,253 | 91 | 1,041 | – | 1,041 |
| NY | 88,541 | (X) | 26,399 | 14,820 | 11,579 | 258 | 1,623 | 1,637 | 877 | 1,152 | 1,772 | 3 | 1,412 | 126 | 56,356 | 52,739 | 3,618 | 4,014 | 1,204 | (X) |

See footnotes at end of table.

## Table 491. State Government Tax Collections by State: 2018-Continued.

See headnote on page 315.

| State | All taxes | Total property taxes | Selective sales and gross receipts — Total | Total general sales and gross receipts — Total | Selective sales tax — Total [1] | Alcoholic beverage sales | Insurance premiums | Motor fuels sales | Public utilities | Tobacco products | License taxes — Total [1] | Corporation | Motor vehicle | Occupancy and business n.e.c. [2] | Income taxes — Total | Individual income | Corporation net income | Other taxes — Total [1] | Death and gift | Severance |
|---|---|---|---|---|---|---|---|---|---|---|---|---|---|---|---|---|---|---|---|---|
| NC..... | 27,855 | (X) | 12,213 | 8,010 | 4,203 | 412 | 589 | 1,975 | – | 292 | 2,197 | 757 | 854 | 350 | 13,352 | 12,610 | 743 | 93 | 11 | 2 |
| ND..... | 4,205 | 5 | 1,396 | 913 | 483 | 9 | 63 | 197 | 50 | 28 | 214 | (X) | 118 | 75 | 475 | 368 | 107 | 2,116 | (X) | 2,116 |
| OH..... | 29,130 | (X) | 18,086 | 12,148 | 5,938 | 105 | 583 | 1,912 | 927 | 941 | 2,270 | 297 | 787 | 908 | 8,708 | 8,699 | 9 | 66 | – | 66 |
| OK..... | 9,564 | (X) | 4,062 | 2,724 | 1,338 | 122 | 329 | 485 | 44 | 313 | 1,050 | 59 | 769 | 1 | 3,730 | 3,495 | 235 | 721 | – | 700 |
| OR..... | 12,645 | 20 | 1,659 | (X) | 1,659 | 19 | 71 | 539 | 9 | 264 | 1,087 | 40 | 539 | 382 | 9,684 | 8,880 | 804 | 194 | 176 | 16 |
| PA..... | 40,710 | 34 | 21,034 | 10,921 | 10,113 | 397 | 836 | 3,375 | 1,155 | 1,373 | 2,722 | 6 | 1,184 | 1,038 | 15,287 | 12,801 | 2,486 | 1,632 | 982 | (X) |
| RI..... | 3,483 | 3 | 1,682 | 1,049 | 633 | 20 | 82 | 80 | 60 | 147 | 102 | 5 | 21 | 62 | 1,447 | 1,329 | 118 | 249 | 133 | (X) |
| SC..... | 10,550 | 37 | 4,948 | 3,303 | 1,645 | 179 | 239 | 647 | 29 | 27 | 582 | 110 | 274 | 127 | 4,856 | 4,432 | 424 | 126 | (X) | (X) |
| SD..... | 1,918 | (X) | 1,585 | 1,104 | 481 | 19 | 92 | 187 | 4 | 59 | 292 | 6 | 83 | 135 | 32 | (X) | 32 | 8 | (X) | 8 |
| TN..... | 14,269 | (X) | 10,343 | 7,470 | 2,874 | 202 | 971 | 1,087 | 9 | 249 | 1,764 | 920 | 358 | 373 | 1,891 | 247 | 1,644 | 272 | – | 1 |
| TX..... | 60,329 | (X) | 51,462 | 36,130 | 15,332 | 1,322 | 2,445 | 3,710 | 630 | 1,440 | 3,635 | 153 | 2,358 | 610 | (X) | (X) | (X) | 5,232 | (X) | 5,232 |
| UT..... | 8,039 | (X) | 3,269 | 2,249 | 1,020 | 51 | 135 | 497 | 24 | 114 | 336 | – | 218 | 56 | 4,392 | 3,991 | 401 | 41 | (X) | 41 |
| VT..... | 3,284 | 1,066 | 1,095 | 398 | 698 | 27 | 59 | 83 | 9 | 71 | 126 | 4 | 73 | 26 | 930 | 819 | 111 | 67 | 23 | (X) |
| VA..... | 23,489 | 32 | 7,087 | 4,077 | 3,011 | 231 | 517 | 1,031 | 117 | 160 | 879 | 64 | 493 | 232 | 14,968 | 14,106 | 862 | 524 | 1 | 3 |
| WA..... | 26,575 | 2,770 | 20,323 | 15,643 | 4,680 | 371 | 631 | 1,714 | 501 | 422 | 2,071 | 42 | 1,130 | 365 | (X) | (X) | (X) | 1,411 | 209 | 41 |
| WV..... | 5,418 | 7 | 2,732 | 1,312 | 1,420 | 18 | 170 | 420 | 120 | 178 | 194 | 1 | 4 | 8 | 2,061 | 1,951 | 110 | 424 | (X) | 412 |
| WI..... | 18,743 | 163 | 8,233 | 5,484 | 2,749 | 62 | 208 | 1,051 | 362 | 617 | 1,182 | 22 | 518 | 465 | 9,062 | 8,151 | 910 | 103 | 2 | 11 |
| WY..... | 1,837 | 250 | 863 | 689 | 174 | 2 | 23 | 114 | 5 | 22 | 188 | 14 | 92 | 40 | (X) | (X) | (X) | 537 | – | 532 |

X Not applicable. – Represents zero or rounds to zero. [1] Includes other items not shown separately. [2] N.e.c. means not elsewhere classified.

Source: U.S. Census Bureau, Census of Governments, "2018 State Government Tax Tables," <https://www.census.gov/programs-surveys/stc.html>, accessed June 2019. See also <https://www.census.gov/govs/index.html>.

# Table 492. State Governments—Expenditures and Debt by State: 2016

[In millions of dollars (2,225,107 represents $2,225,107,000,000) except as indicated. For fiscal year ending in year shown; see text, this section]

| State | Total expend-itures | Inter-govern-mental | Direct expenditures Total | Direct general expenditures Total¹ | Educa-tion | Public welfare | Health | Hospi-tals | High-ways | Police protec-tion | Correc-tions | Parks and recre-ation | Housing and com-munity devel-opment | Sewer-age | Solid waste man-age-ment | Govern-men-tal admin-istra-tion | Inter-est on gen-eral debt | Utility and liquor store | Insur-ance trust | Cash and security holdings | Total debt out-stand-ing |
|---|---|---|---|---|---|---|---|---|---|---|---|---|---|---|---|---|---|---|---|---|---|
| U.S.. | 2,225,107 | 532,699 | 1,692,408 | 1,373,167 | 304,301 | 581,912 | 44,165 | 79,102 | 104,849 | 15,003 | 49,040 | 5,539 | 8,676 | 1,246 | 1,348 | 55,361 | 44,624 | 33,693 | 285,548 | 4,341,959 | 1,160,489 |
| AL... | 29,747 | 6,672 | 23,075 | 19,212 | 5,908 | 7,115 | 421 | 2,000 | 1,616 | 165 | 505 | 15 | 29 | (NA) | (NA) | 573 | 338 | 321 | 3,541 | 45,076 | 8,667 |
| AK.. | 12,360 | 2,038 | 10,322 | 8,759 | 1,619 | 2,231 | 167 | 27 | 1,290 | 117 | 332 | 14 | 164 | (NA) | (NA) | 695 | 182 | 233 | 1,330 | 74,150 | 5,954 |
| AZ.. | 41,770 | 10,904 | 30,866 | 26,569 | 5,353 | 13,906 | 2,561 | 53 | 1,450 | 220 | 1,035 | 79 | 69 | (NA) | 1 | 727 | 637 | 30 | 4,267 | 58,741 | 14,400 |
| AR.. | 22,882 | 5,883 | 16,999 | 15,063 | 3,330 | 6,980 | 295 | 1,022 | 1,183 | 118 | 429 | 71 | 14 | (Z) | 9 | 658 | 131 | (NA) | 1,936 | 34,073 | 4,829 |
| CA.. | 327,898 | 103,512 | 224,386 | 173,735 | 34,785 | 79,810 | 1,874 | 10,969 | 7,654 | 1,902 | 9,382 | 520 | 262 | 484 | 561 | 7,969 | 6,994 | 1,353 | 49,298 | 654,911 | 151,308 |
| CO... | 34,283 | 7,311 | 26,972 | 21,475 | 6,462 | 7,717 | 499 | 914 | 1,369 | 226 | 896 | 94 | 169 | 3 | 17 | 948 | 848 | 13 | 5,483 | 73,261 | 16,687 |
| CT... | 31,919 | 5,438 | 26,481 | 21,208 | 4,127 | 7,404 | 811 | 1,396 | 1,331 | 239 | 684 | 52 | 249 | (NA) | 98 | 1,518 | 1,492 | 759 | 4,514 | 46,950 | 37,025 |
| DE... | 9,400 | 1,512 | 7,888 | 7,050 | 1,712 | 2,446 | 439 | 46 | 598 | 133 | 308 | 52 | 76 | (NA) | 43 | 514 | 198 | 137 | 701 | 15,267 | 5,045 |
| FL... | 87,924 | 20,408 | 67,516 | 58,362 | 11,195 | 25,597 | 3,613 | 957 | 6,856 | 566 | 2,309 | 147 | 234 | (NA) | 148 | 2,300 | 995 | 262 | 8,893 | 215,699 | 33,469 |
| GA... | 47,487 | 11,836 | 35,651 | 29,193 | 7,809 | 11,578 | 1,226 | 1,046 | 2,566 | 404 | 1,194 | 226 | 289 | 9 | 12 | 909 | 635 | 86 | 6,373 | 95,924 | 13,131 |
| HI.... | 12,192 | 135 | 12,057 | 10,672 | 3,386 | 2,758 | 516 | 626 | 454 | 39 | 217 | 63 | 160 | (NA) | (NA) | 555 | 121 | (NA) | 1,385 | 22,383 | 9,217 |
| ID.... | 9,225 | 2,277 | 6,948 | 5,734 | 1,182 | 2,427 | 149 | 48 | 520 | 63 | 259 | 29 | 101 | (NA) | (NA) | 378 | 155 | 120 | 1,094 | 23,793 | 3,543 |
| IL.... | 77,826 | 18,109 | 59,717 | 45,341 | 8,195 | 19,529 | 1,665 | 1,526 | 6,047 | 381 | 1,056 | 74 | 203 | 11 | 22 | 1,188 | 3,236 | (NA) | 14,376 | 156,686 | 65,792 |
| IN.... | 39,223 | 9,712 | 29,511 | 26,629 | 7,622 | 12,654 | 542 | -54 | 1,705 | 218 | 672 | 65 | 398 | 1 | 6 | 701 | 979 | (Z) | 2,882 | 59,778 | 22,471 |
| IA.... | 23,381 | 5,471 | 17,910 | 15,190 | 3,459 | 6,380 | 133 | 1,782 | 1,506 | 98 | 294 | 28 | 26 | 1 | 3 | 552 | 206 | 200 | 2,520 | 42,462 | 5,956 |
| KS.... | 18,665 | 4,800 | 13,865 | 11,973 | 2,936 | 4,148 | 148 | 2,019 | 1,113 | 96 | 310 | 39 | 96 | (NA) | (NA) | 437 | 174 | (NA) | 1,892 | 23,302 | 9,538 |
| KY.... | 35,147 | 4,780 | 30,367 | 25,939 | 6,111 | 11,165 | 364 | 1,857 | 2,271 | 224 | 613 | 123 | 287 | (NA) | 29 | 1,111 | 654 | 31 | 4,396 | 39,481 | 14,453 |
| LA.... | 31,219 | 5,766 | 25,453 | 20,990 | 5,120 | 8,627 | 492 | 461 | 1,541 | 257 | 498 | 292 | 117 | (NA) | (NA) | 918 | 880 | 9 | 4,453 | 59,262 | 17,913 |
| ME... | 9,330 | 1,289 | 8,041 | 7,020 | 1,063 | 3,333 | 222 | 79 | 692 | 90 | 167 | 8 | 167 | (NA) | (NA) | 376 | 183 | 24 | 997 | 18,568 | 4,845 |
| MD... | 43,759 | 9,398 | 34,360 | 29,027 | 5,788 | 11,931 | 1,341 | 549 | 2,371 | 520 | 1,474 | 96 | 372 | 160 | 25 | 1,505 | 1,147 | 990 | 4,343 | 69,648 | 27,871 |
| MA... | 63,569 | 9,081 | 54,488 | 44,568 | 7,221 | 19,875 | 1,848 | 551 | 2,723 | 827 | 1,119 | 187 | 1,208 | 246 | 10 | 1,877 | 2,885 | 3,256 | 6,664 | 90,985 | 76,861 |
| MI.... | 70,110 | 20,818 | 49,292 | 40,698 | 11,248 | 15,736 | 1,472 | 3,789 | 1,308 | 458 | 1,871 | 126 | 637 | (NA) | 5 | 883 | 1,667 | 825 | 7,769 | 99,516 | 33,745 |
| MN... | 46,595 | 13,144 | 33,451 | 27,627 | 6,062 | 14,146 | 418 | 303 | 2,145 | 333 | 549 | 220 | 116 | 161 | 15 | 1,106 | 592 | 471 | 5,353 | 78,477 | 16,213 |
| MS... | 22,108 | 5,252 | 16,856 | 13,931 | 3,019 | 6,227 | 315 | 1,439 | 955 | 120 | 294 | 44 | 36 | (NA) | (NA) | 379 | 263 | 279 | 2,646 | 32,635 | 7,283 |
| MO... | 32,403 | 6,173 | 26,230 | 21,700 | 4,097 | 8,663 | 1,834 | 1,992 | 1,235 | 231 | 775 | 83 | 214 | (NA) | 2 | 549 | 770 | (NA) | 4,530 | 85,170 | 19,103 |
| MT... | 7,084 | 1,094 | 5,990 | 4,945 | 1,012 | 1,697 | 215 | 70 | 629 | 38 | 212 | 17 | 26 | (NA) | (NA) | 424 | 111 | 100 | 945 | 18,743 | 3,052 |
| NE... | 10,942 | 2,418 | 8,524 | 7,784 | 2,326 | 2,595 | 510 | 179 | 892 | 75 | 363 | 49 | 2 | 4 | 11 | 233 | 60 | (NA) | 740 | 19,913 | 1,951 |
| NV... | 15,229 | 4,429 | 10,800 | 8,171 | 1,930 | 3,871 | 229 | 248 | 620 | 82 | 277 | 18 | 21 | (NA) | 5 | 299 | 127 | 51 | 2,579 | 39,695 | 3,222 |
| NH... | 7,611 | 461 | 7,150 | 5,853 | 1,207 | 2,328 | 152 | 55 | 421 | 62 | 122 | 25 | 113 | 18 | 30 | 274 | 329 | 535 | 762 | 13,973 | 7,869 |
| NJ.... | 72,065 | 11,672 | 60,393 | 44,262 | 10,591 | 16,682 | 1,336 | 2,258 | 3,176 | 518 | 1,348 | 226 | 441 | 3 | 5 | 1,758 | 2,179 | 2,992 | 13,139 | 115,619 | 66,722 |
| NM... | 20,030 | 4,986 | 15,044 | 12,735 | 2,652 | 5,629 | 464 | 1,153 | 677 | 138 | 474 | 57 | 52 | (NA) | (Z) | 605 | 298 | (NA) | 2,309 | 52,199 | 6,952 |
| NY... | 194,243 | 61,640 | 132,603 | 97,888 | 12,909 | 54,406 | 3,027 | 5,274 | 4,456 | 813 | 3,247 | 628 | 350 | (NA) | 41 | 5,041 | 4,069 | 13,117 | 21,599 | 362,347 | 137,480 |
| NC... | 53,398 | 12,859 | 40,539 | 34,441 | 9,717 | 11,586 | 1,010 | 2,153 | 3,638 | 713 | 1,257 | 169 | 295 | 1 | 11 | 1,607 | 578 | 181 | 5,916 | 116,224 | 16,919 |

See footnotes at end of table.

# Table 492. State Governments—Expenditures and Debt by State: 2016-Continued.

See headnote on page 317.

| State | Total expenditures | Inter-govern-mental | Direct expenditures Total | Direct general expenditures Total[1] | Educa-tion | Public welfare | Health | Hospi-tals | High-ways | Police protec-tion | Correc-tions | Parks and recre-ation | Hous-ing and com-munity devel-opment | Sewer-age | Solid waste man-age-ment | Gov-ern-men-tal admin-istra-tion | Inter-est on gen-eral debt | Utility and liquor store | Insur-ance trust | Cash and security holdings | Total debt out-stand-ing |
|---|---|---|---|---|---|---|---|---|---|---|---|---|---|---|---|---|---|---|---|---|---|
| ND.. | 8,154 | 2,112 | 6,042 | 5,205 | 1,313 | 1,540 | 259 | 27 | 1,017 | 27 | 101 | 35 | 34 | (NA) | 3 | 197 | 79 | 90 | 747 | 28,849 | 2,356 |
| OH.. | 86,699 | 18,552 | 68,147 | 50,133 | 10,629 | 23,462 | 1,970 | 3,761 | 3,454 | 322 | 1,537 | 192 | 249 | (NA) | 29 | 1,900 | 1,282 | 814 | 17,200 | 216,937 | 33,165 |
| OK.. | 24,746 | 4,459 | 20,287 | 16,565 | 4,726 | 6,536 | 846 | 208 | 1,740 | 229 | 570 | 81 | 165 | (NA) | (Z) | 694 | 345 | 903 | 2,819 | 44,432 | 8,703 |
| OR.. | 33,939 | 5,552 | 28,387 | 22,594 | 4,199 | 10,203 | 574 | 2,281 | 1,152 | 200 | 712 | 68 | 106 | 2 | 7 | 1,389 | 461 | 401 | 5,393 | 91,102 | 13,356 |
| PA... | 96,292 | 20,051 | 76,242 | 62,259 | 12,035 | 26,118 | 2,226 | 4,364 | 7,794 | 1,012 | 2,048 | 313 | 77 | 18 | 43 | 2,722 | 1,506 | 1,819 | 12,163 | 123,378 | 47,099 |
| RI.... | 8,566 | 1,237 | 7,330 | 5,895 | 1,047 | 2,613 | 182 | 67 | 305 | 81 | 202 | 46 | 92 | 52 | 50 | 389 | 439 | 163 | 1,272 | 16,650 | 9,052 |
| SC... | 31,607 | 6,394 | 25,213 | 20,222 | 5,715 | 7,330 | 1,096 | 1,804 | 1,470 | 174 | 501 | 117 | 153 | (NA) | (NA) | 537 | 369 | 1,568 | 3,423 | 44,008 | 16,228 |
| SD... | 5,071 | 775 | 4,296 | 3,758 | 888 | 1,044 | 181 | 23 | 656 | 44 | 125 | 41 | 42 | (NA) | (NA) | 208 | 112 | (NA) | 539 | 15,528 | 3,366 |
| TN... | 32,337 | 7,618 | 24,719 | 22,099 | 4,804 | 11,381 | 583 | 399 | 1,375 | 253 | 709 | 95 | 254 | 1 | 7 | 856 | 266 | 1 | 2,619 | 53,132 | 6,076 |
| TX... | 145,590 | 31,763 | 113,827 | 95,917 | 25,602 | 36,544 | 2,472 | 7,638 | 9,297 | 1,038 | 3,708 | 207 | 39 | 20 | 65 | 2,053 | 1,516 | 10 | 17,899 | 350,719 | 49,357 |
| UT... | 19,285 | 3,512 | 15,773 | 13,728 | 4,935 | 3,382 | 341 | 1,700 | 755 | 148 | 343 | 47 | 91 | (NA) | (Z) | 604 | 240 | 258 | 1,788 | 33,763 | 7,014 |
| VT... | 6,728 | 1,772 | 4,957 | 4,518 | 1,070 | 1,770 | 387 | 20 | 394 | 81 | 137 | 19 | 89 | 2 | 5 | 168 | 103 | 61 | 378 | 7,851 | 2,492 |
| VA.... | 52,932 | 12,467 | 40,465 | 34,882 | 8,797 | 10,595 | 966 | 4,753 | 3,621 | 347 | 1,264 | 121 | 161 | 42 | 1 | 1,392 | 1,105 | 713 | 4,871 | 96,237 | 28,628 |
| WA... | 52,910 | 11,874 | 41,035 | 33,810 | 8,912 | 12,653 | 1,107 | 2,724 | 2,073 | 287 | 1,040 | 86 | 87 | (NA) | 10 | 1,164 | 1,440 | 239 | 6,987 | 102,579 | 33,060 |
| WV... | 14,543 | 2,385 | 12,158 | 10,401 | 2,257 | 4,428 | 230 | 167 | 1,152 | 84 | 301 | 52 | 20 | (NA) | 9 | 482 | 286 | 88 | 1,669 | 21,483 | 7,224 |
| WI.... | 38,231 | 9,032 | 29,198 | 23,832 | 5,431 | 10,311 | 176 | 2,156 | 1,100 | 142 | 1,055 | 58 | 20 | 8 | 6 | 717 | 929 | 40 | 5,326 | 111,056 | 23,052 |
| WY... | 6,454 | 1,868 | 4,587 | 3,609 | 787 | 825 | 256 | 5 | 485 | 48 | 144 | 24 | 8 | (NA) | 4 | 322 | 35 | 151 | 827 | 29,341 | 776 |

NA Not available or not comparable. Z Less than $500,000. [1] Includes other direct general expenditures not shown separately.

Source: U.S. Census Bureau, Federal, State, and Local Governments, Government Finance Statistics, "Annual Surveys of State and Local Government Finances, <https://www.census.gov/programs-surveys/gov-finances.html>, accessed November 2018.

# Table 493. Local Governments—Revenue by State: 2016

[In millions of dollars (1,802,160 represents $1,802,160,000,000). For fiscal year ending in year shown; see text, this section. Minus sign (-) indicates decrease]

| State | Total revenue | General revenue, total | Inter-governmental revenue | General revenue from own sources — Total | Taxes Total [1] | Taxes Property | Taxes Sales and gross receipt | Taxes Individual income | Taxes Other taxes | Current charges and miscellaneous general revenue | Current charges Total [1] | Current charges Education | Current charges Hospitals | Current charges Sewerage | Misc. general revenue Total [1] | Misc. Interest earnings | Misc. Special assessment | Utility revenue | Liquor store revenue | Insurance trust revenue |
|---|---|---|---|---|---|---|---|---|---|---|---|---|---|---|---|---|---|---|---|---|
| U.S... | 1,802,160 | 1,635,605 | 589,857 | 1,045,748 | 676,593 | 487,293 | 117,722 | 32,677 | 30,844 | 369,154 | 289,136 | 23,642 | 87,528 | 54,822 | 80,019 | 14,172 | 8,750 | 150,260 | 1,422 | 14,873 |
| AL. .. | 21,715 | 18,689 | 6,846 | 11,843 | 5,651 | 2,304 | 2,542 | 120 | 685 | 6,193 | 5,261 | 342 | 3,473 | 540 | 932 | 130 | 29 | 2,980 | (NA) | 45 |
| AK. .. | 5,602 | 5,194 | 2,294 | 2,899 | 1,785 | 1,406 | 337 | (NA) | 42 | 1,115 | 939 | 25 | 386 | 115 | 176 | 48 | 9 | 394 | 6 | 8 |
| AZ. .. | 29,448 | 24,503 | 9,153 | 15,350 | 10,067 | 6,392 | 3,237 | (NA) | 437 | 5,283 | 4,058 | 470 | 816 | 916 | 1,225 | 372 | 52 | 4,879 | (NA) | 66 |
| AR. .. | 10,335 | 9,331 | 5,267 | 4,064 | 2,374 | 1,007 | 1,331 | (NA) | 36 | 1,691 | 1,172 | 158 | 173 | 298 | 518 | 162 | 25 | 982 | (NA) | 21 |
| CA. .. | 305,048 | 274,198 | 120,826 | 153,372 | 83,574 | 58,753 | 18,821 | (NA) | 6,000 | 69,798 | 55,789 | 2,204 | 15,994 | 7,606 | 14,009 | 2,662 | 1,674 | 26,913 | (NA) | 3,936 |
| CO. .. | 30,712 | 27,895 | 7,690 | 20,205 | 12,763 | 7,880 | 4,334 | (NA) | 548 | 7,442 | 5,415 | 506 | 1,242 | 894 | 2,028 | 281 | 313 | 2,716 | (NA) | 100 |
| CT. .. | 18,765 | 17,793 | 5,485 | 12,308 | 10,660 | 10,501 | (NA) | (NA) | 158 | 1,648 | 1,189 | 119 | (NA) | 446 | 460 | 66 | 36 | 783 | (NA) | 190 |
| DE. .. | 3,554 | 3,069 | 1,450 | 1,619 | 1,010 | 820 | 16 | 58 | 111 | 609 | 407 | 13 | (NA) | 165 | 202 | 18 | 26 | 467 | (NA) | 19 |
| DC. .. | 14,626 | 13,610 | 4,484 | 9,126 | 7,419 | 2,419 | 1,784 | 1,908 | 751 | 1,708 | 797 | 38 | 147 | 300 | 911 | 61 | (Z) | 1,034 | (NA) | -18 |
| FL. ... | 98,286 | 88,214 | 23,974 | 64,240 | 34,207 | 26,098 | 6,019 | (NA) | 2,090 | 30,033 | 21,981 | 1,913 | 7,092 | 3,432 | 8,052 | 1,094 | 2,863 | 9,540 | (NA) | 532 |
| GA. .. | 44,146 | 39,202 | 12,657 | 26,544 | 16,289 | 10,996 | 4,825 | (NA) | 468 | 10,256 | 8,602 | 519 | 3,827 | 1,561 | 1,654 | 272 | 45 | 4,820 | (NA) | 124 |
| HI. ... | 4,191 | 3,750 | 613 | 3,137 | 2,320 | 1,629 | 450 | (NA) | 241 | 817 | 711 | (NA) | (NA) | 488 | 105 | 21 | 16 | 441 | (NA) | (NA) |
| ID. ... | 5,918 | 5,674 | 2,344 | 3,330 | 1,697 | 1,586 | 44 | (NA) | 67 | 1,633 | 1,384 | 78 | 550 | 250 | 249 | 45 | 27 | 244 | (NA) | (Z) |
| IL. ... | 73,285 | 67,096 | 22,199 | 44,897 | 33,668 | 27,150 | 5,604 | (NA) | 914 | 11,229 | 8,383 | 1,272 | 1,028 | 1,541 | 2,847 | 333 | 405 | 5,160 | (NA) | 1,029 |
| IN. ... | 30,573 | 27,819 | 10,747 | 17,072 | 8,102 | 6,407 | 218 | 1,321 | 156 | 8,970 | 7,336 | 337 | 4,381 | 1,719 | 1,633 | 153 | 17 | 2,710 | (NA) | 43 |
| IA. ... | 17,220 | 16,078 | 6,058 | 10,020 | 5,732 | 4,954 | 580 | 103 | 96 | 4,287 | 3,632 | 517 | 1,756 | 596 | 655 | 95 | 21 | 1,141 | (NA) | 1 |
| KS. ... | 14,975 | 13,409 | 5,116 | 8,293 | 5,010 | 3,667 | 1,216 | 2 | 125 | 3,284 | 2,348 | 410 | 874 | 437 | 936 | 185 | 122 | 1,539 | (NA) | 28 |
| KY. ... | 15,038 | 13,213 | 5,187 | 8,026 | 5,179 | 2,860 | 685 | 1,358 | 94 | 2,847 | 2,229 | 106 | 637 | 645 | 618 | 287 | 11 | 1,805 | (NA) | 21 |
| LA. ... | 22,210 | 20,969 | 6,783 | 14,186 | 8,909 | 4,093 | 4,611 | (NA) | 206 | 5,277 | 4,049 | 56 | 2,256 | 451 | 1,229 | 317 | 12 | 1,219 | (NA) | 21 |
| ME. ... | 5,160 | 5,027 | 1,463 | 3,564 | 2,823 | 2,790 | 10 | (NA) | 23 | 741 | 599 | 39 | 106 | 174 | 141 | 22 | 7 | 133 | (NA) | (NA) |
| MD. ... | 29,302 | 27,858 | 8,059 | 19,799 | 15,416 | 8,571 | 826 | 5,193 | 826 | 4,383 | 3,479 | 518 | 41 | 1,142 | 904 | 103 | 52 | 905 | (NA) | 244 |
| MA. ... | 35,059 | 31,357 | 10,422 | 20,935 | 16,865 | 16,085 | 400 | (NA) | 379 | 4,070 | 3,132 | 381 | 307 | 1,271 | 938 | 61 | 12 | 2,982 | 295 | 720 |
| MI. ... | 46,948 | 43,823 | 20,751 | 23,072 | 13,113 | 12,005 | 276 | 494 | 338 | 9,959 | 7,906 | 1,096 | 723 | 1,959 | 2,054 | 305 | 211 | 2,721 | (NA) | 405 |
| MN. ... | 31,872 | 29,230 | 12,921 | 16,310 | 8,461 | 7,809 | 363 | (NA) | 289 | 7,849 | 5,631 | 533 | 1,855 | 881 | 2,218 | 616 | 430 | 2,245 | 318 | 79 |
| MS. ... | 13,101 | 12,237 | 5,052 | 7,184 | 3,125 | 2,923 | 115 | (NA) | 87 | 4,059 | 3,600 | 337 | 2,488 | 274 | 459 | 67 | 8 | 865 | (NA) | (NA) |
| MO. ... | 26,108 | 23,444 | 7,123 | 16,321 | 10,184 | 5,886 | 3,230 | 390 | 603 | 6,136 | 4,786 | 621 | 1,795 | 1,013 | 1,350 | 255 | 97 | 2,630 | (NA) | 34 |
| MT. ... | 3,903 | 3,762 | 1,546 | 2,216 | 1,344 | 1,297 | 9 | (NA) | 38 | 872 | 635 | 75 | 87 | 119 | 237 | 44 | 76 | 141 | (NA) | 1 |
| NE. ... | 14,387 | 9,775 | 2,751 | 7,024 | 4,587 | 3,642 | 482 | 9 | 464 | 2,436 | 1,934 | 250 | 533 | 280 | 502 | 93 | 45 | 4,532 | (NA) | 80 |
| NV. ... | 14,810 | 13,582 | 5,719 | 7,864 | 4,546 | 2,643 | 1,519 | (NA) | 385 | 3,317 | 2,462 | 34 | 677 | 495 | 855 | 124 | 93 | 1,228 | (NA) | (NA) |
| NH. ... | 6,134 | 6,013 | 1,550 | 4,463 | 3,790 | 3,753 | 3 | (NA) | 34 | 673 | 487 | 49 | (NA) | 132 | 187 | 23 | 3 | 120 | (NA) | (Z) |
| NJ. ... | 49,773 | 48,642 | 13,231 | 35,411 | 28,691 | 28,074 | 195 | (NA) | 422 | 6,720 | 4,856 | 1,156 | 250 | 1,722 | 1,864 | 203 | 2 | 1,126 | (NA) | 5 |
| NM. ... | 8,962 | 8,337 | 4,303 | 4,034 | 2,652 | 1,496 | 1,086 | (NA) | 71 | 1,382 | 971 | 101 | 174 | 200 | 412 | 108 | 28 | 624 | (NA) | (NA) |
| NY. ... | 195,377 | 182,821 | 58,367 | 124,453 | 96,313 | 55,176 | 18,637 | 11,594 | 4,474 | 28,140 | 21,273 | 1,237 | 5,432 | 2,913 | 6,867 | 877 | 130 | 7,759 | (NA) | 4,797 |

See footnotes at end of table.

# Table 493. Local Governments—Revenue by State: 2016-Continued.

See headnote on page 319.

| State | Total revenue | General revenue, total | Inter-govern-mental revenue | General revenue from own sources Total | Taxes Total¹ | Property | Sales and gross receipt | Indi-vidual income | Other taxes | Current charges and miscel-laneous general revenue | Current charges Total¹ | Educa-tion | Hospi-tals | Sewer-age | Miscellaneous general revenue Total¹ | Interest earn-ings | Special assess-ment | Utility rev-enue | Liquor store rev-enue | Insur-ance trust rev-enue |
|---|---|---|---|---|---|---|---|---|---|---|---|---|---|---|---|---|---|---|---|---|
| NC.. | 49,278 | 44,013 | 17,163 | 26,850 | 13,604 | 9,906 | 3,245 | (NA) | 453 | 13,246 | 11,591 | 553 | 7,708 | 1,392 | 1,655 | 170 | 15 | 4,464 | 783 | 18 |
| ND.. | 4,840 | 4,574 | 2,415 | 2,159 | 1,300 | 976 | 290 | (NA) | 35 | 858 | 435 | 68 | (Z) | 66 | 423 | 28 | 131 | 255 | (NA) | 11 |
| OH.. | 56,790 | 53,651 | 19,104 | 34,547 | 23,299 | 14,690 | 2,615 | 5,153 | 577 | 11,249 | 8,461 | 1,228 | 1,447 | 2,401 | 2,788 | 541 | 229 | 3,084 | (NA) | 55 |
| OK.. | 13,912 | 12,623 | 4,215 | 8,407 | 5,067 | 2,741 | 2,227 | (NA) | 99 | 3,340 | 2,588 | 315 | 975 | 416 | 752 | 73 | 34 | 1,240 | (NA) | 49 |
| OR.. | 21,125 | 19,524 | 7,571 | 11,954 | 7,377 | 5,881 | 541 | (Z) | 875 | 4,577 | 3,578 | 517 | 333 | 1,131 | 999 | 270 | 84 | 1,584 | (NA) | 16 |
| PA.. | 66,154 | 62,035 | 24,688 | 37,347 | 27,283 | 18,848 | 1,357 | 4,984 | 1,635 | 10,064 | 7,677 | 871 | 26 | 2,836 | 2,388 | 797 | 93 | 3,026 | (NA) | 1,094 |
| RI.. | 4,833 | 4,563 | 1,365 | 3,198 | 2,616 | 2,552 | 29 | (NA) | 36 | 581 | 438 | 43 | (NA) | 127 | 144 | 14 | 4 | 218 | (NA) | 53 |
| SC.. | 23,270 | 21,442 | 6,379 | 15,063 | 7,482 | 5,735 | 815 | (NA) | 931 | 7,581 | 6,540 | 247 | 4,662 | 683 | 1,041 | 171 | 56 | 1,807 | (NA) | 22 |
| SD.. | 3,675 | 3,283 | 986 | 2,297 | 1,645 | 1,201 | 405 | (NA) | 39 | 651 | 532 | 93 | 85 | 101 | 119 | 18 | 18 | 367 | 21 | 4 |
| TN.. | 32,895 | 23,829 | 8,014 | 15,814 | 8,704 | 5,560 | 2,761 | (NA) | 383 | 7,111 | 5,915 | 468 | 2,864 | 973 | 1,196 | 260 | 114 | 8,934 | (NA) | 133 |
| TX.. | 137,223 | 123,337 | 36,315 | 87,021 | 60,048 | 49,167 | 9,826 | (NA) | 1,055 | 26,973 | 21,220 | 2,259 | 5,718 | 3,847 | 5,753 | 1,561 | 397 | 13,802 | (NA) | 84 |
| UT.. | 12,463 | 10,428 | 3,688 | 6,740 | 4,315 | 3,102 | 1,091 | (NA) | 122 | 2,425 | 1,761 | 177 | 73 | 398 | 664 | 50 | 52 | 2,035 | (NA) | (Z) |
| VT.. | 2,986 | 2,735 | 1,816 | 920 | 594 | 560 | 23 | (NA) | 11 | 325 | 237 | 29 | (NA) | 75 | 89 | 11 | 6 | 245 | (NA) | 6 |
| VA.. | 39,233 | 37,124 | 13,428 | 23,696 | 17,153 | 12,971 | 2,834 | (NA) | 1,348 | 6,543 | 5,160 | 288 | 345 | 1,620 | 1,382 | 263 | 57 | 1,941 | (NA) | 168 |
| WA.. | 47,101 | 40,174 | 14,471 | 25,704 | 14,491 | 8,396 | 5,031 | (NA) | 1,064 | 11,213 | 9,371 | 355 | 2,647 | 2,491 | 1,842 | 215 | 456 | 6,804 | (NA) | 122 |
| WV.. | 5,498 | 5,230 | 1,925 | 3,306 | 2,034 | 1,667 | 118 | (NA) | 250 | 1,272 | 1,023 | 34 | 331 | 275 | 249 | 35 | 25 | 240 | (NA) | 28 |
| WI.. | (S) | (S) | (S) | (S) | (S) | (S) | (S) | (S) | (NA) | (S) | (S) | (S) | (S) | (S) | (S) | (S) | (S) | (S) | (S) | (S) |
| WY.. | 5,386 | 5,150 | 2,140 | 3,010 | 1,329 | 1,061 | 214 | (NA) | 55 | 1,680 | 1,485 | 71 | 1,137 | 76 | 196 | 26 | 16 | 236 | (NA) | (NA) |

S Figure does not meet publication standards. NA Not available or not comparable. Z Less than $500,000. ¹ Includes corporation income, not shown separately.

Source: U.S. Census Bureau, Federal, State, and Local Governments, Government Finance Statistics, "Annual Surveys of State and Local Government Finances," <https://www.census.gov/programs-surveys/gov-finances.html>, accessed December 2018.

# Table 494. Local Governments—Expenditures and Debt by State: 2016

[In millions of dollars (1,830,588 represents $1,830,588,000,000). For fiscal year ending in year shown; see text, this section]

| State | Total expendi- tures [1] | Total [1] | Direct expenditures — Direct general expenditures — Total | Educa- tion | Public welfare | Hospi- tals | Health | High- ways | Police protec- tion | Correc- tions | Parks and recre- ation | Housing and com- munity devel- opment | Sewer- age | Solid waste manage- ment | Govern- mental admini- stration | Interest on general debt | Other | Utility expen- ditures | Insur- ance trust expen- ditures | Debt out- stand- ing |
|---|---|---|---|---|---|---|---|---|---|---|---|---|---|---|---|---|---|---|---|---|
| U.S... | 1,830,588 | 1,814,250 | 1,563,735 | 661,006 | 55,729 | 104,014 | 52,461 | 70,092 | 94,172 | 28,985 | 36,407 | 41,469 | 54,381 | 23,248 | 79,753 | 60,002 | 202,014 | 196,851 | 52,428 | 1,842,231 |
| AL.... | 22,134 | 22,111 | 18,899 | 7,553 | 43 | 3,931 | 402 | 805 | 1,086 | 218 | 374 | 472 | 387 | 280 | 971 | 638 | 1,741 | 2,977 | 235 | 20,201 |
| AK.... | 5,529 | 5,529 | 4,958 | 1,922 | 3 | 435 | 121 | 293 | 253 | 6 | 103 | 215 | 97 | 158 | 299 | 101 | 951 | 534 | 33 | 3,330 |
| AZ. .. | 28,403 | 28,155 | 22,203 | 9,158 | 116 | 946 | 290 | 1,008 | 2,041 | 649 | 580 | 379 | 726 | 423 | 1,669 | 953 | 3,265 | 5,508 | 444 | 34,394 |
| AR.... | 10,312 | 10,292 | 9,240 | 5,088 | 16 | 191 | 63 | 552 | 573 | 169 | 203 | 172 | 319 | 214 | 430 | 348 | 900 | 991 | 62 | 11,058 |
| CA. .. | 307,409 | 306,739 | 253,342 | 87,796 | 18,649 | 15,953 | 18,325 | 9,491 | 15,668 | 6,086 | 5,928 | 7,901 | 8,254 | 2,620 | 13,007 | 9,769 | 33,894 | 40,714 | 12,684 | 282,518 |
| CO... | 30,211 | 30,178 | 25,498 | 9,613 | 786 | 1,440 | 360 | 1,514 | 1,647 | 417 | 1,119 | 723 | 953 | 129 | 1,767 | 1,271 | 3,759 | 4,253 | 426 | 36,238 |
| CT... | 19,175 | 19,170 | 17,218 | 9,436 | 113 | (NA) | 158 | 720 | 998 | (NA) | 237 | 721 | 642 | 201 | 637 | 390 | 2,965 | 969 | 983 | 11,314 |
| DE... | 3,527 | 3,525 | 3,042 | 1,950 | 1 | (NA) | 39 | 160 | 215 | (NA) | 36 | 72 | 178 | 26 | 148 | 71 | 147 | 403 | 80 | 2,543 |
| DC... | 16,585 | 16,585 | 12,762 | 2,757 | 3,785 | 270 | 456 | 355 | 593 | 145 | 328 | 679 | 593 | 118 | 699 | 562 | 1,422 | 3,314 | 509 | 14,521 |
| FL.... | 99,992 | 99,713 | 86,499 | 30,324 | 1,131 | 7,742 | 1,320 | 2,841 | 7,283 | 1,940 | 2,834 | 2,040 | 3,502 | 2,389 | 4,688 | 3,041 | 15,424 | 10,680 | 2,534 | 105,615 |
| GA... | 46,578 | 46,537 | 39,504 | 18,917 | 165 | 3,758 | 1,021 | 1,568 | 2,314 | 725 | 891 | 945 | 1,184 | 642 | 2,781 | 787 | 3,805 | 5,970 | 1,063 | 44,808 |
| HI. ... | 4,160 | 4,160 | 2,955 | (Z) | 97 | (NA) | 29 | 318 | 420 | (NA) | 242 | 88 | 409 | 227 | 301 | 201 | 624 | 1,205 | (NA) | 6,167 |
| ID..... | 5,560 | 5,558 | 5,305 | 2,181 | 29 | 659 | 107 | 322 | 394 | 84 | 123 | 46 | 216 | 163 | 334 | 86 | 561 | 251 | 2 | 2,430 |
| IL..... | 80,116 | 80,116 | 66,093 | 29,538 | 651 | 2,278 | 868 | 3,517 | 4,836 | 796 | 2,557 | 1,765 | 2,120 | 571 | 4,127 | 3,470 | 8,998 | 8,515 | 5,508 | 85,874 |
| IN.... | 28,412 | 28,408 | 25,445 | 9,967 | 57 | 5,134 | 242 | 1,005 | 1,037 | 487 | 497 | 479 | 990 | 285 | 1,300 | 910 | 3,054 | 2,883 | 80 | 28,375 |
| IA.... | 17,051 | 17,006 | 15,704 | 7,536 | 84 | 1,781 | 309 | 1,076 | 681 | 150 | 302 | 139 | 508 | 282 | 584 | 407 | 1,867 | 1,298 | 4 | 12,568 |
| KS.... | 14,900 | 14,899 | 13,202 | 6,452 | 35 | 909 | 261 | 856 | 703 | 205 | 291 | 198 | 363 | 166 | 672 | 571 | 1,519 | 1,590 | 106 | 19,693 |
| KY.... | 15,099 | 15,088 | 12,940 | 6,439 | 44 | 573 | 472 | 496 | 488 | 291 | 223 | 165 | 678 | 197 | 587 | 748 | 1,538 | 2,076 | 72 | 24,376 |
| LA.... | 22,064 | 22,040 | 20,353 | 7,923 | 73 | 2,636 | 232 | 853 | 1,357 | 640 | 446 | 638 | 778 | 352 | 1,250 | 644 | 2,528 | 1,491 | 196 | 19,167 |
| ME.... | 4,926 | 4,923 | 4,741 | 2,402 | 46 | 104 | 35 | 327 | 205 | 97 | 88 | 117 | 191 | 117 | 230 | 101 | 680 | 182 | (NA) | 2,965 |
| MD... | 31,829 | 31,823 | 28,326 | 12,959 | 157 | 52 | 521 | 1,030 | 2,129 | 425 | 1,081 | 1,078 | 1,180 | 977 | 1,416 | 874 | 4,447 | 1,706 | 1,526 | 25,022 |
| MA... | 35,573 | 34,757 | 30,101 | 15,155 | 96 | 867 | 146 | 1,082 | 1,675 | (NA) | 306 | 1,553 | 981 | 408 | 1,109 | 520 | 6,203 | 2,795 | 1,862 | 18,141 |
| MI.... | 47,634 | 47,350 | 42,116 | 18,749 | 1,140 | 839 | 2,901 | 2,525 | 2,051 | 651 | 872 | 501 | 2,354 | 493 | 2,272 | 1,502 | 5,266 | 3,428 | 1,806 | 38,762 |
| MN... | 32,232 | 32,160 | 29,330 | 12,230 | 1,494 | 1,827 | 751 | 2,850 | 1,590 | 464 | 892 | 905 | 797 | 343 | 1,421 | 1,019 | 2,746 | 2,415 | 138 | 34,995 |
| MS.... | 13,075 | 13,074 | 12,174 | 5,303 | 27 | 2,436 | 95 | 704 | 622 | 204 | 172 | 238 | 377 | 193 | 642 | 220 | 939 | 900 | (NA) | 6,727 |
| MO... | 27,372 | 27,370 | 23,784 | 10,981 | 265 | 1,848 | 346 | 1,157 | 1,513 | 186 | 660 | 424 | 1,167 | 168 | 1,140 | 822 | 3,107 | 2,795 | 791 | 26,781 |
| MT... | 4,019 | 4,018 | 3,830 | 1,881 | 61 | 95 | 142 | 235 | 253 | 45 | 77 | 57 | 152 | 81 | 241 | 62 | 447 | 187 | 1 | 2,217 |
| NE. .. | 14,508 | 14,504 | 9,642 | 4,953 | 118 | 646 | 61 | 698 | 383 | 137 | 188 | 215 | 320 | 98 | 453 | 261 | 1,110 | 4,488 | 374 | 13,331 |
| NV. ... | 13,746 | 13,736 | 12,329 | 4,203 | 359 | 698 | 148 | 810 | 1,102 | 435 | 575 | 272 | 600 | 24 | 889 | 652 | 1,563 | 1,406 | (NA) | 25,882 |
| NH... | 5,513 | 5,437 | 5,275 | 2,924 | 223 | (NA) | 21 | 293 | 332 | 76 | 73 | 100 | 145 | 107 | 302 | 106 | 572 | 142 | 19 | 2,567 |
| NJ.... | 49,815 | 49,362 | 48,188 | 25,517 | 1,035 | 277 | 363 | 1,501 | 2,927 | 695 | 566 | 925 | 1,578 | 983 | 1,755 | 1,151 | 8,916 | 1,166 | 8 | 33,411 |
| NM... | 8,559 | 8,547 | 7,786 | 3,995 | 93 | 213 | 74 | 304 | 563 | 222 | 264 | 93 | 204 | 231 | 521 | 198 | 812 | 761 | (NA) | 8,362 |
| NY. ... | 205,126 | 194,593 | 166,403 | 65,516 | 11,201 | 11,255 | 3,719 | 7,298 | 9,109 | 3,277 | 2,420 | 5,552 | 3,407 | 2,806 | 4,899 | 7,813 | 28,132 | 15,880 | 12,310 | 219,039 |

See footnotes at end of table.

# Table 494. Local Governments—Expenditures and Debt by State: 2016-Continued.

See headnote on page 321.

| State | Total expendi-tures [1] | Direct expenditures | | | | | | | | | | | | | | | | Utility expen-ditures | Insur-ance trust expen-ditures | Debt out-stand-ing |
| | | Direct general expenditures | | | | | | | | | | | | | | | | | | |
| | | Total [1] | Total | Educa-tion | Public welfare | Hospi-tals | Health | High-ways | Police protec-tion | Correc-tions | Parks and recre-ation | Housing and com-munity devel-opment | Sewer-age | Solid waste manage-ment | Gov-ern-mental admini-stration | Interest on general debt | Other | | | |
|---|---|---|---|---|---|---|---|---|---|---|---|---|---|---|---|---|---|---|---|---|
| NC... | 48,555 | 48,424 | 42,770 | 15,731 | 1,800 | 8,116 | 3,679 | 625 | 2,558 | 566 | 920 | 1,171 | 1,042 | 774 | 1,664 | 1,247 | 2,875 | 4,928 | 53 | 30,321 |
| ND... | 4,764 | 4,751 | 4,372 | 1,873 | 87 | (Z) | 49 | 797 | 181 | 75 | 214 | 59 | 131 | 68 | 190 | 97 | 552 | 348 | 31 | 4,428 |
| OH... | 57,841 | 57,393 | 53,446 | 23,853 | 2,701 | 1,500 | 2,407 | 2,541 | 3,560 | 469 | 1,196 | 1,885 | 2,175 | 464 | 3,462 | 1,504 | 5,728 | 3,783 | 164 | 52,061 |
| OK... | 14,196 | 14,195 | 12,580 | 5,903 | 27 | 944 | 244 | 826 | 836 | 182 | 413 | 280 | 338 | 218 | 719 | 217 | 1,433 | 1,490 | 124 | 10,016 |
| OR... | 21,272 | 21,268 | 18,780 | 8,392 | 236 | 352 | 863 | 939 | 1,115 | 505 | 583 | 545 | 886 | 139 | 1,036 | 819 | 2,369 | 2,304 | 184 | 20,550 |
| PA... | 67,192 | 67,180 | 59,913 | 29,330 | 4,196 | 17 | 3,036 | 2,628 | 2,705 | 1,468 | 722 | 1,762 | 2,298 | 826 | 3,520 | 2,847 | 4,558 | 4,558 | 2,710 | 74,770 |
| RI... | 4,818 | 4,818 | 4,308 | 2,363 | 8 | (NA) | 21 | 119 | 344 | 21 | 51 | 187 | 131 | 54 | 160 | 102 | 748 | 248 | 262 | 2,679 |
| SC... | 22,372 | 22,321 | 20,666 | 8,638 | 30 | 4,779 | 221 | 510 | 1,020 | 254 | 485 | 341 | 533 | 359 | 1,076 | 616 | 1,805 | 1,638 | 17 | 27,385 |
| SD... | 3,672 | 3,672 | 3,234 | 1,568 | 16 | 78 | 37 | 391 | 157 | 55 | 119 | 59 | 108 | 49 | 192 | 74 | 330 | 375 | 46 | 2,402 |
| TN... | 33,064 | 33,062 | 22,899 | 9,174 | 150 | 3,250 | 391 | 885 | 1,602 | 466 | 500 | 551 | 881 | 373 | 1,407 | 908 | 2,361 | 9,375 | 787 | 36,637 |
| TX... | 140,297 | 138,573 | 119,145 | 57,460 | 402 | 10,189 | 2,797 | 4,742 | 6,577 | 2,213 | 2,289 | 1,948 | 4,128 | 1,360 | 5,967 | 7,714 | 11,360 | 17,308 | 2,120 | 229,953 |
| UT... | 11,565 | 11,557 | 9,562 | 4,817 | 182 | 178 | 246 | 385 | 507 | 184 | 433 | 247 | 273 | 149 | 618 | 193 | 1,149 | 1,983 | 13 | 11,416 |
| VT... | 2,819 | 2,818 | 2,513 | 1,608 | 2 | (Z) | 10 | 229 | 107 | (Z) | 40 | 61 | 84 | 32 | 117 | 31 | 190 | 282 | 23 | 1,138 |
| VA.... | 39,737 | 39,711 | 36,005 | 16,304 | 1,505 | 334 | 1,321 | 1,057 | 1,991 | 1,296 | 961 | 818 | 1,645 | 600 | 2,184 | 1,255 | 4,734 | 2,551 | 1,155 | 37,456 |
| WA.... | 46,031 | 45,842 | 36,786 | 14,875 | 200 | 2,882 | 1,316 | 2,113 | 1,668 | 687 | 1,067 | 1,269 | 1,943 | 755 | 1,810 | 1,272 | 4,929 | 8,768 | 288 | 52,025 |
| WV... | 5,902 | 5,898 | 5,515 | 3,102 | 7 | 312 | 59 | 91 | 303 | 53 | 122 | 119 | 318 | 68 | 451 | 97 | 414 | 326 | 57 | 3,479 |
| WI.... | (S) | (S) | (S) | (S) | (S) | (S) | (S) | (S) | (S) | (S) | (S) | (S) | (S) | (S) | (NA) | (S) | (S) | (S) | (S) | (S) |
| WY... | 5,476 | 5,475 | 5,168 | 2,333 | 18 | 1,199 | 52 | 230 | 194 | 70 | 121 | 7 | 79 | 109 | 321 | 22 | 412 | 306 | (NA) | 1,138 |

NA Not available or not comparable. S Figure does not meet publication standards. Z Less than $500,000. [1] Includes other items not shown separately.

Source: U.S. Census Bureau, Federal, State, and Local Governments, Government Finance Statistics, "Annual Surveys of State and Local Government Finances," <https://www.census.gov/programs-surveys/gov-finances.html>, accessed December 2018.

# Table 495. Government Employment and Payrolls by Level of Government: 1982 to 2017

[Employees in thousands (15,841 represents 15,841,000); payroll in millions of dollars (23,173 represents $23,173,000,000). Data through 1992 are for the month of October. Beginning with the 1997 survey, data are for the month of March. Covers both full-time and part-time employees. Local government data are estimates subject to sampling variation; see Appendix III and source]

| Type of government | 1982 | 1987 | 1992 | 1997 | 2000 | 2005 | 2010 | 2015 | 2016 | 2017 |
|---|---|---|---|---|---|---|---|---|---|---|
| **EMPLOYEES (1,000)** | | | | | | | | | | |
| **Total** | **15,841** | **17,212** | **18,745** | **19,540** | **20,876** | **21,725** | **22,607** | **(NA)** | **(NA)** | **(NA)** |
| Federal (civilian) [1] | 2,848 | 3,091 | 3,047 | 2,807 | 2,899 | 2,720 | 3,008 | (NA) | (NA) | (NA) |
| State and local | 12,993 | 14,121 | 15,698 | 16,733 | 17,976 | 19,004 | 19,599 | 19,293 | 19,406 | 19,544 |
| Percent of total | 82 | 82 | 84 | 86 | 86 | 87 | 87 | (NA) | (NA) | (NA) |
| State | 3,744 | 4,116 | 4,595 | 4,733 | 4,877 | 5,078 | 5,326 | 5,344 | 5,368 | 5,400 |
| Local | 9,249 | 10,005 | 11,103 | 12,000 | 13,099 | 13,926 | 14,274 | 13,949 | 14,038 | 14,144 |
| **PAYROLLS (mil. dol.)** | | | | | | | | | | |
| **Total** | **23,173** | **32,669** | **43,120** | **49,156** | **58,166** | **71,599** | **86,643** | **(NA)** | **(NA)** | **(NA)** |
| Federal (civilian) [1] | 5,959 | 7,924 | 9,937 | 9,744 | 11,485 | 13,475 | 16,238 | (NA) | (NA) | (NA) |
| State and local | 17,214 | 24,745 | 33,183 | 39,412 | 46,681 | 58,123 | 70,404 | 75,072 | 77,325 | 80,276 |
| Percent of total | 74 | 76 | 77 | 80 | 80 | 81 | 81 | (NA) | (NA) | (NA) |
| State | 5,022 | 7,263 | 9,828 | 11,413 | 13,279 | 16,062 | 19,579 | 21,568 | 22,149 | 22,920 |
| Local | 12,192 | 17,482 | 23,355 | 27,999 | 33,402 | 42,062 | 50,825 | 53,503 | 55,176 | 57,356 |

NA Not available. [1] Includes employees outside the United States.

Source: U.S. Census Bureau, Census of Governments, Annual Survey of Public Employment and Payroll, "2017 Government Employment and Payroll Tables," <https://www.census.gov/programs-surveys/apes.html>, accessed April 2019.

# Table 496. State and Local Government Employment and Payrolls by Function: 2017

[Employees in thousands (19,544 represents 19,544,000); payroll in millions of dollars (80,276.2 represents $80,276,200,000). See headnote, Table 495]

| Function | Employees (1,000) | | | Payrolls (mil. dol.) | | |
|---|---|---|---|---|---|---|
| | Total | State | Local | Total | State | Local |
| **Total** | **19,544** | **5,400** | **14,144** | **80,276.2** | **22,920.0** | **57,356.2** |
| Financial administration | 445 | 173 | 271 | 2,059.1 | 865.4 | 1,193.7 |
| Other government administration | 411 | 57 | 355 | 1,332.8 | 259.3 | 1,073.5 |
| Judicial & legal | 440 | 180 | 260 | 2,286.7 | 1,013.8 | 1,273.0 |
| Police protection | 986 | 104 | 882 | 5,593.1 | 645.6 | 4,947.5 |
| Fire protection | 442 | – | 442 | 2,310.6 | – | 2,310.6 |
| Corrections | 720 | 448 | 271 | 3,359.3 | 2,084.1 | 1,275.2 |
| Streets & highways | 505 | 214 | 291 | 2,305.4 | 1,044.0 | 1,261.4 |
| Air transportation | 52 | 3 | 49 | 289.4 | 19.6 | 269.8 |
| Water transport/terminals | 13 | 5 | 9 | 84.0 | 28.5 | 55.5 |
| Public welfare | 535 | 247 | 289 | 2,217.2 | 1,004.0 | 1,213.1 |
| Health | 469 | 192 | 277 | 2,091.1 | 902.0 | 1,189.1 |
| Hospitals | 1,088 | 435 | 653 | 5,497.6 | 2,172.8 | 3,324.7 |
| Social insurance administration | 73 | 72 | 1 | 333.2 | 329.5 | 3.7 |
| Solid waste management | 114 | 2 | 111 | 476.7 | 14.5 | 462.2 |
| Sewerage | 130 | 2 | 128 | 629.2 | 12.0 | 617.2 |
| Parks and recreation | 420 | 41 | 380 | 1,002.4 | 128.8 | 873.6 |
| Housing and community development | 109 | 1 | 108 | 498.8 | 3.8 | 495.1 |
| Natural resources | 191 | 147 | 44 | 811.0 | 633.1 | 177.9 |
| Water supply | 181 | 1 | 180 | 886.7 | 4.6 | 882.1 |
| Electric power | 79 | 4 | 75 | 596.3 | 33.2 | 563.0 |
| Gas supply | 12 | – | 12 | 58.5 | – | 58.5 |
| Transit | 254 | 34 | 220 | 1,496.6 | 235.0 | 1,261.6 |
| Elementary and secondary education | 7,810 | 59 | 7,751 | 29,224.0 | 242.3 | 28,981.7 |
| Higher education | 3,281 | 2,695 | 587 | 11,707.3 | 9,902.1 | 1,805.2 |
| Other education | 90 | 90 | – | 396.7 | 396.7 | – |
| Libraries | 183 | 1 | 182 | 473.6 | 2.3 | 471.3 |
| State liquor stores | 13 | 13 | – | 32.9 | 32.9 | – |
| Other and unallocable | 498 | 180 | 318 | 2,226.0 | 910.0 | 1,316.1 |

– Represents or rounds to zero.

Source: U.S. Census Bureau, Census of Governments, Annual Survey of Public Employment and Payroll, "2017 Government Employment and Payroll Tables," <https://www.census.gov/programs-surveys/apes.html>, accessed April 2019.

# Table 497. State and Local Government—Employer Costs Per Hour Worked: 2019

[In dollars. As of March. Based on a sample; see source for details]

| Occupation and industry | Total compensation | Wages and salaries | Benefit cost | | | | | |
|---|---|---|---|---|---|---|---|---|
| | | | Total | Paid leave | Supplemental pay | Insurance | Retirement and savings | Legally required benefits |
| **Total workers** | **50.89** | **31.75** | **19.14** | **3.80** | **0.50** | **6.05** | **6.00** | **2.80** |
| OCCUPATIONAL GROUP | | | | | | | | |
| Management, professional, and related | 60.98 | 39.35 | 21.63 | 4.27 | 0.40 | 6.62 | 7.19 | 3.15 |
| Professional and related | 59.23 | 38.50 | 20.73 | 3.80 | 0.37 | 6.60 | 6.93 | 3.03 |
| Teachers [1] | 66.93 | 44.66 | 22.27 | 3.36 | 0.25 | 7.19 | 8.26 | 3.22 |
| Primary, secondary, and special education school teachers | 66.72 | 43.89 | 22.82 | 3.07 | 0.23 | 7.59 | 8.87 | 3.06 |
| Sales and office | 35.10 | 20.29 | 14.81 | 3.07 | 0.31 | 5.63 | 3.70 | 2.11 |
| Office and administrative support | 35.25 | 20.34 | 14.92 | 3.08 | 0.31 | 5.70 | 3.73 | 2.10 |
| Service | 37.26 | 21.43 | 15.83 | 3.15 | 0.79 | 4.78 | 4.83 | 2.28 |
| INDUSTRY GROUP | | | | | | | | |
| Education and health services | 53.12 | 34.29 | 18.83 | 3.49 | 0.34 | 6.22 | 6.05 | 2.72 |
| Educational services | 54.45 | 35.37 | 19.08 | 3.36 | 0.25 | 6.34 | 6.40 | 2.73 |
| Elementary and secondary schools | 52.88 | 34.34 | 18.54 | 2.77 | 0.22 | 6.32 | 6.65 | 2.58 |
| Junior colleges, colleges, and universities | 58.86 | 38.31 | 20.55 | 5.10 | 0.35 | 6.29 | 5.65 | 3.16 |
| Health care and social assistance | 44.98 | 27.68 | 17.30 | 4.31 | 0.88 | 5.52 | 3.89 | 2.70 |
| Hospitals | 47.65 | 29.88 | 17.77 | 4.57 | 1.06 | 5.49 | 3.80 | 2.86 |
| Public administration | 49.00 | 28.44 | 20.56 | 4.55 | 0.77 | 5.95 | 6.30 | 2.98 |

[1] Includes postsecondary teachers; primary, secondary, and special education teachers; and other teachers and instructors.

Source: U.S. Bureau of Labor Statistics, National Compensation Survey, *Employer Costs for Employee Compensation–March 2019*, June 2019. See also <http://www.bls.gov/ncs/ect/>.

# Table 498. State and Local Government—Full-Time Employment and Salary by Sex and Race/Ethnicity: 1980 to 2017

[2,350 represents 2,350,000. As of June 30. Excludes school systems and educational institutions. Based on reports from state governments (42 in 1980; 49 in 1984 through 1987; and 50 in 1989 through 1991) and a sample of county, municipal, township, and special district jurisdictions employing 15 or more nonelected, nonappointed full-time employees. Beginning 1993, only for state and local governments with 100 or more employees. For definition of median, see Guide to Tabular Presentation]

| Year and occupation | Employment (1,000) | | | | | | Median annual salary ($1,000) | | | | |
|---|---|---|---|---|---|---|---|---|---|---|---|
| | | | | Minority | | | | | | Minority | |
| | Male | Female | White [1] | Total [2] | Black [1] | Hispanic [3] | Male | Female | White [1] | Black [1] | Hispanic [3] |
| 1980 | 2,350 | 1,637 | 3,146 | 842 | 619 | 163 | 15.2 | 11.4 | 13.8 | 11.5 | 12.3 |
| 1985 | 2,789 | 1,952 | 3,563 | 1,179 | 835 | 248 | 22.3 | 17.3 | 20.6 | 17.5 | 19.2 |
| 1986 | 2,797 | 1,982 | 3,549 | 1,230 | 865 | 259 | 23.4 | 18.1 | 21.5 | 18.7 | 20.2 |
| 1987 | 2,818 | 2,031 | 3,600 | 1,249 | 872 | 268 | 24.2 | 18.9 | 22.4 | 19.3 | 21.1 |
| 1989 | 3,030 | 2,227 | 3,863 | 1,394 | 961 | 308 | 26.1 | 20.6 | 24.1 | 20.7 | 22.7 |
| 1990 | 3,071 | 2,302 | 3,918 | 1,456 | 994 | 327 | 27.3 | 21.8 | 25.2 | 22.0 | 23.8 |
| 1991 | 3,110 | 2,349 | 3,965 | 1,494 | 1,011 | 340 | 28.4 | 22.7 | 26.4 | 22.7 | 24.5 |
| 1993 | 2,820 | 2,204 | 3,588 | 1,436 | 948 | 341 | 30.6 | 24.3 | 28.5 | 24.2 | 26.8 |
| 1995 | 2,960 | 2,355 | 3,781 | 1,534 | 993 | 379 | 33.5 | 27.0 | 31.4 | 26.8 | 28.6 |
| 1997 | 2,898 | 2,307 | 3,676 | 1,529 | 973 | 392 | 34.6 | 27.9 | 32.2 | 27.4 | 29.5 |
| 1999 | 2,939 | 2,393 | 3,723 | 1,609 | 1,012 | 417 | 37.0 | 29.9 | 34.8 | 29.6 | 31.2 |
| 2001 | 3,080 | 2,554 | 3,888 | 1,746 | 1,077 | 471 | 39.8 | 32.1 | 37.5 | 31.5 | 33.8 |
| 2003 | 3,134 | 2,610 | 3,919 | 1,826 | 1,097 | 508 | 42.2 | 34.7 | 40.0 | 33.6 | 36.6 |
| 2005 | 3,185 | 2,644 | 3,973 | 1,856 | 1,100 | 532 | 44.1 | 36.4 | 41.5 | 35.3 | 38.9 |
| 2007 | 3,383 | 2,823 | 4,156 | (NA) | (NA) | (NA) | (NA) | (NA) | (NA) | (NA) | (NA) |
| 2009 | 3,239 | 2,742 | 3,976 | 2,004 | 1,145 | 601 | 50.3 | 41.5 | 47.6 | 40.3 | 44.8 |
| 2011 | 2,924 | 2,477 | 3,561 | 1,839 | 1,015 | 570 | 51.8 | 43.1 | 49.1 | 41.7 | 47.0 |
| 2013 | 3,055 | 2,568 | 3,671 | 1,952 | 1,057 | 634 | 52.5 | 43.8 | 49.9 | 42.0 | 46.8 |
| 2015 | 2,969 | 2,492 | 3,536 | 1,926 | 1,011 | 634 | 54.9 | 46.5 | 52.2 | 44.1 | 49.8 |
| **2017, total** | **3,031** | **2,536** | **3,511** | **2,056** | **1,025** | **698** | **(NA)** | **(NA)** | **54.0** | **46.2** | **52.3** |
| Officials/administrators | 222 | 187 | 295 | 114 | 49 | 37 | (NA) | (NA) | 72.4 | 71.9 | 71.8 |
| Professionals | 637 | 901 | 1,009 | 529 | 254 | 144 | (NA) | (NA) | 64.1 | 55.8 | 65.5 |
| Technicians | 240 | 170 | 267 | 143 | 65 | 50 | (NA) | (NA) | 52.1 | 44.1 | 50.8 |
| Protective service | 951 | 235 | 785 | 401 | 198 | 163 | (NA) | (NA) | 56.8 | 47.7 | 61.3 |
| Paraprofessionals | 98 | 252 | 184 | 166 | 97 | 51 | (NA) | (NA) | (NA) | (NA) | (NA) |
| Administrative support | 129 | 652 | 458 | 323 | 150 | 126 | (NA) | (NA) | 39.4 | 39.0 | 41.3 |
| Skilled craft | 372 | 20 | 271 | 122 | 58 | 47 | (NA) | (NA) | 39.3 | 49.0 | 53.5 |
| Service/maintenance | 381 | 118 | 242 | 257 | 154 | 81 | (NA) | (NA) | 32.2 | 41.0 | 42.1 |

NA Not available. [1] Non-Hispanic. [2] Includes other minority groups, not shown separately. [3] Persons of Hispanic origin may be of any race.

Source: U.S. Equal Employment Opportunity Commission, "Job Patterns for Minorities and Women in State and Local Government," <www.eeoc.gov>, accessed August 2019.

# Table 499. State and Local Government Full-Time Equivalent Employment by Selected Function and State: 2017

[In thousands (1,927.0 represents 1,927,000). For March. Local government amounts are estimates subject to sampling variation; see Appendix III and source]

| State | Total[1] | | Education: Elementary/secondary | | Higher education | | Public welfare | | Health | | Hospitals | | Highways | | Police protection | | Fire protection | | Corrections | | Parks and recreation | |
|---|---|---|---|---|---|---|---|---|---|---|---|---|---|---|---|---|---|---|---|---|---|---|---|
| | State | Local | State | Local | State | Local | State | Local | State | Local | State | Local | State | Local | State | Local | State | Local | State | Local | State | Local |
| U.S. | 1,927.0 | 7,122.5 | 48.2 | 6,782.7 | 1,796.4 | 339.8 | 242.7 | 272.7 | 183.6 | 251.9 | 402.2 | 598.7 | 208.6 | 276.6 | 102.2 | 826.6 | (X) | 358.4 | 444.6 | 264.7 | 35.3 | 238.8 |
| AL | 45.9 | 95.3 | — | 95.3 | 42.9 | 1.1 | 4.2 | 1.1 | 4.3 | 6.4 | 13.4 | 25.8 | 4.3 | 6.1 | 1.3 | 13.1 | (X) | 6.3 | 4.3 | 3.6 | 0.5 | 3.9 |
| AK | 7.9 | 16.8 | 3.0 | 16.8 | 4.7 | 0.1 | 1.8 | 1.1 | 0.7 | 0.3 | 0.2 | 0.9 | 3.0 | 0.7 | 2.0 | 1.3 | (X) | 0.8 | 2.2 | 0.1 | 0.1 | 0.6 |
| AZ | 37.5 | 119.9 | — | 109.4 | 34.8 | 10.5 | 6.1 | 0.1 | 2.2 | 3.9 | 0.6 | 2.9 | 2.5 | 4.1 | 2.0 | 18.1 | (X) | 9.0 | 9.4 | 5.6 | 0.3 | 4.7 |
| AR | 27.3 | 69.3 | — | 69.3 | 26.0 | — | 4.2 | — | 3.2 | 0.6 | 6.6 | 1.3 | 3.7 | 3.6 | 1.2 | 7.5 | (X) | 3.1 | 5.8 | 2.5 | 0.7 | 1.5 |
| CA | 175.1 | 761.8 | — | 688.4 | 170.8 | 73.4 | 4.0 | 78.1 | 15.9 | 49.0 | 48.1 | 69.9 | 18.7 | 22.7 | 11.5 | 89.6 | (X) | 33.6 | 58.5 | 33.4 | 3.4 | 33.1 |
| CO | 52.2 | 108.2 | — | 107.1 | 50.4 | 1.2 | 2.4 | 7.4 | 1.5 | 5.5 | 6.6 | 10.6 | 3.1 | 3.3 | 1.9 | 15.1 | (X) | 7.2 | 7.4 | 4.3 | 1.0 | 8.0 |
| CT | 21.2 | 93.8 | — | 93.8 | 18.3 | — | 5.2 | 1.4 | 3.5 | 1.2 | 6.0 | — | 3.4 | 0.5 | 1.9 | 8.2 | (X) | 4.4 | 5.3 | — | 0.2 | 1.9 |
| DE | 8.2 | 17.7 | — | 17.7 | 7.8 | — | 1.6 | — | 2.2 | 0.3 | 1.3 | — | 1.5 | 0.1 | 1.1 | 1.6 | (X) | 0.2 | 2.8 | — | 0.3 | 0.3 |
| DC | (X) | 9.5 | (X) | 8.7 | (X) | 0.8 | (X) | 2.5 | (X) | 0.8 | (X) | 1.5 | (X) | 0.9 | (X) | 4.8 | (X) | 1.9 | (X) | 1.6 | (X) | 0.8 |
| FL | 69.9 | 389.4 | — | 360.1 | 67.0 | 29.3 | 9.3 | 3.7 | 16.0 | 5.4 | 4.0 | 51.3 | 6.2 | 12.8 | 4.1 | 57.6 | (X) | 29.0 | 23.7 | 16.9 | 1.3 | 18.4 |
| GA | 66.8 | 240.1 | — | 240.1 | 64.2 | — | 7.0 | 1.5 | 3.7 | 7.8 | 7.9 | 20.0 | 4.1 | 7.0 | 2.6 | 25.0 | (X) | 13.6 | 16.1 | 9.9 | 3.5 | 5.8 |
| HI | 37.7 | — | 26.3 | — | 11.3 | — | 0.4 | 0.1 | 2.0 | 0.4 | 4.2 | — | 0.8 | 0.9 | — | 4.0 | (X) | 2.0 | 2.4 | — | 0.2 | 2.2 |
| ID | 9.3 | 36.3 | — | 34.4 | 8.9 | 1.9 | 1.8 | 0.1 | 1.9 | 0.9 | 0.6 | 4.1 | 1.3 | 1.9 | 0.5 | 3.7 | (X) | 1.5 | 2.4 | 1.7 | 0.2 | 1.1 |
| IL | 58.1 | 298.0 | — | 274.7 | 56.3 | 23.3 | 9.0 | 5.0 | 2.1 | 5.5 | 10.3 | 11.7 | 6.4 | 10.1 | 3.1 | 38.4 | (X) | 16.8 | 13.1 | 10.5 | 0.4 | 17.8 |
| IN | 59.9 | 133.8 | — | 133.8 | 59.0 | 1.0 | 6.0 | 1.0 | 1.6 | 2.9 | 1.5 | 23.0 | 3.5 | 5.4 | 1.8 | 13.8 | (X) | 8.1 | 6.1 | 6.3 | 0.2 | 3.4 |
| IA | 24.8 | 86.9 | — | 79.9 | 23.8 | 7.0 | 2.6 | 1.1 | 0.4 | 1.7 | 8.9 | 12.2 | 2.1 | 5.3 | 0.9 | 6.2 | (X) | 2.1 | 2.7 | 1.6 | 0.1 | 2.1 |
| KS | 24.3 | 94.2 | — | 86.3 | 23.7 | 7.9 | 3.0 | 0.5 | 1.0 | 2.9 | 10.7 | 9.0 | 2.6 | 4.7 | 1.1 | 8.0 | (X) | 3.6 | 3.3 | 2.9 | 0.6 | 2.6 |
| KY | 40.3 | 106.2 | — | 106.2 | 38.3 | — | 7.0 | 0.3 | 3.3 | 5.0 | 7.2 | 5.0 | 4.4 | 3.0 | 2.0 | 8.0 | (X) | 4.4 | 4.1 | 4.0 | 0.9 | 1.9 |
| LA | 27.9 | 97.4 | 0.1 | 97.4 | 24.9 | — | 5.4 | 1.2 | 3.6 | 1.3 | 10.1 | 19.2 | 4.3 | 5.5 | 1.8 | 16.1 | (X) | 5.3 | 5.7 | 6.8 | 0.9 | 4.2 |
| ME | 7.2 | 34.0 | — | 34.0 | 6.9 | — | 2.2 | 0.1 | 0.9 | 0.2 | 0.5 | 1.1 | 2.1 | 1.7 | 0.5 | 2.5 | (X) | 1.8 | 1.2 | 0.7 | 0.1 | 0.6 |
| MD | 30.6 | 145.0 | — | 133.1 | 28.6 | 11.9 | 6.2 | 2.5 | 6.1 | 4.8 | 3.3 | 0.3 | 4.3 | 4.6 | 2.2 | 16.2 | (X) | 7.1 | 11.4 | 3.5 | 0.5 | 6.5 |
| MA | 35.0 | 154.3 | 2.3 | 154.2 | 31.6 | — | 7.7 | 2.5 | 7.2 | 2.9 | 5.4 | 1.6 | 2.7 | 5.8 | 2.8 | 17.5 | (X) | 13.1 | 11.7 | — | 0.9 | 2.2 |
| MI | 77.3 | 175.0 | — | 161.9 | 76.7 | 13.1 | 11.3 | 3.7 | 6.5 | 10.0 | 17.1 | 8.1 | 2.7 | 8.0 | 2.9 | 17.9 | (X) | 7.1 | 12.3 | 5.3 | 0.6 | 3.6 |
| MN | 39.9 | 128.7 | — | 128.7 | 36.3 | — | 3.0 | 11.7 | 3.5 | 3.4 | 5.0 | 5.0 | 4.7 | 6.7 | 1.0 | 11.6 | (X) | 3.6 | 4.4 | 5.8 | 0.6 | 4.6 |
| MS | 21.9 | 78.4 | — | 72.1 | 20.4 | 6.3 | 4.3 | 0.5 | 2.9 | 0.2 | 10.4 | 19.0 | 3.2 | 4.3 | 1.2 | 8.5 | (X) | 3.0 | 2.5 | 2.2 | 0.2 | 1.5 |
| MO | 32.2 | 142.3 | — | 136.4 | 30.5 | 5.9 | 6.7 | 3.0 | 2.9 | 4.0 | 10.1 | 12.0 | 5.3 | 6.4 | 2.5 | 16.0 | (X) | 7.5 | 11.9 | 2.9 | 0.5 | 4.7 |
| MT | 7.6 | 22.9 | — | 22.4 | 7.2 | 0.5 | 1.8 | 0.5 | 0.8 | 1.2 | 0.8 | 0.4 | 2.1 | 1.3 | 0.5 | 2.2 | (X) | 0.8 | 1.2 | 0.7 | 0.1 | 0.5 |
| NE | 13.2 | 53.9 | — | 50.4 | 12.6 | 3.5 | 2.6 | 1.4 | 0.6 | 0.5 | 3.7 | 4.7 | 1.8 | 3.1 | 0.7 | 4.3 | (X) | 1.6 | 2.8 | 1.5 | 0.3 | 1.1 |
| NV | 10.0 | 49.5 | — | 49.5 | 9.9 | — | 2.5 | 1.4 | 1.5 | 0.9 | 1.3 | 4.3 | 1.7 | 1.0 | 0.9 | 7.1 | (X) | 2.6 | 3.8 | 2.0 | 0.2 | 3.2 |
| NH | 7.4 | 35.6 | — | 35.6 | 7.1 | — | 2.0 | 2.4 | 0.8 | 0.2 | 0.6 | — | 1.6 | 1.5 | 0.5 | 3.4 | (X) | 2.0 | 1.0 | 0.7 | 0.3 | 0.5 |
| NJ | 53.9 | 218.0 | 16.1 | 208.3 | 35.2 | 10.6 | 9.0 | 8.6 | 3.9 | 4.0 | 13.2 | 1.2 | 5.9 | 8.8 | 0.6 | 30.8 | (X) | 8.0 | 8.7 | 6.1 | 0.6 | 5.7 |
| NM | 18.5 | 48.6 | — | 45.2 | 17.5 | 3.4 | 1.6 | 0.9 | 2.2 | 0.7 | 7.8 | 1.3 | 2.2 | 1.8 | 0.6 | 2.5 | (X) | 2.5 | 3.8 | 2.4 | 0.6 | 2.0 |
| NY | 61.7 | 501.5 | — | 476.0 | 57.6 | 25.3 | 4.7 | 42.7 | 8.4 | 15.6 | 41.8 | 51.2 | 10.7 | 26.2 | 6.2 | 80.8 | (X) | 25.3 | 32.2 | 25.3 | 2.8 | 12.7 |
| NC | 64.7 | 225.3 | — | 203.9 | 61.7 | 21.4 | 1.1 | 16.4 | 2.4 | 16.3 | 22.6 | 55.4 | 8.8 | 3.8 | 3.2 | 25.2 | (X) | 9.9 | 19.4 | 5.5 | 1.4 | 6.4 |
| ND | 8.9 | 17.0 | — | 17.0 | 8.5 | — | 0.5 | 1.0 | 0.9 | — | 0.9 | — | 1.0 | 12.1 | 0.4 | 1.7 | (X) | 0.4 | 0.9 | 0.6 | 0.2 | 1.1 |
| OH | 76.2 | 243.7 | — | 239.0 | 74.0 | 4.7 | 2.8 | 20.8 | 2.8 | 14.6 | 14.6 | 11.8 | 6.2 | 12.1 | 2.6 | 29.4 | (X) | 18.2 | 13.4 | 8.9 | 0.5 | 9.1 |
| OK | 31.1 | 91.2 | — | 91.2 | 29.5 | — | 7.1 | 0.2 | 5.3 | 1.7 | 1.1 | 10.6 | 2.8 | 4.9 | 1.9 | 9.5 | (X) | 4.5 | 4.9 | 1.9 | 0.7 | 1.6 |
| OR | 26.4 | 75.1 | — | 67.0 | 25.5 | 8.1 | 8.4 | 1.2 | 2.1 | 5.1 | 7.5 | 2.5 | 3.7 | 3.4 | 1.5 | 7.6 | (X) | 4.1 | 5.3 | 3.4 | 0.7 | 3.9 |
| PA | 66.2 | 242.6 | — | 232.0 | 60.9 | 10.6 | 11.2 | 16.0 | 1.7 | 5.5 | 12.0 | — | 13.1 | 10.6 | 6.7 | 25.9 | (X) | 6.1 | 17.9 | 13.3 | 0.4 | 3.2 |
| RI | 6.0 | 19.5 | 0.4 | 19.5 | 5.1 | — | 1.3 | 0.2 | 1.0 | 0.1 | 0.7 | — | 0.7 | 0.8 | 0.3 | 2.6 | (X) | 2.1 | 1.5 | — | 2.5 | 0.5 |
| SC | 35.1 | 103.3 | 16.1 | 103.3 | 31.8 | 0.4 | 5.4 | 0.3 | 5.2 | 2.5 | 6.8 | 24.1 | 4.6 | 2.6 | 2.1 | 12.1 | (X) | 6.3 | 7.5 | 3.4 | 0.8 | 4.0 |
| SD | 6.0 | 21.2 | — | 20.8 | 5.6 | — | 1.8 | 0.3 | 0.7 | 0.4 | 0.3 | 0.5 | 1.0 | 1.5 | 0.4 | 1.7 | (X) | 0.5 | 0.7 | 0.7 | 0.2 | 0.7 |
| TN | 36.8 | 129.9 | — | 129.9 | 34.8 | — | 7.4 | 1.8 | 4.2 | 4.6 | 3.5 | 24.0 | 3.2 | 6.7 | 1.8 | 19.3 | (X) | 8.2 | 6.9 | 6.0 | 1.0 | 4.3 |
| TX | 144.5 | 791.3 | — | 746.0 | 142.1 | 45.4 | 24.7 | 3.9 | 19.2 | 29.7 | 23.3 | 58.4 | 11.9 | 20.3 | 6.9 | 69.8 | (X) | 29.0 | 41.8 | 27.8 | 1.2 | 18.2 |
| UT | 30.1 | 55.2 | — | 55.2 | 28.6 | — | 2.9 | 0.7 | 2.1 | 3.6 | 10.5 | 1.0 | 1.6 | 1.7 | 0.9 | 5.7 | (X) | 2.7 | 3.3 | 2.2 | 0.3 | 3.8 |
| VT | 5.2 | 21.1 | — | 21.1 | 4.8 | — | 1.6 | — | 0.5 | 0.1 | 0.5 | — | 1.1 | 1.1 | 0.6 | 0.9 | (X) | 0.4 | 1.1 | — | 0.1 | 0.2 |
| VA | 59.9 | 200.4 | — | 199.1 | 57.7 | 1.2 | 3.1 | 8.6 | 6.9 | 6.2 | 11.5 | 2.3 | 7.8 | 4.1 | 3.1 | 18.8 | (X) | 11.3 | 13.1 | 11.2 | 1.1 | 7.9 |
| WA | 59.8 | 129.9 | — | 129.9 | 57.6 | — | 10.7 | 1.1 | 7.2 | 3.6 | 11.4 | 19.4 | 6.6 | 6.8 | 2.2 | 12.2 | (X) | 9.2 | 8.9 | 4.6 | 0.6 | 5.9 |
| WV | 15.4 | 42.6 | — | 42.6 | 14.2 | — | 3.4 | — | 0.8 | 1.1 | 1.5 | 2.2 | 4.7 | 0.9 | 1.0 | 3.0 | (X) | 1.0 | 3.3 | 0.2 | 0.6 | 0.7 |
| WI | 39.8 | 129.4 | — | 119.6 | 38.7 | 9.8 | 2.3 | 12.0 | 1.6 | 5.7 | 3.6 | 0.8 | 1.5 | 8.4 | 1.0 | 15.0 | (X) | 5.0 | 9.4 | 3.9 | 0.2 | 3.0 |
| WY | 4.1 | 20.4 | — | 18.3 | 3.9 | 2.0 | 0.6 | 0.1 | 0.9 | 0.3 | 0.7 | 7.1 | 1.7 | 0.8 | 0.3 | 1.7 | (X) | 0.5 | 1.2 | 0.7 | 0.2 | 0.8 |

— Represents or rounds to zero. X Not applicable. [1] Includes other categories, not shown separately.

Source: U.S. Census Bureau, Census of Governments, "2017 Government Employment and Payroll Tables," <https://www.census.gov/programs-surveys/apes.html>, accessed April 2019.

# Table 500. State and Local Government Employment and Average Monthly Earnings by State: 2010 to 2017

[4,378 represents 4,378,000. As of March. Full-time equivalent is a computed statistic representing the number of full-time employees that could have been employed if the reported number of hours worked by part-time employees had been worked by full-time employees. This statistic is calculated separately for each function of a government by dividing the "part-time hours paid" by the standard number of hours for full-time employees in the particular government and then adding the resulting quotient to the number of full-time employees]

| State | Full-time equivalent employment (1,000) | | | | | | Average monthly earnings [2] (dol.) | | | | | |
|---|---|---|---|---|---|---|---|---|---|---|---|---|
| | State | | | Local [1] | | | State | | | Local [1] | | |
| | 2010 | 2016 | 2017 | 2010 | 2016 | 2017 | 2010 | 2016 | 2017 | 2010 | 2016 | 2017 |
| United States..... | 4,378 | 4,361 | 4,382 | 12,171 | 12,074 | 12,203 | 4,620 | 5,274 | 5,420 | 4,310 | 4,755 | 4,910 |
| Alabama............ | 90 | 90 | 91 | 198 | 191 | 191 | 4,099 | 4,600 | 4,709 | 3,240 | 3,589 | 3,727 |
| Alaska.............. | 27 | 25 | 24 | 28 | 28 | 27 | 5,176 | 5,884 | 6,026 | 4,935 | 5,507 | 5,693 |
| Arizona............ | 67 | 72 | 73 | 225 | 209 | 208 | 4,365 | 4,907 | 5,029 | 4,163 | 4,414 | 4,509 |
| Arkansas.......... | 63 | 62 | 62 | 106 | 108 | 106 | 3,795 | 4,153 | 4,188 | 3,208 | 3,229 | 3,315 |
| California.......... | 411 | 415 | 424 | 1,381 | 1,400 | 1,437 | 5,740 | 7,043 | 7,258 | 5,787 | 6,596 | 6,855 |
| Colorado........... | 71 | 88 | 88 | 199 | 206 | 211 | 5,033 | 5,716 | 5,836 | 4,230 | 4,763 | 4,874 |
| Connecticut........ | 63 | 63 | 59 | 123 | 130 | 128 | 5,632 | 6,355 | 6,692 | 5,063 | 5,450 | 5,730 |
| Delaware........... | 26 | 26 | 26 | 23 | 23 | 24 | 4,113 | 4,645 | 4,716 | 4,484 | 4,973 | 5,052 |
| District of Columbia......... | (X) | (X) | (X) | 44 | 48 | 51 | (X) | (X) | (X) | 5,900 | 7,053 | 7,147 |
| Florida.............. | 184 | 179 | 180 | 727 | 707 | 711 | 3,861 | 4,379 | 4,430 | 3,986 | 4,217 | 4,335 |
| Georgia............ | 124 | 128 | 130 | 392 | 385 | 391 | 3,795 | 4,260 | 4,455 | 3,439 | 3,737 | 3,920 |
| Hawaii............. | 58 | 59 | 59 | 15 | 17 | 17 | 3,943 | 4,736 | 4,862 | 5,040 | 5,393 | 5,644 |
| Idaho.............. | 22 | 24 | 24 | 55 | 58 | 60 | 4,280 | 5,167 | 5,315 | 3,341 | 3,558 | 3,734 |
| Illinois.............. | 131 | 124 | 122 | 513 | 507 | 497 | 5,324 | 5,829 | 5,877 | 4,716 | 5,233 | 5,391 |
| Indiana............. | 90 | 89 | 90 | 254 | 232 | 234 | 4,023 | 4,408 | 4,542 | 3,547 | 3,835 | 3,956 |
| Iowa............... | 51 | 51 | 51 | 124 | 133 | 135 | 5,326 | 6,324 | 6,579 | 3,831 | 4,314 | 4,505 |
| Kansas............. | 44 | 52 | 54 | 156 | 146 | 147 | 4,178 | 4,672 | 4,694 | 3,361 | 3,695 | 3,827 |
| Kentucky........... | 81 | 86 | 84 | 161 | 159 | 159 | 3,940 | 4,473 | 4,629 | 3,101 | 3,475 | 3,646 |
| Louisiana.......... | 89 | 74 | 73 | 187 | 184 | 186 | 4,282 | 4,743 | 4,767 | 3,397 | 3,514 | 3,616 |
| Maine.............. | 21 | 21 | 20 | 51 | 49 | 49 | 4,063 | 4,366 | 4,521 | 3,545 | 3,925 | 4,049 |
| Maryland........... | 88 | 86 | 85 | 215 | 218 | 222 | 4,650 | 5,255 | 5,451 | 5,190 | 5,503 | 5,754 |
| Massachusetts...... | 95 | 99 | 98 | 233 | 237 | 230 | 4,973 | 5,914 | 6,113 | 4,800 | 5,358 | 5,537 |
| Michigan........... | 146 | 144 | 147 | 329 | 294 | 287 | 5,208 | 5,821 | 5,953 | 4,618 | 4,707 | 4,763 |
| Minnesota.......... | 80 | 83 | 83 | 201 | 209 | 211 | 5,338 | 5,847 | 6,039 | 4,447 | 4,853 | 5,094 |
| Mississippi......... | 57 | 57 | 56 | 136 | 134 | 133 | 3,537 | 3,907 | 3,997 | 2,985 | 3,317 | 3,333 |
| Missouri............ | 89 | 87 | 86 | 234 | 228 | 233 | 3,518 | 3,897 | 4,008 | 3,502 | 3,690 | 3,893 |
| Montana............ | 20 | 20 | 21 | 38 | 37 | 36 | 4,016 | 4,637 | 4,810 | 3,476 | 3,966 | 4,176 |
| Nebraska........... | 33 | 32 | 32 | 88 | 88 | 90 | 4,013 | 4,373 | 4,535 | 3,785 | 4,434 | 4,568 |
| Nevada............. | 28 | 28 | 29 | 86 | 85 | 87 | 4,891 | 4,964 | 5,152 | 5,149 | 5,435 | 5,540 |
| New Hampshire..... | 19 | 19 | 19 | 53 | 51 | 52 | 4,584 | 5,265 | 5,445 | 3,813 | 4,423 | 4,600 |
| New Jersey......... | 152 | 139 | 139 | 356 | 339 | 339 | 5,767 | 6,251 | 6,290 | 5,449 | 6,087 | 6,198 |
| New Mexico........ | 48 | 46 | 45 | 80 | 80 | 78 | 3,978 | 4,674 | 4,761 | 3,440 | 3,798 | 3,882 |
| New York........... | 251 | 242 | 248 | 975 | 941 | 953 | 5,484 | 6,222 | 6,316 | 5,315 | 5,987 | 6,055 |
| North Carolina...... | 146 | 140 | 145 | 402 | 409 | 417 | 3,886 | 4,668 | 4,855 | 3,690 | 3,979 | 4,127 |
| North Dakota........ | 18 | 19 | 19 | 26 | 29 | 28 | 4,103 | 4,865 | 4,975 | 3,550 | 4,309 | 4,471 |
| Ohio................ | 140 | 138 | 138 | 466 | 451 | 451 | 4,995 | 5,393 | 5,559 | 4,101 | 4,305 | 4,507 |
| Oklahoma.......... | 71 | 69 | 66 | 146 | 147 | 145 | 3,864 | 4,260 | 4,346 | 3,119 | 3,384 | 3,516 |
| Oregon............. | 65 | 68 | 70 | 133 | 130 | 131 | 4,452 | 5,131 | 5,655 | 4,348 | 5,068 | 5,246 |
| Pennsylvania....... | 168 | 163 | 164 | 429 | 400 | 402 | 4,564 | 5,104 | 5,299 | 4,290 | 4,909 | 5,007 |
| Rhode Island........ | 19 | 18 | 18 | 31 | 30 | 29 | 5,298 | 5,962 | 6,142 | 4,953 | 5,379 | 5,658 |
| South Carolina...... | 77 | 80 | 80 | 171 | 183 | 186 | 3,810 | 4,245 | 4,347 | 3,557 | 3,779 | 3,891 |
| South Dakota....... | 14 | 14 | 14 | 31 | 32 | 33 | 3,938 | 4,591 | 4,748 | 3,149 | 3,528 | 3,748 |
| Tennessee.......... | 83 | 79 | 79 | 247 | 250 | 249 | 3,822 | 4,364 | 4,482 | 3,358 | 3,666 | 3,871 |
| Texas.............. | 318 | 310 | 313 | 1,134 | 1,176 | 1,200 | 4,280 | 5,146 | 5,206 | 3,604 | 4,030 | 4,147 |
| Utah................ | 51 | 58 | 61 | 90 | 89 | 94 | 4,409 | 5,022 | 5,159 | 3,706 | 4,211 | 4,266 |
| Vermont............ | 14 | 14 | 14 | 26 | 26 | 27 | 4,645 | 5,204 | 5,589 | 3,589 | 4,159 | 4,281 |
| Virginia............. | 125 | 127 | 126 | 319 | 321 | 323 | 4,384 | 5,075 | 5,369 | 3,905 | 4,324 | 4,514 |
| Washington......... | 123 | 127 | 127 | 226 | 226 | 255 | 4,913 | 5,392 | 5,530 | 5,416 | 6,213 | 6,388 |
| West Virginia....... | 39 | 41 | 39 | 62 | 63 | 63 | 3,554 | 3,796 | 3,890 | 3,219 | 3,480 | 3,425 |
| Wisconsin.......... | 72 | 73 | 73 | 211 | 213 | 212 | 4,901 | 5,328 | 5,419 | 4,239 | 4,616 | 4,790 |
| Wyoming........... | 14 | 14 | 13 | 37 | 37 | 37 | 4,240 | 4,624 | 4,664 | 4,068 | 4,700 | 4,743 |

X Not applicable. [1] Estimates subject to sampling variation; see Appendix III and source. [2] For full-time employees.

Source: U.S. Census Bureau, Census of Governments, Annual Survey of Public Employment and Payroll, "2017 Government Employment and Payroll Tables," <https://www.census.gov/programs-surveys/apes.html>, accessed April 2019.

# Federal Government Finances and Employment

This section presents statistics relating to the financial structure and civilian employment of the federal government. The fiscal data cover taxes, other receipts, outlays, and debt. The principal sources of fiscal data are the *Budget of the United States Government* and related documents, published annually by the Office of Management and Budget (OMB), and the U.S. Department of the Treasury's *Combined Statement of Receipts, Outlays, and Balances of the United States Government*. Detailed data on tax returns and collections are published annually by the Internal Revenue Service. The personnel data relate to staffing, payrolls, and retirements are published by the Office of Personnel Management. Data on federally owned land and real property are collected by the General Services Administration and presented in its annual *Federal Real Property Report*.

**Budget concept**—Under the unified budget concept, all federal monies are included in one comprehensive budget. These monies comprise both federal funds and trust funds. Federal funds are derived mainly from taxes and borrowing and are not restricted by law to any specific government purpose. Trust funds, such as the Unemployment Trust Fund, collect certain taxes and other receipts for use in carrying out specific purposes or programs in accordance with the terms of the trust agreement or statute. Fund balances include both cash balances with the Treasury and investments in U.S. securities. Part of the balance is obligated, part unobligated. Prior to 1985, the budget totals, under provisions of law, excluded some federal activities—including the Federal Financing Bank, the Postal Service, the Synthetic Fuels Corporation, and the lending activities of the Rural Electrification Administration. The Balanced Budget and Emergency Deficit Control Act of 1985 (P.L.99-177) repealed the off-budget status of these entities and placed Social Security (Federal Old-Age and Survivors Insurance and the Federal Disability Insurance Trust Funds) off-budget. Though Social Security is now off-budget and, by law excluded from coverage of the congressional budget resolutions, it continues to be a federal program.

Receipts arising from the government's sovereign powers are reported as governmental receipts and all other receipts, i.e., from business or market-oriented activities, are offset against outlays. Outlays are reported on a checks-issued (net) basis (i.e., outlays are recorded at the time the checks to pay bills are issued).

**Debt concept**—For most of U.S. history, the total debt consisted of debt borrowed by the Treasury (i.e., public debt). The present debt series includes both public debt and agency debt. The *gross federal debt* includes money borrowed by the Treasury and by various federal agencies; it is the broadest generally used measure of the federal debt. *Total public debt* is covered by a statutory debt limitation and includes only borrowing by the Treasury.

**Treasury receipts and outlays**—All receipts of the government, with a few exceptions, are deposited to the credit of the U.S. Treasury regardless of ultimate disposition. Under the Constitution, no money may be withdrawn from the Treasury unless appropriated by the Congress.

The day-to-day cash operations of the federal government clearing through the accounts of the U.S. Treasury are reported in the *Daily Treasury Statement*. Extensive detail on the public debt is published in the *Monthly Statement of the Public Debt of the United States*.

Budget receipts such as taxes, customs duties, and miscellaneous receipts, which are collected by government agencies, and outlays represented by checks issued and cash payments made by disbursing officers as well as government agencies are reported in the *Monthly Treasury Statement of Receipts and Outlays of the United States Government* and in the Treasury's *Combined Statement of Receipts, Outlays, and Balances of the United States Government*. These deposits in and payments from accounts maintained by government agencies are on the same basis as the unified budget.

The quarterly *Treasury Bulletin* contains data on fiscal operations and related Treasury activities, including financial statements of government corporations and other business-type activities.

**Income tax returns and tax collections**—Tax data are compiled by the Internal Revenue Service of the Treasury Department. The annual *Internal Revenue Service Data Book* gives a detailed account of tax collections by kind of tax. The agency's annual *Statistics of Income* reports present detailed data from individual income tax returns and corporation income tax returns as well as historical tax data. The quarterly *Statistics of Income Bulletin* presents data on such diverse subjects as tax-exempt organizations, unincorporated businesses, fiduciary income tax and estate tax returns, sales of capital assets by individuals, international income and taxes reported by corporations and individuals, and estate tax wealth.

**Employment and payrolls**—The Office of Personnel Management collects employment, payroll, and retirement data from all departments and agencies of the federal government, except the Central Intelligence Agency, the National Security Agency, the National Geospatial-Intelligence Agency, and the Defense Intelligence Agency. Employment figures represent the number of persons who occupied civilian positions at the end of the report month shown and who are paid for services rendered to the federal government, regardless of the nature of appointment or method of payment. Federal payrolls include all payments for personnel services rendered during the report month and payments for accumulated annual leave of employees who separate from the service. Since most federal employees are paid on a biweekly basis, the calendar month earnings are partially estimated on the basis of the number of work days in each month where payroll periods overlap.

Federal employment and payroll figures are published by the Office of Personnel Management in its *Federal Civilian Workforce Statistics—Employment and Trends* and the FedScope database system. It also publishes employment data on minority groups, white- and blue-collar workers, employment by geographic area, and salary and wage distribution of federal employees. General schedule is primarily white-collar; wage system primarily blue-collar. Data on federal employment are also issued by the Bureau of Labor Statistics in its *Monthly Labor Review* and *Employment and Earnings Online* and by the U.S. Census Bureau in its annual report series *Federal, State, and Local Governments: Public Employment and Payroll Data*.

## Table 501. Federal Budget—Receipts and Outlays: 1960 to 2019

[92.5 represents $92,500,000,000. For fiscal years ending in year shown; See text, Section 8. See also headnote, Table 503]

| Fiscal year | In current dollars (bil. dol.) | | | In constant (2012) dollars (bil. dol.) | | | As percentage of GDP [1] | | |
|---|---|---|---|---|---|---|---|---|---|
| | Receipts | Outlays | Surplus or deficit (-) | Receipts | Outlays | Surplus or deficit (-) | Receipts | Outlays | Surplus or deficit (-) |
| 1960............ | 92.5 | 92.2 | 0.3 | 696.5 | 694.2 | 2.3 | 17.3 | 17.3 | 0.1 |
| 1970............ | 192.8 | 195.6 | -2.8 | 1,080.2 | 1,096.1 | -15.9 | 18.4 | 18.7 | -0.3 |
| 1980............ | 517.1 | 590.9 | -73.8 | 1,393.5 | 1,592.4 | -198.9 | 18.5 | 21.2 | -2.6 |
| 1990............ | 1,032.0 | 1,253.0 | -221.0 | 1,755.0 | 2,130.9 | -375.9 | 17.5 | 21.2 | -3.7 |
| 1995............ | 1,351.8 | 1,515.7 | -164.0 | 1,960.0 | 2,197.7 | -237.7 | 17.9 | 20.0 | -2.2 |
| 1998............ | 1,721.7 | 1,652.5 | 69.3 | 2,374.8 | 2,279.3 | 95.5 | 19.3 | 18.5 | 0.8 |
| 1999............ | 1,827.5 | 1,701.8 | 125.6 | 2,490.1 | 2,318.9 | 171.2 | 19.3 | 18.0 | 1.3 |
| 2000............ | 2,025.2 | 1,789.0 | 236.2 | 2,691.3 | 2,377.3 | 313.9 | 20.0 | 17.7 | 2.3 |
| 2001............ | 1,991.1 | 1,862.8 | 128.2 | 2,578.5 | 2,412.4 | 166.1 | 18.9 | 17.7 | 1.2 |
| 2002............ | 1,853.1 | 2,010.9 | -157.8 | 2,363.4 | 2,564.6 | -201.2 | 17.1 | 18.6 | -1.5 |
| 2003............ | 1,782.3 | 2,159.9 | -377.6 | 2,210.2 | 2,678.4 | -468.2 | 15.8 | 19.1 | -3.3 |
| 2004............ | 1,880.1 | 2,292.8 | -412.7 | 2,272.3 | 2,771.1 | -498.8 | 15.6 | 19.1 | -3.4 |
| 2005............ | 2,153.6 | 2,472.0 | -318.3 | 2,516.5 | 2,888.5 | -372.0 | 16.8 | 19.3 | -2.5 |
| 2006............ | 2,406.9 | 2,655.0 | -248.2 | 2,718.4 | 2,998.7 | -280.3 | 17.6 | 19.5 | -1.8 |
| 2007............ | 2,568.0 | 2,728.7 | -160.7 | 2,822.3 | 2,998.9 | -176.6 | 18.0 | 19.1 | -1.1 |
| 2008............ | 2,524.0 | 2,982.5 | -458.6 | 2,681.1 | 3,168.2 | -487.1 | 17.1 | 20.2 | -3.1 |
| 2009............ | 2,105.0 | 3,517.7 | -1,412.7 | 2,236.3 | 3,737.0 | -1,500.8 | 14.6 | 24.4 | -9.8 |
| 2010............ | 2,162.7 | 3,457.1 | -1,294.4 | 2,257.3 | 3,608.3 | -1,351.0 | 14.6 | 23.3 | -8.7 |
| 2011............ | 2,303.5 | 3,603.1 | -1,299.6 | 2,349.3 | 3,674.7 | -1,325.4 | 15.0 | 23.4 | -8.4 |
| 2012............ | 2,450.0 | 3,526.6 | -1,076.6 | 2,450.0 | 3,526.6 | -1,076.6 | 15.3 | 22.0 | -6.7 |
| 2013............ | 2,775.1 | 3,454.9 | -679.8 | 2,736.3 | 3,406.5 | -670.3 | 16.7 | 20.8 | -4.1 |
| 2014............ | 3,021.5 | 3,506.3 | -484.8 | 2,932.9 | 3,403.5 | -470.6 | 17.4 | 20.2 | -2.8 |
| 2015............ | 3,249.9 | 3,691.8 | -442.0 | 3,137.6 | 3,564.2 | -426.7 | 18.0 | 20.4 | -2.4 |
| 2016............ | 3,268.0 | 3,852.6 | -584.7 | 3,133.2 | 3,693.8 | -560.5 | 17.6 | 20.8 | -3.2 |
| 2017............ | 3,316.2 | 3,981.6 | -665.4 | 3,126.4 | 3,753.8 | -627.4 | 17.2 | 20.7 | -3.5 |
| 2018............ | 3,329.9 | 4,109.0 | -779.1 | 3,062.8 | 3,779.5 | -716.6 | 16.5 | 20.3 | -3.9 |
| 2019, estimate...... | 3,437.7 | 4,529.2 | -1,091.5 | 3,093.9 | 4,076.3 | -982.4 | 16.1 | 21.3 | -5.1 |

[1] Gross domestic product; see text, Section 13.

Source: U.S. Office of Management and Budget, *Budget of the U.S. Government, Fiscal Year 2020: Historical Tables*, March 2019. See also <http://www.whitehouse.gov/omb/budget>.

## Table 502. Federal Budget Debt: 1960 to 2019

[290.5 represents $290,500,000,000. As of the end of the fiscal year. See text, Section 8]

| Fiscal year | Total (bil. dol.) | | | | | As percent of GDP [1] | | | | |
|---|---|---|---|---|---|---|---|---|---|---|
| | Gross federal debt | Federal government accounts | Held by the public | | | Gross federal debt | Federal government accounts | Held by the public | | |
| | | | Total | Federal Reserve System | Other | | | Total | Federal Reserve System | Other |
| 1960.............. | 290.5 | 53.7 | 236.8 | 26.5 | 210.3 | 54.4 | 10.0 | 44.3 | 5.0 | 39.4 |
| 1970.............. | 380.9 | 97.7 | 283.2 | 57.7 | 225.5 | 36.4 | 9.3 | 27.1 | 5.5 | 21.5 |
| 1980.............. | 909.0 | 197.1 | 711.9 | 120.8 | 591.1 | 32.6 | 7.1 | 25.5 | 4.3 | 21.2 |
| 1985.............. | 1,817.4 | 310.2 | 1,507.3 | 169.8 | 1,337.5 | 42.6 | 7.3 | 35.3 | 4.0 | 31.4 |
| 1990.............. | 3,206.3 | 794.7 | 2,411.6 | 234.4 | 2,177.1 | 54.4 | 13.5 | 40.9 | 4.0 | 36.9 |
| 1991.............. | 3,598.2 | 909.2 | 2,689.0 | 258.6 | 2,430.4 | 59.1 | 14.9 | 44.1 | 4.2 | 39.9 |
| 1992.............. | 4,001.8 | 1,002.1 | 2,999.7 | 296.4 | 2,703.3 | 62.4 | 15.6 | 46.8 | 4.6 | 42.1 |
| 1993.............. | 4,351.0 | 1,102.6 | 3,248.4 | 325.7 | 2,922.7 | 64.2 | 16.3 | 47.9 | 4.8 | 43.1 |
| 1994.............. | 4,643.3 | 1,210.2 | 3,433.1 | 355.2 | 3,077.9 | 64.7 | 16.9 | 47.8 | 4.9 | 42.9 |
| 1995.............. | 4,920.6 | 1,316.2 | 3,604.4 | 374.1 | 3,230.3 | 65.1 | 17.4 | 47.7 | 4.9 | 42.7 |
| 1996.............. | 5,181.5 | 1,447.4 | 3,734.1 | 390.9 | 3,343.1 | 65.2 | 18.2 | 47.0 | 4.9 | 42.0 |
| 1997.............. | 5,369.2 | 1,596.9 | 3,772.3 | 424.5 | 3,347.8 | 63.5 | 18.9 | 44.6 | 5.0 | 39.6 |
| 1998.............. | 5,478.2 | 1,757.1 | 3,721.1 | 458.2 | 3,262.9 | 61.3 | 19.7 | 41.7 | 5.1 | 36.5 |
| 1999.............. | 5,605.5 | 1,973.2 | 3,632.4 | 496.6 | 3,135.7 | 59.1 | 20.8 | 38.3 | 5.2 | 33.1 |
| 2000.............. | 5,628.7 | 2,218.9 | 3,409.8 | 511.4 | 2,898.4 | 55.6 | 21.9 | 33.7 | 5.1 | 28.6 |
| 2001.............. | 5,769.9 | 2,450.3 | 3,319.6 | 534.1 | 2,785.5 | 54.8 | 23.3 | 31.5 | 5.1 | 26.5 |
| 2002.............. | 6,198.4 | 2,658.0 | 3,540.4 | 604.2 | 2,936.2 | 57.2 | 24.5 | 32.7 | 5.6 | 27.1 |
| 2003.............. | 6,760.0 | 2,846.6 | 3,913.4 | 656.1 | 3,257.3 | 59.9 | 25.2 | 34.7 | 5.8 | 28.9 |
| 2004.............. | 7,354.7 | 3,059.1 | 4,295.5 | 700.3 | 3,595.2 | 61.2 | 25.4 | 35.7 | 5.8 | 29.9 |
| 2005.............. | 7,905.3 | 3,313.1 | 4,592.2 | 736.4 | 3,855.9 | 61.6 | 25.8 | 35.8 | 5.7 | 30.0 |
| 2006.............. | 8,451.4 | 3,622.4 | 4,829.0 | 768.9 | 4,060.0 | 62.0 | 26.6 | 35.4 | 5.6 | 29.8 |
| 2007.............. | 8,950.7 | 3,915.6 | 5,035.1 | 779.6 | 4,255.5 | 62.6 | 27.4 | 35.2 | 5.5 | 29.8 |
| 2008.............. | 9,986.1 | 4,183.0 | 5,803.1 | 491.1 | 5,311.9 | 67.7 | 28.4 | 39.4 | 3.3 | 36.0 |
| 2009.............. | 11,875.9 | 4,331.1 | 7,544.7 | 769.2 | 6,775.5 | 82.3 | 30.0 | 52.3 | 5.3 | 46.9 |
| 2010.............. | 13,528.8 | 4,509.9 | 9,018.9 | 811.7 | 8,207.2 | 91.2 | 30.4 | 60.8 | 5.5 | 55.3 |
| 2011.............. | 14,764.2 | 4,636.0 | 10,128.2 | 1,664.7 | 8,463.5 | 95.8 | 30.1 | 65.8 | 10.8 | 54.9 |
| 2012.............. | 16,050.9 | 4,769.8 | 11,281.1 | 1,645.3 | 9,635.8 | 100.0 | 29.7 | 70.3 | 10.2 | 60.0 |
| 2013.............. | 16,719.4 | 4,736.7 | 11,982.7 | 2,072.3 | 9,910.4 | 100.7 | 28.5 | 72.2 | 12.5 | 59.7 |
| 2014.............. | 17,794.5 | 5,014.6 | 12,779.9 | 2,451.7 | 10,328.2 | 102.7 | 28.9 | 73.7 | 14.1 | 59.6 |
| 2015.............. | 18,120.1 | 5,003.4 | 13,116.7 | 2,461.9 | 10,654.7 | 100.2 | 27.7 | 72.5 | 13.6 | 58.9 |
| 2016.............. | 19,539.5 | 5,371.8 | 14,167.6 | 2,463.5 | 11,704.2 | 105.3 | 29.0 | 76.4 | 13.3 | 63.1 |
| 2017.............. | 20,205.7 | 5,540.3 | 14,665.4 | 2,465.4 | 12,200.0 | 104.8 | 28.7 | 76.1 | 12.8 | 63.3 |
| 2018.............. | 21,462.3 | 5,712.7 | 15,749.6 | 2,313.2 | 13,436.4 | 106.1 | 28.2 | 77.8 | 11.4 | 66.4 |
| 2019, estimate. .. | 22,775.5 | 5,856.9 | 16,918.6 | (NA) | (NA) | 107.0 | 27.5 | 79.5 | (NA) | (NA) |

NA Not available. [1] Gross domestic product; see text, Section 13.

Source: U.S. Office of Management and Budget, *Budget of the U.S. Government, Fiscal Year 2020: Historical Tables*, March 2019. See also <http://www.whitehouse.gov/omb/budget>.

# Table 503. Federal Budget Outlays by Type: 1990 to 2019

[1,253.0 represents $1,253,000,000,000. For fiscal years ending September 30. Given the inherent imprecision in adjusting outlays for inflation, the data shown in constant dollars present a reasonable perspective, not precision. The deflators and the categories that are deflated are as comparable over time as feasible. Minus sign (-) indicates offset]

| Type | Unit | 1990 | 2000 | 2005 | 2010 | 2017 | 2018 | 2019, est. |
|---|---|---|---|---|---|---|---|---|
| **Current dollar outlays** | **Bil. dol.** | **1,253.0** | **1,789.0** | **2,472.0** | **3,457.1** | **3,981.6** | **4,109.0** | **4,529.2** |
| National defense [1] | Bil. dol. | 299.3 | 294.4 | 495.3 | 693.5 | 598.7 | 631.2 | 684.6 |
| Nondefense, total | Bil. dol. | 953.7 | 1,494.6 | 1,976.7 | 2,763.6 | 3,382.9 | 3,477.9 | 3,844.6 |
| Payments for individuals | Bil. dol. | 592.4 | 1,067.4 | 1,511.9 | 2,305.9 | 2,871.7 | 2,893.1 | 3,150.8 |
| Direct payments [2] | Bil. dol. | 513.5 | 876.6 | 1,229.0 | 1,906.7 | 2,360.0 | 2,363.6 | 2,582.4 |
| Grants to state and local governments.... | Bil. dol. | 78.9 | 190.7 | 282.9 | 399.2 | 511.7 | 529.4 | 568.5 |
| All other grants | Bil. dol. | 56.2 | 95.1 | 145.1 | 209.2 | 163.1 | 167.1 | 181.1 |
| Net interest [2] | Bil. dol. | 184.3 | 222.9 | 184.0 | 196.2 | 262.6 | 325.0 | 393.5 |
| All other [2] | Bil. dol. | 157.4 | 151.7 | 200.9 | 134.4 | 175.5 | 190.6 | 216.1 |
| Undistributed offsetting receipts [2] | Bil. dol. | -36.6 | -42.6 | -65.2 | -82.1 | -89.8 | -97.9 | -96.9 |
| **Constant (2012) dollar outlays** | **Bil. dol.** | **2,130.9** | **2,377.3** | **2,888.5** | **3,608.3** | **3,753.8** | **3,779.5** | **4,076.3** |
| National defense [1] | Bil. dol. | 542.7 | 431.6 | 587.5 | 723.7 | 572.5 | 591.0 | 628.2 |
| Nondefense, total | Bil. dol. | 1,588.4 | 1,945.8 | 2,300.9 | 2,884.5 | 3,181.2 | 3,188.4 | 3,448.1 |
| Payments for individuals | Bil. dol. | 942.4 | 1,367.2 | 1,747.6 | 2,406.3 | 2,707.3 | 2,660.4 | 2,835.3 |
| Direct payments [2] | Bil. dol. | 816.6 | 1,122.2 | 1,420.1 | 1,989.7 | 2,225.0 | 2,173.7 | 2,324.0 |
| Grants to state and local governments.... | Bil. dol. | 125.7 | 245.0 | 327.5 | 416.7 | 482.3 | 486.7 | 511.4 |
| All other grants | Bil. dol. | 112.1 | 143.2 | 183.6 | 220.8 | 150.0 | 148.4 | 156.1 |
| Net interest [2] | Bil. dol. | 290.8 | 285.8 | 211.1 | 203.9 | 243.2 | 294.6 | 349.7 |
| All other [2] | Bil. dol. | 325.5 | 214.4 | 238.1 | 139.6 | 162.2 | 172.0 | 191.4 |
| Undistributed offsetting receipts [2] | Bil. dol. | -82.4 | -64.8 | -79.5 | -86.0 | -81.5 | -86.9 | -84.4 |
| **Outlays as percent of GDP [3]** | **Percent** | **21.2** | **17.7** | **19.3** | **23.3** | **20.7** | **20.3** | **21.3** |
| National defense [1] | Percent | 5.1 | 2.9 | 3.9 | 4.7 | 3.1 | 3.1 | 3.2 |
| Nondefense, total | Percent | 16.2 | 14.8 | 15.4 | 18.6 | 17.6 | 17.2 | 18.1 |
| Payments for individuals | Percent | 10.0 | 10.5 | 11.8 | 15.5 | 14.9 | 14.3 | 14.8 |
| Direct payments [2] | Percent | 8.7 | 8.7 | 9.6 | 12.8 | 12.2 | 11.7 | 12.1 |
| Grants to state and local governments.... | Percent | 1.3 | 1.9 | 2.2 | 2.7 | 2.7 | 2.6 | 2.7 |
| All other grants | Percent | 1.0 | 0.9 | 1.1 | 1.4 | 0.8 | 0.8 | 0.9 |
| Net interest [2] | Percent | 3.1 | 2.2 | 1.4 | 1.3 | 1.4 | 1.6 | 1.8 |
| All other [2] | Percent | 2.7 | 1.5 | 1.6 | 0.9 | 0.9 | 0.9 | 1.0 |
| Undistributed offsetting receipts [2] | Percent | -0.6 | -0.4 | -0.5 | -0.6 | -0.5 | -0.5 | -0.5 |

[1] Includes a small amount of grants to state and local governments and direct payments for individuals. [2] Includes some off-budget amounts; most of the off-budget amounts are direct payments for individuals (social security benefits). [3] Gross domestic product; see text, Section 13.

Source: U.S. Office of Management and Budget, *Budget of the U.S. Government, Fiscal Year 2020: Historical Tables*, March 2019. See also <http://www.whitehouse.gov/omb/budget>.

# Table 504. Federal Budget Outlays by Agency: 1990 to 2019

[In billions of dollars (1,253.0 represents $1,253,000,000,000). For fiscal years ending September 30]

| Department or other unit | 1990 | 2000 | 2005 | 2010 | 2017 | 2018 | 2019, est. |
|---|---|---|---|---|---|---|---|
| **Outlays, total [1]** | **1,253.0** | **1,789.0** | **2,472.0** | **3,457.1** | **3,981.6** | **4,109.0** | **4,529.2** |
| Legislative branch | 2.2 | 2.9 | 4.0 | 5.8 | 4.5 | 4.7 | 5.8 |
| Judicial branch | 1.6 | 4.1 | 5.5 | 7.2 | 7.6 | 7.8 | 8.0 |
| Agriculture | 45.9 | 75.1 | 85.3 | 129.5 | 127.6 | 136.7 | 156.0 |
| Commerce | 3.7 | 7.8 | 6.1 | 13.2 | 10.3 | 8.6 | 14.1 |
| Defense—Military | 289.7 | 281.0 | 474.4 | 666.7 | 568.9 | 600.7 | 652.2 |
| Education | 23.0 | 33.5 | 72.9 | 93.7 | 111.7 | 63.7 | 108.3 |
| Energy | 12.1 | 15.0 | 21.3 | 30.8 | 25.8 | 26.5 | 31.6 |
| Health and Human Services | 175.5 | 382.3 | 581.4 | 854.1 | 1,116.8 | 1,120.5 | 1,230.3 |
| Homeland Security | 7.2 | 13.2 | 38.7 | 44.5 | 50.5 | 68.4 | 62.3 |
| Housing and Urban Development | 20.2 | 30.8 | 42.5 | 60.1 | 55.6 | 54.7 | 32.1 |
| Interior | 5.8 | 8.0 | 9.3 | 13.2 | 12.2 | 13.2 | 12.1 |
| Justice | 5.9 | 16.8 | 22.4 | 29.6 | 31.0 | 34.5 | 41.4 |
| Labor | 26.1 | 31.9 | 46.9 | 173.1 | 40.1 | 39.6 | 37.1 |
| State | 4.8 | 6.7 | 12.7 | 23.8 | 27.1 | 26.4 | 29.7 |
| Transportation | 25.6 | 41.6 | 56.6 | 77.8 | 79.4 | 78.5 | 83.4 |
| Treasury | 253.9 | 390.5 | 410.2 | 444.3 | 546.4 | 629.5 | 709.4 |
| Veterans Affairs | 29.0 | 47.0 | 69.8 | 108.3 | 176.1 | 178.5 | 199.9 |
| Corps of Engineers—Civil Works | 3.3 | 4.2 | 4.7 | 9.9 | 6.5 | 5.1 | 8.5 |
| Other Defense—Civil Programs | 21.7 | 32.8 | 43.5 | 54.0 | 58.7 | 55.4 | 62.2 |
| Environmental Protection Agency | 5.1 | 7.2 | 7.9 | 11.0 | 8.1 | 8.1 | 7.0 |
| Executive Office of the President | 0.2 | 0.3 | 7.7 | 0.6 | 0.4 | 0.4 | 0.4 |
| International Assistance Programs | 10.1 | 12.1 | 15.0 | 20.0 | 18.9 | 21.6 | 24.3 |
| National Aeronautics and Space Administration | 12.4 | 13.4 | 15.6 | 18.9 | 18.7 | 19.8 | 21.0 |
| National Science Foundation | 1.8 | 3.4 | 5.4 | 6.7 | 7.2 | 7.2 | 7.2 |
| Office of Personnel Management | 31.9 | 48.7 | 59.5 | 69.9 | 95.5 | 98.8 | 102.5 |
| Social Security Administration (on-budget) | 17.3 | 45.1 | 54.6 | 70.8 | 93.3 | 87.9 | 93.8 |
| Social Security Administration (off-budget) | 245.0 | 396.2 | 506.8 | 683.4 | 907.5 | 952.0 | 1,010.6 |
| Undistributed offsetting receipts [2] | -98.9 | -173.0 | -226.2 | -267.9 | -236.9 | -248.0 | -245.8 |

[1] Includes other agencies, not shown separately. [2] Includes some off-budget amounts; most of the off-budget amounts are direct payments to individuals (social security benefits).

Source: U.S. Office of Management and Budget, *Budget of the U.S. Government, Fiscal Year 2020: Historical Tables*, March 2019. See also <http://www.whitehouse.gov/omb/budget>.

# Table 505. Federal Budget Outlays by Detailed Function: 1990 to 2019

[In billions of dollars (1,253.0 represents $1,253,000,000,000). For fiscal years ending September 30. Minus sign (-) indicates decrease]

| Superfunction and function | 1990 | 2000 | 2005 | 2010 | 2015 | 2016 | 2017 | 2018 | 2019, est. |
|---|---|---|---|---|---|---|---|---|---|
| **Total outlays** | **1,253.0** | **1,789.0** | **2,472.0** | **3,457.1** | **3,691.8** | **3,852.6** | **3,981.6** | **4,109.0** | **4,529.2** |
| National defense [1] | 299.3 | 294.4 | 495.3 | 693.5 | 589.7 | 593.4 | 598.7 | 631.2 | 684.6 |
| Department of Defense—Military | 289.7 | 281.0 | 474.1 | 666.7 | 562.5 | 565.4 | 568.9 | 600.7 | 652.2 |
| Military personnel | 75.6 | 76.0 | 127.5 | 155.7 | 145.2 | 147.9 | 144.7 | 145.8 | 156.7 |
| Operation and maintenance | 88.3 | 105.8 | 188.1 | 276.0 | 247.2 | 243.2 | 245.2 | 256.7 | 275.8 |
| Procurement | 81.0 | 51.7 | 82.3 | 133.6 | 101.3 | 102.7 | 104.1 | 112.7 | 123.3 |
| Research, development, test, and evaluation | 37.5 | 37.6 | 65.7 | 77.0 | 64.1 | 64.9 | 68.1 | 77.0 | 85.3 |
| Military construction | 5.1 | 5.1 | 5.3 | 21.2 | 8.1 | 6.7 | 6.7 | 6.7 | 7.9 |
| Atomic energy defense activities | 9.0 | 12.1 | 18.0 | 19.3 | 18.7 | 19.4 | 20.5 | 20.9 | 23.6 |
| International affairs [1] | 13.8 | 17.2 | 34.6 | 45.2 | 52.0 | 45.3 | 46.3 | 49.0 | 54.3 |
| International development and humanitarian assistance | 5.5 | 6.5 | 17.7 | 19.0 | 24.1 | 24.1 | 24.5 | 25.1 | 26.0 |
| International security assistance | 8.7 | 6.4 | 7.9 | 11.4 | 12.9 | 11.3 | 12.2 | 11.4 | 13.1 |
| Conduct of foreign affairs | 3.0 | 4.7 | 9.1 | 13.6 | 13.2 | 13.9 | 12.9 | 12.0 | 13.7 |
| General science, space, and technology | 14.4 | 18.6 | 23.6 | 30.1 | 29.4 | 30.2 | 30.4 | 31.5 | 33.8 |
| General science and basic research | 2.8 | 6.2 | 8.8 | 11.7 | 11.7 | 12.0 | 12.3 | 12.4 | 13.6 |
| Space flight, research, and supporting activities | 11.6 | 12.4 | 14.8 | 18.4 | 17.7 | 18.2 | 18.1 | 19.1 | 20.3 |
| Energy [1] | 3.3 | -0.8 | 0.4 | 11.6 | 6.8 | 3.7 | 3.9 | 2.2 | 3.2 |
| Energy supply | 2.0 | -1.8 | -0.9 | 5.8 | 4.7 | 2.0 | 2.8 | 1.4 | 1.7 |
| Natural resources and environment [1] | 17.1 | 25.0 | 28.0 | 43.7 | 36.0 | 39.1 | 37.9 | 39.1 | 39.9 |
| Water resources | 4.4 | 5.1 | 5.7 | 11.7 | 7.8 | 7.4 | 7.5 | 6.0 | 10.3 |
| Conservation and land management | 4.0 | 6.8 | 6.2 | 10.8 | 10.5 | 12.3 | 12.2 | 13.4 | 10.0 |
| Recreational resources | 1.4 | 2.5 | 3.0 | 3.9 | 3.5 | 3.7 | 3.9 | 4.0 | 4.3 |
| Pollution control and abatement | 5.2 | 7.4 | 8.1 | 10.8 | 7.2 | 8.6 | 8.1 | 8.0 | 7.1 |
| Agriculture | 11.6 | 36.5 | 26.6 | 21.4 | 18.5 | 18.3 | 18.9 | 21.8 | 38.1 |
| Farm income stabilization | 9.6 | 33.4 | 22.0 | 16.5 | 13.4 | 13.4 | 14.2 | 16.7 | 31.0 |
| Agricultural research and services | 2.1 | 3.0 | 4.5 | 4.9 | 5.1 | 4.9 | 4.7 | 5.1 | 7.1 |
| Commerce and housing credit [1] | 67.6 | 3.2 | 7.6 | -82.3 | -37.9 | -34.1 | -26.7 | -9.5 | -26.4 |
| Mortgage credit | 3.8 | -3.3 | -0.9 | 35.8 | -35.7 | -34.7 | -30.1 | -7.4 | -48.6 |
| Postal service | 2.1 | 2.1 | -1.2 | -0.7 | -1.6 | -1.3 | -2.2 | -1.4 | -0.9 |
| Deposit insurance | 57.9 | -3.1 | -1.4 | -32.0 | -12.8 | -13.1 | -12.1 | -15.9 | -6.6 |
| Transportation [1] | 29.5 | 46.9 | 67.9 | 92.0 | 89.5 | 92.6 | 93.6 | 92.8 | 98.9 |
| Ground transportation | 19.0 | 31.7 | 42.3 | 60.8 | 59.1 | 62.1 | 62.9 | 61.9 | 63.6 |
| Air transportation | 7.2 | 10.6 | 18.8 | 21.4 | 20.0 | 20.0 | 20.3 | 20.2 | 22.9 |
| Water transportation | 3.2 | 4.4 | 6.4 | 9.4 | 10.0 | 10.1 | 10.1 | 10.2 | 11.8 |
| Community and regional development [1] | 8.5 | 10.6 | 26.3 | 23.9 | 20.7 | 20.1 | 24.9 | 42.2 | 33.0 |
| Community development | 3.5 | 5.5 | 5.9 | 9.9 | 7.8 | 7.1 | 6.7 | 7.1 | 8.1 |
| Disaster relief and insurance | 2.1 | 2.6 | 17.7 | 10.7 | 9.0 | 10.6 | 15.1 | 32.3 | 21.0 |
| Education, training, employment, and social services [1] | 37.2 | 53.8 | 97.6 | 128.6 | 122.1 | 109.7 | 144.0 | 95.5 | 142.5 |
| Elementary, secondary, and vocational education | 9.9 | 20.6 | 38.3 | 73.3 | 40.0 | 39.8 | 40.6 | 39.5 | 45.3 |
| Higher education | 11.1 | 10.1 | 31.4 | 20.9 | 51.3 | 38.8 | 71.8 | 24.6 | 63.7 |
| Research and general education aids | 1.6 | 2.5 | 3.1 | 3.6 | 3.5 | 3.5 | 3.7 | 3.6 | 3.9 |
| Training and employment | 5.6 | 6.8 | 6.9 | 9.9 | 7.1 | 7.0 | 7.0 | 6.8 | 7.4 |
| Social services | 8.1 | 12.6 | 16.3 | 19.2 | 18.3 | 18.8 | 18.9 | 19.1 | 20.3 |
| Health | 57.7 | 154.5 | 250.5 | 369.1 | 482.2 | 511.3 | 533.1 | 551.2 | 601.0 |
| Health care services | 47.6 | 136.2 | 219.6 | 330.7 | 446.4 | 474.8 | 492.8 | 511.6 | 557.4 |
| Health research and training | 8.6 | 16.0 | 28.1 | 34.2 | 31.4 | 31.8 | 34.9 | 35.5 | 38.6 |
| Consumer and occupational health and safety | 1.5 | 2.3 | 2.9 | 4.1 | 4.5 | 4.7 | 5.4 | 4.2 | 4.9 |
| Medicare | 98.1 | 197.1 | 298.6 | 451.6 | 546.2 | 594.5 | 597.3 | 588.7 | 651.2 |
| Income security [1] | 148.8 | 253.7 | 345.8 | 622.2 | 508.8 | 514.1 | 503.5 | 495.3 | 533.2 |
| General retirement and disability insurance (excluding social security) | 5.1 | 5.2 | 7.0 | 6.6 | 7.8 | 3.8 | 4.5 | 6.3 | 6.0 |
| Federal employee retirement and disability | 52.0 | 77.2 | 93.4 | 119.9 | 139.2 | 144.8 | 142.2 | 140.7 | 148.7 |
| Unemployment compensation | 18.9 | 23.0 | 35.4 | 160.1 | 35.0 | 35.2 | 33.3 | 30.9 | 29.1 |
| Housing assistance | 15.9 | 28.9 | 37.9 | 58.7 | 47.8 | 49.1 | 50.0 | 49.5 | 51.4 |
| Food and nutrition assistance | 24.1 | 32.5 | 50.8 | 95.1 | 104.8 | 102.3 | 99.7 | 98.1 | 101.9 |
| Social security | 248.6 | 409.4 | 523.3 | 706.7 | 887.8 | 916.1 | 944.9 | 987.8 | 1,047.0 |
| Veterans' benefits and services [1] | 29.0 | 47.0 | 70.1 | 108.4 | 159.7 | 174.5 | 176.5 | 178.9 | 200.5 |
| Income security for veterans | 15.3 | 24.9 | 35.8 | 49.2 | 76.4 | 86.8 | 86.1 | 85.5 | 101.2 |
| Veterans education, training, and rehabilitation | 0.2 | 1.3 | 2.8 | 8.1 | 13.4 | 14.4 | 13.3 | 12.4 | 13.9 |
| Hospital and medical care for veterans | 12.1 | 19.5 | 28.8 | 45.7 | 61.9 | 65.2 | 69.7 | 73.9 | 79.2 |
| Veterans housing | 0.5 | 0.4 | 0.9 | 0.5 | 0.7 | 0.8 | -0.5 | -1.3 | -3.1 |
| Administration of justice | 10.2 | 28.5 | 40.0 | 54.4 | 51.9 | 55.8 | 57.9 | 60.4 | 71.8 |
| Federal law enforcement activities | 4.8 | 12.1 | 19.9 | 28.7 | 26.9 | 28.9 | 29.8 | 31.3 | 34.6 |
| Federal litigative and judicial activities | 3.6 | 7.8 | 10.7 | 14.5 | 14.7 | 14.9 | 15.1 | 17.0 | 19.3 |
| Federal correctional activities | 1.3 | 3.7 | 4.8 | 6.3 | 7.0 | 7.0 | 7.0 | 6.8 | 7.0 |
| Criminal justice assistance | 0.5 | 4.9 | 4.6 | 4.8 | 3.2 | 5.0 | 6.0 | 5.3 | 10.8 |
| General government | 10.5 | 13.0 | 17.0 | 23.0 | 21.0 | 23.1 | 23.8 | 23.9 | 26.8 |
| Net interest [1] | 184.3 | 222.9 | 184.0 | 196.2 | 223.2 | 240.0 | 262.6 | 325.0 | 393.5 |
| Interest on Treasury debt securities (gross) | 264.7 | 361.9 | 352.3 | 413.9 | 402.4 | 430.0 | 456.9 | 521.6 | 593.1 |
| Interest received by on-budget trust funds | -46.3 | -69.3 | -69.2 | -67.3 | -45.8 | -55.5 | -60.5 | -66.3 | -66.1 |
| Interest received by off-budget trust funds | -16.0 | -59.8 | -91.8 | -118.5 | -96.0 | -90.6 | -86.5 | -83.8 | -82.7 |
| Allowances | – | – | – | – | – | – | – | – | -0.7 |
| Undistributed offsetting receipts [2] | -36.6 | -42.6 | -65.2 | -82.1 | -115.8 | -95.3 | -89.8 | -97.9 | -96.9 |

– Represents or rounds to zero. [1] Includes functions not shown separately. [2] Includes some off-budget amounts; most of the off-budget amounts are direct payments for individuals (social security benefits).

Source: U.S. Office of Management and Budget, *Budget of the U.S. Government, Fiscal Year 2020: Historical Tables*, March 2019. See also <http://www.whitehouse.gov/omb/budget>.

# Table 506. Federal Budget Outlays for Payments for Individuals by Category and Major Program: 1990 to 2019

[In billions of dollars (592.4 represents $592,400,000,000). For fiscal years ending September 30]

| Category and program | 1990 | 2000 | 2005 | 2010 | 2015 | 2016 | 2017 | 2018 | 2019, est. |
|---|---|---|---|---|---|---|---|---|---|
| **Total, payments for individuals** | **592.4** | **1,067.4** | **1,512.6** | **2,307.0** | **2,654.9** | **2,777.8** | **2,873.0** | **2,894.5** | **3,152.3** |
| Social security and railroad retirement | 253.3 | 410.7 | 523.5 | 706.6 | 890.2 | 919.1 | 948.6 | 991.2 | 1,051.5 |
| Social security: | | | | | | | | | |
| Old age and survivors insurance | 221.9 | 351.4 | 434.0 | 576.6 | 738.0 | 766.4 | 795.5 | 837.6 | 893.9 |
| Disability insurance | 24.4 | 54.4 | 84.2 | 123.5 | 143.4 | 143.5 | 143.2 | 143.9 | 146.7 |
| Railroad retirement (excl. social security) | 7.0 | 4.8 | 5.4 | 6.5 | 8.9 | 9.3 | 9.9 | 9.7 | 10.9 |
| Federal employees' retirement and insurance | 64.2 | 100.4 | 127.0 | 166.8 | 212.0 | 228.3 | 225.0 | 224.0 | 247.2 |
| Military retirement | 21.6 | 32.9 | 39.0 | 50.7 | 56.8 | 61.6 | 57.8 | 54.5 | 60.4 |
| Civil service retirement | 31.0 | 45.1 | 54.7 | 69.5 | 81.8 | 82.9 | 83.7 | 85.9 | 87.9 |
| Veterans service-connected compensation | 10.7 | 20.8 | 30.9 | 43.5 | 69.7 | 79.9 | 79.8 | 80.0 | 94.7 |
| Other | 0.8 | 1.7 | 2.4 | 3.2 | 3.7 | 3.9 | 3.7 | 3.6 | 4.1 |
| Unemployment assistance | 17.5 | 21.1 | 33.1 | 158.3 | 32.7 | 32.9 | 30.9 | 28.5 | 27.2 |
| Medical care [1] | 167.4 | 368.6 | 575.4 | 876.8 | 1,111.0 | 1,197.2 | 1,233.5 | 1,264.1 | 1,378.5 |
| Medicare: | | | | | | | | | |
| Hospital insurance | 65.9 | 127.9 | 181.3 | 245.6 | 273.5 | 286.0 | 290.3 | 292.1 | 320.4 |
| Supplementary medical insurance | 41.5 | 87.2 | 150.0 | 264.9 | 348.6 | 391.5 | 399.8 | 400.1 | 442.2 |
| State children's health insurance | – | 1.2 | 5.1 | 7.9 | 9.2 | 14.4 | 16.3 | 17.3 | 18.6 |
| Medicaid | 41.1 | 117.9 | 181.7 | 272.8 | 349.8 | 368.3 | 374.7 | 389.2 | 418.7 |
| Indian health | 1.1 | 2.4 | 3.1 | 4.4 | 4.6 | 4.1 | 4.1 | 4.2 | 5.5 |
| Hospital and medical care for veterans | 12.3 | 20.1 | 30.7 | 48.5 | 63.7 | 65.8 | 67.9 | 72.9 | 77.8 |
| Health resources and services | 1.4 | 3.9 | 5.9 | 7.1 | 7.7 | 8.8 | 9.3 | 9.5 | 9.8 |
| Substance abuse and mental health services | 1.2 | 2.5 | 3.2 | 3.3 | 3.1 | 3.4 | 3.4 | 3.8 | 4.9 |
| Uniformed Services retiree health care fund | – | – | 6.3 | 8.4 | 10.0 | 9.8 | 9.9 | 10.1 | 11.0 |
| Other | 2.9 | 5.4 | 8.2 | 14.0 | 12.7 | 13.3 | 14.0 | 14.3 | 14.8 |
| Assistance to students | 11.2 | 10.9 | 32.1 | 55.5 | 74.7 | 60.2 | 102.0 | 60.9 | 87.8 |
| Veterans' education benefits | 0.8 | 1.6 | 3.3 | 8.8 | 13.6 | 14.6 | 13.5 | 12.7 | 14.2 |
| Student assistance, Department of Education and other | 10.4 | 9.2 | 28.9 | 46.8 | 61.1 | 45.6 | 88.5 | 48.2 | 73.6 |
| Housing assistance | 15.9 | 28.6 | 37.5 | 57.6 | 46.7 | 48.0 | 48.9 | 48.4 | 50.2 |
| Food and nutrition assistance | 24.0 | 32.4 | 50.7 | 95.0 | 104.6 | 102.1 | 99.6 | 97.9 | 101.6 |
| SNAP (including Puerto Rico) [2] | 15.9 | 18.3 | 32.6 | 70.5 | 76.1 | 73.1 | 70.1 | 68.5 | 71.2 |
| Child nutrition and special milk programs | 5.0 | 9.2 | 11.9 | 16.4 | 21.0 | 22.0 | 22.5 | 22.8 | 23.9 |
| Supplemental feeding programs (WIC and CSFP [3]) | 2.1 | 4.0 | 5.0 | 6.5 | 6.3 | 6.0 | 5.7 | 5.4 | 5.4 |
| Commodity donations and other | 1.0 | 0.9 | 1.2 | 1.6 | 1.1 | 1.1 | 1.2 | 1.1 | 1.2 |
| Public assistance and related programs [1] | 34.9 | 88.5 | 123.4 | 183.2 | 175.3 | 180.2 | 174.2 | 169.7 | 195.6 |
| Supplemental security income program | 11.5 | 29.7 | 35.4 | 44.0 | 52.3 | 56.7 | 51.9 | 47.9 | 53.1 |
| Family support payments to states and TANF [4] | 12.2 | 18.4 | 21.3 | 21.9 | 20.0 | 19.7 | 20.0 | 20.6 | 20.8 |
| Low income home energy assistance | 1.3 | 1.5 | 2.1 | 4.6 | 3.4 | 3.3 | 3.2 | 3.4 | 3.7 |
| Earned income tax credit | 4.4 | 26.1 | 34.6 | 54.7 | 60.1 | 60.6 | 59.7 | 58.6 | 60.7 |
| Payments to states for daycare assistance | – | 3.3 | 4.9 | 5.9 | 5.1 | 5.3 | 5.7 | 5.9 | 7.6 |
| Veterans' non-service-connected pensions | 3.6 | 3.0 | 3.7 | 4.4 | 5.3 | 5.8 | 5.5 | 4.8 | 5.2 |
| Payments to states for foster care/adoption assistance | 1.6 | 5.5 | 6.4 | 7.0 | 7.3 | 7.7 | 7.7 | 8.6 | 7.9 |
| Payment where child credit exceeds tax liability | – | 0.8 | 14.6 | 22.7 | 20.6 | 20.2 | 19.4 | 18.6 | 35.5 |
| Other public assistance | 0.3 | 0.3 | 0.4 | 18.1 | 1.2 | 1.0 | 0.9 | 1.4 | 1.2 |
| All other payments for individuals | 4.0 | 6.2 | 9.8 | 7.2 | 7.7 | 9.8 | 10.4 | 9.7 | 12.7 |
| Coal miners and black lung benefits | 1.5 | 1.5 | 1.4 | 0.5 | 0.4 | 0.4 | 0.5 | 0.5 | 0.4 |
| Veterans' insurance and burial benefits | 1.4 | 1.4 | 1.4 | 1.3 | 1.2 | 0.9 | 0.6 | 0.6 | 1.0 |
| Aging services programs | – | 0.9 | 1.4 | 1.5 | 1.7 | 2.0 | 1.9 | 1.9 | 2.2 |
| Energy employees compensation fund | – | – | 0.6 | 1.1 | 1.0 | 1.1 | 1.2 | 1.4 | 1.4 |
| September 11th victim compensation | – | – | (Z) | – | 0.1 | 1.7 | (Z) | (Z) | – |
| Refugee assistance and other | 1.1 | 2.4 | 5.0 | 2.8 | 3.2 | 3.7 | 6.2 | 5.3 | 7.7 |

– Represents zero. Z Less than $50,000,000. [1] Includes other items not shown separately. [2] Supplemental Nutrition Assistance Program, formerly known as food stamps. [3] WIC is Women, Infants, and Children. CSFP is Commodity Supplemental Food Program. [4] TANF is Temporary Assistance for Needy Families.

Source: U.S. Office of Management and Budget, *Budget of the U.S. Government, Fiscal Year 2020: Historical Tables*, March 2019. See also <http://www.whitehouse.gov/omb/budget>.

# Table 507. Federal Budget Receipts by Source: 1990 to 2019

[In billions of dollars (1,032.0 represents $1,032,000,000,000). For fiscal years ending September 30. Receipts reflect collections. Covers both federal funds and trust funds; see text, this section. Minus sign (-) indicates decrease]

| Source | 1990 | 2000 | 2005 | 2010 | 2015 | 2016 | 2017 | 2018 | 2019, est. |
|---|---|---|---|---|---|---|---|---|---|
| **Total federal receipts**............ | **1,032.0** | **2,025.2** | **2,153.6** | **2,162.7** | **3,249.9** | **3,268.0** | **3,316.2** | **3,329.9** | **3,437.7** |
| (On-budget)..................... | 750.3 | 1,544.6 | 1,576.1 | 1,531.0 | 2,479.5 | 2,457.8 | 2,465.6 | 2,475.2 | 2,526.5 |
| (Off-budget)..................... | 281.7 | 480.6 | 577.5 | 631.7 | 770.4 | 810.2 | 850.6 | 854.7 | 911.1 |
| Individual income taxes............ | 466.9 | 1,004.5 | 927.2 | 898.5 | 1,540.8 | 1,546.1 | 1,587.1 | 1,683.5 | 1,698.4 |
| Corporation income taxes.......... | 93.5 | 207.3 | 278.3 | 191.4 | 343.8 | 299.6 | 297.0 | 204.7 | 216.2 |
| Social insurance and retirement receipts....... | 380.0 | 652.9 | 794.1 | 864.8 | 1,065.3 | 1,115.1 | 1,161.9 | 1,170.7 | 1,242.4 |
| Excise taxes..................... | 35.3 | 68.9 | 73.1 | 66.9 | 98.3 | 95.0 | 83.8 | 95.0 | 98.7 |
| Other.......................... | 56.2 | 91.7 | 80.9 | 141.0 | 201.8 | 212.2 | 186.3 | 175.9 | 182.0 |
| **Social insurance and retirement receipts** | **380.0** | **652.9** | **794.1** | **864.8** | **1,065.3** | **1,115.1** | **1,161.9** | **1,170.7** | **1,242.4** |
| Employment and general retirement, total...... | 353.9 | 620.5 | 747.7 | 815.9 | 1,010.4 | 1,062.3 | 1,111.9 | 1,121.2 | 1,193.0 |
| Old-age and survivors insurance (off-budget)................ | 255.0 | 411.7 | 493.6 | 540.0 | 658.5 | 665.7 | 688.0 | 691.2 | 767.7 |
| Disability insurance (off-budget)............... | 26.6 | 68.9 | 83.8 | 91.7 | 111.8 | 144.5 | 162.6 | 163.5 | 143.4 |
| Hospital insurance................ | 68.6 | 135.5 | 166.1 | 180.1 | 234.2 | 246.8 | 255.9 | 260.7 | 276.3 |
| Railroad retirement/pension fund........... | 2.3 | 2.7 | 2.3 | 2.3 | 3.3 | 3.1 | 3.1 | 3.4 | 3.3 |
| Unemployment insurance funds................ | 21.6 | 27.6 | 42.0 | 44.8 | 51.2 | 48.9 | 45.8 | 45.0 | 44.4 |
| Other retirement.................. | 4.5 | 4.8 | 4.5 | 4.1 | 3.7 | 3.9 | 4.2 | 4.5 | 5.0 |
| Federal employees retirement—employee share................. | 4.4 | 4.7 | 4.4 | 4.1 | 3.6 | 3.9 | 4.2 | 4.5 | 5.0 |
| **Excise taxes, total**............... | **35.3** | **68.9** | **73.1** | **66.9** | **98.3** | **95.0** | **83.8** | **95.0** | **98.7** |
| Federal funds [1]................. | 15.6 | 22.7 | 22.5 | 18.3 | 37.8 | 34.0 | 21.2 | 30.1 | 32.9 |
| Alcohol........................ | 5.7 | 8.1 | 8.1 | 9.2 | 9.6 | 9.8 | 9.9 | 10.1 | 10.2 |
| Tobacco....................... | 4.1 | 7.2 | 7.9 | 17.2 | 14.5 | 14.1 | 13.8 | 12.9 | 13.2 |
| Telephone..................... | 3.0 | 5.7 | 6.0 | 1.0 | 0.6 | 0.5 | 0.6 | 0.5 | 0.5 |
| Ozone-depleting chemicals/products......... | 0.4 | 0.1 | – | – | – | – | – | – | – |
| Transportation fuels.............. | – | 0.8 | -0.8 | -11.0 | -3.4 | -4.8 | -3.4 | -1.5 | -3.7 |
| Health insurance providers.................. | – | – | – | – | 11.3 | 11.2 | 0.1 | 4.7 | 9.6 |
| Indoor tanning services............. | – | – | – | – | 0.1 | 0.1 | 0.1 | 0.1 | 0.1 |
| Trust funds [1]................... | 19.8 | 46.2 | 50.5 | 48.7 | 60.5 | 61.0 | 62.6 | 64.9 | 65.8 |
| Transportation.................. | 13.9 | 35.0 | 37.9 | 35.0 | 40.8 | 41.3 | 41.0 | 42.6 | 42.8 |
| Airport and airway............... | 3.7 | 9.7 | 10.3 | 10.6 | 14.3 | 14.4 | 15.1 | 15.8 | 16.3 |
| Black lung disability............. | 0.7 | 0.5 | 0.6 | 0.6 | 0.6 | 0.4 | 0.4 | 0.4 | 0.2 |
| Inland waterway................. | 0.1 | 0.1 | 0.1 | 0.1 | 0.1 | 0.1 | 0.1 | 0.1 | 0.1 |
| Hazardous substance superfund.............. | 0.8 | (Z) | – | – | – | – | – | – | – |
| Oil spill liability................. | 0.1 | 0.2 | – | 0.5 | 0.5 | 0.5 | 0.5 | 0.5 | 0.1 |
| Aquatic resources............... | 0.2 | 0.3 | 0.4 | 0.6 | 0.6 | 0.6 | 0.6 | 0.6 | 0.6 |
| Leaking underground storage tank............ | 0.1 | 0.2 | 0.2 | 0.2 | 0.2 | 0.2 | 0.2 | 0.2 | 0.2 |
| Tobacco assessments............ | – | – | 0.9 | 0.9 | (Z) | (Z) | (Z) | (Z) | – |
| Vaccine Injury compensation.............. | 0.2 | 0.1 | 0.1 | 0.2 | 0.3 | 0.3 | 0.3 | 0.3 | 0.3 |

– Represents zero. Z less than $50,000,000. [1] Includes other funds, not shown separately.

Source: U.S. Office of Management and Budget, *Budget of the U.S. Government, Fiscal Year 2020: Historical Tables*, March 2019. See also <http://www.whitehouse.gov/omb/budget>.


# Table 508. Federal Trust Fund Income, Outlays, and Balances: 2018 to 2020

[In billions of dollars (17.2 represents $17,200,000,000). For fiscal years ending September 30. Income reflects receipts deposited. Outlays are on a checks-issued basis less refunds collected. Balances reflect funds that have not been spent. See text, this section, for discussion of the budget concept and trust funds]

| Description | Income | | | Outlays | | | Balances [1] | | |
|---|---|---|---|---|---|---|---|---|---|
| | 2018 | 2019, est. | 2020, est. | 2018 | 2019, est. | 2020, est. | 2018 | 2019, est. | 2020, est. |
| Airport and airway trust fund...................... | 17.2 | 17.8 | 17.8 | -15.3 | -17.1 | -17.6 | 17.0 | 17.7 | 17.9 |
| Civil service retirement and disability fund...... | 103.9 | 104.4 | 108.7 | -86.0 | -88.0 | -89.6 | 923.0 | 939.4 | 958.5 |
| Federal employees' health benefits fund....... | 54.5 | 56.0 | 58.8 | -53.2 | -55.8 | -58.6 | 27.4 | 27.6 | 27.8 |
| Employee life insurance fund.................... | 4.2 | 4.4 | 4.6 | -3.3 | -3.3 | -3.3 | 46.5 | 47.6 | 48.9 |
| Foreign military sales trust fund................ | 32.2 | 43.1 | 47.4 | -31.7 | -43.1 | -47.4 | 33.6 | 33.6 | 33.6 |
| Foreign service retirement and disability fund.. | 1.4 | 1.4 | 1.4 | -1.0 | -1.0 | -1.0 | 19.2 | 19.6 | 20.0 |
| Highway trust fund.................... | 43.8 | 44.1 | 44.3 | -55.6 | -56.7 | -58.1 | 44.5 | 31.9 | 18.0 |
| Medicare: | | | | | | | | | |
| Hospital insurance (HI) trust fund............. | 308.9 | 324.5 | 339.6 | -303.2 | -331.6 | -336.8 | 203.2 | 196.2 | 199.0 |
| Supplemental medical insurance trust fund... | 437.3 | 459.5 | 496.0 | -408.3 | -450.5 | -491.0 | 96.9 | 106.0 | 111.0 |
| Military retirement fund...................... | 135.4 | 144.9 | 150.6 | -54.5 | -60.3 | -62.1 | 735.2 | 819.7 | 908.2 |
| Railroad retirement trust funds.................. | 13.6 | 12.5 | 12.7 | -13.1 | -14.4 | -13.7 | 24.6 | 22.9 | 22.3 |
| Social security: | | | | | | | | | |
| Disability insurance trust fund.................. | 170.3 | 150.4 | 145.2 | -146.6 | -149.6 | -151.2 | 93.1 | 94 | 88.1 |
| Old-age and survivors trust fund............. | 822.5 | 897.9 | 943.7 | -841.5 | -897.8 | -956.2 | 2,801.1 | 2,801.3 | 2,788.8 |
| Unemployment trust funds...................... | 46.9 | 46.6 | 48.9 | -32.3 | -30.5 | -32.0 | 73.1 | 89.2 | 106.0 |
| Other trust funds.................... | 31.6 | 26.8 | 27.7 | -23.8 | -25.3 | -24.1 | 49.7 | 51.1 | 54.8 |

[1] Balances available on a cash basis (rather than an authorization basis) at the end of the year. Balances are primarily invested in federal debt securities.

Source: U.S. Office of Management and Budget, *Budget of the U.S. Government, Fiscal Year 2020: Analytical Perspectives*, March 2019. See also <http://www.whitehouse.gov/omb/budget>.

# Table 509. Tax Expenditure Estimates Relating to Individual and Corporate Income Taxes by Selected Function: 2018 to 2021

[In millions of dollars (12,030 represents $12,030,000,000). For fiscal years ending September 30. Tax expenditures are defined as revenue losses attributable to provisions of the federal tax laws which allow a special exclusion, exemption, or deduction from gross income or which provide a special credit, a preferential rate of tax, or a deferral of liability. Minus sign (-) indicates decrease]

| Function and provision | 2018 | 2019 | 2020 | 2021 |
|---|---|---|---|---|
| **National defense:** | | | | |
| Exclusion of benefits and allowances to armed forces personnel | 12,030 | 12,450 | 11,220 | 11,240 |
| **International affairs:** | | | | |
| Exclusion of income earned abroad by U.S. citizens | 6,930 | 7,280 | 7,640 | 8,020 |
| Exclusion of certain allowances for Federal employees abroad | 240 | 250 | 260 | 280 |
| Inventory property sales source rules exception | 1,250 | – | – | – |
| Reduced tax rate on active income of controlled foreign corporations | 63,400 | 34,490 | 38,950 | 41,870 |
| **General science, space, and technology:** | | | | |
| Expensing of research and experimentation expenditures (normal tax method) | 8,510 | 6,750 | 7,430 | 8,420 |
| Credit for increasing research activities | 13,310 | 14,480 | 15,870 | 17,310 |
| **Energy:** | | | | |
| Energy production credit | 3,150 | 3,240 | 3,320 | 3,510 |
| Energy investment credit | 3,180 | 4,300 | 5,100 | 5,250 |
| Credit for residential energy efficient property | 1,900 | 1,530 | 1,180 | 770 |
| **Commerce and housing:** | | | | |
| Financial institutions and insurance: | | | | |
| Exclusion of life insurance death benefits | 13,510 | 14,350 | 15,550 | 16,600 |
| Housing: | | | | |
| Deductibility of mortgage interest on owner–occupied homes | 37,160 | 26,850 | 29,820 | 33,090 |
| Deductibility of state and local property tax on owner–occupied homes | 15,360 | 6,250 | 6,650 | 7,100 |
| Capital gains exclusion on home sales | 43,760 | 44,380 | 46,600 | 49,000 |
| Exclusion of net imputed rental income | 116,590 | 121,070 | 125,610 | 129,970 |
| Exception from passive loss rules for $25,000 of rental loss | 5,720 | 6,030 | 6,390 | 6,750 |
| Credit for low–income housing investments | 9,140 | 9,040 | 9,070 | 9,230 |
| Commerce: | | | | |
| Capital gains (except agriculture, timber, iron ore, and coal) | 118,630 | 102,910 | 99,210 | 99,890 |
| Step–up basis of capital gains at death | 46,730 | 49,920 | 51,840 | 53,630 |
| Accelerated depreciation of machinery and equipment (normal tax method) | 67,820 | 68,750 | 65,410 | 63,890 |
| Deduction for U.S. production activities | 3,610 | – | – | – |
| **Transportation:** | | | | |
| Exclusion of reimbursed employee parking expenses | 2,120 | 2,201 | 2,271 | 2,343 |
| **Education, training, employment, and social services:** | | | | |
| Education: | | | | |
| Exclusion of scholarship and fellowship income (normal tax method) | 3,070 | 2,840 | 2,960 | 3,100 |
| Tax credits and deductions for postsecondary education expenses | 17,450 | 16,300 | 16,360 | 16,490 |
| Exclusion of interest on bonds for private nonprofit educational facilities | 1,830 | 1,900 | 1,990 | 2,110 |
| Parental personal exemption for students age 19 years or over | 2,860 | – | – | – |
| Deductibility of charitable contributions (education) | 5,400 | 4,140 | 4,450 | 4,790 |
| Training, employment, and social services: | | | | |
| Exclusion of employee meals and lodging (other than military) | 4,640 | 4,260 | 4,390 | 4,530 |
| Credit for child and dependent care expenses | 4,560 | 4,360 | 4,460 | 4,560 |
| Deductibility of charitable contributions, other than education and health | 45,956 | 36,660 | 39,540 | 42,760 |
| **Health:** | | | | |
| Exclusion of employer contributions for medical insurance premiums and medical care | 205,080 | 203,290 | 214,950 | 227,350 |
| Self–employed medical insurance premiums | 7,420 | 7,430 | 7,910 | 8,440 |
| Medical Savings Accounts/Health Savings Accounts | 7,410 | 7,810 | 8,460 | 9,080 |
| Deductibility of medical expenses | 8,840 | 6,890 | 7,130 | 7,880 |
| Exclusion of interest on hospital construction bonds | 2,700 | 2,810 | 2,930 | 3,120 |
| Refundable Premium Assistance Tax Credit | 6,790 | 5,900 | 5,930 | 6,000 |
| Deductibility of charitable contributions (health) | 4,890 | 3,960 | 4,270 | 4,620 |
| **Income security:** | | | | |
| Child credit | 30,450 | 76,010 | 76,930 | 77,910 |
| Exclusion of workers' compensation benefits | 9,590 | 9,680 | 9,780 | 9,880 |
| Net exclusion of pension contributions and earnings: | | | | |
| Defined benefit employer plans | 69,910 | 71,430 | 73,540 | 75,290 |
| Defined contribution employer plans | 72,260 | 75,720 | 84,590 | 90,670 |
| Individual Retirement Accounts (IRAs) | 19,680 | 20,620 | 23,590 | 24,730 |
| Self-employed plans | 24,940 | 24,120 | 26,680 | 29,680 |
| Exclusion of other employee benefits: | | | | |
| Premiums on group term life insurance | 2,810 | 2,810 | 2,930 | 3,060 |
| Earned income tax credit | 8,050 | 8,110 | 2,660 | 2,710 |
| **Social security:** | | | | |
| Exclusion of social security benefits: | | | | |
| Social security benefits for retired and disabled workers, spouses, dependents, and survivors | 32,970 | 29,980 | 31,020 | 32,090 |
| **Veterans' benefits and services:** | | | | |
| Exclusion of veterans' death benefits and disability compensation | 8,240 | 8,180 | 8,710 | 9,060 |
| **General purpose fiscal assistance:** | | | | |
| Exclusion of interest on public purpose state and local bonds | 23,130 | 24,080 | 25,100 | 26,740 |
| Deductibility of nonbusiness state and local tax, other than owner-occupied homes | 22,330 | 4,610 | 7,520 | 8,000 |
| **Interest:** | | | | |
| Deferral of interest on U.S. savings bonds | 950 | 850 | 840 | 840 |
| **Addendum: Aid to state and local governments:** | | | | |
| Deductibility of: | | | | |
| Property taxes on owner–occupied homes | 15,360 | 6,250 | 6,650 | 7,100 |
| Nonbusiness state and local taxes other than on owner–occupied homes | 22,330 | 4,610 | 7,520 | 8,000 |
| Exclusion of interest on state and local bonds for: | | | | |
| Public purposes | 23,130 | 24,080 | 25,100 | 26,740 |
| Private nonprofit educational facilities | 1,830 | 1,900 | 1,990 | 2,110 |
| Hospital construction | 2,700 | 2,810 | 2,930 | 3,120 |

– Represents or rounds to zero.

Source: U.S. Office of Management and Budget, *Fiscal Year 2020 Budget of the U.S. Government: Analytical Perspectives*, March 2019. See also <http://www.whitehouse.gov/omb/budget/>.

## Table 510. Internal Revenue Gross Collections by Type of Tax: 2005 to 2018

[2,269 represents $2,269,000,000,000, except percent. For fiscal years ending September 30. See text, this section, for information on taxes]

| Type of tax | Gross collections (bil. dol.) | | | | | | Percent of total | | | | | |
|---|---|---|---|---|---|---|---|---|---|---|---|---|
| | 2005 | 2010 | 2015 | 2016 | 2017 | 2018 | 2005 | 2010 | 2015 | 2016 | 2017 | 2018 |
| **United States, total**............ | **2,269** | **2,345** | **3,303** | **3,333** | **3,417** | **3,465** | **100.0** | **100.0** | **100.0** | **100.0** | **100.0** | **100.0** |
| Individual income taxes............ | 1,108 | 1,164 | 1,760 | 1,786 | 1,838 | 1,933 | 48.8 | 49.7 | 53.3 | 53.6 | 53.8 | 55.8 |
| Withheld by employers........... | 787 | 900 | 1,241 | 1,267 | 1,331 | 1,349 | 34.7 | 38.4 | 37.6 | 38.0 | 39.0 | 38.9 |
| Tax payments [1]................... | 321 | 264 | 519 | 519 | 507 | 585 | 14.1 | 11.3 | 15.7 | 15.6 | 14.8 | 16.9 |
| Estate and trust income tax....... | (NA) | 12 | 33 | 30 | 29 | 38 | (NA) | 0.5 | 1.0 | 0.9 | 0.8 | 1.1 |
| Employment taxes................. | 771 | 824 | 1,022 | 1,074 | 1,123 | 1,133 | 34.0 | 35.1 | 31.0 | 32.2 | 32.9 | 32.7 |
| Old-age and disability insurance......................... | 760 | 813 | 1,007 | 1,060 | 1,109 | 1,118 | 33.5 | 34.7 | 30.5 | 31.8 | 32.5 | 32.3 |
| Unemployment insurance........ | 7 | 7 | 9 | 8 | 8 | 9 | 0.3 | 0.3 | 0.3 | 0.3 | 0.2 | 0.3 |
| Railroad retirement............. | 5 | 5 | 6 | 6 | 6 | 6 | 0.2 | 0.2 | 0.2 | 0.2 | 0.2 | 0.2 |
| Business income taxes [2]......... | 307 | 278 | 390 | 346 | 339 | 263 | 13.5 | 11.9 | 11.8 | 10.4 | 9.9 | 7.6 |
| Estate and gift taxes.............. | 26 | 20 | 20 | 22 | 24 | 24 | 1.1 | 0.8 | 0.6 | 0.7 | 0.7 | 0.7 |
| Excise taxes...................... | 57 | 47 | 77 | 76 | 64 | 74 | 2.5 | 2.0 | 2.3 | 2.3 | 1.9 | 2.1 |

NA Not available. [1] Includes collections of estimated income tax and payments made in conjunction with individual income tax return filings. Also includes estate and trust income tax for 2005. [2] Includes corporate income tax and tax-exempt organization unrelated business income tax.

Source: U.S. Internal Revenue Service, *IRS Data Book 2018*, May 2019, and earlier editions. See also <https://www.irs.gov/statistics/soi-tax-stats-irs-data-book>.

## Table 511. Individual Income Tax Returns Filed—Audits Coverage: 1995 to 2018

[In units as indicated (114,683 represents 114,683,000). An IRS audit is a review/examination of an organization's or individual's tax return to determine if income, expenses, and credits are being reported accurately. Includes audits based on an earned income tax credit claim, and the resulting recommended additional taxes]

| Year | Returns filed [1] (1,000) | Returns examined | | Total recommended additional tax [3] ($1,000) | Average recommended additional tax per return [3] (dollars) |
|---|---|---|---|---|---|
| | | Total [2] (1,000) | Percent coverage | | |
| 1995.................. | 114,683 | 1,919 | 1.7 | 7,756,954 | 4,041 |
| 1996.................. | 116,060 | 1,942 | 1.7 | 7,600,191 | 3,915 |
| 1997.................. | 118,363 | 1,519 | 1.3 | 8,363,918 | 5,505 |
| 1998.................. | 120,342 | 1,193 | 1.0 | 6,095,698 | 5,110 |
| 1999.................. | 122,547 | 1,100 | 0.9 | 4,458,474 | 4,052 |
| 2000.................. | 124,887 | 618 | 0.5 | 3,388,905 | 5,486 |
| 2001.................. | 127,097 | 732 | 0.6 | 3,301,860 | 4,512 |
| 2002.................. | 129,445 | 744 | 0.6 | 3,636,486 | 4,889 |
| 2003.................. | 130,341 | 849 | 0.7 | 4,559,902 | 5,369 |
| 2004.................. | 130,134 | 997 | 0.8 | 6,201,693 | 6,220 |
| 2005.................. | 130,577 | 1,199 | 0.9 | 13,355,087 | 11,138 |
| 2006.................. | 132,276 | 1,284 | 1.0 | 13,045,221 | 10,160 |
| 2007.................. | 134,543 | 1,385 | 1.0 | 15,705,155 | 11,343 |
| 2008.................. | 137,850 | 1,392 | 1.0 | 12,462,770 | 8,956 |
| 2009 [4].............. | 138,950 | 1,426 | 1.0 | 14,940,892 | 10,478 |
| 2010.................. | 142,823 | 1,581 | 1.1 | 15,066,486 | 9,527 |
| 2011.................. | 140,837 | 1,565 | 1.1 | 14,652,239 | 9,364 |
| 2012.................. | 143,400 | 1,482 | 1.0 | 15,310,908 | 10,331 |
| 2013.................. | 145,819 | 1,405 | 1.0 | 14,049,657 | 10,000 |
| 2014.................. | 145,236 | 1,242 | 0.9 | 11,885,411 | 9,566 |
| 2015.................. | 146,861 | 1,228 | 0.8 | 12,308,319 | 10,022 |
| 2016.................. | 147,967 | 1,035 | 0.7 | 9,864,674 | 9,532 |
| 2017.................. | 149,919 | 934 | 0.6 | 9,028,417 | 9,669 |
| 2018.................. | 150,043 | 892 | 0.6 | 9,050,651 | 10,144 |

[1] Returns generally filed in previous calendar year. [2] Includes examinations conducted in person and by correspondence (mail). [3] For 1995, amount includes associated penalties. [4] Excludes returns filed by individuals only to receive an economic stimulus payment and who had no other reason to file.

Source: U.S. Internal Revenue Service, *IRS Data Book, 2018*, May 2019, and earlier editions. See also <https://www.irs.gov/statistics/soi-tax-stats-irs-data-book>.

## Table 512. Federal Individual Income Tax Returns—Adjusted Gross Income, Taxable Income, and Total Income Tax: 2010 to 2016

[142,892 represents 142,892,000. For tax years. Based on a sample of returns; see source and Appendix III]

| Year | 2010 | | 2015 | | 2016 | | Percent change in amount, 2015-16 |
|---|---|---|---|---|---|---|---|
| | Number of returns (1,000) | Amount (mil. dol.) | Number of returns (1,000) | Amount (mil. dol.) | Number of returns (1,000) | Amount (mil. dol.) | |
| **Adjusted gross income (less deficit)**..... | **142,892** | **8,089,142** | **150,493** | **10,210,310** | **150,272** | **10,225,938** | **0.2** |
| Exemptions [1]...................... | 287,679 | 1,049,272 | 291,939 | 1,140,740 | 289,753 | 1,146,206 | 0.5 |
| Taxable income..................... | 107,304 | 5,502,001 | 114,872 | 7,350,295 | 115,521 | 7,330,109 | -0.3 |
| Total income tax.................... | 84,476 | 951,674 | 99,041 | 1,457,891 | 100,052 | 1,446,048 | -0.8 |
| Alternative minimum tax.................. | 4,020 | 27,461 | 4,468 | 31,166 | 4,634 | 31,016 | -0.5 |

[1] The number of returns represent the number of exemptions.

Source: U.S. Internal Revenue Service, Statistics of Income, *Individual Income Tax Returns Complete Report 2016,* September 2018. See also <https://www.irs.gov/statistics/soi-tax-stats-individual-income-tax-returns-publication-1304-complete-report>.

# Table 513. Federal Individual Income Tax Returns—Adjusted Gross Income (AGI) by Selected Source of Income and Income Class: 2016

[In millions of dollars (9,578,115 represents $9,578,115,000,000), except as indicated. For the tax year. Minus sign (-) indicates net loss was greater than net income. Based on sample; see Appendix III]

| Item | Total [1] | Under $10,000 [1] | $10,000 to $19,999 | $20,000 to $29,999 | $30,000 to $39,999 | $40,000 to $49,999 | $50,000 to $99,999 | $100,000 and over |
|---|---|---|---|---|---|---|---|---|
| | | | | | Adjusted gross income class | | | |
| Number of taxable returns (1,000)..... | 100,052 | 1,987 | 9,512 | 10,872 | 10,801 | 9,709 | 31,572 | 25,600 |
| Adjusted gross income (AGI) [2]......... | 9,578,115 | 5,098 | 145,917 | 271,822 | 377,978 | 435,534 | 2,264,740 | 6,077,026 |
| Salaries and wages...................... | 6,526,020 | 14,238 | 118,585 | 219,167 | 305,909 | 351,540 | 1,733,825 | 3,782,757 |
| Percent of AGI............................ | 68.1 | 279.3 | 81.3 | 80.6 | 80.9 | 80.7 | 76.6 | 62.2 |
| Interest received......................... | 139,061 | 802 | 1,009 | 1,633 | 2,477 | 2,358 | 16,450 | 114,331 |
| Dividends in AGI.......................... | 415,246 | 1,255 | 1,269 | 2,491 | 4,007 | 4,924 | 40,921 | 360,379 |
| Business, profession, net profit less loss.................... | 262,248 | 172 | 5,462 | 7,582 | 8,534 | 10,093 | 51,133 | 179,272 |
| Sales of property, net gain less loss [3]..................... | 604,647 | 2,849 | 8 | 266 | 452 | 709 | 13,953 | 586,412 |
| Pensions and annuities in AGI.......... | 644,165 | 176 | 14,817 | 27,486 | 36,198 | 39,981 | 226,227 | 299,281 |
| Rents and royalties, net income less loss [4]................. | 55,127 | 40 | 509 | 772 | 1,003 | 801 | 3,729 | 48,273 |
| Number of all returns (1,000)........... | 150,272 | 23,080 | 22,745 | 18,735 | 15,088 | 11,665 | 33,199 | 25,759 |
| Adjusted gross income [2]............... | 10,225,938 | -92,188 | 338,004 | 464,947 | 525,140 | 522,265 | 2,367,475 | 6,100,295 |
| Salaries and wages...................... | 7,217,426 | 111,270 | 253,416 | 382,875 | 436,140 | 426,148 | 1,814,826 | 3,792,751 |
| Interest received......................... | 157,293 | 8,524 | 3,138 | 2,917 | 3,704 | 3,177 | 18,949 | 116,884 |
| Dividends in AGI.......................... | 456,099 | 12,192 | 6,580 | 6,545 | 7,343 | 7,250 | 49,528 | 366,662 |
| Business, profession, net profit less loss........................ | 328,082 | 4,401 | 37,910 | 19,144 | 16,241 | 15,126 | 55,467 | 179,793 |
| Sales of property, net gain less loss [3]..................... | 620,508 | 5,163 | 726 | 1,745 | 1,832 | 2,055 | 18,116 | 590,871 |
| Pensions and annuities in AGI.......... | 693,627 | 12,409 | 31,456 | 36,932 | 39,732 | 42,351 | 229,930 | 300,816 |
| Rents and royalties, net income less loss [4].................. | 51,250 | -3,230 | 1,000 | 826 | 569 | 250 | 3,477 | 48,358 |

[1] Includes a small number of returns with no adjusted gross income. [2] Includes other sources, not shown separately. [3] Includes sales of capital assets and other property. [4] Excludes rental passive losses disallowed in the computation of AGI.

Source: U.S. Internal Revenue Service, *Statistics of Income—Individual Income Tax Returns 2016*, Publication 1304, September 2018. See also <https://www.irs.gov/statistics>.

# Table 514. Federal Individual Income Tax Returns—Total and Selected Sources of Adjusted Gross Income: 2015 and 2016

[In units as indicated (150,493 represents 150,493,000). For tax years. Based on a sample of returns; see source and Appendix III. Minus sign (-) indicates decrease]

| Item | 2015 Number of returns (1,000) | 2015 Amount (mil. dol.) | 2016 Number of returns (1,000) | 2016 Amount (mil. dol.) | Change in amount, 2015-2016 Net change (mil. dol.) | Percent change |
|---|---|---|---|---|---|---|
| Adjusted gross income (less deficit) [1].................... | 150,493 | 10,210,310 | 150,272 | 10,225,938 | 15,628 | 0.2 |
| Salaries and wages................................. | 124,591 | 7,112,223 | 124,472 | 7,217,426 | 105,203 | 1.5 |
| Taxable interest..................................... | 42,637 | 95,881 | 42,583 | 96,640 | 759 | 0.8 |
| Ordinary dividends.................................. | 27,607 | 260,253 | 27,470 | 254,065 | -6,187 | -2.4 |
| Qualified dividends.................................. | 25,756 | 203,188 | 25,630 | 202,034 | -1,154 | -0.6 |
| Business or profession net income (less loss)................. | 24,727 | 331,814 | 25,064 | 328,082 | -3,732 | -1.1 |
| Net capital gain..................................... | 24,278 | 706,515 | 24,043 | 620,975 | -85,540 | -12.1 |
| Capital gain distributions [2]......................... | 14,056 | 74,060 | 13,233 | 42,534 | -31,526 | -42.6 |
| Sales of property other than capital assets, net gain (less loss)................................ | 2,217 | 11,943 | 2,082 | 6,293 | -5,650 | -47.3 |
| Sales of property other than capital assets, net gain....... | 1,064 | 33,037 | 978 | 27,611 | -5,425 | -16.4 |
| Taxable social security benefits........................ | 19,661 | 277,411 | 19,967 | 285,939 | 8,528 | 3.1 |
| Total rental and royalty net income (less net loss) [3].......... | 11,300 | 56,813 | 10,986 | 51,250 | -5,563 | -9.8 |
| Partnership and S corporation net income (less loss)......... | 8,744 | 629,005 | 8,711 | 628,666 | -339 | -0.1 |
| Estate and trust net income (less loss)................... | 688 | 27,420 | 652 | 26,571 | -849 | -3.1 |
| Farm net income (less loss)........................... | 1,800 | -13,964 | 1,751 | -17,666 | -3,702 | 26.5 |
| Farm net income.................................... | 521 | 13,534 | 481 | 11,506 | -2,028 | -15.0 |
| Unemployment compensation.......................... | 6,207 | 27,225 | 5,567 | 25,420 | -1,805 | -6.6 |
| Taxable pensions and annuities........................ | 28,199 | 689,992 | 27,861 | 693,627 | 3,635 | 0.5 |
| Taxable Individual Retirement Account (IRA) distributions.... | 14,159 | 253,213 | 14,387 | 257,508 | 4,295 | 1.7 |
| Other net income (less loss) [4]........................ | 6,454 | 40,075 | 6,228 | 38,245 | -1,830 | -4.6 |
| Gambling earnings................................... | 1,934 | 32,967 | 1,975 | 31,574 | -1,393 | -4.2 |

[1] Includes other sources of income, not shown separately. [2] Includes both Schedule D and Form 1040 or 1040A capital gain distributions. [3] Includes farm rental net income (less loss). [4] Other net income (less loss) represents data reported on Form 1040, line 21, except net operating losses, foreign-earned income exclusions, cancellation of debt, taxable health savings account distributions, and gambling earnings.

Source: U.S. Internal Revenue Service, Statistics of Income, "SOI Tax Stats - Individual Statistical Tables by Size of Adjusted Gross Income," <https://www.irs.gov/statistics/soi-tax-stats-individual-statistical-tables-by-size-of-adjusted-gross-income>, accessed September 2018.

# Table 515. Federal Individual Income Tax Returns—Net Capital Gains and Capital Gain Distributions From Mutual Funds: 1990 to 2016

[14,288 represents 14,288,000. For tax years. Based on a sample of returns; see source and Appendix III. Minus sign (-) indicates decrease]

| Tax year | Net capital gain (less loss) | | | | Capital gain distributions [2] | | | |
|---|---|---|---|---|---|---|---|---|
| | Number of returns (1,000) | Current dollars (mil. dol.) | Constant (1982–1984) dollars [1] | | Number of returns (1,000) | Current dollars (mil. dol.) | Constant (1982–1984) dollars [1] | |
| | | | Amount (mil. dol.) | Percent change | | | Amount (mil. dol.) | Percent change |
| 1990 | 14,288 | 114,231 | 87,399 | -25.6 | 5,069 | 3,905 | 2,988 | -32.4 |
| 1991 | 15,009 | 102,776 | 75,460 | -13.7 | 5,796 | 4,665 | 3,425 | 14.6 |
| 1992 | 16,491 | 118,230 | 84,269 | 11.7 | 5,917 | 7,426 | 5,293 | 54.5 |
| 1993 | 18,409 | 144,172 | 99,773 | 18.4 | 9,998 | 11,995 | 8,301 | 56.8 |
| 1994 | 18,823 | 142,288 | 96,011 | -3.8 | 9,803 | 11,322 | 7,640 | -8.0 |
| 1995 | 19,963 | 170,415 | 111,821 | 16.5 | 10,744 | 14,391 | 9,443 | 23.6 |
| 1996 | 22,065 | 251,817 | 160,495 | 43.5 | 12,778 | 24,722 | 15,757 | 66.9 |
| 1997 | 24,240 | 356,083 | 221,859 | 38.2 | 14,969 | 45,132 | 28,120 | 78.5 |
| 1998 | 25,690 | 446,084 | 273,671 | 23.4 | 16,070 | 46,147 | 28,311 | 0.7 |
| 1999 | 27,701 | 542,758 | 325,785 | 19.0 | 17,012 | 59,473 | 35,698 | 26.1 |
| 2000 | 29,521 | 630,542 | 366,168 | 12.4 | 17,546 | 79,079 | 45,923 | 28.6 |
| 2001 | 25,956 | 326,527 | 184,374 | -49.6 | 12,216 | 13,609 | 7,684 | -83.3 |
| 2002 | 24,189 | 238,789 | 132,734 | -28.0 | 7,567 | 5,343 | 2,970 | -61.4 |
| 2003 | 22,985 | 294,354 | 159,975 | 20.5 | 7,265 | 4,695 | 2,552 | -14.1 |
| 2004 | 25,267 | 473,662 | 250,747 | 56.7 | 10,733 | 15,336 | 8,119 | 218.2 |
| 2005 | 26,196 | 668,015 | 342,046 | 36.4 | 13,393 | 35,581 | 18,219 | 124.4 |
| 2006 | 26,668 | 779,462 | 386,638 | 13.0 | 14,511 | 59,417 | 29,473 | 61.8 |
| 2007 | 27,156 | 907,656 | 437,758 | 13.2 | 15,714 | 86,397 | 41,669 | 41.4 |
| 2008 | 23,731 | 469,273 | 217,959 | -50.2 | 11,544 | 21,954 | 10,197 | -75.5 |
| 2009 | 20,291 | 231,548 | 107,929 | -50.5 | 4,191 | 2,411 | 1,124 | -89.0 |
| 2010 | 21,315 | 364,410 | 167,118 | 54.8 | 6,567 | 6,270 | 2,875 | 155.9 |
| 2011 | 22,154 | 377,037 | 167,617 | 0.3 | 8,859 | 14,171 | 6,300 | 119.1 |
| 2012 | 22,721 | 622,887 | 271,299 | 61.9 | 10,412 | 17,829 | 7,766 | 23.3 |
| 2013 | 23,993 | 489,621 | 210,176 | -22.5 | 12,845 | 44,774 | 19,220 | 147.5 |
| 2014 | 24,268 | 698,649 | 295,117 | 40.4 | 13,665 | 79,059 | 33,396 | 73.8 |
| 2015 | 24,278 | 706,515 | 298,086 | 1.0 | 14,056 | 74,060 | 31,247 | -6.4 |
| 2016 | 24,043 | 620,975 | 258,732 | -13.2 | 13,233 | 42,534 | 17,722 | -43.3 |

[1] Constant dollars were calculated using the U.S. Bureau of Labor Statistics consumer price index for urban consumers (CPI-U, 1982-1984=100). See Table 756. [2] Capital gain distributions are included in net capital gain (less loss). For 1991–1996, and 1999 and later years, capital gain distributions from mutual funds are the sum of the amounts reported on the Form 1040 and Schedule D. For 1997 and 1998, capital gain distributions were reported entirely on the Schedule D.

Source: U.S. Internal Revenue Service, Statistics of Income, "SOI Tax Stats - Individual Statistical Tables by Size of Adjusted Gross Income," <https://www.irs.gov/statistics/soi-tax-stats-individual-statistical-tables-by-size-of-adjusted-gross-income>, accessed September 2018.

# Table 516. Alternative Minimum Tax: 1987 to 2016

[140 represents 140,000. For tax years. Based on a sample of returns; see source and Appendix III]

| Tax year | Highest statutory alternative minimum tax rate (percent) [1] | Alternative minimum tax | | Tax year | Highest statutory alternative minimum tax rate (percent) [1] | Alternative minimum tax | |
|---|---|---|---|---|---|---|---|
| | | Number of returns (1,000) | Amount (mil. dol.) | | | Number of returns (1,000) | Amount (mil. dol.) |
| 1987 | 21 | 140 | 1,675 | 2002 | 28 | 1,911 | 6,854 |
| 1988 | 21 | 114 | 1,028 | 2003 | 28 | 2,358 | 9,470 |
| 1989 | 21 | 117 | 831 | 2004 | 28 | 3,096 | 13,029 |
| 1990 | 21 | 132 | 830 | 2005 | 28 | 4,005 | 17,421 |
| 1991 | 24 | 244 | 1,213 | 2006 | 28 | 3,967 | 21,565 |
| 1992 | 24 | 287 | 1,357 | 2007 | 28 | 4,109 | 24,110 |
| 1993 | 28 | 335 | 2,053 | 2008 | 28 | 3,935 | 25,649 |
| 1994 | 28 | 369 | 2,212 | 2009 | 28 | 3,828 | 22,580 |
| 1995 | 28 | 414 | 2,291 | 2010 | 28 | 4,020 | 27,461 |
| 1996 | 28 | 478 | 2,813 | 2011 | 28 | 4,248 | 30,479 |
| 1997 | 28 | 618 | 4,005 | 2012 | 28 | 4,225 | 32,770 |
| 1998 | 28 | 853 | 5,015 | 2013 | 28 | 3,940 | 27,426 |
| 1999 | 28 | 1,018 | 6,478 | 2014 | 28 | 4,278 | 28,646 |
| 2000 | 28 | 1,304 | 9,601 | 2015 | 28 | 4,468 | 31,166 |
| 2001 | 28 | 1,120 | 6,757 | 2016 | 28 | 4,634 | 31,016 |

[1] Beginning 1997, the top rate on most long-term capital gains was 20 percent; beginning 2003, the rate was 15 percent.

Source: U.S. Internal Revenue Service, Statistics of Income, "SOI Tax Stats - Individual Statistical Tables by Size of Adjusted Gross Income," <https://www.irs.gov/statistics/soi-tax-stats-individual-statistical-tables-by-size-of-adjusted-gross-income>, accessed September 2018.

# Table 517. Federal Individual Income Tax Returns—Sources of Net Losses Included in Adjusted Gross Income: 2015 and 2016

[25,408 represents 25,408,000. For tax years. Based on a sample of returns; see source and Appendix III]

| Item | 2015 Number of returns (1,000) | 2015 Amount (mil. dol.) | 2016 Number of returns (1,000) | 2016 Amount (mil. dol.) | Percent change in amount, 2015–2016 |
|---|---|---|---|---|---|
| Total net losses | 25,408 | 509,503 | 26,002 | 500,834 | -1.7 |
| Business or profession net loss | 5,936 | 60,161 | 6,103 | 60,997 | 1.4 |
| Net capital loss [1] | 8,280 | 18,646 | 9,054 | 20,126 | 7.9 |
| Net loss, sales of property other than capital assets | 1,153 | 21,094 | 1,105 | 21,319 | 1.1 |
| Total rental and royalty net loss [2] | 4,532 | 46,246 | 4,308 | 46,943 | 1.5 |
| Partnership and S corporation net loss | 2,700 | 126,618 | 2,673 | 125,646 | -0.8 |
| Estate and trust net loss | 58 | 5,033 | 49 | 3,857 | -23.4 |
| Farm net loss | 1,279 | 27,498 | 1,270 | 29,172 | 6.1 |
| Net operating loss [3] | 1,138 | 197,513 | 1,110 | 185,805 | -5.9 |
| Other net loss [4] | 333 | 6,694 | 330 | 6,969 | 4.1 |

[1] As reported on Form 1040, Schedule D. Includes only the portion of capital losses allowable in the calculation of adjusted gross income. Only $3,000 of net capital loss per return ($1,500 for married filing separately) are allowed to be included in negative total income. Any excess is carried forward to future years. [2] Includes farm rental net loss. [3] Net operating loss is a carryover of the loss from a business when taxable income from a prior year was less than zero. [4] Other net loss represents losses reported on Form 1040, line 21, except net operating loss and the foreign-earned income exclusion.

Source: U.S. Internal Revenue Service, Statistics of Income, "SOI Tax Stats - Individual Statistical Tables by Size of Adjusted Gross Income," <https://www.irs.gov/statistics/soi-tax-stats-individual-statistical-tables-by-size-of-adjusted-gross-income>, accessed September 2018.

# Table 518. Federal Individual Income Tax Returns—Number, Income Tax, and Average Tax by Size of Adjusted Gross Income: 2015 and 2016

[150,493 represents 150,493,000. Based on sample of returns; see Appendix III. Minus sign (-) indicates net loss was greater than net income]

| Size of adjusted gross income | Number of returns (1,000) | | Adjusted gross income (AGI) (bil. dol.) | | Income tax total [1] (bil. dol.) | | Taxes as percent of AGI (for taxable returns only) | | Average tax (for taxable returns only) (dol.) | |
|---|---|---|---|---|---|---|---|---|---|---|
| | 2015 | 2016 | 2015 | 2016 | 2015 | 2016 | 2015 | 2016 | 2015 | 2016 |
| Total | 150,493 | 150,272 | 10,210 | 10,226 | 1,458 | 1,446 | 15.3 | 15.1 | 14,720 | 14,453 |
| No AGI [2] | 2,072 | 2,093 | -203.8 | -201.5 | 0.2 | 0.1 | (X) | (X) | 36,515 | 21,134 |
| $1 to $4,999 | 10,135 | 9,989 | 26.2 | 25.8 | – | – | 6.6 | 5.4 | 205 | 171 |
| $5,000 to $9,999 | 11,399 | 10,999 | 86.4 | 83.5 | 0.4 | 0.3 | 2.4 | 2.4 | 191 | 192 |
| $10,000 to $14,999 | 12,219 | 11,835 | 152.8 | 147.8 | 1.4 | 1.4 | 2.5 | 2.5 | 319 | 323 |
| $15,000 to $19,999 | 11,228 | 10,910 | 195.9 | 190.2 | 3.5 | 3.5 | 3.9 | 3.8 | 678 | 671 |
| $20,000 to $24,999 | 9,981 | 9,847 | 224.2 | 221.0 | 6.2 | 6.1 | 5.1 | 5.0 | 1,145 | 1,131 |
| $25,000 to $29,999 | 8,833 | 8,888 | 242.6 | 243.9 | 8.8 | 9.0 | 6.0 | 6.0 | 1,645 | 1,646 |
| $30,000 to $39,999 | 14,914 | 15,088 | 519.5 | 525.1 | 25.2 | 25.7 | 6.8 | 6.8 | 2,382 | 2,378 |
| $40,000 to $49,999 | 11,625 | 11,665 | 520.8 | 522.3 | 32.5 | 32.5 | 7.5 | 7.5 | 3,353 | 3,346 |
| $50,000 to $74,999 | 19,980 | 20,224 | 1,228.3 | 1,241.8 | 99.8 | 101.5 | 8.7 | 8.7 | 5,341 | 5,385 |
| $75,000 to $99,999 | 12,822 | 12,975 | 1,111.2 | 1,125.7 | 105.9 | 108.3 | 9.7 | 9.8 | 8,430 | 8,517 |
| $100,000 to $199,999 | 18,533 | 18,858 | 2,506.5 | 2,552.5 | 316.3 | 321.6 | 12.7 | 12.7 | 17,191 | 17,186 |
| $200,000 to $499,999 | 5,428 | 5,583 | 1,546.5 | 1,588.3 | 299.8 | 308.2 | 19.4 | 19.4 | 55,334 | 55,319 |
| $500,000 to $999,999 | 884 | 893 | 597.7 | 599.6 | 154.4 | 154.7 | 25.9 | 25.8 | 174,789 | 173,327 |
| $1,000,000 to $1,499,999 | 196 | 193 | 236.5 | 232.6 | 66.3 | 65.2 | 28.1 | 28.0 | 338,945 | 338,234 |
| $1,500,000 to $1,999,999 | 80 | 78 | 137.7 | 133.6 | 39.7 | 38.6 | 28.8 | 28.9 | 496,618 | 497,142 |
| $2,000,000 to $4,999,999 | 117 | 111 | 346.9 | 329.9 | 101.5 | 96.0 | 29.3 | 29.1 | 870,364 | 864,605 |
| $5,000,000 to $9,999,999 | 29 | 27 | 195.7 | 181.7 | 56.3 | 52.0 | 28.8 | 28.6 | 1,965,939 | 1,952,541 |
| $10,000,000 or more | 18 | 16 | 538.8 | 482.1 | 139.6 | 121.4 | 25.9 | 25.2 | 7,731,699 | 7,548,877 |

X Not applicable. – Represents or rounds to zero [1] Consists of income tax after credits (including alternative minimum tax). [2] In addition to low-income taxpayers, this size class (and others) includes taxpayers with "tax preferences," not reflected in "adjusted gross income" or "taxable income," which are subject to the "alternative minimum tax" (included in "total income tax").

Source: U.S. Internal Revenue Service, Statistics of Income Bulletin, "Historical Data Tables," <https://www.irs.gov/statistics>, accessed May 2019.

# Table 519. Federal Individual Income Tax Returns—Selected Itemized Deductions and the Standard Deduction: 2015 and 2016

[44,567 represents 44,567,000. For tax years. Based on a sample of returns; see source and Appendix III. Minus sign (-) indicates decrease]

| Item | 2015 Number of returns [1] (1,000) | 2015 Amount (mil. dol.) | 2016 Number of returns [1] (1,000) | 2016 Amount (mil. dol.) | Percent change, 2015–2016 Number of returns [1] (1,000) | Percent change, 2015–2016 Amount (percent) |
|---|---|---|---|---|---|---|
| Total itemized deductions................................ | 44,567 | 1,257,437 | 45,153 | 1,293,399 | 1.3 | 2.9 |
| Medical and dental expenses after Adjusted Gross Income (AGI) limitation...................... | 8,777 | 86,931 | 8,934 | 90,195 | 1.8 | 3.8 |
| Taxes paid [2]................................................ | 44,191 | 553,016 | 44,803 | 566,098 | 1.4 | 2.4 |
| State and local income taxes......................... | 33,063 | 335,060 | 33,423 | 337,680 | 1.1 | 0.8 |
| State and local general sales taxes................ | 9,627 | 17,641 | 9,746 | 18,328 | 1.2 | 3.9 |
| Interest paid [3]............................................. | 33,302 | 304,461 | 33,485 | 304,997 | 0.5 | 0.2 |
| Home mortgage interest................................ | 32,716 | 283,004 | 32,933 | 282,953 | 0.7 | – |
| Charitable contributions.................................. | 36,624 | 221,850 | 36,937 | 233,867 | 0.9 | 5.4 |
| Other than cash contributions....................... | 22,542 | 70,870 | 22,969 | 79,569 | 1.9 | 12.3 |
| Casualty and theft losses............................... | 72 | 1,646 | 154 | 5,187 | 113.3 | 215.2 |
| Total limited miscellaneous deductions after 2% AGI limitation.................................. | 12,776 | 113,175 | 13,014 | 115,544 | 1.9 | 2.1 |
| Total unlimited miscellaneous deductions................ | 1,235 | 24,188 | 1,238 | 23,245 | 0.3 | -3.9 |
| Itemized deductions in excess of limitation.................... | 2,931 | 47,831 | 2,981 | 45,734 | 1.7 | -4.4 |
| Basic standard deduction............................... | 103,844 | 872,463 | 103,013 | 865,094 | -0.8 | -0.8 |
| Additional standard deduction.......................... | 15,097 | 28,146 | 15,316 | 28,572 | 1.4 | 1.5 |

– Represents or rounds to zero. [1] Returns with no adjusted gross income are excluded from the deduction counts. For this reason, the sum of the number of returns with total itemized deductions and the number of returns with total standard deduction is less than the total number of returns for all filers. [2] Includes real estate taxes, personal property taxes, and other taxes, not shown separately. [3] Includes investment interest, deductible mortgage "points," and qualified mortgage interest premiums, not shown separately.

Source: U.S. Internal Revenue Service, Statistics of Income, "SOI Tax Stats - Individual Statistical Tables by Size of Adjusted Gross Income," <https://www.irs.gov/statistics/soi-tax-stats-individual-statistical-tables-by-size-of-adjusted-gross-income>, accessed September 2018.

# Table 520. Federal Individual Income Tax Returns—Statutory Adjustments: 2015 and 2016

[38,586 represents 38,586,000. For tax years. Based on a sample of returns; see source and Appendix III. Minus sign (-) indicates decrease]

| Item | 2015 Number of returns (1,000) | 2015 Amount (mil. dol.) | 2016 Number of returns (1,000) | 2016 Amount (mil. dol.) | Percent change in amount, 2015-2016 |
|---|---|---|---|---|---|
| Total statutory adjustments............................. | 38,586 | 150,093 | 38,858 | 153,414 | 2.2 |
| Payments to an Individual Retirement Account (IRA)................... | 2,641 | 13,044 | 2,667 | 13,387 | 2.6 |
| Educator expenses deduction........................ | 3,721 | 950 | 3,853 | 983 | 3.4 |
| Certain business expenses of reservists, performing artists, etc........ | 169 | 579 | 157 | 605 | 4.5 |
| Moving expenses adjustment.......................... | 1,134 | 3,692 | 1,115 | 3,487 | -5.6 |
| Student loan interest deduction....................... | 12,371 | 13,438 | 12,396 | 13,448 | 0.1 |
| Tuition and fees deduction............................. | 1,656 | 3,919 | 1,687 | 3,910 | -0.2 |
| Health savings account deduction................... | 1,392 | 4,323 | 1,721 | 4,967 | 14.9 |
| Self-employment tax deduction....................... | 19,633 | 30,107 | 19,583 | 29,866 | -0.8 |
| Self-employment health insurance deduction...................... | 4,098 | 28,852 | 4,057 | 30,112 | 4.4 |
| Payments to a self-employed retirement (Keogh) plan.................. | 1,012 | 24,378 | 989 | 24,683 | 1.3 |
| Early withdrawal of savings penalty................ | 467 | 77 | 416 | 108 | 40.5 |
| Alimony paid................................................. | 599 | 12,345 | 586 | 12,639 | 2.4 |
| Domestic production activities deduction.......... | 696 | 12,792 | 720 | 13,377 | 4.6 |
| Other adjustments [1]..................................... | 142 | 1,597 | 138 | 1,844 | 15.5 |

[1] Includes foreign housing adjustment, medical savings accounts deduction, and other adjustments.

Source: U.S. Internal Revenue Service, Statistics of Income, "SOI Tax Stats - Individual Statistical Tables by Size of Adjusted Gross Income," <https://www.irs.gov/statistics/soi-tax-stats-individual-statistical-tables-by-size-of-adjusted-gross-income>, accessed September 2018.

## Table 521. Federal Individual Income Tax Returns—Itemized Deductions and Statutory Adjustments by Size of Adjusted Gross Income: 2016

[45,153 represents 45,153,000. Based on a sample of returns; see Appendix III]

| Item | Unit | Total [1] | Adjusted gross income class | | | | | | |
|---|---|---|---|---|---|---|---|---|---|
| | | | Under $10,000 [1] | $10,000 to $19,999 | $20,000 to $29,999 | $30,000 to $39,999 | $40,000 to $49,999 | $50,000 to $99,999 | $100,000 and over |
| **Returns with itemized deductions:** | | | | | | | | | |
| Number of returns [2] | 1,000 | 45,153 | 728 | 1,453 | 2,021 | 2,598 | 2,982 | 14,600 | 20,771 |
| Amount [2,3] | Mil. dol. | 1,293,399 | 11,639 | 23,422 | 33,024 | 41,756 | 49,595 | 281,340 | 852,624 |
| **Medical and dental expenses: [4]** | | | | | | | | | |
| Returns | 1,000 | 8,934 | 525 | 929 | 1,019 | 955 | 857 | 3,100 | 1,550 |
| Amount | Mil. dol. | 90,195 | 4,473 | 9,085 | 8,788 | 8,124 | 7,652 | 29,743 | 22,330 |
| **Taxes paid:** | | | | | | | | | |
| Returns | 1,000 | 44,803 | 698 | 1,396 | 1,958 | 2,545 | 2,945 | 14,516 | 20,745 |
| Amount | Mil. dol. | 566,098 | 2,915 | 4,923 | 7,154 | 9,991 | 13,117 | 93,599 | 434,399 |
| **State and local taxes: [5]** | | | | | | | | | |
| Returns | 1,000 | 43,170 | 590 | 1,259 | 1,815 | 2,390 | 2,797 | 14,018 | 20,301 |
| Amount | Mil. dol. | 356,008 | 612 | 1,125 | 2,205 | 3,519 | 5,307 | 44,904 | 298,337 |
| **Real estate taxes:** | | | | | | | | | |
| Returns | 1,000 | 37,895 | 525 | 1,011 | 1,282 | 1,809 | 2,240 | 12,170 | 18,858 |
| Amount | Mil. dol. | 197,632 | 2,207 | 3,495 | 4,431 | 5,850 | 7,181 | 45,368 | 129,100 |
| **Interest paid:** | | | | | | | | | |
| Returns | 1,000 | 33,485 | 396 | 730 | 1,018 | 1,532 | 1,994 | 10,931 | 16,885 |
| Amount | Mil. dol. | 304,997 | 2,704 | 4,668 | 6,548 | 9,730 | 12,791 | 81,280 | 187,276 |
| **Home mortgage interest:** | | | | | | | | | |
| Returns | 1,000 | 32,933 | 390 | 710 | 999 | 1,511 | 1,965 | 10,821 | 16,538 |
| Amount | Mil. dol. | 282,953 | 2,590 | 4,468 | 6,192 | 9,081 | 11,828 | 76,088 | 172,705 |
| **Charitable contributions:** | | | | | | | | | |
| Returns | 1,000 | 36,937 | 428 | 967 | 1,423 | 1,888 | 2,187 | 11,623 | 18,421 |
| Amount | Mil. dol. | 233,867 | 484 | 1,976 | 3,734 | 5,141 | 6,501 | 38,418 | 177,613 |
| **Unreimbursed employee business expenses:** | | | | | | | | | |
| Returns | 1,000 | 14,735 | 63 | 273 | 668 | 978 | 1,127 | 5,384 | 6,241 |
| Amount | Mil. dol. | 97,109 | 409 | 1,874 | 5,056 | 7,311 | 8,013 | 34,097 | 40,349 |
| **Returns with statutory adjustments:** | | | | | | | | | |
| Number of returns [1] | 1,000 | 38,858 | 4,037 | 4,983 | 3,516 | 3,429 | 3,117 | 10,064 | 9,711 |
| Amount of adjustments [3] | Mil. dol. | 153,414 | 5,914 | 6,232 | 6,241 | 6,991 | 7,045 | 28,596 | 92,395 |
| **Payments to IRAs: [6]** | | | | | | | | | |
| Returns | 1,000 | 2,667 | 59 | 135 | 193 | 256 | 272 | 896 | 856 |
| Amount | Mil. dol. | 13,387 | 216 | 427 | 800 | 949 | 1,088 | 4,360 | 5,547 |
| **Deduction for self-employment tax:** | | | | | | | | | |
| Returns | 1,000 | 19,583 | 3,147 | 3,900 | 1,758 | 1,371 | 1,118 | 3,729 | 4,559 |
| Amount | Mil. dol. | 29,866 | 1,440 | 3,163 | 1,934 | 1,631 | 1,498 | 5,641 | 14,559 |
| **Self-employment health insurance:** | | | | | | | | | |
| Returns | 1,000 | 4,057 | 332 | 279 | 286 | 267 | 230 | 905 | 1,758 |
| Amount | Mil. dol. | 30,112 | 1,328 | 876 | 1,051 | 1,139 | 1,197 | 5,707 | 18,814 |
| **Payments to Keogh plans:** | | | | | | | | | |
| Returns | 1,000 | 989 | [7] 8 | [7] 7 | [7] 6 | 31 | 27 | 139 | 771 |
| Amount | Mil. dol. | 24,683 | [7] 105 | [7] 30 | [7] 85 | 229 | 297 | 1,564 | 22,375 |

[1] For returns with statutory adjustments, includes a small number of taxable returns with no adjusted gross income. [2] After limitations. [3] Includes other deductions and adjustments, not shown separately. [4] Before limitation. [5] State and local taxes include income taxes and sales taxes. [6] Individual retirement accounts. [7] Includes estimates that should be used with caution due to the small number of sample returns on which they are based.

Source: U.S. Internal Revenue Service, Statistics of Income, "SOI Tax Stats - Individual Statistical Tables by Size of Adjusted Gross Income," <https://www.irs.gov/statistics/soi-tax-stats-individual-statistical-tables-by-size-of-adjusted-gross-income>, accessed September 2018.

## Table 522. Federal Individual Income Tax Returns—Selected Tax Credits: 2015 and 2016

[48,981 represents 48,981,000. For tax years. Based on a sample of returns; see source and Appendix III]

| Item | 2015 | | 2016 | | Percent change, 2015-2016 | |
|---|---|---|---|---|---|---|
| | Number of returns (1,000) | Amount (mil. dol.) | Number of returns (1,000) | Amount (mil. dol.) | Number of returns (1,000) | Amount (mil. dol.) |
| **Total tax credits [1]** | **48,981** | **77,927** | **48,478** | **75,381** | **-1.0** | **-3.3** |
| Child care credit | 6,344 | 3,585 | 6,469 | 3,635 | 2.0 | 1.4 |
| Earned income credit [2] | 4,626 | 1,490 | 4,437 | 1,403 | -4.1 | -5.8 |
| Foreign tax credit | 7,968 | 22,560 | 7,798 | 20,090 | -2.1 | -10.9 |
| General business credit | 334 | 3,616 | 352 | 4,131 | 5.4 | 14.2 |
| Minimum tax credit | 307 | 973 | 321 | 907 | 4.7 | -6.8 |
| Child tax credit | 22,377 | 27,100 | 22,097 | 26,800 | -1.3 | -1.1 |
| Education credit [3] | 9,606 | 10,234 | 8,998 | 9,653 | -6.3 | -5.7 |
| Retirement savings contribution credit | 8,109 | 1,441 | 8,458 | 1,536 | 4.3 | 6.6 |
| Residential energy credit | 2,593 | 2,088 | 2,613 | 2,336 | 0.8 | 11.9 |

[1] Includes credits not shown separately. [2] Represents portion of credit used to offset income tax before credits. [3] Excludes refundable portion.

Source: U.S. Internal Revenue Service, Statistics of Income, "SOI Tax Stats - Individual Statistical Tables by Size of Adjusted Gross Income," <https://www.irs.gov/statistics/soi-tax-stats-individual-statistical-tables-by-size-of-adjusted-gross-income>, accessed September 2018.

# Table 523. Federal Individual Income Tax Returns by State: 2016

[In units as indicated (149,853 represents 149,853,000). For tax year. Data may not agree with data in other tables due to differing survey methodology used to derive state data]

| State | Total number of returns (1,000) | Adjusted gross income (mil. dol.) | | | Itemized deductions (mil. dol.) | | | | Income tax (mil. dol.) |
|---|---|---|---|---|---|---|---|---|---|
| | | Total [1] | Salaries and wages | Net capital gain [2] | Total [1] | State and local income tax | Real estate taxes | Home mortgage interest paid | |
| United States...... | 149,853 | 10,200,124 | 7,187,734 | 618,950 | 1,297,101 | 337,502 | 196,081 | 278,521 | 1,439,016 |
| Alabama............. | 2,044 | 113,629 | 81,267 | 4,121 | 12,349 | 2,304 | 653 | 2,742 | 13,639 |
| Alaska.............. | 348 | 23,528 | 16,850 | 695 | 1,676 | 27 | 329 | 627 | 3,272 |
| Arizona............. | 2,944 | 177,717 | 125,023 | 8,717 | 21,397 | 3,659 | 2,153 | 5,766 | 22,948 |
| Arkansas........... | 1,222 | 67,927 | 46,776 | 3,258 | 7,587 | 1,883 | 458 | 1,263 | 8,147 |
| California........... | 17,817 | 1,413,476 | 979,623 | 114,955 | 237,481 | 82,420 | 30,327 | 53,206 | 213,762 |
| Colorado........... | 2,649 | 194,422 | 134,336 | 15,020 | 23,018 | 5,442 | 2,294 | 6,873 | 27,785 |
| Connecticut......... | 1,754 | 162,758 | 111,188 | 11,266 | 24,619 | 8,614 | 5,124 | 4,509 | 27,543 |
| Delaware........... | 456 | 29,342 | 20,437 | 988 | 3,564 | 992 | 380 | 1,018 | 3,757 |
| District of Columbia.. | 343 | 31,911 | 22,589 | 2,184 | 4,744 | 1,823 | 423 | 988 | 5,600 |
| Florida............. | 9,668 | 599,323 | 383,336 | 47,572 | 61,327 | 3,489 | 9,187 | 13,377 | 87,771 |
| Georgia............ | 4,435 | 269,644 | 200,103 | 11,166 | 38,783 | 8,968 | 3,828 | 7,997 | 34,690 |
| Hawaii............. | 685 | 42,823 | 29,706 | 2,472 | 5,461 | 1,620 | 386 | 1,822 | 5,211 |
| Idaho.............. | 740 | 41,690 | 28,704 | 2,662 | 5,308 | 1,380 | 519 | 1,246 | 4,800 |
| Illinois............. | 6,100 | 436,922 | 307,923 | 26,870 | 51,161 | 10,639 | 11,971 | 10,837 | 64,139 |
| Indiana............ | 3,102 | 177,298 | 129,777 | 6,399 | 16,206 | 4,549 | 1,542 | 3,476 | 21,770 |
| Iowa.............. | 1,448 | 88,263 | 62,994 | 2,919 | 9,866 | 2,742 | 1,481 | 1,790 | 10,594 |
| Kansas............ | 1,324 | 82,418 | 58,537 | 3,807 | 8,447 | 1,803 | 1,157 | 1,607 | 10,713 |
| Kentucky.......... | 1,906 | 103,818 | 75,434 | 4,097 | 11,427 | 3,734 | 1,107 | 2,343 | 12,113 |
| Louisiana.......... | 1,968 | 111,968 | 80,639 | 4,443 | 12,994 | 2,127 | 781 | 2,408 | 14,531 |
| Maine............. | 651 | 37,066 | 25,785 | 1,846 | 4,161 | 1,196 | 758 | 941 | 4,351 |
| Maryland.......... | 2,951 | 224,469 | 163,160 | 8,556 | 39,312 | 12,655 | 4,953 | 9,299 | 31,133 |
| Massachusetts...... | 3,410 | 301,415 | 208,762 | 23,051 | 38,852 | 11,998 | 7,332 | 8,701 | 49,146 |
| Michigan.......... | 4,719 | 286,575 | 200,686 | 11,595 | 29,552 | 7,364 | 4,855 | 6,232 | 38,085 |
| Minnesota......... | 2,737 | 195,638 | 141,074 | 9,090 | 25,604 | 8,941 | 3,340 | 5,700 | 26,692 |
| Mississippi......... | 1,230 | 59,499 | 43,625 | 2,085 | 6,858 | 1,155 | 471 | 1,191 | 6,447 |
| Missouri........... | 2,781 | 165,066 | 116,918 | 6,526 | 18,273 | 4,854 | 2,078 | 3,642 | 21,072 |
| Montana........... | 501 | 27,983 | 18,189 | 1,851 | 3,421 | 914 | 388 | 796 | 3,331 |
| Nebraska.......... | 898 | 55,221 | 39,749 | 2,834 | 6,205 | 1,681 | 935 | 1,085 | 6,829 |
| Nevada............ | 1,378 | 88,971 | 57,830 | 9,836 | 9,876 | 568 | 883 | 2,434 | 12,971 |
| New Hampshire...... | 699 | 51,609 | 37,128 | 2,820 | 5,354 | 562 | 1,559 | 1,413 | 7,407 |
| New Jersey......... | 4,385 | 370,382 | 269,203 | 16,594 | 58,265 | 17,236 | 15,249 | 11,163 | 58,453 |
| New Mexico........ | 908 | 46,568 | 32,180 | 1,874 | 4,712 | 923 | 497 | 1,209 | 5,355 |
| New York.......... | 9,589 | 769,644 | 521,574 | 65,595 | 122,382 | 50,426 | 21,319 | 16,995 | 125,742 |
| North Carolina....... | 4,512 | 270,985 | 195,348 | 12,210 | 33,275 | 8,832 | 3,583 | 7,622 | 34,270 |
| North Dakota........ | 360 | 23,859 | 16,555 | 1,275 | 1,623 | 202 | 194 | 371 | 3,244 |
| Ohio.............. | 5,573 | 325,566 | 234,294 | 11,128 | 32,446 | 9,057 | 5,598 | 6,641 | 41,135 |
| Oklahoma.......... | 1,616 | 92,312 | 65,475 | 4,536 | 10,270 | 1,968 | 895 | 1,785 | 11,142 |
| Oregon............ | 1,899 | 123,504 | 83,539 | 7,398 | 18,680 | 6,209 | 2,649 | 4,401 | 15,620 |
| Pennsylvania........ | 6,189 | 404,790 | 287,202 | 19,921 | 44,165 | 11,492 | 8,550 | 9,554 | 55,697 |
| Rhode Island........ | 529 | 33,966 | 24,529 | 1,530 | 4,299 | 1,172 | 878 | 1,019 | 4,511 |
| South Carolina....... | 2,204 | 124,456 | 86,568 | 5,560 | 15,113 | 3,880 | 1,247 | 3,488 | 14,990 |
| South Dakota........ | 416 | 25,555 | 16,444 | 1,545 | 1,894 | 91 | 261 | 377 | 3,426 |
| Tennessee.......... | 2,991 | 174,852 | 125,891 | 9,203 | 14,530 | 628 | 1,528 | 3,567 | 23,285 |
| Texas............. | 12,116 | 779,505 | 581,615 | 42,672 | 76,416 | 1,508 | 15,684 | 15,818 | 110,136 |
| Utah.............. | 1,289 | 83,703 | 60,652 | 5,229 | 12,446 | 2,776 | 1,048 | 3,019 | 10,126 |
| Vermont............ | 326 | 19,311 | 13,281 | 1,168 | 2,248 | 611 | 511 | 478 | 2,317 |
| Virginia............ | 3,910 | 292,085 | 211,033 | 12,626 | 40,803 | 10,695 | 5,397 | 11,327 | 40,907 |
| Washington......... | 3,489 | 276,796 | 190,296 | 24,073 | 29,236 | 955 | 4,810 | 8,802 | 41,033 |
| West Virginia........ | 767 | 38,375 | 27,910 | 812 | 2,982 | 962 | 202 | 661 | 4,153 |
| Wisconsin.......... | 2,843 | 177,941 | 126,766 | 7,995 | 20,917 | 6,428 | 3,890 | 4,126 | 22,769 |
| Wyoming........... | 269 | 18,718 | 11,823 | 2,084 | 1,762 | 118 | 153 | 400 | 2,699 |
| Other [3].............. | 765 | 64,859 | 57,410 | 10,219 | 3,754 | 1,230 | 283 | 371 | 7,754 |

[1] Includes other items, not shown separately. [2] Less loss. [3] Includes returns filed from Army Post Office and Fleet Post Office addresses by members of the armed forces stationed overseas; returns filed by other U.S. citizens abroad; and returns filed by residents of Puerto Rico with income from sources outside of Puerto Rico or with income earned as U.S. government employees.

Source: U.S. Internal Revenue Service, Statistics of Income Bulletin, "Historical Data Tables," <https://www.irs.gov/statistics/soi-tax-stats-historical-data-tables>, accessed September 2018.

## Table 524. Individuals Due an Unclaimed Income Tax Refund by State: 2015

[1,408,482 represents $1,408,482,000. Data are estimates, and are for unclaimed income tax refunds for taxpayers who did not file a 2015 Form 1040 federal income tax return. Taxpayers have a 3-year window in which to claim a tax refund, after which the money becomes the property of the U.S. Treasury]

| State | Total persons (number) | Value of potential refunds ($1,000) [1] | Median potential refund (dol.) | State | Total persons (number) | Value of potential refunds ($1,000) [1] | Median potential refund (dol.) |
|---|---|---|---|---|---|---|---|
| **Total U.S.** | **1,223,000** | **1,408,482** | **879** | Missouri | 27,000 | 29,008 | 825 |
| Alabama | 20,100 | 22,261 | 865 | Montana | 4,100 | 4,521 | 831 |
| Alaska | 5,300 | 6,809 | 921 | Nebraska | 6,300 | 6,923 | 870 |
| Arizona | 27,300 | 29,486 | 780 | Nevada | 13,700 | 15,728 | 867 |
| Arkansas | 11,200 | 12,000 | 824 | New Hampshire | 5,500 | 6,859 | 976 |
| California | 111,200 | 124,397 | 832 | New Jersey | 33,100 | 41,353 | 960 |
| Colorado | 23,500 | 26,173 | 824 | New Mexico | 8,600 | 9,950 | 860 |
| Connecticut | 12,700 | 15,981 | 952 | New York | 62,500 | 77,662 | 964 |
| Delaware | 4,800 | 5,570 | 886 | North Carolina | 37,100 | 39,955 | 831 |
| District of Columbia | 3,400 | 4,219 | 918 | North Dakota | 3,700 | 4,493 | 980 |
| Florida | 84,000 | 95,697 | 887 | Ohio | 43,600 | 47,428 | 852 |
| Georgia | 41,100 | 44,754 | 799 | Oklahoma | 19,100 | 22,006 | 886 |
| Hawaii | 7,000 | 8,523 | 935 | Oregon | 17,900 | 19,118 | 779 |
| Idaho | 5,200 | 5,209 | 712 | Pennsylvania | 46,000 | 53,541 | 934 |
| Illinois | 45,800 | 54,804 | 924 | Rhode Island | 3,300 | 4,025 | 949 |
| Indiana | 26,900 | 30,670 | 895 | South Carolina | 14,600 | 15,701 | 777 |
| Iowa | 12,300 | 13,737 | 913 | South Dakota | 3,300 | 3,646 | 928 |
| Kansas | 12,700 | 14,283 | 874 | Tennessee | 24,000 | 25,976 | 853 |
| Kentucky | 15,700 | 17,246 | 874 | Texas | 129,300 | 158,244 | 929 |
| Louisiana | 22,600 | 26,759 | 884 | Utah | 9,300 | 9,859 | 791 |
| Maine | 4,700 | 4,820 | 806 | Vermont | 2,200 | 2,388 | 876 |
| Maryland | 25,700 | 31,274 | 897 | Virginia | 32,900 | 38,441 | 867 |
| Massachusetts | 26,100 | 32,579 | 973 | Washington | 32,400 | 40,142 | 939 |
| Michigan | 39,700 | 45,535 | 873 | West Virginia | 5,900 | 6,979 | 948 |
| Minnesota | 18,000 | 19,222 | 813 | Wisconsin | 16,100 | 16,532 | 787 |
| Mississippi | 11,200 | 12,032 | 814 | Wyoming | 3,300 | 3,964 | 958 |

[1] Excluding credits.

Source: U.S. Internal Revenue Service, News Release, "Refunds of $1.4 billion waiting to be claimed by individuals who have not filed federal income tax returns for 2015," IR-2019-38, March 2019. See also <https://www.irs.gov/newsroom>.

## Table 525. Federal Employees—Summary Characteristics: 1990 to 2017

[In percent, except as indicated. As of September 30. For civilian employees of executive branch agencies participating in Office of Personnel Management's Central Personnel Data File (CPDF)]

| Characteristics | 1990 | 1995 | 2000 | 2005 | 2010 | 2015 | 2016 | 2017 |
|---|---|---|---|---|---|---|---|---|
| Average age (years) [1] | 42.3 | 44.3 | 46.3 | 46.9 | 46.8 | 47.4 | 47.4 | 47.5 |
| Average length of service (years) | 13.4 | 15.5 | 17.1 | 16.4 | 14.3 | 13.7 | 13.5 | 13.5 |
| Retirement eligible: [2] | | | | | | | | |
| Civil Service Retirement System | 8.0 | 10.0 | 17.0 | 33.0 | 57.0 | 81.1 | 85.7 | 89.5 |
| Bachelor's degree or higher | 35.0 | 39.0 | 41.0 | 43.0 | 46.0 | 51.0 | 51.2 | 51.7 |
| Sex: Male | 57.0 | 56.0 | 55.0 | 56.0 | 55.9 | 56.8 | 56.7 | 56.6 |
| Female | 43.0 | 44.0 | 45.0 | 44.0 | 44.1 | 43.2 | 43.3 | 43.4 |
| Race and national origin: | | | | | | | | |
| Total minorities | 27.4 | 28.9 | 30.4 | 31.7 | 33.3 | 35.3 | 35.9 | 36.7 |
| Black | 16.7 | 16.8 | 17.1 | 17.0 | 17.5 | 17.7 | 17.9 | 18.2 |
| Hispanic | 5.4 | 5.9 | 6.6 | 7.4 | 7.7 | 8.4 | 8.5 | 8.8 |
| Asian/Pacific Islander | 3.5 | 4.2 | 4.5 | 5.1 | 5.6 | 6.2 | 6.4 | 6.5 |
| American Indian/Alaska Native | 1.8 | 2.0 | 2.2 | 2.1 | 2.1 | 1.7 | 1.7 | 1.7 |
| Disabled | 7.0 | 7.0 | 7.0 | 7.0 | 7.0 | 12.5 | 9.5 | 9.9 |
| Veterans preference | 30.0 | 26.0 | 24.0 | 22.0 | 23.1 | 25.9 | 26.2 | 26.3 |
| Vietnam era veterans | 17.0 | 17.0 | 14.0 | 11.0 | 8.0 | 3.2 | 2.7 | 2.2 |
| Retired military | 4.9 | 4.2 | 3.9 | 5.4 | 7.0 | 8.3 | 8.3 | 8.3 |
| Retired officers | 0.5 | 0.5 | 0.5 | 1.0 | 1.6 | 1.9 | 1.9 | 1.9 |
| Average base salary (dollar) [1] | 32,026 | 41,557 | 51,618 | 64,175 | 76,231 | 81,249 | 82,709 | 84,913 |

[1] For full-time permanent employees. [2] Represents full-time permanent employees under the Civil Service Retirement System (excluding hires since January 1984), and the Federal Employees Retirement System (since January 1984).

Source: U.S. Office of Personnel Management, Office of Workforce Information, *The Fact Book, Federal Civilian Workforce Statistics*, annual. Beginning 2008, Central Personnel Data File, "Profile of Federal Civilian Non-Postal Full-Time Employees," <http://www.opm.gov/policy-data-oversight/data-analysis-documentation/federal-employment-reports/reports-publications/profile-of-federal-civilian-non-postal-employees/>, accessed April 2018.

## Table 526. Full-Time Federal Civilian Employment—Employees and Average Pay by Pay System: 2010 to 2018

[1,950 represents 1,950,000. As of September 30. Data are shown for all full-time nonseasonal employees. Includes employees in U.S., U.S. territories, foreign countries, and unspecified locations. Excludes postal employees and other selected agencies; see <http://www.fedscope.opm.gov/datadefn/aboutehri_sdm.asp> for details. See text, this section, for explanation of general schedule and wage system]

| Pay system | Employees (1,000) | | | | Average annual pay (dol.) | | | |
|---|---|---|---|---|---|---|---|---|
| | 2010 | 2016 | 2017 | 2018 | 2010 | 2016 | 2017 | 2018 |
| **Total, excluding postal** | **1,950** | **1,963** | **1,959** | **1,965** | **75,704** | **82,274** | **84,523** | **85,144** |
| General schedule and equivalently graded | 1,410 | 1,429 | 1,418 | 1,414 | 73,656 | 79,852 | 81,976 | 83,744 |
| Prevailing rate pay plans (blue collar) | 195 | 185 | 184 | 183 | 52,051 | 54,415 | 55,829 | 56,954 |
| Other white collar pay plans | 344 | 349 | 357 | 367 | 97,459 | 107,006 | 109,393 | 104,575 |

Source: U.S. Office of Personnel Management, "FedScope," <http://www.fedscope.opm.gov/>, accessed March 2019.

# Table 527. Federal Government Civilian Employment by State: 2010 to 2018

[As of September 30. For agencies excluded from total, see <http://www.fedscope.opm.gov/datadefn/aboutehri_sdm.asp>]

| State | 2010 | 2016 | 2017 | 2018 | State | 2010 | 2016 | 2017 | 2018 |
|---|---|---|---|---|---|---|---|---|---|
| U.S. [1].... | 2,061,320 | 2,053,984 | 2,045,296 | 2,055,698 | MO......... | 38,351 | 34,282 | 34,048 | 34,892 |
| AL......... | 42,267 | 38,445 | 38,147 | 38,226 | MT......... | 12,010 | 10,538 | 10,268 | 10,257 |
| AK......... | 14,072 | 11,571 | 10,988 | 11,043 | NE......... | 10,686 | 9,831 | 9,798 | 9,770 |
| AZ......... | 42,409 | 32,313 | 32,422 | 32,231 | NV......... | 11,475 | 11,042 | 11,479 | 11,528 |
| AR......... | 14,741 | 13,021 | 12,875 | 13,103 | NH......... | 4,436 | 4,393 | 4,287 | 4,424 |
| CA......... | 172,547 | 143,418 | 142,923 | 143,428 | NJ......... | 30,101 | 20,570 | 20,505 | 20,525 |
| CO......... | 40,744 | 37,817 | 37,186 | 36,983 | NM......... | 27,682 | 22,238 | 21,807 | 21,577 |
| CT......... | 8,671 | 8,031 | 7,994 | 7,961 | NY......... | 68,202 | 52,161 | 51,583 | 51,886 |
| DE......... | 3,425 | 3,064 | 3,159 | 3,085 | NC......... | 43,678 | 43,558 | 43,566 | 44,584 |
| DC......... | 167,893 | 172,626 | 170,063 | 140,211 | ND......... | 6,723 | 5,618 | 5,510 | 5,543 |
| FL......... | 88,933 | 78,608 | 79,033 | 80,348 | OH......... | 53,014 | 49,368 | 49,474 | 49,958 |
| GA......... | 80,229 | 71,776 | 71,440 | 72,377 | OK......... | 39,463 | 38,106 | 38,023 | 38,981 |
| HI......... | 25,354 | 22,287 | 22,248 | 22,591 | OR......... | 22,470 | 20,472 | 19,997 | 20,234 |
| ID......... | 10,496 | 9,601 | 9,706 | 9,839 | PA......... | 69,792 | 59,851 | 59,463 | 60,042 |
| IL......... | 51,136 | 41,381 | 41,044 | 40,924 | RI......... | 7,135 | 7,340 | 7,418 | 7,466 |
| IN......... | 24,734 | 23,116 | 23,200 | 23,621 | SC......... | 21,675 | 20,643 | 20,895 | 21,377 |
| IA......... | 9,245 | 8,689 | 8,666 | 8,800 | SD......... | 8,849 | 8,456 | 8,455 | 8,374 |
| KS......... | 17,792 | 16,004 | 15,960 | 16,187 | TN......... | 28,822 | 26,154 | 25,460 | 26,159 |
| KY......... | 26,523 | 22,706 | 22,401 | 22,244 | TX......... | 140,292 | 113,038 | 114,596 | 115,414 |
| LA......... | 21,075 | 18,135 | 18,729 | 18,906 | UT......... | 31,051 | 28,682 | 27,920 | 28,755 |
| ME......... | 11,132 | 10,629 | 10,671 | 11,093 | VT......... | 4,495 | 3,425 | 3,372 | 3,377 |
| MD......... | 128,281 | 130,378 | 130,088 | 129,102 | VA......... | 145,449 | 136,170 | 134,559 | 136,529 |
| MA......... | 29,223 | 24,875 | 24,659 | 24,466 | WA......... | 57,894 | 54,840 | 54,440 | 54,824 |
| MI......... | 30,023 | 25,743 | 25,751 | 25,765 | WV......... | 16,287 | 15,148 | 15,223 | 15,063 |
| MN......... | 18,561 | 16,379 | 16,630 | 16,692 | WI......... | 15,809 | 15,393 | 15,316 | 15,732 |
| MS......... | 19,353 | 17,954 | 17,853 | 17,839 | WY......... | 6,640 | 6,433 | 6,267 | 6,352 |

[1] Total does not include employees based in U.S. Territories or foreign countries and includes data that has been suppressed for security purposes; see source for details.

Source: U.S. Office of Personnel Management, "FedScope," <http://www.fedscope.opm.gov/>, accessed March 2019.

# Table 528. Federal Executive Branch Retirements: 2005 to 2017

[For fiscal years ending September 30. Covers non-postal, executive branch federal civilian employees with personnel records in the Enterprise Human Resources Integration-Statistical Data Mart (EHRI-SDM) and Central Personnel Data File (CPDF). Retiring employees must satisfy the minimum years of service requirement; for more information, see source]

| Characteristic | 2005 | 2010 | 2012 | 2013 | 2014 | 2015 | 2016 | 2017 |
|---|---|---|---|---|---|---|---|---|
| Total retirements.................. | 61,860 | 52,660 | 69,320 | 65,264 | 68,746 | 65,375 | 64,051 | 62,155 |
| Sex: | | | | | | | | |
| Male.............................. | 37,241 | 30,481 | 38,493 | 36,787 | 38,115 | 36,115 | 35,650 | 34,916 |
| Female........................... | 24,619 | 22,179 | 30,827 | 28,477 | 30,631 | 29,260 | 28,401 | 27,238 |
| Race: | | | | | | | | |
| White............................. | 46,687 | 38,947 | 50,259 | 46,816 | 49,454 | 46,243 | 45,472 | 43,779 |
| Black............................. | 8,970 | 7,547 | 10,621 | 9,664 | 10,582 | 10,248 | 9,880 | 9,907 |
| Hispanic.......................... | 3,438 | 3,008 | 4,149 | 3,953 | 4,262 | 4,225 | 4,183 | 4,113 |
| Other............................. | 2,757 | 3,070 | 4,259 | 4,805 | 4,440 | 4,040 | 4,505 | 4,340 |
| Retirement type: | | | | | | | | |
| Mandatory......................... | 557 | 755 | 941 | 965 | 1,024 | 960 | 984 | 1,034 |
| Disability......................... | 5,606 | 3,925 | 3,743 | 3,254 | 3,669 | 4,279 | 2,964 | 1,734 |
| Voluntary......................... | 47,155 | 45,758 | 59,812 | 58,295 | 61,017 | 58,294 | 58,666 | 57,947 |
| Early out.......................... | 7,511 | 1,456 | 4,124 | 2,184 | 2,468 | 1,298 | 954 | 771 |
| Other............................. | 1,031 | 766 | 700 | 566 | 568 | 544 | 483 | 669 |
| Occupational category: | | | | | | | | |
| Administrative..................... | 24,711 | 21,673 | 29,460 | 27,153 | 28,633 | 26,995 | 26,130 | 26,842 |
| Professional....................... | 12,434 | 10,906 | 14,322 | 14,410 | 16,090 | 15,198 | 15,179 | 15,086 |
| Technical.......................... | 11,514 | 9,539 | 12,237 | 11,416 | 11,825 | 11,794 | 10,914 | 10,182 |
| Blue collar........................ | 8,232 | 6,489 | 8,097 | 7,296 | 7,066 | 6,529 | 6,027 | 5,556 |
| Other............................. | 4,934 | 4,033 | 5,194 | 4,982 | 5,122 | 4,845 | 4,638 | 4,480 |
| Veteran status: | | | | | | | | |
| Veteran........................... | 23,828 | 18,686 | 22,738 | 21,276 | 21,752 | 20,507 | 20,117 | 18,906 |
| Exempt........................... | 1,770 | 1,130 | 923 | 611 | 548 | 534 | 548 | 544 |
| Non-veteran....................... | 36,262 | 32,844 | 45,659 | 43,377 | 46,446 | 44,334 | 43,386 | 42,705 |
| Average retirement age (years)..... | 58.9 | 60.3 | 60.8 | 61.3 | 61.4 | 61.5 | 61.8 | 62.0 |
| Average length of service (years)... | 27.9 | 27.7 | 27.9 | 27.5 | 26.9 | 26.3 | 25.6 | 25.3 |

Source: U.S. Office of Personnel Management, *Executive Branch Retirement Statistics: Fiscal Years 2007-2018*, April 2018 and earlier reports. See also <http://www.opm.gov/policy-data-oversight/data-analysis-documentation/federal-employment-reports/>.

# Table 529. Area of Federally Owned Buildings, Excluding Department of Defense, by State: 2017

[1,150.9 represents 1,150,900,000. As of September 30. For executive branch departments and agencies subject to the Chief Financial Officers Act of 1990. Department of Defense Data is under review and is not included in FY 2017 totals]

| State | Total building area (mil. sq. ft.) [2] | Owned building area (mil. sq. ft.) | Leased building area (mil. sq. ft.) | State | Total building area (mil. sq. ft.) [2] | Owned building area (mil. sq. ft.) | Leased building area (mil. sq. ft.) |
|---|---|---|---|---|---|---|---|
| **United States** [1]... | **1,150.9** | **891.8** | **256.9** | Missouri........... | 29.5 | 18.8 | 10.6 |
| Alabama............ | 17.1 | 13.5 | 3.6 | Montana........... | 10.8 | 8.5 | 2.3 |
| Alaska............. | 11.5 | 10.1 | 1.4 | Nebraska.......... | 5.7 | 4.3 | 1.4 |
| Arizona............ | 30.3 | 26.1 | 4.1 | Nevada............ | 10.3 | 8.2 | 2.1 |
| Arkansas........... | 10.2 | 8.8 | 1.3 | New Hampshire... | 3.0 | 2.5 | 0.6 |
| California.......... | 99.3 | 81.0 | 18.1 | New Jersey........ | 18.4 | 13.8 | 4.6 |
| Colorado........... | 23.1 | 16.8 | 6.3 | New Mexico....... | 32.1 | 29.0 | 3.2 |
| Connecticut........ | 6.1 | 5.2 | 0.9 | New York.......... | 51.7 | 43.8 | 7.8 |
| Delaware........... | 1.3 | 0.9 | 0.4 | North Carolina.... | 18.4 | 13.0 | 5.4 |
| Dist. of Columbia. .. | 75.8 | 52.3 | 23.5 | North Dakota...... | 6.3 | 5.7 | 0.7 |
| Florida............. | 41.9 | 31.1 | 10.7 | Ohio............... | 35.5 | 30.5 | 5.0 |
| Georgia............ | 31.7 | 21.8 | 9.9 | Oklahoma......... | 11.8 | 6.7 | 5.1 |
| Hawaii............. | 4.4 | 3.4 | 0.7 | Oregon............ | 17.5 | 14.7 | 2.8 |
| Idaho.............. | 12.4 | 10.8 | 1.6 | Pennsylvania...... | 32.6 | 25.1 | 7.5 |
| Illinois............. | 34.8 | 29.4 | 5.4 | Rhode Island...... | 1.8 | 1.1 | 0.6 |
| Indiana............ | 14.2 | 11.4 | 2.8 | South Carolina.... | 19.5 | 17.7 | 1.8 |
| Iowa............... | 7.4 | 5.9 | 1.4 | South Dakota..... | 10.1 | 9.4 | 0.8 |
| Kansas............. | 9.0 | 6.2 | 2.8 | Tennessee......... | 26.6 | 23.4 | 3.2 |
| Kentucky........... | 20.5 | 17.8 | 2.7 | Texas............. | 61.1 | 44.1 | 16.9 |
| Louisiana.......... | 17.3 | 14.2 | 3.1 | Utah.............. | 9.7 | 7.3 | 2.5 |
| Maine.............. | 4.3 | 3.6 | 0.7 | Vermont........... | 2.7 | 1.5 | 1.2 |
| Maryland........... | 73.2 | 53.9 | 19.3 | Virginia........... | 53.3 | 26.7 | 26.6 |
| Massachusetts...... | 18.7 | 15.5 | 2.6 | Washington....... | 32.2 | 27.0 | 5.1 |
| Michigan........... | 16.6 | 12.2 | 4.2 | West Virginia...... | 17.3 | 14.9 | 2.4 |
| Minnesota.......... | 11.1 | 8.9 | 2.1 | Wisconsin......... | 9.9 | 7.6 | 2.3 |
| Mississippi......... | 13.3 | 11.4 | 1.9 | Wyoming.......... | 9.3 | 8.6 | 0.7 |

[1] Includes property in U.S. territories, not shown separately. [2] Includes museum trust and state government owned. Non-federal government entities hold title to the real property asset but rights for use have been granted to the Federal Government in a method other than a leasehold arrangement; in the case of a museum trust, the trust holds title but Federal funds may be received to cover operational and maintenance costs.

Source: U.S. General Services Administration, "Real Property Management Policy—Asset Management, FRPP Summary Report Library," <http://www.gsa.gov/portal/content/102880>, accessed November 2018.

# National Security and Veterans Affairs

This section displays data for national security (national defense and homeland security) and benefits for veterans. Data are presented on national defense and its human and financial costs; active and reserve military personnel; federally sponsored programs and benefits for veterans; and funding, budget and selected agencies for homeland security. The principal sources of these data are the *Veterans Benefits Administration Annual Benefits Report*, U.S. Department of Veterans Affairs; *Budget in Brief*, U.S. Department of Homeland Security; and *The Budget of the United States Government*, Office of Management and Budget.

**Department of Defense (DoD)**—The U.S. Department of Defense is responsible for providing the military forces of the United States. It includes the Office of the Secretary of Defense, the Joint Chiefs of Staff, the Army, the Navy, the Air Force, and the defense agencies. The President serves as Commander-in-Chief of the Armed Forces; from him, the authority flows to the Secretary of Defense and through the Joint Chiefs of Staff to the commanders of unified and specified commands (e.g., U.S. Strategic Command).

**Reserve components**—The Reserve components of the Armed Forces consist of the Army National Guard of the United States, Army Reserve, Naval Reserve, Marine Corps Reserve, Air National Guard, Air Force Reserve, and Coast Guard Reserve. They provide trained personnel and units available for active duty in the Armed Forces during times of war or national emergency, and at such other times as national security may require. The National Guard has dual federal/state responsibilities and uses jointly provided equipment, facilities, and budget support. The President is empowered to mobilize the National Guard and to use the Armed Forces as he considers necessary to enforce federal authority in any state. There is in each Armed Force a ready reserve, a standby reserve, and a retired reserve. The Ready Reserve includes the Selected Reserve, which provides trained and ready units and individuals to augment the active forces during times of war or national emergency, or at other times when required; and the Individual Ready Reserve, which is a manpower pool that can be called to active duty during times of war or national emergency and would normally be used as individual fillers for active, guard, and reserve units, and as a source of combat replacements. Most of the Ready Reserve serves in an active status.

**Department of Veterans Affairs (VA)**—A veteran is someone 18 years and older (there are a few 17-year-old veterans) who is not currently on active duty, but who once served on active duty in the United States Army, Navy, Air Force, Marine Corps, or Coast Guard, or who served in the Merchant Marine during World War II. There are many groups whose active service makes them veterans including: those who incurred a service-connected disability during active duty for training in the Reserves or National Guard even though that service would not otherwise have counted for veteran status, and members of a national guard or reserve component who have been ordered to active duty by order of the President or those who have a full-time military job. The latter are called AGRs (Active Guard and Reserve). No one who has received a dishonorable discharge is a veteran.

The VA administers laws authorizing benefits for eligible former and present members of the Armed Forces and for the beneficiaries of deceased members. Veterans' benefits available under various acts of Congress include compensation for service-connected disability or death; pensions for non-service-connected disability or death; vocational rehabilitation, education and training; home loan insurance; life insurance; health care; special housing and automobiles or other conveyances for certain disabled veterans; burial and plot allowances; and educational assistance to families of deceased or totally disabled veterans, servicemen missing in action, or prisoners of war. Since these benefits are legislated by Congress, the dates they were enacted and the dates they apply to veterans may be different from the actual dates the conflicts occurred. VA estimates of veterans cover all persons discharged from active U.S. military service under conditions other than dishonorable.

**Department of Homeland Security (DHS)**—The creation of DHS, which began operations in March 2003, represents a fusion of 22 federal agencies from different legacy agencies (the Coast Guard and Secret Service remained intact) to coordinate and centralize the leadership of many homeland security activities under a single department. The largest organizations under DHS include: Customs and Border Protection (CBP), Immigration and Customs Enforcement (ICE), Transportation Security Administration (TSA), Federal Emergency Management Agency (FEMA), and the Coast Guard.

**Coast Guard**—With more than 218 years of service to the Nation, the Coast Guard is a military, multi-mission, maritime organization that promotes safety and safeguards U.S. economic and security interests throughout the maritime environment. As one of the five Armed Services of the United States, it is the only military organization within the DHS. Unlike its sister services in the Department of Defense (DoD), the Coast Guard is also a law enforcement and regulatory agency with broad domestic authorities.

**Federal Emergency Management Agency (FEMA)**—FEMA manages and coordinates the federal response to and recovery from major domestic disasters and emergencies of all types in accordance with the Robert T. Stafford Disaster Relief and Emergency Assistance Act. The agency ensures the effectiveness of emergency response providers at all levels of government in responding to terrorist attacks, major disasters, and other emergencies. Through the Disaster Relief Fund, FEMA provides individual and public assistance to help families and communities impacted by declared disasters rebuild and recover. FEMA is also the principal component for preparing state and local governments to prevent or respond to threats or incidents of terrorism and other catastrophic events, through their state and local programs.

**The Customs and Border Protection (CBP)**—CBP is responsible for managing, securing, and controlling U.S. borders. This includes carrying out traditional border-related responsibilities, such as stemming the tide of illegal drugs and illegal aliens; securing and facilitating legitimate global trade and travel; and protecting the food supply and agriculture industry from pests and disease. CBP is composed of the Border Patrol and Inspections (both moved from Immigration and Naturalization Service) along with Customs (absorbed from the U.S. Department of Treasury) and Animal and Plant Health Inspections Services (absorbed from the U.S. Department of Agriculture).

**The Immigration and Customs Enforcement (ICE)**—ICE's mission is to protect America and uphold public safety by targeting the people, money, and materials crossing the nation's borders that support terrorist and criminal activities. ICE is the largest investigation arm of DHS. ICE is composed of five law enforcement divisions: Investigations, Intelligence, Federal Protective Service, International Affairs, and Detention and Removal Operations. ICE investigates a wide range of national security, financial, and smuggling violations including drug smuggling, human trafficking, illegal arms exports, financial crimes, commercial fraud, human smuggling, document fraud, money laundering, child pornography/exploitation, and immigration fraud.

**The Transportation Security Administration (TSA)**—TSA was created as part of the Aviation and Transportation Security Act on November 19, 2001. TSA was originally part of the U.S. Department of Transportation, but was moved to DHS. TSA's mission is to provide security to our nation's transportation systems with a primary focus on aviation security.

## Table 530. National Defense Outlays and Veterans' Benefits: 1960 to 2020

[In billions of dollars (53.6 represents $53,600,000,000), except percent. For fiscal year ending in year shown; see text, Section 8. Includes outlays of Department of Defense, Department of Veterans Affairs, and other agencies for activities primarily related to national defense and veterans programs. For explanation of average annual percent change, see Guide to Tabular Presentation. Minus sign (-) indicates decrease]

| Year | National defense and veterans' outlays | | | | Annual percent change [1] | | | Defense outlays, percent of— | |
|---|---|---|---|---|---|---|---|---|---|
| | | Defense outlays | | | | | | | |
| | Total outlays | Current dollars | Constant (2012) dollars | Veterans' outlays | Total outlays | Defense outlays | Veterans' outlays | Federal outlays | Gross domestic product [2] |
| 1960 | 53.6 | 48.1 | (NA) | 5.4 | -1.63 | -1.81 | -0.04 | 52.2 | 9.0 |
| 1970 | 90.4 | 81.7 | 498.2 | 8.7 | 0.26 | -0.98 | 13.60 | 41.8 | 7.8 |
| 1980 | 155.2 | 134.0 | 384.5 | 21.2 | 13.88 | 15.17 | 6.30 | 22.7 | 4.8 |
| 1990 | 328.4 | 299.3 | 542.7 | 29.0 | -1.56 | -1.39 | -3.23 | 23.9 | 5.1 |
| 2000 | 341.4 | 294.4 | 431.5 | 47.0 | 7.37 | 7.13 | 8.88 | 16.5 | 2.9 |
| 2001 | 349.7 | 304.7 | 432.0 | 45.0 | 2.45 | 3.52 | -4.29 | 16.4 | 2.9 |
| 2002 | 399.4 | 348.5 | 478.4 | 50.9 | 14.21 | 14.35 | 13.24 | 17.3 | 3.2 |
| 2003 | 461.7 | 404.7 | 521.9 | 57.0 | 15.61 | 16.15 | 11.89 | 18.7 | 3.6 |
| 2004 | 515.6 | 455.8 | 566.5 | 59.7 | 11.66 | 12.62 | 4.85 | 19.9 | 3.8 |
| 2005 | 565.4 | 495.3 | 587.5 | 70.1 | 9.67 | 8.66 | 17.36 | 20.0 | 3.9 |
| 2006 | 591.6 | 521.8 | 593.5 | 69.8 | 4.64 | 5.36 | -0.44 | 19.7 | 3.8 |
| 2007 | 624.1 | 551.3 | 607.0 | 72.8 | 5.48 | 5.64 | 4.31 | 20.2 | 3.9 |
| 2008 | 700.7 | 616.1 | 653.3 | 84.7 | 12.28 | 11.76 | 16.25 | 20.7 | 4.2 |
| 2009 | 756.4 | 661.0 | 702.4 | 95.4 | 7.95 | 7.30 | 12.73 | 18.8 | 4.6 |
| 2010 | 801.9 | 693.5 | 723.6 | 108.4 | 6.01 | 4.91 | 13.58 | 20.1 | 4.7 |
| 2011 | 832.7 | 705.6 | 715.2 | 127.2 | 3.85 | 1.74 | 17.35 | 19.6 | 4.6 |
| 2012 | 802.4 | 677.9 | 677.8 | 124.6 | -3.64 | -3.93 | -2.04 | 19.2 | 4.2 |
| 2013 | 772.4 | 633.4 | 629.0 | 138.9 | -3.75 | -6.55 | 11.51 | 18.3 | 3.8 |
| 2014 | 753.1 | 603.5 | 590.0 | 149.6 | -2.50 | -4.73 | 7.69 | 17.2 | 3.5 |
| 2015 | 749.4 | 589.7 | 574.1 | 159.7 | -0.49 | -2.29 | 6.77 | 16.0 | 3.3 |
| 2016 | 767.9 | 593.4 | 575.8 | 174.5 | 2.47 | 0.63 | 9.25 | 15.4 | 3.2 |
| 2017 | 775.3 | 598.7 | 572.5 | 176.5 | 0.96 | 0.90 | 1.16 | 15.0 | 3.1 |
| **2018** | **810.0** | **631.2** | **590.9** | **178.9** | **4.48** | **5.42** | **1.31** | **15.4** | **3.1** |
| 2019 estimate | 885.0 | 684.6 | 628.2 | 200.5 | 9.26 | 8.46 | 12.08 | 15.1 | 3.2 |
| 2020 estimate | 955.4 | 737.9 | 663.8 | 217.5 | 7.95 | 7.79 | 8.51 | 15.5 | 3.3 |

NA Not available. [1] Change from immediate prior year. [2] Represents fiscal year GDP; for definition, see text, Section 13.

Source: U.S. Office of Management and Budget, *Budget of the U.S. Government, Fiscal Year 2020: Historical Tables*, March 2019. See also <http://www.whitehouse.gov/omb/budget/>.

## Table 531. National Defense Budget Authority and Outlays for Defense Functions: 2000 to 2020

[In billions of dollars (304.0 represents $304,000,000,000). For year ending September 30. Data includes defense budget authority and outlays by other departments. Minus sign (-) indicates decrease]

| Function | 2000 | 2010 | 2012 | 2013 | 2014 | 2015 | 2016 | 2017 | 2018 | 2019 est. | 2020 est. |
|---|---|---|---|---|---|---|---|---|---|---|---|
| **Total budget authority** | **304.0** | **721.2** | **681.4** | **610.2** | **622.3** | **598.4** | **624.1** | **656.3** | **726.8** | **726.2** | **761.8** |
| Department of Defense—Military | 290.3 | 695.6 | 655.4 | 585.2 | 595.7 | 570.8 | 595.7 | 626.2 | 694.5 | 693.1 | 728.0 |
| Military personnel | 73.8 | 157.1 | 158.4 | 153.5 | 150.2 | 145.9 | 145.4 | 146.1 | 150.9 | 158.6 | 165.1 |
| Operation and maintenance | 108.7 | 293.6 | 286.8 | 258.3 | 262.5 | 246.6 | 245.1 | 258.7 | 274.1 | 279.7 | 293.8 |
| Procurement | 55.0 | 135.8 | 118.3 | 97.8 | 100.4 | 102.1 | 118.9 | 124.3 | 147.5 | 147.6 | 143.4 |
| Research, development, test, and evaluation | 38.7 | 80.2 | 72.0 | 63.3 | 63.5 | 63.9 | 69.5 | 74.1 | 92.0 | 95.5 | 104.5 |
| Military construction | 5.1 | 22.6 | 11.4 | 8.1 | 8.4 | 5.7 | 6.9 | 6.9 | 10.4 | 9.7 | 19.8 |
| Family housing | 3.5 | 2.3 | 1.7 | 1.5 | 1.4 | 1.1 | 1.3 | 1.3 | 1.4 | 1.6 | 1.3 |
| Other | 5.4 | 4.0 | 6.9 | 2.8 | 9.4 | 5.6 | 8.5 | 14.7 | 18.3 | 0.4 | 0.1 |
| Atomic energy defense activities | 12.4 | 18.2 | 18.3 | 17.5 | 18.4 | 19.0 | 20.1 | 21.4 | 23.3 | 24.0 | 24.8 |
| Defense-related activities | 1.3 | 7.3 | 7.7 | 7.4 | 8.2 | 8.5 | 8.3 | 8.7 | 9.0 | 9.1 | 9.0 |
| **Total outlays** | **294.4** | **693.5** | **677.9** | **633.4** | **603.5** | **589.7** | **593.4** | **598.7** | **631.2** | **684.6** | **737.9** |
| Department of Defense—Military | 281.0 | 666.7 | 650.9 | 607.8 | 577.9 | 562.5 | 565.4 | 568.9 | 600.7 | 652.2 | 704.3 |
| Military personnel | 76.0 | 155.7 | 152.3 | 150.8 | 148.9 | 145.2 | 147.9 | 144.7 | 145.8 | 156.7 | 163.3 |
| Operation and maintenance | 105.8 | 276.0 | 282.3 | 259.7 | 244.5 | 247.2 | 243.2 | 245.2 | 256.7 | 275.8 | 290.1 |
| Procurement | 51.7 | 133.6 | 124.7 | 114.9 | 107.5 | 101.3 | 102.7 | 104.1 | 112.7 | 123.3 | 138.7 |
| Research, development, test, and evaluation | 37.6 | 77.0 | 70.4 | 66.9 | 64.9 | 64.1 | 64.9 | 68.1 | 77.0 | 85.3 | 99.9 |
| Military construction | 5.1 | 21.2 | 14.6 | 12.3 | 9.8 | 8.1 | 6.7 | 6.7 | 6.7 | 7.9 | 9.0 |
| Family housing | 3.4 | 3.2 | 2.3 | 1.8 | 1.4 | 1.2 | 1.3 | 1.2 | 1.2 | 1.4 | 1.4 |
| Other | 1.4 | 0.1 | 4.3 | 1.4 | 0.9 | -4.7 | -1.2 | -1.1 | 0.7 | 1.9 | 2.0 |
| Atomic energy defense activities | 12.1 | 19.3 | 19.2 | 17.6 | 17.4 | 18.7 | 19.4 | 20.5 | 20.9 | 23.6 | 24.8 |
| Defense-related activities | 1.2 | 7.5 | 7.8 | 8.0 | 8.1 | 8.5 | 8.6 | 9.3 | 9.5 | 8.8 | 8.8 |

Source: U.S. Office of Management and Budget, *Budget of the U.S. Government, Fiscal Year 2020: Historical Tables*, March 2019. See also <http://www.whitehouse.gov/omb/budget/>.

## Table 532. Department of Defense Property—Sites, Land, and Assets: 2017

[In units, as indicated (1,173.2 represents $1,173,200,000,000). Data collected as of September 30, 2017. A site is a physical location owned by, leased to, or otherwise possessed by a DoD component]

| Asset type | Unit | Total | Army | Navy | Air Force | Marine Corps | WHS [1] |
|---|---|---|---|---|---|---|---|
| **DoD sites, total**................................. | **Number** | **4,775** | **1,807** | **970** | **1,710** | **213** | **75** |
| United States............................... | Number | 4,150 | 1,565 | 785 | 1,535 | 190 | 75 |
| Territories................................... | Number | 111 | 40 | 62 | 9 | – | – |
| Overseas.................................... | Number | 514 | 202 | 123 | 166 | 23 | – |
| **Acres of land, total**............................ | **Number** | **26,882,845** | **13,699,399** | **2,213,278** | **8,479,371** | **2,489,833** | **963** |
| Owned........................................ | Number | 8,921,349 | 5,693,971 | 639,550 | 1,528,280 | 1,058,584 | 963 |
| Leased....................................... | Number | 901,879 | 726,370 | 72,488 | 102,533 | 488 | – |
| Other [2]..................................... | Number | 17,059,616 | 7,279,058 | 1,501,240 | 6,848,558 | 1,430,760 | – |
| **Facility assets, total** [3]...................... | **Number** | **585,816** | **288,388** | **116,675** | **128,166** | **51,674** | **913** |
| Buildings.................................... | Number | 279,240 | 138,639 | 63,768 | 49,223 | 27,438 | 172 |
| Structures................................... | Number | 184,508 | 85,468 | 33,891 | 46,679 | 17,958 | 512 |
| Linear structures.......................... | Number | 122,068 | 64,281 | 19,016 | 32,264 | 6,278 | 229 |
| **Plant replacement value of assets, total** [4]. ... | **Bil. dol.** | **1,173.2** | **451.6** | **267.9** | **351.3** | **94.7** | **7.6** |
| Buildings.................................... | Bil. dol. | 748.9 | 293.5 | 162.8 | 216.3 | 69.1 | 7.2 |
| Structures................................... | Bil. dol. | 238.8 | 88.4 | 70.0 | 67.9 | 12.2 | 0.3 |
| Linear structures.......................... | Bil. dol. | 185.5 | 69.7 | 35.2 | 67.1 | 13.4 | 0.1 |

– Represents zero. [1] Washington Headquarters Service. [2] Includes buildings that have been privatized or are operated by private entities in direct support of the DoD mission. [3] Buildings (roofed and floored facilities enclosed by exterior walls); structures (facilities other than buildings or linear structures, constructed on or in the land, such as towers, storage tanks, wharfs, and piers); and linear structures (facilities that traverse land such as runways, roads, rail lines, pipelines, fences, pavements, and electrical distribution line and are reported by a linear unit of measure). [4] Calculated cost to replace the current physical plant (facilities and supporting infrastructure) using today's construction costs (labor and materials) and standards (methodologies and codes).

Source: U.S. Department of Defense, Office of the Deputy Assistant Secretary of Defense (OASD) for Infrastructure, *Base Structure Report Fiscal Year 2018 Baseline, A Summary of the Real Property Inventory*, 2019. See also <http://www.acq.osd.mil/eie/Library.html#BSR>.

## Table 533. Military Personnel and Families by Selected Characteristics: 2005 to 2017

[In units, as indicated. Reserve and National Guard includes Selected Reserve only, unless otherwise noted. Personnel data primarily from Defense Manpower Data Center (DMDC). Family member data is from the Defense Enrollment and Eligibility Reporting System]

| Characteristic | 2005 | | 2010 | | 2016 | | 2017 | |
|---|---|---|---|---|---|---|---|---|
| | Active Duty | Reserve and Guard | Active Duty | Reserve and Guard | Active Duty | Reserve and Guard | Active Duty | Reserve and Guard |
| **MILITARY PERSONNEL** | | | | | | | | |
| **Total (number)**.................. | **1,373,534** | **829,005** | **1,417,370** | **857,261** | **1,288,596** | **818,305** | **1,294,520** | **815,116** |
| Ratio of officers to enlisted members..... | 1 to 5.1 | 1 to 5.6 | 1 to 5.0 | 1 to 5.7 | 1 to 4.6 | 1 to 5.2 | 1 to 4.6 | 1 to 5.2 |
| Separations from duty (number)........... | 217,598 | 160,882 | 176,248 | 133,223 | 186,793 | 125,933 | 174,403 | 119,841 |
| Retired personnel (number) [1]............. | 1,522,532 | 627,424 | 1,540,830 | 716,228 | 1,581,046 | 772,162 | 1,585,220 | 775,598 |
| PERCENT | | | | | | | | |
| Male......................................... | 85.4 | 82.8 | 85.6 | 82.1 | 84.1 | 80.7 | 83.8 | 80.4 |
| Female...................................... | 14.6 | 17.2 | 14.4 | 17.9 | 15.9 | 19.3 | 16.2 | 19.6 |
| Minority race/ethnicity [2]................. | 35.9 | 30.4 | 30.0 | 24.1 | 31.4 | 26.1 | 31.3 | 26.1 |
| Duty location in the U.S., & territories. ... | 85.3 | 96.9 | 86.4 | 99.1 | 88.0 | 98.9 | 87.5 | 98.9 |
| 25 years old and under.................... | 46.6 | 31.2 | 44.2 | 33.3 | 44.2 | 33.0 | 45.0 | 32.5 |
| With bachelor's degree or higher.......... | 17.7 | 19.7 | 17.7 | 19.4 | 21.6 | 23.6 | 21.8 | 23.0 |
| Married...................................... | 54.6 | 51.4 | 56.4 | 48.2 | 53.5 | 44.5 | 52.6 | 44.4 |
| In dual-military marriages................ | 6.9 | 2.6 | 6.7 | 2.6 | 6.6 | 2.7 | 6.6 | 2.7 |
| MILITARY FAMILIES | | | | | | | | |
| **Family members (number)**.............. | **1,865,058** | **1,141,735** | **1,983,236** | **1,161,631** | **1,669,941** | **1,059,220** | **1,623,305** | **1,054,783** |
| Spouses (number)....................... | 679,738 | 415,548 | 725,877 | 413,295 | 623,981 | 371,628 | 612,127 | 369,653 |
| Adult dependents (number)............. | 8,130 | 1,762 | 9,485 | 1,961 | 9,487 | 1,662 | 8,988 | 1,605 |
| PERCENT | | | | | | | | |
| With children................................ | 43.2 | 43.0 | 44.1 | 43.2 | 39.9 | 41.6 | 38.3 | 41.5 |
| With children age 5 & under.............. | 39.8 | 24.8 | 42.3 | 27.9 | 42.2 | 31.2 | 42.2 | 31.3 |
| Single parents............................. | 5.4 | 8.2 | 5.4 | 9.3 | 4.3 | 9.1 | 4.0 | 9.1 |
| Average age at birth of first child (years).................................... | 24.8 | 27.3 | 24.9 | 26.6 | 25.8 | 28.0 | 25.9 | 28.2 |

[1] Retired Reserve and Guard includes ready reserve. [2] Black or African American, Asian, American Indian or Alaska Native, Native Hawaiian or Other Pacific Islander, multi-racial, or other/unknown.

Source: U.S. Department of Defense, Office of the Deputy Assistant Secretary of Defense, Military Community and Family Policy, *2017 Demographics Profile of the Military Community*, and earlier reports. See also <https://www.militaryonesource.mil/reports-and-surveys>.

## Table 534. Military Personnel on Active Duty by Location: 1980 to 2018

[In thousands (2,051 represents 2,051,000). As of September 30. Prior to 2012, data from DOD Statistical Information Analysis Division (SIAD). Beginning 2012, data from Defense Manpower Data Center (DMDC)]

| Location | 1980 | 1990 | 2000 | 2010 | 2013 | 2014 | 2015 | 2016 | 2017 | 2018 [1] |
|---|---|---|---|---|---|---|---|---|---|---|
| **Total**............................... | **2,051** | **2,046** | **1,384** | **1,431** | **1,370** | **1,326** | **1,301** | **1,328** | **1,335** | **1,346** |
| Shore-based [2].................... | 1,840 | 1,794 | 1,237 | 1,328 | (NA) | (NA) | (NA) | (NA) | (NA) | (NA) |
| Afloat [3].......................... | 211 | 252 | 147 | 103 | (NA) | (NA) | (NA) | (NA) | (NA) | (NA) |
| United States [4]................... | 1,562 | 1,437 | 1,127 | 1,134 | 1,209 | 1,168 | 1,146 | 1,130 | 1,120 | 1,173 |
| Foreign countries................ | 489 | 609 | 258 | 297 | 161 | 159 | 156 | 199 | 215 | 172 |

NA Not available. [1] Beginning December 2017, no longer includes personnel on temporary duty, or deployed in support of contingency operations. [2] Includes Navy personnel temporarily on shore. [3] Includes Marine Corps. [4] Includes Puerto Rico and Island Areas.

Source: U.S. Department of Defense, DoD Personnel, Workforce Reports & Publications, data prior to 2016, "Active Duty Military Personnel By Service By Region/Country," November 2015 and earlier reports. Beginning 2016, "Military and Civilian Personnel by Service/Agency by State/Country," <https://www.dmdc.osd.mil/appj/dwp/dwp_reports.jsp>, accessed January 2019.

# Table 535. Department of Defense Personnel by Service Branch and Sex: 1960 to 2018

[In thousands (2,475 represents 2,475,000). As of end of fiscal year; see text, Section 8. Includes National Guard, Reserve, and retired regular personnel on extended or continuous active duty. Excludes Coast Guard. Other officer candidates are included under enlisted personnel]

| Year | Total [1,2] | Army Total [1] | Army Male Officers | Army Male Enlisted | Army Female Officers | Army Female Enlisted | Navy [2] Total [1] | Navy Male Officers | Navy Male Enlisted | Navy Female Officers | Navy Female Enlisted | Marine Corps Total [1] | Marine Male Officers | Marine Male Enlisted | Marine Female Officers | Marine Female Enlisted | Air Force Total [1] | Air Force Male Officers | Air Force Male Enlisted | Air Force Female Officers | Air Force Female Enlisted |
|---|---|---|---|---|---|---|---|---|---|---|---|---|---|---|---|---|---|---|---|---|---|
| 1960 | 2,475 | 873 | 97 | 762 | 4.3 | 8.3 | 617 | 67 | 540 | 2.7 | 5.4 | 171 | 16 | 153 | 0.1 | 1.5 | 815 | 126 | 677 | 3.7 | 5.7 |
| 1965 | 2,654 | 969 | 108 | 846 | 3.8 | 8.5 | 670 | 75 | 583 | 2.6 | 5.3 | 190 | 17 | 172 | 0.1 | 1.4 | 825 | 128 | 685 | 4.1 | 4.7 |
| 1970 | 3,065 | 1,323 | 162 | 1,142 | 5.2 | 11.5 | 691 | 78 | 600 | 2.9 | 5.8 | 260 | 25 | 233 | 0.3 | 2.1 | 791 | 125 | 648 | 4.7 | 9.0 |
| 1975 | 2,128 | 784 | 98 | 640 | 4.6 | 37.7 | 535 | 62 | 449 | 3.7 | 17.5 | 196 | 19 | 174 | 0.3 | 2.8 | 613 | 100 | 478 | 5.0 | 25.2 |
| 1980 | 2,051 | 777 | 91 | 612 | 7.6 | 61.7 | 527 | 58 | 430 | 4.9 | 30.1 | 189 | 18 | 164 | 0.5 | 6.2 | 558 | 90 | 404 | 8.5 | 51.9 |
| 1985 | 2,151 | 781 | 99 | 599 | 10.8 | 68.4 | 571 | 64 | 449 | 6.9 | 45.7 | 198 | 19 | 169 | 0.7 | 9.0 | 602 | 96 | 431 | 11.9 | 58.1 |
| 1986 | 2,169 | 781 | 99 | 597 | 11.3 | 69.7 | 581 | 65 | 457 | 7.3 | 47.2 | 200 | 19 | 170 | 0.6 | 9.2 | 608 | 97 | 434 | 12.4 | 61.2 |
| 1987 | 2,174 | 781 | 96 | 596 | 11.6 | 71.6 | 587 | 65 | 462 | 7.2 | 47.7 | 200 | 19 | 170 | 0.6 | 9.1 | 607 | 94 | 432 | 12.6 | 63.2 |
| 1988 | 2,138 | 772 | 95 | 588 | 11.8 | 72.0 | 593 | 65 | 466 | 7.3 | 49.7 | 197 | 19 | 168 | 0.7 | 9.0 | 576 | 92 | 405 | 12.9 | 61.5 |
| 1989 | 2,130 | 770 | 95 | 584 | 12.2 | 74.3 | 593 | 65 | 464 | 7.5 | 52.1 | 197 | 19 | 168 | 0.7 | 9.0 | 571 | 91 | 399 | 13.4 | 63.7 |
| 1990 | 2,044 | 732 | 92 | 553 | 12.4 | 71.2 | 579 | 64 | 451 | 7.8 | 52.1 | 197 | 19 | 168 | 0.7 | 8.7 | 535 | 87 | 370 | 13.3 | 60.8 |
| 1991 | 1,986 | 711 | 91 | 535 | 12.5 | 67.8 | 570 | 63 | 444 | 8.0 | 51.4 | 194 | 19 | 166 | 0.7 | 8.3 | 510 | 84 | 350 | 13.3 | 59.1 |
| 1992 | 1,807 | 610 | 83 | 449 | 11.7 | 61.7 | 542 | 61 | 417 | 8.3 | 51.0 | 185 | 18 | 157 | 0.6 | 7.9 | 470 | 77 | 320 | 12.7 | 56.1 |
| 1993 | 1,705 | 572 | 77 | 420 | 11.1 | 60.2 | 510 | 58 | 390 | 8.3 | 49.3 | 178 | 17 | 153 | 0.6 | 7.2 | 444 | 72 | 302 | 12.3 | 54.5 |
| 1994 | 1,610 | 541 | 74 | 394 | 10.9 | 59.0 | 469 | 54 | 355 | 8.0 | 47.9 | 174 | 17 | 149 | 0.6 | 7.0 | 426 | 69 | 287 | 12.3 | 54.0 |
| 1995 | 1,518 | 509 | 72 | 365 | 10.8 | 57.3 | 435 | 51 | 324 | 7.9 | 47.9 | 175 | 17 | 150 | 0.7 | 7.4 | 400 | 66 | 266 | 12.1 | 52.1 |
| 1996 | 1,472 | 491 | 70 | 347 | 10.6 | 59.0 | 417 | 50 | 308 | 7.8 | 46.9 | 175 | 17 | 149 | 0.8 | 7.8 | 389 | 64 | 256 | 12.0 | 52.8 |
| 1997 | 1,439 | 492 | 69 | 346 | 10.4 | 62.4 | 396 | 48 | 290 | 7.8 | 44.8 | 174 | 17 | 148 | 0.8 | 8.5 | 377 | 62 | 246 | 12.0 | 53.8 |
| 1998 | 1,407 | 484 | 68 | 340 | 10.4 | 61.4 | 382 | 47 | 280 | 7.8 | 42.9 | 173 | 17 | 146 | 0.9 | 8.9 | 368 | 60 | 237 | 12.0 | 54.2 |
| 1999 | 1,386 | 479 | 67 | 337 | 10.5 | 61.5 | 373 | 46 | 271 | 7.7 | 43.9 | 173 | 17 | 145 | 0.9 | 9.3 | 361 | 58 | 232 | 11.8 | 54.6 |
| 2000 | 1,384 | 482 | 66 | 339 | 10.8 | 62.9 | 373 | 46 | 272 | 7.8 | 43.8 | 173 | 17 | 146 | 0.9 | 9.5 | 356 | 57 | 227 | 11.8 | 55.0 |
| 2001 | 1,385 | 481 | 65 | 337 | 11.0 | 63.4 | 378 | 46 | 273 | 8.0 | 46.6 | 173 | 17 | 145 | 1.0 | 9.6 | 354 | 57 | 224 | 12.0 | 55.6 |
| 2002 | 1,414 | 487 | 66 | 341 | 11.5 | 63.2 | 385 | 47 | 279 | 8.2 | 47.3 | 174 | 17 | 146 | 1.0 | 9.5 | 368 | 59 | 233 | 12.9 | 58.6 |
| 2003 | 1,434 | 499 | 68 | 352 | 12.0 | 63.5 | 382 | 47 | 276 | 8.2 | 47.3 | 178 | 18 | 149 | 1.1 | 9.6 | 375 | 61 | 237 | 13.5 | 60.0 |
| 2004 | 1,427 | 500 | 69 | 358 | 12.3 | 61.0 | 373 | 46 | 273 | 8.1 | 46.1 | 178 | 18 | 149 | 1.1 | 9.7 | 377 | 61 | 242 | 13.6 | 60.2 |
| 2005 | 1,389 | 493 | 69 | 353 | 12.4 | 57.9 | 363 | 45 | 266 | 7.8 | 44.5 | 180 | 18 | 151 | 1.0 | 9.8 | 354 | 60 | 225 | 13.4 | 55.6 |
| 2006 | 1,385 | 505 | 69 | 365 | 12.5 | 58.5 | 350 | 44 | 255 | 7.6 | 43.2 | 180 | 18 | 151 | 1.1 | 10.0 | 349 | 58 | 223 | 12.8 | 55.8 |
| 2007 | 1,380 | 522 | 71 | 379 | 13.0 | 58.8 | 338 | 44 | 244 | 7.6 | 42.2 | 186 | 18 | 156 | 1.1 | 10.5 | 333 | 54 | 214 | 11.8 | 53.4 |
| 2008 | 1,402 | 544 | 74 | 392 | 13.5 | 59.7 | 332 | 44 | 235 | 7.7 | 41.4 | 199 | 19 | 167 | 1.2 | 11.1 | 327 | 53 | 207 | 11.9 | 51.4 |
| 2009 | 1,419 | 553 | 76 | 399 | 14.3 | 59.4 | 329 | 44 | 231 | 7.9 | 42.2 | 203 | 19 | 170 | 1.2 | 11.7 | 333 | 53 | 211 | 12.1 | 52.0 |
| 2010 | 1,431 | 566 | 79 | 407 | 15.1 | 60.3 | 328 | 44 | 228 | 8.2 | 43.4 | 202 | 18 | 169 | 1.3 | 12.2 | 334 | 54 | 212 | 12.4 | 50.9 |
| 2011 | 1,425 | 565 | 82 | 403 | 15.7 | 60.2 | 325 | 44 | 224 | 8.5 | 44.0 | 201 | 21 | 167 | 1.3 | 12.4 | 333 | 53 | 213 | 12.3 | 50.3 |
| 2012 | 1,400 | 550 | 82 | 390 | 16.0 | 57.4 | 318 | 44 | 217 | 8.6 | 44.3 | 198 | 20 | 164 | 1.3 | 12.6 | 333 | 53 | 214 | 12.5 | 49.8 |
| 2013 | 1,383 | 532 | 82 | 373 | 16.2 | 55.7 | 324 | 45 | 219 | 9.0 | 47.0 | 196 | 20 | 162 | 1.4 | 12.8 | 330 | 52 | 213 | 12.7 | 49.1 |
| 2014 | 1,338 | 508 | 81 | 353 | 16.2 | 53.8 | 326 | 45 | 219 | 9.2 | 48.1 | 188 | 19 | 154 | 1.4 | 12.8 | 316 | 50 | 203 | 12.4 | 46.7 |
| 2015 | 1,314 | 491 | 79 | 339 | 15.9 | 53.4 | 328 | 45 | 219 | 9.4 | 49.9 | 183 | 19 | 150 | 1.5 | 12.6 | 311 | 49 | 200 | 12.4 | 46.3 |
| 2016 | 1,301 | 475 | 76 | 326 | 15.7 | 53.2 | 325 | 45 | 216 | 9.8 | 50.2 | 184 | 19 | 149 | 1.5 | 13.3 | 318 | 48 | 204 | 12.6 | 48.3 |
| 2017 | 1,307 | 476 | 76 | 325 | 15.9 | 54.4 | 324 | 44 | 214 | 10.1 | 51.4 | 184 | 20 | 149 | 1.6 | 13.9 | 323 | 49 | 207 | 12.9 | 50.1 |
| 2018 | 1,317 | 476 | 76 | 325 | 16.1 | 54.6 | 330 | 44 | 217 | 10.4 | 53.6 | 185 | 20 | 150 | 1.7 | 14.3 | 326 | 49 | 207 | 13.3 | 51.8 |

[1] Includes cadets, midshipmen, and others, not shown separately. [2] Beginning 1980, excludes Navy Reserve personnel on active duty for Training and Administration of Reserves (TARS).

Source: U.S. Department of Defense, Statistical Information Analysis Division, *Selected Manpower Statistics*, discontinued; and Defense Manpower Data Center, "Active Duty Military Personnel by Service by Rank/Grade," <https://www.dmdc.osd.mil/appj/dwp/dwp_reports.jsp>, accessed November 2018.

## Table 536. Military Personnel on Active Duty by Rank or Grade: 2000 to 2018

[As of September 30]

| Rank/grade | 2000 | 2010 | 2014 | 2015 | 2016 | 2017 | 2018 |
|---|---|---|---|---|---|---|---|
| Total. | **1,384,338** | **1,430,985** | **1,338,487** | **1,313,940** | **1,301,308** | **1,307,364** | **1,317,325** |
| Total officers. | **217,178** | **234,000** | **235,000** | **230,468** | **228,148** | **228,972** | **230,708** |
| General – Admiral. | 34 | 39 | 38 | 38 | 39 | 37 | 40 |
| Lieutenant General – Vice Admiral. | 119 | 150 | 145 | 141 | 137 | 147 | 147 |
| Major General – Rear Admiral (U). | 282 | 310 | 304 | 310 | 307 | 301 | 296 |
| Brigadier General – Rear Admiral (L). | 436 | 482 | 424 | 420 | 420 | 418 | 438 |
| Colonel – Captain. | 11,304 | 12,160 | 11,591 | 11,240 | 11,253 | 11,222 | 10,999 |
| Lieutenant Colonel – Commander. | 27,461 | 28,773 | 27,932 | 27,221 | 27,079 | 27,028 | 27,126 |
| Major – LT Commander. | 43,229 | 45,295 | 45,624 | 43,609 | 42,958 | 42,630 | 43,145 |
| Captain – Lieutenant. | 68,106 | 74,997 | 76,207 | 75,525 | 74,633 | 74,838 | 74,120 |
| 1st Lieutenant – Lieutenant (JG). | 24,713 | 25,523 | 29,863 | 29,484 | 28,303 | 27,642 | 28,250 |
| 2nd Lieutenant – Ensign. | 26,405 | 27,128 | 23,639 | 23,724 | 24,745 | 26,607 | 28,002 |
| Chief Warrant Officer W-5. | 473 | 746 | 836 | 797 | 769 | 739 | 783 |
| Chief Warrant Officer W-4. | 2,029 | 3,233 | 2,937 | 2,782 | 2,631 | 2,756 | 2,761 |
| Chief Warrant Officer W-3. | 3,824 | 4,795 | 5,269 | 5,424 | 5,348 | 5,327 | 5,225 |
| Chief Warrant Officer W-2. | 6,674 | 7,489 | 7,952 | 7,694 | 7,393 | 6,875 | 6,737 |
| Warrant Officer W-1. | 2,089 | 2,880 | 2,239 | 2,059 | 2,133 | 2,405 | 2,639 |
| Total enlisted. | **1,154,624** | **1,183,200** | **1,090,759** | **1,070,546** | **1,060,084** | **1,065,163** | **1,073,324** |
| E-9. | 10,240 | 10,192 | 10,238 | 9,991 | 9,979 | 10,071 | 10,369 |
| E-8. | 26,035 | 27,331 | 27,296 | 26,443 | 25,965 | 26,137 | 26,195 |
| E-7. | 97,717 | 97,070 | 94,076 | 89,580 | 89,428 | 88,408 | 91,086 |
| E-6. | 164,857 | 170,856 | 159,711 | 156,786 | 154,408 | 154,681 | 157,265 |
| E-5. | 229,492 | 249,981 | 227,369 | 219,613 | 214,296 | 218,278 | 221,114 |
| E-4. | 250,999 | 279,315 | 268,701 | 277,371 | 262,254 | 251,734 | 245,602 |
| E-3. | 196,276 | 228,152 | 190,482 | 174,695 | 183,762 | 186,496 | 191,054 |
| E-2. | 98,983 | 75,177 | 65,878 | 66,744 | 67,996 | 71,613 | 70,960 |
| E-1. | 80,025 | 45,126 | 47,008 | 49,323 | 51,996 | 57,745 | 59,679 |
| **Cadets and Midshipmen.** | **12,536** | **13,785** | **12,728** | **12,926** | **13,076** | **13,229** | **13,293** |

Source: U.S. Department of Defense, Statistical Information Analysis Division, *Atlas/Data Abstract for the United States and Selected Areas*, annual, discontinued; and "Active Duty Military Personnel by Rank/Grade," <https://www.dmdc.osd.mil/appj/dwp/dwp_reports.jsp>, accessed March 2019.

## Table 537. Military Retirement System—Disabled and Non-Disabled Personnel and Payments: 2018

[Payment in thousands of dollars (4,593,158 represents $4,593,158,000). As of September 30. The data published in the source report are produced from files maintained by the Defense Manpower Data Center. This report compiles data primarily from the "Retiree Pay and Survivor Pay" files. Any grouping of members by address reflects mailing, not necessarily residence, address. Only those members in plans administered by the Department of Defense (DoD) are included in this table. The data are preliminary because of reporting delays about members who retired or died within one month of the September 30 reporting date. These data were not processed in time to be included in this report. For more information, see Introduction and Overview, source]

| State | Retired military personnel [1] | | | Monthly payment ($1,000) | State | Retired military personnel [1] | | | Monthly payment ($1,000) |
|---|---|---|---|---|---|---|---|---|---|
| | Total | Disabled [2] | Non-disabled | | | Total | Disabled [2] | Non-disabled | |
| **Total [3]** | **2,168,011** | **275,049** | **1,892,962** | **4,593,158** | MS. | 27,811 | 3,094 | 24,717 | 51,001 |
| | | | | | MO. | 39,018 | 5,703 | 33,315 | 71,702 |
| **U.S.** | **2,126,558** | **270,013** | **1,856,545** | **4,513,091** | MT. | 9,590 | 1,206 | 8,384 | 18,928 |
| AL. | 61,866 | 6,982 | 54,884 | 130,667 | NE. | 14,600 | 1,484 | 13,116 | 31,725 |
| AK. | 10,977 | 1,491 | 9,486 | 23,074 | NV. | 29,913 | 2,866 | 27,047 | 64,130 |
| AZ. | 57,457 | 6,508 | 50,949 | 123,200 | NH. | 9,567 | 1,124 | 8,443 | 20,193 |
| AR. | 25,352 | 3,343 | 22,009 | 46,696 | NJ. | 19,225 | 3,161 | 16,064 | 32,253 |
| CA. | 154,736 | 18,970 | 135,766 | 328,349 | NM. | 21,053 | 2,320 | 18,733 | 46,400 |
| CO. | 53,723 | 7,135 | 46,588 | 130,839 | NY. | 40,217 | 7,791 | 32,426 | 62,504 |
| CT. | 10,218 | 1,534 | 8,684 | 19,076 | NC. | 99,354 | 13,228 | 86,126 | 217,133 |
| DE. | 9,148 | 822 | 8,326 | 17,781 | ND. | 5,487 | 518 | 4,969 | 9,814 |
| DC. | 2,405 | 359 | 2,046 | 6,238 | OH. | 47,642 | 7,598 | 40,044 | 89,577 |
| FL. | 202,840 | 21,854 | 180,986 | 463,534 | OK. | 36,475 | 4,746 | 31,729 | 70,370 |
| GA. | 99,645 | 13,803 | 85,842 | 204,596 | OR. | 21,000 | 3,349 | 17,651 | 39,358 |
| HI. | 18,030 | 1,764 | 16,266 | 42,361 | PA. | 51,972 | 7,256 | 44,716 | 95,481 |
| ID. | 14,671 | 1,790 | 12,881 | 29,424 | RI. | 5,305 | 672 | 4,633 | 11,111 |
| IL. | 36,817 | 5,732 | 31,085 | 71,247 | SC. | 61,196 | 6,720 | 54,476 | 126,858 |
| IN. | 26,488 | 4,665 | 21,823 | 43,560 | SD. | 8,679 | 803 | 7,876 | 17,095 |
| IA. | 13,396 | 1,997 | 11,399 | 22,463 | TN. | 57,089 | 7,668 | 49,421 | 113,474 |
| KS. | 22,485 | 3,028 | 19,457 | 46,827 | TX. | 215,818 | 31,725 | 184,093 | 472,762 |
| KY. | 29,017 | 4,581 | 24,436 | 55,172 | UT. | 17,607 | 1,910 | 15,697 | 35,762 |
| LA. | 26,701 | 4,122 | 22,579 | 51,115 | VT. | 3,909 | 544 | 3,365 | 6,680 |
| ME. | 11,912 | 1,453 | 10,459 | 22,255 | VA. | 157,821 | 11,840 | 145,981 | 452,105 |
| MD. | 55,680 | 5,407 | 50,273 | 132,773 | WA. | 74,910 | 8,289 | 66,621 | 163,636 |
| MA. | 18,424 | 2,918 | 15,506 | 32,154 | WV. | 11,004 | 1,610 | 9,394 | 19,201 |
| MI. | 30,940 | 5,962 | 24,978 | 50,294 | WI. | 22,271 | 3,262 | 19,009 | 37,337 |
| MN. | 19,400 | 2,698 | 16,702 | 31,501 | WY. | 5,697 | 608 | 5,089 | 11,305 |

[1] Represents military personnel (officers and enlisted) receiving and not receiving pay from DoD. [2] A disabled military member is entitled to disability retired pay if the disability is not the result of the member's intentional misconduct or willful neglect, was not incurred during a period of unauthorized absence, and either: (1) the member has at least 20 years of service; or (2) at the time of determination, the disability is at least 30 percent (under a standard schedule of rating disabilities by the Veterans Administration) and one of four additional conditions are met. For details on these conditions and additional information, see Overview, source. [3] Includes states, U.S. territories, and retirees living in foreign countries.

Source: U.S. Department of Defense, Office of the Actuary, *Statistical Report on the Military Retirement System, Fiscal Year Ended September 30, 2018*, May 2019. See also <http://actuary.defense.gov>.

## Table 538. U.S. Active Duty Military Deaths and Personnel Wounded in Action by Conflict and Manner of Death: 2001 to 2019

[As of August 9, 2019. See source for details]

| Item | Operation Enduring Freedom (OEF) [1] | Operation Iraqi Freedom (OIF) [2] | Operation New Dawn (OND) [3] | Operation Inherent Resolve (OIR) [4] | Operation Freedom's Sentinel (OFS) [5] |
|---|---|---|---|---|---|
| **Deaths, total** | **2,347** | **4,410** | **74** | **84** | **75** |
| Total hostile deaths | 1,845 | 3,481 | 38 | 16 | 55 |
| Killed in action | 1,370 | 2,675 | 22 | 8 | 32 |
| Died of wounds | 472 | 799 | 16 | 8 | 23 |
| Died while missing in action | (NA) | 1 | – | – | – |
| Died while captured | (NA) | 5 | – | – | – |
| Died while detained | (NA) | 1 | – | – | – |
| Died of terrorist activities | 2 | | | | |
| Total non-hostile deaths | 502 | 929 | 36 | 68 | 20 |
| Accident | 304 | 566 | 7 | 26 | 12 |
| Illness or injury | 61 | 93 | 10 | 13 | 2 |
| Homicide | 13 | 36 | 3 | 2 | 1 |
| Undetermined | 10 | 11 | 3 | 1 | – |
| Self-inflicted | 113 | 223 | 13 | 24 | 4 |
| Pending | 1 | – | – | 2 | 1 |
| **Wounded in action** | **20,103** | **31,957** | **298** | **79** | **428** |

– Represents zero. NA Not available. [1] OEF October 2001-December 2014 combat operations in Afghanistan and against al Qaeda. [2] OIF March 2003-September 2010 combat operations in Iraq. [3] OND September 2010-December 2011 advise and train Iraqi security forces in Iraq. [4] OIR August 2014-present to support Iraqi Security Force operations against the Islamic State of Iraq and the Levant (ISIL). [5] OFS 2015-present to train, advise, and assist Afghan National Defense and Security Forces in Afghanistan and conduct counterterrorism operations against the remnants of al Qaeda.

Source: U.S. Department of Defense, Defense Manpower Data Center, "Defense Casualty Analysis System," <https://dcas.dmdc.osd.mil/>, accessed August 2019.

## Table 539. U.S. Military Personnel on Active Duty Overseas by Selected Country: 2009 to 2018

[As of September 30. Data from Defense Manpower Data Center (DMDC). This data catalogues the history of personnel in the military and their family for purposes of healthcare, retirement funding, and other administrative needs, and may not accurately reflect current force totals]

| Country | 2009 | 2010 | 2011 | 2012 | 2013 | 2014 | 2015 | 2016 | 2017 | 2018 [1] |
|---|---|---|---|---|---|---|---|---|---|---|
| **Total overseas [2]** | **352,603** | **339,360** | **336,645** | **272,623** | **251,737** | **232,790** | **213,067** | **198,557** | **215,249** | **[3] 172,370** |
| Afghanistan | 47,520 | 81,875 | 82,177 | 63,243 | 48,807 | 24,170 | 9,392 | 9,027 | 13,329 | [3] (NA) |
| Australia | 101 | 163 | 176 | 344 | 229 | 1,147 | 1,201 | 187 | 1,239 | 1,496 |
| Bahrain | 4,369 | 4,626 | 4,623 | 5,310 | 6,308 | 5,502 | 5,160 | 5,370 | 8,610 | 4,214 |
| Belgium | 1,244 | 1,157 | 1,176 | 1,159 | 1,155 | 1,202 | 1,202 | 852 | 867 | 1,049 |
| Canada | 93 | 131 | 130 | 149 | 149 | 145 | 146 | 139 | 129 | 144 |
| Cuba (Guantanamo) | 1,484 | 870 | 843 | 996 | 978 | 892 | 782 | 797 | 753 | 831 |
| Diego Garcia [4] | 304 | 484 | 468 | 522 | 451 | 521 | 486 | 294 | 264 | 299 |
| Djibouti | 955 | 990 | 1,417 | 1,837 | 2,084 | 1,984 | 1,970 | 1,702 | 3,132 | 954 |
| Egypt | 264 | 262 | 230 | 280 | 266 | 304 | 350 | 356 | 375 | 280 |
| Germany | 45,654 | 43,911 | 43,393 | 42,891 | 35,849 | 36,855 | 35,216 | 34,612 | 34,516 | 35,116 |
| Greece | 390 | 380 | 378 | 364 | 393 | 380 | 371 | 360 | 433 | 410 |
| Honduras | 425 | 391 | 356 | 408 | 376 | 374 | 660 | 397 | 505 | 467 |
| Hungary | 54 | 50 | 57 | 63 | 65 | 66 | 70 | 207 | 215 | 202 |
| Iraq | 72,368 | 38,591 | 28,675 | 164 | 138 | 498 | 4,231 | 4,626 | 7,402 | [3] (NA) |
| Italy | 11,003 | 8,836 | 10,451 | 9,074 | 10,686 | 11,373 | 11,614 | 12,090 | 11,756 | 12,703 |
| Japan | 47,913 | 46,313 | 48,235 | 49,350 | 52,972 | 52,518 | 55,744 | 38,834 | 44,562 | 54,281 |
| Jordan | 95 | 42 | 195 | 422 | 1,140 | 1,386 | 1,861 | 1,556 | 1,862 | 59 |
| Kenya | 43 | 23 | 62 | 98 | 120 | 104 | 96 | 40 | 208 | 46 |
| Korea, South | 26,605 | 27,869 | 28,271 | 27,724 | 30,252 | 29,074 | 24,934 | 24,190 | 23,635 | 25,813 |
| Kosovo | 28 | 52 | 68 | 58 | 514 | 496 | 87 | 366 | 384 | (NA) |
| Kuwait | 30,974 | 17,584 | 16,881 | 10,006 | 8,109 | 11,377 | 8,809 | 5,818 | 9,241 | 1,863 |
| Kyrgyzstan | 3,169 | 5,483 | 10,194 | 6,857 | 3,222 | 121 | 83 | 67 | 65 | 5 |
| Netherlands | 527 | 433 | 407 | 398 | 378 | 411 | 399 | 382 | 407 | 404 |
| Niger | 3 | 2 | 3 | 16 | 97 | 119 | 139 | 8 | 510 | 8 |
| Norway | 73 | 68 | 80 | 88 | 84 | 81 | 83 | 77 | 344 | 474 |
| Pakistan | 144 | 268 | 121 | 92 | 87 | 94 | 116 | 121 | 111 | 35 |
| Philippines | 473 | 546 | 551 | 416 | 398 | 251 | 234 | 36 | 101 | 145 |
| Poland | 30 | 18 | 33 | 40 | 47 | 51 | 61 | 53 | 173 | 150 |
| Portugal | 719 | 699 | 709 | 733 | 698 | 653 | 464 | 197 | 192 | 233 |
| Qatar | 9,383 | 12,036 | 11,812 | 6,865 | 5,919 | 5,589 | 5,219 | 3,216 | 4,666 | 783 |
| Romania | 10 | 7 | 11 | 76 | 166 | 675 | 611 | 682 | 451 | 294 |
| Saudi Arabia | 351 | 325 | 524 | 471 | 654 | 553 | 515 | 371 | 402 | 323 |
| Singapore | 208 | 216 | 206 | 163 | 214 | 217 | 252 | 176 | 206 | 205 |
| Somalia | 4 | 2 | 178 | 173 | 310 | 53 | 232 | 106 | 285 | 60 |
| Spain | 1,358 | 1,396 | 1,591 | 1,719 | 1,915 | 3,095 | 3,393 | 3,272 | 3,940 | 3,602 |
| Syria | 4 | 3 | 3 | 1 | 1 | (NA) | (NA) | (NA) | 1,547 | [3] (NA) |
| Thailand | 218 | 201 | 233 | 117 | 106 | 110 | 108 | 296 | 309 | 316 |
| Turkey | 1,812 | 1,721 | 1,651 | 1,566 | 1,514 | 1,595 | 2,081 | 2,139 | 1,950 | 1,695 |
| United Arab Emirates | 1,535 | 1,427 | 1,851 | 2,424 | 3,384 | 2,045 | 2,620 | 1,510 | 3,455 | 414 |
| United Kingdom | 8,933 | 8,764 | 8,673 | 8,516 | 9,045 | 8,495 | 8,062 | 8,404 | 8,341 | 9,137 |
| Yemen | 34 | 104 | 30 | 115 | 248 | 161 | 8 | 7 | 14 | 4 |
| Guam | 5,578 | 5,423 | 5,470 | 5,494 | 5,467 | 6,337 | 6,531 | 3,977 | 4,590 | 6,199 |
| Puerto Rico | 643 | 654 | 680 | 704 | 667 | 657 | 725 | 142 | 176 | 158 |

NA Not available. [1] Starting in December 2017, the table no longer includes personnel on temporary duty, or deployed in support of contingency operations. [2] Includes items not shown separately, and also personnel in unknown and classified locations. [3] Data are not shown for Afghanistan, Iraq, and Syria. With ongoing operations, any questions concerning DoD personnel strength numbers are deferred to OSD Public Affairs/Joint Chiefs of Staff. [4] British Indian Ocean Territory.

Source: U.S. Department of Defense, DoD Personnel, Workforce Reports & Publications, "Military and Civilian Personnel by Service/Agency by State/Country," <https://www.dmdc.osd.mil/appj/dwp/stats_reports.jsp>, accessed March 2019.

# Table 540. Suicides of Military Personnel by Selected Characteristics: 2012 to 2017

[Data are shown for suicides reported in Department of Defense Suicide Event Report (DoDSER). Covers all service members in the active component at time of event, including Reserve component service members in active status. Beginning 2013, covers service members in the active component of the military only. DoDSER standardizes suicide surveillance efforts across the military services to support the DoD's suicide prevention mission. Confirmed suicides are those that have been confirmed by the Armed Forces Medical Examiner System (AFMES)]

| Characteristics | Suicides | | | | | |
|---|---|---|---|---|---|---|
| | 2012 | 2013 | 2014 | 2015 | 2016 | 2017 |
| Suicides confirmed/pending confirmation [1] | **319** | **256** | **276** | **266** | **280** | **284** |
| By sex: | | | | | | |
| Male | 295 | 241 | 256 | 252 | 260 | 268 |
| Female | 24 | 15 | 20 | 14 | 20 | 16 |
| By race/ethnicity: | | | | | | |
| White | 244 | 192 | 199 | 186 | 215 | 219 |
| Black or African American | 44 | 32 | 42 | 44 | 33 | 28 |
| Asian or Pacific Islander | 13 | 8 | 8 | 12 | 9 | 13 |
| American Indian or Alaska Native | 4 | 8 | 3 | 4 | 6 | 2 |
| By Hispanic origin: | | | | | | |
| Hispanic or Latino | 27 | 21 | 34 | 29 | 29 | 41 |
| Non-Hispanic or Latino | 287 | 232 | 240 | 231 | 245 | 235 |
| Unknown | (NA) | 3 | 2 | 6 | 6 | 8 |
| By age: | | | | | | |
| Under 25 years old | 130 | 108 | 102 | 107 | 127 | 120 |
| 25-29 years old | 89 | 72 | 72 | 62 | 67 | 75 |
| 30-39 years old | 81 | 57 | 83 | 77 | 62 | 59 |
| 40 years old and over | 19 | 19 | 19 | 20 | 23 | 30 |
| By marital status: | | | | | | |
| Never married | 134 | 106 | 105 | 116 | 120 | 115 |
| Married | 171 | 126 | 145 | 132 | 135 | 140 |
| Legally separated | – | 2 | – | – | 2 | – |
| Divorced | 14 | 22 | 25 | 17 | 22 | 28 |
| Widowed | – | – | – | 1 | 1 | 1 |

NA Not available. – Represents zero. [1] Includes other or unknown race/ethnicity, age, and marital status, not shown separately.

Source: U.S. Department of Defense, National Center for Telehealth and Technology, *Department of Defense Suicide Event Report, Calendar Year 2017 Annual Report*, 2019, and earlier reports. See also <http:/www.dspo.mil>.

# Table 541. Sexual Assault in the Military—Incident Reports and Victims by Type of Report and Selected Characteristics: 2015 to 2018

[Data are for fiscal years. Reports of sexual assault (rape, aggravated sexual assault, sexual assault, aggravated sexual contact, abusive sexual contact, wrongful sexual contact, non-consensual sodomy, and attempts to commit these offenses) by or against Service Members. Restricted Reporting allows victim confidential access to medical care and advocacy services. When a victim makes an Unrestricted Report, the report is also referred to a Military Criminal Investigation Organization for investigation and command is notified]

| Item | Unrestricted | | | | Restricted | | | |
|---|---|---|---|---|---|---|---|---|
| | 2015 | 2016 | 2017 | 2018 | 2015 | 2016 | 2017 | 2018 |
| REPORTS [1] | | | | | | | | |
| Total | **4,510** | **4,499** | **5,032** | **5,685** | **1,499** | **1,581** | **1,659** | **1,818** |
| Service member on service member | 2,379 | 2,232 | 2,450 | 2,853 | 711 | 720 | 851 | 1,006 |
| Service member on non-service member | 779 | 739 | 822 | 900 | 25 | 39 | 43 | 40 |
| Non-service member on service member | 196 | 157 | 199 | 178 | 323 | 407 | 419 | 413 |
| Unidentified subject on service member | 592 | 785 | 843 | 913 | 355 | 345 | 343 | 359 |
| Unknown | 564 | 586 | 718 | 841 | 85 | 70 | 3 | – |
| VICTIMS IN COMPLETED INVESTIGATIONS [2] | | | | | | | | |
| Total | **4,303** | **4,409** | **4,606** | **5,053** | (X) | (X) | (X) | (X) |
| Service member victims | 3,422 | 3,551 | 3,735 | 4,162 | (X) | (X) | (X) | (X) |
| Non-service member victims | 881 | 858 | 871 | 891 | (X) | (X) | (X) | (X) |
| VICTIMS [3, 4] | | | | | | | | |
| By sex: | | | | | | | | |
| Male | 807 | 824 | 832 | 905 | 313 | 312 | 300 | 366 |
| Female | 3,457 | 3,558 | 3,744 | 4,143 | 1,178 | 1,266 | 1,357 | 1,452 |
| By age: | | | | | | | | |
| 0-15 years old | 37 | 45 | 66 | 67 | 157 | 182 | 149 | 150 |
| 16-19 years old | 967 | 1,028 | 1,083 | 1,263 | 346 | 359 | 440 | 434 |
| 20-24 years old | 1,815 | 1,858 | 1,966 | 2,157 | 590 | 616 | 670 | 783 |
| 25-34 years old | 845 | 842 | 869 | 956 | 295 | 307 | 310 | 360 |
| 35-49 years old | 213 | 193 | 205 | 205 | 61 | 68 | 65 | 64 |
| 50-64 years old | 10 | 17 | 16 | 5 | 6 | 4 | 3 | 3 |
| 65 years and older | 2 | 21 | 35 | 86 | – | – | – | – |
| SERVICE MEMBER VICTIMS [4] | | | | | | | | |
| By service branch: | | | | | | | | |
| Army | 1,569 | 1,567 | 1,599 | 1,849 | 470 | 485 | 513 | 569 |
| Navy | 848 | 951 | 1,016 | 1,064 | 361 | 355 | 406 | 423 |
| Marines | 392 | 424 | 444 | 524 | 277 | 303 | 315 | 347 |
| Air Force | 608 | 607 | 674 | 725 | 355 | 392 | 380 | 438 |
| Coast Guard | 3 | 1 | 1 | – | – | – | 1 | 1 |

– Represents zero. X Not applicable. [1] Reports of sexual assault during the fiscal year. [2] Victims in investigations completed during the fiscal year. [3] For unrestricted reports, data shown for victims in investigations completed during the fiscal year. [4] Includes other and unknown, not shown separately.

Source: U.S. Department of Defense, *Annual Report on Sexual Assault in the Military, Fiscal Year 2018*, May 2019, and earlier reports. See also <https://www.sapr.mil/reports>.

## Table 542. U.S. Military Sales and Assistance to Foreign Governments: 1990 to 2017

[In millions of dollars (14,600 represents $14,600,000,000). For year ending September 30. Department of Defense (DoD) sales deliveries cover deliveries against sales orders authorized under Arms Export Control Act, as well as earlier and applicable legislation. For details regarding individual programs, see source]

| Item | 1990 | 2000 | 2010 | 2012 | 2013 | 2014 | 2015 | 2016 | 2017 |
|---|---|---|---|---|---|---|---|---|---|
| Military sales agreements............... | 14,600 | 10,829 | 22,158 | 63,505 | 23,823 | 32,824 | 45,322 | 27,617 | 51,025 |
| Military construction sales agreements.......................... | 628 | 284 | 955 | 790 | 340 | 1,444 | 441 | 102 | 1,655 |
| Military sales deliveries [1]............. | 8,360 | 10,938 | 13,440 | 14,250 | 15,669 | 15,250 | 16,913 | 16,709 | 27,963 |
| Military construction sales deliveries... | 348 | 183 | 459 | 488 | 497 | 389 | 493 | 423 | 491 |
| Military financing program.............. | 4,354 | 4,333 | 5,016 | 5,929 | 4,874 | 4,601 | 5,212 | 5,616 | 5,144 |
| Commercial exports licensed under Arms Export Control Act [2]............. | 6,216 | 478 | – | – | – | – | – | – | – |
| Military assistance program delivery [3]................................. | 125 | 5 | – | – | 60 | 111 | 101 | 35 | – |
| IMET program/deliveries [4]............. | 43 | 50 | 108 | 105 | 99 | 103 | 104 | 111 | 139 |

– Represents or rounds to zero. [1] Includes military construction sales deliveries. [2] The total dollar value of deliveries made for purchases of munitions-controlled items by foreign governments directly from U.S. manufacturers. [3] Includes Military Assistance Service Funded (MASF) program data and Section 506(a) drawdown authority. [4] International Military Education and Training. Includes military assistance services and emergency drawdowns.

Source: U.S. Department of Defense, Defense Security Cooperation Agency, DSCA Historical Facts Book & Fiscal Year Series, *DSCA Fiscal Year Series, as of September 30, 2017*. See also <http://dsca.mil/resources/dsca-historical-facts-book-fiscal-year-series>.

## Table 543. U.S. Military Sales Deliveries by Selected Country: 2000 to 2017

[In millions of dollars (10,938 represents $10,938,000,000). For year ending September 30. Represents Department of Defense military sales]

| Country | 2000 | 2010 | 2011 | 2012 | 2013 | 2014 | 2015 | 2016 | 2017 |
|---|---|---|---|---|---|---|---|---|---|
| Total [1]................................... | 10,938 | 13,440 | 13,726 | 14,250 | 15,669 | 15,250 | 16,913 | 16,709 | 27,963 |
| International organizations............... | 61 | 86 | 147 | 116 | 165 | 167 | 124 | 125 | 140 |
| Afghanistan.............................. | – | 18 | 17 | 4 | 8 | 34 | 87 | 55 | 98 |
| Argentina................................ | 10 | 26 | 12 | 14 | 13 | 16 | 84 | 43 | 31 |
| Australia................................. | 332 | 891 | 726 | 631 | 628 | 804 | 2,301 | 1,158 | 1,224 |
| Bahrain.................................. | 55 | 111 | 51 | 94 | 69 | 56 | 35 | 30 | 65 |
| Belgium................................. | 61 | 26 | 27 | 57 | 22 | 49 | 67 | 30 | 76 |
| Brazil.................................... | 61 | 29 | 36 | 133 | 54 | 52 | 73 | 59 | 39 |
| Canada.................................. | 84 | 381 | 395 | 287 | 289 | 239 | 179 | 284 | 217 |
| Chile.................................... | 1 | 23 | 23 | 81 | 56 | 46 | 74 | 48 | 54 |
| Colombia................................ | 14 | 425 | 149 | 122 | 146 | 91 | 76 | 74 | 55 |
| Denmark................................. | 43 | 43 | 67 | 45 | 91 | 51 | 85 | 147 | 137 |
| Ecuador................................. | 1 | 3 | 1 | 1 | 2 | 1 | – | – | 9 |
| Egypt.................................... | 1,186 | 956 | 908 | 846 | 1,540 | 980 | 448 | 1,242 | 503 |
| El Salvador.............................. | 14 | 6 | 5 | 6 | 4 | 2 | 2 | 2 | 1 |
| Finland.................................. | 690 | 127 | 94 | 82 | 103 | 62 | 135 | 74 | 99 |
| France................................... | 217 | 112 | 132 | 125 | 184 | 143 | 295 | 120 | 217 |
| Georgia.................................. | 3 | 10 | 28 | 18 | 36 | 14 | 9 | 14 | 15 |
| Germany................................. | 136 | 296 | 160 | 141 | 148 | 163 | 139 | 153 | 106 |
| Greece................................... | 389 | 265 | 149 | 163 | 61 | 94 | 112 | 83 | 132 |
| India.................................... | – | 31 | 57 | 167 | 194 | 370 | 656 | 212 | 244 |
| Indonesia................................ | – | 16 | 17 | 35 | 39 | 122 | 165 | 68 | 218 |
| Iraq..................................... | – | 400 | 765 | 610 | 520 | 1,098 | 1,722 | 2,216 | 1,755 |
| Israel.................................... | 550 | 938 | 789 | 925 | 937 | 897 | 661 | 666 | 547 |
| Italy..................................... | 51 | 179 | 101 | 87 | 69 | 78 | 85 | 70 | 65 |
| Japan.................................... | 432 | 779 | 435 | 498 | 352 | 523 | 1,317 | 863 | 1,014 |
| Jordan................................... | 52 | 173 | 211 | 376 | 337 | 281 | 193 | 173 | 166 |
| Kenya.................................... | 2 | 2 | 16 | 29 | 3 | 4 | 3 | 4 | 18 |
| Korea, South............................. | 1,399 | 594 | 712 | 723 | 603 | 600 | 453 | 596 | 10,238 |
| Kuwait................................... | 321 | 242 | 434 | 262 | 303 | 553 | 368 | 474 | 615 |
| Lebanon................................. | 5 | 69 | 19 | 25 | 60 | 89 | 97 | 66 | 57 |
| Malaysia................................. | 411 | 45 | 29 | 35 | 41 | 46 | 93 | 63 | 40 |
| Mexico................................... | 9 | 59 | 38 | 8 | 19 | 195 | 19 | 100 | 118 |
| Morocco................................. | 8 | 28 | 976 | 381 | 213 | 79 | 42 | 79 | 108 |
| Netherlands.............................. | 278 | 200 | 184 | 177 | 134 | 145 | 198 | 195 | 226 |
| Nigeria................................... | – | 5 | 13 | 8 | 14 | 10 | 34 | 5 | 6 |
| Norway................................... | 64 | 127 | 147 | 94 | 166 | 143 | 136 | 193 | 127 |
| Oman.................................... | 1 | 34 | 36 | 49 | 58 | 413 | 178 | 141 | 71 |
| Pakistan................................. | – | 1,129 | 549 | 382 | 275 | 338 | 176 | 255 | 138 |
| Philippines............................... | 10 | 37 | 27 | 26 | 23 | 20 | 76 | 57 | 46 |
| Poland................................... | 13 | 74 | 190 | 162 | 154 | 87 | 126 | 164 | 203 |
| Portugal................................. | 20 | 29 | 36 | 46 | 16 | 18 | 21 | 21 | 21 |
| Saudi Arabia............................. | 1,988 | 1,683 | 1,493 | 1,619 | 3,308 | 2,264 | 2,796 | 3,215 | 5,572 |
| Singapore................................ | 131 | 296 | 250 | 240 | 210 | 222 | 141 | 241 | 186 |
| Spain.................................... | 141 | 152 | 98 | 67 | 98 | 113 | 89 | 87 | 89 |
| Switzerland.............................. | 69 | 80 | 82 | 87 | 82 | 66 | 53 | 62 | 43 |
| Taiwan................................... | 784 | 863 | 767 | 975 | 784 | 1,681 | 1,090 | 1,063 | 1,022 |
| Thailand................................. | 114 | 41 | 89 | 62 | 82 | 100 | 80 | 95 | 106 |
| Tunisia................................... | 4 | 12 | 14 | 12 | 12 | 10 | 20 | 22 | 109 |
| Turkey................................... | 216 | 251 | 876 | 1,240 | 644 | 194 | 420 | 231 | 342 |
| Ukraine.................................. | 1 | 21 | 8 | 4 | 4 | 10 | 19 | 18 | 17 |
| United Arab Emirates..................... | 40 | 594 | 634 | 1,367 | 769 | 797 | 452 | 555 | 376 |
| United Kingdom.......................... | 347 | 261 | 343 | 311 | 1,295 | 403 | 305 | 283 | 275 |
| Yemen................................... | – | 6 | 5 | 4 | 7 | 6 | 3 | 1 | 1 |

– Represents or rounds to zero. [1] Includes countries, programs, and classified totals not shown.

Source: U.S. Department of Defense, Defense Security Cooperation Agency, DSCA Historical Facts Book & Fiscal Year Series, *DSCA Fiscal Year Series, as of September 30, 2017*. See also <https://dsca.mil/resources/dsca-historical-facts-book-fiscal-year-series>.

## Table 544. Arms Transfer Agreements with Developing Nations by Supplier Country: 2008 to 2015

[In millions of constant 2015 U.S. dollars (57,475 is $57,475,000,000). Developing nations category excludes the United States, Europe, Canada, Japan, Australia, and New Zealand. All data are for the calendar year given except for U.S. MAP (Military Assistance Program), IMET (International Military Education and Training), and Excess Defense Article data, which are included for the particular fiscal year. All amounts given include the values of all categories of weapons, spare parts, construction, all associated services, military assistance, excess defense articles, and training programs. Statistics for foreign countries are based upon estimated selling prices. All foreign data are rounded to the nearest $100 million]

| Supplier | 2008 | 2009 | 2010 | 2011 | 2012 | 2013 | 2014 | 2015 [1] | 2008-2015 |
|---|---|---|---|---|---|---|---|---|---|
| Total.............. | 57,475 | 59,841 | 35,029 | 82,700 | 58,276 | 58,234 | 80,699 | 65,243 | 497,496 |
| United States................ | 30,714 | 14,614 | 15,988 | 59,873 | 11,891 | 18,404 | 30,246 | 26,743 | 208,473 |
| Russia...................... | 6,098 | 16,598 | 7,399 | 6,080 | 17,525 | 11,041 | 10,375 | 11,000 | 86,116 |
| France...................... | 6,323 | 10,360 | 2,067 | 5,013 | 3,253 | 3,921 | 5,696 | 15,200 | 51,834 |
| United Kingdom.............. | 0 | 1,225 | 1,306 | 533 | 5,982 | 3,715 | 407 | 700 | 13,868 |
| China...................... | 2,484 | 3,342 | 2,176 | 3,413 | 3,673 | 4,437 | 3,357 | 6,000 | 28,882 |
| Germany.................... | 3,388 | 2,451 | 109 | 107 | 5,142 | 7,223 | 407 | 700 | 19,526 |
| Italy........................ | 1,581 | 1,448 | 1,306 | 1,173 | 1,574 | 929 | 1,119 | 1,000 | 10,130 |
| All other European............. | 4,630 | 5,124 | 3,046 | 3,093 | 6,087 | 3,715 | 24,819 | 2,900 | 53,415 |
| All others...................... | 2,258 | 4,679 | 1,632 | 3,413 | 3,148 | 4,850 | 4,272 | 1,000 | 25,253 |

[1] Data are rounded to the nearest $100 million.

Source: Congressional Research Service, *Conventional Arms Transfers to Developing Nations, 2008-2015*, R44716, December 2016.

## Table 545. Veterans by Selected Period of Service and State and Island Areas: 2017

[In thousands (19,999 represents 19,999,000). As of September 30. The Veteran Population Projection Model 2016 (VetPop2016) is the Department of Veterans Affairs (VA) latest official estimate and projection of the veteran population. It is based on tabulations prepared for the VA Office of the Actuary; recent American Community Survey, Internal Revenue Service, and Social Security Administration data; administrative data and projections of service member separations from active duty provided by the Department of Defense, Defense Manpower Data Center and the Office of the Actuary; and VA data on veterans benefits]

| State and area | Total [1,2] | Gulf War era [3] | Vietnam era [4] | State and area | Total [1,2] | Gulf War era [3] | Vietnam era [4] |
|---|---|---|---|---|---|---|---|
| United States............ | 19,999 | 7,271 | 6,651 | Montana..................... | 91 | 34 | 32 |
| Alabama.................... | 370 | 154 | 123 | Nebraska.................... | 130 | 51 | 42 |
| Alaska...................... | 69 | 38 | 19 | Nevada...................... | 218 | 81 | 77 |
| Arizona..................... | 508 | 170 | 178 | New Hampshire............. | 105 | 31 | 38 |
| Arkansas.................... | 222 | 81 | 77 | New Jersey.................. | 356 | 96 | 115 |
| California................... | 1,682 | 584 | 573 | New Mexico................. | 159 | 59 | 56 |
| Colorado.................... | 403 | 177 | 128 | New York.................... | 777 | 227 | 251 |
| Connecticut................. | 184 | 51 | 61 | North Carolina.............. | 730 | 307 | 229 |
| Delaware.................... | 72 | 24 | 27 | North Dakota................ | 52 | 22 | 16 |
| District of Columbia........ | 28 | 11 | 6 | Ohio......................... | 775 | 242 | 263 |
| Florida...................... | 1,525 | 512 | 520 | Oklahoma................... | 303 | 121 | 106 |
| Georgia..................... | 697 | 306 | 214 | Oregon...................... | 304 | 90 | 117 |
| Hawaii...................... | 112 | 50 | 36 | Pennsylvania................ | 819 | 232 | 281 |
| Idaho....................... | 122 | 46 | 43 | Rhode Island................ | 63 | 20 | 21 |
| Illinois...................... | 628 | 204 | 213 | South Carolina............. | 403 | 162 | 140 |
| Indiana..................... | 410 | 133 | 134 | South Dakota............... | 65 | 27 | 22 |
| Iowa........................ | 206 | 65 | 71 | Tennessee................... | 470 | 174 | 163 |
| Kansas...................... | 194 | 78 | 65 | Texas....................... | 1,585 | 716 | 483 |
| Kentucky.................... | 295 | 106 | 102 | Utah........................ | 134 | 55 | 44 |
| Louisiana................... | 284 | 120 | 89 | Vermont..................... | 43 | 13 | 15 |
| Maine....................... | 114 | 36 | 42 | Virginia..................... | 725 | 374 | 204 |
| Maryland.................... | 390 | 167 | 116 | Washington.................. | 560 | 220 | 195 |
| Massachusetts.............. | 323 | 83 | 112 | West Virginia............... | 143 | 46 | 50 |
| Michigan.................... | 589 | 165 | 211 | Wisconsin................... | 364 | 107 | 126 |
| Minnesota.................. | 328 | 92 | 119 | Wyoming.................... | 47 | 20 | 17 |
| Mississippi.................. | 191 | 78 | 57 | Puerto Rico................. | 79 | 22 | 27 |
| Missouri.................... | 443 | 150 | 155 | Island Areas & Foreign.... | 106 | 41 | 30 |

[1] Veterans serving in more than one period of service are counted only once in the total. [2] Current civilians discharged from active duty, other than for training only without service-connected disability. [3] Service from August 2, 1990 to the present. [4] Service from August 5, 1964 to May 7, 1975.

Source: U.S. Department of Veterans Affairs, National Center for Veterans Analysis and Statistics, "The Veteran Population Projection Model 2016 (VetPop2016)," <http://www.va.gov/vetdata/veteran_population.asp>, accessed July 2019.

# Table 546. Veterans Benefits—Expenditures by Program and Compensation for Service-Connected Disabilities: 2000 to 2018

[In millions of dollars (47,086 represents $47,086,000,000). For years ending September 30]

| Program | 2000 | 2005 | 2010 | 2013 | 2014 | 2015 | 2016 | 2017 | 2018 |
|---|---|---|---|---|---|---|---|---|---|
| **Total expenditures**.......................... | **47,086** | **69,667** | **108,635** | **142,822** | **161,229** | **167,210** | **173,686** | **180,591** | **180,604** |
| Medical programs......................... | 19,637 | 29,433 | 42,372 | 55,994 | 59,424 | 65,561 | 63,473 | 69,710 | 71,303 |
| Construction............................... | 466 | 483 | 1,618 | 1,330 | 1,536 | 1,828 | 1,708 | 1,467 | 1,177 |
| General operating expenses............. | 1,016 | 1,294 | 6,101 | 6,890 | 7,602 | 8,056 | 7,898 | 9,223 | 9,513 |
| Compensation and pension............. | 22,012 | 34,694 | 47,785 | 63,575 | 75,265 | 75,787 | 84,028 | 84,138 | 82,776 |
| Vocational rehabilitation and education..... | 1,610 | 2,937 | 8,260 | 11,949 | 13,681 | 13,408 | 13,838 | 13,182 | 13,178 |
| All other [1]................................ | 2,345 | 826 | 2,499 | 3,085 | 3,721 | 2,570 | 2,740 | 2,871 | 2,656 |
| Compensation for service-connected disabilities............................. | 15,511 | 24,515 | 36,486 | 49,152 | 54,229 | 60,213 | 64,714 | 69,991 | 76,709 |

[1] Includes insurance, indemnities, and miscellaneous funds and expenditures and offsets from public receipts. Excludes expenditures from personal funds of patients.

Source: U.S. Department of Veterans Affairs, "Summary of Expenditures By State," <http://www.va.gov/vetdata/Expenditures.asp>, accessed July 2019; and *Annual Benefits Report*, March 2019, and earlier reports. See also <https://www.benefits.va.gov/REPORTS/abr/>.

# Table 547. Veterans Compensation and Pension Benefits—Number on Rolls by Period of Service and Status: 1990 to 2018

[In thousands (3,584 represents 3,584,000). As of September 30. Living veterans refers to veterans receiving compensation for disability incurred or aggravated while on active duty, and war veterans receiving pension benefits for non-service connected disabilities and/or who are age 65 and older. Survivors include veterans' spouses, dependent children, and (based on need) dependent parents of veterans]

| Period of service and veteran status | 1990 | 2000 | 2010 | 2012 | 2013 | 2014 | 2015 | 2016 | 2017 | 2018 |
|---|---|---|---|---|---|---|---|---|---|---|
| **Total**............................... | **3,584** | **3,236** | **4,070** | **4,425** | **4,639** | **4,848** | **5,061** | **5,247** | **5,442** | **5,619** |
| Living veterans......................... | 2,746 | 2,672 | 3,524 | 3,852 | 4,051 | 4,254 | 4,464 | 4,645 | 4,829 | 5,003 |
| Compensation [1]...................... | 2,184 | 2,308 | 3,210 | 3,537 | 3,743 | 3,949 | 4,169 | 4,356 | 4,553 | 4,743 |
| Pension [2]............................ | 562 | 364 | 314 | 315 | 308 | 305 | 295 | 289 | 277 | 260 |
| Survivors of veterans.................. | 838 | 564 | 546 | 574 | 587 | 594 | 597 | 602 | 613 | 616 |
| Compensation [1]...................... | 320 | 307 | 347 | 366 | 377 | 382 | 390 | 399 | 411 | 423 |
| Pension [2]............................ | 518 | 257 | 199 | 207 | 210 | 212 | 206 | 203 | 201 | 193 |
| World War I and earlier................ | 198 | 34 | 6 | 5 | 4 | 4 | 3 | 3 | 2 | 2 |
| Living veterans..................... | 18 | (Z) | (Z) | (Z) | (Z) | (Z) | (Z) | (Z) | (Z) | (Z) |
| World War II............................ | 1,723 | 968 | 529 | 469 | 434 | 399 | 357 | 320 | 286 | 249 |
| Living veterans..................... | 1,294 | 676 | 298 | 245 | 215 | 189 | 160 | 135 | 112 | 89 |
| Korean conflict [3]..................... | 390 | 323 | 275 | 274 | 271 | 268 | 262 | 256 | 249 | 238 |
| Living veterans..................... | 305 | 255 | 209 | 204 | 199 | 194 | 186 | 178 | 169 | 158 |
| Vietnam era [4]........................ | 774 | 969 | 1,447 | 1,594 | 1,660 | 1,716 | 1,765 | 1,803 | 1,840 | 1,868 |
| Living veterans..................... | 685 | 848 | 1,261 | 1,381 | 1,433 | 1,477 | 1,514 | 1,538 | 1,560 | 1,572 |
| Gulf War era [5]....................... | (X) | 334 | 1,140 | 1,383 | 1,561 | 1,723 | 1,915 | 2,090 | 2,267 | 2,441 |
| Living veterans..................... | (X) | 326 | 1,117 | 1,357 | 1,523 | 1,694 | 1,883 | 2,057 | 2,231 | 2,403 |
| Peacetime............................. | 495 | 607 | 673 | 701 | 709 | 738 | 759 | 775 | 797 | 821 |
| Living veterans..................... | 444 | 567 | 638 | 665 | 683 | 700 | 720 | 737 | 758 | 781 |

X Not applicable. Z Fewer than 500. [1] Compensation is based on military service-connected disability and death. [2] Pension is based on need and includes coverage for veterans with disabilities not connected to military service. [3] Service during period June 27, 1950 to January 31, 1955. [4] Service from August 5, 1964 to May 7, 1975. [5] Service from August 2, 1990 to the present.

Source: U.S. Department of Veterans Affairs, 1990 to 1995, *Annual Report of the Secretary of Veterans Affairs*; 1996 to 2010, *Annual Accountability Report* and unpublished data; and beginning 2011, *Annual Benefits Report, Fiscal Year 2018*, March 2019 and earlier reports. See also <https://www.benefits.va.gov/REPORTS/abr/>.

# Table 548. Veterans Living by Period of Service, Age, and Sex: 2017

[19,999 represents 19,999,000. As of September 30. Includes veterans living outside the United States. Based on the Department of Veterans Affairs' (VA) latest official estimate and projection of the veteran population, the Veteran Population Projection Model 2016 (VetPop2016)]

| Period of service and age | Total | Male | Female | Period of service and age | Total | Male | Female |
|---|---|---|---|---|---|---|---|
| **Total**............................ | **19,999** | **18,116** | **1,883** | 30 to 34 years old.................. | 948 | 772 | 176 |
| PERIOD OF SERVICE | | | | 35 to 39 years old.................. | 1,030 | 833 | 196 |
| Wartime vets [1]..................... | 15,450 | 13,989 | 1,461 | 40 to 44 years old.................. | 998 | 827 | 171 |
| Gulf War Era [2]..................... | 7,271 | 6,090 | 1,181 | 45 to 49 years old.................. | 1,335 | 1,145 | 190 |
| Vietnam Era [3]..................... | 6,651 | 6,418 | 233 | 50 to 54 years old.................. | 1,552 | 1,351 | 201 |
| Korean conflict [4].................. | 1,475 | 1,432 | 44 | 55 to 59 years old.................. | 1,823 | 1,594 | 229 |
| World War II........................ | 624 | 595 | 29 | 60 to 64 years old.................. | 1,893 | 1,700 | 193 |
| Peacetime.......................... | 4,549 | 4,127 | 422 | 65 to 69 years old.................. | 2,308 | 2,194 | 114 |
| AGE | | | | 70 to 74 years old.................. | 2,593 | 2,522 | 71 |
| Under 20 years old................. | 9 | 7 | 3 | 75 to 79 years old.................. | 1,568 | 1,524 | 44 |
| 20 to 24 years old.................. | 274 | 214 | 60 | 80 to 84 years old.................. | 1,287 | 1,249 | 38 |
| 25 to 29 years old.................. | 727 | 591 | 136 | 85 years & over.................... | 1,653 | 1,594 | 59 |

[1] Veterans who served in more than one wartime period are counted only once in the total. [2] Service from August 2, 1990 to the present. [3] Service from August 5, 1964 to May 7, 1975. [4] Service during period June 27, 1950 to January 31, 1955.

Source: U.S. Department of Veterans Affairs, National Center for Veterans Analysis and Statistics, "The Veteran Population Projection Model 2016 (VetPop2016)," <https://www.va.gov/vetdata/Veteran_Population.asp>, accessed July 2019.

## Table 549. Veteran Income, Education, Poverty, and Disability Status Compared to Nonveteran Population: 2016 and 2017

[248,479 represents 248,479,000. Data are based on American Community Survey (ACS). The ACS universe includes the civilian household and group quarters population. Based on a sample and subject to sampling variability]

| Characteristic | 2016 | | | 2017 | | |
|---|---|---|---|---|---|---|
| | Total | Veterans | Nonveterans | Total | Veterans | Nonveterans |
| **Population 18 years old and over (1,000)**....... | **248,479** | **18,497** | **229,982** | **251,048** | **18,205** | **232,843** |
| INCOME | | | | | | |
| Median income in past 12 months (dollars) [1]....... | 29,591 | 39,494 | 28,347 | 30,696 | 40,577 | 30,098 |
| Male........ | (NA) | 40,076 | 35,365 | (NA) | 40,995 | 36,573 |
| Female........ | (NA) | 34,178 | 23,445 | (NA) | 35,517 | 24,653 |
| EDUCATIONAL ATTAINMENT | | | | | | |
| Population 25 years old and over.................... | 217,863 | 18,258 | 199,605 | 220,624 | 17,953 | 202,670 |
| Less than high school graduate (percent)........ | 12.6 | 6.3 | 13.2 | 12.0 | 5.8 | 12.6 |
| High school graduate or equivalency (percent)... | 27.2 | 28.1 | 27.1 | 27.2 | 28.2 | 27.1 |
| Some college or associate's degree (percent).... | 28.9 | 37.3 | 28.2 | 28.8 | 37.2 | 28.1 |
| Bachelor's degree or higher (percent)............ | 31.3 | 28.3 | 31.5 | 32.0 | 28.8 | 32.2 |
| POVERTY AND DISABILITY STATUS | | | | | | |
| Population for whom poverty status is determined........ | 242,019 | 18,164 | 223,855 | 244,592 | 17,884 | 226,708 |
| Below poverty in the past 12 months (percent)... | 12.5 | 6.9 | 12.9 | 11.9 | 6.9 | 12.3 |
| With any disability (percent)........................ | 15.5 | 29.3 | 14.4 | 15.3 | 29.5 | 14.2 |

NA Not available. [1] For population with income.

Source: U.S. Census Bureau, American Community Survey, S2101, "Veteran Status," <http://factfinder.census.gov>, accessed November 2018.

## Table 550. Veterans by Sex, Race, and Hispanic Origin: 2016 and 2017

[See headnote, Table 549]

| Characteristic | 2016 | | | 2017 | | |
|---|---|---|---|---|---|---|
| | Total veterans | 18 to 64 years | 65 years and over | Total veterans | 18 to 64 years | 65 years and over |
| **Total**........................ | **18,496,937** | **9,268,774** | **9,228,163** | **18,204,605** | **9,117,616** | **9,086,989** |
| Male........................ | 16,898,924 | 7,963,616 | 8,935,308 | 16,584,495 | 7,807,552 | 8,776,943 |
| Female........................ | 1,598,013 | 1,305,158 | 292,855 | 1,620,110 | 1,310,064 | 310,046 |
| White alone................. | 15,295,005 | 7,046,286 | 8,248,719 | 14,971,878 | 6,897,994 | 8,073,884 |
| Male........................ | 14,156,703 | 6,159,650 | 7,997,053 | 13,809,369 | 5,992,812 | 7,816,557 |
| Female........................ | 1,138,302 | 886,636 | 251,666 | 1,162,509 | 905,182 | 257,327 |
| Black or African American alone........ | 2,145,866 | 1,490,650 | 655,216 | 2,139,651 | 1,474,012 | 665,639 |
| Male........................ | 1,828,388 | 1,198,511 | 629,877 | 1,826,298 | 1,194,900 | 631,398 |
| Female........................ | 317,478 | 292,139 | 25,339 | 313,353 | 279,112 | 34,241 |
| American Indian/Alaska Native alone.. | 136,487 | 85,175 | 51,312 | 141,494 | 88,423 | 53,071 |
| Male........................ | 120,172 | 71,223 | 48,949 | 125,750 | 75,555 | 50,195 |
| Female........................ | 16,315 | 13,952 | 2,363 | 15,744 | 12,868 | 2,876 |
| Asian alone................. | 297,301 | 185,177 | 112,124 | 297,891 | 181,567 | 116,324 |
| Male........................ | 261,180 | 155,036 | 106,144 | 262,186 | 150,237 | 111,949 |
| Female........................ | 36,121 | 30,141 | 5,980 | 35,705 | 31,330 | 4,375 |
| Native Hawaiian and other Pacific Islander alone................. | 34,098 | 24,795 | 9,303 | 33,981 | 21,530 | 12,451 |
| Male........................ | 27,902 | 19,301 | 8,601 | 28,820 | 17,725 | 11,095 |
| Female........................ | 6,196 | 5,494 | 702 | 5,161 | 3,805 | 1,356 |
| Some other race alone................. | 233,207 | 175,475 | 57,732 | 251,899 | 186,355 | 65,544 |
| Male........................ | 203,288 | 147,845 | 55,443 | 222,528 | 159,914 | 62,614 |
| Female........................ | 29,919 | 27,630 | 2,289 | 29,371 | 26,441 | 2,930 |
| Two or more races................. | 354,973 | 261,216 | 93,757 | 367,811 | 267,735 | 100,076 |
| Male........................ | 301,291 | 212,050 | 89,241 | 309,544 | 216,409 | 93,135 |
| Female........................ | 53,682 | 49,166 | 4,516 | 58,267 | 51,326 | 6,941 |
| Hispanic or Latino origin [1]................ | 1,205,080 | 837,219 | 367,861 | 1,264,460 | 892,464 | 371,996 |
| Male........................ | 1,071,614 | 717,674 | 353,940 | 1,113,263 | 756,128 | 357,135 |
| Female........................ | 133,466 | 119,545 | 13,921 | 151,197 | 136,336 | 14,861 |

[1] Persons of Hispanic or Latino origin may be of any race.

Source: U.S. Census Bureau, American Community Survey, Tables B21001, C21001A, C21001B, C21001C, C21001D, C21001E, C21001F, C21001G, and C21001I, <http://factfinder.census.gov>, accessed November 2018.

## Table 551. Deferred Action for Childhood Arrivals (DACA) Recipients by Selected Characteristics and Top Country of Birth: 2019

[As of April 30, 2019. The active DACA population are individuals who have an approved I-821D Consideration of DACA form with validity as of April 30, 2019. Data are estimates. Individuals who have obtained Lawful Permanent Resident Status or U.S. Citizenship are excluded]

| Characteristic | Number | Top 20 countries of birth | Number |
|---|---|---|---|
| Total............................................ | 669,080 | Mexico..................................... | 535,980 |
| | | El Salvador................................ | 25,590 |
| SEX | | Guatemala................................ | 17,470 |
| Female....................................... | 353,510 | Honduras.................................. | 16,010 |
| Male.......................................... | 315,520 | Peru........................................ | 6,670 |
| Not available............................... | 40 | Korea, South.............................. | 6,620 |
| AGE | | Brazil....................................... | 5,380 |
| Under 16 years old......................... | 190 | Ecuador.................................... | 5,020 |
| 16 to 20 years old.......................... | 120,390 | Colombia................................... | 4,510 |
| 21 to 25 years old.......................... | 251,080 | Argentina.................................. | 3,570 |
| 26 to 30 years old.......................... | 183,940 | Philippines................................ | 3,460 |
| 31 to 35 years old.......................... | 96,560 | Jamaica.................................... | 2,400 |
| 36 to 37 years old.......................... | 16,910 | India....................................... | 2,390 |
| Median age................................. | 25 | Venezuela................................. | 2,270 |
| MARITAL STATUS | | Dominican Republic....................... | 2,140 |
| Single........................................ | 518,990 | Uruguay.................................... | 1,800 |
| Married...................................... | 137,890 | Trinidad And Tobago...................... | 1,660 |
| Divorced..................................... | 9,740 | Bolivia...................................... | 1,530 |
| Widowed..................................... | 320 | Costa Rica................................. | 1,460 |
| Not available............................... | 2,130 | Nicaragua.................................. | 1,340 |

Source: Department of Homeland Security, U.S. Citizenship and Immigration Services, "Immigration and Citizenship Data," <https://www.uscis.gov/tools/reports-studies/immigration-forms-data>, accessed September 2019.

## Table 552. Department of Homeland Security Total Budget Authority and Personnel by Organization: 2018 and 2019

[74,347,857 represents $74,347,857,000. For the fiscal year ending September 30. Not all activities carried out by the Department of Homeland Security (DHS) constitute homeland security funding (e.g., Coast Guard search and rescue activities)]

| Organization or activity | Budget authority (thousand dollars) | | Full-time employees (number) | |
|---|---|---|---|---|
| | 2018 [1] | 2019 | 2018 [1] | 2019 |
| Total............................................ | 74,347,857 | 74,271,019 | 225,746 | 232,121 |
| Departmental management and operations [2]............................ | 923,813 | 1,212,178 | 2,463 | 2,449 |
| Analysis and operations................................ | 245,905 | 253,253 | 837 | 841 |
| Office of the Inspector General........................ | 168,000 | 138,369 | 760 | 715 |
| U.S. Customs & Border Protection..................... | 16,318,190 | 16,690,317 | 58,562 | 60,646 |
| U.S. Immigration & Customs Enforcement............. | 7,452,484 | 8,817,130 | 20,083 | 23,439 |
| Transportation Security Administration................ | 7,885,914 | 7,726,058 | 54,651 | 53,637 |
| U.S. Coast Guard...................................... | 12,328,004 | 11,651,747 | 48,916 | 48,643 |
| U.S. Secret Service.................................... | 2,271,524 | 2,416,624 | 6,934 | 7,334 |
| Cybersecurity and Infrastructure Security Agency [3]..................... | 3,387,457 | 3,348,261 | 3,592 | 3,607 |
| Office of Health Affairs [4].............................. | 121,569 | (X) | 96 | (X) |
| Federal Emergency Management Agency (FEMA)..................... | 17,332,575 | 15,902,829 | 9,859 | 10,482 |
| FEMA Grants [5]........................................ | 3,059,731 | 2,499,961 | ([7]) | ([7]) |
| U.S. Citizenship & Immigration Services.............. | 4,482,039 | 4,719,570 | 17,296 | 18,498 |
| Federal Law Enforcement Training Center............ | 254,000 | 382,134 | 1,068 | 1,167 |
| Science & Technology Directorate (S&T)............. | 840,943 | 583,283 | 485 | 431 |
| Domestic Nuclear Detection Office [4]................. | 335,440 | (X) | 144 | (X) |
| Countering Weapons of Mass Destruction [6]......... | (X) | 429,266 | (X) | 232 |

X Not applicable. [1] Revised enacted. [2] Comprised of the Office of the Secretary & Executive Management, and the Management Directorate, which includes the Under Secretary for Management and its team of chief officers. [3] The Cybersecurity and Infrastructure Security Agency Act of 2018 elevated the mission of the former National Protection and Programs Directorate within DHS and established the Cybersecurity and Infrastructure Security Agency. [4] As of December 2017, the Office of Health Affairs and the Domestic Nuclear Detection Office were consolidated into the newly established Countering Weapons of Mass Destruction Office. [5] Includes State and Local Programs and Emergency Management Performance Grants, and Assistance to Firefighters Grants. [6] The Countering Weapons of Mass Destruction Office was established in December 2017. [7] Employee data are included among FEMA full-time employees.

Source: U.S. Department of Homeland Security, *Budget-in-Brief, Fiscal Year 2020*, 2019. See also <http://www.dhs.gov/dhs-budget>.

## Table 553. Homeland Security Grants by State and Outlying Area: 2018 and 2019

[In thousands of dollars (1,067,000 represents $1,067,000,000). For years ending September 30. The Homeland Security Grant Program consists of the following: State Homeland Security Program (SHSP), Urban Areas Security Initiative (UASI), and Operation Stonegarden]

| State/territory | 2018 | 2019 | State/territory | 2018 | 2019 | State/territory | 2018 | 2019 |
|---|---|---|---|---|---|---|---|---|
| Total......... | 1,067,000 | 1,095,000 | KS............... | 3,980 | 4,078 | OK............... | 3,980 | 4,078 |
|  |  |  | KY............... | 3,980 | 4,078 | OR............... | 6,480 | 7,328 |
| U.S............. | 1,056,776 | 1,084,333 | LA............... | 4,380 | 4,807 | PA............... | 29,777 | 29,525 |
|  |  |  | ME............... | 5,450 | 5,948 | RI............... | 3,980 | 4,078 |
| AL............... | 4,380 | 4,474 | MD............... | 9,882 | 12,000 | SC............... | 3,980 | 4,078 |
| AK............... | 3,980 | 4,078 | MA............... | 22,895 | 23,900 | SD............... | 3,980 | 4,078 |
| AZ............... | 25,580 | 23,863 | MI............... | 13,709 | 13,468 | TN............... | 3,980 | 4,078 |
| AR............... | 3,980 | 4,078 | MN............... | 10,070 | 10,246 | TX............... | 89,860 | 98,437 |
| CA............... | 193,335 | 197,911 | MS............... | 4,288 | 4,389 | UT............... | 3,980 | 4,078 |
| CO............... | 6,980 | 7,328 | MO............... | 6,980 | 7,328 | VT............... | 4,980 | 4,851 |
| CT............... | 3,980 | 4,078 | MT............... | 5,635 | 5,956 | VA............... | 8,620 | 12,450 |
| DE............... | 3,980 | 4,078 | NE............... | 3,980 | 4,078 | WA............... | 13,788 | 15,581 |
| DC............... | 56,730 | 58,500 | NV............... | 8,980 | 9,078 | WV............... | 3,980 | 4,078 |
| FL............... | 23,324 | 27,149 | NH............... | 4,240 | 4,344 | WI............... | 3,980 | 4,078 |
| GA............... | 12,508 | 11,750 | NJ............... | 30,743 | 28,050 | WY............... | 3,980 | 4,078 |
| HI............... | 5,480 | 7,328 | NM............... | 7,151 | 7,587 | AS [1]............... | 1,000 | 1,000 |
| ID............... | 4,180 | 4,430 | NY............... | 258,615 | 258,937 | GU [1]............... | 1,000 | 1,000 |
| IL............... | 83,712 | 83,712 | NC............... | 7,746 | 5,750 | MP [1]............... | 1,000 | 1,000 |
| IN............... | 3,980 | 4,078 | ND............... | 5,543 | 5,787 | PR [1]............... | 5,824 | 5,929 |
| IA............... | 3,980 | 4,078 | OH............... | 9,114 | 8,751 | VI [1]............... | 1,400 | 1,739 |

[1] AS—American Samoa, GU—Guam, MP—Northern Mariana Islands, PR—Puerto Rico, VI—Virgin Islands.

Source: U.S. Department of Homeland Security, Federal Emergency Management Agency, *Grant Programs Directorate Information Bulletin*, No. 443, August 2019, and earlier reports. See also <https://www.fema.gov/grant-programs-directorate>.

## Table 554. Urban Areas Security Initiative (UASI) Grant Program: 2019

[In thousands of dollars (590,000 represents $590,000,000). For year ending September 30. The UASI Program provides financial assistance to address the unique multi-disciplinary planning, operations, equipment, training, and exercise needs of high-threat, high-density urban areas]

| State | Urban area | Amount | State | Urban area | Amount |
|---|---|---|---|---|---|
| Total........ | (X) | 590,000 | MD........... | Baltimore | 4,000 |
| AZ............ | Phoenix | 4,000 | MA........... | Boston | 16,900 |
| CA............ | Anaheim/Santa Ana | 5,000 | MI............ | Detroit | 5,000 |
| CA............ | San Francisco Bay Area | 27,500 | MN........... | Minneapolis-Saint Paul (Twin Cities) | 5,000 |
| CA............ | Los Angeles/Long Beach | 68,000 | MO........... | St. Louis | 3,250 |
| CA............ | Riverside | 3,250 | NV........... | Las Vegas | 5,000 |
| CA............ | Sacramento | 3,250 | NJ............ | Jersey City/Newark | 20,050 |
| CA............ | San Diego | 16,900 | NY........... | New York City | 178,750 |
| CO........... | Denver | 3,250 | OR........... | Portland | 3,250 |
| DC........... | National Capital Region | 52,750 | PA........... | Philadelphia | 16,900 |
| FL............ | Miami/Fort Lauderdale | 7,000 | PA........... | Pittsburgh | 3,250 |
| FL............ | Orlando | 3,250 | TX............ | Dallas/Fort Worth/Arlington | 16,900 |
| FL............ | Tampa | 3,250 | TX............ | Houston | 24,600 |
| GA........... | Atlanta | 6,000 | TX............ | San Antonio Area | 3,250 |
| HI............ | Honolulu | 3,250 | VA........... | Hampton Roads Area | 3,250 |
| IL............. | Chicago | 68,000 | WA........... | Seattle | 6,000 |

X Not applicable.

Source: U.S. Department of Homeland Security, Federal Emergency Management Agency, *Grant Programs Directorate Information Bulletin*, No. 443, August 2019. See also <https://www.fema.gov/grant-programs-directorate>.

## Table 555. Preparedness Grant Programs: 2010 to 2019

[In millions of dollars (2,968 represents $2,968,000,000. For years ending September 30]

| Program | 2010 | 2011 | 2012 | 2013 | 2014 | 2015 | 2016 | 2017 | 2018 | 2019 |
|---|---|---|---|---|---|---|---|---|---|---|
| Total [1]................................ | 2,968 | 2,191 | 1,381 | 1,507 | 1,616 | 1,617 | 1,617 | 1,622 | 1,687 | 1,715 |
| Homeland Security Grant Program [1]................. | 1,786 | 1,289 | 831 | 968 | 1,043 | 1,044 | 1,037 | 1,037 | 1,067 | 1,095 |
| State Homeland Security Program.................. | 842 | 527 | 294 | 355 | 401 | 402 | 402 | 402 | 402 | 415 |
| Urban Areas Security Initiative...................... | 833 | 663 | 490 | 559 | 587 | 587 | 580 | 580 | 580 | 590 |
| Operation Stonegarden............................. | 60 | 55 | 47 | 55 | 55 | 55 | 55 | 55 | 85 | 90 |
| Emergency Management Performance Grants Program............................................. | 330 | 329 | 340 | 332 | 350 | 350 | 350 | 350 | 350 | 350 |
| Tribal Homeland Security Grant Program........... | 10 | 10 | 6 | 10 | 10 | 10 | 10 | 10 | 10 | 10 |
| Nonprofit Security Grant Program.................... | 19 | 19 | 10 | 10 | 13 | 13 | 20 | 25 | 60 | 60 |
| Transit Security Grant Program [1]................... | 253 | 200 | 88 | 84 | 90 | 87 | 87 | 88 | 88 | 88 |
| Port Security Grant Program......................... | 288 | 235 | 98 | 93 | 100 | 100 | 100 | 100 | 100 | 100 |
| Intercity Bus Security Grant Program............... | 12 | 5 | (NA) | (NA) | (NA) | 3 | 3 | 2 | 2 | 2 |

NA Not available. [1] Includes grant programs not listed separately.

Source: U.S. Department of Homeland Security, Federal Emergency Management Agency, *Grant Programs Directorate Information Bulletin*, No. 443, August 2019, and earlier reports. See also <https://www.fema.gov/grant-programs-directorate>.

## Table 556. Aliens Returned or Removed by Leading Crime Category and Country of Nationality: 2010 to 2017

[For year ending September 30. For definitions of immigration enforcement terms, see source. "Crime categories" and "Countries of nationality" are ranked by data for most recent year]

| Crime category and country of nationality | 2010 | 2011 | 2012 | 2013 | 2014 | 2015 | 2016 | 2017 |
|---|---|---|---|---|---|---|---|---|
| **Total aliens returned or removed:**............... | **854,278** | **712,519** | **646,815** | **611,432** | **569,482** | **456,081** | **440,065** | **396,118** |
| Returns [1]....................................... | 471,805 | 322,055 | 231,115 | 178,984 | 163,862 | 129,675 | 106,473 | 100,754 |
| Removals [2]..................................... | 382,473 | 390,464 | 415,700 | 432,448 | 405,620 | 326,406 | 333,592 | 295,364 |
| Noncriminal.................................... | 211,443 | 200,762 | 215,661 | 233,960 | 233,000 | 187,412 | 197,362 | 174,063 |
| Criminal [3].................................... | 171,030 | 189,702 | 200,039 | 198,488 | 172,620 | 138,994 | 136,230 | 121,301 |
| Leading crime category: | | | | | | | | |
| Immigration.................................... | 31,944 | 37,697 | 47,559 | 62,033 | 54,709 | 45,496 | 47,073 | 35,385 |
| Dangerous drugs.............................. | 43,463 | 43,535 | 42,738 | 30,692 | 28,270 | 23,930 | 23,343 | 20,703 |
| Criminal traffic offenses..................... | 31,112 | 43,334 | 46,141 | 29,966 | 24,729 | 18,620 | 18,283 | 17,554 |
| Assault....................................... | 12,291 | 12,835 | 12,993 | 20,192 | 17,754 | 14,518 | 13,345 | 13,130 |
| Weapon offenses.............................. | 2,839 | 2,742 | 2,510 | 5,277 | 4,589 | 3,752 | 3,779 | 3,376 |
| Burglary...................................... | 4,275 | 3,824 | 3,557 | 5,504 | 4,759 | 3,753 | 3,498 | 3,241 |
| Fraudulent activities......................... | 3,903 | 4,271 | 3,870 | 5,186 | 3,940 | 2,966 | 2,458 | 3,128 |
| Larceny....................................... | 5,468 | 5,749 | 5,419 | 5,329 | 4,350 | 3,184 | 2,868 | 2,817 |
| Sexual assault................................ | 3,333 | 3,592 | 3,363 | 3,168 | 2,961 | 2,557 | 2,524 | 2,493 |
| Obstructing police............................ | 1,898 | 2,309 | 2,495 | 2,929 | 2,437 | 1,907 | 2,064 | 1,882 |
| Other, including unknown...................... | 30,504 | 29,814 | 29,394 | 28,212 | 24,122 | 18,311 | 16,995 | 17,592 |
| Leading country of nationality of criminals removed: | | | | | | | | |
| Mexico........................................ | 129,661 | 145,539 | 151,337 | 146,170 | 126,363 | 104,863 | 102,646 | 85,784 |
| Guatemala.................................... | 9,422 | 11,750 | 13,497 | 15,426 | 13,722 | 10,542 | 10,622 | 11,130 |
| Honduras..................................... | 10,416 | 10,883 | 13,824 | 16,598 | 14,064 | 8,565 | 8,595 | 9,288 |
| El Salvador................................... | 8,412 | 8,545 | 8,670 | 9,472 | 8,952 | 7,228 | 6,725 | 6,492 |
| Dominican Republic........................... | 2,292 | 2,151 | 2,187 | 1,821 | 1,642 | 1,522 | 1,485 | 1,515 |
| Jamaica...................................... | 1,168 | 1,230 | 1,157 | 999 | 834 | 641 | 620 | 678 |
| Colombia..................................... | 1,249 | 1,063 | 1,057 | 929 | 876 | 795 | 764 | 640 |
| Ecuador...................................... | 693 | 709 | 708 | 579 | 571 | 488 | 466 | 507 |
| Brazil......................................... | 497 | 552 | 426 | 375 | 281 | 288 | 330 | 407 |
| Nicaragua.................................... | 805 | 712 | 729 | 692 | 643 | 440 | 392 | 381 |
| Haiti.......................................... | 134 | 246 | 565 | 458 | 352 | 268 | 264 | 343 |
| Canada....................................... | 478 | 428 | 385 | 383 | 305 | 265 | 257 | 203 |
| Somalia....................................... | 9 | 8 | (D) | 34 | 24 | 4 | 25 | 179 |

D Data withheld to limit disclosure. [1] Returns are the confirmed movement of an inadmissible or deportable alien out of the U.S. not based on an order of removal. Most voluntary departures are of Mexican nationals who have been apprehended by the U.S. Border Patrol and are returned to Mexico. [2] Removals are the compulsory and confirmed movement of an inadmissible or deportable alien out of the U.S. based on an order of removal. An alien who is removed has administrative or criminal consequences placed on subsequent reentry. [3] Persons removed based on a criminal charge or those with a criminal conviction.

Source: U.S. Department of Homeland Security, Office of Immigration Statistics, "2017 Yearbook of Immigration Statistics," <https://www.dhs.gov/immigration-statistics>, accessed April 2019; and *Immigration Enforcement Actions: 2017*, and previous editions.

## Table 557. Deportable Aliens Apprehended or Arrested by Program and Border Patrol Sector: 2000 to 2017

[As of the end of September. Deportable aliens located refer to Border Patrol apprehensions and Immigration and Customs Enforcement (ICE) administrative arrests]

| Program and sector | 2000 | 2010 | 2014 | 2015 | 2016 | 2017 |
|---|---|---|---|---|---|---|
| **Total**.......................................... | **1,814,729** | **796,587** | **679,996** | **462,388** | **530,250** | **461,540** |
| Investigations................................. | 138,291 | 18,290 | 11,626 | 7,288 | 4,330 | 7,539 |
| Enforcement and Removal Operations (ERO) [1].... | (X) | 314,915 | 181,719 | 117,983 | 110,104 | 143,470 |
| **Border Patrol (apprehensions)**.................. | **1,676,438** | **463,382** | **486,651** | **337,117** | **415,816** | **310,531** |
| **All southwest sectors**........................ | **1,643,679** | **447,731** | **479,371** | **331,333** | **408,870** | **303,916** |
| Rio Grande Valley, Texas..................... | 133,243 | 59,766 | 256,393 | 147,257 | 186,830 | 137,562 |
| Tucson, Arizona.............................. | 616,346 | 212,202 | 87,915 | 63,397 | 64,891 | 38,657 |
| San Diego, California......................... | 151,681 | 68,565 | 29,911 | 26,290 | 31,891 | 26,086 |
| Laredo, Texas................................ | 108,973 | 35,287 | 44,049 | 35,888 | 36,562 | 25,460 |
| El Paso, Texas............................... | 115,696 | 12,251 | 12,339 | 14,495 | 25,634 | 25,193 |
| El Centro, California.......................... | 238,126 | 32,562 | 14,511 | 12,820 | 19,448 | 18,633 |
| Del Rio, Texas............................... | 157,178 | 14,694 | 24,255 | 19,013 | 23,078 | 13,476 |
| Yuma, Arizona............................... | 108,747 | 7,116 | 5,902 | 7,142 | 14,170 | 12,847 |
| Big Bend, Texas [2]........................... | 13,689 | 5,288 | 4,096 | 5,031 | 6,366 | 6,002 |
| **All other sectors**............................ | **32,759** | **15,651** | **7,280** | **5,784** | **6,946** | **6,615** |
| Miami, Florida................................ | 6,237 | 4,651 | 2,034 | 1,752 | 3,205 | 2,280 |
| Detroit, Michigan............................. | 2,057 | 1,669 | 647 | 637 | 716 | 1,070 |
| New Orleans, Louisiana....................... | 6,478 | 3,171 | 950 | 849 | 764 | 920 |
| Grand Forks, North Dakota.................... | 562 | 543 | 767 | 789 | 505 | 496 |
| Swanton, Vermont............................ | 1,957 | 1,422 | 506 | 341 | 291 | 449 |
| Buffalo, New York............................ | 1,570 | 2,422 | 741 | 291 | 226 | 447 |
| Ramey, Puerto Rico.......................... | 1,731 | 398 | 958 | 557 | 694 | 388 |
| Blaine, Washington........................... | 2,581 | 673 | 272 | 282 | 271 | 288 |
| Spokane, Washington......................... | 1,324 | 356 | 269 | 190 | 206 | 208 |
| Havre, Montana.............................. | 1,568 | 290 | 91 | 64 | 43 | 39 |
| Houlton, Maine............................... | 489 | 56 | 45 | 32 | 25 | 30 |
| Livermore, California [3]....................... | 6,205 | (X) | (X) | (X) | (X) | (X) |

X Not applicable. [1] Includes arrests of fugitive and nonfugitive aliens under the Office of Detention and Removal Operations (DRO), National Fugitive Operations Program. Beginning in 2008, includes all administrative arrests conducted by ICE ERO. [2] Formerly known as Marfa, TX. [3] Livermore sector closed August 31, 2004.

Source: U.S. Department of Homeland Security, Office of Immigration Statistics, "2017 Yearbook of Immigration Statistics," and earlier reports, <https://www.dhs.gov/immigration-statistics/yearbook>, accessed April 2019.

# Table 558. Deportable Aliens Apprehended or Arrested: 1925 to 2017

[As of the end of September. Prior to 1952, data refer to Border Patrol Apprehensions. Detention and Removal Operations data are included beginning in 2006. Beginning in 2008, includes all administrative arrests conducted by the ICE, Office of Enforcement and Removal Operations. Beginning in 2009, data also include administrative arrests conducted under the 287(g) program (Delegation of Immigration Authority)]

| Year | Number | Year | Number | Year | Number | Year | Number |
|---|---|---|---|---|---|---|---|
| 1925 | 22,199 | 1965 | 110,371 | 2002 | 1,062,270 | 2010 | 796,587 |
| 1930 | 20,880 | 1970 | 345,353 | 2003 | 1,046,422 | 2011 | 678,606 |
| 1935 | 11,016 | 1975 | 766,600 | 2004 | 1,264,232 | 2012 | 671,327 |
| 1940 | 10,492 | 1980 | 910,361 | 2005 | 1,291,065 | 2013 | 662,483 |
| 1945 | 69,164 | 1985 | 1,348,749 | 2006 | 1,206,408 | 2014 | 679,996 |
| 1950 | 468,339 | 1990 | 1,169,939 | 2007 | 960,673 | 2015 | 462,388 |
| 1955 | 254,096 | 1995 | 1,394,554 | 2008 | 1,043,759 | 2016 [1] | 530,250 |
| 1960 | 70,684 | 2000 | 1,814,729 | 2009 | 889,212 | 2017 | 461,540 |

[1] The counting methodology for administrative arrests by ICE ERO was revised to align with ICE ERO reporting for 2016; prior to 2016, only one administrative arrest could be counted for the same person on the same day.

Source: U.S. Department of Homeland Security, Office of Immigration Statistics, "2017 Yearbook of Immigration Statistics," <https://www.dhs.gov/immigration-statistics/yearbook>, accessed April 2019.

# Table 559. Foreign Visitor Overstays by Country of Citizenship: 2018

[Data shown for foreign nationals entering the U.S. as nonimmigrant visitors for business or pleasure through an air or sea point of entry. For fiscal year ending Sept. 30. An overstay is a nonimmigrant who was lawfully admitted to the U.S. for an authorized period but stayed or remains in the U.S. beyond the lawful admission period. The Visa Waiver Program (VWP) allows citizens of specific countries to travel to the U.S. for tourism, business, or while in transit for up to 90 days without obtaining a visa. Data are generated from Department of Homeland Security's Arrival and Departure Information System (ADIS)]

| Country of citizenship | Expected departures | Overstays (number) | | | Overstay rates | |
|---|---|---|---|---|---|---|
| | | Total | Out-of-country [1] | Suspected in-country [2] | Total | Suspected in-country [2] |
| **Total** | **54,706,966** | **666,582** | **96,978** | **569,604** | **1.22** | **1.04** |
| **North American, total** | **12,810,521** | **141,895** | **12,483** | **129,412** | **1.11** | **1.01** |
| Canada | 9,669,759 | 92,542 | 7,253 | 85,289 | 0.96 | 0.88 |
| Mexico | 3,140,762 | 49,353 | 5,230 | 44,123 | 1.57 | 1.40 |
| VISA WAIVER PROGRAM | | | | | | |
| **Total** | **22,940,801** | **93,323** | **13,573** | **79,750** | **0.41** | **0.35** |
| United Kingdom | 4,745,902 | 14,215 | 1,982 | 12,233 | 0.30 | 0.26 |
| Japan | 3,122,345 | 4,877 | 372 | 4,505 | 0.16 | 0.14 |
| Germany | 2,128,450 | 6,728 | 962 | 5,766 | 0.32 | 0.27 |
| France | 1,907,233 | 11,530 | 1,103 | 10,427 | 0.60 | 0.55 |
| Korea, South | 1,579,221 | 4,551 | 1,027 | 3,524 | 0.29 | 0.22 |
| Australia | 1,418,265 | 3,984 | 829 | 3,155 | 0.28 | 0.22 |
| Italy | 1,304,020 | 7,072 | 1,063 | 6,009 | 0.54 | 0.46 |
| Spain | 1,050,622 | 11,772 | 1,564 | 10,208 | 1.12 | 0.97 |
| Netherlands | 795,308 | 3,180 | 359 | 2,821 | 0.40 | 0.35 |
| Ireland | 558,218 | 1,705 | 218 | 1,487 | 0.31 | 0.27 |
| Sweden | 541,849 | 1,412 | 244 | 1,168 | 0.26 | 0.22 |
| Taiwan | 428,767 | 1,755 | 541 | 1,214 | 0.41 | 0.28 |
| Switzerland | 409,632 | 1,222 | 190 | 1,032 | 0.30 | 0.25 |
| Chile | 403,917 | 6,019 | 655 | 5,364 | 1.49 | 1.33 |
| New Zealand | 345,636 | 1,095 | 252 | 843 | 0.32 | 0.24 |
| Denmark | 340,333 | 770 | 114 | 656 | 0.23 | 0.19 |
| Belgium | 300,319 | 933 | 148 | 785 | 0.31 | 0.26 |
| Norway | 285,524 | 648 | 128 | 520 | 0.23 | 0.18 |
| Austria | 210,050 | 721 | 74 | 647 | 0.34 | 0.31 |
| Portugal | 198,982 | 3,584 | 444 | 3,140 | 1.80 | 1.58 |
| Finland | 151,678 | 352 | 59 | 293 | 0.23 | 0.19 |
| Singapore | 134,505 | 302 | 97 | 205 | 0.22 | 0.15 |
| Czechia | 125,142 | 786 | 174 | 612 | 0.63 | 0.49 |
| Hungary | 98,877 | 1,246 | 268 | 978 | 1.26 | 0.99 |
| NON-VISA WAIVER PROGRAM | | | | | | |
| **Total** | **15,257,468** | **305,215** | **20,945** | **284,270** | **2.00** | **1.86** |
| China | 2,345,850 | 18,314 | 2,575 | 15,739 | 0.78 | 0.67 |
| Brazil | 2,200,440 | 36,289 | 1,720 | 34,569 | 1.65 | 1.57 |
| India | 1,134,436 | 12,986 | 2,216 | 10,770 | 1.14 | 0.95 |
| Argentina | 1,116,017 | 8,185 | 276 | 7,909 | 0.73 | 0.71 |
| Colombia | 929,005 | 21,917 | 935 | 20,982 | 2.36 | 2.26 |
| Venezuela | 477,224 | 35,931 | 1,029 | 34,902 | 7.53 | 7.31 |
| Dominican Republic | 446,451 | 14,641 | 443 | 14,198 | 3.28 | 3.18 |
| Ecuador | 429,106 | 6,997 | 345 | 6,652 | 1.63 | 1.55 |
| Israel | 418,944 | 3,626 | 375 | 3,251 | 0.87 | 0.78 |
| Jamaica | 312,667 | 10,626 | 384 | 10,242 | 3.40 | 3.28 |
| Costa Rica | 306,925 | 3,014 | 184 | 2,830 | 0.98 | 0.92 |
| Philippines | 304,585 | 5,613 | 620 | 4,993 | 1.84 | 1.64 |
| Peru | 302,829 | 4,993 | 340 | 4,653 | 1.65 | 1.54 |
| Guatemala | 276,400 | 5,839 | 291 | 5,548 | 2.11 | 2.01 |
| Bahamas, The | 272,487 | 1,545 | 253 | 1,292 | 0.57 | 0.47 |
| Russia | 265,798 | 4,581 | 347 | 4,234 | 1.72 | 1.59 |
| Honduras | 214,468 | 4,143 | 253 | 3,890 | 1.93 | 1.81 |
| Poland | 211,438 | 1,850 | 215 | 1,635 | 0.87 | 0.77 |
| El Salvador | 199,915 | 3,439 | 210 | 3,229 | 1.72 | 1.62 |
| Nigeria | 195,785 | 29,723 | 719 | 29,004 | 15.18 | 14.81 |
| Trinidad and Tobago | 180,415 | 811 | 83 | 728 | 0.45 | 0.40 |
| Turkey | 165,724 | 3,084 | 280 | 2,804 | 1.86 | 1.69 |

[1] Individuals whose departure was recorded after their lawful admission period expired. [2] Individuals for whom no departure has been recorded.

Source: Department of Homeland Security, *Fiscal Year 2018 Entry/Exit Overstay Report*, April 2019. See also <https://www.dhs.gov/publication/entryexit-overstay-report>.

# Table 560. Terrorism Related Deaths, Injuries, and Kidnappings of Private U.S. Citizens by Selected Country: 2011 to 2017

[Private U.S. citizen refers to any U.S. citizen overseas not acting in an official capacity on behalf of the U.S. government. Includes U.S. government employees' households and U.S. citizens working for contractors hired by the U.S. government. Excludes U.S. military personnel while on active duty or employees of the Department of State and other federal agencies while overseas on U.S. government orders]

| Incident type and location | 2011 | 2012 | 2013 | 2014 | 2015 | 2016 | 2017 |
|---|---|---|---|---|---|---|---|
| **DEATHS** | | | | | | | |
| **Total** | 17 | 10 | 16 | 24 | 20 | 16 | 7 |
| Afghanistan | 15 | 10 | 12 | 20 | 8 | 1 | – |
| Algeria | – | – | 3 | – | – | – | – |
| Bangladesh | – | – | – | – | 1 | 1 | – |
| Belgium | – | – | – | – | – | 4 | – |
| Burkina Faso | – | – | – | – | – | 1 | – |
| Egypt | – | – | – | 1 | – | – | 1 |
| France | – | – | – | – | 1 | 3 | – |
| Iraq | 1 | – | – | – | – | – | – |
| Israel, Jerusalem, West Bank, Gaza | 1 | – | – | 5 | 3 | 3 | – |
| Jordan | – | – | – | – | 2 | – | – |
| Lebanon | – | – | 1 | – | – | – | – |
| Libya | – | – | – | – | 1 | – | – |
| Mali | – | – | – | – | 1 | – | – |
| Pakistan | – | – | – | – | 1 | 1 | 1 |
| Somalia | – | – | – | 3 | 1 | – | 3 |
| Spain | – | – | – | – | – | – | 1 |
| Syria | – | – | – | 4 | 1 | – | – |
| Turkey | – | – | – | – | – | 2 | – |
| United Arab Emirates | – | – | – | 1 | – | – | – |
| United Kingdom | – | – | – | – | – | – | 1 |
| **INJURIES** | | | | | | | |
| **Total** | 14 | 2 | [1]7 | 8 | 22 | 34 | 8 |
| Afghanistan | 10 | 1 | 1 | 2 | 2 | 5 | 1 |
| Bangladesh | – | – | – | – | 1 | – | – |
| Belgium | – | – | – | – | – | 17 | – |
| Burkina Faso | – | – | – | – | – | 1 | – |
| France | – | – | – | – | 6 | 3 | – |
| Germany | – | – | – | – | – | 2 | – |
| Iraq | 1 | 1 | – | – | 1 | – | – |
| Israel, Jerusalem, West Bank, Gaza | 3 | – | – | 5 | 6 | 6 | 1 |
| Jordan | – | – | – | – | 2 | – | – |
| Kenya | – | – | 6 | – | – | – | – |
| Pakistan | – | – | – | – | 1 | – | – |
| Saudi Arabia | – | – | – | 1 | 2 | – | – |
| Somalia | – | – | – | – | 1 | – | – |
| Spain | – | – | – | – | – | – | 1 |
| Turkey | – | – | – | – | – | – | 1 |
| United Kingdom | – | – | – | – | – | – | 4 |
| **KIDNAPPINGS** | | | | | | | |
| **Total** | 3 | 3 | 13 | 3 | – | 6 | 3 |
| Afghanistan | – | – | – | 2 | – | 1 | – |
| Colombia | – | – | 1 | – | – | – | 3 |
| Iraq | 1 | – | – | – | – | 3 | – |
| Libya | – | – | 1 | – | – | – | – |
| Niger | – | – | – | – | – | 1 | – |
| Nigeria | – | 1 | 3 | 1 | – | – | – |
| Pakistan | 1 | – | – | – | – | – | – |
| Somalia | 1 | 1 | – | – | – | – | – |
| Syria | – | – | 7 | – | – | 1 | – |
| Yemen | – | 1 | 1 | – | – | – | – |

– Represents zero. [1] Excludes 2 citizens held hostage in Algeria; and 48 citizens present, but not medically injured, at Westgate Mall in Kenya.

Source: U.S. State Department, Bureau of Counterterrorism, "Country Reports on Terrorism," <http://www.state.gov/j/ct/rls/crt/index.htm>, accessed November 2018.

# Table 561. Customs and Border Protection (CBP)—Processed and Cleared Passengers, Planes, Vehicles, and Containers: 2008 to 2015

[In thousands (93,768 represents 93,768,000). For year ending September 30]

| Item | 2008 | 2009 | 2010 | 2011 | 2012 | 2013 | 2014 | 2015 |
|---|---|---|---|---|---|---|---|---|
| **AIR** | | | | | | | | |
| Passengers | 93,768 | 87,749 | 91,488 | 94,605 | 98,367 | 10,221 | 107,049 | 112,505 |
| Commercial aircraft [1] | 696 | 638 | 657 | 662 | 675 | 870 | 900 | 941 |
| Private aircraft | 138 | 109 | 115 | 121 | 116 | 116 | 117 | 116 |
| **LAND** | | | | | | | | |
| Passengers [2, 3] | 290,146 | 257,476 | 244,322 | 227,965 | 234,898 | 242,064 | 247,813 | 250,449 |
| Privately owned vehicles [2] | 109,548 | 99,017 | 93,966 | 92,673 | 94,952 | 98,460 | 100,909 | 103,022 |
| Truck containers [4] | 11,013 | 9,238 | 10,003 | 10,117 | 10,419 | 10,473 | 10,851 | 10,937 |
| Rail containers | 2,747 | 2,179 | 2,431 | 2,634 | 2,936 | 3,061 | 3,272 | 3,290 |
| **SEA** | | | | | | | | |
| Passengers [5] | 16,636 | 15,967 | 17,170 | 17,796 | 18,335 | 17,883 | 19,713 | 19,796 |
| Vessels [6] | 148 | 146 | 152 | 141 | 139 | 133 | 133 | 136 |
| Vessel containers | 10,886 | 9,300 | 10,282 | 10,721 | 10,975 | 11,044 | 11,549 | 12,119 |

[1] Aircraft transporting passengers and/or cargo for some payment or other consideration, including money or services rendered. [2] See Table 1297 for more details. [3] Includes pedestrians. [4] Number of trucks entering the U.S. [5] Excludes passengers on ferries. [6] Includes every description of water craft or other contrivance used or capable of being used as a means of transportation on water; does not include aircraft.

Source: U.S. Department of Homeland Security, Customs and Border Protection, ProQuest Freedom of Information Act request, received March 2016. See also <http://www.cbp.gov>.

## Table 562. Passengers Screened and Firearms Discovered at TSA Checkpoints: 2015 to 2018

[Number, unless otherwise noted (708,316 represents 708,316,000). Firearms are those found in carry-on bags]

| Item | 2015 | 2016 | 2017 | 2018 | Top 5 airports for found firearms | Firearms found in 2018 |
|---|---|---|---|---|---|---|
| Passengers screened (thousands)... | 708,316 | 738,318 | 771,557 | 813,791 | Atlanta, Hartsfield-Jackson Intl........ | 298 |
| Firearms found........................... | 2,653 | 3,391 | 3,957 | 4,239 | Dallas-Fort Worth Intl.................... | 219 |
| Firearms loaded....................... | 2,198 | 2,815 | 3,324 | 3,656 | Phoenix, Sky Harbor Intl............... | 129 |
| Percentage loaded...... | 83 | 83 | 84 | 86 | Denver Intl................................. | 126 |
| Airports with firearms discovered..... | 236 | 238 | 239 | 249 | Orlando Intl.............................. | 123 |

Source: U.S. Department of Homeland Security, Transportation Security Administration, "TSA Year in Review: A Record Setting 2018," <https://www.tsa.gov/blog>, and earlier releases.

## Table 563. Value of Counterfeit Goods Seized for Intellectual Property Rights Violations by Commodity and Country of Origin: 2017 and 2018

[In thousands of dollars (1,206,382 represents $1,206,382,000), except as indicated. Customs and Border Protection enforces Intellectual Property Rights (IPR), most visibly by seizing products that infringe IPR such as trademarks, copyrights, and patents. Value of goods seized represent Manufacturer's Suggested Retail Price (MSRP), which is the price at which merchandise is sold at retail to the consumer or what the value of the counterfeit goods would have been at retail had they been genuine]

| Commodity | 2017 | 2018 | Country of origin | 2017 | 2018 |
|---|---|---|---|---|---|
| **Number of IPR Seizures...................** | **34,143** | **33,810** | | | |
| **Total MSRP value of IPR seizures..............** | **1,206,382** | **1,399,874** | China................................. | 554,632 | 761,115 |
| Jewelry, watches, and parts..................... | 460,162 | 618,167 | Hong Kong.............................. | 386,242 | 440,345 |
| Handbags/wallets/backpacks............... | 234,452 | 226,506 | India..................................... | 8,342 | 19,952 |
| Consumer electronics/parts.............. | 85,116 | 89,593 | Singapore............................. | 4,997 | (NA) |
| Wearing apparel/accessories.................. | 74,881 | 115,164 | Turkey................................. | 4,983 | 5,759 |
| Pharmaceuticals/personal care............... | 69,759 | 131,458 | Pakistan............................... | (NA) | 2,779 |
| Consumer products........................... | 46,265 | 40,846 | Korea, South........................ | 4,235 | 10,136 |
| Footwear.................................... | 41,490 | 77,501 | Malaysia............................... | (NA) | 4,674 |
| Computers/technology components............ | (NA) | 29,940 | Canada................................. | 3,037 | 7,799 |
| Labels/tags................................. | 80,951 | (NA) | Thailand.............................. | 1,857 | (NA) |
| Optical media............................... | 27,574 | (NA) | Vietnam................................ | 4,392 | 5,192 |
| Toys....................................... | 12,128 | 10,590 | Taiwan................................. | 4,902 | 5,008 |
| Automotive/aerospace........................ | (NA) | 14,862 | | | |
| All other commodities........................ | 73,604 | 45,248 | All other countries..................... | 228,763 | 137,114 |

NA Not available.

Source: U.S. Department of Homeland Security, Customs and Border Protection, *Intellectual Property Rights Seizure Statistics FY2018*, August 2019, and earlier reports. See also <http://www.cbp.gov/trade/priority-issues/ipr/statistics>.

# Section 11
# Social Insurance and Human Services

This section presents data related to government expenditures for social insurance and human services; the population receiving government assistance; government programs for Old-Age, Survivors, and Disability Insurance (OASDI), commonly known as Social Security; government employee retirement; private retirement savings plans; government unemployment and disability insurance; federal supplemental security income payments and aid to the needy; child and other welfare services; and federal food programs. Also included here are selected data on workers' compensation, child support, child care, homelessness, social assistance organizations, charitable contributions, and philanthropic foundations.

A principal source for these data is the Social Security Administration's *Annual Statistical Supplement to the Social Security Bulletin* which presents current data on many of the programs. Additional sources of data include the Census Bureau's Annual Social and Economic Supplement of the Current Population Survey, and the Survey of Income and Program Participation (conducted as a series of surveys over a period of time spanning several years); and the Department of Health and Human Services' Administration for Children and Families.

**Social insurance under the Social Security Act**—Programs established by the Social Security Act provide protection against wage loss resulting from retirement, prolonged disability, death, or unemployment, and protection against the cost of medical care during old age and disability. The federal OASDI program provides monthly benefits to retired or disabled insured workers and their dependents, and to survivors of insured workers. To be eligible, a worker must have had a specified period of employment in which OASDI taxes were paid. The age of eligibility for full retirement benefits had been 65 for many years. For persons born in 1938 or later, however, that age gradually increases until it reaches age 67 for those born in 1960 and later. Reduced benefits may be obtained as early as age 62. The worker's spouse is under the same limitations. Survivor benefits are payable to dependents of deceased insured workers. Disability benefits are payable to an insured worker under full retirement age with a prolonged disability, and to the disabled worker's dependents on the same basis as dependents of retired workers. Disability benefits are provided at age 50 to the disabled widow or widower of a deceased worker who was fully insured at the time of death. Disabled children, age 18 or older, of retired, disabled, or deceased workers are also eligible for benefits. A special lump sum benefit may be payable on the death of an insured worker to a spouse or minor children. For information on the Medicare program, see Section 3, Health and Nutrition.

Retirement, survivors, and disability insurance benefits are funded by a payroll tax on annual earnings (up to a maximum share of earnings set by law) of workers, employers, and the self-employed. The maximum taxable earnings are adjusted annually to reflect increasing wage levels (see Table 569). Tax receipts and benefit payments are administered through federal trust funds. Special benefits for

uninsured persons; hospital benefits for persons age 65 and over with specified amounts of social security coverage less than that required for cash benefit eligibility; and that part of the cost of supplementary medical insurance not financed by contributions from participants are all financed from federal general revenues.

Unemployment insurance is administered by the U.S. Employment and Training Administration and each state's employment security agency. By agreement with the U.S. Secretary of Labor, state agencies also administer unemployment compensation for eligible former military personnel and federal employees. Under state unemployment insurance laws, benefits related to an individual's past earnings are paid to eligible unemployed workers. State laws vary concerning the length of time benefits are paid and their amount. In most states, benefits are payable for 26 weeks and, during periods of high unemployment, extended benefits are payable under a federal-state program to those who have exhausted their regular state benefits. Some states also supplement the basic benefit with allowances for dependents. Unemployment insurance is financed through Federal and state employer payroll taxes. Generally, employers pay both Federal and state unemployment taxes for workers paid $1,500 or more during any quarter of a calendar year, or if they had at least 1 employee during any day of the week during 20 weeks in a calendar year (weeks need not be consecutive).

**Retirement programs for government employees**—The Civil Service Retirement System (CSRS) and the Federal Employees' Retirement System (FERS) are the two major programs providing old-age, disability, and survivor annuities for federal civilian employees. The FERS replaced the CSRS for federal employees who first entered covered service on or after January 1, 1987. CSRS employees were offered the option of transferring to FERS during 1987 and 1998. There are separate retirement systems for the uniformed services (supplementing OASDI) and for certain special groups of federal employees. State and local government employees are covered for the most part by state and local retirement systems similar to the federal programs. In many jurisdictions, these benefits supplement OASDI coverage.

**Workers' compensation**—All states provide protection against work-connected injuries and deaths, although some states exclude certain workers (e.g., domestic workers). Federal laws cover federal employees, private employees in the District of Columbia, and longshoremen and harbor workers. In addition, the Department of Labor administers "black lung" benefit programs for coal miners disabled by pneumoconiosis and for specified dependents and survivors. Specified occupational diseases are compensable to some extent. In most states, benefits are related to the worker's salary. The benefits may or may not be augmented by dependents' allowances or automatically adjusted to prevailing wage levels.

**Income support**—Income support programs are designed to provide benefits that assist persons with limited income and resources. The Supplemental Security Income (SSI) program and Temporary

Assistance for Needy Families (TANF) program are the major programs providing monthly payments. In addition, a number of programs provide money payments or in-kind benefits for special needs or purposes. Several programs offer food and nutritional services. Also, various federal-state programs provide energy assistance, public housing, and subsidized housing to individuals and families with low incomes. General assistance may also be available at the state or local level.

The SSI program, administered by the Social Security Administration, provides income support to persons with low income and few resources who are age 65 and older, or blind or disabled, and children who have limited income and resources. Unlike social security, SSI benefits are not based on a person's work history, and the program is financed by general funds of the U.S. Treasury. Eligibility requirements and federal payment standards are nationally uniform. Most states supplement the basic SSI payment for all or selected categories of persons.

The Personal Responsibility and Work Opportunity Reconciliation Act of 1996 contains provisions that replaced the Aid to Families With Dependent Children (AFDC), Job Opportunities and Basic Skills (JOBS), and Emergency Assistance programs with the TANF block grant program. This law contains strong work requirements, comprehensive child support enforcement, support for families moving from welfare to work, and other features. The TANF program became effective as soon as each state submitted a complete implementation plan, but no later than July 1, 1997. The older AFDC program provided cash assistance based on need, income, resources, and family size.

**Federal nutrition assistance**—Under the Supplemental Nutrition Assistance Program (SNAP), formerly known as the food stamp program, single persons and those living in households meeting nationwide standards for income and assets may receive benefits to assist in purchasing food. Benefits come on an electronic benefits transfer card that recipients use much like a bank debit card for purchasing eligible food items in retail food stores. The monthly amount of benefits, also known as

allotments, is determined by household size and income. Households without income receive the determined monthly cost of a nutritionally adequate diet for their household size. This amount is updated to account for food price increases. Households with income receive the difference between the amount of a nutritionally adequate diet and 30 percent of their income, after certain allowable deductions.

The USDA website has detailed information regarding eligibility for SNAP, including income limits and maximum monthly SNAP allotments by household size, at <https://www.fns.usda.gov/snap/recipient/eligibility>. All households in which all members receive TANF or SSI are categorically eligible for SNAP without meeting these income or resource criteria. Households are certified for varying lengths of time, depending on their income sources and individual circumstances.

**Health and welfare services**—Programs providing health and welfare services are aided through federal grants to states for child welfare services, vocational rehabilitation, activities for the elderly, maternal and child health services, maternity and infant care projects, comprehensive health services, and a variety of public health activities. For information about the Medicaid program, see Section 3, Health and Nutrition.

**Noncash benefits**—The U.S. Census Bureau annually collects data on the characteristics of recipients of noncash (in-kind) benefits to supplement the collection of annual money income data in the Current Population Survey (see text, Section 1, Population, and Section 13, Income, Expenditures, Poverty, and Wealth). Noncash benefits are those benefits received in a form other than money which serve to enhance or improve the economic well-being of the recipient. As for money income, the data for noncash benefits are for the calendar year prior to the date of the interview. The major categories of noncash benefits covered are public transfers (e.g., SNAP, school lunch, public housing, and Medicaid) and employer or union-provided benefits to employees.

**Statistical reliability**—For discussion of statistical collection, estimation, and sampling procedures and measures of statistical reliability applicable to Census Bureau data, see Appendix III.

## Table 564. Government Transfer Payments to Individuals—Summary: 1990 to 2017

[In billions of current dollars (568.1 represents $568,100,000,000)]

| Year | Government transfer payments to individuals, total | Retirement and disability insurance benefits | Medical payments | Income maintenance benefits | Unemployment insurance benefits | Veterans benefits | Education and training assistance payments [1] | Other [2] |
|---|---|---|---|---|---|---|---|---|
| 1990 | 568.1 | 263.9 | 188.8 | 65.4 | 18.2 | 17.7 | 12.3 | 1.7 |
| 2000 | 1,032.4 | 424.5 | 427.2 | 110.6 | 21.0 | 25.0 | 21.9 | 2.3 |
| 2002 | 1,235.4 | 474.5 | 522.4 | 125.0 | 53.7 | 29.5 | 27.8 | 2.4 |
| 2003 | 1,304.2 | 493.4 | 556.5 | 137.6 | 53.6 | 31.8 | 28.3 | 3.0 |
| 2004 | 1,387.1 | 517.0 | 611.4 | 149.1 | 37.1 | 34.1 | 30.8 | 7.7 |
| 2005 | 1,473.5 | 545.5 | 655.6 | 165.9 | 32.3 | 36.4 | 33.0 | 4.9 |
| 2006 | 1,575.4 | 576.9 | 720.4 | 170.4 | 30.9 | 38.9 | 34.8 | 3.1 |
| 2007 | 1,679.8 | 608.8 | 775.9 | 180.6 | 33.4 | 41.7 | 36.8 | 2.6 |
| 2008 | 1,900.5 | 639.0 | 825.5 | 196.0 | 52.0 | 45.0 | 42.5 | 100.4 |
| 2009 | 2,087.4 | 698.5 | 890.4 | 230.8 | 132.0 | 51.5 | 53.5 | 30.6 |
| 2010 | 2,260.4 | 724.9 | 938.4 | 256.0 | 139.7 | 58.0 | 64.5 | 78.8 |
| 2011 | 2,288.7 | 747.4 | 970.1 | 264.1 | 107.9 | 63.3 | 65.0 | 70.9 |
| 2012 | 2,300.2 | 796.2 | 1,001.6 | 267.6 | 84.4 | 70.1 | 63.7 | 16.5 |
| 2013 | 2,363.2 | 832.8 | 1,040.5 | 271.2 | 63.0 | 79.1 | 63.8 | 12.8 |
| 2014 | 2,474.1 | 870.4 | 1,116.4 | 271.0 | 35.8 | 83.7 | 64.7 | 32.2 |
| 2015 | 2,609.8 | 908.3 | 1,196.6 | 272.7 | 32.5 | 89.8 | 64.4 | 45.4 |
| 2016 | 2,694.3 | 931.3 | 1,250.2 | 269.9 | 31.9 | 92.8 | 64.6 | 53.6 |
| 2017 | 2,781.1 | 960.7 | 1,298.9 | 268.1 | 29.5 | 98.5 | 65.1 | 60.3 |

[1] See footnote 9, Table 565. [2] See footnote 10, Table 565.

Source: U.S. Bureau of Economic Analysis, Regional Economic Accounts, Annual State Personal Income and Employment, "SAINC35 Personal Current Transfer Receipts," <http://www.bea.gov/regional/index.htm>, accessed February 2019.

## Table 565. Government Transfer Payments to Individuals by Payment Type: 1990 to 2017

[In millions of current dollars (568,060 represents $568,060,000,000)]

| Item | 1990 | 2000 | 2005 | 2010 | 2015 | 2016 | 2017 |
|---|---|---|---|---|---|---|---|
| Total | 568,060 | 1,032,404 | 1,473,518 | 2,260,351 | 2,609,754 | 2,694,343 | 2,781,115 |
| Retirement & disability insurance benefits | 263,888 | 424,461 | 545,484 | 724,895 | 908,349 | 931,286 | 960,711 |
| Social security | 244,135 | 401,393 | 512,728 | 690,174 | 871,793 | 896,472 | 926,072 |
| Railroad retirement & disability | 7,221 | 8,267 | 9,194 | 10,779 | 12,228 | 12,352 | 12,475 |
| Workers' compensation (federal & state) | 8,618 | 10,898 | 15,863 | 15,505 | 14,090 | 14,004 | 14,041 |
| Other government disability insurance & retirement [1] | 3,914 | 3,903 | 7,699 | 8,437 | 10,238 | 8,458 | 8,123 |
| Medical payments | 188,808 | 427,194 | 655,571 | 938,402 | 1,196,644 | 1,250,218 | 1,298,866 |
| Medicare | 107,638 | 219,117 | 332,127 | 513,390 | 633,969 | 662,150 | 695,265 |
| Public assistance medical care [2] | 78,176 | 205,021 | 315,189 | 410,957 | 547,616 | 573,902 | 589,004 |
| Military medical insurance [3] | 2,994 | 3,056 | 8,255 | 14,055 | 15,059 | 14,166 | 14,597 |
| Income maintenance benefits | 65,441 | 110,582 | 165,905 | 256,034 | 272,711 | 269,922 | 268,123 |
| Supplemental Security Income (SSI) | 16,670 | 31,675 | 38,261 | 49,158 | 56,661 | 56,449 | 56,414 |
| Earned income tax credit | 6,313 | 30,423 | 39,237 | 59,778 | 69,620 | 70,404 | 69,604 |
| Supplemental Nutrition Assistance Program | 14,741 | 14,565 | 29,492 | 66,515 | 68,719 | 65,443 | 63,976 |
| Family assistance [4] | 19,187 | 18,440 | 18,355 | 22,421 | 20,953 | 20,323 | 20,482 |
| Other, excluding family assistance [5] | 8,530 | 15,479 | 40,560 | 58,162 | 56,758 | 57,303 | 57,647 |
| Unemployment insurance compensation | 18,208 | 20,989 | 32,277 | 139,715 | 32,465 | 31,908 | 29,514 |
| State unemployment insurance compensation | 17,644 | 20,223 | 31,001 | 137,016 | 31,431 | 31,056 | 28,529 |
| Unemployment compensation for federal civilian employees | 215 | 226 | 225 | 535 | 203 | 171 | 181 |
| Unemployment compensation for railroad employees | 89 | 81 | 72 | 116 | 90 | 132 | 103 |
| Unemployment compensation for veterans | 144 | 181 | 446 | 1,155 | 389 | 281 | 217 |
| Other unemployment compensation [6] | 116 | 278 | 533 | 893 | 352 | 268 | 484 |
| Veterans benefits | 17,687 | 25,004 | 36,389 | 57,962 | 89,822 | 92,793 | 98,538 |
| Veterans pension & disability | 15,550 | 21,966 | 32,511 | 48,455 | 75,848 | 79,792 | 85,405 |
| Veterans readjustment [7] | 257 | 1,322 | 2,256 | 7,976 | 12,699 | 11,819 | 12,056 |
| Veterans life insurance benefits | 1,868 | 1,706 | 1,597 | 1,442 | 1,185 | 1,096 | 992 |
| Other assistance to veterans [8] | 12 | 10 | 25 | 89 | 90 | 86 | 85 |
| Federal education & training assistance payments [9] | 12,286 | 21,851 | 33,015 | 64,511 | 64,386 | 64,625 | 65,074 |
| Other payments to individuals [10] | 1,742 | 2,323 | 4,877 | 78,832 | 45,377 | 53,591 | 60,289 |

[1] Mostly temporary disability, pension benefit guaranty, black lung, and Panama Canal construction annuity payments. [2] Medicaid and other medical vendor payments. [3] Payments made under TriCare Management Program (formerly called CHAMPUS) for medical care of dependents of active duty and retired military personnel and their dependents at nonmilitary medical facilities. [4] Through 1995, consists of Emergency Assistance and Aid to Families with Dependent Children. Beginning with 1998, consists of Temporary Assistance for Needy Families benefits. [5] Mostly general assistance; food expenditures for Special Supplemental Nutrition Program for Women, Infants, and Children (WIC); Other Needs Assistance; refugee assistance; foster home care and adoption assistance; 2008 Economic Stimulus Act Rebates; Child Tax Credits; American Recovery and Reinvestment Act of 2009 (ARRA) funded tax credits; other tax credits; and energy assistance. [6] Trade readjustment allowance, Redwood Park benefit, public service employment benefit, and transitional benefit. [7] Mostly veterans' readjustment benefit payments, educational assistance to spouses and children of disabled or deceased veterans, and payments to paraplegics and for autos and conveyances for disabled veterans. [8] Mostly state and local government payments to veterans. [9] Mostly federal fellowship payments (National Science Foundation fellowships and traineeships, subsistence payments to state maritime academy cadets, and other fellowships), interest subsidy on higher education loans, Pell Grants, Job Corps payments, education exchange payments, and state education assistance payments. [10] Mostly Bureau of Indian Affairs payments; Alaska Permanent Fund dividend payments; compensation of survivors of public safety officers; compensation of crime victims; disaster relief payments; compensation for Japanese internment; ARRA funded Federal Additional Compensation for unemployment, COBRA premium reduction, and Economic Recovery lump sum payment; and other special payments to individuals.

Source: U.S. Bureau of Economic Analysis, Regional Economic Accounts, Annual State Personal Income and Employment, "SAINC35 Personal Current Transfer Receipts," <http://www.bea.gov/regional/index.htm>, accessed February 2019.

# Table 566. Government Transfer Payments to Individuals by State: 2010 to 2017

[In millions of current dollars not adjusted for inflation (2,260,351 represents $2,260,351,000,000)]

| State | 2010, total | 2016, total | 2017 | | | | | | | |
|---|---|---|---|---|---|---|---|---|---|---|
| | | | Total | Retire-ment and disability insurance benefits | Medical payments | Income mainte-nance benefits | Unem-ployment insurance benefits | Veterans benefits | Educa-tion and training assis-tance [1] | Other [2] |
| **United States**........ | **2,260,351** | **2,694,343** | **2,781,115** | **960,711** | **1,298,866** | **268,123** | **29,514** | **98,538** | **65,074** | **60,289** |
| Alabama................. | 36,885 | 42,827 | 44,417 | 17,142 | 18,017 | 4,503 | 185 | 2,316 | 1,251 | 1,003 |
| Alaska.................. | 5,189 | 6,461 | 6,782 | 1,447 | 3,040 | 872 | 91 | 355 | 74 | 903 |
| Arizona................. | 46,551 | 54,613 | 57,186 | 20,662 | 26,602 | 4,780 | 309 | 2,224 | 1,793 | 818 |
| Arkansas............... | 23,007 | 27,683 | 28,341 | 10,223 | 13,098 | 2,497 | 158 | 1,214 | 789 | 362 |
| California............... | 259,129 | 324,835 | 321,862 | 96,742 | 159,715 | 34,081 | 5,181 | 9,209 | 9,430 | 7,504 |
| Colorado............... | 28,542 | 37,117 | 38,174 | 13,787 | 17,492 | 2,896 | 426 | 2,125 | 955 | 493 |
| Connecticut............ | 28,329 | 31,813 | 32,430 | 11,448 | 15,919 | 2,497 | 635 | 603 | 674 | 654 |
| Delaware............... | 6,972 | 9,100 | 9,709 | 3,484 | 4,676 | 685 | 71 | 278 | 370 | 146 |
| District of Columbia. ... | 5,301 | 6,383 | 6,497 | 1,217 | 4,003 | 900 | 55 | 126 | 162 | 34 |
| Florida................. | 147,547 | 182,892 | 192,516 | 69,980 | 84,211 | 18,181 | 481 | 7,526 | 3,791 | 8,347 |
| Georgia................ | 59,961 | 73,072 | 75,919 | 27,383 | 30,323 | 9,015 | 354 | 4,220 | 2,049 | 2,576 |
| Hawaii................. | 9,006 | 10,940 | 11,407 | 4,093 | 4,975 | 1,224 | 161 | 637 | 221 | 95 |
| Idaho.................. | 9,921 | 11,935 | 12,515 | 5,238 | 4,950 | 977 | 110 | 538 | 267 | 434 |
| Illinois................. | 90,583 | 97,587 | 100,880 | 35,871 | 46,025 | 11,253 | 1,785 | 2,223 | 2,185 | 1,537 |
| Indiana................ | 45,972 | 54,316 | 56,087 | 21,664 | 25,435 | 4,883 | 259 | 1,517 | 1,542 | 787 |
| Iowa................... | 21,092 | 24,507 | 24,468 | 10,064 | 10,329 | 1,931 | 399 | 719 | 723 | 304 |
| Kansas................ | 18,598 | 21,248 | 21,799 | 8,907 | 9,246 | 1,829 | 197 | 816 | 391 | 413 |
| Kentucky.............. | 34,555 | 41,331 | 42,672 | 14,881 | 20,444 | 3,860 | 322 | 1,470 | 1,345 | 351 |
| Louisiana.............. | 33,352 | 42,603 | 44,531 | 13,095 | 22,463 | 4,679 | 226 | 1,468 | 1,413 | 1,187 |
| Maine.................. | 11,056 | 12,827 | 13,311 | 4,911 | 6,078 | 972 | 102 | 620 | 222 | 405 |
| Maryland............... | 37,990 | 47,810 | 49,107 | 16,415 | 24,316 | 4,351 | 572 | 1,823 | 930 | 700 |
| Massachusetts......... | 54,798 | 64,407 | 65,467 | 19,873 | 34,229 | 6,130 | 1,390 | 1,501 | 1,460 | 884 |
| Michigan............... | 80,630 | 91,573 | 92,274 | 35,765 | 41,460 | 8,416 | 823 | 2,406 | 1,961 | 1,442 |
| Minnesota............. | 37,924 | 44,487 | 46,035 | 16,394 | 21,911 | 4,153 | 754 | 1,364 | 1,133 | 326 |
| Mississippi............ | 23,427 | 27,593 | 27,916 | 9,580 | 12,949 | 3,069 | 110 | 995 | 692 | 520 |
| Missouri............... | 44,332 | 51,484 | 52,913 | 19,873 | 24,284 | 4,104 | 330 | 1,979 | 989 | 1,354 |
| Montana............... | 6,854 | 8,461 | 9,084 | 3,609 | 3,937 | 627 | 112 | 397 | 147 | 253 |
| Nebraska.............. | 11,489 | 13,510 | 14,088 | 5,601 | 5,878 | 1,157 | 83 | 662 | 302 | 405 |
| Nevada................ | 16,258 | 21,184 | 22,197 | 8,010 | 9,616 | 2,188 | 321 | 1,098 | 538 | 425 |
| New Hampshire........ | 8,864 | 11,070 | 11,522 | 4,843 | 5,121 | 588 | 71 | 410 | 304 | 185 |
| New Jersey............ | 68,883 | 77,752 | 79,724 | 28,466 | 36,624 | 7,501 | 1,900 | 1,386 | 1,844 | 2,004 |
| New Mexico............ | 15,448 | 18,993 | 19,041 | 6,220 | 8,925 | 2,140 | 158 | 932 | 403 | 263 |
| New York.............. | 178,462 | 200,768 | 221,941 | 58,730 | 129,058 | 22,109 | 2,118 | 3,161 | 4,186 | 2,579 |
| North Carolina......... | 68,663 | 82,980 | 86,459 | 31,695 | 35,964 | 8,343 | 227 | 4,542 | 2,110 | 3,577 |
| North Dakota........... | 4,405 | 5,338 | 5,462 | 2,226 | 2,241 | 459 | 109 | 211 | 97 | 118 |
| Ohio................... | 88,300 | 101,243 | 104,066 | 37,195 | 50,891 | 9,124 | 908 | 2,778 | 2,085 | 1,086 |
| Oklahoma.............. | 26,910 | 31,409 | 32,351 | 11,957 | 13,418 | 3,066 | 258 | 2,179 | 791 | 681 |
| Oregon................ | 28,483 | 35,690 | 36,698 | 13,635 | 16,774 | 3,060 | 510 | 1,551 | 647 | 522 |
| Pennsylvania........... | 108,365 | 125,839 | 126,671 | 45,594 | 60,726 | 11,465 | 1,922 | 3,040 | 2,070 | 1,852 |
| Rhode Island........... | 9,319 | 10,468 | 10,954 | 3,652 | 5,288 | 1,144 | 152 | 285 | 262 | 171 |
| South Carolina......... | 35,399 | 42,989 | 44,438 | 17,374 | 17,906 | 3,906 | 186 | 2,471 | 1,431 | 1,163 |
| South Dakota.......... | 5,212 | 6,124 | 6,330 | 2,601 | 2,571 | 527 | 33 | 290 | 124 | 184 |
| Tennessee............. | 49,089 | 56,838 | 58,624 | 21,908 | 25,361 | 5,936 | 236 | 2,625 | 1,337 | 1,220 |
| Texas.................. | 153,344 | 193,825 | 199,204 | 62,584 | 91,179 | 23,424 | 2,493 | 10,211 | 4,151 | 5,163 |
| Utah................... | 13,185 | 16,042 | 16,637 | 6,428 | 6,332 | 1,721 | 163 | 614 | 754 | 627 |
| Vermont............... | 5,220 | 6,315 | 6,415 | 2,260 | 3,049 | 584 | 64 | 170 | 175 | 113 |
| Virginia................ | 47,926 | 59,738 | 62,496 | 23,972 | 25,440 | 5,234 | 341 | 4,071 | 1,587 | 1,851 |
| Washington............ | 48,772 | 57,994 | 60,197 | 23,317 | 25,453 | 5,382 | 1,021 | 2,789 | 1,570 | 665 |
| West Virginia.......... | 16,457 | 19,070 | 19,644 | 7,444 | 8,812 | 1,714 | 159 | 818 | 479 | 217 |
| Wisconsin............. | 40,869 | 45,053 | 47,263 | 19,264 | 20,445 | 3,756 | 418 | 1,376 | 782 | 1,223 |
| Wyoming.............. | 3,525 | 4,210 | 4,393 | 1,987 | 1,665 | 231 | 65 | 197 | 87 | 162 |

[1] Mostly federal fellowship payments (National Science Foundation fellowships and traineeships, subsistence payments to state maritime academy cadets, and other federal fellowships), interest subsidy on higher education loans, Pell Grants, Job Corps payments, education exchange payments, and state education assistance payments. [2] Mostly Bureau of Indian Affairs payments; Alaska Permanent Fund dividend payments; compensation of survivors of public safety officers; compensation of victims of crime; disaster relief payments; compensation for Japanese internment; the American Recovery and Reinvestment Act of 2009 funded Federal Additional Compensation for unemployment, COBRA premium reduction, and the Economic Recovery lump sum payment; and other special payments to individuals.

Source: U.S. Bureau of Economic Analysis, Regional Economic Accounts, Annual State Personal Income and Employment, "SAINC35 Personal Current Transfer Receipts," <https://www.bea.gov/regional/index.htm>, accessed February 2019.

# Table 567. Number of Persons With Income by Source of Income: 2017

[In thousands (231,467 represents 231,467,000). Persons 15 years old and over as of March of following year. Based on Current Population Survey, Annual Social and Economic Supplement (CPS ASEC); see text, Sections 1 and 13, and Appendix III]

| Source of income | Total persons with income | Under 65 years | 65 years and over | Men | Women | White [1] | Black [1] | Hispanic origin [2] |
|---|---|---|---|---|---|---|---|---|
| **Total** | **231,467** | **182,212** | **49,255** | **114,849** | **116,618** | **182,349** | **28,229** | **35,062** |
| Earnings | 166,296 | 154,560 | 11,736 | 88,101 | 78,196 | 130,013 | 20,367 | 28,190 |
| Wages and salary | 157,184 | 147,071 | 10,113 | 82,404 | 74,780 | 122,350 | 19,679 | 26,591 |
| Nonfarm self-employment | 12,255 | 10,565 | 1,690 | 7,314 | 4,941 | 10,121 | 1,093 | 1,957 |
| Farm self-employment | 2,201 | 1,869 | 332 | 1,326 | 875 | 1,871 | 188 | 211 |
| Unemployment compensation | 3,668 | 3,363 | 305 | 2,139 | 1,529 | 2,906 | 463 | 628 |
| State or local only | 3,387 | 3,129 | 258 | 1,967 | 1,420 | 2,696 | 418 | 584 |
| Combinations | 281 | 234 | 46 | 172 | 109 | 211 | 44 | 43 |
| Workers' compensation | 1,374 | 1,200 | 175 | 827 | 548 | 1,086 | 152 | 226 |
| State payments | 314 | 274 | 40 | 201 | 113 | 247 | 37 | 59 |
| Employment insurance | 622 | 557 | 65 | 408 | 215 | 505 | 58 | 111 |
| Own insurance | 11 | 8 | 2 | 8 | 3 | 7 | 2 | 1 |
| Other | 658 | 574 | 84 | 358 | 300 | 516 | 74 | 90 |
| Social Security | 52,770 | 11,353 | 41,417 | 23,681 | 29,089 | 44,227 | 5,645 | 4,256 |
| SSI (Supplemental Security Income) | 6,474 | 5,030 | 1,444 | 2,773 | 3,701 | 4,121 | 1,714 | 1,124 |
| Public assistance, total | 1,632 | 1,502 | 130 | 357 | 1,275 | 1,003 | 474 | 403 |
| TANF only [3] | 976 | 931 | 45 | 167 | 809 | 563 | 323 | 244 |
| Other assistance only | 621 | 536 | 85 | 186 | 435 | 413 | 147 | 149 |
| Both | 35 | 35 | – | 4 | 31 | 27 | 5 | 10 |
| Veterans' benefits | 4,012 | 1,995 | 2,017 | 3,303 | 709 | 3,175 | 626 | 333 |
| Disability only | 2,607 | 1,419 | 1,189 | 2,348 | 259 | 2,089 | 388 | 221 |
| Survivors only | 287 | 70 | 217 | 15 | 272 | 247 | 26 | 15 |
| Pension only | 706 | 236 | 470 | 600 | 106 | 511 | 158 | 45 |
| Education only | 83 | 83 | – | 67 | 16 | 62 | 12 | 8 |
| Other only | 147 | 70 | 77 | 101 | 46 | 126 | 15 | 19 |
| Combinations | 182 | 118 | 65 | 173 | 9 | 140 | 27 | 25 |
| Means-tested | 561 | 277 | 284 | 472 | 89 | 439 | 81 | 68 |
| Nonmeans-tested | 3,451 | 1,718 | 1,733 | 2,831 | 620 | 2,736 | 545 | 266 |
| Survivors benefits [4] | 3,006 | 1,062 | 1,944 | 749 | 2,256 | 2,688 | 204 | 142 |
| Company or union | 1,147 | 255 | 892 | 148 | 998 | 1,046 | 71 | 57 |
| Federal government | 262 | 66 | 197 | 31 | 232 | 228 | 29 | 17 |
| Military retirement | 183 | 32 | 151 | 16 | 167 | 147 | 13 | 7 |
| State or local government | 319 | 104 | 215 | 75 | 245 | 290 | 21 | 9 |
| Estates or trusts | 348 | 209 | 139 | 166 | 181 | 328 | 11 | 15 |
| Annuities | 228 | 108 | 120 | 98 | 130 | 197 | 10 | 14 |
| Disability benefits [4] | 2,777 | 2,390 | 386 | 1,404 | 1,372 | 2,061 | 517 | 390 |
| Workers' compensation | 326 | 289 | 36 | 203 | 122 | 267 | 28 | 48 |
| Company or union | 531 | 448 | 83 | 233 | 298 | 417 | 76 | 90 |
| Federal government | 195 | 167 | 28 | 103 | 92 | 138 | 47 | 24 |
| Military retirement | 169 | 127 | 41 | 138 | 31 | 128 | 29 | 29 |
| State or local government | 500 | 452 | 47 | 225 | 274 | 382 | 89 | 75 |
| Accident insurance | 232 | 209 | 23 | 103 | 130 | 191 | 24 | 34 |
| Retirement income [4] | 26,646 | 7,471 | 19,175 | 13,533 | 13,114 | 23,272 | 2,167 | 1,448 |
| Pension income | 19,589 | 4,309 | 15,280 | 10,692 | 8,897 | 17,286 | 1,457 | 928 |
| Company or union retirement | 13,465 | 3,122 | 10,344 | 7,320 | 6,145 | 11,717 | 1,157 | 719 |
| Federal government retirement | 2,364 | 782 | 1,582 | 1,384 | 980 | 1,991 | 270 | 132 |
| Military retirement | 1,056 | 473 | 583 | 788 | 268 | 884 | 106 | 76 |
| State or local government retirement | 6,470 | 1,895 | 4,575 | 2,828 | 3,642 | 5,649 | 532 | 369 |
| Annuities | 3,697 | 704 | 2,992 | 1,699 | 1,998 | 3,355 | 180 | 150 |
| IRA, KEOGH, or 401(k) [5] | 5,406 | 869 | 4,536 | 2,778 | 2,628 | 4,955 | 208 | 192 |
| Property income [6] | 139,566 | 107,246 | 32,320 | 68,991 | 70,575 | 115,136 | 12,169 | 14,379 |
| Interest | 136,616 | 105,276 | 31,340 | 67,372 | 69,244 | 112,686 | 11,940 | 14,052 |
| Dividends | 31,174 | 21,726 | 9,448 | 16,830 | 14,344 | 26,944 | 1,577 | 1,523 |
| Rents, royalties, estates or trusts | 12,234 | 7,917 | 4,318 | 6,437 | 5,797 | 10,441 | 700 | 890 |
| Educational assistance [4] | 8,212 | 8,163 | 50 | 3,415 | 4,798 | 5,945 | 1,272 | 1,469 |
| Pell grant only | 2,251 | 2,241 | 9 | 874 | 1,376 | 1,556 | 471 | 524 |
| Other government only | 1,217 | 1,199 | 17 | 555 | 661 | 839 | 222 | 271 |
| Scholarships only | 2,648 | 2,633 | 15 | 1,020 | 1,629 | 1,972 | 292 | 377 |
| Child support | 3,967 | 3,911 | 57 | 304 | 3,664 | 2,932 | 780 | 706 |
| Financial assistance from outside the household | 3,214 | 2,932 | 282 | 1,276 | 1,937 | 2,368 | 355 | 481 |
| Other income, not elsewhere classified | 1,737 | 1,410 | 326 | 888 | 848 | 1,424 | 153 | 156 |
| Combinations of income types: | | | | | | | | |
| Government transfer payments | 70,122 | 26,675 | 43,448 | 32,393 | 37,729 | 56,722 | 8,942 | 7,218 |
| Public assistance or SSI or both | 7,881 | 6,341 | 1,540 | 3,085 | 4,797 | 4,990 | 2,118 | 1,477 |
| Social security or railroad retirement | 52,870 | 11,385 | 41,485 | 23,756 | 29,114 | 44,324 | 5,647 | 4,265 |

– Represents or rounds to zero. [1] Refers to people who reported specified race only and no other race category. [2] Persons of Hispanic origin may be of any race. [3] TANF is Temporary Assistance for Needy Families Program. [4] Includes other sources not shown separately. [5] Individual retirement account, tax-deferred retirement plan for self-employed and unincorporated businesses, and employer-sponsored retirement plan. [6] Includes estates and trusts reported as survivor benefits.

Source: U.S. Census Bureau, *Income and Poverty in the United States: 2017,* Current Population Reports, P60-263, September 2018; and "Current Population Survey Tables for Personal Income: Table PINC-09," <http://www.census.gov/topics/income-poverty/income/data/tables.html>, accessed November 2018.

# Table 568. Persons Living in Households Receiving Selected Benefits by Selected Characteristics: 2017

[322,549 represents 322,549,000, except percent. Based on Current Population Survey, Annual Social and Economic Supplement (CPS ASEC); see text of Section 1 and Appendix III. Persons who lived with someone (a nonrelative or a relative) who received aid. Not every person tallied here received the aid themselves. Persons living in households receiving more than one type of aid are counted only once. Excludes members of the Armed Forces except those living off post or with their families on post. Population controls are based on Census 2010. SNAP = Supplemental Nutrition Assistance Program]

| Characteristic | Total (1,000) | In household receiving means-tested assistance [1] (1,000) | Percent | In household receiving means-tested cash assistance (1,000) | Percent | In household receiving food stamps (SNAP) (1,000) | Percent | In household in which one or more persons are covered by Medicaid (1,000) | Percent | Living in public or authorized housing (1,000) | Percent |
|---|---|---|---|---|---|---|---|---|---|---|---|
| Total.................... | 322,549 | 114,637 | 35.5 | 19,787 | 6.1 | 33,900 | 10.5 | 92,074 | 28.5 | 11,593 | 3.6 |
| Under 18 years................. | 73,356 | 37,908 | 51.7 | 4,584 | 6.2 | 12,269 | 16.7 | 30,424 | 41.5 | 3,566 | 4.9 |
| 18 to 24 years................. | 29,363 | 11,855 | 40.4 | 1,737 | 5.9 | 3,070 | 10.5 | 9,902 | 33.7 | 1,193 | 4.1 |
| 25 to 34 years................. | 44,854 | 16,121 | 35.9 | 2,468 | 5.5 | 4,647 | 10.4 | 13,444 | 30.0 | 1,499 | 3.3 |
| 35 to 44 years................. | 40,659 | 15,030 | 37.0 | 2,093 | 5.1 | 3,776 | 9.3 | 11,860 | 29.2 | 1,174 | 2.9 |
| 45 to 54 years................. | 41,537 | 12,837 | 30.9 | 2,615 | 6.3 | 3,337 | 8.0 | 10,272 | 24.7 | 1,034 | 2.5 |
| 55 to 59 years................. | 21,622 | 5,957 | 27.5 | 1,797 | 8.3 | 1,814 | 8.4 | 5,040 | 23.3 | 630 | 2.9 |
| 60 to 64 years................. | 20,078 | 5,311 | 26.5 | 1,565 | 7.8 | 1,637 | 8.2 | 4,447 | 22.1 | 624 | 3.1 |
| 65 years and over............ | 51,080 | 9,618 | 18.8 | 2,927 | 5.7 | 3,350 | 6.6 | 6,686 | 13.1 | 1,873 | 3.7 |
| Male........................ | 158,116 | 54,597 | 34.5 | 9,131 | 5.8 | 15,001 | 9.5 | 43,904 | 27.8 | 4,885 | 3.1 |
| Female..................... | 164,433 | 60,040 | 36.5 | 10,656 | 6.5 | 18,898 | 11.5 | 48,169 | 29.3 | 6,708 | 4.1 |
| White alone [2]............... | 247,272 | 79,415 | 32.1 | 12,738 | 5.2 | 20,959 | 8.5 | 63,805 | 25.8 | 5,623 | 2.3 |
| Black alone [2]............... | 42,474 | 22,203 | 52.3 | 4,811 | 11.3 | 9,305 | 21.9 | 17,696 | 41.7 | 4,579 | 10.8 |
| Asian alone [2]............... | 19,475 | 6,295 | 32.3 | 969 | 5.0 | 1,159 | 6.0 | 5,341 | 27.4 | 503 | 2.6 |
| Hispanic [3]................. | 59,053 | 33,534 | 56.8 | 4,515 | 7.6 | 9,607 | 16.3 | 27,065 | 45.8 | 2,604 | 4.4 |
| In married couple families....... | 194,037 | 56,630 | 29.2 | 7,476 | 3.9 | 10,560 | 5.4 | 45,093 | 23.2 | 2,192 | 1.1 |
| In families with male householder, no spouse present.... | 18,674 | 9,696 | 51.9 | 1,669 | 8.9 | 2,779 | 14.9 | 8,218 | 44.0 | 631 | 3.4 |
| In families with female householder, no spouse present..... | 47,999 | 31,674 | 66.0 | 6,625 | 13.8 | 14,160 | 29.5 | 26,420 | 55.0 | 5,072 | 10.6 |

[1] Means-tested assistance includes means-tested cash assistance, supplemental nutrition assistance program benefits, Medicaid, and public or authorized housing. [2] Refers to people who reported specific race and did not report any other race category. [3] People of Hispanic origin may be of any race.

Source: U.S. Census Bureau, *Income and Poverty in the United States: 2017*, Current Population Reports, P60-263, September 2018; and "Current Population Survey Detailed Tables for Poverty: Table POV-26," <http://www.census.gov/topics/income-poverty/poverty/data/tables.html>, accessed November 2018.

# Table 569. Social Security—Covered Employment, Earnings, and Contribution Rates: 1990 to 2018

[164.3 represents 164,300,000. Includes the Island Areas of the U.S. Represents all reported employment. Data are estimated. OASDI is Old-age, survivors, and disability insurance; SMI is Supplementary medical insurance. All data are subject to revision by source]

| Item | Unit | 1990 | 2000 | 2010 | 2013 | 2014 | 2015 | 2016 | 2017 | 2018 |
|---|---|---|---|---|---|---|---|---|---|---|
| **Workers with insured status [1]......** | Million | **164.3** | **185.2** | **204.2** | **209.6** | **212.1** | **214.7** | **217.4** | **219.7** | **222.0** |
| Male........................... | Million | 86.8 | 95.5 | 103.5 | 105.9 | 107.0 | 108.2 | 109.4 | 110.4 | 111.4 |
| Female......................... | Million | 77.5 | 89.8 | 100.8 | 103.8 | 105.1 | 106.6 | 108.0 | 109.3 | 110.6 |
| Under 20 years old............. | Million | 4.8 | 4.9 | 2.5 | 2.1 | 2.2 | 2.3 | 2.6 | 2.4 | 2.4 |
| Age 20 to 24................... | Million | 16.6 | 16.0 | 16.0 | 15.6 | 15.7 | 15.8 | 15.9 | 16.0 | 16.1 |
| Age 25 to 29................... | Million | 20.6 | 17.5 | 19.3 | 19.5 | 19.9 | 20.2 | 20.6 | 21.0 | 21.1 |
| Age 30 to 34................... | Million | 21.3 | 19.2 | 18.7 | 19.6 | 19.7 | 19.8 | 19.9 | 20.0 | 20.2 |
| Age 35 to 39................... | Million | 19.3 | 21.2 | 18.2 | 18.1 | 18.3 | 18.8 | 19.2 | 19.5 | 19.7 |
| Age 40 to 44................... | Million | 17.0 | 21.4 | 19.6 | 19.1 | 18.8 | 18.2 | 17.9 | 17.9 | 18.1 |
| Age 45 to 49................... | Million | 12.8 | 19.2 | 21.2 | 19.8 | 19.4 | 19.4 | 19.4 | 19.4 | 19.1 |
| Age 50 to 54................... | Million | 10.1 | 16.6 | 20.9 | 21.2 | 21.1 | 20.8 | 20.3 | 19.8 | 19.4 |
| Age 55 to 59................... | Million | 8.8 | 12.2 | 18.3 | 19.6 | 19.9 | 20.2 | 20.4 | 20.5 | 20.5 |
| Age 60 to 64................... | Million | 8.6 | 9.3 | 15.5 | 16.6 | 17.1 | 17.6 | 18.1 | 18.5 | 18.9 |
| Age 65 to 69................... | Million | 8.0 | 7.8 | 11.1 | 13.3 | 14.0 | 14.8 | 15.3 | 15.5 | 15.9 |
| Age 70 to 74................... | Million | 6.4 | 7.0 | 8.1 | 9.4 | 9.9 | 10.2 | 10.9 | 11.7 | 12.3 |
| Age 75 and older............... | Million | 9.9 | 12.8 | 14.9 | 15.7 | 16.0 | 16.4 | 16.9 | 17.6 | 18.3 |
| Workers reported with— | | | | | | | | | | |
| Taxable earnings [2]........... | Million | 133.0 | 154.7 | 157.1 | 163.0 | 165.4 | 168.3 | 171.0 | 173.0 | 176.0 |
| Maximum earnings [2]......... | Million | 7.6 | 9.2 | 8.6 | 9.9 | 9.8 | 9.9 | 10.5 | 11.1 | 10.5 |
| Earnings in covered employment [2].... | Bil. dol. | 2,716 | 4,832 | 6,294 | 7,067 | 7,432 | 7,811 | 8,019 | 8,377 | 8,776 |
| Reported taxable [2]......... | Bil. dol. | 2,359 | 4,008 | 5,307 | 5,909 | 6,179 | 6,478 | 6,662 | 6,998 | 7,291 |
| Percent of total............. | Percent | 86.9 | 82.9 | 84.3 | 83.6 | 83.1 | 82.9 | 83.1 | 83.5 | 83.1 |
| Average per worker: | | | | | | | | | | |
| Total earnings [2]........... | Dollars | 20,422 | 31,236 | 40,075 | 43,354 | 44,925 | 46,418 | 46,906 | 48,417 | 49,864 |
| Taxable earnings [2]......... | Dollars | 17,737 | 25,907 | 33,789 | 36,251 | 37,350 | 38,498 | 38,970 | 40,447 | 41,425 |
| Annual maximum taxable earnings [3]............... | Dollars | 51,300 | 76,200 | 106,800 | 113,700 | 117,000 | 118,500 | 118,500 | 127,200 | 128,400 |
| Contribution rates for OASDI: [4] | | | | | | | | | | |
| Each employer and employee........ | Percent | 7.65 | 7.65 | 7.65 | 7.65 | 7.65 | 7.65 | 7.65 | 7.65 | 7.65 |
| Self-employed [5]................. | Percent | 15.30 | 15.30 | 15.30 | 15.30 | 15.30 | 15.30 | 15.30 | 15.30 | 15.30 |
| SMI, monthly premium (as of Jan. 1)... | Dollars | 28.60 | 45.50 | 110.50 | 104.90 | 104.90 | 104.90 | 121.80 | 134.00 | 134.00 |

[1] Estimated number fully insured for retirement and/or survivor benefits as of end of year. [2] Includes self-employment. Averages per worker computed with unrounded earnings and worker amounts, and may not agree with rounded table amounts. [3] Beginning in 1994, the upper limit on earnings subject to HI taxes was removed. [4] OASDI tax rates for employees and self-employed workers were reduced by 2 percent for 2011 and 2012. This reduction is being made up by transfers from the General Fund of the Treasury to the OASI and DI trust funds. [5] Half of self-employment tax is deductible for income tax purposes and for computing self-employment income subject to social security tax.

Source: U.S. Social Security Administration, *Annual Statistical Supplement to the Social Security Bulletin, 2019* and unpublished data. See also <https://www.ssa.gov/policy/docs/statcomps/supplement/2019/index.html>.

# Table 570. Social Security (OASDI)—Benefits by Type of Beneficiary: 1990 to 2018

[39,832 represents 39,832,000. A person eligible to receive more than one type of benefit is generally classified or counted only once as a retired-worker beneficiary. OASDI = Old-age, survivors, and disability insurance. See also headnote, Table 571]

| Type of beneficiary | 1990 | 2000 | 2010 | 2012 | 2013 | 2014 | 2015 | 2016 | 2017 | 2018 (P) |
|---|---|---|---|---|---|---|---|---|---|---|
| **Number of benefits [1] (1,000)** | **39,832** | **45,415** | **54,032** | **56,758** | **57,979** | **59,007** | **59,963** | **60,907** | **61,903** | **62,906** |
| Retired workers [2] | 24,838 | 28,499 | 34,593 | 36,720 | 37,893 | 39,009 | 40,089 | 41,233 | 42,447 | 43,721 |
| Disabled workers [3] | 3,011 | 5,042 | 8,204 | 8,827 | 8,941 | 8,955 | 8,909 | 8,809 | 8,695 | 8,537 |
| Wives and husbands [2, 4] | 3,367 | 2,963 | 2,477 | 2,443 | 2,442 | 2,452 | 2,478 | 2,506 | 2,502 | 2,510 |
| Children | 3,187 | 3,803 | 4,313 | 4,419 | 4,413 | 4,355 | 4,297 | 4,222 | 4,169 | 4,108 |
| Under age 18 | 2,497 | 2,976 | 3,209 | 3,258 | 3,237 | 3,166 | 3,096 | 3,007 | 2,938 | 2,858 |
| Disabled children [5] | 600 | 729 | 949 | 1,007 | 1,030 | 1,049 | 1,068 | 1,085 | 1,105 | 1,127 |
| Students [6] | 89 | 98 | 155 | 154 | 146 | 140 | 133 | 129 | 125 | 122 |
| Of retired workers | 422 | 459 | 580 | 612 | 625 | 635 | 649 | 662 | 675 | 690 |
| Of deceased workers | 1,776 | 1,878 | 1,913 | 1,907 | 1,899 | 1,892 | 1,893 | 1,893 | 1,904 | 1,911 |
| Of disabled workers | 989 | 1,466 | 1,820 | 1,900 | 1,888 | 1,828 | 1,755 | 1,667 | 1,590 | 1,507 |
| Widowed mothers and fathers [7] | 304 | 203 | 158 | 154 | 150 | 143 | 140 | 133 | 128 | 121 |
| Widows and widowers [2, 8] | 5,111 | 4,901 | 4,286 | 4,193 | 4,139 | 4,092 | 4,050 | 4,004 | 3,961 | 3,908 |
| Parents [2] | 6 | 3 | 2 | 1 | 1 | 1 | 1 | 1 | 1 | 1 |
| Special benefits [9] | 7 | (Z) | (Z) | (NA) | (NA) | (NA) | (NA) | (NA) | (NA) | (NA) |
| **AVERAGE MONTHLY BENEFIT, CURRENT DOLLARS** | | | | | | | | | | |
| Retired workers [2] | 603 | 844 | 1,176 | 1,262 | 1,294 | 1,329 | 1,342 | 1,360 | 1,404 | 1,461 |
| Retired worker and wife [2] | 1,027 | 1,420 | 1,930 | 2,078 | 2,140 | 2,209 | 2,249 | 2,296 | 2,383 | 2,494 |
| Disabled workers [3] | 587 | 786 | 1,068 | 1,130 | 1,146 | 1,165 | 1,166 | 1,171 | 1,197 | 1,234 |
| Wives and husbands [2, 4] | 298 | 416 | 561 | 605 | 626 | 651 | 669 | 687 | 712 | 744 |
| Children of retired workers | 259 | 395 | 577 | 617 | 632 | 647 | 651 | 657 | 675 | 697 |
| Children of deceased workers | 406 | 550 | 752 | 799 | 814 | 831 | 832 | 837 | 858 | 885 |
| Children of disabled workers | 164 | 228 | 318 | 336 | 341 | 349 | 351 | 355 | 366 | 381 |
| Widowed mothers and fathers [7] | 409 | 595 | 849 | 900 | 918 | 935 | 940 | 947 | 975 | 1,007 |
| Widows and widowers, nondisabled [2] | 556 | 810 | 1,134 | 1,215 | 1,244 | 1,276 | 1,286 | 1,301 | 1,338 | 1,388 |
| Parents [2] | 482 | 704 | 998 | 1,073 | 1,094 | 1,121 | 1,133 | 1,154 | 1,186 | 1,232 |
| Special benefits [9] | 167 | 217 | 276 | (NA) | (NA) | (NA) | (NA) | (NA) | (NA) | (NA) |
| **AVERAGE MONTHLY BENEFIT, CONSTANT (2018) DOLLARS [10]** | | | | | | | | | | |
| Retired workers [2] | 1,132 | 1,219 | 1,347 | 1,380 | 1,395 | 1,421 | 1,424 | 1,415 | 1,438 | 1,461 |
| Retired worker and wife [2] | 1,927 | 2,049 | 2,211 | 2,272 | 2,307 | 2,363 | 2,388 | 2,388 | 2,441 | 2,494 |
| Disabled workers [3] | 1,102 | 1,135 | 1,223 | 1,236 | 1,236 | 1,246 | 1,238 | 1,218 | 1,226 | 1,234 |
| Wives and husbands [2, 4] | 559 | 601 | 643 | 662 | 675 | 697 | 710 | 715 | 729 | 744 |
| Children of deceased workers | 762 | 794 | 861 | 874 | 877 | 888 | 883 | 871 | 879 | 885 |
| Widowed mothers and fathers [7] | 768 | 859 | 972 | 985 | 989 | 1,000 | 998 | 985 | 999 | 1,007 |
| Widows and widowers, nondisabled [2] | 1,043 | 1,169 | 1,299 | 1,329 | 1,341 | 1,364 | 1,366 | 1,353 | 1,371 | 1,388 |
| **Number of benefits awarded (1,000)** | **3,717** | **4,290** | **5,697** | **5,655** | **5,533** | **5,361** | **5,440** | **5,456** | **5,520** | **5,597** |
| Retired workers [2] | 1,665 | 1,961 | 2,634 | 2,735 | 2,794 | 2,772 | 2,839 | 2,911 | 2,975 | 3,082 |
| Disabled workers [3] | 468 | 622 | 1,027 | 960 | 869 | 779 | 741 | 706 | 716 | 687 |
| Wives and husbands [2, 4] | 379 | 385 | 409 | 420 | 420 | 428 | 463 | 476 | 452 | 476 |
| Children | 695 | 777 | 1,045 | 959 | 877 | 810 | 798 | 776 | 777 | 754 |
| Widowed mothers and fathers [7] | 58 | 40 | 32 | 29 | 27 | 25 | 25 | 24 | 23 | 22 |
| Widows and widowers [2, 8] | 452 | 505 | 550 | 552 | 546 | 547 | 573 | 563 | 577 | 577 |
| Parents [2] | (Z) | (Z) | (Z) | (Z) | (Z) | (Z) | (Z) | (Z) | (Z) | (Z) |
| Special benefits [9] | (Z) | (Z) | (Z) | (NA) | (NA) | (NA) | (NA) | (NA) | (NA) | (NA) |
| **BENEFIT PAYMENTS DURING YEAR (bil. dol.)** | | | | | | | | | | |
| **Total [11]** | **247.8** | **407.6** | **701.6** | **774.8** | **812.2** | **848.4** | **886.2** | **911.3** | **941.5** | **988.6** |
| Monthly benefits [12] | 247.6 | 407.4 | 701.4 | 774.6 | 812.0 | 848.2 | 886.0 | 911.1 | 941.3 | 988.4 |
| Retired workers [2] | 156.8 | 253.5 | 443.4 | 497.5 | 528.9 | 560.1 | 592.4 | 616.0 | 644.0 | 686.0 |
| Disabled workers [3] | 22.1 | 49.8 | 115.1 | 127.2 | 130.4 | 132.2 | 133.9 | 143.0 | 134.0 | 144.0 |
| Wives and husbands [2, 4] | 14.5 | 19.4 | 24.6 | 26.0 | 26.9 | 28.1 | 29.3 | 30.0 | 31.0 | 32.0 |
| Children | 12.0 | 19.3 | 30.7 | 32.4 | 32.7 | 33.0 | 33.5 | 33.5 | 33.9 | 34.6 |
| Under age 18 | 9.0 | 14.1 | 21.4 | 22.2 | 22.2 | 22.2 | 22.3 | 22.1 | 22.1 | 22.3 |
| Disabled children [5] | 2.5 | 4.6 | 8.0 | 8.9 | 9.2 | 9.6 | 10.0 | 10.3 | 10.6 | 11.1 |
| Students [6] | 0.5 | 0.7 | 1.3 | 1.3 | 1.3 | 1.3 | 1.2 | 1.2 | 1.2 | 1.2 |
| Of retired workers | 1.3 | 2.1 | 4.1 | 4.6 | 4.8 | 5.0 | 5.2 | 5.4 | 5.6 | 5.8 |
| Of deceased workers | 8.6 | 12.5 | 18.0 | 18.8 | 18.9 | 19.2 | 19.6 | 19.8 | 20.0 | 20.7 |
| Of disabled workers | 2.2 | 4.7 | 8.5 | 9.1 | 9.0 | 8.9 | 8.7 | 8.5 | 8.3 | 8.2 |
| Widowed mothers and fathers [7] | 1.4 | 1.4 | 1.6 | 1.7 | 1.7 | 1.6 | 1.6 | 1.6 | 1.5 | 1.5 |
| Widows and widowers [2, 8] | 40.7 | 63.9 | 86.0 | 89.9 | 91.4 | 93.2 | 95.1 | 95.8 | 96.7 | 99.0 |
| Parents [2] | (Z) | (Z) | (Z) | (Z) | (Z) | (Z) | (Z) | (Z) | (Z) | (Z) |
| Special benefits [9] | (Z) | (Z) | (Z) | (NA) | (NA) | (NA) | (NA) | (NA) | (NA) | (NA) |
| Lump sum | 0.2 | 0.2 | 0.2 | 0.2 | 0.2 | 0.2 | 0.2 | 0.2 | 0.2 | 0.2 |

NA Not available. P Preliminary. Z Fewer than 500 or less than $50 million. [1] Number of benefit payments in current-payment status, i.e., actually being made at a specified time with no deductions or with deductions amounting to less than a month's benefit. [2] Age 62 and over. [3] Disabled workers under full retirement age. [4] Includes spouse beneficiaries with entitled children in their care and entitled divorced spouses. [5] Age 18 and over. Disability began before age 22. [6] Full-time students age 18 and 19. [7] Includes surviving divorced mothers and fathers with entitled children in their care. [8] Includes widows and widowers and surviving divorced widows and widowers age 60 and over, and disabled widows and widowers age 50 and over. [9] Benefits for persons age 72 and over not insured under regular or transitional provisions of Social Security Act. [10] Constant dollar figures are based on the consumer price index (CPI-U) for December as published by the U.S. Bureau of Labor Statistics. [11] Represents total disbursements of benefit checks by the U.S. Department of the Treasury during the years specified. [12] Distribution by type estimated.

Source: U.S. Social Security Administration, *Annual Statistical Supplement to the Social Security Bulletin, 2019*, and earlier editions. See also <http://www.ssa.gov/policy/index.html>.

# Table 571. Social Security—Beneficiaries, Annual Payments, and Average Monthly Benefit, 2000 to 2017, and by State and Other Areas, 2018

[45,417 represents 45,417,000. Number of beneficiaries in current-payment status, and annual and average monthly benefit as of December. Data for 2000 are based on 10-percent sample of administrative records. All other years are 100 percent data. See also headnote, Table 570]

| Year, state, and other area | Number of beneficiaries (1,000) | | | | Annual payments [2] (mil. dol.) | | | | Average monthly benefit (dol.) | | |
|---|---|---|---|---|---|---|---|---|---|---|---|
| | Total | Retired workers and dependents [1] | Survivors | Disabled workers and dependents | Total | Retired workers and dependents [1] | Survivors | Disabled workers and dependents | Retired workers [3] | Disabled workers | Widows and widowers [4] |
| 2000. | 45,417 | 31,761 | 6,981 | 6,675 | 407,431 | 274,645 | 77,848 | 54,938 | 845 | 787 | 810 |
| 2010. | 54,032 | 37,489 | 6,358 | 10,184 | 701,436 | 471,505 | 105,740 | 124,191 | 1,176 | 1,068 | 1,134 |
| 2011. | 55,404 | 38,486 | 6,305 | 10,613 | 724,943 | 489,698 | 106,310 | 128,935 | 1,229 | 1,111 | 1,185 |
| 2012. | 56,758 | 39,613 | 6,256 | 10,889 | 774,626 | 527,402 | 110,346 | 136,878 | 1,262 | 1,130 | 1,215 |
| 2013. | 57,979 | 40,804 | 6,189 | 10,988 | 812,050 | 559,946 | 112,032 | 140,072 | 1,294 | 1,146 | 1,244 |
| 2014. | 59,007 | 41,918 | 6,790 | 10,931 | 848,228 | 592,616 | 114,037 | 141,620 | 1,329 | 1,165 | 1,276 |
| 2015. | 59,963 | 43,073 | 6,084 | 10,806 | 886,012 | 626,378 | 116,352 | 143,282 | 1,342 | 1,166 | 1,286 |
| 2016. | 60,907 | 44,266 | 6,031 | 10,610 | 911,132 | 651,280 | 117,149 | 142,703 | 1,360 | 1,171 | 1,301 |
| 2017. | 61,903 | 45,498 | 5,994 | 10,411 | 941,252 | 680,233 | 118,279 | 142,740 | 1,404 | 1,197 | 1,338 |
| Total, 2018 [5],[6] | 62,906 | 46,803 | 5,940 | 10,162 | 988,373 | 723,542 | 121,175 | 143,656 | 1,461 | 1,234 | 1,388 |
| United States. | 61,363 | 45,679 | 5,725 | 9,959 | 973,139 | 713,781 | 118,234 | 141,124 | (NA) | (NA) | (NA) |
| Alabama. | 1,143 | 753 | 122 | 268 | 17,537 | 11,507 | 2,335 | 3,695 | 1,435 | 1,211 | 1,353 |
| Alaska. | 101 | 77 | 10 | 14 | 1,518 | 1,131 | 187 | 200 | 1,401 | 1,219 | 1,354 |
| Arizona. | 1,349 | 1,057 | 114 | 179 | 21,622 | 16,621 | 2,374 | 2,627 | 1,491 | 1,282 | 1,432 |
| Arkansas. | 697 | 463 | 70 | 163 | 10,347 | 6,875 | 1,304 | 2,168 | 1,387 | 1,176 | 1,317 |
| California. | 5,963 | 4,690 | 520 | 752 | 92,389 | 70,405 | 10,822 | 11,162 | 1,432 | 1,268 | 1,370 |
| Colorado. | 875 | 683 | 74 | 117 | 13,893 | 10,603 | 1,582 | 1,708 | 1,471 | 1,253 | 1,434 |
| Connecticut. | 682 | 532 | 55 | 95 | 11,838 | 9,156 | 1,276 | 1,406 | 1,612 | 1,286 | 1,557 |
| Delaware. | 213 | 164 | 18 | 32 | 3,622 | 2,757 | 385 | 480 | 1,584 | 1,319 | 1,523 |
| District of Columbia. | 83 | 60 | 7 | 15 | 1,242 | 911 | 128 | 203 | 1,413 | 1,089 | 1,248 |
| Florida. | 4,626 | 3,595 | 381 | 650 | 72,670 | 55,416 | 7,898 | 9,356 | 1,452 | 1,254 | 1,409 |
| Georgia. | 1,830 | 1,312 | 181 | 337 | 28,246 | 20,048 | 3,488 | 4,710 | 1,437 | 1,235 | 1,371 |
| Hawaii. | 271 | 225 | 21 | 25 | 4,270 | 3,469 | 433 | 368 | 1,452 | 1,269 | 1,358 |
| Idaho. | 346 | 263 | 30 | 53 | 5,299 | 3,968 | 608 | 723 | 1,430 | 1,208 | 1,428 |
| Illinois. | 2,243 | 1,699 | 217 | 327 | 36,394 | 26,967 | 4,702 | 4,725 | 1,491 | 1,253 | 1,467 |
| Indiana. | 1,350 | 975 | 135 | 241 | 22,129 | 15,854 | 2,872 | 3,403 | 1,522 | 1,236 | 1,504 |
| Iowa. | 647 | 498 | 60 | 90 | 10,296 | 7,800 | 1,277 | 1,219 | 1,468 | 1,177 | 1,442 |
| Kansas. | 553 | 415 | 52 | 86 | 8,971 | 6,685 | 1,102 | 1,184 | 1,512 | 1,207 | 1,484 |
| Kentucky. | 990 | 642 | 113 | 234 | 14,841 | 9,483 | 2,135 | 3,223 | 1,393 | 1,204 | 1,318 |
| Louisiana. | 908 | 593 | 126 | 188 | 13,356 | 8,474 | 2,380 | 2,502 | 1,363 | 1,185 | 1,293 |
| Maine. | 344 | 249 | 29 | 67 | 5,078 | 3,627 | 565 | 886 | 1,371 | 1,158 | 1,345 |
| Maryland. | 1,001 | 763 | 90 | 148 | 16,695 | 12,579 | 1,908 | 2,208 | 1,549 | 1,280 | 1,465 |
| Massachusetts. | 1,273 | 936 | 103 | 234 | 20,560 | 15,020 | 2,213 | 3,327 | 1,509 | 1,241 | 1,450 |
| Michigan. | 2,209 | 1,597 | 211 | 402 | 36,824 | 26,389 | 4,629 | 5,806 | 1,551 | 1,269 | 1,517 |
| Minnesota. | 1,033 | 808 | 82 | 143 | 16,850 | 13,051 | 1,802 | 1,997 | 1,521 | 1,222 | 1,470 |
| Mississippi. | 669 | 441 | 77 | 151 | 9,815 | 6,437 | 1,364 | 2,014 | 1,369 | 1,178 | 1,282 |
| Missouri. | 1,294 | 921 | 125 | 247 | 20,117 | 14,197 | 2,500 | 3,420 | 1,439 | 1,201 | 1,417 |
| Montana. | 234 | 182 | 21 | 31 | 3,518 | 2,677 | 419 | 422 | 1,387 | 1,166 | 1,392 |
| Nebraska. | 346 | 265 | 32 | 48 | 5,464 | 4,145 | 677 | 642 | 1,468 | 1,160 | 1,437 |
| Nevada. | 537 | 418 | 43 | 76 | 8,364 | 6,342 | 889 | 1,133 | 1,429 | 1,295 | 1,415 |
| New Hampshire. | 306 | 225 | 22 | 58 | 5,073 | 3,759 | 489 | 825 | 1,566 | 1,272 | 1,526 |
| New Jersey. | 1,626 | 1,260 | 137 | 228 | 28,449 | 21,708 | 3,158 | 3,583 | 1,617 | 1,360 | 1,538 |
| New Mexico. | 437 | 319 | 42 | 76 | 6,420 | 4,628 | 779 | 1,013 | 1,378 | 1,168 | 1,296 |
| New York. | 3,627 | 2,739 | 307 | 581 | 59,019 | 43,961 | 6,623 | 8,435 | 1,515 | 1,269 | 1,439 |
| North Carolina. | 2,099 | 1,546 | 182 | 371 | 32,999 | 24,167 | 3,563 | 5,269 | 1,462 | 1,231 | 1,390 |
| North Dakota. | 134 | 103 | 15 | 17 | 2,041 | 1,527 | 295 | 219 | 1,404 | 1,154 | 1,349 |
| Ohio. | 2,356 | 1,691 | 260 | 405 | 36,880 | 25,926 | 5,399 | 5,555 | 1,439 | 1,189 | 1,419 |
| Oklahoma. | 789 | 555 | 85 | 149 | 12,103 | 8,430 | 1,670 | 2,003 | 1,425 | 1,187 | 1,380 |
| Oregon. | 872 | 680 | 69 | 122 | 13,837 | 10,579 | 1,508 | 1,750 | 1,465 | 1,224 | 1,456 |
| Pennsylvania. | 2,825 | 2,088 | 269 | 468 | 46,238 | 33,771 | 5,821 | 6,646 | 1,515 | 1,237 | 1,465 |
| Rhode Island. | 225 | 165 | 17 | 44 | 3,597 | 2,630 | 363 | 604 | 1,493 | 1,213 | 1,458 |
| South Carolina. | 1,143 | 835 | 104 | 205 | 18,073 | 13,117 | 2,017 | 2,939 | 1,476 | 1,255 | 1,379 |
| South Dakota. | 179 | 140 | 17 | 22 | 2,697 | 2,081 | 324 | 292 | 1,396 | 1,147 | 1,335 |
| Tennessee. | 1,453 | 1,020 | 146 | 287 | 22,521 | 15,766 | 2,808 | 3,947 | 1,450 | 1,202 | 1,378 |
| Texas. | 4,224 | 3,084 | 465 | 675 | 64,533 | 46,105 | 9,206 | 9,222 | 1,431 | 1,217 | 1,344 |
| Utah. | 407 | 310 | 40 | 56 | 6,488 | 4,873 | 834 | 781 | 1,501 | 1,235 | 1,508 |
| Vermont. | 150 | 113 | 12 | 26 | 2,360 | 1,771 | 242 | 347 | 1,482 | 1,163 | 1,417 |
| Virginia. | 1,530 | 1,145 | 138 | 247 | 24,705 | 18,317 | 2,862 | 3,526 | 1,507 | 1,246 | 1,412 |
| Washington. | 1,347 | 1,038 | 108 | 201 | 22,170 | 16,838 | 2,402 | 2,930 | 1,536 | 1,255 | 1,495 |
| West Virginia. | 476 | 313 | 59 | 103 | 7,385 | 4,736 | 1,184 | 1,465 | 1,437 | 1,237 | 1,367 |
| Wisconsin. | 1,233 | 943 | 102 | 189 | 19,976 | 15,127 | 2,214 | 2,635 | 1,502 | 1,223 | 1,483 |
| Wyoming. | 112 | 87 | 10 | 15 | 1,810 | 1,370 | 219 | 221 | 1,485 | 1,237 | 1,472 |
| American Samoa. | 6 | 3 | 1 | 2 | 60 | 28 | 15 | 17 | 929 | 909 | 821 |
| Guam. | 18 | 13 | 3 | 2 | 196 | 132 | 38 | 26 | 994 | 1,118 | 936 |
| Northern Mariana Islands. | 3 | 2 | 1 | (Z) | 26 | 16 | 7 | 3 | 753 | 834 | 711 |
| Puerto Rico. | 821 | 539 | 98 | 184 | 8,949 | 5,333 | 1,321 | 2,295 | 969 | 1,093 | 853 |
| U.S. Virgin Islands. | 22 | 18 | 2 | 2 | 302 | 243 | 33 | 26 | 1,269 | 1,260 | 1,112 |
| Abroad. | 672 | 548 | 111 | 13 | 5,692 | 3,995 | 1,526 | 171 | 764 | 1,204 | 806 |

NA Not available. Z Less than 500. [1] Data for 1990-2006 include special benefits for persons age 72 years and over not insured under regular or transitional provisions of Social Security Act. [2] Unnegotiated checks not deducted. [3] Excludes persons with special benefits. [4] Nondisabled only. [5] Includes those with state or area unknown. [6] 2018 data are preliminary.

Source: U.S. Social Security Administration, *Annual Statistical Supplement to the Social Security Bulletin, 2019*, and earlier reports. See also <http://www.ssa.gov/policy/index.html>.

## Table 572. Social Security Trust Funds: 1990 to 2018

[In billions of dollars (286.7 represents $286,700,000,000)]

| Type of trust fund | 1990 | 2000 | 2010 | 2013 | 2014 | 2015 | 2016 | 2017 | 2018 |
|---|---|---|---|---|---|---|---|---|---|
| **OLD-AGE AND SURVIVORS INSURANCE (OASI)** | | | | | | | | | |
| Total income [1] | 286.7 | 490.5 | 677.1 | 743.8 | 769.4 | 801.6 | 797.5 | 825.6 | 831.0 |
| Net payroll tax contributions | 266.1 | 421.4 | 544.8 | 620.8 | 646.2 | 679.5 | 678.8 | 706.5 | 715.9 |
| Taxation of benefits | 4.8 | 11.6 | 22.1 | 20.7 | 28.0 | 30.6 | 31.6 | 35.9 | 34.5 |
| Interest received [2] | 16.4 | 57.5 | 108.2 | 98.1 | 94.8 | 91.2 | 87.0 | 83.2 | 80.7 |
| Total expenditures [1] | 227.5 | 358.3 | 584.9 | 679.5 | 714.2 | 750.5 | 776.4 | 806.7 | 853.5 |
| Benefit payments [3] | 223.0 | 352.7 | 577.4 | 672.1 | 706.8 | 742.9 | 768.6 | 798.7 | 844.9 |
| Assets, end of year | 214.2 | 931.0 | 2,429.0 | 2,674.0 | 2,729.2 | 2,780.3 | 2,801.3 | 2,820.3 | 2,797.9 |
| **DISABILITY INSURANCE (DI)** | | | | | | | | | |
| Total income [1] | 28.8 | 77.9 | 104.0 | 111.2 | 114.9 | 118.6 | 160.0 | 171.0 | 172.3 |
| Net payroll tax contributions | 28.4 | 71.1 | 92.5 | 105.4 | 109.7 | 115.4 | 157.4 | 167.1 | 169.2 |
| Taxation of benefits | 0.1 | 0.7 | 1.9 | 0.4 | 1.7 | 1.1 | 1.2 | 2.0 | 0.5 |
| Interest received [2] | 0.9 | 6.9 | 9.3 | 4.7 | 3.4 | 2.1 | 1.4 | 1.9 | 2.6 |
| Total expenditures [1] | 25.6 | 56.8 | 127.7 | 143.5 | 145.1 | 146.6 | 145.9 | 145.8 | 146.8 |
| Benefit payments [3] | 24.8 | 55.0 | 124.2 | 140.1 | 141.7 | 143.4 | 142.8 | 142.8 | 143.7 |
| Assets, end of year | 11.1 | 118.5 | 179.9 | 90.4 | 60.2 | 32.3 | 46.3 | 71.5 | 97.1 |

[1] Includes other income or expenses not shown separately. [2] Includes relatively small amounts of gifts to the fund. [3] Includes payments for vocational rehabilitation services furnished to disabled persons receiving benefits because of their disabilities. Amounts reflect deductions for unnegotiated benefit checks.

Source: U.S. Social Security Administration, Office of the Chief Actuary, "Statistical Tables," <https://www.ssa.gov/oact/STATS/index.html>, accessed June 2019.

## Table 573. Retirement Employee Benefit Participation by Worker Characteristics: 2010 to 2018

[In percent. Based on National Compensation Survey (NCS). The March 2018 NCS obtained data from approximately 6,588 private industry establishments, representing about 118 million workers; see Appendix III. Defined benefit plans provide retirement benefits based on employer benefit formulas that may take into account salary, years of service, and age. Defined contribution plans provide benefits based on employer and employee contributions to individual employee accounts and the rate of return on money invested; the retirement benefit depends on the account balance at retirement. See source for more information]

| Characteristic | Total [1] | | | | Defined benefit | | | | Defined contribution | | | |
|---|---|---|---|---|---|---|---|---|---|---|---|---|
| | 2010 | 2016 | 2017 | 2018 | 2010 | 2016 | 2017 | 2018 | 2010 | 2016 | 2017 | 2018 |
| **All workers** | **50** | **49** | **50** | **51** | **19** | **15** | **15** | **13** | **41** | **44** | **44** | **47** |
| Management, professional, and related | 68 | 69 | 70 | 72 | 25 | 21 | 20 | 19 | 60 | 63 | 64 | 67 |
| Service | 23 | 23 | 22 | 24 | 7 | 6 | 6 | 5 | 18 | 19 | 19 | 22 |
| Sales and office | 53 | 50 | 51 | 52 | 16 | 11 | 11 | 10 | 46 | 46 | 47 | 49 |
| Natural resources, construction, and maintenance | 51 | 49 | 48 | 47 | 26 | 21 | 21 | 19 | 40 | 41 | 41 | 39 |
| Production, transportation, and material moving | 51 | 53 | 53 | 54 | 24 | 19 | 19 | 17 | 38 | 44 | 44 | 47 |
| Full-time | 59 | 60 | 60 | 61 | 22 | 18 | 18 | 16 | 50 | 54 | 54 | 56 |
| Part-time | 21 | 21 | 21 | 22 | 8 | 5 | 5 | 5 | 15 | 17 | 17 | 18 |
| Union | 82 | 81 | 82 | 82 | 67 | 65 | 66 | 61 | 44 | 44 | 44 | 46 |
| Nonunion | 46 | 46 | 47 | 48 | 13 | 10 | 9 | 8 | 41 | 44 | 45 | 47 |

[1] Total is less than the sum of the individual retirement items because many employees participate in both types of plans.

Source: U.S. Bureau of Labor Statistics, *National Compensation Survey: Employee Benefits in the United States, March 2018*, Bulletin 2789, September 2018, and previous editions. See also <https://www.bls.gov/ncs/ebs/benefits/2018/home.htm>.

## Table 574. Households Owning Individual Retirement Accounts (IRAs): 2000 to 2018

[In percent. Prior to 2014, incidence of individual retirement account (IRA) ownership is based on an annual tracking survey of approximately 4,000 randomly selected, representative U.S. households conducted via landline telephones only. Beginning in 2014, the survey was expanded and is based on a dual frame sample of landline and cell phone numbers, for a total of approximately 5,000 U.S. households. See source for details]

| Year and characteristic | Any type of IRA [1] | Traditional IRA | Roth IRA | Employer-sponsored IRA [2] | Year and characteristic | Any type of IRA [1] | Traditional IRA | Roth IRA | Employer-sponsored IRA [2] |
|---|---|---|---|---|---|---|---|---|---|
| 2000 | 35.7 | 28.7 | 9.2 | 6.8 | 2016 [3] | 33.8 | 25.5 | 17.4 | 5.7 |
| 2005 | 37.9 | 30.0 | 12.8 | 7.4 | 2017 [3] | 34.8 | 27.8 | 19.7 | 6.0 |
| 2009 | 39.3 | 31.2 | 14.5 | 8.2 | | | | | |
| 2010 | 41.4 | 32.8 | 16.6 | 8.0 | **2018, total [3, 4]** | **33.4** | **26.0** | **17.6** | **5.9** |
| 2011 | 38.8 | 31.2 | 15.7 | 7.5 | Under 35 years | 24.0 | 16.0 | 14.0 | 5.0 |
| 2012 | 40.4 | 32.5 | 16.8 | 7.6 | 35 to 44 years | 34.0 | 24.0 | 21.0 | 6.0 |
| 2013 | 37.6 | 29.4 | 15.6 | 7.5 | 45 to 54 years | 38.0 | 30.0 | 24.0 | 7.0 |
| 2014 [3] | 33.7 | 25.3 | 15.6 | 6.0 | 55 to 64 years | 37.0 | 28.0 | 18.0 | 8.0 |
| 2015 [3] | 32.3 | 24.4 | 16.3 | 5.4 | 65 years and over | 35.0 | 31.0 | 14.0 | 5.0 |

[1] Excludes ownership of Coverdell Education Savings Accounts, which were referred to as Education IRAs before July 2001. [2] Employer-sponsored IRAs include SEP IRAs, SARSEP IRAs, and SIMPLE IRAs. [3] Beginning 2014, lower incidence likely results in part from a revised sampling methodology. See source for details. [4] Age is based on the age of the sole or co-decision maker for household saving and investing.

Source: Investment Company Institute, Washington, DC, Holden, Sarah, and Daniel Schrass, "Appendix: The Role of IRAs in US Households' Saving for Retirement, 2018," *ICI Research Perspective* 24, No. 10, December 2018 ©. See also <https://www.ici.org/research/retirement>.

## Table 575. State and Local Government Retirement Systems—Beneficiaries and Finances: 1990 to 2018

[In billions of dollars (111.3 represents $111,300,000,000), except as indicated. For fiscal years closed during the 12 months ending June 30. Minus sign (-) indicates negative earnings on investment. Based on the Annual Survey of Public Pensions]

| Year and level of government | Number of beneficiaries (1,000) | Receipts | | | | | Benefits and withdrawals | | | Cash and security holdings |
|---|---|---|---|---|---|---|---|---|---|---|
| | | Total [1] | Employee contributions | Government contributions | | Earnings on investments | Total [1] | Benefits | Withdrawals | |
| | | | | State | Local | | | | | |
| 1990: All systems.............. | 4,026 | 111.3 | 13.9 | 14.0 | 18.6 | 64.9 | 38.4 | 36.0 | 2.4 | 721 |
| State-administered............ | 3,232 | 89.2 | 11.6 | 14.0 | 11.5 | 52.0 | 29.6 | 27.6 | 2.0 | 575 |
| Locally administered.......... | 794 | 22.2 | 2.2 | (Z) | 7.0 | 12.9 | 8.8 | 8.4 | 0.4 | 145 |
| 2000: All systems.............. | 6,292 | 297.0 | 25.0 | 17.5 | 22.6 | 231.9 | 95.7 | 91.3 | 4.4 | 2,169 |
| State-administered............ | 4,786 | 247.4 | 20.7 | 17.2 | 16.7 | 192.8 | 76.0 | 72.2 | 3.8 | 1,798 |
| Locally administered.......... | 1,506 | 49.7 | 4.3 | 0.4 | 5.9 | 39.1 | 19.8 | 19.1 | 0.7 | 371 |
| 2010: All systems.............. | 8,271 | 125.8 | 39.3 | 36.2 | 50.3 | 347.5 | 216.5 | 200.6 | 4.2 | 2,671 |
| State-administered............ | 7,020 | 98.0 | 33.2 | 35.6 | 29.2 | 291.1 | 176.5 | 163.4 | 3.5 | 2,218 |
| Locally administered.......... | 1,252 | 27.9 | 6.1 | 0.6 | 21.2 | 56.5 | 40.0 | 37.2 | 0.7 | 453 |
| **2018: All systems [2]** | **11,018** | **218.9** | **56.5** | **72.3** | **90.0** | **436.1** | **335.3** | **308.7** | **7.6** | **4,339** |
| State-administered............ | 9,424 | 172.2 | 47.4 | 71.3 | 53.5 | 347.0 | 274.1 | 253.9 | 6.3 | 3,528 |
| Locally administered.......... | 1,594 | 46.6 | 9.1 | 1.0 | 36.5 | 89.1 | 61.1 | 54.8 | 1.3 | 811 |

Z Less than $50 million. [1] May include items not shown separately. [2] Beginning 2015: 1) the universe of local pension systems was enhanced compared to prior survey years, and 2) data for state systems refer to funds rather than entire systems; changes to accounting standards provide actuarial data on a fund basis and not a system basis.

Source: U.S. Census Bureau, through 1995, *Finances of Employee-Retirement Systems of State and Local Governments*, Series GF, No. 2, annual; and, beginning 2000, "Federal, State, and Local Governments—Annual Survey of Public Pensions," <https://www.census.gov/programs-surveys/aspp.html>, accessed July 2019.

## Table 576. Defined Benefit Retirement Plan Participation Among Workers by Plan Status: 2018

[In percent. All workers participating in defined benefit plans = 100 percent. Based on the March 2018 National Compensation Survey; survey drew responses from 6,588 private industry establishments of all sizes, representing about 118 million workers. Excludes farm and private households, the self-employed, Federal government, and establishments with no workers in the survey scope. For more information, see Appendix III, and source <https://www.bls.gov/ncs/ebs/benefits/2018/home.htm>]

| Characteristics | Open plans [1] | Frozen plans [2] | | | Workers in plans frozen over 5 years |
|---|---|---|---|---|---|
| | | No participants accrue benefits [3] | All participants accrue benefits | Some participants accrue benefits | |
| **All workers**.......................... | **61** | **14** | **22** | **3** | **89** |
| OCCUPATION | | | | | |
| Management, professional, and related............................ | 54 | 19 | 23 | 4 | 90 |
| Management, business, and financial............................ | 58 | 21 | 17 | 3 | 93 |
| Professional and related............................ | 51 | 17 | 27 | 5 | 88 |
| Service.................... | 75 | (S) | (S) | (S) | 62 |
| Sales and office.................... | 57 | 17 | 24 | 2 | 93 |
| Sales and related.................... | 58 | 20 | 20 | 2 | 98 |
| Office and administrative support.................... | 56 | 16 | 25 | 3 | 92 |
| Natural resources, construction, and maintenance.............. | 77 | 4 | 17 | 2 | 85 |
| Construction, extraction, farming, fishing, and forestry.......... | 92 | (S) | 4 | (S) | 93 |
| Installation, maintenance, and repair.......... | 58 | 5 | 33 | 3 | 83 |
| Production, transportation, and material moving................. | 61 | 11 | 24 | 4 | 90 |
| Production.......... | 44 | 19 | 34 | 3 | 89 |
| Transportation and material moving.................... | 74 | 5 | 17 | 4 | 92 |
| WORK STATUS | | | | | |
| Full time.................... | 60 | 15 | 22 | 3 | 90 |
| Part time.................... | 69 | (S) | 23 | (S) | 80 |
| UNION STATUS | | | | | |
| Union.................... | 78 | 4 | 17 | 1 | 87 |
| Nonunion.................... | 49 | 21 | 25 | 5 | 89 |
| AVERAGE WAGE PERCENTILE [4] | | | | | |
| Lowest 25 percent.................... | 67 | (S) | 20 | (S) | 78 |
| Lowest 10 percent.................... | 88 | (S) | (S) | (S) | (NA) |
| Second 25 percent.................... | 64 | 14 | 18 | 4 | 90 |
| Third 25 percent.................... | 61 | 14 | 22 | 3 | 87 |
| Highest 25 percent.................... | 59 | 14 | 23 | 3 | 91 |
| Highest 10 percent.................... | 57 | 17 | 22 | 4 | 91 |
| INDUSTRY | | | | | |
| Goods-producing industries............................ | 57 | 14 | 23 | 6 | 90 |
| Manufacturing.................... | 38 | 19 | 34 | 8 | 90 |
| Service-providing industries.................... | 62 | 14 | 21 | 2 | 88 |
| Trade, transportation, and utilities.................... | 70 | 4 | 24 | 2 | 92 |
| Information.................... | 33 | (S) | 49 | (S) | 95 |
| Financial activities.................... | 53 | 28 | 17 | 2 | 92 |
| Professional and business services.................... | 62 | 17 | (S) | (S) | 95 |
| Education and health services.................... | 62 | (S) | 21 | (S) | 73 |

NA Not available. S No workers in this category or data do not meet publication standards. [1] Plans open to new participants. [2] New employees are not allowed in the plan. Benefit accruals may continue for existing participants. [3] Participants in these plans stopped accruing benefits on the date the plan was frozen. The benefit the employee receives is calculated as of the day the plan was frozen. [4] Based on the average wage for the occupation, which may include workers with earnings both above and below the threshold. For values, see "Technical Note" in source.

Source: U.S. Bureau of Labor Statistics, *National Compensation Survey: Employee Benefits in the United States, March 2018*, Bulletin 2789, September 2018. See also <https://www.bls.gov/ncs/ebs/benefits/2018/home.htm>.

# Table 577. Private Pension Plans—Summary by Type of Plan: 2000 to 2016

[In units as indicated (735.7 represents 735,700). Pension plans include defined benefit plans, and defined contribution plans. A defined benefit plan, funded by the employer, promises a specific monthly benefit at retirement, often determined by a formula that includes factors such as salary, age, and job tenure. A defined contribution plan requires the employee to make contributions to an individual account; employers may add contributions to accounts for each employee. The retirement benefit is dependent upon the account balance at retirement, which will reflect contributions, investment gains or losses, and fees charged to the account. Employee Stock Ownership Plans (ESOP) and 401(k) plans are included among defined contribution plans. Data are based on Form 5500 series reports filed with the Department of Labor and exclude (1) selected pension plans qualified under sections 403(b), 457(b) and 457(f) of the Internal Revenue Code, (2) most SARSEP, SEP and SIMPLE IRA plans, (3) unfunded excess benefit plans, (4) selected church plans, (5) unfunded pension plan for select group of management or highly compensated employees, (6) individual retirement accounts (IRAs), and (7) governmental plans]

| Item | Unit | Total | | | | Defined contribution plan | | | | Defined benefit plan | | | |
|---|---|---|---|---|---|---|---|---|---|---|---|---|---|
| | | 2000 | 2005 | 2010 | 2016 | 2000 | 2005 | 2010 | 2016 | 2000 | 2005 | 2010 | 2016 |
| Number of plans [1] | 1,000 | 735.7 | 679.1 | 701.0 | 702.5 | 686.9 | 631.5 | 654.5 | 656.2 | 48.8 | 47.6 | 46.5 | 46.3 |
| Total participants [2] | Million | 103.3 | 117.4 | 129.7 | 136.2 | 61.7 | 75.5 | 88.3 | 100.2 | 41.6 | 41.9 | 41.4 | 36.0 |
| Active participants [3] | Million | 73.1 | 82.7 | 90.6 | 93.9 | 50.9 | 62.4 | 73.4 | 80.0 | 22.2 | 20.3 | 17.2 | 13.9 |
| Assets [4] | Bil. dol. | 4,203 | 5,062 | 6,282 | 8,615 | 2,216 | 2,808 | 3,833 | 5,692 | 1,986 | 2,254 | 2,448 | 2,923 |
| Contributions [5] | Bil. dol. | 231.9 | 341.4 | 445.3 | 584.4 | 198.5 | 248.8 | 314.3 | 459.0 | 33.4 | 92.7 | 131.1 | 125.5 |
| Benefits [6] | Bil. dol. | 341.0 | 354.5 | 456.9 | 687.3 | 213.5 | 218.0 | 287.3 | 454.9 | 127.5 | 136.6 | 169.6 | 232.4 |

[1] Excludes all plans covering only one participant. [2] Includes active, retired, and separated vested participants not yet in pay status. Also includes double counting of workers in more than one plan. [3] Active participants includes individuals who are eligible to elect to have the employer make payments to a 401(k) type plan (even if individuals are not contributing) and nonvested former employees who have not yet incurred a break in service. [4] Asset amounts shown exclude funds held by life insurance companies under allocated group insurance contracts for payment of retirement benefits. [5] Includes both employer and employee contributions. [6] Includes benefits paid directly from trust funds and premium payments made from plans to insurance carriers. Excludes benefits paid directly by insurance carriers.

Source: U.S. Department of Labor, Employee Benefits Security Administration, Retirement Bulletins, *Private Pension Plan Bulletin Historical Tables and Graphs, 1975-2016,* December 2018. See also <https://www.dol.gov/agencies/ebsa/researchers/statistics/retirement-bulletins/private-pension-plan>.

# Table 578. Characteristics of U.S. Households Owning Individual Retirement Accounts (IRAs): 2018

[Data are based on a 2018 mutual fund shareholder tracking survey of 2,251 households conducted via landline telephone and of 2,750 households conducted via cell phone; and a 2018 IRA owners survey of 3,219 U.S. households owning traditional or Roth IRAs, conducted via a self-administered survey online. See source for details and changes in methodology]

| Characteristic | Unit | Households owning IRAs | | | | House-holds not own-ing IRAs |
|---|---|---|---|---|---|---|
| | | Total | Tradi-tional IRA | Roth IRA | Employer-spon-sored [1] | |
| **MEDIAN PER HOUSEHOLD** | | | | | | |
| Age of household sole or co-decision maker for saving & investing | Years | 54 | 55 | 52 | 53 | 51 |
| Household income [2] | Dollars | 93,300 | 92,500 | 112,500 | 100,000 | 45,000 |
| Household financial assets [3] | Dollars | 300,000 | 425,000 | 425,000 | 375,000 | 33,000 |
| Household financial assets in traditional or Roth IRAs | Dollars | 65,000 | 87,500 | 75,000 | (NA) | (X) |
| Share of household financial assets in type of IRA indicated | Percent | 34 | 31 | 14 | (NA) | (X) |
| **PERCENT OF HOUSEHOLDS** | | | | | | |
| Household has defined contribution account or defined benefit plan coverage (total) [4] | Percent | 82 | 82 | 86 | 90 | 43 |
| Defined contribution retirement plan account | Percent | 74 | 72 | 79 | 83 | 34 |
| Defined benefit plan coverage | Percent | 38 | 45 | 43 | 38 | 21 |
| Types of IRAs owned: [4] | | | | | | |
| Traditional IRA | Percent | 78 | 100 | 66 | 66 | (X) |
| Roth IRA | Percent | 53 | 44 | 100 | 53 | (X) |
| Employer-sponsored IRA [1] | Percent | 18 | 15 | 18 | 100 | (X) |

X Not applicable. NA Not available. [1] Employer-sponsored IRAs include SEP IRAs, SAR-SEP IRAs, and SIMPLE IRAs. [2] Total reported is household income before taxes in 2017. [3] Household financial assets include assets in employer-sponsored retirement plans but exclude the household's primary residence. [4] Multiple responses are included.

Source: Investment Company Institute, Washington, DC. Holden, Sarah, and Daniel Schrass, "Appendix: The Role of IRAs in US Households' Saving for Retirement, 2018," *ICI Research Perspective* 24, No. 10, December 2018 ©. See also <https://www.ici.org/pubs/research>.

## Table 579. Households with Assets in Individual Retirement Accounts (IRAs) by Type of IRA: 2017 and 2018

[Shown as percent of households with assets in IRAs, by household asset size group. Data are based on an annual survey of approximately 3,200 U.S. households owning traditional IRAs and Roth IRAs, conducted via a self-administered survey online. The IRA Owners Survey excludes households owning only employer-sponsored IRAs (SEP, SAR-SEP, and SIMPLE IRAs) or Coverdell Education Savings Accounts (education IRAs). See source for details]

| Size of assets | Unit | 2017 | | | 2018 | | |
| | | Total assets in IRAs | Type of IRA owned | | Total assets in IRAs | Type of IRA owned | |
| | | | Traditional IRAs | Roth IRAs | | Traditional IRAs | Roth IRAs |
|---|---|---|---|---|---|---|---|
| PERCENT DISTRIBUTION OF HOUSEHOLDS | | | | | | | |
| Less than $10,000............................. | Percent | 15 | 16 | 26 | 17 | 16 | 27 |
| $10,000 to $24,999............................. | Percent | 14 | 15 | 19 | 14 | 15 | 21 |
| $25,000 to $49,999............................. | Percent | 13 | 13 | 19 | 13 | 12 | 15 |
| $50,000 to $99,999............................. | Percent | 16 | 18 | 18 | 13 | 15 | 14 |
| $100,000 to $249,999......................... | Percent | 19 | 18 | 14 | 18 | 19 | 15 |
| $250,000 or more.............................. | Percent | 23 | 20 | 4 | 25 | 23 | 8 |
| TOTAL ASSETS IN IRAs | | | | | | | |
| Mean............................................. | Dollars | 177,600 | 160,600 | 63,800 | 191,200 | 178,600 | 77,400 |
| Median........................................... | Dollars | 62,500 | 60,000 | 30,000 | 65,000 | 62,500 | 25,000 |

Source: Investment Company Institute, Washington, DC. Holden, Sarah, and Daniel Schrass, "Appendix: The Role of IRAs in US Households' Saving for Retirement, 2018," *ICI Research Perspective,* 24, No. 10, December 2018 ©. See also <https://www.ici.org/pubs/research>.

## Table 580. Defined Contribution 401(k) Type Plans, Active Participants, Assets, Contributions, Benefits, and Return Rates: 1990 to 2016

[Participants in thousands (19,466 represents 19,466,000); values in millions of dollars (384,854 represents $384,854,000,000). Excludes "one-participant plans." Based on Form 5500 filings with Department of Labor. See source for methodology]

| Year | Number of 401(k) type plans | Active participants (1,000) [1] | Total assets (mil. dol.) [2] | Total contributions (mil. dol.) [3] | Total benefits (mil. dol.) [4] | Investment rates of return [5] |
|---|---|---|---|---|---|---|
| 1990................ | 97,614 | 19,466 | 384,854 | 48,998 | 32,028 | (NA) |
| 2000................ | 348,053 | 39,847 | 1,724,549 | 169,238 | 172,211 | -3.8 |
| 2005................ | 436,207 | 54,623 | 2,395,792 | 223,533 | 189,822 | 6.3 |
| 2006................ | 465,653 | 58,351 | 2,768,242 | 251,233 | 229,217 | 12.4 |
| 2007................ | 490,917 | 59,566 | 2,981,522 | 273,235 | 262,108 | 7.6 |
| 2008................ | 511,583 | 59,976 | 2,230,188 | 285,773 | 233,452 | -24.9 |
| 2009................ | 512,464 | 60,285 | 2,734,064 | 258,357 | 208,467 | 18.8 |
| 2010................ | 518,675 | 60,510 | 3,142,141 | 267,584 | 245,474 | 12.0 |
| 2011................ | 513,496 | 61,371 | 3,146,851 | 285,679 | 252,692 | 0.1 |
| 2012................ | 516,293 | 63,088 | 3,530,122 | 306,092 | 284,677 | 11.2 |
| 2013................ | 527,047 | 64,495 | 4,179,351 | 327,886 | 328,680 | 18.3 |
| 2014................ | 533,769 | 62,651 | 4,399,891 | 349,216 | 365,657 | 6.7 |
| 2015................ | 546,896 | 65,307 | 4,382,033 | 377,743 | 385,907 | 0.1 |
| 2016................ | 560,373 | 67,121 | 4,738,481 | 398,920 | 391,540 | 7.6 |

NA Not available. [1] Since 2005, includes individuals who are merely eligible to elect to have the employer make payments to a 401(k) type plan, and nonvested former employees who have not yet incurred a break in service. Prior to 2005, active participants were adjusted to exclude individuals who were not contributing to the retirement plan and not entitled to receive benefits. Between 2009 and 2013, all participants reported on the Form 5500-SF were assumed to be active. Since 2014, active participants are separately reported on the Form 5500-SF. [2] Excludes funds held by life insurance companies under allocated group insurance contracts for payment of retirement benefits. [3] Includes both employer and employee contributions. [4] Includes both benefits paid directly from trust funds and premium payments made by plans to insurance carriers. Amounts exclude benefits paid directly by insurance carriers. [5] For plans with 100 or more participants.

Source: U.S. Department of Labor, Employee Benefits Security Administration, Retirement Bulletins, *Private Pension Plan Bulletin Historical Tables and Graphs, 1975-2016,* December 2018. See also <https://www.dol.gov/agencies/ebsa/researchers/statistics/retirement-bulletins/private-pension-plan>.

# Table 581. State Unemployment Insurance—Summary: 2000 to 2017

[In units as indicated (2,110 represents 2,110,000). Includes unemployment compensation for state and local government employees where covered by state law]

| Item | Unit | 2000 | 2005 | 2010 | 2012 | 2013 | 2014 | 2015 | 2016 | 2017 |
|---|---|---|---|---|---|---|---|---|---|---|
| Insured unemployment, average weekly......... | 1,000 | 2,110 | 2,661 | 4,487 | 3,297 | 2,947 | 2,574 | 2,237 | 2,099 | 1,948 |
| Percent of covered employment [1]............... | Percent | 1.7 | 2.1 | 3.6 | 2.5 | 2.2 | 1.9 | 1.6 | 1.5 | 1.4 |
| Percent of civilian unemployed................. | Percent | 37.1 | 35.1 | 30.3 | 26.4 | 25.7 | 26.8 | 27.0 | 27.1 | 27.9 |
| Unemployment benefits, average weekly........ | Dollars | 221 | 267 | 299 | 303 | 309 | 315 | 329 | 344 | 351 |
| Percent of weekly wage......................... | Percent | 32.9 | 34.6 | 33.7 | 32.2 | 32.6 | 32.2 | 32.6 | 33.7 | 33.3 |
| Weeks compensated.............................. | Million | 96.0 | 121.2 | 203.1 | 147.6 | 132.2 | 115.1 | 100.7 | 94.8 | 87.6 |
| Beneficiaries, first payments.................... | 1,000 | 7,033 | 7,917 | 10,727 | 8,656 | 7,819 | 7,043 | 6,506 | 6,097 | 5,696 |
| Average duration of benefits [2].................. | Weeks | 13.7 | 15.3 | 18.9 | 17.1 | 16.9 | 16.3 | 15.5 | 15.5 | 15.4 |
| Claimants exhausting benefits.................... | 1,000 | 2,144 | 2,856 | 6,365 | 4,228 | 3,689 | 3,029 | 2,510 | 2,324 | 2,120 |
| Exhaustion rate (percent of first payments) [3]... | Percent | 31.8 | 35.9 | 53.4 | 47.2 | 44.6 | 40.3 | 37.6 | 36.7 | 36.4 |
| Contributions collected [4]......................... | Bil. dol. | 19.9 | 34.8 | 35.9 | 50.4 | 47.2 | 43.9 | 41.8 | 38.9 | 36.9 |
| Benefits paid.................................... | Bil. dol. | 19.4 | 29.3 | 53.9 | 39.4 | 36.3 | 32.4 | 29.8 | 29.5 | 27.8 |
| Unemployment trust fund reserves [5]............. | Bil. dol. | 54.1 | 29.0 | 9.5 | 16.7 | 23.0 | 30.4 | 38.8 | 47.0 | 55.2 |
| Average employer tax rate [6]...................... | Percent | 1.8 | 2.9 | 3.0 | 3.5 | 3.3 | 2.9 | 2.7 | 2.4 | 2.2 |

[1] Insured unemployment as percent of average covered employment. [2] Weeks compensated during the year divided by the number of first payments. May include more than one period of continuous unemployment. [3] Percent of claimants who started receiving unemployment insurance benefits who also received the maximum benefits they were entitled to before the end of their benefit year. Based on first payments for 12-month period ending June 30. [4] Contributions collected through unemployment taxes paid by employers and by employees in states that tax workers. [5] Reserves as of December 31 are the funds on deposit in a State's account, as reported by the U.S. Treasury. Trust fund balances are the major portion of reserves. The reserves for all States have been adjusted to contain amounts loaned or advanced from the Federal Unemployment Account. These advances, which can be used only for the payment of unemployment benefits, must be repaid. [6] As percent of taxable wages.

Source: U.S. Department of Labor, Employment and Training Administration, Unemployment Insurance Data, "Benefits and Claims: Annual Program and Financial Data (Handbook 394)," <https://ows.doleta.gov/unemploy/DataDashboard.asp>, accessed March 2019.

# Table 582. State Unemployment Insurance by State and Island Area: 2017

[In units, as indicated (5,696 represents 5,696,000). See headnote, Table 581. For state data on insured unemployment, see Table 656]

| State and Island Areas | Beneficiaries, first payments (1,000) | Benefits paid (mil. dol.) | Avg. weekly unemployment benefits (dol.) | Average duration of benefits (weeks) | State and Island Areas | Beneficiaries, first payments (1,000) | Benefits paid (mil. dol.) | Avg. weekly unemployment benefits (dol.) | Average duration of benefits (weeks) |
|---|---|---|---|---|---|---|---|---|---|
| Total [1]..... | 5,696 | 27,846 | 351 | 15.4 | MT........... | 22 | 98 | 340 | 15.7 |
| AL.......... | 54 | 158 | 221 | 13.7 | NE........... | 18 | 73 | 328 | 12.2 |
| AK.......... | 24 | 100 | 274 | 18.2 | NV........... | 63 | 294 | 339 | 14.8 |
| AZ.......... | 70 | 242 | 228 | 15.5 | NH........... | 13 | 53 | 327 | 12.6 |
| AR.......... | 42 | 120 | 267 | 12.1 | NJ........... | 261 | 1,877 | 440 | 18.4 |
| CA.......... | 942 | 5,101 | 324 | 17.8 | NM........... | 27 | 136 | 330 | 17.9 |
| CO.......... | 73 | 425 | 421 | 14.6 | NY........... | 415 | 2,054 | 339 | 16.9 |
| CT.......... | 110 | 625 | 302 | 17.2 | NC........... | 83 | 179 | 257 | 9.3 |
| DE.......... | 16 | 64 | 261 | 17.6 | ND........... | 19 | 119 | 482 | 13.4 |
| DC.......... | 21 | 115 | 347 | 18.2 | OH........... | 175 | 852 | 363 | 14.6 |
| FL.......... | 173 | 381 | 246 | 9.2 | OK........... | 41 | 231 | 363 | 17.2 |
| GA.......... | 139 | 309 | 288 | 8.4 | OR........... | 84 | 481 | 383 | 15.0 |
| HI.......... | 23 | 160 | 495 | 15.6 | PA........... | 337 | 1,744 | 382 | 15.8 |
| ID.......... | 29 | 90 | 318 | 11.0 | RI........... | 29 | 120 | 355 | 15.2 |
| IL.......... | 291 | 1,712 | 376 | 17.3 | SC........... | 58 | 163 | 257 | 11.8 |
| IN.......... | 74 | 258 | 282 | 13.2 | SD........... | 6 | 29 | 326 | 14.4 |
| IA.......... | 79 | 398 | 392 | 13.4 | TN........... | 67 | 215 | 237 | 13.1 |
| KS.......... | 43 | 130 | 381 | 11.2 | TX........... | 432 | 2,272 | 399 | 15.2 |
| KY.......... | 48 | 274 | 326 | 18.7 | UT........... | 32 | 146 | 392 | 12.6 |
| LA.......... | 48 | 205 | 213 | 16.9 | VT........... | 15 | 61 | 355 | 13.4 |
| ME.......... | 21 | 84 | 324 | 13.3 | VA........... | 72 | 320 | 309 | 15.5 |
| MD.......... | 81 | 466 | 340 | 19.0 | WA........... | 147 | 926 | 495 | 15.0 |
| MA.......... | 177 | 1,367 | 507 | 17.2 | WV........... | 36 | 141 | 285 | 15.1 |
| MI.......... | 224 | 802 | 308 | 12.0 | WI........... | 115 | 400 | 317 | 13.0 |
| MN.......... | 111 | 697 | 446 | 16.5 | WY........... | 11 | 60 | 382 | 15.6 |
| MS.......... | 28 | 76 | 206 | 14.1 | PR........... | 81 | 145 | 118 | 15.3 |
| MO.......... | 93 | 288 | 261 | 12.1 | VI........... | 4 | 12 | 307 | 11.9 |

[1] Includes all States, District of Columbia, Puerto Rico, and Virgin Islands.

Source: U.S. Department of Labor, Employment and Training Administration, Unemployment Insurance Data, "Benefits and Claims: Annual Program and Financial Data (Handbook 394)," <https://ows.doleta.gov/unemploy/DataDashboard.asp>, accessed March 2019.

# Table 583. Workers' Compensation Costs and Payments: 2000 to 2016

[In units as indicated (127.1 represents 127,100,000). See headnote, Table 584]

| Item | 2000 | 2005 | 2009 | 2010 | 2011 | 2012 | 2013 | 2014 | 2015 | 2016 |
|---|---|---|---|---|---|---|---|---|---|---|
| Workers covered (mil.)................ | 127.1 | 128.2 | 124.9 | 124.6 | 125.9 | 128.1 | 130.4 | 132.9 | 135.9 | 138.3 |
| Covered wages (bil. dol.)............... | 4,495 | 5,213 | 5,675 | 5,834 | 6,058 | 6,326 | 6,501 | 6,831 | 7,198 | 7,422 |
| **Employer costs [1] (bil. dol.)**............ | **60.7** | **89.8** | **73.9** | **72.8** | **78.9** | **84.7** | **88.8** | **93.0** | **95.5** | **96.5** |
| Private carriers [1]................... | 36.0 | 51.0 | 43.0 | 42.8 | 46.6 | 51.3 | 54.7 | 56.9 | 58.9 | 59.9 |
| State funds...................... | 8.9 | 18.2 | 10.6 | 9.6 | 10.4 | 11.0 | 12.1 | 13.3 | 13.3 | 13.0 |
| Federal programs [2]............... | 3.6 | 4.1 | 4.1 | 4.2 | 4.4 | 4.5 | 4.6 | 4.9 | 5.4 | 5.7 |
| Self-insured employers................ | 12.1 | 16.5 | 16.3 | 16.2 | 17.5 | 17.9 | 17.5 | 17.9 | 17.9 | 18.0 |
| **Benefits paid [3] (bil. dol.)**........... | **47.7** | **57.1** | **58.4** | **58.5** | **61.4** | **62.6** | **63.2** | **62.9** | **62.0** | **61.9** |
| By private carriers................. | 26.9 | 29.0 | 30.9 | 31.1 | 33.0 | 33.9 | 35.0 | 34.8 | 34.3 | 34.4 |
| From state funds.................. | 7.4 | 11.1 | 10.0 | 9.8 | 9.8 | 10.0 | 9.6 | 9.3 | 9.1 | 8.9 |
| Federal programs [2]............... | 3.0 | 3.3 | 3.5 | 3.7 | 3.8 | 3.8 | 3.7 | 3.7 | 3.7 | 3.6 |
| Self-insured employers............... | 10.5 | 13.7 | 14.0 | 13.9 | 14.8 | 15.0 | 15.0 | 15.1 | 15.0 | 15.0 |
| Type of benefit: | | | | | | | | | | |
| Medical......................... | 20.9 | 26.4 | 28.2 | 28.7 | 30.8 | 31.3 | 32.0 | 32.0 | 31.2 | 31.1 |
| Cash............................ | 26.8 | 30.7 | 30.3 | 29.8 | 30.6 | 31.4 | 31.3 | 30.9 | 30.8 | 30.8 |
| Per $100 of covered wages: (dol.) | | | | | | | | | | |
| Employer costs.................. | 1.35 | 1.72 | 1.30 | 1.25 | 1.30 | 1.34 | 1.37 | 1.36 | 1.33 | 1.30 |
| Benefits paid.................... | 1.06 | 1.09 | 1.03 | 1.00 | 1.01 | 0.99 | 0.97 | 0.92 | 0.86 | 0.83 |

[1] Costs are employer expenditures in the calendar year for workers' compensation benefits, administrative costs, and/or insurance premiums; for private carriers, includes benefit payments made under deductible provisions. [2] Federal costs and benefits include costs to the federal government and benefits paid, under the Federal Employees' Compensation Act, and costs associated with and benefits paid via the Federal Black Lung Disability Trust Fund. Beginning 1997, data also account for the Longshore and Harbor Workers' Compensation Act. [3] Benefits are payments in the calendar year to injured workers and to providers of their medical care, including benefits paid by employers under deductible provisions in their workers' compensation insurance.

Source: National Academy of Social Insurance, Washington, DC, *Workers' Compensation: Benefits, Costs, and Coverage, 2016,* October 2018, and earlier reports ©. See also <http://www.nasi.org>.

# Table 584. Workers' Compensation Payments by State: 2000 to 2016

[In millions of dollars (47,699 represents $47,699,000,000). Calendar-year data. Workers' compensation provides medical care, rehabilitation, and cash benefits for workers who are injured on the job or who contract work-related illnesses. It also pays benefits to families of workers who die of work-related causes. Workers' compensation benefits are paid by private insurance carriers, by state or federal workers' compensation funds, or by self-insured employers. See source for data estimation methodology]

| State | 2000 | 2010 | 2014 | 2015 | 2016 | State | 2000 | 2010 | 2014 | 2015 | 2016 |
|---|---|---|---|---|---|---|---|---|---|---|---|
| **Total...............** | **47,699** | **58,939** | **62,866** | **62,018** | **61,918** | Missouri.................. | 780 | 801 | 917 | 983 | 1,016 |
| | | | | | | Montana................. | 155 | 266 | 246 | 253 | 261 |
| Alabama............... | 529 | 629 | 637 | 617 | 601 | Nebraska............... | 230 | 316 | 318 | 301 | 314 |
| Alaska................. | 139 | 222 | 232 | 235 | 228 | Nevada................. | 347 | 430 | 353 | 340 | 354 |
| Arizona................ | 498 | 702 | 735 | 737 | 752 | New Hampshire......... | 177 | 252 | 213 | 214 | 206 |
| Arkansas.............. | 214 | 214 | 210 | 199 | 207 | New Jersey............ | 1,378 | 2,067 | 2,335 | 2,346 | 2,357 |
| California............. | 9,449 | 10,099 | 12,093 | 12,038 | 12,139 | New Mexico........... | 144 | 276 | 299 | 303 | 288 |
| Colorado.............. | 810 | 800 | 789 | 831 | 801 | New York............. | 2,761 | 4,617 | 5,640 | 5,772 | 5,964 |
| Connecticut........... | 638 | 795 | 989 | 982 | 897 | North Carolina........ | 865 | 1,357 | 1,278 | 1,216 | 1,203 |
| Delaware.............. | 118 | 212 | 249 | 228 | 225 | North Dakota.......... | 70 | 120 | 192 | 180 | 166 |
| District of Columbia..... | 78 | 105 | 118 | 120 | 120 | Ohio.................. | 2,099 | 2,209 | 2,089 | 1,978 | 1,866 |
| Florida................ | 2,577 | 2,777 | 3,371 | 3,188 | 3,175 | Oklahoma............. | 485 | 843 | 760 | 708 | 618 |
| Georgia............... | 965 | 1,459 | 1,378 | 1,313 | 1,375 | Oregon............... | 425 | 681 | 656 | 632 | 633 |
| Hawaii................ | 231 | 242 | 271 | 298 | 306 | Pennsylvania......... | 2,379 | 2,935 | 2,998 | 2,975 | 3,119 |
| Idaho................. | 114 | 240 | 254 | 263 | 268 | Rhode Island......... | 127 | 160 | 165 | 162 | 157 |
| Illinois................ | 1,944 | 3,003 | 2,723 | 2,399 | 2,354 | South Carolina........ | 515 | 891 | 896 | 890 | 903 |
| Indiana............... | 545 | 599 | 590 | 566 | 576 | South Dakota......... | 63 | 100 | 97 | 105 | 103 |
| Iowa.................. | 343 | 564 | 641 | 617 | 664 | Tennessee............ | 774 | 781 | 670 | 659 | 622 |
| Kansas............... | 323 | 405 | 433 | 424 | 421 | Texas................ | 2,160 | 1,491 | 1,499 | 1,536 | 1,468 |
| Kentucky.............. | 584 | 663 | 644 | 684 | 653 | Utah................. | 172 | 275 | 259 | 269 | 275 |
| Louisiana............. | 547 | 802 | 784 | 774 | 795 | Vermont.............. | 101 | 137 | 151 | 150 | 140 |
| Maine................. | 245 | 252 | 252 | 232 | 241 | Virginia.............. | 597 | 786 | 920 | 923 | 951 |
| Maryland.............. | 641 | 954 | 980 | 965 | 908 | Washington........... | 1,527 | 2,309 | 2,393 | 2,404 | 2,431 |
| Massachusetts......... | 801 | 1,016 | 1,127 | 1,097 | 1,145 | West Virginia......... | 661 | 543 | 420 | 414 | 414 |
| Michigan.............. | 1,474 | 1,272 | 1,109 | 1,078 | 955 | Wisconsin............ | 765 | 1,072 | 1,204 | 1,170 | 1,171 |
| Minnesota............. | 798 | 1,035 | 1,087 | 1,033 | 1,029 | Wyoming............. | 89 | 154 | 184 | 178 | 175 |
| Mississippi............ | 293 | 338 | 337 | 332 | 306 | **Federal, total [1]**........ | **2,957** | **3,672** | **3,681** | **3,706** | **3,603** |

[1] Federal benefits include: those paid under the Federal Employees' Compensation Act for civilian employees; the portion of the black lung benefit program that is financed by employers; and a portion of benefits under the Longshore and Harbor Workers' Compensation Act (LHWCA) that are not reflected in state data, namely, benefits paid by self-insured employers and by special funds under the LHWCA. See Appendix B in source for more information about federal programs.

Source: National Academy of Social Insurance, Washington, DC, *Workers' Compensation: Benefits, Costs, and Coverage, 2016*, October 2018, and earlier reports ©. See also <http://www.nasi.org>.

**Table 585. Supplemental Security Income—Recipients and Payments: 1990 to 2017**

[In units as indicated (4,817 represents 4,817,000). Recipients and monthly payment as of December. Payments are federally administered, for the calendar year. Includes persons with a federal SSI payment and/or state supplementation]

| Program | Unit | 1990 | 2000 | 2005 | 2010 | 2013 | 2014 | 2015 | 2016 | 2017 |
|---|---|---|---|---|---|---|---|---|---|---|
| **Recipients, total**............... | **1,000** | **4,817** | **6,602** | **7,114** | **7,912** | **8,363** | **8,336** | **8,310** | **8,251** | **8,228** |
| Aged................................ | 1,000 | 1,454 | 1,289 | 1,214 | 1,184 | 1,157 | 1,152 | 1,157 | 1,165 | 1,176 |
| Blind................................ | 1,000 | 84 | 79 | 75 | 69 | 68 | 67 | 68 | 68 | 69 |
| Disabled.......................... | 1,000 | 3,279 | 5,234 | 5,825 | 6,659 | 7,139 | 7,116 | 7,084 | 7,018 | 6,982 |
| **Payments, total** [1]............. | **Mil. dol.** | **16,133** | **30,672** | **37,236** | **48,195** | **53,900** | **54,693** | **54,966** | **54,799** | **54,516** |
| Aged................................ | Mil. dol. | 3,559 | 4,540 | 4,965 | 5,454 | 5,592 | 5,688 | 5,729 | 5,797 | 5,838 |
| Blind................................ | Mil. dol. | 329 | 386 | 414 | 423 | 432 | 440 | 448 | 455 | 458 |
| Disabled.......................... | Mil. dol. | 12,245 | 25,746 | 31,857 | 42,317 | 47,875 | 48,565 | 48,788 | 48,547 | 48,220 |
| **Average monthly payment, total**............... | **Dollars** | **276** | **379** | **439** | **501** | **529** | **532** | **541** | **542** | **542** |
| Aged................................ | Dollars | 208 | 300 | 360 | 400 | 417 | 420 | 428 | 429 | 429 |
| Blind................................ | Dollars | 319 | 413 | 475 | 522 | 542 | 548 | 558 | 560 | 560 |
| Disabled.......................... | Dollars | 303 | 398 | 455 | 518 | 547 | 550 | 560 | 561 | 561 |

[1] Totals for Aged, Blind, and Disabled are derived. The derivation creates slight discrepancies between the sum of the group totals and total payments.

Source: U.S. Social Security Administration, *Annual Statistical Supplement to the Social Security Bulletin, 2018,* <https://www.ssa.gov/policy/docs/statcomps/supplement/2018/index.html>, accessed April 2019.

**Table 586. Supplemental Security Income (SSI)—Recipients and Payments by State and Other Area: 2010 to 2017**

[In units as indicated (7,912 represents 7,912,000). Recipients as of December; payments for calendar year. Data cover federal SSI payments and/or federally administered state supplementation]

| State and other area | Recipients (1,000) 2010 | Recipients (1,000) 2017 | Payments for the year (mil. dol.) 2010 | Payments for the year (mil. dol.) 2016 | Payments for the year (mil. dol.) 2017 | State and other area | Recipients (1,000) 2010 | Recipients (1,000) 2017 | Payments for the year (mil. dol.) 2010 | Payments for the year (mil. dol.) 2016 | Payments for the year (mil. dol.) 2017 |
|---|---|---|---|---|---|---|---|---|---|---|---|
| **Total** [1].... | **7,912** | **8,228** | **48,195** | **54,799** | **54,516** | MO......... | 134 | 138 | 785 | 886 | 875 |
| **U.S.**...... | **7,911** | **8,227** | **48,189** | **54,792** | **54,509** | MT......... | 18 | 18 | 98 | 112 | 110 |
| AL.......... | 172 | 165 | 996 | 1,066 | 1,049 | NE......... | 26 | 28 | 144 | 174 | 175 |
| AK......... | 12 | 13 | 70 | 77 | 78 | NV......... | 41 | 56 | 241 | 368 | 374 |
| AZ.......... | 110 | 119 | 644 | 782 | 781 | NH......... | 18 | 19 | 103 | 121 | 120 |
| AR......... | 107 | 108 | 603 | 699 | 695 | NJ......... | 169 | 182 | 1,001 | 1,169 | 1,158 |
| CA......... | 1,269 | 1,263 | 8,870 | 9,525 | 9,442 | NM......... | 60 | 64 | 340 | 403 | 402 |
| CO......... | 66 | 73 | 377 | 466 | 470 | NY......... | 681 | 638 | 4,445 | 4,167 | 4,123 |
| CT......... | 58 | 66 | 340 | 423 | 429 | NC......... | 219 | 232 | 1,243 | 1,496 | 1,497 |
| DE......... | 16 | 17 | 91 | 110 | 111 | ND......... | 8 | 8 | 43 | 48 | 50 |
| DC......... | 24 | 27 | 153 | 190 | 187 | OH......... | 286 | 310 | 1,784 | 2,089 | 2,072 |
| FL.......... | 484 | 579 | 2,760 | 3,676 | 3,688 | OK......... | 94 | 97 | 541 | 625 | 624 |
| GA......... | 228 | 260 | 1,317 | 1,687 | 1,692 | OR......... | 75 | 89 | 439 | 569 | 580 |
| HI.......... | 25 | 24 | 157 | 166 | 162 | PA......... | 358 | 361 | 2,229 | 2,484 | 2,459 |
| ID.......... | 27 | 31 | 155 | 196 | 196 | RI......... | 33 | 33 | 201 | 213 | 213 |
| IL.......... | 273 | 271 | 1,662 | 1,821 | 1,805 | SC......... | 112 | 117 | 635 | 745 | 743 |
| IN.......... | 118 | 128 | 716 | 866 | 863 | SD......... | 14 | 15 | 75 | 90 | 91 |
| IA.......... | 48 | 51 | 266 | 318 | 317 | TN......... | 175 | 179 | 1,023 | 1,176 | 1,164 |
| KS......... | 46 | 48 | 269 | 308 | 309 | TX......... | 617 | 658 | 3,316 | 4,064 | 4,026 |
| KY......... | 192 | 178 | 1,116 | 1,151 | 1,128 | UT......... | 28 | 32 | 160 | 205 | 207 |
| LA......... | 175 | 177 | 989 | 1,143 | 1,136 | VT......... | 15 | 15 | 87 | 99 | 98 |
| ME......... | 35 | 37 | 196 | 233 | 233 | VA......... | 148 | 158 | 832 | 1,000 | 1,007 |
| MD......... | 107 | 122 | 658 | 826 | 840 | WA......... | 137 | 150 | 881 | 1,022 | 1,016 |
| MA......... | 193 | 186 | 1,211 | 1,192 | 1,186 | WV......... | 80 | 74 | 472 | 483 | 478 |
| MI.......... | 254 | 275 | 1,581 | 1,868 | 1,861 | WI......... | 107 | 118 | 625 | 772 | 779 |
| MN......... | 86 | 94 | 516 | 625 | 623 | WY......... | 6 | 7 | 35 | 41 | 41 |
| MS......... | 126 | 120 | 699 | 756 | 746 | MP [2]...... | 1 | 1 | 6 | 7 | 7 |

[1] Includes Northern Mariana Islands and recipients whose residence was "unknown." Total may not equal sum due to rounding. [2] Northern Marianas.

Source: U.S. Social Security Administration, *Annual Statistical Supplement to the Social Security Bulletin, 2018,* <https://www.ssa.gov/policy/docs/statcomps/supplement/2018/index.html>, accessed April 2019, and previous editions. See also <https://www.ssa.gov/policy/>.

## Table 587. Temporary Assistance for Needy Families (TANF)—Families and Recipients: 1980 to 2018

[In thousands (3,712 represents 3,712,000). Average monthly families and recipients for calendar year. Prior to TANF, the cash assistance program to families was called Aid to Families with Dependent Children (1980–1996). Under the Personal Responsibility and Work Opportunity Reconciliation Act of 1996, the program became TANF. See text, this section. Includes Puerto Rico, Guam, and Virgin Islands]

| Year | Families | Recipients | Year | Families | Recipients | Year | Families | Recipients |
|---|---|---|---|---|---|---|---|---|
| 1980 | 3,712 | 10,774 | 2003 | 2,024 | 4,929 | 2011 | 1,846 | 4,363 |
| 1990 | 4,057 | 11,695 | 2004 | 1,979 | 4,748 | 2012 | 1,723 | 4,017 |
| 1997 | 3,740 | 10,376 | 2005 | 1,894 | 4,469 | 2013 | 1,612 | 3,713 |
| 1998 | 3,050 | 8,347 | 2006 | 1,777 | 4,148 | 2014 | 1,476 | 3,407 |
| 1999 | 2,554 | 6,824 | 2007 | 1,674 | 3,897 | 2015 | 1,300 | 3,010 |
| 2000 | 2,215 | 5,778 | 2008 | 1,633 | 3,795 | 2016 | 1,174 | 2,678 |
| 2001 | 2,104 | 5,359 | 2009 | 1,769 | 4,154 | 2017 | 1,075 | 2,486 |
| 2002 | 2,048 | 5,069 | 2010 | 1,858 | 4,403 | 2018 | 984 | 2,197 |

Source: U.S. Department of Health and Human Services, Administration for Children and Families, "Temporary Assistance for Needy Families, Caseload Data," <http://www.acf.hhs.gov/programs/ofa/programs/tanf>, accessed April 2019.

## Table 588. Temporary Assistance for Needy Families (TANF)—Recipients by State and Island Area: 2010 to 2018

[In thousands (1,858.2 represents 1,858,200). Average monthly families and recipients for calendar year. See headnote, Table 587]

| State and Island Area | Families | | | Recipients | | | State and Island Area | Families | | | Recipients | | |
|---|---|---|---|---|---|---|---|---|---|---|---|---|---|
| | 2010 | 2017 | 2018 | 2010 | 2017 | 2018 | | 2010 | 2017 | 2018 | 2010 | 2017 | 2018 |
| Total [1] | 1,858.2 | 1,075.2 | 983.8 | 4,402.9 | 2,485.8 | 2,197.5 | MT | 3.7 | 4.3 | 3.9 | 9.4 | 10.9 | 9.7 |
| U.S. | 1,842.9 | 1,067.3 | 977.5 | 4,361.3 | 2,464.5 | 2,180.6 | NE | 7.6 | 4.5 | 4.2 | 18.3 | 10.6 | 10.0 |
| AL | 22.0 | 9.4 | 8.2 | 53.5 | 21.4 | 18.4 | NV | 10.5 | 9.5 | 9.3 | 27.1 | 24.3 | 23.6 |
| AK | 3.4 | 3.1 | 2.7 | 9.3 | 8.5 | 7.2 | NH | 5.3 | 2.6 | 3.3 | 11.0 | 5.1 | 6.8 |
| AZ | 27.7 | 8.4 | 7.3 | 60.3 | 17.6 | 14.9 | NJ | 33.9 | 13.2 | 10.9 | 80.7 | 29.9 | 24.8 |
| AR | 8.5 | 3.2 | 2.9 | 19.3 | 7.0 | 6.2 | NM | 20.3 | 10.9 | 10.4 | 53.5 | 27.5 | 25.9 |
| CA | 583.9 | 350.7 | 316.6 | 1,437.4 | 857.7 | 767.1 | NY | 121.8 | 97.3 | 89.8 | 272.3 | 220.5 | 203.0 |
| CO | 11.4 | 16.1 | 14.4 | 29.3 | 42.3 | 36.1 | NC | 23.9 | 16.2 | 14.9 | 45.8 | 79.6 | 25.5 |
| CT | 17.1 | 10.3 | 9.6 | 34.0 | 23.2 | 23.0 | ND | 2.0 | 1.1 | 1.0 | 5.1 | 2.7 | 2.5 |
| DE | 5.4 | 3.9 | 3.7 | 15.4 | 11.0 | 10.3 | OH | 103.5 | 54.8 | 49.9 | 238.4 | 101.4 | 90.7 |
| DC | 8.1 | 3.8 | 5.0 | 18.5 | 9.4 | 13.7 | OK | 9.3 | 6.8 | 6.3 | 21.0 | 15.1 | 13.9 |
| FL | 57.6 | 45.1 | 41.9 | 105.5 | 72.9 | 66.3 | OR | 28.0 | 15.8 | 15.0 | 72.2 | 34.4 | 33.3 |
| GA | 20.4 | 11.7 | 10.7 | 37.8 | 14.9 | 20.7 | PA | 53.6 | 51.1 | 45.7 | 130.4 | 126.9 | 113.0 |
| HI | 9.1 | 5.1 | 4.5 | 25.9 | 14.1 | 12.2 | RI | 7.2 | 4.6 | 4.2 | 16.8 | 10.8 | 10.0 |
| ID | 1.8 | 1.9 | 2.0 | 2.7 | 2.8 | 3.0 | SC | 18.6 | 8.7 | 8.1 | 43.8 | 18.8 | 17.6 |
| IL | 23.4 | 13.0 | 11.3 | 66.2 | 27.8 | 22.2 | SD | 3.2 | 3.0 | 3.0 | 6.8 | 6.0 | 6.0 |
| IN | 35.1 | 7.0 | 6.1 | 86.2 | 13.9 | 12.1 | TN | 61.5 | 25.5 | 21.8 | 157.2 | 56.5 | 47.3 |
| IA | 17.9 | 9.5 | 8.4 | 45.7 | 23.0 | 20.0 | TX | 51.2 | 28.1 | 25.7 | 116.7 | 61.6 | 55.3 |
| KS | 14.8 | 4.5 | 4.2 | 38.3 | 8.7 | 4.2 | UT | 6.5 | 3.7 | 3.5 | 17.6 | 9.1 | 8.3 |
| KY | 30.5 | 21.2 | 19.2 | 62.0 | 53.0 | 37.9 | VT | 2.9 | 2.8 | 2.4 | 6.3 | 6.0 | 4.9 |
| LA | 10.6 | 5.5 | 5.6 | 23.7 | 13.4 | 13.8 | VA | 35.2 | 18.9 | 20.1 | 79.3 | 35.3 | 33.9 |
| ME | 11.1 | 3.3 | 3.3 | 26.2 | 7.0 | 7.5 | WA | 66.7 | 26.8 | 25.4 | 161.7 | 58.6 | 55.1 |
| MD | 24.7 | 18.9 | 17.5 | 59.6 | 46.8 | 43.1 | WV | 10.0 | 7.1 | 6.6 | 22.5 | 14.1 | 12.9 |
| MA | 49.7 | 28.8 | 27.9 | 97.5 | 53.4 | 52.3 | WI | 22.9 | 16.2 | 15.1 | 53.2 | 34.4 | 31.9 |
| MI | 68.1 | 14.1 | 12.5 | 178.5 | 33.9 | 30.4 | WY | 0.3 | 0.5 | 0.5 | 0.7 | 1.3 | 1.2 |
| MN | 23.1 | 18.7 | 17.2 | 49.5 | 44.3 | 40.8 | GU | 1.3 | 0.6 | 0.5 | 3.0 | 1.2 | 1.1 |
| MS | 12.0 | 5.1 | 4.2 | 25.3 | 10.1 | 8.3 | PR | 13.5 | 7.1 | 5.6 | 37.1 | 19.4 | 15.2 |
| MO | 35.8 | 11.1 | 9.6 | 86.2 | 24.8 | 21.5 | VI | 0.5 | 0.2 | 0.2 | 1.5 | 0.7 | 0.5 |

[1] Includes Puerto Rico (PR), Guam (GU), and the Virgin Islands (VI).

Source: U.S. Department of Health and Human Services, Administration for Children and Families, "Temporary Assistance for Needy Families, Caseload Data," <http://www.acf.hhs.gov/programs/ofa/programs/tanf/data-reports>, accessed April 2019.

## Table 589. Household Use of Food Pantries and Emergency (Soup) Kitchens: 2017

[In thousands (126,724 represents 126,724,000), except percent. Based on the 2017 Current Population Survey Food Security Supplement that asked questions about use of food pantries and emergency kitchens among households with incomes below 185 percent of the Federal poverty level, and households above this level that indicated difficulty in meeting food needs. Covers the use of food pantries and emergency kitchens at least once during the 12-month period ended December 2017, for persons occupying housing units; survey excludes homeless persons, and may also miss persons in tenuous housing arrangements (such as temporarily living with another family)]

| Category | Food pantries | | | Emergency (soup) kitchens | | |
|---|---|---|---|---|---|---|
| | Total households [1] | Number of users | Percent using | Total households [1] | Number of users | Percent using |
| All households | 126,724 | 5,919 | 4.7 | 126,736 | 726 | 0.6 |
| All persons in households | 319,023 | 15,917 | 5.0 | 319,093 | 1,508 | 0.5 |
| Adults in households | 245,559 | 10,923 | 4.4 | 245,622 | 1,147 | 0.5 |
| Children in households | 73,464 | 4,994 | 6.8 | 73,471 | 361 | 0.5 |
| Households by food security status: [2] | | | | | | |
| Food-secure households | 111,889 | 2,064 | 1.8 | 111,895 | 242 | 0.2 |
| Food-insecure households | 14,811 | 3,849 | 26.0 | 14,794 | 483 | 3.3 |
| Households with low food security | 9,140 | 1,909 | 20.9 | 9,138 | 176 | 1.9 |
| Households with very low food security | 5,671 | 1,939 | 34.2 | 5,656 | 308 | 5.5 |

[1] Totals exclude households that did not answer questions about using food pantries and emergency kitchens, and also households that did not answer questions about food security. [2] Food secure households report zero or 1-2 indications, typically anxiety over food sufficiency or supply, with little or no indication of changes in diets or food intake. Households with low food security report reduced quality, variety, or desirability of diet, with little or no indication of reduced food intake. Households with very low food security report multiple indications of disrupted eating patterns and reduced food intake. See also headnote, Table 215.

Source: U.S. Department of Agriculture, Economic Research Service, *Statistical Supplement to Household Food Security in the United States in 2017,* No. 079, September 2018. See also <https://www.ers.usda.gov/topics/food-nutrition-assistance/food-security-in-the-us.aspx>.

## Table 590. Temporary Assistance for Needy Families (TANF)—Expenditures by State: Fiscal Years 2000 to 2017

[In millions of dollars (24,781 represents $24,781,000,000). Represents federal and state funds expended in fiscal year. Negative values occur when contracted obligations are fulfilled or terminated and the actual cost for the service is less than the obligated amount. Expenditures on basic assistance includes cash, payments, vouchers, and other forms of benefits designed to meet a family's ongoing basic needs (food, clothing, shelter, utilities, household goods, personal care items, and general incidental expenses)]

| State | 2000, Total | 2010, Total | 2017 Total [1] | 2017 Expenditures on basic assistance | State | 2000, Total | 2010, Total | 2017 Total [1] | 2017 Expenditures on basic assistance |
|---|---|---|---|---|---|---|---|---|---|
| U.S. | 24,781 | 33,255 | 28,701 | 7,060 | MO | 321 | 405 | 335 | 42 |
| AL | 96 | 191 | 202 | 22 | MT | 44 | 47 | 54 | 26 |
| AK | 93 | 62 | 73 | 53 | NE | 79 | 98 | 89 | 27 |
| AZ | 261 | 350 | 340 | 38 | NV | 69 | 108 | 102 | 39 |
| AR | 139 | 233 | 161 | 6 | NH | 73 | 86 | 62 | 19 |
| CA | 6,481 | 7,239 | 6,237 | 2,539 | NJ | 321 | 1,446 | 1,283 | 97 |
| CO | 205 | 323 | 410 | 90 | NM | 149 | 237 | 256 | 55 |
| CT | 436 | 500 | 460 | 52 | NY | 3,512 | 5,347 | 4,664 | 1,456 |
| DE | 55 | 75 | 115 | 17 | NC | 440 | 563 | 491 | 42 |
| DC | 157 | 251 | 313 | 122 | ND | 33 | 37 | 32 | 4 |
| FL | 781 | 901 | 768 | 163 | OH | 995 | 1,331 | 1,067 | 247 |
| GA | 386 | 563 | 486 | 87 | OK | 130 | 179 | 137 | 43 |
| HI | 162 | 378 | 195 | 40 | OR | 169 | 392 | 304 | 89 |
| ID | 43 | 35 | 40 | 8 | PA | 1,327 | 964 | 979 | 187 |
| IL | 879 | 1,255 | 1,065 | 43 | RI | 172 | 149 | 143 | 24 |
| IN | 342 | 344 | 449 | 17 | SC | 245 | 180 | 163 | 38 |
| IA | 163 | 194 | 188 | 37 | SD | 21 | 31 | 27 | 14 |
| KS | 151 | 207 | 163 | 14 | TN | 293 | 338 | 183 | 62 |
| KY | 203 | 281 | 269 | 171 | TX | 727 | 908 | 869 | 51 |
| LA | 118 | 264 | 196 | 19 | UT | 100 | 132 | 107 | 25 |
| ME | 108 | 141 | 79 | 26 | VT | 62 | 78 | 83 | 15 |
| MD | 336 | 564 | 475 | 116 | VA | 418 | 299 | 235 | 68 |
| MA | 690 | 1,022 | 961 | 207 | WA | 535 | 1,494 | 924 | 144 |
| MI | 1,264 | 1,703 | 1,165 | 133 | WV | 134 | 199 | 128 | 27 |
| MN | 381 | 475 | 536 | 98 | WI | 382 | 524 | 504 | 86 |
| MS | 62 | 106 | 105 | 9 | WY | 34 | 29 | 28 | 7 |

[1] Includes expenditures for other items not shown separately, including work subsidies, education and training, and other services and programs; and funds transferred to support other funds and programs.

Source: U.S. Department of Health and Human Services, Administration for Children and Families, "Temporary Assistance for Needy Families, Expenditure Data," <http://www.acf.hhs.gov/programs/ofa/programs/tanf/data-reports>, accessed April 2019.

## Table 591. Federal Food Programs: Fiscal Years 1990 to 2018

[20.0 represents 20,000,000, except as noted. For fiscal years ending September 30. Program data include Puerto Rico, Virgin Islands, Guam, American Samoa, Northern Marianas, and the former Trust Territory when a federal food program was operated in these areas. Participation data are average monthly figures except as noted. Participants are not reported for The Emergency Food Assistance Program (TEFAP)]

| Program | Unit | 1990 | 2000 | 2005 | 2010 | 2015 | 2016 | 2017 | 2018 (P) |
|---|---|---|---|---|---|---|---|---|---|
| Supplemental nutrition assistance program: [1] | | | | | | | | | |
| Participants | Million | 20.0 | 17.2 | 25.6 | 40.3 | 45.8 | 44.2 | 42.1 | 40.3 |
| Value of benefits | Mil. dol. | 14,143 | 14,983 | 28,568 | 64,702 | 69,645 | 66,539 | 63,601 | 60,608 |
| Average monthly benefit value per recipient | Dollars | 59 | 73 | 93 | 134 | 127 | 125 | 126 | 125 |
| Nutrition assistance program for Puerto Rico: [2] | | | | | | | | | |
| Federal grant | Mil. dol. | 937 | 1,268 | 1,495 | 2,001 | 1,951 | 1,959 | 1,949 | 1,920 |
| National school lunch program (NSLP): | | | | | | | | | |
| Children participating [3] | Million | 24.1 | 27.3 | 29.6 | 31.8 | 30.5 | 30.4 | 30.0 | 29.7 |
| Free lunches served | Million | 1,662 | 2,205 | 2,477 | 2,948 | 3,274 | 3,366 | 3,282 | 3,329 |
| Reduced-price lunches served | Million | 273 | 409 | 479 | 498 | 360 | 336 | 315 | 288 |
| Federal cost (cash payments) | Mil. dol. | 3,214 | 5,493 | 7,055 | 9,752 | 11,696 | 12,259 | 12,251 | 12,576 |
| School breakfast (SB): | | | | | | | | | |
| Children participating [3] | Million | 4.1 | 7.6 | 9.4 | 11.7 | 14.0 | 14.6 | 14.7 | 14.7 |
| Federal cash payments | Mil. dol. | 599 | 1,393 | 1,927 | 2,859 | 3,892 | 4,212 | 4,252 | 4,393 |
| Special supplemental food program (WIC): [4] | | | | | | | | | |
| Participants | Million | 4.5 | 7.2 | 8.0 | 9.2 | 8.0 | 7.7 | 7.3 | 6.9 |
| Federal cost for food | Mil. dol. | 1,637 | 2,853 | 3,603 | 4,562 | 4,176 | 3,950 | 3,606 | 3,376 |
| Child and adult care (CACFP): [5] | | | | | | | | | |
| Participants [6] | Million | 1.5 | 2.7 | 3.1 | 3.4 | 4.2 | 4.4 | 4.5 | 4.6 |
| Federal cash payments | Mil. dol. | 719 | 1,500 | 1,904 | 2,398 | 3,009 | 3,217 | 3,240 | 3,318 |
| Federal cost of food commodities for: [7] | | | | | | | | | |
| School food programs [8] | Mil. dol. | 617 | 655 | 975 | 1,128 | 1,307 | 1,311 | 1,393 | 1,243 |
| TEFAP [9] | Mil. dol. | 282 | 182 | 314 | 566 | 451 | 586 | 578 | 540 |

P Preliminary. [1] The program name was changed from Food Stamp to Supplemental Nutrition Assistance (SNAP) in October 2008. [2] Puerto Rico receives a grant in lieu of SNAP benefits. [3] Average participation per day are 9-month averages (excludes summer months). Includes children in public and nonprofit private elementary and secondary schools and in residential child care institutions. [4] WIC serves pregnant and postpartum women, infants, and children up to age 5. [5] CACFP provides year-round subsidies to feed preschool children and elderly and disabled adults in day care centers, and children and youth in emergency shelters for the homeless and eligible afterschool care programs. [6] Average quarterly daily attendance at participating institutions. [7] Includes the federal cost of commodity entitlements, cash-in-lieu of commodities, and bonus foods. [8] National school lunch and breakfast programs, and special milk program. [9] Emergency food assistance is food made available to hunger relief organizations such as food banks and soup kitchens. It is not disaster relief.

Source: U.S. Department of Agriculture, Food and Nutrition Service, "Program Data, Overview," <https://www.fns.usda.gov/pd/overview>, accessed February 2019.

## Table 592. Supplemental Nutrition Assistance Program (SNAP) by State: 2000 to 2018

[17,194 represents 17,194,000; 14,983 represents $14,983,000,000. Participation data are average monthly number participating in fiscal year ending September 30. The Food Stamp Program was renamed the Supplemental Nutrition Assistance Program (SNAP) in October 2008]

| State | Persons (1,000) | | | Benefits (mil. dol.) | | | State | Persons (1,000) | | | Benefits (mil. dol.) | | |
|---|---|---|---|---|---|---|---|---|---|---|---|---|---|
| | 2000 | 2010 | 2018 | 2000 | 2010 | 2018 | | 2000 | 2010 | 2018 | 2000 | 2010 | 2018 |
| Total [1].... | 17,194 | 40,302 | 40,324 | 14,983 | 64,702 | 60,608 | MS........... | 276 | 576 | 505 | 226 | 847 | 680 |
| | | | | | | | MO........... | 423 | 901 | 737 | 358 | 1,361 | 1,061 |
| U.S........... | 17,156 | 40,245 | 40,247 | 14,927 | 64,562 | 60,415 | MT........... | 59 | 114 | 115 | 51 | 177 | 158 |
| AL........... | 396 | 805 | 767 | 344 | 1,226 | 1,085 | NE........... | 82 | 163 | 170 | 61 | 238 | 229 |
| AK........... | 38 | 76 | 92 | 46 | 159 | 187 | NV........... | 61 | 278 | 440 | 57 | 415 | 614 |
| AZ........... | 259 | 1,018 | 846 | 240 | 1,588 | 1,210 | NH........... | 36 | 104 | 87 | 28 | 152 | 101 |
| AR........... | 247 | 467 | 372 | 206 | 686 | 480 | NJ........... | 345 | 622 | 760 | 304 | 1,030 | 1,013 |
| CA........... | 1,831 | 3,239 | 3,950 | 1,639 | 5,692 | 6,333 | NM........... | 169 | 357 | 456 | 140 | 542 | 638 |
| CO........... | 156 | 405 | 450 | 127 | 688 | 669 | NY........... | 1,439 | 2,758 | 2,797 | 1,361 | 4,985 | 4,527 |
| CT........... | 165 | 336 | 387 | 138 | 570 | 615 | NC........... | 488 | 1,346 | 1,075 | 403 | 2,072 | 1,871 |
| DE........... | 32 | 113 | 140 | 31 | 171 | 197 | ND........... | 32 | 60 | 53 | 25 | 95 | 75 |
| DC........... | 81 | 118 | 111 | 77 | 196 | 188 | OH........... | 610 | 1,607 | 1,421 | 520 | 2,734 | 2,078 |
| FL........... | 882 | 2,603 | 3,348 | 771 | 4,417 | 5,764 | OK........... | 253 | 582 | 585 | 208 | 900 | 833 |
| GA........... | 559 | 1,591 | 1,539 | 489 | 2,565 | 2,337 | OR........... | 234 | 705 | 634 | 198 | 1,067 | 938 |
| HI........... | 118 | 138 | 164 | 166 | 358 | 469 | PA........... | 777 | 1,575 | 1,819 | 656 | 2,333 | 2,592 |
| ID........... | 58 | 194 | 158 | 46 | 300 | 200 | RI........... | 74 | 139 | (NA) | 59 | 238 | (NA) |
| IL........... | 817 | 1,646 | 1,826 | 777 | 2,784 | 2,778 | SC........... | 295 | 797 | 658 | 249 | 1,256 | 944 |
| IN........... | 300 | 813 | 617 | 268 | 1,291 | 868 | SD........... | 43 | 95 | 87 | 37 | 153 | 131 |
| IA........... | 123 | 340 | 345 | 100 | 526 | 446 | TN........... | 496 | 1,224 | 971 | 415 | 1,966 | 1,425 |
| KS........... | 117 | 270 | 217 | 83 | 403 | 294 | TX........... | 1,333 | 3,552 | 3,895 | 1,215 | 5,447 | 5,525 |
| KY........... | 403 | 778 | 610 | 337 | 1,186 | 854 | UT........... | 82 | 247 | 189 | 68 | 367 | 259 |
| LA........... | 500 | 826 | 867 | 448 | 1,286 | 1,297 | VT........... | 41 | 86 | 73 | 32 | 124 | 107 |
| ME........... | 102 | 230 | 168 | 81 | 356 | 218 | VA........... | 336 | 786 | 736 | 263 | 1,213 | 1,052 |
| MD........... | 219 | 561 | 646 | 199 | 878 | 910 | WA........... | 295 | 956 | 877 | 241 | 1,387 | 1,269 |
| MA........... | 232 | 749 | 771 | 182 | 1,166 | 1,159 | WV........... | 227 | 341 | 321 | 185 | 487 | 440 |
| MI........... | 603 | 1,776 | 1,282 | 457 | 2,809 | 1,894 | WI........... | 193 | 715 | 653 | 129 | 1,000 | 817 |
| MN........... | 196 | 430 | 429 | 165 | 625 | 544 | WY........... | 22 | 35 | 29 | 19 | 52 | 41 |

NA Not available. [1] Includes Guam and the Virgin Islands. Puerto Rico, American Samoa, and the Northern Marianas receive nutrition assistance grants in lieu of SNAP.

Source: U.S. Department of Agriculture, Food and Nutrition Service, Supplemental Nutrition Assistance Program (SNAP), "National and/or State Level Monthly and/or Annual Data," <https://www.fns.usda.gov/pd/supplemental-nutrition-assistance-program-snap>, accessed March 2019.

## Table 593. Supplemental Nutrition Assistance Program (SNAP) Households and Participants by Type: 1990 to 2017

[7,811 represents 7,811,000. For fiscal years ending September 30. Data for 1990 exclude Guam and the Virgin Islands. The Food Stamp Program was renamed Supplemental Nutrition Assistance Program (SNAP) in October 2008. Based on a sample of households from the SNAP Quality Control System]

| Fiscal year | Households | | | | Participants | | |
|---|---|---|---|---|---|---|---|
| | Total [1] (1,000) | Percent of total | | | Total (1,000) | Percent of total | |
| | | With children | With elderly [2] | With disabled [3] | | Children | Elderly [2] |
| 1990................. | 7,811 | 60.3 | 18.1 | 8.9 | 20,440 | 49.6 | 7.7 |
| 1995................. | 10,883 | 59.7 | 16.0 | 18.9 | 26,955 | 51.5 | 7.1 |
| 1996................. | 10,552 | 59.5 | 16.2 | 20.2 | 25,926 | 51.0 | 7.3 |
| 1997................. | 9,452 | 58.3 | 17.6 | 22.3 | 23,117 | 51.4 | 7.9 |
| 1998................. | 8,246 | 58.3 | 18.2 | 24.4 | 19,969 | 52.8 | 8.2 |
| 1999................. | 7,670 | 55.7 | 20.1 | 26.4 | 18,149 | 51.5 | 9.4 |
| 2000................. | 7,335 | 53.9 | 21.0 | 27.5 | 17,091 | 51.3 | 10.0 |
| 2001................. | 7,450 | 53.6 | 20.4 | 27.7 | 17,297 | 51.1 | 9.6 |
| 2002................. | 8,201 | 54.1 | 18.7 | 27.0 | 19,041 | 51.0 | 8.9 |
| 2003................. | 8,971 | 55.1 | 17.1 | 22.1 | 20,764 | 50.8 | 8.1 |
| 2004................. | 10,069 | 54.3 | 17.3 | 22.7 | 23,279 | 50.0 | 8.2 |
| 2005................. | 10,852 | 53.7 | 17.1 | 23.0 | 24,794 | 49.9 | 8.3 |
| 2006................. | 11,313 | 52.0 | 17.9 | 23.1 | 25,472 | 49.1 | 8.7 |
| 2007................. | 11,561 | 51.0 | 17.8 | 23.8 | 25,775 | 48.9 | 8.8 |
| 2008................. | 12,464 | 50.6 | 18.5 | 22.6 | 27,607 | 48.4 | 9.1 |
| 2009................. | 14,981 | 49.9 | 16.6 | 21.2 | 32,889 | 47.5 | 8.3 |
| 2010................. | 18,369 | 48.7 | 15.5 | 19.8 | 39,759 | 46.6 | 7.9 |
| 2011................. | 20,803 | 47.1 | 16.5 | 20.2 | 44,148 | 45.1 | 8.5 |
| 2012................. | 22,046 | 45.3 | 17.2 | 20.0 | 46,022 | 44.5 | 9.0 |
| 2013................. | 22,802 | 44.8 | 17.4 | 20.3 | 47,098 | 44.4 | 9.3 |
| 2014................. | 22,445 | 43.6 | 19.0 | 20.4 | 45,874 | 44.2 | 10.1 |
| 2015................. | 22,293 | 42.7 | 19.6 | 20.2 | 45,184 | 44.0 | 10.6 |
| 2016................. | 21,511 | 42.9 | 21.8 | 20.3 | 43,539 | 44.1 | 11.8 |
| 2017................. | 20,597 | 41.7 | 24.1 | 20.8 | 41,491 | 43.5 | 13.1 |

[1] Total does not include those who are ineligible or those receiving disaster benefits. [2] Persons 60 years old and over. [3] Non-elderly individuals with disabilities. The substantial increase in 1995 and decrease in 2003 are in part a result of changes in the definition of a household with an individual with a disability. Changes involve primarily raising and lowering the age to be considered "nonelderly," and the inclusion of households receiving supplemental security income and/or other government benefits due to a disability. Additional changes in definitions were made in 2015 and 2016. See source, appendix A, for details.

Source: U.S. Department of Agriculture, Food and Nutrition Service, *Characteristics of Supplemental Nutrition Assistance Program Households: Fiscal Year 2017*, Report No. SNAP-18-CHAR, February 2019. See also <http://www.fns.usda.gov/ops/supplemental-nutrition-assistance-program-snap-research>.

# Table 594. Supplemental Nutrition Assistance Program (SNAP) Households and Participants—Summary: 2017

[20,597 represents 20,597,000. For fiscal year ending September 30. Based on a sample of households from the SNAP Quality Control System. Figures are lower than official participation counts because they do not include ineligible participants or those receiving disaster food stamp assistance]

| Household type and income source | Households Number (1,000) | Percent | Age, sex, race, and ethnicity | Participants Number (1,000) | Percent |
|---|---|---|---|---|---|
| Total | 20,597 | 100.0 | Total | 41,491 | 100.0 |
| With children | 8,588 | 41.7 | Children | 18,033 | 43.5 |
| Single-parent households | 5,041 | 24.5 | Under age 5 | 5,573 | 13.4 |
| Married-couple households | 1,551 | 7.5 | Age 5 to 17 | 12,460 | 30.0 |
| Other [1] | 1,997 | 9.7 | Nonelderly adults | 18,011 | 43.4 |
| With elderly | 4,955 | 24.1 | Age 18 to 35 | 8,475 | 20.4 |
| Living alone | 4,047 | 19.6 | Age 36 to 59 | 9,536 | 23.0 |
| Not living alone | 908 | 4.4 | Elderly, age 60 and over | 5,447 | 13.1 |
| Disabled nonelderly | 4,289 | 20.8 | | | |
| Living alone | 2,716 | 13.2 | Male | 17,777 | 42.8 |
| Not living alone | 1,573 | 7.6 | Female | 23,714 | 57.2 |
| With earned income | 6,477 | 31.4 | White, non-Hispanic | 14,847 | 35.8 |
| Wages and salaries | 5,612 | 27.2 | Black, non-Hispanic | 10,555 | 25.4 |
| Unearned income | 12,225 | 59.4 | Hispanic | 6,832 | 16.5 |
| TANF [2] | 1,006 | 4.9 | Asian, non-Hispanic | 1,308 | 3.2 |
| Supplemental security income | 4,514 | 21.9 | Native American, non-Hispanic | 562 | 1.4 |
| Social security | 5,883 | 28.6 | Multiracial, non-Hispanic | 403 | 1.0 |
| No income | 3,910 | 19.0 | Race unknown | 6,984 | 16.8 |

[1] Other households with children include other multiple-adult households and children-only households. [2] Temporary Assistance for Needy Families (TANF) program.

Source: U.S. Department of Agriculture, Food and Nutrition Service, *Characteristics of Supplemental Nutrition Assistance Program Households: Fiscal Year 2017*, Report No. SNAP-18-CHAR, February 2019. See also <https://www.fns.usda.gov/ops/supplemental-nutrition-assistance-program-snap-research>.

# Table 595. Children Under Age 6 in Child Care by Type of Arrangement and Hours in Nonparental Care by Child and Family Characteristics: 2016

[In percent except as indicated (21,362 represents 21,362,000). Covers children under age 6 not enrolled in kindergarten who are in a nonparental care arrangement on a weekly basis. A child's primary arrangement is the regular care arrangement or early childhood education program in which the child spends the most time per week. Based on the Early Childhood Program Participation Survey of the National Household Education Surveys Program. Detail may not sum to totals because of rounding]

| Selected child or family characteristic | Number of children (1,000) | Children in parental care only | Non-parental care, total | Center-based care | Relative | Non-relative home-based care | Multiple arrange-ments [1] | Average hours in non-parental care per week [2] |
|---|---|---|---|---|---|---|---|---|
| Total children under age 6 | 21,362 | 40.3 | 59.7 | 29.4 | 18.5 | 10.0 | 1.8 | 30.6 |
| Age of child: | | | | | | | | |
| Under 1 year old | 4,724 | 52.6 | 47.4 | 10.7 | 23.2 | 11.8 | 1.6 | 33.0 |
| 1 to 2 years old | 8,552 | 46.0 | 54.0 | 21.4 | 19.9 | 11.4 | 1.3 | 30.8 |
| 3 to 5 years old | 8,087 | 27.1 | 72.9 | 48.7 | 14.4 | 7.6 | 2.3 | 29.5 |
| Non-Hispanic race of child: | | | | | | | | |
| White | 10,731 | 37.8 | 62.2 | 31.4 | 16.4 | 12.4 | 2.0 | 30.5 |
| Black | 2,837 | 32.5 | 67.5 | 31.6 | 24.9 | 8.8 | [6] 2.3 | 33.5 |
| Asian | 995 | 43.1 | 56.9 | 30.6 | 19.9 | 5.8 | (B) | 30.3 |
| Two or more races | 1,235 | 39.2 | 60.8 | 33.7 | 17.7 | 9.0 | (B) | 33.6 |
| Hispanic, any race | 5,418 | 48.5 | 51.5 | 23.1 | 19.7 | 7.2 | 1.5 | 28.1 |
| Number of parents in household: [3] | | | | | | | | |
| Two parents | 16,428 | 42.9 | 57.1 | 30.0 | 15.5 | 9.8 | 1.8 | 29.3 |
| One parent | 4,449 | 32.3 | 67.7 | 27.5 | 27.1 | 11.5 | 1.7 | 34.2 |
| Mother's employment status: [4] | | | | | | | | |
| Currently employed | 12,154 | 21.1 | 78.9 | 36.5 | 24.6 | 15.2 | 2.6 | 33.2 |
| 35 or more hours per week | 8,884 | 15.9 | 84.1 | 39.9 | 24.2 | 17.5 | 2.6 | 35.9 |
| Less than 35 hours per week | 3,270 | 35.3 | 64.7 | 27.2 | 25.9 | 9.1 | 2.5 | 23.6 |
| Not in labor force | 7,811 | 69.0 | 31.0 | 20.4 | 7.9 | 2.3 | [6] 0.4 | 20.6 |
| Mother's highest education: [4] | | | | | | | | |
| Less than high school | 2,716 | 60.4 | 39.6 | 18.0 | 15.4 | 5.5 | (B) | 27.6 |
| High school/GED [5] | 4,085 | 51.0 | 49.0 | 18.5 | 21.8 | 6.1 | 2.5 | 29.4 |
| Vocational/technical/some college | 3,698 | 41.1 | 58.9 | 27.6 | 20.9 | 9.2 | [6] 1.2 | 28.8 |
| Associate's degree | 1,752 | 39.0 | 61.0 | 26.2 | 22.1 | 10.8 | [6] 1.9 | 33.3 |
| Bachelor's degree | 5,675 | 33.9 | 66.1 | 38.1 | 15.4 | 10.9 | 1.7 | 30.3 |
| Graduate/professional degree | 2,835 | 20.5 | 79.5 | 44.5 | 14.2 | 18.6 | 2.2 | 33.0 |
| Household income: | | | | | | | | |
| $20,000 or less | 3,049 | 52.3 | 47.7 | 22.5 | 17.4 | 5.7 | [6] 2.2 | 31.3 |
| $20,001 to $50,000 | 5,706 | 50.2 | 49.8 | 21.3 | 20.8 | 6.5 | 1.3 | 30.0 |
| $50,001 to $75,000 | 3,821 | 43.9 | 56.1 | 21.6 | 21.0 | 11.6 | 1.9 | 29.1 |
| $75,001 to $100,000 | 2,882 | 34.2 | 65.8 | 31.9 | 21.8 | 10.4 | 1.7 | 29.9 |
| Over $100,000 | 5,904 | 25.3 | 74.7 | 44.6 | 13.8 | 14.5 | 1.9 | 31.7 |

B Reporting standards not met. Either there are too few cases for a reliable estimate or the coefficient of variation (CV) is 50 percent or greater. [1] Children who spent an equal number of hours per week in multiple nonparental care arrangements. [2] Mean hours per week per child, among preschool children enrolled in any type of nonparental care arrangement. For children with more than one arrangement, the hours of each weekly arrangement were summed to calculate the total amount of time in child care per week. [3] Excludes children living apart from their parents. [4] Excludes children living in households with no mother or female guardian present. [5] GED (General Educational Development diploma). [6] Interpret data with caution. The coefficient of variation (CV) for this estimate is between 30 and 50 percent.

Source: U.S. National Center for Education Statistics, *Digest of Education Statistics*, "Advance Release of Selected 2017 Digest Tables," <https://nces.ed.gov/programs/digest/>, accessed May 2018.

## Table 596. Child Support—Award and Recipient Status of Custodial Parents: 2015

[In thousands (13,573 represents 13,573,000), except as noted. Income and support received in 2015 dollars. Based on the Child Support Supplement to the April 2016 Current Population Survey. Custodial parents aged 15 years and older with own children under age 21 years living with them, and receiving support from noncustodial parents living outside the household. Covers civilian noninstitutional population]

| Award and recipient status | All custodial parents | | | | Custodial parents below poverty level | | | |
|---|---|---|---|---|---|---|---|---|
| | Total | | | | Total | | | |
| | Number | Percent distri-bution | Mothers | Fathers | Number | Percent distri-bution | Mothers | Fathers |
| **Total**.................................... | **13,573** | (X) | **10,918** | **2,655** | **3,631** | (X) | **3,187** | **444** |
| With child support agreement or award [1]........ | 6,807 | (X) | 5,756 | 1,051 | 1,788 | (X) | 1,586 | 202 |
| Supposed to receive payments in 2015......... | 5,845 | 100.0 | 4,961 | 884 | 1,560 | 100.0 | 1,381 | 178 |
| Actually received payments in 2015........... | 4,049 | 69.3 | 3,530 | 519 | 1,051 | 67.4 | 955 | 96 |
| Received full amount..................... | 2,543 | 43.5 | 2,229 | 314 | 612 | 39.2 | 552 | 59 |
| Received partial payments............... | 1,506 | 25.8 | 1,301 | 205 | 439 | 28.1 | 402 | 36 |
| Did not receive payments in 2015.............. | 1,796 | 30.7 | 1,431 | 365 | 509 | 32.6 | 427 | 82 |
| Child support not awarded........................ | 6,766 | (X) | 5,162 | 1,604 | 1,843 | (X) | 1,601 | 242 |
| **MEAN INCOME AND CHILD SUPPORT** | | | | | | | | |
| Received child support payments in 2015: | | | | | | | | |
| Mean total money income (dol.)............... | 36,263 | (X) | 33,646 | 54,075 | 8,483 | (X) | 8,367 | 9,634 |
| Mean child support received (dol.)............ | 4,976 | (X) | 4,906 | 5,453 | 4,006 | (X) | 4,004 | 4,030 |
| Received the full amount due: | | | | | | | | |
| Mean total money income (dol.)............... | 39,031 | (X) | 36,138 | 59,558 | 9,395 | (X) | 9,301 | 10,273 |
| Mean child support received (dol.)............ | 6,398 | (X) | 6,209 | 7,741 | 5,445 | (X) | 5,402 | 5,840 |
| Received partial payments: | | | | | | | | |
| Mean total money income (dol.)............... | 31,587 | (X) | 29,377 | 45,652 | 7,211 | (X) | 7,087 | 8,590 |
| Mean child support received (dol.)............ | 2,575 | (X) | 2,675 | 1,938 | 1,999 | (X) | 2,083 | 1,071 |
| Received no payments in 2015: | | | | | | | | |
| Mean total money income (dol.)................ | 31,542 | (X) | 29,036 | 41,358 | 7,312 | (X) | 7,388 | 6,919 |
| Without child support agreement or award: | | | | | | | | |
| Mean total money income (dol.)................. | 33,143 | (X) | 27,877 | 50,097 | 8,589 | (X) | 8,269 | 10,700 |

X Not applicable. [1] Child support award status as of April 2016.

Source: U.S. Census Bureau, *Custodial Mothers and Fathers and Their Child Support: 2015*, Current Population Report P60-262, January 2018; and "2015 Child Support Detailed Tables," <https://www.census.gov/topics/families/child-support.Tables.html>. See also <https://www.census.gov/topics/families/child-support.html>.

## Table 597. Child Support Enforcement Program—Caseload and Finances: 2010 to 2018

[In units as indicated (15,859 represents 15,859,000). For fiscal years ending September 30. Includes Puerto Rico, Guam, and the Virgin Islands. The Child Support Program is a federal/state/tribal/local partnership that operates under Title IV-D of the Social Security Act. The Office of Child Support (OCSE) locates absent parents, establishes paternity of children, and establishes and enforces support orders. The OCSE does not assist families directly but rather helps child support agencies in the states and tribes to develop, manage and operate their programs. Case types include IV-A cases in which children are eligible for Temporary Assistance for Needy Families (TANF); and IV-E cases in which children are entitled to foster care maintenance; case types reflect Social Security Act Titles IV-A and IV-E. Child support collected for families not receiving TANF goes to the family to help it remain self-sufficient. Most child support collected on behalf of TANF and foster care families goes to Federal and State governments to offset program payments. Some States pass-through a portion of their collections to help families become self-sufficient. Based on data reported by state agencies. Minus sign (-) indicates net outlay]

| Item | Unit | 2010 | 2014 | 2015 | 2016 | 2017 | 2018 (P) |
|---|---|---|---|---|---|---|---|
| **Total cases**....................................... | **1,000** | **15,859** | **15,124** | **14,745** | **14,522** | **14,229** | **13,924** |
| Number of children..................................... | 1,000 | 17,509 | 16,338 | 15,899 | 15,562 | 15,147 | 14,728 |
| Paternities established or acknowledged, total.... | 1,000 | 1,734 | 1,542 | 1,484 | 1,479 | 1,435 | 1,413 |
| Support orders established, total.................... | 1,000 | 1,297 | 1,069 | 1,016 | 981 | 936 | 872 |
| **FINANCES** | | | | | | | |
| **Total distributed collections**...................... | **Mil. dol.** | **26,556** | **28,199** | **28,559** | **28,834** | **28,625** | **28,584** |
| Total payments to families or foster care.......... | Mil. dol. | 24,474 | 26,211 | 26,592 | 26,880 | 26,725 | 26,703 |
| Total medical support................................ | Mil. dol. | 303 | 483 | 511 | 540 | 559 | 593 |
| Total passed through................................ | Mil. dol. | 135 | 118 | 112 | 105 | 102 | 98 |
| Total fees withheld by state......................... | Mil. dol. | 37 | 52 | 53 | 53 | 54 | 53 |
| Total assistance reimbursement [1]................. | Mil. dol. | 1,607 | 1,335 | 1,292 | 1,256 | 1,185 | 1,137 |
| State share........................................ | Mil. dol. | 704 | 592 | 574 | 559 | 526 | 504 |
| Federal share..................................... | Mil. dol. | 903 | 743 | 717 | 697 | 658 | 633 |
| Current Assistance Collections [2]................. | Mil. dol. | 1,015 | 847 | 808 | 771 | 711 | 681 |
| Former Assistance Collections [3].................. | Mil. dol. | 8,971 | 8,819 | 8,959 | 8,868 | 8,615 | 8,445 |
| Medicaid Never Assistance Collections [4]........ | Mil. dol. | 4,729 | 7,072 | 7,368 | 7,904 | 8,368 | 8,724 |
| Never Assistance Collections [5]................... | Mil. dol. | 11,840 | 11,461 | 11,425 | 11,291 | 10,932 | 10,734 |
| Total administrative expenditures.................... | Mil. dol. | 5,776 | 5,690 | 5,749 | 5,728 | 5,880 | 5,877 |
| Federal share....................................... | Mil. dol. | 3,811 | 3,446 | 3,474 | 3,444 | 3,560 | 3,551 |
| State share......................................... | Mil. dol. | 1,964 | 2,244 | 2,275 | 2,284 | 2,320 | 2,326 |
| Cost effectiveness ratio............................. | Dol. | 4.88 | 5.25 | 5.26 | 5.33 | 5.15 | 5.14 |

P Preliminary. [1] Equals collections that will be divided between State and Federal governments to reimburse their respective shares of either Title IV-A (TANF) payments or Title IV-E (foster care) maintenance payments. [2] Made on behalf of families currently receiving Title IV-A (TANF) or Title IV-E (foster care) assistance. [3] Made on behalf of families formerly receiving Title IV-A (TANF) or Title IV-E (foster care) assistance. [4] Collections received and distributed on behalf of children who are receiving Child Support Enforcement services under Title IV-D of the Social Security Act, and who either currently receive or formerly received Medicaid payments, but who do not and never did receive assistance under either Title IV-A (TANF or AFDC) or Title IV-E (Foster Care) of the Social Security Act. [5] Made on behalf of families never receiving public assistance under Medicaid, TANF, or Foster Care.

Source: U.S. Department of Health and Human Services, Administration for Children & Families, Office of Child Support Enforcement, *Preliminary Report FY2018*, June 2019, and earlier editions. See also <https://www.acf.hhs.gov/css/data>.

# Table 598. Children in Foster Care and Awaiting Adoption: 2017

[Data cover fiscal year ending September 30 of year shown, and are current as of August 2018. Data are preliminary. States may resubmit data, and therefore estimates may change. Due to missing data for some characteristics, data may not sum to totals]

| Characteristic | In foster care [1] | Entered foster care | Exited foster care | Waiting to be adopted [1,2] | Adopted [3] |
|---|---|---|---|---|---|
| **Total** | **442,995** | **269,690** | **247,631** | **123,437** | **59,430** |
| *SEX* | | | | | |
| Male | 228,707 | (NA) | (NA) | 64,390 | 30,482 |
| Female | 214,236 | (NA) | (NA) | 59,039 | 28,940 |
| *AGE* | | | | | |
| Under 1 year | 32,247 | 50,076 | 11,115 | 4,639 | 1,252 |
| 1 to 5 years | 151,772 | 82,653 | 89,543 | 50,467 | 32,078 |
| 6 to 10 years | 103,087 | 58,184 | 58,983 | 33,413 | 16,398 |
| 11 to 15 years | 92,551 | 54,619 | 43,976 | 26,702 | 7,841 |
| 16 to 17 years | 48,646 | 22,680 | 21,505 | 8,216 | 1,734 |
| 18 to 20 years | 13,091 | 1,451 | 21,594 | (X) | 118 |
| Mean age, years | 8.4 | 7.1 | 8.7 | 7.6 | 6.3 |
| Median age, years | 7.7 | 6.1 | 7.8 | 6.8 | 5.2 |
| *RACE/ETHNICITY [4]* | | | | | |
| American Indian/Alaska Native | 10,529 | 6,153 | 5,655 | 2,442 | 1,114 |
| Asian | 2,175 | 1,423 | 1,421 | 491 | 207 |
| Black | 100,607 | 56,614 | 52,430 | 27,388 | 10,332 |
| White | 193,828 | 124,937 | 112,881 | 53,440 | 28,868 |
| Hispanic origin [5] | 93,507 | 54,411 | 52,627 | 27,416 | 12,621 |
| Two or more races | 32,126 | 18,756 | 17,803 | 9,896 | 5,351 |
| *TIME IN CARE* | | | | | |
| Mean months | 20.1 | (X) | 19.2 | 30.9 | (NA) |
| Median months | 12.9 | (X) | 14.3 | 25.1 | (NA) |

NA Not available. X Not applicable. [1] As of September 30. [2] Includes children whose goal is adoption and/or whose parents' parental rights have been terminated. Excludes children age 16 and older whose parents' parental rights have been terminated and whose goal is emancipation. [3] Children adopted with public agency involvement. Data are from the Adoption and Foster Care Analysis and Reporting System (AFCARS) Adoption file; the number of adoptions reported here may not equal the number reported as discharges to adoption from foster care. [4] All races exclude children of Hispanic origin. [5] Children of Hispanic origin may be of any race.

Source: U.S. Department of Health and Human Services, Administration for Children and Families, *The Adoption and Foster Care Analysis and Reporting System Report, Preliminary FY2017 Estimates as of August 10, 2018,* No. 25. See also <http://www.acf.hhs.gov/cb>.

# Table 599. Child Care Expenses by Type of Child Care Arrangement and Child and Family Characteristics: 2016

[8,311 represents 8,311,000. Covers children from birth through age 5, who are not in kindergarten, and who have at least one regularly scheduled weekly nonparental care arrangement with an out-of-pocket expense. Excludes children for whom no fee was charged, or for whom another source paid the entire fee. Data cover the primary care arrangement where the child spends the most time. Some children have multiple primary care arrangements; a single child may be represented in multiple columns of this table. Based on the Early Childhood Program Participation Survey of the National Household Education Surveys Program. Detail may not sum to totals because of rounding]

| Selected child and family characteristics | Number of children whose families paid for child care (1,000) | Hourly out-of-pocket expense by type of primary care (2016-17 dollars) | | |
|---|---|---|---|---|
| | | Relative care | Nonrelative care | Center-based care [1] |
| **Total children under 6 years old** | **8,311** | **4.99** | **6.54** | **7.60** |
| Age of child: | | | | |
| Under 1 year old | 1,280 | 4.55 | 6.57 | 7.89 |
| 1 to 2 years old | 3,051 | 5.54 | 7.16 | 7.67 |
| 3 to 5 years old | 3,979 | 4.78 | 5.68 | 7.52 |
| Non-Hispanic race of child: | | | | |
| White | 4,758 | 3.95 | 6.08 | 7.36 |
| Black | 1,072 | 4.82 | [5] 10.19 | 5.92 |
| Asian or Pacific Islander | 368 | [5] 10.41 | 9.18 | 11.59 |
| Other race | 498 | 3.27 | 5.35 | 7.42 |
| Hispanic, any race | 1,614 | 5.61 | 5.74 | 8.66 |
| Family type: | | | | |
| Two parents or guardians | 6,835 | 5.16 | 6.26 | 8.15 |
| One parent or guardian | 1,476 | 4.43 | [5] 7.74 | 4.83 |
| Parents' highest education: [2] | | | | |
| Less than high school | 369 | 5.65 | [5] 4.79 | [5] 2.21 |
| High school/GED [3] | 873 | 4.83 | 4.77 | 5.22 |
| Vocational/technical or some college | 1,892 | 4.02 | 4.25 | 6.07 |
| Bachelor's degree | 2,820 | 5.54 | 7.51 | 7.78 |
| Graduate/professional degree | 2,357 | 6.65 | 7.94 | 9.41 |
| Household income: | | | | |
| $20,000 or less | 608 | 3.80 | (B) | 4.29 |
| $20,001 to $50,000 | 1,537 | 5.22 | 5.43 | 5.33 |
| $50,001 to $75,000 | 1,313 | 5.50 | 4.20 | 6.04 |
| $75,001 to $100,000 | 1,283 | 4.02 | 5.54 | 7.13 |
| Over $100,000 | 3,569 | 6.06 | 7.83 | 9.27 |
| Poverty status of household: [4] | | | | |
| At or above poverty threshold | 7,535 | 5.42 | 6.32 | 7.87 |
| Below poverty threshold | 776 | 3.47 | (B) | 4.01 |

B Reporting standards not met. There are too few cases for a reliable estimate. [1] Includes day care centers, Head Start programs, preschools, and prekindergartens. [2] Parents or guardians. [3] GED, General Educational Development diploma. [4] Children are considered poor if living in households with incomes below the poverty threshold, which is a dollar amount determined by the federal government, given household size and composition. Income is reported in categories rather than in exact amounts, and therefore the poverty measures used in this report are approximations. [5] Interpret data with caution. The coefficient of variation for this estimate is 30 percent or greater.

Source: U.S. National Center for Education Statistics, *Early Childhood Program Participation, Results from the National Household Education Surveys Program of 2016,* No. NCES 2017101REV, January 2019 (revised). See also <https://nces.ed.gov/nhes/young_children.asp>.

## Table 600. Head Start—Summary: 2010 to 2018

[Funding data in millions of dollars (7,234.8 represents $7,234,800,000); all other data in thousands (904.1 represents 904,100). For fiscal years. The Head Start program serves children, families, and pregnant women in all 50 states, DC, and six territories. Data on cumulative enrollment, staff, and volunteers are submitted by Head Start grantees and delegates. Federal funding covers all Head Start programs, including American Indian and Alaska Native programs, Migrant and Seasonal Head Start Programs, and support activities]

| Item | 2010 | 2013 | 2014 | 2015 | 2016 | 2017 | 2018 |
|---|---|---|---|---|---|---|---|
| Federal funding (million dollars) | 7,234.8 | 7,573.1 | [3] 8,598.1 | 8,285.5 | 8,438.9 | 8,877.4 | 9,127.2 |
| Funded enrollment slots [1] | 904.1 | 903.7 | 927.3 | 944.6 | 915.6 | 899.4 | 887.1 |
| Cumulative enrollment [2] | 1,117.7 | 1,129.8 | 1,076.1 | 1,100.4 | 1,097.4 | 1,074.2 | 1,054.7 |
| Children age 2 and under | 146.3 | 177.0 | 173.2 | 193.2 | 230.3 | 243.4 | 258.0 |
| Children age 3 | 386.7 | 392.4 | 375.9 | 399.4 | 383.9 | 374.0 | 364.1 |
| Children age 4 | 548.0 | 531.9 | 497.1 | 480.1 | 455.9 | 427.6 | 404.8 |
| Children age 5 and older | 23.2 | 12.9 | 15.3 | 12.2 | 11.9 | 13.9 | 12.4 |
| Hispanic/Latino | 405.4 | 419.9 | 406.6 | 414.0 | 411.4 | 400.4 | 385.7 |
| Non-Hispanic/non-Latino | 712.3 | 709.8 | 669.5 | 686.3 | 686.0 | 673.7 | 669.0 |
| American Indian/Alaska Native | 41.7 | 44.1 | 45.2 | 45.4 | 42.1 | 42.1 | 41.3 |
| Asian | 19.0 | 19.9 | 19.8 | 21.8 | 22.6 | 22.6 | 22.8 |
| Black/African American | 326.5 | 326.8 | 309.9 | 318.3 | 319.9 | 313.5 | 312.7 |
| Native Hawaiian/Pacific Islander | 6.9 | 6.5 | 7.0 | 9.8 | 7.4 | 7.7 | 7.1 |
| White | 450.3 | 476.4 | 458.0 | 473.5 | 477.8 | 469.6 | 461.2 |
| Biracial/multiracial | 83.9 | 104.4 | 102.2 | 107.2 | 107.5 | 106.2 | 103.3 |
| Other/unspecified | 189.4 | 152.1 | 134.1 | 124.3 | 120.1 | 112.5 | 106.2 |
| Total staff | 228.3 | 236.7 | 226.0 | 230.0 | 241.5 | 240.0 | 246.1 |
| Total volunteers | 1,335.9 | 1,234.6 | 1,167.1 | 1,141.5 | 1,118.8 | 1,086.4 | 1,046.4 |
| Parent volunteers | 881.1 | 817.8 | 800.2 | 782.2 | 783.6 | 769.6 | 738.7 |

[1] Funded enrollment is the number of children and pregnant women supported by federal Head Start funds at any one time during the year. Data are derived from the annual Administration for Children and Families budget and congressional documents, and do not reflect changes made during the year. [2] Cumulative enrollment refers to actual number of children and pregnant women served, including enrollees who left during the year and enrollees who filled those empty slots. More children and families may receive Head Start services cumulatively throughout the year than indicated by funded enrollment numbers. [3] Represents funding available after Congress restored funds in the amount of the previous year's fiscal sequestration.

Source: U.S. Department of Health and Human Services, Administration for Children and Families, Early Childhood Learning & Knowledge Center, "Head Start Program Facts Sheets," <https://eclkc.ohs.acf.hhs.gov/about-us/article/office-head-start-ohs>; and "Office of Head Start Enterprise System," <https://hses.ohs.acf.hhs.gov/pir/home>; accessed June 2019.

## Table 601. Social Assistance Services—Nonemployer Establishments and Receipts: 2010 to 2017

[Receipts in millions of dollars (12,753 represents $12,753,000,000). Includes only firms subject to federal income tax. Nonemployers are businesses with no paid employees. Nonemployer firm receipts may include commissions or earnings]

| Kind of business | NAICS code [1] | 2010 | 2012 | 2013 | 2014 | 2015 | 2016 | 2017 |
|---|---|---|---|---|---|---|---|---|
| ESTABLISHMENTS | | | | | | | | |
| Social assistance, total | 624 | 912,247 | 864,345 | 861,579 | 850,786 | 822,350 | 782,320 | 729,150 |
| Individual and family services | 6241 | 141,971 | 151,564 | 154,024 | 160,562 | 163,337 | 164,218 | 170,672 |
| Community/emergency and other relief services | 6242 | 6,080 | 6,470 | 6,058 | 6,399 | 6,355 | 6,384 | 6,512 |
| Vocational rehabilitation services | 6243 | 11,984 | 12,986 | 12,769 | 12,938 | 12,916 | 12,700 | 12,510 |
| Child day care services | 6244 | 752,212 | 693,325 | 688,728 | 670,887 | 639,742 | 599,018 | 539,456 |
| RECEIPTS (mil. dol) | | | | | | | | |
| Social assistance, total | 624 | 12,753 | 12,804 | 12,813 | 13,114 | 13,238 | 13,099 | 12,992 |
| Individual and family services | 6241 | 2,599 | 2,915 | 3,016 | 3,275 | 3,492 | 3,641 | 3,881 |
| Community/emergency and other relief services | 6242 | 96 | 105 | 98 | 106 | 111 | 114 | 114 |
| Vocational rehabilitation services | 6243 | 287 | 320 | 312 | 318 | 341 | 345 | 343 |
| Child day care services | 6244 | 9,772 | 9,464 | 9,387 | 9,415 | 9,294 | 8,999 | 8,653 |

[1] North American Industry Classification System; see text, Section 15. Data for 2010 based on NAICS 2007; data for 2016 based on NAICS 2012; and data for 2017 based on 2017 NAICS.

Source: U.S. Census Bureau, Nonemployer Statistics, "NES Datasets," <https://www.census.gov/programs-surveys/nonemployer-statistics/data/datasets.html>, accessed July 2019.

## Table 602. Social Assistance Services—Revenue for Employer Firms: 2016 and 2017

[In millions of dollars (174,247 represents $174,247,000,000). Based on Census Bureau's Service Annual Survey and administrative data. Estimates have been adjusted to the results of the 2012 Economic Census. See Appendix III]

| Kind of business | NAICS code [1] | 2016 | | | 2017 | | |
|---|---|---|---|---|---|---|---|
| | | Total | Taxable firms | Tax-exempt firms | Total | Taxable firms | Tax-exempt firms |
| Social assistance, total............ | 624 | 174,247 | 51,506 | 122,741 | 187,064 | 56,087 | 130,977 |
| Child and youth services............... | 62411 | 14,052 | 1,246 | 12,806 | 14,734 | 1,357 | 13,377 |
| Services for elderly and disabled persons......... | 62412 | 44,013 | 18,175 | 25,838 | 47,953 | 19,811 | 28,142 |
| Other individual and family services............... | 62419 | 32,329 | 4,500 | 27,829 | 33,322 | 4,766 | 28,556 |
| Community food services............ | 62421 | 10,865 | (S) | 10,809 | 11,447 | 56 | 11,391 |
| Community housing services........... | 62422 | 12,199 | 110 | 12,089 | 12,709 | 133 | 12,576 |
| Emergency and other relief services.............. | 62423 | 9,208 | (S) | 9,089 | 11,332 | 156 | 11,176 |
| Vocational rehabilitation services.................. | 6243 | 13,486 | 2,268 | 11,218 | 14,012 | 2,381 | 11,631 |
| Child day care services............... | 6244 | 38,095 | 25,032 | 13,063 | 41,555 | 27,427 | 14,128 |

S Figure does not meet publication standards. [1] 2012 North American Industry Classification System.

Source: U.S. Census Bureau, Service Annual Survey, "Service Annual Survey Latest Data (NAICS-basis): 2017," <https://www.census.gov/programs-surveys/sas/data.html>, accessed December 2018.

## Table 603. Emergency and Transitional Beds in Homeless Assistance Systems: 2018

[Data cover all States, DC, Guam, Northern Marianas, Puerto Rico, and the Virgin Islands. Data were reported by approximately 400 Continuums of Care, and were collected for a point-in-time during the last week of January 2018. Data were not independently verified by Department of Housing and Urban Development (HUD)]

| Homeless programs | Total year-round beds | Year-round units/beds [1] | | | | Other beds | |
|---|---|---|---|---|---|---|---|
| | | Family units | Family beds | Adult-only beds | Child-only beds | Seasonal beds [2] | Overflow/ voucher [3] |
| Total...................... | 896,893 | 135,370 | 420,424 | 472,526 | 3,943 | 21,776 | 18,216 |
| Emergency, safe haven, and transitional housing................. | 389,622 | 60,432 | 193,277 | 192,678 | 3,667 | 21,776 | 18,216 |
| Emergency shelters..................... | 286,203 | 44,155 | 144,632 | 138,648 | 2,923 | 21,776 | 18,216 |
| Safe haven [4]............................. | 2,390 | (X) | (X) | 2,390 | (X) | (X) | (X) |
| Transitional housing [5].................. | 101,029 | 16,277 | 48,645 | 51,640 | 744 | (X) | (X) |
| Permanent housing....................... | 507,271 | 74,938 | 227,147 | 279,848 | 276 | (X) | (X) |
| Permanent supportive housing [6]........ | 361,386 | 42,774 | 125,586 | 235,680 | 120 | (X) | (X) |
| Rapid re-housing.......................... | 109,095 | 25,548 | 81,102 | 27,899 | 94 | (X) | (X) |
| Other permanent housing [7].............. | 36,790 | 6,616 | 20,459 | 16,269 | 62 | (X) | (X) |

X Not applicable. [1] Year-round beds are available for use throughout the year and are considered part of the stable inventory of beds for homeless persons. [2] Seasonal beds are typically available during particularly high-demand seasons of the year (e.g. winter months in the North or summer months in the South) to accommodate increased need for emergency shelters to prevent illness or death due to the weather. [3] Overflow beds are typically used during unanticipated emergencies (e.g., precipitous temperature drops or a natural disaster that displaces residents). Voucher beds are made available in a hotel or motel, and often function like overflow beds. [4] A safe haven provides temporary shelter and services for hard-to-reach homeless persons with severe mental illness who come primarily from the streets and have been unable or unwilling to participate in housing or supportive services. Accommodations are private or semi-private. [5] Provides a place to stay with supportive services for up to 24 months. [6] Provides long-term housing with supportive services for formerly homeless people with disabilities, and often also those with chronic homelessness. [7] May or may not include services, and does not require people to have a disability.

Source: U.S. Department of Housing and Urban Development, *2018 Continuum of Care Homeless Assistance Programs: Housing Inventory Count Report,* November 2018. See also <https://www.hudexchange.info/manage-a-program/coc-housing-inventory-count-reports/>.

## Table 604. Homeless Population by Type and Shelter Status: 2010 to 2018

[Data are point-in-time (PIT) counts made on a single night in January by Continuums of Care (CoCs) in all States, DC, and U.S. territories. Data are not independently verified by the Department of Housing and Urban Development (HUD). CoCs are required to provide an unduplicated count of homeless persons according to HUD standards. See HUD's Point-in-Time Count Methodology Guide at <https://www.hudexchange.info/programs/hdx/guides/pit-hic/#general-pit-guides-and-tools>. Sheltered homeless people may be staying in emergency shelters, hotels/motels paid for by charities or government programs, transitional housing programs, or safe havens (temporary shelter for people with severe mental illness). People staying in places not designed for use as regular accommodations, including cars, abandoned buildings, transit stations, and campgrounds, are considered unsheltered]

| Homeless population by type | 2010 | 2013 | 2014 | 2015 | 2016 | 2017 | 2018 |
|---|---|---|---|---|---|---|---|
| Total | 637,077 | 590,364 | 576,450 | 564,708 | 549,928 | 550,996 | 552,830 |
| Sheltered | 403,543 | 394,698 | 401,051 | 391,440 | 373,571 | 360,867 | 358,363 |
| Unsheltered | 233,534 | 195,666 | 175,399 | 173,268 | 176,357 | 190,129 | 194,467 |
| Individuals [1] | 395,140 | 368,174 | 360,189 | 358,422 | 355,212 | 366,585 | 372,417 |
| Sheltered | 212,218 | 203,127 | 209,148 | 205,616 | 198,008 | 193,144 | 194,340 |
| Unsheltered | 182,922 | 165,047 | 151,041 | 152,806 | 157,204 | 173,441 | 178,077 |
| Persons in families with children | 241,937 | 222,190 | 216,261 | 206,286 | 194,716 | 184,411 | 180,413 |
| Sheltered | 191,325 | 191,571 | 191,903 | 185,824 | 175,563 | 167,723 | 164,023 |
| Unsheltered | 50,612 | 30,619 | 24,358 | 20,462 | 19,153 | 16,688 | 16,390 |
| Chronically homeless individuals [2] | 106,062 | 86,289 | 83,989 | 83,170 | 77,486 | 86,705 | 88,640 |
| Sheltered | 43,329 | 29,418 | 31,203 | 28,355 | 24,596 | 26,629 | 30,754 |
| Unsheltered | 62,733 | 56,871 | 52,786 | 54,815 | 52,890 | 60,076 | 57,886 |
| Chronically homeless people in families [2] | (NA) | 16,539 | 15,143 | 13,105 | 8,646 | 8,387 | 8,273 |
| Sheltered | (NA) | 8,150 | 9,362 | 8,412 | 5,512 | 5,980 | 5,821 |
| Unsheltered | (NA) | 8,389 | 5,781 | 4,693 | 3,134 | 2,407 | 2,452 |
| Veterans | 74,087 | 55,619 | 49,689 | 47,725 | 39,471 | 40,020 | 37,878 |
| Sheltered | 43,437 | 34,909 | 32,119 | 31,505 | 26,404 | 24,690 | 23,312 |
| Unsheltered | 30,650 | 20,710 | 17,570 | 16,220 | 13,067 | 15,330 | 14,566 |
| Children under age 18, unaccompanied | 8,153 | (NA) | (NA) | 4,667 | 3,824 | 4,635 | 4,093 |
| Sheltered | 4,349 | (NA) | (NA) | 2,287 | 2,218 | 2,122 | 2,014 |
| Unsheltered | 3,804 | (NA) | (NA) | 2,380 | 1,606 | 2,513 | 2,079 |
| Severely mentally ill | 107,539 | (NA) | 116,363 | 104,083 | 107,801 | (NA) | 111,122 |
| Sheltered | 71,989 | (NA) | 70,253 | 59,394 | 61,846 | (NA) | 58,942 |
| Unsheltered | 35,550 | (NA) | 46,110 | 44,689 | 45,955 | (NA) | 52,180 |
| Chronic substance abuse | 139,853 | (NA) | 116,516 | 103,888 | 94,496 | (NA) | 86,647 |
| Sheltered | 95,049 | (NA) | 70,500 | 60,071 | 52,290 | (NA) | 45,372 |
| Unsheltered | 44,804 | (NA) | 46,016 | 43,817 | 42,206 | (NA) | 41,275 |
| Persons with HIV/AIDS | 14,498 | (NA) | 12,223 | 9,294 | 9,240 | (NA) | 10,064 |
| Sheltered | 10,590 | (NA) | 9,638 | 6,532 | 6,860 | (NA) | 7,244 |
| Unsheltered | 3,908 | (NA) | 2,585 | 2,762 | 2,380 | (NA) | 2,820 |
| Domestic violence victims | 66,878 | (NA) | 59,352 | 67,690 | 68,464 | (NA) | 48,666 |
| Sheltered | 49,709 | (NA) | 42,893 | 41,015 | 41,779 | (NA) | 30,607 |
| Unsheltered | 17,169 | (NA) | 16,459 | 26,675 | 26,685 | (NA) | 18,059 |

NA Not available. [1] People who are not part of a family with children. Includes homeless single adults, unaccompanied youth, or individuals in multiple-adult or multiple-child households. [2] An individual or household head of a family with a disability, and continuously homeless for a year or more, or with at least four episodes of homelessness in the last 3 years.

Source: U.S. Department of Housing and Urban Development, HUD Exchange, "PIT and HIC Data Since 2007: 2007 - 2018 PIT Counts by State," December 2018, <https://www.hudexchange.info/resource/3031/pit-and-hic-data-since-2007/>, accessed February 2019; and *2018 CoC (Continuum of Care) Homeless Populations and Subpopulations Report,* November 2018 and earlier reports. See also <https://www.hudexchange.info/programs/coc/coc-homeless-populations-and-subpopulations-reports/>.

## Table 605. Volunteers by Selected Characteristics: 2017

[In percent. Covers adults age 16 and over who performed unpaid volunteer activities for an organization at any time during the 12-month period from September 1 to the week of the survey. Data were collected by the September 2017 Volunteering and Civic Life Supplement to the Current Population Survey (CPS)]

| Volunteer characteristics | Percent volun- teering | Percent of volunteers by main organization type [1] | | | | | | | |
|---|---|---|---|---|---|---|---|---|---|
| | | Civic and political [2] | Educational or youth service | Environ- mental or animal care | Hospital or other health | Public safety | Religious | Sport, hobby, cultural, or arts | Other |
| Total [3] | 30.3 | 6.2 | 19.2 | 5.0 | 6.0 | 6.0 | 32.0 | 25.7 | 3.6 |
| Men | 26.5 | 7.8 | 16.2 | 4.7 | 4.3 | 3.1 | 30.3 | 29.6 | 4.0 |
| Women | 33.8 | 5.1 | 21.4 | 5.1 | 7.2 | 1.7 | 33.3 | 22.8 | 3.3 |
| Age 16 to 19 | 28.3 | 3.7 | 24.1 | 4.5 | 4.7 | 1.5 | 22.9 | 35.5 | 3.0 |
| Age 20 to 24 | 22.7 | 8.7 | 19.9 | 9.5 | 10.1 | 2.4 | 25.6 | 20.6 | 3.2 |
| Age 25 to 34 | 27.8 | 6.8 | 24.6 | 7.2 | 7.3 | 2.7 | 25.5 | 22.7 | 3.3 |
| Age 35 to 44 | 36.9 | 5.1 | 27.1 | 3.7 | 4.3 | 2.7 | 24.2 | 29.7 | 3.2 |
| Age 45 to 54 | 34.0 | 4.9 | 19.7 | 4.2 | 5.5 | 2.0 | 30.7 | 29.8 | 3.3 |
| Age 55 to 64 | 30.2 | 7.3 | 12.7 | 5.3 | 6.0 | 2.5 | 40.0 | 22.1 | 4.2 |
| Age 65 and older | 28.0 | 7.5 | 9.4 | 3.5 | 6.2 | 1.9 | 45.7 | 21.5 | 4.4 |
| Less than high school | 10.1 | 4.0 | 25.3 | 2.8 | 3.2 | 1.7 | 32.6 | 26.7 | 3.7 |
| High school [4] | 18.8 | 4.6 | 19.4 | 4.6 | 5.4 | 2.4 | 39.1 | 19.8 | 4.5 |
| Some college [5] | 32.1 | 6.3 | 17.8 | 5.0 | 6.1 | 3.4 | 34.0 | 23.7 | 3.8 |
| College graduate | 45.7 | 7.0 | 19.1 | 5.4 | 6.5 | 1.7 | 28.6 | 28.6 | 3.2 |

[1] Main organization is the organization for which the volunteer worked the most hours. [2] Includes organizations involved in professional and/or international activities. [3] Data by education cover persons age 25 and over. [4] Includes high school diploma or equivalent. [5] Includes "some college, no degree" and "associate degree."

Source: Corporation for National and Community Service, "Volunteering in America," <https://www.nationalservice.gov/serve/via>, accessed April 2019.

# Table 606. Charitable Giving by Source and Type of Recipient Organization: 1990 to 2018

[In billions of dollars (98.5 represents $98,500,000,000). Individual giving is estimated using Internal Revenue Service information from individual tax returns, and from a study of approximately 8,000 to 9,000 households participating in the Philanthropy Panel Study conducted by Indiana University Lilly Family School of Philanthropy. Data on foundation giving are provided by Candid (formerly the Foundation Center). Corporate giving data are based on itemized contributions claimed on federal tax returns, and also from Candid. Data on contributions by bequest are primarily based on data from the Council for Aid to Education, with additional calculations performed by Giving USA using IRS tax data on charitable bequest deductions. Giving to recipient organizations are from various research organizations, including the Evangelical Council for Financial Accountability and other nonprofit research organizations]

| Source and allocation | 1990 | 2000 | 2005 | 2010 | 2011 | 2012 | 2013 | 2014 | 2015 | 2016 | 2017 | 2018 |
|---|---|---|---|---|---|---|---|---|---|---|---|---|
| **Total charitable giving** | **98.5** | **229.7** | **292.4** | **288.2** | **298.5** | **332.6** | **332.5** | **357.6** | **375.9** | **396.5** | **424.7** | **427.7** |
| Individuals | 79.0 | 174.1 | 220.8 | 208.0 | 213.9 | 244.4 | 242.4 | 252.3 | 264.7 | 279.4 | 295.3 | 292.1 |
| Foundations [1] | 7.2 | 24.6 | 32.4 | 41.0 | 43.8 | 46.4 | 49.9 | 54.9 | 57.3 | 63.1 | 70.7 | 75.9 |
| Corporations | 5.5 | 10.7 | 15.2 | 15.8 | 15.6 | 17.2 | 15.9 | 18.3 | 18.3 | 19.4 | 19.0 | 20.1 |
| Charitable bequests | 6.8 | 20.3 | 24.0 | 23.4 | 25.2 | 24.6 | 24.4 | 32.2 | 35.6 | 34.6 | 39.7 | 39.7 |
| Giving by recipient organization: | | | | | | | | | | | | |
| Religion | 49.8 | 77.0 | 90.9 | 97.5 | 101.8 | 105.8 | 110.4 | 116.0 | 119.2 | 123.8 | 126.5 | 124.5 |
| Education | 11.8 | 28.8 | 35.0 | 42.2 | 42.9 | 46.9 | 44.5 | 49.4 | 53.1 | 53.7 | 59.5 | 58.7 |
| Human services | 6.7 | 20.8 | 30.4 | 36.8 | 37.4 | 41.1 | 41.1 | 43.6 | 46.7 | 48.7 | 51.7 | 51.5 |
| Health | 7.8 | 15.3 | 20.3 | 27.7 | 25.9 | 26.2 | 32.3 | 33.2 | 34.2 | 37.7 | 40.7 | 40.8 |
| Public/societal benefit | 6.6 | 15.0 | 20.8 | 19.2 | 21.4 | 22.9 | 24.3 | 25.7 | 26.9 | 30.6 | 32.4 | 31.2 |
| Arts, culture, and humanities | 3.7 | 10.6 | 12.4 | 13.4 | 12.8 | 13.9 | 14.6 | 15.9 | 17.6 | 17.1 | 19.4 | 19.5 |
| International affairs | 2.1 | 6.3 | 12.7 | 13.9 | 15.2 | 16.0 | 19.4 | 20.3 | 23.7 | 21.8 | 20.9 | 22.9 |
| Environment/animals | 1.3 | 4.9 | 6.5 | 7.9 | 8.2 | 8.9 | 8.6 | 9.6 | 10.6 | 11.2 | 12.3 | 12.7 |
| Gifts to foundations [1] | 3.8 | 24.7 | 24.5 | 26.1 | 30.2 | 40.1 | 40.8 | 43.8 | 38.5 | 39.7 | 54.0 | 50.3 |
| Gifts to individuals | (NA) | (NA) | 3.1 | 4.9 | 6.1 | 5.8 | 7.2 | 6.8 | 6.9 | 9.9 | 9.3 | 9.1 |
| Unallocated [2] | 5.0 | 26.4 | 36.0 | -1.4 | -3.3 | 5.0 | -10.7 | -6.5 | -1.4 | 2.4 | -2.0 | 6.5 |

NA Not available. [1] Data are from Candid, formerly the Foundation Center. [2] Money deducted as a charitable contribution by donors but not allocated to sources. May include gifts to governmental entities, in-kind giving, or gifts to new charities.

Source: Giving USA Foundation, Chicago, IL, *Giving USA 2019: The Annual Report on Philanthropy for the Year 2018* ©, researched and written at the Indiana University Lilly Family School of Philanthropy. See also <https://givingusa.org/>.

# Table 607. Domestic Private Foundations—Financial Information: 2000 to 2015

[Financial data in billions of dollars (409.5 represents $409,500,000,000). Minus sign (-) indicates loss]

| Item | 2000 | 2005 | 2007 | 2008 | 2009 | 2010 | 2011 | 2012 | 2013 | 2014 | 2015 |
|---|---|---|---|---|---|---|---|---|---|---|---|
| Number of tax returns | 66,738 | 79,535 | 84,613 | 90,850 | 92,624 | 93,436 | 92,990 | 93,542 | 95,121 | 97,484 | 99,683 |
| Nonoperating foundations [1] | 61,501 | 72,800 | 77,457 | 83,024 | 84,660 | 86,254 | 85,500 | 85,447 | 86,584 | 88,878 | 90,699 |
| Operating foundations [2] | 5,238 | 6,734 | 7,156 | 7,826 | 7,964 | 7,181 | 7,490 | 8,095 | 8,537 | 8,606 | 8,984 |
| Total assets, book value [3] | 409.5 | 481.8 | 591.2 | 531.4 | 550.9 | 584.2 | 594.3 | 633.1 | 693.3 | 738.4 | 754.3 |
| Total assets, fair market value [3] | 471.6 | 545.9 | 652.4 | 526.5 | 588.5 | 641.0 | 641.3 | 698.6 | 791.0 | 830.3 | 829.4 |
| Investments in securities | 361.4 | 373.1 | 400.3 | 287.6 | 324.7 | 353.3 | 344.8 | 373.3 | 430.9 | 459.3 | 451.7 |
| Total revenue | 72.8 | 76.4 | 107.3 | 49.7 | 52.2 | 72.5 | 79.4 | 95.3 | 106.1 | 119.5 | 107.0 |
| Total expenses | 37.4 | 42.8 | 58.8 | 60.3 | 56.2 | 60.1 | 64.3 | 64.8 | 73.7 | 79.2 | 81.0 |
| Contributions, gifts, and grants paid | 27.6 | 31.9 | 42.6 | 42.8 | 40.9 | 44.7 | 46.9 | 48.6 | 54.2 | 57.6 | 58.7 |
| Excess of revenue over expenses (net) | 35.3 | 33.5 | 48.6 | -10.6 | -4.0 | 12.3 | 15.1 | 30.5 | 32.4 | 40.3 | 26.0 |
| Net investment income [4] | 48.8 | 44.3 | 62.8 | 23.1 | 17.6 | 29.8 | 34.2 | 38.4 | 50.4 | 59.9 | 48.8 |

[1] Generally provide charitable support through grants and other financial means to charitable organizations; the majority of foundations are nonoperating. [2] Generally conduct their own charitable activities, e.g., museums. [3] Data for book and fair market value of assets were reduced to avoid overstating the joint assets of the Bill and Melinda Gates Foundation and the Bill and Melinda Gates Foundation Trust, by tax year as follows: 2007, $38.7 billion; 2008, $29.6 billion; 2009, $33.4 billion; 2010, $36.7 billion; 2011, $33.8 billion; 2012, $36.4 billion; 2013, $40.5 billion; 2014, $43.4 billion; and 2015, $39.3 billion. [4] This equals gross investment income less allowable deductions. Represents income not considered related to a foundation's charitable purpose, e.g., interest, dividends, and capital gains. Foundations could be subject to an excise tax on such income.

Source: Internal Revenue Service, *Statistics of Income Bulletin*, "SOI Tax Stats – Domestic Private Foundation and Charitable Trust Statistics," <https://www.irs.gov/statistics>, accessed April 2019.

# Table 608. Foundations—Number and Finances by Foundation Type: 2000 to 2017

[In millions of dollars (486,085 represents $486,085,000,000), except number of foundations. Figures are for fiscal years, and cover only grantmaking foundations. Covers nongovernmental nonprofit organizations with funds and programs managed by their own trustees or directors, whose goals were to maintain or aid social, educational, religious, or other activities deemed to serve the common good. Excludes organizations that make general appeals to the public for funds, act as trade associations for industrial or other special groups, or do not currently award grants]

| Year | Number | Assets (million dollars) | Gifts received (million dollars) | Total giving [1] (million dollars) |
|---|---|---|---|---|
| 2000 | 56,582 | 486,085 | 27,614 | 24,563 |
| 2010 | 76,610 | 643,974 | 37,961 | 45,858 |
| 2015 | 86,203 | 890,061 | 53,157 | 62,794 |
| **Total, 2016** | **85,987** | **907,625** | **57,500** | **68,948** |
| Independent | 79,132 | 741,859 | 33,413 | 47,204 |
| Operating | 3,377 | 46,578 | 9,456 | 8,107 |
| Corporate | 2,683 | 29,622 | 4,982 | 5,823 |
| Community | 795 | 89,565 | 9,648 | 7,814 |
| **Total, 2017** | **86,124** | **1,013,523** | **72,993** | **77,183** |
| Independent | 79,351 | 827,082 | 41,574 | 50,385 |
| Operating | 3,311 | 52,142 | 12,616 | 11,092 |
| Corporate | 2,670 | 31,673 | 7,286 | 6,457 |
| Community | 792 | 102,626 | 11,518 | 9,249 |

[1] Includes grants, scholarships, and employee matching gifts; excludes set-asides, loans, program-related investments (PRIs), and program expenses.

Source: Candid, New York, NY ©, "Foundation Stats," <http://data.foundationcenter.org/>, accessed August 2019, and unpublished data.

# Table 609. Nonprofit Charitable Organizations—Financial Information: 2000 to 2015

[In billions of dollars (1,562.5 represents $1,562,500,000,000), except as indicated. Includes data reported by organizations described in Internal Revenue Code, Section 501(c)(3), excluding private foundations and most religious organizations. Prior to 2010, organizations with receipts under $25,000 were not required to file. Beginning with 2010, organizations with receipts under $50,000 were not required to file]

| Year | Number of tax returns (1,000) | Total assets | Net assets | Revenue Total [1] | Revenue Program service revenue [2] | Revenue Contributions, gifts, and grants | Total expenses | Excess of revenue over expenses (net) |
|---|---|---|---|---|---|---|---|---|
| 2000 | 230.2 | 1,562.5 | 1,023.2 | 866.2 | 579.1 | 199.1 | 796.4 | 69.8 |
| 2001 | 240.6 | 1,631.7 | 1,020.3 | 897.0 | 630.8 | 212.4 | 862.7 | 34.3 |
| 2002 | 251.7 | 1,733.9 | 1,040.3 | 955.3 | 691.8 | 214.5 | 934.7 | 20.6 |
| 2003 | 263.4 | 1,899.9 | 1,164.3 | 1,072.2 | 754.6 | 230.0 | 1,009.7 | 62.5 |
| 2004 | 276.2 | 2,058.6 | 1,276.1 | 1,153.0 | 801.2 | 248.6 | 1,058.5 | 94.5 |
| 2005 | 286.6 | 2,241.9 | 1,411.3 | 1,252.9 | 852.6 | 276.3 | 1,137.9 | 115.0 |
| 2006 | 301.2 | 2,549.7 | 1,617.7 | 1,370.9 | 920.2 | 303.2 | 1,230.4 | 140.5 |
| 2007 | 313.1 | 2,683.4 | 1,674.4 | 1,445.9 | 980.3 | 324.5 | 1,317.2 | 128.7 |
| 2008 | 315.2 | 2,521.2 | 1,434.7 | 1,378.3 | 1,038.0 | 320.7 | 1,396.4 | -18.1 |
| 2009 | 320.8 | 2,697.1 | 1,564.2 | 1,481.1 | 1,085.9 | 327.4 | 1,433.9 | 47.2 |
| 2010 | 269.5 | 2,946.5 | 1,772.4 | 1,593.0 | 1,147.3 | 344.9 | 1,497.2 | 95.8 |
| 2011 | 274.3 | 3,030.1 | 1,781.9 | 1,647.9 | 1,194.2 | 357.4 | 1,558.4 | 89.5 |
| 2012 | 279.4 | 3,274.0 | 1,970.4 | 1,734.2 | 1,248.2 | 371.1 | 1,624.1 | 110.1 |
| 2013 | 285.9 | 3,507.6 | 2,184.0 | 1,828.2 | 1,296.1 | 394.1 | 1,700.4 | 127.8 |
| 2014 | 201.8 | 3,703.1 | 2,280.9 | 1,941.5 | 1,382.2 | 417.6 | 1,793.3 | 148.2 |
| 2015 | 208.9 | 3,793.3 | 2,296.2 | 2,004.6 | 1,466.0 | 425.8 | 1,900.6 | 104.0 |

[1] Includes other sources of revenue not shown separately. [2] Represents fees collected by organizations in support of their tax-exempt purposes, such as tuition and fees at educational institutions, hospital patient charges, and admission and activity fees collected by museums and other nonprofit organizations or institutions.

Source: U.S. Internal Revenue Service, Statistics of Income, "SOI Tax Stats – Charities & Other Tax-Exempt Organizations Statistics," <https://www.irs.gov/uac/tax-stats>, accessed August 2018.

# Table 610. Individual Charitable Contributions by State: 2016

[In units, as indicated (235,734 represents $235,734,000,000). Covers returns primarily for 2016 tax year that were filed during 2017, but may also include a limited number of returns for earlier tax years that were also received during 2017. Data will not agree with data in other tables due to differing survey methodology used to derive state data]

| State | Charitable contributions Number of returns (1,000) | Charitable contributions Amount (mil. dol.) | State | Charitable contributions Number of returns (1,000) | Charitable contributions Amount (mil. dol.) | State | Charitable contributions Number of returns (1,000) | Charitable contributions Amount (mil. dol.) | State | Charitable contributions Number of returns (1,000) | Charitable contributions Amount (mil. dol.) |
|---|---|---|---|---|---|---|---|---|---|---|---|
| Total [1] | 37,128 | 235,734 | ID | 173 | 1,211 | MO | 595 | 3,850 | PA | 1,455 | 7,333 |
| AL | 470 | 3,546 | IL | 1,595 | 9,240 | MT | 112 | 629 | RI | 145 | 487 |
| AK | 57 | 327 | IN | 570 | 3,487 | NE | 209 | 1,243 | SC | 524 | 3,377 |
| AZ | 730 | 3,701 | IA | 352 | 1,694 | NV | 293 | 1,771 | SD | 58 | 582 |
| AR | 224 | 2,455 | KS | 281 | 1,952 | NH | 171 | 807 | TN | 504 | 4,361 |
| CA | 5,154 | 36,634 | KY | 408 | 2,198 | NJ | 1,547 | 6,694 | TX | 2,276 | 16,691 |
| CO | 713 | 4,269 | LA | 374 | 2,487 | NM | 159 | 814 | UT | 402 | 4,082 |
| CT | 607 | 3,319 | ME | 135 | 492 | NY | 2,784 | 19,583 | VT | 66 | 302 |
| DE | 122 | 558 | MD | 1,143 | 5,999 | NC | 1,127 | 6,881 | VA | 1,213 | 6,717 |
| DC | 113 | 912 | MA | 1,048 | 6,093 | ND | 49 | 365 | WA | 855 | 7,166 |
| FL | 1,854 | 13,087 | MI | 1,064 | 5,712 | OH | 1,147 | 5,778 | WV | 95 | 499 |
| GA | 1,262 | 10,151 | MN | 812 | 3,947 | OK | 306 | 2,440 | WI | 716 | 3,142 |
| HI | 163 | 671 | MS | 250 | 1,786 | OR | 557 | 2,747 | WY | 42 | 542 |

[1] Includes returns filed by members of the armed forces stationed overseas, other U.S. citizens abroad, and residents of Puerto Rico with income from sources outside Puerto Rico or with income earned as U.S. government employees.

Source: U.S. Internal Revenue Service, Statistics of Income, Individual Income Tax Return (Form 1040) Statistics: State Data, "SOI Tax Stats - Historic Table 2," <https://www.irs.gov/uac/soi-tax-stats-individual-income-tax-return-form-1040-statistics>, accessed September 2018.

# Labor Force, Employment, and Earnings

This section presents statistics on the labor force; its distribution by occupation and industry affiliation; and the supply of, demand for, and conditions of labor. The chief source of these data is the Current Population Survey (CPS) conducted by the U.S. Census Bureau for the Bureau of Labor Statistics (BLS). Comprehensive historical and current data are available from the BLS internet site at <http://www.bls.gov/cps/>. These data are published on a current basis in the BLS monthly publication *Employment and Earnings Online*. Detailed data on the labor force are also available from the Census Bureau's decennial census of population.

**Types of data**—Most statistics in this section are obtained by two methods: household interviews or questionnaires and reports of establishment payroll records. Each method provides data that the other cannot suitably supply. Population characteristics, for example, are readily obtainable only from the household survey, while detailed industrial classifications can be readily derived only from establishment records.

CPS data are obtained from a monthly sample survey of the population. The CPS is used to gather data for the calendar week, generally the week including the 12th of the month, and provides current comprehensive data on the labor force (see text, Section 1, Population). The CPS provides information on the work status of the population without duplication since each person is classified as employed, unemployed, or not in the labor force. Employed persons holding more than one job are counted only once, according to the job at which they worked the most hours during the survey week.

*Employment and Earnings Online* presents data including national totals of the number of persons in the civilian labor force by sex, disability status, race, Hispanic origin, and age; the number employed; hours of work; industry and occupational groups; usual weekly earnings; and the number unemployed, as well as reasons for and duration of unemployment. Annual data shown in this section are averages of monthly figures for each calendar year, unless otherwise specified.

The CPS also produces annual estimates of employment and unemployment for each state, 50 large metropolitan statistical areas, and selected cities. These estimates are published annually in *Geographic Profile of Employment and Unemployment* available at <https://www.bls.gov/opub/geographic-profile/home.htm>.

Data based on establishment records are compiled by the BLS and cooperating state agencies as part of an ongoing Current Employment Statistics (CES) program. The BLS collects survey data monthly from a probability-based sample of nonfarm, business establishments. Data collection centers perform initial enrollment of each firm via telephone, collect the data for several months via Computer Assisted Telephone Interviewing (CATI), and where possible transfer respondents to a self-reporting mode such as touch-tone data entry, fax, or web collection. Very large, multi-establishment firms' ongoing reporting is established via Electronic Data Interchange (EDI). CES data are adjusted annually to data from government unemployment insurance administrative records, which are supplemented by data from other government agencies. The estimates exclude self-employed persons, private household workers, unpaid family workers, agricultural workers, and members of the Armed Forces.

The CES counts workers each time they appear on a payroll during the reference period (the payroll period that includes the 12th of the month). Thus, unlike the CPS, a person with two jobs is counted twice. The establishment survey is designed to provide estimates of nonfarm wage and salary employment, average weekly hours, and average hourly and weekly earnings by detailed industry for the nation, states, and selected metropolitan areas. Establishment survey data also are published in *Employment and Earnings Online*. Historical national data are available at <http://www.bls.gov/ces/>. Historical data for states and metropolitan areas are available at <http://www.bls.gov/sae/>. CES estimates are currently classified by the 2017 North American Industry Classification System (NAICS). All published series for the nation have a NAICS-based history extending back to at least 1990. Employment series for total nonfarm and other high-level aggregates start in 1939.

For more information on data concepts, sample design, and estimating methods for the CES Survey, see the BLS Handbook of Methods, Chapter 2 <http://www.bls.gov/opub/hom/>. For information regarding revisions and collection rates, see <https://www.bls.gov/web/empsit/cesbmart.htm>.

**Labor force**—According to the CPS definitions, the civilian labor force comprises all civilians in the noninstitutionalized population aged 16 years and over classified as "employed" or "unemployed" according to specific criteria. *Employed* civilians comprise (a) all civilians, who, during the reference week, did any work for pay or profit (minimum of an hour's work) or worked 15 hours or more as unpaid workers in a family enterprise and (b) all civilians who were not working but who had jobs or businesses from which they were temporarily absent for noneconomic reasons (illness, weather conditions, vacation, labor-management dispute, etc.) whether they were paid for the time off or were seeking other jobs. *Unemployed* persons comprise all civilians who had no employment during the reference week, who made specific efforts to find a job within the previous 4 weeks (such as applying directly to an employer or to a public employment service or checking with friends) and who were available for work during that week, except for temporary illness. Persons on layoff from a job and expecting recall also are classified as unemployed. All other civilian persons, 16 years old and over, are classified as "not in the labor force."

Various breaks in the CPS data series have occurred over time due to the introduction of population adjustments and other changes. For details on these breaks in series and the effect that they had on the CPS data, see the BLS website at <www.bls.gov/cps/documentation.htm#concepts>.

Beginning in January of each year, the CPS data reflect the introduction of revised population controls. For additional information on the effects of revised population controls on estimates from the CPS, see <www.bls.gov/cps/documentation.htm#pop>.

**Hours and earnings**—Average hourly earnings, based on establishment data, are gross earnings (i.e., earnings before payroll deductions) and include overtime premiums; they exclude irregular bonuses and value of payments in kind. Hours are those for which pay was received. Annual wages and salaries from the CPS consist of total monies received for work performed by an employee during the income year. It includes wages, salaries, commissions, tips, piece-rate payments, and cash bonuses earned before deductions were made for taxes, bonds, union dues, etc. Persons who worked 35 hours or more are classified as working full-time.

**Industry and occupational groups**—Industry data derived from the CPS for 1983-91 utilize the 1980 census industrial classification developed from the 1972 Standard Industrial Classification (SIC). CPS data from 1971 to 1982 were based on the 1970 census classification system, which was developed from the 1967 SIC. Most of the industry categories were not affected by the change in classification.

The occupational classification system used in the 1980 census and in the CPS for 1983-91, evolved from the 1980 Standard Occupational Classification (SOC) system, first introduced in 1977. Occupational categories used in the 1980 census classification system are so radically different from the 1970 census system used in the CPS through 1982 that their implementation represented a break in historical data series.

Beginning in January 1992, the occupational and industrial classification systems used in the 1990 census were introduced into the CPS. (These systems were largely based on the 1980 SOC and the 1987 SIC systems, respectively.)

Beginning in 2003, the 2002 occupational and industrial classification systems were introduced into the CPS. These systems were derived from the 2000 SOC and the 2002 NAICS. The composition of detailed occupational and industrial classifications in the new classification systems was substantially changed from the previous systems in use, as was the structure for aggregating them into broad groups. Consequently, the use of the new classification systems created breaks in existing data series at all levels of aggregation. CPS data using the new classification systems are available for data from 2000. Additional information on the occupational and industrial classifications systems used in the CPS, including changes over time, appear on the BLS website at <www.bls.gov/cps/documentation.htm#oi>. Establishments responding to the establishment survey are classified according to the 2012 NAICS. Previously they were classified according to the SIC manual. See text, Section 15, Business Enterprise, for information about the SIC manual and NAICS.

**Productivity**—BLS publishes data on output per hour (labor productivity), output per combined unit of labor and capital input (multifactor productivity), and, for industry groups and industries, output per combined unit of capital, labor, energy, materials, and purchased service inputs. Labor productivity and related indexes are published for the business sector as a whole and its major subsectors: nonfarm business, manufacturing, and nonfinancial corporations, and for over 200 detailed industries. Productivity indexes that take into account capital, labor, energy, materials, and service inputs are published for 18 major manufacturing industry groups, 86 detailed manufacturing industries, utility services, and air and railroad transportation. The major sector data are published in the BLS quarterly news release *Productivity and Costs* and in the annual *Multifactor Productivity Trends* release. Industry productivity measures are updated and published annually in the news releases *Productivity and Costs by Industry* and *Multifactor Productivity Trends by Industry*. The latest data are available at the Labor Productivity and Costs website at <http://www.bls.gov/lpc/> and the Multifactor Productivity website at <http://www.bls.gov/mfp>. Detailed information on methods, limitations, and data sources appears in the BLS *Handbook of Methods*, Chapters 10 and 11 at <http://www.bls.gov/opub/hom/home.htm> and <http://www.bls.gov/lpc/lpcmethods.htm>.

**Unions**—As defined here, unions include traditional labor unions and employee associations similar to labor unions. Data on union membership status provided by BLS are for employed wage and salary workers and relate to their principal job. Earnings by union membership status are usual weekly earnings of full-time wage and salary workers. The information is collected through the Current Population Survey.

**Work stoppages**—Work stoppages include all strikes and lockouts known to BLS that last for at least 1 full day or shift and involve 1,000 or more workers. All stoppages, whether or not authorized by a union, legal or illegal, are counted. Excluded are work slowdowns and instances where employees report to work late or leave early to attend meetings or rallies.

**Seasonal adjustment**—Many economic statistics reflect a regularly recurring seasonal movement that can be estimated on the basis of past experience. By eliminating that part of the change which can be ascribed to usual seasonal variation (e.g., climate or school openings and closings), it is possible to observe the cyclical and other nonseasonal movements in the series. However, in evaluating deviations from the seasonal pattern—that is, changes in a seasonally adjusted series—it is important to note that seasonal adjustment is merely an approximation based on past experience. Seasonally adjusted estimates have a broader margin of possible error than the original data on which they are based, since they are subject not only to sampling and other errors, but also are affected by the uncertainties of the adjustment process itself. Consistent with BLS practices, annual estimates will be published only for not seasonally-adjusted data.

**Statistical reliability**—For discussion of statistical collection, estimation, sampling procedures, and measures of statistical reliability applicable to Census Bureau and BLS data, see Appendix III.

# Table 611. Civilian Population—Employment Status: 1970 to 2018

[In thousands (137,085 represents 137,085,000), except as indicated. Annual averages of monthly figures. Civilian noninstitutionalized population 16 years old and over. Data not strictly comparable with data for earlier years; see BLS Handbook of Methods, <http://www.bls.gov/opub/hom/>. Based on Current Population Survey; see text, Section 1 and Appendix III]

| Year | Civilian noninstitutional population | Civilian labor force | | | | Unemployed | | Not in labor force | |
|---|---|---|---|---|---|---|---|---|---|
| | | Total | Percent of population | Employed | Employment/population ratio [1] | Number | Percent of labor force | Number | Percent of population |
| 1970 | 137,085 | 82,771 | 60.4 | 78,678 | 57.4 | 4,093 | 4.9 | 54,315 | 39.6 |
| 1980 | 167,745 | 106,940 | 63.8 | 99,303 | 59.2 | 7,637 | 7.1 | 60,806 | 36.2 |
| 1990 | 189,164 | 125,840 | 66.5 | 118,793 | 62.8 | 7,047 | 5.6 | 63,324 | 33.5 |
| 2000 | 212,577 | 142,583 | 67.1 | 136,891 | 64.4 | 5,692 | 4.0 | 69,994 | 32.9 |
| 2001 | 215,092 | 143,734 | 66.8 | 136,933 | 63.7 | 6,801 | 4.7 | 71,359 | 33.2 |
| 2002 | 217,570 | 144,863 | 66.6 | 136,485 | 62.7 | 8,378 | 5.8 | 72,707 | 33.4 |
| 2003 | 221,168 | 146,510 | 66.2 | 137,736 | 62.3 | 8,774 | 6.0 | 74,658 | 33.8 |
| 2004 | 223,357 | 147,401 | 66.0 | 139,252 | 62.3 | 8,149 | 5.5 | 75,956 | 34.0 |
| 2005 | 226,082 | 149,320 | 66.0 | 141,730 | 62.7 | 7,591 | 5.1 | 76,762 | 34.0 |
| 2006 | 228,815 | 151,428 | 66.2 | 144,427 | 63.1 | 7,001 | 4.6 | 77,387 | 33.8 |
| 2007 | 231,867 | 153,124 | 66.0 | 146,047 | 63.0 | 7,078 | 4.6 | 78,743 | 34.0 |
| 2008 | 233,788 | 154,287 | 66.0 | 145,362 | 62.2 | 8,924 | 5.8 | 79,501 | 34.0 |
| 2009 | 235,801 | 154,142 | 65.4 | 139,877 | 59.3 | 14,265 | 9.3 | 81,659 | 34.6 |
| 2010 | 237,830 | 153,889 | 64.7 | 139,064 | 58.5 | 14,825 | 9.6 | 83,941 | 35.3 |
| 2011 | 239,618 | 153,617 | 64.1 | 139,869 | 58.4 | 13,747 | 8.9 | 86,001 | 35.9 |
| 2012 | 243,284 | 154,975 | 63.7 | 142,469 | 58.6 | 12,506 | 8.1 | 88,310 | 36.3 |
| 2013 | 245,679 | 155,389 | 63.2 | 143,929 | 58.6 | 11,460 | 7.4 | 90,290 | 36.8 |
| 2014 | 247,947 | 155,922 | 62.9 | 146,305 | 59.0 | 9,617 | 6.2 | 92,025 | 37.1 |
| 2015 | 250,801 | 157,130 | 62.7 | 148,834 | 59.3 | 8,296 | 5.3 | 93,671 | 37.3 |
| 2016 | 253,538 | 159,187 | 62.8 | 151,436 | 59.7 | 7,751 | 4.9 | 94,351 | 37.2 |
| 2017 | 255,079 | 160,320 | 62.9 | 153,337 | 60.1 | 6,982 | 4.4 | 94,759 | 37.1 |
| 2018 | 257,791 | 162,075 | 62.9 | 155,761 | 60.4 | 6,314 | 3.9 | 95,716 | 37.1 |

[1] Civilian employed as a percent of the civilian noninstitutional population.

Source: U.S. Bureau of Labor Statistics, "Employment and Earnings Online," <www.bls.gov/opub/ee/home.htm>, accessed January 2019.

# Table 612. Civilian Labor Force and Participation Rates Projections: 2016 to 2026

[159.2 represents 159,200,000. Civilian noninstitutionalized population 16 years old and over. Based on Current Population Survey; see text, Section 1 and Appendix III]

| Race, Hispanic origin, sex, and age | Civilian labor force (mil.) | | | | | | Participation rate (percent) [1] | | | | | |
|---|---|---|---|---|---|---|---|---|---|---|---|---|
| | 2016 [2] | 2022 | 2023 | 2024 | 2025 | 2026 | 2016 [2] | 2022 | 2023 | 2024 | 2025 | 2026 |
| Total [3] | 159.2 | 165.5 | 166.6 | 167.6 | 168.6 | 169.7 | 62.8 | 61.6 | 61.4 | 61.3 | 61.1 | 61.0 |
| White | 124.7 | 127.6 | 128.0 | 128.4 | 128.8 | 129.2 | 62.9 | 61.7 | 61.5 | 61.4 | 61.2 | 61.1 |
| Male | 67.6 | 68.7 | 68.8 | 69.0 | 69.1 | 69.3 | 69.8 | 67.8 | 67.5 | 67.2 | 67.0 | 66.8 |
| Female | 57.1 | 58.9 | 59.2 | 59.4 | 59.7 | 60.0 | 56.3 | 55.9 | 55.8 | 55.7 | 55.6 | 55.6 |
| Black | 19.6 | 20.8 | 21.0 | 21.2 | 21.4 | 21.6 | 61.6 | 60.6 | 60.4 | 60.2 | 60.0 | 59.9 |
| Male | 9.3 | 9.8 | 9.9 | 10.0 | 10.0 | 10.1 | 64.1 | 62.4 | 62.0 | 61.7 | 61.4 | 61.1 |
| Female | 10.3 | 11.0 | 11.1 | 11.2 | 11.3 | 11.4 | 59.4 | 59.1 | 59.0 | 58.9 | 58.9 | 58.8 |
| Asian | 9.6 | 11.1 | 11.4 | 11.7 | 11.9 | 12.2 | 63.2 | 62.9 | 62.9 | 62.9 | 62.8 | 62.8 |
| Male | 5.1 | 5.9 | 6.1 | 6.2 | 6.3 | 6.5 | 72.1 | 71.6 | 71.6 | 71.5 | 71.4 | 71.4 |
| Female | 4.5 | 5.2 | 5.3 | 5.5 | 5.6 | 5.7 | 55.5 | 55.3 | 55.3 | 55.3 | 55.3 | 55.3 |
| All others [4] | 5.3 | 6.0 | 6.2 | 6.3 | 6.5 | 6.7 | 64.1 | 60.0 | 59.9 | 59.8 | 59.7 | 59.7 |
| Male | 2.8 | 3.1 | 3.2 | 3.3 | 3.3 | 3.4 | 68.8 | 62.7 | 62.4 | 62.1 | 61.9 | 61.7 |
| Female | 2.5 | 2.9 | 3.0 | 3.1 | 3.2 | 3.3 | 59.7 | 57.4 | 57.4 | 57.5 | 57.6 | 57.6 |
| Hispanic [5] | 26.8 | 31.6 | 32.4 | 33.3 | 34.1 | 34.9 | 65.8 | 65.9 | 65.8 | 65.8 | 65.9 | 65.9 |
| Male | 15.4 | 18.0 | 18.4 | 18.9 | 19.3 | 19.7 | 76.0 | 75.0 | 74.8 | 74.6 | 74.5 | 74.4 |
| Female | 11.4 | 13.6 | 14.0 | 14.4 | 14.8 | 15.2 | 55.8 | 56.8 | 56.9 | 57.0 | 57.2 | 57.4 |
| Male | 84.8 | 87.5 | 88.0 | 88.4 | 88.8 | 89.3 | 69.2 | 67.2 | 66.9 | 66.6 | 66.4 | 66.2 |
| 16 to 19 years | 3.0 | 2.7 | 2.7 | 2.7 | 2.6 | 2.6 | 35.3 | 32.3 | 31.8 | 31.4 | 31.1 | 30.8 |
| 20 to 24 years | 8.0 | 7.5 | 7.5 | 7.5 | 7.4 | 7.4 | 73.0 | 70.9 | 70.7 | 70.5 | 70.2 | 70.0 |
| 25 to 34 years | 19.2 | 20.2 | 20.3 | 20.2 | 20.2 | 20.1 | 88.8 | 88.0 | 87.9 | 87.8 | 87.7 | 87.6 |
| 35 to 44 years | 17.7 | 19.2 | 19.5 | 19.8 | 20.1 | 20.4 | 90.6 | 90.2 | 90.1 | 90.0 | 89.9 | 89.8 |
| 45 to 54 years | 17.9 | 16.8 | 16.8 | 16.8 | 16.8 | 16.9 | 86.3 | 85.6 | 85.5 | 85.3 | 85.3 | 85.2 |
| 55 to 64 years | 13.9 | 14.3 | 14.2 | 14.1 | 14.0 | 14.0 | 70.2 | 69.8 | 69.8 | 69.9 | 70.0 | 70.1 |
| 65 years and over | 5.1 | 6.8 | 7.1 | 7.3 | 7.6 | 7.9 | 24.0 | 25.3 | 25.5 | 25.6 | 25.8 | 25.9 |
| Female | 74.4 | 78.0 | 78.6 | 79.2 | 79.8 | 80.4 | 56.8 | 56.3 | 56.3 | 56.2 | 56.1 | 56.1 |
| 16 to 19 years | 2.9 | 2.8 | 2.7 | 2.7 | 2.7 | 2.7 | 35.1 | 33.5 | 33.2 | 32.9 | 32.8 | 32.7 |
| 20 to 24 years | 7.4 | 7.2 | 7.2 | 7.2 | 7.2 | 7.2 | 68.0 | 67.4 | 67.5 | 67.5 | 67.5 | 67.6 |
| 25 to 34 years | 16.4 | 17.3 | 17.4 | 17.5 | 17.4 | 17.4 | 74.5 | 75.5 | 75.6 | 75.7 | 75.8 | 76.0 |
| 35 to 44 years | 15.1 | 16.2 | 16.5 | 16.7 | 16.9 | 17.2 | 74.5 | 74.7 | 74.8 | 74.8 | 74.8 | 74.8 |
| 45 to 54 years | 16.0 | 15.4 | 15.5 | 15.5 | 15.6 | 15.7 | 73.9 | 75.4 | 75.7 | 75.9 | 76.2 | 76.4 |
| 55 to 64 years | 12.5 | 13.5 | 13.4 | 13.4 | 13.5 | 13.5 | 58.4 | 61.3 | 61.8 | 62.3 | 62.8 | 63.4 |
| 65 years and over | 4.1 | 5.7 | 5.9 | 6.2 | 6.5 | 6.7 | 15.5 | 17.4 | 17.7 | 17.9 | 18.1 | 18.3 |

[1] Civilian labor force as a percent of the civilian noninstitutional population projections. [2] Data for 2016 are actual. [3] Includes other races, not shown separately. [4] Includes persons classified as multi-racial, American Indian and Alaska Native, or Native Hawaiian and Other Pacific Islander. [5] Persons of Hispanic origin may be of any race.

Source: U.S. Bureau of Labor Statistics, "Employment Projections Program," <http://www.bls.gov/emp/ep_data_labor_force.htm>, accessed February 2018.

## Table 613. Civilian Population—Employment Status by Sex, Race, and Ethnicity: 1980 to 2018

[In thousands (79,398 represents 79,398,000), except as indicated. Annual averages of monthly figures. Data not strictly comparable with data for earlier years; see BLS Handbook of Methods, <https://www.bls.gov/opub/hom/>. For U.S. totals see Table 611]

| Year, sex, race, and Hispanic origin | Civilian noninstitu-tionalized population | Civilian labor force | | | | Unemployed | | Not in labor force | |
|---|---|---|---|---|---|---|---|---|---|
| | | Total | Percent of population | Employed | Employ-ment/ population ratio [1] | Number | Percent of labor force | Number | Percent of population |
| **Male:** | | | | | | | | | |
| 1980 | 79,398 | 61,453 | 77.4 | 57,186 | 72.0 | 4,267 | 6.9 | 17,945 | 22.6 |
| 1990 | 90,377 | 69,011 | 76.4 | 65,104 | 72.0 | 3,906 | 5.7 | 21,367 | 23.6 |
| 2000 | 101,964 | 76,280 | 74.8 | 73,305 | 71.9 | 2,975 | 3.9 | 25,684 | 25.2 |
| 2010 | 115,174 | 81,985 | 71.2 | 73,359 | 63.7 | 8,626 | 10.5 | 33,189 | 28.8 |
| 2016 | 122,497 | 84,755 | 69.2 | 80,568 | 65.8 | 4,187 | 4.9 | 37,743 | 30.8 |
| 2017 | 123,275 | 85,145 | 69.1 | 81,402 | 66.0 | 3,743 | 4.4 | 38,130 | 30.9 |
| 2018 | 124,678 | 86,096 | 69.1 | 82,698 | 66.3 | 3,398 | 3.9 | 38,582 | 30.9 |
| **Female:** | | | | | | | | | |
| 1980 | 88,348 | 45,487 | 51.5 | 42,117 | 47.7 | 3,370 | 7.4 | 42,861 | 48.5 |
| 1990 | 98,787 | 56,829 | 57.5 | 53,689 | 54.3 | 3,140 | 5.5 | 41,957 | 42.5 |
| 2000 | 110,613 | 66,303 | 59.9 | 63,586 | 57.5 | 2,717 | 4.1 | 44,310 | 40.1 |
| 2010 | 122,656 | 71,904 | 58.6 | 65,705 | 53.6 | 6,199 | 8.6 | 50,752 | 41.4 |
| 2016 | 131,040 | 74,432 | 56.8 | 70,868 | 54.1 | 3,564 | 4.8 | 56,608 | 43.2 |
| 2017 | 131,804 | 75,175 | 57.0 | 71,936 | 54.6 | 3,239 | 4.3 | 56,629 | 43.0 |
| 2018 | 133,112 | 75,978 | 57.1 | 73,063 | 54.9 | 2,916 | 3.8 | 57,134 | 42.9 |
| **White:** [2] | | | | | | | | | |
| 1980 | 146,122 | 93,600 | 64.1 | 87,715 | 60.0 | 5,884 | 6.3 | 52,523 | 35.9 |
| 1990 | 160,625 | 107,447 | 66.9 | 102,261 | 63.7 | 5,186 | 4.8 | 53,178 | 33.1 |
| 2000 | 176,220 | 118,545 | 67.3 | 114,424 | 64.9 | 4,121 | 3.5 | 57,675 | 32.7 |
| 2010 | 192,075 | 125,084 | 65.1 | 114,168 | 59.4 | 10,916 | 8.7 | 66,991 | 34.9 |
| 2016 | 198,215 | 124,658 | 62.9 | 119,313 | 60.2 | 5,345 | 4.3 | 73,557 | 37.1 |
| 2017 | 198,942 | 124,941 | 62.8 | 120,176 | 60.4 | 4,765 | 3.8 | 74,001 | 37.2 |
| 2018 | 200,221 | 125,815 | 62.8 | 121,461 | 60.7 | 4,354 | 3.5 | 74,407 | 37.2 |
| **Black:** [2] | | | | | | | | | |
| 1980 | 17,824 | 10,865 | 61.0 | 9,313 | 52.2 | 1,553 | 14.3 | 6,959 | 39.0 |
| 1990 | 21,477 | 13,740 | 64.0 | 12,175 | 56.7 | 1,565 | 11.4 | 7,737 | 36.0 |
| 2000 | 24,902 | 16,397 | 65.8 | 15,156 | 60.9 | 1,241 | 7.6 | 8,505 | 34.2 |
| 2010 | 28,708 | 17,862 | 62.2 | 15,010 | 52.3 | 2,852 | 16.0 | 10,846 | 37.8 |
| 2016 | 31,889 | 19,637 | 61.6 | 17,982 | 56.4 | 1,655 | 8.4 | 12,252 | 38.4 |
| 2017 | 32,247 | 20,088 | 62.3 | 18,587 | 57.6 | 1,501 | 7.5 | 12,159 | 37.7 |
| 2018 | 32,761 | 20,414 | 62.3 | 19,091 | 58.3 | 1,322 | 6.5 | 12,347 | 37.7 |
| **Asian:** [2, 3] | | | | | | | | | |
| 2000 | 9,330 | 6,270 | 67.2 | 6,043 | 64.8 | 227 | 3.6 | 3,060 | 32.8 |
| 2010 | 11,199 | 7,248 | 64.7 | 6,705 | 59.9 | 543 | 7.5 | 3,951 | 35.3 |
| 2016 | 15,121 | 9,562 | 63.2 | 9,213 | 60.9 | 349 | 3.6 | 5,559 | 36.8 |
| 2017 | 15,368 | 9,781 | 63.6 | 9,448 | 61.5 | 333 | 3.4 | 5,587 | 36.4 |
| 2018 | 15,961 | 10,137 | 63.5 | 9,832 | 61.6 | 304 | 3.0 | 5,825 | 36.5 |
| **Hispanic:** [4] | | | | | | | | | |
| 1980 | 9,598 | 6,146 | 64.0 | 5,527 | 57.6 | 620 | 10.1 | 3,451 | 36.0 |
| 1990 | 15,904 | 10,720 | 67.4 | 9,845 | 61.9 | 876 | 8.2 | 5,184 | 32.6 |
| 2000 | 23,938 | 16,689 | 69.7 | 15,735 | 65.7 | 954 | 5.7 | 7,249 | 30.3 |
| 2010 | 33,713 | 22,748 | 67.5 | 19,906 | 59.0 | 2,843 | 12.5 | 10,964 | 32.5 |
| 2016 | 40,697 | 26,797 | 65.8 | 25,249 | 62.0 | 1,548 | 5.8 | 13,900 | 34.2 |
| 2017 | 41,371 | 27,339 | 66.1 | 25,938 | 62.7 | 1,401 | 5.1 | 14,032 | 33.9 |
| 2018 | 42,734 | 28,336 | 66.3 | 27,012 | 63.2 | 1,323 | 4.7 | 14,398 | 33.7 |
| **Mexican:** | | | | | | | | | |
| 1990 | 9,752 | 6,707 | 68.8 | 6,146 | 63.0 | 561 | 8.4 | 3,045 | 31.2 |
| 2000 | 15,333 | 10,783 | 70.3 | 10,144 | 66.2 | 639 | 5.9 | 4,550 | 29.7 |
| 2010 | 21,267 | 14,403 | 67.7 | 12,622 | 59.4 | 1,781 | 12.4 | 6,864 | 32.3 |
| 2016 | 24,960 | 16,458 | 65.9 | 15,502 | 62.1 | 955 | 5.8 | 8,503 | 34.1 |
| 2017 | 25,455 | 16,808 | 66.0 | 15,958 | 62.7 | 849 | 5.1 | 8,647 | 34.0 |
| 2018 | 26,031 | 17,312 | 66.5 | 16,497 | 63.4 | 815 | 4.7 | 8,718 | 33.5 |
| **Puerto Rican:** | | | | | | | | | |
| 1990 | 1,718 | 960 | 55.9 | 870 | 50.6 | 91 | 9.5 | 758 | 44.1 |
| 2000 | 2,193 | 1,411 | 64.3 | 1,318 | 60.1 | 92 | 6.6 | 783 | 35.7 |
| 2010 | 3,110 | 1,906 | 61.3 | 1,612 | 51.8 | 293 | 15.4 | 1,204 | 38.7 |
| 2016 | 3,835 | 2,305 | 60.1 | 2,146 | 56.0 | 159 | 6.9 | 1,530 | 39.9 |
| 2017 | 3,902 | 2,409 | 61.7 | 2,265 | 58.1 | 144 | 6.0 | 1,493 | 38.3 |
| 2018 | 3,938 | 2,408 | 61.2 | 2,272 | 57.7 | 136 | 5.7 | 1,529 | 38.8 |
| **Cuban:** | | | | | | | | | |
| 1990 | 918 | 603 | 65.7 | 559 | 60.9 | 44 | 7.2 | 315 | 34.3 |
| 2000 | 1,174 | 740 | 63.1 | 707 | 60.3 | 33 | 4.5 | 434 | 37.0 |
| 2010 | 1,549 | 970 | 62.6 | 850 | 54.9 | 120 | 12.4 | 579 | 37.4 |
| 2016 | 1,819 | 1,149 | 63.2 | 1,088 | 59.8 | 61 | 5.3 | 670 | 36.8 |
| 2017 | 1,723 | 1,063 | 61.7 | 1,019 | 59.2 | 43 | 4.1 | 660 | 38.3 |
| 2018 | 1,905 | 1,181 | 62.0 | 1,139 | 59.8 | 41 | 3.5 | 725 | 38.1 |

[1] Civilian employed as a percent of the civilian noninstitutional population. [2] Beginning with the 2003 CPS, respondents could choose more than one race. Beginning in 2003, data represent persons who selected this race group only and exclude persons reporting more than one race. The CPS in prior years allowed respondents to report only one race group. See also comments on race in text for section 1. [3] Prior to 2003, Asian includes Pacific Islanders. [4] Persons of Hispanic origin may be of any race. Includes persons of other Hispanic or Latino ethnicity, not shown separately.

Source: U.S. Bureau of Labor Statistics, CPS Tables, "Employment status of the civilian noninstitutional population by age, sex, and race" and "Employment status of the Hispanic or Latino population by sex, age, and detailed ethnic group," February 2019, and earlier releases, <https://www.bls.gov/cps/tables.htm>.

# Table 614. Foreign-Born and Native-Born Populations—Employment Status by Selected Characteristics: 2018

[257,791 represents 257,791,000. For civilian noninstitutional population 16 years old and over, except as indicated. The foreign born are persons who reside in the United States but who were born outside the country or in one of its outlying areas to parents who were not U.S. citizens. The foreign born include legally admitted immigrants, refugees, temporary residents such as students and temporary workers, and undocumented immigrants. Annual averages of monthly figures. Based on Current Population Survey; see text, Section 1 and Appendix III]

| Characteristic | Civilian noninstitutionalized population (1,000) | Civilian labor force | | | | | Not in the labor force (1,000) |
|---|---|---|---|---|---|---|---|
| | | Total (1,000) | Participation rate [1] | Employed (1,000) | Unemployed | | |
| | | | | | Number (1,000) | Unemployment rate | |
| **Total**............................... | **257,791** | **162,075** | **62.9** | **155,761** | **6,314** | **3.9** | **95,716** |
| Male............................... | 124,678 | 86,096 | 69.1 | 82,698 | 3,398 | 3.9 | 38,582 |
| Female........................... | 133,112 | 75,978 | 57.1 | 73,063 | 2,916 | 3.8 | 57,134 |
| **FOREIGN BORN** | | | | | | | |
| **Total [2]**........................... | **42,898** | **28,202** | **65.7** | **27,217** | **986** | **3.5** | **14,696** |
| Male............................... | 20,803 | 16,203 | 77.9 | 15,714 | 488 | 3.0 | 4,600 |
| Female........................... | 22,095 | 12,000 | 54.3 | 11,502 | 497 | 4.1 | 10,095 |
| Age: | | | | | | | |
| 16 to 24 years old............... | 3,443 | 1,761 | 51.2 | 1,638 | 124 | 7.0 | 1,682 |
| 25 to 34 years old............... | 7,946 | 6,092 | 76.7 | 5,877 | 215 | 3.5 | 1,854 |
| 35 to 44 years old............... | 9,499 | 7,520 | 79.2 | 7,302 | 219 | 2.9 | 1,979 |
| 45 to 54 years old............... | 8,715 | 7,044 | 80.8 | 6,844 | 200 | 2.8 | 1,671 |
| 55 to 64 years old............... | 6,542 | 4,425 | 67.6 | 4,255 | 170 | 3.8 | 2,117 |
| 65 years old and over........... | 6,754 | 1,360 | 20.1 | 1,301 | 58 | 4.3 | 5,394 |
| Race and Hispanic ethnicity: | | | | | | | |
| White, non-Hispanic............. | 7,837 | 4,676 | 59.7 | 4,517 | 160 | 3.4 | 3,161 |
| Black, non-Hispanic............. | 3,786 | 2,682 | 70.8 | 2,560 | 122 | 4.6 | 1,104 |
| Asian, non-Hispanic............. | 11,118 | 7,082 | 63.7 | 6,895 | 187 | 2.6 | 4,036 |
| Hispanic [3]......................... | 19,683 | 13,457 | 68.4 | 12,950 | 507 | 3.8 | 6,226 |
| Educational attainment: | | | | | | | |
| Total, 25 years old and over..... | 39,455 | 26,441 | 67.0 | 25,579 | 862 | 3.3 | 13,014 |
| Less than a high school diploma.. | 9,616 | 5,607 | 58.3 | 5,378 | 229 | 4.1 | 4,009 |
| High school graduates, no college [4]..... | 10,127 | 6,629 | 65.5 | 6,415 | 214 | 3.2 | 3,498 |
| Some college or associate's degree............ | 6,366 | 4,448 | 69.9 | 4,301 | 147 | 3.3 | 1,918 |
| Bachelor's degree and higher [5]................. | 13,347 | 9,758 | 73.1 | 9,485 | 273 | 2.8 | 3,589 |
| **NATIVE BORN** | | | | | | | |
| **Total [2]**........................... | **214,892** | **133,872** | **62.3** | **128,544** | **5,328** | **4.0** | **81,020** |
| Male............................... | 103,875 | 69,894 | 67.3 | 66,984 | 2,910 | 4.2 | 33,981 |
| Female........................... | 111,018 | 63,979 | 57.6 | 61,560 | 2,418 | 3.8 | 47,039 |
| Age: | | | | | | | |
| 16 to 24 years old............... | 34,561 | 19,223 | 55.6 | 17,539 | 1,684 | 8.8 | 15,338 |
| 25 to 34 years old............... | 36,635 | 30,682 | 83.8 | 29,447 | 1,235 | 4.0 | 5,953 |
| 35 to 44 years old............... | 31,071 | 26,099 | 84.0 | 25,315 | 784 | 3.0 | 4,972 |
| 45 to 54 years old............... | 32,525 | 26,267 | 80.8 | 25,529 | 738 | 2.8 | 6,258 |
| 55 to 64 years old............... | 35,572 | 22,929 | 64.5 | 22,310 | 619 | 2.7 | 12,643 |
| 65 years old and over........... | 44,529 | 8,673 | 19.5 | 8,404 | 269 | 3.1 | 35,856 |
| Race and Hispanic ethnicity: | | | | | | | |
| White, non-Hispanic............. | 154,396 | 95,991 | 62.2 | 92,952 | 3,038 | 3.2 | 58,405 |
| Black, non-Hispanic............. | 27,076 | 16,484 | 60.9 | 15,355 | 1,129 | 6.8 | 10,592 |
| Asian, non-Hispanic............. | 4,408 | 2,761 | 62.6 | 2,657 | 104 | 3.8 | 1,647 |
| Hispanic [3]......................... | 23,051 | 14,879 | 64.5 | 14,063 | 816 | 5.5 | 8,172 |
| Educational attainment: | | | | | | | |
| Total, 25 years and over......... | 180,332 | 114,650 | 63.6 | 111,005 | 3,644 | 3.2 | 65,682 |
| Less than a high school diploma.. | 12,635 | 4,671 | 37.0 | 4,323 | 347 | 7.4 | 7,964 |
| High school graduates, no college [4]..... | 52,465 | 29,382 | 56.0 | 28,135 | 1,247 | 4.2 | 23,083 |
| Some college or associate's degree............ | 51,038 | 33,138 | 64.9 | 32,036 | 1,101 | 3.3 | 17,900 |
| Bachelor's degree and higher [5]................. | 64,193 | 47,459 | 73.9 | 46,511 | 949 | 2.0 | 16,734 |

[1] Civilian labor force as a percent of the civilian noninstitutionalized population. [2] Includes other races, not shown separately. [3] Persons of Hispanic origin may be of any race. [4] Includes persons with a high school diploma or equivalent. [5] Includes persons with bachelor's, master's, professional, and doctoral degrees.

Source: U.S. Bureau of Labor Statistics, *Foreign-Born Workers: Labor Force Characteristics—2018*, USDL 19-0812, May 2019. See also <http://www.bls.gov/news.release/forbrn.toc.htm>.

# Table 615. Employment Status of Veterans by Period of Service and Sex: 2018

[In thousands (248,874 represents 248,874,000). For civilian noninstitutional population 18 years old and over. Veterans are defined as men and women who have previously served on active duty in the U.S. Armed Forces and who were civilians at the time they were surveyed. Veterans are counted in only one period of service, their most recent wartime period; veterans who served in both a wartime period and any other service period are classified in the wartime period. See text, Section 10. Annual averages of monthly figures. Beginning with 2014, estimates for veterans incorporate updated weighting procedures. The primary impact of the change was an increase in the "Gulf War-era I" veteran population and a decrease in the number of veterans in the "Other service periods" category. For more information, see <http://www.bls.gov/cps/vetsweights2014.pdf>. Based on Current Population Survey; see text, Section 1 and Appendix III]

| Veteran status, period of service, and sex | Civilian non-institu-tionalized popula-tion | Civilian labor force | | | | | | | Not in labor force |
|---|---|---|---|---|---|---|---|---|---|
| | | Total | Percent of popula-tion | Employed | | Unemployed | | | |
| | | | | Total | Percent of popula-tion | Total | Percent of labor force | | |
| Total, 18 years and over................. | 248,874 | 159,942 | 64.3 | 153,923 | 61.8 | 6,019 | 3.8 | | 88,932 |
| **Veterans**.......................... | **19,201** | **9,453** | **49.2** | **9,127** | **47.5** | **326** | **3.5** | | **9,748** |
| Gulf War era, total........................ | 7,238 | 5,784 | 79.9 | 5,588 | 77.2 | 197 | 3.4 | | 1,454 |
| Gulf War era II [1]....................... | 4,149 | 3,358 | 80.9 | 3,229 | 77.8 | 129 | 3.8 | | 791 |
| Gulf War era I [2]....................... | 3,089 | 2,427 | 78.6 | 2,358 | 76.3 | 68 | 2.8 | | 662 |
| WWII, Korean War, and Vietnam era [3]...... | 7,626 | 1,594 | 20.9 | 1,537 | 20.2 | 57 | 3.6 | | 6,033 |
| Other service periods [4]................... | 4,336 | 2,075 | 47.9 | 2,002 | 46.2 | 73 | 3.5 | | 2,261 |
| Nonveterans [5]......................... | 229,673 | 150,489 | 65.5 | 144,797 | 63.0 | 5,693 | 3.8 | | 79,184 |
| Male, 18 years and over................. | 120,152 | 85,094 | 70.8 | 81,852 | 68.1 | 3,242 | 3.8 | | 35,058 |
| **Veterans**.......................... | **17,335** | **8,320** | **48.0** | **8,027** | **46.3** | **292** | **3.5** | | **9,015** |
| Gulf War era, total........................ | 6,043 | 4,919 | 81.4 | 4,748 | 78.6 | 171 | 3.5 | | 1,124 |
| Gulf War era II [1]....................... | 3,444 | 2,853 | 82.8 | 2,742 | 79.6 | 111 | 3.9 | | 592 |
| Gulf War era I [2]....................... | 2,599 | 2,066 | 79.5 | 2,005 | 77.2 | 61 | 2.9 | | 533 |
| WWII, Korean War, and Vietnam era [3]...... | 7,366 | 1,541 | 20.9 | 1,485 | 20.2 | 56 | 3.6 | | 5,826 |
| Other service periods [4]................... | 3,925 | 1,860 | 47.4 | 1,795 | 45.7 | 65 | 3.5 | | 2,065 |
| Nonveterans [5]......................... | 102,817 | 76,774 | 74.7 | 73,824 | 71.8 | 2,950 | 3.8 | | 26,043 |
| Female, 18 years and over................. | 128,722 | 74,849 | 58.1 | 72,072 | 56.0 | 2,777 | 3.7 | | 53,874 |
| **Veterans**.......................... | **1,866** | **1,133** | **60.7** | **1,099** | **58.9** | **34** | **3.0** | | **732** |
| Gulf War era, total........................ | 1,194 | 865 | 72.4 | 840 | 70.3 | 25 | 2.9 | | 329 |
| Gulf War era II [1]....................... | 704 | 505 | 71.7 | 487 | 69.1 | 18 | 3.5 | | 200 |
| Gulf War era I [2]....................... | 490 | 360 | 73.5 | 353 | 72.0 | 7 | 2.1 | | 130 |
| WWII, Korean War, and Vietnam era [3]...... | 260 | 53 | 20.3 | 52 | 19.9 | 1 | 1.7 | | 207 |
| Other service periods [4]................... | 412 | 215 | 52.3 | 208 | 50.5 | 8 | 3.6 | | 196 |
| Nonveterans [5]......................... | 126,857 | 73,715 | 58.1 | 70,972 | 55.9 | 2,743 | 3.7 | | 53,141 |

[1] Gulf War era II: September 2001–present. [2] Gulf War era I: August 1990–August 2001. [3] World War II: December 1941–December 1946. Korean War: July 1950–January 1955. Vietnam era: August 1964–April 1975. [4] Other service periods; all other time periods. [5] Nonveterans are men and women who never served on active duty in the U.S. Armed Forces.

Source: U.S. Bureau of Labor Statistics, *Employment Situation of Veterans—2018*, USDL 19-0451, March 2019. See also <http://www.bls.gov/news.release/vet.nr0.htm>.

# Table 616. Labor Force Status of Persons With and Without a Disability: 2018

[30,136 represents 30,136,000. For civilian noninstitutionalized population 16 years old and over. Persons with a disability are those who have a physical, mental, or emotional condition that causes serious difficulty with their daily activities. Annual averages of monthly figures. Based on Current Population Survey; see text, Section 1 and Appendix III]

| Characteristic | Civilian non-institutional-ized popula-tion (1,000) | Civilian labor force | | | | | Not in the labor force (1,000) |
|---|---|---|---|---|---|---|---|
| | | Total (1,000) | Participation rate [1] | Employed (1,000) | Unemployed | | |
| | | | | | Number (1,000) | Unemploy-ment rate | |
| **WITH DISABILITY** | | | | | | | |
| **Total**........................ | **30,136** | **6,266** | **20.8** | **5,767** | **499** | **8.0** | **23,870** |
| Sex: | | | | | | | |
| Male......................... | 13,997 | 3,389 | 24.2 | 3,122 | 267 | 7.9 | 10,608 |
| Female....................... | 16,139 | 2,877 | 17.8 | 2,645 | 232 | 8.1 | 13,262 |
| Age: | | | | | | | |
| 16 to 64 years................... | 15,325 | 5,111 | 33.3 | 4,666 | 445 | 8.7 | 10,215 |
| 16 to 19 years................... | 644 | 151 | 23.5 | 112 | 39 | 26.1 | 493 |
| 20 to 24 years................... | 867 | 384 | 44.3 | 328 | 56 | 14.6 | 483 |
| 25 to 34 years................... | 1,914 | 930 | 48.6 | 828 | 101 | 10.9 | 984 |
| 35 to 44 years................... | 2,140 | 861 | 40.2 | 795 | 67 | 7.7 | 1,279 |
| 45 to 54 years................... | 3,537 | 1,204 | 34.0 | 1,123 | 81 | 6.7 | 2,333 |
| 55 to 64 years................... | 6,223 | 1,580 | 25.4 | 1,480 | 100 | 6.3 | 4,643 |
| 65 years and over............... | 14,810 | 1,155 | 7.8 | 1,101 | 54 | 4.7 | 13,655 |
| **WITHOUT DISABILITY** | | | | | | | |
| **Total**........................ | **227,655** | **155,809** | **68.4** | **149,994** | **5,815** | **3.7** | **71,846** |
| Sex: | | | | | | | |
| Male......................... | 110,681 | 82,707 | 74.7 | 79,576 | 3,131 | 3.8 | 27,974 |
| Female....................... | 116,974 | 73,102 | 62.5 | 70,418 | 2,684 | 3.7 | 43,872 |
| Age: | | | | | | | |
| 16 to 64 years................... | 191,182 | 146,932 | 76.9 | 141,390 | 5,542 | 3.8 | 44,250 |
| 16 to 19 years................... | 16,121 | 5,734 | 35.6 | 5,014 | 720 | 12.6 | 10,387 |
| 20 to 24 years................... | 20,372 | 14,715 | 72.2 | 13,723 | 992 | 6.7 | 5,657 |
| 25 to 34 years................... | 42,667 | 35,844 | 84.0 | 34,496 | 1,348 | 3.8 | 6,823 |
| 35 to 44 years................... | 38,429 | 32,758 | 85.2 | 31,822 | 936 | 2.9 | 5,671 |
| 45 to 54 years................... | 37,703 | 32,107 | 85.2 | 31,250 | 857 | 2.7 | 5,596 |
| 55 to 64 years................... | 35,890 | 25,773 | 71.8 | 25,085 | 689 | 2.7 | 10,117 |
| 65 years and over............... | 36,472 | 8,877 | 24.3 | 8,604 | 273 | 3.1 | 27,595 |

[1] Civilian labor force as a percent of the civilian noninstitutional population.

Source: U.S. Bureau of Labor Statistics, "Persons with A Disability: Labor Force Characteristics—2018," USDL 19-0326, <http://www.bls.gov/cps/demographics.htm#disability>, accessed June 2019.

# Table 617. Civilian Labor Force—Percent Distribution by Sex and Age: 1980 to 2018

[106,940 represents 106,940,000. Civilian noninstitutionalized population 16 years old and over. Annual averages of monthly figures. Data not strictly comparable with data for earlier years; see BLS Handbook of Methods, <https://www.bls.gov/opub/hom/>. Based on Current Population Survey; see text, Section 1 and Appendix III]

| Year and sex | Civilian labor force (1,000) | Percent distribution | | | | | | |
| | | 16 to 19 years | 20 to 24 years | 25 to 34 years | 35 to 44 years | 45 to 54 years | 55 to 64 years | 65 years and over |
|---|---|---|---|---|---|---|---|---|
| **Total:** | | | | | | | | |
| 1980................. | 106,940 | 8.8 | 14.9 | 27.3 | 19.1 | 15.8 | 11.2 | 2.9 |
| 1990................. | 125,840 | 6.2 | 11.7 | 28.6 | 25.5 | 16.1 | 9.2 | 2.7 |
| 2000................. | 142,583 | 5.8 | 10.0 | 23.0 | 26.3 | 21.8 | 10.1 | 3.0 |
| 2010................. | 153,889 | 3.8 | 9.8 | 21.8 | 21.7 | 23.4 | 15.1 | 4.4 |
| 2018................. | 162,075 | 3.6 | 9.3 | 22.7 | 20.7 | 20.6 | 16.9 | 6.2 |
| **Male:** | | | | | | | | |
| 1980................. | 61,453 | 8.1 | 14.0 | 27.6 | 19.3 | 16.1 | 11.8 | 3.1 |
| 1990................. | 69,011 | 5.9 | 11.4 | 28.8 | 25.3 | 16.1 | 9.6 | 2.9 |
| 2000................. | 76,280 | 5.6 | 9.9 | 23.4 | 26.3 | 21.3 | 10.2 | 3.3 |
| 2010................. | 81,985 | 3.6 | 9.6 | 22.4 | 22.1 | 23.0 | 14.8 | 4.5 |
| 2018................. | 86,096 | 3.4 | 9.0 | 23.0 | 21.0 | 20.4 | 16.8 | 6.4 |
| **Female:** | | | | | | | | |
| 1980................. | 45,487 | 9.6 | 16.1 | 26.9 | 19.0 | 15.4 | 10.4 | 2.6 |
| 1990................. | 56,829 | 6.5 | 12.0 | 28.3 | 25.8 | 16.1 | 8.7 | 2.6 |
| 2000................. | 66,303 | 6.0 | 10.2 | 22.5 | 26.4 | 22.3 | 9.9 | 2.7 |
| 2010................. | 71,904 | 4.1 | 10.0 | 21.2 | 21.2 | 23.8 | 15.6 | 4.2 |
| 2018................. | 75,978 | 3.9 | 9.6 | 22.4 | 20.4 | 20.8 | 17.0 | 5.9 |

Source: U.S. Bureau of Labor Statistics, CPS Tables, "Employment status of the civilian noninstitutional population by age, sex, and race," February 2019, and earlier releases, <https://www.bls.gov/cps/tables.htm>.

# Table 618. Civilian Labor Force and Participation Rates by Educational Attainment, Sex, Race, and Hispanic Origin: 2005 to 2018

[127,030 represents 127,030,000. Civilian noninstitutional population 25 years old and over. Annual averages of monthly figures. Revisions to population controls and other changes can affect the comparability of data over time; see BLS Handbook of Methods, <https://www.bls.gov/opub/hom/>. See Table 654 for unemployment data. Rates are based on annual average civilian noninstitutional population of each specified group and represent proportion of each specified group in the civilian labor force]

| Year, sex, and race/ethnicity | Civilian labor force | | | | | Participation rate (percent) [1] | | | | |
| | | Percent distribution | | | | | | | | |
| | Total (1,000) | Less than a high school diploma | High school graduate, no college | Less than a bachelor's degree | College graduate | Total | Less than a high school diploma | High school graduate, no college | Less than a bachelor's degree | College graduate |
|---|---|---|---|---|---|---|---|---|---|---|
| **Total:** [2] | | | | | | | | | | |
| 2005.............. | 127,030 | 10.0 | 30.1 | 27.5 | 32.4 | 67.1 | 45.5 | 63.2 | 72.5 | 77.9 |
| 2010.............. | 132,955 | 8.9 | 28.8 | 27.7 | 34.6 | 66.5 | 46.3 | 61.6 | 70.5 | 76.7 |
| 2015.............. | 135,907 | 8.1 | 26.0 | 27.6 | 38.4 | 64.0 | 45.4 | 57.2 | 66.6 | 74.4 |
| 2018.............. | 141,090 | 7.3 | 25.5 | 26.6 | 40.6 | 64.2 | 46.2 | 57.5 | 65.5 | 73.8 |
| **Male:** | | | | | | | | | | |
| 2005.............. | 68,389 | 11.7 | 30.9 | 25.4 | 32.1 | 75.4 | 58.6 | 73.6 | 79.3 | 82.9 |
| 2010.............. | 71,129 | 10.6 | 30.4 | 25.6 | 33.4 | 74.1 | 59.1 | 71.4 | 76.7 | 81.3 |
| 2015.............. | 72,698 | 9.7 | 28.1 | 25.8 | 36.4 | 71.5 | 58.3 | 67.2 | 73.1 | 79.0 |
| 2018.............. | 75,402 | 8.7 | 28.0 | 25.3 | 38.0 | 71.4 | 58.8 | 67.7 | 71.9 | 78.1 |
| **Female:** | | | | | | | | | | |
| 2005.............. | 58,641 | 8.0 | 29.2 | 30.0 | 32.8 | 59.4 | 32.9 | 53.8 | 66.8 | 72.9 |
| 2010.............. | 61,825 | 7.0 | 26.9 | 30.1 | 36.0 | 59.5 | 33.5 | 52.4 | 65.4 | 72.4 |
| 2015.............. | 63,209 | 6.2 | 23.6 | 29.6 | 40.7 | 57.2 | 32.3 | 47.6 | 61.1 | 70.2 |
| 2018.............. | 65,690 | 5.7 | 22.6 | 28.2 | 43.5 | 57.5 | 33.6 | 47.4 | 60.0 | 69.9 |
| **White:** [3] | | | | | | | | | | |
| 2005.............. | 104,240 | 9.8 | 29.9 | 27.6 | 32.7 | 66.9 | 46.4 | 62.5 | 72.0 | 77.5 |
| 2010.............. | 108,274 | 8.9 | 28.7 | 27.5 | 34.9 | 66.5 | 47.7 | 61.2 | 70.1 | 76.5 |
| 2015.............. | 107,366 | 8.1 | 25.9 | 27.5 | 38.5 | 63.8 | 46.7 | 56.7 | 65.9 | 74.0 |
| 2018.............. | 109,855 | 7.4 | 25.4 | 26.6 | 40.7 | 63.7 | 48.1 | 56.8 | 64.5 | 73.1 |
| **Black:** [3] | | | | | | | | | | |
| 2005.............. | 14,252 | 11.2 | 36.4 | 30.2 | 22.2 | 67.2 | 39.8 | 67.9 | 75.6 | 82.0 |
| 2010.............. | 15,114 | 9.4 | 33.3 | 32.8 | 24.5 | 65.8 | 38.8 | 63.8 | 73.5 | 79.5 |
| 2015.............. | 16,279 | 7.5 | 30.9 | 33.3 | 28.3 | 63.9 | 37.5 | 58.8 | 70.2 | 77.7 |
| 2018.............. | 17,478 | 6.4 | 30.6 | 31.8 | 31.2 | 64.5 | 35.9 | 59.8 | 69.4 | 77.7 |
| **Asian:** [3] | | | | | | | | | | |
| 2005.............. | 5,805 | 8.0 | 17.7 | 17.3 | 57.0 | 69.4 | 45.3 | 61.8 | 71.6 | 77.5 |
| 2010.............. | 6,601 | 7.3 | 18.8 | 17.1 | 56.7 | 68.7 | 44.1 | 62.8 | 70.6 | 75.9 |
| 2015.............. | 8,200 | 6.1 | 17.1 | 16.0 | 60.9 | 66.7 | 40.8 | 58.8 | 68.1 | 73.7 |
| 2018.............. | 9,236 | 5.3 | 16.3 | 15.3 | 63.1 | 67.6 | 40.5 | 59.0 | 67.7 | 74.6 |
| **Hispanic:** [4] | | | | | | | | | | |
| 2005.............. | 16,135 | 35.5 | 29.4 | 20.9 | 14.2 | 70.8 | 61.4 | 74.3 | 78.8 | 81.7 |
| 2010.............. | 18,987 | 31.4 | 30.8 | 21.7 | 16.0 | 71.4 | 61.9 | 73.9 | 77.8 | 81.7 |
| 2015.............. | 21,618 | 27.7 | 29.8 | 23.6 | 18.9 | 69.3 | 59.3 | 69.6 | 75.5 | 80.1 |
| 2018.............. | 23,657 | 24.3 | 31.4 | 23.5 | 20.8 | 69.5 | 59.1 | 69.9 | 74.2 | 79.2 |

[1] Civilian labor force as a percent of the civilian noninstitutional population. [2] Includes other races, not shown separately. [3] Beginning in 2003, data represent persons who selected this race group only and exclude persons reporting more than one race. See footnote 2, Table 613. [4] Persons of Hispanic origin may be of any race.

Source: U.S. Bureau of Labor Statistics, CPS Tables, "Employment status of the civilian noninstitutional population 25 years and over by educational attainment, sex, race, and Hispanic or Latino ethnicity," February 2019, and earlier releases, <https://www.bls.gov/cps/tables.htm>.

# Table 619. Civilian Labor Force by Employment Status and Sex by State: 2018

[In thousands (162,075 represents 162,075,000), except ratio and rate. Preliminary data. Civilian noninstitutionalized population 16 years old and over. Annual averages of monthly figures. Data for states may not sum to national totals due to rounding]

| State | Labor force | | Employed | | Employ-ment/ population ratio [1] | Unemployed | | | | | Participation rate [3] | |
|---|---|---|---|---|---|---|---|---|---|---|---|---|
| | | | | | | Number | | Rate [2] | | | | |
| | Total | Female | Total | Female | | Total | Female | Total | Male | Female | Male | Female |
| **United States** | **162,075** | **75,978** | **155,761** | **73,063** | **60.4** | **6,314** | **2,916** | **3.9** | **3.9** | **3.8** | **69.1** | **57.1** |
| Alabama | 2,208 | 1,027 | 2,121 | 986 | 55.1 | 87 | 42 | 3.9 | 3.8 | 4.1 | 64.9 | 50.7 |
| Alaska | 355 | 164 | 332 | 156 | 60.7 | 23 | 8 | 6.6 | 8.2 | 4.7 | 68.7 | 61.1 |
| Arizona | 3,409 | 1,580 | 3,250 | 1,510 | 58.4 | 159 | 70 | 4.7 | 4.9 | 4.4 | 67.3 | 55.4 |
| Arkansas | 1,342 | 634 | 1,291 | 611 | 55.2 | 50 | 23 | 3.8 | 3.9 | 3.6 | 62.8 | 52.2 |
| California | 19,479 | 8,848 | 18,666 | 8,448 | 59.8 | 813 | 400 | 4.2 | 3.9 | 4.5 | 69.6 | 55.4 |
| Colorado | 3,091 | 1,414 | 2,988 | 1,379 | 66.9 | 103 | 35 | 3.3 | 4.0 | 2.5 | 75.7 | 62.7 |
| Connecticut | 1,907 | 920 | 1,828 | 887 | 63.1 | 79 | 33 | 4.1 | 4.6 | 3.6 | 70.8 | 61.3 |
| Delaware | 488 | 238 | 469 | 228 | 60.5 | 19 | 9 | 3.8 | 3.7 | 3.9 | 68.0 | 58.3 |
| District of Columbia | 406 | 206 | 383 | 194 | 66.5 | 23 | 12 | 5.6 | 5.6 | 5.6 | 74.7 | 66.8 |
| Florida | 10,248 | 4,868 | 9,879 | 4,679 | 57.3 | 369 | 190 | 3.6 | 3.3 | 3.9 | 65.1 | 54.2 |
| Georgia | 5,125 | 2,453 | 4,927 | 2,352 | 60.7 | 198 | 101 | 3.9 | 3.6 | 4.1 | 69.6 | 57.3 |
| Hawaii | 680 | 330 | 663 | 322 | 60.5 | 18 | 7 | 2.6 | 3.0 | 2.2 | 66.3 | 58.2 |
| Idaho | 857 | 384 | 831 | 372 | 62.3 | 26 | 13 | 3.0 | 2.8 | 3.3 | 71.4 | 57.1 |
| Illinois | 6,482 | 3,070 | 6,207 | 2,950 | 61.7 | 275 | 120 | 4.2 | 4.6 | 3.9 | 70.1 | 59.2 |
| Indiana | 3,412 | 1,575 | 3,293 | 1,518 | 63.1 | 119 | 57 | 3.5 | 3.4 | 3.6 | 72.5 | 58.8 |
| Iowa | 1,691 | 792 | 1,649 | 772 | 66.8 | 43 | 20 | 2.5 | 2.5 | 2.5 | 73.8 | 63.4 |
| Kansas | 1,485 | 689 | 1,434 | 664 | 64.4 | 51 | 25 | 3.4 | 3.3 | 3.6 | 73.0 | 60.6 |
| Kentucky | 2,067 | 974 | 1,977 | 933 | 56.6 | 90 | 42 | 4.4 | 4.4 | 4.3 | 64.7 | 54.0 |
| Louisiana | 2,113 | 1,013 | 2,009 | 960 | 55.8 | 104 | 54 | 4.9 | 4.6 | 5.3 | 64.4 | 53.6 |
| Maine | 698 | 338 | 674 | 327 | 60.9 | 25 | 11 | 3.5 | 3.8 | 3.2 | 67.2 | 59.2 |
| Maryland | 3,207 | 1,547 | 3,074 | 1,482 | 64.2 | 133 | 64 | 4.2 | 4.2 | 4.2 | 73.3 | 61.3 |
| Massachusetts | 3,819 | 1,864 | 3,689 | 1,810 | 65.6 | 130 | 54 | 3.4 | 3.9 | 2.9 | 72.4 | 63.7 |
| Michigan | 4,903 | 2,306 | 4,699 | 2,219 | 58.9 | 203 | 87 | 4.1 | 4.5 | 3.8 | 67.0 | 56.2 |
| Minnesota | 3,073 | 1,479 | 2,986 | 1,446 | 67.7 | 88 | 33 | 2.8 | 3.4 | 2.2 | 73.2 | 66.3 |
| Mississippi | 1,277 | 620 | 1,215 | 589 | 53.0 | 62 | 31 | 4.8 | 4.7 | 5.0 | 61.0 | 51.0 |
| Missouri | 3,066 | 1,491 | 2,966 | 1,455 | 61.7 | 99 | 37 | 3.2 | 4.0 | 2.5 | 67.9 | 60.0 |
| Montana | 525 | 245 | 506 | 238 | 60.0 | 19 | 7 | 3.7 | 4.4 | 2.9 | 66.7 | 58.0 |
| Nebraska | 1,032 | 485 | 1,003 | 472 | 67.9 | 29 | 13 | 2.8 | 3.0 | 2.6 | 75.1 | 64.7 |
| Nevada | 1,523 | 697 | 1,454 | 664 | 60.5 | 69 | 33 | 4.5 | 4.3 | 4.7 | 69.6 | 57.4 |
| New Hampshire | 762 | 358 | 742 | 349 | 66.9 | 20 | 9 | 2.6 | 2.6 | 2.6 | 74.1 | 63.5 |
| New Jersey | 4,487 | 2,129 | 4,298 | 2,034 | 59.8 | 189 | 95 | 4.2 | 4.0 | 4.5 | 68.2 | 57.0 |
| New Mexico | 946 | 446 | 902 | 427 | 55.4 | 44 | 19 | 4.7 | 5.1 | 4.3 | 63.3 | 53.3 |
| New York | 9,704 | 4,647 | 9,302 | 4,474 | 58.2 | 402 | 173 | 4.1 | 4.5 | 3.7 | 66.3 | 55.7 |
| North Carolina | 4,991 | 2,409 | 4,801 | 2,310 | 59.0 | 190 | 99 | 3.8 | 3.5 | 4.1 | 66.9 | 56.2 |
| North Dakota | 398 | 179 | 387 | 175 | 66.8 | 11 | 4 | 2.8 | 3.3 | 2.3 | 74.2 | 63.1 |
| Ohio | 5,755 | 2,730 | 5,494 | 2,625 | 59.5 | 261 | 105 | 4.5 | 5.2 | 3.8 | 67.9 | 57.2 |
| Oklahoma | 1,844 | 828 | 1,781 | 799 | 59.2 | 63 | 29 | 3.4 | 3.4 | 3.5 | 69.6 | 53.5 |
| Oregon | 2,089 | 991 | 2,002 | 953 | 59.2 | 87 | 38 | 4.1 | 4.4 | 3.8 | 66.3 | 57.4 |
| Pennsylvania | 6,441 | 3,055 | 6,165 | 2,929 | 59.9 | 276 | 126 | 4.3 | 4.5 | 4.1 | 68.3 | 57.3 |
| Rhode Island | 559 | 270 | 537 | 259 | 62.0 | 23 | 11 | 4.1 | 4.2 | 4.0 | 69.9 | 59.8 |
| South Carolina | 2,320 | 1,096 | 2,238 | 1,056 | 55.8 | 82 | 40 | 3.5 | 3.4 | 3.6 | 64.7 | 51.7 |
| South Dakota | 458 | 213 | 445 | 207 | 66.8 | 14 | 7 | 2.9 | 2.9 | 3.0 | 73.7 | 63.9 |
| Tennessee | 3,248 | 1,518 | 3,133 | 1,459 | 58.7 | 114 | 59 | 3.5 | 3.2 | 3.9 | 67.7 | 54.5 |
| Texas | 13,876 | 6,237 | 13,342 | 5,985 | 61.7 | 534 | 253 | 3.8 | 3.7 | 4.1 | 72.6 | 56.2 |
| Utah | 1,553 | 684 | 1,503 | 659 | 65.3 | 51 | 25 | 3.3 | 2.9 | 3.7 | 76.1 | 59.1 |
| Vermont | 346 | 166 | 337 | 161 | 65.1 | 9 | 5 | 2.7 | 2.4 | 3.0 | 70.9 | 63.2 |
| Virginia | 4,362 | 2,065 | 4,235 | 2,007 | 63.6 | 128 | 58 | 2.9 | 3.0 | 2.8 | 71.9 | 59.6 |
| Washington | 3,779 | 1,704 | 3,611 | 1,634 | 60.8 | 168 | 69 | 4.4 | 4.7 | 4.1 | 70.9 | 56.6 |
| West Virginia | 782 | 363 | 741 | 347 | 51.0 | 41 | 16 | 5.3 | 5.9 | 4.5 | 59.1 | 48.8 |
| Wisconsin | 3,123 | 1512 | 3,031 | 1,468 | 65.6 | 92 | 44 | 3.0 | 3.0 | 2.9 | 70.9 | 64.4 |
| Wyoming | 287 | 130 | 275 | 124 | 62.0 | 12 | 6 | 4.2 | 4.0 | 4.3 | 70.4 | 58.8 |

[1] Civilian employment as a percent of civilian noninstitutionalized population. [2] Percent unemployed of the civilian labor force. [3] Percent of civilian noninstitutionalized population of each specified group in the civilian labor force.

Source: U.S. Bureau of Labor Statistics, Labor Force Statistics from the Current Population Survey, "Employment status of the civilian noninstitutional population by sex, age, and race," <http://www.bls.gov/cps/tables.htm>; and Local Area Unemployment Statistics, "Expanded State Employment Status Demographic Data," <https://www.bls.gov/lau/#tables>; accessed August 2019.

## Table 620. Civilian Labor Force Status by Selected Metropolitan Area: 2018

[162,075 represents 162,075,000. Civilian noninstitutional population 16 years old and over. Annual averages of monthly figures. Data are derived from the Local Area Unemployment Statistics program, a Federal-State cooperative effort in which monthly estimates of total employment and unemployment are prepared for approximately 7,300 areas. For definitions of metropolitan areas, see Appendix II]

| Metropolitan area ranked by 2010 population | Civilian labor force (1,000) | Unemployment rate [1] | Metropolitan area ranked by 2010 population | Civilian labor force (1,000) | Unemployment rate [1] |
|---|---|---|---|---|---|
| **United States, total**................................... | **162,075** | **3.9** | San Antonio-New Braunfels, TX.................... | 1,190 | 3.3 |
| New York-Newark-Jersey City, NY-NJ-PA........... | 9,935 | 4.0 | Orlando-Kissimmee-Sanford, FL.................. | 1,338 | 3.3 |
| Los Angeles-Long Beach-Anaheim, CA............... | 6,762 | 4.2 | Cincinnati, OH-KY-IN............................. | 1,116 | 4.0 |
| Chicago-Naperville-Elgin, IL-IN-WI.................. | 4,876 | 4.0 | Cleveland-Elyria, OH.............................. | 1,035 | 5.1 |
| Dallas-Fort Worth-Arlington, TX..................... | 3,900 | 3.5 | Kansas City, MO-KS.............................. | 1,134 | 3.4 |
| Philadelphia-Camden-Wilmington, PA-NJ-DE-MD... | 3,082 | 4.2 | Las Vegas-Henderson-Paradise, NV.............. | 1,098 | 4.8 |
| Houston-The Woodlands-Sugar Land, TX.......... | 3,391 | 4.3 | Columbus, OH................................... | 1,081 | 3.8 |
| Washington-Arlington-Alexandria, DC-VA-MD-WV... | 3,393 | 3.3 | Indianapolis-Carmel-Anderson, IN................ | 1,062 | 3.2 |
| Miami-Fort Lauderdale-West Palm Beach, FL...... | 3,151 | 3.6 | San Jose-Sunnyvale-Santa Clara, CA............ | 1,080 | 2.7 |
| Atlanta-Sandy Springs-Roswell, GA................. | 3,072 | 3.8 | Austin-Round Rock, TX........................... | 1,197 | 2.9 |
| Boston-Cambridge-Nashua, MA-NH NECTA [2]....... | 2,811 | 3.0 | Virginia Beach-Norfolk-Newport News, VA-NC... | 850 | 3.3 |
| San Francisco-Oakland-Hayward, CA............... | 2,584 | 2.7 | Nashville-Davidson-Murfreesboro-Franklin, TN... | 1,043 | 2.7 |
| Detroit-Warren-Dearborn, MI........................ | 2,131 | 4.3 | Providence-Warwick, RI-MA NECTA [2]............ | 690 | 4.1 |
| Riverside-San Bernardino-Ontario, CA............. | 2,053 | 4.2 | Milwaukee-Waukesha-West Allis, WI.............. | 825 | 3.2 |
| Phoenix-Mesa-Scottsdale, AZ....................... | 2,408 | 4.2 | Jacksonville, FL.................................. | 773 | 3.4 |
| Seattle-Tacoma-Bellevue, WA....................... | 2,113 | 3.9 | Memphis, TN-MS-AR.............................. | 635 | 4.1 |
| Minneapolis-St. Paul-Bloomington, MN-WI......... | 2,001 | 2.7 | Oklahoma City, OK................................ | 682 | 3.1 |
| San Diego-Carlsbad, CA............................ | 1,592 | 3.3 | Louisville-Jefferson County, KY-IN............... | 671 | 3.9 |
| St. Louis, MO-IL.................................... | 1,459 | 3.4 | Hartford-W. Hartford-E. Hartford, CT NECTA [2]... | 626 | 4.1 |
| Tampa-St. Petersburg-Clearwater, FL............... | 1,531 | 3.5 | Richmond, VA.................................... | 676 | 3.2 |
| Baltimore-Columbia-Towson, MD..................... | 1,493 | 4.0 | New Orleans-Metairie, LA......................... | 595 | 4.6 |
| Denver-Aurora-Lakewood, CO....................... | 1,646 | 3.2 | Buffalo-Cheektowaga-Niagara Falls, NY.......... | 543 | 4.6 |
| Pittsburgh, PA..................................... | 1,204 | 4.3 | Raleigh, NC...................................... | 711 | 3.4 |
| Portland-Vancouver-Hillsboro, OR-WA.............. | 1,313 | 3.9 | Birmingham-Hoover, AL........................... | 545 | 3.5 |
| Charlotte-Concord-Gastonia, NC-SC................ | 1,333 | 3.6 | Salt Lake City, UT................................ | 654 | 3.0 |
| Sacramento-Roseville-Arden-Arcade, CA........... | 1,096 | 3.7 | Rochester, NY.................................... | 522 | 4.2 |

[1] Percent of the civilian labor force unemployed. [2] New England City and Town Areas. See Appendix II.

Source: U.S. Bureau of Labor Statistics, "Local Area Unemployment Statistics," <http://www.bls.gov/lau/>, accessed May 2019.

## Table 621. School Enrollment and Labor Force Status of Teenagers and Young Adults: 2018

[In thousands (37,962 represents 37,962,000), except percent rate. As of October. Covers civilian noninstitutional population age 16 to 24. Based on Current Population Survey; see text, Section 1 and Appendix III]

| Characteristic | Population | Civilian labor force | Employed | Unemployed Total | Unemployed Rate [1] | Not in labor force |
|---|---|---|---|---|---|---|
| **Total, 16 to 24 years [2]**......................... | **37,962** | **20,829** | **19,120** | **1,709** | **8.2** | **17,134** |
| **Enrolled in school [2]**........................... | **21,698** | **7,962** | **7,429** | **533** | **6.7** | **13,735** |
| Enrolled in high school............................. | 9,435 | 2,137 | 1,912 | 225 | 10.5 | 7,298 |
| Male......................................... | 4,970 | 1,037 | 919 | 118 | 11.4 | 3,933 |
| Female....................................... | 4,465 | 1,100 | 993 | 107 | 9.7 | 3,365 |
| Enrolled in college................................ | 12,263 | 5,825 | 5,517 | 308 | 5.3 | 6,437 |
| Male......................................... | 5,644 | 2,535 | 2,385 | 150 | 5.9 | 3,110 |
| Female....................................... | 6,618 | 3,290 | 3,132 | 159 | 4.8 | 3,328 |
| Enrolled in two-year college.................... | 3,008 | 1,663 | 1,564 | 99 | 6.0 | 1,345 |
| Enrolled in four-year college................... | 9,254 | 4,162 | 3,953 | 209 | 5.0 | 5,092 |
| White: | | | | | | |
| Enrolled in high school......................... | 6,860 | 1,654 | 1,495 | 159 | 9.6 | 5,207 |
| Enrolled in college............................ | 8,913 | 4,494 | 4,285 | 209 | 4.7 | 4,420 |
| Black or African American: | | | | | | |
| Enrolled in high school......................... | 1,416 | 240 | 199 | 40 | 16.8 | 1,176 |
| Enrolled in college............................ | 1,683 | 793 | 734 | 59 | 7.4 | 890 |
| Asian: | | | | | | |
| Enrolled in high school......................... | 449 | 52 | 47 | 4 | (NA) | 398 |
| Enrolled in college............................ | 1,082 | 306 | 283 | 23 | 7.4 | 777 |
| Hispanic: [3] | | | | | | |
| Enrolled in high school......................... | 2,193 | 360 | 307 | 53 | 14.8 | 1,833 |
| Enrolled in college............................ | 2,482 | 1,303 | 1,256 | 47 | 3.6 | 1,179 |
| **Not enrolled in school [2]**....................... | **16,264** | **12,866** | **11,691** | **1,175** | **9.1** | **3,398** |
| White......................................... | 12,057 | 9,634 | 8,900 | 735 | 7.6 | 2,423 |
| Black......................................... | 2,547 | 1,934 | 1,644 | 290 | 15.0 | 613 |
| Asian......................................... | 734 | 549 | 480 | 69 | 12.6 | 185 |
| Hispanic [3]................................... | 4,049 | 3,093 | 2,815 | 277 | 9.0 | 956 |

NA Not available. [1] Percent unemployed of civilian labor force in each category. [2] Includes other races, not shown separately. [3] Persons of Hispanic origin may be of any race.

Source: U.S. Bureau of Labor Statistics, *College Enrollment and Work Activity of Recent High School and College Graduates—2018*, USDL 19-0697, April 2019. See also <http://www.bls.gov/news.release/hsgec.toc.htm>.

# Table 622. Labor Force Participation Rates by Marital Status, Sex, and Age: 1970 to 2018

[In percent. For the civilian noninstitutional population 16 years old and over. Annual averages of monthly figures. Participation rate is the civilian labor force as a percent of the civilian noninstitutional population. Based on Current Population Survey; see text, Section 1 and Appendix III]

| Marital status and year | Male participation rate | | | | | | | Female participation rate | | | | | | |
|---|---|---|---|---|---|---|---|---|---|---|---|---|---|---|
| | Total | 16–19 years | 20–24 years | 25–34 years | 35–44 years | 45–64 years | 65 years and over | Total | 16–19 years | 20–24 years | 25–34 years | 35–44 years | 45–64 years | 65 years and over |
| **Single:** [1] | | | | | | | | | | | | | | |
| 1970 | 65.5 | 54.6 | 73.8 | 87.9 | 86.2 | 75.7 | 25.2 | 56.8 | 44.7 | 73.0 | 81.4 | 78.6 | 73.0 | 19.7 |
| 1980 | 72.6 | 59.9 | 81.3 | 89.2 | 82.2 | 66.9 | 16.8 | 64.4 | 53.6 | 75.2 | 83.3 | 76.9 | 65.6 | 13.9 |
| 1990 | 74.8 | 55.1 | 81.6 | 89.9 | 84.5 | 67.3 | 15.7 | 66.7 | 51.7 | 74.5 | 80.9 | 80.8 | 66.2 | 12.1 |
| 2000 | 73.6 | 52.5 | 80.5 | 89.4 | 82.9 | 69.7 | 17.3 | 68.9 | 51.1 | 76.1 | 83.9 | 80.9 | 69.9 | 10.8 |
| 2010 | 67.3 | 34.6 | 73.1 | 85.8 | 83.7 | 67.6 | 25.0 | 63.3 | 34.9 | 69.8 | 81.3 | 78.2 | 69.4 | 20.1 |
| 2011 | 67.0 | 33.4 | 73.3 | 85.4 | 82.6 | 67.4 | 23.8 | 62.8 | 34.3 | 69.1 | 79.9 | 77.8 | 67.8 | 21.7 |
| 2012 | 66.8 | 33.7 | 72.9 | 85.8 | 81.7 | 67.1 | 23.6 | 62.8 | 34.5 | 68.5 | 79.8 | 78.1 | 68.2 | 20.5 |
| 2013 | 66.9 | 34.0 | 72.5 | 85.4 | 82.2 | 66.9 | 24.5 | 63.0 | 34.5 | 69.2 | 79.2 | 77.5 | 67.3 | 22.7 |
| 2014 | 66.7 | 33.3 | 72.5 | 85.1 | 82.4 | 64.4 | 25.9 | 62.9 | 34.4 | 69.1 | 79.9 | 77.6 | 65.5 | 21.3 |
| 2015 | 66.8 | 33.9 | 71.7 | 85.6 | 81.2 | 64.6 | 26.6 | 62.9 | 34.1 | 69.3 | 79.7 | 77.6 | 65.8 | 20.9 |
| 2016 | 67.3 | 35.1 | 71.8 | 85.5 | 82.5 | 65.2 | 26.1 | 63.4 | 35.0 | 69.2 | 80.9 | 77.3 | 65.4 | 22.6 |
| 2017 | 67.4 | 34.4 | 72.9 | 85.6 | 82.8 | 64.2 | 26.3 | 64.3 | 35.7 | 69.8 | 81.7 | 78.9 | 66.0 | 23.7 |
| 2018 | 67.7 | 34.0 | 72.1 | 85.9 | 83.4 | 66.4 | 25.9 | 64.5 | 35.9 | 70.2 | 81.4 | 78.4 | 66.3 | 25.2 |
| **Married:** [2] | | | | | | | | | | | | | | |
| 1970 | 86.1 | 92.3 | 94.7 | 98.0 | 98.1 | 91.2 | 29.9 | 40.5 | 37.8 | 47.9 | 38.8 | 46.8 | 44.0 | 7.3 |
| 1980 | 80.9 | 91.3 | 96.9 | 97.5 | 97.2 | 84.3 | 20.5 | 49.8 | 49.3 | 61.4 | 58.8 | 61.8 | 46.9 | 7.3 |
| 1990 | 78.6 | 92.1 | 95.6 | 96.9 | 96.7 | 82.6 | 17.5 | 58.4 | 49.5 | 66.1 | 69.6 | 74.0 | 56.5 | 8.5 |
| 2000 | 77.3 | 79.5 | 94.1 | 96.7 | 95.8 | 83.0 | 19.2 | 61.1 | 53.2 | 63.8 | 70.3 | 74.8 | 65.4 | 10.1 |
| 2010 | 75.8 | 78.2 | 89.3 | 94.3 | 94.5 | 83.6 | 23.5 | 61.0 | 40.2 | 60.6 | 68.8 | 72.8 | 68.8 | 15.2 |
| 2011 | 74.9 | 75.9 | 90.2 | 93.9 | 94.3 | 82.8 | 24.5 | 60.2 | 44.7 | 60.6 | 68.2 | 72.5 | 68.0 | 15.3 |
| 2012 | 74.6 | 83.7 | 91.3 | 94.2 | 94.3 | 83.0 | 25.6 | 59.5 | 42.1 | 60.5 | 68.5 | 72.3 | 67.3 | 15.9 |
| 2013 | 74.2 | 81.7 | 90.1 | 94.0 | 94.1 | 83.0 | 25.7 | 58.9 | 46.3 | 58.4 | 67.8 | 71.3 | 67.1 | 16.5 |
| 2014 | 73.5 | 76.8 | 92.0 | 93.4 | 94.0 | 82.9 | 24.9 | 58.4 | 45.1 | 58.9 | 67.7 | 71.3 | 66.6 | 16.8 |
| 2015 | 73.4 | 75.9 | 89.7 | 93.5 | 94.2 | 83.1 | 25.2 | 58.1 | 47.1 | 61.6 | 67.1 | 71.9 | 66.0 | 16.8 |
| 2016 | 73.1 | 71.5 | 89.3 | 93.7 | 94.2 | 83.2 | 25.5 | 57.9 | 43.8 | 59.9 | 67.9 | 71.8 | 66.3 | 16.6 |
| 2017 | 72.9 | 80.1 | 89.1 | 93.4 | 94.1 | 83.5 | 25.4 | 58.2 | 50.6 | 61.0 | 68.4 | 72.3 | 67.0 | 17.0 |
| 2018 | 73.1 | 89.5 | 88.9 | 94.4 | 94.4 | 83.9 | 25.7 | 58.2 | 48.7 | 61.7 | 69.4 | 72.4 | 67.2 | 17.1 |
| **Other:** [3] | | | | | | | | | | | | | | |
| 1970 | 60.7 | (B) | 90.4 | 93.7 | 91.1 | 78.5 | 19.3 | 40.3 | 48.6 | 60.3 | 64.6 | 68.8 | 61.9 | 10.0 |
| 1980 | 67.5 | (B) | 92.6 | 94.1 | 91.9 | 73.3 | 13.7 | 43.6 | 50.0 | 68.4 | 76.5 | 77.1 | 60.2 | 8.2 |
| 1990 | 68.9 | (B) | 93.1 | 93.0 | 90.7 | 74.9 | 12.0 | 47.2 | 53.9 | 65.4 | 77.0 | 82.1 | 65.0 | 8.4 |
| 2000 | 66.8 | 60.5 | 88.1 | 93.2 | 89.9 | 73.9 | 12.9 | 49.0 | 46.0 | 74.0 | 83.1 | 82.9 | 69.8 | 8.7 |
| 2010 | 63.0 | 37.6 | 78.8 | 89.0 | 88.5 | 71.8 | 17.2 | 48.8 | 35.2 | 66.3 | 77.7 | 80.7 | 68.8 | 12.1 |
| 2011 | 62.4 | 39.7 | 76.2 | 88.3 | 87.2 | 71.1 | 17.8 | 48.8 | 39.9 | 65.6 | 77.1 | 79.2 | 68.3 | 12.3 |
| 2012 | 61.7 | 35.1 | 78.3 | 88.5 | 87.4 | 70.9 | 17.6 | 48.3 | 34.9 | 68.4 | 77.4 | 79.8 | 67.6 | 12.6 |
| 2013 | 60.2 | 29.2 | 74.1 | 89.4 | 88.3 | 69.4 | 16.8 | 47.3 | 36.6 | 63.8 | 76.4 | 79.7 | 66.6 | 12.8 |
| 2014 | 59.6 | 31.2 | 80.3 | 88.8 | 87.1 | 70.4 | 16.9 | 47.3 | 38.2 | 66.3 | 77.2 | 80.1 | 66.8 | 13.0 |
| 2015 | 58.8 | 36.6 | 73.0 | 87.0 | 86.8 | 70.3 | 17.7 | 46.7 | 42.9 | 67.0 | 75.4 | 79.0 | 66.4 | 13.4 |
| 2016 | 59.6 | 37.7 | 71.0 | 88.2 | 87.1 | 71.0 | 19.1 | 46.9 | 40.4 | 67.5 | 76.1 | 80.6 | 66.4 | 13.8 |
| 2017 | 59.0 | 34.7 | 77.5 | 88.7 | 87.9 | 71.1 | 19.0 | 46.0 | 31.8 | 63.5 | 79.0 | 79.7 | 66.0 | 13.5 |
| 2018 | 58.3 | 33.3 | 75.3 | 87.0 | 87.6 | 71.7 | 19.1 | 45.9 | 31.9 | 64.3 | 79.8 | 80.6 | 66.4 | 13.8 |

B Percentage not shown where base is less than 50,000. [1] Never married. [2] Spouse present. [3] Widowed, divorced, and separated (married, spouse absent).

Source: U.S. Bureau of Labor Statistics, unpublished data. See also <http://www.bls.gov/cps/home.htm>.

# Table 623. Marital Status of Women in the Civilian Labor Force: 1970 to 2018

[31,543 represents 31,543,000. For civilian noninstitutional population 16 years and over. Annual averages of monthly figures. Based on the Current Population Survey; see text, Section 1 and Appendix III]

| Year | Female civilian labor force (1,000) | | | | Female participation rate (percent) [3] | | | |
|---|---|---|---|---|---|---|---|---|
| | Total | Never married | Married [1] | Other [2] | Total | Never married | Married [1] | Other [2] |
| 1970 | 31,543 | 7,265 | 18,475 | 5,804 | 43.3 | 56.8 | 40.5 | 40.3 |
| 1980 | 45,487 | 11,865 | 24,980 | 8,643 | 51.5 | 64.4 | 49.8 | 43.6 |
| 1990 | 56,829 | 14,612 | 30,901 | 11,315 | 57.5 | 66.7 | 58.4 | 47.2 |
| 2000 | 66,303 | 17,849 | 35,146 | 13,308 | 59.9 | 68.9 | 61.1 | 49.0 |
| 2005 | 69,288 | 19,183 | 35,941 | 14,163 | 59.3 | 66.0 | 60.7 | 49.4 |
| 2010 | 71,904 | 20,592 | 36,742 | 14,570 | 58.6 | 63.3 | 61.0 | 48.8 |
| 2011 | 71,642 | 20,878 | 36,141 | 14,623 | 58.1 | 62.8 | 60.2 | 48.8 |
| 2012 | 72,648 | 21,506 | 36,436 | 14,706 | 57.7 | 62.8 | 59.5 | 48.3 |
| 2013 | 72,722 | 22,070 | 36,137 | 14,515 | 57.2 | 63.0 | 58.9 | 47.3 |
| 2014 | 73,039 | 22,320 | 36,082 | 14,637 | 57.0 | 62.9 | 58.4 | 47.3 |
| 2015 | 73,510 | 22,738 | 36,135 | 14,637 | 56.7 | 62.9 | 58.1 | 46.7 |
| 2016 | 74,433 | 23,321 | 36,387 | 14,725 | 56.8 | 63.4 | 57.9 | 46.9 |
| 2017 | 75,174 | 23,993 | 36,776 | 14,405 | 57.0 | 64.3 | 58.2 | 46.0 |
| 2018 | 75,979 | 24,556 | 36,885 | 14,538 | 57.1 | 64.5 | 58.2 | 45.9 |

[1] Spouse present. [2] Widowed, divorced, and separated (married, spouse absent). [3] Civilian labor force as a percent of the civilian noninstitutional population.

Source: U.S. Bureau of Labor Statistics, unpublished data. See also <http://www.bls.gov/cps/home.htm>.

# Table 624. Employment Status of Women by Marital Status and Presence and Age of Children: 1970 to 2018

[7.0 represents 7,000,000. As of March. Data are from the Current Population Survey, Annual Social and Economic Supplement (ASEC), which includes civilian noninstitutionalized population, age 16 years old and over. For more information; see text, Section 1 and Appendix III]

| Item | Total | | | With any children under age 18 | | | | | | | | |
|---|---|---|---|---|---|---|---|---|---|---|---|---|
| | | | | Total | | | Children 6 to 17 years | | | Children under 6 years | | |
| | Single [1] | Mar-ried [2] | Other [3] | Single [1] | Mar-ried [2] | Other [3] | Single [1] | Mar-ried [2] | Other [3] | Single [1] | Mar-ried [2] | Other [3] |
| **IN LABOR FORCE (millions)** | | | | | | | | | | | | |
| 1970 | 7.0 | 18.4 | 5.9 | (NA) | 10.2 | 1.9 | (NA) | 6.3 | 1.3 | (NA) | 3.9 | 0.6 |
| 1980 | 11.2 | 24.9 | 8.8 | 0.6 | 13.7 | 3.6 | 0.2 | 8.4 | 2.6 | 0.3 | 5.2 | 1.0 |
| 1990 | 14.0 | 31.0 | 11.2 | 1.5 | 16.5 | 4.2 | 0.6 | 9.3 | 3.0 | 0.9 | 7.2 | 1.2 |
| 2000 | 17.8 | 35.0 | 13.2 | 3.1 | 18.2 | 4.5 | 1.2 | 10.8 | 3.4 | 1.8 | 7.3 | 1.1 |
| 2010 | 20.0 | 37.2 | 14.7 | 3.6 | 17.6 | 4.5 | 1.6 | 10.4 | 3.3 | 2.1 | 7.2 | 1.2 |
| 2016 | 23.2 | 36.9 | 14.7 | 4.1 | 16.9 | 4.1 | 1.9 | 10.2 | 3.0 | 2.2 | 6.7 | 1.1 |
| 2017 | 23.7 | 37.4 | 14.4 | 4.0 | 16.9 | 3.9 | 2.0 | 10.2 | 2.9 | 2.1 | 6.7 | 1.0 |
| 2018 | 24.4 | 37.1 | 14.5 | 4.0 | 16.9 | 3.9 | 2.0 | 10.1 | 3.0 | 2.1 | 6.8 | 0.9 |
| **PARTICIPATION RATE [4]** | | | | | | | | | | | | |
| 1970 | 53.0 | 40.8 | 39.1 | (NA) | 39.7 | 60.7 | (NA) | 49.2 | 66.9 | (NA) | 30.3 | 52.2 |
| 1980 | 61.5 | 50.1 | 44.0 | 52.0 | 54.1 | 69.4 | 67.6 | 61.7 | 74.6 | 44.1 | 45.1 | 60.3 |
| 1990 | 66.4 | 58.2 | 46.8 | 55.2 | 66.3 | 74.2 | 69.7 | 73.6 | 79.7 | 48.7 | 58.9 | 63.6 |
| 2000 | 68.6 | 62.0 | 50.2 | 73.9 | 70.6 | 82.7 | 79.7 | 77.2 | 84.9 | 70.5 | 62.8 | 76.6 |
| 2010 | 62.3 | 61.7 | 49.2 | 70.1 | 69.7 | 79.2 | 77.0 | 75.9 | 81.8 | 65.6 | 62.5 | 73.1 |
| 2016 | 62.7 | 58.9 | 47.2 | 72.8 | 68.6 | 79.3 | 78.3 | 73.0 | 80.6 | 68.6 | 62.9 | 75.5 |
| 2017 | 63.9 | 59.1 | 46.4 | 73.4 | 69.3 | 79.0 | 78.9 | 74.3 | 80.8 | 68.9 | 62.9 | 74.1 |
| 2018 | 64.5 | 58.3 | 46.3 | 75.0 | 69.0 | 79.7 | 79.5 | 74.7 | 81.2 | 71.3 | 61.8 | 75.1 |
| **EMPLOYMENT (millions)** | | | | | | | | | | | | |
| 1970 | 6.5 | 17.5 | 5.6 | (NA) | 9.6 | 1.8 | (NA) | 6.0 | 1.2 | (NA) | 3.6 | 0.6 |
| 1980 | 10.1 | 23.6 | 8.2 | 0.4 | 12.8 | 3.3 | 0.2 | 8.1 | 2.4 | 0.2 | 4.8 | 0.9 |
| 1990 | 12.9 | 29.9 | 10.5 | 1.2 | 15.8 | 3.8 | 0.5 | 8.9 | 2.7 | 0.7 | 6.9 | 1.1 |
| 2000 | 16.4 | 34.0 | 12.7 | 2.7 | 17.6 | 4.3 | 1.1 | 10.6 | 3.2 | 1.6 | 7.1 | 1.1 |
| 2010 | 17.5 | 35.0 | 13.3 | 3.0 | 16.5 | 4.0 | 1.3 | 9.8 | 2.9 | 1.6 | 6.7 | 1.1 |
| 2016 | 21.4 | 35.7 | 14.0 | 3.7 | 16.3 | 3.9 | 1.8 | 9.9 | 2.9 | 1.9 | 6.5 | 1.0 |
| 2017 | 22.3 | 36.4 | 13.6 | 3.7 | 16.4 | 3.7 | 1.8 | 9.9 | 2.8 | 1.9 | 6.5 | 0.9 |
| 2018 | 23.0 | 36.2 | 13.9 | 3.7 | 16.5 | 3.7 | 1.8 | 9.9 | 2.8 | 1.9 | 6.6 | 0.8 |
| **UNEMPLOYMENT RATE [5]** | | | | | | | | | | | | |
| 1970 | 7.1 | 4.8 | 4.8 | (NA) | 6.0 | 7.2 | (NA) | 4.8 | 5.9 | (NA) | 7.9 | 9.8 |
| 1980 | 10.3 | 5.3 | 6.4 | 23.2 | 5.9 | 9.2 | 15.6 | 4.4 | 7.9 | 29.2 | 8.3 | 12.8 |
| 1990 | 8.2 | 3.5 | 5.7 | 18.4 | 4.2 | 8.5 | 14.5 | 3.8 | 7.7 | 20.8 | 4.8 | 10.2 |
| 2000 | 7.3 | 2.7 | 4.3 | 11.0 | 2.9 | 5.1 | 8.7 | 2.6 | 4.8 | 12.6 | 3.5 | 5.9 |
| 2010 | 12.3 | 6.0 | 9.7 | 18.1 | 6.3 | 11.1 | 14.4 | 6.0 | 10.3 | 20.9 | 6.7 | 13.4 |
| 2016 | 8.0 | 3.1 | 4.7 | 10.4 | 3.2 | 5.5 | 8.7 | 3.1 | 4.5 | 11.9 | 3.4 | 8.2 |
| 2017 | 6.3 | 2.8 | 5.1 | 9.4 | 3.1 | 5.4 | 7.3 | 3.1 | 4.8 | 11.3 | 3.1 | 7.3 |
| 2018 | 5.6 | 2.6 | 4.2 | 8.0 | 2.5 | 5.2 | 6.6 | 2.3 | 4.7 | 9.3 | 2.8 | 6.6 |

NA Not available. [1] Never married. [2] Spouse present. [3] Widowed, divorced, or separated (married, spouse absent). [4] Percent of women in each specific category in the labor force. [5] Unemployed as a percent of civilian labor force in specified group.

Source: U.S. Bureau of Labor Statistics, unpublished data. See also <http://www.bls.gov/cps/home.htm>.

# Table 625. Labor Force Participation Rates for Wives, Spouse Present, by Age of Own Youngest Child: 1990 to 2018

[In percent. As of March. Based on Current Population Survey, Annual Social and Economic Supplement (ASEC), which includes civilian noninstitutionalized population, 16 years old and over, and military personnel who live in households with at least one other civilian adult. Armed Forces includes only those Armed Forces members living on or off post with their families; all other members of the Armed Forces are excluded. Data refer to persons in primary families. For more information; see text, Section 1 and Appendix III]

| Presence and age of child | 1990 | 2000 | 2010 | 2016 | 2017 | 2018 | | | | |
|---|---|---|---|---|---|---|---|---|---|---|
| | | | | | | Total | White [1] | Black [1] | Asian [1, 2] | His-panic [3] |
| **Wives, total** | 58.3 | 62.2 | 61.9 | 59.1 | 59.3 | 58.5 | 58.2 | 62.7 | 56.9 | 55.0 |
| No children under 18 years | 51.1 | 54.8 | 56.0 | 52.7 | 52.8 | 51.8 | 51.3 | 54.6 | 52.9 | 52.1 |
| With children under 18 years | 66.5 | 70.9 | 70.1 | 68.9 | 69.5 | 69.2 | 69.9 | 75.0 | 60.4 | 57.2 |
| Under 6 years, total | 59.1 | 63.1 | 62.9 | 63.1 | 63.1 | 62.1 | 63.5 | 68.3 | 50.0 | 47.2 |
| Under 3 years | 55.9 | 59.4 | 59.5 | 62.3 | 62.1 | 60.0 | 61.7 | 62.1 | 46.6 | 43.3 |
| Under 1 year | 53.9 | 58.4 | 59.0 | 60.0 | 60.4 | 59.2 | 60.6 | 64.1 | 46.6 | 30.4 |
| 1 year | (NA) | (NA) | 57.6 | 62.3 | 62.3 | 59.7 | 62.5 | 54.6 | 43.1 | 47.9 |
| 2 years | 60.9 | 61.9 | 62.4 | 64.9 | 63.7 | 61.3 | 62.0 | 69.3 | 49.3 | 51.1 |
| 3 to 5 years | 64.1 | 68.6 | 67.7 | 64.2 | 64.5 | 64.9 | 66.0 | 76.3 | 53.7 | 51.6 |
| 3 years | 63.0 | 66.0 | 66.4 | 61.2 | 62.2 | 64.3 | 67.0 | 70.1 | 44.4 | 49.4 |
| 4 years | 65.0 | 69.6 | 68.9 | 65.7 | 65.4 | 65.0 | 65.3 | 76.6 | 57.5 | 57.2 |
| 5 years | 64.4 | 70.7 | 68.1 | 66.2 | 66.5 | 65.7 | 65.4 | 83.7 | 59.9 | 48.2 |
| 6 to 13 years | 73.1 | 76.0 | 74.8 | 72.2 | 73.5 | 74.1 | 74.0 | 81.4 | 69.3 | 63.5 |
| 14 to 17 years | 75.0 | 80.8 | 79.0 | 75.8 | 76.8 | 76.6 | 77.1 | 77.4 | 71.8 | 68.8 |

NA Not available. [1] Persons in this race group only. See footnote 2, Table 613. [2] Excludes Pacific Islanders. [3] Persons of Hispanic origin may be of any race.

Source: U.S. Bureau of Labor Statistics, unpublished data. See also <http://www.bls.gov/cps/home.htm>.

# Table 626. Married Couples by Labor Force Status of Spouses: 1990 to 2018

[52,317 represents 52,317,000. As of March. Based on the Annual Social and Economic Supplement (ASEC) to the Current Population Survey; for details see source and Appendix III]

| Year | Number (1,000) | | | | | Percent distribution | | | | |
|---|---|---|---|---|---|---|---|---|---|---|
| | All married couples | In labor force | | | Husband & wife not in labor force | All married couples | In labor force | | | Husband & wife not in labor force |
| | | Husband and wife | Husband only | Wife only | | | Husband and wife | Husband only | Wife only | |
| **TOTAL** | | | | | | | | | | |
| 1990 | 52,317 | 28,056 | 13,013 | 2,453 | 8,794 | 100.0 | 53.6 | 24.9 | 4.7 | 16.8 |
| 2000 | 55,311 | 31,095 | 11,815 | 3,301 | 9,098 | 100.0 | 56.2 | 21.4 | 6.0 | 16.4 |
| 2010 | 60,384 | 32,731 | 13,074 | 4,526 | 10,053 | 100.0 | 54.2 | 21.7 | 7.5 | 16.6 |
| 2012 | 61,047 | 31,803 | 13,820 | 4,595 | 10,830 | 100.0 | 52.1 | 22.6 | 7.5 | 17.7 |
| 2013 | 61,295 | 31,673 | 13,901 | 4,656 | 11,065 | 100.0 | 51.7 | 22.7 | 7.6 | 18.1 |
| 2014 | 61,850 | 31,666 | 13,913 | 4,708 | 11,563 | 100.0 | 51.2 | 22.5 | 7.6 | 18.7 |
| 2015 | 62,230 | 31,688 | 14,164 | 4,757 | 11,622 | 100.0 | 50.9 | 22.8 | 7.6 | 18.7 |
| 2016 | 62,628 | 32,120 | 13,885 | 4,790 | 11,833 | 100.0 | 51.3 | 22.2 | 7.6 | 18.9 |
| 2017 | 63,325 | 32,658 | 13,803 | 4,797 | 12,068 | 100.0 | 51.6 | 21.8 | 7.6 | 19.1 |
| 2018 | 63,739 | 32,373 | 14,202 | 4,826 | 12,339 | 100.0 | 50.8 | 22.3 | 7.6 | 19.4 |
| **WITH CHILDREN UNDER AGE 18** | | | | | | | | | | |
| 1990 | 24,537 | 15,768 | 7,667 | 558 | 544 | 100.0 | 64.3 | 31.2 | 2.3 | 2.2 |
| 2000 | 25,248 | 17,116 | 6,950 | 795 | 387 | 100.0 | 67.8 | 27.5 | 3.1 | 1.5 |
| 2010 | 25,317 | 16,710 | 7,220 | 962 | 425 | 100.0 | 66.0 | 28.5 | 3.8 | 1.7 |
| 2012 | 24,445 | 15,752 | 7,226 | 1,009 | 457 | 100.0 | 64.4 | 29.6 | 4.1 | 1.9 |
| 2013 | 24,677 | 15,755 | 7,408 | 1,051 | 462 | 100.0 | 63.8 | 30.0 | 4.3 | 1.9 |
| 2014 | 24,775 | 15,945 | 7,336 | 949 | 545 | 100.0 | 64.4 | 29.6 | 3.8 | 2.2 |
| 2015 | 24,857 | 15,828 | 7,454 | 987 | 589 | 100.0 | 63.7 | 30.0 | 4.0 | 2.4 |
| 2016 | 24,638 | 15,873 | 7,176 | 1,042 | 546 | 100.0 | 64.4 | 29.1 | 4.2 | 2.2 |
| 2017 | 24,465 | 15,895 | 7,029 | 1,058 | 483 | 100.0 | 65.0 | 28.7 | 4.3 | 2.0 |
| 2018 | 24,555 | 15,903 | 7,132 | 1,043 | 476 | 100.0 | 64.8 | 29.0 | 4.2 | 1.9 |
| **WITH CHILDREN UNDER AGE 6** | | | | | | | | | | |
| 1990 | 12,051 | 6,932 | 4,692 | 192 | 235 | 100.0 | 57.5 | 38.9 | 1.6 | 2.0 |
| 2000 | 11,393 | 6,984 | 4,077 | 211 | 121 | 100.0 | 61.3 | 35.8 | 1.9 | 1.1 |
| 2010 | 11,599 | 6,924 | 4,181 | 335 | 159 | 100.0 | 59.7 | 36.0 | 2.9 | 1.4 |
| 2012 | 11,055 | 6,509 | 3,986 | 383 | 176 | 100.0 | 58.9 | 36.1 | 3.5 | 1.6 |
| 2013 | 10,867 | 6,347 | 3,951 | 403 | 166 | 100.0 | 58.4 | 36.4 | 3.7 | 1.5 |
| 2014 | 10,887 | 6,378 | 3,965 | 340 | 204 | 100.0 | 58.6 | 36.4 | 3.1 | 1.9 |
| 2015 | 10,862 | 6,351 | 3,969 | 320 | 222 | 100.0 | 58.5 | 36.5 | 2.9 | 2.0 |
| 2016 | 10,688 | 6,349 | 3,759 | 383 | 197 | 100.0 | 59.4 | 35.2 | 3.6 | 1.8 |
| 2017 | 10,727 | 6,410 | 3,811 | 339 | 166 | 100.0 | 59.8 | 35.5 | 3.2 | 1.5 |
| 2018 | 11,001 | 6,464 | 4,025 | 356 | 157 | 100.0 | 58.8 | 36.6 | 3.2 | 1.4 |

Source: U.S. Census Bureau, Families and Living Arrangements, Detailed Table MC-1, "Married Couples by Labor Force Status of Spouses: 1986 to Present," <https://www.census.gov/data/tables/time-series/demo/families/families.html>, accessed April 2019.

# Table 627. Employed Civilians and Weekly Hours: 1990 to 2018

[In thousands (118,793 represents 118,793,000), except as indicated. Annual averages of monthly figures. Civilian noninstitutionalized population 16 years old and over. Based on Current Population Survey; see text, Section 1 and Appendix III]

| Item | 1990 | 2000 | 2010 | 2014 | 2015 | 2016 | 2017 | 2018 |
|---|---|---|---|---|---|---|---|---|
| **Total employed** | **118,793** | **136,891** | **139,064** | **146,305** | **148,834** | **151,436** | **153,337** | **155,761** |
| Age: | | | | | | | | |
| 16 to 19 years old | 6,581 | 7,189 | 4,378 | 4,548 | 4,734 | 4,965 | 5,074 | 5,126 |
| 20 to 24 years old | 13,401 | 13,229 | 12,699 | 13,894 | 14,022 | 14,027 | 14,132 | 14,051 |
| 25 to 34 years old | 33,935 | 31,549 | 30,229 | 31,975 | 32,742 | 33,722 | 34,439 | 35,324 |
| 35 to 44 years old | 30,817 | 36,433 | 30,663 | 30,966 | 31,252 | 31,562 | 31,892 | 32,616 |
| 45 to 54 years old | 19,525 | 30,310 | 33,191 | 32,556 | 32,643 | 32,720 | 32,503 | 32,373 |
| 55 to 64 years old | 11,189 | 14,002 | 21,636 | 24,395 | 24,975 | 25,524 | 26,064 | 26,565 |
| 65 years old and over | 3,346 | 4,179 | 6,268 | 7,971 | 8,465 | 8,916 | 9,234 | 9,705 |
| Sex: | | | | | | | | |
| Male | 65,104 | 73,305 | 73,359 | 77,692 | 79,131 | 80,568 | 81,402 | 82,698 |
| Female | 53,689 | 63,586 | 65,705 | 68,613 | 69,703 | 70,868 | 71,936 | 73,063 |
| Marital status: | | | | | | | | |
| Married, spouse present | 70,543 | 78,287 | 77,874 | 79,097 | 79,935 | 80,621 | 81,487 | 81,920 |
| Single (never married) | 30,741 | 36,967 | 38,800 | 43,757 | 45,148 | 46,823 | 47,995 | 49,566 |
| Widowed, divorced, separated | 17,510 | 21,636 | 22,390 | 23,452 | 23,751 | 23,993 | 23,856 | 24,276 |
| Class of worker: | | | | | | | | |
| Nonagricultural industries | 115,570 | 134,427 | 136,858 | 144,068 | 146,411 | 148,976 | 150,883 | 153,336 |
| Wage and salary worker [1] | 106,598 | 125,114 | 127,914 | 135,402 | 137,678 | 140,161 | 142,096 | 144,326 |
| Self-employed | 8,719 | 9,205 | 8,860 | 8,602 | 8,665 | 8,751 | 8,736 | 8,941 |
| Unpaid family workers | 253 | 108 | 84 | 64 | 68 | 65 | 52 | 69 |
| Agriculture and related industries | 3,223 | 2,464 | 2,206 | 2,237 | 2,422 | 2,460 | 2,454 | 2,425 |
| Wage and salary worker [1] | 1,740 | 1,421 | 1,353 | 1,459 | 1,547 | 1,583 | 1,640 | 1,632 |
| Self-employed | 1,378 | 1,010 | 821 | 756 | 844 | 853 | 790 | 766 |
| Unpaid family workers | 105 | 33 | 33 | 22 | 32 | 23 | 24 | 27 |
| Weekly hours: | | | | | | | | |
| Nonagricultural industries: | | | | | | | | |
| Wage and salary workers [1] | 39.2 | 39.6 | 38.3 | 38.7 | 38.7 | 38.8 | 38.6 | 38.9 |
| Self-employed | 40.8 | 39.7 | 35.6 | 35.9 | 36.1 | 36.1 | 36.0 | 36.4 |
| Unpaid family workers | 34.0 | 32.5 | 33.3 | 33.3 | 28.9 | 30.6 | 31.0 | 32.4 |

[1] Includes the incorporated self-employed.

Source: U.S. Bureau of Labor Statistics, "Labor Force Statistics from the Current Population Survey," <http://www.bls.gov/cps>, accessed May 2019.

## Table 628. Persons at Work by Hours Worked: 2018

[In thousands (150,394 represents 150,394,000), except as indicated. Annual averages of monthly figures. Persons "at work" are a subgroup of employed persons. This subgroup excludes those absent from their jobs during reference period for reasons such as vacation, illness, or industrial dispute. Civilian noninstitutionalized population 16 years old and over. Based on Current Population Survey; see text, Section 1, and Appendix III]

| Hours of work | Persons at work (1,000) | | | Percent distribution | | |
|---|---|---|---|---|---|---|
| | Total | Agriculture and related industries | Non-agricultural industries | Total | Agriculture and related industries | Non-agricultural industries |
| **Total** | **150,394** | **2,328** | **148,066** | **100.0** | **100.0** | **100.0** |
| 1 to 34 hours | 34,025 | 589 | 33,436 | 22.6 | 25.3 | 22.6 |
| 1 to 4 hours | 1,485 | 44 | 1,441 | 1.0 | 1.9 | 1.0 |
| 5 to 14 hours | 5,212 | 140 | 5,072 | 3.5 | 6.0 | 3.4 |
| 15 to 29 hours | 17,039 | 274 | 16,765 | 11.3 | 11.8 | 11.3 |
| 30 to 34 hours | 10,290 | 132 | 10,158 | 6.8 | 5.7 | 6.9 |
| 35 hours and over | 116,369 | 1,739 | 114,630 | 77.4 | 74.7 | 77.4 |
| 35 to 39 hours | 9,359 | 99 | 9,260 | 6.2 | 4.2 | 6.3 |
| 40 hours | 69,340 | 703 | 68,637 | 46.1 | 30.2 | 46.4 |
| 41 hours and over | 37,670 | 937 | 36,733 | 25.0 | 40.3 | 24.8 |
| 41 to 48 hours | 13,060 | 192 | 12,867 | 8.7 | 8.3 | 8.7 |
| 49 to 59 hours | 14,734 | 292 | 14,442 | 9.8 | 12.5 | 9.8 |
| 60 hours and over | 9,877 | 453 | 9,424 | 6.6 | 19.5 | 6.4 |
| Average weekly hours of: | | | | | | |
| Total persons at work | 38.9 | 42.1 | 38.9 | (X) | (X) | (X) |
| Persons usually working full-time [1] | 42.5 | 47.6 | 42.5 | (X) | (X) | (X) |

X Not applicable. [1] Full-time workers are those who usually worked 35 hours or more (at all jobs).

Source: U.S. Bureau of Labor Statistics, CPS Tables, "Persons at Work in Agriculture and Nonagricultural Industries by Hours of Work," <http://www.bls.gov/cps/tables.htm>, accessed February 2019.

## Table 629. Persons With a Job, But Not at Work by Reason: 1990 to 2018

[In thousands (6,160 represents 6,160,000), except percent. For civilian noninstitutionalized population 16 years old and over. Annual averages of monthly figures. Based on Current Population Survey; see text, Section 1 and Appendix III]

| Reason for not working | 1990 | 2000 | 2010 | 2011 | 2012 | 2013 | 2014 | 2015 | 2016 | 2017 | 2018 |
|---|---|---|---|---|---|---|---|---|---|---|---|
| **Total not at work** | **6,160** | **5,681** | **5,060** | **4,990** | **5,132** | **5,003** | **5,029** | **5,066** | **5,284** | **5,607** | **5,367** |
| Percent of employed | 5.2 | 4.2 | 3.6 | 3.6 | 3.6 | 3.5 | 3.4 | 3.4 | 3.5 | 3.7 | 3.4 |
| Reason for not working: | | | | | | | | | | | |
| Vacation | 3,529 | 3,109 | 2,487 | 2,500 | 2,633 | 2,501 | 2,512 | 2,563 | 2,671 | 2,893 | 2,724 |
| Illness | 1,341 | 1,156 | 942 | 921 | 906 | 940 | 953 | 907 | 1,001 | 951 | 981 |
| Child care problems | (NA) | (NA) | (NA) | 23 | 20 | 22 | 28 | 32 | 29 | 30 | 33 |
| Other family/personal obligations | (NA) | (NA) | (NA) | 229 | 253 | 245 | 258 | 259 | 284 | 266 | 269 |
| Labor/industrial dispute | 24 | 14 | 8 | 9 | 6 | 6 | 3 | 5 | 5 | 5 | 6 |
| Bad weather | 90 | 89 | 172 | 169 | 107 | 112 | 138 | 119 | 130 | 241 | 179 |
| Maternity or paternity leave | (NA) | (NA) | (NA) | 254 | 286 | 279 | 288 | 322 | 303 | 315 | 331 |
| School/training | (NA) | (NA) | (NA) | 114 | 119 | 113 | 120 | 134 | 125 | 135 | 131 |
| Civic/military duty | (NA) | (NA) | (NA) | 6 | 11 | 9 | 7 | 8 | 7 | 9 | 6 |
| All other | 1,177 | 1,313 | 1,451 | 766 | 792 | 775 | 721 | 718 | 729 | 762 | 707 |

NA Not available.

Source: U.S. Bureau of Labor Statistics, Current Population Survey, unpublished data. See also <http://www.bls.gov/cps/>.

## Table 630. Class of Worker by Sex and Selected Characteristics: 2016

[In percent, except as indicated (9,604 represents 9,604,000). Civilian noninstitutionalized population 16 years old and over. Annual averages of monthly figures. Based on Current Population Survey; see text, Section 1 and Appendix III]

| Characteristic | Unincorporated self-employed | | | Incorporated self-employed | | | Wage and salary workers [1] | | |
|---|---|---|---|---|---|---|---|---|---|
| | Total | Male | Female | Total | Male | Female | Total | Male | Female |
| **Total (1,000)** | **9,604** | **5,980** | **3,624** | **5,643** | **3,963** | **1,680** | **136,111** | **70,600** | **65,511** |
| PERCENT DISTRIBUTION | 100.0 | 100.0 | 100.0 | 100.0 | 100.0 | 100.0 | 100.0 | 100.0 | 100.0 |
| Age: | | | | | | | | | |
| 16 to 19 years old | 0.8 | 0.8 | 0.9 | 0.2 | 0.1 | 0.3 | 3.6 | 3.4 | 3.7 |
| 20 to 24 years old | 2.8 | 2.9 | 2.5 | 1.0 | 1.1 | 1.0 | 10.1 | 9.9 | 10.2 |
| 25 to 34 years old | 14.2 | 14.1 | 14.4 | 10.6 | 10.3 | 11.1 | 23.3 | 24.0 | 22.6 |
| 35 to 44 years old | 19.8 | 19.5 | 20.4 | 20.1 | 19.6 | 21.5 | 21.0 | 21.4 | 20.5 |
| 45 to 54 years old | 23.6 | 23.1 | 24.3 | 29.0 | 28.5 | 30.1 | 21.2 | 20.9 | 21.4 |
| 55 to 64 years old | 23.6 | 23.7 | 23.5 | 26.0 | 26.0 | 25.9 | 16.0 | 15.5 | 16.5 |
| 65 years old and over | 15.2 | 16.0 | 14.0 | 13.2 | 14.5 | 10.2 | 4.9 | 4.8 | 5.0 |
| Race/ethnicity: | | | | | | | | | |
| White [2] | 85.4 | 85.4 | 85.3 | 85.1 | 86.4 | 82.0 | 78.1 | 79.4 | 76.6 |
| Black [2] | 6.8 | 6.8 | 6.7 | 5.5 | 5.3 | 6.1 | 12.5 | 11.1 | 14.0 |
| Asian [2] | 5.1 | 5.0 | 5.4 | 7.3 | 6.4 | 9.4 | 6.1 | 6.2 | 6.0 |
| Hispanic [3] | 16.3 | 17.7 | 14.0 | 9.5 | 9.6 | 9.3 | 17.0 | 18.6 | 15.3 |
| Country of birth: | | | | | | | | | |
| U.S. born | 80.1 | 78.7 | 82.3 | 82.1 | 82.4 | 81.4 | 83.2 | 81.6 | 85.0 |
| Foreign-born | 19.9 | 21.3 | 17.7 | 17.9 | 17.6 | 18.6 | 16.8 | 18.4 | 15.0 |

[1] Excludes the incorporated self-employed. [2] For persons in this race group only. [3] Persons of Hispanic origin may be of any race.

Source: U.S. Bureau of Labor Statistics, Current Population Survey, unpublished data. See also <http://www.bls.gov/cps>.

## Table 631. Self-Employed Workers by Industry and Occupation: 2000 to 2018

[In thousands (10,214 represents 10,214,000). Civilian noninstitutionalized population 16 years old and over. Annual averages of monthly figures. Data represent the unincorporated self-employed. Excludes the incorporated self-employed who are considered wage and salary workers. Based on the occupational and industrial classification derived from those used in the 2000 census. See text, this section. Based on the Current Population Survey (CPS); see text, Section 1 and Appendix III]

| Item | 2000 | 2010 | 2013 | 2014 | 2015 | 2016 | 2017 | 2018 |
|---|---|---|---|---|---|---|---|---|
| Total self-employed............... | **10,214** | **9,681** | **9,408** | **9,358** | **9,509** | **9,604** | **9,526** | **9,707** |
| INDUSTRY | | | | | | | | |
| Agriculture and related industries............ | 1,010 | 821 | 789 | 756 | 844 | 853 | 790 | 766 |
| Mining........ | 12 | 20 | 16 | 20 | 21 | 17 | 11 | 10 |
| Construction........ | 1,728 | 1,699 | 1,530 | 1,595 | 1,603 | 1,628 | 1,567 | 1,650 |
| Manufacturing........ | 334 | 304 | 275 | 278 | 288 | 267 | 280 | 258 |
| Wholesale and retail trade........ | 1,221 | 962 | 825 | 851 | 870 | 888 | 842 | 812 |
| Transportation and utilities........ | 348 | 360 | 340 | 368 | 397 | 417 | 453 | 443 |
| Information........ | 139 | 139 | 126 | 132 | 161 | 120 | 143 | 144 |
| Financial activities........ | 735 | 641 | 651 | 628 | 625 | 687 | 666 | 724 |
| Professional and business services........ | 1,927 | 1,999 | 2,057 | 1,984 | 1,944 | 2,073 | 2,102 | 2,054 |
| Education and health services........ | 1,107 | 1,100 | 1,072 | 1,074 | 1,069 | 1,037 | 985 | 1,072 |
| Leisure and hospitality........ | 660 | 610 | 671 | 658 | 698 | 668 | 682 | 701 |
| Other services........ | 993 | 1,028 | 1,055 | 1,014 | 988 | 949 | 1,005 | 1,075 |
| OCCUPATION | | | | | | | | |
| Management, professional, and related occupations........ | 4,169 | 3,928 | 3,963 | 3,878 | 3,958 | 3,953 | 3,985 | 4,109 |
| Service occupations........ | 1,775 | 1,885 | 2,030 | 1,969 | 1,948 | 1,943 | 1,984 | 2,023 |
| Sales and office occupations........ | 1,982 | 1,586 | 1,449 | 1,438 | 1,470 | 1,463 | 1,448 | 1,432 |
| Natural resources, construction, and maintenance occupations........ | 1,591 | 1,635 | 1,365 | 1,462 | 1,482 | 1,548 | 1,418 | 1,463 |
| Production, transportation, and material moving occupations........ | 698 | 647 | 602 | 610 | 650 | 697 | 691 | 679 |

Source: U.S. Bureau of Labor Statistics, "Labor Force Statistics from the Current Population Survey," <http://www.bls.gov/cps/tables.htm>, accessed September 2019; and unpublished CPS data.

## Table 632. Type of Work Flexibility Provided to Employees: 2016

[In percent. The National Study of Employers does not ask employers to report on whether they have "written policies," but rather whether their organization "allows employees to" or "provides the following benefits or programs." The wording is used for two reasons. First, employers may have written policies, but not allow employees to use them. Second, smaller employers are less likely to have written policies than larger ones. For methodology, see source]

| Type of work flexibility provided to employees | Organizations allowing flexibility to all or most employees | | |
|---|---|---|---|
| | Total employers | Employers with 50 to 99 employees | Employers with 1,000 or more employees |
| FLEX TIME AND PLACE | | | |
| Periodically change starting and quitting times within some range of hours........ | 32 | 36 | 17 |
| Change starting and quitting times on a daily basis........ | 11 | 12 | 4 |
| Compress workweek by working longer hours on fewer days for at least part of the year...... | 9 | 10 | 4 |
| Work some regular paid hours at home occasionally........ | 8 | 9 | 1 |
| Work some regular paid hours at home on regular basis........ | 2 | 2 | 3 |
| CHOICES IN MANAGING TIME | | | |
| Have control over when to take breaks........ | 59 | 63 | 47 |
| Have choices about and control over which shifts to work........ | 10 | 10 | 14 |
| Have control over paid and unpaid overtime hours........ | 21 | 22 | 11 |
| REDUCED TIME | | | |
| Move from full time to part time and back again while remaining in same position or level........ | 8 | 8 | 10 |
| Work part year (work reduced time on annual basis)........ | 2 | 2 | 3 |
| CAREGIVING LEAVE | | | |
| Return to work gradually after childbirth or adoption........ | 52 | 57 | 42 |
| TIME OFF | | | |
| Family or personal time off without loss of pay........ | 47 | 51 | 33 |
| Do volunteer work during regular work hours........ | 23 | 26 | 21 |
| FLEX CAREERS | | | |
| Phase into retirement by working reduced hours over time prior to full retirement........ | 21 | 25 | 17 |
| Take sabbaticals (paid or unpaid for six months or more)........ | 11 | 12 | 10 |
| Take extended career breaks for caregiving or other personal or family reasons........ | 35 | 42 | 27 |
| Receive special consideration when returning to the organization after an extended career break........ | 13 | 18 | 10 |

Source: Society for Human Resource Management, Families and Work Institute, *2016 National Study of Employers* ©. See also <http://www.whenworkworks.org/be-effective/guides-tools/2016-national-study-of-employers>.

## Table 633. Multiple Jobholders: 2018

[7,769 represents 7,769,000. Annual average of monthly figures. Civilian noninstitutionalized population 16 years old and over. Multiple jobholders are employed persons who either had jobs as wage or salary workers with two employers or more; were self-employed and also held a wage and salary job; or were unpaid family workers and also held a wage and salary job. Based on the Current Population Survey; see text, Section 1 and Appendix III]

| Characteristic | Total Number (1,000) | Total Percent of employed | Male Number (1,000) | Male Percent of employed | Female Number (1,000) | Female Percent of employed |
|---|---|---|---|---|---|---|
| **Total [1], [2]** | **7,769** | **5.0** | **3,835** | **4.6** | **3,934** | **5.4** |
| Age: | | | | | | |
| 16 to 19 years old | 183 | 3.6 | 61 | 2.4 | 122 | 4.6 |
| 20 to 24 years old | 780 | 5.6 | 328 | 4.6 | 452 | 6.6 |
| 25 to 54 years old | 5,197 | 5.2 | 2,597 | 4.8 | 2,600 | 5.6 |
| 55 to 64 years old | 1,220 | 4.6 | 629 | 4.5 | 591 | 4.7 |
| 65 years old and over | 390 | 4.0 | 221 | 4.1 | 169 | 3.9 |
| Race and ethnicity: | | | | | | |
| White | 6,166 | 5.1 | 3,057 | 4.7 | 3,110 | 5.6 |
| Black | 993 | 5.2 | 469 | 5.2 | 523 | 5.2 |
| Asian | 307 | 3.1 | 162 | 3.1 | 145 | 3.1 |
| Hispanic [3] | 951 | 3.5 | 538 | 3.5 | 413 | 3.6 |
| Marital status: | | | | | | |
| Married, spouse present | 3,842 | 4.7 | 2,191 | 4.8 | 1,651 | 4.6 |
| Widowed, divorced, or separated | 1,348 | 5.6 | 484 | 4.7 | 864 | 6.2 |
| Single, never married | 2,579 | 5.2 | 1,160 | 4.4 | 1,419 | 6.1 |
| Full- or part-time status: [4] | | | | | | |
| Primary job full-time, secondary job part-time | 4,290 | (X) | 2,327 | (X) | 1,963 | (X) |
| Both jobs part-time | 2,031 | (X) | 717 | (X) | 1,314 | (X) |
| Both jobs full-time | 316 | (X) | 196 | (X) | 120 | (X) |
| Hours vary on primary or secondary job | 1,080 | (X) | 570 | (X) | 510 | (X) |

X Not applicable. [1] Includes a small number of persons who work part-time on their primary job and full-time on their secondary job(s), not shown separately. [2] Includes other races, not shown separately. [3] Persons of Hispanic origin may be of any race. [4] Full-time work is 35 or more hours per week; part-time work is less than 35 hours per week.

Source: U.S. Bureau of Labor Statistics, CPS Tables, "Multiple Jobholders by Selected Characteristics," <http://www.bls.gov/cps/tables.htm>, accessed February 2019.

## Table 634. Average Number of Jobs Held From Ages 18 to 52 during 1978 to 2016

[For persons ages 51 to 60 in 2016-17 (and who were ages 14 to 22 when first interviewed in 1979). A job is an uninterrupted period of work with a particular employer. Educational attainment as of 2016-2017 survey. Based on the National Longitudinal Survey of Youth 1979; see source for details]

| Sex, race, ethnicity and educational attainment | Average jobs held [1] | Average number of jobs held by age 18 to 24 years | 25 to 34 years | 35 to 44 years | 45 to 52 years |
|---|---|---|---|---|---|
| **Total [2]** | **12.3** | **5.7** | **4.5** | **2.9** | **1.9** |
| Less than a high school diploma | 11.9 | 5.1 | 4.6 | 2.8 | 1.5 |
| High school graduate, no college | 12.0 | 5.3 | 4.5 | 3.0 | 1.9 |
| Some college or associate's degree | 12.8 | 5.7 | 4.6 | 3.0 | 2.1 |
| Bachelor's degree or more | 12.4 | 6.3 | 4.4 | 2.8 | 2.1 |
| Male | 12.5 | 5.9 | 4.7 | 2.9 | 1.9 |
| Less than a high school diploma | 13.3 | 6.0 | 5.5 | 3.1 | 1.6 |
| High school graduate, no college | 12.6 | 5.8 | 4.8 | 2.9 | 1.9 |
| Some college or associate's degree | 13.0 | 6.0 | 4.7 | 2.9 | 2.0 |
| Bachelor's degree or more | 11.6 | 5.9 | 4.3 | 2.8 | 2.0 |
| Female | 12.1 | 5.4 | 4.3 | 2.9 | 2.0 |
| Less than a high school diploma | 9.9 | 3.8 | 3.5 | 2.5 | 1.3 |
| High school graduate, no college | 11.4 | 4.8 | 4.0 | 3.0 | 1.8 |
| Some college or associate's degree | 12.6 | 5.6 | 4.5 | 3.0 | 2.1 |
| Bachelor's degree or more | 13.1 | 6.6 | 4.5 | 2.8 | 2.1 |
| White, non-Hispanic | 12.4 | 5.9 | 4.5 | 2.9 | 1.9 |
| Less than a high school diploma | 12.6 | 5.6 | 5.0 | 3.0 | 1.5 |
| High school graduate, no college | 12.2 | 5.5 | 4.5 | 2.9 | 1.8 |
| Some college or associate's degree | 12.8 | 5.9 | 4.5 | 2.9 | 2.1 |
| Bachelor's degree or more | 12.3 | 6.4 | 4.4 | 2.8 | 2.0 |
| Black, non-Hispanic | 11.8 | 4.8 | 4.6 | 3.1 | 1.9 |
| Less than a high school diploma | 10.3 | 3.9 | 4.0 | 2.5 | 1.3 |
| High school graduate, no college | 11.4 | 4.5 | 4.6 | 3.1 | 1.9 |
| Some college or associate's degree | 12.5 | 5.0 | 4.8 | 3.4 | 2.1 |
| Bachelor's degree or more | 12.8 | 5.6 | 4.7 | 3.2 | 2.4 |
| Hispanic [3] | 12.1 | 5.1 | 4.3 | 3.0 | 1.9 |
| Less than a high school diploma | 11.4 | 4.5 | 4.1 | 2.8 | 1.6 |
| High school graduate, no college | 11.7 | 5.1 | 4.2 | 3.0 | 1.9 |
| Some college or associate's degree | 13.3 | 5.4 | 4.5 | 3.2 | 2.1 |
| Bachelor's degree or more | 11.7 | 5.3 | 4.5 | 2.8 | 1.9 |

[1] Jobs held in more than one age category were counted in each category, but only once in the total. [2] Includes other races, not shown separately. [3] Persons of Hispanic origin may be of any race.

Source: U.S. Bureau of Labor Statistics, *Number of Jobs Held, Labor Market Experience, and Earnings Growth: Results from a National Longitudinal Survey,* USDL 19-1520, August 2019. See also <http://www.bls.gov/news.release/nlsoy.nr0.htm>.

## Table 635. Distribution of Workers by Tenure With Current Employer by Selected Characteristics: 2018

[137,442 represents 137,442,000. As of January. From the 2018 Displaced Worker Supplement to the Current Population Survey. For employed wage and salary workers 16 years old and over. Data exclude the incorporated and unincorporated self-employed; see source and Appendix III]

| Characteristic | Number employed (1,000) | Percent distribution by tenure with current employer | | | | | | | | Median years [1] |
|---|---|---|---|---|---|---|---|---|---|---|
| | | 12 months or less | 13-23 months | 2 years | 3-4 years | 5-9 years | 10-14 years | 15-19 years | 20 years or more | |
| **Total [2]** | **137,442** | **22.3** | **6.9** | **5.6** | **17.6** | **18.8** | **11.6** | **6.9** | **10.3** | **4.2** |
| AGE AND SEX | | | | | | | | | | |
| 16 to 19 years old | 4,597 | 74.0 | 11.9 | 7.4 | 6.2 | 0.4 | – | – | – | (NA) |
| 20 years old and over | 132,845 | 20.5 | 6.7 | 5.5 | 18.0 | 19.5 | 12.1 | 7.2 | 10.6 | (NA) |
| 20 to 24 years old | 13,455 | 53.6 | 12.6 | 11.0 | 18.3 | 4.5 | 0.1 | – | – | 1.2 |
| 25 to 34 years old | 32,512 | 27.7 | 9.5 | 7.9 | 26.2 | 21.8 | 6.3 | 0.7 | – | 2.8 |
| 35 to 44 years old | 29,110 | 17.1 | 6.0 | 4.8 | 18.5 | 23.8 | 17.3 | 8.8 | 3.8 | 4.9 |
| 45 to 54 years old | 28,528 | 11.9 | 4.7 | 3.5 | 14.5 | 20.5 | 15.9 | 11.9 | 17.2 | 7.6 |
| 55 to 64 years old | 22,367 | 9.2 | 3.5 | 3.2 | 11.5 | 18.5 | 14.9 | 11.9 | 27.4 | 10.1 |
| 65 years old and over | 6,872 | 8.4 | 4.0 | 2.9 | 11.5 | 18.8 | 15.4 | 10.4 | 28.6 | 10.2 |
| **Male** | **71,178** | **21.8** | **6.6** | **5.5** | **17.5** | **19.1** | **11.8** | **6.9** | **10.9** | **4.3** |
| 16 to 19 years old | 2,217 | 72.9 | 12.2 | 6.5 | 8.0 | 0.4 | – | – | – | (NA) |
| 20 years old and over | 68,960 | 20.2 | 6.4 | 5.5 | 17.8 | 19.7 | 12.1 | 7.1 | 11.2 | (NA) |
| 20 to 24 years old | 6,838 | 52.2 | 12.0 | 11.3 | 19.9 | 4.5 | 0.2 | – | – | 1.3 |
| 25 to 34 years old | 17,374 | 27.2 | 9.1 | 7.6 | 25.0 | 23.6 | 6.9 | 0.6 | – | 2.9 |
| 35 to 44 years old | 15,334 | 16.2 | 6.0 | 4.8 | 18.2 | 23.4 | 17.8 | 9.3 | 4.3 | 5.0 |
| 45 to 54 years old | 14,673 | 12.2 | 4.0 | 3.4 | 14.2 | 19.4 | 16.0 | 12.2 | 18.6 | 8.1 |
| 55 to 64 years old | 11,202 | 9.5 | 3.5 | 3.0 | 11.4 | 18.8 | 13.3 | 10.9 | 29.7 | 10.2 |
| 65 years old and over | 3,539 | 7.9 | 3.7 | 3.3 | 11.5 | 18.2 | 16.6 | 9.7 | 29.1 | 10.2 |
| **Female** | **66,264** | **22.8** | **7.1** | **5.7** | **17.7** | **18.6** | **11.5** | **7.0** | **9.6** | **4.0** |
| 16 to 19 years old | 2,380 | 75.1 | 11.6 | 8.3 | 4.6 | 0.3 | – | – | – | (NA) |
| 20 years old and over | 63,884 | 20.9 | 7.0 | 5.6 | 18.2 | 19.3 | 12.0 | 7.2 | 9.9 | (NA) |
| 20 to 24 years old | 6,617 | 55.0 | 13.1 | 10.8 | 16.6 | 4.5 | – | – | – | 1.2 |
| 25 to 34 years old | 15,138 | 28.4 | 9.9 | 8.2 | 27.6 | 19.7 | 5.5 | 0.7 | – | 2.7 |
| 35 to 44 years old | 13,776 | 18.1 | 5.9 | 4.7 | 18.9 | 24.3 | 16.8 | 8.1 | 3.2 | 4.7 |
| 45 to 54 years old | 13,856 | 11.6 | 5.4 | 3.7 | 14.8 | 21.7 | 15.7 | 11.5 | 15.7 | 7.1 |
| 55 to 64 years old | 11,165 | 8.9 | 3.4 | 3.4 | 11.6 | 18.2 | 16.5 | 12.9 | 25.1 | 10.1 |
| 65 years old and over | 3,333 | 8.9 | 4.4 | 2.4 | 11.6 | 19.3 | 14.2 | 11.1 | 28.1 | 10.1 |
| RACE AND HISPANIC ORIGIN | | | | | | | | | | |
| White [3] | 106,391 | 21.6 | 6.7 | 5.3 | 17.0 | 19.1 | 11.9 | 7.3 | 11.2 | (NA) |
| Male | 56,112 | 20.9 | 6.4 | 5.2 | 17.0 | 19.4 | 12.0 | 7.2 | 11.9 | (NA) |
| Female | 50,280 | 22.3 | 7.0 | 5.4 | 17.0 | 18.7 | 11.8 | 7.4 | 10.4 | (NA) |
| Black [3] | 16,978 | 25.6 | 6.7 | 6.7 | 18.7 | 17.6 | 10.5 | 6.4 | 7.7 | (NA) |
| Male | 7,764 | 26.8 | 6.8 | 7.0 | 17.5 | 17.4 | 10.5 | 6.6 | 7.3 | (NA) |
| Female | 9,214 | 24.6 | 6.6 | 6.5 | 19.8 | 17.8 | 10.5 | 6.3 | 8.0 | (NA) |
| Asian [3] | 8,941 | 20.4 | 7.7 | 6.1 | 20.6 | 20.3 | 12.6 | 5.7 | 6.6 | (NA) |
| Male | 4,725 | 19.8 | 7.3 | 6.1 | 21.5 | 20.2 | 12.6 | 5.6 | 6.7 | (NA) |
| Female | 4,216 | 21.1 | 8.1 | 6.1 | 19.6 | 20.4 | 12.6 | 5.7 | 6.5 | (NA) |
| Hispanic [4] | 23,720 | 25.6 | 5.9 | 7.5 | 19.1 | 19.4 | 10.4 | 5.7 | 6.5 | (NA) |
| Male | 13,206 | 23.7 | 5.4 | 7.9 | 19.9 | 20.1 | 10.9 | 5.2 | 6.9 | (NA) |
| Female | 10,514 | 28.0 | 6.5 | 6.9 | 18.0 | 18.5 | 9.8 | 6.2 | 6.0 | (NA) |

– Represents or rounds to zero. NA Not available. [1] Median definition, see Guide to Tabular Presentation. [2] Includes other races, not shown separately. [3] For persons in this race group only. See footnote 2, Table 613. [4] Persons of Hispanic origin may be of any race.

Source: U.S. Bureau of Labor Statistics, "Employee Tenure in 2018," USDL 18-1500, September 2018, <http://www.bls.gov/news.release/tenure.toc.htm>.

## Table 636. Part-Time Workers by Reason: 2018

[34,025 represents 34,025,000, except hours. For persons working 1 to 34 hours during the reference week of the survey. For civilian noninstitutionalized population 16 years old and over. Annual average of monthly figures. Based on the Current Population Survey; see text, Section 1 and Appendix III]

| Reason | All industries | | | Nonagricultural industries | | |
|---|---|---|---|---|---|---|
| | | Usually work— | | | Usually work— | |
| | Total | Full-time | Part-time | Total | Full-time | Part-time |
| **Total working fewer than 35 hours** | **34,025** | **9,357** | **24,668** | **33,436** | **9,187** | **24,249** |
| Economic reasons | 4,778 | 1,407 | 3,371 | 4,698 | 1,366 | 3,333 |
| Slack work or business conditions | 2,933 | 1,152 | 1,782 | 2,885 | 1,124 | 1,761 |
| Could find only part time work | 1,510 | (S) | 1,510 | 1,500 | (S) | 1,500 |
| Seasonal work | 221 | 142 | 79 | 201 | 129 | 72 |
| Job started or ended during the week | 113 | 113 | (S) | 113 | 113 | (S) |
| Non-economic reasons | 29,247 | 7,950 | 21,297 | 28,737 | 7,822 | 20,916 |
| Child-care problems | 1,106 | 75 | 1,031 | 1,098 | 74 | 1,024 |
| Other family or personal obligations | 5,029 | 651 | 4,379 | 4,947 | 637 | 4,310 |
| Health or medical limitations | 1,072 | (S) | 1,072 | 1,044 | (S) | 1,044 |
| In school or training | 6,186 | 91 | 6,095 | 6,123 | 90 | 6,033 |
| Retired or social security limit on earnings | 2,741 | (S) | 2,741 | 2,617 | (S) | 2,617 |
| Vacation or personal day | 3,595 | 3,595 | (S) | 3,559 | 3,559 | (S) |
| Holiday, legal, or religious | 507 | 507 | (S) | 503 | 503 | (S) |
| Weather-related curtailment | 647 | 647 | (S) | 618 | 618 | (S) |
| Other | 8,364 | 2,383 | 5,981 | 8,228 | 2,340 | 5,888 |
| Average hours per week: | | | | | | |
| Economic reasons | 23.2 | 23.8 | 22.9 | 23.2 | 23.8 | 23.0 |
| Noneconomic reasons | 21.3 | 24.7 | 20.1 | 21.4 | 24.8 | 20.1 |

S No data or data do not meet publication standards.

Source: U.S. Bureau of Labor Statistics, CPS Tables, "Persons at work 1 to 34 hours in all and in nonagricultural industries by reason for working less than 35 hours and usual full- or part-time status," <http://www.bls.gov/cps/tables.htm>, accessed February 2019.

## Table 637. Displaced Workers by Selected Characteristics: 2018

[In percent, except total (2,981 represents 2,981,000). As of January 2018. For persons 20 years old and over with job tenure of 3 years or more who lost or left a job between January 2015 and December 2017 because of plant closings or moves, insufficient work for workers to do, or the abolishment of their positions. Based on Current Population Survey; see source and Appendix III]

| Characteristic | Total (1,000) | Employment status in January 2018 | | | Reason for job loss, 2015-2017 | | |
|---|---|---|---|---|---|---|---|
| | | Employed | Unemployed | Not in the labor force | Plant or company closed down or moved | Insufficient work | Position or shift abolished |
| **Total** [1]............... | **2,981** | **66.4** | **14.4** | **19.3** | **36.7** | **26.3** | **37.0** |
| 20 to 24 years old.................. | 73 | ( [2] ) | ( [2] ) | ( [2] ) | ( [2] ) | ( [2] ) | ( [2] ) |
| 25 to 54 years old.................. | 1,759 | 75.6 | 14.9 | 9.4 | 36.4 | 28.6 | 35.0 |
| 55 to 64 years old.................. | 798 | 60.2 | 14.9 | 24.8 | 35.9 | 20.3 | 43.8 |
| 65 years old and over............... | 351 | 30.7 | 12.2 | 57.2 | 37.1 | 28.9 | 33.9 |
| Males...................... | 1,681 | 67.4 | 14.8 | 17.7 | 33.0 | 31.8 | 35.2 |
| 20 to 24 years old.................. | 33 | ( [2] ) | ( [2] ) | ( [2] ) | ( [2] ) | ( [2] ) | ( [2] ) |
| 25 to 54 years old.................. | 988 | 75.1 | 17.2 | 7.7 | 31.9 | 35.3 | 32.8 |
| 55 to 64 years old.................. | 483 | 61.5 | 12.0 | 26.4 | 37.1 | 22.2 | 40.6 |
| 65 years old and over............... | 176 | 37.0 | 9.4 | 53.5 | 32.1 | 35.9 | 32.0 |
| Females...................... | 1,301 | 65.0 | 13.8 | 21.3 | 41.4 | 19.4 | 39.3 |
| 20 to 24 years old.................. | 40 | ( [2] ) | ( [2] ) | ( [2] ) | ( [2] ) | ( [2] ) | ( [2] ) |
| 25 to 54 years old.................. | 771 | 76.3 | 12.0 | 11.7 | 42.1 | 20.0 | 37.9 |
| 55 to 64 years old.................. | 315 | 58.2 | 19.3 | 22.4 | 34.1 | 17.3 | 48.6 |
| 65 years old and over............... | 175 | 24.3 | 14.9 | 60.8 | 42.2 | 21.9 | 35.9 |
| White only.................... | 2,435 | 65.3 | 14.3 | 20.4 | 36.4 | 26.6 | 37.0 |
| Male......................... | 1,390 | 66.0 | 14.7 | 19.3 | 33.3 | 32.1 | 34.7 |
| Female....................... | 1,045 | 64.4 | 13.6 | 22.0 | 40.6 | 19.4 | 40.0 |
| Black only.................... | 285 | 65.9 | 21.2 | 12.9 | 33.2 | 30.3 | 36.4 |
| Male......................... | 139 | 68.3 | 21.8 | 10.0 | 26.2 | 33.1 | 40.6 |
| Female....................... | 146 | 63.7 | 20.7 | 15.6 | 39.9 | 27.6 | 32.5 |
| Asian only.................... | 157 | 69.9 | 7.5 | 22.5 | 46.5 | 14.2 | 39.3 |
| Male......................... | 83 | 78.2 | 5.8 | 16.0 | 39.9 | 21.8 | 38.3 |
| Female....................... | 74 | ( [2] ) | ( [2] ) | ( [2] ) | ( [2] ) | ( [2] ) | ( [2] ) |
| Hispanic [3].................... | 404 | 68.6 | 21.8 | 9.6 | 52.0 | 28.0 | 20.0 |
| Male......................... | 238 | 72.1 | 18.1 | 9.9 | 53.5 | 33.4 | 13.1 |
| Female....................... | 167 | 63.7 | 27.1 | 9.2 | 49.8 | 20.3 | 29.9 |

[1] Includes other races, not shown separately. [2] Data not shown where base is less than 75,000. [3] Persons of Hispanic or Latino origin may be of any race.

Source: U.S. Bureau of Labor Statistics, *Worker Displacement: 2015-2017*, USDL 18-1370, August 2018. See also <http://www.bls.gov/news.release/disp.toc.htm>.

## Table 638. Persons Not in the Labor Force By Age, Sex, and Reason: 2018

[In thousands (95,716 represents 95,716,000). For civilian noninstitutional population 16 years old and over. Persons who are neither employed nor unemployed are not in the labor force. This includes retired persons, students, those taking care of children or other family members, and others who are neither working nor seeking work. Annual average of monthly figures. Based on the Current Population Survey; see text, Section 1, and Appendix III]

| Status and reason | Total | Age | | | Sex | |
|---|---|---|---|---|---|---|
| | | 16 to 24 years old | 25 to 54 years old | 55 years old and over | Male | Female |
| **Total not in the labor force**........................... | **95,716** | **17,020** | **22,685** | **56,010** | **38,582** | **57,134** |
| Do not want a job now [1]............................... | 90,467 | 15,430 | 20,513 | 54,524 | 36,133 | 54,334 |
| Want a job now [1]...................................... | 5,249 | 1,590 | 2,172 | 1,487 | 2,448 | 2,800 |
| In the previous year: | | | | | | |
| Did not search for a job......................... | 3,161 | 925 | 1,195 | 1,040 | 1,399 | 1,762 |
| Did search for a job, but not in past 4 weeks [2]...... | 2,088 | 665 | 977 | 447 | 1,049 | 1,039 |
| Not available for work now....................... | 571 | 232 | 267 | 72 | 232 | 338 |
| Available for work now, but not looking for work [3]............. | 1,517 | 433 | 709 | 375 | 817 | 700 |
| Reason for not currently looking for work: | | | | | | |
| Discouraged over job prospects [4]............ | 423 | 93 | 211 | 120 | 266 | 158 |
| Family responsibilities....................... | 173 | 25 | 114 | 35 | 50 | 123 |
| In school or training......................... | 184 | 144 | 36 | 4 | 99 | 85 |
| Ill health or disability........................ | 152 | 16 | 64 | 72 | 85 | 67 |
| Other [5]................................... | 584 | 156 | 285 | 143 | 317 | 267 |

[1] Includes some persons who are not asked if they want a job. [2] Persons who had a job in previous 12 months must have searched since the end of that job. [3] Persons who want a job, have searched for work during the previous 12 months, and were available to take a job during the reference week, but had not looked for work in the past 4 weeks; persons are referred to as "marginally attached to the labor force." [4] Includes such things as believes no work available, could not find work, lacks necessary schooling or training, employer thinks too young or old, and other types of discrimination. [5] Includes such things as child care and transportation problems.

Source: U.S. Bureau of Labor Statistics, CPS Tables, "Persons not in the labor force by desire and availability for work, age, and sex," <http://www.bls.gov/cps/tables.htm>, accessed February 2019.

# Table 639. Employment Status of Parents by Age of Youngest Child and Family Type: 2015 to 2018

[In thousands (34,363 represents 34,363,000), except percent distribution. Annual average of monthly figures. For families with own children (sons, daughters, step-children, and adopted children). Based on the Current Population Survey, see text, Section 1, and Appendix III]

| Characteristic | Number | | | | Percent distribution | | | |
|---|---|---|---|---|---|---|---|---|
| | 2015 | 2016 | 2017 | 2018 | 2015 | 2016 | 2017 | 2018 |
| **WITH OWN CHILDREN UNDER 18 YEARS OLD** | | | | | | | | |
| Total families.................... | **34,363** | **34,206** | **33,615** | **33,632** | **100.0** | **100.0** | **100.0** | **100.0** |
| Parent(s) employed..................... | 30,672 | 30,671 | 30,318 | 30,522 | 89.3 | 89.7 | 90.2 | 90.8 |
| No parent employed.................... | 3,692 | 3,534 | 3,297 | 3,109 | 10.7 | 10.3 | 9.8 | 9.2 |
| Married-couple families................ | 23,401 | 23,125 | 22,855 | 22,883 | 100.0 | 100.0 | 100.0 | 100.0 |
| Parent(s) employed................. | 22,631 | 22,379 | 22,158 | 22,296 | 96.7 | 96.8 | 96.9 | 97.4 |
| Mother employed................. | 15,420 | 15,377 | 15,389 | 15,545 | 65.9 | 66.5 | 67.3 | 67.9 |
| Both parents employed......... | 14,174 | 14,123 | 14,151 | 14,407 | 60.6 | 61.1 | 61.9 | 63.0 |
| Mother employed, not father........... | 1,246 | 1,254 | 1,238 | 1,138 | 5.3 | 5.4 | 5.4 | 5.0 |
| Father employed, not mother........... | 7,211 | 7,001 | 6,769 | 6,751 | 30.8 | 30.3 | 29.6 | 29.5 |
| Neither parent employed............. | 771 | 746 | 697 | 586 | 3.3 | 3.2 | 3.1 | 2.6 |
| Families maintained by women [1]........... | 8,505 | 8,538 | 8,259 | 8,125 | 100.0 | 100.0 | 100.0 | 100.0 |
| Mother employed................. | 6,024 | 6,191 | 6,043 | 6,018 | 70.8 | 72.5 | 73.2 | 74.1 |
| Mother not employed.............. | 2,481 | 2,347 | 2,216 | 2,108 | 29.2 | 27.5 | 26.8 | 25.9 |
| Families maintained by men [1]............ | 2,457 | 2,544 | 2,500 | 2,624 | 100.0 | 100.0 | 100.0 | 100.0 |
| Father employed.................. | 2,017 | 2,102 | 2,117 | 2,209 | 82.1 | 82.6 | 84.7 | 84.2 |
| Father not employed............... | 440 | 442 | 383 | 416 | 17.9 | 17.4 | 15.3 | 15.8 |
| **WITH OWN CHILDREN 6 to 17 YEARS OLD** | | | | | | | | |
| Total families.................... | **19,774** | **19,774** | **19,621** | **19,377** | **100.0** | **100.0** | **100.0** | **100.0** |
| Parent(s) employed..................... | 17,762 | 17,814 | 17,742 | 17,627 | 89.8 | 90.1 | 90.4 | 91.0 |
| No parent employed.................... | 2,012 | 1,960 | 1,879 | 1,751 | 10.2 | 9.9 | 9.6 | 9.0 |
| Married-couple families................ | 13,306 | 13,105 | 13,032 | 12,859 | 100.0 | 100.0 | 100.0 | 100.0 |
| Parent(s) employed................. | 12,842 | 12,649 | 12,595 | 12,488 | 96.5 | 96.5 | 96.6 | 97.1 |
| Mother employed................. | 9,363 | 9,284 | 9,362 | 9,384 | 70.4 | 70.8 | 71.8 | 73.0 |
| Both parents employed......... | 8,565 | 8,483 | 8,553 | 8,643 | 64.4 | 64.7 | 65.6 | 67.2 |
| Mother employed, not father........... | 798 | 801 | 810 | 741 | 6.0 | 6.1 | 6.2 | 5.8 |
| Father employed, not mother........... | 3,479 | 3,365 | 3,233 | 3,104 | 26.1 | 25.7 | 24.8 | 24.1 |
| Neither parent employed............. | 464 | 456 | 437 | 370 | 3.5 | 3.5 | 3.4 | 2.9 |
| Families maintained by women [1]........... | 5,080 | 5,189 | 5,093 | 5,028 | 100.0 | 100.0 | 100.0 | 100.0 |
| Mother employed................. | 3,790 | 3,955 | 3,890 | 3,887 | 74.6 | 76.2 | 76.4 | 77.3 |
| Mother not employed.............. | 1,290 | 1,234 | 1,204 | 1,141 | 25.4 | 23.8 | 23.6 | 22.7 |
| Families maintained by men [1]............ | 1,388 | 1,481 | 1,496 | 1,491 | 100.0 | 100.0 | 100.0 | 100.0 |
| Father employed.................. | 1,130 | 1,211 | 1,257 | 1,251 | 81.4 | 81.8 | 84.1 | 83.9 |
| Father not employed............... | 258 | 270 | 239 | 240 | 18.6 | 18.2 | 15.9 | 16.1 |
| **WITH OWN CHILDREN UNDER 6 YEARS OLD** | | | | | | | | |
| Total families.................... | **14,589** | **14,432** | **13,994** | **14,254** | **100.0** | **100.0** | **100.0** | **100.0** |
| Parent(s) employed..................... | 12,910 | 12,857 | 12,576 | 12,896 | 88.5 | 89.1 | 89.9 | 90.5 |
| No parent employed.................... | 1,680 | 1,575 | 1,418 | 1,359 | 11.5 | 10.9 | 10.1 | 9.5 |
| Married-couple families................ | 10,096 | 10,020 | 9,823 | 10,024 | 100.0 | 100.0 | 100.0 | 100.0 |
| Parent(s) employed................. | 9,789 | 9,730 | 9,562 | 9,808 | 97.0 | 97.1 | 97.3 | 97.8 |
| Mother employed................. | 6,057 | 6,093 | 6,027 | 6,161 | 60.0 | 60.8 | 61.4 | 61.5 |
| Both parents employed......... | 5,609 | 5,640 | 5,598 | 5,764 | 55.6 | 56.3 | 57.0 | 57.5 |
| Mother employed, not father........... | 448 | 453 | 428 | 396 | 4.4 | 4.5 | 4.4 | 4.0 |
| Father employed, not mother........... | 3,732 | 3,637 | 3,536 | 3,647 | 37.0 | 36.3 | 36.0 | 36.4 |
| Neither parent employed............. | 307 | 290 | 261 | 216 | 3.0 | 2.9 | 2.7 | 2.2 |
| Families maintained by women [1]........... | 3,425 | 3,349 | 3,166 | 3,097 | 100.0 | 100.0 | 100.0 | 100.0 |
| Mother employed................. | 2,234 | 2,236 | 2,154 | 2,130 | 65.2 | 66.8 | 68.0 | 68.8 |
| Mother not employed.............. | 1,191 | 1,113 | 1,013 | 967 | 34.8 | 33.2 | 32.0 | 31.2 |
| Families maintained by men [1]............ | 1,069 | 1,063 | 1,005 | 1,133 | 100.0 | 100.0 | 100.0 | 100.0 |
| Father employed.................. | 887 | 891 | 860 | 957 | 83.0 | 83.8 | 85.6 | 84.5 |
| Father not employed............... | 182 | 172 | 145 | 176 | 17.0 | 16.2 | 14.4 | 15.5 |

[1] No spouse present.

Source: U.S. Bureau of Labor Statistics, *Employment Characteristics of Families—2018,* USDL 19-0666, April 2019, and earlier releases. See also <http://www.bls.gov/news.release/famee.toc.htm>.

# Table 640. Working Poor and People and Families in the Labor Force by Poverty Status: 2008 to 2017

[In thousands (147,838 represents 147,838,000), except rate. The labor force includes people working or looking for work for at least 27 weeks during the year. The working poor rate is the number of individuals in the labor force (working or looking for work) whose incomes are below the official poverty level, as a percent of all people in the labor force. Based on the Current Population Survey, Annual Social and Economic Supplement]

| Characteristic | 2008 | 2009 | 2010 | 2011 | 2012 | 2013 | 2014 | 2015 | 2016 | 2017 |
|---|---|---|---|---|---|---|---|---|---|---|
| **Total in the labor force [1]** ... | **147,838** | **147,902** | **146,859** | **147,475** | **148,735** | **149,483** | **150,319** | **152,230** | **153,364** | **154,762** |
| In poverty......................... | 8,883 | 10,391 | 10,512 | 10,382 | 10,612 | 10,450 | 9,487 | 8,560 | 7,572 | 6,946 |
| Working poor rate.............. | 6.0 | 7.0 | 7.2 | 7.0 | 7.1 | 7.0 | 6.3 | 5.6 | 4.9 | 4.5 |
| Unrelated individuals........... | 32,785 | 33,798 | 34,099 | 33,731 | 34,810 | 35,061 | 35,018 | 35,953 | 35,789 | 36,959 |
| In poverty......................... | 3,275 | 3,947 | 3,947 | 3,621 | 3,851 | 4,141 | 3,395 | 3,137 | 2,792 | 2,524 |
| Working poor rate.............. | 10.0 | 11.7 | 11.6 | 10.7 | 11.1 | 11.8 | 9.7 | 8.7 | 7.8 | 6.8 |
| Primary families [2].............. | 65,907 | 65,467 | 64,931 | 66,225 | 66,541 | 66,462 | 66,732 | 67,193 | 67,628 | 67,588 |
| In poverty......................... | 4,538 | 5,193 | 5,269 | 5,469 | 5,478 | 5,137 | 5,108 | 4,607 | 4,082 | 3,854 |
| Working poor rate.............. | 6.9 | 7.9 | 8.1 | 8.3 | 8.2 | 7.7 | 7.7 | 6.9 | 6.0 | 5.7 |

[1] Includes individuals in families, not shown separately. [2] Primary families with at least one member in the labor force for more than half the year.

Source: U.S. Bureau of Labor Statistics, "A Profile of the Working Poor, 2017," <https://www.bls.gov/opub/reports/working-poor/2017/home.htm>, accessed April 2019.

# Table 641. Employed Civilians by Occupation, Sex, Race, and Hispanic Origin: 2018

[155,761 represents 155,761,000. Civilian noninstitutionalized population 16 years old and over. Annual average of monthly figures. Based on Current Population Survey; see text, Section 1 and Appendix III. Occupational classifications are those used in the 2010 Census]

| Occupation | Total employed | Percent of total | | | |
|---|---|---|---|---|---|
| | | Female | Black [1] | Asian [1] | Hispanic [2] |
| **Total, 16 years and over**......................... | **155,761** | **46.9** | **12.3** | **6.3** | **17.3** |
| **Management, professional and related occupations**.................... | **62,436** | **51.5** | **9.6** | **8.5** | **9.7** |
| Management, business, and financial operations occupations.............. | 25,850 | 44.0 | 8.2 | 6.8 | 9.8 |
| Management occupations [3].................................... | 18,263 | 40.0 | 7.6 | 5.9 | 10.3 |
| Chief executives............................................ | 1,573 | 26.9 | 3.5 | 5.9 | 6.1 |
| General and operations managers............................. | 1,037 | 31.7 | 7.5 | 4.8 | 10.5 |
| Marketing and sales managers................................ | 1,083 | 47.6 | 6.7 | 5.4 | 9.7 |
| Administrative services managers............................. | 161 | 34.2 | 7.4 | 3.0 | 13.0 |
| Computer and information systems managers.................. | 623 | 27.0 | 5.8 | 14.3 | 6.6 |
| Financial managers.......................................... | 1,231 | 55.2 | 8.1 | 7.4 | 9.4 |
| Human resources managers.................................. | 313 | 77.9 | 12.8 | 6.3 | 10.2 |
| Industrial production managers................................ | 264 | 22.0 | 6.3 | 6.0 | 12.5 |
| Purchasing managers........................................ | 219 | 45.3 | 9.0 | 4.0 | 10.7 |
| Transportation, storage, and distribution managers............. | 303 | 16.0 | 7.2 | 4.4 | 13.7 |
| Farmers, ranchers, and other agricultural managers............. | 991 | 25.8 | 0.9 | 1.4 | 5.1 |
| Construction managers....................................... | 1,021 | 7.7 | 3.1 | 2.4 | 15.3 |
| Education administrators..................................... | 955 | 66.9 | 14.4 | 3.4 | 10.5 |
| Architectural and engineering managers....................... | 156 | 11.5 | 5.0 | 9.9 | 4.6 |
| Food service managers....................................... | 1,273 | 49.2 | 10.7 | 10.0 | 18.5 |
| Lodging managers........................................... | 153 | 56.0 | 11.1 | 10.2 | 11.5 |
| Medical and health services managers......................... | 639 | 72.0 | 11.5 | 5.0 | 9.0 |
| Property, real estate, and community association managers.............. | 717 | 49.7 | 7.3 | 4.6 | 13.6 |
| Social and community service managers....................... | 437 | 69.1 | 13.8 | 4.0 | 7.6 |
| Business and financial operations occupations [3]...................... | 7,587 | 53.8 | 9.8 | 9.1 | 8.7 |
| Wholesale and retail buyers, except farm products.................. | 193 | 50.7 | 10.7 | 5.7 | 11.1 |
| Purchasing agents, except wholesale, retail, and farm products........ | 244 | 46.7 | 8.0 | 5.0 | 7.6 |
| Claims adjusters, appraisers, examiners, and investigators............. | 344 | 57.4 | 19.1 | 3.7 | 10.9 |
| Compliance officers......................................... | 281 | 53.7 | 11.3 | 5.4 | 6.9 |
| Cost estimators............................................. | 117 | 14.1 | 1.9 | 4.0 | 10.5 |
| Human resources workers.................................... | 664 | 70.7 | 10.5 | 7.0 | 13.2 |
| Management analysts........................................ | 944 | 41.3 | 8.3 | 12.3 | 6.5 |
| Accountants and auditors.................................... | 1,929 | 60.6 | 9.3 | 12.7 | 7.6 |
| Appraisers and assessors of real estate....................... | 84 | 45.3 | 10.7 | 4.0 | 4.2 |
| Financial analysts........................................... | 307 | 40.7 | 8.1 | 14.1 | 5.5 |
| Personal financial advisors................................... | 537 | 33.5 | 5.0 | 6.9 | 6.6 |
| Insurance underwriters....................................... | 119 | 59.7 | 13.7 | 5.3 | 6.2 |
| Credit counselors and loan officers........................... | 350 | 54.1 | 7.6 | 4.3 | 13.0 |
| Tax preparers.............................................. | 113 | 56.8 | 16.7 | 5.1 | 13.1 |
| Professional and related occupations........................... | 36,586 | 56.8 | 10.5 | 9.6 | 9.6 |
| Computer and mathematical occupations [3].................... | 5,126 | 25.6 | 8.4 | 22.0 | 7.5 |
| Computer systems analysts.................................. | 652 | 37.5 | 10.0 | 20.4 | 7.9 |
| Computer programmers...................................... | 477 | 21.2 | 9.3 | 19.4 | 7.8 |
| Software developers, applications and systems software........... | 1,682 | 19.3 | 3.9 | 35.4 | 5.3 |
| Computer support specialists................................. | 566 | 28.1 | 12.6 | 12.0 | 9.8 |
| Database administrators..................................... | 108 | 37.9 | 8.2 | 16.7 | 9.5 |
| Network and computer systems administrators.................. | 204 | 21.2 | 12.1 | 8.5 | 9.3 |
| Operations research analysts................................. | 131 | 49.1 | 10.9 | 9.8 | 9.9 |
| Architecture and engineering occupations [3]................... | 3,263 | 15.9 | 6.5 | 11.9 | 8.9 |
| Architects, except naval..................................... | 239 | 29.7 | 4.5 | 11.5 | 10.1 |
| Aerospace engineers........................................ | 147 | 13.4 | 7.1 | 17.6 | 7.8 |
| Civil engineers............................................. | 456 | 14.8 | 4.4 | 9.3 | 7.9 |
| Computer hardware engineers................................ | 71 | 18.9 | 6.9 | 30.9 | 14.1 |
| Electrical and electronics engineers........................... | 269 | 9.4 | 8.4 | 17.8 | 8.1 |
| Industrial engineers, including health and safety.................. | 246 | 23.0 | 4.9 | 9.0 | 7.4 |
| Mechanical engineers....................................... | 333 | 10.9 | 3.5 | 15.0 | 5.5 |
| Drafters................................................... | 133 | 20.6 | 4.8 | 4.6 | 11.0 |
| Engineering technicians, except drafters....................... | 439 | 18.1 | 12.0 | 6.2 | 11.1 |
| Life, physical, and social science occupations [3]................ | 1,529 | 46.7 | 7.1 | 12.8 | 8.7 |
| Biological scientists......................................... | 104 | 47.5 | 1.6 | 13.7 | 3.6 |
| Medical scientists.......................................... | 169 | 52.1 | 9.5 | 20.7 | 8.6 |
| Chemists and materials scientists............................ | 118 | 37.7 | 4.2 | 16.8 | 7.7 |
| Environmental scientists and geoscientists..................... | 100 | 33.1 | 7.8 | 1.1 | 8.4 |
| Psychologists.............................................. | 224 | 75.9 | 7.7 | 3.0 | 11.2 |
| Community and social services occupations [3]................. | 2,680 | 66.5 | 20.4 | 3.9 | 12.1 |
| Counselors................................................ | 895 | 72.0 | 22.2 | 3.9 | 12.7 |
| Social workers............................................. | 835 | 81.6 | 23.6 | 3.5 | 13.4 |
| Miscellaneous community and social service specialists.............. | 71 | 76.3 | 21.5 | 3.3 | 12.4 |
| Clergy..................................................... | 415 | 22.4 | 12.5 | 4.3 | 6.4 |
| Legal occupations............................................ | 1,891 | 51.6 | 7.3 | 4.7 | 9.9 |
| Lawyers................................................... | 1,199 | 37.4 | 5.5 | 4.9 | 6.1 |
| Judges, magistrates, and other judicial workers................. | 80 | 32.3 | 13.3 | 1.2 | 6.7 |
| Paralegals and legal assistants............................... | 444 | 86.4 | 11.3 | 5.3 | 18.5 |
| Miscellaneous legal support workers.......................... | 156 | 73.1 | 7.2 | 2.9 | 16.6 |
| Education, training, and library occupations [3].................. | 9,313 | 73.2 | 10.6 | 5.2 | 10.7 |
| Postsecondary teachers..................................... | 1,417 | 49.0 | 7.9 | 13.7 | 7.3 |
| Preschool and kindergarten teachers.......................... | 716 | 97.6 | 16.0 | 4.0 | 14.5 |
| Elementary and middle school teachers........................ | 3,421 | 79.8 | 11.1 | 3.3 | 10.3 |
| Secondary school teachers.................................. | 1,062 | 58.0 | 7.3 | 2.6 | 9.0 |
| Special education teachers.................................. | 369 | 87.5 | 8.5 | 1.6 | 7.6 |
| Other teachers and instructors............................... | 905 | 61.9 | 11.4 | 6.1 | 10.5 |
| Librarians................................................. | 178 | 78.5 | 6.6 | 4.7 | 8.4 |
| Teacher assistants.......................................... | 994 | 88.9 | 12.9 | 4.6 | 17.4 |

See footnotes at end of table.

| Occupation | Total employed | Percent of total | | | |
|---|---|---|---|---|---|
| | | Female | Black [1] | Asian [1] | Hispanic [2] |
| Arts, design, entertainment, sports, and media occupations [3] | 3,362 | 46.8 | 7.4 | 5.5 | 11.8 |
| Artists and related workers | 232 | 52.2 | 6.0 | 5.8 | 9.6 |
| Designers | 984 | 53.0 | 3.7 | 7.2 | 13.1 |
| Producers and directors | 201 | 29.2 | 11.3 | 2.3 | 7.1 |
| Athletes, coaches, umpires, and related workers | 359 | 34.9 | 10.7 | 2.4 | 11.8 |
| Musicians, singers, and related workers | 202 | 35.0 | 15.1 | 5.9 | 10.5 |
| News analysts, reporters and correspondents | 79 | 51.7 | 8.7 | 4.1 | 15.2 |
| Public relations specialists | 140 | 65.7 | 7.1 | 4.9 | 10.0 |
| Editors | 160 | 52.2 | 1.7 | 4.4 | 10.3 |
| Writers and authors | 227 | 59.6 | 5.4 | 4.0 | 4.5 |
| Miscellaneous media and communication workers | 111 | 70.8 | 6.0 | 16.0 | 24.9 |
| Broadcast and sound engineering technicians and radio operators | 120 | 12.4 | 11.5 | 5.7 | 16.3 |
| Photographers | 208 | 47.8 | 6.8 | 5.8 | 11.4 |
| Healthcare practitioner and technical occupations [3] | 9,420 | 75.0 | 12.6 | 9.9 | 8.5 |
| Dentists | 162 | 35.7 | 1.6 | 17.6 | 4.3 |
| Dietitians and nutritionists | 104 | 93.1 | 9.6 | 9.1 | 9.6 |
| Pharmacists | 348 | 63.4 | 7.2 | 23.1 | 4.4 |
| Physicians and surgeons | 1,094 | 40.3 | 7.6 | 19.8 | 7.4 |
| Physician assistants | 132 | 72.1 | 2.9 | 5.1 | 8.2 |
| Occupational therapists | 116 | 86.8 | 2.5 | 6.4 | 4.2 |
| Physical therapists | 286 | 69.5 | 7.4 | 14.3 | 4.3 |
| Speech-language pathologists | 152 | 96.0 | 3.5 | 1.2 | 4.8 |
| Veterinarians | 102 | 71.2 | – | 4.1 | 2.3 |
| Registered nurses | 3,213 | 88.6 | 13.1 | 9.0 | 7.2 |
| Clinical laboratory technologists and technicians | 318 | 75.2 | 18.6 | 8.5 | 12.9 |
| Dental hygienists | 178 | 97.1 | 5.6 | 3.8 | 8.6 |
| Diagnostic-related technologists and technicians | 346 | 67.9 | 11.8 | 5.6 | 14.7 |
| Emergency medical technicians and paramedics | 214 | 33.9 | 11.9 | 2.2 | 13.9 |
| Health practitioner support technologists and technicians | 694 | 80.6 | 14.1 | 6.9 | 15.0 |
| Licensed practical and licensed vocational nurses | 658 | 87.8 | 30.4 | 5.1 | 11.5 |
| Medical records and health information technicians | 171 | 93.6 | 15.5 | 9.2 | 9.2 |
| **Service occupations** | **26,854** | **57.5** | **17.3** | **6.1** | **24.4** |
| Healthcare support occupations [3] | 3,629 | 87.1 | 26.2 | 5.7 | 18.3 |
| Nursing, psychiatric, and home health aides | 2,035 | 89.3 | 35.8 | 5.4 | 16.3 |
| Massage therapists | 155 | 83.2 | 9.2 | 10.2 | 13.9 |
| Dental assistants | 293 | 96.0 | 9.9 | 3.5 | 27.7 |
| Medical assistants | 570 | 90.6 | 15.3 | 4.5 | 28.6 |
| Protective service occupations [3] | 3,203 | 22.5 | 20.1 | 2.4 | 13.8 |
| First-line supervisors of police and detectives | 88 | 17.0 | 9.2 | 0.4 | 9.4 |
| Firefighters | 306 | 5.1 | 8.9 | 1.1 | 7.4 |
| Bailiffs, correctional officers, and jailers | 406 | 29.6 | 29.0 | 1.2 | 13.7 |
| Detectives and criminal investigators | 164 | 24.4 | 10.2 | 1.0 | 11.2 |
| Police and sheriff's patrol officers | 728 | 15.4 | 12.7 | 2.1 | 13.5 |
| Private detectives and investigators | 96 | 49.5 | 15.7 | 3.3 | 20.2 |
| Security guards and gaming surveillance officers | 958 | 22.4 | 30.7 | 3.9 | 16.8 |
| Lifeguards and other protective service workers | 117 | 46.3 | 6.5 | 4.0 | 9.7 |
| Food preparation and serving related occupations | 8,220 | 55.5 | 14.8 | 6.5 | 25.9 |
| Chefs and head cooks | 427 | 22.0 | 17.2 | 16.6 | 26.6 |
| First-line supervisors of food preparation and serving workers | 563 | 57.2 | 17.8 | 2.8 | 16.8 |
| Cooks | 2,067 | 41.8 | 17.6 | 6.3 | 34.7 |
| Food-preparation workers | 988 | 61.0 | 15.9 | 6.2 | 26.2 |
| Bartenders | 474 | 57.2 | 7.3 | 2.9 | 15.1 |
| Combined food preparation and serving workers, including fast food | 322 | 63.0 | 17.8 | 3.5 | 21.0 |
| Counter attendants, cafeteria, food concession, and coffee shop | 202 | 68.8 | 15.3 | 4.9 | 18.0 |
| Waiters and waitresses | 2,020 | 69.9 | 10.7 | 7.6 | 22.6 |
| Food servers, nonrestaurant | 226 | 70.2 | 25.5 | 8.4 | 22.2 |
| Dining room and cafeteria attendants and bartender helpers | 309 | 45.7 | 13.5 | 6.0 | 29.2 |
| Dishwashers | 263 | 24.3 | 13.2 | 5.7 | 27.9 |
| Hosts and hostesses, restaurant, lounge, and coffee shop | 354 | 81.6 | 12.9 | 4.5 | 27.0 |
| Building and grounds cleaning and maintenance occupations | 5,854 | 41.3 | 14.8 | 3.1 | 38.8 |
| First-line supervisors of housekeeping and janitorial workers | 339 | 42.4 | 15.9 | 3.6 | 25.1 |
| First-line supervisors of landscaping, lawn service, and groundskeeping workers | 254 | 8.0 | 6.5 | 1.5 | 26.2 |
| Janitors and building cleaners | 2,342 | 34.1 | 19.1 | 3.5 | 32.8 |
| Maids and housekeeping cleaners | 1,512 | 90.1 | 16.1 | 4.5 | 49.3 |
| Pest control workers | 79 | 8.4 | 10.6 | – | 12.2 |
| Grounds maintenance workers | 1,328 | 6.7 | 7.5 | 1.0 | 45.0 |
| Personal care and service occupations [3] | 5,947 | 76.9 | 16.3 | 10.5 | 17.8 |
| First-line supervisors of gaming workers | 187 | 44.4 | 10.4 | 4.1 | 10.2 |
| First-line supervisors of personal service workers | 208 | 73.3 | 11.9 | 17.8 | 9.5 |
| Nonfarm animal caretakers | 268 | 77.6 | 3.8 | 1.8 | 9.8 |
| Gaming services workers | 102 | 47.8 | 10.6 | 30.3 | 6.7 |
| Barbers | 132 | 21.0 | 30.2 | 5.3 | 27.3 |
| Hairdressers, hairstylists, and cosmetologists | 834 | 92.1 | 14.2 | 7.3 | 17.6 |
| Miscellaneous personal appearance workers | 449 | 83.6 | 9.1 | 57.2 | 10.8 |
| Baggage porters, bellhops, and concierges | 92 | 22.6 | 37.7 | 10.3 | 26.1 |
| Child care workers | 1,193 | 94.0 | 15.5 | 4.1 | 24.3 |
| Personal care aides | 1,354 | 84.4 | 24.6 | 8.3 | 22.4 |
| Recreation and fitness workers | 497 | 60.5 | 15.6 | 4.3 | 9.2 |
| **Sales and office occupations** | **33,461** | **61.1** | **12.8** | **4.9** | **16.6** |
| Sales and related occupations [3] | 15,806 | 49.4 | 11.0 | 5.3 | 16.3 |

See footnotes at end of table.

## Table 641. Employed Civilians by Occupation, Sex, Race, and Hispanic Origin: 2018-Continued.

See headnote on page 407.

| Occupation | Total employed | Percent of total | | | |
|---|---|---|---|---|---|
| | | Female | Black [1] | Asian [1] | Hispanic [2] |
| First-line supervisors of retail sales workers.................... | 3,366 | 44.6 | 10.2 | 5.3 | 13.9 |
| First-line supervisors of non-retail sales workers.................... | 1,257 | 28.5 | 6.9 | 6.4 | 15.0 |
| Cashiers.................... | 3,200 | 73.8 | 17.3 | 6.6 | 24.5 |
| Counter and rental clerks.................... | 114 | 40.6 | 20.4 | 5.8 | 24.6 |
| Parts salespersons.................... | 127 | 10.4 | 9.2 | 2.8 | 19.3 |
| Retail salespersons.................... | 3,147 | 48.7 | 12.6 | 5.1 | 18.2 |
| Advertising sales agents.................... | 221 | 50.4 | 10.4 | 4.8 | 14.9 |
| Insurance sales agents.................... | 619 | 51.4 | 8.7 | 5.3 | 11.6 |
| Securities, commodities, and financial services sales agents.............. | 231 | 31.8 | 6.3 | 6.8 | 11.9 |
| Travel agents.................... | 79 | 85.5 | 17.7 | 4.4 | 9.9 |
| Sales representatives, services, all other.................... | 516 | 30.0 | 6.5 | 2.9 | 7.5 |
| Sales representatives, wholesale and manufacturing.................... | 1,273 | 27.6 | 4.1 | 2.9 | 11.2 |
| Real estate brokers and sales agents.................... | 1,072 | 56.2 | 6.4 | 6.1 | 10.8 |
| Telemarketers.................... | 58 | 65.3 | 23.3 | 3.7 | 22.9 |
| Door-to-door sales, news and street vendors, and related workers........ | 158 | 60.9 | 10.6 | 1.3 | 22.8 |
| Office and administrative support occupations [3].................... | 17,655 | 71.6 | 14.4 | 4.6 | 16.9 |
| First-line supervisors of office and administrative support workers......... | 1,450 | 71.7 | 11.2 | 3.5 | 13.5 |
| Bill and account collectors.................... | 122 | 71.1 | 24.0 | 1.4 | 21.3 |
| Billing and posting clerks.................... | 490 | 87.1 | 13.8 | 5.2 | 18.0 |
| Bookkeeping, accounting, and auditing clerks.................... | 1,045 | 86.7 | 7.0 | 3.7 | 10.2 |
| Payroll and timekeeping clerks.................... | 121 | 89.8 | 13.3 | 6.6 | 14.9 |
| Tellers.................... | 300 | 85.4 | 12.7 | 6.1 | 17.8 |
| Court, municipal, and license clerks.................... | 83 | 76.5 | 12.6 | 2.9 | 16.1 |
| Customer service representatives.................... | 2,563 | 63.7 | 17.8 | 4.7 | 19.1 |
| File clerks.................... | 161 | 76.8 | 15.1 | 5.5 | 15.5 |
| Hotel, motel, and resort desk clerks.................... | 131 | 68.6 | 13.7 | 5.9 | 21.8 |
| Interviewers, except eligibility and loan.................... | 152 | 81.6 | 21.7 | 3.1 | 16.4 |
| Library assistants, clerical.................... | 103 | 78.0 | 9.5 | 3.8 | 8.3 |
| Loan interviewers and clerks.................... | 117 | 80.8 | 13.9 | 9.5 | 11.7 |
| Order clerks.................... | 78 | 49.1 | 13.2 | 8.2 | 17.7 |
| Receptionists and information clerks.................... | 1,324 | 90.5 | 13.2 | 3.2 | 20.4 |
| Reservation and transportation ticket agents and travel clerks.............. | 128 | 59.4 | 17.3 | 5.3 | 21.9 |
| Couriers and messengers.................... | 293 | 21.1 | 21.1 | 4.3 | 20.3 |
| Dispatchers.................... | 293 | 60.7 | 15.2 | 2.8 | 13.3 |
| Postal service clerks.................... | 120 | 54.9 | 40.9 | 8.3 | 8.6 |
| Postal service mail carriers.................... | 302 | 39.8 | 23.6 | 6.9 | 13.3 |
| Postal service mail sorters, processors, and processing machine operators.................... | 58 | 56.6 | 41.1 | 4.4 | 11.7 |
| Production, planning, and expediting clerks.................... | 269 | 54.0 | 9.4 | 7.3 | 12.5 |
| Shipping, receiving, and traffic clerks.................... | 578 | 29.1 | 15.2 | 3.1 | 23.6 |
| Stock clerks and order fillers.................... | 1,527 | 37.4 | 19.7 | 4.5 | 22.9 |
| Weighers, measurers, checkers, and samplers, recordkeeping.............. | 56 | 38.9 | 9.5 | 4.0 | 18.1 |
| Secretaries and administrative assistants.................... | 2,569 | 94.0 | 8.9 | 3.3 | 13.5 |
| Computer operators.................... | 73 | 63.8 | 16.8 | 9.5 | 10.7 |
| Data entry keyers.................... | 270 | 77.2 | 17.0 | 9.1 | 18.1 |
| Word processors and typists.................... | 67 | 85.1 | 22.2 | 8.0 | 15.9 |
| Insurance claims and policy processing clerks.................... | 244 | 82.5 | 14.9 | 2.6 | 14.8 |
| Mail clerks and mail machine operators, except postal service.............. | 63 | 41.5 | 20.6 | 2.5 | 20.5 |
| Office clerks, general.................... | 1,309 | 84.5 | 14.2 | 7.0 | 19.1 |
| **Natural resources, construction, and maintenance occupations**........ | **14,471** | **5.1** | **7.6** | **2.2** | **31.9** |
| Farming, fishing, and forestry occupations [3].................... | 1,121 | 24.3 | 3.8 | 2.2 | 46.0 |
| Construction and extraction occupations [3].................... | 8,338 | 3.4 | 7.1 | 1.6 | 37.0 |
| First-line supervisors of construction trades and extraction workers.................... | 634 | 3.5 | 4.2 | 0.8 | 23.0 |
| Brickmasons, blockmasons, and stonemasons.................... | 143 | 1.9 | 9.3 | 1.5 | 35.5 |
| Carpenters.................... | 1,375 | 2.2 | 6.2 | 2.3 | 39.1 |
| Carpet, floor, and tile installers and finishers.................... | 164 | 1.9 | 8.4 | 0.7 | 46.4 |
| Cement masons, concrete finishers, and terrazzo workers.................... | 50 | – | 12.5 | – | 46.6 |
| Construction laborers.................... | 2,110 | 3.7 | 7.5 | 1.6 | 47.6 |
| Operating engineers and other construction equipment operators......... | 342 | 2.0 | 7.5 | 0.3 | 17.4 |
| Drywall installers, ceiling tile installers, and tapers.................... | 164 | 1.6 | 4.6 | 0.6 | 70.2 |
| Electricians.................... | 887 | 2.4 | 8.2 | 1.8 | 23.3 |
| Painters, construction and maintenance.................... | 607 | 7.2 | 5.7 | 2.3 | 54.9 |
| Pipelayers, plumbers, pipefitters, and steamfitters.................... | 641 | 3.5 | 8.2 | 1.3 | 26.6 |
| Roofers.................... | 201 | 2.6 | 6.6 | 1.8 | 56.3 |
| Sheet metal workers.................... | 147 | 2.8 | 7.7 | 1.3 | 23.3 |
| Construction and building inspectors.................... | 108 | 14.0 | 7.7 | 2.2 | 8.4 |
| Highway maintenance workers.................... | 105 | 3.9 | 12.2 | 0.7 | 12.7 |
| Installation, maintenance, and repair occupations [3].................... | 5,012 | 3.7 | 9.4 | 3.3 | 20.1 |
| First-line supervisors of mechanics, installers, and repairers.............. | 280 | 5.9 | 7.4 | 1.6 | 12.9 |
| Computer, automated teller, and office machine repairers.................... | 185 | 13.7 | 14.0 | 7.6 | 14.7 |
| Radio and telecommunications equipment installers and repairers........ | 136 | 13.6 | 16.0 | 8.8 | 19.1 |
| Aircraft mechanics and service technicians.................... | 164 | 3.6 | 9.1 | 5.0 | 19.4 |
| Automotive body and related repairers.................... | 152 | 1.8 | 5.0 | 1.6 | 30.9 |
| Automotive service technicians and mechanics.................... | 916 | 2.1 | 8.8 | 4.1 | 26.0 |
| Bus and truck mechanics and diesel engine specialists.................... | 389 | 0.9 | 8.1 | 1.8 | 18.7 |
| Heavy vehicle and mobile equip. service technicians and mechanics..... | 211 | 0.8 | 6.4 | 2.1 | 12.4 |
| Heating, air conditioning, and refrigeration mechanics and installers.................... | 472 | 1.4 | 7.6 | 2.9 | 21.5 |
| Industrial and refractory machinery mechanics.................... | 442 | 2.4 | 9.3 | 3.3 | 15.4 |
| Maintenance and repair workers, general.................... | 507 | 3.5 | 12.7 | 3.1 | 19.0 |
| Electrical power-line installers and repairers.................... | 137 | 4.1 | 10.0 | 0.9 | 12.1 |
| Telecommunications line installers and repairers.................... | 210 | 3.9 | 13.1 | 4.2 | 19.2 |

See footnotes at end of table.

## Table 641. Employed Civilians by Occupation, Sex, Race, and Hispanic Origin: 2018-Continued.

See headnote on page 407.

| Occupation | Total employed | Female | Black [1] | Asian [1] | Hispanic [2] |
|---|---|---|---|---|---|
| **Production, transportation, and material moving occupations**........... | **18,539** | **23.1** | **16.6** | **5.1** | **22.8** |
| Production occupations [3].......................... | 8,621 | 28.8 | 13.5 | 5.8 | 23.4 |
| First-line supervisors of production and operating workers............. | 832 | 19.6 | 10.2 | 4.3 | 18.9 |
| Electrical, electronics, and electromechanical assemblers.............. | 124 | 49.2 | 12.2 | 15.1 | 22.5 |
| Bakers.................................... | 219 | 61.1 | 12.8 | 7.3 | 29.5 |
| Butchers and other meat, poultry, and fish processing workers............ | 265 | 28.3 | 20.8 | 6.4 | 32.4 |
| Food batchmakers............................. | 80 | 63.3 | 11.2 | 7.3 | 22.0 |
| Machinists................................. | 344 | 6.4 | 7.2 | 5.8 | 13.6 |
| Welding, soldering, and brazing workers................... | 633 | 5.4 | 8.3 | 1.4 | 25.0 |
| Metal workers and plastic workers, all other................ | 373 | 18.3 | 15.0 | 7.0 | 22.9 |
| Printing press operators......................... | 164 | 22.7 | 10.2 | 3.6 | 20.6 |
| Laundry and dry-cleaning workers.................... | 143 | 71.5 | 20.1 | 7.1 | 43.1 |
| Sewing machine operators........................ | 174 | 73.4 | 9.4 | 12.7 | 44.3 |
| Tailors, dressmakers, and sewers.................... | 85 | 75.1 | 3.6 | 25.3 | 23.5 |
| Stationary engineers and boiler operators................ | 79 | 1.3 | 8.8 | 9.4 | 10.6 |
| Water and wastewater treatment plant and system operators.......... | 101 | 7.2 | 7.6 | 1.4 | 9.4 |
| Crushing, grinding, polishing, mixing, and blending workers.............. | 79 | 9.1 | 15.7 | 0.3 | 20.0 |
| Inspectors, testers, sorters, samplers, and weighers................ | 807 | 36.6 | 13.9 | 6.0 | 19.1 |
| Medical, dental, and ophthalmic laboratory technicians.............. | 87 | 54.2 | 10.1 | 13.2 | 19.9 |
| Packaging and filling machine operators and tenders............. | 277 | 55.8 | 22.3 | 7.6 | 38.9 |
| Painting workers............................. | 165 | 9.4 | 11.2 | 1.8 | 36.0 |
| Transportation and material-moving occupations [3].......... | 9,918 | 18.1 | 19.2 | 4.5 | 22.3 |
| Supervisors, transportation and material-moving workers............. | 217 | 23.2 | 19.5 | 6.7 | 14.2 |
| Aircraft pilots and flight engineers.................... | 119 | 9.0 | 2.7 | 4.2 | 6.8 |
| Bus drivers................................. | 599 | 43.8 | 29.4 | 3.8 | 15.1 |
| Driver/sales workers and truck drivers.................. | 3,549 | 6.6 | 16.3 | 3.2 | 20.9 |
| Taxi drivers and chauffeurs........................ | 777 | 18.0 | 27.9 | 14.9 | 18.3 |
| Parking lot attendants.......................... | 87 | 9.7 | 17.1 | 7.8 | 44.2 |
| Automotive and water craft service attendants.............. | 102 | 20.5 | 9.5 | 7.7 | 20.8 |
| Industrial truck and tractor operators.................. | 631 | 8.1 | 21.5 | 1.7 | 30.2 |
| Cleaners of vehicles and equipment.................... | 329 | 15.2 | 19.8 | 2.0 | 32.9 |
| Laborers and freight, stock, and material movers, hand.................... | 2,106 | 21.4 | 18.9 | 3.1 | 22.0 |
| Packers and packagers, hand....................... | 607 | 54.5 | 19.8 | 7.9 | 42.6 |
| Refuse and recyclable material collectors................. | 91 | 14.5 | 23.5 | 2.8 | 28.6 |

− Represents or rounds to zero. [1] Data represent persons who selected this race group only and exclude persons reporting more than one race. See also comments on race in the text for Section 1. [2] Persons of Hispanic origin may be of any race. [3] Includes other occupations, not shown separately.

Source: U.S. Bureau of Labor Statistics, CPS Tables, "Employed persons by detailed occupation, sex, race, and Hispanic or Latino ethnicity," <http://www.bls.gov/cps/tables.htm>, accessed February 2019.

## Table 642. Employed Workers With Contract, On-Call, Temporary, and Traditional Work Arrangements: 2017

[In thousands (153,331 represents 153,331,000). As of February. For employed workers 16 years old and over. Based on the Current Population Survey; see text, Section 1 and Appendix III]

| Characteristic | Total employed [1] | Workers with alternative arrangements | | | | Workers with traditional arrangements |
|---|---|---|---|---|---|---|
| | | Independent contractors | On-call workers | Temporary help agency workers | Workers provided by contract firms | |
| **Total employed**........................ | **153,331** | **10,614** | **2,579** | **1,356** | **933** | **137,853** |
| 16 to 19 years old.................... | 4,842 | 43 | 107 | 25 | 14 | 4,647 |
| 20 to 24 years old.................... | 14,212 | 330 | 263 | 195 | 53 | 13,370 |
| 25 to 34 years old.................... | 33,991 | 1,593 | 516 | 303 | 224 | 31,361 |
| 35 to 44 years old.................... | 32,065 | 2,160 | 565 | 283 | 207 | 28,849 |
| 45 to 54 years old.................... | 32,745 | 2,562 | 446 | 276 | 206 | 29,263 |
| 55 to 64 years old.................... | 26,236 | 2,426 | 399 | 170 | 124 | 23,110 |
| 65 years old and over................ | 9,240 | 1,500 | 283 | 105 | 106 | 7,253 |
| Male.................................... | 81,545 | 6,820 | 1,355 | 709 | 625 | 72,035 |
| 16 to 19 years old.................... | 2,365 | 42 | 53 | 20 | 9 | 2,235 |
| 20 to 24 years old.................... | 7,412 | 187 | 169 | 100 | 28 | 6,931 |
| 25 to 34 years old.................... | 18,169 | 1,016 | 271 | 170 | 157 | 16,554 |
| 35 to 44 years old.................... | 17,585 | 1,430 | 329 | 122 | 144 | 15,557 |
| 45 to 54 years old.................... | 17,099 | 1,611 | 208 | 166 | 146 | 14,971 |
| 55 to 64 years old.................... | 13,840 | 1,547 | 209 | 81 | 81 | 11,914 |
| 65 years old and over................ | 5,076 | 986 | 117 | 50 | 60 | 3,873 |
| Female.................................... | 71,785 | 3,794 | 1,224 | 647 | 308 | 65,818 |
| 16 to 19 years old.................... | 2,477 | 1 | 55 | 5 | 5 | 2,412 |
| 20 to 24 years old.................... | 6,800 | 143 | 94 | 95 | 25 | 6,439 |
| 25 to 34 years old.................... | 15,823 | 577 | 245 | 133 | 67 | 14,807 |
| 35 to 44 years old.................... | 14,480 | 730 | 237 | 161 | 63 | 13,292 |
| 45 to 54 years old.................... | 15,646 | 951 | 238 | 110 | 60 | 14,292 |
| 55 to 64 years old.................... | 12,396 | 878 | 190 | 88 | 44 | 11,196 |
| 65 years old and over................ | 4,164 | 514 | 166 | 55 | 45 | 3,380 |
| Full-time workers.................... | 125,240 | 7,485 | 1,428 | 1,042 | 785 | 114,496 |
| Part-time workers.................... | 28,091 | 3,129 | 1,151 | 314 | 148 | 23,357 |

[1] Includes day laborers (an alternative arrangement) and a small number of workers who were both "on call" and "provided by contract firms," not shown separately.

Source: U.S. Bureau of Labor Statistics, *Contingent and Alternative Employment Arrangements, May 2017*, USDL 18–0942, June 2018. See also <https://www.bls.gov/cps/lfcharacteristics.htm#contingent>.

# Table 643. Employment and Annual and Hourly Wages by Occupation: 2018

[In dollars, except employment. As of May. Data shown for occupations with over 1,500,000 employees. Data from the Occupational Employment Statistics survey. For definition of mean and median, see Guide to Tabular Presentation]

| Occupation | Employment (number) | Mean hourly wage | Annual wages [1] | Median hourly wage |
|---|---|---|---|---|
| **All occupations [2]**............................................ | **144,733,270** | **24.98** | **51,960** | **18.58** |
| Management occupations............................... | 7,616,650 | 58.44 | 121,560 | 50.11 |
| Top executives........................................ | 2,535,640 | 61.66 | 128,240 | 49.73 |
| General and operations managers............... | 2,289,770 | 59.56 | 123,880 | 48.52 |
| Operations specialties managers.................. | 1,853,660 | 63.79 | 132,680 | 57.01 |
| Other management occupations................... | 2,510,140 | 48.51 | 100,900 | 43.33 |
| Business and financial operations occupations.... | 7,721,300 | 36.98 | 76,910 | 32.86 |
| Business operations specialists..................... | 5,022,640 | 35.52 | 73,890 | 32.27 |
| Financial specialists.................................. | 2,698,660 | 39.69 | 82,550 | 34.02 |
| Computer and mathematical occupations........... | 4,384,300 | 44.01 | 91,530 | 41.51 |
| Computer occupations............................... | 4,214,820 | 43.98 | 91,480 | 41.50 |
| Software developers and programmers........... | 1,666,270 | 50.23 | 104,480 | 48.04 |
| Architecture and engineering occupations......... | 2,556,220 | 42.01 | 87,370 | 38.55 |
| Engineers............................................... | 1,700,880 | 47.71 | 99,230 | 44.75 |
| Community and social service occupations......... | 2,171,820 | 23.69 | 49,280 | 21.62 |
| Counselors, social workers, and other community and social service specialists........ | 2,090,700 | 23.69 | 49,270 | 21.62 |
| Education, training, and library occupations....... | 8,779,780 | 27.22 | 56,620 | 23.89 |
| Postsecondary teachers............................. | 1,517,100 | ([3]) | 85,190 | ([3]) |
| Preschool, primary, secondary, and special education school teachers................. | 4,193,290 | ([3]) | 59,980 | ([3]) |
| Elementary and middle school teachers......... | 2,032,880 | ([3]) | 62,150 | ([3]) |
| Arts, design, entertainment, sports, and media occupations.... | 1,951,170 | 28.74 | 59,780 | 23.70 |
| Healthcare practitioners and technical occupations.... | 8,646,730 | 39.42 | 82,000 | 31.94 |
| Health diagnosing and treating practitioners....... | 5,367,930 | 49.02 | 101,960 | 38.94 |
| Registered nurses................................... | 2,951,960 | 36.30 | 75,510 | 34.48 |
| Health technologists and technicians.............. | 3,110,180 | 23.26 | 48,380 | 21.49 |
| Healthcare support occupations..................... | 4,117,450 | 15.57 | 32,380 | 14.30 |
| Nursing, psychiatric, and home health aides..... | 2,355,640 | 13.55 | 28,180 | 12.89 |
| Protective service occupations...................... | 3,437,410 | 23.36 | 48,580 | 19.54 |
| Food preparation and serving related occupations.... | 13,374,620 | 12.30 | 25,580 | 11.09 |
| Cooks and food preparation workers............... | 3,218,110 | 12.56 | 26,120 | 11.91 |
| Cooks................................................. | 2,403,510 | 12.77 | 26,560 | 12.12 |
| Food and beverage serving workers................ | 7,630,110 | 11.51 | 23,940 | 10.43 |
| Fast food and counter workers..................... | 4,150,030 | 10.70 | 22,260 | 10.32 |
| Combined food preparation and serving workers, including fast food.......... | 3,676,180 | 10.64 | 22,140 | 10.22 |
| Waiters and waitresses.............................. | 2,582,410 | 12.42 | 25,830 | 10.47 |
| Building and grounds cleaning and maintenance occupations.... | 4,421,980 | 14.43 | 30,020 | 12.91 |
| Building cleaning and pest control workers........ | 3,171,520 | 13.56 | 28,200 | 12.17 |
| Building cleaning workers........................... | 3,094,210 | 13.44 | 27,960 | 12.10 |
| Janitors and cleaners, except maids and housekeeping cleaners.................... | 2,156,270 | 13.92 | 28,950 | 12.55 |
| Personal care and service occupations............. | 5,451,330 | 13.51 | 28,090 | 11.74 |
| Other personal care and service workers.......... | 3,605,950 | 13.07 | 27,190 | 11.70 |
| Sales and related occupations...................... | 14,542,290 | 20.09 | 41,790 | 13.55 |
| Retail sales workers................................. | 8,787,270 | 12.75 | 26,520 | 11.33 |
| Cashiers............................................... | 3,657,570 | 11.19 | 23,270 | 10.79 |
| Retail salespersons................................. | 4,448,120 | 13.61 | 28,310 | 11.63 |
| Sales representatives, services..................... | 2,046,120 | 34.37 | 71,490 | 26.13 |
| Sales representatives, wholesale and manufacturing.... | 1,663,160 | 35.43 | 73,680 | 20.64 |
| Office and administrative support occupations..... | 21,828,990 | 18.75 | 38,990 | 17.19 |
| Financial clerks...................................... | 2,978,640 | 19.07 | 39,660 | 18.02 |
| Bookkeeping, accounting, and auditing clerks.... | 1,530,430 | 20.25 | 42,110 | 19.35 |
| Information and record clerks....................... | 5,773,540 | 17.19 | 35,750 | 15.91 |
| Customer service representatives.................. | 2,871,400 | 17.53 | 36,470 | 16.23 |
| Material recording, scheduling, dispatching, and distributing workers.... | 4,149,140 | 17.28 | 35,950 | 15.45 |
| Stock clerks and order fillers....................... | 2,056,030 | 13.71 | 28,520 | 12.36 |
| Secretaries and administrative assistants......... | 3,498,120 | 20.34 | 42,320 | 18.69 |
| Secretaries and administrative assistants, except legal, medical, and executive...... | 2,165,310 | 18.28 | 38,030 | 17.61 |
| Other office and administrative support workers.... | 3,873,130 | 17.28 | 35,940 | 16.16 |
| Office clerks, general................................. | 2,972,930 | 16.92 | 35,200 | 15.74 |
| Construction and extraction occupations........... | 5,962,640 | 24.62 | 51,220 | 22.12 |
| Construction trades workers........................ | 4,497,490 | 23.97 | 49,850 | 21.54 |
| Installation, maintenance, and repair occupations.... | 5,628,880 | 23.54 | 48,960 | 21.89 |
| Vehicle and mobile equipment mechanics, installers, and repairers...................... | 1,614,070 | 22.21 | 46,200 | 20.83 |
| Other installation, maintenance, and repair occupations.... | 2,959,670 | 22.30 | 46,380 | 20.68 |
| Production occupations.............................. | 9,115,530 | 18.84 | 39,190 | 16.86 |
| Assemblers and fabricators......................... | 1,831,200 | 17.14 | 35,650 | 15.78 |
| Metal workers and plastic workers.................. | 1,940,370 | 19.94 | 41,480 | 18.70 |
| Other production occupations....................... | 2,537,090 | 17.92 | 37,270 | 16.35 |
| Transportation and material moving occupations.... | 10,244,260 | 18.41 | 38,290 | 15.74 |
| Motor vehicle operators............................. | 4,088,870 | 18.94 | 39,400 | 17.85 |
| Driver/sales workers and truck drivers............ | 3,130,500 | 19.68 | 40,920 | 18.66 |
| Heavy and tractor-trailer truck drivers........... | 1,800,330 | 21.91 | 45,570 | 21.00 |
| Material moving workers............................. | 4,911,060 | 15.17 | 31,560 | 13.74 |
| Laborers and material movers, hand............... | 4,002,390 | 14.32 | 29,790 | 13.02 |
| Laborers and freight, stock, and material movers, hand........ | 2,893,180 | 14.85 | 30,890 | 13.59 |

[1] Annual wages have been calculated by multiplying the hourly mean wage by a "year-round, full-time" hours figure of 2,080 hours; for those occupations where there is not an hourly mean wage published, the annual wage has been directly calculated from the reported survey data. [2] Includes occupations not shown separately. [3] Wages for some occupations that do not generally work year-round full-time are reported as either hourly wages or as annual salaries, depending on how they are typically paid.

Source: U.S. Bureau of Labor Statistics, Occupational Employment Statistics, *Occupational Employment and Wages—May 2018*, USDL 19-0493, March 2019. See also <http://www.bls.gov/oes/>.

# Table 644. Employed Civilians by Occupation—States: 2017

[In thousands (153,337 represents 153,337,000). Excludes persons with no previous work experience. Based on the Current Population Survey see text, Section 1 and Appendix III]

| State | Total employed | Management, professional, and related occupations | | Service occupations | Sales and office occupations | | Natural resources, construction, and maintenance occupations | | | Production, transportation, and material-moving occupations | |
| | | Management, business, and financial | Professional and related | | Sales and related | Office and administrative | Farming, fishing, and forestry | Construction and extraction occupations | Installation, maintenance, and repair | Production | Transportation and material-moving |
|---|---|---|---|---|---|---|---|---|---|---|---|
| Total U.S. | 153,337 | 25,379 | 35,522 | 26,751 | 15,815 | 17,751 | 1,184 | 8,031 | 4,977 | 8,482 | 9,445 |
| AL | 2,066 | 273 | 436 | 314 | 213 | 248 | (S) | 115 | 89 | 192 | 168 |
| AK | 338 | 54 | 74 | 59 | 33 | 50 | (S) | 20 | 14 | (S) | 21 |
| AZ | 3,138 | 541 | 708 | 608 | 339 | 409 | (S) | 157 | (S) | 104 | 155 |
| AR | 1,311 | 178 | 285 | 221 | 147 | 161 | (S) | 68 | 46 | 106 | 80 |
| CA | 18,340 | 3,044 | 4,329 | 3,300 | 1,856 | 2,057 | 283 | 862 | 525 | 921 | 1,162 |
| CO | 2,922 | 614 | 715 | 460 | 321 | 292 | (S) | 181 | (S) | (S) | 143 |
| CT | 1,831 | 316 | 467 | 344 | 187 | 208 | (S) | 83 | (S) | 104 | 74 |
| DE | 456 | 80 | 103 | 80 | 45 | 55 | (S) | 25 | (S) | 19 | 30 |
| DC | 377 | 110 | 143 | 50 | 20 | 31 | (S) | 7 | (S) | (S) | 11 |
| FL | 9,713 | 1,535 | 2,005 | 1,941 | 1,217 | 1,191 | (S) | 550 | 327 | 328 | 573 |
| GA | 4,836 | 769 | 1,062 | 783 | 550 | 604 | (S) | 241 | 176 | 268 | 344 |
| HI | 668 | 98 | 141 | 153 | 73 | 74 | (S) | 42 | (S) | (S) | 41 |
| ID | 808 | 134 | 171 | 133 | 80 | 100 | (S) | 42 | (S) | 43 | 50 |
| IL | 6,156 | 1,040 | 1,406 | 1,028 | 643 | 720 | (S) | 241 | 175 | 424 | 444 |
| IN | 3,199 | 476 | 675 | 529 | 312 | 373 | (S) | 132 | 131 | 329 | 224 |
| IA | 1,622 | 277 | 345 | 269 | 166 | 186 | (S) | (S) | (S) | 102 | 116 |
| KS | 1,428 | 213 | 344 | 230 | 135 | 169 | (S) | 86 | (S) | 117 | 80 |
| KY | 1,966 | 298 | 393 | 302 | 208 | 260 | (S) | 121 | 83 | 141 | 143 |
| LA | 2,002 | 275 | 426 | 381 | 229 | 218 | (S) | 160 | 75 | 99 | 130 |
| ME | 680 | 113 | 156 | 113 | 71 | 77 | (S) | (S) | (S) | (S) | (S) |
| MD | 3,088 | 586 | 914 | 539 | 265 | 344 | (S) | 160 | (S) | (S) | 134 |
| MA | 3,535 | 658 | 1,050 | 584 | 325 | 390 | (S) | 152 | 86 | 116 | 169 |
| MI | 4,650 | 745 | 1,100 | 782 | 432 | 515 | (S) | 191 | 148 | 436 | 273 |
| MN | 3,004 | 557 | 729 | 493 | 314 | 308 | (S) | 135 | (S) | 212 | 162 |
| MS | 1,213 | 131 | 246 | 213 | 125 | 152 | (S) | 80 | 54 | 115 | 87 |
| MO | 2,894 | 522 | 605 | 492 | 299 | 341 | (S) | 170 | 97 | 176 | 177 |
| MT | 500 | 90 | 109 | 94 | 50 | 57 | (S) | 31 | (S) | 18 | 25 |
| NE | 976 | 169 | 217 | 158 | 96 | 111 | (S) | 52 | (S) | 71 | 56 |
| NV | 1,387 | 165 | 234 | 373 | 149 | 172 | (S) | 90 | 45 | 48 | 103 |
| NH | 723 | 130 | 173 | 115 | 76 | 78 | (S) | 38 | (S) | 49 | 41 |
| NJ | 4,305 | 871 | 1,075 | 720 | 436 | 490 | (S) | 157 | 130 | 152 | 271 |
| NM | 875 | 117 | 202 | 189 | 91 | 101 | (S) | 57 | 33 | 31 | 46 |
| NY | 9,295 | 1,427 | 2,449 | 1,843 | 891 | 1,096 | (S) | 469 | 251 | 328 | 511 |
| NC | 4,706 | 737 | 1,104 | 786 | 472 | 533 | (S) | 266 | 166 | 352 | 259 |
| ND | 404 | 76 | 85 | 66 | 38 | 42 | (S) | 24 | 19 | 18 | 30 |
| OH | 5,496 | 899 | 1,199 | 907 | 545 | 628 | (S) | 240 | 196 | 449 | 407 |
| OK | 1,753 | 293 | 378 | 270 | 179 | 207 | (S) | 127 | 73 | 108 | 103 |
| OR | 2,030 | 369 | 491 | 365 | 194 | 207 | (S) | 78 | (S) | 95 | 131 |
| PA | 6,092 | 941 | 1,437 | 1,060 | 626 | 722 | (S) | 301 | 204 | 360 | 409 |
| RI | 532 | 91 | 140 | 99 | 49 | 55 | (S) | (S) | (S) | 36 | 28 |
| SC | 2,191 | 316 | 519 | 344 | 221 | 266 | (S) | 128 | 98 | 165 | 122 |
| SD | 441 | 75 | 86 | 77 | 44 | 47 | (S) | (S) | (S) | 35 | (S) |
| TN | 3,078 | 481 | 648 | 522 | 334 | 340 | (S) | 157 | 113 | 237 | 230 |
| TX | 12,935 | 2,167 | 2,731 | 2,181 | 1,452 | 1,539 | (S) | 959 | 460 | 607 | 796 |
| UT | 1,515 | 259 | 363 | 220 | 153 | 199 | (S) | 84 | (S) | 99 | 83 |
| VT | 335 | 57 | 84 | 55 | 32 | 35 | (S) | 20 | (S) | 22 | 15 |
| VA | 4,148 | 780 | 1,135 | 720 | 374 | 442 | (S) | 197 | 125 | 154 | 208 |
| WA | 3,551 | 654 | 810 | 576 | 360 | 392 | 74 | 181 | 116 | 157 | 230 |
| WV | 738 | 101 | 158 | 131 | 66 | 82 | (S) | 48 | 36 | 48 | 62 |
| WI | 3,069 | 479 | 675 | 475 | 283 | 377 | (S) | 125 | 117 | 275 | 221 |
| WY | 280 | 42 | 55 | 49 | 24 | 33 | (S) | 25 | 15 | 11 | 21 |

S Data are not shown when the labor force base does not meet publication standard of reliability for the particular area, as determined by the sample size.

Source: U.S. Bureau of Labor Statistics, "Geographic Profile of Employment and Unemployment, 2017," January 2019. See also <https://www.bls.gov/opub/geographic-profile/>.

# Table 645. Fastest Growing and Largest Occupations Projected with Education Needed and Median Wages: 2016 to 2026

[In thousands (11.3 represents 11,300), except percent and wage. Estimates based on the Current Employment Statistics Program, the Occupational Employment Statistics Survey, and the Current Population Survey. See source for methodological assumptions. Occupations based on the 2010 Standard Occupational Classification system. Additional occupation information in the Occupational Outlook Handbook <http://www.bls.gov/ooh>]

| Occupation | Employment (1,000) | | Change, 2016–2026 | | Median annual wage (in dollars), 2016 | Typical education needed for entry [1] |
|---|---|---|---|---|---|---|
| | 2016 | 2026 | Number (1,000) | Percent | | |
| **FASTEST GROWING** | | | | | | |
| Solar photovoltaic installers | 11.3 | 23.2 | 11.9 | 105.3 | 39,240 | High school diploma or equivalent |
| Wind turbine service technicians | 5.8 | 11.3 | 5.5 | 96.1 | 52,260 | Postsecondary nondegree award |
| Home health aides | 911.5 | 1,337.0 | 425.6 | 46.7 | 22,600 | High school diploma or equivalent |
| Personal care aides | 2,016.1 | 2,770.1 | 754.0 | 37.4 | 21,920 | High school diploma or equivalent |
| Physician assistants | 106.2 | 145.9 | 39.7 | 37.4 | 101,480 | Master's degree |
| Nurse practitioners | 155.5 | 211.5 | 56.0 | 36.0 | 100,910 | Master's degree |
| Statisticians | 37.2 | 49.6 | 12.4 | 33.4 | 80,500 | Master's degree |
| Physical therapist assistants | 88.3 | 115.5 | 27.2 | 30.8 | 56,610 | Associate's degree |
| Software developers, applications | 831.3 | 1,084.6 | 253.4 | 30.5 | 100,080 | Bachelor's degree |
| Mathematicians | 3.1 | 4.0 | 0.9 | 29.4 | 105,810 | Master's degree |
| Bicycle repairers | 12.4 | 16.1 | 3.7 | 29.4 | 27,630 | High school diploma or equivalent |
| Medical assistants | 634.4 | 819.0 | 184.6 | 29.1 | 31,540 | Postsecondary nondegree award |
| Physical therapist aides | 52.0 | 67.1 | 15.1 | 29.1 | 25,680 | High school diploma or equivalent |
| Occupational therapy assistants | 39.3 | 50.7 | 11.4 | 28.9 | 59,010 | Associate's degree |
| Information security analysts | 100.0 | 128.5 | 28.4 | 28.4 | 92,600 | Bachelor's degree |
| Genetic counselors | 3.1 | 3.9 | 0.9 | 28.3 | 74,120 | Master's degree |
| Operations research analysts | 114.0 | 145.3 | 31.3 | 27.4 | 79,200 | Bachelor's degree |
| Forest fire inspectors and prevention specialists | 1.7 | 2.2 | 0.5 | 26.6 | 36,230 | High school diploma or equivalent |
| Health specialties teachers, postsecondary | 233.5 | 294.0 | 60.5 | 25.9 | 99,360 | Doctoral or professional degree |
| Derrick operators, oil and gas | 11.1 | 13.9 | 2.8 | 25.7 | 48,130 | No formal educational credential |
| Physical therapists | 239.8 | 299.8 | 60.0 | 25.0 | 85,400 | Doctoral or professional degree |
| Occupational therapy aides | 7.5 | 9.3 | 1.8 | 24.7 | 28,330 | High school diploma or equivalent |
| Roustabouts, oil and gas | 50.0 | 62.3 | 12.2 | 24.5 | 37,340 | No formal educational credential |
| Phlebotomists | 122.7 | 152.6 | 30.0 | 24.4 | 32,710 | Postsecondary nondegree award |
| Rotary drill operators, oil and gas | 16.7 | 20.8 | 4.0 | 24.2 | 54,430 | No formal educational credential |
| Nursing instructors and teachers, postsecondary | 67.9 | 84.2 | 16.3 | 24.0 | 69,130 | Doctoral or professional degree |
| Massage therapists | 160.3 | 198.1 | 37.7 | 23.5 | 39,860 | Postsecondary nondegree award |
| Service unit operators, oil, gas, and mining | 41.4 | 51.1 | 9.7 | 23.4 | 48,610 | No formal educational credential |
| Respiratory therapists | 130.2 | 160.6 | 30.4 | 23.4 | 58,670 | Associate's degree |
| Diagnostic medical sonographers | 67.3 | 82.9 | 15.6 | 23.2 | 69,650 | Associate's degree |
| **LARGEST JOB GROWTH** | | | | | | |
| Personal care aides | 2,016.1 | 2,770.1 | 754.0 | 37.4 | 21,920 | High school diploma or equivalent |
| Combined food preparation and serving workers, including fast food | 3,452.2 | 4,032.1 | 579.9 | 16.8 | 19,440 | No formal educational credential |
| Registered nurses | 2,955.2 | 3,392.2 | 437.0 | 14.8 | 68,450 | Bachelor's degree |
| Home health aides | 911.5 | 1,337.0 | 425.6 | 46.7 | 22,600 | High school diploma or equivalent |
| Software developers, applications | 831.3 | 1,084.6 | 253.4 | 30.5 | 100,080 | Bachelor's degree |
| Janitors and cleaners, except maids and housekeeping cleaners | 2,384.6 | 2,617.7 | 233.0 | 9.8 | 24,190 | No formal educational credential |
| General and operations managers | 2,263.1 | 2,469.0 | 205.9 | 9.1 | 99,310 | Bachelor's degree |
| Laborers and freight, stock, and material movers, hand | 2,628.4 | 2,829.2 | 200.8 | 7.6 | 25,980 | No formal educational credential |
| Medical assistants | 634.4 | 819.0 | 184.6 | 29.1 | 31,540 | Postsecondary nondegree award |
| Waiters and waitresses | 2,600.5 | 2,783.0 | 182.5 | 7.0 | 19,990 | No formal educational credential |
| Nursing assistants | 1,510.3 | 1,674.4 | 164.0 | 10.9 | 26,590 | Postsecondary nondegree award |
| Construction laborers | 1,216.7 | 1,370.0 | 153.3 | 12.6 | 33,430 | No formal educational credential |
| Cooks, restaurant | 1,231.9 | 1,377.2 | 145.3 | 11.8 | 24,140 | No formal educational credential |
| Accountants and auditors | 1,397.7 | 1,538.0 | 140.3 | 10.0 | 68,150 | Bachelor's degree |
| Customer service representatives | 2,784.5 | 2,920.5 | 136.0 | 4.9 | 32,300 | High school diploma or equivalent |
| Market research analysts and marketing specialists | 595.4 | 731.4 | 136.0 | 22.8 | 62,560 | Bachelor's degree |
| Medical secretaries | 574.2 | 703.2 | 129.1 | 22.5 | 33,730 | High school diploma or equivalent |
| Landscaping and groundskeeping workers | 1,197.9 | 1,321.2 | 123.3 | 10.3 | 26,320 | No formal educational credential |
| Heavy and tractor-trailer truck drivers | 1,871.7 | 1,985.5 | 113.8 | 6.1 | 41340 | Postsecondary nondegree award |
| Maintenance and repair workers, general | 1,432.6 | 1,545.3 | 112.7 | 7.9 | 36,940 | High school diploma or equivalent |
| Teacher assistants | 1,308.1 | 1,417.6 | 109.5 | 8.4 | 25,410 | Some college, no degree |
| Financial managers | 580.4 | 688.8 | 108.4 | 18.7 | 121,750 | Bachelor's degree |
| Elementary school teachers, except special education | 1,410.9 | 1,514.9 | 104.1 | 7.4 | 55,800 | Bachelor's degree |
| Stock clerks and order fillers | 2,008.6 | 2,109.9 | 101.3 | 5.0 | 23,840 | High school diploma or equivalent |
| Management analysts | 806.4 | 902.8 | 96.5 | 12.0 | 81,330 | Bachelor's degree |
| Receptionists and information clerks | 1,053.7 | 1,149.4 | 95.7 | 9.1 | 27,920 | High school diploma or equivalent |
| Sales representatives, services, all other | 983.0 | 1,077.2 | 94.2 | 9.6 | 52,490 | High school diploma or equivalent |
| Teachers and instructors, all other | 993.9 | 1,086.4 | 92.5 | 9.3 | 30,110 | Bachelor's degree |
| Business operations specialists, all other | 1,023.9 | 1,114.1 | 90.2 | 8.8 | 69,040 | Bachelor's degree |
| Licensed practical and licensed vocational nurses | 724.5 | 813.1 | 88.6 | 12.2 | 44,090 | Postsecondary nondegree award |

[1] An occupation is placed into 1 of 8 categories that best describe the typical education needed by most workers to enter that occupation. For more information, see "Measures of Education and Training" at <http://www.bls.gov/emp/ep_education_tech.htm>.

Source: U.S. Bureau of Labor Statistics, Employment Projections, "EP Tables—Occupations," <https://www.bls.gov/emp/tables.htm>, accessed November 2017.

# Table 646. Employment Projections by Industry: 2016 to 2026

[11,438.7 represents 11,438,700. Estimates based on the Current Employment Statistics program. See source for methodological assumptions. Minus sign (-) indicates decline]

| Industry | 2012 NAICS code [1] | Employment (1,000) | | Change, 2016–2026 (1,000) | Average annual rate of change 2016–2026 |
|---|---|---|---|---|---|
| | | 2016 | 2026 | | |
| **LARGEST GROWTH** | | | | | |
| Food services and drinking places | 722 | 11,438.7 | 12,515.7 | 1,077.0 | 0.9 |
| Individual and family services | 6241 | 2,229.4 | 3,100.8 | 871.4 | 3.4 |
| Construction | 23 | 6,711.0 | 7,575.7 | 864.7 | 1.2 |
| Home health care services | 6216 | 1,362.0 | 2,100.2 | 738.2 | 4.4 |
| Offices of physicians | 6211 | 2,527.7 | 3,076.5 | 548.8 | 2.0 |
| Nursing and residential care facilities | 623 | 3,313.6 | 3,742.7 | 429.1 | 1.2 |
| Computer systems design and related services | 5415 | 1,990.7 | 2,415.7 | 425.0 | 2.0 |
| Hospitals | 622 | 5,025.0 | 5,444.0 | 419.0 | 0.8 |
| Local government educational services compensation | (X) | 7,920.0 | 8,333.1 | 413.1 | 0.5 |
| Outpatient care centers | 6214 | 856.3 | 1,178.9 | 322.6 | 3.2 |
| Management, scientific, and technical consulting services | 5416 | 1,372.5 | 1,691.5 | 319.0 | 2.1 |
| Offices of other health practitioners | 6213 | 858.5 | 1,122.5 | 264.0 | 2.7 |
| Services to buildings and dwellings | 5617 | 2,070.3 | 2,322.6 | 252.3 | 1.2 |
| Junior colleges, colleges, universities, and professional schools | 6112, 6113 | 1,818.9 | 2,058.0 | 239.1 | 1.2 |
| Warehousing and storage | 493 | 915.1 | 1,110.8 | 195.7 | 2.0 |
| Employment services | 5613 | 3,566.5 | 3,760.9 | 194.4 | 0.5 |
| Offices of dentists | 6212 | 925.8 | 1,101.2 | 175.4 | 1.8 |
| Motor vehicle and parts dealers | 441 | 1,981.8 | 2,145.7 | 163.9 | 0.8 |
| Wholesale trade | 42 | 5,867.0 | 6,012.8 | 145.8 | 0.2 |
| Agencies, brokerages, and other insurance related activities | 5242 | 1,098.1 | 1,241.6 | 143.5 | 1.2 |
| **FASTEST GROWTH** | | | | | |
| Home health care services | 6216 | 1,362.0 | 2,100.2 | 738.2 | 4.4 |
| Other information services | 519 | 259.3 | 384.7 | 125.4 | 4.0 |
| Individual and family services | 6241 | 2,229.4 | 3,100.8 | 871.4 | 3.4 |
| Outpatient care centers | 6214 | 856.3 | 1,178.9 | 322.6 | 3.2 |
| Offices of other health practitioners | 6213 | 858.5 | 1,122.5 | 264.0 | 2.7 |
| Medical and diagnostic laboratories | 6215 | 262.8 | 334.9 | 72.1 | 2.5 |
| Other ambulatory health care services | 6219 | 288.6 | 365.0 | 76.4 | 2.4 |
| Support activities for mining | 213 | 265.0 | 334.3 | 69.3 | 2.4 |
| Other personal services | 8129 | 320.2 | 401.5 | 81.3 | 2.3 |
| Management, scientific, and technical consulting services | 5416 | 1,372.5 | 1,691.5 | 319.0 | 2.1 |
| Office administrative services | 5611 | 495.1 | 608.4 | 113.3 | 2.1 |
| Offices of physicians | 6211 | 2,527.7 | 3,076.5 | 548.8 | 2.0 |
| Warehousing and storage | 493 | 915.1 | 1,110.8 | 195.7 | 2.0 |
| Computer systems design and related services | 5415 | 1,990.7 | 2,415.7 | 425.0 | 2.0 |
| Software publishers | 5112 | 355.6 | 425.5 | 69.9 | 1.8 |
| Offices of dentists | 6212 | 925.8 | 1,101.2 | 175.4 | 1.8 |
| Oil and gas extraction | 211 | 180.0 | 214.0 | 34.0 | 1.7 |
| Other educational services | 6114-7 | 730.3 | 867.4 | 137.1 | 1.7 |
| Local government passenger transit | (X) | 284.1 | 332.3 | 48.2 | 1.6 |
| Museums, historical sites, and similar institutions | 712 | 159.7 | 185.9 | 26.2 | 1.5 |
| **MOST RAPIDLY DECLINING** | | | | | |
| Tobacco manufacturing | 3122 | 12.9 | 8.0 | -4.9 | -4.7 |
| Federal electric utilities | (X) | 15.5 | 10.8 | -4.7 | -3.5 |
| Apparel, leather and allied product manufacturing | 315, 316 | 160.8 | 112.6 | -48.2 | -3.5 |
| Communications equipment manufacturing | 3342 | 85.6 | 61.9 | -23.7 | -3.2 |
| Newspaper, periodical, book, and directory publishers | 5111 | 374.4 | 286.4 | -88.0 | -2.6 |
| Manufacturing and reproducing magnetic and optical media | 3346 | 15.4 | 11.9 | -3.5 | -2.6 |
| Cable and other subscription programming | 5152 | 52.8 | 40.9 | -11.9 | -2.5 |
| Logging | 1133 | 51.2 | 40.3 | -10.9 | -2.4 |
| Foundries | 3315 | 117.5 | 92.4 | -25.1 | -2.4 |
| Pulp, paper, and paperboard mills | 3221 | 100.0 | 79.2 | -20.8 | -2.3 |
| Textile mills and textile product mills | 313, 314 | 228.9 | 184.7 | -44.2 | -2.1 |
| Other chemical product and preparation manufacturing | 3259 | 80.2 | 65.8 | -14.4 | -2.0 |
| Wired telecommunications carriers | 5171 | 588.5 | 486.0 | -102.5 | -1.9 |
| Satellite, telecommunications resellers, and all other telecommunications | 5174, 5179 | 85.3 | 70.5 | -14.8 | -1.9 |
| Printing and related support activities | 323 | 446.7 | 373.5 | -73.2 | -1.8 |
| Rubber product manufacturing | 3262 | 133.1 | 111.6 | -21.5 | -1.7 |
| Iron and steel mills and ferroalloy manufacturing | 3311 | 83.6 | 70.6 | -13.0 | -1.7 |
| Spring and wire product manufacturing | 3326 | 43.0 | 36.5 | -6.5 | -1.6 |
| Computer and peripheral equipment manufacturing, excluding digital camera manufacturing | 3341 | 164.1 | 141.0 | -23.1 | -1.5 |
| Industrial machinery manufacturing | 3332 | 113.6 | 97.8 | -15.8 | -1.5 |

X Not applicable. [1] Based on the North American Industry Classification System, 2012; see text, Section 15.

Source: U.S. Bureau of Labor Statistics, Employment Projections, "EP Tables—Industries," <https://www.bls.gov/emp/tables.htm>, accessed December 2017.

# Table 647. Occupations of the Employed by Race/Ethnicity and Educational Attainment: 2018

[In thousands (136,584 represents 136,584,000). Annual averages of monthly figures. Civilian noninstitutional population 25 years old and over. Based on Current Population Survey; see text, Section 1 and Appendix III]

| Race/ethnicity and educational attainment | Total employed | Managerial, professional, and related | Service | Sales and office | Natural resources, construction, and maintenance | Production, transportation, and material-moving |
|---|---|---|---|---|---|---|
| **Total** [1]............... | **136,584** | **58,641** | **21,095** | **27,753** | **12,874** | **16,221** |
| Less than a high school diploma.......... | 9,701 | 681 | 3,119 | 1,102 | 2,500 | 2,299 |
| High school graduate, no college......... | 34,550 | 5,619 | 7,729 | 8,159 | 5,447 | 7,595 |
| Some college or associate degree........ | 36,338 | 11,870 | 6,670 | 9,690 | 3,685 | 4,423 |
| Bachelor's degree or higher............... | 55,995 | 40,470 | 3,577 | 8,801 | 1,243 | 1,904 |
| White....... | 106,704 | 46,599 | 14,949 | 22,058 | 11,073 | 12,024 |
| Less than a high school diploma......... | 7,713 | 571 | 2,313 | 841 | 2,209 | 1,779 |
| High school graduate, no college....... | 26,870 | 4,673 | 5,231 | 6,558 | 4,709 | 5,699 |
| Some college or associate degree...... | 28,348 | 9,606 | 4,767 | 7,659 | 3,124 | 3,192 |
| Bachelor's degree or higher.............. | 43,772 | 31,750 | 2,637 | 7,000 | 1,031 | 1,354 |
| Black....... | 16,556 | 5,577 | 3,861 | 3,369 | 1,022 | 2,727 |
| Less than a high school diploma......... | 1,009 | 54 | 431 | 133 | 123 | 268 |
| High school graduate, no college........ | 4,986 | 598 | 1,639 | 1,024 | 444 | 1,280 |
| Some college or associate degree...... | 5,271 | 1,440 | 1,283 | 1,319 | 339 | 890 |
| Bachelor's degree or higher.............. | 5,291 | 3,485 | 507 | 893 | 117 | 288 |
| Asian....... | 9,006 | 5,016 | 1,405 | 1,415 | 303 | 868 |
| Less than a high school diploma......... | 479 | 26 | 207 | 69 | 41 | 136 |
| High school graduate, no college........ | 1,468 | 178 | 554 | 286 | 102 | 347 |
| Some college or associate degree...... | 1,373 | 441 | 314 | 346 | 92 | 181 |
| Bachelor's degree or higher.............. | 5,687 | 4,371 | 330 | 714 | 68 | 204 |
| Hispanic [2]....... | 22,758 | 5,478 | 5,341 | 4,142 | 4,114 | 3,683 |
| Less than a high school diploma......... | 5,488 | 246 | 1,814 | 443 | 1,771 | 1,215 |
| High school graduate, no college........ | 7,145 | 820 | 1,884 | 1,417 | 1,466 | 1,558 |
| Some college or associate degree...... | 5,354 | 1,431 | 1,138 | 1,482 | 664 | 639 |
| Bachelor's degree or higher.............. | 4,770 | 2,981 | 505 | 801 | 212 | 271 |

[1] Includes other races, not shown separately. [2] Persons of Hispanic origin may be of any race.

Source: U.S. Bureau of Labor Statistics, Current Population Survey, unpublished data. See also <http://www.bls.gov/cps/>.

# Table 648. Employment by Industry, Sex, Race, and Hispanic Origin: 2000 to 2018

[In thousands (136,891 represents 136,891,000), except percent. Civilian noninstitutional population 16 years old and over. Annual average of monthly figures. Based on Current Population Survey; see text, Section 1, Population, and Appendix III]

| Industry | Total | | | | 2018, percent | | | |
|---|---|---|---|---|---|---|---|---|
| | 2000 | 2005 | 2010 | 2018 | Female | Black [1] | Asian [1] | Hispanic [2] |
| **Total employed**................ | **136,891** | **141,730** | **139,064** | **155,761** | **46.9** | **12.3** | **6.3** | **17.3** |
| Agriculture and related industries............ | 2,464 | 2,197 | 2,206 | 2,425 | 25.9 | 2.6 | 1.6 | 26.0 |
| Mining and related industries................. | 475 | 624 | 731 | 784 | 13.8 | 6.4 | 2.8 | 20.7 |
| Construction......................... | 9,931 | 11,197 | 9,077 | 11,181 | 9.9 | 6.2 | 2.0 | 30.7 |
| Manufacturing............................ | 19,644 | 16,253 | 14,081 | 15,560 | 29.2 | 10.4 | 6.9 | 16.7 |
| Durable goods........................ | 12,519 | 10,333 | 8,789 | 9,831 | 25.1 | 9.3 | 7.5 | 14.3 |
| Nondurable goods.................... | 7,125 | 5,919 | 5,293 | 5,729 | 36.2 | 12.4 | 5.9 | 20.8 |
| Wholesale trade........................ | 4,216 | 4,579 | 3,805 | 3,671 | 28.5 | 8.9 | 5.2 | 19.2 |
| Retail trade........................ | 15,763 | 16,825 | 15,934 | 16,599 | 48.3 | 12.6 | 5.6 | 17.7 |
| Transportation and utilities................. | 7,380 | 7,360 | 7,134 | 8,551 | 24.4 | 19.2 | 5.5 | 18.3 |
| Transportation and warehousing........... | 6,096 | 6,184 | 5,880 | 7,207 | 24.9 | 21.1 | 5.9 | 19.7 |
| Utilities........................ | 1,284 | 1,176 | 1,253 | 1,345 | 21.4 | 9.0 | 3.0 | 11.0 |
| Information......................... | 4,059 | 3,402 | 3,149 | 2,919 | 38.3 | 11.6 | 7.3 | 12.2 |
| Financial activities..................... | 9,374 | 10,203 | 9,350 | 10,649 | 52.6 | 10.2 | 7.5 | 12.6 |
| Finance and insurance.................... | 6,641 | 7,035 | 6,605 | 7,376 | 55.0 | 10.2 | 8.4 | 11.4 |
| Real estate and rental and leasing......... | 2,734 | 3,168 | 2,745 | 3,273 | 47.0 | 10.2 | 5.2 | 15.4 |
| Professional and business services......... | 13,649 | 14,294 | 15,253 | 18,950 | 41.5 | 9.9 | 9.0 | 15.9 |
| Professional and technical services........ | 8,266 | 8,584 | 9,115 | 12,105 | 42.2 | 6.6 | 12.1 | 8.7 |
| Management, administrative, and waste services................. | 5,383 | 5,709 | 6,138 | 6,845 | 40.3 | 15.7 | 3.4 | 28.8 |
| Education and health services............... | 26,188 | 29,174 | 32,062 | 35,043 | 74.4 | 15.1 | 6.4 | 12.9 |
| Educational services..................... | 11,255 | 12,264 | 13,155 | 13,910 | 68.3 | 11.5 | 5.2 | 11.9 |
| Health care and social assistance.......... | 14,933 | 16,910 | 18,907 | 21,133 | 78.4 | 17.5 | 7.1 | 13.6 |
| Hospitals........................ | 5,202 | 5,719 | 6,249 | 7,108 | 75.0 | 15.4 | 8.9 | 10.9 |
| Health services, except hospitals......... | 7,009 | 8,332 | 9,406 | 10,636 | 78.7 | 18.4 | 6.6 | 13.8 |
| Social assistance.................... | 2,722 | 2,860 | 3,252 | 3,389 | 84.2 | 19.5 | 4.8 | 18.6 |
| Leisure and hospitality.................... | 11,186 | 12,071 | 12,530 | 14,268 | 51.5 | 13.4 | 6.8 | 23.1 |
| Arts, entertainment, and recreation........ | 2,539 | 2,765 | 2,966 | 3,362 | 44.7 | 11.4 | 5.1 | 14.0 |
| Accommodation and food services......... | 8,647 | 9,306 | 9,564 | 10,905 | 53.6 | 14.0 | 7.4 | 25.9 |
| Other services........................ | 6,450 | 7,020 | 6,769 | 7,742 | 53.6 | 10.8 | 8.4 | 20.3 |
| Other services, except private households......................... | 5,731 | 6,208 | 6,102 | 6,965 | 49.1 | 11.0 | 9.0 | 17.7 |
| Private households.................... | 718 | 812 | 667 | 777 | 93.2 | 9.4 | 3.0 | 43.6 |
| Public administration.................... | 6,113 | 6,530 | 6,983 | 7,419 | 45.8 | 16.9 | 4.4 | 11.7 |

[1] Persons in this race group only. See footnote 2, Table 613. [2] Persons of Hispanic origin may be of any race.

Source: U.S. Bureau of Labor Statistics, CPS Tables, "Employed persons by detailed industry, sex, race, and Hispanic or Latino ethnicity," February 2019, and earlier releases, <http://www.bls.gov/cps/tables.htm>.

# Table 649. Unemployed Workers—Summary: 1990 to 2018

[In thousands (7,047 represents 7,047,000), except as indicated. For civilian noninstitutionalized population 16 years old and over. Annual averages of monthly figures. Revisions to population controls and other changes can affect the comparability of data over time. Based on the Current Population Survey; see text, Section 1 and Appendix III]

| Item | 1990 | 2000 | 2010 | 2013 | 2014 | 2015 | 2016 | 2017 | 2018 |
|---|---|---|---|---|---|---|---|---|---|
| **UNEMPLOYED** | | | | | | | | | |
| **Total** [1] | **7,047** | **5,692** | **14,825** | **11,460** | **9,617** | **8,296** | **7,751** | **6,982** | **6,314** |
| 16 to 19 years old | 1,212 | 1,081 | 1,528 | 1,327 | 1,106 | 966 | 925 | 827 | 759 |
| 20 to 24 years old | 1,299 | 1,022 | 2,329 | 1,997 | 1,747 | 1,501 | 1,286 | 1,127 | 1,048 |
| 25 to 34 years old | 1,995 | 1,207 | 3,386 | 2,504 | 2,224 | 1,905 | 1,797 | 1,647 | 1,450 |
| 35 to 44 years old | 1,328 | 1,133 | 2,703 | 1,913 | 1,539 | 1,351 | 1,258 | 1,143 | 1,003 |
| 45 to 54 years old | 723 | 762 | 2,769 | 1,945 | 1,507 | 1,259 | 1,189 | 1,060 | 938 |
| 55 to 64 years old | 386 | 355 | 1,660 | 1,340 | 1,107 | 978 | 941 | 835 | 789 |
| 65 years and over | 105 | 132 | 449 | 435 | 387 | 337 | 355 | 343 | 327 |
| Male | 3,906 | 2,975 | 8,626 | 6,314 | 5,190 | 4,490 | 4,187 | 3,743 | 3,398 |
| 16 to 19 years old | 667 | 599 | 863 | 746 | 605 | 531 | 512 | 457 | 422 |
| 20 to 24 years old | 715 | 547 | 1,398 | 1,143 | 996 | 865 | 742 | 667 | 596 |
| 25 to 34 years old | 1,092 | 602 | 1,993 | 1,381 | 1,185 | 1,030 | 966 | 884 | 763 |
| 35 to 44 years old | 711 | 557 | 1,534 | 1,015 | 813 | 695 | 644 | 575 | 515 |
| 45 to 54 years old | 413 | 398 | 1,614 | 1,039 | 782 | 649 | 602 | 537 | 490 |
| 55 to 64 years old | 249 | 189 | 962 | 741 | 600 | 536 | 528 | 445 | 435 |
| 65 years and over | 59 | 83 | 262 | 250 | 210 | 184 | 193 | 179 | 177 |
| Female | 3,140 | 2,717 | 6,199 | 5,146 | 4,426 | 3,807 | 3,564 | 3,239 | 2,916 |
| 16 to 19 years old | 544 | 483 | 665 | 581 | 501 | 435 | 413 | 371 | 338 |
| 20 to 24 years old | 584 | 475 | 931 | 854 | 751 | 636 | 545 | 460 | 452 |
| 25 to 34 years old | 902 | 604 | 1,392 | 1,123 | 1,039 | 874 | 832 | 763 | 687 |
| 35 to 44 years old | 617 | 577 | 1,169 | 898 | 726 | 656 | 614 | 568 | 488 |
| 45 to 54 years old | 310 | 364 | 1,156 | 906 | 725 | 610 | 586 | 523 | 448 |
| 55 to 64 years old | 137 | 165 | 698 | 600 | 507 | 442 | 413 | 389 | 354 |
| 65 years and over | 46 | 50 | 187 | 185 | 177 | 153 | 162 | 164 | 150 |
| White [2] | 5,186 | 4,121 | 10,916 | 8,033 | 6,540 | 5,662 | 5,345 | 4,765 | 4,354 |
| Black [2,3] | 1,565 | 1,241 | 2,852 | 2,429 | 2,141 | 1,846 | 1,655 | 1,501 | 1,322 |
| Asian [2,3] | (NA) | 227 | 543 | 448 | 436 | 347 | 349 | 333 | 304 |
| Hispanic [4] | 876 | 954 | 2,843 | 2,257 | 1,878 | 1,726 | 1,548 | 1,401 | 1,323 |
| **UNEMPLOYMENT RATE** [5] (percent) | | | | | | | | | |
| **Total** [1] | **5.6** | **4.0** | **9.6** | **7.4** | **6.2** | **5.3** | **4.9** | **4.4** | **3.9** |
| 16 to 19 years old | 15.5 | 13.1 | 25.9 | 22.9 | 19.6 | 16.9 | 15.7 | 14.0 | 12.9 |
| 20 to 24 years old | 8.8 | 7.2 | 15.5 | 12.8 | 11.2 | 9.7 | 8.4 | 7.4 | 6.9 |
| 25 to 34 years old | 5.6 | 3.7 | 10.1 | 7.4 | 6.5 | 5.5 | 5.1 | 4.6 | 3.9 |
| 35 to 44 years old | 4.1 | 3.0 | 8.1 | 5.9 | 4.7 | 4.1 | 3.8 | 3.5 | 3.0 |
| 45 to 54 years old | 3.6 | 2.5 | 7.7 | 5.6 | 4.4 | 3.7 | 3.5 | 3.2 | 2.8 |
| 55 to 64 years old | 3.3 | 2.5 | 7.1 | 5.3 | 4.3 | 3.8 | 3.6 | 3.1 | 2.9 |
| 65 years and over | 3.0 | 3.1 | 6.7 | 5.4 | 4.6 | 3.8 | 3.8 | 3.6 | 3.3 |
| Male | 5.7 | 3.9 | 10.5 | 7.6 | 6.3 | 5.4 | 4.9 | 4.4 | 3.9 |
| 16 to 19 years old | 16.3 | 14.0 | 28.8 | 25.5 | 21.4 | 18.4 | 17.1 | 15.5 | 14.5 |
| 20 to 24 years old | 9.1 | 7.3 | 17.8 | 14.0 | 12.2 | 10.8 | 9.3 | 8.4 | 7.7 |
| 25 to 34 years old | 5.5 | 3.4 | 10.9 | 7.6 | 6.4 | 5.5 | 5.0 | 4.6 | 3.9 |
| 35 to 44 years old | 4.1 | 2.8 | 8.5 | 5.8 | 4.6 | 4.0 | 3.6 | 3.2 | 2.8 |
| 45 to 54 years old | 3.7 | 2.4 | 8.6 | 5.7 | 4.4 | 3.6 | 3.4 | 3.0 | 2.8 |
| 55 to 64 years old | 3.8 | 2.4 | 8.0 | 5.6 | 4.5 | 3.9 | 3.8 | 3.1 | 3.0 |
| 65 years and over | 3.0 | 3.3 | 7.1 | 5.5 | 4.6 | 3.8 | 3.8 | 3.4 | 3.2 |
| Female | 5.5 | 4.1 | 8.6 | 7.1 | 6.1 | 5.2 | 4.8 | 4.3 | 3.8 |
| 16 to 19 years old | 14.7 | 12.1 | 22.8 | 20.3 | 17.7 | 15.5 | 14.3 | 12.5 | 11.3 |
| 20 to 24 years old | 8.5 | 7.1 | 13.0 | 11.5 | 10.1 | 8.5 | 7.4 | 6.3 | 6.2 |
| 25 to 34 years old | 5.6 | 4.1 | 9.1 | 7.3 | 6.6 | 5.5 | 5.1 | 4.6 | 4.0 |
| 35 to 44 years old | 4.2 | 3.3 | 7.7 | 6.0 | 4.9 | 4.4 | 4.1 | 3.7 | 3.2 |
| 45 to 54 years old | 3.4 | 2.5 | 6.8 | 5.5 | 4.5 | 3.8 | 3.7 | 3.3 | 2.8 |
| 55 to 64 years old | 2.8 | 2.5 | 6.2 | 5.0 | 4.2 | 3.6 | 3.3 | 3.1 | 2.7 |
| 65 years and over | 3.1 | 2.7 | 6.2 | 5.1 | 4.7 | 3.9 | 3.9 | 3.8 | 3.3 |
| White [2] | 4.8 | 3.5 | 8.7 | 6.5 | 5.3 | 4.6 | 4.3 | 3.8 | 3.5 |
| Black [2] | 11.4 | 7.6 | 16.0 | 13.1 | 11.3 | 9.6 | 8.4 | 7.5 | 6.5 |
| Asian [2,3] | (NA) | 3.6 | 7.5 | 5.2 | 5.0 | 3.8 | 3.6 | 3.4 | 3.0 |
| Hispanic [4] | 8.2 | 5.7 | 12.5 | 9.1 | 7.4 | 6.6 | 5.8 | 5.1 | 4.7 |
| **PERCENT WITHOUT WORK FOR—** | | | | | | | | | |
| Fewer than 5 weeks | 46.3 | 44.9 | 18.7 | 22.5 | 25.7 | 28.9 | 30.5 | 32.5 | 34.4 |
| 5 to 14 weeks | 32.0 | 31.9 | 22.0 | 24.1 | 25.3 | 27.7 | 28.7 | 28.8 | 29.7 |
| 15 weeks and over | 21.6 | 23.2 | 59.3 | 53.4 | 49.0 | 43.3 | 40.8 | 38.7 | 35.9 |
| 15 to 26 weeks | 11.7 | 11.8 | 16.0 | 15.8 | 15.6 | 15.3 | 14.9 | 14.6 | 14.5 |
| 27 weeks and over | 10.0 | 11.4 | 43.3 | 37.6 | 33.5 | 28.1 | 25.9 | 24.2 | 21.4 |
| Unemployment duration, average (weeks) [6] | 12.0 | 12.6 | 33.0 | 36.5 | 33.7 | 29.2 | 27.5 | 25.0 | 22.7 |

NA Not available. [1] Includes other races not shown separately. [2] For persons reporting this race group only. [3] Prior to 2003, includes Pacific Islanders. [4] Persons of Hispanic or Latino origin may be of any race. [5] Unemployed as percent of civilian labor force in specified group. [6] Beginning 2011, the CPS increased the maximum duration of unemployment that respondents could report from 2 years to 5 years. For more information, see <http://www.bls.gov/cps/duration.htm>.

Source: U.S. Bureau of Labor Statistics, "Labor Force Statistics from the Current Population Survey," <http://www.bls.gov/cps>, accessed April 2019.

# Table 650. Unemployed Jobseekers' Job Search Methods: 2018

[6,314 represents 6,314,000. For the civilian noninstitutionalized population 16 years old and over. Annual averages of monthly data. Based on the Current Population Survey; see text, Section 1 and Appendix III]

| Characteristic | Population (1,000) | | Jobseekers' job search methods (percent) | | | | | | | Average number of methods used |
|---|---|---|---|---|---|---|---|---|---|---|
| | Total unemployed | Total jobseekers [1] | Contact employer directly | Sent out a resume or filled out applications | Placed or answered ads | Friends or relatives | Public employment agency | Private employment agency | Other activities | |
| **Total, 16 years and over [2]** | **6,314** | **5,461** | **50.2** | **55.0** | **14.1** | **23.8** | **14.5** | **8.1** | **13.5** | **1.8** |
| AGE | | | | | | | | | | |
| 16 to 19 years old | 759 | 710 | 48.3 | 59.6 | 10.3 | 18.0 | 6.8 | 3.0 | 9.4 | 1.6 |
| 20 to 24 years old | 1,048 | 959 | 52.7 | 57.1 | 14.4 | 21.3 | 11.9 | 6.4 | 13.1 | 1.8 |
| 25 to 34 years old | 1,450 | 1,274 | 50.5 | 56.1 | 13.9 | 22.8 | 15.1 | 8.5 | 12.5 | 1.8 |
| 35 to 44 years old | 1,003 | 840 | 49.5 | 54.3 | 14.0 | 25.7 | 19.0 | 9.8 | 13.7 | 1.9 |
| 45 to 54 years old | 938 | 786 | 51.1 | 54.5 | 15.6 | 27.5 | 17.2 | 10.5 | 16.0 | 1.9 |
| 55 to 64 years old | 789 | 648 | 49.3 | 49.5 | 16.0 | 28.7 | 17.3 | 10.5 | 16.2 | 1.9 |
| 65 years old and over | 327 | 245 | 47.1 | 46.2 | 15.0 | 24.0 | 12.3 | 8.3 | 15.7 | 1.7 |
| SEX | | | | | | | | | | |
| Male, total | 3,398 | 2,899 | 51.7 | 52.6 | 14.3 | 25.1 | 14.8 | 8.3 | 13.6 | 1.8 |
| 16 to 19 years old | 422 | 395 | 47.7 | 58.0 | 9.9 | 18.4 | 6.8 | 2.9 | 8.4 | 1.5 |
| 20 to 24 years old | 596 | 544 | 52.6 | 54.5 | 14.9 | 23.7 | 11.9 | 7.1 | 12.1 | 1.8 |
| 25 to 34 years old | 763 | 651 | 52.3 | 53.5 | 14.3 | 26.1 | 15.3 | 8.7 | 13.1 | 1.8 |
| 35 to 44 years old | 515 | 420 | 52.8 | 51.3 | 14.2 | 27.1 | 21.1 | 10.4 | 13.8 | 1.9 |
| 45 to 54 years old | 490 | 403 | 53.8 | 52.6 | 16.9 | 27.0 | 18.4 | 10.1 | 16.8 | 2.0 |
| 55 to 64 years old | 435 | 352 | 51.4 | 46.3 | 14.8 | 29.2 | 17.1 | 10.7 | 17.8 | 1.9 |
| 65 years old and over | 177 | 133 | 48.5 | 44.5 | 15.6 | 23.0 | 11.0 | 8.0 | 16.6 | 1.7 |
| Female, total | 2,916 | 2,562 | 48.6 | 57.8 | 13.9 | 22.3 | 14.2 | 8.0 | 13.3 | 1.8 |
| 16 to 19 years old | 338 | 316 | 49.1 | 61.6 | 10.7 | 17.5 | 6.8 | 3.1 | 10.5 | 1.6 |
| 20 to 24 years old | 452 | 414 | 52.8 | 60.6 | 13.9 | 18.3 | 12.0 | 5.5 | 14.5 | 1.8 |
| 25 to 34 years old | 687 | 623 | 48.7 | 58.8 | 13.5 | 19.4 | 15.0 | 8.2 | 11.9 | 1.8 |
| 35 to 44 years old | 488 | 420 | 46.1 | 57.4 | 13.8 | 24.3 | 17.0 | 9.3 | 13.6 | 1.8 |
| 45 to 54 years old | 448 | 383 | 48.2 | 56.4 | 14.2 | 28.0 | 16.0 | 11.0 | 15.1 | 1.9 |
| 55 to 64 years old | 354 | 295 | 46.9 | 53.3 | 17.4 | 28.1 | 17.6 | 10.3 | 14.2 | 1.9 |
| 65 years old and over | 150 | 112 | 45.5 | 48.3 | 14.3 | 25.2 | 13.8 | 8.7 | 14.5 | 1.7 |
| RACE/ETHNICITY | | | | | | | | | | |
| White [3] | 4,354 | 3,672 | 50.6 | 54.3 | 14.4 | 24.4 | 13.4 | 8.0 | 14.0 | 1.8 |
| Male | 2,380 | 1,979 | 52.2 | 52.4 | 14.7 | 26.1 | 14.0 | 8.3 | 14.3 | 1.8 |
| Female | 1,973 | 1,693 | 48.7 | 56.5 | 14.0 | 22.5 | 12.7 | 7.6 | 13.6 | 1.8 |
| Black [3] | 1,322 | 1,214 | 49.9 | 54.4 | 13.0 | 22.0 | 19.4 | 8.7 | 11.8 | 1.8 |
| Male | 676 | 616 | 51.8 | 49.1 | 12.8 | 22.4 | 18.9 | 7.9 | 11.0 | 1.7 |
| Female | 646 | 598 | 48.0 | 59.8 | 13.2 | 21.5 | 19.9 | 9.6 | 12.6 | 1.9 |
| Asian [3] | 304 | 281 | 49.8 | 60.1 | 13.9 | 27.6 | 10.3 | 10.3 | 15.4 | 1.9 |
| Male | 159 | 145 | 51.4 | 58.4 | 14.0 | 27.3 | 11.0 | 11.2 | 16.0 | 1.9 |
| Female | 146 | 135 | 48.0 | 61.9 | 13.7 | 27.9 | 9.5 | 9.3 | 14.8 | 1.9 |
| Hispanic [4] | 1,323 | 1,117 | 49.8 | 52.0 | 11.8 | 29.2 | 13.5 | 7.4 | 10.6 | 1.7 |
| Male | 695 | 569 | 52.4 | 49.1 | 11.8 | 31.4 | 14.7 | 7.7 | 11.0 | 1.8 |
| Female | 628 | 547 | 47.0 | 55.1 | 11.9 | 26.9 | 12.2 | 7.2 | 10.2 | 1.7 |

[1] Excludes persons on temporary layoff. [2] Includes other races not shown separately. [3] Data for this race group only. [4] Persons of Hispanic or Latino origin may be of any race.

Source: U.S. Bureau of Labor Statistics, CPS Tables, "Unemployed jobseekers by sex, age, race, Hispanic or Latino ethnicity, and active jobsearch methods used," February 2019, <http://www.bls.gov/cps/tables.htm>.

# Table 651. Unemployed Persons by Sex and Reason: 2000 to 2018

[In thousands (2,975 represents 2,975,000). For civilian noninstitutionalized population 16 years old and over. Annual averages of monthly figures. Revisions to population controls and other changes affect comparability of data over time. Based on Current Population Survey; see text, Section 1 and Appendix III]

| Sex and reason | 2000 | 2008 | 2009 | 2010 | 2011 | 2012 | 2013 | 2014 | 2015 | 2016 | 2017 | 2018 |
|---|---|---|---|---|---|---|---|---|---|---|---|---|
| **Male, total** | **2,975** | **5,033** | **8,453** | **8,626** | **7,684** | **6,771** | **6,314** | **5,190** | **4,490** | **4,187** | **3,743** | **3,398** |
| Job losers [1] | 1,516 | 3,055 | 5,967 | 5,919 | 4,968 | 4,103 | 3,690 | 2,926 | 2,441 | 2,232 | 2,038 | 1,772 |
| Job leavers | 387 | 458 | 438 | 457 | 494 | 487 | 465 | 416 | 397 | 414 | 382 | 413 |
| Reentrants | 854 | 1128 | 1,504 | 1,608 | 1,545 | 1481 | 1,491 | 1,279 | 1,178 | 1108 | 961 | 896 |
| New entrants | 217 | 393 | 545 | 641 | 678 | 699 | 668 | 569 | 474 | 433 | 362 | 317 |
| **Female, total** | **2,717** | **3,891** | **5,811** | **6,199** | **6,063** | **5,734** | **5,146** | **4,426** | **3,807** | **3,564** | **3,239** | **2,916** |
| Job losers [1] | 1,001 | 1,735 | 3,193 | 3,331 | 3,139 | 2,774 | 2,383 | 1,952 | 1,622 | 1,508 | 1,397 | 1,218 |
| Job leavers | 393 | 438 | 444 | 432 | 463 | 480 | 467 | 408 | 423 | 444 | 396 | 381 |
| Reentrants | 1,107 | 1,345 | 1,683 | 1,858 | 1,857 | 1,864 | 1,716 | 1,550 | 1,357 | 1,222 | 1,118 | 1,032 |
| New entrants | 217 | 374 | 491 | 579 | 605 | 617 | 579 | 517 | 405 | 390 | 328 | 285 |

[1] Includes persons who completed temporary jobs.

Source: U.S. Bureau of Labor Statistics, CPS Tables, "Unemployed jobseekers by sex, reason for unemployment, and active jobsearch methods used," February 2019, and earlier releases, <http://www.bls.gov/cps/tables.htm>.

## Table 652. Unemployment Rates by Industry and by Sex: 2010 to 2018

[In percent. Civilian noninstitutionalized population 16 years old and over. Annual averages of monthly figures. Rate represents unemployment as a percent of labor force in each specified group. Based on Current Population Survey; see text, Section 1 and Appendix III. See also headnote, Table 631, regarding industries]

| Industry | Total | | | | Male | | Female | |
|---|---|---|---|---|---|---|---|---|
| | 2010 | 2016 | 2017 | 2018 | 2017 | 2018 | 2017 | 2018 |
| **All employed** [1] | **9.6** | **4.9** | **4.4** | **3.9** | **4.4** | **3.9** | **4.3** | **3.8** |
| Wage and salary workers: | | | | | | | | |
| Agriculture and related industries | 13.9 | 8.3 | 7.2 | 7.2 | 5.7 | 6.4 | 11.7 | 9.8 |
| Mining, quarrying, and oil and gas extraction | 9.4 | 8.0 | 4.1 | 3.4 | 4.0 | 3.5 | 4.8 | 3.2 |
| Construction | 20.6 | 6.3 | 6.0 | 5.1 | 6.0 | 5.2 | 6.0 | 4.2 |
| Manufacturing | 10.6 | 4.3 | 3.6 | 3.3 | 3.3 | 3.0 | 4.3 | 3.9 |
| Wholesale trade | 7.3 | 3.6 | 3.2 | 3.1 | 2.8 | 3.1 | 4.3 | 3.0 |
| Retail trade | 10.0 | 5.3 | 4.9 | 4.6 | 4.5 | 4.2 | 5.4 | 5.0 |
| Transportation and utilities | 8.4 | 4.2 | 4.1 | 3.4 | 3.7 | 3.2 | 5.2 | 3.8 |
| Transportation and warehousing | 9.4 | 4.4 | 4.4 | 3.6 | 4.1 | 3.6 | 5.3 | 3.9 |
| Utilities | 3.4 | 3.1 | 2.6 | 1.8 | 2.1 | 1.3 | 4.5 | 3.3 |
| Information | 9.7 | 4.6 | 4.5 | 3.7 | 4.4 | 4.0 | 4.6 | 3.1 |
| Telecommunications | 9.2 | 3.3 | 4.5 | 2.7 | 4.2 | 3.0 | 5.1 | 2.0 |
| Financial activities | 6.9 | 2.7 | 2.4 | 2.2 | 2.7 | 2.3 | 2.2 | 2.0 |
| Finance and insurance | 6.6 | 2.4 | 2.3 | 1.9 | 2.6 | 1.9 | 2.1 | 1.9 |
| Real estate and rental and leasing | 7.6 | 3.6 | 2.8 | 2.8 | 3.0 | 3.1 | 2.5 | 2.3 |
| Professional and business services | 10.8 | 5.1 | 4.5 | 3.9 | 4.3 | 3.7 | 4.9 | 4.2 |
| Professional and technical services | 6.5 | 2.8 | 2.8 | 2.3 | 2.5 | 2.1 | 3.2 | 2.7 |
| Management, administrative, and waste services | 16.8 | 8.6 | 7.4 | 6.7 | 7.1 | 6.6 | 7.8 | 6.8 |
| Education and health services | 5.8 | 3.3 | 3.0 | 2.6 | 2.9 | 2.4 | 3.1 | 2.7 |
| Educational services | 6.4 | 4.1 | 3.5 | 3.4 | 3.5 | 3.0 | 3.5 | 3.6 |
| Health care and social assistance | 5.6 | 3.1 | 2.9 | 2.4 | 2.6 | 2.1 | 3.0 | 2.5 |
| Leisure and hospitality | 12.2 | 6.8 | 6.1 | 5.7 | 6.0 | 5.8 | 6.1 | 5.6 |
| Arts, entertainment, and recreation | 11.6 | 6.3 | 5.6 | 5.6 | 5.9 | 6.0 | 5.3 | 5.1 |
| Accommodation and food services | 12.3 | 6.9 | 6.2 | 5.7 | 6.1 | 5.7 | 6.3 | 5.7 |
| Other services | 8.5 | 4.4 | 3.8 | 3.3 | 4.2 | 3.2 | 3.4 | 3.5 |
| Government workers | 4.4 | 2.7 | 2.5 | 2.3 | 2.4 | 2.3 | 2.5 | 2.4 |

[1] Includes a small amount of persons whose last job was in the Armed Forces.

Source: U.S. Bureau of Labor Statistics, CPS Tables, "Unemployed persons by industry, class of worker, and sex," February 2019, and earlier releases, <http://www.bls.gov/cps/tables.htm>.

## Table 653. Unemployment by Occupation: 2010 to 2018

[14,825 represents 14,825,000. Civilian noninstitutionalized population 16 years old and over. Annual averages of monthly data. Rate represents unemployment as a percent of the labor force for each specified group. Based on Current Population Survey; see text, Section 1 and Appendix III. See also headnote, Table 631, regarding occupations]

| Occupation | Number unemployed (1,000) | | | | Unemployment rate | | | | |
|---|---|---|---|---|---|---|---|---|---|
| | | | | | | | 2018 | | |
| | 2010 | 2016 | 2017 | 2018 | 2010 | 2017 | Total | Male | Female |
| **Total** [1] | **14,825** | **7,751** | **6,982** | **6,314** | **9.6** | **4.4** | **3.9** | **3.9** | **3.8** |
| Management, professional, and related occupations | 2,566 | 1,513 | 1,383 | 1,346 | 4.7 | 2.2 | 2.1 | 2.0 | 2.2 |
| Management, business, and financial operations | 1,117 | 629 | 558 | 523 | 5.1 | 2.2 | 2.0 | 1.9 | 2.1 |
| Management | 762 | 404 | 341 | 328 | 4.8 | 1.9 | 1.8 | 1.7 | 1.8 |
| Business and financial operations | 355 | 225 | 217 | 196 | 5.6 | 2.8 | 2.5 | 2.3 | 2.7 |
| Professional and related occupations | 1,449 | 884 | 825 | 822 | 4.5 | 2.3 | 2.2 | 2.1 | 2.3 |
| Computer and mathematical | 195 | 120 | 119 | 113 | 5.2 | 2.4 | 2.1 | 2.1 | 2.3 |
| Architecture and engineering | 173 | 78 | 79 | 59 | 6.2 | 2.4 | 1.8 | 1.7 | 2.2 |
| Life, physical, and social science | 69 | 34 | 36 | 31 | 4.6 | 2.4 | 2.0 | 1.7 | 2.4 |
| Community and social services | 114 | 70 | 48 | 62 | 4.6 | 1.8 | 2.2 | 2.6 | 2.1 |
| Legal | 48 | 23 | 27 | 31 | 2.7 | 1.4 | 1.6 | 1.7 | 1.5 |
| Education, training, and library | 379 | 271 | 251 | 286 | 4.2 | 2.7 | 3.0 | 2.5 | 3.2 |
| Arts, design, entertainment, sports, and media | 269 | 155 | 135 | 107 | 8.9 | 4.0 | 3.1 | 3.1 | 3.0 |
| Healthcare practitioner and technical | 203 | 133 | 129 | 133 | 2.5 | 1.4 | 1.4 | 1.2 | 1.4 |
| Service occupations | 2,819 | 1,655 | 1,530 | 1,353 | 10.3 | 5.4 | 4.8 | 5.1 | 4.6 |
| Healthcare support | 276 | 168 | 165 | 129 | 7.6 | 4.5 | 3.4 | 3.0 | 3.5 |
| Protective service | 207 | 119 | 106 | 89 | 5.9 | 3.3 | 2.7 | 2.6 | 3.0 |
| Food preparation and serving-related | 1,079 | 627 | 572 | 530 | 12.4 | 6.4 | 6.1 | 6.7 | 5.6 |
| Building and grounds cleaning and maintenance | 780 | 430 | 387 | 338 | 12.8 | 6.2 | 5.5 | 5.8 | 4.9 |
| Personal care and service | 477 | 312 | 300 | 266 | 8.7 | 4.8 | 4.3 | 3.9 | 4.4 |
| Sales and office occupations | 3,315 | 1,623 | 1,443 | 1,337 | 9.0 | 4.1 | 3.8 | 3.6 | 4.0 |
| Sales and related | 1,596 | 799 | 699 | 669 | 9.4 | 4.2 | 4.1 | 3.3 | 4.8 |
| Office and administrative support | 1,719 | 825 | 744 | 668 | 8.7 | 4.0 | 3.6 | 4.2 | 3.4 |
| Natural resources, construction, and maintenance | 2,504 | 953 | 903 | 780 | 16.1 | 6.0 | 5.1 | 4.9 | 8.2 |
| Farming, fishing, and forestry | 193 | 127 | 113 | 114 | 16.3 | 8.7 | 9.2 | 8.0 | 12.6 |
| Construction and extraction | 1,809 | 618 | 611 | 530 | 20.1 | 7.1 | 6.0 | 6.0 | 6.4 |
| Installation, maintenance, and repair | 503 | 207 | 179 | 136 | 9.3 | 3.5 | 2.6 | 2.6 | 4.1 |
| Production, transportation, and material moving | 2,365 | 1,160 | 1,014 | 881 | 12.8 | 5.4 | 4.5 | 4.3 | 5.3 |
| Production | 1,206 | 516 | 435 | 361 | 13.1 | 4.9 | 4.0 | 3.7 | 4.8 |
| Transportation and material moving | 1,159 | 644 | 579 | 520 | 12.4 | 5.8 | 5.0 | 4.8 | 5.9 |

[1] Includes a small amount of persons whose last job was in the Armed Forces.

Source: U.S. Bureau of Labor Statistics, CPS Tables, "Unemployed persons by occupation and sex," February 2019, and earlier releases, <http://www.bls.gov/cps/tables.htm>.

## Table 654. Unemployed and Unemployment Rates by Educational Attainment, Sex, Race, and Hispanic Origin: 2000 to 2018

[3,589 represents 3,589,000. Annual averages of monthly figures. Civilian noninstitutionalized population 25 years old and over. See Table 618 for civilian labor force and participation rate data. Revisions to population controls and other changes can affect the comparability of data over time. Based on Current Population Survey; see text, Section 1 and Appendix III]

| Year, sex, and race/ethnicity | Unemployed (1,000) | | | | | Unemployment rate [1] | | | | |
|---|---|---|---|---|---|---|---|---|---|---|
| | Total | Less than a high school diploma | High school graduate, no college | Some college or associate's degree | Bachelor's degree or higher | Total | Less than a high school diploma | High school graduate, no college | Some college or associate's degree | Bachelor's degree or higher |
| Total: [2] | | | | | | | | | | |
| 2000 | 3,589 | 791 | 1,298 | 890 | 610 | 3.0 | 6.3 | 3.4 | 2.7 | 1.7 |
| 2010 | 10,968 | 1,765 | 3,943 | 3,093 | 2,167 | 8.2 | 14.9 | 10.3 | 8.4 | 4.7 |
| 2018 | 4,507 | 576 | 1,461 | 1,248 | 1,222 | 3.2 | 5.6 | 4.1 | 3.3 | 2.1 |
| Male: | | | | | | | | | | |
| 2000 | 1,829 | 411 | 682 | 427 | 309 | 2.8 | 5.4 | 3.4 | 2.6 | 1.5 |
| 2010 | 6,365 | 1,137 | 2,452 | 1,646 | 1,130 | 8.9 | 15.0 | 11.3 | 9.0 | 4.8 |
| 2018 | 2,380 | 336 | 850 | 590 | 604 | 3.2 | 5.1 | 4.0 | 3.1 | 2.1 |
| Female: | | | | | | | | | | |
| 2000 | 1,760 | 380 | 616 | 463 | 301 | 3.2 | 7.8 | 3.5 | 2.8 | 1.8 |
| 2010 | 4,603 | 628 | 1,492 | 1,447 | 1,037 | 7.4 | 14.6 | 9.0 | 7.8 | 4.7 |
| 2018 | 2,127 | 240 | 610 | 658 | 619 | 3.2 | 6.4 | 4.1 | 3.5 | 2.2 |
| White: [3] | | | | | | | | | | |
| 2000 | 2,644 | 564 | 924 | 667 | 489 | 2.6 | 5.6 | 2.9 | 2.4 | 1.6 |
| 2010 | 8,174 | 1,337 | 2,937 | 2,278 | 1,622 | 7.5 | 13.9 | 9.5 | 7.6 | 4.3 |
| 2018 | 3,152 | 413 | 989 | 853 | 897 | 2.9 | 5.1 | 3.5 | 2.9 | 2.0 |
| Black: [3] | | | | | | | | | | |
| 2000 | 731 | 179 | 315 | 169 | 68 | 5.4 | 10.7 | 6.4 | 4.0 | 2.5 |
| 2010 | 2,022 | 321 | 795 | 614 | 292 | 13 4 | 22.5 | 15.8 | 12.4 | 7.9 |
| 2018 | 922 | 117 | 357 | 287 | 161 | 5.3 | 10.4 | 6.7 | 5.2 | 2.9 |
| Asian: [3, 4] | | | | | | | | | | |
| 2000 | 146 | 28 | 34 | 35 | 49 | 2.7 | 5.7 | 3.0 | 3.2 | 1.8 |
| 2010 | 446 | 54 | 95 | 92 | 205 | 6.8 | 11.1 | 7.6 | 8.1 | 5.5 |
| 2018 | 228 | 14 | 36 | 39 | 139 | 2.5 | 2.9 | 2.4 | 2.8 | 2.4 |
| Hispanic: [5] | | | | | | | | | | |
| 2000 | 569 | 297 | 150 | 85 | 38 | 4.4 | 6.2 | 3.9 | 3.2 | 2.2 |
| 2010 | 2,041 | 787 | 674 | 399 | 182 | 10.8 | 13.2 | 11.5 | 9.7 | 6.0 |
| 2018 | 899 | 265 | 293 | 200 | 141 | 3.8 | 4.6 | 3.9 | 3.6 | 2.9 |

[1] Unemployed as percent of the civilian labor force. [2] Includes other races, not shown separately. [3] Beginning 2003, data are for persons in this race group only; 2000 data reflect the primary race persons identified with. [4] 2000 data include Pacific Islanders. [5] Persons of Hispanic origin may be of any race.

Source: U.S. Bureau of Labor Statistics, CPS Tables, "Employment status of the civilian noninstitutional population 25 years and over by educational attainment, sex, race, and Hispanic or Latino ethnicity," February 2019, and earlier releases, <http://www.bls.gov/cps/tables.htm>.

## Table 655. Unemployed Persons by Reason for Unemployment and Duration: 2018

[6,314 represents 6,314,000. Annual averages of monthly data. Based on Current Population Survey; see text, Section 1 and Appendix III]

| Age, sex, and reason | Total unemployed (1,000) | Percent distribution by duration | | | | |
|---|---|---|---|---|---|---|
| | | Less than 5 weeks | 5 to 14 weeks | 15 weeks and over | | |
| | | | | Total | 15 to 26 weeks | 27 weeks or longer |
| **Total 16 years old and over** | **6,314** | **34.4** | **29.7** | **35.9** | **14.5** | **21.4** |
| 16 to 19 years old | 759 | 47.2 | 32.5 | 20.4 | 11.1 | 9.3 |
| **Males, 20 years old and over** | **2,976** | **31.7** | **29.0** | **39.4** | **15.9** | **23.5** |
| Job losers and persons who completed temporary jobs | 1,706 | 34.3 | 29.9 | 35.8 | 16.2 | 19.6 |
| On temporary layoff | 472 | 54.0 | 30.9 | 15.1 | 10.6 | 4.4 |
| Not on temporary layoff | 1,234 | 26.8 | 29.5 | 43.7 | 18.3 | 25.4 |
| Permanent job losers | 826 | 24.5 | 29.3 | 46.2 | 18.8 | 27.4 |
| Persons who completed temporary jobs | 408 | 31.4 | 29.9 | 38.7 | 17.4 | 21.4 |
| Job leavers | 381 | 37.9 | 31.1 | 31.1 | 13.0 | 18.0 |
| Reentrants | 759 | 23.7 | 26.7 | 49.7 | 16.7 | 32.9 |
| New entrants | 130 | 25.2 | 24.5 | 50.3 | 14.4 | 35.9 |
| **Females, 20 years old and over** | **2,578** | **33.7** | **29.7** | **36.5** | **14.0** | **22.5** |
| Job losers and persons who completed temporary jobs | 1,173 | 37.8 | 30.2 | 32.0 | 13.1 | 18.9 |
| On temporary layoff | 332 | 59.6 | 30.8 | 9.6 | 6.7 | 3.0 |
| Not on temporary layoff | 841 | 29.2 | 30.0 | 40.8 | 15.7 | 25.1 |
| Permanent job losers | 595 | 27.4 | 30.2 | 42.4 | 16.0 | 26.4 |
| Persons who completed temporary jobs | 246 | 33.6 | 29.4 | 37.0 | 15.0 | 22.0 |
| Job leavers | 361 | 35.2 | 34.5 | 30.3 | 14.3 | 15.9 |
| Reentrants | 912 | 29.2 | 26.9 | 44.0 | 14.8 | 29.2 |
| New entrants | 132 | 25.2 | 32.6 | 42.2 | 15.5 | 26.7 |

NA Not available.

Source: U.S. Bureau of Labor Statistics, CPS Tables, "Unemployed persons by reason for unemployment, sex, age, and duration of unemployment," <http://www.bls.gov/cps/tables.htm>, accessed March 2019.

# Table 656. Total Unemployed and Insured Unemployed by State: 2000 to 2018

[5,692 represents 5,692,000. Civilian noninstitutionalized population 16 years old and over. Annual averages of monthly figures, except as noted. State total unemployment estimates come from the Local Area Unemployment Statistics program, while U.S. totals come from the Current Population Survey; see text, Section 1 and Appendix III. U.S. totals derived by independent population controls; therefore, state data may not add to U.S. totals. Unemployment data are based on population controls from Census 2010]

| State | Total unemployed | | | | | | | | Insured unemployed [2,4] | | | |
|-------|------------------|---|---|---|---|---|---|---|---|---|---|---|
| | Number (1,000) | | | | Percent [1] | | | | Number (1,000) | | Percent [3] | |
| | 2000 | 2010 | 2017 | 2018 | 2000 | 2010 | 2017 | 2018 | 2010 | 2018 | 2010 | 2018 |
| **United States**.......... | **5,692** | **14,825** | **6,982** | **6,314** | **4.0** | **9.6** | **4.4** | **3.9** | **4,487** | **1,755** | **3.6** | **1.2** |
| Alabama................. | 98 | 231 | 97 | 86 | 4.6 | 10.5 | 4.4 | 3.9 | 53 | 17 | 3.0 | 0.9 |
| Alaska................. | 20 | 28 | 25 | 24 | 6.4 | 7.9 | 7.0 | 6.6 | 14 | 7 | 4.6 | 2.3 |
| Arizona................. | 99 | 320 | 163 | 166 | 4.0 | 10.4 | 4.9 | 4.8 | 79 | 25 | 3.5 | 0.9 |
| Arkansas............... | 54 | 111 | 50 | 50 | 4.3 | 8.2 | 3.7 | 3.7 | 44 | 12 | 4.0 | 1.0 |
| California.............. | 835 | 2,244 | 920 | 815 | 4.9 | 12.2 | 4.8 | 4.2 | 655 | 329 | 4.6 | 1.9 |
| Colorado............... | 65 | 238 | 81 | 102 | 2.8 | 8.7 | 2.7 | 3.3 | 64 | 20 | 3.0 | 0.8 |
| Connecticut............ | 42 | 174 | 89 | 78 | 2.4 | 9.1 | 4.7 | 4.1 | 67 | 35 | 4.3 | 2.1 |
| Delaware............... | 15 | 37 | 21 | 18 | 3.7 | 8.4 | 4.5 | 3.8 | 13 | 5 | 3.4 | 1.2 |
| District of Columbia..... | 17 | 33 | 24 | 22 | 5.6 | 9.4 | 6.1 | 5.6 | 5 | 4 | 1.1 | 0.8 |
| Florida................. | 291 | 1,018 | 424 | 365 | 3.7 | 11.1 | 4.2 | 3.6 | 225 | 40 | 3.2 | 0.5 |
| Georgia................ | 151 | 495 | 237 | 201 | 3.6 | 10.5 | 4.7 | 3.9 | 117 | 27 | 3.2 | 0.6 |
| Hawaii................. | 26 | 45 | 17 | 17 | 4.2 | 6.9 | 2.4 | 2.4 | 17 | 7 | 3.1 | 1.1 |
| Idaho................. | 31 | 68 | 27 | 24 | 4.7 | 9.0 | 3.2 | 2.8 | 26 | 6 | 4.5 | 0.9 |
| Illinois................ | 282 | 688 | 319 | 278 | 4.3 | 10.4 | 4.9 | 4.3 | 220 | 98 | 4.1 | 1.7 |
| Indiana................ | 97 | 330 | 119 | 116 | 3.1 | 10.4 | 3.6 | 3.4 | 79 | 21 | 3.0 | 0.7 |
| Iowa.................. | 42 | 101 | 52 | 43 | 2.6 | 6.0 | 3.1 | 2.5 | 40 | 19 | 2.9 | 1.3 |
| Kansas................ | 50 | 106 | 54 | 50 | 3.6 | 7.1 | 3.7 | 3.4 | 37 | 10 | 2.9 | 0.7 |
| Kentucky.............. | 82 | 210 | 101 | 89 | 4.2 | 10.2 | 4.9 | 4.3 | 50 | 19 | 3.0 | 1.0 |
| Louisiana.............. | 108 | 166 | 108 | 103 | 5.3 | 8.0 | 5.1 | 4.9 | 55 | 13 | 3.1 | 0.7 |
| Maine................. | 23 | 57 | 24 | 24 | 3.4 | 8.1 | 3.4 | 3.4 | 18 | 6 | 3.2 | 0.9 |
| Maryland.............. | 100 | 235 | 136 | 125 | 3.6 | 7.7 | 4.3 | 3.9 | 73 | 30 | 3.1 | 1.2 |
| Massachusetts.......... | 90 | 289 | 139 | 127 | 2.7 | 8.3 | 3.8 | 3.3 | 116 | 63 | 3.7 | 1.8 |
| Michigan.............. | 186 | 605 | 225 | 203 | 3.6 | 12.6 | 4.6 | 4.1 | 160 | 54 | 4.3 | 1.3 |
| Minnesota............. | 89 | 218 | 104 | 89 | 3.2 | 7.4 | 3.4 | 2.9 | 81 | 41 | 3.2 | 1.5 |
| Mississippi............ | 71 | 136 | 65 | 61 | 5.4 | 10.4 | 5.1 | 4.8 | 36 | 9 | 3.4 | 0.8 |
| Missouri............... | 106 | 293 | 115 | 98 | 3.6 | 9.6 | 3.8 | 3.2 | 75 | 24 | 3.0 | 0.9 |
| Montana............... | 23 | 37 | 21 | 20 | 5.0 | 7.3 | 3.9 | 3.7 | 17 | 7 | 4.2 | 1.6 |
| Nebraska.............. | 27 | 46 | 29 | 29 | 2.8 | 4.6 | 2.9 | 2.8 | 19 | 5 | 2.1 | 0.5 |
| Nevada................ | 45 | 184 | 74 | 68 | 4.2 | 13.5 | 5.1 | 4.6 | 54 | 20 | 4.9 | 1.4 |
| New Hampshire......... | 18 | 43 | 20 | 19 | 2.7 | 5.8 | 2.7 | 2.5 | 18 | 4 | 3.1 | 0.6 |
| New Jersey............. | 158 | 434 | 206 | 183 | 3.7 | 9.5 | 4.6 | 4.1 | 166 | 95 | 4.5 | 2.4 |
| New Mexico............ | 42 | 76 | 55 | 47 | 4.9 | 8.1 | 5.9 | 4.9 | 25 | 9 | 3.4 | 1.1 |
| New York.............. | 415 | 826 | 448 | 394 | 4.5 | 8.6 | 4.7 | 4.1 | 290 | 139 | 3.5 | 1.5 |
| North Carolina......... | 152 | 501 | 221 | 195 | 3.7 | 10.9 | 4.5 | 3.9 | 156 | 20 | 4.2 | 0.5 |
| North Dakota........... | 10 | 14 | 11 | 11 | 3.0 | 3.8 | 2.7 | 2.6 | 5 | 4 | 1.5 | 0.9 |
| Ohio.................. | 231 | 600 | 287 | 263 | 4.0 | 10.3 | 5.0 | 4.6 | 144 | 53 | 3.0 | 1.0 |
| Oklahoma.............. | 50 | 120 | 78 | 63 | 3.0 | 6.8 | 4.2 | 3.4 | 34 | 12 | 2.4 | 0.8 |
| Oregon................ | 93 | 211 | 86 | 87 | 5.1 | 10.6 | 4.1 | 4.2 | 83 | 27 | 5.3 | 1.4 |
| Pennsylvania........... | 252 | 540 | 314 | 276 | 4.1 | 8.5 | 4.9 | 4.3 | 265 | 113 | 4.9 | 2.0 |
| Rhode Island........... | 22 | 63 | 24 | 23 | 4.1 | 11.2 | 4.4 | 4.1 | 18 | 9 | 4.1 | 1.9 |
| South Carolina......... | 75 | 241 | 99 | 80 | 3.8 | 11.2 | 4.3 | 3.4 | 71 | 16 | 4.1 | 0.8 |
| South Dakota........... | 10 | 22 | 15 | 14 | 2.5 | 5.0 | 3.2 | 3.0 | 4 | 2 | 1.2 | 0.4 |
| Tennessee............. | 110 | 299 | 120 | 113 | 3.9 | 9.7 | 3.8 | 3.5 | 68 | 16 | 2.7 | 0.5 |
| Texas................. | 445 | 997 | 586 | 534 | 4.3 | 8.1 | 4.3 | 3.9 | 216 | 120 | 2.2 | 1.0 |
| Utah.................. | 38 | 106 | 50 | 49 | 3.3 | 7.8 | 3.3 | 3.1 | 28 | 9 | 2.5 | 0.6 |
| Vermont............... | 9 | 22 | 10 | 9 | 2.8 | 6.1 | 3.0 | 2.7 | 10 | 4 | 3.6 | 1.2 |
| Virginia............... | 83 | 297 | 159 | 129 | 2.3 | 7.1 | 3.7 | 3.0 | 62 | 21 | 1.8 | 0.6 |
| Washington............ | 158 | 351 | 175 | 171 | 5.2 | 10.0 | 4.7 | 4.5 | 109 | 45 | 4.0 | 1.4 |
| West Virginia........... | 44 | 70 | 41 | 41 | 5.5 | 8.7 | 5.2 | 5.3 | 21 | 10 | 3.2 | 1.5 |
| Wisconsin............. | 105 | 267 | 103 | 94 | 3.5 | 8.7 | 3.3 | 3.0 | 122 | 32 | 4.7 | 1.1 |
| Wyoming.............. | 10 | 20 | 12 | 12 | 3.9 | 6.4 | 4.2 | 4.1 | 7 | 2 | 2.6 | 0.9 |

[1] Total unemployment as percent of civilian labor force. [2] Number of average weekly jobless workers who are receiving state unemployment benefits. Source: U.S. Employment and Training Administration, "Unemployment Insurance, Financial Data Handbook 394," <https://workforcesecurity.doleta.gov/unemply/hb394.asp>, accessed September 2019. [3] Those currently collecting unemployment insurance as a percent of the total number of eligible workers. [4] U.S. totals include Puerto Rico and the Virgin Islands.

Source: Except as noted, U.S. Bureau of Labor Statistics, "Local Area Unemployment Statistics," <http://www.bls.gov/lau/>, accessed September 2019.

# Table 657. Nonfarm Establishments—Employees, Hours, and Earnings by Industry: 1990 to 2018

[109,527 represents 109,527,000. Annual averages of monthly data. Based on data from establishment reports. Includes all full- and part-time employees who worked during, or received pay for, any part of the pay period including the 12th of the month. Excludes proprietors, the self-employed, farm workers, unpaid family workers, private household workers, and Armed Forces. Establishment data shown here conform to industry definitions in the 2017 North American Industry Classification System (NAICS) and are adjusted to March employment benchmarks. Based on the Current Employment Statistics Program; see source and Appendix III]

| Item and year | Total nonfarm | Private industry Total [1] | Construction | Manufacturing | Wholesale trade | Retail trade | Transportation and warehousing | Utilities | Information | Finance and insurance | Real estate and rental and leasing | Professional and technical services | Administrative and waste services | Educational services | Health care and social assistance | Arts entertainment and recreation | Accommodations and food services | Government |
|---|---|---|---|---|---|---|---|---|---|---|---|---|---|---|---|---|---|---|
| **EMPLOYEES (1,000)** | | | | | | | | | | | | | | | | | | |
| 1990 | 109,527 | 91,112 | 5,263 | 17,695 | 5,230 | 13,186 | 3,479 | 740 | 2,688 | 4,976 | 1,637 | 4,565 | 4,646 | 1,688 | 9,336 | 1,132 | 8,156 | 18,415 |
| 2000 | 132,024 | 111,235 | 6,787 | 17,263 | 5,888 | 15,284 | 4,414 | 601 | 3,630 | 5,773 | 2,011 | 6,732 | 8,172 | 2,390 | 12,861 | 1,788 | 10,074 | 20,790 |
| 2005 | 134,051 | 112,247 | 7,336 | 14,227 | 5,706 | 15,285 | 4,365 | 554 | 3,061 | 6,063 | 2,134 | 7,065 | 8,175 | 2,836 | 14,840 | 1,892 | 10,923 | 21,804 |
| 2010 | 130,362 | 107,871 | 5,518 | 11,528 | 5,387 | 14,446 | 4,196 | 553 | 2,707 | 5,761 | 1,934 | 7,486 | 7,419 | 3,155 | 16,820 | 1,913 | 11,135 | 22,490 |
| 2014 | 138,958 | 117,076 | 6,151 | 12,185 | 5,740 | 15,363 | 4,667 | 552 | 2,726 | 5,931 | 2,046 | 8,386 | 8,564 | 3,417 | 18,022 | 2,103 | 12,593 | 21,882 |
| 2015 | 141,843 | 119,814 | 6,461 | 12,336 | 5,780 | 15,611 | 4,877 | 556 | 2,750 | 6,035 | 2,083 | 8,658 | 8,823 | 3,472 | 18,557 | 2,166 | 12,994 | 22,029 |
| 2016 | 144,352 | 122,128 | 6,728 | 12,354 | 5,787 | 15,832 | 5,020 | 556 | 2,794 | 6,148 | 2,139 | 8,881 | 8,981 | 3,570 | 19,069 | 2,252 | 13,408 | 22,224 |
| 2017 | 146,624 | 124,275 | 6,969 | 12,439 | 5,814 | 15,846 | 5,195 | 555 | 2,814 | 6,262 | 2,189 | 9,058 | 9,142 | 3,668 | 19,520 | 2,333 | 13,718 | 22,350 |
| 2018 | 149,074 | 126,625 | 7,289 | 12,689 | 5,853 | 15,833 | 5,419 | 555 | 2,828 | 6,314 | 2,255 | 9,300 | 9,327 | 3,728 | 19,939 | 2,394 | 13,955 | 22,449 |
| **WEEKLY EARNINGS [2] (dol.)** | | | | | | | | | | | | | | | | | | |
| 1990 | (NA) | 349.63 | 513.43 | 436.13 | 443.61 | 235.72 | 471.85 | 670.80 | 479.50 | (NA) | (NA) | 505.13 | 273.81 | (NA) | 319.26 | 219.02 | 147.92 | (NA) |
| 2000 | (NA) | 480.99 | 685.78 | 591.01 | 630.09 | 333.48 | 562.59 | 955.09 | 700.92 | (NA) | (NA) | 746.12 | 387.72 | (NA) | 447.45 | 273.79 | 207.44 | (NA) |
| 2005 | (NA) | 544.02 | 750.37 | 673.30 | 683.99 | 377.58 | 618.70 | 1,095.91 | 805.11 | (NA) | (NA) | 862.36 | 432.08 | (NA) | 555.82 | 330.31 | 226.48 | (NA) |
| 2010 | (NA) | 636.19 | 891.83 | 765.18 | 814.04 | 400.38 | 711.22 | 1,262.89 | 939.85 | (NA) | (NA) | 1,073.43 | 536.08 | (NA) | 652.07 | 363.91 | 266.78 | (NA) |
| 2014 | (NA) | 694.85 | 977.11 | 822.03 | 894.06 | 431.97 | 789.61 | 1,383.91 | 1,030.17 | (NA) | (NA) | 1,171.49 | 568.57 | (NA) | 706.15 | 388.40 | 290.05 | (NA) |
| 2015 | (NA) | 708.90 | 998.02 | 832.25 | 907.72 | 446.01 | 804.95 | 1,444.03 | 1,038.10 | (NA) | (NA) | 1,201.23 | 569.06 | (NA) | 722.49 | 379.22 | 300.17 | (NA) |
| 2016 | (NA) | 723.31 | 1031.88 | 855.77 | 929.09 | 447.69 | 810.89 | 1,502.09 | 1,068.23 | (NA) | (NA) | 1,223.97 | 585.46 | (NA) | 737.17 | 380.57 | 310.02 | (NA) |
| 2017 | (NA) | 742.62 | 1,061.98 | 876.10 | 957.95 | 463.10 | 817.13 | 1,540.27 | 1,100.03 | (NA) | (NA) | 1,254.18 | 605.86 | (NA) | 755.48 | 387.40 | 323.66 | (NA) |
| 2018 | (NA) | 767.08 | 1,108.49 | 908.08 | 980.54 | 482.90 | 838.89 | 1,569.90 | 1,137.84 | (NA) | (NA) | 1,294.29 | 622.71 | (NA) | 777.27 | 389.84 | 337.85 | (NA) |
| **WEEKLY HOURS [2]** | | | | | | | | | | | | | | | | | | |
| 1990 | (NA) | 34.3 | 38.3 | 40.5 | 38.4 | 30.6 | 37.7 | 41.6 | 35.8 | (NA) | (NA) | 36.1 | 32.3 | (NA) | 31.8 | 26.1 | 25.9 | (NA) |
| 2000 | (NA) | 34.3 | 39.2 | 41.3 | 38.8 | 30.7 | 37.4 | 42.0 | 36.8 | (NA) | (NA) | 36.2 | 33.1 | (NA) | 32.1 | 25.6 | 26.2 | (NA) |
| 2005 | (NA) | 33.8 | 38.6 | 40.7 | 37.7 | 30.6 | 37.0 | 41.1 | 36.5 | (NA) | (NA) | 35.7 | 32.8 | (NA) | 32.8 | 25.7 | 25.7 | (NA) |
| 2010 | (NA) | 33.4 | 38.4 | 41.1 | 37.9 | 30.2 | 37.1 | 42.0 | 36.3 | (NA) | (NA) | 35.9 | 33.9 | (NA) | 32.2 | 23.8 | 25.0 | (NA) |
| 2014 | (NA) | 33.7 | 39.6 | 42.0 | 38.6 | 30.0 | 38.5 | 42.3 | 35.9 | (NA) | (NA) | 36.4 | 34.5 | (NA) | 32.2 | 24.1 | 25.3 | (NA) |
| 2015 | (NA) | 33.7 | 39.6 | 41.8 | 38.6 | 30.1 | 38.8 | 42.4 | 35.7 | (NA) | (NA) | 36.4 | 34.0 | (NA) | 32.3 | 23.7 | 25.3 | (NA) |
| 2016 | (NA) | 33.6 | 39.7 | 41.9 | 38.6 | 29.7 | 38.8 | 42.5 | 35.5 | (NA) | (NA) | 36.3 | 33.9 | (NA) | 32.3 | 23.2 | 25.2 | (NA) |
| 2017 | (NA) | 33.7 | 39.7 | 41.9 | 39.0 | 30.2 | 38.4 | 42.5 | 35.8 | (NA) | (NA) | 36.5 | 34.0 | (NA) | 32.4 | 22.9 | 25.2 | (NA) |
| 2018 | (NA) | 33.8 | 40.0 | 42.2 | 38.9 | 30.4 | 38.4 | 42.7 | 35.6 | (NA) | (NA) | 36.6 | 34.0 | (NA) | 32.4 | 22.5 | 25.3 | (NA) |
| **HOURLY EARNINGS [2] (dol.)** | | | | | | | | | | | | | | | | | | |
| 1990 | (NA) | 10.20 | 13.42 | 10.78 | 11.55 | 7.71 | 12.50 | 15.14 | 13.40 | (NA) | (NA) | 14.00 | 8.48 | (NA) | 10.03 | 8.41 | 5.70 | (NA) |
| 2000 | (NA) | 14.02 | 17.48 | 14.32 | 16.24 | 10.87 | 15.05 | 22.75 | 19.07 | (NA) | (NA) | 20.62 | 11.70 | (NA) | 13.93 | 10.68 | 7.92 | (NA) |
| 2005 | (NA) | 16.12 | 19.46 | 16.56 | 18.13 | 12.36 | 16.71 | 25.68 | 22.06 | (NA) | (NA) | 24.13 | 13.17 | (NA) | 16.94 | 12.85 | 8.80 | (NA) |
| 2010 | (NA) | 19.05 | 23.22 | 18.61 | 21.46 | 13.25 | 19.17 | 30.04 | 25.87 | (NA) | (NA) | 29.93 | 15.81 | (NA) | 20.23 | 15.27 | 10.68 | (NA) |
| 2014 | (NA) | 20.61 | 24.67 | 19.56 | 23.14 | 14.40 | 20.52 | 32.86 | 28.70 | (NA) | (NA) | 32.23 | 16.49 | (NA) | 21.96 | 16.14 | 11.47 | (NA) |
| 2015 | (NA) | 21.03 | 25.20 | 19.91 | 23.52 | 14.83 | 20.75 | 34.02 | 29.05 | (NA) | (NA) | 32.96 | 16.73 | (NA) | 22.41 | 15.97 | 11.87 | (NA) |
| 2016 | (NA) | 21.54 | 25.97 | 20.44 | 24.07 | 15.05 | 20.91 | 35.33 | 30.05 | (NA) | (NA) | 33.72 | 17.26 | (NA) | 22.83 | 16.38 | 12.32 | (NA) |
| 2017 | (NA) | 22.06 | 26.74 | 20.90 | 24.58 | 15.33 | 21.30 | 35.22 | 30.74 | (NA) | (NA) | 34.41 | 17.82 | (NA) | 23.35 | 16.94 | 12.85 | (NA) |
| 2018 | (NA) | 22.71 | 27.74 | 21.54 | 25.18 | 15.91 | 21.84 | 35.77 | 31.93 | (NA) | (NA) | 35.41 | 18.32 | (NA) | 23.98 | 17.30 | 13.37 | (NA) |

NA Not available. [1] Includes other industries not shown separately. [2] Average hours and earnings of production and nonsupervisory employees.

Source: U.S. Bureau of Labor Statistics, Current Employment Statistics, "Employment, Hours, and Earnings—National," <https://www.bls.gov/ces/data.htm>, accessed July 2019.

# Table 658. Employees in Nonfarm Establishments by State and Industry: 2018

[In thousands (148,836.5 represents 148,836,500). Includes all full- and part-time employees who worked during, or received pay for, any part of the pay period reported. Excludes proprietors, the self-employed, farm workers, unpaid family workers, private household workers, and Armed Forces. Compiled from data supplied by cooperating state agencies. Based on North American Industry Classification System, 2017; see text, section 15]

| State | Total [1] | Con-struction | Manu-facturing | Trade, transpor-tation and utilities | Infor-mation | Fin-ancial activi-ties [2] | Profes-sional and business ser-vices [3] | Educa-tion and health ser-vices [4] | Leisure and hospi-tality [5] | Other ser-vices [6] | Govern-ment |
|---|---|---|---|---|---|---|---|---|---|---|---|
| U.S........ | 148,836.5 | 7,236.1 | 12,665.3 | 27,653.8 | 2,840.9 | 8,469.2 | 20,885.5 | 23,616.3 | 16,207.0 | 5,763.9 | 22,778.2 |
| AL.......... | 2,042.0 | 89.1 | 267.1 | 380.7 | 21.1 | 96.4 | 244.0 | 245.3 | 205.9 | 96.7 | 385.9 |
| AK.......... | 327.3 | 15.9 | 12.5 | 64.3 | 5.6 | 11.8 | 27.1 | 50.4 | 35.6 | 11.0 | 80.4 |
| AZ.......... | 2,856.0 | 158.8 | 170.1 | 534.5 | 47.4 | 220.8 | 431.1 | 445.7 | 326.6 | 92.7 | 415.2 |
| AR.......... | 1,261.9 | 50.6 | 160.5 | 251.5 | 11.2 | 60.5 | 146.2 | 191.2 | 118.6 | 53.4 | 212.2 |
| CA.......... | 17,175.2 | 859.6 | 1,325.4 | 3,051.6 | 543.7 | 836.3 | 2,663.7 | 2,726.5 | 1,986.1 | 572.1 | 2,587.4 |
| CO........ | 2,725.3 | 172.3 | 147.6 | 469.8 | 74.9 | 170.5 | 425.6 | 340.6 | 339.9 | 110.8 | 445.0 |
| CT........ | 1,689.0 | 58.6 | 160.3 | 296.5 | 31.9 | 126.1 | 220.5 | 334.9 | 157.7 | 65.4 | 236.7 |
| DE........ | 461.3 | 22.3 | 27.1 | 80.1 | 4.1 | 47.5 | 63.6 | 80.1 | 51.5 | 18.6 | 66.4 |
| DC........ | 792.2 | 15.7 | 1.3 | 33.2 | 19.3 | 29.7 | 167.7 | 130.8 | 79.7 | 76.3 | 238.5 |
| FL.......... | 8,781.9 | 540.9 | 372.0 | 1,780.9 | 139.7 | 576.7 | 1,366.8 | 1,305.3 | 1,227.1 | 354.4 | 1,112.5 |
| GA........ | 4,540.0 | 196.2 | 408.0 | 943.0 | 114.6 | 248.2 | 692.4 | 584.5 | 490.6 | 159.3 | 693.8 |
| HI.......... | 656.6 | 36.1 | 14.2 | 122.6 | 9.1 | 28.8 | 82.5 | 85.8 | 123.9 | 28.0 | 125.6 |
| ID.......... | 737.3 | 49.1 | 68.2 | 142.5 | 8.9 | 36.4 | 94.2 | 105.6 | 78.5 | 25.5 | 124.9 |
| IL.......... | 6,117.4 | 225.8 | 588.3 | 1,216.1 | 94.4 | 401.8 | 951.4 | 934.0 | 617.3 | 254.4 | 826.3 |
| IN.......... | 3,144.0 | 141.3 | 542.0 | 597.5 | 29.4 | 138.7 | 342.7 | 475.2 | 309.5 | 131.8 | 429.7 |
| IA.......... | 1,584.2 | 77.5 | 223.0 | 312.6 | 22.0 | 109.1 | 141.0 | 234.7 | 143.6 | 57.5 | 260.7 |
| KS.......... | 1,415.8 | 61.1 | 165.1 | 268.7 | 18.7 | 77.1 | 180.0 | 199.5 | 129.7 | 50.9 | 258.3 |
| KY.......... | 1,931.6 | 78.1 | 252.1 | 403.8 | 22.0 | 93.0 | 217.4 | 278.3 | 197.6 | 65.6 | 313.7 |
| LA.......... | 1,981.5 | 151.1 | 134.9 | 379.5 | 22.9 | 91.1 | 213.0 | 315.5 | 236.1 | 73.9 | 327.6 |
| ME.......... | 628.5 | 28.9 | 52.0 | 119.1 | 7.3 | 31.9 | 69.3 | 127.2 | 68.3 | 22.2 | 100.1 |
| MD.......... | 2,744.3 | 163.1 | 108.3 | 467.4 | 36.5 | 144.4 | 451.0 | 471.5 | 281.5 | 114.7 | 504.6 |
| MA.......... | 3,642.9 | 157.2 | 244.1 | 579.4 | 91.5 | 221.5 | 583.9 | 797.9 | 373.0 | 138.9 | 454.5 |
| MI.......... | 4,418.6 | 169.2 | 629.8 | 791.4 | 55.8 | 219.0 | 660.6 | 679.0 | 433.6 | 166.6 | 606.5 |
| MN.......... | 2,954.4 | 122.5 | 321.4 | 537.0 | 49.3 | 184.1 | 378.1 | 543.4 | 272.8 | 113.6 | 425.5 |
| MS.......... | 1,154.8 | 43.7 | 144.9 | 231.1 | 11.0 | 44.4 | 109.8 | 145.0 | 135.5 | 41.3 | 241.3 |
| MO........ | 2,887.4 | 122.5 | 272.8 | 543.7 | 50.5 | 173.3 | 386.5 | 478.8 | 305.9 | 115.5 | 433.7 |
| MT.......... | 477.6 | 28.6 | 20.5 | 94.8 | 6.3 | 24.9 | 42.7 | 77.2 | 66.0 | 18.9 | 90.4 |
| NE.......... | 1,023.1 | 52.3 | 99.7 | 201.3 | 17.7 | 73.9 | 119.2 | 155.6 | 92.2 | 36.8 | 173.5 |
| NV.......... | 1,386.5 | 89.7 | 55.5 | 255.5 | 15.6 | 68.2 | 190.6 | 140.6 | 353.4 | 42.0 | 161.0 |
| NH.......... | 681.0 | 26.9 | 70.5 | 139.3 | 12.4 | 34.4 | 83.2 | 125.8 | 72.1 | 25.4 | 90.0 |
| NJ.......... | 4,154.8 | 157.9 | 247.4 | 888.1 | 69.7 | 250.5 | 672.3 | 708.2 | 387.2 | 171.5 | 600.5 |
| NM.......... | 842.2 | 47.2 | 27.0 | 137.6 | 11.9 | 34.2 | 106.4 | 139.7 | 98.0 | 28.9 | 186.8 |
| NY.......... | 9,669.9 | 398.4 | 443.1 | 1,563.0 | 275.2 | 719.1 | 1,340.7 | 2,064.6 | 957.8 | 413.6 | 1,488.9 |
| NC.......... | 4,488.2 | 219.5 | 474.2 | 833.3 | 80.0 | 239.6 | 634.5 | 611.6 | 502.6 | 154.3 | 733.0 |
| ND.......... | 433.4 | 25.9 | 25.9 | 94.2 | 6.2 | 24.3 | 34.6 | 63.7 | 40.2 | 15.2 | 82.5 |
| OH.......... | 5,559.9 | 219.3 | 698.9 | 1,024.3 | 70.8 | 307.9 | 731.2 | 936.1 | 566.4 | 213.7 | 779.2 |
| OK.......... | 1,687.4 | 80.3 | 137.7 | 299.2 | 19.9 | 79.2 | 190.4 | 236.3 | 171.9 | 71.5 | 347.8 |
| OR.......... | 1,909.5 | 104.8 | 194.9 | 352.2 | 34.2 | 102.0 | 249.0 | 295.1 | 210.7 | 64.5 | 295.0 |
| PA.......... | 6,006.0 | 255.8 | 569.4 | 1,126.8 | 85.8 | 325.5 | 804.5 | 1,274.8 | 571.6 | 260.4 | 702.9 |
| RI.......... | 496.1 | 19.2 | 40.3 | 77.4 | 5.9 | 35.4 | 68.5 | 106.5 | 58.7 | 23.1 | 61.0 |
| SC.......... | 2,145.3 | 102.5 | 247.8 | 406.3 | 28.2 | 104.2 | 292.9 | 252.9 | 260.3 | 76.8 | 369.0 |
| SD.......... | 438.9 | 22.9 | 44.4 | 86.8 | 5.6 | 29.2 | 32.6 | 72.8 | 47.3 | 16.8 | 79.6 |
| TN.......... | 3,060.3 | 124.8 | 350.7 | 627.2 | 45.5 | 162.5 | 416.9 | 435.6 | 338.9 | 118.3 | 435.5 |
| TX.......... | 12,503.4 | 739.1 | 881.1 | 2,485.3 | 204.1 | 776.9 | 1,732.9 | 1,696.8 | 1,355.6 | 433.5 | 1,951.8 |
| UT.......... | 1,516.5 | 104.1 | 133.1 | 285.8 | 38.6 | 87.7 | 215.1 | 204.2 | 149.4 | 41.2 | 247.9 |
| VT.......... | 315.5 | 15.1 | 29.8 | 54.3 | 4.3 | 12.1 | 28.9 | 66.1 | 37.5 | 10.2 | 56.4 |
| VA.......... | 4,000.6 | 197.4 | 240.1 | 659.7 | 67.2 | 207.4 | 748.6 | 541.1 | 407.8 | 201.1 | 722.5 |
| WA.......... | 3,406.0 | 213.6 | 287.9 | 637.7 | 133.9 | 158.0 | 425.3 | 491.8 | 342.6 | 122.1 | 586.7 |
| WV.......... | 726.0 | 41.1 | 47.1 | 130.0 | 8.2 | 29.1 | 68.9 | 128.2 | 74.0 | 24.3 | 152.6 |
| WI.......... | 2,971.5 | 122.2 | 475.5 | 543.2 | 47.3 | 152.9 | 326.8 | 456.1 | 282.6 | 152.3 | 407.8 |
| WY.......... | 285.5 | 20.3 | 9.8 | 52.0 | 3.6 | 11.0 | 18.7 | 28.2 | 36.1 | 16.4 | 68.9 |

[1] Includes mining and logging, not shown separately. [2] Finance and insurance; and real estate and rental and leasing. [3] Professional, scientific, and technical services; management of companies and enterprises; and administrative and support, and waste management and remediation services. [4] Education services; and health care and social assistance. [5] Arts, entertainment, and recreation; and accommodations and food services. [6] Includes repair and maintenance; personal and laundry services; and membership associations and organizations.

Source: U.S. Bureau of Labor Statistics, State and Metro Area Employment, Hours, and Earnings, "Employees on nonfarm payrolls in States and selected areas by major industry," <http://www.bls.gov/sae/tables.htm>, accessed July 2019.

# Table 659. Nonfarm Industries—Employees and Earnings: 1990 to 2018

[Annual averages of monthly figures (109,527 represents 109,527,000). Covers all full- and part-time employees who worked during, or received pay for, any part of the pay period including the 12th of the month. See also headnote, Table 657]

| Industry | 2017 NAICS code [1] | All employees (1,000) | | | | | Average hourly earnings [2] (dol.) | | |
|---|---|---|---|---|---|---|---|---|---|
| | | 1990 | 2000 | 2010 | 2017 | 2018 | 2000 | 2010 | 2018 |
| **Total nonfarm** | (X) | **109,527** | **132,024** | **130,362** | **146,624** | **149,074** | **(NA)** | **(NA)** | **(NA)** |
| Goods-producing [3] | (X) | 23,723 | 24,649 | 17,751 | 20,084 | 20,710 | 15.27 | 20.28 | 24.00 |
| Service-providing [4] | (X) | 85,804 | 107,375 | 112,611 | 126,540 | 128,365 | (NA) | (NA) | (NA) |
| **Total private** | (X) | **91,112** | **111,235** | **107,871** | **124,275** | **126,625** | **14.02** | **19.05** | **22.71** |
| **Mining and logging** | (X) | **765** | **599** | **705** | **676** | **732** | **16.55** | **23.82** | **28.30** |
| Logging | 1133 | 85 | 79 | 50 | 50 | 49 | 13.70 | 18.85 | 20.94 |
| **Mining** | 21 | **680** | **520** | **655** | **626** | **683** | **16.94** | **24.24** | **28.82** |
| Oil and gas extraction | 211 | 190 | 125 | 159 | 144 | 145 | 19.43 | 27.36 | 35.71 |
| Mining, except oil and gas | 212 | 302 | 225 | 205 | 186 | 192 | 18.07 | 24.63 | 26.65 |
| Support activities for mining | 213 | 188 | 171 | 292 | 296 | 346 | 14.55 | 22.95 | 28.15 |
| **Construction** | **23** | **5,263** | **6,787** | **5,518** | **6,969** | **7,289** | **17.48** | **23.22** | **27.74** |
| Construction of buildings | 236 | 1,413 | 1,633 | 1,230 | 1,545 | 1,626 | 16.74 | 22.73 | 27.50 |
| Residential building | 2361 | 673 | 823 | 572 | 753 | 804 | 15.18 | 19.80 | 24.66 |
| Nonresidential building | 2362 | 741 | 809 | 658 | 793 | 822 | 18.18 | 25.13 | 29.84 |
| Heavy and civil engineering construction | 237 | 813 | 937 | 825 | 996 | 1,052 | 16.80 | 23.76 | 29.72 |
| Highway, street, and bridge construction | 2373 | 289 | 340 | 287 | 328 | 344 | 18.17 | 23.76 | 28.60 |
| Specialty trade contractors | 238 | 3,037 | 4,217 | 3,463 | 4,427 | 4,612 | 17.91 | 23.22 | 27.29 |
| Building foundation and exterior contractors | 2381 | 703 | 919 | 680 | 878 | 910 | 16.93 | 21.20 | 25.32 |
| Building equipment contractors | 2382 | 1,282 | 1,897 | 1,634 | 2,093 | 2,180 | 19.52 | 24.89 | 29.02 |
| Building finishing contractors | 2383 | 665 | 857 | 634 | 802 | 837 | 16.44 | 22.06 | 26.29 |
| **Manufacturing** | 31-33 | **17,695** | **17,263** | **11,528** | **12,439** | **12,689** | **14.32** | **18.61** | **21.54** |
| **Durable goods** | (X) | **10,737** | **10,877** | **7,064** | **7,741** | **7,945** | **14.93** | **19.81** | **22.51** |
| Wood products | 321 | 543 | 615 | 342 | 397 | 406 | 11.63 | 14.85 | 17.88 |
| Nonmetallic mineral products | 327 | 528 | 554 | 371 | 410 | 415 | 14.53 | 17.48 | 21.41 |
| Cement and concrete products | 3273 | 195 | 234 | 170 | 192 | 192 | 14.64 | 17.84 | 22.13 |
| Primary metals | 331 | 689 | 622 | 362 | 371 | 378 | 16.64 | 20.13 | 23.31 |
| Iron and steel mills and ferroalloy production | 3311 | 187 | 135 | 87 | 82 | 83 | (NA) | (NA) | (NA) |
| Foundries | 3315 | 214 | 217 | 112 | 117 | 120 | 14.72 | 18.22 | 21.34 |
| Fabricated metal products | 332 | 1,610 | 1,753 | 1,282 | 1,425 | 1,467 | 13.77 | 17.94 | 20.55 |
| Architectural and structural metals | 3323 | 357 | 428 | 321 | 373 | 390 | 13.43 | 17.47 | 19.95 |
| Machine shops and threaded products | 3327 | 309 | 365 | 313 | 353 | 362 | 14.53 | 18.68 | 21.91 |
| Machinery | 333 | 1,410 | 1,457 | 996 | 1,079 | 1,120 | 15.21 | 18.96 | 23.06 |
| Agricultural, construction, and mining machinery | 3331 | 229 | 222 | 208 | 206 | 220 | 14.21 | 18.95 | 22.48 |
| Heating, ventilation and air conditioning, and commercial refrigeration equipment | 3334 | 165 | 194 | 125 | 130 | 133 | 13.10 | 16.16 | 20.35 |
| Metalworking machinery | 3335 | 267 | 274 | 155 | 180 | 182 | 16.66 | 20.00 | 23.40 |
| Computer and electronic products | 334 | 1,903 | 1,820 | 1,095 | 1,039 | 1,055 | 14.73 | 22.78 | 25.09 |
| Computer and peripheral equipment | 3341 | 367 | 302 | 158 | 156 | 156 | (NA) | (NA) | (NA) |
| Communications equipment | 3342 | 223 | 239 | 117 | 87 | 86 | 14.39 | 23.88 | 20.42 |
| Semiconductors and electronic components | 3344 | 574 | 676 | 369 | 362 | 369 | 13.46 | 20.35 | 22.25 |
| Electronic instruments | 3345 | 635 | 488 | 400 | 401 | 410 | 15.00 | 24.02 | 20.70 |
| Electrical equipment and appliances | 335 | 633 | 591 | 360 | 386 | 399 | 13.23 | 16.87 | 20.59 |
| Household appliances | 3352 | 114 | 106 | 60 | 63 | 63 | (NA) | (NA) | (NA) |
| Electrical equipment | 3353 | 244 | 210 | 136 | 138 | 141 | 13.28 | 16.51 | 20.73 |
| Transportation equipment | 336 | 2,135 | 2,057 | 1,333 | 1,643 | 1,702 | 18.89 | 25.23 | 26.32 |
| Motor vehicles | 3361 | 271 | 291 | 153 | 219 | 234 | 24.45 | 29.05 | 29.76 |
| Motor vehicle parts | 3363 | 653 | 840 | 419 | 589 | 597 | 17.95 | 20.66 | 20.88 |
| Aerospace products and parts | 3364 | 841 | 517 | 478 | 488 | 509 | 20.52 | 33.65 | 37.84 |
| Ship and boat building | 3366 | 174 | 154 | 125 | 135 | 139 | (NA) | (NA) | (NA) |
| Furniture and related products | 337 | 602 | 680 | 357 | 395 | 395 | 11.73 | 15.06 | 17.86 |
| Household and institutional furniture | 3371 | 398 | 441 | 223 | 249 | 249 | 11.39 | 14.75 | 17.51 |
| Miscellaneous durable goods manufacturing | 339 | 686 | 728 | 567 | 595 | 608 | 11.93 | 16.56 | 19.14 |
| Medical equipment and supplies | 3391 | 283 | 284 | 303 | 311 | 317 | 12.70 | 17.56 | 20.60 |
| **Nondurable goods** | (X) | **6,958** | **6,386** | **4,464** | **4,699** | **4,743** | **13.31** | **16.80** | **19.96** |
| Food manufacturing | 311 | 1,507 | 1,553 | 1,451 | 1,598 | 1,620 | 11.77 | 14.41 | 17.49 |
| Fruit and vegetable preserving | 3114 | 218 | 197 | 173 | 174 | 172 | 11.90 | 14.56 | 16.74 |
| Dairy products | 3115 | 145 | 136 | 130 | 146 | 149 | 14.85 | 18.92 | 22.82 |
| Animal slaughtering and processing | 3116 | 427 | 507 | 489 | 513 | 521 | 10.27 | 12.69 | 15.48 |
| Bakeries and tortilla manufacturing | 3118 | 292 | 306 | 277 | 311 | 313 | 11.45 | 14.44 | 16.92 |
| Textile mills | 313 | 492 | 378 | 119 | 113 | 113 | 11.23 | 13.56 | 16.46 |
| Textile product mills | 314 | 236 | 230 | 119 | 116 | 116 | 10.31 | 11.79 | 15.31 |
| Apparel | 315 | 903 | 484 | 157 | 119 | 113 | 8.61 | 11.43 | 15.32 |
| Cut and sew apparel | 3152 | 750 | 380 | 124 | 96 | 91 | (NA) | (NA) | (NA) |
| Leather and allied products | 316 | (NA) | (NA) | (NA) | (NA) | (NA) | (NA) | (NA) | (NA) |
| Paper and paper products | 322 | 647 | 605 | 395 | 366 | 367 | 15.91 | 20.04 | 21.88 |
| Pulp, paper, and paperboard mills | 3221 | 238 | 191 | 112 | 97 | 95 | (NA) | (NA) | (NA) |
| Converted paper products | 3222 | 409 | 413 | 282 | 269 | 272 | (NA) | (NA) | (NA) |
| Printing and related support activities | 323 | 809 | 807 | 488 | 440 | 431 | 14.09 | 16.91 | 18.74 |
| Petroleum and coal products | 324 | 153 | 123 | 114 | 115 | 116 | 22.80 | 31.31 | 40.32 |
| Chemicals | 325 | 1,036 | 980 | 787 | 824 | 838 | 17.09 | 21.07 | 25.46 |
| Basic chemicals | 3251 | 249 | 188 | 142 | 151 | 153 | 21.06 | 24.93 | 28.83 |
| Resin, rubber, and artificial fibers | 3252 | 158 | 136 | 89 | 93 | 94 | 17.09 | 21.11 | 27.74 |
| Pharmaceuticals and medicines | 3254 | 207 | 274 | 277 | 293 | 296 | 17.27 | 21.95 | 27.81 |
| Plastics and rubber products | 326 | 825 | 951 | 625 | 717 | 731 | 12.70 | 15.71 | 18.49 |
| Plastics products | 3261 | 618 | 737 | 502 | 581 | 593 | 12.04 | 15.47 | 18.39 |
| Rubber products | 3262 | 207 | 214 | 123 | 136 | 138 | 14.83 | 16.64 | 18.94 |
| **Trade, transportation, and utilities** | (X) | **22,634** | **26,187** | **24,581** | **27,409** | **27,659** | **13.29** | **16.80** | **19.90** |
| **Wholesale trade** | **42** | **5,230** | **5,888** | **5,387** | **5,814** | **5,853** | **16.24** | **21.46** | **25.18** |
| Durable goods | 423 | 2,913 | 3,342 | 2,848 | 3,108 | 3,153 | 16.83 | 21.30 | 25.81 |
| Motor vehicles and parts | 4231 | 314 | 361 | 317 | 346 | 349 | 14.37 | 17.86 | 21.64 |
| Lumber and construction supplies | 4233 | 186 | 233 | 196 | 235 | 242 | 13.79 | 18.87 | 23.55 |
| Commercial equipment | 4234 | 628 | 758 | 657 | 676 | 682 | 20.35 | 25.29 | 31.01 |

See footnotes at end of table.

| Industry | 2017 NAICS code [1] | All employees (1,000) | | | | | Average hourly earnings [2] (dol.) | | |
|---|---|---|---|---|---|---|---|---|---|
| | | 1990 | 2000 | 2010 | 2017 | 2018 | 2000 | 2010 | 2018 |
| Electric goods........................ | 4236 | 369 | 438 | 328 | 352 | 353 | 19.51 | 23.42 | 27.53 |
| Hardware and plumbing.............. | 4237 | 221 | 253 | 227 | 267 | 277 | 15.21 | 20.14 | 25.16 |
| Machinery and supplies.............. | 4238 | 703 | 739 | 629 | 686 | 699 | 16.57 | 21.27 | 26.25 |
| Nondurable goods..................... | 424 | 1,958 | 2,131 | 2,026 | 2,153 | 2,152 | 14.54 | 20.03 | 22.69 |
| Paper and paper products........... | 4241 | 168 | 184 | 135 | 132 | 129 | 15.87 | 22.96 | 24.52 |
| Druggists' goods..................... | 4242 | 154 | 212 | 219 | 233 | 235 | 19.22 | 24.08 | 28.81 |
| Apparel and piece goods............ | 4243 | 154 | 166 | 141 | 153 | 151 | 14.70 | 21.54 | 21.99 |
| Grocery and related products....... | 4244 | 636 | 704 | 726 | 787 | 792 | 13.73 | 19.33 | 20.81 |
| Alcoholic beverages................. | 4248 | 117 | 130 | 166 | 201 | 200 | 15.80 | 20.14 | 23.41 |
| Electronic markets and agents and brokers... | 425 | 359 | 415 | 513 | 553 | 548 | 20.38 | 28.21 | 31.79 |
| **Retail trade**........................... | **44, 45** | **13,186** | **15,284** | **14,446** | **15,846** | **15,833** | **10.87** | **13.25** | **15.91** |
| Motor vehicle and parts dealers............ | 441 | 1,494 | 1,847 | 1,629 | 2,005 | 2,021 | 14.94 | 17.06 | 20.24 |
| Automobile dealers................... | 4411 | 983 | 1,217 | 1,012 | 1,293 | 1,299 | 16.95 | 18.22 | 21.87 |
| Auto parts, accessories, and tire stores...... | 4413 | 418 | 499 | 489 | 555 | 563 | 11.04 | 14.54 | 16.45 |
| Furniture and home furnishings stores......... | 442 | 432 | 544 | 438 | 476 | 481 | 12.33 | 15.25 | 18.59 |
| Furniture stores..................... | 4421 | 244 | 289 | 217 | 223 | 228 | 13.37 | 16.17 | 19.60 |
| Home furnishings stores............. | 4422 | 188 | 254 | 221 | 253 | 253 | 11.06 | 14.03 | 17.41 |
| Electronics and appliance stores............... | 443 | 451 | 648 | 523 | 503 | 488 | 13.17 | 16.84 | 22.65 |
| Building material and garden supply stores... | 444 | 891 | 1,143 | 1,133 | 1,277 | 1,307 | 11.26 | 14.12 | 16.56 |
| Building material and supplies dealers.... | 4441 | 753 | 983 | 1,006 | 1,121 | 1,147 | 11.31 | 14.14 | 16.62 |
| Food and beverage stores................ | 445 | 2,779 | 2,993 | 2,808 | 3,086 | 3,087 | 9.76 | 12.03 | 13.41 |
| Grocery stores....................... | 4451 | 2,406 | 2,582 | 2,461 | 2,705 | 2,698 | 9.71 | 12.12 | 13.39 |
| Specialty food stores................ | 4452 | 232 | 270 | 211 | 223 | 229 | 9.97 | 11.13 | 13.49 |
| Beer, wine, and liquor stores........ | 4453 | 141 | 141 | 136 | 158 | 161 | 10.40 | 11.89 | 13.67 |
| Health and personal care stores........... | 446 | 792 | 928 | 981 | 1,067 | 1,061 | 11.68 | 16.99 | 18.99 |
| Gasoline stations..................... | 447 | 910 | 936 | 819 | 930 | 934 | 8.05 | 10.25 | 11.66 |
| Clothing & clothing accessories stores......... | 448 | 1,313 | 1,322 | 1,353 | 1,374 | 1,366 | 9.96 | 11.59 | 14.87 |
| Clothing stores...................... | 4481 | 930 | 954 | 1,040 | 1,029 | 1,028 | 9.88 | 10.91 | 14.06 |
| Shoe stores.......................... | 4482 | 216 | 193 | 182 | 212 | 202 | 8.96 | 11.80 | 15.35 |
| Jewelry, luggage, and leather goods stores.. | 4483 | 167 | 175 | 131 | 134 | 136 | 11.48 | 15.56 | 18.91 |
| Sporting goods, hobby, book, and music stores...... | 451 | 464 | 603 | 579 | 606 | 576 | 9.38 | 11.69 | 14.97 |
| Sporting goods and musical instrument stores...... | 4511 | 352 | 437 | 459 | 525 | 500 | 9.55 | 11.82 | 15.02 |
| Book stores and news dealers...... | 4512 | 111 | 166 | 120 | 81 | 76 | 8.91 | 11.10 | 14.53 |
| General merchandise stores................. | 452 | 2,500 | 2,820 | 2,998 | 3,126 | 3,105 | 9.22 | 10.98 | 13.76 |
| Department stores................... | 4522 | 1,481 | 1,740 | 1,485 | 1,174 | 1,151 | (NA) | (NA) | (NA) |
| Miscellaneous store retailers................. | 453 | 738 | 1,007 | 762 | 828 | 834 | 10.20 | 12.50 | 14.03 |
| Florists.............................. | 4531 | 121 | 130 | 69 | 60 | 60 | 8.95 | 11.05 | 13.23 |
| Office supplies, stationery, and gift stores.... | 4532 | 358 | 471 | 303 | 257 | 249 | 10.46 | 13.06 | 14.27 |
| Used merchandise stores............ | 4533 | 56 | 107 | 125 | 175 | 175 | 8.07 | 10.72 | 12.49 |
| Nonstore retailers...................... | 454 | 422 | 495 | 425 | 567 | 573 | 13.27 | 17.83 | 20.01 |
| Electronic shopping and mail-order houses.. | 4541 | 159 | 258 | 250 | 392 | 399 | 13.43 | 18.34 | 19.72 |
| **Transportation and warehousing**............. | **48,49** | **3,479** | **4,414** | **4,196** | **5,195** | **5,419** | **15.05** | **19.17** | **21.84** |
| Air transportation...................... | 481 | 529 | 614 | 458 | 492 | 501 | 13.57 | 24.56 | 33.60 |
| Scheduled air transportation........ | 4811 | 503 | 570 | 417 | 448 | 455 | (NA) | (NA) | (NA) |
| Rail transportation..................... | 482 | 272 | 232 | 216 | 215 | 214 | (NA) | (NA) | (NA) |
| Water transportation................... | 483 | 57 | 56 | 62 | 65 | 65 | (NA) | (NA) | (NA) |
| Truck transportation................... | 484 | 1,123 | 1,406 | 1,251 | 1,457 | 1,492 | 15.86 | 18.62 | 22.17 |
| General freight trucking............. | 4841 | 807 | 1,013 | 868 | 1,002 | 1,030 | 16.37 | 18.51 | 22.09 |
| Specialized freight trucking......... | 4842 | 315 | 393 | 383 | 455 | 462 | 14.52 | 18.89 | 22.33 |
| Transit and ground passenger transport....... | 485 | 274 | 372 | 430 | 489 | 488 | 11.88 | 14.98 | 17.76 |
| Urban, interurban, rural, and charter bus transportation.......... | 4851, 2,5 | 72 | 97 | 94 | 103 | 104 | (NA) | (NA) | (NA) |
| Taxi and limousine service.......... | 4853 | 57 | 72 | 68 | 79 | 75 | (NA) | (NA) | (NA) |
| School and employee bus transportation. . . | 4854 | 114 | 152 | 186 | 200 | 200 | 11.42 | 14.90 | 18.06 |
| Pipeline transportation................. | 486 | 60 | 46 | 42 | 49 | 49 | 19.86 | 29.54 | 40.95 |
| Scenic and sightseeing transportation......... | 487 | 16 | 28 | 27 | 35 | 34 | (NA) | (NA) | (NA) |
| Support activities for transportation...... | 488 | 364 | 537 | 543 | 690 | 712 | 14.57 | 21.09 | 21.86 |
| Support activities for air transportation....... | 4881 | 96 | 141 | 154 | 212 | 221 | 13.42 | 17.04 | 18.22 |
| Support activities for water transportation.... | 4883 | 91 | 97 | 91 | 92 | 95 | 19.57 | 35.16 | 37.10 |
| Support activities for road transportation..... | 4884 | 35 | 66 | 80 | 102 | 103 | 13.98 | 15.68 | 17.15 |
| Freight transportation arrangement........... | 4885 | 111 | 178 | 169 | 217 | 227 | 13.46 | 21.24 | 22.36 |
| Couriers and messengers................. | 492 | 375 | 605 | 528 | 676 | 725 | 13.51 | 17.67 | 18.92 |
| Couriers and express delivery services...... | 4921 | 340 | 546 | 480 | 598 | 634 | (NA) | (NA) | (NA) |
| Warehousing and storage.............. | 493 | 409 | 518 | 638 | 1,027 | 1,140 | 14.49 | 15.57 | 17.84 |
| **Utilities**............................. | **22** | **740** | **601** | **553** | **555** | **555** | **22.75** | **30.04** | **36.77** |
| Power generation and supply.............. | 2211 | 550 | 434 | 398 | 393 | 393 | 23.13 | 31.25 | 38.62 |
| Natural gas distribution............ | 2212 | 155 | 121 | 108 | 112 | 110 | 23.41 | 28.36 | 35.54 |
| Water, sewage and other systems...... | 2213 | 35 | 46 | 47 | 51 | 52 | 16.93 | 23.73 | 23.70 |
| **Information**......................... | **51** | **2,688** | **3,630** | **2,707** | **2,814** | **2,828** | **19.07** | **25.87** | **31.93** |
| Publishing industries, except internet........... | 511 | 871 | 1,035 | 759 | 729 | 733 | (NA) | 26.78 | 34.92 |
| Newspaper, book, and directory publishers. . | 5111 | 773 | 774 | 498 | 347 | 325 | (NA) | 20.98 | 23.83 |
| Software publishers................. | 5112 | 98 | 261 | 261 | 381 | 408 | 28.48 | 36.41 | 43.02 |
| Motion picture and sound recording........... | 512 | 255 | 383 | 370 | 433 | 436 | 21.25 | 22.11 | 25.14 |
| Broadcasting, except internet.............. | 515 | 284 | 344 | 290 | 268 | 270 | 16.74 | 24.01 | 29.90 |
| Radio and television broadcasting............. | 5151 | 232 | 253 | 210 | 215 | 217 | (NA) | (NA) | (NA) |
| Cable and other subscription programming. . . | 5152 | 52 | 91 | 80 | 53 | 54 | (NA) | (NA) | (NA) |
| Telecommunications.................... | 517 | 1,009 | 1,397 | 903 | 781 | 751 | 18.59 | 26.24 | 30.91 |
| Wired telecommunications carriers............ | 517311 | 760 | 922 | 603 | 575 | 547 | (NA) | (NA) | (NA) |
| Wireless telecommunications carriers (except satellite)...... | 517312 | 36 | 186 | 170 | 117 | 114 | (NA) | (NA) | (NA) |
| Data processing, hosting and related services.......... | 518 | 211 | 316 | 243 | 318 | 330 | 16.97 | 27.03 | 32.93 |
| **Financial activities**.................... | **(X)** | **6,614** | **7,783** | **7,695** | **8,451** | **8,569** | **15.04** | **21.55** | **26.94** |

See footnotes at end of table.

| Industry | 2017 NAICS code [1] | All employees (1,000) | | | | | Average hourly earnings [2] (dol.) | | |
|---|---|---|---|---|---|---|---|---|---|
| | | 1990 | 2000 | 2010 | 2017 | 2018 | 2000 | 2010 | 2018 |
| **Finance and insurance** | **52** | **4,976** | **5,773** | **5,761** | **6,262** | **6,314** | **(NA)** | **(NA)** | **(NA)** |
| Monetary authorities—central bank | 521 | 24 | 23 | 20 | 19 | 20 | (NA) | (NA) | (NA) |
| Credit intermediation and related activities | 522 | 2,425 | 2,548 | 2,550 | 2,645 | 2,647 | 13.14 | 18.25 | 23.72 |
| Depository credit intermediation | 5221 | 1,909 | 1,681 | 1,729 | 1,713 | 1,715 | 11.97 | 17.55 | 22.04 |
| Commercial banking | 52211 | 1,362 | 1,251 | 1,306 | 1,324 | 1,320 | 11.83 | 17.56 | 22.20 |
| Nondepository credit intermediation | 5222 | 398 | 644 | 562 | 622 | 623 | 15.30 | 20.14 | 27.35 |
| Activities related to credit intermediation | 5223 | 119 | 222 | 259 | 309 | 309 | 15.39 | 18.29 | 25.01 |
| Securities, commodity contracts, and investments, and funds and trusts | 523, 5 | 489 | 851 | 850 | 938 | 957 | 20.04 | 31.21 | 40.42 |
| Securities and commodity contracts brokerage and exchanges | 5231,2 | 341 | 569 | 471 | 457 | 461 | 20.05 | 31.72 | 40.08 |
| Other financial investment activities, incl. funds trusts | 5239, 525 | 148 | 282 | 379 | 481 | 496 | 20.03 | 30.51 | 40.74 |
| Insurance carriers and related activities | 524 | 2,039 | 2,351 | 2,341 | 2,660 | 2,690 | 17.47 | 24.58 | 29.67 |
| Insurance carriers | 5241 | 1,349 | 1,544 | 1,445 | 1,517 | 1,522 | 18.03 | 25.95 | 30.99 |
| Insurance agencies, brokerages, and related services | 5242 | 690 | 807 | 896 | 1,143 | 1,169 | 16.32 | 22.18 | 27.82 |
| **Real estate and rental and leasing** | **53** | **1,637** | **2,011** | **1,934** | **2,189** | **2,255** | **(NA)** | **(NA)** | **(NA)** |
| Real estate | 531 | 1,109 | 1,316 | 1,396 | 1,606 | 1,661 | 12.26 | 17.37 | 21.69 |
| Lessors of real estate | 5311 | 566 | 610 | 565 | 596 | 604 | 11.19 | 16.52 | 20.45 |
| Offices of real estate agents and brokers | 5312 | 217 | 281 | 286 | 318 | 343 | 12.57 | 17.10 | 22.52 |
| Activities related to real estate | 5313 | 327 | 424 | 544 | 691 | 714 | 13.60 | 18.37 | 22.36 |
| Rental and leasing services | 532 | 514 | 667 | 514 | 560 | 571 | 11.69 | 15.96 | 20.45 |
| Automotive equipment rental and leasing | 5321 | 163 | 208 | 161 | 213 | 220 | (NA) | (NA) | (NA) |
| Consumer goods rental | 5322 | 220 | 292 | 198 | 156 | 147 | (NA) | (NA) | (NA) |
| Machinery/equipment rental and leasing | 5324 | 84 | 103 | 114 | 156 | 168 | 14.95 | 19.83 | 26.54 |
| Lessors of nonfinancial intangible assets | 533 | 14 | 28 | 25 | 24 | 23 | (NA) | (NA) | (NA) |
| **Professional and business services** | **(X)** | **10,881** | **16,704** | **16,783** | **20,508** | **20,999** | **15.53** | **22.80** | **26.81** |
| **Professional and technical services** | **54** | **4,565** | **6,732** | **7,486** | **9,058** | **9,300** | **20.62** | **29.93** | **35.41** |
| Legal services | 5411 | 944 | 1,066 | 1,114 | 1,137 | 1,141 | 21.38 | 31.04 | 35.77 |
| Accounting and bookkeeping services | 5412 | 665 | 867 | 887 | 997 | 1,014 | 14.42 | 21.03 | 26.02 |
| Architectural and engineering services | 5413 | 942 | 1,239 | 1,276 | 1,435 | 1,476 | 20.49 | 30.22 | 34.51 |
| Specialized design services | 5414 | 82 | 132 | 113 | 140 | 144 | 15.32 | 22.36 | 28.98 |
| Computer systems design and related | 5415 | 414 | 1,259 | 1,456 | 2,051 | 2,122 | 27.11 | 37.12 | 43.04 |
| Management and technical consulting | 5416 | 324 | 694 | 1,031 | 1,433 | 1,483 | 20.87 | 28.54 | 34.79 |
| Scientific research and development | 5417 | 495 | 517 | 623 | 665 | 693 | 21.39 | 35.63 | 40.13 |
| Advertising and related services | 5418 | 383 | 498 | 410 | 491 | 490 | 17.01 | 24.64 | 29.20 |
| **Management of companies and enterprises** | **55** | **1,671** | **1,800** | **1,878** | **2,308** | **2,372** | **15.30** | **23.81** | **28.86** |
| **Administrative and waste services** | **56** | **4,646** | **8,172** | **7,419** | **9,142** | **9,327** | **11.70** | **15.81** | **18.32** |
| Administrative and support services | 561 | 4,416 | 7,859 | 7,062 | 8,726 | 8,890 | 11.53 | 15.60 | 18.05 |
| Office administrative services | 5611 | 211 | 264 | 407 | 507 | 515 | 14.68 | 23.56 | 27.93 |
| Facilities support services | 5612 | 58 | 97 | 133 | 151 | 153 | 16.73 | 20.97 | 19.98 |
| Employment services | 5613 | 1,513 | 3,850 | 2,724 | 3,595 | 3,679 | 11.90 | 16.19 | 18.09 |
| Temporary help services | 56132 | 1,156 | 2,636 | 2,094 | 2,940 | 3,012 | 11.79 | 14.23 | 17.61 |
| Business support services | 5614 | 506 | 788 | 811 | 904 | 899 | 11.10 | 14.53 | 17.70 |
| Travel arrangement and reservation | 5615 | 250 | 299 | 186 | 218 | 219 | 12.72 | 17.10 | 23.19 |
| Investigation and security services | 5616 | 508 | 690 | 782 | 920 | 945 | 9.79 | 14.15 | 16.45 |
| Services to buildings and dwellings | 5617 | 1,175 | 1,571 | 1,745 | 2,111 | 2,153 | 10.02 | 12.97 | 15.00 |
| Waste management and remediation services | 562 | 229 | 313 | 357 | 415 | 438 | 15.29 | 19.32 | 23.08 |
| Waste collection | 5621 | 82 | 100 | 141 | 175 | 183 | 12.97 | 17.50 | 19.81 |
| Waste treatment and disposal | 5622 | 77 | 119 | 96 | 97 | 99 | 15.02 | 20.29 | 26.61 |
| **Education and health services** | **(X)** | **11,024** | **15,252** | **19,975** | **23,188** | **23,667** | **13.91** | **19.95** | **23.65** |
| **Educational services** | **61** | **1,688** | **2,390** | **3,155** | **3,668** | **3,728** | **(NA)** | **(NA)** | **(NA)** |
| Elementary and secondary schools | 6111 | 461 | 716 | 849 | 1,065 | 1,083 | (NA) | (NA) | (NA) |
| Junior colleges | 6112 | 44 | 79 | 99 | 58 | 53 | (NA) | (NA) | (NA) |
| Colleges and universities | 6113 | 939 | 1,196 | 1,591 | 1,793 | 1,811 | (NA) | (NA) | (NA) |
| Business, computer, and management training | 6114 | 60 | 86 | 78 | 69 | 74 | (NA) | (NA) | (NA) |
| Technical and trade schools | 6115 | 72 | 91 | 126 | 113 | 114 | (NA) | (NA) | (NA) |
| Other schools and instruction | 6116 | 96 | 184 | 309 | 424 | 440 | (NA) | (NA) | (NA) |
| Educational support services | 6117 | 17 | 39 | 103 | 146 | 152 | (NA) | (NA) | (NA) |
| **Health care and social assistance** | **62** | **9,336** | **12,861** | **16,820** | **19,520** | **19,939** | **13.93** | **20.23** | **23.98** |
| Health care | 621,2,3 | 8,211 | 10,858 | 13,777 | 15,717 | 16,006 | 14.63 | 21.71 | 25.92 |
| Ambulatory health care services | 621 | 2,842 | 4,320 | 5,975 | 7,297 | 7,499 | 15.00 | 21.68 | 25.93 |
| Offices of physicians | 6211 | 1,251 | 1,801 | 2,264 | 2,581 | 2,621 | 15.65 | 24.03 | 31.23 |
| Offices of dentists | 6212 | 513 | 688 | 828 | 936 | 956 | 15.96 | 22.65 | 25.79 |
| Offices of other health practitioners | 6213 | 276 | 438 | 671 | 889 | 930 | 14.24 | 20.48 | 23.07 |
| Outpatient care centers | 6214 | 287 | 425 | 649 | 897 | 934 | 15.36 | 22.81 | 26.39 |
| Medical and diagnostic laboratories | 6215 | 129 | 162 | 228 | 269 | 278 | 15.74 | 23.48 | 25.69 |
| Home health care services | 6216 | 288 | 633 | 1,085 | 1,420 | 1,473 | 12.86 | 16.64 | 18.00 |
| Hospitals | 622 | 3,513 | 3,954 | 4,679 | 5,072 | 5,145 | 16.71 | 26.11 | 31.31 |
| General medical and surgical hospitals | 6221 | 3,305 | 3,745 | 4,357 | 4,669 | 4,724 | 16.75 | 26.33 | 31.56 |
| Psychiatric and substance abuse hospitals | 6222 | 113 | 86 | 109 | 140 | 152 | (NA) | (NA) | (NA) |
| Nursing and residential care facilities | 623 | 1,856 | 2,583 | 3,124 | 3,348 | 3,362 | 10.67 | 14.21 | 16.42 |
| Nursing care facilities | 6231 | 1,170 | 1,514 | 1,657 | 1,627 | 1,609 | 11.08 | 15.26 | 17.27 |
| Residential mental health facilities | 6232 | 269 | 437 | 565 | 632 | 644 | 9.96 | 13.06 | 15.66 |
| Community care facilities for the elderly | 6233 | 330 | 478 | 741 | 922 | 944 | 9.83 | 12.89 | 15.45 |
| Social assistance | 624 | 1,125 | 2,003 | 3,043 | 3,803 | 3,933 | 9.72 | 12.75 | 14.84 |
| Individual and family services | 6241 | 429 | 821 | 1,664 | 2,353 | 2,464 | 10.30 | 13.07 | 15.26 |
| Emergency and other relief services | 6242 | 67 | 117 | 143 | 169 | 175 | 10.95 | 14.41 | 17.90 |
| Vocational rehabilitation services | 6243 | 242 | 370 | 388 | 338 | 330 | 9.57 | 12.47 | 14.31 |
| Child day care services | 6244 | 388 | 696 | 848 | 943 | 964 | 8.88 | 11.99 | 13.50 |
| **Leisure and hospitality** | **(X)** | **9,288** | **11,862** | **13,049** | **16,051** | **16,348** | **8.32** | **11.31** | **13.87** |
| **Arts, entertainment, and recreation** | **71** | **1,132** | **1,788** | **1,913** | **2,333** | **2,394** | **10.68** | **15.27** | **17.30** |

See footnotes at end of table.

# Table 659. Nonfarm Industries—Employees and Earnings: 1990 to 2018-Continued.

| Industry | 2017 NAICS code [1] | All employees (1,000) | | | | | Average hourly earnings [2] (dol.) | | |
|---|---|---|---|---|---|---|---|---|---|
| | | 1990 | 2000 | 2010 | 2017 | 2018 | 2000 | 2010 | 2018 |
| Performing arts and spectator sports........... | 711 | 273 | 382 | 406 | 494 | 506 | 13.11 | 21.01 | 25.62 |
| Museums, historical sites, zoos, and parks.... | 712 | 68 | 110 | 128 | 166 | 170 | 12.20 | 15.60 | 17.83 |
| Amusements, gambling, and recreation....... | 713 | 791 | 1,296 | 1,379 | 1,674 | 1,717 | 9.86 | 13.38 | 14.60 |
| **Accommodation and food services**........... | **72** | **8,156** | **10,074** | **11,135** | **13,718** | **13,955** | **7.92** | **10.68** | **13.37** |
| Accommodation........................ | 721 | 1,616 | 1,884 | 1,760 | 2,003 | 2,028 | 9.48 | 13.02 | 14.82 |
| Traveler accommodation.................. | 7211 | 1,582 | 1,837 | 1,703 | 1,934 | 1,957 | 9.49 | 13.07 | 14.87 |
| Food services and drinking places........... | 722 | 6,540 | 8,189 | 9,376 | 11,715 | 11,926 | 7.49 | 10.15 | 13.07 |
| Full-service restaurants.................. | 722511 | 3,070 | 3,845 | 4,482 | 5,450 | 5,539 | 7.78 | 10.93 | 14.35 |
| Limited-service restaurants.............. | 722513 | 2,429 | 3,042 | 3,418 | 4,380 | 4,447 | 6.80 | 8.86 | 11.11 |
| Special food services.................... | 7223 | 392 | 491 | 543 | 698 | 715 | 9.45 | 11.83 | 14.91 |
| Drinking places, alcoholic beverages...... | 7224 | 312 | 391 | 341 | 391 | 397 | 7.24 | 10.15 | 15.10 |
| **Other services**................................ | **81** | **4,261** | **5,168** | **5,331** | **5,770** | **5,845** | **12.73** | **17.06** | **20.78** |
| Repair and maintenance.................... | 811 | 1,009 | 1,242 | 1,139 | 1,311 | 1,329 | 13.28 | 16.82 | 20.91 |
| Automotive repair and maintenance........... | 8111 | 659 | 888 | 801 | 926 | 938 | 12.45 | 15.55 | 19.56 |
| Electronic equipment repair and maintenance.................... | 8112 | 100 | 107 | 98 | 103 | 103 | 16.31 | 19.41 | 24.09 |
| Commercial machinery repair and maintenance.................... | 8113 | 161 | 161 | 172 | 205 | 211 | 15.53 | 21.03 | 25.39 |
| Personal and laundry services................ | 812 | 1,120 | 1,243 | 1,265 | 1,478 | 1,510 | 10.18 | 13.42 | 15.96 |
| Personal care services................... | 8121 | 430 | 490 | 601 | 711 | 728 | 10.18 | 13.97 | 16.59 |
| Death care services.................... | 8122 | 123 | 136 | 131 | 137 | 136 | 13.04 | 17.46 | 20.34 |
| Dry-cleaning and laundry services........... | 8123 | 371 | 388 | 302 | 299 | 297 | 9.17 | 11.80 | 13.63 |
| Dry-cleaning and laundry services, except coin-operated............... | 81232 | 215 | 211 | 146 | 131 | 127 | 8.14 | 10.56 | 12.42 |
| Other personal services.................... | 8129 | 196 | 229 | 232 | 332 | 348 | 10.52 | 12.43 | 15.58 |
| Pet care services, except veterinary......... | 81291 | 23 | 31 | 63 | 116 | 122 | 12.12 | 12.83 | 14.72 |
| Parking lots and garages................. | 81293 | 68 | 93 | 111 | 141 | 147 | 8.81 | 11.18 | 14.22 |
| Membership associations & organizations...... | 813 | 2,132 | 2,683 | 2,926 | 2,981 | 3,006 | 13.66 | 18.76 | 23.00 |
| Grantmaking and giving services............... | 8132 | 113 | 116 | 178 | 184 | 183 | 14.65 | 23.51 | 31.95 |
| Social advocacy organizations............. | 8133 | 126 | 143 | 202 | 228 | 233 | 12.08 | 17.36 | 23.79 |
| Civic and social organizations.................. | 8134 | 377 | 404 | 392 | 391 | 391 | 9.85 | 12.16 | 15.94 |
| Professional and similar organizations........ | 8139 | 379 | 473 | 477 | 471 | 478 | 15.98 | 22.67 | 27.64 |
| **Government**................................ | **(X)** | **18,415** | **20,790** | **22,490** | **22,350** | **22,449** | **(NA)** | **(NA)** | **(NA)** |
| Federal.................................. | (X) | 3,196 | 2,865 | 2,977 | 2,805 | 2,796 | (NA) | (NA) | (NA) |
| Federal, except U.S. Postal Service............. | (X) | 2,371 | 1,985 | 2,318 | 2,189 | 2,188 | (NA) | (NA) | (NA) |
| U.S. Postal Service....................... | (X) | 825 | 880 | 659 | 615 | 609 | (NA) | (NA) | (NA) |
| State.................................... | (X) | 4,305 | 4,786 | 5,137 | 5,165 | 5,176 | (NA) | (NA) | (NA) |
| Local.................................... | (X) | 10,914 | 13,139 | 14,376 | 14,379 | 14,477 | (NA) | (NA) | (NA) |

NA Not available. X Not applicable. [1] Based on the North American Industry Classification System, 2017. See text, Section 15. [2] Production employees in the goods-producing industries and nonsupervisory employees in service-providing industries. [3] Mining and logging, construction, and manufacturing. [4] Trade, transportation and utilities, information, financial activities, professional and business services, education and health services, leisure and hospitality, other services, and government.

Source: U.S. Bureau of Labor Statistics, Current Employment Statistics, "Employment, Hours, and Earnings—National," <http://www.bls.gov/ces/data.htm>, accessed April 2019.

# Table 660. Women Employed by Nonfarm Industry: 1990 to 2018

[51,619 represents 51,619,000. Annual averages of monthly data. For coverage, see headnote, Table 657]

| Industry | Women employees (1,000) | | | | Percent of total employees | | | |
|---|---|---|---|---|---|---|---|---|
| | 1990 | 2000 | 2010 | 2018 | 1990 | 2000 | 2010 | 2018 |
| **Total nonfarm**...................... | **51,619** | **63,399** | **65,087** | **74,015** | **47.1** | **48.0** | **49.9** | **49.7** |
| **Total private**........................ | **41,764** | **51,629** | **52,258** | **61,089** | **45.8** | **46.4** | **48.4** | **48.2** |
| Construction........................... | 656 | 846 | 723 | 935 | 12.5 | 12.5 | 13.1 | 12.8 |
| Manufacturing.......................... | 5,702 | 5,359 | 3,268 | 3,550 | 32.2 | 31.0 | 28.3 | 28.0 |
| Trade, transportation, and utilities.......... | 9,352 | 10,847 | 9,989 | 11,098 | 41.3 | 41.4 | 40.6 | 40.1 |
| Wholesale trade....................... | 1,598 | 1,812 | 1,619 | 1,744 | 30.6 | 30.8 | 30.1 | 29.8 |
| Retail trade........................... | 6,697 | 7,681 | 7,228 | 7,880 | 50.8 | 50.3 | 50.0 | 49.8 |
| Transportation and warehousing........... | 880 | 1,203 | 1,004 | 1,345 | 25.3 | 27.3 | 23.9 | 24.8 |
| Utilities.............................. | 177 | 151 | 139 | 129 | 24.0 | 25.1 | 25.1 | 23.3 |
| Information............................. | 1,324 | 1,697 | 1,104 | 1,115 | 49.3 | 46.7 | 40.8 | 39.4 |
| Financial activities...................... | 4,055 | 4,697 | 4,530 | 4,846 | 61.3 | 60.3 | 58.9 | 56.6 |
| Professional and business services.............. | 5,116 | 7,693 | 7,472 | 9,506 | 47.0 | 46.1 | 44.5 | 45.3 |
| Professional and technical services........... | 2,217 | 3,156 | 3,537 | 4,321 | 48.6 | 46.9 | 47.2 | 46.5 |
| Management of companies and enterprises...... | 850 | 925 | 940 | 1,181 | 50.9 | 51.4 | 50.1 | 49.8 |
| Administrative and waste services........... | 2,049 | 3,612 | 2,995 | 4,005 | 44.1 | 44.2 | 40.4 | 42.9 |
| Education and health services.................. | 8,455 | 11,703 | 15,435 | 18,249 | 76.7 | 76.7 | 77.3 | 77.1 |
| Educational services.................... | 958 | 1,417 | 1,929 | 2,319 | 56.8 | 59.3 | 61.2 | 62.2 |
| Health care and social assistance............. | 7,496 | 10,286 | 13,505 | 15,930 | 80.3 | 80.0 | 80.3 | 79.9 |
| Leisure and hospitality.................... | 4,829 | 6,082 | 6,819 | 8,591 | 52.0 | 51.3 | 52.3 | 52.6 |
| Arts, entertainment, and recreation.............. | 516 | 815 | 886 | 1,155 | 45.6 | 45.6 | 46.3 | 48.3 |
| Accommodation and food services........... | 4,312 | 5,267 | 5,933 | 7,436 | 52.9 | 52.3 | 53.3 | 53.3 |
| Other services......................... | 2,164 | 2,614 | 2,820 | 3,106 | 50.8 | 50.6 | 52.9 | 53.1 |
| **Government**......................... | **9,855** | **11,771** | **12,829** | **12,926** | **53.5** | **56.6** | **57.0** | **57.6** |
| Federal............................... | 1,378 | 1,231 | 1,326 | 1,248 | 43.1 | 43.0 | 44.5 | 44.6 |
| State government....................... | 2,137 | 2,464 | 2,639 | 2,799 | 49.6 | 51.5 | 51.4 | 54.1 |
| Local government....................... | 6,340 | 8,076 | 8,864 | 8,879 | 58.1 | 61.5 | 61.7 | 61.3 |

Source: U.S. Bureau of Labor Statistics, Current Employment Statistics, "Employment, Hours, and Earnings—National," <http://www.bls.gov/ces/data.htm>, accessed February 2019.

## Table 661. Job Gains and Job Losses of Private Sector Establishments by Industry Sector: 2000 to 2018

[In thousands (16,145 represents 16,145,000). For year ending in March. Based on the Quarterly Census of Employment and Wages (QCEW). Excludes self-employed and certain nonprofit organizations. Minus sign (-) indicates a decrease in employment and comes from either closing establishments or contracting establishments. For more information, see source]

| Year and industry | Gross job gains | | | Gross job losses | | | Net change [1] |
|---|---|---|---|---|---|---|---|
| | Total | Expanding establishments | Opening establishments | Total | Contracting establishments | Closing establishments | |
| 2000 | 16,145 | 10,620 | 5,525 | 13,160 | 8,291 | 4,869 | 2,985 |
| 2005 | 13,829 | 9,406 | 4,423 | 11,826 | 7,675 | 4,151 | 2,003 |
| 2006 | 14,096 | 9,629 | 4,467 | 11,494 | 7,715 | 3,779 | 2,602 |
| 2007 | 13,517 | 9,243 | 4,274 | 12,002 | 8,249 | 3,753 | 1,515 |
| 2008 | 12,786 | 8,718 | 4,068 | 12,674 | 8,776 | 3,898 | 112 |
| 2009 | 10,149 | 6,668 | 3,481 | 15,969 | 11,706 | 4,263 | -5,820 |
| 2010 | 10,075 | 6,839 | 3,236 | 12,760 | 9,142 | 3,618 | -2,685 |
| 2011 | 11,629 | 8,295 | 3,334 | 9,721 | 6,623 | 3,098 | 1,908 |
| 2012 | 12,216 | 8,662 | 3,554 | 9,546 | 6,508 | 3,038 | 2,670 |
| 2013 | 12,045 | 8,553 | 3,492 | 9,924 | 6,829 | 3,095 | 2,121 |
| 2014 | 12,282 | 8,700 | 3,582 | 10,008 | 6,945 | 3,063 | 2,274 |
| 2015 | 12,834 | 9,143 | 3,691 | 10,115 | 6,940 | 3,175 | 2,719 |
| 2016 | 13,168 | 9,394 | 3,774 | 10,656 | 7,426 | 3,230 | 2,512 |
| 2017 | 12,953 | 9,156 | 3,797 | 10,921 | 7,638 | 3,283 | 2,032 |
| **2018, Total private** | **13,117** | **9,349** | **3,768** | **10,898** | **7,618** | **3,280** | **2,219** |
| Goods producing | 2,383 | 1,905 | 478 | 1,875 | 1,415 | 460 | 508 |
| Natural resources and mining | 268 | 207 | 61 | 224 | 166 | 58 | 44 |
| Construction | 1,195 | 891 | 304 | 927 | 666 | 261 | 268 |
| Manufacturing | 920 | 807 | 113 | 724 | 583 | 141 | 196 |
| Service providing | 10,735 | 7,444 | 3,291 | 9,024 | 6,204 | 2,820 | 1,711 |
| Wholesale trade | 569 | 438 | 131 | 489 | 329 | 160 | 80 |
| Retail trade | 1,341 | 959 | 382 | 1,321 | 930 | 391 | 20 |
| Transportation and warehousing | 550 | 426 | 124 | 360 | 255 | 105 | 190 |
| Utilities | 24 | 20 | 4 | 26 | 22 | 4 | -2 |
| Information | 305 | 227 | 78 | 304 | 225 | 79 | 1 |
| Financial activities | 785 | 576 | 209 | 690 | 476 | 214 | 95 |
| Professional and business services | 2,622 | 1,979 | 643 | 2,203 | 1,579 | 624 | 419 |
| Education and health services | 1,915 | 1,391 | 524 | 1,482 | 999 | 483 | 433 |
| Leisure and hospitality | 1,881 | 1,088 | 793 | 1,641 | 1,089 | 552 | 240 |
| Other services | 493 | 327 | 166 | 452 | 291 | 161 | 41 |

[1] Net change is the difference between total gross job gains and total gross job losses.

Source: U.S. Bureau of Labor Statistics, Business Employment Dynamics, "Annual Business Employment Dynamics Data," <http://www.bls.gov/bdm/bdmann.htm#TOTAL>, accessed July 2019.

## Table 662. Private Sector Gross Job Gains and Job Losses by State: 2018

[In thousands (13,117 represents 13,117,000). For year ending in March. Based on the Quarterly Census of Employment and Wages (QCEW). Excludes self-employed and certain nonprofit organizations. Minus sign (-) indicates a decrease in employment and comes from either closing establishments or contracting establishments. For more information, see source]

| State | Gross job gains | | | Gross job losses | | | Net change [1] | State | Gross job gains | | | Gross job losses | | | Net change [1] |
|---|---|---|---|---|---|---|---|---|---|---|---|---|---|---|---|
| | Total | Expanding establishments | Opening establishments | Total | Contracting establishments | Closing establishments | | | Total | Expanding establishments | Opening establishments | Total | Contracting establishments | Closing establishments | |
| **U.S.** | **13,117** | **9,349** | **3,768** | **10,898** | **7,618** | **3,280** | **2,219** | MO | 224 | 155 | 69 | 210 | 141 | 69 | 14 |
| AL | 166 | 118 | 48 | 148 | 104 | 44 | 18 | MT | 40 | 28 | 12 | 34 | 24 | 11 | 5 |
| AK | 23 | 16 | 7 | 24 | 18 | 6 | -1 | NE | 73 | 52 | 21 | 69 | 50 | 19 | 4 |
| AZ | 280 | 205 | 75 | 199 | 138 | 61 | 81 | NV | 143 | 101 | 42 | 104 | 75 | 29 | 39 |
| AR | 98 | 68 | 30 | 86 | 61 | 25 | 11 | NH | 52 | 38 | 14 | 47 | 34 | 12 | 5 |
| CA | 1,761 | 1,208 | 553 | 1,445 | 966 | 478 | 316 | NJ | 356 | 245 | 111 | 302 | 219 | 83 | 54 |
| CO | 262 | 183 | 79 | 202 | 137 | 65 | 60 | NM | 72 | 50 | 21 | 60 | 40 | 19 | 12 |
| CT | 127 | 93 | 34 | 123 | 91 | 32 | 4 | NY | 838 | 603 | 234 | 708 | 469 | 239 | 130 |
| DE | 41 | 27 | 15 | 35 | 24 | 11 | 6 | NC | 400 | 285 | 115 | 324 | 229 | 95 | 76 |
| DC | 59 | 39 | 20 | 46 | 32 | 14 | 14 | ND | 36 | 26 | 10 | 33 | 23 | 9 | 3 |
| FL | 925 | 608 | 317 | 746 | 486 | 260 | 179 | OH | 411 | 320 | 91 | 362 | 269 | 93 | 49 |
| GA | 459 | 313 | 146 | 370 | 247 | 123 | 89 | OK | 160 | 106 | 54 | 127 | 84 | 43 | 33 |
| HI | 51 | 34 | 17 | 47 | 33 | 14 | 5 | OR | 190 | 126 | 64 | 131 | 94 | 37 | 59 |
| ID | 70 | 49 | 21 | 49 | 34 | 15 | 21 | PA | 451 | 348 | 103 | 374 | 274 | 99 | 78 |
| IL | 500 | 369 | 131 | 437 | 304 | 133 | 63 | RI | 40 | 28 | 13 | 36 | 24 | 12 | 4 |
| IN | 252 | 192 | 60 | 215 | 158 | 57 | 37 | SC | 200 | 142 | 58 | 153 | 115 | 38 | 47 |
| IA | 113 | 84 | 29 | 105 | 81 | 24 | 8 | SD | 31 | 23 | 8 | 27 | 21 | 7 | 4 |
| KS | 107 | 79 | 28 | 105 | 75 | 30 | 2 | TN | 243 | 179 | 64 | 203 | 156 | 47 | 41 |
| KY | 160 | 116 | 44 | 147 | 108 | 40 | 13 | TX | 1,190 | 856 | 334 | 945 | 674 | 271 | 245 |
| LA | 181 | 130 | 51 | 168 | 119 | 50 | 13 | UT | 155 | 108 | 46 | 110 | 77 | 33 | 44 |
| ME | 48 | 34 | 14 | 41 | 28 | 13 | 6 | VT | 23 | 16 | 6 | 21 | 15 | 7 | 2 |
| MD | 229 | 168 | 62 | 207 | 143 | 64 | 23 | VA | 338 | 242 | 96 | 288 | 198 | 90 | 50 |
| MA | 290 | 210 | 80 | 242 | 169 | 72 | 49 | WA | 324 | 230 | 94 | 234 | 172 | 63 | 90 |
| MI | 342 | 262 | 79 | 288 | 204 | 84 | 54 | WV | 62 | 42 | 20 | 53 | 37 | 16 | 9 |
| MN | 206 | 157 | 49 | 190 | 134 | 56 | 17 | WI | 207 | 158 | 49 | 178 | 137 | 41 | 29 |
| MS | 86 | 62 | 24 | 81 | 60 | 22 | 5 | WY | 23 | 17 | 7 | 21 | 15 | 6 | 3 |

[1] Net change is the difference between total gross job gains and total gross job losses.

Source: U.S. Bureau of Labor Statistics, Business Employment Dynamics, "Annual Business Employment Dynamics Data," <http://www.bls.gov/bdm/bdmann.htm>, accessed July 2019.

## Table 663. Hires and Separations Affecting Establishment Payrolls By Industry: 2015 to 2018

[62,616 represents 62,616,000. Hires represent any additions to payrolls, including new and rehired employees, full- and part-time workers, short-term and seasonal workers, and other hires. Separations represent terminations of employment, including quits, layoffs, and discharges, and other separations. Based on a monthly survey of private nonfarm establishments and governmental entities]

| Industry | Annual hires (1,000) | | | | Annual separations (1,000) | | | |
|---|---|---|---|---|---|---|---|---|
| | 2015 | 2016 | 2017 | 2018 | 2015 | 2016 | 2017 | 2018 |
| Total | 62,616 | 63,724 | 65,669 | 68,949 | 59,925 | 61,509 | 63,454 | 66,097 |
| Total private industry | 58,548 | 59,515 | 61,526 | 64,569 | 56,008 | 57,439 | 59,400 | 61,907 |
| Mining and logging | 302 | 292 | 373 | 470 | 452 | 395 | 328 | 406 |
| Construction | 3,987 | 4,067 | 4,593 | 4,544 | 3,644 | 3,923 | 4,281 | 4,227 |
| Manufacturing | 3,223 | 3,351 | 3,986 | 4,403 | 3,159 | 3,366 | 3,812 | 4,137 |
| Durable goods | 1,880 | 1,924 | 2,238 | 2,517 | 1,884 | 1,980 | 2,120 | 2,297 |
| Nondurable goods | 1,342 | 1,426 | 1,750 | 1,886 | 1,276 | 1,386 | 1,694 | 1,841 |
| Trade, transportation, and utilities | 13,072 | 12,866 | 12,659 | 13,870 | 12,659 | 12,482 | 12,502 | 13,564 |
| Wholesale trade | 1,643 | 1,644 | 1,653 | 1,754 | 1,626 | 1,614 | 1,625 | 1,684 |
| Retail trade | 9,095 | 8,798 | 8,487 | 9,242 | 8,906 | 8,626 | 8,534 | 9,236 |
| Transportation, warehousing, and utilities | 2,332 | 2,425 | 2,515 | 2,874 | 2,127 | 2,244 | 2,341 | 2,642 |
| Information | 979 | 982 | 1,020 | 1,084 | 950 | 929 | 1,009 | 1,086 |
| Financial activities | 2,370 | 2,402 | 2,531 | 2,516 | 2,227 | 2,218 | 2,386 | 2,401 |
| Finance and insurance | 1,589 | 1,598 | 1,657 | 1,651 | 1,481 | 1,468 | 1,579 | 1,602 |
| Real estate and rental and leasing | 781 | 803 | 870 | 865 | 745 | 751 | 807 | 797 |
| Professional and business services | 12,947 | 13,332 | 13,440 | 13,866 | 12,430 | 13,013 | 13,018 | 13,301 |
| Education and health services | 7,511 | 7,687 | 8,010 | 8,260 | 6,874 | 7,102 | 7,550 | 7,694 |
| Educational services | 1,095 | 1,114 | 1,141 | 1,184 | 1,017 | 1,034 | 1,063 | 1,107 |
| Health care and social assistance | 6,416 | 6,573 | 6,866 | 7,073 | 5,858 | 6,070 | 6,487 | 6,589 |
| Leisure and hospitality | 11,646 | 12,219 | 12,227 | 12,920 | 11,149 | 11,762 | 11,900 | 12,545 |
| Arts, entertainment, and recreation | 1,845 | 1,907 | 2,037 | 2,227 | 1,771 | 1,824 | 1,956 | 2,092 |
| Accommodation and food services | 9,798 | 10,312 | 10,189 | 10,694 | 9,378 | 9,938 | 9,942 | 10,452 |
| Other services | 2,513 | 2,313 | 2,692 | 2,636 | 2,460 | 2,246 | 2,610 | 2,549 |
| Government workers | 4,069 | 4,211 | 4,143 | 4,378 | 3,915 | 4,072 | 4,055 | 4,188 |
| Federal | 413 | 414 | 382 | 420 | 382 | 372 | 402 | 410 |
| State and local | 3,652 | 3,796 | 3,762 | 3,962 | 3,531 | 3,699 | 3,653 | 3,780 |

Source: U.S. Bureau of Labor Statistics, *Job Openings and Labor Turnover—January 2019*, USDL 19-0404, March 2019. See also <http://www.bls.gov/jlt/news.htm>.

## Table 664. Type of Separations Affecting Establishment Payrolls: 2018

[40,073 represents 40,073,000. Covers all private nonfarm establishments. Separations are the total number of terminations of employment occurring at any time during the reference month, and are reported by type of separation—quits, layoffs and discharges, and other separations. Annual rate estimates are computed by dividing annual levels by the Current Employment Statistics (CES) annual average employment level and multiplying that quotient by 100]

| Industry | Number (1,000) | | | Rate (percent) [1] | | |
|---|---|---|---|---|---|---|
| | Annual quits [2] | Annual layoffs and discharges [3] | Annual other separations [4] | Annual quits [2] | Annual layoffs and discharges [3] | Annual other separations [4] |
| Total | 40,073 | 21,888 | 4,136 | 26.9 | 14.7 | 2.8 |
| Total private industry | 37,913 | 20,581 | 3,413 | 29.9 | 16.3 | 2.7 |
| Mining and logging | 243 | 141 | 21 | 33.2 | 19.3 | 2.9 |
| Construction | 2,055 | 2,016 | 154 | 28.2 | 27.7 | 2.1 |
| Manufacturing | 2,498 | 1,387 | 255 | 19.7 | 10.9 | 2.0 |
| Durable goods | 1,385 | 750 | 161 | 17.4 | 9.4 | 2.0 |
| Nondurable goods | 1,113 | 638 | 90 | 23.5 | 13.5 | 1.9 |
| Trade, transportation, and utilities | 8,548 | 4,190 | 829 | 30.9 | 15.1 | 3.0 |
| Wholesale trade | 1,049 | 493 | 143 | 17.9 | 8.4 | 2.4 |
| Retail trade | 6,020 | 2,681 | 538 | 38.0 | 16.9 | 3.4 |
| Transportation, warehousing, and utilities | 1,478 | 1,017 | 149 | 24.7 | 17.0 | 2.5 |
| Information | 575 | 430 | 81 | 20.3 | 15.2 | 2.9 |
| Financial activities | 1,391 | 711 | 298 | 16.2 | 8.3 | 3.5 |
| Finance and insurance | 845 | 497 | 259 | 13.4 | 7.9 | 4.1 |
| Real estate and rental and leasing | 544 | 216 | 37 | 24.1 | 9.6 | 1.6 |
| Professional and business services | 7,595 | 4,936 | 773 | 36.2 | 23.5 | 3.7 |
| Education and health services | 5,042 | 2,087 | 567 | 21.3 | 8.8 | 2.4 |
| Educational services | 567 | 469 | 69 | 15.2 | 12.6 | 1.9 |
| Health care and social assistance | 4,474 | 1,616 | 498 | 22.4 | 8.1 | 2.5 |
| Leisure and hospitality | 8,470 | 3,762 | 314 | 51.8 | 23.0 | 1.9 |
| Arts, entertainment, and recreation | 912 | 1,134 | 49 | 38.1 | 47.4 | 2.0 |
| Accommodation and food services | 7,557 | 2,631 | 267 | 54.2 | 18.9 | 1.9 |
| Other services | 1,501 | 921 | 128 | 25.7 | 15.8 | 2.2 |
| Government workers | 2,159 | 1,308 | 725 | 9.6 | 5.8 | 3.2 |
| Federal | 189 | 92 | 130 | 6.8 | 3.3 | 4.6 |
| State and local | 1,974 | 1,213 | 592 | 10.0 | 6.2 | 3.0 |

[1] As a percent of total employment. [2] Quits are voluntary separations by employees (except for retirements, which are reported as other separations). [3] Layoffs and discharges are involuntary separations initiated by the employer and include layoffs with no intent to rehire; formal layoffs lasting or expected to last more than seven days; discharges resulting from mergers, downsizing, or closings, firings or other discharges for cause; terminations of permanent or short term employees; and terminations of seasonal employees. [4] Other separations include retirements, transfers to other locations, deaths, and separations due to disability.

Source: U.S. Bureau of Labor Statistics, *Job Openings and Labor Turnover—January 2019*, USDL 19-0404, March 2019. See also <https://www.bls.gov/jlt/news.htm>.

## Table 665. Private Nonprofit Establishments, Employees, and Average Annual Wages by Selected Industry: 2017

[In units, as indicated. 122,387 represents 122,387,000. Data from Bureau of Labor Statistics' Quarterly Census of Employment and Wages and IRS Exempt Organization Business Master File]

| Industry | NAICS code | All establishments | | | 501(c)(3) nonprofit establishments | | | 501(c)(3) percent of total employment |
|---|---|---|---|---|---|---|---|---|
| | | Establishments (number) | Annual average employment (1,000s) | Annual wages per employee (dollars) | Establishments (number) | Annual average employment (1,000s) | Annual wages per employee (dollars) | |
| **Total private** | (X) | **9,536,831** | **122,387** | **55,338** | **299,457** | **12,489** | **53,667** | **10.2** |
| Agriculture, forestry, fishing and hunting | 11 | 104,445 | 1,261 | 34,464 | 338 | 3 | 34,981 | 0.2 |
| Construction | 23 | 784,852 | 6,919 | 60,735 | 930 | 9 | 46,364 | 0.1 |
| Manufacturing | 31-33 | 346,723 | 12,407 | 66,840 | 267 | 7 | 38,240 | 0.1 |
| Wholesale trade | 42 | 612,359 | 5,899 | 75,904 | 732 | 4 | 57,227 | 0.1 |
| Retail trade | 44-45 | 1,042,096 | 15,854 | 31,217 | 5,750 | 93 | 22,467 | 0.6 |
| Transportation and warehousing | 48-49 | 242,932 | 4,947 | 51,726 | 893 | 21 | 34,523 | 0.4 |
| Information | 51 | 162,702 | 2,793 | 105,722 | 4,705 | 68 | 52,650 | 2.4 |
| Finance and insurance | 52 | 484,801 | 5,909 | 106,185 | 1,301 | 44 | 95,789 | 0.7 |
| Real estate and rental and leasing | 53 | 385,826 | 2,180 | 56,970 | 3,916 | 36 | 38,779 | 1.7 |
| Professional, scientific, and technical services | 54 | 1,183,104 | 8,996 | 93,687 | 11,944 | 270 | 80,686 | 3.0 |
| Management of companies and enterprises | 55 | 64,772 | 2,278 | 119,885 | 4,633 | 281 | 69,142 | 12.3 |
| Administrative and support and waste management and remediation services | 56 | 534,038 | 9,065 | 39,621 | 5,098 | 101 | 53,689 | 1.1 |
| Educational services | 61 | 117,479 | 2,824 | 50,053 | 32,832 | 2,004 | 55,389 | 70.9 |
| Elementary and secondary schools | 6111 | 17,969 | 811 | 41,234 | 12,879 | 684 | 41,766 | 84.3 |
| Colleges, universities, and professional schools | 6113 | 8,934 | 1,242 | 64,605 | 5,331 | 1,138 | 66,097 | 91.6 |
| Health care and social assistance | 62 | 1,532,134 | 19,322 | 49,076 | 138,319 | 8,307 | 54,742 | 43.0 |
| Hospitals | 622 | 10,024 | 5,018 | 62,595 | 5,171 | 4,207 | 63,923 | 83.8 |
| Other residential care facilities | 6239 | 6,585 | 165 | 31,853 | 3,680 | 112 | 33,615 | 67.8 |
| Community food and housing, and emergency and other relief services | 6242 | 11,389 | 169 | 37,870 | 9,871 | 154 | 37,301 | 91.2 |
| Vocational rehabilitation services | 6243 | 9,574 | 335 | 26,599 | 6,940 | 289 | 25,542 | 86.1 |
| Arts, entertainment, and recreation | 71 | 141,502 | 2,294 | 37,759 | 15,261 | 356 | 29,810 | 15.5 |
| Performing arts companies | 7111 | 10,026 | 123 | 49,541 | 3,498 | 70 | 38,353 | 57.0 |
| Museums, historical sites, and similar institutions | 712 | 6,475 | 163 | 34,795 | 4,960 | 141 | 35,759 | 86.5 |
| Accommodation and food services | 72 | 697,728 | 13,607 | 20,731 | 1,909 | 38 | 20,838 | 0.3 |
| Other services (except public administration) | 81 | 839,795 | 4,435 | 37,320 | 66,719 | 838 | 39,198 | 18.9 |
| Religious, grantmaking, civic, professional, and similar organizations | 813 | 146,264 | 1,370 | 43,941 | 64,730 | 819 | 39,353 | 59.8 |
| Religious organizations | 8131 | 23,174 | 192 | 28,976 | 18,324 | 163 | 29,495 | 84.9 |
| Grantmaking and giving services | 8132 | 16,042 | 143 | 66,667 | 14,118 | 131 | 66,130 | 91.5 |
| Social advocacy organizations | 8133 | 22,277 | 212 | 48,115 | 18,070 | 185 | 47,191 | 87.6 |
| Civic and social organizations | 8134 | 25,771 | 392 | 19,976 | 8,992 | 280 | 18,957 | 71.3 |

Source: U.S. Bureau of Labor Statistics, Business Employment Dynamics, "Research Data on the Nonprofit Sector," <https://www.bls.gov/bdm/nonprofits/nonprofits.htm>, accessed May 2019.

## Table 666. Indexes of Multifactor Productivity and Related Measures: 1990 to 2018

[2012=100. Data shown for private nonfarm business. Multifactor productivity (MFP) is a measure of economic performance comparing the amount of goods and services produced (output) to the amount of combined inputs used to produce those goods and services. Measured using output and compensation data published by the Bureau of Economic Analysis (BEA), hours data published by other BLS programs, and capital data supplied by BEA and U.S. Department of Agriculture. See source for details]

| Year | Labor productivity (output per hour worked) | Output per unit of capital services | Multifactor productivity [1] | Value added output [2] | Labor [3] | Capital services [4] | Combined units of labor and capital services | Capital intensity (capital services per hour) |
|---|---|---|---|---|---|---|---|---|
| 1990 | 60.1 | 117.3 | 80.6 | 53.4 | 80.2 | 45.5 | 66.3 | 51.2 |
| 1995 | 65.4 | 114.1 | 82.9 | 61.7 | 87.7 | 54.1 | 74.5 | 57.3 |
| 2000 | 75.3 | 109.5 | 88.8 | 79.1 | 99.5 | 72.3 | 89.1 | 68.8 |
| 2005 | 88.6 | 106.1 | 96.9 | 90.9 | 98.9 | 85.7 | 93.8 | 83.5 |
| 2010 | 99.4 | 98.6 | 99.5 | 95.0 | 94.9 | 96.4 | 95.5 | 100.8 |
| 2015 | 102.6 | 100.5 | 101.4 | 109.2 | 107.1 | 108.7 | 107.7 | 102.1 |
| 2017 | 103.9 | 98.9 | 101.2 | 114.0 | 111.1 | 115.2 | 112.6 | 105.0 |
| 2018 | 105.3 | 99.6 | 102.1 | 118.0 | 113.8 | 118.5 | 115.5 | 105.7 |
| ANNUAL PERCENT CHANGE | | | | | | | | |
| 1990 | 1.8 | -1.9 | 0.1 | 1.5 | 0.3 | 3.5 | 1.3 | 3.9 |
| 1995 | 1.2 | -0.9 | 0.3 | 3.5 | 2.6 | 4.5 | 3.2 | 2.2 |
| 2000 | 3.4 | -1.6 | 1.5 | 4.7 | 1.6 | 6.5 | 3.1 | 5.1 |
| 2005 | 2.2 | 0.5 | 1.5 | 4.0 | 1.8 | 3.4 | 2.4 | 1.7 |
| 2010 | 3.3 | 2.5 | 2.6 | 3.3 | 0.6 | 0.8 | 0.7 | 0.8 |
| 2015 | 1.3 | 0.5 | 0.9 | 3.5 | 2.4 | 3.0 | 2.7 | 0.8 |
| 2017 | 1.1 | -0.2 | 0.4 | 2.7 | 1.9 | 2.9 | 2.3 | 1.3 |
| 2018 | 1.3 | 0.6 | 1.0 | 3.5 | 2.4 | 2.9 | 2.6 | 0.7 |

[1] Output per combined units of labor input and capital services. [2] Gross domestic product originating in the sector. [3] Index of hours worked of all persons including employees, proprietors, and unpaid family workers, classified by age, education, and gender. [4] Measures the services derived from the stock of physical assets and intellectual property products.

Source: U.S. Bureau of Labor Statistics, Multifactor Productivity, "Multifactor Productivity Trends, 2018," March 2019. See also <https://www.bls.gov/mfp/home.htm>

# Table 667. Productivity and Related Measures for Selected NAICS Industries: 1987 to 2018

[For a discussion of productivity measures and methodology, see text, this section and BLS Handbook of Methods, Chapter 11, <http://www.bls.gov/opub/hom/homch11.htm>. Minus sign (-) indicates decrease]

| Industry | 2012 NAICS code [1] | Average annual percent change [2] | | | | | | | |
|---|---|---|---|---|---|---|---|---|---|
| | | 1987-2018 [3] | | | | 2017-2018 | | | |
| | | Labor productivity | Unit labor costs | Output | Hours | Labor productivity | Unit labor costs | Output | Hours |
| Mining | 21 | 1.3 | 2.5 | 1.4 | 0.1 | 2.1 | -1.6 | 11.8 | 9.5 |
| Oil and gas extraction | 211 | 2.9 | 2.2 | 1.7 | -1.2 | 12.1 | -12.4 | 15.6 | 3.1 |
| Mining, except oil and gas | 212 | 1.4 | 1.6 | 0.1 | -1.3 | -3.5 | 7.6 | 0.2 | 3.8 |
| Coal mining | 2121 | 1.7 | 1.0 | -1.4 | -3.0 | -4.9 | 7.6 | -2.0 | 3.0 |
| Utilities | 22 | 2.0 | 1.6 | 1.3 | -0.7 | 4.5 | -2.3 | 4.5 | – |
| Power generation and supply | 2211 | 2.8 | 0.8 | 1.9 | -0.9 | 2.6 | -0.9 | 3.2 | 0.7 |
| Natural gas distribution | 2212 | 0.7 | 3.6 | -0.3 | -1.0 | 13.5 | -9.7 | 10.7 | -2.4 |
| Water, sewage and other systems | 2213 | -1.8 | 4.7 | 0.7 | 2.5 | -0.5 | 6.6 | -0.5 | – |
| Manufacturing: | | | | | | | | | |
| Food | 311 | 0.6 | 1.9 | 1.2 | 0.6 | -3.1 | 4.1 | -0.6 | 2.6 |
| Fruit and vegetable preserving and specialty | 3114 | 0.9 | 1.8 | 0.9 | – | -2.8 | 6.1 | -4.6 | -1.8 |
| Dairy products | 3115 | 1.1 | 2.2 | 1.0 | – | -5.7 | 3.8 | -1.5 | 4.4 |
| Animal slaughtering and processing | 3116 | 0.3 | 2.0 | 1.5 | 1.2 | -1.8 | 6.3 | -0.3 | 1.6 |
| Bakeries and tortilla manufacturing | 3118 | 0.1 | 1.8 | 0.4 | 0.3 | -4.4 | 1.8 | 0.7 | 5.3 |
| Beverages and tobacco products | 312 | -0.6 | 2.6 | -0.3 | 0.4 | -7.2 | 6.6 | -2.3 | 5.2 |
| Textile mills | 313 | 2.8 | -0.1 | -2.1 | -4.8 | -3.4 | -1.0 | 2.1 | 5.7 |
| Apparel | 315 | -0.5 | 1.8 | -6.7 | -6.2 | 1.5 | 0.4 | -3.3 | -4.7 |
| Leather and allied products | 316 | 0.9 | 1.9 | -4.1 | -4.9 | 0.3 | 3.4 | -3.5 | -3.8 |
| Wood products | 321 | 0.9 | 2.2 | -0.1 | -1.0 | -4.6 | 7.9 | -1.3 | 3.4 |
| Paper and paper products | 322 | 1.6 | 1.3 | -0.2 | -1.8 | -2.5 | 1.7 | -1.0 | 1.5 |
| Converted paper products | 3222 | 1.3 | 1.7 | 0.1 | -1.2 | -2.2 | 3.8 | -0.9 | 1.3 |
| Printing and related support activities | 323 | 1.3 | 1.2 | -0.6 | -1.8 | 2.0 | 2.0 | -1.5 | -3.5 |
| Petroleum and coal products | 324 | 1.9 | 2.6 | 1.0 | -0.9 | -7.8 | 7.7 | -3.3 | 4.9 |
| Chemicals | 325 | 1.2 | 2.0 | 0.8 | -0.4 | -1.4 | 2.0 | 0.6 | 2.1 |
| Pharmaceuticals and medicines | 3254 | -0.5 | 3.7 | 1.2 | 1.6 | -3.4 | 2.4 | -1.0 | 2.5 |
| Plastics and rubber products | 326 | 1.3 | 1.6 | 1.1 | -0.2 | -3.3 | 7.2 | -2.5 | 0.9 |
| Plastics products | 3261 | 1.3 | 1.7 | 1.4 | 0.1 | -3.3 | 7.3 | -2.5 | 0.9 |
| Nonmetallic mineral products | 327 | 0.7 | 1.9 | 0.1 | -0.6 | -3.0 | 4.9 | -0.5 | 2.6 |
| Primary metals | 331 | 2.3 | 0.7 | 0.5 | -1.7 | -3.0 | 3.9 | 2.6 | 5.7 |
| Fabricated metal products | 332 | 0.8 | 1.9 | 0.6 | -0.2 | -1.4 | 5.2 | 1.0 | 2.4 |
| Forging and stamping | 3321 | 1.9 | 1.0 | 0.9 | -1.0 | -0.5 | 6.0 | -0.3 | 0.3 |
| Cutlery and hand tools | 3322 | 1.4 | 1.3 | -0.7 | -2.1 | -0.3 | -7.0 | 10.3 | 10.7 |
| Architectural and structural metals | 3323 | 0.4 | 2.4 | 0.8 | 0.4 | -1.8 | 7.0 | 1.0 | 2.9 |
| Machine shops and threaded products | 3327 | 1.3 | 1.6 | 2.0 | 0.7 | -2.8 | 5.1 | 0.8 | 3.7 |
| Other fabricated metal products | 3329 | 0.4 | 2.1 | -0.1 | -0.5 | -0.7 | 6.1 | – | 0.7 |
| Machinery | 333 | 1.7 | 1.1 | 1.1 | -0.6 | – | 4.0 | 2.8 | 2.9 |
| Agriculture, construction, and mining machinery | 3331 | 1.7 | 1.0 | 1.8 | 0.1 | 1.0 | 3.2 | 6.5 | 5.5 |
| Industrial machinery | 3332 | 1.2 | 1.5 | 0.6 | -0.6 | -2.5 | 9.7 | -1.7 | 0.8 |
| Computer and electronic products | 334 | 8.2 | -4.7 | 6.0 | -2.0 | -0.6 | 5.4 | -0.7 | -0.1 |
| Semiconductors and electronic components | 3344 | 11.6 | -7.6 | 9.9 | -1.5 | -1.2 | 5.9 | -0.2 | 1.0 |
| Electronic instruments | 3345 | 2.7 | 0.7 | 1.2 | -1.5 | -1.5 | 7.0 | -1.4 | 0.1 |
| Electrical equipment and appliances | 335 | 1.6 | 1.4 | -0.1 | -1.6 | -1.3 | 4.6 | -1.1 | 0.3 |
| Transportation equipment | 336 | 2.2 | 0.3 | 1.5 | -0.6 | -4.7 | 7.5 | -1.0 | 3.9 |
| Motor vehicles | 3361 | 2.4 | 0.1 | 1.8 | -0.7 | -7.6 | 7.2 | -0.1 | 8.2 |
| Motor vehicle parts | 3363 | 2.7 | -1.0 | 2.6 | – | -1.2 | 5.4 | 0.2 | 1.5 |
| Aerospace products and parts | 3364 | 1.6 | 1.3 | 0.2 | -1.4 | -8.1 | 10.3 | -3.2 | 5.3 |
| Ship and boat building | 3366 | 1.5 | 1.9 | 0.7 | -0.9 | -1.0 | 6.4 | -1.0 | 0.1 |
| Furniture and related products | 337 | 1.2 | 1.7 | -0.1 | -1.4 | -2.3 | 4.7 | -1.7 | 0.6 |
| Household and institutional furniture | 3371 | 1.1 | 1.8 | -0.4 | -1.5 | -2.0 | 3.7 | -0.2 | 1.8 |
| Miscellaneous manufacturing | 339 | 1.6 | 1.6 | 1.5 | -0.2 | -1.9 | 7.0 | -1.5 | 0.4 |
| Medical equipment and supplies | 3391 | 2.0 | 1.5 | 2.9 | 0.9 | -1.8 | 7.8 | -2.3 | -0.5 |
| Wholesale trade | 42 | 2.7 | 0.9 | 3.1 | 0.3 | 1.6 | 1.4 | 2.3 | 0.7 |
| Durable goods | 423 | 4.3 | -0.4 | 4.5 | 0.2 | 3.6 | 0.2 | 5.1 | 1.4 |
| Nondurable goods | 424 | 1.0 | 2.8 | 1.3 | 0.2 | -1.3 | 5.0 | -1.0 | 0.3 |
| Electronic markets and agents and brokers | 425 | 1.6 | 0.6 | 3.3 | 1.7 | 5.2 | -7.6 | 2.6 | -2.4 |
| Retail trade | 44-45 | 2.9 | – | 3.3 | 0.5 | 3.2 | – | 3.3 | 0.2 |
| Motor vehicle and parts dealers | 441 | 2.2 | 0.6 | 3.0 | 0.8 | 2.2 | 0.7 | 2.2 | – |
| Automobile dealers | 4411 | 2.3 | 0.5 | 3.1 | 0.8 | 2.6 | -0.5 | 2.7 | 0.1 |
| Other motor vehicle dealers | 4412 | 2.5 | 1.0 | 3.7 | 1.2 | -8.1 | 14.1 | -3.2 | 5.4 |
| Auto parts, accessories, and tire stores | 4413 | 1.1 | 1.3 | 1.8 | 0.7 | 2.3 | 2.0 | 0.7 | -1.6 |
| Furniture and home furnishings stores | 442 | 3.8 | -0.9 | 3.8 | – | 1.3 | 3.5 | 3.0 | 1.7 |
| Furniture stores | 4421 | 3.3 | -0.8 | 3.4 | – | 3.4 | -0.7 | 6.5 | 3.0 |
| Home furnishings stores | 4422 | 4.4 | -1.2 | 4.4 | – | -1.1 | 8.6 | -0.8 | 0.3 |
| Electronics and appliance stores | 443 | 10.7 | -7.2 | 11.1 | 0.4 | 8.8 | -3.9 | 7.0 | -1.7 |
| Building material and garden supply stores | 444 | 2.6 | -0.1 | 3.3 | 0.7 | -0.6 | 1.7 | 0.8 | 1.5 |
| Building material and supplies dealers | 4441 | 2.5 | – | 3.3 | 0.8 | 0.4 | 0.9 | 2.0 | 1.6 |
| Lawn and garden equipment and supplies stores | 4442 | 3.0 | -0.6 | 2.9 | – | -8.1 | 7.9 | -7.1 | 1.1 |
| Food and beverage stores | 445 | 0.7 | 2.1 | 0.7 | – | 3.1 | -1.7 | 3.1 | – |
| Grocery stores | 4451 | 0.6 | 2.3 | 0.6 | 0.1 | 4.2 | -2.3 | 3.1 | -1.0 |
| Specialty food stores | 4452 | 0.1 | 2.0 | -0.3 | -0.4 | -7.4 | 7.0 | 0.3 | 8.3 |
| Beer, wine and liquor stores | 4453 | 2.2 | 0.6 | 1.5 | -0.6 | -0.6 | -0.1 | 4.3 | 5.0 |
| Health and personal care stores | 446 | 1.6 | 1.6 | 2.7 | 1.1 | 2.4 | -0.7 | 2.2 | -0.2 |
| Gasoline stations | 447 | 1.4 | 1.6 | 1.1 | -0.2 | -1.6 | 4.0 | 0.5 | 2.1 |
| Clothing and clothing accessories stores | 448 | 3.9 | -1.1 | 3.7 | -0.2 | 4.3 | -3.2 | 5.6 | 1.2 |
| Clothing stores | 4481 | 4.3 | -1.3 | 4.1 | -0.1 | 4.2 | -2.6 | 5.0 | 0.7 |
| Shoe stores | 4482 | 2.9 | -0.7 | 2.5 | -0.3 | 0.9 | -3.4 | 4.6 | 3.7 |
| Jewelry, luggage, and leather goods stores | 4483 | 3.3 | -0.2 | 2.7 | -0.6 | 9.1 | -6.5 | 9.8 | 0.7 |
| Sporting goods, hobby, book, and music stores | 451 | 3.5 | -0.6 | 3.7 | 0.2 | 4.1 | 3.2 | -3.2 | -7.0 |

See footnotes at end of table.

# Table 667. Productivity and Related Measures for Selected NAICS Industries: 1987 to 2018-Continued.

See headnote on page 430.

| Industry | 2012 NAICS code [1] | Average annual percent change [2] | | | | | | | |
|---|---|---|---|---|---|---|---|---|---|
| | | 1987-2018 [3] | | | | 2017-2018 | | | |
| | | Labor produc-tivity | Unit labor costs | Output | Hours | Labor produc-tivity | Unit labor costs | Output | Hours |
| Sporting goods and musical instrument stores.. | 4511 | 4.0 | -1.1 | 4.5 | 0.5 | 1.8 | 3.4 | -2.9 | -4.6 |
| Book, periodical, and music stores.............. | 4512 | 1.9 | 1.0 | 0.3 | -1.6 | 23.0 | 1.9 | -5.4 | -23.1 |
| General merchandise stores........................ | 452 | 2.9 | -0.7 | 4.2 | 1.3 | 2.2 | -0.3 | 3.0 | 0.9 |
| Department stores............................. | 4521 | 0.6 | 0.9 | 0.5 | -0.1 | 0.7 | 0.2 | -0.1 | -0.8 |
| Other general merchandise stores.............. | 4529 | 4.9 | -1.8 | 7.4 | 2.3 | 2.1 | 0.3 | 3.9 | 1.8 |
| Miscellaneous store retailers....................... | 453 | 3.3 | -0.8 | 3.1 | -0.2 | 3.1 | 1.5 | 3.5 | 0.4 |
| Florists...................................... | 4531 | 3.3 | -0.1 | 0.1 | -3.1 | 15.5 | -7.8 | 4.9 | -9.2 |
| Office supplies, stationery and gift stores........ | 4532 | 5.6 | -2.5 | 3.8 | -1.7 | 9.0 | -9.0 | 5.9 | -2.8 |
| Used merchandise stores..................... | 4533 | 4.7 | -2.0 | 5.9 | 1.1 | 8.3 | 3.6 | – | -7.7 |
| Other miscellaneous store retailers............ | 4539 | 0.9 | 0.6 | 2.4 | 1.5 | -4.8 | 8.5 | 3.3 | 8.4 |
| Nonstore retailers................................. | 454 | 8.1 | -3.6 | 8.9 | 0.7 | 11.5 | 1.1 | 9.8 | -1.5 |
| Electronic shopping and mail-order houses..... | 4541 | 9.9 | -4.6 | 14.1 | 3.8 | 11.0 | 3.4 | 10.6 | -0.4 |
| Vending machine operators................... | 4542 | 0.5 | 3.0 | -1.9 | -2.4 | 10.3 | 1.3 | 6.1 | -3.8 |
| Direct selling establishments................. | 4543 | 2.4 | 0.3 | 1.0 | -1.3 | 7.7 | -3.0 | 4.3 | -3.2 |
| Transportation and warehousing: | | | | | | | | | |
| Air transportation................................ | 481 | 3.0 | 0.9 | 2.7 | -0.3 | 5.1 | – | 5.1 | – |
| Line-haul railroads............................... | 482111 | 3.6 | -0.4 | 1.8 | -1.7 | -0.6 | 5.3 | – | 0.6 |
| Truck transportation............................. | 484 | 0.7 | 1.0 | 2.0 | 1.3 | -0.3 | 5.0 | 2.4 | 2.7 |
| General freight trucking..................... | 4841 | 1.1 | 1.0 | 2.3 | 1.2 | 1.5 | 3.1 | 4.0 | 2.5 |
| Used household and office goods moving....... | 48421 | -0.4 | 2.6 | -0.1 | 0.3 | (NA) | (NA) | (NA) | (NA) |
| Postal service.................................... | 491 | 0.4 | 2.9 | -0.6 | -1.0 | – | 5.5 | -1.5 | -1.5 |
| Couriers and messengers......................... | 492 | -1.9 | 3.2 | 0.6 | 2.6 | -1.6 | 4.1 | 2.7 | 4.4 |
| Warehousing and storage......................... | 493 | 1.4 | 0.3 | 5.6 | 4.1 | -7.6 | 11.2 | 2.0 | 10.4 |
| General warehousing and storage............. | 49311 | 2.5 | -0.5 | 6.9 | 4.3 | (NA) | (NA) | (NA) | (NA) |
| Refrigerated warehousing and storage......... | 49312 | -0.2 | 1.5 | 2.9 | 3.1 | (NA) | (NA) | (NA) | (NA) |
| Information: | | | | | | | | | |
| Publishing........................................ | 511 | 3.8 | 1.6 | 3.3 | -0.5 | 7.3 | 1.2 | 9.7 | 2.3 |
| Newspaper, book, and directory publishers..... | 5111 | 0.1 | 4.0 | -2.5 | -2.6 | (NA) | (NA) | (NA) | (NA) |
| Software publishers............................ | 5112 | 10.8 | -5.2 | 17.2 | 5.8 | 4.0 | 0.5 | 15.5 | 11.0 |
| Motion picture and video exhibition.............. | 51213 | 1.4 | 2.0 | 1.8 | 0.4 | (NA) | (NA) | (NA) | (NA) |
| Broadcasting, except internet..................... | 515 | 3.0 | 1.7 | 2.9 | -0.1 | 4.5 | – | 4.9 | 0.4 |
| Radio and television broadcasting............. | 5151 | 2.2 | 1.7 | 1.8 | -0.4 | 5.7 | -2.5 | 5.7 | – |
| Cable and other subscription programming..... | 5152 | 5.2 | 2.9 | 6.4 | 1.2 | 2.1 | 4.5 | 3.8 | 1.6 |
| Wired telecommunications carriers............... | 5171 | 3.6 | -0.7 | 2.6 | -0.9 | 3.1 | 1.6 | -4.6 | -7.5 |
| Wireless telecommunications carriers........... | 5172 | 11.9 | -6.9 | 18.5 | 5.9 | 10.1 | -7.9 | 6.6 | -3.1 |
| Finance and insurance: | | | | | | | | | |
| Commercial banking............................... | 52211 | 3.0 | 2.0 | 3.0 | – | 1.5 | 2.3 | 1.7 | 0.3 |
| Real estate and rental and leasing: | | | | | | | | | |
| Passenger car rental.............................. | 532111 | 2.1 | 1.4 | 3.1 | 1.0 | (NA) | (NA) | (NA) | (NA) |
| Truck, trailer and RV rental and leasing........... | 53212 | 1.9 | 1.1 | 2.7 | 0.7 | 2.8 | 6.2 | 7.2 | 4.3 |
| Video tape and disc rental........................ | 53223 | 6.7 | -2.3 | -2.3 | -8.4 | (NA) | (NA) | (NA) | (NA) |
| Professional and technical services: | | | | | | | | | |
| Accounting and bookkeeping services.............. | 5412 | 2.6 | 1.0 | 3.3 | 0.6 | -0.9 | 5.5 | 0.1 | 1.0 |
| Architectural services............................ | 54131 | 1.4 | 1.9 | 2.6 | 1.2 | (NA) | (NA) | (NA) | (NA) |
| Engineering services............................. | 54133 | 1.2 | 2.7 | 2.8 | 1.6 | 1.9 | 2.0 | 3.4 | 1.4 |
| Advertising agencies............................. | 54181 | 1.9 | 2.1 | 2.4 | 0.5 | (NA) | (NA) | (NA) | (NA) |
| Photography studios, portrait..................... | 541921 | 0.3 | 1.7 | 1.2 | 1.0 | (NA) | (NA) | (NA) | (NA) |
| Administrative and waste services: | | | | | | | | | |
| Employment placement agencies.................. | 56131 | 4.3 | – | 5.3 | 1.0 | (NA) | (NA) | (NA) | (NA) |
| Travel arrangement and reservation services..... | 5615 | 6.0 | -1.0 | 4.1 | -1.8 | 7.3 | -1.4 | 3.1 | -3.9 |
| Janitorial services................................ | 56172 | 1.7 | 1.8 | 3.4 | 1.8 | (NA) | (NA) | (NA) | (NA) |
| Health care and social assistance: | | | | | | | | | |
| Medical and diagnostic laboratories............... | 6215 | 1.9 | 0.5 | 5.0 | 3.0 | -0.8 | 4.0 | 1.0 | 1.8 |
| Arts, entertainment, and recreation: | | | | | | | | | |
| Amusement parks and arcades................... | 7131 | -1.4 | 5.3 | -0.7 | 0.8 | 4.8 | 3.6 | 3.8 | -1.0 |
| Fitness and recreational sports centers........... | 71394 | 3.7 | -0.7 | 4.4 | 0.7 | (NA) | (NA) | (NA) | (NA) |
| Accommodation and food services: | | | | | | | | | |
| Food services and drinking places............... | 722 | 0.5 | 3.0 | 2.3 | 1.8 | 1.6 | 2.0 | 3.6 | 2.0 |
| Special food services........................... | 7223 | 1.2 | 1.4 | 2.6 | 1.4 | 0.7 | -0.5 | 5.6 | 4.8 |
| Drinking places, alcoholic beverages............. | 7224 | -0.3 | 3.1 | – | 0.3 | -0.7 | 2.2 | 2.5 | 3.2 |
| Restaurants and other eating places............. | 7225 | 0.5 | 3.2 | 2.4 | 1.9 | 1.7 | 2.2 | 3.5 | 1.7 |
| Other services: | | | | | | | | | |
| Automotive repair and maintenance.............. | 8111 | 1.1 | 2.1 | 1.5 | 0.4 | -3.9 | 8.6 | 0.4 | 4.6 |
| Reupholstery and furniture repair................. | 81142 | -0.9 | 3.8 | -2.8 | -2.0 | (NA) | (NA) | (NA) | (NA) |
| Personal care services........................... | 8121 | 2.2 | 1.7 | 3.4 | 1.2 | (NA) | (NA) | (NA) | (NA) |
| Funeral homes and funeral services.............. | 81221 | -0.2 | 3.9 | -0.3 | – | (NA) | (NA) | (NA) | (NA) |
| Dry cleaning and laundry services............... | 8123 | 2.0 | 1.5 | 1.1 | -0.9 | 10.9 | -4.9 | 7.3 | -3.3 |
| Coin-operated laundries and drycleaners......... | 81231 | 2.3 | 1.8 | 0.4 | -1.9 | (NA) | (NA) | (NA) | (NA) |
| Dry cleaning and laundry services............... | 81232 | 0.8 | 2.2 | -1.2 | -1.9 | (NA) | (NA) | (NA) | (NA) |
| Photofinishing................................... | 81292 | 3.4 | 1.8 | -4.0 | -7.1 | (NA) | (NA) | (NA) | (NA) |

NA Not available. – Represents zero or rounds to less than half the unit of measurement shown. [1] North American Industry Classification System, 2012 (NAICS); see text, Section 15. [2] Average annual percent changes based on compound rate formula. Rates of change are calculated using index numbers to three decimal places. [3] For NAICS industries 22, 48-71, and 81 average annual percent changes are for 1987-2017. For NAICS industries 484, 4841, 493, 49311, and 49312, annual percent changes are for 1992-2017. For NAICS industries 48421, 71391 and 71394, average annual percent changes are for 2002-2017. For NAICS industries 5412, and 5615 average annual percent changes are for 1997-2017. For NAICS industries 56131, and 6215 average annual percent changes are for 1994-2017. For NAICS industry 7131 average annual percent change is for 2007-2017.

Source: U.S. Bureau of Labor Statistics. Labor Productivity and Costs, "Productivity and Costs by Industry," <http://www.bls.gov/lpc/data.htm>, accessed September 2019.

## Table 668. Productivity and Related Measures: 1980 to 2018

[See text, this section. Minus sign (-) indicates decrease]

| Item | 1980 | 1990 | 2000 | 2010 | 2014 | 2015 | 2016 | 2017 | 2018 |
|---|---|---|---|---|---|---|---|---|---|
| **INDEXES (2012=100)** | | | | | | | | | |
| Output per hour, business sector................ | 50.8 | 60.8 | 76.1 | 99.3 | 101.6 | 102.8 | 103.0 | 104.1 | 105.6 |
| Nonfarm business................................ | 51.9 | 61.2 | 76.2 | 99.2 | 101.3 | 102.6 | 102.8 | 104.0 | 105.4 |
| Manufacturing................................ | (NA) | 47.7 | 69.8 | 100.4 | 101.2 | 99.6 | 99.5 | 100.7 | 101.5 |
| Output [1], business sector.................... | 38.1 | 54.0 | 79.8 | 95.2 | 105.6 | 109.3 | 111.1 | 114.0 | 117.9 |
| Nonfarm business................................ | 38.2 | 53.9 | 79.7 | 95.0 | 105.4 | 109.0 | 110.8 | 113.8 | 117.8 |
| Manufacturing................................ | (NA) | 68.3 | 99.5 | 96.2 | 103.6 | 103.0 | 102.9 | 105.2 | 108.0 |
| Hours [2], business sector.................... | 75.1 | 88.8 | 104.8 | 95.9 | 103.9 | 106.3 | 107.9 | 109.5 | 111.7 |
| Nonfarm business................................ | 73.6 | 88.2 | 104.6 | 95.8 | 104.0 | 106.2 | 107.8 | 109.4 | 111.8 |
| Manufacturing................................ | (NA) | 143.2 | 142.5 | 95.8 | 102.4 | 103.4 | 103.4 | 104.5 | 106.4 |
| Compensation per hour [3], business sector...... | 27.3 | 46.5 | 69.2 | 95.3 | 104.1 | 107.1 | 108.3 | 112.0 | 115.0 |
| Nonfarm business................................ | 27.6 | 46.7 | 69.3 | 95.3 | 104.1 | 107.3 | 108.5 | 112.2 | 115.1 |
| Manufacturing................................ | (NA) | 48.3 | 70.0 | 96.5 | 103.3 | 105.9 | 106.6 | 110.1 | 111.9 |
| Real hourly compensation [3], business sector.... | 72.5 | 79.3 | 92.4 | 100.4 | 100.9 | 103.6 | 103.4 | 104.7 | 105.0 |
| Nonfarm business................................ | 73.3 | 79.7 | 92.5 | 100.4 | 100.9 | 103.8 | 103.6 | 104.9 | 105.0 |
| Manufacturing................................ | (NA) | 82.4 | 93.4 | 101.7 | 100.1 | 102.4 | 101.8 | 103.0 | 102.2 |
| Unit labor costs [4], business sector............... | 53.8 | 76.5 | 90.9 | 95.9 | 102.5 | 104.2 | 105.2 | 107.5 | 108.9 |
| Nonfarm business................................ | 53.1 | 76.4 | 91.0 | 96.1 | 102.8 | 104.6 | 105.5 | 107.9 | 109.2 |
| Manufacturing................................ | (NA) | 101.3 | 100.3 | 96.2 | 102.1 | 106.3 | 107.1 | 109.4 | 110.3 |
| **ANNUAL PERCENT CHANGE [5]** | | | | | | | | | |
| Output per hour, business sector............... | – | 2.0 | 3.4 | 3.3 | 0.7 | 1.2 | 0.2 | 1.1 | 1.4 |
| Nonfarm business................................ | – | 1.7 | 3.3 | 3.4 | 0.8 | 1.3 | 0.2 | 1.2 | 1.3 |
| Manufacturing................................ | (NA) | 3.5 | 3.7 | 6.1 | -0.2 | -1.6 | -0.1 | 1.2 | 0.8 |
| Output [1], business sector.................... | -0.9 | 1.6 | 4.9 | 3.2 | 3.0 | 3.5 | 1.7 | 2.6 | 3.4 |
| Nonfarm business................................ | -0.9 | 1.5 | 4.7 | 3.3 | 3.1 | 3.5 | 1.6 | 2.7 | 3.5 |
| Manufacturing................................ | (NA) | 0.3 | 2.8 | 6.1 | 1.3 | -0.6 | -0.1 | 2.2 | 2.7 |
| Hours [2], business sector.................... | -0.9 | -0.4 | 1.4 | -0.1 | 2.4 | 2.3 | 1.5 | 1.5 | 2.0 |
| Nonfarm business................................ | -0.8 | -0.2 | 1.4 | -0.1 | 2.3 | 2.2 | 1.4 | 1.5 | 2.1 |
| Manufacturing................................ | (NA) | -3.1 | -0.8 | – | 1.6 | 1.0 | – | 1.0 | 1.9 |
| Compensation per hour [3], business sector....... | 10.7 | 6.3 | 6.9 | 1.8 | 2.6 | 2.8 | 1.1 | 3.4 | 2.7 |
| Nonfarm business................................ | 10.8 | 6.0 | 7.0 | 1.9 | 2.8 | 3.1 | 1.1 | 3.4 | 2.6 |
| Manufacturing................................ | (NA) | 5.4 | 6.5 | 1.3 | 2.8 | 2.5 | 0.6 | 3.3 | 1.6 |
| Real hourly compensation [3], business sector.... | -0.4 | 1.3 | 3.4 | 0.1 | 0.9 | 2.7 | -0.2 | 1.3 | 0.3 |
| Nonfarm business................................ | -0.4 | 1.0 | 3.5 | 0.2 | 1.1 | 2.9 | -0.2 | 1.2 | 0.2 |
| Manufacturing................................ | (NA) | 0.5 | 3.0 | -0.4 | 1.1 | 2.3 | -0.7 | 1.2 | -0.8 |
| Unit labor costs [4], business sector............... | 10.7 | 4.2 | 3.4 | -1.5 | 1.9 | 1.7 | 0.9 | 2.3 | 1.3 |
| Nonfarm business................................ | 10.8 | 4.2 | 3.6 | -1.5 | 2.0 | 1.8 | 0.9 | 2.2 | 1.2 |
| Manufacturing................................ | (NA) | 1.9 | 2.7 | -4.5 | 3.0 | 4.1 | 0.7 | 2.1 | 0.8 |

– Represents or rounds to zero. NA Not available. [1] Refers to gross sectoral product, a chain–type, current–weighted index. [2] Hours at work of all persons engaged in the business and nonfarm business sectors (employees, proprietors, and unpaid family workers), and employees' and proprietors' hours in manufacturing. [3] Wages and salaries of employees plus employers' contributions for social insurance and private benefit plans. Also includes an estimate of same for self-employed. Real compensation deflated by the Consumer Price Index research series; see text, Section 14. [4] Hourly compensation divided by output per hour. [5] All changes are from the immediate prior year.

Source: U.S. Bureau of Labor Statistics, Labor Productivity and Costs, "Major Sector Productivity and Costs," <http://www.bls.gov/lpc/home.htm>, accessed June 2019.

## Table 669. Employed Persons and Average Hours Worked Per Day at Workplace and at Home: 2018

[165,269 represents 165,269,000. Civilian noninstitutionalized population 15 years old and over, except as indicated. Includes work at main job and any other jobs. Excludes travel related to work. Based on the American Time Use Survey]

| Characteristic | Total employed (1,000) | Employed persons who worked on an average day [1] | | | | | | | | |
|---|---|---|---|---|---|---|---|---|---|---|
| | | Total | | | Worked at workplace | | | Worked at home [2] | | |
| | | Number (1,000) | Percent of employed | Hours of work | Number (1,000) | Percent of those who worked | Hours of work | Number (1,000) | Percent of those who worked | Hours of work |
| **Total.....................** | **165,269** | **110,785** | **67.0** | **7.62** | **90,515** | **81.7** | **7.94** | **26,240** | **23.7** | **2.94** |
| Work status: [3] | | | | | | | | | | |
| Full-time workers [4]........ | 130,608 | 92,999 | 71.2 | 8.10 | 78,334 | 84.2 | 8.28 | 21,091 | 22.7 | 3.11 |
| Part-time workers [4]........ | 34,662 | 17,785 | 51.3 | 5.10 | 12,181 | 68.5 | 5.75 | 5,149 | 28.9 | 2.25 |
| Male [3]...................... | 85,959 | 60,191 | 70.0 | 7.88 | 50,443 | 83.8 | 8.04 | 14,017 | 23.3 | 3.11 |
| Full-time workers [4]........ | 72,929 | 52,922 | 72.6 | 8.23 | 45,178 | 85.4 | 8.30 | 12,435 | 23.5 | 3.17 |
| Part-time workers [4]........ | 13,030 | 7,269 | 55.8 | 5.32 | 5,265 | 72.4 | 5.78 | 1,581 | 21.8 | 2.64 |
| Female [3]...................... | 79,311 | 50,594 | 63.8 | 7.31 | 40,072 | 79.2 | 7.82 | 12,223 | 24.2 | 2.74 |
| Full-time workers [4]........ | 57,679 | 40,077 | 69.5 | 7.93 | 33,156 | 82.7 | 8.26 | 8,656 | 21.6 | 3.02 |
| Part-time workers [4]........ | 21,632 | 10,517 | 48.6 | 4.96 | 6,916 | 65.8 | 5.73 | 3,567 | 33.9 | 2.08 |
| Jobholding status: | | | | | | | | | | |
| Single jobholders......... | 151,967 | 100,420 | 66.1 | 7.59 | 82,453 | 82.1 | 7.90 | 23,025 | 22.9 | 2.90 |
| Multiple jobholders........ | 13,302 | 10,364 | 77.9 | 7.90 | 8,062 | 77.8 | 8.32 | 3,215 | 31.0 | 3.24 |
| Educational attainment: [5] | | | | | | | | | | |
| Less than high school.... | 8,126 | 4,824 | 59.4 | 7.50 | 4,362 | 90.4 | 7.64 | 620 | 12.9 | (S) |
| High school diploma [6].... | 37,439 | 24,300 | 64.9 | 8.07 | 21,910 | 90.2 | 8.15 | 2,883 | 11.9 | 2.65 |
| Some college........... | 33,763 | 23,386 | 69.3 | 7.90 | 19,875 | 85.0 | 8.05 | 4,876 | 20.8 | 3.09 |
| Bachelor's degree or higher................... | 63,427 | 46,035 | 72.6 | 7.36 | 33,585 | 73.0 | 7.96 | 16,950 | 36.8 | 2.97 |

S Estimate is suppressed because it does not meet publication standards. [1] Individuals may have worked at more than one location. [2] "Working at home" includes any time persons did work at home and is not restricted to persons whose usual workplace is their home. [3] Includes workers whose hours vary. [4] Full-time workers usually worked 35 or more hours per week at all jobs combined; part-time workers worked fewer than 35 hours per week. [5] For persons 25 years old and over. [6] Includes persons with a high school diploma or equivalent.

Source: U.S. Bureau of Labor Statistics, American Time Use Survey—2018 Results, USDL 19-1003, June 2019. See also <http://www.bls.gov/tus/home.htm#news>.

## Table 670. Annual Total Compensation and Wages and Salary Accruals Per Full-Time Equivalent Employee by Industry: 2000 to 2018

[In dollars. Compensation is equal to the sum of wages and salaries and of supplements to wages and salaries; supplements are made on behalf of employees but are not included in regular wage payments to employees, such as contributions for employee pension and insurance funds, and employer contributions for government social insurance. Wages and salaries consist of cash remuneration of labor, including sick or vacation pay, severance pay, commissions, tips, and bonuses. Based on the 2012 North American Industry Classification System (NAICS); see text, Section 15]

| Industry | Total annual compensation | | | | Annual salary and wages | | | |
|---|---|---|---|---|---|---|---|---|
| | 2000 | 2010 | 2017 | 2018 | 2000 | 2010 | 2017 | 2018 |
| Compensation of employees............... | 47,550 | 66,208 | 77,107 | 79,521 | 39,238 | 53,235 | 62,669 | 64,678 |
| Domestic industries................................ | 47,450 | 65,823 | 76,379 | 78,778 | 39,166 | 52,939 | 62,095 | 64,090 |
| Private industries.............................. | 46,136 | 62,441 | 73,049 | 75,381 | 38,862 | 51,913 | 61,348 | 63,305 |
| Agriculture, forestry, fishing, and hunting........ | 25,814 | 37,634 | 45,567 | 48,709 | 22,146 | 30,610 | 36,816 | 38,828 |
| Mining....... | 70,434 | 107,738 | 124,920 | 126,843 | 58,134 | 91,837 | 104,112 | 106,279 |
| Utilities.... | 84,821 | 123,905 | 151,415 | 156,132 | 64,772 | 89,603 | 110,819 | 113,665 |
| Construction......... | 46,201 | 63,648 | 74,937 | 77,083 | 38,551 | 52,757 | 63,431 | 65,487 |
| Manufacturing.......... | 54,167 | 75,485 | 86,784 | 89,176 | 43,957 | 59,997 | 69,418 | 71,281 |
| Wholesale trade......... | 59,068 | 78,065 | 92,796 | 95,404 | 50,896 | 67,167 | 79,609 | 81,527 |
| Retail trade......... | 31,224 | 38,464 | 43,802 | 45,460 | 26,589 | 32,028 | 36,879 | 38,223 |
| Transportation and warehousing............. | 48,462 | 62,458 | 71,715 | 73,423 | 39,055 | 49,744 | 57,851 | 59,458 |
| Information......... | 72,135 | 98,952 | 133,622 | 143,187 | 62,571 | 81,295 | 114,769 | 123,534 |
| Finance and insurance......... | 76,234 | 104,130 | 128,873 | 132,385 | 64,574 | 88,165 | 109,581 | 112,335 |
| Real estate and rental and leasing............. | 43,235 | 58,043 | 72,430 | 75,204 | 37,150 | 49,209 | 62,876 | 65,349 |
| Professional, scientific, and technical services.. | 71,592 | 95,391 | 114,236 | 117,947 | 62,472 | 82,570 | 99,308 | 102,676 |
| Management of companies and enterprises [1]... | 90,766 | 126,701 | 148,880 | 152,631 | 74,253 | 103,873 | 127,625 | 130,777 |
| Administrative and waste management services.......... | 28,921 | 44,896 | 51,891 | 53,700 | 25,035 | 37,374 | 43,747 | 45,221 |
| Educational services.......... | 34,164 | 50,711 | 58,254 | 59,424 | 29,244 | 41,367 | 47,606 | 48,404 |
| Health care and social assistance............. | 42,009 | 59,618 | 66,592 | 68,262 | 35,249 | 48,977 | 54,761 | 56,061 |
| Arts, entertainment, and recreation............. | 37,384 | 49,745 | 58,977 | 59,876 | 32,482 | 42,672 | 50,418 | 51,204 |
| Accommodation and food services............. | 20,819 | 27,965 | 33,646 | 34,910 | 18,045 | 24,138 | 29,241 | 30,403 |
| Other services, except government............. | 30,412 | 41,739 | 50,691 | 52,016 | 25,990 | 35,876 | 43,894 | 45,069 |
| Government......... | 54,624 | 82,264 | 95,428 | 98,468 | 40,824 | 57,925 | 66,369 | 68,638 |
| Federal......... | 61,449 | 104,416 | 118,746 | 122,895 | 46,749 | 74,664 | 82,935 | 85,556 |
| State and local......... | 52,718 | 76,234 | 89,441 | 92,191 | 39,169 | 53,369 | 62,116 | 64,290 |

[1] Consists of offices of bank and other holding companies and of corporate, subsidiary, and regional managing offices.

Source: U.S. Bureau of Economic Analysis, National Income and Product Accounts Tables, "Table 6.2D. Compensation of Employees by Industry," "Table 6.5D. Full-Time Equivalent Employees by Industry," and "Table 6.6D. Wages and Salaries Per Full-Time Equivalent Employee by Industry," <http://www.bea.gov/itable/>, accessed September 2019.

## Table 671. Average Hourly and Weekly Earnings of Employees by Private Industry Group: 2000 to 2018

[In dollars. Average earnings include overtime. Data are for production and nonsupervisory employees. See headnote, Table 657]

| Private industry group | Current dollars | | | | | Constant (1982–84) dollars [1] | | | | |
|---|---|---|---|---|---|---|---|---|---|---|
| | 2000 | 2010 | 2010 | 2017 | 2018 | 2000 | 2010 | 2010 | 2017 | 2010 |
| **AVERAGE HOURLY EARNINGS** | | | | | | | | | | |
| Total private.................... | 14.02 | 19.05 | 21.54 | 22.06 | 22.71 | 8.30 | 8.90 | 9.20 | 9.23 | 9.26 |
| Mining and logging........................... | 16.55 | 23.82 | 26.97 | 27.44 | 28.30 | 9.80 | 11.13 | 11.52 | 11.48 | 11.54 |
| Construction........................... | 17.48 | 23.22 | 25.97 | 26.74 | 27.74 | 10.35 | 10.85 | 11.09 | 11.19 | 11.32 |
| Manufacturing........................... | 14.32 | 18.61 | 20.44 | 20.90 | 21.54 | 8.48 | 8.70 | 8.73 | 8.74 | 8.79 |
| Trade, transportation, and utilities [2]........ | 13.29 | 16.80 | 18.95 | 19.31 | 19.90 | 7.87 | 7.85 | 8.10 | 8.08 | 8.12 |
| Information........................... | 19.07 | 25.87 | 30.05 | 30.74 | 31.93 | 11.29 | 12.09 | 12.84 | 12.86 | 13.02 |
| Financial activities [2]........................... | 15.04 | 21.55 | 26.12 | 26.57 | 26.94 | 8.90 | 10.07 | 11.16 | 11.11 | 10.99 |
| Professional and business services [2]..... | 15.53 | 22.80 | 25.43 | 26.05 | 26.81 | 9.19 | 10.66 | 10.86 | 10.90 | 10.94 |
| Education and health services [2]........... | 13.91 | 19.95 | 22.52 | 23.03 | 23.65 | 8.24 | 9.32 | 9.62 | 9.63 | 9.65 |
| Leisure and hospitality [2]................... | 8.32 | 11.31 | 12.85 | 13.38 | 13.87 | 4.93 | 5.29 | 5.49 | 5.60 | 5.66 |
| Other services.................... | 12.73 | 17.06 | 19.36 | 20.10 | 20.78 | 7.54 | 7.97 | 8.27 | 8.41 | 8.48 |
| **AVERAGE WEEKLY EARNINGS** | | | | | | | | | | |
| Total private.................... | 481 | 636 | 723 | 743 | 767 | 285 | 297 | 309 | 311 | 313 |
| Mining and logging........................... | 735 | 1,063 | 1,222 | 1,266 | 1,323 | 435 | 497 | 522 | 530 | 540 |
| Construction........................... | 686 | 892 | 1,032 | 1,062 | 1,108 | 406 | 417 | 441 | 444 | 452 |
| Manufacturing........................... | 591 | 765 | 856 | 876 | 908 | 350 | 358 | 366 | 366 | 370 |
| Trade, transportation, and utilities........ | 450 | 559 | 635 | 653 | 675 | 266 | 261 | 271 | 273 | 275 |
| Information........................... | 701 | 940 | 1,068 | 1,100 | 1,138 | 415 | 439 | 456 | 460 | 464 |
| Financial activities [2]........................... | 540 | 780 | 963 | 983 | 997 | 320 | 365 | 411 | 411 | 407 |
| Professional and business services [2]..... | 536 | 799 | 900 | 923 | 949 | 317 | 374 | 384 | 386 | 387 |
| Education and health services [2]........... | 448 | 639 | 724 | 742 | 762 | 265 | 299 | 309 | 310 | 311 |
| Leisure and hospitality [2]................... | 217 | 281 | 320 | 333 | 345 | 129 | 131 | 137 | 139 | 141 |
| Other services.................... | 413 | 524 | 596 | 618 | 640 | 245 | 245 | 254 | 258 | 261 |

[1] Earnings in current dollars divided by the Consumer Price Index (CPI-W) on a 1982–84 base; see text, Section 14. [2] For composition of industries, see Table 659.

Source: U.S. Bureau of Labor Statistics, Current Employment Statistics, "Employment, Hours, and Earnings—National," <http://www.bls.gov/ces/data.htm>, accessed July 2019.

## Table 672. Employment and Wages of Private Sector and Government Employees: 2000 to 2018

[7,879 represents 7,879,000. Based on federal-state cooperative program, The Quarterly Census of Employment and Wages (QCEW), also referenced as ES-202. Includes workers covered by state unemployment insurance laws and federal civilian workers covered by unemployment compensation for federal employees. Excludes most agricultural workers on small farms, all Armed Forces, elected officials in most states, railroad employees, most domestic workers, most student workers at school, value of meals and lodging, and tips and other gratuities]

| Employment and wages | Unit | 2000 | 2010 | 2014 | 2015 | 2016 | 2017 | 2018 |
|---|---|---|---|---|---|---|---|---|
| **Establishments:** | | | | | | | | |
| **Total** | **1,000** | **7,879** | **8,993** | **9,361** | **9,523** | **9,717** | **9,835** | **10,011** |
| Excluding federal | 1,000 | 7,829 | 8,926 | 9,300 | 9,462 | 9,656 | 9,775 | 9,952 |
| Private | 1,000 | 7,622 | 8,696 | 9,067 | 9,224 | 9,418 | 9,537 | 9,712 |
| State government | 1,000 | 65 | 67 | 68 | 69 | 69 | 69 | 70 |
| Local governments | 1,000 | 141 | 164 | 165 | 169 | 169 | 169 | 170 |
| Federal government | 1,000 | 50 | 67 | 61 | 61 | 60 | 60 | 59 |
| **Average annual employment:** | | | | | | | | |
| **Total** | **1,000** | **129,877** | **127,820** | **136,614** | **139,492** | **141,870** | **143,860** | **146,132** |
| Excluding federal | 1,000 | 127,006 | 124,840 | 133,884 | 136,735 | 139,077 | 141,057 | 143,337 |
| Private | 1,000 | 110,015 | 106,201 | 115,569 | 118,308 | 120,505 | 122,387 | 124,552 |
| State government | 1,000 | 4,370 | 4,606 | 4,545 | 4,567 | 4,570 | 4,629 | 4,625 |
| Local governments | 1,000 | 12,620 | 14,032 | 13,770 | 13,861 | 14,003 | 14,042 | 14,160 |
| Federal government | 1,000 | 2,871 | 2,981 | 2,730 | 2,756 | 2,793 | 2,803 | 2,795 |
| **Annual wages:** | | | | | | | | |
| **Total** | **Bil. dol.** | **4,588** | **5,976** | **7,017** | **7,385** | **7,607** | **7,968** | **8,368** |
| Excluding federal | Bil. dol. | 4,455 | 5,769 | 6,810 | 7,170 | 7,388 | 7,743 | 8,135 |
| Private | Bil. dol. | 3,888 | 4,934 | 5,928 | 6,256 | 6,449 | 6,773 | 7,124 |
| State government | Bil. dol. | 159 | 226 | 246 | 255 | 261 | 272 | 281 |
| Local governments | Bil. dol. | 409 | 610 | 636 | 659 | 678 | 698 | 729 |
| Federal government | Bil. dol. | 133 | 206 | 207 | 215 | 219 | 225 | 234 |
| **Average annual wage per employee:** | | | | | | | | |
| **Total** | **Dol.** | **35,323** | **46,751** | **51,364** | **52,942** | **53,621** | **55,390** | **57,266** |
| Excluding federal | Dol. | 35,077 | 46,215 | 50,866 | 52,439 | 53,124 | 54,892 | 56,752 |
| Private | Dol. | 35,337 | 46,455 | 51,296 | 52,876 | 53,515 | 55,338 | 57,198 |
| State government | Dol. | 36,296 | 48,960 | 54,179 | 55,878 | 57,168 | 58,802 | 60,751 |
| Local governments | Dol. | 32,387 | 43,493 | 46,155 | 47,573 | 48,440 | 49,720 | 51,515 |
| Federal government | Dol. | 46,228 | 69,198 | 75,797 | 77,900 | 78,379 | 80,432 | 83,657 |
| **Average weekly wage per employee:** | | | | | | | | |
| **Total** | **Dol.** | **679** | **899** | **988** | **1,018** | **1,031** | **1,065** | **1,101** |
| Excluding federal | Dol. | 675 | 889 | 978 | 1,008 | 1,022 | 1,056 | 1,091 |
| Private | Dol. | 680 | 893 | 986 | 1,017 | 1,029 | 1,064 | 1,100 |
| State government | Dol. | 698 | 942 | 1,042 | 1,075 | 1,099 | 1,131 | 1,168 |
| Local governments | Dol. | 623 | 836 | 888 | 915 | 932 | 956 | 991 |
| Federal government | Dol. | 889 | 1,331 | 1,458 | 1,498 | 1,507 | 1,547 | 1,609 |

Source: U.S. Bureau of Labor Statistics, Quarterly Census of Employment and Wages, "QCEW Data Viewer," and earlier releases, <http://www.bls.gov/cew/>, accessed September 2019.

## Table 673. Average Annual Wage by State: 2017 and 2018

[In dollars, except percent change. See headnote, Table 672]

| State/area | Average wage per employee 2017 | Average wage per employee 2018 | Percent change, 2017-18 | State/area | Average wage per employee 2017 | Average wage per employee 2018 | Percent change, 2017-18 |
|---|---|---|---|---|---|---|---|
| **United States** | **55,390** | **57,266** | **3.4** | Montana | 42,045 | 43,407 | 3.2 |
| Alabama | 45,997 | 47,414 | 3.1 | Nebraska | 44,851 | 46,262 | 3.1 |
| Alaska | 53,714 | 55,668 | 3.6 | Nevada | 48,126 | 50,041 | 4.0 |
| Arizona | 50,146 | 51,865 | 3.4 | New Hampshire | 55,138 | 56,782 | 3.0 |
| Arkansas | 42,959 | 43,950 | 2.3 | New Jersey | 64,042 | 65,727 | 2.6 |
| California | 65,857 | 68,478 | 4.0 | New Mexico | 43,535 | 45,167 | 3.7 |
| Colorado | 56,914 | 58,941 | 3.6 | New York | 70,682 | 72,900 | 3.1 |
| Connecticut | 66,636 | 67,742 | 1.7 | North Carolina | 48,920 | 50,756 | 3.8 |
| Delaware | 55,828 | 56,814 | 1.8 | North Dakota | 50,313 | 52,356 | 4.1 |
| District of Columbia | 92,544 | 95,909 | 3.6 | Ohio | 49,153 | 50,573 | 2.9 |
| Florida | 48,455 | 50,094 | 3.4 | Oklahoma | 45,121 | 46,727 | 3.6 |
| Georgia | 52,189 | 53,496 | 2.5 | Oregon | 51,118 | 53,053 | 3.8 |
| Hawaii | 49,671 | 50,977 | 2.6 | Pennsylvania | 54,000 | 55,628 | 3.0 |
| Idaho | 41,345 | 42,882 | 3.7 | Rhode Island | 52,840 | 53,736 | 1.7 |
| Illinois | 57,971 | 59,941 | 3.4 | South Carolina | 44,177 | 44,729 | 1.2 |
| Indiana | 46,192 | 47,590 | 3.0 | South Dakota | 42,432 | 43,694 | 3.0 |
| Iowa | 46,074 | 47,511 | 3.1 | Tennessee | 48,820 | 50,450 | 3.3 |
| Kansas | 45,116 | 46,607 | 3.3 | Texas | 55,795 | 57,747 | 3.5 |
| Kentucky | 45,166 | 46,302 | 2.5 | Utah | 46,575 | 48,513 | 4.2 |
| Louisiana | 46,500 | 48,116 | 3.5 | Vermont | 46,186 | 47,640 | 3.1 |
| Maine | 43,911 | 45,370 | 3.3 | Virginia | 56,503 | 58,239 | 3.1 |
| Maryland | 59,603 | 61,151 | 2.6 | Washington | 62,041 | 66,119 | 6.6 |
| Massachusetts | 69,929 | 72,606 | 3.8 | West Virginia | 43,419 | 46,120 | 6.2 |
| Michigan | 52,487 | 53,803 | 2.5 | Wisconsin | 47,238 | 48,872 | 3.5 |
| Minnesota | 56,140 | 58,007 | 3.3 | Wyoming | 46,270 | 48,059 | 3.9 |
| Mississippi | 38,788 | 39,762 | 2.5 | Puerto Rico | 27,549 | 28,784 | 4.5 |
| Missouri | 47,364 | 49,053 | 3.6 | Virgin Islands | 41,106 | 47,535 | 15.6 |

Source: U.S. Bureau of Labor Statistics, Quarterly Census of Employment and Wages, "Employment and Wages Online Annual Averages, 2018," and earlier editions, <http://www.bls.gov/cew/home.htm>, accessed September 2019.

## Table 674. Full-Time Wage and Salary Workers—Number and Earnings: 2010 to 2018

[99,531 represents 99,531,000. Earnings shown in current dollars; data represent annual averages of usual weekly earnings. Full time workers are those who usually worked 35 hours or more per week at all jobs combined. Based on the Current Population Survey; see text, Section 1 and Appendix III. For definition of median, see Guide to Tabular Presentation]

| Characteristic | Number of workers (1,000) | | | Median weekly earnings (dollars) | | |
|---|---|---|---|---|---|---|
| | 2010 | 2017 | 2018 | 2010 | 2017 | 2018 |
| **All workers** [1] | **99,531** | **113,272** | **115,567** | **747** | **860** | **886** |
| Male | 55,059 | 62,980 | 64,142 | 824 | 941 | 973 |
| Female | 44,472 | 50,291 | 51,425 | 669 | 770 | 789 |
| White [2] | 80,656 | 87,730 | 88,953 | 765 | 890 | 916 |
| Black [2] | 11,658 | 14,521 | 15,041 | 611 | 682 | 694 |
| Asian [2] | 4,946 | 7,320 | 7,643 | 855 | 1,043 | 1,095 |
| Hispanic [3] | 14,837 | 19,615 | 20,297 | 535 | 655 | 680 |
| OCCUPATION | | | | | | |
| Management, professional and related occupations | 39,145 | 47,207 | 48,808 | 1,063 | 1,224 | 1,246 |
| Management, business, and financial operations | 15,648 | 19,414 | 19,863 | 1,155 | 1,327 | 1,355 |
| Professional and related occupations | 23,497 | 27,794 | 28,945 | 1,008 | 1,160 | 1,176 |
| Computer and mathematical occupations | 3,202 | 4,350 | 4,755 | 1,289 | 1,465 | 1,539 |
| Architecture and engineering occupations | 2,366 | 2,936 | 2,994 | 1,255 | 1,478 | 1,484 |
| Life, physical, and social science occupations | 1,127 | 1,238 | 1,308 | 1,062 | 1,286 | 1,270 |
| Community and social services occupations | 1,909 | 2,165 | 2,223 | 802 | 900 | 913 |
| Legal occupations | 1,248 | 1,379 | 1,466 | 1,213 | 1,443 | 1,467 |
| Education, training, and library occupations | 6,535 | 6,978 | 7,166 | 913 | 1,002 | 1,002 |
| Arts, design, entertainment, sports, and media | 1,431 | 1,778 | 1,880 | 920 | 1,066 | 1,086 |
| Healthcare practitioner and technical occupations | 5,678 | 6,970 | 7,154 | 986 | 1,124 | 1,140 |
| Service occupations | 14,424 | 16,044 | 16,288 | 479 | 544 | 569 |
| Healthcare support occupations | 2,219 | 2,500 | 2,595 | 471 | 542 | 561 |
| Protective service occupations | 2,872 | 2,739 | 2,836 | 747 | 852 | 848 |
| Food preparation and serving-related occupations | 3,823 | 4,465 | 4,394 | 406 | 484 | 501 |
| Building and grounds cleaning and maintenance | 3,310 | 3,641 | 3,695 | 446 | 522 | 551 |
| Personal care and service occupations | 2,199 | 2,699 | 2,768 | 455 | 520 | 544 |
| Sales and office occupations | 23,060 | 23,686 | 23,714 | 631 | 718 | 742 |
| Sales and related occupations | 9,121 | 9,953 | 10,077 | 666 | 763 | 798 |
| Office and administrative support occupations | 13,939 | 13,733 | 13,637 | 619 | 701 | 717 |
| Natural resources, construction, and maintenance | 9,869 | 11,509 | 11,546 | 719 | 801 | 824 |
| Farming, fishing, and forestry occupations | 729 | 962 | 850 | 416 | 539 | 581 |
| Construction and extraction occupations | 5,020 | 6,147 | 6,414 | 709 | 796 | 808 |
| Installation, maintenance, and repair occupations | 4,120 | 4,400 | 4,282 | 794 | 878 | 934 |
| Production, transportation, and material-moving | 13,034 | 14,825 | 15,210 | 599 | 692 | 707 |
| Production occupations | 6,861 | 7,589 | 7,668 | 599 | 701 | 723 |
| Transportation and material-moving occupations | 6,172 | 7,236 | 7,542 | 599 | 681 | 689 |

[1] Includes other races, not shown separately. [2] For persons in this race group only. [3] Persons of Hispanic origin may be of any race.

Source: U.S. Bureau of Labor Statistics, CPS Tables, "Median weekly earnings of full-time wage and salary workers by selected characteristics," and "Median weekly earnings of full-time wage and salary workers by detailed occupation and sex," February 2019, and earlier releases, <http://www.bls.gov/cps/tables.htm>.

## Table 675. Median Usual Weekly Earnings of Full-Time Wage and Salary Workers by Sex and Education: 1980 to 2018

[In current dollars. For wage and salary workers 25 years old and over. Based on Current Population Survey; see text, Section 1 and Appendix III. Wages and salaries are collected before taxes and other deductions and include overtime pay, commissions, or tips usually received at principal job. Earnings reported on basis other than weekly are converted to a weekly equivalent. Excludes all incorporated and unincorporated self employed. Data not strictly comparable to data for earlier years. See text this section and <http://www.bls.gov/cps/eetech_methods.pdf>]

| Year and sex | Total | Less than a high school diploma | High school, no college [1] | Some college or associate's degree | Bachelor's degree and higher [2] |
|---|---|---|---|---|---|
| CURRENT DOLLARS | | | | | |
| Male: | | | | | |
| 1980 | 339 | 267 | 327 | 358 | 427 |
| 1990 | 512 | 349 | 459 | 542 | 741 |
| 2000 | 693 | 406 | 591 | 691 | 1,020 |
| 2010 | 874 | 486 | 710 | 845 | 1,330 |
| 2017 | 996 | 584 | 797 | 917 | 1,481 |
| 2018 | 1,026 | 607 | 819 | 951 | 1,524 |
| Female: | | | | | |
| 1980 | 213 | 164 | 201 | 231 | 290 |
| 1990 | 369 | 240 | 315 | 395 | 535 |
| 2000 | 516 | 304 | 420 | 505 | 756 |
| 2010 | 704 | 388 | 543 | 638 | 986 |
| 2017 | 810 | 447 | 610 | 700 | 1,131 |
| 2018 | 830 | 469 | 616 | 717 | 1,145 |
| WOMEN'S EARNINGS AS PERCENT OF MEN'S | | | | | |
| 1980 | 62.8 | 61.4 | 61.5 | 64.5 | 67.9 |
| 1990 | 72.1 | 68.8 | 68.6 | 72.9 | 72.2 |
| 2000 | 74.5 | 74.9 | 71.1 | 73.1 | 74.1 |
| 2010 | 80.5 | 79.8 | 76.5 | 75.5 | 74.1 |
| 2017 | 81.3 | 76.5 | 76.5 | 76.3 | 76.4 |
| 2018 | 80.9 | 77.3 | 75.2 | 75.4 | 75.1 |

[1] Includes persons with a high school diploma or equivalent. [2] Includes bachelor's, master's, professional, or doctoral degree.

Source: U.S. Bureau of Labor Statistics, "Labor Force Statistics from the Current Population Survey," <http://www.bls.gov/cps/data.htm>, accessed January 2019.

# Table 676. Workers With Earnings by Occupation of Longest Held Job and Sex: 2017

[78,196 represents 78,196,000. As of March. For definition of median, see Guide to Tabular Presentation. Based on the Current Population Survey, Annual Social and Economic Supplement (CPS ASEC); includes civilian noninstitutional population 15 years old and over, and military personnel who live in households with at least one other civilian adult. See text, Section 1, and Appendix III]

| Major occupation group of longest job held in 2017 | All workers | | | | Full-time, year-round | | | |
|---|---|---|---|---|---|---|---|---|
| | Female | | Male | | Female | | Male | |
| | Number (1,000) | Median earnings (dol.) | Number (1,000) | Median earnings (dol.) | Number (1,000) | Median earnings (dol.) | Number (1,000) | Median earnings (dol.) |
| Total......................... | 78,196 | 31,610 | 88,101 | 44,408 | 49,293 | 41,977 | 66,379 | 52,146 |
| Management, business, and financial occupations.............. | 11,954 | 53,542 | 14,565 | 75,678 | 9,555 | 61,046 | 12,638 | 81,043 |
| Professional and related occupations........................ | 22,008 | 46,250 | 16,750 | 68,182 | 14,548 | 55,384 | 13,039 | 77,346 |
| Service occupations.................. | 16,652 | 18,515 | 12,565 | 25,635 | 8,152 | 26,748 | 7,883 | 35,430 |
| Sales and office occupations.............. | 21,874 | 27,688 | 13,932 | 37,055 | 13,453 | 37,078 | 10,012 | 48,437 |
| Natural resources, construction, and maintenance...................... | 904 | 21,548 | 14,384 | 37,763 | 459 | 37,520 | 10,960 | 42,193 |
| Production, transportation, and material-moving occupations.............. | 4,730 | 25,015 | 15,198 | 36,544 | 1,996 | 31,970 | 11,202 | 42,036 |
| Armed Forces.................... | 74 | (B) | 706 | 47,426 | 66 | (B) | 644 | 50,946 |

B Base less than 75,000.

Source: U.S. Census Bureau, *Income and Poverty in the United States: 2017*, September 2018, Current Population Reports, P60-263; and "Detailed Tables: Person Table PINC-06," <https://www.census.gov/data/tables/time-series/demo/income-poverty/cps-pinc.html>, accessed November 2018.

# Table 677. Employment Cost Index (ECI) for Total Compensation by Occupation and Industry: 2010 to 2018

[As of December (2005 = 100). The ECI is a measure of the rate of change in compensation (wages, salaries, and employer costs for employee benefits). Data are not seasonally adjusted. Industry classifications based on North American Industry Classification System (NAICS); occupation classifications based on the 2010 Standard Occupational Classification (SOC)]

| Occupational group and industry | Indexes (December 2005 = 100) | | | | Annual percent change from immediate prior year | | | |
|---|---|---|---|---|---|---|---|---|
| | 2010 | 2016 | 2017 | 2018 | 2010 | 2016 | 2017 | 2018 |
| **Civilian workers** [1]........................ | **113.2** | **127.9** | **131.2** | **135.0** | **2.0** | **2.2** | **2.6** | **2.9** |
| **State and local government**........................ | **116.2** | **130.9** | **134.2** | **137.7** | **1.8** | **2.4** | **2.5** | **2.6** |
| Workers, by occupational group: | | | | | | | | |
| Management, professional and related occupations... | 115.5 | 129.8 | 133.0 | 136.4 | 1.5 | 2.4 | 2.5 | 2.6 |
| Sales and office occupations........................ | 116.6 | 132.4 | 135.7 | 140.0 | 1.9 | 2.5 | 2.5 | 3.2 |
| Service occupations........................ | 118.0 | 133.5 | 137.0 | 140.8 | 2.3 | 2.7 | 2.6 | 2.8 |
| Workers, by industry division: | | | | | | | | |
| Service-providing industries: [2] | | | | | | | | |
| Education and health services [2]........................ | 115.6 | 129.8 | 132.9 | 136.5 | 1.5 | 2.4 | 2.4 | 2.7 |
| Schools........................ | 115.3 | 129.4 | 132.4 | 136.0 | 1.4 | 2.5 | 2.3 | 2.7 |
| Health care and social assistance [2]................ | 117.9 | 132.8 | 135.8 | 139.3 | 2.2 | 2.2 | 2.3 | 2.6 |
| Hospitals........................ | 117.0 | 130.5 | 133.4 | 136.5 | 2.4 | 2.4 | 2.2 | 2.3 |
| Public administration........................ | 116.8 | 132.0 | 135.7 | 139.2 | 1.9 | 2.2 | 2.8 | 2.6 |
| **Private industry workers** [3]........................ | **112.5** | **127.2** | **130.5** | **134.4** | **2.1** | **2.2** | **2.6** | **3.0** |
| Workers, by occupational group: | | | | | | | | |
| Management, professional, and related occupations... | 113.0 | 127.4 | 130.5 | 133.8 | 2.1 | 1.7 | 2.4 | 2.5 |
| Sales and office occupations........................ | 111.6 | 126.8 | 130.1 | 135.0 | 2.2 | 2.3 | 2.6 | 3.8 |
| Natural resources, construction, and maintenance occupations........................ | 113.3 | 127.7 | 131.2 | 134.5 | 1.9 | 2.2 | 2.7 | 2.5 |
| Production, transportation, and material moving occupations........................ | 111.5 | 127.0 | 131.0 | 134.7 | 2.4 | 2.7 | 3.1 | 2.8 |
| Service occupations........................ | 113.5 | 127.2 | 130.9 | 135.6 | 1.5 | 3.2 | 2.9 | 3.6 |
| Workers, by industry division: | | | | | | | | |
| Goods-producing industries [2]........................ | 111.1 | 125.8 | 128.9 | 131.9 | 2.3 | 2.1 | 2.5 | 2.3 |
| Construction........................ | 112.7 | 125.8 | 128.8 | 132.4 | 0.9 | 1.9 | 2.4 | 2.8 |
| Manufacturing........................ | 110.0 | 125.5 | 128.9 | 131.6 | 2.8 | 2.2 | 2.7 | 2.1 |
| Service-providing industries [2]........................ | 113.0 | 127.7 | 131.0 | 135.2 | 2.0 | 2.2 | 2.6 | 3.2 |
| Trade, transportation, and utilities........................ | 111.4 | 128.5 | 132.3 | 136.8 | 2.4 | 2.8 | 3.0 | 3.4 |
| Information........................ | 110.0 | 125.4 | 128.4 | 134.3 | 1.6 | 2.2 | 2.4 | 4.6 |
| Financial activities........................ | 111.4 | 127.4 | 129.9 | 134.2 | 2.6 | 2.9 | 2.0 | 3.3 |
| Professional and business services........................ | 114.6 | 128.0 | 131.9 | 135.2 | 2.0 | 1.2 | 3.0 | 2.5 |
| Education and health services........................ | 114.7 | 127.8 | 130.4 | 134.1 | 1.7 | 1.9 | 2.0 | 2.8 |
| Leisure and hospitality........................ | 114.1 | 125.8 | 130.3 | 135.7 | 1.2 | 3.3 | 3.6 | 4.1 |
| Bargaining status: | | | | | | | | |
| Union........................ | 114.8 | 130.6 | 134.5 | 138.8 | 3.3 | 1.5 | 3.0 | 3.2 |
| Nonunion........................ | 112.1 | 126.6 | 129.9 | 133.7 | 1.8 | 2.3 | 2.6 | 2.9 |

[1] Includes workers in the private nonfarm economy except those in private households, and workers in the public sector, except the federal government. [2] Includes all other items not shown separately. [3] Excludes farm and household workers.

Source: U.S. Bureau of Labor Statistics, Employment Cost Trends, "Employment Cost Index," <http://www.bls.gov/ncs/ect/home.htm#data>, accessed July 2019.

# Table 678. Federal and State Minimum Wage Rates: 1940 to 2019

[In current dollars. Wage rates are as of January 1, except as noted. Where an employee is subject to both the state and federal minimum wage laws, the employee is entitled to the higher minimum wage rate]

| Year | Federal minimum wage rates per hour | State | 2019 minimum wage rates per hour | State | 2019 minimum wage rates per hour | State | 2019 minimum wage rates per hour |
|---|---|---|---|---|---|---|---|
| 1940 | 0.30 | AL | (X) | KY | 7.25 | ND | 7.25 |
| 1945 (as of Oct. 24) | 0.40 | AK | 9.89 | LA | (X) | OH | [7] 7.25/8.55 |
| 1950 (as of Jan. 25) | 0.75 | AZ | 11.00 | ME | 11.00 | OK | [8] 2.00/7.25 |
| 1960 | 1.00 | AR | [2] 9.25 | MD | 10.10 | OR | 11.25 |
| 1965 (as of Sept. 3) | 1.25 | CA | [9] 11.00/12.00 | MA | 12.00 | PA | 7.25 |
| 1970 (as of Feb. 1) | 1.45 | CO | 11.10 | MI | [1] 9.45 | RI | 10.50 |
| 1975 | 2.10 | CT | 10.10 | MN | [4] 8.04/9.86 | SC | (X) |
| 1980 | 3.10 | DE | 8.75 | MS | (X) | SD | 9.10 |
| 1985 | 3.35 | DC | 14.00 | MO | 8.60 | TN | (X) |
| 1990 (as of Apr. 1) | 3.80 | FL | 8.46 | MT | [5] 4.00/8.50 | TX | 7.25 |
| 1995 | 4.25 | GA | [3] 5.15 | NE | [2] 9.00 | UT | 7.25 |
| 2000 | 5.15 | HI | 10.10 | NV | [6] 7.25/8.25 | VT | [1] 10.78 |
| 2005 | 5.15 | ID | 7.25 | NH | 7.25 | VA | [2] 7.25 |
| 2007 (as of Jul. 24) | 5.85 | IL | [2] 8.25 | NJ | 10.00 | WA | 12.00 |
| 2008 (as of Jul. 24) | 6.55 | IN | [1] 7.25 | NM | 7.50 | WV | [3] 8.75 |
| 2009 (as of Jul. 24) | 7.25 | IA | 7.25 | NY | [10] 11.10 | WI | 7.25 |
| **2019 (as of July 1)** | **7.25** | KS | 7.25 | NC | 7.25 | WY | 5.15 |

X Not applicable. [1] Employers of 2 or more. [2] Employers of 4 or more. [3] Employers of 6 or more. [4] Large employer (receipts of $500,000 or more) and small employer (with annual receipts of less than $500,000). [5] Lower rate for businesses with gross annual sales of $110,000 or less. [6] Nevada: $8.25 with no health insurance benefits provided by employer. $7.25 with health insurance provided by employer and received by employee. [7] Ohio: $7.25 for those employers grossing $305,000 or less. [8] Oklahoma: employers of 10 or more full time employees at any one location, and employers with gross sales over $100,000 regardless of number of full-time employees. All other employers $2.00. [9] California: $11.00 minimum wage for employers with 25 or fewer employees, and $12.00 minimum wage for employers with 26 or more employees. [10] Basic minimum rate: $11.10; $12.00 (Long Island & Westchester); $13.50 (NYC- Small Employers of 10 or less); and $15.00 (NYC- Large Employers of 11 or more).

Source: U.S. Department of Labor, Wage and Hour Division, "History of Federal Minimum Wage Rates Under the Fair Labor Standards Act," and "State Minimum Wage Laws," <https://www.dol.gov/whd/minwage/america.htm>, accessed September 2019.

# Table 679. Workers Paid Hourly Rates At or Below Federal Minimum Wage by Selected Characteristics: 2018

[81,915 represents 81,915,000. Data are annual averages. For employed wage and salary workers, excluding all self-employed. Based on the Current Population Survey; see text, Section 1 and Appendix III]

| Characteristic | Number of workers paid hourly rates (1,000) | | | | Percent of workers paid hourly rates at or below federal minimum wage | | |
|---|---|---|---|---|---|---|---|
| | | At or below federal minimum wage | | | | | |
| | Total | Total | At prevailing federal minimum wage | Below prevailing federal minimum wage | Total | At prevailing federal minimum wage | Below prevailing federal minimum wage |
| **Total, 16 years and over** [1] | **81,915** | **1,711** | **434** | **1,276** | **2.1** | **0.5** | **1.6** |
| 16 to 24 years | 15,963 | 805 | 271 | 534 | 5.0 | 1.7 | 3.3 |
| 25 years and over | 65,952 | 905 | 163 | 742 | 1.4 | 0.2 | 1.1 |
| Male, 16 years old and over | 40,691 | 632 | 168 | 464 | 1.6 | 0.4 | 1.1 |
| 16 to 24 years | 7,994 | 301 | 115 | 186 | 3.8 | 1.4 | 2.3 |
| 25 years and over | 32,698 | 331 | 52 | 278 | 1.0 | 0.2 | 0.9 |
| Female, 16 years old and over | 41,223 | 1,078 | 267 | 812 | 2.6 | 0.6 | 2.0 |
| 16 to 24 years | 7,969 | 504 | 156 | 348 | 6.3 | 2.0 | 4.4 |
| 25 years and over | 33,254 | 575 | 110 | 464 | 1.7 | 0.3 | 1.4 |
| White [2] | 62,204 | 1,242 | 283 | 958 | 2.0 | 0.5 | 1.5 |
| Men | 31,509 | 434 | 101 | 333 | 1.4 | 0.3 | 1.1 |
| Women | 30,695 | 808 | 182 | 626 | 2.6 | 0.6 | 2.0 |
| Black [2] | 12,135 | 313 | 114 | 198 | 2.6 | 0.9 | 1.6 |
| Men | 5,537 | 137 | 52 | 85 | 2.5 | 0.9 | 1.5 |
| Women | 6,598 | 175 | 63 | 113 | 2.7 | 0.9 | 1.7 |
| Asian [2] | 4,130 | 69 | 16 | 53 | 1.7 | 0.4 | 1.3 |
| Men | 1,909 | 23 | 6 | 17 | 1.2 | 0.3 | 0.9 |
| Women | 2,221 | 46 | 10 | 36 | 2.1 | 0.4 | 1.6 |
| Hispanic [3] | 17,452 | 324 | 78 | 246 | 1.9 | 0.4 | 1.4 |
| Men | 9,543 | 131 | 26 | 105 | 1.4 | 0.3 | 1.1 |
| Women | 7,909 | 194 | 52 | 141 | 2.4 | 0.7 | 1.8 |
| Full-time workers | 61,650 | 742 | 121 | 621 | 1.2 | 0.2 | 1.0 |
| Men | 33,736 | 288 | 45 | 244 | 0.9 | 0.1 | 0.7 |
| Women | 27,913 | 454 | 76 | 377 | 1.6 | 0.3 | 1.4 |
| Part-time workers [4] | 20,155 | 965 | 312 | 653 | 4.8 | 1.5 | 3.2 |
| Men | 6,895 | 341 | 122 | 219 | 4.9 | 1.8 | 3.2 |
| Women | 13,260 | 624 | 190 | 434 | 4.7 | 1.4 | 3.3 |
| Private sector industries | 72,234 | 1,622 | 403 | 1,219 | 2.2 | 0.6 | 1.7 |
| Public sector industries | 9,681 | 89 | 32 | 57 | 0.9 | 0.3 | 0.6 |

[1] Includes other races, not shown separately. Also includes a small number of multiple jobholders whose full- or part-time status cannot be determined for their principal job. [2] For persons in this race group only. See footnote 3, Table 613. [3] Persons of Hispanic or Latino origin may be of any race. [4] Working fewer than 35 hours per week.

Source: U.S. Bureau of Labor Statistics, *Characteristics of Minimum Wage Workers: 2018*, March 2019. See also <https://www.bls.gov/cps/earnings.htm#minwage>.

## Table 680. Earnings by Sex and Women's Earnings as a Percent of Men's Earnings by Occupation: 2016 and 2017

[Median earnings inflation-adjusted dollars for the full-time, year round civilian employed population age 16 years and over. Estimates subject to sampling variability. Based on the American Community Survey]

| Occupation | 2016 | | | 2017 | | |
|---|---|---|---|---|---|---|
| | Median earnings 2016 inflation-adjusted | | Women's earnings as a percent of men's earnings | Median earnings 2017 inflation-adjusted | | Women's earnings as a percent of men's earnings |
| | Female | Male | | Female | Male | |
| **Total:** | **40,675** | **50,741** | **80.2** | **41,512** | **51,421** | **80.7** |
| Management, business, science, and arts | 55,474 | 76,692 | 72.3 | 56,743 | 77,953 | 72.8 |
| Management, business, and financial | 60,751 | 80,473 | 75.5 | 61,683 | 81,395 | 75.8 |
| Management | 62,254 | 81,829 | 76.1 | 64,266 | 83,387 | 77.1 |
| Business and financial operations | 56,897 | 74,011 | 76.9 | 59,584 | 75,902 | 78.5 |
| Computer, engineering, and science | 70,044 | 82,347 | 85.1 | 71,502 | 84,802 | 84.3 |
| Computer and mathematical | 72,472 | 85,427 | 84.8 | 75,555 | 87,012 | 86.8 |
| Architecture and engineering | 71,072 | 82,192 | 86.5 | 72,047 | 83,593 | 86.2 |
| Life, physical, and social science | 60,646 | 70,191 | 86.4 | 62,345 | 71,799 | 86.8 |
| Education, legal, community service, arts, and media | 47,103 | 59,998 | 78.5 | 48,245 | 60,609 | 79.6 |
| Community and social service | 42,947 | 45,984 | 93.4 | 44,800 | 47,178 | 95.0 |
| Legal | 65,014 | 121,654 | 53.4 | 67,050 | 122,231 | 54.9 |
| Education, training, and library | 46,403 | 56,876 | 81.6 | 47,033 | 57,802 | 81.4 |
| Arts, design, entertainment, sports, and media | 48,440 | 55,625 | 87.1 | 50,300 | 57,128 | 88.0 |
| Healthcare practitioners and technical | 58,404 | 81,023 | 72.1 | 60,334 | 80,092 | 75.3 |
| Health diagnosing and treating practitioners and other technical | 68,240 | 105,798 | 64.5 | 70,039 | 102,039 | 68.6 |
| Health technologists and technicians | 40,125 | 46,947 | 85.5 | 41,031 | 46,933 | 87.4 |
| Service | 24,575 | 31,738 | 77.4 | 25,558 | 33,232 | 76.9 |
| Healthcare support | 27,470 | 31,269 | 87.9 | 29,262 | 32,119 | 91.1 |
| Protective service | 41,504 | 52,217 | 79.5 | 41,728 | 55,080 | 75.8 |
| Fire fighting and prevention, and other protective service workers including supervisors | 34,689 | 42,438 | 81.7 | 35,044 | 45,068 | 77.8 |
| Law enforcement workers including supervisors | 49,192 | 61,126 | 80.5 | 49,793 | 62,220 | 80.0 |
| Food preparation and serving related | 21,224 | 24,935 | 85.1 | 21,710 | 26,046 | 83.4 |
| Building and grounds cleaning and maintenance | 21,933 | 30,043 | 73.0 | 22,449 | 31,124 | 72.1 |
| Personal care and service | 23,318 | 30,831 | 75.6 | 24,682 | 31,141 | 79.3 |
| Sales and office | 35,368 | 46,408 | 76.2 | 36,103 | 47,360 | 76.2 |
| Sales and related | 34,226 | 51,791 | 66.1 | 35,512 | 52,335 | 67.9 |
| Office and administrative support | 35,548 | 40,053 | 88.8 | 36,261 | 40,709 | 89.1 |
| Natural resources, construction, and maintenance | 31,194 | 41,612 | 75.0 | 31,725 | 42,203 | 75.2 |
| Farming, fishing, and forestry | 21,214 | 28,231 | 75.1 | 21,200 | 30,115 | 70.4 |
| Construction and extraction | 35,859 | 40,926 | 87.6 | 35,760 | 41,422 | 86.3 |
| Installation, maintenance, and repair | 40,827 | 46,092 | 88.6 | 41,113 | 47,168 | 87.2 |
| Production, transportation, and material moving | 27,925 | 40,181 | 69.5 | 28,993 | 40,690 | 71.3 |
| Production | 28,241 | 40,898 | 69.1 | 29,317 | 41,565 | 70.5 |
| Transportation | 31,991 | 42,389 | 75.5 | 31,941 | 44,173 | 72.3 |
| Material moving | 25,006 | 31,564 | 79.2 | 25,935 | 31,790 | 81.6 |

Source: U.S. Census Bureau, 2016 and 2017 American Community Survey, B24022, "Sex by Occupation and Median Earnings in the Past 12 Months (in 2016 and 2017 Inflation-Adjusted Dollars) for the Full-time, Year-Round Civilian Employed Population 16 Years and Over," <http://factfinder.census.gov/>, accessed November 2018.

## Table 681. Workers' Earnings by Certification and License Status and Selected Characteristics: 2018

[In dollars, unless otherwise noted (115,567 represents 115,567,000). Data shown for wage and salary workers aged 16 years old and over, unless otherwise noted. Excludes self-employed workers. Certifications are issued by a non-governmental certification body and convey that an individual has the knowledge or skill to perform a specific job. A license is awarded by a government agency and conveys a legal authority to work in an occupation. For definition of median, see Guide to Tabular Presentation]

| Characteristic | Full-time wage and salary workers (1,000) | Median weekly earnings | | | | |
|---|---|---|---|---|---|---|
| | | | With a certification or license [1] | | | Without a certification or license |
| | | Total | Total | Certification only | With a license [2] | |
| **Total workers, 16 years old and over** | **115,567** | **886** | **1,106** | **1,196** | **1,093** | **818** |
| AGE | | | | | | |
| 16 to 24 years old | 10,428 | 548 | 634 | 597 | 638 | 532 |
| 25 to 54 years old | 80,891 | 917 | 1,110 | 1,206 | 1,098 | 858 |
| 55 years old and over | 24,247 | 985 | 1,205 | 1,326 | 1,195 | 916 |
| SEX | | | | | | |
| Men | 64,142 | 973 | 1,231 | 1,283 | 1,226 | 907 |
| Women | 51,425 | 789 | 990 | 1,071 | 985 | 726 |
| RACE/ETHNICITY | | | | | | |
| White | 88,953 | 916 | 1,133 | 1,202 | 1,127 | 847 |
| Black or African American | 15,041 | 694 | 838 | 945 | 831 | 657 |
| Asian | 7,643 | 1,095 | 1,342 | 1,668 | 1,297 | 1,021 |
| Hispanic or Latino | 20,297 | 680 | 899 | 880 | 902 | 648 |
| EDUCATIONAL ATTAINMENT | | | | | | |
| Workers, 25 years old and over | 105,138 | 932 | 1,134 | 1,231 | 1,127 | 871 |
| Less than a high school diploma | 6,999 | 553 | 636 | 683 | 629 | 546 |
| High school graduates, no college [3] | 26,237 | 730 | 837 | 872 | 831 | 715 |
| Some college or associate degree | 27,476 | 826 | 902 | 1,003 | 890 | 803 |
| Bachelor's degree and higher | 44,427 | 1,324 | 1,356 | 1,553 | 1,339 | 1,284 |

[1] A person may have more than one certification or license. [2] Persons with a license may also have a certification. [3] Includes persons with a high school diploma or equivalent.

Source: U.S. Bureau of Labor Statistics, "Labor Force Statistics from the Current Population Survey," <http://www.bls.gov/cps/certifications-and-licenses.htm>, accessed August 2019.

## Table 682. Average Hours Spent Per Day on Primary Activities by Married Mothers and Fathers by Employment Status: 2013 to 2017

[Data are shown for households with own children under age 18. Data are averages for the 2013-2017 period and cover an individual's main activity. Does not include secondary activities done simultaneously]

| Activity | Both spouses work full time | | Mother employed part time and father employed full time | | Mother not employed and father employed full time | |
|---|---|---|---|---|---|---|
| | Mothers | Fathers | Mothers | Fathers | Mothers | Fathers |
| Total, all activities........................... | 24.00 | 24.00 | 24.00 | 24.00 | 24.00 | 24.00 |
| Personal care activities...................... | 9.16 | 8.63 | 9.23 | 8.61 | 9.60 | 8.82 |
| Sleeping....................................... | 8.33 | 8.04 | 8.46 | 7.98 | 8.92 | 8.21 |
| Household activities........................... | 1.87 | 1.35 | 2.67 | 1.29 | 3.69 | 1.02 |
| Housework.................................. | 0.73 | 0.28 | 1.09 | 0.20 | 1.59 | 0.18 |
| Food preparation and cleanup............ | 0.82 | 0.42 | 1.14 | 0.39 | 1.69 | 0.30 |
| Lawn and garden care.................... | 0.06 | 0.24 | 0.11 | 0.24 | 0.10 | 0.19 |
| Purchasing goods and services............. | 0.51 | 0.32 | 0.60 | 0.29 | 0.67 | 0.35 |
| Grocery shopping.......................... | 0.14 | 0.07 | 0.18 | 0.05 | 0.22 | 0.07 |
| Consumer goods purchases, except grocery shopping........ | 0.29 | 0.20 | 0.32 | 0.20 | 0.34 | 0.23 |
| Caring for and helping household members...... | 1.38 | 0.95 | 1.84 | 0.90 | 2.71 | 0.87 |
| Caring for and helping household children......... | 1.36 | 0.92 | 1.82 | 0.89 | 2.69 | 0.86 |
| Physical care............................ | 0.57 | 0.30 | 0.67 | 0.27 | 1.01 | 0.25 |
| Education-related activities................. | 0.11 | 0.09 | 0.22 | 0.07 | 0.27 | 0.06 |
| Reading to/with children.................. | 0.04 | 0.04 | 0.09 | 0.03 | 0.09 | 0.03 |
| Playing/doing hobbies with children......... | 0.27 | 0.27 | 0.34 | 0.28 | 0.62 | 0.34 |
| Working and work-related activities [1]....... | 5.13 | 6.22 | 2.84 | 6.12 | 0.06 | 6.42 |
| Working [1]................................. | 5.10 | 6.19 | 2.82 | 6.09 | 0.02 | 6.40 |
| Leisure and sports........................... | 2.94 | 3.57 | 3.26 | 3.62 | 3.79 | 3.39 |
| Socializing and communicating.............. | 0.61 | 0.54 | 0.68 | 0.58 | 0.83 | 0.69 |
| Watching television........................ | 1.50 | 2.03 | 1.48 | 1.98 | 1.92 | 1.74 |
| Participating in sports, exercise, and recreation........ | 0.18 | 0.28 | 0.25 | 0.33 | 0.25 | 0.27 |
| Travel......................................... | 1.35 | 1.38 | 1.45 | 1.46 | 1.19 | 1.42 |
| Travel related to caring for/helping household children....... | 0.25 | 0.16 | 0.32 | 0.12 | 0.35 | 0.09 |
| Other activities, not elsewhere classified....... | 1.66 | 1.59 | 2.11 | 1.71 | 2.29 | 1.69 |

[1] Estimates include a small amount of work time done by persons who do not meet the American Time Use Survey definition of employed.

Source: U.S. Bureau of Labor Statistics, "American Time Use Survey," <http://www.bls.gov/tus/#tables>, accessed November 2018.

## Table 683. Workers With Access to Unmarried Domestic Partner Benefits for Partners of Same and Opposite Sex by Selected Characteristics: 2011 to 2018

[In percent. All workers = 100 percent. As of March. For employees in private industry. Based on National Compensation Survey (NCS). See headnote, Table 686, and Appendix III. See Table 168 for data on health benefit program participation]

| Characteristic | Defined benefit retirement survivor benefits for partners | | | | | | Healthcare benefits for partners | | | | | |
|---|---|---|---|---|---|---|---|---|---|---|---|---|
| | Same sex | | | Opposite sex | | | Same sex | | | Opposite sex | | |
| | 2011 | 2017 | 2018 | 2011 | 2017 | 2018 | 2011 | 2017 | 2018 | 2011 | 2017 | 2018 |
| Total........................................ | 7 | 11 | 11 | 7 | 10 | 10 | 29 | 39 | 40 | 25 | 35 | 36 |
| WORKER CHARACTERISTICS | | | | | | | | | | | | |
| Management, professional, and related........ | 11 | 17 | 17 | 10 | 17 | 17 | 46 | 57 | 58 | 38 | 51 | 54 |
| Service...................................... | 3 | 4 | 4 | 3 | 4 | 4 | 17 | 21 | 22 | 14 | 18 | 21 |
| Sales and office............................. | 8 | 10 | 10 | 7 | 10 | 10 | 30 | 42 | 41 | 26 | 38 | 38 |
| Natural resources, construction, and maintenance........ | 8 | 9 | 10 | 7 | 7 | 8 | 22 | 28 | 32 | 18 | 24 | 29 |
| Production, transportation, and material moving............ | 8 | 10 | 12 | 7 | 10 | 11 | 25 | 33 | 35 | 21 | 30 | 31 |
| Full-time [1]................................. | 9 | 13 | 13 | 8 | 12 | 12 | 36 | 47 | 48 | 31 | 42 | 44 |
| Part-time [1]................................ | 4 | 5 | 5 | 4 | 5 | 5 | 9 | 17 | 16 | 8 | 16 | 16 |
| Union [2].................................... | 25 | 33 | 36 | 22 | 28 | 30 | 46 | 58 | 60 | 31 | 44 | 46 |
| Nonunion [2]................................ | 6 | 8 | 8 | 5 | 9 | 8 | 28 | 37 | 38 | 24 | 34 | 35 |
| AVERAGE HOURLY WAGE [3] | | | | | | | | | | | | |
| Lowest 25 percent (under $12.75)......... | 2 | 3 | 3 | 2 | 3 | 3 | 11 | 17 | 19 | 9 | 16 | 18 |
| Lowest 10 percent (under $10.00)....... | 1 | 1 | 1 | 1 | 2 | 1 | 6 | 8 | 10 | 4 | 7 | 10 |
| Second 25 percent ($12.75 to $18.78).... | 5 | 8 | 8 | 5 | 8 | 8 | 26 | 37 | 38 | 23 | 35 | 36 |
| Third 25 percent ($18.78 to $30.08)....... | 9 | 12 | 13 | 8 | 11 | 12 | 35 | 45 | 47 | 30 | 40 | 42 |
| Highest 25 percent ($30.08 and over)...... | 15 | 22 | 22 | 14 | 21 | 21 | 50 | 61 | 62 | 41 | 53 | 56 |
| Highest 10 percent ($46.73 and over). .. | 16 | 23 | 24 | 15 | 23 | 23 | 59 | 69 | 69 | 49 | 62 | 61 |
| ESTABLISHMENT CHARACTERISTICS | | | | | | | | | | | | |
| 1 to 99 workers............................. | 3 | 5 | 5 | 3 | 5 | 5 | 18 | 26 | 27 | 16 | 25 | 26 |
| 100 or more workers........................ | 12 | 17 | 18 | 12 | 17 | 17 | 42 | 54 | 55 | 34 | 47 | 48 |
| Goods producing [4]......................... | 6 | 10 | 10 | 6 | 9 | 9 | 27 | 34 | 37 | 24 | 32 | 35 |
| Service producing [4]........................ | 8 | 11 | 11 | 7 | 11 | 11 | 30 | 39 | 41 | 25 | 35 | 37 |

[1] Employees are classified as working either a full-time or part-time schedule based on the definition used by each establishment. [2] See footnote 6, Table 686. [3] The National Compensation Survey—Benefits program presents wage data in percentiles rather than dollar amounts; 2018 average wages shown here; for calculation detail, see "Technical Note" in source. [4] See Table 659 for composition of goods- and service-producing industries.

Source: U.S. Bureau of Labor Statistics, *National Compensation Survey: Employee Benefits in the United States, March 2018*, Bulletin 2789, September 2018, and earlier reports. See also <https://www.bls.gov/ncs/ebs/benefits/2018/home.htm>.

# Table 684. Employer Costs for Employee Compensation Per Hour Worked: 2018

[In dollars. As of December. Based on the National Compensation Survey (NCS). See Appendix III]

| Compensation component | Total civilian workers | State and local government workers | Private industry workers | | | | | | |
|---|---|---|---|---|---|---|---|---|---|
| | | | Total | Goods producing[1] | Service providing[2] | Union workers | Non-union workers | 1–99 workers | 100 workers or more |
| **Total compensation** | **36.32** | **50.55** | **34.05** | **39.49** | **32.95** | **47.29** | **32.81** | **28.14** | **41.08** |
| Wages and salaries | 24.91 | 31.59 | 23.85 | 26.35 | 23.34 | 27.85 | 23.47 | 20.80 | 27.47 |
| Total benefits | 11.41 | 18.96 | 10.20 | 13.14 | 9.61 | 19.45 | 9.33 | 7.34 | 13.60 |
| Paid leave[3] | 2.62 | 3.79 | 2.44 | 2.55 | 2.42 | 3.36 | 2.35 | 1.70 | 3.32 |
| Vacation | 1.28 | 1.44 | 1.26 | 1.31 | 1.24 | 1.71 | 1.21 | 0.86 | 1.73 |
| Holiday | 0.78 | 1.08 | 0.73 | 0.87 | 0.70 | 0.99 | 0.71 | 0.54 | 0.96 |
| Sick | 0.40 | 0.97 | 0.31 | 0.28 | 0.32 | 0.48 | 0.30 | 0.21 | 0.44 |
| Supplemental pay[3] | 1.01 | 0.50 | 1.09 | 1.68 | 0.98 | 1.56 | 1.05 | 0.68 | 1.59 |
| Overtime[4] | 0.28 | 0.21 | 0.29 | 0.65 | 0.22 | 0.77 | 0.25 | 0.22 | 0.37 |
| Insurance[3] | 3.16 | 5.95 | 2.71 | 3.63 | 2.53 | 6.61 | 2.34 | 1.85 | 3.73 |
| Health insurance | 3.00 | 5.79 | 2.56 | 3.43 | 2.38 | 6.27 | 2.21 | 1.76 | 3.51 |
| Retirement and savings | 1.95 | 5.95 | 1.32 | 1.94 | 1.19 | 4.31 | 1.04 | 0.74 | 2.00 |
| Defined benefit | 1.22 | 5.52 | 0.54 | 0.96 | 0.45 | 3.16 | 0.29 | 0.26 | 0.87 |
| Defined contributions | 0.73 | 0.43 | 0.78 | 0.97 | 0.74 | 1.15 | 0.74 | 0.48 | 1.13 |
| Legally required | 2.66 | 2.78 | 2.64 | 3.34 | 2.50 | 3.60 | 2.55 | 2.36 | 2.96 |
| Social Security and Medicare | 2.03 | 2.18 | 2.01 | 2.26 | 1.95 | 2.46 | 1.96 | 1.73 | 2.33 |
| Social Security[5] | 1.62 | 1.66 | 1.61 | 1.82 | 1.57 | 1.98 | 1.57 | 1.40 | 1.86 |
| Medicare | 0.41 | 0.52 | 0.40 | 0.44 | 0.39 | 0.48 | 0.39 | 0.34 | 0.47 |
| Federal unemployment | 0.03 | (6) | 0.04 | 0.03 | 0.04 | 0.04 | 0.04 | 0.04 | 0.03 |
| State unemployment | 0.14 | 0.06 | 0.15 | 0.19 | 0.14 | 0.18 | 0.14 | 0.15 | 0.15 |
| Workers' compensation | 0.46 | 0.54 | 0.45 | 0.85 | 0.37 | 0.93 | 0.41 | 0.44 | 0.46 |

[1] Based on the 2012 North American Industry Classification System (NAICS). See text, this section. Includes mining, construction, and manufacturing. The agriculture, forestry, farming, and hunting sector is excluded. [2] Based on the 2012 NAICS. Includes utilities; wholesale and retail trade; transportation and warehousing; information; finance and insurance; real estate and rental and leasing; professional and technical services; management of companies and enterprises, administrative and waste services; education services; health care and social assistance; arts, entertainment, and recreation; accommodations and food services; and other services, except public administration. [3] Includes costs for other items not shown separately. [4] Includes premium pay for work in addition to regular work schedule, such as, overtime, weekends, and holidays. [5] Comprises the Old-Age, Survivors, and Disability Insurance Program (OASDI). [6] Cost per hour worked is $0.01 or less.

Source: U.S. Bureau of Labor Statistics, *Employer Costs for Employee Compensation—December 2018*, USDL 19-0449, March 2019. See also <http://www.bls.gov/ncs/ect/home.htm>.

# Table 685. Workers With Access to Retirement and Health Care Benefits by Selected Characteristics: 2018

[In percent. All workers = 100 percent. As of March. For employees in private industry. Based on National Compensation Survey (NCS). See headnote, Table 686, and Appendix III. See Table 168 for data on health benefit program participation]

| Characteristic | Retirement benefits | | | Healthcare benefits | | | |
|---|---|---|---|---|---|---|---|
| | All plans[1] | Defined benefit[2] | Defined contribution[2] | Medical care | Dental care | Vision care | Outpatient prescription drug coverage |
| **Total** | **68** | **17** | **64** | **69** | **42** | **24** | **68** |
| WORKER CHARACTERISTICS | | | | | | | |
| Management, professional, and related | 83 | 24 | 80 | 87 | 61 | 36 | 86 |
| Service | 44 | 6 | 41 | 42 | 23 | 13 | 40 |
| Sales and office | 71 | 14 | 68 | 66 | 38 | 21 | 65 |
| Natural resources, construction, and maintenance | 62 | 20 | 56 | 73 | 38 | 25 | 71 |
| Production, transportation, and material moving | 71 | 21 | 64 | 77 | 45 | 27 | 76 |
| Full-time[3] | 77 | 20 | 74 | 86 | 53 | 30 | 84 |
| Part-time[3] | 39 | 9 | 34 | 21 | 11 | 7 | 20 |
| Union[4] | 92 | 68 | 58 | 94 | 74 | 56 | 94 |
| Nonunion[4] | 65 | 12 | 64 | 66 | 39 | 21 | 65 |
| AVERAGE HOURLY WAGE[5] | | | | | | | |
| Lowest 25 percent (under $12.75) | 44 | 5 | 41 | 35 | 16 | 9 | 34 |
| Lowest 10 percent (under $10.00) | 32 | 3 | 30 | 24 | 10 | 6 | 23 |
| Second 25 percent ($12.75 to $18.78) | 67 | 12 | 64 | 72 | 40 | 22 | 71 |
| Third 25 percent ($18.78 to $30.08) | 79 | 20 | 75 | 86 | 53 | 31 | 84 |
| Highest 25 percent ($30.08 and over) | 87 | 33 | 82 | 92 | 67 | 41 | 91 |
| Highest 10 percent ($46.73 and over) | 88 | 35 | 84 | 93 | 70 | 42 | 93 |
| ESTABLISHMENT CHARACTERISTICS | | | | | | | |
| 1 to 99 workers | 53 | 7 | 51 | 55 | 28 | 16 | 54 |
| 100 or more workers | 85 | 28 | 79 | 85 | 58 | 34 | 84 |
| Goods producing[6] | 75 | 22 | 71 | 85 | 51 | 31 | 83 |
| Service producing[6] | 66 | 16 | 62 | 66 | 40 | 23 | 64 |

[1] Employees may have access to defined benefit and/or defined contribution plans. Total excludes duplication. [2] A defined benefit plan is a retirement plan that uses a specific, predetermined formula to calculate the amount of an employee's guaranteed future benefit. A defined contribution plan provides benefits based on employer and employee contributions to individual employee accounts and the rate of return on money invested; the retirement benefit depends on the account balance at retirement. [3] Employees are classified as working either a full-time or part-time schedule based on the definition used by each establishment. [4] See footnote 6, Table 686. [5] The National Compensation Survey—Benefits program presents wage data in percentiles rather than dollar amounts; for calculation detail, see "Technical Note" in source. [6] See Table 659 for composition of goods- and service-producing industries.

Source: U.S. Bureau of Labor Statistics, *National Compensation Survey: Employee Benefits in the United States, March 2018*, Bulletin 2789, September 2018. See also <http://www.bls.gov/ncs/ebs/benefits/2018/home.htm>.

# Table 686. Workers With Access to Selected Employee Benefits: 2018

[In percent. All workers = 100 percent. As of March. For employees in private industry. Based on National Compensation Survey (NCS). The NCS benefits survey obtained data from 6,588 private industry establishments of all sizes, representing approximately 118.1 million workers. Excludes agricultural establishments, private households, and the self-employed. An employee has access to a benefit plan if the plan is made available by the employer, regardless of whether the employee participates in the plan. See Appendix III. See also <https://www.bls.gov/ncs/ebs/national-compensation-survey-glossary-of-employee-benefit-terms.htm> for glossary of terms]

| Characteristic | Leave benefits | | | | | | Quality of life benefits | | | Nonproduction bonuses | |
|---|---|---|---|---|---|---|---|---|---|---|---|
| | Paid holidays | Paid sick leave | Paid vacation | Paid jury duty leave | Family leave[1] Paid | Family leave[1] Unpaid | Employer assistance for child care[2] | Flexible workplace[3] | Subsidized commuting | All nonproduction bonuses[4] | End of year bonus |
| **Total** | **78** | **71** | **77** | **57** | **16** | **88** | **10** | **7** | **7** | **39** | **11** |
| **WORKER CHARACTERISTIC** | | | | | | | | | | | |
| Management, professional, and related occupations | 91 | 90 | 89 | 77 | 28 | 94 | 19 | 17 | 14 | 49 | 15 |
| Service occupations | 54 | 52 | 57 | 35 | 9 | 81 | 6 | 1 | 4 | 24 | 6 |
| Sales and office occupations | 82 | 74 | 80 | 57 | 17 | 89 | 8 | 7 | 6 | 42 | 11 |
| Natural resources, construction, and maintenance occupations | 79 | 63 | 75 | 45 | 9 | 83 | 7 | 1 | 3 | 40 | 13 |
| Production, transportation, and material moving occupations | 85 | 65 | 83 | 59 | 8 | 87 | 4 | 3 | 2 | 40 | 9 |
| Full-time[5] | 90 | 82 | 90 | 68 | 19 | 90 | 12 | 9 | 8 | 46 | 13 |
| Part-time[5] | 44 | 39 | 40 | 26 | 6 | 80 | 4 | 2 | 3 | 22 | 5 |
| Union[6] | 90 | 83 | 89 | 78 | 15 | 92 | 16 | 2 | 8 | 34 | 4 |
| Nonunion[6] | 77 | 70 | 76 | 55 | 16 | 87 | 9 | 8 | 7 | 40 | 12 |
| **AVERAGE HOURLY WAGE[7]** | | | | | | | | | | | |
| Lowest 25 percent (under $12.75) | 54 | 45 | 52 | 31 | 7 | 31 | 4 | 1 | 3 | 24 | 5 |
| Lowest 10 percent (under $10.00) | 40 | 31 | 41 | 25 | 4 | 76 | 3 | (S) | (S) | 20 | 6 |
| Second 25 percent ($12.75 to $18.78) | 82 | 73 | 83 | 56 | 15 | 88 | 6 | 4 | 4 | 41 | 11 |
| Third 25 percent ($18.78 to $30.08) | 91 | 83 | 90 | 69 | 18 | 90 | 11 | 7 | 7 | 46 | 14 |
| Highest 25 percent ($30.08 and over) | 93 | 90 | 91 | 79 | 27 | 94 | 21 | 18 | 15 | 51 | 16 |
| Highest 10 percent ($46.73 and over) | 93 | 92 | 92 | 82 | 31 | 95 | 25 | 24 | 18 | 52 | 17 |
| **ESTABLISHMENT CHARACTERISTICS** | | | | | | | | | | | |
| 1 to 99 workers | 71 | 62 | 70 | 45 | 12 | 82 | 5 | 6 | 4 | 37 | 14 |
| 100 or more workers | 87 | 82 | 86 | 71 | 21 | 95 | 16 | 9 | 10 | 43 | 8 |
| Goods producing[8] | 90 | 68 | 87 | 60 | 10 | 88 | 9 | 6 | 3 | 47 | 15 |
| Service producing[8] | 76 | 71 | 75 | 56 | 17 | 88 | 10 | 7 | 8 | 38 | 10 |
| **GEOGRAPHIC AREA[9]** | | | | | | | | | | | |
| New England | 80 | 78 | 78 | 71 | 20 | 93 | 17 | 12 | 13 | 37 | 16 |
| Middle Atlantic | 79 | 74 | 78 | 70 | 23 | 86 | 14 | 8 | 9 | 42 | 14 |
| South Atlantic | 78 | 67 | 77 | 57 | 13 | 87 | 10 | 7 | 6 | 44 | 12 |
| East South Central | 79 | 62 | 78 | 57 | 14 | 82 | (S) | 5 | 2 | 43 | (S) |
| West South Central | 81 | 71 | 79 | 61 | 17 | 83 | 9 | 7 | 6 | 44 | 13 |
| East North Central | 76 | 64 | 76 | 53 | 13 | 88 | 8 | 7 | 5 | 41 | 11 |
| West North Central | 76 | 65 | 76 | 55 | 11 | 91 | 6 | 5 | 4 | 35 | 8 |
| Mountain | 79 | 69 | 81 | 56 | 18 | 90 | 10 | 8 | 8 | 36 | 10 |
| Pacific | 78 | 86 | 76 | 42 | 18 | 90 | 9 | 6 | 8 | 30 | 7 |

S Indicates no workers in this category or data did not meet publication criteria. [1] Some workers may have access to both types of plans. [2] A workplace program that provides for either the full or partial cost of caring for an employee's children in a nursery, day care center, or a babysitter in facilities either on or off the employer's premises. [3] Permits employees to work an agreed-upon portion of their work schedule at home or at some other approved location. [4] Includes cash profit-sharing, employee recognition, end-of-year, holiday, payment in lieu of benefits, longevity, referral, and all other bonuses. [5] Employees are classified as working either a full-time or part-time schedule based on the definition used by each establishment. [6] Union workers are those whose wages are determined through collective bargaining. [7] The National Compensation Survey—Benefits program presents wage data in percentiles rather than dollar amounts; see "Technical Note" in source. [8] See Table 659, for composition of goods- and service-producing industries. [9] For composition of census divisions, see inside front cover.

Source: U.S. Bureau of Labor Statistics, *National Compensation Survey: Employee Benefits in the United States, March 2018*, Bulletin 2789, September 2018. See also <http://www.bls.gov/ncs/ebs/benefits/2018/home.htm>.

# Table 687. Industries With the Highest Total Case Incidence Rates for Nonfatal Injuries and Illnesses: 2017

[Rates per 100 full-time employees. Private industry unless otherwise noted. Incidence rates refer to any Occupational Safety & Health Administration (OSHA)-recordable occupational injury or illness, whether or not it resulted in days away from work, job transfer, or restriction. Incidence rates were calculated as: number of injuries and illnesses divided by total hours worked by all employees during the year multiplied by 200,000 as base for 100 full-time equivalent workers (working 40 hours per week, 50 weeks per year)]

| Industry | 2012 NAICS code [1] | Incidence rate | Industry | 2012 NAICS code [1] | Incidence rate |
|---|---|---|---|---|---|
| **All industries, including State and local government** [2] | **(X)** | **3.1** | Beet sugar manufacturing | 311313 | 7.8 |
| Nursing and residential care facilities [3] | 623 | 10.9 | Psychiatric and substance abuse hospitals | 6222 | 7.8 |
| Motor home manufacturing | 336213 | 10.3 | Hog and pig farming | 1122 | 7.7 |
| Skiing facilities | 71392 | 10.2 | Hospitals [3] | 622 | 7.7 |
| Veterinary services | 54194 | 9.8 | Framing contractors | 23813 | 7.5 |
| Materials recovery facilities | 56292 | 9.8 | Steel foundries (except investment) | 331513 | 7.4 |
| Iron foundries | 331511 | 8.5 | Used household and office goods moving | 48421 | 7.4 |
| Wood container and pallet manufacturing | 32192 | 8.3 | Roasted nuts and peanut butter manufacturing | 311911 | 7.3 |
| Manufactured home (mobile home) manufacturing | 321991 | 8.2 | Light truck and utility vehicle manufacturing | 336112 | 7.2 |
| Couriers and express delivery services | 4921 | 8.2 | Police protection [3] | 92212 | 7.2 |
| Travel trailer and camper manufacturing | 336214 | 8.0 | Ambulance services | 62191 | 7.1 |
| Pet and pet supplies stores | 45391 | 8.0 | Seafood product preparation and packaging | 3117 | 7.0 |
| Correctional institutions [3] | 92214 | 7.9 | Nonferrous forging | 332112 | 7.0 |
| | | | Truck trailer manufacturing | 336212 | 7.0 |

X Not applicable. [1] Based on the North American Industry Classification System, 2012 (NAICS). See text, this section. [2] Excludes farms with fewer than 11 employees. [3] State government.

Source: U.S. Bureau of Labor Statistics, Industry Injury and Illness Data, "Supplemental News Release Tables," <http://www.bls.gov/iif/oshsum.htm>, accessed November 2018.

# Table 688. Nonfatal Occupational Injuries and Illnesses by Industry: 2016 and 2017

[3,534.6 represents 3,534,600. Rates per 100 full-time employees. Except as noted, data refer to any Occupational Safety and Health Administration (OSHA) recordable occupational injury or illness, whether or not it resulted in days away from work, job transfer, or restriction. Incidence rates were calculated as: number of injuries and illnesses divided by total hours worked by all employees during the year multiplied by 200,000 as base for 100 full-time equivalent workers (working 40 hours, per week, 50 weeks per year)]

| Industry | 2012 NAICS code [1] | Number of cases (1,000) | | Incidence rate of cases | |
|---|---|---|---|---|---|
| | | 2016 | 2017 | 2016 | 2017 |
| **Total** | **(X)** | **3,534.6** | **3,475.9** | **3.2** | **3.1** |
| **Private industry** [2] | **(X)** | **2,857.4** | **2,811.5** | **2.9** | **2.8** |
| Agriculture, forestry, fishing, hunting [2] | 11 | 58.3 | 50.2 | 6.1 | 5.0 |
| Mining [3] | 21 | 10.1 | 10.2 | 1.5 | 1.5 |
| Construction | 23 | 203.5 | 198.1 | 3.2 | 3.1 |
| Manufacturing | 31–33 | 449.8 | 428.9 | 3.6 | 3.5 |
| Wholesale trade | 42 | 157.1 | 157.9 | 2.8 | 2.8 |
| Retail trade | 44–45 | 395.9 | 395.7 | 3.3 | 3.3 |
| Transportation and warehousing [4] | 48–49 | 210.2 | 215.7 | 4.6 | 4.6 |
| Utilities | 22 | 11.5 | 11.2 | 2.1 | 2.0 |
| Information | 51 | 32.5 | 33.7 | 1.3 | 1.3 |
| Finance and insurance | 52 | 30.8 | 27.5 | 0.6 | 0.5 |
| Real estate and rental and leasing | 53 | 51.1 | 46.6 | 2.7 | 2.4 |
| Professional, scientific, and technical services | 54 | 71.6 | 69.6 | 0.9 | 0.8 |
| Management of companies and enterprises | 55 | 20.3 | 20.6 | 0.9 | 0.9 |
| Administrative and support & waste management and remediation services | 56 | 119.5 | 116.9 | 2.3 | 2.2 |
| Educational services | 61 | 37.5 | 38.5 | 2.0 | 1.9 |
| Health care and social assistance | 62 | 585.8 | 582.8 | 4.2 | 4.1 |
| Arts, entertainment, and recreation | 71 | 58.6 | 58.9 | 4.4 | 4.2 |
| Accommodation and food services | 72 | 279.9 | 282.6 | 3.3 | 3.2 |
| Other services, except public administration | 81 | 73.3 | 66.0 | 2.3 | 2.1 |
| **State and local government** [2] | **(X)** | **677.2** | **664.3** | **4.7** | **4.6** |
| State government | (X) | 148.4 | 143.9 | 3.7 | 3.6 |
| Local government | (X) | 528.8 | 520.4 | 5.0 | 5.0 |

X Not applicable. [1] North American Industry Classification System, 2012; see text, this section. [2] Excludes farms with fewer than 11 employees. [3] Data for Mining (2012 NAICS Sector 21) include establishments not governed by the Mine Safety and Health Administration rules and reporting, such as those in Oil and Gas Extraction and related support activities. Data for mining operators in coal, metal, and nonmetal mining are provided to BLS by the Mine Safety and Health Administration, U.S. Department of Labor. Independent mining contractors are excluded from the coal, metal, and nonmetal mining industries. These data do not reflect the changes the Occupational Safety and Health Administration made to its recordkeeping requirements effective January 1, 2002; therefore, estimates for these industries are not comparable to estimates in other industries. [4] Data for employers in railroad transportation are provided to BLS by the Federal Railroad Administration, U.S. Department of Transportation.

Source: U.S. Bureau of Labor Statistics, "Employer-Reported Workplace Injuries and Illnesses – 2017, Supplemental Files, Summary Tables," <https://www.bls.gov/news.release/osh.toc.htm>, accessed January 2019.

## Table 689. Fatal Work Injuries by Event or Exposure: 2017

[For the 50 states and the District of Columbia. Based on the Census of Fatal Occupational Injuries. For details, see source]

| Event or exposure | Number of fatalities | Percent distribution | Event or exposure | Number of fatalities | Percent distribution |
|---|---|---|---|---|---|
| Total [1] | 5,147 | 100 | Contacts with objects and equipment [1] | 695 | 14 |
| Transportation incidents [1] | 2,077 | 40 | Struck by object or equipment [1] | 503 | 10 |
| Roadway incident [1] | 1,299 | 25 | Struck by falling object or equipment | 237 | 5 |
| Collision between motor vehicles [2] | 663 | 13 | Struck by flying object | 28 | 1 |
| Noncollision incidents | 252 | 5 | Caught in or compressed by equipment | | |
| Nonroadway incident | 209 | 4 | or objects | 108 | 2 |
| Aircraft accidents | 126 | 2 | Caught in or crushed in collapsing materials | 70 | 1 |
| Pedestrians struck by a vehicle [2] | 313 | 6 | Falls | 887 | 17 |
| Water vehicle accidents | 68 | 1 | Exposure to harmful substances or | | |
| Railway accidents | 48 | 1 | environments [1] | 531 | 10 |
| Assaults and violent acts [1] | 807 | 16 | Contact with electric current | 136 | 3 |
| Homicides [1] | 458 | 9 | Exposure to caustic, noxious or allergenic | | |
| Shooting | 351 | 7 | substances | 317 | 6 |
| Stabbing | 47 | 1 | Oxygen deficiency | 39 | 1 |
| Self-inflicted injury | 275 | 5 | Fires and explosions | 123 | 2 |

[1] Includes other causes, not shown separately. [2] Including mobile equipment.

Source: U.S. Bureau of Labor Statistics, "Census of Fatal Occupational Injuries—Current and Revised Data," <http://www.bls.gov/iif/oshcfoi1.htm>, accessed August 2019.

## Table 690. Worker Fatalities on the Job by Industry and Occupation: 2017

[Excludes homicides and suicides]

| Industry group | Deaths Number | Deaths Rate [1] | Occupations with highest fatal work injury rates | Deaths Number | Deaths Rate [1] |
|---|---|---|---|---|---|
| Total | 5,147 | 3.5 | Fishers and related fishing workers | 41 | 99.8 |
| | | | Logging workers | 55 | 84.3 |
| | | | Aircraft pilots and flight engineers | 59 | 48.6 |
| Agriculture [2] | 581 | 23.0 | Roofers | 91 | 45.2 |
| Mining [3] | 112 | 12.9 | Refuse and recyclable material collectors | 30 | 35.0 |
| Construction | 971 | 9.5 | Structural iron and steel workers | 14 | 33.4 |
| Manufacturing | 303 | 1.9 | Driver/sales workers and truck drivers | 987 | 26.8 |
| Wholesale trade | 174 | 4.8 | Farmers, ranchers, and other agricultural managers | 258 | 24.0 |
| Retail trade | 287 | 2.0 | First-line supervisors of landscaping, | | |
| Transportation and warehousing | 882 | 15.1 | lawn service, and groundskeeping workers | 53 | 21.0 |
| Utilities | 28 | 2.6 | Electrical power-line installers and repairers | 26 | 18.7 |
| Information | 43 | 1.6 | First-line supervisors of construction | | |
| Financial activities [4] | 101 | 1.0 | trades and extraction workers | 121 | 17.4 |
| Professional & business services [4] | 532 | 3.0 | Maintenance and repair workers, general | 87 | 16.6 |
| Educational & health services | 189 | 0.8 | Miscellaneous agricultural workers | 154 | 16.4 |
| Leisure & hospitality [4] | 262 | 2.2 | Transportation and material moving occupations | 1,443 | 15.9 |
| Other services [5] | 205 | 2.9 | Helpers, construction trades | 11 | 15.7 |
| Government | 473 | 2.0 | Grounds maintenance workers | 191 | 15.5 |

[1] The rate represents the number of fatal occupational injuries per 100,000 full-time equivalent workers. [2] Includes forestry, fishing, and hunting. [3] Includes oil and gas extraction. [4] For composition of industry, see Table 659. [5] Excludes public service administration.

Source: U.S. Bureau of Labor Statistics, Census of Fatal Occupational Injuries, "Fatal Injury Rates," <http://stats.bls.gov/iif/oshcfoi1.htm#rates>, accessed August 2019.

## Table 691. Nonfatal Occupational Injury and Illness Cases in Private Industry by Type of Injury or Illness and Days Away from Work: 2017

[882.7 represents 882,700. Covers work-related injuries and illnesses involving one or more days of missed work]

| Type of work-related injury or illness | Number of injury or illness cases (1,000) | | | | | | | | Median number of days away from work |
|---|---|---|---|---|---|---|---|---|---|
| | All cases | 1 day | 2 days | 3-5 days | 6-10 days | 11-20 days | 21-30 days | 31 days or more | |
| Total [1] | 882.7 | 121.0 | 94.4 | 159.5 | 103.1 | 94.7 | 56.8 | 253.2 | 8 |
| Traumatic injuries and disorders | 856.7 | 118.4 | 92.2 | 155.0 | 100.1 | 92.1 | 54.9 | 244.0 | 8 |
| Fractures | 83.6 | 4.6 | 3.6 | 9.2 | 7.6 | 8.9 | 7.8 | 41.9 | 31 |
| Sprains, strains, tears | 311.3 | 31.8 | 30.7 | 57.1 | 38.3 | 36.0 | 20.7 | 96.7 | 10 |
| Hernia | 11.2 | 0.1 | 0.2 | 0.5 | 1.2 | 2.5 | 1.7 | 4.9 | 28 |
| Concussions | 14.5 | 1.7 | 1.8 | 3.2 | 2.1 | 1.4 | 0.7 | 3.5 | 6 |
| Soreness, pain, hurt-nonspecified injury | 143.3 | 19.9 | 16.3 | 26.4 | 15.6 | 15.5 | 8.3 | 41.3 | 8 |
| Disease and disorders of body systems | 16.0 | 1.1 | 1.1 | 2.0 | 2.1 | 1.7 | 1.5 | 6.5 | 21 |
| Carpal tunnel syndrome | 5.5 | 0.2 | 0.2 | 0.5 | 0.5 | 0.5 | 0.9 | 2.8 | 33 |
| Disorders of the eye, adnexa, vision | 0.9 | 0.4 | 0.1 | 0.2 | 0.1 | 0.1 | (Z) | 0.1 | 2 |
| Infectious and parasitic diseases | 1.2 | 0.2 | 0.2 | 0.3 | 0.2 | 0.1 | (Z) | 0.1 | 4 |
| Mental disorders or syndromes | 3.3 | 0.1 | 0.1 | 0.6 | 0.2 | 0.5 | 0.2 | 1.5 | 27 |

Z Less than 50 cases. [1] Total includes unclassified and ill-defined conditions.

Source: U.S. Bureau of Labor Statistics, Survey of Occupational Injuries and Illnesses, 2017 Resource Tables, "R.67. Detailed nature by number of days away from work," <https://stats.bls.gov/iif/oshcdnew2017.htm>, accessed September 2019.

## Table 692. Labor Union Membership by Sector: 1990 to 2018

[16,740 represents 16,740,000. Annual averages of monthly figures. For wage and salary workers in agriculture and non-agriculture. Data represent union members by place of residence. Based on the Current Population Survey and subject to sampling error. For methodological details, see source]

| Sector | 1990 | 2000 | 2010 | 2012 | 2013 | 2014 | 2015 | 2016 | 2017 | 2018 |
|---|---|---|---|---|---|---|---|---|---|---|
| **TOTAL (1,000)** | | | | | | | | | | |
| **Wage and salary workers:** | | | | | | | | | | |
| Union members.............. | 16,740 | 16,258 | 14,715 | 14,349 | 14,516 | 14,570 | 14,786 | 14,550 | 14,812 | 14,740 |
| Covered by unions............ | 19,058 | 17,944 | 16,290 | 15,906 | 16,016 | 16,142 | 16,433 | 16,265 | 16,436 | 16,374 |
| **Public sector workers:** | | | | | | | | | | |
| Union members.............. | 6,485 | 7,111 | 7,623 | 7,319 | 7,203 | 7,214 | 7,234 | 7,113 | 7,211 | 7,162 |
| Covered by unions............ | 7,691 | 7,976 | 8,406 | 8,062 | 7,894 | 7,923 | 8,023 | 7,827 | 7,945 | 7,862 |
| **Private sector workers:** | | | | | | | | | | |
| Union members.............. | 10,255 | 9,148 | 7,092 | 7,030 | 7,313 | 7,356 | 7,552 | 7,436 | 7,600 | 7,578 |
| Covered by unions............ | 11,366 | 9,969 | 7,884 | 7,844 | 8,122 | 8,219 | 8,410 | 8,438 | 8,491 | 8,512 |
| **PERCENT** | | | | | | | | | | |
| **Wage and salary workers:** | | | | | | | | | | |
| Union members.............. | 16.1 | 13.5 | 11.9 | 11.2 | 11.2 | 11.1 | 11.1 | 10.7 | 10.7 | 10.5 |
| Covered by unions............ | 18.3 | 14.9 | 13.1 | 12.5 | 12.4 | 12.3 | 12.3 | 11.9 | 11.9 | 11.7 |
| **Public sector workers:** | | | | | | | | | | |
| Union members.............. | 36.5 | 37.5 | 36.2 | 35.9 | 35.3 | 35.7 | 35.2 | 34.4 | 34.4 | 33.9 |
| Covered by unions............ | 43.3 | 42.0 | 40.0 | 39.6 | 38.7 | 39.2 | 39.0 | 37.9 | 37.9 | 37.2 |
| **Private sector workers:** | | | | | | | | | | |
| Union members.............. | 11.9 | 9.0 | 6.9 | 6.6 | 6.7 | 6.6 | 6.7 | 6.4 | 6.5 | 6.4 |
| Covered by unions............ | 13.2 | 9.8 | 7.7 | 7.3 | 7.5 | 7.4 | 7.4 | 7.3 | 7.3 | 7.2 |

Source: Bloomberg BNA, *2019 Union Membership and Earnings Data Book*, by Barry Hirsch and David Macpherson, Bloomberg Law, <https://www.bloomberglaw.com/product/labor/document/XAOCRE0G000000?documentName=ORCA122534.PDF&fmt=pdf>. Copyright 2019 by The Bureau of National Affairs, Inc. (800-372-1033) <http://www.bna.com>.

## Table 693. Labor Union Members by Selected Characteristics: 2018

[In units as indicated (140,099 represents 140,099,000). Annual averages of monthly data. Covers employed wage and salary workers 16 years old and over. Excludes self-employed workers whose businesses are incorporated and not incorporated. Based on Current Population Survey; see text, Section 1 and Appendix III]

| Characteristic | Employed wage and salary workers | | | Median usual usual weekly earnings [3] (dollars) | | | |
|---|---|---|---|---|---|---|---|
| | | Percent | | | | | |
| | Total (1,000) | Union members [1] | Represented by union [2] | Total | Union members [1] | Represented by union [2] | Not represented by union |
| **Total [4]**............ | **140,099** | **10.5** | **11.7** | **886** | **1,051** | **1,042** | **860** |
| SEX | | | | | | | |
| Men....................... | 72,632 | 11.1 | 12.2 | 973 | 1,123 | 1,121 | 948 |
| Women.................... | 67,467 | 9.9 | 11.1 | 789 | 968 | 958 | 764 |
| AGE | | | | | | | |
| 16 to 24 years old........ | 18,698 | 4.4 | 5.2 | 548 | 676 | 668 | 536 |
| 25 to 34 years old........ | 33,232 | 9.3 | 10.4 | 808 | 921 | 913 | 791 |
| 35 to 44 years old........ | 29,433 | 11.7 | 12.9 | 986 | 1,154 | 1,146 | 959 |
| 45 to 54 years old........ | 28,525 | 12.8 | 14.1 | 1,002 | 1,144 | 1,144 | 978 |
| 55 to 64 years old........ | 22,839 | 13.3 | 14.7 | 994 | 1,107 | 1,107 | 972 |
| 65 years and over........ | 7,372 | 9.3 | 10.5 | 944 | 1,059 | 1,053 | 928 |
| RACE/ETHNICITY | | | | | | | |
| White [5]................. | 108,164 | 10.4 | 11.5 | 916 | 1,098 | 1,090 | 889 |
| Men...................... | 57,132 | 11.0 | 12.1 | 1,002 | 1,157 | 1,154 | 978 |
| Women................... | 51,032 | 9.6 | 10.9 | 817 | 1,007 | 1,001 | 786 |
| Black [5]................. | 17,994 | 12.5 | 13.8 | 694 | 826 | 815 | 673 |
| Men...................... | 8,330 | 13.3 | 14.7 | 735 | 890 | 879 | 714 |
| Women................... | 9,664 | 11.9 | 13.1 | 654 | 782 | 766 | 635 |
| Asian [5]................. | 8,973 | 8.4 | 9.5 | 1,095 | 1,119 | 1,121 | 1,092 |
| Men...................... | 4,652 | 8.1 | 8.9 | 1,241 | 1,196 | 1,228 | 1,243 |
| Women................... | 4,321 | 8.9 | 10.2 | 937 | 1,033 | 999 | 929 |
| Hispanic [6]............... | 24,591 | 9.1 | 10.1 | 680 | 912 | 900 | 657 |
| Men...................... | 13,775 | 9.5 | 10.5 | 720 | 978 | 962 | 698 |
| Women................... | 10,815 | 8.6 | 9.6 | 617 | 836 | 824 | 601 |
| INDUSTRY [7] | | | | | | | |
| Private sector............ | 118,968 | 6.4 | 7.2 | 861 | 999 | 989 | 848 |
| Mining................... | 721 | 4.7 | 5.3 | 1,291 | (B) | (B) | 1,269 |
| Construction............. | 8,169 | 12.8 | 13.8 | 868 | 1,220 | 1,210 | 819 |
| Manufacturing........... | 14,861 | 9.0 | 9.7 | 917 | 992 | 992 | 908 |
| Wholesale and retail trade.... | 18,736 | 4.3 | 5.0 | 722 | 759 | 743 | 721 |
| Transportation and utilities.... | 6,467 | 17.3 | 18.3 | 901 | 1,106 | 1,091 | 864 |
| Information.............. | 2,536 | 9.6 | 10.3 | 1,169 | 1,355 | 1,336 | 1,157 |
| Financial activities...... | 9,148 | 2.1 | 2.8 | 1,047 | 937 | 940 | 1,052 |
| Professional and business services...... | 15,228 | 2.6 | 3.2 | 1,094 | 888 | 906 | 1,105 |
| Education and health services.......... | 22,982 | 8.1 | 9.3 | 860 | 984 | 978 | 845 |
| Leisure and hospitality......... | 12,582 | 2.9 | 3.5 | 584 | 700 | 695 | 579 |
| Other services.......... | 6,192 | 2.6 | 3.0 | 735 | 1,165 | 1,186 | 725 |
| Public sector............ | 21,131 | 33.9 | 37.2 | 999 | 1,099 | 1,094 | 936 |

B Base is less than 50,000. [1] Members of a labor union or an employee association similar to a labor union. [2] Members of a labor union or an employee association similar to a union as well as workers who report no union affiliation but whose jobs are covered by a union or an employee association contract. [3] For full-time employed wage and salary workers. [4] Includes other races not shown separately. Also includes a small number of multiple jobholders whose full- and part-time status cannot be determined for their principal job. [5] For persons in this race group only. [6] Persons of Hispanic origin may be of any race. [7] For composition of industries, see Table 659.

Source: U.S. Bureau of Labor Statistics, *Union Members—2018*, USDL 19-0079, January 2019. See also <http://www.bls.gov/news.release/union2.toc.htm>.

# Table 694. Labor Union Membership by State: 2010 and 2018

[Annual averages of monthly figures (14,715.1 represents 14,715,100). For wage and salary workers in agriculture and non-agriculture. Data represent union members by place of residence. Based on the Current Population Survey and subject to sampling error. For methodological details, see source]

| State | Union members (1,000) | | Workers covered by unions (1,000) | | Percent of workers | | | | | |
|---|---|---|---|---|---|---|---|---|---|---|
| | | | | | Union members | | Covered by unions | | Private sector union members | |
| | 2010 | 2018 | 2010 | 2018 | 2010 | 2018 | 2010 | 2018 | 2010 | 2018 |
| **United States......** | **14,715.1** | **14,740.2** | **16,289.5** | **16,374.4** | **11.9** | **10.5** | **13.1** | **11.7** | **6.9** | **6.4** |
| Alabama [1]............ | 183.3 | 180.6 | 202.8 | 196.3 | 10.1 | 9.3 | 11.2 | 10.1 | 5.7 | 6.0 |
| Alaska............... | 67.6 | 55.1 | 73.0 | 59.9 | 22.9 | 18.4 | 24.8 | 20.0 | 11.2 | 9.0 |
| Arizona [1]............ | 161.0 | 156.6 | 203.0 | 191.0 | 6.4 | 5.3 | 8.1 | 6.5 | 3.6 | 2.4 |
| Arkansas [1]........... | 43.6 | 56.2 | 58.6 | 61.8 | 4.0 | 4.8 | 5.4 | 5.3 | 2.7 | 4.1 |
| California............. | 2,431.3 | 2,404.9 | 2,577.8 | 2,586.6 | 17.5 | 14.7 | 18.6 | 15.8 | 9.3 | 8.3 |
| Colorado............. | 140.4 | 281.1 | 170.9 | 306.9 | 6.6 | 11.0 | 8.0 | 12.0 | 3.8 | 8.1 |
| Connecticut.......... | 258.3 | 267.2 | 269.7 | 280.1 | 16.7 | 15.9 | 17.4 | 16.7 | 8.3 | 8.3 |
| Delaware............. | 40.2 | 44.8 | 43.9 | 46.9 | 11.4 | 10.3 | 12.5 | 10.8 | 5.8 | 5.9 |
| District of Columbia.. | 25.9 | 35.2 | 30.0 | 41.3 | 9.0 | 9.9 | 10.5 | 11.6 | 5.9 | 5.9 |
| Florida [1]............. | 391.8 | 484.2 | 488.0 | 587.6 | 5.6 | 5.6 | 6.9 | 6.7 | 2.3 | 2.4 |
| Georgia [1]............ | 153.3 | 200.1 | 191.3 | 247.7 | 4.0 | 4.5 | 5.0 | 5.5 | 2.5 | 2.7 |
| Hawaii............... | 111.3 | 138.9 | 120.3 | 145.8 | 21.8 | 23.1 | 23.5 | 24.3 | 14.6 | 15.1 |
| Idaho [1].............. | 41.5 | 34.2 | 50.1 | 41.4 | 7.1 | 4.7 | 8.6 | 5.6 | 3.6 | 2.6 |
| Illinois............... | 843.8 | 786.0 | 891.2 | 839.2 | 15.5 | 13.8 | 16.4 | 14.7 | 9.5 | 8.7 |
| Indiana [3]............ | 278.6 | 269.0 | 312.8 | 283.2 | 10.9 | 8.8 | 12.2 | 9.3 | 8.2 | 7.0 |
| Iowa [1].............. | 158.2 | 112.8 | 191.8 | 129.1 | 11.4 | 7.7 | 13.8 | 8.8 | 7.1 | 5.2 |
| Kansas [1]............ | 83.7 | 90.6 | 111.0 | 129.3 | 6.8 | 7.0 | 9.1 | 10.1 | 4.5 | 4.9 |
| Kentucky [6].......... | 146.5 | 160.2 | 166.1 | 206.1 | 8.9 | 8.8 | 10.1 | 11.4 | 7.2 | 6.8 |
| Louisiana [1].......... | 75.6 | 89.0 | 96.0 | 103.9 | 4.3 | 5.0 | 5.5 | 5.8 | 3.2 | 3.1 |
| Maine................ | 62.9 | 73.9 | 70.7 | 84.7 | 11.6 | 12.9 | 13.0 | 14.8 | 5.1 | 5.8 |
| Maryland............. | 296.1 | 306.3 | 328.8 | 334.6 | 11.6 | 11.0 | 12.9 | 12.0 | 6.1 | 5.8 |
| Massachusetts....... | 414.8 | 462.7 | 446.4 | 491.0 | 14.5 | 13.6 | 15.6 | 14.5 | 7.0 | 7.2 |
| Michigan [3].......... | 627.3 | 624.6 | 658.7 | 662.5 | 16.5 | 14.5 | 17.3 | 15.3 | 11.1 | 11.0 |
| Minnesota........... | 384.6 | 395.4 | 397.3 | 421.2 | 15.6 | 15.0 | 16.1 | 16.0 | 8.4 | 8.9 |
| Mississippi [1]........ | 46.3 | 57.7 | 58.3 | 79.9 | 4.5 | 5.1 | 5.6 | 7.1 | 3.7 | 3.6 |
| Missouri [6].......... | 244.3 | 251.8 | 274.4 | 283.1 | 9.9 | 9.4 | 11.1 | 10.6 | 8.5 | 6.4 |
| Montana............. | 46.1 | 50.4 | 52.2 | 59.9 | 12.7 | 11.8 | 14.4 | 14.0 | 5.6 | 5.7 |
| Nebraska [1].......... | 75.3 | 58.4 | 95.6 | 70.9 | 9.3 | 6.6 | 11.8 | 8.0 | 4.8 | 3.7 |
| Nevada [1]............ | 151.3 | 190.8 | 169.9 | 215.5 | 15.0 | 13.9 | 16.8 | 15.6 | 10.8 | 11.1 |
| New Hampshire...... | 63.2 | 67.7 | 72.6 | 77.1 | 10.2 | 10.2 | 11.7 | 11.6 | 4.4 | 4.9 |
| New Jersey.......... | 636.9 | 587.2 | 660.0 | 638.8 | 17.1 | 14.9 | 17.7 | 16.2 | 9.0 | 7.8 |
| New Mexico.......... | 54.8 | 55.3 | 72.4 | 66.3 | 7.3 | 6.8 | 9.7 | 8.2 | 2.6 | 4.1 |
| New York............ | 1,958.7 | 1,873.9 | 2,098.6 | 2,028.3 | 24.2 | 22.3 | 26.0 | 24.1 | 13.7 | 13.2 |
| North Carolina [1]...... | 116.7 | 117.1 | 179.6 | 172.8 | 3.2 | 2.7 | 4.9 | 4.0 | 1.8 | 2.0 |
| North Dakota [1]....... | 23.0 | 17.9 | 28.4 | 23.0 | 7.4 | 5.2 | 9.1 | 6.7 | 4.6 | 3.5 |
| Ohio................. | 654.9 | 639.9 | 701.9 | 722.1 | 13.7 | 12.7 | 14.7 | 14.3 | 8.4 | 7.4 |
| Oklahoma [2].......... | 77.4 | 90.1 | 98.5 | 117.6 | 5.5 | 5.7 | 6.9 | 7.4 | 3.5 | 2.4 |
| Oregon.............. | 245.1 | 241.2 | 267.9 | 255.2 | 16.2 | 13.9 | 17.7 | 14.7 | 9.1 | 7.1 |
| Pennsylvania......... | 770.2 | 700.1 | 831.4 | 747.8 | 14.7 | 12.5 | 15.9 | 13.4 | 9.3 | 8.0 |
| Rhode Island........ | 74.9 | 83.2 | 79.4 | 88.5 | 16.4 | 17.3 | 17.4 | 18.5 | 8.4 | 8.8 |
| South Carolina [1]..... | 79.6 | 55.4 | 106.8 | 71.8 | 4.6 | 2.7 | 6.2 | 3.6 | 2.7 | 1.6 |
| South Dakota [1]....... | 20.0 | 21.7 | 23.5 | 27.5 | 5.6 | 5.6 | 6.6 | 7.1 | 3.0 | 3.0 |
| Tennessee [1].......... | 115.5 | 154.1 | 142.5 | 178.6 | 4.7 | 5.5 | 5.8 | 6.3 | 2.2 | 3.2 |
| Texas [1]............. | 545.4 | 511.9 | 676.7 | 653.6 | 5.4 | 4.3 | 6.7 | 5.5 | 3.2 | 2.6 |
| Utah [1].............. | 74.6 | 55.6 | 95.6 | 75.9 | 6.5 | 4.1 | 8.4 | 5.6 | 3.9 | 2.5 |
| Vermont............. | 34.2 | 30.6 | 39.5 | 33.8 | 11.8 | 10.5 | 13.6 | 11.6 | 5.3 | 4.7 |
| Virginia [1]........... | 160.6 | 167.8 | 196.4 | 213.2 | 4.6 | 4.3 | 5.7 | 5.5 | 2.9 | 3.2 |
| Washington.......... | 551.8 | 648.1 | 605.2 | 669.9 | 19.4 | 19.8 | 21.3 | 20.5 | 10.7 | 12.9 |
| West Virginia [5]....... | 99.9 | 68.5 | 111.4 | 73.8 | 14.8 | 10.0 | 16.5 | 10.8 | 11.2 | 7.7 |
| Wisconsin [4].......... | 354.9 | 218.6 | 379.8 | 233.3 | 14.2 | 8.1 | 15.1 | 8.6 | 8.4 | 5.5 |
| Wyoming [1]........... | 18.1 | 15.4 | 20.7 | 18.0 | 7.4 | 6.5 | 8.4 | 7.6 | 4.9 | 4.5 |

[1] Right to work state as of 2000. [2] Passed right to work law in 2001. [3] Passed right to work law in 2012. [4] Passed right to work law in 2015. [5] Passed right to work law in 2016. [6] Passed right to work law in 2017.

Source: Bloomberg BNA, *2019 Union Membership and Earnings Data Book*, by Barry Hirsch and David Macpherson, Bloomberg Law, <https://www.bloomberglaw.com/product/labor/document/XAOCRE0G000000?documentName=ORCA122534.PDF&fmt=pdf>. Copyright 2019 by The Bureau of National Affairs, Inc. (800-372-1033) <http://www.bna.com>.

## Table 695. Work Stoppages: 1960 to 2018

[896 represents 896,000. Excludes work stoppages involving fewer than 1,000 workers and lasting less than 1 day. The term "major work stoppage" includes both worker-initiated strikes and employer-initiated lockouts that involve 1,000 or more workers. Information is based on reports of labor disputes appearing in daily newspapers, trade journals, and other public sources]

| Year | Number of work stoppages [1] | Workers involved [2] (1,000) | Days idle total Number [3] (1,000) | Days idle total Percent estimated working time [4] | Year | Number of work stoppages [1] | Workers involved [2] (1,000) | Days idle total Number [3] (1,000) | Days idle total Percent estimated working time [4] |
|---|---|---|---|---|---|---|---|---|---|
| 1960 | 222 | 896 | 13,260 | 0.09 | 2000 | 39 | 394 | 20,419 | 0.06 |
| 1970 | 381 | 2,468 | 52,761 | 0.29 | 2001 | 29 | 99 | 1,151 | (Z) |
| 1980 | 187 | 795 | 20,844 | 0.09 | 2002 | 19 | 46 | 660 | (Z) |
| 1984 | 62 | 376 | 8,499 | 0.04 | 2003 | 14 | 129 | 4,091 | 0.01 |
| 1985 | 54 | 324 | 7,079 | 0.03 | 2004 | 17 | 171 | 3,344 | 0.01 |
| 1986 | 69 | 533 | 11,861 | 0.05 | 2005 | 22 | 100 | 1,736 | 0.01 |
| 1987 | 46 | 174 | 4,481 | 0.02 | 2006 | 20 | 70 | 2,688 | 0.01 |
| 1988 | 40 | 118 | 4,381 | 0.02 | 2007 | 21 | 189 | 1,265 | (Z) |
| 1989 | 51 | 452 | 16,996 | 0.07 | 2008 | 15 | 72 | 1,954 | 0.01 |
| 1990 | 44 | 185 | 5,926 | 0.02 | 2009 | 5 | 13 | 124 | (Z) |
| 1991 | 40 | 392 | 4,584 | 0.02 | 2010 | 11 | 45 | 302 | (Z) |
| 1992 | 35 | 364 | 3,989 | 0.01 | 2011 | 19 | 113 | 1,020 | (Z) |
| 1993 | 35 | 182 | 3,981 | 0.01 | 2012 | 19 | 148 | 1,131 | (Z) |
| 1994 | 45 | 322 | 5,021 | 0.02 | 2013 | 15 | 55 | 290 | (Z) |
| 1995 | 31 | 192 | 5,771 | 0.02 | 2014 | 11 | 34 | 200 | (Z) |
| 1996 | 37 | 273 | 4,889 | 0.02 | 2015 | 12 | 47 | 740 | (Z) |
| 1997 | 29 | 339 | 4,497 | 0.01 | 2016 | 15 | 99 | 1,543 | (Z) |
| 1998 | 34 | 387 | 5,116 | 0.02 | 2017 | 7 | 25 | 440 | (Z) |
| 1999 | 17 | 73 | 1,996 | 0.01 | 2018 | 20 | 485 | 2,815 | 0.01 |

Z Less than 0.005 percent. [1] Beginning in year indicated. [2] Workers counted more than once if involved in more than one stoppage during the year. [3] Resulting from all stoppages in effect in a year, including those that began in an earlier year. The number of total days of idleness is computed by multiplying the number of workers idled by the number of lost workdays during the reference period. [4] Agricultural and government employees are included in the total working time; private household and forestry and fishery employees are excluded.

Source: U.S. Bureau of Labor Statistics, *Major Work Stoppages in 2018*, USDL 19-0189, February 2019. See also <http://www.bls.gov/wsp>.

# Section 13
# Income, Expenditures, Poverty, and Wealth

This section presents data on gross domestic product (GDP), gross national product (GNP), national and personal income, savings and investment, money income, poverty, and national and personal wealth. The data on income and expenditures measure two aspects of the U.S. economy. One aspect relates to the National Income and Product Accounts (NIPA), a summation reflecting the entire complex of the nation's economic income and output and the interaction of its major components; the other relates to personal and household income and wealth, and consumer expenditures.

The primary source for data on GDP, GNP, national and personal income, gross saving and investment, and fixed assets and consumer durables is the *Survey of Current Business*, issued monthly by the Bureau of Economic Analysis (BEA). These data are also available in tables accessible through an interactive tool on the BEA's website, <http://www.bea.gov/iTable/index.cfm>. Revisions occur annually. The BEA conducts a comprehensive revision using data from the Census Bureau's Economic Census approximately every 5 years. The most recent comprehensive revision to the NIPA was released beginning in July 2018. Discussions of the revision are available at the BEA's website.

Sources of income distribution data are the decennial censuses of population, the Annual Social and Economic Supplement of the Current Population Survey (CPS), and the American Community Survey, all products of the U.S. Census Bureau (see text, Section 1). Annual data on income of families, individuals, and households are presented in *Current Population Reports, Income and Poverty in the United States*, in print and online. Detailed statistics and historical data are available on the Census Bureau's website at <http://www.census.gov/topics/income-poverty.html>.

Data on the household sector's savings and assets are published by the Board of Governors of the Federal Reserve System in the quarterly statistical release, *Financial Accounts of the United States*. The Federal Reserve Board also periodically conducts the *Survey of Consumer Finances*, which presents financial information on family assets and net worth. The most recent survey is available online at <http://www.federalreserve.gov/econresdata/scf/scfindex.htm>. Detailed information on personal wealth is published periodically by the Internal Revenue Service (IRS) in the *SOI (Statistics of Income) Bulletin*.

**National income and product**—*GDP,* or value added, is the value of the goods and services produced by the nation's economy less the value of the goods and services used up in production. GDP is equal to the sum of personal consumption expenditures, gross private domestic investment, net exports of goods and services, and government consumption expenditures and gross investment. The goods and services included are largely those bought for final use (excluding illegal transactions) in the market economy. A number of inclusions, however, represent imputed values, the most important of which is the rental value of owner-occupied housing. GDP, in this broad context, measures the output attributable to the factors of production located in the United States. GDP

by state is the gross market value of the goods and services attributable to labor and property located in a state. It is the state counterpart of the nation's GDP.

The BEA releases GDP and related data in current dollar estimates, which reflect the value when transactions occurred, and in real values that are inflation-adjusted estimates that exclude the effects of price changes. Quantities, or "real" volume measures, and prices are expressed as index numbers with a specified reference year equal to 100 (currently 2012). Quantity and price indexes are calculated using a Fisher-chained weighted formula that incorporates weights from two adjacent periods (years for annual data). Chained-dollar values are calculated by multiplying the quantity index by the current dollar value in the reference year (2012) and then dividing by 100. Percent changes calculated from real quantity indexes and chained-dollar levels are conceptually the same; any differences are due to rounding. Chained-dollar values are not additive because the relative weights for a given period differ from those of the reference year. In tables that display chained-dollar values, a "residual" line shows the difference between the sum of detailed chained-dollar series and its corresponding aggregate.

*Gross national product* measures the output attributable to all labor and property supplied by United States residents, including residents working abroad. The GNP takes into account net income payments to the rest of the world. In brief, the GNP is the result of subtracting net income payments to the rest of the world from GDP.

*National income* includes all net incomes, net of consumption of fixed capital (CFC), earned in production. National income is also the sum of compensation of employees, proprietors' income with inventory valuation adjustment (IVA) and capital consumption adjustment (CCAdj), rental income of persons with CCAdj, corporate profits with IVA and CCAdj, net interest and miscellaneous payments, taxes on production and imports less subsidies, business current transfer payments (net), and current surplus of government enterprises, less subsidies.

*Capital consumption adjustment* for corporations and for nonfarm sole proprietorships and partnerships is the difference between capital consumption based on income tax returns and capital consumption measured using empirical evidence on prices of used equipment and structures in resale markets, which have shown that depreciation for most types of assets approximates a geometric pattern. The tax return data are valued at historical costs and reflect changes over time in service lives and depreciation patterns as permitted by tax regulations. Inventory valuation adjustment represents the difference between the book value of inventories used up in production and the cost of replacing them.

*Personal income* is the current income that persons receive in return for their provision of labor, land, and capital used in current production, plus current transfer receipts less contributions for government social insurance (domestic). Classified as "persons" are individuals (including owners of unincorporated firms), nonprofit institutions that primarily serve individuals, private trust funds, and private noninsured welfare funds. Personal income includes personal current transfer receipts (payments not resulting from current production) from government and business such as social security benefits, public assistance, etc., but excludes transfers among persons. Also included are certain nonmonetary types of income; chiefly, estimated net rental value to owner-occupants of their homes and the value of services furnished without payment by financial intermediaries. Capital gains (and losses) are excluded.

*Disposable personal income* is personal income less personal current taxes. It is the income available to persons for spending or saving. Personal current taxes are tax payments (net of refunds) by persons (except personal contributions for government social insurance) that are not chargeable to business expense. Personal taxes include income taxes, personal property taxes, motor vehicle licenses, and other miscellaneous taxes.

**Gross domestic product by industry**—The BEA also prepares estimates of value added by industry. *Value added* is a measure of the contribution of each private industry and of government to the nation's GDP. It is defined as an industry's gross output (which consists of sales or receipts and other operating income, commodity taxes, and inventory change) minus its intermediate inputs (which consist of energy, raw materials, semi-finished goods, and purchased services). Data are available by industry, for private industries and for Federal and state and local government. Industries are classified according to the North American Industry Classification System.

The estimates by industry are available in current dollars and are derived from the estimates of gross domestic income, which consists of three components—the compensation of employees, gross operating surplus, and taxes on production and imports, less subsidies. Real, or inflation-adjusted, estimates are also available.

**Regional Economic Accounts**—These accounts consist of estimates of state and local area personal income and of gross domestic product by state and are consistent with estimates of personal income and gross domestic product in the BEA's national economic accounts. BEA's estimates of state and local area personal income provide a framework for analyzing individual state and local economies, and they show how the economies compare with each other. The *personal income* of a state and/or local area is the income received by, or on behalf of, the residents of that state or area. Estimates of labor and proprietors' earnings by place of work indicate the economic activity of business and government within that area, and estimates of personal income by place of residence indicate the income within the area that is available for spending. BEA prepares estimates for states, counties, metropolitan areas, and BEA economic areas.

Gross domestic product by state estimates measure the value added to the nation's production by the labor and property in each state. GDP by state is often considered the state counterpart of the nation's GDP. The GDP by state estimates provide the basis for analyzing the regional impacts of national economic trends. GDP by state is measured as the sum of the distributions by industry and state of the components of gross domestic income; that is, the sum of the costs incurred and incomes earned in the production of GDP by state. GDP estimates are available in current dollars and in real (chained dollars) by industry.

**Consumer Expenditure Survey**—The Consumer Expenditure Survey program began in 1980. The principal objective of the survey is to collect current consumer expenditure data, which provide a continuous flow of data on the buying habits of American consumers. The data are necessary for revisions of the Consumer Price Index.

The survey conducted by the Census Bureau for the Bureau of Labor Statistics consists of two components: (1) an interview panel survey in which the expenditures of consumer units are obtained over 4 quarters, and (2) a diary or recordkeeping survey completed by participating households for two consecutive 1-week periods. See Appendix III for more information.

**Money income of households, families, and individuals**—Money income statistics are based on data collected in various field surveys of income conducted since 1936. Since 1947, the Census Bureau has collected the data on an annual basis and published them in *Current Population Reports*, P60 Series. In each of the surveys, field representatives interview samples of the population with respect to income received during the previous year. *Money income* as defined by the Census Bureau differs from the BEA concept of "personal income." Data on consumer income collected in the CPS by the Census Bureau cover money income received (exclusive of certain money receipts such as capital gains) before payments for personal income taxes, social security, union dues, Medicare deductions, etc. Money income does not reflect the fact that some families receive part of their income in the form of noncash benefits (see Section 11) such as food stamps, health benefits, and subsidized housing; that some farm families receive noncash benefits in the form of goods produced and consumed on the farm; or that noncash benefits are also received by some nonfarm residents, which often take the form of the use of business transportation and facilities, full or partial payments by business for retirement programs, medical and educational expenses, etc. These elements should be considered when comparing income levels. None of the aggregate income concepts (GDP, national income, or personal income) is exactly comparable with money income, although personal income is the closest. For a definition of families and households, see text, Section 1.

**Poverty**—Families and unrelated individuals are classified as being above or below poverty following the Office of Management and Budget's Statistical Policy Directive 14. The Census Bureau uses a set of thresholds that vary by family size and composition.

The official poverty thresholds do not vary geographically, but they are updated every year to reflect changes in the consumer price index (CPI-U). The official poverty definition uses money income before taxes and does not include capital gains or noncash benefits (such as public housing, Medicaid, and food stamps).

The original thresholds were based on the U.S. Department of Agriculture's 1961 Economy Food Plan and reflected the different consumption requirements of families. The following technical changes to the thresholds were made in 1981: (1) distinctions based on sex of householder were eliminated, (2) separate thresholds for farm families were dropped, and (3) the matrix was expanded to families of nine or more persons from the old cutoff of seven or more persons. These changes were incorporated in the calculation of poverty data beginning with data for 1981. Besides the Census Bureau website at <http://www.census.gov /topics/income-poverty/poverty.html>, information on poverty guidelines and research may be found at the U.S. Department of Human Services website at <https://aspe.hhs.gov/poverty-guidelines>.

**Statistical reliability**—For a discussion of statistical collection and estimation, sampling procedures, and measures of statistical reliability pertaining to Census Bureau data, see Appendix III.

# Table 696. Gross Domestic Product in Current and Chained (2012) Dollars: 1990 to 2018

[In billions of dollars (5,963 represents $5,963,000,000,000). For explanation of gross domestic product and chained dollars, see text, this section. Minus sign (-) indicates decline in inventories or net imports]

| Item | 1990 | 2000 | 2005 | 2006 | 2007 | 2008 | 2009 | 2010 | 2011 | 2012 | 2013 | 2014 | 2015 | 2016 | 2017 | 2018 |
|---|---|---|---|---|---|---|---|---|---|---|---|---|---|---|---|---|
| **CURRENT DOLLARS** | | | | | | | | | | | | | | | | |
| **Gross domestic product** | 5,963 | 10,252 | 13,037 | 13,815 | 14,452 | 14,713 | 14,449 | 14,992 | 15,543 | 16,197 | 16,785 | 17,527 | 18,225 | 18,715 | 19,519 | 20,580 |
| Personal consumption expenditures | 3,809 | 6,762 | 8,747 | 9,260 | 9,706 | 9,976 | 9,842 | 10,186 | 10,641 | 11,007 | 11,317 | 11,823 | 12,284 | 12,748 | 13,312 | 13,999 |
| Durable goods | 497 | 913 | 1,129 | 1,158 | 1,188 | 1,099 | 1,012 | 1,049 | 1,093 | 1,144 | 1,189 | 1,242 | 1,306 | 1,353 | 1,413 | 1,476 |
| Nondurable goods | 994 | 1,541 | 1,954 | 2,081 | 2,179 | 2,264 | 2,168 | 2,269 | 2,425 | 2,494 | 2,541 | 2,621 | 2,614 | 2,643 | 2,752 | 2,889 |
| Services | 2,318 | 4,309 | 5,664 | 6,021 | 6,339 | 6,613 | 6,662 | 6,868 | 7,123 | 7,369 | 7,587 | 7,960 | 8,364 | 8,753 | 9,147 | 9,634 |
| Gross private domestic investment | 993 | 2,038 | 2,535 | 2,701 | 2,673 | 2,478 | 1,930 | 2,165 | 2,333 | 2,622 | 2,826 | 3,044 | 3,223 | 3,179 | 3,371 | 3,628 |
| Fixed investment | 979 | 1,984 | 2,477 | 2,632 | 2,639 | 2,507 | 2,080 | 2,112 | 2,286 | 2,551 | 2,721 | 2,960 | 3,091 | 3,152 | 3,340 | 3,574 |
| Nonresidential | 739 | 1,498 | 1,621 | 1,794 | 1,949 | 1,991 | 1,690 | 1,735 | 1,907 | 2,119 | 2,211 | 2,400 | 2,457 | 2,453 | 2,585 | 2,787 |
| Residential | 240 | 485 | 856 | 838 | 690 | 516 | 390 | 377 | 379 | 432 | 510 | 560 | 634 | 698 | 756 | 787 |
| Change in private inventories | 15 | 55 | 58 | 69 | 34 | -29 | -151 | 54 | 46 | 71 | 105 | 84 | 132 | 27 | 30 | 55 |
| Net exports of goods and services | -78 | -375 | -721 | -771 | -718 | -723 | -396 | -514 | -579 | -569 | -491 | -508 | -520 | -519 | -575 | -638 |
| Exports | 552 | 1,096 | 1,305 | 1,473 | 1,661 | 1,837 | 1,582 | 1,846 | 2,103 | 2,191 | 2,273 | 2,372 | 2,267 | 2,221 | 2,357 | 2,510 |
| Imports | 630 | 1,471 | 2,026 | 2,244 | 2,379 | 2,560 | 1,978 | 2,360 | 2,682 | 2,760 | 2,764 | 2,879 | 2,787 | 2,739 | 2,932 | 3,148 |
| Government consumption expenditures and gross investment | 1,239 | 1,827 | 2,476 | 2,624 | 2,791 | 2,982 | 3,074 | 3,155 | 3,148 | 3,137 | 3,132 | 3,168 | 3,237 | 3,307 | 3,412 | 3,591 |
| Federal | 562 | 634 | 947 | 1,001 | 1,051 | 1,151 | 1,218 | 1,298 | 1,299 | 1,287 | 1,227 | 1,215 | 1,222 | 1,234 | 1,269 | 1,347 |
| National defense | 405 | 393 | 609 | 641 | 679 | 750 | 788 | 828 | 834 | 814 | 764 | 743 | 730 | 728 | 746 | 794 |
| Nondefense | 157 | 241 | 338 | 360 | 371 | 400 | 431 | 470 | 465 | 472 | 462 | 472 | 491 | 506 | 523 | 554 |
| State and local | 676 | 1,193 | 1,529 | 1,624 | 1,740 | 1,831 | 1,855 | 1,857 | 1,849 | 1,850 | 1,906 | 1,953 | 2,016 | 2,073 | 2,143 | 2,244 |
| **CHAINED (2012) DOLLARS [1]** | | | | | | | | | | | | | | | | |
| **Gross domestic product** | 9,365 | 13,131 | 14,913 | 15,338 | 15,626 | 15,605 | 15,209 | 15,599 | 15,841 | 16,197 | 16,495 | 16,912 | 17,404 | 17,689 | 18,108 | 18,638 |
| Personal consumption expenditures | 6,012 | 8,643 | 10,076 | 10,385 | 10,615 | 10,593 | 10,460 | 10,643 | 10,844 | 11,007 | 11,167 | 11,497 | 11,921 | 12,247 | 12,567 | 12,945 |
| Durable goods | (NA) | (NA) | 1,005 | 1,049 | 1,100 | 1,036 | 973 | 1,027 | 1,080 | 1,144 | 1,214 | 1,302 | 1,399 | 1,484 | 1,586 | 1,686 |
| Nondurable goods | (NA) | (NA) | 2,383 | 2,462 | 2,503 | 2,464 | 2,423 | 2,461 | 2,483 | 2,494 | 2,538 | 2,605 | 2,693 | 2,757 | 2,825 | 2,910 |
| Services | (NA) | (NA) | 6,689 | 6,872 | 7,004 | 7,093 | 7,070 | 7,157 | 7,282 | 7,369 | 7,415 | 7,595 | 7,838 | 8,021 | 8,182 | 8,388 |
| Gross private domestic investment | 1,223 | 2,347 | 2,671 | 2,752 | 2,684 | 2,463 | 1,942 | 2,216 | 2,362 | 2,622 | 2,801 | 2,959 | 3,104 | 3,064 | 3,199 | 3,361 |
| Fixed investment | (NA) | 2,294 | 2,619 | 2,687 | 2,653 | 2,499 | 2,100 | 2,164 | 2,318 | 2,551 | 2,692 | 2,869 | 2,967 | 3,024 | 3,150 | 3,293 |
| Nonresidential | (NA) | 1,616 | 1,716 | 1,854 | 1,982 | 1,994 | 1,704 | 1,781 | 1,935 | 2,119 | 2,206 | 2,365 | 2,408 | 2,425 | 2,531 | 2,692 |
| Residential | (NA) | 647 | 885 | 819 | 666 | 505 | 395 | 383 | 382 | 432 | 485 | 504 | 555 | 591 | 612 | 603 |
| Change in private inventories | (NA) | 79 | 64 | 87 | 41 | -33 | -177 | 57 | 47 | 71 | 109 | 86 | 132 | 23 | 32 | 48 |
| Net exports of goods and services | (NA) | (NA) | -888 | -905 | -824 | -662 | -485 | -566 | -568 | -569 | -533 | -577 | -722 | -784 | -850 | -920 |
| Exports | 693 | 1,380 | 1,533 | 1,676 | 1,822 | 1,925 | 1,764 | 1,978 | 2,119 | 2,191 | 2,270 | 2,365 | 2,376 | 2,376 | 2,459 | 2,533 |
| Imports | 795 | 1,930 | 2,421 | 2,581 | 2,646 | 2,587 | 2,249 | 2,544 | 2,687 | 2,760 | 2,802 | 2,942 | 3,098 | 3,160 | 3,309 | 3,453 |
| Government consumption expenditures and gross investment | 2,377 | 2,663 | 3,015 | 3,064 | 3,119 | 3,196 | 3,307 | 3,307 | 3,203 | 3,137 | 3,061 | 3,033 | 3,092 | 3,148 | 3,170 | 3,224 |
| Federal | (NA) | (NA) | 1,099 | 1,125 | 1,147 | 1,219 | 1,293 | 1,346 | 1,311 | 1,287 | 1,215 | 1,184 | 1,183 | 1,188 | 1,197 | 1,232 |
| National defense | (NA) | (NA) | 709 | 720 | 740 | 791 | 837 | 861 | 843 | 814 | 760 | 728 | 713 | 709 | 714 | 737 |
| Nondefense | (NA) | (NA) | 391 | 405 | 407 | 427 | 456 | 485 | 468 | 472 | 456 | 455 | 469 | 478 | 482 | 494 |
| State and local | (NA) | (NA) | 1,920 | 1,942 | 1,975 | 1,979 | 2,016 | 1,961 | 1,892 | 1,850 | 1,845 | 1,849 | 1,907 | 1,958 | 1,971 | 1,990 |
| Residual | -166 | -50 | 35 | 32 | 26 | -2 | -15 | -11 | -4 | — | -(Z) | 1 | 11 | 21 | 17 | 2 |

— Represents zero. NA Not available. Z Less than $500 million. [1] Chained (2012) dollar series are calculated as the product of the chain-type quantity index and the 2012 current-dollar value of the corresponding series, divided by 100. Because the formula for the chain-type quantity indexes uses weights of more than one period, the corresponding chained-dollar estimates are usually not additive. The residual line is the difference between the first line and the sum of the most detailed lines.

Source: U.S. Bureau of Economic Analysis, National Income and Product Accounts Tables, "Table 1.1.5. Gross Domestic Product," and "Table 1.1.6. Real Gross Domestic Product, Chained Dollars," <http://www.bea.gov/iTable/>, accessed July 2019.

## Table 697. Real Gross Domestic Product, Chained (2012) Dollars—Annual Percent Change: 1990 to 2018

[Percent change from immediate previous year; for example, 1990, change from 1989. Minus sign (-) indicates decrease]

| Component | 1990 | 2000 | 2010 | 2012 | 2013 | 2014 | 2015 | 2016 | 2017 | 2018 |
|---|---|---|---|---|---|---|---|---|---|---|
| **Gross domestic product (GDP)**............ | **1.9** | **4.1** | **2.6** | **2.2** | **1.8** | **2.5** | **2.9** | **1.6** | **2.4** | **2.9** |
| Personal consumption expenditures........... | 2.0 | 5.1 | 1.7 | 1.5 | 1.5 | 3.0 | 3.7 | 2.7 | 2.6 | 3.0 |
| Durable goods.......................... | -0.4 | 8.6 | 5.6 | 6.0 | 6.1 | 7.2 | 7.5 | 6.1 | 6.9 | 6.3 |
| Nondurable goods..................... | 1.2 | 3.2 | 1.6 | 0.4 | 1.8 | 2.6 | 3.4 | 2.4 | 2.5 | 3.0 |
| Services.............................. | 2.9 | 5.0 | 1.2 | 1.2 | 0.6 | 2.4 | 3.2 | 2.3 | 2.0 | 2.5 |
| Gross private domestic investment.......... | -2.6 | 6.7 | 14.1 | 11.0 | 6.9 | 5.6 | 4.9 | -1.3 | 4.4 | 5.1 |
| Fixed investment........................ | -1.4 | 7.1 | 3.1 | 10.0 | 5.6 | 6.6 | 3.4 | 1.9 | 4.2 | 4.6 |
| Nonresidential...................... | 1.1 | 9.3 | 4.5 | 9.5 | 4.1 | 7.2 | 1.8 | 0.7 | 4.4 | 6.4 |
| Structures..................... | 1.5 | 8.1 | -16.1 | 13.0 | 1.3 | 11.0 | -3.0 | -5.0 | 4.7 | 4.1 |
| Equipment.................... | -2.1 | 9.7 | 20.2 | 11.0 | 4.7 | 7.0 | 3.2 | -1.3 | 4.7 | 6.8 |
| Intellectual property products.............. | 8.4 | 9.5 | 2.7 | 5.0 | 5.4 | 4.8 | 3.6 | 7.9 | 3.7 | 7.4 |
| Residential........................ | -8.5 | 0.7 | -3.1 | 13.0 | 12.4 | 3.8 | 10.2 | 6.5 | 3.5 | -1.5 |
| Exports................................... | 8.8 | 8.3 | 12.1 | 3.4 | 3.6 | 4.2 | 0.5 | – | 3.5 | 3.0 |
| Goods................................ | 8.6 | 9.9 | 15.0 | 3.8 | 3.2 | 4.6 | -0.4 | 0.6 | 3.9 | 4.3 |
| Services............................. | 9.5 | 4.3 | 6.3 | 2.4 | 4.5 | 3.3 | 2.2 | -1.1 | 2.7 | 0.7 |
| Imports.................................. | 3.6 | 12.9 | 13.1 | 2.7 | 1.5 | 5.0 | 5.3 | 2.0 | 4.7 | 4.4 |
| Goods................................ | 2.9 | 13.0 | 15.4 | 2.6 | 1.8 | 5.6 | 5.7 | 1.5 | 4.8 | 5.0 |
| Services............................. | 6.5 | 12.5 | 3.6 | 3.1 | 0.5 | 2.3 | 3.5 | 4.4 | 4.4 | 1.6 |
| Government consumption expenditures and gross investment........................ | 3.2 | 1.8 | – | -2.1 | -2.4 | -0.9 | 1.9 | 1.8 | 0.7 | 1.7 |
| Federal............................... | 2.1 | 0.3 | 4.1 | -1.9 | -5.5 | -2.6 | -0.1 | 0.4 | 0.8 | 2.9 |
| National defense.................. | 0.3 | -0.9 | 2.9 | -3.4 | -6.7 | -4.1 | -2.1 | -0.6 | 0.7 | 3.3 |
| Nondefense...................... | 7.3 | 2.3 | 6.2 | 0.9 | -3.5 | -0.1 | 3.1 | 2.0 | 0.8 | 2.4 |
| State and local....................... | 4.1 | 2.7 | -2.7 | -2.2 | -0.3 | 0.2 | 3.2 | 2.6 | 0.6 | 1.0 |

– Represents or rounds to zero.

Source: U.S. Bureau of Economic Analysis, National Income and Product Accounts Tables, "Table 1.1.1. Percent Change From Preceding Period in Real Gross Domestic Product," <http://www.bea.gov/iTable/index_nipa.cfm>, accessed July 2019.

## Table 698. Gross Domestic Product in Current and Chained (2012) Dollars by Type of Product and Sector: 1990 to 2018

[In billions of dollars (5,963 represents $5,963,000,000,000). For explanation of chained dollars, see text, this section]

| Type of product and sector | 1990 | 2000 | 2010 | 2013 | 2014 | 2015 | 2016 | 2017 | 2018 |
|---|---|---|---|---|---|---|---|---|---|
| **CURRENT DOLLARS** | | | | | | | | | |
| **Gross domestic product**............... | **5,963** | **10,252** | **14,992** | **16,785** | **17,527** | **18,225** | **18,715** | **19,519** | **20,580** |
| Product: | | | | | | | | | |
| Goods.................................. | 2,121 | 3,439 | 4,396 | 5,150 | 5,323 | 5,479 | 5,495 | 5,708 | 6,039 |
| Durable goods...................... | 1,176 | 2,084 | 2,478 | 2,896 | 2,991 | 3,037 | 3,074 | 3,195 | 3,409 |
| Nondurable goods.................. | 946 | 1,355 | 1,918 | 2,254 | 2,332 | 2,443 | 2,421 | 2,513 | 2,630 |
| Services [1]............................. | 3,293 | 5,826 | 9,537 | 10,366 | 10,794 | 11,254 | 11,682 | 12,170 | 12,809 |
| Structures............................ | 549 | 987 | 1,060 | 1,269 | 1,410 | 1,492 | 1,538 | 1,641 | 1,732 |
| Sector: | | | | | | | | | |
| Business [2]............................ | 4,542 | 7,876 | 11,140 | 12,671 | 13,281 | 13,826 | 14,181 | 14,831 | 15,681 |
| Nonfarm [3]......................... | 4,464 | 7,800 | 11,023 | 12,486 | 13,112 | 13,680 | 14,052 | 14,691 | 15,551 |
| Farm............................. | 78 | 76 | 118 | 185 | 168 | 146 | 129 | 139 | 130 |
| Households and institutions................. | 636 | 1,192 | 1,905 | 2,075 | 2,159 | 2,256 | 2,349 | 2,446 | 2,570 |
| General government [4]................. | 785 | 1,184 | 1,946 | 2,039 | 2,088 | 2,142 | 2,185 | 2,243 | 2,330 |
| Federal............................. | 307 | 360 | 640 | 658 | 667 | 675 | 686 | 702 | 729 |
| State and local....................... | 478 | 824 | 1,306 | 1,381 | 1,421 | 1,467 | 1,499 | 1,541 | 1,601 |
| **CHAINED (2012) DOLLARS** | | | | | | | | | |
| **Gross domestic product**............... | **9,365** | **13,131** | **15,599** | **16,495** | **16,912** | **17,404** | **17,689** | **18,108** | **18,638** |
| Product: | | | | | | | | | |
| Goods.................................. | 2,228 | 3,468 | 4,510 | 5,143 | 5,317 | 5,477 | 5,545 | 5,756 | 6,046 |
| Durable goods...................... | (NA) | (NA) | 2,491 | 2,898 | 3,000 | 3,037 | 3,103 | 3,237 | 3,451 |
| Nondurable goods.................. | (NA) | (NA) | 2,022 | 2,245 | 2,317 | 2,440 | 2,441 | 2,519 | 2,595 |
| Services [1]............................. | 6,133 | 8,137 | 9,969 | 10,123 | 10,296 | 10,583 | 10,783 | 10,958 | 11,203 |
| Structures............................ | 1,154 | 1,543 | 1,122 | 1,231 | 1,301 | 1,346 | 1,362 | 1,403 | 1,414 |
| Sector: | | | | | | | | | |
| Business [2]............................ | 6,584 | 9,729 | 11,607 | 12,487 | 12,877 | 13,332 | 13,568 | 13,950 | 14,425 |
| Nonfarm [3]......................... | 6,494 | 9,594 | 11,444 | 12,307 | 12,695 | 13,139 | 13,366 | 13,748 | 14,224 |
| Farm............................. | 92 | 138 | 165 | 180 | 182 | 194 | 206 | 202 | 196 |
| Households and institutions................. | 1,232 | 1,641 | 1,975 | 2,033 | 2,065 | 2,100 | 2,132 | 2,161 | 2,203 |
| General government [4]................. | 1,660 | 1,770 | 2,016 | 1,976 | 1,972 | 1,976 | 1,994 | 2,005 | 2,022 |
| Federal............................. | 613 | 532 | 658 | 652 | 647 | 642 | 645 | 645 | 648 |
| State and local....................... | 1,042 | 1,240 | 1,358 | 1,324 | 1,325 | 1,333 | 1,348 | 1,359 | 1,373 |

NA Not available. [1] Includes government consumption expenditures, which are for services (such as education and national defense) produced by government. In current dollars, these services are valued at their cost of production. [2] Equals gross domestic product excluding gross value added of households and institutions and of general government. [3] Equals gross domestic business value added excluding gross farm value added. [4] Equals compensation of general government employees plus general government consumption of fixed capital.

Source: U.S. Bureau of Economic Analysis, "National Income and Product Accounts Tables," <http://www.bea.gov/iTable/index_nipa.cfm>, accessed July 2019.

# Table 699. Gross Domestic Product in Current and Chained (2012) Dollars by Industry: 2000 to 2018

[In billions of dollars (10,252 represents $10,252,000,000,000). Based on 2012 North American Industry Classification System (NAICS); see text, Section 15. GDP by industry is the contribution of each private industry and of government to the nation's output, or GDP. An industry's GDP, or its "value added," is equal to its gross output (sales or receipts and other operating income, commodity taxes, and inventory change) minus its intermediate inputs (energy, raw materials, semifinished goods, and services that are purchased from domestic industries or from foreign sources). Detail may not add to total due to rounding]

| Industry | Current dollars | | | | Chained (2012) dollars [1] | | | |
|---|---|---|---|---|---|---|---|---|
| | 2000 | 2010 | 2017 | 2018 | 2000 | 2010 | 2017 | 2018 |
| **Gross domestic product**............... | **10,252** | **14,992** | **19,485** | **20,494** | **13,131** | **15,599** | **18,051** | **18,566** |
| Private industries................... | 8,929 | 12,884 | 17,032 | 17,989 | 11,384 | 13,467 | 15,718 | 16,189 |
| Agriculture, forestry, fishing, and hunting.......... | 98 | 146 | 169 | 164 | 162 | 194 | 223 | 214 |
| Farms.......................... | 76 | 118 | 133 | 127 | 138 | 165 | 190 | 182 |
| Forestry, fishing, and related activities............ | 22 | 29 | 36 | 37 | 25 | 29 | 32 | 32 |
| Mining.......................... | 111 | 306 | 269 | 321 | 236 | 309 | 429 | 436 |
| Oil and gas extraction............. | 68 | 189 | 175 | 219 | 138 | 182 | 363 | 358 |
| Mining, except oil and gas........ | 29 | 69 | 54 | 56 | 94 | 75 | 66 | 68 |
| Mining support activities.......... | 14 | 48 | 40 | 46 | 19 | 52 | 39 | 45 |
| Utilities........................ | 180 | 279 | 307 | 319 | 261 | 266 | 274 | 280 |
| Construction.................... | 461 | 525 | 781 | 840 | 783 | 547 | 624 | 642 |
| Manufacturing.................. | 1,550 | 1,797 | 2,180 | 2,335 | 1,679 | 1,933 | 2,042 | 2,134 |
| Durable goods................. | 925 | 964 | 1,227 | 1,301 | 753 | 968 | 1,140 | 1,201 |
| Wood products.............. | 28 | 23 | 38 | 40 | 25 | 23 | 29 | 28 |
| Nonmetallic mineral products........ | 43 | 38 | 60 | 62 | 49 | 39 | 46 | 46 |
| Primary metals.............. | 47 | 51 | 60 | 65 | 62 | 51 | 69 | 63 |
| Fabricated metal products........ | 121 | 120 | 152 | 162 | 156 | 126 | 138 | 146 |
| Machinery.................. | 113 | 127 | 150 | 162 | 130 | 132 | 129 | 139 |
| Computer and electronic products...... | 225 | 240 | 281 | 296 | 68 | 227 | 303 | 321 |
| Electrical equipment, appliances, and components........ | 46 | 51 | 59 | 62 | 54 | 53 | 57 | 58 |
| Motor vehicles, bodies & trailers, & parts....... | 138 | 89 | 159 | 169 | 100 | 87 | 129 | 145 |
| Other transportation equipment......... | 71 | 121 | 148 | 158 | 95 | 124 | 135 | 143 |
| Furniture and related products........ | 34 | 22 | 31 | 33 | 40 | 23 | 28 | 30 |
| Miscellaneous manufacturing........ | 59 | 83 | 89 | 92 | 61 | 84 | 83 | 87 |
| Nondurable goods........... | 625 | 833 | 953 | 1,034 | 967 | 972 | 901 | 931 |
| Food & beverage & tobacco....... | 163 | 223 | 270 | 279 | 225 | 233 | 233 | 243 |
| Textile mills and textile product mills....... | 28 | 16 | 18 | 19 | 31 | 17 | 17 | 18 |
| Apparel and leather and allied products......... | 22 | 10 | 9 | 9 | 20 | 11 | 8 | 8 |
| Paper products............. | 62 | 56 | 59 | 61 | 71 | 56 | 51 | 51 |
| Printing and related support activities........ | 44 | 39 | 39 | 40 | 38 | 38 | 36 | 37 |
| Petroleum and coal products........ | 53 | 123 | 121 | 165 | 185 | 213 | 178 | 190 |
| Chemical products........... | 188 | 303 | 354 | 374 | 289 | 347 | 297 | 303 |
| Plastics and rubber products....... | 66 | 62 | 83 | 86 | 77 | 68 | 77 | 79 |
| Wholesale trade................ | 623 | 889 | 1,174 | 1,234 | 809 | 948 | 1,115 | 1,151 |
| Retail trade.................... | 686 | 852 | 1,087 | 1,132 | 820 | 900 | 1,061 | 1,102 |
| Transportation and warehousing......... | 308 | 433 | 609 | 648 | 425 | 461 | 531 | 544 |
| Air transportation............. | 58 | 84 | 136 | 142 | 77 | 92 | 117 | 122 |
| Rail transportation............ | 23 | 34 | 40 | 43 | 42 | 38 | 37 | 38 |
| Water transportation.......... | 8 | 15 | 14 | 15 | 5 | 12 | 10 | 10 |
| Truck transportation.......... | 98 | 113 | 153 | 163 | 129 | 121 | 133 | 129 |
| Transit & ground passenger transport.......... | 18 | 31 | 44 | 47 | 31 | 33 | 39 | 41 |
| Pipeline transportation......... | 9 | 20 | 41 | 44 | 16 | 22 | 35 | 36 |
| Other transportation & support........ | 66 | 90 | 117 | 124 | 106 | 101 | 98 | 102 |
| Warehousing and storage........ | 27 | 45 | 64 | 70 | 27 | 41 | 64 | 67 |
| Information.................... | 471 | 753 | 1,051 | 1,126 | 422 | 750 | 1,114 | 1,209 |
| Publishing industries (except internet, includes software)... | 116 | 187 | 267 | 287 | 126 | 189 | 259 | 278 |
| Motion picture and sound recording........ | 54 | 91 | 91 | 96 | 45 | 92 | 93 | 97 |
| Broadcasting and telecommunications........ | 277 | 375 | 429 | 441 | 225 | 369 | 485 | 512 |
| Data processing, internet publishing, & related services.... | 24 | 101 | 264 | 302 | 24 | 100 | 277 | 321 |
| Finance and insurance............ | 743 | 1,004 | 1,466 | 1,514 | 905 | 1,078 | 1,164 | 1,128 |
| Real estate and rental and leasing........ | 1,232 | 1,939 | 2,591 | 2,725 | 1,546 | 1,987 | 2,285 | 2,342 |
| Professional, scientific, and technical services......... | 652 | 1,064 | 1,450 | 1,548 | 845 | 1,093 | 1,363 | 1,438 |
| Legal services............... | 129 | 204 | 258 | 271 | 237 | 222 | 211 | 213 |
| Computer systems design, related services....... | 114 | 203 | 323 | 344 | 86 | 199 | 346 | 372 |
| Miscellaneous services......... | 409 | 657 | 869 | 934 | 545 | 673 | 813 | 862 |
| Management of companies & enterprises........ | 171 | 265 | 369 | 387 | 277 | 270 | 369 | 387 |
| Administrative and waste management services........ | 282 | 438 | 607 | 641 | 338 | 445 | 541 | 561 |
| Educational services.............. | 95 | 199 | 246 | 254 | 153 | 212 | 213 | 216 |
| Health care and social assistance........... | 600 | 1,112 | 1,455 | 1,526 | 836 | 1,149 | 1,347 | 1,390 |
| Ambulatory health care services......... | 288 | 532 | 708 | 746 | 375 | 545 | 693 | 727 |
| Hospitals................... | 190 | 370 | 473 | 493 | 279 | 385 | 419 | 426 |
| Nursing and residential care facilities........ | 69 | 121 | 146 | 152 | 108 | 125 | 130 | 131 |
| Social assistance............ | 53 | 90 | 127 | 135 | 76 | 94 | 107 | 111 |
| Arts, entertainment, and recreation........ | 99 | 152 | 214 | 223 | 138 | 159 | 189 | 193 |
| Performing arts, spectator sports, museums, & related..... | 49 | 88 | 126 | 132 | 72 | 90 | 109 | 113 |
| Amusements, gambling, & recreation........ | 50 | 65 | 88 | 92 | 66 | 69 | 80 | 80 |
| Accommodation and food services.......... | 288 | 404 | 591 | 616 | 425 | 427 | 497 | 500 |
| Accommodation............. | 93 | 112 | 163 | 168 | 127 | 119 | 140 | 138 |
| Food services and drinking places........ | 194 | 291 | 427 | 448 | 298 | 308 | 357 | 362 |
| Other services, except government.......... | 280 | 328 | 416 | 435 | 431 | 346 | 357 | 362 |
| Government.................... | 1,323 | 2,108 | 2,454 | 2,505 | 1,978 | 2,182 | 2,177 | 2,177 |
| Federal..................... | 424 | 697 | 760 | 764 | 624 | 716 | 701 | 699 |
| State and local.............. | 899 | 1,411 | 1,694 | 1,741 | 1,355 | 1,466 | 1,475 | 1,478 |

[1] Chained (2012) dollar series are calculated as the product of the chain-type quantity index and the 2012 current-dollar value of the corresponding series, divided by 100. Because the formula for the chain-type quantity indexes uses weights of more than one period, the corresponding chained-dollar estimates are usually not additive.

Source: U.S. Bureau of Economic Analysis, Industry Economic Accounts, "GDP by Industry Data," <http://www.bea.gov/industry/index.htm>, accessed April 2019.

## Table 700. Relation of GDP, GNP, Net National Product, National Income, Personal Income, Disposable Personal Income, and Personal Saving: 2000 to 2018

[In billions of dollars (10,252 represents $10,252,000,000,000). For definitions, see text, this section. Minus sign (-) indicates deficit or net disbursement]

| Item | 2000 | 2010 | 2013 | 2014 | 2015 | 2016 | 2017 | 2018 |
|---|---|---|---|---|---|---|---|---|
| **Gross domestic product (GDP)**................. | **10,252** | **14,992** | **16,785** | **17,527** | **18,225** | **18,715** | **19,519** | **20,580** |
| Plus: Income receipts from the rest of the world.. | 381 | 715 | 823 | 854 | 838 | 862 | 958 | 1,106 |
| Less: Income payments to the rest of the world.. | 346 | 519 | 593 | 612 | 613 | 644 | 715 | 838 |
| **Equals: Gross national product (GNP)**......... | **10,287** | **15,188** | **17,016** | **17,768** | **18,449** | **18,933** | **19,763** | **20,848** |
| Less: Consumption of fixed capital................ | 1,511 | 2,391 | 2,681 | 2,815 | 2,916 | 2,992 | 3,121 | 3,291 |
| **Equals: Net national product**.................... | **8,776** | **12,797** | **14,334** | **14,953** | **15,533** | **15,942** | **16,641** | **17,557** |
| Less: Statistical discrepancy...................... | -96 | 61 | -160 | -289 | -255 | -112 | -68 | 11 |
| **Equals: National income**........................... | **8,873** | **12,736** | **14,495** | **15,242** | **15,788** | **16,054** | **16,709** | **17,546** |
| Less: Corporate profits [1]............................ | 787 | 1,729 | 2,011 | 2,120 | 2,062 | 2,011 | 2,006 | 2,075 |
| Taxes on production and imports less subsidies............................................. | 663 | 1,007 | 1,129 | 1,183 | 1,220 | 1,251 | 1,303 | 1,377 |
| Contributions for government social insurance.. | 706 | 984 | 1,104 | 1,154 | 1,205 | 1,240 | 1,300 | 1,356 |
| Net interest and miscellaneous payments on assets................................................. | 541 | 465 | 466 | 516 | 587 | 560 | 608 | 673 |
| Business current transfer payments (net )....... | 85 | 127 | 110 | 133 | 157 | 168 | 145 | 154 |
| Current surplus of government enterprises...... | 11 | -20 | -16 | -11 | -6 | -3 | -2 | -6 |
| Plus: Personal income receipts on assets......... | 1,486 | 1,782 | 2,066 | 2,302 | 2,471 | 2,521 | 2,682 | 2,930 |
| Personal current transfer receipts............... | 1,087 | 2,325 | 2,424 | 2,542 | 2,683 | 2,774 | 2,848 | 2,971 |
| **Equals: Personal income**.......................... | **8,653** | **12,552** | **14,181** | **14,992** | **15,718** | **16,121** | **16,879** | **17,819** |
| Less: Personal current taxes...................... | 1,236 | 1,237 | 1,676 | 1,784 | 1,938 | 1,956 | 2,046 | 2,078 |
| **Equals: Disposable personal income**........... | **7,416** | **11,314** | **12,505** | **13,208** | **13,780** | **14,165** | **14,833** | **15,742** |
| Less: Personal outlays.............................. | 7,058 | 10,573 | 11,704 | 12,237 | 12,731 | 13,206 | 13,802 | 14,531 |
| **Equals: Personal saving**.......................... | **358** | **741** | **801** | **971** | **1,049** | **959** | **1,031** | **1,210** |

[1] Corporate profits with inventory valuation and capital consumption adjustments.

Source: U.S. Bureau of Economic Analysis, National Income and Product Accounts Tables, "Table 1.7.5. Relation of Gross Domestic Product, Gross National Product, Net National Product, National Income, and Personal Income," and "Table 2.1. Personal Income and Its Disposition," <http://www.bea.gov/iTable/index_nipa.cfm>, accessed July 2019.

## Table 701. Gross Saving and Investment: 2000 to 2018

[In billions of dollars (2,127 represents $2,127,000,000,000), except as noted. Minus (-) sign indicates deficit]

| Item | 2000 | 2010 | 2013 | 2014 | 2015 | 2016 | 2017 | 2018 |
|---|---|---|---|---|---|---|---|---|
| **Gross saving**........................................ | **2,127** | **2,312** | **3,218** | **3,560** | **3,675** | **3,485** | **3,626** | **3,795** |
| Net saving............................................ | 616 | -79 | 537 | 745 | 758 | 493 | 505 | 504 |
| Net private saving................................. | 501 | 1,554 | 1,440 | 1,588 | 1,549 | 1,417 | 1,478 | 1,753 |
| Domestic business................................. | 143 | 813 | 639 | 617 | 500 | 458 | 447 | 542 |
| Undistributed corporate profits................. | 103 | 918 | 780 | 761 | 575 | 564 | 574 | 531 |
| Inventory valuation adjustment, corporate....... | -17 | -48 | 14 | 2 | 53 | -1 | -49 | -52 |
| Capital consumption adjustment, corporate..... | 57 | -58 | -155 | -146 | -129 | -105 | -78 | 63 |
| Households and institutions........................ | 358 | 741 | 801 | 971 | 1,049 | 959 | 1,031 | 1,210 |
| Personal saving.................................. | 358 | 741 | 801 | 971 | 1,049 | 959 | 1,031 | 1,210 |
| Net government saving............................. | 115 | -1,633 | -903 | -842 | -790 | -924 | -973 | -1,249 |
| Federal............................................ | 155 | -1,325 | -638 | -604 | -570 | -677 | -725 | -1,010 |
| State and local................................... | -41 | -307 | -265 | -238 | -220 | -247 | -248 | -239 |
| Consumption of fixed capital....................... | 1,511 | 2,391 | 2,681 | 2,815 | 2,916 | 2,992 | 3,121 | 3,291 |
| Private............................................... | 1,232 | 1,934 | 2,177 | 2,298 | 2,394 | 2,463 | 2,578 | 2,726 |
| Domestic business................................. | 1,005 | 1,537 | 1,739 | 1,831 | 1,908 | 1,954 | 2,041 | 2,151 |
| Households and institutions...................... | 227 | 397 | 438 | 467 | 486 | 509 | 537 | 574 |
| Government......................................... | 280 | 457 | 505 | 517 | 523 | 528 | 543 | 566 |
| Federal............................................ | 163 | 244 | 266 | 270 | 271 | 272 | 277 | 286 |
| State and local................................... | 117 | 213 | 239 | 246 | 251 | 257 | 266 | 280 |
| **Gross domestic investment, capital account transactions, and net lending**....... | **2,031** | **2,373** | **3,058** | **3,271** | **3,420** | **3,373** | **3,559** | **3,806** |
| Gross domestic investment......................... | 2,427 | 2,810 | 3,426 | 3,647 | 3,844 | 3,814 | 4,025 | 4,315 |
| Gross private domestic investment............... | 2,038 | 2,165 | 2,826 | 3,044 | 3,223 | 3,179 | 3,371 | 3,628 |
| Gross government investment..................... | 389 | 645 | 600 | 603 | 621 | 635 | 655 | 687 |
| Capital account transactions (net) [1]............... | (Z) | 1 | 1 | (Z) | (Z) | 1 | 9 | -3 |
| Net lending or net borrowing........................ | -397 | -437 | -369 | -376 | -425 | -442 | -476 | -507 |
| Statistical discrepancy.............................. | -96 | 61 | -160 | -289 | -255 | -112 | -68 | 11 |
| Addenda: | | | | | | | | |
| Gross private saving................................ | 1,733 | 3,488 | 3,617 | 3,886 | 3,942 | 3,880 | 4,056 | 4,478 |
| Gross government saving........................... | 395 | -1,175 | -399 | -326 | -268 | -395 | -430 | -683 |
| Federal............................................... | 319 | -1,081 | -372 | -334 | -299 | -405 | -448 | -724 |
| State and local...................................... | 76 | -94 | -27 | 8 | 31 | 10 | 18 | 40 |
| Net domestic investment........................... | 916 | 419 | 745 | 832 | 928 | 822 | 904 | 1,024 |
| Gross saving as a percent of gross national income................................... | 20.5 | 15.3 | 18.7 | 19.7 | 19.6 | 18.3 | 18.3 | 18.2 |
| Net saving as a percent of gross national income................................... | 5.9 | -0.5 | 3.1 | 4.1 | 4.1 | 2.6 | 2.5 | 2.4 |
| Disaster losses [2]................................... | – | – | – | – | – | – | 104 | 51 |

– Represents zero. Z Less than $500 million. [1] Consists of capital transfers and the acquisition and disposal of nonproduced nonfinancial assets. [2] Consists of damages to fixed assets.

Source: U.S. Bureau of Economic Analysis, National Income and Product Accounts Tables, "Table 5.1 Saving and Investment by Sector," <http://www.bea.gov/iTable/index_nipa.cfm>, accessed July 2019.

# Table 702. Gross Domestic Product by State in Current and Chained (2012) Dollars: 2000 to 2018

[In billions of dollars (10,252.3 represents $10,252,300,000,000). For definition of gross domestic product by state or chained dollars, see text, this section]

| State | Current dollars | | | | | Chained (2012) dollars [2] | | | | |
|---|---|---|---|---|---|---|---|---|---|---|
| | 2000 | 2010 | 2016 | 2017 | 2018 | 2000 | 2010 | 2016 | 2017 | 2018 |
| United States [1] | 10,252.3 | 14,992.1 | 18,707.2 | 19,485.4 | 20,494.1 | 13,131.0 | 15,598.8 | 17,659.2 | 18,050.7 | 18,566.4 |
| Alabama | 119.2 | 174.8 | 203.4 | 211.7 | 221.1 | 156.6 | 182.3 | 189.6 | 193.1 | 196.9 |
| Alaska | 26.8 | 52.9 | 49.4 | 51.7 | 54.0 | 39.5 | 54.2 | 52.6 | 52.5 | 52.3 |
| Arizona | 164.6 | 248.2 | 311.4 | 326.5 | 346.8 | 207.8 | 257.5 | 288.7 | 297.2 | 309.1 |
| Arkansas | 68.8 | 101.7 | 120.1 | 123.7 | 128.1 | 90.2 | 105.9 | 113.8 | 114.9 | 115.9 |
| California | 1,366.6 | 1,974.6 | 2,663.4 | 2,809.9 | 2,968.1 | 1,709.9 | 2,058.1 | 2,498.8 | 2,587.6 | 2,677.9 |
| Colorado | 180.6 | 255.1 | 329.1 | 347.2 | 368.8 | 232.8 | 264.8 | 315.4 | 325.1 | 336.4 |
| Connecticut | 165.9 | 237.7 | 263.0 | 265.5 | 274.2 | 216.4 | 247.5 | 241.4 | 239.9 | 242.2 |
| Delaware | 43.4 | 57.4 | 70.4 | 72.2 | 75.0 | 56.1 | 60.0 | 63.7 | 63.7 | 63.9 |
| District of Columbia | 61.1 | 106.1 | 129.8 | 134.9 | 140.3 | 85.3 | 110.0 | 119.4 | 121.4 | 124.0 |
| Florida | 489.5 | 737.8 | 938.4 | 979.5 | 1,036.3 | 642.7 | 766.2 | 864.0 | 885.9 | 917.0 |
| Georgia | 307.6 | 416.9 | 538.2 | 562.1 | 588.2 | 393.2 | 433.0 | 495.2 | 509.4 | 522.4 |
| Hawaii | 41.5 | 68.2 | 85.9 | 89.0 | 92.0 | 56.4 | 71.0 | 78.8 | 80.0 | 80.8 |
| Idaho | 38.0 | 55.2 | 69.3 | 72.4 | 77.0 | 47.3 | 57.9 | 65.6 | 67.2 | 69.9 |
| Illinois | 487.2 | 662.6 | 805.4 | 825.8 | 864.6 | 641.7 | 695.0 | 743.8 | 748.2 | 764.2 |
| Indiana | 203.1 | 280.1 | 338.2 | 351.1 | 366.7 | 263.7 | 295.1 | 315.1 | 320.1 | 326.1 |
| Iowa | 93.0 | 141.5 | 180.4 | 183.0 | 190.2 | 122.2 | 149.5 | 168.9 | 168.3 | 170.7 |
| Kansas | 85.9 | 127.7 | 155.7 | 160.1 | 167.0 | 114.0 | 134.9 | 148.2 | 149.4 | 152.3 |
| Kentucky | 114.3 | 164.6 | 195.1 | 201.0 | 208.3 | 152.1 | 172.0 | 181.6 | 183.6 | 186.1 |
| Louisiana | 132.8 | 225.7 | 228.1 | 238.1 | 252.1 | 206.7 | 247.4 | 228.5 | 228.7 | 231.2 |
| Maine | 36.8 | 51.7 | 59.6 | 61.7 | 64.4 | 48.5 | 53.8 | 54.7 | 55.6 | 56.7 |
| Maryland | 192.1 | 316.5 | 384.2 | 398.4 | 412.9 | 251.0 | 327.2 | 355.1 | 362.0 | 367.9 |
| Massachusetts | 289.9 | 409.8 | 519.7 | 540.9 | 567.3 | 359.5 | 424.6 | 477.9 | 488.3 | 501.3 |
| Michigan | 351.6 | 386.6 | 490.2 | 505.8 | 528.0 | 438.3 | 400.9 | 448.7 | 456.0 | 468.4 |
| Minnesota | 190.0 | 271.8 | 338.6 | 352.3 | 368.3 | 246.0 | 284.9 | 317.6 | 324.3 | 331.4 |
| Mississippi | 65.6 | 95.2 | 106.9 | 109.9 | 114.1 | 88.1 | 100.0 | 100.1 | 100.6 | 101.6 |
| Missouri | 187.3 | 258.5 | 296.1 | 304.1 | 317.7 | 246.0 | 269.7 | 273.2 | 275.8 | 282.2 |
| Montana | 21.9 | 38.1 | 45.6 | 47.1 | 49.0 | 31.4 | 40.5 | 44.2 | 44.4 | 44.8 |
| Nebraska | 56.5 | 91.8 | 116.1 | 118.5 | 123.0 | 76.6 | 97.9 | 110.2 | 110.5 | 112.2 |
| Nevada | 76.6 | 123.6 | 150.4 | 157.0 | 165.8 | 105.3 | 128.8 | 138.3 | 141.7 | 146.2 |
| New Hampshire | 45.2 | 64.2 | 78.4 | 81.2 | 84.7 | 56.7 | 66.4 | 72.5 | 74.0 | 75.6 |
| New Jersey | 362.0 | 495.1 | 581.3 | 599.3 | 624.9 | 473.0 | 516.6 | 537.1 | 544.0 | 554.7 |
| New Mexico | 55.2 | 84.0 | 91.0 | 94.2 | 99.4 | 72.0 | 87.0 | 91.0 | 91.0 | 92.6 |
| New York | 838.7 | 1,213.9 | 1,541.5 | 1,598.5 | 1,676.4 | 1,088.0 | 1,269.5 | 1,388.3 | 1,407.2 | 1,437.0 |
| North Carolina | 275.7 | 415.2 | 518.2 | 537.9 | 565.8 | 354.8 | 433.4 | 472.9 | 482.0 | 496.1 |
| North Dakota | 18.0 | 35.4 | 50.8 | 51.6 | 54.7 | 24.6 | 37.7 | 50.8 | 49.9 | 51.2 |
| Ohio | 391.1 | 497.2 | 621.4 | 645.8 | 676.2 | 509.0 | 521.1 | 581.6 | 590.9 | 601.5 |
| Oklahoma | 90.8 | 152.9 | 178.5 | 187.3 | 200.0 | 124.1 | 159.2 | 189.1 | 189.6 | 193.0 |
| Oregon | 117.3 | 163.8 | 215.2 | 226.1 | 238.7 | 137.8 | 169.0 | 200.3 | 206.7 | 213.7 |
| Pennsylvania | 407.7 | 599.3 | 724.3 | 752.3 | 788.5 | 537.2 | 622.5 | 685.5 | 697.2 | 712.1 |
| Rhode Island | 34.5 | 49.6 | 57.7 | 59.3 | 61.0 | 45.2 | 51.5 | 53.0 | 53.4 | 53.7 |
| South Carolina | 115.2 | 163.9 | 212.7 | 221.9 | 230.4 | 150.5 | 170.2 | 194.5 | 199.5 | 202.8 |
| South Dakota | 22.7 | 37.5 | 48.5 | 49.6 | 51.6 | 29.4 | 40.1 | 45.4 | 45.3 | 45.9 |
| Tennessee | 181.6 | 255.9 | 334.4 | 347.8 | 365.6 | 233.2 | 266.7 | 306.3 | 313.6 | 322.9 |
| Texas | 738.9 | 1,237.2 | 1,564.4 | 1,654.5 | 1,775.8 | 998.3 | 1,301.7 | 1,593.1 | 1,624.9 | 1,676.7 |
| Utah | 70.3 | 118.0 | 157.9 | 165.7 | 177.3 | 92.5 | 123.3 | 146.9 | 150.8 | 157.2 |
| Vermont | 18.3 | 27.1 | 31.6 | 32.6 | 33.7 | 23.0 | 28.1 | 29.3 | 29.6 | 30.0 |
| Virginia | 266.9 | 422.9 | 493.9 | 510.4 | 534.4 | 346.2 | 437.3 | 455.4 | 463.4 | 476.4 |
| Washington | 237.8 | 365.6 | 492.9 | 522.4 | 563.2 | 312.2 | 381.3 | 460.1 | 479.2 | 506.7 |
| West Virginia | 42.6 | 65.3 | 69.8 | 73.1 | 77.5 | 62.1 | 68.4 | 68.7 | 69.6 | 71.3 |
| Wisconsin | 180.5 | 254.4 | 312.1 | 321.6 | 337.0 | 233.1 | 264.8 | 288.4 | 292.5 | 299.8 |
| Wyoming | 17.2 | 37.4 | 35.9 | 37.6 | 39.4 | 27.7 | 39.8 | 38.1 | 38.3 | 38.4 |

[1] The difference between the United States and sum-of-states reflects overseas activity, economic activity taking place outside the borders of the United States by the military and associated federal civilian support staff. [2] Chained (2012) dollar series are calculated as the product of the chain-type quantity index and the 2012 current-dollar value of the corresponding series, divided by 100. Because the formula for the chain-type quantity indexes uses weights of more than one period, the corresponding chained-dollar estimates are usually not additive.

Source: U.S. Bureau of Economic Analysis, Regional Economic Accounts, "Gross Domestic Product by State," <https://www.bea.gov/data/economic-accounts/regional>, accessed May 2019.

# Table 703. Gross Domestic Product by Selected Industry and State: 2018

[In billions of dollars (20,494.1 represents $20,494,100,000,000). Data are subject to revision. For definition of gross domestic product by state, see text, this section. Industries based on 2012 North American Industry Classification System; see text, Section 15]

| State | Total [1] | Manu-facturing | Whole-sale trade | Retail trade | Infor-mation | Finance and insur-ance | Real estate, rental, and leasing | Profes-sional and technical services | Health care and social assist-ance | Govern-ment [2] |
|---|---|---|---|---|---|---|---|---|---|---|
| **United States [3]** | **20,494.1** | **2,334.6** | **1,234.0** | **1,132.5** | **1,125.9** | **1,514.2** | **2,725.1** | **1,548.3** | **1,526.1** | **2,504.7** |
| Alabama | 221.1 | 38.0 | 13.0 | 14.8 | 5.0 | 12.3 | 24.2 | 13.9 | 16.4 | 36.0 |
| Alaska | 54.0 | 1.7 | 1.4 | 2.3 | 1.3 | 1.2 | 5.6 | 1.9 | 4.3 | 10.9 |
| Arizona | 346.8 | 29.9 | 20.2 | 24.7 | 12.2 | 23.8 | 53.6 | 19.7 | 30.0 | 42.4 |
| Arkansas | 128.1 | 19.8 | 10.0 | 9.1 | 3.2 | 5.7 | 13.7 | 4.8 | 11.3 | 16.2 |
| California | 2,968.1 | 316.8 | 149.6 | 152.0 | 306.7 | 145.3 | 497.2 | 262.2 | 186.7 | 332.6 |
| Colorado | 368.8 | 25.1 | 21.4 | 19.4 | 21.7 | 20.4 | 54.1 | 35.4 | 23.3 | 43.6 |
| Connecticut | 274.2 | 30.8 | 18.1 | 13.7 | 13.8 | 35.1 | 40.6 | 19.1 | 21.9 | 27.8 |
| Delaware | 75.0 | 4.7 | 2.1 | 2.8 | 1.2 | 23.4 | 10.6 | 4.9 | 5.6 | 7.1 |
| District of Columbia | 140.3 | (D) | 1.2 | 1.7 | 7.9 | 5.6 | 12.8 | 30.4 | 6.5 | 44.6 |
| Florida | 1,036.3 | 55.9 | 73.2 | 74.6 | 44.9 | 61.9 | 171.6 | 76.5 | 88.3 | 112.5 |
| Georgia | 588.2 | 64.6 | 43.8 | 32.3 | 48.5 | 46.6 | 69.9 | 39.6 | 38.4 | 67.9 |
| Hawaii | 92.0 | 1.9 | 2.8 | 6.1 | 2.0 | 2.9 | 19.2 | 3.7 | 6.2 | 18.0 |
| Idaho | 77.0 | 9.2 | 4.9 | 6.0 | 1.6 | 3.2 | 10.2 | 4.2 | 6.3 | 10.0 |
| Illinois | 864.6 | 108.4 | 68.6 | 41.5 | 32.7 | 87.5 | 110.0 | 72.6 | 61.6 | 82.6 |
| Indiana | 366.7 | 102.1 | 22.0 | 20.7 | 6.2 | 20.3 | 35.5 | 16.1 | 31.0 | 33.1 |
| Iowa | 190.2 | 35.7 | 11.8 | 9.9 | 4.8 | 25.8 | 19.4 | 6.5 | 12.6 | 21.5 |
| Kansas | 167.0 | 27.2 | 11.5 | 10.2 | 5.8 | 9.6 | 19.8 | 9.3 | 12.6 | 21.5 |
| Kentucky | 208.3 | 38.7 | 14.4 | 12.2 | 4.7 | 11.3 | 22.0 | 8.6 | 18.1 | 28.2 |
| Louisiana | 252.1 | 49.2 | 14.0 | 16.0 | 5.0 | 10.6 | 26.4 | 12.6 | 19.3 | 28.1 |
| Maine | 64.4 | 6.3 | 3.6 | 5.2 | 1.2 | 3.7 | 9.5 | 3.7 | 7.6 | 8.8 |
| Maryland | 412.9 | 24.3 | 17.9 | 20.1 | 17.6 | 21.4 | 72.1 | 41.3 | 31.0 | 81.8 |
| Massachusetts | 567.3 | 53.3 | 28.5 | 22.5 | 34.4 | 49.0 | 80.8 | 73.8 | 51.4 | 54.7 |
| Michigan | 528.0 | 102.3 | 35.6 | 31.4 | 13.8 | 27.4 | 63.2 | 41.4 | 44.7 | 54.8 |
| Minnesota | 368.3 | 52.7 | 26.0 | 19.8 | 13.8 | 31.3 | 40.7 | 25.8 | 35.4 | 36.2 |
| Mississippi | 114.1 | 18.5 | 6.3 | 9.1 | 2.3 | 5.4 | 12.2 | 3.8 | 9.0 | 19.6 |
| Missouri | 317.7 | 40.7 | 22.4 | 18.6 | 13.3 | 23.8 | 35.7 | 22.8 | 28.5 | 36.9 |
| Montana | 49.0 | 3.1 | 2.8 | 3.2 | 1.2 | 2.5 | 6.8 | 2.5 | 5.1 | 7.3 |
| Nebraska | 123.0 | 14.1 | 7.7 | 6.6 | 3.9 | 12.3 | 12.3 | 5.4 | 9.4 | 15.3 |
| Nevada | 165.8 | 8.1 | 7.2 | 11.3 | 6.0 | 8.9 | 24.7 | 8.2 | 10.3 | 18.0 |
| New Hampshire | 84.7 | 9.9 | 5.7 | 5.5 | 3.8 | 6.5 | 12.5 | 6.6 | 7.8 | 8.7 |
| New Jersey | 624.9 | 52.7 | 51.0 | 35.0 | 28.9 | 39.6 | 106.2 | 57.6 | 49.6 | 63.2 |
| New Mexico | 99.4 | 4.0 | 3.3 | 5.7 | 2.7 | 3.4 | 13.2 | 7.5 | 7.6 | 22.9 |
| New York | 1,676.4 | 74.6 | 76.8 | 75.0 | 140.7 | 304.5 | 235.2 | 146.3 | 121.9 | 177.2 |
| North Carolina | 565.8 | 103.6 | 33.4 | 28.9 | 21.0 | 49.6 | 63.2 | 36.7 | 37.7 | 72.1 |
| North Dakota | 54.7 | 4.0 | 4.9 | 3.0 | 1.4 | 2.5 | 6.4 | 1.8 | 4.3 | 6.1 |
| Ohio | 676.2 | 112.2 | 43.1 | 39.7 | 18.5 | 61.3 | 74.7 | 35.0 | 58.6 | 72.1 |
| Oklahoma | 200.0 | 19.1 | 11.4 | 11.1 | 4.7 | 7.5 | 19.2 | 8.2 | 14.2 | 30.2 |
| Oregon | 238.7 | 34.8 | 13.1 | 12.0 | 9.2 | 10.6 | 37.3 | 13.8 | 20.5 | 30.0 |
| Pennsylvania | 788.5 | 93.8 | 45.1 | 37.6 | 54.9 | 50.5 | 96.3 | 58.0 | 76.4 | 74.9 |
| Rhode Island | 61.0 | 5.3 | 3.7 | 3.3 | 1.6 | 5.7 | 9.1 | 3.7 | 6.0 | 7.9 |
| South Carolina | 230.4 | 38.7 | 13.2 | 15.0 | 6.6 | 10.3 | 29.3 | 13.2 | 15.1 | 35.1 |
| South Dakota | 51.6 | 5.3 | 3.9 | 3.6 | 1.2 | 8.2 | 5.1 | 1.6 | 5.0 | 5.8 |
| Tennessee | 365.6 | 56.0 | 25.6 | 24.7 | 11.6 | 20.7 | 39.4 | 20.1 | 37.7 | 40.4 |
| Texas | 1,775.8 | 230.4 | 146.7 | 98.1 | 64.8 | 99.1 | 174.6 | 125.9 | 108.7 | 184.7 |
| Utah | 177.3 | 19.2 | 9.4 | 12.7 | 9.0 | 15.4 | 23.1 | 12.4 | 10.2 | 21.6 |
| Vermont | 33.7 | 3.2 | 1.7 | 2.5 | 0.9 | 1.7 | 5.0 | 2.2 | 3.6 | 4.8 |
| Virginia | 534.4 | 47.8 | 23.0 | 26.5 | 18.9 | 27.2 | 76.3 | 69.8 | 34.0 | 96.3 |
| Washington | 563.2 | 63.1 | 29.9 | 49.2 | 74.7 | 20.4 | 72.1 | 37.4 | 35.4 | 71.0 |
| West Virginia | 77.5 | 7.9 | 3.6 | 5.1 | 1.5 | 2.7 | 8.1 | 3.5 | 8.1 | 11.9 |
| Wisconsin | 337.0 | 63.3 | 21.7 | 18.6 | 12.3 | 27.2 | 39.8 | 15.0 | 29.2 | 35.0 |
| Wyoming | 39.4 | (D) | 1.6 | 2.1 | 0.6 | 1.0 | 4.5 | 1.2 | 1.7 | 6.2 |

D Figure withheld to avoid disclosure of confidential information. [1] Includes industries not shown separately. [2] Includes federal civilian and military, and state and local government. [3] The difference between the United States and sum-of-states reflects overseas activity, economic activity taking place outside the borders of the United States by the military and associated federal civilian support staff.

Source: U.S. Bureau of Economic Analysis, Regional Economic Accounts, "Gross Domestic Product by State," <http://www.bea.gov/regional/index.htm>, accessed May 2019.

# Table 704. Household Production Value: 1965 to 2017

[In billions of dollars (277.4 represents $277,400,000,000). Measures the value of time spent on the unpaid work of household production tasks. Household production hours are aggregated across seven categories: housework, cooking, odd jobs, gardening, shopping, child care, and domestic travel related to these tasks. The value of these nonmarket services is the product of the wage rate of general purpose domestic workers and the number of hours worked]

| Year | Household production value (bil. dol.) | Year | Household production value (bil. dol.) | Year | Household production value (bil. dol.) |
|---|---|---|---|---|---|
| 1965 | 277.4 | 1996 | 2,465.1 | 2007 | 3,630.4 |
| 1970 | 428.0 | 1997 | 2,488.7 | 2008 | 3,828.1 |
| 1975 | 707.4 | 1998 | 2,701.4 | 2009 | 3,691.7 |
| 1980 | 1,106.9 | 1999 | 2,601.5 | 2010 | 3,643.1 |
| 1985 | 1,467.0 | 2000 | 2,921.2 | 2011 | 3,706.0 |
| 1990 | 1,902.6 | 2001 | 2,799.3 | 2012 | 3,781.5 |
| 1991 | 1,908.1 | 2002 | 2,780.1 | 2013 | 4,097.2 |
| 1992 | 1,984.7 | 2003 | 3,043.3 | 2014 | 4,228.4 |
| 1993 | 2,119.3 | 2004 | 3,183.3 | 2015 | 4,405.0 |
| 1994 | 2,272.5 | 2005 | 3,208.3 | 2016 | 4,594.6 |
| 1995 | 2,395.9 | 2006 | 3,405.5 | 2017 | 4,516.1 |

Source: U.S. Bureau of Economic Analysis, Special Topics, "Household Production Satellite Account," <https://www.bea.gov/data/special-topics/household-production>, accessed August 2019.

Income, Expenditures, Poverty, and Wealth    455

## Table 705. Financial Accounts of the United States—Composition of Individuals' Savings: 1990 to 2018

[In billions of dollars (667.9 represents $667,900,000,000). Combined statement for households, nonprofit organizations, and nonfinancial noncorporate business. Minus sign (-) indicates decrease]

| Composition of savings | 1990 | 2000 | 2010 | 2014 | 2015 | 2016 | 2017 | 2018 |
|---|---|---|---|---|---|---|---|---|
| **Net acquisition of financial assets** | **667.9** | **873.1** | **925.3** | **1,561.5** | **1,650.0** | **1,568.7** | **1,735.7** | **2,369.1** |
| Foreign deposits | 1.4 | 7.6 | 4.5 | -6.4 | -13.8 | -5.6 | 12.8 | 2.2 |
| Checkable deposits and currency | 3.5 | -95.4 | -88.9 | 143.7 | 67.3 | -34.9 | 81.1 | 186.2 |
| Time and savings deposits | 42.4 | 355.0 | 279.2 | 442.2 | 552.5 | 705.6 | 292.5 | 489.5 |
| Money market fund shares | 43.1 | 184.1 | -301.6 | -20.6 | -14.3 | 8.7 | 64.3 | 132.5 |
| Debt securities | 211.6 | -51.1 | 170.8 | -167.5 | 281.3 | -3.5 | 20.0 | 691.8 |
| Treasury securities | 97.0 | -204.7 | 297.5 | -250.1 | 311.0 | 131.7 | 24.8 | 586.5 |
| Agency and GSE-backed securities [1] | 36.4 | 28.2 | -8.7 | 97.1 | 215.7 | -63.3 | 100.1 | 113.1 |
| Municipal securities | 35.9 | 16.6 | 74.4 | -59.4 | -40.7 | 10.7 | -50.5 | -72.0 |
| Corporate and foreign bonds | 42.2 | 108.8 | -192.5 | 44.8 | -204.8 | -82.6 | -54.4 | 64.3 |
| Loans | 16.4 | 111.4 | 21.3 | 39.0 | -55.7 | -0.5 | -60.8 | -13.9 |
| Corporate equities [2] | -61.9 | -396.0 | -196.0 | 95.1 | -137.9 | -150.6 | 225.9 | 190.5 |
| Mutual fund shares | 28.9 | 76.8 | 222.9 | 250.1 | 100.3 | 189.7 | 292.9 | -63.5 |
| Trade receivables | 5.9 | 10.1 | 6.3 | 27.5 | 0.2 | 10.2 | 9.8 | 8.3 |
| Life insurance reserves | 27.0 | 43.7 | 14.9 | 49.6 | 47.3 | 41.8 | 19.0 | 29.1 |
| Pension entitlements | 331.6 | 444.5 | 654.9 | 334.7 | 412.0 | 341.0 | 375.9 | 312.6 |
| Miscellaneous and other assets | 18.1 | 182.4 | 137.0 | 374.2 | 410.8 | 466.8 | 402.4 | 403.9 |
| **Gross investment in nonfinancial assets** | **829.7** | **1,592.6** | **1,675.2** | **2,146.7** | **2,287.1** | **2,381.5** | **2,512.0** | **2,639.9** |
| Minus: Consumption of fixed capital | 617.7 | 1,010.5 | 1,568.4 | 1,741.0 | 1,793.5 | 1,854.8 | 1,928.2 | 1,978.4 |
| **Equals: Net investment in nonfinancial assets** | **212.0** | **582.1** | **106.8** | **405.7** | **493.6** | **526.7** | **583.8** | **661.5** |
| **Net increase in liabilities** | **238.7** | **923.5** | **-153.5** | **709.0** | **608.4** | **911.4** | **970.8** | **904.5** |
| Home mortgages | 206.9 | 423.0 | -129.4 | 32.7 | 146.9 | 248.3 | 328.7 | 300.4 |
| Other mortgages | -4.4 | 106.3 | -33.2 | 188.8 | 177.2 | 212.4 | 196.4 | 204.3 |
| Consumer credit | 15.1 | 176.5 | -28.2 | 221.2 | 234.4 | 233.6 | 183.9 | 187.0 |
| Other loans and advances | 3.6 | 8.6 | 77.6 | 33.2 | -76.5 | -10.2 | 60.9 | -26.9 |
| Other liabilities | 17.4 | 209.1 | -40.4 | 233.1 | 126.3 | 227.2 | 200.9 | 239.7 |
| Personal saving, FOF concept (FOF) [3] | 656.9 | 567.4 | 1,157.5 | 1,267.5 | 1,556.6 | 1,198.6 | 1,313.4 | 2,129.3 |
| Personal saving, NIPA concept (FOF) [3] | 580.1 | 324.1 | 1,101.4 | 1,094.0 | 1,355.3 | 988.7 | 1,079.2 | 1,843.5 |
| Personal saving, NIPA concept (NIPA) [4] | 361.1 | 358.3 | 740.9 | 970.3 | 1,044.2 | 948.2 | 986.8 | 1,043.4 |

[1] GSE = government-sponsored enterprises. [2] Only directly held and those in closed-end and exchange-traded funds. Other equities are included in mutual funds, life insurance reserves, and pension entitlements. [3] Flow of Funds measure. [4] National Income and Product Accounts measure.

Source: Board of Governors of the Federal Reserve System, "Z.1 Financial Accounts of the United States: Summary Table F.6 Derivation of Measures of Personal Saving," March 2019, <https://www.federalreserve.gov/releases/Z1/current/default.htm>, accessed March 2019.

## Table 706. Government Consumption Expenditures and Gross Investment by Level of Government and Type: 2002 to 2018

[In billions of dollars (2,089 represents $2,089,000,000,000). Government consumption expenditures are services (such as education and national defense) produced by government that are valued at their cost of production; excludes government sales to other sectors and government own-account investment (construction, software, and research and development). Gross government investment consists of general government and government enterprise expenditures for fixed assets; inventory investment is included in government consumption expenditures. For explanation of national income and chained dollars, see text, Section 13]

| Level of government and type | Current dollars | | | | Chained (2012) dollars | | | |
|---|---|---|---|---|---|---|---|---|
| | 2002 | 2010 | 2017 | 2018 | 2002 | 2010 | 2017 | 2018 |
| **Government consumption expenditures and gross investment, total** | **2,089** | **3,155** | **3,412** | **3,591** | **2,885** | **3,307** | **3,170** | **3,224** |
| Consumption expenditures | 1,645 | 2,510 | 2,757 | 2,904 | 2,300 | 2,633 | 2,553 | 2,596 |
| Gross investment | 444 | 645 | 655 | 687 | 585 | 675 | 616 | 628 |
| Structures | 220 | 312 | 311 | 325 | 358 | 335 | 282 | 283 |
| Equipment | 96 | 148 | 143 | 153 | 95 | 150 | 142 | 151 |
| Intellectual property products | 127 | 184 | 200 | 208 | 147 | 190 | 192 | 195 |
| **Federal** | **743** | **1,298** | **1,269** | **1,347** | **970** | **1,346** | **1,197** | **1,232** |
| Consumption expenditures | 561 | 1,001 | 993 | 1,057 | 761 | 1,040 | 930 | 957 |
| Gross investment | 182 | 297 | 277 | 290 | 210 | 306 | 267 | 275 |
| Structures | 16 | 33 | 16 | 16 | 24 | 35 | 15 | 14 |
| Equipment | 58 | 108 | 97 | 106 | 61 | 111 | 97 | 105 |
| Intellectual property products | 108 | 156 | 163 | 169 | 127 | 161 | 156 | 157 |
| **National defense** | **459** | **828** | **746** | **794** | **606** | **861** | **714** | **737** |
| Consumption expenditures | 359 | 652 | 600 | 637 | 491 | 679 | 571 | 588 |
| Gross investment | 100 | 176 | 146 | 156 | 116 | 182 | 143 | 150 |
| Structures | 6 | 17 | 4 | 4 | 9 | 18 | 3 | 3 |
| Equipment | 46 | 89 | 77 | 84 | 50 | 91 | 77 | 84 |
| Intellectual property products | 48 | 70 | 66 | 69 | 57 | 73 | 62 | 63 |
| **Nondefense** | **284** | **470** | **523** | **554** | **363** | **485** | **482** | **494** |
| Consumption expenditures | 202 | 349 | 393 | 420 | 269 | 361 | 358 | 369 |
| Gross investment | 82 | 121 | 130 | 134 | 94 | 124 | 124 | 125 |
| Structures | 10 | 16 | 13 | 12 | 15 | 17 | 11 | 11 |
| Equipment | 12 | 19 | 20 | 22 | 11 | 19 | 20 | 21 |
| Intellectual property products | 60 | 86 | 98 | 100 | 70 | 88 | 93 | 93 |
| **State and local** | **1,346** | **1,857** | **2,143** | **2,244** | **1,928** | **1,961** | **1,971** | **1,990** |
| Consumption expenditures | 1,084 | 1,509 | 1,765 | 1,847 | 1,545 | 1,593 | 1,622 | 1,637 |
| Gross investment | 262 | 347 | 378 | 397 | 383 | 368 | 349 | 353 |
| Structures | 204 | 280 | 295 | 309 | 334 | 301 | 268 | 269 |
| Equipment | 38 | 40 | 46 | 48 | 34 | 40 | 45 | 46 |
| Intellectual property products | 19 | 28 | 37 | 40 | 21 | 28 | 36 | 39 |

Source: U.S. Bureau of Economic Analysis, National Income and Product Accounts Tables, "Table 3.9.5. Government Consumption Expenditures and Gross Investment" and "Table 3.9.6. Real Government Consumption Expenditures and Gross Investment, Chained Dollars," <http://www.bea.gov/iTable/index_nipa.cfm>, accessed July 2019.

# Table 707. Personal Consumption Expenditures by Function: 2002 to 2018

[In billions of dollars (7,343 represents $7,343,000,000,000). In current and chained (2012) dollars. For definition of chained dollars, see text, this section. Minus sign (-) indicates decrease]

| Function | Current dollars | | | | Chained (2012) dollars | | | |
|---|---|---|---|---|---|---|---|---|
| | 2002 | 2010 | 2017 | 2018 | 2002 | 2010 | 2017 | 2018 |
| **Personal consumption expenditures** [1] | **7,343** | **10,186** | **13,312** | **13,999** | **9,089** | **10,643** | **12,567** | **12,945** |
| Food and nonalcoholic beverages purchased for off-premises consumption | 490 | 679 | 831 | 862 | 645 | 728 | 809 | 835 |
| Alcoholic beverages purchased for off-premises consumption | 84 | 108 | 136 | 141 | 99 | 109 | 131 | 135 |
| Clothing, footwear, and related services | 295 | 332 | 392 | 408 | 298 | 349 | 394 | 409 |
| Clothing (garments, cleaning, repair, and rental) | 249 | 269 | 313 | 326 | 248 | 285 | 317 | 329 |
| Footwear [2] | 46 | 62 | 79 | 82 | 50 | 64 | 76 | 80 |
| Housing [1] | 1,133 | 1,604 | 2,130 | 2,224 | 1,415 | 1,662 | 1,841 | 1,858 |
| Rental of tenant-occupied nonfarm housing [3] | 250 | 373 | 571 | 592 | 324 | 389 | 486 | 486 |
| Imputed rental of owner-occupied nonfarm housing [4] | 869 | 1,214 | 1,539 | 1,610 | 1,072 | 1,253 | 1,336 | 1,353 |
| Household utilities and fuels | 215 | 324 | 342 | 365 | 334 | 336 | 320 | 333 |
| Water supply and sanitation | 55 | 78 | 99 | 102 | 92 | 87 | 82 | 82 |
| Electricity, gas, and other fuels | 160 | 246 | 244 | 263 | 243 | 249 | 238 | 252 |
| Furnishings, household equipment, and routine household maintenance [1] | 366 | 411 | 542 | 573 | 351 | 409 | 586 | 617 |
| Furniture, furnishings, and floor coverings [5] | 122 | 128 | 180 | 190 | 104 | 125 | 204 | 219 |
| Household appliances [6] | 42 | 50 | 63 | 65 | 45 | 52 | 75 | 75 |
| Tools and equipment for house and garden | 18 | 20 | 30 | 32 | 18 | 20 | 31 | 32 |
| Medical products, appliances, and equipment [1] | 234 | 379 | 557 | 581 | 305 | 401 | 493 | 507 |
| Pharmaceutical and other medical products [7] | 200 | 326 | 491 | 512 | 267 | 347 | 429 | 440 |
| Outpatient services | 515 | 775 | 1,012 | 1,063 | 639 | 795 | 977 | 1,016 |
| Physician services [8] | 269 | 411 | 536 | 560 | 324 | 422 | 535 | 554 |
| Dental services | 76 | 104 | 126 | 133 | 112 | 109 | 112 | 114 |
| Paramedical services [9] | 170 | 260 | 349 | 371 | 205 | 264 | 331 | 349 |
| Hospital and nursing home services | 568 | 925 | 1,231 | 1,289 | 804 | 967 | 1,143 | 1,167 |
| Transportation | 807 | 962 | 1,232 | 1,312 | 1,162 | 1,085 | 1,364 | 1,400 |
| Motor vehicles | 360 | 288 | 429 | 446 | 359 | 300 | 438 | 458 |
| New motor vehicles | 244 | 182 | 282 | 289 | 250 | 191 | 274 | 283 |
| Net purchases of used motor vehicles | 116 | 106 | 147 | 157 | 109 | 109 | 166 | 179 |
| Motor vehicle operation [1] | 371 | 570 | 651 | 705 | 688 | 671 | 773 | 782 |
| Motor vehicle fuels, lubricants, and fluids | 154 | 312 | 290 | 328 | 411 | 406 | 422 | 421 |
| Motor vehicle maintenance and repair | 121 | 137 | 181 | 190 | 164 | 142 | 166 | 171 |
| Public transportation | 76 | 104 | 152 | 161 | 110 | 115 | 149 | 155 |
| Telephone and related communication equipment | 6 | 18 | 30 | 31 | 2 | 15 | 79 | 86 |
| Postal and delivery services | 9 | 15 | 13 | 13 | 14 | 16 | 11 | 11 |
| Telecommunication services | 131 | 148 | 152 | 159 | 130 | 145 | 195 | 209 |
| Internet access | 14 | 40 | 71 | 71 | 11 | 40 | 71 | 71 |
| Recreation [1] | 669 | 884 | 1,157 | 1,203 | 590 | 863 | 1,210 | 1,267 |
| Video and audio equipment | 86 | 83 | 81 | 84 | 28 | 66 | 128 | 149 |
| Information processing equipment | 44 | 95 | 134 | 142 | 16 | 81 | 178 | 195 |
| Services related to video/audio goods and computers | 61 | 97 | 130 | 133 | 78 | 103 | 114 | 115 |
| Sports and recreational goods and related services | 156 | 177 | 248 | 250 | 134 | 171 | 283 | 295 |
| Magazines, newspapers, books, and stationery | 81 | 75 | 89 | 95 | 89 | 76 | 84 | 89 |
| Gambling | 74 | 109 | 136 | 143 | 95 | 115 | 127 | 130 |
| Pets, pet products, and related services | 45 | 76 | 111 | 115 | 64 | 80 | 106 | 108 |
| Education [1] | 150 | 240 | 293 | 304 | 269 | 263 | 252 | 255 |
| Higher education | 87 | 155 | 184 | 189 | 164 | 171 | 157 | 158 |
| Food services | 383 | 537 | 768 | 822 | 514 | 567 | 681 | 710 |
| Accommodations [10] | 53 | 99 | 145 | 152 | 67 | 104 | 129 | 133 |
| Financial services | 319 | 465 | 661 | 709 | 407 | 507 | 496 | 498 |
| Insurance [1] | 215 | 289 | 380 | 402 | 294 | 304 | 340 | 348 |
| Life insurance | 59 | 78 | 83 | 85 | 74 | 80 | 73 | 74 |
| Net health insurance | 107 | 143 | 213 | 229 | 155 | 151 | 198 | 205 |
| Net motor vehicle and other transportation insurance | 46 | 60 | 73 | 78 | 60 | 65 | 61 | 62 |
| Personal care [11] | 143 | 207 | 271 | 285 | 169 | 211 | 258 | 269 |
| Personal items [12] | 63 | 85 | 100 | 107 | 73 | 90 | 101 | 111 |
| Social services and religious activities [13] | 93 | 139 | 193 | 203 | 120 | 145 | 170 | 175 |
| Professional and other services [1] | 127 | 159 | 196 | 199 | 181 | 167 | 171 | 167 |
| Legal services | 74 | 87 | 107 | 107 | 106 | 92 | 94 | 90 |
| Accounting and other business services | 20 | 28 | 37 | 39 | 29 | 30 | 31 | 31 |
| Funeral and burial services | 17 | 24 | 28 | 27 | 25 | 25 | 25 | 24 |
| Tobacco | 70 | 98 | 97 | 99 | 130 | 104 | 81 | 80 |
| Net foreign travel and expenditures abroad by: | | | | | | | | |
| U.S. residents [1] | -12 | -29 | -37 | -21 | -4 | -35 | -20 | -4 |
| Foreign travel by U.S. residents | 67 | 103 | 170 | 187 | 105 | 108 | 176 | 189 |
| Less: Expenditures in the United States by nonresidents | 83 | 140 | 214 | 218 | 117 | 151 | 203 | 202 |
| Final consumption expenditures of nonprofit institutions serving households (NPISHs) [14] | 198 | 294 | 414 | 443 | 194 | 299 | 351 | 369 |

[1] Includes other expenditures not shown separately. [2] Also includes repair and hire of footwear. [3] Rent for space (see footnote 4), and for appliances, furnishings, and furniture. [4] Rent for space and for heating and plumbing facilities, water heaters, lighting fixtures, kitchen cabinets, linoleum, storm windows and doors, window screens, and screen doors; excludes rent for appliances and furniture and purchases of fuel and electricity. [5] Includes clocks, lamps, lighting fixtures, other household decorative items, and repair of furniture, furnishings, and floor coverings. [6] Includes appliance repair. [7] Excludes drug preparations and related products dispensed by physicians, hospitals, and other medical services. [8] Offices of physicians, HMO medical centers, and freestanding ambulatory surgical and emergency centers. [9] Includes home health care, medical laboratories, and other health professionals (except physicians) and services. [10] Hotels, motels, other traveler accommodations, clubs, and housing at schools. [11] Cosmetics, toiletries, and personal care appliances and services. [12] Jewelry, watches, luggage, and similar items. [13] Household purchases from business, government, and nonprofit institutions providing social services and religious activities. Purchases from nonprofit establishments exclude unrelated sales, secondary sales, and sales to businesses, government, and the rest of the world, but include membership dues and fees. [14] Net expenses of NPISHs, defined as their gross operating expenses less primary sales to households.

Source: U.S. Bureau of Economic Analysis, National Income and Product Accounts, "2.5.5 Personal Consumption Expenditures by Function," and "2.5.6 Real Personal Consumption Expenditures by Function, Chained Dollars," <https://www.bea.gov/iTable/index_nipa.cfm>, accessed July 2019.

Income, Expenditures, Poverty, and Wealth **457**

# Table 708. Personal Income By Source and Disposition: 2000 to 2018

[In billions of dollars (8,653 represents $8,653,000,000,000), except as indicated. For definition of personal income and chained dollars, see text, this section]

| Item | 2000 | 2010 | 2013 | 2014 | 2015 | 2016 | 2017 | 2018 |
|---|---|---|---|---|---|---|---|---|
| **Personal income**.......... | **8,653** | **12,552** | **14,181** | **14,992** | **15,718** | **16,121** | **16,879** | **17,819** |
| Compensation of employees, received........... | 5,848 | 7,925 | 8,834 | 9,249 | 9,698 | 9,960 | 10,412 | 10,928 |
| Wages and salaries.......... | 4,826 | 6,372 | 7,113 | 7,475 | 7,857 | 8,083 | 8,462 | 8,888 |
| Supplements to wages and salaries.......... | 1,022 | 1,553 | 1,721 | 1,774 | 1,841 | 1,877 | 1,950 | 2,040 |
| Proprietors' income [1].......... | 754 | 1,109 | 1,404 | 1,448 | 1,422 | 1,424 | 1,518 | 1,589 |
| Farm.......... | 31 | 39 | 88 | 70 | 56 | 36 | 38 | 27 |
| Nonfarm.......... | 722 | 1,070 | 1,315 | 1,378 | 1,366 | 1,388 | 1,480 | 1,562 |
| Rental income of persons [2].......... | 183 | 394 | 557 | 605 | 648 | 681 | 719 | 757 |
| Personal income receipts on assets.......... | 1,486 | 1,782 | 2,066 | 2,302 | 2,471 | 2,521 | 2,682 | 2,930 |
| Personal interest income.......... | 1,102 | 1,238 | 1,273 | 1,349 | 1,438 | 1,457 | 1,552 | 1,703 |
| Personal dividend income.......... | 384 | 544 | 793 | 953 | 1,033 | 1,064 | 1,130 | 1,227 |
| Personal current transfer receipts.......... | 1,087 | 2,325 | 2,424 | 2,542 | 2,683 | 2,774 | 2,848 | 2,971 |
| Government social benefits to persons [3].......... | 1,045 | 2,281 | 2,386 | 2,499 | 2,633 | 2,715 | 2,800 | 2,918 |
| Social security [4].......... | 401 | 690 | 799 | 835 | 872 | 896 | 926 | 972 |
| Unemployment insurance.......... | 21 | 139 | 62 | 35 | 32 | 32 | 30 | 27 |
| Veterans' benefits.......... | 25 | 58 | 79 | 84 | 93 | 96 | 104 | 110 |
| Other current transfer receipts, from business (net).......... | 42 | 44 | 38 | 43 | 50 | 60 | 48 | 53 |
| Less: Contributions for government social insurance....... | 706 | 984 | 1,104 | 1,154 | 1,205 | 1,240 | 1,300 | 1,356 |
| Less: Personal current taxes.......... | 1,236 | 1,237 | 1,676 | 1,784 | 1,938 | 1,956 | 2,046 | 2,078 |
| **Equals: Disposable personal income**.......... | **7,416** | **11,314** | **12,505** | **13,208** | **13,780** | **14,165** | **14,833** | **15,742** |
| Less: Personal outlays.......... | 7,058 | 10,573 | 11,704 | 12,237 | 12,731 | 13,206 | 13,802 | 14,531 |
| Personal consumption expenditures.......... | 6,762 | 10,186 | 11,317 | 11,823 | 12,284 | 12,748 | 13,312 | 13,999 |
| Personal interest payments [5].......... | 215 | 243 | 230 | 244 | 264 | 274 | 299 | 337 |
| Personal current transfer payments.......... | 81 | 145 | 157 | 170 | 183 | 184 | 191 | 196 |
| **Equals: Personal saving**.......... | **358** | **741** | **801** | **971** | **1,049** | **959** | **1,031** | **1,210** |
| Personal saving as a percentage of disposable personal income.......... | 4.8 | 6.5 | 6.4 | 7.3 | 7.6 | 6.8 | 7.0 | 7.7 |
| *Addenda:* | | | | | | | | |
| Disposable personal income: | | | | | | | | |
| Total, billions of chained (2012) dollars [6].......... | 9,479 | 11,822 | 12,339 | 12,844 | 13,373 | 13,608 | 14,003 | 14,556 |
| Per capita: | | | | | | | | |
| Current dollars.......... | 26,262 | 36,524 | 39,521 | 41,440 | 42,925 | 43,812 | 45,583 | 48,075 |
| Chained (2012) dollars.......... | 33,568 | 38,163 | 38,996 | 40,300 | 41,656 | 42,090 | 43,031 | 44,455 |

[1] With inventory valuation and capital consumption adjustments. [2] Includes capital consumption adjustment. [3] Includes other benefits not shown separately. [4] Social security benefits include benefits distributed from the Old-Age and Survivors Insurance Trust Fund and the Disability Insurance Trust Fund. [5] Consists of nonmortgage interest paid by households. [6] The current-dollar measure is deflated by the implicit price deflator for personal consumption expenditures.

Source: U.S. Bureau of Economic Analysis, National Income and Product Accounts Tables, "Table 2.1 Personal Income and Its Disposition," <http://www.bea.gov/iTable/index_nipa.cfm>, accessed July 2019.

# Table 709. Selected Per Capita Income and Product Measures in Current and Chained (2012) Dollars: 1970 to 2018

[In dollars. Based on U.S. Census Bureau estimated population including Armed Forces abroad, and institutionalized population; based on monthly averages. For explanation of chained dollars, see text, this section]

| Year | Current dollars | | | | | Chained (2012) dollars | | | | |
|---|---|---|---|---|---|---|---|---|---|---|
| | Gross domestic product | Gross national product | Personal income | Disposable personal income | Personal consumption expenditures | Gross domestic product | Gross national product | Disposable personal income | Personal consumption expenditures |
| 1970.......... | 5,233 | 5,265 | 4,218 | 3,715 | 3,153 | 24,142 | 24,329 | 17,734 | 15,051 |
| 1980.......... | 12,547 | 12,697 | 10,204 | 8,888 | 7,688 | 29,681 | 30,079 | 21,542 | 18,631 |
| 1990.......... | 23,835 | 23,974 | 19,641 | 17,264 | 15,225 | 37,435 | 37,673 | 27,250 | 24,031 |
| 2000.......... | 36,305 | 36,429 | 30,640 | 26,262 | 23,945 | 46,498 | 46,672 | 33,568 | 30,607 |
| 2001.......... | 37,100 | 37,271 | 31,574 | 27,230 | 24,772 | 46,497 | 46,726 | 34,149 | 31,067 |
| 2002.......... | 37,980 | 38,137 | 31,807 | 28,153 | 25,499 | 46,858 | 47,067 | 34,848 | 31,563 |
| 2003.......... | 39,426 | 39,627 | 32,645 | 29,192 | 26,574 | 47,756 | 48,013 | 35,446 | 32,267 |
| 2004.......... | 41,648 | 41,914 | 34,219 | 30,643 | 28,004 | 49,125 | 49,454 | 36,302 | 33,176 |
| 2005.......... | 44,044 | 44,307 | 35,806 | 31,710 | 29,552 | 50,381 | 50,697 | 36,527 | 34,041 |
| 2006.......... | 46,231 | 46,400 | 38,089 | 33,549 | 30,990 | 51,330 | 51,532 | 37,621 | 34,752 |
| 2007.......... | 47,902 | 48,263 | 39,801 | 34,855 | 32,173 | 51,794 | 52,199 | 38,119 | 35,186 |
| 2008.......... | 48,311 | 48,819 | 40,855 | 35,906 | 32,758 | 51,240 | 51,788 | 38,125 | 34,783 |
| 2009.......... | 47,028 | 47,490 | 39,250 | 35,500 | 32,034 | 49,501 | 49,991 | 37,728 | 34,045 |
| 2010.......... | 48,396 | 49,028 | 40,518 | 36,524 | 32,881 | 50,354 | 51,017 | 38,163 | 34,357 |
| 2011.......... | 49,811 | 50,568 | 42,709 | 38,052 | 34,102 | 50,766 | 51,538 | 38,777 | 34,752 |
| 2012.......... | 51,541 | 52,280 | 44,582 | 39,780 | 35,025 | 51,541 | 52,280 | 39,780 | 35,025 |
| 2013.......... | 53,046 | 53,775 | 44,817 | 39,521 | 35,766 | 52,131 | 52,848 | 38,996 | 35,291 |
| 2014.......... | 54,993 | 55,750 | 47,038 | 41,440 | 37,095 | 53,063 | 53,799 | 40,300 | 36,074 |
| 2015.......... | 56,770 | 57,470 | 48,961 | 42,925 | 38,266 | 54,213 | 54,901 | 41,656 | 37,135 |
| 2016.......... | 57,885 | 58,559 | 49,862 | 43,812 | 39,430 | 54,711 | 55,371 | 42,090 | 37,881 |
| 2017.......... | 59,984 | 60,732 | 51,869 | 45,583 | 40,909 | 55,647 | 56,374 | 43,031 | 38,619 |
| 2018.......... | 62,853 | 63,671 | 54,420 | 48,075 | 42,752 | 56,922 | 57,715 | 44,455 | 39,533 |

Source: U.S. Bureau of Economic Analysis, National Income and Product Accounts Tables, "Table 7.1. Selected Per Capita Product and Income Series in Current and Chained Dollars," <http://www.bea.gov/iTable/index_nipa.cfm>, accessed July 2019.

# Table 710. Personal Income in Current and Constant (2012) Dollars by State: 2000 to 2018

[In billions of dollars (8,650.3 represents $8,650,300,000,000). Represents income that all persons who are state residents receive from all sources. Data exclude income of foreign nationals employed in the U.S. by their home governments, and income earned by U.S. citizens while living abroad. Data also exclude the earnings of federal civilian and military personnel stationed abroad. Totals may differ from those in Table 700, Table 708, and Table 709]

| State | Current dollars | | | | | Constant (2012) dollars [1] | | | | |
|---|---|---|---|---|---|---|---|---|---|---|
| | 2000 | 2005 | 2010 | 2017 | 2018 | 2000 | 2005 | 2010 | 2017 | 2018 |
| United States.............. | 8,650.3 | 10,593.9 | 12,542.0 | 16,820.3 | 17,572.9 | 11,056.8 | 12,203.3 | 13,104.8 | 15,857.2 | 16,236.4 |
| Alabama...................... | 108.5 | 136.2 | 162.0 | 198.9 | 206.9 | 138.7 | 156.9 | 169.2 | 187.5 | 191.2 |
| Alaska........................ | 20.0 | 25.9 | 35.2 | 42.3 | 44.0 | 25.6 | 29.8 | 36.7 | 39.9 | 40.7 |
| Arizona....................... | 135.0 | 188.1 | 215.0 | 296.6 | 313.0 | 172.5 | 216.7 | 224.7 | 279.7 | 289.2 |
| Arkansas..................... | 61.1 | 78.1 | 93.1 | 123.3 | 128.3 | 78.1 | 90.0 | 97.3 | 116.3 | 118.5 |
| California.................... | 1,135.3 | 1,409.0 | 1,627.8 | 2,364.1 | 2,475.7 | 1,451.2 | 1,623.0 | 1,700.9 | 2,228.8 | 2,287.4 |
| Colorado..................... | 147.2 | 174.8 | 204.7 | 306.4 | 323.8 | 188.2 | 201.3 | 213.9 | 288.9 | 299.1 |
| Connecticut.................. | 147.0 | 175.7 | 222.6 | 257.7 | 266.4 | 187.9 | 202.4 | 232.6 | 243.0 | 246.1 |
| Delaware..................... | 26.6 | 33.2 | 36.7 | 47.8 | 49.8 | 34.0 | 38.2 | 38.4 | 45.0 | 46.0 |
| District of Columbia....... | 24.8 | 30.3 | 38.5 | 55.5 | 57.5 | 31.7 | 34.9 | 40.2 | 52.3 | 53.1 |
| Florida....................... | 471.1 | 641.6 | 725.8 | 1,000.6 | 1,052.6 | 602.1 | 739.1 | 758.4 | 943.3 | 972.5 |
| Georgia...................... | 236.8 | 296.7 | 335.3 | 460.4 | 481.2 | 302.7 | 341.8 | 350.4 | 434.0 | 444.6 |
| Hawaii........................ | 35.9 | 47.4 | 57.1 | 75.4 | 77.5 | 45.8 | 54.6 | 59.7 | 71.0 | 71.6 |
| Idaho......................... | 32.6 | 41.8 | 50.1 | 71.8 | 75.7 | 41.7 | 48.1 | 52.4 | 67.7 | 69.9 |
| Illinois....................... | 413.4 | 477.0 | 540.5 | 693.9 | 725.4 | 528.5 | 549.5 | 564.7 | 654.2 | 670.2 |
| Indiana....................... | 171.4 | 196.8 | 229.5 | 301.0 | 312.2 | 219.1 | 226.7 | 239.8 | 283.8 | 288.4 |
| Iowa.......................... | 80.7 | 96.4 | 116.4 | 148.0 | 154.1 | 103.1 | 111.0 | 121.6 | 139.6 | 142.4 |
| Kansas....................... | 76.2 | 88.5 | 112.7 | 141.5 | 146.0 | 97.5 | 101.9 | 117.7 | 133.4 | 134.9 |
| Kentucky..................... | 100.9 | 121.5 | 144.0 | 180.8 | 186.7 | 129.0 | 140.0 | 150.5 | 170.5 | 172.5 |
| Louisiana.................... | 107.1 | 135.7 | 170.5 | 204.5 | 212.2 | 136.9 | 156.3 | 178.1 | 192.8 | 196.1 |
| Maine........................ | 35.1 | 43.2 | 50.3 | 62.1 | 64.6 | 44.8 | 49.7 | 52.5 | 58.5 | 59.7 |
| Maryland..................... | 188.9 | 244.3 | 288.6 | 368.3 | 380.2 | 241.5 | 281.5 | 301.6 | 347.2 | 351.3 |
| Massachusetts.............. | 245.4 | 285.6 | 348.4 | 463.9 | 483.7 | 313.7 | 329.0 | 364.1 | 437.4 | 446.9 |
| Michigan..................... | 301.7 | 329.2 | 348.7 | 460.3 | 475.6 | 385.6 | 379.2 | 364.3 | 433.9 | 439.5 |
| Minnesota.................... | 159.1 | 193.8 | 225.6 | 303.1 | 316.3 | 203.4 | 223.3 | 235.7 | 285.8 | 292.3 |
| Mississippi.................. | 61.8 | 77.8 | 91.9 | 109.3 | 113.5 | 79.0 | 89.6 | 96.1 | 103.1 | 104.8 |
| Missouri...................... | 157.2 | 186.9 | 220.5 | 275.0 | 285.7 | 200.9 | 215.3 | 230.4 | 259.2 | 264.0 |
| Montana...................... | 21.0 | 28.0 | 35.6 | 47.7 | 50.1 | 26.8 | 32.2 | 37.2 | 44.9 | 46.2 |
| Nebraska..................... | 49.9 | 60.7 | 74.8 | 97.6 | 100.5 | 63.8 | 69.9 | 78.1 | 92.0 | 92.9 |
| Nevada....................... | 64.6 | 93.3 | 101.2 | 138.4 | 146.3 | 82.5 | 107.5 | 105.7 | 130.5 | 135.2 |
| New Hampshire.............. | 44.1 | 52.9 | 62.3 | 80.1 | 83.3 | 56.3 | 61.0 | 65.1 | 75.5 | 77.0 |
| New Jersey................... | 331.3 | 386.9 | 452.3 | 581.2 | 602.3 | 423.5 | 445.7 | 472.6 | 547.9 | 556.5 |
| New Mexico.................. | 42.2 | 55.8 | 69.3 | 83.1 | 86.3 | 54.0 | 64.3 | 72.4 | 78.4 | 79.8 |
| New York..................... | 684.9 | 787.3 | 954.4 | 1,281.1 | 1,341.9 | 875.4 | 906.9 | 997.2 | 1,207.7 | 1,239.9 |
| North Carolina.............. | 221.9 | 281.1 | 340.8 | 454.3 | 475.9 | 283.6 | 323.8 | 356.1 | 428.3 | 439.7 |
| North Dakota................ | 16.8 | 20.4 | 29.4 | 39.5 | 41.3 | 21.5 | 23.5 | 30.8 | 37.2 | 38.1 |
| Ohio.......................... | 326.0 | 374.1 | 423.1 | 544.8 | 563.9 | 416.6 | 430.9 | 442.0 | 513.6 | 521.0 |
| Oklahoma.................... | 83.4 | 111.1 | 137.3 | 174.4 | 181.9 | 106.6 | 127.9 | 143.5 | 164.4 | 168.1 |
| Oregon....................... | 97.8 | 117.1 | 138.3 | 199.4 | 209.1 | 125.0 | 134.9 | 144.5 | 188.0 | 193.2 |
| Pennsylvania................ | 374.4 | 451.9 | 533.8 | 682.5 | 708.9 | 478.6 | 520.5 | 557.8 | 643.5 | 654.9 |
| Rhode Island................ | 32.0 | 39.6 | 45.2 | 55.9 | 57.6 | 40.8 | 45.6 | 47.2 | 52.7 | 53.3 |
| South Carolina.............. | 101.2 | 124.5 | 150.5 | 209.2 | 217.3 | 129.3 | 143.4 | 157.2 | 197.2 | 200.7 |
| South Dakota................ | 20.3 | 26.1 | 33.5 | 42.5 | 44.2 | 26.0 | 30.0 | 35.0 | 40.0 | 40.9 |
| Tennessee................... | 155.6 | 188.9 | 227.8 | 305.7 | 319.4 | 198.9 | 217.5 | 238.0 | 288.2 | 295.1 |
| Texas......................... | 589.6 | 747.1 | 966.9 | 1,340.6 | 1,411.0 | 753.7 | 860.6 | 1,010.3 | 1,263.8 | 1,303.7 |
| Utah.......................... | 55.1 | 71.4 | 89.3 | 134.8 | 143.3 | 70.4 | 82.2 | 93.4 | 127.1 | 132.4 |
| Vermont...................... | 17.6 | 21.5 | 25.8 | 32.6 | 33.6 | 22.5 | 24.7 | 26.9 | 30.7 | 31.0 |
| Virginia....................... | 232.0 | 304.7 | 364.4 | 466.7 | 485.1 | 296.6 | 351.0 | 380.7 | 440.0 | 448.2 |
| Washington.................. | 194.2 | 235.2 | 286.7 | 428.8 | 458.0 | 248.2 | 271.0 | 299.6 | 404.2 | 423.2 |
| West Virginia................ | 40.5 | 48.8 | 60.1 | 69.9 | 73.3 | 51.7 | 56.3 | 62.8 | 65.9 | 67.7 |
| Wisconsin................... | 158.9 | 190.5 | 221.9 | 283.6 | 295.1 | 203.1 | 219.5 | 231.9 | 267.4 | 272.6 |
| Wyoming..................... | 14.5 | 19.6 | 26.0 | 33.2 | 34.7 | 18.6 | 22.5 | 27.1 | 31.3 | 32.1 |

[1] Constant dollar estimates are computed by ProQuest using the national implicit price deflator for personal consumption expenditures from the Bureau of Economic Analysis' National Income and Product Accounts Tables. Any regional differences in the rate of inflation are not reflected in these constant dollar estimates.

Source: Except as noted, U.S. Bureau of Economic Analysis, Regional Economic Accounts, Personal Income by State, Interactive Data, "Table SAINC1 Personal Income Summary," <https://www.bea.gov/data/economic-accounts/regional>, accessed March 2019.

# Table 711. Personal Income Per Capita in Current and Constant (2012) Dollars by State: 2000 to 2018

[In dollars, except as indicated. Represents income that all persons who are state residents receive from all sources. Data exclude income of foreign nationals employed in the U.S. by their home governments, and income earned by U.S. citizens while living abroad. Data also exclude the earnings of federal civilian and military personnel stationed abroad. Totals may differ from those in Table 700, Table 708, and Table 709]

| State | Current dollars | | | | Constant (2012) dollars [1] | | | | Income rank [2] | |
|---|---|---|---|---|---|---|---|---|---|---|
| | 2000 | 2010 | 2017 | 2018 (P) | 2000 | 2010 | 2017 | 2018 (P) | 2010 | 2018 (P) |
| **United States** | **30,657** | **40,546** | **51,731** | **53,712** | **39,186** | **42,366** | **48,769** | **49,627** | (X) | (X) |
| Alabama | 24,372 | 33,845 | 40,802 | 42,334 | 31,152 | 35,364 | 38,466 | 39,114 | 42 | 47 |
| Alaska | 31,881 | 49,254 | 57,180 | 59,687 | 40,750 | 51,464 | 53,906 | 55,147 | 6 | 11 |
| Arizona | 26,151 | 33,555 | 42,085 | 43,650 | 33,426 | 35,061 | 39,676 | 40,330 | 43 | 43 |
| Arkansas | 22,824 | 31,863 | 41,063 | 42,566 | 29,174 | 33,293 | 38,712 | 39,328 | 50 | 46 |
| California | 33,403 | 43,617 | 60,004 | 62,586 | 42,696 | 45,574 | 56,569 | 57,826 | 12 | 7 |
| Colorado | 34,027 | 40,547 | 54,561 | 56,846 | 43,493 | 42,367 | 51,437 | 52,522 | 23 | 14 |
| Connecticut | 43,091 | 62,203 | 72,110 | 74,561 | 55,079 | 64,995 | 67,981 | 68,890 | 2 | 2 |
| Delaware | 33,862 | 40,804 | 49,925 | 51,449 | 43,282 | 42,635 | 47,067 | 47,536 | 22 | 22 |
| District of Columbia | 43,329 | 63,650 | 79,792 | 81,882 | 55,383 | 66,506 | 75,224 | 75,654 | 1 | 1 |
| Florida | 29,355 | 38,513 | 47,701 | 49,417 | 37,522 | 40,241 | 44,970 | 45,658 | 26 | 27 |
| Georgia | 28,783 | 34,527 | 44,214 | 45,745 | 36,790 | 36,076 | 41,683 | 42,266 | 41 | 40 |
| Hawaii | 29,544 | 41,864 | 52,910 | 54,565 | 37,763 | 43,743 | 49,881 | 50,415 | 18 | 17 |
| Idaho | 25,089 | 31,923 | 41,778 | 43,155 | 32,069 | 33,356 | 39,386 | 39,873 | 49 | 44 |
| Illinois | 33,251 | 42,090 | 54,271 | 56,933 | 42,501 | 43,979 | 51,164 | 52,603 | 16 | 13 |
| Indiana | 28,138 | 35,356 | 45,196 | 46,646 | 35,966 | 36,943 | 42,608 | 43,098 | 39 | 36 |
| Iowa | 27,535 | 38,139 | 47,093 | 48,823 | 35,195 | 39,851 | 44,397 | 45,110 | 28 | 29 |
| Kansas | 28,304 | 39,424 | 48,600 | 50,155 | 36,178 | 41,193 | 45,818 | 46,340 | 24 | 24 |
| Kentucky | 24,918 | 33,119 | 40,600 | 41,779 | 31,850 | 34,605 | 38,276 | 38,601 | 45 | 48 |
| Louisiana | 23,943 | 37,513 | 43,786 | 45,542 | 30,604 | 39,196 | 41,279 | 42,078 | 30 | 41 |
| Maine | 27,450 | 37,852 | 46,485 | 48,241 | 35,087 | 39,551 | 43,824 | 44,572 | 29 | 31 |
| Maryland | 35,572 | 49,857 | 61,123 | 62,914 | 45,468 | 52,094 | 57,624 | 58,129 | 5 | 6 |
| Massachusetts | 38,577 | 53,061 | 67,596 | 70,073 | 49,309 | 55,442 | 63,726 | 64,743 | 3 | 3 |
| Michigan | 30,310 | 35,300 | 46,136 | 47,582 | 38,742 | 36,884 | 43,495 | 43,963 | 40 | 33 |
| Minnesota | 32,252 | 42,478 | 54,442 | 56,374 | 41,225 | 44,384 | 51,325 | 52,086 | 15 | 15 |
| Mississippi | 21,696 | 30,947 | 36,567 | 37,994 | 27,732 | 32,336 | 34,473 | 35,104 | 51 | 51 |
| Missouri | 28,028 | 36,782 | 45,014 | 46,635 | 35,825 | 38,433 | 42,437 | 43,088 | 32 | 37 |
| Montana | 23,195 | 35,891 | 45,274 | 47,120 | 29,648 | 37,502 | 42,682 | 43,536 | 36 | 35 |
| Nebraska | 29,115 | 40,878 | 50,875 | 52,110 | 37,215 | 42,713 | 47,962 | 48,147 | 21 | 21 |
| Nevada | 31,988 | 37,449 | 46,557 | 48,225 | 40,887 | 39,130 | 43,891 | 44,557 | 31 | 32 |
| New Hampshire | 35,547 | 47,317 | 59,360 | 61,405 | 45,436 | 49,440 | 55,961 | 56,735 | 8 | 8 |
| New Jersey | 39,298 | 51,402 | 65,387 | 67,609 | 50,231 | 53,709 | 61,643 | 62,467 | 4 | 5 |
| New Mexico | 23,178 | 33,548 | 39,709 | 41,198 | 29,626 | 35,054 | 37,436 | 38,065 | 44 | 49 |
| New York | 36,044 | 49,194 | 65,392 | 68,667 | 46,071 | 51,402 | 61,648 | 63,444 | 7 | 4 |
| North Carolina | 27,453 | 35,592 | 44,233 | 45,834 | 35,090 | 37,189 | 41,701 | 42,348 | 38 | 39 |
| North Dakota | 26,175 | 43,643 | 52,284 | 54,306 | 33,457 | 45,602 | 49,291 | 50,176 | 11 | 19 |
| Ohio | 28,684 | 36,663 | 46,710 | 48,242 | 36,664 | 38,308 | 44,036 | 44,573 | 33 | 30 |
| Oklahoma | 24,133 | 36,527 | 44,356 | 46,128 | 30,847 | 38,166 | 41,816 | 42,620 | 34 | 38 |
| Oregon | 28,508 | 36,046 | 48,093 | 49,908 | 36,439 | 37,664 | 45,340 | 46,112 | 35 | 26 |
| Pennsylvania | 30,479 | 41,997 | 53,363 | 55,349 | 38,958 | 43,882 | 50,308 | 51,139 | 17 | 16 |
| Rhode Island | 30,424 | 42,844 | 52,943 | 54,523 | 38,888 | 44,767 | 49,912 | 50,376 | 13 | 18 |
| South Carolina | 25,138 | 32,455 | 41,659 | 42,736 | 32,131 | 33,911 | 39,274 | 39,486 | 46 | 45 |
| South Dakota | 26,890 | 41,061 | 48,616 | 50,141 | 34,371 | 42,904 | 45,833 | 46,327 | 20 | 25 |
| Tennessee | 27,276 | 35,838 | 45,566 | 47,179 | 34,864 | 37,446 | 42,957 | 43,591 | 37 | 34 |
| Texas | 28,151 | 38,304 | 47,332 | 49,161 | 35,983 | 40,023 | 44,622 | 45,422 | 27 | 28 |
| Utah | 24,531 | 32,193 | 43,441 | 45,340 | 31,356 | 33,638 | 40,954 | 41,891 | 48 | 42 |
| Vermont | 28,915 | 41,201 | 52,152 | 53,598 | 36,959 | 43,050 | 49,166 | 49,521 | 19 | 20 |
| Virginia | 32,654 | 45,413 | 55,137 | 56,952 | 41,738 | 47,451 | 51,980 | 52,620 | 10 | 12 |
| Washington | 32,858 | 42,524 | 57,743 | 60,781 | 41,999 | 44,432 | 54,437 | 56,158 | 14 | 9 |
| West Virginia | 22,386 | 32,392 | 38,454 | 40,578 | 28,614 | 33,846 | 36,252 | 37,492 | 47 | 50 |
| Wisconsin | 29,573 | 38,994 | 48,970 | 50,756 | 37,800 | 40,744 | 46,166 | 46,896 | 25 | 23 |
| Wyoming | 29,363 | 46,002 | 57,384 | 60,095 | 37,532 | 48,066 | 54,099 | 55,524 | 9 | 10 |

P Preliminary. X Not applicable. [1] Constant dollar estimates are computed by ProQuest using the national implicit price deflator for personal consumption expenditures from the Bureau of Economic Analysis' National Income and Product Accounts tables. Any regional differences in the rate of inflation are not reflected in these constant dollar estimates. [2] Ranking based on current dollar income.

Source: Except as noted, U.S. Bureau of Economic Analysis, Regional Economic Accounts, Personal Income by State, Interactive Data, "Table SAINC1 Personal Income Summary," <https://www.bea.gov/data/economic-accounts/regional>, accessed March 2019.

# Table 712. Disposable Personal Income Per Capita in Current and Constant (2012) Dollars by State: 2000 to 2018

[In dollars, except as indicated. Per capita disposable personal income is total disposable personal income divided by total midyear population. Disposable personal income is total personal income minus personal current taxes. It is the portion of personal income that is available for saving and spending. The estimate of personal income in the United States is derived as the sum of the state estimates and the estimate for the District of Columbia; it differs from the estimate of personal income in the national income and product accounts (NIPAs) because of differences in coverage, in the methodologies used to prepare the estimates, and in the timing of the availability of source data. See text, Section 13]

| State | Current dollars | | | | Constant (2012) dollars [1] | | | | Index, compared to U.S. average [2] | |
|---|---|---|---|---|---|---|---|---|---|---|
| | 2000 | 2010 | 2017 | 2018 (P) | 2000 | 2010 | 2017 | 2018 (P) | 2010 | 2018 (P) |
| United States........... | 26,279 | 36,550 | 45,480 | 47,451 | 33,590 | 38,190 | 42,876 | 43,842 | 100.0 | 100.0 |
| Alabama.................. | 21,640 | 31,086 | 36,831 | 38,369 | 27,660 | 32,481 | 34,722 | 35,451 | 85.1 | 80.9 |
| Alaska.................... | 28,443 | 45,514 | 52,384 | 54,951 | 36,356 | 47,557 | 49,385 | 50,771 | 124.5 | 115.8 |
| Arizona................... | 22,811 | 30,838 | 37,804 | 39,345 | 29,157 | 32,222 | 35,640 | 36,352 | 84.4 | 82.9 |
| Arkansas................. | 20,261 | 29,214 | 37,000 | 38,540 | 25,898 | 30,525 | 34,882 | 35,609 | 79.9 | 81.2 |
| California................. | 27,653 | 38,843 | 51,481 | 53,944 | 35,346 | 40,586 | 48,534 | 49,841 | 106.3 | 113.7 |
| Colorado................. | 28,895 | 36,242 | 47,524 | 49,801 | 36,934 | 37,868 | 44,803 | 46,013 | 99.2 | 105.0 |
| Connecticut.............. | 35,000 | 54,421 | 61,267 | 63,893 | 44,737 | 56,863 | 57,759 | 59,033 | 148.9 | 134.7 |
| Delaware................. | 29,270 | 36,848 | 44,172 | 45,786 | 37,413 | 38,502 | 41,643 | 42,304 | 100.8 | 96.5 |
| District of Columbia...... | 36,293 | 55,909 | 67,850 | 70,045 | 46,390 | 58,418 | 63,965 | 64,717 | 153.0 | 147.6 |
| Florida.................... | 25,648 | 35,407 | 42,869 | 44,609 | 32,783 | 36,996 | 40,415 | 41,216 | 96.9 | 94.0 |
| Georgia.................. | 24,839 | 31,322 | 39,319 | 40,870 | 31,749 | 32,728 | 37,068 | 37,761 | 85.7 | 86.1 |
| Hawaii.................... | 25,963 | 38,367 | 47,215 | 48,905 | 33,186 | 40,089 | 44,512 | 45,185 | 105.0 | 103.1 |
| Idaho..................... | 21,965 | 29,378 | 37,473 | 38,826 | 28,076 | 30,696 | 35,328 | 35,873 | 80.4 | 81.8 |
| Illinois.................... | 28,478 | 37,798 | 47,532 | 50,157 | 36,401 | 39,494 | 44,811 | 46,342 | 103.4 | 105.7 |
| Indiana................... | 24,650 | 32,193 | 40,437 | 41,915 | 31,508 | 33,638 | 38,122 | 38,727 | 88.1 | 88.3 |
| Iowa...................... | 24,367 | 34,759 | 42,020 | 43,770 | 31,146 | 36,319 | 39,614 | 40,441 | 95.1 | 92.2 |
| Kansas................... | 24,658 | 35,737 | 43,615 | 45,171 | 31,518 | 37,341 | 41,118 | 41,735 | 97.8 | 95.2 |
| Kentucky................. | 21,842 | 30,139 | 36,219 | 37,441 | 27,918 | 31,492 | 34,145 | 34,593 | 82.5 | 78.9 |
| Louisiana................. | 21,428 | 34,566 | 39,734 | 41,487 | 27,389 | 36,117 | 37,459 | 38,332 | 94.6 | 87.4 |
| Maine.................... | 23,965 | 34,568 | 41,541 | 43,291 | 30,632 | 36,119 | 39,163 | 39,998 | 94.6 | 91.2 |
| Maryland................. | 30,111 | 44,172 | 52,939 | 54,780 | 38,488 | 46,154 | 49,908 | 50,613 | 120.9 | 115.4 |
| Massachusetts........... | 31,142 | 46,562 | 57,223 | 59,681 | 39,806 | 48,652 | 53,947 | 55,142 | 127.4 | 125.8 |
| Michigan................. | 26,191 | 32,162 | 40,730 | 42,202 | 33,477 | 33,605 | 38,398 | 38,992 | 88.0 | 88.9 |
| Minnesota................ | 27,424 | 37,824 | 46,895 | 48,858 | 35,053 | 39,521 | 44,210 | 45,142 | 103.5 | 103.0 |
| Mississippi............... | 19,609 | 28,636 | 33,504 | 34,949 | 25,064 | 29,921 | 31,586 | 32,291 | 78.3 | 73.7 |
| Missouri.................. | 24,459 | 33,518 | 39,963 | 41,589 | 31,264 | 35,022 | 37,675 | 38,426 | 91.7 | 87.6 |
| Montana.................. | 20,490 | 32,838 | 40,448 | 42,341 | 26,190 | 34,312 | 38,132 | 39,121 | 89.8 | 89.2 |
| Nebraska................. | 25,576 | 37,311 | 45,591 | 46,879 | 32,691 | 38,985 | 42,981 | 43,313 | 102.1 | 98.8 |
| Nevada................... | 27,874 | 34,355 | 41,418 | 43,102 | 35,629 | 35,897 | 39,047 | 39,824 | 94.0 | 90.8 |
| New Hampshire.......... | 30,720 | 43,472 | 53,049 | 55,165 | 39,266 | 45,423 | 50,012 | 50,969 | 118.9 | 116.3 |
| New Jersey.............. | 32,954 | 45,528 | 56,462 | 58,760 | 42,122 | 47,571 | 53,229 | 54,291 | 124.6 | 123.8 |
| New Mexico.............. | 20,694 | 31,022 | 36,187 | 37,655 | 26,451 | 32,414 | 34,115 | 34,791 | 84.9 | 79.4 |
| New York................. | 30,019 | 42,472 | 55,114 | 58,256 | 38,370 | 44,378 | 51,959 | 53,825 | 116.2 | 122.8 |
| North Carolina........... | 23,778 | 32,354 | 39,181 | 40,779 | 30,393 | 33,806 | 36,938 | 37,677 | 88.5 | 85.9 |
| North Dakota............. | 23,662 | 39,820 | 47,006 | 49,056 | 30,245 | 41,607 | 44,315 | 45,325 | 108.9 | 103.4 |
| Ohio...................... | 24,735 | 33,124 | 41,541 | 43,093 | 31,616 | 34,611 | 39,163 | 39,815 | 90.6 | 90.8 |
| Oklahoma................ | 21,233 | 33,580 | 40,264 | 42,011 | 27,140 | 35,087 | 37,959 | 38,816 | 91.9 | 88.5 |
| Oregon................... | 24,312 | 32,357 | 41,687 | 43,460 | 31,076 | 33,809 | 39,300 | 40,154 | 88.5 | 91.6 |
| Pennsylvania............. | 26,356 | 37,812 | 47,069 | 49,042 | 33,688 | 39,509 | 44,374 | 45,312 | 103.5 | 103.4 |
| Rhode Island............. | 26,267 | 38,860 | 46,872 | 48,577 | 33,574 | 40,604 | 44,188 | 44,882 | 106.3 | 102.4 |
| South Carolina........... | 22,205 | 29,840 | 37,341 | 38,487 | 28,382 | 31,179 | 35,203 | 35,560 | 81.6 | 81.1 |
| South Dakota............. | 24,331 | 38,320 | 44,131 | 45,731 | 31,100 | 40,040 | 41,604 | 42,253 | 104.8 | 96.4 |
| Tennessee............... | 24,577 | 33,485 | 41,581 | 43,218 | 31,414 | 34,988 | 39,200 | 39,931 | 91.6 | 91.1 |
| Texas.................... | 24,793 | 35,224 | 42,879 | 44,720 | 31,690 | 36,805 | 40,424 | 41,319 | 96.4 | 94.2 |
| Utah...................... | 21,458 | 29,374 | 38,469 | 40,291 | 27,428 | 30,692 | 36,267 | 37,227 | 80.4 | 84.9 |
| Vermont.................. | 25,239 | 37,750 | 46,716 | 48,206 | 32,260 | 39,444 | 44,041 | 44,540 | 103.3 | 101.6 |
| Virginia................... | 27,783 | 40,530 | 48,048 | 49,886 | 35,512 | 42,349 | 45,297 | 46,092 | 110.9 | 105.1 |
| Washington............... | 28,392 | 39,083 | 51,222 | 54,103 | 36,291 | 40,837 | 48,289 | 49,988 | 106.9 | 114.0 |
| West Virginia............. | 20,014 | 29,640 | 34,829 | 36,805 | 25,582 | 30,970 | 32,835 | 34,006 | 81.1 | 77.6 |
| Wisconsin................ | 25,502 | 35,231 | 43,169 | 44,953 | 32,597 | 36,812 | 40,697 | 41,534 | 96.4 | 94.7 |
| Wyoming................. | 25,402 | 41,861 | 51,944 | 54,657 | 32,469 | 43,740 | 48,970 | 50,500 | 114.5 | 115.2 |

P Preliminary. [1] Constant dollar estimates are computed by ProQuest using the national implicit price deflator for personal consumption expenditures from the Bureau of Economic Analysis' National Income and Product Accounts Tables. Any regional differences in the rate of inflation are not reflected in these constant dollar estimates. [2] Indexes calculated using disposable personal income per capita in current dollars.

Source: Except as noted, U.S. Bureau of Economic Analysis, Regional Economic Accounts, Personal Income by State, Interactive Data, "Table SAINC51 Disposable Personal Income Summary," <https://www.bea.gov/data/economic-accounts/regional>, accessed March 2019.

# Table 713. Personal Income by Selected Large Metropolitan Area: 2001 to 2017

[7,936,326 represents $7,936,326,000,000. MSA=Metropolitan Statistical Area. The MSAs used by the Bureau of Economic Analysis are defined in the Office of Management and Budget Bulletin No. 18-03, issued April 10, 2018. Per capita personal income was computed using Census Bureau midyear population estimates. Estimates for 2010-2017 reflect county population estimates available as of March 2018]

| Metropolitan statistical areas ranked by 2017 population | Personal income | | | Personal income per capita | | | Index (U.S.= 100), 2017 |
|---|---|---|---|---|---|---|---|
| | 2001 (mil. dol.) | 2010 (mil. dol.) | 2017 (mil. dol.) | 2001 (dol.) | 2010 (dol.) | 2017 (dol.) | |
| United States, metro portion.................. | 7,936,326 | 11,060,411 | 15,002,534 | 33,031 | 42,024 | 53,617 | 100.0 |
| New York-Newark-Jersey City, NY-NJ-PA MSA..... | 801,530 | 1,064,877 | 1,443,163 | 41,945 | 54,322 | 71,019 | 132.5 |
| Los Angeles-Long Beach-Anaheim, CA MSA........ | 411,089 | 578,118 | 802,394 | 32,857 | 45,019 | 60,087 | 112.1 |
| Chicago-Naperville-Elgin, IL-IN-WI MSA............. | 339,345 | 418,599 | 555,922 | 37,008 | 44,196 | 58,315 | 108.8 |
| Dallas-Fort Worth-Arlington, TX MSA................ | 183,848 | 264,557 | 392,146 | 34,195 | 41,005 | 52,995 | 98.8 |
| Houston-The Woodlands-Sugar Land, TX MSA..... | 164,766 | 267,817 | 363,677 | 34,199 | 45,031 | 52,765 | 98.4 |
| Washington-Arlington-Alexandria, DC-VA-MD-WV MSA................ | 217,441 | 330,571 | 432,558 | 43,748 | 58,345 | 69,581 | 129.8 |
| Miami-Fort Lauderdale-West Palm Beach, FL MSA.................. | 170,916 | 239,772 | 330,929 | 33,442 | 42,940 | 53,732 | 100.2 |
| Philadelphia-Camden-Wilmington, PA-NJ-DE-MD MSA................ | 209,871 | 287,193 | 377,223 | 36,730 | 48,096 | 61,879 | 115.4 |
| Atlanta-Sandy Springs-Roswell, GA MSA.......... | 153,395 | 203,544 | 292,221 | 34,843 | 38,380 | 49,657 | 92.6 |
| Boston-Cambridge-Newton, MA-NH MSA.......... | 193,272 | 265,319 | 358,021 | 43,607 | 58,117 | 74,024 | 138.1 |
| Phoenix-Mesa-Scottsdale, AZ MSA.............. | 96,749 | 146,616 | 208,896 | 28,762 | 34,874 | 44,096 | 82.2 |
| San Francisco-Oakland-Hayward, CA MSA........ | 207,254 | 265,878 | 432,360 | 49,644 | 61,194 | 91,459 | 170.6 |
| Riverside-San Bernardino-Ontario, CA MSA....... | 83,354 | 127,901 | 178,883 | 24,680 | 30,142 | 39,052 | 72.8 |
| Detroit-Warren-Dearborn, MI MSA................. | 155,389 | 162,618 | 219,372 | 34,826 | 37,895 | 50,863 | 94.9 |
| Seattle-Tacoma-Bellevue, WA MSA............... | 120,829 | 167,668 | 267,654 | 39,066 | 48,627 | 69,214 | 129.1 |
| Minneapolis-St. Paul-Bloomington, MN-WI MSA.... | 116,048 | 154,445 | 215,087 | 37,597 | 46,032 | 59,736 | 111.4 |
| San Diego-Carlsbad, CA MSA.................... | 98,574 | 136,919 | 193,296 | 34,350 | 44,113 | 57,913 | 108.0 |
| Tampa-St. Petersburg-Clearwater, FL MSA......... | 72,566 | 107,213 | 139,319 | 29,691 | 38,448 | 45,067 | 84.1 |
| Denver-Aurora-Lakewood, CO MSA................. | 85,941 | 111,189 | 172,311 | 38,734 | 43,528 | 59,660 | 111.3 |
| Baltimore-Columbia-Towson, MD MSA............. | 92,278 | 131,922 | 167,921 | 35,830 | 48,581 | 59,797 | 111.5 |
| St. Louis, MO-IL MSA............................ | 88,244 | 118,255 | 147,100 | 32,803 | 42,387 | 52,398 | 97.7 |
| Charlotte-Concord-Gastonia, NC-SC MSA........ | 52,022 | 86,143 | 125,654 | 29,400 | 38,747 | 49,758 | 92.8 |
| Orlando-Kissimmee-Sanford, FL MSA............. | 47,026 | 71,183 | 104,107 | 27,495 | 33,274 | 41,480 | 77.4 |
| San Antonio-New Braunfels, TX MSA............. | 48,316 | 77,285 | 110,855 | 27,639 | 35,897 | 44,808 | 83.6 |
| Portland-Vancouver-Hillsboro, OR-WA MSA........ | 63,930 | 88,949 | 131,861 | 32,433 | 39,854 | 53,751 | 100.2 |
| Pittsburgh, PA MSA.............................. | 76,711 | 100,906 | 125,649 | 31,732 | 42,812 | 53,849 | 100.4 |
| Sacramento-Roseville-Arden Arcade, CA MSA..... | 62,332 | 88,560 | 125,039 | 33,398 | 41,116 | 53,783 | 100.3 |
| Las Vegas-Henderson-Paradise, NV MSA.......... | 46,367 | 70,001 | 97,457 | 31,747 | 35,845 | 44,217 | 82.5 |
| Cincinnati, OH-KY-IN MSA......................... | 64,880 | 85,716 | 112,302 | 32,243 | 40,475 | 51,536 | 96.1 |
| Kansas City, MO-KS MSA......................... | 58,612 | 82,558 | 108,374 | 31,897 | 41,004 | 50,906 | 94.9 |
| Austin-Round Rock, TX MSA....................... | 46,277 | 70,429 | 115,982 | 35,023 | 40,769 | 54,817 | 102.2 |
| Columbus, OH MSA............................... | 53,173 | 73,623 | 103,195 | 31,154 | 38,620 | 49,644 | 92.6 |
| Cleveland-Elyria, OH MSA......................... | 68,537 | 82,445 | 106,555 | 32,000 | 39,722 | 51,755 | 96.5 |
| Indianapolis-Carmel-Anderson, IN MSA............ | 56,383 | 78,042 | 106,415 | 33,418 | 41,238 | 52,457 | 97.8 |
| San Jose-Sunnyvale-Santa Clara, CA MSA......... | 88,366 | 111,488 | 193,098 | 50,706 | 60,523 | 96,623 | 180.2 |
| Nashville-Davidson-Murfreesboro-Franklin, TN MSA.................. | 45,400 | 69,922 | 106,464 | 32,217 | 41,725 | 55,944 | 104.3 |
| Virginia Beach-Norfolk-Newport News, VA-NC MSA.................. | 46,633 | 68,179 | 83,678 | 29,265 | 40,584 | 48,502 | 90.5 |
| Providence-Warwick, RI-MA MSA.................. | 50,148 | 67,519 | 84,737 | 31,432 | 42,137 | 52,271 | 97.5 |
| Milwaukee-Waukesha-West Allis, WI MSA.......... | 53,265 | 67,891 | 85,032 | 35,339 | 43,613 | 53,946 | 100.6 |
| Jacksonville, FL MSA............................. | 35,252 | 52,262 | 71,707 | 30,704 | 38,744 | 47,647 | 88.9 |
| Oklahoma City, OK MSA........................... | 31,427 | 48,669 | 65,170 | 28,342 | 38,695 | 47,097 | 87.8 |
| Memphis, TN-MS-AR MSA......................... | 38,104 | 49,047 | 60,614 | 31,115 | 36,981 | 44,958 | 83.9 |
| Raleigh, NC MSA................................. | 29,536 | 48,592 | 70,016 | 35,453 | 42,722 | 52,444 | 97.8 |
| Richmond, VA MSA............................... | 36,460 | 51,651 | 70,660 | 34,048 | 42,686 | 54,597 | 101.8 |
| Louisville/Jefferson County, KY-IN MSA............. | 34,769 | 46,460 | 61,197 | 30,709 | 37,541 | 47,294 | 88.2 |
| New Orleans-Metairie, LA MSA..................... | 38,815 | 50,719 | 62,683 | 28,869 | 42,426 | 49,134 | 91.6 |
| Hartford-West Hartford-East Hartford, CT MSA..... | 45,254 | 61,539 | 74,253 | 39,062 | 50,677 | 61,353 | 114.4 |
| Salt Lake City, UT MSA........................... | 26,725 | 39,391 | 58,525 | 28,011 | 36,090 | 48,645 | 90.7 |
| Birmingham-Hoover, AL MSA....................... | 31,467 | 44,042 | 55,312 | 29,712 | 39,017 | 48,105 | 89.7 |
| Buffalo-Cheektowaga-Niagara Falls, NY MSA....... | 32,981 | 44,089 | 54,926 | 28,308 | 38,820 | 48,314 | 90.1 |
| Rochester, NY MSA............................... | 32,655 | 42,862 | 52,968 | 30,570 | 39,677 | 49,138 | 91.6 |
| Grand Rapids-Wyoming, MI MSA................... | 28,677 | 36,096 | 51,538 | 30,361 | 36,482 | 48,661 | 90.8 |
| Tucson, AZ MSA................................. | 22,709 | 33,359 | 42,585 | 26,428 | 33,986 | 41,637 | 77.7 |
| Tulsa, OK MSA.................................. | 23,940 | 38,834 | 51,359 | 27,593 | 41,322 | 51,841 | 96.7 |
| Fresno, CA MSA................................. | 19,280 | 29,562 | 41,024 | 23,714 | 31,711 | 41,470 | 77.3 |
| Honolulu, HI MSA................................ | 28,738 | 43,342 | 56,084 | 32,555 | 45,328 | 56,728 | 105.8 |
| Bridgeport-Stamford-Norwalk, CT MSA............. | 59,025 | 95,622 | 104,590 | 66,390 | 103,965 | 110,104 | 205.4 |
| Worcester, MA-CT MSA........................... | 28,941 | 39,450 | 50,647 | 33,224 | 42,932 | 53,738 | 100.2 |
| Omaha-Council Bluffs, NE-IA MSA.................. | 26,241 | 38,935 | 50,973 | 33,808 | 44,853 | 54,615 | 101.9 |
| Albuquerque, NM MSA............................ | 20,600 | 30,640 | 37,209 | 27,766 | 34,443 | 40,856 | 76.2 |

Source: U.S. Bureau of Economic Analysis, Regional Economic Accounts, Personal Income by County, Metro, and Other Areas, "Table MAINC1 Personal Income Summary," <https://www.bea.gov/data/economic-accounts/regional>, accessed February 2019.

# Table 714. Households by Income Level and Median Income by State: 2017

[In thousands (120,063 represents 120,063,000), except as indicated. The American Community Survey universe includes the household population and the population living in institutions, college dormitories, and other group quarters. Based on a sample and subject to sampling variability; see text, Section 1 and Appendix III. For definition of median, see Guide to Tabular Presentation]

| State | Number of households (1,000) | | | | | | | | Median income (dollars) |
|---|---|---|---|---|---|---|---|---|---|
| | Total | Under $25,000 | $25,000 to $49,999 | $50,000 to $74,999 | $75,000 to $99,999 | $100,000 to $149,999 | $150,000 to $199,999 | $200,000 or more | |
| **United States........** | **120,063** | **24,400** | **26,131** | **21,128** | **15,031** | **17,528** | **7,520** | **8,325** | **60,336** |
| Alabama............... | 1,842 | 503 | 443 | 325 | 207 | 225 | 72 | 67 | 48,123 |
| Alaska................. | 251 | 35 | 46 | 47 | 34 | 49 | 21 | 18 | 73,181 |
| Arizona................ | 2,553 | 527 | 602 | 477 | 323 | 355 | 132 | 137 | 56,581 |
| Arkansas.............. | 1,153 | 312 | 307 | 210 | 126 | 118 | 46 | 34 | 45,869 |
| California.............. | 13,005 | 2,248 | 2,405 | 2,076 | 1,603 | 2,136 | 1,097 | 1,441 | 71,805 |
| Colorado............... | 2,139 | 331 | 435 | 383 | 291 | 368 | 163 | 168 | 69,117 |
| Connecticut............ | 1,357 | 213 | 252 | 219 | 171 | 230 | 118 | 154 | 74,168 |
| Delaware.............. | 358 | 68 | 75 | 64 | 48 | 52 | 26 | 24 | 62,852 |
| District of Columbia. .. | 281 | 58 | 36 | 36 | 31 | 46 | 26 | 47 | 82,372 |
| Florida................. | 7,690 | 1,704 | 1,922 | 1,416 | 925 | 940 | 368 | 414 | 52,594 |
| Georgia................ | 3,745 | 810 | 867 | 673 | 466 | 507 | 205 | 216 | 56,183 |
| Hawaii................. | 458 | 70 | 78 | 74 | 68 | 85 | 42 | 42 | 77,765 |
| Idaho.................. | 625 | 129 | 165 | 128 | 79 | 79 | 25 | 20 | 52,225 |
| Illinois................. | 4,809 | 947 | 973 | 839 | 618 | 742 | 330 | 359 | 62,992 |
| Indiana................ | 2,557 | 549 | 623 | 492 | 338 | 339 | 115 | 100 | 54,181 |
| Iowa................... | 1,258 | 243 | 295 | 242 | 176 | 188 | 63 | 51 | 58,570 |
| Kansas................ | 1,129 | 222 | 277 | 218 | 146 | 159 | 54 | 52 | 56,422 |
| Kentucky.............. | 1,725 | 457 | 429 | 300 | 203 | 208 | 66 | 62 | 48,375 |
| Louisiana.............. | 1,737 | 510 | 411 | 285 | 181 | 207 | 74 | 70 | 46,145 |
| Maine.................. | 541 | 116 | 126 | 104 | 73 | 75 | 25 | 22 | 56,277 |
| Maryland............... | 2,207 | 304 | 377 | 353 | 287 | 415 | 222 | 249 | 80,776 |
| Massachusetts......... | 2,605 | 457 | 436 | 373 | 311 | 459 | 250 | 318 | 77,385 |
| Michigan............... | 3,930 | 842 | 951 | 724 | 492 | 532 | 202 | 188 | 54,909 |
| Minnesota............. | 2,162 | 340 | 436 | 400 | 302 | 370 | 158 | 155 | 68,388 |
| Mississippi............ | 1,092 | 333 | 272 | 190 | 124 | 110 | 35 | 29 | 43,529 |
| Missouri............... | 2,385 | 523 | 586 | 453 | 302 | 309 | 111 | 101 | 53,578 |
| Montana............... | 423 | 93 | 105 | 82 | 53 | 56 | 20 | 15 | 53,386 |
| Nebraska.............. | 754 | 137 | 177 | 151 | 106 | 111 | 39 | 33 | 59,970 |
| Nevada................ | 1,095 | 207 | 258 | 219 | 145 | 157 | 57 | 52 | 58,003 |
| New Hampshire....... | 529 | 79 | 98 | 93 | 74 | 97 | 44 | 44 | 73,381 |
| New Jersey............ | 3,219 | 505 | 535 | 481 | 400 | 569 | 310 | 419 | 80,088 |
| New Mexico........... | 768 | 208 | 197 | 133 | 83 | 90 | 32 | 26 | 46,744 |
| New York.............. | 7,304 | 1,527 | 1,386 | 1,149 | 866 | 1,102 | 555 | 718 | 64,894 |
| North Carolina........ | 3,955 | 902 | 967 | 726 | 476 | 495 | 196 | 193 | 52,752 |
| North Dakota.......... | 316 | 60 | 67 | 58 | 47 | 49 | 18 | 16 | 61,843 |
| Ohio................... | 4,667 | 1,036 | 1,124 | 862 | 596 | 626 | 222 | 201 | 54,021 |
| Oklahoma.............. | 1,470 | 359 | 375 | 272 | 178 | 174 | 60 | 53 | 50,061 |
| Oregon................ | 1,604 | 316 | 354 | 300 | 212 | 235 | 96 | 91 | 60,212 |
| Pennsylvania.......... | 5,009 | 1,066 | 1,080 | 898 | 645 | 723 | 292 | 304 | 59,195 |
| Rhode Island.......... | 409 | 88 | 78 | 67 | 54 | 67 | 28 | 27 | 63,870 |
| South Carolina........ | 1,905 | 466 | 475 | 351 | 224 | 227 | 82 | 80 | 50,570 |
| South Dakota.......... | 344 | 71 | 82 | 66 | 48 | 49 | 15 | 13 | 56,521 |
| Tennessee............. | 2,589 | 612 | 646 | 491 | 305 | 312 | 107 | 114 | 51,340 |
| Texas................. | 9,624 | 1,953 | 2,148 | 1,726 | 1,179 | 1,398 | 585 | 635 | 59,206 |
| Utah................... | 975 | 138 | 199 | 200 | 145 | 174 | 63 | 56 | 68,358 |
| Vermont............... | 257 | 53 | 58 | 50 | 35 | 37 | 11 | 13 | 57,513 |
| Virginia................ | 3,121 | 512 | 581 | 528 | 413 | 518 | 260 | 309 | 71,535 |
| Washington............ | 2,840 | 452 | 542 | 503 | 387 | 495 | 220 | 242 | 70,979 |
| West Virginia.......... | 715 | 216 | 178 | 129 | 78 | 72 | 24 | 19 | 43,469 |
| Wisconsin............. | 2,350 | 452 | 545 | 448 | 327 | 349 | 126 | 103 | 59,305 |
| Wyoming.............. | 226 | 43 | 50 | 43 | 32 | 38 | 11 | 8 | 60,434 |
| Puerto Rico........... | 1,191 | 710 | 273 | 116 | 45 | 30 | 7 | 10 | 19,343 |

Source: U.S. Census Bureau, 2017 American Community Survey, B19001, "Household Income in the Past 12 Months (In 2017 Inflation-Adjusted Dollars)"; and B19013, "Median Household Income in the Past 12 Months (In 2017 Inflation-Adjusted Dollars)"; <http://factfinder.census.gov/>, accessed November 2018.

# Table 715. Families by Income Level and Median Income by State: 2017

[In thousands (78,631 represents 78,631,000), except as indicated. The American Community Survey universe includes the household population and the population living in institutions, college dormitories, and other group quarters. Based on a sample and subject to sampling variability; see text, Section 1 and Appendix III. For definition of median, see Guide to Tabular Presentation]

| State | Number of families (1,000) | | | | | | | | Median income (dollars) |
|---|---|---|---|---|---|---|---|---|---|
| | Total | Less than $25,000 | $25,000 to $49,999 | $50,000 to $74,999 | $75,000 to $99,999 | $100,000 to $149,999 | $150,000 to $199,999 | $200,000 and over | |
| United States........ | 78,631 | 10,178 | 15,432 | 14,234 | 11,255 | 14,104 | 6,321 | 7,106 | 73,891 |
| Alabama.............. | 1,204 | 212 | 273 | 234 | 168 | 193 | 64 | 60 | 61,512 |
| Alaska................ | 167 | 16 | 26 | 31 | 24 | 38 | 18 | 15 | 86,831 |
| Arizona.............. | 1,652 | 230 | 354 | 325 | 239 | 282 | 108 | 113 | 67,886 |
| Arkansas............ | 755 | 124 | 199 | 154 | 105 | 100 | 41 | 31 | 57,421 |
| California............ | 8,911 | 1,104 | 1,577 | 1,416 | 1,140 | 1,621 | 874 | 1,179 | 82,009 |
| Colorado............ | 1,367 | 123 | 233 | 237 | 210 | 285 | 136 | 143 | 84,918 |
| Connecticut.......... | 877 | 78 | 136 | 129 | 121 | 181 | 97 | 135 | 93,870 |
| Delaware............ | 236 | 28 | 43 | 43 | 35 | 42 | 22 | 21 | 77,082 |
| District of Columbia. .. | 119 | 20 | 13 | 11 | 12 | 19 | 14 | 31 | 106,528 |
| Florida.............. | 4,944 | 723 | 1,171 | 953 | 695 | 752 | 304 | 346 | 64,003 |
| Georgia.............. | 2,526 | 380 | 534 | 468 | 355 | 422 | 178 | 189 | 67,983 |
| Hawaii............... | 320 | 30 | 45 | 50 | 52 | 72 | 37 | 34 | 91,460 |
| Idaho................ | 420 | 48 | 103 | 96 | 66 | 66 | 22 | 19 | 64,178 |
| Illinois.............. | 3,084 | 370 | 551 | 542 | 447 | 588 | 278 | 308 | 79,168 |
| Indiana.............. | 1,660 | 214 | 352 | 351 | 265 | 287 | 103 | 88 | 68,085 |
| Iowa................. | 795 | 82 | 156 | 160 | 137 | 159 | 56 | 46 | 75,076 |
| Kansas.............. | 734 | 78 | 155 | 152 | 115 | 139 | 49 | 47 | 72,057 |
| Kentucky............ | 1,130 | 197 | 257 | 218 | 162 | 180 | 60 | 55 | 61,593 |
| Louisiana............ | 1,107 | 223 | 247 | 193 | 139 | 176 | 66 | 63 | 60,510 |
| Maine................ | 330 | 34 | 70 | 68 | 56 | 62 | 22 | 18 | 72,177 |
| Maryland............ | 1,470 | 122 | 214 | 210 | 201 | 318 | 185 | 220 | 98,393 |
| Massachusetts....... | 1,652 | 165 | 233 | 224 | 212 | 345 | 204 | 268 | 98,758 |
| Michigan............ | 2,518 | 332 | 528 | 493 | 381 | 442 | 176 | 164 | 69,664 |
| Minnesota........... | 1,389 | 109 | 227 | 249 | 220 | 310 | 135 | 137 | 86,416 |
| Mississippi.......... | 716 | 147 | 173 | 144 | 101 | 95 | 32 | 26 | 55,937 |
| Missouri............. | 1,527 | 205 | 335 | 306 | 233 | 263 | 95 | 89 | 67,317 |
| Montana............. | 263 | 31 | 58 | 54 | 42 | 48 | 17 | 13 | 68,994 |
| Nebraska............ | 485 | 48 | 95 | 99 | 83 | 95 | 35 | 30 | 75,112 |
| Nevada.............. | 700 | 87 | 149 | 147 | 108 | 121 | 46 | 42 | 68,276 |
| New Hampshire....... | 346 | 28 | 50 | 60 | 53 | 80 | 38 | 37 | 91,029 |
| New Jersey........... | 2,235 | 218 | 322 | 314 | 291 | 457 | 261 | 373 | 97,300 |
| New Mexico.......... | 479 | 92 | 113 | 91 | 62 | 73 | 26 | 22 | 58,308 |
| New York............ | 4,620 | 628 | 813 | 736 | 605 | 824 | 438 | 577 | 80,114 |
| North Carolina....... | 2,590 | 383 | 574 | 502 | 373 | 418 | 168 | 173 | 65,964 |
| North Dakota......... | 190 | 18 | 29 | 37 | 35 | 42 | 16 | 14 | 81,869 |
| Ohio................. | 2,951 | 397 | 624 | 575 | 456 | 527 | 194 | 177 | 69,632 |
| Oklahoma............ | 964 | 151 | 231 | 194 | 142 | 146 | 53 | 47 | 61,471 |
| Oregon.............. | 1,011 | 119 | 200 | 198 | 155 | 185 | 78 | 75 | 73,202 |
| Pennsylvania........ | 3,177 | 364 | 599 | 603 | 495 | 592 | 255 | 268 | 75,949 |
| Rhode Island......... | 252 | 29 | 41 | 42 | 38 | 55 | 25 | 23 | 84,557 |
| South Carolina........ | 1,253 | 200 | 292 | 246 | 177 | 194 | 73 | 70 | 62,432 |
| South Dakota......... | 213 | 27 | 38 | 44 | 38 | 41 | 13 | 11 | 73,236 |
| Tennessee........... | 1,707 | 262 | 392 | 349 | 242 | 265 | 97 | 100 | 62,926 |
| Texas................ | 6,696 | 969 | 1,391 | 1,210 | 911 | 1,151 | 505 | 559 | 70,136 |
| Utah................. | 723 | 62 | 129 | 152 | 123 | 151 | 56 | 50 | 77,940 |
| Vermont............. | 154 | 18 | 29 | 31 | 25 | 30 | 10 | 11 | 74,426 |
| Virginia............. | 2,091 | 211 | 339 | 349 | 298 | 406 | 219 | 270 | 86,279 |
| Washington.......... | 1,834 | 177 | 294 | 326 | 275 | 377 | 182 | 203 | 84,594 |
| West Virginia........ | 462 | 92 | 110 | 96 | 62 | 63 | 21 | 17 | 56,086 |
| Wisconsin........... | 1,478 | 155 | 287 | 292 | 251 | 292 | 111 | 91 | 75,413 |
| Wyoming............. | 146 | 15 | 28 | 30 | 24 | 32 | 10 | 7 | 74,868 |
| Puerto Rico.......... | 806 | 426 | 212 | 92 | 37 | 25 | 6 | 8 | 23,190 |

Source: U.S. Census Bureau, 2017 American Community Survey, B19101, "Family Income in the Past 12 Months (In 2017 Inflation-Adjusted Dollars)"; and B19113, "Median Family Income in the Past 12 Months (In 2017 Inflation-Adjusted Dollars)"; <http://factfinder.census.gov/>, accessed November 2018.

## Table 716. Average Annual Expenditures of All Consumer Units by Major Type of Expenditure: 1990 to 2017

[Consumer units in thousands (96,968 represents 96,968,000); expenditures in dollars. Based on Consumer Expenditure Survey. Data are averages for the noninstitutional population. Expenditures are direct out-of-pocket expenditures. Consumers units may be all members in a housing unit (families), a person living alone or sharing a household with others and financially independent, or 2 or more unrelated persons living together who share expenses]

| Type of expenditure | 1990 | 2000 | 2005 | 2010 | 2014 | 2015 | 2016 | 2017 |
|---|---|---|---|---|---|---|---|---|
| Number of consumer units (1,000)............ | 96,968 | 109,367 | 117,356 | 121,107 | 127,006 | 128,437 | 129,549 | 130,001 |
| **Expenditures, avg. (dol.)** [1]................. | **28,381** | **38,045** | **46,409** | **48,109** | **53,495** | **55,978** | **57,311** | **60,060** |
| Food........................................... | 4,296 | 5,158 | 5,931 | 6,129 | 6,759 | 7,023 | 7,203 | 7,729 |
| Food at home [1]........................... | 2,485 | 3,021 | 3,297 | 3,624 | 3,971 | 4,015 | 4,049 | 4,363 |
| Cereals and bakery products............. | 368 | 453 | 445 | 502 | 519 | 518 | 524 | 564 |
| Meats, poultry, fish, and eggs........... | 668 | 795 | 764 | 784 | 892 | 896 | 890 | 944 |
| Dairy products........................... | 295 | 325 | 378 | 380 | 423 | 413 | 410 | 450 |
| Fruits and vegetables.................... | 408 | 521 | 552 | 679 | 756 | 769 | 783 | 837 |
| Other food at home...................... | 746 | 927 | 1,158 | 1,278 | 1,382 | 1,419 | 1,442 | 1,568 |
| Food away from home........................ | 1,811 | 2,137 | 2,634 | 2,505 | 2,787 | 3,008 | 3,154 | 3,365 |
| Alcoholic beverages.......................... | 293 | 372 | 426 | 412 | 463 | 515 | 484 | 558 |
| Housing [1]................................... | 8,703 | 12,319 | 15,167 | 16,557 | 17,798 | 18,409 | 18,886 | 19,884 |
| Shelter.................................... | 4,836 | 7,114 | 8,805 | 9,812 | 10,491 | 10,742 | 11,128 | 11,895 |
| Utilities, fuels, and public services............ | 1,890 | 2,489 | 3,183 | 3,660 | 3,921 | 3,885 | 3,884 | 3,836 |
| Apparel and services........................ | 1,618 | 1,856 | 1,886 | 1,700 | 1,786 | 1,846 | 1,803 | 1,833 |
| Transportation [1]........................... | 5,120 | 7,417 | 8,344 | 7,677 | 9,073 | 9,503 | 9,049 | 9,576 |
| Vehicle purchases........................ | 2,129 | 3,418 | 3,544 | 2,588 | 3,301 | 3,997 | 3,634 | 4,054 |
| Gasoline and motor oil.................... | 1,047 | 1,291 | 2,013 | 2,132 | 2,468 | 2,090 | 1,909 | 1,968 |
| Other vehicle expenses................... | 1,642 | 2,281 | 2,339 | 2,464 | 2,723 | 2,756 | 2,884 | 2,842 |
| Public transportation..................... | 302 | 427 | 448 | 493 | 581 | 661 | 623 | 712 |
| Health care [2]............................... | 1,480 | 2,066 | 2,664 | 3,157 | 4,290 | 4,342 | 4,612 | 4,928 |
| Entertainment............................... | 1,422 | 1,863 | 2,388 | 2,504 | 2,728 | 2,842 | 2,913 | 3,203 |
| Personal care products and services........... | 364 | 564 | 541 | 582 | 645 | 683 | 707 | 762 |
| Reading...................................... | 153 | 146 | 126 | 100 | 103 | 114 | 118 | 110 |
| Education.................................... | 406 | 632 | 940 | 1,074 | 1,236 | 1,315 | 1,329 | 1,491 |
| Tobacco products, smoking supplies........... | 274 | 319 | 319 | 362 | 319 | 349 | 337 | 332 |
| Personal insurance and pensions.............. | 2,592 | 3,365 | 5,204 | 5,373 | 5,726 | 6,349 | 6,831 | 6,771 |
| Life and other personal insurance............ | 345 | 399 | 381 | 318 | 327 | 333 | 322 | 418 |
| Pensions and Social Security................. | 2,248 | 2,966 | 4,823 | 5,054 | 5,399 | 6,016 | 6,509 | 6,353 |

[1] Includes expenditures not shown separately. [2] Due to changes implemented with the 2014 questionnaire on health insurance, 2014 and subsequent data are not directly comparable to data from previous years.

Source: U.S. Bureau of Labor Statistics, Consumer Expenditure Survey program, "Annual Calendar Year Tables, 2017," <http://www.bls.gov/cex/tables.htm>, accessed December 2018; and previous releases.

## Table 717. Average Annual Expenditures of All Consumer Units by Metropolitan Statistical Area: 2016 to 2017

[In dollars. Covers 2-year period, 2016 to 2017. MSA = Metropolitan Statistical Area. See text, Section 1 and Appendix II. See headnote, Table 716]

| Metropolitan statistical area | Total expenditures [1] | Food | Housing Total [1] | Housing Shelter | Housing Utility, fuels [2] | Transportation Total [1] | Transportation Vehicle purchases | Transportation Gasoline and motor oil | Health care |
|---|---|---|---|---|---|---|---|---|---|
| Anchorage, Alaska............................ | 71,606 | 8,306 | 23,039 | 14,231 | 4,590 | 12,446 | 5,850 | 2,307 | 4,557 |
| Atlanta, Georgia............................. | 62,250 | 6,683 | 20,965 | 12,346 | 4,363 | 11,747 | 5,287 | 2,494 | 4,447 |
| Baltimore, Maryland.......................... | 69,126 | 8,964 | 23,247 | 14,800 | 4,021 | 11,049 | 5,491 | 2,117 | 4,926 |
| Boston, Massachusetts....................... | 74,316 | 8,264 | 29,015 | 18,887 | 4,125 | 8,463 | 2,961 | 1,746 | 5,261 |
| Chicago, Illinois............................. | 60,582 | 8,170 | 21,254 | 13,546 | 3,755 | 7,717 | 2,850 | 1,770 | 5,154 |
| Dallas-Fort Worth, Texas..................... | 63,207 | 6,571 | 22,350 | 13,869 | 4,182 | 10,507 | 4,482 | 2,117 | 4,479 |
| Denver, Colorado............................ | 74,088 | 8,855 | 25,059 | 15,452 | 4,015 | 11,841 | 5,261 | 2,028 | 6,046 |
| Detroit, Michigan............................ | 60,183 | 7,397 | 18,794 | 10,429 | 4,131 | 10,426 | 3,409 | 1,943 | 5,079 |
| Honolulu, Hawaii............................. | 65,099 | 10,036 | 24,355 | 16,502 | 4,203 | 7,391 | [3] 1,954 | 1,794 | 3,977 |
| Houston, Texas.............................. | 67,304 | 9,153 | 21,818 | 12,823 | 4,226 | 12,232 | 5,469 | 2,241 | 4,517 |
| Los Angeles, California...................... | 66,971 | 8,727 | 24,331 | 16,454 | 3,757 | 9,741 | 3,346 | 2,601 | 3,956 |
| Miami, Florida............................... | 59,947 | 7,040 | 22,620 | 14,759 | 3,845 | 7,963 | 2,179 | 2,160 | 4,405 |
| Minneapolis-St. Paul, Minnesota............. | 70,487 | 8,571 | 22,782 | 13,901 | 3,554 | 9,409 | 3,769 | 1,976 | 6,242 |
| New York City............................... | 67,782 | 7,689 | 26,113 | 18,174 | 4,000 | 7,907 | 1,777 | 1,378 | 4,681 |
| Philadelphia, Pennsylvania................... | 65,436 | 8,203 | 20,932 | 12,413 | 4,380 | 9,505 | 3,617 | 1,843 | 5,540 |
| Phoenix, Arizona............................ | 62,072 | 6,856 | 19,491 | 10,634 | 4,071 | 9,985 | 4,430 | 1,914 | 5,328 |
| San Diego, California........................ | 79,585 | 9,984 | 28,595 | 18,677 | 3,760 | 10,592 | 3,188 | 2,432 | 5,272 |
| San Francisco, California.................... | 79,291 | 8,918 | 32,656 | 22,885 | 4,258 | 7,994 | [3] 1,904 | 1,927 | 5,013 |
| Seattle, Washington......................... | 83,790 | 10,958 | 26,965 | 17,241 | 3,964 | 12,810 | 5,363 | 2,032 | 5,546 |
| St. Louis, Missouri.......................... | 62,394 | 7,300 | 20,154 | 10,350 | 4,222 | 9,958 | 4,408 | 1,981 | 4,828 |
| Tampa, Florida.............................. | 48,654 | 6,289 | 17,131 | 10,220 | 3,365 | 8,307 | 3,697 | 1,555 | 3,782 |
| Washington, DC............................. | 79,921 | 9,188 | 29,101 | 19,571 | 4,154 | 10,748 | 4,069 | 1,894 | 5,594 |

[1] Includes expenditures not shown separately. [2] Includes public services. [3] Data are likely to have large sampling errors.

Source: U.S. Bureau of Labor Statistics, Consumer Expenditure Survey program, "Metropolitan Statistical Area Tables," <http://www.bls.gov/cex/tables.htm>, accessed December 2018.

## Table 718. Personal Consumption Expenditures—Total and Per Capita by State: 2000 to 2017

[Total in millions of current dollars (6,758,606 represents $6,758,606,000,000); per capita amounts in current dollars. Per capita data reflect Census Bureau midyear population estimates for years 2010-2017, available as of December 2017]

| State | Total personal consumption expenditures (million dollars) | | | | | Per capita personal consumption expenditures (dollars) | | | | |
|---|---|---|---|---|---|---|---|---|---|---|
| | 2000 | 2010 | 2015 | 2016 | 2017 | 2000 | 2010 | 2015 | 2016 | 2017 |
| **United States......** | **6,758,606** | **10,177,465** | **12,287,647** | **12,760,282** | **13,314,863** | **23,953** | **32,901** | **38,275** | **39,456** | **40,878** |
| Alabama............. | 87,080 | 130,834 | 149,745 | 153,457 | 158,375 | 19,559 | 27,339 | 30,870 | 31,572 | 32,489 |
| Alaska.............. | 16,578 | 27,841 | 33,504 | 34,332 | 35,537 | 26,400 | 38,992 | 45,400 | 46,299 | 48,036 |
| Arizona............. | 116,522 | 186,603 | 221,711 | 229,756 | 242,400 | 22,579 | 29,125 | 32,594 | 33,256 | 34,548 |
| Arkansas............ | 49,704 | 77,005 | 91,201 | 94,713 | 98,766 | 18,556 | 26,356 | 30,649 | 31,695 | 32,875 |
| California........... | 853,510 | 1,279,143 | 1,589,353 | 1,671,196 | 1,754,083 | 25,112 | 34,268 | 40,719 | 42,528 | 44,366 |
| Colorado............ | 117,009 | 172,803 | 214,032 | 224,732 | 236,839 | 27,042 | 34,232 | 39,341 | 40,638 | 42,239 |
| Connecticut......... | 102,017 | 149,077 | 172,445 | 176,372 | 181,992 | 29,902 | 41,640 | 47,983 | 49,160 | 50,720 |
| Delaware............ | 19,864 | 32,002 | 38,240 | 39,353 | 40,739 | 25,260 | 35,569 | 40,504 | 41,307 | 42,351 |
| Dist. of Columbia.... | 20,447 | 31,247 | 38,917 | 40,440 | 42,273 | 35,744 | 51,644 | 57,849 | 59,094 | 60,914 |
| Florida.............. | 386,622 | 609,693 | 763,109 | 794,066 | 829,402 | 24,092 | 32,351 | 37,650 | 38,441 | 39,525 |
| Georgia............. | 181,590 | 276,668 | 335,349 | 349,126 | 365,321 | 22,072 | 28,485 | 32,879 | 33,851 | 35,028 |
| Hawaii.............. | 29,315 | 48,197 | 60,117 | 62,807 | 65,768 | 24,157 | 35,340 | 42,148 | 43,961 | 46,071 |
| Idaho............... | 26,034 | 42,495 | 53,641 | 56,771 | 60,675 | 20,035 | 27,051 | 32,523 | 33,792 | 35,339 |
| Illinois.............. | 313,177 | 440,902 | 512,854 | 529,435 | 549,556 | 25,187 | 34,335 | 39,873 | 41,247 | 42,927 |
| Indiana............. | 132,488 | 190,954 | 223,375 | 231,331 | 242,041 | 21,748 | 29,423 | 33,790 | 34,870 | 36,305 |
| Iowa................ | 63,727 | 93,260 | 110,453 | 114,223 | 118,444 | 21,757 | 30,575 | 35,419 | 36,483 | 37,652 |
| Kansas.............. | 58,190 | 85,462 | 100,215 | 103,082 | 106,429 | 21,603 | 29,898 | 34,488 | 35,451 | 36,534 |
| Kentucky............ | 81,301 | 119,806 | 140,416 | 145,612 | 150,485 | 20,079 | 27,555 | 31,753 | 32,824 | 33,785 |
| Louisiana........... | 86,643 | 131,421 | 154,318 | 157,893 | 161,794 | 19,375 | 28,916 | 33,036 | 33,694 | 34,539 |
| Maine............... | 31,242 | 48,019 | 54,289 | 55,839 | 57,930 | 24,464 | 36,170 | 40,887 | 41,977 | 43,364 |
| Maryland............ | 137,125 | 214,790 | 252,958 | 262,066 | 272,556 | 25,819 | 37,109 | 42,156 | 43,498 | 45,034 |
| Massachusetts...... | 195,220 | 282,701 | 338,224 | 350,556 | 365,405 | 30,690 | 43,062 | 49,783 | 51,373 | 53,267 |
| Michigan............ | 238,774 | 313,221 | 363,927 | 377,305 | 390,895 | 23,991 | 31,713 | 36,693 | 37,983 | 39,237 |
| Minnesota........... | 135,428 | 191,103 | 230,061 | 240,189 | 252,923 | 27,450 | 35,984 | 41,957 | 43,473 | 45,354 |
| Mississippi.......... | 48,686 | 74,667 | 85,073 | 87,164 | 89,604 | 17,093 | 25,137 | 28,497 | 29,197 | 30,027 |
| Missouri............ | 131,533 | 190,110 | 221,232 | 227,513 | 236,100 | 23,457 | 31,708 | 36,431 | 37,351 | 38,619 |
| Montana............ | 18,848 | 31,759 | 39,333 | 40,840 | 43,023 | 20,855 | 32,064 | 38,250 | 39,320 | 40,955 |
| Nebraska........... | 38,744 | 59,503 | 71,168 | 74,127 | 77,111 | 22,607 | 32,516 | 37,584 | 38,859 | 40,160 |
| Nevada............. | 48,155 | 89,587 | 109,976 | 114,473 | 119,339 | 23,854 | 33,146 | 38,146 | 38,946 | 39,806 |
| New Hampshire..... | 34,807 | 54,545 | 63,087 | 64,966 | 67,496 | 28,073 | 41,425 | 47,429 | 48,663 | 50,265 |
| New Jersey......... | 242,214 | 363,204 | 422,789 | 435,617 | 449,477 | 28,730 | 41,256 | 47,186 | 48,518 | 49,911 |
| New Mexico......... | 36,477 | 58,724 | 68,838 | 70,517 | 72,447 | 20,029 | 28,443 | 33,059 | 33,814 | 34,696 |
| New York........... | 502,799 | 739,393 | 901,711 | 936,872 | 978,399 | 26,461 | 38,103 | 45,497 | 47,230 | 49,291 |
| North Carolina...... | 171,052 | 263,160 | 320,334 | 334,022 | 350,857 | 21,166 | 27,486 | 31,900 | 32,887 | 34,152 |
| North Dakota........ | 13,954 | 24,090 | 34,856 | 34,587 | 35,286 | 21,734 | 35,714 | 46,175 | 45,778 | 46,713 |
| Ohio................ | 262,645 | 365,848 | 431,733 | 443,301 | 459,381 | 23,113 | 31,705 | 37,199 | 38,141 | 39,403 |
| Oklahoma........... | 65,057 | 102,404 | 123,750 | 126,518 | 129,937 | 18,833 | 27,238 | 31,695 | 32,265 | 33,056 |
| Oregon............. | 83,046 | 123,275 | 152,837 | 160,525 | 169,046 | 24,214 | 32,127 | 38,052 | 39,287 | 40,805 |
| Pennsylvania....... | 299,506 | 448,280 | 514,867 | 529,000 | 548,321 | 24,381 | 35,267 | 40,252 | 41,370 | 42,819 |
| Rhode Island........ | 25,120 | 37,393 | 43,164 | 44,348 | 45,770 | 23,918 | 35,505 | 40,878 | 41,934 | 43,193 |
| South Carolina...... | 81,492 | 129,331 | 155,879 | 162,424 | 169,281 | 20,250 | 27,898 | 31,861 | 32,748 | 33,692 |
| South Dakota....... | 15,992 | 27,043 | 33,896 | 35,390 | 37,012 | 21,157 | 33,131 | 39,689 | 41,078 | 42,558 |
| Tennessee.......... | 123,295 | 179,916 | 214,151 | 223,278 | 234,422 | 21,617 | 28,307 | 32,493 | 33,579 | 34,905 |
| Texas.............. | 474,925 | 756,111 | 971,144 | 1,010,548 | 1,061,038 | 22,675 | 29,955 | 35,372 | 36,214 | 37,486 |
| Utah................ | 46,452 | 77,743 | 98,616 | 105,035 | 111,002 | 20,696 | 28,013 | 33,038 | 34,502 | 35,786 |
| Vermont............ | 15,405 | 23,755 | 28,340 | 28,997 | 29,839 | 25,269 | 37,957 | 45,383 | 46,518 | 47,845 |
| Virginia............. | 174,097 | 288,202 | 342,143 | 354,902 | 368,875 | 24,501 | 35,912 | 40,893 | 42,178 | 43,551 |
| Washington......... | 153,764 | 235,508 | 294,627 | 309,831 | 328,645 | 26,015 | 34,935 | 41,190 | 42,554 | 44,377 |
| West Virginia........ | 33,653 | 51,738 | 59,958 | 61,428 | 63,115 | 18,624 | 27,902 | 32,590 | 33,592 | 34,758 |
| Wisconsin........... | 126,171 | 187,741 | 218,629 | 226,219 | 235,644 | 23,478 | 32,993 | 37,958 | 39,186 | 40,660 |
| Wyoming............ | 11,111 | 19,190 | 23,060 | 23,192 | 23,773 | 22,479 | 34,003 | 39,345 | 39,650 | 41,036 |

Source: U.S. Bureau of Economic Analysis, Regional Economic Accounts, "Personal Consumption Expenditures (PCE) by State," <http://bea.gov/regional/index.htm>, accessed February 2019.

# Table 719. Average Annual Expenditures of All Consumer Units by Race, Hispanic Origin, and Age of Householder: 2017

[In dollars. See headnote, Table 716. See source for definitions, standard errors, and other information]

| Expenditure type | All consumer units [1] | White and all other races [2] | Asian | Black or African American | His-panic [3] | Age of householder: Under 25 years | Age of householder: 65 years old and over |
|---|---|---|---|---|---|---|---|
| **Expenditures, total** | **60,060** | **62,032** | **72,850** | **43,117** | **49,190** | **33,629** | **49,542** |
| Food | 7,729 | 7,995 | 9,469 | 5,422 | 7,300 | 4,759 | 6,326 |
| Food at home | 4,363 | 4,470 | 5,385 | 3,323 | 4,354 | 2,397 | 3,815 |
| Cereals and bakery products | 564 | 580 | 687 | 418 | 561 | 326 | 506 |
| Cereals and cereal products | 176 | 174 | 299 | 147 | 194 | 120 | 138 |
| Bakery products | 388 | 406 | 387 | 271 | 367 | 206 | 369 |
| Meats, poultry, fish, and eggs [4] | 944 | 938 | 1,245 | 874 | 1,069 | 532 | 800 |
| Beef | 253 | 261 | 265 | 202 | 302 | 155 | 221 |
| Pork | 181 | 182 | 217 | 165 | 188 | 87 | 163 |
| Poultry | 186 | 181 | 231 | 205 | 249 | 127 | 132 |
| Fish and seafood | 140 | 130 | 321 | 142 | 154 | 68 | 128 |
| Eggs | 55 | 54 | 85 | 52 | 69 | 40 | 44 |
| Dairy products [4] | 450 | 479 | 428 | 276 | 403 | 245 | 409 |
| Fresh milk and cream | 147 | 152 | 172 | 103 | 167 | 95 | 126 |
| Fruits and vegetables [4] | 837 | 843 | 1,315 | 629 | 908 | 457 | 756 |
| Fresh fruits | 314 | 319 | 529 | 208 | 347 | 176 | 287 |
| Fresh vegetables | 274 | 277 | 526 | 170 | 310 | 138 | 250 |
| Processed fruits | 112 | 111 | 116 | 115 | 119 | 64 | 99 |
| Other food at home [4] | 1,568 | 1,630 | 1,710 | 1,126 | 1,413 | 836 | 1,345 |
| Sugar and other sweets | 150 | 158 | 136 | 97 | 106 | 65 | 146 |
| Nonalcoholic beverages | 423 | 437 | 434 | 326 | 414 | 222 | 361 |
| Food away from home | 3,365 | 3,524 | 4,084 | 2,099 | 2,946 | 2,362 | 2,511 |
| Alcoholic beverages | 558 | 623 | 488 | 170 | 313 | 317 | 459 |
| Housing | 19,884 | 20,154 | 26,412 | 15,808 | 18,165 | 11,255 | 16,668 |
| Shelter | 11,895 | 11,918 | 17,729 | 9,613 | 11,388 | 7,553 | 9,270 |
| Owned dwellings | 6,947 | 7,248 | 10,466 | 3,808 | 4,954 | 964 | 5,950 |
| Mortgage interest and charges | 3,265 | 3,350 | 5,433 | 1,949 | 2,653 | 520 | 1,574 |
| Property taxes | 2,065 | 2,153 | 3,391 | 1,041 | 1,208 | 287 | 2,315 |
| Maintenance, repair, insurance, other expenses | 1,616 | 1,745 | 1,642 | 818 | 1,093 | 157 | 2,061 |
| Rented dwellings | 4,167 | 3,836 | 6,204 | 5,447 | 6,127 | 6,279 | 2,530 |
| Other lodging | 782 | 835 | 1,058 | 358 | 307 | 310 | 790 |
| Utilities, fuels, and public services | 3,836 | 3,900 | 3,685 | 3,497 | 3,645 | 1,853 | 3,572 |
| Natural gas | 381 | 375 | 427 | 395 | 309 | 116 | 392 |
| Electricity | 1,420 | 1,443 | 1,174 | 1,364 | 1,297 | 741 | 1,392 |
| Fuel oil and other fuels | 97 | 110 | 63 | 32 | 44 | 14 | 134 |
| Telephone | 1,356 | 1,374 | 1,347 | 1,248 | 1,421 | 771 | 1,063 |
| Water and other public services | 583 | 598 | 674 | 457 | 574 | 210 | 591 |
| Household operations | 1,412 | 1,438 | 2,082 | 1,004 | 923 | 528 | 1,235 |
| Personal services | 439 | 430 | 973 | 298 | 316 | 161 | 110 |
| Other household expenses | 973 | 1,008 | 1,108 | 706 | 607 | 367 | 1,125 |
| Housekeeping supplies [4] | 755 | 790 | 587 | 584 | 610 | 316 | 861 |
| Laundry and cleaning supplies | 177 | 179 | 128 | 184 | 187 | 96 | 163 |
| Postage and stationery | 150 | 162 | 95 | 92 | 95 | 73 | 195 |
| Household furnishings and equipment [4] | 1,987 | 2,107 | 2,330 | 1,110 | 1,599 | 1,005 | 1,729 |
| Household textiles | 114 | 118 | 182 | 65 | 85 | 55 | 126 |
| Furniture | 515 | 535 | 609 | 360 | 554 | 318 | 427 |
| Major appliances | 280 | 298 | 269 | 174 | 280 | 110 | 268 |
| Miscellaneous household equipment | 916 | 984 | 1,086 | 423 | 570 | 439 | 787 |
| Apparel and services [4] | 1,833 | 1,853 | 2,243 | 1,557 | 2,079 | 1,315 | 1,193 |
| Men and boys | 442 | 446 | 633 | 354 | 549 | 306 | 258 |
| Women and girls | 694 | 726 | 726 | 472 | 607 | 466 | 490 |
| Footwear | 379 | 369 | 404 | 436 | 541 | 331 | 211 |
| Other apparel products and services | 241 | 236 | 293 | 257 | 262 | 162 | 200 |
| Transportation | 9,576 | 9,932 | 11,031 | 6,841 | 8,173 | 6,655 | 7,513 |
| Vehicle purchases (net outlay) [4] | 4,054 | 4,286 | 4,448 | 2,484 | 3,211 | 3,366 | 2,856 |
| Cars and trucks, new | 1,900 | 1,983 | 3,523 | 794 | 1,010 | 1,289 | 1,693 |
| Cars and trucks, used | 2,101 | 2,239 | 916 | 1,687 | 2,169 | 2,053 | 1,119 |
| Gasoline and motor oil | 1,968 | 2,016 | 1,999 | 1,661 | 2,191 | 1,417 | 1,290 |
| Other vehicle expenses | 2,842 | 2,943 | 2,889 | 2,187 | 2,159 | 1,467 | 2,774 |
| Vehicle finance charges | 220 | 228 | 172 | 194 | 200 | 134 | 112 |
| Maintenance and repair | 954 | 1,012 | 793 | 650 | 779 | 471 | 1,046 |
| Vehicle insurance | 967 | 990 | 914 | 835 | 718 | 502 | 1,003 |
| Vehicle rental, leases, licenses, other charges | 700 | 713 | 1,011 | 508 | 462 | 361 | 612 |
| Public transportation | 712 | 687 | 1,695 | 509 | 612 | 405 | 594 |
| Health care | 4,928 | 5,244 | 4,658 | 3,079 | 2,946 | 1,547 | 6,620 |
| Entertainment [5] | 3,203 | 3,475 | 2,797 | 1,643 | 1,878 | 1,488 | 2,636 |
| Personal care products and services | 762 | 781 | 720 | 653 | 717 | 473 | 670 |
| Reading | 110 | 121 | 97 | 47 | 48 | 42 | 147 |
| Education | 1,491 | 1,470 | 3,314 | 953 | 897 | 2,333 | 388 |
| Tobacco products and smoking supplies | 332 | 355 | 122 | 268 | 120 | 220 | 219 |
| Miscellaneous | 1,010 | 1,081 | 835 | 638 | 606 | 358 | 1,043 |
| Cash contributions | 1,873 | 1,961 | 1,627 | 1,419 | 979 | 299 | 2,430 |
| Personal insurance and pensions | 6,771 | 6,986 | 9,035 | 4,620 | 4,968 | 2,567 | 3,230 |
| Life and other personal insurance | 418 | 433 | 411 | 327 | 190 | 42 | 467 |
| Pensions and social security | 6,353 | 6,553 | 8,624 | 4,293 | 4,778 | 2,525 | 2,762 |
| **Personal taxes** | **9,967** | **10,396** | **15,672** | **5,246** | **4,035** | **1,791** | **5,046** |

[1] Includes other races not shown separately. [2] All other races includes Native Hawaiian/Pacific Islander, Native American/Alaskan, and about 1 percent reporting more than one race. [3] People of Hispanic origin may be of any race. [4] Includes other types, not shown separately. [5] For additional recreation expenditures, see Section 26.

Source: U.S. Bureau of Labor Statistics, Consumer Expenditure Survey Program, "Annual Calendar Year Tables, 2017," <http://www.bls.gov/cex/tables.htm>, accessed December 2018.

# Table 720. Average Annual Expenditures of All Consumer Units by Region and Size of Unit: 2017

[In dollars. For composition of regions, see map, inside front cover. See headnote, Table 716. See source for definitions, standard errors, and other information]

| Expenditure type | Region | | | | Size of consumer unit | | | | |
|---|---|---|---|---|---|---|---|---|---|
| | North-east | Mid-west | South | West | One person | Two persons | Three persons | Four persons | Five or more |
| **Expenditures, total**................... | **64,016** | **57,303** | **54,815** | **68,602** | **35,960** | **64,513** | **70,927** | **80,151** | **73,421** |
| Food............................... | 8,059 | 7,249 | 7,117 | 8,982 | 4,425 | 7,865 | 9,019 | 10,995 | 10,962 |
| Food at home.................... | 4,707 | 4,100 | 3,988 | 4,987 | 2,323 | 4,417 | 5,126 | 6,194 | 6,738 |
| Cereals and bakery products............. | 629 | 530 | 516 | 628 | 289 | 548 | 665 | 835 | 943 |
| Cereals and cereal products......... | 191 | 166 | 154 | 212 | 83 | 158 | 215 | 265 | 344 |
| Bakery products.................. | 438 | 364 | 362 | 415 | 205 | 389 | 450 | 570 | 599 |
| Meats, poultry, fish, and eggs [1]........... | 1,027 | 838 | 906 | 1,045 | 469 | 956 | 1,126 | 1,343 | 1,522 |
| Beef............................. | 273 | 227 | 245 | 278 | 118 | 267 | 293 | 341 | 433 |
| Pork............................. | 161 | 168 | 185 | 203 | 83 | 190 | 206 | 266 | 294 |
| Poultry.......................... | 205 | 145 | 182 | 218 | 99 | 168 | 219 | 276 | 340 |
| Fish and seafood................. | 176 | 112 | 131 | 154 | 74 | 147 | 177 | 189 | 190 |
| Dairy products.................... | 496 | 450 | 391 | 514 | 236 | 453 | 526 | 655 | 699 |
| Fresh milk and cream............. | 167 | 137 | 136 | 159 | 76 | 135 | 178 | 225 | 253 |
| Other dairy products............. | 328 | 313 | 256 | 354 | 160 | 319 | 347 | 430 | 447 |
| Fruits and vegetables [1]............. | 952 | 741 | 736 | 1,009 | 452 | 856 | 966 | 1,217 | 1,236 |
| Fresh fruits...................... | 348 | 277 | 271 | 397 | 171 | 318 | 356 | 477 | 455 |
| Fresh vegetables................. | 332 | 235 | 231 | 341 | 147 | 289 | 328 | 372 | 396 |
| Processed fruits.................. | 127 | 102 | 98 | 133 | 63 | 111 | 126 | 167 | 174 |
| Other food at home [1].............. | 1,603 | 1,540 | 1,438 | 1,791 | 878 | 1,605 | 1,844 | 2,145 | 2,337 |
| Sugar and other sweets........... | 150 | 157 | 136 | 165 | 77 | 158 | 179 | 206 | 220 |
| Nonalcoholic beverages.......... | 418 | 414 | 418 | 443 | 256 | 434 | 505 | 536 | 603 |
| Food away from home.............. | 3,352 | 3,149 | 3,129 | 3,995 | 2,101 | 3,448 | 3,893 | 4,801 | 4,225 |
| Alcoholic beverages................ | 554 | 545 | 454 | 754 | 390 | 737 | 577 | 574 | 389 |
| Housing............................ | 22,667 | 17,797 | 17,800 | 23,271 | 13,529 | 20,354 | 23,319 | 26,051 | 23,850 |
| Shelter.......................... | 14,503 | 9,868 | 10,155 | 14,772 | 8,735 | 11,950 | 14,014 | 15,253 | 13,491 |
| Owned dwellings................. | 8,490 | 6,385 | 5,914 | 8,031 | 3,574 | 7,410 | 8,944 | 10,417 | 7,772 |
| Mortgage interest and charges.......... | 3,350 | 2,814 | 2,975 | 4,138 | 1,373 | 3,034 | 4,570 | 5,809 | 4,404 |
| Property taxes.................. | 3,503 | 2,107 | 1,388 | 2,033 | 1,168 | 2,416 | 2,333 | 2,876 | 2,031 |
| Maintenance, repair, insurance, other expenses................. | 1,636 | 1,464 | 1,551 | 1,860 | 1,033 | 1,960 | 2,041 | 1,732 | 1,338 |
| Rented dwellings................. | 4,916 | 2,752 | 3,608 | 5,906 | 4,710 | 3,503 | 4,158 | 3,978 | 5,147 |
| Other lodging................... | 1,097 | 731 | 632 | 835 | 451 | 1,037 | 912 | 859 | 571 |
| Utilities, fuels, and public services.......... | 4,003 | 3,715 | 3,805 | 3,870 | 2,353 | 3,999 | 4,492 | 5,001 | 5,142 |
| Natural gas..................... | 548 | 569 | 216 | 346 | 249 | 404 | 427 | 482 | 484 |
| Electricity....................... | 1,328 | 1,254 | 1,633 | 1,286 | 938 | 1,479 | 1,629 | 1,789 | 1,838 |
| Fuel oil and other fuels.......... | 309 | 72 | 44 | 42 | 67 | 117 | 118 | 98 | 81 |
| Telephone services.............. | 1,407 | 1,304 | 1,329 | 1,410 | 747 | 1,399 | 1,641 | 1,843 | 1,942 |
| Water and other public services........... | 412 | 515 | 584 | 786 | 352 | 600 | 677 | 788 | 798 |
| Household operations.............. | 1,451 | 1,303 | 1,354 | 1,586 | 738 | 1,276 | 1,812 | 2,549 | 1,805 |
| Personal services.............. | 462 | 448 | 442 | 406 | 68 | 132 | 792 | 1,391 | 851 |
| Other household expenses....... | 989 | 855 | 911 | 1,179 | 670 | 1,144 | 1,020 | 1,158 | 954 |
| Housekeeping supplies [1]........... | 735 | 716 | 701 | 900 | 463 | 826 | 871 | 867 | 1,042 |
| Laundry and cleaning supplies...... | 165 | 173 | 179 | 188 | 103 | 168 | 229 | 231 | 280 |
| Postage and stationery.......... | 155 | 131 | 143 | 175 | 107 | 187 | 131 | 146 | 180 |
| Household furnishings and equipment [1].... | 1,974 | 2,195 | 1,784 | 2,143 | 1,240 | 2,303 | 2,129 | 2,381 | 2,370 |
| Household textiles.............. | 95 | 123 | 117 | 116 | 75 | 137 | 117 | 115 | 144 |
| Furniture....................... | 587 | 551 | 470 | 501 | 243 | 624 | 590 | 623 | 684 |
| Major appliances............... | 266 | 283 | 264 | 317 | 134 | 320 | 325 | 389 | 366 |
| Miscellaneous household equipment...... | 889 | 1,031 | 801 | 1,023 | 685 | 1,019 | 941 | 1,079 | 995 |
| Apparel and services [1]................ | 1,951 | 1,717 | 1,675 | 2,121 | 1,007 | 1,821 | 1,941 | 2,788 | 2,956 |
| Men and boys.................... | 514 | 420 | 394 | 489 | 235 | 415 | 515 | 751 | 659 |
| Women and girls................. | 693 | 647 | 621 | 865 | 388 | 716 | 708 | 992 | 1,123 |
| Footwear........................ | 397 | 364 | 352 | 425 | 197 | 341 | 391 | 612 | 735 |
| Other apparel products and services....... | 278 | 214 | 228 | 260 | 173 | 309 | 197 | 250 | 261 |
| Transportation..................... | 8,867 | 9,548 | 9,347 | 10,570 | 5,155 | 10,170 | 11,695 | 13,230 | 12,624 |
| Vehicle purchases (net outlay) [1]............ | 3,210 | 3,843 | 4,241 | 4,619 | 1,761 | 4,401 | 5,042 | 5,800 | 5,855 |
| Cars and trucks, new............ | 1,668 | 1,512 | 2,065 | 2,179 | 832 | 2,282 | 2,442 | 2,520 | 2,087 |
| Cars and trucks, used........... | 1,507 | 2,271 | 2,139 | 2,351 | 896 | 2,050 | 2,541 | 3,207 | 3,746 |
| Gasoline and motor oil.............. | 1,739 | 1,920 | 1,953 | 2,228 | 999 | 1,979 | 2,399 | 2,839 | 3,014 |
| Other vehicle expenses............ | 2,878 | 3,172 | 2,625 | 2,863 | 1,961 | 2,955 | 3,517 | 3,656 | 2,982 |
| Vehicle finance charges......... | 185 | 223 | 240 | 212 | 83 | 228 | 277 | 350 | 347 |
| Maintenance and repair......... | 891 | 1,178 | 813 | 1,028 | 794 | 938 | 1,103 | 1,116 | 1,048 |
| Vehicle insurance.............. | 801 | 930 | 1,119 | 876 | 695 | 981 | 1,246 | 1,266 | 927 |
| Vehicle rental, leases, licenses, other charges................. | 1,001 | 840 | 454 | 747 | 390 | 809 | 892 | 924 | 659 |
| Public transportation............. | 1,040 | 613 | 529 | 860 | 435 | 835 | 737 | 935 | 774 |
| Health care [2]....................... | 5,126 | 5,262 | 4,669 | 4,892 | 2,967 | 6,218 | 5,529 | 5,558 | 4,467 |
| Entertainment [3]................... | 3,133 | 3,341 | 2,832 | 3,763 | 1,660 | 3,750 | 3,378 | 4,465 | 3,962 |
| Personal care products and services........ | 741 | 788 | 689 | 879 | 496 | 806 | 870 | 1,041 | 882 |
| Reading........................... | 123 | 110 | 98 | 120 | 80 | 127 | 127 | 133 | 86 |
| Education.......................... | 2,341 | 1,287 | 1,156 | 1,581 | 743 | 1,329 | 2,290 | 2,307 | 2,010 |
| Tobacco products/smoking supplies.......... | 357 | 384 | 336 | 255 | 240 | 331 | 447 | 362 | 398 |
| Miscellaneous...................... | 1,176 | 859 | 846 | 1,305 | 773 | 1,109 | 1,282 | 1,096 | 832 |
| Cash contributions................. | 1,523 | 1,855 | 1,828 | 2,251 | 1,403 | 2,491 | 1,589 | 1,704 | 1,737 |
| Personal insurance and pensions...... | 7,399 | 6,562 | 5,968 | 7,858 | 3,093 | 7,404 | 8,865 | 9,845 | 8,265 |
| Life and other personal insurance........... | 489 | 443 | 408 | 351 | 187 | 527 | 502 | 549 | 417 |
| Pensions and social security............. | 6,910 | 6,119 | 5,559 | 7,507 | 2,906 | 6,877 | 8,364 | 9,297 | 7,848 |
| **Personal taxes**..................... | **12,516** | **8,831** | **8,114** | **12,221** | **4,793** | **12,669** | **12,528** | **13,976** | **6,704** |

[1] Includes other types not shown separately. [2] For additional health care expenditures, see Table 149. [3] For additional recreation expenditures, see Section 26.

Source: U.S. Bureau of Labor Statistics, Consumer Expenditure Survey Program, "Annual Calendar Year Tables, 2017," <http://www.bls.gov/cex/tables.htm>, accessed December 2018.

## Table 721. Average Annual Expenditures of All Consumer Units by Income Level: 2017

[In dollars. See headnote, Table 716. See source for definitions, standard errors, and other information]

| Income level | Total expenditures [1] | Food | Housing | | | Transportation | | | Health care | Pensions and social security |
|---|---|---|---|---|---|---|---|---|---|---|
| | | | Total [1] | Shelter | Utilities, fuels [2] | Total [1] | Vehicle purchases | Gasoline and motor oil | | |
| **All consumer units**.......... | **60,060** | **7,729** | **19,884** | **11,895** | **3,836** | **9,576** | **4,054** | **1,968** | **4,928** | **6,353** |
| BY INCOME | | | | | | | | | | |
| Less than $15,000............. | 24,607 | 3,938 | 9,783 | 5,982 | 2,163 | 3,401 | 1,176 | 864 | 2,193 | 391 |
| $15,000 to $29,999........... | 33,300 | 4,806 | 12,817 | 7,662 | 2,872 | 4,930 | 1,966 | 1,218 | 3,360 | 1,405 |
| $30,000 to $39,999........... | 41,550 | 5,878 | 14,585 | 8,471 | 3,457 | 7,191 | 3,097 | 1,652 | 4,249 | 2,459 |
| $40,000 to $49,999........... | 46,258 | 6,598 | 16,216 | 9,550 | 3,600 | 7,529 | 2,580 | 1,818 | 4,558 | 3,116 |
| $50,000 to $69,999........... | 54,216 | 7,443 | 18,446 | 10,789 | 3,851 | 9,545 | 4,218 | 2,045 | 4,733 | 4,780 |
| $70,000 to $99,999........... | 66,116 | 8,385 | 21,933 | 13,018 | 4,348 | 10,795 | 4,322 | 2,488 | 5,639 | 7,586 |
| $100,000 to $149,999........ | 86,170 | 10,918 | 26,684 | 15,737 | 4,910 | 14,041 | 6,397 | 2,833 | 6,850 | 11,502 |
| $150,000 to $199,999........ | 115,404 | 12,171 | 35,589 | 22,062 | 5,510 | 18,753 | 7,707 | 2,974 | 7,431 | 17,595 |
| $200,000 and over............. | 161,247 | 16,309 | 47,410 | 29,602 | 6,302 | 23,342 | 11,212 | 3,155 | 9,689 | 25,355 |

[1] Includes expenditures not shown separately. [2] Includes public services.

Source: U.S. Bureau of Labor Statistics, Consumer Expenditure Survey, "Annual Calendar Year Tables, 2017," <http://stats.bls.gov/cex/tables.htm>, accessed December 2018.

## Table 722. Annual Expenditures Per Child by Married-Couple Families by Family Income and Expenditure Type: 2015

[In dollars. Excludes expenses for college. Estimates are based on 2011-2015 Consumer Expenditure Survey data updated to 2015 dollars by using the Consumer Price Index. Data are for the younger child in a two-child family. Estimates are about the same for the older child, so to calculate expenses for two children, figures should be summed for the appropriate age categories. To estimate expenses for an only child, multiply the total expense for the appropriate age category by 1.27. To estimate expenses for each child in a family with three or more children, multiply the total expense for each appropriate age category by 0.76; for expenses on all children in a family, these totals should be summed. Please note that estimates for 2015 are not directly comparable to estimates published for 2013 due to the change in using base data from the 2005-2006 vs. 2011-2015 Consumer Expenditure surveys. For methodology, see source]

| Family income and age of child | Total | Expenditure type | | | | | Child care and education [1] | Miscellaneous [2] |
|---|---|---|---|---|---|---|---|---|
| | | Housing | Food | Transportation | Clothing | Health care | | |
| INCOME: LESS THAN $59,200 (Average – $36,300) | | | | | | | | |
| Less than 2 years old........................ | 9,690 | 3,160 | 1,310 | 1,200 | 670 | 820 | 2,080 | 450 |
| 3 to 5 years old.............................. | 9,700 | 3,160 | 1,350 | 1,250 | 540 | 760 | 2,080 | 560 |
| 6 to 8 years old.............................. | 9,330 | 3,160 | 1,930 | 1,310 | 540 | 790 | 920 | 680 |
| 9 to 11 years old............................. | 9,960 | 3,160 | 2,200 | 1,350 | 690 | 900 | 920 | 740 |
| 12 to 14 years old........................... | 9,570 | 3,160 | 2,290 | 1,500 | 740 | 860 | 440 | 580 |
| 15 to 17 years old........................... | 9,980 | 3,160 | 2,300 | 1,690 | 720 | 910 | 640 | 560 |
| INCOME: $59,200 to $107,400 (Average = $81,700) | | | | | | | | |
| Less than 2 years old........................ | 12,680 | 3,680 | 1,580 | 1,790 | 750 | 1,180 | 2,870 | 830 |
| 3 to 5 years old.............................. | 12,730 | 3,680 | 1,690 | 1,840 | 600 | 1,110 | 2,870 | 940 |
| 6 to 8 years old.............................. | 12,350 | 3,680 | 2,280 | 1,900 | 600 | 1,130 | 1,710 | 1,050 |
| 9 to 11 years old............................. | 13,180 | 3,680 | 2,680 | 1,940 | 780 | 1,280 | 1,710 | 1,110 |
| 12 to 14 years old........................... | 13,030 | 3,680 | 2,780 | 2,090 | 860 | 1,240 | 1,430 | 950 |
| 15 to 17 years old........................... | 13,900 | 3,680 | 2,790 | 2,270 | 830 | 1,300 | 2,090 | 940 |
| INCOME: MORE THAN $107,400 (Average = $185,400) | | | | | | | | |
| Less than 2 years old........................ | 19,770 | 5,460 | 2,210 | 2,590 | 1,110 | 1,580 | 5,170 | 1,650 |
| 3 to 5 years old.............................. | 19,790 | 5,460 | 2,320 | 2,640 | 940 | 1,490 | 5,170 | 1,770 |
| 6 to 8 years old.............................. | 19,380 | 5,460 | 2,960 | 2,690 | 940 | 1,440 | 4,010 | 1,880 |
| 9 to 11 years old............................. | 20,700 | 5,460 | 3,570 | 2,740 | 1,180 | 1,800 | 4,010 | 1,940 |
| 12 to 14 years old........................... | 21,050 | 5,460 | 3,560 | 2,890 | 1,310 | 1,740 | 4,310 | 1,780 |
| 15 to 17 years old........................... | 23,380 | 5,460 | 3,720 | 3,070 | 1,280 | 1,820 | 6,270 | 1,760 |

[1] Includes only families with child care and education expenses. [2] Expenses include personal care items, entertainment, and reading materials.

Source: U.S. Department of Agriculture, Center for Nutrition Policy and Promotion, *Expenditures on Children by Families, 2015*, March 2017 (revised). See also <https://www.cnpp.usda.gov/ExpendituresonChildrenbyFamilies>.

## Table 723. Money Income of Households—Percent Distribution by Income Level, Race, and Hispanic Origin, in Constant (2017) Dollars: 2000 to 2017

[In percent except as noted (108,209 represents 108,209,000). Households as of March of following year. Constant dollars based on CPI-U-RS deflator. Based on Current Population Survey, Annual Social and Economic Supplement (CPS ASEC); see text, this section and Section 1, and Appendix III. For definition of median, see Guide to Tabular Presentation. A household consists of all the persons who occupy a housing unit. Household count excludes persons living in group quarters and institutions. For 2001 data and earlier, the CPS allowed respondents to report only one race group. Beginning with the 2003 CPS covering data for 2002, refers to respondents reporting only one race. Two basic ways of defining a race group are possible: a group such as Asian may be defined as 1) those who reported Asian and no other race (the race-alone concept), or 2) those who reported Asian regardless of whether they also reported another race (the race-alone-or-in-combination concept). Please note that the 2014 CPS ASEC covering data for 2013 included redesigned questions for income; use caution when comparing 2013 and subsequent data to data for previous years. See source for more information]

| Year | Number of house-holds (1,000) | Percent distribution | | | | | | | Median income (dollars) |
|---|---|---|---|---|---|---|---|---|---|
| | | Under $15,000 | $15,000 to $24,999 | $25,000 to $34,999 | $35,000 to $49,999 | $50,000 to $74,999 | $75,000 to $99,999 | $100,000 and over | |
| ALL HOUSEHOLDS [1] | | | | | | | | | |
| 2000 [4] | 108,209 | 9.9 | 9.6 | 9.3 | 13.5 | 17.9 | 13.1 | 26.5 | 59,938 |
| 2010 [5] | 119,927 | 12.0 | 11.0 | 10.2 | 12.9 | 17.3 | 12.0 | 24.7 | 55,520 |
| 2016 [6] | 126,224 | 11.0 | 9.5 | 9.3 | 12.6 | 16.9 | 12.2 | 28.4 | 60,309 |
| 2017 [6] | 127,586 | 10.7 | 9.6 | 9.2 | 12.3 | 16.5 | 12.5 | 29.2 | 61,372 |
| WHITE [2] | | | | | | | | | |
| 2000 [4] | 90,030 | 8.7 | 9.3 | 9.0 | 13.4 | 18.0 | 13.5 | 28.1 | 62,688 |
| 2010 [5] | 96,306 | 10.1 | 10.7 | 9.9 | 12.9 | 17.6 | 12.5 | 26.2 | 58,261 |
| 2016 [6] | 99,400 | 9.4 | 9.0 | 9.1 | 12.7 | 17.0 | 12.7 | 30.1 | 63,188 |
| 2017 [6] | 100,065 | 9.1 | 9.2 | 9.0 | 12.1 | 16.7 | 12.9 | 31.1 | 65,273 |
| BLACK [2] | | | | | | | | | |
| 2000 [4] | 13,174 | 18.4 | 12.2 | 11.8 | 14.9 | 18.1 | 10.3 | 14.3 | 42,348 |
| 2010 [5] | 15,265 | 23.3 | 13.7 | 12.0 | 14.0 | 15.5 | 9.3 | 12.1 | 36,195 |
| 2016 [6] | 16,733 | 20.4 | 13.1 | 11.6 | 13.7 | 16.3 | 9.6 | 15.5 | 40,339 |
| 2017 [6] | 16,997 | 19.9 | 12.7 | 11.6 | 14.1 | 15.7 | 9.8 | 16.1 | 40,258 |
| ASIAN AND PACIFIC ISLANDER [2] | | | | | | | | | |
| 2000 [4] | 3,963 | 8.0 | 6.3 | 6.5 | 11.2 | 15.6 | 13.8 | 38.5 | 79,590 |
| 2010 [5] | 5,212 | 10.0 | 8.1 | 7.6 | 8.9 | 17.3 | 11.3 | 36.8 | 72,402 |
| 2016 [6] | 6,392 | 8.9 | 6.4 | 6.4 | 8.1 | 15.4 | 13.3 | 41.6 | 83,182 |
| 2017 [6] | 6,735 | 9.0 | 6.6 | 5.8 | 9.6 | 14.5 | 12.9 | 41.7 | 81,331 |
| HISPANIC [3] | | | | | | | | | |
| 2000 [4] | 10,034 | 11.9 | 12.6 | 11.7 | 16.7 | 19.7 | 11.7 | 15.7 | 47,345 |
| 2010 [5] | 14,435 | 15.5 | 13.2 | 13.5 | 14.7 | 18.2 | 10.3 | 14.7 | 42,399 |
| 2016 [6] | 16,915 | 12.4 | 11.5 | 11.2 | 15.8 | 17.9 | 12.0 | 19.1 | 48,700 |
| 2017 [6] | 17,318 | 12.0 | 11.1 | 11.3 | 15.0 | 18.1 | 12.6 | 19.8 | 50,486 |

[1] Includes other races not shown separately. [2] Beginning with 2002, data represent White alone, Black alone, or Asian alone. [3] People of Hispanic origin may be of any race. Data for Hispanics overlap with data for racial groups. [4] Data reflect implementation of Census 2000-based population controls and a 28,000 household sample expansion to 78,000 households. [5] Beginning with 2009 income data, the Census Bureau expanded the upper income intervals used to calculate medians to $250,000 or more. Medians falling in the upper open-ended interval are plugged with "$250,000." Before 2009, the upper open-ended interval was $100,000 and a plug of "$100,000" was used. Data reflect implementation of Census 2010-based population controls. [6] Beginning with 2013, data are based on redesigned questions on income.

Source: U.S. Census Bureau, *Income and Poverty in the United States: 2017,* Current Population Reports, P60-263, September 2018; and "Historical Income Tables: Households, Table H-17," <http://www.census.gov/topics/income-poverty/income/data/tables.html>, accessed November 2018.

## Table 724. Money Income of Households—Median Income by Race and Hispanic Origin, in Current and Constant (2017) Dollars: 1990 to 2017

[In dollars. See headnote, Table 723]

| Year | Median income in current dollars | | | | | Median income in constant (2017) dollars | | | | |
|---|---|---|---|---|---|---|---|---|---|---|
| | All house-holds [1] | White [2] | Black [2] | Asian, Pacific Islander [2] | His-panic [3] | All house-holds [1] | White [2] | Black [2] | Asian, Pacific Islander [2] | His-panic [3] |
| 1990 | 29,943 | 31,231 | 18,676 | 38,450 | 22,330 | 54,621 | 56,970 | 34,068 | 70,139 | 40,733 |
| 2000 [4,5] | 41,990 | 43,916 | 29,667 | 55,757 | 33,168 | 59,938 | 62,688 | 42,348 | 79,590 | 47,345 |
| 2005 | 46,326 | 48,554 | 30,858 | 61,094 | 35,967 | 58,291 | 61,094 | 38,828 | 76,873 | 45,256 |
| 2010 [6] | 49,276 | 51,709 | 32,124 | 64,259 | 37,631 | 55,520 | 58,261 | 36,195 | 72,402 | 42,399 |
| 2011 [7] | 50,054 | 52,214 | 32,229 | 65,129 | 38,624 | 54,673 | 57,033 | 35,203 | 71,139 | 42,188 |
| 2012 | 51,017 | 53,706 | 33,321 | 68,636 | 39,005 | 54,569 | 57,446 | 35,641 | 73,415 | 41,721 |
| 2013 [8] | 53,585 | 56,745 | 35,324 | 72,383 | 39,687 | 56,479 | 59,810 | 37,232 | 76,293 | 41,831 |
| 2014 [8] | 53,657 | 56,866 | 35,398 | 74,297 | 42,491 | 55,613 | 58,939 | 36,689 | 77,006 | 44,040 |
| 2015 [8] | 56,516 | 60,109 | 36,898 | 77,166 | 45,148 | 58,476 | 62,194 | 38,178 | 79,842 | 46,714 |
| 2016 [8] | 59,039 | 61,858 | 39,490 | 81,431 | 47,675 | 60,309 | 63,188 | 40,339 | 83,182 | 48,700 |
| 2017 [8] | 61,372 | 65,273 | 40,258 | 81,331 | 50,486 | 61,372 | 65,273 | 40,258 | 81,331 | 50,486 |

[1] Includes other races, not shown separately. [2] Beginning with 2002, data represent White alone, Black alone, or Asian alone. [3] People of Hispanic origin may be of any race. [4] Implementation of Census 2000-based population controls. [5] Implementation of a 28,000 household sample expansion. [6] Median income is calculated using $2,500 income intervals. Beginning with 2009 income data, the Census Bureau expanded the upper income intervals used to calculate medians to $250,000 or more. Before 2009, the upper open-ended interval was $100,000 and a plug of "$100,000" was used. [7] Implementation of Census 2010-based population controls. [8] Data are based on redesigned questions on income.

Source: U.S. Census Bureau, *Income and Poverty in the United States: 2017,* Current Population Reports, P60-263, September 2018; and "Historical Income Tables: Households, Table H-5," <http://www.census.gov/topics/income-poverty/income/data/tables.html>, accessed November 2018.

# Table 725. Money Income of Households—Households by Income Level and Selected Characteristics: 2017

[127,586 represents 127,586,000. Households as of March of the following year. Based on Current Population Survey, Annual Social and Economic Supplement (CPS ASEC); see text, this section and Section 1, and Appendix III. For definition of median, see Guide to Tabular Presentation. See headnote, Table 723]

| Characteristic | Number of households (1,000) | | | | | | | | Median house-hold income (dollars) [1] |
|---|---|---|---|---|---|---|---|---|---|
| | Total house-holds | Under $15,000 | $15,000 to $24,999 | $25,000 to $34,999 | $35,000 to $49,999 | $50,000 to $74,999 | $75,000 to $99,999 | $100,000 and over | |
| **Total**........... | **127,586** | **13,590** | **12,218** | **11,770** | **15,726** | **20,988** | **15,974** | **37,319** | **61,372** |
| Region: [2] | | | | | | | | | |
| Northeast.............. | 22,513 | 2,425 | 2,000 | 1,951 | 2,475 | 3,494 | 2,723 | 7,443 | 66,450 |
| Midwest.............. | 27,635 | 2,832 | 2,631 | 2,538 | 3,432 | 4,768 | 3,653 | 7,780 | 61,136 |
| South.............. | 48,591 | 5,591 | 5,086 | 4,959 | 6,429 | 7,951 | 5,838 | 12,739 | 55,709 |
| West.............. | 28,847 | 2,741 | 2,501 | 2,321 | 3,389 | 4,775 | 3,761 | 9,360 | 67,517 |
| Age of householder: | | | | | | | | | |
| 15 to 24 years.............. | 6,211 | 1,034 | 823 | 832 | 1,022 | 1,098 | 586 | 815 | 40,093 |
| 25 to 34 years.............. | 20,264 | 1,741 | 1,411 | 1,999 | 2,705 | 4,123 | 2,968 | 5,316 | 62,294 |
| 35 to 44 years.............. | 21,576 | 1,529 | 1,352 | 1,528 | 2,372 | 3,514 | 3,127 | 8,152 | 78,368 |
| 45 to 54 years.............. | 22,542 | 1,693 | 1,343 | 1,480 | 2,366 | 3,592 | 3,051 | 9,016 | 80,671 |
| 55 to 64 years.............. | 24,020 | 2,739 | 1,944 | 1,677 | 2,775 | 3,742 | 3,064 | 8,081 | 68,567 |
| 65 years and over.............. | 32,973 | 4,852 | 5,345 | 4,254 | 4,485 | 4,919 | 3,178 | 5,938 | 41,125 |
| Type of household: | | | | | | | | | |
| Family household.............. | 83,088 | 4,651 | 5,176 | 6,394 | 9,573 | 14,101 | 12,145 | 31,049 | 77,713 |
| Married-couple.............. | 61,241 | 1,817 | 2,629 | 3,796 | 6,058 | 10,124 | 9,523 | 27,295 | 90,386 |
| Male householder, spouse absent.............. | 6,424 | 440 | 527 | 607 | 1,019 | 1,285 | 958 | 1,586 | 60,843 |
| Female householder, spouse absent.............. | 15,423 | 2,393 | 2,020 | 1,991 | 2,496 | 2,693 | 1,664 | 2,167 | 41,703 |
| Nonfamily household......... | 44,498 | 8,939 | 7,042 | 5,376 | 6,152 | 6,887 | 3,829 | 6,271 | 36,650 |
| Male householder.............. | 21,017 | 3,498 | 2,640 | 2,358 | 2,924 | 3,646 | 2,005 | 3,947 | 44,250 |
| Female householder........ | 23,481 | 5,442 | 4,403 | 3,019 | 3,229 | 3,241 | 1,825 | 2,322 | 30,748 |
| Size of household: | | | | | | | | | |
| One person.............. | 35,740 | 8,375 | 6,525 | 4,702 | 5,139 | 5,210 | 2,546 | 3,242 | 30,828 |
| Two people.............. | 44,038 | 2,832 | 3,370 | 4,096 | 5,629 | 7,992 | 6,350 | 13,772 | 68,374 |
| Three people.............. | 19,333 | 1,173 | 1,040 | 1,270 | 2,180 | 3,352 | 2,821 | 7,497 | 80,053 |
| Four people.............. | 16,468 | 680 | 729 | 935 | 1,528 | 2,405 | 2,396 | 7,798 | 94,876 |
| Five people.............. | 7,442 | 317 | 355 | 474 | 704 | 1,211 | 1,142 | 3,241 | 88,726 |
| Six people.............. | 2,851 | 121 | 116 | 178 | 351 | 501 | 456 | 1,130 | 82,182 |
| Seven or more people....... | 1,714 | 92 | 83 | 116 | 195 | 320 | 263 | 644 | 78,426 |
| Number of earners: | | | | | | | | | |
| No earners.............. | 30,382 | 9,950 | 6,401 | 4,080 | 3,508 | 3,043 | 1,517 | 1,885 | 22,746 |
| One earner.............. | 46,733 | 3,358 | 5,074 | 6,205 | 8,320 | 9,353 | 5,580 | 8,846 | 50,607 |
| Two earners and more....... | 50,472 | 281 | 744 | 1,485 | 3,900 | 8,593 | 8,877 | 26,588 | 103,827 |
| Two earners.............. | 40,099 | 266 | 694 | 1,362 | 3,501 | 7,443 | 7,161 | 19,676 | 98,331 |
| Three earners.............. | 7,676 | 15 | 49 | 113 | 360 | 979 | 1,320 | 4,840 | 121,697 |
| Four earners or more....... | 2,697 | – | 2 | 9 | 38 | 173 | 399 | 2,076 | 150,986 |
| Work experience of householder: | | | | | | | | | |
| **Total**.............. | **127,586** | **13,590** | **12,218** | **11,770** | **15,726** | **20,988** | **15,974** | **37,319** | **61,372** |
| Worked.............. | 83,801 | 3,129 | 4,898 | 6,358 | 10,073 | 15,086 | 12,496 | 31,763 | 78,963 |
| Worked at full-time jobs.... | 70,211 | 1,476 | 3,281 | 4,859 | 8,267 | 12,949 | 11,034 | 28,342 | 83,215 |
| 50 weeks or more.......... | 61,502 | 686 | 2,428 | 3,986 | 7,160 | 11,324 | 9,934 | 25,985 | 86,590 |
| 27 to 49 weeks.......... | 5,665 | 223 | 498 | 579 | 713 | 1,132 | 772 | 1,750 | 67,644 |
| 26 weeks or less.......... | 3,044 | 567 | 355 | 294 | 393 | 492 | 328 | 613 | 45,909 |
| Worked at part-time jobs... | 13,590 | 1,653 | 1,617 | 1,499 | 1,807 | 2,136 | 1,460 | 3,418 | 52,258 |
| 50 weeks or more.......... | 7,784 | 710 | 889 | 880 | 1,053 | 1,212 | 846 | 2,194 | 56,510 |
| 27 to 49 weeks.......... | 2,758 | 282 | 336 | 309 | 351 | 496 | 311 | 672 | 54,595 |
| 26 weeks or less.......... | 3,048 | 660 | 392 | 309 | 401 | 428 | 305 | 550 | 41,216 |
| Did not work.............. | 43,785 | 10,461 | 7,320 | 5,413 | 5,652 | 5,904 | 3,479 | 5,557 | 32,178 |
| Educational attainment of householder: [3] | | | | | | | | | |
| **Total**.............. | **121,375** | **12,555** | **11,395** | **10,939** | **14,703** | **19,890** | **15,388** | **36,506** | **62,625** |
| Less than 9th grade.......... | 4,094 | 1,115 | 824 | 566 | 525 | 531 | 277 | 258 | 26,587 |
| 9th to 12th grade (no diploma).............. | 7,467 | 1,856 | 1,345 | 1,022 | 987 | 1,095 | 585 | 580 | 30,100 |
| High school graduate......... | 32,111 | 4,472 | 4,260 | 3,899 | 4,940 | 5,572 | 3,738 | 5,228 | 44,970 |
| Some college, no degree..... | 21,162 | 2,197 | 2,236 | 2,264 | 2,875 | 3,847 | 2,722 | 5,020 | 55,563 |
| Associate's degree.......... | 12,868 | 975 | 1,038 | 1,165 | 1,776 | 2,442 | 1,894 | 3,578 | 64,263 |
| Bachelor's degree or more.... | 43,673 | 1,942 | 1,691 | 2,022 | 3,600 | 6,402 | 6,173 | 21,843 | 100,021 |
| Bachelor's degree.......... | 26,727 | 1,258 | 1,126 | 1,435 | 2,453 | 4,285 | 3,976 | 12,197 | 91,772 |
| Master's degree.......... | 12,545 | 523 | 468 | 485 | 911 | 1,652 | 1,713 | 6,793 | 108,231 |
| Professional degree.......... | 1,744 | 67 | 39 | 51 | 96 | 195 | 174 | 1,122 | 139,069 |
| Doctoral degree.......... | 2,657 | 93 | 58 | 50 | 139 | 271 | 311 | 1,735 | 140,110 |
| Housing tenure: | | | | | | | | | |
| Owner occupied.............. | 82,105 | 5,614 | 6,197 | 6,206 | 8,973 | 13,440 | 11,424 | 30,254 | 76,046 |
| Renter occupied.............. | 43,826 | 7,586 | 5,736 | 5,385 | 6,530 | 7,306 | 4,414 | 6,866 | 41,315 |
| Occupier paid no cash rent.. | 1,656 | 391 | 285 | 180 | 222 | 243 | 136 | 202 | 32,874 |

– Represents or rounds to zero. [1] Median income calculated using $2,500 income intervals. Medians falling in the upper open-ended interval are plugged with "$250,000." [2] For composition of regions, see map, inside front cover. [3] Data shown for householders age 25 and over.

Source: U.S. Census Bureau, *Income and Poverty in the United States: 2017*, Current Population Reports, P60-263, September 2018; and "Current Population Survey Tables for Household Income: Table HINC-01," <http://www.census.gov/topics/income-poverty/income/data/tables.html>, accessed November 2018.

## Table 726. Money Income of Households—Households by Income Level, Race, and Hispanic Origin: 2017

[127,586 represents 127,586,000. Households as of March of the following year. Based on Current Population Survey, Annual Social and Economic Supplement (ASEC); see text, this section and Section 1, and Appendix III]

| Income interval | Number of households (1,000) | | | | | Percent distribution | | | | |
|---|---|---|---|---|---|---|---|---|---|---|
| | All races [1] | White alone | Black alone | Asian alone | His-panic [2] | All races [1] | White alone | Black alone | Asian alone | His-panic [2] |
| **All households..............** | **127,586** | **100,065** | **16,997** | **6,735** | **17,318** | **100.0** | **100.0** | **100.0** | **100.0** | **100.0** |
| Under $10,000................ | 7,715 | 4,922 | 2,094 | 400 | 1,203 | 6.0 | 4.9 | 12.3 | 5.9 | 6.9 |
| $10,000 to $14,999........... | 5,875 | 4,153 | 1,290 | 205 | 883 | 4.6 | 4.2 | 7.6 | 3.0 | 5.1 |
| $15,000 to $19,999........... | 6,091 | 4,571 | 1,108 | 202 | 912 | 4.8 | 4.6 | 6.5 | 3.0 | 5.3 |
| $20,000 to $24,999........... | 6,127 | 4,652 | 1,050 | 242 | 1,006 | 4.8 | 4.6 | 6.2 | 3.6 | 5.8 |
| $25,000 to $29,999........... | 5,818 | 4,453 | 948 | 195 | 982 | 4.6 | 4.5 | 5.6 | 2.9 | 5.7 |
| $30,000 to $34,999........... | 5,952 | 4,507 | 1,027 | 195 | 984 | 4.7 | 4.5 | 6.0 | 2.9 | 5.7 |
| $35,000 to $39,999........... | 5,644 | 4,332 | 926 | 191 | 940 | 4.4 | 4.3 | 5.4 | 2.8 | 5.4 |
| $40,000 to $44,999........... | 5,184 | 3,913 | 845 | 237 | 804 | 4.1 | 3.9 | 5.0 | 3.5 | 4.6 |
| $45,000 to $49,999........... | 4,898 | 3,902 | 624 | 217 | 846 | 3.8 | 3.9 | 3.7 | 3.2 | 4.9 |
| $50,000 to $59,999........... | 9,092 | 7,205 | 1,245 | 366 | 1,354 | 7.1 | 7.2 | 7.3 | 5.4 | 7.8 |
| $60,000 to $74,999........... | 11,896 | 9,490 | 1,426 | 613 | 1,786 | 9.3 | 9.5 | 8.4 | 9.1 | 10.3 |
| $75,000 to $84,999........... | 7,420 | 5,939 | 818 | 434 | 977 | 5.8 | 5.9 | 4.8 | 6.4 | 5.6 |
| $85,000 to $99,999........... | 8,554 | 7,016 | 854 | 434 | 1,205 | 6.7 | 7.0 | 5.0 | 6.4 | 7.0 |
| $100,000 to $149,999......... | 18,481 | 15,360 | 1,620 | 1,096 | 1,988 | 14.5 | 15.4 | 9.5 | 16.3 | 11.5 |
| $150,000 to $199,999......... | 8,964 | 7,485 | 595 | 723 | 782 | 7.0 | 7.5 | 3.5 | 10.7 | 4.5 |
| $200,000 to $249,999......... | 4,310 | 3,554 | 243 | 415 | 320 | 3.4 | 3.6 | 1.4 | 6.2 | 1.8 |
| $250,000 and above........... | 5,564 | 4,609 | 286 | 571 | 344 | 4.4 | 4.6 | 1.7 | 8.5 | 2.0 |

[1] Includes other races, not shown separately. [2] Persons of Hispanic origin may be of any race.

Source: U.S. Census Bureau, *Income and Poverty in the United States: 2017*, Current Population Reports, P60-263, September 2018; and "Current Population Survey Tables for Household Income: Table HINC-06," <http://www.census.gov/topics/income-poverty/income/data/tables.html>, accessed November 2018.

## Table 727. Share of Aggregate Income Received by Each Fifth and Top 5 Percent of Households: 1990 to 2017

[In units as indicated (94,312 represents 94,312,000). Households as of March of the following year. Income in constant 2017 CPI-U-RS-adjusted dollars. The shares method ranks households from highest to lowest on the basis of income and then divides them into groups of equal population size, typically quintiles. The aggregate income of each group is then divided by the overall aggregate income to derive shares. Based on the Current Population Survey, Annual Social and Economic Supplement (CPS ASEC); see text, this section and Section 1, and Appendix III. For data collection changes over time, see source. See also headnote, Table 723]

| Year | Number of house-holds (1,000) | Income at selected positions in constant (2017) dollars | | | | | Percent distribution of aggregate income | | | | | |
|---|---|---|---|---|---|---|---|---|---|---|---|---|
| | | Upper limit of each fifth | | | | Top 5 percent, lower limit | Lowest 5th | Second 5th | Third 5th | Fourth 5th | Highest 5th | Top 5 percent |
| | | Lowest | Second | Third | Fourth | | | | | | | |
| 1990............ | 94,312 | 22,802 | 43,163 | 66,034 | 100,702 | 172,835 | 3.8 | 9.6 | 15.9 | 24.0 | 46.6 | 18.5 |
| 1995 [1]........ | 99,627 | 23,073 | 43,125 | 67,300 | 104,349 | 181,061 | 3.7 | 9.1 | 15.2 | 23.3 | 48.7 | 21.0 |
| 2000 [2, 3]...... | 108,209 | 25,580 | 47,106 | 74,475 | 116,716 | 207,293 | 3.6 | 8.9 | 14.8 | 23.0 | 49.8 | 22.1 |
| 2005............ | 114,384 | 24,131 | 45,298 | 72,552 | 115,390 | 208,874 | 3.4 | 8.6 | 14.6 | 23.0 | 50.4 | 22.2 |
| 2006............ | 116,011 | 24,418 | 46,038 | 73,126 | 118,260 | 212,081 | 3.4 | 8.6 | 14.5 | 22.9 | 50.5 | 22.3 |
| 2007............ | 116,783 | 24,048 | 46,340 | 73,480 | 118,516 | 209,773 | 3.4 | 8.7 | 14.8 | 23.4 | 49.7 | 21.2 |
| 2008............ | 117,181 | 23,639 | 44,512 | 71,589 | 114,406 | 205,438 | 3.4 | 8.6 | 14.7 | 23.3 | 50.0 | 21.5 |
| 2009 [4].......... | 117,538 | 23,425 | 44,151 | 70,781 | 114,530 | 206,156 | 3.4 | 8.6 | 14.6 | 23.2 | 50.3 | 21.7 |
| 2010 [5].......... | 119,927 | 22,534 | 42,815 | 69,293 | 112,704 | 203,355 | 3.3 | 8.5 | 14.6 | 23.4 | 50.3 | 21.3 |
| 2011............ | 121,084 | 22,132 | 42,075 | 68,196 | 110,956 | 203,165 | 3.2 | 8.4 | 14.3 | 23.0 | 51.1 | 22.3 |
| 2012............ | 122,459 | 22,033 | 42,533 | 69,079 | 111,344 | 204,466 | 3.2 | 8.3 | 14.4 | 23.0 | 51.0 | 22.3 |
| 2013 [6].......... | 123,931 | 22,134 | 43,251 | 70,830 | 116,186 | 216,208 | 3.1 | 8.2 | 14.3 | 23.0 | 51.4 | 22.2 |
| 2014 [6].......... | 124,587 | 22,213 | 42,688 | 70,699 | 116,355 | 214,100 | 3.1 | 8.2 | 14.3 | 23.2 | 51.2 | 21.9 |
| 2015 [6].......... | 125,819 | 23,591 | 45,020 | 74,498 | 121,060 | 221,900 | 3.1 | 8.2 | 14.3 | 23.2 | 51.1 | 22.1 |
| 2016 [6].......... | 126,224 | 24,518 | 46,581 | 76,479 | 123,621 | 230,095 | 3.1 | 8.3 | 14.2 | 22.9 | 51.5 | 22.6 |
| 2017 [6].......... | 127,586 | 24,638 | 47,110 | 77,552 | 126,855 | 237,034 | 3.1 | 8.2 | 14.3 | 23.0 | 51.5 | 22.3 |

[1] Data reflect full implementation of the 1990 Census-based sample design and metropolitan definitions, 7,000 household sample reduction, and revised race edits. [2] Implementation of Census 2000-based population controls. [3] Implementation of a 28,000 household sample expansion. [4] Beginning with 2009 income data, the Census Bureau expanded the upper income interval used to calculate medians and Gini indexes to $250,000 or more. Medians falling in the upper open-ended interval are plugged with "$250,000." [5] Implementation of Census 2010-based population controls. [6] Data are based on redesigned questions on income. See source for more information.

Source: U.S. Census Bureau, *Income and Poverty in the United States: 2017,* Current Population Reports, P60-263, September 2018; and "Historical Income Tables: Households, Tables H1 and H2," <http://www.census.gov/topics/income-poverty/income/data/tables.html>, accessed November 2018.

## Table 728. Money Income of Families—Families by Income Level, Race, and Hispanic Origin: 2017

[83,103 represents 83,103,000. Families as of March of the following year. Based on Current Population Survey, Annual Social and Economic Supplement (CPS ASEC); see text, this section, Section 1, and Appendix III. A family is a group of persons residing together and related by birth, marriage, or adoption. See also headnote in Table 723 regarding changes in the CPS ASEC]

| Income interval | Number of families (1,000) | | | | | Percent distribution | | | | |
|---|---|---|---|---|---|---|---|---|---|---|
| | All races | White alone | Black alone | Asian alone | His-panic [1] | All races | White alone | Black alone | Asian alone | His-panic [1] |
| **All families**................ | **83,103** | **65,678** | **10,024** | **4,922** | **13,201** | **100.0** | **100.0** | **100.0** | **100.0** | **100.0** |
| Under $10,000.................. | 3,429 | 2,179 | 918 | 182 | 737 | 4.1 | 3.3 | 9.2 | 3.7 | 5.6 |
| $10,000 to $14,999............. | 1,877 | 1,309 | 420 | 69 | 483 | 2.3 | 2.0 | 4.2 | 1.4 | 3.7 |
| $15,000 to $19,999............. | 2,365 | 1,671 | 481 | 106 | 625 | 2.8 | 2.5 | 4.8 | 2.2 | 4.7 |
| $20,000 to $24,999............. | 3,102 | 2,233 | 578 | 159 | 755 | 3.7 | 3.4 | 5.8 | 3.2 | 5.7 |
| $25,000 to $29,999............. | 3,139 | 2,330 | 517 | 142 | 790 | 3.8 | 3.5 | 5.2 | 2.9 | 6.0 |
| $30,000 to $34,999............. | 3,508 | 2,656 | 598 | 121 | 744 | 4.2 | 4.0 | 6.0 | 2.5 | 5.6 |
| $35,000 to $39,999............. | 3,350 | 2,529 | 546 | 133 | 738 | 4.0 | 3.9 | 5.4 | 2.7 | 5.6 |
| $40,000 to $44,999............. | 3,240 | 2,462 | 494 | 178 | 602 | 3.9 | 3.7 | 4.9 | 3.6 | 4.6 |
| $45,000 to $49,999............. | 3,120 | 2,483 | 399 | 155 | 659 | 3.8 | 3.8 | 4.0 | 3.1 | 5.0 |
| $50,000 to $59,999............. | 5,675 | 4,492 | 762 | 240 | 1,054 | 6.8 | 6.8 | 7.6 | 4.9 | 8.0 |
| $60,000 to $74,999............. | 8,184 | 6,544 | 937 | 445 | 1,468 | 9.8 | 10.0 | 9.3 | 9.0 | 11.1 |
| $75,000 to $84,999............. | 5,288 | 4,192 | 578 | 330 | 788 | 6.4 | 6.4 | 5.8 | 6.7 | 6.0 |
| $85,000 to $99,999............. | 6,551 | 5,413 | 618 | 344 | 967 | 7.9 | 8.2 | 6.2 | 7.0 | 7.3 |
| $100,000 to $149,999............ | 14,492 | 12,065 | 1,263 | 860 | 1,591 | 17.4 | 18.4 | 12.6 | 17.5 | 12.1 |
| $150,000 to $199,999............ | 7,428 | 6,207 | 475 | 614 | 614 | 8.9 | 9.5 | 4.7 | 12.5 | 4.7 |
| $200,000 to $249,999............ | 3,610 | 2,965 | 211 | 361 | 285 | 4.3 | 4.5 | 2.1 | 7.3 | 2.2 |
| $250,000 and above.............. | 4,743 | 3,948 | 227 | 485 | 303 | 5.7 | 6.0 | 2.3 | 9.9 | 2.3 |

[1] Persons of Hispanic origin may be of any race.

Source: U.S. Census Bureau, *Income and Poverty in the United States: 2017*, Current Population Reports, P60-263, September 2018; and "Current Population Survey Tables for Family Income: Table FINC-07," <https://www.census.gov/topics/income-poverty/income/data/tables.html>, accessed November 2018.

## Table 729. Money Income of Families—Percent Distribution of Families by Income Level in Constant (2017) Dollars: 2000 to 2017

[73,778 represents 73,778,000. Income in 2017 Consumer Price Index Research Series Using Current Methods (CPI-U-RS) adjusted dollars. Families as of March of the following year. Based on Current Population Survey, Annual Social and Economic Supplement (CPS ASEC); see text, this section and Section 1, and Appendix III. For definition of median, see Guide to Tabular Presentation. For comments on race, see headnote, Table 723, and also text for Section 1, Population. Data users should exercise caution when comparing 2013 and subsequent data to data from previous year surveys due the use of redesigned income questions. See source for more information]

| Year | Number of families (1,000) | Percent distribution | | | | | | | Median income (dollars) |
|---|---|---|---|---|---|---|---|---|---|
| | | Under $15,000 | $15,000 to $24,999 | $25,000 to $34,999 | $35,000 to $49,999 | $50,000 to $74,999 | $75,000 to $99,999 | $100,000 and over | |
| **ALL FAMILIES [1]** | | | | | | | | | |
| 2000 [4]............................ | 73,778 | 5.7 | 6.9 | 8.0 | 12.9 | 18.5 | 15.1 | 32.9 | 72,417 |
| 2010 [5]............................ | 79,559 | 7.8 | 7.8 | 9.0 | 12.4 | 18.0 | 13.8 | 31.2 | 67,869 |
| 2016 [6]............................ | 82,854 | 6.8 | 6.7 | 7.9 | 11.6 | 17.4 | 13.9 | 35.7 | 74,271 |
| 2017 [6]............................ | 83,103 | 6.4 | 6.6 | 8.0 | 11.7 | 16.7 | 14.2 | 36.4 | 75,938 |
| **WHITE [2]** | | | | | | | | | |
| 2000 [4]............................ | 61,330 | 4.6 | 6.2 | 7.5 | 12.6 | 18.6 | 15.6 | 34.7 | 75,696 |
| 2010 [5]............................ | 63,976 | 6.4 | 7.0 | 8.6 | 12.4 | 18.2 | 14.4 | 33.0 | 70,886 |
| 2016 [6]............................ | 65,750 | 5.7 | 6.1 | 7.5 | 11.5 | 17.4 | 14.4 | 37.4 | 77,904 |
| 2017 [6]............................ | 65,678 | 5.3 | 5.9 | 7.6 | 11.4 | 16.8 | 14.6 | 38.4 | 79,749 |
| **BLACK [2]** | | | | | | | | | |
| 2000 [4]............................ | 8,731 | 13.3 | 11.5 | 11.7 | 15.4 | 18.8 | 11.7 | 17.6 | 48,071 |
| 2010 [5]............................ | 9,571 | 17.1 | 12.4 | 12.3 | 14.4 | 17.0 | 11.1 | 15.7 | 43,485 |
| 2016 [6]............................ | 9,975 | 14.0 | 10.8 | 11.3 | 13.6 | 18.0 | 11.8 | 20.7 | 50,427 |
| 2017 [6]............................ | 10,024 | 13.4 | 10.6 | 11.1 | 14.4 | 17.0 | 11.9 | 21.7 | 50,597 |
| **ASIAN AND PACIFIC ISLANDER [2]** | | | | | | | | | |
| 2000 [4]............................ | 2,982 | 4.7 | 5.5 | 5.6 | 10.3 | 15.3 | 14.6 | 44.0 | 89,382 |
| 2010 [5]............................ | 3,879 | 6.1 | 6.7 | 6.6 | 9.1 | 16.4 | 12.5 | 42.7 | 84,748 |
| 2016 [6]............................ | 4,725 | 4.8 | 5.3 | 5.6 | 7.4 | 14.9 | 14.0 | 48.0 | 95,509 |
| 2017 [6]............................ | 4,922 | 5.1 | 5.4 | 5.3 | 9.4 | 13.9 | 13.7 | 47.2 | 92,784 |
| **HISPANIC ORIGIN [3]** | | | | | | | | | |
| 2000 [4]............................ | 8,017 | 10.1 | 12.0 | 12.1 | 17.3 | 19.8 | 12.1 | 16.5 | 49,164 |
| 2010 [5]............................ | 11,284 | 14.1 | 12.8 | 13.6 | 14.7 | 18.9 | 10.4 | 15.5 | 44,280 |
| 2016 [6]............................ | 13,017 | 9.9 | 10.8 | 11.6 | 15.7 | 18.8 | 12.6 | 20.6 | 52,204 |
| 2017 [6]............................ | 13,201 | 9.2 | 10.5 | 11.6 | 15.1 | 19.1 | 13.3 | 21.2 | 53,614 |

[1] Includes other races not shown separately. [2] Beginning with data for 2002, represents White alone, Black alone, or Asian alone. [3] People of Hispanic origin may be of any race. [4] Data reflect implementation of Census 2000-based population controls and a 28,000 household sample expansion to 78,000 households. [5] Median income is calculated using $2,500 income intervals. Beginning with 2009 income data, the Census Bureau expanded the upper income intervals used to calculate medians to $250,000 or more. Medians falling in the upper open-ended interval are plugged with "$250,000." Before 2009, the upper open-ended interval was $100,000 and a plug of "$100,000" was used. Implementation of Census 2010-based population controls. [6] Data are based on redesigned questions on income. See source for more information.

Source: U.S. Census Bureau, *Income and Poverty in the United States: 2017*, Current Population Reports, P60-263, September 2018; and "Historical Income Tables: Families, Table F-23," <https://www.census.gov/topics/income-poverty/income/data/tables.html>, accessed November 2018.

# Table 730. Money Income of Families—Median Income by Race and Hispanic Origin in Current and Constant (2017) Dollars: 1990 to 2017

[In dollars. For 2001 and earlier data, the CPS allowed respondents to report only one race group. Beginning with the 2003 CPS covering data for 2002, respondents could choose more than one race. The CPS uses two basic ways to define a race group. A group such as Asian may be defined as those who reported Asian and no other race (the race-alone or single-race concept), or as those who reported Asian regardless of whether they also reported another race (the race-alone-or-in-combination concept). See also comments on race in the text for Section 1, Population. See also headnote, Table 729]

| Year | Median income in current dollars | | | | | Median income in constant (2017) dollars | | | | |
|---|---|---|---|---|---|---|---|---|---|---|
| | All races [1] | White [2] | Black [2] | Asian, Pacific Islander [2] | His-panic [3] | All races [1] | White [2] | Black [2] | Asian, Pacific Islander [2] | His-panic [3] |
| 1990 [4] | 35,353 | 36,915 | 21,423 | 42,246 | 23,431 | 64,489 | 67,339 | 39,079 | 77,063 | 42,742 |
| 2000 [4] | 50,732 | 53,029 | 33,676 | 62,617 | 34,442 | 72,417 | 75,696 | 48,071 | 89,382 | 49,164 |
| 2005 | 56,194 | 59,317 | 35,464 | 68,957 | 37,867 | 70,708 | 74,637 | 44,624 | 86,767 | 47,647 |
| 2010 [5] | 60,236 | 62,914 | 38,594 | 75,217 | 39,300 | 67,869 | 70,886 | 43,485 | 84,748 | 44,280 |
| 2011 | 60,974 | 64,081 | 40,495 | 72,996 | 40,061 | 66,601 | 69,995 | 44,232 | 79,732 | 43,758 |
| 2012 | 62,241 | 65,880 | 40,517 | 77,864 | 40,764 | 66,575 | 70,467 | 43,338 | 83,286 | 43,602 |
| 2013 [6] | 65,471 | 68,802 | 41,890 | 82,793 | 40,939 | 69,007 | 72,518 | 44,153 | 87,265 | 43,150 |
| 2014 [6] | 66,632 | 70,609 | 43,151 | 82,732 | 45,114 | 69,062 | 73,184 | 44,724 | 85,749 | 46,759 |
| 2015 [6] | 70,697 | 74,291 | 45,781 | 90,847 | 47,328 | 73,149 | 76,867 | 47,369 | 93,998 | 48,969 |
| 2016 [6] | 72,707 | 76,264 | 49,365 | 93,498 | 51,105 | 74,271 | 77,904 | 50,427 | 95,509 | 52,204 |
| 2017 [6] | 75,938 | 79,749 | 50,597 | 92,784 | 53,614 | 75,938 | 79,749 | 50,597 | 92,784 | 53,614 |

[1] Includes other races not shown separately. [2] Beginning 2002, data represent White alone, Black alone, or Asian alone. [3] People of Hispanic origin may be of any race. [4] Implementation of Census 2000-based population controls and 28,000 household sample expansion. [5] Median income calculated using $2,500 income intervals. Beginning 2009, Census Bureau expanded upper income intervals used to calculate medians to $250,000 or more. Medians falling in the upper open-ended interval are plugged with "$250,000." Before 2009, the upper open-ended interval was $100,000 and a plug of "$100,000" was used. Implementation of Census 2010-based population controls. [6] Based on redesigned questions on income.

Source: U.S. Census Bureau, *Income and Poverty in the United States: 2017*, Current Population Reports, P60-263, September 2018; and "Historical Income Tables: Families, Table F-05," <https://www.census.gov/topics/income-poverty/income/data/tables.html>, accessed November 2018.

# Table 731. Money Income of Families—Distribution of Families by Income Level and Selected Characteristics: 2017

[83,103 represents 83,103,000. See headnote, Table 729. Median income is calculated using $2,500 income intervals. Medians falling in the upper open-ended interval are plugged with "$250,000." For composition of regions, see map inside front cover]

| Characteristic | Number of families (1,000) | | | | | | | | Median income (dollars) |
|---|---|---|---|---|---|---|---|---|---|
| | Total | Under $15,000 | $15,000 to $24,999 | $25,000 to $34,999 | $35,000 to $49,999 | $50,000 to $74,999 | $75,000 to $99,999 | $100,000 and over | |
| **All families** | **83,103** | **5,307** | **5,466** | **6,647** | **9,711** | **13,858** | **11,840** | **30,274** | **75,938** |
| Region: | | | | | | | | | |
| Northeast | 14,254 | 830 | 816 | 1,084 | 1,473 | 2,167 | 1,925 | 5,962 | 83,641 |
| Midwest | 17,593 | 999 | 982 | 1,354 | 2,045 | 2,967 | 2,777 | 6,467 | 78,118 |
| South | 32,033 | 2,383 | 2,379 | 2,809 | 4,033 | 5,483 | 4,447 | 10,500 | 69,278 |
| West | 19,223 | 1,093 | 1,291 | 1,401 | 2,160 | 3,241 | 2,690 | 7,345 | 78,346 |
| Type of family: | | | | | | | | | |
| Married-couple families | 61,254 | 1,837 | 2,642 | 3,816 | 6,096 | 10,159 | 9,503 | 27,201 | 90,148 |
| Male householder, no spouse present | 6,424 | 550 | 617 | 735 | 1,111 | 1,251 | 849 | 1,309 | 52,950 |
| Female householder, no spouse present | 15,425 | 2,919 | 2,206 | 2,096 | 2,504 | 2,448 | 1,489 | 1,762 | 37,098 |
| Unrelated subfamilies | 446 | 118 | 76 | 57 | 79 | 51 | 23 | 42 | 30,558 |
| Age of householder: | | | | | | | | | |
| 15 to 24 years old | 3,017 | 512 | 388 | 363 | 476 | 512 | 327 | 437 | 41,855 |
| 25 to 34 years old | 12,910 | 1,254 | 989 | 1,237 | 1,593 | 2,460 | 1,870 | 3,504 | 63,088 |
| 35 to 44 years old | 17,031 | 1,102 | 999 | 1,143 | 1,805 | 2,604 | 2,516 | 6,861 | 82,452 |
| 45 to 54 years old | 16,645 | 777 | 729 | 872 | 1,513 | 2,558 | 2,386 | 7,809 | 93,891 |
| 55 to 64 years old | 15,750 | 757 | 861 | 921 | 1,634 | 2,484 | 2,311 | 6,782 | 86,575 |
| 65 years old and over | 17,751 | 903 | 1,498 | 2,111 | 2,691 | 3,242 | 2,428 | 4,877 | 61,946 |
| Number of earners: | | | | | | | | | |
| No earners | 13,558 | 3,124 | 1,999 | 2,011 | 2,049 | 1,871 | 1,060 | 1,446 | 33,029 |
| One earner | 27,257 | 1,955 | 2,897 | 3,492 | 4,521 | 5,180 | 3,404 | 5,810 | 52,237 |
| Two earners or more | 42,288 | 227 | 570 | 1,144 | 3,141 | 6,810 | 7,376 | 23,018 | 106,807 |
| Educational attainment of householder: **Persons age 25 and over, total** | **80,086** | **4,794** | **5,077** | **6,284** | **9,236** | **13,348** | **11,510** | **29,836** | **77,246** |
| Less than 9th grade | 2,679 | 421 | 486 | 427 | 443 | 444 | 248 | 213 | 35,155 |
| 9th to 12th grade (no diploma) | 4,739 | 703 | 748 | 730 | 716 | 835 | 507 | 501 | 38,973 |
| High school graduate (includes equivalency) | 20,577 | 1,714 | 1,805 | 2,281 | 3,307 | 4,115 | 2,966 | 4,387 | 56,063 |
| Some college, no degree | 13,735 | 847 | 974 | 1,227 | 1,842 | 2,614 | 2,123 | 4,111 | 68,442 |
| Associate's degree | 8,770 | 368 | 475 | 690 | 1,116 | 1,653 | 1,436 | 3,031 | 76,075 |
| Bachelor's degree or more | 29,586 | 742 | 591 | 929 | 1,812 | 3,687 | 4,232 | 17,595 | 119,115 |
| Bachelor's degree | 18,064 | 520 | 421 | 657 | 1,319 | 2,560 | 2,799 | 9,788 | 107,112 |
| Master's degree | 8,425 | 164 | 144 | 222 | 366 | 866 | 1,129 | 5,533 | 131,893 |
| Professional degree | 1,190 | 25 | 15 | 18 | 54 | 101 | 112 | 867 | 175,163 |
| Doctoral degree | 1,906 | 34 | 10 | 32 | 72 | 161 | 191 | 1,404 | 156,409 |

Source: U.S. Census Bureau, *Income and Poverty in the United States: 2017*, Current Population Reports, P60-263, September 2018; and "Current Population Survey Tables for Family Income: Table FINC-01," <https://www.census.gov/topics/income-poverty/income/data/tables.html>, accessed November 2018.

## Table 732. Median Income of Families by Type of Family in Current and Constant (2017) Dollars: 1990 to 2017

[In dollars. See headnote, Table 729. For definition of median, see Guide to Tabular Presentation]

| Year | Current dollars | | | | | | Constant (2017) dollars | | | | | |
| | All families | Married-couple families | | | Male house-holder, no spouse present | Female house-holder, no spouse present | All families | Married-couple families | | | Male house-holder, no spouse present | Female house-holder, no spouse present |
| | | Total | Wife in paid labor force | Wife not in paid labor force | | | | Total | Wife in paid labor force | Wife not in paid labor force | | |
|---|---|---|---|---|---|---|---|---|---|---|---|---|
| 1990......... | 35,353 | 39,895 | 46,777 | 30,265 | 29,046 | 16,932 | 64,489 | 72,775 | 85,328 | 55,208 | 52,984 | 30,887 |
| 2000 [1]....... | 50,732 | 59,099 | 69,235 | 39,982 | 37,727 | 25,716 | 72,417 | 84,360 | 98,829 | 57,072 | 53,853 | 36,708 |
| 2005......... | 56,194 | 65,906 | 78,755 | 44,457 | 41,111 | 27,244 | 70,708 | 82,928 | 99,096 | 55,939 | 51,729 | 34,281 |
| 2010 [2]....... | 60,236 | 72,241 | 87,397 | 48,733 | 43,206 | 29,155 | 67,869 | 81,395 | 98,472 | 54,908 | 48,681 | 32,849 |
| 2013 [3]....... | 65,471 | 78,614 | 96,062 | 54,231 | 47,191 | 31,131 | 69,007 | 82,860 | 101,251 | 57,160 | 49,740 | 32,813 |
| 2014 [3]....... | 66,632 | 80,814 | 99,983 | 54,779 | 47,597 | 31,770 | 69,062 | 83,761 | 103,629 | 56,776 | 49,333 | 32,928 |
| 2015 [3]....... | 70,697 | 84,324 | 103,699 | 56,010 | 49,772 | 34,126 | 73,149 | 87,248 | 107,295 | 57,952 | 51,498 | 35,310 |
| 2016 [3]....... | 72,707 | 86,811 | 106,082 | 58,694 | 51,568 | 36,658 | 74,271 | 88,678 | 108,363 | 59,956 | 52,677 | 37,446 |
| 2017 [3]....... | 75,938 | 90,148 | 110,893 | 61,901 | 52,950 | 37,098 | 75,938 | 90,148 | 110,893 | 61,901 | 52,950 | 37,098 |

[1] Implementation of Census 2000-based population controls, and of a 28,000 household sample expansion. [2] Median income calculated using $2,500 income intervals. Beginning with 2009 income data, the Census Bureau expanded from $100,000 the upper income intervals used to calculate medians to $250,000 or more. Implementation of Census 2010-based population controls. [3] Based on redesigned income questions; see source for details.

Source: U.S. Census Bureau, *Income and Poverty in the United States: 2017*, Current Population Reports, P60-263, September 2018; and "Historical Income Tables: Families, Table F-7," <https://www.census.gov/topics/income-poverty/income/data/tables.html>, accessed November 2018.

## Table 733. Married-Couple Families—Number and Median Income by Work Experience of Husbands and Wives and Presence of Related Children: 2017

[61,254 represents 61,254,000. Children are related by birth, marriage, or adoption. Based on the Current Population Survey, Annual Social and Economic Supplement; see text, Sections 1 and 13, and Appendix III. See headnote, Table 735]

| Work experience of husband or wife | Number (1,000) | | | | | Median income (dollars) | | | | |
| | All married-couple families | With no related children | One or more related children under 18 years old | | | All married-couple families | With no related children | One or more related children under 18 years old | | |
| | | | Total | One child | Two children or more | | | Total | One child | Two children or more |
|---|---|---|---|---|---|---|---|---|---|---|
| **All married-couple families**........ | **61,254** | **36,026** | **25,229** | **9,854** | **15,375** | **90,148** | **84,717** | **97,622** | **101,168** | **95,343** |
| Husband worked [1].................... | 45,845 | 22,523 | 23,322 | 8,976 | 14,346 | 104,311 | 107,520 | 101,354 | 105,827 | 98,899 |
| Wife worked....................... | 32,444 | 16,026 | 16,418 | 6,742 | 9,676 | 116,716 | 117,251 | 116,190 | 117,748 | 114,828 |
| Wife did not work.................. | 13,401 | 6,497 | 6,904 | 2,235 | 4,669 | 75,424 | 81,775 | 66,971 | 73,546 | 65,022 |
| Husband worked year-round, full time [1]........................ | 38,417 | 17,808 | 20,608 | 7,915 | 12,693 | 109,680 | 113,038 | 105,225 | 110,695 | 102,145 |
| Wife worked....................... | 27,673 | 13,135 | 14,538 | 5,961 | 8,577 | 121,095 | 121,977 | 120,206 | 121,452 | 118,970 |
| Wife did not work.................. | 10,744 | 4,674 | 6,070 | 1,954 | 4,116 | 78,851 | 85,817 | 71,861 | 77,733 | 69,023 |
| Husband did not work [1]............ | 15,409 | 13,502 | 1,907 | 877 | 1,029 | 50,538 | 50,672 | 49,580 | 52,186 | 46,081 |
| Wife worked....................... | 4,612 | 3,462 | 1,150 | 505 | 646 | 66,702 | 69,134 | 60,436 | 62,193 | 56,480 |
| Wife did not work.................. | 10,797 | 10,041 | 756 | 372 | 384 | 43,893 | 44,521 | 31,151 | 36,278 | 21,679 |

[1] Spouse has any work status.

Source: U.S. Census Bureau, *Income and Poverty in the United States: 2017*, Current Population Reports, P60-263, September 2018; and "Current Population Survey Tables for Family Income: Table FINC-04," <http://www.census.gov/topics/income-poverty/income/data/tables.html>, accessed November 2018.

## Table 734. Median Income of People in Constant (2017) Dollars by Sex, Race, and Hispanic Origin: 2000 to 2017

[In dollars. People as of March of following year. People age 15 and over. Constant dollars based on CPI-U-RS deflator. Based on the Current Population Survey, Annual Social and Economic Supplement (CPS ASEC); see text, this section and Section 1 and Appendix III. For 2001 and earlier data, the CPS allowed respondents to report only one race group. Beginning with the 2003 CPS covering data for 2002, respondents could choose more than one race. The CPS uses two basic ways of defining a race group. A group such as Asian may be defined as 1) those who reported Asian and no other race (the race-alone or single-race concept), or 2) those who reported Asian regardless of whether they also reported another race (the race-alone-or-in-combination concept). See also headnote, Table 729]

| Race and Hispanic origin | Male | | | | | Female | | | | |
| | 2000 [1] | 2005 | 2010 [2] | 2016 [3] | 2017 [3] | 2000 [1] | 2005 | 2010 [2] | 2016 [3] | 2017 [3] |
|---|---|---|---|---|---|---|---|---|---|---|
| **All races [4]**.................... | **40,458** | **39,353** | **36,286** | **39,705** | **40,396** | **22,929** | **23,374** | **23,408** | **25,427** | **25,486** |
| White [5]......................... | 42,533 | 40,490 | 38,730 | 41,506 | 41,578 | 22,952 | 23,491 | 23,544 | 25,763 | 25,793 |
| Black [5]......................... | 30,466 | 28,504 | 26,248 | 30,275 | 30,112 | 22,669 | 22,185 | 22,135 | 23,326 | 23,639 |
| Asian [5]......................... | 44,012 | 43,052 | 40,362 | 47,592 | 48,842 | 24,775 | 27,230 | 26,549 | 27,347 | 28,260 |
| Hispanic [6]...................... | 27,832 | 27,794 | 25,261 | 31,168 | 30,691 | 17,483 | 18,919 | 18,356 | 20,334 | 20,312 |
| White non-Hispanic........... | 44,976 | 44,474 | 41,862 | 44,333 | 45,836 | 23,788 | 24,475 | 24,467 | 27,065 | 27,116 |

[1] Implementation of Census 2000-based population controls and sample expanded by 28,000 households. [2] See footnote 2, Table 732. [3] Based on redesigned questions on income. [4] Includes other races not shown separately. [5] Data for 2002 and later refer to people reporting White alone, Black alone, or Asian alone ("Asian alone" replaced "Asian and Pacific Islander"). [6] People of Hispanic origin may be of any race.

Source: U.S. Census Bureau, *Income and Poverty in the United States: 2017*, Current Population Reports, P60-263, September 2018; and "Historical Income Tables: People, Tables P-2 and P-5," <https://www.census.gov/topics/income-poverty/income/data/tables.html>, accessed November 2018.

## Table 735. Money Income of People—People by Income Level and by Sex and Selected Characteristics: 2017

[127,288 represents 127,288,000. People age 15 and over as of March of following year. Based on the Current Population Survey, Annual Social and Economic Supplement (CPS ASEC), see text, this section and Section 1, and Appendix III. Median income is calculated using $2,500 income intervals. Medians falling in the upper open-ended interval are plugged with "$250,000." For definition of median, see Guide to Tabular Presentation]

| Characteristic | All persons (1,000) | People with income Number (1,000) Total (1,000) | Under $5,000 or loss | $5,000 to $9,999 | $10,000 to $14,999 | $15,000 to $24,999 | $25,000 to $34,999 | $35,000 to $49,999 | $50,000 to $74,999 | $75,000 and over | Median income (current dollars) |
|---|---|---|---|---|---|---|---|---|---|---|---|
| **MALE** | | | | | | | | | | | |
| Total | 127,288 | 114,849 | 7,221 | 5,952 | 7,350 | 15,428 | 14,351 | 17,250 | 19,515 | 27,782 | 40,396 |
| 15 to 24 years old | 21,426 | 13,809 | 3,658 | 1,978 | 1,571 | 2,648 | 1,717 | 1,127 | 664 | 446 | 13,734 |
| 25 to 34 years old | 22,490 | 20,982 | 785 | 934 | 943 | 2,650 | 3,341 | 4,232 | 4,180 | 3,916 | 40,575 |
| 35 to 44 years old | 20,071 | 19,204 | 574 | 518 | 618 | 1,829 | 2,107 | 3,159 | 4,044 | 6,354 | 52,403 |
| 45 to 54 years old | 20,340 | 19,394 | 656 | 547 | 757 | 1,704 | 1,986 | 3,090 | 3,972 | 6,681 | 53,985 |
| 55 to 64 years old | 19,902 | 19,007 | 844 | 759 | 1,171 | 2,266 | 1,970 | 2,621 | 3,451 | 5,925 | 48,863 |
| 65 years old and over | 23,059 | 22,454 | 702 | 1,215 | 2,290 | 4,330 | 3,230 | 3,021 | 3,204 | 4,461 | 32,654 |
| Educational attainment: | | | | | | | | | | | |
| Total [1] | 105,862 | 101,040 | 3,563 | 3,973 | 5,780 | 12,781 | 12,634 | 16,123 | 18,851 | 27,336 | 45,256 |
| Less than 9th grade | 4,256 | 3,903 | 181 | 444 | 570 | 1,030 | 666 | 542 | 324 | 144 | 21,899 |
| 9th to 12th grade [2] | 6,939 | 6,249 | 352 | 696 | 779 | 1,401 | 1,057 | 864 | 686 | 414 | 24,085 |
| High school graduate [3] | 31,325 | 29,381 | 1,106 | 1,349 | 2,273 | 4,851 | 4,950 | 5,684 | 5,314 | 3,855 | 35,276 |
| Some college, no degree | 16,981 | 16,300 | 677 | 609 | 863 | 2,276 | 2,310 | 2,958 | 3,396 | 3,211 | 40,912 |
| Associate's degree | 9,687 | 9,401 | 315 | 236 | 436 | 1,072 | 1,184 | 1,785 | 2,165 | 2,208 | 46,518 |
| Bachelor's degree or more | 36,674 | 35,807 | 932 | 640 | 859 | 2,150 | 2,466 | 4,290 | 6,966 | 17,504 | 72,315 |
| Bachelor's degree | 23,080 | 22,462 | 630 | 413 | 638 | 1,556 | 1,853 | 3,133 | 4,655 | 9,585 | 65,325 |
| Master's degree | 9,217 | 9,059 | 208 | 168 | 165 | 443 | 447 | 834 | 1,666 | 5,128 | 82,722 |
| Professional degree | 1,780 | 1,724 | 38 | 19 | 28 | 44 | 88 | 125 | 263 | 1,120 | 110,651 |
| Doctoral degree | 2,597 | 2,561 | 56 | 41 | 29 | 107 | 78 | 197 | 382 | 1,671 | 102,423 |
| Housing tenure: | | | | | | | | | | | |
| Owner-occupied | 87,130 | 79,293 | 4,973 | 3,523 | 4,606 | 9,424 | 8,831 | 11,466 | 14,026 | 22,444 | 45,302 |
| Renter-occupied | 38,726 | 34,268 | 2,166 | 2,320 | 2,633 | 5,710 | 5,340 | 5,596 | 5,321 | 5,183 | 31,933 |
| Occupier paid no cash rent | 1,432 | 1,289 | 82 | 109 | 112 | 294 | 180 | 189 | 168 | 156 | 27,328 |
| Region: | | | | | | | | | | | |
| Northeast | 22,391 | 20,427 | 1,379 | 1,052 | 1,262 | 2,514 | 2,329 | 2,854 | 3,391 | 5,645 | 42,300 |
| Midwest | 26,677 | 24,509 | 1,715 | 1,202 | 1,494 | 3,077 | 3,021 | 3,779 | 4,574 | 5,647 | 40,915 |
| South | 47,514 | 42,370 | 2,546 | 2,284 | 2,889 | 5,997 | 5,663 | 6,518 | 6,962 | 9,512 | 37,838 |
| West | 30,706 | 27,543 | 1,581 | 1,413 | 1,706 | 3,839 | 3,338 | 4,100 | 4,587 | 6,979 | 40,727 |
| **FEMALE** | | | | | | | | | | | |
| Total | 134,885 | 116,618 | 12,968 | 10,996 | 12,951 | 20,432 | 15,159 | 16,020 | 14,282 | 13,811 | 25,486 |
| 15 to 24 years old | 20,916 | 13,266 | 3,894 | 2,251 | 1,688 | 2,476 | 1,469 | 960 | 395 | 131 | 11,185 |
| 25 to 34 years old | 22,364 | 19,392 | 2,091 | 1,275 | 1,319 | 3,083 | 3,425 | 3,376 | 2,842 | 1,982 | 30,601 |
| 35 to 44 years old | 20,588 | 18,244 | 1,970 | 1,068 | 1,279 | 2,427 | 2,311 | 3,060 | 2,884 | 3,245 | 35,216 |
| 45 to 54 years old | 21,196 | 19,170 | 1,654 | 1,203 | 1,424 | 2,725 | 2,440 | 3,060 | 3,146 | 3,519 | 35,444 |
| 55 to 64 years old | 21,799 | 19,745 | 1,955 | 1,761 | 1,981 | 3,111 | 2,262 | 2,917 | 2,701 | 3,057 | 29,531 |
| 65 years old and over | 28,021 | 26,802 | 1,404 | 3,439 | 5,260 | 6,610 | 3,251 | 2,646 | 2,314 | 1,876 | 19,180 |
| Educational attainment: | | | | | | | | | | | |
| Total [1] | 113,969 | 103,352 | 9,074 | 8,745 | 11,262 | 17,956 | 13,690 | 15,060 | 13,887 | 13,680 | 27,709 |
| Less than 9th grade | 4,472 | 3,294 | 403 | 729 | 787 | 809 | 334 | 143 | 64 | 25 | 12,365 |
| 9th to 12th grade [2] | 6,743 | 5,471 | 569 | 1,148 | 1,225 | 1,359 | 590 | 327 | 182 | 72 | 13,801 |
| High school graduate [3] | 31,360 | 27,672 | 2,557 | 3,324 | 4,119 | 6,716 | 4,293 | 3,687 | 2,134 | 842 | 20,199 |
| Some college, no degree | 18,461 | 16,919 | 1,522 | 1,333 | 2,124 | 3,421 | 2,922 | 2,638 | 1,906 | 1,053 | 25,161 |
| Associate's degree | 12,682 | 11,905 | 911 | 775 | 1,168 | 2,072 | 1,937 | 2,204 | 1,777 | 1,062 | 30,406 |
| Bachelor's degree or more | 40,251 | 38,092 | 3,113 | 1,436 | 1,840 | 3,578 | 3,613 | 6,061 | 7,825 | 10,627 | 48,223 |
| Bachelor's degree | 25,155 | 23,562 | 2,219 | 1,018 | 1,307 | 2,581 | 2,619 | 4,115 | 4,629 | 5,073 | 41,827 |
| Master's degree | 11,831 | 11,379 | 737 | 318 | 442 | 802 | 830 | 1,663 | 2,690 | 3,897 | 56,806 |
| Professional degree | 1,393 | 1,335 | 69 | 41 | 39 | 85 | 67 | 116 | 222 | 695 | 77,090 |
| Doctoral degree | 1,872 | 1,817 | 87 | 59 | 51 | 110 | 97 | 168 | 283 | 962 | 77,766 |
| Housing tenure: | | | | | | | | | | | |
| Owner-occupied | 91,149 | 80,152 | 8,968 | 6,876 | 8,252 | 13,217 | 9,714 | 11,060 | 10,905 | 11,159 | 27,213 |
| Renter-occupied | 42,241 | 35,224 | 3,848 | 3,932 | 4,492 | 6,930 | 5,315 | 4,828 | 3,305 | 2,574 | 21,994 |
| Occupier paid no cash rent | 1,495 | 1,242 | 152 | 189 | 207 | 284 | 130 | 131 | 71 | 77 | 17,056 |
| Region: | | | | | | | | | | | |
| Northeast | 23,936 | 21,213 | 2,160 | 2,038 | 2,347 | 3,382 | 2,758 | 2,794 | 2,801 | 2,934 | 26,879 |
| Midwest | 28,017 | 25,107 | 2,639 | 2,375 | 2,651 | 4,466 | 3,423 | 3,581 | 3,299 | 2,671 | 25,966 |
| South | 51,324 | 43,577 | 5,001 | 4,164 | 5,030 | 8,071 | 5,647 | 6,026 | 5,021 | 4,617 | 24,144 |
| West | 31,607 | 26,721 | 3,168 | 2,419 | 2,923 | 4,513 | 3,331 | 3,618 | 3,161 | 3,588 | 25,761 |

[1] Population age 25 and over. [2] No diploma attained. [3] Includes high school equivalency.

Source: U.S. Census Bureau, *Income and Poverty in the United States: 2017*, Current Population Reports, P60-263, September 2018; and "Current Population Survey Tables for Personal Income: Table PINC-01," <https://www.census.gov/topics/income-poverty/income/data/tables.html>, accessed November 2018.

## Table 736. Average Earnings of Year-Round, Full-Time Workers by Educational Attainment: 2017

[In dollars. For people 18 years old and over, as of March of the following year. Based on the Current Population Survey, Annual Social and Economic Supplement (ASEC); see text, this section and Section 1, and Appendix III]

| Sex and age | All workers | Less than 9th grade | High school | | College | | |
| | | | 9th to 12th grade (no diploma) | High school graduate [1] | Some college, no degree | Associate degree | Bachelor's degree or more |
|---|---|---|---|---|---|---|---|
| **Male, total**.............. | **73,413** | **35,689** | **41,024** | **51,493** | **59,183** | **63,961** | **105,663** |
| 18 to 24 years old.......... | 37,043 | (B) | 37,258 | 34,292 | 34,184 | 33,673 | 54,277 |
| 25 to 34 years old.......... | 58,661 | 31,033 | 36,564 | 42,604 | 48,402 | 52,611 | 80,520 |
| 35 to 44 years old.......... | 77,399 | 34,759 | 40,338 | 55,901 | 62,767 | 70,113 | 105,687 |
| 45 to 54 years old.......... | 81,872 | 39,598 | 43,154 | 55,088 | 69,581 | 71,226 | 117,807 |
| 55 to 64 years old.......... | 85,557 | 36,305 | 46,265 | 62,964 | 68,623 | 69,210 | 123,473 |
| 65 years old and over...... | 90,784 | 43,835 | 47,402 | 52,712 | 67,941 | 69,965 | 128,060 |
| **Female, total**.............. | **55,049** | **25,584** | **28,500** | **36,927** | **40,969** | **46,849** | **74,274** |
| 18 to 24 years old.......... | 29,817 | (B) | 25,065 | 23,762 | 26,036 | 27,754 | 44,293 |
| 25 to 34 years old.......... | 48,576 | (B) | 27,499 | 31,393 | 35,964 | 40,041 | 61,498 |
| 35 to 44 years old.......... | 61,115 | 23,698 | 29,002 | 39,262 | 41,046 | 49,245 | 80,997 |
| 45 to 54 years old.......... | 59,235 | 25,586 | 29,310 | 40,651 | 45,903 | 50,177 | 80,189 |
| 55 to 64 years old.......... | 58,429 | 28,875 | 28,352 | 40,643 | 46,442 | 51,519 | 82,473 |
| 65 years old and over...... | 61,231 | (B) | 30,965 | 39,617 | 64,522 | 53,864 | 79,870 |

B Base figure too small to meet statistical standards for reliability of derived figure. [1] Includes general educational development equivalency.

Source: U.S. Census Bureau, *Income and Poverty in the United States: 2017,* Current Population Reports, P60-263, September 2018; and "Current Population Survey Tables for Personal Income: Table PINC-04," <https://www.census.gov/topics/income-poverty/income/data/tables.html>, accessed November 2018.

## Table 737. Per Capita Money Income in Current and Constant (2017) Dollars by Race and Hispanic Origin: 1990 to 2017

[In dollars. Constant dollars based on 2017 CPI-U-RS deflator. People as of March of following year. Based on the Current Population Survey, Annual Social and Economic Supplement (ASEC); see text, this section, Section 1, and Appendix III. See headnote, Table 729]

| Year | Current dollars | | | | | Constant (2017) dollars | | | | |
| | All races [1] | White [2] | Black [2] | Asian [2] | His-panic [3] | All races [1] | White [2] | Black [2] | Asian [2] | His-panic [3] |
|---|---|---|---|---|---|---|---|---|---|---|
| 1990............... | 14,387 | 15,265 | 9,017 | (NA) | 8,424 | 26,244 | 27,846 | 16,448 | (NA) | 15,367 |
| 2000 [4]............. | 22,346 | 23,582 | 14,796 | 23,350 | 12,651 | 31,898 | 33,662 | 21,120 | 33,331 | 18,059 |
| 2005 [5]............. | 25,036 | 26,496 | 16,874 | 27,331 | 14,483 | 31,502 | 33,339 | 21,232 | 34,390 | 18,224 |
| 2010 [6]............. | 26,558 | 28,356 | 18,019 | 28,673 | 15,044 | 29,923 | 31,949 | 20,302 | 32,306 | 16,950 |
| 2013 [7]............. | 30,027 | 31,759 | 20,658 | 34,843 | 17,354 | 31,649 | 33,474 | 21,774 | 36,725 | 18,291 |
| 2014 [7]............. | 30,176 | 32,089 | 21,066 | 34,096 | 17,699 | 31,276 | 33,259 | 21,834 | 35,339 | 18,344 |
| 2015 [7]............. | 31,653 | 33,564 | 22,452 | 36,280 | 19,457 | 32,751 | 34,728 | 23,231 | 37,538 | 20,132 |
| 2016 [7]............. | 33,205 | 35,168 | 23,622 | 38,156 | 20,430 | 33,919 | 35,924 | 24,130 | 38,977 | 20,869 |
| 2017 [7]............. | 34,489 | 36,521 | 24,298 | 40,767 | 20,937 | 34,489 | 36,521 | 24,298 | 40,767 | 20,937 |

NA Not available. [1] Includes other races, not shown separately. [2] As of 2002, data refer to people reporting specified race alone ("Asian alone" replaced "Asian and Pacific Islander"). [3] People of Hispanic origin may be of any race. [4] Implementation of Census 2000-based population controls, and of a 28,000 household sample expansion. [5] Data have been revised to reflect a correction to the weights in the 2005 ASEC. [6] Implementation of Census 2010-based population controls. [7] As of 2013, data based on redesigned income questions.

Source: U.S. Census Bureau, *Income and Poverty in the United States: 2017,* Current Population Reports, P60-263, September 2018; and "Historical Income Tables: People, Table P-1," <https://www.census.gov/topics/income-poverty/income/data/tables.html>, accessed November 2018.

## Table 738. Money Income of People—People by Income Level and by Sex, Race, and Hispanic Origin: 2017

[In thousands (127,288 represents 127,288,000). People age 15 years and over as of March of the following year. Based on Current Population Survey, Annual Social and Economic Supplement (ASEC); see text, this section, Section 1, and Appendix III]

| Income interval | Male | | | | | Female | | | | |
| | All races [1] | White alone | Black alone | Asian alone | His-panic [2] | All races [1] | White alone | Black alone | Asian alone | His-panic [2] |
|---|---|---|---|---|---|---|---|---|---|---|
| **Total**................... | **127,288** | **100,096** | **15,304** | **7,685** | **21,710** | **134,885** | **103,674** | **18,055** | **8,531** | **21,784** |
| Under $10,000 [3]................ | 25,610 | 18,017 | 4,580 | 1,725 | 5,548 | 42,230 | 31,313 | 5,825 | 3,274 | 9,460 |
| $10,000 to $19,999............. | 14,967 | 11,423 | 2,289 | 667 | 2,989 | 23,709 | 18,326 | 3,438 | 1,125 | 3,948 |
| $20,000 to $29,999............. | 15,263 | 12,055 | 1,963 | 699 | 3,545 | 17,522 | 13,508 | 2,585 | 827 | 2,959 |
| $30,000 to $39,999............. | 13,300 | 10,522 | 1,695 | 674 | 2,786 | 13,347 | 10,287 | 1,962 | 649 | 1,949 |
| $40,000 to $49,999............. | 10,849 | 8,754 | 1,145 | 585 | 1,945 | 9,984 | 7,862 | 1,318 | 510 | 1,145 |
| $50,000 to $59,999............. | 9,106 | 7,509 | 971 | 407 | 1,297 | 7,217 | 5,801 | 846 | 395 | 667 |
| $60,000 to $74,999............. | 10,409 | 8,488 | 1,043 | 617 | 1,297 | 7,065 | 5,663 | 805 | 422 | 625 |
| $75,000 to $84,999............. | 5,359 | 4,466 | 364 | 404 | 576 | 3,381 | 2,713 | 333 | 256 | 278 |
| $85,000 to $99,999............. | 4,810 | 4,001 | 366 | 322 | 509 | 3,101 | 2,483 | 271 | 289 | 255 |
| $100,000 to $149,999........... | 9,816 | 8,219 | 537 | 883 | 743 | 4,707 | 3,607 | 473 | 535 | 314 |
| $150,000 to $199,999........... | 3,941 | 3,306 | 196 | 386 | 239 | 1,348 | 1,079 | 105 | 137 | 81 |
| $200,000 to $249,999........... | 1,731 | 1,491 | 78 | 135 | 123 | 538 | 441 | 24 | 56 | 41 |
| $250,000 and above............ | 2,125 | 1,843 | 77 | 179 | 113 | 736 | 590 | 68 | 57 | 59 |

[1] Includes other races not shown separately. [2] Persons of Hispanic origin may be of any race. [3] Includes persons without income.

Source: U.S. Census Bureau, *Income and Poverty in the United States: 2017,* Current Population Reports, P60-263, September 2018; and "Current Population Survey Tables for Personal Income: Table PINC-11," <https://www.census.gov/topics/income-poverty/income/data/tables.html>, accessed November 2018.

# Table 739. Household, Family, and Per Capita Income, and Individuals and Families Below Poverty Level, by City: 2017

[The American Community Survey universe includes the household population and the population living in institutions, college dormitories, and other group quarters. Based on a sample and subject to sampling variability; see text, Section 1 and Appendix III. For definition of median, see Guide to Tabular Presentation. CDP is Census designated place]

| City | Median household income (dol.) | Median family income (dol.) | Per capita income (dol.) | Number below poverty level [1] | | Percent below poverty level | |
|---|---|---|---|---|---|---|---|
| | | | | Individuals [1] | Families | Individuals [1] | Families |
| Albuquerque, NM. | 50,456 | 67,301 | 28,732 | 84,169 | 13,520 | 15.2 | 10.5 |
| Anaheim, CA. | 70,395 | 72,477 | 26,538 | 55,296 | 9,784 | 15.9 | 13.4 |
| Anchorage, AK. | 79,166 | 91,590 | 37,992 | 28,300 | 4,026 | 9.9 | 5.7 |
| Arlington, TX. | 57,083 | 66,985 | 25,807 | 61,478 | 11,385 | 15.7 | 12.3 |
| Atlanta, GA. | 57,597 | 78,645 | 44,690 | 88,065 | 13,279 | 19.3 | 14.6 |
| Aurora, CO. | 63,055 | 74,160 | 29,099 | 38,820 | 7,132 | 10.7 | 8.4 |
| Austin, TX. | 67,755 | 87,200 | 40,323 | 121,955 | 16,934 | 13.1 | 8.7 |
| Bakersfield, CA. | 57,105 | 60,183 | 24,170 | 66,911 | 11,359 | 17.8 | 13.0 |
| Baltimore, MD. | 47,131 | 58,613 | 29,242 | 130,980 | 20,496 | 22.2 | 16.9 |
| Boston, MA. | 66,758 | 76,603 | 42,236 | 119,925 | 17,813 | 18.7 | 13.9 |
| Charlotte, NC. | 61,350 | 75,564 | 37,300 | 104,780 | 18,100 | 12.4 | 9.3 |
| Chicago, IL. | 55,295 | 64,441 | 34,269 | 495,511 | 81,770 | 18.6 | 14.8 |
| Cincinnati, OH. | 38,938 | 55,434 | 29,465 | 79,976 | 11,523 | 27.7 | 19.6 |
| Cleveland, OH. | 28,974 | 35,053 | 19,401 | 124,234 | 22,822 | 33.1 | 28.3 |
| Colorado Springs, CO. | 59,514 | 71,772 | 31,585 | 58,335 | 11,578 | 12.8 | 10.1 |
| Columbus, OH. | 51,708 | 61,094 | 27,544 | 169,323 | 27,665 | 19.8 | 14.4 |
| Corpus Christi, TX. | 53,605 | 64,649 | 27,593 | 46,110 | 8,488 | 14.5 | 10.8 |
| Dallas, TX. | 50,627 | 55,540 | 32,114 | 245,123 | 45,366 | 18.5 | 15.4 |
| Denver, CO. | 65,224 | 85,166 | 42,271 | 84,458 | 12,399 | 12.2 | 8.7 |
| Detroit, MI. | 30,344 | 36,939 | 17,667 | 227,766 | 39,531 | 34.5 | 28.0 |
| El Paso, TX. | 44,754 | 50,933 | 21,908 | 130,692 | 27,239 | 19.3 | 16.4 |
| Fort Worth, TX. | 60,205 | 69,973 | 28,174 | 111,101 | 19,798 | 12.9 | 9.8 |
| Fresno, CA. | 48,600 | 53,428 | 22,870 | 122,772 | 22,591 | 23.7 | 19.3 |
| Greensboro, NC. | 47,043 | 60,993 | 28,556 | 46,597 | 8,670 | 16.8 | 13.0 |
| Henderson, NV. | 69,667 | 85,567 | 39,234 | 25,043 | 4,398 | 8.3 | 5.7 |
| Honolulu (Urban) CDP, HI. | 69,193 | 87,905 | 37,303 | 35,080 | 6,147 | 10.3 | 8.1 |
| Houston, TX. | 50,896 | 56,751 | 31,175 | 469,187 | 87,986 | 20.6 | 17.1 |
| Indianapolis, IN. | 47,225 | 59,275 | 27,304 | 146,863 | 22,782 | 17.5 | 12.4 |
| Jacksonville, FL. | 51,497 | 64,742 | 28,531 | 132,022 | 25,248 | 15.1 | 11.8 |
| Kansas City, MO. | 51,330 | 68,780 | 31,767 | 74,400 | 11,500 | 15.5 | 10.6 |
| Las Vegas, NV. | 56,699 | 67,201 | 30,121 | 91,538 | 16,225 | 14.5 | 10.9 |
| Lexington-Fayette, KY. | 56,137 | 75,756 | 32,927 | 51,096 | 7,678 | 16.6 | 10.4 |
| Lincoln, NE. | 56,160 | 75,146 | 30,012 | 33,554 | 5,122 | 12.4 | 7.8 |
| Long Beach, CA. | 60,557 | 67,882 | 32,006 | 76,862 | 12,689 | 16.6 | 12.5 |
| Los Angeles, CA. | 60,197 | 67,685 | 33,496 | 683,382 | 108,232 | 17.4 | 13.2 |
| Louisville/Jefferson County, KY [2]. | 51,960 | 67,965 | 29,336 | 91,778 | 16,873 | 15.1 | 11.3 |
| Memphis, TN. | 39,333 | 46,985 | 24,143 | 156,871 | 27,546 | 24.6 | 19.9 |
| Mesa, AZ. | 55,014 | 67,826 | 27,808 | 73,484 | 12,906 | 15.0 | 11.1 |
| Miami, FL. | 40,327 | 41,874 | 27,250 | 103,445 | 19,672 | 22.7 | 20.2 |
| Milwaukee, WI. | 39,098 | 46,302 | 22,098 | 144,727 | 24,584 | 25.0 | 20.2 |
| Minneapolis, MN. | 60,789 | 82,994 | 38,131 | 74,432 | 8,882 | 18.3 | 11.6 |
| Nashville-Davidson, TN [2]. | 57,737 | 67,088 | 33,028 | 93,800 | 16,693 | 14.6 | 10.8 |
| New Orleans, LA. | 36,999 | 55,138 | 28,297 | 99,735 | 13,695 | 26.2 | 18.9 |
| New York, NY. | 60,879 | 68,353 | 37,447 | 1,522,962 | 277,207 | 18.0 | 14.7 |
| Newark, NJ. | 35,167 | 39,624 | 18,812 | 76,159 | 15,539 | 27.8 | 25.4 |
| Oakland, CA. | 70,577 | 77,401 | 40,262 | 64,305 | 10,159 | 15.3 | 11.6 |
| Oklahoma City, OK. | 52,062 | 67,201 | 28,507 | 99,844 | 17,151 | 15.8 | 11.7 |
| Omaha, NE. | 56,406 | 72,055 | 31,655 | 59,133 | 10,193 | 13.0 | 9.1 |
| Philadelphia, PA. | 39,759 | 54,431 | 26,039 | 395,664 | 54,684 | 25.7 | 18.3 |
| Phoenix, AZ. | 56,696 | 65,509 | 27,999 | 268,855 | 45,526 | 16.8 | 12.8 |
| Pittsburgh, PA. | 45,851 | 66,263 | 32,602 | 56,543 | 7,649 | 20.2 | 13.0 |
| Plano, TX. | 94,306 | 105,512 | 46,412 | 14,412 | 3,386 | 5.1 | 4.5 |
| Portland, OR. | 66,187 | 85,262 | 37,876 | 93,386 | 14,091 | 14.7 | 10.2 |
| Raleigh, NC. | 64,660 | 82,597 | 35,484 | 56,263 | 8,762 | 12.6 | 8.4 |
| Riverside, CA. | 66,928 | 73,467 | 24,733 | 40,209 | 6,030 | 12.8 | 9.3 |
| Sacramento, CA. | 56,943 | 64,554 | 31,207 | 76,886 | 13,090 | 15.6 | 11.6 |
| San Antonio, TX. | 50,044 | 59,810 | 24,625 | 257,166 | 44,234 | 17.3 | 13.6 |
| San Diego, CA. | 76,662 | 90,695 | 39,325 | 182,267 | 25,891 | 13.1 | 8.5 |
| San Francisco, CA. | 110,816 | 131,244 | 64,597 | 86,695 | 8,694 | 10.0 | 5.1 |
| San Jose, CA. | 104,675 | 119,331 | 43,593 | 86,282 | 13,604 | 8.4 | 5.8 |
| San Juan, Puerto Rico. | 21,533 | 29,778 | 19,138 | 126,215 | 26,842 | 39.8 | 36.1 |
| Santa Ana, CA. | 65,655 | 64,156 | 20,326 | 50,830 | 8,026 | 15.4 | 13.2 |
| Seattle, WA. | 86,822 | 121,256 | 55,276 | 78,605 | 9,036 | 11.1 | 6.0 |
| St. Louis, MO. | 41,441 | 56,652 | 28,913 | 61,212 | 9,291 | 20.3 | 14.0 |
| St. Paul, MN. | 54,290 | 67,552 | 29,198 | 55,782 | 8,645 | 18.7 | 13.7 |
| Stockton, CA. | 51,336 | 58,014 | 22,831 | 58,956 | 9,760 | 19.3 | 14.8 |
| Tampa, FL. | 50,489 | 64,692 | 34,278 | 69,559 | 11,581 | 18.6 | 14.0 |
| Tucson, AZ. | 41,613 | 51,296 | 22,511 | 112,670 | 19,024 | 22.1 | 16.4 |
| Tulsa, OK. | 45,894 | 56,706 | 28,743 | 76,804 | 14,405 | 19.5 | 15.4 |
| Virginia Beach, VA. | 72,586 | 86,305 | 36,608 | 35,394 | 5,874 | 8.0 | 5.1 |
| Washington, DC. | 82,372 | 106,528 | 52,500 | 109,920 | 15,929 | 16.6 | 13.3 |
| Wichita, KS. | 50,504 | 63,834 | 26,900 | 63,888 | 12,011 | 16.6 | 12.5 |

[1] Poverty status was determined for all people except institutionalized people, people in military group quarters, people in college dormitories, and unrelated individuals under 15 years old. [2] Represents metropolitan government (balance) of locality.

Source: U.S. Census Bureau, 2017 American Community Survey: DP03, B01003, B17001, and B17019, <http://factfinder.census.gov>, accessed November 2018. See also <http://www.census.gov/programs-surveys/acs/>.

# Table 740. Individuals and Families Below Poverty Level—Number and Rate by State: 2007 and 2017

[In thousands (38,052 represents 38,052,000), except as indicated. Represents number and percent below poverty in the past 12 months. Poverty status was determined for all people except institutionalized people, people in military group quarters, people in college dormitories, and unrelated individuals under 15 years old. These groups were excluded from the numerator and denominator when calculating poverty rates. Based on a sample and subject to sampling variability; see Appendix III]

| State | Number below poverty (1,000) | | | | Percent below poverty | | | |
| | Individuals | | Families | | Individuals | | Families | |
| | 2007 | 2017 | 2007 | 2017 | 2007 | 2017 | 2007 | 2017 |
|---|---|---|---|---|---|---|---|---|
| United States.......... | 38,052 | 42,584 | 7,162 | 7,501 | 13.0 | 13.4 | 9.5 | 9.5 |
| Alabama................. | 760 | 803 | 163 | 154 | 16.9 | 16.9 | 13.1 | 12.8 |
| Alaska.................. | 60 | 80 | 10 | 12 | 8.9 | 11.1 | 6.5 | 7.4 |
| Arizona................. | 881 | 1,019 | 152 | 176 | 14.2 | 14.9 | 10.2 | 10.7 |
| Arkansas................ | 492 | 478 | 104 | 88 | 17.9 | 16.4 | 13.7 | 11.6 |
| California.............. | 4,433 | 5,160 | 774 | 858 | 12.4 | 13.3 | 9.3 | 9.6 |
| Colorado................ | 569 | 564 | 101 | 92 | 12.0 | 10.3 | 8.4 | 6.7 |
| Connecticut............. | 269 | 334 | 50 | 56 | 7.9 | 9.6 | 5.7 | 6.4 |
| Delaware................ | 88 | 127 | 17 | 22 | 10.5 | 13.6 | 7.5 | 9.2 |
| District of Columbia..... | 92 | 110 | 14 | 16 | 16.4 | 16.6 | 13.0 | 13.3 |
| Florida................. | 2,159 | 2,890 | 398 | 499 | 12.1 | 14.0 | 8.6 | 10.1 |
| Georgia................. | 1,324 | 1,518 | 249 | 280 | 14.3 | 14.9 | 10.7 | 11.1 |
| Hawaii.................. | 100 | 133 | 16 | 24 | 8.0 | 9.5 | 5.4 | 7.4 |
| Idaho................... | 178 | 216 | 35 | 36 | 12.1 | 12.8 | 8.9 | 8.6 |
| Illinois................ | 1,496 | 1,570 | 280 | 278 | 11.9 | 12.6 | 8.8 | 9.0 |
| Indiana................. | 758 | 871 | 145 | 153 | 12.3 | 13.5 | 8.7 | 9.2 |
| Iowa.................... | 318 | 327 | 58 | 53 | 11.0 | 10.7 | 7.4 | 6.7 |
| Kansas.................. | 300 | 336 | 56 | 58 | 11.2 | 11.9 | 7.7 | 7.9 |
| Kentucky................ | 714 | 744 | 147 | 146 | 17.3 | 17.2 | 13.2 | 12.9 |
| Louisiana............... | 775 | 899 | 158 | 163 | 18.6 | 19.7 | 14.6 | 14.7 |
| Maine................... | 154 | 144 | 28 | 21 | 12.0 | 11.1 | 7.9 | 6.3 |
| Maryland................ | 454 | 549 | 76 | 92 | 8.3 | 9.3 | 5.4 | 6.2 |
| Massachusetts........... | 621 | 692 | 113 | 120 | 9.9 | 10.5 | 7.3 | 7.2 |
| Michigan................ | 1,377 | 1,378 | 257 | 245 | 14.0 | 14.2 | 10.1 | 9.7 |
| Minnesota............... | 482 | 517 | 87 | 80 | 9.5 | 9.5 | 6.5 | 5.8 |
| Mississippi............. | 582 | 571 | 123 | 107 | 20.6 | 19.8 | 16.3 | 14.9 |
| Missouri................ | 742 | 796 | 146 | 141 | 13.0 | 13.4 | 9.5 | 9.2 |
| Montana................. | 132 | 128 | 23 | 20 | 14.1 | 12.5 | 9.7 | 7.7 |
| Nebraska................ | 193 | 201 | 38 | 35 | 11.2 | 10.8 | 8.2 | 7.2 |
| Nevada.................. | 270 | 384 | 47 | 64 | 10.7 | 13.0 | 7.5 | 9.1 |
| New Hampshire........... | 90 | 100 | 16 | 17 | 7.1 | 7.7 | 4.6 | 4.9 |
| New Jersey.............. | 729 | 883 | 138 | 163 | 8.6 | 10.0 | 6.3 | 7.3 |
| New Mexico.............. | 349 | 402 | 69 | 73 | 18.1 | 19.7 | 14.2 | 15.2 |
| New York................ | 2,570 | 2,722 | 474 | 482 | 13.7 | 14.1 | 10.3 | 10.4 |
| North Carolina.......... | 1,259 | 1,471 | 252 | 275 | 14.3 | 14.7 | 10.6 | 10.6 |
| North Dakota............ | 74 | 75 | 13 | 12 | 12.1 | 10.3 | 7.5 | 6.1 |
| Ohio.................... | 1,464 | 1,583 | 287 | 290 | 13.1 | 14.0 | 9.7 | 9.8 |
| Oklahoma................ | 557 | 604 | 111 | 112 | 15.9 | 15.8 | 11.9 | 11.6 |
| Oregon.................. | 474 | 538 | 83 | 89 | 12.9 | 13.2 | 8.9 | 8.8 |
| Pennsylvania............ | 1,393 | 1,549 | 259 | 256 | 11.6 | 12.5 | 8.1 | 8.1 |
| Rhode Island............ | 122 | 118 | 21 | 20 | 12.0 | 11.6 | 8.3 | 7.9 |
| South Carolina.......... | 642 | 752 | 129 | 141 | 15.0 | 15.4 | 11.2 | 11.3 |
| South Dakota............ | 101 | 109 | 18 | 18 | 13.1 | 13.0 | 8.9 | 8.4 |
| Tennessee............... | 954 | 980 | 192 | 187 | 15.9 | 15.0 | 12.0 | 10.9 |
| Texas................... | 3,791 | 4,077 | 738 | 758 | 16.3 | 14.7 | 12.8 | 11.3 |
| Utah.................... | 251 | 297 | 43 | 48 | 9.7 | 9.7 | 6.9 | 6.7 |
| Vermont................. | 61 | 68 | 11 | 11 | 10.1 | 11.3 | 6.4 | 7.0 |
| Virginia................ | 743 | 874 | 140 | 149 | 9.9 | 10.6 | 7.1 | 7.1 |
| Washington.............. | 725 | 802 | 127 | 130 | 11.4 | 11.0 | 7.8 | 7.1 |
| West Virginia........... | 298 | 336 | 64 | 65 | 16.9 | 19.1 | 13.0 | 14.1 |
| Wisconsin............... | 588 | 640 | 104 | 105 | 10.8 | 11.3 | 7.1 | 7.1 |
| Wyoming................. | 44 | 64 | 7 | 11 | 8.7 | 11.3 | 5.2 | 7.6 |
| Puerto Rico............. | 1,763 | 1,469 | 372 | 330 | 45.5 | 44.4 | 41.4 | 40.9 |

Source: U.S. Census Bureau, 2017 American Community Survey: B17001, "Poverty Status in the Past 12 Months by Sex By Age," and B17019, "Poverty Status in the Past 12 Months of Families by Household Type by Tenure"; <http://factfinder.census.gov>, accessed November 2018. See also <http://www.census.gov/programs-surveys/acs/>.

## Table 741. Poverty Thresholds by Size of Family Unit: 1980 to 2017

[In dollars per year. The official poverty definition uses money income before taxes and does not include capital gains and noncash benefits (such as public housing and food stamps). For information on the official poverty thresholds, see text, this section. For more on poverty, see <http://www.census.gov/topics/income-poverty/poverty.html>. See also headnote, Table 742]

| Size of family unit | 1980 | 1990 | 1995 | 2000 [2] | 2005 | 2010 [3] | 2015 [4] | 2016 [4] | 2017 [4] |
|---|---|---|---|---|---|---|---|---|---|
| One person (unrelated individual) [1]...... | 4,190 | 6,652 | 7,763 | 8,791 | 9,973 | 11,137 | 12,082 | 12,228 | 12,488 |
| Under 65 years old...................... | 4,290 | 6,800 | 7,929 | 8,959 | 10,160 | 11,344 | 12,331 | 12,486 | 12,752 |
| 65 years old and over.................. | 3,949 | 6,268 | 7,309 | 8,259 | 9,367 | 10,458 | 11,367 | 11,511 | 11,756 |
| Two persons.................... | 5,363 | 8,509 | 9,933 | 11,235 | 12,755 | 14,216 | 15,391 | 15,569 | 15,877 |
| Householder under 65 years old........ | 5,537 | 8,794 | 10,259 | 11,589 | 13,145 | 14,676 | 15,952 | 16,151 | 16,493 |
| Householder 65 years old and over..... | 4,983 | 7,905 | 9,219 | 10,418 | 11,815 | 13,194 | 14,342 | 14,522 | 14,828 |
| Three persons.................... | 6,565 | 10,419 | 12,158 | 13,740 | 15,577 | 17,373 | 18,871 | 19,105 | 19,515 |
| Four persons.................... | 8,414 | 13,359 | 15,569 | 17,604 | 19,971 | 22,315 | 24,257 | 24,563 | 25,094 |
| Five persons.................... | 9,966 | 15,792 | 18,408 | 20,815 | 23,613 | 26,442 | 28,741 | 29,111 | 29,714 |
| Six persons.................... | 11,269 | 17,839 | 20,804 | 23,533 | 26,683 | 29,904 | 32,542 | 32,928 | 33,618 |
| Seven persons.................... | 12,761 | 20,241 | 23,552 | 26,750 | 30,249 | 34,019 | 36,998 | 37,458 | 38,173 |
| Eight persons.................... | 14,199 | 22,582 | 26,237 | 29,701 | 33,610 | 37,953 | 41,029 | 41,781 | 42,684 |
| Nine or more persons.................... | 16,896 | 26,848 | 31,280 | 35,150 | 40,288 | 45,224 | 49,177 | 49,721 | 50,681 |

[1] A person living alone or with non-relatives. [2] Implementation of Census 2000-based population controls and sample expanded by 28,000 households. [3] Implementation of Census 2010-based population controls. [4] Based on redesigned questions on income; see source for more information.

Source: U.S. Census Bureau, *Income and Poverty in the United States: 2017,* Current Population Reports, P60-263, September 2018; and "Poverty Thresholds," <https://www.census.gov/topics/income-poverty/poverty/data/tables.html>, accessed November 2018.

## Table 742. People Below Poverty Level by Race and Hispanic Origin, and Below 125 Percent of Poverty Level: 1990 to 2017

[33,585 represents 33,585,000. People as of March of the following year. Based on Current Population Survey, Annual Social and Economic Supplement (ASEC); see text, this section, Section 1, and Appendix III. Beginning with 2003 CPS ASEC covering data for 2002, refers to persons of specified race only and who did not report any other race category; "Asian" replaced "Asian Pacific Islander." For information on measuring poverty, see <http://www.census.gov/topics/income-poverty/poverty/guidance/poverty-measures.html>. Data users should exercise caution when comparing 2014 and subsequent data to data from previous year surveys due the use of redesigned income questions. See source for more information]

| Year | Number of persons below poverty (1,000) | | | | | Percent of persons below poverty | | | | | Below 125 percent of poverty level [1] | |
|---|---|---|---|---|---|---|---|---|---|---|---|---|
| | All races [2] | White | Black | Asian | His-panic [3] | All races [2] | White | Black | Asian | His-panic [3] | Number (1,000) | Percent of total pop-ulation |
| 1990......... | 33,585 | 22,326 | 9,837 | 858 | 6,006 | 13.5 | 10.7 | 31.9 | 12.2 | 28.1 | 44,837 | 18.0 |
| 1991......... | 35,708 | 23,747 | 10,242 | 996 | 6,339 | 14.2 | 11.3 | 32.7 | 13.8 | 28.7 | 47,527 | 18.9 |
| 1992 [4]......... | 38,014 | 25,259 | 10,827 | 985 | 7,592 | 14.8 | 11.9 | 33.4 | 12.7 | 29.6 | 50,592 | 19.7 |
| 1993 [5]......... | 39,265 | 26,226 | 10,877 | 1,134 | 8,126 | 15.1 | 12.2 | 33.1 | 15.3 | 30.6 | 51,801 | 20.0 |
| 1994......... | 38,059 | 25,379 | 10,196 | 974 | 8,416 | 14.5 | 11.7 | 30.6 | 14.6 | 30.7 | 50,401 | 19.3 |
| 1995......... | 36,425 | 24,423 | 9,872 | 1,411 | 8,574 | 13.8 | 11.2 | 29.3 | 14.6 | 30.3 | 48,761 | 18.5 |
| 1996......... | 36,529 | 24,650 | 9,694 | 1,454 | 8,697 | 13.7 | 11.2 | 28.4 | 14.5 | 29.4 | 49,310 | 18.5 |
| 1997......... | 35,574 | 24,396 | 9,116 | 1,468 | 8,308 | 13.3 | 11.0 | 26.5 | 14.0 | 27.1 | 47,853 | 17.8 |
| 1998......... | 34,476 | 23,454 | 9,091 | 1,360 | 8,070 | 12.7 | 10.5 | 26.1 | 12.5 | 25.6 | 46,036 | 17.0 |
| 1999 [6]......... | 32,791 | 22,169 | 8,441 | 1,285 | 7,876 | 11.9 | 9.8 | 23.6 | 10.7 | 22.7 | 45,030 | 16.3 |
| 2000 [7]......... | 31,581 | 21,645 | 7,982 | 1,258 | 7,747 | 11.3 | 9.5 | 22.5 | 9.9 | 21.5 | 43,612 | 15.6 |
| 2001......... | 32,907 | 22,739 | 8,136 | 1,275 | 7,997 | 11.7 | 9.9 | 22.7 | 10.2 | 21.4 | 45,320 | 16.1 |
| 2002......... | 34,570 | 23,466 | 8,602 | 1,161 | 8,555 | 12.1 | 10.2 | 24.1 | 10.1 | 21.8 | 47,084 | 16.5 |
| 2003......... | 35,861 | 24,272 | 8,781 | 1,401 | 9,051 | 12.5 | 10.5 | 24.4 | 11.8 | 22.5 | 48,687 | 16.9 |
| 2004 [8]......... | 37,040 | 25,327 | 9,014 | 1,201 | 9,122 | 12.7 | 10.8 | 24.7 | 9.8 | 21.9 | 49,693 | 17.1 |
| 2005......... | 36,950 | 24,872 | 9,168 | 1,402 | 9,368 | 12.6 | 10.6 | 24.9 | 11.1 | 21.8 | 49,327 | 16.8 |
| 2006......... | 36,460 | 24,416 | 9,048 | 1,353 | 9,243 | 12.3 | 10.3 | 24.3 | 10.3 | 20.6 | 49,688 | 16.8 |
| 2007......... | 37,276 | 25,120 | 9,237 | 1,349 | 9,890 | 12.5 | 10.5 | 24.5 | 10.2 | 21.5 | 50,876 | 17.0 |
| 2008......... | 39,829 | 26,990 | 9,379 | 1,576 | 10,987 | 13.2 | 11.2 | 24.7 | 11.8 | 23.2 | 53,805 | 17.9 |
| 2009......... | 43,569 | 29,830 | 9,944 | 1,746 | 12,350 | 14.3 | 12.3 | 25.8 | 12.5 | 25.3 | 56,840 | 18.7 |
| 2010 [9]......... | 46,343 | 31,083 | 10,746 | 1,899 | 13,522 | 15.1 | 13.0 | 27.4 | 12.2 | 26.5 | 60,669 | 19.8 |
| 2011......... | 46,247 | 30,849 | 10,929 | 1,973 | 13,244 | 15.0 | 12.8 | 27.6 | 12.3 | 25.3 | 60,949 | 19.8 |
| 2012......... | 46,496 | 30,816 | 10,911 | 1,921 | 13,616 | 15.0 | 12.7 | 27.2 | 11.7 | 25.6 | 61,202 | 19.7 |
| 2013 [10]......... | 46,269 | 31,287 | 10,186 | 2,255 | 13,356 | 14.8 | 12.9 | 25.2 | 13.1 | 24.7 | 60,396 | 19.3 |
| 2014 [10]......... | 46,657 | 31,089 | 10,755 | 2,137 | 13,104 | 14.8 | 12.7 | 26.2 | 12.0 | 23.6 | 61,339 | 19.4 |
| 2015 [10]......... | 43,123 | 28,566 | 10,020 | 2,078 | 12,133 | 13.5 | 11.6 | 24.1 | 11.4 | 21.4 | 56,912 | 17.9 |
| 2016 [10]......... | 40,616 | 27,113 | 9,234 | 1,908 | 11,137 | 12.7 | 11.0 | 22.0 | 10.1 | 19.4 | 54,430 | 17.0 |
| 2017 [10]......... | 39,698 | 26,436 | 8,993 | 1,953 | 10,790 | 12.3 | 10.7 | 21.2 | 10.0 | 18.3 | 54,010 | 16.7 |

[1] People with incomes below 125 percent of poverty level. [2] Includes other races, not shown separately. [3] People of Hispanic origin may be of any race. [4] Implementation of 1990 Census population controls. [5] The March 1994 income supplement was revised to allow for the coding of different income amounts on selected questionnaire items. Limits either increased or decreased in the following categories: earnings increased to $999,999; Social Security increased to $49,999; Supplemental Security Income and public assistance increased to $24,999; veterans' benefits increased to $99,999; child support and alimony decreased to $49,999. [6] Implementation of Census-2000-based population controls. [7] Implementation of sample expansion by 28,000 households. [8] Data have been revised to reflect a correction to the weights in the 2005 ASEC. [9] Implementation of Census 2010-based population controls. [10] Data based on redesigned income questions. See source for more information.

Source: U.S. Census Bureau, *Income and Poverty in the United States: 2017,* Current Population Reports, P60-263, September 2018; and "Historical Poverty Tables: People and Families, Tables 2 and 6," <https://www.census.gov/topics/income-poverty/poverty/data/tables.html>, accessed November 2018.

# Table 743. Children Below Poverty Level by Race and Hispanic Origin: 1990 to 2017

[12,715 represents 12,715,000. Persons as of March of the following year. Covers only related children under age 18, in families. Based on Current Population Survey, Annual Social and Economic Supplement (CPS ASEC); see text, this section, Section 1, and Appendix III. See headnote, Table 742]

| Year | Number of children below poverty level (1,000) | | | | | Percent of children below poverty level | | | | |
|---|---|---|---|---|---|---|---|---|---|---|
| | All races [1] | White | Black | Asian | His-panic [2] | All races [1] | White | Black | Asian | His-panic [2] |
| 1990............ | 12,715 | 7,696 | 4,412 | 356 | 2,750 | 19.9 | 15.1 | 44.2 | 17.0 | 37.7 |
| 1991............ | 13,658 | 8,316 | 4,637 | 348 | 2,977 | 21.1 | 16.1 | 45.6 | 17.1 | 39.8 |
| 1992 [3]........ | 14,521 | 8,752 | 5,015 | 352 | 3,440 | 21.6 | 16.5 | 46.3 | 16.0 | 39.0 |
| 1993 [4]........ | 14,961 | 9,123 | 5,030 | 358 | 3,666 | 22.0 | 17.0 | 45.9 | 17.6 | 39.9 |
| 1994............ | 14,610 | 8,826 | 4,787 | 308 | 3,956 | 21.2 | 16.3 | 43.3 | 17.9 | 41.1 |
| 1995............ | 13,999 | 8,474 | 4,644 | 532 | 3,938 | 20.2 | 15.5 | 41.5 | 18.6 | 39.3 |
| 1996............ | 13,764 | 8,488 | 4,411 | 553 | 4,090 | 19.8 | 15.5 | 39.5 | 19.1 | 39.9 |
| 1997............ | 13,422 | 8,441 | 4,116 | 608 | 3,865 | 19.2 | 15.4 | 36.8 | 19.9 | 36.4 |
| 1998............ | 12,845 | 7,935 | 4,073 | 542 | 3,670 | 18.3 | 14.4 | 36.4 | 17.5 | 33.6 |
| 1999 [5]........ | 11,678 | 7,194 | 3,698 | 367 | 3,561 | 16.6 | 13.1 | 32.8 | 11.5 | 29.9 |
| 2000 [6]........ | 11,005 | 6,834 | 3,495 | 407 | 3,342 | 15.6 | 12.4 | 30.9 | 12.5 | 27.6 |
| 2001............ | 11,175 | 7,086 | 3,423 | 353 | 3,433 | 15.8 | 12.8 | 30.0 | 11.1 | 27.4 |
| 2002............ | 11,646 | 7,203 | 3,570 | 302 | 3,653 | 16.3 | 13.1 | 32.1 | 11.4 | 28.2 |
| 2003............ | 12,340 | 7,624 | 3,750 | 331 | 3,982 | 17.2 | 13.9 | 33.6 | 12.1 | 29.5 |
| 2004 [7]........ | 12,473 | 7,876 | 3,702 | 265 | 3,985 | 17.3 | 14.3 | 33.4 | 9.4 | 28.6 |
| 2005............ | 12,335 | 7,652 | 3,743 | 312 | 3,977 | 17.1 | 13.9 | 34.2 | 11.0 | 27.7 |
| 2006............ | 12,299 | 7,522 | 3,690 | 351 | 3,959 | 16.9 | 13.6 | 33.0 | 12.0 | 26.6 |
| 2007............ | 12,802 | 8,002 | 3,838 | 345 | 4,348 | 17.6 | 14.4 | 34.3 | 11.8 | 28.3 |
| 2008............ | 13,507 | 8,441 | 3,781 | 430 | 4,888 | 18.5 | 15.3 | 34.4 | 14.2 | 30.3 |
| 2009............ | 14,774 | 9,440 | 3,919 | 444 | 5,419 | 20.1 | 17.0 | 35.3 | 13.6 | 32.5 |
| 2010 [8]........ | 15,598 | 9,590 | 4,271 | 477 | 5,815 | 21.5 | 17.9 | 39.0 | 14.0 | 34.3 |
| 2011............ | 15,539 | 9,643 | 4,247 | 466 | 5,820 | 21.4 | 18.1 | 38.6 | 13.0 | 33.7 |
| 2012............ | 15,437 | 9,547 | 4,097 | 470 | 5,773 | 21.3 | 17.9 | 37.5 | 13.3 | 33.3 |
| 2013 [9]........ | 15,116 | 9,702 | 3,678 | 538 | 5,638 | 20.9 | 18.4 | 33.8 | 14.4 | 32.2 |
| 2014 [9]........ | 14,987 | 9,172 | 4,036 | 492 | 5,522 | 20.7 | 17.4 | 37.1 | 13.4 | 31.3 |
| 2015 [9]........ | 13,962 | 8,838 | 3,571 | 420 | 5,139 | 19.2 | 16.7 | 32.7 | 11.4 | 28.6 |
| 2016 [9]........ | 12,803 | 7,963 | 3,382 | 412 | 4,764 | 17.6 | 15.1 | 30.6 | 10.7 | 26.3 |
| 2017 [9]........ | 12,439 | 7,772 | 3,134 | 442 | 4,519 | 17.1 | 14.8 | 28.8 | 11.1 | 24.7 |

[1] Includes other races, not shown separately. [2] People of Hispanic origin may be of any race. [3] Implementation of 1990 Census population controls. [4] See Table 742, footnote 5. [5] Implementation of Census 2000-based population controls. [6] Sample expanded to 28,000 households. [7] Data have been revised to reflect a correction to the weights in the 2005 ASEC. [8] Implementation of Census 2010-based population controls. [9] Data based on redesigned income questions. See source for more information.

Source: U.S. Census Bureau, *Income and Poverty in the United States: 2017*, Current Population Reports, P60-263, September 2018; and "Historical Poverty Tables: People and Families, Table 3," <https://www.census.gov/topics/income-poverty/poverty/data/tables.html>, accessed November 2018.

# Table 744. People Below Poverty Level by Selected Characteristics: 2017

[39,698 represents 39,698,000. People as of March of the following year. Based on the Current Population Survey, Annual Social and Economic and Supplement (CPS ASEC). Data by education cover people age 25 and over, based on the highest grade completed]

| Sex, age, education, region, nativity | Number below poverty level (1,000) | | | | | Percent below poverty level | | | | |
|---|---|---|---|---|---|---|---|---|---|---|
| | All races [1] | White alone | Black alone | Asian alone | His-panic [2] | All races [1] | White alone | Black alone | Asian alone | His-panic [2] |
| **Total**........................... | **39,698** | **26,436** | **8,993** | **1,953** | **10,790** | **12.3** | **10.7** | **21.2** | **10.0** | **18.3** |
| Male........................... | 17,365 | 11,572 | 3,832 | 869 | 4,785 | 11.0 | 9.5 | 19.2 | 9.3 | 16.1 |
| Female......................... | 22,333 | 14,864 | 5,161 | 1,084 | 6,005 | 13.6 | 11.9 | 22.9 | 10.7 | 20.4 |
| AGE | | | | | | | | | | |
| Under 18 years old.............. | 12,808 | 8,041 | 3,184 | 455 | 4,639 | 17.5 | 15.2 | 29.0 | 11.3 | 25.0 |
| 18 to 24 years old.............. | 4,727 | 3,018 | 1,053 | 363 | 1,177 | 16.1 | 14.0 | 23.7 | 20.4 | 17.8 |
| 25 to 34 years old.............. | 5,348 | 3,531 | 1,227 | 346 | 1,428 | 11.9 | 10.7 | 18.9 | 10.3 | 15.4 |
| 35 to 44 years old.............. | 4,168 | 2,915 | 838 | 199 | 1,378 | 10.3 | 9.5 | 15.5 | 6.3 | 16.3 |
| 45 to 54 years old.............. | 3,748 | 2,620 | 820 | 158 | 821 | 9.0 | 8.1 | 15.3 | 6.0 | 11.8 |
| 55 to 59 years old.............. | 2,130 | 1,490 | 472 | 78 | 304 | 9.9 | 8.5 | 18.6 | 7.3 | 11.5 |
| 60 to 64 years old.............. | 2,088 | 1,452 | 468 | 100 | 308 | 10.4 | 9.0 | 19.4 | 9.1 | 14.0 |
| 65 years old and over.......... | 4,681 | 3,368 | 932 | 255 | 736 | 9.2 | 7.8 | 19.3 | 10.8 | 17.0 |
| 65 to 74 years old............. | 2,484 | 1,748 | 535 | 126 | 415 | 8.2 | 6.9 | 17.7 | 8.9 | 15.6 |
| 75 years old and over......... | 2,197 | 1,620 | 397 | 129 | 321 | 10.6 | 9.2 | 22.0 | 13.8 | 19.3 |
| EDUCATION | | | | | | | | | | |
| No high school diploma........ | 5,485 | 3,751 | 1,208 | 253 | 2,265 | 24.5 | 22.2 | 37.0 | 19.5 | 23.5 |
| High school, no college........ | 7,942 | 5,463 | 1,883 | 296 | 1,482 | 12.7 | 11.1 | 21.3 | 11.4 | 14.2 |
| Some college, less than 4-year degree....... | 5,075 | 3,492 | 1,195 | 143 | 773 | 8.8 | 7.6 | 14.7 | 7.0 | 10.1 |
| College, 4-year degree or higher....... | 3,661 | 2,671 | 471 | 443 | 454 | 4.8 | 4.4 | 6.9 | 5.7 | 7.3 |
| REGION | | | | | | | | | | |
| Northeast...................... | 6,373 | 4,032 | 1,465 | 561 | 1,739 | 11.4 | 9.4 | 19.8 | 13.5 | 22.1 |
| Midwest........................ | 7,647 | 5,143 | 1,806 | 275 | 968 | 11.4 | 9.2 | 25.3 | 11.8 | 17.7 |
| South.......................... | 16,609 | 10,490 | 4,987 | 433 | 4,318 | 13.6 | 11.7 | 20.8 | 10.0 | 19.2 |
| West........................... | 9,069 | 6,771 | 734 | 685 | 3,765 | 11.8 | 11.5 | 18.9 | 7.9 | 16.2 |
| NATIVITY | | | | | | | | | | |
| Native......................... | 33,095 | 22,091 | 8,237 | 638 | 7,257 | 11.9 | 10.0 | 21.9 | 8.6 | 18.8 |
| Foreign born................... | 6,603 | 4,345 | 756 | 1,315 | 3,533 | 14.5 | 16.0 | 15.8 | 10.9 | 17.3 |
| Naturalized citizen............ | 2,213 | 1,303 | 327 | 538 | 912 | 10.1 | 11.0 | 12.2 | 7.9 | 12.1 |
| Not a citizen.................. | 4,390 | 3,042 | 429 | 776 | 2,621 | 18.6 | 19.8 | 20.2 | 14.7 | 20.4 |

[1] Includes other races, not shown separately. [2] Persons of Hispanic origin may be of any race.

Source: U.S. Census Bureau, *Income and Poverty in the United States: 2017*, Current Population Reports, P60-263, September 2018; and "Current Population Survey Detailed Tables for Poverty: Tables POV01, POV29, and POV41," <https://www.census.gov/topics/income-poverty/poverty/data/tables.html>, accessed November 2018.

## Table 745. Work Experience of People During Year by Poverty Status by Sex and Age: 2017

[115,671 represents 115,671,000. Covers persons age 16 and over. Based on the Current Population Survey, Annual Social and Economic Supplement (ASEC); see text, this section, Section 1, and Appendix III]

| Sex and age | Worked full-time year-round | | | Did not work full-time year-round | | | Did not work | | |
|---|---|---|---|---|---|---|---|---|---|
| | Number (1,000) | Below poverty level | | Number (1,000) | Below poverty level | | Number (1,000) | Below poverty level | |
| | | Number (1,000) | Percent | | Number (1,000) | Percent | | Number (1,000) | Percent |
| **BOTH SEXES** | | | | | | | | | |
| **Total** | **115,671** | **2,468** | **2.1** | **50,373** | **6,035** | **12.0** | **92,007** | **19,664** | **21.4** |
| 16 to 17 years old | 149 | 8 | 5.1 | 1,937 | 156 | 8.0 | 6,773 | 1,113 | 16.4 |
| 18 to 64 years old | 109,700 | 2,422 | 2.2 | 42,499 | 5,714 | 13.4 | 45,914 | 14,073 | 30.7 |
| 18 to 24 years old | 7,844 | 270 | 3.4 | 11,726 | 1,670 | 14.2 | 9,793 | 2,787 | 28.5 |
| 25 to 34 years old | 27,454 | 819 | 3.0 | 9,537 | 1,587 | 16.6 | 7,863 | 2,942 | 37.4 |
| 35 to 54 years old | 53,521 | 1,116 | 2.1 | 13,772 | 1,813 | 13.2 | 14,903 | 4,987 | 33.5 |
| 55 to 64 years old | 20,882 | 216 | 1.0 | 7,464 | 644 | 8.6 | 13,355 | 3,358 | 25.1 |
| 65 years old and over | 5,822 | 39 | 0.7 | 5,938 | 166 | 2.8 | 39,320 | 4,477 | 11.4 |
| **MALE** | | | | | | | | | |
| **Total** | **66,373** | **1,295** | **2.0** | **21,566** | **2,438** | **11.3** | **37,242** | **7,808** | **21.0** |
| 16 to 17 years old | 102 | 4 | 4.2 | 938 | 76 | 8.2 | 3,435 | 553 | 16.1 |
| 18 to 64 years old | 62,664 | 1,272 | 2.0 | 17,641 | 2,282 | 12.9 | 17,341 | 5,626 | 32.4 |
| 18 to 24 years old | 4,470 | 131 | 2.9 | 5,593 | 678 | 12.1 | 4,780 | 1,284 | 26.9 |
| 25 to 34 years old | 15,736 | 394 | 2.5 | 4,115 | 550 | 13.4 | 2,639 | 1,033 | 39.1 |
| 35 to 54 years old | 30,782 | 613 | 2.0 | 4,878 | 743 | 15.2 | 4,752 | 1,957 | 41.2 |
| 55 to 64 years old | 11,676 | 133 | 1.1 | 3,055 | 311 | 10.2 | 5,170 | 1,352 | 26.1 |
| 65 years old and over | 3,607 | 19 | 0.5 | 2,987 | 80 | 2.7 | 16,465 | 1,628 | 9.9 |
| **FEMALE** | | | | | | | | | |
| **Total** | **49,299** | **1,173** | **2.4** | **28,807** | **3,597** | **12.5** | **54,765** | **11,856** | **21.6** |
| 16 to 17 years old | 48 | 3 | (B) | 998 | 79 | 7.9 | 3,337 | 560 | 16.8 |
| 18 to 64 years old | 47,037 | 1,150 | 2.4 | 24,858 | 3,432 | 13.8 | 28,573 | 8,447 | 29.6 |
| 18 to 24 years old | 3,373 | 138 | 4.1 | 6,133 | 993 | 16.2 | 5,013 | 1,503 | 30.0 |
| 25 to 34 years old | 11,718 | 425 | 3.6 | 5,422 | 1,036 | 19.1 | 5,224 | 1,909 | 36.5 |
| 35 to 54 years old | 22,740 | 503 | 2.2 | 8,894 | 1,069 | 12.0 | 10,151 | 3,030 | 29.8 |
| 55 to 64 years old | 9,206 | 83 | 0.9 | 4,409 | 333 | 7.6 | 8,185 | 2,006 | 24.5 |
| 65 years old and over | 2,214 | 20 | 0.9 | 2,951 | 86 | 2.9 | 22,855 | 2,849 | 12.5 |

B Base figure too small to meet statistical standards for reliability of a derived figure.

Source: U.S. Census Bureau, *Income and Poverty in the United States: 2017*, Current Population Reports, P60-263, September 2018; "Current Population Survey Detailed Tables for Poverty: Table POV22," <https://www.census.gov/topics/income-poverty/poverty/data/tables.html>, accessed November 2018.

## Table 746. Families Below Poverty Level by Race and Hispanic Origin, and Below 125 Percent of Poverty Level: 1990 to 2017

[7,098 represents 7,098,000. Families as of March of the following year. Based on Current Population Survey, Annual Social and Economic Supplement (ASEC); see text, this section and Section 1, and Appendix III. For data collection changes over time, see "Changes in Methodology for the March Current Population Survey" at <https://www.census.gov/topics/income-poverty/income/guidance/cps-methodology-changes.html>. Beginning with the 2003 CPS covering data for 2002, respondents were allowed to choose more than one race. Two basic ways of defining a race group are possible: a group such as Asian may be defined as those who reported Asian and no other race (the race-alone concept), or as those who reported Asian regardless of whether they also reported another race (the race-alone-or-in-combination concept). For 2001 data and earlier, the CPS allowed respondents to report only one race group. See also comments on race in the text for Section 1, Population. See comments on changes to the CPS ASEC in headnote, Table 742]

| Year | Number of families below poverty (1,000) | | | | | Percent of families below poverty | | | | | Below 125 percent of poverty level | |
|---|---|---|---|---|---|---|---|---|---|---|---|---|
| | All races [1] | White [2] | Black [2] | Asian [2] | His-panic [3] | All races [1] | White [2] | Black [2] | Asian [2] | His-panic [3] | Number (1,000) | Percent |
| 1990 | 7,098 | 4,622 | 2,193 | 169 | 1,244 | 10.7 | 8.1 | 29.3 | 11.0 | 25.0 | 9,564 | 14.4 |
| 1995 | 7,532 | 4,994 | 2,127 | 264 | 1,695 | 10.8 | 8.5 | 26.4 | 12.4 | 27.0 | 10,223 | 14.7 |
| 2000 [4] | 6,400 | 4,333 | 1,686 | 233 | 1,540 | 8.7 | 7.1 | 19.3 | 7.8 | 19.2 | 9,032 | 12.2 |
| 2005 | 7,657 | 5,068 | 1,997 | 289 | 1,948 | 9.9 | 8.0 | 22.1 | 9.0 | 19.7 | 10,442 | 13.5 |
| 2006 | 7,668 | 5,118 | 2,007 | 260 | 1,922 | 9.8 | 8.0 | 21.6 | 7.8 | 18.9 | 10,531 | 13.4 |
| 2007 | 7,623 | 5,046 | 2,045 | 261 | 2,045 | 9.8 | 7.9 | 22.1 | 7.9 | 19.7 | 10,551 | 13.5 |
| 2008 | 8,147 | 5,414 | 2,055 | 341 | 2,239 | 10.3 | 8.4 | 22.0 | 9.8 | 21.3 | 11,164 | 14.2 |
| 2009 | 8,792 | 5,994 | 2,125 | 337 | 2,369 | 11.1 | 9.3 | 22.7 | 9.4 | 22.7 | 11,620 | 14.7 |
| 2010 [5] | 9,400 | 6,305 | 2,311 | 362 | 2,739 | 11.8 | 9.9 | 24.1 | 9.3 | 24.3 | 12,448 | 15.6 |
| 2011 | 9,497 | 6,334 | 2,334 | 401 | 2,651 | 11.8 | 9.8 | 24.2 | 9.7 | 22.9 | 12,500 | 15.5 |
| 2012 | 9,520 | 6,299 | 2,327 | 387 | 2,807 | 11.8 | 9.7 | 23.7 | 9.4 | 23.5 | 12,669 | 15.7 |
| 2013 [6] | 9,645 | 6,526 | 2,204 | 448 | 2,865 | 11.7 | 9.9 | 22.4 | 10.2 | 23.1 | 12,605 | 15.3 |
| 2014 [6] | 9,467 | 6,310 | 2,265 | 401 | 2,684 | 11.6 | 9.7 | 22.9 | 8.9 | 21.5 | 12,635 | 15.5 |
| 2015 [6] | 8,589 | 5,743 | 2,082 | 374 | 2,502 | 10.4 | 8.8 | 21.1 | 8.0 | 19.6 | 11,603 | 14.1 |
| 2016 [6] | 8,081 | 5,433 | 1,893 | 340 | 2,253 | 9.8 | 8.3 | 19.0 | 7.2 | 17.3 | 11,083 | 13.4 |
| 2017 [6] | 7,758 | 5,170 | 1,825 | 382 | 2,156 | 9.3 | 7.9 | 18.2 | 7.8 | 16.3 | 10,758 | 12.9 |

[1] Includes other races, not shown separately. [2] Beginning 2002, data refer to persons who reported specified race only and no other race category; prior to 2002, Asian included Pacific Islander. [3] People of Hispanic origin may be of any race. [4] Implementation of Census 2000 based population controls and sample expanded by 28,000 households. [5] Implementation of Census 2010-based population controls. [6] Data are based on redesigned income questions. See source for more information.

Source: U.S. Census Bureau, *Income and Poverty in the United States: 2017*, Current Population Reports, P60-263, September 2018; and "Historical Poverty Tables: People and Families, Table 4," and "Current Population Survey Detailed Tables for Poverty: Table POV04," <https://www.census.gov/topics/income-poverty/poverty/data/tables.html>, accessed November 2018.

# Table 747. Families Below Poverty Level by Selected Characteristics: 2017

[In thousands (7,758 represents 7,758,000), except as noted. All families as of March of the following year. Based on the Current Population Survey, Annual Social and Economic Supplement (CPS ASEC); see text, this section and Section 1, and Appendix III. Data below represent persons who selected each race group only and exclude persons reporting more than one race. See also comments on race in the text for Section 1. For composition of regions, see map, inside front cover]

| Characteristic | Number below poverty level (1,000) | | | | | Percent below poverty level | | | | |
|---|---|---|---|---|---|---|---|---|---|---|
| | All races[1] | White alone | Black alone | Asian alone | His-panic[2] | All races[1] | White alone | Black alone | Asian alone | His-panic[2] |
| **Total families** | **7,758** | **5,170** | **1,825** | **382** | **2,156** | **9.3** | **7.9** | **18.2** | **7.8** | **16.3** |
| Age of householder: | | | | | | | | | | |
| 18 to 24 years old | 648 | 364 | 208 | 31 | 182 | 22.6 | 18.0 | 40.4 | 21.2 | 21.1 |
| 25 to 34 years old | 1,987 | 1,285 | 524 | 86 | 616 | 15.4 | 13.3 | 27.3 | 11.1 | 21.8 |
| 35 to 44 years old | 1,905 | 1,290 | 414 | 96 | 665 | 11.2 | 10.1 | 18.2 | 7.1 | 19.4 |
| 45 to 54 years old | 1,175 | 814 | 234 | 63 | 305 | 7.1 | 6.3 | 11.3 | 6.0 | 11.2 |
| 55 to 64 years old | 993 | 696 | 198 | 55 | 200 | 6.3 | 5.4 | 12.3 | 6.2 | 10.6 |
| 65 years old and over | 1,013 | 697 | 237 | 52 | 172 | 5.7 | 4.6 | 14.7 | 7.4 | 12.2 |
| Region: | | | | | | | | | | |
| Northeast | 1,199 | 765 | 282 | 101 | 355 | 8.4 | 6.8 | 16.2 | 9.7 | 19.8 |
| Midwest | 1,456 | 983 | 371 | 43 | 178 | 8.3 | 6.5 | 22.3 | 7.6 | 15.7 |
| South | 3,400 | 2,149 | 1,040 | 94 | 861 | 10.6 | 8.8 | 18.2 | 8.4 | 16.8 |
| West | 1,702 | 1,274 | 133 | 143 | 763 | 8.9 | 8.4 | 14.6 | 6.6 | 14.8 |
| Type of family: | | | | | | | | | | |
| Married couple | 3,005 | 2,287 | 323 | 261 | 861 | 4.9 | 4.5 | 6.8 | 6.5 | 10.3 |
| Male householder, no spouse present | 793 | 520 | 194 | 29 | 206 | 12.4 | 11.0 | 18.5 | 9.0 | 13.8 |
| Female householder, no spouse present | 3,959 | 2,363 | 1,309 | 91 | 1,089 | 25.7 | 23.9 | 30.8 | 15.5 | 32.7 |
| Families with children[3] | 5,435 | 3,561 | 1,352 | 232 | 1,736 | 14.3 | 12.5 | 24.7 | 8.9 | 21.4 |

[1] Includes other races, not shown separately. [2] Hispanic persons may be of any race. [3] Children under age 18 related to the householder.

Source: U.S. Census Bureau, *Income and Poverty in the United States: 2017*, Current Population Reports, P60-263, September 2018; and "Current Population Survey Detailed Tables for Poverty: Tables POV04 and POV44," <https://www.census.gov/topics/income-poverty/poverty/data/tables.html>, accessed November 2018.

# Table 748. Top Wealth Holders With Gross Assets of $5 Million or More—Debts, Mortgages, and Net Worth: 2013

[7,289,626 represents $7,289,626,000,000. Figures are estimates from the Personal Wealth Study, based on a sample of Federal estate tax returns (Form 706). Covers the segment of the population for whom personal wealth is at least equal to the estate tax filing threshold in effect for the estimation period. Based on the estate multiplier technique; for more information on this methodology, see source]

| Sex and net worth | Total assets[1] | | Debts and mortgages | | Net worth[2] | |
|---|---|---|---|---|---|---|
| | Number of top wealth holders | Amount (mil. dol.) | Number of top wealth holders | Amount (mil. dol.) | Number of top wealth holders | Amount (mil. dol.) |
| **Both sexes, total** | **584,194** | **7,289,626** | **442,290** | **432,333** | **584,194** | **6,857,292** |
| Size of net worth: | | | | | | |
| Under $5 million[3] | 102,954 | 437,172 | 88,466 | 122,350 | 102,954 | 314,823 |
| $5 million to under $10 million | 325,371 | 2,358,888 | 232,032 | 115,554 | 325,371 | 2,243,334 |
| $10 million to under $20 million | 103,903 | 1,458,237 | 80,269 | 69,199 | 103,903 | 1,389,038 |
| $20 million to under $50 million | 37,596 | 1,163,133 | 28,766 | 59,877 | 37,596 | 1,103,255 |
| $50 million or more | 14,369 | 1,872,193 | 12,756 | 65,352 | 14,369 | 1,806,841 |
| **Males, total** | **356,549** | **4,540,744** | **268,058** | **327,470** | **356,549** | **4,213,273** |
| Size of net worth: | | | | | | |
| Under $5 million[3] | 73,415 | 321,029 | 61,536 | 104,926 | 73,415 | 216,102 |
| $5 million to under $10 million | 189,343 | 1,359,306 | 132,853 | 78,395 | 189,343 | 1,280,911 |
| $10 million to under $20 million | 60,875 | 851,278 | 47,186 | 47,931 | 60,875 | 803,346 |
| $20 million to under $50 million | 24,132 | 756,426 | 18,744 | 49,080 | 24,132 | 707,345 |
| $50 million or more | 8,784 | 1,252,704 | 7,739 | 47,136 | 8,784 | 1,205,567 |
| **Females, total** | **227,645** | **2,748,882** | **174,232** | **104,865** | **227,645** | **2,644,019** |
| Size of net worth: | | | | | | |
| Under $5 million[3] | 29,540 | 116,144 | 26,930 | 17,424 | 29,540 | 98,720 |
| $5 million to under $10 million | 136,028 | 999,582 | 99,178 | 37,159 | 136,028 | 962,423 |
| $10 million to under $20 million | 43,029 | 606,959 | 33,084 | 21,267 | 43,029 | 585,692 |
| $20 million to under $50 million | 13,463 | 406,708 | 10,022 | 10,800 | 13,463 | 395,910 |
| $50 million or more | 5,586 | 619,489 | 5,017 | 18,216 | 5,586 | 601,274 |

[1] Total assets is the sum of all assets owned by the individual before subtracting debts, mortgages, and liens owed to others. It differs from gross assets, which is a Federal estate tax concept of wealth, in that it includes the cash value of life insurance instead of the full face value of life insurance minus indebtedness. [2] Net worth is defined as total assets minus debts and mortgages. [3] Includes individuals with zero net worth.

Source: U.S. Internal Revenue Service, Statistics of Income Division, "SOI Tax Stats - Personal Wealth Statistics," August 2017. See also <https://www.irs.gov/uac/soi-tax-stats-personal-wealth-statistics>.

## Table 749. Top Wealth Holders With Gross Assets of $5 Million or More by Type of Property, Sex, and Size of Net Worth: 2013

[7,289,626 represents $7,289,626,000,000. Figures are estimates from the Personal Wealth Study, based on a sample of Federal estate tax returns (Form 706). Covers the segment of the population for whom personal wealth is at least equal to the estate tax filing threshold in effect for the estimation period. Based on the estate multiplier technique; for more information on this methodology, see source]

| Sex and net worth | Number of top wealth holders | Assets (mil. dol.) | | | | |
|---|---|---|---|---|---|---|
| | | Total [1] | Personal residences | Other real estate | Closely held stock | Publicly traded stock |
| **Both sexes, total** | **584,194** | **7,289,626** | **458,121** | **618,807** | **888,688** | **1,348,302** |
| Size of net worth: | | | | | | |
| Under $5 million [2] | 102,954 | 437,172 | 55,285 | 51,141 | 27,611 | 46,999 |
| $5 million to under $10 million | 325,371 | 2,358,888 | 215,480 | 255,585 | 173,468 | 389,202 |
| $10 million to under $20 million | 103,903 | 1,458,237 | 94,574 | 138,159 | 169,026 | 267,517 |
| $20 million to under $50 million | 37,596 | 1,163,133 | 54,624 | 88,287 | 184,229 | 235,082 |
| $50 million or more | 14,369 | 1,872,193 | 38,156 | 85,633 | 334,353 | 409,499 |
| **Males, total** | **356,549** | **4,540,744** | **238,165** | **369,694** | **659,317** | **742,460** |
| Size of net worth: | | | | | | |
| Under $5 million [2] | 73,415 | 321,029 | 33,892 | 39,347 | 20,802 | 31,674 |
| $5 million to under $10 million | 189,343 | 1,359,306 | 97,826 | 136,043 | 121,452 | 202,227 |
| $10 million to under $20 million | 60,875 | 851,278 | 50,755 | 77,898 | 120,811 | 137,956 |
| $20 million to under $50 million | 24,132 | 756,426 | 33,883 | 57,061 | 146,894 | 133,897 |
| $50 million or more | 8,784 | 1,252,704 | 21,809 | 59,343 | 249,356 | 236,705 |
| **Females, total** | **227,645** | **2,748,882** | **219,956** | **249,113** | **229,371** | **605,842** |
| Size of net worth: | | | | | | |
| Under $5 million [2] | 29,540 | 116,144 | 21,393 | 11,794 | 6,809 | 15,325 |
| $5 million to under $10 million | 136,028 | 999,582 | 117,655 | 119,542 | 52,015 | 186,976 |
| $10 million to under $20 million | 43,029 | 606,959 | 43,819 | 60,261 | 48,214 | 129,562 |
| $20 million to under $50 million | 13,463 | 406,708 | 20,742 | 31,226 | 37,335 | 101,185 |
| $50 million or more | 5,586 | 619,489 | 16,347 | 26,290 | 84,997 | 172,794 |

[1] Total assets is the sum of all assets owned by the individual before subtracting debts, mortgages, and liens owed to others. Includes other types of assets, not shown separately. [2] Includes individuals with zero or negative net worth.

Source: U.S. Internal Revenue Service, Statistics of Income Division, "SOI Tax Stats - Personal Wealth Statistics," August 2017. See also <https://www.irs.gov/uac/soi-tax-stats-personal-wealth-statistics>.

## Table 750. Top Wealth Holders With Net Worth of $5 Million or More—Number and Net Worth by State: 2013

[6,542,469 represents $6,542,469,000,000. Estimates based on a sample of federal estate tax returns (Form 706). Estimates of wealth by state can be subject to significant year-to-year fluctuations, especially for individuals at the extreme tail of the net worth distribution and for states with relatively small decedent populations. Based on the estate multiplier technique; for more information on this methodology, see source]

| State | Number of top wealth holders | Net worth (mil. dol.) | State | Number of top wealth holders | Net worth (mil. dol.) |
|---|---|---|---|---|---|
| **Total [1]** | **481,239** | **6,542,469** | Missouri | 3,899 | 113,689 |
| | | | Montana | 1,073 | 45,527 |
| Alabama | 4,115 | 55,864 | Nebraska | 3,299 | 59,527 |
| Alaska | 2,648 | 19,056 | Nevada | 3,383 | 78,822 |
| Arizona | 5,345 | 65,383 | New Hampshire | 1,684 | 20,798 |
| Arkansas | 1,342 | 19,783 | New Jersey | 13,957 | 200,859 |
| California | 78,413 | 1,123,895 | New Mexico | 4,763 | 34,411 |
| Colorado | 4,962 | 92,484 | New York | 53,038 | 712,276 |
| Connecticut | 12,316 | 207,003 | North Carolina | 11,931 | 113,321 |
| Delaware | 350 | 3,571 | North Dakota | 2,877 | 22,144 |
| District of Columbia | 4,993 | 46,716 | Ohio | 10,861 | 116,394 |
| Florida | 36,703 | 617,817 | Oklahoma | 9,960 | 80,432 |
| Georgia | 10,149 | 108,776 | Oregon | 3,115 | 33,312 |
| Hawaii | 826 | 13,066 | Pennsylvania | 13,428 | 194,665 |
| Idaho | 2,660 | 28,187 | Rhode Island | 2,322 | 21,151 |
| Illinois | 17,597 | 240,630 | South Carolina | 7,889 | 91,076 |
| Indiana | 5,416 | 66,877 | South Dakota | 1,165 | 14,388 |
| Iowa | 4,448 | 75,025 | Tennessee | 4,716 | 48,567 |
| Kansas | 5,643 | 61,054 | Texas | 41,736 | 530,581 |
| Kentucky | 3,288 | 55,828 | Utah | 1,701 | 27,181 |
| Louisiana | 3,611 | 40,627 | Vermont | 2,287 | 26,514 |
| Maine | 4,335 | 37,156 | Virginia | 11,208 | 137,868 |
| Maryland | 7,792 | 118,316 | Washington | 10,303 | 128,356 |
| Massachusetts | 12,383 | 158,892 | West Virginia | 613 | 6,653 |
| Michigan | 8,535 | 98,191 | Wisconsin | 4,722 | 63,550 |
| Minnesota | 11,323 | 145,541 | Wyoming | 1,412 | 21,746 |
| Mississippi | 2,340 | 32,678 | Other areas [1] | 2,365 | 66,245 |

[1] Includes U.S. territories and possessions.

Source: U.S. Internal Revenue Service, Statistics of Income Division, "SOI Tax Stats - Personal Wealth Statistics," August 2017, <https://www.irs.gov/uac/soi-tax-stats-personal-wealth-statistics>.

# Table 751. Nonfinancial Assets Held by Families by Type of Asset: 2016

[Value of assets in thousands of constant (2016) dollars (189.9 represents $189,900). Families include one-person units and, as used in this table, are comparable to the U.S. Census Bureau's household concept. Based on internal data from the Survey of Consumer Finances; see Appendix III. All dollar amounts are adjusted to 2016 dollars using the "current methods" version of the consumer price index (CPI) for all urban consumers. For definition of median, see Guide to Tabular Presentation. For data on financial assets, see Table 1202]

| Family characteristic | Any financial or non-financial asset | Any non-financial asset | Vehicles | Primary residence | Other residential property | Equity in nonresidential property | Business equity | Other asset |
|---|---|---|---|---|---|---|---|---|
| **PERCENT OF FAMILIES HOLDING ASSET** | | | | | | | | |
| All families, total.................... | **99.4** | **90.8** | **85.2** | **63.7** | **13.8** | **6.2** | **13.0** | **6.5** |
| Age of family head: | | | | | | | | |
| Under 35 years old................... | 99.1 | 84.2 | 80.2 | 33.1 | 4.0 | 2.3 | 5.6 | 5.2 |
| 35 to 44 years old................... | 98.7 | 91.3 | 86.7 | 57.8 | 12.0 | 3.8 | 15.0 | 3.9 |
| 45 to 54 years old................... | 99.9 | 93.6 | 89.1 | 68.8 | 13.2 | 5.5 | 17.3 | 6.4 |
| 55 to 64 years old................... | 99.5 | 91.4 | 86.1 | 73.7 | 19.2 | 9.3 | 17.3 | 7.2 |
| 65 to 74 years old................... | 99.9 | 93.6 | 86.8 | 79.1 | 21.4 | 8.7 | 13.3 | 9.9 |
| 75 years old and over............... | 99.4 | 93.2 | 82.2 | 83.1 | 16.3 | 9.9 | 8.5 | 7.8 |
| Race or ethnicity of respondent: | | | | | | | | |
| White, non-Hispanic................. | 99.7 | 94.6 | 89.6 | 72.5 | 16.3 | 7.5 | 15.5 | 8.5 |
| Black/African-American, non-Hispanic......................... | 99.1 | 81.2 | 73.1 | 44.7 | 8.3 | 4.1 | 6.6 | 1.8 |
| Hispanic or Latino................... | 98.1 | 84.4 | 80.0 | 45.5 | 6.3 | 2.3 | 5.8 | 2.2 |
| Other or multiple race............... | 99.1 | 87.5 | 80.4 | 53.6 | 13.3 | 5.2 | 13.4 | 5.2 |
| Tenure: | | | | | | | | |
| Owner occupied...................... | 100.0 | 100.0 | 92.9 | 100.0 | 18.5 | 8.4 | 17.0 | 8.0 |
| Renter occupied or other............ | 98.3 | 74.7 | 71.8 | (B) | 5.6 | 2.3 | 6.0 | 4.0 |
| **MEDIAN VALUE [1] ($1,000)** | | | | | | | | |
| All families, total.................... | **189.9** | **158.9** | **17.3** | **185.0** | **145.7** | **70.0** | **79.9** | **13.0** |
| Age of family head: | | | | | | | | |
| Under 35 years old................... | 31.7 | 24.0 | 14.0 | 160.0 | 85.0 | 13.0 | 20.0 | 7.5 |
| 35 to 44 years old................... | 159.1 | 144.6 | 19.5 | 200.0 | 115.0 | 32.0 | 40.0 | 6.0 |
| 45 to 54 years old................... | 239.3 | 182.7 | 19.3 | 200.0 | 150.0 | 100.0 | 100.0 | 12.0 |
| 55 to 64 years old................... | 286.7 | 210.0 | 19.8 | 200.0 | 200.0 | 121.0 | 100.0 | 25.0 |
| 65 to 74 years old................... | 291.8 | 200.3 | 17.7 | 180.0 | 130.0 | 45.0 | 57.4 | 20.0 |
| 75 years old and over............... | 304.1 | 201.1 | 13.6 | 175.0 | 170.8 | 125.0 | 235.8 | 15.0 |
| Race or ethnicity of respondent: | | | | | | | | |
| White, non-Hispanic................. | 264.7 | 193.5 | 18.4 | 200.0 | 180.0 | 89.6 | 100.0 | 15.0 |
| Black/African-American, non-Hispanic......................... | 46.6 | 62.4 | 13.0 | 124.0 | 50.0 | 12.0 | 27.2 | 6.8 |
| Hispanic or Latino................... | 54.0 | 68.0 | 15.2 | 158.0 | 100.0 | 50.0 | 30.0 | 10.0 |
| Other or multiple race............... | 134.2 | 145.6 | 17.9 | 240.0 | 141.3 | 50.0 | 67.5 | 10.3 |
| Tenure: | | | | | | | | |
| Owner occupied...................... | 341.7 | 237.4 | 21.4 | 185.0 | 150.0 | 90.0 | 100.0 | 20.0 |
| Renter occupied or other............ | 14.5 | 11.7 | 10.1 | (B) | 115.0 | 12.0 | 30.0 | 6.8 |

B Base too small to meet statistical standards for reliability of derived figure. [1] Median value of asset for families holding such assets.

Source: Board of Governors of the Federal Reserve System, 2016 Survey of Consumer Finances, *Changes in U.S. Family Finances From 2013 to 2016: Evidence from the Survey of Consumer Finances,* Federal Reserve Bulletin, Vol. 103, No. 3, September 2017. See also <http://www.federalreserve.gov/econresdata/scf/scfindex.htm>.

# Table 752. Family Net Worth—Median and Mean Net Worth in Constant (2016) Dollars by Selected Family Characteristics: 2007 to 2016

[Net worth in thousands of constant (2016) dollars (139.7 represents $139,700). Constant dollar figures are based on Consumer Price Index for all urban consumers published by U.S. Bureau of Labor Statistics. Families include one-person units and as used in this table are comparable to the U.S. Census Bureau's household concept. Based on internal data from the Survey of Consumer Finances; see Appendix III. For definition of mean and median, see Guide to Tabular Presentation]

| Family characteristic | 2007 | | 2010 | | 2013 | | 2016 | |
|---|---|---|---|---|---|---|---|---|
| | Median | Mean | Median | Mean | Median | Mean | Median | Mean |
| All families............................. | **139.7** | **645.9** | **85.4** | **551.3** | **83.7** | **551.3** | **97.3** | **692.0** |
| Age of family head: | | | | | | | | |
| Under 35 years old................... | 13.7 | 122.8 | 10.3 | 72.2 | 10.7 | 77.8 | 11.0 | 76.1 |
| 35 to 44 years old................... | 102.2 | 377.9 | 46.6 | 240.3 | 48.2 | 358.0 | 59.8 | 288.6 |
| 45 to 54 years old................... | 214.1 | 766.9 | 130.3 | 633.4 | 108.6 | 546.6 | 124.2 | 727.5 |
| 55 to 64 years old................... | 294.3 | 1,090.7 | 198.3 | 973.2 | 171.1 | 823.3 | 187.3 | 1,167.4 |
| 65 to 74 years old................... | 277.3 | 1,176.2 | 228.4 | 937.7 | 239.3 | 1,089.8 | 223.4 | 1,066.0 |
| 75 years old and over............... | 247.3 | 739.2 | 239.6 | 749.3 | 200.8 | 665.3 | 264.8 | 1,066.9 |
| Race or ethnicity of respondent: | | | | | | | | |
| White, non-Hispanic................. | 198.3 | 803.7 | 144.3 | 723.5 | 146.4 | 727.8 | 171.0 | 933.7 |
| Black or African-American, non-Hispanic......................... | 24.4 | 155.7 | 17.6 | 109.8 | 13.6 | 102.1 | 17.1 | 138.0 |
| Hispanic or Latino................... | 24.4 | 215.6 | 17.9 | 127.8 | 14.2 | 111.0 | 20.6 | 191.2 |
| Other or multiple race............... | 70.3 | 457.0 | 47.1 | 370.7 | 42.5 | 383.6 | 64.7 | 457.7 |
| Tenure: | | | | | | | | |
| Owner occupied...................... | 271.9 | 903.4 | 192.8 | 788.6 | 201.5 | 807.3 | 231.4 | 1,034.2 |
| Renter occupied or other............ | 5.9 | 82.5 | 5.6 | 63.3 | 5.5 | 72.5 | 5.0 | 91.0 |

Source: Board of Governors of the Federal Reserve System, 2016 Survey of Consumer Finances, *Changes in U.S. Family Finances From 2013 to 2016: Evidence from the Survey of Consumer Finances,* Federal Reserve Bulletin, Vol. 103, No. 3, September 2017. See also <https://www.federalreserve.gov/econres/scfindex.htm>.

## Table 753. Household and Nonprofit Organization Sector Balance Sheet: 1990 to 2018

[In billions of dollars (25,962 represents $25,962,000,000,000), unless otherwise noted. As of December 31. Sector includes domestic hedge funds, private equity funds, and personal trusts. For details of financial assets and liabilities, see Table 1201 and Table 1203]

| Item | 1990 | 2000 | 2005 | 2010 | 2015 | 2016 | 2017 | 2018 |
|---|---|---|---|---|---|---|---|---|
| **Assets** | **25,962** | **51,487** | **75,672** | **78,739** | **104,159** | **110,106** | **119,054** | **120,390** |
| Nonfinancial assets [1] | 9,750 | 16,910 | 28,629 | 23,046 | 30,012 | 31,791 | 33,780 | 35,374 |
| Real estate [2] | 7,605 | 13,517 | 24,243 | 18,108 | 24,456 | 26,064 | 27,877 | 29,196 |
| Households [3] | 6,812 | 12,203 | 22,170 | 16,254 | 21,615 | 23,029 | 24,584 | 25,877 |
| Consumer durable goods [4] | 2,039 | 3,202 | 4,106 | 4,535 | 5,006 | 5,149 | 5,294 | 5,531 |
| Financial assets [1] | 16,212 | 34,577 | 47,043 | 55,692 | 74,147 | 78,314 | 85,274 | 85,016 |
| Time and savings deposits | 2,674 | 3,068 | 4,882 | 6,464 | 8,450 | 9,108 | 9,298 | 9,724 |
| Money market fund shares | 421 | 1,296 | 1,262 | 1,658 | 1,552 | 1,551 | 1,608 | 1,731 |
| Debt securities [1] | 1,529 | 2,048 | 3,224 | 5,266 | 4,640 | 4,512 | 4,539 | 5,435 |
| Treasury securities | 505 | 536 | 286 | 1,081 | 1,081 | 1,182 | 1,205 | 1,901 |
| Municipal securities | 660 | 475 | 1,702 | 1,914 | 1,886 | 1,862 | 1,858 | 1,767 |
| Corporate and foreign bonds | 249 | 463 | 851 | 1,993 | 1,168 | 1,025 | 928 | 1,096 |
| Corporate equities [2] | 1,707 | 7,213 | 8,122 | 8,695 | 13,348 | 14,807 | 17,703 | 16,128 |
| Mutual fund shares | 466 | 2,465 | 3,297 | 4,501 | 6,746 | 7,219 | 8,529 | 7,811 |
| Life insurance reserves | 391 | 839 | 1,136 | 1,273 | 1,511 | 1,568 | 1,627 | 1,636 |
| Pension entitlements [5] | 4,970 | 11,058 | 14,562 | 18,351 | 23,505 | 24,376 | 25,820 | 25,640 |
| Equity in noncorporate business [6] | 3,064 | 5,019 | 8,466 | 6,893 | 10,831 | 11,622 | 12,508 | 13,055 |
| **Liabilities [1]** | **3,714** | **7,407** | **12,260** | **14,037** | **14,546** | **15,005** | **15,570** | **16,061** |
| Loans [1] | 3,538 | 7,102 | 11,817 | 13,467 | 13,954 | 14,398 | 14,940 | 15,409 |
| Home mortgages [7] | 2,489 | 4,817 | 8,942 | 9,994 | 9,583 | 9,785 | 10,071 | 10,337 |
| Consumer credit | 824 | 1,741 | 2,321 | 2,647 | 3,414 | 3,647 | 3,831 | 4,018 |
| **Net worth** | **22,248** | **44,080** | **63,412** | **64,702** | **89,614** | **95,101** | **103,484** | **104,329** |
| Replacement cost value of structures: | | | | | | | | |
| Residential [1] | 4,287 | 7,732 | 12,245 | 12,732 | 15,425 | 16,442 | 17,190 | 18,366 |
| Households | 4,184 | 7,596 | 12,053 | 12,529 | 15,175 | 16,175 | 16,910 | 18,067 |
| Nonresidential (nonprofits) | 469 | 808 | 1,181 | 1,415 | 1,673 | 1,721 | 1,789 | 1,890 |
| Disposable personal income | 4,319 | 7,416 | 9,386 | 11,314 | 13,784 | 14,171 | 14,796 | 15,531 |
| Owners' equity in real estate | 4,323 | 7,386 | 13,228 | 6,260 | 12,032 | 13,244 | 14,513 | 15,540 |
| Owners' equity as percent of real estate | 63.5 | 60.5 | 59.7 | 38.5 | 55.7 | 57.5 | 59.0 | 60.1 |

[1] Includes other types of assets and/or liabilities not shown separately. [2] At market value. [3] Includes all types of owner-occupied housing, including farm houses, mobile homes, second homes that are not rented, vacant homes for sale, and vacant land. [4] At replacement (current) cost. [5] Includes public and private defined benefit and defined contribution pension plans and annuities, including those in IRAs (individual retirement accounts) and at life insurance companies. Excludes social security. [6] Net worth of nonfinancial noncorporate business and owners' equity in unincorporated security brokers and dealers. [7] Includes loans made under home equity lines of credit and home equity loans secured by junior liens.

Source: Board of Governors of the Federal Reserve System, "Z.1 Financial Accounts of the United States: B.101 Balance Sheet of Households and Nonprofit Organizations," March 2019, <https://www.federalreserve.gov/releases/Z1/Current/>, accessed March 2019.

## Table 754. Net Stock of Fixed Assets and Consumer Durable Goods in Current and Chained (2012) Dollars: 1990 to 2017

[In billions of dollars (18,925 represents $18,925,000,000,000)]

| Item | 1990 | 2000 | 2005 | 2010 | 2014 | 2015 | 2016 | 2017 |
|---|---|---|---|---|---|---|---|---|
| **CURRENT DOLLARS** | | | | | | | | |
| **Net stock, total** | **18,925** | **31,025** | **43,481** | **50,635** | **58,830** | **60,085** | **62,400** | **64,874** |
| Fixed assets | 16,886 | 27,824 | 39,375 | 46,099 | 53,970 | 55,079 | 57,251 | 59,580 |
| Private | 12,803 | 21,483 | 30,662 | 34,582 | 40,733 | 41,652 | 43,443 | 45,272 |
| Nonresidential | 7,101 | 11,672 | 15,512 | 18,799 | 22,167 | 22,637 | 23,211 | 24,120 |
| Equipment | 2,424 | 3,805 | 4,423 | 5,224 | 6,133 | 6,298 | 6,447 | 6,679 |
| Structures | 4,055 | 6,468 | 9,311 | 11,286 | 13,248 | 13,453 | 13,733 | 14,222 |
| Intellectual property products | 621 | 1,399 | 1,777 | 2,289 | 2,785 | 2,886 | 3,031 | 3,218 |
| Residential | 5,702 | 9,810 | 15,150 | 15,783 | 18,566 | 19,015 | 20,232 | 21,153 |
| Government | 4,083 | 6,341 | 8,713 | 11,517 | 13,237 | 13,427 | 13,808 | 14,308 |
| Nonresidential | 3,941 | 6,111 | 8,381 | 11,185 | 12,852 | 13,035 | 13,393 | 13,879 |
| Equipment | 535 | 655 | 735 | 923 | 990 | 988 | 997 | 1,009 |
| Structures | 2,908 | 4,800 | 6,842 | 9,249 | 10,751 | 10,932 | 11,257 | 11,697 |
| Intellectual property products | 498 | 656 | 803 | 1,012 | 1,111 | 1,115 | 1,139 | 1,173 |
| Residential | 142 | 230 | 332 | 333 | 385 | 392 | 416 | 429 |
| Consumer durable goods | 2,039 | 3,202 | 4,106 | 4,535 | 4,861 | 5,006 | 5,149 | 5,294 |
| Motor vehicles and parts | 650 | 1,051 | 1,313 | 1,288 | 1,445 | 1,501 | 1,554 | 1,585 |
| Furnishings and durable household equipment | 649 | 977 | 1,259 | 1,396 | 1,458 | 1,490 | 1,521 | 1,558 |
| Recreational goods and vehicles | 419 | 724 | 964 | 1,061 | 1,089 | 1,123 | 1,140 | 1,185 |
| Other | 322 | 449 | 570 | 792 | 869 | 891 | 935 | 966 |
| **CHAINED (2012) DOLLARS** | | | | | | | | |
| **Net stock, total** | **(NA)** | **41,512** | **47,828** | **52,140** | **54,937** | **55,832** | **56,718** | **57,564** |
| Fixed assets | (NA) | 39,037 | 43,998 | 47,606 | 49,863 | 50,555 | 51,232 | 51,850 |
| Private | (NA) | 29,071 | 32,935 | 35,477 | 37,284 | 37,882 | 38,458 | 38,984 |
| Nonresidential | (NA) | 15,942 | 17,728 | 19,458 | 21,015 | 21,454 | 21,837 | 22,232 |
| Equipment | (NA) | 3,970 | 4,668 | 5,311 | 6,172 | 6,413 | 6,602 | 6,809 |
| Structures | (NA) | 10,669 | 11,271 | 11,927 | 12,274 | 12,391 | 12,481 | 12,569 |
| Intellectual property products | (NA) | 1,482 | 1,830 | 2,228 | 2,577 | 2,667 | 2,780 | 2,892 |
| Residential | (NA) | 13,142 | 15,190 | 16,017 | 16,281 | 16,449 | 16,648 | 16,793 |
| Government | (NA) | 9,994 | 11,063 | 12,129 | 12,575 | 12,667 | 12,765 | 12,854 |
| Nonresidential | (NA) | 9,689 | 10,742 | 11,793 | 12,236 | 12,327 | 12,424 | 12,512 |
| Equipment | (NA) | 740 | 800 | 944 | 972 | 972 | 975 | 983 |
| Structures | (NA) | 8,159 | 9,041 | 9,819 | 10,185 | 10,270 | 10,356 | 10,426 |
| Intellectual property products | (NA) | 794 | 907 | 1,030 | 1,078 | 1,084 | 1,091 | 1,101 |
| Residential | (NA) | 300 | 319 | 336 | 340 | 341 | 342 | 343 |
| Consumer durable goods | (NA) | 2,757 | 3,863 | 4,535 | 5,088 | 5,308 | 5,541 | 5,803 |

NA Not available.

Source: U.S. Bureau of Economic Analysis, National Data, "Fixed Assets Accounts Tables," <https://www.bea.gov/iTable/index_FA.cfm>, accessed July 2019.

# Section 14
# Prices

The Prices section contains producer and consumer price indexes and actual prices for selected commodities. The primary sources of the data are monthly publications of the U.S. Department of Labor, Bureau of Labor Statistics (BLS), which include *Consumer Price Index Detailed Report*, *Producer Price Index Detailed Report*, and *U.S. Import and Export Price Indexes*. Additionally, BLS provides comprehensive databases for the respective price indexes at <www.bls.gov/data/>. The Bureau of Economic Analysis (BEA) is the source for gross domestic product measures. Table 759 on housing price indexes contains data from the Federal Housing Finance Agency's Housing Price Index. Other commodity, housing, and energy prices may be found in the Energy and Utilities; Forestry, Fishing and Mining; and Construction and Housing sections.

Most price data is measured by an index. An index is a tool that simplifies the measurement of movements in a numerical series. An index allows you to properly compare two or more values in different time periods or places by comparing both to a base year. An index of 110, for example, means there has been a 10-percent increase in price since the reference period; similarly, an index of 90 means a 10-percent decrease. Movements of the index from one date to another can be expressed as changes in index points (simply, the difference between index levels), but it is more useful to express the movements as percent changes. This is because index points are affected by the level of the index in relation to its reference period, while percent changes are not.

**Consumer price indexes (CPI)**—The CPI is a measure of the average change in prices over time in a "market basket" of goods and services purchased either by urban wage earners and clerical workers or by all urban consumers. The all urban consumer group represents approximately 93 percent of the total U.S. population and is based on the expenditures of residents of urban or metropolitan areas, including wage earners and clerical workers; professional, managerial, and technical workers; the self-employed; short-term workers; the unemployed; and retirees and others not in the labor force. Not included in the CPI are the spending patterns of people living in rural nonmetropolitan areas, farm families, people in the Armed Forces, and those in institutions, such as prisons and mental hospitals. Consumer inflation for all urban consumers is measured by two indexes, the Consumer Price Index for All Urban Consumers (CPI-U) and the Chained Consumer Price Index for All Urban Consumers (C-CPI-U). The broadest and most comprehensive CPI is called the All Items Consumer Price Index for All Urban Consumers (CPI-U) for the U.S. City Average. CPIs in this section generally have a base of 1982–84 = 100.

The CPI is a product of a series of interrelated samples. Data from the 2010 Decennial Census determines the urban areas from which data on prices are collected and the housing units within each area that are eligible for use in the shelter component of the CPI. The Census of Population also provides data on the number of consumers represented by each area selected as a CPI price collection area. A sample of about 14,500 families each year serves as the basis

for a Point-of-Purchase Survey that identifies the places where households purchase various types of goods and services. The CPI market basket is developed from detailed expenditure information provided by families and individuals on what they actually bought. There is a time lag between the expenditure survey and its use in the CPI. For example, CPI data in 2016 and 2017 was based on data collected from the Consumer Expenditure Surveys for 2013 and 2014. In each of those years, about 24,000 consumers from around the country provided information each quarter on their spending habits in the interview survey. To collect information on frequently purchased items, such as food and personal care products, another 12,000 consumers in each of these years kept diaries listing everything they bought during a 2-week period. Over that period, expenditure information came from approximately 24,000 weekly diaries and 48,000 quarterly interviews used to determine the importance, or weight, of the item categories in the CPI index structure.

The CPI represents all goods and services purchased for consumption by the reference population. BLS has classified all expenditure items into more than 200 categories, arranged into eight major groups which are food and beverages, housing, apparel, transportation, medical care, recreation, education and communication, and other goods and services. The CPI does not include investment items, such as stocks, bonds, real estate, and life insurance, as these items relate to savings and not to day-to-day consumption expenses.

**Producer price index (PPI)**—Dating from 1890, the PPI is the oldest continuous statistical series published by BLS. The PPI is a family of indexes that measures the average change over time in the selling prices received by domestic producers of goods and services. Imports are excluded. The target set of goods and services included in the PPI is the entire marketed output of U.S. producers. The set includes both goods and services purchased by other producers as inputs to their operations or as capital investment, as well as goods and services purchased by consumers either directly from the service producer or indirectly from a retailer. About 10,000 PPIs for individual products and groups of products are released each month.

PPIs are published for the output of almost all industries in the goods-producing sectors of the U.S. economy, and, while more indexes are gradually being introduced, are currently available for approximately 72 percent of the service sector. For any given industry, producers are usually selected for the PPI survey using a systematic sampling from a listing of all firms that file with the Unemployment Insurance System. Establishments are asked to report their prices as of Tuesday of the week containing the 13th of the month. Each month over 100,000 prices are solicited from roughly 25,000 reporters. Currently, some PPIs have an index base set at 1982 = 100, while the remainder have an index base that corresponds with the month prior to the month that the index was introduced. For further detail regarding the PPI, see the BLS Handbook of Methods, Chapter 14, <https://www.bls.gov/opub/hom/pdf/ppi-20111028.pdf>.

In January 2014, PPI transitioned from the Stage of Processing (SOP) system to the Final Demand–Intermediate Demand (FD-ID) system as its primary index aggregation structure. The transition to the FD-ID system is the culmination of a long-standing PPI objective to improve the SOP system (domestically produced goods for domestic, nongovernment consumption) by incorporating PPIs for services, construction, government purchases, and exports. The FD portion of the FD-ID system expands coverage relative to the finished goods stage of the SOP system by including indexes that examine inflation from the producer perspective for goods, services, and construction sold as personal consumption, capital investment, government purchase, and export. The ID portion of the system allows data users to examine inflation from the producer perspective for goods, services, and construction sold to businesses as inputs to production, excluding capital investment.

**BEA price indexes**—BEA chain-weighted price indexes are weighted averages of the detailed price indexes used in the deflation of the goods and services that make up the gross domestic product (GDP) and its major components. Growth rates are constructed for years and quarters using quantity weights for the current and preceding year or quarter; these growth rates are used to move the index for the preceding period forward a year or quarter at a time. All chain-weighted price indexes are expressed in terms of the reference year value 2012 = 100.

Personal consumption expenditures (PCE) price and quantity indexes are based on market transactions for which there are corresponding price measures. The price index provides a measure of the prices paid by persons for domestic purchases of goods and services. PCEs are defined as market value of spending by individuals and not-for-profit institutions on all goods and services. Personal consumption expenditures also include the value of certain imputed goods and services—such as the rental value of owner-occupied homes and compensation paid in kind—such as employer-paid health and life insurance premiums. The PCE price index is known for capturing inflation (or deflation) across a wide range of consumer expenses and for reflecting changes in consumer behavior. More information on this index may be found at <https://www.bea.gov/data/personal-consumption-expenditures-price-index>.

**Measures of inflation**—Inflation is a period of rising price levels for goods and factors of production. Inflation results in a decline in the purchasing power of the dollar. It is suggested that changes in price levels be compared from the same month of the prior year and not as a change from the prior month. The BLS offers several indexes that measure different aspects of inflation, three of which are included in this section. The CPI measures inflation as experienced by consumers in their day-to-day living expenses. The PPI measures prices at the producer level only. The International Price Program measures change in the prices of imports and exports of nonmilitary goods between the United States and other countries.

Whereas the CPI and PPI measure a benchmark approach to price levels, the BEA's Personal Consumption Expenditures uses a chain-weight approach which links weighted averages from adjoining years.

Other measures of inflation include spot market price indexes from the Commodity Research Bureau and the employment cost, hourly compensation, and unit labor cost indexes from the BLS. Found in Section 12, Labor Force, Employment, and Earnings, these BLS indexes are used as a measure of the change in cost of the labor factor of production and changes in long-term interest rates that are often used to measure changes in the cost of the capital factor of production.

**International price indexes**—The BLS International Price Program produces Import/Export Price Indexes (MXP) for nonmilitary goods traded between the United States and the rest of the world.

The U.S. Import and U.S. Export Price Indexes measure the change over time in the prices of goods or services purchased from abroad by U.S. residents (imports) or sold to foreign buyers by U.S. residents (exports). The reference period for the indexes is 2000 = 100, unless otherwise indicated. The product universe for both the import and export indexes includes raw materials, agricultural products, semifinished manufactures, and finished manufactures, including both capital and consumer goods. Price data for these items are collected primarily by mail questionnaire. In nearly all cases, the data are collected directly from the exporter or importer.

To the extent possible, the data gathered refer to prices at the U.S. border for exports and at either the foreign border or the U.S. border for imports. For nearly all products, the prices refer to transactions completed during the first week of the month. Survey respondents are asked to indicate all discounts, allowances, and rebates applicable to the reported prices, so that the price used in the calculation of the indexes is the actual price for which the product was bought or sold.

## Table 755. Purchasing Power of the Dollar: 1950 to 2018

[Indexes: PPI, 1982=$1.00; CPI, 1982-84=$1.00. Producer prices prior to 1961 and consumer prices prior to 1964 exclude Alaska and Hawaii. Producer prices based on final demand, finished goods index. Data is obtained by dividing the average price index for the 1982=100, PPI and the 1982-84=100, CPI base periods (100.0) by the price index for a given period and expressing the result in dollars and cents. Annual figures are based on average of monthly data]

| Year | Annual average as measured by— | | Year | Annual average as measured by— | |
|---|---|---|---|---|---|
| | Producer prices | Consumer prices | | Producer prices | Consumer prices |
| 1950. | 3.546 | 4.149 | 1989. | 0.880 | 0.806 |
| 1955. | 3.279 | 3.731 | 1990. | 0.839 | 0.765 |
| 1960. | 2.994 | 3.378 | 1991. | 0.822 | 0.734 |
| 1962. | 2.985 | 3.311 | 1992. | 0.812 | 0.713 |
| 1963. | 2.994 | 3.268 | 1993. | 0.802 | 0.692 |
| 1964. | 2.985 | 3.226 | 1994. | 0.797 | 0.675 |
| 1965. | 2.933 | 3.175 | 1995. | 0.782 | 0.656 |
| 1966. | 2.841 | 3.086 | 1996. | 0.762 | 0.637 |
| 1967. | 2.809 | 2.994 | 1997. | 0.759 | 0.623 |
| 1968. | 2.732 | 2.874 | 1998. | 0.765 | 0.613 |
| 1969. | 2.632 | 2.725 | 1999. | 0.752 | 0.600 |
| 1970. | 2.545 | 2.577 | 2000. | 0.725 | 0.581 |
| 1971. | 2.469 | 2.469 | 2001. | 0.711 | 0.565 |
| 1972. | 2.392 | 2.392 | 2002. | 0.720 | 0.556 |
| 1973. | 2.193 | 2.252 | 2003. | 0.698 | 0.543 |
| 1974. | 1.901 | 2.028 | 2004. | 0.673 | 0.529 |
| 1975. | 1.718 | 1.859 | 2005. | 0.642 | 0.512 |
| 1976. | 1.645 | 1.757 | 2006. | 0.623 | 0.496 |
| 1977. | 1.546 | 1.650 | 2007. | 0.600 | 0.482 |
| 1978. | 1.433 | 1.534 | 2008. | 0.565 | 0.464 |
| 1979. | 1.289 | 1.377 | 2009. | 0.580 | 0.466 |
| 1980. | 1.136 | 1.214 | 2010. | 0.556 | 0.459 |
| 1981. | 1.041 | 1.100 | 2011. | 0.524 | 0.445 |
| 1982. | 1.000 | 1.036 | 2012. | 0.515 | 0.436 |
| 1983. | 0.984 | 1.004 | 2013. | 0.508 | 0.429 |
| 1984. | 0.964 | 0.962 | 2014. | 0.499 | 0.422 |
| 1985. | 0.955 | 0.929 | 2015. | 0.516 | 0.422 |
| 1986. | 0.969 | 0.912 | 2016. | 0.521 | 0.417 |
| 1987. | 0.949 | 0.880 | 2017. | 0.505 | 0.408 |
| 1988. | 0.926 | 0.845 | 2018. | 0.490 | 0.398 |

Source: U.S. Bureau of Labor Statistics, "CPI Databases," <http://www.bls.gov/cpi/#data>, and "PPI Databases," <http://www.bls.gov/ppi/#data>; accessed May 2019.

## Table 756. Consumer Price Indexes (CPI-U) by Major Group: 1990 to 2018

[1982-84=100, except as indicated. Represents annual averages of monthly figures. Reflects buying patterns of all urban consumers. Minus sign (-) indicates decrease. See text, this section]

| Year | All items | Com-modities | Services | Food | Food and bever-ages | Energy | All items less food and energy | Hous-ing | Apparel | Trans-porta-tion | Medical care | Educa-tion and com-munica-tion [1] |
|---|---|---|---|---|---|---|---|---|---|---|---|---|
| 1990. | 130.7 | 122.8 | 139.2 | 132.4 | 132.1 | 102.1 | 135.5 | 128.5 | 124.1 | 120.5 | 162.8 | (NA) |
| 1995. | 152.4 | 136.4 | 168.7 | 148.4 | 148.9 | 105.2 | 161.2 | 148.5 | 132.0 | 139.1 | 220.5 | 92.2 |
| 2000. | 172.2 | 149.2 | 195.3 | 167.8 | 168.4 | 124.6 | 181.3 | 169.6 | 129.6 | 153.3 | 260.8 | 102.5 |
| 2005. | 195.3 | 160.2 | 230.1 | 190.7 | 191.2 | 177.1 | 200.9 | 195.7 | 119.5 | 173.9 | 323.2 | 113.7 |
| 2007. | 207.3 | 167.5 | 246.8 | 202.9 | 203.3 | 207.7 | 210.7 | 209.6 | 119.0 | 184.7 | 351.1 | 119.6 |
| 2008. | 215.3 | 174.8 | 255.5 | 214.1 | 214.2 | 236.7 | 215.6 | 216.3 | 118.9 | 195.5 | 364.1 | 123.6 |
| 2009. | 214.5 | 169.7 | 259.2 | 218.0 | 218.2 | 193.1 | 219.2 | 217.1 | 120.1 | 179.3 | 375.6 | 127.4 |
| 2010. | 218.1 | 174.6 | 261.3 | 219.6 | 220.0 | 211.4 | 221.3 | 216.3 | 119.5 | 193.4 | 388.4 | 129.9 |
| 2011. | 224.9 | 183.9 | 265.8 | 227.8 | 227.9 | 243.9 | 225.0 | 219.1 | 122.1 | 212.4 | 400.3 | 131.5 |
| 2012. | 229.6 | 187.6 | 271.4 | 233.8 | 233.7 | 246.1 | 229.8 | 222.7 | 126.3 | 217.3 | 414.9 | 133.8 |
| 2013. | 233.0 | 187.7 | 277.9 | 237.0 | 237.0 | 244.4 | 233.8 | 227.4 | 127.4 | 217.4 | 425.1 | 135.9 |
| 2014. | 236.7 | 187.9 | 285.1 | 242.7 | 242.4 | 243.6 | 237.9 | 233.2 | 127.5 | 215.9 | 435.3 | 137.5 |
| 2015. | 237.0 | 181.7 | 291.7 | 247.2 | 246.8 | 202.9 | 242.2 | 238.1 | 125.9 | 199.1 | 446.8 | 138.2 |
| 2016. | 240.0 | 179.2 | 299.9 | 247.9 | 247.7 | 189.5 | 247.6 | 244.0 | 126.0 | 194.9 | 463.7 | 139.1 |
| 2017. | 245.1 | 181.2 | 308.1 | 250.1 | 249.8 | 204.5 | 252.2 | 251.2 | 125.6 | 201.6 | 475.3 | 136.5 |
| 2018. | 251.1 | 184.6 | 316.6 | 253.6 | 253.3 | 219.9 | 257.6 | 258.5 | 125.7 | 210.7 | 484.7 | 136.8 |
| PERCENT CHANGE [2] | | | | | | | | | | | | |
| 1990. | 5.4 | 5.2 | 5.5 | 5.8 | 5.8 | 8.3 | 5.0 | 4.5 | 4.6 | 5.6 | 9.0 | (NA) |
| 1995. | 2.8 | 1.9 | 3.4 | 2.8 | 2.8 | 0.6 | 3.0 | 2.6 | -1.0 | 3.6 | 4.5 | 3.8 |
| 2000. | 3.4 | 3.3 | 3.4 | 2.3 | 2.3 | 16.9 | 2.4 | 3.5 | -1.3 | 6.2 | 4.1 | 1.3 |
| 2005. | 3.4 | 3.6 | 3.3 | 2.4 | 2.5 | 17.0 | 2.2 | 3.3 | -0.7 | 6.6 | 4.2 | 1.9 |
| 2007. | 2.8 | 2.1 | 3.3 | 4.0 | 3.9 | 5.5 | 2.3 | 3.1 | -0.4 | 2.1 | 4.4 | 2.4 |
| 2008. | 3.8 | 4.3 | 3.5 | 5.5 | 5.4 | 13.9 | 2.3 | 3.2 | -0.1 | 5.9 | 3.7 | 3.4 |
| 2009. | -0.4 | -2.9 | 1.4 | 1.8 | 1.9 | -18.4 | 1.7 | 0.4 | 1.0 | -8.3 | 3.2 | 3.0 |
| 2010. | 1.6 | 2.9 | 0.8 | 0.8 | 0.8 | 9.5 | 1.0 | -0.4 | -0.5 | 7.9 | 3.4 | 2.0 |
| 2011. | 3.2 | 5.3 | 1.7 | 3.7 | 3.6 | 15.4 | 1.7 | 1.3 | 2.2 | 9.8 | 3.0 | 1.2 |
| 2012. | 2.1 | 2.0 | 2.1 | 2.6 | 2.5 | 0.9 | 2.1 | 1.6 | 3.4 | 2.3 | 3.7 | 1.8 |
| 2013. | 1.5 | – | 2.4 | 1.4 | 1.4 | -0.7 | 1.8 | 2.1 | 0.9 | – | 2.5 | 1.5 |
| 2014. | 1.6 | 0.1 | 2.6 | 2.4 | 2.3 | -0.3 | 1.7 | 2.6 | 0.1 | -0.7 | 2.4 | 1.2 |
| 2015. | 0.1 | -3.3 | 2.3 | 1.9 | 1.8 | -16.7 | 1.8 | 2.1 | -1.3 | -7.8 | 2.6 | 0.5 |
| 2016. | 1.3 | -1.4 | 2.8 | 0.3 | 0.3 | -6.6 | 2.2 | 2.5 | 0.1 | -2.1 | 3.8 | 0.7 |
| 2017. | 2.1 | 1.1 | 2.7 | 0.9 | 0.9 | 7.9 | 1.8 | 3.0 | -0.3 | 3.4 | 2.5 | -1.9 |
| 2018. | 2.4 | 1.9 | 2.8 | 1.4 | 1.4 | 7.5 | 2.1 | 2.9 | – | 4.5 | 2.0 | 0.2 |

– Represents or rounds to zero. NA Not available. [1] Dec. 1997=100. [2] Change from immediate prior year. 1990 change from 1989.
Source: U.S. Bureau of Labor Statistics, "CPI Databases," <http://www.bls.gov/cpi/#data>, April 2019.

# Table 757. Consumer Price Indexes (CPI-U) and Annual Percent Change for Selected Urban Areas: 2018

[1982–84=100. Percent changes computed from annual averages of monthly figures published by source. In January 2018, BLS introduced a new geographic area sample for the Consumer Price Index (CPI) which utilizes the 2010 Decennial Census and incorporates an updated area sample design; see source for more information. Local area CPI indexes are by-products of the national CPI program. Each local index has a smaller sample size than the national index and is therefore subject to substantially more sampling and other measurement error. As a result, local area indexes show greater volatility than the national index, although their long-term trends are similar. Minus sign (-) indicates decrease. See also text, this section and Appendix III]

| Urban area | Consumer Price Index | | | | | | | |
| --- | --- | --- | --- | --- | --- | --- | --- | --- |
| | All items | Food and beverage | Food | Housing | Apparel | Transportation | Medical care | Fuel and other utilities |
| U.S. city average | 251.1 | 253.3 | 253.6 | 258.5 | 125.7 | 210.7 | 484.7 | 241.6 |
| Atlanta-Sandy Springs-Roswell, GA | 238.6 | 253.3 | 263.7 | 242.0 | 140.0 | 210.6 | 448.9 | 291.8 |
| Baltimore-Columbia-Towson, MD | 253.4 | 259.1 | 258.9 | 258.2 | 134.8 | 203.7 | 424.9 | 229.9 |
| Boston-Cambridge-Newton, MA-NH | 275.8 | 264.6 | 266.0 | 284.7 | 139.3 | 196.0 | 651.6 | 294.6 |
| Chicago-Naperville-Elgin, IL-IN-WI | 237.7 | 248.3 | 247.4 | 247.7 | 84.6 | 187.0 | 503.2 | 205.4 |
| Dallas-Fort Worth-Arlington, TX | 232.8 | 252.1 | 246.3 | 224.3 | 110.3 | 209.5 | 436.6 | 236.8 |
| Denver-Aurora-Lakewood, CO | 262.0 | 235.3 | 239.2 | 261.8 | 99.5 | 257.1 | 595.1 | 245.0 |
| Detroit-Warren-Dearborn, MI | 232.3 | 223.6 | 222.8 | 218.1 | 119.9 | 242.6 | 440.8 | 247.2 |
| Houston-The Woodlands-Sugar Land, TX | 225.9 | 229.0 | 229.0 | 219.8 | 188.3 | 186.5 | 494.8 | 180.7 |
| Los Angeles-Long Beach-Anaheim, CA | 266.0 | 259.4 | 259.8 | 301.4 | 109.1 | 213.1 | 475.7 | 321.3 |
| Miami-Fort Lauderdale-West Palm Beach, FL | 265.1 | 263.3 | 265.6 | 275.0 | 141.0 | 226.5 | 554.7 | 178.0 |
| Minneapolis-St. Paul-Bloomington, MN-WI | 245.0 | 279.8 | 269.0 | 228.9 | 130.3 | 203.5 | 535.2 | 216.8 |
| New York-Newark-Jersey City, NY-NJ-PA | 273.6 | 266.4 | 266.5 | 297.7 | 125.7 | 221.7 | 488.3 | 197.6 |
| Philadelphia-Camden-Wilmington, PA-NJ-DE-MD | 251.6 | 233.7 | 233.8 | 259.5 | 110.4 | 213.7 | 521.7 | 206.6 |
| Phoenix-Mesa-Scottsdale, AZ | 138.9 | 144.8 | 145.6 | 141.5 | 142.5 | 127.8 | (NA) | 165.6 |
| San Diego-Carlsbad, CA | 292.5 | 257.2 | 254.6 | 343.6 | 165.0 | 227.6 | (NA) | 334.9 |
| San Francisco-Oakland-Hayward, CA | 285.6 | 277.7 | 275.8 | 337.0 | 112.7 | 203.8 | 508.6 | 396.0 |
| Seattle-Tacoma-Bellevue, WA | 271.1 | 270.3 | 273.0 | 316.8 | 127.6 | 227.3 | 399.0 | 269.2 |
| St. Louis, MO-IL | 228.9 | 253.7 | 253.2 | 222.2 | 157.3 | 192.0 | 454.4 | 220.4 |
| Tampa-St. Petersburg-Clearwater, FL | 224.3 | 226.1 | 226.7 | 223.5 | 149.8 | 201.6 | 389.3 | 211.9 |
| Urban Alaska | 225.5 | 209.6 | 215.1 | 206.9 | 167.1 | 226.8 | 579.4 | 333.3 |
| Urban Hawaii | 277.1 | 281.8 | 282.6 | 300.7 | 110.3 | 227.7 | (NA) | 362.4 |
| Washington-Arlington-Alexandria, DC-VA-MD-WV | 261.4 | 247.9 | 252.7 | 272.1 | 165.2 | 217.1 | 450.0 | 228.8 |

## PERCENT CHANGE, 2017-2018

| Urban area | All items | Food and beverage | Food | Housing | Apparel | Transportation | Medical care | Fuel and other utilities |
| --- | --- | --- | --- | --- | --- | --- | --- | --- |
| U.S. city average | 2.4 | 1.4 | 1.4 | 2.9 | – | 4.5 | 2.0 | 1.8 |
| Atlanta-Sandy Springs-Roswell, GA | 2.4 | 0.9 | 0.8 | 3.0 | 0.7 | 6.5 | -1.1 | 0.5 |
| Baltimore-Columbia-Towson, MD | 1.9 | 1.6 | 1.3 | 1.4 | 0.7 | 2.9 | 6.3 | -5.9 |
| Boston-Cambridge-Newton, MA-NH | 3.3 | 1.8 | 2.0 | 4.7 | -3.3 | 4.8 | 1.9 | 8.7 |
| Chicago-Naperville-Elgin, IL-IN-WI | 1.8 | 1.8 | 1.6 | 2.6 | -2.5 | 2.5 | 1.3 | 0.4 |
| Dallas-Fort Worth-Arlington, TX | 3.0 | – | -0.1 | 4.3 | 2.0 | 3.7 | 1.4 | 5.9 |
| Denver-Aurora-Lakewood, CO | 2.7 | 2.3 | 2.3 | 2.7 | -3.2 | 4.5 | 6.4 | 3.9 |
| Detroit-Warren-Dearborn, MI | 2.4 | 0.7 | 0.6 | 2.3 | 1.3 | 5.1 | 1.9 | 1.0 |
| Houston-The Woodlands-Sugar Land, TX | 2.4 | 1.2 | 1.2 | 2.8 | – | 3.0 | 3.3 | 8.4 |
| Los Angeles-Long Beach-Anaheim, CA | 3.8 | 1.6 | 1.7 | 4.5 | 2.1 | 7.2 | 0.9 | 4.8 |
| Miami-Fort Lauderdale-West Palm Beach, FL | 3.3 | 1.0 | 0.9 | 3.1 | -0.9 | 5.6 | 9.8 | 0.8 |
| Minneapolis-St. Paul-Bloomington, MN-WI | 2.4 | 1.8 | 1.9 | 3.3 | 2.4 | 1.6 | 1.6 | 1.7 |
| New York-Newark-Jersey City, NY-NJ-PA | 1.9 | 2.3 | 2.2 | 2.1 | -1.3 | 3.5 | 2.5 | 4.7 |
| Philadelphia-Camden-Wilmington, PA-NJ-DE-MD | 1.3 | 0.4 | 0.5 | 1.6 | -1.2 | 2.9 | 2.5 | 2.2 |
| Phoenix-Mesa-Scottsdale, AZ | 4.2 | 0.7 | 0.8 | 5.0 | 0.7 | 8.8 | (NA) | -1.2 |
| San Diego-Carlsbad, CA | 3.4 | 2.0 | 2.1 | 4.7 | 1.3 | 6.6 | (NA) | 7.3 |
| San Francisco-Oakland-Hayward, CA | 3.9 | 3.4 | 2.7 | 3.9 | -3.2 | 6.5 | 3.6 | 2.4 |
| Seattle-Tacoma-Bellevue, WA | 3.2 | 2.0 | 2.0 | 4.7 | -2.5 | 4.6 | 0.8 | 1.5 |
| St. Louis, MO-IL | 1.8 | 2.3 | 1.1 | 1.8 | -0.9 | 3.9 | 3.3 | -0.7 |
| Tampa-St. Petersburg-Clearwater, FL | 2.2 | 0.5 | 2.4 | 3.3 | -1.8 | 4.8 | -3.9 | 2.5 |
| Urban Alaska | 3.0 | 1.6 | 0.6 | 1.8 | 2.0 | 7.0 | 7.6 | 3.8 |
| Urban Hawaii | 1.9 | 1.6 | 1.6 | 2.1 | -4.8 | 4.6 | (NA) | 8.4 |
| Washington-Arlington-Alexandria, DC-VA-MD-WV | 2.0 | 1.2 | 1.2 | 1.7 | 6.3 | 3.4 | 0.9 | -2.6 |

– Represents or rounds to zero. NA Not available.

Source: U.S. Bureau of Labor Statistics, CPI Databases, "All Urban Consumers (Current Series)," <https://www.bls.gov/cpi/data.htm>, accessed April 2019.

# Table 758. Consumer Price Indexes for All Urban Consumers (CPI-U) for Selected Items and Groups: 2000 to 2018

[1982-1984=100, unless otherwise noted. Annual averages of monthly figures. Reflects buying patterns of all urban consumers. For information about the CPI methodology, see the U.S. Bureau of Labor Statistics Handbook of Methods, Chapter 17, Consumer Price Index at <http://www.bls.gov/opub/hom/pdf/homch17.pdf>]

| Item | 2000 | 2010 | 2013 | 2014 | 2015 | 2016 | 2017 | 2018 |
|---|---|---|---|---|---|---|---|---|
| **All items** | **172.2** | **218.1** | **233.0** | **236.7** | **237.0** | **240.0** | **245.1** | **251.1** |
| **Food and beverages** | **168.4** | **220.0** | **237.0** | **242.4** | **246.8** | **247.7** | **249.8** | **253.3** |
| Food | 167.8 | 219.6 | 237.0 | 242.7 | 247.2 | 247.9 | 250.1 | 253.6 |
| Food at home | 167.9 | 215.8 | 233.9 | 239.5 | 242.3 | 239.1 | 238.6 | 239.7 |
| Cereals and bakery products | 188.3 | 250.4 | 270.4 | 271.1 | 274.1 | 273.1 | 271.7 | 272.8 |
| Cereals and cereal products | 175.9 | 217.6 | 232.7 | 232.9 | 234.1 | 231.2 | 227.7 | 226.6 |
| Rice, pasta, and cornmeal | 150.7 | 224.4 | 239.4 | 238.1 | 241.6 | 239.1 | 234.3 | 236.2 |
| Rice [1,2] | 99.3 | 156.9 | 170.2 | 170.7 | 167.2 | 163.1 | 160.0 | 161.7 |
| Bakery products | 194.1 | 268.0 | 291.5 | 292.5 | 296.6 | 296.9 | 296.8 | 299.3 |
| Bread [2] | 107.4 | 159.8 | 176.8 | 176.4 | 178.7 | 178.5 | 178.3 | 179.4 |
| Cakes, cupcakes, and cookies | 187.9 | 251.7 | 271.0 | 273.5 | 278.8 | 281.6 | 282.7 | 287.5 |
| Other bakery products | 191.5 | 247.1 | 263.5 | 264.8 | 266.4 | 265.4 | 264.9 | 264.7 |
| Meats, poultry, fish and eggs | 154.5 | 207.7 | 236.0 | 253.0 | 260.3 | 247.7 | 245.8 | 248.9 |
| Meats, poultry, and fish | 155.5 | 208.6 | 236.7 | 253.7 | 258.5 | 249.4 | 249.0 | 250.7 |
| Meats | 150.7 | 206.2 | 234.8 | 256.5 | 264.2 | 252.5 | 251.0 | 252.1 |
| Beef and veal | 148.1 | 224.5 | 268.3 | 300.7 | 322.5 | 302.1 | 298.4 | 302.6 |
| Uncooked ground beef | 125.2 | 203.6 | 246.8 | 276.0 | 295.3 | 268.2 | 266.6 | 268.2 |
| Uncooked beef steaks [2] | 109.1 | 153.3 | 179.9 | 199.9 | 214.6 | 206.2 | 201.1 | 203.7 |
| Pork | 156.5 | 190.0 | 208.6 | 227.6 | 218.7 | 209.9 | 211.1 | 210.2 |
| Poultry | 159.8 | 204.0 | 231.7 | 236.3 | 237.3 | 230.9 | 231.3 | 232.1 |
| Chicken [2] | 102.5 | 131.8 | 148.2 | 151.7 | 152.1 | 147.5 | 148.6 | 150.3 |
| Fish and seafood | 190.4 | 243.2 | 273.3 | 289.0 | 286.3 | 284.2 | 287.7 | 293.8 |
| Eggs | 131.9 | 192.8 | 224.2 | 243.0 | 286.2 | 226.0 | 204.5 | 226.6 |
| Dairy products [2] | 160.7 | 199.2 | 217.6 | 225.3 | 222.4 | 217.3 | 217.5 | 216.5 |
| Milk [2] | 107.8 | 133.6 | 149.2 | 156.6 | 147.5 | 140.7 | 139.7 | 137.0 |
| Cheese and related products | 162.8 | 204.8 | 221.9 | 234.1 | 233.6 | 228.0 | 228.5 | 229.2 |
| Ice cream and related products | 164.4 | 195.0 | 215.5 | 215.4 | 219.2 | 219.4 | 219.9 | 220.6 |
| Fruits and vegetables | 204.6 | 273.5 | 290.0 | 294.4 | 293.8 | 296.3 | 295.7 | 297.8 |
| Fresh fruits and vegetables | 238.8 | 314.8 | 332.8 | 339.2 | 337.7 | 341.7 | 342.4 | 346.1 |
| Fresh fruits | 258.3 | 322.3 | 343.2 | 359.7 | 352.0 | 359.8 | 361.4 | 365.2 |
| Fresh vegetables | 219.4 | 305.5 | 320.5 | 316.3 | 321.4 | 321.5 | 321.1 | 324.7 |
| Processed fruits and vegetables [2] | 105.6 | 146.6 | 157.2 | 157.3 | 158.5 | 157.9 | 155.4 | 154.5 |
| Nonalcoholic beverages and beverage materials | 137.8 | 161.6 | 166.9 | 166.0 | 167.9 | 167.3 | 167.6 | 167.6 |
| Juices and nonalcoholic drinks [2] | 105.6 | 124.5 | 127.8 | 127.1 | 128.5 | 128.6 | 129.0 | 129.7 |
| Carbonated drinks | 123.4 | 154.7 | 159.5 | 150.8 | 159.0 | 161.1 | 161.0 | 163.7 |
| Nonfrozen noncarbonated juices and drinks [2] | 104.2 | 114.8 | 117.0 | 116.2 | 117.9 | 117.4 | 117.7 | 117.7 |
| Beverage materials including coffee and tea [2] | 97.9 | 114.0 | 119.8 | 118.9 | 120.4 | 118.3 | 118.3 | 116.7 |
| Coffee | 154.0 | 186.4 | 204.7 | 201.0 | 205.5 | 199.3 | 199.2 | 194.9 |
| Other food at home | 155.6 | 191.1 | 204.8 | 206.2 | 209.3 | 209.5 | 209.9 | 210.2 |
| Sugar and sweets | 154.0 | 201.2 | 211.0 | 209.3 | 216.1 | 215.3 | 215.1 | 215.9 |
| Candy and chewing gum [2] | 103.8 | 132.5 | 139.6 | 139.7 | 145.4 | 145.1 | 144.3 | 145.7 |
| Fats and oils | 147.4 | 200.6 | 229.3 | 229.7 | 227.3 | 225.9 | 227.7 | 228.0 |
| Other foods | 172.2 | 204.0 | 217.7 | 219.9 | 223.4 | 224.1 | 224.4 | 224.7 |
| Frozen and freeze dried prepared food | 148.5 | 165.3 | 167.8 | 168.7 | 170.9 | 169.7 | 167.9 | 166.8 |
| Snacks | 166.3 | 216.6 | 242.8 | 244.3 | 250.6 | 252.2 | 251.8 | 253.4 |
| Spices, seasonings, condiments, sauces | 175.6 | 214.4 | 226.4 | 229.7 | 235.6 | 237.7 | 239.6 | 241.7 |
| Other miscellaneous food [2] | 107.5 | 121.7 | 129.2 | 130.4 | 131.8 | 131.6 | 131.9 | 131.5 |
| Food away from home | 169.0 | 226.1 | 243.1 | 249.0 | 256.1 | 262.7 | 268.8 | 275.9 |
| Full service meals and snacks [2] | 106.8 | 141.1 | 151.5 | 155.3 | 159.4 | 163.1 | 167.1 | 171.0 |
| Limited service meals and snacks [2] | 106.3 | 143.9 | 154.6 | 158.4 | 163.3 | 167.7 | 171.8 | 176.6 |
| At employee sites and schools [2] | 104.4 | 141.0 | 155.3 | 158.2 | 161.7 | 170.0 | 172.1 | 178.1 |
| From vending machines and mobile vendors [2] | 102.4 | 133.1 | 143.3 | 143.1 | 146.3 | 150.8 | 154.8 | 159.5 |
| Other food away from home [2] | 109.0 | 159.3 | 169.6 | 173.8 | 179.6 | 182.7 | 184.5 | 191.8 |
| Alcoholic beverages | 174.7 | 223.3 | 234.6 | 237.3 | 239.5 | 242.5 | 245.4 | 249.1 |
| Alcoholic beverages at home | 158.1 | 191.0 | 195.7 | 197.0 | 197.3 | 199.0 | 200.3 | 202.5 |
| Beer, ale, and other malt beverages at home | 156.8 | 201.0 | 211.1 | 213.8 | 215.0 | 218.9 | 222.9 | 226.0 |
| Distilled spirits at home | 162.3 | 188.8 | 191.0 | 192.4 | 192.6 | 193.3 | 192.5 | 192.0 |
| Wine at home | 151.6 | 169.7 | 169.2 | 169.0 | 168.5 | 168.4 | 167.9 | 170.0 |
| Alcoholic beverages away from home | 207.1 | 291.9 | 317.9 | 323.8 | 330.5 | 336.6 | 343.5 | 350.9 |
| **Housing** | **169.6** | **216.3** | **227.4** | **233.2** | **238.1** | **244.0** | **251.2** | **258.5** |
| Shelter | 193.4 | 248.4 | 263.1 | 270.5 | 278.8 | 288.2 | 297.8 | 307.7 |
| Rent of primary residence | 183.9 | 249.4 | 267.7 | 276.2 | 286.0 | 296.8 | 308.1 | 319.3 |
| Lodging away from home [2] | 117.5 | 133.7 | 142.4 | 148.5 | 153.0 | 158.1 | 159.4 | 161.1 |
| Other lodging away from home including hotels and motels | 252.4 | 280.4 | 294.8 | 307.8 | 317.4 | 325.3 | 327.1 | 329.4 |
| Owners' equivalent rent of primary residence [3] | 198.7 | 256.6 | 270.7 | 277.8 | 285.9 | 295.3 | 305.1 | 315.2 |
| Tenants' and household insurance [2] | 103.7 | 125.7 | 135.4 | 141.9 | 146.4 | 147.7 | 148.8 | 150.7 |
| Fuels and utilities | 137.9 | 214.2 | 225.2 | 234.6 | 230.1 | 228.9 | 237.3 | 241.6 |
| Household energy | 122.8 | 189.3 | 193.8 | 202.2 | 194.7 | 191.1 | 198.3 | 200.8 |
| Fuel oil and other fuels | 129.7 | 275.1 | 332.0 | 338.9 | 256.2 | 226.3 | 254.4 | 293.0 |
| Fuel oil | 130.3 | 282.9 | 370.2 | 365.0 | 254.3 | 209.2 | 241.7 | 296.1 |
| Propane, kerosene, and firewood [4] | 155.5 | 320.6 | 327.6 | 358.4 | 305.9 | 295.5 | 322.1 | 340.9 |
| Energy services | 128.0 | 192.9 | 194.8 | 203.4 | 198.7 | 196.1 | 202.7 | 203.8 |
| Electricity | 128.5 | 193.1 | 200.8 | 208.0 | 209.2 | 207.0 | 211.4 | 212.9 |
| Utility (piped) gas service | 132.0 | 189.7 | 174.5 | 186.8 | 164.6 | 160.6 | 173.4 | 173.6 |
| Water and sewer and trash collection services [2] | 106.5 | 170.9 | 197.6 | 204.9 | 214.0 | 221.7 | 229.1 | 237.1 |
| Water and sewerage maintenance | 227.5 | 380.7 | 449.7 | 468.1 | 492.9 | 513.7 | 532.8 | 550.7 |
| Garbage and trash collection [5] | 269.8 | 384.4 | 416.2 | 425.8 | 432.0 | 439.4 | 449.1 | 466.9 |
| **Household furnishings and operations** | **128.2** | **125.5** | **124.8** | **123.1** | **122.6** | **121.6** | **120.7** | **121.6** |
| Furniture and bedding | 134.4 | 119.7 | 118.7 | 115.5 | 114.7 | 112.1 | 111.0 | 111.1 |
| Living room, kitchen, and dining room furniture [2] | 102.4 | 88.9 | 90.1 | 87.1 | 86.8 | 85.3 | 84.6 | 85.2 |
| Appliances [2] | 96.3 | 86.9 | 86.3 | 82.5 | 79.3 | 76.6 | 74.7 | 75.8 |
| Other household equipment and furnishings [2] | 98.0 | 70.8 | 63.5 | 60.7 | 59.1 | 57.1 | 54.4 | 51.5 |
| Clocks, lamps, and decorator items | 111.7 | 62.9 | 52.8 | 49.4 | 47.1 | 44.8 | 41.0 | 37.7 |

See footnotes at end of table.

# Table 758. Consumer Price Indexes for All Urban Consumers (CPI-U) for Selected Items and Groups: 2000 to 2018-Continued.

See headnote on page 491.

| Item | 2000 | 2010 | 2013 | 2014 | 2015 | 2016 | 2017 | 2018 |
|---|---|---|---|---|---|---|---|---|
| Nonelectric cookware and tableware [2] | 98.4 | 96.6 | 97.2 | 93.3 | 90.4 | 88.7 | 86.3 | 83.9 |
| Tools, hardware, outdoor equipment and supplies [2] | 97.0 | 91.6 | 92.0 | 91.3 | 91.1 | 90.1 | 89.6 | 89.5 |
| Tools, hardware, and supplies [2] | 97.3 | 96.5 | 100.7 | 100.2 | 100.1 | 98.3 | 97.9 | 98.5 |
| Outdoor equipment and supplies [2] | 96.8 | 88.9 | 87.9 | 87.0 | 86.8 | 86.2 | 85.7 | 85.3 |
| Housekeeping supplies | 153.4 | 183.3 | 189.1 | 187.6 | 186.8 | 186.3 | 184.9 | 186.4 |
| Household cleaning products [2] | 105.1 | 120.6 | 121.3 | 119.1 | 118.9 | 119.4 | 118.2 | 118.7 |
| Household paper products [2] | 113.8 | 158.0 | 170.3 | 170.3 | 169.2 | 169.2 | 168.7 | 169.6 |
| Miscellaneous household products [2] | 104.3 | 116.9 | 120.1 | 119.8 | 119.0 | 117.5 | 116.4 | 118.3 |
| Household operations [2] | 110.5 | 150.3 | 157.6 | 161.6 | 166.9 | 171.6 | 176.3 | 186.0 |
| Domestic services [2] | 109.7 | 144.4 | 150.1 | 153.7 | 155.6 | 157.2 | 160.9 | 165.8 |
| Gardening and lawncare services [2] | 111.4 | 155.3 | 160.6 | 165.0 | 171.8 | 174.4 | 179.3 | 193.1 |
| **Apparel** | **129.6** | **119.5** | **127.4** | **127.5** | **125.9** | **126.0** | **125.6** | **125.7** |
| Men's and boy's apparel | 129.7 | 111.9 | 121.6 | 120.6 | 119.6 | 118.8 | 117.2 | 118.1 |
| Men's apparel | 133.1 | 117.5 | 126.7 | 125.0 | 124.0 | 122.6 | 121.5 | 120.7 |
| Men's shirts and sweaters [2] | 98.3 | 78.6 | 82.9 | 81.0 | 79.5 | 79.5 | 78.6 | 78.2 |
| Boys' apparel | 116.2 | 91.5 | 102.6 | 103.9 | 103.0 | 103.8 | 100.8 | 106.7 |
| Women's and girl's apparel | 121.5 | 107.1 | 113.3 | 114.4 | 111.2 | 111.2 | 111.0 | 110.4 |
| Women's apparel | 121.9 | 109.5 | 116.2 | 117.6 | 114.4 | 114.6 | 114.2 | 113.5 |
| Women's suits and separates [2] | 98.2 | 83.9 | 86.7 | 85.3 | 81.8 | 81.5 | 80.1 | 79.1 |
| Women's underwear, nightwear, swimwear, and accessories [2] | 101.8 | 96.0 | 103.2 | 106.3 | 105.2 | 106.4 | 107.1 | 105.6 |
| Girls' apparel | 119.7 | 95.4 | 99.6 | 99.0 | 96.0 | 95.6 | 95.8 | 95.0 |
| Footwear | 123.8 | 128.0 | 135.0 | 135.5 | 136.8 | 137.3 | 136.7 | 136.1 |
| Men's footwear | 129.5 | 127.6 | 136.8 | 138.0 | 137.9 | 138.8 | 138.6 | 139.7 |
| Women's footwear | 119.6 | 125.3 | 130.4 | 128.0 | 128.9 | 128.6 | 127.1 | 124.9 |
| Jewelry and watches [4] | 137.0 | 152.4 | 168.2 | 163.6 | 160.0 | 169.1 | 174.2 | 172.7 |
| Jewelry [4] | 141.2 | 161.2 | 177.6 | 170.6 | 165.5 | 175.8 | 179.4 | 175.0 |
| **Transportation** | **153.3** | **193.4** | **217.4** | **215.9** | **199.1** | **194.9** | **201.6** | **210.7** |
| Private transportation | 149.1 | 188.7 | 212.4 | 211.0 | 193.7 | 189.5 | 196.6 | 206.4 |
| New and used motor vehicles [2] | 100.8 | 97.1 | 100.9 | 100.8 | 100.8 | 100.2 | 98.9 | 99.1 |
| New vehicles | 142.8 | 138.0 | 145.8 | 146.3 | 147.1 | 147.4 | 147.0 | 146.3 |
| Used cars and trucks | 155.8 | 143.1 | 149.9 | 149.1 | 147.1 | 143.5 | 138.3 | 138.4 |
| Leased cars and trucks [6] | (NA) | 97.0 | 86.7 | 84.8 | 84.2 | 84.5 | 84.8 | 89.2 |
| Motor fuel | 129.3 | 239.2 | 303.9 | 292.4 | 213.1 | 188.4 | 212.7 | 241.9 |
| Gasoline (all types) | 128.6 | 238.6 | 302.6 | 290.9 | 212.0 | 187.6 | 211.8 | 240.6 |
| Motor vehicle parts and equipment | 101.5 | 137.0 | 146.4 | 144.8 | 144.2 | 143.6 | 143.0 | 143.7 |
| Motor vehicle maintenance and repair | 177.3 | 248.0 | 261.6 | 266.0 | 270.7 | 275.4 | 280.8 | 286.4 |
| Motor vehicle insurance | 256.7 | 375.2 | 419.4 | 437.2 | 460.6 | 489.1 | 526.9 | 566.0 |
| Motor vehicle fees [2] | 107.3 | 165.5 | 174.8 | 176.5 | 178.9 | 182.6 | 185.0 | 188.7 |
| Public transportation | 209.6 | 251.4 | 278.9 | 276.4 | 268.7 | 265.4 | 263.1 | 258.8 |
| Airline fare | 239.4 | 278.2 | 312.7 | 307.7 | 292.2 | 282.6 | 275.8 | 264.9 |
| **Medical care** | **260.8** | **388.4** | **425.1** | **435.3** | **446.8** | **463.7** | **475.3** | **484.7** |
| Medical care commodities | 238.1 | 314.7 | 335.1 | 343.4 | 354.6 | 366.8 | 377.0 | 381.4 |
| Prescription drugs | 285.4 | 407.8 | 442.6 | 458.3 | 479.3 | 502.5 | 519.6 | 528.0 |
| Nonprescription drugs [10] | (NA) | 100.0 | 99.4 | 98.5 | 97.8 | 96.6 | 97.4 | 96.9 |
| Medical care services | 266.0 | 411.2 | 454.0 | 464.8 | 476.2 | 494.8 | 506.8 | 517.8 |
| Professional medical services | 237.7 | 328.2 | 349.5 | 355.2 | 361.5 | 371.5 | 375.1 | 378.4 |
| Physicians' services | 244.7 | 331.3 | 354.2 | 359.1 | 366.1 | 378.1 | 380.1 | 380.5 |
| Dental services | 258.5 | 398.8 | 431.8 | 441.0 | 452.2 | 465.0 | 472.6 | 485.5 |
| Eyeglasses and eye care [4] | 149.7 | 176.7 | 180.8 | 183.9 | 184.0 | 187.0 | 187.3 | 189.6 |
| Services by other medical professionals [4] | 161.9 | 214.4 | 223.3 | 226.4 | 228.2 | 231.0 | 236.6 | 237.4 |
| Hospital and related services | 317.3 | 607.7 | 701.3 | 733.8 | 761.9 | 795.1 | 831.7 | 866.9 |
| Hospital services [7] | 115.9 | 227.2 | 265.4 | 278.8 | 290.1 | 303.3 | 318.2 | 332.2 |
| Nursing homes and adult day services [7] | 117.0 | 177.0 | 194.5 | 200.1 | 206.4 | 213.7 | 220.3 | 227.8 |
| Health insurance [9] | (NA) | 106.2 | 123.0 | 122.1 | 123.6 | 131.8 | 133.9 | 135.5 |
| **Recreation [2]** | **103.3** | **113.3** | **115.3** | **115.5** | **115.9** | **117.0** | **118.5** | **119.1** |
| Video and audio [2] | 101.0 | 99.1 | 99.7 | 99.8 | 99.6 | 100.9 | 104.2 | 104.2 |
| Cable and satellite television and radio service [5] | 266.8 | 372.4 | 406.5 | 416.1 | 422.8 | 438.3 | 462.2 | 470.5 |
| Pets, pet products and services [2] | 106.1 | 154.4 | 164.6 | 165.7 | 167.3 | 169.6 | 170.3 | 172.4 |
| Sporting goods | 119.0 | 118.8 | 118.1 | 116.5 | 114.6 | 113.1 | 111.0 | 111.0 |
| Other recreational goods [2] | 87.8 | 57.8 | 51.9 | 49.4 | 47.0 | 43.9 | 40.6 | 37.4 |
| Other recreation services [2] | 111.7 | 145.1 | 150.5 | 152.7 | 156.2 | 159.9 | 164.1 | 167.9 |
| Club membership for shopping clubs, fraternal or other organizations & participant sports fees [2] | 108.9 | 123.5 | 127.5 | 129.3 | 130.1 | 132.2 | 135.3 | 139.2 |
| Admissions | 230.5 | 322.8 | 336.2 | 341.9 | 354.1 | 365.8 | 374.8 | 381.6 |
| Recreational reading materials [2] | 188.3 | 220.7 | 232.0 | 236.7 | 240.7 | 240.7 | 241.5 | 246.3 |
| **Education and communication [2]** | **102.5** | **129.9** | **135.9** | **137.5** | **138.2** | **139.1** | **136.5** | **136.8** |
| Education [2] | 112.5 | 199.3 | 224.5 | 231.9 | 240.5 | 247.5 | 253.2 | 258.8 |
| Educational books and supplies | 279.9 | 505.6 | 594.7 | 615.4 | 648.2 | 678.8 | 689.5 | 696.1 |
| Tuition, other school fees, and childcare | 324.0 | 573.2 | 643.7 | 664.8 | 688.8 | 708.1 | 724.7 | 741.3 |
| College tuition and fees | 331.9 | 638.2 | 732.4 | 759.5 | 785.9 | 807.0 | 823.1 | 841.3 |
| Child care and nursery school [11] | 156.3 | 240.4 | 259.4 | 264.9 | 275.4 | 283.1 | 290.4 | 295.0 |
| Communication [2] | 93.6 | 84.7 | 82.6 | 82.1 | 80.2 | 79.2 | 75.0 | 73.9 |
| Postage and delivery services [2] | 103.2 | 145.9 | 167.3 | 174.2 | 174.6 | 175.6 | 180.3 | 184.9 |
| Information and information processing [2] | 92.8 | 81.5 | 78.9 | 78.2 | 76.4 | 75.4 | 71.1 | 70.0 |
| Telephone services [2] | 98.5 | 102.4 | 101.6 | 101.1 | 99.3 | 98.8 | 91.8 | 90.4 |
| Wireless telephone services [2] | 76.0 | 62.4 | 58.6 | 57.4 | 55.2 | 54.7 | 48.8 | 47.6 |
| Land-line telephone services [10] | (NA) | 101.6 | 108.1 | 111.1 | 113.4 | 114.5 | 116.1 | 117.2 |
| Information technology, hardware, and services [8] | 25.9 | 9.4 | 8.5 | 8.4 | 8.1 | 7.8 | 7.6 | 7.5 |
| **Other goods and services** | **271.1** | **381.3** | **401.0** | **408.1** | **414.9** | **423.1** | **432.6** | **442.3** |
| Tobacco and smoking products | 394.9 | 807.3 | 876.8 | 903.3 | 930.8 | 963.4 | 1,022.8 | 1,063.5 |
| Cigarettes [2] | 159.9 | 329.0 | 357.1 | 368.4 | 380.0 | 393.5 | 418.3 | 434.9 |
| Personal care | 165.6 | 206.6 | 215.0 | 218.0 | 220.8 | 224.3 | 227.0 | 231.1 |
| Personal care products | 153.7 | 161.1 | 161.8 | 163.4 | 163.3 | 163.1 | 161.7 | 161.5 |
| Hair, dental, shaving, and miscellaneous personal care products [2] | 103.3 | 104.3 | 102.8 | 103.4 | 103.7 | 103.1 | 102.3 | 102.3 |

See footnotes at end of table.

## Table 758. Consumer Price Indexes for All Urban Consumers (CPI-U) for Selected Items and Groups: 2000 to 2018-Continued.

See headnote on page 491.

| Item | 2000 | 2010 | 2013 | 2014 | 2015 | 2016 | 2017 | 2018 |
|---|---|---|---|---|---|---|---|---|
| Cosmetics, perfume, bath, nail preparations and implements... | 166.8 | 182.2 | 186.4 | 189.3 | 188.2 | 188.8 | 187.0 | 186.3 |
| Personal care services... | 178.1 | 229.6 | 238.8 | 242.0 | 247.2 | 252.9 | 257.4 | 264.2 |
| Haircuts and other personal care services [2]... | 108.7 | 140.1 | 145.7 | 147.7 | 150.8 | 154.3 | 157.0 | 161.2 |
| Miscellaneous personal services... | 252.3 | 354.1 | 381.9 | 389.7 | 399.3 | 411.8 | 424.0 | 439.8 |
| Legal services [4]... | 189.3 | 288.1 | 311.8 | 318.5 | 323.6 | 334.5 | 346.4 | 361.2 |
| Funeral expenses [4]... | 187.8 | 282.0 | 301.6 | 307.1 | 313.7 | 319.4 | 325.6 | 331.7 |
| **SPECIAL AGGREGATE INDEXES** | | | | | | | | |
| Commodities... | 149.2 | 174.6 | 187.7 | 187.9 | 181.7 | 179.2 | 181.2 | 184.6 |
| Commodities less food and beverages... | 137.7 | 150.4 | 161.5 | 159.6 | 149.2 | 145.4 | 147.2 | 150.3 |
| Nondurables less food and beverages... | 147.4 | 189.9 | 212.2 | 210.0 | 189.4 | 183.8 | 190.6 | 199.0 |
| Nondurables less food, beverages, and apparel... | 162.5 | 238.1 | 269.8 | 266.2 | 233.3 | 223.9 | 235.3 | 249.0 |
| Durables... | 125.4 | 111.3 | 111.9 | 110.3 | 109.1 | 107.3 | 105.3 | 104.4 |
| Services [3]... | 195.3 | 261.3 | 277.9 | 285.1 | 291.7 | 299.9 | 308.1 | 316.6 |
| Rent of shelter [3]... | 201.3 | 258.8 | 274.0 | 281.8 | 290.4 | 300.3 | 310.3 | 320.7 |
| Transportation services... | 196.1 | 259.8 | 280.0 | 285.3 | 291.0 | 299.4 | 309.9 | 321.8 |
| Other services... | 229.9 | 309.6 | 328.7 | 334.4 | 339.4 | 346.0 | 347.8 | 352.7 |
| All items less food... | 173.0 | 217.8 | 232.3 | 235.8 | 235.4 | 238.8 | 244.3 | 250.7 |
| All items less shelter... | 165.7 | 208.6 | 223.8 | 226.2 | 223.3 | 223.8 | 227.2 | 231.8 |
| All items less medical care... | 167.3 | 209.7 | 223.6 | 227.1 | 226.9 | 229.3 | 234.1 | 239.9 |
| Commodities less food... | 139.2 | 153.0 | 164.1 | 162.3 | 152.2 | 148.6 | 150.5 | 153.6 |
| Nondurables less food... | 149.1 | 191.9 | 213.6 | 211.7 | 192.3 | 187.2 | 193.8 | 201.9 |
| Nondurables less food and apparel... | 162.9 | 235.6 | 265.4 | 262.3 | 232.7 | 224.5 | 235.0 | 247.8 |
| Nondurables... | 158.2 | 205.3 | 225.3 | 226.7 | 217.6 | 215.0 | 219.6 | 225.8 |
| Apparel less footwear [3]... | 126.2 | 113.3 | 121.1 | 121.1 | 118.8 | 118.9 | 118.5 | 118.7 |
| Services less rent of shelter [3]... | 202.9 | 284.4 | 304.1 | 311.2 | 315.8 | 322.8 | 329.3 | 336.4 |
| Services less medical care services... | 188.9 | 249.6 | 264.5 | 271.5 | 277.7 | 285.2 | 293.0 | 301.3 |
| Energy... | 124.6 | 211.4 | 244.4 | 243.6 | 202.9 | 189.5 | 204.5 | 219.9 |
| All items less energy... | 178.6 | 220.5 | 233.6 | 238.0 | 242.3 | 247.0 | 251.2 | 256.3 |
| All items less food and energy... | 181.3 | 221.3 | 233.8 | 237.9 | 242.2 | 247.6 | 252.2 | 257.6 |
| Commodities less food and energy commodities... | 144.9 | 143.6 | 147.3 | 146.8 | 146.1 | 145.4 | 144.4 | 144.1 |
| Energy commodities... | 129.5 | 242.6 | 307.4 | 296.9 | 216.7 | 191.6 | 216.3 | 246.2 |
| Services less energy services... | 202.1 | 268.3 | 286.4 | 293.5 | 301.1 | 310.4 | 318.7 | 328.0 |
| Domestically produced farm food... | 170.1 | 221.6 | 241.4 | 247.9 | 251.0 | 247.3 | 246.6 | 247.7 |
| Utilities and public transportation... | 152.6 | 203.1 | 212.1 | 216.7 | 214.8 | 215.2 | 216.4 | 217.2 |

NA Not available. [1] Special indexes based on a substantially smaller sample. [2] December 1997=100. [3] December 1982–100. [4] December 1986=100. [5] December 1983=100. [6] December 2001=100. [7] December 1996=100. [8] December 1988=100. [9] December 2005=100. [10] December 2009=100. [11] December 1990=100.

Source: U.S. Bureau of Labor Statistics, CPI Databases, "All Urban Consumers (Current Series)," <https://www.bls.gov/cpi/data.htm>, accessed April 2019.

## Table 759. Single-Family Housing Price Indexes by State: 2000 to 2018

[Data are for the fourth quarter of the year shown. Index 1991, 1st quarter = 100. Purchase only indexes. Data are seasonally adjusted. The index reflects average price changes in repeat sales or refinancings on the same properties. The information is obtained by reviewing repeat mortgage transactions on single-family properties whose mortgages have been purchased or securitized by either Fannie Mae or Freddie Mac; for more information on methodology, see source]

| State | 2000 | 2005 | 2010 | 2015 | 2018 | State | 2000 | 2005 | 2010 | 2015 | 2018 |
|---|---|---|---|---|---|---|---|---|---|---|---|
| **U.S.** | **143.9** | **216.5** | **182.5** | **221.5** | **265.8** | MO | 150.3 | 197.5 | 178.3 | 204.1 | 244.5 |
| AL | 142.9 | 182.9 | 176.0 | 193.3 | 223.4 | MT | 179.3 | 275.6 | 280.7 | 338.8 | 406.6 |
| AK | 137.1 | 208.2 | 220.0 | 247.7 | 264.0 | NE | 162.0 | 193.8 | 187.4 | 224.4 | 268.0 |
| AZ | 155.8 | 304.3 | 171.7 | 258.4 | 326.2 | NV | 128.3 | 269.8 | 125.0 | 194.4 | 266.4 |
| AR | 141.3 | 185.5 | 175.8 | 197.0 | 225.1 | NH | 146.2 | 237.9 | 194.9 | 215.9 | 257.3 |
| CA | 123.6 | 284.3 | 159.9 | 233.3 | 285.3 | NJ | 133.4 | 253.6 | 214.1 | 216.4 | 241.6 |
| CO | 216.9 | 269.9 | 257.8 | 360.9 | 467.8 | NM | 145.3 | 214.4 | 209.1 | 214.0 | 245.6 |
| CT | 117.8 | 194.3 | 166.1 | 164.3 | 174.2 | NY | 128.4 | 212.6 | 202.9 | 211.5 | 246.8 |
| DE | 121.5 | 208.7 | 187.2 | 189.4 | 208.0 | NC | 146.1 | 182.5 | 181.6 | 203.7 | 248.6 |
| DC | 133.0 | 322.8 | 317.5 | 464.5 | 578.8 | ND | 137.9 | 191.4 | 223.2 | 300.6 | 311.1 |
| FL | 139.8 | 300.5 | 173.1 | 244.5 | 312.5 | OH | 148.2 | 174.3 | 151.1 | 172.2 | 205.5 |
| GA | 151.7 | 191.1 | 152.9 | 198.5 | 246.7 | OK | 144.2 | 177.6 | 191.9 | 221.2 | 242.9 |
| HI | 92.3 | 203.7 | 177.0 | 222.6 | 265.9 | OR | 184.1 | 296.5 | 252.8 | 342.6 | 431.7 |
| ID | 154.0 | 228.1 | 189.2 | 252.0 | 338.3 | PA | 121.1 | 189.5 | 185.4 | 199.4 | 229.8 |
| IL | 145.5 | 203.2 | 173.0 | 182.8 | 205.1 | RI | 120.2 | 236.3 | 183.0 | 196.3 | 235.3 |
| IN | 142.4 | 165.4 | 156.0 | 177.4 | 213.3 | SC | 145.0 | 185.6 | 178.9 | 206.8 | 250.0 |
| IA | 157.4 | 190.7 | 193.7 | 219.0 | 249.1 | SD | 160.1 | 207.7 | 215.5 | 257.3 | 300.3 |
| KS | 154.3 | 188.2 | 188.7 | 212.1 | 251.2 | TN | 147.0 | 185.3 | 180.4 | 215.8 | 269.0 |
| KY | 150.8 | 184.5 | 186.7 | 208.2 | 244.7 | TX | 143.0 | 172.3 | 184.8 | 241.9 | 293.7 |
| LA | 157.1 | 213.1 | 224.8 | 256.7 | 280.7 | UT | 194.1 | 256.0 | 249.2 | 321.1 | 421.6 |
| ME | 133.0 | 220.4 | 201.1 | 214.6 | 256.4 | VT | 127.2 | 207.6 | 201.8 | 214.6 | 240.3 |
| MD | 121.9 | 254.6 | 206.3 | 224.1 | 253.2 | VA | 131.2 | 234.4 | 206.8 | 230.6 | 263.6 |
| MA | 156.8 | 251.9 | 213.2 | 243.9 | 293.7 | WA | 154.5 | 242.4 | 219.5 | 277.1 | 369.8 |
| MI | 173.2 | 200.2 | 143.7 | 188.5 | 233.5 | WV | 137.4 | 180.3 | 186.7 | 209.7 | 213.9 |
| MN | 172.2 | 252.4 | 204.7 | 243.9 | 292.8 | WI | 166.4 | 222.3 | 203.8 | 220.9 | 266.0 |
| MS | 143.0 | 178.4 | 173.0 | 191.1 | 209.9 | WY | 169.0 | 258.0 | 277.6 | 322.1 | 349.0 |

Source: Federal Housing Finance Agency, "House Price Index Datasets, Quarterly Data, Purchase-Only Indexes," <https://www.fhfa.gov/DataTools/Downloads/Pages/House-Price-Index-Datasets.aspx#qpo>, accessed March 2019.

## Table 760. Average Prices of Selected Fuels and Electricity: 1990 to 2018

[Fuels in dollars per unit; electricity in cents per kWh. Represents price to end-users, except as noted]

| Item | Unit | 1990 | 2000 | 2010 | 2013 | 2014 | 2015 | 2016 | 2017 | 2018 |
|---|---|---|---|---|---|---|---|---|---|---|
| Crude oil, composite [1] | Barrel | 22.22 | 28.26 | 76.69 | 100.49 | 92.02 | 48.39 | 40.66 | 50.68 | 64.37 |
| Motor gasoline: [2] | | | | | | | | | | |
| Unleaded regular | Gallon | 1.16 | 1.51 | 2.79 | 3.53 | 3.37 | 2.45 | 2.14 | 2.41 | 2.74 |
| Unleaded premium | Gallon | 1.35 | 1.69 | 3.05 | 3.84 | 3.71 | 2.87 | 2.61 | 2.91 | 3.27 |
| No. 2 fuel oil (heating oil) | Gallon | 0.73 | 0.93 | 2.46 | 3.34 | 3.33 | 2.02 | 1.72 | 2.01 | 2.38 |
| No. 2 diesel fuel | Gallon | 0.73 | 0.94 | 2.31 | 3.12 | 2.92 | 1.82 | 1.51 | 1.81 | 2.26 |
| Propane, consumer grade | Gallon | 0.75 | 0.60 | 1.48 | 1.03 | 1.10 | 0.48 | 0.50 | 0.77 | 0.93 |
| Residual fuel oil | Gallon | 0.44 | 0.60 | 1.71 | 2.48 | 2.33 | 1.29 | 0.95 | 1.29 | 1.66 |
| Natural gas, residential | 1,000 cu/ft | 5.80 | 7.76 | 11.39 | 10.32 | 10.97 | 10.38 | 10.05 | 10.91 | 10.53 |
| Electricity, residential | kWh | 7.83 | 8.24 | 11.54 | 12.13 | 12.52 | 12.65 | 12.55 | 12.89 | 12.89 |

[1] Refiner acquisition cost. [2] Average, all service.

Source: U.S. Energy Information Administration, *Monthly Energy Review*, April 2019. See also <http://www.eia.gov/totalenergy/data/monthly/>.

## Table 761. Retail Gasoline Prices—U.S. Total and Selected Cities: 2015 to 2018

[In dollars per gallon. Prices are annual averages]

| Area | Regular | | | | Midgrade | | | | Premium | | | |
|---|---|---|---|---|---|---|---|---|---|---|---|---|
| | 2015 | 2016 | 2017 | 2018 | 2015 | 2016 | 2017 | 2018 | 2015 | 2016 | 2017 | 2018 |
| **U.S. total** | **2.43** | **2.14** | **2.42** | **2.72** | **2.65** | **2.40** | **2.68** | **3.06** | **2.83** | **2.62** | **2.92** | **3.29** |
| Boston, MA | 2.36 | 2.11 | 2.40 | 2.73 | 2.59 | 2.36 | 2.66 | 3.01 | 2.75 | 2.57 | 2.86 | 3.20 |
| Chicago, IL | 2.62 | 2.24 | 2.49 | 2.78 | 2.90 | 2.57 | 2.82 | 3.16 | 3.17 | 2.91 | 3.20 | 3.55 |
| Cleveland, OH | 2.33 | 2.07 | 2.28 | 2.56 | 2.54 | 2.36 | 2.58 | 2.88 | 2.76 | 2.65 | 2.87 | 3.20 |
| Denver, CO | 2.32 | 2.02 | 2.31 | 2.60 | 2.54 | 2.30 | 2.61 | 2.92 | 2.74 | 2.56 | 2.89 | 3.21 |
| Houston, TX | 2.13 | 1.87 | 2.12 | 2.42 | 2.40 | 2.16 | 2.43 | 2.78 | 2.65 | 2.44 | 2.71 | 3.02 |
| Los Angeles, CA | 3.29 | 2.80 | 3.05 | 3.51 | 3.40 | 2.91 | 3.17 | 3.68 | 3.50 | 3.01 | 3.29 | 3.78 |
| Miami, FL | 2.56 | 2.31 | 2.70 | 2.73 | 2.84 | 2.62 | 3.00 | 3.03 | 3.05 | 2.90 | 3.25 | 3.30 |
| New York, NY | 2.40 | 2.12 | 2.47 | 2.77 | 2.67 | 2.43 | 2.76 | 3.05 | 2.85 | 2.62 | 2.96 | 3.22 |
| San Francisco, CA | 3.14 | 2.75 | 3.08 | 3.54 | 3.26 | 2.89 | 3.24 | 3.72 | 3.37 | 3.01 | 3.35 | 3.85 |
| Seattle, WA | 2.77 | 2.50 | 2.87 | 3.27 | 2.90 | 2.66 | 3.05 | 3.53 | 3.01 | 2.77 | 3.16 | 3.61 |

Source: U.S. Energy Information Administration, "Weekly Retail Gasoline and Diesel Prices," <http://www.eia.gov/petroleum/data.cfm#prices>, accessed January 2019.

## Table 762. Weekly Food Cost of a Nutritious Diet by Type of Family and Individual: 2010 and 2018

[In dollars. As of December. Suggested plans assume that food for all meals and snacks is purchased at the store and prepared at home. All four Food Plans are based on 2001-02 data and updated to current dollars by using the Consumer Price Index for specific food items. See source for details]

| Family and individual type | Thrifty plan | | Low-cost plan | | Moderate plan | | Liberal plan | |
|---|---|---|---|---|---|---|---|---|
| | 2010 | 2018 | 2010 | 2018 | 2010 | 2018 | 2010 | 2018 |
| **FAMILIES** | | | | | | | | |
| Family of two (male & female): | | | | | | | | |
| 19 to 50 years old | 81.10 | 88.90 | 103.40 | 113.80 | 128.40 | 141.30 | 160.80 | 176.90 |
| 51 to 70 years old | 76.90 | 84.30 | 99.20 | 109.10 | 122.60 | 135.80 | 148.00 | 164.70 |
| Family of four: | | | | | | | | |
| Couple (male & female), | | | | | | | | |
| 19 to 50 years old and children aged— | | | | | | | | |
| 2 to 3 and 4 to 5 years old | 118.10 | 129.80 | 150.20 | 165.90 | 185.50 | 205.10 | 229.90 | 253.80 |
| 6 to 8 and 9 to 11 years old | 135.60 | 148.90 | 176.60 | 195.50 | 221.00 | 245.00 | 268.50 | 297.30 |
| **INDIVIDUALS** [1] | | | | | | | | |
| Child: | | | | | | | | |
| 1 year old | 20.10 | 21.70 | 26.80 | 29.30 | 30.60 | 33.30 | 37.10 | 40.50 |
| 2 to 3 years old | 21.70 | 23.90 | 27.50 | 30.80 | 33.30 | 37.10 | 40.50 | 45.00 |
| 4 to 5 years old | 22.70 | 25.10 | 28.70 | 31.60 | 35.50 | 39.60 | 43.30 | 48.00 |
| 6 to 8 years old | 28.80 | 31.90 | 39.20 | 44.20 | 48.20 | 53.80 | 56.90 | 63.70 |
| 9 to 11 years old | 33.00 | 36.20 | 43.40 | 47.90 | 56.10 | 62.70 | 65.50 | 72.90 |
| Male: | | | | | | | | |
| 12 to 13 years old | 35.10 | 38.70 | 49.50 | 55.00 | 61.70 | 69.00 | 72.70 | 81.20 |
| 14 to 18 years old | 36.20 | 39.80 | 50.80 | 55.70 | 63.80 | 70.70 | 73.40 | 81.60 |
| 19 to 50 years old | 39.00 | 42.80 | 50.30 | 55.40 | 62.90 | 69.30 | 77.10 | 85.00 |
| 51 to 70 years old | 35.60 | 39.00 | 47.60 | 52.40 | 58.60 | 65.10 | 71.10 | 79.00 |
| 71 years old and over | 35.80 | 39.20 | 47.00 | 51.30 | 58.50 | 64.20 | 71.90 | 79.20 |
| Female: | | | | | | | | |
| 12 to 13 years old | 35.30 | 38.50 | 42.90 | 47.30 | 51.90 | 57.60 | 63.00 | 70.10 |
| 14 to 18 years old | 34.80 | 38.00 | 43.10 | 47.30 | 52.00 | 56.60 | 63.90 | 70.20 |
| 19 to 50 years old | 34.70 | 38.00 | 43.70 | 48.10 | 53.80 | 59.10 | 69.00 | 75.70 |
| 51 to 70 years old | 34.30 | 37.60 | 42.50 | 46.80 | 52.90 | 58.40 | 63.50 | 70.70 |
| 71 years old and over | 33.80 | 37.00 | 42.10 | 46.10 | 52.50 | 57.70 | 63.40 | 69.70 |

[1] The costs given are for individuals in 4-person families. For individuals in other size families, the following adjustments are suggested: 1-person, add 20 percent; 2-person, add 10 percent; 3-person, add 5 percent; 5- or 6-person, subtract 5 percent; and 7-or-more person, subtract 10 percent.

Source: U.S. Department of Agriculture, Center for Nutrition Policy and Promotion, *Official USDA Food Plans: Cost of Food at Home at Four Levels, U.S. Average, December 2018*, January 2019, and earlier reports. See also <https://www.cnpp.usda.gov/USDAFoodPlansCostofFood/reports>.

## Table 763. Food—Retail Prices of Selected Items: 1990 to 2018

[In dollars per pound, except as indicated. As of December. See Appendix III]

| Food | 1990 | 2000 | 2005 | 2010 | 2014 | 2015 | 2016 | 2017 | 2018 |
|---|---|---|---|---|---|---|---|---|---|
| **Cereals and bakery products:** | | | | | | | | | |
| Flour, white, all purpose...................... | 0.24 | 0.28 | 0.30 | 0.44 | 0.51 | 0.50 | 0.50 | 0.46 | 0.44 |
| Rice, white, long grain, raw.................... | 0.49 | (NA) | 0.52 | 0.73 | 0.70 | 0.71 | 0.69 | 0.71 | 0.71 |
| Spaghetti and macaroni.................... | 0.85 | 0.88 | 0.87 | 1.19 | 1.16 | 1.29 | 1.29 | 1.24 | 1.16 |
| Bread, white, pan............................. | 0.70 | 0.99 | 1.05 | 1.39 | 1.47 | 1.43 | 1.36 | 1.32 | 1.29 |
| Bread, whole wheat........................... | (NA) | 1.36 | 1.29 | 1.88 | 1.99 | 1.95 | 1.96 | 1.97 | 1.92 |
| **Beef:** | | | | | | | | | |
| Ground beef, 100% beef...................... | 1.63 | 1.63 | 2.30 | 2.38 | 4.16 | 4.06 | 3.56 | 3.71 | 3.73 |
| Ground chuck, 100% beef.................... | 2.02 | 1.98 | 2.61 | 2.93 | 4.22 | 4.03 | 3.62 | 3.73 | 3.71 |
| Ground beef, lean and extra lean............ | (NA) | 2.33 | 2.91 | 3.49 | 6.08 | 5.89 | 5.54 | 5.52 | 5.26 |
| Beef roasts (all, uncooked)................. | (NA) | 2.93 | 3.73 | 4.15 | 5.85 | 5.48 | 5.16 | 5.21 | 5.20 |
| Beef steaks (all, uncooked).................. | (NA) | 4.09 | 5.03 | 5.60 | 7.54 | 7.51 | 7.12 | 7.36 | 7.58 |
| Round steak, USDA Choice.................. | 3.42 | 3.28 | 4.12 | 4.30 | 6.26 | 5.93 | 5.56 | 5.83 | 5.69 |
| Sirloin steak, boneless....................... | 4.24 | 4.81 | 5.93 | 6.07 | 8.15 | 8.29 | 7.91 | 7.93 | 8.31 |
| **Pork:** | | | | | | | | | |
| Bacon, sliced................................ | 2.28 | 3.03 | 3.33 | 4.16 | 5.53 | 5.73 | 5.10 | 5.63 | 5.50 |
| Chops, center cut, bone-in.................. | 3.32 | 3.46 | 3.28 | 3.58 | 4.26 | 4.09 | 3.63 | 3.81 | 3.95 |
| Ham, boneless, excluding canned............ | (NA) | 2.75 | 3.09 | 3.47 | 4.35 | 4.03 | 3.93 | 3.87 | 3.88 |
| **Poultry, fish, and eggs:** | | | | | | | | | |
| Chicken, fresh, whole........................ | 0.86 | 1.08 | 1.06 | 1.28 | 1.54 | 1.44 | 1.46 | 1.47 | 1.47 |
| Chicken breast, boneless.................... | (NA) | (NA) | (NA) | 3.32 | 3.48 | 3.28 | 3.20 | 3.19 | 3.11 |
| Chicken legs, bone-in....................... | 1.17 | 1.26 | 1.33 | 1.48 | 1.61 | 1.57 | 1.43 | 1.46 | 1.40 |
| Turkey, frozen, whole........................ | 0.96 | 0.99 | 1.07 | 1.38 | 1.33 | 1.45 | 1.50 | 1.50 | 1.41 |
| Tuna, light, chunk, canned.................. | 2.11 | 1.92 | (NA) | (NA) | (NA) | 3.26 | 3.15 | (NA) | (NA) |
| Eggs, grade A large (dozen)................. | 1.00 | 0.96 | 1.35 | 1.79 | 2.21 | 2.75 | 1.38 | 1.82 | 1.60 |
| **Dairy products:** | | | | | | | | | |
| Milk, fresh, whole, fortified (per gal.)......... | (NA) | 2.79 | 3.24 | 3.32 | 3.82 | 3.31 | 3.29 | 3.16 | 2.85 |
| Milk, low-fat, reduced fat, skim, per gallon... | (NA) | (NA) | (NA) | (NA) | (NA) | (NA) | (NA) | (NA) | 2.63 |
| Yogurt, per 8 ounce.......................... | (NA) | (NA) | (NA) | (NA) | (NA) | (NA) | (NA) | (NA) | 1.08 |
| Butter, in sticks.............................. | (NA) | (NA) | (NA) | (NA) | (NA) | (NA) | (NA) | (NA) | 3.93 |
| American processed cheese................. | (NA) | 3.69 | 3.92 | 3.80 | 4.71 | 4.35 | 4.21 | 4.13 | 3.94 |
| Cheddar cheese, natural..................... | (NA) | 3.76 | 4.43 | 4.93 | 5.44 | 5.33 | 4.90 | 4.95 | 5.36 |
| Ice cream, prepack., bulk, reg. (1/2 gal.)..... | 2.54 | 3.66 | 3.69 | 4.58 | 5.04 | 4.73 | 4.68 | 4.76 | 4.81 |
| **Fresh fruits and vegetables:** | | | | | | | | | |
| Apples, Red Delicious....................... | 0.77 | 0.82 | 0.97 | 1.20 | 1.29 | 1.40 | 1.31 | (NA) | (NA) |
| Bananas..................................... | 0.43 | 0.49 | 0.48 | 0.59 | 0.59 | 0.58 | 0.58 | 0.56 | 0.58 |
| Oranges, navel............................... | 0.56 | 0.62 | 0.89 | 1.02 | 1.25 | 1.23 | 1.17 | 1.32 | 1.39 |
| Grapefruit.................................... | 0.56 | 0.58 | 1.10 | 0.99 | 1.10 | 1.09 | 1.25 | 1.33 | 1.35 |
| Grapes, Thompson seedless................. | (NA) | 2.36 | 2.76 | 2.87 | 2.96 | 2.83 | 2.88 | 2.61 | 2.28 |
| Lemons...................................... | 0.97 | 1.11 | 1.51 | 1.60 | 1.97 | 1.98 | 1.99 | 1.99 | 2.39 |
| Pears, Anjou................................. | 0.79 | (NA) | 1.00 | 1.42 | (NA) | (NA) | 1.63 | 1.55 | 1.57 |
| Strawberries, dry pint, per 12 ounces........ | (NA) | (NA) | 2.67 | 3.07 | 3.56 | 3.50 | 3.28 | 3.09 | 3.17 |
| Lettuce, iceberg............................. | 0.58 | 0.85 | 0.85 | 0.99 | 1.11 | 1.48 | 1.02 | 1.01 | 1.25 |
| Tomatoes, field grown........................ | 0.86 | 1.57 | 1.85 | 1.59 | 2.19 | 1.93 | 1.97 | 2.24 | 2.18 |
| Peppers, sweet.............................. | (NA) | (NA) | (NA) | 2.40 | 2.62 | (NA) | 2.20 | 2.42 | 2.65 |
| Potatoes, white.............................. | 0.32 | 0.35 | 0.50 | 0.58 | 0.64 | 0.64 | 0.69 | 0.73 | 0.72 |
| **Sugar and fats and oils:** | | | | | | | | | |
| Sugar, white, all sizes....................... | 0.43 | 0.41 | 0.45 | 0.64 | 0.61 | 0.64 | 0.61 | 0.65 | 0.57 |
| Margarine, tubs, soft......................... | (NA) | 0.84 | 0.91 | 1.62 | 1.96 | 1.86 | 1.78 | 1.70 | 1.57 |
| Peanut butter, creamy, all sizes............. | 2.07 | 1.96 | 1.70 | 1.99 | 2.70 | 2.68 | 2.62 | 2.48 | (NA) |
| **Nonalcoholic beverages:** | | | | | | | | | |
| All soft drinks, 2 liter........................ | (NA) | (NA) | (NA) | (NA) | (NA) | (NA) | (NA) | (NA) | 1.47 |
| All soft drinks, per 12 oz can in 12-pack..... | (NA) | (NA) | (NA) | (NA) | (NA) | (NA) | (NA) | (NA) | 0.33 |
| Coffee, 100% ground roast, all sizes......... | 2.94 | 3.21 | 3.24 | 4.15 | 4.59 | 4.49 | 4.28 | 4.29 | (NA) |
| **Prepared foods:** | | | | | | | | | |
| Potato chips, per 16 ounces................. | 2.97 | 3.44 | 3.46 | 4.74 | 4.27 | 4.41 | 4.35 | 4.43 | 4.45 |

NA Not available.

Source: U.S. Bureau of Labor Statistics, CPI Databases, "Average Price Indexes," <http://www.bls.gov/cpi/data.htm>, accessed February 2019.


## Table 764. Employment Cost Index for Total Compensation, Wages and Salaries, and Benefits: 2008 to 2018

[As of December (2005=100). Data are not seasonally adjusted. For data by industry, see Table 677]

| Compensation type and occupation | 2008 | 2009 | 2010 | 2011 | 2012 | 2013 | 2014 | 2015 | 2016 | 2017 | 2018 |
|---|---|---|---|---|---|---|---|---|---|---|---|
| **Total compensation:** | | | | | | | | | | | |
| All civilian workers [1]...................... | 109.5 | 111.0 | 113.2 | 115.5 | 117.7 | 120.0 | 122.7 | 125.1 | 127.9 | 131.2 | 135.0 |
| Private industry workers................ | 108.9 | 110.2 | 112.5 | 115.0 | 117.1 | 119.4 | 122.2 | 124.5 | 127.2 | 130.5 | 134.4 |
| State and local government workers... | 111.6 | 114.2 | 116.2 | 117.7 | 119.9 | 122.2 | 124.7 | 127.8 | 130.9 | 134.2 | 137.7 |
| **Wages and salaries:** | | | | | | | | | | | |
| All civilian workers [1]...................... | 109.6 | 111.2 | 113.0 | 114.6 | 116.5 | 118.7 | 121.2 | 123.7 | 126.6 | 129.8 | 133.8 |
| Private industry workers................ | 109.4 | 110.8 | 112.8 | 114.6 | 116.6 | 119.0 | 121.6 | 124.2 | 127.1 | 130.6 | 134.7 |
| State and local government workers... | 110.4 | 112.5 | 113.8 | 114.9 | 116.2 | 117.5 | 119.4 | 121.6 | 124.1 | 126.7 | 129.7 |
| **Benefits:** | | | | | | | | | | | |
| All civilian workers [1]...................... | 109.1 | 110.7 | 113.9 | 117.5 | 120.3 | 123.0 | 126.2 | 128.4 | 131.1 | 134.4 | 138.1 |
| Private industry workers................ | 107.7 | 108.7 | 111.9 | 115.9 | 118.2 | 120.5 | 123.5 | 125.1 | 127.3 | 130.2 | 133.6 |
| State and local government workers... | 114.2 | 117.7 | 121.1 | 123.6 | 127.8 | 132.0 | 135.8 | 140.6 | 145.0 | 149.7 | 154.4 |

[1] Includes workers in the private nonfarm economy except those in private households and workers in the public sector except the federal government.

Source: U.S. Bureau of Labor Statistics, Employment Cost Trends, "Employment Cost Index," <http://www.bls.gov/ncs/ect/#data>, accessed February 2019.

## Table 765. Indexes of Spot Primary Market Prices: 1990 to 2018

[1967=100. Represents unweighted geometric average of price quotations of 23 commodities. The indexes are computed daily and therefore are much more sensitive to changes in market conditions than a monthly producer price index]

| Items and number | 1990 | 1995 | 2000 | 2005 | 2010 | 2012 | 2013 | 2014 | 2015 | 2016 | 2017 | 2018 |
|---|---|---|---|---|---|---|---|---|---|---|---|---|
| **All commodities (23)** | **258.1** | **289.1** | **224.0** | **303.3** | **520.3** | **482.1** | **456.2** | **438.0** | **374.8** | **423.1** | **432.5** | **409.2** |
| Foodstuffs (10) | 206.4 | 236.4 | 184.7 | 241.7 | 440.3 | 423.9 | 364.7 | 369.4 | 335.0 | 338.8 | 336.0 | 324.2 |
| Raw industrials (13) | 301.2 | 332.2 | 255.8 | 354.7 | 583.8 | 526.8 | 532.4 | 492.6 | 404.9 | 493.2 | 514.7 | 480.4 |
| Livestock and products (5) | 292.7 | 307.4 | 265.5 | 326.6 | 528.0 | 599.7 | 547.8 | 556.2 | 392.2 | 446.2 | 437.3 | 396.4 |
| Metals (5) | 283.2 | 300.6 | 214.0 | 440.9 | 1,006.2 | 918.7 | 935.2 | 824.4 | 556.0 | 803.9 | 911.6 | 829.9 |
| Textiles and fibers (4) | 257.6 | 274.3 | 245.7 | 252.5 | 342.1 | 276.8 | 278.2 | 257.7 | 271.9 | 287.3 | 304.5 | 286.9 |
| Fats and oils (4) | 188.7 | 226.7 | 163.6 | 223.4 | 478.3 | 471.5 | 387.3 | 364.0 | 315.2 | 393.3 | 380.8 | 357.4 |

Source: cmdty by Barchart, Chicago, IL, *CRB Commodity Index Report*, weekly ©. See also <http://www.barchart.com/cmdty>.

## Table 766. Producer Price Indexes—Final and Intermediate Demand: 2010 to 2018

[November 2009=100. Minus sign (-) indicates decrease. For information on producer prices, see Bureau of Labor Statistics, <http://www.bls.gov/ppi/>]

| Commodity type | Index | | | | | | |
|---|---|---|---|---|---|---|---|
| | 2010 | 2013 | 2014 | 2015 | 2016 | 2017 | 2018 |
| **FINAL DEMAND** | | | | | | | |
| Total | **101.8** | **109.1** | **110.9** | **109.9** | **110.4** | **113.0** | **116.2** |
| Final demand goods | 102.8 | 112.6 | 114.0 | 109.1 | 107.6 | 111.2 | 115.0 |
| Final demand foods | 103.7 | 117.8 | 121.6 | 118.4 | 115.1 | 116.5 | 116.7 |
| Final demand energy | 107.2 | 125.3 | 124.2 | 98.6 | 90.4 | 99.8 | 110.0 |
| Final demand goods less foods and energy | 101.4 | 107.9 | 109.5 | 109.9 | 110.7 | 113.2 | 116.0 |
| Final demand services | 101.3 | 107.1 | 109.0 | 110.0 | 111.5 | 113.5 | 116.5 |
| Final demand trade services | 101.7 | 108.2 | 110.2 | 111.6 | 113.1 | 114.8 | 116.9 |
| Final demand transportation and warehousing services | 103.2 | 115.3 | 117.7 | 115.3 | 113.5 | 115.9 | 122.0 |
| Final demand services less trade, transportation, and warehousing | 100.9 | 105.8 | 107.5 | 108.7 | 110.6 | 112.8 | 115.8 |
| **INTERMEDIATE DEMAND** | | | | | | | |
| Processed goods for intermediate demand | 183.4 | 200.8 | 201.9 | 188.0 | 182.2 | 190.7 | 200.9 |
| Processed foods and feeds | 171.7 | 204.3 | 210.8 | 197.7 | 188.4 | 190.3 | 191.6 |
| Processed energy goods | 187.8 | 213.7 | 211.5 | 168.9 | 152.6 | 171.0 | 190.8 |
| Processed materials less foods and energy | 180.8 | 193.8 | 195.2 | 189.4 | 186.9 | 193.3 | 201.8 |
| Unprocessed goods for intermediate demand | 212.2 | 246.7 | 249.3 | 189.1 | 173.4 | 190.8 | 200.1 |
| Unprocessed foodstuffs and feedstuffs | 152.4 | 200.2 | 210.1 | 181.4 | 162.4 | 167.1 | 163.9 |
| Unprocessed energy materials | 216.7 | 234.7 | 233.1 | 141.1 | 128.1 | 150.7 | 168.7 |
| Unprocessed nonfood materials less energy | 329.1 | 351.2 | 345.7 | 296.0 | 288.0 | 324.1 | 340.7 |
| Services for intermediate demand | 101.1 | 107.2 | 108.9 | 110.2 | 112.1 | 115.0 | 118.6 |
| Trade services for intermediate demand | 100.8 | 109.2 | 110.4 | 113.1 | 112.1 | 115.3 | 120.0 |
| Transportation and warehousing services for intermediate demand | 103.3 | 116.1 | 119.4 | 119.1 | 118.2 | 120.6 | 125.4 |
| Services less trade, transportation, and warehousing for intermediate demand | 100.7 | 105.0 | 106.5 | 107.8 | 110.9 | 113.8 | 117.0 |
| **PERCENT CHANGE [1]** | | | | | | | |
| **FINAL DEMAND** | | | | | | | |
| Total | **(NA)** | **1.3** | **1.6** | **-0.9** | **0.5** | **2.4** | **2.8** |
| Final demand goods | (NA) | 0.8 | 1.2 | -4.3 | -1.4 | 3.3 | 3.4 |
| Final demand foods | (NA) | 1.6 | 3.2 | -2.6 | -2.8 | 1.2 | 0.2 |
| Final demand energy | (NA) | -0.8 | -0.9 | -20.6 | -8.3 | 10.4 | 10.2 |
| Final demand goods less foods and energy | (NA) | 1.0 | 1.5 | 0.4 | 0.7 | 2.3 | 2.5 |
| Final demand services | (NA) | 1.6 | 1.8 | 0.9 | 1.4 | 1.8 | 2.6 |
| Final demand trade services | (NA) | 1.4 | 1.8 | 1.3 | 1.3 | 1.5 | 1.8 |
| Final demand transportation and warehousing services | (NA) | 1.0 | 2.1 | -2.0 | -1.6 | 2.1 | 5.3 |
| Final demand services less trade, transportation, and warehousing | (NA) | 1.8 | 1.6 | 1.1 | 1.7 | 2.0 | 2.7 |
| **INTERMEDIATE DEMAND** | | | | | | | |
| Processed goods for intermediate demand | 6.3 | (Z) | 0.5 | -6.9 | -3.1 | 4.7 | 5.3 |
| Processed foods and feeds | 3.4 | 1.4 | 3.2 | -6.2 | -4.7 | 1.0 | 0.7 |
| Processed energy goods | 15.6 | -2.2 | -1.0 | -20.1 | -9.7 | 12.1 | 11.6 |
| Processed materials less foods and energy | 4.3 | 0.6 | 0.7 | -3.0 | -1.3 | 3.4 | 4.4 |
| Unprocessed goods for intermediate demand | 21.1 | 2.2 | 1.1 | -24.1 | -8.3 | 10.0 | 4.9 |
| Unprocessed foodstuffs and feedstuffs | 13.3 | 1.9 | 4.9 | -13.7 | -10.5 | 2.9 | -1.9 |
| Unprocessed energy materials | 22.6 | 7.5 | -0.7 | -39.5 | -9.2 | 17.6 | 11.9 |
| Unprocessed nonfood materials less energy | 32.5 | -5.0 | -1.6 | -14.4 | -2.7 | 12.5 | 5.1 |
| Services for intermediate demand | (NA) | 1.8 | 1.6 | 1.2 | 1.7 | 2.6 | 3.1 |
| Trade services for intermediate demand | (NA) | 2.2 | 1.1 | 2.4 | -0.9 | 2.9 | 4.1 |
| Transportation and warehousing services for intermediate demand | (NA) | 2.5 | 2.8 | -0.3 | -0.8 | 2.0 | 4.0 |
| Services less trade, transportation, and warehousing for intermediate demand | (NA) | 1.5 | 1.4 | 1.2 | 2.9 | 2.6 | 2.8 |

NA Not available. Z less than 0.05 percent. [1] Change from immediate prior year. 2010, change from 2009.

Source: U.S. Bureau of Labor Statistics, PPI Databases, "Commodity Data including "headline" FD-ID Indexes," <http://www.bls.gov/ppi/data.htm>, accessed May 2019.

# Table 767. Producer Price Indexes—Final and Intermediate Demand by Commodity: 2000 to 2018

[1982=100, unless otherwise noted. For information on producer prices, see Bureau of Labor Statistics, <http://www.bls.gov/ppi/>]

| Item | 2000 | 2005 | 2010 | 2015 | 2016 | 2017 | 2018 |
|---|---|---|---|---|---|---|---|
| **Final demand (Nov. 2009=100)** | **(NA)** | **(NA)** | **101.8** | **109.9** | **110.4** | **113.0** | **116.2** |
| **Final demand goods (Nov. 2009=100)** | **(NA)** | **(NA)** | **102.8** | **109.1** | **107.6** | **111.2** | **115.0** |
| **Final demand foods (Nov. 2009=100)** | **(NA)** | **(NA)** | **103.7** | **118.4** | **115.1** | **116.5** | **116.7** |
| Fresh fruits & melons | 91.4 | 102.8 | 123.8 | 124.2 | 138.7 | 147.9 | 145.1 |
| Fresh & dry vegetables | 126.7 | 142.6 | 178.5 | 200.2 | 202.2 | 215.2 | 211.6 |
| Grains | 78.3 | 83.4 | 160.2 | 151.9 | 135.1 | 135.6 | 144.9 |
| Eggs for fresh use (Dec. 1991=100) | 84.9 | 79.6 | 123.4 | 219.3 | 107.5 | 123.8 | 162.9 |
| Oilseeds | 93.8 | 113.4 | 191.0 | 176.6 | 180.5 | 176.6 | 168.3 |
| Bakery products | 182.3 | 201.1 | 244.8 | 275.0 | 277.7 | 279.6 | 286.5 |
| Milled rice | 101.2 | 120.1 | 183.6 | 199.0 | 189.2 | 184.0 | 204.0 |
| Dry macaroni, spaghetti, and egg noodle products (June 1985=100) | 121.6 | 127.9 | 170.7 | 216.2 | 207.2 | 201.2 | 202.9 |
| Beef & veal | 113.7 | 147.4 | 157.1 | 243.6 | 202.9 | 201.5 | 204.9 |
| Pork | 113.4 | 131.9 | 142.6 | 145.6 | 142.6 | 147.1 | 137.8 |
| Processed young chickens | 110.4 | 136.2 | 149.0 | 174.0 | 168.7 | 174.6 | 160.1 |
| Processed turkeys | 98.7 | 105.1 | 132.1 | 164.3 | 147.2 | 137.2 | 139.9 |
| Unprocessed and prepared seafood | 198.1 | 222.6 | 272.4 | 322.0 | 327.6 | 337.9 | 344.5 |
| Dairy products | 133.7 | 154.5 | 174.0 | 193.6 | 190.4 | 196.9 | 192.3 |
| Processed fruits & vegetables | 128.6 | 140.4 | 176.6 | 197.7 | 198.7 | 202.8 | 207.6 |
| Confectionery end products | 170.6 | 205.1 | 236.4 | 282.8 | 277.7 | 275.3 | 278.5 |
| Soft drinks | 144.1 | 159.1 | 183.9 | 196.7 | 205.5 | 203.3 | 205.6 |
| Coffee (whole bean, ground, & instant) | 133.5 | 151.1 | 190.2 | 204.7 | 196.3 | 193.9 | 194.1 |
| Shortening, cooking oil, and margarine | 132.4 | 176.7 | 233.6 | 243.3 | 242.3 | 256.9 | 250.7 |
| Frozen specialty food | 143.5 | 152.7 | 176.4 | 189.5 | 187.4 | 186.5 | 186.1 |
| **Final demand energy (Nov. 2009=100)** | **(NA)** | **(NA)** | **107.2** | **98.6** | **90.4** | **99.8** | **110.0** |
| Liquefied petroleum gas | 127.1 | 244.7 | 301.8 | 109.8 | 106.0 | 154.3 | 196.0 |
| Residential electric power (Dec. 1990=100) | 110.8 | 126.4 | 154.7 | 172.2 | 172.2 | 177.1 | 179.4 |
| Residential natural gas (Dec. 1990=100) | 135.5 | 216.8 | 201.7 | 184.4 | 182.1 | 198.0 | 198.2 |
| Gasoline | 94.6 | 168.6 | 225.3 | 177.2 | 145.2 | 171.5 | 202.5 |
| Home heating oil & distillates | 93.5 | 178.4 | 207.5 | 160.9 | 122.9 | 155.9 | 203.7 |
| No. 2 diesel fuel | 93.3 | 189.1 | 232.9 | 181.4 | 143.5 | 185.6 | 247.3 |
| **Other final demand goods (Nov. 2009=100)** | **(NA)** | **(NA)** | **101.4** | **109.9** | **110.7** | **113.2** | **116.0** |
| Alcoholic beverages | 140.6 | 158.5 | 175.1 | 192.6 | 193.4 | 195.6 | 199.6 |
| Women's, girls', and infants' apparel (December 2003=100) | (NA) | 100.3 | 101.6 | 105.2 | 106.0 | 107.7 | 109.0 |
| Men's and boys' apparel (December 2003=100) | (NA) | 98.7 | 101.5 | 113.0 | 113.1 | 114.2 | 115.6 |
| Textile house furnishings | 122.0 | 122.9 | 131.7 | 162.8 | 164.6 | 167.5 | 167.9 |
| Footwear | 144.9 | 148.1 | 162.4 | 196.0 | 199.5 | 201.9 | 203.5 |
| Industrial chemicals | 129.1 | 188.5 | 269.2 | 242.2 | 228.1 | 254.0 | 274.0 |
| Pharmaceutical preparations (June 2001=100) | (NA) | 117.9 | 155.1 | 212.8 | 231.5 | 246.5 | 259.2 |
| Soaps and synthetic detergents | 128.2 | 134.6 | 161.2 | 175.7 | 177.0 | 177.9 | 181.3 |
| Cosmetics and other toilet preparations | 137.4 | 143.0 | 149.9 | 161.4 | 162.4 | 162.8 | 165.1 |
| Tires, tubes, tread, & repair materials | 93.0 | 108.1 | 138.1 | 149.3 | 147.1 | 148.7 | 150.5 |
| Agricultural machinery and equipment | 153.7 | 174.7 | 203.5 | 222.2 | 224.4 | 226.6 | 230.4 |
| Construction machinery and equipment | 148.6 | 168.3 | 191.4 | 217.0 | 219.0 | 220.9 | 223.1 |
| Industrial material handling equipment | 134.7 | 150.6 | 183.1 | 207.0 | 209.2 | 212.7 | 219.2 |
| Electronic computers (December 2004=100) | 261.6 | 85.5 | 30.3 | 20.4 | 19.5 | 18.4 | 17.8 |
| Textile machinery and equipment | 156.2 | 160.5 | 165.9 | 176.1 | 173.0 | 171.3 | 171.7 |
| Paper industries machinery (June 1982=100) | 164.7 | 178.1 | 197.2 | 216.2 | 219.8 | 219.5 | 222.3 |
| Printing trades machinery and equipment | 142.1 | 144.3 | 155.4 | 162.3 | 163.8 | 163.0 | 164.0 |
| Transformers and power regulators | 135.8 | 150.3 | 223.1 | 212.8 | 208.0 | 214.6 | 225.9 |
| Oil field and gas field machinery | 128.2 | 155.9 | 200.7 | 216.5 | 214.9 | 214.3 | 216.7 |
| Mining machinery and equipment | 146.1 | 175.9 | 221.5 | 260.6 | 263.9 | 266.3 | 277.4 |
| Office and store machines and equipment | 112.7 | 115.1 | 121.0 | 122.7 | 123.1 | 122.5 | 121.1 |
| Household furniture | 152.7 | 166.5 | 187.4 | 203.9 | 205.3 | 209.1 | 215.2 |
| Household appliances | 107.3 | 103.3 | 110.5 | 116.8 | 115.8 | 116.0 | 119.0 |
| Home electronic equipment | 71.8 | 62.6 | 52.9 | 51.3 | 51.5 | 51.6 | 51.3 |
| Lawn and garden equipment | 132.0 | 134.5 | 141.7 | 143.7 | 143.8 | 144.4 | 146.9 |
| Passenger cars | 132.8 | 131.8 | 129.0 | 133.4 | 133.5 | 134.1 | 134.0 |
| Light motor trucks | 157.6 | 148.4 | 153.3 | 171.4 | 173.1 | 176.1 | 178.0 |
| Heavy motor trucks | 148.0 | 162.4 | 195.7 | 218.1 | 222.6 | 227.1 | 229.9 |
| Truck trailers | 139.4 | 157.1 | 181.5 | 201.0 | 201.5 | 202.7 | 213.1 |
| Aircraft | 184.2 | 223.5 | 263.0 | 290.8 | 292.5 | 296.2 | 301.3 |
| Ships (December 1985=100) | 146.9 | 176.6 | 215.1 | 225.2 | 224.0 | 223.8 | 224.2 |
| Railroad equipment | 135.7 | 160.4 | 184.4 | 201.9 | 203.3 | 203.2 | 202.1 |
| **Final demand services (Nov. 2009=100)** | **(NA)** | **(NA)** | **101.3** | **110.0** | **111.5** | **113.5** | **116.5** |
| **Final demand trade services (Nov. 2009=100)** | **(NA)** | **(NA)** | **101.7** | **111.6** | **113.1** | **114.8** | **116.9** |
| Machinery & equipment wholesaling (Mar. 2009=100) | (NA) | (NA) | 101.2 | 110.7 | 117.9 | 119.3 | 124.2 |
| Furnishings wholesaling (Mar. 2009=100) | (NA) | (NA) | 78.5 | 89.1 | 93.4 | 95.2 | 96.8 |
| Apparel wholesaling (Mar. 2009=100) | (NA) | (NA) | 97.3 | 117.9 | 117.6 | 117.5 | 119.1 |
| Food & alcohol wholesaling (June 2009=100) | (NA) | (NA) | 105.7 | 105.2 | 106.5 | 107.3 | 110.0 |
| Food & alcohol retailing (Mar. 2009=100) | (NA) | (NA) | 98.9 | 126.4 | 129.5 | 129.9 | 131.9 |
| Health, beauty, & optical goods retailing (Mar. 2009=100) | (NA) | (NA) | 107.8 | 118.9 | 119.1 | 117.4 | 119.5 |
| Apparel, jewelry, footwear, & accessories retailing (June 2009=100) | (NA) | (NA) | 104.2 | 113.9 | 114.0 | 113.5 | 112.2 |
| Automobiles & automobile parts retailing (June 2009=100) | (NA) | (NA) | 105.9 | 101.2 | 95.8 | 94.4 | 94.7 |
| Sporting goods, including boats, retailing (Mar. 2009=100) | (NA) | (NA) | 96.6 | 108.9 | 112.2 | 112.6 | 113.2 |
| Furniture retailing (Mar. 2009=100) | (NA) | (NA) | 99.7 | 102.2 | 105.1 | 106.5 | 103.5 |
| Major household appliances retailing (Mar. 2009=100) | (NA) | (NA) | 97.3 | 80.5 | 78.2 | 84.7 | 91.2 |
| Book retailing (Mar. 2009=100) | (NA) | (NA) | 104.8 | 110.3 | 108.7 | 107.1 | 109.5 |
| **Final demand transportation & warehousing services (Nov. 2009=100)** | **(NA)** | **(NA)** | **103.2** | **115.3** | **113.5** | **115.9** | **122.0** |
| Rail transportation of freight & mail (Dec. 2008=100) | (NA) | (NA) | 101.6 | 116.5 | 113.7 | 117.8 | 124.6 |
| Truck transportation of freight (June 2009=100) | (NA) | (NA) | 102.0 | 113.4 | 112.2 | 114.9 | 122.6 |
| Air transportation of freight (Dec. 2008=100) | (NA) | (NA) | 100.1 | 112.5 | 110.7 | 109.7 | 112.1 |

See footnotes at end of table.

**Table 767. Producer Price Indexes—Final and Intermediate Demand by Commodity: 2000 to 2018**-Continued.

See headnote on page 497.

| Item | 2000 | 2005 | 2010 | 2015 | 2016 | 2017 | 2018 |
|---|---|---|---|---|---|---|---|
| Courier, messenger, & U.S. postal services (June 2009=100)....... | (NA) | (NA) | 105.5 | 131.5 | 131.2 | 134.3 | 139.9 |
| Rail transportation of passengers (Dec. 2008=100).................. | (NA) | (NA) | 100.7 | 115.2 | 117.1 | 119.8 | 122.1 |
| Airline passenger services (Dec. 2008=100)........................ | (NA) | (NA) | 102.8 | 112.3 | 109.3 | 110.7 | 113.6 |
| **Other final demand services (Nov. 2009=100)**.................... | **(NA)** | **(NA)** | **100.9** | **108.7** | **110.6** | **112.8** | **115.8** |
| Sales of books................................................... | 218.2 | 264.0 | 317.1 | 363.9 | 370.6 | 376.3 | 384.7 |
| Cellphone & other wireless telecom services (Mar. 2009=100)...... | (NA) | (NA) | 94.4 | 77.6 | 71.6 | 66.2 | 63.7 |
| Cable & satellite subscriber services (Dec. 2008=100).............. | (NA) | (NA) | 103.7 | 112.7 | 118.3 | 122.3 | 129.9 |
| Internet access services (Mar. 2009=100)......................... | (NA) | (NA) | 98.3 | 98.2 | 97.8 | 96.0 | 93.8 |
| **Processed goods for intermediate demand**................ | **129.2** | **154.0** | **183.4** | **188.0** | **182.2** | **190.7** | **200.9** |
| **Processed materials less foods & feeds**.................... | **130.1** | **155.1** | **184.4** | **187.2** | **181.8** | **190.9** | **201.9** |
| Synthetic fibers................................................. | 107.2 | 112.3 | 111.6 | 121.3 | 118.9 | 121.9 | 130.2 |
| Processed yarns & threads...................................... | 107.9 | 111.7 | 130.0 | 135.6 | 133.2 | 136.4 | 143.2 |
| Finished fabrics................................................. | 122.5 | 124.1 | 137.1 | 154.0 | 153.7 | 154.1 | 157.4 |
| Commercial electric power..................................... | 131.5 | 149.8 | 182.5 | 195.8 | 193.9 | 199.4 | 199.9 |
| Industrial electric power....................................... | 131.5 | 156.2 | 193.1 | 223.7 | 213.6 | 240.6 | 247.0 |
| Commercial natural gas (Dec. 1990=100)....................... | 134.7 | 232.5 | 208.0 | 176.6 | 172.0 | 189.0 | 190.7 |
| Industrial natural gas (Dec. 1990=100)......................... | 139.0 | 249.4 | 202.0 | 158.6 | 146.7 | 159.5 | 157.8 |
| Natural gas to electric utilities (Dec. 1990=100)................. | 120.7 | 204.0 | 174.8 | 159.6 | 157.7 | 168.1 | 169.6 |
| Jet fuels........................................................ | 88.5 | 169.6 | 225.5 | 171.3 | 134.4 | 167.9 | 221.3 |
| Prepared paint.................................................. | 160.8 | 187.9 | 237.1 | 273.0 | 271.6 | 274.6 | 285.6 |
| Medicinal and botanical chemicals, drugs, and other products...... | 146.2 | 136.0 | 175.2 | 177.1 | 176.0 | 174.6 | 181.1 |
| Biological products, including diagnostics........................ | 172.2 | 195.1 | 223.7 | 256.4 | 263.7 | 262.6 | 265.9 |
| Fats & oils, inedible............................................. | 70.1 | 146.9 | 244.3 | 204.9 | 209.1 | 225.2 | 198.6 |
| Plastic resins & materials....................................... | 141.6 | 193.0 | 210.1 | 228.0 | 218.5 | 232.7 | 243.9 |
| Synthetic rubber................................................ | 119.1 | 151.3 | 215.5 | 197.6 | 193.5 | 210.4 | 215.9 |
| Plastic construction products.................................... | 135.8 | 158.8 | 190.9 | 213.1 | 211.9 | 217.3 | 226.1 |
| Softwood lumber................................................ | 178.6 | 203.6 | 160.8 | 192.7 | 198.8 | 223.7 | 241.9 |
| Hardwood lumber............................................... | 185.9 | 196.6 | 187.3 | 221.1 | 218.1 | 219.6 | 230.1 |
| Millwork........................................................ | 176.4 | 197.2 | 207.0 | 237.2 | 240.6 | 247.6 | 259.5 |
| Plywood......................................................... | 157.6 | 186.8 | 176.7 | 198.9 | 192.3 | 204.2 | 230.2 |
| Paper........................................................... | 149.8 | 159.6 | 182.1 | 189.8 | 186.7 | 186.4 | 197.6 |
| Paperboard..................................................... | 176.7 | 175.5 | 224.9 | 243.1 | 233.4 | 257.5 | 273.5 |
| Paper boxes & containers....................................... | 172.6 | 183.7 | 219.4 | 247.3 | 248.1 | 259.5 | 264.8 |
| Foundry & forge shop products................................. | 136.5 | 156.2 | 191.2 | 209.2 | 207.0 | 206.4 | 210.3 |
| Steel mill products.............................................. | 108.4 | 159.7 | 191.7 | 177.1 | 167.8 | 187.4 | 211.1 |
| Primary nonferrous metals...................................... | 113.6 | 158.2 | 210.3 | 170.7 | 167.1 | 186.5 | 193.7 |
| Aluminum mill shapes.......................................... | 149.0 | 161.1 | 171.9 | 172.4 | 164.5 | 180.8 | 202.8 |
| Copper & brass mill shapes..................................... | 162.3 | 235.8 | 421.3 | 356.9 | 331.0 | 393.0 | 408.8 |
| Nonferrous wire & cable........................................ | 143.7 | 169.4 | 258.1 | 238.2 | 224.1 | 235.6 | 248.6 |
| Hardware....................................................... | 151.2 | 168.0 | 194.0 | 209.7 | 210.6 | 213.8 | 218.1 |
| Plumbing fixtures & brass fittings............................... | 180.4 | 197.6 | 231.4 | 257.1 | 257.8 | 262.4 | 270.2 |
| Heating equipment............................................. | 155.6 | 179.9 | 221.5 | 248.2 | 253.1 | 255.9 | 266.5 |
| Fabricated structural metal products............................ | 144.9 | 175.1 | 201.1 | 215.6 | 214.0 | 218.9 | 234.2 |
| Air conditioning & refrigeration equipment...................... | 135.3 | 146.2 | 163.8 | 179.2 | 180.9 | 184.6 | 192.6 |
| Motors, generators, motor generator sets....................... | 146.2 | 157.8 | 190.6 | 211.6 | 209.4 | 211.1 | 216.8 |
| Electronic components & accessories............................ | 97.1 | 87.0 | 73.5 | 68.2 | 67.2 | 66.8 | 65.9 |
| Internal combustion engines.................................... | 143.8 | 147.7 | 161.7 | 168.4 | 164.3 | 166.0 | 168.1 |
| Machine shop products......................................... | 138.0 | 151.0 | 174.7 | 184.0 | 184.4 | 184.9 | 189.9 |
| Cement......................................................... | 150.1 | 176.4 | 193.5 | 223.4 | 235.2 | 246.0 | 252.1 |
| Concrete products.............................................. | 147.8 | 177.2 | 210.6 | 239.4 | 247.0 | 254.1 | 263.7 |
| Motor vehicle parts............................................. | 113.6 | 113.1 | 121.8 | 125.9 | 124.9 | 125.2 | 126.9 |
| Aircraft engines & engine parts (Dec. 1985=100)................. | 141.0 | 165.9 | 197.4 | 221.2 | 224.1 | 224.3 | 226.7 |
| Aircraft parts & auxiliary equipment (June 1985=100)............ | 145.7 | 155.3 | 167.7 | 183.3 | 184.7 | 185.0 | 186.4 |
| Medical/surgical/personal aid devices........................... | 146.0 | 159.2 | 169.0 | 176.2 | 177.4 | 178.5 | 180.5 |
| **Unprocessed goods for intermediate demand**.............. | **120.6** | **182.2** | **212.2** | **189.1** | **173.4** | **190.8** | **200.1** |
| **Unprocessed foodstuffs & feedstuffs**..................... | **100.2** | **122.7** | **152.4** | **181.4** | **162.4** | **167.1** | **163.9** |
| Wheat.......................................................... | 80.3 | 102.7 | 157.2 | 153.3 | 122.1 | 131.6 | 150.3 |
| Corn............................................................ | 76.4 | 75.9 | 160.8 | 149.6 | 137.7 | 136.1 | 141.0 |
| Slaughter cattle................................................. | 104.1 | 131.5 | 139.8 | 225.6 | 181.9 | 178.8 | 172.4 |
| Slaughter hogs.................................................. | 72.7 | 82.7 | 92.6 | 80.6 | 81.0 | 88.5 | 80.1 |
| Broilers and other meat type chickens........................... | 127.6 | 181.0 | 221.3 | 246.8 | 228.5 | 257.2 | 270.1 |
| Slaughter turkeys............................................... | 120.7 | 131.1 | 173.0 | 234.3 | 242.4 | 201.7 | 170.5 |
| Raw milk....................................................... | 92.0 | 113.5 | 121.9 | 127.7 | 123.9 | 134.5 | 123.4 |
| Hay and hayseeds.............................................. | 156.3 | 190.1 | 214.3 | 309.2 | 253.4 | 274.7 | 327.8 |
| Raw cane sugar & byproducts................................... | 100.2 | 124.9 | 179.9 | 149.4 | 158.0 | 161.9 | 151.9 |
| **Unprocessed nonfood materials**............................ | **130.4** | **223.4** | **249.3** | **183.7** | **171.6** | **198.3** | **217.0** |
| Raw cotton...................................................... | 95.2 | 78.9 | 117.9 | 101.6 | 103.2 | 114.8 | 124.1 |
| Hides & skins................................................... | 174.0 | 189.9 | 224.9 | 258.8 | 213.2 | 204.3 | 171.0 |
| Coal............................................................ | 87.9 | 116.8 | 189.5 | 194.0 | 189.6 | 195.8 | 199.6 |
| Natural gas..................................................... | 155.5 | 335.4 | 185.8 | 105.4 | 96.2 | 118.7 | 112.1 |
| Crude petroleum................................................ | 85.2 | 150.1 | 218.6 | 129.5 | 111.2 | 138.3 | 182.0 |
| Logs, bolts, timber, pulpwood and wood chips................... | 196.4 | 197.4 | 213.4 | 241.9 | 239.2 | 239.8 | 248.7 |
| Wastepaper..................................................... | 282.5 | 230.9 | 421.5 | 291.8 | 312.5 | 399.9 | 276.9 |
| Iron ore......................................................... | 94.8 | 116.9 | 147.1 | 132.0 | 124.3 | 131.9 | 136.8 |
| Iron & steel scrap............................................... | 142.1 | 289.8 | 541.1 | 342.8 | 328.5 | 440.4 | 523.5 |
| Nonferrous metal ores (Dec. 1983=100)......................... | 68.0 | 150.0 | 298.6 | 272.6 | 262.4 | 309.4 | 330.6 |
| Copper base scrap.............................................. | 123.7 | 258.6 | 548.2 | 427.6 | 369.0 | 428.9 | 460.7 |
| Aluminum base scrap........................................... | 177.0 | 210.1 | 241.6 | 208.7 | 186.2 | 210.2 | 215.6 |
| Construction sand, gravel, & crushed stone..................... | 163.1 | 195.8 | 262.2 | 299.9 | 312.6 | 323.2 | 334.7 |

NA Not available.

Source: U.S. Bureau of Labor Statistics, PPI Databases, "Commodity Data including "headline" FD-ID Indexes," <http://www.bls.gov/ppi/data.htm>, accessed May 2019.

# Table 768. Chain-Type Price Indexes for Personal Consumption Expenditures by Type of Expenditure: 1990 to 2018

[2012=100. For explanation of "chain-type," see text, Section 13. See also Table 707]

| Type of Expenditure | 1990 | 2000 | 2005 | 2010 | 2015 | 2016 | 2017 | 2018 |
|---|---|---|---|---|---|---|---|---|
| **Personal consumption expenditures** | **63.4** | **78.2** | **86.8** | **95.7** | **103.0** | **104.1** | **105.9** | **108.1** |
| Household consumption expenditures [1] | 62.7 | 77.8 | 86.5 | 95.6 | 102.8 | 103.8 | 105.6 | 107.8 |
| Food and beverages purchased for off-premises consumption | 61.1 | 73.9 | 82.6 | 93.9 | 104.1 | 103.0 | 102.9 | 103.4 |
| Food and nonalcoholic beverages purchased for off-premises consumption | 60.5 | 72.8 | 81.6 | 93.2 | 104.4 | 103.0 | 102.7 | 103.2 |
| Alcoholic beverages purchased for off-premises consumption | 64.6 | 81.7 | 89.3 | 98.7 | 102.1 | 103.0 | 103.7 | 104.7 |
| Food produced and consumed on farms | 76.5 | 64.1 | 75.6 | 81.7 | 101.8 | 89.4 | 92.9 | 91.9 |
| Clothing, footwear, and related services | 109.2 | 103.0 | 95.9 | 95.0 | 100.3 | 100.2 | 99.7 | 99.9 |
| Clothing | 111.8 | 105.0 | 96.6 | 94.5 | 99.5 | 99.2 | 98.7 | 99.0 |
| Garments | 117.3 | 108.0 | 97.7 | 94.4 | 99.1 | 98.7 | 98.1 | 98.3 |
| Women's and girls' clothing | 122.9 | 107.5 | 98.0 | 94.8 | 98.5 | 98.5 | 98.3 | 97.8 |
| Men's and boys' clothing | 109.9 | 108.5 | 97.1 | 93.6 | 100.1 | 99.4 | 98.1 | 98.8 |
| Children's and infants' clothing | 111.2 | 109.0 | 97.5 | 95.4 | 100.0 | 96.9 | 96.0 | 100.5 |
| Footwear [2] | 96.8 | 93.6 | 92.9 | 97.1 | 103.8 | 104.2 | 103.8 | 103.3 |
| Housing, utilities, and fuels | 54.5 | 71.8 | 85.3 | 96.5 | 107.6 | 110.5 | 114.4 | 118.1 |
| Housing | 55.4 | 74.1 | 86.4 | 96.5 | 108.2 | 111.9 | 115.7 | 119.7 |
| Rental of tenant-occupied nonfarm housing [3] | 53.7 | 71.2 | 83.7 | 95.8 | 109.4 | 113.4 | 117.6 | 121.8 |
| Imputed rental of owner-occupied nonfarm housing [4] | 56.1 | 75.0 | 86.9 | 96.9 | 108.0 | 111.5 | 115.2 | 119.0 |
| Household utilities and fuels | 49.9 | 61.9 | 80.5 | 96.6 | 103.9 | 102.9 | 106.9 | 109.5 |
| Water supply and sanitation | 37.1 | 56.2 | 68.9 | 90.5 | 112.8 | 116.8 | 120.7 | 124.9 |
| Electricity, gas, and other fuels | 54.3 | 63.9 | 84.7 | 98.8 | 100.8 | 98.2 | 102.2 | 104.3 |
| Electricity | 59.8 | 65.3 | 76.7 | 98.2 | 106.4 | 105.3 | 107.5 | 108.3 |
| Natural gas | 58.4 | 80.1 | 128.9 | 113.9 | 99.2 | 96.6 | 104.3 | 104.3 |
| Fuel oil and other fuels | 27.1 | 35.8 | 58.7 | 77.5 | 69.8 | 58.0 | 66.9 | 80.8 |
| Furnishings, household equipment, and routine household maintenance | 97.4 | 105.3 | 102.2 | 100.3 | 95.4 | 94.2 | 92.6 | 92.7 |
| Furniture, furnishings, and floor coverings [5] | 114.3 | 121.8 | 112.9 | 102.5 | 92.8 | 90.6 | 88.2 | 87.0 |
| Household textiles | 179.3 | 161.9 | 134.5 | 106.4 | 89.4 | 87.2 | 83.9 | 82.6 |
| Household appliances [6] | 95.8 | 93.2 | 91.4 | 96.3 | 90.2 | 86.5 | 83.9 | 87.1 |
| Glassware, tableware, and household utensils [7] | 126.5 | 126.6 | 113.1 | 106.3 | 92.8 | 90.4 | 88.3 | 83.6 |
| Health | 48.8 | 70.9 | 83.4 | 96.1 | 103.7 | 105.4 | 107.2 | 109.1 |
| Medical products, appliances, and equipment | 51.9 | 71.0 | 83.1 | 94.5 | 106.4 | 110.1 | 113.0 | 114.4 |
| Pharmaceutical and other medical products [8] | 49.1 | 68.5 | 81.5 | 93.9 | 107.2 | 111.3 | 114.7 | 116.2 |
| Pharmaceutical products | 48.8 | 68.2 | 81.3 | 93.8 | 107.3 | 111.5 | 114.9 | 116.4 |
| Other medical products | 76.4 | 95.2 | 96.6 | 98.5 | 99.2 | 98.7 | 99.0 | 99.6 |
| Therapeutic appliances and equipment | 70.0 | 88.2 | 93.4 | 98.3 | 100.9 | 101.6 | 101.9 | 102.8 |
| Outpatient services | 54.3 | 77.0 | 86.4 | 97.4 | 101.7 | 102.5 | 103.6 | 104.7 |
| Physician services [9] | 57.5 | 80.8 | 87.4 | 97.4 | 99.5 | 99.8 | 100.2 | 101.0 |
| Dental services | 37.5 | 61.9 | 77.6 | 95.5 | 108.3 | 111.4 | 113.2 | 116.3 |
| Paramedical services | 58.3 | 78.3 | 88.6 | 98.3 | 102.5 | 103.7 | 105.5 | 106.3 |
| Hospital and nursing home services | 43.8 | 65.9 | 81.1 | 95.7 | 104.3 | 105.8 | 107.7 | 110.5 |
| Hospitals [10] | 44.2 | 65.8 | 81.0 | 95.5 | 104.4 | 105.6 | 107.4 | 110.0 |
| Nursing homes | 42.5 | 66.2 | 81.5 | 96.3 | 104.1 | 106.8 | 109.5 | 113.3 |
| Transportation | 57.8 | 70.8 | 78.9 | 88.6 | 90.6 | 87.9 | 90.4 | 93.7 |
| Motor vehicles | 80.7 | 100.7 | 97.2 | 96.0 | 100.7 | 99.4 | 98.0 | 97.4 |
| New motor vehicles | 83.8 | 99.5 | 95.8 | 95.6 | 102.6 | 102.9 | 102.8 | 102.3 |
| Net purchases of used motor vehicles | 74.3 | 103.9 | 100.6 | 97.0 | 96.2 | 91.9 | 88.4 | 87.5 |
| Motor vehicle operation | 44.4 | 54.5 | 70.4 | 84.9 | 83.2 | 79.4 | 84.2 | 90.2 |
| Motor vehicle parts and accessories | 73.7 | 72.3 | 78.3 | 94.0 | 99.8 | 99.7 | 99.7 | 100.7 |
| Motor vehicle fuels, lubricants, and fluids | 32.3 | 41.3 | 62.3 | 76.9 | 68.7 | 61.0 | 68.9 | 78.0 |
| Public transportation | 67.5 | 77.5 | 76.1 | 90.4 | 101.5 | 100.9 | 101.9 | 103.4 |
| Ground transportation [11] | 49.7 | 63.3 | 77.2 | 93.7 | 104.9 | 107.4 | 108.9 | 110.2 |
| Air transportation | 75.8 | 82.9 | 74.5 | 88.5 | 99.9 | 97.6 | 98.3 | 100.1 |
| Water transportation | 130.4 | 145.3 | 115.3 | 103.2 | 100.4 | 104.0 | 105.0 | 105.3 |
| Communication | 111.9 | 111.8 | 105.2 | 102.6 | 88.6 | 84.4 | 78.5 | 76.6 |
| Telecommunication services | 106.4 | 102.9 | 97.9 | 101.9 | 89.7 | 85.8 | 78.1 | 75.9 |
| Internet access | 180.7 | 125.9 | 125.1 | 100.7 | 101.3 | 101.2 | 100.1 | 99.3 |
| Recreation | 120.6 | 116.7 | 109.4 | 102.4 | 97.0 | 96.1 | 95.6 | 95.0 |
| Video and audio equipment, computers, and related services | 398.7 | 216.5 | 156.1 | 110.7 | 89.5 | 86.1 | 84.6 | 81.8 |
| Video and audio equipment | 508.7 | 343.5 | 241.3 | 126.1 | 76.7 | 69.0 | 63.1 | 56.4 |
| Sports and recreational goods and related services | 124.4 | 120.8 | 110.5 | 104.1 | 92.9 | 90.6 | 87.6 | 85.0 |
| Sports and recreational vehicles | 78.0 | 90.4 | 92.4 | 96.3 | 100.3 | 101.8 | 101.4 | 103.0 |
| Other sporting and recreational goods | 145.1 | 133.3 | 117.0 | 106.4 | 90.7 | 87.3 | 83.6 | 79.7 |
| Magazines, newspapers, books, and stationery | 65.7 | 87.8 | 91.9 | 98.6 | 104.8 | 104.7 | 105.4 | 106.8 |
| Education | 27.8 | 49.4 | 69.3 | 91.3 | 110.9 | 113.9 | 116.6 | 119.3 |
| Higher education | 24.9 | 47.2 | 67.6 | 90.8 | 111.8 | 114.8 | 117.1 | 119.7 |
| Net foreign travel and expenditures abroad by U.S. residents: | | | | | | | | |
| Foreign travel by U.S. residents | 48.8 | 60.1 | 78.7 | 94.6 | 98.4 | 95.9 | 96.6 | 99.1 |
| Less: Expenditures in the United States by nonresidents | 54.2 | 70.5 | 80.4 | 92.4 | 102.4 | 103.3 | 105.3 | 107.7 |

[1] Consists of household purchases of goods and services from business, government, nonprofit institutions, and the rest of the world. [2] Consists of shoes and other footwear, and of repair and hire of footwear. [3] Consists of rent for space (see footnote 4) and rent for appliances, furnishings, and furniture. [4] Consists of rent for space and for heating and plumbing facilities, water heaters, lighting fixtures, kitchen cabinets, linoleum, storm windows and doors, window screens, and screen doors, but excludes rent for appliances and furniture and purchases of fuel and electricity. [5] Includes clocks, lamps, lighting fixtures, and other household decorative items; also includes repair of furniture, furnishings, and floor coverings. [6] Consists of major household appliances, small electric household appliances, and repair of household appliances. [7] Consists of dishes, flatware, and non-electric cookware and tableware. [8] Excludes drug preparations and related products dispensed by physicians, hospitals, and other medical services. [9] Consists of offices of physicians, health maintenance organization medical centers, and freestanding ambulatory surgical and emergency centers. [10] Consists of nonprofit hospitals, proprietary hospitals, and government hospitals. Consists of primary sales of these hospitals for personal consumption. [11] Includes railway transportation, taxicab services, school and employee services, limousine services, and airport bus fares.

Source: U.S. Bureau of Economic Analysis, National Income and Product Accounts Tables, "Table 2.5.4. Price Indexes for Personal Consumption Expenditures by Function," <https://apps.bea.gov/iTable/index_nipa.cfm>, accessed August 2019.

## Table 769. Chain-Type Price Indexes for Gross Domestic Product: 1990 to 2018

[2012=100. For explanation of "chain-type," see text, Section 13]

| Component | 1990 | 2000 | 2005 | 2010 | 2014 | 2015 | 2016 | 2017 | 2018 |
|---|---|---|---|---|---|---|---|---|---|
| **Gross domestic product** | **63.7** | **78.1** | **87.4** | **96.1** | **103.6** | **104.7** | **105.8** | **107.8** | **110.4** |
| **Personal consumption expenditures** | **63.4** | **78.2** | **86.8** | **95.7** | **102.8** | **103.0** | **104.1** | **105.9** | **108.1** |
| Goods | 81.9 | 89.1 | 91.1 | 95.2 | 98.9 | 95.9 | 94.3 | 94.6 | 95.2 |
| Durable goods | 131.9 | 125.7 | 112.3 | 102.1 | 95.4 | 93.4 | 91.1 | 89.0 | 87.5 |
| Nondurable goods | 63.1 | 74.0 | 82.0 | 92.2 | 100.6 | 97.1 | 95.9 | 97.4 | 99.3 |
| Services | 54.8 | 72.9 | 84.7 | 96.0 | 104.8 | 106.7 | 109.1 | 111.8 | 114.9 |
| **Gross private domestic investment** | **81.3** | **86.8** | **94.8** | **97.7** | **102.9** | **103.7** | **103.6** | **105.4** | **107.8** |
| Fixed investment | 80.3 | 86.5 | 94.6 | 97.6 | 103.2 | 104.2 | 104.2 | 106.1 | 108.5 |
| Nonresidential | 92.5 | 92.7 | 94.4 | 97.4 | 101.5 | 102.0 | 101.1 | 102.1 | 103.5 |
| Structures | 40.9 | 55.3 | 75.7 | 92.0 | 107.2 | 109.6 | 110.0 | 113.0 | 117.1 |
| Equipment | 135.0 | 114.2 | 104.6 | 99.5 | 99.2 | 98.7 | 97.4 | 97.3 | 97.4 |
| Intellectual property products | 88.1 | 97.8 | 96.0 | 98.3 | 100.8 | 101.7 | 100.5 | 101.7 | 103.3 |
| Residential | 56.3 | 75.0 | 96.7 | 98.3 | 111.1 | 114.1 | 118.1 | 123.5 | 130.5 |
| Net exports of goods and services: | | | | | | | | | |
| Exports | 79.7 | 79.5 | 85.1 | 93.3 | 100.3 | 95.4 | 93.5 | 95.9 | 99.1 |
| Goods | 85.7 | 80.0 | 84.9 | 93.0 | 98.3 | 91.3 | 87.7 | 90.0 | 93.2 |
| Services | 65.7 | 78.2 | 85.6 | 94.2 | 104.7 | 104.6 | 106.3 | 109.1 | 112.4 |
| Imports | 79.2 | 76.2 | 83.7 | 92.8 | 97.9 | 89.9 | 86.7 | 88.6 | 91.2 |
| Goods | 83.1 | 76.6 | 83.2 | 92.1 | 96.7 | 87.6 | 83.8 | 85.7 | 88.2 |
| Services | 63.7 | 74.3 | 86.7 | 96.4 | 103.6 | 102.3 | 101.9 | 103.9 | 107.0 |
| **Government consumption expenditures and gross investment** | **52.1** | **68.6** | **82.1** | **95.4** | **104.4** | **104.7** | **105.1** | **107.6** | **111.4** |
| Federal | 57.3 | 72.9 | 86.2 | 96.4 | 102.6 | 103.3 | 103.9 | 106.0 | 109.3 |
| National defense | 57.2 | 71.9 | 86.0 | 96.1 | 102.1 | 102.4 | 102.8 | 104.5 | 107.6 |
| Nondefense | 57.1 | 74.6 | 86.5 | 96.9 | 103.6 | 104.7 | 105.7 | 108.4 | 112.0 |
| State and local | 49.2 | 66.0 | 79.6 | 94.7 | 105.6 | 105.7 | 105.9 | 108.7 | 112.8 |

Source: U.S. Bureau of Economic Analysis, National Income and Product Accounts Tables, "Table 1.1.4. Price Indexes for Gross Domestic Product," <https://apps.bea.gov/iTable/index_nipa.cfm>, accessed July 2019.

## Table 770. Import and Export Price Indexes by End-Use Category: 1990 to 2019

[As of June. Import indexes are weighted by the 2000 Tariff Schedule of the United States Annotated, a scheme for describing and reporting product composition and value of U.S. imports. Import prices are based on U.S. dollar prices paid by importer. Export indexes are weighted by 2000 export values according to the Schedule B classification system of the U.S. Census Bureau. Prices used in these indexes were collected from a sample of U.S. manufacturers of exports and are factory transaction prices, except as noted. Minus sign (-) indicates decrease]

| Year | Index (2000 = 100) | | | | | | Percent change [1] | | | | | |
|---|---|---|---|---|---|---|---|---|---|---|---|---|
| | Imports | | | Exports | | | Imports | | | Exports | | |
| | Total | Petro-leum imports | Non–petro-leum imports | Total | Agri-cultural exports | Non–agri-cultural exports | Total | Petro-leum imports | Non–petro-leum imports | Total | Agri-cultural exports | Non–agri-cultural exports |
| 1990 | 90.8 | 55.4 | 96.4 | 95.1 | 107.7 | 93.5 | -0.8 | -13.4 | 0.5 | -0.1 | -4.0 | 0.5 |
| 1991 | 93.4 | 63.2 | 98.3 | 96.1 | 104.3 | 95.3 | 2.9 | 14.1 | 2.0 | 1.1 | -3.2 | 1.9 |
| 1992 | 94.8 | 66.0 | 99.5 | 96.5 | 104.0 | 95.8 | 1.5 | 4.4 | 1.2 | 0.4 | -0.3 | 0.5 |
| 1993 | 95.0 | 60.4 | 100.5 | 96.9 | 100.3 | 96.7 | 0.2 | -8.5 | 1.0 | 0.4 | -3.6 | 0.9 |
| 1994 | 96.3 | 57.6 | 102.6 | 98.5 | 109.3 | 97.5 | 1.4 | -4.6 | 2.1 | 1.7 | 9.0 | 0.8 |
| 1995 | 101.4 | 62.9 | 107.6 | 104.5 | 117.0 | 103.3 | 5.3 | 9.2 | 4.9 | 6.1 | 7.0 | 5.9 |
| 1996 | 100.7 | 66.4 | 106.2 | 105.4 | 140.8 | 101.7 | -0.7 | 5.6 | -1.3 | 0.9 | 20.3 | -1.5 |
| 1997 | 98.8 | 62.5 | 104.3 | 103.2 | 120.5 | 101.5 | -1.9 | -5.9 | -1.8 | -2.1 | -14.4 | -0.2 |
| 1998 | 93.1 | 44.3 | 100.5 | 99.9 | 110.8 | 98.8 | -5.8 | -29.1 | -3.6 | -3.2 | -8.0 | -2.7 |
| 1999 | 92.9 | 54.5 | 98.8 | 98.2 | 101.1 | 97.9 | -0.2 | 23.0 | -1.7 | -1.7 | -8.8 | -0.9 |
| 2000 [2] | 100.2 | 101.9 | 99.9 | 100.1 | 100.5 | 100.0 | 7.9 | 87.0 | 1.1 | 1.9 | -0.6 | 2.1 |
| 2001 | 97.6 | 89.4 | 98.9 | 99.4 | 100.9 | 99.3 | -2.6 | -12.3 | -1.0 | -0.7 | 0.4 | -0.7 |
| 2002 | 94.1 | 85.3 | 96.2 | 98.0 | 100.7 | 97.8 | -3.6 | -4.6 | -2.7 | -1.4 | -0.2 | -1.5 |
| 2003 | 96.2 | 96.4 | 97.3 | 99.5 | 110.0 | 98.7 | 2.2 | 13.0 | 1.1 | 1.5 | 9.2 | 0.9 |
| 2004 | 101.7 | 129.7 | 99.7 | 103.4 | 127.4 | 101.5 | 5.7 | 34.5 | 2.5 | 3.9 | 15.8 | 2.8 |
| 2005 | 109.2 | 181.5 | 102.0 | 106.7 | 123.9 | 105.4 | 7.4 | 39.9 | 2.3 | 3.2 | -2.7 | 3.8 |
| 2006 | 117.3 | 242.6 | 104.2 | 111.2 | 124.1 | 110.3 | 7.4 | 33.7 | 2.2 | 4.2 | 0.2 | 4.6 |
| 2007 | 120.0 | 245.6 | 107.1 | 116.0 | 146.7 | 113.8 | 2.3 | 1.2 | 2.8 | 4.3 | 18.2 | 3.2 |
| 2008 | 145.5 | 450.3 | 114.9 | 126.1 | 195.2 | 121.2 | 21.3 | 83.3 | 7.3 | 8.7 | 33.1 | 6.5 |
| 2009 | 120.0 | 241.5 | 107.4 | 117.8 | 169.7 | 114.1 | -17.5 | -46.4 | -6.5 | -6.6 | -13.1 | -5.9 |
| 2010 | 125.2 | 267.4 | 110.7 | 122.2 | 165.3 | 119.1 | 4.3 | 10.7 | 3.1 | 3.7 | -2.6 | 4.4 |
| 2011 | 142.2 | 397.8 | 116.4 | 134.5 | 217.2 | 128.6 | 13.6 | 48.8 | 5.1 | 10.1 | 31.4 | 8.0 |
| 2012 | 138.7 | 357.2 | 116.3 | 131.7 | 204.5 | 126.5 | -2.5 | -10.2 | -0.1 | -2.1 | -5.8 | -1.6 |
| 2013 | 138.8 | 364.9 | 115.7 | 132.8 | 224.2 | 126.2 | 0.1 | 2.2 | -0.5 | 0.8 | 9.6 | -0.2 |
| 2014 | 140.5 | 387.9 | 115.8 | 133.0 | 221.4 | 126.6 | 1.2 | 6.3 | 0.1 | 0.2 | -1.2 | 0.3 |
| 2015 | 126.6 | 229.7 | 112.8 | 125.3 | 184.3 | 120.9 | -9.9 | -40.8 | -2.6 | -5.8 | -16.8 | -4.5 |
| 2016 | 120.7 | 173.1 | 110.5 | 120.9 | 181.9 | 116.3 | -4.7 | -24.6 | -2.0 | -3.5 | -1.3 | -3.8 |
| 2017 | 122.4 | 178.7 | 112.0 | 121.6 | 174.9 | 117.5 | 1.4 | 3.2 | 1.4 | 0.6 | -3.8 | 1.0 |
| 2018 | 128.2 | 255.4 | 113.5 | 128.0 | 184.2 | 123.7 | 4.7 | 42.9 | 1.3 | 5.3 | 5.3 | 5.3 |
| 2019 | 125.6 | 237.1 | 111.9 | 125.9 | 180.4 | 121.7 | -2.0 | -7.2 | -1.4 | -1.6 | -2.1 | -1.6 |

[1] Percent change from immediate prior year. [2] June 2000 may not equal 100 because indexes were reweighted to an "average" trade value in 2000.

Source: U.S. Bureau of Labor Statistics, U.S. Import and Export Price Indexes, "History Tables: Complete Historical Index Information," <http://www.bls.gov/mxp/>, accessed August 2019.

# Table 771. Export Price Indexes—Selected Commodities: 2000 to 2019

[2000=100. As of June. Indexes are weighted by 2000 export values according to the Schedule B commodity classification system of the U.S. Census Bureau. Prices used in these indexes were collected from a sample of U.S. manufacturers of exports and are factory transaction prices; see source]

| Commodity | 2000 [1] | 2005 | 2010 | 2015 | 2016 | 2017 | 2018 | 2019 |
|---|---|---|---|---|---|---|---|---|
| **All commodities** | **100.1** | **106.7** | **122.2** | **125.3** | **120.9** | **121.6** | **128.0** | **125.9** |
| Live animals and animal products | 102.2 | 130.9 | 172.2 | 193.5 | 186.3 | 207.2 | 208.0 | 217.9 |
| Vegetable products | 100.0 | 130.3 | 177.5 | 206.1 | 208.0 | 187.1 | 203.5 | 199.1 |
| Fruit and nuts | 94.8 | 126.5 | 131.0 | 175.1 | 158.2 | 133.2 | 142.6 | 139.7 |
| Cereals | 100.0 | 118.1 | 171.4 | 194.4 | 192.4 | 177.4 | 203.0 | 205.7 |
| Wheat and meslin | 99.4 | 130.0 | 151.6 | 198.3 | 174.2 | 169.9 | 206.1 | 197.0 |
| Corn (maize) | 101.0 | 111.8 | 174.3 | 181.1 | 197.1 | 175.6 | 192.0 | 204.7 |
| Oilseeds | 102.8 | 136.2 | 196.2 | 204.7 | 220.2 | 190.4 | 212.3 | 187.0 |
| Prepared foodstuffs, beverages, and tobacco | 100.0 | 110.3 | 139.3 | 153.2 | 150.0 | 147.7 | 153.3 | 153.3 |
| Mineral products | 97.8 | 182.3 | 247.9 | 211.3 | 167.6 | 190.8 | 245.8 | 215.3 |
| Fuels | 97.4 | 172.8 | 239.2 | 205.0 | 160.1 | 182.4 | 237.0 | 206.8 |
| Petroleum oils | 97.4 | 184.8 | 231.5 | 228.8 | 179.3 | 181.2 | 244.4 | 217.2 |
| Chemicals and related products | 100.3 | 115.3 | 144.5 | 143.9 | 136.3 | 132.7 | 139.2 | 138.3 |
| Plastics and rubber products | 101.5 | 118.4 | 136.8 | 143.0 | 136.3 | 137.1 | 145.0 | 143.9 |
| Woodpulp and paper products | 101.6 | 101.9 | 117.6 | 123.7 | 121.2 | 128.0 | 133.8 | 124.6 |
| Textiles | 100.2 | 100.8 | 115.7 | 122.2 | 119.5 | 120.2 | 126.0 | 121.4 |
| Stone and glass products | 100.7 | 103.5 | 115.9 | 122.4 | 122.8 | 122.7 | 124.2 | 127.5 |
| Gems and precious metals | 98.1 | 106.5 | 211.0 | 233.8 | 229.6 | 233.4 | 238.7 | 245.3 |
| Base metals | 100.5 | 131.8 | 160.4 | 153.1 | 143.3 | 151.3 | 165.1 | 159.1 |
| Iron and steel | 101.7 | 164.0 | 194.3 | 165.5 | 144.7 | 153.6 | (NA) | (NA) |
| Copper | 98.7 | 143.1 | 217.0 | 191.3 | 150.1 | 167.6 | 205.5 | 178.6 |
| Aluminum | 98.4 | 113.2 | 117.8 | 115.5 | 104.7 | 111.3 | 123.8 | 104.2 |
| Machinery | 99.9 | 94.9 | 95.5 | 97.1 | 95.9 | 96.1 | 97.6 | 98.0 |
| Nonelectrical machinery | 100.0 | 100.5 | 106.8 | 113.5 | 112.9 | 113.8 | 115.1 | 116.3 |
| Computer equipment | 99.9 | 76.6 | 53.1 | 43.8 | 40.6 | 37.7 | 36.8 | 35.5 |
| Electrical machinery | 99.8 | 88.6 | 83.2 | 79.3 | 77.5 | 77.0 | 78.7 | 78.3 |
| Transportation equipment | 100.0 | 108.8 | 121.4 | 130.8 | 131.7 | 132.7 | 135.2 | 137.2 |
| Motor vehicles and their parts | 100.0 | 103.2 | 108.5 | 115.0 | 114.9 | 115.1 | 116.3 | 116.7 |
| Instruments | 100.0 | 101.3 | 106.2 | 107.8 | 106.1 | 106.3 | 109.5 | 109.0 |
| Miscellaneous manufactured articles | 100.4 | 100.6 | 108.1 | 111.3 | 111.6 | 112.4 | 112.1 | 112.9 |

NA Not available. [1] June 2000 may not equal 100 because indexes were reweighted to an "average" trade value in 2000.

Source: U.S. Bureau of Labor Statistics, U.S. Import and Export Price Indexes, "History Tables: Complete Historical Index Information," <http://www.bls.gov/mxp/>, accessed August 2019.

# Table 772. Import Price Indexes—Selected Commodities: 2000 to 2019

[2000=100. As of June. Indexes are weighted by the 2000 Tariff Schedule of the United States Annotated, a scheme for describing and reporting product composition and value of U.S. imports. Import prices are based on U.S. dollar prices paid by importer]

| Commodity | 2000 [1] | 2005 | 2010 | 2015 | 2016 | 2017 | 2018 | 2019 |
|---|---|---|---|---|---|---|---|---|
| **All commodities** | **100.2** | **109.2** | **125.2** | **126.6** | **120.7** | **122.4** | **128.2** | **125.6** |
| Live animals and animal products | 99.9 | 112.7 | 143.0 | 185.2 | 189.4 | 198.2 | 192.4 | 196.0 |
| Meat | 100.5 | 138.7 | 183.2 | 234.5 | 236.0 | 254.9 | 248.3 | 265.7 |
| Fish | 100.2 | 88.3 | 107.1 | 127.3 | 139.8 | 143.9 | 138.5 | 139.9 |
| Vegetable products | 97.1 | 116.9 | 169.5 | 201.8 | 185.9 | 222.6 | 201.4 | 215.3 |
| Vegetables | 93.9 | 136.8 | 326.2 | 459.9 | 406.7 | 467.6 | 357.4 | 506.8 |
| Fruit and nuts | 96.9 | 89.7 | 106.8 | 95.5 | 82.1 | 134.7 | 124.0 | 124.5 |
| Prepared foodstuffs, beverages and tobacco | 100.0 | 114.0 | 141.2 | 160.7 | 163.6 | 160.7 | 167.1 | 164.9 |
| Mineral products | 101.3 | 178.1 | 248.5 | 210.9 | 157.9 | 166.6 | 230.5 | 215.9 |
| Fuels | 101.3 | 177.5 | 244.9 | 208.1 | 155.5 | 163.8 | 228.6 | 213.2 |
| Chemicals and related products | 99.8 | 111.3 | 139.3 | 148.3 | 146.8 | 152.0 | 158.2 | 156.1 |
| Organic chemicals | 100.6 | 109.6 | 133.8 | 123.7 | 120.3 | 123.6 | 133.6 | 127.3 |
| Pharmaceutical products | 99.8 | 111.0 | 117.9 | 136.7 | 142.4 | 149.2 | 151.6 | 152.3 |
| Plastics and rubber products | 99.9 | 113.5 | 136.7 | 142.1 | 136.6 | 139.4 | 141.4 | 140.8 |
| Hides, skins, and leather products | 100.2 | 104.0 | 114.5 | 128.1 | 123.5 | 123.6 | 125.8 | 124.6 |
| Wood products | 100.5 | 124.2 | 134.3 | 138.6 | 140.6 | 154.3 | 180.3 | 143.6 |
| Woodpulp and paper products | 100.0 | 102.3 | 112.5 | 111.9 | 109.9 | 110.5 | 117.9 | 120.0 |
| Textiles | 99.7 | 100.4 | 103.1 | 114.5 | 113.2 | 113.1 | 114.3 | 114.2 |
| Footwear | 99.6 | 100.3 | 106.1 | 122.3 | 122.0 | 121.4 | 121.1 | 121.3 |
| Stone and glass products | 99.5 | 105.4 | 123.8 | 132.8 | 131.7 | 130.0 | 132.3 | 132.1 |
| Gems and precious metals | 99.3 | 98.3 | 161.5 | 170.8 | 167.6 | 170.6 | 174.2 | 177.6 |
| Gold | 98.3 | 150.7 | 430.5 | 424.4 | 437.0 | 458.8 | 464.3 | 476.6 |
| Base metals | 101.5 | 132.1 | 180.2 | 168.1 | 155.1 | 166.9 | 185.3 | 174.1 |
| Iron and steel | 104.1 | 170.6 | 238.8 | 181.6 | 169.5 | 196.5 | 231.5 | 216.2 |
| Articles of iron and steel | 100.6 | 122.7 | 149.9 | 148.2 | 138.0 | 144.0 | 153.1 | 149.8 |
| Copper | 97.2 | 142.7 | 313.8 | 299.8 | 241.1 | 266.1 | 316.2 | 271.5 |
| Aluminum | 97.9 | 113.2 | 132.8 | 131.5 | 120.9 | 128.4 | 144.0 | 130.6 |
| Machinery | 100.2 | 89.7 | 86.5 | 82.5 | 80.8 | 80.4 | 80.5 | 79.2 |
| Nonelectrical machinery | 99.8 | 90.1 | 87.9 | 87.7 | 85.8 | 85.8 | 86.9 | 85.3 |
| Electrical machinery | 100.5 | 89.4 | 85.2 | 77.6 | 76.0 | 75.3 | 74.6 | 73.5 |
| Transportation equipment | 100.0 | 104.4 | 109.7 | 114.6 | 114.2 | 114.1 | 114.3 | 113.4 |
| Motor vehicles and their parts | 100.1 | 103.8 | 108.8 | 113.2 | 112.9 | 113.1 | 113.3 | 112.5 |
| Instruments | 99.8 | 100.1 | 100.8 | 103.7 | 103.4 | 101.4 | 102.5 | 101.7 |
| Miscellaneous manufactured articles | 99.7 | 99.4 | 106.5 | 112.8 | 112.2 | 110.9 | 112.3 | 112.2 |
| Furniture | 99.5 | 103.4 | 109.4 | 117.3 | 116.8 | 116.4 | 118.1 | 118.3 |

[1] June 2000 may not equal 100 because indexes were reweighted to an "average" trade value in 2000.

Source: U.S. Bureau of Labor Statistics, U.S. Import and Export Price Indexes, "History Tables: Complete Historical Index Information," <http://www.bls.gov/mxp/>, accessed August 2019.

# Section 15
# Business Enterprise

This section relates to the place and behavior of the business firm and to business initiative in the American economy. It includes data on the number, type, and size of businesses; financial data of domestic and multinational U.S. corporations; business investments, expenditures, and profits; and sales and inventories.

The principal sources of these data are the *Survey of Current Business*, published online by the Bureau of Economic Analysis (BEA); the web site of the Board of Governors of the Federal Reserve System at <https://www.federalreserve.gov/data.htm>; the annual *Statistics of Income (SOI)* reports of the Internal Revenue Service (IRS); and the U.S. Census Bureau's Economic Census, *County Business Patterns, Quarterly Financial Report for Manufacturing, Mining, and Trade Corporations (QFR), Annual Survey of Entrepreneurs, Survey of Business Owners*, and *Annual Capital Expenditures Survey*. The Census Bureau has announced that they will replace the *Annual Survey of Entrepreneurs* and *Survey of Business Owners* with the *Annual Business Survey*. Data collection for this new survey began in June 2018 and the first set of data scheduled to be released in December 2019. See also BEA Interactive Tables <http://www.bea.gov/iTable/index.cfm>.

**Business firms**—A firm is generally defined as a business organization or entity consisting of one or more domestic establishment locations under common ownership or control. The terms firm, business, company, and enterprise are used interchangeably throughout this section. A firm doing business in more than one industry is classified by industry according to the major activity of the firm as a whole.

The IRS concept of a business firm relates primarily to the legal entity used for tax reporting purposes. A sole proprietorship is an unincorporated business owned by one person and may include large enterprises with many employees and hired managers and part-time operators. A partnership is an unincorporated business owned by two or more persons, each of whom has a financial interest in the business. A corporation is a business that is legally incorporated under state laws. While many corporations file consolidated tax returns, most corporate tax returns represent individual corporations, some of which are affiliated through common ownership or control with other corporations filing separate returns.

**Economic Census**—The Economic Census is the major source of facts about the structure and functioning of the nation's economy. It provides essential information for government, business, industry, and the general public. It establishes benchmarks for economic indicators such as the gross domestic product estimates, production and price indexes, business sales, and other statistical series that measure short-term changes in economic conditions. The Census Bureau takes the Economic Census every 5 years, covering years ending in "2" and "7."

The Economic Census is collected on an establishment basis. A company operating at more than one location is required to file a separate report for each store, factory, shop, or other location. Companies engaged in distinctly different lines of activity at one location are requested to submit separate reports, if the business records permit such a separation, and if the activities are substantial in size. Each establishment is assigned a separate industry classification based on its primary activity and not that of its parent company. Establishments responding to the establishment survey are classified into industries on the basis of their principal product or activity (determined by self-reporting, annual sales volume, or products manufactured by a plant). The statistics issued by industry in the 2012 Economic Census are classified primarily on the 2012 North American Industry Classification System (NAICS).

Data from the 2012 Economic Census have been fully released as of September 2016 through the Census Bureau's American FactFinder® service on the Census Bureau Web site at <factfinder.census.gov>. Data from the 2017 Economic Census will be released on a flow basis between September 2019 and December 2021. Data will be released via the Census Bureau's new dissemination platform at <https://data.census.gov>. The American FactFinder® service will be discontinued in 2020. More detailed information about the scope, coverage, methodology, classification system, data items, and publications for the Economic Censuses and related surveys is available at <https://www.census.gov/programs-surveys/economic-census.html>.

**Survey of Business Owners**—The Survey of Business Owners (SBO) provides statistics that describe the composition of U.S. businesses by gender, ethnicity, race and veteran status. Data from SBO are published in a series of releases: *American Indian- and Alaska Native-Owned Firms, Asian-Owned Firms, Black-Owned Firms, Hispanic-Owned Firms, Native Hawaiian- and Other Pacific Islander-Owned Firms, Women-Owned Firms, Veteran-Owned Firms, Characteristics of Business Owners*, and *Company Summary*. Data are presented by industry classifications, geographic area, and size of firm (employment and receipts). Each owner had the option of selecting more than one race and therefore is included in each race selected. For more information, see <https://www.census.gov/programs-surveys/sbo.html>. Data collection for this survey had been discontinued and will be replaced by the *Annual Business Survey*.

**Annual Survey of Entrepreneurs**— The Annual Survey of Entrepreneurs provides statistics that describe the economic and demographic characteristics of employer businesses and their owners by gender, ethnicity, race and veteran status. Data from ASE is published in a series of releases: Company Summary Tables, Characteristics of Businesses, and Characteristics of Business Owners. For more information see <https://www.census.gov/programs-surveys/ase.html>. Data collection for this survey had been discontinued and will be replaced by the *Annual Business Survey*.

**North American Industry Classification System (NAICS)**—NAICS is the standard used by federal statistical agencies in classifying business establishments for the purpose of collecting, analyzing, and publishing statistical data related to the U.S. business economy. NAICS was developed under the auspices of the Office of Management and Budget (OMB), and adopted in 1997 to replace the Standard Industrial Classification (SIC) system. The official *2017 NAICS Manual* includes definitions for each industry, background information, tables showing changes between the 2012 and 2017 revisions, and a comprehensive index. Noticeable changes were made to six of the twenty NAICS sectors during the 2012 revision of NAICS. Those sectors are 22 (utilities), 23 (construction), 31-33 (manufacturing), 42 (wholesale trade), 44-45 (retail trade) and 72 (accommodation and food services). The 2017 revision impacted 28 of the 2012 NAICS 6-digit industries. For more information, see <http://www.census.gov/eos/www/naics/>.

**Quarterly Financial Report**—The Quarterly Financial Report (QFR) program publishes quarterly aggregate statistics on the financial conditions of U.S. corporations. The QFR requests companies to report estimates from their statements of income and retained earnings, and balance sheets. The statistical data are classified and aggregated by type of industry and asset size. The QFR sample includes corporations that have a plurality of business activity in manufacturing industries with domestic assets of $250,000 and above, and mining, wholesale, retail, and selected service industries with assets of $50 million and above. The data are available quarterly in the *Quarterly Financial Report for Manufacturing, Mining, Trade, and Selected Service Industries* at <https://www.census.gov/econ/qfr/>.

**Multinational enterprises**—BEA collects financial and operating data on U.S. multinational enterprises. These data provide a picture of the overall activities of foreign affiliates and U.S. parent enterprises, using a variety of indicators of their financial structure and operations. The data on foreign affiliates cover the entire operations of the affiliate, irrespective of the percentage of U.S. ownership. These data cover items such as sales, value added, employment and compensation of employees, capital expenditures, exports and imports, and research and development expenditures. Separate tabulations are available for all affiliates and for affiliates that are majority-owned by their U.S. parent(s). More information is available at <http://www.bea.gov/international/index.htm#omc>.

**Statistical reliability**—For a discussion of statistical collection, estimation, and sampling procedures and measures of reliability applicable to data from the Census Bureau and the Internal Revenue Service, see Appendix III.

# Table 773. Number of Tax Returns, Receipts, and Net Income by Type of Business: 1990 to 2016

[14,783 represents 14,783,000. Covers active enterprises only. Nonfarm sole proprietorship and partnership data are for tax year shown, which covers returns processed by the IRS during the following calendar year. Corporation data are for tax year shown which, covers (a) corporate returns with accounting periods for the calendar year ending December of year shown and (b) those returns with accounting periods for the noncalendar year ending between July of year shown and June of the following year. Figures are estimates based on sample of unaudited tax returns; see Appendix III]

| Year | Number of returns (1,000) | | | Business receipts [2] (bil. dol.) | | | Net income (less loss) [3] (bil. dol.) | | |
|---|---|---|---|---|---|---|---|---|---|
| | Nonfarm proprietor-ships [1] | Partner-ships | Corpora-tions | Nonfarm proprietor-ships [1] | Partner-ships | Corpora-tions | Nonfarm proprietor-ships [1] | Partner-ships | Corpora-tions |
| 1990........... | 14,783 | 1,554 | 3,717 | 731 | 483 | 9,860 | 141 | 17 | 383 |
| 1991........... | 15,181 | 1,515 | 3,803 | 713 | 483 | 9,966 | 142 | 21 | 361 |
| 1992........... | 15,495 | 1,485 | 3,869 | 737 | 515 | 10,360 | 154 | 43 | 414 |
| 1993........... | 15,848 | 1,468 | 3,965 | 757 | 561 | 10,866 | 156 | 67 | 510 |
| 1994........... | 16,154 | 1,494 | 4,342 | 791 | 656 | 11,884 | 167 | 82 | 595 |
| 1995........... | 16,424 | 1,581 | 4,474 | 807 | 761 | 12,786 | 169 | 107 | 736 |
| 1996........... | 16,955 | 1,654 | 4,631 | 843 | 916 | 13,659 | 177 | 145 | 839 |
| 1997........... | 17,176 | 1,759 | 4,710 | 870 | 1,142 | 14,461 | 187 | 168 | 957 |
| 1998........... | 17,409 | 1,855 | 4,849 | 918 | 1,357 | 15,010 | 202 | 187 | 895 |
| 1999........... | 17,576 | 1,937 | 4,936 | 969 | 1,616 | 16,314 | 208 | 228 | 985 |
| 2000........... | 17,903 | 2,058 | 5,045 | 1,021 | 2,062 | 17,637 | 215 | 269 | 987 |
| 2001........... | 18,338 | 2,132 | 5,136 | 1,017 | 2,278 | 17,504 | 217 | 276 | 649 |
| 2002........... | 18,926 | 2,242 | 5,267 | 1,030 | 2,414 | 17,297 | 221 | 271 | 597 |
| 2003........... | 19,710 | 2,375 | 5,401 | 1,050 | 2,546 | 18,264 | 230 | 301 | 822 |
| 2004........... | 20,591 | 2,547 | 5,558 | 1,140 | 2,819 | 19,976 | 248 | 385 | 1,170 |
| 2005........... | 21,468 | 2,764 | 5,671 | 1,223 | 3,280 | 21,800 | 270 | 546 | 2,027 |
| 2006........... | 22,075 | 2,947 | 5,841 | 1,278 | 3,571 | 23,310 | 278 | 667 | 2,024 |
| 2007........... | 23,123 | 3,096 | 5,869 | 1,324 | 3,847 | 24,217 | 281 | 683 | 1,950 |
| 2008........... | 22,614 | 3,146 | 5,847 | 1,317 | 4,344 | 24,718 | 265 | 458 | 1,061 |
| 2009........... | 22,660 | 3,169 | 5,825 | 1,178 | 3,562 | 21,585 | 245 | 410 | 971 |
| 2010........... | 23,004 | 3,248 | 5,814 | 1,196 | 3,946 | 23,058 | 268 | 594 | 1,422 |
| 2011........... | 23,427 | 3,285 | 5,823 | 1,266 | 4,455 | 25,198 | 283 | 581 | 1,406 |
| 2012........... | 23,554 | 3,389 | 5,841 | 1,302 | 4,690 | 26,029 | 305 | 778 | 1,872 |
| 2013........... | 24,075 | 3,461 | 5,888 | 1,342 | 5,069 | 26,850 | 302 | 769 | 1,994 |
| 2014........... | 24,632 | 3,611 | 6,001 | 1,394 | 5,186 | 28,075 | 317 | 837 | 2,145 |
| 2015........... | 25,226 | 3,715 | (NA) | 1,444 | 4,877 | (NA) | 332 | 781 | (NA) |
| 2016........... | 25,526 | 3,763 | (NA) | 1,422 | 4,919 | (NA) | 328 | 792 | (NA) |

NA Not available. [1] Number of returns represents returns with nonfarm business net income or deficit. [2] Excludes investment income for S corporations; for definition, see footnote 1, Table 782. [3] Net income (less loss) is defined differently by form of organization, basically as follows: (a) Proprietorships: Total taxable receipts less total business deductions, including cost of sales and operations, depletion, and certain capital expensing, excluding charitable contributions and owners' salaries; (b) Partnerships: Total taxable receipts (including investment income except capital gains) less deductions, including cost of sales and operations and certain payments to partners, excluding charitable contributions, oil and gas depletion, and certain capital expensing; and (c) Corporations: Includes "Total net income (less deficit)" from S Corporations; net income is before income tax.

Source: U.S. Internal Revenue Service, "Tax Statistics," <https://www.irs.gov/statistics>, accessed August 2019.

# Table 774. Number of Business Tax Returns by Size of Receipts: 2000 to 2016

[In thousands (5,045 represents 5,045,000). Covers active enterprises only. Figures are estimates based on sample of unaudited tax returns; see Appendix III]

| Size-class of receipts | 2000 | 2005 | 2009 | 2010 | 2011 | 2012 | 2013 | 2014 | 2015 | 2016 |
|---|---|---|---|---|---|---|---|---|---|---|
| **Corporations, total**.............. | **5,045** | **5,671** | **5,825** | **5,814** | **5,823** | **5,841** | **5,888** | **6,001** | **(NA)** | **(NA)** |
| Under $25,000 [1]..................... | 1,220 | 1,300 | 1,501 | 1,484 | 1,449 | 1,409 | 1,419 | 1,419 | (NA) | (NA) |
| $25,000 to $49,999................... | 305 | 340 | 399 | 385 | 379 | 396 | (NA) | (NA) | (NA) | (NA) |
| $50,000 to $99,999................... | 477 | 544 | 576 | 592 | 582 | 556 | (NA) | (NA) | (NA) | (NA) |
| $100,000 to $499,999................ | 1,515 | 1,755 | 1,714 | 739 | 1,743 | 1,761 | 1,800 | 1,810 | (NA) | (NA) |
| $500,000 to $999,999................ | 582 | 644 | 641 | 618 | 624 | 646 | 644 | 670 | (NA) | (NA) |
| $1,000,000 or more.................. | 946 | 1,088 | 994 | 1,005 | 1,047 | 1,073 | 1,103 | 1,151 | (NA) | (NA) |
| **Partnerships, total**............... | **2,058** | **2,764** | **3,169** | **3,249** | **3,285** | **3,389** | **3,461** | **3,611** | **3,715** | **3,763** |
| Under $25,000 [1]..................... | 1,105 | 1,465 | 1,746 | 1,788 | 1,774 | 1,815 | 1,845 | 1,951 | 2,031 | 1,993 |
| $25,000 to $49,999................... | 183 | 218 | 241 | 238 | 254 | 272 | 297 | 267 | 275 | 345 |
| $50,000 to $99,999................... | 187 | 233 | 279 | 289 | 289 | 293 | 274 | 316 | 293 | 278 |
| $100,000 to $499,999................ | 353 | 489 | 511 | 531 | 556 | 565 | 580 | 590 | 621 | 645 |
| $500,000 to $999,999................ | 92 | 131 | 148 | 151 | 150 | 164 | 171 | 175 | 171 | 171 |
| $1,000,000 or more.................. | 137 | 227 | 244 | 252 | 262 | 280 | 294 | 312 | 325 | 331 |
| **Nonfarm proprietorships, total**............................... | **17,903** | **21,468** | **22,660** | **23,004** | **23,427** | **23,554** | **24,075** | **24,632** | **25,226** | **25,526** |
| Under $25,000 [1]..................... | 11,997 | 14,456 | 15,951 | 16,258 | 16,468 | 16,450 | 16,843 | 17,181 | 17,528 | 14,703 |
| $25,000 to $49,999................... | 2,247 | 2,587 | 2,722 | 2,652 | 2,740 | 2,838 | 2,816 | 2,886 | 2,991 | 3,080 |
| $50,000 to $99,999................... | 1,645 | 1,981 | 1,825 | 1,892 | 1,869 | 1,899 | 1,969 | 2,034 | 2,107 | 2,215 |
| $100,000 to $499,999................ | 1,733 | 2,091 | 1,834 | 1,869 | 2,002 | 1,999 | 2,067 | 2,130 | 2,181 | 2,087 |
| $500,000 to $999,999................ | 190 | 235 | 211 | 219 | 222 | 234 | 239 | 251 | 265 | 271 |
| $1,000,000 or more.................. | 92 | 117 | 116 | 114 | 126 | 134 | 140 | 150 | 154 | 155 |

NA Not available. [1] Includes firms with no receipts.

Source: U.S. Internal Revenue Service, Statistics of Income Tax Stats, "Historical Table 12," <https://www.irs.gov/statistics/soi-tax-stats-historical-data-tables>, accessed September 2019; and *Corporation Income Tax Returns Complete Report, 2014,* Publication 16 (Rev. 6-2019). See also <https://www.irs.gov/statistics/soi-tax-stats-corporation-complete-report>.

# Table 775. Number of Tax Returns, Receipts, and Net Income by Type of Business and Industry: 2016

[Tax returns in thousands (25,526 represents 25,526,000); receipts and income in billions of dollars (1,422 represents $1,422,000,000,000). Covers active enterprises only. Nonfarm sole proprietorship and partnership data are for tax year shown, which covers returns processed by the IRS during 2017. Figures are estimates based on sample of unaudited tax returns; see Appendix III. Based on the North American Industry Classification System (NAICS); see text, this section. Minus sign (-) indicates net loss]

| Industry | NAICS code | Number of returns (1,000) | | Business receipts [1] (bil. dol.) | | Net income (less loss) [2] (bil. dol.) | |
|---|---|---|---|---|---|---|---|
| | | Non-farm proprietor-ships | Part-ner-ships | Non-farm proprietor-ships | Part-ner-ships | Non-farm proprietor-ships | Part-ner-ships |
| **Total** | (X) | **25,526** | **3,763** | **1,422** | **4,919** | **328** | **792** |
| Agriculture, forestry, fishing, and hunting | 11 | 297 | 137 | 21 | 35 | 2 | 1 |
| Mining | 21 | 113 | 42 | 7 | 116 | (Z) | 10 |
| Utilities | 22 | 14 | 6 | 1 | 159 | (Z) | -16 |
| Construction | 23 | 2,840 | (Z) | 242 | 322 | 41 | 18 |
| Special trade contractors | 238 | 2,202 | (NA) | 163 | (NA) | 31 | (NA) |
| Manufacturing | 31–33 | 370 | 71 | 33 | 851 | 4 | 63 |
| Wholesale trade | 42 | 343 | 70 | 48 | 624 | 5 | 16 |
| Retail trade [3] | 44–45 | 2,329 | 175 | 175 | 542 | 11 | 10 |
| Motor vehicle and parts dealers | 441 | 132 | (NA) | 39 | (NA) | 1 | (NA) |
| Food and beverage stores | 445 | 92 | (NA) | 25 | (NA) | 1 | (NA) |
| Gasoline stations | 447 | 13 | (NA) | 15 | (NA) | (Z) | (NA) |
| Transportation and warehousing | 48–49 | 1,985 | 42 | 103 | 201 | 15 | 8 |
| Information | 51 | 368 | 44 | 12 | 371 | 2 | 64 |
| Finance and insurance | 52 | 609 | 379 | 76 | 243 | 21 | 341 |
| Real estate and rental and leasing | 53 | 1,282 | 1,878 | 83 | 183 | 29 | 106 |
| Professional, scientific, and technical services [3] | 54 | 3,467 | 241 | 189 | 487 | 78 | 98 |
| Legal services | 5411 | 348 | (NA) | 41 | (NA) | 18 | (NA) |
| Management, scientific, and technical consulting services | 5416 | 930 | (NA) | 50 | (NA) | 26 | (NA) |
| Management of companies and enterprises | 55 | (NA) | 29 | (NA) | 22 | (NA) | 21 |
| Administrative and support and waste management and remediation services | 56 | 2,558 | 61 | 76 | 117 | 21 | 6 |
| Educational services | 61 | 823 | (NA) | 13 | (NA) | 5 | (NA) |
| Health care and social assistance | 62 | 2,127 | 83 | 121 | 293 | 48 | 35 |
| Arts, entertainment, and recreation | 71 | 1,643 | 48 | 44 | 79 | 11 | 3 |
| Accommodation and food services | 72 | 487 | 158 | 63 | 227 | 4 | 6 |
| Accommodation | 721 | 71 | (NA) | 7 | (NA) | (Z) | (NA) |
| Food services and drinking places | 722 | 417 | (NA) | 56 | (NA) | 3 | (NA) |
| Other services [3] | 81 | 3,450 | (NA) | 112 | (NA) | 31 | (NA) |
| Auto repair and maintenance | 8111 | 394 | (NA) | 28 | (NA) | 4 | (NA) |
| Personal and laundry services | 812 | 2,375 | (NA) | 61 | (NA) | 21 | (NA) |
| Religious, grantmaking, civic, professional, and similar organizations | 813 | 282 | (NA) | 5 | (NA) | 2 | (NA) |
| Unclassified | (X) | 420 | – | 5 | – | 2 | – |

– Represents zero. NA Not available. X Not applicable. Z Less than 500 or $500 million. [1] Excludes investment income for S corporations; for definition, see footnote 1, Table 782. [2] Net income (less loss) is defined differently by form of organization, basically as follows: (a) Proprietorships: Total taxable receipts less total business deductions, including cost of sales and operations, depletion, and certain capital expensing, excluding charitable contributions and owners' salaries; (b) Partnerships: Total taxable receipts (including investment income except capital gains) less deductions, including cost of sales and operations and certain payments to partners, excluding charitable contributions, oil and gas depletion, and certain capital expensing; and (c) Corporations: Total taxable receipts (including investment income, capital gains, and income from foreign subsidiaries deemed received for tax purposes, except for S corporations) less business deductions, including cost of sales and operations, depletion, certain capital expensing, and officers' compensation excluding S corporation charitable contributions and investment expenses; net income is before income tax. [3] Includes other industries, not shown separately.

Source: U.S. Internal Revenue Service, "SOI Tax Stats - Business Tax Statistics," <http://www.irs.gov/uac/SOI-Tax-Stats-Business-Tax-Statistics>, accessed August 2019.

# Table 776. Nonfarm Sole Proprietorships—Selected Income and Deduction Items: 2000 to 2016

[In billions of dollars (1,021 represents $1,021,000,000,000), except as indicated. Data are for tax year shown which covers returns processed by the IRS during the following calendar year. All figures are estimates based on samples. Tax law changes have affected the comparability of the data over time; see Statistics of Income reports for a description. See Appendix III]

| Item | 2000 | 2005 | 2010 | 2011 | 2012 | 2013 | 2014 | 2015 | 2016 |
|---|---|---|---|---|---|---|---|---|---|
| Number of returns (1,000) | 17,905 | 21,468 | 23,004 | 23,427 | 23,554 | 24,075 | 24,632 | 25,226 | 25,526 |
| Returns with net income (1,000) | 13,308 | 15,750 | 17,007 | 17,360 | 17,571 | 17,972 | 18,294 | 18,785 | 18,959 |
| Business receipts | 1,021 | 1,223 | 1,196 | 1,266 | 1,302 | 1,342 | 1,394 | 1,444 | 1,422 |
| Income from sales and operations | 1,008 | 1,205 | 1,176 | 1,246 | 1,281 | 1,323 | 1,375 | 1,423 | 1,404 |
| Business deductions [1] | 806 | 953 | 929 | 984 | 998 | 1,040 | 1,078 | 1,113 | 1,095 |
| Cost of sales and operations [1] | 387 | 397 | 367 | 394 | 390 | 406 | 417 | 432 | 411 |
| Purchases | 269 | 253 | 240 | 256 | 251 | 260 | 256 | 265 | 239 |
| Labor costs | 29 | 32 | 27 | 28 | 31 | 33 | 33 | 37 | 36 |
| Materials and supplies | 43 | 56 | 45 | 49 | 50 | 52 | 57 | 61 | 64 |
| Advertising | 10 | 14 | 13 | 13 | 14 | 15 | 15 | 16 | 16 |
| Car and truck expenses | 46 | 71 | 73 | 83 | 86 | 89 | 92 | 90 | 89 |
| Commissions | 12 | 15 | 12 | 13 | 14 | 14 | 14 | 17 | 16 |
| Contract labor | (NA) | 28 | 34 | 38 | 42 | 48 | 54 | 54 | 57 |
| Depreciation | 32 | 39 | 35 | 36 | 34 | 35 | 37 | 38 | (Z) |
| Insurance | 14 | 19 | 16 | 17 | 17 | 18 | 19 | 20 | 20 |
| Interest paid [2] | 12 | 12 | 11 | 10 | 9 | 9 | 9 | 9 | 9 |
| Legal and professional services | 7 | 10 | 10 | 11 | 11 | 12 | 12 | 13 | 13 |
| Office expenses | 10 | 13 | 12 | 12 | 12 | 12 | 13 | 13 | 13 |
| Rent paid [3] | 33 | 39 | 42 | 43 | 43 | 45 | 47 | 48 | 48 |
| Repairs | 12 | 15 | 15 | 16 | 17 | 18 | 18 | 19 | 18 |
| Salaries and wages (net) | 63 | 75 | 74 | 78 | 80 | 83 | 87 | 89 | 91 |
| Supplies | 22 | 29 | 30 | 32 | 34 | 35 | 37 | 38 | 39 |
| Taxes paid | 14 | 17 | 18 | 18 | 18 | 19 | 19 | 20 | 20 |
| Travel | 8 | 11 | 12 | 13 | 13 | 14 | 15 | 17 | 17 |
| Utilities | 19 | 23 | 24 | 27 | 28 | 31 | 32 | 31 | 32 |
| Net income (less loss) [4] | 215 | 270 | 268 | 283 | 305 | 302 | 317 | 332 | 328 |
| Net income [4] | 245 | 315 | 323 | 337 | 357 | 357 | 375 | 392 | 389 |
| **Constant (2009) Dollars [5]** | | | | | | | | | |
| Business receipts | 1,247 | 1,329 | 1,181 | 1,225 | 1,237 | 1,255 | 1,281 | 1,312 | 1,276 |
| Business deductions | 985 | 1,036 | 918 | 953 | 948 | 973 | 991 | 1,012 | 983 |
| Net income (less loss) | 262 | 293 | 265 | 274 | 290 | 283 | 291 | 302 | 295 |
| Net Income | 300 | 342 | 319 | 326 | 339 | 334 | 344 | 357 | 349 |

NA Not available. Z represents less than $500,000. [1] Includes other amounts not shown separately. [2] Interest paid includes "mortgage interest" and "other interest paid on business indebtedness." [3] Rent paid includes "Rent on machinery and equipment" and "Rent on other business property." [4] After adjustment for the passive loss carryover from prior years. Therefore, "business receipts" minus "total deductions" do not equal "net income." [5] Based on the overall implicit price deflator for gross domestic product.

Source: U.S. Internal Revenue Service, "SOI Tax Stats - Nonfarm Sole Proprietorship Statistics," <http://www.irs.gov/uac/SOI-Tax-Stats-Nonfarm-Sole-Proprietorship-Statistics>, accessed July 2019.

# Table 777. Partnerships—Selected Income and Balance Sheet Items: 2000 to 2016

[In billions of dollars (6,694 represents $6,694,000,000,000), except as indicated. Covers active partnerships only. Data are for tax year shown which covers returns processed by the IRS during the following calendar year. All figures are estimates based on samples. See Appendix III]

| Item | 2000 | 2005 | 2010 | 2011 | 2012 | 2013 | 2014 | 2015 | 2016 |
|---|---|---|---|---|---|---|---|---|---|
| Number of returns (1,000) | 2,058 | 2,764 | 3,248 | 3,285 | 3,389 | 3,461 | 3,611 | 3,715 | 3,763 |
| Returns with net income (1,000) | 1,261 | 1,580 | 1,635 | 1,725 | 1,869 | 1,944 | 2,019 | 2,152 | 2,196 |
| Number of partners (1,000) | 13,660 | 16,212 | 22,428 | 24,390 | 25,334 | 27,491 | 27,714 | 27,093 | 28,164 |
| Assets [1,2] | 6,694 | 13,734 | 19,820 | 20,574 | 22,015 | 24,163 | 26,129 | 27,366 | 28,950 |
| Depreciable assets (net) | 1,487 | 2,176 | 3,263 | 3,337 | 3,570 | 3,798 | 4,093 | 4,423 | 4,751 |
| Inventories, end of year | 150 | 315 | 277 | 285 | 304 | 313 | 331 | 343 | 367 |
| Land | 359 | 607 | 913 | 922 | 957 | 1,001 | 1,069 | 1,143 | 1,200 |
| Liabilities [1,2] | 3,696 | 7,483 | 8,994 | 8,939 | 9,277 | 9,841 | 10,625 | 11,019 | 12,022 |
| Accounts payable | 230 | 400 | 492 | 504 | 509 | 533 | 537 | 529 | 583 |
| Short-term debt [3] | 252 | 373 | 481 | 394 | 326 | 306 | 328 | 351 | 407 |
| Long-term debt [4] | 1,132 | 1,772 | 2,693 | 2,559 | 2,706 | 2,717 | 2,993 | 3,222 | 3,477 |
| Nonrecourse loans | 639 | 914 | 1,225 | 1,213 | 1,212 | 1,225 | 1,254 | 1,270 | 1,318 |
| Partners' capital accounts [2] | 2,999 | 6,251 | 10,826 | 11,636 | 12,738 | 14,322 | 15,504 | 16,347 | 16,928 |
| Total receipts [1] | 2,405 | 3,863 | 4,721 | 5,212 | 5,557 | 5,921 | 6,100 | 5,798 | 5,886 |
| Business receipts | 2,062 | 3,280 | 3,946 | 4,455 | 4,690 | 5,069 | 5,186 | 4,877 | 4,919 |
| Deductions from a trade or business [1] | 2,136 | 3,317 | 4,128 | 4,631 | 4,779 | 5,152 | 5,263 | 5,018 | 5,094 |
| Cost of goods sold/operations | 1,226 | 1,976 | 2,336 | 2,732 | 2,828 | 3,087 | 3,066 | 2,696 | 2,660 |
| Salaries and wages | 201 | 293 | 405 | 436 | 463 | 502 | 541 | 578 | 607 |
| Taxes paid | 31 | 47 | 63 | 69 | 73 | 79 | 83 | 87 | 89 |
| Interest paid | 93 | 103 | 86 | 81 | 81 | 78 | 83 | 85 | 97 |
| Depreciation [5] | 116 | 140 | 247 | 305 | 261 | 288 | 304 | 325 | 352 |
| Net income (less loss) | 269 | 546 | 594 | 581 | 778 | 769 | 837 | 781 | 792 |
| Net income | 410 | 724 | 904 | 913 | 1,068 | 1,080 | 1,156 | 1,137 | 1,173 |

[1] Includes items not shown separately. [2] Assets, liabilities, and partners' capital accounts are understated because not all partnerships file complete balance sheets. [3] Mortgages, notes, and bonds payable in less than 1 year. [4] Mortgages, notes, and bonds payable in 1 year or more. [5] Represents the more complete amounts reported in depreciation computation schedules, rather than the amounts reported as the depreciation deduction.

Source: U.S. Internal Revenue Service, "SOI Tax Stats - Partnership Statistics," <http://www.irs.gov/uac/SOI-Tax-Stats-Partnership-Statistics>, accessed July 2019.

## Table 778. Partnerships—Selected Items by Industry: 2016

[In billions of dollars (28,950 represents $28,950,000,000,000), except as indicated. Covers active partnerships only. Data are for tax year shown, which covers returns processed by the IRS during 2017. Figures are estimates based on samples. Based on the North American Industry Classification System (NAICS), 2012; see text, this section. Minus sign (-) indicates net loss.]

| Industry and year | 2012 NAICS code | Partnerships (1,000) | | | Total assets [1] | Business receipts | Total deduc-tions | Net income less loss | Net income | Net loss |
| | | Total | With net income | With net loss | | | | | | |
|---|---|---|---|---|---|---|---|---|---|---|
| Total [2] | (X) | 3,763 | 2,196 | 1,567 | 28,950 | 4,919 | 4,981 | 792 | 1,173 | 382 |
| Agriculture, forestry, fishing, and hunting | 11 | 137 | 70 | 67 | 254 | 35 | 48 | 1 | 12 | 11 |
| Mining | 21 | 42 | 23 | 19 | 563 | 116 | 129 | 10 | 32 | 22 |
| Utilities | 22 | 6 | 1 | 4 | 443 | 159 | 182 | -16 | 9 | 25 |
| Construction | 23 | 170 | 108 | 62 | 257 | 322 | 312 | 18 | 25 | 7 |
| Manufacturing | 31–33 | 71 | 32 | 39 | 900 | 851 | 835 | 63 | 85 | 22 |
| Wholesale trade | 42 | 70 | 35 | 36 | 343 | 624 | 617 | 16 | 25 | 9 |
| Retail trade | 44–45 | 175 | 103 | 72 | 224 | 542 | 547 | 10 | 18 | 7 |
| Transportation and warehousing | 48–49 | 42 | 23 | 18 | 792 | 201 | 207 | 8 | 22 | 14 |
| Information | 51 | 44 | 17 | 26 | 975 | 371 | 342 | 64 | 80 | 16 |
| Finance and insurance | 52 | 379 | 239 | 140 | 15,639 | 243 | 343 | 341 | 401 | 60 |
| Real estate and rental and leasing | 53 | 1,878 | 1,095 | 782 | 6,571 | 183 | 210 | 106 | 229 | 123 |
| Professional, scientific, and technical services | 54 | 241 | 150 | 91 | 337 | 487 | 407 | 98 | 112 | 15 |
| Management of companies and enterprises | 55 | 29 | 13 | 16 | 856 | 22 | 40 | 21 | 34 | 13 |
| Administrative and support & waste management and remediation services | 56 | 61 | 47 | 14 | 106 | 117 | 122 | 6 | 11 | 5 |
| Educational and other services [3] | 61/81 | 132 | 71 | 61 | 39 | 45 | 45 | 2 | 5 | 3 |
| Health care and social assistance | 62 | 83 | 49 | 34 | 202 | 293 | 279 | 35 | 44 | 9 |
| Arts, entertainment, and recreation | 71 | 48 | 35 | 13 | 152 | 79 | 88 | 3 | 11 | 8 |
| Accommodation and food services | 72 | 158 | 84 | 74 | 297 | 227 | 228 | 6 | 19 | 13 |

X Not applicable. [1] Total assets are understated because not all partnerships file complete balance sheets. [2] Includes businesses not allocable to individual industries. [3] The educational and other services sectors were combined due to disclosure concerns.

Source: U.S. Internal Revenue Service, "SOI Tax Stats - Partnership Statistics," <http://www.irs.gov/uac/SOI-Tax-Stats-Partnership-Statistics-by-Sector-or-Industry>, accessed July 2019.

## Table 779. Nonfinancial Noncorporate Business-Sector Balance Sheet: 2000 to 2018

[In billions of dollars (7,802 represents $7,802,000,000,000), except as noted. Represents year-end (4th quarter) outstandings]

| Item | 2000 | 2005 | 2010 | 2013 | 2014 | 2015 | 2016 | 2017 | 2018 |
|---|---|---|---|---|---|---|---|---|---|
| **Assets** | 7,802 | 12,629 | 12,540 | 15,259 | 16,406 | 17,494 | 18,689 | 19,953 | 20,885 |
| Nonfinancial assets | 6,329 | 10,032 | 8,811 | 10,728 | 11,432 | 12,122 | 12,828 | 13,657 | 14,152 |
| Real estate [1] | 5,579 | 9,092 | 7,684 | 9,470 | 10,120 | 10,822 | 11,516 | 12,303 | 12,723 |
| Residential | 3,269 | 5,730 | 4,319 | 5,259 | 5,592 | 6,003 | 6,451 | 6,937 | 7,313 |
| Nonresidential | 2,310 | 3,362 | 3,366 | 4,211 | 4,528 | 4,819 | 5,066 | 5,367 | 5,410 |
| Equipment [2] | 447 | 562 | 682 | 757 | 786 | 796 | 805 | 827 | 896 |
| Residential [3] | 35 | 42 | 43 | 47 | 47 | 48 | 48 | 50 | 57 |
| Nonresidential | 412 | 521 | 639 | 710 | 739 | 748 | 757 | 776 | 839 |
| Intellectual property products [2] | 119 | 160 | 200 | 223 | 234 | 244 | 256 | 267 | 277 |
| Inventories [2] | 185 | 218 | 244 | 277 | 291 | 260 | 250 | 259 | 256 |
| Financial assets | 1,473 | 2,597 | 3,728 | 4,531 | 4,974 | 5,372 | 5,860 | 6,296 | 6,734 |
| Checkable deposits and currency | 181 | 224 | 182 | 178 | 247 | 254 | 279 | 280 | 312 |
| Time and savings deposits | 248 | 474 | 706 | 834 | 850 | 861 | 909 | 973 | 1,037 |
| Money market fund shares | 49 | 69 | 77 | 83 | 86 | 88 | 97 | 105 | 114 |
| Debt securities [4] | 43 | 61 | 54 | 60 | 61 | 66 | 73 | 79 | 86 |
| Treasury securities | 40 | 56 | 48 | 55 | 57 | 62 | 68 | 74 | 80 |
| Municipal securities | 2 | 4 | 6 | 4 | 4 | 4 | 5 | 5 | 6 |
| Loans [4] | 23 | 36 | 42 | 35 | 34 | 42 | 46 | 49 | 54 |
| Mortgages | 23 | 36 | 42 | 35 | 34 | 42 | 46 | 49 | 54 |
| Trade receivables | 342 | 431 | 533 | 648 | 669 | 663 | 729 | 787 | 861 |
| Miscellaneous assets | 587 | 1,302 | 2,135 | 2,695 | 3,027 | 3,398 | 3,728 | 4,023 | 4,270 |
| Insurance receivables | 77 | 99 | 132 | 117 | 129 | 119 | 116 | 121 | 122 |
| Equity investment in GSEs [5] | 3 | 4 | 7 | 8 | 9 | 9 | 10 | 12 | 12 |
| Other | 506 | 1,198 | 1,996 | 2,571 | 2,889 | 3,270 | 3,602 | 3,889 | 4,135 |
| **Liabilities** | 2,796 | 4,180 | 5,673 | 6,071 | 6,449 | 6,708 | 7,128 | 7,507 | 7,900 |
| Loans | 1,912 | 2,898 | 3,951 | 4,164 | 4,446 | 4,692 | 4,976 | 5,229 | 5,485 |
| Depository institution loans n.e.c. [6] | 402 | 671 | 928 | 991 | 1,078 | 1,142 | 1,205 | 1,251 | 1,288 |
| Other loans and advances | 129 | 135 | 171 | 187 | 196 | 200 | 203 | 206 | 215 |
| Mortgages | 1,381 | 2,093 | 2,853 | 2,986 | 3,172 | 3,350 | 3,569 | 3,771 | 3,981 |
| Trade payables | 267 | 335 | 428 | 528 | 537 | 521 | 602 | 678 | 767 |
| Taxes payable | 65 | 87 | 99 | 111 | 117 | 123 | 130 | 136 | 144 |
| Miscellaneous liabilities | 549 | 858 | 1,189 | 1,262 | 1,339 | 1,360 | 1,406 | 1,447 | 1,486 |
| **Net worth** | 5,006 | 8,449 | 6,867 | 9,188 | 9,957 | 10,786 | 11,561 | 12,446 | 12,985 |
| Debt/net worth (percent) | 38 | 34 | 58 | 45 | 45 | 44 | 43 | 42 | 42 |

[1] At market value. [2] At replacement (current) cost. [3] Durable goods in rental properties. [4] Includes other items not shown separately. [5] Government-sponsored enterprises (GSEs). Equity in the Farm Credit System. [6] Not elsewhere classified.

Source: Board of Governors of the Federal Reserve System, "Z.1, Financial Accounts of the United States," March 2019, <http://www.federalreserve.gov/releases/z1/>, accessed April 2019.

## Table 780. Nonfinancial Corporate Business-Sector Balance Sheet: 2000 to 2018

[In billions of dollars (20,609 represents $20,609,000,000,000). Represents year-end (4th quarter) outstandings]

| Item | 2000 | 2005 | 2010 | 2013 | 2014 | 2015 | 2016 | 2017 | 2018 |
|---|---|---|---|---|---|---|---|---|---|
| **Assets** | **20,609** | **26,288** | **28,965** | **34,412** | **36,638** | **39,315** | **41,861** | **44,574** | **45,195** |
| Nonfinancial assets | 10,810 | 14,323 | 14,878 | 18,086 | 19,299 | 20,493 | 21,455 | 22,835 | 23,318 |
| Real estate [1] | 5,443 | 8,012 | 7,342 | 9,460 | 10,359 | 11,357 | 12,045 | 12,999 | 13,018 |
| Equipment [2] | 2,889 | 3,258 | 3,835 | 4,323 | 4,483 | 4,591 | 4,685 | 4,857 | 5,055 |
| Intellectual property products [2] | 1,138 | 1,435 | 1,841 | 2,129 | 2,224 | 2,299 | 2,410 | 2,561 | 2,717 |
| Inventories [2] | 1,340 | 1,619 | 1,860 | 2,174 | 2,233 | 2,247 | 2,314 | 2,419 | 2,527 |
| Financial assets [3] | 9,799 | 11,965 | 14,087 | 16,325 | 17,339 | 18,822 | 20,406 | 21,739 | 21,878 |
| Checkable deposits and currency | 226 | 331 | 529 | 716 | 771 | 838 | 998 | 1,095 | 1,074 |
| Time and savings deposits | 272 | 380 | 177 | 175 | 152 | 144 | 163 | 167 | 155 |
| Money market fund shares | 214 | 359 | 555 | 535 | 558 | 577 | 464 | 475 | 502 |
| Debt securities | 123 | 213 | 204 | 179 | 209 | 206 | 199 | 232 | 219 |
| Mutual fund shares [1] | 118 | 134 | 186 | 210 | 234 | 235 | 237 | 277 | 262 |
| Trade receivables | 1,939 | 2,108 | 2,203 | 2,611 | 2,718 | 2,750 | 2,974 | 3,247 | 3,532 |
| U.S. direct investment abroad | 1,371 | 2,381 | 3,517 | 4,471 | 4,921 | 5,068 | 5,334 | 5,725 | 5,561 |
| **Liabilities [3]** | **9,632** | **11,182** | **13,226** | **15,395** | **16,569** | **17,886** | **19,124** | **20,150** | **20,501** |
| Debt securities | 2,721 | 3,010 | 3,964 | 4,811 | 5,133 | 5,559 | 5,848 | 6,153 | 6,240 |
| Commercial paper | 278 | 90 | 83 | 145 | 182 | 179 | 181 | 207 | 181 |
| Municipal securities [4] | 154 | 242 | 503 | 524 | 523 | 536 | 553 | 566 | 562 |
| Corporate bonds | 2,288 | 2,678 | 3,378 | 4,142 | 4,428 | 4,844 | 5,115 | 5,381 | 5,497 |
| Loans | 1,958 | 2,264 | 2,106 | 2,290 | 2,393 | 2,528 | 2,642 | 3,011 | 3,519 |
| Depository institution loans n.e.c. [5] | 901 | 591 | 482 | 786 | 863 | 970 | 1,025 | 1,065 | 1,192 |
| Other loans and advances | 701 | 904 | 947 | 1,063 | 1,126 | 1,090 | 1,102 | 1,388 | 1,721 |
| Mortgages | 356 | 769 | 676 | 441 | 404 | 469 | 515 | 558 | 606 |
| Trade payables | 1,542 | 1,701 | 1,746 | 1,938 | 2,088 | 2,111 | 2,305 | 2,516 | 2,752 |
| Taxes payable | 78 | 86 | 43 | 45 | 43 | 42 | 33 | 246 | 224 |
| Foreign direct investment in U.S | 1,218 | 1,651 | 2,296 | 2,753 | 2,946 | 3,271 | 3,643 | 3,893 | 4,125 |
| **Net worth (market value)** | **10,977** | **15,106** | **15,739** | **19,017** | **20,069** | **21,429** | **22,737** | **24,424** | **24,695** |
| Debt/net worth (percent) | 42.6 | 34.9 | 38.6 | 37.3 | 37.5 | 37.7 | 37.3 | 37.5 | 39.5 |

[1] At market value. [2] At replacement (current) cost. [3] Includes items not shown separately. [4] Industrial revenue bonds. Issued by state and local governments to finance private investment and secured in interest and principal by the industrial user of the funds. [5] Not elsewhere classified.

Source: Board of Governors of the Federal Reserve System, "Z.1, Financial Accounts of the United States," March 2019 <http://www.federalreserve.gov/releases/z1/>, accessed April 2019.

## Table 781. Corporate Funds—Sources and Uses: 2000 to 2018

[In billions of dollars (451 represents $451,000,000,000)]

| Item | 2000 | 2005 | 2010 | 2013 | 2014 | 2015 | 2016 | 2017 | 2018 |
|---|---|---|---|---|---|---|---|---|---|
| Profits before tax | 451 | 1,030 | 1,042 | 1,322 | 1,375 | 1,294 | 1,254 | 1,264 | 1,257.0 |
| - Taxes on corporate income | 165 | 263 | 204 | 264 | 291 | 284 | 271 | 247 | 166.4 |
| - Net dividends | 251 | 171 | 375 | 532 | 598 | 641 | 699 | 704 | 241.9 |
| + Inventory valuation adjustment (IVA) | -17 | -36 | -48 | 14 | 4 | 53 | -1 | -46 | -62.9 |
| + Capital consumption allowance [1] | 786 | 805 | 1,087 | 1,163 | 1,239 | 1,317 | 1,368 | 1,475 | 1,698.1 |
| + Foreign earnings retained abroad | 103 | -29 | 212 | 216 | 206 | 201 | 200 | 212 | -216.4 |
| - Net capital transfers | (Z) | -16 | 21 | -6 | -7 | -3 | 3 | 180 | -6.4 |
| =Gross saving less net capital transfers paid | 907 | 1,352 | 1,693 | 1,925 | 1,941 | 1,943 | 1,849 | 1,774 | 2,273.9 |
| Gross investment | 1,798 | 1,168 | 1,385 | 1,584 | 1,283 | 2,001 | 1,805 | 1,680 | 1,906.5 |
| Capital expenditures [2] | 1,147 | 1,206 | 1,300 | 1,676 | 1,819 | 1,916 | 1,770 | 1,890 | 2,075.9 |
| Fixed investment [3] | 1,098 | 1,154 | 1,247 | 1,592 | 1,742 | 1,777 | 1,735 | 1,864 | 2,027.1 |
| Inventory change + IVA | 50 | 51 | 54 | 83 | 75 | 110 | 28 | 25 | 50.0 |
| Nonproduced nonfinancial assets | -1 | 1 | -1 | 1 | 2 | 29 | 7 | 1 | -1.2 |
| Net lending (+) or net borrowing (-) | 649 | -38 | 85 | -92 | -536 | 85 | 35 | -209 | -169.4 |
| Net acquisition of financial assets [2] | 1,887 | 927 | 572 | 834 | 846 | 1,498 | 1,420 | 968 | 364.5 |
| Foreign deposits | -7 | 10 | 9 | 69 | -11 | -20 | 4 | 145 | -140.1 |
| Checkable deposits and currency | 35 | 100 | 184 | 51 | 55 | 67 | 160 | 97 | -21.2 |
| Time and savings deposits | 35 | 10 | -51 | 25 | -23 | -8 | 19 | 4 | -12.1 |
| Money market fund shares | 17 | 53 | -170 | 31 | 22 | 19 | -113 | 12 | 26.4 |
| Debt securities [2] | 19 | 40 | -16 | -1 | 30 | -3 | -6 | 33 | -13.0 |
| Municipal securities | 7 | (Z) | -3 | -2 | (Z) | 1 | -3 | 9 | -4.6 |
| Loans | 8 | 2 | -4 | -4 | 2 | 2 | 1 | -3 | -2.3 |
| Mutual fund shares | (Z) | 1 | 8 | 3 | 15 | 8 | -11 | 5 | 5.5 |
| Trade receivables | 282 | 278 | 142 | 268 | 107 | 33 | 223 | 273 | 285.4 |
| U.S. direct investment abroad | 136 | 15 | 299 | 297 | 317 | 264 | 255 | 277 | -160.3 |
| Miscellaneous assets [2] | 1,523 | 596 | 226 | 84 | 262 | 1,168 | 798 | 265 | 519.1 |
| Net increase in liabilities [2] | 1,238 | 965 | 487 | 926 | 1,382 | 1,413 | 1,385 | 1,178 | 533.8 |
| Debt securities [2] | 201 | -6 | 237 | 293 | 323 | 426 | 289 | 305 | 86.8 |
| Commercial paper | 48 | -8 | 25 | 14 | 38 | -3 | 2 | 26 | -25.5 |
| Corporate bonds | 151 | -41 | 180 | 278 | 286 | 416 | 271 | 266 | 116.1 |
| Loans | 157 | 271 | -299 | 96 | 102 | 157 | 119 | 211 | 187.8 |
| Depository institution loans n.e.c. [4] | 55 | -27 | -85 | 73 | 77 | 105 | 56 | 40 | 126.2 |
| Other loans and advances [5] | 78 | 110 | -108 | 38 | 63 | -6 | 12 | 127 | 6.9 |
| Mortgages | 24 | 187 | -106 | -14 | -38 | 59 | 51 | 43 | 54.7 |
| Corporate equities | -118 | -300 | -251 | -353 | -394 | -550 | -577 | -319 | -513.5 |
| Trade payables | 313 | 199 | 156 | 101 | 150 | 22 | 195 | 211 | 235.7 |
| Foreign direct investment in U.S | 249 | 103 | 162 | 187 | 185 | 413 | 408 | 248 | 260.3 |
| Miscellaneous liabilities [2] | 431 | 701 | 475 | 610 | 1,017 | 945 | 960 | 309 | 299.0 |
| Claims of pension fund on sponsor | 118 | 93 | -21 | 126 | 42 | 59 | 63 | 16 | 5.4 |

Z Less than $500 million. [1] Consumption of fixed capital plus capital consumption adjustment. [2] Includes other items not shown separately. [3] Nonresidential fixed investment plus residential fixed investment. [4] Not elsewhere classified. [5] Loans from rest of the world, U.S. government, and nonbank financial institutions.

Source: Board of Governors of the Federal Reserve System, "Z.1, Financial Accounts of the United States," March 2019, <http://www.federalreserve.gov/releases/z1/>, accessed May 2019.

# Table 782. Corporations—Selected Financial Items: 2000 to 2014

[In billions of dollars (47,027 represents $47,027,000,000,000), except as noted. Covers active corporations only. Corporation data are for tax year shown which covers (a) corporate returns with accounting periods for the calendar year ending December of year shown and (b) those returns with accounting periods for the noncalendar year ending between July of year shown and June of the following year. All corporations are required to file returns except those specifically exempt. See source for changes in law affecting comparability of historical data. Based on samples; see Appendix III]

| Item | 2000 | 2005 | 2008 | 2009 | 2010 | 2011 | 2012 | 2013 | 2014 |
|---|---|---|---|---|---|---|---|---|---|
| Number of returns (1,000) | 5,045 | 5,671 | 5,847 | 5,825 | 5,814 | 5,823 | 5,841 | 5,888 | 6,001 |
| Number with net income (1,000) | 2,819 | 3,324 | 3,184 | 3,149 | 3,265 | 3,385 | 3,549 | 3,581 | 3,725 |
| S Corporation returns [1] (1,000) | 2,860 | 3,684 | 4,050 | 4,095 | 4,128 | 4,159 | 4,205 | 4,258 | 4,380 |
| Assets [2] | 47,027 | 66,445 | 76,799 | 75,965 | 79,905 | 81,280 | 84,952 | 88,214 | 95,864 |
| Cash | 1,820 | 2,823 | 4,384 | 4,853 | 3,893 | 4,196 | 4,404 | 4,871 | 5,578 |
| Notes and accounts receivable | 8,754 | 11,962 | 13,855 | 12,544 | 12,718 | 13,089 | 13,016 | 12,714 | 14,090 |
| Inventories | 1,272 | 1,505 | 1,619 | 1,474 | 1,544 | 1,653 | 1,750 | 1,836 | 1,945 |
| Investments in government obligations | 1,236 | 1,613 | 2,193 | 2,501 | 2,730 | 2,859 | 3,002 | 2,958 | 3,237 |
| Mortgage and real estate | 2,822 | 4,777 | 5,450 | 4,847 | 7,914 | 7,615 | 7,579 | 7,533 | 7,506 |
| Other investments | 17,874 | 25,162 | 27,169 | 27,574 | 29,389 | 29,745 | 32,158 | 34,758 | 37,093 |
| Depreciable assets | 7,292 | 8,416 | 9,467 | 9,613 | 9,875 | 10,226 | 10,672 | 11,210 | 11,852 |
| Depletable assets | 191 | 310 | 587 | 629 | 661 | 757 | 855 | 922 | 1,031 |
| Land | 303 | 407 | 509 | 517 | 548 | 567 | 584 | 601 | 633 |
| Liabilities [2] | 47,027 | 66,445 | 76,799 | 75,965 | 79,905 | 81,280 | 84,952 | 88,214 | 95,864 |
| Accounts payable | 3,758 | 6,029 | 6,822 | 5,694 | 5,768 | 5,343 | 5,288 | 5,063 | 6,337 |
| Short-term debt [3] | 4,020 | 4,192 | 4,726 | 4,542 | 3,752 | 3,839 | 3,557 | 3,682 | 3,757 |
| Long-term debt [4] | 6,184 | 8,332 | 11,062 | 10,718 | 14,680 | 14,489 | 14,473 | 13,579 | 14,304 |
| Net worth [5] | 17,349 | 23,525 | 25,469 | 24,567 | 28,938 | 29,250 | 31,804 | 35,079 | 37,998 |
| Capital stock | 3,966 | 2,482 | 3,184 | 3,019 | 3,064 | 2,983 | 3,067 | 2,982 | 3,118 |
| Paid-in or capital surplus | 12,265 | 17,828 | 23,574 | 24,110 | 24,283 | 24,859 | 26,243 | 27,642 | 30,068 |
| Retained earnings [6] | 3,627 | 4,331 | 613 | 2,024 | 3,534 | 3,586 | 4,804 | 6,969 | 7,623 |
| Receipts [2, 7] | 20,606 | 25,505 | 28,590 | 24,773 | 26,199 | 28,336 | 29,404 | 30,192 | 31,563 |
| Business receipts [7, 8] | 17,637 | 21,800 | 24,718 | 21,585 | 23,058 | 25,198 | 26,029 | 26,850 | 28,075 |
| Interest [9] | 1,628 | 1,773 | 2,179 | 1,540 | 1,366 | 1,344 | 1,209 | 1,109 | 1,100 |
| Rents and royalties | 254 | 290 | 317 | 296 | 307 | 315 | 332 | 355 | 369 |
| Deductions [2, 7] | 19,692 | 23,613 | 27,687 | 23,944 | 24,944 | 27,093 | 27,713 | 28,357 | 29,522 |
| Cost of goods sold [8] | 11,135 | 13,816 | 16,080 | 13,286 | 14,502 | 16,180 | 16,579 | 17,141 | 17,850 |
| Compensation of officers | 401 | 445 | 467 | 428 | 435 | 454 | 479 | 479 | 488 |
| Rent paid on business property | 380 | 439 | 491 | 476 | 467 | 471 | 484 | 495 | 513 |
| Taxes paid | 390 | 473 | 469 | 473 | 493 | 519 | 546 | 564 | 581 |
| Interest paid | 1,272 | 1,287 | 1,659 | 1,070 | 888 | 860 | 814 | 711 | 706 |
| Depreciation | 614 | 531 | 759 | 712 | 728 | 874 | 709 | 730 | 769 |
| Advertising | 234 | 253 | 267 | 241 | 256 | 264 | 275 | 285 | 295 |
| Net income (less loss) [7, 10] | 928 | 1,949 | 984 | 919 | 1,356 | 1,323 | 1,774 | 1,929 | 2,145 |
| Net income | 1,337 | 2,235 | 1,807 | 1,615 | 1,836 | 1,829 | 2,175 | 2,329 | 2,561 |
| Deficit | 409 | 286 | 823 | 696 | 480 | 506 | 401 | 401 | 416 |
| Income subject to tax | 760 | 1,201 | 978 | 895 | 1,022 | 994 | 1,150 | 1,258 | 1,401 |
| Income tax before credits [11] | 266 | 419 | 342 | 313 | 358 | 349 | 403 | 442 | 491 |
| Income tax after credits [12] | 204 | 312 | 229 | 205 | 223 | 221 | 268 | 293 | 336 |

[1] Represents certain small corporations with a limit on the number of shareholders, mostly individuals, electing to be taxed at the shareholder level. [2] Includes items not shown separately. [3] Payable in less than 1 year. [4] Payable in 1 year or more. [5] Net worth is the sum of capital stock, additional paid-in capital, retained earnings, appropriated, retained earnings, unappropriated, adjustments to shareholders' equity, minus cost of treasury stock. [6] Appropriated and unappropriated and adjustments to shareholders' equity. [7] Receipts, deductions, and net income of S corporations are limited to those from trade or business. Those from investments are excluded. [8] Includes gross sales and cost of sales of securities, commodities, and real estate by exchanges, brokers, or dealers selling on their own accounts. Excludes investment income. [9] Includes tax-exempt interest in state and local government obligations. [10] Excludes regulated investment companies. [11] Consists of regular (and alternative tax) only. [12] Includes minimum tax, alternative minimum tax, adjustments for prior year credits, and other income-related taxes.

Source: U.S. Internal Revenue Service, "SOI Tax Stats - Corporation Complete Report," <https://www.irs.gov/statistics/soi-tax-stats-corporation-complete-report>, accessed August 2019.

# Table 783. Economic Census Summary (NAICS 2007 Basis): 2007 and 2012

[23 represents 23,000. Covers establishments with payroll. Data are based on the 2007 and 2012 Economic Censuses which are subject to nonsampling error. Data for the construction sector are also subject to sampling errors. For details on survey methodology and nonsampling and sampling errors, see Appendix III]

| Kind of business | 2007 NAICS code [1] | Establishments (1,000) | | Sales, receipts, or shipments (bil. dol.) | | Annual payroll (bil. dol.) | | Paid employees [2] (1,000) | |
|---|---|---|---|---|---|---|---|---|---|
| | | 2007 | 2012 | 2007 | 2012 | 2007 | 2012 | 2007 | 2012 |
| Mining, quarrying, and oil and gas extraction.... | 21 | 23 | 25 | 414 | 529 | 41 | 59 | 730 | 848 |
| Oil & gas extraction................................. | 211 | 6 | 7 | 255 | 311 | 10 | 15 | 150 | 176 |
| Mining (except oil & gas).......................... | 212 | 6 | 6 | 86 | 98 | 12 | 14 | 211 | 212 |
| Support activities for mining....................... | 213 | 10 | 13 | 73 | 120 | 19 | 30 | 369 | 460 |
| Utilities....................................................... | 22 | 17 | 18 | 584 | 532 | 52 | 59 | 637 | 651 |
| Construction............................................... | 23 | 729 | 598 | 1,732 | 1,366 | 331 | 273 | 7,316 | 5,670 |
| Construction of buildings............................ | 236 | 212 | 164 | 748 | 508 | 78 | 55 | 1,541 | 1,085 |
| Heavy and civil engineering construction........ | 237 | 39 | 33 | 260 | 256 | 54 | 55 | 1,044 | 961 |
| Specialty trade contractors........................ | 238 | 478 | 401 | 723 | 603 | 199 | 163 | 4,731 | 3,623 |
| Manufacturing............................................. | 31-33 | 333 | 297 | 5,319 | 5,697 | 614 | 593 | 13,396 | 11,214 |
| Wholesale trade.......................................... | 42 | 435 | 419 | 6,516 | 7,900 | 336 | 362 | 6,227 | 5,882 |
| Merchant wholesalers, durable goods.......... | 423 | 255 | 245 | 2,898 | 3,152 | 207 | 217 | 3,619 | 3,355 |
| Merchant wholesalers, nondurable goods...... | 424 | 135 | 131 | 2,991 | 4,108 | 116 | 132 | 2,320 | 2,244 |
| Wholesale electronic markets and agents and brokers........................................... | 425 | 45 | 43 | 627 | 639 | 13 | 14 | 289 | 283 |
| Retail trade................................................. | 44-45 | 1,128 | 1,062 | 3,918 | 4,220 | 363 | 369 | 15,515 | 14,704 |
| Motor vehicle & parts dealers..................... | 441 | 127 | 116 | 891 | 869 | 73 | 70 | 1,914 | 1,710 |
| Furniture & home furnishings stores............. | 442 | 65 | 52 | 108 | 89 | 15 | 11 | 557 | 425 |
| Electronics & appliance stores.................... | 443 | 51 | 47 | 109 | 101 | 11 | 10 | 486 | 416 |
| Building material & garden equipment & supplies dealers..................................... | 444 | 91 | 78 | 318 | 279 | 38 | 34 | 1331.3 | 1,145 |
| Food & beverage stores............................ | 445 | 146 | 148 | 539 | 620 | 55 | 61 | 2,827 | 2,865 |
| Health & personal care stores..................... | 446 | 88 | 91 | 234 | 270 | 28 | 31 | 1,068 | 1,002 |
| Gasoline stations..................................... | 447 | 119 | 114 | 450 | 554 | 15 | 16 | 891 | 857 |
| Clothing & clothing accessories stores.......... | 448 | 156 | 148 | 216 | 234 | 27 | 28 | 1,644 | 1,664 |
| Sporting goods, hobby, musical instrument, and book stores..................................... | 451 | 57 | 48 | 81 | 79 | 9 | 9 | 619 | 535 |
| General merchandise stores....................... | 452 | 46 | 49 | 577 | 641 | 54 | 58 | 2,763 | 2,773 |
| Miscellaneous store retailers..................... | 453 | 122 | 107 | 104 | 98 | 14 | 14 | 792 | 713 |
| Nonstore retailers.................................... | 454 | 59 | 64 | 290 | 386 | 23 | 27 | 621 | 600 |
| Transportation & warehousing [3]................... | 48-49 | 220 | 214 | 640 | 731 | 173 | 184 | 4,454 | 4,305 |
| Truck transportation................................. | 484 | 120 | 112 | 218 | 238 | 58 | 58 | 1,508 | 1,363 |
| Information................................................. | 51 | 142 | 138 | 1,072 | 1,238 | 229 | 269 | 3,497 | 3,321 |
| Publishing industries (except internet)........... | 511 | 31 | 28 | 282 | 272 | 81 | 80 | 1,093 | 876 |
| Motion picture & sound recording industries.... | 512 | 24 | 25 | 95 | 92 | 18 | 16 | 336 | 304 |
| Broadcasting (except internet)..................... | 515 | 10 | 10 | 100 | 127 | 18 | 20 | 295 | 278 |
| Telecommunications................................. | 517 | 52 | 51 | 491 | 546 | 75 | 76 | 1,251 | 1,134 |
| Data processing, hosting, and related services.............................................. | 518 | 17 | 15 | 67 | 108 | 26 | 41 | 394 | 497 |
| Other information services.......................... | 519 | 7 | 11 | 37 | 94 | 10 | 35 | 128 | 231 |
| Finance & insurance [4]................................ | 52 | 502 | 460 | 3,669 | 3,636 | 502 | 524 | 6,000 | 6,041 |
| Credit intermediation & related activities........ | 522 | 231 | 196 | 1,343 | 1,095 | 181 | 184 | 3,280 | 2,815 |
| Insurance carriers & related activities............ | 524 | 185 | 176 | 1,669 | 1,925 | 154 | 169 | 2,423 | 2,304 |
| Real estate & rental & leasing [4].................... | 53 | 384 | 354 | 485 | 488 | 85 | 85 | 2,188 | 1,924 |
| Professional, scientific, & technical services..... | 54 | 847 | 856 | 1,251 | 1,480 | 502 | 581 | 7,870 | 8,204 |
| Management of companies & enterprises........ | 55 | 51 | 54 | 104 | 116 | 250 | 309 | 2,664 | 3,082 |
| Admin/support waste management/remediation services.............................................. | 56 | 395 | 386 | 631 | 673 | 301 | 329 | 10,251 | 9,774 |
| Administrative & support services............... | 561 | 374 | 363 | 556 | 594 | 285 | 311 | 9,865 | 9,406 |
| Waste management & remediation services.... | 562 | 22 | 23 | 75 | 79 | 17 | 18 | 386 | 368 |
| Educational services.................................... | 61 | 61 | 68 | 45 | 53 | 14 | 17 | 540 | 642 |
| Health care and social assistance................. | 62 | 785 | 831 | 1,668 | 2,040 | 663 | 801 | 16,792 | 18,415 |
| Ambulatory health care services................. | 621 | 548 | 583 | 668 | 814 | 275 | 340 | 5,703 | 6,475 |
| Hospitals............................................... | 622 | 7 | 6 | 703 | 877 | 265 | 317 | 5,529 | 5,751 |
| Nursing & residential care facilities.............. | 623 | 76 | 81 | 169 | 203 | 75 | 87 | 3,071 | 3,364 |
| Social assistance.................................... | 624 | 154 | 161 | 128 | 146 | 48 | 58 | 2,489 | 2,824 |
| Arts, entertainment, & recreation................... | 71 | 125 | 125 | 189 | 201 | 58 | 64 | 2,061 | 2,082 |
| Performing arts, spectator sports, & related industries................................. | 711 | 44 | 46 | 78 | 86 | 28 | 32 | 438 | 434 |
| Museums, historical sites, & like institutions.... | 712 | 7 | 7 | 13 | 14 | 4 | 4 | 130 | 135 |
| Amusement, gambling, & recreation industries........................................... | 713 | 74 | 72 | 98 | 101 | 27 | 28 | 1,494 | 1,513 |
| Accommodation & food services................... | 72 | 634 | 662 | 614 | 708 | 171 | 196 | 11,601 | 12,008 |
| Accommodation...................................... | 721 | 63 | 64 | 180 | 196 | 46 | 50 | 1,971 | 1,950 |
| Food services & drinking places................. | 722 | 572 | 599 | 433 | 512 | 124 | 146 | 9,630 | 10,058 |
| Other services (except public administration).... | 81 | 540 | 530 | 405 | 427 | 99 | 108 | 3,479 | 3,431 |
| Repair & maintenance.............................. | 811 | 222 | 210 | 138 | 144 | 40 | 41 | 1,261 | 1,194 |
| Personal and laundry services.................... | 812 | 210 | 213 | 82 | 87 | 27 | 29 | 1,338 | 1,349 |
| Religious, grantmaking, civic, professional, and similar organizations........ | 813 | 108 | 107 | 185 | 196 | 32 | 38 | 880 | 887 |

[1] Based on North American Industry Classification System, 2007; see text, this section. [2] For pay period including March 12. [3] For detailed industries, see Table 1088. [4] For detailed industries, see Table 1194.

Source: U.S. Census Bureau, 2012 Economic Census, Table EC1200CCOMP1, "All sectors: Core Business Statistics Series: Comparative Statistics for the U.S. (2007 NAICS Basis): 2012 and 2007," <http://factfinder.census.gov>, accessed September 2016.

# Table 784. Nonemployer Establishments and Receipts by Industry: 2010 to 2017

[22,111 represents 22,111,000. Includes only firms subject to federal income tax. Nonemployers are businesses with no paid employees. Data originate chiefly from administrative records of the Internal Revenue Service; see Appendix III. Data for 2010 based on the North American Industry Classification System (NAICS), 2007; data for 2015 and 2016 based on NAICS 2012; and data for 2017 based on NAICS 2017]

| Kind of business | NAICS code | Establishments (1,000) | | | Receipts (mil. dol.) | | |
|---|---|---|---|---|---|---|---|
| | | 2010 | 2016 | 2017 | 2010 | 2016 | 2017 |
| **All industries**.......... | (X) | **22,111** | **24,813** | **25,702** | **950,814** | **1,165,668** | **1,231,393** |
| Agriculture, forestry, fishing and hunting.......... | 11 | 237 | 236 | 251 | 10,115 | 11,136 | 11,644 |
| Mining, quarrying, and oil and gas extraction.......... | 21 | 106 | 87 | 89 | 6,923 | 4,921 | 5,630 |
| Utilities.......... | 22 | 17 | 20 | 14 | 698 | 978 | 855 |
| Construction.......... | 23 | 2,424 | 2,471 | 2,494 | 120,151 | 150,825 | 159,580 |
| Manufacturing.......... | 31–33 | 318 | 349 | 348 | 14,572 | 17,337 | 17,964 |
| Wholesale trade.......... | 42 | 393 | 407 | 399 | 34,082 | 36,861 | 37,568 |
| Retail trade.......... | 44–45 | 1,822 | 2,004 | 2,093 | 75,720 | 87,804 | 90,617 |
| Transportation & warehousing.......... | 48–49 | 1,021 | 1,865 | 2,206 | 60,746 | 86,974 | 99,482 |
| Information.......... | 51 | 311 | 337 | 350 | 10,739 | 12,920 | 13,478 |
| Finance & insurance.......... | 52 | 717 | 717 | 732 | 50,626 | 54,267 | 58,376 |
| Real estate & rental & leasing.......... | 53 | 2,343 | 2,678 | 2,785 | 209,549 | 266,037 | 279,569 |
| Professional, scientific, & technical services.......... | 54 | 3,121 | 3,441 | 3,535 | 130,613 | 159,177 | 166,944 |
| Admin/support waste mgmt/remediation services...... | 56 | 1,937 | 2,083 | 2,143 | 39,111 | 47,214 | 50,102 |
| Educational services.......... | 61 | 567 | 718 | 742 | 7,703 | 10,197 | 10,803 |
| Health care & social assistance.......... | 62 | 1,935 | 1,954 | 1,941 | 57,686 | 65,605 | 68,026 |
| Arts, entertainment, & recreation.......... | 71 | 1,154 | 1,384 | 1,436 | 26,756 | 35,407 | 37,396 |
| Accommodation & food services.......... | 72 | 329 | 383 | 403 | 14,355 | 17,628 | 18,580 |
| Other services (except public administration).......... | 81 | 3,358 | 3,680 | 3,740 | 80,669 | 100,380 | 104,780 |

X Not applicable.

Source: U.S. Census Bureau, Nonemployer Statistics, "Geographic Area Series: Nonemployer Statistics for the U.S., States, Metropolitan Areas, and Counties," <https://data.census.gov/cedsci/>, accessed July 2019. See also <https://www.census.gov/programs-surveys/nonemployer-statistics.html>.

# Table 785. Establishments, Employees, and Payroll by Employment-Size Class: 1990 to 2016

[In units as noted (6,176 represents 6,176,000). Excludes self-employed individuals, employees of private households, railroad employees, agricultural production employees, and most government employees. Employees are for the week including March 12. Covers establishments with payroll. An establishment is a single physical location where business is conducted or where services or industrial operations are performed. For statement on methodology, see Appendix III]

| Employment-size class | Unit | 1990 | 2000 | 2005 | 2010 | 2013 | 2014 | 2015 | 2016 |
|---|---|---|---|---|---|---|---|---|---|
| **Establishments, total**.......... | 1,000 | **6,176** | **7,070** | **7,500** | **7,397** | **7,488** | **7,563** | **7,664** | **7,758** |
| Under 20 employees.......... | 1,000 | 5,354 | 6,069 | 6,468 | 6,408 | 6,440 | 6,492 | 6,559 | 6,627 |
| 20 to 99 employees.......... | 1,000 | 684 | 826 | 856 | 824 | 873 | 891 | 919 | 941 |
| 100 to 499 employees.......... | 1,000 | 122 | 157 | 157 | 148 | 156 | 161 | 166 | 169 |
| 500 to 999 employees.......... | 1,000 | 10 | 12 | 12 | 11 | 12 | 12 | 13 | 13 |
| 1,000 or more employees.......... | 1,000 | 6 | 7 | 7 | 7 | 7 | 7 | 7 | 8 |
| **Employees, total**.......... | 1,000 | **93,476** | **114,065** | **116,317** | **111,970** | **118,266** | **121,080** | **124,086** | **126,752** |
| Under 20 employees.......... | 1,000 | 24,373 | 27,569 | 28,874 | 28,958 | 29,128 | 29,379 | 29,406 | 29,815 |
| 20 to 99 employees.......... | 1,000 | 27,414 | 33,147 | 34,302 | 32,730 | 34,799 | 35,494 | 36,640 | 37,545 |
| 100 to 499 employees.......... | 1,000 | 22,926 | 29,736 | 29,591 | 27,718 | 29,545 | 30,460 | 31,416 | 32,050 |
| 500 to 999 employees.......... | 1,000 | 6,551 | 8,291 | 8,053 | 7,331 | 8,063 | 8,270 | 8,550 | 8,647 |
| 1,000 or more employees.......... | 1,000 | 12,212 | 15,322 | 15,497 | 15,233 | 16,732 | 17,477 | 18,074 | 18,695 |
| **Annual payroll, total**.......... | Bil. dol. | **2,104** | **3,879** | **4,483** | **4,941** | **5,622** | **5,940** | **6,253** | **6,435** |
| Under 20 employees.......... | Bil. dol. | 485 | 818 | 970 | 1,057 | 1,142 | 1,187 | 1,235 | 1,262 |
| 20 to 99 employees.......... | Bil. dol. | 547 | 1,006 | 1,177 | 1,281 | 1,435 | 1,505 | 1,584 | 1,630 |
| 100 to 499 employees.......... | Bil. dol. | 518 | 1,031 | 1,176 | 1,280 | 1,469 | 1,565 | 1,651 | 1,697 |
| 500 to 999 employees.......... | Bil. dol. | 174 | 336 | 376 | 410 | 486 | 516 | 550 | 563 |
| 1,000 or more employees.......... | Bil. dol. | 381 | 690 | 784 | 913 | 1,090 | 1,167 | 1,235 | 1,283 |

Source: U.S. Census Bureau, County Business Patterns, "Geographic Area Series: County Business Patterns by Employment Size Class," <http://factfinder.census.gov>, accessed April 2018. See also <https://www.census.gov/programs-surveys/cbp.html>.

## Table 786. Employer Firms by Industry, Owner's Education and Age, and Whether Family-Owned: 2016

[In thousands, (5,602 represents 5,602,000). Includes all U.S. firms with paid employees operating during 2016 with receipts of $1,000 or more and classified in the 2012 North American Industry Classification System (NAICS) sectors 11 through 99, except for NAICS 111, 112, 482, 491, 521, 525, 813, 814, and 92. Firms with more than one domestic establishment are counted in each industry in which they operate, but only once in the total. Additionally, detail may not add to total due to nonresponse on selected survey items and because the survey asked for information for up to four persons owning the largest percentage(s) of the business. Based on the 2016 Annual Survey of Entrepreneurs]

| Industry | NAICS code | Total firms | Owner's highest level of education | | | | | Age of owner | | | Family owned firms |
|---|---|---|---|---|---|---|---|---|---|---|---|
| | | | High school or less | Some college, no degree | Associate's or technical degree | Bachelor's degree | Advanced degree | Under 35 | 35 to 64 | 65 or over | |
| **All industries** | (X) | 5,602 | 1,187 | 756 | 596 | 1,505 | 1,178 | 311 | 3,887 | 1,024 | 1,036 |
| Agriculture, forestry, fishing and hunting | 11 | 27 | 11 | 4 | 3 | 6 | 2 | 2 | 18 | 7 | 8 |
| Mining, quarrying, and oil and gas extraction | 21 | 22 | 7 | 4 | 3 | 8 | 3 | 2 | 16 | 7 | 6 |
| Utilities | 22 | 6 | (Z) | (Z) | (Z) | 1 | (Z) | (Z) | 2 | 1 | (Z) |
| Construction | 23 | 665 | 241 | 120 | 122 | 127 | 30 | 38 | 508 | 94 | 140 |
| Manufacturing | 31-33 | 250 | 72 | 46 | 37 | 88 | 32 | 12 | 194 | 69 | 64 |
| Wholesale trade | 42 | 306 | 66 | 52 | 31 | 125 | 39 | 13 | 222 | 78 | 65 |
| Retail trade | 44-45 | 650 | 189 | 112 | 74 | 192 | 67 | 42 | 462 | 131 | 152 |
| Transportation & warehousing | 48-49 | 182 | 68 | 29 | 21 | 32 | 9 | 11 | 120 | 29 | 36 |
| Information | 51 | 74 | 7 | 9 | 4 | 31 | 16 | 5 | 48 | 14 | 11 |
| Finance & insurance | 52 | 235 | 23 | 32 | 16 | 106 | 42 | 12 | 154 | 52 | 36 |
| Real estate & rental & leasing | 53 | 290 | 47 | 45 | 26 | 114 | 51 | 13 | 183 | 86 | 61 |
| Professional, scientific, & technical services | 54 | 800 | 40 | 62 | 41 | 267 | 361 | 37 | 574 | 161 | 109 |
| Management of companies & enterprises | 55 | 26 | 3 | 2 | 1 | 10 | 4 | 1 | 13 | 6 | 4 |
| Administrative & support and waste management & remediation services | 56 | 334 | 89 | 59 | 39 | 87 | 32 | 21 | 232 | 52 | 64 |
| Educational services | 61 | 91 | 6 | 8 | 5 | 22 | 18 | 5 | 44 | 10 | 12 |
| Health care & social assistance | 62 | 646 | 22 | 21 | 22 | 58 | 395 | 26 | 404 | 88 | 64 |
| Arts, entertainment, & recreation | 71 | 121 | 16 | 14 | 8 | 39 | 15 | 8 | 67 | 17 | 18 |
| Accommodation & food services | 72 | 518 | 163 | 79 | 52 | 142 | 47 | 40 | 368 | 75 | 112 |
| Other services (except public administration) | 81 | 385 | 118 | 59 | 90 | 66 | 21 | 24 | 273 | 56 | 77 |

X Not applicable. Z Less than 500.

Source: U.S. Census Bureau, 2016 Annual Survey of Entrepreneurs, Tables "SE1600CSA01," "SE1600CSCB02," "SE1600CSCBO07," and "SE1600CSCBO08," <http://factfinder.census.gov>, accessed August 2018.

## Table 787. Employer Firms by Industry and Whether Franchised: 2016

[In thousands, except as noted (5,601.8 represents 5,601,800). Includes all U.S. firms with paid employees operating during 2016 with receipts of $1,000 or more and classified in the 2012 North American Industry Classification System (NAICS) sectors 11 through 99, except for NAICS 111, 112, 482, 491, 521, 525, 813, 814, and 92. Firms with more than one domestic establishment are counted in each industry in which they operate, but only once in the U.S. industries total. Based on the 2016 Annual Survey of Entrepreneurs]

| Industry | NAICS code | Total firms [1] | All or part of the business operated as a franchise | | | Did not operate as a franchise | | |
|---|---|---|---|---|---|---|---|---|
| | | | Firms | Paid employees [2] | Payroll (mil. dol.) | Firms | Paid employees [2] | Payroll (mil. dol.) |
| **All industries** | (X) | 5,601.8 | 188.0 | 6,360 | 189,927 | 3,322.8 | 53,584 | 2,764,590 |
| Agriculture, forestry, fishing and hunting | 11 | 27.2 | 0.2 | 4 | 115 | 16.8 | 166 | 5,414 |
| Mining, quarrying, and oil and gas extraction | 21 | 22.4 | 0.4 | 3 | 128 | 14.4 | 271 | 21,561 |
| Utilities | 22 | 6.1 | 0.1 | ([3]) | (S) | 2.0 | 71 | 6,356 |
| Construction | 23 | 665.4 | 8.4 | 81 | 3,913 | 422.9 | 4,074 | 235,931 |
| Manufacturing | 31-33 | 250.0 | 4.0 | 94 | 4,320 | 158.7 | 5,813 | 305,605 |
| Wholesale trade | 42 | 306.1 | 5.2 | 129 | 6,630 | 196.5 | 3,281 | 203,927 |
| Retail trade | 44-45 | 650.3 | 37.5 | 974 | 36,720 | 365.6 | 5,601 | 155,104 |
| Transportation & warehousing | 48-49 | 182.2 | 4.4 | ([4]) | (S) | 104.8 | 1,889 | 89,738 |
| Information | 51 | 73.7 | 0.8 | 261 | 21,552 | 41.9 | 1,055 | 82,847 |
| Finance & insurance | 52 | 235.4 | 9.2 | 104 | 7,285 | 151.9 | 3,216 | 286,753 |
| Real estate & rental & leasing | 53 | 290.2 | 7.9 | 130 | 4,983 | 176.1 | 1,089 | 57,676 |
| Professional, scientific, & technical services | 54 | 800.2 | 8.1 | 185 | 3,606 | 533.9 | 4,866 | 389,663 |
| Management of companies and enterprises | 55 | 25.8 | 2.0 | 126 | 10,668 | 12.2 | 1,190 | 124,035 |
| Administrative & support and waste management & remediation services | 56 | 334.3 | 12.4 | 342 | 9,314 | 200.0 | 5,581 | 227,192 |
| Educational services | 61 | 90.8 | 4.0 | 40 | 587 | 39.1 | 559 | 19,786 |
| Health care & social assistance | 62 | 646.0 | 10.2 | 275 | 6,108 | 383.3 | 7,857 | 379,709 |
| Arts, entertainment, & recreation | 71 | 121.3 | 5.9 | 74 | 3,874 | 56.8 | 789 | 27,177 |
| Accommodation & food services | 72 | 517.7 | 57.9 | 3,001 | 47,038 | 230.5 | 4,706 | 97,457 |
| Other services (except public administration) | 81 | 385.4 | 12.7 | 179 | 4,684 | 229.8 | 1,481 | 48,139 |

X Not applicable. S Figure does not meet publication standards. [1] Includes firms that did not indicate franchise status. [2] For pay period ending March 12. [3] 250 to 499 employees. [4] 100,000 employees or more.

Source: U.S. Census Bureau, 2016 Annual Survey of Entrepreneurs, Table "SE1600CSCB06," <http://factfinder.census.gov>, accessed August 2018.

## Table 788. Franchised Businesses by Type of Business: 2012

[129,242 represents $129,242,000,000. Data shown for franchisor- and franchisee-owned establishments with paid employees. Covers franchised businesses with over 3,500 establishments. Data are based on the 2012 Economic Census, for details see Appendix III]

| Kind of business | 2012 NAICS code [1] | Number of establish-ments | Revenue (mil. dol.) | Annual payroll (mil. dol.) | Paid employees (number) |
|---|---|---|---|---|---|
| Limited-service restaurants............................. | 722513 | 122,042 | 129,242 | 31,726 | 2,630,074 |
| Gasoline stations with convenience stores............................ | 447110 | 32,845 | 158,109 | 4,267 | 251,960 |
| Full-service restaurants............................ | 722511 | 28,940 | 36,070 | 11,828 | 879,771 |
| Hotels (except casino hotels) and motels............................ | 721110 | 23,305 | 51,556 | 11,645 | 601,424 |
| New car dealers........................... | 441110 | 21,292 | 672,550 | 47,524 | 973,745 |
| Snack and nonalcoholic beverage bars.......................... | 722515 | 16,494 | 9,614 | 2,275 | 195,342 |
| Offices of real estate agents and brokers.......................... | 531210 | 14,588 | 16,241 | 1,406 | 41,156 |
| Fitness and recreational sports centers.......................... | 713940 | 7,340 | 2,584 | 729 | 60,957 |
| Beauty salons........................ | 812112 | 6,326 | 1,873 | 839 | 49,174 |
| Janitorial services........................ | 561720 | 6,194 | 3,987 | 1,457 | 81,833 |
| Optical goods stores........................ | 446130 | 5,982 | 5,492 | 928 | 40,343 |
| Tax preparation services........................ | 541213 | 5,702 | 1,331 | 395 | 55,215 |
| Other gasoline stations........................ | 447190 | 5,212 | 32,855 | 918 | 45,866 |
| General automotive repair........................ | 811111 | 3,956 | 2,961 | 797 | 23,484 |
| Convenience stores........................ | 445120 | 3,894 | 5,713 | 507 | 27,599 |

[1] Based on the 2012 North American Industry Classification System (NAICS); see text, this section.

Source: U.S. Census Bureau, 2012 Economic Census, Table "EC1200CFRA1: Economic Census: Core Business Statistics Series, 2012: Franchise Status for Selected Industries and States: 2012," <http://factfinder.census.gov>, accessed February 2016.

## Table 789. Employer Firms by Industry and Amount and Source of Capital to Start or Acquire Business: 2016

[In thousands (5,602 represents 5,602,000). Includes all U.S. firms with paid employees operating during 2016 with receipts of $1,000 or more and classified in the 2012 North American Industry Classification System (NAICS) sectors 11 through 99, except for NAICS 111, 112, 482, 491, 521, 525, 813, 814, and 92. Firms with more than one domestic establishment are counted in each industry in which they operate, but only once in the U.S. industries total. Based on the 2016 Annual Survey of Entrepreneurs]

| Industry | NAICS code | Total firms [2] | Source of capital [1] | | | Amount of capital | | | | |
|---|---|---|---|---|---|---|---|---|---|---|
| | | | Personal savings, assets, or home equity loan | Credit cards [3] | Busi-ness loan [4] | Under $10,000 | $10,000 to $49,000 | $50,000 to $249,999 | $250,000 to $999,999 | $1 mil-lion & over |
| **All industries**.................... | (X) | 5,602 | 2,788 | 493 | 817 | 832 | 727 | 691 | 236 | 78 |
| Agriculture, forestry, fishing and hunting.......................... | 11 | 27 | 13 | 2 | 6 | 3 | 3 | 4 | 1 | 1 |
| Mining, quarrying, and oil & gas extraction...................... | 21 | 22 | 10 | 1 | 4 | 2 | 2 | 2 | 1 | 1 |
| Utilities................................ | 22 | 6 | 1 | (Z) | (Z) | (Z) | (Z) | (Z) | (Z) | (Z) |
| Construction.......................... | 23 | 665 | 345 | 69 | 65 | 141 | 96 | 50 | 11 | 3 |
| Manufacturing......................... | 31-33 | 250 | 127 | 21 | 47 | 26 | 30 | 31 | 14 | 7 |
| Wholesale trade..................... | 42 | 306 | 154 | 24 | 40 | 38 | 37 | 39 | 15 | 6 |
| Retail trade.......................... | 44-45 | 650 | 337 | 59 | 122 | 58 | 85 | 114 | 36 | 10 |
| Transportation & warehousing.... | 48-49 | 182 | 81 | 17 | 29 | 21 | 30 | 22 | 5 | 2 |
| Information.......................... | 51 | 74 | 33 | 6 | 6 | 11 | 7 | 7 | 3 | 2 |
| Finance & insurance............... | 52 | 235 | 125 | 22 | 24 | 36 | 34 | 30 | 8 | 5 |
| Real estate & rental & leasing..... | 53 | 290 | 140 | 14 | 31 | 50 | 30 | 25 | 12 | 8 |
| Professional, scientific, & technical services................. | 54 | 800 | 436 | 73 | 70 | 203 | 114 | 66 | 16 | 6 |
| Management of companies and enterprises...................... | 55 | 26 | 7 | (Z) | 3 | 1 | 1 | 1 | 1 | 2 |
| Administrative & support and waste management & remediation services.............. | 56 | 334 | 170 | 34 | 35 | 74 | 48 | 29 | 6 | 2 |
| Educational services.............. | 61 | 91 | 35 | 7 | 7 | 12 | 11 | 8 | 2 | (Z) |
| Health care & social assistance... | 62 | 646 | 273 | 52 | 147 | 69 | 72 | 98 | 44 | 8 |
| Arts, entertainment, & recreation......................... | 71 | 121 | 47 | 8 | 13 | 15 | 9 | 11 | 6 | 3 |
| Accommodation & food services.. | 72 | 518 | 256 | 43 | 100 | 20 | 54 | 100 | 39 | 12 |
| Other services (except public administration)............. | 81 | 385 | 202 | 40 | 66 | 51 | 62 | 54 | 15 | 3 |

X Not applicable. Z Less than 500. [1] Not all sources of capital are shown separately. [2] Includes firms that did not respond to survey questions regarding amount and source of capital. [3] Includes personal and business credit cards carrying balances. [4] Includes loans from federal/state/local government, banks/financial institutions (including government guaranteed business loans), and loans/investments from family and friends.

Source: U.S. Census Bureau, 2016 Annual Survey of Entrepreneurs, Tables "SE1600CSCB07" and "SE1600CSCB08," <http://factfinder.census.gov>, accessed August 2018.

# Table 790. Establishments, Employees, and Payroll by Employment-Size Class and Industry: 2000 to 2016

[Establishments and employees in thousands (7,070.0 represents 7,070,000); payroll in billions of dollars (3,879 represents $3,879,000,000,000). See headnote, Table 785. Data for 2000 based on the North American Industry Classification System (NAICS), 1997; 2010 data based on NAICS 2007; and 2016 data based on NAICS 2012. See text, this section]

| Industry | NAICS code | 2000, total | 2010, total | 2016 | | | | | |
|---|---|---|---|---|---|---|---|---|---|
| | | | | Total | Under 20 employees | 20 to 99 employees | 100 to 499 employees | 500 to 999 or employees | 1,000 more employees |
| **Establishments, total** [1] | (X) | 7,070.0 | 7,396.6 | 7,757.8 | 6,627.4 | 941.3 | 168.8 | 12.7 | 7.7 |
| Agriculture, forestry, fishing & hunting | 113–115 | 26.1 | 21.7 | 22.6 | 21.1 | 1.3 | 0.2 | (Z) | (Z) |
| Mining, quarrying, & oil and gas extraction | 21 | 23.7 | 27.1 | 27.2 | 21.9 | 4.4 | 0.9 | 0.1 | (Z) |
| Utilities | 22 | 17.3 | 17.6 | 18.2 | 12.8 | 4.1 | 1.1 | 0.1 | 0.1 |
| Construction | 23 | 709.6 | 682.7 | 696.7 | 634.3 | 54.8 | 7.1 | 0.4 | 0.1 |
| Manufacturing | 31–33 | 354.5 | 300.0 | 291.5 | 202.2 | 64.5 | 21.8 | 2.1 | 0.9 |
| Wholesale trade | 42 | 446.2 | 414.6 | 412.5 | 349.7 | 53.7 | 8.4 | 0.6 | 0.2 |
| Retail trade | 44–45 | 1,113.6 | 1,068.0 | 1,069.1 | 907.2 | 131.9 | 29.7 | 0.3 | (Z) |
| Transportation and warehousing | 48–49 | 190.0 | 208.5 | 231.0 | 192.7 | 29.9 | 7.3 | 0.8 | 0.3 |
| Information | 51 | 133.6 | 135.4 | 146.4 | 119.9 | 20.4 | 5.3 | 0.6 | 0.2 |
| Finance and insurance | 52 | 423.7 | 473.5 | 477.0 | 437.5 | 31.2 | 6.6 | 1.0 | 0.6 |
| Real estate and rental and leasing | 53 | 300.2 | 347.3 | 390.5 | 373.8 | 14.9 | 1.6 | 0.1 | (Z) |
| Professional, scientific, & technical services | 54 | 722.7 | 851.5 | 903.5 | 831.8 | 59.7 | 10.8 | 0.8 | 0.5 |
| Management of companies and enterprises | 55 | 47.4 | 50.9 | 55.4 | 36.3 | 12.8 | 5.1 | 0.8 | 0.5 |
| Administrative/support waste management/ remediation services | 56 | 351.5 | 381.8 | 409.5 | 345.0 | 46.6 | 15.0 | 1.7 | 1.1 |
| Educational services | 61 | 68.0 | 90.1 | 103.4 | 79.8 | 18.9 | 3.8 | 0.4 | 0.5 |
| Health care and social assistance | 62 | 658.6 | 812.9 | 890.5 | 742.6 | 117.5 | 26.3 | 2.1 | 2.1 |
| Arts, entertainment, and recreation | 71 | 103.8 | 123.2 | 137.2 | 115.0 | 18.2 | 3.6 | 0.2 | 0.1 |
| Accommodation and food services | 72 | 542.4 | 644.0 | 703.5 | 481.8 | 210.6 | 10.5 | 0.5 | 0.2 |
| Other services [2] | 81 | 723.3 | 725.5 | 754.2 | 704.3 | 45.8 | 3.8 | 0.2 | 0.1 |
| Unclassified establishments | 99 | 99.0 | 20.5 | 17.8 | 17.7 | (Z) | – | – | – |
| **Employees, total** [1] | (X) | 114,065 | 111,970 | 126,752.2 | 29,815.2 | 37,544.8 | 32,049.5 | 8,647.5 | 18,695.2 |
| Agriculture, forestry, fishing & hunting | 113–115 | 184 | 156 | 160.4 | 72.2 | 49.5 | 27.9 | 4.9 | 5.9 |
| Mining, quarrying, & oil and gas extraction | 21 | 456 | 582 | 587.0 | 103.9 | 174.9 | 178.7 | 50.9 | 78.7 |
| Utilities | 22 | 655 | 638 | 638.9 | 69.9 | 179.6 | 214.5 | 81.5 | 93.3 |
| Construction | 23 | 6,573 | 5,389 | 6,311.3 | 2,326.5 | 2,125 | 1,294.6 | 253.2 | 311.9 |
| Manufacturing | 31–33 | 16,474 | 10,863 | 11,590.4 | 1,146.2 | 2,836.9 | 4,379.3 | 1,406.1 | 1,821.9 |
| Wholesale trade | 42 | 6,112 | 5,599 | 6,110.7 | 1,680.0 | 2,125 | 1,567.1 | 381.4 | 357.2 |
| Retail trade | 44–45 | 14,841 | 14,497 | 15,967.9 | 5,022.1 | 5,226.3 | 5,484.3 | 161.1 | 74.0 |
| Transportation and warehousing | 48–49 | 3,790 | 4,012 | 4,729.7 | 770.9 | 1,242.6 | 1,410.0 | 539.4 | 766.7 |
| Information | 51 | 3,546 | 3,124 | 3,448.0 | 517.4 | 856.1 | 1,051.5 | 422.4 | 600.5 |
| Finance and insurance | 52 | 5,963 | 5,929 | 6,336.8 | 1,840.5 | 1,219.1 | 1,360.3 | 664.8 | 1,252.1 |
| Real estate and rental and leasing | 53 | 1,942 | 1,946 | 2,111.4 | 1,152.3 | 558.4 | 295.1 | 55.4 | 50.3 |
| Professional, scientific, & technical services | 54 | 6,816 | 7,822 | 8,799.9 | 2,743.2 | 2,358.1 | 2,071.4 | 565.4 | 1,061.8 |
| Management of companies and enterprises | 55 | 2,874 | 2,833 | 3,380.4 | 197.6 | 578.8 | 1,066.5 | 530.9 | 1,006.7 |
| Administrative/support waste management/ remediation services | 56 | 9,138 | 8,977 | 11,628.5 | 1,322.8 | 2,016.4 | 3,048.5 | 1,190.2 | 4,051.5 |
| Educational services | 61 | 2,532 | 3,274 | 3,677.3 | 390.4 | 799.1 | 716.7 | 317.6 | 1,453.5 |
| Health care and social assistance | 62 | 14,109 | 17,788 | 19,735.7 | 3,847.4 | 4,736.2 | 4,886.7 | 1,434.0 | 4,831.4 |
| Arts, entertainment, and recreation | 71 | 1,741 | 2,004 | 2,311.4 | 419.8 | 771.7 | 685.9 | 159.7 | 274.4 |
| Accommodation and food services | 72 | 9,881 | 11,312 | 13,704.0 | 3,243.7 | 8,022.5 | 1,659.1 | 313.3 | 465.4 |
| Other services [2] | 81 | 5,293 | 5,204 | 5,499.2 | 2,925.9 | 1,668.7 | 651.4 | 115.3 | 137.9 |
| Unclassified establishments | 99 | 144 | (NA) | 23.2 | 22.4 | 0.8 | – | – | – |
| **Annual payroll, total** [1] | (X) | 3,879 | 4,941 | 6,435.1 | 1,262.5 | 1,629.6 | 1,696.7 | 563.0 | 1,283.4 |
| Agriculture, forestry, fishing & hunting | 113–115 | 5 | 5 | 6.6 | 3.1 | 2.2 | 1.0 | 0.2 | 0.1 |
| Mining, quarrying, & oil and gas extraction | 21 | 22 | 46 | 49.4 | 7.0 | 13.3 | 16.3 | 4.8 | 8.0 |
| Utilities | 22 | 41 | 55 | 65.4 | 5.6 | 16.6 | 21.7 | 10.1 | 11.4 |
| Construction | 23 | 240 | 261 | 371.3 | 110.4 | 130.7 | 90.7 | 18.7 | 20.7 |
| Manufacturing | 31–33 | 644 | 550 | 663.7 | 49.9 | 143.7 | 244.1 | 86.4 | 139.6 |
| Wholesale trade | 42 | 270 | 339 | 427.9 | 99.6 | 136.4 | 111.1 | 34.9 | 45.9 |
| Retail trade | 44–45 | 303 | 359 | 437.7 | 130.1 | 141.2 | 156.7 | 6.0 | 3.7 |
| Transportation and warehousing | 48–49 | 126 | 167 | 229.2 | 34.5 | 57.1 | 64.9 | 25.4 | 47.2 |
| Information | 51 | 209 | 224 | 317.5 | 35.4 | 61.5 | 100.1 | 47.0 | 73.5 |
| Finance and insurance | 52 | 347 | 472 | 611.7 | 122.3 | 130.0 | 148.8 | 66.8 | 143.9 |
| Real estate and rental and leasing | 53 | 59 | 80 | 110.5 | 53.6 | 31.9 | 18.3 | 3.5 | 3.1 |
| Professional, scientific, & technical services | 54 | 362 | 543 | 720.3 | 175.1 | 194.3 | 195.0 | 56.3 | 99.5 |
| Management of companies and enterprises | 55 | 211 | 282 | 367.2 | 22.4 | 56.5 | 112.5 | 59.4 | 116.4 |
| Administrative/support waste management/ remediation services | 56 | 210 | 304 | 460.4 | 57.8 | 81.9 | 103.5 | 37.8 | 179.5 |
| Educational services | 61 | 62 | 110 | 138.6 | 10.5 | 25.4 | 28.5 | 9.8 | 64.4 |
| Health care and social assistance | 62 | 431 | 753 | 940.0 | 182.8 | 198.2 | 190.8 | 71.8 | 296.4 |
| Arts, entertainment, and recreation | 71 | 43 | 62 | 81.1 | 18.6 | 17.9 | 26.2 | 9.1 | 9.4 |
| Accommodation and food services | 72 | 126 | 186 | 261.3 | 59.9 | 136.8 | 39.8 | 9.3 | 15.5 |
| Other services [2] | 81 | 110 | 140 | 174.9 | 83.4 | 54.0 | 26.7 | 5.6 | 5.2 |
| Unclassified establishments | 99 | 4 | (Z) | 0.5 | 0.5 | (Z) | – | – | – |

– Represents zero. NA Not available. X Not applicable. Z Less than 50 establishments, 500 employees, or $500 million. [1] Totals for 2000 include auxiliaries. Beginning 2010, cases previously classified under NAICS code 95 (auxiliaries) are coded in the operating NAICS sector of the establishment. [2] Except public administration.

Source: U.S. Census Bureau, County Business Patterns, "Geographic Area Series: County Business Patterns by Employment Size Class," <http://factfinder.census.gov>, accessed April 2018. See also <https://www.census.gov/programs-surveys/cbp.html>.

# Table 791. Employer Firms, Employment, and Annual Payroll by Employment Size of Firm and Industry: 2016

[5,955 represents 5,955,000. A firm is an aggregation of all establishments owned by a parent company (within a geographic location and/or industry) with some annual payroll. A firm may be a single location or it can include multiple locations. Employment is measured in March and payroll is annual leading to some firms with zero employment. Numbers in parentheses represent 2012 North American Industry Classification System codes; see text, this section]

| Industry and data type | Unit | Total | All industries—employment size of firm | | | | | | |
|---|---|---|---|---|---|---|---|---|---|
| | | | 0 to 4 | 5 to 9 | 10 to 19 | 20 to 99 | 100 to 499 | Less than 500 | 500 or more |
| **Total, all industries [1]:** | | | | | | | | | |
| Firms | 1,000 | 5,955 | 3,665 | 1,014 | 627 | 538 | 91 | 5,935 | 20 |
| Employment | 1,000 | 126,752 | 5,923 | 6,682 | 8,433 | 21,094 | 17,784 | 59,915 | 66,837 |
| Annual payroll | Bil. dol. | 6,435 | 268 | 249 | 329 | 899 | 871 | 2,616 | 3,819 |
| **Construction (23):** | | | | | | | | | |
| Firms | 1,000 | 683 | 455 | 109 | 63 | 49 | 6 | 682 | 1 |
| Employment | 1,000 | 6,311 | 709 | 715 | 843 | 1,861 | 1,069 | 5,197 | 1,115 |
| Annual payroll | Bil. dol. | 371 | 32 | 31 | 43 | 111 | 72 | 289 | 83 |
| **Manufacturing (31–33):** | | | | | | | | | |
| Firms | 1,000 | 250 | 103 | 46 | 38 | 47 | 12 | 246 | 4 |
| Employment | 1,000 | 11,590 | 189 | 309 | 517 | 1,915 | 2,178 | 5,108 | 6,482 |
| Annual payroll | Bil. dol. | 664 | 9 | 12 | 22 | 92 | 113 | 247 | 417 |
| **Wholesale trade (42):** | | | | | | | | | |
| Firms | 1,000 | 303 | 173 | 50 | 35 | 34 | 8 | 300 | 3 |
| Employment | 1,000 | 6,111 | 290 | 332 | 464 | 1,257 | 1,102 | 3,446 | 2,665 |
| Annual payroll | Bil. dol. | 428 | 16 | 18 | 26 | 76 | 70 | 206 | 222 |
| **Retail trade (44–45):** | | | | | | | | | |
| Firms | 1,000 | 651 | 388 | 133 | 71 | 48 | 8 | 649 | 2 |
| Employment | 1,000 | 15,968 | 715 | 878 | 936 | 1,831 | 1,219 | 5,579 | 10,389 |
| Annual payroll | Bil. dol. | 438 | 20 | 23 | 27 | 65 | 49 | 183 | 255 |
| **Transportation & warehousing (48–49):** | | | | | | | | | |
| Firms | 1,000 | 181 | 118 | 25 | 17 | 15 | 4 | 179 | 2 |
| Employment | 1,000 | 4,730 | 171 | 164 | 226 | 576 | 530 | 1,667 | 3,063 |
| Annual payroll | Bil. dol. | 229 | 7 | 6 | 9 | 25 | 24 | 70 | 159 |
| **Information (51):** | | | | | | | | | |
| Firms | 1,000 | 76 | 47 | 11 | 7 | 7 | 2 | 75 | 1 |
| Employment | 1,000 | 3,448 | 67 | 70 | 98 | 296 | 376 | 907 | 2,541 |
| Annual payroll | Bil. dol. | 318 | 5 | 4 | 6 | 20 | 31 | 66 | 251 |
| **Finance & insurance (52):** | | | | | | | | | |
| Firms | 1,000 | 238 | 171 | 35 | 13 | 13 | 4 | 236 | 2 |
| Employment | 1,000 | 6,337 | 296 | 223 | 177 | 515 | 708 | 1,920 | 4,417 |
| Annual payroll | Bil. dol. | 612 | 16 | 13 | 14 | 45 | 66 | 154 | 457 |
| **Professional, scientific and technical services (54):** | | | | | | | | | |
| Firms | 1,000 | 806 | 592 | 103 | 57 | 42 | 8 | 802 | 3 |
| Employment | 1,000 | 8,800 | 858 | 674 | 760 | 1,595 | 1,294 | 5,182 | 3,618 |
| Annual payroll | Bil. dol. | 720 | 52 | 39 | 50 | 123 | 111 | 376 | 344 |
| **Management of companies and enterprises (55):** | | | | | | | | | |
| Firms | 1,000 | 27 | 3 | 1 | 1 | 6 | 9 | 19 | 8 |
| Employment | 1,000 | 3,380 | 3 | 3 | 6 | 71 | 318 | 401 | 2,979 |
| Annual payroll | Bil. dol. | 367 | 1 | (Z) | 1 | 5 | 26 | 32 | 335 |
| **Administrative & support and waste management & remediation services (56):** | | | | | | | | | |
| Firms | 1,000 | 341 | 217 | 51 | 31 | 29 | 8 | 337 | 4 |
| Employment | 1,000 | 11,629 | 324 | 334 | 418 | 1,166 | 1,448 | 3,690 | 7,938 |
| Annual payroll | Bil. dol. | 460 | 15 | 12 | 16 | 46 | 50 | 138 | 322 |
| **Educational services (61):** | | | | | | | | | |
| Firms | 1,000 | 92 | 45 | 15 | 12 | 15 | 4 | 90 | 1 |
| Employment | 1,000 | 3,677 | 69 | 98 | 165 | 635 | 663 | 1,631 | 2,047 |
| Annual payroll | Bil. dol. | 139 | 2 | 2 | 4 | 20 | 26 | 54 | 85 |
| **Health care and social assistance (62):** | | | | | | | | | |
| Firms | 1,000 | 662 | 346 | 141 | 85 | 68 | 18 | 657 | 4 |
| Employment | 1,000 | 19,736 | 597 | 935 | 1,138 | 2,716 | 3,443 | 8,828 | 10,908 |
| Annual payroll | Bil. dol. | 940 | 33 | 40 | 49 | 109 | 127 | 358 | 582 |
| **Accommodation and food services (72):** | | | | | | | | | |
| Firms | 1,000 | 528 | 199 | 103 | 103 | 110 | 10 | 525 | 2 |
| Employment | 1,000 | 13,704 | 326 | 690 | 1,414 | 4,091 | 1,791 | 8,311 | 5,393 |
| Annual payroll | Bil. dol. | 261 | 10 | 11 | 23 | 73 | 33 | 149 | 112 |
| **Other services (except public administration) (81):** | | | | | | | | | |
| Firms | 1,000 | 690 | 442 | 137 | 65 | 41 | 5 | 689 | 1 |
| Employment | 1,000 | 5,499 | 810 | 891 | 853 | 1,470 | 666 | 4,690 | 809 |
| Annual payroll | Bil. dol. | 175 | 22 | 24 | 25 | 45 | 26 | 142 | 33 |

Z Less than $500 million. [1] Includes other industries, not shown separately.

Source: U.S. Census Bureau, Statistics of U.S. Businesses (SUSB), "2016 SUSB Annual Data Tables by Establishment Industry," <https://www.census.gov/data/tables/2016/econ/susb/2016-susb-annual.html>, accessed May 2019.

# Table 792. Employer Firms, Employment, and Payroll by Employment Size of Firm and State: 2015 and 2016

[5,901 represents 5,901,000. A firm is an aggregation of all establishments owned by a parent company (within a state) with some annual payroll. A firm may be a single location or it can include multiple locations]

| State | Employer firms (1,000) | | | | | Employment, 2016 (1,000) | | | Annual payroll, 2016 (bil. dol.) | | |
|---|---|---|---|---|---|---|---|---|---|---|---|
| | 2015 | | 2016 | | | | | | | | |
| | Total | Less than 20 employees | Total | Less than 20 employees | Less than 500 employees | Total | Less than 20 employees | Less than 500 employees | Total | Less than 20 employees | Less than 500 employees |
| U.S. | 5,901 | 5,266 | 5,955 | 5,306 | 5,935 | 126,752 | 21,038 | 59,915 | 6,435 | 846 | 2,616 |
| AL | 73 | 62 | 74 | 62 | 71 | 1,673 | 273 | 789 | 69 | 9 | 30 |
| AK | 17 | 15 | 17 | 15 | 16 | 266 | 57 | 141 | 15 | 3 | 7 |
| AZ | 105 | 89 | 107 | 91 | 104 | 2,379 | 349 | 1,039 | 106 | 14 | 41 |
| AR | 50 | 43 | 51 | 43 | 49 | 1,024 | 176 | 490 | 41 | 6 | 17 |
| CA | 740 | 657 | 752 | 667 | 746 | 14,600 | 2,579 | 7,129 | 887 | 121 | 358 |
| CO | 134 | 117 | 136 | 119 | 133 | 2,318 | 424 | 1,117 | 120 | 18 | 50 |
| CT | 72 | 61 | 72 | 60 | 69 | 1,534 | 258 | 750 | 95 | 12 | 38 |
| DE | 20 | 16 | 20 | 16 | 19 | 400 | 65 | 188 | 21 | 3 | 8 |
| DC | 18 | 13 | 18 | 13 | 17 | 527 | 58 | 247 | 40 | 4 | 17 |
| FL | 436 | 395 | 445 | 403 | 440 | 8,170 | 1,354 | 3,398 | 363 | 52 | 137 |
| GA | 175 | 151 | 177 | 153 | 173 | 3,804 | 578 | 1,638 | 183 | 22 | 67 |
| HI | 25 | 21 | 25 | 21 | 24 | 528 | 89 | 275 | 23 | 4 | 11 |
| ID | 38 | 32 | 38 | 33 | 37 | 562 | 128 | 316 | 22 | 4 | 11 |
| IL | 256 | 222 | 257 | 222 | 252 | 5,513 | 833 | 2,486 | 295 | 36 | 117 |
| IN | 109 | 91 | 109 | 91 | 105 | 2,720 | 397 | 1,222 | 117 | 14 | 46 |
| IA | 62 | 53 | 63 | 53 | 61 | 1,354 | 220 | 652 | 57 | 7 | 25 |
| KS | 58 | 49 | 58 | 49 | 56 | 1,185 | 203 | 604 | 51 | 7 | 23 |
| KY | 69 | 58 | 69 | 58 | 66 | 1,603 | 243 | 702 | 65 | 8 | 25 |
| LA | 82 | 68 | 81 | 68 | 79 | 1,709 | 297 | 903 | 75 | 11 | 35 |
| ME | 34 | 29 | 34 | 30 | 33 | 512 | 112 | 289 | 21 | 4 | 11 |
| MD | 109 | 92 | 110 | 93 | 107 | 2,283 | 382 | 1,143 | 122 | 17 | 55 |
| MA | 142 | 121 | 143 | 122 | 140 | 3,255 | 499 | 1,490 | 205 | 24 | 81 |
| MI | 173 | 149 | 173 | 149 | 170 | 3,806 | 631 | 1,869 | 183 | 25 | 79 |
| MN | 119 | 101 | 119 | 101 | 116 | 2,662 | 393 | 1,255 | 137 | 16 | 54 |
| MS | 44 | 37 | 44 | 37 | 43 | 939 | 162 | 440 | 34 | 5 | 15 |
| MO | 124 | 108 | 126 | 109 | 123 | 2,495 | 401 | 1,169 | 112 | 14 | 45 |
| MT | 32 | 29 | 32 | 29 | 32 | 378 | 107 | 245 | 15 | 4 | 9 |
| NE | 43 | 36 | 43 | 37 | 42 | 884 | 146 | 412 | 38 | 5 | 15 |
| NV | 51 | 42 | 52 | 43 | 49 | 1,165 | 169 | 487 | 49 | 7 | 20 |
| NH | 31 | 26 | 31 | 25 | 29 | 594 | 108 | 296 | 29 | 5 | 14 |
| NJ | 194 | 170 | 194 | 170 | 191 | 3,636 | 664 | 1,810 | 215 | 29 | 89 |
| NM | 35 | 29 | 34 | 28 | 33 | 629 | 122 | 335 | 25 | 4 | 12 |
| NY | 463 | 415 | 465 | 416 | 460 | 8,118 | 1,521 | 4,106 | 522 | 68 | 213 |
| NC | 171 | 148 | 174 | 150 | 171 | 3,795 | 601 | 1,672 | 171 | 21 | 63 |
| ND | 20 | 17 | 20 | 17 | 19 | 347 | 69 | 199 | 16 | 3 | 8 |
| OH | 185 | 156 | 185 | 155 | 181 | 4,790 | 698 | 2,193 | 218 | 25 | 87 |
| OK | 73 | 62 | 73 | 62 | 70 | 1,360 | 249 | 713 | 57 | 9 | 26 |
| OR | 92 | 80 | 94 | 81 | 91 | 1,551 | 331 | 853 | 74 | 12 | 34 |
| PA | 230 | 197 | 230 | 197 | 226 | 5,355 | 847 | 2,498 | 261 | 32 | 104 |
| RI | 24 | 20 | 24 | 20 | 23 | 435 | 82 | 230 | 20 | 3 | 10 |
| SC | 80 | 68 | 81 | 69 | 78 | 1,716 | 286 | 795 | 69 | 10 | 28 |
| SD | 22 | 19 | 22 | 19 | 21 | 358 | 76 | 211 | 14 | 3 | 7 |
| TN | 97 | 81 | 98 | 81 | 95 | 2,593 | 361 | 1,096 | 115 | 14 | 44 |
| TX | 428 | 369 | 434 | 374 | 428 | 10,430 | 1,559 | 4,707 | 527 | 64 | 204 |
| UT | 63 | 54 | 65 | 56 | 62 | 1,239 | 202 | 573 | 54 | 7 | 23 |
| VT | 18 | 15 | 18 | 16 | 17 | 263 | 62 | 161 | 11 | 2 | 6 |
| VA | 151 | 129 | 152 | 130 | 148 | 3,254 | 532 | 1,535 | 170 | 21 | 71 |
| WA | 150 | 131 | 152 | 133 | 149 | 2,685 | 526 | 1,380 | 157 | 21 | 64 |
| WV | 28 | 23 | 27 | 22 | 26 | 559 | 101 | 275 | 22 | 3 | 9 |
| WI | 109 | 91 | 109 | 91 | 106 | 2,524 | 400 | 1,259 | 116 | 14 | 49 |
| WY | 18 | 16 | 18 | 15 | 17 | 208 | 60 | 131 | 9 | 2 | 5 |

Source: U.S. Census Bureau, Statistics of U.S. Businesses (SUSB), "2016 SUSB Annual Data Tables by Establishment Industry," and earlier releases, <https://www.census.gov/programs-surveys/susb/data/tables.html>, accessed June 2019.

# Table 793. Employer Firms, Establishments, Employment, and Annual Payroll by Firm Size: 1990 to 2016

[5,074 represents 5,074,000. Firms are an aggregation of all establishments owned by a parent company with some annual payroll. Establishments are locations with active payroll in any quarter. This table illustrates the changing importance of enterprise sizes over time, not job growth, as enterprises can grow or decline and change enterprise size cells over time]

| Item | Total | Employment size of firm | | | | | | |
|---|---|---|---|---|---|---|---|---|
| | | 0 to 4 [1] | 5 to 9 | 10 to 19 | 20 to 99 | 100 to 499 | Less than 500 | 500 or more |
| **Firms (1,000):** | | | | | | | | |
| 1990 | 5,074 | 3,021 | 952 | 563 | 454 | 70 | 5,060 | 14 |
| 2000 | 5,653 | 3,397 | 1,021 | 617 | 516 | 84 | 5,635 | 17 |
| 2005 | 5,984 | 3,678 | 1,050 | 630 | 521 | 87 | 5,966 | 17 |
| 2010 | 5,735 | 3,575 | 968 | 617 | 475 | 82 | 5,717 | 17 |
| 2015 | 5,901 | 3,644 | 1,005 | 617 | 526 | 89 | 5,881 | 19 |
| 2016 | 5,955 | 3,665 | 1,014 | 627 | 538 | 91 | 5,935 | 20 |
| **Establishments (1,000):** | | | | | | | | |
| 1990 | 6,176 | 3,032 | 971 | 600 | 590 | 255 | 5,448 | 728 |
| 2000 | 7,070 | 3,406 | 1,035 | 652 | 674 | 312 | 6,080 | 990 |
| 2005 | 7,500 | 3,684 | 1,063 | 662 | 679 | 332 | 6,421 | 1,079 |
| 2010 | 7,397 | 3,583 | 982 | 653 | 648 | 354 | 6,220 | 1,176 |
| 2015 | 7,664 | 3,650 | 1,016 | 649 | 698 | 367 | 6,380 | 1,284 |
| 2016 | 7,758 | 3,672 | 1,026 | 658 | 705 | 367 | 6,428 | 1,330 |
| **Employment (1,000):** | | | | | | | | |
| 1990 | 93,469 | 5,117 | 6,252 | 7,543 | 17,710 | 13,545 | 50,167 | 43,302 |
| 2000 | 114,065 | 5,593 | 6,709 | 8,286 | 20,277 | 16,260 | 57,124 | 56,941 |
| 2005 | 116,317 | 5,937 | 6,898 | 8,454 | 20,444 | 16,911 | 58,645 | 57,672 |
| 2010 | 111,970 | 5,926 | 6,359 | 8,288 | 18,554 | 15,869 | 54,997 | 56,973 |
| 2015 | 124,086 | 5,877 | 6,614 | 8,298 | 20,645 | 17,503 | 58,938 | 65,148 |
| 2016 | 126,752 | 5,923 | 6,682 | 8,433 | 21,094 | 17,784 | 59,915 | 66,837 |
| **Annual payroll (bil. dol.):** | | | | | | | | |
| 1990 | 2,104 | 117 | 114 | 144 | 352 | 279 | 1,007 | 1,097 |
| 2000 | 3,879 | 186 | 174 | 231 | 608 | 528 | 1,727 | 2,152 |
| 2005 | 4,483 | 220 | 206 | 269 | 700 | 617 | 2,013 | 2,470 |
| 2010 | 4,941 | 227 | 212 | 283 | 719 | 666 | 2,107 | 2,834 |
| 2015 | 6,253 | 263 | 244 | 322 | 876 | 846 | 2,551 | 3,702 |
| 2016 | 6,435 | 268 | 249 | 329 | 899 | 871 | 2,616 | 3,819 |

[1] Employment is measured in March, thus some firms (start-ups after March, closures before March, and seasonal firms) will have zero employment and some annual payroll.

Source: U.S. Census Bureau, Statistics of U.S. Businesses (SUSB), "SUSB Historical Data," <https://www.census.gov/data/tables/time-series/econ/susb/susb-historical.html>, accessed June 2019.

# Table 794. Job Creation and Job Destruction of Active Establishments by Firm Age: 2016

[6,886 represents 6,886,000. An establishment is a single physical location where business is conducted or where services or industrial operations are performed. A firm is a business organization consisting of one or more domestic establishments that are under common ownership or control. Firms may have one or more establishments. The firm and the establishment are the same for single-establishment firms. Data cover nonfarm private establishments with paid employees; exclusions include self–employed individuals, employees of private households, and railroad, agricultural production, and most government employees. Data are from the Business Dynamics Statistics (BDS) program and compiled from the Longitudinal Business Database. The BDS program is based on the same basic source data as the Census Bureau's County Business Patterns and Statistics of U.S. Business programs, but differences in how the source data are processed lead to differences in published statistics. For more information about concepts and methodology, see <https://www.census.gov/programs-surveys/bds/documentation/methodology.html>]

| Firm age [1] | Establish-ments | Employ-ees | Percent of employ-ment | Job creation [2] | | Job destruction [3] | | Net job creation | | |
|---|---|---|---|---|---|---|---|---|---|---|
| | | | | Total | Rate | Total | Rate | Total | Rate | Percent of net job creation |
| **Total** | **6,886** | **124,231** | **100.0** | **16,453** | **13.4** | **13,528** | **11.0** | **2,925** | **2.4** | **100.0** |
| Startups | 439 | 2,573 | 2.1 | 2,573 | 200.0 | – | – | 2,573 | 200.0 | 88.0 |
| 1 year | 328 | 2,370 | 1.9 | 591 | 24.5 | 672 | 27.9 | -81 | -3.4 | -2.8 |
| 2 years | 286 | 2,337 | 1.9 | 476 | 20.2 | 519 | 22.0 | -43 | -1.8 | -1.5 |
| 3 years | 251 | 2,084 | 1.7 | 377 | 17.9 | 416 | 19.8 | -38 | -1.9 | -1.3 |
| 4 years | 231 | 2,085 | 1.7 | 363 | 17.2 | 408 | 19.4 | -46 | -2.2 | -1.6 |
| 5 years | 210 | 2,077 | 1.7 | 329 | 15.7 | 361 | 17.2 | -32 | -1.5 | -1.1 |
| 6 to 10 years | 937 | 9,777 | 7.9 | 1,360 | 13.8 | 1,465 | 14.9 | -105 | -1.1 | -3.6 |
| 11 to 15 years | 742 | 9,051 | 7.3 | 1,095 | 12.1 | 1,156 | 12.7 | -60 | -0.6 | -2.1 |
| 16 to 20 years | 584 | 8,285 | 6.7 | 920 | 11.1 | 956 | 11.5 | -36 | -0.4 | -1.2 |
| 21 to 25 years | 432 | 6,863 | 5.5 | 782 | 11.4 | 808 | 11.8 | -27 | -0.4 | -0.9 |
| 26 years and older | 1,096 | 25,501 | 20.5 | 2,662 | 10.5 | 2,460 | 9.7 | 201 | 0.8 | 6.9 |
| Unknown\left censored [4] | 1,351 | 51,229 | 41.2 | 4,926 | 9.7 | 4,308 | 8.5 | 618 | 1.2 | 21.1 |

– Represents zero. [1] Establishment age is computed by taking the difference between the current year of operation and the birth year. Firm age is computed from the age of the establishments belonging to that particular firm. [2] Job creation is employment gains from expanding establishments, including establishment startups. [3] Job destruction is all employment losses from contracting establishments, including establishments shutting down. [4] Within the BDS, all firms/establishments born prior to 1976 have an unknown birth year and are therefore of an unknown age and are grouped into the age category "left censored."

Source: U.S. Census Bureau, Center for Economic Studies, "Business Dynamics Statistics (BDS)," <https://www.census.gov/programs-surveys/bds.html>, accessed July 2019.

## Table 795. Establishments and Employment Changes from Births, Deaths, Expansions, and Contractions by Employment Size of Enterprise: 2015 to 2016

[In thousands (6,872 represents 6,872,000), except percent. Data represent activity from March of the beginning year to March of the ending year. This table provides the number of births and deaths of initial establishments (based on Census ID) as an approximation of firm births and deaths. An establishment is a single physical location at which business is conducted or where services or industrial operations are performed. An enterprise is a business organization consisting of one or more domestic establishments under common ownership or control. Minus sign (-) indicates decrease]

| Employment size of firm | Establishments | | | Employment | | Percent change in employment due to— | | | |
|---|---|---|---|---|---|---|---|---|---|
| | Number in initial year | Births [1] | Deaths [2] | Number in initial year | Change in employ-ment | Births [1] | Deaths [2] | Births and expan-sions [3] | Deaths and con-tractions [4] |
| **Total** | **6,872** | **705** | **598** | **124,067** | **2,685** | **4.4** | **-3.6** | **13.2** | **-11.0** |
| 1 to 4 | 2,896 | 453 | 396 | 5,873 | 830 | 13.5 | -11.6 | 32.0 | -17.9 |
| 5 to 9 | 1,016 | 66 | 59 | 6,610 | 192 | 6.5 | -5.7 | 18.4 | -15.5 |
| 10 to 19 | 648 | 33 | 32 | 8,294 | 179 | 5.2 | -4.8 | 15.3 | -13.2 |
| 20 to 99 | 697 | 30 | 29 | 20,641 | 311 | 4.3 | -4.0 | 12.7 | -11.2 |
| 100 to 499 | 364 | 20 | 15 | 17,502 | 260 | 3.4 | -3.0 | 11.5 | -10.0 |
| Less than 500 | 5,621 | 603 | 531 | 58,920 | 1,772 | 5.3 | -4.8 | 15.3 | -12.3 |
| 500 or more | 1,252 | 102 | 67 | 65,147 | 913 | 3.5 | -2.5 | 11.3 | -9.9 |

[1] Births are establishments that have zero employment in the first quarter of the initial year and positive employment in the first quarter of the subsequent year. [2] Deaths are establishments that have positive employment in the first quarter of the initial year and zero employment in the first quarter of the subsequent year. [3] Expansions are establishments that have positive first quarter employment in both the initial and subsequent years and increase employment during the time period between the first quarter of the initial year and the first quarter of the subsequent year. [4] Contractions are establishments that have positive first quarter employment in both the initial and subsequent years and decrease employment during the time period between the first quarter of the initial year and the first quarter of the subsequent year.

Source: U.S. Census Bureau, "Statistics of U.S. Businesses," <https://www.census.gov/programs-surveys/susb.html>, accessed March 2019.

## Table 796. Small Business Administration Loans to Minority-Owned Small Businesses: 1980 to 2018

[381 represents $381,000,000. For year ending September 30. A small business must be independently owned and operated, must not be dominant in its particular industry, and must meet standards set by the Small Business Administration as to its annual receipts or number of employees]

| Year | Number of loans | | | | | Amount (mil. dol.) | | | | |
|---|---|---|---|---|---|---|---|---|---|---|
| | Total minority loans [1] | Black | Asian or Pacific Islander | Hispanic (incl. Puerto Rican) | Amer-ican Indian | Total minority loans [1] | Black | Asian or Pacific Islander | Hispanic (incl. Puerto Rican) | Amer-ican Indian |
| 1980 | 4,276 | 1,732 | 659 | 1,715 | 170 | 381 | 146 | 70 | 149 | 15 |
| 1985 | 2,028 | 608 | 657 | 689 | 74 | 291 | 64 | 115 | 102 | 10 |
| 1990 | 2,368 | 515 | 1,074 | 694 | 85 | 576 | 97 | 316 | 149 | 14 |
| 1995 | 10,879 | 2,775 | 3,768 | 3,936 | 400 | 1,839 | 294 | 946 | 539 | 61 |
| 1990 | 9,903 | 2,337 | 3,829 | 3,355 | 442 | 2,088 | 301 | 1,174 | 529 | 83 |
| 1997 | 10,247 | 1,929 | 4,533 | 3,378 | 407 | 2,507 | 299 | 1,501 | 626 | 81 |
| 1998 | 10,890 | 1,955 | 5,194 | 3,279 | 462 | 2,718 | 315 | 1,693 | 633 | 77 |
| 1999 | 12,081 | 2,217 | 5,578 | 3,749 | 537 | 3,389 | 402 | 2,149 | 754 | 84 |
| 2000 | 12,041 | 2,183 | 5,827 | 3,491 | 540 | 3,675 | 415 | 2,390 | 767 | 102 |
| 2001 | 11,926 | 2,025 | 5,711 | 3,619 | 571 | 3,510 | 409 | 2,257 | 740 | 103 |
| 2002 | 14,417 | 2,298 | 7,226 | 4,259 | 634 | 4,287 | 458 | 2,808 | 893 | 128 |
| 2003 | 20,483 | 4,138 | 9,469 | 6,089 | 787 | 4,307 | 462 | 2,770 | 957 | 119 |
| 2004 | 25,906 | 5,451 | 12,007 | 7,656 | 792 | 5,271 | 582 | 3,408 | 1,167 | 115 |
| 2005 | 30,226 | 7,302 | 13,353 | 8,748 | 823 | 6,294 | 756 | 4,072 | 1,341 | 125 |
| 2006 | 34,374 | 8,056 | 14,336 | 11,116 | 866 | 6,803 | 862 | 4,249 | 1,576 | 116 |
| 2007 | 36,962 | 9,812 | 15,312 | 10,918 | 920 | 7,020 | 1,072 | 4,331 | 1,490 | 127 |
| 2008 | 24,995 | 7,475 | 10,732 | 6,130 | 658 | 5,730 | 1,081 | 3,510 | 1,027 | 112 |
| 2009 | 11,072 | 3,067 | 5,142 | 2,537 | 293 | 3,371 | 612 | 2,100 | 600 | 47 |
| 2010 | 11,235 | 1,707 | 5,942 | 3,192 | 387 | 3,982 | 345 | 2,743 | 806 | 86 |
| 2011 | 13,151 | 1,643 | 7,119 | 3,915 | 470 | 6,000 | 446 | 4,369 | 1,053 | 131 |
| 2012 | 11,883 | 1,308 | 6,490 | 3,665 | 420 | 5,385 | 349 | 3,920 | 1,032 | 85 |
| 2013 | 12,777 | 1,415 | 7,178 | 3,831 | 353 | 6,336 | 491 | 4,679 | 1,072 | 94 |
| 2014 | 13,746 | 1,790 | 7,321 | 4,253 | 382 | 6,627 | 502 | 4,775 | 1,245 | 105 |
| 2015 | 17,123 | 2,330 | 8,787 | 5,545 | 461 | 8,033 | 653 | 5,600 | 1,631 | 149 |
| 2016 | 18,131 | 2,585 | 9,135 | 5,984 | 427 | 8,756 | 703 | 6,261 | 1,650 | 142 |
| 2017 | 17,991 | 2,636 | 9,182 | 5,714 | 457 | 9,589 | 739 | 6,983 | 1,721 | 142 |
| 2018 | 17,567 | 2,855 | 8,629 | 5,641 | 441 | 9,687 | 857 | 6,808 | 1,840 | 181 |

[1] Beginning 2010, includes other minority loans not shown separately.

Source: U.S. Small Business Administration, "SBA Lending Statistics for Major Programs (as of 9/30/2018)," <https://www.sba.gov/about-sba/sba-newsroom/weekly-lending-report/archive>, accessed April 2019.

## Table 797. U.S. Firms—Ownership by Gender, Ethnicity, Race, and Veteran Status: 2012

[27,626 represents 27,626,000. Based on the 2012 Survey of Business Owners; see text, this section and Appendix III. Firm ownership type is determined by the group owning 51 percent or more of the equity, interest, or stock of the business. A minority-owned firm is one in which Black or African Americans, American Indians and Alaska Natives, Asians, Native Hawaiians and Other Pacific Islanders, and/or Hispanics own 51 percent or more of the interest or stock of the business. Detail may not add to total due to rounding, because Hispanic persons may be of any race, and because each owner had the option of selecting more than one race and is therefore included in each race selected]

| Firm ownership type | All firms [1] | | Firms with paid employees | | | |
|---|---|---|---|---|---|---|
| | Firms (1,000) | Sales and receipts (bil. dol.) | Firms (1,000) | Sales and receipts (bil. dol.) | Employees (1,000) | Annual payroll (bil. dol.) |
| **All firms** | **27,626** | **33,537** | **5,424** | **32,495** | **115,249** | **5,236** |
| Female | 9,878 | 1,420 | 1,036 | 1,191 | 8,432 | 264 |
| Male | 14,845 | 9,466 | 3,336 | 8,813 | 41,132 | 1,644 |
| Equally male/female | 2,456 | 1,078 | 765 | 961 | 6,495 | 189 |
| Hispanic [2] | 3,306 | 474 | 288 | 380 | 2,330 | 71 |
| Equally Hispanic/non-Hispanic [2] | 130 | 54 | 39 | 48 | 360 | 10 |
| Non-Hispanic | 23,743 | 11,436 | 4,810 | 10,537 | 53,369 | 2,015 |
| Minority | 7,952 | 1,380 | 909 | 1,161 | 7,165 | 219 |
| Equally minority/nonminority | 239 | 101 | 71 | 89 | 638 | 21 |
| Nonminority | 18,988 | 10,483 | 4,157 | 9,714 | 48,256 | 1,856 |
| Veteran | 2,522 | 1,141 | 442 | 1,049 | 5,026 | 195 |
| Equally veteran/nonveteran | 587 | 306 | 174 | 276 | 1,681 | 55 |
| Nonveteran | 24,071 | 10,517 | 4,519 | 9,640 | 49,352 | 1,847 |
| White | 21,540 | 10,951 | 4,438 | 10,105 | 50,568 | 1,929 |
| Black or African American | 2,584 | 150 | 109 | 103 | 975 | 28 |
| American Indian and Alaska Native | 273 | 39 | 26 | 32 | 208 | 7 |
| Asian | 1,918 | 699 | 481 | 628 | 3,573 | 111 |
| Native Hawaiian and Other Pacific Islander | 55 | 8 | 5 | 6 | 39 | 1 |
| Some other race | 1,174 | 110 | 79 | 77 | 596 | 16 |

[1] Both firms with paid employees and firms with no paid employees. [2] Persons of Hispanic origin may be of any race and therefore may be included in more than one race group.

Source: U.S. Census Bureau, 2012 Economic Census, Survey of Business Owners, Tables "SB1200CSA01" and "SB1200CSA02," <http://factfinder.census.gov/>, accessed January 2016. See also <https://www.census.gov/programs-surveys/sbo.html>.

## Table 798. Women-Owned Firms by Kind of Business: 2012

[9,878 represents 9,878,000. See headnote, Table 797]

| Kind of business | 2012 NAICS code [1] | All firms [2] | | Firms with paid employees | | | |
|---|---|---|---|---|---|---|---|
| | | Firms (1,000) | Sales and receipts (mil. dol.) | Firms (1,000) | Sales and receipts (mil. dol.) | Employees (1,000) | Annual payroll (mil. dol.) |
| **Total [3]** | (X) | **9,878** | **1,419,834** | **1,036** | **1,190,586** | **8,432** | **263,720** |
| Forestry, fishing and hunting, and agricultural support services | 113–115 | 37 | 2,918 | 2 | 2,055 | 20 | 438 |
| Mining, quarrying, and oil & gas extraction | 21 | 22 | 12,689 | 2 | 11,674 | 27 | 1,763 |
| Utilities | 22 | 4 | 1,173 | (Z) | 1,105 | 2 | 97 |
| Construction | 23 | 266 | 93,002 | 55 | 85,116 | 436 | 20,265 |
| Manufacturing | 31–33 | 139 | 123,984 | 36 | 121,094 | 559 | 23,741 |
| Wholesale trade | 42 | 155 | 275,903 | 42 | 269,336 | 374 | 18,091 |
| Retail trade | 44–45 | 1,045 | 208,976 | 132 | 185,476 | 792 | 18,813 |
| Transportation and warehousing [4] | 48–49 | 159 | 44,216 | 22 | 38,671 | 250 | 8,971 |
| Information | 51 | 114 | 28,816 | 10 | 26,499 | 124 | 6,663 |
| Finance and insurance [5] | 52 | 218 | 36,136 | 34 | 28,379 | 159 | 7,932 |
| Real estate and rental and leasing | 53 | 712 | 72,714 | 58 | 33,392 | 194 | 7,026 |
| Professional, scientific, and technical services | 54 | 1,335 | 138,670 | 165 | 102,552 | 775 | 38,060 |
| Management of companies and enterprises | 55 | 2 | 4,854 | 2 | 4,854 | 51 | 3,874 |
| Administrative and support and waste management and remediation services | 56 | 1,080 | 80,329 | 68 | 65,147 | 1,142 | 29,982 |
| Educational services | 61 | 367 | 14,168 | 23 | 10,128 | 170 | 3,606 |
| Health care and social assistance | 62 | 1,603 | 131,361 | 171 | 101,370 | 1,581 | 43,478 |
| Arts, entertainment, and recreation | 71 | 471 | 20,383 | 19 | 12,447 | 134 | 4,394 |
| Accommodation and food services | 72 | 266 | 69,029 | 103 | 63,856 | 1,203 | 17,432 |
| Other services (except public administration) [6] | 81 | 1,885 | 60,246 | 93 | 27,207 | 437 | 9,051 |
| Industries not classified | 99 | 3 | 268 | 3 | 227 | 2 | 45 |

X Not applicable. Z Less than 500. [1] Based on the 2012 North American Industry Classification System (NAICS); see text, this section. [2] Both firms with paid employees and firms with no paid employees. [3] Firms with more than one establishment are counted in each industry in which they operate, but only once in the total. [4] Excludes rail transportation (NAICS 482), and the postal service (NAICS 491). [5] Excludes monetary authorities-central banks (NAICS 521) and funds, trusts, and other financial vehicles (NAICS 525). [6] Excludes religious, grantmaking, civic, professional, and similar organizations (NAICS 813) and private households (NAICS 814).

Source: U.S. Census Bureau, 2012 Economic Census, Survey of Business Owners, Table "SB1200CSA01," <http://factfinder.census.gov/>, accessed January 2016. See also <https://www.census.gov/programs-surveys/sbo.html>.

# Table 799. Minority-Owned Firms by Kind of Business: 2012

[1,380,149 represents $1,380,149,000,000. See headnote, Table 797]

| Kind of business | 2012 NAICS code [1] | All firms [2] | | Firms with paid employees | | | |
|---|---|---|---|---|---|---|---|
| | | Firms | Sales and receipts (mil. dol.) | Firms | Sales and receipts (mil. dol.) | Employ-ees | Annual payroll (mil. dol.) |
| Total [3] | (X) | 7,952,386 | 1,380,149 | 908,800 | 1,161,431 | 7,165,151 | 219,298 |
| Forestry, fishing and hunting, and agricultural support services | 113–115 | 36,552 | 2,326 | 1,140 | 1,218 | 14,187 | 321 |
| Mining, quarrying, and oil & gas extraction | 21 | 8,450 | 4,193 | 1,190 | 3,487 | 16,334 | 875 |
| Utilities | 22 | 5,461 | 1,281 | 205 | 1,179 | 961 | 98 |
| Construction | 23 | 712,348 | 90,342 | 61,694 | 67,131 | 349,466 | 14,116 |
| Manufacturing | 31–33 | 106,357 | 80,011 | 25,304 | 77,132 | 331,920 | 13,315 |
| Wholesale trade | 42 | 160,511 | 296,999 | 54,863 | 286,906 | 403,154 | 18,177 |
| Retail trade | 44–45 | 650,346 | 277,901 | 138,487 | 255,949 | 750,432 | 16,849 |
| Transportation and warehousing [4] | 48–49 | 525,734 | 59,169 | 29,561 | 31,014 | 208,569 | 6,818 |
| Information | 51 | 83,915 | 17,540 | 6,931 | 15,525 | 71,880 | 4,962 |
| Finance and insurance [5] | 52 | 152,062 | 22,059 | 21,609 | 15,626 | 85,680 | 4,522 |
| Real estate and rental and leasing | 53 | 383,081 | 38,409 | 25,911 | 15,269 | 81,701 | 2,810 |
| Professional, scientific, and technical services | 54 | 783,716 | 121,409 | 98,528 | 99,072 | 625,797 | 37,609 |
| Management of companies and enterprises | 55 | 1,138 | 3,829 | 1,138 | 3,829 | 47,854 | 3,771 |
| Administrative and support and waste management and remediation services | 56 | 920,463 | 57,283 | 48,614 | 43,553 | 733,549 | 18,838 |
| Educational services | 61 | 167,585 | 6,875 | 9,539 | 5,110 | 78,984 | 1,789 |
| Health care and social assistance | 62 | 1,049,683 | 118,039 | 135,899 | 98,415 | 1,139,737 | 38,180 |
| Arts, entertainment, and recreation | 71 | 289,684 | 11,309 | 7,091 | 6,180 | 46,407 | 2,063 |
| Accommodation and food services | 72 | 320,808 | 115,475 | 163,160 | 109,428 | 1,857,539 | 27,407 |
| Other services (except public administration) [6] | 81 | 1,595,222 | 55,542 | 78,925 | 25,307 | 319,741 | 6,760 |
| Industries not classified | 99 | 1,567 | 159 | 1,303 | 101 | 1,256 | 20 |

X Not applicable. [1] Based on the 2012 North American Industry Classification System (NAICS); see text, this section. [2] Both firms with paid employees and firms with no paid employees. [3] Firms with more than one establishment are counted in each industry in which they operate, but only once in the total. [4] Excludes rail transportation (NAICS 482), and the postal service (NAICS 491). [5] Excludes monetary authorities-central banks (NAICS 521) and funds, trusts, and other financial vehicles (NAICS 525). [6] Excludes religious, grantmaking, civic, professional, and similar organizations (NAICS 813) and private households (NAICS 814).

Source: U.S. Census Bureau, 2012 Economic Census, Survey of Business Owners, Table "SB1200CSA01," <http://factfinder.census.gov/>, accessed January 2016. See also <https://www.census.gov/programs-surveys/sbo.html>.

# Table 800. Hispanic-Owned Firms by Kind of Business: 2012

[473,636 represents $473,636,000,000. See headnote, Table 797]

| Kind of business | 2012 NAICS code [1] | All firms [2] | | Firms with paid employees | | | |
|---|---|---|---|---|---|---|---|
| | | Firms | Sales and receipts (mil. dol.) | Firms | Sales and receipts (mil. dol.) | Employ-ees | Annual payroll (mil. dol.) |
| Total [3] | (X) | 3,305,873 | 473,636 | 287,501 | 379,995 | 2,329,553 | 70,856 |
| Forestry, fishing and hunting, and agricultural support services | 113–115 | 17,590 | 1,137 | 631 | 659 | 11,214 | 213 |
| Mining, quarrying, and oil & gas extraction | 21 | 4,849 | 2,395 | 700 | 1,876 | 10,297 | 515 |
| Utilities | 22 | 3,188 | 305 | 135 | 236 | 559 | 18 |
| Construction | 23 | 475,472 | 55,830 | 38,704 | 38,901 | 222,161 | 8,437 |
| Manufacturing | 31–33 | 51,380 | 25,269 | 10,475 | 23,737 | 122,302 | 4,630 |
| Wholesale trade | 42 | 64,063 | 96,238 | 17,036 | 92,525 | 126,660 | 5,450 |
| Retail trade | 44–45 | 255,837 | 91,683 | 33,136 | 83,644 | 202,134 | 5,250 |
| Transportation and warehousing [4] | 48–49 | 243,123 | 31,178 | 15,291 | 16,924 | 111,642 | 3,814 |
| Information | 51 | 30,315 | 4,085 | 2,312 | 3,360 | 20,353 | 1,028 |
| Finance and insurance [5] | 52 | 55,392 | 7,680 | 8,529 | 5,553 | 33,547 | 1,480 |
| Real estate and rental and leasing | 53 | 142,696 | 12,542 | 9,995 | 5,052 | 30,005 | 1,015 |
| Professional, scientific, and technical services | 54 | 278,066 | 33,525 | 29,582 | 25,584 | 170,953 | 8,858 |
| Management of companies and enterprises | 55 | 376 | 1,713 | 376 | 1,713 | 20,529 | 2,018 |
| Administrative and support and waste management and remediation services | 56 | 527,608 | 26,545 | 25,243 | 18,171 | 326,767 | 7,721 |
| Educational services | 61 | 53,510 | 1,964 | 2,142 | 1,423 | 21,222 | 539 |
| Health care and social assistance | 62 | 347,955 | 28,937 | 30,335 | 23,210 | 302,521 | 9,407 |
| Arts, entertainment, and recreation | 71 | 101,624 | 3,891 | 2,350 | 2,097 | 16,986 | 701 |
| Accommodation and food services | 72 | 100,176 | 28,424 | 37,825 | 26,423 | 484,750 | 7,331 |
| Other services (except public administration) [6] | 81 | 553,065 | 20,250 | 23,214 | 8,885 | 94,671 | 2,430 |
| Industries not classified | 99 | 366 | 44 | 269 | 23 | 278 | 4 |

X Not applicable. [1] Based on the 2012 North American Industry Classification System (NAICS); see text, this section. [2] Both firms with paid employees and firms with no paid employees. [3] Firms with more than one establishment are counted in each industry in which they operate, but only once in the total. [4] Excludes rail transportation (NAICS 482), and the postal service (NAICS 491). [5] Excludes monetary authorities-central banks (NAICS 521) and funds, trusts, and other financial vehicles (NAICS 525). [6] Excludes religious, grantmaking, civic, professional, and similar organizations (NAICS 813) and private households (NAICS 814).

Source: U.S. Census Bureau, 2012 Economic Census, Survey of Business Owners, Table "SB1200CSA01," <http://factfinder.census.gov/>, accessed January 2016. See also <https://www.census.gov/programs-surveys/sbo.html>.

# Table 801. Black-Owned Firms by Kind of Business: 2012

[150,203 represents $150,203,000,000. See headnote, Table 797]

| Kind of business | 2012 NAICS code [1] | All firms [2] | | Firms with paid employees | | | |
|---|---|---|---|---|---|---|---|
| | | Firms | Sales and receipts (mil. dol.) | Firms | Sales and receipts (mil. dol.) | Employ-ees | Annual payroll (mil dol.) |
| Total [3] | (X) | 2,584,403 | 150,203 | 109,137 | 103,452 | 975,052 | 27,690 |
| Forestry, fishing and hunting, and agricultural support services | 113–115 | 5,465 | 234 | 126 | 114 | 655 | 20 |
| Mining | 21 | 1,026 | 64 | 40 | 37 | 223 | 8 |
| Utilities | 22 | 1,646 | 29 | 5 | 7 | 14 | 1 |
| Construction | 23 | 136,729 | 11,142 | 7,594 | 8,326 | 39,883 | 1,708 |
| Manufacturing | 31–33 | 22,649 | 8,217 | 1,299 | 7,797 | 18,917 | 725 |
| Wholesale trade | 42 | 24,465 | 12,938 | 2,338 | 12,003 | 18,486 | 876 |
| Retail trade | 44–45 | 160,276 | 17,188 | 8,274 | 14,090 | 43,154 | 1,167 |
| Transportation and warehousing [4] | 48–49 | 184,777 | 12,248 | 6,467 | 4,099 | 38,917 | 1,025 |
| Information | 51 | 28,459 | 2,497 | 976 | 2,024 | 10,556 | 619 |
| Finance and insurance [5] | 52 | 43,649 | 3,665 | 4,295 | 2,661 | 16,423 | 889 |
| Real estate and rental and leasing | 53 | 78,011 | 4,468 | 2,812 | 1,858 | 10,845 | 373 |
| Professional, scientific, and technical services | 54 | 206,942 | 15,683 | 13,822 | 11,282 | 81,170 | 4,457 |
| Management of companies and enterprises | 55 | 196 | 453 | 196 | 453 | 7,957 | 395 |
| Administrative and support and waste management and remediation services | 56 | 294,977 | 12,349 | 10,485 | 8,979 | 169,660 | 4,476 |
| Educational services | 61 | 67,399 | 1,582 | 1,586 | 940 | 14,360 | 345 |
| Health care and social assistance | 62 | 492,983 | 24,244 | 32,055 | 16,904 | 309,855 | 7,311 |
| Arts, entertainment, and recreation | 71 | 124,286 | 3,713 | 1,890 | 1,704 | 8,666 | 549 |
| Accommodation and food services | 72 | 60,329 | 8,538 | 6,938 | 7,657 | 153,306 | 2,085 |
| Other services (except public administration) [6] | 81 | 649,896 | 10,906 | 7,769 | 2,490 | 31,543 | 656 |
| Industries not classified | 99 | 606 | 46 | 536 | 28 | 462 | 5 |

X Not applicable. [1] Based on the 2012 North American Industry Classification System (NAICS); see text, this section. [2] Both firms with paid employees and firms with no paid employees. [3] Firms with more than one establishment are counted in each industry in which they operate, but only once in the total. [4] Excludes rail transportation (NAICS 482), and the postal service (NAICS 491). [5] Excludes monetary authorities-central banks (NAICS 521) and funds, trusts, and other financial vehicles (NAICS 525). [6] Excludes religious, grantmaking, civic, professional, and similar organizations (NAICS 813) and private households (NAICS 814).

Source: U.S. Census Bureau, 2012 Economic Census, Survey of Business Owners, Table "SB1200CSA01," <http://factfinder.census.gov/>, accessed January 2016. See also <https://www.census.gov/programs-surveys/sbo.html>.

# Table 802. Asian–Owned Firms by Kind of Business: 2012

[699,492 represents $699,492,000,000. See headnote, Table 797]

| Kind of business | 2012 NAICS code [1] | All firms [2] | | Firms with paid employees | | | |
|---|---|---|---|---|---|---|---|
| | | Firms | Sales and receipts (mil. dol.) | Firms | Sales and receipts (mil. dol.) | Employ-ees | Annual payroll (mil. dol.) |
| Total [3] | (X) | 1,917,902 | 699,492 | 481,026 | 627,532 | 3,572,577 | 110,544 |
| Forestry, fishing and hunting, and agricultural support services | 113–115 | 6,385 | 500 | 129 | 177 | 736 | 28 |
| Mining, quarrying, and oil & gas extraction | 21 | 1,144 | 995 | 135 | 934 | 2,663 | 177 |
| Utilities | 22 | 525 | 756 | 32 | 746 | 194 | 67 |
| Construction | 23 | 76,883 | 15,362 | 10,567 | 12,919 | 54,404 | 2,473 |
| Manufacturing | 31–33 | 27,590 | 42,596 | 12,212 | 41,801 | 172,485 | 7,148 |
| Wholesale trade | 42 | 67,062 | 177,956 | 34,152 | 172,843 | 244,854 | 11,131 |
| Retail trade | 44–45 | 218,054 | 156,835 | 93,021 | 146,868 | 477,684 | 9,688 |
| Transportation and warehousing [4] | 48–49 | 93,554 | 14,157 | 6,767 | 8,726 | 48,424 | 1,663 |
| Information | 51 | 23,031 | 10,260 | 3,207 | 9,490 | 38,095 | 3,135 |
| Finance and insurance [5] | 52 | 48,148 | 9,700 | 7,634 | 6,719 | 30,511 | 1,908 |
| Real estate and rental and leasing | 53 | 149,452 | 19,868 | 11,975 | 7,766 | 36,762 | 1,257 |
| Professional, scientific, and technical services | 54 | 276,960 | 67,766 | 50,834 | 58,666 | 345,376 | 23,067 |
| Management of companies and enterprises | 55 | 481 | 1,494 | 481 | 1,494 | 17,446 | 1,249 |
| Administrative and support and waste management and remediation services | 56 | 86,064 | 15,386 | 10,891 | 13,724 | 191,550 | 5,378 |
| Educational services | 61 | 42,744 | 3,047 | 5,440 | 2,508 | 40,051 | 785 |
| Health care and social assistance | 62 | 203,471 | 60,879 | 69,953 | 54,631 | 497,812 | 20,162 |
| Arts, entertainment, and recreation | 71 | 54,857 | 2,962 | 2,403 | 1,817 | 17,351 | 537 |
| Accommodation and food services | 72 | 156,391 | 76,004 | 115,634 | 72,950 | 1,176,725 | 17,400 |
| Other services (except public administration) [6] | 81 | 385,583 | 22,903 | 46,128 | 12,705 | 178,974 | 3,281 |
| Industries not classified | 99 | 549 | 66 | 455 | 48 | 480 | 9 |

X Not applicable. [1] Based on the 2012 North American Industry Classification System (NAICS); see text, this section. [2] Both firms with paid employees and firms with no paid employees. [3] Firms with more than one establishment are counted in each industry in which they operate, but only once in the total. [4] Excludes rail transportation (NAICS 482), and the postal service (NAICS 491). [5] Excludes monetary authorities-central banks (NAICS 521) and funds, trusts, and other financial vehicles (NAICS 525). [6] Excludes religious, grantmaking, civic, professional, and similar organizations (NAICS 813) and private households (NAICS 814).

Source: U.S. Census Bureau, 2012 Economic Census, Survey of Business Owners, Table "SB1200CSA01," <http://factfinder.census.gov/>, accessed January 2016. See also <https://www.census.gov/programs-surveys/sbo.html>.

## Table 803. Native Hawaiian- and Other Pacific Islander-Owned Firms by Kind of Business: 2012

[8,136 represents $8,136,000,000. See headnote, Table 797]

| Kind of business | 2012 NAICS code [1] | All firms [2] Firms | All firms [2] Sales and receipts (mil. dol.) | Firms with paid employees Firms | Firms with paid employees Sales and receipts (mil. dol.) | Firms with paid employees Employees | Firms with paid employees Annual payroll (mil. dol.) |
|---|---|---|---|---|---|---|---|
| **Total [3]**................................ | (X) | **54,749** | **8,136** | **4,706** | **6,470** | **39,001** | **1,431** |
| Forestry, fishing and hunting, and agricultural support services..................... | 113–115 | 632 | 17 | 1 | (S) | ( [4] ) | (S) |
| Mining, quarrying, and oil & gas extraction............... | 21 | 44 | (S) | 24 | (S) | ( [5] ) | (S) |
| Utilities.................................... | 22 | 23 | (Z) | 1 | (S) | ( [4] ) | (S) |
| Construction................................ | 23 | 5,551 | 1,508 | 724 | 1,254 | 4,803 | 240 |
| Manufacturing............................... | 31–33 | 962 | 535 | 249 | 517 | 2,645 | 102 |
| Wholesale trade............................ | 42 | 1,283 | 1,080 | 151 | 1,023 | 1,696 | 81 |
| Retail trade................................ | 44–45 | 4,702 | 816 | 485 | 698 | 2,894 | 72 |
| Transportation and warehousing [6]............ | 48–49 | 2,566 | 545 | 226 | (S) | ( [5] ) | (S) |
| Information................................. | 51 | 626 | 107 | 54 | 91 | 328 | 17 |
| Finance and insurance [8]...................... | 52 | 1,227 | 160 | 127 | 70 | 382 | 24 |
| Real estate and rental and leasing........... | 53 | 2,791 | 196 | 168 | 69 | 564 | 20 |
| Professional, scientific, and technical services.. | 54 | 6,292 | 932 | 600 | 765 | 3,680 | 255 |
| Management of companies and enterprises....... | 55 | 8 | 12 | 8 | 12 | 183 | 13 |
| Administrative and support and waste management and remediation services...................... | 56 | 6,435 | 449 | 283 | 331 | 5,968 | 151 |
| Educational services....................... | 61 | 1,316 | 38 | 89 | (S) | ( [9] ) | (S) |
| Health care and social assistance............ | 62 | 6,635 | 457 | 548 | 319 | 2,788 | 92 |
| Arts, entertainment, and recreation........... | 71 | 3,541 | 285 | 169 | 218 | 1,174 | 72 |
| Accommodation and food services............. | 72 | 1,454 | 351 | 448 | 307 | 5,327 | 80 |
| Other services (except public administration) [10].......... | 81 | 8,674 | 458 | 367 | (S) | ( [7] ) | (S) |
| Industries not classified................... | 99 | 11 | (Z) | 11 | 1 | 13 | (Z) |

X Not applicable. S Withheld because estimate did not meet publication standards. Z Less than $500,000. [1] Based on the 2012 North American Industry Classification System (NAICS); see text, this section. [2] Both firms with paid employees and firms with no paid employees. [3] Firms with more than one establishment are counted in each industry in which they operate, but only once in the total. [4] 0 to 19 employees. [5] 1,000 to 2,499 employees. [6] Excludes rail transportation (NAICS 482), and the postal service (NAICS 491). [7] 2,500 to 4,999 employees. [8] Excludes monetary authorities-central banks (NAICS 521) and funds, trusts, and other financial vehicles (NAICS 525). [9] 100 to 249 employees. [10] Excludes religious, grantmaking, civic, professional, and similar organizations (NAICS 813) and private households (NAICS 814).

Source: U.S. Census Bureau, 2012 Economic Census, Survey of Business Owners, Table "SB1200CSA01," <http://factfinder.census.gov/>, accessed January 2016. See also <https://www.census.gov/programs-surveys/sbo.html>.

## Table 804. American Indian- and Alaska Native-Owned Firms by Kind of Business: 2012

[38,838 represents $38,838,000,000. See headnote, Table 797]

| Kind of business | 2012 NAICS code [1] | All firms [2] Firms | All firms [2] Sales and receipts (mil. dol.) | Firms with paid employees Firms | Firms with paid employees Sales and receipts (mil. dol.) | Firms with paid employees Employees | Firms with paid employees Annual payroll (mil. dol.) |
|---|---|---|---|---|---|---|---|
| **Total [3]**................................ | (X) | **272,919** | **38,838** | **26,179** | **31,654** | **208,178** | **6,995** |
| Forestry, fishing and hunting, and agricultural support services..................... | 113–115 | 6,998 | 399 | 250 | 229 | 1,590 | 53 |
| Mining, quarrying, and oil & gas extraction............ | 21 | 1,407 | 532 | 289 | 434 | 1,953 | 103 |
| Utilities.................................... | 22 | 296 | 195 | 14 | 187 | 154 | 8 |
| Construction................................ | 23 | 35,969 | 7,401 | 4,836 | 6,124 | 29,700 | 1,329 |
| Manufacturing............................... | 31–33 | 5,991 | 2,513 | 1,146 | 2,349 | 13,133 | 519 |
| Wholesale trade............................ | 42 | 5,946 | 5,645 | 1,022 | 5,281 | 8,270 | 419 |
| Retail trade................................ | 44–45 | 22,433 | 6,535 | 2,655 | 5,962 | 18,524 | 476 |
| Transportation and warehousing [4]............ | 48–49 | 11,370 | 1,467 | 939 | 884 | 5,692 | 190 |
| Information................................. | 51 | 3,457 | 445 | 286 | 380 | 2,931 | 108 |
| Finance and insurance [5]...................... | 52 | 6,199 | 889 | 1,225 | 602 | 4,901 | 200 |
| Real estate and rental and leasing........... | 53 | 10,925 | 918 | 873 | 440 | 2,678 | 123 |
| Professional, scientific, and technical services.. | 54 | 30,966 | 3,168 | 3,627 | 2,193 | 17,882 | 787 |
| Management of companies and enterprises....... | 55 | 56 | 152 | 56 | 152 | 1,173 | 75 |
| Administrative and support and waste management and remediation services...................... | 56 | 29,100 | 2,681 | 2,035 | 2,263 | 39,133 | 1,096 |
| Educational services....................... | 61 | 7,437 | 264 | 266 | 196 | 2,813 | 109 |
| Health care and social assistance............ | 62 | 29,099 | 2,200 | 3,010 | 1,712 | 27,822 | 675 |
| Arts, entertainment, and recreation........... | 71 | 15,980 | 679 | 281 | 428 | 2,112 | 208 |
| Accommodation and food services............. | 72 | 5,770 | 1,048 | 1,462 | 934 | 18,591 | 250 |
| Other services (except public administration) [6]....... | 81 | 43,573 | 1,704 | 1,963 | 902 | 9,096 | 266 |
| Industries not classified................... | 99 | 37 | 2 | 35 | 2 | 32 | (Z) |

X Not applicable. Z Less than $500,000. [1] Based on the 2012 North American Industry Classification System (NAICS); see text, this section. [2] Both firms with paid employees and firms with no paid employees. [3] Firms with more than one establishment are counted in each industry in which they operate, but only once in the total. [4] Excludes rail transportation (NAICS 482), and the postal service (NAICS 491). [5] Excludes monetary authorities-central banks (NAICS 521) and funds, trusts, and other financial vehicles (NAICS 525). [6] Excludes religious, grantmaking, civic, professional, and similar organizations (NAICS 813) and private households (NAICS 814).

Source: U.S. Census Bureau, 2012 Economic Census, Survey of Business Owners, Table "SBO1200CSA01," <http://factfinder.census.gov/>, accessed January 2016. See also <https://www.census.gov/programs-surveys/sbo.html>.

## Table 805. Employer Firm Ownership by Industry and Sex, Race/Ethnicity, and Veteran Status: 2016

[In thousands (3,434.8 represents 3,434,800). Includes all U.S. firms with paid employees operating during 2016 with receipts of $1,000 or more and classified in the 2012 North American Industry Classification System (NAICS) sectors 11 through 99, except for NAICS 111, 112, 482, 491, 521, 525, 813, 814, and 92. Firms with more than one domestic establishment are counted in each industry in which they operate, but only once in the U.S. industries total. Additionally, each owner had the option of selecting more than one race and is therefore included in each race selected. Based on the 2016 Annual Survey of Entrepreneurs]

| Industry | NAICS code | Sex | | Race/ethnicity [1] | | | | | | Veteran owned |
|---|---|---|---|---|---|---|---|---|---|---|
| | | Male | Fe-male | White | Black | American Indian and Alaska Native | Asian | Native Hawaiian and other Pacific Islander | His-panic [2] | |
| All industries | (X) | 3,434.8 | 1,118.9 | 4,534.3 | 121.5 | 29.1 | 555.3 | 5.2 | 337.5 | 379.6 |
| Agriculture, forestry, fishing and hunting | 11 | 16.7 | 3.2 | 25.2 | 0.2 | 0.2 | 0.3 | – | 1.4 | 1.7 |
| Mining, quarrying, and oil and gas extraction | 21 | 14.6 | 2.3 | 20.1 | (Z) | 0.2 | 0.1 | (Z) | 0.8 | 1.9 |
| Utilities | 22 | 1.9 | 0.3 | 2.4 | (Z) | (Z) | (Z) | – | 0.1 | 0.2 |
| Construction | 23 | 519.1 | 58.5 | 622.3 | 7.9 | 5.9 | 13.2 | 0.9 | 49.9 | 52.1 |
| Manufacturing | 31-33 | 165.1 | 36.3 | 217.0 | 1.5 | 1.2 | 12.5 | 0.2 | 12.4 | 20.2 |
| Wholesale trade | 42 | 207.8 | 43.8 | 245.6 | 2.0 | 0.9 | 37.9 | 0.1 | 16.6 | 21.6 |
| Retail trade | 44-45 | 383.7 | 134.6 | 509.8 | 8.7 | 2.6 | 104.9 | 0.4 | 35.4 | 35.7 |
| Transportation & warehousing | 48-49 | 123.2 | 25.2 | 152.8 | 7.6 | 1.1 | 9.8 | 0.1 | 19.8 | 13.9 |
| Information | 51 | 46.3 | 11.4 | 57.9 | 1.7 | 0.3 | 4.0 | 0.1 | 2.7 | 4.6 |
| Finance & insurance | 52 | 156.8 | 37.3 | 201.1 | 4.9 | 1.5 | 8.2 | 0.2 | 11.1 | 21.6 |
| Real estate & rental & leasing | 53 | 158.0 | 65.6 | 250.3 | 3.1 | 1.0 | 15.9 | 0.3 | 11.9 | 20.5 |
| Professional, scientific, & technical services | 54 | 519.8 | 178.4 | 691.1 | 15.9 | 4.9 | 62.1 | 0.6 | 35.6 | 65.9 |
| Management of companies and enterprises | 55 | 11.5 | 1.9 | 14.0 | 0.1 | (Z) | 0.6 | (Z) | 0.2 | 1.5 |
| Administrative & support and waste management & remediation services | 56 | 205.6 | 70.5 | 288.5 | 10.5 | 2.3 | 12.0 | 0.4 | 29.6 | 23.6 |
| Educational services | 61 | 24.1 | 25.2 | 49.1 | 2.3 | 0.1 | 6.8 | (Z) | 2.8 | 3.1 |
| Health care & social assistance | 62 | 328.2 | 187.0 | 446.4 | 36.8 | 2.7 | 76.9 | 0.9 | 33.6 | 43.8 |
| Arts, entertainment, & recreation | 71 | 56.6 | 21.8 | 87.3 | 2.2 | 0.4 | 2.7 | 0.2 | 2.7 | 5.2 |
| Accommodation & food services | 72 | 298.4 | 109.1 | 350.2 | 7.4 | 1.5 | 129.7 | 0.3 | 43.5 | 20.2 |
| Other services (except public administration) | 81 | 209.1 | 103.4 | 303.7 | 7.7 | 2.1 | 58.1 | 0.4 | 26.7 | 23.0 |

X Not applicable. – Represents zero. Z Less than 50. [1] Includes other, not shown separately. [2] A Hispanic firm may be of any race and therefore may be included in more than one race group.

Source: U.S. Census Bureau, 2016 Annual Survey of Entrepreneurs, Table "SE1600CSA01," <http://factfinder.census.gov>, accessed August 2018.

## Table 806. Bankruptcy Petitions Filed and Pending by Type and Chapter: 2000 to 2018

[For years ending June 30. Covers only bankruptcy cases filed under the Bankruptcy Reform Act of 1978. Bankruptcy: legal recognition that a company or individual is insolvent and must restructure or liquidate. Section 101 of the U.S. Bankruptcy Code defines consumer (nonbusiness) debt as that incurred by an individual primarily for a personal, family, or household purpose. If the debtor is a corporation or partnership, or if debt related to operation of a business predominates, the nature of the debt is business. Petitions "filed" means the commencement of a proceeding through the presentation of a petition to the clerk of the court; "pending" is a proceeding in which the administration has not been completed]

| Item | 2000 | 2005 | 2010 | 2013 | 2014 | 2015 | 2016 | 2017 | 2018 |
|---|---|---|---|---|---|---|---|---|---|
| Total filed | 1,276,922 | 1,637,254 | 1,572,597 | 1,137,978 | 1,000,083 | 879,736 | 819,159 | 796,037 | 775,578 |
| Chapter 7 [1] | 885,447 | 1,196,212 | 1,133,320 | 778,845 | 669,976 | 568,679 | 509,769 | 489,011 | 479,151 |
| Chapter 9 [2] | 8 | 6 | 12 | 16 | 13 | 7 | 5 | 9 | 6 |
| Chapter 11 [3] | 9,947 | 6,703 | 14,272 | 9,633 | 8,347 | 6,672 | 7,928 | 6,999 | 7,141 |
| Chapter 12 [4] | 732 | 290 | 660 | 426 | 394 | 357 | 459 | 482 | 475 |
| Chapter 13 [5] | 380,770 | 433,945 | 424,242 | 348,994 | 321,278 | 303,945 | 300,858 | 299,398 | 288,741 |
| Section 304 [6] | 18 | 98 | (X) | (X) | (X) | (X) | (X) | (X) | (X) |
| Chapter 15 [7] | (X) | (X) | 91 | 64 | 74 | 76 | 140 | 138 | 64 |
| Business [8] | 36,910 | 32,406 | 59,608 | 36,061 | 30,113 | 25,046 | 25,227 | 23,443 | 22,245 |
| Nonbusiness [9] | 1,240,012 | 1,604,848 | 1,512,989 | 1,101,917 | 969,970 | 854,690 | 793,932 | 772,594 | 753,333 |
| Chapter 7 [1] | 864,183 | 1,174,681 | 1,091,322 | 754,391 | 649,975 | 551,808 | 494,218 | 474,258 | 465,472 |
| Chapter 11 [3] | 722 | 847 | 1,827 | 1,417 | 1,211 | 1,078 | 1,146 | 1,099 | 1,071 |
| Chapter 13 [5] | 375,107 | 429,315 | 419,836 | 346,105 | 318,781 | 301,802 | 298,566 | 297,237 | 286,790 |
| Total pending | 1,400,416 | 1,750,562 | 1,659,399 | 1,584,972 | 1,461,132 | 1,316,672 | 1,194,843 | 1,100,309 | 1,050,518 |

X Not applicable. [1] Chapter 7, liquidation of nonexempt assets of businesses or individuals. [2] Chapter 9, adjustment of debts of a municipality. [3] Chapter 11, individual or business reorganization. [4] Chapter 12, adjustment of debts of a family farmer with regular income, effective November 26, 1986. [5] Chapter 13, adjustment of debts of an individual with regular income. [6] Chapter 11, U.S.C., Section 304, cases ancillary to foreign proceedings. [7] Chapter 15 was added and Section 304 was terminated by changes in Bankruptcy Laws effective October 2005. [8] Business bankruptcies include those filed under Chapters 7, 9, 11, 12, 13, or 15. [9] Includes other petitions, not shown separately.

Source: Administrative Office of the United States Courts, "Caseload Statistics Data Tables," <http://www.uscourts.gov/statistics-reports/caseload-statistics-data-tables>, accessed March 2019.

# Table 807. Bankruptcy Cases Filed by State: 2000 to 2018

[In thousands (1,276.9 represents 1,276,900). For years ending June 30. See headnote, Table 806]

| State | 2000 | 2005 | 2010 | 2012 | 2013 | 2014 | 2015 | 2016 | 2017 | 2018 |
|---|---|---|---|---|---|---|---|---|---|---|
| Total [1] | 1,276.9 | 1,637.3 | 1,572.6 | 1,311.6 | 1,138.0 | 1,000.1 | 879.7 | 819.2 | 796.0 | 775.6 |
| Alabama | 31.4 | 42.6 | 34.9 | 29.2 | 27.7 | 26.1 | 25.2 | 26.1 | 27.2 | 26.7 |
| Alaska | 1.4 | 1.6 | 1.1 | 0.9 | 0.7 | 0.5 | 0.4 | 0.5 | 0.5 | 0.4 |
| Arizona | 21.7 | 32.4 | 40.7 | 32.1 | 25.1 | 21.9 | 18.0 | 16.5 | 15.4 | 16.1 |
| Arkansas | 16.3 | 25.5 | 16.9 | 13.6 | 12.6 | 11.8 | 10.4 | 10.4 | 10.7 | 10.5 |
| California | 160.6 | 122.6 | 242.0 | 213.5 | 161.2 | 116.7 | 91.9 | 77.8 | 73.4 | 69.5 |
| Colorado | 15.6 | 30.2 | 31.9 | 28.6 | 24.3 | 20.3 | 16.0 | 13.8 | 12.5 | 11.8 |
| Connecticut | 11.4 | 11.8 | 11.3 | 8.9 | 7.5 | 7.1 | 6.6 | 6.1 | 5.7 | 5.9 |
| Delaware | 4.9 | 3.6 | 4.5 | 4.1 | 3.5 | 3.4 | 2.7 | 2.9 | 2.8 | 3.2 |
| District of Columbia | 2.6 | 1.9 | 1.9 | 1.0 | 0.8 | 0.8 | 0.8 | 0.7 | 0.7 | 0.8 |
| Florida | 74.0 | 85.8 | 107.4 | 87.7 | 78.5 | 73.3 | 62.4 | 50.3 | 44.7 | 41.3 |
| Georgia | 57.9 | 77.3 | 77.8 | 69.3 | 61.6 | 55.2 | 51.1 | 49.4 | 48.1 | 45.7 |
| Hawaii | 5.0 | 3.2 | 3.7 | 2.9 | 2.4 | 1.9 | 1.6 | 1.5 | 1.4 | 1.5 |
| Idaho | 7.3 | 9.7 | 8.3 | 7.0 | 5.9 | 5.1 | 4.4 | 3.9 | 3.8 | 3.7 |
| Illinois | 62.3 | 83.6 | 80.8 | 70.7 | 69.1 | 62.9 | 58.8 | 55.8 | 52.3 | 49.7 |
| Indiana | 37.5 | 55.9 | 49.3 | 37.3 | 35.1 | 31.2 | 28.0 | 25.1 | 24.0 | 23.0 |
| Iowa | 8.2 | 14.3 | 10.4 | 7.2 | 5.9 | 5.5 | 4.7 | 4.4 | 4.2 | 4.6 |
| Kansas | 11.4 | 17.3 | 11.4 | 9.6 | 8.7 | 8.0 | 7.2 | 6.5 | 6.8 | 6.8 |
| Kentucky | 20.8 | 29.2 | 26.0 | 21.1 | 18.9 | 17.9 | 15.8 | 15.4 | 15.5 | 15.4 |
| Louisiana | 23.1 | 31.1 | 19.5 | 16.9 | 15.9 | 15.6 | 14.3 | 14.0 | 13.4 | 13.5 |
| Maine | 4.1 | 4.7 | 4.1 | 3.3 | 2.7 | 2.2 | 2.0 | 1.7 | 1.4 | 1.5 |
| Maryland | 31.1 | 28.5 | 29.1 | 24.3 | 23.2 | 21.9 | 19.0 | 17.9 | 17.5 | 17.5 |
| Massachusetts | 16.7 | 19.6 | 22.9 | 18.8 | 14.0 | 11.4 | 9.6 | 8.9 | 8.6 | 8.5 |
| Michigan | 36.4 | 68.5 | 71.0 | 53.5 | 45.4 | 38.6 | 33.6 | 32.1 | 30.6 | 30.2 |
| Minnesota | 15.4 | 19.4 | 22.6 | 18.2 | 15.4 | 13.4 | 11.3 | 10.1 | 9.6 | 9.9 |
| Mississippi | 17.9 | 21.8 | 14.8 | 13.2 | 12.4 | 12.4 | 10.9 | 11.1 | 11.9 | 12.6 |
| Missouri | 26.3 | 39.2 | 32.9 | 27.7 | 27.1 | 22.3 | 19.9 | 18.8 | 18.4 | 17.8 |
| Montana | 3.3 | 4.4 | 3.1 | 2.3 | 2.0 | 1.7 | 1.4 | 1.4 | 1.3 | 1.3 |
| Nebraska | 5.6 | 9.6 | 7.9 | 6.0 | 5.6 | 4.9 | 4.3 | 4.2 | 4.0 | 4.0 |
| Nevada | 14.3 | 16.3 | 31.0 | 21.0 | 15.7 | 12.3 | 10.2 | 9.2 | 8.9 | 9.0 |
| New Hampshire | 3.9 | 4.9 | 5.7 | 4.4 | 3.6 | 2.9 | 2.3 | 2.0 | 1.8 | 1.8 |
| New Jersey | 38.7 | 40.7 | 39.7 | 34.8 | 29.3 | 28.4 | 26.1 | 25.7 | 26.5 | 26.7 |
| New Mexico | 7.1 | 10.1 | 6.6 | 5.1 | 4.6 | 4.0 | 3.6 | 3.3 | 3.4 | 3.3 |
| New York | 61.7 | 81.7 | 58.2 | 45.7 | 38.3 | 34.6 | 30.9 | 30.2 | 31.6 | 34.2 |
| North Carolina | 25.8 | 37.5 | 27.7 | 22.7 | 20.0 | 17.6 | 16.2 | 15.4 | 14.7 | 14.3 |
| North Dakota | 2.0 | 2.5 | 1.6 | 1.1 | 0.9 | 0.7 | 0.6 | 0.6 | 0.8 | 0.8 |
| Ohio | 53.6 | 95.8 | 72.9 | 53.8 | 49.8 | 43.6 | 39.9 | 37.7 | 37.4 | 37.9 |
| Oklahoma | 19.3 | 28.2 | 15.1 | 12.7 | 11.3 | 10.2 | 9.4 | 9.1 | 9.5 | 9.6 |
| Oregon | 18.1 | 25.3 | 20.1 | 16.7 | 14.0 | 13.1 | 11.5 | 9.9 | 9.1 | 9.0 |
| Pennsylvania | 43.8 | 62.3 | 38.8 | 31.1 | 27.5 | 25.9 | 22.7 | 22.2 | 22.4 | 21.7 |
| Rhode Island | 4.8 | 4.4 | 5.4 | 4.5 | 3.6 | 3.3 | 2.7 | 2.4 | 2.2 | 2.3 |
| South Carolina | 11.7 | 15.2 | 9.7 | 8.0 | 7.7 | 7.6 | 7.1 | 6.7 | 6.6 | 6.6 |
| South Dakota | 2.1 | 2.9 | 2.0 | 1.7 | 1.4 | 1.3 | 1.2 | 1.1 | 1.0 | 1.1 |
| Tennessee | 47.1 | 60.8 | 52.5 | 45.6 | 43.3 | 40.7 | 37.3 | 36.5 | 35.8 | 34.5 |
| Texas | 62.9 | 97.5 | 57.8 | 50.3 | 44.0 | 38.9 | 34.7 | 33.7 | 35.6 | 33.5 |
| Utah | 14.4 | 20.5 | 17.0 | 17.1 | 15.2 | 14.0 | 13.0 | 11.8 | 11.7 | 10.3 |
| Vermont | 1.6 | 1.7 | 1.7 | 1.1 | 0.9 | 0.8 | 0.7 | 0.6 | 0.5 | 0.6 |
| Virginia | 37.1 | 38.8 | 37.8 | 31.8 | 27.2 | 25.1 | 23.2 | 23.3 | 22.8 | 22.8 |
| Washington | 31.2 | 37.7 | 33.5 | 30.0 | 26.5 | 22.9 | 19.7 | 17.4 | 15.5 | 13.9 |
| West Virginia | 8.2 | 12.6 | 6.6 | 4.3 | 3.8 | 3.5 | 3.3 | 3.3 | 3.4 | 3.1 |
| Wisconsin | 18.0 | 29.0 | 30.0 | 26.5 | 23.9 | 22.0 | 19.9 | 17.7 | 17.1 | 16.9 |
| Wyoming | 2.0 | 2.5 | 1.5 | 1.3 | 1.3 | 1.1 | 0.9 | 0.9 | 1.0 | 1.0 |

[1] Includes Island Areas, not shown separately.

Source: Administrative Office of the United States Courts, "Caseload Statistics Data Tables," <http://www.uscourts.gov/statistics-reports/caseload-statistics-data-tables>, accessed March 2019.

## Table 808. Patents and Trademarks: 2000 to 2017

[In thousands (176.0 represents 176,000), unless otherwise noted. Calendar year data. Covers U.S. patents issued to citizens of the United States and residents of foreign countries. For data on foreign countries, see Table 1411]

| Type | 2000 | 2005 | 2010 | 2012 | 2013 | 2014 | 2015 | 2016 | 2017 |
|---|---|---|---|---|---|---|---|---|---|
| **Patents issued**............................ | **176.0** | **157.7** | **244.3** | **276.8** | **302.9** | **326.0** | **326.0** | **333.6** | **351.4** |
| Inventions.............................. | 157.5 | 143.8 | 219.6 | 253.2 | 277.8 | 300.7 | 298.4 | 303.0 | 318.8 |
| Individuals.......................... | 22.4 | 14.7 | 16.6 | 17.2 | 18.7 | 19.3 | 18.9 | 18.7 | 19.3 |
| Corporations: | | | | | | | | | |
| United States..................... | 70.9 | 65.2 | 97.8 | 111.8 | 124.7 | 136.4 | 133.4 | 136.8 | 145.3 |
| Foreign [1]......................... | 63.3 | 63.2 | 104.3 | 123.2 | 133.4 | 144.0 | 145.1 | 146.7 | 153.3 |
| U.S. government...................... | 0.9 | 0.7 | 0.9 | 1.0 | 1.0 | 1.0 | 1.0 | 0.9 | 0.9 |
| Designs................................. | 17.4 | 13.0 | 22.8 | 22.0 | 23.5 | 23.7 | 26.0 | 28.9 | 30.9 |
| Botanical plants...................... | 0.5 | 0.7 | 1.0 | 0.9 | 0.8 | 1.1 | 1.1 | 1.2 | 1.3 |
| Reissues............................... | 0.5 | 0.2 | 0.9 | 0.8 | 0.8 | 0.6 | 0.5 | 0.4 | 0.4 |
| U.S. residents.......................... | 96.9 | 82.6 | 121.2 | 134.2 | 147.7 | 158.7 | 156.0 | 160.5 | 169.2 |
| Foreign country residents................ | 79.1 | 75.2 | 123.2 | 142.6 | 155.3 | 167.3 | 170.0 | 173.0 | 182.2 |
| Percent of total....................... | 44.9 | 47.6 | 50.4 | 51.5 | 51.3 | 51.3 | 52.1 | 51.9 | 51.8 |
| Trademarks: | | | | | | | | | |
| Applications filed........................ | 361.8 | 334.7 | 368.9 | 415.0 | 433.7 | 455.0 | 503.9 | 530.3 | 594.1 |

[1] Includes patents to foreign governments.

Source: U.S. Patent and Trademark Office, "General Patent Statistics Reports Available for Viewing," <http://www.uspto.gov/web/offices/ac/ido/oeip/taf/reports_stco.htm>, accessed September 2018; and unpublished data.

## Table 809. Patents by State and Island Areas: 2017

[Includes only U.S. patents granted to residents of the United States and U.S. territories]

| State | Total | Inventions | Designs | Botanical plants | Reissues | State | Total | Inventions | Designs | Botanical plants | Reissues |
|---|---|---|---|---|---|---|---|---|---|---|---|
| **Total [1]**................ | **169,208** | **150,949** | **17,539** | **516** | **204** | Missouri............ | 1,383 | 1,234 | 146 | 2 | 1 |
| | | | | | | Montana........... | 183 | 150 | 33 | 0 | 0 |
| Alabama.............. | 569 | 496 | 69 | 2 | 2 | Nebraska........... | 351 | 307 | 44 | 0 | 0 |
| Alaska................ | 59 | 50 | 9 | 0 | 0 | Nevada............ | 880 | 782 | 92 | 0 | 6 |
| Arizona............... | 3,070 | 2,841 | 222 | 1 | 6 | New Hampshire. .. | 1,127 | 1,029 | 92 | 0 | 6 |
| Arkansas............. | 347 | 266 | 79 | 2 | 0 | New Jersey........ | 5,126 | 4,530 | 584 | 5 | 7 |
| California.............. | 46,172 | 42,012 | 3,945 | 173 | 42 | New Mexico........ | 552 | 496 | 51 | 1 | 4 |
| Colorado.............. | 3,519 | 3,141 | 370 | 0 | 8 | New York.......... | 10,465 | 9,189 | 1,263 | 4 | 9 |
| Connecticut........... | 2,697 | 2,487 | 204 | 5 | 1 | North Carolina..... | 3,951 | 3,662 | 266 | 16 | 7 |
| Delaware............. | 340 | 323 | 17 | 0 | 0 | North Dakota....... | 133 | 123 | 10 | 0 | 0 |
| District of Columbia. .. | 212 | 180 | 32 | 0 | 0 | Ohio.............. | 4,506 | 3,767 | 730 | 2 | 7 |
| Florida................ | 5,256 | 4,396 | 815 | 37 | 8 | Oklahoma.......... | 642 | 560 | 80 | 0 | 2 |
| Georgia............... | 3,116 | 2,654 | 434 | 23 | 5 | Oregon............ | 4,019 | 2,904 | 1,070 | 45 | 0 |
| Hawaii................ | 153 | 120 | 30 | 3 | 0 | Pennsylvania...... | 4,784 | 4,246 | 519 | 11 | 8 |
| Idaho................. | 758 | 716 | 42 | 0 | 0 | Rhode Island...... | 435 | 359 | 73 | 0 | 3 |
| Illinois................ | 6,043 | 5,133 | 897 | 8 | 5 | South Carolina..... | 1,200 | 1,047 | 148 | 5 | 0 |
| Indiana............... | 2,535 | 2,289 | 245 | 0 | 1 | South Dakota...... | 151 | 138 | 13 | 0 | 0 |
| Iowa.................. | 1,155 | 1,086 | 69 | 0 | 0 | Tennessee......... | 1,311 | 1,094 | 211 | 2 | 4 |
| Kansas............... | 892 | 797 | 94 | 0 | 1 | Texas............. | 11,469 | 10,563 | 862 | 25 | 19 |
| Kentucky.............. | 801 | 724 | 73 | 4 | 0 | Utah.............. | 1,840 | 1,560 | 280 | 0 | 0 |
| Louisiana............. | 511 | 452 | 47 | 12 | 0 | Vermont........... | 461 | 427 | 31 | 1 | 2 |
| Maine................. | 211 | 196 | 14 | 0 | 1 | Virginia............ | 2,384 | 2,205 | 178 | 0 | 1 |
| Maryland.............. | 2,180 | 1,980 | 190 | 6 | 4 | Washington........ | 7,943 | 7,284 | 629 | 20 | 10 |
| Massachusetts........ | 7,929 | 7,430 | 479 | 10 | 10 | West Virginia....... | 122 | 110 | 12 | 0 | 0 |
| Michigan.............. | 7,213 | 6,384 | 748 | 77 | 4 | Wisconsin.......... | 2,728 | 2,233 | 478 | 13 | 4 |
| Minnesota............ | 4,906 | 4,456 | 445 | 0 | 5 | Wyoming........... | 122 | 103 | 18 | 0 | 1 |
| Mississippi............ | 235 | 193 | 42 | 0 | 0 | Island areas........ | 58 | 42 | 15 | 1 | 0 |

[1] Includes unspecified areas.

Source: U.S. Patent and Trademark Office, "General Patent Statistics Reports Available for Viewing," <http://www.uspto.gov/web/offices/ac/ido/oeip/taf/reports_stco.htm>, accessed September 2018; and unpublished data.

## Table 810. Copyright Registration by Subject Matter: 1990 to 2017

[In thousands (590.7 represents 590,700). For years ending September 30. Comprises claims to copyrights registered for both U.S. and foreign works. Semiconductor chips and renewals are not considered copyright registration claims]

| Subject matter | 1990 | 2000 | 2005 | 2010 | 2012 | 2013 | 2014 | 2015 | 2016 | 2017 |
|---|---|---|---|---|---|---|---|---|---|---|
| **Total copyright basic registrations..** | **590.7** | **497.6** | **515.2** | **636.0** | **508.7** | **496.2** | **476.0** | **443.0** | **414.1** | **452.1** |
| Monographs [1]............................ | 179.7 | 169.7 | 191.4 | 245.8 | 198.5 | 180.6 | 175.4 | 175.5 | 168.8 | 153.0 |
| Serials............................... | 111.5 | 69.0 | 57.7 | 90.5 | 48.2 | 44.2 | 43.2 | 55.1 | 33.9 | 39.6 |
| Sound recordings......................... | 37.5 | 34.2 | 49.9 | 77.9 | 74.3 | 72.4 | 65.5 | 43.0 | 42.4 | 59.2 |
| Performing arts [2]........................ | 185.3 | 138.9 | 133.7 | 124.5 | 114.8 | 116.1 | 103.3 | 80.1 | 75.3 | 103.5 |
| Works of the visual arts [3]................ | 76.7 | 85.8 | 82.5 | 97.2 | 72.8 | 82.9 | 88.7 | 89.2 | 85.6 | 86.5 |
| Renewals.............................. | 51.8 | 16.8 | 15.8 | 0.1 | 0.2 | 0.2 | 0.1 | 0.8 | 0.2 | 0.4 |
| Mask work (semiconductor chip products)........................... | 1.0 | 0.7 | 0.5 | 0.3 | 2.6 | 0.3 | 0.1 | 0.1 | (Z) | (Z) |

Z Less than 50. [1] Includes computer software and machine readable works. [2] Includes musical works, dramatic works, choreography, pantomimes, motion pictures, and filmstrips. [3] Two-dimensional works of fine and graphic art, including prints and art reproductions; sculptural works; technical drawings and models; photographs; commercial prints and labels; and works of applied arts, cartographic works, and multimedia works.

Source: The Library of Congress, *Annual Report of the Librarian of Congress, For the Fiscal Year Ending September 30, 2017*, 2018. See also <http://www.loc.gov/about/reports-and-budgets/annual-reports/>.

# Table 811. Net Stock of Private Fixed Assets by Industry: 2000 to 2017

[In billions of dollars (21,483 represents $21,483,000,000,000). Estimates as of Dec. 31. Fixed assets are assets that are used repeatedly, or continuously, in processes of production for more than a year. Net stock estimates are presented in terms of current-cost, and cover equipment, structures, and intellectual property products. (pt) = part]

| Industry | NAICS code [1] | 2000 | 2005 | 2010 | 2016 | 2017 |
|---|---|---|---|---|---|---|
| **Private fixed assets**.... | (X) | **21,483** | **30,662** | **34,582** | **43,443** | **45,272** |
| Agriculture, forestry, fishing, and hunting.... | 11 | 338 | 431 | 487 | 652 | 666 |
| Farms [2].... | 111, 112 | 311 | 394 | 438 | 587 | 595 |
| Forestry, fishing, and related activities.... | 113-115 | 27 | 37 | 49 | 65 | 70 |
| Mining.... | 21 | 576 | 1,225 | 1,575 | 2,138 | 2,147 |
| Oil and gas extraction.... | 211 | 442 | 1,054 | 1,328 | 1,795 | 1,804 |
| Mining, except oil and gas.... | 212 | 90 | 104 | 138 | 201 | 205 |
| Support activities for mining.... | 213 | 44 | 67 | 109 | 142 | 138 |
| Utilities.... | 22 | 1,039 | 1,371 | 1,859 | 2,347 | 2,438 |
| Construction.... | 23 | 174 | 228 | 264 | 324 | 340 |
| Manufacturing.... | 31-33 | 2,315 | 2,704 | 3,215 | 3,822 | 3,965 |
| Durable goods.... | (X) | 1,289 | 1,457 | 1,664 | 1,935 | 1,991 |
| Wood products.... | 321 | 32 | 36 | 38 | 43 | 45 |
| Nonmetallic mineral products.... | 327 | 67 | 79 | 90 | 97 | 100 |
| Primary metals.... | 331 | 134 | 140 | 162 | 174 | 176 |
| Fabricated metal products.... | 332 | 124 | 141 | 162 | 192 | 198 |
| Machinery.... | 333 | 166 | 177 | 203 | 237 | 242 |
| Computer and electronic products.... | 334 | 360 | 411 | 482 | 558 | 573 |
| Electrical equipment, appliances, and components.... | 335 | 58 | 62 | 68 | 77 | 79 |
| Motor vehicles, bodies and trailers, and parts.... | 3361-3363 | 156 | 186 | 190 | 249 | 257 |
| Other transportation equipment.... | 3364, 3365, 3369 | 112 | 128 | 158 | 182 | 190 |
| Furniture and related products.... | 337 | 17 | 21 | 22 | 23 | 24 |
| Miscellaneous manufacturing.... | 339 | 64 | 77 | 91 | 105 | 108 |
| Nondurable goods.... | (X) | 1,026 | 1,247 | 1,551 | 1,887 | 1,974 |
| Food and beverage and tobacco products.... | 311, 312 | 201 | 242 | 287 | 336 | 350 |
| Textile mills and textile product mills.... | 313, 314 | 45 | 44 | 42 | 40 | 40 |
| Apparel and leather and allied products.... | 315, 316 | 18 | 19 | 18 | 18 | 18 |
| Paper products.... | 322 | 105 | 107 | 110 | 119 | 122 |
| Printing and related support activities.... | 323 | 42 | 48 | 50 | 47 | 47 |
| Petroleum and coal products.... | 324 | 117 | 144 | 198 | 244 | 252 |
| Chemical products.... | 325 | 422 | 558 | 755 | 977 | 1,033 |
| Plastics and rubber products.... | 326 | 75 | 85 | 92 | 107 | 112 |
| Wholesale trade.... | 42 | 348 | 432 | 491 | 616 | 654 |
| Retail trade.... | 44-45 | 656 | 958 | 1,132 | 1,324 | 1,372 |
| Transportation and warehousing [3].... | 48-49 | 821 | 957 | 1,095 | 1,368 | 1,427 |
| Air transportation.... | 481 | 184 | 206 | 219 | 259 | 272 |
| Railroad transportation.... | 482 | 288 | 318 | 359 | 419 | 426 |
| Water transportation.... | 483 | 37 | 37 | 43 | 58 | 61 |
| Truck transportation.... | 484 | 71 | 96 | 106 | 150 | 157 |
| Transit and ground passenger transportation.... | 485 | 37 | 39 | 42 | 45 | 45 |
| Pipeline transportation.... | 486 | 73 | 111 | 161 | 249 | 273 |
| Warehousing and storage.... | 493 | 21 | 30 | 40 | 52 | 55 |
| Information.... | 51 | 1,201 | 1,471 | 1,830 | 2,202 | 2,336 |
| Publishing industries (includes software).... | 511, 516 (pt) | 118 | 184 | 258 | 336 | 351 |
| Motion picture and sound recording industries.... | 512 | 186 | 234 | 258 | 269 | 275 |
| Broadcasting and telecommunications.... | 515, 517 | 858 | 986 | 1,215 | 1,357 | 1,427 |
| Information and data processing services.... | 516 (pt), 518, 519 | 40 | 66 | 99 | 240 | 283 |
| Finance and insurance.... | 52 | 782 | 1,024 | 1,154 | 1,392 | 1,440 |
| Federal Reserve banks.... | 521 | 9 | 10 | 10 | 10 | 10 |
| Credit intermediation and related activities.... | 522 | 487 | 645 | 717 | 898 | 927 |
| Securities, commodity contracts, and investments.... | 523 | 92 | 118 | 152 | 172 | 181 |
| Insurance carriers and related activities.... | 524 | 177 | 221 | 236 | 271 | 282 |
| Funds, trusts, and other financial vehicles.... | 525 | 18 | 31 | 40 | 40 | 40 |
| Real estate and rental and leasing.... | 53 | 10,739 | 16,382 | 17,227 | 22,041 | 23,042 |
| Real estate.... | 531 | 10,512 | 16,086 | 16,880 | 21,540 | 22,524 |
| Rental and leasing services and lessors of intangible assets [4].... | 532, 533 | 227 | 296 | 347 | 501 | 518 |
| Professional, scientific, and technical services [3].... | 54 | 313 | 447 | 576 | 690 | 723 |
| Legal services.... | 5411 | 23 | 35 | 43 | 45 | 46 |
| Computer systems design and related services.... | 5415 | 52 | 74 | 96 | 100 | 101 |
| Management of companies and enterprises [5].... | 55 | 266 | 317 | 355 | 388 | 397 |
| Administrative and support and waste management.... | 56 | 151 | 202 | 245 | 313 | 329 |
| Administrative and support services.... | 561 | 85 | 122 | 153 | 210 | 223 |
| Waste management and remediation services.... | 562 | 67 | 80 | 92 | 103 | 106 |
| Educational services.... | 61 | 217 | 331 | 469 | 584 | 611 |
| Health care and social assistance.... | 62 | 694 | 993 | 1,221 | 1,500 | 1,560 |
| Ambulatory health care services.... | 621 | 208 | 272 | 317 | 378 | 393 |
| Hospitals.... | 622 | 428 | 623 | 773 | 954 | 992 |
| Nursing and residential care facilities.... | 623 | 33 | 58 | 77 | 100 | 105 |
| Social assistance.... | 624 | 26 | 41 | 53 | 68 | 71 |
| Arts, entertainment, and recreation.... | 71 | 164 | 241 | 289 | 390 | 420 |
| Performing arts, spectator sports, museums, and related activities.... | 711, 712 | 84 | 117 | 142 | 184 | 195 |
| Amusements, gambling, and recreation industries.... | 713 | 80 | 123 | 147 | 206 | 225 |
| Accommodation and food services.... | 72 | 342 | 455 | 542 | 683 | 714 |
| Accommodation.... | 721 | 188 | 262 | 327 | 433 | 458 |
| Food services and drinking places.... | 722 | 154 | 193 | 215 | 250 | 256 |
| Other services, except government.... | 81 | 347 | 493 | 557 | 669 | 694 |

X Not applicable. [1] Based on North American Industry Classification System; see text this section. [2] NAICS crop and animal production. [3] Includes other activities, not shown separately. [4] Intangible assets include patents, trademarks, and franchise agreements, but not copyrights. [5] Consists of bank and other holding companies.

Source: U.S. Bureau of Economic Analysis, National Economic Accounts, "Table 3.1ESI. Current-Cost Net Stock of Private Fixed Assets by Industry," <http://www.bea.gov/itable/>, accessed November 2018.

# Table 812. Capital Expenditures: 2000 to 2017

[In billions of dollars (1,161 represents $1,161,000,000,000). Based on the Annual Capital Expenditure Survey, which is a sample survey and subject to sampling error; see source for details]

| Item | All companies | | | | Companies with employees | | | | Companies without employees | | | |
|---|---|---|---|---|---|---|---|---|---|---|---|---|
| | 2000 | 2010 | 2016 | 2017 | 2000 | 2010 | 2016 | 2017 | 2000 | 2010 | 2016 | 2017 |
| **Capital expenditures, total**......... | **1,161** | **1,106** | **1,575** | **1,683** | **1,090** | **1,036** | **1,479** | **1,582** | **71** | **70** | **95** | **101** |
| Structures...................... | 364 | 430 | 600 | 666 | 338 | 396 | 553 | 613 | 26 | 33 | 47 | 54 |
| New......................... | 329 | 395 | 544 | 617 | 309 | 368 | 509 | 577 | 20 | 28 | 35 | 40 |
| Used........................ | 35 | 34 | 56 | 49 | 29 | 29 | 44 | 36 | 6 | 6 | 12 | 13 |
| Equipment..................... | 797 | 676 | 975 | 1,016 | 752 | 640 | 927 | 969 | 45 | 36 | 48 | 47 |
| New......................... | 751 | 638 | 925 | 959 | 718 | 612 | 888 | 923 | 32 | 27 | 37 | 36 |
| Used........................ | 46 | 38 | 50 | 57 | 34 | 28 | 39 | 46 | 12 | 10 | 11 | 12 |
| Capitalized computer software [1]......... | (NA) | (NA) | (NA) | (NA) | (NA) | (NA) | 100 | 102 | (NA) | (NA) | (NA) | (NA) |
| Capital leases [1].................... | 20 | 16 | 36 | 37 | 19 | 15 | 35 | 36 | (Z) | 1 | 1 | 1 |

NA Not available. Z Less than $500 million. [1] Included in structures and equipment data shown above.

Source: U.S. Census Bureau, "Annual Capital Expenditures: 2017," and earlier reports, <http://www.census.gov/programs-surveys/aces.html>, accessed March 2019.

# Table 813. Capital Expenditures by Industry: 2000 to 2017

[In billions of dollars (1,090 represents $1,090,000,000,000). Covers only companies with employees. Data from 2000 based on the North American Industry Classification System (NAICS), 1997; 2005 data based on NAICS 2002; 2010 through 2013 based on NAICS 2007; 2014 through 2017 data based on NAICS 2012; see text this section. Based on the Annual Capital Expenditure Survey, which is a sample survey and subject to sampling error; see source for details]

| Industry | NAICS code | 2000 | 2005 | 2010 | 2013 | 2014 | 2015 | 2016 | 2017 |
|---|---|---|---|---|---|---|---|---|---|
| **Total expenditures**.......................... | (X) | **1,090** | **1,063** | **1,036** | **1,401** | **1,507** | **1,548** | **1,479** | **1,582** |
| Forestry, fishing, and agricultural services...... | 113–115 | 1 | 3 | 3 | 3 | 4 | 3 | 5 | 5 |
| Mining............................... | 21 | 43 | 67 | 116 | 202 | 231 | 174 | 93 | 133 |
| Utilities.............................. | 22 | 61 | 58 | 94 | 111 | 119 | 131 | 133 | 134 |
| Construction......................... | 23 | 25 | 30 | 18 | 28 | 30 | 33 | 36 | 35 |
| Manufacturing........................ | 31–33 | 215 | 166 | 161 | 221 | 231 | 245 | 244 | 248 |
| Durable goods...................... | 321, 327, 33 | 134 | 92 | 87 | 121 | 125 | 128 | 123 | 130 |
| Nondurable goods.................. | 31, 322–326 | 81 | 73 | 74 | 100 | 106 | 117 | 121 | 118 |
| Wholesale trade...................... | 42 | 34 | 41 | 31 | 38 | 45 | 42 | 44 | 43 |
| Retail trade.......................... | 44–45 | 70 | 74 | 65 | 78 | 82 | 86 | 87 | 92 |
| Transportation and warehousing............. | 48–49 | 60 | 57 | 59 | 93 | 111 | 117 | 110 | 110 |
| Information.......................... | 51 | 160 | 91 | 97 | 124 | 132 | 133 | 143 | 159 |
| Finance and insurance.................. | 52 | 134 | 161 | 103 | 138 | 153 | 165 | 162 | 167 |
| Real estate and rental and leasing.......... | 53 | 92 | 103 | 81 | 114 | 122 | 152 | 151 | 158 |
| Professional, scientific, & technical services. .. | 54 | 34 | 33 | 28 | 36 | 30 | 33 | 32 | 38 |
| Management of companies and enterprises. .. | 55 | 5 | 3 | 5 | 6 | 5 | 5 | 6 | 8 |
| Administrative & support and waste management & remediation services.......... | 56 | 18 | 18 | 17 | 22 | 23 | 26 | 28 | 27 |
| Educational services.................... | 61 | 18 | 17 | 23 | 23 | 26 | 33 | 30 | 37 |
| Health care and social assistance.............. | 62 | 52 | 74 | 78 | 94 | 89 | 94 | 94 | 105 |
| Arts, entertainment, and recreation............. | 71 | 19 | 14 | 12 | 15 | 20 | 16 | 23 | 22 |
| Accommodation and food services............. | 72 | 26 | 31 | 20 | 35 | 30 | 33 | 30 | 36 |
| Other services (except public administration)... | 81 | 21 | 20 | 21 | 19 | 20 | 23 | 27 | 22 |
| Structure and equipment expenditures serving multiple industry categories............ | (X) | 2 | 2 | 2 | 3 | 3 | 4 | 4 | 5 |

X Not applicable.

Source: U.S. Census Bureau, "Annual Capital Expenditures: 2017," and earlier reports, <http://www.census.gov/programs-surveys/aces.html>, accessed March 2019.

# Table 814. Private Domestic Investment in Current and Chained (2012) Dollars: 2000 to 2017

[In billions of dollars (2,038 represents $2,038,000,000,000). Covers equipment, structures, and intellectual property products. For explanation of chained dollars; see text, Section 13]

| Item | 2000 | 2005 | 2010 | 2013 | 2014 | 2015 | 2016 | 2017 |
|---|---|---|---|---|---|---|---|---|
| **CURRENT DOLLARS** | | | | | | | | |
| **Gross private domestic investment**............ | **2,038** | **2,535** | **2,166** | **2,826** | **3,039** | **3,212** | **3,170** | **3,368** |
| Less: Consumption of fixed capital................ | 1,232 | 1,623 | 1,934 | 2,177 | 2,301 | 2,395 | 2,464 | 2,575 |
| Equals: Net private domestic investment......... | 807 | 912 | 232 | 649 | 738 | 817 | 706 | 793 |
| Fixed investment............................... | 1,984 | 2,477 | 2,112 | 2,722 | 2,954 | 3,083 | 3,141 | 3,343 |
| Less: Consumption of fixed capital.............. | 1,232 | 1,623 | 1,934 | 2,177 | 2,301 | 2,395 | 2,464 | 2,575 |
| Equals: Net fixed investment.................... | 752 | 855 | 178 | 545 | 654 | 688 | 677 | 768 |
| Nonresidential.............................. | 1,498 | 1,621 | 1,735 | 2,212 | 2,394 | 2,450 | 2,442 | 2,588 |
| Residential................................. | 485 | 856 | 377 | 510 | 560 | 634 | 699 | 755 |
| Change in private inventories.................... | 55 | 58 | 54 | 105 | 85 | 129 | 29 | 25 |
| **CHAINED (2012) DOLLARS** | | | | | | | | |
| **Gross private domestic investment**............ | **2,347** | **2,671** | **2,217** | **2,802** | **2,952** | **3,092** | **3,051** | **3,197** |
| Less: Consumption of fixed capital................ | 1,414 | 1,732 | 1,986 | 2,152 | 2,223 | 2,295 | 2,363 | 2,449 |
| Equals: Net private domestic investment......... | 933 | 938 | 230 | 650 | 729 | 797 | 688 | 748 |
| Fixed investment............................... | 2,294 | 2,619 | 2,164 | 2,692 | 2,862 | 2,959 | 3,010 | 3,155 |
| Nonresidential.............................. | 1,616 | 1,716 | 1,781 | 2,206 | 2,357 | 2,400 | 2,411 | 2,538 |
| Residential................................. | 647 | 885 | 383 | 486 | 504 | 555 | 591 | 611 |
| Change in private inventories.................... | 79 | 64 | 57 | 109 | 87 | 129 | 23 | 23 |

Source: U.S. Bureau of Economic Analysis, National Economic Accounts, "Table 5.2.5. Gross and Net Domestic Investment by Major Type" and "Table 5.2.6. Real Gross and Net Domestic Investment by Major Type, Chained Dollars," <http://www.bea.gov/itable/>, accessed November 2018.

# Table 815. Business Cycle Expansions and Contractions—Months of Duration: 1945 to 2009

[A trough is the low point of a business cycle; a peak is the high point. Contraction, or recession, is the period from peak to subsequent trough; expansion is the period from trough to subsequent peak. Business cycle reference dates are determined by the National Bureau of Economic Research, Inc]

| Business cycle reference date | | | | Contraction (Peak to trough) | Expansion (Previous trough to peak) | Length of cycle | |
|---|---|---|---|---|---|---|---|
| Peak | | Trough | | | | Trough from previous trough | Peak from previous peak |
| Month | Year | Month | Year | | | | |
| February...................... | 1945 | October | 1945 | 8 | [1] 80 | [1] 88 | [2] 93 |
| November.................... | 1948 | October | 1949 | 11 | 37 | 48 | 45 |
| July........................... | 1953 | May | 1954 | 10 | 45 | 55 | 56 |
| August....................... | 1957 | April | 1958 | 8 | 39 | 47 | 49 |
| April.......................... | 1960 | February | 1961 | 10 | 24 | 34 | 32 |
| December................... | 1969 | November | 1970 | 11 | 106 | 117 | 116 |
| November.................... | 1973 | March | 1975 | 16 | 36 | 52 | 47 |
| January...................... | 1980 | July | 1980 | 6 | 58 | 64 | 74 |
| July........................... | 1981 | November | 1982 | 16 | 12 | 28 | 18 |
| July........................... | 1990 | March | 1991 | 8 | 92 | 100 | 108 |
| March........................ | 2001 | November | 2001 | 8 | 120 | 128 | 128 |
| December................... | 2007 | June | 2009 | 18 | 73 | 91 | 81 |
| Average, all cycles: 1945 to 2009 (11 cycles)... | (X) | (X) | (X) | 11.1 | 59.4 | 69.5 | 68.5 |

X Not applicable. [1] Previous trough: June 1938. [2] Previous peak: May 1937.

Source: National Bureau of Economic Research, Inc., Cambridge, MA, "US Business Cycle Expansions and Contractions," <http://www.nber.org/cycles.html>, accessed September 2019 ©.

# Table 816. The Conference Board Leading, Coincident, and Lagging Economic Indexes®: 2000 to 2018

[299.4 represents 299,400]

| Item | Unit | 2000 | 2005 | 2010 | 2017 | 2018 |
|---|---|---|---|---|---|---|
| *The Conference Board Leading Economic Index*® (LEI) for the U.S., composite....................................... | 2016=100 | 91.3 | 100.9 | 82.1 | 104.0 | 109.9 |
| Average weekly hours, manufacturing........................... | Hours | 41.2 | 40.6 | 41.1 | 41.9 | 42.1 |
| Average weekly initial claims for unemployment insurance........................................... | 1,000 | 299.4 | 330.6 | 458.5 | 244.7 | 220.8 |
| Manufacturers' new orders, consumer goods and materials (1982 dollars)..................................... | Mil. dol. | 152,070 | 150,555 | 122,223 | 132,566 | 135,347 |
| Building permits, new private housing units..................... | 1,000 | 1,598 | 2,160 | 604 | 1,286 | 1,313 |
| Manufacturers' new orders, nondefense capital goods excluding aircraft (1982 dollars)..................... | Mil. dol. | 45,991 | 40,545 | 36,351 | 37,776 | 39,394 |
| Leading Credit Index ™ (standard deviation from the mean).. | Std. dev. | 1.5 | -0.6 | -1.0 | -0.6 | -0.6 |
| Interest rate spread, 10-year Treasury bonds less federal funds........................................................ | Percent | -0.21 | 1.08 | 3.04 | 1.33 | 1.08 |
| *The Conference Board Coincident Economic Index*® (CEI) for the U.S., composite..................................... | 2016=100 | 86.8 | 90.6 | 88.5 | 102.0 | 104.3 |
| Employees on nonagricultural payrolls.......................... | 1,000 | 132,031 | 134,040 | 130,354 | 146,611 | 149,064 |
| Index of industrial production..................................... | 2012=100 | 95.2 | 99.6 | 94.1 | 104.4 | 108.6 |
| Personal income less transfer payments (2012 dollars)....... | Bil. dol. | 9,669 | 10,460 | 10,685 | 13,171 | 13,479 |
| Manufacturing and trade sales (2012 dollars).................. | Mil. dol. | 1,127,075 | 1,248,214 | 1,198,692 | 1,452,109 | 1,488,332 |
| *Composite index of 7 lagging indicators* ........................ | 2016=100 | 75.4 | 78.9 | 82.6 | 102.5 | 104.9 |
| Inventories to sales ratio, manufacturing and trade............ | Ratio | 1.4 | 1.3 | 1.4 | 1.4 | 1.4 |
| Average duration of unemployment.............................. | Weeks | 12.7 | 18.4 | 33.1 | 25.0 | 22.7 |
| Consumer installment credit to personal income ratio......... | Percent | 18.7 | 21.2 | 20.2 | 22.2 | 22.3 |
| Commercial and industrial loans outstanding (2012 dollars)............................................. | Mil. dol. | 1,130,657 | 785,778 | 796,479 | 1,353,914 | 1,399,282 |
| Change in labor cost per unit of output, manufacturing........ | Percent | 2.3 | -1.8 | -2.4 | 2.2 | 1.0 |
| Change in consumer price index for services.................. | Percent | 3.8 | 3.5 | 0.9 | 2.6 | 2.8 |
| Average prime rate............................................... | Percent | 9.2 | 6.2 | 3.3 | 4.1 | 4.9 |

Source: The Conference Board, New York, NY 10022-6601, *Business Cycle Indicators*, monthly. Reproduced with permission from The Conference Board, Inc. © 2019, The Conference Board, Inc. For more information, see <http://www.conference-board.org/data/>.

# Table 817. Manufacturing and Trade—Sales and Inventories: 1992 to 2018

[In billions of dollars (540 represents $540,000,000,000), except ratios. Based on North American Industry Classification System (NAICS); see text, this section]

| Year | Sales, average monthly [1] | | | | Inventories [2] | | | | Inventory-sales ratio [3] | | | |
|------|-------|-------------------|--------------|---------------------------|-------|-------------------|--------------|---------------------------|-------|-------------------|--------------|---------------------------|
| | Total | Manufac-turing | Retail trade | Mer-chant whole-salers | Total | Manufac-turing | Retail trade | Mer-chant whole-salers | Total | Manufac-turing | Retail trade | Mer-chant whole-salers |
| 1992...... | 540 | 242 | 151 | 147 | 836 | 379 | 260 | 197 | 1.53 | 1.57 | 1.67 | 1.31 |
| 1993...... | 567 | 252 | 161 | 154 | 863 | 380 | 278 | 205 | 1.50 | 1.50 | 1.68 | 1.30 |
| 1994...... | 610 | 270 | 175 | 165 | 926 | 400 | 304 | 222 | 1.46 | 1.44 | 1.66 | 1.29 |
| 1995...... | 655 | 290 | 185 | 180 | 985 | 425 | 322 | 238 | 1.48 | 1.44 | 1.72 | 1.29 |
| 1996...... | 687 | 300 | 197 | 190 | 1,005 | 430 | 333 | 241 | 1.45 | 1.44 | 1.67 | 1.27 |
| 1997...... | 723 | 320 | 206 | 198 | 1,045 | 443 | 344 | 258 | 1.42 | 1.37 | 1.64 | 1.26 |
| 1998...... | 742 | 325 | 215 | 202 | 1,077 | 448 | 357 | 272 | 1.44 | 1.39 | 1.62 | 1.32 |
| 1999...... | 786 | 336 | 234 | 217 | 1,137 | 463 | 384 | 290 | 1.40 | 1.35 | 1.59 | 1.30 |
| 2000...... | 834 | 351 | 249 | 235 | 1,196 | 481 | 406 | 309 | 1.41 | 1.35 | 1.59 | 1.29 |
| 2001...... | 818 | 331 | 255 | 232 | 1,119 | 427 | 394 | 298 | 1.42 | 1.38 | 1.58 | 1.32 |
| 2002...... | 823 | 326 | 261 | 236 | 1,140 | 423 | 415 | 301 | 1.36 | 1.29 | 1.55 | 1.26 |
| 2003...... | 855 | 335 | 272 | 248 | 1,148 | 408 | 431 | 308 | 1.34 | 1.25 | 1.56 | 1.22 |
| 2004...... | 926 | 359 | 289 | 278 | 1,242 | 441 | 460 | 340 | 1.30 | 1.19 | 1.56 | 1.17 |
| 2005...... | 1,006 | 395 | 307 | 303 | 1,314 | 475 | 472 | 368 | 1.27 | 1.17 | 1.51 | 1.17 |
| 2006...... | 1,069 | 418 | 323 | 328 | 1,409 | 523 | 486 | 399 | 1.28 | 1.20 | 1.49 | 1.17 |
| 2007...... | 1,128 | 443 | 333 | 352 | 1,488 | 563 | 501 | 424 | 1.28 | 1.22 | 1.49 | 1.17 |
| 2008...... | 1,161 | 456 | 328 | 377 | 1,466 | 543 | 477 | 446 | 1.31 | 1.26 | 1.52 | 1.20 |
| 2009...... | 989 | 369 | 301 | 319 | 1,332 | 505 | 429 | 398 | 1.38 | 1.39 | 1.47 | 1.29 |
| 2010...... | 1,089 | 409 | 318 | 361 | 1,451 | 554 | 455 | 442 | 1.27 | 1.28 | 1.39 | 1.15 |
| 2011...... | 1,207 | 458 | 342 | 407 | 1,566 | 607 | 471 | 488 | 1.26 | 1.29 | 1.35 | 1.15 |
| 2012...... | 1,267 | 475 | 359 | 434 | 1,655 | 625 | 506 | 524 | 1.28 | 1.30 | 1.38 | 1.17 |
| 2013...... | 1,303 | 484 | 372 | 448 | 1,719 | 630 | 544 | 545 | 1.29 | 1.29 | 1.41 | 1.19 |
| 2014...... | 1,341 | 491 | 387 | 464 | 1,778 | 640 | 561 | 577 | 1.31 | 1.31 | 1.43 | 1.22 |
| 2015...... | 1,295 | 460 | 394 | 441 | 1,809 | 636 | 588 | 585 | 1.39 | 1.39 | 1.46 | 1.33 |
| 2016...... | 1,287 | 446 | 405 | 436 | 1,840 | 631 | 612 | 596 | 1.42 | 1.41 | 1.49 | 1.35 |
| 2017...... | 1,353 | 467 | 423 | 463 | 1,902 | 659 | 626 | 616 | 1.38 | 1.37 | 1.47 | 1.30 |
| 2018...... | 1,438 | 500 | 443 | 495 | 1,995 | 683 | 653 | 660 | 1.36 | 1.35 | 1.44 | 1.29 |

[1] Averages of monthly not-seasonally-adjusted figures. [2] Seasonally adjusted end-of-year data. [3] Averages of seasonally adjusted monthly ratios.

Source: U.S. Census Bureau, "Manufacturing & Trade Inventories & Sales," <https://www.census.gov/mtis/index.html>, accessed June 2019.

# Table 818. Industrial Production Indexes by Industry: 2000 to 2018

[2012 = 100]

| Industry | NAICS code [1] | 2000 | 2005 | 2010 | 2014 | 2015 | 2016 | 2017 | 2018 |
|----------|------------|------|------|------|------|------|------|------|------|
| **Total index**.................. | ( [2] ) | **95.2** | **99.6** | **94.1** | **105.2** | **104.1** | **102.1** | **104.4** | **108.6** |
| **Manufacturing (SIC)** [3]................ | ( [4] ) | **98.2** | **103.4** | **94.7** | **102.0** | **101.5** | **100.7** | **102.7** | **105.0** |
| Manufacturing (NAICS)................ | 31–33 | 95.1 | 101.2 | 94.2 | 102.3 | 101.9 | 101.1 | 103.2 | 106.0 |
| Durable goods.................. | ( [5] ) | 85.0 | 93.4 | 89.2 | 105.1 | 103.9 | 101.7 | 104.0 | 107.5 |
| Wood products.................. | 321 | 138.3 | 147.7 | 94.1 | 108.4 | 112.7 | 116.9 | 124.1 | 127.1 |
| Nonmetallic mineral products.............. | 327 | 132.8 | 138.6 | 95.9 | 109.1 | 109.8 | 111.3 | 115.3 | 119.5 |
| Primary metals.................. | 331 | 105.0 | 99.1 | 95.1 | 104.0 | 96.8 | 92.5 | 93.7 | 97.6 |
| Fabricated metal products.............. | 332 | 110.7 | 104.4 | 90.7 | 103.6 | 100.2 | 96.5 | 97.9 | 102.5 |
| Machinery.................. | 333 | 94.8 | 88.9 | 82.1 | 96.7 | 89.0 | 82.2 | 87.9 | 92.6 |
| Computers and electronic products.................. | 334 | 37.6 | 59.7 | 85.6 | 107.4 | 108.1 | 110.4 | 115.2 | 120.9 |
| Electrical equipment, appliances, and components.................. | 335 | 134.9 | 112.9 | 93.1 | 101.8 | 101.3 | 101.0 | 101.8 | 103.7 |
| Motor vehicles and parts.................. | 3361–3363 | 103.3 | 108.8 | 82.7 | 117.1 | 123.2 | 124.8 | 124.7 | 129.9 |
| Aerospace and other misc. transportation equipment.................. | 3364–3369 | 73.2 | 77.3 | 90.6 | 106.8 | 106.8 | 99.5 | 99.9 | 100.2 |
| Furniture and related products.................. | 337 | 147.2 | 149.8 | 91.9 | 101.3 | 106.3 | 106.6 | 106.3 | 106.3 |
| Miscellaneous products.................. | 339 | 91.6 | 105.3 | 103.4 | 100.0 | 100.4 | 100.7 | 99.5 | 99.3 |
| Nondurable goods.................. | ( [6] ) | 107.8 | 110.5 | 99.8 | 99.3 | 99.6 | 100.4 | 102.3 | 104.2 |
| Food, beverage, and tobacco products.................. | 311–312 | 98.1 | 102.7 | 99.8 | 101.6 | 103.8 | 105.0 | 107.6 | 109.7 |
| Textile and product mills.................. | 313–314 | 204.1 | 176.6 | 105.4 | 105.8 | 100.9 | 99.0 | 99.7 | 100.9 |
| Apparel and leather.................. | 315–316 | 408.0 | 225.7 | 107.8 | 88.8 | 84.7 | 80.9 | 74.6 | 72.4 |
| Paper.................. | 322 | 120.1 | 112.4 | 97.4 | 99.3 | 98.6 | 97.7 | 97.0 | 96.0 |
| Printing and related support.................. | 323 | 144.2 | 131.0 | 103.5 | 98.5 | 97.5 | 99.2 | 99.8 | 97.5 |
| Petroleum and coal products.................. | 324 | 89.2 | 100.1 | 97.9 | 100.2 | 98.1 | 104.4 | 107.1 | 106.9 |
| Chemical.................. | 325 | 96.2 | 109.3 | 101.3 | 95.6 | 95.2 | 94.7 | 96.6 | 100.4 |
| Plastics and rubber products.................. | 326 | 116.7 | 116.6 | 94.2 | 103.9 | 105.8 | 107.1 | 109.3 | 110.2 |
| Other manufacturing (non-NAICS) [7].......... | 1133, 5111 | 192.5 | 169.2 | 111.3 | 93.8 | 90.4 | 88.0 | 87.5 | 78.8 |
| **Mining**.................. | **21** | **88.8** | **84.0** | **87.2** | **117.8** | **113.9** | **102.6** | **110.1** | **123.7** |
| **Electric and gas utilities**.................. | **2211–2212** | **92.0** | **99.5** | **102.8** | **103.5** | **102.7** | **102.3** | **101.5** | **106.0** |
| Electric power generation, transmission, and distribution.................. | 2211 | 90.4 | 99.2 | 102.3 | 102.0 | 101.9 | 101.8 | 100.8 | 104.0 |
| Natural gas distribution.................. | 2212 | 103.6 | 102.0 | 106.2 | 115.7 | 109.6 | 105.9 | 106.7 | 119.1 |

[1] Except as noted, based on North American Industry Classification System, 2012; see text, this section. [2] Includes NAICS codes 31–33, 1133, 5111, 21, 2211, and 2212. [3] Standard Industrial Classification (SIC); see text, this section. [4] Includes NAICS codes 31–33, 1133, and 5111. [5] Includes NAICS codes 321, 327, and 331–339. [6] Includes NAICS codes 311–316, and 322–326. [7] Those industries—logging and newspaper, periodical, book, and directory publishing—that have traditionally been considered to be manufacturing.

Source: Board of Governors of the Federal Reserve System, "Industrial Production and Capacity Utilization, G.17," <http://www.federalreserve.gov/econresdata/default.htm>, accessed April 2019.

# Table 819. Index of Industrial Capacity and Utilization Rate: 1990 to 2018

[2012 output = 100. Annual figures are averages of monthly data. The capacity index is an indicator of the maximum sustainable output a plant can maintain under realistic circumstances; capacity here is expressed as a proportion of 2012 actual output. Capacity utilization rate is a measure of output as a proportion of capacity; this is the output index divided by the capacity index]

| Year | Index of capacity | | Utilization rate | | | | |
| | Total industry | Manufacturing [1] | Total industry | Stage of process | | | Manufacturing [1] |
| | | | | Crude [2] | Primary and semifinished [3] | Finished [4] | |
|---|---|---|---|---|---|---|---|
| 1990 | 77.9 | 77.4 | 82.4 | 87.9 | 82.6 | 80.5 | 81.5 |
| 1995 | 88.2 | 89.0 | 83.9 | 89.0 | 86.4 | 79.7 | 83.1 |
| 2000 | 116.9 | 123.2 | 81.5 | 88.5 | 84.0 | 76.9 | 79.7 |
| 2005 | 124.3 | 131.8 | 80.1 | 86.7 | 81.9 | 75.7 | 78.5 |
| 2010 | 128.0 | 134.1 | 73.5 | 83.2 | 71.8 | 71.2 | 70.7 |
| 2011 | 127.5 | 132.6 | 76.1 | 84.5 | 74.4 | 73.7 | 73.5 |
| 2012 | 130.0 | 134.1 | 76.9 | 85.5 | 74.7 | 74.8 | 74.5 |
| 2013 | 132.2 | 135.6 | 77.2 | 86.0 | 75.5 | 73.8 | 74.4 |
| 2014 | 133.8 | 135.6 | 78.6 | 88.4 | 76.7 | 74.6 | 75.2 |
| 2015 | 135.4 | 134.8 | 76.9 | 82.7 | 76.3 | 75.1 | 75.3 |
| 2016 | 136.0 | 135.7 | 75.0 | 78.4 | 75.2 | 73.6 | 74.2 |
| 2017 | 136.6 | 136.6 | 76.5 | 83.7 | 75.7 | 74.2 | 75.1 |
| 2018 | 137.9 | 137.2 | 78.7 | 88.8 | 77.5 | 75.3 | 76.6 |

[1] Manufacturing consists of those industries included in the North American Industry Classification System (NAICS) definition of manufacturing plus those industries—logging and newspaper, periodical, book, and directory publishing—that have traditionally been considered to be a part of manufacturing and are included in the industrial sector under the Standard Industrial Classification (SIC) system. [2] Crude processing covers a relatively small portion of total industrial capacity and consists of logging (NAICS 1133), much of mining (excluding stone, sand, and gravel mining, and oil and gas drilling, NAICS 21231, 21221–2, and 213111) and some basic manufacturing industries, including basic chemicals (NAICS 3251); fertilizers, pesticides, and other agricultural chemicals (NAICS 32531, 2); pulp, paper, and paperboard mills (NAICS 3221); and alumina, aluminum, and other nonferrous production and processing mills (NAICS 3313, 4). [3] Primary and semifinished processing loosely corresponds to the previously published aggregate, primary processing. Includes utilities and portions of several 2-digit SIC industries included in the former advanced processing group. These include printing and related support activities (NAICS 3231); paints and adhesives (NAICS 3255); and newspaper, periodical, book, and directory publishers (NAICS 5111). [4] Finished processing generally corresponds to the previously published aggregate, advanced processing. Includes oil and gas well drilling and carpet and rug mills.

Source: Board of Governors of the Federal Reserve System, "Industrial Production and Capacity Utilization, G.17," <https://www.federalreserve.gov/data.htm>, accessed April 2019.

# Table 820. Corporate Profits, Taxes, and Dividends: 2000 to 2018

[In billions of dollars (786.6 represents $786,600,000,000). Covers corporations organized for profit and other entities treated as corporations. Represents profits to U.S. residents, without deduction of depletion charges and exclusive of capital gains and losses; intercorporate dividends from profits of domestic corporations are eliminated; and net receipts of dividends, reinvested earnings of incorporated foreign affiliates, and earnings of unincorporated foreign affiliates are added. Minus (-) sign indicates loss]

| Item | 2000 | 2005 | 2010 | 2013 | 2014 | 2015 | 2016 | 2017 | 2018 |
|---|---|---|---|---|---|---|---|---|---|
| Corporate profits with IVA and CCAdj [1] | 786.6 | 1,488.6 | 1,728.7 | 2,010.7 | 2,118.8 | 2,057.3 | 2,035.0 | 2,099.3 | 2,262.8 |
| Taxes on corporate income | 233.4 | 379.8 | 272.5 | 362.8 | 407.4 | 397.2 | 392.9 | 350.7 | 231.3 |
| Profits after tax with IVA and CCAdj [1] | 553.2 | 1,108.8 | 1,456.2 | 1,647.9 | 1,711.5 | 1,660.1 | 1,642.1 | 1,748.6 | 2,031.5 |
| Net dividends | 410.2 | 602.0 | 643.2 | 1,009.0 | 1,096.1 | 1,164.9 | 1,187.4 | 1,215.3 | 1,241.6 |
| Undistributed profits with IVA and CCAdj [1] | 142.9 | 506.8 | 813.0 | 638.9 | 615.4 | 495.2 | 454.7 | 533.3 | 789.9 |
| Addenda for corporate cash flow: | | | | | | | | | |
| Net cash flow with IVA and CCAdj [1] | 981.6 | 1,536.6 | 2,104.7 | 2,094.8 | 2,140.4 | 2,091.8 | 2,080.5 | 1,941.4 | 2,571.5 |
| Undistributed profits with IVA and CCAdj [1] | 142.9 | 506.8 | 813.0 | 638.9 | 615.4 | 495.2 | 454.7 | 533.3 | 789.9 |
| Consumption of fixed capital | 838.6 | 1,042.0 | 1,271.2 | 1,450.2 | 1,528.3 | 1,593.4 | 1,630.3 | 1,699.6 | 1,785.9 |
| Less: Capital transfers paid (net) | – | 12.2 | -20.6 | -5.7 | 3.3 | -3.2 | 4.4 | 291.5 | 4.3 |

– Represents or rounds to zero. [1] Inventory valuation adjustment (IVA) and capital consumption adjustment (CCAdj).

Source: U.S. Bureau of Economic Analysis, National Income and Product Accounts Tables, "Table 1.12. National Income by Type of Income," <http://www.bea.gov/itable/>, accessed April 2019.

# Table 821. Corporate Profits With Inventory Valuation and Capital Consumption Adjustments—Financial and Nonfinancial Industries: 2000 to 2018

[In billions of dollars (787 represents $787,000,000,000). Based on the North American Industry Classification System, 2012; see text, this section. Minus sign (-) indicates loss. See headnote, Table 820]

| Industry group | 2000 | 2005 | 2010 | 2015 | 2016 | 2017 | 2018 |
|---|---|---|---|---|---|---|---|
| **Corporate profits with IVA/CCAdj [1]** | **787** | **1,489** | **1,729** | **2,057** | **2,035** | **2,099** | **2,263** |
| Domestic industries | 641 | 1,263 | 1,343 | 1,655 | 1,629 | 1,650 | 1,778 |
| Rest of the world | 146 | 226 | 386 | 403 | 407 | 449 | 484 |
| **Corporate profits with IVA [1]** | **730** | **1,629** | **1,786** | **2,187** | **2,129** | **2,136** | **2,129** |
| Domestic industries | 584 | 1,403 | 1,401 | 1,785 | 1,722 | 1,688 | 1,645 |
| Financial [2] | 150 | 410 | 406 | 438 | 469 | 469 | 448 |
| Nonfinancial | 434 | 994 | 995 | 1,347 | 1,253 | 1,219 | 1,197 |
| Utilities | 24 | 32 | 31 | 20 | 7 | 4 | -2 |
| Manufacturing | 176 | 280 | 282 | 423 | 323 | 293 | 282 |
| Wholesale trade | 60 | 96 | 99 | 152 | 128 | 112 | 104 |
| Retail trade | 51 | 123 | 116 | 169 | 174 | 163 | 154 |
| Transportation and warehousing | 10 | 28 | 45 | 62 | 63 | 59 | 56 |
| Information | -12 | 101 | 102 | 140 | 172 | 149 | 156 |
| Other nonfinancial [3] | 126 | 334 | 320 | 380 | 388 | 440 | 446 |
| Rest of the world | 146 | 226 | 386 | 403 | 407 | 449 | 484 |

[1] Inventory valuation adjustment (IVA) and capital consumption adjustment (CCAdj). [2] Consists of finance and insurance and bank and other holding companies. [3] Consists of agriculture, forestry, fishing, and hunting; mining; construction; real estate and rental and leasing; professional, scientific, and technical services; administrative and waste management services; educational services; health care and social assistance; arts, entertainment, and recreation; accommodation and food services; and other services, except government.

Source: U.S. Bureau of Economic Analysis, National Income and Product Accounts Tables, "Table 6.16D. Corporate Profits by Industry," <http://www.bea.gov/itable/>, accessed April 2019.

## Table 822. Corporate Profits Before Taxes by Industry: 2000 to 2018

[In billions of dollars (747 represents $747,000,000,000). Profits are without inventory valuation and capital consumption adjustments. Minus sign (-) indicates loss. See headnote, Table 820]

| Industry | 2012 NAICS code [1] | 2000 | 2010 | 2015 | 2016 | 2017 | 2018 |
|---|---|---|---|---|---|---|---|
| **Corporate profits before tax** | (X) | **747** | **1,834** | **2,137** | **2,117** | **2,133** | **2,063** |
| Domestic industries | (X) | 601 | 1,448 | 1,734 | 1,706 | 1,679 | 1,562 |
| Agriculture, forestry, fishing, and hunting | 11 | 1 | 8 | 12 | 8 | 8 | 4 |
| Mining | 21 | 15 | 33 | -9 | -25 | -5 | 20 |
| Utilities | 221 | 25 | 31 | 19 | 10 | 12 | -4 |
| Construction | 23 | 36 | 27 | 76 | 94 | 100 | 109 |
| Manufacturing | 31-33 | 186 | 299 | 393 | 333 | 344 | 310 |
| Wholesale trade | 42 | 63 | 117 | 136 | 126 | 137 | 122 |
| Retail trade | 44–45 | 53 | 126 | 167 | 171 | 161 | 139 |
| Transportation and warehousing | 48–49 | 10 | 45 | 60 | 64 | 59 | 45 |
| Information | 51 | -12 | 102 | 136 | 158 | 141 | 122 |
| Finance and insurance | 52 | 46 | 220 | 290 | 303 | 292 | 279 |
| Real estate and rental and leasing | 53 | 9 | 14 | 20 | 24 | 19 | 11 |
| Professional, scientific, and technical services | 54 | 9 | 82 | 75 | 75 | 69 | 62 |
| Management of companies and enterprises [2] | 551111, 2 | 103 | 186 | 158 | 153 | 122 | 126 |
| Administrative and waste management services | 56 | 9 | 28 | 34 | 37 | 40 | 37 |
| Educational services | 61 | 2 | 11 | 5 | 5 | 5 | 5 |
| Health care and social assistance | 62 | 23 | 78 | 86 | 96 | 99 | 103 |
| Arts, entertainment, and recreation | 71 | 3 | 8 | 11 | 14 | 15 | 15 |
| Accommodation and food services | 72 | 14 | 18 | 44 | 41 | 39 | 33 |
| Other services, except public administration | 81 | 6 | 15 | 21 | 21 | 21 | 22 |
| Rest of the world [3] | (X) | 146 | 386 | 403 | 412 | 454 | 502 |

X Not applicable. [1] Based on North American Industry Classification System, 2012; see text, this section. [2] Consists of bank and other holding companies. [3] Consists of receipts by all U.S. residents, including both corporations and persons, of dividends from foreign corporations, and, for U.S. corporations, their share of reinvested earnings of their incorporated foreign affiliates, and earnings of unincorporated foreign affiliates, net of corresponding payments.

Source: U.S. Bureau of Economic Analysis, National Income and Product Accounts Tables, "Table 6.17D. Corporate Profits Before Tax by Industry," <http://www.bea.gov/itable/>, accessed August 2019.

## Table 823. Manufacturing, Mining, and Trade Corporations—Profits and Stockholders' Equity by Industry: 2017 and 2018

[Averages of quarterly figures at annual rates. Manufacturing data exclude estimates for corporations with less than $250,000 in assets at time of sample selection. Mining, and wholesale and retail trade data excludes estimates for corporations with less than $50 million in assets at time of sample selection. Based on sample; see source for discussion of methodology. Based on North American Industry Classification System (NAICS), 2017; see text, this section]

| Industry | 2017 NAICS code | Ratio of profits after taxes to stockholders' equity (percent) | | Profits after taxes per dollar of sales (cents) | | Ratio of stockholders' equity to debt | |
|---|---|---|---|---|---|---|---|
| | | 2017 | 2018 | 2017 | 2018 | 2017 | 2018 |
| **Manufacturing** | **31–33** | **12.6** | **14.4** | **8.4** | **9.3** | **1.4** | **1.4** |
| Nondurable manufacturing | (X) | 12.4 | 12.4 | 8.8 | 8.6 | 1.2 | 1.3 |
| Food | 311 | 14.5 | 6.6 | 7.6 | 3.9 | 1.4 | 1.3 |
| Beverage and tobacco products | 312 | 19.8 | 19.9 | 21.8 | 24.0 | 0.8 | 0.9 |
| Textile mills and textile product mills | 313, 314 | 12.6 | 9.5 | 7.0 | 5.3 | 2.4 | 2.2 |
| Apparel and leather products | 315, 316 | 22.4 | 26.0 | 10.0 | 9.8 | 1.6 | 1.4 |
| Paper | 322 | 19.1 | 15.9 | 7.8 | 7.0 | 0.8 | 1.0 |
| Printing and related support activities | 323 | 18.7 | 21.2 | 3.6 | 4.2 | 0.5 | 0.5 |
| Petroleum and coal products | 324 | 8.7 | 10.9 | 5.5 | 6.2 | 2.2 | 2.4 |
| Chemicals | 325 | 10.8 | 13.3 | 10.7 | 13.2 | 1.0 | 1.1 |
| Plastics and rubber products | 326 | 16.3 | 7.9 | 7.1 | 3.7 | 1.2 | 1.2 |
| Durable manufacturing | (X) | 12.7 | 16.5 | 8.1 | 9.9 | 1.5 | 1.5 |
| Wood products | 321 | 14.7 | 17.2 | 5.4 | 6.6 | 1.4 | 1.5 |
| Nonmetallic mineral products | 327 | 9.2 | 10.0 | 7.0 | 7.7 | 2.1 | 1.9 |
| Primary metals | 331 | 11.3 | 12.3 | 7.3 | 7.9 | 1.8 | 2.4 |
| Fabricated metal products | 332 | 16.9 | 19.0 | 7.3 | 8.1 | 1.4 | 1.4 |
| Machinery | 333 | 16.9 | 15.5 | 7.4 | 9.0 | 1.6 | 1.8 |
| Computer and electronic products | 334 | 14.3 | 20.7 | 17.1 | 23.0 | 1.5 | 1.5 |
| Electrical equipment, appliances, & components | 335 | 14.3 | -10.1 | 1.3 | -5.2 | 1.5 | 1.2 |
| Transportation equipment | 336 | 15.7 | 20.7 | 4.9 | 6.3 | 1.5 | 1.4 |
| Furniture and related products | 337 | 26.4 | 23.5 | 6.9 | 5.7 | 1.2 | 1.0 |
| Miscellaneous manufacturing | 339 | 8.1 | 12.0 | 8.1 | 12.3 | 1.5 | 1.5 |
| **All mining** | **21** | **2.0** | **5.9** | **3.1** | **8.0** | **1.4** | **1.5** |
| **All wholesale trade** | **42** | **11.7** | **11.2** | **1.9** | **1.8** | **1.3** | **1.3** |
| Durable goods | 423 | 9.3 | 11.8 | 2.0 | 2.5 | 1.5 | 1.5 |
| Nondurable goods | 424, 425 | 15.3 | 10.2 | 1.7 | 1.1 | 1.0 | 1.0 |
| **All retail trade** | **44–45** | **17.7** | **16.4** | **3.0** | **2.9** | **1.1** | **1.1** |
| Food and beverage stores | 445 | 12.5 | 10.2 | 1.6 | 1.4 | 1.3 | 1.3 |
| Clothing and general merchandise stores | 448, 452 | 17.6 | 13.9 | 3.2 | 2.5 | 1.3 | 1.3 |
| All other retail trade | (X) | 19.0 | 19.4 | 3.3 | 3.6 | 1.0 | 0.9 |

X Not applicable.

Source: U.S. Census Bureau, *Quarterly Financial Report for Manufacturing, Mining, Trade, and Selected Service Industries*, <http://www.census.gov/econ/qfr/index.html>.

# Table 824. U.S. Multinational Enterprises—Value Added, Employment, and Capital Expenditures: 1989 to 2016

[Value added and capital expenditures in billions of dollars (1,401 represents $1,401,000,000,000); employees in thousands. For the years shown prior to 2007, the data items needed to calculate value added and capital expenditures for individual U.S. parents and foreign affiliates were collected for nonbank businesses only. The value added and capital expenditures statistics for bank parents and affiliates for those years are estimates. See headnote, Table 825. MNE = Multinational enterprise. MOFA = Majority-owned foreign affiliate]

| Item | 1989 | 1994 | 1999 | 2004 | 2009 | 2010 | 2014 | 2015 | 2016 (P) |
|---|---|---|---|---|---|---|---|---|---|
| **VALUE ADDED** | | | | | | | | | |
| MNEs worldwide: | | | | | | | | | |
| Parents and MOFAs................ | 1,401 | 1,773 | 2,645 | 3,221 | 3,741 | 4,191 | 5,380 | 5,308 | 5,226 |
| Parents.................................. | 1,077 | 1,362 | 2,064 | 2,366 | 2,596 | 2,949 | 3,889 | 3,949 | 3,926 |
| MOFAs.................................. | 324 | 411 | 580 | 854 | 1,145 | 1,242 | 1,490 | 1,359 | 1,300 |
| **EMPLOYEES** | | | | | | | | | |
| MNEs worldwide: | | | | | | | | | |
| Parents and all affiliates............ | 26,370 | 26,571 | 33,398 | 32,892 | 35,962 | 36,287 | 43,988 | 44,685 | 44,762 |
| Parents and MOFAs................ | 24,826 | 25,142 | 31,913 | 31,466 | 33,727 | 34,105 | 41,640 | 42,127 | 42,279 |
| Parents.................................. | 19,617 | 19,330 | 23,985 | 22,446 | 22,933 | 22,791 | 27,587 | 28,046 | 28,023 |
| Affiliates, total......................... | 6,753 | 7,241 | 9,412 | 10,445 | 13,029 | 13,496 | 16,401 | 16,639 | 16,739 |
| MOFAs.................................. | 5,209 | 5,812 | 7,928 | 9,020 | 10,794 | 11,313 | 14,052 | 14,081 | 14,256 |
| Other..................................... | 1,544 | 1,429 | 1,484 | 1,426 | 2,235 | 2,182 | 2,349 | 2,558 | 2,483 |
| **CAPITAL EXPENDITURES** | | | | | | | | | |
| MNEs worldwide: | | | | | | | | | |
| Parents and all affiliates............ | 279 | 331 | 563 | 500 | 653 | (NA) | 1,018 | (NA) | (NA) |
| Parents and MOFAs................ | 263 | 306 | 531 | 476 | 599 | 607 | 968 | 927 | 857 |
| Parents.................................. | 204 | 235 | 417 | 351 | 432 | 441 | 722 | 713 | 657 |
| Affiliates, total......................... | 75 | 96 | 146 | 149 | 221 | (NA) | 296 | (NA) | (NA) |
| MOFAs.................................. | 59 | 72 | 115 | 125 | 167 | 166 | 245 | 215 | 199 |
| Other..................................... | 16 | 25 | 31 | 24 | 54 | (NA) | 51 | (NA) | (NA) |

P Preliminary. NA Not available.

Source: U.S. Bureau of Economic Analysis, "Activities of U.S. Multinational Enterprises in 2016," *Survey of Current Business*, Vol. 98, No. 9, September 2018. See also <https://apps.bea.gov/scb/issues.htm>.

# Table 825. U.S. Multinational Enterprises—Selected Characteristics: 2016

[In billions of dollars (40,407 represents $40,407,000,000,000), except as indicated. Data for 2016 are preliminary. Consists of U.S. parent enterprises and their foreign affiliates. U.S. parent comprises the domestic operations of a multinational and is a U.S. person that owns or controls, directly or indirectly, 10 percent or more of the voting securities of an incorporated foreign business enterprise, or an equivalent interest in an unincorporated foreign business enterprise. A U.S. person can be an incorporated business enterprise. A majority-owned foreign affiliate (MOFA) is a foreign business enterprise in which a U.S. parent enterprise owns or controls more than 50 percent of the voting securities]

| Industry | 2007 NAICS code [1] | U.S. parents [2] Total assets | U.S. parents [2] Capital expenditures | U.S. parents [2] Value added | U.S. parents [2] Employment (1,000) | Majority-owned foreign affiliates [3] Capital expenditures | Majority-owned foreign affiliates [3] Value added | Majority-owned foreign affiliates [3] Employment (1,000) |
|---|---|---|---|---|---|---|---|---|
| All industries........................ | (X) | 40,407 | 657 | 3,026 | 28,023 | 100 | 1,300 | 14,266 |
| Mining [4]................................ | 21 | 559 | 39 | 68 | 258 | 46 | 81 | 231 |
| Oil and gas extraction............... | 211 | 289 | 24 | 33 | 46 | 36 | 54 | 53 |
| Manufacturing [4]...................... | 31-33 | 8,284 | 213 | 1,387 | 7,276 | 64 | 558 | 5,411 |
| Food...................................... | 311 | 687 | 14 | 108 | 848 | 6 | 32 | 456 |
| Beverages and tobacco products.................. | 312 | 366 | 4 | 68 | 144 | 4 | 53 | 242 |
| Petroleum and coal products............ | 324 | 1,114 | 36 | 125 | 272 | 2 | 38 | 15 |
| Chemicals [4]........................... | 325 | 1,895 | 32 | 281 | 905 | 13 | 127 | 677 |
| Pharmaceuticals and medicines.................. | 3254 | 1,312 | 13 | 185 | 424 | 6 | 67 | 274 |
| Machinery............................... | 333 | 455 | 11 | 79 | 565 | 4 | 59 | 524 |
| Computers and electronic products [4]............. | 334 | 1,093 | 25 | 220 | 900 | 13 | 86 | 860 |
| Computers and peripheral equipment........... | 3341 | 329 | 7 | 80 | 183 | 2 | 37 | 246 |
| Transportation equipment [4]........................ | 336 | 1,347 | 57 | 232 | 1,424 | 9 | 54 | 1,106 |
| Motor vehicles, bodies and trailers, & parts..... | 3361-3363 | 669 | 46 | 103 | 636 | 8 | 47 | 1,011 |
| Wholesale trade......................... | 42 | 1,585 | 46 | 236 | 1,684 | 9 | 158 | 944 |
| Retail trade [4]........................... | 44, 45 | 977 | 44 | 387 | 5,928 | 7 | 79 | 1,576 |
| General merchandise stores.................. | 452 | 280 | 13 | 147 | 2,472 | 4 | 33 | 929 |
| Information [4]........................... | 51 | 2,685 | 93 | 469 | 2,184 | 16 | 85 | 643 |
| Publishing industries.................. | 511 | 447 | 9 | 91 | 464 | 2 | 36 | 185 |
| Broadcasting (except internet)..................... | 515 | 622 | 18 | 107 | 507 | 1 | 6 | 24 |
| Telecommunications.................. | 517 | 968 | 48 | 162 | 565 | 9 | 15 | 106 |
| Finance and insurance [4]............................. | 52 | 22,694 | 64 | 513 | 2,853 | 7 | 88 | 704 |
| Insurance carriers and related activities.......... | 524 | 7,156 | 14 | 132 | 1,144 | 1 | 22 | 211 |
| Professional, scientific, & technical services [4]..... | 54 | 799 | 12 | 249 | 1,642 | 6 | 124 | 1,428 |
| Computer systems design & related services.... | 5415 | 394 | 6 | 78 | 490 | 4 | 55 | 779 |
| Other industries [4]..................................... | (X) | 2,824 | 147 | 617 | 6,197 | 43 | 129 | 3,319 |
| Utilities.................................... | 22 | 728 | 46 | 70 | 179 | 8 | 12 | 36 |
| Transportation and warehousing.................. | 48-49 | 570 | 36 | 180 | 1,364 | 5 | 24 | 333 |
| Real estate & rental and leasing................... | 53 | 476 | 37 | 70 | 354 | 19 | 44 | 175 |
| Administration, support, and waste management................. | 56 | 195 | 6 | 68 | 1,141 | 1 | 40 | 1,156 |

X Not applicable. [1] Based on North American Industry Classification System, 2007; see text, this section. [2] Data are by industry of U.S. parent. [3] Data are by industry of foreign affiliate. [4] Includes other industries, not shown separately.

Source: U.S. Bureau of Economic Analysis, International Economic Accounts, "Direct Investment and Multinational Enterprises," <http://www.bea.gov/iTable/index_MNC.cfm>, accessed November 2018.

# Table 826. U.S. Multinational Enterprises—Value Added: 2010 and 2016

[In billions of dollars (4,191 represents $4,191,000,000,000). See headnote, Table 825. Data are by industry of U.S. parent]

| Industry | 2007 NAICS code[1] | U.S. multinationals | | U.S. parents | | Majority-owned foreign affiliates | |
|---|---|---|---|---|---|---|---|
| | | 2010 | 2016 | 2010 | 2016 | 2010 | 2016 |
| **All industries**........................ | (X) | **4,191** | **5,226** | **2,949** | **3,926** | **1,242** | **1,300** |
| Mining[2]................................ | 21 | 118 | 94 | 75 | 68 | 43 | 26 |
| Oil and gas extraction................ | 211 | 58 | 43 | 41 | 33 | 18 | 9 |
| Manufacturing[2]....................... | 31-33 | 1,900 | 2,061 | 1,147 | 1,387 | 753 | 675 |
| Food.................................... | 311 | 145 | 147 | 96 | 108 | 49 | 39 |
| Beverages and tobacco products...... | 312 | 67 | 84 | 49 | 68 | 18 | 16 |
| Petroleum and coal products.......... | 324 | 383 | 243 | 135 | 125 | 248 | 118 |
| Chemicals[2]........................... | 325 | 337 | 431 | 197 | 281 | 140 | 151 |
| Pharmaceuticals and medicines...... | 3254 | 187 | 276 | 113 | 185 | 74 | 91 |
| Machinery.............................. | 333 | 104 | 115 | 69 | 79 | 35 | 37 |
| Computers and electronic products[2].. | 334 | 235 | 338 | 155 | 220 | 80 | 118 |
| Computers and peripheral equipment.. | 3341 | 68 | 132 | 38 | 80 | 31 | 52 |
| Semiconductors and other electronic components..... | 3344 | 79 | 80 | 51 | 53 | 28 | 27 |
| Transportation equipment[2]........... | 336 | 314 | 329 | 229 | 232 | 85 | 97 |
| Motor vehicles, bodies and trailers, and parts........ | 3361-3363 | 133 | 155 | 83 | 103 | 49 | 53 |
| Wholesale trade....................... | 42 | 174 | 282 | 143 | 236 | 32 | 47 |
| Retail trade[2]......................... | 44, 45 | 303 | 442 | 257 | 387 | 46 | 55 |
| General merchandise stores.......... | 452 | (NA) | (NA) | 122 | 147 | (D) | (D) |
| Information[2].......................... | 51 | 392 | 558 | 333 | 469 | 58 | 89 |
| Publishing industries................. | 511 | 100 | 125 | 72 | 91 | 27 | 34 |
| Broadcasting (except internet)........ | 515 | 49 | 115 | 41 | 107 | 8 | 8 |
| Telecommunications................... | 517 | 172 | 174 | 162 | 162 | 10 | 13 |
| Finance and insurance[2].............. | 52 | 480 | 677 | 357 | 513 | 123 | 164 |
| Depository credit intermediation (banking)...... | 5221 | 157 | 224 | 139 | 206 | 18 | 18 |
| Insurance carriers and related activities............ | 524 | 101 | 158 | 84 | 132 | 17 | 26 |
| Professional, scientific, and technical services[2]........ | 54 | 275 | 344 | 196 | 249 | 79 | 95 |
| Computer systems design and related services......... | 5415 | 133 | 138 | 80 | 78 | 53 | 59 |
| Other industries[2]..................... | (X) | 548 | 767 | 440 | 617 | 108 | 150 |
| Utilities................................ | 22 | 66 | 78 | 61 | 70 | 5 | 7 |
| Transportation and warehousing...... | 48-49 | 132 | 200 | 116 | 180 | 17 | 19 |
| Real estate and rental and leasing.... | 53 | 44 | 87 | 35 | 70 | 9 | 17 |
| Administration, support, and waste management....... | 56 | 99 | 96 | 73 | 68 | 26 | 28 |
| Accommodation and food services.... | 72 | 75 | 96 | 54 | 66 | 22 | 29 |

X Not applicable. NA Not available. D Data withheld to avoid disclosure. [1] Based on North American Industry Classification System, 2007; see text, this section. [2] Includes other industries, not shown separately.

Source: U.S. Bureau of Economic Analysis, International Economic Accounts, "Direct Investment and Multinational Enterprises," <http://www.bea.gov/iTable/index_MNC.cfm>, accessed November 2018.

# Table 827. U.S. Majority-Owned Foreign Affiliates—Value Added by Industry of Affiliate and Country: 2016

[In millions of dollars (1,300,419 represents $1,300,419,000,000). Data are preliminary. See headnote, Table 825. Numbers in parentheses represent North American Industry Classification System 2007 codes; see text, this section]

| Country | All industries[1] | Mining (21) | Manufacturing (31-33) | | Wholesale trade (42) | Finance and insurance (52) | Professional, scientific, and technical services (54) |
|---|---|---|---|---|---|---|---|
| | | | Total[1] | Chemicals (325) | | | |
| **All countries[2]**.............. | **1,300,419** | **80,696** | **557,619** | **127,344** | **157,574** | **87,966** | **123,643** |
| United Kingdom................ | 166,067 | 3,528 | 53,735 | 5,449 | 12,041 | 26,565 | 19,825 |
| Canada........................ | 118,863 | 5,359 | 45,013 | 6,651 | 13,270 | 3,656 | 8,560 |
| Ireland........................ | 90,971 | (D) | 41,095 | 14,107 | 5,093 | 2,281 | 6,684 |
| Germany....................... | 80,697 | 685 | 40,929 | 8,411 | 12,198 | 2,022 | 7,145 |
| China.......................... | 65,141 | 853 | 37,244 | 9,522 | 10,024 | 1,073 | 4,696 |
| Netherlands.................... | 56,987 | 430 | 29,911 | 7,442 | 4,852 | 3,798 | 3,087 |
| Switzerland.................... | 55,648 | 181 | 18,614 | 9,155 | 18,596 | 1,214 | 1,984 |
| France......................... | 49,765 | 38 | 25,473 | 5,857 | 6,703 | 1,774 | 4,806 |
| Japan.......................... | 46,795 | – | 17,015 | 5,954 | 6,907 | 5,460 | 7,755 |
| Mexico......................... | 45,108 | 2,397 | 25,579 | 3,209 | 2,267 | 3,039 | 1,946 |
| Singapore...................... | 44,512 | 306 | 19,356 | 7,659 | 8,597 | 4,360 | 2,655 |
| Australia....................... | 41,499 | 4,406 | 14,332 | 2,005 | 6,432 | 1,589 | 5,554 |
| Brazil.......................... | 34,785 | 1,338 | 19,579 | 4,881 | 1,924 | 3,116 | 2,905 |
| India........................... | 29,079 | 43 | 6,373 | 2,036 | 2,031 | 2,544 | 13,362 |
| Italy........................... | 28,485 | 128 | 11,225 | 2,832 | 3,313 | 465 | 2,217 |
| Belgium........................ | 25,313 | (Z) | 13,272 | 6,950 | 5,586 | 2,047 | 1,153 |
| Hong Kong..................... | 17,245 | 5 | 3,952 | 629 | 4,588 | 4,811 | 2,248 |
| Spain.......................... | 16,202 | 15 | 9,593 | 2,259 | 2,339 | 352 | 884 |
| Korea, South................... | 16,066 | (D) | 10,386 | 1,303 | 1,557 | 1,209 | 772 |

– Represents or rounds to zero. D Data withheld to avoid disclosure. Z A non-zero value between -$500,000 and $500,000. [1] Includes other industries, not shown separately. [2] Includes other countries, not shown separately.

Source: U.S. Bureau of Economic Analysis, International Economic Accounts, "Activities of U.S. Multinational Enterprises, Majority-owned Foreign Affiliates, Value Added by Country and Industry 2009-2016," <http://www.bea.gov/international/di1usdop.htm>, accessed November 2018.

# Section 16
# Science and Technology

This section presents statistics on scientific, engineering, and technological resources, with emphasis on patterns of research and development (R&D) funding and on scientific, engineering, and technical personnel; education; and employment.

The National Science Foundation (NSF) gathers data chiefly through recurring surveys and reports the data via detailed statistical tables; information briefs; and annual, biennial, and special reports; see <http://www.nsf.gov/statistics>. Areas of coverage include R&D expenditures; Federal R&D funding; scientific employment; graduate enrollment and support in academic science and engineering; characteristics of doctoral scientists and engineers; and of recent graduates in the United States. Report titles include: *Science and Engineering Indicators; National Patterns of R&D Resources; Federal Funds for Research and Development; Federal R&D Funding by Budget Function; Federal Support for S&E to Universities, Colleges, and Selected Nonprofit Institutions;* and *Business Research and Development and Innovation.* Statistical surveys in these areas pose problems of concept and definition and the data should therefore be regarded as broad estimates rather than precise, quantitative statements. See sources for methodological and technical details.

The National Science Board's biennial *Science and Engineering Indicators* at <http://www.nsf.gov/statistics/seind/> contains data and analysis of international and domestic science and technology, including education and workforce statistics.

**Research and development outlays**—NSF defines research as "systematic study directed toward fuller scientific knowledge of the subject studied" and development as "the systematic use of scientific knowledge directed toward the production of useful materials, devices, systems, or methods, including design and development of prototypes and processes."

National coverage of R&D expenditures is developed primarily from periodic surveys in four principal economic sectors: (1) *government*, made up primarily of federal executive agencies; (2) *industry*, consisting of manufacturing and nonmanufacturing firms and the federally funded research and development centers (FFRDCs) they administer; (3) *universities and colleges*, composed of universities, colleges, and their affiliated institutions, agricultural experiment stations, and associated schools of agriculture and of medicine, and FFRDCs administered by educational institutions; and (4) *other nonprofit institutions*, consisting of such organizations as private philanthropic foundations, nonprofit research institutes, voluntary health agencies, and FFRDCs administered by nonprofit organizations.

The R&D funds reported consist of current operating costs, including planning and administration costs, except as otherwise noted. They exclude funds for routine testing, mapping and surveying, collection of general purpose data, dissemination of scientific information, and training of scientific personnel.

**Scientists, engineers, and technicians**—Scientists and engineers are defined as persons engaged in scientific and engineering work at a level requiring a knowledge of sciences equivalent at least to that acquired through completion of a 4-year college course. Technicians are defined as persons engaged in technical work at a level requiring knowledge acquired through a technical institute, junior college, or other type of training less extensive than 4-year college training. Craftsmen and skilled workers are excluded.

[In millions of dollars (13,711 represents $13,711,000,000), except percent]

| Year | Total | Sources of funds — Federal government | Industry | Universities/ colleges [1] | Non-profit | Non-federal government [2] | Percent of total — Federal government | Industry | Universities/ colleges [1] | Non-profit | Non-federal government [2] |
|---|---|---|---|---|---|---|---|---|---|---|---|
| 1960...... | 13,711 | 8,915 | 4,516 | 67 | 123 | 90 | 65.0 | 32.9 | 0.5 | 0.9 | 0.7 |
| 1970...... | 26,271 | 14,984 | 10,449 | 259 | 343 | 237 | 57.0 | 39.8 | 1.0 | 1.3 | 0.9 |
| 1980...... | 63,224 | 29,986 | 30,929 | 920 | 871 | 519 | 47.4 | 48.9 | 1.5 | 1.4 | 0.8 |
| 1985...... | 114,671 | 52,641 | 57,962 | 1,743 | 1,491 | 834 | 45.9 | 50.5 | 1.5 | 1.3 | 0.7 |
| 1986...... | 120,249 | 54,622 | 60,991 | 2,019 | 1,647 | 969 | 45.4 | 50.7 | 1.7 | 1.4 | 0.8 |
| 1987...... | 126,360 | 58,609 | 62,576 | 2,262 | 1,849 | 1,065 | 46.4 | 49.5 | 1.8 | 1.5 | 0.8 |
| 1988...... | 133,881 | 60,131 | 67,977 | 2,527 | 2,081 | 1,165 | 44.9 | 50.8 | 1.9 | 1.6 | 0.9 |
| 1989...... | 141,891 | 60,465 | 74,966 | 2,852 | 2,333 | 1,274 | 42.6 | 52.8 | 2.0 | 1.6 | 0.9 |
| 1990...... | 151,993 | 61,610 | 83,208 | 3,187 | 2,589 | 1,399 | 40.5 | 54.7 | 2.1 | 1.7 | 0.9 |
| 1991...... | 160,876 | 60,783 | 92,300 | 3,458 | 2,852 | 1,483 | 37.8 | 57.4 | 2.1 | 1.8 | 0.9 |
| 1992...... | 165,350 | 60,915 | 96,229 | 3,569 | 3,113 | 1,525 | 36.8 | 58.2 | 2.2 | 1.9 | 0.9 |
| 1993...... | 165,730 | 60,528 | 96,549 | 3,709 | 3,388 | 1,557 | 36.5 | 58.3 | 2.2 | 2.0 | 0.9 |
| 1994...... | 169,207 | 60,777 | 99,204 | 3,938 | 3,665 | 1,623 | 35.9 | 58.6 | 2.3 | 2.2 | 1.0 |
| 1995...... | 183,625 | 62,969 | 110,871 | 4,110 | 3,925 | 1,751 | 34.3 | 60.4 | 2.2 | 2.1 | 1.0 |
| 1996...... | 197,346 | 63,394 | 123,417 | 4,436 | 4,239 | 1,861 | 32.1 | 62.5 | 2.2 | 2.1 | 0.9 |
| 1997...... | 211,894 | 64,362 | 136,208 | 4,852 | 4,571 | 1,902 | 30.4 | 64.3 | 2.3 | 2.2 | 0.9 |
| 1998...... | 225,759 | 65,908 | 147,774 | 5,193 | 4,963 | 1,920 | 29.2 | 65.5 | 2.3 | 2.2 | 0.9 |
| 1999...... | 244,451 | 66,817 | 164,545 | 5,654 | 5,399 | 2,036 | 27.3 | 67.3 | 2.3 | 2.2 | 0.8 |
| 2000...... | 267,950 | 67,238 | 185,975 | 6,270 | 6,285 | 2,182 | 25.1 | 69.4 | 2.3 | 2.3 | 0.8 |
| 2001...... | 278,539 | 73,793 | 188,408 | 6,874 | 7,122 | 2,341 | 26.5 | 67.6 | 2.5 | 2.6 | 0.8 |
| 2002...... | 277,911 | 78,873 | 180,704 | 7,673 | 8,109 | 2,553 | 28.4 | 65.0 | 2.8 | 2.9 | 0.9 |
| 2003...... | 291,365 | 85,133 | 186,171 | 8,286 | 8,988 | 2,788 | 29.2 | 63.9 | 2.8 | 3.1 | 1.0 |
| 2004...... | 302,731 | 90,795 | 191,346 | 8,637 | 9,028 | 2,926 | 30.0 | 63.2 | 2.9 | 3.0 | 1.0 |
| 2005...... | 325,288 | 95,413 | 207,775 | 9,353 | 9,771 | 2,977 | 29.3 | 63.9 | 2.9 | 3.0 | 0.9 |
| 2006...... | 350,908 | 99,938 | 227,182 | 10,176 | 10,320 | 3,293 | 28.5 | 64.7 | 2.9 | 2.9 | 0.9 |
| 2007...... | 377,890 | 105,128 | 246,815 | 10,933 | 11,420 | 3,594 | 27.8 | 65.3 | 2.9 | 3.0 | 1.0 |
| 2008...... | 404,773 | 117,615 | 258,016 | 11,738 | 13,184 | 4,221 | 29.1 | 63.7 | 2.9 | 3.3 | 1.0 |
| 2009...... | 402,931 | 125,765 | 246,610 | 12,056 | 14,205 | 4,295 | 31.2 | 61.2 | 3.0 | 3.5 | 1.1 |
| 2010...... | 406,580 | 126,617 | 248,124 | 12,262 | 15,275 | 4,302 | 31.1 | 61.0 | 3.0 | 3.8 | 1.1 |
| 2011...... | 426,161 | 127,015 | 266,421 | 13,104 | 15,235 | 4,386 | 29.8 | 62.5 | 3.1 | 3.6 | 1.0 |
| 2012...... | 433,619 | 123,838 | 275,717 | 14,300 | 15,607 | 4,158 | 28.6 | 63.6 | 3.3 | 3.6 | 1.0 |
| 2013...... | 453,964 | 120,130 | 297,167 | 15,378 | 17,045 | 4,244 | 26.5 | 65.5 | 3.4 | 3.8 | 0.9 |
| 2014...... | 475,418 | 118,364 | 318,382 | 16,209 | 18,250 | 4,214 | 24.9 | 67.0 | 3.4 | 3.8 | 0.9 |
| 2015...... | 493,687 | 119,495 | 333,207 | 17,320 | 19,386 | 4,280 | 24.2 | 67.5 | 3.5 | 3.9 | 0.9 |
| 2016 [3].... | 515,305 | 116,120 | 355,545 | 18,462 | 20,637 | 4,542 | 22.5 | 69.0 | 3.6 | 4.0 | 0.9 |
| 2017 [4].... | 542,222 | 117,955 | 378,022 | 19,511 | 21,986 | 4,748 | 21.8 | 69.7 | 3.6 | 4.1 | 0.9 |

[1] Figures for university and college (U&C) R&D prior to 2003 cover only science and engineering (S&E) fields; in 2003 and later years, R&D in non-S&E fields is also included. Also, adjustments have been made to U&C R&D for 1998 and later years to eliminate double counting of funds passed through from one academic institution to another. [2] Nonfederal R&D expenditures to university and college performers. [3] Some data for 2016 are preliminary. [4] Estimated.

Source: U.S. National Science Foundation, *National Patterns of R&D Resources, 2016-17 Data Update*, NSF 19-309, February 2019. See also <http://www.nsf.gov/statistics/natlpatterns/>.

## Table 829. National Research and Development (R&D) Expenditures as a Percent of Gross Domestic Product by Country: 1990 to 2017

| Year | United States | Japan [1] | Germany [2] | France | United Kingdom | Italy | Canada | South Korea | OECD total [3] | Russia | China |
|---|---|---|---|---|---|---|---|---|---|---|---|
| 1990.... | [4] 2.56 | [7] 2.71 | [7] 2.61 | 2.27 | 1.95 | [8] 1.21 | 1.48 | (NA) | [7] 2.16 | 1.89 | (NA) |
| 1995.... | [4] 2.41 | [7] 2.61 | 2.13 | 2.24 | 1.66 | 0.94 | 1.65 | [9] 2.20 | [5,7] 1.95 | 0.79 | [10] 0.57 |
| 2000.... | [4] 2.63 | 2.91 | 2.40 | [5] 2.09 | 1.63 | 1.01 | 1.86 | [9] 2.18 | [7] 2.12 | 0.98 | [5] 0.89 |
| 2005.... | [4] 2.52 | 3.18 | 2.43 | 2.05 | 1.56 | 1.05 | 1.97 | [9] 2.63 | [7] 2.14 | 0.99 | 1.31 |
| 2006.... | [4] 2.56 | 3.28 | 2.46 | 2.05 | 1.58 | 1.09 | 1.94 | [9] 2.83 | [7] 2.17 | 1.00 | 1.37 |
| 2007.... | [4] 2.63 | 3.34 | 2.45 | 2.02 | 1.62 | 1.13 | 1.90 | [5] 3.00 | [7] 2.20 | 1.04 | 1.37 |
| 2008.... | [4] 2.77 | [5] 3.34 | 2.60 | 2.06 | [7] 1.62 | 1.16 | 1.86 | 3.12 | [7] 2.27 | 0.97 | 1.45 |
| 2009.... | [4] 2.81 | 3.23 | 2.73 | 2.21 | [7] 1.68 | 1.22 | 1.92 | 3.29 | [7] 2.32 | 1.16 | [5] 1.66 |
| 2010.... | [4] 2.74 | 3.14 | 2.71 | [5] 2.18 | [7] 1.66 | 1.22 | 1.83 | 3.47 | [7] 2.28 | 1.05 | 1.71 |
| 2011.... | [4] 2.77 | 3.24 | 2.80 | 2.19 | 1.66 | 1.21 | 1.79 | 3.74 | [7] 2.31 | 1.01 | 1.78 |
| 2012.... | [4] 2.68 | 3.21 | 2.87 | 2.23 | [7] 1.59 | 1.27 | [5] 1.77 | 4.03 | [7] 2.31 | 1.03 | 1.91 |
| 2013.... | [4] 2.71 | [5] 3.31 | 2.82 | 2.24 | 1.64 | 1.31 | 1.71 | 4.15 | [7] 2.33 | 1.03 | 2.00 |
| 2014.... | [4] 2.72 | 3.40 | 2.87 | [5] 2.28 | [7] 1.66 | [7] 1.34 | [5] 1.71 | 4.29 | [7] 2.35 | 1.07 | 2.03 |
| 2015.... | [4] 2.72 | 3.28 | 2.91 | 2.27 | 1.67 | 1.34 | 1.69 | 4.22 | [7] 2.34 | 1.10 | 2.07 |
| 2016.... | [4,6] 2.76 | 3.16 | 2.92 | [6] 2.22 | [7] 1.68 | [5] 1.37 | 1.69 | 4.23 | [7] 2.34 | 1.10 | 2.12 |
| 2017.... | [4,7] 2.79 | 3.21 | 3.04 | [7] 2.19 | [6] 1.66 | [6] 1.35 | [6] 1.59 | 4.55 | [7] 2.37 | [7] 1.11 | 2.15 |

NA Not available. [1] Data on Japanese research and development after 1996 may not be consistent with data in earlier years because of changes in methodology. [2] Data for 1990 are for West Germany only. [3] Organisation for Economic Cooperation and Development. [4] Excludes most or all capital expenditure. [5] Time series break. [6] Provisional. [7] Estimated value. [8] Excluding extramural R&D expenditure. [9] Excluding R&D in the social sciences and humanities. [10] Underestimated or based on underestimated data.

Source: Organisation for Economic Co-operation and Development (OECD), 2019, "Main Science and Technology Indicators," OECD Science, Technology and R&D Statistics (database) ©, <http://dx.doi.org/10.1787/data-00182-en>, accessed September 2019.

# Table 830. Research and Development (R&D) Expenditures By Performing Sector and Source of Funds: 1990 to 2017

[In millions of dollars (151,993 represents $151,993,000,000). For calendar year. FFRDCs are federally funded research and development centers]

| Year | Total | All federal research | Federal intramural[1] | FFRDCs[2] | Non-federal government | Industry: Total | Industry: Federal government | Industry: Industry[3] | Universities and colleges: Total | Univ: Federal government | Univ: Non-federal government[3] | Univ: Industry | Univ: Universities & colleges | Univ: Non-profits | Other nonprofit institutions: Total | Other: Federal government | Other: Industry | Other: Non-profits |
|---|---|---|---|---|---|---|---|---|---|---|---|---|---|---|---|---|---|---|
| **RESEARCH AND DEVELOPMENT TOTAL** | | | | | | | | | | | | | | | | | | |
| 1990 | 151,993 | 23,524 | 15,671 | 7,853 | (NA) | 107,404 | 25,802 | 81,602 | 16,939 | 9,939 | 1,399 | 1,166 | 3,187 | 1,249 | 4,126 | 2,346 | 440 | 1,340 |
| 2000 | 267,950 | 28,516 | 19,247 | 9,269 | (NA) | 199,961 | 17,117 | 182,844 | 29,916 | 17,095 | 2,182 | 2,112 | 6,270 | 2,258 | 9,557 | 4,510 | 1,020 | 4,027 |
| 2010 | 406,580 | 50,798 | 31,970 | 18,828 | 691 | 278,977 | 34,199 | 244,778 | 58,084 | 34,682 | 3,673 | 2,953 | 12,262 | 4,515 | 18,030 | 7,093 | 1,265 | 9,672 |
| 2012 | 433,619 | 52,144 | 34,017 | 18,128 | 665 | 302,251 | 30,621 | 271,630 | 60,896 | 34,968 | 3,560 | 3,169 | 14,300 | 4,899 | 17,664 | 6,239 | 1,366 | 10,059 |
| 2013 | 453,964 | 51,086 | 33,406 | 17,680 | 620 | 322,528 | 29,362 | 293,166 | 61,546 | 33,839 | 3,643 | 3,375 | 15,378 | 5,312 | 18,185 | 5,970 | 1,444 | 10,770 |
| 2014 | 475,418 | 52,687 | 34,783 | 17,903 | 583 | 340,728 | 26,554 | 314,174 | 62,346 | 33,121 | 3,714 | 3,601 | 16,209 | 5,701 | 19,075 | 6,135 | 1,520 | 11,420 |
| 2015[4] | 493,687 | 52,847 | 34,199 | 18,649 | 608 | 355,821 | 26,990 | 328,831 | 64,642 | 33,554 | 3,772 | 3,842 | 17,320 | 6,154 | 19,769 | 6,219 | 1,572 | 11,979 |
| 2016[5] | 515,305 | 51,140 | 31,715 | 19,424 | 651 | 374,685 | 23,772 | 350,913 | 67,813 | 34,677 | 3,953 | 4,042 | 18,462 | 6,679 | 21,017 | 6,641 | 1,649 | 12,728 |
| 2017[5] | 542,222 | 51,326 | 31,168 | 20,159 | 688 | 397,064 | 23,785 | 373,279 | 70,826 | 35,736 | 4,103 | 4,266 | 19,511 | 7,210 | 22,319 | 7,212 | 1,725 | 13,382 |
| **BASIC RESEARCH** | | | | | | | | | | | | | | | | | | |
| 1990 | 23,029 | 5,352 | 2,319 | 3,033 | (NA) | 4,629 | 869 | 3,760 | 11,126 | 6,889 | 847 | 705 | 1,929 | 756 | 1,922 | 947 | 245 | 730 |
| 2000 | 42,033 | 7,801 | 3,765 | 4,037 | (NA) | 7,040 | 925 | 6,115 | 22,290 | 13,469 | 1,501 | 1,453 | 4,314 | 1,553 | 4,902 | 2,099 | 566 | 2,236 |
| 2010 | 75,907 | 11,748 | 5,111 | 6,637 | 98 | 16,371 | 1,406 | 14,964 | 38,203 | 23,412 | 2,251 | 1,750 | 7,882 | 2,910 | 9,487 | 3,414 | 702 | 5,370 |
| 2012 | 73,285 | 11,150 | 5,489 | 5,661 | 95 | 13,294 | 644 | 12,650 | 39,311 | 23,111 | 2,176 | 1,828 | 9,083 | 3,113 | 9,436 | 3,092 | 758 | 5,585 |
| 2013 | 78,486 | 9,519 | 5,330 | 4,188 | 88 | 19,508 | 1,196 | 18,312 | 39,558 | 22,313 | 2,188 | 1,939 | 9,765 | 3,354 | 9,813 | 3,031 | 802 | 5,980 |
| 2014 | 82,054 | 9,875 | 5,705 | 4,170 | 97 | 21,936 | 2,044 | 19,891 | 39,871 | 21,812 | 2,227 | 2,057 | 10,214 | 3,562 | 10,275 | 3,090 | 844 | 6,341 |
| 2015[4] | 83,456 | 10,017 | 5,890 | 4,127 | 100 | 21,792 | 2,038 | 19,754 | 40,989 | 21,900 | 2,277 | 2,176 | 10,875 | 3,761 | 10,558 | 3,034 | 873 | 6,651 |
| 2016[5] | 88,567 | 10,315 | 6,119 | 4,196 | 123 | 24,644 | 2,005 | 22,639 | 42,279 | 22,260 | 2,351 | 2,252 | 11,468 | 3,949 | 11,206 | 3,224 | 915 | 7,067 |
| 2017[5] | 92,231 | 10,358 | 6,222 | 4,136 | 161 | 26,176 | 2,006 | 24,170 | 43,772 | 22,819 | 2,415 | 2,344 | 12,001 | 4,193 | 11,765 | 3,377 | 958 | 7,430 |
| **APPLIED RESEARCH** | | | | | | | | | | | | | | | | | | |
| 1990 | 34,897 | 4,808 | 3,652 | 1,156 | (NA) | 24,399 | 5,967 | 18,432 | 4,406 | 2,140 | 453 | 377 | 1,031 | 404 | 1,284 | 780 | 120 | 384 |
| 2000 | 56,503 | 7,856 | 6,105 | 1,750 | (NA) | 39,176 | 2,682 | 36,494 | 6,361 | 3,081 | 558 | 540 | 1,604 | 578 | 3,110 | 1,831 | 258 | 1,021 |
| 2010 | 79,258 | 13,203 | 8,016 | 5,187 | 577 | 44,906 | 4,705 | 40,201 | 14,759 | 8,762 | 1,015 | 778 | 3,141 | 1,064 | 5,813 | 3,041 | 321 | 2,451 |
| 2012 | 87,070 | 14,328 | 8,587 | 5,741 | 555 | 50,755 | 4,137 | 46,618 | 15,908 | 9,170 | 1,007 | 877 | 3,693 | 1,162 | 5,524 | 2,629 | 346 | 2,549 |
| 2013 | 88,335 | 15,132 | 8,309 | 6,823 | 518 | 51,013 | 6,028 | 44,985 | 16,112 | 8,876 | 1,063 | 935 | 3,943 | 1,296 | 5,561 | 2,465 | 366 | 2,730 |
| 2014 | 91,890 | 15,727 | 8,775 | 6,952 | 473 | 53,415 | 6,445 | 46,971 | 16,422 | 8,708 | 1,085 | 997 | 4,214 | 1,418 | 5,853 | 2,574 | 385 | 2,894 |
| 2015[4] | 97,323 | 16,698 | 9,347 | 7,351 | 494 | 56,472 | 6,102 | 50,370 | 17,463 | 9,095 | 1,093 | 1,107 | 4,562 | 1,606 | 6,197 | 2,762 | 398 | 3,036 |
| 2016[5] | 104,629 | 17,416 | 9,788 | 7,628 | 509 | 61,019 | 5,181 | 55,839 | 19,060 | 9,805 | 1,179 | 1,224 | 4,998 | 1,855 | 6,625 | 2,981 | 418 | 3,226 |
| 2017[5] | 110,352 | 17,784 | 9,805 | 7,979 | 505 | 64,764 | 5,184 | 59,580 | 20,164 | 10,224 | 1,244 | 1,308 | 5,357 | 2,031 | 7,136 | 3,307 | 437 | 3,391 |
| **DEVELOPMENT** | | | | | | | | | | | | | | | | | | |
| 1990 | 94,067 | 13,363 | 9,700 | 3,663 | (NA) | 78,376 | 18,966 | 59,410 | 1,407 | 910 | 99 | 83 | 226 | 89 | 920 | 619 | 75 | 226 |
| 2000 | 169,414 | 12,859 | 9,377 | 3,482 | (NA) | 153,745 | 13,510 | 140,235 | 1,265 | 545 | 123 | 119 | 352 | 127 | 1,545 | 580 | 195 | 771 |
| 2010 | 251,415 | 25,847 | 18,844 | 7,004 | 15 | 217,700 | 28,089 | 189,611 | 5,122 | 2,509 | 408 | 425 | 1,240 | 541 | 2,730 | 638 | 242 | 1,850 |
| 2012 | 273,264 | 26,666 | 19,941 | 6,725 | 15 | 238,202 | 25,840 | 212,362 | 5,677 | 2,687 | 378 | 464 | 1,524 | 625 | 2,704 | 518 | 261 | 1,925 |
| 2013 | 287,144 | 26,436 | 19,767 | 6,668 | 14 | 252,007 | 22,137 | 229,870 | 5,877 | 2,650 | 393 | 502 | 1,670 | 663 | 2,811 | 474 | 276 | 2,061 |
| 2014 | 301,474 | 27,084 | 20,303 | 6,781 | 13 | 265,377 | 18,065 | 247,312 | 6,053 | 2,602 | 402 | 548 | 1,781 | 721 | 2,947 | 471 | 291 | 2,185 |
| 2015[4] | 312,909 | 26,132 | 18,961 | 7,171 | 14 | 277,557 | 18,850 | 258,707 | 6,191 | 2,559 | 403 | 559 | 1,883 | 787 | 3,015 | 422 | 301 | 2,292 |
| 2016[5] | 322,109 | 23,409 | 15,808 | 7,601 | 18 | 289,021 | 16,586 | 272,434 | 6,475 | 2,613 | 424 | 567 | 1,997 | 875 | 3,187 | 436 | 315 | 2,435 |
| 2017[5] | 339,638 | 23,184 | 15,140 | 8,044 | 22 | 306,124 | 16,595 | 289,528 | 6,890 | 2,693 | 444 | 614 | 2,153 | 985 | 3,418 | 528 | 330 | 2,560 |

NA Not available. [1] Includes expenditures for federal intramural R&D as well as cost associated with administering extramural R&D. [2] The R&D expenditures of FFRDC's are chiefly federally funded, the small remainder reflects funding from state or local government, businesses, other nonprofit organizations, and other sources. [3] Includes all nonfederal sources. [4] Some data for 2016 are preliminary. [5] Estimates.

Source: National Science Foundation, National Center for Science and Engineering Statistics, *National Patterns of R&D Resources: 2016-17 Data Update*, NSF 19-309, February 2019. See also <http://www.nsf.gov/statistics/natlpatterns/>.

# Table 831. Federal Obligations for Research by Field of Science: 2010 to 2018

[In millions of dollars (63,728 represents $63,728,000,000). For years ending September 30. Excludes research and development (R&D) plant (facilities and fixed equipment)]

| Field of science | 2010 | 2012 | 2013 | 2014 | 2015 | 2016 | 2017 | 2018 (P) |
|---|---|---|---|---|---|---|---|---|
| **Research, total**......................... | **63,728** | **61,986** | **59,533** | **63,191** | **63,825** | **66,874** | **69,642** | **71,263** |
| Basic................................... | 31,795 | 30,959 | 29,779 | 31,588 | 31,527 | 32,287 | 33,265 | 33,712 |
| Applied................................ | 31,933 | 31,027 | 29,753 | 31,604 | 32,298 | 34,587 | 36,376 | 37,551 |
| Computer sciences and mathematics....... | 3,412 | 3,528 | 3,427 | 3,883 | 3,863 | 4,223 | 3,894 | 4,184 |
| Engineering............................ | 11,081 | 11,403 | 10,948 | 11,888 | 11,984 | 12,799 | 12,978 | 14,726 |
| Environmental sciences.................. | 3,339 | 3,884 | 4,041 | 4,366 | 4,414 | 4,428 | 4,470 | 4,291 |
| Life sciences.......................... | 33,909 | 31,006 | 29,663 | 30,951 | 30,625 | 32,045 | 34,090 | 33,459 |
| Physical sciences...................... | 5,871 | 6,408 | 6,282 | 6,483 | 6,510 | 6,670 | 6,582 | 6,931 |
| Psychology............................. | 2,156 | 2,087 | 1,935 | 1,968 | 1,995 | 2,021 | 2,081 | 2,092 |
| Social sciences........................ | 1,197 | 1,125 | 1,237 | 1,435 | 1,136 | 1,227 | 1,027 | 1,044 |
| Other sciences, n.e.c. [1]............... | 2,763 | 2,546 | 1,999 | 2,218 | 3,299 | 3,461 | 4,521 | 4,536 |

P Data are preliminary. [1] Not elsewhere classified.

Source: U.S. National Science Foundation, *Federal Funds for Research and Development, Fiscal Years 2017-18; Data Tables*, June 2019, and earlier reports. See also <http://www.nsf.gov/statistics/fedfunds/>.

# Table 832. Federal Budget Authority for Research and Development (R&D) by Selected Budget Function: 2000 to 2018

[In millions of current dollars (78,664 represents $78,664,000,000). For year ending September 30. Excludes R&D plant. Represents budget authority. Functions shown are those for which $1 billion or more was authorized in 2018]

| Function | 2000 | 2010 | 2013 | 2014 | 2015 | 2016 | 2017 | 2018 (P) |
|---|---|---|---|---|---|---|---|---|
| **Total** [1]............................ | **78,664** | **146,596** | **130,861** | **133,547** | **136,090** | **147,813** | **124,710** | **128,107** |
| National defense....................... | 42,580 | 86,517 | 70,620 | 70,611 | 72,560 | 79,828 | 57,055 | 60,775 |
| Health................................. | 17,869 | 31,488 | 30,044 | 30,927 | 30,331 | 32,365 | 34,255 | 34,379 |
| General science and basic research..... | 4,977 | 9,280 | 8,802 | 9,482 | 10,068 | 10,042 | 9,947 | 10,050 |
| Space flight, research, and supporting activities...................... | 5,363 | 8,232 | 10,476 | 11,055 | 10,875 | 12,789 | 10,134 | 9,713 |
| Energy................................. | 996 | 2,455 | 2,269 | 2,387 | 3,153 | 3,473 | 3,519 | 3,483 |
| Natural resources and environment...... | 1,999 | 2,237 | 2,020 | 2,172 | 2,161 | 2,294 | 2,378 | 2,389 |
| Agriculture............................ | 1,426 | 2,043 | 1,753 | 1,967 | 1,989 | 2,030 | 2,090 | 1,994 |
| Transportation......................... | 1,636 | 1,496 | 1,337 | 1,261 | 1,363 | 1,326 | 1,444 | 1,439 |
| Veterans benefits and services......... | 645 | 1,034 | 1,164 | 1,101 | 1,178 | 1,222 | 1,346 | 1,338 |

P Preliminary [1] Includes other functions, not shown separately.

Source: U.S. National Science Foundation, *Federal R&D Funding by Budget Function: Fiscal Years 2017-19*, NSF 19-312, February 2019, and earlier reports. See also <http://www.nsf.gov/statistics/fedbudget/>.

# Table 833. Federal Research and Development (R&D) Budget by Federal Agency: 2010 to 2019

[In millions of dollars (149,595 represents $149,595,000,000). For fiscal years ending September 30. R&D refers to actual research and development activities as well as R&D facilities. R&D facilities (also known as R&D plants) includes construction, repair, or alteration of physical plant used in the conduct of R&D. Based on Office of Management and Budget data]

| Federal agency | 2010 | 2013 | 2014 | 2015 | 2016 | 2017 | 2018 [2] | 2019 [3,4] |
|---|---|---|---|---|---|---|---|---|
| **Total research and development** [1].......... | **149,595** | **131,483** | **136,565** | **138,959** | **149,520** | **128,540** | **142,888** | **133,251** |
| Defense R&D........................... | 86,756 | 69,766 | 71,469 | 72,344 | 79,109 | 57,447 | 66,132 | 65,972 |
| Nondefense R&D........................ | 62,840 | 61,716 | 65,096 | 66,615 | 70,411 | 71,093 | 76,757 | 67,278 |
| Department of Defense.................. | 82,902 | 65,540 | 66,505 | 66,146 | 72,801 | 51,062 | 58,557 | 59,085 |
| NASA.................................. | 9,262 | 10,999 | 11,754 | 12,145 | 13,273 | 12,170 | 11,214 | 10,841 |
| Department of Energy.................. | 10,836 | 10,705 | 11,994 | 14,385 | 15,007 | 14,800 | 18,359 | 14,196 |
| Office of Science.................... | 4,528 | 4,291 | 4,724 | 5,099 | 5,305 | 5,342 | 6,204 | 5,335 |
| Health and Human Services.............. | 31,758 | 29,802 | 30,669 | 30,453 | 32,243 | 34,222 | 37,057 | 34,196 |
| National Institutes of Health........ | 30,189 | 28,341 | 29,251 | 29,026 | 30,843 | 32,542 | 35,647 | 33,138 |
| National Science Foundation............ | 5,392 | 5,329 | 5,800 | 5,990 | 6,022 | 5,946 | 6,279 | 6,121 |
| Department of Agriculture.............. | 2,611 | 2,116 | 2,380 | 2,454 | 2,657 | 2,584 | 2,776 | 2,106 |
| Department of Interior................. | 776 | 785 | 840 | 864 | 973 | 941 | 1,016 | 735 |
| Department of Transportation........... | 1,073 | 818 | 797 | 887 | 948 | 921 | 1,022 | 817 |
| Environmental Protection Agency........ | 597 | 530 | 538 | 521 | 513 | 499 | 518 | 275 |
| Department of Commerce................. | 1,337 | 1,297 | 1,552 | 1,527 | 1,675 | 1,796 | 2,473 | 1,365 |
| NIST [5]............................... | 588 | 596 | 655 | 669 | 762 | 750 | 1,055 | 563 |
| Department of Homeland Security........ | 887 | 684 | 1,032 | 919 | 582 | 723 | 735 | 546 |
| Department of Veterans Affairs......... | 1,034 | 1,164 | 1,101 | 1,178 | 1,222 | 1,346 | 1,340 | 1,345 |
| All other............................. | 1,131 | 1,714 | 1,604 | 1,491 | 1,604 | 1,529 | 1,541 | 1,623 |

[1] Includes data for agencies not shown. [2] Estimated. [3] Proposed budget outlay estimates based on official Office of Management and Budget and agency data and source estimates. See source for details. [4] Beginning in FY 2019, federal agencies changed what is counted as R&D, excluding user demonstrations of a system for a specific use case and preproduction development. Therefore FY 2019 R&D figures are not fully compatible with earlier data. [5] National Institute of Standards and Technology.

Source: American Association for the Advancement of Science (AAAS), "Updated FY 2019 Budget Tables," *Guide to the President's Budget: Research and Development FY 2019* ©, May 2018, and earlier reports. See also <http://www.aaas.org/program/rd-budget-and-policy-program/>.

# Table 834. Funds for Domestic Business Research and Development (R&D) Performed by Companies by Industry: 2015

[In millions of dollars (404,594 represents $404,594,000,000), except percent. For calendar years. The data represents for-profit companies that have five or more paid employees in the United States, have at least one establishment that is in business during the survey year, and is located in the United States. Covers basic research, applied research, and development performed by the company and others. Based on the Business R&D Innovation Survey. For information, see <http://www.nsf.gov/statistics/srvyindustry/>]

| Industry | NAICS [1] code | Domestic R&D paid for by the company and others | | Domestic R&D paid for by the company | |
|---|---|---|---|---|---|
| | | Value (million dollars) | As a percent of domestic sales [2] | Value (million dollars) | As a percent of domestic sales [2] |
| **All industries, total [3]** | (X) | **404,594** | **4.5** | **296,677** | **3.3** |
| **All manufacturing industries, total [3]** | (X) | **278,782** | **5.2** | **195,792** | **3.7** |
| Chemicals | 325 | 99,369 | 9.7 | 58,769 | 5.7 |
| Pharmaceuticals and medicines | 3254 | 89,308 | 19.6 | 50,242 | 11.0 |
| Machinery | 333 | 13,965 | 3.9 | 12,544 | 3.5 |
| Semiconductor machinery | 333242 | 3,261 | 30.4 | 2,917 | 27.2 |
| Computer and electronic products | 334 | 74,036 | 10.1 | 63,765 | 8.7 |
| Electrical equipment, appliances, and components | 335 | 4,523 | 3.0 | 3,852 | 2.6 |
| Transportation equipment | 336 | 56,534 | 4.8 | 29,224 | 2.5 |
| Aerospace products and parts | 3364 | 32,220 | 9.9 | 11,138 | 3.4 |
| **All nonmanufacturing industries, total [3]** | (X) | **125,811** | **3.4** | **100,885** | **2.7** |
| Mining, extraction, and support activities | 21 | 4,484 | 1.5 | 3,393 | 1.2 |
| Information | 51 | 67,372 | 6.1 | 64,578 | 5.8 |
| Software publishing | 5112 | 34,508 | 8.6 | 32,500 | 8.1 |
| Professional, scientific, and technical services | 54 | 41,744 | 9.9 | 21,915 | 5.2 |
| Computer systems design and related services | 5415 | 14,431 | 9.5 | 12,418 | 8.2 |
| Scientific research and development services | 5417 | 18,861 | 31.0 | 3,896 | 6.4 |

X Not applicable. [1] North American Industry Classification System (NAICS); see text, Section 15. [2] Includes companies located in the United States that performed or funded R&D. [3] Includes industries not shown separately.

Source: U.S. National Science Foundation, National Center for Science and Engineering Statistics, *Business Research and Development and Innovation: 2015*, NSF 18-313, August 2018. See also <http://www.nsf.gov/statistics/industry/>.

# Table 835. Academic and Industrial Research and Development (R&D) Expenditures by State: 2016

[In millions of dollars (67,813 represents $67,813,000,000). Industry R&D data refer to calendar years; other R&D data refer to fiscal years but are used here as approximations to calendar year data. For definition of research and development see text this section]

| State | Academic R&D [2] (mil. dol.) | Academic R&D per $1,000 of state GDP | Industry-performed R&D (mil. dol.) | Industry R&D per $1,000 of state GDP | State | Academic R&D [2] (mil. dol.) | Academic R&D per $1,000 of state GDP | Industry-performed R&D (mil. dol.) | Industry R&D per $1,000 of state GDP |
|---|---|---|---|---|---|---|---|---|---|
| **U.S. [1]** | **67,813** | **3.62** | **374,685** | **20.03** | MO | 1,119 | 3.77 | 5,958 | 20.06 |
| AL | 950 | 4.65 | 1,694 | 8.30 | MT | 195 | 4.20 | 140 | 3.01 |
| AK | 167 | 3.30 | 34 | 0.67 | NE | 481 | 4.04 | 604 | 5.08 |
| AZ | 1,162 | 3.82 | 6,472 | 21.26 | NV | 191 | 1.29 | 574 | 3.87 |
| AR | 298 | 2.46 | 366 | 3.02 | NH | 380 | 4.88 | 1,919 | 24.65 |
| CA | 8,889 | 3.39 | 117,569 | 44.88 | NJ | 1,158 | 2.01 | 15,715 | 27.27 |
| CO | 1,379 | 4.26 | 4,355 | 13.45 | NM | 375 | 4.02 | 487 | 5.22 |
| CT | 1,176 | 4.58 | 7,987 | 31.07 | NY | 6,090 | 4.06 | 15,714 | 10.47 |
| DE | 198 | 2.79 | 2,069 | 29.17 | NC | 2,938 | 5.67 | 10,064 | 19.41 |
| DC | 556 | 4.42 | 328 | 2.61 | ND | 227 | 4.26 | 254 | 4.76 |
| FL | 2,527 | 2.72 | 6,273 | 6.74 | OH | 2,193 | 3.51 | 8,892 | 14.24 |
| GA | 2,180 | 4.09 | 5,245 | 9.85 | OK | 489 | 2.69 | 692 | 3.81 |
| HI | 318 | 3.75 | 164 | 1.93 | OR | 759 | 3.34 | 6,523 | 28.73 |
| ID | 155 | 2.26 | 1,590 | 23.17 | PA | 3,951 | 5.46 | 12,300 | 16.99 |
| IL | 2,401 | 3.01 | 13,733 | 17.23 | RI | 463 | 8.05 | 875 | 15.22 |
| IN | 1,410 | 4.08 | 5,949 | 17.23 | SC | 687 | 3.26 | 1,301 | 6.17 |
| IA | 814 | 4.37 | 2,862 | 15.37 | SD | 107 | 2.20 | 151 | 3.10 |
| KS | 559 | 3.61 | 2,204 | 14.24 | TN | 1,092 | 3.29 | 1,610 | 4.85 |
| KY | 556 | 2.84 | 1,070 | 5.47 | TX | 5,257 | 3.28 | 17,353 | 10.84 |
| LA | 683 | 2.87 | 274 | 1.15 | UT | 573 | 3.64 | 3,453 | 21.94 |
| ME | 100 | 1.68 | 290 | 4.88 | VT | 121 | 3.87 | 248 | 7.93 |
| MD | 3,800 | 9.98 | 5,676 | 14.91 | VA | 1,463 | 2.98 | 3,773 | 7.68 |
| MA | 3,797 | 7.51 | 21,560 | 42.63 | WA | 1,646 | 3.45 | 19,673 | 41.25 |
| MI | 2,468 | 5.07 | 18,847 | 38.71 | WV | 199 | 2.74 | 182 | 2.51 |
| MN | 961 | 2.84 | 7,084 | 20.91 | WI | 1,459 | 4.64 | 4,972 | 15.82 |
| MS | 455 | 4.17 | 222 | 2.04 | WY | 112 | 2.95 | 172 | 4.54 |

[1] U.S. totals will not equal state totals because the U.S. totals include data for outlying areas (Puerto Rico, Guam, and Virgin Islands), R&D expenditures that cannot be allocated to specific states, and double counting of U&C (universities and colleges) data (see footnote 2). [2] State level university R&D data have not been adjusted to eliminate double counting of funds passed through from one academic institution to another. See source for more information.

Source: National Science Foundation, *National Patterns of R&D Resources: 2016-17 Data Update*, NSF 19-309, February 2019. See also <http://www.nsf.gov/statistics/natlpatterns/>.

## Table 836. Research and Development (R&D) Expenditures in Science and Engineering at Universities and Colleges: 2010 to 2017

[In millions of dollars (61,287 represents $61,287,000,000). Data include R&D expenditures for both science and engineering (S&E) as well as non S&E fields, except for data by field. Beginning with FY2012, includes institutions reporting $1 million or more in total R&D expenditures; prior to FY2012 includes all institutions. Totals may not add due to rounding. Reference period is the fiscal year of the surveyed institutions. Data are based on the Higher Education R&D (HERD) Survey, which in 2010 succeeded the Survey of Research and Development Expenditures at Colleges and Universities; see source for details]

| Characteristic | 2010 | 2012 | 2013 | 2014 | 2015 | 2016 | 2017 |
|---|---|---|---|---|---|---|---|
| **Expenditures, total** | **61,287** | **65,729** | **67,013** | **67,197** | **68,551** | **71,795** | **75,175** |
| Basic research | 40,416 | 42,402 | 43,305 | 42,989 | 43,851 | 45,103 | 46,465 |
| Applied research & development (R&D) | 20,870 | 23,327 | 23,708 | 24,207 | 24,699 | 26,692 | 28,710 |
| SOURCE OF FUNDS | | | | | | | |
| Federal government | 37,478 | 40,142 | 39,446 | 37,960 | 37,849 | 38,778 | 40,238 |
| State and local government | 3,887 | 3,734 | 3,696 | 3,903 | 3,855 | 4,024 | 4,237 |
| Institutions' own funds | 11,943 | 13,587 | 14,936 | 15,735 | 16,592 | 17,964 | 18,884 |
| Industry | 3,202 | 3,274 | 3,511 | 3,727 | 4,002 | 4,211 | 4,425 |
| Nonprofit organizations | 3,730 | 4,022 | 3,889 | 3,964 | 4,220 | 4,615 | 5,117 |
| Other | 1,048 | 969 | 1,535 | 1,908 | 2,033 | 2,203 | 2,274 |
| FIELD | | | | | | | |
| Total science and engineering | 58,388 | 62,199 | 63,354 | 63,764 | 64,940 | 67,648 | 70,829 |
| Physical sciences | 4,622 | 4,710 | 4,647 | 4,616 | 4,659 | 4,889 | 5,049 |
| Geosciences | 2,992 | 3,173 | 3,195 | 3,228 | 3,247 | 3,086 | 3,154 |
| Mathematics and statistics | 592 | 674 | 671 | 658 | 641 | 682 | 701 |
| Computer and information sciences | 1,638 | 1,822 | 2,068 | 1,928 | 1,963 | 2,078 | 2,192 |
| Life sciences | 34,984 | 37,200 | 37,565 | 37,955 | 38,782 | 40,868 | 43,095 |
| Psychology | 1,078 | 1,179 | 1,128 | 1,142 | 1,182 | 1,219 | 1,243 |
| Social sciences | 2,000 | 2,054 | 2,173 | 2,216 | 2,317 | 2,368 | 2,550 |
| Other sciences | 1,156 | 1,102 | 1,172 | 1,044 | 1,078 | 1,077 | 947 |
| Engineering | 9,326 | 10,284 | 10,734 | 10,977 | 11,071 | 11,381 | 11,897 |

Source: U.S. National Science Foundation, "Higher Education Research and Development: Fiscal Year 2017, Data Tables," and earlier editions, <http://www.nsf.gov/statistics/herd/>, accessed January 2019.

## Table 837. Federal Research and Development (R&D) Obligations to Selected Universities and Colleges: 1990 to 2017

[In millions of dollars (9,031.4 represents $9,031,400,000). Year ending September 30. Top 40 institutions receiving Federal Research & Development (R&D) funds in FY2017. From the Survey of Federal Science and Engineering Support to Universities, Colleges, and Nonprofit Institutions. Included are colleges of liberal arts; schools of arts and sciences; professional schools, as in engineering and medicine, including affiliate hospitals and associated research institutes; and agricultural experiment stations. Does not cover academic Federally Funded Research and Development Centers (FFRDC) administered by higher education institutions. Includes administrative expenses for R&D and excludes investments in physical assets, routine testing, quality control, and monitoring, and training of scientific and technical personnel, see <http://ncsesdata.nsf.gov/fedsupport/2017/fss17-tech-notes.pdf>. Data not comparable to previous editions]

| Major institution ranked by 2017 obligations | 1990 | 2000 | 2010 [2] | 2015 | 2016 | 2017 |
|---|---|---|---|---|---|---|
| **Total, all institutions** [1] | **9,031.4** | **17,271.7** | **30,748.2** | **26,772.3** | **28,199.5** | **29,462.9** |
| Johns Hopkins University | 469.5 | 795.5 | 1,515.8 | 1,340.7 | 1,805.4 | 1,658.3 |
| University of Michigan, all campuses | 176.4 | 346.7 | 686.6 | 606.1 | 626.1 | 656.7 |
| University of Washington—Seattle | 217.2 | 396.1 | 736.6 | 611.9 | 590.3 | 612.7 |
| University of California—San Diego | 164.8 | 314.4 | 613.2 | 536.6 | 554.5 | 586.7 |
| University of California—San Francisco | 167.3 | 289.2 | 531.3 | 528.5 | 547.2 | 573.5 |
| Stanford University | 248.0 | 355.0 | 516.8 | 504.0 | 513.9 | 550.2 |
| Columbia University in the City of New York | 154.1 | 284.6 | 497.6 | 476.1 | 522.6 | 534.7 |
| University of Pennsylvania | 142.5 | 348.5 | 609.0 | 494.6 | 512.1 | 509.3 |
| University of Pittsburgh, all campuses | 116.6 | 246.2 | 497.1 | 450.0 | 493.6 | 503.6 |
| University of California—Los Angeles | 176.7 | 372.4 | 548.8 | 481.8 | 490.8 | 492.4 |
| Duke University | 116.1 | 232.2 | 496.8 | 428.5 | 467.8 | 490.3 |
| Georgia Institute of Technology—Atlanta | 54.3 | 58.4 | 234.9 | 295.2 | 156.9 | 465.7 |
| University of Wisconsin—Madison | 155.2 | 263.4 | 461.9 | 386.6 | 411.8 | 453.8 |
| Washington University | 117.9 | 287.3 | 445.5 | 391.6 | 408.9 | 447.8 |
| Harvard University | 148.1 | 299.9 | 548.7 | 425.5 | 448.1 | 447.5 |
| University of Colorado—Boulder | 116.4 | 272.3 | 427.0 | 416.7 | 438.8 | 442.2 |
| Yale University | 142.5 | 260.0 | 470.5 | 370.8 | 425.6 | 431.6 |
| University of North Carolina at Chapel Hill | 100.2 | 232.7 | 429.7 | 416.8 | 452.4 | 430.3 |
| Pennsylvania State University, all campuses | 136.4 | 230.1 | 413.1 | 362.9 | 362.1 | 428.9 |
| University of Southern California | 122.7 | 203.9 | 378.9 | 289.2 | 325.2 | 405.8 |
| Cornell University, all campuses | 144.7 | 240.1 | 359.8 | 296.4 | 303.6 | 369.1 |
| Vanderbilt University | 70.6 | 138.4 | 399.1 | 329.3 | 379.8 | 368.6 |
| Northwestern University | 61.1 | 151.5 | 282.0 | 337.0 | 367.4 | 357.8 |
| University of Minnesota, all campuses | 137.5 | 276.8 | 420.3 | 359.5 | 349.8 | 355.1 |
| Emory University | 49.6 | 145.6 | 303.1 | 324.2 | 320.6 | 340.0 |
| New York University | 80.0 | 130.0 | 257.1 | 263.8 | 273.0 | 328.5 |
| Massachusetts Institute of Technology | 218.3 | 248.9 | 340.2 | 350.5 | 340.6 | 319.5 |
| University of California—Davis | 68.9 | 148.5 | 313.2 | 315.4 | 278.7 | 315.3 |
| Mount Sinai School of Medicine | 44.0 | 119.5 | 216.5 | 262.4 | 277.2 | 303.7 |
| University of Texas at Austin | 91.8 | 135.0 | 192.9 | 203.4 | 279.0 | 299.2 |
| Case Western Reserve University | 71.3 | 179.4 | 287.0 | 273.3 | 290.3 | 287.4 |
| Carnegie Mellon University | 50.0 | 88.3 | 132.1 | 104.3 | 110.7 | 263.3 |
| Ohio State University, all campuses | 80.1 | 140.8 | 313.6 | 232.5 | 246.2 | 261.8 |
| University of Florida | 55.5 | 129.2 | 228.2 | 239.0 | 227.8 | 254.7 |
| University of California—Berkeley | 121.7 | 196.2 | 306.0 | 295.0 | 261.1 | 254.6 |
| Baylor College of Medicine | 72.3 | 172.3 | 251.3 | 227.5 | 234.1 | 254.5 |
| University of Alabama at Birmingham | 74.5 | 182.9 | 236.0 | 254.2 | 247.4 | 249.2 |
| University of Illinois at Urbana-Champaign | 99.7 | 156.1 | 230.3 | 216.5 | 242.7 | 246.5 |
| University of Rochester | 102.5 | 153.2 | 293.8 | 232.2 | 168.5 | 243.1 |
| Oregon Health & Science University | 25.3 | 113.2 | 225.3 | 198.9 | 187.2 | 219.3 |

[1] Includes other institutions, not shown separately. [2] Includes American Recovery and Reinvestment Act of 2009 obligations.

Source: U.S. National Science Foundation, National Center for Science and Engineering Statistics, "NCES Interactive Tool," <https://ncsesdata.nsf.gov/ids/>, accessed February 2019. See also <http://www.nsf.gov/statistics/fedsupport/>.

## Table 838. Research and Development (R&D) Spending and Employment by Company Size: 2010 to 2015

[Expenditures in millions of dollars (278,977 represents $278,977,000,000). Data are from the Business R&D and Innovation Survey. Data represent all for-profit, nonfarm companies that are publicly or privately held and have five or more employees in the United States]

| Company size | R&D expenditures [1] (million dollars) | | | R&D intensity (R&D as a percent of sales) | | | R&D employment as percent of total employment | | |
|---|---|---|---|---|---|---|---|---|---|
| | 2010 | 2014 | 2015 | 2010 | 2014 | 2015 | 2010 | 2014 | 2015 |
| **All companies............** | **278,977** | **340,728** | **355,821** | **(NA)** | **(NA)** | **(NA)** | **7.6** | **7.0** | **8.2** |
| Micro companies: | | | | | | | | | |
| 5–9 employees................. | 3,851 | 3,295 | 2,988 | 12.9 | 10.1 | 10.7 | 28.2 | 22.9 | 26.3 |
| Small companies: | | | | | | | | | |
| 10–19 employees.............. | 5,721 | 5,063 | 5,680 | 11.6 | 9.1 | 8.7 | 25.3 | 21.5 | 22.7 |
| 20–49 employees.............. | 11,626 | 10,542 | 10,249 | 8.0 | 6.3 | 5.7 | 16.0 | 16.7 | 17.0 |
| Medium companies: | | | | | | | | | |
| 50–99 employees.............. | 8,855 | 10,178 | 11,509 | 6.0 | 5.4 | 6.7 | 14.1 | 14.1 | 14.4 |
| 100–249 employees........... | 11,866 | 13,492 | 13,602 | 4.1 | 3.7 | 4.3 | 10.0 | 10.5 | 11.7 |
| Large companies: | | | | | | | | | |
| 250–499 employees........... | 10,283 | 12,203 | 13,553 | 3.1 | 4.2 | 4.8 | 9.6 | 10.7 | 10.7 |
| 500–999 employees........... | 10,116 | 13,262 | 15,217 | 3.2 | 3.5 | 4.4 | 7.8 | 8.5 | 9.6 |
| 1,000–4,999 employees........ | 48,227 | 57,551 | 58,094 | 4.0 | 4.5 | 4.5 | 8.3 | 9.8 | 9.5 |
| 5,000–9,999 employees........ | 27,463 | 38,202 | 38,838 | 2.0 | 4.3 | 3.9 | 7.9 | 9.8 | 8.8 |
| 10,000–24,999 employees..... | 41,835 | 54,445 | 59,328 | 2.5 | 2.7 | 3.6 | 6.9 | 5.7 | 7.8 |
| 25,000 or more employees.... | 99,133 | 122,495 | 126,763 | 3.0 | 3.0 | 3.4 | 5.0 | 4.2 | 5.2 |

NA Not available. [1] Domestic R&D paid for by the company and others and performed by the company.

Source: U.S. National Science Foundation, *Indicators of R&D in Small Businesses: Data from the 2009–15 Business R&D and Innovation Survey*, NSF 19-316, April 2019. See also <https://www.nsf.gov/statistics/2019/nsf19316/>.

## Table 839. Graduate Science and Engineering Students in Doctorate-Granting Colleges by Characteristic and Field: 2000 to 2017

[In thousands (443.5 represents 443,500). As of Fall. Includes outlying areas. Based on the Survey of Graduate Students and Postdoctorates in Science and Engineering (GSS). In 2017, the GSS underwent a redesign, which included a reorganization of the taxonomy of academic disciplines; therefore, 2017 data are not fully comparable to earlier data. See source for more information]

| Field of science or engineering | Total | | | Characteristic | | | | | | | | |
|---|---|---|---|---|---|---|---|---|---|---|---|---|
| | | | | Female | | | Foreign [1] | | | Part-time | | |
| | 2000 | 2010 | 2017 [2] | 2000 | 2010 | 2017 [2] | 2000 | 2010 | 2017 [2] | 2000 | 2010 | 2017 [2] |
| **Total, all surveyed fields...........** | **443.5** | **575.8** | **577.1** | **201.8** | **265.0** | **253.0** | **123.3** | **165.9** | **217.3** | **123.6** | **142.5** | **135.14** |
| Science/engineering......... | 374.8 | 508.1 | 521.9 | 150.3 | 215.3 | 212.2 | 118.0 | 158.3 | 210.1 | 99.3 | 121.7 | 118.4 |
| Engineering, total........... | 98.8 | 141.8 | 157.6 | 19.7 | 32.9 | 38.8 | 46.3 | 64.2 | 86.3 | 28.2 | 35.4 | 38.7 |
| Sciences, total [3]........... | 275.9 | 366.3 | 364.3 | 130.7 | 182.4 | 173.3 | 71.7 | 94.1 | 123.8 | 71.1 | 86.4 | 79.7 |
| Physical sciences......... | 29.6 | 37.9 | 40.7 | 8.8 | 12.4 | 13.5 | 11.5 | 15.0 | 16.2 | 3.5 | 3.6 | 4.1 |
| Geosciences [4]............. | 13.0 | 14.8 | 11.8 | 5.3 | 6.7 | 5.3 | 2.6 | 2.9 | 2.7 | 2.8 | 2.9 | 2.3 |
| Math sciences............. | 14.4 | 21.3 | 26.6 | 5.2 | 7.4 | 9.6 | 5.9 | 8.4 | 14.0 | 3.0 | 4.4 | 4.6 |
| Computer sciences........ | 40.3 | 45.9 | 73.4 | 11.7 | 11.2 | 21.6 | 19.7 | 22.6 | 45.3 | 16.7 | 15.8 | 24.8 |
| Agricultural sciences [5].... | 11.3 | 14.6 | 8.9 | 4.8 | 7.2 | 4.7 | 2.4 | 3.2 | 2.8 | 2.4 | 4.1 | 2.4 |
| Natural resources and conservation............. | (NA) | (NA) | 9.5 | (NA) | (NA) | 5.2 | (NA) | (NA) | 1.5 | (NA) | (NA) | 2.6 |
| Biological sciences........ | 53.1 | 69.5 | 78.3 | 27.8 | 39.3 | 44.2 | 11.6 | 16.9 | 17.0 | 7.6 | 9.5 | 10.4 |
| Psychology [6].............. | 40.3 | 45.2 | 37.2 | 29.0 | 33.8 | 27.6 | 2.1 | 2.9 | 2.8 | 10.8 | 11.7 | 9.1 |
| Social sciences.......... | 73.9 | 95.9 | 69.2 | 38.1 | 51.0 | 37.1 | 15.8 | 18.8 | 19.0 | 24.3 | 28.1 | 16.6 |
| Health fields, total [6].......... | 68.8 | 67.7 | 55.3 | 51.5 | 49.7 | 40.8 | 5.4 | 7.6 | 7.2 | 24.3 | 20.8 | 16.7 |

NA Not available. [1] Temporary residents. [2] Data for 2017 are not comparable with earlier data. The list of GSS-eligible disciplinary fields was updated in 2017 to align with the National Center for Science and Engineering Statistics Taxonomy of Disciplines. Natural resources and conservation was split from agricultural sciences; neurosciences are included in biological and biomedical sciences; physical sciences adds materials sciences; social sciences no longer includes public administration; and multidisciplinary and interdisciplinary studies no longer includes nanoscience. See source for more information. [3] Beginning in 2010, sciences includes communication, family and consumer/human science, multidisciplinary/interdisciplinary studies, and neuroscience, not shown separately. In 2017, communication and family and consumer/human science became ineligible. [4] Earth or geosciences, atmospheric, and ocean sciences. [5] Through 2016, agricultural sciences includes data for natural resources and conservation. [6] Beginning in 2010, the numbers for psychology and health reflect more rigorous follow-up with institutions regarding the exclusion of practitioner-oriented graduate degree programs and may not reflect changes in actual enrollments.

Source: U.S. National Science Foundation, National Center for Science and Engineering Statistics, "NCSES Interactive Data Tool," <https://ncsesdata.nsf.gov/ids/>, accessed August 2019. See also <http://www.nsf.gov/statistics/gradpostdoc/>.

## Table 840. Temporary Visa Holders Awarded Doctorates in Science and Engineering For Top 10 Countries of Origin: 2007 to 2017

[Based on the Survey of Earned Doctorates; for information, see <http://www.nsf.gov/statistics/srvydoctorates/>]

| Country of origin | 2007 | 2008 | 2009 | 2010 | 2011 | 2012 | 2013 | 2014 | 2015 | 2016 | 2017 |
|---|---|---|---|---|---|---|---|---|---|---|---|
| **All temporary visa holders** [1] | **15,123** | **15,261** | **14,736** | **13,636** | **14,235** | **14,784** | **15,674** | **15,839** | **16,130** | **16,491** | **16,323** |
| Science | 8,171 | 8,553 | 8,349 | 7,809 | 8,021 | 8,374 | 8,676 | 8,764 | 8,903 | 9,481 | 9,096 |
| Engineering | 4,591 | 4,492 | 4,221 | 3,866 | 4,164 | 4,355 | 4,759 | 4,961 | 5,108 | 4,844 | 5,070 |
| COUNTRY | | | | | | | | | | | |
| China [2] | 4,320 | 4,148 | 3,753 | 3,457 | 3,652 | 3,906 | 4,443 | 4,650 | 4,970 | 5,144 | 5,157 |
| India | 1,923 | 2,158 | 2,112 | 1,994 | 2,036 | 2,142 | 2,074 | 2,208 | 2,119 | 2,089 | 1,887 |
| South Korea | 1,129 | 1,153 | 1,179 | 1,076 | 1,085 | 1,132 | 1,012 | 928 | 920 | 891 | 815 |
| Taiwan | 478 | 462 | 544 | 501 | 570 | 581 | 571 | 558 | 514 | 499 | 435 |
| Turkey | 410 | 467 | 445 | 405 | 422 | 352 | 391 | 360 | 386 | 380 | 396 |
| Canada | 353 | 370 | 387 | 339 | 307 | 299 | 332 | 321 | 318 | 272 | 289 |
| Iran | (D) | 132 | (D) | (D) | 193 | 278 | 380 | 463 | 608 | 664 | 732 |
| Thailand | 236 | 291 | 220 | 182 | 235 | 240 | 227 | 200 | 193 | 168 | 154 |
| Japan | 211 | 209 | 193 | 173 | 179 | 179 | 166 | 129 | 120 | 129 | 92 |
| Mexico | 172 | 161 | 171 | 169 | 159 | 185 | 146 | 161 | 155 | 191 | 146 |

D Data is suppressed to avoid disclosure of confidential information. [1] Total includes doctorates awarded to temporary visa holders from other countries, not shown separately. [2] Includes Hong Kong.

Source: U.S. National Science Foundation, National Center for Science and Engineering Statistics, "Doctorate Recipients from U.S. Universities: 2017, Data Tables," <https://ncses.nsf.gov/pubs/nsf19301/data>, accessed February 2019.

## Table 841. Science and Engineering (S&E) Degrees Awarded by Degree Level and Sex of Recipient: 2000 to 2015

[Includes degrees in the following science and engineering (S&E) fields: astronomy, chemistry, physics, atmospheric sciences, earth sciences, ocean sciences, mathematics and statistics, computer sciences, agricultural sciences, biological sciences, psychology, social sciences, and engineering. For doctoral degrees, medical and health sciences are included under S&E because these data correspond to the doctor's research/scholarship degree level which are research focused degrees]

| Academic year ending | Bachelor's degree | | | | Master's degree | | | | Doctoral degree [1,2] | | | |
|---|---|---|---|---|---|---|---|---|---|---|---|---|
| | Total S&E | Men | Women | Percent women | Total S&E | Men | Women | Percent women | Total S&E | Men | Women | Percent women |
| 2000 | 398,602 | 197,650 | 200,952 | 50.4 | 96,230 | 54,560 | 41,670 | 43.3 | 27,862 | 17,024 | 10,838 | 38.9 |
| 2001 | 400,435 | 197,771 | 202,664 | 50.6 | 99,528 | 55,884 | 43,644 | 43.9 | 28,096 | 16,873 | 11,223 | 39.9 |
| 2002 | 415,983 | 204,675 | 211,308 | 50.8 | 99,650 | 55,939 | 43,711 | 43.9 | 27,588 | 16,164 | 11,424 | 41.4 |
| 2003 | 442,755 | 219,815 | 222,940 | 50.4 | 108,355 | 61,183 | 47,172 | 43.5 | 28,746 | 16,569 | 12,177 | 42.4 |
| 2004 | 458,658 | 227,861 | 230,797 | 50.3 | 119,296 | 67,215 | 52,081 | 43.7 | 30,979 | 17,532 | 13,447 | 43.4 |
| 2005 | 470,214 | 233,924 | 236,290 | 50.3 | 120,870 | 67,244 | 53,626 | 44.4 | 34,468 | 18,970 | 15,498 | 45.0 |
| 2006 | 478,858 | 238,029 | 240,829 | 50.3 | 120,999 | 66,249 | 54,750 | 45.2 | 37,541 | 20,254 | 17,287 | 46.0 |
| 2007 | 485,772 | 241,697 | 244,075 | 50.2 | 120,278 | 65,353 | 54,925 | 45.7 | 40,980 | 21,653 | 19,327 | 47.2 |
| 2008 | 496,168 | 246,719 | 249,449 | 50.3 | 126,404 | 68,810 | 57,594 | 45.6 | 41,480 | 21,995 | 19,485 | 47.0 |
| 2009 | 505,435 | 250,742 | 254,693 | 50.4 | 134,517 | 73,489 | 61,028 | 45.4 | 41,111 | 21,743 | 19,368 | 47.1 |
| 2010 | 525,374 | 261,091 | 264,283 | 50.3 | 139,926 | 76,266 | 63,660 | 45.5 | 36,711 | 20,361 | 16,350 | 44.5 |
| 2011 | 554,365 | 275,258 | 279,107 | 50.3 | 150,653 | 82,451 | 68,202 | 45.3 | 38,470 | 21,377 | 17,093 | 44.4 |
| 2012 | 589,330 | 291,791 | 297,539 | 50.5 | 161,371 | 87,810 | 73,561 | 45.6 | 39,828 | 22,101 | 17,727 | 44.5 |
| 2013 | 615,475 | 305,777 | 309,698 | 50.3 | 166,397 | 90,046 | 76,351 | 45.9 | 41,563 | 23,021 | 18,542 | 44.6 |
| 2014 | 635,915 | 318,015 | 317,900 | 50.0 | 171,228 | 92,457 | 78,771 | 46.0 | 43,995 | 24,072 | 19,923 | 45.3 |
| 2015 | 650,057 | 327,122 | 322,935 | 49.7 | 180,955 | 99,282 | 81,673 | 45.1 | 44,521 | 24,371 | 20,150 | 45.3 |

[1] Prior to 2008, the National Center for Education Statistics (NCES) used two doctoral degree categories (doctor's and first professional). Data in this table for those years include only the doctor's category. In 2008 and 2009, NCES allowed optional reporting in three new doctoral degree categories (doctor's research/scholarship, doctor's professional practice, and doctor's other) in addition to the doctor's category. For those 2 years, data in this table include only doctorates reported in the doctor's category plus those reported in doctor's research/scholarship. In 2010, NCES required institutions to use only the three new doctoral degree categories, and data in this table for 2010 and later include only doctorates reported in the category doctor's research/scholarship.

Source: U.S. National Science Foundation, *Science and Engineering Indicators, 2018*, NSB-2018-1, January 2018. See also <http://www.nsf.gov/statistics/seind/>.

## Table 842. Science and Engineering (S&E) Degrees as Percent of Higher Education Degrees Conferred by State: 2016

[Includes bachelor's, master's, and doctorate degrees. S&E degrees include degrees in physical, computer, agricultural, biological, earth, atmospheric, ocean, and social sciences; psychology; mathematics; and engineering]

| State | S&E degrees conferred | All higher education degrees | S&E higher education degrees (percent) | State | S&E degrees conferred | All higher education degrees | S&E higher education degrees (percent) | State | S&E degrees conferred | All higher education degrees | S&E higher education degrees (percent) |
|---|---|---|---|---|---|---|---|---|---|---|---|
| U.S.[1] | 903,376 | 2,802,969 | 32.2 | IA | 12,929 | 49,427 | 26.2 | NC | 25,627 | 73,945 | 34.7 |
| | | | | KS | 6,983 | 28,572 | 24.4 | ND | 2,188 | 8,114 | 27.0 |
| | | | | KY | 8,377 | 33,307 | 25.2 | OH | 28,655 | 97,263 | 29.5 |
| AL | 10,922 | 43,841 | 24.9 | LA | 8,502 | 30,826 | 27.6 | OK | 7,832 | 28,179 | 27.8 |
| AK | 1,000 | 2,759 | 36.2 | ME | 3,385 | 10,010 | 33.8 | OR | 11,129 | 33,138 | 33.6 |
| AZ | 21,814 | 87,928 | 24.8 | MD | 22,528 | 55,180 | 40.8 | PA | 43,242 | 132,450 | 32.6 |
| AR | 5,495 | 21,604 | 25.4 | MA | 36,782 | 102,716 | 35.8 | RI | 5,218 | 15,374 | 33.9 |
| CA | 111,631 | 274,860 | 40.6 | MI | 27,811 | 84,071 | 33.1 | SC | 9,950 | 31,975 | 31.1 |
| CO | 18,815 | 50,597 | 37.2 | MN | 18,596 | 63,937 | 29.1 | SD | 2,504 | 7,833 | 32.0 |
| CT | 12,332 | 34,375 | 35.9 | MS | 5,049 | 20,321 | 24.8 | TN | 12,193 | 48,562 | 25.1 |
| DE | 3,375 | 11,277 | 29.9 | MO | 18,099 | 65,240 | 27.7 | TX | 56,326 | 183,360 | 30.7 |
| DC | 9,170 | 23,093 | 39.7 | MT | 2,689 | 7,325 | 36.7 | UT | 11,634 | 45,415 | 25.6 |
| FL | 41,698 | 138,611 | 30.1 | NE | 5,443 | 20,253 | 26.9 | VT | 3,445 | 8,559 | 40.3 |
| GA | 22,494 | 70,981 | 31.7 | NV | 3,426 | 11,163 | 30.7 | VA | 29,590 | 83,967 | 35.2 |
| HI | 2,955 | 8,524 | 34.7 | NH | 5,597 | 19,519 | 28.7 | WA | 17,730 | 44,099 | 40.2 |
| ID | 3,973 | 13,429 | 29.6 | NJ | 22,020 | 60,918 | 36.1 | WV | 6,854 | 22,992 | 29.8 |
| IL | 35,568 | 121,537 | 29.3 | NM | 3,993 | 12,331 | 32.4 | WI | 16,066 | 47,971 | 33.5 |
| IN | 19,104 | 64,141 | 29.8 | NY | 71,509 | 216,790 | 33.0 | WY | 1,128 | 2,688 | 42.0 |

[1] Total higher education degrees and S&E degrees include U.S. territories.

Source: U.S. National Science Foundation, *Science and Engineering Indicators, 2018*, NSB-2018-1, January 2018. See also <http://www.nsf.gov/statistics/seind/>.

## Table 843. Doctorates Conferred in Science and Engineering by Field, Sex, Citizenship Status, Race, and Hispanic Origin: 2017

[In percent, except as indicated. Based on the Survey of Earned Doctorates. For description of methodology, see <https://www.nsf.gov/statistics/srvydoctorates/>]

| Characteristic | Total [1] | Life sciences | | | Physical sciences | | | Social sciences | | | Engineering |
|---|---|---|---|---|---|---|---|---|---|---|---|
| | | Total [2] | Biological sciences | Health sciences | Total [2] | Chemistry | Physics [3] | Total [2] | Psychology | Economics [4] | |
| **Total conferred (number)** | 54,664 | 12,592 | 8,477 | 2,509 | 6,081 | 2,697 | 2,219 | 9,079 | 3,960 | 1,237 | 9,843 |
| SEX | | | | | | | | | | | |
| Male | 53.3 | 44.7 | 47.4 | 32.1 | 66.9 | 61.9 | 79.0 | 40.7 | 28.7 | 65.6 | 75.1 |
| Female | 46.6 | 55.3 | 52.6 | 67.8 | 33.1 | 38.0 | 21.0 | 59.3 | 71.0 | 34.2 | 24.0 |
| CITZENSHIP | | | | | | | | | | | |
| U.S. citizen or permanent resident | 65.5 | 70.3 | 71.7 | 74.7 | 61.1 | 62.7 | 55.8 | 75.7 | 85.9 | 43.6 | 44.1 |
| Temporary visa holders | 29.9 | 26.4 | 25.5 | 21.5 | 35.5 | 34.1 | 40.7 | 18.5 | 7.4 | 52.3 | 51.5 |
| RACE/ETHNICITY [5] | | | | | | | | | | | |
| **Total conferred (number)** | 35,791 | 8,857 | 6,082 | 1,873 | 3,717 | 1,691 | 1,239 | 6,874 | 3,403 | 539 | 4,339 |
| Non-Hispanic (number): | | | | | | | | | | | |
| White | 45.5 | 48.1 | 49.4 | 47.6 | 46.4 | 46.2 | 42.8 | 52.5 | 61.9 | 27.6 | 28.6 |
| Asian [6] | 6.4 | 8.1 | 9.1 | 7.3 | 5.9 | 6.7 | 5.9 | 5.9 | 5.6 | 7.0 | 7.4 |
| Black | 4.4 | 4.6 | 3.5 | 9.5 | 1.5 | 2.0 | 1.1 | 5.8 | 5.8 | 1.5 | 1.7 |
| American Indian/Alaska Native | 0.2 | 0.2 | 0.2 | 0.4 | 0.1 | 0.1 | 0.0 | 0.3 | 0.3 | 0.1 | 0.1 |
| Two or more races | 1.9 | 2.3 | 2.4 | 2.4 | 1.8 | 2.2 | 1.5 | 2.3 | 2.7 | 1.5 | 1.2 |
| Hispanic [7] | 4.6 | 4.8 | 5.2 | 4.6 | 3.6 | 3.6 | 3.0 | 6.4 | 7.3 | 2.6 | 2.9 |
| Other/unknown [8] | 2.4 | 2.3 | 1.9 | 2.9 | 1.8 | 1.9 | 1.5 | 2.6 | 2.4 | 3.3 | 2.1 |

[1] Total includes non-Science and Engineering degrees, including education, humanities, and business doctorates. [2] Includes other fields, not shown separately. [3] Includes astronomy. [4] Includes econometrics and natural resource/environmental economics. [5] Covers U.S. citizens and permanent residents only. [6] Excludes Native Hawaiians or Other Pacific Islanders. [7] Persons reporting Hispanic ethnicity may be of any race or combination of races. [8] Includes other non-Hispanic race, and individuals who did not report race nor ethnicity.

Source: U.S. National Science Foundation, National Center for Science and Engineering Statistics, "Doctorate Recipients from U.S. Universities: 2017, Data Tables," <https://ncses.nsf.gov/pubs/nsf19301/data>, accessed March 2019.

# Table 844. Doctorates Awarded by Field of Study and Year of Doctorate: 2010 to 2017

[Based on the Survey of Earned Doctorates. For description of methodology, see <http://www.nsf.gov/statistics/srvydoctorates/>]

| Field of study | 2010 | 2011 | 2012 | 2013 | 2014 | 2015 | 2016 | 2017 |
|---|---|---|---|---|---|---|---|---|
| **Total, all fields** | **48,029** | **48,911** | **50,944** | **52,704** | **53,992** | **54,901** | **54,862** | **54,664** |
| **Science and engineering, total** | **34,998** | **36,332** | **37,846** | **39,032** | **40,635** | **41,189** | **41,280** | **41,438** |
| Science, total | 27,420 | 28,300 | 29,377 | 30,032 | 31,008 | 31,313 | 31,822 | 31,595 |
| Life sciences | 11,319 | 11,535 | 11,964 | 12,208 | 12,484 | 12,499 | 12,554 | 12,592 |
| Agricultural sciences & natural resources | 1,100 | 1,206 | 1,255 | 1,324 | 1,338 | 1,434 | 1,381 | 1,606 |
| Biological/biomedical sciences | 8,046 | 8,152 | 8,322 | 8,355 | 8,868 | 8,788 | 8,873 | 8,477 |
| Health sciences | 2,173 | 2,177 | 2,387 | 2,529 | 2,278 | 2,277 | 2,300 | 2,509 |
| Physical and earth sciences | 4,995 | 5,271 | 5,419 | 5,584 | 5,911 | 5,918 | 6,252 | 6,081 |
| Chemistry | 2,304 | 2,432 | 2,416 | 2,484 | 2,673 | 2,668 | 2,704 | 2,697 |
| Geosciences, atmospheric & ocean sciences | 862 | 852 | 941 | 989 | 1,099 | 1,057 | 1,227 | 1,165 |
| Physics and astronomy | 1,829 | 1,987 | 2,062 | 2,111 | 2,139 | 2,193 | 2,321 | 2,219 |
| Mathematics and computer sciences | 3,223 | 3,273 | 3,496 | 3,660 | 3,862 | 3,818 | 3,956 | 3,843 |
| Computer and information sciences | 1,633 | 1,667 | 1,793 | 1,843 | 1,988 | 2,003 | 2,084 | 1,987 |
| Mathematics & statistics | 1,590 | 1,606 | 1,703 | 1,817 | 1,874 | 1,815 | 1,872 | 1,856 |
| Psychology & social sciences | 7,883 | 8,221 | 8,498 | 8,580 | 8,751 | 9,078 | 9,060 | 9,079 |
| Psychology | 3,421 | 3,576 | 3,599 | 3,592 | 3,724 | 3,776 | 3,931 | 3,960 |
| Anthropology | 507 | 553 | 547 | 550 | 524 | 492 | 460 | 455 |
| Economics | 1,073 | 1,121 | 1,243 | 1,183 | 1,195 | 1,255 | 1,236 | 1,237 |
| Political science & government | 728 | 685 | 724 | 803 | 777 | 859 | 745 | 752 |
| Sociology | 639 | 657 | 633 | 636 | 679 | 742 | 615 | 689 |
| Other social sciences | 1,515 | 1,629 | 1,752 | 1,816 | 1,852 | 1,954 | 2,073 | 1,986 |
| Engineering, total | 7,578 | 8,032 | 8,469 | 9,000 | 9,627 | 9,876 | 9,458 | 9,843 |
| Aerospace, aeronautical & astronautical | 252 | 262 | 307 | 348 | 386 | 361 | 370 | 378 |
| Bioengineering & biomedical | 824 | 898 | 943 | 1,039 | 1,046 | 1,126 | 1,090 | 1041 |
| Chemical | 822 | 823 | 840 | 824 | 973 | 1,002 | 921 | 936 |
| Civil | 643 | 634 | 495 | 542 | 617 | 632 | 563 | 741 |
| Electrical, electronics & communications | 1,778 | 1,886 | 1,938 | 1,897 | 1,953 | 1,997 | 1,822 | 1,900 |
| Industrial & manufacturing | 215 | 258 | 226 | 241 | 298 | 243 | 256 | 253 |
| Materials science | 670 | 662 | 743 | 815 | 832 | 871 | 984 | 958 |
| Mechanical | 983 | 1,084 | 1,220 | 1,277 | 1,331 | 1,466 | 1,296 | 1,409 |
| Other | 1,391 | 1,525 | 1,757 | 2,017 | 2,191 | 2,178 | 2,156 | 2,227 |
| **Non-science and engineering, total** | **13,031** | **12,579** | **13,098** | **13,672** | **13,357** | **13,712** | **13,582** | **13,226** |
| Education | 5,287 | 4,670 | 4,803 | 4,934 | 4,789 | 5,098 | 5,146 | 4,823 |
| Humanities | 5,015 | 5,226 | 5,561 | 5,715 | 5,524 | 5,594 | 5,480 | 5,290 |
| Professional/other/unknown | 2,729 | 2,683 | 2,734 | 3,023 | 3,044 | 3,020 | 2,956 | 3,113 |

Source: U.S. National Science Foundation, National Center for Science and Engineering Statistics, "Doctorate Recipients from U.S. Universities: 2017, Data Tables," <https://ncses.nsf.gov/pubs/nsf19301/data>, accessed February 2019.

# Table 845. Employed Scientists and Engineers by Sex, Race/Ethnicity, and Selected Characteristics: 2017

[In thousands (27,273 represents 27,273,000). Scientists and engineers are individuals who have a bachelor's or higher degree, and have an S&E (Science and Engineer) or S&E-related degree or occupation. Data based on various NSF (National Science Foundation) and non-NSF surveys; see <https://ncses.nsf.gov/pubs/nsf19304/technical-notes> for details]

| Characteristic | Total [1] | Female | Male | Hispanic or Latino [2] | Asian [3] | Black or African American [3] | White [3] | More than one race [3] |
|---|---|---|---|---|---|---|---|---|
| **All employed scientists and engineers** | **27,273** | **13,002** | **14,271** | **2,328** | **3,546** | **2,008** | **18,750** | **495** |
| Age: | | | | | | | | |
| Under 30 years | 4,029 | 2,273 | 1,756 | 481 | 578 | 269 | 2,559 | 125 |
| 30-39 years | 7,208 | 3,571 | 3,638 | 672 | 1,154 | 572 | 4,589 | 185 |
| 40-49 years | 6,254 | 3,022 | 3,231 | 562 | 950 | 496 | 4,103 | 94 |
| 50-75 years | 9,783 | 4,136 | 5,647 | 614 | 864 | 671 | 7,499 | 90 |
| Employment status: | | | | | | | | |
| Employed, full-time | 22,866 | 10,102 | 12,764 | 1,964 | 3,083 | 1,772 | 15,512 | 407 |
| Employed, part-time | 4,407 | 2,900 | 1,508 | 364 | 463 | 236 | 3,239 | 88 |
| Highest degree attained: | | | | | | | | |
| Bachelor's | 15,198 | 7,197 | 8,001 | 1,438 | 1,655 | 1,146 | 10,550 | 310 |
| Master's | 8,236 | 4,246 | 3,990 | 610 | 1,273 | 663 | 5,534 | 128 |
| Doctorate | 1,503 | 590 | 913 | 88 | 323 | 69 | 998 | 19 |
| Professional | 2,336 | 969 | 1,367 | 192 | 295 | 130 | 1,668 | 38 |
| By occupation: | | | | | | | | |
| S&E occupations | 6,769 | 1,966 | 4,803 | 505 | 1,338 | 382 | 4,397 | 109 |
| Science occupations | 5,041 | 1,697 | 3,344 | 362 | 1,056 | 320 | 3,201 | 78 |
| Engineering occupations | 1,728 | 269 | 1,459 | 143 | 283 | 62 | 1,196 | 31 |
| S&E related occupations | 8,271 | 4,764 | 3,507 | 702 | 1,042 | 610 | 5,726 | 147 |
| Non-S&E related occupations | 12,233 | 6,271 | 5,962 | 1,121 | 1,166 | 1,016 | 8,628 | 239 |
| By employment sector: | | | | | | | | |
| Business or industry | 14,541 | 5,611 | 8,930 | 1,189 | 2,270 | 873 | 9,903 | 241 |
| Federal government | 1,287 | 542 | 746 | 120 | 135 | 170 | 816 | 34 |
| Nonprofit | 3,226 | 2,201 | 1,026 | 251 | 326 | 297 | 2,270 | 67 |
| Self-employed | 1,652 | 777 | 875 | 142 | 137 | 68 | 1,274 | 25 |
| State or local government | 1,614 | 804 | 809 | 198 | 157 | 214 | 994 | 37 |
| Universities and 4-year colleges | 2,168 | 1,166 | 1,002 | 147 | 371 | 124 | 1,462 | 40 |
| Other educational institutions | 2,785 | 1,901 | 884 | 282 | 151 | 262 | 2,032 | 51 |

[1] Total includes other races, not shown separately. [2] Persons of Hispanic origin may be of any race. [3] Non-Hispanic.

Source: U.S. National Science Foundation, National Center for Science and Engineering Statistics, "Women, Minorities, and Persons with Disabilities in Science and Engineering - Data Tables," <https://ncses.nsf.gov/pubs/nsf19304/data>, accessed April 2019.

# Table 846. Science and Engineering (S&E) Degree Holders by Occupation: 2015

[In thousands (19,688 represents 19,688,000). Data represents all workers who attained their highest degree (bachelor's or higher) in an S&E or S&E-related field. Detail may not add to total due to rounding]

| Occupation | Total S&E and S&E-related degree holders | Employees by field of highest degree [1] | | | | | | S&E related fields [5] |
|---|---|---|---|---|---|---|---|---|
| | | Total S&E fields | Computer and mathematical sciences | Biological, agricultural, and environmental life sciences [2] | Physical and related sciences [3] | Social and related sciences [4] | Engineering | |
| All occupations.............................. | 19,688 | 13,497 | 2,346 | 2,116 | 789 | 5,056 | 3,190 | 6,191 |
| **S&E occupations**............................ | 5,221 | 4,854 | 1,350 | 624 | 386 | 660 | 1,834 | 367 |
| Computer & mathematical scientists..... | 2,335 | 2,178 | 1,280 | 116 | 67 | 203 | 512 | 157 |
| Computer & information scientists [6].... | 2,092 | 1,951 | 1,159 | 65 | 60 | 181 | 486 | 141 |
| Computer engineers—software.............. | 537 | 499 | 279 | 7 | 8 | 11 | 194 | 38 |
| Software developers....................... | 506 | 485 | 288 | 10 | 23 | 27 | 137 | 21 |
| Computer system analysts.................. | 234 | 213 | 139 | 7 | 5 | 23 | 39 | 21 |
| Computer support specialists.............. | 149 | 130 | 82 | 6 | 4 | 19 | 19 | 19 |
| Network/computer systems administrators..... | 140 | 133 | 84 | 7 | (S) | 13 | 25 | 7 |
| Mathematical scientists.................... | (S) | 139 | 45 | (S) | 5 | 17 | 21 | (S) |
| Biological, agricultural, & environmental life scientists [6]..... | 568 | 496 | 4 | 422 | 37 | 19 | 13 | 72 |
| Biological & medical scientists [6].............. | 411 | 346 | 4 | 290 | 27 | 13 | 11 | 65 |
| Biological scientists [7].................... | 125 | 121 | (S) | 111 | 5 | 4 | (Z) | 4 |
| Medical scientists (excluding practitioners)..... | 129 | 85 | 4 | 65 | 5 | 5 | 6 | 44 |
| Physical & related scientists [6]................. | 321 | 309 | 1 | 41 | 232 | 9 | 26 | 12 |
| Chemists, except biochemists.............. | 102 | 96 | (S) | 15 | 74 | 1 | 5 | 6 |
| Physicists & astronomers.................. | 49 | 47 | (Z) | (S) | 41 | (S) | 4 | 2 |
| Social & related scientists [6]................. | 454 | 423 | 8 | 10 | 1 | 400 | 2 | 31 |
| Psychologists, including clinical.............. | 193 | 189 | (S) | (S) | (S) | 187 | (S) | 4 |
| Postsecondary teachers—social sciences... | 110 | 106 | 3 | (S) | (S) | 101 | (S) | 4 |
| Engineers [6]................................ | 1,542 | 1,448 | 56 | 34 | 48 | 28 | 1,281 | 94 |
| Electrical or computer hardware engineers.. | 334 | 321 | 23 | (S) | 10 | (S) | 281 | 13 |
| Mechanical engineers...................... | 307 | 292 | 8 | (S) | 2 | (S) | 280 | 15 |
| Civil, architectural, or sanitary engineers. ... | 234 | 217 | 3 | 3 | 3 | 5 | 204 | 17 |
| Aerospace, aeronautical, or astronautical engineers..... | 86 | 83 | 4 | (S) | 5 | (S) | 73 | 3 |
| **S&E-related occupations**.................... | 6,390 | 1,953 | 326 | 600 | 160 | 390 | 477 | 4,437 |
| Health-related occupations [6].............. | 4,351 | 666 | 24 | 341 | 63 | 223 | 15 | 3,685 |
| Diagnosing/treating practitioners [8]............ | 1,192 | 58 | (S) | 44 | 6 | 7 | (S) | 1,134 |
| Registered nurses, pharmacists, dieticians, therapists, physician assistants, & nurse practitioners.............. | 2,139 | 168 | (S) | 67 | 13 | 71 | (S) | 1,971 |
| S&E managers............................... | 758 | 477 | 99 | 56 | 26 | 54 | 242 | 281 |
| Medical & health services managers......... | 264 | 51 | (S) | 24 | (S) | 23 | (S) | 213 |
| Engineering managers...................... | 297 | 244 | 13 | 5 | 11 | 7 | 208 | 53 |
| Computer & information systems managers..... | 155 | 144 | 85 | 3 | (S) | 22 | 30 | 11 |
| S&E precollege teachers [9]................. | 502 | 269 | 63 | 103 | 33 | 62 | 7 | 233 |
| S&E technicians & technologists [6]................. | 589 | 506 | 124 | 98 | 37 | 44 | 202 | 83 |
| Computer programmers...................... | 140 | 130 | 87 | 7 | 5 | 4 | 28 | 10 |
| Electrical, electronic, industrial, & mechanical technicians..... | 147 | 125 | 6 | 4 | 8 | 5 | 102 | 22 |
| Other S&E-related occupations [6].............. | 190 | 36 | 15 | (S) | (S) | 7 | 12 | 154 |
| Architects................................ | 158 | 19 | 3 | (S) | (S) | 3 | 11 | 139 |
| **Non-S&E occupations**......................... | 8,053 | 6,666 | 670 | 893 | 242 | 3,983 | 879 | 1,387 |
| Non-S&E managers.......................... | 1,306 | 1,105 | 138 | 124 | 48 | 494 | 301 | 201 |
| Management-related occupations [6]............ | 1,552 | 1,345 | 197 | 161 | 40 | 770 | 177 | 207 |
| Accountants, auditors, & other financial specialists..... | 531 | 483 | 85 | 37 | 10 | 303 | 49 | 48 |
| Personnel, training, & labor relations specialists..... | 219 | 191 | 23 | 24 | (S) | 126 | 17 | 28 |
| Non-S&E precollege teachers [6]................ | 520 | 339 | 20 | 24 | 15 | 270 | 10 | 181 |
| Prekindergarten and kindergarten............ | 108 | 60 | (S) | (S) | (S) | 53 | (S) | 48 |
| Elementary.............................. | 236 | 168 | 15 | 9 | 13 | 126 | 4 | 68 |
| Secondary—other subjects.................. | 76 | 47 | 1 | 6 | (S) | 37 | 2 | 29 |
| Special education—primary & secondary.... | 61 | 40 | (Z) | 2 | (S) | 35 | (S) | 21 |
| Non-S&E postsecondary teachers.......... | 94 | 65 | 8 | 2 | (S) | 51 | 4 | 29 |
| Social services & related occupations [6]....... | 544 | 429 | 8 | 21 | (S) | 391 | 7 | 115 |
| Counselors [10]............................ | 301 | 224 | (S) | 10 | (S) | 208 | (S) | 77 |
| Social workers............................ | 201 | 167 | (S) | 5 | (S) | 157 | (S) | 34 |
| Sales & marketing occupations................ | 1,239 | 1,053 | 84 | 178 | 54 | 614 | 123 | 186 |
| Arts, humanities, & related occupations....... | 256 | 224 | 20 | 27 | 11 | 143 | 23 | 32 |
| Other non-S&E occupations [6]................ | 2,540 | 2,105 | 195 | 355 | 71 | 1,251 | 233 | 435 |

Z Entry would amount to less than 500. S Data suppressed for reasons of confidentiality and/or reliability. [1] Includes bachelor's, master's, and doctorate degrees. [2] Biological sciences include biology, ecology, nutritional sciences, pharmacology, zoology, and related fields. [3] Physical sciences include chemistry; earth, atmospheric, and ocean sciences; physics and astronomy; and related fields. [4] Social sciences include economics, political science, psychology, sociology and anthropology, linguistics, geography, history and philosophy of science, and related fields. [5] S&E-related fields include health fields, science and math teacher education, technology and technical fields, architecture, and actuarial science. [6] Includes other occupations not shown separately. [7] Includes botanists, ecologists, zoologists, etc. [8] Includes dentists, optometrists, physicians, psychiatrists, podiatrists, surgeons, and veterinarians. [9] Secondary teachers in computer, mathematics, sciences, and social sciences. [10] Includes educational, vocational, mental health, substance abuse, etc.

Source: U.S. National Science Foundation, *Science and Engineering Indicators, 2018*, NSB-2018-1, January 2018. See also <http://www.nsf.gov/statistics/seind/>.

## Table 847. Civilian Employment of Scientists, Engineers, and Related Occupations by Occupation and Industry: 2016

[In thousands (367.6 represents 367,600). Standard Occupational Classification (SOC) system classifies workers into 840 detailed occupations. Industry classifications correspond to 2012 North American Industry Classification (NAICS) industrial groups]

| Occupation | Total employment, all workers | Wage and salary workers | | | | | | Self employed [2] |
|---|---|---|---|---|---|---|---|---|
| | | Mining (NAICS 21) [1] | Construction (NAICS 23) | Manufacturing (NAICS 31–33) | Information (NAICS 51) | Professional, scientific, technical services (NAICS 54) | Government | |
| Computer and information systems............ | 367.6 | 0.9 | 1.1 | 29.9 | 40.4 | 116.2 | 22.2 | 3.1 |
| Architectural and engineering managers........ | 180.1 | 2.2 | 5.0 | 65.3 | 3.3 | 63.3 | 16.8 | (NA) |
| Natural science managers.................... | 56.7 | 0.3 | (NA) | 6.4 | (NA) | 23.2 | 16.0 | (NA) |
| Computer and mathematical scientists [3]......... | 4,419.0 | 10.6 | 15.4 | 288.8 | 564.6 | 1,517.8 | 271.8 | 116.2 |
| Computer occupations..................... | 4,238.4 | 10.3 | 15.3 | 277.3 | 557.8 | 1,476.6 | 249.4 | 114.7 |
| Mathematical science occupations............. | 180.7 | 0.3 | (NA) | 11.5 | 6.8 | 41.2 | 22.4 | 1.4 |
| Surveyors, cartographers, and photogrammetrists.................... | 57.4 | 0.9 | 3.7 | 0.2 | 0.2 | 37.6 | 10.5 | 1.3 |
| Engineers [3]................................. | 1,681.0 | 29.4 | 50.9 | 578.4 | 34.9 | 523.9 | 203.2 | 25.0 |
| Aerospace engineers.................... | 69.6 | (NA) | (NA) | 34.4 | 0.1 | 20.7 | 10.0 | (NA) |
| Civil engineers......................... | 303.5 | 1.0 | 31.3 | 4.0 | 0.5 | 162.5 | 76.1 | 10.2 |
| Computer hardware engineers.............. | 73.6 | (NA) | 0.1 | 27.4 | 3.3 | 29.8 | 5.1 | (NA) |
| Electrical and electronics engineers............ | 324.6 | 0.5 | 6.2 | 102.4 | 28.9 | 93.4 | 28.7 | 3.9 |
| Industrial engineers [4]...................... | 283.8 | 2.8 | 6.5 | 188.1 | 0.9 | 37.1 | 5.9 | 1.4 |
| Mechanical engineers.................... | 288.8 | 2.0 | 4.3 | 138.1 | 0.3 | 90.1 | 15.1 | 1.4 |
| Drafters, engineering, and mapping technicians [3].................... | 709.2 | 7.1 | 26.4 | 216.4 | 5.5 | 265.6 | 91.1 | 12.1 |
| Engineering technicians, except drafters....... | 441.3 | (NA) | 5.3 | 165.0 | 3.9 | 122.7 | 78.4 | 3.0 |
| Surveying and mapping technicians........... | 60.2 | 1.5 | 1.5 | 0.2 | 0.2 | 35.0 | 8.9 | 5.5 |
| Life, physical, and social science occupations... | 1,299.5 | 19.5 | 1.1 | 119.1 | 1.7 | 334.8 | 319.1 | 64.0 |
| Life scientists........................... | 325.4 | 0.1 | (NA) | 27.3 | 0.1 | 92.6 | 70.1 | 8.6 |
| Physical scientists...................... | 278.2 | 9.2 | 0.3 | 42.5 | 1.0 | 94.6 | 76.2 | 4.8 |
| Social scientists and related occupations...... | 303.8 | 0.1 | 0.3 | 4.0 | 0.3 | 39.5 | 86.7 | 46.9 |
| Life, physical, & social science technicians.... | 392.1 | 10.1 | 0.4 | 49.0 | 0.3 | 108.1 | 86.0 | 3.7 |

NA Not available. [1] Includes oil and gas extraction. [2] Includes unpaid family workers. [3] Includes other occupations not shown separately. [4] Includes health and safety engineers.

Source: U.S. Bureau of Labor Statistics, National Employment Matrix, "Employment Projections," <http://www.bls.gov/emp/tables.htm>, accessed February 2018.

## Table 848. Top 20 Metropolitan Areas with the Largest Proportion of Workers in Science and Engineering Occupations: 2014 and 2016

[As of May. Ranked for top 20 metro areas with highest percent of S&E (science and engineering) workforce in 2016. Data are from U.S. Bureau of Labor Statistics' Occupational Employment Statistics Survey. Excludes metropolitan statistical areas where S&E proportions were suppressed. Differences among employment estimates may not be statistically significant; see source for details]

| Metropolitan statistical area | 2014 | | | 2016 | | |
|---|---|---|---|---|---|---|
| | Workers employed | | Percent of area workforce in S&E occupations | Workers employed | | Percent of area workforce in S&E occupations |
| | All occupations | S&E occupations | | All occupations | S&E occupations | |
| **U.S. total**.............. | **135,128,260** | **6,318,580** | **4.7** | **140,400,040** | **6,746,600** | **4.8** |
| California-Lexington Park, MD.............. | (X) | (X) | (X) | 44,000 | 8,250 | 18.8 |
| San Jose-Sunnyvale-Santa Clara, CA................ | 973,480 | 163,460 | 16.8 | 1,045,430 | 179,820 | 17.2 |
| Boulder, CO.............. | 167,200 | 22,620 | 13.5 | 176,230 | 25,780 | 14.6 |
| Framingham, MA NECTA division [1]............. | 162,170 | 21,010 | 13.0 | 174,430 | 22,680 | 13.0 |
| Huntsville, AL.............. | 208,480 | 27,820 | 13.3 | 218,260 | 28,250 | 12.9 |
| San Francisco-Redwood City-South San Francisco, CA.............. | (X) | (X) | (X) | 1,067,130 | 117,500 | 11.0 |
| Washington-Arlington-Alexandria, DC-VA-MD-WV....... | 2,378,260 | 259,080 | 10.9 | 2,490,690 | 267,000 | 10.7 |
| Seattle-Bellevue-Everett, WA,.............. | 1,492,650 | 154,480 | 10.3 | 1,588,590 | 169,210 | 10.7 |
| Durham-Chapel Hill, NC.............. | 284,480 | 33,020 | 11.6 | 292,860 | 30,620 | 10.5 |
| Lowell-Billerica-Chelmsford, MA-NH, NECTA division [1].. | 118,980 | 10,420 | 8.8 | 151,310 | 15,730 | 10.4 |
| Silver Spring-Frederick-Rockville, MD.............. | (X) | (X) | (X) | 581,380 | 58,830 | 10.1 |
| Corvallis, OR.............. | 33,450 | 3,920 | 11.7 | 32,930 | 3,270 | 9.9 |
| Ann Arbor, MI.............. | 204,840 | 17,810 | 8.7 | 210,990 | 19,100 | 9.1 |
| Trenton, NJ.............. | (X) | (X) | (X) | 225,950 | 20,180 | 8.9 |
| Madison, WI.............. | 347,750 | 27,250 | 7.8 | 381,890 | 34,080 | 8.9 |
| Raleigh, NC.............. | (X) | (X) | (X) | 595,370 | 52,690 | 8.8 |
| Boston-Cambridge-Newton, MA NECTA division [1]........ | (X) | (X) | (X) | 1,803,030 | 159,430 | 8.8 |
| Ames, IA.............. | 42,250 | 3,740 | 8.9 | 43,690 | 3,850 | 8.8 |
| Ithaca, NY.............. | 49,430 | 4,380 | 8.9 | 50,590 | 4,450 | 8.8 |
| Austin-Round Rock, TX.............. | (X) | (X) | (X) | 965,100 | 81,190 | 8.4 |
| Bethesda-Rockville-Frederick, MD,.............. | 566,300 | 55,860 | 9.9 | (X) | (X) | (X) |
| San Francisco-San Mateo-Redwood City, CA,.............. | 1,086,660 | 105,430 | 9.7 | (X) | (X) | (X) |
| Boston-Cambridge-Quincy, MA, NECTA division [1]........ | 1,795,230 | 157,300 | 8.8 | (X) | (X) | (X) |
| Columbus, IN.............. | 48,120 | 4,090 | 8.5 | (X) | (X) | (X) |

X Not applicable. [1] NECTA = New England City and Town Area.

Source: U.S. National Science Foundation, *Science and Engineering Indicators, 2018*, NSB-2018-1, January 2018, and earlier reports. See also <http://www.nsf.gov/statistics/seind/>.

# Table 849. High-Technology Establishments, Business Formations, and Employment by State: 2014

[Employment in thousands (121,058 represents 121,058,000). High-technology industries are those industries for which employment in technology-oriented occupations accounts for a proportion of that industry's total employment that is at least twice the 4.9% average for all industries. Includes only private-sector businesses. For a complete list of included industries, see source. Minus sign (-) indicates loss]

| State | All establishments | | High technology establishments | | | | | |
|---|---|---|---|---|---|---|---|---|
| | | | Establishments | | Net business formations | | Employment | |
| | Total | Employment (1,000) | Total | Percent of all establishments | Total | Percent of all establishments | Total (1,000) | Percent of total employment |
| **United States** | **7,547,983** | **121,058** | **688,985** | **9.1** | **13,409** | **0.2** | **14,792** | **12.2** |
| Alabama | 97,522 | 1,604 | 7,025 | 7.2 | 146 | 0.1 | 163 | 10.1 |
| Alaska | 20,696 | 267 | 1,720 | 8.3 | 39 | 0.2 | 39 | 14.6 |
| Arizona | 134,235 | 2,241 | 12,408 | 9.2 | 242 | 0.2 | 246 | 11.0 |
| Arkansas | 64,571 | 992 | 4,963 | 7.7 | 58 | 0.1 | 102 | 10.3 |
| California | 887,221 | 13,836 | 93,710 | 10.6 | 1,908 | 0.2 | 1,904 | 13.8 |
| Colorado | 157,826 | 2,181 | 19,926 | 12.6 | 499 | 0.3 | 341 | 15.6 |
| Connecticut | 88,337 | 1,484 | 7,455 | 8.4 | 8 | – | 198 | 13.3 |
| Delaware | 24,281 | 392 | 3,131 | 12.9 | 75 | 0.3 | 55 | 14.0 |
| District of Columbia | 22,185 | 496 | 3,942 | 17.8 | 88 | 0.4 | 83 | 16.7 |
| Florida | 518,959 | 7,441 | 49,232 | 9.5 | 1,421 | 0.3 | 653 | 8.8 |
| Georgia | 220,314 | 3,551 | 22,355 | 10.1 | 287 | 0.1 | 486 | 13.7 |
| Hawaii | 31,772 | 519 | 2,260 | 7.1 | 35 | 0.1 | 31 | 5.9 |
| Idaho | 43,732 | 530 | 3,095 | 7.1 | 76 | 0.2 | 57 | 10.8 |
| Illinois | 315,593 | 5,313 | 29,704 | 9.4 | 357 | 0.1 | 681 | 12.8 |
| Indiana | 143,549 | 2,603 | 10,377 | 7.2 | 215 | 0.1 | 241 | 9.3 |
| Iowa | 80,285 | 1,316 | 4,844 | 6.0 | 4 | – | 116 | 8.8 |
| Kansas | 73,891 | 1,178 | 6,273 | 8.5 | 75 | 0.1 | 160 | 13.6 |
| Kentucky | 91,297 | 1,535 | 6,266 | 6.9 | 173 | 0.2 | 130 | 8.5 |
| Louisiana | 104,891 | 1,718 | 8,621 | 8.2 | 278 | 0.3 | 161 | 9.4 |
| Maine | 40,314 | 492 | 2,704 | 6.7 | -38 | -0.1 | 40 | 8.0 |
| Maryland | 136,248 | 2,217 | 16,806 | 12.3 | 380 | 0.3 | 374 | 16.9 |
| Massachusetts | 173,213 | 3,087 | 18,018 | 10.4 | 89 | 0.1 | 470 | 15.2 |
| Michigan | 217,916 | 3,611 | 16,648 | 7.6 | 23 | – | 433 | 12.0 |
| Minnesota | 147,240 | 2,566 | 13,645 | 9.3 | 151 | 0.1 | 395 | 15.4 |
| Mississippi | 58,427 | 912 | 3,684 | 6.3 | 93 | 0.2 | 67 | 7.3 |
| Missouri | 153,620 | 2,404 | 10,069 | 6.6 | 146 | 0.1 | 285 | 11.9 |
| Montana | 36,707 | 364 | 2,774 | 7.6 | 9 | – | 26 | 7.3 |
| Nebraska | 52,905 | 851 | 3,529 | 6.7 | -7 | – | 71 | 8.3 |
| Nevada | 61,542 | 1,091 | 6,476 | 10.5 | 142 | 0.2 | 74 | 6.8 |
| New Hampshire | 37,330 | 563 | 3,483 | 9.3 | -45 | -0.1 | 68 | 12.1 |
| New Jersey | 230,272 | 3,526 | 23,645 | 10.3 | -111 | – | 525 | 14.9 |
| New Mexico | 43,650 | 603 | 3,577 | 8.2 | 46 | 0.1 | 65 | 10.8 |
| New York | 535,045 | 7,855 | 40,942 | 7.7 | 783 | 0.1 | 795 | 10.1 |
| North Carolina | 219,532 | 3,560 | 19,287 | 8.8 | 395 | 0.2 | 395 | 11.1 |
| North Dakota | 24,650 | 361 | 1,510 | 6.1 | 65 | 0.3 | 29 | 8.0 |
| Ohio | 250,113 | 4,635 | 20,367 | 8.1 | 456 | 0.2 | 506 | 10.9 |
| Oklahoma | 92,279 | 1,361 | 8,093 | 8.8 | 235 | 0.3 | 159 | 11.7 |
| Oregon | 109,558 | 1,443 | 8,926 | 8.1 | 77 | 0.1 | 170 | 11.8 |
| Pennsylvania | 297,850 | 5,255 | 24,854 | 8.3 | 426 | 0.1 | 636 | 12.1 |
| Rhode Island | 28,090 | 422 | 2,175 | 7.7 | 29 | 0.1 | 41 | 9.6 |
| South Carolina | 102,144 | 1,619 | 7,264 | 7.1 | 83 | 0.1 | 176 | 10.9 |
| South Dakota | 26,141 | 348 | 1,552 | 5.9 | 7 | – | 28 | 8.0 |
| Tennessee | 131,227 | 2,454 | 9,024 | 6.9 | 77 | 0.1 | 244 | 9.9 |
| Texas | 556,676 | 9,918 | 56,855 | 10.2 | 2,360 | 0.4 | 1,349 | 13.6 |
| Utah | 73,264 | 1,148 | 7,914 | 10.8 | 212 | 0.3 | 139 | 12.1 |
| Vermont | 21,017 | 261 | 1,579 | 7.5 | -3 | – | 25 | 9.4 |
| Virginia | 195,370 | 3,160 | 25,565 | 13.1 | 687 | 0.4 | 554 | 17.5 |
| Washington | 178,458 | 2,529 | 16,331 | 9.2 | 420 | 0.2 | 455 | 18.0 |
| West Virginia | 37,283 | 575 | 2,441 | 6.5 | -13 | – | 51 | 8.9 |
| Wisconsin | 137,977 | 2,451 | 9,906 | 7.2 | 127 | 0.1 | 281 | 11.5 |
| Wyoming | 20,768 | 220 | 2,035 | 9.8 | 124 | 0.6 | 20 | 9.3 |

– Represents or rounds to zero.

Source: U.S. National Science Foundation, *Science and Engineering Indicators, 2018*, NSB-2018-1, January 2018. See <http://www.nsf.gov/statistics/seind/>.

## Table 850. Employment and Median Salary of Worker With Highest Degree in Science and Engineering (S&E) Field by Sex and Occupation: 2015

[Rounded to the nearest 1,000. Data are for full-time workers who typically work 35 or more hours weekly in their principal job. Data are from National Science Foundation's Scientists and Engineers Statistical Data System (SESTAT)]

| Occupation | Total | | Female | | | Male | | |
|---|---|---|---|---|---|---|---|---|
| | Number | Median salary (dollars) | Number | Percent | Median salary (dollars) | Number | Percent | Median salary (dollars) |
| **All occupations**..................... | **11,555,000** | **75,000** | **4,222,000** | **36.5** | **57,000** | **7,334,000** | **63.5** | **86,000** |
| S&E................................. | 4,383,000 | 90,000 | 1,071,000 | 24.4 | 75,000 | 3,312,000 | 75.6 | 95,000 |
| Engineers.................................... | 1,362,000 | 92,000 | 198,000 | 14.5 | 88,000 | 1,164,000 | 85.5 | 95,000 |
| Computer and mathematical scientists.. | 1,988,000 | 97,000 | 422,000 | 21.2 | 85,000 | 1,565,000 | 78.7 | 100,000 |
| Biological, agricultural, and other life scientists...................... | 439,000 | 62,000 | 186,000 | 42.4 | 55,000 | 252,000 | 57.4 | 68,000 |
| Physical scientists........................ | 273,000 | 78,000 | 69,000 | 25.3 | 60,000 | 204,000 | 74.7 | 83,000 |
| Social scientists........................... | 321,000 | 69,000 | 196,000 | 61.1 | 63,000 | 125,000 | 38.9 | 82,000 |
| S&E related occupations................... | 1,678,000 | 73,000 | 707,000 | 42.1 | 56,000 | 972,000 | 57.9 | 90,000 |
| Health-related occupations................ | 468,000 | 55,000 | 329,000 | 70.3 | 55,000 | 139,000 | 29.7 | 51,000 |
| Non-S&E related occupations.............. | 5,471,000 | 60,000 | 2,427,000 | 44.4 | 50,000 | 3,044,000 | 55.6 | 75,000 |

Source: U.S. National Science Foundation, Science and Engineering Indicators 2018, NSB-2018-1, January 2018. See also <http://www.nsf.gov/statistics/seind/>.

## Table 851. Federal Discretionary Outlays for General Science and Space and Other Technology: 1970 to 2018, and Projections for 2019 and 2020

[In billions of dollars (4.5 represents $4,500,000,000). For fiscal years ending in year shown; see text, Section 8]

| Year | Current dollars | | | Constant (2012) dollars | | |
|---|---|---|---|---|---|---|
| | Total | General science and research | Space/other technologies | Total | General science and research | Space/other technologies |
| 1970............. | 4.5 | 0.9 | 3.6 | 26.0 | 5.5 | 20.6 |
| 1980............. | 5.8 | 1.4 | 4.5 | 16.9 | 4.0 | 12.9 |
| 1990............. | 14.4 | 2.8 | 11.6 | 29.8 | 5.8 | 24.0 |
| 2000 [1]......... | 18.6 | 6.2 | 12.4 | 26.3 | 8.7 | 17.6 |
| 2005............. | 23.6 | 8.8 | 14.8 | 27.9 | 10.4 | 17.5 |
| 2006............. | 23.5 | 9.0 | 14.5 | 27.0 | 10.3 | 16.6 |
| 2007............. | 24.4 | 9.1 | 15.3 | 27.0 | 10.1 | 16.9 |
| 2008............. | 26.7 | 9.5 | 17.2 | 28.9 | 10.3 | 18.6 |
| 2009............. | 28.3 | 9.9 | 18.4 | 30.3 | 10.6 | 19.7 |
| 2010............. | 30.0 | 11.6 | 18.4 | 31.1 | 12.1 | 19.1 |
| 2011............. | 29.4 | 12.3 | 17.0 | 29.8 | 12.5 | 17.3 |
| 2012............. | 28.9 | 12.3 | 16.6 | 28.9 | 12.3 | 16.6 |
| 2013............. | 28.8 | 12.4 | 16.4 | 28.4 | 12.2 | 16.2 |
| 2014............. | 28.5 | 11.9 | 16.6 | 27.6 | 11.5 | 16.0 |
| 2015............. | 29.4 | 11.7 | 17.7 | 27.9 | 11.1 | 16.8 |
| 2016............. | 30.1 | 11.9 | 18.2 | 28.4 | 11.2 | 17.2 |
| 2017............. | 30.3 | 12.2 | 18.1 | 28.0 | 11.3 | 16.7 |
| 2018............. | 31.4 | 12.3 | 19.1 | 28.3 | 11.1 | 17.2 |
| 2019, proj...... | 33.7 | 13.4 | 20.3 | 29.8 | 11.9 | 17.9 |
| 2020, proj...... | 34.4 | 13.2 | 21.2 | 29.8 | 11.5 | 18.4 |

[1] Due to the effects of the Credit Reform Act of 1990 on the measurement and classification of Federal credit activities, the discretionary outlays for years prior to 1992 are not strictly comparable to those for 1992 and beyond.

Source: U.S. Office of Management and Budget, Budget of the U.S. Government, Fiscal Year 2020: Historical Tables, March 2019. See also <http://www.whitehouse.gov/omb/budget>.

## Table 852. Space Launch Events Worldwide: 2000 to 2017

[2,729 represents $2,729,000,000.) Data show all U.S. and international orbital launches. Launch data includes launch failures; launch failures happen when the payload does not reach a usable orbit or is destroyed as the result of a launch vehicle malfunction. In 2017 there were 5 launch failures; these included four government launches and New Zealand's commercial test launch]

| Country/region | Non-commercial launches | | | | Commercial launches | | | | Launch revenues for commercial launch events (mil. dol.) | | | |
|---|---|---|---|---|---|---|---|---|---|---|---|---|
| | 2000 | 2010 | 2015 | 2017 | 2000 | 2010 | 2015 | 2017 | 2000 | 2010 | 2015 | 2017 |
| **Total**.............. | **50** | **51** | **64** | **57** | **35** | **23** | **22** | **33** | **2,729** | **2,453** | **2,150** | **3,018** |
| United States...... | 21 | 11 | 12 | 8 | 7 | 4 | 8 | 21 | 370 | 307 | 617 | 1,731 |
| Russia.............. | 23 | 18 | 21 | 16 | 13 | 13 | 5 | 3 | 671 | 826 | 289 | 195 |
| Europe............. | – | – | 5 | 3 | 12 | 6 | 6 | 8 | 1,433 | 1,320 | 1,066 | 1,092 |
| New Zealand...... | – | – | – | – | – | – | – | 1 | (X) | (X) | (X) | – |
| China.............. | 5 | 15 | 19 | 18 | – | – | – | – | (X) | (X) | (X) | (X) |
| India.............. | – | 3 | 3 | 5 | – | – | 2 | – | (X) | (X) | 66 | (X) |
| Japan.............. | 1 | 2 | 3 | 7 | – | – | 1 | – | (X) | (X) | 113 | (X) |
| Israel.............. | – | 1 | – | – | – | – | – | – | (X) | (X) | (X) | (X) |
| Iran................ | – | – | 1 | – | – | – | – | – | (X) | (X) | (X) | (X) |
| Korea, North...... | – | – | – | – | – | – | – | – | (X) | (X) | (X) | (X) |
| Korea, South...... | – | 1 | – | – | – | – | – | – | (X) | (X) | (X) | (X) |
| Multinational...... | – | – | – | – | 3 | – | – | – | 255 | (X) | (X) | (X) |

– Represents zero. X Not applicable.

Source: Federal Aviation Administration, Commercial Space Transportation: 2014 Year in Review, February 2015, and earlier editions; and The Annual Compendium of Commercial Space Transportation: 2018, January 2018, and earlier editions. See also <http://www.faa.gov/about/office_org/headquarters_offices/ast/reports_studies/>.

# Section 17
# Agriculture

This section presents statistics on farms and farm operators; farm income, expenditures, and debt; farm output, productivity, and marketings; foreign trade in agricultural products; specific crops; livestock, poultry, and their products; and direct marketing to consumers.

The principal sources are the data collected by the National Agricultural Statistics Service (NASS), the Economic Research Service (ERS), and the Foreign Agricultural Service (FAS) of the U.S. Department of Agriculture (USDA) and published in reports or databases. The ERS publishes data on farm assets, debt, and income on the internet at <http://www.ers.usda.gov/data-products/farm-income-and-wealth-statistics>. The ERS also provides data on commodity supply and disappearance via commodity outlook reports, yearbooks, and databases, available on the ERS site at <http://www.ers.usda.gov/data-products.aspx>. Sources of current data on agricultural exports and imports include the Global Agricultural Trade System database provided by the FAS at <http://www.fas.usda.gov/gats> and the "Foreign Agricultural Trade of the United States (FATUS)" data, published by the ERS, available on the ERS site at <https://www.ers.usda.gov/data-products/foreign-agricultural-trade-of-the-united-states-fatus/>.

The field offices of the NASS collect data on crops, livestock and products, agricultural prices, farm employment, and other related subjects mainly through sample surveys. Information is obtained on crops, livestock, and products pertaining to agricultural production and marketing. State estimates and supporting information are sent to the Agricultural Statistics Board of NASS, which reviews the estimates and issues reports containing state and national data. Among these reports are annual summaries such as *Crop Production, Crop Values, Agricultural Prices,* and *Meat Animals Production, Disposition and Income.* The NASS also provides data through the QuickStats database at <http://quickstats.nass.usda.gov>.

The USDA conducts the Census of Agriculture every 5 years and collects information concerning all areas of farming and ranching operations, including production expenses, market value of products, and operator characteristics. The information from the 2017 Census of Agriculture is available in print form in the Volume 1, Geographic Area Series; and on the internet at <https://www.nass.usda.gov/Publications/AgCensus/2017/>. An evaluation of coverage has been conducted for each census of agriculture since 1945 to provide estimates of the completeness of census farm counts. Beginning with the 1997 Census of Agriculture, census farm counts and totals were statistically adjusted for coverage and reported at the county level. The size of the adjustments varies considerably by state. In general, farms not on the census mail list tended to be small in acreage, production, and sales of farm products.

For more explanation about census mail list compilation, collection methods, coverage measurement, and adjustments, see Appendix A,

*2017 Census of Agriculture,* Volume 1, <https://www.nass.usda.gov/Publications/AgCensus/2017/>.

**Farms and farmland**—The definitions of a farm have varied through time. Since 1850, when minimum criteria defining a farm for census purposes first were established, the farm definition has changed nine times. The current definition, first used for the 1974 census, is any place from which $1,000 or more of agricultural products were produced and sold, or normally would have been sold, during the census year.

Acreage designated as "land in farms" consists primarily of agricultural land used for crops, pasture, or grazing. It also includes woodland and wasteland not actually under cultivation or used for pasture or grazing, provided it was part of the farm operator's total operation. Land in farms includes acres set aside under annual commodity acreage programs as well as acres idled by federal conservation programs for places meeting the farm definition. Land in farms is an operating unit concept and includes land owned and operated as well as land rented from others. All grazing land, except land used under government permits on a per-head basis, was included as "land in farms" provided it was part of a farm or ranch.

**Farm income**—The final agricultural sector output comprises cash receipts from farm marketings of crops and livestock, federal government payments made directly to farmers for farm-related activities, rental value of farm homes, value of farm products consumed in farm homes, and other farm-related income such as machine hire and custom work. Farm marketings represent quantities of agricultural products sold by farmers multiplied by prices received per unit of production at the local market. Information on prices received for farm products is generally obtained by the NASS Agricultural Statistics Board from surveys of firms (such as grain elevators, packers, and processors) purchasing agricultural commodities directly from producers. In some cases, the price information is obtained directly from the producers.

**Crops**—Estimates of crop acreage and production by the NASS are based on current sample survey data obtained from individual producers and objective yield counts, reports of carlot shipments, market records, personal field observations by field statisticians, and reports from other sources.

Prices received by farmers are marketing year average prices and do not include allowances for outstanding loans, government purchases, deficiency payments or disaster payments. These averages are based on monthly prices weighted by monthly sales during specific periods. All state marketing year average prices are based on individual state marketing years, while U.S. marketing year average prices are based on standard U.S. marketing years for each crop. For a description of how U.S. prices are computed as well as a listing of the crop marketing years, see *Crop Values Annual Summary.*

Value of production is computed by multiplying state prices by each state's production. The U.S. value of production is the sum of state values for all states. Value of production figures should not be confused with cash receipts from farm marketings which relate to sales during a calendar year, irrespective of the year of production.

**Livestock**—Annual inventory numbers of livestock and estimates of livestock, dairy, and poultry production prepared by the Department of Agriculture are based on information from farmers and ranchers obtained by probability survey sampling methods.

**Statistical reliability**—For a discussion of statistical collection and estimation, sampling procedures, and measures of statistical reliability pertaining to Department of Agriculture data, see Appendix III.

# Table 853. Selected Characteristics of Farms by North American Industry Classification System (NAICS): 2017

[388,522,695 represents $388,522,695,000. See text this section and Appendix III]

| Industry | 2012 NAICS code [1] | Farms | Land in farms (acres) | Harvested cropland (acres) | Market value of agricultural products sold ($1,000) Total | Crops | Livestock [2] |
|---|---|---|---|---|---|---|---|
| **Total**............................. | (X) | **2,042,220** | **900,217,576** | **320,041,858** | **388,522,695** | **193,546,699** | **194,975,996** |
| Crop production............... | 111 | 967,090 | 421,544,023 | 262,718,038 | 189,264,224 | 181,697,779 | 7,566,445 |
| Oilseed and grain farming............ | 1111 | 325,033 | 275,696,715 | 209,754,358 | 102,018,657 | 96,275,715 | 5,742,943 |
| Soybean farming............ | 11111 | 105,832 | 53,532,004 | 44,561,866 | 20,411,246 | 20,077,387 | 333,859 |
| Oilseed (except soybean) farming.......... | 11112 | 849 | 1,488,090 | 1,073,701 | 251,972 | 248,984 | 2,988 |
| Dry pea and bean farming........... | 11113 | 1,296 | 1,782,380 | 1,173,169 | 321,225 | 316,886 | 4,339 |
| Wheat farming................ | 11114 | 18,312 | 29,720,570 | 15,595,523 | 3,125,617 | 2,993,054 | 132,563 |
| Corn farming................. | 11115 | 133,981 | 97,079,475 | 81,479,149 | 46,437,032 | 45,435,179 | 1,001,853 |
| Rice farming.................. | 11116 | 2,680 | 3,323,806 | 2,451,234 | 1,893,094 | 1,860,141 | 32,953 |
| Other grain farming............. | 11119 | 62,083 | 88,770,390 | 63,419,716 | 29,578,471 | 25,344,085 | 4,234,387 |
| Vegetable and melon farming......... | 1121 | 45,165 | 9,310,059 | 6,008,800 | 19,731,533 | 19,627,511 | 104,022 |
| Potato farming................. | 111211 | 2,568 | 3,189,793 | 2,516,571 | 4,605,952 | 4,587,516 | 18,435 |
| Other vegetable (except potato) and melon farming............ | 111219 | 42,597 | 6,120,266 | 3,492,229 | 15,125,582 | 15,039,994 | 85,587 |
| Fruit and tree nut farming................ | 1113 | 95,441 | 13,357,346 | 6,173,016 | 28,336,564 | 28,211,310 | 125,254 |
| Orange groves................. | 11131 | 4,500 | 1,093,218 | 562,704 | 1,589,218 | 1,563,214 | 26,004 |
| Citrus (except orange) groves.............. | 11132 | 3,451 | 513,909 | 277,376 | 1,621,780 | 1,613,949 | 7,831 |
| Noncitrus fruit and tree nut farming......... | 11133 | 87,490 | 11,750,219 | 5,332,936 | 25,125,566 | 25,034,147 | 91,419 |
| Apple orchards.............. | 111331 | 10,087 | 2,226,789 | 472,433 | 3,518,947 | 3,512,021 | 6,926 |
| Grape vineyards............ | 111332 | 17,949 | 2,254,802 | 1,143,044 | 6,073,378 | 6,059,901 | 13,477 |
| Strawberry farming.......... | 111333 | 1,391 | 137,455 | 60,565 | 2,018,159 | 2,017,404 | 755 |
| Berry (except strawberry) farming.......... | 111334 | 11,005 | 1,073,431 | 254,450 | 1,359,836 | 1,355,865 | 3,971 |
| Tree nut farming............ | 111335 | 24,174 | 4,493,273 | 2,620,517 | 8,391,403 | 8,344,887 | 46,516 |
| Fruit and tree nut combination farming.................. | 111336 | 1,477 | 250,421 | 140,631 | 516,724 | 510,459 | 6,265 |
| Other noncitrus fruit farming.............. | 111339 | 21,407 | 1,314,048 | 641,296 | 3,247,118 | 3,233,609 | 13,509 |
| Greenhouse, nursery, and floriculture production................. | 1114 | 45,477 | 3,934,004 | 1,364,516 | 16,496,154 | 16,460,012 | 36,142 |
| Food crops grown under cover.............. | 11141 | 4,199 | 155,700 | 22,701 | 2,081,839 | 2,076,997 | 4,841 |
| Nursery and floriculture production.......... | 11142 | 41,278 | 3,778,304 | 1,341,815 | 14,414,316 | 14,383,015 | 31,301 |
| Nursery and tree production........... | 111421 | 26,174 | 3,294,378 | 1,202,706 | 8,175,668 | 8,150,549 | 25,119 |
| Floriculture production...................... | 111422 | 15,104 | 483,926 | 139,109 | 6,238,648 | 6,232,466 | 6,182 |
| Other crop farming................ | 1119 | 455,974 | 119,245,899 | 39,417,348 | 22,681,315 | 21,123,231 | 1,558,084 |
| Tobacco farming.................. | 11191 | 3,757 | 1,586,381 | 938,702 | 1,413,240 | 1,365,986 | 47,253 |
| Cotton farming................... | 11192 | 8,815 | 15,874,682 | 11,237,600 | 6,011,120 | 5,908,080 | 103,040 |
| Sugarcane farming............... | 11193 | 467 | 1,351,038 | 940,656 | 967,695 | 965,173 | 2,522 |
| Hay farming...................... | 11194 | 244,035 | 46,273,222 | 16,001,743 | 5,585,232 | 5,124,522 | 460,710 |
| All other crop farming............ | 11199 | 198,900 | 54,160,576 | 10,298,647 | 8,704,028 | 7,759,469 | 944,559 |
| Animal production................. | 112 | 1,075,130 | 478,673,553 | 57,323,820 | 199,258,471 | 11,848,920 | 187,409,551 |
| Cattle ranching and farming................ | 1121 | 692,625 | 394,097,473 | 48,045,215 | 114,809,219 | 7,935,980 | 106,873,239 |
| Beef cattle ranching and farming including feedlots............ | 11211 | 654,875 | 376,699,018 | 36,258,728 | 72,426,397 | 5,259,911 | 67,166,486 |
| Beef cattle ranching and farming.......... | 112111 | 641,496 | 362,543,006 | 31,777,036 | 33,370,653 | 3,454,114 | 29,916,539 |
| Cattle feedlots............. | 112112 | 13,379 | 14,156,012 | 4,481,692 | 39,055,744 | 1,805,797 | 37,249,947 |
| Dairy cattle and milk production............ | 11212 | 37,750 | 17,398,455 | 11,786,487 | 42,382,822 | 2,676,069 | 39,706,753 |
| Hog and pig farming................. | 1122 | 23,048 | 5,793,498 | 4,308,268 | 27,143,555 | 2,386,171 | 24,757,384 |
| Poultry and egg production................. | 1123 | 44,260 | 5,916,544 | 2,087,155 | 50,155,733 | 875,539 | 49,280,194 |
| Chicken egg production............. | 11231 | 19,785 | 1,295,219 | 371,262 | 8,905,165 | 161,201 | 8,743,964 |
| Broilers and other meat-type chicken production................. | 11232 | 15,609 | 3,394,774 | 1,223,669 | 31,068,699 | 482,203 | 30,586,497 |
| Turkey production................. | 11233 | 2,517 | 763,815 | 410,201 | 5,972,474 | 197,628 | 5,774,846 |
| Poultry hatcheries................. | 11234 | 264 | 12,237 | 878 | 3,402,867 | 188 | 3,402,679 |
| Other poultry production................. | 11239 | 6,085 | 450,499 | 81,145 | 806,527 | 34,319 | 772,208 |
| Sheep and goat farming................. | 1124 | 92,974 | 13,975,994 | 383,580 | 877,791 | 49,649 | 828,143 |
| Sheep farming................. | 11241 | 46,799 | 9,952,322 | 275,661 | 638,150 | 37,251 | 600,899 |
| Goat farming................. | 11242 | 46,175 | 4,023,672 | 107,919 | 239,641 | 12,398 | 227,244 |
| Animal aquaculture................. | 1125 | 3,981 | 1,008,935 | 53,195 | 1,778,231 | 26,807 | 1,751,425 |
| Other animal production................. | 1129 | 218,242 | 57,881,109 | 2,446,407 | 4,493,942 | 574,774 | 3,919,168 |
| Apiculture................. | 11291 | 10,517 | 439,719 | 15,109 | 357,124 | 3,590 | 353,534 |
| Horse and other equine production........ | 11292 | 157,237 | 22,695,698 | 829,208 | 1,444,757 | 30,969 | 1,413,788 |
| Fur-bearing animal and rabbit production................. | 11293 | 773 | 30,476 | 5,662 | 140,297 | 2,235 | 138,062 |
| All other animal production................. | 11299 | 49,715 | 34,715,216 | 1,596,428 | 2,551,764 | 537,981 | 2,013,784 |

X Not applicable. [1] Based on the North American Industry Classification System (NAICS) 2012; see text, Section 15. [2] Includes poultry and poultry products sold.

Source: U.S. Department of Agriculture, National Agricultural Statistics Service, *2017 Census of Agriculture*, Vol. 1, April 2019. See also <https://www.nass.usda.gov/AgCensus/index.php>.

## Table 854. Farms—Number and Acreage: 2000 to 2018

[2,167 represents 2,167,000. As of June. Based on 1974 census definition; for definition of farms and farmland, see text, this section. Data for census years have been adjusted for underenumeration]

| Item | Unit | 2000 | 2005 | 2010 | 2013 | 2014 | 2015 | 2016 | 2017 | 2018 |
|------|------|------|------|------|------|------|------|------|------|------|
| Number of farms.......... | 1,000 | 2,167 | 2,099 | 2,150 | 2,100 | 2,082 | 2,064 | 2,055 | 2,042 | 2,029 |
| Land in farms.............. | Million acres | 945 | 928 | 916 | 912 | 909 | 906 | 903 | 900 | 900 |
| Average per farm........ | Acres | 436 | 442 | 426 | 434 | 436 | 439 | 439 | 441 | 443 |

Source: U.S. Department of Agriculture, National Agricultural Statistics Service, *Farm Numbers and Land in Farms, Final Estimates, 2013–2017* and earlier reports; and *Farms and Land in Farms 2018 Summary*, April 2019. See also <http://www.nass.usda.gov/Publications/index.asp>.

## Table 855. Farms—Number and Acreage by State: 2010 and 2018

[2,150 represents 2,150,000. See headnote, Table 854]

| State | Farms (1,000) 2010 | Farms (1,000) 2018 | Land in farms (mil. acres) 2010 | Land in farms (mil. acres) 2018 | Acreage per farm 2010 | Acreage per farm 2018 | State | Farms (1,000) 2010 | Farms (1,000) 2018 | Land in farms (mil. acres) 2010 | Land in farms (mil. acres) 2018 | Acreage per farm 2010 | Acreage per farm 2018 |
|-------|------|------|------|------|------|------|-------|------|------|------|------|------|------|
| **United States.....** | **2,150** | **2,029** | **915.7** | **899.5** | **426** | **443** | Missouri............ | 103 | 95 | 28.7 | 27.7 | 279 | 292 |
| | | | | | | | Montana............ | 29 | 27 | 60.6 | 58.0 | 2,082 | 2,156 |
| Alabama........... | 46 | 40 | 8.9 | 8.5 | 193 | 214 | Nebraska........... | 50 | 46 | 45.4 | 45.0 | 917 | 980 |
| Alaska............. | 1 | 1 | 0.9 | 0.9 | 1,181 | 850 | Nevada............. | 4 | 3 | 5.9 | 6.1 | 1,579 | 1,794 |
| Arizona............ | 18 | 19 | 24.8 | 26.2 | 1,378 | 1,365 | New Hampshire.... | 4 | 4 | 0.5 | 0.4 | 109 | 105 |
| Arkansas........... | 47 | 43 | 13.7 | 13.9 | 291 | 327 | New Jersey......... | 10 | 10 | 0.7 | 0.8 | 74 | 76 |
| California.......... | 79 | 69 | 25.5 | 24.3 | 322 | 350 | New Mexico......... | 22 | 25 | 43.4 | 40.5 | 1,973 | 1,640 |
| Colorado........... | 36 | 39 | 31.5 | 31.8 | 868 | 817 | New York........... | 36 | 33 | 7.1 | 6.9 | 197 | 207 |
| Connecticut........ | 6 | 6 | 0.4 | 0.4 | 75 | 69 | North Carolina...... | 52 | 46 | 8.4 | 8.4 | 163 | 181 |
| Delaware.......... | 3 | 2 | 0.5 | 0.5 | 200 | 230 | North Dakota....... | 31 | 26 | 39.5 | 39.3 | 1,262 | 1,506 |
| Florida............ | 48 | 48 | 9.4 | 9.7 | 197 | 204 | Ohio............... | 75 | 78 | 13.8 | 13.9 | 184 | 179 |
| Georgia............ | 44 | 42 | 9.7 | 10.1 | 219 | 243 | Oklahoma.......... | 83 | 77 | 34.7 | 34.2 | 417 | 442 |
| Hawaii............. | 7 | 7 | 1.1 | 1.1 | 153 | 151 | Oregon............ | 37 | 37 | 16.2 | 16.0 | 439 | 430 |
| Idaho............. | 25 | 25 | 11.5 | 11.6 | 453 | 468 | Pennsylvania....... | 61 | 53 | 7.7 | 7.3 | 126 | 138 |
| Illinois............ | 76 | 72 | 26.9 | 27.0 | 354 | 375 | Rhode Island....... | 1 | 1 | 0.1 | 0.1 | 56 | 55 |
| Indiana............ | 61 | 56 | 14.8 | 15.0 | 242 | 267 | South Carolina..... | 26 | 25 | 5.0 | 4.8 | 192 | 195 |
| Iowa.............. | 89 | 86 | 30.6 | 30.6 | 343 | 356 | South Dakota...... | 32 | 30 | 43.4 | 43.2 | 1,361 | 1,459 |
| Kansas............ | 63 | 59 | 46.2 | 45.8 | 732 | 778 | Tennessee.......... | 73 | 70 | 10.8 | 10.9 | 148 | 156 |
| Kentucky.......... | 80 | 75 | 13.4 | 12.9 | 167 | 172 | Texas............. | 249 | 247 | 131.6 | 127.0 | 530 | 514 |
| Louisiana.......... | 29 | 27 | 8.0 | 8.0 | 274 | 292 | Utah.............. | 18 | 18 | 11.0 | 10.7 | 629 | 591 |
| Maine............. | 8 | 8 | 1.4 | 1.3 | 173 | 171 | Vermont........... | 7 | 7 | 1.2 | 1.2 | 172 | 176 |
| Maryland.......... | 13 | 12 | 2.1 | 2.0 | 164 | 161 | Virginia............ | 47 | 43 | 8.2 | 7.8 | 176 | 184 |
| Massachusetts..... | 8 | 7 | 0.5 | 0.5 | 69 | 69 | Washington......... | 38 | 36 | 14.6 | 14.7 | 382 | 412 |
| Michigan........... | 53 | 47 | 10.0 | 9.8 | 187 | 209 | West Virginia....... | 22 | 23 | 3.6 | 3.6 | 161 | 154 |
| Minnesota.......... | 77 | 69 | 26.3 | 25.5 | 342 | 372 | Wisconsin.......... | 73 | 65 | 14.7 | 14.3 | 201 | 221 |
| Mississippi......... | 40 | 35 | 10.9 | 10.4 | 275 | 300 | Wyoming........... | 12 | 12 | 30.0 | 29.0 | 2,586 | 2,437 |

Source: U.S. Department of Agriculture, National Agricultural Statistics Service, "Quick Stats," <http://quickstats.nass.usda.gov/>, accessed May 2019. See also <http://www.nass.usda.gov/Statistics_by_Subject/>.

## Table 856. Farms by Size and Type of Organization: 1982 to 2017

[2,241 represents 2,241,000. For comments on adjustment, see text, this section]

| Size and type of organization | Unit | Not adjusted for coverage 1982 | Not adjusted for coverage 1987 | Not adjusted for coverage 1992 | Adjusted for coverage [1] 1997 | Adjusted for coverage [1] 2002 | Adjusted for coverage [1] 2007 | Adjusted for coverage [1] 2012 | Adjusted for coverage [1] 2017 |
|---|---|---|---|---|---|---|---|---|---|
| Farms........................................ | 1,000 | 2,241 | 2,088 | 1,925 | 2,216 | 2,129 | 2,205 | 2,109 | 2,042 |
| Land in farms............................... | Mil. acres | 987 | 964 | 946 | 955 | 938 | 922 | 915 | 900 |
| Average size of farm...................... | Acres | 440 | 462 | 491 | 431 | 441 | 418 | 434 | 441 |
| Farms by size: | | | | | | | | | |
| 1 to 9 acres............................... | 1,000 | 188 | 183 | 166 | 205 | 179 | 233 | 224 | 273 |
| 10 to 49 acres............................ | 1,000 | 449 | 412 | 388 | 531 | 564 | 620 | 590 | 583 |
| 50 to 179 acres........................... | 1,000 | 712 | 645 | 584 | 694 | 659 | 661 | 634 | 565 |
| 180 to 499 acres.......................... | 1,000 | 527 | 478 | 428 | 428 | 389 | 368 | 346 | 315 |
| 500 to 999 acres.......................... | 1,000 | 204 | 200 | 186 | 179 | 162 | 150 | 143 | 133 |
| 1,000 to 1,999 acres...................... | 1,000 | 97 | 102 | 102 | 103 | 99 | 93 | 91 | 88 |
| 2,000 acres or more...................... | 1,000 | 65 | 67 | 71 | 74 | 78 | 80 | 82 | 85 |
| Farms by type of organization: | | | | | | | | | |
| Family or individual....................... | 1,000 | 1,946 | 1,809 | 1,653 | 1,923 | 1,910 | 1,906 | 1,829 | 1,751 |
| Partnership................................ | 1,000 | 223 | 200 | 187 | 186 | 130 | 174 | 138 | 130 |
| Corporation............................... | 1,000 | 60 | 67 | 73 | 90 | 74 | 96 | 107 | 117 |
| Other [2].................................. | 1,000 | 12 | 12 | 12 | 17 | 16 | 28 | 36 | 44 |

[1] Data have been adjusted for coverage; see text, this section. [2] Cooperative, estate or trust, institutional, etc.

Source: U.S. Department of Agriculture, National Agricultural Statistics Service, *2017 Census of Agriculture*, Vol. 1, April 2019, and earlier reports. See also <https://www.nass.usda.gov/AgCensus/>.

## Table 857. Farms—Number and Acreage by Size of Farm: 2012 and 2017

[2,109 represents 2,109,000. Data have been adjusted for coverage; see text, this section]

| Size of farm | Number of farms (1,000) | | Land in farms (mil. acres) | | Cropland harvested (mil. acres) | | Percent distribution, 2017 | | |
|---|---|---|---|---|---|---|---|---|---|
| | 2012 | 2017 | 2012 | 2017 | 2012 | 2017 | Number of farms | All land in farms | Cropland harvested |
| Total.......................... | 2,109 | 2,042 | 914.5 | 900.2 | 315.0 | 320.0 | 100.0 | 100.0 | 100.0 |
| Under 10 acres................ | 224 | 273 | 1.0 | 1.3 | 0.3 | 0.4 | 13.4 | 0.1 | 0.1 |
| 10 to 49 acres................. | 590 | 583 | 15.1 | 14.8 | 4.1 | 4.1 | 28.5 | 1.6 | 1.3 |
| 50 to 69 acres................. | 154 | 135 | 8.9 | 7.8 | 2.5 | 2.2 | 6.6 | 0.9 | 0.7 |
| 70 to 99 acres................. | 185 | 163 | 15.2 | 13.4 | 4.4 | 3.9 | 8.0 | 1.5 | 1.2 |
| 100 to 139 acres.............. | 166 | 149 | 19.3 | 17.3 | 5.7 | 5.2 | 7.3 | 1.9 | 1.6 |
| 140 to 179 acres.............. | 129 | 117 | 20.3 | 18.4 | 6.3 | 5.8 | 5.7 | 2.0 | 1.8 |
| 180 to 219 acres.............. | 84 | 74 | 16.7 | 14.6 | 5.6 | 5.0 | 3.6 | 1.6 | 1.6 |
| 220 to 259 acres.............. | 64 | 57 | 15.1 | 13.6 | 5.5 | 5.0 | 2.8 | 1.5 | 1.6 |
| 260 to 499 acres.............. | 198 | 184 | 70.6 | 65.8 | 28.8 | 27.0 | 9.0 | 7.3 | 8.4 |
| 500 to 999 acres.............. | 143 | 133 | 99.0 | 92.9 | 49.5 | 45.9 | 6.5 | 10.3 | 14.3 |
| 1,000 to 1,999 acres........... | 91 | 88 | 125.1 | 120.7 | 68.7 | 66.2 | 4.3 | 13.4 | 20.7 |
| 2,000 acres or more........... | 82 | 85 | 508.2 | 519.6 | 133.6 | 149.4 | 4.2 | 57.7 | 46.7 |

Source: U.S. Department of Agriculture, National Agricultural Statistics Service, *2017 Census of Agriculture*, Vol. 1, April 2019. See also <https://www.nass.usda.gov/AgCensus/>.

## Table 858. Farms—Number, Acreage, and Value by Tenure of Principal Operator and Type of Organization: 2012 and 2017

[2,109 represents 2,109,000. Full owners own all the land they operate. Part owners own a part and rent from others the rest of the land they operate. A principal operator is the person primarily responsible for the on-site, day-to-day operation of the farm or ranch business. Data have been adjusted for coverage; see text, this section]

| Item and year | Unit | Total [1] | Tenure of operator | | | Type of organization | | |
|---|---|---|---|---|---|---|---|---|
| | | | Full owner | Part owner | Tenant | Family or individual | Partner-ship | Corpora-tion |
| **NUMBER OF FARMS** | | | | | | | | |
| 2012............................. | 1,000 | 2,109 | 1,428 | 533 | 148 | 1,829 | 138 | 107 |
| 2017............................. | 1,000 | 2,042 | 1,409 | 493 | 140 | 1,751 | 130 | 117 |
| Under 50 acres................. | 1,000 | 856 | 740 | 62 | 54 | 779 | 29 | 33 |
| 50 to 179 acres................ | 1,000 | 565 | 419 | 113 | 33 | 499 | 29 | 24 |
| 180 to 499 acres............... | 1,000 | 315 | 167 | 126 | 23 | 262 | 25 | 19 |
| 500 to 999 acres............... | 1,000 | 133 | 45 | 76 | 12 | 101 | 15 | 14 |
| 1,000 acres or more............ | 1,000 | 173 | 37 | 117 | 19 | 110 | 31 | 27 |
| **LAND IN FARMS** | | | | | | | | |
| 2012............................. | Mil. acres | 915 | 336 | 491 | 87 | 562 | 156 | 131 |
| 2017............................. | Mil. acres | 900 | 310 | 503 | 87 | 541 | 158 | 140 |
| Value of land and buildings, 2017.............. | Bil. dol. | 2,679 | 907 | 1,538 | 234 | 1,732 | 451 | 418 |
| Value of farm products sold, 2017.............. | Bil. dol. | 389 | 142 | 207 | 40 | 182 | 89 | 111 |

[1] Includes other types, not shown separately.

Source: U.S. Department of Agriculture, National Agricultural Statistics Service, *2017 Census of Agriculture*, Vol. 1, April 2019, and earlier reports. See also <https://www.nass.usda.gov/AgCensus/>.

## Table 859. Corporate Farms—Characteristics by Type: 2002 to 2017

[139.6 represents 139,600,000. Data have been adjusted for coverage; see text, this section and Appendix III]

| Item | Unit | All corpora-tions | Family held corporations | | | Other corporations | | |
|---|---|---|---|---|---|---|---|---|
| | | | Total | 1 to 10 stock-holders | 11 or more stock-holders | Total | 1 to 10 stock-holders | 11 or more stock-holders |
| Farms: | | | | | | | | |
| 2002............................. | Number | 73,752 | 66,667 | 65,017 | 1,650 | 7,085 | 6,010 | 1,075 |
| 2007............................. | Number | 96,074 | 85,837 | 83,796 | 2,041 | 10,237 | 9,330 | 907 |
| 2012............................. | Number | 106,716 | 95,142 | 92,834 | 2,308 | 11,574 | 10,438 | 1,136 |
| **2017** | | | | | | | | |
| Farms............................. | Number | 116,840 | 104,155 | 101,851 | 2,304 | 12,685 | 11,541 | 1,144 |
| Percent distribution...................... | Percent | 100.0 | 89.1 | 87.2 | 2.0 | 10.9 | 9.9 | 1.0 |
| Land in farms.............................. | Mil. acres | 139.6 | 126.7 | 119.6 | 7.1 | 12.9 | 10.5 | 2.4 |
| Average per farm........................ | Acres | 1,194 | 1,216 | 1,174 | 3,084 | 1,016 | 910 | 2,090 |
| Value of— | | | | | | | | |
| Land and buildings.................... | Bil. dol. | 417.6 | 378.7 | 360.8 | 18.0 | 38.8 | 30.0 | 8.8 |
| Average per farm..................... | $1,000 | 3,574 | 3,636 | 3,542 | 7,798 | 3,062 | 2,601 | 7,712 |
| Farm products sold..................... | Bil. dol. | 111.0 | 89.1 | 83.2 | 5.9 | 22.0 | 13.8 | 8.2 |
| Average per farm..................... | $1,000 | 950 | 855 | 817 | 2,547 | 1,733 | 1,197 | 7,133 |

Source: U.S. Department of Agriculture, National Agricultural Statistics Service, *2017 Census of Agriculture*, Vol. 1, April 2019, and earlier reports. See also <https://www.nass.usda.gov/AgCensus/>.

## Table 860. Farms—Number, Acreage, and Value by State: 2012 and 2017

[2,109 represents 2,109,000. Data have been adjusted for coverage; see text, this section and Appendix III]

| State | Number of farms (1,000) 2012 | Number of farms (1,000) 2017 | Land in farms (mil. acres) 2012 | Land in farms (mil. acres) 2017 | Average size of farm (acres) 2012 | Average size of farm (acres) 2017 | Total value of land and buildings (bil. dol.) 2012 | Total value of land and buildings (bil. dol.) 2017 | Market value of agricultural products sold and government payments (mil. dol.) 2012 | Market value of agricultural products sold and government payments (mil. dol.) 2017 |
|---|---|---|---|---|---|---|---|---|---|---|
| U.S. | 2,109 | 2,042 | 914.5 | 900.2 | 434 | 441 | 2,268.5 | 2,679.0 | 402,698 | 397,466 |
| AL. | 43 | 41 | 8.9 | 8.6 | 206 | 211 | 23.7 | 25.6 | 5,659 | 6,115 |
| AK. | 1 | 1 | 0.8 | 0.8 | 1,094 | 858 | 0.5 | 0.6 | 61 | 73 |
| AZ. | 20 | 19 | 26.2 | 26.1 | 1,312 | 1,369 | 16.9 | 21.2 | 3,763 | 3,874 |
| AR. | 45 | 43 | 13.8 | 13.9 | 306 | 326 | 36.4 | 43.9 | 10,039 | 9,973 |
| CA. | 78 | 71 | 25.6 | 24.5 | 328 | 348 | 160.5 | 229.4 | 42,774 | 45,282 |
| CO. | 36 | 39 | 31.9 | 31.8 | 881 | 818 | 40.8 | 51.2 | 7,946 | 7,690 |
| CT. | 6 | 6 | 0.4 | 0.4 | 73 | 69 | 4.8 | 4.8 | 555 | 582 |
| DE. | 2 | 2 | 0.5 | 0.5 | 208 | 228 | 4.2 | 4.4 | 1,284 | 1,481 |
| FL. | 48 | 48 | 9.5 | 9.7 | 200 | 204 | 49.7 | 57.4 | 7,742 | 7,416 |
| GA. | 42 | 42 | 9.6 | 10.0 | 228 | 235 | 29.7 | 34.9 | 9,397 | 9,821 |
| HI. | 7 | 7 | 1.1 | 1.1 | 161 | 155 | 10.2 | 10.6 | 667 | 572 |
| ID. | 25 | 25 | 11.8 | 11.7 | 474 | 468 | 26.1 | 33.5 | 7,901 | 7,697 |
| IL. | 75 | 73 | 26.9 | 27.0 | 359 | 372 | 169.8 | 196.5 | 17,740 | 17,531 |
| IN. | 59 | 57 | 14.7 | 15.0 | 251 | 264 | 78.8 | 98.4 | 11,478 | 11,450 |
| IA. | 89 | 86 | 30.6 | 30.6 | 345 | 355 | 195.6 | 215.8 | 31,604 | 29,639 |
| KS. | 62 | 59 | 46.1 | 45.8 | 747 | 781 | 75.3 | 84.6 | 18,903 | 19,292 |
| KY. | 77 | 76 | 13.0 | 13.0 | 169 | 171 | 39.5 | 48.8 | 5,237 | 5,865 |
| LA. | 28 | 27 | 7.9 | 8.0 | 281 | 292 | 20.2 | 24.4 | 3,948 | 3,350 |
| ME. | 8 | 8 | 1.5 | 1.3 | 178 | 172 | 3.4 | 3.4 | 773 | 676 |
| MD. | 12 | 12 | 2.0 | 2.0 | 166 | 160 | 14.1 | 15.6 | 2,307 | 2,517 |
| MA. | 8 | 7 | 0.5 | 0.5 | 68 | 68 | 5.5 | 5.4 | 500 | 479 |
| MI. | 52 | 48 | 9.9 | 9.8 | 191 | 205 | 40.0 | 48.4 | 8,834 | 8,388 |
| MN. | 75 | 69 | 26.0 | 25.5 | 349 | 371 | 109.9 | 123.8 | 21,748 | 18,790 |
| MS. | 38 | 35 | 10.9 | 10.4 | 287 | 298 | 24.8 | 28.6 | 6,622 | 6,410 |
| MO. | 99 | 95 | 28.3 | 27.8 | 285 | 291 | 78.9 | 94.0 | 9,489 | 10,850 |
| MT. | 28 | 27 | 59.8 | 58.1 | 2,134 | 2,149 | 46.9 | 53.2 | 4,440 | 3,805 |
| NE. | 50 | 46 | 45.3 | 45.0 | 907 | 971 | 107.9 | 123.9 | 23,461 | 22,623 |
| NV. | 4 | 3 | 5.9 | 6.1 | 1,429 | 1,790 | 5.5 | 5.6 | 767 | 671 |
| NH. | 4 | 4 | 0.5 | 0.4 | 108 | 103 | 2.0 | 2.2 | 194 | 191 |
| NJ. | 9 | 10 | 0.7 | 0.7 | 79 | 74 | 9.1 | 9.9 | 1,015 | 1,105 |
| NM. | 25 | 25 | 43.2 | 40.7 | 1,748 | 1,624 | 18.7 | 21.2 | 2,621 | 2,646 |
| NY. | 36 | 33 | 7.2 | 6.9 | 202 | 205 | 18.7 | 22.2 | 5,490 | 5,428 |
| NC. | 50 | 46 | 8.4 | 8.4 | 168 | 182 | 36.5 | 39.1 | 12,708 | 13,008 |
| ND. | 31 | 26 | 39.3 | 39.3 | 1,268 | 1,492 | 56.0 | 67.1 | 11,332 | 8,701 |
| OH. | 75 | 78 | 14.0 | 14.0 | 185 | 179 | 67.5 | 86.6 | 10,293 | 9,692 |
| OK. | 80 | 79 | 34.4 | 34.2 | 428 | 435 | 46.0 | 59.2 | 7,386 | 7,698 |
| OR. | 35 | 38 | 16.3 | 16.0 | 460 | 424 | 30.7 | 38.8 | 4,970 | 5,099 |
| PA. | 59 | 53 | 7.7 | 7.3 | 130 | 137 | 41.8 | 47.7 | 7,487 | 7,833 |
| RI. | 1 | 1 | 0.1 | 0.1 | 56 | 55 | 1.0 | 0.9 | 62 | 59 |
| SC. | 25 | 25 | 5.0 | 4.7 | 197 | 191 | 14.8 | 17.0 | 3,087 | 3,064 |
| SD. | 32 | 30 | 43.3 | 43.2 | 1,352 | 1,443 | 73.0 | 89.4 | 10,454 | 10,141 |
| TN. | 68 | 70 | 10.9 | 10.9 | 160 | 155 | 38.7 | 42.6 | 3,679 | 3,915 |
| TX. | 249 | 248 | 130.2 | 127.0 | 523 | 511 | 218.1 | 243.5 | 26,020 | 25,673 |
| UT. | 18 | 18 | 11.0 | 10.8 | 609 | 587 | 16.0 | 19.6 | 1,840 | 1,866 |
| VT. | 7 | 7 | 1.3 | 1.2 | 171 | 175 | 4.0 | 4.2 | 790 | 787 |
| VA. | 46 | 43 | 8.3 | 7.8 | 180 | 180 | 35.8 | 36.1 | 3,836 | 4,021 |
| WA. | 37 | 36 | 14.7 | 14.7 | 396 | 410 | 33.9 | 40.9 | 9,280 | 9,803 |
| WV. | 21 | 24 | 3.6 | 3.7 | 168 | 155 | 8.9 | 9.7 | 814 | 763 |
| WI. | 70 | 65 | 14.6 | 14.3 | 209 | 221 | 57.2 | 70.2 | 11,982 | 11,554 |
| WY. | 12 | 12 | 30.4 | 29.0 | 2,587 | 2,430 | 20.6 | 22.6 | 1,718 | 1,502 |

Source: U.S. Department of Agriculture, National Agricultural Statistics Service, *2017 Census of Agriculture*, Vol. 1, April 2019. See also <https://www.nass.usda.gov/AgCensus/>.

## Table 861. Farms—Number, Value of Sales, and Government Payments by Economic Class of Farm: 2012 and 2017

[2,109 represents 2,109,000. Economic class of farm is a combination of market value of agricultural products sold and federal farm program payments. Data have been adjusted for coverage; see text, this section and Appendix III]

| Economic class | Number of farms (1,000) 2012, total | Number of farms (1,000) 2017 Total | Number of farms (1,000) 2017 Receiving government payments | Market value of agricultural products sold and government payments (mil. dol.) 2012, total | Market value of agricultural products sold and government payments (mil. dol.) 2017 Total | Market value of agricultural products sold and government payments (mil. dol.) 2017 Agricultural products sold | Market value of agricultural products sold and government payments (mil. dol.) 2017 Government payments |
|---|---|---|---|---|---|---|---|
| Total. | 2,109 | 2,042 | 643 | 402,698 | 397,466 | 388,523 | 8,944 |
| Less than $1,000. | 429 | 472 | 17 | 80 | 97 | 88 | 8 |
| $1,000 to $2,499. | 237 | 217 | 44 | 393 | 360 | 295 | 65 |
| $2,500 to $4,999. | 231 | 211 | 47 | 832 | 757 | 629 | 128 |
| $5,000 to $9,999. | 249 | 234 | 59 | 1,769 | 1,666 | 1,415 | 251 |
| $10,000 to $24,999. | 272 | 253 | 83 | 4,323 | 4,041 | 3,505 | 536 |
| $25,000 to $49,999. | 162 | 155 | 67 | 5,736 | 5,494 | 4,915 | 578 |
| $50,000 to $99,999. | 134 | 126 | 68 | 9,575 | 8,934 | 8,255 | 679 |
| $100,000 to $249,999. | 142 | 134 | 86 | 23,196 | 21,730 | 20,614 | 1,116 |
| $250,000 to $499,999. | 96 | 89 | 64 | 34,463 | 31,718 | 30,478 | 1,241 |
| $500,000 to $999,999. | 78 | 72 | 54 | 55,663 | 50,677 | 49,011 | 1,666 |
| $1,000,000 to $2,499,999. | 58 | 56 | 39 | 90,534 | 86,284 | 84,438 | 1,846 |
| $2,500,000 to $4,999,999. | 15 | 15 | 9 | 50,511 | 50,087 | 49,521 | 567 |
| $5 million or more. | 9 | 9 | 4 | 125,624 | 135,622 | 135,359 | 263 |

Source: U.S. Department of Agriculture, National Agricultural Statistics Service, *2017 Census of Agriculture*, Vol. 1, April 2019.

## Table 862. Farms—Number, Acreage, and Value of Sales by Size of Sales: 2012 and 2017

[2,109 represents 2,109,000. Data have been adjusted for coverage; see text, this section and Appendix III]

| Market value of agricultural products sold | Farms (1,000) | Acreage Total (mil.) | Acreage Average per farm | Value of sales Total (mil. dol.) | Value of sales Average per farm (dol.) | Percent distribution Farms | Percent distribution Acreage | Percent distribution Value of sales |
|---|---|---|---|---|---|---|---|---|
| **2012** | | | | | | | | |
| **Total**................................ | **2,109** | **914.5** | **434** | **394,644** | **187,097** | **100.0** | **100.0** | **100.0** |
| Less than $2,500...................... | 788 | 118.4 | 150 | 380 | 483 | 37.4 | 12.9 | 0.1 |
| $2,500 to $4,999..................... | 191 | 19.6 | 102 | 688 | 3,592 | 9.1 | 2.1 | 0.2 |
| $5,000 to $9,999..................... | 214 | 25.4 | 119 | 1,522 | 7,104 | 10.2 | 2.8 | 0.4 |
| $10,000 to $24,999................... | 245 | 59.4 | 243 | 3,908 | 15,954 | 11.6 | 6.5 | 1.0 |
| $25,000 to $49,999................... | 153 | 48.4 | 316 | 5,418 | 35,440 | 7.2 | 5.3 | 1.4 |
| $50,000 to $99,999................... | 129 | 64.0 | 495 | 9,251 | 71,507 | 6.1 | 7.0 | 2.3 |
| $100,000 to $249,999................ | 139 | 115.9 | 835 | 22,822 | 164,328 | 6.6 | 12.7 | 5.8 |
| $250,000 to $499,999................ | 94 | 121.1 | 1,288 | 33,964 | 361,045 | 4.5 | 13.2 | 8.6 |
| $500,000 to $999,999................ | 76 | 129.4 | 1,704 | 54,686 | 719,996 | 3.6 | 14.2 | 13.9 |
| $1,000,000 or more.................. | 79 | 212.9 | 2,687 | 262,006 | 3,307,109 | 3.8 | 23.3 | 66.4 |
| **2017** | | | | | | | | |
| **Total**................................ | **2,042** | **900.2** | **441** | **388,523** | **190,245** | **100.0** | **100.0** | **100.0** |
| Less than $2,500...................... | 792 | 103.6 | 131 | 404 | 510 | 38.8 | 11.5 | 0.1 |
| $2,500 to $4,999..................... | 185 | 16.1 | 87 | 663 | 3,577 | 9.1 | 1.8 | 0.2 |
| $5,000 to $9,999..................... | 208 | 24.7 | 119 | 1,478 | 7,101 | 10.2 | 2.7 | 0.4 |
| $10,000 to $24,999................... | 228 | 50.0 | 219 | 3,650 | 15,994 | 11.2 | 5.6 | 0.9 |
| $25,000 to $49,999................... | 144 | 50.0 | 347 | 5,100 | 35,389 | 7.1 | 5.6 | 1.3 |
| $50,000 to $99,999................... | 119 | 66.3 | 555 | 8,478 | 70,982 | 5.8 | 7.4 | 2.2 |
| $100,000 to $249,999................ | 131 | 119.6 | 914 | 21,171 | 161,697 | 6.4 | 13.3 | 5.4 |
| $250,000 to $499,999................ | 88 | 126.6 | 1,441 | 31,319 | 356,545 | 4.3 | 14.1 | 8.1 |
| $500,000 to $999,999................ | 70 | 131.7 | 1,889 | 49,339 | 707,846 | 3.4 | 14.6 | 12.7 |
| $1,000,000 or more.................. | 77 | 211.6 | 2,752 | 266,922 | 3,472,604 | 3.8 | 23.5 | 68.7 |

Source: U.S. Department of Agriculture, National Agricultural Statistics Service, *2017 Census of Agriculture*, Vol. 1, April 2019, and earlier reports. See also <https://www.nass.usda.gov/AgCensus/>.

## Table 863. Farmers by Selected Producer Characteristics: 2017

[A producer is a person who is involved in making decisions for the farm operation including decisions about planting, harvesting, livestock management, and marketing. A producer may be the owner, a household member of the owner, hired manager, tenant, renter, or sharecropper. Demographic information was collected for up to four producers per farm. The primary producer is the producer designated as the person who made the most decisions for the farm; if equal decisions were made, the primary was designed as the person who worked off the farm the least. See source for more details]

| Characteristics | All producers | Primary producers | Characteristics | All producers | Primary producers |
|---|---|---|---|---|---|
| **Total**............................ | **3,399,834** | **2,042,220** | Primary occupation: | | |
| By sex: | | | Farming............................... | 1,416,848 | 964,477 |
| Male............................... | 2,172,373 | 1,553,220 | Other................................. | 1,982,986 | 1,077,743 |
| Female............................ | 1,227,461 | 489,000 | By place of residence: | | |
| | | | On farm operated................... | 2,530,442 | 1,562,320 |
| By age: | | | Not on farm operated............... | 869,392 | 479,900 |
| Under 25 years..................... | 50,943 | 10,518 | Days of work off farm: | | |
| 25 to 34 years....................... | 234,496 | 111,236 | None.................................. | 1,311,334 | 859,347 |
| 35 to 44 years....................... | 390,345 | 207,348 | Any................................... | 2,088,500 | 1,182,873 |
| 45 to 54 years....................... | 614,654 | 351,677 | 1 to 49 days........................ | 285,477 | 172,209 |
| 55 to 64 years....................... | 955,354 | 580,769 | 50 to 99 days....................... | 151,972 | 92,576 |
| 65 to 74 years....................... | 757,936 | 498,595 | 100 to 199 days..................... | 282,056 | 168,777 |
| 75 years and older.................. | 396,106 | 282,077 | 200 days or more................... | 1,368,995 | 749,311 |
| Average age.......................... | 57.5 | 59.4 | Years on present farm: | | |
| | | | 2 years or less...................... | 201,061 | 100,947 |
| By race/ethnicity: | | | 3 or 4 years......................... | 268,316 | 140,359 |
| American Indian/Alaska Native.... | 58,199 | 35,494 | 5 to 9 years......................... | 495,022 | 269,230 |
| Asian................................ | 22,016 | 11,955 | 10 years or more.................... | 2,435,435 | 1,531,684 |
| Black or African American.......... | 45,508 | 31,071 | Years operating any farm: | | |
| Native Hawaiian or other | | | 5 years or less...................... | 474,198 | 237,838 |
| Pacific Islander..................... | 3,018 | 1,662 | 6 to 10 years........................ | 434,076 | 234,522 |
| White................................ | 3,244,344 | 1,945,696 | 11 years or more.................... | 2,491,560 | 1,569,860 |
| More than one race reported....... | 26,749 | 16,342 | Military service: | | |
| | | | Never served........................ | 3,029,215 | 1,768,912 |
| Hispanic or Latino [1]............... | 112,451 | 66,727 | Served [2]............................ | 370,619 | 273,308 |

[1] Persons of Hispanic origin may be of any race. [2] Includes producers who currently or previously served on active duty in the U.S. Armed Forces.

Source: U.S. Department of Agriculture, National Agricultural Statistics Service, *2017 Census of Agriculture*, Vol. 1, April 2019. See also <https://www.nass.usda.gov/AgCensus/>.

# Table 864. Family Farm Household Income and Wealth: 2013 to 2017, and by Farm Type, 2017

[In dollars, except for number of farms. Based on Agricultural Resource Management Survey (ARMS) Phase III. A family farm is defined as one in which the majority of the ownership of the farm business is held by related individuals. Nearly all farms (98 percent in 2017) are family farms. The farm operator is the person who runs the farm, making the day-to-day management decisions. The operator could be an owner, hired manager, cash tenant, share tenant, and/or a partner. If land is rented or worked on shares, the tenant or renter is the operator. For multiple-operator farms, a principal operator is identified as the individual making most of the day-to-day decisions about the operation. If secondary operators are the spouses of principal operators, both operators are considered part of the principal operator household. Minus sign (-) indicates loss]

| Item | 2013 | 2014 | 2015 | 2016 | 2017 Total | Rural residence farms [1] | Intermediate farms [2] | Commercial farms [3] |
|---|---|---|---|---|---|---|---|---|
| | | | | | | ERS farm typology | | |
| **Number of family farms** | **2,045,352** | **2,053,008** | **2,032,300** | **2,027,269** | **1,996,252** | **1,049,995** | **761,925** | **184,332** |
| INCOME PER FAMILY FARM HOUSEHOLD | | | | | | | | |
| Net earnings from farming activities | 30,639 | 31,025 | 24,740 | 24,731 | 23,678 | -91 | 7,665 | 225,264 |
| Off-farm income of the household | 90,481 | 103,140 | 95,140 | 93,187 | 89,817 | 107,693 | 68,197 | 77,355 |
| Earned income | 66,053 | 71,754 | 65,814 | 65,680 | 61,458 | 81,463 | 35,143 | 56,279 |
| Unearned income | 24,428 | 31,386 | 29,326 | 27,506 | 28,359 | 26,230 | 33,054 | 21,075 |
| Total household income, mean [4] | 121,120 | 134,164 | 119,880 | 117,918 | 113,495 | 107,602 | 75,862 | 302,619 |
| WEALTH PER FAMILY FARM HOUSEHOLD | | | | | | | | |
| Assets, mean [4] | 1,466,569 | 1,674,467 | 1,590,217 | 1,751,763 | 1,787,408 | 1,321,551 | 1,637,816 | 5,059,359 |
| Farm assets | 948,116 | 998,082 | 1,003,551 | 1,131,480 | 1,093,067 | 595,310 | 1,027,479 | 4,199,504 |
| Non-farm assets | 518,453 | 676,385 | 586,666 | 620,283 | 694,341 | 726,241 | 610,337 | 859,855 |
| Debt, mean [4] | 153,593 | 205,024 | 190,885 | 185,679 | 219,681 | 132,010 | 174,905 | 904,153 |
| Farm debt | 80,655 | 100,288 | 101,430 | 99,664 | 110,587 | 34,803 | 66,153 | 725,931 |
| Non-farm debt | 72,938 | 104,736 | 89,454 | 86,014 | 109,095 | 97,207 | 108,752 | 178,222 |
| Net worth, mean [4] | 1,312,976 | 1,469,443 | 1,399,332 | 1,566,084 | 1,567,727 | 1,189,541 | 1,462,911 | 4,155,206 |
| Farm net worth | 867,461 | 897,794 | 902,121 | 1,031,816 | 982,480 | 560,507 | 961,326 | 3,473,573 |
| Non-farm net worth | 445,515 | 571,649 | 497,212 | 534,269 | 585,246 | 629,034 | 501,584 | 681,634 |

[1] Farms in which the principal operator is retired or has a major occupation other than farming. [2] Farms with farming as the operator's major occupation, but with less than $350,000 in gross sales. [3] Farms with more than $350,000 in gross sales. [4] For definition of mean see Guide to Tabular Presentation.

Source: U.S. Department of Agriculture, Economic Research Service, "Farm Household Income and Characteristics," <http://www.ers.usda.gov/data-products/farm-household-income-and-characteristics.aspx>, accessed January 2019.

# Table 865. Farm Type, Acreage, and Production: 2000 to 2017

[2,166 represents 2,166,000. Based on Agricultural Resource Management Survey (ARMS). The farm typology used by the Economic Research Service was revised in 2013, and has been applied to data beginning in 2011. For more information, see <https://www.ers.usda.gov/publications/pub-details/?pubid=43744>]

| Type of farm | Unit | 2000 | 2005 | 2010 | 2012 | 2013 | 2014 | 2015 | 2016 | 2017 |
|---|---|---|---|---|---|---|---|---|---|---|
| Total farms: | | | | | | | | | | |
| Number of farms | 1,000 | 2,166 | 2,095 | 2,193 | 2,102 | 2,095 | 2,076 | 2,059 | 2,052 | 2,040 |
| Total value of production | Mil. dol. | 177,286 | 215,295 | 286,792 | 372,545 | 383,407 | 420,251 | 368,144 | 353,164 | 365,766 |
| Total acres operated | Mil. | 995 | 916 | 912 | 870 | 897 | 933 | 850 | 897 | 860 |
| Acres operated per farm | Acres | 459 | 437 | 416 | 414 | 428 | 449 | 413 | 437 | 422 |
| Commercial farms: [1] | | | | | | | | | | |
| Number of farms | 1,000 | 178 | 216 | 264 | 243 | 241 | 220 | 212 | 208 | 228 |
| Total value of production | Mil. dol. | 121,202 | 166,566 | 240,751 | 288,342 | 296,218 | 329,903 | 279,081 | 273,505 | 271,547 |
| Total acres operated | Mil. | 392 | 418 | 482 | 410 | 468 | 510 | 439 | 443 | 414 |
| Acres operated per farm | Acres | 2,205 | 1,939 | 1,829 | 1,691 | 1,947 | 2,319 | 2,066 | 2,129 | 1,811 |
| Intermediate farms: [2] | | | | | | | | | | |
| Number of farms | 1,000 | 668 | 550 | 618 | 701 | 695 | 632 | 632 | 617 | 762 |
| Total value of production | Mil. dol. | 41,813 | 33,872 | 30,325 | 64,403 | 62,494 | 62,630 | 61,283 | 56,277 | 71,447 |
| Total acres operated | Mil. | 392 | 307 | 242 | 278 | 257 | 229 | 232 | 255 | 266 |
| Acres operated per farm | Acres | 587 | 558 | 392 | 397 | 370 | 363 | 367 | 414 | 349 |
| Residence farms: [3] | | | | | | | | | | |
| Number of farms | 1,000 | 1,320 | 1,329 | 1,311 | 1,158 | 1,160 | 1,225 | 1,215 | 1,228 | 1,050 |
| Total value of production | Mil. dol. | 14,272 | 14,856 | 15,716 | 19,801 | 24,695 | 27,717 | 27,780 | 23,382 | 22,772 |
| Total acres operated | Mil. | 211 | 191 | 187 | 182 | 172 | 194 | 179 | 198 | 181 |
| Acres operated per farm | Acres | 160 | 144 | 143 | 157 | 148 | 158 | 147 | 161 | 172 |

[1] Data for 2010 and earlier include farms with sales of $250,000 or more. Beginning in 2011, data are for farms with $350,000 or more gross cash farm income and nonfamily farms. [2] Data for 2010 and earlier include small family farms whose operators report farming as their major occupation. Beginning in 2011, data are for farms with less than $350,000 in gross cash farm income and a principal operator whose primary occupation is farming. [3] Data for 2010 and earlier include retirement and residential farms. Beginning in 2011, data are for farms with less than $350,000 in gross cash farm income and where the principal operator is either retired or has a primary occupation other than farming.

Source: U.S. Department of Agriculture, Economic Research Service, "ARMS Farm Financial and Crop Production Practices," <http://www.ers.usda.gov/data-products/arms-farm-financial-and-crop-production-practices.aspx>, accessed March 2019.

## Table 866. Farms with Renewable Energy Systems by Type of Farm: 2012

[Farms reporting renewable energy systems on their operation. Based on the 1974 definition of farms and farmland, see text, this section. Farm types are based on the USDA's Economic Research Service typology. Family farms, farms in which the majority of the business is owned by the operator and individuals related to the operator, are classified based on the gross cash farm income (GCFI). GCFI includes sales of crops and livestock, fees for delivering commodities under production contracts, government payments, and farm-related income]

| Energy system | All farms | Small family farms (GCFI less than $350,000) | | | | Mid-sized family farms (GCFI $350,000 to $999,999) | Large-scale family farms (GCFI greater than $1,000,000) | Non-family farms [3] |
| | | Total small family farms | Retirement or off-farm occupa-tion [1] | Farm-occupation farms [2] | | | | |
| | | | | Low sales (GCFI less than $150,000) | Moderate sales (GCFI $350,00 to $999,999) | | | |
|---|---|---|---|---|---|---|---|---|
| Number of farms, total................. | 2,109,303 | 1,861,216 | 1,423,432 | 342,440 | 95,344 | 118,340 | 59,537 | 70,210 |
| **Number of farms with any renewable energy system.........** | **57,299** | **48,307** | **34,473** | **10,476** | **3,358** | **4,391** | **2,281** | **2,320** |
| Percent of all farms.................... | 2.7 | 2.6 | 2.4 | 3.1 | 3.5 | 3.7 | 3.8 | 3.3 |
| By type of system: | | | | | | | | |
| Solar panels............................. | 36,331 | 32,217 | 23,005 | 7,464 | 1,748 | 1,742 | 802 | 1,570 |
| Wind turbines........................... | 9,054 | 6,646 | 4,460 | 1,485 | 701 | 1,253 | 713 | 442 |
| Methane digesters...................... | 537 | 344 | 258 | 68 | 18 | 32 | 111 | 50 |
| Geoexchange systems................ | 9,403 | 7,809 | 6,122 | 1,107 | 580 | 906 | 446 | 242 |
| Small hydro systems................... | 1,323 | 1,168 | 843 | 275 | 50 | 51 | 21 | 83 |
| Biodiesel................................ | 4,099 | 3,061 | 1,958 | 734 | 369 | 547 | 283 | 208 |
| Ethanol................................. | 2,364 | 1,623 | 1,021 | 338 | 264 | 443 | 211 | 87 |
| Other.................................... | 1243 | 1121 | 755 | 305 | 61 | 47 | 9 | 66 |
| Wind rights leased to others........... | 10,181 | 6,851 | 4,402 | 1,372 | 1,077 | 1,893 | 939 | 498 |

[1] Farms in which the principal operator is retired or has a major occupation other than farming. [2] Small family farms with farming as the operator's major occupation. [3] Any farm where the operator and persons related to the operator do not own a majority of the business.

Source: U.S. Department of Agriculture, National Agricultural Statistics Service, *2012 Census of Agriculture, Farm Typology*, Volume 2, January 2015. See also <https://www.nass.usda.gov/AgCensus/>.

## Table 867. Sales of Agricultural Products Direct to Consumers: 2007 to 2017

[1,211,270 represents $1,211,270,000. Farm operations who sell directly to consumers for human consumption at roadside stands, farmers' markets, pick-your-own, on-farm stores, and community support agricultural arrangements. Excludes non-edible products such as nursery crops, cut flowers, and wool, but includes livestock sales. Sales of agricultural products by vertically integrated operations through their own processing and marketing operations are also excluded]

| Item | Number of farms with direct sales | | Number of farms with direct and value added sales | Value of direct sales ($1,000) | | Value of direct and value added sales ($1,000) |
| | 2007 | 2012 | 2017 [4] | 2007 | 2012 | 2017 [4] |
|---|---|---|---|---|---|---|
| **Total, all farms with direct sales................** | **136,817** | **144,530** | **130,056** | **1,211,270** | **1,309,827** | **2,805,310** |
| Percent of all farms.............................. | 0.2 | 0.9 | 6.4 | 0.4 | 0.3 | 0.7 |
| BY VALUE OF SALES | | | | | | |
| $1 to $499............................................ | 35,440 | 37,398 | 30,695 | 7,217 | 7,770 | 6,559 |
| $500 to $999........................................ | 20,547 | 20,170 | 17,318 | 14,013 | 13,605 | 11,615 |
| $1,000 to $4,999.................................... | 49,957 | 52,750 | 43,934 | 113,960 | 121,750 | 101,770 |
| $5,000 to $9,999.................................... | 13,060 | 14,452 | 13,707 | 88,174 | 97,308 | 92,663 |
| $10,000 to $24,999................................. | 10,032 | 11,045 | 11,669 | 151,063 | 164,774 | 176,745 |
| $25,000 to $49,999................................. | 3,903 | 4,244 | 5,068 | 133,328 | 143,722 | 172,716 |
| $50,000 or more..................................... | 3,878 | 4,471 | 7,665 | 703,515 | 760,819 | 2,243,242 |
| BY PRIMARY ACTIVITY OF FARM [1,2] | | | | | | |
| Oilseed and grains................................. | 7,052 | 8,715 | 5,143 | 37,930 | 63,321 | 64,610 |
| Vegetables and melons............................ | 17,961 | 23,218 | 20,013 | 335,311 | 420,466 | 632,095 |
| Fruit and tree nuts.................................. | 17,161 | 18,399 | 19,724 | 343,878 | 319,523 | 1,267,029 |
| Greenhouse and nursery [3]....................... | 3,834 | 6,031 | 6,105 | 50,169 | 59,845 | 107,661 |
| Beef cattle ranching and farming.................. | 35,984 | 35,980 | 28,156 | 141,427 | 147,315 | 179,653 |
| Dairy cattle and milk production................... | 3,221 | 2,982 | 2,264 | 52,594 | 43,546 | 152,584 |
| Hog and pig farming................................ | 5,227 | 3,897 | 3,552 | 18,970 | 15,970 | 20,662 |
| Poultry and egg production........................ | 8,833 | 9,999 | 8,107 | 54,898 | 36,782 | 88,818 |
| Sheep and goat farming........................... | 9,127 | 10,198 | 9,538 | 16,613 | 19,647 | 32,240 |

[1] Based on the farms' North American Industry Classification (NAICS) codes, indicating main commodity type produced. [2] Includes other types, not shown separately. [3] Includes floriculture. [4] 2017 data includes value added sales and is not directly comparable to prior data.

Source: U.S. Department of Agriculture, National Agricultural Statistics Service, *2017 Census of Agriculture*, Vol. 1, April 2019, and earlier reports. See also <https://www.nass.usda.gov/AgCensus/>.

## Table 868. Organic Agriculture—Number of Farms, Acreage, and Value of Sales, 2008 and 2014, and for Leading States, 2014

[3,164,995 represents $3,164,995,000. Includes all known organic producers that are either certified organic or exempt from certification in the United States (those grossing less than $5,000 annually from organic sales). Organic food must be produced without the use of conventional pesticides, petroleum-based or sewage sludge-based fertilizers, herbicides, pesticides, genetic engineering (biotechnology), antibiotics, growth hormones, or irradiation. Animals raised on an organic operation must be fed organic feed and given access to the outdoors. Land must have no prohibited substances applied to it for at least 3 years before the harvest of an organic crop]

| Year and leading states | Organic farms (number) | Organic land (acres) | Value of sales ($1,000) [1] | | | |
| | | | Total product sales | Crops [2] | Livestock and poultry | Livestock and poultry products |
|---|---|---|---|---|---|---|
| 2008................ | 14,540 | 4,077,337 | 3,164,995 | 1,942,317 | 316,470 | 906,207 |
| **2014, U.S. total [3]**.... | **14,093** | **3,670,560** | **5,454,979** | **3,290,188** | **660,340** | **1,504,452** |
| California............... | 2,805 | 687,168 | 2,231,241 | 1,659,305 | 271,354 | 300,582 |
| Washington........... | 716 | 73,841 | 514,897 | 386,701 | (D) | (D) |
| Pennsylvania......... | 679 | 97,617 | 313,456 | 91,362 | 112,467 | 109,627 |
| Oregon............... | 525 | 204,166 | 237,121 | 127,568 | 17,630 | 91,923 |
| Wisconsin.............. | 1,228 | 228,605 | 200,800 | 48,513 | 24,908 | 127,379 |
| Texas................. | 234 | 126,639 | 199,094 | 78,169 | 17,680 | 103,245 |
| New York.............. | 917 | 212,701 | 164,203 | 52,698 | 16,011 | 95,494 |
| Colorado.............. | 157 | 115,116 | 146,799 | 52,198 | (D) | (D) |
| Michigan.............. | 332 | 58,085 | 124,612 | (D) | (D) | 70,698 |
| Iowa.................. | 612 | 97,448 | 102,626 | 50,741 | (D) | (D) |

D Data withheld to limit disclosure. [1] Value of sales of commodities; excludes value-added organic products. [2] Includes nursery and greenhouse. [3] Includes other states, not shown separately.

Source: U.S. Department of Agriculture, National Agricultural Statistics Service, *2012 Census of Agriculture: Organic Survey (2014)*, Vol. 3, Special Studies, Part 4, September 2015, and earlier reports. See also <https://www.nass.usda.gov/Surveys/Guide_to_NASS_Surveys/Organic_Production/>.

## Table 869. Adoption of Genetically Engineered Crops: 2000 to 2018

[As percent of all crops planted. As of June. Based on June Agricultural Survey conducted by National Agricultural Statistical Services (NASS). Excludes conventionally bred herbicide tolerant varieties. Insect resistant varieties include only those containing bacillus thuringiensis (Bt). The Bt varieties include those that contain more than one gene that can resist different types of insects. Stacked gene varieties include only those varieties containing biotech traits for both herbicide tolerance and insect resistance]

| Genetically engineered crop | 2000 | 2005 | 2010 | 2011 | 2012 | 2013 | 2014 | 2015 | 2016 | 2017 | 2018 |
|---|---|---|---|---|---|---|---|---|---|---|---|
| **Corn**............................ | **25** | **52** | **86** | **88** | **88** | **90** | **93** | **92** | **92** | **92** | **92** |
| Insect resistant.................... | 18 | 26 | 16 | 16 | 15 | 5 | 4 | 4 | 3 | 3 | 2 |
| Herbicide tolerant................ | 6 | 17 | 23 | 23 | 21 | 14 | 13 | 12 | 13 | 12 | 10 |
| Stacked gene.................... | 1 | 9 | 47 | 49 | 52 | 71 | 76 | 77 | 76 | 77 | 80 |
| **Cotton**............................ | **61** | **79** | **93** | **90** | **94** | **90** | **96** | **94** | **93** | **96** | **94** |
| Insect resistant.................... | 15 | 18 | 15 | 17 | 14 | 8 | 5 | 5 | 4 | 5 | 3 |
| Herbicide tolerant................ | 26 | 27 | 20 | 15 | 17 | 15 | 12 | 10 | 9 | 11 | 9 |
| Stacked gene.................... | 20 | 34 | 58 | 58 | 63 | 67 | 79 | 79 | 80 | 80 | 82 |
| **Soybean**........................... | **54** | **87** | **93** | **94** | **93** | **93** | **94** | **94** | **94** | **94** | **94** |
| Insect resistant.................... | (X) | (X) | (X) | (X) | (X) | (X) | (X) | (X) | (X) | (X) | (X) |
| Herbicide tolerant................ | 54 | 87 | 93 | 94 | 93 | 93 | 94 | 94 | 94 | 94 | 94 |
| Stacked gene.................... | (X) | (X) | (X) | (X) | (X) | (X) | (X) | (X) | (X) | (X) | (X) |

X Not applicable.

Source: U.S. Department of Agriculture, Economic Research Service, "Adoption of Genetically Engineered Crops in the U.S.," <http://www.ers.usda.gov/data-products/adoption-of-genetically-engineered-crops-in-the-us.aspx>, accessed July 2018.

## Table 870. Farm Production Expenses: 2012 and 2017

[2,109 represents 2,109,000. Data have been adjusted for coverage; see text, this section and Appendix III]

| Production expenses | 2012 | | | 2017 | | |
| | Farms (1,000) | Expenses (mil. dol.) | Percent of total | Farms (1,000) | Expenses (mil. dol.) | Percent of total |
|---|---|---|---|---|---|---|
| **Total**...................................... | **2,109** | **328,939** | **100.0** | **2,042** | **326,391** | **100.0** |
| Fertilizer....................................... | 1,012 | 28,533 | 8.7 | 1,025 | 23,543 | 7.2 |
| Chemicals..................................... | 1,000 | 16,460 | 5.0 | 894 | 17,585 | 5.4 |
| Seeds, plants, vines, and trees.................. | 829 | 19,493 | 5.9 | 703 | 20,970 | 6.4 |
| Livestock and poultry........................... | 545 | 41,586 | 12.6 | 556 | 44,934 | 13.8 |
| Feed........................................... | 1,256 | 75,706 | 23.0 | 1,262 | 62,625 | 19.2 |
| Gasoline and fuel.............................. | 1,988 | 16,573 | 5.0 | 1,922 | 13,474 | 4.1 |
| Utilities......................................... | 1,353 | 8,262 | 2.5 | 1,339 | 9,009 | 2.8 |
| Supplies, repairs, and maintenance............. | 1,663 | 18,868 | 5.7 | 1,665 | 19,671 | 6.0 |
| Farm labor [1].................................. | 784 | 33,461 | 10.2 | 709 | 39,231 | 12.0 |
| Customwork and custom hauling................ | 462 | 6,611 | 2.0 | 428 | 7,555 | 2.3 |
| Cash rent for land, buildings and grazing fees.... | 560 | 21,001 | 6.4 | 482 | 21,060 | 6.5 |
| Rent and lease for machinery, equipment, and farm share.. | 133 | 2,332 | 0.7 | 138 | 2,424 | 0.7 |
| Interest expense............................... | 784 | 12,124 | 3.7 | 669 | 12,396 | 3.8 |
| Property taxes................................. | 1,980 | 7,429 | 2.3 | 1,920 | 9,415 | 2.9 |
| Medical supplies, veterinary, custom services for livestock.. | (NA) | (NA) | (NA) | 944 | 4,446 | 1.4 |
| Other production expenses [2]................... | 1,135 | 20,501 | 6.2 | 849 | 18,052 | 5.5 |

NA Not available. [1] Includes hired and contract labor. [2] Data for 2012 include expenses for medical supplies, veterinary, and custom services for animals. Starting 2017, these data are reported separately.

Source: U.S. Department of Agriculture, National Agricultural Statistics Service, *2017 Census of Agriculture*, Vol. 1, April 2019. See also <https://www.nass.usda.gov/AgCensus/>.

## Table 871. Balance Sheet of the Farming Sector: 1990 to 2018

[In billions of dollars, except as indicated (841 represents $841,000,000,000). As of December 31. Balance sheet estimates exclude the personal portion of farm households' assets and debts]

| Item | 1990 | 2000 | 2010 | 2011 | 2012 | 2013 | 2014 | 2015 | 2016 | 2017 | 2018 |
|---|---|---|---|---|---|---|---|---|---|---|---|
| **Assets** | **841** | **1,203** | **2,171** | **2,319** | **2,638** | **2,768** | **2,931** | **2,879** | **2,913** | **3,006** | **3,021** |
| Investments and other financial assets | 38 | 57 | 135 | 107 | 139 | 86 | 111 | 88 | 78 | 83 | 73 |
| Investment in cooperatives | (NA) | (NA) | 6 | 6 | 7 | 8 | 8 | 7 | 7 | 9 | 7 |
| Financial assets and net accounts receivable | (NA) | (NA) | 130 | 102 | 132 | 78 | 103 | 80 | 71 | 74 | 65 |
| Inventories | 97 | 110 | 168 | 185 | 182 | 192 | 210 | 187 | 180 | 180 | 173 |
| Crops | 23 | 28 | 57 | 62 | 65 | 60 | 62 | 53 | 56 | 57 | 60 |
| Livestock and poultry | 71 | 77 | 91 | 101 | 96 | 111 | 128 | 118 | 109 | 107 | 97 |
| Purchased inputs [1] | 3 | 5 | 20 | 21 | 21 | 21 | 20 | 16 | 15 | 16 | 16 |
| Real estate [2] | 619 | 946 | 1,660 | 1,803 | 2,074 | 2,243 | 2,365 | 2,364 | 2,400 | 2,471 | 2,510 |
| Value of machinery and motor vehicles [3] | 86 | 90 | 208 | 224 | 244 | 247 | 246 | 240 | 255 | 272 | 265 |
| **Debt [4]** | **131** | **164** | **279** | **294** | **298** | **315** | **345** | **357** | **374** | **393** | **402** |
| Real estate | 68 | 85 | 154 | 167 | 173 | 185 | 197 | 209 | 226 | 238 | 246 |
| Commercial banks [5] | 15 | 30 | 51 | 53 | 65 | 69 | 73 | 79 | 84 | 89 | 93 |
| Farm Credit System | 23 | 30 | 72 | 75 | 80 | 85 | 89 | 97 | 104 | 108 | 113 |
| Farm Service Agency | 7 | 3 | 3 | 3 | 4 | 4 | 4 | 5 | 6 | 6 | 7 |
| Farmer Mac [6] | (NA) | (NA) | 4 | 4 | 4 | 4 | 5 | 5 | 5 | 6 | 7 |
| Individuals and others [5] | 14 | 11 | 10 | 18 | 9 | 10 | 13 | 10 | 12 | 13 | 10 |
| Storage facility loans | – | (NA) | 1 | 1 | 1 | 1 | 1 | 1 | 1 | 1 | 1 |
| Life insurance companies | 9 | 11 | 12 | 13 | 11 | 12 | 12 | 13 | 13 | 15 | 16 |
| Nonreal estate | 63 | 79 | 125 | 127 | 124 | 130 | 148 | 148 | 148 | 155 | 156 |
| Commercial banks [5] | 31 | 45 | 56 | 59 | 60 | 64 | 71 | 73 | 73 | 73 | 75 |
| Farm Credit System | 10 | 17 | 39 | 41 | 43 | 44 | 48 | 48 | 49 | 51 | 53 |
| Farm Service Agency | 10 | 4 | 4 | 4 | 3 | 3 | 4 | 4 | 4 | 4 | 4 |
| Individuals and others [5] | 12 | 13 | 26 | 23 | 18 | 20 | 26 | 23 | 22 | 27 | 24 |
| **Equity** | **709** | **1,039** | **1,892** | **2,024** | **2,341** | **2,452** | **2,585** | **2,522** | **2,539** | **2,813** | **2,619** |
| **FINANCIAL RATIOS (percent)** | | | | | | | | | | | |
| Farm debt/asset ratio | 15.60 | 13.62 | 12.85 | 12.70 | 11.28 | 11.39 | 11.78 | 12.39 | 12.84 | 13.07 | 13.31 |
| Farm debt/equity ratio | 18.48 | 15.77 | 14.74 | 14.55 | 12.71 | 12.86 | 13.35 | 14.15 | 14.74 | 15.04 | 15.35 |

– Represents or rounds to zero. NA Not available. [1] Purchased inputs represent value of prepaid expenses on supplies such as fertilizer and lime applied, seed, feed and other inputs purchased for next year's production. It also includes the seed, fertilizer, fuel, and other expenses already invested in crops. [2] Includes farmland, buildings and other service structures. Includes farm real estate assets leased from non-operator landlords. [3] Includes automobiles, trucks and farm machinery leased to farm operators. [4] Reflects outstanding agricultural sector debt where it is held rather than where it originated. Excludes debt on operator dwellings and for nonfarm purposes. Sector-level estimates of farm debt report aggregate data by lender type and therefore does not identify who owes the debt. [5] Beginning with 2012, farm sector debt held by savings associations is reported with the commercial bank lender group instead of the individuals and others grouping. [6] The Federal Agricultural Mortgage Corporation (known as Farmer Mac) operates as a federally sponsored enterprise providing a secondary market for agricultural real estate mortgage loans, rural housing mortgage loans, and rural utility cooperative loans.

Source: U.S. Department of Agriculture, Economic Research Service, "U.S. and State Farm Income and Wealth Statistics," <http://www.ers.usda.gov/data-products/farm-income-and-wealth-statistics.aspx>, accessed September 2019.

## Table 872. Farm Sector Output and Value Added: 1990 to 2018

[In billions of dollars (179.9 represents $179,900,000,000). For definition of value added and explanation of chained dollars, see text, Section 13. Minus sign (-) indicates decrease]

| Item | 1990 | 2000 | 2005 | 2010 | 2012 | 2013 | 2014 | 2015 | 2016 | 2017 | 2018 |
|---|---|---|---|---|---|---|---|---|---|---|---|
| **CURRENT DOLLARS** | | | | | | | | | | | |
| **Farm output** | **179.9** | **204.3** | **251.9** | **323.2** | **405.7** | **439.1** | **445.2** | **402.4** | **375.1** | **391.5** | **389.2** |
| Cash receipts from farm marketings | 171.9 | 197.6 | 241.4 | 321.7 | 401.9 | 404.1 | 424.9 | 377.8 | 358.7 | 372.2 | 373.7 |
| Farm products consumed on farms | 0.6 | 0.3 | 0.4 | 0.4 | 0.4 | 0.5 | 0.6 | 0.6 | 0.5 | 0.4 | 0.4 |
| Other farm income | 4.9 | 8.4 | 10.2 | 14.4 | 23.2 | 23.9 | 24.0 | 23.5 | 20.1 | 23.8 | 23.6 |
| Change in farm finished goods inventories | 2.4 | -2.0 | -0.1 | -13.3 | -19.8 | 10.6 | -4.3 | 0.5 | -4.3 | -5.0 | -8.4 |
| Less: Intermediate goods and services consumed | 102.1 | 128.3 | 147.4 | 205.6 | 256.8 | 254.5 | 277.0 | 256.3 | 246.1 | 252.0 | 259.6 |
| **Equals: Gross farm value added** | **77.8** | **76.0** | **104.5** | **117.6** | **148.9** | **184.6** | **168.1** | **146.0** | **129.0** | **139.4** | **129.6** |
| Less: Consumption of fixed capital | 17.9 | 22.8 | 27.5 | 33.1 | 37.1 | 40.3 | 44.4 | 47.2 | 47.8 | 48.4 | 50.1 |
| **Equals: Net farm value added** | **59.8** | **53.2** | **77.0** | **84.6** | **111.8** | **144.4** | **123.7** | **98.8** | **81.2** | **91.0** | **79.5** |
| Compensation of employees | 13.4 | 19.6 | 22.0 | 24.3 | 28.3 | 28.6 | 29.1 | 27.3 | 29.4 | 30.4 | 32.7 |
| Taxes on production and imports | 3.8 | 4.6 | 5.3 | 7.5 | 8.2 | 8.5 | 9.9 | 9.3 | 8.8 | 9.6 | 10.3 |
| Less: Subsidies to operators | 7.6 | 20.0 | 20.9 | 10.5 | 8.8 | 8.9 | 7.5 | 8.9 | 11.2 | 9.8 | 12.1 |
| Net operating surplus | 50.3 | 48.8 | 70.5 | 63.3 | 84.1 | 116.1 | 92.2 | 71.1 | 54.2 | 60.8 | 48.6 |
| **CHAINED (2012) DOLLARS** | | | | | | | | | | | |
| **Farm output, total** | **(NA)** | **(NA)** | **400.8** | **416.1** | **405.7** | **431.4** | **442.6** | **449.4** | **470.7** | **477.4** | **474.6** |
| Cash receipts from farm marketings | (NA) | (NA) | 384.4 | 415.5 | 401.9 | 396.5 | 417.2 | 417.7 | 446.4 | 449.8 | 451.2 |
| Farm products consumed on farms | (NA) | (NA) | 0.5 | 0.5 | 0.4 | 0.5 | 0.5 | 0.6 | 0.6 | 0.5 | 0.5 |
| Other farm income | (NA) | (NA) | 17.5 | 18.6 | 23.2 | 23.9 | 27.7 | 29.3 | 26.5 | 30.9 | 30.2 |
| Change in farm finished goods inventories | (NA) | (NA) | -0.2 | -19.5 | -19.8 | 9.3 | -4.3 | 0.3 | -5.1 | -6.0 | -9.6 |
| Less: Intermediate goods and services consumed | (NA) | (NA) | 231.6 | 251.1 | 256.8 | 251.3 | 260.6 | 256.5 | 267.2 | 275.6 | 277.4 |
| **Equals: Gross farm value added** | **(NA)** | **(NA)** | **168.8** | **165.1** | **148.9** | **179.8** | **181.6** | **194.4** | **205.8** | **202.3** | **196.5** |
| Less: Consumption of fixed capital | (NA) | (NA) | 32.0 | 34.4 | 37.1 | 39.7 | 43.0 | 45.2 | 45.3 | 45.2 | 46.0 |
| **Equals: Net farm value added** | **(NA)** | **(NA)** | **139.5** | **131.4** | **111.8** | **140.0** | **138.3** | **149.2** | **162.8** | **158.6** | **150.1** |

NA Not available.

Source: U.S. Bureau of Economic Analysis, National Income and Product Accounts, "Table 7.3.5 Farm Sector Output, Gross Value Added, and Net Value Added," and "Table 7.3.6 Real Farm Sector Output, Real Gross Value Added, and Real Net Value Added, Chained Dollars," <http://www.bea.gov/itable/>, accessed August 2019.

# Table 873. Value Added to Economy by Agricultural Sector: 1990 to 2018

[In billions of dollars (188.5 represents $188,500,000,000). Value of agricultural sector production is the gross value of the commodities and services produced within a year. Net value-added is the sector's contribution to the national economy and is the value of farm sector production minus the value of intermediate goods used. Net farm income is the farm operators' share of income from the sector's production activities. Minus sign (-) indicates decrease]

| Item | 1990 | 2000 | 2010 | 2011 | 2012 | 2013 | 2014 | 2015 | 2016 | 2017 | 2018 |
|---|---|---|---|---|---|---|---|---|---|---|---|
| **Value of agricultural production** | **188.5** | **218.4** | **344.1** | **410.0** | **439.2** | **473.1** | **473.5** | **430.0** | **399.3** | **415.7** | **415.0** |
| Value of crop production | 83.2 | 95.0 | 168.1 | 199.3 | 212.9 | 233.8 | 206.3 | 184.3 | 189.3 | 187.9 | 189.6 |
| Crop cash receipts | 80.2 | 92.5 | 180.4 | 201.0 | 231.6 | 220.9 | 211.7 | 187.9 | 195.8 | 194.9 | 197.0 |
| Cotton | 5.5 | 2.9 | 7.5 | 7.3 | 8.2 | 6.5 | 7.1 | 4.8 | 5.5 | 7.6 | 8.1 |
| Feed crops | 18.7 | 20.5 | 55.1 | 71.7 | 82.1 | 70.8 | 65.9 | 56.9 | 55.4 | 53.9 | 56.0 |
| Food grains | 7.5 | 6.5 | 14.3 | 16.5 | 19.3 | 17.2 | 16.1 | 12.3 | 11.3 | 11.2 | 11.5 |
| Fruits and tree nuts | 9.4 | 12.3 | 21.6 | 24.2 | 28.1 | 30.2 | 32.2 | 28.4 | 29.7 | 30.6 | 29.0 |
| Oil crops | 12.3 | 13.5 | 36.5 | 35.3 | 46.9 | 47.3 | 42.6 | 35.5 | 44.0 | 41.1 | 42.2 |
| Tobacco | 2.7 | 2.3 | 1.3 | 1.1 | 1.3 | 1.6 | 1.7 | 1.6 | 1.3 | 1.4 | 1.2 |
| Vegetables and melons | 11.3 | 15.8 | 17.4 | 17.6 | 17.4 | 19.5 | 19.0 | 20.4 | 19.5 | 20.5 | 18.5 |
| All other crops | 12.9 | 18.6 | 26.5 | 27.2 | 28.2 | 27.8 | 27.1 | 28.0 | 28.9 | 28.6 | 30.4 |
| Home consumption | 0.1 | 0.2 | 0.1 | 0.1 | 0.1 | 0.2 | 0.2 | 0.3 | 0.2 | 0.2 | 0.2 |
| Value of inventory adjustment [1] | 2.8 | 2.2 | -12.3 | -1.8 | -18.8 | 12.7 | -5.6 | -3.8 | -6.6 | -7.1 | -7.5 |
| Value of livestock production | 90.0 | 99.1 | 140.2 | 163.8 | 169.1 | 181.1 | 214.3 | 194.1 | 165.4 | 176.9 | 177.5 |
| Animals and products cash receipts | 89.1 | 99.6 | 140.9 | 164.9 | 169.8 | 183.1 | 212.3 | 189.5 | 162.7 | 175.6 | 176.5 |
| Milk | 20.2 | 20.6 | 31.4 | 39.5 | 37.1 | 40.3 | 49.4 | 35.7 | 34.5 | 37.9 | 35.2 |
| Meat animals | 51.1 | 53.0 | 69.1 | 84.0 | 88.2 | 91.6 | 107.6 | 98.8 | 82.7 | 88.0 | 88.2 |
| Miscellaneous livestock | 2.5 | 4.1 | 5.7 | 6.0 | 6.3 | 6.9 | 6.9 | 6.7 | 6.7 | 6.9 | 6.8 |
| Poultry and eggs | 15.3 | 21.9 | 34.7 | 35.4 | 38.3 | 44.4 | 48.5 | 48.3 | 38.8 | 42.8 | 46.3 |
| Home consumption | 0.5 | 0.1 | 0.3 | 0.3 | 0.3 | 0.3 | 0.3 | 0.4 | 0.3 | 0.3 | 0.3 |
| Value of inventory adjustment [1] | 0.4 | -0.6 | -0.9 | -1.4 | -1.0 | -2.4 | 1.7 | 4.3 | 2.4 | 1.1 | 0.7 |
| Farm-related income | 15.3 | 24.4 | 35.8 | 46.9 | 57.1 | 58.2 | 52.9 | 51.5 | 44.5 | 50.8 | 47.8 |
| Forest products sold | 1.8 | 0.8 | 0.5 | 0.5 | 0.5 | 0.6 | 0.6 | 0.7 | 0.7 | 0.7 | 0.7 |
| Gross imputed rental value of farm dwellings | 7.2 | 12.7 | 15.8 | 16.2 | 17.9 | 17.2 | 16.3 | 17.1 | 16.6 | 18.1 | 18.7 |
| Machine hire and custom work | 1.8 | 2.2 | 3.8 | 4.0 | 3.9 | 4.4 | 4.4 | 4.7 | 3.6 | 4.8 | 3.9 |
| Other farm income | 4.5 | 8.7 | 15.7 | 26.3 | 34.9 | 36.0 | 31.5 | 29.0 | 23.6 | 27.1 | 24.5 |
| Less: Intermediate product expenses [2] | 90.7 | 119.1 | 189.1 | 215.9 | 237.4 | 239.9 | 255.5 | 235.7 | 221.6 | 228.3 | 230.0 |
| Farm origin | 39.5 | 47.9 | 82.2 | 96.2 | 106.3 | 109.9 | 117.0 | 110.1 | 99.5 | 104.5 | 104.8 |
| Feed purchased | 20.4 | 24.5 | 45.4 | 54.6 | 60.5 | 62.4 | 63.7 | 58.5 | 55.6 | 54.5 | 53.8 |
| Livestock and poultry purchased | 14.6 | 15.9 | 20.4 | 23.7 | 24.8 | 25.5 | 31.2 | 30.3 | 22.1 | 27.4 | 29.1 |
| Seed purchased | 4.5 | 7.5 | 16.3 | 17.8 | 20.9 | 21.9 | 22.1 | 21.3 | 21.8 | 22.5 | 21.9 |
| Manufactured inputs | 22.0 | 28.7 | 50.1 | 58.1 | 64.8 | 65.8 | 67.5 | 59.1 | 56.5 | 56.3 | 57.9 |
| Electricity | 2.6 | 3.0 | 4.6 | 4.9 | 5.4 | 5.5 | 5.9 | 5.7 | 5.6 | 5.8 | 6.1 |
| Fertilizers, lime, and soil conditioners | 8.2 | 10.0 | 21.0 | 25.1 | 28.9 | 28.3 | 28.1 | 25.5 | 23.5 | 22.0 | 23.2 |
| Pesticides | 5.4 | 8.5 | 10.7 | 11.8 | 14.0 | 14.6 | 15.8 | 14.6 | 15.2 | 15.7 | 15.4 |
| Petroleum fuel and oils | 5.8 | 7.2 | 13.8 | 16.2 | 16.5 | 17.3 | 17.7 | 13.2 | 12.2 | 12.8 | 13.2 |
| Other intermediate expenses [2] | 29.2 | 42.5 | 56.8 | 61.7 | 66.3 | 64.2 | 70.9 | 66.5 | 65.6 | 67.5 | 67.3 |
| Machine hire and custom work | 3.0 | 4.1 | 4.3 | 4.0 | 4.9 | 4.6 | 5.9 | 4.8 | 4.4 | 4.6 | 4.3 |
| Marketing, storage, and transportation expenses | 4.2 | 7.5 | 9.0 | 9.0 | 9.2 | 8.0 | 10.8 | 9.2 | 9.7 | 9.8 | 11.9 |
| Repair and maintenance of capital items | 8.6 | 10.9 | 14.6 | 15.3 | 16.5 | 17.2 | 17.8 | 16.6 | 15.9 | 16.6 | 15.3 |
| Miscellaneous expenses [2] | 13.4 | 19.9 | 29.0 | 33.4 | 35.7 | 34.5 | 36.5 | 35.9 | 35.5 | 36.5 | 35.7 |
| Total insurance premiums [3] | 3.4 | 4.8 | 7.5 | 9.9 | 10.4 | 10.6 | 10.6 | 10.0 | 9.6 | 10.3 | 9.9 |
| Less: Contract labor | 1.6 | 2.7 | 3.9 | 4.4 | 4.8 | 4.6 | 6.4 | 5.7 | 6.0 | 5.9 | 6.0 |
| Plus: Net government transactions [4] | 3.1 | 15.8 | 0.9 | -1.6 | -1.5 | -1.4 | -4.6 | -2.7 | 0.3 | -1.9 | 0.1 |
| Direct government payments [5] | 9.3 | 23.2 | 12.4 | 10.4 | 10.6 | 11.0 | 9.8 | 10.8 | 13.0 | 11.5 | 13.7 |
| Property taxes [2] | 6.2 | 7.4 | 11.5 | 12.0 | 12.2 | 12.4 | 14.3 | 13.5 | 12.6 | 13.5 | 13.6 |
| Motor vehicle registration and licensing fees | 0.4 | 0.5 | 0.6 | 0.7 | 0.7 | 0.7 | 0.7 | 0.7 | 0.7 | 0.7 | 0.7 |
| **Equals: Gross value added** | **99.3** | **112.5** | **152.1** | **188.1** | **195.5** | **227.2** | **207.0** | **185.8** | **171.9** | **179.6** | **179.1** |
| Less: Capital consumption [2] | 18.1 | 20.1 | 17.6 | 18.5 | 34.3 | 38.1 | 50.4 | 41.6 | 44.7 | 35.3 | 30.9 |
| **Equals: Net value added** | **81.2** | **92.4** | **134.6** | **169.6** | **161.2** | **189.1** | **156.6** | **144.3** | **127.2** | **144.3** | **148.1** |
| Less: Factor payments to stakeholders [6] | 35.0 | 41.7 | 57.4 | 56.0 | 64.8 | 65.5 | 64.5 | 62.8 | 65.2 | 66.6 | 64.1 |
| Employee compensation [7] | 12.4 | 17.9 | 23.6 | 22.6 | 27.4 | 27.7 | 28.1 | 26.4 | 28.4 | 30.4 | 28.1 |
| Net rent paid to operator landlords | (NA) | (NA) | 2.1 | 2.1 | 2.6 | 2.8 | 4.7 | 4.7 | 4.5 | 4.1 | 3.6 |
| Net rent paid to nonoperator landlords | 9.0 | 9.2 | 14.8 | 15.3 | 18.0 | 20.0 | 15.9 | 15.4 | 14.9 | 13.5 | 11.7 |
| Total interest expenses | 13.5 | 14.6 | 16.9 | 16.0 | 16.9 | 14.9 | 15.7 | 16.4 | 17.3 | 18.7 | 20.7 |
| **Equals: Net farm income** | **46.3** | **50.7** | **77.1** | **113.6** | **96.4** | **123.7** | **92.1** | **81.4** | **62.0** | **77.7** | **84.0** |

NA Not available. [1] A positive value of inventory change represents current-year production not sold by December 31. A negative value is an offset to production from prior years included in current-year sales. [2] Including expenses associated with operator dwellings. [3] Includes federal and private crop and livestock insurance premiums as well as casualty, hail, motor vehicle and all other insurance premiums. [4] Direct government payments minus motor vehicle registration and licensing fees and property taxes. [5] Government payments reflect payments made directly to all recipients in the farm sector, including landlords. The nonoperator landlords share is offset by its inclusion in rental expenses paid to these landlords and thus is not reflected in net farm income or net cash income. [6] Prior to 2008, factor payments to stakeholders only includes net rent paid to nonoperator landlords. [7] Includes hired labor and non-cash employee compensation.

Source: U.S. Department of Agriculture, Economic Research Service, "U.S. and State Farm Income and Wealth Statistics," <http://www.ers.usda.gov/data-products/farm-income-and-wealth-statistics.aspx>, accessed September 2019.

# Table 874. Value of Agricultural Production, Income, and Government Payments by State: 2016 and 2017

[In millions of dollars (398,782 represents $398,782,000,000). See headnote, Table 873. Minus sign (-) indicates loss]

| State | Value of agricultural production 2016 | 2017 | Net farm income 2016 | 2017 | Government payments, 2017 | State | Value of agricultural production 2016 | 2017 | Net farm income 2016 | 2017 | Government payments, 2017 |
|---|---|---|---|---|---|---|---|---|---|---|---|
| U.S. | 398,782 | 418,127 | 61,542 | 75,381 | 11,532 | MO | 10,997 | 11,513 | 1,471 | 1,750 | 423 |
| | | | | | | MT | 4,323 | 4,029 | 707 | 362 | 375 |
| AL | 5,723 | 6,402 | 930 | 1,724 | 205 | NE | 22,498 | 23,044 | 3,836 | 2,686 | 803 |
| AK | 49 | 52 | -4 | -9 | 7 | NV | 704 | 767 | 22 | -4 | 9 |
| AZ | 4,545 | 5,159 | 1,332 | 1,514 | 35 | NH | 262 | 278 | 2 | 25 | 6 |
| AR | 8,987 | 9,806 | 849 | 1,579 | 650 | NJ | 1,252 | 1,335 | 219 | 356 | 12 |
| CA | 50,711 | 55,501 | 15,230 | 17,813 | 179 | NM | 3,208 | 3,378 | 816 | 794 | 96 |
| CO | 7,264 | 7,803 | 1,135 | 884 | 269 | NY | 5,559 | 5,956 | 694 | 1,166 | 76 |
| CT | 641 | 694 | 8 | 85 | 5 | NC | 12,404 | 13,418 | 2,457 | 3,191 | 156 |
| DE | 1,359 | 1,537 | 356 | 571 | 22 | ND | 9,454 | 9,044 | 868 | 658 | 588 |
| FL | 8,262 | 8,895 | 1,911 | 2,636 | 92 | OH | 9,613 | 9,953 | 423 | 1,240 | 358 |
| GA | 9,284 | 10,072 | 1,839 | 2,671 | 392 | OK | 7,278 | 7,532 | 1,171 | 1,390 | 289 |
| HI | 826 | 843 | 66 | 103 | 12 | OR | 5,350 | 5,388 | 919 | 625 | 124 |
| ID | 7,681 | 7,814 | 1,679 | 1,233 | 162 | PA | 7,347 | 8,214 | 694 | 1,755 | 88 |
| IL | 17,747 | 17,826 | 2,209 | 2,055 | 609 | RI | 92 | 97 | 10 | 20 | 3 |
| IN | 11,515 | 11,475 | 1,413 | 1,576 | 373 | SC | 2,673 | 2,815 | 120 | 302 | 85 |
| IA | 28,215 | 28,876 | 2,512 | 3,420 | 691 | SD | 10,193 | 10,161 | 1,315 | 1,448 | 566 |
| KS | 16,656 | 16,977 | 2,257 | 1,159 | 622 | TN | 3,986 | 4,244 | 182 | 648 | 150 |
| KY | 6,319 | 6,835 | 993 | 1,743 | 169 | TX | 24,105 | 26,288 | 2,956 | 4,440 | 937 |
| LA | 3,255 | 3,515 | 563 | 851 | 293 | UT | 1,863 | 1,957 | 290 | 314 | 47 |
| ME | 772 | 812 | 88 | 144 | 13 | VT | 890 | 943 | 165 | 229 | 11 |
| MD | 2,490 | 2,715 | 358 | 679 | 58 | VA | 4,168 | 4,387 | 279 | 691 | 76 |
| MA | 524 | 580 | -78 | 5 | 7 | WA | 10,809 | 11,172 | 2,770 | 3,189 | 213 |
| MI | 8,163 | 8,113 | 12 | 611 | 201 | WV | 901 | 909 | 17 | 60 | 18 |
| MN | 18,203 | 18,335 | 989 | 1,852 | 461 | WI | 12,200 | 12,662 | 1,637 | 1,801 | 134 |
| MS | 5,743 | 6,234 | 716 | 1,263 | 312 | WY | 1,718 | 1,771 | 144 | 86 | 48 |

Source: U.S. Department of Agriculture, Economic Research Service, "U.S. and State Farm Income and Wealth Statistics," <http://www.ers.usda.gov/data-products/farm-income-and-wealth-statistics.aspx>, accessed February 2019.

# Table 875. Farm Income—Cash Receipts From Farm Marketings: 2010 to 2018

[In millions of dollars (321,237 represents $321,237,000,000). Represents gross receipts from commercial market sales as well as net Commodity Credit Corporation loans. The source estimates and publishes individual cash receipt values only for major commodities and major producing states. The U.S. receipts for individual commodities, computed as the sum of the reported states, may understate the value of sales for some commodities, with the balance included in the appropriate category labeled "other" or "miscellaneous." The degree of underestimation in some of the minor commodities can be substantial]

| Commodities | 2010 | 2015 | 2017 | 2018 | Commodities | 2010 | 2015 | 2017 | 2018 |
|---|---|---|---|---|---|---|---|---|---|
| Total [1] | 321,237 | 377,431 | 370,423 | 373,499 | Broccoli | 727 | 1,059 | 926 | 739 |
| Animals and products | 140,871 | 189,516 | 175,560 | 176,530 | Carrots | 647 | 820 | 696 | 732 |
| Meat animals | 69,144 | 98,806 | 87,975 | 88,203 | Corn, sweet | 952 | 1,043 | 892 | 859 |
| Cattle and calves | 51,246 | 78,253 | 66,937 | 67,105 | Lettuce | 2,213 | 3,150 | 4,236 | 2,706 |
| Hogs | 17,898 | 20,553 | 21,038 | 21,098 | Lettuce, head | 1,058 | 1,253 | 1,775 | 1,220 |
| Dairy products, milk | 31,372 | 35,717 | 37,941 | 35,244 | Onions | 1,050 | 1,039 | 1,042 | 817 |
| Poultry/eggs [1] | 34,690 | 48,292 | 42,788 | 46,257 | Peppers, bell | 592 | 733 | 626 | 533 |
| Broilers | 23,692 | 28,716 | 30,232 | 31,746 | Tomatoes | 2,281 | 2,603 | 1,678 | 1,856 |
| Chicken eggs | 6,553 | 13,763 | 7,635 | 10,586 | Tomatoes, fresh | 1,355 | 1,221 | 772 | 814 |
| Turkeys | 4,372 | 5,708 | 4,874 | 3,875 | Cantaloupes | 305 | 264 | 296 | 332 |
| Miscellaneous animals [1] | 5,664 | 6,701 | 6,856 | 6,825 | Watermelons | 499 | 488 | 594 | 655 |
| Aquaculture | 474 | 468 | 491 | 460 | Fruits/nuts [1] | 21,613 | 28,447 | 30,589 | 28,983 |
| Honey | 282 | 329 | 333 | 333 | Grapefruit | 291 | 216 | 257 | 221 |
| Crops | 180,366 | 187,916 | 194,864 | 196,969 | Lemons | 395 | 697 | 763 | 716 |
| Food grains [1] | 14,314 | 12,296 | 11,201 | 11,533 | Oranges | 1,997 | 1,963 | 1,944 | 1,770 |
| Rice | 3,263 | 2,803 | 2,423 | 2,515 | Apples | 2,311 | 3,366 | 3,601 | 3,014 |
| Wheat | 11,021 | 9,427 | 8,703 | 8,934 | Cherries | 756 | 838 | 949 | 694 |
| Feed crops [1] | 55,143 | 56,930 | 53,916 | 56,044 | Grapes | 4,024 | 5,914 | 6,508 | 6,615 |
| Corn | 47,540 | 47,023 | 45,555 | 47,241 | Peaches | 617 | 602 | 600 | 511 |
| Hay | 5,217 | 6,961 | 6,380 | 6,931 | Pears | 387 | 494 | 519 | 429 |
| Sorghum grain | 1,487 | 1,837 | 1,153 | 1,142 | Blueberries | 644 | 867 | 833 | 820 |
| Cotton | 7,465 | 4,756 | 7,574 | 8,083 | Cranberries | 299 | 262 | 252 | 222 |
| Tobacco | 1,336 | 1,607 | 1,379 | 1,247 | Raspberries | 259 | 721 | 494 | 367 |
| Oil crops [1] | 36,544 | 35,519 | 41,094 | 42,214 | Strawberries | 2,261 | 2,239 | 2,896 | 2,671 |
| Peanuts | 824 | 1,275 | 1,440 | 1,420 | Almonds | 2,903 | 5,869 | 5,604 | 5,468 |
| Soybeans | 34,665 | 33,118 | 38,522 | 39,772 | Pistachios | 1,159 | 888 | 1,015 | 2,616 |
| Sunflower | 507 | 568 | 420 | 369 | Walnuts | 1,028 | 1,012 | 1,569 | 879 |
| Vegetables and melons [1] | 17,405 | 20,359 | 20,494 | 18,507 | All other crops [1] | 26,546 | 28,001 | 28,616 | 30,359 |
| Beans, dry | 780 | 915 | 966 | 967 | Sugarcane | 1,075 | 1,017 | 1,001 | 985 |
| Potatoes | 3,336 | 3,708 | 3,875 | 3,691 | Sugar beets | 1,734 | 1,503 | 1,364 | 1,543 |
| Sweet potatoes | 472 | 676 | 657 | 654 | Floriculture | 4,149 | 4,374 | 4,450 | 4,766 |
| Beans, snap | 434 | 414 | 349 | 364 | Mushrooms | 924 | 1,124 | 1,156 | 1,163 |

[1] Includes other commodities not shown separately.

Source: U.S. Department of Agriculture, Economic Research Service, "U.S. and State Farm Income and Wealth Statistics," <http://www.ers.usda.gov/data-products/farm-income-and-wealth-statistics.aspx>, accessed September 2019.

## Table 876. Cash Receipts for Cattle, Corn, Soybeans, and Milk—Total and for Leading States: 2018

[In millions of dollars (67,105 represents $67,105,000,000). See headnote Table 875]

| State | Value | State | Value | State | Value | State | Value |
|---|---|---|---|---|---|---|---|
| **Cattle and calves...** | **67,105** | **Corn...** | **47,241** | **Soybeans...** | **39,772** | **Milk...** | **35,244** |
| Nebraska... | 10,584 | Iowa... | 8,063 | Illinois... | 6,015 | California... | 6,372 |
| Texas... | 8,624 | Illinois... | 7,589 | Iowa... | 5,038 | Wisconsin... | 5,003 |
| Kansas... | 8,286 | Nebraska... | 5,595 | Minnesota... | 3,424 | New York... | 2,476 |
| Iowa... | 4,075 | Minnesota... | 4,422 | Indiana... | 3,062 | Idaho... | 2,373 |
| Colorado... | 3,460 | Indiana... | 3,316 | Nebraska... | 2,841 | Texas... | 2,167 |

Source: U.S. Department of Agriculture, Economic Research Service, "U.S. and State Farm Income and Wealth Statistics," <http://www.ers.usda.gov/data-products/farm-income-and-wealth-statistics.aspx>, accessed September 2019.

## Table 877. Farm Marketings: 2017 and 2018; and Principal Commodities, 2018, by State

[In millions of dollars (370,423 represents $370,423,000,000). See headnote Table 875]

| State | 2017 Total | 2017 Animals and products | 2017 Crops | 2018 Total | 2018 Animals and products | 2018 Crops | State rank for total farm marketings and three principal commodities in order of marketing receipts |
|---|---|---|---|---|---|---|---|
| **U.S....** | **370,423** | **175,560** | **194,864** | **373,499** | **176,530** | **196,969** | **Cattle and calves, corn, soybeans** |
| AL... | 5,555 | 4,406 | 1,149 | 5,774 | 4,544 | 1,230 | 25—Broilers, cattle and calves, chicken eggs |
| AK... | 35 | 7 | 29 | 38 | 8 | 30 | 50—Floriculture, hay, cattle and calves |
| AZ... | 4,534 | 1,750 | 2,783 | 4,298 | 1,735 | 2,563 | 29—Lettuce, cattle and calves, milk |
| AR... | 8,962 | 5,372 | 3,590 | 9,167 | 5,570 | 3,597 | 13—Broilers, soybeans, rice |
| CA... | 49,608 | 11,192 | 38,415 | 49,915 | 11,740 | 38,175 | 1—Milk, grapes, almonds |
| CO... | 6,892 | 4,702 | 2,190 | 7,074 | 4,699 | 2,375 | 21—Cattle and calves, milk, corn |
| CT... | 601 | 172 | 429 | 598 | 181 | 417 | 45—Floriculture, milk, chicken eggs |
| DE... | 1,340 | 1,064 | 276 | 1,409 | 1,135 | 275 | 39—Broilers, corn, soybeans |
| FL... | 7,874 | 1,676 | 6,198 | 7,187 | 1,593 | 5,594 | 20—Floriculture, oranges, sugarcane |
| GA... | 8,966 | 5,866 | 3,100 | 9,128 | 6,036 | 3,092 | 14—Broilers, cotton lint, peanuts |
| HI... | 645 | 158 | 488 | 593 | 165 | 428 | 46—Coffee, cattle and calves, macadamia nuts |
| ID... | 7,328 | 4,369 | 2,959 | 7,391 | 4,326 | 3,065 | 19—Milk, cattle and calves, potatoes |
| IL... | 15,928 | 2,574 | 13,354 | 16,795 | 2,330 | 14,465 | 6—Corn, soybeans, hogs |
| IN... | 10,692 | 3,824 | 6,868 | 10,711 | 3,796 | 6,915 | 10—Corn, soybeans, hogs |
| IA... | 26,619 | 13,449 | 13,170 | 27,669 | 14,269 | 13,399 | 2—Corn, hogs, soybeans |
| KS... | 15,714 | 9,581 | 6,134 | 15,950 | 9,515 | 6,435 | 7—Cattle and calves, corn, soybeans |
| KY... | 5,568 | 3,185 | 2,383 | 5,904 | 3,367 | 2,537 | 24—Broilers, soybeans, cattle and calves |
| LA... | 3,051 | 1,099 | 1,951 | 3,141 | 1,147 | 1,995 | 33—Soybeans, broilers, sugarcane |
| ME... | 674 | 287 | 386 | 667 | 293 | 375 | 43—Potatoes, milk, chicken eggs |
| MD... | 2,297 | 1,386 | 911 | 2,245 | 1,355 | 889 | 36—Broilers, corn, soybeans |
| MA... | 440 | 108 | 332 | 434 | 103 | 331 | 47—Cranberries, milk, turkeys |
| MI... | 7,462 | 3,238 | 4,224 | 7,564 | 3,291 | 4,272 | 18—Milk, corn, soybeans |
| MN... | 17,191 | 7,657 | 9,534 | 17,256 | 7,473 | 9,783 | 5—Corn, soybeans, hogs |
| MS... | 5,597 | 3,316 | 2,280 | 5,728 | 3,401 | 2,326 | 26—Broilers, soybeans, cotton lint |
| MO... | 9,902 | 4,574 | 5,328 | 10,099 | 4,709 | 5,390 | 11—Soybeans, cattle and calves, corn |
| MT... | 3,539 | 1,721 | 1,818 | 3,494 | 1,606 | 1,888 | 32—Cattle and calves, wheat, hay |
| NE... | 20,300 | 11,451 | 8,849 | 21,318 | 11,914 | 9,404 | 4—Cattle and calves, corn, soybeans |
| NV... | 643 | 467 | 176 | 660 | 484 | 176 | 44—Cattle and calves, milk, hay |
| NH... | 226 | 106 | 120 | 229 | 112 | 117 | 48—Milk, chicken eggs, turkeys |
| NJ... | 1,143 | 112 | 1,031 | 1,108 | 127 | 981 | 40—Floriculture, blueberries, chicken eggs |
| NM... | 2,961 | 2,206 | 755 | 2,919 | 2,210 | 709 | 34—Milk, cattle and calves, pecans |
| NY... | 5,229 | 3,301 | 1,928 | 5,025 | 3,084 | 1,941 | 27—Milk, cattle and calves, corn |
| NC... | 11,403 | 7,729 | 3,674 | 11,139 | 7,634 | 3,505 | 8—Broilers, hogs, turkeys |
| ND... | 7,844 | 1,245 | 6,599 | 7,966 | 1,265 | 6,701 | 17—Soybeans, wheat, corn |
| OH... | 8,537 | 3,478 | 5,059 | 8,928 | 3,518 | 5,409 | 16—Soybeans, corn, milk |
| OK... | 6,823 | 5,410 | 1,413 | 6,736 | 5,288 | 1,447 | 23—Cattle and calves, hogs, broilers |
| OR... | 4,979 | 1,575 | 3,404 | 4,897 | 1,451 | 3,446 | 28—Cattle and calves, milk, hay |
| PA... | 6,770 | 4,297 | 2,472 | 6,792 | 4,225 | 2,567 | 22—Milk, chicken eggs, broilers |
| RI... | 73 | 29 | 44 | 76 | 33 | 44 | 49—Chicken eggs, turkeys, milk |
| SC... | 2,363 | 1,358 | 1,005 | 2,521 | 1,391 | 1,129 | 35—Broilers, corn, cotton lint |
| SD... | 8,985 | 3,943 | 5,042 | 9,114 | 4,072 | 5,042 | 15—Cattles and calves, corn, soybeans |
| TN... | 3,533 | 1,429 | 2,104 | 3,542 | 1,409 | 2,132 | 30—Soybeans, cattle and calves, broilers |
| TX... | 22,231 | 14,425 | 7,806 | 21,816 | 14,426 | 7,390 | 3—Cattle and calves, cotton lint, broilers |
| UT... | 1,808 | 1,349 | 458 | 1,686 | 1,200 | 486 | 37—Cattle and calves, milk, hay |
| VT... | 789 | 602 | 187 | 740 | 557 | 183 | 41—Milk, cattle and calves, maple products |
| VA... | 3,585 | 2,334 | 1,251 | 3,530 | 2,232 | 1,297 | 31—Broilers, cattle and calves, milk |
| WA... | 9,688 | 2,463 | 7,225 | 9,401 | 2,485 | 6,916 | 12—Apples, milk, wheat |
| WV... | 727 | 572 | 155 | 684 | 523 | 161 | 42—Broilers, cattle and calves, chicken eggs |
| WI... | 11,317 | 7,833 | 3,484 | 10,895 | 7,346 | 3,548 | 9—Milk, cattle and calves, corn |
| WY... | 1,455 | 1,112 | 343 | 1,547 | 1,151 | 396 | 38—Cattle and calves, hay, hogs |

Source: U.S. Department of Agriculture, Economic Research Service, "U.S. and State Farm Income and Wealth Statistics," <http://www.ers.usda.gov/data-products/farm-income-and-wealth-statistics.aspx>, accessed September 2019.

## Table 878. Indexes of Prices Received and Paid by Farmers: 2000 to 2018

[2011=100]

| Item | 2000 | 2010 | 2015 | 2018 | Item | 2000 | 2010 | 2015 | 2018 |
|---|---|---|---|---|---|---|---|---|---|
| **Prices received, all products....** | **59** | **87** | **99** | **91** | Livestock and poultry............ | 71 | 86 | 147 | 106 |
| Crops................................ | 54 | 87 | 87 | 87 | Seed and plants.................. | 37 | 93 | 125 | 119 |
| Food grains...................... | 36 | 74 | 76 | 75 | Fertilizer [2]...................... | 34 | 77 | 87 | 67 |
| Feed grains...................... | 35 | 66 | 63 | 58 | Agricultural chemicals........... | 83 | 100 | 107 | 101 |
| Cotton........................... | 57 | 81 | (NA) | (NA) | Fuels.............................. | 36 | 78 | 64 | 71 |
| Tobacco.......................... | 99 | 99 | (NA) | (NA) | Supplies and repairs............. | 73 | 96 | 106 | 112 |
| Oil-bearing crops................ | 40 | 81 | 76 | 74 | Autos and trucks.................. | 103 | 97 | 106 | 106 |
| Fruits and nuts.................. | 59 | 89 | 139 | 133 | Farm machinery................... | 57 | 94 | 115 | 120 |
| Commercial vegetables......... | 77 | 104 | 109 | 107 | Building materials................ | 71 | 97 | 107 | 116 |
| Potatoes and dry beans......... | 55 | 82 | (NA) | (NA) | Agricultural services............. | 72 | 98 | 114 | 115 |
| Animals and products............. | 64 | 86 | 113 | 94 | Rent.............................. | 54 | 93 | 130 | 120 |
| Livestock....................... | 62 | 82 | 120 | 96 | | | | | |
| Dairy products................... | 61 | 81 | 85 | 81 | Interest........................... | 78 | 92 | 98 | 118 |
| Poultry and eggs................ | 71 | 102 | 128 | 116 | Taxes.............................. | 55 | 96 | 110 | 117 |
| **Prices paid, total [1]................** | **59** | **90** | **111** | **109** | Wage rates........................ | 73 | 99 | 112 | 126 |
| Production........................ | 54 | 88 | 112 | 106 | | | | | |
| Feed................................ | 45 | 80 | 106 | 100 | Parity ratio [3]...................... | 101 | 96 | 90 | 83 |

NA Not available. [1] Includes production items, interest, taxes, wage rates, and a family living component. The family living component is the Consumer Price Index for all urban consumers from the Bureau of Labor Statistics. See text, Section 14 and Table 755. [2] Includes lime and soil conditioners. [3] Ratio of prices received by farmers to prices paid.

Source: U.S. Department of Agriculture, National Agricultural Statistics Service, "Quick Stats," <http://quickstats.nass.usda.gov/>, accessed July 2019.

## Table 879. Farm and Marketing Bill Share of the U.S. Food Dollar (Nominal) by Selected Characteristics: 2000 to 2017

[In percent. The food dollar series measures annual expenditures by U.S. consumers on domestically produced food; a food dollar represents the average $1 expenditure. Farm share is measured as the average payment from each food dollar expenditure that farmers receive for their raw food dollar commodities. The food marketing bill is measured as the average value added to the raw food dollar from each consumer food dollar expenditure. Based on input-output data from the Bureau of Labor Statistics and Bureau of Economic Analysis]

| Item | 2000 | 2005 | 2010 | 2012 | 2013 | 2014 | 2015 | 2016 | 2017 |
|---|---|---|---|---|---|---|---|---|---|
| **SHARE OF FOOD DOLLAR** | | | | | | | | | |
| Food dollar, total: | | | | | | | | | |
| Farm share........................ | 15.8 | 15.8 | 16.4 | 17.4 | 17.3 | 17.2 | 15.5 | 14.8 | 14.6 |
| Marketing bill share.............. | 84.2 | 84.2 | 83.6 | 82.6 | 82.7 | 82.8 | 84.5 | 85.2 | 85.4 |
| Food at home dollar: | | | | | | | | | |
| Farm share........................ | 22.5 | 23.6 | 24.2 | 26.1 | 25.8 | 26.2 | 24.3 | 23.6 | 23.4 |
| Marketing bill share.............. | 77.5 | 76.4 | 75.8 | 73.9 | 74.2 | 73.8 | 75.7 | 76.4 | 76.6 |
| Food away from home dollar: | | | | | | | | | |
| Farm share........................ | 6.2 | 5.1 | 5.5 | 5.9 | 6.1 | 5.8 | 4.9 | 4.4 | 4.4 |
| Marketing bill share.............. | 93.8 | 94.9 | 94.5 | 94.1 | 93.9 | 94.2 | 95.1 | 95.6 | 95.6 |
| Food and beverage dollar: [1] | | | | | | | | | |
| Farm share........................ | 13.1 | 13.2 | 13.6 | 14.6 | 14.5 | 14.5 | 13.0 | 12.5 | 12.3 |
| Marketing bill share.............. | 86.9 | 86.8 | 86.4 | 85.4 | 85.5 | 85.5 | 87.0 | 87.5 | 87.7 |
| Home food and beverage dollar: [1] | | | | | | | | | |
| Farm share........................ | 18.0 | 18.9 | 19.4 | 21.1 | 20.8 | 21.2 | 19.4 | 18.9 | 18.7 |
| Marketing bill share.............. | 82.0 | 81.1 | 80.6 | 78.9 | 79.2 | 78.8 | 80.6 | 81.1 | 81.3 |
| Away food and beverage dollar: [1] | | | | | | | | | |
| Farm share........................ | 5.4 | 4.5 | 4.7 | 5.1 | 5.2 | 5.1 | 4.3 | 4.0 | 4.0 |
| Marketing bill share.............. | 94.6 | 95.5 | 95.3 | 94.9 | 94.8 | 94.9 | 95.7 | 96.0 | 96.0 |
| **MARKETING BILL COST COMPONENTS** | | | | | | | | | |
| Primary factors: | | | | | | | | | |
| Salary and benefits [2]............ | 52.9 | 50.4 | 49.0 | 48.9 | 48.5 | 48.7 | 50.3 | 50.6 | 50.5 |
| Output taxes [3]................... | 7.3 | 8.0 | 9.3 | 8.9 | 8.8 | 8.8 | 8.7 | 8.8 | 9.2 |
| Property income [4]............... | 34.6 | 35.6 | 35.9 | 35.8 | 36.7 | 36.6 | 35.9 | 35.6 | 35.3 |
| Imports [5]........................ | 5.1 | 6.0 | 5.8 | 6.4 | 5.9 | 5.9 | 5.1 | 5.0 | 5.0 |
| Industry groups: [6] | | | | | | | | | |
| Farm and agribusiness [7]......... | 10.6 | 10.9 | 11.6 | 12.1 | 12.5 | 12.4 | 11.0 | 10.0 | 9.9 |
| Food processing.................. | 18.2 | 15.8 | 16.7 | 15.8 | 15.8 | 15.3 | 15.7 | 15.2 | 15.0 |
| Packaging......................... | 4.2 | 3.6 | 2.8 | 2.7 | 2.6 | 2.5 | 2.4 | 2.4 | 2.3 |
| Transportation.................... | 3.8 | 3.6 | 3.3 | 3.3 | 3.3 | 3.2 | 3.4 | 3.6 | 3.5 |
| Wholesale trade.................. | 9.4 | 9.2 | 9.4 | 9.3 | 9.3 | 9.1 | 8.9 | 9.1 | 9.1 |
| Retail trade....................... | 13.0 | 13.7 | 13.9 | 13.0 | 13.1 | 12.9 | 12.6 | 12.4 | 12.6 |
| Food services..................... | 28.4 | 30.6 | 30.2 | 31.1 | 31.2 | 32.7 | 35.0 | 36.3 | 36.7 |
| Energy............................ | 4.7 | 5.5 | 5.0 | 5.6 | 5.2 | 5.1 | 3.8 | 3.9 | 3.8 |
| Finance and insurance........... | 3.8 | 3.3 | 3.4 | 3.3 | 3.3 | 3.1 | 3.3 | 3.3 | 3.2 |
| Advertising....................... | 2.5 | 2.5 | 2.4 | 2.5 | 2.5 | 2.5 | 2.6 | 2.6 | 2.6 |
| Legal and accounting............ | 1.5 | 1.5 | 1.4 | 1.3 | 1.3 | 1.2 | 1.3 | 1.3 | 1.3 |

[1] Includes alcoholic beverages and soft drinks. [2] Pre-tax employee wages plus employer and employee costs for employee benefits. [3] Value of excise, sales, property, and severance taxes (less subsidies), customs duties, and other non-tax government fees levied on establishments. [4] Allocated compensation to various owners for services on behalf of a domestic establishment that directs sales to the U.S. food supply. Includes machinery, equipment, structures, natural resources, product inventory, and other tangible or intangible assets. [5] Food and non-food commodities imported from international sources and used by U.S. food supply chain industries producing for the U.S. market. [6] For each industry group, the amount shown excludes value-added contributions to the food dollar that trace back to other supply chain industry groups. For example, the value of energy used by the transportation and packaging industries is deducted from those groups and included with the energy group. [7] Farm and agribusiness value-added contributions from non-farm supply chain industry groups, such as energy, transportation, and financial services, are deducted from the farm share and therefore the industry group series value for farms and agribusiness is smaller than the farm share value of the marketing bill series.

Source: U.S. Department of Agriculture, Economic Research Service, "Food Dollar Series," <http://www.ers.usda.gov/data-products/food-dollar-series.aspx>, accessed July 2019.

## Table 880. Agricultural Exports and Imports—Volume by Principal Commodity: 2000 to 2018

[In thousands (1,436 represents 1,436,000). 1 kiloliter equals 264.17 gallons. Includes Puerto Rico, U.S. territories, and shipments under foreign aid programs. Commodity and commodity grouping definitions used are Foreign Agricultural Trade of the United States (FATUS) groupings. See source for details]

| Commodity | Unit | 2000 | 2005 | 2010 | 2015 | 2016 | 2017 | 2018 |
|---|---|---|---|---|---|---|---|---|
| **EXPORTS** | | | | | | | | |
| Fruit juices and wine | Kiloliters | 1,436 | 1,398 | 1,498 | 1,286 | 1,082 | 1,038 | 928 |
| Beef, pork, lamb, and poultry meats [1] | Metric tons | 4,431 | 4,343 | 6,366 | 6,457 | 6,932 | 7,213 | 7,405 |
| Wheat, unmilled | Metric tons | 27,568 | 27,040 | 27,608 | 21,258 | 23,885 | 27,171 | 22,244 |
| Wheat products | Metric tons | 844 | 313 | 446 | 440 | 461 | 393 | 379 |
| Rice, paddy, milled | Metric tons | 3,241 | 4,388 | 4,464 | 3,880 | 3,878 | 3,826 | 3,184 |
| Feed grains | Metric tons | 54,946 | 50,865 | 54,504 | 54,604 | 62,625 | 58,598 | 73,881 |
| Feed grain products | Metric tons | 657 | 3,442 | 1,081 | 851 | 888 | 967 | 922 |
| Feeds and fodders [2] | Metric tons | 13,065 | 11,422 | 19,024 | 22,725 | 22,295 | 21,791 | 22,186 |
| Fresh fruits and nuts | Metric tons | 3,452 | 3,675 | 4,308 | 4,566 | 4,749 | 4,765 | 4,647 |
| Fruit products [3] | Metric tons | 387 | 394 | 570 | 570 | 525 | 546 | 466 |
| Vegetables, fresh | Metric tons | 2,100 | 2,077 | 2,140 | 2,236 | 2,435 | 2,453 | 2,434 |
| Vegetables, frozen and canned | Metric tons | 1,110 | 1,086 | 1,410 | 1,889 | 1,976 | 1,882 | 1,815 |
| Oilcake and meal | Metric tons | 6,760 | 6,905 | 10,004 | 11,689 | 10,823 | 10,839 | 13,168 |
| Oilseeds | Metric tons | 27,715 | 26,462 | 43,282 | 48,914 | 58,786 | 56,281 | 47,208 |
| Vegetable oils | Metric tons | 2,043 | 1,937 | 3,544 | 2,646 | 2,643 | 2,721 | 2,527 |
| Tobacco, unmanufactured | Metric tons | 180 | 154 | 179 | 156 | 164 | 144 | 149 |
| Cotton, excluding linters | Metric tons | 1,485 | 3,405 | 2,956 | 2,396 | 2,469 | 3,252 | 3,575 |
| **IMPORTS** | | | | | | | | |
| Fruit juices | Kiloliters | 3,114 | 4,149 | 4,274 | 4,477 | 4,627 | 4,718 | 5,198 |
| Wine | Kiloliters | 458 | 726 | 959 | 1,157 | 1,166 | 1,257 | 1,197 |
| Malt beverages | Kiloliters | 2,346 | 2,995 | 3,161 | 3,675 | 3,915 | 4,038 | 4,183 |
| Coffee, including products | Metric tons | 1,370 | 1,307 | 1,390 | 1,584 | 1,647 | 1,676 | 1,643 |
| Rubber and allied gums, crude | Metric tons | 1,232 | 1,169 | 945 | 950 | 946 | 972 | 997 |
| Beef, pork, lamb, and poultry meats [1] | Metric tons | 1,564 | 1,778 | 1,351 | 1,918 | 1,799 | 1,819 | 1,791 |
| Grains [4] | Metric tons | 4,622 | 3,726 | 5,166 | 6,328 | 6,202 | 6,542 | 6,456 |
| Biscuits, pasta, and noodles | Metric tons | 711 | 1,001 | 1,097 | 1,445 | 1,643 | 1,754 | 1,906 |
| Feeds and fodders [2] | Metric tons | 1,224 | 963 | 1,423 | 2,221 | 1,894 | 1,706 | 1,844 |
| Fruits, nuts, and preparations [5] | Metric tons | 8,357 | 9,570 | 10,934 | 13,874 | 14,256 | 14,685 | 15,119 |
| Vegetables, fresh and frozen | Metric tons | 3,804 | 5,183 | 6,861 | 8,221 | 9,051 | 9,376 | 9,840 |
| Tobacco, unmanufactured | Metric tons | 216 | 233 | 164 | 155 | 172 | 142 | 135 |
| Oilseeds and oilnuts | Metric tons | 951 | 818 | 1,223 | 1,643 | 1,420 | 1,485 | 1,409 |
| Vegetable oils and waxes | Metric tons | 1,846 | 2,386 | 3,730 | 4,890 | 5,314 | 5,531 | 5,575 |
| Oilcake and meal | Metric tons | 1,254 | 1,541 | 1,504 | 4,020 | 3,970 | 3,756 | 3,713 |

[1] Includes variety meats. [2] Excluding oilcake and meal. [3] Includes canned, dried, and frozen fruits. [4] Includes wheat, corn, oats, barley, and rice. [5] Includes bananas and plantains.

Source: U.S. Department of Agriculture, Foreign Agricultural Service, "Global Agricultural Trade System," <http://www.fas.usda.gov/gats/>, accessed August 2019.

## Table 881. Agricultural Chemical and Fertilizer Exports and General Imports by Type: 2000 to 2018

[In thousands of metric tons (21,480 represents 21,480,000). Metric ton = 1.102 short tons or .984 long tons. Includes Puerto Rico, U.S. territories, and shipments under foreign aid programs. Commodity and commodity grouping definitions used are Foreign Agricultural Trade of the United States (FATUS) groupings. See source for details]

| Commodity | 2000 | 2005 | 2010 | 2013 | 2014 | 2015 | 2016 | 2017 | 2018 |
|---|---|---|---|---|---|---|---|---|---|
| **GENERAL IMPORTS [1]** | | | | | | | | | |
| **Fertilizers, total** | **21,480** | **30,397** | **43,657** | **33,663** | **35,612** | **35,676** | **31,894** | **33,432** | **34,486** |
| Nitrogen | 10,552 | 17,901 | 17,171 | 17,374 | 17,914 | 18,304 | 16,134 | 13,999 | 12,787 |
| Potassium | 9,324 | 10,215 | 10,230 | 9,685 | 10,646 | 10,275 | 8,878 | 12,288 | 12,903 |
| Phosphate | 1,592 | 2,243 | 16,200 | 6,538 | 6,965 | 6,975 | 6,798 | 7,028 | 8,695 |
| Mixed/organic fertilizer | 13 | 37 | 56 | 65 | 87 | 122 | 83 | 117 | 101 |
| **Agricultural chemicals, total** | **58** | **80** | **90** | **116** | **100** | **115** | **125** | **141** | **142** |
| Herbicides | 12 | 23 | 15 | 19 | 14 | 19 | 27 | 34 | 33 |
| Fungicides | 17 | 21 | 25 | 26 | 28 | 33 | 35 | 38 | 40 |
| Insecticides | 10 | 7 | 1 | 1 | 1 | 1 | 1 | 2 | 2 |
| Other pesticides | 19 | 29 | 49 | 70 | 57 | 61 | 60 | 68 | 68 |
| **EXPORTS** | | | | | | | | | |
| **Fertilizers, total** | **21** | **32** | **10,310** | **11,165** | **10,598** | **9,916** | **10,569** | **11,865** | **10,796** |
| Nitrogen | 19 | 26 | 1,741 | 2,588 | 2,564 | 2,346 | 2,842 | 4,001 | 3,891 |
| Potassium | – | – | 333 | 320 | 96 | 54 | 56 | 83 | 61 |
| Phosphate | 2 | 6 | 7,820 | 7,580 | 7,119 | 6,467 | 6,660 | 6,647 | 6,083 |
| Mixed/organic fertilizer | – | – | 416 | 678 | 819 | 1,048 | 1,011 | 1,134 | 762 |
| **Agricultural chemicals, total** | **154** | **127** | **146** | **170** | **159** | **150** | **156** | **1,170** | **1,151** |
| Herbicides | 60 | 56 | 83 | 95 | 84 | 81 | 91 | 117 | 93 |
| Fungicides | 14 | 18 | 15 | 22 | 24 | 19 | 18 | 19 | 20 |
| Insecticides | 62 | 23 | 27 | 27 | 27 | 24 | 20 | – | – |
| Other pesticides | 19 | 29 | 22 | 25 | 23 | 26 | 27 | 1,035 | 1,038 |

– Represents or rounds to zero. [1] Total shipments arriving in the U.S., including both merchandise that enters consumption channels immediately and merchandise entered into bonded warehouses or Foreign Trade Zones under Customs custody.

Source: U.S. Department of Agriculture, Foreign Agricultural Service, "Global Agricultural Trade System," <http://www.fas.usda.gov/gats>, accessed May 2019.

## Table 882. Agricultural Exports and Imports—Value: 1990 to 2017

[In billions of dollars, except percent (16.6 represents $16,600,000,000). Includes Puerto Rico, U.S. territories, and shipments under foreign aid programs. Excludes fish, forest products, distilled liquors, manufactured tobacco, and products made from cotton; but includes raw tobacco, raw cotton, rubber, beer and wine, and processed agricultural products]

| Year | Trade balance | Exports, domestic products | Percent of all exports | Imports for con-sumption | Percent of all imports | Year | Trade balance | Exports, domestic products | Percent of all exports | Imports for con-sumption | Percent of all imports |
|---|---|---|---|---|---|---|---|---|---|---|---|
| 1990......... | 16.6 | 39.5 | 11.0 | 22.9 | 5.0 | 2011......... | 37.5 | 136.4 | 10.5 | 99.0 | 4.5 |
| 2000......... | 12.3 | 51.3 | 7.2 | 39.0 | 3.2 | 2012......... | 38.6 | 141.6 | 10.5 | 102.9 | 4.6 |
| 2005......... | 3.9 | 63.2 | 7.8 | 59.3 | 3.6 | 2013......... | 40.1 | 144.4 | 10.5 | 104.2 | 4.7 |
| 2007......... | 18.1 | 90.0 | 8.6 | 71.9 | 3.7 | 2014......... | 38.1 | 150.0 | 10.7 | 111.8 | 4.8 |
| 2008......... | 34.3 | 114.8 | 9.8 | 80.5 | 3.8 | 2015......... | 19.4 | 133.1 | 10.3 | 113.6 | 5.2 |
| 2009......... | 26.8 | 98.5 | 10.3 | 71.7 | 4.6 | 2016......... | 20.3 | 134.7 | 11.0 | 114.5 | 5.3 |
| 2010......... | 34.0 | 115.8 | 10.3 | 81.9 | 4.3 | 2017......... | 17.4 | 138.4 | 10.6 | 121.0 | 5.2 |

Source: U.S. Department of Agriculture, Economic Research Service, "Foreign Agricultural Trade of the United States (FATUS)," <https://www.ers.usda.gov/data-products/foreign-agricultural-trade-of-the-united-states-fatus/>, accessed April 2018.

## Table 883. Agricultural Imports—Value by Selected Commodity: 2000 to 2018

[In millions of dollars (38,974 represents $38,974,000,000). For calendar year. Includes Puerto Rico, U.S. territories, and shipments under foreign aid programs. Excludes fish, forest products, distilled liquors, manufactured tobacco, and products made from cotton; but includes raw tobacco, raw cotton, rubber, beer and wine, and processed agricultural products]

| Commodity [1] | Value (mil. dol.) | | | | | | | Percent distribution | | |
|---|---|---|---|---|---|---|---|---|---|---|
| | 2000 | 2005 | 2010 | 2015 | 2016 | 2017 | 2018 | 2000 | 2010 | 2018 |
| Total [2]................... | 38,974 | 59,291 | 81,863 | 113,633 | 114,453 | 120,966 | 128,762 | 100.0 | 100.0 | 100.0 |
| Cattle, live...................... | 1,152 | 1,039 | 1,575 | 2,195 | 1,619 | 1,533 | 1,587 | 3.0 | 1.9 | 1.2 |
| Beef and veal................... | 2,399 | 3,651 | 2,830 | 6,655 | 5,259 | 5,258 | 5,618 | 6.2 | 3.5 | 4.4 |
| Pork............................ | 997 | 1,281 | 1,185 | 1,622 | 1,626 | 1,734 | 1,602 | 2.6 | 1.4 | 1.2 |
| Dairy products.................. | 1,671 | 2,686 | 2,619 | 3,493 | 3,428 | 2,813 | 2,946 | 4.3 | 3.2 | 2.3 |
| Grains and feeds............... | 3,075 | 4,527 | 7,788 | 11,085 | 11,088 | 12,194 | 13,661 | 7.9 | 9.5 | 10.6 |
| Fruits and preparations......... | 3,851 | 5,842 | 9,168 | 14,047 | 15,257 | 16,323 | 17,237 | 9.9 | 11.2 | 13.4 |
| Vegetables and preparations [3]. | 3,958 | 6,410 | 9,318 | 12,063 | 13,270 | 13,578 | 14,504 | 10.2 | 11.4 | 11.3 |
| Sugar and related products...... | 1,555 | 2,494 | 4,047 | 4,600 | 4,625 | 4,656 | 4,673 | 4.0 | 4.9 | 3.6 |
| Cocoa and products............. | 1,404 | 2,751 | 4,295 | 4,860 | 5,081 | 5,012 | 4,714 | 3.6 | 5.2 | 3.7 |
| Coffee and products............. | 2,700 | 2,976 | 4,943 | 6,303 | 6,004 | 6,618 | 6,053 | 6.9 | 6.0 | 4.7 |
| Rubber, crude natural........... | 842 | 1,552 | 2,820 | 1,499 | 1,308 | 1,768 | 1,538 | 2.2 | 3.4 | 1.2 |
| Wine........................... | 2,207 | 3,762 | 4,279 | 5,478 | 5,646 | 6,022 | 6,340 | 5.7 | 5.2 | 4.9 |
| Malt beverages................. | 2,179 | 3,096 | 3,506 | 4,547 | 4,868 | 5,084 | 5,352 | 5.6 | 4.3 | 4.2 |
| Oilseeds and products.......... | 1,773 | 2,998 | 5,390 | 8,319 | 8,462 | 9,225 | 9,242 | 4.5 | 6.6 | 7.2 |

[1] Commodity and commodity grouping definitions used are the Foreign Agricultural Trade of the United States (FATUS) commodity code groupings. See source for more details. [2] Includes other commodities, not shown separately. [3] Includes pulses.

Source: U.S. Department of Agriculture, Foreign Agricultural Service, "Global Agricultural Trade System (GATS)," <http://www.fas.usda.gov/gats>, accessed May 2019.

## Table 884. Agricultural Imports—Value by Selected Country of Origin: 2000 to 2018

[In millions of dollars (38,974 represents $38,974,000,000). Totals include transshipments through Canada, but transshipments are not distributed by country after 1998. See headnote Table 882]

| Country | Value (mil. dol.) | | | | | | | Percent distribution | | |
|---|---|---|---|---|---|---|---|---|---|---|
| | 2000 | 2005 | 2010 | 2015 | 2016 | 2017 | 2018 | 2000 | 2010 | 2018 |
| Total............................ | 38,974 | 59,291 | 81,863 | 113,633 | 114,453 | 120,966 | 128,762 | 100.0 | 100.0 | 100.0 |
| Mexico.......................... | 5,077 | 8,331 | 13,578 | 21,034 | 22,944 | 24,568 | 25,945 | 13.0 | 16.6 | 20.1 |
| European Union [1].............. | 8,312 | 13,426 | 14,370 | 20,000 | 20,589 | 22,066 | 23,817 | 21.3 | 17.6 | 18.5 |
| Canada......................... | 8,661 | 12,270 | 16,244 | 21,821 | 21,526 | 22,306 | 23,049 | 22.2 | 19.8 | 17.9 |
| China........................... | 812 | 1,872 | 3,367 | 4,356 | 4,331 | 4,501 | 4,910 | 2.1 | 4.1 | 3.8 |
| Indonesia....................... | 998 | 1,702 | 2,887 | 2,882 | 2,884 | 3,710 | 3,362 | 2.6 | 3.5 | 2.6 |
| Brazil........................... | 1,144 | 1,952 | 2,894 | 3,482 | 3,395 | 3,294 | 3,340 | 2.9 | 3.5 | 2.6 |
| Australia [2].................... | 1,592 | 2,421 | 2,307 | 4,274 | 3,166 | 3,238 | 3,209 | 4.1 | 2.8 | 2.5 |
| Chile............................ | 1,026 | 1,521 | 2,293 | 2,854 | 3,130 | 2,887 | 3,072 | 2.6 | 2.8 | 2.4 |
| India............................ | 826 | 923 | 1,592 | 2,670 | 2,108 | 2,606 | 2,679 | 2.1 | 1.9 | 2.1 |
| Thailand........................ | 779 | 1,094 | 2,034 | 2,274 | 2,340 | 2,455 | 2,673 | 2.0 | 2.5 | 2.1 |
| Colombia........................ | 1,123 | 1,437 | 1,977 | 2,428 | 2,348 | 2,609 | 2,617 | 2.9 | 2.4 | 2.0 |
| New Zealand [2]................. | 1,132 | 1,712 | 1,666 | 2,884 | 2,576 | 2,589 | 2,564 | 2.9 | 2.0 | 2.0 |
| Vietnam......................... | 200 | 422 | 970 | 1,841 | 2,153 | 2,402 | 2,329 | 0.5 | 1.2 | 1.8 |
| Peru............................ | 196 | 448 | 974 | 1,677 | 1,830 | 1,984 | 2,229 | 0.5 | 1.2 | 1.7 |
| Guatemala...................... | 710 | 920 | 1,387 | 1,928 | 1,913 | 2,070 | 2,186 | 1.8 | 1.7 | 1.7 |
| Costa Rica...................... | 812 | 916 | 1,295 | 1,484 | 1,625 | 1,616 | 1,590 | 2.1 | 1.6 | 1.2 |
| Argentina....................... | 672 | 831 | 1,159 | 1,536 | 1,386 | 1,390 | 1,395 | 1.7 | 1.4 | 1.1 |
| Philippines...................... | 468 | 568 | 884 | 1,146 | 1,130 | 1,242 | 1,134 | 1.2 | 1.1 | 0.9 |
| Ecuador......................... | 451 | 596 | 869 | 1,226 | 1,202 | 1,002 | 1,077 | 1.2 | 1.1 | 0.8 |
| Malaysia........................ | 353 | 666 | 1,729 | 1,171 | 1,013 | 991 | 998 | 0.9 | 2.1 | 0.8 |
| Rest of world.................... | 3,627 | 5,264 | 7,390 | 10,665 | 10,866 | 11,441 | 14,586 | 9.3 | 9.0 | 11.3 |

[1] For consistency, data for all years are shown on the basis of 28 countries in the European Union; see footnote 3, Table 1396. [2] Data is a summarization of component countries.

Source: U.S. Department of Agriculture, Foreign Agricultural Service, "Global Agricultural Trade System (GATS)," <http://www.fas.usda.gov/gats>, accessed May 2019.

## Table 885. Selected Farm Products—U.S. and World Production and Exports: 2010 to 2018

[58.9 represents 58,900,000. Metric ton = 1.102 short tons or .984 long tons]

| Commodity | Unit | Quantity | | | | | | United States as percent of world | | |
|---|---|---|---|---|---|---|---|---|---|---|
| | | United States | | | World | | | | | |
| | | 2010 | 2015 | 2018 | 2010 | 2015 | 2018 | 2010 | 2015 | 2018 |
| PRODUCTION [1] | | | | | | | | | | |
| Wheat....................... | Mil. metric tons | 58.9 | 56.1 | 51.3 | 650.7 | 738.2 | 730.9 | 9.0 | 7.6 | 7.0 |
| Corn for grain............... | Mil. metric tons | 315.6 | 345.5 | 366.3 | 849.5 | 1,014.2 | 1,122.7 | 37.2 | 34.1 | 32.6 |
| Soybeans................... | Mil. metric tons | 90.7 | 106.9 | 123.7 | 264.7 | 316.6 | 362.9 | 34.3 | 33.8 | 34.1 |
| Rice, milled................. | Mil. metric tons | 7.6 | 6.1 | 7.1 | 451.6 | 476.7 | 498.7 | 1.7 | 1.3 | 1.4 |
| Cotton...................... | Million bales [2] | 18.1 | 12.9 | 18.4 | 117.3 | 96.2 | 119.3 | 15.4 | 13.4 | 15.4 |
| EXPORTS [3] | | | | | | | | | | |
| Wheat [4]..................... | Mil. metric tons | 35.1 | 21.2 | 25.5 | 133.0 | 172.8 | 175.3 | 26.4 | 12.3 | 14.5 |
| Corn....................... | Mil. metric tons | 46.5 | 48.2 | 53.3 | 91.6 | 119.9 | 172.4 | 50.8 | 40.2 | 30.9 |
| Soybeans................... | Mil. metric tons | 41.0 | 52.9 | 46.3 | 91.6 | 132.6 | 150.2 | 44.7 | 39.9 | 30.8 |
| Rice, milled basis.......... | Mil. metric tons | 3.5 | 3.4 | 2.9 | 35.2 | 40.4 | 46.2 | 10.0 | 8.4 | 6.3 |
| Cotton...................... | Million bales [2] | 14.4 | 9.2 | 14.5 | 34.9 | 34.7 | 41.1 | 41.2 | 26.4 | 35.3 |

[1] Production years vary by commodity. In most cases, includes harvests from July 1 of the year shown through June 30 of the following year. [2] Bales of 480 lb. net weight. [3] Data are for local marketing year beginning in year shown. See source for more information. [4] Includes wheat flour on a grain equivalent.

Source: U.S. Department of Agriculture, Foreign Agricultural Service, "Production, Supply and Distribution Online," <http://www.fas.usda.gov/psdonline/>, accessed August 2019.

## Table 886. Percent of U.S. Agricultural Commodity Output Exported: 2008 to 2016

[In percent. All export shares are estimated from export and production values]

| Commodity group | 2008 | 2009 | 2010 | 2011 | 2012 | 2013 | 2014 | 2015 | 2016 |
|---|---|---|---|---|---|---|---|---|---|
| **Total agriculture**...................... | **19.8** | **17.3** | **19.2** | **20.8** | **20.6** | **20.7** | **20.7** | **19.4** | **19.9** |
| Total food and beverages.............. | 19.2 | 16.8 | 18.4 | 19.7 | 19.8 | 19.9 | 20.1 | 19.1 | 19.3 |
| Animal foods [1]......................... | 9.9 | 8.8 | 9.7 | 11.0 | 11.3 | 11.3 | 10.5 | 9.5 | 9.8 |
| Plant foods [2]......................... | 30.3 | 25.4 | 28.3 | 29.8 | 28.3 | 28.8 | 31.7 | 29.6 | 29.7 |
| Non-manufactured products........... | 26.2 | 22.0 | 23.3 | 23.5 | 21.3 | 21.0 | 22.3 | 21.3 | 23.7 |
| Crops................................ | 38.4 | 31.4 | 34.5 | 35.4 | 30.9 | 31.5 | 36.3 | 35.2 | 36.5 |
| Food grains........................ | 76.0 | 49.5 | 63.6 | 80.2 | 52.9 | 73.3 | 59.9 | 62.0 | 63.0 |
| Feed grains........................ | 26.5 | 19.9 | 20.7 | 21.8 | 13.4 | 11.6 | 20.3 | 20.4 | 22.2 |
| Oilseeds........................... | 56.6 | 46.7 | 52.5 | 51.4 | 54.2 | 47.6 | 57.8 | 55.3 | 53.8 |
| Vegetables and melons.............. | 15.8 | 14.9 | 16.4 | 16.5 | 17.1 | 16.8 | 17.6 | 15.9 | 17.5 |
| Fruits and tree nuts................. | 37.4 | 37.4 | 38.7 | 40.4 | 40.1 | 41.9 | 42.8 | 45.2 | 42.7 |
| Sweeteners......................... | 6.5 | 5.0 | 6.5 | 6.3 | 5.7 | 5.9 | 6.6 | 5.2 | 3.8 |
| Livestock............................ | 0.9 | 0.9 | 0.8 | 0.8 | 1.0 | 0.7 | 0.6 | 0.5 | 0.5 |
| Manufactured products................. | 18.8 | 16.3 | 18.8 | 21.3 | 23.4 | 24.5 | 24.4 | 21.6 | 19.9 |
| Grain & oilseed milling products..... | 41.2 | 36.5 | 45.4 | 43.8 | 53.7 | 59.0 | 62.8 | 54.7 | 49.8 |
| Sugar & confections................. | 14.8 | 13.8 | 14.0 | 16.1 | 18.0 | 19.6 | 20.2 | 18.7 | 17.9 |
| Preserved fruit & vegetables......... | 17.0 | 15.5 | 17.1 | 20.1 | 19.5 | 19.4 | 20.5 | 19.1 | 18.8 |
| Dairy products...................... | 14.6 | 8.6 | 12.3 | 15.5 | 17.4 | 22.7 | 23.7 | 17.0 | 14.3 |
| Meat products....................... | 32.5 | 26.5 | 31.9 | 39.4 | 41.3 | 40.0 | 38.5 | 33.1 | 30.8 |
| Bakery products..................... | 4.1 | 4.1 | 4.3 | 5.0 | 5.6 | 5.8 | 5.6 | 5.3 | 4.9 |
| Other foods.......................... | 14.4 | 13.8 | 14.9 | 15.9 | 19.2 | 20.0 | 19.2 | 18.7 | 18.2 |
| Beverages........................... | 7.6 | 7.5 | 9.2 | 10.4 | 11.1 | 13.1 | 12.7 | 13.1 | 11.1 |

[1] Animal products include red meats, poultry meat and eggs, and dairy products. [2] Plant or crop food products include food grains, vegetable oils, fruits, nuts, vegetables, sweeteners (sugarcane, sugar beets, honey), tropical products (coffee, cocoa, spices), grain and oilseed milling products, sugar and confections, and bakery products.

Source: U.S. Department of Agriculture, Economic Research Service, "U.S. Agricultural Trade," <https://www.ers.usda.gov/topics/international-markets-trade/us-agricultural-trade/>, accessed February 2018.

## Table 887. Top 10 U.S. Export Markets for Soybeans, Corn, Wheat, and Poultry: 2018

[In thousands of metric tons (46,196 represents 46,196,000). Commodity and commodity grouping definitions used are the Foreign Agricultural Trade of the United States (FATUS) commodity code groupings. See source for details]

| Country | Soybeans | Country | Corn | Country | Wheat [1] | Country | Poultry meat |
|---|---|---|---|---|---|---|---|
| **World, total**....... | **46,196** | **World, total**....... | **69,749** | **World, total**....... | **22,244** | **World, total**....... | **3,636** |
| China............... | 8,235 | Mexico.............. | 16,699 | Japan.............. | 2,861 | Mexico.............. | 858 |
| Mexico.............. | 4,814 | Japan.............. | 15,267 | Mexico.............. | 2,803 | Angola.............. | 209 |
| Netherlands........ | 3,483 | Korea, South........ | 7,264 | Philippines.......... | 2,645 | Taiwan.............. | 201 |
| Egypt............... | 3,187 | Colombia............ | 5,512 | Korea, South........ | 1,533 | Cuba................ | 195 |
| Indonesia........... | 2,637 | Taiwan.............. | 3,209 | Taiwan.............. | 983 | Canada............. | 155 |
| Japan.............. | 2,269 | Peru............... | 3,074 | Iraq............... | 882 | Hong Kong......... | 135 |
| Taiwan.............. | 2,262 | Canada............. | 1,971 | Nigeria............. | 814 | Guatemala......... | 128 |
| Argentina........... | 1,986 | Vietnam............ | 1,909 | Indonesia........... | 779 | Philippines........... | 115 |
| Spain............... | 1,737 | Egypt.............. | 1,865 | Thailand........... | 696 | Vietnam............. | 107 |
| Pakistan............ | 1,733 | Saudi Arabia........ | 1,724 | Guatemala......... | 548 | South Africa........ | 103 |
| Rest of world....... | 13,852 | Rest of world....... | 11,255 | Rest of world....... | 7,700 | Rest of world........ | 1,429 |

[1] Unmilled.

Source: U.S. Department of Agriculture, Foreign Agricultural Service, "Global Agricultural Trade System (GATS)," <http://www.fas.usda.gov/gats/>, accessed August 2019.

## Table 888. Agricultural Exports—Value by Principal Commodity: 2000 to 2018

[In millions of dollars (51,265 represents $51,265,000,000). Includes Puerto Rico, U.S. territories, and shipments under foreign aid programs. Excludes fish, forest products, distilled liquors, manufactured tobacco, and products made from cotton; but includes raw tobacco, raw cotton, rubber, beer and wine, and processed agricultural products. Commodity and commodity grouping definitions used are the Foreign Agricultural Trade of the United States (FATUS) commodity code groupings. See source for more details]

| Commodity | Value (mil. dol.) | | | | | | | Percent distribution | | |
|---|---|---|---|---|---|---|---|---|---|---|
| | 2000 | 2005 | 2010 | 2015 | 2016 | 2017 | 2018 | 2000 | 2010 | 2018 |
| **Total agricultural exports**...... | **51,265** | **63,182** | **115,820** | **133,057** | **134,678** | **138,160** | **139,597** | **100.0** | **100.0** | **100.0** |
| Animals and animal products [1].... | 11,600 | 12,227 | 22,340 | 26,719 | 25,844 | 28,892 | 29,615 | 22.6 | 19.3 | 21.2 |
| Red meat and meat products..... | 5,276 | 4,299 | 9,336 | 12,407 | 12,862 | 14,446 | 15,284 | 10.3 | 8.1 | 10.9 |
| Poultry and poultry products...... | 2,235 | 3,139 | 4,806 | 4,915 | 4,654 | 5,092 | 5,140 | 4.4 | 4.1 | 3.7 |
| Grains and feeds [1].................. | 13,620 | 16,364 | 29,224 | 31,277 | 30,388 | 29,780 | 33,001 | 26.6 | 25.2 | 23.6 |
| Wheat and products.............. | 3,578 | 4,520 | 7,061 | 5,977 | 5,667 | 6,340 | 5,682 | 7.0 | 6.1 | 4.1 |
| Corn.................................. | 4,469 | 4,789 | 9,792 | 8,271 | 9,879 | 9,112 | 12,467 | 8.7 | 8.5 | 8.9 |
| Fruits and preparations............ | 2,743 | 3,468 | 5,262 | 6,285 | 6,178 | 6,369 | 6,302 | 5.4 | 4.5 | 4.5 |
| Nuts and preparations............. | 1,322 | 2,992 | 4,795 | 9,058 | 8,586 | 9,105 | 9,168 | 2.6 | 4.1 | 6.6 |
| Vegetables and preparations [2]..... | 3,112 | 3,571 | 5,375 | 6,995 | 7,208 | 7,306 | 6,930 | 6.1 | 4.6 | 5.0 |
| Oilseeds and products [1]........... | 8,584 | 10,229 | 27,265 | 28,319 | 31,571 | 30,004 | 26,620 | 16.7 | 23.5 | 19.1 |
| Soybeans......................... | 5,258 | 6,274 | 18,611 | 18,862 | 22,839 | 21,456 | 17,063 | 10.3 | 16.1 | 12.2 |
| Vegetable oils and waxes....... | 1,259 | 1,656 | 3,903 | 3,128 | 3,030 | 3,124 | 2,925 | 2.5 | 3.4 | 2.1 |
| Tobacco, unmanufactured......... | 1,204 | 990 | 1,168 | 1,109 | 1,085 | 1,010 | 1,049 | 2.3 | 1.0 | 0.8 |
| Cotton, excluding linters............ | 1,873 | 3,921 | 5,734 | 3,889 | 3,959 | 5,827 | 6,546 | 3.7 | 5.0 | 4.7 |
| Other................................. | 7,207 | 9,421 | 14,658 | 19,407 | 19,859 | 19,867 | 20,366 | 14.1 | 12.7 | 14.6 |

[1] Includes commodities not shown separately. [2] Includes pulses (legumes).

Source: U.S. Department of Agriculture, Foreign Agricultural Service, "Global Agricultural Trade System (GATS)," <http://www.fas.usda.gov/gats>, accessed August 2019.

## Table 889. Agricultural Exports—Value by World Region and Selected Country of Destination: 2000 to 2018

[51,265 represents $51,265,000,000. Includes Puerto Rico, U.S. territories, and shipments under foreign aid programs. Excludes fish, forest products, distilled liquors, manufactured tobacco, and products made from cotton; but includes raw tobacco, raw cotton, rubber, beer and wine, and processed agricultural products]

| Country | Value (mil. dol.) | | | | | | | Percent distribution | | |
|---|---|---|---|---|---|---|---|---|---|---|
| | 2000 | 2005 | 2010 | 2015 | 2016 | 2017 | 2018 | 2000 | 2010 | 2018 |
| **Total agricultural exports [1]**...... | **51,265** | **63,182** | **115,820** | **133,057** | **134,678** | **138,160** | **139,597** | **100.0** | **100.0** | **100.0** |
| Canada................................ | 7,643 | 10,619 | 16,897 | 20,988 | 20,307 | 20,608 | 20,871 | 14.9 | 14.6 | 15.0 |
| Mexico................................ | 6,410 | 9,429 | 14,585 | 17,695 | 17,827 | 18,598 | 19,096 | 12.5 | 12.6 | 13.7 |
| Caribbean............................ | 1,408 | 1,913 | 3,172 | 3,299 | 3,378 | 3,527 | 3,589 | 2.7 | 2.7 | 2.6 |
| Central America..................... | 1,121 | 1,589 | 2,904 | 3,728 | 3,864 | 3,742 | 4,203 | 2.2 | 2.5 | 3.0 |
| South America....................... | 1,704 | 1,943 | 4,240 | 6,405 | 6,605 | 6,447 | 7,652 | 3.3 | 3.7 | 5.5 |
| Asia, excluding Middle East [2]....... | 19,877 | 22,543 | 49,766 | 56,477 | 59,386 | 61,217 | 56,700 | 38.8 | 43.0 | 40.6 |
| Japan............................... | 9,292 | 7,931 | 11,784 | 11,135 | 11,030 | 11,897 | 12,930 | 18.1 | 10.2 | 9.3 |
| Korea, South...................... | 2,546 | 2,233 | 5,307 | 6,028 | 6,183 | 6,868 | 8,312 | 5.0 | 4.6 | 6.0 |
| Taiwan.............................. | 1,996 | 2,301 | 3,190 | 3,150 | 3,226 | 3,317 | 3,949 | 3.9 | 2.8 | 2.8 |
| China [3]............................ | 1,716 | 5,233 | 17,564 | 20,230 | 21,394 | 19,476 | 9,147 | 3.3 | 15.2 | 6.6 |
| Indonesia........................... | 668 | 958 | 2,246 | 2,190 | 2,678 | 2,892 | 3,097 | 1.3 | 1.9 | 2.2 |
| Europe [2]............................ | 7,654 | 8,361 | 11,365 | 14,096 | 13,461 | 13,807 | 15,472 | 14.9 | 9.8 | 11.1 |
| European Union [4].................. | 6,516 | 7,059 | 8,925 | 12,133 | 11,523 | 11,438 | 13,510 | 12.7 | 7.7 | 9.7 |
| Russia.............................. | 580 | 972 | 1,132 | 426 | 250 | 193 | 233 | 1.1 | 1.0 | 0.2 |
| Middle East.......................... | 2,323 | 2,844 | 5,993 | 5,516 | 5,625 | 6,083 | 6,281 | 4.5 | 5.2 | 4.5 |
| Africa [2]............................. | 2,308 | 2,773 | 5,725 | 3,553 | 3,355 | 3,501 | 4,545 | 4.5 | 4.9 | 3.3 |
| Egypt............................... | 1,050 | 819 | 2,095 | 1,052 | 741 | 770 | 1,914 | 2.0 | 1.8 | 1.4 |
| Oceania.............................. | 490 | 742 | 1,389 | 1,996 | 1,800 | 1,953 | 2,036 | 1.0 | 1.2 | 1.5 |

[1] Totals include transshipments through Canada, but transshipments are not distributed by country after 2000. [2] Includes areas not shown separately. [3] China includes Macao; however, Hong Kong remains separate economically until 2050 and is not included. [4] For consistency, data for all years are shown on the basis of 28 countries in the European Union; see footnote 3, Table 1396.

Source: U.S. Department of Agriculture, Foreign Agricultural Service, "Global Agricultural Trade System (GATS)," <http://www.fas.usda.gov/gats>, accessed August 2019.

## Table 890. Cropland Used for Crops and Acres Harvested: 1990 to 2018

[In millions of acres, except as indicated (341 represents 341,000,000)]

| Item | 1990 | 2000 | 2010 | 2013 | 2014 | 2015 | 2016 | 2017 | 2018 (P) |
|---|---|---|---|---|---|---|---|---|---|
| **Cropland used for crops**.................. | **341** | **345** | **335** | **336** | **341** | **337** | **336** | **338** | **339** |
| Index (1977 = 100).......................... | 90 | 91 | 89 | 89 | 90 | (NA) | (NA) | (NA) | (NA) |
| Cropland harvested [1]......................... | 310 | 314 | 315 | 311 | 318 | 316 | 317 | 314 | 312 |
| Crop failure................................... | 6 | 11 | 5 | 12 | 10 | 7 | 7 | 9 | 11 |
| Cultivated summer fallow.................... | 25 | 20 | 14 | 13 | 14 | 13 | 12 | 15 | 16 |
| Cropland idled by all federal programs [2,3]................................ | 62 | 31 | 31 | 27 | 25 | 24 | 24 | 23 | 23 |
| **Acres of crops harvested [4]**............... | **322** | **325** | **322** | **321** | **325** | **323** | **323** | **320** | **318** |

NA Not available. P Preliminary. [1] Land supporting one or more harvested crops. [2] Beginning in 2000, includes only the Conservation Reserve Program; all other federal acreage reduction programs were eliminated by the Federal Agricultural Improvement Act of 1996. [3] Data are for fiscal years. [4] Area in principal crops harvested plus acreages in fruits, vegetables for sale, tree nuts, and other minor crops. Acres are counted twice for land that is double cropped.

Source: U.S. Department of Agriculture, Economic Research Service, *Agricultural Resources and Environmental Indicators*, 2006, and earlier reports; "Major Land Uses," <http://www.ers.usda.gov/data-products/major-land-uses.aspx>, accessed September 2019; and Farm Service Agency, "CRP Enrollment and Rental Payments by State, 1986-2017," <http://www.fsa.usda.gov/programs-and-services/conservation-programs/reports-and-statistics/index>, accessed September 2019.

## Table 891. Cotton, Hay, and Potatoes—Supply and Use: 2000 to 2018

[13.1 represents 13,100,000. Marketing year beginning January 1 for potatoes, May 1 for hay, and August 1 for cotton. Acreage, production, and yield of all crops periodically revised on basis of census data]

| Item | Unit | 2000 | 2005 | 2010 | 2015 | 2016 | 2017 | 2018 |
|---|---|---|---|---|---|---|---|---|
| COTTON | | | | | | | | |
| Acreage harvested............... | Million | 13.1 | 13.8 | 10.7 | 8.1 | 9.5 | 11.1 | 10.2 |
| Yield per acre..................... | Pounds | 632 | 831 | 812 | 766 | 867 | 905 | 864 |
| Production...................... | Mil. bales [4] | 17.2 | 23.9 | 18.1 | 12.9 | 17.2 | 20.9 | 18.4 |
| Imports......................... | Mil. bales [4] | – | – | | | | | |
| Total supply [1]................. | Mil. bales [4] | 21.1 | 29.4 | 21.1 | 16.6 | 21.0 | 23.7 | [8] 22.7 |
| Exports........................ | Mil. bales [4] | 6.7 | 17.7 | 14.4 | 9.2 | 14.9 | 15.8 | [8] 15.0 |
| Total use [2]..................... | Mil. bales [4] | 15.6 | 23.5 | 18.3 | 12.6 | 18.2 | 19.1 | [8] 18.3 |
| Ending stocks.................. | Mil. bales [4] | 6.0 | 6.1 | 2.6 | 3.8 | 2.8 | 4.3 | [8] 4.3 |
| Price per unit [3]................ | Cents/lb. | 51.6 | 49.7 | 84.6 | 64.5 | 70.5 | 71.9 | 76.0 |
| Value of production............. | Mil. dol. | 4,260 | 5,695 | 7,347 | 3,989 | 5,814 | 7,223 | 6,712 |
| HAY | | | | | | | | |
| Acreage harvested............... | Million | 60.4 | 61.6 | 59.6 | 54.5 | 53.2 | 52.8 | 52.8 |
| Yield per acre..................... | Sh. tons | 2.5 | 2.4 | 2.4 | 2.5 | 2.5 | 2.4 | 2.3 |
| Production....................... | Mil. sh. tons | 154 | 150 | 145 | 135 | 134 | 128 | 124 |
| Price per unit [5, 6]................ | Dol./ton | 84.6 | 98.2 | 114.0 | 145.0 | 129.0 | 142.0 | 164.0 |
| Value of production............. | Mil. dol. | 11,557 | 12,534 | 14,607 | 16,568 | 15,477 | 16,109 | 17,048 |
| POTATOES | | | | | | | | |
| Acreage harvested............... | Million | 1.3 | 1.1 | 1.0 | 1.1 | 1.0 | 1.0 | 1.0 |
| Yield per acre..................... | Cwt. [7] | 381 | 390 | 401 | 419 | 434 | 432 | 444 |
| Production...................... | Mil. cwt. [7] | 514 | 424 | 405 | 449 | 450 | 451 | 454 |
| Price per unit [3].................. | Dol./cwt. [7] | 5.08 | 7.04 | 9.20 | 8.79 | 9.08 | 9.17 | 8.48 |
| Value of production............. | Mil. dol. | 2,590 | 2,982 | 3,725 | 3,942 | 4,091 | 4,133 | 3,853 |

– Represents zero or rounds to less than half the unit of measurement shown. [1] Comprises beginning stocks, production, and imports. [2] Includes feed, residual, and other domestic uses not shown separately. [3] Marketing year average price. U.S. prices are computed by weighting U.S. monthly prices by estimated monthly marketings and do not include an allowance for outstanding loans and government purchases and payments. [4] Bales of 480 pounds, net weight. [5] Prices are for hay sold baled. [6] Season average prices received by farmers. U.S. prices are computed by weighting state prices by estimated sales. [7] Cwt = hundredweight (100 pounds). [8] Preliminary estimates.

Source: U.S. Department of Agriculture, National Agricultural Statistics Service, "Quick Stats," <http://quickstats.nass.usda.gov/>; and U.S. Department of Agriculture, Economic Research Service, "Feed Grains Database" and "Cotton and Wool Yearbook," <http://www.ers.usda.gov/data-products.aspx>; accessed August 2019.

## Table 892. Horticultural Specialty Crop Operations, Value of Sales, and Total Land Area Used to Grow Horticultural Crops: 2014

[Horticultural specialty operation is defined as any place that produced and sold $10,000 or more of horticultural specialty products. Excludes mushrooms as well as grass seeds, vegetables, and fruits grown in the open. See source for more information]

| Item | Operations | Value of sales (1,000) | Total land area [1] | | | |
|---|---|---|---|---|---|---|
| | | | Green-houses (1,000 square feet) | Shade structures (1,000 square feet) | Natural shade (acres) | Area in open (acres) [2] |
| **Horticultural specialty crops, total**..................... | **23,221** | **13,789,048** | **894,907** | **429,708** | **5,404** | **497,339** |
| Annual bedding/garden plants............................. | 7,964 | 2,567,534 | 282,790 | 17,537 | 195 | 7,294 |
| Herbaceous perennial plants.............................. | 6,291 | 944,850 | 31,262 | 8,857 | 292 | 5,397 |
| Potted flowering plants for indoor or patio use............ | 4,059 | 1,084,274 | 63,039 | 21,576 | 16 | 1,794 |
| Foliage plants for indoor or patio use..................... | 2,644 | 721,889 | 40,164 | 104,013 | 47 | 1,828 |
| Cut flowers............................................. | 1,998 | 462,098 | 57,514 | 11,378 | 97 | 15,931 |
| Cut cultivated greens................................... | 728 | 99,040 | 3,269 | 166,717 | 2,159 | 2,295 |
| Nursery stock sold...................................... | 8,226 | 4,266,631 | 203,861 | 83,640 | 2,224 | 302,202 |
| Propagative material [3]................................. | 1,067 | 695,126 | 29,492 | 2,459 | 94 | 12,346 |
| Sod, sprigs, or plugs.................................... | 1,289 | 1,138,465 | 707 | 36 | 13 | 55,019 |
| Dried bulbs, corms, rhizomes, and tubers................. | 204 | 74,014 | 359 | 186 | 8 | 5,309 |
| Food crops grown under protection....................... | 2,521 | 796,664 | 84,507 | 2,366 | 75 | 5,330 |
| Transplants for commercial vegetable production [4]...... | 693 | 371,817 | 26,638 | (D) | (D) | 7,618 |
| Vegetable seeds........................................ | 385 | 135,122 | 510 | (D) | (D) | 32,620 |
| Flower seeds........................................... | 169 | 31,607 | 172 | 14 | (D) | 4,869 |
| Aquatic plants.......................................... | 345 | 20,205 | 878 | 45 | 2 | 1,274 |
| Cut Christmas trees..................................... | 3,352 | 366,632 | 516 | 170 | 29 | 26,500 |
| Short rotation woody crops............................... | 49 | 1,845 | (NA) | (NA) | (NA) | (NA) |
| Tobacco transplants [5].................................. | 183 | 11,236 | (NA) | (NA) | (NA) | (NA) |

D Withheld to avoid disclosure. NA Not available. [1] Total land area represents the land utilized on the operation as the area used for horticultural production. Includes volume of stacked benches and stacked pots and the area used to produce multiple crop types. [2] Excludes acres in production for Christmas trees or sod, sprigs, or plugs. [3] Includes cuttings, plug seedlings, liners, tissue cultured plantlets, and prefinished plants. As of 2014, this data includes seedlings for reforestation and may not be comparable to 2009 data. [4] Includes strawberries. [5] Includes transplants grown for sale; excludes transplants for the farmer's own use.

Source: U.S. Department of Agriculture, National Agricultural Statistics Service, *2014 Census of Horticultural Specialties,* Vol. 3, December 2015. See also <http://www.agcensus.usda.gov/Publications/Census_of_Horticulture_Specialties/>.

## Table 893. Corn—Acreage, Production, and Value by Leading States: 2016 to 2018

[86,748 represents 86,748,000. One bushel of corn (bu.) = 56 pounds. State value of production is computed by multiplying the state price by its production; acreage harvested and production value for the United States is the sum of state values]

| State | Acreage harvested (1,000 acres) | | | Yield per acre (bu.) | | | Production (mil. bu.) | | | Price per unit ($/bu.) | | | Value of production (mil. dol.) | | |
|---|---|---|---|---|---|---|---|---|---|---|---|---|---|---|---|
| | 2016 | 2017 | 2018 | 2016 | 2017 | 2018 | 2016 | 2017 | 2018 | 2016 | 2017 | 2018 | 2016 | 2017 | 2018 |
| U.S. [1].... | 86,748 | 82,733 | 81,740 | 175 | 177 | 176 | 15,148 | 14,609 | 14,420 | 3.36 | 3.36 | 3.55 | 51,304 | 49,568 | 51,481 |
| IA......... | 13,500 | 12,900 | 12,800 | 203 | 202 | 196 | 2,741 | 2,606 | 2,509 | 3.30 | 3.31 | 3.50 | 9,044 | 8,625 | 8,781 |
| IL......... | 11,450 | 10,950 | 10,850 | 197 | 201 | 210 | 2,256 | 2,201 | 2,279 | 3.43 | 3.41 | 3.60 | 7,737 | 7,505 | 8,203 |
| NE........ | 9,550 | 9,300 | 9,310 | 178 | 181 | 192 | 1,700 | 1,683 | 1,788 | 3.32 | 3.35 | 3.55 | 5,644 | 5,639 | 6,346 |
| MN........ | 8,000 | 7,630 | 7,490 | 193 | 194 | 182 | 1,544 | 1,480 | 1,363 | 3.21 | 3.18 | 3.40 | 4,956 | 4,707 | 4,635 |
| IN......... | 5,470 | 5,200 | 5,200 | 173 | 180 | 189 | 946 | 936 | 983 | 3.63 | 3.56 | 3.60 | 3,435 | 3,332 | 3,538 |
| SD......... | 5,130 | 5,080 | 4,860 | 161 | 145 | 160 | 826 | 737 | 778 | 3.09 | 3.09 | 3.30 | 2,552 | 2,276 | 2,566 |
| KS........ | 4,920 | 5,200 | 5,000 | 142 | 132 | 129 | 699 | 686 | 645 | 3.20 | 3.28 | 3.60 | 2,236 | 2,251 | 2,322 |
| OH........ | 3,300 | 3,150 | 3,300 | 159 | 177 | 187 | 525 | 558 | 617 | 3.61 | 3.61 | 3.65 | 1,894 | 2,013 | 2,252 |
| WI........ | 3,220 | 2,930 | 3,170 | 178 | 174 | 172 | 573 | 510 | 545 | 3.28 | 3.30 | 3.50 | 1,880 | 1,682 | 1,908 |
| MO........ | 3,500 | 3,250 | 3,330 | 163 | 170 | 140 | 571 | 553 | 466 | 3.40 | 3.41 | 3.60 | 1,940 | 1,884 | 1,678 |
| ND........ | 3,270 | 3,230 | 2,930 | 158 | 139 | 153 | 517 | 449 | 448 | 3.01 | 3.04 | 3.30 | 1,555 | 1,365 | 1,479 |
| MI........ | 2,040 | 1,890 | 1,940 | 157 | 159 | 153 | 320 | 301 | 297 | 3.44 | 3.46 | 3.55 | 1,102 | 1,040 | 1,054 |
| KY........ | 1,400 | 1,220 | 1,230 | 159 | 178 | 175 | 223 | 217 | 215 | 3.74 | 3.69 | 3.80 | 833 | 801 | 818 |
| TX........ | 2,550 | 2,240 | 1,750 | 127 | 140 | 108 | 324 | 314 | 189 | 3.71 | 3.70 | 4.10 | 1,201 | 1,160 | 775 |
| CO........ | 1,170 | 1,300 | 1,200 | 137 | 143 | 130 | 160 | 186 | 156 | 3.42 | 3.37 | 3.75 | 548 | 626 | 585 |
| PA........ | 950 | 920 | 950 | 129 | 161 | 140 | 123 | 148 | 133 | 4.04 | 3.87 | 4.05 | 495 | 573 | 539 |
| TN........ | 830 | 710 | 690 | 151 | 171 | 168 | 125 | 121 | 116 | 3.66 | 3.55 | 3.75 | 459 | 431 | 435 |
| AR........ | 745 | 595 | 645 | 171 | 183 | 181 | 127 | 109 | 117 | 3.69 | 3.64 | 3.70 | 470 | 396 | 432 |
| NY........ | 570 | 485 | 645 | 129 | 161 | 159 | 74 | 78 | 103 | 3.90 | 4.07 | 4.10 | 287 | 318 | 420 |
| NC........ | 940 | 840 | 830 | 129 | 142 | 113 | 121 | 119 | 94 | 4.07 | 4.24 | 4.35 | 494 | 506 | 408 |

[1] Includes other states, not shown separately.

Source: U.S. Department of Agriculture, National Agricultural Statistics Service, "Quick Stats," <http://quickstats.nass.usda.gov/>, accessed May 2019. See also <http://www.nass.usda.gov/Publications>.

## Table 894. Soybeans—Acreage, Production, and Value by Leading States: 2016 to 2018

[82,706 represents 82,706,000. One bushel of soybeans (bu.) = 60 pounds. State value of production is computed by multiplying the state price by its production; value for the United States is the sum of state values]

| State | Acreage harvested (1,000 acres) | | | Yield per acre (bu.) | | | Production (mil. bu.) | | | Price per unit ($/bu.) | | | Value of production (mil. dol.) | | |
|---|---|---|---|---|---|---|---|---|---|---|---|---|---|---|---|
| | 2016 | 2017 | 2018 | 2016 | 2017 | 2018 | 2016 | 2017 | 2018 | 2016 | 2017 | 2018 | 2016 | 2017 | 2018 |
| U.S. [1]... | 82,706 | 89,542 | 88,110 | 52 | 49 | 52 | 4,296 | 4,412 | 4,544 | 9.47 | 9.33 | 8.60 | 40,695 | 41,309 | 39,134 |
| IL........ | 10,050 | 10,550 | 10,750 | 59 | 58 | 65 | 593 | 612 | 699 | 9.78 | 9.60 | 8.95 | 5,799 | 5,874 | 6,254 |
| IA........ | 9,440 | 9,940 | 9,910 | 60 | 57 | 57 | 566 | 567 | 565 | 9.34 | 9.25 | 8.60 | 5,290 | 5,241 | 4,858 |
| MN....... | 7,490 | 8,090 | 7,710 | 52 | 48 | 51 | 389 | 384 | 389 | 9.23 | 9.17 | 8.55 | 3,595 | 3,524 | 3,329 |
| IN........ | 5,630 | 5,940 | 5,920 | 58 | 54 | 59 | 324 | 321 | 346 | 9.69 | 9.61 | 8.75 | 3,137 | 3,083 | 3,030 |
| NE........ | 5,150 | 5,670 | 5,650 | 61 | 58 | 59 | 314 | 326 | 333 | 9.18 | 9.08 | 8.30 | 2,884 | 2,960 | 2,767 |
| OH....... | 4,840 | 5,090 | 4,980 | 55 | 50 | 58 | 264 | 252 | 289 | 9.66 | 9.62 | 8.75 | 2,548 | 2,424 | 2,527 |
| MO...... | 5,540 | 5,910 | 5,800 | 49 | 50 | 45 | 271 | 293 | 261 | 9.60 | 9.48 | 8.60 | 2,606 | 2,773 | 2,245 |
| SD....... | 5,170 | 5,610 | 5,580 | 50 | 43 | 46 | 256 | 241 | 257 | 9.03 | 8.94 | 8.05 | 2,311 | 2,157 | 2,066 |
| ND....... | 5,990 | 7,050 | 6,860 | 42 | 35 | 36 | 249 | 243 | 244 | 8.97 | 8.88 | 8.30 | 2,230 | 2,160 | 2,021 |
| KS....... | 4,010 | 5,110 | 4,700 | 48 | 38 | 44 | 192 | 192 | 204 | 9.26 | 9.00 | 7.95 | 1,782 | 1,725 | 1,625 |
| AR....... | 3,090 | 3,500 | 3,240 | 47 | 51 | 51 | 145 | 179 | 165 | 9.83 | 9.77 | 9.00 | 1,428 | 1,744 | 1,487 |
| MS....... | 2,020 | 2,170 | 2,190 | 48 | 53 | 55 | 97 | 115 | 119 | 9.94 | 9.74 | 9.25 | 964 | 1,120 | 1,104 |
| MI....... | 2,060 | 2,270 | 2,280 | 51 | 43 | 48 | 104 | 96 | 109 | 9.51 | 9.39 | 8.60 | 989 | 906 | 941 |
| KY....... | 1,780 | 1,940 | 1,990 | 50 | 53 | 52 | 89 | 103 | 103 | 9.87 | 9.70 | 8.80 | 878 | 997 | 911 |
| WI....... | 1,950 | 2,140 | 2,160 | 55 | 48 | 49 | 107 | 102 | 106 | 9.36 | 9.34 | 8.60 | 1,004 | 949 | 910 |

[1] Includes other states, not shown separately.

Source: U.S. Department of Agriculture, National Agricultural Statistics Service, "Quick Stats," <http://quickstats.nass.usda.gov/>, accessed May 2019. See also <http://www.nass.usda.gov/Publications>.

## Table 895. Wheat—Acreage, Production, and Value by Leading States: 2016 to 2018

[43,848 represents 43,848,000. One bushel of wheat (bu.) = 60 pounds. State value of production is computed by multiplying the price per unit by total production, for each state; value for the United States is the sum of production values for all states]

| State | Acreage harvested (1,000 acres) | | | Yield per acre (bu.) | | | Production (mil. bu.) | | | Price per unit ($/bu.) | | | Value of production (mil. dol.) | | |
|---|---|---|---|---|---|---|---|---|---|---|---|---|---|---|---|
| | 2016 | 2017 | 2018 | 2016 | 2017 | 2018 | 2016 | 2017 | 2018 | 2016 | 2017 | 2018 | 2016 | 2017 | 2018 |
| U.S. [1]...... | 43,848 | 37,555 | 39,605 | 53 | 46 | 48 | 2,309 | 1,741 | 1,884 | 3.89 | 4.72 | 5.15 | 9,151 | 8,235 | 9,693 |
| ND......... | 7,405 | 6,260 | 7,635 | 45 | 38 | 48 | 333 | 237 | 363 | 4.68 | 5.74 | 5.15 | 1,558 | 1,361 | 1,872 |
| KS......... | 8,200 | 6,950 | 7,300 | 57 | 48 | 38 | 467 | 334 | 277 | 3.20 | 4.07 | 4.95 | 1,496 | 1,358 | 1,373 |
| MT......... | 4,975 | 4,665 | 5,165 | 42 | 27 | 38 | 211 | 127 | 198 | 4.43 | 5.34 | 5.30 | 934 | 680 | 1,047 |
| WA......... | 2,200 | 2,140 | 2,165 | 72 | 67 | 71 | 157 | 143 | 153 | 4.16 | 4.85 | 5.45 | 654 | 691 | 835 |
| ID......... | 1,125 | 1,109 | 1,136 | 91 | 82 | 92 | 103 | 91 | 104 | 4.10 | 4.64 | 5.10 | 421 | 421 | 532 |
| MN......... | 1,268 | 1,135 | 1,575 | 59 | 67 | 59 | 75 | 76 | 93 | 4.69 | 5.76 | 5.35 | 351 | 437 | 497 |
| SD......... | 2,157 | 1,196 | 1,628 | 52 | 35 | 44 | 111 | 42 | 72 | 4.15 | 5.52 | 5.30 | 462 | 230 | 383 |
| OK......... | 3,500 | 2,900 | 2,500 | 39 | 34 | 28 | 137 | 99 | 70 | 3.44 | 3.98 | 5.15 | 470 | 392 | 361 |
| CO......... | 2,200 | 2,029 | 1,954 | 48 | 43 | 36 | 106 | 88 | 71 | 3.08 | 3.88 | 4.65 | 326 | 340 | 328 |

[1] Includes other states, not shown separately.

Source: U.S. Department of Agriculture, National Agricultural Statistics Service, "Quick Stats," <http://quickstats.nass.usda.gov/>, accessed May 2019. See also <http://www.nass.usda.gov/Publications>.

# Table 896. Commercial Vegetable and Other Specified Crops—Area, Production, and Value: 2016 to 2018

[7 represents 7,000. Except as noted, relates to commercial production for fresh market and processing combined. Includes market garden areas but excludes minor producing acreage in minor producing states. Excludes production for home use in farm and nonfarm gardens. Value is for season or crop year and should not be confused with calendar-year income. Hundredweight (cwt.) is the unit used for fresh market yield and production and is equal to one hundred pounds]

| Crop | Area harvested (1,000 acres) | | | Utilized production [1] (1,000 cwt.) | | | Value of production [2] (mil. dol.) | | |
|---|---|---|---|---|---|---|---|---|---|
| | 2016 | 2017 | 2018 | 2016 | 2017 | 2018 | 2016 | 2017 | 2018 |
| Artichokes............... | 7 | 7 | 7 | 986 | 936 | 1,001 | 78 | 66 | 63 |
| Asparagus............... | 26 | 26 | 22 | 833 | 839 | 775 | 92 | 101 | 88 |
| Beans, snap............. | 237 | 212 | 222 | 20,001 | 18,040 | 17,565 | 404 | 349 | 364 |
| Beans, dry edible............. | 1,558 | 2,023 | 2,016 | [3] 28,703 | [3] 35,961 | [3] 37,494 | 863 | 1,006 | 978 |
| Broccoli................. | 131 | 129 | 114 | 22,466 | 20,384 | 17,273 | 847 | 926 | 739 |
| Cabbage................. | 57 | 61 | 54 | 18,918 | 19,765 | 17,391 | 448 | 431 | 409 |
| Cantaloupes............. | 59 | 63 | 61 | 15,125 | 15,392 | 14,603 | 261 | 296 | 332 |
| Carrots.................. | 78 | 76 | 80 | 31,739 | 30,996 | 32,936 | 787 | 696 | 732 |
| Cauliflower.............. | 42 | 46 | 44 | 7,461 | 9,050 | 9,278 | 416 | 416 | 425 |
| Celery.................. | 33 | 32 | 30 | 17,676 | 16,045 | 17,782 | 319 | 322 | 444 |
| Corn, sweet............. | 478 | 465 | 473 | 72,637 | 75,369 | 73,201 | 871 | 892 | 859 |
| Fresh market........... | (NA) | (NA) | (NA) | 23,037 | 23,613 | 22,368 | 654 | 689 | 656 |
| Processed............. | (NA) | (NA) | (NA) | 49,600 | 51,756 | 50,833 | 217 | 203 | 203 |
| Cucumbers.............. | 115 | 117 | 111 | 17,321 | 18,887 | 15,421 | 345 | 392 | 333 |
| Lettuce, head........... | 142 | 141 | 120 | 53,841 | 49,396 | 40,561 | 1,435 | 1,775 | 1,220 |
| Lettuce, leaf............ | 69 | 67 | 69 | 15,486 | 13,675 | 11,277 | 715 | 833 | 585 |
| Lettuce, Romaine........... | 105 | 117 | 100 | 33,894 | 36,308 | 29,029 | 1,032 | 1,628 | 901 |
| Onions................. | 148 | 152 | 130 | 77,225 | 80,561 | 70,886 | 1,059 | 1,042 | 817 |
| Peas, green............. | 139 | 134 | 131 | 6,124 | 6,012 | 5,069 | 83 | 85 | 65 |
| Peppers, bell............ | 44 | 42 | 40 | 14,699 | 14,193 | 12,864 | 486 | 626 | 533 |
| Pumpkins............... | 75 | 72 | 66 | 17,097 | 15,601 | 14,792 | 232 | 197 | 190 |
| Spinach................ | 58 | 65 | 61 | 8,581 | 8,091 | 8,481 | 378 | 471 | 423 |
| Squash................. | 46 | 46 | 45 | 8,156 | 7,970 | 7,250 | 200 | 236 | 193 |
| Tomatoes............... | 349 | 311 | 322 | 283,912 | 240,055 | 275,476 | 2,017 | 1,678 | 1,856 |
| Fresh market........... | (NA) | (NA) | (NA) | 20,496 | 20,970 | 19,623 | 867 | 772 | 814 |
| Processed............. | (NA) | (NA) | (NA) | 263,416 | 219,085 | 255,853 | 1,150 | 906 | 1,042 |
| Watermelons............ | 112 | 108 | 111 | 39,950 | 40,286 | 38,849 | 547 | 594 | 657 |

NA Not available. [1] Utilized production is the amount of a crop sold plus the quantities used at home or held in storage. It is equal to the difference between the total production and what was harvested but not sold. [2] Fresh market vegetables valued at f.o.b. (free on board) shipping point. Processing vegetables are equivalent returns at packinghouse door. [3] Total production.

Source: U.S. Department of Agriculture, National Agricultural Statistics Service, "Quick Stats," <http://quickstats.nass.usda.gov/>, accessed May 2019.

# Table 897. Fruits and Nuts: Utilized Production and Value, 2010 to 2018; and Leading Producing States, 2018

[4,603 represents 4,603,000]

| Fruits and nuts | Utilized production [1] (1,000 tons) | | | | Value of utilized production (mil. dol.) | | | | Leading states in order of production, 2018 |
|---|---|---|---|---|---|---|---|---|---|
| | 2010 | 2015 | 2017 | 2018 | 2010 | 2015 | 2017 | 2018 | |
| **FRUITS** | | | | | | | | | |
| Apples [2]............................. | 4,603 | 4,983 | 5,605 | 4,945 | 2,311 | 3,350 | 3,601 | 3,014 | WA, NY, MI |
| Avocados.......................... | 174 | 229 | 187 | 184 | 479 | 433 | 392 | 400 | CA, FL, HI |
| Blackberries, cultivated (OR).... | 22 | 26 | 20 | (NA) | 33 | 38 | 31 | (NA) | OR |
| Blueberries......................... | 247 | 330 | 290 | 303 | 644 | 873 | 833 | 820 | WA, OR, MI |
| Cherries, sweet.................... | 308 | 334 | 433 | 342 | 716 | 751 | 892 | 638 | WA, OR, CA |
| Cranberries........................ | 340 | 423 | 417 | 442 | 299 | 262 | 252 | 222 | WI, MA, OR |
| Dates.............................. | 29 | 39 | 43 | 40 | 37 | 61 | 151 | 152 | CA, AZ |
| Figs (fresh) (CA).................. | 41 | 32 | 31 | (NA) | 22 | 25 | 29 | (NA) | (NA) |
| Grapefruit......................... | 1,238 | 910 | 698 | 509 | 291 | 216 | 257 | 208 | TX, FL, CA |
| Grapes............................ | 7,430 | 7,621 | 7,383 | 7,596 | 4,024 | 5,914 | 6,508 | 6,615 | CA, WA |
| Kiwifruit (CA)...................... | 33 | 21 | 33 | 38 | 25 | 31 | 35 | 33 | CA |
| Lemons............................ | 882 | 904 | 882 | 888 | 395 | 697 | 763 | 716 | CA, AZ |
| Nectarines......................... | 233 | 173 | 141 | 120 | 129 | 158 | 128 | 105 | CA, WA |
| Olives (CA)........................ | 206 | 179 | 192 | 53 | 137 | 160 | 187 | 41 | CA |
| Oranges........................... | 8,243 | 6,353 | 5,088 | 3,875 | 1,997 | 1,963 | 1,944 | 1,830 | FL, CA, TX |
| Peaches........................... | 1,130 | 825 | 694 | 638 | 617 | 606 | 600 | 511 | CA, SC, GA |
| Pears.............................. | 813 | 803 | 731 | 800 | 387 | 494 | 519 | 429 | WA, OR, CA |
| Plums (CA)........................ | 142 | 105 | 115 | 99 | 79 | 105 | 115 | 93 | CA |
| Prunes (dried basis) (CA)........ | 390 | 319 | 326 | 280 | 176 | 226 | 208 | 195 | CA |
| Raspberries........................ | 75 | 145 | 113 | 109 | 259 | 670 | 494 | 367 | CA, WA |
| Strawberries....................... | 1,426 | 1,533 | 1,359 | 1,428 | 2,261 | 2,239 | 2,896 | 2,671 | CA, FL, NC |
| Tangelos (FL)...................... | 41 | 30 | (NA) | (NA) | 7 | 9 | (NA) | (NA) | (NA) |
| Tangerines and mandarins....... | 596 | 863 | 1,029 | 804 | 275 | 468 | 568 | 576 | CA, FL |
| **NUTS [3]** | | | | | | | | | |
| Almonds (CA)...................... | 1,414 | 1,630 | 1,846 | 1,840 | 2,903 | 5,869 | 5,604 | 5,468 | CA |
| Hazelnuts (OR)..................... | 28 | 31 | 32 | 51 | 67 | 87 | 74 | 92 | OR |
| Macadamia nuts (HI).............. | 20 | 24 | 25 | 18 | 30 | 46 | 54 | 42 | HI |
| Pecans............................ | 147 | 127 | 152 | 122 | 675 | 560 | 709 | 425 | NM, GA, TX |
| Pistachios (CA).................... | 261 | 135 | 300 | 494 | 1,159 | 888 | 1,015 | 2,616 | CA |
| Walnuts (CA)...................... | 504 | 606 | 630 | 676 | 1,028 | 1,012 | 1,569 | 879 | CA |

NA Not available. [1] Excludes quantities not harvested or not marketed. Utilized production is the amount sold plus the quantities used at home or held in storage. [2] Production in commercial orchards with 100 or more bearing-age trees. [3] In-shell equivalent.

Source: U.S. Department of Agriculture, National Agricultural Statistics Service, *Noncitrus Fruits and Nuts Final Estimates 2007-2012*, October 2014; *Citrus Fruits Final Estimates, 2008-2012*, August 2014; *Citrus Fruits 2019 Summary*, August 2019; and *Noncitrus Fruits and Nuts 2018 Summary*, June 2019. See also <https://www.nass.usda.gov/Data_and_Statistics/index.php>.

## Table 898. Tree Nuts—Supply and Use: 2000 to 2017

[In thousands of pounds (shelled) (331,466 represents 331,466,000). Season begins in July for hazelnuts, August for almonds, September for pistachios, and October for pecans. For walnuts, season began in August through 2007; as of 2008, season begins September 1]

| Year | Beginning stocks | Marketable production [1] | Imports | Supply, total | Consumption | Exports | Ending stocks |
|---|---|---|---|---|---|---|---|
| Total nuts: | | | | | | | |
| 2000 | 331,466 | 1,127,940 | 293,047 | 1,752,452 | 733,765 | 780,988 | 237,699 |
| 2010 | 422,055 | 2,482,242 | 485,098 | 3,389,395 | 1,195,946 | 1,786,058 | 407,391 |
| 2015 | 585,250 | 2,665,812 | 668,081 | 3,919,144 | 1,308,364 | 2,035,232 | 575,549 |
| 2016 | 575,549 | 3,328,244 | 697,217 | 4,601,009 | 1,572,145 | 2,381,451 | 647,413 |
| 2017, total [2,3] | **647,413** | **3,182,268** | **737,727** | **4,567,408** | **1,635,520** | **2,396,353** | **535,535** |
| Almonds | 398,677 | 2,215,266 | 32,528 | 2,637,443 | 743,835 | 1,534,595 | 359,013 |
| Pecans | 69,489 | (NA) | 136,000 | 341,542 | 147,014 | 115,000 | 79,527 |
| Pistachios | 126,769 | 226,915 | 1,582 | 355,266 | 136,796 | 178,922 | 39,548 |
| Hazelnuts | 3,106 | 25,515 | 13,775 | 42,396 | 20,967 | 20,028 | 1,401 |
| Walnuts | 49,372 | 556,259 | 12,740 | 618,370 | 162,715 | 399,609 | 56,046 |

NA Not available. [1] Utilized production minus inedibles and noncommercial usage. [2] Includes macadamia nuts, Brazil nuts, cashew nuts, pine nuts, chestnuts, and mixed nuts, not shown separately. [3] Data are preliminary.

Source: U.S. Department of Agriculture, Economic Research Service, "Fruit and Tree Nut Yearbook Tables," <http://www.ers.usda.gov/data-products/fruit-and-tree-nut-data/yearbook-tables.aspx>, accessed November 2018. See also <http://www.ers.usda.gov/data-products/fruit-and-tree-nut-data.aspx>.

## Table 899. Honey—Number of Bee Colonies, Yield, and Production: 1990 to 2018

[3,220 represents 3,220,000. Includes only beekeepers with five or more colonies. Colonies were not included if honey was not harvested]

| Year | Honey-producing colonies [1] (1,000) | Yield per colony (pounds) | Production (1,000 pounds) | Average price per pound (cents) | Value of production (1,000 dollars) |
|---|---|---|---|---|---|
| 1990 | 3,220 | 61.7 | 198,674 | 54 | 106,688 |
| 2000 | 2,622 | 84.0 | 220,286 | 60 | 132,865 |
| 2005 | 2,409 | 72.5 | 174,614 | 92 | 160,994 |
| 2010 | 2,692 | 65.6 | 176,462 | 162 | 285,692 |
| 2013 | 2,641 | 56.6 | 149,550 | 214 | 320,037 |
| 2014 | 2,741 | 65.1 | 178,310 | 217 | 386,933 |
| 2015 | 2,661 | 58.9 | 156,705 | 208 | 325,946 |
| 2016 | 2,780 | 58.4 | 162,246 | 212 | 343,962 |
| 2017 | 2,684 | 55.5 | 149,025 | 220 | 327,855 |
| 2018 | 2,803 | 54.4 | 152,348 | 217 | 333,482 |

[1] Honey producing colonies are the maximum number of colonies from which honey was taken during the year. It is possible to take honey from colonies which did not survive the entire year.

Source: U.S. Department of Agriculture, National Agricultural Statistics Service, *Honey–Final Estimates 2013-2017*, June 2019, and earlier editions; and *Honey*, May 2019. See also <http://www.nass.usda.gov/Surveys/Guide_to_NASS_Surveys/Bee_and_Honey>.

## Table 900. Vegetables and Dry Edible Beans—Supply and Utilization: 2000 to 2018

[40,556 represents 40,556,000,000. Data for calendar year except where noted. Food availability is a proxy for food consumption. Vegetable data excludes melons]

| Item | Unit | 2000 | 2005 | 2010 | 2015 | 2016 | 2017 | 2018 (P) |
|---|---|---|---|---|---|---|---|---|
| VEGETABLES, FRESH MARKET | | | | | | | | |
| Production | Mil. lbs. | 40,556 | 40,332 | 38,028 | 35,983 | 39,964 | 39,681 | 35,890 |
| Imports | Mil. lbs. | 5,499 | 7,783 | 10,931 | 13,183 | 14,617 | 15,019 | 15,079 |
| Total supply | Mil. lbs. | 47,400 | 49,606 | 50,529 | 50,913 | 56,266 | 56,478 | 52,673 |
| Exports | Mil. lbs. | 3,718 | 3,721 | 3,388 | 3,069 | 3,286 | 3,089 | 3,137 |
| Ending stocks [1] | Mil. lbs. | 1,266 | 1,280 | 1,488 | 1,685 | 1,778 | 1,704 | 1,710 |
| Domestic availability | Mil. lbs. | 41,460 | 43,864 | 44,819 | 45,509 | 50,373 | 51,193 | 47,376 |
| Per capita availability | Lbs. | 146.8 | 148.1 | 144.9 | 141.9 | 155.9 | 157.4 | 144.8 |
| VEGETABLES, PROCESSED MARKET [2] | | | | | | | | |
| Production | Mil. lbs. | 35,369 | 33,265 | 36,570 | 40,142 | 37,169 | 33,257 | 35,708 |
| Imports | Mil. lbs. | 3,581 | 5,555 | 6,393 | 7,192 | 7,622 | 7,845 | 8,247 |
| Total supply | Mil. lbs. | 62,174 | 62,646 | 71,320 | 73,265 | 75,434 | 72,013 | 72,898 |
| Exports | Mil. lbs. | 4,479 | 4,889 | 6,627 | 10,220 | 10,228 | 8,914 | 8,305 |
| Ending stocks | Mil. lbs. | 23,291 | 20,838 | 27,999 | 30,642 | 30,911 | 28,944 | 27,733 |
| Domestic availability | Mil. lbs. | 34,404 | 36,919 | 36,695 | 32,402 | 34,294 | 34,156 | 36,861 |
| Per capita availability | Lbs. | 121.8 | 124.6 | 118.6 | 101.0 | 106.2 | 104.7 | 112.8 |
| POTATOES, FRESH MARKET | | | | | | | | |
| Utilized production [3] | Mil. lbs. | 13,185 | 12,075 | 11,342 | 10,982 | 10,857 | 11,275 | 10,148 |
| Imports | Mil. lbs. | 805 | 788 | 916 | 882 | 1,093 | 1,106 | 1,073 |
| Total supply | Mil. lbs. | 13,990 | 12,863 | 12,258 | 11,864 | 11,950 | 12,381 | 11,221 |
| Exports | Mil. lbs. | 677 | 639 | 856 | 905 | 1,078 | 1,204 | 1,057 |
| Domestic availability | Mil. lbs. | 13,314 | 12,224 | 11,402 | 10,960 | 10,872 | 11,177 | 10,164 |
| Per capita availability | Lbs. | 47.1 | 41.3 | 36.9 | 34.2 | 33.7 | 34.4 | 31.1 |
| DRY EDIBLE BEANS | | | | | | | | |
| Production | Mil. lbs. | 2,654 | 2,658 | 3,180 | 3,006 | 2,871 | 3,596 | 3,785 |
| Imports | Mil. lbs. | 129 | 225 | 289 | 342 | 325 | 335 | 377 |
| Exports | Mil. lbs. | 788 | 564 | 1,001 | 947 | 1,023 | 1,212 | 918 |
| Domestic availability | Mil. lbs. | 2,170 | 1,813 | 2,094 | 2,304 | 2,196 | 2,534 | 3,154 |
| Per capita availability | Lbs. | 7.7 | 6.1 | 6.8 | 7.2 | 6.8 | 7.8 | 9.6 |

P Preliminary. [1] Applies only to brussel sprouts, onions, and okra. [2] Includes vegetables for canning and freezing. Excludes mushrooms for canning, and potatoes. [3] Crop year utilization for the past season and the current season distributed on a calendar year basis using National Agricultural Statistics Service potato marketing distributions.

Source: U.S. Department of Agriculture, Economic Research Service, *Vegetable and Pulses Yearbook*, April 2019. See also <http://www.ers.usda.gov/data-products/vegetables-and-pulses-data.aspx>.

## Table 901. Organic Vegetable, Fruit, and Field Crops—Farms, Production, and Value of Sales: 2016

[Unit column indicates quantity harvested and sales. Includes certified organic producers who have been certified by state or private agencies accredited by the USDA. Organic food must be produced without the use of conventional pesticides, petroleum-based or sewage sludge-based fertilizers, herbicides, pesticides, genetic engineering (biotechnology), antibiotics, growth hormones, or irradiation. Land must have no prohibited substances applied to it for at least 3 years before the harvest of an organic crop. Cwt = hundredweight (100 pounds)]

| Commodity | Unit | Farms (number) | Acres harvested (number) | Quantity harvested | Sales Quantity | Sales Value of sales (1,000 dollars) |
|---|---|---|---|---|---|---|
| Vegetables, potatoes, and melons [1,2] | | 3,121 | 186,178 | (X) | (X) | 1,644,431 |
| Beans, snap | Cwt | 538 | 5,136 | (X) | (X) | 27,660 |
| Broccoli | Cwt | 518 | 7,785 | 891,931 | 891,891 | 70,651 |
| Cabbage, all | Cwt | 577 | 1,831 | 392,151 | 392,147 | 19,560 |
| Cantaloupes and muskmelons | Cwt | 229 | 1,444 | 336,004 | 336,004 | 14,509 |
| Carrots | Cwt | 594 | 9,942 | 2,365,710 | 2,365,710 | 88,349 |
| Cauliflower | Cwt | 279 | 2,997 | 418,428 | 418,428 | 32,383 |
| Celery | Cwt | 138 | 2,741 | 1,042,224 | 1,042,223 | 37,655 |
| Garlic | Cwt | 711 | 1,669 | 147,286 | 147,276 | 28,655 |
| Herbs | Pounds | 440 | 1,744 | 11,465,439 | 11,465,439 | 26,992 |
| Lettuce | Cwt | 819 | 37,641 | 3,628,863 | 3,628,863 | 277,345 |
| Onions, all | Cwt | 555 | 2,574 | 1,038,112 | 1,038,104 | 33,815 |
| Peas, green | Tons | 332 | 9,207 | 16,799 | 16,799 | 15,731 |
| Peppers, bell | Cwt | 675 | 1,270 | 259,806 | 259,805 | 20,962 |
| Potatoes | Cwt | 681 | 17,244 | 4,668,037 | 4,667,978 | 150,579 |
| Spinach | Cwt | 344 | 17,547 | 1,178,182 | 1,177,948 | 118,162 |
| Squash | Cwt | 1,117 | 6,891 | 1,084,403 | 1,084,402 | 48,280 |
| Sweet corn | Cwt | 335 | 11,916 | 1,525,668 | 1,525,668 | 27,215 |
| Sweet potatoes | Cwt | 285 | 9,647 | 2,913,020 | 2,913,020 | 100,993 |
| Tomatoes | Cwt | 1,057 | 12,435 | (X) | (X) | 174,973 |
| Watermelon | Cwt | 254 | 731 | 146,283 | 146,283 | 6,562 |
| Apples, all | Pounds | 583 | 15,037 | 521,256,053 | 521,191,807 | 327,423 |
| Grapes, all | Tons | 712 | 27,358 | 149,965 | 144,403 | 218,401 |
| Citrus fruits, all | Tons | 579 | 12,154 | 123,318 | 123,119 | 122,817 |
| Lemons | Tons | 252 | 3,339 | 38,784 | 38,784 | 56,956 |
| Oranges, all | Tons | 273 | 5,866 | 60,630 | 60,431 | 41,933 |
| Other fruits and berries [1] | (X) | 2,366 | 39,886 | (X) | (X) | 659,863 |
| Avocado | Tons | 305 | 4,025 | 11,938 | 11,936 | 31,412 |
| Peaches | Tons | 191 | 2,520 | 15,775 | 15,775 | 27,639 |
| Pears | Tons | 173 | 1,963 | 21,444 | 21,444 | 20,804 |
| Plums | Tons | 151 | 1,425 | 5,949 | 5,949 | 11,040 |
| Blueberries, cultivated, all | Pounds | 455 | 5,359 | 42,375,017 | 42,374,189 | 100,482 |
| Strawberries | Cwt | 611 | 6,249 | 1,493,500 | 1,490,954 | 241,621 |
| Tree nuts [1] | (X) | 345 | 21,183 | (X) | (X) | 78,900 |
| Almonds | Pounds | 76 | 5,897 | 6,641,324 | 6,641,324 | 32,014 |
| Walnuts, English | Tons | 186 | 5,975 | 5,814 | 5,814 | 24,415 |
| Field crops [1] | (X) | 7,403 | 1,684,047 | (X) | (X) | 762,613 |
| Barley for grain or seed | Bushels | 510 | 51,254 | 2,717,771 | 1,937,653 | 16,866 |
| Corn for grain or seed | Bushels | 3,275 | 213,934 | 25,562,804 | 18,217,993 | 163,878 |
| Corn for silage or greenchop | Tons | 1,109 | 47,074 | 726,014 | 91,733 | 5,859 |
| Hay, all dry | Tons | 3,956 | 490,187 | 1,432,174 | 699,350 | 129,922 |
| Oats for grain or seed | Bushels | 1,206 | 50,732 | 3,051,226 | 2,097,703 | 13,343 |
| Soybeans for beans | Bushels | 1,748 | 124,591 | 4,602,376 | 3,829,144 | 78,491 |
| Wheat, all | Bushels | 1,139 | 336,550 | 10,551,643 | 8,938,312 | 107,130 |

X Not applicable. [1] Includes commodities not shown separately. [2] Vegetable grown in the open.

Source: U.S. Department of Agriculture, National Agricultural Statistics Service, *Certified Organic Survey, 2016 Summary*, September 2017. See also <https://www.nass.usda.gov/Surveys/Guide_to_NASS_Surveys/Organic_Production/index.php>.

## Table 902. Organic Livestock and Poultry—Farms, Inventory, and Value of Sales: 2016

[Includes all known organic producers that are certified organic. Animals raised on an organic operation must be fed organic feed and given access to the outdoors]

| Type of livestock and poultry | Farms (number) | Inventory [1] (number) | Value of sales (dollars) |
|---|---|---|---|
| Milk cows | 2,559 | 267,523 | 57,801,387 |
| Beef cows | 490 | 42,554 | 10,531,380 |
| Other cattle [2] | 3,048 | 218,268 | 164,407,528 |
| Hogs and pigs | 151 | 14,707 | 6,891,039 |
| Sheep and lambs | 102 | 9,446 | 1,199,815 |
| Goats and kids | 70 | 3,609 | 227,551 |
| Other livestock [3] | 42 | (X) | 659,340 |
| Chickens, layers | 818 | 15,475,570 | 2,462,123 |
| Chickens, broilers | 215 | 19,437,579 | 749,929,661 |
| Turkeys | 103 | 410,711 | 83,129,395 |
| Other poultry [4] | 130 | (X) | 79,265,683 |

X Not applicable. [1] As of December 31, 2016. [2] Includes organic bulls, beef calves, replacement milk heifers, etc. [3] Includes organic livestock not listed separately on the report form, such as farm raised bison, deer, rabbits, and fish. [4] Includes organic poultry not listed separately on the report form, including ducks, quail, etc.

Source: U.S. Department of Agriculture, National Agricultural Statistics Service, *Certified Organic Survey, 2016 Summary*, September 2017. See also <https://www.nass.usda.gov/Surveys/Guide_to_NASS_Surveys/Organic_Production/index.php>.

# Table 903. Meat Supply and Consumption: 2000 to 2018

[In millions of pounds, carcass weight equivalent (82,372 represents 82,372,000,000). Carcass weight equivalent is the weight of the animal minus entrails, head, hide, and internal organs; includes fat and bone. Covers federal and state inspected, and farm slaughtered]

| Year and type of meat | Production | Imports | Supply [1] | Exports | Consump- tion [2] | Ending stocks |
|---|---|---|---|---|---|---|
| RED MEAT AND POULTRY [3] | | | | | | |
| 2000 | 82,372 | 4,144 | 88,460 | 9,343 | 77,073 | 2,044 |
| 2005 | 86,783 | 4,856 | 93,787 | 9,274 | 82,328 | 2,185 |
| 2010 | 91,769 | 3,459 | 97,222 | 13,961 | 81,147 | 2,113 |
| 2015 | 94,289 | 4,875 | 101,230 | 14,275 | 84,593 | 2,361 |
| 2016 | 97,271 | 4,503 | 104,135 | 15,173 | 86,593 | 2,369 |
| 2017 | 99,810 | 4,515 | 106,694 | 16,035 | 88,242 | 2,416 |
| 2018, preliminary | 102,069 | 4,473 | 108,958 | 16,807 | 89,732 | 2,419 |
| RED MEATS, TOTAL | | | | | | |
| 2000 | 46,299 | 4,127 | 51,313 | 3,760 | 46,556 | 996 |
| 2005 | 45,849 | 4,803 | 51,805 | 3,373 | 47,367 | 1,066 |
| 2010 | 49,180 | 3,323 | 53,617 | 6,538 | 45,934 | 1,145 |
| 2015 | 48,520 | 4,698 | 54,408 | 7,282 | 45,806 | 1,320 |
| 2016 | 50,481 | 4,319 | 56,120 | 7,801 | 47,015 | 1,304 |
| 2017 | 52,078 | 4,361 | 57,743 | 8,497 | 48,000 | 1,246 |
| 2018, preliminary | 53,507 | 4,313 | 59,066 | 9,043 | 48,757 | 1,266 |
| Beef: [4] | | | | | | |
| 2000 | 26,888 | 3,032 | 30,332 | 2,468 | 27,338 | 525 |
| 2005 | 24,787 | 3,599 | 29,022 | 697 | 27,754 | 571 |
| 2010 | 26,412 | 2,298 | 29,275 | 2,300 | 26,390 | 585 |
| 2015 | 23,760 | 3,368 | 27,719 | 2,267 | 24,769 | 683 |
| 2016 | 25,288 | 3,012 | 28,983 | 2,557 | 25,669 | 757 |
| 2017 | 26,250 | 2,993 | 30,000 | 2,859 | 26,492 | 649 |
| 2018, preliminary | 26,938 | 2,998 | 30,585 | 3,161 | 26,762 | 662 |
| Pork: | | | | | | |
| 2000 | 18,952 | 965 | 20,378 | 1,287 | 18,639 | 453 |
| 2005 | 20,705 | 1,024 | 22,239 | 2,666 | 19,093 | 480 |
| 2010 | 22,456 | 859 | 23,840 | 4,223 | 19,077 | 541 |
| 2015 | 24,517 | 1,116 | 26,191 | 5,010 | 20,592 | 590 |
| 2016 | 24,957 | 1,091 | 26,638 | 5,239 | 20,892 | 507 |
| 2017 | 25,598 | 1,116 | 27,221 | 5,632 | 21,034 | 554 |
| 2018, preliminary | 26,330 | 1,042 | 27,926 | 5,876 | 21,491 | 559 |
| Veal: | | | | | | |
| 2000 | 225 | ([4]) | 230 | ([4]) | 225 | 5 |
| 2005 | 165 | ([4]) | 169 | ([4]) | 164 | 5 |
| 2010 | 145 | ([4]) | 154 | ([4]) | 150 | 4 |
| 2015 | 88 | ([4]) | 94 | ([4]) | 88 | 6 |
| 2016 | 81 | ([4]) | 87 | ([4]) | 73 | 14 |
| 2017 | 80 | ([4]) | 95 | ([4]) | 78 | 16 |
| 2018, preliminary | 81 | ([4]) | 97 | ([4]) | 89 | 8 |
| Lamb and mutton: | | | | | | |
| 2000 | 234 | 130 | 372 | 5 | 354 | 13 |
| 2005 | 191 | 180 | 375 | 9 | 356 | 10 |
| 2010 | 168 | 166 | 348 | 16 | 317 | 15 |
| 2015 | 155 | 214 | 400 | 4 | 357 | 41 |
| 2016 | 155 | 216 | 413 | 5 | 381 | 26 |
| 2017 | 150 | 252 | 428 | 6 | 396 | 27 |
| 2018, preliminary | 158 | 273 | 458 | 6 | 415 | 36 |
| POULTRY, TOTAL [3] | | | | | | |
| 2000 | 36,073 | 16 | 37,147 | 5,583 | 30,516 | 1,048 |
| 2005 | 40,935 | 54 | 41,981 | 5,902 | 34,961 | 1,119 |
| 2010 | 42,589 | 136 | 43,605 | 7,423 | 35,214 | 968 |
| 2015 | 45,768 | 177 | 46,822 | 6,994 | 38,787 | 1,041 |
| 2016 | 46,790 | 184 | 48,014 | 7,372 | 39,578 | 1,065 |
| 2017 | 47,732 | 154 | 48,950 | 7,538 | 40,242 | 1,170 |
| 2018, preliminary | 48,562 | 160 | 49,892 | 7,764 | 40,975 | 1,153 |
| Broilers: | | | | | | |
| 2000 | 30,209 | 13 | 31,017 | 4,918 | 25,302 | 798 |
| 2005 | 34,986 | 42 | 35,730 | 5,203 | 29,617 | 910 |
| 2010 | 36,515 | 107 | 37,238 | 6,762 | 29,703 | 773 |
| 2015 | 39,620 | 131 | 40,430 | 6,321 | 33,278 | 832 |
| 2016 | 40,261 | 131 | 41,224 | 6,645 | 33,802 | 778 |
| 2017 | 41,217 | 126 | 42,120 | 6,786 | 34,479 | 856 |
| 2018, preliminary | 42,145 | 139 | 43,140 | 7,069 | 35,227 | 845 |
| Other chicken: | | | | | | |
| 2000 | 531 | 2 | 541 | 220 | 312 | 9 |
| 2005 | 516 | 3 | 522 | 130 | 390 | 2 |
| 2010 | 504 | 4 | 510 | 79 | 427 | 4 |
| 2015 | 522 | 2 | 527 | 144 | 375 | 8 |
| 2016 | 548 | 3 | 558 | 158 | 392 | 8 |
| 2017 | 535 | 3 | 546 | 130 | 411 | 5 |
| 2018, preliminary | 539 | 2 | 546 | 84 | 456 | 6 |
| Turkeys: | | | | | | |
| 2000 | 5,333 | 1 | 5,589 | 445 | 4,902 | 241 |
| 2005 | 5,432 | 9 | 5,730 | 570 | 4,954 | 206 |
| 2010 | 5,570 | 25 | 5,857 | 581 | 5,084 | 192 |
| 2015 | 5,627 | 45 | 5,865 | 529 | 5,135 | 201 |
| 2016 | 5,981 | 50 | 6,232 | 569 | 5,384 | 279 |
| 2017 | 5,981 | 25 | 6,284 | 622 | 5,352 | 310 |
| 2018, preliminary | 5,878 | 19 | 6,206 | 611 | 5,293 | 303 |

[1] Total supply equals production plus imports plus ending stocks of previous year. [2] Includes shipments to territories. [3] Poultry production is ready-to-cook production; prior to 2001, includes other production (not federally inspected). [4] Veal exports and imports included with beef.

Source: U.S. Department of Agriculture, Economic Research Service, "Livestock and Meat Domestic Data," <http://www.ers.usda.gov/data-products/livestock-meat-domestic-data.aspx>, accessed July 2019.

## Table 904. Livestock Inventory and Production: 2000 to 2018

[98.2 represents 98,200,000. Production in live weight; includes animals-for-slaughter market, younger animals shipped to other states for feeding or breeding purposes, farm slaughter and custom slaughter consumed on farms where produced, minus livestock shipped into states for feeding or breeding with an adjustment for changes in inventory. Prices are for the marketing year, which for cattle and sheep and lambs starts January 1; for hogs the marketing year starts December 1]

| Type of livestock | Unit | 2000 | 2010 | 2011 | 2012 | 2013 | 2014 | 2015 | 2016 | 2017 | 2018 |
|---|---|---|---|---|---|---|---|---|---|---|---|
| **ALL CATTLE** [1] | | | | | | | | | | | |
| Inventory (number on farms): [2] | Mil. | 98.2 | 94.1 | 92.9 | 91.2 | 90.1 | 88.2 | 89.2 | 91.9 | 93.6 | 94.3 |
| Total value | Bil. dol. | 67.1 | 78.3 | 88.0 | 101.3 | 102.6 | 107.9 | 141.3 | 129.6 | 103.8 | 108.1 |
| Value per head | Dol. | 683 | 833 | 947 | 1,111 | 1,139 | 1,223 | 1,584 | 1,410 | 1,109 | 1,146 |
| Production: Quantity | Bil. lb. | 43.0 | 41.4 | 41.5 | 40.9 | 40.8 | 40.3 | 41.5 | 42.7 | 44.2 | 46.3 |
| Cattle, price per 100 pounds [3] | Dol. | (NA) | 92.2 | 113.0 | 121.0 | 125.0 | 152.0 | 147.0 | 119.0 | 120.0 | 115.0 |
| Calves, price per 100 pounds | Dol. | (NA) | 117.0 | 142.0 | 172.0 | 181.0 | 261.0 | 247.0 | 158.0 | 168.0 | 170.0 |
| Value of production | Bil. dol. | 28.5 | 36.9 | 45.1 | 48.1 | 48.6 | 60.1 | 60.1 | 48.6 | 50.4 | 49.8 |
| **HOGS AND PIGS** | | | | | | | | | | | |
| Inventory (number on farms): [4] | Mil. | 59.3 | 64.7 | 64.7 | 66.3 | 66.2 | 64.8 | 67.6 | 69.0 | 71.3 | 73.1 |
| Total value | Bil. dol. | 4.3 | 5.4 | 6.9 | 8.1 | 7.7 | 8.9 | 9.7 | 6.6 | 6.6 | 7.2 |
| Value per head | Dol. | 72 | 83 | 106 | 123 | 116 | 138 | 144 | 96 | 92 | 99 |
| Production: Quantity | Bil. lb. | 25.7 | 30.3 | 30.8 | 32.1 | 32.5 | 32.1 | 34.7 | 35.9 | 37.0 | 38.8 |
| Price per 100 pounds | Dol. | (NA) | 54.1 | 65.3 | 64.2 | 67.2 | 76.5 | 55.3 | 49.3 | 53.1 | 50.2 |
| Value of production | Bil. dol. | 10.8 | 16.0 | 20.0 | 20.3 | 21.6 | 24.2 | 18.8 | 17.4 | 19.2 | 19.1 |
| **SHEEP AND LAMBS** | | | | | | | | | | | |
| Inventory (number on farms): [2] | Mil. | 7.0 | 5.6 | 5.5 | 5.4 | 5.4 | 5.2 | 5.3 | 5.3 | 5.3 | 5.3 |
| Total value | Mil. dol. | 670 | 761 | 929 | 1,188 | 951 | 982 | 1,127 | 1,071 | 1,068 | 1,071 |
| Value per head | Dol. | 95 | 135 | 170 | 221 | 177 | 188 | 214 | 202 | 203 | 204 |
| Production: Quantity | Mil. lb. | 512 | 405 | (NA) | (NA) | (NA) | (NA) | (NA) | (NA) | (NA) | (NA) |
| Value of production | Mil. dol. | 365 | 443 | (NA) | (NA) | (NA) | (NA) | (NA) | (NA) | (NA) | (NA) |

NA Not available. [1] Includes milk cows. [2] As of January 1. [3] Cattle weighing 500 pounds or more. [4] As of December 1 of preceding year.

Source: U.S. Department of Agriculture, National Agricultural Statistics Service, "Quick Stats," <http://quickstats.nass.usda.gov/>, accessed June 2019. See also *Meat Animals Production, Disposition, and Income Annual Summary*, <http://www.nass.usda.gov/Publications>.

## Table 905. Livestock Operations by Size of Herd: 2000 to 2017

[In thousands (1,076 represents 1,076,000). Prior to 2007, an operation is any place having one or more head on hand at any time during the year. Beginning 2007, operations are any place having one or more head on hand on December 31]

| Size of herd | 2000 | 2010 | 2012 | 2017 | Size of herd | 2000 | 2010 | 2012 | 2017 |
|---|---|---|---|---|---|---|---|---|---|
| **CATTLE** [1] | | | | | **MILK COWS** [2] | | | | |
| **Total operations** | **1,076** | **935** | **913** | **883** | **Total operations** | **105** | **63** | **64** | **55** |
| 1 to 49 head | 671 | 635 | 637 | 599 | 1 to 49 head | 53 | 31 | 34 | 28 |
| 50 to 99 head | 186 | 129 | 118 | 119 | 50 to 99 head | 31 | 16 | 15 | 12 |
| 100 to 499 head | 192 | 142 | 130 | 136 | 100 head or more | 21 | 16 | 14 | 14 |
| 500 to 999 head | 19 | 19 | 17 | 18 | | | | | |
| 1,000 head or more | 10 | 11 | 11 | 11 | **HOGS AND PIGS** | | | | |
| | | | | | **Total operations** | **87** | **69** | **63** | **66** |
| **BEEF COWS** [2] | | | | | 1 to 99 head | 50 | 49 | 47 | 52 |
| **Total operations** | **831** | **742** | **728** | **729** | 100 to 499 head | 17 | 5 | 4 | 3 |
| 1 to 49 head | 655 | 588 | 594 | 577 | 500 to 999 head | 8 | 3 | 2 | 1 |
| 50 to 99 head | 100 | 82 | 71 | 80 | 1,000 to 1,999 head | 6 | 4 | 3 | 2 |
| 100 to 499 head | 71 | 66 | 57 | 66 | 2,000 to 4,999 head | 5 | 5 | 5 | 5 |
| 500 head or more | 6 | 6 | 5 | 6 | 5,000 or more head | 2 | 3 | 3 | 4 |

[1] Includes calves. [2] Included in operations with cattle.

Source: U.S. Department of Agriculture, National Agricultural Statistics Service, *Livestock Operations Final Estimates 2003–2007*, March 2009; and *Farms, Land in Farms, and Livestock Operations 2012 Summary*, February 2013. Beginning with 2012 data, *Census of Agriculture*, Vol. 1, April 2019, and earlier reports. See also <http://www.agcensus.usda.gov/Publications/index.php>.

## Table 906. Hogs and Pigs—Number, Production, and Slaughter by Leading States: 2016 to 2018

[71,345 represents 71,345,000. Production in live weight. See headnote Table 904]

| State | Number on farms [1] (1,000) | | | Quantity produced (mil. lb.) | | | Value of production (mil. dol.) | | | Commercial slaughter [2] (mil. lb.) | |
|---|---|---|---|---|---|---|---|---|---|---|---|
| | 2016 | 2017 | 2018 | 2016 | 2017 | 2018 | 2016 | 2017 | 2018 | 2017 | 2018 |
| **U.S.** [3] | **71,345** | **73,145** | **74,915** | **35,899** | **36,963** | **38,829** | **17,363** | **19,159** | **19,060** | **34,241** | **35,233** |
| IA | 22,200 | 22,800 | 23,500 | 12,732 | 12,791 | 14,487 | 5,686 | 6,158 | 6,603 | 9,294 | 9,909 |
| NC | 9,300 | 9,000 | 9,100 | 4,134 | 4,248 | 4,159 | 2,067 | 2,269 | 2,077 | (D) | (D) |
| MN | 8,500 | 8,500 | 9,000 | 4,344 | 4,442 | 4,553 | 2,022 | 2,238 | 2,163 | 3,167 | 3,247 |
| IL | 5,100 | 5,400 | 5,350 | 2,118 | 2,184 | 2,166 | 1,132 | 1,228 | 1,144 | 3,476 | 3,494 |
| IN | 4,050 | 4,000 | 4,200 | 1,950 | 2,198 | 2,212 | 910 | 1,092 | 1,028 | 2,481 | 2,373 |
| MO | 3,100 | 3,400 | 3,600 | 1,624 | 1,496 | 1,232 | 829 | 850 | 723 | 2,680 | 2,613 |
| NE | 3,400 | 3,600 | 3,500 | 1,322 | 1,379 | 1,395 | 718 | 801 | 776 | 2,235 | 2,216 |

D Data withheld to limit disclosure. [1] As of December 1. [2] Includes slaughter in federally inspected and other slaughter plants; excludes animals slaughtered on farms. [3] Includes other states, not shown separately.

Source: U.S. Department of Agriculture, National Agricultural Statistics Service, "Quick Stats," <http://quickstats.nass.usda.gov/>, accessed July 2019. See also *Meat Animals Production, Disposition, and Income Annual Summary* and *Livestock Slaughter Annual Summary*, <http://www.nass.usda.gov/Publications>.

## Table 907. Cattle and Calves—Number, Production, and Value by Leading States: 2016 to 2019

[93,625 represents 93,625,000. Includes milk cows. See headnote, Table 904]

| State | Number on farms [1] (1,000) | | | Production (mil. lb.) | | | Value of production (mil. dol.) | | | Commercial slaughter [2] (mil. lb.) | |
|---|---|---|---|---|---|---|---|---|---|---|---|
| | 2017 | 2018 | 2019 | 2016 | 2017 | 2018 | 2016 | 2017 | 2018 | 2017 | 2018 |
| U.S. [3]...... | 93,625 | 94,298 | 94,760 | 42,694 | 44,197 | 46,319 | 48,573 | 50,398 | 49,845 | 43,315 | 44,460 |
| TX............ | 12,300 | 12,500 | 13,000 | 6,111 | 6,303 | 6,537 | 7,240 | 7,508 | 7,584 | 7,344 | 7,553 |
| NE............ | 6,450 | 6,800 | 6,800 | 5,696 | 5,292 | 5,607 | 6,331 | 5,791 | 5,306 | 10,463 | 10,484 |
| KS............ | 6,400 | 6,300 | 6,350 | 4,234 | 4,301 | 4,408 | 4,590 | 4,578 | 4,472 | 8,814 | 9,091 |
| OK............ | 5,000 | 5,100 | 5,300 | 2,073 | 2,451 | 2,308 | 2,554 | 3,048 | 2,794 | 29 | 30 |
| CA............ | 5,150 | 5,200 | 5,150 | 1,840 | 1,945 | 2,411 | 2,003 | 2,098 | 2,494 | 1,768 | 1,868 |
| MO............ | 4,300 | 4,350 | 4,250 | 1,281 | 1,373 | 1,534 | 1,653 | 1,839 | 1,976 | 48 | 54 |
| SD............ | 3,850 | 4,000 | 4,050 | 1,520 | 1,727 | 1,830 | 1,905 | 2,219 | 2,267 | 568 | 606 |
| IA............. | 3,900 | 4,000 | 3,950 | 2,126 | 2,099 | 2,188 | 2,537 | 2,568 | 2,566 | (D) | (D) |
| WI............ | 3,550 | 3,500 | 3,450 | 1,405 | 1,527 | 1,510 | 1,621 | 1,711 | 1,620 | 1,842 | 1,852 |
| CO............ | 2,850 | 2,850 | 2,850 | 1,653 | 1,775 | 1,845 | 1,900 | 2,070 | 1,974 | 3,467 | 3,450 |
| ID............ | 2,370 | 2,420 | 2,500 | 1,207 | 1,199 | 1,280 | 1,384 | 1,379 | 1,410 | 227 | 543 |

D Data withheld to limit disclosure. [1] As of January 1. [2] Data cover cattle only. Includes slaughter in federally inspected and other slaughter plants; excludes animals slaughtered on farms. [3] Includes other states, not shown separately.

Source: U.S. Department of Agriculture, National Agricultural Statistics Service, "Quick Stats," <http://quickstats.nass.usda.gov/>, accessed July 2019. See also *Meat Animals Production, Disposition, and Income Annual Summary* and *Livestock Slaughter Annual Summary*, <http://www.nass.usda.gov/Publications>.

## Table 908. Milk Cows—Number, Production, and Value by Leading States: 2016 to 2018

[9,334 represents 9,334,000]

| State | Number on farms [1] (1,000) | | | Milk produced on farms [2] (mil. lb.) | | | Milk produced per milk cow (pounds) [2] | | | Value of production [3] (mil. dol.) | | |
|---|---|---|---|---|---|---|---|---|---|---|---|---|
| | 2016 | 2017 | 2018 | 2016 | 2017 | 2018 | 2016 | 2017 | 2018 | 2016 | 2017 | 2018 |
| U.S. [4]...... | 9,334 | 9,406 | 9,399 | 212,451 | 215,527 | 217,575 | 22,761 | 22,914 | 23,149 | 34,712 | 38,119 | 35,411 |
| CA............ | 1,762 | 1,749 | 1,734 | 40,469 | 39,798 | 40,413 | 22,968 | 22,755 | 23,306 | 6,070 | 6,567 | 6,377 |
| WI............ | 1,279 | 1,278 | 1,274 | 30,110 | 30,333 | 30,579 | 23,542 | 23,735 | 24,002 | 5,058 | 5,490 | 5,046 |
| NY............ | 620 | 624 | 623 | 14,777 | 14,929 | 14,882 | 23,834 | 23,925 | 23,888 | 2,512 | 2,717 | 2,485 |
| ID............ | 595 | 600 | 609 | 14,665 | 14,633 | 15,149 | 24,647 | 24,388 | 24,875 | 2,361 | 2,517 | 2,378 |
| TX............ | 477 | 515 | 537 | 10,773 | 12,054 | 12,852 | 22,585 | 23,406 | 23,933 | 1,853 | 2,218 | 2,172 |
| PA............ | 529 | 525 | 519 | 10,812 | 10,893 | 10,665 | 20,439 | 20,749 | 20,549 | 1,860 | 2,026 | 1,792 |
| MN............ | 461 | 458 | 453 | 9,666 | 9,867 | 9,868 | 20,967 | 21,544 | 21,784 | 1,624 | 1,756 | 1,628 |
| MI............ | 419 | 427 | 424 | 10,876 | 11,231 | 11,168 | 25,957 | 26,302 | 26,340 | 1,642 | 1,842 | 1,664 |
| NM............ | 315 | 329 | 330 | 7,711 | 8,212 | 8,285 | 24,479 | 24,960 | 25,106 | 1,203 | 1,339 | 1,218 |

[1] Average number during year. Represents cows and heifers that have calved, kept for milk; excluding heifers not yet fresh. [2] Excludes milk sucked by calves. [3] Valued at average returns per 100 pounds of milk in combined marketings of milk and cream. Includes value of milk fed to calves. [4] Includes other states, not shown separately.

Source: U.S. Department of Agriculture, National Agricultural Statistics Service, "Quick Stats," <http://quickstats.nass.usda.gov/>, accessed July 2019. See also *Milk: Production, Disposition, and Income Annual Summary*, <http://www.nass.usda.gov/Publications>.

## Table 909. Milk Production and Manufactured Dairy Products: 2000 to 2018

[105 represents 105,000]

| Item | Unit | 2000 | 2005 | 2010 | 2013 | 2014 | 2015 | 2016 | 2017 | 2018 |
|---|---|---|---|---|---|---|---|---|---|---|
| **Number of farms with milk cows**.............. | 1,000 | 105 | 78 | 63 | (NA) | (NA) | (NA) | (NA) | 55 | (NA) |
| Cows and heifers that have calved, kept for milk [1]...................... | Mil. head | 9.2 | 9.1 | 9.1 | 9.2 | 9.3 | 9.3 | 9.3 | 9.4 | 9.4 |
| Milk produced on farms......................... | Bil. lb. | 167 | 177 | 193 | 201 | 206 | 209 | 212 | 216 | 218 |
| Production per cow......................... | 1,000 lb. | 18.2 | 19.6 | 21.1 | 21.8 | 22.2 | 22.4 | 22.8 | 22.9 | 23.1 |
| Milk marketed by producers [2].................. | Bil. lb. | 166 | 176 | 192 | 200 | 205 | 208 | 211 | 215 | 217 |
| Value of milk produced........................... | Bil. dol. | 20.7 | 26.9 | 31.5 | 40.5 | 49.6 | 35.9 | 34.7 | 38.1 | 35.4 |
| Cash receipts from marketing of milk and cream [2]......................... | Bil. dol. | 20.6 | 26.7 | 31.4 | 40.3 | 49.4 | 35.7 | 34.5 | 37.9 | 35.2 |
| **Number of dairy manufacturing plants**....... | **Number** | **1,164** | **1,088** | **1,250** | **1,265** | **1,269** | **1,273** | **1,298** | **1,305** | **1,273** |
| Manufactured dairy products: | | | | | | | | | | |
| Butter (including whey butter).................. | Mil. lb. | 1,256 | 1,347 | 1,564 | 1,863 | 1,855 | 1,850 | 1,839 | 1,847 | 1,891 |
| Cheese, total [3]................................. | Mil. lb. | 8,258 | 9,149 | 10,443 | 11,102 | 11,512 | 11,831 | 12,182 | 12,640 | 13,025 |
| American (excl. full-skim American).......... | Mil. lb. | 3,642 | 3,808 | 4,289 | 4,420 | 4,588 | 4,694 | 4,769 | 5,072 | 5,254 |
| Cream and Neufchatel...................... | Mil. lb. | 687 | 715 | 745 | 842 | 852 | 876 | 909 | 918 | 915 |
| All Italian varieties............................. | Mil. lb. | 3,289 | 3,803 | 4,416 | 4,735 | 4,950 | 5,082 | 5,304 | 5,395 | 5,557 |
| Cottage cheese—creamed and lowfat........ | Mil. lb. | 735 | 785 | 719 | 678 | 668 | 681 | 697 | 675 | 695 |
| Nonfat dry milk [4].............................. | Mil. lb. | 1,457 | 1,210 | 1,563 | 1,478 | 1,765 | 1,822 | 1,753 | 1,835 | 1,774 |
| Dry whey [5]..................................... | Mil. lb. | 1,188 | 1,041 | 1,013 | 953 | 870 | 978 | 955 | 1,035 | 999 |
| Yogurt, plain and fruit-flavored.................. | Mil. lb. | 1,837 | 3,058 | 4,181 | 4,715 | 4,757 | 4,646 | 4,458 | 4,478 | 4,388 |
| Ice cream, regular.............................. | Mil. gal. | 980 | 960 | 929 | 897 | 866 | 897 | 907 | 871 | 840 |
| Ice cream, lowfat [6]............................ | Mil. gal. | 373 | 360 | 415 | 401 | 412 | 439 | 436 | 461 | 451 |

NA Not available. [1] Average number during year, excluding heifers not yet fresh. [2] Comprises sales to plants and dealers, and retail sales by farmers direct to consumers. [3] Includes varieties not shown separately. [4] Data for 2000 includes dry skim milk for animal feed. [5] Includes animal but excludes modified whey production. [6] Includes freezer-made milkshake in most states.

Source: U.S. Department of Agriculture, National Agricultural Statistics Service, "Quick Stats," <http://quickstats.nass.usda.gov/>, accessed June 2019; *Dairy Products Annual Summary*; *Milk Production, Disposition, and Income Annual Summary*; and *Farms, Land in Farms, And Livestock Operations, Summary*, annual. See also <http://www.nass.usda.gov/Publications/index.asp>.

## Table 910. Milk Production and Commercial Use in All Products: 2000 to 2018

[In billions of pounds, milkfat basis (167.4 represents 167,400,000,000) except as noted. Changes have been made to conversion factors used for dairy stocks, trade, and commercial use estimates; data have been revised and are not comparable to data previously shown. See <https://www.ers.usda.gov/data-products/dairy-data/documentation>]

| Year | Farm milk supply use | | | Beginning stocks | Imports | Commercial supply, total | Commercial use | | Ending stocks [1] | Milk price per 100 pounds [2] (dollars) |
|------|---------|----------|---------------|-----------|---------|---------|--------------------|-------------|---------|---------|
| | Production | Farm use | Farm marketings | | | | USDA net removals | Disappearance | | |
| 2000...... | 167.4 | 1.3 | 166.1 | 5.8 | 4.5 | 176.4 | 0.3 | 169.5 | 6.5 | 12.30 |
| 2005...... | 176.9 | 1.1 | 175.8 | 6.9 | 7.4 | 190.2 | – | 182.6 | 7.5 | 15.10 |
| 2010...... | 192.9 | 1.0 | 191.9 | 10.7 | 4.0 | 206.6 | 0.2 | 196.4 | 10.1 | 16.30 |
| 2013...... | 201.3 | 1.0 | 200.3 | 11.4 | 3.8 | 215.4 | – | 205.1 | 10.3 | 20.10 |
| 2014...... | 206.0 | 1.0 | 205.1 | 10.3 | 4.4 | 219.8 | – | 209.3 | 10.4 | 24.00 |
| 2015...... | 208.5 | 1.0 | 207.5 | 10.4 | 5.8 | 223.7 | – | 211.5 | 12.3 | 17.10 |
| 2016...... | 212.5 | 1.0 | 211.5 | 12.3 | 6.9 | 230.7 | – | 218.0 | 12.7 | 16.30 |
| 2017...... | 215.5 | 1.0 | 214.5 | 12.7 | 6.0 | 233.2 | – | 219.8 | 13.4 | 17.70 |
| 2018...... | 217.6 | 1.0 | 216.6 | 13.4 | 6.3 | 236.3 | – | 222.5 | 13.8 | 16.20 |

– Represents or rounds to zero. [1] Includes commercial stocks of butter, cheese, canned milk, dry milk products, whey products, and lactose. [2] Wholesale price received by farmers for all milk delivered to plants and dealers.

Source: U.S. Department of Agriculture, Economic Research Service, "Dairy Data," <http://www.ers.usda.gov/data-products/dairy-data.aspx>, accessed July 2019.

## Table 911. Chicken, Turkey, and Egg Production: 1990 to 2018

[353 represents 353,000,000. For years ending November 30, except as noted]

| Item | Unit | 1990 | 1995 | 2000 | 2005 | 2010 | 2014 | 2015 | 2016 | 2017 | 2018 |
|------|------|------|------|------|------|------|------|------|------|------|------|
| Chickens: [1] | | | | | | | | | | | |
| Number [2]............... | Million | 353 | 388 | 437 | 456 | 457 | 489 | 484 | 501 | 515 | 528 |
| Value per head [2]........ | Dollars | 2.29 | 2.41 | 2.44 | 2.52 | 3.58 | 4.13 | 4.38 | 4.23 | 4.20 | 4.33 |
| Value, total [2]............. | Mil. dol. | 808 | 935 | 1,064 | 1,150 | 1,637 | 2,021 | 2,116 | 2,115 | 2,163 | 2,284 |
| Number sold............ | Million | 208 | 180 | 218 | 194 | 173 | 192 | 199 | 208 | 190 | 190 |
| Value of sales........... | Mil. dol. | 94 | 60 | 64 | 65 | 73 | 97 | 105 | 88 | 47 | 49 |
| PRODUCTION | | | | | | | | | | | |
| Broiler chickens: [3] | | | | | | | | | | | |
| Number................. | Million | 5,864 | 7,326 | 8,284 | 8,872 | 8,624 | 8,545 | 8,689 | 8,777 | 8,914 | 9,037 |
| Weight................. | Bil. lb. | 25.6 | 34.2 | 41.6 | 47.9 | 49.2 | 51.4 | 53.4 | 54.3 | 55.6 | 56.8 |
| Production value........ | Mil. dol. | 8,366 | 11,762 | 13,989 | 20,878 | 23,692 | 32,728 | 28,716 | 25,936 | 30,232 | 31,746 |
| Turkeys: [4] | | | | | | | | | | | |
| Number................. | Million | 282 | 292 | 270 | 250 | 244 | 238 | 233 | 244 | 245 | 245 |
| Weight................. | Bil. lb. | 6.0 | 6.8 | 7.0 | 7.0 | 7.1 | 7.2 | 7.0 | 7.5 | 7.5 | 7.6 |
| Production value........ | Mil. dol. | 2,393 | 2,769 | 2,828 | 3,108 | 4,372 | 5,305 | 5,708 | 6,184 | 4,874 | 3,875 |
| Eggs: | | | | | | | | | | | |
| Average number of layers................. | Thousand | 270,946 | 294,350 | 329,067 | 345,027 | 341,505 | 368,193 | 356,370 | 369,949 | 381,175 | 391,311 |
| Eggs per layer.......... | Number | 251 | 254 | 257 | 262 | 269 | 277 | 276 | 279 | 281 | 279 |
| Total production........ | Billion | 68.1 | 74.8 | 84.7 | 90.3 | 91.8 | 101.8 | 98.3 | 103.2 | 107.2 | 109.2 |
| In dozens............. | Million | (NA) | (NA) | (NA) | (NA) | (NA) | 8,485 | 8,191 | 8,600 | 8,937 | 9,099 |
| Production value....... | Mil. dol. | 4,021 | 3,893 | 4,359 | 4,067 | 6,553 | 10,343 | 13,763 | 6,591 | 7,635 | 10,586 |

NA Not available. [1] Excludes commercial broilers. [2] As of December 1. [3] Young chickens of the heavy breeds and other meat-type birds, to be marketed at 2-5 lbs. live weight and from which no pullets are kept for egg production. Not included in sales of chickens. [4] Data for turkeys are for year ending August 31.

Source: U.S. Department of Agriculture, National Agricultural Statistics Service, "Quick Stats," <http://quickstats.nass.usda.gov/>, accessed July 2019; *Poultry Production and Value Final Estimates 2008-2012*, October 2014, and earlier reports; *Chickens and Eggs Final Estimates 2008-2012*, September 2014, and earlier reports; *Poultry—Production and Value*, annual; and *Chickens and Eggs*, annual. See also <http://www.nass.usda.gov/Publications>.

## Table 912. Broiler Chicken and Turkey Production by Leading States: 2016 to 2018

[In millions of pounds, live weight production (54,259 represents 54,259,000,000)]

| State | Broiler chickens | | | Turkeys | | | State | Broiler chickens | | | Turkeys | | |
|-------|------|------|------|------|------|------|-------|------|------|------|------|------|------|
| | 2016 | 2017 | 2018 | 2016 | 2017 | 2018 | | 2016 | 2017 | 2018 | 2016 | 2017 | 2018 |
| U.S. [1]..... | 54,259 | 55,574 | 56,791 | 7,487 | 7,544 | 7,598 | MS...... | 4,658 | 4,743 | 4,711 | (NA) | (NA) | (NA) |
| | | | | | | | MO...... | 1,436 | 1,426 | 1,466 | 626 | 614 | 640 |
| AL.......... | 5,993 | 6,134 | 6,180 | (NA) | (NA) | (NA) | NC...... | 6,468 | 6,563 | 6,901 | 1,203 | 1,144 | 1,196 |
| AR.......... | 6,561 | 6,989 | 7,316 | 525 | 587 | 595 | OH...... | 475 | 526 | 561 | 237 | 281 | 282 |
| CA.......... | (NA) | (NA) | (NA) | 324 | 320 | 318 | OK...... | 1,363 | 1,370 | 1,319 | (NA) | (NA) | (NA) |
| DE.......... | 1,843 | 1,871 | 1,924 | (NA) | (NA) | (NA) | PA...... | 1,040 | 1,037 | 1,141 | 190 | 205 | 195 |
| FL.......... | 367 | 372 | 386 | (NA) | (NA) | (NA) | SC...... | 1,811 | 1,799 | 1,807 | (NA) | (NA) | (NA) |
| GA.......... | 8,066 | 8,044 | 8,168 | (NA) | (NA) | (NA) | SD...... | (NA) | (NA) | (NA) | 180 | 176 | 179 |
| IN........... | (NA) | (NA) | (NA) | 759 | 792 | 768 | TN...... | 929 | 909 | 940 | (NA) | (NA) | (NA) |
| IA........... | (NA) | (NA) | (NA) | 461 | 485 | 477 | TX...... | 3,840 | 4,103 | 4,248 | (NA) | (NA) | (NA) |
| KY.......... | 1,832 | 1,893 | 1,972 | (NA) | (NA) | (NA) | UT...... | (NA) | (NA) | (NA) | 122 | 134 | (D) |
| MD.......... | 1,851 | 1,840 | 1,736 | (NA) | (NA) | (NA) | VA...... | 1,534 | 1,609 | 1,673 | 468 | 459 | 462 |
| MI.......... | (NA) | (NA) | (NA) | 217 | 206 | 222 | WV...... | 352 | 336 | 317 | 111 | 111 | 96 |
| MN.......... | 295 | 358 | 361 | 1,104 | 1,058 | 1,113 | WI...... | 227 | 226 | 229 | (NA) | (NA) | (NA) |

NA Not available. D Data withheld to avoid disclosing data for individual operations. Data are included in U.S. total. [1] Includes other states, not shown separately.

Source: U.S. Department of Agriculture, National Agricultural Statistics Service, "Quick Stats," <http://quickstats.nass.usda.gov/>, accessed July 2019. See also *Poultry—Production and Value*, <http://www.nass.usda.gov/Publications>.

# Forestry, Fishing, and Mining

This section presents data on the area, ownership, production, trade, reserves, and disposition of natural resources, defined here as including forestry, fisheries, and mining and mineral products.

**Forestry**—This section presents data on the area, ownership, and timber resource of commercial timberland; forestry statistics covering the National Forests and Forest Service cooperative programs; product data for lumber, pulpwood, woodpulp, paper and paperboard; and similar data.

The principal sources of data relating to forests and forest products are *Forest Resources of the United States, 2017; U.S. Timber Production, Trade, Consumption, and Price Statistics, 1965 to 2013; Land Areas of the National Forest System*, issued annually by the Forest Service of the U.S. Department of Agriculture; *Agricultural Statistics*, issued by the Department of Agriculture; and reports of the Annual Survey of Manufactures issued by the U.S. Census Bureau, see <http://www.census.gov/programs-surveys/asm.html>. Further sources used in this section and issued by the U.S. Census Bureau include the annual *County Business Patterns* reports, and the 2012 Economic Census. Additional information is published in the *Paper Industry Annual Statistical Summary* of the American Forest and Paper Association, Washington, DC.

The completeness and reliability of statistics on forests and forest products vary considerably. The data for forest land area and stand volumes are much more reliable for areas that have been recently surveyed than for those for which only estimates are available. In general, more data are available for lumber and other manufactured products such as particle board and softwood panels, etc., than for the primary forest products such as poles and piling and fuelwood.

**Fisheries**—The principal source of data relating to fisheries is data issued annually by the National Marine Fisheries Service (NMFS), National Oceanic and Atmospheric Administration (NOAA). The NMFS collects and disseminates data on commercial landings of fish and shellfish. Annual reports include quantity and value of commercial landings of fish and shellfish, disposition of landings, and number and kinds of fishing vessels and fishing gear. Reports for the fish-processing industry include annual output for wholesaling, and fish processing establishments and annual and seasonal employment. The principal source for these data is the annual *Fisheries of the United States*. Additional government sources include *Agricultural Statistics*, issued annually by the Department of Agriculture; and *Trout Production* and *Catfish Production*, issued by the National Agricultural Statistics service of the U.S. Department of Agriculture.

**Mining and mineral products**—This section presents data relating to mineral industries and their products, summary measures of production and employment, and more detailed data on production, prices, imports and exports, consumption, and distribution for specific industries and products. Data on mining and mineral products may also be found in Sections 19,

21, 28, and 30 of this *Abstract*; data on mining employment may be found in Section 12.

Mining comprises the extraction of minerals occurring naturally (coal, ores, crude petroleum, natural gas) and quarrying, well operation, milling, refining and processing, and other preparation customarily done at the mine or well site or as a part of extraction activity. (Mineral preparation plants are usually operated together with mines or quarries.) Exploration for minerals is included as is the development of mineral properties.

The principal governmental sources of these data are the *Minerals Yearbook* and *Mineral Commodity Summaries*, published by the U.S. Geological Survey, U.S. Department of the Interior, and various monthly and annual publications of the Energy Information Administration, U.S. Department of Energy. See text, Section 19, for a list of Department of Energy publications.

Mineral statistics, with principal emphasis on commodity detail, have been collected by the U.S. Geological Survey and the former Bureau of Mines since 1880. Current data in U.S. Geological Survey publications include quantity and value of nonfuel minerals produced, sold, or used by producers, or shipped; quantity of minerals stocked; crude materials treated and prepared minerals recovered; and consumption of mineral raw materials.

The Economic Census, conducted by the Census Bureau at various intervals since 1840, collects data on mineral industries. Beginning with the 1967 census, legislation provides for a census to be conducted every 5 years for years ending in "2" and "7." Data from the 2012 Economic Census have been fully released as of September 2016 through the Census Bureau's American FactFinder® service on the Census Bureau web site at <factfinder.census.gov>. Data from the 2017 Economic Census will be released on a flow basis between September 2019 and December 2021. Economic Census data are based on the North American Industry Classification System (NAICS). The Census provides, for the various types of mineral establishments, information on operating costs, capital expenditures, labor, equipment, and energy requirements in relation to their value of shipments and other receipts.

# Table 913. Natural Resource–Related Industries—Establishments, Employees, and Annual Payroll by Industry: 2015 and 2016

[In units as indicated (1,633.3 represents 1,633,300; 104.90 represents $104,900,000,000). Excludes most government employees, railroad employees, and self-employed persons. See source for definitions and statement on reliability of data. An establishment is a single physical location where business is conducted or where services or industrial operations are performed. See Appendix III]

| Industry | 2012 NAICS Code [1] | Establishments (number) | | Number of employees [2] (1,000) | | Annual payroll (bil. dol.) | |
|---|---|---|---|---|---|---|---|
| | | 2015 | 2016 | 2015 | 2016 | 2015 | 2016 |
| Natural resource–related industries, total............. | (X) | 69,881 | 68,170 | 1,633.3 | 1,487.3 | 104.90 | 93.32 |
| Forestry, fishing, hunting, and agriculture support..... | 11 | 22,368 | 22,594 | 160.1 | 160.4 | 6.53 | 6.60 |
| Forestry and logging................................. | 113 | 8,754 | 8,739 | 56.2 | 55.7 | 2.54 | 2.46 |
| Timber tract operations............................ | 1131 | 473 | 480 | 3.7 | 4.2 | 0.23 | 0.22 |
| Forest nurseries and gathering forest products........... | 1132 | 183 | 183 | 1.4 | 1.4 | 0.06 | 0.05 |
| Logging.............................................. | 1133 | 8,098 | 8,076 | 51.1 | 50.2 | 2.24 | 2.19 |
| Fishing, hunting and trapping.......................... | 114 | 2,688 | 2,807 | 7.5 | 7.1 | 0.40 | 0.40 |
| Fishing................................................ | 1141 | 2,343 | 2,449 | 5.9 | 5.5 | 0.35 | 0.35 |
| Hunting and trapping.............................. | 1142 | 345 | 358 | 1.6 | 1.7 | 0.05 | 0.05 |
| Agriculture and forestry support activities.................. | 115 | 10,926 | 11,048 | 96.5 | 97.6 | 3.59 | 3.74 |
| Crop production support activities..................... | 1151 | 4,761 | 4,848 | 65.3 | 66.0 | 2.46 | 2.58 |
| Animal production support activities..................... | 1152 | 4,485 | 4,488 | 19.5 | 19.9 | 0.65 | 0.67 |
| Forestry support activities........................... | 1153 | 1,680 | 1,712 | 11.7 | 11.7 | 0.49 | 0.49 |
| Mining, quarrying and oil, and gas extraction............ | 21 | 29,225 | 27,234 | 743.7 | 587.0 | 61.65 | 49.40 |
| Oil and gas extraction.................................. | 211 | 7,906 | 7,330 | 135.5 | 122.1 | 17.28 | 15.30 |
| Mining (except oil and gas)................................. | 212 | 6,324 | 6,204 | 191.9 | 173.9 | 13.99 | 12.26 |
| Coal mining.......................................... | 2121 | 881 | 800 | 69.9 | 55.0 | 5.40 | 4.08 |
| Metal ore mining..................................... | 2122 | 330 | 331 | 40.2 | 37.9 | 3.56 | 3.19 |
| Nonmetallic mineral mining and quarrying............... | 2123 | 5,113 | 5,073 | 81.8 | 81.0 | 5.03 | 4.99 |
| Mining support activities................................ | 213 | 14,995 | 13,700 | 416.2 | 291.0 | 30.37 | 21.84 |
| Timber–related manufacturing............................ | (X) | 18,288 | 18,342 | 729.5 | 739.8 | 36.72 | 37.33 |
| Wood product manufacturing............................ | 321 | 14,071 | 14,251 | 378.5 | 391.4 | 15.24 | 16.04 |
| Sawmills and wood preservation....................... | 3211 | 3,165 | 3,213 | 84.1 | 84.8 | 3.57 | 3.79 |
| Veneer, plywood and engineered wood product manufacturing.......................................... | 3212 | 1,407 | 1,412 | 69.8 | 75.0 | 3.22 | 3.43 |
| Other wood product manufacturing........................ | 3219 | 9,499 | 9,626 | 224.6 | 231.5 | 8.45 | 8.82 |
| Paper manufacturing..................................... | 322 | 4,217 | 4,091 | 351.0 | 348.5 | 21.48 | 21.28 |
| Pulp, paper and paperboard mills......................... | 3221 | 460 | 453 | 105.7 | 103.0 | 8.07 | 7.80 |
| Converted paper product manufacturing................... | 3222 | 3,757 | 3,638 | 245.3 | 245.4 | 13.41 | 13.48 |

X Not applicable. [1] Data based on North American Industry Classification System (NAICS), 2012. [2] Covers full- and part-time employees who are on the payroll in the pay period including March 12.

Source: U.S. Census Bureau, County Business Patterns, "Geography Area Series: County Business Patterns," <http://factfinder.census.gov>, accessed April 2018. See also <https://www.census.gov/programs-surveys/cbp.html>.

# Table 914. Natural Resource–Related Industries—Establishments, Sales, Payroll, and Employees by Industry: 2007 and 2012

[414 represents $414,000,000,000. Includes only establishments with payroll. Data are based on the 2007 and 2012 economic censuses, which are subject to nonsampling error. For details on methodology and nonsampling and sampling errors, see Appendix III]

| Industry | 2007 NAICS code [1] | Establishments (number) | | Value of shipments (bil. dol.) | | Annual payroll (bil. dol.) | | Paid employees [2] (1,000) | |
|---|---|---|---|---|---|---|---|---|---|
| | | 2007 | 2012 | 2007 | 2012 | 2007 | 2012 | 2007 | 2012 |
| Mining............................................. | 21 | 22,667 | 25,417 | 414 | 529 | 41 | 59 | 730 | 848 |
| Oil & gas extraction.............................. | 211 | 6,260 | 6,735 | 255 | 311 | 10 | 15 | 150 | 176 |
| Mining (except oil & gas)...................... | 212 | 6,472 | 6,091 | 86 | 98 | 12 | 14 | 211 | 212 |
| Mining support activities....................... | 213 | 9,935 | 12,591 | 73 | 120 | 19 | 30 | 369 | 460 |
| Manufacturing [3]................................ | 31–33 | 332,536 | 297,191 | 5,319 | 5,697 | 614 | 593 | 13,396 | 11,214 |
| Wood product manufacturing................. | 321 | 16,868 | 13,579 | 102 | 78 | 17 | 12 | 524 | 337 |
| Paper manufacturing........................... | 322 | 4,988 | 4,425 | 177 | 181 | 21 | 20 | 418 | 350 |
| Petroleum & coal products manufacturing... | 324 | 2,283 | 2,193 | 615 | 851 | 9 | 9 | 106 | 101 |

[1] Data based on North American Industry Classification System (NAICS), 2007. [2] For pay period including March 12. [3] Includes other industries, not shown separately.

Source: U.S. Census Bureau, 2012 Economic Census, "EC1200CCOMP1: All sectors: Core Business Statistics Series: Comparative Statistics for the U.S. (2007 NAICS Basis): 2012 and 2007," <http://factfinder.census.gov>, accessed September 2016.

## Table 915. Gross Domestic Product of Natural Resource-Related Industries in Current and Chained (2012) Dollars by Industry: 2010 to 2018

[In billions of dollars (14,992.1 represents $14,992,100,000,000). Data are based on the North American Industry Classification System (NAICS); see text, Section 15. Data include nonfactor charges (capital consumption allowances, indirect business taxes, etc.) as well as factor charges against gross product; corporate profits and capital consumption allowances have been shifted from a company to an establishment basis]

| Industry | Current dollars | | | | Chained (2012) dollars | | | |
|---|---|---|---|---|---|---|---|---|
| | 2010 | 2016 | 2017 | 2018 | 2010 | 2016 | 2017 | 2018 |
| **All industries, total** [1] | **14,992.1** | **18,707.2** | **19,485.4** | **20,494.1** | **15,598.8** | **17,659.2** | **18,050.7** | **18,566.4** |
| Industries covered [2] | 531.7 | 473.8 | 534.8 | 586.6 | 581.9 | 736.4 | 731.7 | 729.2 |
| Percent of all industries | 3.5 | 2.5 | 2.7 | 2.9 | 3.7 | 4.2 | 4.1 | 3.9 |
| Private industries | 12,884.1 | 16,319.4 | 17,031.7 | 17,989.4 | 13,467.3 | 15,387.5 | 15,718.2 | 16,188.9 |
| Agriculture, forestry, fishing, and hunting | 146.3 | 164.9 | 169.2 | 164.2 | 193.9 | 234.2 | 223.0 | 213.8 |
| Farms | 117.6 | 129.5 | 132.8 | 126.7 | 165.1 | 203.3 | 190.2 | 181.5 |
| Forestry, fishing, and related activities | 28.7 | 35.5 | 36.4 | 37.5 | 29.1 | 31.9 | 32.3 | 31.5 |
| Mining | 305.8 | 216.2 | 268.6 | 321.1 | 309.3 | 423.1 | 429.3 | 435.9 |
| Oil and gas extraction | 188.8 | 133.6 | 174.8 | 218.8 | 181.7 | 378.4 | 363.1 | 357.6 |
| Mining, except oil and gas | 69.5 | 49.8 | 54.2 | 56.3 | 75.3 | 62.6 | 66.5 | 67.5 |
| Support activities for mining | 47.5 | 32.8 | 39.6 | 46.1 | 52.3 | 32.3 | 38.6 | 45.2 |
| Timber-related manufacturing | 79.6 | 92.7 | 97.0 | 101.3 | 78.7 | 79.1 | 79.4 | 79.5 |
| Wood products | 23.3 | 35.0 | 38.1 | 40.4 | 22.9 | 27.2 | 28.8 | 28.0 |
| Paper products | 56.3 | 57.7 | 58.9 | 60.9 | 55.8 | 51.9 | 50.6 | 51.5 |

[1] Includes industries not shown separately. [2] Sum of agriculture/forestry/fishing/hunting, mining, and timber-related manufacturing.

Source: U.S. Bureau of Economic Analysis, Industry Economic Data, GDP-by-Industry, "Value Added by Industry" and "Real Value Added by Industry," <http://www.bea.gov/itable/>, accessed April 2019.

## Table 916. Timber–Based Manufacturing Industries—Establishments, Shipments, Payroll, and Employees: 2012

[78,123,546 represents $78,123,546,000. Includes only establishments or firms with payroll. Data for industries with NAICS codes less than 6-digits were derived by summing values with the corresponding 6-digit NAICS codes. See Appendix III]

| Industry | 2012 NAICS code [1] | Establish- ments (number) | Value of shipments ($1,000) | Annual payroll ($1,000) | Paid employees [2] |
|---|---|---|---|---|---|
| **Wood product manufacturing** | **321** | **13,741** | **78,123,546** | **12,520,235** | **338,773** |
| Saw mills | 321113 | 2,928 | 18,785,567 | 2,629,715 | 64,743 |
| Wood preservation | 321114 | 421 | 4,285,259 | 367,257 | 8,061 |
| Hardwood veneer and plywood manufacturing | 321211 | 240 | 2,532,796 | 439,647 | 11,734 |
| Softwood veneer and plywood manufacturing | 321212 | 100 | 4,221,047 | 623,881 | 13,739 |
| Engineered wood member (except truss) manufacturing | 321213 | 107 | 901,798 | 120,672 | 2,854 |
| Truss manufacturing | 321214 | 772 | 3,084,288 | 696,224 | 18,828 |
| Reconstituted wood product manufacturing | 321219 | 218 | 6,365,849 | 661,850 | 13,531 |
| Wood window and door manufacturing | 321911 | 1,139 | 9,196,661 | 1,815,229 | 46,713 |
| Cut stock, resawing lumber, and planing | 321912 | 989 | 5,979,132 | 838,000 | 24,358 |
| Other millwork (including flooring) | 321918 | 1,502 | 4,994,874 | 920,332 | 26,738 |
| Wood container and pallet manufacturing | 321920 | 2,687 | 6,889,954 | 1,438,803 | 49,003 |
| Manufactured home (mobile home) manufacturing | 321991 | 271 | 3,492,514 | 686,290 | 20,912 |
| Prefabricated wood building manufacturing | 321992 | 615 | 2,323,210 | 441,883 | 12,012 |
| All other miscellaneous wood product manufacturing | 321999 | 1,752 | 5,070,597 | 840,362 | 25,547 |
| **Paper manufacturing** | **322** | **4,425** | **180,610,366** | **19,910,069** | **350,185** |
| Pulp mills | 322110 | 32 | 5,985,071 | 590,813 | 7,728 |
| Paper (except newsprint) mills | 322121 | 166 | 44,026,857 | 4,193,576 | 60,217 |
| Newsprint mills | 322122 | 17 | 2,720,026 | 255,201 | 3,573 |
| Paperboard mills | 322130 | 156 | 28,441,347 | 2,612,294 | 34,910 |
| Corrugated and solid fiber box manufacturing | 322211 | 1,264 | 33,604,124 | 4,146,346 | 76,372 |
| Folding paperboard box manufacturing | 322212 | 507 | 12,596,499 | 1,991,529 | 39,456 |
| Other paperboard container manufacturing | 322219 | 344 | 7,604,741 | 909,918 | 21,047 |
| Paper bag and coated and treated paper manufacturing | 322220 | 816 | 21,304,814 | 2,601,905 | 50,481 |
| Stationery product manufacturing | 322230 | 460 | 6,944,097 | 913,180 | 21,876 |
| Sanitary paper product manufacturing | 322291 | 142 | 12,175,509 | 949,647 | 18,071 |
| All other converted paper product manufacturing | 322299 | 521 | 5,207,281 | 745,660 | 16,455 |

[1] North American Industry Classification System, 2012. [2] For pay period including March 12.

Source: U.S. Census Bureau, 2012 Economic Census, "EC1200A1: All sectors: Geographic Area Series: Economy-Wide Key Statistics: 2012," <http://factfinder.census.gov>, accessed September 2016.

## Table 917. Timber-Based Manufacturing Industries—Employees, Payroll, and Shipments: 2016

[In thousands (11,113 represents 11,113,000). Based on the Annual Survey of Manufactures, see Appendix III]

| Selected industry | 2012 NAICS code [1] | All employees Number (1,000) | All employees Payroll Total (mil. dol.) | All employees Payroll Per employee (dol.) | Produc- tion workers, total (1,000) | Value added by manufactures Total (mil. dol.) | Value added by manufactures Per produc- tion worker (dol.) | Value of ship- ments (mil. dol.) |
|---|---|---|---|---|---|---|---|---|
| **Manufacturing, all industries [2]**............ | 31–33 | **11,113** | **643,406** | **57,898** | **7,733** | **2,408,996** | **311,515** | **5,354,694** |
| **Timber-based manufacturing, total**..... | 321–322 | **711** | **36,761** | **51,676** | **560** | **128,709** | **229,718** | **283,713** |
| Percent of total manufacturing.......... | (X) | 6.4 | 5.7 | (X) | 7.2 | 5.3 | (X) | 5.3 |
| Wood product manufacturing.................. | 321 | 378 | 16,072 | 42,466 | 302 | 44,245 | 146,462 | 102,047 |
| Sawmills and wood preservation........... | 3211 | 77 | 3,742 | 48,477 | 65 | 11,663 | 179,908 | 30,556 |
| Veneer, plywood, and engineered wood product..................................... | 3212 | 73 | 3,380 | 46,362 | 58 | 9,721 | 168,120 | 22,074 |
| Other wood product........................ | 3219 | 228 | 8,950 | 39,191 | 179 | 22,862 | 127,401 | 49,417 |
| Millwork.................................... | 32191 | 105 | 4,374 | 41,724 | 83 | 11,992 | 144,339 | 25,198 |
| Wood container and pallet................. | 32192 | 55 | 1,903 | 34,900 | 43 | 3,956 | 91,743 | 9,287 |
| All other wood products.................... | 32199 | 69 | 2,673 | 38,734 | 53 | 6,914 | 129,844 | 14,932 |
| Manufactured (mobile) home............ | 321991 | 23 | 831 | 36,411 | 19 | 2,351 | 125,143 | 5,117 |
| Prefabricated wood building.............. | 321992 | 16 | 688 | 44,128 | 11 | 1,364 | 128,727 | 3,201 |
| All other misc. wood product............. | 321999 | 31 | 1,154 | 37,716 | 24 | 3,199 | 134,046 | 6,615 |
| Paper manufacturing......................... | 322 | 333 | 20,689 | 62,145 | 258 | 84,464 | 327,130 | 181,667 |
| Pulp, paper, and paperboard mills........... | 3221 | 99 | 7,640 | 77,136 | 78 | 41,418 | 531,239 | 76,435 |
| Pulp mills.................................. | 32211 | 8 | 671 | 84,191 | 6 | 2,769 | 431,522 | 5,501 |
| Paper mills................................. | 32212 | 57 | 4,200 | 73,945 | 45 | 21,708 | 478,628 | 41,937 |
| Paperboard mills........................... | 32213 | 34 | 2,770 | 80,782 | 26 | 16,941 | 646,766 | 28,997 |
| Converted paper product.................... | 3222 | 234 | 13,049 | 55,796 | 180 | 43,046 | 238,837 | 105,232 |
| Paperboard container....................... | 32221 | 138 | 7,817 | 56,442 | 107 | 23,409 | 217,887 | 61,797 |
| Paper bag and coated and treated paper............................... | 32222 | 46 | 2,627 | 57,488 | 35 | 9,368 | 271,194 | 20,660 |
| Stationery product.......................... | 32223 | 17 | 793 | 47,992 | 13 | 2,206 | 175,173 | 6,291 |
| Other converted paper products........... | 32229 | 33 | 1,812 | 54,651 | 26 | 8,064 | 314,234 | 16,483 |

X Not applicable. [1] North American Industry Classification System, 2012; see text, Section 15. [2] Includes other industries, not shown separately.

Source: U.S. Census Bureau, Annual Survey of Manufactures, "Statistics for Industry Groups and Industries: 2016 and 2015," <http://factfinder.census.gov>, accessed February 2018.

## Table 918. Forest Land and Timberland by Type of Owner and Region: 2017

[In thousands of acres (765,493 represents 765,493,000). As of January 1. Data are from the U.S. Forest Service's Forest Inventory and Analysis National Program. Forest land is land at least 10 percent stocked by forest trees of any size, including land that formerly had such tree cover and that will be naturally or artificially regenerated. The minimum area for classification of forest land is 1 acre or strips of timber with a crown width of at least 120 feet wide. Timberland is forest land that is producing or is capable of producing crops of industrial wood and that is not withdrawn from timber utilization by statute or administrative regulation]

| Region | Forest land, total | Timberland Total | Timberland Federal Total | Timberland Federal National forest | Timberland Federal Bureau of Land Manage- ment lands | Timberland Federal Other | State, county, and municipal | Private [1] |
|---|---|---|---|---|---|---|---|---|
| **Total**........................ | **765,493** | **514,425** | **108,178** | **96,138** | **6,109** | **5,931** | **47,095** | **359,152** |
| North.......................... | 175,789 | 164,894 | 11,348 | 10,146 | 12 | 1,190 | 25,650 | 127,896 |
| Northeast.................... | 84,727 | 78,539 | 2,852 | 2,355 | 0 | 498 | 10,102 | 65,586 |
| North Central................ | 91,062 | 86,355 | 8,495 | 7,792 | 12 | 692 | 15,549 | 62,310 |
| South......................... | 245,513 | 208,092 | 16,397 | 12,258 | 0 | 4,138 | 9,561 | 182,135 |
| Southeast.................... | 89,692 | 85,754 | 7,016 | 5,061 | 0 | 1,955 | 5,618 | 73,119 |
| South Central............... | 155,821 | 122,338 | 9,380 | 7,197 | 0 | 2,183 | 3,942 | 109,016 |
| Rocky Mountains.............. | 130,641 | 69,654 | 47,111 | 44,206 | 2,688 | 217 | 3,193 | 19,350 |
| Great Plains................. | 6,797 | 6,084 | 1,217 | 1,051 | 18 | 148 | 265 | 4,602 |
| Intermountain................ | 123,844 | 63,569 | 45,894 | 43,154 | 2,670 | 70 | 2,927 | 14,748 |
| Pacific Coast.................. | 213,549 | 71,784 | 33,323 | 29,527 | 3,409 | 386 | 8,691 | 29,771 |
| Alaska........................ | 128,735 | 12,996 | 4,874 | 3,848 | 812 | 213 | 4,810 | 3,313 |
| Pacific Northwest........... | 51,827 | 41,462 | 19,200 | 16,802 | 2,299 | 98 | 3,637 | 18,625 |
| Pacific Southwest [2]......... | 32,986 | 17,326 | 9,249 | 8,877 | 297 | 75 | 245 | 7,833 |

[1] Includes Indian lands. [2] Includes Hawaii.

Source: U.S. Forest Service, National Assessment - Resources Planning Act (RPA), *Forest Resources of the United States, 2017: A Technical Document Supporting the Forest Service 2020 Update of the RPA Assessment,* May 2018. See also <https://www.fia.fs.fed.us/program-features/rpa/>.

# Table 919. National Forest System Lands by State: 2018

[In thousands of acres (232,421 represents 232,421,000). As of September 30, 2018. Data do not include Delaware, District of Columbia, Hawaii, Iowa, Maryland, Massachusetts, New Jersey, or Rhode Island]

| State | Total lands | National Forest System lands [1] | Other lands [2] | State | Total lands | National Forest System lands [1] | Other lands [2] |
|---|---|---|---|---|---|---|---|
| **United States**....... | **232,421** | **192,948** | **39,473** | Nevada................ | 6,288 | 5,761 | 527 |
| Alabama.............. | 1,290 | 671 | 620 | New Hampshire...... | 851 | 754 | 97 |
| Alaska................ | 23,930 | 22,139 | 1,791 | New Mexico.......... | 10,250 | 9,225 | 1,024 |
| Arizona.............. | 11,813 | 11,179 | 633 | New York............. | 17 | 16 | (Z) |
| Arkansas............ | 3,549 | 2,593 | 956 | North Carolina........ | 3,027 | 1,256 | 1,770 |
| California............ | 24,288 | 20,792 | 3,496 | North Dakota......... | 1,103 | 1,103 | (Z) |
| Colorado............ | 15,960 | 14,487 | 1,473 | Ohio................. | 856 | 244 | 612 |
| Connecticut.......... | (Z) | (Z) | – | Oklahoma............ | 759 | 400 | 359 |
| Florida.............. | 1,423 | 1,203 | 220 | Oregon.............. | 17,654 | 15,697 | 1,957 |
| Georgia............. | 1,796 | 868 | 929 | Pennsylvania........ | 741 | 514 | 227 |
| Idaho............... | 21,714 | 20,448 | 1,266 | South Carolina........ | 1,381 | 635 | 747 |
| Illinois.............. | 958 | 305 | 653 | South Dakota........ | 2,436 | 2,006 | 430 |
| Indiana.............. | 647 | 204 | 443 | Tennessee........... | 1,291 | 722 | 569 |
| Kansas............. | 109 | 109 | (Z) | Texas............... | 2,002 | 757 | 1,245 |
| Kentucky............ | 2,205 | 818 | 1,387 | Utah................ | 9,211 | 8,193 | 1,018 |
| Louisiana............ | 1,032 | 609 | 423 | Vermont............. | 837 | 411 | 426 |
| Maine............... | 94 | 54 | 41 | Virginia.............. | 3,254 | 1,668 | 1,586 |
| Michigan............ | 4,887 | 2,875 | 2,013 | Washington.......... | 11,990 | 9,335 | 2,654 |
| Minnesota........... | 5,488 | 2,845 | 2,643 | West Virginia......... | 1,893 | 1,046 | 846 |
| Mississippi.......... | 2,374 | 1,191 | 1,183 | Wisconsin........... | 2,003 | 1,525 | 478 |
| Missouri............. | 3,093 | 1,508 | 1,585 | Wyoming............ | 9,726 | 9,216 | 510 |
| Montana............. | 19,189 | 17,186 | 2,002 | Puerto Rico.......... | 56 | 29 | 27 |
| Nebraska............ | 562 | 351 | 211 | Virgin Islands........ | (Z) | (Z) | – |

– Represents zero. Z Less than 500 acres. [1] National Forest System is a nationally significant system of federally owned units of forest, range, and related land consisting of national forests, purchase units, national grasslands, land utilization project areas, experimental forest areas, experimental range areas, designated experimental areas, and other land areas; water areas; and interests in lands that are administered by USDA Forest Service or designated for administration through the Forest Service. [2] Other lands are lands within the unit boundaries in private, state, county, and municipal ownership and the federal lands over which the Forest Service has no jurisdiction. Also includes lands offered to the United States and approved for acquisition and subsequent Forest Service administration, but to which title has not yet been accepted by the United States.

Source: U.S. Forest Service, *Land Areas of the National Forest System as of September 30, 2018*, November 2018. See also <https://www.fs.fed.us/land/staff/lar/LAR2018/lar2018index.html>.

# Table 920. Timber Volume, Growth, and Removal on Timberland by Species Group and Region: 2016 and 2017

[In millions of cubic feet (1,116,012 represents 1,116,012,000,000). Data are from the U.S. Forest Service's Forest Inventory and Analysis National Program]

| Region | 2017 Net volume [1] | | | | | | 2016 Net growth and removals of growing stock | | | | | |
|---|---|---|---|---|---|---|---|---|---|---|---|---|
| | All timber [2] | | | Growing stock [3] | | | Timber growth [4] | | | Timber removals [5] | | |
| | All species | Soft-woods | Hard-woods | All species | Soft-woods | Hard-woods | All species | Soft-woods | Hard-woods | All species | Soft-woods | Hard-woods |
| **Total**................ | **1,116,012** | **598,873** | **517,139** | **985,238** | **560,526** | **424,712** | **25,009** | **15,468** | **9,542** | **13,041** | **8,901** | **4,140** |
| North................ | 314,204 | 68,278 | 245,926 | 270,041 | 60,601 | 209,440 | 5,932 | 1,546 | 4,386 | 2,491 | 654 | 1,837 |
| Northeast............ | 172,556 | 41,465 | 131,091 | 152,780 | 37,108 | 115,672 | 3,264 | 917 | 2,347 | 1,176 | 377 | 799 |
| North Central......... | 141,647 | 26,813 | 114,834 | 117,261 | 23,494 | 93,768 | 2,668 | 629 | 2,039 | 1,315 | 277 | 1,038 |
| South............... | 377,781 | 149,800 | 227,981 | 319,088 | 141,307 | 177,781 | 13,764 | 9,268 | 4,496 | 7,859 | 5,647 | 2,212 |
| Southeast............ | 167,894 | 71,539 | 96,355 | 142,603 | 67,540 | 75,063 | 6,393 | 4,285 | 2,108 | 3,527 | 2,736 | 790 |
| South Central........ | 209,887 | 78,261 | 131,626 | 176,485 | 73,767 | 102,717 | 7,371 | 4,983 | 2,388 | 4,333 | 2,911 | 1,422 |
| Rocky Mountains.... | 144,222 | 128,750 | 15,472 | 130,005 | 119,102 | 10,903 | 299 | 189 | 109 | 405 | 396 | 8,626 |
| Great Plains......... | 8,476 | 2,537 | 5,938 | 4,487 | 1,885 | 2,601 | 57 | -2 | 59 | 34 | 29 | 6 |
| Intermountain........ | 135,747 | 126,213 | 9,534 | 125,518 | 117,217 | 8,301 | 242 | 192 | 50 | 370 | 367 | 3 |
| Pacific Coast........ | 279,805 | 252,044 | 27,760 | 266,104 | 239,515 | 26,589 | 5,015 | 4,465 | 550 | 2,286 | 2,204 | 82 |
| Alaska.............. | 39,229 | 35,639 | 3,590 | 37,140 | 33,761 | 3,379 | 254 | 133 | 121 | 39 | 39 | (Z) |
| Pacific Northwest.... | 166,844 | 153,680 | 13,163 | 159,238 | 146,480 | 12,758 | 3,707 | 3,423 | 284 | 1,892 | 1,811 | 81 |
| Pacific Southwest [6].. | 73,732 | 62,725 | 11,007 | 69,726 | 59,273 | 10,452 | 1,054 | 909 | 145 | 355 | 355 | (Z) |

Z Less than 500,000. [1] As of January 1. [2] Includes growing stock, live cull and sound dead. [3] Live trees of commercial species meeting specified standards of quality or vigor. Cull trees are excluded. Includes only trees 5.0-inches in diameter or larger at 4 1/2 feet above ground. [4] The net increase in the volume of trees during a specified year. Components include the increment in net volume of trees at the beginning of the specific year surviving to its end, plus the net volume of trees reaching the minimum size class during the year, minus the volume of trees that died during the year, and minus the net volume of trees that became cull trees during the year. [5] The net volume of trees removed from the inventory during a specified year by harvesting, cultural operations such as timber stand improvement, or land clearing. [6] Includes Hawaii.

Source: U.S. Forest Service, National Assessment - Resources Planning Act (RPA), *Forest Resources of the United States, 2017: A Technical Document Supporting the Forest Service 2020 Update of the RPA Assessment,* May 2018. See also <https://www.fia.fs.fed.us/program-features/rpa/>.

## Table 921. Timber Removals—Roundwood Product Output by Source and Species Group: 2016

[In millions of cubic feet (13,972 represents 13,972,000,000). Data are from U.S. Forest Service's Forest Inventory and Analysis National Program]

| Source and species group | Total | Sawlogs | Pulpwood | Veneer logs | Other products [1] | Fuelwood [2] |
|---|---|---|---|---|---|---|
| **Total** | **13,972** | **5,521** | **5,368** | **660** | **728** | **1,695** |
| Softwoods | 9,480 | 4,075 | 3,640 | 590 | 576 | 599 |
| Hardwoods | 4,493 | 1,446 | 1,728 | 69 | 153 | 1,096 |
| Growing stock [3] | 11,650 | 5,334 | 4,773 | 648 | 563 | 332 |
| Softwoods | 8,393 | 3,959 | 3,280 | 582 | 423 | 149 |
| Hardwoods | 3,257 | 1,374 | 1,493 | 65 | 141 | 183 |
| Other sources [4] | 2,323 | 187 | 596 | 12 | 165 | 1,363 |
| Softwoods | 1,086 | 115 | 360 | 8 | 153 | 450 |
| Hardwoods | 1,236 | 72 | 235 | 4 | 12 | 913 |

[1] Includes poles, pilings, posts, cooperage and miscellaneous products. [2] Downed and dead wood volume left on the ground after trees have been cut on timberland and used for conversion to some form of energy, primarily in residential use. [3] Includes live trees of commercial species meeting specified standards of quality or vigor. Cull trees are excluded. Includes only trees 5.0 inches in diameter or larger at 4.5 feet above the ground. [4] Includes salvable dead trees, rough and rotten trees, trees of noncommercial species, trees less than 5.0 inches in diameter at 4.5 feet above the ground, tops, and roundwood harvested from nonforest land (for example, fence rows).

Source: U.S. Forest Service, National Assessment - Resources Planning Act (RPA), *Forest Resources of the United States, 2017: A Technical Document Supporting the Forest Service 2020 Update of the RPA Assessment,* May 2018. See also <https://www.fia.fs.fed.us/program-features/rpa/>.


## Table 922. Timber Products—Production, Foreign Trade, and Consumption by Type of Product: 1990 to 2013

[In millions of cubic feet, roundwood equivalent (15,577 represents 15,577,000,000)]

| Type of product | 1990 | 1995 | 2000 | 2005 | 2008 | 2009 | 2010 | 2011 | 2012 | 2013 |
|---|---|---|---|---|---|---|---|---|---|---|
| **Industrial roundwood:** | | | | | | | | | | |
| Domestic production | 15,577 | 15,454 | 15,528 | 14,075 | 11,721 | 10,384 | 10,727 | 11,299 | 11,611 | 11,971 |
| Softwoods | 10,968 | 10,166 | 10,327 | 10,406 | 8,880 | 7,716 | 8,218 | 8,640 | 8,978 | 9,225 |
| Hardwoods | 4,609 | 5,288 | 5,201 | 3,669 | 2,841 | 2,668 | 2,509 | 2,660 | 2,633 | 2,746 |
| Imports | 3,044 | 3,929 | 4,619 | 5,511 | 3,148 | 2,388 | 2,496 | 2,466 | 2,577 | 2,597 |
| Exports | 2,306 | 2,284 | 2,039 | 1,470 | 1,751 | 1,571 | 1,840 | 2,040 | 1,960 | 2,161 |
| Consumption | 16,315 | 17,099 | 18,108 | 18,116 | 13,117 | 11,201 | 11,384 | 11,725 | 12,228 | 12,407 |
| Softwoods | 11,736 | 11,955 | 12,830 | 14,021 | 10,278 | 8,520 | 8,895 | 9,097 | 9,598 | 9,925 |
| Hardwoods | 4,579 | 5,144 | 5,278 | 4,095 | 2,840 | 2,681 | 2,489 | 2,629 | 2,630 | 2,482 |
| **Lumber:** | | | | | | | | | | |
| Domestic production | 7,317 | 6,857 | 7,384 | 7,680 | 5,395 | 4,576 | 4,569 | 5,005 | 5,219 | 5,607 |
| Imports | 1,905 | 2,545 | 2,943 | 3,744 | 1,894 | 1,347 | 1,422 | 1,403 | 1,480 | 1,699 |
| Exports | 589 | 462 | 435 | 362 | 345 | 288 | 341 | 387 | 374 | 406 |
| Consumption | 8,633 | 8,939 | 9,892 | 11,063 | 6,945 | 5,636 | 5,650 | 6,022 | 6,324 | 6,901 |
| **Plywood and veneer:** | | | | | | | | | | |
| Domestic production | 1,423 | 1,303 | 1,187 | 1,068 | 745 | 616 | 655 | 653 | 679 | 702 |
| Imports | 97 | 107 | 154 | 373 | 184 | 146 | 161 | 163 | 160 | 171 |
| Exports | 109 | 89 | 51 | 37 | 45 | 34 | 55 | 52 | 57 | 57 |
| Consumption | 1,410 | 1,321 | 1,290 | 1,403 | 884 | 728 | 760 | 764 | 782 | 815 |
| **Pulp products:** | | | | | | | | | | |
| Domestic production | 5,313 | 6,079 | 5,881 | 4,498 | 4,720 | 4,423 | 4,617 | 4,682 | 4,824 | 4,766 |
| Imports | 1,038 | 1,245 | 1,448 | 1,272 | 1,029 | 857 | 873 | 861 | 879 | 672 |
| Exports | 645 | 904 | 776 | 560 | 791 | 731 | 802 | 881 | 875 | 1,033 |
| Consumption | 5,705 | 6,420 | 6,553 | 5,211 | 4,959 | 4,550 | 4,688 | 4,661 | 4,842 | 4,406 |
| **Logs:** [1] | | | | | | | | | | |
| Imports | 4 | 13 | 72 | 113 | 35 | 28 | 32 | 30 | 49 | 47 |
| Exports | 674 | 451 | 422 | 345 | 313 | 322 | 407 | 485 | 432 | 432 |
| Pulpwood chips, exports | 288 | 377 | 355 | 166 | 257 | 196 | 235 | 235 | 235 | 234 |
| **Other industrial timber products:** [2] | | | | | | | | | | |
| Production and consumption | 562 | 387 | 300 | 318 | 290 | 250 | 245 | 239 | 222 | 230 |
| **Fuelwood:** | | | | | | | | | | |
| Production and consumption | 2,900 | 2,150 | 1,622 | 1,550 | 1,510 | 1,400 | 1,380 | 1,366 | 1,440 | 1,520 |

[1] Prior to 2010, pulpwood logs are not included in logs. [2] Includes cooperage logs, poles and piling, fence posts, hewn ties, round mine timbers, box bolts, etc.

Source: U.S. Forest Service, *U.S. Timber Production, Trade, Consumption, and Price Statistics, 1965-2013,* February 2016. See also <https://www.treesearch.fs.fed.us/pubs/50895>.

# Table 923. Selected Timber Products—Imports and Exports: 1990 to 2013

[In million board feet (13,107 represents 13,107,000,000), except as indicated]

| Product | Unit | 1990 | 1995 | 2000 | 2005 | 2009 | 2010 | 2011 | 2012 | 2013 |
|---|---|---|---|---|---|---|---|---|---|---|
| IMPORTS | | | | | | | | | | |
| Lumber, total............... | Mil. bd. ft. | 13,107 | 17,556 | 20,243 | 25,753 | 9,236 | 9,769 | 9,633 | 10,172 | 11,666 |
| Softwood................. | Mil. bd. ft. | 12,875 | 17,202 | 19,449 | 24,678 | 8,855 | 9,468 | 9,289 | 9,864 | 11,358 |
| Hardwood............... | Mil. bd. ft. | 232 | 354 | 795 | 1,075 | 381 | 301 | 344 | 308 | 308 |
| From Canada............ | Mil. bd. ft. | 11,918 | 16,990 | 18,616 | 21,841 | 8,393 | 9,151 | 8,946 | 9,633 | 11,020 |
| Logs, total [1]............... | Mil. bd. ft. [2] | 23 | 80 | 450 | 704 | 178 | 199 | 188 | 307 | 291 |
| Softwood................. | Mil. bd. ft. | 13 | 55 | 390 | 609 | 90 | 99 | 91 | 136 | 120 |
| Hardwood............... | Mil. bd. ft. | 10 | 26 | 59 | 95 | 88 | 100 | 97 | 171 | 171 |
| From Canada............ | Mil. bd. ft. | 19 | 56 | 426 | 605 | 89 | 90 | 84 | 133 | 120 |
| Paper and board [3]........... | 1,000 tons | 12,195 | 14,238 | 17,356 | 17,958 | 11,218 | 11,144 | 10,670 | 10,490 | 11,007 |
| Woodpulp................... | 1,000 tons | 4,893 | 5,969 | 7,227 | 6,762 | 5,044 | 6,163 | 6,117 | 5,599 | 6,112 |
| Plywood................... | Mil. sq. ft. [4] | 1,687 | 1,951 | 2,902 | 6,964 | 2,751 | 3,042 | 3,081 | 3,029 | 3,219 |
| EXPORTS | | | | | | | | | | |
| Lumber, total............... | Mil. bd. ft. | 4,614 | 2,958 | 2,700 | 2,191 | 1,784 | 2,148 | 2,468 | 2,383 | 2,601 |
| To: Canada.............. | Mil. bd. ft. | 658 | 650 | 701 | 649 | 455 | 621 | 573 | 634 | 640 |
| Japan................. | Mil. bd. ft. | 1,270 | 978 | 325 | 80 | 128 | 179 | 196 | 189 | 208 |
| European Union........... | Mil. bd. ft. | 686 | 513 | 507 | 346 | 175 | 209 | 196 | 166 | 166 |
| Softwood................. | Mil. bd. ft. | 3,753 | 1,872 | 1,400 | 897 | 983 | 1,347 | 1,667 | 1,582 | 1,788 |
| Hardwood............... | Mil. bd. ft. | 813 | 1,057 | 1,300 | 1,294 | 801 | 801 | 801 | 801 | 801 |
| Logs, total [1]............... | Mil. bd. ft. [2] | 4,213 | 2,820 | 2,638 | 2,157 | 2,014 | 2,542 | 3,031 | 2,698 | 2,698 |
| To: Canada.............. | Mil. bd. ft. [2] | 396 | 716 | 1,350 | 1,168 | 876 | 835 | 719 | 754 | 811 |
| Japan................. | Mil. bd. ft. [2] | 2,626 | 1,728 | 934 | 574 | 435 | 425 | 458 | 469 | 523 |
| China................. | Mil. bd. ft. [2] | 362 | 20 | 22 | 94 | 270 | 780 | 1,384 | 1,052 | 1,291 |
| Softwood................. | Mil. bd. ft. | 3,994 | 2,552 | 2,066 | 1,607 | 1,644 | 2,074 | 2,501 | 2,110 | 2,546 |
| Hardwood............... | Mil. bd. ft. | 220 | 268 | 573 | 550 | 369 | 468 | 409 | 418 | 418 |
| Paper and board [3]........... | 1,000 tons | 5,163 | 7,621 | 8,701 | 7,125 | 7,750 | 8,781 | 9,331 | 9,036 | 12,890 |
| Woodpulp................... | 1,000 tons | 5,905 | 8,261 | 6,409 | 6,413 | 7,519 | 8,265 | 9,068 | 8,125 | 8,146 |
| Plywood................... | Mil. sq. ft. [4] | 1,766 | 1,517 | 916 | 686 | 619 | 1,004 | 949 | 1,039 | 1,035 |

[1] Prior to 2000, pulpwood logs are not included. [2] Log scale. [3] Includes paper and board products. Excludes hardboard. [4] 3/8 inch basis.

Source: U.S. Forest Service. *U.S. Timber Production, Trade, Consumption, and Price Statistics, 1965-2013*, February 2016. See also <http://www.treesearch.fs.fed.us/pubs/50895>.

# Table 924. Lumber Production and Consumption by Species Group: 1990 to 2013

[In billion board feet (48.1 represents 48,100,000,000), except per capita in board feet. Per capita consumption based on estimated resident population as of July 1]

| Item | 1990 | 1995 | 2000 | 2005 | 2006 | 2007 | 2008 | 2009 | 2010 | 2011 | 2012 | 2013 |
|---|---|---|---|---|---|---|---|---|---|---|---|---|
| **Production, total**................. | **48.1** | **44.9** | **48.6** | **50.9** | **49.7** | **45.8** | **36.0** | **30.2** | **30.5** | **33.3** | **34.8** | **37.3** |
| By species: | | | | | | | | | | | | |
| Softwoods........................ | 35.8 | 32.2 | 36.0 | 39.8 | 38.7 | 35.2 | 29.2 | 23.2 | 24.8 | 26.8 | 28.3 | 30.0 |
| Hardwoods........................ | 12.0 | 12.6 | 12.6 | 11.2 | 11.0 | 10.6 | 6.8 | 7.0 | 5.7 | 6.6 | 6.5 | 7.3 |
| **Consumption, total**............... | **57.4** | **59.5** | **66.1** | **74.5** | **70.9** | **62.5** | **46.9** | **37.7** | **38.1** | **40.5** | **42.4** | **45.6** |
| Per capita........................ | 230 | 226 | 234 | 251 | 245 | 207 | 154 | 123 | 123 | 130 | 135 | 144 |
| By species: | | | | | | | | | | | | |
| Softwoods........................ | 45.7 | 47.6 | 54.0 | 63.6 | 60.6 | 52.6 | 40.7 | 31.1 | 32.9 | 34.4 | 36.4 | 39.6 |
| Hardwoods........................ | 11.7 | 11.9 | 12.1 | 10.9 | 10.3 | 9.9 | 6.2 | 6.6 | 5.2 | 6.1 | 6.0 | 6.0 |

Source: U.S. Forest Service, *U.S. Timber Production, Trade, Consumption, and Price Statistics, 1965-2013*, February 2016. See also <https://www.treesearch.fs.fed.us/pubs/50895>.

# Table 925. Pulpwood Consumption, Woodpulp Production, and Paper and Board Production and Consumption: 1990 to 2013

[In thousands (99,361 represents 99,361,000) except where otherwise indicated]

| Item | Unit | 1990 | 1995 | 2000 | 2005 | 2009 | 2010 | 2011 | 2012 | 2013 |
|---|---|---|---|---|---|---|---|---|---|---|
| Pulpwood consumption......... | 1,000 cords [1] | 99,361 | 97,052 | 95,904 | 108,513 | 87,424 | 89,774 | 89,158 | 90,649 | 86,164 |
| Woodpulp production [2]......... | 1,000 tons | 60,311 | 63,507 | 62,599 | 59,121 | 50,598 | 52,832 | 53,175 | 53,001 | 53,099 |
| Paper and board: [3] | | | | | | | | | | |
| Production..................... | 1,000 tons | 78,679 | 89,509 | 94,491 | 91,031 | 78,299 | 82,968 | 82,003 | 81,051 | 80,477 |
| Consumption [4]................. | 1,000 tons | 85,711 | 96,126 | 103,147 | 101,864 | 81,767 | 85,331 | 83,342 | 82,565 | 78,594 |
| Per capita..................... | Pounds | 686 | 731 | 731 | 687 | 532 | 551 | 534 | 525 | 498 |

[1] One cord equals 128 cubic feet. [2] Includes dissolving and special alpha pulps; excludes defibrated/exploded pulps and screenings. [3] Excludes wet machine board and construction grades. [4] Production plus imports, minus exports.

Source: U.S. Forest Service. *U.S. Timber Production, Trade, Consumption, and Price Statistics, 1965-2013*, February 2016. See also <https://www.treesearch.fs.fed.us/pubs/50895>.

## Table 926. Selected Timber Products—Producer Price Indexes: 1990 to 2018

[1982=100, unless otherwise noted. For information about producer prices, see text, Section 14]

| Product | 1990 | 1995 | 2000 | 2005 | 2010 | 2015 | 2016 | 2017 | 2018 |
|---|---|---|---|---|---|---|---|---|---|
| **Lumber and wood products**..................... | **129.7** | **178.1** | **178.2** | **196.5** | **192.7** | **221.9** | **222.7** | **230.4** | **243.9** |
| Lumber............................................. | 124.6 | 173.4 | 178.8 | 198.6 | 167.3 | 199.3 | 201.8 | 217.2 | 232.3 |
| Softwood lumber................................ | 123.8 | 178.5 | 178.6 | 203.6 | 160.8 | 192.7 | 198.8 | 223.7 | 241.9 |
| Softwood cut stock and dimension.......... | 129.7 | 183.6 | 195.3 | 205.1 | 206.0 | 199.7 | 200.0 | 214.2 | 228.1 |
| Softwood lumber, not edge worked [1]...... | (NA) | (NA) | (NA) | 115.0 | 85.8 | 104.9 | 108.6 | 121.9 | 131.0 |
| Softwood lumber, MFPL [1, 2]............... | (NA) | (NA) | (NA) | 111.2 | 111.5 | 128.3 | 130.5 | 152.3 | 171.4 |
| Hardwood lumber................................ | 131.0 | 167.0 | 185.9 | 196.6 | 187.3 | 221.1 | 218.1 | 219.6 | 230.1 |
| Millwork.......................................... | 130.4 | 163.8 | 176.4 | 197.2 | 207.0 | 237.2 | 240.6 | 247.6 | 259.5 |
| General millwork............................... | 132.0 | 165.4 | 178.0 | 196.1 | 211.2 | 238.0 | 241.0 | 245.7 | 251.4 |
| Prefabricated structural members........... | 122.3 | 163.5 | 175.1 | 206.9 | 185.6 | 232.6 | 237.6 | 255.5 | 299.2 |
| Plywood.......................................... | 114.2 | 165.3 | 157.6 | 186.8 | 176.7 | 198.9 | 192.3 | 204.2 | 230.2 |
| Softwood veneer and plywood................ | 119.6 | 188.1 | 173.3 | 223.5 | 197.1 | 234.5 | 214.5 | 234.8 | 274.5 |
| Hardwood veneer and plywood [3]........... | (NA) | (NA) | (NA) | (NA) | 103.6 | 108.6 | 112.9 | 115.3 | 123.5 |
| Other wood products........................... | 114.7 | 143.7 | 130.5 | 139.2 | 142.5 | 161.4 | 159.3 | 160.5 | 169.3 |
| Wood pallets and pallet containers......... | 127.6 | 169.7 | 178.5 | 196.3 | 206.6 | 242.1 | 239.7 | 242.2 | 262.8 |
| Wood boxes..................................... | 119.1 | 145.0 | 155.2 | 164.9 | 183.0 | 199.4 | 199.7 | 201.3 | 205.4 |
| **Pulp, paper, and allied products**............... | **141.2** | **172.2** | **183.7** | **202.6** | **236.9** | **248.8** | **247.7** | **254.6** | **260.0** |
| Pulp, paper, and products, excl. building paper..... | 132.9 | 163.4 | 161.4 | 169.8 | 206.8 | 218.4 | 216.3 | 223.9 | 229.7 |
| Woodpulp....................................... | 151.3 | 183.2 | 145.3 | 138.0 | 186.0 | 181.6 | 171.6 | 179.3 | 216.0 |
| Wastepaper..................................... | 138.9 | 371.1 | 282.5 | 230.9 | 421.5 | 291.8 | 312.5 | 399.9 | 276.9 |
| Paper............................................. | 128.8 | 159.0 | 149.8 | 159.6 | 182.1 | 189.8 | 186.7 | 186.4 | 197.6 |
| Writing and printing papers.................. | 129.1 | 158.4 | 146.6 | 156.1 | 179.5 | 183.6 | 180.4 | 176.7 | 188.5 |
| Newsprint....................................... | 119.6 | 161.8 | 127.5 | 138.5 | 125.6 | 113.6 | 114.7 | 118.5 | 138.5 |
| Paperboard..................................... | 135.7 | 183.1 | 176.7 | 175.5 | 224.9 | 243.1 | 233.4 | 257.5 | 273.5 |
| Converted paper and paperboard products....... | 135.2 | 157.0 | 162.7 | 176.1 | 209.0 | 228.2 | 228.5 | 233.8 | 237.4 |
| Sanitary paper products, including stock......... | 135.3 | 144.4 | 146.7 | 154.6 | 181.8 | 182.2 | 182.4 | 181.4 | 179.5 |
| Paper, plastic, and foil bags................. | 156.6 | 172.4 | 173.7 | 210.8 | 246.0 | 280.5 | 275.9 | 279.1 | 287.0 |
| Paper boxes and containers................. | 129.9 | 163.8 | 172.6 | 183.7 | 219.4 | 247.3 | 248.1 | 259.5 | 264.8 |
| Paperboard fiber drums................... | 130.6 | 150.6 | 180.6 | (NA) | 293.4 | 354.7 | 372.1 | 391.7 | 414.9 |
| Office supplies and accessories........... | 121.4 | 134.9 | 133.8 | 143.1 | 159.9 | 174.0 | 176.1 | 177.2 | 186.6 |
| Die-cut paper & paperboard office supplies [1].... | (NA) | (NA) | (NA) | 108.8 | 125.2 | 143.8 | 144.6 | 147.0 | 150.3 |
| Fiber cans, tubes, and similar fiber products...... | 147.8 | 178.3 | 205.5 | 235.2 | 268.6 | 283.0 | 287.9 | 307.6 | 323.8 |
| Building paper & building board mill products........ | 112.2 | 144.9 | 138.8 | 184.9 | 168.4 | 186.3 | 201.0 | 221.3 | 222.9 |
| Hardboard, particleboard & fiberboard products. .. | 107.5 | 139.6 | 132.8 | 176.9 | 158.5 | 175.2 | 189.5 | 209.1 | 210.5 |

NA Not available. [1] December 2003=100. [2] Made from purchased lumber. [3] December 2005=100.

Source: U.S. Bureau of Labor Statistics, "Producer Price Indexes," <http://www.bls.gov/ppi/>, accessed June 2019.

## Table 927. Paper and Paperboard—Production and New Supply: 1990 to 2018

[In millions of short tons (80.55 represents 80,550,000). 1 short ton = 2,000 lbs]

| Item | 1990 | 1995 | 2000 | 2005 | 2010 | 2015 | 2016 | 2017 | 2018 |
|---|---|---|---|---|---|---|---|---|---|
| **Production, total**.................... | **80.55** | **91.21** | **96.05** | **92.61** | **83.70** | **79.80** | **79.15** | **79.17** | **78.87** |
| Paper, total........................... | 39.36 | 42.90 | 45.52 | 41.40 | 35.51 | 29.60 | 28.61 | 27.34 | 26.25 |
| Paperboard, total.................... | 39.42 | 46.55 | 48.97 | 49.71 | 47.46 | 49.40 | 49.73 | 51.07 | 51.86 |
| Unbleached kraft................. | 20.36 | 22.73 | 21.80 | 22.58 | 21.36 | 22.41 | 22.63 | 23.31 | (NA) |
| Semichemical..................... | 5.64 | 5.67 | 5.95 | 6.41 | 5.44 | 4.75 | 4.42 | 4.61 | 4.61 |
| Bleached kraft.................... | 4.26 | 5.16 | 5.30 | 5.58 | 5.62 | 5.35 | 5.21 | 5.29 | 5.40 |
| Recycled.......................... | 9.03 | 12.84 | 15.79 | 15.06 | 15.05 | 16.89 | 17.48 | 17.86 | (NA) |
| Wet machine board and construction grades.............. | 1.82 | 1.82 | 1.56 | 1.50 | 0.73 | 0.80 | 0.81 | 0.76 | 0.76 |
| **New supply, all grades, excluding products**.............. | **87.68** | **98.08** | **105.02** | **101.81** | **84.16** | **79.99** | **79.46** | **78.94** | **79.41** |
| Paper, total........................... | 49.49 | 52.77 | 57.13 | 53.69 | 40.34 | 34.43 | 33.54 | 31.86 | 31.38 |
| Newsprint........................... | 13.41 | 12.76 | 12.92 | 10.12 | 5.00 | 3.51 | 3.35 | 2.91 | 2.54 |
| Printing/writing papers............ | 25.46 | 29.55 | 32.99 | 31.99 | 23.73 | 19.08 | 18.13 | 16.79 | 16.53 |
| Packaging and industrial converting papers............... | 4.72 | 4.24 | 4.27 | 4.05 | 4.18 | 4.17 | 4.23 | 4.36 | 4.41 |
| Tissue.............................. | 5.90 | 6.22 | 6.95 | 7.54 | 7.43 | 7.68 | 7.83 | 7.80 | 7.90 |
| Paperboard, total.................... | 36.30 | 43.39 | 46.02 | 46.51 | 43.06 | 44.77 | 45.13 | 46.33 | 47.29 |

NA Not available.

Source: American Forest and Paper Association, Washington, DC, *Paper Industry Annual Statistical Summary* ©.

## Table 928. Fishery Products—Domestic Catch, Imports, and Disposition: 1990 to 2017

[Live weight, in millions of pounds (16,349 represents 16,349,000,000)]

| Item | 1990 | 1995 | 2000 | 2005 | 2010 | 2014 | 2015 | 2016 | 2017 (P) |
|---|---|---|---|---|---|---|---|---|---|
| **Total supply**........... | **16,349** | **16,484** | **17,340** | **20,612** | **19,748** | **21,431** | **21,426** | **21,542** | **22,266** |
| For human food........... | 12,662 | 13,584 | 14,740 | 18,155 | 17,560 | 19,115 | 18,848 | 18,780 | 19,805 |
| For industrial use [1]........ | 3,687 | 2,900 | 2,600 | 2,457 | 2,188 | 2,317 | 2,579 | 2,762 | 2,461 |
| **Domestic catch**............ | **9,404** | **9,788** | **9,069** | **9,707** | **8,231** | **9,486** | **9,718** | **9,572** | **9,916** |
| For human food........... | 7,041 | 7,667 | 6,912 | 7,997 | 6,526 | 7,828 | 7,750 | 7,484 | 8,228 |
| For industrial use [1]........ | 2,363 | 2,121 | 2,157 | 1,710 | 1,705 | 1,658 | 1,968 | 2,088 | 1,688 |
| **Imports [2]**.............. | **6,945** | **6,696** | **8,271** | **10,905** | **11,517** | **11,945** | **11,709** | **11,970** | **12,350** |
| For human food........... | 5,621 | 5,917 | 7,828 | 10,158 | 11,034 | 11,286 | 11,098 | 11,295 | 11,577 |
| For industrial use [1]........ | 1,324 | 779 | 443 | 747 | 483 | 659 | 611 | 675 | 773 |
| **Exports**............... | **4,627** | **5,166** | **5,758** | **8,420** | **6,129** | **9,344** | **8,771** | **8,675** | **8,921** |
| For human food........... | 3,832 | 4,175 | 4,587 | 6,385 | 5,170 | 7,365 | 6,936 | 6,772 | 6,984 |
| For industrial use [1]........ | 795 | 991 | 1,171 | 2,035 | 959 | 1,979 | 1,835 | 1,903 | 1,938 |
| **Disposition of domestic catch**.......... | **9,404** | **9,788** | **9,069** | **9,707** | **8,231** | **9,486** | **9,718** | **9,572** | **9,916** |
| Fresh and frozen [3]........... | 6,501 | 7,099 | 6,657 | 7,776 | 6,515 | 7,916 | 7,622 | 7,509 | 8,091 |
| Canned [3]............... | 751 | 769 | 530 | 563 | 373 | 196 | 364 | 186 | 289 |
| Cured................ | 126 | 90 | 119 | 160 | 102 | 63 | 65 | 57 | 136 |
| Reduced to meal, oil, etc......... | 2,026 | 1,830 | 1,763 | 1,208 | 1,241 | 1,311 | 1,667 | 1,820 | 1,400 |

P Preliminary. [1] Processed into meal, oil, solubles, and shell products, or used as bait and animal food. [2] Includes landings of tuna caught by foreign vessels in American Samoa. [3] Includes for human food, and bait and animal food.

Source: U.S. National Oceanic and Atmospheric Administration, National Marine Fisheries Service, *Fisheries of the United States 2017*, September 2018, and earlier editions. See also <https://www.fisheries.noaa.gov/resource/document/fisheries-united-states-2017-report>.

## Table 929. Fisheries—Quantity and Value of Domestic Catch: 1980 to 2017

[In millions of pounds (6,482 represents 6,482,000,000), except as noted]

| Year | Quantity [1] (mil. lbs.) Total | For human food | For industrial products [2] | Value (mil. dol.) | Average price per lb. (cents) | Year | Quantity [1] (mil. lbs.) Total | For human food | For industrial products [2] | Value (mil. dol.) | Average price per lb. (cents) |
|---|---|---|---|---|---|---|---|---|---|---|---|
| 1980...... | 6,482 | 3,654 | 2,828 | 2,237 | 34.5 | 2009...... | 8,031 | 6,198 | 1,833 | 3,891 | 48.4 |
| 1985...... | 6,258 | 3,294 | 2,964 | 2,326 | 37.2 | 2010...... | 8,231 | 6,526 | 1,705 | 4,520 | 54.9 |
| 1990...... | 9,404 | 7,041 | 2,363 | 3,522 | 37.5 | 2011...... | 9,858 | 7,909 | 1,949 | 5,289 | 53.7 |
| 1995...... | 9,788 | 7,667 | 2,121 | 3,770 | 38.5 | 2012...... | 9,634 | 7,477 | 2,157 | 5,103 | 53.0 |
| 2000...... | 9,069 | 6,912 | 2,157 | 3,550 | 39.1 | 2013...... | 9,870 | 8,043 | 1,827 | 5,466 | 55.4 |
| 2005...... | 9,707 | 7,997 | 1,710 | 3,942 | 40.6 | 2014...... | 9,486 | 7,828 | 1,658 | 5,448 | 57.4 |
| 2006...... | 9,483 | 7,842 | 1,641 | 4,024 | 42.4 | 2015...... | 9,718 | 7,750 | 1,968 | 5,203 | 53.5 |
| 2007...... | 9,309 | 7,490 | 1,819 | 4,192 | 45.0 | 2016...... | 9,572 | 7,404 | 2,088 | 5,312 | 55.5 |
| 2008...... | 8,325 | 6,633 | 1,692 | 4,383 | 52.6 | 2017 (P).. | 9,916 | 8,228 | 1,688 | 5,421 | 54.7 |

P Preliminary. [1] Live weight. [2] Processed into meal, oil, solubles, and shell products, or used as bait and animal food.

Source: U.S. National Oceanic and Atmospheric Administration, National Marine Fisheries Service, *Fisheries of the United States 2017*, September 2018, and earlier editions. See also <https://www.fisheries.noaa.gov/resource/document/fisheries-united-states-2017-report>.

## Table 930. Domestic Fish and Shellfish Catch and Value by Major Species Caught: 2000 to 2017

[In thousands (9,068,985 represents 9,068,985,000)]

| Species | Quantity (1,000 lbs.) 2000 | 2010 | 2016 | 2017 (P) | Value ($1,000) 2000 | 2010 | 2016 | 2017 (P) |
|---|---|---|---|---|---|---|---|---|
| **Total [1]**............... | **9,068,985** | **8,230,587** | **9,572,037** | **9,915,924** | **3,549,481** | **4,519,510** | **5,311,696** | **5,421,425** |
| **Fish, total [1]**............ | **7,689,661** | **6,918,013** | **8,442,812** | **8,773,469** | **1,594,815** | **2,155,593** | **2,288,300** | **2,541,922** |
| Cod, Atlantic.......... | 25,060 | 17,714 | 3,221 | 1,857 | 26,384 | 28,119 | 6,140 | 4,444 |
| Cod, Pacific........... | 530,505 | 539,635 | 708,572 | 657,321 | 142,330 | 146,941 | 171,400 | 156,371 |
| Flatfish, Atlantic and Pacific [2]............ | 412,723 | 624,358 | 565,447 | 544,866 | 109,910 | 146,243 | 141,391 | 141,228 |
| Halibut............. | 75,190 | 56,497 | 25,166 | 26,466 | 143,826 | 206,553 | 127,008 | 125,785 |
| Herring, Atlantic........ | 160,269 | 144,513 | 139,263 | 110,804 | 9,972 | 21,275 | 29,675 | 28,244 |
| Herring, Pacific........ | 74,835 | 108,868 | 52,287 | 69,116 | 12,043 | 23,308 | 5,528 | 8,152 |
| Menhaden............ | 1,760,498 | 1,471,803 | 1,727,502 | 1,413,104 | 112,403 | 107,193 | 179,791 | 125,495 |
| Pollock, Alaska......... | 2,606,802 | 1,947,580 | 3,355,068 | 3,388,620 | 160,525 | 282,399 | 417,207 | 413,273 |
| Salmon............. | 628,638 | 787,740 | 561,036 | 1,008,198 | 270,213 | 554,816 | 420,233 | 687,770 |
| Tuna............... | 50,779 | 48,047 | 55,973 | 54,904 | 95,176 | 108,453 | 157,477 | 154,392 |
| Whiting (Atlantic, silver)........ | 26,855 | 17,564 | 13,929 | 11,800 | 11,370 | 10,862 | 10,615 | 9,009 |
| Whiting (Pacific, hake)......... | 452,718 | 355,272 | 558,047 | 773,885 | 18,809 | 27,316 | 46,639 | 60,373 |
| **Shellfish, total [1]**........ | **1,379,324** | **1,276,366** | **1,092,930** | **1,108,041** | **1,954,666** | **2,341,902** | **2,997,868** | **2,855,955** |
| Clams............... | 118,482 | 88,891 | 88,886 | 84,883 | 153,973 | 200,657 | 234,856 | 210,755 |
| Crabs............... | 299,006 | 349,604 | 317,348 | 274,578 | 405,006 | 572,797 | 704,288 | 610,377 |
| Lobsters: American........... | 83,180 | 115,433 | 158,561 | 132,973 | 301,300 | 396,757 | 666,679 | 552,057 |
| Oysters.............. | 41,146 | 28,080 | 33,295 | 31,805 | 90,667 | 117,590 | 217,170 | 236,418 |
| Scallops, sea.......... | 32,747 | 57,454 | 40,514 | 51,461 | 164,609 | 455,088 | 486,101 | 506,531 |
| Shrimp.............. | 332,486 | 258,972 | 270,787 | 283,272 | 690,453 | 413,980 | 483,430 | 530,977 |
| Squid, Pacific.......... | 259,508 | 286,403 | 84,501 | 137,482 | 27,077 | 70,706 | 40,315 | 68,635 |

P Preliminary. [1] Includes other species not shown separately. [2] Includes flounders, soles, and other flatfish. Excludes halibut.

Source: U.S. National Oceanic and Atmospheric Administration, National Marine Fisheries Service, *Fisheries of the United States 2017*, September 2018, and earlier editions. See also <https://www.fisheries.noaa.gov/resource/document/fisheries-united-states-2017-report>.

## Table 931. U.S. Private Aquaculture—Trout and Catfish Production and Value: 1990 to 2018

[67.8 represents 67,800,000. Data are for calendar year and foodsize fish (trout at least 12 inches long; catfish weighing at least three quarters of a pound)]

| Item | Unit | 1990 | 1995 | 2000 | 2005 | 2010 | 2016 | 2017 | 2018 |
|---|---|---|---|---|---|---|---|---|---|
| TROUT FOODSIZE | | | | | | | | | |
| Number sold............................ | Mil. | 67.8 | 60.2 | 58.4 | 55.6 | 38.7 | 46.3 | 41.0 | 35.8 |
| Total weight............................ | Mil. lb. | 56.8 | 55.6 | 59.0 | 59.9 | 45.3 | 59.1 | 53.9 | 47.4 |
| Total value of sales................... | Mil. dol. | 64.6 | 60.8 | 63.3 | 63.5 | 63.2 | 97.1 | 102.7 | 90.8 |
| Avg. price received by processors.... | Dol./lb. | 1.14 | 1.09 | 1.07 | 1.06 | 1.40 | 1.64 | 1.91 | 1.91 |
| Percent sold to processors............ | Percent | 58.0 | 68.0 | 69.7 | 66.0 | 63.4 | 60.9 | 59.4 | 40.5 |
| CATFISH FOODSIZE | | | | | | | | | |
| Number sold............................ | Mil. | 272.9 | 321.8 | 420.1 | 395.6 | 263.4 | 190.6 | 199.8 | 208.8 |
| Total weight............................ | Mil. lb. | 392.4 | 481.5 | 633.8 | 605.5 | 478.9 | 320.2 | 330.4 | 343.6 |
| Total value of sales................... | Mil. dol. | 305.1 | 378.1 | 468.8 | 427.8 | 375.1 | 363.4 | 355.4 | 335.0 |
| Avg. price received by processors.... | Dol./lb. | 0.78 | 0.79 | 0.74 | 0.71 | 0.78 | 1.14 | 1.08 | 0.97 |

Source: U.S. Department of Agriculture, National Agricultural Statistics Service, *Trout Production*, April 2019, and *Catfish Production*, February 2019. See also <https://www.nass.usda.gov/Publications/Reports_by_Release_Day/index.php>.

## Table 932. Supply of Selected Shellfish and Fish Products: 1990 to 2017

[In millions of pounds (734 represents 734,000,000). Totals available for U.S. consumption are supply minus exports plus imports. Round weight is the complete or full weight as caught]

| Species | Unit | 1990 | 1995 | 2000 | 2005 | 2010 | 2014 | 2015 | 2016 | 2017 (P) |
|---|---|---|---|---|---|---|---|---|---|---|
| Shrimp.................. | Heads-off weight | 734 | 832 | 1,173 | 1,559 | 1,739 | 1,733 | 1,797 | 1,819 | 2,053 |
| Tuna, canned........... | Canned weight | 856 | 875 | 980 | 895 | 834 | 728 | 704 | 671 | 670 |
| Snow crab.............. | Round weight | 37 | 42 | 122 | 171 | 197 | 194 | 239 | 205 | 194 |
| Clams.................. | Meat weight | 152 | 144 | 133 | 120 | 105 | 109 | 105 | 109 | 101 |
| Salmon, canned [1]...... | Canned weight | 148 | 147 | 95 | 123 | 73 | 16 | 101 | -11 | 92 |
| American lobster....... | Round weight | 95 | 94 | 125 | 144 | 186 | 210 | 222 | 230 | 198 |
| Spiny lobster........... | Round weight | 89 | 89 | 99 | 83 | 60 | 12 | 13 | 28 | 46 |
| Scallops............... | Meat weight | 74 | 62 | 78 | 86 | 85 | 68 | 62 | 68 | 71 |
| Oysters................. | Meat weight | 56 | 63 | 71 | 65 | 57 | 58 | 57 | 64 | 66 |
| King crab.............. | Round weight | 19 | 21 | 41 | 78 | 44 | 54 | 53 | 50 | 46 |
| Crab meat, canned.... | Canned weight | 9 | 12 | 29 | 59 | 66 | 62 | 63 | 61 | 64 |

P Preliminary. [1] The method of calculating canned salmon supply does not incorporate annual beginning and ending warehouse stock. Due to the biennial nature of the pink salmon fishery, some salmon canned in one year may be exported in the following year.

Source: U.S. National Oceanic and Atmospheric Administration, National Marine Fisheries Service, *Fisheries of the United States 2017*, September 2018, and earlier editions. See also <https://www.fisheries.noaa.gov/resource/document/fisheries-united-states-2017-report>.

## Table 933. Canned, Fresh, and Frozen Fishery Products—Production and Value: 1990 to 2017

[Production in millions of pounds (1,178 represents 1,178,000,000); value in millions of dollars (1,562 represents $1,562,000,000). Canned fishery products data are for natural pack only]

| Product | Production (mil. lbs.) | | | | | Value (mil. dol.) | | | | |
|---|---|---|---|---|---|---|---|---|---|---|
| | 1990 | 2000 | 2010 | 2016 | 2017 (P) | 1990 | 2000 | 2010 | 2016 | 2017 (P) |
| **Canned, total**..................... | **1,178** | **1,747** | **956** | **869** | **882** | **1,562** | **1,626** | **1,414** | **1,239** | **1,395** |
| Tuna........................ | 581 | 671 | 395 | 383 | 363 | 902 | 856 | 724 | 699 | 736 |
| Salmon...................... | 196 | 171 | 146 | 52 | 134 | 366 | 288 | 356 | 142 | 310 |
| Clam products............... | 110 | 127 | 110 | 118 | 63 | 76 | 120 | 98 | 145 | 106 |
| Sardines, Maine............. | 13 | (Z) | (D) | (D) | (D) | 17 | (Z) | (D) | (D) | (D) |
| Shrimp...................... | 1 | 2 | (D) | (D) | (D) | 3 | 11 | (D) | (D) | (D) |
| Crab [1].................... | 1 | (Z) | 1 | (Z) | (Z) | 4 | (Z) | 8 | 1 | 1 |
| Oysters [2].................. | 1 | (Z) | (D) | (D) | (D) | 1 | 1 | (D) | (D) | (D) |
| Other....................... | 275 | 776 | 303 | 316 | 322 | 193 | 350 | 228 | 251 | 243 |
| **Fish fillets and steaks** [3]........ | **441** | **368** | **585** | **778** | **793** | **843** | **823** | **1,486** | **2,102** | **2,130** |
| Cod......................... | 65 | 56 | 49 | 76 | 72 | 132 | 167 | 131 | 321 | 315 |
| Flounder.................... | 54 | 27 | 32 | 11 | 12 | 154 | 71 | 53 | 45 | 50 |
| Haddock..................... | 7 | 6 | 23 | 9 | 11 | 24 | 24 | 89 | 49 | 53 |
| Ocean perch, Atlantic........ | 1 | (Z) | 1 | 1 | 1 | 1 | 1 | 3 | 3 | 3 |
| Rockfish.................... | 33 | 11 | 2 | 2 | 3 | 53 | 25 | 6 | 7 | 9 |
| Pollock, Atlantic............ | 12 | 2 | 2 | 1 | 10 | 21 | 4 | 7 | 4 | 16 |
| Pollock, Alaska............. | 164 | 160 | 290 | 473 | 455 | 174 | 178 | 368 | 656 | 582 |
| Other....................... | 105 | 106 | 186 | 205 | 229 | 284 | 353 | 829 | 1,018 | 1,103 |

P Preliminary. D Figure withheld to avoid disclosure pertaining to a specific organization or individual. Data is included in "other". Z Less than 500,000 pounds or $500,000. [1] Includes crab meat specialties. [2] Includes oyster specialties. [3] Fresh and frozen.

Source: U.S. National Oceanic and Atmospheric Administration, National Marine Fisheries Service, *Fisheries of the United States 2017*, September 2018, and earlier editions. See also <https://www.fisheries.noaa.gov/resource/document/fisheries-united-states-2017-report>.

# Table 934. Mineral and Mining Industries—Employment, Hours, and Earnings: 1990 to 2018

[In thousands (680 represents 680,000), except as noted. Industries based on North American Classification System (NAICS) 2017. Based on the Current Employment Statistics Program, see Appendix III]

| Industry and item | Unit | 1990 | 1995 | 2000 | 2005 | 2010 | 2015 | 2017 | 2018 |
|---|---|---|---|---|---|---|---|---|---|
| All mining: [1] | | | | | | | | | |
|   All employees | 1,000 | 680 | 558 | 520 | 562 | 655 | 760 | 626 | 683 |
|   Production workers | 1,000 | 469 | 391 | 383 | 419 | 483 | 550 | 450 | 503 |
|   Avg. weekly hours | Number | 46.1 | 46.8 | 45.5 | 46.4 | 44.8 | 46.1 | 46.6 | 47.2 |
|   Avg. weekly earnings | Dollars | 630 | 711 | 770 | 884 | 1,086 | 1,238 | 1,304 | 1,361 |
| Oil and gas extraction: | | | | | | | | | |
|   All employees | 1,000 | 190 | 152 | 125 | 126 | 159 | 193 | 144 | 145 |
|   Production workers | 1,000 | 84 | 73 | 67 | 72 | 89 | 108 | 74 | 80 |
|   Avg. weekly hours | Number | 44.4 | 43.6 | 41.3 | 44.3 | 39.0 | 43.9 | 41.5 | 43.0 |
|   Avg. weekly earnings | Dollars | 591 | 677 | 802 | 856 | 1,066 | 1,323 | 1,448 | 1,534 |
| Coal mining: | | | | | | | | | |
|   All employees | 1,000 | 136 | 97 | 72 | 74 | 81 | 64 | 52 | 52 |
|   Production workers | 1,000 | 110 | 78 | 59 | 61 | 70 | 54 | 43 | 44 |
|   Avg. weekly hours | Number | 44.7 | 45.7 | 45.6 | 48.5 | 48.4 | 45.3 | 46.7 | 47.3 |
|   Avg. weekly earnings | Dollars | 822 | 929 | 945 | 1,071 | 1,366 | 1,386 | 1,434 | 1,440 |
| Metal ore mining: | | | | | | | | | |
|   All employees | 1,000 | 53 | 48 | 38 | 29 | 37 | 42 | 40 | 41 |
|   Production workers | 1,000 | 43 | 39 | 29 | 22 | 28 | (NA) | (NA) | (NA) |
|   Avg. weekly hours | Number | 42.5 | 43.4 | 43.4 | 44.2 | 42.5 | (NA) | (NA) | (NA) |
|   Avg. weekly earnings | Dollars | 646 | 788 | 871 | 1,001 | 1,158 | (NA) | (NA) | (NA) |
| Nonmetallic minerals mining, and quarrying: | | | | | | | | | |
|   All employees | 1,000 | 113 | 108 | 115 | 110 | 87 | 92 | 95 | 99 |
|   Production workers | 1,000 | 85 | 81 | 87 | 84 | 65 | (NA) | (NA) | (NA) |
|   Avg. weekly hours | Number | 45.0 | 46.3 | 46.1 | 45.9 | 43.8 | (NA) | (NA) | (NA) |
|   Avg. weekly earnings | Dollars | 532 | 632 | 722 | 830 | 848 | (NA) | (NA) | (NA) |

NA Not available. [1] Includes other industries not shown separately.

Source: U.S. Bureau of Labor Statistics, Current Employment Statistics, "Employment, Hours, and Earnings—National," <https://www.bls.gov/ces/data.htm>, accessed May 2019.

# Table 935. Mine Safety: 2010 to 2018

[Calendar year data]

| Item | Total | | | Coal | | | Metal and non-metal | | |
|---|---|---|---|---|---|---|---|---|---|
| | 2010 | 2017 | 2018 | 2010 | 2017 | 2018 | 2010 | 2017 | 2018 |
| Number of mines | 14,283 | 13,103 | 13,059 | 1,942 | 1,215 | 1,191 | 12,341 | 11,888 | 11,868 |
| Number of miners | 362,028 | 321,287 | 331,980 | 136,071 | 82,939 | 82,817 | 225,957 | 238,347 | 249,163 |
| Fatalities | 72 | 28 | 28 | 48 | 15 | 12 | 24 | 13 | 16 |
| Fatal injury rate [1] | 0.024 | 0.010 | 0.010 | 0.038 | 0.020 | 0.016 | 0.013 | 0.007 | 0.008 |
| All injury rate [1] | 2.83 | 2.17 | 2.04 | 3.47 | 3.19 | 2.85 | 2.38 | 1.79 | 1.73 |
| Total mining area inspection hours per mine [2] | 63 | 56 | 52 | 259 | 252 | 240 | 23 | 24 | 23 |
| Citations and orders [3] | 170,034 | 104,616 | 97,788 | 96,337 | 46,764 | 46,852 | 73,697 | 57,852 | 50,936 |
| S&S citations and orders [4] (percent) | 32 | 21 | 21 | 32 | 21 | 21 | 31 | 22 | 21 |
| Amount assessed [5] (mil. dol.) | 162.3 | 55.9 | 54.7 | 110.2 | 27.2 | 31.6 | 52.1 | 28.7 | 23.1 |
| Coal production (mil. tons) | (X) | (X) | (X) | 1,086 | 775 | 756 | (X) | (X) | (X) |

X Not applicable. [1] Reported injury rates per 200,000 employees. [2] Total Mining Area Time includes: On-site Inspection Time (metal/non-metal), MMU Pit Time (Coal), Outby Area Time (Coal), Surface Area Time (Coal), Citation/Order writing On-Site. On-site inspection hours represent hours entered by Authorized Representatives of the Secretary (AR) for certain inspection activities and task codes. [3] Citations and orders are those not vacated. [4] A violation that "significantly and substantially" contributes to the cause and effect of a coal or other mine safety or health hazard. [5] Government penalties or fines.

Source: U.S. Mine Safety and Health Administration, Office of Program Education and Outreach Services, "Mine Safety and Health At a Glance," <https://www.msha.gov/msha-glance>, accessed June 2019.

# Table 936. Mining and Primary Metal Production Indexes: 1990 to 2018

[Index 2012=100]

| Industry group | 2012 NAICS [1] code | 1990 | 1995 | 2000 | 2005 | 2010 | 2015 | 2016 | 2017 | 2018 |
|---|---|---|---|---|---|---|---|---|---|---|
| **Mining** [2] | 21 | **92.2** | **89.9** | **88.8** | **84.0** | **87.2** | **113.9** | **102.6** | **110.1** | **123.8** |
|   Oil and gas extraction [2] | 211 | 87.7 | 85.3 | 82.9 | 76.0 | 85.6 | 134.1 | 128.7 | 135.0 | 155.8 |
|     Crude oil and natural gas | 211111 | 89.5 | 86.1 | 83.0 | 76.3 | 85.5 | 134.2 | 128.2 | 134.3 | 154.9 |
|   Coal mining | 2121 | 108.4 | 106.7 | 109.4 | 113.1 | 106.9 | 86.9 | 70.0 | 74.9 | 73.6 |
|   Metal ore mining | 2122 | 110.3 | 120.7 | 117.1 | 102.0 | 97.1 | 99.9 | 100.3 | 98.0 | 93.4 |
|     Iron ore | 21221 | 106.6 | 118.1 | 118.5 | 102.1 | 93.4 | 85.3 | 77.3 | 88.7 | 95.5 |
|     Gold ore and silver ore | 21222 | 127.7 | 136.6 | 152.2 | 110.0 | 99.6 | 91.9 | 97.7 | 100.8 | 88.4 |
|     Copper, nickel, lead, and zinc | 21223 | 122.5 | 140.5 | 122.6 | 99.0 | 96.0 | 116.8 | 119.6 | 106.8 | 105.0 |
|   Oil and gas drilling | 213111 | 65.3 | 49.8 | 60.2 | 75.8 | 71.5 | 77.3 | 45.2 | 65.2 | 75.8 |
| **Primary metal manufacturing** [2] | 331 | **91.3** | **100.5** | **105.0** | **99.1** | **95.1** | **96.8** | **92.5** | **93.7** | **97.6** |
|   Iron and steel | 3311, 3312 | 86.0 | 95.5 | 99.8 | 96.6 | 91.8 | 91.6 | 87.4 | 91.7 | 96.6 |
|   Aluminum | 3313 | 99.1 | 95.6 | 101.2 | 103.9 | 89.0 | 107.1 | 106.0 | 102.6 | 107.0 |
|   Nonferrous metals [2] | 3314 | 88.7 | 100.8 | 90.6 | 80.4 | 108.2 | 98.2 | 95.3 | 91.3 | 90.8 |

[1] Based on the 2012 North American Industry Classification System (NAICS). [2] Includes other industries not shown separately.

Source: Board of Governors of the Federal Reserve System, "Industrial Production and Capacity Utilization, Statistical Release G.17," <http://www.federalreserve.gov/datadownload/default.htm>, accessed June 2019.

# Table 937. Mineral Production: 1990 to 2017

[In units as indicated (1,029.1 represents 1,029,100,000). Data represent production as measured by mine shipments, mine sales, or marketable production. See Appendix IV for information on weights and measures]

| Minerals and metals | Unit | 1990 | 2000 | 2010 | 2016 | 2017 |
|---|---|---|---|---|---|---|
| FUEL MINERALS | | | | | | |
| Coal, total.................................... | Mil. short tons | 1,029.1 | 1,073.6 | 1,084.4 | 728.4 | 774.6 |
| Bituminous................................ | Mil. short tons | 693.2 | 574.3 | 489.5 | 325.1 | 353.5 |
| Subbituminous........................... | Mil. short tons | 244.3 | 409.2 | 514.8 | 330.2 | 351.5 |
| Lignite...................................... | Mil. short tons | 88.1 | 85.6 | 78.2 | 71.3 | 67.7 |
| Anthracite................................. | Mil. short tons | 3.5 | 4.6 | 1.8 | 1.7 | 1.9 |
| Natural gas (marketed production)................. | Tril. cu. ft. | 18.6 | 20.2 | 22.4 | 28.4 | 29.2 |
| Petroleum (crude)............................... | Mil. barrels [1] | 2,685 | 2,131 | 1,999 | 3,232 | 3,413 |
| Uranium concentrate (recoverable content)......... | Mil. lb. | 8.9 | 4.0 | 4.2 | 2.9 | 2.4 |
| NONFUEL MINERALS | | | | | | |
| Asbestos (sales)................................ | 1,000 metric tons | (D) | 5 | – | – | – |
| Barite, primary, sold/used by producers............ | 1,000 metric tons | 430 | 392 | 662 | 232 | 334 |
| Boron minerals, sold or used by producers......... | 1,000 metric tons | 1,090 | 1,070 | (D) | (D) | (D) |
| Bromine, sold or used by producers................ | 1,000 metric tons | 177 | 228 | (D) | (D) | (D) |
| Cement (excludes Puerto Rico): [2]................ | Mil. metric tons | (NA) | (NA) | 66.4 | 84.7 | 86.1 |
| Clays.......................................... | 1,000 metric tons | 42,900 | 40,800 | 25,600 | 23,900 | 28,000 |
| Diatomite....................................... | 1,000 metric tons | 631 | 677 | 595 | 686 | 768 |
| Feldspar....................................... | 1,000 metric tons | 630 | 790 | 500 | 470 | 440 |
| Fluorspar, finished shipments..................... | 1,000 metric tons | 64 | – | (NA) | (NA) | (NA) |
| Garnet (industrial).............................. | 1,000 metric tons | 47 | 60 | 53 | 81 | 107 |
| Gypsum, crude................................. | Mil. metric tons | 15 | 20 | 10 | 19.8 | 21 |
| Helium [3]...................................... | Mil. cu. meters | 65 | 98 | 75 | 66 | 63 |
| Lime, sold or used by producers [4]............... | Mil. metric tons | 16 | 20 | 18 | 18 | 18 |
| Mica, scrap/flake, sold or used by producers....... | 1,000 metric tons | 109 | 101 | 56 | 28 | 40 |
| Peat, sales by producers......................... | 1,000 metric tons | 721 | 847 | 628 | 441 | 498 |
| Perlite, processed, sold or used................... | 1,000 metric tons | 576 | 672 | 414 | 437 | 479 |
| Phosphate rock, marketable...................... | Mil. metric tons | 46 | 39 | 26 | 27 | 28 |
| Potash (K2O equivalent), marketable.............. | 1,000 metric tons | 1,710 | 1,300 | 930 | 510 | 480 |
| Pumice & pumicite, sold and used................. | 1,000 metric tons | 443 | 1,050 | 241 | 374 | 383 |
| Salt (excludes Puerto Rico) [2]................... | Mil. metric tons | 37 | 46 | 43 | 42 | 40 |
| Sand & gravel: | | | | | | |
| Construction.............................. | Mil. metric tons | 829 | 1,120 | 807 | 888 | 900 |
| Industrial................................. | 1,000 metric tons | 26 | 28 | 32 | 79 | 102 |
| Soda ash (sodium carbonate)..................... | 1,000 metric tons | 9,100 | 10,200 | 10,600 | 11,800 | 12,000 |
| Stone: | | | | | | |
| Crushed and broken....................... | Mil. metric tons | 1,110 | 1,560 | 1,160 | 1,360 | 1,350 |
| Dimension [4]............................. | 1,000 metric tons | 1,120 | 1,250 | 1,670 | 2,790 | 2,810 |
| Sulfur: total shipments.......................... | 1,000 metric tons | 11,500 | 10,700 | 9,170 | 9,740 | 9,640 |
| Talc and pyrophyllite, crude [5].................. | 1,000 metric tons | 1,270 | 851 | 604 | 578 | 610 |
| Vermiculite concentrate.......................... | 1,000 metric tons | 209 | 150 | 100 | 100 | 100 |
| METALS | | | | | | |
| Aluminum...................................... | 1,000 metric tons | 4,048 | 3,668 | 1,726 | 818 | 741 |
| Copper (recoverable content)..................... | 1,000 metric tons | 1,590 | 1,450 | 1,110 | 1,430 | 1,260 |
| Gold (recoverable content)....................... | Metric tons | 294 | 353 | 231 | 228 | 237 |
| Iron ore, usable (gross weight)................... | Mil. metric tons | 57 | 61 | 50 | 42 | 48 |
| Lead (recoverable content)....................... | 1,000 metric tons | 484 | 449 | 369 | 346 | 310 |
| Magnesium metal............................... | 1,000 metric tons | 139 | (D) | (D) | (D) | (D) |
| Molybdenum, mine.............................. | 1,000 metric tons | 62 | 41 | 59 | 36 | 41 |
| Nickel ore, refinery byproduct.................... | 1,000 metric tons | 330 | (D) | (D) | (D) | (D) |
| Palladium metal................................ | Kilograms | 5,930 | 10,300 | 11,600 | 13,100 | 13,600 |
| Platinum metal................................. | Kilograms | 1,810 | 3,110 | 3,450 | 3,890 | 3,980 |
| Silicon (Si content) [6].......................... | 1,000 metric tons | 418 | 367 | 176 | 384 | 415 |
| Silver (recoverable content)...................... | Metric tons | 2,120 | 1,860 | 1,280 | 1,140 | 1,030 |
| Titanium concentrate, (TiO2 content).............. | 1,000 metric tons | (D) | 300 | 200 | 100 | 100 |
| Vanadium (recoverable content)................... | Metric tons | 2,310 | – | 1,060 | – | – |
| Zinc, ore and concentrate........................ | 1,000 metric tons | 508 | 796 | 748 | 805 | 774 |

NA Not available. D Withheld to avoid disclosing individual company data. – Represents or rounds to zero. [1] 42-gallon barrels. [2] Data for 2017 are estimates. [3] Extracted from natural gas. Both grade A and crude helium. [4] Includes Puerto Rico. [5] After 1990, includes only talc. [6] For 2006-2010, ferrosilicon only; silicon metal withheld to avoid disclosing proprietary data. Beginning in 2011, silicon alloys and metal. Beginning 2012, includes statistics for ferrosilicon and silicon metal containing less than 99.9% silicon.

Source: Nonfuels, through 1994, U.S. Bureau of Mines; thereafter, U.S. Geological Survey, *Mineral Commodity Summaries 2019,* February 2019, and earlier reports; see also <https://www.usgs.gov/centers/nmic/publications>. Fuels, U.S. Energy Information Administration, *Annual Energy Review 2011,* September 2012, and earlier reports; *Annual Coal Report, 2017,* November 2018; and "Natural Gas Gross Withdrawals and Production," <https://www.eia.gov/naturalgas/data.php>, "Uranium & Nuclear Fuel Summary Production Statistics," <https://www.eia.gov/nuclear/data.php>, and "Crude Oil Production," <https://www.eia.gov/petroleum/data.php>, accessed July 2019.

Table 938. Nonfuel Mineral Commodities—Summary: 2017

# Table 938. Nonfuel Mineral Commodities—Summary: 2017

[1,430 represents 1,430,000. Except as noted, data are for mine or crude production, and average price or value are in dollars per metric ton]

| Mineral | Unit | Mineral disposition | | | | Average price per unit (dollars) | Employment (number) |
|---|---|---|---|---|---|---|---|
| | | Production | Exports | Net import reliance [1,2] (percent) | Consumption, apparent | | |
| Alumina (metal equivalent)....... | 1,000 metric tons | 1,430 | 516 | 38 | 2,300 | [3] 487 | [21] 31,700 |
| Aluminum.................... | 1,000 metric tons | 741 | 2,900 | 59 | 5,670 | [4] 0.98 | [21] 31,700 |
| Antimony (contained)............ | Metric tons | – | [5] 2,253 | 83 | 26,800 | [4] 3.98 | 27 |
| Asbestos...................... | Metric tons | (NA) | – | 100 | 332 | (NA) | (NA) |
| Barite........................ | 1,000 metric tons | 334 | 116 | 86 | 2,440 | [6] 179 | 350 |
| Bauxite (metal equiv.)............ | 1,000 metric tons | (D) | 29 | >75 | (D) | [7] 32 | (NA) |
| Beryllium (contained)............ | Metric tons | 150 | 38 | 17 | 181 | [8] 640 | (NA) |
| Bismuth (contained)............. | Metric tons | – | 392 | 97 | 2,530 | [4] 4.93 | (NA) |
| Boron (B2O3 content)............ | 1,000 metric tons | (D) | [9] 228 | ([10]) | (D) | [11] 392 | 1,310 |
| Bromine (contained)............. | Metric tons | (D) | [12] 43,400 | <25 | (D) | (NA) | 1,050 |
| Cadmium (contained)............ | Metric tons | (D) | [13] 223 | <25 | (D) | [8, 15] 1.75 | (NA) |
| Cement........................ | 1,000 metric tons | [14] 86,100 | 1,035 | 13 | 97,400 | 121 | 10,500 |
| Chromium..................... | 1,000 metric tons | [16] 158 | 256 | 71 | 542 | [17] 259 | (NA) |
| Clays......................... | 1,000 metric tons | [18] 28,000 | 4,050 | ([10]) | 25,000 | (NA) | 5,590 |
| Cobalt (contained)............... | Metric tons | [19] 2,750 | 5,730 | 69 | 8,910 | [4] 26.97 | (NA) |
| Copper (mine, recoverable)...... | 1,000 metric tons | 1,260 | 237 | 37 | 1,870 | [4] 2.85 | 10,600 |
| Diamond, stones (industrial)..... | Million carats | 87 | – | 1 | 88.6 | [20] 12.9 | (NA) |
| Diatomite..................... | 1,000 metric tons | 768 | 87 | ([10]) | 690 | 360 | 750 |
| Feldspar...................... | 1,000 metric tons | 440 | 5 | 39 | 730 | 64 | 240 |
| Fluorspar..................... | 1,000 metric tons | (NA) | 11 | 100 | 390 | [11] 262 | 4 |
| Garnet (industrial)............... | Metric tons | 107,000 | 23,300 | 22 | 138,000 | 260 | 120 |
| Gemstones.................... | Million dollars | [22] 64.3 | [23] 21,100 | 99 | 4,060 | (NA) | 1,120 |
| Germanium (contained).......... | Kilograms | (D) | 3,670 | >50 | (NA) | [8] 1,082 | (NA) |
| Gold (contained)............... | Metric tons | 237 | 461 | ([10]) | (NA) | [24] 1,261 | 12,000 |
| Graphite (natural)............... | metric tons | – | 13,900 | 100 | 38,000 | [25] 1,390 | (NA) |
| Gypsum (crude)................ | 1,000 metric tons | 20,700 | 36 | 10 | 46,300 | 7.5 | 4,500 |
| Iodine........................ | Metric tons | (D) | 1,230 | >50 | (D) | [27] 19.55 | 60 |
| Iron ore (usable)................ | Million metric tons | 47.9 | 10.6 | ([10]) | 39.5 | 80.15 | 4,630 |
| Iron and steel scrap (metal)...... | Million metric tons | [28] 60.5 | 15 | ([10]) | 50 | 265 | 27,000 |
| Iron and steel slag (metal)....... | Million metric tons | 16 | (Z) | 13 | 16 | 25 | 1,500 |
| Lead (contained)............... | 1,000 metric tons | 310 | 269 | 36 | 1,760 | [4] 1.145 | 3,740 |
| Lime......................... | 1,000 metric tons | [30] 17,800 | 391 | <1 | 17,800 | [30] 121.80 | (NA) |
| Lithium....................... | Metric tons | (D) | 1,960 | >50 | (NA) | 15,000 | 70 |
| Magnesium compounds.......... | 1,000 metric tons | [26] 438 | 103 | 43 | 771 | (NA) | 260 |
| Magnesium metal............... | 1,000 metric tons | (D) | 14 | <25 | (D) | [4] 2.15 | 400 |
| Manganese (gross weight)....... | 1,000 metric tons | – | 1 | 100 | 715 | [31] 6.19 | (NA) |
| Mercury [32].................... | Metric tons | [19] (NA) | – | (NA) | (NA) | [33] 1,041 | (NA) |
| Mica, scrap and flake............ | Metric tons | 40,000 | 6,790 | 36 | 62,900 | 165 | (NA) |
| Molybdenum (contained)........ | Metric tons | 40,700 | 43,200 | ([10]) | 33,300 | [8] 18.06 | 940 |
| Nickel (contained) [34]............ | Metric tons | 22,100 | 62,500 | 53 | 262,000 | 10,403 | (NA) |
| Niobium (columbium)............ | Metric tons | – | 1,490 | 100 | 7,820 | [8] 20 | (NA) |
| Nitrogen (fixed)-ammonia......... | 1,000 metric tons | 11,600 | 612 | 18 | 14,100 | [35] 247 | 1,500 |
| Peat.......................... | 1,000 metric tons | 498 | 30 | 67 | 1,520 | 27.55 | 540 |
| Perlite........................ | 1,000 metric tons | 570 | 32 | 21 | 603 | 73 | 130 |
| Phosphate rock................ | 1,000 metric tons | 27,900 | (NA) | 5 | 28,800 | 73.67 | 2,000 |
| Platinum-group metals.......... | Kilograms | [36] 17,580 | [36] 69,000 | [37] 71 | (NA) | [24] 951.23 | 1,513 |
| Potash (K2O equivalent)......... | 1,000 metric tons | 480 | 128 | 92 | 6,200 | [38] 775 | 900 |
| Pumice and pumicite............ | 1,000 metric tons | 383 | 11 | 29 | 538 | 39 | 140 |
| Salt.......................... | 1,000 metric tons | 40,000 | 1,120 | 23 | 49,000 | [39] 200 | 4,100 |
| Silicon, metal................. | 1,000 metric tons | [40] 415 | 71 | <50 | [40] 616 | [4] 1.17 | (NA) |
| Silver (contained)............... | Metric tons | 1,030 | 157 | 58 | 5,180 | [24] 17.07 | (NA) |
| Soda ash (sodium carbonate).... | 1,000 metric tons | 12,000 | 6,990 | ([10]) | 5,040 | [41] 132.68 | 2,600 |
| Stone (crushed)................ | Million metric tons | 1,350 | 1 | 1 | 1,420 | 11.50 | 68,600 |
| Sulfur (all forms)................ | 1,000 metric tons | 9,070 | 2,423 | 4 | 10,000 | [42] 46.40 | 2,400 |
| Talc.......................... | 1,000 metric tons | 610 | 220 | 20 | 662 | 214 | 206 |
| Thallium (contained)............. | Kilograms | – | 1,958 | (NA) | (NA) | [8] 4,200 | (NA) |
| Tin (contained)................. | Metric tons | [19] 11,200 | 5,986 | 76 | 43,000 | [4] 9.37 | (NA) |
| Titanium dioxide................ | 1,000 metric tons | 1,260 | 634 | ([10]) | 870 | (NA) | 3,110 |
| Tungsten (contained)............ | Metric tons | [19] (D) | 3,542 | >50 | (D) | [43] 245 | (NA) |
| Vermiculite.................... | 1,000 metric tons | 100 | 2 | 30 | 150 | 140–575 | 70 |
| Zinc (contained)................ | 1,000 metric tons | 774 | 682 | 84 | 829 | [4, 44] 1.39 | 2,660 |
| Zirconium (ZrO2)................ | Metric tons | 50,000 | 5,099 | ([10]) | 40,000 | [29] 916 | (NA) |

– Represents or rounds to zero. < Less than. > Greater than. D Withheld to avoid disclosing company proprietary data. NA Not available. Z Less than .05 million metric tons or less than half a unit shown. [1] Net imports calculated as imports minus exports and may include adjustments for industry stock changes. [2] Calculated as percent of apparent consumption. [3] Alumina, average value, U.S. imports (f.a.s.). [4] Dollars per pound. [5] Ore and concentrates not included. [6] Estimated price, ground, average value, f.o.b. mill. [7] Bauxite, average value, U.S. imports (f.a.s.). [8] Dollars per kilogram. [9] Boric acid, gross weight. [10] Net exporter. [11] Average value of imports (cost, insurance, and freight, c.i.f.). [12] Elemental bromine and compounds. [13] Unwrought cadmium and powders. [14] Production for Portland and masonry cement includes cement made from imported clinker; excludes Puerto Rico. [15] Average free market price for 99.95% purity in 10-ton lots; cost, insurance, and freight; global ports. Source: Metal Bulletin. [16] Recycling production. [17] Unit value of imported chromite ore, gross weight. [18] Excludes attapulgite. [19] Secondary production. [20] Value of imports, dollars per carat. [21] Alumina and aluminum production workers Source: U.S. Department of Labor, Bureau of Labor Statistics. [22] Natural gemstone production, 9.2 million dollars; laboratory-created (synthetic) gemstone production, 55.1 million dollars. [23] Includes reexports. [24] Dollars per troy ounce. [25] Price of flake imports (average at foreign ports). Graphite lump/chip (Sri Lankan) price, $1,880 per ton. [26] Magnesium compounds shipments. [27] Average value of imports (c.i.f.), dollars per kilogram. [28] Iron and steel scrap production includes receipts for purchased scrap. Exports excludes rails for rerolling and other uses, and ships, boats, and other vessels for scrapping. [29] Unit value based on annual imports for consumption from Australia, Senegal, and South Africa. [30] Lime production data are sold or used by producers. Price data are for quicklime only. [31] 46% to 48% Mn metallurgical ore, per metric ton unit, contained Mn; cost, insurance, and freight (c.i.f.) value, U.S. ports. [32] Mercury not produced as principal commodity in U.S. since 1992; secondary production (recycled) not reported. [33] Dollars per 76-pound flask. [34] Primary and secondary materials. [35] Dollars per short ton, average, f.o.b. Gulf Coast. [36] Platinum and palladium. [37] Platinum. [38] Price of K2O, all products. [39] Vacuum and open pan, bulk, pellets and packaged, f.o.b. mine and plant. [40] Combined for ferrosilicon and silicon metal. [41] Dollars per short ton, f.o.b., mine or plant. [42] Elemental sulfur, f.o.b., mine or plant. [43] A metric ton unit of tungsten trioxide (WO3) contains 7.93 kilograms of tungsten. Platts Metals Week. [44] Platts Metals Week North American price for Special High Grade zinc.

Source: U.S. Geological Survey, *Mineral Commodity Summaries 2019*, February 2019. See also <https://www.usgs.gov/centers/nmic/mineral-commodity-summaries>.

# Table 939. Selected Fuel and Nonfuel Mineral Products—Average Prices: 1990 to 2018

| Year | Nonfuel minerals | | | | | | | | | Fuels | | |
|---|---|---|---|---|---|---|---|---|---|---|---|---|
| | Copper, cathode (cents/lb.) | Platinum [1] (dol./troy oz.) | Gold (dol./troy oz.) [2] | Silver (dol./troy oz.) [2] | Lead [3] (cents/lb.) | Nickel [4] (cents/lb.) | Tin (New York) [4] (cents/lb.) | Zinc [5] (cents/lb.) | Sulfur, crude [6] (dol./metric ton) | Bituminous coal [7] (dol./short ton) | Crude petroleum [7] (dol./bbl.) | Natural gas [8] (dol./1,000 cu. ft.) |
| 1990......... | 123 | 467 | 385 | 4.82 | 46 | 402 | 386 | 75 | 80 | 27.43 | 20.03 | 3.03 |
| 1995......... | 138 | 425 | 386 | 5.15 | 42 | 373 | 416 | 56 | 44 | 25.56 | 14.62 | 2.78 |
| 2000......... | 88 | 549 | 280 | 5.00 | 44 | 392 | 370 | 56 | 25 | 24.15 | 26.72 | 4.62 |
| 2001......... | 77 | 533 | 272 | 4.39 | 44 | 270 | 315 | 44 | 10 | 25.36 | 21.84 | 5.72 |
| 2002......... | 76 | 543 | 311 | 4.62 | 44 | 307 | 292 | 39 | 12 | 26.57 | 22.51 | 4.12 |
| 2003......... | 85 | 694 | 365 | 4.91 | 44 | 437 | 340 | 41 | 29 | 26.57 | 27.56 | 5.85 |
| 2004......... | 134 | 849 | 411 | 6.69 | 55 | 627 | 547 | 52 | 33 | 30.56 | 36.77 | 6.65 |
| 2005......... | 174 | 900 | 446 | 7.34 | 61 | 669 | 483 | 67 | 31 | 36.80 | 50.28 | 8.67 |
| 2006......... | 315 | 1,144 | 606 | 11.61 | 77 | 1,100 | 565 | 159 | 33 | 39.32 | 59.69 | 8.61 |
| 2007......... | 328 | 1,308 | 699 | 13.43 | 124 | 1,688 | 899 | 154 | 36 | 40.80 | 66.52 | 8.16 |
| 2008......... | 319 | 1,578 | 874 | 15.00 | 120 | 957 | 1,129 | 89 | 264 | 51.39 | 94.04 | 9.18 |
| 2009......... | 241 | 1,208 | 975 | 14.69 | 87 | 665 | 837 | 78 | 2 | 55.44 | 56.35 | 6.48 |
| 2010......... | 348 | 1,616 | 1,228 | 20.20 | 109 | 989 | 1,240 | 102 | 70 | 60.88 | 74.71 | 6.18 |
| 2011......... | 406 | 1,725 | 1,572 | 35.28 | 122 | 1,038 | 1,575 | 106 | 160 | 68.50 | 95.73 | 5.63 |
| 2012......... | 367 | 1,555 | 1,673 | 31.22 | 114 | 795 | 1,283 | 96 | 124 | 66.04 | 94.52 | 4.73 |
| 2013......... | 340 | 1,490 | 1,415 | 23.89 | 110 | 681 | 1,352 | 96 | 69 | 60.61 | 95.99 | 4.88 |
| 2014......... | 318 | 1,388 | 1,269 | 19.09 | 106 | 765 | 1,023 | 107 | 80 | 55.99 | 87.39 | 5.71 |
| 2015......... | 256 | 1,056 | 1,163 | 15.72 | 91 | 537 | 756 | 96 | 88 | 51.57 | 44.39 | 4.26 |
| 2016......... | 225 | 990 | 1,252 | 17.20 | 94 | 435 | 839 | 101 | 38 | 48.40 | 38.29 | 3.71 |
| 2017......... | 285 | 951 | 1,261 | 17.07 | 115 | 472 | 937 | 139 | 46 | 55.60 | 48.05 | 4.16 |
| 2018 [9]....... | 300 | 900 | 1,270 | 15.30 | 115 | 620 | 930 | 145 | 70 | (NA) | 61.41 | 4.21 |

NA Not available. [1] Average annual dealer prices. [2] 99.95 percent purity. [3] North American delivered basis. 1990-2012, North American producer price. Beginning 2013, North American market price. [4] Nickel: London Metal Exchange. Tin: Metals Week composite. [5] Platt's Metals Week price for North American Special High Grade zinc. Average prices for 1990 are for U.S. High Grade Zinc. [6] F.o.b. (Free on Board) works. [7] Average value at the point of production or domestic first purchase price. [8] Citygate price. Citygate is a point or measuring station at which a distributing gas utility receives gas from a natural gas pipeline company or transmission system. [9] Estimated.

Source: Nonfuels, through 1994, U.S. Bureau of Mines; thereafter, U.S. Geological Survey, *Mineral Commodity Summaries 2019*, February 2019 and earlier reports. Fuels, U.S. Energy Information Administration, *Monthly Energy Review*, March 2019 and earlier reports; and *Annual Coal Report, 2017*, November 2018 and earlier reports. See also <http://minerals.usgs.gov/minerals/pubs/mcs/> and <http://www.eia.gov/totalenergy/data/monthly/>.

# Table 940. Value of Domestic Nonfuel Mineral Production by State: 2000 to 2018

[In millions of dollars (39,400 represents $39,400,000,000)]

| State | 2000 | 2010 | 2017 [1] | 2018 [1] | State | 2000 | 2010 | 2017 [1] | 2018 [1] |
|---|---|---|---|---|---|---|---|---|---|
| **United States [2]**........ | **39,400** | **66,400** | **75,200** | **82,200** | | | | | |
| Alabama............. | 930 | 969 | 1,310 | 1,450 | Montana............ | 596 | 1,140 | 1,050 | 1,130 |
| Alaska................. | 1,140 | 3,400 | 3,530 | 3,440 | Nebraska............ | [3] 84 | 234 | [3] 192 | [3] 209 |
| Arizona.............. | 2,510 | 6,790 | 6,610 | 6,690 | Nevada.............. | 2,980 | 7,700 | 8,680 | 7,880 |
| Arkansas............ | 484 | 709 | 771 | 903 | New Hampshire..... | [3] 57 | [3] 94 | 78 | 162 |
| California............. | 3,270 | 2,890 | 3,520 | 4,560 | New Jersey.......... | [3] 291 | [3] 258 | 265 | 295 |
| Colorado.............. | 592 | 1,850 | 1,680 | 1,380 | New Mexico......... | 786 | 1,020 | 1,310 | 1,160 |
| Connecticut.......... | [3] 112 | [3] 148 | [3] 183 | [3] 200 | New York............ | 1,020 | 1,310 | [3] 1,280 | 1,790 |
| Delaware............. | [3] 14 | [3] 12 | [3] 25 | [3] 31 | North Carolina...... | 744 | 880 | [3] 1,110 | [3] 1,210 |
| Florida................. | 1,820 | 2,680 | 3,150 | 3,550 | North Dakota........ | 35 | [3] 70 | [3] 72 | [3] 136 |
| Georgia............... | 1,620 | 1,430 | 1,840 | 1,960 | Ohio................. | 999 | 1,170 | [3] 1,080 | [3] 1,200 |
| Hawaii............... | [3] 92 | 106 | 105 | 141 | Oklahoma........... | 473 | 702 | 700 | 894 |
| Idaho................. | 358 | 1,180 | [3] 191 | [3] 208 | Oregon............. | 299 | 312 | 474 | 530 |
| Illinois................. | 913 | 924 | [3] 1,380 | [3] 1,780 | Pennsylvania....... | [3] 1,250 | [3] 1,670 | [3] 1,850 | [3] 1,920 |
| Indiana............... | 695 | 782 | 1,020 | 1,060 | Rhode Island........ | [3] 20 | [3] 33 | [3] 63 | [3] 56 |
| Iowa................. | 503 | 583 | [3] 583 | [3] 680 | South Carolina...... | [3] 551 | [3] 468 | [3] 784 | [3] 1,050 |
| Kansas............... | 629 | 1,090 | [3] 598 | [3] 672 | South Dakota....... | 233 | 258 | 372 | 339 |
| Kentucky............. | 501 | 762 | [3] 592 | [3] 513 | Tennessee.......... | 737 | 831 | 1,140 | 1,460 |
| Louisiana............. | 325 | 549 | [3] 477 | [3] 536 | Texas................ | 1,950 | 2,780 | 5,220 | 6,030 |
| Maine................. | 96 | 110 | [3] 104 | [3] 135 | Utah................. | 1,430 | 4,380 | 2,610 | 2,940 |
| Maryland............. | [3] 358 | [3] 305 | [3] 379 | [3] 410 | Vermont............. | [3] 67 | [3] 121 | [3] 149 | [3] 104 |
| Massachusetts......... | [3] 200 | [3] 233 | [3] 296 | [3] 340 | Virginia.............. | 710 | 1,040 | 1,250 | 1,290 |
| Michigan............. | 1,640 | 2,190 | 2,450 | 2,470 | Washington.......... | 607 | 712 | 901 | 1,090 |
| Minnesota............. | 1,460 | [3] 4,180 | [3] 3,180 | [3] 4,050 | West Virginia........ | 172 | 272 | [3] 245 | [3] 263 |
| Mississippi............. | 149 | 198 | 216 | 404 | Wisconsin........... | [3] 372 | 509 | [3] 1,490 | [3] 2,730 |
| Missouri............... | 1,370 | 2,010 | 2,540 | 2,930 | Wyoming............ | 978 | 1,860 | 2,410 | 2,410 |

[1] Preliminary. [2] Includes data not distributed to States, not shown separately. [3] Partial data only; excludes values withheld to avoid disclosing individual company data.

Source: U.S. Geological Survey, *Minerals Yearbook, 2015*, March 2019, and earlier reports; and *Mineral Commodities Summaries 2019*, February 2019, and earlier reports. See also <http://minerals.er.usgs.gov/minerals/pubs/mcs/>.

## Table 941. Principal Fuels, Nonmetals, and Metals—World Production, 2000 to 2017, and the U.S. Share, 2017

[In units as indicated (5,127 represents 5,127,000,000), except as indicated; see Appendix IV]

| Mineral | Unit | World production | | | | | U.S. share |
|---|---|---|---|---|---|---|---|
| | | 2000 | 2010 | 2015 | 2016 | 2017 | 2017 |
| **FUELS** | | | | | | | |
| Coal.................................. | Mil. sh. tons | 5,127 | 8,155 | 8,737 | 8,150 | (NA) | (NA) |
| Petroleum (crude) [1]..................... | million barrels | 25,012 | 27,334 | 29,476 | 29,507 | 29,600 | 11.5 |
| Natural gas (dry, marketable)............... | billion cubic feet | 86,770 | 113,085 | 124,611 | 125,740 | 130,751 | 20.9 |
| Natural gas plant liquids................... | million barrels | 2,327 | 3,157 | 3,695 | 3,762 | 3,871 | 35.7 |
| **NONMETALS** | | | | | | | |
| Asbestos............................ | 1,000 metric tons | 2,110 | 2,010 | 1,310 | 1,280 | 1,170 | – |
| Barite............................... | 1,000 metric tons | 6,560 | 6,820 | 8,390 | 7,320 | 8,670 | 3.9 |
| Cement, hydraulic.................... | Mil. metric tons | 1,660 | 3,290 | 4,100 | 4,140 | 4,050 | 2.1 |
| Feldspar............................ | 1,000 metric tons | 9,540 | 21,600 | 23,100 | 23,400 | 24,700 | 1.8 |
| Fluorspar........................... | 1,000 metric tons | 4,450 | 7,000 | 6,090 | 5,930 | 5,680 | (NA) |
| Gypsum............................. | Mil. metric tons | 108 | 241 | 260 | 261 | 141 | 14.7 |
| Mica (incl. scrap)................... | 1,000 metric tons | (NA) | (NA) | 275 | 294 | 360 | 11.1 |
| Nitrogen (N content)................. | Mil. metric tons | 108 | 132 | 147 | 144 | 142 | 8.2 |
| Phosphate rock (gross wt.)........... | Mil. metric tons | 132 | 183 | 263 | 255 | 269 | 10.4 |
| Sulfur, elemental basis.............. | Mil. metric tons | 59 | 70 | 74 | 74 | 80 | 12.0 |
| **METALS, mine basis** | | | | | | | |
| Copper............................. | 1,000 metric tons | 13,200 | 16,100 | 19,100 | 20,100 | 20,000 | 6.3 |
| Gold................................ | Metric tons | 2,590 | 2,590 | 3,090 | 3,120 | 3,230 | 7.3 |
| Iron ore (gross wt.)................. | Mil. metric tons | 969 | 1,870 | 2,320 | 2,350 | 2,430 | 2.0 |
| Lead [2]............................ | 1,000 metric tons | 3,200 | 4,160 | 4,950 | 4,710 | 4,580 | 6.8 |
| Mercury............................ | Metric tons | 1,360 | 2,180 | 3,300 | 3,670 | 3,790 | (NA) |
| Molybdenum........................ | 1,000 metric tons | 135 | 246 | 288 | 278 | 297 | 13.7 |
| Nickel [2].......................... | 1,000 metric tons | 1,290 | 1,710 | 2,180 | 2,040 | 2,160 | 1.0 |
| Silver.............................. | 1,000 metric tons | 18 | 23 | 27 | 27 | 27 | 3.8 |
| Tantalum concentrates (Ta content)....... | Metric tons | 1,070 | 922 | 1,200 | 1,220 | 1,810 | (NA) |
| Titanium mineral concentrates [3]....... | 1,000 metric tons | 4,940 | 7,760 | 6,980 | 7,000 | 5,540 | 1.8 |
| Tungsten [2]........................ | 1,000 metric tons | 44 | 68 | 90 | 88 | 82 | – |
| Vanadium [2]........................ | 1,000 metric tons | 41 | 72 | 82 | 70 | 71 | – |
| Zinc [2]............................ | 1,000 metric tons | 8,770 | 12,300 | 13,500 | 12,600 | 12,500 | 6.2 |
| **METALS, smelter basis** | | | | | | | |
| Aluminum........................... | 1,000 metric tons | 24,300 | 41,800 | 57,700 | 58,600 | 59,400 | 1.2 |
| Cadmium............................ | 1,000 metric tons | 20 | 24 | 25 | 26 | 25 | (D) |
| Copper............................. | 1,000 metric tons | 11,000 | 15,600 | 18,500 | 20,100 | 20,000 | 6.3 |
| Iron, pig........................... | Mil. metric tons | 573 | 1,040 | 1,160 | 1,160 | 1,170 | 1.9 |
| Magnesium [4,5]..................... | 1,000 metric tons | 422 | 765 | 980 | 999 | 1,050 | (D) |
| Raw steel........................... | Mil. metric tons | 850 | 1,430 | 1,620 | 1,630 | 1,690 | 4.8 |
| Tin [4]............................. | 1,000 metric tons | 272 | 318 | 330 | 306 | (NA) | (NA) |
| Zinc................................ | 1,000 metric tons | 9,137 | 12,800 | 13,900 | 13,800 | (NA) | (NA) |

– Represents zero. NA Not available. D Figure withheld. [1] Includes lease condensate. [2] Content of ore and concentrate. [3] Production from ilmenite only, but includes U.S. rutile and ilmenite production. [4] Primary production. [5] Starting 2005, excludes U.S. production.

Source: U.S. Energy Information Administration, Open Data, "International Energy Data," <http://www.eia.gov/opendata/>, accessed September 2019; and U.S. Geological Survey, *Minerals Commodity Survey 2019*, Feb 2019, and "Minerals Yearbook Metals and Minerals," <https://www.usgs.gov/centers/nmic/publications>, accessed September 2019.

## Table 942. Net U.S. Imports of Selected Minerals and Metals as Percent of Apparent Consumption: 1980 to 2018

[In percent. Based on net imports which equal the difference between imports and exports plus or minus government stockpile and industry stock changes]

| Minerals and metals | 1980 | 1990 | 2000 | 2005 | 2010 | 2015 | 2016 | 2017 | 2018 [1] |
|---|---|---|---|---|---|---|---|---|---|
| Fluorspar........................... | 87 | 91 | 100 | 100 | 100 | 100 | 100 | 100 | 100 |
| Manganese......................... | 98 | 100 | 100 | 100 | 100 | 100 | 100 | 100 | 100 |
| Niobium............................ | 100 | 100 | 100 | 100 | 100 | 100 | 100 | 100 | 100 |
| Strontium.......................... | 100 | 100 | 100 | 100 | 100 | 100 | 100 | 100 | 100 |
| Tantalum........................... | 90 | 86 | 80 | 100 | 100 | 100 | 100 | 100 | 100 |
| Mica (sheet)........................ | 100 | 100 | 100 | 100 | 100 | 100 | 100 | 100 | 100 |
| Vanadium.......................... | 35 | (D) | 100 | 100 | 82 | 100 | 100 | 100 | 100 |
| Potash............................. | 65 | 68 | 80 | 80 | 83 | 87 | 90 | 92 | 92 |
| Titanium........................... | (NA) | (NA) | 79 | 71 | 65 | 85 | 91 | 92 | 91 |
| Zinc................................ | 60 | 64 | 72 | 67 | 73 | 81 | 84 | 84 | 85 |
| Barite.............................. | 44 | 71 | 84 | 84 | 75 | 78 | 84 | 86 | 84 |
| Tin................................. | 79 | 71 | 88 | 78 | 73 | 76 | 76 | 76 | 78 |
| Bauxite [2]......................... | (NA) | 98 | 100 | 100 | 100 | >75 | >75 | >75 | >75 |
| Platinum............................ | (NA) | (NA) | 78 | 93 | 91 | 66 | 66 | 71 | 73 |
| Chromium.......................... | 67 | 80 | 77 | 68 | 63 | 67 | 66 | 71 | 71 |
| Silver.............................. | 7 | (NA) | 43 | 72 | 65 | 71 | 68 | 58 | 65 |
| Cobalt.............................. | 93 | 84 | 78 | 83 | 81 | 73 | 76 | 69 | 61 |
| Nickel.............................. | 76 | 64 | 54 | 48 | 41 | 52 | 46 | 53 | 52 |
| Tungsten........................... | 53 | 81 | 66 | 68 | 63 | >25 | >25 | >50 | >50 |
| Aluminum........................... | ([3]) | ([3]) | 33 | 41 | 14 | 41 | 53 | 59 | 50 |
| Palladium........................... | (NA) | (NA) | 84 | 84 | 49 | 53 | 53 | 38 | 33 |
| Copper............................. | 16 | 15 | 37 | 42 | 32 | 31 | 29 | 37 | 32 |
| Iron and steel...................... | 13 | 13 | 18 | 15 | 6 | 22 | 24 | 25 | 24 |
| Gypsum............................ | 21 | 27 | 27 | 27 | 12 | 10 | 11 | 10 | 11 |
| Sulfur.............................. | 14 | 15 | 18 | 24 | 19 | 14 | 7 | 4 | 5 |

D Withheld to avoid disclosure. NA Not available. > Greater than. [1] Preliminary. [2] Includes alumina. [3] Net exporter.

Source: Through 1990, U.S. Bureau of Mines; thereafter, U.S. Geological Survey, *Mineral Commodity Summaries 2019*, February 2019, and earlier reports. See also <http://minerals.usgs.gov/minerals/pubs/mcs/>.

# Table 943. Petroleum Industry—Production, Foreign Trade, Reserves, and Refineries: 1990 to 2018

[In units as indicated (2,685 represents 2,685,000,000); mil. bbl.= millions of barrels. For definitions, see source below]

| Item | Unit | 1990 | 2000 | 2005 | 2010 | 2015 | 2016 | 2017 | 2018 |
|---|---|---|---|---|---|---|---|---|---|
| Crude oil production, total [1] | Mil. bbl. | 2,685 | 2,125 | 1,892 | 1,999 | 3,442 | 3,223 | 3,413 | 4,012 |
| Average price per barrel | Dollars | 20 | 27 | 50 | 75 | 44 | 38 | 48 | 61 |
| Lower 48 states [2] | Mil. bbl. | 2,037 | 1,771 | 1,577 | 1,780 | 3,266 | 3,045 | 3,233 | 3,837 |
| Alaska | Mil. bbl. | 647 | 354 | 315 | 219 | 176 | 179 | 180 | 175 |
| Imports: Crude oil [1, 3] | Mil. bbl. | 2,151 | 3,320 | 3,696 | 3,363 | 2,687 | 2,873 | 2,909 | 2,831 |
| Refined petroleum products | Mil. bbl. | 775 | 874 | 1,310 | 942 | 761 | 807 | 794 | 792 |
| Exports: Crude oil [1] | Mil. bbl. | 40 | 18 | 12 | 15 | 170 | 216 | 423 | 731 |
| Proved reserves | Bil. bbl. | 26 | 22 | 22 | 23 | 32 | 33 | 39 | (NA) |
| Operable refineries | Number | 205 | 158 | 148 | 148 | 140 | 141 | 141 | 135 |
| Daily capacity (Jan. 1) | 1,000 bbl. | 15,572 | 16,512 | 17,125 | 17,584 | 17,967 | 18,317 | 18,617 | 18,598 |
| Refinery input, total | Mil. bbl. | 5,325 | 5,964 | 6,136 | 6,345 | 6,871 | 6,940 | 7,003 | 7,135 |
| Crude oil [1] | Mil. bbl. | 4,894 | 5,514 | 5,555 | 5,374 | 5,909 | 5,924 | 6,055 | 6,193 |
| Hydrocarbon gas liquids | Mil. bbl. | 171 | 139 | 161 | 161 | 189 | 196 | 207 | 210 |
| Other liquids [4] | Mil. bbl. | 260 | 311 | 420 | 810 | 773 | 819 | 741 | 732 |
| Refinery output, total [5] | Mil. bbl. | 5,574 | 6,311 | 6,497 | 6,735 | 7,258 | 7,349 | 7,409 | 7,551 |
| Motor gasoline [6] | Mil. bbl. | 2,540 | 2,910 | 3,036 | 3,306 | 3,560 | 3,658 | 3,633 | 3,671 |
| Jet fuel (kerosene type) | Mil. bbl. | 478 | 588 | 564 | 517 | 580 | 604 | 621 | 660 |
| Distillate fuel oil | Mil. bbl. | 1,067 | 1,310 | 1,443 | 1,542 | 1,819 | 1,769 | 1,834 | 1,886 |
| Residual fuel oil | Mil. bbl. | 347 | 255 | 229 | 213 | 152 | 153 | 156 | 155 |
| Hydrocarbon gas liquids | Mil. bbl. | 182 | 258 | 209 | 240 | 224 | 231 | 229 | 231 |
| Utilization rate | Percent | 87.1 | 92.6 | 90.6 | 86.4 | 91.0 | 89.7 | 91.1 | 93.2 |

NA Not available. [1] Includes lease condensate. [2] Excluding Alaska and Hawaii. [3] Includes imports for the Strategic Petroleum Reserve. [4] Unfinished oils (net), other hydrocarbons, hydrogen, aviation and motor gasoline blending components (net). Beginning 1995, also includes oxygenates (net). [5] Includes other products not shown separately. [6] Finished motor gasoline. Beginning 1995, also includes ethanol blended into motor gasoline.

Source: U.S. Energy Information Administration, *Annual Energy Review 2011*, September 2012; and "Petroleum & Other Liquids Data," <http://www.eia.gov/naturalgas/data.cfm> and "Monthly Energy Review, Petroleum," <http://www.eia.gov/totalenergy/data/monthly/#petroleum>, accessed September 2019.

# Table 944. Crude Oil and Petroleum Products Supply, Disposition, and Ending Stocks: 2018

[In millions of barrels (4,011.5 represents 4,011,500,000). Minus sign (-) indicates decrease]

| Commodity | Supply | | | | Disposition | | | | Ending stocks |
|---|---|---|---|---|---|---|---|---|---|
| | Field production [1] | Refinery and blender net production | Imports | Adjustments [2] | Stock change | Refinery and blender net inputs | Exports | Products supplied [3] | |
| Crude oil | 4,011.5 | (X) | 2,831.3 | 89.0 | 7.0 | 6,193.4 | 731.4 | – | 1,090.9 |
| Hydrocarbon gas liquids | 1,587.4 | 231.4 | 71.1 | (X) | -2.4 | 209.8 | 584.7 | 1,090.2 | 188.5 |
| Natural gasoline | 182.9 | (X) | 0.1 | (X) | 0.7 | 60.5 | 65.8 | 48.3 | 20.8 |
| Ethane | 622.9 | 2.2 | – | (X) | -6.0 | (X) | 93.2 | 537.9 | 49.6 |
| Propane | 508.7 | 110.0 | 49.9 | (X) | 1.3 | (X) | 354.7 | 312.7 | 63.7 |
| Normal butane | 132.0 | 16.4 | 8.5 | (X) | -0.6 | 69.3 | 69.3 | 18.8 | 37.7 |
| Isobutane | 140.8 | -4.9 | 4.1 | (X) | 0.1 | 79.9 | 1.6 | 58.3 | 8.5 |
| Finished motor gasoline | (X) | 3,671.4 | 16.4 | 37.3 | 1.1 | (X) | 324.3 | 3,401.5 | 25.7 |
| Kerosene-type jet fuel | (X) | 659.8 | 46.3 | (X) | 0.4 | (X) | 81.2 | 624.5 | 41.6 |
| Distillate fuel oil [4] | (X) | 1,886.3 | 63.7 | 27.9 | -5.6 | (X) | 474.7 | 1,508.8 | 140.0 |

– Represents or rounds to zero. X Not applicable. [1] Represents crude oil production on leases, natural gas liquids production at natural gas processing plants, new supply of other hydrocarbons/oxygenates and motor gasoline blending components, fuel ethanol, and distillate fuel oil. [2] Includes an adjustment for crude oil, previously referred to as "Unaccounted For Crude Oil." Also included is an adjustment for motor gasoline blending components, fuel ethanol, and distillate fuel oil. [3] Products supplied is equal to field production, plus refinery and blender net production, plus import, plus adjustments, minus stock change, minus refinery and blender net inputs, minus export. [4] Distillate stocks located in the "Northeast Heating Oil Reserve" are not included.

Source: U.S. Energy Information Administration, Petroleum & Other Liquids, "Supply and Disposition," <http://www.eia.gov/petroleum/>, accessed September 2019.

# Table 945. Natural Gas Plant Liquids—Production and Value: 1990 to 2018

[In units, as indicated. Barrels of 42 gallons (569 represents 569,000,000)]

| Item | Unit | 1990 | 1995 | 2000 | 2005 | 2010 | 2015 | 2016 | 2017 | 2018 |
|---|---|---|---|---|---|---|---|---|---|---|
| Field production [1] | Mil. bbl. | 569 | 643 | 699 | 627 | 757 | 1,220 | 1,284 | 1,381 | 1,587 |
| Pentanes plus | Mil. bbl. | 113 | 122 | 112 | 97 | 101 | 158 | 159 | 165 | 183 |
| Liquefied petroleum gases | Mil. bbl. | 456 | 521 | 587 | 529 | 656 | 1,062 | 1,126 | 1,215 | 1,404 |
| Natural gas processed | Tril. cu. ft. | 15 | 17 | 17 | 15 | 16 | 21 | 20 | 20 | (NA) |

NA Not available. [1] Includes other finished petroleum products, not shown separately.

Source: U.S. Energy Information Administration, "Natural Gas Plant Processing," <https://www.eia.gov/naturalgas/data.php>, and "Natural Gas Plant Field Production," <https://www.eia.gov/petroleum/data.php>; accessed September 2019.

# Table 946. Crude Petroleum and Natural Gas—Production and Value for Major Producing States: 2010 to 2018

[In units as indicated (1,999 represents 1,999,000,000 barrels)]

| State | Crude petroleum Quantity (mil. bbl.) | | | | Value (mil. dol.) [2] | | | | Natural gas marketed production [1] Quantity (bil. cu. ft.) | | | |
|---|---|---|---|---|---|---|---|---|---|---|---|---|
| | 2010 | 2015 | 2017 | 2018 | 2010 | 2015 | 2017 | 2018 | 2010 | 2015 | 2017 | 2018 |
| Total [3]............... | 1,999 | 3,442 | 3,413 | 4,012 | 149,372 | 152,799 | 164,011 | 246,307 | 22,382 | 28,772 | 29,197 | 32,735 |
| Alabama................ | 7 | 10 | 7 | 6 | 540 | 432 | 330 | 382 | 223 | 168 | 150 | (NA) |
| Alaska [4]............... | 215 | 170 | 175 | 169 | 15,561 | 6,970 | 7,921 | 10,529 | 374 | 344 | 344 | 341 |
| Arkansas............... | 6 | 6 | 5 | 5 | 407 | 268 | 236 | 295 | 927 | 1,010 | 707 | 595 |
| California.............. | 200 | 201 | 173 | 169 | 14,930 | 9,185 | 8,590 | 11,524 | 287 | 237 | 209 | 199 |
| Colorado.............. | 33 | 123 | 133 | 178 | 2,402 | 4,974 | 6,168 | 10,646 | 1,578 | 1,689 | 1,683 | 1,826 |
| Florida................. | 2 | 2 | 2 | 2 | (NA) | (NA) | (NA) | (NA) | 12 | 1 | 1 | (NA) |
| Illinois................. | 9 | 10 | 8 | 8 | 664 | 419 | 391 | 516 | 2 | 2 | 2 | (NA) |
| Indiana................ | 2 | 2 | 2 | 2 | 134 | 99 | 83 | 103 | 7 | 7 | 6 | (NA) |
| Kansas................ | 40 | 45 | 36 | 35 | 2,931 | 1,962 | 1,646 | 2,098 | 325 | 284 | 214 | 203 |
| Kentucky.............. | 3 | 3 | 2 | 2 | 178 | 130 | 117 | 140 | 135 | 96 | 89 | (NA) |
| Louisiana.............. | 67 | 64 | 52 | 49 | 5,264 | 3,081 | 2,632 | 3,255 | 2,210 | 1,805 | 2,139 | 2,818 |
| Michigan.............. | 7 | 7 | 6 | 5 | 523 | 302 | 283 | 354 | 131 | 108 | 97 | (NA) |
| Mississippi............ | 24 | 25 | 18 | 17 | 1,840 | 1,166 | 855 | 1,092 | 74 | 58 | 38 | (NA) |
| Montana.............. | 25 | 29 | 21 | 22 | 1,779 | 1,153 | 930 | 1,250 | 88 | 51 | 46 | 43 |
| Nebraska.............. | 2 | 3 | 2 | 2 | 162 | 117 | 94 | 121 | 2 | (Z) | (Z) | (NA) |
| New Mexico........... | 66 | 148 | 173 | 249 | 4,960 | 6,556 | 8,267 | 13,957 | 1,292 | 1,245 | 1,293 | 1,488 |
| New York.............. | (Z) | (Z) | (Z) | (Z) | (NA) | (NA) | (NA) | (NA) | 36 | 17 | 11 | (NA) |
| North Dakota.......... | 113 | 430 | 391 | 462 | 7,906 | 17,793 | 18,378 | 27,816 | 82 | 471 | 594 | 739 |
| Ohio................... | 5 | 27 | 20 | 23 | 352 | 1,025 | 923 | 1,408 | 78 | 1,007 | 1,773 | 2,385 |
| Oklahoma............. | 68 | 167 | 164 | 201 | 5,120 | 7,499 | 7,935 | 12,633 | 1,827 | 2,500 | 2,514 | 2,946 |
| Pennsylvania.......... | 3 | 7 | 7 | 6 | 226 | 276 | 301 | 386 | 573 | 4,813 | 5,464 | 6,207 |
| Texas................. | 427 | 1,257 | 1,271 | 1,609 | 32,529 | 56,501 | 61,739 | 96,400 | 6,715 | 7,890 | 7,135 | 7,866 |
| Utah.................. | 25 | 37 | 34 | 37 | 1,679 | 1,511 | 1,524 | 2,107 | 432 | 417 | 315 | 297 |
| West Virginia.......... | 2 | 12 | 9 | 12 | 130 | 390 | 410 | 666 | 265 | 1,315 | 1,601 | 1,799 |
| Wyoming.............. | 54 | 86 | 76 | 88 | 3,670 | 3,512 | 3,531 | 5,220 | 2,306 | 1,809 | 1,585 | 1,512 |
| Federal offshore....... | 588 | 564 | 619 | 646 | (NA) | (NA) | (NA) | (NA) | (NA) | (NA) | (NA) | (NA) |
| Lower 48 states........ | 1,784 | 3,273 | 3,238 | 3,842 | 133,887 | 145,894 | 156,176 | 235,723 | 22,008 | 28,428 | 28,853 | 32,394 |

Z Less than 500,000. NA Not available. [1] Excludes nonhydrocarbon gases. [2] Crude petroleum production value calculated using production quantity and domestic crude oil first purchase price. [3] Includes other states, not shown separately. State production includes state offshore production, as well as extractions from the Gulf not distributed to states. U.S. level totals shown in Table 943 and Table 948 may contain revisions not carried to state level. [4] Alaska crude oil production and value for North Slope only.

Source: U.S. Energy Information Administration, "Petroleum & Other Liquids Data," <http://www.eia.gov/petroleum/data.cfm>; and "Natural Gas Data," <http://www.eia.gov/naturalgas/data.cfm>; accessed September 2019.

# Table 947. Crude Oil and Natural Gas—Reserves by State: 2010 to 2017

[23,267 mil. bbl. represents 23,267,000,000 barrels. As of December 31. Proved reserves are estimated quantities of the mineral, which geological and engineering data demonstrate with reasonable certainty, to be recoverable in future years from known reservoirs under existing economic and operating conditions. Based on a sample of operators of oil and gas wells]

| Area | 2010 | | 2015 | | 2016 | | 2017 | |
|---|---|---|---|---|---|---|---|---|
| | Crude oil proved reserves (mil. bbl.) | Natural gas (bil. cu. ft.) | Crude oil proved reserves (mil. bbl.) | Natural gas (bil. cu. ft.) | Crude oil proved reserves (mil. bbl.) | Natural gas (bil. cu. ft.) | Crude oil proved reserves (mil. bbl.) | Natural gas (bil. cu. ft.) |
| United States [1]......... | 23,267 | 304,625 | 32,318 | 307,730 | 32,773 | 322,234 | 39,160 | 438,460 |
| Alabama................ | 42 | 2,629 | 64 | 2,182 | 43 | 1,791 | 43 | 1,510 |
| Alaska................. | 3,722 | 8,838 | 2,034 | 4,566 | 1,572 | 3,316 | 2,016 | 6,521 |
| Arkansas............... | 40 | 14,178 | 51 | 8,339 | 40 | 7,416 | 37 | 8,267 |
| California.............. | 2,938 | 2,647 | 2,333 | 1,832 | 1,933 | 1,340 | 2,209 | 1,560 |
| Colorado.............. | 386 | 24,119 | 1,212 | 17,139 | 1,267 | 17,761 | 1,528 | 26,573 |
| Florida................. | 18 | 56 | 16 | – | 14 | 1 | (NA) | (NA) |
| Illinois................. | 64 | (NA) | 31 | (NA) | 36 | (NA) | 38 | (NA) |
| Indiana................ | 8 | (NA) | 8 | (NA) | 4 | (NA) | 5 | (NA) |
| Kansas................ | 295 | 3,673 | 337 | 3,183 | 358 | 2,821 | 304 | 2,654 |
| Kentucky.............. | 15 | 2,613 | 10 | 1,362 | 10 | 1,123 | 8 | 1,136 |
| Louisiana.............. | 424 | 29,277 | 424 | 16,097 | 408 | 17,816 | 418 | 36,119 |
| Michigan.............. | 40 | 2,919 | 43 | 1,386 | 51 | 1,286 | 54 | 1,489 |
| Mississippi............ | 247 | 853 | 158 | 480 | 126 | 357 | 121 | 350 |
| Montana.............. | 369 | 944 | 326 | 692 | 285 | 569 | 302 | 611 |
| Nebraska.............. | 10 | (NA) | 17 | (NA) | 14 | (NA) | 13 | (NA) |
| New Mexico........... | 823 | 15,412 | 1,486 | 14,364 | 1,549 | 13,527 | 2,581 | 19,365 |
| New York.............. | (NA) | 281 | (NA) | 104 | (NA) | 120 | (NA) | 104 |
| North Dakota.......... | 1,814 | 1,667 | 5,193 | 6,203 | 5,256 | 7,030 | 5,473 | 8,445 |
| Ohio................... | 42 | 832 | 62 | 12,104 | 38 | 15,143 | 47 | 26,123 |
| Oklahoma............. | 710 | 26,345 | 1,262 | 28,486 | 1,693 | 31,712 | 1,917 | 35,491 |
| Pennsylvania.......... | 22 | 13,960 | 13 | 55,894 | 2 | 61,841 | 11 | 89,589 |
| Texas................. | 5,674 | 88,997 | 11,759 | 78,866 | 12,859 | 81,224 | 15,936 | 105,618 |
| Utah.................. | 449 | 6,981 | 389 | 3,547 | 372 | 3,494 | 285 | 3,752 |
| Virginia............... | (NA) | 3,215 | (NA) | 2,496 | (NA) | 2,447 | (NA) | 2,741 |
| West Virginia.......... | 17 | 7,000 | 12 | 20,553 | 6 | 23,025 | 9 | 32,785 |
| Wyoming.............. | 567 | 35,074 | 725 | 20,436 | 791 | 20,818 | 943 | 21,549 |
| Federal offshore......... | 4,496 | 11,765 | 4,335 | 7,296 | 4,033 | 6,144 | 4,789 | 5,945 |
| Lower 48 states.......... | 19,545 | 295,787 | 30,284 | 303,164 | 31,201 | 318,918 | 37,144 | 431,939 |

– Represents zero. NA Not available. [1] Includes other states, not shown separately.

Source: U.S. Energy Information Administration, "Petroleum & Other Liquids Data," <http://www.eia.gov/petroleum/data.cfm>; and "Natural Gas Data," <http://www.eia.gov/naturalgas/data.cfm>; accessed February 2019.

## Table 948. Dry Natural Gas—Supply, Consumption, Reserves, and Marketed Production: 1990 to 2018

[270 represents 270,000. Data are for dry natural gas, plus a small amount of supplemental gaseous fuels. Minus sign (-) indicates debit]

| Item | Unit | 1990 | 2000 | 2005 | 2010 | 2015 | 2016 | 2017 | 2018 (P) |
|---|---|---|---|---|---|---|---|---|---|
| Producing wells (year-end)............ | 1,000 | 270 | 342 | 426 | 488 | 575 | 572 | 486 | (NA) |
| Production value at wells............... | Bil. dol. | 31.8 | 74.3 | 138.8 | (NA) | (NA) | (NA) | (NA) | (NA) |
| Avg. per 1,000 cu. ft.................... | Dollars | 1.71 | 3.68 | 7.33 | 4.48 | (NA) | (NA) | (NA) | (NA) |
| Proved reserves [1]...................... | Tril. cu. ft. | 169.3 | 177.4 | 204.4 | 304.6 | 307.7 | 322.2 | 438.5 | (NA) |
| **Marketed production [2]**................ | **Bil. cu. ft.** | **18,593.8** | **20,197.5** | **18,927.1** | **22,381.9** | **28,772.0** | **28,400.0** | **29,197.0** | **32,735.1** |
| Minus: Extraction losses [3]............ | Bil. cu. ft. | 784.1 | 1,015.5 | 876.5 | 1,066.4 | 1,706.6 | 1,807.9 | 1,905.8 | 2,296.5 |
| Equals: Dry production................. | Bil. cu. ft. | 17,809.7 | 19,182.0 | 18,050.6 | 21,315.5 | 27,065.5 | 26,592.1 | 27,291.2 | 30,438.6 |
| Plus: Supplemental gas supplies..... | Bil. cu. ft. | 122.8 | 90.0 | 63.7 | 64.6 | 58.6 | 57.2 | 65.7 | 67.7 |
| Equals: Dry production with supplemental gas...................... | Bil. cu. ft. | 17,932.5 | 19,272.0 | 18,114.3 | 21,380.1 | 27,124.1 | 26,649.3 | 27,356.9 | 30,506.3 |
| Plus: Withdrawals from storage [4]..... | Bil. cu. ft. | 1,933.8 | 3,498.2 | 3,056.6 | 3,274.4 | 3,099.7 | 3,324.9 | 3,590.5 | 3,999.4 |
| Plus: Imports........................... | Bil. cu. ft. | 1,532.3 | 3,781.6 | 4,341.0 | 3,740.8 | 2,718.1 | 3,006.5 | 3,042.4 | 2,888.8 |
| Plus: Balancing item [5]................. | Bil. cu. ft. | 307.3 | -305.7 | 236.1 | 115.5 | -267.9 | -216.5 | -359.8 | -154.0 |
| Equals: Total supply.................... | Bil. cu. ft. | 21,705.8 | 26,246.1 | 25,748.0 | 28,510.7 | 32,674.0 | 32,764.2 | 33,630.0 | 37,239.8 |
| Minus: Exports.......................... | Bil. cu. ft. | 85.6 | 243.7 | 728.6 | 1,136.8 | 1,783.5 | 2,335.4 | 3,167.9 | 3,607.4 |
| Minus: Additions to storage [4]......... | Bil. cu. ft. | 2,433.5 | 2,684.3 | 3,001.6 | 3,291.4 | 3,638.3 | 2,976.7 | 3,336.6 | 3,675.9 |
| **Equals: Consumption, total**......... | **Bil. cu. ft.** | **19,173.6** | **23,333.1** | **22,014.4** | **24,086.8** | **27,243.9** | **27,444.2** | **27,110.3** | **29,956.5** |
| Lease and plant fuel................... | Bil. cu. ft. | 1,236.4 | 1,150.9 | 1,111.5 | 1,285.6 | 1,576.4 | 1,545.3 | 1,564.5 | 1,754.0 |
| Pipeline fuel [6]........................ | Bil. cu. ft. | (NA) | 642.2 | 584.0 | 674.1 | 678.2 | 686.7 | 721.5 | 797.3 |
| Residential.............................. | Bil. cu. ft. | 4,391.3 | 4,996.2 | 4,826.8 | 4,782.4 | 4,612.9 | 4,346.6 | 4,412.3 | 4,974.0 |
| Commercial [7]......................... | Bil. cu. ft. | 2,622.7 | 3,182.5 | 2,998.9 | 3,102.6 | 3,201.7 | 3,109.6 | 3,164.1 | 3,476.3 |
| Industrial............................... | Bil. cu. ft. | (NA) | 8,142.2 | 6,601.2 | 6,826.2 | 7,521.9 | 7,728.7 | 7,949.2 | 8,285.8 |
| Vehicle fuel............................ | Bil. cu. ft. | (NA) | 12.8 | 22.9 | 28.7 | 39.4 | 42.0 | 48.7 | 43.4 |
| Electric power sector.................. | Bil. cu. ft. | (NA) | 5,206.3 | 5,869.1 | 7,387.2 | 9,613.4 | 9,985.3 | 9,250.1 | 10,625.7 |
| World production (dry)................. | Tril. cu. ft. | 73.4 | 86.8 | 98.6 | 113.1 | 124.6 | 125.7 | 130.8 | (NA) |
| U.S. production (dry)................. | Tril. cu. ft. | 17.8 | 19.2 | 18.1 | 21.3 | 27.1 | 26.6 | 27.3 | 30.4 |
| U.S. percent of world............... | Percent | 24.3 | 22.1 | 18.3 | 18.8 | 21.7 | 21.1 | 20.9 | (NA) |

P Preliminary. NA Not available. [1] Estimated, end of year. [2] Gross withdrawals less gas used for repressuring, quantities vented and flared, and nonhydrocarbon gases removed in treating or processing operations. Includes all quantities of gas used in field and processing plant operations. [3] Volumetric reduction in natural gas resulting from the removal of natural gas plant liquids, which are transferred to petroleum supply. [4] Underground storage. [5] Quantities lost and imbalances in data due to differences among data sources. Since 1980, excludes in-transit shipments that cross U.S.-Canada border (i.e., natural gas delivered to its destination via the other country). [6] Natural gas consumed in the operation of pipelines, primarily in compressors. [7] Includes gas used by local, State, and Federal agencies engaged in nonmanufacturing activities.

Source: U.S. Energy Information Administration, "Natural Gas Data," <http://www.eia.gov/naturalgas/data.cfm>; "Monthly Energy Review, Natural Gas," <http://www.eia.gov/totalenergy/data/monthly/#naturalgas>; and "International Energy Statistics," <http://www.eia.gov/countries/data.cfm>; accessed August 2019.

## Table 949. Unconventional Dry Natural Gas Production and Proved Reserves: 2016 and 2017

[In billions of cubic feet (1,020 represents 1,020,000,000,000). For states not listed, no production or reserves were reported]

| State | Production Coalbed methane [2] 2016 | Coalbed methane [2] 2017 | Shale gas [3] 2016 | Shale gas [3] 2017 | Proved reserves [1] Coalbed methane [2] 2016 | Coalbed methane [2] 2017 | Shale gas [3] 2016 | Shale gas [3] 2017 |
|---|---|---|---|---|---|---|---|---|
| **United States.........** | **1,020** | **980** | **17,032** | **18,589** | **10,585** | **11,878** | **209,809** | **307,903** |
| Alabama................. | 45 | 62 | (NA) | (NA) | 985 | 789 | (NA) | (NA) |
| Alaska................... | – | – | – | – | – | – | – | – |
| Arkansas............... | 1 | 1 | 733 | 618 | 9 | 10 | 6,262 | 7,090 |
| California............... | – | – | 6 | 6 | – | – | 41 | 62 |
| Colorado............... | 352 | 338 | 164 | 97 | 3,265 | 3,275 | 2,032 | 1,885 |
| Florida................... | – | – | (NA) | (NA) | – | – | (NA) | (NA) |
| Kansas.................. | 11 | 15 | – | – | 55 | 46 | – | – |
| Kentucky............... | – | (NA) | – | (NA) | 6 | (NA) | 12 | (NA) |
| Louisiana............... | – | – | 1,111 | 1,450 | 1 | – | 9,637 | 26,484 |
| Michigan................ | – | – | 84 | 63 | – | – | 1,128 | 942 |
| Mississippi............. | – | – | 2 | 2 | – | – | 7 | 8 |
| Montana................ | – | – | 19 | 18 | 7 | 1 | 213 | 258 |
| New Mexico............ | 253 | 234 | 497 | 592 | 2,210 | 3,175 | 5,581 | 9,451 |
| New York............... | – | – | (NA) | (NA) | – | – | (NA) | (NA) |
| North Dakota........... | – | – | 582 | 664 | – | – | 8,259 | 9,984 |
| Ohio..................... | (NA) | (NA) | 1,386 | 1,747 | (NA) | (NA) | 15,472 | 26,468 |
| Oklahoma............... | 43 | 36 | 1,082 | 1,290 | 320 | 318 | 20,327 | 22,675 |
| Pennsylvania.......... | 10 | (NA) | 5,049 | 5,365 | 206 | (NA) | 60,979 | 89,478 |
| Texas.................... | 11 | 8 | 5,029 | 5,171 | 84 | 74 | 56,577 | 78,666 |
| Utah..................... | 39 | 36 | (NA) | (NA) | 332 | 438 | (NA) | (NA) |
| Virginia.................. | 102 | 99 | 4 | 4 | 2,117 | 2,465 | 45 | 66 |
| West Virginia.......... | 9 | 7 | 1,270 | 1,486 | 99 | 89 | 23,146 | 34,296 |
| Wyoming............... | 143 | 135 | 5 | 6 | 882 | 1,014 | 17 | 28 |

– Represents or rounds to zero. NA Not available. [1] Proved reserves of natural gas as of December 31 of the report year are the estimated quantities which analysis of geological and engineering data demonstrate with reasonable certainty to be recoverable in future years from known reservoirs under existing economic and operating conditions. [2] Methane is generated during coal formation and is contained in the coal microstructure. Typical recovery entails pumping water out of the coal to allow the gas to escape. Methane is the principal component of natural gas. Coal bed methane can be added to natural gas pipelines without any special treatment. [3] Natural gas produced from organic (black) shale formations.

Source: U.S. Energy Information Administration, "Natural Gas Data," <http://www.eia.gov/naturalgas/data.cfm>, accessed February 2019.

# Table 950. Coal Production, Supply, Disposition, and Prices: 2000 to 2018

[In millions of short tons (1,073.6 represents 1,073,600,000). 1 short ton = 2,000 lbs]

| Item | 2000 | 2005 | 2010 | 2015 | 2016 | 2017 | 2018 |
|---|---|---|---|---|---|---|---|
| **United States, total production** | **1,073.6** | **1,131.5** | **1,084.4** | **896.9** | **728.4** | **774.6** | **756.1** |
| Consumption by sector: | | | | | | | |
| Total | 1,084.1 | 1,126.0 | 1,048.5 | 798.1 | 731.1 | 716.9 | 687.3 |
| Residential [1] | 0.5 | 0.4 | (NA) | (NA) | (NA) | (NA) | (NA) |
| Commercial | 3.7 | 4.3 | 3.1 | 1.5 | 1.2 | 1.1 | 1.0 |
| Industrial | 94.1 | 83.8 | 70.4 | 58.2 | 51.3 | 50.8 | 49.8 |
| Coke plants | 28.9 | 23.4 | 21.1 | 19.7 | 16.5 | 17.5 | 18.3 |
| Other industrial plants | 65.2 | 60.3 | 49.3 | 38.5 | 34.8 | 33.3 | 31.5 |
| Combined heat and power (CHP) | 28.0 | 25.9 | 24.6 | 17.0 | 14.7 | 13.0 | 12.5 |
| Noncombined heat and power | 37.2 | 34.5 | 24.7 | 21.5 | 20.1 | 20.3 | 19.0 |
| Electric power | 985.8 | 1,037.5 | 975.1 | 738.4 | 678.6 | 665.0 | 636.5 |
| Year-end coal stocks: | | | | | | | |
| Total | 140.3 | 144.3 | 231.7 | 238.4 | 193.0 | 167.0 | 132.1 |
| Residential and commercial | (NA) | (NA) | 0.6 | 0.4 | 0.4 | 0.3 | 0.3 |
| Industrial | 6.1 | 8.2 | 6.5 | 6.6 | 5.3 | 5.0 | 5.1 |
| Coke plants | 1.5 | 2.6 | 1.9 | 2.2 | 1.7 | 1.7 | 1.8 |
| Other industrial plants | 4.6 | 5.6 | 4.5 | 4.4 | 3.6 | 3.2 | 3.3 |
| Electric power | 102.3 | 101.1 | 174.9 | 195.5 | 162.0 | 137.7 | 102.8 |
| Producers/distributors | 31.9 | 35.0 | 49.8 | 35.9 | 25.3 | 24.0 | 24.0 |
| U.S. coal trade: | | | | | | | |
| Net exports [2] | 46.0 | 19.5 | 62.4 | 62.6 | 50.4 | 89.2 | 109.7 |
| Exports | 58.5 | 49.9 | 81.7 | 74.0 | 60.3 | 97.0 | 115.6 |
| Steam coal | 25.7 | 21.3 | 25.6 | 28.0 | 19.3 | 41.7 | (NA) |
| Metallurgical coal | 32.8 | 28.7 | 56.1 | 46.0 | 40.9 | 55.3 | (NA) |
| Coke | 1.3 | 1.7 | 1.5 | 0.9 | 1.0 | 1.2 | (NA) |
| Imports | 12.5 | 30.5 | 19.4 | 11.3 | 9.8 | 7.8 | 6.0 |
| Average delivered price (dollars per short ton) to: | | | | | | | |
| Electric power sector | 24.28 | 31.22 | 44.27 | 42.6 | 40.64 | 39.18 | (NA) |

NA Not available. [1] Beginning in 2008, residential coal consumption data are not collected by Energy Information Administration. [2] Exports minus imports.

Source: U.S. Energy Information Administration, *Annual Coal Report 2017*, November 2018, and earlier reports; and "Coal Data," <http://www.eia.gov/coal/data.cfm> and "Monthly Energy Review, Coal," <http://www.eia.gov/totalenergy/data/monthly/#coal>, accessed August 2019.

# Table 951. Coal and Coke—Summary: 1990 to 2017

[In millions of short tons (1,029 represents 1,029,000,000), except as indicated. Includes coal consumed at mines. Recoverability varies between 40 and 90 percent for individual deposits; 50 percent or more of overall U.S. coal reserve base is believed to be recoverable]

| Item | Unit | 1990 | 2000 | 2005 | 2010 | 2014 | 2015 | 2016 | 2017 |
|---|---|---|---|---|---|---|---|---|---|
| COAL | | | | | | | | | |
| **Production, total [1,2]** | Mil. sh. tons | **1,029** | **1,074** | **1,131** | **1,084** | **1,000** | **897** | **728** | **775** |
| Average price per short ton | Dollars | 21.76 | 16.78 | 23.34 | 35.61 | 34.83 | 31.81 | 30.57 | 33.72 |
| Anthracite production [2] | Mil. sh. tons | 4 | 5 | 2 | 2 | 2 | 2 | 2 | 2 |
| Bituminous coal and lignite [3] | Mil. sh. tons | 1,026 | 1,069 | 1,130 | 1,083 | 998 | 895 | 727 | 773 |
| Underground | Mil. sh. tons | 425 | 374 | 369 | 337 | 355 | 307 | 252 | 273 |
| Surface [2] | Mil. sh. tons | 605 | 700 | 763 | 747 | 645 | 590 | 476 | 501 |
| Exports | Mil. sh. tons | 106 | 58 | 50 | 82 | 97 | 74 | 60 | 97 |
| Imports | Mil. sh. tons | 3 | 13 | 30 | 19 | 11 | 11 | 10 | 8 |
| Consumption [4] | Mil. sh. tons | 904 | 1,084 | 1,126 | 1,049 | 918 | 798 | 731 | 717 |
| Electric power sector [5] | Mil. sh. tons | 783 | 985.821 | 1,037 | 975 | 852 | 738 | 679 | 665 |
| Industrial | Mil. sh. tons | 115 | 94 | 84 | 70 | 64 | 58 | 51 | 51 |
| Number of mines | Number | 3,243 | 1,453 | 1,415 | 1,285 | 985 | 853 | 710 | 680 |
| Daily employment | 1,000 | 131 | 72 | 79 | 86 | 75 | 66 | 52 | 53 |
| Production, by state: | | | | | | | | | |
| Alabama | Mil. sh. tons | 29 | 19 | 21 | 20 | 16 | 13 | 10 | 13 |
| Illinois | Mil. sh. tons | 60 | 33 | 32 | 33 | 58 | 56 | 43 | 48 |
| Indiana | Mil. sh. tons | 36 | 28 | 34 | 35 | 39 | 34 | 29 | 31 |
| Kentucky | Mil. sh. tons | 173 | 131 | 120 | 105 | 77 | 61 | 43 | 42 |
| Montana | Mil. sh. tons | 38 | 38 | 40 | 45 | 45 | 42 | 32 | 35 |
| Ohio | Mil. sh. tons | 35 | 22 | 25 | 27 | 22 | 17 | 13 | 9 |
| Pennsylvania | Mil. sh. tons | 71 | 75 | 67 | 59 | 61 | 50 | 46 | 49 |
| Virginia | Mil. sh. tons | 47 | 33 | 28 | 22 | 15 | 14 | 13 | 13 |
| West Virginia | Mil. sh. tons | 169 | 158 | 154 | 135 | 112 | 96 | 80 | 93 |
| Wyoming | Mil. sh. tons | 184 | 339 | 404 | 443 | 396 | 376 | 297 | 316 |
| Other states | Mil. sh. tons | 187 | 197 | 205 | 159 | 157 | 136 | 122 | 123 |
| World production | Mil. sh. tons | 5,280 | 5,127 | 6,644 | 8,155 | 8,981 | 8,737 | 8,150 | (NA) |
| U.S. percent of world | Percent | 19.5 | 20.9 | 17.0 | 13.3 | 11.1 | 10.3 | 8.9 | (NA) |
| COKE | | | | | | | | | |
| Production | Mil. sh. tons | 27.6 | 20.8 | 16.7 | 15.0 | 15.2 | 13.8 | 11.9 | 12.9 |
| Imports | Mil. sh. tons | 0.8 | 3.8 | 3.5 | 1.2 | 0.1 | 0.1 | 0.2 | 0.1 |
| Exports | Mil. sh. tons | 0.6 | 1.1 | 1.7 | 1.5 | 0.9 | 0.9 | 1.0 | 1.2 |
| Consumption [6] | Mil. sh. tons | 27.8 | 23.2 | 18.2 | 14.8 | 14.4 | 13.1 | 11.2 | 11.8 |

NA Not available. [1] Includes bituminous coal, subbituminous coal, lignite, and anthracite. [2] Beginning 2005, includes a small amount of refuse recovery. [3] Includes subbituminous. [4] Includes other categories not shown separately. [5] Electricity-only and combined-heat-and-power (CHP) plants whose primary business is to sell electricity and/or heat to the public. [6] Consumption is calculated as the sum of production and imports minus exports and stock change.

Source: U.S. Energy Information Administration, *Annual Energy Review 2011*, September 2012; *Annual Coal Report 2017*, November 2018; *Quarterly Coal Report*, April 2019; and Open Data, "International Energy Data," <http://www.eia.gov/opendata/>, accessed August 2019. See also <http://www.eia.gov/totalenergy> and <http://www.eia.gov/coal/annual/>.

# Table 952. Demonstrated Coal Reserves by Major Producing State: 2016 and 2017

[Reserves in millions of short tons (475,990 represents 475,990,000,000). As of January 1 the following year. The demonstrated reserve base represents the sum of coal in both measured and indicated resource categories of reliability. Measured resources of coal are estimates that have a high degree of geologic assurance from sample analyses and measurements from closely spaced and geologically well-known sample sites. Indicated resources are estimates based partly from sample and analyses and measurements and partly from reasonable geologic projections]

| State | 2016 Number of mines | 2016 Total reserves | 2016 Under-ground | 2016 Surface | 2017 Number of mines | 2017 Total reserves | 2017 Under-ground | 2017 Surface |
|---|---|---|---|---|---|---|---|---|
| **United States** [1] | **710** | **475,990** | **327,282** | **148,707** | **680** | **474,828** | **326,731** | **148,097** |
| Alabama | 30 | 3,869 | 757 | 3,112 | 30 | 3,845 | 736 | 3,109 |
| Alaska | 1 | 6,088 | 5,423 | 665 | 1 | 6,087 | 5,423 | 664 |
| Arkansas | 3 | 415 | 271 | 144 | 3 | 415 | 271 | 144 |
| Colorado | 8 | 15,687 | 10,933 | 4,754 | 7 | 15,660 | 10,906 | 4,754 |
| Illinois | 21 | 103,589 | 87,108 | 16,481 | 18 | 103,495 | 87,018 | 16,477 |
| Indiana | 20 | 8,876 | 8,430 | 446 | 18 | 8,826 | 8,402 | 424 |
| Iowa | (NA) | 2,189 | 1,732 | 457 | (NA) | 2,189 | 1,732 | 457 |
| Kansas | 1 | 970 | (NA) | 970 | (NA) | 970 | (NA) | 970 |
| Kentucky | 158 | 28,248 | 15,763 | 12,485 | 151 | 28,172 | 15,700 | 12,472 |
| Kentucky, Eastern | 142 | 9,453 | 519 | 8,934 | 138 | 9,423 | 500 | 8,924 |
| Kentucky, Western | 16 | 18,794 | 15,243 | 3,551 | 13 | 18,749 | 15,200 | 3,548 |
| Maryland | 17 | 601 | 558 | 42 | 14 | 598 | 557 | 41 |
| Missouri | 1 | 5,984 | 1,479 | 4,505 | 1 | 5,984 | 1,479 | 4,505 |
| Montana | 6 | 118,629 | 70,867 | 47,761 | 6 | 118,580 | 70,856 | 47,725 |
| New Mexico | 3 | 11,776 | 6,022 | 5,754 | 3 | 11,755 | 6,011 | 5,744 |
| North Dakota | 5 | 8,655 | (NA) | 8,655 | 5 | 8,619 | (NA) | 8,619 |
| Ohio | 19 | 22,847 | 17,197 | 5,651 | 18 | 22,831 | 17,183 | 5,647 |
| Oklahoma | 4 | 1,535 | 1,222 | 313 | 5 | 1,534 | 1,221 | 313 |
| Pennsylvania | 172 | 26,277 | 22,156 | 4,121 | 153 | 26,182 | 22,068 | 4,114 |
| Anthracite [2] | 53 | 7,173 | 3,840 | 3,333 | 57 | 7,171 | 3,840 | 3,330 |
| Bituminous | 119 | 19,103 | 18,315 | 788 | 96 | 19,012 | 18,228 | 784 |
| Tennessee | 6 | 747 | 495 | 251 | 6 | 746 | 495 | 251 |
| Texas | 14 | 11,817 | (NA) | 11,817 | 10 | 11,772 | (NA) | 11,772 |
| Utah | 8 | 4,967 | 4,703 | 264 | 8 | 4,938 | 4,675 | 263 |
| Virginia | 54 | 1,303 | 836 | 467 | 52 | 1,279 | 817 | 463 |
| Washington | (NA) | 1,340 | 1,332 | 8 | (NA) | 1,340 | 1,332 | 8 |
| West Virginia | 123 | 30,555 | 27,410 | 3,145 | 140 | 30,385 | 27,265 | 3,120 |
| Wyoming | 16 | 58,121 | 42,432 | 15,689 | 17 | 57,724 | 42,429 | 15,296 |

NA Not available. [1] Includes other states not shown separately. [2] All of the anthracite mines in the United States are located in northeastern Pennsylvania.

Source: U.S. Energy Information Administration, *Annual Coal Report 2017*, November 2018, and earlier reports. See also <http://www.eia.gov/coal/annual/>.

# Table 953. Uranium Concentrate Industry—Summary: 1990 to 2018

[In units as indicated (1.7 represents 1,700,000). See also Section 19, Table 975]

| Item | Unit | 1990 | 1995 | 2000 | 2010 | 2014 | 2015 | 2016 | 2017 | 2018 |
|---|---|---|---|---|---|---|---|---|---|---|
| Exploration and development, surface drilling | Mil. ft. | 1.7 | 1.3 | 1.0 | 4.9 | 1.3 | 0.9 | 0.8 | 0.2 | (D) |
| Expenditures | Mil. dol. | (NA) | 2.6 | 5.6 | 44.6 | 28.2 | 28.7 | 22.3 | 4.0 | (D) |
| Number of mines operated | Number | 39 | 12 | 10 | 9 | 11 | 9 | 9 | 7 | 7 |
| Underground | Number | 27 | – | 1 | 4 | 2 | 1 | – | – | – |
| Open pit | Number | 2 | – | – | – | – | – | – | – | – |
| In situ leaching | Number | 7 | 5 | 4 | 4 | 8 | 7 | 8 | 6 | 6 |
| Other sources [1] | Number | 3 | 7 | 5 | 1 | 1 | 1 | 1 | 1 | 1 |
| Mine production | 1,000 pounds | 5,876 | 3,528 | 3,123 | 4,237 | 4,912 | 3,711 | 2,545 | 1,150 | 721 |
| Underground | 1,000 pounds | (D) | – | (D) | (D) | (D) | (D) | (D) | (D) | (D) |
| Open pit | 1,000 pounds | 1,881 | – | – | – | – | – | – | – | – |
| In situ leaching | 1,000 pounds | (D) | 3,372 | 2,995 | (D) | (D) | (D) | (D) | (D) | (D) |
| Other sources [1] | 1,000 pounds | 3,995 | 156 | 128 | (D) | (D) | (D) | (D) | (D) | (D) |
| Uranium concentrate production | 1,000 pounds | 8,886 | 6,043 | 3,958 | 4,228 | 4,891 | 3,343 | 2,916 | 2,443 | 1,647 |
| Concentrate shipments from mills and plants | 1,000 pounds | 12,957 | 5,500 | 3,187 | 5,137 | 4,593 | 4,023 | 3,018 | 2,277 | 1,489 |
| Employment | Person-years [2] | 1,335 | 1,107 | 627 | 1,073 | 787 | 625 | 560 | 424 | 372 |

– Represents zero. D Data withheld to avoid disclosing figures for individual companies. NA Not available. [1] Includes mine water, mill site cleanup and mill tailings, and well field restoration as sources of uranium. [2] A person-year is defined as one whole year, or fraction thereof, worked by an employee, including contracted man power. 12 months worked is 1 person year.

Source: U.S. Energy Information Administration, through 2002, *Uranium Industry*, annual. Thereafter, *Domestic Uranium Production Report*, May 2019, and earlier reports. See also <http://www.eia.gov/uranium/production/annual/>.

# Table 954. Crude Petroleum and Natural Gas Extraction Industry Establishments, Employees, and Payroll by State: 2016

[14,364,998 represents $14,364,998,000. Excludes self-employed individuals, employees of private households, railroad employees, agricultural production employees, and most government employees. See source for definitions and statement on reliability of data. An establishment is a single physical location where business is conducted or where services or industrial operations are performed. See Appendix III]

| State | Crude petroleum and natural gas extraction (NAICS 211111) [1] | | | State | Crude petroleum and natural gas extraction (NAICS 211111) [1] | | |
|---|---|---|---|---|---|---|---|
| | Establish-ments | Number of employees [2] | Annual payroll ($1,000) | | Establish-ments | Number of employees [2] | Annual payroll ($1,000) |
| United States........ | 6,878 | 113,404 | 14,364,998 | Missouri.............. | 69 | 697 | 79,500 |
| | | | | Montana............. | 13 | 31 | 1,485 |
| Alabama................ | 28 | 269 | 25,255 | Nebraska............ | 73 | 842 | 100,984 |
| Alaska.................. | 23 | 2,181 | 444,643 | Nevada............. | 20 | 90 | 4,483 |
| Arizona................. | 15 | 38 | 2,858 | New Hampshire..... | 13 | 56 | 3,910 |
| Arkansas............... | 100 | 1,638 | 122,975 | New Mexico......... | 3 | 13 | 1,004 |
| California.............. | 201 | 5,317 | 694,788 | New York............ | 2 | ( [3] ) | (D) |
| Colorado.............. | 377 | 6,357 | 896,572 | North Carolina..... | 153 | 3,568 | 337,165 |
| Connecticut........... | 4 | 7 | 883 | North Dakota........ | 37 | 259 | 22,511 |
| Delaware.............. | 5 | 20 | 3,527 | Ohio................. | 5 | 24 | 3,616 |
| District of Columbia.... | 2 | ( [3] ) | (D) | Oklahoma........... | 66 | 3,392 | 393,318 |
| Florida................ | 19 | 165 | 13,514 | Oregon.............. | 175 | 1,638 | 99,650 |
| Georgia................ | 4 | 35 | 1,211 | Pennsylvania........ | 1,041 | 13,235 | 1,481,924 |
| Idaho................. | 1 | ( [3] ) | (D) | Rhode Island........ | 3 | 4 | 185 |
| Illinois................. | 154 | 789 | 39,350 | South Carolina...... | 194 | 4,963 | 572,785 |
| Indiana................ | 38 | 209 | 12,032 | South Dakota...... | 7 | 45 | 3,347 |
| Kansas................ | 358 | 2,300 | 155,066 | Tennessee.......... | 14 | 105 | 10,949 |
| Kentucky.............. | 70 | 504 | 41,888 | Texas............... | 2,780 | 51,109 | 7,335,484 |
| Louisiana............. | 354 | 6,942 | 833,130 | Utah................ | 49 | 1,384 | 131,133 |
| Maryland............. | 1 | ( [3] ) | (D) | Virginia.............. | 22 | 396 | 26,604 |
| Massachusetts........ | 2 | ( [3] ) | (D) | Washington.......... | 7 | 22 | 1,690 |
| Michigan.............. | 2 | ( [3] ) | (D) | West Virginia........ | 164 | 1,955 | 173,903 |
| Minnesota............ | 69 | 757 | 59,882 | Wisconsin........... | 1 | ( [3] ) | (D) |
| Mississippi............ | 7 | 19 | 1,703 | Wyoming............ | 133 | 2,010 | 225,587 |

D Withheld to avoid disclosing data for individual companies; data are included in higher level totals. NA Not available. [1] North American Industry Classification System, 2012. [2] Covers full-time and part-time employees who are on the payroll in the pay period including March 12. [3] 0 to 19 employees.

Source: U.S. Census Bureau, County Business Patterns, "Geography Area Series: County Business Patterns," <http://factfinder.census.gov>, accessed April 2018. See also <https://www.census.gov/programs-surveys/cbp.html>.

# Table 955. Natural Gas Liquid Extraction Industry—Establishments, Employees, and Payroll by State: 2016

[930,717 represents $930,717,000. Excludes self-employed individuals, employees of private households, railroad employees, agricultural production employees, and most government employees. See source for definitions and statement on reliability of data. An establishment is a single physical location where business is conducted or where services or industrial operations are performed. See Appendix III]

| State | Natural gas liquid extraction (NAICS 211112) [1] | | | State | Natural gas liquid extraction (NAICS 211112) [1] | | |
|---|---|---|---|---|---|---|---|
| | Establish-ments | Number of employees [2] | Annual payroll ($1,000) | | Establish-ments | Number of employees [2] | Annual payroll ($1,000) |
| United States...... | 452 | 8,736 | 930,717 | Missouri.............. | 3 | ( [5] ) | (D) |
| | | | | Montana............. | 3 | 77 | 6,048 |
| Alabama.............. | 2 | ( [4] ) | (D) | Nebraska............ | 1 | ( [3] ) | (D) |
| Alaska................ | 3 | ( [6] ) | (D) | New Mexico......... | 22 | 434 | 42,095 |
| Arizona............... | 1 | ( [3] ) | (D) | New York............ | 1 | ( [4] ) | (D) |
| Arkansas............. | 1 | ( [4] ) | (D) | North Dakota........ | 4 | 538 | 65,660 |
| California............. | 8 | 323 | 34,313 | Ohio................. | 13 | 321 | 31,680 |
| Colorado............. | 21 | 423 | 46,491 | Oklahoma........... | 69 | 712 | 65,492 |
| Florida............... | 1 | ( [4] ) | (D) | Pennsylvania........ | 10 | 275 | 24,747 |
| Illinois................ | 3 | ( [5] ) | (D) | South Carolina...... | 1 | ( [3] ) | (D) |
| Indiana............... | 2 | ( [4] ) | (D) | Tennessee........... | 1 | ( [3] ) | (D) |
| Kansas............... | 23 | 177 | 14,749 | Texas................ | 162 | 2,672 | 272,897 |
| Kentucky............. | 4 | ( [4] ) | (D) | Utah................ | 4 | 117 | 5,092 |
| Louisiana............. | 46 | 672 | 67,577 | Virginia.............. | 1 | ( [3] ) | (D) |
| Michigan............. | 10 | 101 | 8,921 | West Virginia........ | 9 | 161 | 17,930 |
| Mississippi............ | 4 | 155 | 15,587 | Wyoming............. | 19 | 632 | 56,544 |

D Withheld to avoid disclosing data for individual companies; data are included in higher level totals. [1] North American Industry Classification System, 2012. [2] Covers full- and part-time employees who are on the payroll in the pay period including March 12. [3] 0 to 19 employees. [4] 20 to 99 employees. [5] 100 to 249 employees. [6] 250 to 499 employees.

Source: U.S. Census Bureau, County Business Patterns, "Geography Area Series: County Business Patterns," <http://factfinder.census.gov>, accessed April 2018. See also <https://www.census.gov/programs-surveys/cbp.html>.

# Energy and Utilities

This section presents statistics on fuel resources, energy production and consumption, electric energy, renewable energy, and the electric and gas utility industries. The principal sources are the U.S. Department of Energy's Energy Information Administration (EIA), the Edison Electric Institute, Washington, DC, and the American Gas Association, Arlington, VA. The Department of Energy was created in October 1977 and assumed and centralized the responsibilities of all or part of several agencies including the Federal Power Commission (FPC), the U.S. Bureau of Mines, the Federal Energy Administration, and the U.S. Energy Research and Development Administration. For additional data on transportation, see Section 23; on fuels, see Section 18; and on energy-related housing characteristics, see Section 20.

The EIA, in its *Annual Energy Review*, provides statistics and trend data on energy supply, demand, and prices. Information is included on petroleum and natural gas, coal, electricity, hydroelectric power, nuclear power, solar, wind, wood, and geothermal energy. Due to budget constraints, in 2013 the EIA suspended publication of the *Annual Energy Review*. In order to continue publishing similar data, In the *Monthly Energy Review*, the EIA presents data on current supply, disposition, and price data for energy resources and monthly publications on petroleum, coal, natural gas, and electric power. This publication continues coverage of data previously covered the *Annual Energy Review*, which was suspended in 2013 due to budget constraints. Additional EIA reports include the *Electric Power Annual*; *Natural Gas Annual*; *Petroleum Supply Annual*, *U.S. Crude Oil, Natural Gas, and Natural Gas Liquids Reserves Annual Report*; *Electric Sales, Revenue, and Price*; *State Energy Consumption, Price, and Expenditure Data*; *Annual Energy Outlook*; *Uranium Marketing Annual Report*; *Domestic Uranium Production Report—Quarterly*; and *International Energy Statistics*. These various reports contain state, national, and international data on the production of electricity, net summer capability of generating plants, fuels used in energy production, energy sales and consumption, and hydroelectric power. The EIA also provides access to regular data updates through its Open Data program. For more information, please refer to the EIA's Open Data program's web site <http://www.eia.gov/opendata/>.

Data on residential energy consumption, expenditures, and conservation activities are available from EIA's Residential Energy Consumption Survey (RECS) and are published every 4 years. The Commercial Buildings Energy Consumption Survey (CBECS), conducted on a quadrennial basis, collects information on the stock of U.S. commercial buildings, their energy-related characteristics, and their energy consumption and expenditures. Data on manufacturing energy consumption, use, and expenditures are also collected every 4 years from EIA's Manufacturing Energy Consumption Survey (MECS). Due to the long gaps between the RECS, CBECS, and MECS, tables are rotated in and out of Section 19 in an effort to keep the data as current as possible. The results from these surveys are published at <http://www.eia.gov/consumption/>.

The Edison Electric Institute's annual *Statistical Yearbook of the Electric Power Industry* contains data on the distribution of electric energy by public utilities. The American Gas Association, in its annual yearbook, *Gas Facts*, presents data on gas utilities and financial and operating statistics.

**Btu conversion factors**—Various energy sources are converted from original units to the thermal equivalent using British thermal units (Btu). A Btu is the amount of energy required to raise the temperature of 1 pound of water 1 degree Fahrenheit (F) at or near 39.2 degrees F. Factors are calculated annually from the latest final annual data available; some are revised as a result.

**Electric power industry**—In recent years, EIA has restructured the industry categories it once used to gather and report electricity statistics. The electric power industry, previously divided into electric utilities and non-utilities, now consists of the Electric Power Sector, the Commercial Sector, and the Industrial Sector.

The Electric Power Sector is composed of electricity-only and combined-heat-and-power plants (CHPs) whose primary business is to sell electricity, or electricity and heat, to the public.

Electricity-only plants are composed of traditional electric utilities, and nontraditional participants, including energy service providers, power marketers, independent power producers (IPPs), and the portion of CHPs that produce only electricity.

A utility is defined as a corporation, person, agency, authority, or other legal entity or instrumentality aligned with distribution facilities for delivery of electric energy for use primarily by the public. Electric utilities include investor-owned electric utilities, municipal and state utilities, federal electric utilities, and rural electric cooperatives.

An independent power producer is an entity defined as a corporation, person, agency, authority, or other legal entity or instrumentality that owns or operates facilities whose primary business is to produce electricity for use by the public. They are not generally aligned with distribution facilities and are not considered electric utilities.

Combined-heat-and-power producers are plants designed to produce both heat and electricity from a single heat source. These types of electricity producers can be independent power producers or industrial or commercial establishments. As some independent power producers are CHPs, their information is included in the data for the combined-heat-and-power sector.

The Commercial Sector consists of commercial CHPs and commercial electricity-only plants. Industrial CHPs and industrial electricity-only plants make up the Industrial Sector. For more information, please refer to the *Electric Power Annual* web site at <http://www.eia.gov/electricity/annual/>.

## Table 956. Utilities—Establishments, Revenue, Payroll, and Employees by Kind of Business: 2012

[531,891 represents $531,891,000,000. Includes only establishments or firms with payroll. Data based on the 2012 Economic Census. See Appendix III]

| Kind of business | 2012 NAICS code [1] | Establish-ments (number) | Revenue Total (mil. dol.) | Revenue Per paid employee (dol.) | Annual payroll Total (mil. dol.) | Annual payroll Per paid employee (dol.) | Paid employees for pay period including March 12 (number) |
|---|---|---|---|---|---|---|---|
| Utilities............................ | 22 | 17,595 | 531,891 | 816,743 | 58,923 | 90,479 | 651,234 |
| Electric power generation, transmission, & distribution............... | 2211 | 10,330 | 430,079 | 823,891 | 49,937 | 95,663 | 522,010 |
| Electric power generation................ | 22111 | 2,678 | 120,025 | 818,164 | 14,847 | 101,207 | 146,701 |
| Hydroelectric power generation............... | 221111 | 405 | 2,452 | 707,938 | 274 | 79,151 | 3,464 |
| Fossil fuel electric power generation............ | 221112 | 1,416 | 81,474 | 992,721 | 7,998 | 97,451 | 82,071 |
| Nuclear electric power generation............ | 221113 | 141 | 28,868 | 562,132 | 5,698 | 110,961 | 51,354 |
| Solar electric power generation.............. | 221114 | 136 | 428 | 270,276 | 118 | 74,492 | 1,582 |
| Wind electric power generation............. | 221115 | 410 | 5,058 | 946,000 | 510 | 95,437 | 5,347 |
| Geothermal electric power generation......... | 221116 | 45 | 981 | 794,491 | 124 | 100,785 | 1,235 |
| Biomass electric power generation............. | 221117 | 107 | 721 | 506,643 | 106 | 74,218 | 1,424 |
| Other electric power generation.............. | 221118 | 18 | 43 | 193,594 | 19 | 82,888 | 224 |
| Electric power transmission, control & distribution....................... | 22112 | 7,652 | 310,054 | 826,129 | 35,090 | 93,495 | 375,309 |
| Electric bulk power transmission & control....................... | 221121 | 250 | 9,959 | 798,970 | 1,408 | 112,949 | 12,465 |
| Electric power distribution.................... | 221122 | 7,402 | 300,095 | 827,062 | 33,682 | 92,827 | 362,844 |
| Natural gas distribution..................... | 2212 | 2,419 | 89,568 | 1,067,088 | 6,682 | 79,603 | 83,937 |
| Water, sewage, & other systems............ | 2213 | 4,846 | 12,243 | 270,348 | 2,304 | 50,883 | 45,287 |
| Water supply & irrigation systems............ | 22131 | 4,039 | 9,438 | 259,623 | 1,842 | 50,664 | 36,352 |
| Sewage treatment facilities............... | 22132 | 712 | 1,377 | 201,056 | 301 | 43,951 | 6,849 |
| Steam & air-conditioning supply.............. | 22133 | 95 | 1,428 | 684,768 | 162 | 77,473 | 2,086 |

[1] North American Industry Classification System, 2012; see text, Section 15.

Source: U.S. Census Bureau, 2012 Economic Census, EC1200A1, "All sectors: Geographic Area Series: Economy-Wide Key Statistics: 2012," <http://factfinder.census.gov/>, accessed May 2017.

## Table 957. Utilities—Employees, Annual Payroll, and Establishments by Utility Type: 2016

[65,403 represents $65,403,000,000. Excludes most government employees, railroad employees, and self-employed persons. An establishment is a single physical location where business is conducted or where services or industrial operations are performed. See Appendix III]

| Industry | 2012 NAICS code [1] | Number of employ-ees [2] | Annual payroll (mil. dol.) | Average payroll per employ-ee (dol.) | Establishments by employment size-class Total | Under 20 employ-ees | 20 to 99 employ-ees | 100 to 499 employ-ees | 500 employ-ees and over |
|---|---|---|---|---|---|---|---|---|---|
| Utilities, total............................ | 22 | 638,917 | 65,403 | 102,365 | 18,159 | 12,776 | 4,108 | 1,090 | 185 |
| Electric power generation, transmission and distribution............ | 2211 | 507,431 | 54,668 | 107,735 | 10,802 | 6,704 | 3,076 | 850 | 172 |
| Electric power generation................ | 22111 | 135,196 | 15,281 | 113,028 | 2,984 | 2,074 | 650 | 200 | 60 |
| Hydroelectric power....................... | 221111 | 3,298 | 300 | 90,874 | 488 | 442 | 45 | 1 | – |
| Fossil fuel electric power.............. | 221112 | 74,253 | 8,220 | 110,709 | 1,490 | 842 | 456 | 182 | 10 |
| Nuclear electric power................... | 221113 | 47,551 | 5,786 | 121,677 | 153 | 75 | 19 | 9 | 50 |
| Solar electric power.................... | 221114 | 1,564 | 157 | 100,276 | 153 | 129 | 23 | 1 | – |
| Wind electric power..................... | 221115 | 3,179 | 357 | 112,223 | 264 | 238 | 21 | 5 | – |
| Geothermal electric power............. | 221116 | 1,066 | 105 | 98,560 | 33 | 18 | 13 | 2 | – |
| Biomass electric power................ | 221117 | 1,292 | 101 | 78,189 | 112 | 83 | 29 | – | – |
| Other electric power generation....... | 221118 | 2,993 | 255 | 85,279 | 291 | 247 | 44 | – | – |
| Electric power transmission, control & distribution............ | 22112 | 372,235 | 39,387 | 105,812 | 7,818 | 4,630 | 2,426 | 650 | 112 |
| Electric bulk power transmission & control.................... | 221121 | 13,719 | 1,954 | 142,424 | 261 | 159 | 66 | 29 | 7 |
| Electric power distribution.............. | 221122 | 358,516 | 37,433 | 104,411 | 7,557 | 4,471 | 2,360 | 621 | 105 |
| Natural gas distribution.................... | 2212 | 88,366 | 8,088 | 91,523 | 2,578 | 1,717 | 655 | 193 | 13 |
| Water, sewage, & other systems......... | 2213 | 43,120 | 2,647 | 61,396 | 4,779 | 4,355 | 377 | 47 | – |
| Water supply & irrigation systems...... | 22131 | 34,948 | 2,140 | 61,244 | 3,987 | 3,664 | 281 | 42 | – |
| Sewage treatment facilities............ | 22132 | 6,194 | 323 | 52,186 | 681 | 617 | 60 | 4 | – |
| Steam & air-conditioning supply........ | 22133 | 1,978 | 184 | 92,929 | 111 | 74 | 36 | 1 | – |

– Represents zero. [1] North American Industry Classification System, 2012; see text, Section 15. [2] Covers full- and part-time employees who are on the payroll in the pay period including March 12.

Source: U.S. Census Bureau, County Business Patterns, "Geography Area Series: County Business Patterns by Employment Size Class," <http://factfinder.census.gov>, accessed April 2018. See also <https://www.census.gov/programs-surveys/cbp.html>.

## Table 958. Energy Supply and Disposition by Type of Fuel: 1973 to 2018

[In quadrillion British thermal units (Btu) (63.56 represents 63,560,000,000,000,000). For definition of Btu, see source and text, this section]

| Year | Production Total¹ | Crude oil² | Dry natural gas | Coal³ | Nuclear electric power | Renewable energy⁴ Total¹ | Hydroelectric power⁵ | Biomass⁶ | Solar/photovoltaic | Wind | Net imports, total⁷ | Consumption Total¹,⁸ | Petroleum⁹ | Dry natural gas¹⁰ | Coal | Nuclear electric power | Renewable energy⁴ total |
|---|---|---|---|---|---|---|---|---|---|---|---|---|---|---|---|---|---|
| 1973 | 63.56 | 19.49 | 22.19 | 13.99 | 0.91 | 4.41 | 2.86 | 1.53 | (NA) | (NA) | 12.58 | 75.68 | 34.84 | 22.51 | 12.97 | 0.91 | 4.41 |
| 1975 | 61.32 | 17.73 | 19.64 | 14.99 | 1.90 | 4.69 | 3.15 | 1.50 | (NA) | (NA) | 11.71 | 71.96 | 32.73 | 19.95 | 12.66 | 1.90 | 4.69 |
| 1980 | 67.18 | 18.25 | 19.91 | 18.60 | 2.74 | 5.43 | 2.90 | 2.48 | (NA) | (NA) | 12.10 | 78.07 | 34.20 | 20.24 | 15.42 | 2.74 | 5.43 |
| 1985 | 67.70 | 18.99 | 16.98 | 19.33 | 4.08 | 6.08 | 2.97 | 3.02 | (Z) | (Z) | 7.58 | 76.39 | 30.92 | 17.70 | 17.48 | 4.08 | 6.08 |
| 1990 | 70.70 | 15.57 | 18.33 | 22.49 | 6.10 | 6.04 | 3.05 | 2.74 | 0.06 | 0.03 | 14.06 | 84.48 | 33.55 | 19.60 | 19.17 | 6.10 | 6.04 |
| 1995 | 71.17 | 13.89 | 19.08 | 22.13 | 7.08 | 6.56 | 3.21 | 3.10 | 0.07 | 0.03 | 17.68 | 90.99 | 34.40 | 22.67 | 20.09 | 7.08 | 6.56 |
| 1996 | 72.48 | 13.72 | 19.34 | 22.79 | 7.09 | 7.01 | 3.59 | 3.16 | 0.07 | 0.03 | 19.02 | 94.00 | 35.65 | 23.08 | 21.00 | 7.09 | 7.01 |
| 1997 | 72.47 | 13.66 | 19.39 | 23.31 | 6.60 | 7.02 | 3.64 | 3.11 | 0.07 | 0.03 | 20.63 | 94.57 | 36.13 | 23.22 | 21.45 | 6.60 | 7.01 |
| 1998 | 72.87 | 13.24 | 19.61 | 24.05 | 7.07 | 6.49 | 3.30 | 2.93 | 0.07 | 0.03 | 22.24 | 94.98 | 36.78 | 22.83 | 21.66 | 7.07 | 6.49 |
| 1999 | 71.74 | 12.45 | 19.34 | 23.30 | 7.61 | 6.52 | 3.27 | 2.97 | 0.07 | 0.05 | 23.48 | 96.61 | 37.80 | 22.91 | 21.62 | 7.61 | 6.51 |
| 2000 | 71.33 | 12.36 | 19.66 | 22.74 | 7.86 | 6.10 | 2.81 | 3.01 | 0.06 | 0.06 | 24.90 | 98.78 | 38.23 | 23.82 | 22.58 | 7.86 | 6.10 |
| 2001 | 71.73 | 12.28 | 20.17 | 23.55 | 8.03 | 5.16 | 2.24 | 2.62 | 0.06 | 0.07 | 26.32 | 96.13 | 38.15 | 22.77 | 21.91 | 8.03 | 5.16 |
| 2002 | 70.71 | 12.16 | 19.38 | 22.73 | 8.15 | 5.73 | 2.69 | 2.71 | 0.06 | 0.11 | 25.72 | 97.60 | 38.19 | 23.51 | 21.90 | 8.15 | 5.73 |
| 2003 | 69.93 | 11.96 | 19.63 | 22.09 | 7.96 | 5.94 | 2.79 | 2.80 | 0.06 | 0.11 | 26.99 | 97.90 | 38.77 | 22.83 | 22.32 | 7.96 | 5.94 |
| 2004 | 70.23 | 11.55 | 19.07 | 22.85 | 8.22 | 6.06 | 2.69 | 3.00 | 0.06 | 0.14 | 29.14 | 100.07 | 40.21 | 22.92 | 22.47 | 8.22 | 6.07 |
| 2005 | 69.43 | 10.97 | 18.56 | 23.19 | 8.16 | 6.22 | 2.70 | 3.10 | 0.06 | 0.18 | 30.20 | 100.17 | 40.28 | 22.57 | 22.80 | 8.16 | 6.23 |
| 2006 | 70.73 | 10.77 | 19.02 | 23.79 | 8.21 | 6.59 | 2.87 | 3.21 | 0.06 | 0.26 | 29.92 | 99.46 | 39.80 | 22.24 | 22.45 | 8.21 | 6.64 |
| 2007 | 71.40 | 10.74 | 19.79 | 23.49 | 8.46 | 6.51 | 2.45 | 3.47 | 0.07 | 0.34 | 29.34 | 100.97 | 39.45 | 23.66 | 22.75 | 8.46 | 6.52 |
| 2008 | 73.20 | 10.61 | 20.70 | 23.85 | 8.43 | 7.19 | 2.51 | 3.87 | 0.07 | 0.55 | 26.02 | 98.82 | 36.84 | 23.84 | 22.39 | 8.43 | 7.17 |
| 2009 | 72.64 | 11.32 | 21.14 | 21.62 | 8.36 | 7.62 | 2.67 | 3.96 | 0.08 | 0.72 | 22.77 | 94.02 | 34.86 | 23.42 | 19.69 | 8.36 | 7.61 |
| 2010 | 74.97 | 11.60 | 21.81 | 22.04 | 8.43 | 8.31 | 2.54 | 4.55 | 0.09 | 0.92 | 21.69 | 97.61 | 35.42 | 24.57 | 20.83 | 8.43 | 8.27 |
| 2011 | 78.13 | 11.97 | 23.41 | 22.22 | 8.27 | 9.30 | 3.10 | 4.70 | 0.11 | 1.17 | 13.38 | 96.95 | 34.73 | 24.95 | 19.66 | 8.27 | 9.20 |
| 2012 | 79.28 | 13.80 | 24.61 | 20.68 | 8.06 | 8.88 | 2.63 | 4.55 | 0.16 | 1.34 | 15.80 | 94.48 | 33.94 | 26.09 | 17.38 | 8.06 | 8.85 |
| 2013 | 81.86 | 15.81 | 24.86 | 20.00 | 8.24 | 9.42 | 2.56 | 4.82 | 0.22 | 1.60 | 12.84 | 97.22 | 34.50 | 26.81 | 18.04 | 8.24 | 9.45 |
| 2014 | 87.75 | 18.54 | 26.72 | 20.29 | 8.34 | 9.77 | 2.47 | 5.02 | 0.34 | 1.73 | 10.97 | 98.38 | 34.76 | 27.38 | 18.00 | 8.34 | 9.74 |
| 2015 | 88.32 | 19.68 | 28.07 | 17.95 | 8.34 | 9.73 | 2.32 | 4.99 | 0.43 | 1.78 | 10.89 | 97.48 | 35.48 | 28.19 | 15.55 | 8.34 | 9.72 |
| 2016 | 84.36 | 18.49 | 27.58 | 14.67 | 8.43 | 10.43 | 2.47 | 5.08 | 0.57 | 2.10 | 11.26 | 97.44 | 35.82 | 28.40 | 14.23 | 8.43 | 10.37 |
| 2017 | 88.26 | 19.53 | 28.27 | 15.63 | 8.42 | 11.30 | 2.77 | 5.20 | 0.77 | 2.34 | 7.51 | 97.81 | 36.17 | 28.03 | 13.84 | 8.42 | 11.18 |
| 2018 | 95.53 | 22.80 | 31.52 | 15.21 | 8.44 | 11.72 | 2.66 | 5.33 | 0.95 | 2.53 | 3.61 | 101.27 | 36.95 | 30.96 | 13.28 | 8.44 | 11.51 |

NA Not available. Z Less than 5 trillion. ¹ Includes other types of fuel, not shown separately. ² Includes lease condensate. ³ Beginning 1989, includes waste coal supplied. Beginning 2001, also includes a small amount of refuse recovery. ⁴ Electricity net generation from conventional hydroelectric power, geothermal, solar, and wind. Consumption of electricity from wood, biomass waste, and alcohol fuels; geothermal heat pump and direct use energy; and solar thermal direct use energy. ⁵ Conventional hydroelectric net generation. ⁶ Organic nonfossil material of biological origin constituting a renewable energy source. ⁷ Imports minus exports. ⁸ Includes coal coke net imports and electricity net imports, not shown separately. ⁹ Petroleum products supplied, including natural gas plant liquids and crude oil burned as fuel. ¹⁰ Excludes supplemental gaseous fuels. Does not include biofuels that have been blended with petroleum.

Source: U.S. Energy Information Administration, *Monthly Energy Review*, March 2019. See also <http://www.eia.gov/totalenergy/data/monthly/>.

## Table 959. Energy Supply and Disposition by Type of Fuel—Estimates, 2017 and 2018, and Projections, 2019 to 2035

[Quadrillion Btu (89.36 represents 89,360,000,000,000,000) per year. Btu = British thermal unit. For definition of Btu, see source and text, this section. Projections are "reference" or mid-level forecasts. See report for methodology and assumptions used in generating projections]

| Type of fuel | 2017 | 2018 | Projections | | | | |
|---|---|---|---|---|---|---|---|
| | | | 2019 | 2020 | 2025 | 2030 | 2035 |
| **Production, total** | **89.36** | **95.18** | **100.28** | **103.95** | **109.19** | **112.11** | **112.58** |
| Crude oil and lease condensate | 19.54 | 22.42 | 24.94 | 27.23 | 29.31 | 30.01 | 29.73 |
| Natural gas plant liquids | 5.04 | 5.86 | 6.54 | 6.92 | 7.58 | 8.01 | 8.08 |
| Natural gas, dry | 28.18 | 30.56 | 33.45 | 34.79 | 37.98 | 39.92 | 41.05 |
| Coal [1] | 15.90 | 15.69 | 15.07 | 14.30 | 13.57 | 13.29 | 12.46 |
| Nuclear power | 8.42 | 8.46 | 8.34 | 8.21 | 7.03 | 6.95 | 6.87 |
| Renewable energy [2] | 10.75 | 11.06 | 11.20 | 11.65 | 12.81 | 13.22 | 13.67 |
| Other [3] | 1.53 | 1.13 | 0.74 | 0.84 | 0.91 | 0.72 | 0.72 |
| **Imports, total** | **25.47** | **25.72** | **23.63** | **22.09** | **20.10** | **17.72** | **18.24** |
| Crude oil | 17.60 | 17.32 | 15.69 | 14.39 | 12.43 | 10.71 | 11.49 |
| Petroleum and other liquids [4] | 4.43 | 5.07 | 4.87 | 4.64 | 4.54 | 4.05 | 3.85 |
| Natural gas | 3.11 | 2.99 | 2.72 | 2.71 | 2.89 | 2.72 | 2.65 |
| Other imports [5] | 0.34 | 0.34 | 0.35 | 0.35 | 0.25 | 0.25 | 0.25 |
| **Exports, total** | **17.92** | **21.49** | **22.84** | **26.13** | **29.91** | **30.56** | **31.41** |
| Petroleum and other liquids [6] | 12.18 | 15.16 | 15.09 | 17.71 | 19.64 | 19.43 | 20.33 |
| Natural gas | 3.19 | 3.72 | 5.18 | 5.94 | 8.14 | 9.23 | 9.37 |
| Coal | 2.54 | 2.61 | 2.57 | 2.48 | 2.13 | 1.91 | 1.72 |
| **Consumption, total** | **97.41** | **100.13** | **100.26** | **100.18** | **99.30** | **99.16** | **99.27** |
| Petroleum and other liquids [7] | 37.64 | 38.34 | 38.80 | 38.26 | 36.89 | 35.85 | 35.30 |
| Natural gas | 28.08 | 30.42 | 30.69 | 31.36 | 32.33 | 32.96 | 33.86 |
| Coal | 13.76 | 13.17 | 12.58 | 11.92 | 11.47 | 11.37 | 10.73 |
| Nuclear power | 8.42 | 8.46 | 8.34 | 8.21 | 7.03 | 6.95 | 6.87 |
| Renewable energy [8] | 9.19 | 9.43 | 9.53 | 10.11 | 11.27 | 11.68 | 12.14 |
| Other [9] | 0.32 | 0.31 | 0.32 | 0.32 | 0.31 | 0.36 | 0.36 |
| **Net imports of petroleum** | **9.85** | **7.23** | **5.47** | **1.32** | **-2.67** | **-4.67** | **-4.99** |
| **Prices (2018 dollars per unit):** | | | | | | | |
| Crude oil spot prices (dol. per barrel) | | | | | | | |
| Brent spot price | 55.21 | 74.43 | 73.26 | 73.27 | 81.73 | 92.98 | 100.25 |
| West Texas Intermediate spot price | 51.79 | 68.46 | 67.88 | 69.72 | 77.92 | 87.34 | 95.20 |
| Natural gas at Henry Hub (dol. per mil. Btu) | 3.08 | 2.99 | 3.03 | 3.08 | 3.53 | 3.76 | 4.02 |
| Coal minemouth price (dol. per ton) [10] | 36.70 | 33.63 | 32.70 | 32.85 | 32.77 | 32.00 | 32.30 |
| Electricity price (cents per kWh) | 10.8 | 10.6 | 10.5 | 10.2 | 10.3 | 10.4 | 10.6 |

[1] Includes waste coal. [2] Includes grid-connected electricity from conventional hydroelectric power; biomass (including wood and wood waste, and other biomass); landfill gas; biogenic municipal waste; wind; photovoltaic and solar thermal sources; and nonelectric energy from renewable sources, such as active and passive solar systems, and wood. Excludes electricity imports using renewable sources and nonmarketed renewable energy. [3] Includes nonbiogenic municipal waste, hydrogen, methanol, and some domestic inputs to refineries. [4] Includes imports of finished petroleum products, unfinished oils, alcohols, ethers, blending components, and renewable fuels such as ethanol. [5] Includes coal, coal coke (net), and electricity (net). Excludes imports of fuel used in nuclear power plants. [6] Includes crude oil, petroleum products, ethanol, and biodiesel. [7] Includes petroleum-derived fuels and non-petroleum-derived fuels, such as ethanol, biodiesel, and coal-based synthetic liquids. Petroleum coke, which is a solid, is included. Also included are hydrocarbon gas liquids and crude oil consumed as a fuel. [8] Includes grid-connected electricity from wood and wood waste, non-electric energy from wood, and biofuels heat and coproducts used in the production of liquid fuels, but excludes the energy content of the liquid fuels. See also footnote 2. [9] Includes non-biogenic municipal waste, hydrogen, and net electricity imports. [10] Includes reported prices for both open market and captive mines.

Source: U.S. Energy Information Administration, *Annual Energy Outlook 2019*, January 2019. See also <https://www.eia.gov/outlooks/aeo/>.

## Table 960. Energy Consumption by End-Use Sector: 1977 to 2018

[Trillion Btu (15,661.7 represents 15,661,700,000,000,000). Btu=British thermal unit. Represents consumption of fossil fuels and renewable energy, plus electricity retail sales and electrical system energy losses. For definition of Btu, see source and text, this section. See Appendix III]

| Year | Residential | Commer-cial [1] | Industrial [2] | Trans-portation | Year | Residential | Commer-cial [1] | Industrial [2] | Trans-portation |
|---|---|---|---|---|---|---|---|---|---|
| 1977 | 15,661.7 | 10,207.6 | 32,263.0 | 19,821.6 | 1998 | 18,951.9 | 15,967.4 | 34,841.1 | 25,224.5 |
| 1978 | 16,132.3 | 10,511.9 | 32,687.6 | 20,617.1 | 1999 | 19,553.5 | 16,376.2 | 34,762.5 | 25,916.0 |
| 1979 | 15,812.7 | 10,648.0 | 33,924.7 | 20,471.5 | 2000 | 20,421.0 | 17,175.3 | 34,662.1 | 26,515.5 |
| 1980 | 15,753.4 | 10,578.3 | 32,039.4 | 19,696.7 | 2001 | 20,037.6 | 17,136.7 | 32,718.5 | 26,242.1 |
| 1981 | 15,261.5 | 10,615.9 | 30,711.6 | 19,514.0 | 2002 | 20,785.8 | 17,345.6 | 32,660.4 | 26,807.8 |
| 1982 | 15,530.9 | 10,860.3 | 27,614.5 | 19,089.2 | 2003 | 21,119.3 | 17,346.0 | 32,552.7 | 26,881.1 |
| 1983 | 15,425.0 | 10,938.4 | 27,427.8 | 19,176.6 | 2004 | 21,081.4 | 17,655.4 | 33,515.3 | 27,826.5 |
| 1984 | 15,959.6 | 11,443.9 | 29,569.9 | 19,655.6 | 2005 | 21,612.6 | 17,853.3 | 32,441.1 | 28,260.8 |
| 1985 | 16,041.3 | 11,451.2 | 28,815.8 | 20,087.9 | 2006 | 20,670.3 | 17,707.1 | 32,390.3 | 28,696.9 |
| 1986 | 15,975.1 | 11,606.1 | 28,273.6 | 20,788.8 | 2007 | 21,519.0 | 18,252.7 | 32,384.5 | 28,815.2 |
| 1987 | 16,263.2 | 11,946.0 | 29,378.9 | 21,468.9 | 2008 | 21,667.6 | 18,401.9 | 31,333.3 | 27,421.6 |
| 1988 | 17,132.6 | 12,578.1 | 30,677.4 | 22,317.7 | 2009 | 21,081.4 | 17,887.1 | 28,465.3 | 26,588.9 |
| 1989 | 17,789.7 | 13,196.3 | 31,327.8 | 22,478.6 | 2010 | 21,894.2 | 18,058.0 | 30,668.6 | 26,980.1 |
| 1990 | 16,940.1 | 13,317.3 | 31,801.6 | 22,419.0 | 2011 | 21,381.2 | 17,980.3 | 30,978.6 | 26,601.1 |
| 1991 | 17,419.3 | 13,500.0 | 31,399.3 | 22,118.0 | 2012 | 19,869.6 | 17,419.6 | 31,057.0 | 26,129.1 |
| 1992 | 17,354.8 | 13,441.1 | 32,570.9 | 22,415.1 | 2013 | 21,051.2 | 17,929.4 | 31,624.9 | 26,614.2 |
| 1993 | 18,211.6 | 13,816.9 | 32,618.5 | 22,670.8 | 2014 | 21,444.5 | 18,264.5 | 31,795.9 | 26,870.9 |
| 1994 | 18,110.3 | 14,097.3 | 33,519.7 | 23,318.7 | 2015 | 20,615.9 | 18,156.7 | 31,468.7 | 27,240.9 |
| 1995 | 18,516.7 | 14,689.9 | 33,969.2 | 23,811.9 | 2016 | 20,179.8 | 18,030.2 | 31,450.2 | 27,788.2 |
| 1996 | 19,501.8 | 15,171.9 | 34,903.0 | 24,419.3 | 2017 | 19,897.1 | 17,897.5 | 31,994.2 | 28,017.4 |
| 1997 | 18,962.3 | 15,681.1 | 35,199.0 | 24,722.6 | 2018 | 21,651.5 | 18,630.8 | 32,613.1 | 28,393.3 |

[1] Commercial sector fuel use, including use at commercial combined-heat-and-power (CHP) and commercial electricity-only plants. [2] Industrial sector fuel use, including use at industrial combined-heat-and-power (CHP) and industrial electricity-only plants.

Source: U.S. Energy Information Administration, *Monthly Energy Review*, March 2019. See also <http://www.eia.gov/totalenergy/data/monthly/>.

## Table 961. Energy Consumption by Mode of Transportation: 2010 to 2016

[27 represents 27,000,000,000,000. Btu = British thermal unit. For conversion rates for each fuel type, see source]

| Mode | Trillion Btu | | | Unit | Physical units | | |
|---|---|---|---|---|---|---|---|
| | 2010 | 2015 | 2016 | | 2010 | 2015 | 2016 |
| AIR [1] | | | | | | | |
| Aviation gasoline............................................. | 27 | 24 | 25 | Mil. gal. | 221 | 196 | 206 |
| Jet fuel............................................................ | 1,686 | 1,637 | 1,702 | Mil. gal. | 12,492 | 12,124 | 12,604 |
| HIGHWAY | | | | | | | |
| Light duty vehicle, short wheel base & motorcycle [2]... | 10,902 | 11,254 | 11,436 | Mil. gal. | 87,215 | 90,031 | 91,488 |
| Light duty vehicle, long wheel base [2].................... | 4,531 | 4,555 | 4,727 | Mil. gal. | 36,251 | 36,437 | 37,819 |
| Single-unit 2-axle 6-tire or more truck.................... | 1,887 | 1,856 | 1,917 | Mil. gal. | 15,097 | 14,851 | 15,338 |
| Combination truck [3].......................................... | 3,741 | 3,611 | 3,694 | Mil. gal. | 29,927 | 28,886 | 29,555 |
| Bus................................................................. | 240 | 279 | 278 | Mil. gal. | 1,921 | 2,228 | 2,226 |
| TRANSIT [4] | | | | | | | |
| Electricity......................................................... | 22 | 23 | 23 | Mil. kWh | 6,414 | 6,668 | 6,604 |
| Diesel (includes bio-diesel)................................. | 88 | 80 | 82 | Mil. gal. | 633 | 576 | 590 |
| Gasoline and other nondiesel fuels [5].................... | 12 | 14 | 15 | Mil. gal. | 98 | 114 | 116 |
| Compressed natural gas..................................... | 18 | 22 | 23 | Mil. gal. | 126 | 156 | 167 |
| RAIL [6] | | | | | | | |
| Distillate/diesel fuel........................................... | 493 | 521 | 478 | Mil. gal. | 3,557 | 3,754 | 3,445 |
| Electricity......................................................... | 2 | 2 | 2 | Mil. kWh | 559 | 504 | 516 |
| WATER | | | | | | | |
| Residual fuel oil................................................ | 770 | 503 | 439 | Mil. gal. | 5,143 | 3,358 | 2,930 |
| Distillate/diesel fuel oil....................................... | 278 | 335 | 311 | Mil. gal. | 2,003 | 2,417 | 2,245 |
| Gasoline.......................................................... | 146 | 258 | 290 | Mil. gal. | 1,167 | 2,066 | 2,323 |
| PIPELINE | | | | | | | |
| Natural gas....................................................... | 695 | 699 | 719 | Mil. cu. ft. | 674,124 | 678,183 | 697,432 |

[1] Includes general aviation and certified carriers, domestic operations only; and fuel used in air taxi operations, but not commuter operations. [2] "Light duty vehicle, short wheel base" includes passenger cars, light trucks, vans and sport utility vehicles with a wheelbase (WB) equal to or less than 121 inches. "Light duty vehicle, long wheel base" includes large passenger cars, vans, pickup trucks, and sport/utility vehicles with wheelbases (WB) larger than 121 inches. [3] A power unit (truck tractor) and one or more trailing units (a semitrailer or trailer). [4] Includes light, heavy, and commuter rail; motor bus; trolley bus; van pools; automated guideway; and demand-responsive vehicles. [5] Includes gasoline, liquefied petroleum gas, liquefied natural gas, methane, ethanol, bunker fuel, kerosene, grain additive, and other fuel. [6] Includes Amtrak and freight service carriers that have an annual operating revenue of $250 million or more.

Source: U.S. Department of Transportation, Bureau of Transportation Statistics, "National Transportation Statistics," <https://www.bts.gov/topics/national-transportation-statistics>, accessed February 2019.

## Table 962. Renewable Energy Consumption by Source and Sector: 1990 to 2018

[In trillion Btu (6,040.0 represents 6,040,000,000,000,000). For definition of Btu, see source and text, this section. Renewable energy is obtained from sources that are essentially inexhaustible, unlike fossil fuels of which there is a finite supply]

| Source and sector | 1990 | 2000 | 2010 | 2015 | 2016 | 2017 | 2018 |
|---|---|---|---|---|---|---|---|
| **Consumption, total**............... | **6,040.0** | **6,104.2** | **8,266.3** | **9,719.4** | **10,366.5** | **11,178.8** | **11,514.6** |
| Conventional hydroelectric power [1]......... | 3,046.4 | 2,811.1 | 2,538.5 | 2,321.2 | 2,472.4 | 2,767.0 | 2,687.7 |
| Geothermal energy [2]........................... | 170.7 | 164.4 | 208.0 | 211.8 | 209.6 | 210.2 | 217.3 |
| Biomass energy [3].............................. | 2,735.1 | 3,008.2 | 4,505.9 | 4,983.4 | 5,020.2 | 5,084.3 | 5,127.8 |
| Solar energy [4]................................... | 58.8 | 63.4 | 90.5 | 425.7 | 568.7 | 774.5 | 948.6 |
| Wind energy [5]................................... | 29.0 | 57.1 | 923.4 | 1,777.3 | 2,095.6 | 2,342.9 | 2,533.1 |
| **Residential [6]**................................. | **640.2** | **486.3** | **642.0** | **679.5** | **647.4** | **663.6** | **777.7** |
| Wood [7]........................................... | 580.0 | 420.0 | 540.5 | 512.7 | 447.8 | 433.0 | 517.2 |
| Geothermal [2].................................... | 5.5 | 8.6 | 36.8 | 39.6 | 39.0 | 39.6 | 39.6 |
| Solar [4]............................................ | 54.7 | 57.7 | 64.7 | 127.2 | 160.0 | 191.0 | 220.8 |
| **Commercial [8]**................................ | **98.4** | **128.3** | **141.8** | **229.9** | **242.3** | **255.2** | **272.7** |
| Biomass [3]........................................ | 94.0 | 119.1 | 110.9 | 151.9 | 157.7 | 156.4 | 153.3 |
| Geothermal [2].................................... | 2.8 | 7.6 | 18.5 | 19.7 | 19.7 | 19.7 | 19.7 |
| Hydroelectric [1].................................. | 1.4 | 1.0 | 0.8 | 0.3 | 2.0 | 2.2 | 2.2 |
| Solar energy [4]................................... | 0.2 | 0.6 | 11.5 | 56.9 | 61.7 | 75.6 | 95.7 |
| Wind energy [5]................................... | (NA) | (NA) | 0.2 | 1.1 | 1.2 | 1.3 | 1.8 |
| **Industrial [9]**.................................... | **1,717.1** | **1,928.2** | **2,343.3** | **2,491.4** | **2,502.7** | **2,586.7** | **2,592.6** |
| Biomass [3]........................................ | 1,684.2 | 1,881.5 | 2,320.3 | 2,459.8 | 2,466.9 | 2,546.8 | 2,549.3 |
| Geothermal [2].................................... | 1.9 | 4.4 | 4.2 | 4.2 | 4.2 | 4.2 | 4.2 |
| Hydroelectric [1].................................. | 30.9 | 42.2 | 16.3 | 13.1 | 11.7 | 12.7 | 12.9 |
| Solar energy [4]................................... | (Z) | 0.1 | 2.5 | 13.7 | 19.3 | 22.2 | 25.2 |
| Wind energy [5]................................... | (NA) | (NA) | (NA) | 0.5 | 0.7 | 0.8 | 1.0 |
| **Transportation [12]**........................... | **60.4** | **134.9** | **1,074.8** | **1,334.0** | **1,442.7** | **1,438.5** | **1,412.8** |
| Fuel ethanol....................................... | 60.4 | 134.9 | 1,041.4 | 1,109.9 | 1,143.0 | 1,155.6 | 1,150.1 |
| Biodiesel [10]...................................... | (NA) | (NA) | 33.2 | 190.6 | 266.1 | 253.3 | 241.9 |
| **Electric power [11]**............................ | **3,523.9** | **3,426.5** | **4,064.4** | **4,984.5** | **5,531.3** | **6,234.8** | **6,458.8** |
| Biomass [3]........................................ | 316.5 | 452.8 | 459.4 | 524.9 | 505.1 | 509.5 | 495.1 |
| Geothermal [2].................................... | 160.5 | 143.8 | 148.5 | 148.3 | 146.1 | 146.7 | 153.8 |
| Hydroelectric [1].................................. | 3,014.0 | 2,767.9 | 2,521.5 | 2,307.7 | 2,458.7 | 2,752.0 | 2,672.5 |
| Solar [4]............................................ | 3.8 | 5.0 | 11.8 | 227.9 | 327.7 | 485.7 | 607.0 |
| Wind [5]............................................ | 29.0 | 57.1 | 923.3 | 1,775.7 | 2,093.7 | 2,340.8 | 2,530.4 |

NA Not available. Z Less than 500 billion. [1] Power produced from the kinetic energy of falling water. [2] As used at electric power plants, hot water or steam extracted from geothermal reservoirs supplied to steam turbines at electric power plants that drive generators to produce electricity. [3] Wood and wood-derived fuels, municipal solid waste, fuel ethanol, and biodiesel. [4] The radiant energy of the sun, which can be converted into other forms of energy. Solar thermal and photovoltaic electricity net generation and solar thermal direct use energy. [5] Energy present in wind motion that can be converted to mechanical energy for driving pumps, mills, and electric power generators. [6] Living quarters for private households; excludes institutional living quarters. [7] Wood and wood-derived fuels. [8] Service-providing facilities and equipment of businesses, governments, and other private and public organizations. Includes commercial combined-heat-and-power and commercial electricity-only plants. [9] All facilities and equipment used for producing, processing, or assembling goods. Includes industrial combined-heat-and-power and industrial electricity-only plants. [10] Any liquid biofuel suitable as a diesel fuel substitute, additive, or extender. [11] Electricity-only and combined-heat-and-power plants whose primary business is to sell electricity and/or heat to the public. Includes sources not shown separately. [12] Beginning in 2009, includes other renewable diesel fuel and other renewable fuels consumption, not shown separately.

Source: U.S. Energy Information Administration, *Monthly Energy Review*, March 2019. See also <http://www.eia.gov/totalenergy/data/monthly/>.

# Table 963. Energy Consumption—End-Use Sector and Selected Source by State: 2017

[In trillions of British thermal units (97,622 represents 97,622,000,000,000,000 Btu), except as indicated. For definition of Btu, see source and text, this section. U.S. totals may not equal sum of states due to independent rounding and/or interstate flows of electricity that are not allocated to the states. For technical notes and documentation, see source <https://www.eia.gov/state/seds/seds-technical-notes-complete.php?sid=US>]

| State | Total [1,2] | Per capita [3] (mil. Btu) | End-use sector [4] | | | | Source | | | | |
|---|---|---|---|---|---|---|---|---|---|---|---|
| | | | Resi-dential | Com-mercial | Indus-trial [2] | Trans-portation | Petro-leum [5] | Natural gas (dry) [6] | Coal | Hydro-electric power [7] | Nuclear electric power |
| U.S. .......... | 97,622 | 300 | 19,864 | 17,864 | 31,873 | 28,020 | 37,461 | 28,111 | 13,840 | 2,767 | 8,419 |
| AL. ........... | 1,901 | 390 | 323 | 254 | 822 | 501 | 560 | 682 | 379 | 85 | 446 |
| AK. ........... | 608 | 822 | 53 | 59 | 333 | 163 | 224 | 344 | 16 | 15 | – |
| AZ. ........... | 1,475 | 209 | 401 | 355 | 230 | 489 | 557 | 336 | 335 | 63 | 338 |
| AR. ........... | 1,058 | 352 | 202 | 173 | 397 | 286 | 340 | 318 | 268 | 27 | 133 |
| CA. ........... | 7,881 | 200 | 1,416 | 1,473 | 1,818 | 3,175 | 3,667 | 2,189 | 34 | 390 | 187 |
| CO. ........... | 1,463 | 261 | 343 | 291 | 407 | 422 | 501 | 466 | 316 | 17 | – |
| CT. ........... | 726 | 203 | 230 | 188 | 79 | 229 | 311 | 246 | 3 | 3 | 173 |
| DE. ........... | 270 | 282 | 60 | 56 | 84 | 70 | 107 | 103 | 5 | – | – |
| DC. ........... | 168 | 241 | 38 | 104 | 6 | 19 | 18 | 31 | (Z) | – | – |
| FL. ........... | 4,209 | 201 | 1,176 | 991 | 493 | 1,548 | 1,707 | 1,418 | 408 | 2 | 305 |
| GA. ........... | 2,802 | 269 | 666 | 533 | 759 | 844 | 957 | 709 | 344 | 22 | 353 |
| HI. ........... | 283 | 199 | 34 | 43 | 60 | 147 | 242 | 3 | 15 | 1 | – |
| ID. ........... | 554 | 322 | 134 | 92 | 168 | 159 | 184 | 116 | 3 | 98 | – |
| IL. ........... | 3,872 | 303 | 892 | 796 | 1,176 | 1,008 | 1,282 | 1,048 | 685 | 1 | 1,017 |
| IN. ........... | 2,700 | 406 | 498 | 357 | 1,232 | 614 | 761 | 751 | 929 | 3 | – |
| IA. ........... | 1,559 | 496 | 221 | 190 | 848 | 300 | 426 | 413 | 300 | 10 | 55 |
| KS. ........... | 1,073 | 369 | 206 | 213 | 388 | 267 | 349 | 279 | 217 | (Z) | 111 |
| KY. ........... | 1,658 | 372 | 332 | 257 | 598 | 471 | 599 | 297 | 639 | 42 | – |
| LA. ........... | 4,482 | 960 | 312 | 269 | 3,123 | 777 | 2,022 | 1,718 | 142 | 8 | 161 |
| ME. ........... | 392 | 294 | 100 | 66 | 104 | 123 | 191 | 45 | 2 | 31 | – |
| MD. ........... | 1,315 | 218 | 386 | 407 | 108 | 413 | 465 | 233 | 107 | 18 | 158 |
| MA. ........... | 1,424 | 208 | 410 | 402 | 155 | 458 | 577 | 463 | 12 | 10 | 53 |
| MI. ........... | 2,775 | 278 | 725 | 599 | 716 | 735 | 885 | 909 | 499 | 15 | 339 |
| MN. ........... | 1,832 | 329 | 386 | 357 | 628 | 461 | 609 | 467 | 258 | 12 | 145 |
| MS. ........... | 1,176 | 394 | 178 | 153 | 402 | 444 | 509 | 544 | 54 | – | 77 |
| MO. ........... | 1,726 | 283 | 471 | 403 | 301 | 551 | 630 | 265 | 710 | 11 | 87 |
| MT. ........... | 421 | 399 | 96 | 81 | 127 | 117 | 177 | 83 | 156 | 101 | – |
| NE. ........... | 876 | 457 | 146 | 135 | 392 | 202 | 245 | 176 | 234 | 14 | 72 |
| NV. ........... | 707 | 238 | 165 | 142 | 172 | 228 | 267 | 306 | 27 | 17 | – |
| NH. ........... | 317 | 235 | 100 | 70 | 46 | 102 | 159 | 54 | 4 | 13 | 104 |
| NJ. ........... | 2,135 | 240 | 536 | 559 | 257 | 783 | 942 | 734 | 16 | (Z) | 356 |
| NM. ........... | 683 | 327 | 112 | 122 | 229 | 220 | 260 | 250 | 199 | 2 | – |
| NY. ........... | 3,684 | 188 | 1,055 | 1,117 | 388 | 1,124 | 1,339 | 1,280 | 20 | 278 | 441 |
| NC. ........... | 2,503 | 244 | 649 | 567 | 562 | 725 | 856 | 520 | 350 | 35 | 443 |
| ND. ........... | 631 | 836 | 69 | 88 | 343 | 131 | 190 | 118 | 398 | 24 | – |
| OH. ........... | 3,644 | 312 | 839 | 682 | 1,197 | 926 | 1,152 | 1,015 | 811 | 3 | 185 |
| OK. ........... | 1,644 | 418 | 274 | 250 | 637 | 483 | 570 | 692 | 198 | 19 | – |
| OR. ........... | 1,032 | 249 | 264 | 202 | 261 | 305 | 349 | 263 | 19 | 353 | – |
| PA. ........... | 3,808 | 298 | 871 | 631 | 1,355 | 951 | 1,242 | 1,404 | 670 | 29 | 870 |
| RI. ........... | 184 | 174 | 57 | 45 | 23 | 60 | 80 | 95 | – | (Z) | – |
| SC. ........... | 1,644 | 327 | 351 | 274 | 536 | 483 | 552 | 286 | 193 | 17 | 568 |
| SD. ........... | 385 | 441 | 67 | 63 | 157 | 98 | 116 | 85 | 26 | 48 | – |
| TN. ........... | 2,167 | 323 | 497 | 433 | 600 | 637 | 743 | 332 | 335 | 80 | 333 |
| TX. ........... | 13,366 | 472 | 1,641 | 1,601 | 6,754 | 3,370 | 6,636 | 3,994 | 1,452 | 10 | 404 |
| UT. ........... | 829 | 267 | 175 | 170 | 222 | 261 | 309 | 231 | 275 | 12 | – |
| VT. ........... | 135 | 216 | 43 | 25 | 19 | 48 | 81 | 12 | – | 12 | – |
| VA. ........... | 2,303 | 272 | 554 | 612 | 435 | 701 | 792 | 597 | 160 | 10 | 320 |
| WA. ........... | 2,097 | 282 | 504 | 378 | 535 | 679 | 819 | 351 | 62 | 757 | 85 |
| WV. ........... | 756 | 416 | 144 | 108 | 333 | 172 | 200 | 203 | 710 | 15 | – |
| WI. ........... | 1,806 | 312 | 414 | 365 | 600 | 426 | 542 | 504 | 389 | 24 | 101 |
| WY. ........... | 512 | 885 | 51 | 60 | 286 | 115 | 161 | 134 | 458 | 10 | – |

– Represents zero. Z Less than 500 billion Btu. [1] Includes other sources, not shown separately. [2] U.S. total energy and U.S. industrial sector include net imports of coal coke that are not allocated to the states. [3] Based on estimated resident population as of July 1. [4] End-use sector data include electricity sales and associated electrical system energy losses. [5] Includes fuel ethanol blended into motor gasoline. [6] Includes supplemental gaseous fuels. [7] Conventional hydroelectric power. Does not include pumped-storage hydroelectricity.

Source: U.S. Energy Information Administration, "State Energy Data System," <http://www.eia.gov/state/seds/>, accessed August 2019.

# Table 964. Energy-related Carbon Dioxide Emissions by Sector and State: 2016

[In millions of metric tons (5,161.0 represents 5,161,000,000), except percent. Total state CO2 emissions include those from direct fuel use across all sectors as well as primary fuels consumed for electricity generation. Covers emissions released at the location where fossil fuels are consumed. Regarding fuels that are used in one state to generate electricity consumed in another state, emissions are attributed to the state in which the electricity is generated and fuels are combusted. Data are derived from EIA's State Energy Data System]

| State | Total carbon dioxide emissions | Percent of carbon dioxide emissions by sector | | | | | Per capita |
|---|---|---|---|---|---|---|---|
| | | Commercial | Electric Power | Residential | Industrial | Transpor-tation | |
| **Total** [1] | **5,161.0** | **4.5** | **34.8** | **5.8** | **18.2** | **36.7** | **16.0** |
| Alabama | 115.1 | 1.9 | 48.0 | 1.6 | 18.3 | 30.1 | 23.7 |
| Alaska | 34.9 | 5.8 | 7.9 | 4.3 | 48.1 | 33.9 | 47.0 |
| Arizona | 87.0 | 3.3 | 50.9 | 2.5 | 5.3 | 38.0 | 12.6 |
| Arkansas | 62.4 | 4.7 | 48.4 | 2.7 | 13.2 | 31.1 | 20.9 |
| California | 361.4 | 5.2 | 10.1 | 6.7 | 19.1 | 58.9 | 9.2 |
| Colorado | 89.0 | 4.4 | 39.6 | 8.4 | 16.0 | 31.6 | 16.1 |
| Connecticut | 34.3 | 11.4 | 20.4 | 18.3 | 5.4 | 44.6 | 9.6 |
| Delaware | 13.3 | 7.0 | 26.9 | 6.3 | 25.2 | 34.6 | 14.0 |
| District of Columbia | 2.8 | 34.1 | – | 23.2 | 1.1 | 41.7 | 4.0 |
| Florida | 230.1 | 3.2 | 46.0 | 0.5 | 5.2 | 45.0 | 11.1 |
| Georgia | 136.2 | 3.4 | 42.2 | 5.0 | 9.8 | 39.7 | 13.2 |
| Hawaii | 18.4 | 1.8 | 35.7 | 0.2 | 7.2 | 55.2 | 12.9 |
| Idaho | 18.4 | 7.5 | 6.8 | 8.9 | 18.3 | 58.5 | 10.9 |
| Illinois | 204.1 | 6.5 | 32.5 | 10.8 | 16.6 | 33.5 | 15.9 |
| Indiana | 181.9 | 2.9 | 46.0 | 4.2 | 23.1 | 23.8 | 27.4 |
| Iowa | 73.1 | 4.8 | 33.8 | 5.6 | 26.6 | 29.2 | 23.4 |
| Kansas | 62.1 | 3.9 | 40.0 | 5.4 | 20.6 | 30.1 | 21.3 |
| Kentucky | 123.9 | 2.2 | 58.6 | 2.3 | 10.9 | 26.0 | 27.9 |
| Louisiana | 209.1 | 1.0 | 17.3 | 0.9 | 58.2 | 22.6 | 44.6 |
| Maine | 16.5 | 9.8 | 9.1 | 17.7 | 9.1 | 54.2 | 12.4 |
| Maryland | 57.6 | 8.9 | 29.8 | 9.5 | 3.8 | 47.9 | 9.6 |
| Massachusetts | 64.2 | 10.9 | 16.7 | 17.7 | 5.3 | 49.4 | 9.4 |
| Michigan | 151.8 | 6.7 | 36.3 | 12.3 | 11.6 | 33.1 | 15.3 |
| Minnesota | 89.3 | 7.1 | 29.6 | 9.0 | 19.1 | 35.1 | 16.2 |
| Mississippi | 68.9 | 2.3 | 37.6 | 2.1 | 14.8 | 43.3 | 23.1 |
| Missouri | 117.7 | 3.6 | 52.4 | 4.8 | 6.9 | 32.3 | 19.3 |
| Montana | 30.5 | 4.5 | 52.4 | 4.8 | 12.5 | 25.8 | 29.3 |
| Nebraska | 48.6 | 3.7 | 43.6 | 4.5 | 19.7 | 28.5 | 25.4 |
| Nevada | 36.7 | 6.2 | 37.9 | 6.3 | 8.7 | 40.9 | 12.5 |
| New Hampshire | 13.8 | 10.1 | 17.2 | 18.3 | 5.5 | 48.9 | 10.3 |
| New Jersey | 110.8 | 9.1 | 17.7 | 12.2 | 8.6 | 52.4 | 12.3 |
| New Mexico | 48.4 | 3.5 | 47.6 | 4.3 | 15.3 | 29.2 | 23.2 |
| New York | 163.7 | 13.2 | 16.9 | 18.7 | 5.1 | 46.1 | 8.3 |
| North Carolina | 120.6 | 4.4 | 42.1 | 4.2 | 8.6 | 40.7 | 11.9 |
| North Dakota | 54.3 | 1.8 | 53.2 | 1.7 | 27.9 | 15.3 | 71.8 |
| Ohio | 206.3 | 5.3 | 39.1 | 7.8 | 17.2 | 30.5 | 17.7 |
| Oklahoma | 96.9 | 3.1 | 36.5 | 3.3 | 23.5 | 33.6 | 24.7 |
| Oregon | 38.0 | 5.6 | 20.5 | 6.6 | 13.5 | 53.8 | 9.3 |
| Pennsylvania | 217.4 | 4.9 | 37.7 | 8.5 | 21.0 | 27.9 | 17.0 |
| Rhode Island | 9.8 | 8.8 | 26.4 | 18.6 | 6.5 | 39.7 | 9.2 |
| South Carolina | 71.7 | 3.0 | 38.4 | 2.5 | 10.6 | 45.5 | 14.5 |
| South Dakota | 15.0 | 4.9 | 17.4 | 6.3 | 25.9 | 45.5 | 17.4 |
| Tennessee | 103.1 | 3.6 | 34.8 | 3.5 | 15.7 | 42.3 | 15.5 |
| Texas | 653.8 | 1.9 | 31.7 | 1.7 | 30.3 | 34.4 | 23.4 |
| Utah | 58.8 | 4.5 | 46.7 | 6.2 | 12.5 | 30.1 | 19.3 |
| Vermont | 6.0 | 14.3 | – | 21.8 | 7.1 | 56.6 | 9.6 |
| Virginia | 104.2 | 5.5 | 32.2 | 5.5 | 11.2 | 45.6 | 12.4 |
| Washington | 78.9 | 5.5 | 12.1 | 6.4 | 13.9 | 62.0 | 10.8 |
| West Virginia | 94.6 | 1.8 | 72.8 | 1.7 | 10.8 | 12.9 | 51.7 |
| Wisconsin | 95.6 | 6.2 | 40.3 | 9.0 | 13.6 | 30.8 | 16.6 |
| Wyoming | 60.7 | 1.8 | 66.4 | 1.4 | 17.6 | 12.8 | 103.7 |

– Represents zero. [1] For the United States as a whole, see, EIA's *Monthly Energy Review*, Section 12: Environment. The total for all states is different from the national-level estimate because of differing methodologies. These values are unadjusted. See source for details on the data series differences.

Source: U.S. Energy Information Agency, *Energy-Related Carbon Dioxide Emissions by State, 2005-2016*, February 2019. See also <https://www.eia.gov/environment/emissions/state/analysis/>.

# Table 965. Energy Expenditures and Average Fuel Prices by Source and Sector: 1980 to 2017

[In millions of dollars (374,350 represents $374,350,000,000), except as indicated. Btu = British thermal units. For definition of Btu, see text, this section. End-use sector and electric utilities exclude expenditures and prices on energy sources such as hydropower, solar, wind, and geothermal. Also excludes expenditures for reported amounts of energy consumed by the energy industry for production, transportation, and processing operations]

| Source and sector | 1980 | 1990 | 2000 | 2010 | 2013 | 2014 | 2015 | 2016 | 2017 |
|---|---|---|---|---|---|---|---|---|---|
| **EXPENDITURES (mil. dol.)** | | | | | | | | | |
| **Total** [1,2,3] | **374,350** | **474,652** | **687,711** | **1,214,034** | **1,376,134** | **1,394,919** | **1,128,063** | **1,038,121** | **1,136,496** |
| Natural gas [4] | 51,062 | 65,278 | 119,094 | 161,303 | 151,672 | 174,398 | 140,294 | 127,618 | 142,245 |
| Petroleum products | 237,679 | 237,677 | 359,403 | 716,854 | 879,231 | 863,523 | 623,127 | 549,318 | 631,717 |
| Motor gasoline [5] | 124,408 | 126,558 | 192,153 | 376,492 | 467,328 | 452,821 | 342,578 | 310,961 | 348,456 |
| Coal | 22,607 | 28,419 | 27,959 | 50,245 | 45,260 | 44,873 | 36,578 | 31,694 | 30,326 |
| Retail electricity | 98,095 | 176,691 | 231,578 | 365,913 | 372,068 | 389,872 | 388,344 | 383,567 | 387,222 |
| Residential sector [6] | 69,280 | 110,910 | 155,299 | 249,772 | 248,460 | 264,712 | 248,045 | 238,560 | 246,110 |
| Commercial sector [2,3] | 47,074 | 79,602 | 113,421 | 177,662 | 178,184 | 190,720 | 185,971 | 178,884 | 184,761 |
| Industrial sector [2,3] | 94,316 | 103,351 | 140,963 | 221,443 | 236,718 | 242,471 | 186,716 | 169,288 | 190,934 |
| Transportation sector [2] | 163,680 | 180,790 | 278,028 | 565,158 | 712,771 | 697,016 | 507,331 | 451,388 | 514,692 |
| Motor gasoline [5] | 121,809 | 123,845 | 189,836 | 369,433 | 458,655 | 445,572 | 329,609 | 299,361 | 335,666 |
| Electric utilities [3] | 38,027 | 40,627 | 60,053 | 94,791 | 89,112 | 95,827 | 76,352 | 68,327 | 69,775 |
| **AVERAGE FUEL PRICES (dol. per mil. Btu)** | | | | | | | | | |
| **All sectors** | **6.89** | **8.29** | **10.33** | **18.92** | **21.42** | **21.33** | **17.30** | **15.94** | **17.30** |
| Residential sector [6] | 7.46 | 11.87 | 14.21 | 22.37 | 22.59 | 23.35 | 22.93 | 22.92 | 23.77 |
| Commercial sector [3] | 7.83 | 11.87 | 13.90 | 20.92 | 20.64 | 21.43 | 20.72 | 20.17 | 20.86 |
| Industrial sector [3] | 4.72 | 5.30 | 6.50 | 12.13 | 12.51 | 12.71 | 9.87 | 8.99 | 9.91 |
| Transportation sector | 8.61 | 8.33 | 10.77 | 21.53 | 27.73 | 26.71 | 19.15 | 16.70 | 18.91 |
| Electric utilities [3] | 1.77 | 1.48 | 1.71 | 2.63 | 2.62 | 2.80 | 2.28 | 2.09 | 2.21 |

[1] Includes other sources not shown separately. [2] There is a discontinuity in this time series between 1988 and 1989 due to the expanded coverage of the use of wood and biomass waste beginning in 1989. [3] There are no direct fuel costs for hydroelectric, geothermal, wind, photovoltaic, or solar thermal energy. [4] Natural gas as it is consumed; includes supplemental gaseous fuels that are commingled with natural gas. [5] Beginning 1995, includes fuel ethanol blended into motor gasoline. [6] There are no direct fuel costs for geothermal, photovoltaic, or solar thermal energy.

Source: U.S. Energy Information Administration, "State Energy Data System (SEDS)," <http://www.eia.gov/state/seds/>, accessed August 2019.

# Table 966. Fuel Ethanol and Biodiesel—Summary: 2000 to 2018

[233.1 represents 233,100,000,000,000. Btu=British thermal units. For definition of Btu, see source and text, this section. Minus sign (-) indicates an excess of exports over imports, except where noted]

| Fuel | 2000 | 2005 | 2010 | 2013 | 2014 | 2015 | 2016 | 2017 | 2018 |
|---|---|---|---|---|---|---|---|---|---|
| **FUEL ETHANOL** | | | | | | | | | |
| Feedstock [1] (tril. Btu) | 233.1 | 549.5 | 1,823.5 | 1,805.1 | 1,938.0 | 1,998.0 | 2,072.2 | 2,137.9 | 2,152.2 |
| Production: | | | | | | | | | |
| 1,000 barrels | 38,627 | 92,961 | 316,617 | 316,493 | 340,781 | 352,553 | 366,981 | 379,435 | 382,400 |
| Tril. Btu | 137.6 | 331.2 | 1,127.5 | 1,126.4 | 1,212.5 | 1,254.4 | 1,305.7 | 1,349.3 | 1,358.7 |
| Net imports [2] (1,000 barrels) | 116 | 3,234 | -9,115 | -5,761 | -18,371 | -17,632 | -27,002 | -31,268 | -39,682 |
| Stocks [3] (1,000 barrels) | 3,400 | 5,563 | 17,941 | 16,424 | 18,739 | 21,596 | 19,758 | 23,043 | 23,338 |
| Stock change [4] (1,000 barrels) | -624 | -439 | 1,347 | -3,926 | 2,315 | 2,857 | -1,838 | 3,285 | 290 |
| Consumption: | | | | | | | | | |
| 1,000 barrels | 39,367 | 96,634 | 306,155 | 314,658 | 320,095 | 332,064 | 341,817 | 344,882 | 342,428 |
| Tril. Btu | 140.3 | 344.3 | 1,090.2 | 1,119.9 | 1,138.9 | 1,181.5 | 1,216.2 | 1,226.4 | 1,216.6 |
| **BIODIESEL** | | | | | | | | | |
| Feedstock [5] (tril. Btu) | (NA) | 11.7 | 44.4 | 175.9 | 165.4 | 163.4 | 202.8 | 206.4 | 237.0 |
| Production: | | | | | | | | | |
| 1,000 barrels | (NA) | 2,162 | 8,177 | 32,368 | 30,452 | 30,080 | 37,327 | 37,993 | 43,616 |
| Tril. Btu | (NA) | 11.6 | 43.8 | 173.46 | 163.19 | 161.20 | 200.04 | 203.61 | 233.74 |
| Net imports (1,000 barrels) | (NA) | 1 | -2,024 | 3,477 | 2,604 | 6,308 | 14,781 | 7,146 | 1,460 |
| Stocks [6] (1,000 barrels) | (NA) | (NA) | 672 | 3,810 | 3,131 | 3,943 | 6,398 | 4,268 | 4,684 |
| Stock change [4] (1,000 barrels) | (NA) | (NA) | -39 | 1,825 | -679 | 813 | 2,455 | -2,130 | -65 |
| Consumption: | | | | | | | | | |
| 1,000 barrels | (NA) | 2,163 | 6,192 | 34,020 | 33,735 | 35,575 | 49,653 | 47,269 | 45,141 |
| Tril. Btu | (NA) | 11.6 | 33.2 | 182.3 | 180.8 | 190.6 | 266.1 | 253.3 | 241.9 |

NA Not available. [1] Total corn and other biomass inputs to the production of undenatured ethanol used for fuel ethanol. [2] Through 2009, data are for fuel ethanol imports only; data for fuel ethanol exports are not available. Beginning in 2010, data are for fuel ethanol imports minus fuel ethanol exports. [3] Stocks are at end of year. [4] A negative number indicates a decrease in stocks. [5] Total vegetable oil and other biomass inputs to the production of biodiesel. [6] Stocks are at end of period. Includes biodiesel stocks at (or in) refineries, pipelines, and bulk terminals. Beginning in 2011, also includes stocks at biodiesel production plants.

Source: U.S. Energy Information Administration, *Monthly Energy Review*, March 2019. See also <http://www.eia.gov/totalenergy/data/monthly/>.

# Table 967. Energy Expenditures—End-Use Sector and Selected Source by State: 2017

[In millions of dollars (1,136,496 represents $1,136,496,000,000). End-use sector and electric utilities exclude expenditures on energy sources such as hydroelectric, photovoltaic, solar thermal, wind, and geothermal. Also excludes expenditures for reported amounts of energy consumed by the energy industry for production, transportation, and processing operations. For technical notes and documentation, see source, <https://www.eia.gov/state/seds/seds-technical-notes-complete.php>]

| State | Total [1,2] | End-use sector | | | | Source | | | |
|---|---|---|---|---|---|---|---|---|---|
| | | Residential | Commercial | Industrial [2] | Transportation | Petroleum products [3] | Natural gas [4] | Coal | Electricity sales |
| U.S............... | 1,136,496 | 246,110 | 184,761 | 190,934 | 514,692 | 631,717 | 142,245 | 30,326 | 387,222 |
| AL............... | 20,436 | 4,343 | 3,106 | 4,236 | 8,752 | 9,851 | 2,805 | 917 | 8,455 |
| AK............... | 5,112 | 829 | 861 | 674 | 2,748 | 3,570 | 603 | 105 | 1,172 |
| AZ............... | 20,521 | 4,909 | 3,712 | 2,015 | 9,885 | 11,284 | 1,778 | 750 | 8,260 |
| AR............... | 11,305 | 2,171 | 1,520 | 2,437 | 5,178 | 5,970 | 1,788 | 547 | 3,791 |
| CA............... | 124,724 | 22,640 | 22,426 | 14,242 | 65,416 | 71,487 | 14,480 | 127 | 40,960 |
| CO............... | 16,391 | 3,513 | 2,690 | 2,438 | 7,750 | 9,082 | 2,151 | 563 | 5,449 |
| CT............... | 12,536 | 4,322 | 2,725 | 880 | 4,610 | 6,265 | 1,718 | 11 | 4,938 |
| DE............... | 3,336 | 849 | 602 | 445 | 1,440 | 1,681 | 591 | 13 | 1,191 |
| DC............... | 1,970 | 461 | 1,122 | 57 | 330 | 350 | 332 | – | 1,288 |
| FL............... | 57,074 | 14,666 | 10,428 | 3,901 | 28,079 | 30,926 | 6,743 | 1,216 | 24,286 |
| GA............... | 34,011 | 8,621 | 5,506 | 4,429 | 15,455 | 17,369 | 4,389 | 962 | 13,115 |
| HI............... | 5,550 | 826 | 1,005 | 947 | 2,772 | 3,757 | 91 | 46 | 2,416 |
| ID............... | 6,311 | 1,272 | 738 | 1,131 | 3,171 | 3,711 | 584 | 6 | 1,965 |
| IL............... | 40,511 | 9,345 | 6,629 | 6,129 | 18,408 | 21,138 | 6,744 | 1,359 | 12,813 |
| IN............... | 27,101 | 5,268 | 3,300 | 7,253 | 11,280 | 12,984 | 4,300 | 2,335 | 9,559 |
| IA............... | 13,890 | 2,484 | 1,665 | 4,179 | 5,562 | 7,339 | 2,255 | 529 | 4,273 |
| KS............... | 11,180 | 2,445 | 2,107 | 1,927 | 4,700 | 5,641 | 1,436 | 373 | 4,172 |
| KY............... | 17,338 | 3,337 | 2,352 | 3,113 | 8,536 | 9,771 | 1,571 | 1,303 | 6,172 |
| LA............... | 32,041 | 3,306 | 2,591 | 15,968 | 10,177 | 20,841 | 5,085 | 427 | 6,567 |
| ME............... | 5,624 | 1,613 | 873 | 649 | 2,491 | 3,703 | 338 | 10 | 1,460 |
| MD............... | 18,541 | 5,038 | 4,163 | 1,001 | 8,339 | 9,499 | 2,036 | 283 | 7,106 |
| MA............... | 23,206 | 7,092 | 5,576 | 1,846 | 8,693 | 11,092 | 3,732 | 54 | 8,991 |
| MI............... | 32,394 | 8,441 | 5,741 | 4,626 | 13,587 | 15,926 | 5,336 | 1,200 | 11,462 |
| MN............... | 20,067 | 4,403 | 3,393 | 3,519 | 8,751 | 10,678 | 2,602 | 565 | 6,795 |
| MS............... | 13,142 | 2,289 | 1,735 | 2,048 | 7,071 | 7,824 | 1,999 | 143 | 4,290 |
| MO............... | 21,162 | 5,124 | 3,599 | 2,314 | 10,124 | 11,469 | 2,077 | 1,332 | 7,672 |
| MT............... | 4,578 | 945 | 730 | 583 | 2,320 | 2,820 | 453 | 276 | 1,262 |
| NE............... | 8,244 | 1,442 | 1,075 | 1,935 | 3,792 | 4,549 | 926 | 327 | 2,756 |
| NV............... | 9,214 | 1,990 | 1,230 | 1,437 | 4,557 | 5,322 | 1,341 | 85 | 3,212 |
| NH............... | 5,193 | 1,713 | 943 | 503 | 2,034 | 3,105 | 415 | 16 | 1,744 |
| NJ............... | 29,541 | 6,894 | 6,397 | 2,138 | 14,113 | 16,178 | 4,475 | 52 | 9,708 |
| NM............... | 7,368 | 1,254 | 1,127 | 946 | 4,041 | 4,676 | 736 | 392 | 2,187 |
| NY............... | 54,108 | 16,448 | 14,348 | 3,005 | 20,307 | 24,594 | 9,315 | 69 | 21,366 |
| NC............... | 30,734 | 7,458 | 5,006 | 3,950 | 14,319 | 16,652 | 3,109 | 1,053 | 11,881 |
| ND............... | 5,352 | 677 | 749 | 1,704 | 2,221 | 3,239 | 291 | 600 | 1,744 |
| OH............... | 40,371 | 9,481 | 6,132 | 7,560 | 17,198 | 20,381 | 5,849 | 1,775 | 14,297 |
| OK............... | 15,610 | 3,040 | 2,169 | 2,656 | 7,745 | 9,183 | 2,230 | 374 | 4,879 |
| OR............... | 13,020 | 2,845 | 1,960 | 1,754 | 6,460 | 7,311 | 1,364 | 44 | 4,409 |
| PA............... | 43,927 | 11,858 | 5,863 | 7,919 | 18,287 | 23,221 | 8,890 | 1,676 | 14,376 |
| RI............... | 3,229 | 1,053 | 736 | 298 | 1,143 | 1,557 | 654 | – | 1,213 |
| SC............... | 18,962 | 4,315 | 2,731 | 3,086 | 8,830 | 9,946 | 1,508 | 639 | 7,783 |
| SD............... | 3,836 | 722 | 565 | 751 | 1,799 | 2,187 | 417 | 58 | 1,238 |
| TN............... | 24,094 | 4,950 | 4,225 | 3,405 | 11,514 | 13,035 | 1,889 | 795 | 9,149 |
| TX............... | 128,571 | 18,561 | 13,398 | 41,408 | 55,205 | 87,311 | 12,441 | 2,557 | 32,929 |
| UT............... | 9,278 | 1,722 | 1,422 | 1,203 | 4,930 | 5,540 | 1,237 | 542 | 2,604 |
| VT............... | 2,589 | 860 | 443 | 286 | 1,000 | 1,636 | 104 | – | 792 |
| VA............... | 27,218 | 6,537 | 5,047 | 2,682 | 12,953 | 14,695 | 3,060 | 478 | 10,234 |
| WA............... | 23,938 | 5,000 | 3,397 | 2,454 | 13,087 | 14,546 | 2,158 | 149 | 7,225 |
| WV............... | 7,470 | 1,555 | 979 | 1,829 | 3,107 | 3,981 | 536 | 1,621 | 2,853 |
| WI............... | 20,408 | 4,655 | 3,414 | 3,865 | 8,474 | 10,248 | 2,867 | 893 | 7,421 |
| WY............... | 4,442 | 532 | 512 | 1,446 | 1,952 | 2,599 | 412 | 783 | 1,347 |

– Represents or rounds to zero. [1] Total expenditures are the sum of purchases for each source (including electricity sales) less electric power sector purchases of fuel. There are no direct fuel costs for hydroelectric, geothermal, wind, photovoltaic, or solar thermal energy. The U.S. total includes -$269 million for coal coke net imports, which are not allocated to the states. [2] U.S. total includes sources not shown separately, such as electricity imports and exports and coal coke net imports, which are not allocated to the states. [3] Includes fuel ethanol blended into motor gasoline. [4] Includes supplemental gaseous fuels.

Source: U.S. Energy Information Administration, "State Energy Data System," <http://www.eia.gov/state/seds/>, accessed August 2019.

## Table 968. Energy Imports and Exports by Type of Fuel: 1980 to 2018

[In quadrillion Btu (12.10 represents 12,100,000,000,000,000 Btu). Btu=British thermal units; for definition, see text, this section]

| Type of fuel | 1980 | 1990 | 1995 | 2000 | 2005 | 2010 | 2014 | 2015 | 2016 | 2017 | 2018 |
|---|---|---|---|---|---|---|---|---|---|---|---|
| **Net imports, total** [1] | **12.10** | **14.06** | **17.68** | **24.90** | **30.20** | **21.69** | **10.97** | **10.89** | **11.26** | **7.51** | **3.61** |
| Coal | -2.39 | -2.70 | -2.08 | -1.21 | -0.51 | -1.62 | -2.18 | -1.60 | -1.33 | -2.22 | -2.72 |
| Natural gas (dry) | 0.96 | 1.46 | 2.74 | 3.62 | 3.71 | 2.69 | 1.23 | 0.99 | 0.73 | -0.08 | -0.66 |
| Petroleum [2] | 13.50 | 15.29 | 16.82 | 22.31 | 26.85 | 20.58 | 11.79 | 11.29 | 11.71 | 9.77 | 7.06 |
| Other [3] | 0.04 | 0.01 | 0.20 | 0.18 | 0.14 | 0.04 | 0.13 | 0.21 | 0.15 | 0.04 | -0.07 |
| Imports, total | 15.80 | 18.82 | 22.18 | 28.87 | 34.66 | 29.87 | 23.24 | 23.79 | 25.38 | 25.47 | 24.84 |
| Coal | 0.03 | 0.07 | 0.24 | 0.31 | 0.76 | 0.48 | 0.25 | 0.26 | 0.22 | 0.17 | 0.13 |
| Natural gas (dry) | 1.01 | 1.55 | 2.90 | 3.87 | 4.45 | 3.83 | 2.76 | 2.79 | 3.08 | 3.12 | 2.98 |
| Petroleum [2] | 14.66 | 17.12 | 18.80 | 24.42 | 29.20 | 25.36 | 19.95 | 20.41 | 21.70 | 21.87 | 21.48 |
| Other [3] | 0.10 | 0.08 | 0.24 | 0.26 | 0.25 | 0.19 | 0.28 | 0.34 | 0.38 | 0.31 | 0.25 |
| Exports, total | 3.69 | 4.75 | 4.50 | 3.96 | 4.46 | 8.18 | 12.27 | 12.90 | 14.12 | 17.96 | 21.23 |
| Coal | 2.42 | 2.77 | 2.32 | 1.53 | 1.27 | 2.10 | 2.43 | 1.85 | 1.55 | 2.39 | 2.85 |
| Natural gas (dry) | 0.05 | 0.09 | 0.16 | 0.25 | 0.74 | 1.15 | 1.53 | 1.80 | 2.36 | 3.20 | 3.64 |
| Petroleum | 1.16 | 1.82 | 1.98 | 2.11 | 2.34 | 4.78 | 8.16 | 9.12 | 9.99 | 12.11 | 14.42 |
| Other [3] | 0.07 | 0.07 | 0.05 | 0.08 | 0.11 | 0.15 | 0.15 | 0.13 | 0.23 | 0.27 | 0.32 |

[1] Net imports equals imports minus exports. Minus sign (-) indicates exports are greater than imports. [2] Includes imports into the Strategic Petroleum Reserve. [3] Coal coke, small amounts of electricity transmitted across U.S. borders with Canada and Mexico, and small amounts of biomass fuel.

Source: U.S. Energy Information Administration, *Monthly Energy Review*, March 2019. See also <http://www.eia.gov/totalenergy/>.

## Table 969. U.S. Foreign Trade in Natural Gas, Crude Oil, Petroleum Products, and Coal: 1980 to 2018

[985 represents 985,000,000,000 cu. ft. Minus sign (-) indicates trade deficit]

| Mineral fuel | Unit | 1980 | 1990 | 1995 | 2000 | 2005 | 2010 | 2015 | 2017 | 2018 (P) |
|---|---|---|---|---|---|---|---|---|---|---|
| **Natural gas:** | | | | | | | | | | |
| Imports | Bil. cu. ft. | 985 | 1,532 | 2,841 | 3,782 | 4,341 | 3,741 | 2,718 | 3,042 | 2,889 |
| Exports | Bil. cu. ft. | 49 | 86 | 154 | 244 | 729 | 1,137 | 1,784 | 3,168 | 3,607 |
| Net trade [1] | Bil. cu. ft. | -936 | -1,447 | -2,687 | -3,538 | -3,612 | -2,604 | -935 | 125 | 719 |
| **Crude oil:** [2] | | | | | | | | | | |
| Imports [3] | Mil. barrels | 1,926 | 2,151 | 2,639 | 3,320 | 3,696 | 3,363 | 2,687 | 2,909 | 2,831 |
| Exports | Mil. barrels | 105 | 40 | 35 | 18 | 12 | 15 | 170 | 423 | 731 |
| Net trade [1] | Mil. barrels | -1,821 | -2,112 | -2,604 | -3,301 | -3,684 | -3,348 | -2,518 | -2,486 | -2,100 |
| **Petroleum products:** | | | | | | | | | | |
| Imports | Mil. barrels | (NA) | 775 | 586 | 874 | 1,310 | 942 | 761 | 794 | 792 |
| Exports | Mil. barrels | (NA) | 273 | 312 | 362 | 414 | 843 | 1,560 | 1,905 | 2,038 |
| Net trade [1] | Mil. barrels | (NA) | -502 | -274 | -512 | -896 | -98 | 798 | 1,111 | 1,246 |
| **Coal:** | | | | | | | | | | |
| Imports | Mil. sh. tons | 1 | 3 | 9 | 13 | 30 | 19 | 11 | 8 | 6 |
| Exports | Mil. sh. tons | 92 | 106 | 89 | 58 | 50 | 82 | 74 | 97 | 116 |
| Net trade [1] | Mil. sh. tons | 91 | 103 | 79 | 46 | 19 | 62 | 63 | 89 | 110 |

P Preliminary. NA Not available. [1] Exports minus imports. [2] Includes lease condensate. [3] Includes Strategic Petroleum Reserve imports.

Source: U.S. Energy Information Administration, *Monthly Energy Review*, August 2019; and "Petroleum and Other Liquids, Imports/Exports & Movements," <http://www.eia.gov/petroleum/data.cfm#imports>, accessed September 2019.

## Table 970. Crude Oil Imports Into the U.S. by Country of Origin: 1993 to 2018

[In millions of barrels (2,477 represents 2,477,000,000). A barrel contains 42 gallons. Crude oil imports are reported by the Petroleum Administration for Defense (PAD) District in which they are to be processed. A PAD District is a geographic aggregation of the 50 states and D.C. into 5 districts. Includes crude oil imported for storage in the Strategic Petroleum Reserve (SPR). Total Organization of Petroleum Exporting Countries (OPEC) excludes, and non-OPEC includes, petroleum imported into the United States indirectly from members of OPEC, primarily from Caribbean and West European areas, as petroleum products that were refined from crude oil produced by OPEC]

| Country of origin | 1993 | 1995 | 2000 | 2005 | 2010 | 2013 | 2014 | 2015 | 2016 | 2017 | 2018 |
|---|---|---|---|---|---|---|---|---|---|---|---|
| **Total imports** | **2,477** | **2,639** | **3,320** | **3,696** | **3,363** | **2,821** | **2,681** | **2,687** | **2,873** | **2,909** | **2,831** |
| **OPEC, total** [1,2] | **1,346** | **1,303** | **1,663** | **1,758** | **1,662** | **1,275** | **1,097** | **976** | **1,164** | **1,138** | **943** |
| Algeria | 9 | 10 | (Z) | 83 | 120 | 10 | 2 | 1 | 19 | 24 | 29 |
| Angola | 123 | 131 | 108 | 166 | 140 | 73 | 51 | 45 | 58 | 47 | 33 |
| Ecuador | 28 | 35 | 46 | 101 | 76 | 85 | 78 | 82 | 87 | 75 | 64 |
| Iraq | (NA) | (NA) | 227 | 193 | 152 | 124 | 135 | 84 | 154 | 219 | 189 |
| Kuwait | 126 | 78 | 96 | 83 | 71 | 119 | 113 | 74 | 76 | 53 | 28 |
| Nigeria | 264 | 227 | 320 | 393 | 359 | 87 | 21 | 20 | 76 | 113 | 64 |
| Saudi Arabia | 468 | 460 | 558 | 527 | 395 | 484 | 423 | 384 | 402 | 347 | 318 |
| Venezuela | 369 | 420 | 448 | 453 | 333 | 275 | 268 | 283 | 271 | 226 | 185 |
| **Non-OPEC, total** [2] | **1,131** | **1,336** | **1,657** | **1,938** | **1,701** | **1,546** | **1,584** | **1,712** | **1,709** | **1,771** | **1,888** |
| Brazil | (NA) | (NA) | 2 | 34 | 93 | 40 | 53 | 69 | 53 | 72 | 46 |
| Canada | 329 | 380 | 493 | 596 | 719 | 941 | 1,052 | 1,157 | 1,181 | 1,258 | 1,348 |
| Colombia | 52 | 75 | 116 | 57 | 124 | 134 | 107 | 136 | 162 | 121 | 108 |
| Egypt | 25 | 12 | 2 | 1 | 3 | 2 | (NA) | 1 | 4 | 3 | 8 |
| Indonesia | 24 | 23 | 13 | 7 | 12 | 7 | 7 | 13 | 12 | 14 | 15 |
| Mexico | 315 | 375 | 480 | 568 | 421 | 310 | 285 | 251 | 213 | 222 | 243 |
| Norway | 50 | 94 | 111 | 43 | 9 | 6 | 3 | 3 | 13 | 14 | 20 |
| Russia | (NA) | 5 | 3 | 73 | 98 | 15 | 7 | 14 | 14 | 18 | 27 |
| United Kingdom | 114 | 124 | 106 | 82 | 44 | 8 | 3 | 4 | 7 | 9 | 21 |

NA Not available. Z Represents less than 500,000 barrels. [1] Countries listed under OPEC and non-OPEC are based on current affiliations. OPEC and non-OPEC totals are based on affiliations for the stated period of time which may differ from current affiliations. Indonesia withdrew from OPEC in January 2009, rejoined in 2016 and withdrew again in December 2016; Angola joined OPEC in January 2007; Ecuador withdrew from OPEC in January 1993 and rejoined in November 2007; Gabon terminated its membership in 1995 and rejoined in July 2016; Equatorial Guinea joined OPEC in May 2017; Congo (Republic of) joined OPEC in June 2018; and Qatar withdrew from OPEC in January 2019. [2] Includes countries not shown separately.

Source: U.S. Energy Information Administration, Petroleum & Other Liquids, "U.S. Imports by Country of Origin," <https://www.eia.gov/petroleum/data.php#imports>, accessed September 2019.

## Table 971. Crude Oil and Refined Products—Summary: 1980 to 2018

[13,481 represents 13,481,000 bbl. One barrel (bbl.) contains 42 gallons. Data are averages]

| Year | Crude oil [1] (1,000 bbl. per day) Refinery and blender input | Domestic production | Imports Total [3] | Imports Strategic reserve [4] | Exports | Refined oil products (1,000 bbl. per day) Domestic demand | Imports | Exports | Total oil imports [5] (1,000 bbl. per day) | Crude oil stocks [1,2] (mil. bbl.) Total [6] | Strategic reserve [7] |
|---|---|---|---|---|---|---|---|---|---|---|---|
| 1980.... | 13,481 | 8,597 | 5,263 | 44 | 287 | 17,056 | 1,646 | 258 | 6,909 | 466 | 108 |
| 1981.... | 12,470 | 8,572 | 4,396 | 256 | 228 | 16,058 | 1,599 | 367 | 5,996 | 594 | 230 |
| 1982.... | 11,774 | 8,649 | 3,488 | 165 | 236 | 15,296 | 1,625 | 579 | 5,113 | 644 | 294 |
| 1983.... | 11,685 | 8,688 | 3,329 | 234 | 164 | 15,231 | 1,722 | 575 | 5,051 | 723 | 379 |
| 1984.... | 12,044 | 8,879 | 3,426 | 197 | 181 | 15,726 | 2,011 | 541 | 5,437 | 796 | 451 |
| 1985.... | 12,002 | 8,971 | 3,201 | 118 | 204 | 15,726 | 1,866 | 577 | 5,067 | 814 | 493 |
| 1986.... | 12,716 | 8,680 | 4,178 | 48 | 154 | 16,281 | 2,045 | 631 | 6,224 | 843 | 512 |
| 1987.... | 12,854 | 8,349 | 4,674 | 73 | 151 | 16,665 | 2,004 | 613 | 6,678 | 890 | 541 |
| 1988.... | 13,246 | 8,140 | 5,107 | 51 | 155 | 17,283 | 2,295 | 661 | 7,402 | 890 | 560 |
| 1989.... | 13,401 | 7,613 | 5,843 | 56 | 142 | 17,325 | 2,217 | 717 | 8,061 | 921 | 580 |
| 1990.... | 13,409 | 7,355 | 5,894 | 27 | 109 | 16,988 | 2,123 | 748 | 8,018 | 908 | 586 |
| 1991.... | 13,301 | 7,417 | 5,782 | (NA) | 116 | 16,714 | 1,844 | 885 | 7,627 | 893 | 569 |
| 1992.... | 13,411 | 7,171 | 6,083 | 10 | 89 | 17,033 | 1,805 | 861 | 7,888 | 893 | 575 |
| 1993.... | 13,613 | 6,847 | 6,787 | 15 | 98 | 17,237 | 1,833 | 904 | 8,620 | 922 | 587 |
| 1994.... | 13,866 | 6,662 | 7,063 | 12 | 99 | 17,718 | 1,933 | 843 | 8,996 | 929 | 592 |
| 1995.... | 13,973 | 6,560 | 7,230 | (NA) | 95 | 17,725 | 1,605 | 855 | 8,835 | 895 | 592 |
| 1996.... | 14,195 | 6,465 | 7,508 | (NA) | 110 | 18,309 | 1,971 | 871 | 9,478 | 850 | 566 |
| 1997.... | 14,662 | 6,452 | 8,225 | (NA) | 108 | 18,620 | 1,936 | 896 | 10,162 | 868 | 563 |
| 1998.... | 14,889 | 6,252 | 8,706 | (NA) | 110 | 18,917 | 2,002 | 835 | 10,708 | 895 | 571 |
| 1999.... | 14,804 | 5,881 | 8,731 | 8 | 118 | 19,519 | 2,122 | 822 | 10,852 | 852 | 567 |
| 2000.... | 15,067 | 5,822 | 9,071 | 8 | 50 | 19,701 | 2,389 | 990 | 11,459 | 826 | 541 |
| 2001.... | 15,128 | 5,801 | 9,328 | 11 | 20 | 19,649 | 2,543 | 951 | 11,871 | 862 | 550 |
| 2002.... | 14,947 | 5,744 | 9,140 | 16 | 9 | 19,761 | 2,390 | 975 | 11,530 | 877 | 599 |
| 2003.... | 15,304 | 5,649 | 9,665 | (NA) | 12 | 20,034 | 2,599 | 1,014 | 12,264 | 907 | 638 |
| 2004.... | 15,475 | 5,441 | 10,088 | 77 | 27 | 20,731 | 3,057 | 1,021 | 13,145 | 961 | 676 |
| 2005.... | 15,220 | 5,184 | 10,126 | 52 | 32 | 20,802 | 3,588 | 1,133 | 13,714 | 992 | 685 |
| 2006.... | 15,242 | 5,086 | 10,118 | 8 | 25 | 20,687 | 3,589 | 1,292 | 13,707 | 984 | 689 |
| 2007.... | 15,156 | 5,074 | 10,031 | 7 | 27 | 20,680 | 3,437 | 1,405 | 13,468 | 965 | 697 |
| 2008.... | 14,648 | 5,000 | 9,783 | 19 | 29 | 19,498 | 3,132 | 1,773 | 12,915 | 1,010 | 702 |
| 2009.... | 14,336 | 5,349 | 9,013 | 56 | 44 | 18,771 | 2,678 | 1,980 | 11,691 | 1,034 | 727 |
| 2010.... | 14,724 | 5,478 | 9,213 | (NA) | 42 | 19,180 | 2,580 | 2,311 | 11,793 | 1,039 | 727 |
| 2011.... | 14,806 | 5,654 | 8,935 | (NA) | 47 | 18,887 | 2,501 | 2,939 | 11,436 | 1,004 | 696 |
| 2012.... | 14,999 | 6,502 | 8,527 | (NA) | 67 | 18,487 | 2,071 | 3,137 | 10,598 | 1,033 | 695 |
| 2013.... | 15,312 | 7,467 | 7,730 | (NA) | 134 | 18,967 | 2,129 | 3,487 | 9,859 | 1,023 | 696 |
| 2014.... | 15,848 | 8,759 | 7,344 | (NA) | 351 | 19,100 | 1,897 | 3,824 | 9,241 | 1,052 | 691 |
| 2015.... | 16,188 | 9,431 | 7,363 | (NA) | 465 | 19,534 | 2,086 | 4,273 | 9,449 | 1,144 | 695 |
| 2016.... | 16,187 | 8,831 | 7,850 | (NA) | 591 | 19,687 | 2,205 | 4,670 | 10,055 | 1,180 | 695 |
| 2017.... | 16,590 | 9,352 | 7,969 | (NA) | 1,158 | 19,958 | 2,175 | 5,218 | 10,144 | 1,084 | 663 |
| 2018.... | 16,900 | 10,050 | 7,757 | (NA) | 2,004 | 20,453 | 2,171 | 5,584 | 9,928 | 1,091 | 649 |

NA Not available. [1] Includes lease condensate. [2] Crude oil at end of period. Includes commercial and Strategic Petroleum Reserve (SPR) stocks. [3] Includes Strategic Petroleum Reserve. [4] Through 2000, includes imports by SPR only; beginning in 2004, includes imports by SPR, and imports into SPR by others. [5] Crude oil (including Strategic Petroleum Reserve imports) plus refined products. [6] Beginning in 1981, includes stocks of Alaskan crude oil in transit. [7] Crude oil stocks in the Strategic Petroleum Reserve include non-U.S. stocks held under foreign or commercial storage agreements.

Source: U.S. Energy Information Administration, *Monthly Energy Review*, March 2019, and earlier reports. See also <http://www.eia.gov/totalenergy/data/monthly/>.

## Table 972. Petroleum and Coal Products Corporations—Sales, Net Profit, and Profit Per Dollar of Sales: 1990 to 2018

[318.5 represents $318,500,000,000. Through 2000, covers Standard Industrial Classification (SIC) group 29. Beginning 2001, covers North American Industry Classification System (NAICS) 324. Profit rates are averages of quarterly figures at annual rates]

| Item | Unit | 1990 | 1995 | 2000 | 2005 | 2010 | 2014 | 2015 | 2016 | 2017 | 2018 |
|---|---|---|---|---|---|---|---|---|---|---|---|
| Sales..................... | Bil. dol. | 318.5 | 283.1 | 455.2 | 956.0 | 1,077.1 | 1,283.8 | 834.3 | 681.9 | 850.1 | 1,027.9 |
| Net profit: | | | | | | | | | | | |
| Before income taxes............... | Bil. dol. | 23.1 | 16.5 | 55.5 | 120.2 | 56.0 | 82.3 | 21.0 | 1.2 | 34.0 | 71.2 |
| After income taxes................. | Bil. dol. | 17.8 | 13.9 | 42.6 | 96.3 | 54.2 | 74.2 | 24.0 | 11.2 | 8.0 | 63.6 |
| Depreciation [1]........................ | Bil. dol. | 18.7 | 16.7 | 15.5 | 18.6 | 30.8 | 32.0 | 33.6 | 34.6 | 35.2 | 34.8 |
| Profits per dollar of sales: | | | | | | | | | | | |
| Before income taxes............... | Cents | 7.3 | 5.8 | 12.2 | 12.6 | 5.3 | 6.3 | 2.4 | 0.1 | 4.1 | 6.9 |
| After income taxes................. | Cents | 5.6 | 4.9 | 9.4 | 10.1 | 5.1 | 5.7 | 2.8 | 1.6 | 5.5 | 6.2 |
| Profits on stockholders' equity: | | | | | | | | | | | |
| Before income taxes............... | Percent | 16.4 | 12.6 | 29.4 | 38.0 | 12.2 | 14.3 | 3.8 | 0.2 | 6.2 | 12.2 |
| After income taxes................. | Percent | 12.7 | 10.6 | 22.6 | 30.4 | 11.8 | 12.9 | 4.4 | 2.1 | 8.7 | 10.9 |

[1] Includes depletion and accelerated amortization of emergency facilities.

Source: U.S. Census Bureau, *Quarterly Financial Report for Manufacturing, Mining, Trade, and Selected Service Industries*. See also <http://www.census.gov/econ/qfr/>.

## Table 973. Nuclear Power Plants—Number, Capacity, and Generation: 1980 to 2018

[51.8 represents 51,800,000 kilowatts (kW)]

| Item | 1980 | 1990 | 1995 | 2000 | 2005 | 2010 | 2015 | 2016 | 2017 | 2018 (P) |
|---|---|---|---|---|---|---|---|---|---|---|
| Operable generating units [1, 2] | 71 | 112 | 109 | 104 | 104 | 104 | 99 | 99 | 99 | 98 |
| Net summer capacity [2, 3] (mil. kW) | 51.8 | 99.6 | 99.5 | 97.9 | 100.0 | 101.2 | 98.7 | 99.6 | 99.6 | 99.4 |
| Net generation (bil. kWh) | 251.1 | 576.9 | 673.4 | 753.9 | 782.0 | 807.0 | 797.2 | 805.7 | 805.0 | 807.1 |
| Percent of total electricity net generation | 11.0 | 19.0 | 20.1 | 19.8 | 19.3 | 19.6 | 19.6 | 19.8 | 20.0 | 19.3 |
| Capacity factor [4] (percent) | 56.3 | 66.0 | 77.4 | 88.1 | 89.3 | 91.1 | 92.3 | 92.3 | 92.2 | 92.6 |

P Preliminary. [1] Total of nuclear generating units holding full-power licenses, or equivalent permission to operate, at the end of the year. Includes units retaining full-power licenses during long, non-routine shutdowns that for a time rendered them unable to generate electricity. [2] As of year-end. [3] Net summer capacity is the peak steady hourly output that generating equipment is expected to supply to system load, exclusive of auxiliary and other power plant, as demonstrated by a test at the time of summer peak demand. [4] Weighted average of monthly capacity factors. Monthly factors are derived by dividing actual monthly generation by the maximum possible generation for the month (number of hours in the month multiplied by the net summer capacity at the end of the month). Please note that as of 2008, the methodology changed; see U.S. Energy Information Administration, *Electric Power Monthly,* Appendix C, under "Average Capacity Factors."

Source: U.S. Energy Information Administration, *Monthly Energy Review,* March 2019. See also <http://www.eia.gov/totalenergy/data/monthly/>.

## Table 974. Nuclear Power Plants—Number of Reactors, Net Generation, and Net Summer Capacity by State: 2017

[804,950 represents 804,950,000,000 kilowatt hours (kWh)]

| State | Number of reactors | Nuclear net generation Total (mil. kWh) | Nuclear net generation Percent of total [1] | Nuclear net summer capacity Total (mil. kWh) | Nuclear net summer capacity Percent of total [2] | State | Number of reactors | Nuclear net generation Total (mil. kWh) | Nuclear net generation Percent of total [1] | Nuclear net summer capacity Total (mil. kWh) | Nuclear net summer capacity Percent of total [2] |
|---|---|---|---|---|---|---|---|---|---|---|---|
| U.S. | 99 | 804,950 | 20.0 | 99.6 | 9.2 | MN | 3 | 13,904 | 23.7 | 1.7 | 10.0 |
| | | | | | | MS | 1 | 7,365 | 12.3 | 1.4 | 8.9 |
| AL | 5 | 42,652 | 30.5 | 5.1 | 17.0 | MO | 1 | 8,304 | 9.8 | 1.2 | 5.5 |
| AZ | 3 | 32,340 | 30.6 | 3.9 | 13.8 | NE | 1 | 6,913 | 19.5 | 0.8 | 8.9 |
| AR | 2 | 12,691 | 20.9 | 1.8 | 12.4 | NH | 1 | 9,991 | 57.3 | 1.2 | 28.1 |
| CA | 2 | 17,901 | 8.7 | 2.2 | 2.9 | NJ | 4 | 34,033 | 45.0 | 4.1 | 23.0 |
| CT | 2 | 16,500 | 47.7 | 2.1 | 23.4 | NY | 6 | 42,167 | 32.9 | 5.4 | 13.4 |
| FL | 4 | 29,146 | 12.2 | 3.6 | 6.1 | NC | 5 | 42,374 | 33.0 | 5.1 | 15.5 |
| GA | 4 | 33,709 | 26.4 | 4.1 | 11.0 | OH | 2 | 17,688 | 14.8 | 2.1 | 7.1 |
| IL | 11 | 97,191 | 52.9 | 11.6 | 25.6 | PA | 9 | 83,200 | 38.9 | 9.8 | 22.2 |
| IA | 1 | 5,214 | 9.0 | 0.6 | 3.4 | SC | 7 | 54,345 | 58.4 | 6.6 | 28.7 |
| KS | 1 | 10,648 | 20.9 | 1.2 | 7.6 | TN | 4 | 31,818 | 40.3 | 4.5 | 21.6 |
| LA | 2 | 15,410 | 15.8 | 2.1 | 9.0 | TX | 4 | 38,581 | 8.5 | 5.0 | 4.0 |
| MD | 2 | 15,107 | 44.3 | 1.7 | 13.0 | VA | 4 | 30,554 | 33.8 | 3.6 | 12.9 |
| MA | 1 | 5,047 | 15.7 | 0.7 | 5.6 | WA | 1 | 8,128 | 7.0 | 1.2 | 3.8 |
| MI | 4 | 32,381 | 28.8 | 4.1 | 13.9 | WI | 2 | 9,649 | 14.8 | 1.2 | 7.0 |

[1] Percent of total electric power generation, see Table 980. [2] Percent of total net summer capacity, see Table 980.

Source: U.S. Energy Information Administration, *Electric Power Annual,* and "Electricity: Detailed State Data," <http://www.eia.gov/electricity/data/state/>, accessed January 2019.

## Table 975. Uranium Concentrate—Supply, Inventories, and Average Prices: 1990 to 2018

[8.89 represents 8,890,000 pounds (lbs.). Years ending December 31. For additional data on uranium, see Table 937 and Table 953]

| Item | Unit | 1990 | 1995 | 2000 | 2005 | 2010 | 2015 | 2016 | 2017 | 2018 |
|---|---|---|---|---|---|---|---|---|---|---|
| Production [1] | Mil. lbs. | 8.9 | 6.0 | 4.0 | 2.7 | 4.2 | 3.3 | 2.9 | 2.4 | [5] 1.5 |
| Exports [2] | Mil. lbs. | 2.0 | 9.8 | 13.6 | 20.5 | 23.1 | 25.7 | 17.2 | 14.0 | 13.9 |
| Imports [2] | Mil. lbs. | 23.7 | 41.3 | 44.9 | 65.5 | 55.3 | 64.1 | 50.7 | 42.1 | 41.5 |
| Electric plant purchases from domestic suppliers | Mil. lbs. | 20.5 | 22.3 | 24.3 | 27.3 | 16.2 | 19.6 | 18.8 | 14.0 | 11.1 |
| Loaded into U.S. nuclear reactors [3] | Mil. lbs. | (NA) | 51.1 | 51.5 | 58.3 | 44.3 | 47.4 | 42.5 | 45.5 | 50.2 |
| Inventories, total | Mil. lbs. | 129.1 | 72.5 | 111.3 | 93.8 | 111.3 | 135.5 | 144.6 | 141.7 | 131.5 |
| At domestic suppliers | Mil. lbs. | 26.4 | 13.7 | 56.5 | 29.1 | 24.7 | 14.3 | 16.7 | 17.8 | 19.9 |
| At electric plants | Mil. lbs. | 102.7 | 58.7 | 54.8 | 64.7 | 86.5 | 121.1 | 128.0 | 123.9 | 111.6 |
| Average price per pound: Purchased imports [4] | Dollars | 12.55 | 10.20 | 9.84 | 14.83 | 47.01 | 42.96 | 40.45 | 37.09 | 35.70 |
| Domestic purchases | Dollars | 15.70 | 11.11 | 11.45 | 13.98 | 44.88 | 43.03 | 41.64 | 38.57 | 42.98 |

NA Not available. [1] Data are for uranium concentrate, a yellow or brown powder obtained by the milling of uranium ore, processing of in situ leach mining solutions, or as a by-product of phosphoric acid production. [2] Includes transactions by uranium buyers (consumers). Buyer imports and exports prior to 1990 are believed to be small. [3] Does not include any fuel rods removed from reactors and later reloaded into the reactor. [4] For purchases made by U.S. suppliers and by U.S. owners and operators of civilian nuclear power plants. [5] Preliminary.

Source: U.S. Energy Information Administration, through 2010, *Annual Energy Review;* thereafter, *Uranium Marketing Annual Report,* May 2019, and *Domestic Uranium Production Report–Quarterly,* May 2019. See also <http://www.eia.gov/nuclear/>.

# Table 976. Renewable Energy Generating Capacity and Generation Projections: 2018 to 2050

[In gigawatts, unless otherwise noted. Reference case projections are business-as-usual trend estimates, given known technology, as well as market, demographic, and technological trends. Based on results from EIA's National Energy Modeling System]

| Net summer capacity and generation | Reference case | | | | | | | | Annual growth 2018-2050 (percent) |
|---|---|---|---|---|---|---|---|---|---|
| | 2018 | 2020 | 2025 | 2030 | 2035 | 2040 | 2045 | 2050 | |
| **ELECTRIC POWER SECTOR** [1] | | | | | | | | | |
| **Total net summer capacity**.................. | **215.24** | **242.63** | **286.49** | **305.11** | **328.39** | **367.64** | **398.12** | **447.18** | **2.3** |
| Conventional hydroelectric power................ | 78.98 | 79.22 | 79.24 | 79.24 | 79.31 | 79.32 | 79.32 | 79.54 | – |
| Geothermal [2]............................. | 2.46 | 2.61 | 3.46 | 4.86 | 6.37 | 7.29 | 7.74 | 8.37 | 3.9 |
| Municipal waste [3]......................... | 3.69 | 3.69 | 3.68 | 3.68 | 3.68 | 3.68 | 3.68 | 3.68 | – |
| Wood and other biomass [4]................... | 3.31 | 3.52 | 3.52 | 3.52 | 3.52 | 3.55 | 3.55 | 3.56 | 0.2 |
| Solar thermal.............................. | 1.76 | 1.76 | 1.76 | 1.76 | 1.76 | 1.76 | 1.76 | 1.76 | – |
| Solar photovoltaic [5]....................... | 30.29 | 40.98 | 76.72 | 92.28 | 113.05 | 148.95 | 175.14 | 215.50 | 6.3 |
| Wind.................................... | 94.73 | 110.82 | 118.06 | 119.70 | 120.64 | 123.03 | 126.87 | 134.71 | 1.1 |
| Offshore wind............................. | 0.03 | 0.05 | 0.06 | 0.06 | 0.06 | 0.06 | 0.06 | 0.06 | 2.2 |
| **Total generation (bil. kWh)**.................. | **670.29** | **752.37** | **909.48** | **969.34** | **1,035.80** | **1,151.00** | **1,238.37** | **1,382.64** | **2.3** |
| Conventional hydroelectric power............. | 281.60 | 292.33 | 308.45 | 306.83 | 306.05 | 306.43 | 307.29 | 307.76 | 0.3 |
| Geothermal [2]............................ | 16.33 | 17.22 | 24.87 | 36.14 | 48.35 | 56.02 | 60.32 | 65.63 | 4.4 |
| Biogenic municipal waste [6].................. | 19.54 | 19.59 | 19.48 | 19.83 | 19.91 | 19.89 | 20.11 | 20.45 | 0.1 |
| Wood and other biomass..................... | 13.61 | 14.60 | 14.72 | 14.94 | 14.91 | 15.41 | 15.37 | 16.31 | 0.6 |
| Dedicated plants.......................... | 13.11 | 14.35 | 14.47 | 14.83 | 14.69 | 14.99 | 15.15 | 15.86 | 0.6 |
| Co-firing................................ | 0.51 | 0.24 | 0.24 | 0.11 | 0.23 | 0.41 | 0.22 | 0.44 | -0.4 |
| Solar thermal............................. | 3.57 | 3.44 | 3.29 | 3.18 | 3.28 | 3.21 | 3.26 | 3.21 | -0.3 |
| Solar photovoltaic [5]....................... | 63.04 | 83.93 | 174.57 | 219.53 | 271.21 | 370.11 | 436.96 | 543.64 | 7.0 |
| Wind.................................... | 272.50 | 321.16 | 363.95 | 368.74 | 371.94 | 379.79 | 394.91 | 425.49 | 1.4 |
| Offshore wind............................. | 0.10 | 0.11 | 0.15 | 0.15 | 0.15 | 0.15 | 0.15 | 0.15 | 1.3 |
| **END-USE SECTORS** [7] | | | | | | | | | |
| **Total net summer capacity**.................. | **29.84** | **39.50** | **58.90** | **76.01** | **97.77** | **124.90** | **157.02** | **195.54** | **6.1** |
| Conventional hydropower.................... | 0.32 | 0.32 | 0.32 | 0.32 | 0.32 | 0.32 | 0.32 | 0.32 | – |
| Geothermal............................... | – | – | – | – | – | – | – | – | (X) |
| Municipal waste [3]......................... | 0.55 | 0.55 | 0.55 | 0.55 | 0.55 | 0.55 | 0.55 | 0.55 | – |
| Biomass.................................. | 4.34 | 4.71 | 4.90 | 5.09 | 5.38 | 5.73 | 6.03 | 6.36 | 1.2 |
| Solar photovoltaic [5]....................... | 24.03 | 33.32 | 52.52 | 69.45 | 90.81 | 117.11 | 148.35 | 185.88 | 6.6 |
| Wind.................................... | 0.61 | 0.61 | 0.61 | 0.61 | 0.71 | 1.18 | 1.78 | 2.43 | 4.4 |
| **Total generation (bil. kWh)**.................. | **63.89** | **76.97** | **105.13** | **130.65** | **163.69** | **205.17** | **254.11** | **313.24** | **5.1** |
| Conventional hydropower ................... | 1.69 | 1.69 | 1.69 | 1.69 | 1.69 | 1.69 | 1.69 | 1.69 | – |
| Geothermal............................... | – | – | – | – | – | – | – | – | (X) |
| Municipal waste [3]......................... | 3.85 | 3.85 | 3.85 | 3.85 | 3.85 | 3.85 | 3.85 | 3.85 | – |
| Biomass.................................. | 23.97 | 24.01 | 25.12 | 26.26 | 27.92 | 29.88 | 31.46 | 33.32 | 1.0 |
| Solar photovoltaic [5]....................... | 33.60 | 46.65 | 73.69 | 98.07 | 129.32 | 168.19 | 214.74 | 271.13 | 6.7 |
| Wind.................................... | 0.78 | 0.78 | 0.78 | 0.78 | 0.91 | 1.56 | 2.38 | 3.26 | 4.6 |
| **ALL SECTORS** | | | | | | | | | |
| **Total net summer capacity**.................. | **245.09** | **282.13** | **345.39** | **381.12** | **426.16** | **492.53** | **555.15** | **642.72** | **3.1** |
| Conventional hydropower.................... | 79.29 | 79.53 | 79.56 | 79.56 | 79.62 | 79.64 | 79.64 | 79.86 | – |
| Geothermal............................... | 2.46 | 2.61 | 3.46 | 4.86 | 6.37 | 7.29 | 7.74 | 8.37 | 3.9 |
| Municipal waste........................... | 4.24 | 4.24 | 4.23 | 4.23 | 4.23 | 4.23 | 4.23 | 4.23 | – |
| Wood and other biomass [4]................... | 7.65 | 8.22 | 8.42 | 8.61 | 8.90 | 9.28 | 9.58 | 9.92 | 0.8 |
| Solar [5]................................. | 56.07 | 76.05 | 131.00 | 163.49 | 205.62 | 267.83 | 325.25 | 403.14 | 6.4 |
| Wind.................................... | 95.37 | 111.48 | 118.73 | 120.37 | 121.41 | 124.27 | 128.71 | 137.20 | 1.1 |
| **Total generation (bil. kWh)**.................. | **734.18** | **829.35** | **1,014.61** | **1,099.99** | **1,199.49** | **1,356.17** | **1,492.48** | **1,695.88** | **2.7** |
| Conventional hydropower.................... | 283.29 | 294.01 | 310.13 | 308.51 | 307.73 | 308.11 | 308.98 | 309.44 | 0.3 |
| Geothermal............................... | 16.33 | 17.22 | 24.87 | 36.14 | 48.35 | 56.02 | 60.32 | 65.63 | 4.4 |
| Municipal waste........................... | 23.39 | 23.44 | 23.33 | 23.68 | 23.76 | 23.74 | 23.96 | 24.30 | 0.1 |
| Wood and other biomass..................... | 37.58 | 38.61 | 39.84 | 41.20 | 42.83 | 45.29 | 46.83 | 49.62 | 0.9 |
| Solar [5]................................. | 100.21 | 134.02 | 251.55 | 320.78 | 403.81 | 541.51 | 654.95 | 817.98 | 6.8 |
| Wind.................................... | 273.37 | 322.05 | 364.88 | 369.67 | 373.01 | 381.50 | 397.45 | 428.90 | 1.4 |

– Represents or rounds to zero. X Not applicable. [1] Includes electricity-only and combined heat and power plants that have a regulatory status. [2] Includes both hydrothermal resources and near-field enhanced geothermal systems (EGS). [3] Includes municipal waste, landfill gas, and municipal sewage sludge. [4] Facilities co-firing biomass and coal are classified as coal. [5] Does not include off-grid photovoltaics (PV). [6] Includes biogenic municipal waste, landfill gas, and municipal sludge. [7] Includes combined heat and power plants and electricity-only plants in the commercial and industrial sectors with nonregulatory status, and small on-site generating systems in the residential, commercial, and industrial sectors used primarily for own-use generation, but which many also sell some power to the grid.

Source: U.S. Energy Information Administration, *Annual Energy Outlook 2019*, January 2019. See also <http://www.eia.gov/forecasts/aeo/>.

## Table 977. Electricity Net Generation by Sector and Fuel Type: 1990 to 2018

[3,037.8 represents 3,037,800,000,000 kilowatt hours (kWh). Data are for fuels consumed to produce electricity. Also includes fuels consumed to produce useful thermal output at a small number of electric utility combined-heat-and-power (CHP) plants]

| Source and sector | Unit | 1990 | 1995 | 2000 | 2005 | 2010 | 2015 | 2016 | 2017 | 2018 (P) |
|---|---|---|---|---|---|---|---|---|---|---|
| **Net generation, total** | **Bil. kWh.** | **3,037.8** | **3,353.5** | **3,802.1** | **4,055.4** | **4,125.1** | **4,077.6** | **4,076.7** | **4,034.3** | **4,177.8** |
| Electric power sector, total | Bil. kWh. | 2,901.3 | 3,194.2 | 3,637.5 | 3,902.2 | 3,972.4 | 3,919.3 | 3,918.1 | 3,877.5 | 4,018.3 |
| Commercial sector [1] | Bil. kWh. | 5.8 | 8.2 | 7.9 | 8.5 | 8.6 | 12.6 | 12.7 | 13.1 | 13.3 |
| Industrial sector [2] | Bil. kWh. | 130.8 | 151.0 | 156.7 | 144.7 | 144.1 | 145.7 | 145.9 | 143.8 | 146.2 |
| Net generation by source, all sectors: | | | | | | | | | | |
| Fossil fuels, total | Bil. kWh. | 2,103.6 | 2,293.9 | 2,692.5 | 2,909.5 | 2,883.4 | 2,727.2 | 2,654.5 | 2,536.1 | 2,651.2 |
| Coal [3] | Bil. kWh. | 1,594.0 | 1,709.4 | 1,966.3 | 2,012.9 | 1,847.3 | 1,352.4 | 1,239.1 | 1,205.8 | 1,146.4 |
| Petroleum [4] | Bil. kWh. | 126.5 | 74.6 | 111.2 | 122.2 | 37.1 | 28.2 | 24.2 | 21.4 | 24.6 |
| Natural gas [5] | Bil. kWh. | 372.8 | 496.1 | 601.0 | 761.0 | 987.7 | 1,333.5 | 1,378.3 | 1,296.4 | 1,468.0 |
| Other gases [6] | Bil. kWh. | 10.4 | 13.9 | 14.0 | 13.5 | 11.3 | 13.1 | 12.8 | 12.5 | 12.2 |
| Nuclear electric power | Bil. kWh. | 576.9 | 673.4 | 753.9 | 782.0 | 807.0 | 797.2 | 805.7 | 804.9 | 807.1 |
| Hydroelectric pumped storage [7] | Bil. kWh. | -3.5 | -2.7 | -5.5 | -6.6 | -5.5 | -5.1 | -6.7 | -6.5 | -5.9 |
| Renewable energy, total | Bil. kWh. | 357.1 | 384.8 | 356.5 | 357.7 | 427.4 | 544.2 | 609.4 | 686.6 | 712.8 |
| Conventional hydroelectric power | Bil. kWh. | 292.9 | 310.8 | 275.6 | 270.3 | 260.2 | 249.1 | 267.8 | 300.3 | 291.7 |
| Biomass, total | Bil. kWh. | 45.8 | 56.9 | 60.7 | 54.3 | 56.1 | 63.6 | 62.8 | 62.8 | 62.8 |
| Wood [8] | Bil. kWh. | 32.5 | 36.5 | 37.6 | 38.9 | 37.2 | 41.9 | 40.9 | 41.2 | 41.4 |
| Waste [9] | Bil. kWh. | 13.3 | 20.4 | 23.1 | 15.4 | 18.9 | 21.7 | 21.8 | 21.6 | 21.4 |
| Geothermal | Bil. kWh. | 15.4 | 13.4 | 14.1 | 14.7 | 15.2 | 15.9 | 15.8 | 15.9 | 16.7 |
| Solar [10] | Bil. kWh. | 0.4 | 0.5 | 0.5 | 0.6 | 1.2 | 24.9 | 36.1 | 53.3 | 66.6 |
| Wind | Bil. kWh. | 2.8 | 3.2 | 5.6 | 17.8 | 94.7 | 190.7 | 227.0 | 254.3 | 275.0 |
| Other [11] | Bil. kWh. | 3.6 | 4.1 | 4.8 | 12.8 | 12.9 | 14.0 | 13.8 | 13.1 | 12.7 |
| Consumption of fuels for electricity generation: | | | | | | | | | | |
| Coal [3] | Mil. short tons | 792.5 | 860.6 | 994.9 | 1,041.4 | 979.7 | 739.6 | 677.4 | 663.9 | 635.8 |
| Petroleum, total [3] | Mil. bbl. | 218.8 | 132.6 | 195.2 | 206.8 | 65.1 | 49.1 | 43.7 | 39.1 | 43.8 |
| Distillate fuel oil [12] | Mil. bbl. | 18.1 | 19.6 | 31.7 | 20.7 | 14.1 | 12.4 | 9.7 | 9.7 | 13.0 |
| Residual fuel oil [13] | Mil. bbl. | 190.7 | 95.5 | 143.4 | 141.5 | 24.0 | 14.1 | 11.2 | 10.4 | 12.2 |
| Other liquids [14] | Mil. bbl. | 0.4 | 0.7 | 1.4 | 3.0 | 2.1 | 2.4 | 1.5 | 1.5 | 2.1 |
| Petroleum coke | Mil. short tons | 1.9 | 3.4 | 3.7 | 8.3 | 5.0 | 4.0 | 4.3 | 3.5 | 3.3 |
| Natural gas [5] | Bil. cu. ft. | 3,691.6 | 4,737.9 | 5,691.5 | 6,036.4 | 7,680.2 | 10,016.6 | 10,170.1 | 9,507.8 | 10,855.2 |
| Other gases [6] | Tril. Btu. | 111.8 | 132.5 | 126.0 | 109.9 | 90.1 | 106.0 | 73.8 | 70.7 | 69.4 |
| Biomass | Tril. Btu. | 653.5 | 795.6 | 825.9 | 585.3 | 630.3 | 719.6 | 665.1 | 668.3 | 652.6 |
| Wood [8] | Tril. Btu. | 442.3 | 479.9 | 495.8 | 355.3 | 349.5 | 406.7 | 360.0 | 364.0 | 351.2 |
| Waste [9] | Tril. Btu. | 211.2 | 315.7 | 330.1 | 230.1 | 280.8 | 313.0 | 305.1 | 304.3 | 301.4 |
| Other [11] | Tril. Btu. | 36.0 | 42.0 | 46.2 | 173.0 | 184.4 | 203.6 | 198.6 | 189.7 | 184.2 |

P Preliminary. [1] Commercial combined-heat-and-power (CHP) and commercial electricity-only plants. [2] Industrial CHP and industrial electricity-only plants. [3] Anthracite, bituminous coal, subbituminous coal, lignite, waste coal, and coal synfuel. [4] Distillate fuel oil, residual fuel oil, petroleum coke, jet fuel, kerosene, other petroleum, waste oil, and beginning in 2011, propane. [5] Includes a small amount of supplemental gaseous fuels that cannot be identified separately. [6] Blast furnace gas and other manufactured and waste gases derived from fossil fuels. Through 2010, also includes propane. [7] Pumped storage facility production minus energy used for pumping. [8] Wood and wood-derived fuels. [9] Municipal solid waste from non-biogenic sources, landfill gas, sludge waste, agricultural byproducts, and other biomass. Through 2000, also includes nonrenewable waste (municipal solid waste from biogenic sources and tire-derived fuels). [10] Solar thermal and photovoltaic energy. Does not include estimated distributed solar photovoltaic generation, which was 14,139 million kilowatthours in 2015, 18,812 million kilowatthours in 2016, 23,990 million kilowatthours in 2017, and 29,543 million kilowatthours in 2018. [11] Batteries, chemicals, hydrogen, pitch, purchased steam, sulfur, miscellaneous technologies, and beginning 2001, nonrenewable waste (municipal solid waste from nonbiogenic sources, and tire-derived fuels). [12] Fuel oil numbers 1, 2, and 4. For 1990 through 2000, electric utility data also include small amounts of kerosene and jet fuel. [13] Fuel oil numbers 5 and 6. For 1990 through 2000, electric utility data also include a small amount of fuel oil number 4. [14] Jet fuel, kerosene, other petroleum liquids, waste oil, and beginning in 2011, propane.

Source: U.S. Energy Information Administration, *Monthly Energy Review*, April 2019. See also <http://www.eia.gov/totalenergy/data/monthly>.

## Table 978. Total Electric Net Summer Capacity for All Sectors by Energy Source: 1990 to 2017

[In million kilowatts (734.1 represents 734,100,000). Data are at end of year. For plants that use multiple sources of energy, capacity is assigned to the predominant energy source]

| Source | 1990 | 1995 | 2000 | 2005 | 2010 | 2014 | 2015 | 2016 | 2017 |
|---|---|---|---|---|---|---|---|---|---|
| **Net summer capacity, total** | **734.1** | **769.5** | **811.7** | **978.0** | **1,039.1** | **1,068.4** | **1,064.1** | **1,074.3** | **1,084.4** |
| Fossil fuels, total | 527.8 | 554.2 | 598.9 | 757.1 | 782.2 | 774.3 | 758.5 | 750.3 | 748.2 |
| Coal [1] | 307.4 | 311.4 | 315.1 | 313.4 | 316.8 | 299.1 | 279.7 | 266.6 | 256.5 |
| Petroleum [2] | 77.9 | 66.6 | 61.8 | 58.5 | 55.6 | 41.1 | 36.8 | 34.4 | 33.3 |
| Natural gas [3] | 140.8 | 174.5 | 219.6 | 383.1 | 407.0 | 432.2 | 439.4 | 446.8 | 456.0 |
| Other gases [4] | 1.6 | 1.7 | 2.3 | 2.1 | 2.7 | 1.9 | 2.5 | 2.5 | 2.4 |
| Nuclear electric power | 99.6 | 99.5 | 97.9 | 100.0 | 101.2 | 98.6 | 98.7 | 99.6 | 99.6 |
| Hydroelectric pumped storage | 19.5 | 21.4 | 19.5 | 21.3 | 22.2 | 22.5 | 22.6 | 22.8 | 22.8 |
| Renewable energy, total | 86.8 | 93.9 | 94.9 | 98.7 | 132.6 | 177.6 | 192.3 | 212.5 | 227.0 |
| Conventional hydroelectric power | 73.9 | 78.6 | 79.4 | 77.5 | 78.8 | 79.7 | 79.7 | 79.9 | 79.8 |
| Biomass, total | 8.1 | 10.3 | 10.0 | 9.8 | 11.4 | 13.5 | 14.1 | 14.0 | 14.0 |
| Wood [5] | 5.5 | 6.7 | 6.1 | 6.2 | 7.0 | 8.4 | 9.0 | 8.9 | 8.8 |
| Waste [6] | 2.5 | 3.5 | 3.9 | 3.6 | 4.4 | 5.2 | 5.1 | 5.1 | 5.1 |
| Geothermal | 2.7 | 3.0 | 2.8 | 2.3 | 2.4 | 2.5 | 2.5 | 2.5 | 2.5 |
| Solar [7] | 0.3 | 0.3 | 0.4 | 0.4 | 0.9 | 17.6 | 23.4 | 34.7 | 43.1 |
| Wind | 1.8 | 1.7 | 2.4 | 8.7 | 39.1 | 64.2 | 72.6 | 81.3 | 87.6 |
| Other [8] | 0.5 | 0.5 | 0.5 | 0.9 | 0.9 | 2.8 | 1.8 | 2.0 | 2.9 |

[1] Coal includes anthracite, bituminous, subbituminous, lignite, and waste coal; coal synfuel and refined coal; and beginning in 2011, coal-derived synthesis gas. Prior to 2011, coal-derived synthesis gas was included in other gases. [2] Distillate fuel oil, residual fuel oil, petroleum coke, jet fuel, kerosene, other petroleum, waste oil, and beginning in 2011, synthetic gas and propane. Prior to 2011, synthetic gas and propane were included in other gases. [3] Includes a small amount of supplemental gaseous fuels that cannot be identified separately. [4] Blast furnace gas, propane gas, and other manufactured and waste gases derived from fossil fuels. [5] Wood and wood-derived fuels. [6] Municipal solid waste, landfill gas, sludge waste, agricultural byproducts, other biomass solids, other biomass liquids, and other biomass gases (including digester gases, methane, and other biomass gases). [7] Solar thermal and photovoltaic energy. [8] Batteries, hydrogen, purchased steam, sulfur, tire-derived fuels and other miscellaneous energy sources.

Source: U.S. Energy Information Administration, *Electric Power Annual 2017*, October 2018, and earlier reports. See also <http://www.eia.gov/electricity/annual/>.

## Table 979. Electricity—End Use and Average Retail Prices: 1990 to 2017

[2,837.1 represents 2,837,100,000,000. Beginning 2003, the category "other" has been replaced by "transportation," and the categories "commercial" and "industrial" have been redefined. Data represent revenue from electricity retail sales divided by the amount of retail electricity sold (in kilowatt-hours). Prices include state and local taxes, energy or demand charges, customer service charges, environmental surcharges, franchise fees, fuel adjustments, and other miscellaneous charges applied to end-use customers during normal billing operations. Prices do not include deferred charges, credits, or other adjustments, such as fuel or revenue from purchased power, from previous reporting periods. Data are for a census of electric utilities. Beginning in 2000, data also include energy service providers selling to retail customers]

| Item | 1990 | 1995 | 2000 | 2005 | 2010 | 2014 | 2015 | 2016 | 2017 |
|---|---|---|---|---|---|---|---|---|---|
| **END USE** (Billion kilowatt-hours) | | | | | | | | | |
| **Total end use [1]** | **2,837.1** | **3,164.0** | **3,592.4** | **3,811.0** | **3,886.8** | **3,903.3** | **3,900.2** | **3,902.3** | **3,864.9** |
| Direct use [2] | 124.5 | 150.7 | 170.9 | 150.0 | 131.9 | 138.6 | 141.2 | 139.8 | 141.1 |
| **Retail sales, total [3]** | **2,712.6** | **3,013.3** | **3,421.4** | **3,661.0** | **3,754.8** | **3,764.7** | **3,759.0** | **3,762.5** | **3,723.8** |
| Residential | 924.0 | 1,042.5 | 1,192.4 | 1,359.2 | 1,445.7 | 1,407.2 | 1,404.1 | 1,411.1 | 1,378.6 |
| Commercial [4] | 838.3 | 953.1 | 1,159.3 | 1,275.1 | 1,330.2 | 1,352.2 | 1,360.8 | 1,367.2 | 1,353.4 |
| Industrial [5] | 945.5 | 1,012.7 | 1,064.2 | 1,019.2 | 971.2 | 997.6 | 986.5 | 976.7 | 984.3 |
| Transportation [6] | 4.8 | 5.0 | 5.4 | 7.5 | 7.7 | 7.8 | 7.6 | 7.5 | 7.5 |
| **AVERAGE RETAIL PRICES** (Cents per kilowatt-hour) | | | | | | | | | |
| **Total** | **6.57** | **6.89** | **6.81** | **8.14** | **9.83** | **10.44** | **10.41** | **10.27** | **10.48** |
| Residential | 7.83 | 8.40 | 8.24 | 9.45 | 11.54 | 12.52 | 12.65 | 12.55 | 12.89 |
| Commercial [7] | 7.34 | 7.69 | 7.43 | 8.67 | 10.19 | 10.74 | 10.64 | 10.43 | 10.66 |
| Industrial [5] | 4.74 | 4.66 | 4.64 | 5.73 | 6.77 | 7.10 | 6.91 | 6.76 | 6.88 |
| Transportation [6] | (NA) | (NA) | (NA) | 8.57 | 10.56 | 10.45 | 10.09 | 9.63 | 9.68 |
| Other [8] | 6.40 | 6.88 | 6.56 | (NA) | (NA) | (NA) | (NA) | (NA) | (NA) |

NA Not available. [1] The sum of "total retail sales" and "direct use." [2] Use of electricity that is 1) self-generated, 2) produced by either the same entity that consumes the power or an affiliate, and 3) used in direct support of a service or industrial process located within the same facility or group of facilities that house the generating equipment. Direct use is exclusive of station use. [3] Electricity retail sales to ultimate customers reported by electric utilities and, beginning in 2000, other energy service providers. [4] Includes public street and highway lighting, interdepartmental sales, and other sales to public authorities. [5] Beginning 2003, includes agriculture and irrigation. [6] Includes sales to railroads and railways. [7] Beginning 2003, includes public street and highway lighting, interdepartmental sales, and other sales to public authorities. [8] Public street and highway lighting, interdepartmental sales, other sales to public authorities, agriculture and irrigation, and transportation including railroads and railways.

Source: U.S. Energy Information Administration, *Electric Power Annual 2017*, October 2018, and earlier reports. See also <http://www.eia.gov/electricity/>.

## Table 980. Electric Power Industry—Net Generation and Net Summer Capacity by State: 2010 to 2017

[4,125.1 represents 4,125,100,000,000. Capacity as of December 31. Covers utilities for public use]

| State | Net generation (billion kilowatt-hours) | | 2017 | | | | | | Net summer capacity (million kilowatts) | |
|---|---|---|---|---|---|---|---|---|---|---|
| | | | Total [1] (bil. kWh) | Percent from— | | | | | | |
| | 2010 | 2016 | | Petro-leum | Natural gas | Hydro-electric | Nuclear | Coal | 2016 | 2017 |
| United States | 4,125.1 | 4,076.7 | 4,034.3 | 0.5 | 32.1 | 7.4 | 20.0 | 29.9 | 1,074.3 | 1,084.4 |
| Alabama | 152.2 | 142.4 | 140.0 | (Z) | 37.9 | 6.6 | 30.5 | 22.5 | 29.1 | 29.7 |
| Alaska | 6.8 | 6.3 | 6.5 | 13.6 | 49.8 | 25.3 | – | 8.6 | 2.7 | 2.7 |
| Arizona | 111.8 | 108.8 | 105.9 | 0.1 | 28.0 | 6.5 | 30.6 | 29.7 | 28.5 | 28.6 |
| Arkansas | 61.0 | 60.4 | 60.8 | 0.1 | 28.5 | 4.8 | 20.9 | 43.3 | 14.7 | 14.6 |
| California | 204.1 | 197.0 | 206.1 | (Z) | 42.9 | 20.6 | 8.7 | 0.1 | 76.5 | 76.4 |
| Colorado | 50.7 | 54.4 | 53.8 | (Z) | 23.3 | 3.5 | – | 54.3 | 16.1 | 16.0 |
| Connecticut | 33.3 | 36.5 | 34.6 | 0.5 | 46.2 | 1.0 | 47.7 | 0.6 | 8.8 | 8.9 |
| Delaware | 5.6 | 8.7 | 7.5 | 0.3 | 89.7 | – | – | 4.8 | 3.4 | 3.4 |
| District of Columbia | 0.2 | 0.1 | 0.1 | – | 29.5 | – | – | – | (Z) | (Z) |
| Florida | 229.1 | 238.3 | 238.4 | 0.6 | 67.6 | 0.1 | 12.2 | 15.7 | 58.4 | 59.0 |
| Georgia | 137.6 | 133.4 | 127.5 | 0.2 | 41.4 | 1.9 | 26.4 | 25.5 | 37.1 | 36.9 |
| Hawaii | 10.8 | 9.9 | 9.8 | 67.6 | – | 0.7 | – | 14.0 | 2.6 | 2.7 |
| Idaho | 12.0 | 15.7 | 17.4 | (Z) | 17.7 | 61.3 | – | 0.1 | 5.1 | 5.2 |
| Illinois | 201.4 | 187.3 | 183.6 | (Z) | 8.2 | 0.1 | 52.9 | 31.6 | 44.8 | 45.1 |
| Indiana | 125.2 | 101.8 | 98.9 | 0.1 | 18.2 | 0.3 | – | 73.2 | 25.3 | 25.7 |
| Iowa | 57.5 | 54.4 | 57.9 | 0.3 | 7.9 | 1.8 | 9.0 | 43.8 | 17.0 | 17.7 |
| Kansas | 47.9 | 47.6 | 50.9 | 0.1 | 4.2 | 0.1 | 20.9 | 38.1 | 15.4 | 16.1 |
| Kentucky | 98.2 | 80.3 | 73.2 | 0.7 | 14.2 | 6.2 | – | 78.2 | 20.2 | 20.1 |
| Louisiana | 102.9 | 107.3 | 97.7 | 4.7 | 60.3 | 0.9 | 15.8 | 12.6 | 24.2 | 23.7 |
| Maine | 17.0 | 11.5 | 11.3 | 1.2 | 19.9 | 30.1 | – | 0.6 | 4.9 | 4.9 |
| Maryland | 43.6 | 37.2 | 34.1 | 0.3 | 19.7 | 5.8 | 44.3 | 25.0 | 12.3 | 13.1 |
| Massachusetts | 42.8 | 32.0 | 32.2 | 0.8 | 68.8 | 3.2 | 15.7 | 3.5 | 13.3 | 12.1 |
| Michigan | 111.6 | 112.1 | 112.3 | 1.0 | 23.3 | 1.5 | 28.8 | 37.4 | 29.1 | 29.6 |
| Minnesota | 53.7 | 59.5 | 58.7 | 0.1 | 11.4 | 2.1 | 23.7 | 38.8 | 16.0 | 16.6 |
| Mississippi | 54.5 | 62.9 | 59.7 | (Z) | 77.3 | – | 12.3 | 7.7 | 16.0 | 15.8 |
| Missouri | 92.3 | 78.6 | 84.6 | 0.1 | 6.2 | 1.4 | 9.8 | 79.8 | 21.7 | 21.8 |
| Montana | 29.8 | 27.8 | 28.2 | 1.6 | 1.5 | 38.8 | – | 49.1 | 6.2 | 6.2 |
| Nebraska | 36.6 | 36.5 | 35.4 | (Z) | 1.8 | 4.2 | 19.5 | 59.8 | 8.5 | 8.6 |
| Nevada | 35.1 | 39.8 | 38.2 | (Z) | 69.7 | 4.7 | – | 4.9 | 11.8 | 11.4 |
| New Hampshire | 22.2 | 19.3 | 17.4 | 0.6 | 20.5 | 8.1 | 57.3 | 1.6 | 4.4 | 4.4 |
| New Jersey | 65.7 | 77.6 | 75.6 | 0.2 | 49.8 | (Z) | 45.0 | 1.6 | 18.9 | 17.8 |
| New Mexico | 36.3 | 32.9 | 33.6 | 0.1 | 27.2 | 0.6 | – | 54.8 | 8.5 | 8.3 |
| New York | 137.0 | 134.4 | 128.1 | 0.5 | 36.9 | 23.5 | 32.9 | 0.6 | 40.1 | 40.1 |
| North Carolina | 128.7 | 130.8 | 128.5 | 0.2 | 30.0 | 3.0 | 33.0 | 26.8 | 32.3 | 33.0 |
| North Dakota | 34.7 | 37.9 | 41.5 | 0.1 | 1.6 | 6.2 | – | 64.5 | 8.0 | 8.2 |
| Ohio | 143.6 | 118.9 | 119.6 | 1.0 | 24.1 | 0.2 | 14.8 | 57.2 | 28.8 | 30.0 |
| Oklahoma | 72.3 | 78.7 | 73.7 | (Z) | 41.3 | 2.8 | – | 23.6 | 26.0 | 26.7 |
| Oregon | 55.1 | 60.2 | 62.7 | (Z) | 24.0 | 61.1 | – | 2.8 | 16.3 | 16.5 |
| Pennsylvania | 229.8 | 215.1 | 213.6 | 0.2 | 33.9 | 1.5 | 38.9 | 22.3 | 44.1 | 44.1 |
| Rhode Island | 7.7 | 6.6 | 7.6 | 0.8 | 94.4 | (Z) | – | – | 1.9 | 1.9 |
| South Carolina | 104.2 | 97.0 | 93.1 | 0.1 | 18.4 | 2.0 | 58.4 | 19.5 | 22.7 | 22.9 |
| South Dakota | 10.0 | 11.5 | 10.9 | (Z) | 6.0 | 48.1 | – | 18.9 | 4.4 | 4.1 |
| Tennessee | 82.3 | 79.3 | 79.0 | 0.2 | 13.0 | 11.0 | 40.3 | 35.1 | 21.4 | 21.0 |
| Texas | 411.7 | 454.0 | 452.8 | (Z) | 45.2 | 0.2 | 8.5 | 29.7 | 118.7 | 123.5 |
| Utah | 42.2 | 38.1 | 37.4 | 0.1 | 15.7 | 3.5 | – | 70.5 | 9.0 | 9.0 |
| Vermont | 6.6 | 1.9 | 2.1 | 0.3 | 0.1 | 59.8 | – | – | 0.7 | 0.7 |
| Virginia | 73.0 | 92.6 | 90.4 | 0.5 | 49.2 | 1.2 | 33.8 | 11.9 | 26.6 | 27.7 |
| Washington | 103.5 | 114.1 | 115.9 | (Z) | 9.4 | 70.9 | 7.0 | 4.7 | 31.0 | 31.0 |
| West Virginia | 80.8 | 75.9 | 73.4 | 0.2 | 2.1 | 2.3 | – | 93.2 | 15.3 | 14.9 |
| Wisconsin | 64.3 | 65.0 | 65.1 | 0.2 | 21.0 | 4.1 | 14.8 | 55.1 | 16.8 | 17.0 |
| Wyoming | 48.1 | 46.7 | 46.7 | 0.1 | 1.7 | 2.4 | – | 85.7 | 8.6 | 8.6 |

– Represents zero. Z Represents less than .05 percent of net electricity generation, or less than .05 million kilowatts summer capacity. [1] Includes other sources not shown separately.

Source: U.S. Energy Information Administration, *Electric Power Annual*, "Data Tables" and "Detailed State Data," <http://www.eia.gov/electricity/annual/>, accessed November 2018.

## Table 981. Electric Power Industry—Capability, Peak Load, and Capacity Margin: 1980 to 2016

[558,237 represents 558,237,000 kilowatts (kW). Excludes Alaska and Hawaii. Capability represents the maximum kilowatt output with all power sources available and with hydraulic equipment under actual water conditions, allowing for maintenance, emergency outages, and system operating requirements. Capacity margin is the difference between capability and peak load. Minus sign (-) indicates decrease]

| Year | Capability at the time of— Summer peak load (1,000 kW) Amount | Change from prior year | Winter peak load (1,000 kW) Amount | Change from prior year | Noncoincident peak load Summer (1,000 kW) | Winter (1,000 kW) | Capacity margin Summer Amount (1,000 kW) | Percent of capability | Winter Amount (1,000 kW) | Percent of capability |
|---|---|---|---|---|---|---|---|---|---|---|
| 1980 | 558,237 | 13,731 | 572,195 | 17,670 | 427,058 | 384,567 | 131,179 | 23.5 | 187,628 | 32.8 |
| 1985 | 621,597 | 17,357 | 636,475 | 14,350 | 460,503 | 423,660 | 161,094 | 25.9 | 212,815 | 33.4 |
| 1990 | 685,091 | 11,775 | 696,757 | 11,508 | 546,331 | 484,231 | 138,760 | 20.3 | 212,526 | 30.5 |
| 1991 | 690,915 | 5,824 | 703,212 | 6,455 | 551,418 | 485,761 | 139,497 | 20.2 | 217,451 | 30.9 |
| 1992 | 695,436 | 4,521 | 707,752 | 4,540 | 548,707 | 492,983 | 146,729 | 21.1 | 214,769 | 30.3 |
| 1993 | 694,250 | -1,186 | 711,957 | 4,205 | 575,356 | 521,733 | 118,894 | 17.1 | 190,224 | 26.7 |
| 1994 | 702,985 | 8,735 | 715,090 | 3,133 | 585,320 | 518,253 | 117,665 | 16.7 | 196,837 | 27.5 |
| 1995 | 714,222 | 11,237 | 727,679 | 12,589 | 620,249 | 544,684 | 93,973 | 13.2 | 182,995 | 25.1 |
| 1996 | 730,376 | 16,154 | 737,637 | 9,958 | 616,790 | 554,081 | 113,586 | 15.6 | 183,556 | 24.9 |
| 1997 | 737,855 | 7,479 | 736,666 | -971 | 637,677 | 529,874 | 100,178 | 13.6 | 206,792 | 28.1 |
| 1998 | 744,670 | 6,815 | 735,090 | -1,576 | 660,293 | 567,558 | 84,377 | 11.3 | 167,532 | 22.8 |
| 1999 | 765,744 | 21,074 | 748,271 | 13,181 | 682,122 | 570,915 | 83,622 | 10.9 | 177,356 | 23.7 |
| 2000 | 808,054 | 42,310 | 767,505 | 19,234 | 678,413 | 588,426 | 129,641 | 16.0 | 179,079 | 23.3 |
| 2001 | 788,990 | -19,064 | 806,598 | 39,093 | 687,812 | 576,312 | 101,178 | 12.8 | 230,286 | 28.6 |
| 2002 | 833,380 | 44,390 | 850,984 | 44,386 | 714,565 | 604,986 | 118,815 | 14.3 | 245,998 | 28.9 |
| 2003 | 856,131 | 22,751 | 882,120 | 31,136 | 709,375 | 593,874 | 146,756 | 17.1 | 288,246 | 32.7 |
| 2004 | 875,870 | 19,739 | 864,849 | -17,271 | 704,459 | 618,701 | 171,411 | 19.6 | 246,148 | 28.5 |
| 2005 | 882,125 | 6,255 | 878,110 | 13,261 | 758,876 | 626,365 | 123,249 | 14.0 | 251,745 | 28.7 |
| 2006 | 891,226 | 9,101 | 899,551 | 21,441 | 789,475 | 640,981 | 101,751 | 11.4 | 258,570 | 28.7 |
| 2007 | 914,397 | 23,171 | 913,650 | 14,099 | 782,227 | 637,905 | 132,170 | 14.5 | 275,745 | 30.2 |
| 2008 | 909,504 | -4,893 | 927,781 | 14,131 | 752,470 | 643,557 | 157,034 | 17.3 | 284,224 | 30.6 |
| 2009 | 916,449 | 6,945 | 920,002 | -7,779 | 725,958 | 668,818 | 190,491 | 20.8 | 251,184 | 27.3 |
| 2010 | 923,559 | 7,110 | 935,262 | 15,260 | 767,948 | 651,418 | 155,611 | 16.8 | 283,844 | 30.3 |
| 2011 | 892,426 | -31,133 | 893,206 | -42,056 | 782,469 | 648,190 | 109,957 | 12.3 | 245,016 | 27.4 |
| 2012 | 931,893 | 39,467 | 947,156 | 53,950 | 767,762 | 618,570 | 164,131 | 17.6 | 328,586 | 34.7 |
| 2013 | 944,515 | 12,622 | 956,984 | 9,828 | 758,953 | 686,202 | 185,562 | 19.6 | 270,782 | 28.3 |
| 2014 | 917,167 | -27,348 | 928,477 | -28,507 | 723,411 | 677,005 | 193,756 | 21.1 | 251,472 | 27.1 |
| 2015 | 916,439 | -728 | 920,599 | -7,878 | 741,056 | 636,387 | 175,383 | 19.1 | 284,212 | 30.9 |
| 2016 | 923,873 | 7,434 | 935,447 | 14,848 | 768,510 | 649,538 | 155,363 | 16.8 | 285,909 | 30.6 |

Source: Edison Electric Institute, Washington, DC, *Statistical Yearbook of the Electric Power Industry*, annual ©. See also <http://www.eei.org>.

## Table 982. Electric Energy Retail Sales by Class of Service and State: 2017

[In billions of kilowatt-hours (3,723.8 represents 3,723,800,000,000). Data include both bundled and unbundled consumers]

| State | Total [1] | Residential | Commercial | Industrial | State | Total [1] | Residential | Commercial | Industrial |
|---|---|---|---|---|---|---|---|---|---|
| **United States** | **3,723.8** | **1,378.6** | **1,353.4** | **984.3** | Missouri | 76.5 | 33.1 | 30.2 | 13.2 |
| Alabama | 86.2 | 30.2 | 22.7 | 33.3 | Montana | 14.7 | 5.2 | 5.0 | 4.5 |
| Alaska | 6.2 | 2.1 | 2.7 | 1.4 | Nebraska | 30.4 | 9.7 | 9.3 | 11.4 |
| Arizona | 77.6 | 34.3 | 29.7 | 13.7 | Nevada | 36.7 | 12.9 | 11.1 | 12.6 |
| Arkansas | 46.1 | 17.0 | 11.9 | 17.1 | New Hampshire | 10.8 | 4.4 | 4.4 | 2.0 |
| California | 257.3 | 90.1 | 117.7 | 48.6 | New Jersey | 73.4 | 27.8 | 38.0 | 7.3 |
| Colorado | 54.8 | 18.6 | 20.6 | 15.5 | New Mexico | 23.0 | 6.5 | 8.8 | 7.7 |
| Connecticut | 28.1 | 12.4 | 12.3 | 3.2 | New York | 145.0 | 49.1 | 75.3 | 17.8 |
| Delaware | 11.1 | 4.7 | 4.2 | 2.3 | North Carolina | 131.4 | 56.1 | 47.9 | 27.4 |
| District of Columbia | 10.9 | 2.4 | 8.0 | 0.2 | North Dakota | 20.1 | 4.8 | 6.5 | 8.8 |
| Florida | 233.2 | 121.5 | 95.0 | 16.6 | Ohio | 146.6 | 49.8 | 46.2 | 50.7 |
| Georgia | 133.5 | 54.8 | 46.3 | 32.3 | Oklahoma | 60.5 | 21.8 | 20.5 | 18.2 |
| Hawaii | 9.3 | 2.6 | 3.1 | 3.6 | Oregon | 50.0 | 20.1 | 16.6 | 13.4 |
| Idaho | 23.8 | 8.7 | 6.4 | 8.6 | Pennsylvania | 143.0 | 51.7 | 42.6 | 47.9 |
| Illinois | 137.2 | 43.7 | 50.0 | 43.0 | Rhode Island | 7.4 | 3.0 | 3.6 | 0.7 |
| Indiana | 99.0 | 31.6 | 23.7 | 43.7 | South Carolina | 78.1 | 29.2 | 21.8 | 27.1 |
| Iowa | 48.9 | 13.7 | 12.1 | 23.1 | South Dakota | 12.3 | 4.7 | 4.7 | 2.9 |
| Kansas | 40.3 | 13.0 | 15.7 | 11.5 | Tennessee | 97.2 | 39.3 | 33.7 | 24.2 |
| Kentucky | 72.6 | 24.9 | 19.3 | 28.5 | Texas | 401.9 | 144.2 | 137.5 | 120.0 |
| Louisiana | 91.2 | 29.5 | 24.5 | 37.2 | Utah | 30.6 | 9.5 | 11.7 | 9.3 |
| Maine | 11.2 | 4.6 | 3.9 | 2.7 | Vermont | 5.9 | 2.0 | 2.4 | 1.4 |
| Maryland | 59.3 | 26.1 | 28.9 | 3.8 | Virginia | 111.5 | 44.0 | 50.2 | 17.2 |
| Massachusetts | 52.5 | 19.3 | 26.0 | 6.9 | Washington | 91.9 | 37.3 | 29.8 | 24.9 |
| Michigan | 101.9 | 33.0 | 38.3 | 30.6 | West Virginia | 31.7 | 10.6 | 7.5 | 13.6 |
| Minnesota | 67.2 | 21.6 | 23.3 | 22.3 | Wisconsin | 69.1 | 21.2 | 23.6 | 24.2 |
| Mississippi | 47.8 | 17.4 | 14.3 | 16.1 | Wyoming | 16.8 | 2.8 | 3.8 | 10.2 |

[1] Includes transportation, not shown separately.

Source: U.S. Energy Information Administration, "Electric Sales, Revenue, and Average Price," <http://www.eia.gov/electricity/sales_revenue_price/index.cfm>, accessed November 2018.

## Table 983. Electric Energy Average Retail Price by Class of Service and State: 2017

[In cents per kilowatt-hour (kWh). Data include both bundled and unbundled consumers]

| State | Total [1] | Residential | Commercial | Industrial | State | Total [1] | Residential | Commercial | Industrial |
|---|---|---|---|---|---|---|---|---|---|
| **United States** | **10.48** | **12.89** | **10.66** | **6.88** | Missouri | 10.03 | 11.63 | 9.47 | 7.33 |
| Alabama | 9.83 | 12.55 | 11.60 | 6.16 | Montana | 8.92 | 10.95 | 10.12 | 5.25 |
| Alaska | 19.10 | 21.27 | 18.89 | 16.34 | Nebraska | 9.08 | 10.97 | 8.85 | 7.66 |
| Arizona | 10.64 | 12.44 | 10.50 | 6.45 | Nevada | 8.76 | 11.99 | 7.96 | 6.15 |
| Arkansas | 8.26 | 10.28 | 8.51 | 6.07 | New Hampshire | 16.17 | 19.20 | 14.81 | 12.34 |
| California | 16.06 | 18.31 | 15.76 | 12.73 | New Jersey | 13.32 | 15.65 | 12.28 | 10.12 |
| Colorado | 9.99 | 12.17 | 9.89 | 7.50 | New Mexico | 9.59 | 12.88 | 10.19 | 6.15 |
| Connecticut | 17.55 | 20.29 | 16.06 | 13.10 | New York | 14.74 | 18.03 | 14.75 | 5.92 |
| Delaware | 10.90 | 13.35 | 9.89 | 7.78 | North Carolina | 9.04 | 10.94 | 8.44 | 6.20 |
| District of Columbia | 11.80 | 12.94 | 11.66 | 8.23 | North Dakota | 8.78 | 10.29 | 9.19 | 7.63 |
| Florida | 10.42 | 11.61 | 9.35 | 7.83 | Ohio | 9.84 | 12.63 | 10.05 | 6.92 |
| Georgia | 9.83 | 11.90 | 10.09 | 5.96 | Oklahoma | 8.20 | 10.61 | 8.11 | 5.42 |
| Hawaii | 26.05 | 29.50 | 26.77 | 22.92 | Oregon | 8.81 | 10.66 | 8.86 | 5.98 |
| Idaho | 8.26 | 10.04 | 7.98 | 6.66 | Pennsylvania | 10.13 | 14.23 | 8.98 | 6.77 |
| Illinois | 9.49 | 12.95 | 9.09 | 6.47 | Rhode Island | 16.42 | 18.32 | 15.20 | 14.57 |
| Indiana | 9.77 | 12.29 | 10.54 | 7.54 | South Carolina | 9.97 | 13.02 | 10.57 | 6.19 |
| Iowa | 8.73 | 12.34 | 9.46 | 6.21 | South Dakota | 10.05 | 11.77 | 9.74 | 7.84 |
| Kansas | 10.60 | 13.31 | 10.59 | 7.54 | Tennessee | 9.45 | 10.72 | 10.55 | 5.83 |
| Kentucky | 8.57 | 10.85 | 9.85 | 5.72 | Texas | 8.38 | 11.01 | 8.26 | 5.35 |
| Louisiana | 7.79 | 9.74 | 8.95 | 5.48 | Utah | 8.60 | 10.95 | 8.64 | 6.13 |
| Maine | 13.02 | 15.97 | 12.12 | 9.20 | Vermont | 13.74 | 17.68 | 12.54 | 10.21 |
| Maryland | 11.98 | 13.96 | 10.75 | 8.37 | Virginia | 9.18 | 11.55 | 8.01 | 6.51 |
| Massachusetts | 17.12 | 20.06 | 15.93 | 13.88 | Washington | 7.94 | 9.66 | 8.57 | 4.60 |
| Michigan | 11.28 | 15.40 | 11.00 | 7.19 | West Virginia | 9.00 | 11.63 | 9.58 | 6.64 |
| Minnesota | 10.27 | 13.04 | 10.48 | 7.37 | Wisconsin | 10.76 | 14.35 | 10.87 | 7.49 |
| Mississippi | 9.09 | 11.08 | 10.17 | 5.99 | Wyoming | 8.28 | 11.37 | 9.70 | 6.92 |

[1] Includes transportation, not shown separately.

Source: U.S. Energy Information Administration, "Electric Sales, Revenue, and Average Price," <http://www.eia.gov/electricity/sales_revenue_price/index.cfm>, accessed November 2018.

## Table 984. Total Electric Power Industry—Generation, Sales, Revenue, and Customers: 1990 to 2017

[2,808 represents 2,808,000,000,000 Kilowatt hours (kWh). Sales and revenue are to and from ultimate customers. Commercial and Industrial are not wholly comparable on a year-to-year basis due to changes from one classification to another. Beginning 2003, the Energy Information Administration replaced the "Other" sector with the Transportation sector. The Transportation sector consists entirely of electrified rail and urban transit systems. Data previously reported in "Other" have been relocated to the Commercial sector, except for Agriculture (i.e., irrigation load), which have been relocated to the Industrial sector]

| Class | Unit | 1990 | 2000 | 2005 | 2010 | 2013 | 2014 | 2015 | 2016 | 2017 [1] |
|---|---|---|---|---|---|---|---|---|---|---|
| Generation [2] | Bil. kWh | 2,808 | 3,802 | 4,055 | 4,125 | 4,066 | 4,094 | 4,078 | 4,079 | 4,012 |
| Sales [3] | Bil. kWh | 2,713 | 3,421 | 3,661 | 3,755 | 3,752 | 3,792 | 3,759 | 3,762 | 3,723 |
| Residential or domestic | Bil. kWh | 924 | 1,192 | 1,359 | 1,446 | 1,395 | 1,407 | 1,404 | 1,411 | 1,379 |
| Percent of total | Percent | 34.1 | 34.9 | 37.1 | 38.5 | 37.2 | 37.1 | 37.4 | 37.5 | 37.0 |
| Commercial [4] | Bil. kWh | 751 | 1,055 | 1,275 | 1,330 | 1,337 | 1,352 | 1,361 | 1,367 | 1,353 |
| Industrial [5] | Bil. kWh | 946 | 1,064 | 1,019 | 971 | 985 | 998 | 987 | 977 | 984 |
| Revenue [3] | Bil. dol. | 178.2 | 233.2 | 298.0 | 368.9 | 375.1 | 396.3 | 391.3 | 386.5 | 390.3 |
| Residential or domestic | Bil. dol. | 72.4 | 98.2 | 128.4 | 166.8 | 169.1 | 176.2 | 177.6 | 177.1 | 177.7 |
| Percent of total | Percent | 40.6 | 42.1 | 43.1 | 45.2 | 45.1 | 44.5 | 45.4 | 45.8 | 45.5 |
| Commercial [4] | Bil. dol. | 55.1 | 78.4 | 110.5 | 135.6 | 137.2 | 145.3 | 144.8 | 142.6 | 144.2 |
| Industrial [5] | Bil. dol. | 44.9 | 49.4 | 58.5 | 65.8 | 67.9 | 70.9 | 68.2 | 66.1 | 67.7 |
| Ultimate customers [3] | Million | 110.6 | 127.6 | 138.4 | 144.1 | 146.3 | 147.4 | 148.6 | 150.1 | 151.8 |
| Residential or domestic | Million | 97.1 | 111.7 | 120.8 | 125.7 | 127.8 | 128.7 | 129.8 | 131.1 | 132.6 |
| Commercial [4] | Million | 12.1 | 14.3 | 16.9 | 17.7 | 17.7 | 17.9 | 18.0 | 18.1 | 18.4 |
| Industrial [5] | Million | 0.5 | 0.5 | 0.7 | 0.7 | 0.8 | 0.9 | 0.8 | 0.8 | 0.8 |
| Avg. kWh used per customer | 1,000 | 24.5 | 26.8 | 26.5 | 26.1 | 25.5 | 25.5 | 25.2 | 25.1 | 24.1 |
| Residential | 1,000 | 9.5 | 10.7 | 11.3 | 11.5 | 10.9 | 10.9 | 10.8 | 10.8 | 10.3 |
| Commercial [4] | 1,000 | 62.2 | 73.5 | 75.4 | 75.1 | 75.6 | 75.7 | 75.2 | 75.3 | 73.3 |
| Avg. annual bill per customer | Dollar | 1,612 | 1,828 | 2,153 | 2,560 | 2,556 | 2,660 | 2,628 | 2,576 | 2,545 |
| Residential | Dollar | 745 | 879 | 1,063 | 1,327 | 1,321 | 1,366 | 1,367 | 1,351 | 1,334 |
| Commercial [4] | Dollar | 4,562 | 5,464 | 6,538 | 7,661 | 7,732 | 8,092 | 8,008 | 7,860 | 7,827 |
| Avg. revenue per kWh sold | Cents | 6.6 | 6.8 | 8.1 | 9.8 | 10.1 | 10.4 | 10.4 | 10.3 | 10.5 |
| Residential | Cents | 7.8 | 8.2 | 9.4 | 11.5 | 12.1 | 12.5 | 12.7 | 12.6 | 12.9 |
| Commercial [4] | Cents | 7.3 | 7.4 | 8.7 | 10.2 | 10.3 | 10.7 | 10.6 | 10.4 | 10.7 |
| Industrial [5] | Cents | 4.7 | 4.6 | 5.7 | 6.8 | 6.9 | 7.1 | 6.9 | 6.8 | 6.9 |

[1] Preliminary. [2] Includes batteries, chemicals, hydrogen, pitch, sulfur, purchased steam, and miscellaneous technologies, which are not separately displayed. [3] Includes other types, not shown separately. Data for 1990 are as of December 31; beginning 2000, data are yearly averages. [4] Small light and power. [5] Large light and power.

Source: Edison Electric Institute, Washington, DC, *Statistical Yearbook of the Electric Power Industry*, annual ©. See also <http://www.eei.org>.

## Table 985. Revenue and Expense Statistics for Major U.S. Investor-Owned Electric Utilities: 1995 to 2017

[In millions of dollars (199,967 represents $199,967,000,000). Covers investor-owned electric utilities that met any one or more of the following conditions, during each of the last 3 years: 1 million megawatt-hours of total sales, 100 megawatt-hours of annual sales for resale, 500 megawatt-hours of annual power exchange delivered, or 500 megawatt-hours of annual wheeling for others. Missing or erroneous respondent data may result in slight imbalances in some of the expense account subtotals]

| Item | 1995 | 2000 | 2005 | 2010 | 2014 | 2015 | 2016 | 2017 |
|---|---|---|---|---|---|---|---|---|
| **Utility operating revenues**.......... | **199,967** | **233,915** | **265,652** | **285,512** | **298,430** | **282,695** | **282,499** | **286,501** |
| Electric utility........................... | 183,655 | 213,634 | 234,909 | 260,119 | 271,832 | 260,121 | 261,047 | 263,265 |
| Other utility............................. | 16,312 | 20,281 | 30,743 | 25,393 | 26,598 | 22,574 | 21,451 | 23,235 |
| **Utility operating expenses**.......... | **165,321** | **210,250** | **236,786** | **253,022** | **258,936** | **242,728** | **239,037** | **240,041** |
| Electric utility........................... | 150,599 | 191,564 | 207,830 | 234,173 | 240,643 | 228,366 | 226,457 | 226,110 |
| Operation................................ | 91,881 | 132,607 | 150,645 | 166,922 | 165,989 | 149,939 | 145,077 | 142,000 |
| Production............................. | 68,983 | 107,554 | 120,586 | 128,831 | 123,366 | 107,201 | 100,852 | 98,859 |
| Cost of fuel......................... | 29,122 | 32,407 | 36,106 | 44,138 | 42,545 | 34,711 | 32,621 | 32,165 |
| Purchased power.................. | 29,981 | 62,608 | 77,902 | 67,284 | 62,066 | 52,970 | 49,962 | 49,030 |
| Other................................. | 9,880 | 12,561 | 6,599 | 17,409 | 18,755 | 19,521 | 18,269 | 17,664 |
| Transmission........................ | 1,425 | 2,713 | 5,664 | 6,948 | 8,902 | 9,624 | 10,447 | 10,804 |
| Distribution.......................... | 2,561 | 3,092 | 3,502 | 4,007 | 4,331 | 4,406 | 4,734 | 4,358 |
| Customer accounts................. | 3,613 | 4,239 | 4,229 | 5,091 | 5,255 | 5,184 | 5,077 | 4,789 |
| Customer service................... | 1,922 | 1,826 | 2,291 | 4,741 | 6,396 | 6,445 | 6,187 | 5,961 |
| Sales.................................. | 348 | 405 | 219 | 185 | 208 | 201 | 205 | 213 |
| Administrative and general........ | 13,028 | 12,768 | 14,130 | 17,120 | 17,532 | 16,878 | 17,575 | 17,016 |
| Maintenance............................ | 11,767 | 12,064 | 12,033 | 14,957 | 16,801 | 16,392 | 16,982 | 17,996 |
| Depreciation............................ | 19,885 | 20,636 | 17,123 | 20,951 | 25,919 | 26,847 | 30,097 | 30,323 |
| Taxes and other....................... | 27,065 | 24,479 | 26,805 | 31,343 | 31,934 | 35,188 | 34,301 | 35,791 |
| Other utility.............................. | 14,722 | 18,686 | 28,956 | 18,849 | 18,293 | 14,362 | 12,579 | 13,931 |
| **Net utility operating income**........ | **34,646** | **23,665** | **28,866** | **32,490** | **39,494** | **39,968** | **43,462** | **46,460** |

Source: U.S. Energy Information Administration, *Electric Power Annual 2017*, October 2018, and earlier reports. See also <http://www.eia.gov/electricity/annual/>.

## Table 986. Renewable Energy Net Generation of Electricity by Source and State: 2018

[In millions of kilowatt-hours (291,724 represents 291,724,000,000). Data based on results from the Energy Information Agency's annual survey form EIA-923. For more on net generation, see Table 980]

| State | Hydro-electric | Other renewable Total [1] | Wind | Bio-mass [2] | Solar | State | Hydro-electric | Other renewable Total [1] | Wind | Bio-mass [2] | Solar |
|---|---|---|---|---|---|---|---|---|---|---|---|
| **U.S.**...... | **291,724** | **450,592** | **274,952** | **62,765** | **96,147** | MO........ | 1,399 | 3,438 | 2,941 | 155 | 342 |
| AL........ | 11,058 | 3,837 | (NA) | 3,440 | 397 | MT........ | 10,729 | 2,260 | 2,181 | 21 | 58 |
| AK........ | 1,630 | 194 | 147 | 44 | 3 | NE........ | 1,482 | 5,313 | 5,178 | 93 | 42 |
| AZ........ | 6,950 | 8,246 | 586 | 183 | 7,477 | NV........ | 1,888 | 9,211 | 368 | 69 | 5,144 |
| AR........ | 3,536 | 1,681 | (NA) | 1,454 | 227 | NH........ | 1,641 | 2,100 | 434 | 1,558 | 108 |
| CA........ | 25,898 | 71,450 | 13,650 | 5,770 | 39,907 | NJ........ | 36 | 4,199 | 23 | 957 | 3,219 |
| CO........ | 1,922 | 11,660 | 9,819 | 167 | 1,674 | NM........ | 193 | 7,754 | 6,168 | 20 | 1,550 |
| CT........ | 395 | 1,338 | 13 | 714 | 611 | NY........ | 30,911 | 8,581 | 4,383 | 2,299 | 1,899 |
| DE........ | (NA) | 241 | 5 | 63 | 173 | NC........ | 5,001 | 10,412 | 543 | 2,660 | 7,209 |
| DC........ | (NA) | 128 | (NA) | 57 | 71 | ND........ | 2,523 | 10,768 | 10,764 | 4 | – |
| FL........ | 239 | 8,015 | (NA) | 5,111 | 2,904 | OH........ | 565 | 2,761 | 1,772 | 687 | 302 |
| GA........ | 2,878 | 7,418 | (NA) | 4,979 | 2,439 | OK........ | 2,392 | 27,997 | 27,593 | 327 | 77 |
| HI......... | 103 | 2,410 | 543 | 307 | 1,238 | OR........ | 36,729 | 9,155 | 7,137 | 1,029 | 801 |
| ID........ | 10,486 | 3,730 | 2,561 | 514 | 576 | PA........ | 3,530 | 6,470 | 3,615 | 2,345 | 510 |
| IL........ | 144 | 13,420 | 12,812 | 453 | 155 | RI........ | 4 | 509 | 163 | 211 | 135 |
| IN........ | 342 | 6,549 | 5,597 | 472 | 480 | SC........ | 2,555 | 3,441 | (NA) | 2,583 | 858 |
| IA........ | 999 | 22,049 | 21,685 | 218 | 146 | SD........ | 5,165 | 2,769 | 2,766 | – | 3 |
| KS........ | 26 | 19,390 | 19,295 | 59 | 36 | TN........ | 9,685 | 1,281 | 52 | 974 | 255 |
| KY........ | 4,723 | 575 | (NA) | 490 | 85 | TX........ | 1,433 | 81,386 | 75,753 | 1,570 | 4,063 |
| LA........ | 959 | 2,955 | (NA) | 2,726 | 229 | UT........ | 1,273 | 3,980 | 855 | 81 | 2,575 |
| ME........ | 3,600 | 5,007 | 2,412 | 2,527 | 68 | VT........ | 1,392 | 1,087 | 393 | 421 | 273 |
| MD........ | 2,829 | 2,381 | 550 | 533 | 1,298 | VA........ | 1,450 | 5,134 | (NA) | 4,153 | 981 |
| MA........ | 1,135 | 4,629 | 238 | 1,197 | 3,194 | WA........ | 81,576 | 9,309 | 7,356 | 1,798 | 155 |
| MI........ | 1,634 | 8,089 | 5,330 | 2,518 | 241 | WV........ | 1,788 | 1,789 | 1,779 | (NA) | 10 |
| MN........ | 1,206 | 14,496 | 11,346 | 1,765 | 1,385 | WI........ | 2,583 | 3,598 | 1,959 | 1,517 | 122 |
| MS........ | (NA) | 1,808 | (NA) | 1,467 | 341 | WY........ | 1,109 | 4,194 | 4,187 | (NA) | 7 |

– Represents or rounds to zero. NA Not available. [1] Includes generation from geothermal energy, not shown separately. [2] Includes wood and wood derived fuels, landfill gas, biogenic municipal solid waste, and other biomass waste.

Source: Energy Information Administration, "Electricity Data Browser," <http://www.eia.gov/electricity/data/browser/>, accessed April 2019.

## Table 987. Major Power Outages by Type of Disturbance and Duration: 2018

[Data shown for power outages lasting longer than 46 hours]

| Type of disturbance | Month | Area affected | Duration | Number of customers affected [1] |
|---|---|---|---|---|
| Fuel supply deficiency...... | January | Niagara County, New York | 982 Hours, 0 Minutes | (NA) |
| Natural disaster/transmission interruption........ | November | Butte County, California | 489 Hours, 16 Minutes | 11,844 |
| Severe weather............. | October | Florida | 206 Hours, 0 Minutes | 55,000 |
| Severe weather............. | September | North Carolina, South Carolina | 166 Hours, 4 Minutes | 1,457,583 |
| Severe weather............. | September | North Carolina | 140 Hours, 30 Minutes | 325,000 |
| Severe weather............. | March | Atlantic, Camden, Cape May, Gloucester, Salem, Cumberland, and Burlington Counties, New Jersey | 107 Hours, 30 Minutes | 124,000 |
| Fuel supply deficiency...... | November | Wisconsin | 93 Hours, 58 Minutes | – |
| Severe weather............. | March | Delaware, Maryland | 90 Hours, 0 Minutes | 60,000 |
| Severe weather............. | March | Ohio | 85 Hours, 47 Minutes | 249,322 |
| Severe weather............. | November | Tennessee | 76 Hours, 16 Minutes | 61,000 |
| Severe weather............. | January | Texas | 73 Hours, 28 Minutes | (NA) |
| Severe weather............. | April | Michigan | 72 Hours, 0 Minutes | 389,591 |
| Severe weather............. | March | Connecticut, Massachusetts, Rhode Island | 71 Hours, 27 Minutes | 325,000 |
| Severe weather............. | November | Will, DuPage, Kane, McHenry, Winnebago, Ogle, DeKalb, Lee, Grundy, Lake, Cook, Livingston, Stephenson, LaSalle, Kankakee, Kendall and Boone Counties, Illinois | 69 Hours, 47 Minutes | 313,448 |
| Severe weather............. | March | Wayne County, Washtenaw County, Oakland County, Macomb County, Monroe County, Michigan | 69 Hours, 40 Minutes | 95,000 |
| Severe weather............. | May | Connecticut, Massachusetts, Rhode Island | 69 Hours, 22 Minutes | 120,000 |
| Severe weather............. | March | Connecticut, Massachusetts, Maine, New Hampshire, Rhode Island, Vermont | 68 Hours, 58 Minutes | 102,000 |
| Severe weather............. | March | New Jersey | 67 Hours, 22 Minutes | 216,800 |
| Severe weather............. | September | Horry, Chesterfield, Dillon, Georgetown, Marlboro, and Darlington Counties, South Carolina | 62 Hours, 55 Minutes | 50,100 |
| Severe weather............. | April | New York | 61 Hours, 40 Minutes | 72,896 |
| Severe weather............. | June | Missouri, Illinois | 60 Hours, 24 Minutes | 112,000 |
| Severe weather............. | March | Pennsylvania | 60 Hours, 0 Minutes | 630,000 |
| Severe weather............. | September | North Carolina, South Carolina | 59 Hours, 40 Minutes | 50,000 |
| Severe weather............. | December | King, Kitsap, Island, Pierce, Thurston, Whatcom, Skagit, and Kittitas Counties, Washington | 58 Hours, 0 Minutes | 150,000 |
| Severe weather............. | March | New York County, Westchester County, New York | 52 Hours, 0 Minutes | 72,353 |
| Severe weather............. | November | Virginia, West Virginia | 50 Hours, 22 Minutes | 50,600 |
| Severe weather............. | May | Michigan | 49 Hours, 0 Minutes | 300,000 |
| Severe weather............. | March | Pennsylvania | 46 Hours, 20 Minutes | 233,136 |
| System operations.......... | January | Shelby County, Tennessee | 46 Hours, 0 Minutes | (NA) |
| Severe weather............. | January | Tennessee | 46 Hours, 0 Minutes | (NA) |

NA Not available. – Rounds to or equals zero. [1] Number of customers affected are preliminary estimates.

Source: U.S. Energy Information Administration, *Electric Power Monthly*, March 2019. See also <http://www.eia.gov/electricity/monthly/>.

## Table 988. Gas Utility Industry—Summary: 1990 to 2017

[54,261 represents 54,261,000. Covers natural, manufactured, mixed, and liquid petroleum gas. Based on a questionnaire mailed to all privately and municipally owned gas utilities in the United States, except those with annual revenues less than $25,000]

| Item | Unit | 1990 | 1995 | 2000 | 2005 | 2010 | 2015 | 2016 | 2017 |
|---|---|---|---|---|---|---|---|---|---|
| **End users** [1] ........................ | 1,000 | **54,261** | **58,728** | **61,262** | **64,395** | **64,960** | **65,612** | **66,205** | **66,844** |
| Residential.......................... | 1,000 | 49,802 | 53,955 | 56,494 | 59,569 | 60,246 | 60,922 | 61,496 | 62,133 |
| Commercial.......................... | 1,000 | 4,246 | 4,530 | 4,610 | 4,678 | 4,582 | 4,559 | 4,579 | 4,581 |
| Industrial............................ | 1,000 | 166 | 181 | 157 | 145 | 129 | 120 | 120 | 119 |
| Other................................ | 1,000 | 48 | 61 | 2 | 2 | 3 | 10 | 10 | 11 |
| **Sales** [2] .............................. | Tril. Btu [3] | **9,842** | **9,221** | **9,232** | **8,848** | **7,980** | **7,602** | **7,382** | **7,473** |
| Residential.......................... | Tril. Btu | 4,468 | 4,803 | 4,741 | 4,516 | 4,371 | 4,080 | 3,875 | 3,944 |
| Percent of total................... | Percent | 45.4 | 52.1 | 51.4 | 51.0 | 54.8 | 53.7 | 52.5 | 52.8 |
| Commercial.......................... | Tril. Btu | 2,192 | 2,281 | 2,077 | 2,056 | 1,842 | 1,766 | 1,693 | 1,747 |
| Industrial............................ | Tril. Btu | 3,010 | 1,919 | 1,698 | 1,654 | 1,209 | 1,172 | 1,178 | 1,194 |
| Other................................ | Tril. Btu | 171 | 218 | 715 | 622 | 558 | 584 | 636 | 589 |
| **Revenues** [2] .......................... | Mil. dol. | **45,153** | **46,436** | **59,243** | **96,909** | **72,886** | **60,923** | **55,449** | **61,869** |
| Residential.......................... | Mil. dol. | 25,000 | 28,742 | 35,828 | 55,680 | 47,231 | 40,451 | 37,128 | 41,046 |
| Percent of total................... | Percent | 55.4 | 61.9 | 60.5 | 57.5 | 64.8 | 66.4 | 67.0 | 66.3 |
| Commercial.......................... | Mil. dol. | 10,604 | 11,573 | 13,339 | 22,653 | 16,578 | 14,057 | 12,440 | 13,909 |
| Industrial............................ | Mil. dol. | 8,996 | 5,571 | 7,432 | 13,751 | 6,437 | 4,434 | 4,003 | 4,725 |
| Other................................ | Mil. dol. | 553 | 549 | 2,645 | 4,825 | 2,640 | 1,982 | 1,878 | 2,189 |
| **Prices per mil. Btu** [3] .............. | Dollars | **4.59** | **5.05** | **6.42** | **10.95** | **9.13** | **7.99** | **7.51** | **8.28** |
| Residential.......................... | Dollars | 5.60 | 6.00 | 7.56 | 12.33 | 10.81 | 9.91 | 9.58 | 10.41 |
| Commercial.......................... | Dollars | 4.84 | 5.07 | 6.42 | 11.02 | 9.00 | 7.96 | 7.35 | 7.96 |
| Industrial............................ | Dollars | 2.99 | 2.98 | 4.38 | 8.31 | 5.32 | 3.78 | 3.40 | 3.96 |
| **Gas mains mileage**............... | 1,000 | **1,189** | **1,278** | **1,369** | **1,438** | **1,531** | **1,594** | **1,604** | **1,615** |
| Field and gathering................. | 1,000 | 32 | 31 | 27 | 23 | 19 | 18 | 18 | 18 |
| Transmission........................ | 1,000 | 292 | 297 | 297 | 297 | 308 | 301 | 300 | 301 |
| Distribution......................... | 1,000 | 865 | 950 | 1,046 | 1,118 | 1,204 | 1,276 | 1,286 | 1,296 |
| **Construction expenditures**....... | Mil. dol. | **7,899** | **10,760** | **8,624** | **10,089** | **11,042** | **21,074** | **25,124** | **27,593** |
| Transmission........................ | Mil. dol. | 2,886 | 3,380 | 1,590 | 3,368 | 3,524 | 6,578 | 7,559 | 9,161 |
| Distribution......................... | Mil. dol. | 3,714 | 5,394 | 5,437 | 5,129 | 5,674 | 11,614 | 13,432 | 14,878 |
| Production and storage............ | Mil. dol. | 309 | 367 | 138 | 179 | 151 | 135 | 337 | 467 |
| General.............................. | Mil. dol. | 770 | 1,441 | 1,273 | 1,070 | 1,185 | 1,928 | 3,187 | 2,102 |
| Underground storage.............. | Mil. dol. | 219 | 177 | 185 | 343 | 509 | 819 | 607 | 984 |

[1] Annual average. [2] Excludes sales for resale. [3] For definition of Btu (British thermal unit), see text, this section.

Source: American Gas Association, Washington, DC, *Annual Statistics* ©. See also <http://www.aga.org>.

## Table 989. Gas Utility Industry—Customers, Sales, and Revenues by State: 2017

[66,844 represents 66,844,000. See headnote, Table 988. For definition of Btu, see text, this section]

| State | Customers[1] (1,000) Total | Resi-dential | Sales[2] (tril. Btu) Total | Resi-dential | Revenues[2] (mil. dol.) Total | Resi-dential | State | Customers[1] (1,000) Total | Resi-dential | Sales[2] (tril. Btu) Total | Resi-dential | Revenues[2] (mil. dol.) Total | Resi-dential |
|---|---|---|---|---|---|---|---|---|---|---|---|---|---|
| U.S.... | 66,844 | 62,133 | 7,473 | 3,944 | 61,869 | 41,046 | MO...... | 1,524 | 1,387 | 144 | 90 | 1,435 | 1,023 |
| AL........ | 850 | 779 | 99 | 27 | 854 | 426 | MT....... | 310 | 274 | 35 | 22 | 251 | 163 |
| AK........ | 146 | 132 | 62 | 21 | 532 | 213 | NE....... | 509 | 466 | 55 | 31 | 402 | 269 |
| AZ........ | 1,292 | 1,235 | 65 | 34 | 783 | 518 | NV....... | 899 | 855 | 66 | 42 | 489 | 361 |
| AR........ | 623 | 554 | 46 | 27 | 486 | 333 | NH....... | 121 | 106 | 13 | 8 | 168 | 107 |
| CA........ | 11,034 | 10,604 | 610 | 425 | 6,602 | 5,121 | NJ....... | 2,837 | 2,638 | 296 | 217 | 2,568 | 1,918 |
| CO...... | 1,914 | 1,759 | 193 | 123 | 1,398 | 958 | NM...... | 635 | 587 | 46 | 31 | 370 | 277 |
| CT........ | 608 | 548 | 103 | 48 | 1,108 | 649 | NY....... | 4,042 | 3,760 | 449 | 328 | 4,771 | 3,806 |
| DE........ | 186 | 172 | 17 | 10 | 184 | 127 | NC....... | 1,382 | 1,256 | 121 | 62 | 1,273 | 796 |
| DC........ | 142 | 135 | 12 | 9 | 145 | 110 | ND....... | 168 | 145 | 36 | 11 | 192 | 84 |
| FL........ | 761 | 722 | 47 | 14 | 556 | 288 | OH...... | 636 | 603 | 63 | 48 | 574 | 449 |
| GA...... | 354 | 320 | 64 | 14 | 472 | 187 | OK...... | 1,035 | 943 | 84 | 53 | 764 | 582 |
| HI........ | 32 | 29 | 3 | 1 | 91 | 22 | OR...... | 824 | 740 | 90 | 50 | 818 | 507 |
| ID........ | 433 | 391 | 47 | 30 | 326 | 220 | PA....... | 2,615 | 2,434 | 258 | 199 | 2,708 | 2,186 |
| IL........ | 3,818 | 3,570 | 433 | 340 | 3,559 | 2,893 | RI........ | 263 | 241 | 26 | 19 | 329 | 258 |
| IN........ | 1,817 | 1,670 | 181 | 123 | 1,474 | 1,061 | SC....... | 711 | 652 | 151 | 25 | 960 | 358 |
| IA........ | 1,023 | 923 | 129 | 63 | 916 | 561 | SD....... | 213 | 188 | 24 | 13 | 164 | 99 |
| KS........ | 951 | 868 | 83 | 56 | 793 | 596 | TN....... | 1,287 | 1,151 | 137 | 59 | 1,123 | 584 |
| KY........ | 836 | 752 | 90 | 43 | 810 | 488 | TX....... | 4,958 | 4,633 | 1,269 | 170 | 6,235 | 2,229 |
| LA........ | 963 | 903 | 94 | 30 | 723 | 379 | UT....... | 964 | 927 | 102 | 69 | 839 | 604 |
| ME...... | 45 | 34 | 10 | 3 | 113 | 40 | VT....... | 51 | 45 | 12 | 4 | 104 | 50 |
| MD...... | 964 | 910 | 79 | 59 | 937 | 736 | VA....... | 1,239 | 1,149 | 118 | 72 | 1,181 | 855 |
| MA...... | 1,614 | 1,485 | 241 | 123 | 2,389 | 1,586 | WA...... | 1,281 | 1,174 | 154 | 94 | 1,439 | 967 |
| MI........ | 3,319 | 3,085 | 397 | 290 | 3,054 | 2,342 | WV...... | 370 | 336 | 37 | 23 | 304 | 211 |
| MN....... | 1,665 | 1,524 | 251 | 128 | 1,796 | 1,049 | WI....... | 1,932 | 1,758 | 257 | 136 | 1,750 | 1,100 |
| MS........ | 517 | 464 | 57 | 19 | 422 | 218 | WY...... | 132 | 118 | 18 | 9 | 134 | 81 |

[1] Averages for the year. [2] Excludes sales for resale.

Source: American Gas Association, Washington, DC, *Annual Statistics* ©. See also <http://www.aga.org>.

## Table 990. Privately Owned Gas Utility Industry—Balance Sheet and Income Account: 1990 to 2017

[In millions of dollars (121,686 represents $121,686,000,000). The gas utility industry consists of pipeline and distribution companies. Excludes operations of companies distributing gas in bottles or tanks]

| Item | 1990 | 1995 | 2000 | 2005 | 2010 | 2014 | 2015 | 2016 | 2017 |
|---|---|---|---|---|---|---|---|---|---|
| COMPOSITE BALANCE SHEET | | | | | | | | | |
| **Assets, total**........................ | **121,686** | **141,965** | **165,709** | **196,215** | **220,860** | **255,928** | **262,805** | **286,565** | **300,631** |
| Total utility plant........................ | 112,863 | 143,636 | 162,206 | 207,976 | 239,718 | 276,999 | 292,252 | 315,710 | 335,599 |
| Depreciation and amortization........ | 49,483 | 62,723 | 69,366 | 91,794 | 92,012 | 99,388 | 104,615 | 109,089 | 112,416 |
| Utility plant (net)........................ | 63,380 | 80,912 | 92,839 | 116,183 | 147,707 | 177,611 | 187,637 | 206,621 | 223,183 |
| Investment and fund accounts........ | 23,872 | 26,489 | 10,846 | 16,331 | 7,132 | 14,518 | 12,202 | 10,028 | 10,854 |
| Current and accrued assets.......... | 23,268 | 18,564 | 35,691 | 32,325 | 27,288 | 23,319 | 21,309 | 22,218 | 23,677 |
| Deferred debits [1]...................... | 9,576 | 13,923 | 24,279 | 29,574 | 37,307 | 38,930 | 40,253 | 46,355 | 41,240 |
| **Liabilities, total**.................... | **121,686** | **141,965** | **165,709** | **196,215** | **220,860** | **255,928** | **262,805** | **286,565** | **300,631** |
| Capitalization, total.................... | 74,958 | 90,581 | 96,079 | 120,949 | 133,414 | 153,555 | 157,916 | 172,911 | 199,086 |
| Capital stock.......................... | 43,810 | 54,402 | 47,051 | 62,470 | 74,157 | 86,458 | 87,760 | 96,933 | 111,722 |
| Long-term debts...................... | 31,148 | 35,548 | 48,267 | 58,264 | 59,223 | 67,894 | 70,194 | 75,826 | 86,862 |
| Current and accrued liabilities........ | 29,550 | 28,272 | 42,312 | 34,936 | 28,564 | 26,615 | 26,408 | 28,075 | 36,216 |
| Deferred income taxes [2]............ | 11,360 | 14,393 | 17,157 | 24,937 | 34,401 | 39,598 | 43,688 | 50,644 | 39,708 |
| Other liabilities and credits........... | 5,818 | 8,715 | 10,161 | 15,393 | 24,515 | 36,161 | 34,793 | 34,935 | 25,621 |
| COMPOSITE INCOME ACCOUNT | | | | | | | | | |
| **Operating revenues, total**........ | **66,027** | **58,390** | **72,042** | **102,018** | **82,315** | **77,774** | **72,298** | **69,605** | **74,040** |
| Minus: Operating expenses [3]......... | 60,137 | 50,760 | 64,988 | 89,385 | 71,761 | 66,990 | 61,229 | 57,227 | 61,058 |
| Operation and maintenance......... | 51,627 | 37,966 | 54,602 | 77,673 | 57,758 | 51,444 | 45,746 | 41,307 | 43,746 |
| Federal, state, and local taxes...... | 4,957 | 6,182 | 6,163 | 7,513 | 7,569 | 8,396 | 7,872 | 7,835 | 9,111 |
| Equals: Operating income............ | 5,890 | 7,630 | 7,053 | 12,632 | 10,554 | 10,784 | 11,069 | 12,378 | 12,983 |
| Utility operating income.............. | 6,077 | 7,848 | 7,166 | 12,812 | 11,045 | 11,040 | 11,620 | 12,849 | 13,359 |
| Income before interest charges...... | 8,081 | 9,484 | 7,589 | 13,972 | 12,368 | 11,413 | 12,049 | 12,139 | 13,575 |
| Net income............................ | 4,410 | 5,139 | 4,245 | 9,777 | 8,619 | 8,024 | 8,719 | 8,442 | 9,808 |
| Dividends............................... | 3,191 | 4,037 | 3,239 | 2,419 | 2,080 | 1,107 | 1,487 | 1,329 | 1,805 |

[1] Includes capital stock discount and expense and reacquired securities. [2] Includes reserves for deferred income taxes. [3] Includes expenses not shown separately.

Source: American Gas Association, Washington, DC, *Annual Statistics* ©. See also <http://www.aga.org>.

# Table 991. Sewage Treatment Facilities and Employees: 2015 and 2016

[Data based on the North American Industry Classification System (NAICS), 2012; see text, Section 15]

| State | Sewage treatment facilities (NAICS 22132) | | | | State | Sewage treatment facilities (NAICS 22132) | | | |
|---|---|---|---|---|---|---|---|---|---|
| | 2015 | | 2016 | | | 2015 | | 2016 | |
| | Number of establishments | Paid employees | Number of establishments | Paid employees | | Number of establishments | Paid employees | Number of establishments | Paid employees |
| **U.S.** | **695** | **6,171** | **681** | **6,194** | MO. | 20 | 89 | 20 | 102 |
| AL. | 18 | 254 | 17 | 243 | MT. | 6 | 41 | 6 | 40 |
| AK. | 3 | ([1]) | 4 | ([2]) | NE. | 2 | ([2]) | 2 | ([2]) |
| AZ. | 21 | 133 | 20 | 132 | NV. | 1 | ([1]) | 2 | ([1]) |
| AR. | 4 | 18 | 6 | 25 | NH. | 5 | 21 | 5 | 21 |
| CA. | 45 | 330 | 42 | 340 | NJ. | 12 | 83 | 10 | 80 |
| CO. | 8 | 44 | 8 | 94 | NM. | 4 | 37 | 2 | ([1]) |
| CT. | 13 | 99 | 12 | 106 | NY. | 27 | 328 | 28 | 379 |
| DE. | 4 | 59 | 3 | 56 | NC. | 21 | 108 | 22 | 108 |
| DC. | (NA) | (NA) | (NA) | (NA) | ND. | 1 | ([1]) | 1 | ([1]) |
| FL. | 53 | 574 | 45 | 511 | OH. | 13 | 227 | 13 | 268 |
| GA. | 13 | 61 | 12 | 86 | OK. | 19 | 206 | 20 | ([3]) |
| HI. | 18 | 91 | 19 | 94 | OR. | 7 | 37 | 6 | 33 |
| ID. | 5 | 33 | 5 | 35 | PA. | 46 | 485 | 46 | 499 |
| IL. | 32 | 262 | 34 | 278 | RI. | 5 | ([2]) | 5 | ([2]) |
| IN. | 36 | 397 | 33 | 380 | SC. | 7 | 49 | 9 | 54 |
| IA. | 6 | ([2]) | 6 | ([2]) | SD. | (NA) | (NA) | (NA) | (NA) |
| KS. | 2 | ([2]) | 1 | ([2]) | TN. | 10 | 97 | 11 | 92 |
| KY. | 7 | ([2]) | 9 | ([2]) | TX. | 69 | 379 | 65 | 372 |
| LA. | 26 | 356 | 27 | 282 | UT. | (NA) | (NA) | (NA) | (NA) |
| ME. | 1 | ([1]) | 1 | ([1]) | VT. | 2 | ([1]) | 2 | ([1]) |
| MD. | 7 | 71 | 8 | 59 | VA. | 7 | 42 | 6 | 43 |
| MA. | 17 | 311 | 17 | 274 | WA. | 4 | 67 | 5 | 25 |
| MI. | 24 | 145 | 23 | 160 | WV. | 10 | 61 | 10 | 55 |
| MN. | 10 | 90 | 13 | 101 | WI. | 6 | 14 | 4 | 9 |
| MS. | 17 | 218 | 15 | 207 | WY. | 1 | ([1]) | 1 | ([1]) |

NA Not available. [1] 0 to 19 employees. [2] 20 to 99 employees. [3] 100 to 249 employees.

Source: U.S. Census Bureau, County Business Patterns, "Geography Area Series: County Business Patterns," <http://factfinder.census.gov/>, accessed April 2018. See also <https://www.census.gov/programs-surveys/cbp.html>.

# Section 20
# Construction and Housing

This section presents data on the construction industry and on various indicators of its activity and costs; on housing units and their characteristics and occupants; and on the characteristics and vacancy rates for commercial buildings.

The principal source of these data is the U.S. Census Bureau, which issues a variety of current publications, as well as data from the decennial census. Current construction statistics compiled by the Census Bureau appear in its *New Residential Construction* and *New Residential Sales* press releases and web sites at <www.census.gov/construction/nrc/> and <www.census.gov/construction/nrs/>. *Construction Spending* , available at <https://www.census.gov/construction/c30/c30index.html> presents data on all types of construction. Reports of the censuses of construction industries (see below) are also issued on various topics.

Other Census Bureau publications include the quarterly *Housing Vacancies and Homeownership*, the quarterly *Survey of Market Absorption*, the biennial *American Housing Survey* (formerly *Annual Housing Survey*), and other reports of the censuses of housing and of construction industries.

Other sources include Dodge Data & Analytics, New York, NY, which presents national and state data on construction contracts; the National Association of Home Builders with data on housing starts; the NATIONAL ASSOCIATION OF REALTORS®, which presents data on existing home sales; the Bureau of Economic Analysis, which presents data on residential fixed assets; the U.S. Energy Information Administration, which provides data on commercial buildings through its periodic sample surveys; and the Federal Financial Institutions Examination Council, which provide data on home loans and home improvement loans.

**Censuses and surveys**—Censuses of the construction industry were first conducted by the Census Bureau for 1929, 1935, and 1939; beginning in 1967, a census has been taken every 5 years (through 2012, for years ending in "2" and "7"). Release of data from the 2012 Economic Census was completed in 2016. Data from the 2017 Economic Census will be released on a flow basis between September 2019 and December 2021. The construction sector of the Economic Census covers all employer establishments primarily engaged in (1) building construction by general contractors or operative builders; (2) heavy (nonbuilding) construction by general contractors; and (3) construction by special trade contractors. This sector includes construction management and land subdividers and developers. The 20012 census was conducted in accordance with the 2012 North American Industrial Classification System (NAICS). See text, Section 15, Business Enterprise.

The *American Housing Survey* (*Current Housing Reports* Series H-150 and H-170), which began in 1973, provided an annual and ongoing series of data on selected housing and demographic characteristics until 1983. In 1984, the name of the survey was changed from the *Annual Housing Survey*. Currently, national data are collected every other year, and data for selected metropolitan areas are collected on a rotating basis. The supplemental sample of housing units is selected for 25 metropolitan units and combined with the national sample in order to produce metropolitan estimates using the national survey. All samples represent a cross section of the housing stock in their respective areas. Estimates are subject to both sampling and nonsampling errors; caution should therefore be used in making comparisons between years.

Data on residential mortgages were collected continuously from 1890 to 1970, except 1930, as part of the decennial census by the Census Bureau. Since 1973, mortgage status data have been presented in the *American Housing Survey*. Data on mortgage activity are covered in Section 25, Banking and Finance.

**Housing units**—In general, a housing unit is a house, an apartment, a group of rooms or a single room occupied or intended for occupancy as separate living quarters; that is, the occupants live separately from any other individual in the building, and there is direct access from the outside or through a common hall. Transient accommodations, barracks for workers, and institutional-type quarters are not counted as housing units.

**Statistical reliability**—For a discussion of statistical collection and estimation, sampling procedures, and measures of statistical reliability applicable to Census Bureau data, see Appendix III.

## Table 992. Construction—Establishments, Employees, and Payroll by Kind of Business (NAICS Basis): 2015 and 2016

[6,008 represents 6,008,000. Covers establishments with payroll. Excludes most government employees, railroad employees, and self-employed persons. For statement on methodology, see Appendix III]

| Kind of business | 2012 NAICS code [1] | Establishments 2015 | Establishments 2016 | Paid employees [2] (1,000) 2015 | Paid employees [2] (1,000) 2016 | Annual payroll (mil. dol.) 2015 | Annual payroll (mil. dol.) 2016 |
|---|---|---|---|---|---|---|---|
| **Construction** | **23** | **682,390** | **696,733** | **6,008** | **6,311** | **348,599** | **371,256** |
| Construction of buildings | 236 | 206,286 | 210,469 | 1,252 | 1,314 | 75,878 | 80,912 |
| Residential building construction | 2361 | 164,519 | 168,202 | 635 | 664 | 32,280 | 34,416 |
| New single-family housing construction (except for-sale builders) | 236115 | 50,262 | 48,515 | 179 | 176 | 8,459 | 8,608 |
| New multifamily housing construction (except for-sale builders) | 236116 | 2,818 | 2,885 | 33 | 34 | 2,430 | 2,573 |
| New housing for-sale builders | 236117 | 12,878 | 12,924 | 104 | 108 | 7,994 | 8,592 |
| Residential remodelers | 236118 | 98,561 | 103,878 | 319 | 346 | 13,398 | 14,643 |
| Nonresidential building construction | 2362 | 41,767 | 42,267 | 616 | 649 | 43,598 | 46,497 |
| Industrial building construction | 23621 | 3,202 | 3,277 | 88 | 90 | 5,715 | 5,658 |
| Commercial and institutional building construction | 23622 | 38,565 | 38,990 | 528 | 560 | 37,883 | 40,839 |
| Heavy and civil engineering construction | 237 | 38,959 | 38,477 | 922 | 942 | 65,266 | 67,508 |
| Utility system construction | 2371 | 19,585 | 19,315 | 549 | 552 | 37,218 | 38,307 |
| Water and sewer line and related structures | 23711 | 11,017 | 11,107 | 159 | 166 | 9,845 | 10,592 |
| Oil and gas pipeline and related structures | 23712 | 2,166 | 2,126 | 178 | 164 | 13,260 | 12,842 |
| Power and communication line and related structures | 23713 | 6,402 | 6,082 | 211 | 222 | 14,113 | 14,873 |
| Land subdivision | 2372 | 5,239 | 5,063 | 25 | 26 | 1,742 | 1,830 |
| Highway, street, and bridge construction | 2373 | 9,804 | 9,760 | 261 | 275 | 20,429 | 21,284 |
| Other heavy and civil engineering construction | 2379 | 4,331 | 4,339 | 87 | 89 | 5,877 | 6,087 |
| Specialty trade contractors | 238 | 437,145 | 447,787 | 3,835 | 4,056 | 207,455 | 222,836 |
| Foundation, structure, and building exterior contractors | 2381 | 87,703 | 90,244 | 759 | 812 | 37,888 | 41,421 |
| Poured concrete foundation and structures contractors | 23811 | 19,120 | 19,790 | 198 | 218 | 10,430 | 11,766 |
| Structural steel and precast concrete contractors | 23812 | 3,332 | 3,424 | 69 | 71 | 4,069 | 4,259 |
| Framing contractors | 23813 | 10,650 | 10,975 | 71 | 75 | 2,755 | 3,043 |
| Masonry contractors | 23814 | 18,263 | 18,461 | 130 | 140 | 6,090 | 6,556 |
| Glass and glazing contractors | 23815 | 5,305 | 5,583 | 53 | 57 | 2,866 | 3,195 |
| Roofing contractors | 23816 | 18,193 | 18,677 | 158 | 168 | 7,739 | 8,366 |
| Siding contractors | 23817 | 7,491 | 7,844 | 31 | 34 | 1,307 | 1,452 |
| Other foundation, structure, and building exterior contractors | 23819 | 5,349 | 5,490 | 49 | 48 | 2,633 | 2,785 |
| Building equipment contractors | 2382 | 176,142 | 178,345 | 1,824 | 1,917 | 106,922 | 113,799 |
| Electrical contractors | 23821 | 71,848 | 72,784 | 762 | 800 | 44,521 | 47,479 |
| Plumbing, heating, and air-conditioning contractors | 23822 | 97,181 | 98,434 | 934 | 992 | 53,521 | 57,311 |
| Other building equipment contractors | 23829 | 7,113 | 7,127 | 128 | 125 | 8,880 | 9,009 |
| Building finishing contractors | 2383 | 106,961 | 111,822 | 705 | 752 | 32,168 | 35,302 |
| Drywall and insulation contractors | 23831 | 17,857 | 18,148 | 216 | 229 | 10,526 | 11,729 |
| Painting and wall covering contractors | 23832 | 31,943 | 33,824 | 184 | 193 | 7,859 | 8,374 |
| Flooring contractors | 23833 | 14,601 | 15,382 | 68 | 73 | 3,078 | 3,397 |
| Tile and terrazzo contractors | 23834 | 9,160 | 9,489 | 50 | 54 | 2,177 | 2,450 |
| Finish carpentry contractors | 23835 | 26,795 | 28,165 | 125 | 136 | 5,614 | 6,147 |
| Other building finishing contractors | 23839 | 6,605 | 6,814 | 62 | 67 | 2,914 | 3,205 |
| Other specialty trade contractors | 2389 | 66,339 | 67,376 | 547 | 575 | 30,478 | 32,315 |
| Site preparation contractors | 23891 | 34,413 | 34,498 | 318 | 330 | 18,234 | 19,095 |
| All other specialty trade contractors | 23899 | 31,926 | 32,878 | 229 | 244 | 12,243 | 13,220 |

[1] Data based on North American Industry Classification System (NAICS) 2012. See text, Section 15. [2] Employees on the payroll for the pay period including March 12.

Source: U.S. Census Bureau, County Business Patterns, "Geography Area Series: County Business Patterns," <http://factfinder.census.gov/>, accessed April 2018. See also <https://www.census.gov/programs-surveys/cbp.html>.

## Table 993. Value of New Construction Put in Place: 1980 to 2018

[In millions of dollars (273,936 represents $273,936,000,000). Represents value of construction put in place during year; differs from building permit and construction contract data in timing and coverage. Includes installed cost of normal building service equipment and selected types of industrial production equipment (largely site fabricated). Excludes cost of shipbuilding, land, and most types of machinery and equipment. For methodology, see Appendix III]

| Year | Total | Private Total | Private Residential buildings | Private Non-residential | Public Total | Public Federal | Public State and local |
|---|---|---|---|---|---|---|---|
| 1980 | 273,936 | 210,290 | 100,381 | 109,909 | 63,646 | 9,642 | 54,004 |
| 1990 | 476,778 | 369,300 | 191,103 | 178,197 | 107,478 | 12,099 | 95,379 |
| 2000 | 802,756 | 621,431 | 346,138 | 275,293 | 181,325 | 14,168 | 167,157 |
| 2005 | 1,116,811 | 882,651 | 624,574 | 258,077 | 234,160 | 17,300 | 216,860 |
| 2010 | 809,256 | 505,290 | 242,035 | 263,255 | 303,966 | 31,133 | 272,833 |
| 2014 | 1,005,628 | 729,500 | 369,793 | 359,707 | 276,128 | 22,416 | 253,712 |
| 2015 | 1,113,648 | 823,303 | 422,143 | 401,160 | 290,345 | 22,455 | 267,890 |
| 2016 | 1,191,812 | 899,342 | 467,173 | 432,169 | 292,470 | 22,158 | 270,313 |
| 2017 | 1,246,000 | 962,780 | 524,947 | 437,833 | 283,220 | 21,515 | 261,705 |
| 2018 | 1,293,982 | 992,528 | 539,800 | 452,728 | 301,455 | 21,612 | 279,843 |

Source: U.S. Census Bureau, "Construction Spending," <http://www.census.gov/construction/c30/c30index.html>, accessed August 2019.

# Table 994. New Privately Owned Housing Units Authorized by State: 2017 and 2018

[1,282.0 represents 1,282,000. Based on the 2014 Universe, which includes approximately 20,100 places in the United States that have building permit systems in 2014]

| State | Housing units (1,000) 2017 | Housing units (1,000) 2018 Total | Housing units (1,000) 2018 1-unit [1] | Valuation (mil. dol.) 2017 | Valuation (mil. dol.) 2018 Total | Valuation (mil. dol.) 2018 1-unit [1] | State | Housing units (1,000) 2017 | Housing units (1,000) 2018 Total | Housing units (1,000) 2018 1-unit [1] | Valuation (mil. dol.) 2017 | Valuation (mil. dol.) 2018 Total | Valuation (mil. dol.) 2018 1-unit [1] |
|---|---|---|---|---|---|---|---|---|---|---|---|---|---|
| U.S. | 1,282.0 | 1,328.8 | 855.3 | 258,505 | 271,120 | 210,850 | MO. | 18.8 | 16.9 | 11.4 | 3,452 | 3,167 | 2,663 |
| AL. | 14.8 | 14.8 | 13.0 | 2,773 | 3,047 | 2,754 | MT. | 4.9 | 5.1 | 3.2 | 847 | 870 | 649 |
| AK. | 1.5 | 1.7 | 1.2 | 396 | 429 | 357 | NE. | 8.9 | 7.9 | 4.9 | 1,446 | 1,310 | 1,078 |
| AZ. | 39.5 | 41.7 | 32.1 | 8,701 | 9,728 | 8,344 | NV. | 19.5 | 17.6 | 13.0 | 2,846 | 3,401 | 2,964 |
| AR. | 10.8 | 10.2 | 7.4 | 1,766 | 1,829 | 1,557 | NH. | 3.6 | 4.4 | 2.7 | 758 | 875 | 702 |
| CA. | 114.8 | 113.5 | 58.8 | 27,782 | 27,845 | 17,844 | NJ. | 28.5 | 27.9 | 10.3 | 4,142 | 4,220 | 2,120 |
| CO. | 40.7 | 42.6 | 26.1 | 9,525 | 10,231 | 7,879 | NM. | 4.7 | 4.8 | 4.4 | 942 | 1,038 | 1,007 |
| CT. | 4.5 | 4.8 | 2.6 | 1,186 | 1,112 | 855 | NY. | 39.4 | 37.8 | 10.0 | 6,956 | 6,692 | 2,964 |
| DE. | 6.6 | 6.0 | 5.5 | 806 | 789 | 736 | NC. | 67.0 | 71.7 | 51.2 | 12,694 | 13,582 | 11,588 |
| DC. | 6.0 | 4.6 | 0.1 | 690 | 518 | 26 | ND. | 3.4 | 3.2 | 1.9 | 607 | 608 | 464 |
| FL. | 122.7 | 144.4 | 97.1 | 28,095 | 31,544 | 25,454 | OH. | 23.9 | 24.2 | 16.3 | 5,021 | 5,189 | 4,342 |
| GA. | 51.2 | 59.3 | 42.3 | 9,920 | 11,146 | 9,080 | OK. | 11.1 | 10.5 | 9.4 | 2,192 | 2,181 | 2,066 |
| HI. | 4.0 | 4.7 | 2.6 | 1,132 | 1,360 | 935 | OR. | 20.1 | 20.1 | 11.2 | 4,154 | 4,181 | 3,010 |
| ID. | 14.2 | 15.8 | 12.2 | 2,791 | 3,099 | 2,718 | PA. | 22.6 | 23.3 | 15.3 | 4,434 | 4,684 | 3,593 |
| IL. | 25.0 | 21.5 | 10.0 | 4,605 | 4,036 | 2,619 | RI. | 1.2 | 1.3 | 0.9 | 247 | 260 | 223 |
| IN. | 21.7 | 21.5 | 16.4 | 4,583 | 4,880 | 4,269 | SC. | 35.5 | 35.5 | 30.6 | 8,038 | 8,144 | 7,738 |
| IA. | 13.9 | 11.5 | 7.3 | 2,518 | 2,249 | 1,801 | SD. | 5.4 | 5.0 | 3.0 | 894 | 854 | 651 |
| KS. | 9.0 | 9.5 | 5.4 | 1,782 | 1,889 | 1,383 | TN. | 37.9 | 37.2 | 28.0 | 7,043 | 7,048 | 6,239 |
| KY. | 12.6 | 13.8 | 7.8 | 1,974 | 2,268 | 1,692 | TX. | 175.1 | 192.9 | 126.0 | 32,514 | 34,690 | 27,650 |
| LA. | 15.2 | 15.8 | 13.7 | 2,986 | 3,108 | 2,837 | UT. | 24.7 | 25.6 | 18.5 | 5,242 | 5,611 | 4,725 |
| ME. | 4.4 | 4.7 | 3.7 | 828 | 959 | 844 | VT. | 1.7 | 2.1 | 1.1 | 326 | 365 | 263 |
| MD. | 16.2 | 18.6 | 13.0 | 3,257 | 3,702 | 2,872 | VA. | 33.8 | 32.0 | 21.4 | 5,747 | 5,831 | 4,798 |
| MA. | 17.7 | 17.0 | 7.2 | 4,092 | 4,158 | 2,351 | WA. | 45.8 | 47.7 | 23.7 | 9,913 | 9,808 | 6,950 |
| MI. | 23.6 | 19.6 | 15.6 | 4,888 | 4,569 | 4,068 | WV. | 2.7 | 2.9 | 2.3 | 463 | 500 | 450 |
| MN. | 22.0 | 25.7 | 13.6 | 4,818 | 5,721 | 3,755 | WI. | 19.5 | 19.1 | 12.0 | 3,911 | 4,008 | 3,220 |
| MS. | 7.5 | 6.9 | 6.1 | 1,255 | 1,194 | 1,135 | WY. | 1.9 | 1.8 | 1.5 | 526 | 593 | 564 |

[1] The 1-unit structure category is a single-family home. It includes fully detached, semi-detached (semi-attached, side-by-side), row houses, and townhouses.

Source: U.S. Census Bureau, Construction Reports, "Building Permits Survey," <http://www.census.gov/construction/bps/>, accessed August 2019.

# Table 995. Construction Contracts Started—Value of Construction and Floor Space of Buildings by Class of Construction: 2014 to 2018

[607 1 represents $607,100,000,000. Dollar value data includes new construction, additions, and alterations. Square footage data includes new construction and additions; alterations which create no net new square footage are not included]

| Year | Total | Residential buildings | Nonresidential buildings Total | Commer-cial [1] | Manu-facturing | Educa-tion [2] | Health | Public | Reli-gious | Social and recrea-tional | Miscell-aneous | Non-building con-struction |
|---|---|---|---|---|---|---|---|---|---|---|---|---|
| VALUE (bil. dol.) | | | | | | | | | | | | |
| 2014 | 607.1 | 234.6 | 225.0 | 83.9 | 35.8 | 50.9 | 23.1 | 7.8 | 1.7 | 13.9 | 7.8 | 147.5 |
| 2015 | 689.9 | 273.7 | 228.9 | 93.5 | 25.3 | 54.7 | 23.5 | 8.1 | 2.1 | 14.2 | 7.5 | 187.4 |
| 2016 | 738.7 | 297.5 | 258.0 | 115.3 | 20.3 | 56.6 | 26.7 | 9.1 | 1.8 | 18.6 | 9.5 | 183.2 |
| 2017 | 787.1 | 306.9 | 287.2 | 116.7 | 26.1 | 64.9 | 28.3 | 9.6 | 2.2 | 18.0 | 21.6 | 193.0 |
| 2018 | 811.1 | 329.1 | 294.3 | 122.4 | 32.1 | 67.9 | 27.4 | 9.6 | 1.8 | 20.2 | 12.9 | 187.7 |
| FLOOR SPACE (mil. sq. ft.) | | | | | | | | | | | | |
| 2014 | 2,965 | 1,952 | 1,013 | 624 | 80 | 149 | 68 | 16 | 10 | 45 | 21 | (X) |
| 2015 | 3,288 | 2,240 | 1,047 | 664 | 72 | 150 | 73 | 15 | 11 | 41 | 21 | (X) |
| 2016 | 3,583 | 2,448 | 1,135 | 743 | 72 | 148 | 78 | 16 | 10 | 48 | 22 | (X) |
| 2017 | 3,832 | 2,642 | 1,190 | 770 | 71 | 156 | 85 | 20 | 11 | 47 | 29 | (X) |
| 2018 | 4,004 | 2,829 | 1,174 | 755 | 81 | 156 | 81 | 19 | 9 | 48 | 24 | (X) |

X Not applicable. [1] Includes nonindustrial warehouses. [2] Includes science facilities.
Source: Dodge Data & Analytics (copyright) 1-800-591-4462, as of July 25, 2019.

# Table 996. Construction Contracts Started—Value by Region: 2014 to 2017

[In millions of dollars (607,101 represents $607,101,000,000). Includes new construction, additions and alterations]

| Region | 2014 | 2015 | 2016 | 2017 | 2018 Total [1] | 2018 Residential | 2018 Nonresidential |
|---|---|---|---|---|---|---|---|
| United States | 607,101 | 689,932 | 738,734 | 787,112 | 811,117 | 329,083 | 294,343 |
| New England | 22,608 | 27,530 | 30,012 | 30,807 | 33,375 | 12,013 | 14,163 |
| Middle Atlantic | 71,285 | 84,854 | 85,179 | 107,577 | 86,769 | 30,154 | 37,827 |
| East North Central | 64,748 | 69,679 | 78,447 | 79,407 | 83,718 | 27,716 | 32,851 |
| West North Central | 43,959 | 48,397 | 54,509 | 51,131 | 55,824 | 18,288 | 20,889 |
| South Atlantic | 125,307 | 138,444 | 162,648 | 176,745 | 181,745 | 90,559 | 54,834 |
| East South Central | 28,348 | 29,717 | 35,748 | 33,978 | 46,251 | 16,184 | 23,014 |
| West South Central | 110,767 | 139,894 | 116,835 | 120,127 | 127,556 | 50,060 | 39,783 |
| Mountain | 53,860 | 57,946 | 64,586 | 61,295 | 77,126 | 36,711 | 26,426 |
| Pacific | 86,219 | 93,470 | 110,770 | 126,047 | 118,753 | 47,399 | 44,556 |

[1] Includes nonbuilding construction, not shown separately.
Source: Dodge Data & Analytics (copyright) 1-800-591-4462, as of July 25, 2019.

# Table 997. Value of Private Construction Put in Place: 2010 to 2018

[In millions of dollars (505,290 represents $505,290,000,000). Represents value of construction put in place during year; differs from building permit and construction contract data in timing and coverage. See Appendix III]

| Type of construction | 2010 | 2011 | 2012 | 2013 | 2014 | 2015 | 2016 | 2017 | 2018 |
|---|---|---|---|---|---|---|---|---|---|
| **Total private construction** [1] | **505,290** | **501,925** | **571,145** | **635,669** | **729,500** | **823,303** | **899,342** | **962,780** | **992,528** |
| Residential | 242,035 | 244,122 | 269,784 | 323,381 | 369,793 | 422,143 | 467,173 | 524,947 | 539,800 |
| New single family | 112,569 | 108,178 | 132,015 | 170,768 | 193,600 | 221,128 | 242,476 | 270,163 | 284,295 |
| New multifamily | 14,686 | 15,037 | 22,510 | 31,500 | 41,553 | 52,531 | 61,097 | 59,945 | 60,117 |
| Improvements [2] | 114,780 | 120,907 | 115,260 | 121,113 | 134,639 | 148,484 | 163,600 | 194,839 | 195,388 |
| Nonresidential | 263,255 | 257,803 | 301,360 | 312,288 | 359,707 | 401,160 | 432,169 | 437,833 | 452,728 |
| Lodging | 11,201 | 8,395 | 10,197 | 13,028 | 16,306 | 21,324 | 26,516 | 27,985 | 30,761 |
| Office [1] | 24,368 | 23,738 | 27,448 | 30,133 | 38,864 | 47,449 | 59,608 | 58,564 | 63,419 |
| General | 22,203 | 21,231 | 25,111 | 28,419 | 36,958 | 45,675 | 57,386 | 55,874 | 61,478 |
| Financial | 2,122 | 2,284 | 1,945 | 1,597 | 1,867 | 1,629 | 1,851 | 2,432 | 1,773 |
| Commercial | 37,154 | 39,153 | 44,312 | 50,947 | 60,890 | 63,404 | 75,012 | 84,637 | 85,899 |
| Automotive [1] | 3,546 | 4,270 | 4,834 | 4,639 | 4,830 | 5,527 | 7,507 | 8,215 | 7,657 |
| Sales | 1,355 | 1,816 | 2,079 | 1,956 | 2,117 | 2,123 | 3,102 | 3,178 | 3,277 |
| Service/parts | 1,679 | 1,977 | 2,221 | 2,313 | 2,047 | 2,646 | 3,417 | 3,930 | 3,230 |
| Parking | 511 | 478 | 534 | 370 | 666 | 758 | 988 | 1,108 | 1,150 |
| Food/beverage | 4,605 | 5,268 | 5,845 | 6,594 | 7,230 | 7,212 | 8,153 | 8,224 | 8,188 |
| Food | 2,027 | 2,840 | 2,430 | 2,937 | 3,447 | 3,103 | 3,524 | 3,316 | 2,716 |
| Dining/drinking | 1,911 | 1,650 | 2,436 | 2,141 | 2,170 | 2,574 | 2,861 | 3,362 | 3,661 |
| Fast food [1] | 667 | 779 | 979 | 1,516 | 1,613 | 1,535 | 1,768 | 1,546 | 1,811 |
| Multi-retail [1] | 12,486 | 13,361 | 14,904 | 16,686 | 19,543 | 19,629 | 22,099 | 24,703 | 22,159 |
| General merchandise | 3,794 | 3,368 | 3,773 | 2,942 | 2,792 | 2,331 | 2,612 | 1,827 | 2,344 |
| Shopping center | 6,725 | 6,748 | 7,934 | 9,806 | 12,946 | 13,433 | 15,508 | 17,934 | 15,924 |
| Shopping mall | 1,332 | 2,356 | 2,288 | 2,938 | 2,868 | 2,988 | 3,242 | 4,163 | 3,170 |
| Other commercial [1] | 4,220 | 3,720 | 3,934 | 4,786 | 4,586 | 5,205 | 6,389 | 5,331 | 5,362 |
| Drug store | 1,077 | 721 | 765 | 893 | 943 | 531 | 495 | 329 | 273 |
| Building supply store | 772 | 611 | 493 | 506 | 495 | 596 | 537 | 655 | 578 |
| Other stores | 1,741 | 1,743 | 2,069 | 2,468 | 2,409 | 2,866 | 4,157 | 3,225 | 2,666 |
| Warehouse [1] | 5,661 | 6,543 | 7,047 | 8,766 | 13,698 | 16,552 | 22,561 | 29,628 | 33,755 |
| General commercial | 5,229 | 6,219 | 6,575 | 8,107 | 12,894 | 15,478 | 20,247 | 25,243 | 28,268 |
| Ministorage | 401 | 241 | 365 | 472 | 589 | 954 | 2,100 | 4,077 | 5,215 |
| Farm | 6,637 | 5,991 | 7,748 | 9,476 | 11,005 | 9,280 | 8,303 | 8,537 | 8,772 |
| Health care | 29,552 | 28,906 | 31,429 | 29,696 | 28,885 | 30,518 | 31,500 | 32,645 | 32,859 |
| Hospital | 21,528 | 20,483 | 21,223 | 19,199 | 17,680 | 19,348 | 19,729 | 20,064 | 20,772 |
| Medical building | 5,276 | 5,429 | 6,415 | 7,015 | 7,167 | 6,983 | 7,848 | 8,701 | 8,559 |
| Special care | 2,748 | 2,995 | 3,791 | 3,482 | 4,039 | 4,188 | 3,924 | 3,881 | 3,528 |
| Educational [1] | 13,418 | 14,081 | 16,625 | 16,919 | 16,583 | 17,559 | 19,793 | 20,263 | 20,832 |
| Preschool | 492 | 349 | 396 | 420 | 462 | 353 | 502 | 485 | 532 |
| Primary/secondary | 2,585 | 2,973 | 2,795 | 2,997 | 3,599 | 3,615 | 3,833 | 4,331 | 4,574 |
| Higher education [1] | 8,322 | 8,477 | 10,879 | 10,868 | 10,501 | 11,834 | 13,151 | 12,390 | 12,802 |
| Instructional | 4,993 | 4,658 | 5,786 | 4,928 | 4,944 | 5,394 | 5,941 | 5,506 | 5,301 |
| Dormitory | 1,654 | 2,165 | 2,902 | 3,924 | 3,559 | 3,931 | 4,594 | 4,323 | 4,408 |
| Sports/recreation | 790 | 660 | 709 | 981 | 974 | 1,056 | 1,144 | 1,284 | 1,510 |
| Other educational [1] | 1,687 | 1,869 | 2,206 | 2,226 | 1,656 | 1,488 | 1,878 | 2,362 | 2,143 |
| Gallery/museum | 1,522 | 1,468 | 1,407 | 1,486 | 1,224 | 1,054 | 1,463 | 1,695 | 1,646 |
| Religious | 5,237 | 4,205 | 3,819 | 3,565 | 3,380 | 3,568 | 3,721 | 3,366 | 3,021 |
| House of worship | 4,214 | 3,256 | 3,143 | 3,055 | 2,853 | 3,012 | 3,254 | 2,865 | 2,531 |
| Other religious | 1,023 | 950 | 675 | 510 | 527 | 556 | 466 | 501 | 490 |
| Auxiliary building | 795 | 651 | 521 | 419 | 391 | 466 | 377 | 452 | 382 |
| Public safety | 241 | 205 | 103 | 125 | 227 | 224 | 104 | 96 | 135 |
| Amusement and recreation [1] | 6,483 | 6,744 | 6,217 | 6,916 | 7,719 | 9,855 | 12,557 | 13,757 | 14,605 |
| Theme/amusement park | 353 | 472 | 512 | 670 | 943 | 1,225 | 2,090 | 1,874 | 1,815 |
| Sports | 1,596 | 1,096 | 1,043 | 1,336 | 1,889 | 3,456 | 4,474 | 5,797 | 5,340 |
| Fitness | 1,150 | 1,067 | 1,251 | 1,310 | 1,182 | 1,157 | 1,291 | 1,233 | 1,597 |
| Performance/meeting center | 565 | 510 | 517 | 673 | 657 | 566 | 932 | 1,170 | 1,778 |
| Social center | 914 | 662 | 614 | 789 | 757 | 868 | 953 | 789 | 1,086 |
| Movie theater/studio | 426 | 510 | 362 | 618 | 717 | 832 | 1,030 | 764 | 935 |
| Transportation [1] | 9,894 | 9,537 | 10,883 | 11,029 | 12,151 | 13,575 | 13,070 | 14,779 | 17,007 |
| Air | 259 | 535 | 1,044 | 921 | 729 | 828 | 2,054 | 3,514 | 5,568 |
| Land | 9,503 | 8,944 | 9,810 | 9,988 | 11,035 | 12,480 | 10,903 | 10,962 | 10,829 |
| Railroad | 8,973 | 8,546 | 9,279 | 9,272 | 10,225 | 11,653 | 9,900 | 10,087 | 9,978 |
| Communication | 17,689 | 17,536 | 15,952 | 17,619 | 17,105 | 21,505 | 22,014 | 24,701 | 24,455 |
| Power | 66,117 | 64,262 | 86,402 | 81,278 | 98,206 | 91,503 | 91,736 | 90,615 | 94,167 |
| Electricity | 48,972 | 50,291 | 68,967 | 54,411 | 69,970 | 67,123 | 71,356 | 69,898 | 70,881 |
| Gas | 8,297 | 10,357 | 10,317 | 10,897 | 11,033 | 12,546 | 14,474 | 13,241 | 14,639 |
| Oil | 8,848 | 3,614 | 7,118 | 15,970 | 17,203 | 11,834 | 5,906 | 7,476 | 8,647 |
| Sewage and waste disposal | 439 | 520 | 597 | 356 | 241 | 369 | 372 | 226 | 383 |
| Water supply | 717 | 635 | 373 | 591 | 573 | 539 | 206 | 186 | 208 |
| Manufacturing | 40,607 | 39,768 | 46,774 | 49,863 | 58,142 | 79,287 | 75,698 | 65,796 | 64,715 |
| Food/beverage/tobacco | 4,000 | 4,792 | 4,380 | 4,934 | 6,387 | 6,833 | 7,376 | 8,000 | 9,121 |
| Textile/apparel/leather/furniture | 591 | 301 | 171 | 377 | 799 | 605 | 957 | 825 | 525 |
| Wood | 438 | 369 | 335 | 732 | 619 | 335 | 451 | 1,048 | 1,645 |
| Paper/printing/publishing | 634 | 684 | 1,190 | 1,016 | 633 | 827 | 1,161 | 1,443 | 1,840 |
| Petroleum/coal | 11,612 | 5,453 | 4,777 | 4,036 | 5,048 | 4,274 | 3,991 | 3,878 | 3,737 |
| Chemical | 7,580 | 7,345 | 10,848 | 15,483 | 22,744 | 36,616 | 34,383 | 30,192 | 27,454 |
| Plastic/rubber | 728 | 947 | 1,686 | 1,537 | 2,173 | 3,200 | 3,478 | 2,998 | 4,060 |
| Nonmetallic mineral | 1,150 | 896 | 857 | 916 | 944 | 1,158 | 1,423 | 1,018 | 596 |
| Primary metal | 4,738 | 3,130 | 4,691 | 4,487 | 3,836 | 5,943 | 4,069 | 2,741 | 1,473 |
| Fabricated metal | 1,104 | 1,593 | 1,726 | 1,484 | 819 | 1,170 | 2,164 | 1,879 | 1,412 |
| Machinery | 1,030 | 1,373 | 1,631 | 1,442 | 1,163 | 1,855 | 1,453 | 809 | 936 |
| Computer/electronic/electrical | 4,614 | 8,815 | 9,592 | 7,312 | 4,962 | 3,376 | 1,932 | 1,988 | 5,134 |
| Transportation equipment | 1,962 | 3,260 | 3,869 | 5,132 | 6,988 | 12,136 | 11,961 | 8,340 | 6,064 |

[1] Includes other types of construction, not shown separately. [2] Private residential improvement does not include expenditures on rental, vacant, or seasonal properties.

Source: U.S. Census Bureau, "Construction Spending," <http://www.census.gov/construction/c30/c30index.html>, accessed August 2019.

# Table 998. Value of State and Local Government Construction Put in Place: 2010 to 2018

[In millions of dollars (272,833 represents $272,833,000,000)]

| Type of construction | 2010 | 2011 | 2012 | 2013 | 2014 | 2015 | 2016 | 2017 | 2018 |
|---|---|---|---|---|---|---|---|---|---|
| Total construction [1] | 272,833 | 254,753 | 252,378 | 246,955 | 253,712 | 267,890 | 270,313 | 261,705 | 279,843 |
| Residential | 7,576 | 5,962 | 4,672 | 4,537 | 4,128 | 5,701 | 6,059 | 6,207 | 5,868 |
| Multifamily | 6,536 | 5,182 | 3,935 | 3,574 | 3,444 | 4,907 | 5,366 | 5,929 | 5,528 |
| Nonresidential | 265,256 | 248,791 | 247,705 | 242,418 | 249,585 | 262,189 | 264,253 | 255,499 | 273,975 |
| Office | 8,317 | 7,440 | 6,055 | 5,220 | 5,424 | 5,873 | 5,564 | 5,539 | 6,630 |
| Commercial [1] | 1,456 | 1,682 | 1,412 | 1,119 | 898 | 1,404 | 1,660 | 1,415 | 1,931 |
| Automotive | 769 | 840 | 942 | 696 | 499 | 844 | 675 | 607 | 942 |
| Parking | 675 | 680 | 799 | 621 | 443 | 800 | 549 | 590 | 930 |
| Warehouse | 286 | 319 | 171 | 133 | 184 | 244 | 414 | 358 | 345 |
| Health care | 6,193 | 7,009 | 7,040 | 6,928 | 6,174 | 5,440 | 5,575 | 5,999 | 6,312 |
| Hospital | 4,789 | 5,317 | 5,522 | 5,439 | 4,762 | 4,190 | 4,048 | 4,207 | 4,661 |
| Medical building | 747 | 906 | 982 | 970 | 990 | 808 | 909 | 1,079 | 971 |
| Special care | 657 | 785 | 536 | 520 | 422 | 442 | 618 | 714 | 680 |
| Educational [1] | 71,948 | 67,965 | 65,622 | 60,027 | 61,176 | 65,346 | 68,873 | 69,457 | 71,750 |
| Primary/secondary [1] | 44,559 | 40,760 | 39,389 | 36,050 | 35,936 | 38,022 | 41,938 | 44,012 | 46,873 |
| Elementary | 13,171 | 10,795 | 11,195 | 10,580 | 11,887 | 10,433 | 12,706 | 13,839 | 15,375 |
| Middle/junior high | 7,029 | 8,116 | 7,557 | 7,730 | 6,781 | 7,458 | 8,802 | 9,023 | 9,163 |
| High | 24,055 | 21,389 | 20,276 | 17,339 | 16,475 | 19,733 | 19,705 | 19,973 | 20,889 |
| Higher education [1] | 24,384 | 24,315 | 23,328 | 21,790 | 22,722 | 24,895 | 24,420 | 23,088 | 22,481 |
| Instructional | 14,138 | 13,373 | 11,931 | 11,755 | 11,948 | 13,365 | 13,535 | 13,110 | 13,380 |
| Parking | 593 | 717 | 532 | 398 | 391 | 548 | 449 | 386 | 365 |
| Administration | 357 | 433 | 430 | 409 | 528 | 588 | 652 | 470 | 420 |
| Dormitory | 3,371 | 3,965 | 4,435 | 3,845 | 3,468 | 4,109 | 4,158 | 3,079 | 2,685 |
| Library | 662 | 568 | 322 | 157 | 279 | 643 | 460 | 451 | 503 |
| Student union/cafeteria | 1147 | 1227 | 1,464 | 1,378 | 1,412 | 1,241 | 1,305 | 1,356 | 1,294 |
| Sports/recreation | 2398 | 2,358 | 2,356 | 2,594 | 2,901 | 2,844 | 2,595 | 2,836 | 2,621 |
| Infrastructure | 1381 | 1,461 | 1,735 | 1,065 | 1,683 | 1,549 | 1,228 | 1,227 | 1,174 |
| Other educational [1] | 2,223 | 1,831 | 2,054 | 1,500 | 2,062 | 1,895 | 1,846 | 1,506 | 1,533 |
| Library/archive | 1386 | 1,159 | 1,385 | 1,016 | 1,079 | 1,143 | 1,305 | 910 | 988 |
| Public safety [1] | 7,586 | 7,245 | 7,641 | 6,592 | 6,414 | 5,829 | 5,671 | 5,928 | 6,977 |
| Correctional | 4,624 | 4,929 | 5,126 | 4,395 | 4,249 | 3,612 | 3,395 | 3,598 | 4,319 |
| Detention | 2,789 | 3,166 | 3,306 | 2,554 | 2,171 | 1,981 | 1,938 | 2,023 | 2,632 |
| Police/sheriff | 1836 | 1,762 | 1,820 | 1,841 | 2,079 | 1,631 | 1,457 | 1,575 | 1,687 |
| Other public safety | 2,962 | 2,316 | 2,515 | 2,197 | 2,165 | 2,217 | 2,276 | 2,330 | 2,658 |
| Fire/rescue | 1747 | 1,477 | 1,627 | 1,403 | 1,496 | 1,553 | 1,664 | 1,902 | 2,148 |
| Amusement and recreation [1] | 9,668 | 8,542 | 8,876 | 8,001 | 8,713 | 9,954 | 10,218 | 10,613 | 11,465 |
| Sports | 1,819 | 1,223 | 1,127 | 1,289 | 1,856 | 1,749 | 1,614 | 1,500 | 2,145 |
| Performance/meeting center | 1,841 | 1,805 | 1,804 | 1,474 | 1,780 | 1,588 | 1,708 | 1,939 | 2,563 |
| Convention center | 1,119 | 1,112 | 1,316 | 917 | 1,154 | 864 | 856 | 1,109 | 1,620 |
| Social center | 1,561 | 1,054 | 1,008 | 1,127 | 887 | 1,102 | 1,227 | 1,497 | 1,405 |
| Neighborhood center | 1395 | 887 | 890 | 1,050 | 774 | 1,040 | 1,018 | 1,261 | 1,118 |
| Park/camp | 4,259 | 4,277 | 4,825 | 4,098 | 4,070 | 5,230 | 5,441 | 5,570 | 5,144 |
| Transportation | 26,493 | 23,340 | 24,797 | 25,871 | 27,757 | 29,087 | 27,825 | 28,337 | 32,408 |
| Air [1] | 11,897 | 9,867 | 9,799 | 9,768 | 10,821 | 10,828 | 10,575 | 11,658 | 15,829 |
| Passenger terminal | 6,503 | 5,681 | 4,992 | 5,310 | 4,922 | 5,005 | 5,936 | 7,616 | 11,080 |
| Runway | 4,710 | 3,760 | 4,313 | 3,780 | 4,980 | 5,244 | 3,915 | 3,337 | 4,228 |
| Land [1] | 12,954 | 11,811 | 13,047 | 13,984 | 15,106 | 16,597 | 15,655 | 15,160 | 14,991 |
| Passenger terminal | 3,380 | 3223 | 2,978 | 2,946 | 3,666 | 4,558 | 4,471 | 3,683 | 3,125 |
| Mass transit | 6,447 | 5,846 | 7,033 | 7,189 | 7,161 | 7,559 | 7,075 | 7,427 | 7,867 |
| Railroad | 751 | 662 | 850 | 1,459 | 1,695 | 1,641 | 1,131 | 1,120 | 1,262 |
| Water | 1,642 | 1,661 | 1,952 | 2,118 | 1,829 | 1,662 | 1,595 | 1,519 | 1,570 |
| Dock/marina | 1115 | 1247 | 1,502 | 1,583 | 1,360 | 1,232 | 1,258 | 1,211 | 1,203 |
| Dry dock/marine terminal | 527 | 414 | 450 | 536 | 469 | 430 | 337 | 308 | 366 |
| Power [1] | 10,770 | 9,492 | 9,794 | 10,951 | 10,732 | 9,822 | 8,384 | 5,098 | 5,356 |
| Electrical | 9,972 | 7,886 | 7,136 | 8,334 | 8,946 | 8,551 | 7,281 | 4,316 | 4,476 |
| Distribution | 3,253 | 2,486 | 2,046 | 2,151 | 3,120 | 2,607 | 2,798 | 2,323 | 2,678 |
| Highway and street | 81,309 | 78,369 | 79,722 | 80,610 | 84,014 | 89,719 | 91,696 | 87,716 | 91,363 |
| Pavement | 51,433 | 47,954 | 47,566 | 46,282 | 50,509 | 53,266 | 55,221 | 53,839 | 56,460 |
| Lighting | 1975 | 1,754 | 1,738 | 1,525 | 1,221 | 1,512 | 1,834 | 1,844 | 2,318 |
| Retaining wall | 1,250 | 1033 | 845 | 895 | 878 | 1,048 | 842 | 747 | 1,464 |
| Tunnel | 810 | 873 | 1,359 | 1,477 | 1,038 | 825 | 1,182 | 1,139 | 747 |
| Bridge | 24,222 | 25,545 | 27,050 | 28,811 | 29,234 | 31,576 | 30,838 | 29,167 | 29,075 |
| Toll/weigh | 214 | 238 | 338 | 129 | 137 | 209 | 296 | 289 | 322 |
| Maintenance building | 275 | 237 | 187 | 373 | 282 | 392 | 461 | 265 | 280 |
| Rest facility/streetscape | 1130 | 735 | 640 | 1,119 | 715 | 892 | 1,023 | 427 | 697 |
| Sewage and waste disposal | 24,555 | 21,196 | 20,946 | 21,037 | 21,870 | 23,182 | 22,167 | 19,903 | 21,392 |
| Sewage/dry waste [1] | 13,234 | 11,975 | 12,077 | 11,591 | 12,517 | 13,846 | 13,256 | 11,459 | 11,675 |
| Plant | 3,755 | 3,260 | 3,022 | 2,376 | 2,565 | 2,813 | 2,471 | 2,490 | 2,578 |
| Line/pump station | 9,375 | 8,619 | 8,956 | 9,072 | 9,815 | 10,855 | 10,561 | 8,807 | 8,969 |
| Waste water | 11,321 | 9,222 | 8,869 | 9,446 | 9,353 | 9,336 | 8,911 | 8,444 | 9,718 |
| Plant | 9,428 | 7,836 | 7,414 | 7,861 | 7,354 | 6,980 | 6,730 | 6,583 | 6,944 |
| Line/drain | 1,893 | 1,386 | 1,455 | 1,585 | 1,999 | 2,356 | 2,181 | 1,861 | 2,774 |
| Water supply | 14,420 | 13,393 | 12,746 | 12,919 | 12,731 | 12,560 | 12,742 | 11,443 | 13,320 |
| Plant | 5,683 | 5,391 | 4,833 | 4,358 | 4,221 | 4,379 | 4,216 | 4,476 | 4,845 |
| Well | 383 | 389 | 336 | 480 | 513 | 290 | 325 | 338 | 435 |
| Line | 6,246 | 5,867 | 5,631 | 5,777 | 5,816 | 6,026 | 5,715 | 4,650 | 5,605 |
| Pump station | 970 | 744 | 633 | 734 | 817 | 624 | 922 | 779 | 1,042 |
| Reservoir | 393 | 427 | 639 | 804 | 618 | 386 | 709 | 784 | 845 |
| Tank/tower | 744 | 574 | 674 | 765 | 747 | 855 | 856 | 415 | 548 |
| Conservation and development [1] | 2035 | 2,289 | 2,225 | 2,500 | 3,071 | 3,095 | 3,129 | 3,106 | 3,679 |
| Dam/levee | 783 | 874 | 727 | 822 | 1,096 | 946 | 960 | 986 | 1,303 |
| Breakwater/jetty | 675 | 649 | 853 | 1,022 | 1,098 | 1,383 | 1,385 | 1,005 | 1,081 |
| Dredging | 173 | 198 | 184 | 214 | 259 | 298 | 309 | 285 | 277 |

[1] Includes other types of construction, not shown separately.

Source: U.S. Census Bureau, "Construction Spending," <http://www.census.gov/construction/c30/c30index.html>, accessed August 2019.

## Table 999. Construction of New Privately Owned Housing Units Started: 1960 to 2018

[In thousands of units (1,252 represents 1,252,000). For composition of regions, see map inside front cover]

| Year | Total | 1 unit structures | Northeast | Midwest | South | West |
|---|---|---|---|---|---|---|
| 1960............................. | 1,252 | 995 | 221 | 292 | 429 | 309 |
| 1970............................. | 1,434 | 813 | 218 | 294 | 612 | 311 |
| 1980............................. | 1,292 | 852 | 125 | 218 | 643 | 306 |
| 1990............................. | 1,193 | 895 | 131 | 253 | 479 | 329 |
| 1995............................. | 1,354 | 1,076 | 118 | 290 | 615 | 331 |
| 1996............................. | 1,477 | 1,161 | 132 | 322 | 662 | 361 |
| 1997............................. | 1,474 | 1,134 | 137 | 304 | 670 | 363 |
| 1998............................. | 1,617 | 1,271 | 149 | 331 | 743 | 395 |
| 1999............................. | 1,641 | 1,302 | 156 | 347 | 746 | 392 |
| 2000............................. | 1,569 | 1,231 | 155 | 318 | 714 | 383 |
| 2001............................. | 1,603 | 1,273 | 149 | 330 | 732 | 391 |
| 2002............................. | 1,705 | 1,359 | 158 | 350 | 782 | 416 |
| 2003............................. | 1,848 | 1,499 | 163 | 374 | 839 | 472 |
| 2004............................. | 1,956 | 1,611 | 175 | 356 | 909 | 516 |
| 2005............................. | 2,068 | 1,716 | 190 | 357 | 996 | 525 |
| 2006............................. | 1,801 | 1,465 | 167 | 280 | 910 | 444 |
| 2007............................. | 1,355 | 1,046 | 143 | 210 | 681 | 321 |
| 2008............................. | 906 | 622 | 121 | 135 | 453 | 196 |
| 2009............................. | 554 | 445 | 62 | 97 | 278 | 117 |
| 2010............................. | 587 | 471 | 72 | 98 | 298 | 120 |
| 2011............................. | 609 | 431 | 68 | 101 | 308 | 133 |
| 2012............................. | 781 | 535 | 80 | 128 | 398 | 175 |
| 2013............................. | 925 | 618 | 97 | 150 | 464 | 215 |
| 2014............................. | 1,003 | 648 | 110 | 163 | 496 | 235 |
| 2015............................. | 1,112 | 715 | 138 | 153 | 556 | 266 |
| 2016............................. | 1,174 | 782 | 116 | 182 | 585 | 291 |
| 2017............................. | 1,203 | 849 | 111 | 180 | 599 | 313 |
| 2018............................. | 1,250 | 876 | 111 | 173 | 630 | 336 |

Source: U.S. Census Bureau, "New Residential Construction," <http://www.census.gov/construction/nrc/historical_data/>, accessed May 2019.

## Table 1000. Characteristics of New Privately Owned Single-Family Houses Completed: 2000 to 2018

[Percent distribution, except as noted (1,242 represents 1,242,000). Data are percent distribution of characteristics for all houses completed (includes new houses completed, houses built for sale completed, contractor-built and owner-built houses completed, and houses completed for rent). Percents exclude houses for which characteristics specified were not reported, and are computed using unrounded data]

| Characteristic | 2000 | 2010 | 2017 | 2018 | Characteristic | 2000 | 2010 | 2017 | 2018 |
|---|---|---|---|---|---|---|---|---|---|
| Total houses (1,000)....... | 1,242 | 496 | 795 | 840 | Bedrooms........................ | 100 | 100 | 100 | 100 |
| Construction type.............. | 100 | 100 | 100 | 100 | 2 or less......................... | 11 | 13 | 10 | 10 |
| Site built........................ | 94 | 95 | 97 | 97 | 3................................ | 54 | 52 | 45 | 45 |
| Modular......................... | 3 | 2 | 2 | 1 | 4 or more......................... | 35 | 35 | 46 | 45 |
| Other............................ | 3 | 2 | 2 | 2 | Bathrooms........................ | 100 | 100 | 100 | 100 |
| Exterior wall material............ | 100 | 100 | 100 | 100 | 1-1/2 or less..................... | 7 | 8 | 4 | 4 |
| Brick............................ | 20 | 23 | 22 | 21 | 2................................ | 39 | 36 | 31 | 31 |
| Wood............................ | 14 | 8 | 5 | 5 | 2-1/2 or more..................... | 34 | 32 | 29 | 29 |
| Stucco........................... | 17 | 17 | 24 | 25 | 3 baths or more................... | 20 | 25 | 37 | 36 |
| Vinyl siding..................... | 39 | 36 | 27 | 26 | Heating fuel...................... | 100 | 100 | 100 | 100 |
| Fiber cement..................... | (NA) | 13 | 20 | 20 | Gas.............................. | 70 | 54 | 59 | 60 |
| Other............................ | 8 | 2 | 2 | 2 | Electricity....................... | 27 | 43 | 40 | 39 |
| Floor area....................... | 100 | 100 | 100 | 100 | Oil [3]........................... | 3 | 1 | (NA) | (NA) |
| Under 1,400 sq. ft................ | 14 | 13 | 7 | 7 | Other [3]......................... | 1 | 2 | 1 | 1 |
| 1,400 to 1,799 sq. ft............. | 22 | 19 | 15 | 16 | Heating system................... | 100 | 100 | 100 | 100 |
| 1,800 to 2,399 sq. ft............. | 29 | 27 | 27 | 28 | Forced air furnace.............. | 71 | 56 | 57 | 58 |
| 2,400 to 2,999 sq. ft............. | 17 | 18 | 21 | 22 | Electric heat pump............. | 23 | 38 | 41 | 40 |
| 3,000 to 3,999 sq. ft............. | 13 | 15 | 20 | 19 | Other............................ | 6 | 5 | 3 | 3 |
| 4,000 or more.................... | 5 | 7 | 10 | 9 | Central air-conditioning........ | 100 | 100 | 100 | 100 |
| Average (sq. ft.)................. | 2,266 | 2,392 | 2,631 | 2,588 | With............................ | 85 | 88 | 93 | 93 |
| Median (sq. ft.).................. | 2,057 | 2,169 | 2,426 | 2,386 | Without.......................... | 15 | 12 | 7 | 7 |
| Number of stories.............. | 100 | 100 | 100 | 100 | Fireplaces........................ | 100 | 100 | 100 | 100 |
| 1................................ | 47 | 47 | 44 | 46 | No fireplace..................... | 40 | 51 | 55 | 56 |
| 2 or more [1]..................... | 52 | 53 | 55 | 54 | 1 or more........................ | 59 | 49 | 45 | 44 |
| Foundation....................... | 100 | 100 | 100 | 100 | Parking facilities................ | 100 | 100 | 100 | 100 |
| Full or partial basement...... | 37 | 30 | 26 | 25 | Garage.......................... | 89 | 85 | 91 | 92 |
| Slab and other [2]............... | 46 | 52 | 60 | 60 | Carport.......................... | 1 | 1 | 1 | 1 |
| Crawl space...................... | 17 | 18 | 15 | 14 | No garage or carport.......... | 11 | 13 | 7 | 7 |

NA Not available. [1] Includes houses with 1-1/2 and 2-1/2 stories and split-level houses. [2] Includes raised supports such as pilings and piers, and other types. [3] Beginning in 2014, heating oil and kerosene are included in Other heating fuel.

Source: U.S. Census Bureau and U.S. Department of Housing and Urban Development, "Characteristics of New Housing," <http://www.census.gov/construction/chars/>, accessed August 2019.

# Table 1001. Construction Materials—Producer Price Indexes: 2005 to 2018

[1982=100, except as noted. This index, more formally known as the special commodity grouping index for construction materials, covers materials incorporated as integral parts of a building or normally installed during construction and not readily removable. Excludes consumer durables such as kitchen ranges, refrigerators, etc. For discussion of producer price indexes, see text, Section 14]

| Commodity | 2005 | 2010 | 2013 | 2014 | 2015 | 2016 | 2017 | 2018 |
|---|---|---|---|---|---|---|---|---|
| **Construction materials** | **169.6** | **194.5** | **209.3** | **214.4** | **213.6** | **213.9** | **221.6** | **235.7** |
| Architectural coatings | 203.3 | 264.1 | 308.4 | 309.4 | 302.3 | 303.0 | 306.1 | 320.7 |
| Plastic construction products | 158.8 | 190.9 | 208.1 | 211.1 | 213.1 | 211.9 | 217.3 | 226.1 |
| Softwood cut stock and dimension | 205.1 | 206.0 | 203.9 | 207.4 | 199.7 | 200.0 | 214.2 | 228.1 |
| Softwood lumber, not edge worked [1] | 115.0 | 85.8 | 110.4 | 113.4 | 104.9 | 108.6 | 121.9 | 131.0 |
| Softwood lumber, made from purchased lumber [1] | 111.2 | 111.5 | 121.2 | 126.4 | 128.3 | 130.5 | 152.3 | 171.4 |
| Hardwood cut stock and dimension | 198.4 | 186.2 | 221.7 | 275.8 | 246.6 | 239.8 | 250.9 | 262.9 |
| Hardwood flooring [2] | 168.0 | 161.2 | 184.8 | 199.6 | 195.8 | 188.5 | 179.1 | 184.7 |
| Millwork | 197.2 | 207.0 | 225.8 | 232.3 | 237.2 | 240.6 | 247.6 | 259.5 |
| Softwood veneer and plywood | 223.5 | 197.1 | 236.8 | 245.3 | 234.5 | 214.5 | 234.8 | 274.5 |
| Hardwood veneer and plywood [3] | (NA) | 103.6 | 108.0 | 108.4 | 108.6 | 112.9 | 115.3 | 123.5 |
| Prefabricated wood buildings and components [4] | 206.1 | 215.6 | 231.6 | 236.4 | 240.4 | 243.3 | 251.6 | 263.7 |
| Building paper and building board mill products | 184.9 | 168.4 | 207.9 | 188.9 | 186.3 | 201.0 | 221.3 | 222.9 |
| Pressure and soil pipe and fittings, cast iron | 240.8 | 348.4 | 389.9 | 390.6 | 392.9 | 396.4 | 384.4 | 398.5 |
| Hot rolled steel sheet and strip, incl. tin mill products [5] | 125.4 | 150.7 | 136.1 | 140.3 | 115.9 | 107.2 | 126.9 | 149.6 |
| Hot rolled steel bars, plates, and structural shapes [5] | 159.8 | 192.9 | 199.8 | 206.8 | 185.2 | 164.5 | 178.7 | 205.9 |
| Aluminum extruded and drawn pipe and tube [6] | 102.2 | 98.1 | 96.0 | 101.1 | 95.6 | 90.2 | 102.2 | 111.2 |
| Builders' hardware [7] | 179.2 | 219.4 | 235.0 | 242.2 | 244.5 | 246.8 | 251.0 | 256.7 |
| Plumbing fixtures and fittings | 197.6 | 231.4 | 245.7 | 252.6 | 257.1 | 257.8 | 262.4 | 270.2 |
| Heating equipment | 179.9 | 221.5 | 239.8 | 243.6 | 248.2 | 253.1 | 255.9 | 266.5 |
| Metal doors, sash, and trim | 184.9 | 208.1 | 226.3 | 228.1 | 233.6 | 235.5 | 243.1 | 260.1 |
| Sheet metal products | 169.4 | 191.0 | 196.3 | 198.6 | 199.3 | 197.6 | 202.3 | 212.7 |
| Fabricated structural metal bar joists and concrete reinforcing bars | 163.0 | 176.1 | 183.3 | 187.9 | 190.5 | 194.0 | 199.5 | 216.4 |
| Fabricated metal pipe, tube, and fittings [8] | (NA) | (NA) | 101.0 | 101.9 | 101.5 | 100.3 | 100.9 | 104.9 |
| Residential electric lighting fixtures, except portable [9] | 106.9 | 121.1 | 127.2 | 128.1 | 130.4 | 131.5 | 130.2 | 133.9 |
| Elevators, escalators, and other lifts | 123.5 | 133.8 | 140.1 | 143.1 | 145.4 | 147.1 | 151.2 | 155.0 |
| Air purification equipment/industrial and commercial fans and blowers | 170.9 | 192.2 | 206.0 | 211.7 | 217.3 | 218.4 | 220.9 | 228.6 |
| Plumbing and heating valves (low pressure) [10] | 182.2 | 249.5 | 277.6 | 285.8 | 292.6 | 296.9 | 310.8 | (NA) |
| Electric switches [11] | 101.9 | 124.4 | 147.8 | 152.4 | 153.4 | 151.0 | 150.8 | 149.9 |
| Wire connectors for electrical circuitry [11] | 106.9 | 132.1 | 139.1 | 141.8 | 138.8 | 132.8 | 134.6 | 137.7 |
| Current-carrying wiring devices not elsewhere classified [12] | (NA) | 105.2 | 111.1 | 112.1 | 111.3 | 108.8 | 109.3 | 111.3 |
| Noncurrent-carrying electrical conduit and fittings [6, 13] | 106.6 | 119.2 | 134.6 | 135.4 | 134.1 | 134.1 | 136.1 | 141.8 |
| Other noncurrent-carrying wiring devices [6, 14] | 102.3 | 126.4 | 133.3 | 135.1 | 135.6 | 136.1 | 138.1 | 141.7 |
| Carpets and rugs | 145.3 | 167.5 | 178.4 | 182.8 | 184.1 | 183.9 | 184.5 | 193.1 |
| Resilient (hard surface) floor coverings | 169.0 | 203.2 | (NA) | (NA) | (NA) | (NA) | 232.8 | 236.8 |
| Flat glass (float, sheet, and plate process) | 96.0 | 88.2 | 85.8 | 88.8 | 91.0 | 97.3 | 98.5 | 105.3 |
| Construction sand, gravel, and crushed stone | 195.8 | 262.2 | 278.8 | 289.3 | 299.9 | 312.6 | 323.2 | 334.7 |
| Cement, hydraulic | 176.4 | 193.5 | 199.3 | 208.1 | 223.4 | 235.2 | 246.0 | 252.1 |
| Concrete products | 177.2 | 210.6 | 221.0 | 230.3 | 239.4 | 247.0 | 254.1 | 263.7 |
| Clay construction products excluding refractories | 165.4 | 179.4 | 175.8 | 178.1 | 182.4 | 184.7 | 184.5 | 187.7 |
| Prepared asphalt and tar roofing and siding products | 125.0 | 218.9 | 229.7 | 224.5 | 223.2 | 221.6 | 220.5 | 233.8 |
| Roofing asphalts, pitches, coatings, and cement | 155.0 | 227.5 | 265.7 | 265.8 | 234.3 | 201.3 | 210.5 | 221.4 |
| Gypsum products | 229.6 | 206.6 | 268.7 | 290.6 | 293.1 | 297.1 | 322.9 | 342.6 |
| Insulation materials | 142.2 | 146.6 | 173.4 | 182.9 | 182.6 | 187.8 | 189.1 | 194.7 |
| Paving mixtures and blocks | 156.9 | 279.4 | 317.9 | 323.6 | 313.0 | 294.6 | 293.4 | 313.4 |
| Cut stone and stone products [4] | 145.1 | 147.8 | 148.8 | 152.3 | 156.8 | 161.6 | 163.3 | 168.1 |

NA Not available. [1] December 2003=100. [2] June 1984=100. [3] December 2005=100. [4] June 1984=100. [5] June 1982=100. [6] December 2004=100. [7] Includes lock units, key blanks, door and window hardware, cabinet hardware, etc. [8] December 2011=100. [9] June 1998=100. [10] December 1982=100. [11] December 1999=100. [12] June 2006=100. [13] Includes plastic conduit and fittings. [14] Includes boxes, covers, bar hangers, etc.

Source: U.S. Bureau of Labor Statistics, "Producer Price Indexes," <http://www.bls.gov/ppi/data.htm>, accessed May 2019.

# Table 1002. Subsidized Apartments Completed: 1970 to 2016, and by Type of Subsidy, 2016

[Data shown for rental apartments in buildings with five units or more. Details may not sum to totals because of rounding. Based on sample and subject to sampling variability; see source for details]

| Year | Total apartments completed | Subsidized apartments completed | Percent subsidized | Year and type of subsidy | Number |
|---|---|---|---|---|---|
| 1970 | 526,000 | 55,900 | 11 | **2016** | |
| 1980 | 418,900 | 79,900 | 19 | Total apartments completed | 311,000 |
| 1990 | 294,400 | 13,800 | 5 | **Subsidized apartments completed [1]** | **20,200** |
| 2000 | 300,000 | 24,400 | 8 | Section 8 | 6,000 |
| 2005 | 258,000 | 44,000 | 17 | Housing for Elderly Direct Loan Program | 1,300 |
| 2010 | 146,500 | 31,400 | 21 | Low Income Housing Tax Credit (LHITC) | 13,300 |
| 2014 | 255,700 | 26,400 | 10 | Federal tax exempt multifamily bond financing | 1,000 |
| 2015 | 310,300 | 29,200 | 9 | Other subsidized programs | 6,000 |

[1] Respondents were instructed to select all subsidies that applied to the building.

Source: U.S. Census Bureau, "Survey of Market Absorption of New Multifamily Units, Table Creator" <https://www.census.gov/programs-surveys/soma.html>, accessed April 2018.

# Table 1003. Housing Starts and Average Length of Time to Completion of New Privately Owned Single-Family Homes: 1990 to 2018

[895 represents 895,000. For buildings started in permit-issuing places]

| Year | Total [1] | Purpose of construction | | | Region [2] | | | |
|---|---|---|---|---|---|---|---|---|
| | | Built for sale | Contractor built | Owner built | North-east | Mid-west | South | West |
| STARTS (1,000) | | | | | | | | |
| 1990 | 895 | 529 | 196 | 147 | 104 | 193 | 371 | 226 |
| 1996 | 1,161 | 774 | 218 | 144 | 112 | 254 | 524 | 271 |
| 1997 | 1,134 | 784 | 189 | 131 | 111 | 238 | 507 | 278 |
| 1998 | 1,271 | 882 | 209 | 144 | 122 | 273 | 574 | 303 |
| 1999 | 1,302 | 912 | 208 | 142 | 126 | 289 | 580 | 308 |
| 2000 | 1,231 | 871 | 195 | 128 | 118 | 260 | 556 | 297 |
| 2001 | 1,273 | 919 | 186 | 129 | 111 | 269 | 590 | 303 |
| 2002 | 1,359 | 999 | 198 | 125 | 118 | 277 | 628 | 336 |
| 2003 | 1,499 | 1,120 | 205 | 127 | 116 | 309 | 686 | 388 |
| 2004 | 1,611 | 1,240 | 198 | 130 | 128 | 306 | 743 | 433 |
| 2005 | 1,716 | 1,358 | 197 | 129 | 138 | 306 | 831 | 441 |
| 2006 | 1,465 | 1,121 | 189 | 119 | 118 | 235 | 757 | 356 |
| 2007 | 1,046 | 760 | 151 | 104 | 93 | 171 | 540 | 242 |
| 2008 | 622 | 408 | 107 | 74 | 63 | 102 | 324 | 133 |
| 2009 | 445 | 297 | 83 | 51 | 44 | 76 | 232 | 93 |
| 2010 | 471 | 306 | 83 | 55 | 52 | 79 | 247 | 93 |
| 2011 | 431 | 287 | 74 | 47 | 41 | 74 | 229 | 86 |
| 2012 | 535 | 373 | 82 | 47 | 46 | 92 | 283 | 114 |
| 2013 | 618 | 457 | 91 | 45 | 55 | 102 | 326 | 134 |
| 2014 | 648 | 460 | 110 | 50 | 51 | 106 | 346 | 145 |
| 2015 | 715 | 526 | 109 | 50 | 55 | 107 | 387 | 165 |
| 2016 | 782 | 579 | 116 | 49 | 60 | 121 | 421 | 179 |
| 2017 | 849 | 635 | 116 | 55 | 62 | 130 | 453 | 204 |
| 2018 | 871 | 657 | 118 | 51 | 64 | 123 | 463 | 221 |
| COMPLETION (months) | | | | | | | | |
| 1990 | 6.4 | 5.9 | 5.3 | 10.3 | 9.3 | 5.6 | 5.7 | 6.9 |
| 1996 | 6.0 | 5.2 | 5.8 | 9.9 | 8.2 | 6.1 | 5.6 | 5.6 |
| 1997 | 6.0 | 5.2 | 5.9 | 9.8 | 7.3 | 6.2 | 5.6 | 5.8 |
| 1998 | 6.0 | 5.4 | 6.0 | 9.5 | 7.1 | 6.2 | 5.5 | 6.1 |
| 1999 | 6.1 | 5.5 | 6.4 | 9.2 | 7.0 | 6.4 | 5.7 | 6.3 |
| 2000 | 6.2 | 5.6 | 6.5 | 9.2 | 7.5 | 6.4 | 5.9 | 6.0 |
| 2001 | 6.2 | 5.6 | 7.0 | 9.2 | 7.6 | 6.5 | 5.8 | 6.3 |
| 2002 | 6.1 | 5.5 | 6.6 | 9.6 | 7.3 | 6.4 | 5.6 | 6.2 |
| 2003 | 6.2 | 5.5 | 6.8 | 9.9 | 7.5 | 6.7 | 5.7 | 6.2 |
| 2004 | 6.2 | 5.7 | 7.0 | 9.1 | 7.3 | 6.7 | 5.8 | 6.3 |
| 2005 | 6.4 | 5.9 | 7.6 | 9.8 | 7.7 | 6.6 | 6.0 | 6.8 |
| 2006 | 6.9 | 6.3 | 7.8 | 10.7 | 8.3 | 7.1 | 6.3 | 7.4 |
| 2007 | 7.1 | 6.5 | 7.9 | 10.2 | 8.5 | 7.4 | 6.5 | 8.0 |
| 2008 | 7.7 | 6.8 | 8.5 | 11.1 | 8.9 | 8.2 | 6.7 | 9.0 |
| 2009 | 7.9 | 6.6 | 8.7 | 11.9 | 10.7 | 8.2 | 6.7 | 9.0 |
| 2010 | 6.9 | 5.8 | 7.6 | 11.0 | 10.1 | 7.3 | 5.9 | 7.3 |
| 2011 | 6.6 | 5.4 | 7.7 | 10.8 | 8.9 | 6.9 | 5.9 | 6.8 |
| 2012 | 6.0 | 4.9 | 7.3 | 10.5 | 8.5 | 6.5 | 5.2 | 6.1 |
| 2013 | 6.0 | 5.0 | 7.5 | 11.0 | 8.4 | 6.7 | 5.5 | 5.6 |
| 2014 | 6.2 | 5.4 | 7.5 | 10.8 | 8.6 | 6.9 | 5.7 | 6.2 |
| 2015 | 6.3 | 5.5 | 7.6 | 11.1 | 8.9 | 7.0 | 5.8 | 6.1 |
| 2016 | 6.6 | 5.8 | 7.8 | 11.5 | 9.6 | 6.9 | 6.0 | 6.7 |
| 2017 | 6.5 | 5.7 | 8.1 | 11.2 | 9.5 | 7.2 | 5.9 | 6.7 |
| 2018 | 6.7 | 5.9 | 8.4 | 11.4 | 9.3 | 7.5 | 6.0 | 7.1 |

[1] Includes units built for rent not shown separately. [2] For composition of regions, see map, inside front cover.

Source: U.S. Census Bureau, "New Residential Construction," <http://www.census.gov/construction/nrc/>, accessed May 2019.

# Table 1004. Price Indexes of New Single-Family Houses Sold by Region: 1970 to 2018

[2005=100. Based on kinds of homes sold in 2005. Includes value of the lot. For composition of regions, see map, inside front cover]

| Year | Total | North-east | Midwest | South | West | Year | Total | North-east | Midwest | South | West |
|---|---|---|---|---|---|---|---|---|---|---|---|
| 1970 | 14.9 | 13.4 | 17.9 | 18.2 | 10.2 | 2004 | 92.8 | 91.6 | 96.7 | 94.4 | 88.2 |
| 1975 | 22.1 | 19.6 | 25.4 | 26.4 | 15.9 | 2005 | 100.0 | 100.0 | 100.0 | 100.0 | 100.0 |
| 1980 | 38.9 | 30.2 | 41.2 | 44.4 | 31.9 | 2006 | 104.7 | 102.6 | 102.9 | 105.4 | 105.2 |
| 1985 | 46.2 | 43.1 | 48.2 | 53.9 | 36.4 | 2007 | 104.9 | 101.5 | 102.8 | 107.4 | 102.6 |
| 1990 | 55.7 | 58.0 | 58.6 | 60.6 | 46.2 | 2008 | 99.5 | 100.8 | 98.9 | 103.7 | 92.7 |
| 1994 | 62.9 | 62.0 | 69.4 | 68.1 | 51.9 | 2009 | 95.1 | 97.1 | 96.0 | 101.1 | 84.8 |
| 1995 | 64.3 | 62.3 | 70.9 | 70.1 | 52.7 | 2010 | 95.0 | 101.1 | 96.9 | 99.5 | 85.4 |
| 1996 | 66.0 | 63.2 | 72.5 | 71.2 | 55.3 | 2011 | 94.3 | 100.0 | 97.8 | 99.6 | 83.1 |
| 1997 | 67.5 | 65.9 | 74.3 | 72.7 | 56.5 | 2012 | 97.6 | 102.1 | 101.5 | 102.7 | 86.3 |
| 1998 | 69.2 | 66.1 | 76.0 | 74.4 | 58.4 | 2013 | 104.7 | 108.2 | 105.3 | 110.1 | 94.7 |
| 1999 | 72.8 | 69.1 | 79.5 | 78.1 | 62.0 | 2014 | 110.2 | 115.2 | 112.6 | 115.4 | 99.5 |
| 2000 | 75.6 | 73.0 | 83.5 | 80.6 | 64.4 | 2015 | 112.9 | 115.7 | 116.4 | 118.3 | 101.9 |
| 2001 | 77.9 | 76.7 | 84.4 | 82.8 | 67.1 | 2016 | 120.4 | 121.0 | 118.7 | 125.1 | 113.3 |
| 2002 | 81.4 | 80.2 | 86.1 | 86.3 | 71.5 | 2017 | 126.8 | 130.5 | 126.5 | 131.9 | 117.9 |
| 2003 | 86.0 | 84.3 | 90.6 | 89.4 | 78.2 | 2018 | 132.4 | 127.6 | 128.9 | 136.2 | 128.9 |

Source: U.S. Census Bureau, "Construction Price Indexes," <http://www.census.gov/construction/cpi/>, accessed June 2019.

# Table 1005. New Privately Owned Single-Family Houses Sold by Region and Type of Financing, 2005 to 2018, and by Sales-Price Group, 2018

[In thousands (1,283 represents 1,283,000). Based on a national probability sample of monthly interviews with builders or owners of single-family houses for which building permits have been issued or, for nonpermit areas, on which construction has started. For details, see source and Appendix III. For composition of regions, see map inside front cover]

| Year and sales-price group | Total sold | Region | | | | Financing type | | | |
|---|---|---|---|---|---|---|---|---|---|
| | | Northeast | Midwest | South | West | Conventional [1] | FHA insured [2] | VA guaranteed [3] | Cash |
| 2005 | 1,283 | 81 | 205 | 638 | 358 | 1,150 | 51 | 28 | 52 |
| 2010 | 323 | 31 | 45 | 173 | 74 | 189 | 81 | 35 | 19 |
| 2012 | 368 | 29 | 47 | 195 | 97 | 234 | 75 | 35 | 24 |
| 2013 | 429 | 31 | 61 | 233 | 105 | 296 | 67 | 36 | 31 |
| 2014 | 437 | 28 | 59 | 243 | 108 | 311 | 51 | 38 | 37 |
| 2015 | 501 | 24 | 61 | 286 | 130 | 348 | 81 | 42 | 30 |
| 2016 | 561 | 32 | 69 | 318 | 142 | 396 | 88 | 48 | 29 |
| 2017 | 613 | 40 | 72 | 339 | 163 | 442 | 86 | 49 | 36 |
| **2018** | **617** | **32** | **76** | **348** | **160** | **461** | **74** | **43** | **39** |
| Under $125,000 | 7 | (Z) | (Z) | 6 | 1 | 5 | 1 | (Z) | (Z) |
| $125,000 to $149,999 | 11 | (Z) | 1 | 10 | (Z) | 9 | 1 | 1 | (Z) |
| $150,000 to $199,999 | 54 | 1 | 12 | 39 | 3 | 34 | 14 | 4 | 2 |
| $200,000 to $249,999 | 89 | 2 | 15 | 64 | 9 | 48 | 24 | 10 | 7 |
| $250,000 to $299,999 | 98 | 4 | 12 | 63 | 19 | 65 | 17 | 10 | 7 |
| $300,000 to $399,999 | 153 | 5 | 19 | 86 | 43 | 121 | 13 | 11 | 9 |
| $400,000 to $499,999 | 90 | 6 | 8 | 38 | 38 | 76 | 3 | 6 | 5 |
| $500,000 to $749,999 | 78 | 8 | 5 | 33 | 32 | 70 | 1 | 2 | 5 |
| $750,000 and over | 36 | 7 | 3 | 11 | 15 | 32 | (Z) | (Z) | 3 |

Z Less than 500 units. [1] Includes houses reporting other types of financing, not shown separately. [2] Federal Housing Administration. [3] U.S. Department of Veterans Affairs.

Source: U.S. Census Bureau, "New Residential Sales—Annual Characteristics of New Housing," <https://www.census.gov/construction/nrs/index.html>, accessed July 2019.

# Table 1006. Median Sales Price of New Privately Owned Single-Family Houses Sold by Region: 1980 to 2018

[In dollars. For definition of median, see Guide to Tabular Presentation. For composition of regions, see map inside front cover. Based on a national probability sample of monthly interviews with builders or owners of single-family houses selected from building permits and a canvassing of areas not requiring permits. For more details, see source]

| Year | U.S. | Northeast | Midwest | South | West | Year | U.S. | Northeast | Midwest | South | West |
|---|---|---|---|---|---|---|---|---|---|---|---|
| 1980 | 64,600 | 69,500 | 63,400 | 59,600 | 72,300 | 2012 | 245,200 | 368,800 | 230,600 | 227,000 | 270,000 |
| 1985 | 84,300 | 103,300 | 80,300 | 75,000 | 92,600 | 2013 | 268,900 | 371,200 | 255,300 | 246,600 | 310,500 |
| 1990 | 122,900 | 159,000 | 107,900 | 99,000 | 147,500 | 2014 | 288,500 | 398,000 | 273,800 | 264,000 | 339,000 |
| 1995 | 133,900 | 180,000 | 134,000 | 124,500 | 141,000 | 2015 | 294,200 | 442,800 | 276,700 | 271,500 | 348,500 |
| 2000 | 169,000 | 227,400 | 169,700 | 140,000 | 196,400 | 2016 | 307,800 | 428,300 | 277,100 | 281,400 | 367,700 |
| 2005 | 240,900 | 343,800 | 216,900 | 197,300 | 332,600 | 2017 | 323,100 | 490,400 | 284,400 | 291,200 | 390,000 |
| 2010 | 221,800 | 329,900 | 197,700 | 196,800 | 259,300 | 2018 | 326,400 | 484,600 | 290,900 | 291,600 | 410,600 |

Source: U.S. Census Bureau, "New Residential Sales—Annual Characteristics of New Housing," <https://www.census.gov/construction/nrs/index.html>, accessed July 2019.

# Table 1007. New Manufactured (Mobile) Homes Placed for Residential Use and Average Sales Price by Region: 1990 to 2018

[195.4 represents 195,400. A mobile home is a moveable dwelling, 8 feet or more wide and 40 feet or more long, designed to be towed on its own chassis, with transportation gear integral to the unit when it leaves the factory, and without need of permanent foundation. Excluded are travel trailers, motor homes, and modular housing. Data are based on a probability sample and subject to sampling variability; see source. For composition of regions, see map inside front cover]

| Year | Units placed (1,000) | | | | | Average sales price (dollars) | | | | |
|---|---|---|---|---|---|---|---|---|---|---|
| | Total | Northeast | Midwest | South | West | U.S. | Northeast | Midwest | South | West |
| 1990 | 195.4 | 18.8 | 37.7 | 108.4 | 30.6 | 27,800 | 30,000 | 27,000 | 24,500 | 39,300 |
| 1995 | 319.4 | 15.0 | 57.5 | 203.2 | 43.7 | 35,300 | 35,800 | 35,700 | 33,300 | 44,100 |
| 2000 | 280.9 | 14.9 | 48.7 | 178.7 | 38.6 | 46,400 | 47,000 | 47,900 | 44,300 | 54,100 |
| 2005 | 122.9 | 9.2 | 17.1 | 68.1 | 28.5 | 62,600 | 67,000 | 60,600 | 55,700 | 79,900 |
| 2006 | 112.4 | 7.9 | 14.5 | 66.1 | 23.9 | 64,300 | 65,300 | 59,100 | 58,900 | 83,400 |
| 2007 | 94.8 | 7.0 | 10.8 | 59.4 | 17.7 | 65,400 | 66,100 | 64,900 | 59,900 | 85,500 |
| 2008 | 80.5 | 5.0 | 8.2 | 54.0 | 13.3 | 64,700 | 68,400 | 65,700 | 59,600 | 84,900 |
| 2009 | 54.5 | 3.5 | 5.3 | 37.8 | 7.9 | 63,100 | 61,600 | 65,400 | 59,300 | 81,500 |
| 2010 | 50.7 | 3.8 | 5.8 | 34.6 | 6.6 | 62,800 | 65,200 | 60,700 | 60,000 | 79,000 |
| 2011 | 47.6 | 3.3 | 6.3 | 31.5 | 6.5 | 60,500 | 62,700 | 60,800 | 58,400 | 70,600 |
| 2012 | 52.8 | 3.9 | 7.9 | 34.4 | 6.6 | 62,200 | 63,400 | 60,900 | 60,100 | 75,300 |
| 2013 | 56.3 | 4.0 | 7.5 | 37.4 | 7.5 | 64,000 | 66,500 | 62,900 | 61,200 | 79,100 |
| 2014 [1] | 44.1 | 3.0 | 6.8 | 27.5 | 6.8 | 65,300 | 67,900 | 60,600 | 63,000 | 80,700 |
| 2015 | 45.6 | 3.1 | 6.6 | 28.5 | 7.5 | 68,000 | 72,100 | 60,800 | 65,100 | 88,200 |
| 2016 | 51.5 | 3.1 | 8.2 | 32.3 | 7.8 | 70,600 | 77,600 | 61,500 | 68,500 | 88,500 |
| 2017 | 53.9 | 3.6 | 7.7 | 34.9 | 7.8 | 71,900 | 78,400 | 65,400 | 68,200 | 97,600 |
| 2018 | 55.1 | 4.0 | 8.6 | 33.8 | 8.7 | 78,500 | 80,100 | 72,100 | 75,700 | 99,000 |

[1] Beginning 2014, data not comparable to prior years due to a change in methodology. See source for details.

Source: U.S. Census Bureau, "Manufactured Housing Survey (MHS) Tables," <https://www.census.gov/programs-surveys/mhs/data/tables.All.html>, accessed June 2019.

## Table 1008. Existing Single-Family Homes Sold and Price by Region: 1990 to 2018

[2,914 represents 2,914,000. Includes existing detached single-family homes and townhomes. Based on data (adjusted and aggregated to regional and national totals) reported by participating real estate multiple listing services. For definition of median, see Guide to Tabular Presentation. See Table 1010 for data on condominiums and cooperatives. For composition of regions, see map inside front cover]

| Year | Homes sold (1,000) | | | | | Median sales price (dollars) | | | | |
|---|---|---|---|---|---|---|---|---|---|---|
| | U.S. | Northeast | Midwest | South | West | U.S. | Northeast | Midwest | South | West |
| 1990 | 2,914 | 513 | 804 | 1,008 | 589 | 97,300 | 146,200 | 76,700 | 86,300 | 141,200 |
| 1995 | 3,519 | 615 | 940 | 1,212 | 752 | 117,000 | 146,500 | 96,500 | 99,200 | 153,600 |
| 1996 | 3,797 | 656 | 986 | 1,283 | 872 | 122,600 | 147,800 | 102,800 | 105,000 | 160,200 |
| 1997 | 3,964 | 683 | 1,004 | 1,356 | 921 | 129,000 | 152,400 | 108,900 | 111,300 | 169,000 |
| 1998 | 4,495 | 745 | 1,129 | 1,592 | 1,029 | 136,000 | 157,100 | 116,300 | 118,000 | 179,500 |
| 1999 | 4,649 | 728 | 1,145 | 1,704 | 1,072 | 141,200 | 160,700 | 121,600 | 122,100 | 189,400 |
| 2000 | 4,603 | 715 | 1,116 | 1,707 | 1,065 | 147,300 | 161,200 | 125,600 | 130,300 | 199,200 |
| 2001 | 4,735 | 710 | 1,154 | 1,795 | 1,076 | 156,600 | 169,400 | 132,300 | 139,600 | 211,700 |
| 2002 | 4,974 | 730 | 1,217 | 1,872 | 1,155 | 167,600 | 190,100 | 138,300 | 149,700 | 234,300 |
| 2003 | 5,446 | 770 | 1,323 | 2,073 | 1,280 | 180,200 | 220,300 | 143,700 | 159,700 | 254,700 |
| 2004 | 5,958 | 821 | 1,389 | 2,310 | 1,438 | 195,200 | 254,400 | 151,500 | 171,800 | 289,100 |
| 2005 | 6,180 | 838 | 1,411 | 2,457 | 1,474 | 219,000 | 281,600 | 168,300 | 181,100 | 340,300 |
| 2006 | 5,677 | 787 | 1,314 | 2,352 | 1,224 | 221,900 | 280,300 | 164,800 | 183,700 | 350,500 |
| 2007 | 4,398 | 587 | 1,091 | 1,819 | 901 | 217,900 | 288,100 | 161,400 | 178,800 | 342,500 |
| 2008 | 3,665 | 471 | 882 | 1,439 | 873 | 196,600 | 271,500 | 150,500 | 169,400 | 276,100 |
| 2009 | 3,870 | 480 | 918 | 1,460 | 1,012 | 172,100 | 243,200 | 142,900 | 155,000 | 215,400 |
| 2010 | 3,708 | 465 | 859 | 1,426 | 958 | 173,100 | 243,900 | 140,800 | 153,700 | 220,700 |
| 2011 | 3,787 | 449 | 863 | 1,471 | 1,004 | 166,200 | 237,500 | 135,800 | 149,300 | 204,500 |
| 2012 | 4,128 | 492 | 1,002 | 1,605 | 1,029 | 177,200 | 237,200 | 143,700 | 158,400 | 234,300 |
| 2013 | 4,484 | 540 | 1,122 | 1,775 | 1,047 | 197,400 | 248,900 | 155,700 | 174,200 | 276,400 |
| 2014 | 4,344 | 533 | 1,060 | 1,789 | 962 | 208,900 | 252,200 | 164,200 | 182,900 | 294,400 |
| 2015 | 4,646 | 576 | 1,162 | 1,885 | 1,023 | 223,900 | 262,500 | 175,500 | 196,400 | 319,100 |
| 2016 | 4,838 | 617 | 1,222 | 1,955 | 1,044 | 235,500 | 265,400 | 184,400 | 209,200 | 342,900 |
| 2017 | 4,892 | 615 | 1,222 | 1,989 | 1,066 | 248,800 | 275,700 | 196,200 | 222,700 | 369,400 |
| 2018 | 4,742 | 581 | 1,192 | 1,972 | 997 | 261,600 | 289,200 | 201,700 | 231,600 | 388,600 |

Source: NATIONAL ASSOCIATION OF REALTORS ®. See also <http://www.realtor.org/research-and-statistics>.

## Table 1009. Median Sales Price of Existing Single-Family Homes by Selected Metropolitan Area: 2010 and 2018

[In thousands of dollars (173.1 represents $173,100). Covers existing detached single-family homes and townhouses. Areas are metropolitan statistical areas defined by Office of Management and Budget, though in some areas an exact match is not possible from available data]

| Metropolitan area | 2010 | 2018 | Metropolitan area | 2010 | 2018 |
|---|---|---|---|---|---|
| United States, total | 173.1 | 261.6 | New Orleans-Metairie, LA | 159.7 | 210.1 |
| Allentown-Bethlehem-Easton, PA-NJ | 224.0 | 199.3 | New York-Jersey City-White Plains, NY-NJ | 450.0 | 377.8 |
| Anaheim-Santa Ana-Irvine, CA | 546.4 | 820.0 | New York-Newark-Jersey City, NY-NJ-PA | 393.7 | 410.0 |
| Atlanta-Sandy Springs-Marietta, GA | 114.8 | 219.9 | Oklahoma City, OK | 145.7 | 159.5 |
| Atlantic City-Hammonton, NJ | 226.4 | 192.8 | Omaha-Council Bluffs, NE-IA | 137.3 | 191.7 |
| Baltimore-Columbia-Towson, MD | 246.1 | 285.6 | Orlando-Kissimmee-Sanford, FL | 137.0 | 265.0 |
| Boston-Cambridge-Newton, MA-NH | 357.3 | 477.4 | Philadelphia-Camden- | | |
| Boulder, CO | 358.1 | 607.4 | Wilmington, PA-NJ-DE-MD | 214.9 | 229.0 |
| Bridgeport-Stamford-Norwalk, CT | 408.6 | 451.5 | Phoenix-Mesa-Scottsdale, AZ | 139.2 | 269.8 |
| Charleston-North Charleston, SC | 200.5 | 283.0 | Portland-South Portland, ME | 218.0 | 289.7 |
| Chicago-Naperville-Elgin, IL | 191.4 | 259.4 | Portland-Vancouver-Hillsboro, OR-WA | 237.3 | 395.7 |
| Cincinnati, OH-KY-IN | 128.0 | 174.3 | Providence-Warwick, RI-MA | 228.5 | 292.5 |
| Cleveland-Elyria, OH | 114.5 | 153.3 | Raleigh, NC | 190.4 | 283.6 |
| Colorado Springs, CO | 195.5 | 312.2 | Reno, NV | 179.5 | 383.1 |
| Dallas-Fort Worth-Arlington, TX | 143.8 | 260.0 | Richmond, VA | (NA) | 258.8 |
| Deltona-Daytona Beach-Ormond Beach, FL | 115.0 | 209.9 | Riverside-San Bernardino-Ontario, CA | 179.3 | 360.0 |
| Denver-Aurora-Lakewood, CO | 232.4 | 449.9 | Sacramento-Roseville-Arden-Arcade, CA | 184.2 | 365.0 |
| Des Moines-West Des Moines, IA | 150.9 | 204.8 | Saint Louis, MO-IL | 131.1 | 177.5 |
| Eugene-Springfield, OR | 196.3 | 291.7 | Salem, OR | 173.5 | 294.8 |
| Hartford-West Hartford-East Hartford, CT | 235.8 | 235.0 | Salt Lake City, UT | 206.5 | 331.7 |
| Houston-The Woodlands-Sugar Land, TX | 155.0 | 238.8 | San Diego-Carlsbad, CA | 385.7 | 634.0 |
| Indianapolis-Carmel-Anderson, IN | 123.3 | 187.1 | San Francisco-Oakland-Hayward, CA | 525.6 | 987.5 |
| Las Vegas-Henderson-Paradise, NV | 138.0 | 288.8 | San Jose-Sunnyvale-Santa Clara, CA | 595.0 | 1,340.0 |
| Little Rock-North Little Rock-Conway, AR | 132.5 | 146.4 | Seattle-Tacoma-Bellevue, WA | 295.7 | 501.4 |
| Los Angeles-Long Beach-Glendale, CA | 323.3 | 590.8 | Tampa-St. Petersburg-Clearwater, FL | 130.0 | 235.0 |
| Louisville/Jefferson County, KY-IN | 134.6 | 180.1 | Trenton, NJ | 250.7 | 245.5 |
| Madison, WI | 217.7 | 283.7 | Tucson, AZ | 156.6 | 223.0 |
| Memphis, TN-MS-AR | 120.2 | 177.9 | Urban Honolulu, HI | 607.6 | 802.7 |
| Miami-Fort Lauderdale-West Palm Beach, FL | 199.9 | 350.0 | Virginia Beach-Norfolk- | | |
| Milwaukee-Waukesha-West Allis, WI | 205.9 | 250.3 | Newport News, VA-NC | 205.0 | 219.0 |
| Minneapolis-St. Paul-Bloomington, MN-WI | 170.6 | 273.4 | Washington-Arlington- | | |
| New Haven-Milford, CT | 231.0 | 232.9 | Alexandria, DC-VA-MD-WV | 325.3 | 424.0 |

NA Not available.

Source: NATIONAL ASSOCIATION OF REALTORS ®. See also <http://www.realtor.org/research-and-statistics>.

# Table 1010. Existing Apartment Condominiums and Cooperatives—Units Sold and Median Sales Price by Region: 1990 to 2018

[272 represents 272,000. Data shown here reflect revisions from prior estimates. For definition of median, see Guide to Tabular Presentation. For composition of regions, see map inside front cover]

| Year | Units sold (1,000) | | | | | Median sales price (dollars) | | | | |
|------|------|-----------|---------|-------|------|------|-----------|---------|--------|---------|
| | U.S. | Northeast | Midwest | South | West | U.S. | Northeast | Midwest | South | West |
| 1990 | 272 | 73 | 55 | 80 | 64 | 86,900 | 107,500 | 70,200 | 64,200 | 114,600 |
| 1991 | 261 | 76 | 55 | 75 | 55 | 87,500 | 104,600 | 73,900 | 65,600 | 114,500 |
| 1992 | 282 | 88 | 61 | 77 | 56 | 87,700 | 100,600 | 79,000 | 66,600 | 117,400 |
| 1993 | 312 | 98 | 66 | 89 | 59 | 86,000 | 96,800 | 78,900 | 66,500 | 112,000 |
| 1994 | 343 | 108 | 68 | 101 | 66 | 88,800 | 97,100 | 86,200 | 66,700 | 118,600 |
| 1995 | 333 | 108 | 66 | 96 | 63 | 89,000 | 92,500 | 90,700 | 67,800 | 114,800 |
| 1996 | 370 | 120 | 72 | 105 | 73 | 92,600 | 95,100 | 95,200 | 70,600 | 119,800 |
| 1997 | 407 | 134 | 79 | 111 | 83 | 97,300 | 98,600 | 99,100 | 73,300 | 128,900 |
| 1998 | 470 | 157 | 92 | 126 | 95 | 102,500 | 100,900 | 106,400 | 76,800 | 137,700 |
| 1999 | 534 | 182 | 102 | 145 | 105 | 110,100 | 109,800 | 114,600 | 80,700 | 143,900 |
| 2000 | 571 | 197 | 106 | 160 | 108 | 114,000 | 108,500 | 121,700 | 84,200 | 149,100 |
| 2001 | 601 | 203 | 116 | 174 | 108 | 125,600 | 121,200 | 134,800 | 93,200 | 160,400 |
| 2002 | 657 | 221 | 129 | 193 | 114 | 144,900 | 143,500 | 148,600 | 109,900 | 187,000 |
| 2003 | 732 | 250 | 146 | 211 | 125 | 168,500 | 178,100 | 162,600 | 126,900 | 222,400 |
| 2004 | 820 | 292 | 161 | 230 | 137 | 197,100 | 214,100 | 181,000 | 156,600 | 258,000 |
| 2005 | 896 | 331 | 177 | 245 | 143 | 223,900 | 245,100 | 189,100 | 187,300 | 283,800 |
| 2006 | 801 | 299 | 169 | 211 | 122 | 221,900 | 249,700 | 190,900 | 184,000 | 264,700 |
| 2007 | 624 | 126 | 100 | 236 | 162 | 226,300 | 256,100 | 195,200 | 185,100 | 263,300 |
| 2008 | 459 | 103 | 71 | 164 | 121 | 209,800 | 252,500 | 188,200 | 166,800 | 218,500 |
| 2009 | 464 | 105 | 58 | 180 | 121 | 175,600 | 232,800 | 157,100 | 132,700 | 162,100 |
| 2010 | 474 | 95 | 53 | 202 | 124 | 171,700 | 242,200 | 150,500 | 118,500 | 154,700 |
| 2011 | 477 | 89 | 52 | 210 | 126 | 165,100 | 237,700 | 129,000 | 107,800 | 176,000 |
| 2012 | 528 | 104 | 66 | 229 | 129 | 173,700 | 240,100 | 127,800 | 123,900 | 196,700 |
| 2013 | 603 | 118 | 79 | 265 | 141 | 194,900 | 250,200 | 138,300 | 147,900 | 249,200 |
| 2014 | 591 | 112 | 76 | 262 | 141 | 204,300 | 254,900 | 149,300 | 154,700 | 273,300 |
| 2015 | 608 | 115 | 78 | 266 | 149 | 210,700 | 249,300 | 157,900 | 162,900 | 294,500 |
| 2016 | 614 | 116 | 82 | 263 | 153 | 220,700 | 256,600 | 166,200 | 172,600 | 321,300 |
| 2017 | 619 | 116 | 80 | 271 | 152 | 234,300 | 271,700 | 175,200 | 183,800 | 345,600 |
| 2018 | 601 | 110 | 77 | 273 | 141 | 241,000 | 284,600 | 177,600 | 184,500 | 361,500 |

Source: NATIONAL ASSOCIATION OF REALTORS ®. See also <http://www.realtor.org/research-and-statistics>.

# Table 1011. New Unfurnished Apartments Completed and Rented in 3 Months by Region: 1990 to 2017

[214.3 represents 214,300. Structures with five or more units, privately financed, nonsubsidized, unfurnished rental apartments. Based on sample and subject to sampling variability; see source for details. For composition of regions, see map, inside front cover]

| Year and rent | Number (1,000) | | | | | Percent rented in 3 months | | | | |
|---------------|------|-----------|---------|-------|------|------|-----------|---------|-------|------|
| | U.S. | North-east | Midwest | South | West | U.S. | North-east | Midwest | South | West |
| 1990 | 214.3 | 12.7 | 44.3 | 77.2 | 80.0 | 67 | 66 | 75 | 64 | 65 |
| 1995 | 155.0 | 7.1 | 31.7 | 78.5 | 37.7 | 73 | 74 | 75 | 72 | 73 |
| 2000 | 226.2 | 14.8 | 39.5 | 125.9 | 45.9 | 72 | 85 | 76 | 67 | 77 |
| 2005 | 113.0 | 4.7 | 20.5 | 57.8 | 30.0 | 64 | 75 | 64 | 62 | 64 |
| 2006 | 116.4 | 5.8 | 13.6 | 68.4 | 28.6 | 58 | 41 | 58 | 60 | 56 |
| 2007 | 104.8 | 5.6 | 9.5 | 61.8 | 28.0 | 55 | 66 | 58 | 52 | 58 |
| 2008 | 146.4 | 8.9 | 17.2 | 88.2 | 32.1 | 50 | 52 | 58 | 48 | 51 |
| 2009 | 163.0 | 10.0 | 17.2 | 93.3 | 42.4 | 51 | 56 | 74 | 49 | 44 |
| 2010 | 89.1 | 5.9 | 16.2 | 42.8 | 24.1 | 61 | 79 | 68 | 60 | 55 |
| 2011 | 74.7 | 10.9 | 18.6 | 38.8 | 6.4 | 59 | 67 | 53 | 60 | 54 |
| 2012 | 104.5 | 8.9 | 17.8 | 54.3 | 23.5 | 63 | 88 | 60 | 61 | 61 |
| 2013 | 134.2 | 14.2 | 14.3 | 75.8 | 29.9 | 63 | 63 | 78 | 60 | 64 |
| 2014 | 210.8 | 28.1 | 35.6 | 93.6 | 53.4 | 61 | 54 | 60 | 61 | 66 |
| 2015 | 261.8 | 29.9 | 47.1 | 114.9 | 69.9 | 60 | 62 | 67 | 53 | 66 |
| 2016 | 262.5 | 30.2 | 40.0 | 126.8 | 65.4 | 55 | 49 | 56 | 51 | 63 |
| **2017** | **286.0** | **42.0** | **41.9** | **136.0** | **66.1** | **55** | **56** | **55** | **51** | **63** |
| Less than $850 | 18.0 | 0.3 | 3.0 | 13.3 | 1.4 | 55 | 100 | 78 | 46 | 81 |
| $850 to $1,049 | 29.6 | 1.1 | 8.9 | 16.9 | 2.7 | 62 | 95 | 68 | 54 | 75 |
| $1,050 to $1,249 | 37.7 | 0.9 | 8.0 | 21.6 | 7.2 | 61 | 77 | 53 | 59 | 74 |
| $1,250 to $1,449 | 41.4 | 2.2 | 6.1 | 23.4 | 9.8 | 61 | 66 | 55 | 55 | 77 |
| $1,450 to $1,649 | 32.5 | 2.0 | 3.6 | 19.9 | 7.0 | 55 | 54 | 43 | 52 | 67 |
| $1,650 to $1,849 | 26.0 | 4.6 | 2.2 | 13.0 | 6.2 | 56 | 63 | 54 | 49 | 65 |
| $1,850 to $2,409 | 21.1 | 4.7 | 2.5 | 9.2 | 4.8 | 54 | 63 | 69 | 48 | 48 |
| $2,050 to $2,249 | 13.3 | 2.2 | 1.1 | 4.9 | 5.1 | 52 | 74 | 27 | 46 | 54 |
| $2,250 to $2,449 | 16.1 | 6.3 | 0.7 | 3.5 | 4.6 | 44 | 54 | 20 | 40 | 42 |
| $2,450 or more | 50.1 | 17.7 | 4.8 | 10.3 | 17.3 | 47 | 46 | 46 | 32 | 56 |
| Median asking rent (dol.) | 1,550 | 2,344 | 1,285 | 1,387 | 1,811 | 1,478 | 2,222 | 1,205 | 1,351 | 1,651 |

Source: U.S. Census Bureau, "Survey of Market Absorption of New Multifamily Units, Characteristics of Apartments: 2018 (Apartments Completed in 2017 and Absorbed During Their First 3 Months After Completion) Tables," and earlier releases, <https://www.census.gov/programs-surveys/soma.html>, accessed August 2019.

## Table 1012. Total Housing Inventory for the United States: 2000 to 2018

[In thousands (116,264 represents 116,264,000), except percent. Data for 2000-2009 have been revised based on Vintage 2010 estimates. Data for 2010-2018 are based on Vintage 2017 estimates. Based on the Current Population Survey/Housing Vacancy Survey and subject to sampling error; see source and Appendix III for details]

| Item | 2000 | 2005 | 2010 | 2012 | 2013 | 2014 | 2015 | 2016 | 2017 | 2018 |
|---|---|---|---|---|---|---|---|---|---|---|
| All housing units............... | 116,264 | 125,363 | 131,807 | 132,840 | 133,535 | 134,371 | 135,274 | 136,279 | 137,356 | 138,449 |
| Vacant....................... | 13,680 | 15,880 | 18,907 | 18,271 | 18,225 | 17,955 | 17,428 | 17,391 | 17,396 | 16,991 |
| Year-round vacant............... | 10,315 | 12,060 | 14,422 | 13,805 | 13,769 | 13,488 | 13,031 | 13,026 | 13,220 | 12,997 |
| For rent...................... | 2,980 | 3,763 | 4,322 | 3,825 | 3,695 | 3,434 | 3,294 | 3,244 | 3,401 | 3,233 |
| For sale only................. | 1,088 | 1,468 | 2,000 | 1,557 | 1,538 | 1,453 | 1,422 | 1,350 | 1,258 | 1,193 |
| Rented or sold................ | 935 | 1,073 | 915 | 987 | 1,075 | 1,074 | 1,084 | 1,059 | 1,164 | 1,109 |
| Held off market.............. | 5,313 | 5,755 | 7,182 | 7,435 | 7,461 | 7,529 | 7,231 | 7,372 | 7,399 | 7,463 |
| Occasional use.............. | 1,901 | 1,909 | 2,264 | 2,285 | 2,392 | 2,248 | 2,021 | 2,106 | 2,184 | 2,116 |
| Usual residence elsewhere..... | 1,050 | 1,142 | 1,266 | 1,262 | 1,256 | 1,365 | 1,356 | 1,453 | 1,355 | 1,366 |
| Other...................... | 2,363 | 2,703 | 3,654 | 3,888 | 3,812 | 3,918 | 3,855 | 3,814 | 3,859 | 3,980 |
| Seasonal [1].................... | 3,364 | 3,820 | 4,485 | 4,467 | 4,456 | 4,467 | 4,398 | 4,364 | 4,174 | 3,993 |
| Total occupied.................. | 102,584 | 109,484 | 112,899 | 114,568 | 115,309 | 116,415 | 117,846 | 118,887 | 119,962 | 121,458 |
| Owner........................ | 69,223 | 75,411 | 75,460 | 74,966 | 75,077 | 75,038 | 75,022 | 75,401 | 76,605 | 78,211 |
| Renter........................ | 33,362 | 34,073 | 37,440 | 39,603 | 40,232 | 41,376 | 42,823 | 43,486 | 43,357 | 43,247 |
| PERCENT DISTRIBUTION | | | | | | | | | | |
| All housing units.................. | 100.0 | 100.0 | 100.0 | 100.0 | 100.0 | 100.0 | 100.0 | 100.0 | 100.0 | 100.0 |
| Vacant......................... | 11.8 | 12.7 | 14.3 | 13.8 | 13.6 | 13.4 | 12.9 | 12.8 | 12.7 | 12.3 |
| Total occupied.................. | 88.2 | 87.3 | 85.7 | 86.2 | 86.4 | 86.6 | 87.1 | 87.2 | 87.3 | 87.7 |
| Owner........................ | 59.5 | 60.2 | 57.3 | 56.4 | 56.2 | 55.8 | 55.5 | 55.3 | 55.8 | 56.5 |
| Renter........................ | 28.7 | 27.2 | 28.4 | 29.8 | 30.1 | 30.8 | 31.7 | 31.9 | 31.6 | 31.2 |

[1] Includes vacant seasonal mobile homes.

Source: U.S. Census Bureau, "Housing Vacancies and Home Ownership," <http://www.census.gov/housing/hvs/>, accessed April 2019.

## Table 1013. Occupied Housing Inventory by Age of Householder: 2000 to 2018

[In thousands (102,584 represents 102,584,000). Data for 2000-2009 have been revised based on Vintage 2010 estimates. Data for 2010-2018 are based on Vintage 2017 estimates. Based on the Current Population Survey/Housing Vacancy Survey; see source for details]

| Age of householder | 2000 | 2005 | 2010 | 2012 | 2013 | 2014 | 2015 | 2016 | 2017 | 2018 |
|---|---|---|---|---|---|---|---|---|---|---|
| Total.................... | 102,584 | 109,484 | 112,899 | 114,568 | 115,309 | 116,415 | 117,846 | 118,887 | 119,962 | 121,458 |
| Under 25 years old....... | 5,966 | 6,614 | 6,116 | 6,075 | 6,160 | 6,161 | 6,148 | 6,189 | 5,965 | 6,028 |
| 25 to 29 years old........ | 8,199 | 8,893 | 9,124 | 8,782 | 8,778 | 8,885 | 9,047 | 9,123 | 9,312 | 9,538 |
| 30 to 34 years old........ | 9,941 | 9,696 | 9,568 | 9,973 | 10,018 | 10,127 | 10,133 | 10,189 | 10,198 | 10,240 |
| 35 to 39 years old........ | 11,576 | 10,648 | 9,887 | 9,570 | 9,556 | 9,739 | 9,864 | 10,133 | 10,395 | 10,582 |
| 40 to 44 years old........ | 12,016 | 11,858 | 10,624 | 10,674 | 10,408 | 10,205 | 10,129 | 9,912 | 9,772 | 9,675 |
| 45 to 49 years old........ | 10,837 | 11,916 | 11,798 | 10,973 | 10,765 | 10,596 | 10,608 | 10,561 | 10,579 | 10,498 |
| 50 to 54 years old........ | 9,416 | 10,716 | 11,828 | 11,851 | 11,902 | 11,771 | 11,497 | 11,273 | 10,931 | 10,849 |
| 55 to 59 years old........ | 7,457 | 9,614 | 10,534 | 11,294 | 11,373 | 11,428 | 11,614 | 11,734 | 11,649 | 11,541 |
| 60 to 64 years old........ | 6,013 | 7,422 | 9,431 | 9,954 | 10,022 | 10,224 | 10,538 | 10,688 | 11,034 | 11,314 |
| 65 to 69 years old........ | 5,680 | 5,968 | 7,103 | 7,988 | 8,357 | 8,766 | 9,338 | 9,671 | 9,808 | 10,008 |
| 70 to 74 years old........ | 5,421 | 5,073 | 5,499 | 5,816 | 6,205 | 6,482 | 6,719 | 6,975 | 7,595 | 8,023 |
| 75 years old and over.... | 10,061 | 11,066 | 11,387 | 11,619 | 11,767 | 12,032 | 12,211 | 12,442 | 12,724 | 13,163 |

Source: U.S. Census Bureau, "Housing Vacancies and Home Ownership," <http://www.census.gov/housing/hvs/>, accessed April 2019.

## Table 1014. Vacancy Rates for Housing Units—Characteristics: 2000 to 2018

[In percent. Rate is the proportion of vacant housing for rent or for sale to the total rental and homeowner supply, which comprises occupied units, units rented or sold and awaiting occupancy, and vacant units available for rent or sale. Based on the Current Population Survey/Housing Vacancy Survey; see source for details. For composition of regions, see map inside front cover]

| Characteristic | Rental units | | | | | Homeowner units | | | | |
|---|---|---|---|---|---|---|---|---|---|---|
| | 2000 | 2010 | 2015 | 2017 | 2018 | 2000 | 2010 | 2015 | 2017 | 2018 |
| Total units.............. | 8.0 | 10.2 | 7.1 | 7.2 | 6.9 | 1.6 | 2.6 | 1.8 | 1.6 | 1.5 |
| Northeast................. | 5.6 | 7.6 | 5.5 | 5.5 | 5.3 | 1.2 | 1.7 | 1.9 | 1.7 | 1.5 |
| Midwest.................. | 8.8 | 10.8 | 7.6 | 7.9 | 7.5 | 1.3 | 2.6 | 1.7 | 1.5 | 1.3 |
| South.................... | 10.5 | 12.7 | 8.9 | 9.0 | 8.6 | 1.9 | 2.8 | 2.1 | 1.8 | 1.7 |
| West.................... | 5.8 | 8.2 | 5.1 | 5.3 | 5.0 | 1.5 | 2.7 | 1.4 | 1.2 | 1.3 |
| Units in structure: | | | | | | | | | | |
| 1 unit.................... | 7.0 | 9.2 | 7.1 | 6.1 | 5.7 | 1.5 | 2.2 | 1.7 | 1.5 | 1.3 |
| 2 units or more.......... | 8.7 | 11.1 | 7.2 | 8.2 | 7.9 | 4.7 | 9.2 | 5.1 | 4.3 | 4.1 |
| 5 units or more.......... | 9.2 | 11.7 | 7.4 | 8.6 | 8.4 | 5.8 | 9.2 | 4.5 | 3.7 | 3.7 |
| Units with: | | | | | | | | | | |
| 3 rooms or fewer........ | 10.3 | 13.8 | 9.9 | 10.8 | 10.5 | 10.4 | 14.8 | 13.6 | 12.2 | 10.5 |
| 4 rooms................. | 8.2 | 10.5 | 7.0 | 6.9 | 6.6 | 2.9 | 5.7 | 4.4 | 3.4 | 3.1 |
| 5 rooms................. | 6.9 | 8.9 | 6.1 | 5.7 | 5.4 | 2.0 | 3.0 | 2.2 | 1.7 | 1.7 |
| 6 rooms or more........ | 5.2 | 7.1 | 5.6 | 5.8 | 5.5 | 1.1 | 1.7 | 1.2 | 1.1 | 1.0 |

Source: U.S. Census Bureau, "Housing Vacancies and Home Ownership," <http://www.census.gov/housing/hvs/>, accessed April 2019.

# Table 1015. Housing Units and Tenure—States: 2017

[137,407 represents 137,407,000. The American Community Survey universe includes the household population and the population living in institutions, college dormitories, and other group quarters. Based on a sample and subject to sampling variability; see Appendix III]

| State | Housing units (1,000) | | | | | | Housing tenure | | | |
|---|---|---|---|---|---|---|---|---|---|---|
| | | | Vacant | | | | Owner-occupied units | | Renter-occupied units | |
| | Total | Occu-pied | Total [1] | For sea-sonal use [2] | For rent only | For sale only | Total (1,000) | Average house-hold size (persons) | Total (1,000) | Average house-hold size (persons) |
| United States............ | 137,407 | 120,063 | 17,344 | 5,704 | 2,898 | 1,240 | 76,684 | 2.72 | 43,379 | 2.51 |
| Alabama.................... | 2,259 | 1,842 | 417 | 84 | 74 | 23 | 1,253 | 2.65 | 588 | 2.43 |
| Alaska...................... | 317 | 251 | 66 | 33 | 8 | 3 | 159 | 2.96 | 91 | 2.64 |
| Arizona..................... | 2,999 | 2,553 | 446 | 217 | 59 | 33 | 1,652 | 2.71 | 901 | 2.65 |
| Arkansas................... | 1,370 | 1,153 | 217 | 58 | 36 | 15 | 752 | 2.58 | 401 | 2.44 |
| California................... | 14,177 | 13,005 | 1,172 | 417 | 215 | 73 | 7,125 | 3.03 | 5,880 | 2.91 |
| Colorado................... | 2,385 | 2,139 | 246 | 123 | 41 | 15 | 1,395 | 2.64 | 744 | 2.42 |
| Connecticut............... | 1,517 | 1,357 | 161 | 32 | 35 | 19 | 898 | 2.69 | 459 | 2.31 |
| Delaware................... | 433 | 358 | 75 | 43 | 8 | 7 | 254 | 2.65 | 104 | 2.53 |
| District of Columbia....... | 315 | 281 | 33 | 4 | 10 | 2 | 119 | 2.50 | 163 | 2.19 |
| Florida..................... | 9,442 | 7,690 | 1,752 | 913 | 275 | 108 | 5,010 | 2.66 | 2,680 | 2.71 |
| Georgia.................... | 4,282 | 3,745 | 537 | 105 | 102 | 45 | 2,355 | 2.77 | 1,390 | 2.62 |
| Hawaii..................... | 543 | 458 | 85 | 38 | 19 | 3 | 268 | 3.19 | 190 | 2.78 |
| Idaho...................... | 722 | 625 | 97 | 52 | 13 | 7 | 435 | 2.77 | 190 | 2.53 |
| Illinois..................... | 5,359 | 4,809 | 551 | 56 | 125 | 61 | 3,182 | 2.71 | 1,626 | 2.39 |
| Indiana.................... | 2,885 | 2,557 | 328 | 50 | 62 | 27 | 1,766 | 2.62 | 792 | 2.33 |
| Iowa....................... | 1,398 | 1,258 | 140 | 23 | 29 | 15 | 900 | 2.53 | 357 | 2.16 |
| Kansas.................... | 1,274 | 1,129 | 145 | 18 | 32 | 14 | 744 | 2.63 | 385 | 2.27 |
| Kentucky.................. | 1,984 | 1,725 | 259 | 43 | 34 | 19 | 1,147 | 2.59 | 578 | 2.34 |
| Louisiana.................. | 2,062 | 1,737 | 324 | 61 | 59 | 18 | 1,132 | 2.68 | 605 | 2.51 |
| Maine...................... | 743 | 541 | 202 | 143 | 14 | 8 | 396 | 2.51 | 145 | 2.11 |
| Maryland................... | 2,449 | 2,207 | 242 | 58 | 47 | 25 | 1,473 | 2.76 | 735 | 2.51 |
| Massachusetts............. | 2,895 | 2,605 | 290 | 129 | 40 | 18 | 1,624 | 2.70 | 981 | 2.27 |
| Michigan................... | 4,595 | 3,930 | 665 | 295 | 58 | 43 | 2,803 | 2.57 | 1,127 | 2.26 |
| Minnesota................. | 2,438 | 2,162 | 276 | 153 | 28 | 16 | 1,548 | 2.64 | 615 | 2.21 |
| Mississippi................ | 1,324 | 1,092 | 232 | 49 | 42 | 15 | 748 | 2.65 | 344 | 2.63 |
| Missouri................... | 2,792 | 2,385 | 407 | 103 | 55 | 31 | 1,597 | 2.59 | 788 | 2.28 |
| Montana................... | 510 | 423 | 87 | 48 | 9 | 4 | 293 | 2.53 | 131 | 2.16 |
| Nebraska.................. | 838 | 754 | 83 | 19 | 17 | 5 | 500 | 2.60 | 254 | 2.24 |
| Nevada.................... | 1,250 | 1,095 | 155 | 50 | 36 | 15 | 619 | 2.75 | 475 | 2.65 |
| New Hampshire........... | 635 | 529 | 106 | 75 | 6 | 5 | 369 | 2.61 | 160 | 2.12 |
| New Jersey................ | 3,616 | 3,219 | 397 | 139 | 55 | 36 | 2,054 | 2.84 | 1,165 | 2.57 |
| New Mexico............... | 938 | 768 | 170 | 60 | 23 | 11 | 521 | 2.72 | 246 | 2.54 |
| New York.................. | 8,328 | 7,304 | 1,023 | 363 | 149 | 66 | 3,930 | 2.78 | 3,374 | 2.47 |
| North Carolina............ | 4,623 | 3,955 | 668 | 212 | 101 | 46 | 2,587 | 2.58 | 1,368 | 2.43 |
| North Dakota.............. | 375 | 316 | 58 | 16 | 17 | 4 | 201 | 2.47 | 116 | 2.03 |
| Ohio....................... | 5,202 | 4,667 | 535 | 50 | 96 | 44 | 3,070 | 2.53 | 1,597 | 2.24 |
| Oklahoma................. | 1,734 | 1,470 | 264 | 40 | 48 | 20 | 962 | 2.65 | 508 | 2.50 |
| Oregon.................... | 1,769 | 1,604 | 165 | 69 | 24 | 13 | 1,007 | 2.63 | 597 | 2.36 |
| Pennsylvania.............. | 5,694 | 5,009 | 606 | 199 | 100 | 54 | 3,421 | 2.60 | 1,588 | 2.20 |
| Rhode Island.............. | 468 | 409 | 60 | 19 | 8 | 4 | 249 | 2.65 | 160 | 2.24 |
| South Carolina............ | 2,285 | 1,905 | 380 | 138 | 60 | 24 | 1,310 | 2.60 | 595 | 2.50 |
| South Dakota............. | 393 | 344 | 48 | 16 | 8 | 2 | 233 | 2.55 | 111 | 2.17 |
| Tennessee................ | 2,959 | 2,589 | 370 | 70 | 65 | 23 | 1,694 | 2.59 | 895 | 2.43 |
| Texas...................... | 10,933 | 9,624 | 1,310 | 256 | 345 | 104 | 5,964 | 3.02 | 3,660 | 2.64 |
| Utah....................... | 1,085 | 975 | 109 | 52 | 20 | 8 | 682 | 3.27 | 294 | 2.81 |
| Vermont................... | 335 | 257 | 79 | 59 | 3 | 3 | 178 | 2.45 | 78 | 2.06 |
| Virginia.................... | 3,513 | 3,121 | 392 | 89 | 73 | 35 | 2,077 | 2.70 | 1,043 | 2.52 |
| Washington................ | 3,103 | 2,840 | 263 | 97 | 41 | 17 | 1,784 | 2.67 | 1,057 | 2.37 |
| West Virginia.............. | 892 | 715 | 177 | 49 | 18 | 12 | 519 | 2.53 | 196 | 2.31 |
| Wisconsin................. | 2,695 | 2,350 | 345 | 198 | 43 | 20 | 1,566 | 2.53 | 785 | 2.15 |
| Wyoming.................. | 277 | 226 | 51 | 17 | 13 | 3 | 160 | 2.56 | 66 | 2.36 |

[1] Includes other reasons not shown separately. [2] For seasonal, recreational, or occasional use.

Source: U.S. Census Bureau, 2017 American Community Survey, B25002, "Occupancy Status"; B25003, "Tenure"; B25004, "Vacancy Status"; and B25010, "Average Household Size of Units by Tenure"; <http://factfinder.census.gov/>, accessed November 2018.

# Table 1016. Net Stock of Residential Fixed Assets: 1990 to 2017

[In billions of dollars (5,844 represents $5,844,000,000,000). End of year estimates]

| Item | 1990 | 1995 | 2000 | 2005 | 2010 | 2014 | 2015 | 2016 | 2017 |
|---|---|---|---|---|---|---|---|---|---|
| **Total residential fixed assets............** | **5,844** | **7,407** | **10,040** | **15,482** | **16,116** | **18,951** | **19,407** | **20,648** | **21,581** |
| By type of owner and legal form of organization: | | | | | | | | | |
| Private....................................... | 5,702 | 7,228 | 9,810 | 15,150 | 15,783 | 18,566 | 19,015 | 20,232 | 21,153 |
| Corporate................................. | 63 | 73 | 100 | 151 | 169 | 195 | 206 | 219 | 234 |
| Noncorporate............................ | 5,640 | 7,155 | 9,710 | 14,999 | 15,614 | 18,371 | 18,808 | 20,013 | 20,919 |
| Government.................................. | 142 | 179 | 230 | 332 | 333 | 385 | 392 | 416 | 429 |
| Federal.................................... | 52 | 62 | 75 | 103 | 98 | 107 | 107 | 111 | 113 |
| State and local............................ | 90 | 117 | 154 | 229 | 234 | 278 | 285 | 305 | 315 |
| By tenure group: [1] | | | | | | | | | |
| Owner-occupied............................. | 4,184 | 5,485 | 7,596 | 12,053 | 12,529 | 14,864 | 15,175 | 16,176 | 16,910 |
| Tenant-occupied............................ | 1,634 | 1,893 | 2,408 | 3,377 | 3,531 | 4,013 | 4,156 | 4,389 | 4,583 |

[1] Excludes stocks of other nonfarm residential assets, which consists primarily of dormitories and of fraternity and sorority houses.

Source: U.S. Bureau of Economic Analysis, Fixed Assets Accounts Tables, "Table 5.1 Current-Cost Net Stock of Residential Fixed Assets by Type of Owner, Legal Form of Organization, and Tenure Group," <http://www.bea.gov/iTable/index_FA.cfm>, accessed February 2019.

## Table 1017. Homeowner and Rental Vacancy Rates by State: 2018

[In percent. From the Current Population Survey/Housing Vacancy Survey, and includes the civilian noninstitutionalized population, people in noninstitutional group quarters, and military households off post or with families on post (must include 1 household member who is a civilian adult). Based on a sample and subject to sampling variability, see Appendix III]

| State | Homeowner vacancy rate | Rental vacancy rate | State | Homeowner vacancy rate | Rental vacancy rate | State | Homeowner vacancy rate | Rental vacancy rate |
|---|---|---|---|---|---|---|---|---|
| **United States** | **1.5** | **6.9** | Iowa | 1.5 | 7.4 | North Carolina | 1.4 | 7.1 |
| | | | Kansas | 1.6 | 10.5 | North Dakota | 2.4 | 14.3 |
| | | | Kentucky | 1.3 | 6.2 | Ohio | 1.1 | 7.1 |
| Alabama | 1.9 | 13.2 | Louisiana | 1.9 | 10.1 | Oklahoma | 2.5 | 11.6 |
| Alaska | 1.8 | 11.1 | Maine | 1.1 | 4.4 | Oregon | 1.3 | 4.6 |
| Arizona | 1.9 | 6.0 | Maryland | 1.4 | 9.0 | Pennsylvania | 1.6 | 6.7 |
| Arkansas | 2.1 | 9.9 | Massachusetts | 1.0 | 4.2 | Rhode Island | 1.2 | 3.2 |
| California | 1.2 | 4.4 | Michigan | 1.2 | 7.4 | South Carolina | 1.9 | 11.0 |
| Colorado | 0.9 | 3.4 | Minnesota | 0.4 | 5.0 | South Dakota | 1.3 | 7.3 |
| Connecticut | 1.7 | 6.1 | Mississippi | 1.6 | 9.7 | Tennessee | 1.4 | 8.6 |
| Delaware | 1.1 | 7.1 | Missouri | 1.6 | 10.0 | Texas | 1.4 | 8.9 |
| Dist. of Columbia | 1.2 | 7.9 | Montana | 1.4 | 5.9 | Utah | 1.0 | 5.4 |
| Florida | 2.2 | 8.2 | Nebraska | 1.2 | 7.3 | Vermont | 1.1 | 4.2 |
| Georgia | 1.6 | 7.1 | Nevada | 1.1 | 6.2 | Virginia | 1.5 | 6.5 |
| Hawaii | 1.7 | 8.5 | New Hampshire | 0.9 | 3.7 | Washington | 1.1 | 5.1 |
| Idaho | 1.2 | 5.5 | New Jersey | 1.5 | 5.0 | West Virginia | 2.2 | 7.4 |
| Illinois | 1.7 | 7.4 | New Mexico | 2.0 | 9.1 | Wisconsin | 1.4 | 4.6 |
| Indiana | 1.3 | 9.0 | New York | 1.7 | 5.2 | Wyoming | 2.6 | 13.0 |

Source: U.S. Census Bureau, "Housing Vacancies and Home Ownership," <http://www.census.gov/housing/hvs/>, accessed April 2019.

## Table 1018. Homeowner and Rental Vacancy Rates by Metropolitan Area: 2018

[In percent. From the Current Population Survey/Housing Vacancy Survey, and includes the civilian noninstitutionalized population, people in noninstitutional group quarters, and military households off post or with families on post (must include 1 household member who is a civilian adult). Data are based on 2010 metropolitan/nonmetropolitan definitions. Subject to sampling error; see source and Appendix III for details]

| Metropolitan area | Homeowner vacancy rate | Rental vacancy rate | Metropolitan area | Homeowner vacancy rate | Rental vacancy rate |
|---|---|---|---|---|---|
| **Inside metropolitan areas** | **1.4** | **6.7** | Memphis, TN-AR-MS | 1.6 | 11.7 |
| Akron, OH | 0.1 | 3.3 | Miami-Fort Lauderdale-West Palm Beach, FL | 1.9 | 7.4 |
| Albany-Schenectady-Troy, NY | 1.7 | 10.8 | Milwaukee-Waukesha-West Allis, WI | 1.4 | 5.9 |
| Albuquerque, NM | 1.8 | 7.8 | Minneapolis-St. Paul-Bloomington, MN-WI | 0.4 | 4.1 |
| Allentown-Bethlehem-Easton, PA-NJ | 0.9 | 5.7 | Nashville-Davidson-Murfreesboro-Franklin, TN | 0.8 | 7.5 |
| Atlanta-Sandy Springs-Roswell, GA | 1.1 | 6.6 | New Haven-Milford, CT | 1.4 | 5.6 |
| Austin-Round Rock, TX | 1.2 | 7.0 | New Orleans-Metairie, LA | 1.7 | 9.7 |
| Baltimore-Columbia-Towson, MD | 1.6 | 9.4 | New York-Newark-Jersey City, NY-NJ-PA | 1.6 | 4.5 |
| Baton Rouge, LA | 1.4 | 7.6 | North Port-Bradenton-Sarasota, FL | 2.1 | 7.3 |
| Birmingham-Hoover, AL | 1.8 | 11.9 | Oklahoma City, OK | 2.7 | 11.8 |
| Boston-Cambridge-Newton, MA-NH | 1.0 | 3.8 | Omaha-Council Bluffs, NE-IA | 0.7 | 7.1 |
| Bridgeport-Stamford-Norwalk, CT | 1.6 | 8.2 | Orlando-Kissimmee-Sanford, FL | 2.6 | 5.8 |
| Buffalo-Cheektowaga-Niagara Falls, NY | 2.1 | 6.9 | Philadelphia-Camden-Wilmington, PA-NJ-DE-MD | 1.2 | 6.4 |
| Cape Coral-Fort Myers, FL | 3.0 | 5.8 | Phoenix-Mesa-Scottsdale, AZ | 1.4 | 6.2 |
| Charleston-N. Charleston-Summerville, SC | 3.4 | 17.0 | Pittsburgh, PA | 2.2 | 6.3 |
| Charlotte-Concord-Gastonia, NC-SC | 1.7 | 5.6 | Portland-Vancouver-Hillsboro, OR-WA | 1.4 | 3.8 |
| Chicago-Naperville-Elgin, IL | 1.6 | 7.0 | Providence-Warwick, RI-MA | 1.1 | 5.0 |
| Cincinnati, OH-KY-IN | 1.5 | 4.4 | Raleigh, NC | 0.9 | 6.4 |
| Cleveland-Elyria, OH | 0.9 | 6.9 | Richmond, VA | 2.1 | 5.4 |
| Columbia, SC | 1.9 | 9.4 | Riverside-San Bernardino-Ontario, CA | 1.6 | 5.1 |
| Columbus, OH | 1.5 | 8.6 | Rochester, NY | 2.0 | 5.7 |
| Dallas-Ft. Worth-Arlington, TX | 1.4 | 7.4 | Sacramento-Roseville-Arden-Arcade, CA | 1.5 | 5.1 |
| Dayton, OH | 1.0 | 11.2 | St. Louis, MO-IL | 0.9 | 7.4 |
| Denver-Aurora-Lakewood, CO | 0.9 | 3.8 | Salt Lake City, UT | 0.5 | 6.1 |
| Detroit-Warren-Dearborn, MI | 1.0 | 6.8 | San Antonio-New Braunfels, TX | 0.6 | 7.4 |
| Fresno, CA | 1.2 | 1.8 | San Diego-Carlsbad, CA | 0.7 | 4.5 |
| Grand Rapids-Wyoming, MI | 0.3 | 6.8 | San Francisco-Oakland-Hayward, CA | 0.9 | 5.4 |
| Greensboro-High Point, NC | 1.0 | 11.4 | San Jose-Sunnyvale-Santa Clara, CA | 0.5 | 4.6 |
| Hartford-West Hartford-East Hartford, CT | 1.9 | 4.5 | Seattle-Tacoma-Bellevue, WA | 0.8 | 4.8 |
| Houston-The Woodlands-Sugar Land, TX | 2.0 | 8.8 | Syracuse, NY | 1.0 | 5.8 |
| Indianapolis-Carmel-Anderson, IN | 1.5 | 9.9 | Tampa-St. Petersburg-Clearwater, FL | 2.1 | 9.9 |
| Jacksonville, FL | 1.3 | 5.6 | Toledo, OH | 3.3 | 12.6 |
| Kansas City, MO-KS | 1.2 | 7.9 | Tucson, AZ | 1.8 | 4.4 |
| Knoxville, TN | 1.6 | 7.4 | Tulsa, OK | 2.6 | 10.1 |
| Las Vegas-Henderson-Paradise, NV | 0.9 | 6.8 | Urban Honolulu, HI | 1.4 | 6.5 |
| Little Rock-North Little Rock-Conway, AR | 1.8 | 10.9 | Virginia Beach-Norfolk-Newport News, VA | 1.2 | 7.1 |
| Los Angeles-Long Beach-Anaheim, CA | 1.2 | 4.0 | Washington-Arlington-Alexandria, DC-VA-MD-WV | 1.1 | 6.2 |
| Louisville/Jefferson County, KY-IN | 1.4 | 7.7 | Worcester, MA | 0.7 | 2.6 |

Source: U.S. Census Bureau, "Housing Vacancies and Home Ownership," <http://www.census.gov/housing/hvs/>, accessed April 2019.

# Table 1019. Housing Units—Characteristics by Tenure and Region: 2017

[In thousands of units (137,400 represents 137,400,000), except as indicated. As of Fall. Based on the American Housing Survey; see Appendix III. For composition of regions, see map, inside front cover]

| Characteristic | Total housing units | Sea-sonal units | Year-round units | | | | | | | Vacant units |
|---|---|---|---|---|---|---|---|---|---|---|
| | | | Occupied | | | | | | | |
| | | | Total | Owner | Renter | North-east | Mid-west | South | West | |
| **Total units** | **137,400** | **2,793** | **121,600** | **77,570** | **43,990** | **21,829** | **27,047** | **45,457** | **27,226** | **13,050** |
| Percent distribution | 100.0 | 2.0 | 88.5 | 56.5 | 32.0 | 15.9 | 19.7 | 33.1 | 19.8 | 9.5 |
| Units in structure: | | | | | | | | | | |
| Single family detached | 84,830 | 1,685 | 76,830 | 64,380 | 12,450 | 11,676 | 18,778 | 29,624 | 16,752 | 6,310 |
| Single family attached | 10,040 | 154 | 8,958 | 4,735 | 4,223 | 2,295 | 1,763 | 2,920 | 1,981 | 928 |
| 2 to 4 units | 9,744 | 133 | 8,363 | 1,120 | 7,243 | 2,709 | 1,588 | 2,306 | 1,760 | 1,248 |
| 5 to 9 units | 6,645 | 59 | 5,780 | 528 | 5,253 | 1,004 | 1,140 | 2,124 | 1,512 | 805 |
| 10 to 19 units | 6,180 | 73 | 5,282 | 413 | 4,869 | 765 | 1024 | 2,132 | 1,361 | 826 |
| 20 or more units | 11,496 | 213 | 9,543 | 1,346 | 8,196 | 2,879 | 1,732 | 2,577 | 2,354 | 1,740 |
| Manufactured/mobile home [1] | 8,397 | 477 | 6,727 | 4,969 | 1,758 | 494 | 1,016 | 3,751 | 1,468 | 1,192 |
| Year structure built: | | | | | | | | | | |
| Median year (est.) | 1977 | 1978 | 1977 | 1978 | 1974 | (NA) | (NA) | (NA) | (NA) | 1975 |
| 2016 to 2017 | 1,007 | 21 | 841 | 621 | 220 | 79 | 130 | 392 | 241 | 145 |
| 2010 to 2015 | 5,772 | 103 | 5,113 | 3,105 | 2,007 | 532 | 844 | 2,630 | 1,105 | 557 |
| 2005 to 2009 | 9,046 | 232 | 7,936 | 5,449 | 2,487 | 789 | 1,350 | 3,908 | 1,890 | 877 |
| 2000 to 2004 | 10,520 | 248 | 9,448 | 6,325 | 3,123 | 870 | 1,834 | 4,495 | 2,248 | 827 |
| 1995 to 1999 | 10,000 | 154 | 9,132 | 6,537 | 2,596 | 786 | 2,023 | 4,322 | 2,000 | 718 |
| 1990 to 1994 | 7,271 | 153 | 6,564 | 4,825 | 1,739 | 799 | 1,507 | 2,633 | 1,627 | 554 |
| 1985 to 1989 | 10,120 | 239 | 8,952 | 5,749 | 3,203 | 1,119 | 1,548 | 4,059 | 2,225 | 934 |
| 1980 to 1984 | 8,851 | 193 | 7,736 | 4,843 | 2,893 | 916 | 1,311 | 3,521 | 1,989 | 922 |
| 1970 to 1979 | 20,460 | 465 | 17,950 | 11,110 | 6,846 | 2,386 | 3,902 | 7,014 | 4,651 | 2,038 |
| 1960 to 1969 | 14,290 | 254 | 12,680 | 8,167 | 4,518 | 2,407 | 2,913 | 4,524 | 2,840 | 1,350 |
| 1950 to 1959 | 14,250 | 254 | 12,820 | 8,436 | 4,382 | 2,950 | 3,325 | 3,809 | 2,732 | 1,182 |
| 1940 to 1949 | 6,617 | 142 | 5,740 | 3,490 | 2,250 | 1,346 | 1,394 | 1,704 | 1,297 | 735 |
| 1930 to 1939 | 4,205 | 124 | 3,620 | 2,012 | 1,608 | 1,159 | 954 | 881 | 626 | 461 |
| 1920 to 1929 | 5,409 | 66 | 4,682 | 2,417 | 2,265 | 1,827 | 1,296 | 713 | 847 | 662 |
| 1919 or earlier | 9,575 | 146 | 8,340 | 4,483 | 3,857 | 3,863 | 2,717 | 856 | 904 | 1,088 |
| Stories in structure: [2] | | | | | | | | | | |
| 1 story | 42,830 | 1,046 | 37,750 | 26,100 | 11,650 | 1,497 | 4,477 | 20,832 | 10,945 | 4,038 |
| 2 stories | 46,570 | 725 | 41,630 | 26,120 | 15,510 | 6,667 | 11,065 | 13,432 | 10,471 | 4,208 |
| 3 stories | 29,210 | 348 | 26,470 | 16,940 | 9,532 | 8,699 | 8,816 | 5,694 | 3,262 | 2,395 |
| 4 or more stories | 10,315 | 198 | 8,901 | 3,360 | 5,541 | 4,464 | 1,671 | 1,728 | 1037 | 1,217 |
| Foundation: [3] | | | | | | | | | | |
| Full basement | 29,130 | 351 | 26,950 | 23,220 | 3,738 | 8,952 | 11,818 | 4,015 | 2,168 | 1,830 |
| Partial building | 9,895 | 126 | 9,139 | 7,991 | 1149 | 2,612 | 3,555 | 1,759 | 1,214 | 629 |
| Crawlspace | 20,390 | 461 | 18,130 | 14,150 | 3,988 | 804 | 2,759 | 8,872 | 5,701 | 1,796 |
| Concrete slab | 33,460 | 756 | 29,940 | 22,610 | 7,331 | 1,446 | 2,184 | 17,013 | 9,297 | 2,766 |
| Equipment: | | | | | | | | | | |
| With complete facilities [4] | 133,000 | 2,444 | 120,100 | 77,220 | 42,930 | 21,492 | 26,759 | 45,004 | 26,894 | 10,380 |
| Lacking complete facilities [4] | 4,436 | 349 | 1,416 | 351 | 1,064 | 337 | 294 | 454 | 330 | 2,671 |
| Kitchen sink | 136,300 | 2,643 | 121,300 | 77,500 | 43,760 | 21,741 | 26,998 | 45,368 | 27,156 | 12,360 |
| Refrigerator | 134,300 | 2,493 | 121,100 | 77,350 | 43,720 | 21,743 | 26,925 | 45,283 | 27,124 | 10,720 |
| Cooking stove or range | 133,500 | 2,487 | 120,100 | 76,960 | 43,130 | 21,567 | 26,686 | 44,938 | 26,909 | 10,960 |
| Microwave oven only | 863 | 24 | 703 | 271 | 431 | 115 | 210 | 252 | 126 | 136 |
| Dishwasher | 95,690 | 1,487 | 87,080 | 62,160 | 24,920 | 13,961 | 18,464 | 34,034 | 20,624 | 7,117 |
| Washing machine | 110,500 | 1,680 | 102,900 | 75,210 | 27,690 | 16,337 | 23,134 | 40,793 | 22,635 | 5,966 |
| Clothes dryer | 108,700 | 1,656 | 101,100 | 74,340 | 26,770 | 15,779 | 23,005 | 40,034 | 22,286 | 5,894 |
| Main heating equipment: | | | | | | | | | | |
| Warm-air furnace | 88,920 | 1,474 | 79,380 | 53,310 | 26,070 | 10,392 | 22,131 | 28,557 | 18,297 | 8,063 |
| Steam or hot water system | 12,250 | 143 | 11,100 | 6,335 | 4,761 | 8,061 | 1,815 | 589 | 630 | 1,011 |
| Electric heat pump | 16,260 | 383 | 14,130 | 9,751 | 4,377 | 475 | 919 | 11,155 | 1,579 | 1,744 |
| Built-in electric units | 5,667 | 185 | 4,925 | 1,898 | 3,026 | 1,426 | 1,061 | 781 | 1,658 | 557 |
| Floor, wall, or pipeless furnace | 6,324 | 128 | 5,616 | 2,481 | 3,135 | 843 | 610 | 1,438 | 2,726 | 579 |
| Room heaters with flue | 884 | 32 | 740 | 398 | 342 | 165 | 92 | 299 | 184 | 112 |
| Room heaters without flue | 903 | 37 | 749 | 476 | 273 | 26 | 48 | 589 | 86 | 117 |
| Portable electric heaters | 2,268 | 99 | 2,018 | 950 | 1068 | 53 | 75 | 1296 | 594 | 150 |
| Stoves | 1,527 | 79 | 1,348 | 1081 | 267 | 287 | 215 | 291 | 557 | 100 |
| Fireplaces, with and without inserts | 351 | 31 | 295 | 245 | 51 | 26 | 42 | 112 | 117 | 25 |
| Cooking stove | 66 | 5 | 58 | 32 | 26 | 17 | 4 | 21 | 15 | 3 |
| None | 1,459 | 160 | 848 | 453 | 395 | 10 | 6 | 164 | 667 | 451 |
| Main cooling equipment: | | | | | | | | | | |
| Central air conditioning | 93,840 | 1,566 | 84,480 | 58,680 | 25,800 | 8,550 | 20,386 | 39,849 | 15,703 | 7,794 |
| One or more room units | 27,360 | 384 | 25,400 | 12,740 | 12,660 | 10,809 | 5,262 | 4,825 | 4,508 | 1,568 |
| Source of water: | | | | | | | | | | |
| Public system or private company | (NA) | (NA) | 107,800 | 65,820 | 41,950 | 18,478 | 22,939 | 41,095 | 25,257 | (NA) |
| Individual well | (NA) | (NA) | 13,530 | 11,540 | 1,981 | 3,319 | 4,086 | 4,309 | 1,811 | (NA) |
| Means of sewage disposal: | | | | | | | | | | |
| Public sewer | (NA) | (NA) | 99,570 | 58,520 | 41,050 | 17,515 | 22,219 | 35,725 | 24,100 | (NA) |
| Septic tank or cesspool | (NA) | (NA) | 21,720 | 18,860 | 2,858 | 4,252 | 4,741 | 9,643 | 3,081 | (NA) |

NA Not available. [1] Includes trailers. Includes width not reported, not shown separately. [2] Excludes mobile homes; includes basements and finished attics. [3] Includes only single family homes (1 unit, attached or detached). [4] A complete kitchen includes sink, refrigerator, oven or burners.

Source: U.S. Census Bureau, "American Housing Survey: AHS Table Creator," <http://www.census.gov/programs-surveys/ahs/data.html>, accessed February 2019.

# Table 1020. Housing Units by Units in Structure and State: 2017

[In percent, except as indicated (137,407 represents 137,407,000). The American Community Survey universe includes the household population and the population living in institutions, college dormitories, and other group quarters. Based on a sample and subject to sampling variability; see Appendix III]

| State | Total housing units (1,000) | 1-unit detached | 1-unit attached | 2 units | 3 or 4 units | 5 or 9 units | 10 or 19 units | 20 or more units | Mobile homes | Boat, RV, van, etc. |
|---|---|---|---|---|---|---|---|---|---|---|
| **United States......** | **137,407** | **61.7** | **5.9** | **3.6** | **4.4** | **4.7** | **4.4** | **9.2** | **6.2** | **0.1** |
| Alabama............. | 2,259 | 67.8 | 1.5 | 2.3 | 3.0 | 4.3 | 3.5 | 4.0 | 13.5 | 0.1 |
| Alaska................ | 317 | 62.6 | 8.1 | 5.4 | 7.0 | 4.3 | 2.8 | 5.0 | 4.6 | 0.2 |
| Arizona.............. | 2,999 | 64.7 | 4.9 | 1.3 | 3.3 | 4.0 | 4.4 | 7.0 | 10.0 | 0.4 |
| Arkansas........... | 1,370 | 69.9 | 1.4 | 2.9 | 3.3 | 3.6 | 3.9 | 2.6 | 12.2 | 0.1 |
| California............ | 14,177 | 57.8 | 7.1 | 2.4 | 5.4 | 6.0 | 5.2 | 12.3 | 3.7 | 0.1 |
| Colorado............ | 2,385 | 63.1 | 6.9 | 1.8 | 3.1 | 4.7 | 5.6 | 10.8 | 4.0 | 0.1 |
| Connecticut......... | 1,517 | 59.3 | 5.5 | 7.9 | 8.7 | 5.3 | 3.5 | 9.1 | 0.7 | (Z) |
| Delaware............ | 433 | 58.4 | 15.9 | 1.8 | 2.2 | 3.8 | 6.2 | 4.5 | 7.2 | 0.1 |
| District of Columbia.. | 315 | 12.7 | 24.3 | 3.0 | 6.3 | 7.2 | 8.6 | 37.6 | 0.2 | (Z) |
| Florida................ | 9,442 | 54.4 | 6.2 | 2.1 | 4.0 | 4.9 | 5.7 | 13.7 | 8.9 | 0.1 |
| Georgia............. | 4,282 | 66.6 | 3.9 | 2.1 | 3.0 | 4.6 | 4.5 | 6.4 | 8.8 | 0.1 |
| Hawaii................ | 543 | 52.5 | 9.4 | 1.9 | 4.0 | 6.8 | 5.4 | 19.7 | 0.2 | 0.1 |
| Idaho................. | 722 | 74.9 | 2.7 | 2.1 | 4.3 | 2.6 | 2.1 | 3.9 | 7.4 | 0.1 |
| Illinois................ | 5,359 | 59.0 | 5.6 | 5.6 | 6.5 | 6.3 | 3.7 | 10.7 | 2.4 | (Z) |
| Indiana............... | 2,885 | 73.0 | 3.8 | 2.5 | 3.4 | 4.4 | 3.6 | 4.4 | 4.7 | (Z) |
| Iowa................. | 1,398 | 73.8 | 4.0 | 2.3 | 3.3 | 3.4 | 3.9 | 5.7 | 3.6 | (Z) |
| Kansas.............. | 1,274 | 72.6 | 4.8 | 2.5 | 3.7 | 3.8 | 3.5 | 4.8 | 4.3 | (Z) |
| Kentucky............ | 1,984 | 67.2 | 2.6 | 3.3 | 4.4 | 4.2 | 3.3 | 3.2 | 11.7 | 0.1 |
| Louisiana........... | 2,062 | 65.2 | 2.8 | 4.2 | 4.1 | 3.2 | 2.8 | 4.6 | 13.2 | 0.1 |
| Maine................ | 743 | 70.6 | 2.5 | 4.4 | 5.4 | 3.6 | 1.6 | 3.6 | 8.3 | (Z) |
| Maryland............ | 2,449 | 51.2 | 21.5 | 1.5 | 2.1 | 5.3 | 7.8 | 9.0 | 1.5 | (Z) |
| Massachusetts....... | 2,895 | 52.1 | 5.3 | 9.9 | 10.9 | 5.8 | 4.2 | 10.9 | 0.8 | (Z) |
| Michigan............ | 4,595 | 72.5 | 4.4 | 2.3 | 2.6 | 4.3 | 3.5 | 5.1 | 5.2 | (Z) |
| Minnesota........... | 2,438 | 67.2 | 7.2 | 2.0 | 2.2 | 2.3 | 3.6 | 12.3 | 3.3 | (Z) |
| Mississippi.......... | 1,324 | 68.6 | 1.0 | 2.4 | 3.0 | 4.0 | 2.6 | 2.4 | 15.8 | 0.1 |
| Missouri............. | 2,792 | 70.5 | 3.2 | 3.4 | 4.6 | 3.7 | 3.6 | 4.7 | 6.1 | 0.1 |
| Montana............. | 510 | 69.9 | 3.6 | 2.8 | 4.2 | 3.1 | 2.2 | 3.3 | 10.7 | 0.2 |
| Nebraska............ | 838 | 72.6 | 4.0 | 1.9 | 2.8 | 4.3 | 4.4 | 6.9 | 3.1 | (Z) |
| Nevada.............. | 1,250 | 60.0 | 4.5 | 1.2 | 6.4 | 8.7 | 5.0 | 9.0 | 5.1 | 0.1 |
| New Hampshire...... | 635 | 64.2 | 5.6 | 5.2 | 5.8 | 4.4 | 2.8 | 7.1 | 4.9 | 0.1 |
| New Jersey.......... | 3,616 | 53.7 | 9.6 | 9.4 | 6.6 | 4.6 | 4.7 | 10.6 | 0.9 | (Z) |
| New Mexico......... | 938 | 63.8 | 3.3 | 1.9 | 3.9 | 2.9 | 2.5 | 4.0 | 17.5 | 0.2 |
| New York............ | 8,328 | 41.9 | 5.1 | 10.2 | 6.9 | 5.2 | 4.2 | 24.1 | 2.3 | (Z) |
| North Carolina....... | 4,623 | 65.5 | 4.2 | 2.0 | 2.8 | 4.1 | 4.1 | 4.5 | 12.7 | 0.1 |
| North Dakota........ | 375 | 56.7 | 5.6 | 2.3 | 3.8 | 3.5 | 6.0 | 14.8 | 7.3 | (Z) |
| Ohio................. | 5,202 | 68.5 | 4.6 | 4.2 | 4.4 | 4.7 | 4.0 | 5.7 | 3.8 | (Z) |
| Oklahoma........... | 1,734 | 72.6 | 2.0 | 1.9 | 2.6 | 3.8 | 3.5 | 3.8 | 9.6 | 0.2 |
| Oregon.............. | 1,769 | 64.1 | 4.5 | 2.6 | 4.4 | 4.3 | 3.8 | 8.5 | 7.6 | 0.3 |
| Pennsylvania........ | 5,694 | 56.8 | 18.8 | 4.4 | 4.0 | 3.2 | 2.6 | 6.3 | 4.0 | (Z) |
| Rhode Island........ | 468 | 55.2 | 3.0 | 11.7 | 12.0 | 4.6 | 3.9 | 8.5 | 1.0 | 0.1 |
| South Carolina...... | 2,285 | 62.7 | 2.8 | 1.9 | 3.1 | 4.2 | 3.3 | 5.4 | 16.5 | 0.1 |
| South Dakota........ | 393 | 67.3 | 3.5 | 2.0 | 3.6 | 4.1 | 4.5 | 6.6 | 8.3 | (Z) |
| Tennessee........... | 2,959 | 68.4 | 2.9 | 2.7 | 3.2 | 4.8 | 4.1 | 4.6 | 9.2 | 0.1 |
| Texas................ | 10,933 | 65.0 | 2.6 | 1.9 | 3.2 | 4.8 | 6.3 | 8.8 | 7.3 | 0.2 |
| Utah................. | 1,085 | 68.3 | 6.2 | 2.7 | 4.7 | 3.5 | 4.1 | 7.0 | 3.4 | 0.1 |
| Vermont............. | 335 | 65.6 | 3.8 | 6.4 | 6.0 | 5.2 | 2.0 | 4.2 | 6.8 | 0.1 |
| Virginia.............. | 3,513 | 61.6 | 11.0 | 1.5 | 2.7 | 4.8 | 5.6 | 7.5 | 5.2 | (Z) |
| Washington.......... | 3,103 | 63.2 | 4.0 | 2.3 | 3.7 | 4.4 | 5.1 | 11.0 | 6.1 | 0.2 |
| West Virginia........ | 892 | 70.3 | 2.2 | 2.2 | 3.0 | 2.9 | 1.6 | 2.7 | 15.0 | 0.1 |
| Wisconsin........... | 2,695 | 66.4 | 4.3 | 6.3 | 3.8 | 4.9 | 3.5 | 7.4 | 3.4 | (Z) |
| Wyoming............ | 277 | 66.6 | 4.3 | 2.4 | 4.0 | 3.6 | 2.4 | 2.6 | 14.0 | 0.1 |

Z Less than .05 percent.

Source: U.S. Census Bureau, 2017 American Community Survey, B25024, "Units in Structure," <http://factfinder.census.gov/>, accessed November 2018.

## Table 1021. Housing Units—Size of Units and Lot: 2017

[In thousands (137,400 represents 137,400,000), except as indicated. As of Fall. Based on the American Housing Survey; see Appendix III. For composition of regions, see map inside front cover]

| Item | Total housing units | Sea-sonal units | Year-round units Occupied Total | Owner | Renter | North-east | Mid-west | South | West | Vacant units |
|---|---|---|---|---|---|---|---|---|---|---|
| **Total units** | **137,400** | **2,793** | **121,600** | **77,570** | **43,990** | **21,829** | **27,047** | **45,457** | **27,226** | **13,050** |
| Rooms: | | | | | | | | | | |
| 1 room | 732 | 53 | 530 | 19 | 511 | 127 | 134 | 86 | 183 | 149 |
| 2 rooms | 1,474 | 62 | 1,181 | 98 | 1,083 | 293 | 216 | 259 | 412 | 231 |
| 3 rooms | 11,650 | 360 | 9,597 | 1,145 | 8,452 | 2,309 | 1,926 | 2,972 | 2,390 | 1,692 |
| 4 rooms | 23,960 | 878 | 19,460 | 6,109 | 13,350 | 3,678 | 4,193 | 6,891 | 4,697 | 3,621 |
| 5 rooms | 31,320 | 629 | 27,560 | 16,640 | 10,920 | 4,256 | 6,117 | 11,231 | 5,957 | 3,125 |
| 6 rooms | 28,510 | 457 | 25,830 | 20,070 | 5,753 | 4,610 | 5,625 | 10,213 | 5,379 | 2,227 |
| 7 rooms | 18,720 | 194 | 17,440 | 15,080 | 2,359 | 3,025 | 4,067 | 6,549 | 3,797 | 1,092 |
| 8 or more rooms | 21,044 | 159 | 19,970 | 18,403 | 1,565 | 3,532 | 4,770 | 7,260 | 4,406 | 914 |
| Complete bathrooms: | | | | | | | | | | |
| No bathrooms | 339 | 100 | 149 | 32 | 117 | 56 | 30 | 24 | 40 | 90 |
| 1 bathroom | 46,500 | 1,128 | 39,080 | 13,230 | 25,840 | 9,633 | 9,553 | 11,818 | 8,076 | 6,291 |
| 1 and one-half bathrooms | 16,070 | 251 | 14,430 | 9,989 | 4,444 | 3,693 | 4,307 | 4,057 | 2,374 | 1,384 |
| 2 or more bathrooms | 74,493 | 1,313 | 67,899 | 54,313 | 13,592 | 8,447 | 13,159 | 29,561 | 16,732 | 5,285 |
| Square footage of unit: | | | | | | | | | | |
| Less than 500 | 3,409 | 160 | 2,765 | 490 | 2,275 | 719 | 528 | 705 | 814 | 484 |
| 500 to 749 | 9,527 | 292 | 7,702 | 1,246 | 6,457 | 1,548 | 1,442 | 2,553 | 2,160 | 1,533 |
| 750 to 999 | 16,510 | 420 | 13,810 | 4,257 | 9,551 | 2,422 | 3,070 | 5,023 | 3,294 | 2,277 |
| 1,000 to 1,499 | 31,570 | 668 | 27,730 | 17,020 | 10,710 | 4,236 | 6,147 | 10,727 | 6,620 | 3,170 |
| 1,500 to 1,999 | 24,340 | 405 | 22,200 | 18,350 | 3,851 | 3,228 | 4,785 | 8,983 | 5,207 | 1,734 |
| 2,000 to 2,499 | 15,670 | 230 | 14,550 | 12,930 | 1,621 | 2,409 | 3,363 | 5,554 | 3,227 | 883 |
| 2,500 to 2,999 | 8,352 | 124 | 7,828 | 7,299 | 529 | 1,343 | 1,712 | 3,030 | 1,744 | 400 |
| 3,000 to 3,999 | 7,875 | 126 | 7,333 | 6,919 | 414 | 1,065 | 1,917 | 2,828 | 1,522 | 417 |
| 4,000 or more | 3,926 | 73 | 3,555 | 3,260 | 294 | 593 | 922 | 1,335 | 705 | 298 |
| Not reported | 16,230 | 295 | 14,080 | 5,784 | 8,297 | 4,267 | 3,164 | 4,720 | 1,930 | 1,855 |
| Median square footage | 1,473 | 1,200 | 1,500 | 1,800 | 974 | 2,900 | 3,100 | 4,500 | 2,990 | 1,144 |
| Lot size: | | | | | | | | | | |
| Single detached and attached units and mobile homes [1] | 99,750 | 2,164 | 89,490 | 71,880 | 17,620 | 13,899 | 20,838 | 35,401 | 19,349 | 8,094 |
| Less than one-eighth acre | 14,700 | 358 | 12,860 | 8,811 | 4,053 | 3,097 | 2,668 | 3,511 | 3,589 | 1,476 |
| One-eighth to one-quarter acre | 33,400 | 452 | 30,640 | 23,670 | 6,964 | 2,985 | 6,695 | 11,228 | 9,730 | 2,311 |
| One-quarter to one-half acre | 19,930 | 395 | 18,220 | 15,510 | 2,718 | 2,880 | 5,064 | 7,763 | 2,518 | 1,314 |
| One-half up to one acre | 9,455 | 298 | 8,369 | 7,229 | 1,140 | 1,662 | 1,765 | 4,042 | 900 | 787 |
| 1 up to 5 acres | 15,160 | 385 | 13,330 | 11,370 | 1,958 | 2,384 | 2,767 | 6,438 | 1,744 | 1,439 |
| 5 up to 10 acres | 3,079 | 75 | 2,696 | 2,412 | 285 | 377 | 839 | 1,104 | 376 | 308 |
| 10 or more acres | 4,028 | 201 | 3,368 | 2,869 | 499 | 518 | 1,045 | 1,315 | 490 | 459 |

[1] Does not include cooperatives or condominiums.

Source: U.S. Census Bureau, "American Housing Survey: AHS Table Creator," <http://www.census.gov/programs-surveys/ahs/data.html>, accessed February 2019.

## Table 1022. Occupied Housing Units—Tenure by Race of Householder: 2003 to 2017

[In thousands (105,842 represents 105,842,000), except percent. As of Fall. Based on the American Housing Survey; see Appendix III]

| Race of householder and tenure | 2003 | 2005 | 2007 | 2009 | 2011 | 2013 | 2015 | 2017 |
|---|---|---|---|---|---|---|---|---|
| **ALL RACES [1]** | | | | | | | | |
| **Occupied units, total** | **105,842** | **108,871** | **110,692** | **111,806** | **114,907** | **115,852** | **118,290** | **121,600** |
| Owner-occupied | 72,238 | 74,931 | 75,647 | 76,428 | 76,091 | 75,650 | 74,299 | 77,570 |
| Percent of occupied | 68.3 | 68.8 | 68.3 | 68.4 | 66.2 | 65.3 | 62.8 | 63.8 |
| Renter-occupied | 33,604 | 33,940 | 35,045 | 35,378 | 38,816 | 40,201 | 43,991 | 43,990 |
| **WHITE [2]** | | | | | | | | |
| **Occupied units, total** | **87,483** | **89,449** | **90,413** | **91,137** | **92,820** | **93,284** | **93,748** | **95,320** |
| Owner-occupied | 63,126 | 65,023 | 65,554 | 65,935 | 65,357 | 65,088 | 63,049 | 65,230 |
| Percent of occupied | 72.2 | 72.7 | 72.5 | 72.3 | 70.4 | 69.8 | 67.3 | 68.4 |
| Renter-occupied | 24,357 | 24,426 | 24,859 | 25,202 | 27,463 | 28,196 | 30,699 | 30,090 |
| **BLACK [2]** | | | | | | | | |
| **Occupied units, total** | **13,004** | **13,447** | **13,856** | **13,993** | **14,694** | **15,015** | **16,002** | **16,550** |
| Owner-occupied | 6,193 | 6,471 | 6,464 | 6,547 | 6,662 | 6,480 | 6,665 | 7,131 |
| Percent of occupied | 47.6 | 48.1 | 46.7 | 46.8 | 45.3 | 43.2 | 41.7 | 43.1 |
| Renter-occupied | 6,811 | 6,975 | 7,392 | 7,446 | 8,033 | 8,535 | 9,337 | 9,421 |
| **HISPANIC ORIGIN [3]** | | | | | | | | |
| **Occupied units, total** | **11,038** | **11,651** | **12,609** | **12,739** | **13,841** | **14,675** | **15,620** | **16,500** |
| Owner-occupied | 5,106 | 5,752 | 6,364 | 6,439 | 6,530 | 6,897 | 7,109 | 7,763 |
| Percent of occupied | 46.3 | 49.4 | 50.5 | 50.5 | 47.2 | 47.0 | 45.5 | 47.0 |
| Renter-occupied | 5,931 | 5,899 | 6,244 | 6,300 | 7,311 | 7,778 | 8,511 | 8,733 |

[1] Includes other races not shown separately. [2] The 2003 American Housing Survey (AHS) allowed respondents to choose more than one race. Beginning in 2003, data represent householders who selected this race group only and exclude householders reporting more than one race. See also comments on race in the text for Section 1 and the below cited source. [3] Persons of Hispanic origin may be of any race.

Source: U.S. Census Bureau, "American Housing Survey: AHS Table Creator," <http://www.census.gov/programs-surveys/ahs/data.html>, accessed February 2019.

## Table 1023. Homeownership Rates by Age of Householder and Household Type: 2000 to 2018

[In percent. Represents the proportion of owner households to the total number of occupied households. Based on the Current Population Survey/Housing Vacancy Survey, and includes the civilian noninstitutionalized population, people in noninstitutional group quarters, and military in households off post or with their families on post (must have 1 household member who is a civilian adult). See source and Appendix III for details]

| Age of householder and household type | 2000 | 2005 | 2010 | 2012 | 2013 | 2014 | 2015 | 2016 | 2017 | 2018 |
|---|---|---|---|---|---|---|---|---|---|---|
| **United States** | **67.4** | **68.9** | **66.9** | **65.4** | **65.1** | **64.5** | **63.7** | **63.4** | **63.9** | **64.4** |
| AGE OF HOUSEHOLDER | | | | | | | | | | |
| Less than 25 years old | 21.7 | 25.7 | 22.8 | 21.7 | 22.2 | 21.7 | 21.8 | 21.9 | 22.6 | 22.7 |
| 25 to 29 years old | 38.1 | 40.9 | 36.8 | 34.3 | 34.1 | 32.7 | 31.7 | 30.9 | 32.1 | 32.5 |
| 30 to 34 years old | 54.6 | 56.8 | 51.6 | 47.9 | 48.1 | 47.1 | 45.9 | 45.4 | 45.7 | 47.7 |
| 35 to 39 years old | 65.0 | 66.6 | 61.9 | 56.9 | 55.8 | 56.0 | 55.3 | 55.3 | 56.4 | 57.6 |
| 40 to 44 years old | 70.6 | 71.7 | 67.9 | 65.5 | 65.0 | 63.2 | 61.6 | 62.0 | 61.8 | 62.9 |
| 45 to 49 years old | 74.7 | 75.0 | 72.0 | 69.9 | 69.6 | 68.5 | 68.0 | 66.7 | 67.5 | 68.4 |
| 50 to 54 years old | 78.5 | 78.3 | 75.0 | 73.4 | 72.6 | 72.6 | 71.8 | 71.6 | 71.1 | 71.7 |
| 55 to 59 years old | 80.4 | 80.6 | 77.7 | 76.2 | 75.8 | 75.4 | 74.7 | 74.0 | 73.8 | 74.0 |
| 60 to 64 years old | 80.3 | 81.9 | 80.4 | 78.6 | 77.6 | 77.2 | 76.2 | 76.1 | 76.9 | 76.8 |
| 65 to 69 years old | 83.0 | 82.8 | 81.6 | 81.1 | 80.5 | 80.3 | 79.3 | 79.0 | 79.1 | 79.3 |
| 70 to 74 years old | 82.6 | 82.9 | 82.4 | 83.5 | 82.8 | 81.6 | 81.3 | 81.7 | 81.4 | 80.6 |
| 75 years old and over | 77.7 | 78.4 | 78.9 | 80.0 | 80.0 | 78.6 | 77.2 | 77.0 | 76.8 | 76.6 |
| Less than 35 years old | 40.8 | 43.0 | 39.1 | 36.7 | 36.8 | 35.8 | 35.0 | 34.5 | 35.3 | 36.2 |
| 35 to 44 years old | 67.9 | 69.3 | 65.0 | 61.4 | 60.6 | 59.7 | 58.5 | 58.6 | 59.0 | 60.1 |
| 45 to 54 years old | 76.5 | 76.6 | 73.5 | 71.7 | 71.2 | 70.7 | 70.0 | 69.3 | 69.3 | 70.1 |
| 55 to 64 years old | 80.3 | 81.2 | 79.0 | 77.3 | 76.6 | 76.3 | 75.4 | 75.0 | 75.3 | 75.4 |
| 65 years and over | 80.4 | 80.6 | 80.5 | 81.1 | 80.8 | 79.9 | 78.9 | 78.8 | 78.7 | 78.5 |
| TYPE OF HOUSEHOLD | | | | | | | | | | |
| Family households: | | | | | | | | | | |
| Married-couple families | 82.4 | 84.2 | 82.1 | 80.8 | 80.7 | 80.3 | 79.6 | 80.0 | 80.1 | 80.8 |
| Male householder, no spouse present | 57.5 | 59.1 | 56.9 | 55.9 | 55.3 | 54.5 | 53.8 | 53.7 | 55.6 | 56.3 |
| Female householder, no spouse present | 49.1 | 51.0 | 48.6 | 46.7 | 46.7 | 46.2 | 45.9 | 45.7 | 46.7 | 47.9 |
| Nonfamily households: | | | | | | | | | | |
| One-person | 53.6 | 55.6 | 55.3 | 54.5 | 53.9 | 53.3 | 52.2 | 51.3 | 51.5 | 51.8 |
| Male householder | 47.4 | 50.3 | 51.3 | 49.8 | 49.8 | 49.1 | 48.5 | 47.2 | 47.3 | 47.4 |
| Female householder | 58.1 | 59.6 | 58.6 | 58.3 | 57.2 | 56.6 | 55.3 | 54.6 | 54.9 | 55.4 |
| Other: | | | | | | | | | | |
| Male householder | 38.0 | 41.7 | 40.7 | 39.8 | 39.8 | 37.7 | 36.6 | 36.1 | 37.2 | 38.6 |
| Female householder | 40.6 | 44.7 | 41.9 | 41.0 | 41.9 | 41.4 | 40.7 | 38.4 | 39.4 | 41.5 |

Source: U.S. Census Bureau, "Housing Vacancies and Home Ownership," <http://www.census.gov/housing/hvs/>, accessed April 2019.

## Table 1024. Homeownership Rates by State: 2000 to 2018

[In percent. Represents the proportion of owner households to the total number of occupied households. Based on the Current Population Survey/Housing Vacancy Survey, and includes the civilian noninstitutionalized population, people in noninstitutional group quarters, and military in households off post or with their families on post (must have 1 household member who is a civilian adult). See source and Appendix III for details]

| State | 2000 | 2005 | 2010 | 2015 | 2017 | 2018 | State | 2000 | 2005 | 2010 | 2015 | 2017 | 2018 |
|---|---|---|---|---|---|---|---|---|---|---|---|---|---|
| **United States** | **67.4** | **68.9** | **66.9** | **63.7** | **63.9** | **64.4** | Missouri | 74.2 | 72.3 | 71.2 | 68.5 | 67.6 | 69.7 |
| Alabama | 73.2 | 76.6 | 73.2 | 70.0 | 70.0 | 70.3 | Montana | 70.2 | 70.4 | 68.1 | 66.4 | 67.6 | 67.4 |
| Alaska | 66.4 | 66.0 | 65.7 | 62.3 | 65.5 | 63.7 | Nebraska | 70.2 | 70.2 | 70.4 | 68.1 | 66.1 | 66.4 |
| Arizona | 68.0 | 71.1 | 66.6 | 61.7 | 64.4 | 65.7 | Nevada | 64.0 | 63.4 | 59.7 | 54.8 | 55.0 | 57.8 |
| Arkansas | 68.9 | 69.2 | 67.9 | 67.1 | 65.0 | 64.7 | New Hampshire | 69.2 | 74.0 | 74.9 | 71.6 | 71.6 | 73.4 |
| California | 57.1 | 59.7 | 56.1 | 54.3 | 54.4 | 55.1 | New Jersey | 66.2 | 70.1 | 66.5 | 64.0 | 64.1 | 65.0 |
| Colorado | 68.3 | 71.0 | 68.5 | 63.6 | 63.7 | 64.4 | New Mexico | 73.7 | 71.4 | 68.6 | 66.5 | 66.6 | 68.0 |
| Connecticut | 70.0 | 70.5 | 70.8 | 66.5 | 66.1 | 65.3 | New York | 53.4 | 55.9 | 54.5 | 51.5 | 51.1 | 51.0 |
| Delaware | 72.0 | 75.8 | 74.7 | 73.3 | 70.0 | 70.8 | North Carolina | 71.1 | 70.9 | 69.5 | 65.2 | 66.3 | 65.2 |
| Dist. of Columbia | 41.9 | 45.8 | 45.6 | 40.4 | 40.3 | 39.9 | North Dakota | 70.7 | 68.5 | 67.1 | 61.8 | 62.6 | 61.9 |
| Florida | 68.4 | 72.4 | 69.3 | 64.8 | 64.1 | 65.5 | Ohio | 71.3 | 73.3 | 69.7 | 66.4 | 66.0 | 67.3 |
| Georgia | 69.8 | 67.9 | 67.1 | 62.9 | 62.8 | 63.8 | Oklahoma | 72.7 | 72.9 | 69.2 | 67.4 | 68.9 | 69.5 |
| Hawaii | 55.2 | 59.8 | 56.1 | 59.3 | 55.9 | 59.5 | Oregon | 65.3 | 68.2 | 66.3 | 61.1 | 61.8 | 62.0 |
| Idaho | 70.5 | 74.2 | 72.4 | 70.0 | 69.9 | 69.2 | Pennsylvania | 74.7 | 73.3 | 72.2 | 69.6 | 68.6 | 69.9 |
| Illinois | 67.9 | 70.9 | 68.8 | 65.4 | 65.4 | 66.0 | Rhode Island | 61.5 | 63.1 | 62.8 | 58.9 | 56.6 | 60.7 |
| Indiana | 74.9 | 75.0 | 71.2 | 69.4 | 70.0 | 69.8 | South Carolina | 76.5 | 73.9 | 74.8 | 67.1 | 72.8 | 72.0 |
| Iowa | 75.2 | 73.9 | 71.1 | 68.8 | 70.0 | 68.9 | South Dakota | 71.2 | 68.4 | 70.6 | 70.1 | 67.8 | 69.1 |
| Kansas | 69.3 | 69.5 | 67.4 | 64.9 | 66.0 | 67.3 | Tennessee | 70.9 | 72.4 | 71.0 | 66.5 | 67.2 | 68.0 |
| Kentucky | 73.4 | 71.6 | 70.3 | 67.9 | 70.1 | 69.8 | Texas | 63.8 | 65.9 | 65.3 | 61.9 | 61.7 | 62.7 |
| Louisiana | 68.1 | 72.5 | 70.4 | 63.3 | 66.1 | 65.7 | Utah | 72.7 | 73.9 | 72.5 | 69.9 | 71.0 | 72.2 |
| Maine | 76.5 | 73.9 | 73.8 | 69.9 | 71.0 | 71.2 | Vermont | 68.7 | 74.2 | 73.6 | 71.8 | 71.1 | 71.4 |
| Maryland | 69.9 | 71.2 | 68.9 | 67.1 | 66.9 | 66.6 | Virginia | 73.9 | 71.2 | 68.7 | 67.1 | 67.5 | 66.0 |
| Massachusetts | 59.9 | 63.4 | 65.3 | 60.5 | 60.0 | 61.5 | Washington | 63.6 | 67.6 | 64.4 | 62.6 | 63.6 | 64.9 |
| Michigan | 77.2 | 76.4 | 74.5 | 74.6 | 72.9 | 73.0 | West Virginia | 75.9 | 81.3 | 79.0 | 74.9 | 75.1 | 74.7 |
| Minnesota | 76.1 | 76.5 | 72.6 | 70.1 | 72.7 | 69.8 | Wisconsin | 71.8 | 71.1 | 71.0 | 66.6 | 68.0 | 67.9 |
| Mississippi | 75.2 | 78.8 | 74.8 | 70.7 | 71.0 | 72.5 | Wyoming | 71.0 | 72.8 | 73.4 | 69.9 | 70.4 | 71.1 |

Source: U.S. Census Bureau, "Housing Vacancies and Home Ownership," <http://www.census.gov/housing/hvs/>, accessed April 2019.

## Table 1025. Occupied Housing Units—Costs by Region: 2017

[77,570 represents 77,570,000. As of Fall. See headnote, Table 1026, for an explanation of housing costs. Based on the American Housing Survey; see Appendix III. For composition of regions, see map inside front cover]

| Category | Number (1,000) | | | | | Percent distribution | | | | |
|---|---|---|---|---|---|---|---|---|---|---|
| | Total units | North-east | Mid-west | South | West | Total units | North-east | Mid-west | South | West |
| **OWNER-OCCUPIED UNITS** | | | | | | | | | | |
| **Total** | **77,570** | **13,457** | **18,491** | **29,402** | **16,225** | **100.0** | **100.0** | **100.0** | **100.0** | **100.0** |
| Monthly housing costs: | | | | | | | | | | |
| Less than $200 | 1,512 | 85 | 201 | 949 | 279 | 1.9 | 0.6 | 1.1 | 3.2 | 1.7 |
| $200 to $299 | 3,234 | 168 | 641 | 1,934 | 492 | 4.2 | 1.2 | 3.5 | 6.6 | 3.0 |
| $300 to $399 | 5,004 | 386 | 1,256 | 2,605 | 756 | 6.5 | 2.9 | 6.8 | 8.9 | 4.7 |
| $400 to $499 | 5,210 | 641 | 1,388 | 2,336 | 845 | 6.7 | 4.8 | 7.5 | 7.9 | 5.2 |
| $500 to $699 | 9,446 | 1,384 | 2,730 | 3,636 | 1,697 | 12.2 | 10.3 | 14.8 | 12.4 | 10.5 |
| $700 to $999 | 11,832 | 2,068 | 3,361 | 4,329 | 2,074 | 15.3 | 15.4 | 18.2 | 14.7 | 12.8 |
| $1,000 to $1,499 | 15,577 | 2,814 | 4,180 | 5,696 | 2,888 | 20.1 | 20.9 | 22.6 | 19.4 | 17.8 |
| $1,500 to $2,499 | 16,001 | 3,272 | 3,491 | 5,234 | 4,005 | 20.6 | 24.3 | 18.9 | 17.8 | 24.7 |
| $2,500 or more | 9,750 | 2,641 | 1,240 | 2,684 | 3,184 | 12.6 | 19.6 | 6.7 | 9.1 | 19.6 |
| **RENTER-OCCUPIED UNITS** | | | | | | | | | | |
| **Total** | **43,990** | **8,371** | **8,561** | **16,060** | **11,001** | **100.0** | **100.0** | **100.0** | **100.0** | **100.0** |
| Monthly housing costs: | | | | | | | | | | |
| Less than $200 | 1,099 | 230 | 274 | 389 | 207 | 2.5 | 2.7 | 3.2 | 2.4 | 1.9 |
| $200 to $299 | 1,577 | 411 | 353 | 527 | 286 | 3.6 | 4.9 | 4.1 | 3.3 | 2.6 |
| $300 to $399 | 1,453 | 373 | 306 | 486 | 286 | 3.3 | 4.5 | 3.6 | 3.0 | 2.6 |
| $400 to $499 | 1,581 | 262 | 411 | 672 | 235 | 3.6 | 3.1 | 4.8 | 4.2 | 2.1 |
| $500 to $699 | 5,393 | 696 | 1,581 | 2,339 | 777 | 12.3 | 8.3 | 18.5 | 14.6 | 7.1 |
| $700 to $999 | 10,189 | 1,554 | 2,707 | 4,105 | 1,822 | 23.2 | 18.6 | 31.6 | 25.6 | 16.6 |
| $1,000 to $1,499 | 11,224 | 2,228 | 1,707 | 4,134 | 3,156 | 25.5 | 26.6 | 19.9 | 25.7 | 28.7 |
| $1,500 to $2,499 | 7,137 | 1,679 | 619 | 2,004 | 2,836 | 16.2 | 20.1 | 7.2 | 12.5 | 25.8 |
| $2,500 or more | 2,379 | 640 | 209 | 468 | 1,062 | 5.4 | 7.6 | 2.4 | 2.9 | 9.7 |
| No cash rent | 1,961 | 299 | 395 | 933 | 334 | 4.5 | 3.6 | 4.6 | 5.8 | 3.0 |

Source: U.S. Census Bureau, "American Housing Survey: AHS Table Creator," <http://www.census.gov/programs-surveys/ahs/data.html>, accessed February 2019.

## Table 1026. Occupied Housing Units—Financial Summary by Selected Characteristics of the Householder: 2017

[In thousands of units (121,600 represents 121,600,000), except as indicated. As of Fall. Housing costs include real estate taxes, property insurance, utilities, fuel, water, garbage collection, homeowner association fees, cooperative or condominium fees, mobile home fees, routine maintenance, mortgages, other charges in mortgages, and mortgage insurance. Based on the American Housing Survey; see Appendix III]

| Characteristic | Total occupied units | Tenure | | Black [1] | | Hispanic origin [2] | | Elderly [3] | | Households below poverty level [4] | |
|---|---|---|---|---|---|---|---|---|---|---|---|
| | | Owner | Renter | Owner | Renter | Owner | Renter | Owner | Renter | Owner | Renter |
| **Total units [5]** | **121,600** | **77,570** | **43,990** | **7,131** | **9,421** | **7,763** | **8,733** | **23,983** | **6,686** | **6,722** | **10,293** |
| Monthly housing costs: | | | | | | | | | | | |
| Less than $200 | 2,612 | 1,512 | 1,099 | 254 | 400 | 154 | 137 | 713 | 211 | 569 | 755 |
| $200 to $299 | 4,811 | 3,234 | 1,577 | 500 | 520 | 305 | 291 | 1,536 | 503 | 705 | 1,135 |
| $300 to $399 | 6,456 | 5,004 | 1,453 | 594 | 418 | 539 | 271 | 2,645 | 489 | 794 | 643 |
| $400 to $499 | 6,791 | 5,210 | 1,581 | 456 | 421 | 439 | 217 | 2,572 | 382 | 664 | 575 |
| $500 to $699 | 14,839 | 9,446 | 5,393 | 876 | 1,305 | 903 | 858 | 4,459 | 841 | 1,114 | 1,643 |
| $700 to $999 | 22,024 | 11,832 | 10,189 | 1,077 | 2,543 | 1,062 | 2,093 | 4,252 | 1,352 | 1,149 | 2,257 |
| $1,000 to $1,499 | 26,800 | 15,577 | 11,224 | 1,353 | 2,208 | 1,582 | 2,615 | 3,838 | 1,184 | 959 | 1,731 |
| $1,500 to $2,499 | 23,145 | 16,001 | 7,137 | 1,367 | 1,086 | 1,818 | 1,683 | 2,643 | 686 | 505 | 683 |
| $2,500 or more | 12,130 | 9,750 | 2,379 | 655 | 204 | 959 | 285 | 1,321 | 486 | 260 | 293 |
| Median amount (dol.) [6] | 1,036 | 1,071 | 991 | 947 | 872 | 1,131 | 1,056 | (NA) | (NA) | 1,203 | 1,426 |
| Monthly housing costs as percent of income: [7] | | | | | | | | | | | |
| Less than 5 percent | 3,476 | 2,984 | 492 | 263 | 106 | 250 | 83 | 761 | 51 | 12 | 32 |
| 5 to 9 percent | 12,330 | 10,760 | 1,569 | 836 | 298 | 870 | 273 | 3,364 | 145 | 41 | 36 |
| 10 to 14 percent | 16,260 | 13,040 | 3,215 | 1,015 | 563 | 1,128 | 565 | 3,840 | 209 | 133 | 71 |
| 15 to 19 percent | 17,410 | 12,660 | 4,749 | 975 | 888 | 1,169 | 844 | 3,309 | 324 | 182 | 114 |
| 20 to 24 percent | 14,630 | 9,528 | 5,100 | 850 | 926 | 875 | 907 | 2,338 | 520 | 217 | 191 |
| 25 to 29 percent | 11,310 | 6,755 | 4,553 | 627 | 989 | 717 | 818 | 1,845 | 598 | 241 | 452 |
| 30 to 34 percent | 8,594 | 4,718 | 3,876 | 478 | 812 | 588 | 848 | 1,553 | 626 | 239 | 496 |
| 35 to 39 percent | 6,214 | 3,232 | 2,982 | 334 | 686 | 384 | 655 | 1,163 | 405 | 195 | 363 |
| 40 percent or more | 27,300 | 12,938 | 14,361 | 1,578 | 3,484 | 1,678 | 3,265 | 5,509 | 3,153 | 4,513 | 6,825 |
| Median amount (percent) [6,8] | 22 | 19 | 30 | 21 | 33 | 22 | 33 | (NA) | (NA) | (NA) | (NA) |
| Median monthly costs (dol.): [6] | | | | | | | | | | | |
| Electricity | 106 | 119 | 84 | 121 | 84 | 121 | 85 | (NA) | (NA) | (NA) | (NA) |
| Piped gas | 55 | 60 | 42 | 58 | 44 | 51 | 37 | (NA) | (NA) | (NA) | (NA) |
| Fuel oil | 100 | 100 | 83 | 108 | 83 | 106 | 83 | (NA) | (NA) | (NA) | (NA) |

NA Not available. [1] For persons who selected this race group only. [2] Persons of Hispanic origin may be of any race. [3] Householders 65 years old and over. [4] Based on household income of families or of individuals living without relatives. Refers to money income in the 12 months before the survey. Threshold reflects changes in the Consumer Price Index, see source for more information. [5] Include units with no cash rents, not shown separately. [6] For explanation of median, see Guide to Tabular Presentation. [7] Money income before taxes. [8] Excludes households with zero or negative income and those with no cash rent.

Source: U.S. Census Bureau, "American Housing Survey: AHS Table Creator," <http://www.census.gov/programs-surveys/ahs/data.html>, accessed February 2019.

# Table 1027. Owner-Occupied Housing Units—Value and Costs by State: 2017

[In percent, except as indicated (76,684 represents 76,684,000). The American Community Survey universe includes the household population and excludes the population living in institutions, college dormitories, and other group quarters. Based on a sample and subject to sampling variability; see Appendix III. For definition of median, see Guide to Tabular Presentation]

| State | Total (1,000) | Percent of units with value of— $99,999 or less | $100,000 to $199,999 | $200,000 or more | Median value (dol.) | Median selected monthly owner costs [1] (dol.) | Selected monthly owner costs as a percent income in the past 12 months Less than 15.0 percent | 15.0 to 24.9 percent | 25.0 to 29.9 percent | 30.0 percent or more |
|---|---|---|---|---|---|---|---|---|---|---|
| U.S. | 76,684 | 18.8 | 27.4 | 53.8 | 217,600 | 1,513 | 25.5 | 36.1 | 10.4 | 27.4 |
| AL. | 1,253 | 34.3 | 34.7 | 31.0 | 141,300 | 1,123 | 31.6 | 36.6 | 8.2 | 23.0 |
| AK. | 159 | 11.5 | 17.9 | 70.6 | 273,100 | 1,844 | 21.9 | 39.2 | 9.3 | 29.2 |
| AZ. | 1,652 | 15.2 | 28.3 | 56.5 | 223,400 | 1,365 | 25.8 | 35.4 | 9.9 | 27.9 |
| AR. | 752 | 37.6 | 37.1 | 25.3 | 128,500 | 1,025 | 34.6 | 35.7 | 7.9 | 21.1 |
| CA. | 7,125 | 4.9 | 6.4 | 88.7 | 509,400 | 2,269 | 16.9 | 32.1 | 12.2 | 38.2 |
| CO. | 1,395 | 6.4 | 11.9 | 81.7 | 348,900 | 1,681 | 23.9 | 37.6 | 10.9 | 27.1 |
| CT. | 898 | 4.9 | 25.0 | 70.1 | 273,100 | 1,976 | 21.3 | 36.2 | 11.4 | 30.8 |
| DE. | 254 | 8.7 | 22.6 | 68.7 | 252,800 | 1,507 | 25.8 | 34.9 | 10.3 | 27.5 |
| DC. | 119 | 2.2 | 2.0 | 95.8 | 607,200 | 2,432 | 26.6 | 35.0 | 11.2 | 26.6 |
| FL. | 5,010 | 18.4 | 28.1 | 53.5 | 214,000 | 1,423 | 22.1 | 33.8 | 10.5 | 32.7 |
| GA. | 2,355 | 22.9 | 34.4 | 42.7 | 173,700 | 1,341 | 29.0 | 36.1 | 9.1 | 25.0 |
| HI. | 268 | 2.1 | 3.9 | 94.1 | 617,400 | 2,337 | 19.4 | 29.0 | 12.2 | 38.8 |
| ID. | 435 | 13.0 | 34.8 | 52.2 | 207,100 | 1,213 | 24.0 | 38.0 | 11.1 | 25.9 |
| IL. | 3,182 | 20.4 | 30.9 | 48.7 | 195,300 | 1,603 | 24.6 | 37.1 | 10.6 | 27.1 |
| IN. | 1,766 | 31.2 | 40.4 | 28.4 | 141,100 | 1,089 | 36.1 | 36.1 | 8.4 | 18.9 |
| IA. | 900 | 29.5 | 38.5 | 32.0 | 149,100 | 1,205 | 32.5 | 39.1 | 9.1 | 18.9 |
| KS. | 744 | 31.8 | 34.7 | 33.5 | 150,600 | 1,314 | 29.3 | 40.1 | 10.4 | 19.8 |
| KY. | 1,147 | 32.5 | 38.1 | 29.4 | 141,000 | 1,123 | 32.8 | 36.5 | 8.5 | 21.8 |
| LA. | 1,132 | 27.8 | 35.6 | 36.6 | 162,500 | 1,233 | 30.6 | 33.5 | 9.7 | 25.2 |
| ME. | 396 | 19.2 | 33.6 | 47.2 | 191,200 | 1,313 | 26.6 | 37.3 | 9.5 | 26.1 |
| MD. | 1,473 | 6.8 | 16.1 | 77.1 | 312,500 | 1,915 | 23.7 | 38.2 | 10.8 | 27.0 |
| MA. | 1,624 | 2.6 | 10.4 | 87.0 | 385,400 | 2,108 | 22.1 | 37.3 | 10.9 | 29.3 |
| MI. | 2,803 | 29.4 | 35.7 | 34.9 | 155,700 | 1,231 | 30.9 | 36.6 | 9.2 | 22.7 |
| MN. | 1,548 | 12.2 | 30.2 | 57.6 | 224,000 | 1,500 | 28.3 | 39.4 | 10.4 | 21.7 |
| MS. | 748 | 42.0 | 34.0 | 24.0 | 120,200 | 1,090 | 28.8 | 35.9 | 9.4 | 25.4 |
| MO. | 1,597 | 27.4 | 37.6 | 35.0 | 156,700 | 1,207 | 30.9 | 38.1 | 9.0 | 21.5 |
| MT. | 293 | 15.6 | 25.4 | 59.0 | 231,300 | 1,367 | 24.1 | 36.9 | 11.0 | 27.3 |
| NE. | 500 | 25.1 | 41.4 | 33.5 | 155,800 | 1,334 | 28.1 | 40.4 | 10.3 | 20.9 |
| NV. | 619 | 9.0 | 21.7 | 69.3 | 258,200 | 1,428 | 24.2 | 34.6 | 10.9 | 29.9 |
| NH. | 369 | 8.3 | 21.5 | 70.2 | 263,600 | 1,874 | 20.0 | 40.5 | 12.3 | 26.8 |
| NJ. | 2,054 | 5.0 | 15.1 | 79.8 | 334,900 | 2,348 | 17.7 | 35.3 | 12.4 | 34.2 |
| NM. | 521 | 23.3 | 36.5 | 40.2 | 171,300 | 1,244 | 25.9 | 32.8 | 10.3 | 29.4 |
| NY. | 3,930 | 14.3 | 20.2 | 65.5 | 314,500 | 2,036 | 23.3 | 32.6 | 10.6 | 33.1 |
| NC. | 2,587 | 23.2 | 35.1 | 41.7 | 171,200 | 1,242 | 30.3 | 35.6 | 9.6 | 24.0 |
| ND. | 201 | 21.8 | 29.7 | 48.5 | 194,700 | 1,356 | 32.7 | 39.6 | 10.8 | 16.8 |
| OH. | 3,070 | 30.3 | 39.5 | 30.2 | 144,200 | 1,214 | 31.5 | 38.9 | 8.8 | 20.5 |
| OK. | 962 | 34.6 | 37.8 | 27.6 | 137,400 | 1,183 | 30.0 | 36.3 | 9.4 | 23.8 |
| OR. | 1,007 | 8.2 | 14.5 | 77.3 | 319,200 | 1,629 | 20.6 | 35.5 | 11.8 | 31.6 |
| PA. | 3,421 | 21.7 | 33.8 | 44.6 | 181,200 | 1,438 | 27.9 | 37.3 | 10.1 | 24.3 |
| RI. | 249 | 4.1 | 24.1 | 71.8 | 257,800 | 1,782 | 19.9 | 36.2 | 12.0 | 31.5 |
| SC. | 1,310 | 27.8 | 33.9 | 38.3 | 161,800 | 1,195 | 29.9 | 35.5 | 9.0 | 25.0 |
| SD. | 233 | 26.6 | 34.9 | 38.6 | 167,600 | 1,283 | 28.9 | 39.9 | 11.8 | 19.0 |
| TN. | 1,694 | 25.1 | 35.1 | 39.8 | 167,500 | 1,184 | 29.5 | 36.4 | 9.8 | 23.7 |
| TX. | 5,964 | 25.3 | 32.5 | 42.2 | 172,200 | 1,513 | 25.8 | 37.4 | 10.6 | 25.6 |
| UT. | 682 | 5.8 | 20.3 | 73.9 | 275,100 | 1,467 | 24.3 | 40.2 | 11.4 | 23.9 |
| VT. | 178 | 11.4 | 30.2 | 58.4 | 226,300 | 1,527 | 18.0 | 38.1 | 11.7 | 32.1 |
| VA. | 2,077 | 11.0 | 22.8 | 66.3 | 273,400 | 1,718 | 24.8 | 37.5 | 11.2 | 26.0 |
| WA. | 1,784 | 6.8 | 13.8 | 79.4 | 339,000 | 1,806 | 20.6 | 37.8 | 12.4 | 28.8 |
| WV. | 519 | 41.8 | 33.9 | 24.4 | 119,800 | 984 | 35.7 | 32.7 | 9.2 | 22.0 |
| WI. | 1,566 | 17.4 | 39.5 | 43.1 | 178,900 | 1,358 | 26.8 | 40.4 | 10.1 | 22.3 |
| WY. | 160 | 15.3 | 30.1 | 54.5 | 214,300 | 1,386 | 24.9 | 39.3 | 11.5 | 23.9 |

[1] For homes with a mortgage. Selected monthly owner costs are the sum of payments for mortgages, deeds of trust, contracts to purchase, or similar debts on the property (including payments for the first mortgage, second mortgages, home equity loans, and other junior mortgages); real estate taxes; fire, hazard, and flood insurance on the property; utilities; and fuels. It also includes, where appropriate, the monthly condominium fee for condominiums and mobile home costs.

Source: U.S. Census Bureau, 2017 American Community Survey, B25075, "Value"; B25077, "Median Value"; B25088, "Median Selected Monthly Owner Costs by Mortgage Status"; and B25091, "Mortgage Status by Selected Monthly Owner Cost as a Percentage of Household Income in the Past 12 Months"; <http://factfinder.census.gov>, accessed November 2018. See also <https://www.census.gov/programs-surveys/acs/>.

# Table 1028. Renter-Occupied Housing Units—Gross Rent by State: 2017

[In percent, except as indicated (43,379 represents 43,379,000). The American Community Survey universe includes the household population, and excludes the population living in institutions, college dormitories, and other group quarters. For definition of median, see Guide to Tabular Presentation. Based on a sample and subject to sampling variability; see Appendix III]

| State | Total [1] (1,000) | Percent of units with gross rent of— | | | | | Median gross rent (dol.) | Gross rent as a percent of household income in the past 12 months [2] | | | |
|---|---|---|---|---|---|---|---|---|---|---|---|
| | | $299 or less | $300 to $499 | $500 to $749 | $750 to $999 | $1,000 or more | | Less than 15.0 percent | 15.0 to 24.9 percent | 25.0 to 29.9 percent | 30.0 percent or more |
| **U.S.** | **43,379** | **4.0** | **5.6** | **16.1** | **21.0** | **48.3** | **1,012** | **12.2** | **23.8** | **10.8** | **46.0** |
| AL. | 588 | 6.3 | 10.2 | 28.1 | 23.2 | 21.5 | 750 | 13.2 | 21.6 | 10.4 | 40.8 |
| AK. | 91 | 1.1 | 4.7 | 9.2 | 17.6 | 59.8 | 1,201 | 12.9 | 26.4 | 10.3 | 42.0 |
| AZ. | 901 | 2.2 | 4.0 | 16.1 | 23.7 | 49.5 | 1,020 | 11.5 | 25.9 | 10.6 | 44.8 |
| AR. | 401 | 5.5 | 12.0 | 33.6 | 24.5 | 15.6 | 711 | 15.2 | 24.1 | 10.0 | 39.5 |
| CA. | 5,880 | 2.2 | 2.7 | 6.0 | 11.6 | 74.4 | 1,447 | 9.5 | 22.1 | 11.0 | 52.5 |
| CO. | 744 | 3.1 | 3.2 | 8.7 | 16.2 | 65.2 | 1,240 | 9.7 | 24.2 | 11.8 | 49.2 |
| CT. | 459 | 5.0 | 4.8 | 8.9 | 18.4 | 58.7 | 1,125 | 11.4 | 22.6 | 11.7 | 48.3 |
| DE. | 104 | 3.5 | 4.5 | 8.2 | 23.2 | 56.8 | 1,086 | 11.8 | 22.8 | 11.4 | 43.6 |
| DC. | 163 | 6.3 | 3.5 | 5.3 | 8.7 | 73.7 | 1,499 | 12.9 | 24.4 | 11.5 | 44.9 |
| FL. | 2,680 | 2.4 | 2.9 | 10.4 | 21.1 | 58.8 | 1,128 | 8.3 | 21.4 | 10.9 | 52.4 |
| GA. | 1,390 | 3.6 | 5.8 | 18.1 | 24.0 | 43.5 | 958 | 12.9 | 24.4 | 10.8 | 44.4 |
| HI. | 190 | 3.8 | 3.1 | 3.8 | 8.4 | 74.3 | 1,573 | 9.7 | 20.4 | 10.2 | 51.7 |
| ID. | 190 | 4.1 | 7.7 | 26.4 | 28.5 | 27.1 | 822 | 14.4 | 23.3 | 11.7 | 41.7 |
| IL. | 1,626 | 4.6 | 5.9 | 16.2 | 23.7 | 45.3 | 974 | 13.4 | 24.0 | 10.4 | 45.2 |
| IN. | 792 | 4.2 | 7.4 | 29.5 | 31.0 | 22.3 | 793 | 14.5 | 24.4 | 10.6 | 41.7 |
| IA. | 357 | 3.8 | 10.9 | 30.7 | 27.2 | 21.2 | 760 | 16.5 | 26.6 | 10.2 | 38.8 |
| KS. | 385 | 3.7 | 8.6 | 27.6 | 27.6 | 27.4 | 815 | 14.7 | 26.4 | 11.1 | 41.0 |
| KY. | 578 | 7.0 | 10.9 | 30.6 | 24.4 | 17.8 | 724 | 15.9 | 23.3 | 10.6 | 38.4 |
| LA. | 605 | 5.5 | 8.5 | 21.1 | 26.9 | 27.2 | 836 | 10.4 | 19.1 | 8.8 | 47.5 |
| ME. | 145 | 9.2 | 9.5 | 21.8 | 23.8 | 27.9 | 806 | 11.4 | 26.4 | 12.3 | 40.4 |
| MD. | 735 | 3.9 | 3.6 | 5.9 | 11.8 | 71.5 | 1,337 | 10.8 | 25.2 | 11.4 | 47.5 |
| MA. | 981 | 6.8 | 7.0 | 9.0 | 13.3 | 60.8 | 1,208 | 12.7 | 23.4 | 12.0 | 46.5 |
| MI. | 1,127 | 5.0 | 7.1 | 25.2 | 27.9 | 29.8 | 835 | 13.3 | 23.7 | 11.0 | 44.6 |
| MN. | 615 | 5.7 | 7.3 | 16.4 | 24.3 | 42.5 | 939 | 13.6 | 25.6 | 12.1 | 43.7 |
| MS. | 344 | 7.7 | 10.5 | 26.4 | 24.7 | 17.9 | 742 | 12.0 | 21.1 | 10.6 | 40.2 |
| MO. | 788 | 4.4 | 9.4 | 26.8 | 27.1 | 26.1 | 800 | 14.2 | 25.8 | 10.8 | 41.0 |
| MT. | 131 | 5.3 | 10.1 | 29.5 | 22.3 | 24.6 | 759 | 15.9 | 24.2 | 10.3 | 40.2 |
| NE. | 254 | 4.7 | 8.9 | 27.2 | 28.3 | 25.0 | 801 | 17.8 | 27.9 | 9.6 | 36.8 |
| NV. | 475 | 1.4 | 2.7 | 12.9 | 27.0 | 53.3 | 1,051 | 11.6 | 26.8 | 11.1 | 45.5 |
| NH. | 160 | 4.2 | 3.8 | 10.4 | 23.2 | 55.0 | 1,072 | 10.7 | 28.2 | 12.0 | 44.5 |
| NJ. | 1,165 | 4.7 | 3.5 | 4.4 | 12.9 | 71.4 | 1,284 | 11.4 | 23.8 | 10.7 | 49.0 |
| NM. | 246 | 4.6 | 8.1 | 26.1 | 23.4 | 29.0 | 813 | 12.9 | 21.8 | 10.3 | 43.3 |
| NY. | 3,374 | 5.1 | 5.7 | 10.5 | 14.1 | 61.1 | 1,226 | 13.0 | 21.8 | 9.9 | 49.7 |
| NC. | 1,368 | 4.0 | 8.7 | 23.5 | 25.7 | 33.6 | 861 | 13.3 | 24.6 | 11.0 | 42.4 |
| ND. | 116 | 4.7 | 8.5 | 29.0 | 26.6 | 24.3 | 785 | 20.3 | 25.7 | 9.1 | 36.6 |
| OH. | 1,597 | 5.8 | 8.5 | 30.3 | 27.7 | 22.6 | 772 | 15.2 | 25.9 | 10.0 | 41.1 |
| OK. | 508 | 4.3 | 8.4 | 29.3 | 27.2 | 22.1 | 780 | 14.5 | 24.5 | 9.6 | 40.5 |
| OR. | 597 | 2.7 | 4.3 | 12.4 | 21.9 | 54.7 | 1,079 | 9.9 | 25.0 | 10.7 | 48.6 |
| PA. | 1,588 | 5.4 | 7.1 | 19.8 | 24.9 | 36.7 | 893 | 13.4 | 23.8 | 10.2 | 42.5 |
| RI. | 160 | 10.4 | 8.9 | 11.3 | 24.3 | 41.9 | 941 | 15.3 | 21.9 | 14.1 | 43.0 |
| SC. | 595 | 3.9 | 7.2 | 23.6 | 26.6 | 30.4 | 848 | 12.1 | 22.5 | 9.7 | 44.8 |
| SD. | 111 | 6.2 | 14.0 | 30.3 | 25.0 | 18.7 | 722 | 18.0 | 26.8 | 9.9 | 37.8 |
| TN. | 895 | 5.0 | 8.0 | 24.4 | 24.9 | 30.3 | 833 | 12.7 | 24.6 | 11.8 | 40.9 |
| TX. | 3,660 | 2.6 | 4.2 | 15.9 | 26.3 | 46.2 | 987 | 11.9 | 25.3 | 11.0 | 44.5 |
| UT. | 294 | 2.6 | 5.2 | 16.6 | 24.8 | 46.7 | 986 | 13.3 | 27.9 | 11.1 | 41.7 |
| VT. | 78 | 5.1 | 5.9 | 17.5 | 22.7 | 42.7 | 950 | 9.7 | 23.3 | 12.9 | 46.9 |
| VA. | 1,043 | 3.8 | 4.6 | 11.4 | 16.9 | 58.1 | 1,179 | 12.1 | 26.1 | 11.3 | 43.7 |
| WA. | 1,057 | 3.3 | 3.7 | 9.7 | 16.2 | 62.9 | 1,216 | 10.6 | 26.4 | 12.2 | 45.2 |
| WV. | 196 | 8.0 | 12.9 | 28.7 | 21.2 | 13.8 | 690 | 13.5 | 18.5 | 9.8 | 39.6 |
| WI. | 785 | 4.1 | 7.2 | 26.4 | 31.0 | 27.1 | 819 | 15.5 | 26.9 | 10.6 | 41.0 |
| WY. | 66 | 5.3 | 7.0 | 24.2 | 25.5 | 28.9 | 832 | 13.8 | 26.2 | 11.3 | 38.0 |

[1] Includes units with no cash rent. [2] Percent distribution of rental units by gross rent as a percent of household income. Percentage calculated from totals which include units "not computed"; therefore, rows will not total 100 percent.

Source: U.S. Census Bureau, 2017 American Community Survey, B25063, "Gross Rent"; B25064, "Median Gross Rent"; and B25070, "Gross Rent as a Percentage of Household Income in Past 12 Months"; <http://factfinder.census.gov>, accessed November 2018.

# Table 1029. Mortgage Characteristics—Owner-Occupied Units: 2017

[In thousands (77,570 represents 77,570,000). As of Fall. Based on the American Housing Survey; see Appendix III]

| Mortgage characteristic | Total owner occupied units | Housing unit characteristics | | Household characteristics | | | |
|---|---|---|---|---|---|---|---|
| | | New construc-tion [1] | Mobile homes | Black [2] | His-panic [3] | Elderly [4] | Below poverty level [5] |
| **ALL OWNERS** | | | | | | | |
| **Total**............................ | **77,570** | **621** | **4,969** | **7,131** | **7,763** | **23,983** | **6,722** |
| Mortgages currently on property: | | | | | | | |
| None, owned free and clear.................... | 31,380 | (S) | (S) | (S) | 2,868 | (S) | 4,279 |
| Reverse mortgage............................. | 351 | (S) | (S) | (S) | 20 | (S) | 43 |
| Regular or home equity lump sum mortgage(s) [6]... | 42,000 | (S) | (S) | (S) | 4,692 | (S) | 2,245 |
| 1 regular/lump sum mortgage..................... | 40,100 | (S) | (S) | (S) | 4,488 | (S) | 2,177 |
| 2 or more regular/lump sum mortgages............ | 1,898 | (S) | (S) | (S) | 203 | (S) | 67 |
| Regular/home equity lump sum mortgage(s) and home equity line(s) of credit.................. | 2,246 | (S) | (S) | (S) | 95 | (S) | 67 |
| Home equity line(s) of credit.................... | 1,593 | (S) | (S) | (S) | 87 | (S) | 88 |
| Type of loan: [7, 8] | | | | | | | |
| Primary regular mortgage [6]................. | 44,240 | 476 | 1,309 | 4,266 | 4,787 | 7,635 | 2,312 |
| Secondary regular mortgage [6]................. | 1,975 | 16 | 8 | (S) | 213 | 296 | 72 |
| Home equity line of credit...................... | 3,881 | 11 | 44 | 197 | 191 | 1,200 | 156 |
| **OWNERS WITH ONE OR MORE REGULAR OR LUMP SUM HOME EQUITY MORTGAGES** | | | | | | | |
| **Total**............................ | **44,240** | **476** | **1,309** | **4,266** | **4,787** | **7,635** | **2,312** |
| Mortgage origination: | | | | | | | |
| Placed new mortgage(s)......................... | 43,530 | (S) | (S) | (S) | 4,622 | (S) | (S) |
| Primary obtained when property acquired......... | 26,190 | (S) | (S) | (S) | 3,238 | (S) | (S) |
| Obtained later................................. | 17,340 | (S) | (S) | (S) | 1,384 | (S) | (S) |
| Assumed...................................... | 287 | (S) | (S) | (S) | 79 | (S) | (S) |
| Wrap-around.................................. | 43 | (S) | (S) | (S) | 19 | (S) | (S) |
| Not reported.................................. | 373 | (S) | (S) | (S) | 67 | (S) | (S) |
| Payment plan of primary mortgage: | | | | | | | |
| Fixed payment, self amortizing.................. | 41,710 | (S) | (S) | (S) | (S) | (S) | (S) |
| Payment option............................... | 61 | (S) | (S) | (S) | (S) | (S) | (S) |
| Interest only.................................. | 122 | (S) | (S) | (S) | (S) | (S) | (S) |
| Balloon....................................... | 76 | (S) | (S) | (S) | (S) | (S) | (S) |
| Graduated payment mortgage.................... | 255 | (S) | (S) | (S) | (S) | (S) | (S) |
| Adjustable rate mortgage....................... | 1,234 | (S) | (S) | (S) | (S) | (S) | (S) |
| Other......................................... | 573 | (S) | (S) | (S) | (S) | (S) | (S) |
| Interest only adjustable rate.................... | 13 | (S) | (S) | (S) | (S) | (S) | (S) |
| Not reported.................................. | 196 | (S) | (S) | (S) | (S) | (S) | (S) |
| Type of mortgage insurance: | | | | | | | |
| FHA [9]....................................... | 10,160 | (S) | (S) | (S) | 1,685 | 1,309 | 589 |
| VA........................................... | 2,793 | (S) | (S) | (S) | 283 | 544 | 107 |
| RHS/RD [10].................................. | 608 | (S) | (S) | (S) | 60 | 42 | 37 |
| Other types................................... | 29,040 | (S) | (S) | (S) | 2,510 | 5,380 | 1,435 |
| Not reported.................................. | 1,634 | (S) | (S) | (S) | 249 | 360 | 144 |
| Reason primary refinanced: | | | | | | | |
| Units with a refinanced primary mortgage [6]......... | 14,960 | 24 | 212 | 1,070 | 1,167 | 3,076 | 554 |
| To get a lower interest rate...................... | 10,100 | 14 | (S) | 652 | 688 | 1,941 | 320 |
| To reduce monthly payment...................... | 3,672 | (S) | (S) | 312 | 404 | (S) | 127 |
| To reduce payment period....................... | 2,486 | (S) | (S) | 114 | 181 | (S) | 58 |
| To increase payment period..................... | 432 | – | (S) | (S) | 42 | (S) | 15 |
| To receive cash............................... | 1,911 | – | (S) | (S) | 188 | (S) | 85 |
| To suspend or temporarily reduce payments...... | 323 | – | (S) | (S) | 37 | 95 | 17 |
| Other reason.................................. | 1,679 | (S) | (S) | 114 | 121 | 350 | 62 |
| Cash received in primary mortgage refinance: | | | | | | | |
| Units receiving refinance cash.................... | 1,911 | – | (S) | (S) | 188 | (S) | 85 |
| Median amount received (dol.)................... | 30,000 | – | (S) | 30,000 | 30,000 | (NA) | (NA) |

– Represents or rounds to zero. S Represents estimates that did not meet publication standards. NA Not available. [1] Constructed in the 2016-2017 period. [2] For persons who selected this race group only. [3] Persons of Hispanic origin may be of any race. [4] Householders age 65 years old and over. [5] Those households below the poverty threshold based on household income of families or of individuals living without relatives. Income in the AHS refers to money income in the 12 months before the survey. The threshold is updated every year to reflect changes in the Consumer Price Index. See source for more information. [6] Regular mortgages include all mortgages not classified as home-equity line of credit or reverse. [7] Figures may not add to total because more than one category may apply to a unit. [8] A household can have more than one secondary and/or home-equity credit line. [9] Federal Housing Administration. [10] Rural Housing Service/Rural Development.

Source: U.S. Census Bureau, "American Housing Survey: AHS Table Creator," <http://www.census.gov/programs-surveys/ahs/data.html>, accessed February 2019.

# Table 1030. Home Purchase Loans by Race/Ethnicity and Sex: 2017

[Amount in millions of dollars (1,156,592 represents $1,156,592,000,000). Includes applications for conventional home-purchase loans 1- to 4-family and manufactured home dwellings. Applicants are only shown in one race and one gender category]

| Race/ethnicity and gender | Applications received | | Loans originated | | Applications approved, not accepted | | Applications denied | | Applications withdrawn | | Files closed for incompleteness | |
|---|---|---|---|---|---|---|---|---|---|---|---|---|
| | Number | Amount (million dollars) | Number | Amount (million dollars) | Number | Amount (million dollars) | Number | Amount (million dollars) | Number | Amount (million dollars) | Number | Amount (million dollars) |
| **Total [1,2]** | **4,141,715** | **1,156,592** | **2,902,072** | **834,108** | **135,283** | **37,607** | **483,643** | **112,339** | **482,130** | **143,668** | **138,587** | **28,870** |
| White | 2,955,150 | 772,314 | 2,136,259 | 575,204 | 97,242 | 25,247 | 305,618 | 62,909 | 327,590 | 91,753 | 88,441 | 17,201 |
| Male | 992,040 | 254,573 | 702,080 | 184,312 | 32,539 | 7,895 | 112,714 | 24,832 | 112,465 | 31,219 | 32,242 | 6,315 |
| Female | 653,481 | 132,927 | 458,421 | 97,748 | 21,420 | 4,339 | 79,763 | 11,980 | 73,348 | 15,785 | 20,529 | 3,075 |
| Joint (male/female) | 1,300,441 | 382,557 | 970,187 | 291,675 | 43,012 | 12,948 | 111,560 | 25,818 | 140,484 | 44,384 | 35,198 | 7,732 |
| Black | 190,552 | 36,850 | 101,772 | 22,691 | 6,461 | 1,124 | 48,201 | 6,294 | 22,336 | 5,224 | 1,782 | 1,518 |
| Male | 66,310 | 13,422 | 36,794 | 8,268 | 2,350 | 430 | 15,141 | 2,137 | 8,272 | 2,081 | 3,753 | 504 |
| Female | 81,854 | 13,990 | 43,051 | 8,505 | 2,667 | 400 | 21,912 | 2,605 | 9,399 | 1,963 | 4,825 | 517 |
| Joint (male/female) | 40,495 | 9,171 | 21,397 | 5,802 | 1,394 | 288 | 10,261 | 1,459 | 4,501 | 1,148 | 2,942 | 474 |
| Hispanic or Latino | 318,213 | 66,930 | 197,129 | 45,305 | 11,201 | 2,038 | 55,609 | 9,080 | 38,026 | 8,143 | 16,248 | 2,365 |
| Male | 144,311 | 29,783 | 90,107 | 19,745 | 5,077 | 937 | 24,610 | 4,268 | 17,336 | 3,757 | 7,181 | 1,075 |
| Female | 82,185 | 15,417 | 50,187 | 10,249 | 2,760 | 445 | 15,435 | 2,338 | 10,044 | 1,876 | 3,759 | 509 |
| Joint (male/female) | 90,047 | 20,639 | 56,167 | 14,344 | 3,311 | 647 | 15,003 | 2,413 | 10,437 | 2,471 | 5,129 | 763 |
| Asian | 313,472 | 123,015 | 223,906 | 86,390 | 10,428 | 4,192 | 27,946 | 12,577 | 41,913 | 16,396 | 9,279 | 3,461 |
| Male | 137,116 | 53,109 | 97,544 | 36,437 | 4,523 | 1,745 | 11,881 | 6,344 | 18,913 | 7,039 | 4,255 | 1,543 |
| Female | 68,311 | 21,514 | 48,662 | 15,349 | 2,261 | 737 | 6,612 | 1,973 | 8,764 | 2,827 | 2,012 | 628 |
| Joint (male/female) | 106,976 | 47,971 | 77,031 | 34,336 | 3,611 | 1,696 | 9,338 | 4,216 | 14,043 | 6,452 | 2,953 | 1,271 |
| Native Hawaiian/Other Pacific Islander | 10,410 | 3,106 | 6,910 | 2,259 | 356 | 89 | 1,385 | 294 | 1,383 | 379 | 376 | 84 |
| Male | 4,629 | 1,524 | 3,033 | 1,145 | 158 | 41 | 627 | 132 | 639 | 168 | 172 | 39 |
| Female | 2,938 | 677 | 1,915 | 465 | 113 | 24 | 418 | 76 | 379 | 89 | 113 | 23 |
| Joint (male/female) | 2,770 | 888 | 1,925 | 639 | 84 | 25 | 322 | 84 | 352 | 119 | 87 | 22 |
| American Indian/Alaska Native | 17,711 | 3,193 | 8,960 | 1,897 | 574 | 101 | 4,748 | 521 | 1,977 | 527 | 1,452 | 146 |
| Male | 7,887 | 1,428 | 4,217 | 887 | 247 | 43 | 1,892 | 227 | 931 | 207 | 600 | 63 |
| Female | 6,045 | 1,008 | 2,960 | 550 | 202 | 34 | 1,756 | 163 | 680 | 221 | 447 | 40 |
| Joint (male/female) | 3,411 | 698 | 1,633 | 429 | 123 | 24 | 966 | 117 | 329 | 89 | 360 | 37 |
| Two or more minority races | 3,302 | 855 | 1,941 | 558 | 92 | 24 | 610 | 109 | 511 | 138 | 148 | 25 |
| Male | 1,361 | 359 | 799 | 222 | 37 | 10 | 229 | 50 | 235 | 65 | 61 | 12 |
| Female | 1,262 | 265 | 704 | 171 | 36 | 7 | 268 | 35 | 197 | 44 | 57 | 8 |
| Joint (male/female) | 651 | 225 | 424 | 162 | 19 | 6 | 105 | 24 | 73 | 28 | 30 | 5 |
| Joint [3] | 72,441 | 25,644 | 51,047 | 18,565 | 2,210 | 763 | 7,669 | 2,496 | 9,078 | 3,241 | 2,437 | 580 |
| Race not available [4] | 435,652 | 146,389 | 267,817 | 93,399 | 13,911 | 4,488 | 67,321 | 22,143 | 64,713 | 21,428 | 21,890 | 4,931 |
| Male | 69,327 | 20,884 | 40,653 | 12,519 | 2,390 | 726 | 12,471 | 3,949 | 9,469 | 2,897 | 4,344 | 793 |
| Female | 41,895 | 10,053 | 24,256 | 6,137 | 1,242 | 289 | 8,184 | 1,854 | 5,890 | 1,423 | 2,323 | 350 |
| Joint (male/female) | 75,863 | 26,000 | 48,664 | 17,603 | 2,429 | 880 | 10,186 | 2,956 | 10,342 | 3,597 | 4,242 | 874 |

[1] Total includes those cases in which gender was reported and in those in which gender information was not available. [2] Includes all loans from other race/ethnicities not shown separately. [3] "Joint" means with two applicants, one reported a single designation of "White" and the other applicant reported one or more minority racial designations. [4] "Not available" includes situations in which information was reported as not provided or not applicable.

Source: Bureau of Consumer Financial Protection, Federal Financial Institutions Examination Council, "Home Mortgage Disclosure Act: National Aggregate Reports," <https://ffiec.cfpb.gov/>, accessed August 2019.

## Table 1031. Heating Equipment and Fuels for Occupied Units: 2005 to 2017

[108,871 represents 108,871,000. As of Fall. Data for 2005 to 2009 based on population controls from Census 2000. Beginning 2011, data based on Census 2010 controls. Based on American Housing Survey. See Appendix III]

| Type of equipment or fuel | Number (1,000) | | | | | Percent distribution | |
|---|---|---|---|---|---|---|---|
| | 2005 | 2011 | 2013 | 2015 | 2017 | 2015 | 2017 |
| **Occupied units, total**......................... | **108,871** | **114,907** | **115,852** | **118,290** | **121,600** | **100.0** | **100.0** |
| Heating equipment: | | | | | | | |
| Warm air furnace........................... | 68,275 | 73,687 | 74,712 | 76,207 | 79,380 | 64.4 | 65.3 |
| Steam or hot water........................ | 12,880 | 12,624 | 12,448 | 10,919 | 11,100 | 9.2 | 9.1 |
| Heat pumps.................................. | 12,484 | 13,523 | 13,526 | 13,980 | 14,130 | 11.8 | 11.6 |
| Built-in electric units..................... | 4,699 | 4,865 | 5,064 | 4,616 | 4,925 | 3.9 | 4.1 |
| Floor, wall, or pipeless furnace........ | 5,102 | 4,505 | 4,571 | 5,963 | 5,616 | 5.0 | 4.6 |
| Room heaters with flue................... | 1,294 | 932 | 851 | 776 | 740 | 0.7 | 0.6 |
| Room heaters without flue.............. | 1,327 | 1,094 | 1,034 | 647 | 749 | 0.5 | 0.6 |
| Fireplaces, stoves, portable heaters or other........... | 2,411 | 3,208 | 3,260 | 4,362 | 4,076 | 3.7 | 3.4 |
| None.......................................... | 399 | 468 | 386 | 818 | 848 | 0.7 | 0.7 |
| House main heating fuel: | | | | | | | |
| Electricity.................................... | 34,263 | 40,385 | 42,041 | 48,323 | 52,330 | 40.9 | 43.0 |
| Utility gas.................................... | 56,317 | 57,721 | 58,225 | 54,791 | 54,090 | 46.3 | 44.5 |
| Bottled, tank, or liquid propane gas... | 6,228 | 5,415 | 5,198 | 4,703 | 5,074 | 4.0 | 4.2 |
| Fuel oil, kerosene, etc.................... | 9,929 | 8,599 | 7,623 | 6,654 | 6,421 | 5.6 | 5.3 |
| Coal or coke................................. | 95 | 79 | 98 | 80 | 89 | 0.1 | 0.1 |
| Wood and other fuel....................... | 1,640 | 2,240 | 2,280 | 2,921 | 2,335 | 2.5 | 1.9 |
| None.......................................... | 398 | 468 | 387 | 818 | 372 | 0.7 | 0.3 |
| Cooking fuel: | | | | | | | |
| Electricity.................................... | 65,297 | 68,879 | 69,330 | 71,262 | 72,870 | 60.2 | 59.9 |
| Gas [1]........................................ | 43,316 | 45,759 | 46,294 | 46,386 | 48,217 | 39.2 | 39.7 |
| Other fuel.................................... | 51 | 92 | 71 | 200 | 92 | 0.2 | 0.1 |
| None.......................................... | 206 | 177 | 158 | 441 | 21 | 0.4 | (Z) |

Z Less than 0.05 percent. [1] Includes utility, bottled, tank, and liquid propane gas.

Source: U.S. Census Bureau, "American Housing Survey: AHS Table Creator," <http://www.census.gov/programs-surveys/ahs/data.html>, accessed February 2019.

## Table 1032. Occupied Housing Units—Housing Amenities and Deficiencies by Selected Characteristics of the Householder: 2017

[In thousands of units (121,600 represents 121,600,000). As of Fall. Based on the American Housing Survey; see Appendix III]

| Characteristic | Total occupied units | Tenure | | Black [1] | | Hispanic origin [2] | | Elderly [3] | | Households below poverty level [4] | |
|---|---|---|---|---|---|---|---|---|---|---|---|
| | | Owner | Renter | Owner | Renter | Owner | Renter | Owner | Renter | Owner | Renter |
| **Total units**..................... | **121,600** | **77,570** | **43,990** | **7,131** | **9,421** | **7,763** | **8,733** | **23,983** | **6,686** | **6,722** | **10,293** |
| Selected amenities: | | | | | | | | | | | |
| Porch, deck, balcony or patio......... | 103,700 | 71,990 | 31,720 | 6,277 | 6,389 | 6,890 | 5,862 | 22,337 | 4,291 | 5,966 | 6,758 |
| Usable fireplace...................... | 44,530 | 38,050 | 6,482 | 2,952 | 1,078 | 2,760 | 1,076 | 11,307 | 808 | 2,136 | 839 |
| Separate dining room................. | 59,190 | 44,900 | 14,290 | 4,582 | 3,362 | 4,374 | 3,035 | 13,896 | 1,808 | 3,428 | 2,974 |
| With 2 or more living rooms or recreation rooms................... | 39,870 | 35,280 | 4,594 | 2,773 | 741 | 2,331 | 623 | 10,755 | 610 | 1,862 | 618 |
| Garage or carport with home......... | 79,840 | 62,550 | 17,290 | 4,893 | 2,627 | 5,829 | 3,484 | 19,723 | 2,322 | 4,571 | 2,741 |
| Selected deficiencies: | | | | | | | | | | | |
| Signs of mice or rats in last 12 months.............................. | 15,620 | 10,260 | 5,355 | 914 | 1,291 | 728 | 1,176 | 3,140 | 640 | 987 | 1,572 |
| Signs of cockroaches in last 12 months.............................. | 15,300 | 7,424 | 7,877 | 1,092 | 2,134 | 1,358 | 2,342 | 2,219 | 904 | 913 | 2,305 |
| Holes in floors........................ | 1,449 | 654 | 794 | 95 | 201 | 89 | 168 | 179 | 57 | 133 | 254 |
| Open cracks or holes (interior)....... | 6,600 | 3,518 | 3,082 | 467 | 790 | 424 | 608 | 909 | 210 | 511 | 968 |
| Broken/peeling paint or plaster (interior)............................ | 2,525 | 1,253 | 1,272 | 185 | 292 | 165 | 308 | 353 | 104 | 193 | 393 |
| No electrical wiring................... | 119 | 76 | 42 | – | 3 | 10 | 17 | 10 | 3 | 29 | 32 |
| Exposed wiring........................ | 3,267 | 1,833 | 1,434 | 216 | 311 | 249 | 355 | 631 | 208 | 251 | 390 |
| Rooms without electric outlet........ | 2,094 | 1,091 | 1,003 | 131 | 292 | 129 | 193 | 337 | 117 | 199 | 305 |
| Water leakage from inside structure [5]................... | 9,952 | 5,252 | 4,699 | 571 | 1,148 | 499 | 822 | 1,241 | 499 | 427 | 1,161 |
| Water leakage from outside structure [5].................. | 12,320 | 8,146 | 4,176 | 840 | 920 | 767 | 730 | 2,250 | 436 | 745 | 1,030 |
| Sagging roof [6]....................... | 1,739 | 1,256 | 483 | 174 | 67 | 170 | 80 | 338 | 69 | 228 | 171 |
| Missing roof material [6].............. | 3,326 | 2,547 | 779 | 378 | 165 | 330 | 109 | 690 | 81 | 334 | 262 |
| Hole in roof [6]........................ | 1,352 | 921 | 431 | 188 | 102 | 190 | 84 | 252 | 45 | 157 | 168 |
| Missing bricks, siding, or other outside wall material [5]............. | 2,556 | 1,826 | 730 | 262 | 153 | 229 | 102 | 437 | 65 | 270 | 254 |
| Boarded up windows [6]............... | 1,061 | 733 | 328 | 81 | 55 | 126 | 74 | 196 | 12 | 149 | 113 |
| Broken windows [6].................... | 3,913 | 2,799 | 1,113 | 332 | 227 | 363 | 191 | 643 | 88 | 386 | 360 |
| Foundation crumbling or has open crack or hole [6]...................... | 4,969 | 3,605 | 1,364 | 400 | 280 | 411 | 218 | 1,029 | 141 | 509 | 383 |
| Units with mold in the last 12 months.............................. | 3,775 | 1,721 | 2,054 | 220 | 509 | 234 | 482 | 401 | 168 | 272 | 654 |

– Represents or rounds to zero. [1] For persons who selected this race group only. [2] Persons of Hispanic origin may be of any race. [3] Householders 65 years old and over. [4] Based on household income of families or of individuals living without relatives. Refers to money income in the 12 months before the survey. Threshold reflects changes in the Consumer Price Index, see source for more information. [5] During the 12 months prior to the survey. [6] Excludes multiunit structures.

Source: U.S. Census Bureau, "American Housing Survey: AHS Table Creator," <http://www.census.gov/programs-surveys/ahs/data.html>, accessed February 2019.

# Table 1033. Household Energy Consumption and Expenditures by Selected Characteristics: 2015

[118.2 represents 118,200,000. Btu=British thermal units; for definition, see text, Section 19. Includes all primary occupied housing units in the 50 states and the District of Columbia. Vacant housing units, seasonal units, second homes, military houses, and group quarters are excluded. Consumption and expenditures for biomass (wood), coal, district steam, and solar thermal are excluded. Electricity consumption from on-site solar photovoltaic generation (i.e., solar panels) is included. Data from the Residential Energy Consumption Survey (RECS). Data were collected between August 2015 and April 2016]

| Characteristic | Total housing units (millions) | Energy consumption | | | | Energy expenditures | | | |
|---|---|---|---|---|---|---|---|---|---|
| | | Total (trillion Btu) | Per household (million Btu) | Per household member (million Btu) | Per square foot (thousand Btu) | Total (billion dollars) | Per household (dollars) | Per household member (dollars) | Per square foot (dollars) |
| **All homes** | **118.2** | **9,114** | **77.1** | **30.3** | **38.4** | **219.3** | **1,856** | **728** | **0.92** |
| Region: | | | | | | | | | |
| Northeast | 21.0 | 1,984 | 94.4 | 38.1 | 45.2 | 47.7 | 2,269 | 915 | 1.09 |
| Midwest | 26.4 | 2,486 | 94.3 | 37.8 | 41.4 | 46.4 | 1,760 | 706 | 0.77 |
| South | 44.4 | 3,064 | 68.9 | 27.3 | 35.6 | 85.2 | 1,917 | 758 | 0.99 |
| West | 26.4 | 1,581 | 59.9 | 22.3 | 33.4 | 40.1 | 1,518 | 565 | 0.85 |
| Housing unit type: | | | | | | | | | |
| Single-family detached | 73.9 | 6,991 | 94.6 | 34.6 | 37.1 | 161.7 | 2,188 | 801 | 0.86 |
| Single-family attached | 7.0 | 491 | 70.0 | 28.6 | 39.5 | 11.2 | 1,602 | 655 | 0.90 |
| Apartment buildings with 2-4 units | 9.4 | 503 | 53.5 | 22.3 | 52.5 | 12.5 | 1,329 | 555 | 1.30 |
| Apartment buildings with 5 or more units | 21.1 | 724 | 34.2 | 17.3 | 38.8 | 22.1 | 1,045 | 529 | 1.18 |
| Mobile homes | 6.8 | 406 | 59.8 | 22.8 | 50.0 | 11.9 | 1,750 | 666 | 1.46 |
| Housing tenure: | | | | | | | | | |
| Owned | 74.5 | 6,825 | 91.6 | 35.4 | 37.1 | 159.9 | 2,146 | 829 | 0.87 |
| Single-family | 66.2 | 6,347 | 95.9 | 36.5 | 36.5 | 146.2 | 2,208 | 840 | 0.84 |
| Apartments | 3.3 | 175 | 52.4 | 26.6 | 45.5 | 4.9 | 1,476 | 748 | 1.28 |
| Mobile homes | 5.0 | 304 | 61.1 | 24.6 | 49.9 | 8.8 | 1,768 | 712 | 1.44 |
| Rented [1] | 43.7 | 2,289 | 52.4 | 21.2 | 42.7 | 59.4 | 1,360 | 550 | 1.11 |
| Single-family | 14.7 | 1,135 | 77.4 | 25.3 | 41.8 | 26.7 | 1,818 | 594 | 0.98 |
| Apartments | 27.2 | 1,052 | 38.7 | 18.2 | 43.1 | 29.7 | 1,090 | 514 | 1.22 |
| Mobile homes | 1.8 | 103 | 56.3 | 18.7 | 50.2 | 3.1 | 1,702 | 565 | 1.52 |
| Year of construction: | | | | | | | | | |
| Before 1950 | 20.8 | 1,842 | 88.7 | 35.5 | 44.1 | 39.5 | 1,901 | 762 | 0.94 |
| 1950 to 1959 | 12.6 | 1,067 | 84.4 | 34.5 | 45.2 | 23.5 | 1,861 | 760 | 1.00 |
| 1960 to 1969 | 12.8 | 961 | 75.0 | 32.0 | 40.0 | 22.5 | 1,756 | 750 | 0.94 |
| 1970 to 1979 | 18.3 | 1,290 | 70.3 | 27.9 | 39.8 | 32.4 | 1,765 | 700 | 1.00 |
| 1980 to 1989 | 16.0 | 1,053 | 65.7 | 27.3 | 35.9 | 28.0 | 1,747 | 725 | 0.95 |
| 1990 to 1999 | 16.8 | 1,317 | 78.3 | 29.1 | 35.9 | 32.6 | 1,937 | 719 | 0.89 |
| 2000 to 2009 | 17.0 | 1,328 | 78.2 | 28.0 | 32.7 | 34.2 | 2,013 | 721 | 0.84 |
| 2010 to 2015 | 3.8 | 257 | 67.0 | 23.9 | 28.5 | 6.7 | 1,755 | 626 | 0.75 |
| Total square footage: [2] | | | | | | | | | |
| Fewer than 1,000 | 26.6 | 1,072 | 40.3 | 19.9 | 53.8 | 29.9 | 1,126 | 554 | 1.50 |
| 1,000 to 1,499 | 26.1 | 1,542 | 59.0 | 23.2 | 48.2 | 41.0 | 1,569 | 618 | 1.28 |
| 1,500 to 1,999 | 17.5 | 1,359 | 77.8 | 30.4 | 44.6 | 33.5 | 1,919 | 750 | 1.10 |
| 2,000 to 2,499 | 14.1 | 1,268 | 89.8 | 32.7 | 40.3 | 29.5 | 2,088 | 759 | 0.94 |
| 2,500 to 2,999 | 10.8 | 1,111 | 102.9 | 38.5 | 37.7 | 24.7 | 2,282 | 854 | 0.84 |
| 3,000 or greater | 23.1 | 2,762 | 119.6 | 40.4 | 29.4 | 60.8 | 2,631 | 888 | 0.65 |
| Number of household members: | | | | | | | | | |
| 1 member | 28.7 | 1,591 | 55.3 | 55.3 | 36.6 | 37.9 | 1,319 | 1,319 | 0.87 |
| 2 members | 42.7 | 3,229 | 75.6 | 37.8 | 36.6 | 79.0 | 1,849 | 924 | 0.90 |
| 3 members | 19.4 | 1,643 | 84.6 | 28.2 | 39.9 | 39.0 | 2,009 | 670 | 0.95 |
| 4 members | 15.5 | 1,472 | 94.9 | 23.7 | 40.2 | 35.3 | 2,274 | 569 | 0.96 |
| 5 members | 7.2 | 698 | 97.1 | 19.4 | 42.2 | 16.8 | 2,338 | 468 | 1.02 |
| 6 or more members | 4.6 | 481 | 103.8 | 15.7 | 42.0 | 11.4 | 2,457 | 371 | 0.99 |
| Annual household income: | | | | | | | | | |
| Less than $20,000 | 22.9 | 1,303 | 57.0 | 25.9 | 43.1 | 32.5 | 1,421 | 645 | 1.08 |
| $20,000 to $39,999 | 27.3 | 1,882 | 68.9 | 29.3 | 40.7 | 44.5 | 1,629 | 692 | 0.96 |
| $40,000 to $59,999 | 18.4 | 1,354 | 73.6 | 29.9 | 38.7 | 32.7 | 1,778 | 723 | 0.93 |
| $60,000 to $79,999 | 15.2 | 1,218 | 80.0 | 29.9 | 37.0 | 29.6 | 1,940 | 725 | 0.90 |
| $80,000 to $99,999 | 9.7 | 827 | 85.4 | 31.5 | 37.4 | 19.5 | 2,014 | 741 | 0.88 |
| $100,000 to $119,999 | 8.1 | 733 | 90.4 | 30.6 | 34.2 | 17.7 | 2,187 | 739 | 0.83 |
| $120,000 to $139,999 | 5.4 | 552 | 101.7 | 33.7 | 37.1 | 13.0 | 2,396 | 794 | 0.87 |
| $140,000 or more | 11.2 | 1,244 | 111.2 | 36.8 | 36.0 | 29.9 | 2,669 | 884 | 0.86 |
| Main heating fuel | | | | | | | | | |
| Natural gas | 57.7 | 5,517 | 95.7 | 37.0 | 43.1 | 108.1 | 1,875 | 726 | 0.84 |
| Electricity | 40.9 | 2,096 | 51.2 | 20.6 | 30.5 | 68.4 | 1,672 | 672 | 1.00 |
| Fuel oil/kerosene | 5.8 | 645 | 111.2 | 43.6 | 47.9 | 16.9 | 2,919 | 1,144 | 1.26 |
| Propane | 5.0 | 468 | 93.4 | 37.6 | 37.4 | 13.3 | 2,645 | 1,066 | 1.06 |

[1] Rented includes households that occupy their primary housing units without paying rent. [2] Total square footage includes all basements, finished or conditioned (heated or cooled) areas of attics, and conditioned garage space that is attached to the home. Unconditioned and unfinished areas in attics and attached garages are excluded.

Source: U.S. Energy Information Administration, 2015 RECS Survey Data, "Consumption & Energy Expenditures (C&E) Tables," <https://www.eia.gov/consumption/residential/index.php>, accessed May 2019.

# Table 1034. Household Energy Insecurity By Selected Characteristics: 2015

[In percent, except total units (118.2 represents 118,200,000). Data are from the Residential Energy Consumption Survey (RECS). Energy insecurity defined in this table includes only those issues collected as part of the RECS questionnaire. Other factors, such as energy costs as a percentage of household income, could be considered as household energy insecurity, but are not included here. Respondents may report more than one energy insecurity issue. Data were collected between August 2015 and April 2016. Includes all primary occupied housing units in the 50 states and the District of Columbia. Vacant housing units, seasonal units, second homes, military houses, and group quarters are excluded. For composition of regions, see map inside front cover]

| Characteristic | Total housing units (millions) | Percent of households reporting: | | | | | |
| --- | --- | --- | --- | --- | --- | --- | --- |
| | | Any household energy insecurity | Reducing or forgoing food or medicine to pay energy costs | Leaving home at unhealthy temperature | Receiving disconnect or delivery stop notice | Unable to use heating equipment [1] | Unable to use cooling equipment [1] |
| **All homes** | **118.2** | **31.3** | **21.4** | **10.8** | **14.6** | **5.2** | **5.8** |
| Region: | | | | | | | |
| Northeast | 21.0 | 29.5 | 19.0 | 11.9 | 12.9 | 6.7 | 2.9 |
| Midwest | 26.4 | 28.0 | 18.9 | 8.3 | 14.4 | 4.2 | 4.2 |
| South | 44.4 | 34.7 | 24.3 | 11.3 | 16.9 | 6.3 | 8.8 |
| West | 26.4 | 30.7 | 20.8 | 11.7 | 12.1 | 3.0 | 4.9 |
| Housing unit type: | | | | | | | |
| Single-family detached | 73.9 | 27.1 | 18.1 | 8.4 | 12.9 | 4.3 | 5.3 |
| Single-family attached | 7.0 | 34.3 | 22.9 | 14.3 | 15.7 | 5.7 | 5.7 |
| Apartment buildings with 2-4 units | 9.4 | 45.7 | 33.0 | 18.1 | 20.2 | 8.5 | 5.3 |
| Apartment buildings with 5 or more units | 21.1 | 30.8 | 21.3 | 11.4 | 12.3 | 2.8 | 4.3 |
| Mobile homes | 6.8 | 55.9 | 41.2 | 23.5 | 30.9 | 16.2 | 16.2 |
| Number of household members: | | | | | | | |
| 1 member | 28.7 | 29.3 | 18.8 | 12.9 | 11.8 | 4.5 | 4.5 |
| 2 members | 42.7 | 23.9 | 16.6 | 8.4 | 9.6 | 3.0 | 4.7 |
| 3 members | 19.4 | 35.6 | 25.3 | 11.3 | 16.0 | 6.2 | 7.2 |
| 4 members | 15.5 | 38.7 | 28.4 | 11.0 | 21.3 | 7.7 | 7.1 |
| 5 members | 7.2 | 45.8 | 30.6 | 12.5 | 25.0 | 8.3 | 8.3 |
| 6 or more members | 4.6 | 50.0 | 28.3 | 15.2 | 32.6 | 13.0 | 13.0 |
| Annual household income: | | | | | | | |
| Less than $20,000 | 22.9 | 49.8 | 38.4 | 20.1 | 23.1 | 10.5 | 10.0 |
| $20,000 to $39,999 | 27.3 | 40.3 | 29.3 | 13.9 | 19.8 | 7.0 | 8.1 |
| $40,000 to $59,999 | 18.4 | 34.2 | 22.8 | 10.3 | 15.8 | 5.4 | 5.4 |
| $60,000 to $79,999 | 15.2 | 25.7 | 14.5 | 7.2 | 11.8 | 3.3 | 5.3 |
| $80,000 to $99,999 | 9.7 | 18.6 | 8.2 | 4.1 | 8.2 | 1.0 | 2.1 |
| $100,000 to $119,999 | 8.1 | 12.3 | 7.4 | 3.7 | 4.9 | 1.2 | 1.2 |
| $120,000 to $139,999 | 5.4 | 13.0 | 7.4 | 5.6 | 5.6 | (S) | (S) |
| $140,000 or more | 11.2 | 8.0 | 2.7 | 2.7 | 3.6 | 0.9 | 1.8 |
| Householder age 60 or older: [2] | | | | | | | |
| Yes | 39.0 | 20.3 | 13.1 | 8.5 | 6.4 | 2.3 | 3.8 |
| No | 76.7 | 36.9 | 25.7 | 12.0 | 18.6 | 6.4 | 6.6 |
| Children under age 18 in household: | | | | | | | |
| Yes | 37.7 | 41.4 | 28.9 | 11.7 | 23.1 | 7.4 | 7.7 |
| No | 80.5 | 26.6 | 18.0 | 10.4 | 10.6 | 4.2 | 5.0 |
| Ethnicity of householder: [2] | | | | | | | |
| Hispanic or Latino | 15.0 | 45.3 | 32.0 | 16.7 | 18.7 | 7.3 | 8.7 |
| Not Hispanic or Latino | 103.2 | 29.3 | 20.0 | 10.0 | 14.0 | 4.8 | 5.3 |
| Race of householder: [2, 3] | | | | | | | |
| White | 95.4 | 28.1 | 19.1 | 10.1 | 12.6 | 4.4 | 5.1 |
| Hispanic or Latino | 13.8 | 44.2 | 30.4 | 15.9 | 18.8 | 6.5 | 8.7 |
| Not Hispanic or Latino | 81.6 | 25.4 | 17.2 | 8.9 | 11.6 | 3.9 | 4.5 |
| Black or African American | 13.6 | 52.2 | 36.0 | 16.9 | 27.9 | 10.3 | 10.3 |
| Hispanic or Latino | 0.5 | 60.0 | 60.0 | (S) | (S) | (S) | (S) |
| Not Hispanic or Latino | 13.1 | 51.9 | 35.9 | 16.8 | 28.2 | 10.7 | 10.7 |
| Asian | 4.9 | 20.4 | 16.3 | 6.1 | 4.1 | 4.1 | 2.0 |
| American Indian or Alaska Native | 1.3 | 53.8 | 38.5 | (S) | 38.5 | 7.7 | 15.4 |
| Native Hawaiian or Other Pacific Islander | 0.4 | 75.0 | (S) | (S) | (S) | (S) | (S) |
| More than one race | 2.5 | 44.0 | 28.0 | 16.0 | 24.0 | 8.0 | 12.0 |
| Housing tenure: [4] | | | | | | | |
| Owned | 74.5 | 24.2 | 15.6 | 8.1 | 10.1 | 4.4 | 5.1 |
| Rented | 43.7 | 43.5 | 31.4 | 15.6 | 22.2 | 6.4 | 6.9 |

S Data withheld because either the relative standard error was greater than 50% or fewer than 10 cases responded. [1] Includes inability to use equipment because equipment was broken and household could not have it repaired; or electricity, natural gas, or bulk fuel disruption due to lack of payment. [2] A householder is a person in whose name the home is owned or rented. These characteristics refer to the householder that completed the RECS questionnaire. [3] Householders were permitted to select more than one racial category to describe themselves. These householders are only included as "more than one race." [4] Rented includes households that occupy their primary housing units without paying rent.

Source: U.S. Energy Information Administration, 2015 RECS Survey Data, "Housing Characteristics Tables," <https://www.eia.gov/consumption/residential/index.php>, accessed May 2019.

# Table 1035. Home Remodeling—Number of Households With Work Done by Amount Spent: 2018

[In thousands (2,685 represents 2,685,000), except percent. As of Fall 2018. For work done in the prior 12 months. Based on a household survey and subject to sampling error; see source]

| Remodeling project | Total households with work done [1] Number | Total households with work done [1] Percent of households | Households with work done by outside contractor | Number of households by amount spent Under $1,000 | Number of households by amount spent $1,000 to $2,999 | Number of households by amount spent Over $3,000 |
|---|---|---|---|---|---|---|
| Conversion of garage/attic/basement into living space............... | 2,685 | 1.08 | 893 | 548 | 464 | 943 |
| Remodel bathroom........................ | 13,261 | 5.35 | 4,693 | 4,374 | 2,615 | 3,785 |
| Remodel kitchen........................... | 9,427 | 3.80 | 2,659 | 2,088 | 1,856 | 3,246 |
| Remodel bedroom......................... | 6,133 | 2.48 | 840 | 2,539 | 949 | 694 |
| Convert room to home office............. | 2,433 | 0.98 | 227 | 1,282 | 223 | 160 |
| Convert room to home theater........... | 786 | 0.32 | 124 | 319 | 99 | 75 |
| Remodel other rooms..................... | 5,448 | 2.20 | 1,020 | 2,386 | 779 | 893 |
| Add bathroom.............................. | 1,413 | 0.57 | 455 | 227 | 133 | 648 |
| Add/extend garage........................ | 869 | 0.35 | 230 | 35 | 86 | 465 |
| Add other rooms - exterior addition............. | 988 | 0.40 | 305 | 58 | 209 | 471 |
| Add deck/porch/patio...................... | 5,232 | 2.11 | 1,920 | 1,356 | 1,048 | 1,777 |
| Roofing..................................... | 8,369 | 3.38 | 5,175 | 1,208 | 1,185 | 4,254 |
| Siding - vinyl/metal....................... | 1,902 | 0.77 | 982 | 267 | 300 | 716 |
| Aluminum windows........................ | 996 | 0.40 | 471 | 222 | 115 | 368 |
| Clad-wood/wood windows................. | 1,017 | 0.41 | 336 | 101 | 132 | 300 |
| Vinyl windows............................. | 4,177 | 1.69 | 2,442 | 927 | 780 | 1,623 |
| Ceramic tile floors........................ | 3,646 | 1.47 | 1,296 | 1,348 | 588 | 811 |
| Hardwood floors.......................... | 4,870 | 1.97 | 2,414 | 910 | 1,367 | 1,469 |
| Laminate flooring......................... | 5,046 | 2.04 | 1,585 | 2,065 | 1,301 | 630 |
| Vinyl flooring.............................. | 3,159 | 1.27 | 851 | 1,518 | 541 | 356 |
| Carpeting.................................. | 6,408 | 2.59 | 3,626 | 1,998 | 1,810 | 1,026 |
| Kitchen cabinets.......................... | 4,338 | 1.75 | 1,169 | 1,199 | 698 | 1,152 |
| Kitchen counter tops...................... | 4,722 | 1.91 | 2,057 | 1,005 | 999 | 1,564 |
| Skylights................................... | 1,109 | 0.45 | 615 | 337 | 111 | 267 |
| Exterior doors............................. | 4,863 | 1.96 | 2,063 | 2,479 | 939 | 471 |
| Interior doors.............................. | 3,930 | 1.59 | 873 | 2,131 | 381 | 165 |
| Garage doors............................. | 2,995 | 1.21 | 1,270 | 1,120 | 605 | 215 |
| Concrete or masonry work............... | 3,595 | 1.45 | 1,788 | 1,169 | 647 | 1,043 |
| Swimming pool - in ground............... | 888 | 0.36 | 354 | 103 | 7 | 399 |
| Ceramic wall tile.......................... | 2,042 | 0.82 | 876 | 998 | 327 | 98 |

[1] Includes no response and amount unknown.

Source: MRI Survey of the American Consumer. © Courtesy of MRI-Simmons. See also <https://www.mrisimmons.com/>.

# Table 1036. Home Improvement Loans by Race/Ethnicity: 2017

[Applications in thousands (1,051.1 represents 1,051,100); values in millions of dollars (351,534.4 represents $351,534,400,000). Includes applications for home improvement loans, 1- to 4- family and manufactured home dwellings. Applicants are categorized by the race of the first person listed on the application unless the 'joint' designation applies]

| Item | Unit | Total [1, 2] | White, total [1] | Black, total [1] | Asian, total [1] | Joint, total [3] | Hispanic or Latino [4] |
|---|---|---|---|---|---|---|---|
| Applications received: | | | | | | | |
| Number........................... | 1,000 | 1,051.1 | 729.7 | 95.9 | 30.3 | 14.5 | 107.1 |
| Amount........................... | Mil. dol. | 351,534.4 | 296,379.7 | 9,269.3 | 6,366.3 | 2,143.5 | 15,153.7 |
| Loans originated: | | | | | | | |
| Number........................... | 1,000 | 547.0 | 413.1 | 34.2 | 14.4 | 8.2 | 42.8 |
| Amount........................... | Mil. dol. | 166,897.4 | 144,296.1 | 5,250.0 | 3,298.7 | 1,289.0 | 7,719.7 |
| Applications approved but not accepted: | | | | | | | |
| Number........................... | 1,000 | 33.9 | 23.7 | 2.1 | 1.1 | 0.4 | 4.0 |
| Amount........................... | Mil. dol. | 7,888.9 | 6,613.7 | 177.8 | 221.8 | 56.2 | 329.3 |
| Applications denied: | | | | | | | |
| Number........................... | 1,000 | 347.4 | 210.7 | 51.4 | 10.1 | 4.1 | 48.6 |
| Amount........................... | Mil. dol. | 40,897.6 | 28,617.2 | 2,280.5 | 1,239.7 | 420.4 | 4,049.5 |
| Applications withdrawn: | | | | | | | |
| Number........................... | 1,000 | 91.1 | 61.8 | 5.8 | 3.4 | 1.4 | 8.2 |
| Amount........................... | Mil. dol. | 130,036.3 | 113,093.5 | 1,258.8 | 1,279.1 | 282.5 | 2,251.6 |
| Files closed for incompleteness: | | | | | | | |
| Number........................... | 1,000 | 31.6 | 20.4 | 2.4 | 1.4 | 0.4 | 3.4 |
| Amount........................... | Mil. dol. | 5,814.1 | 3,759.2 | 302.1 | 327.0 | 95.5 | 803.6 |

[1] Applicants are shown in only one race category. [2] Total includes other races, not shown separately. [3] Joint means one applicant on an application reports a single designation of "White" and the other applicant reports one or more minority racial designations. [4] Persons of Hispanic origin may be of any race.

Source: Bureau of Consumer Financial Protection, Federal Financial Institutions Examination Council, "Home Mortgage Disclosure Act: National Aggregate Reports," <https://ffiec.cfpb.gov/>, accessed August 2019.

## Table 1037. Commercial Buildings—Summary: 2012

[5,557 represents 5,557,000. Includes mall buildings. Building type based on predominant activity in which the occupants were engaged. Based on the Commercial Buildings Energy Consumption Survey (CBECS), a sample survey of building representatives conducted in 2012; subject to sampling variability]

| Characteristic | All buildings (1,000) | Total floor-space (mil. sq. ft.) | Total workers in all buildings (1,000) | Mean square foot per building [1] (1,000) | Mean square foot per worker [1] | Mean operating hours per week [1] |
|---|---|---|---|---|---|---|
| **All buildings** | **5,557** | **87,043** | **88,182** | **15.7** | **987** | **62** |
| Building floorspace (sq. ft.): | | | | | | |
| 1,001 to 5,000 | 2,777 | 8,036 | 10,232 | 2.9 | 785 | 56 |
| 5,001 to 10,000 | 1,231 | 8,910 | 9,231 | 7.2 | 965 | 62 |
| 10,001 to 25,000 | 882 | 14,083 | 14,183 | 16.0 | 993 | 65 |
| 25,001 to 50,000 | 332 | 11,917 | 11,327 | 35.9 | 1,052 | 72 |
| 50,001 to 100,000 | 199 | 13,938 | 12,354 | 69.9 | 1,128 | 80 |
| 100,001 to 200,000 | 90 | 12,415 | 11,310 | 137.9 | 1,098 | 89 |
| 200,001 to 500,000 | 38 | 10,670 | 10,347 | 284.3 | 1,031 | 100 |
| Over 500,000 | 8 | 7,074 | 9,196 | 885.0 | 769 | 117 |
| Principal activity within building: | | | | | | |
| Education | 389 | 12,237 | 10,885 | 31.5 | 1,124 | 53 |
| Food sales | 177 | 1,252 | 1,172 | 7.1 | 1,067 | 121 |
| Food service | 380 | 1,819 | 3,431 | 4.8 | 530 | 82 |
| Health care | 157 | 4,155 | 7,613 | 26.5 | 546 | 60 |
| Inpatient | 10 | 2,374 | 4,281 | 247.8 | 555 | 168 |
| Outpatient | 147 | 1,781 | 3,333 | 12.1 | 535 | 53 |
| Lodging | 158 | 5,826 | 3,066 | 36.9 | 1,900 | 165 |
| Mercantile | 602 | 11,330 | 9,117 | 18.8 | 1,243 | 64 |
| Retail (other than mall) | 438 | 5,439 | 4,023 | 12.4 | 1,352 | 62 |
| Enclosed and strip malls | 164 | 5,890 | 5,094 | 35.9 | 1,156 | 69 |
| Office | 1,012 | 15,952 | 33,756 | 15.8 | 473 | 55 |
| Public assembly | 352 | 5,559 | 3,108 | 15.8 | 1,789 | 56 |
| Public order and safety | 84 | 1,440 | 1,854 | 17.2 | 776 | 113 |
| Religious worship | 412 | 4,557 | 1,940 | 11.1 | 2,350 | 31 |
| Service | 619 | 4,627 | 4,031 | 7.5 | 1,148 | 56 |
| Warehouse and storage | 796 | 13,032 | 6,362 | 16.4 | 2,048 | 67 |
| Other | 125 | 2,002 | 1,611 | 16.0 | 1,242 | 61 |
| Vacant | 296 | 3,256 | 236 | 11.0 | 13,811 | 8 |
| Number of establishments: | | | | | | |
| One | 4,205 | 54,944 | 52,072 | 13.1 | 1,055 | 64 |
| 2 to 5 | 862 | 17,756 | 18,916 | 20.6 | 939 | 65 |
| 6 to 10 | 147 | 4,425 | 5,890 | 30.1 | 751 | 77 |
| 11 to 20 | 68 | 3,704 | 5,276 | 54.8 | 702 | 70 |
| More than 20 | 27 | 3,821 | 6,028 | 140.9 | 634 | 84 |
| Currently unoccupied | 248 | 2,393 | – | 9.6 | (X) | – |
| Year constructed: | | | | | | |
| Before 1920 | 362 | 3,980 | 3,309 | 11.0 | 1,203 | 48 |
| 1920 to 1945 | 488 | 6,020 | 6,003 | 12.3 | 1,003 | 52 |
| 1946 to 1959 | 599 | 7,381 | 6,566 | 12.3 | 1,124 | 51 |
| 1960 to 1969 | 639 | 10,362 | 9,851 | 16.2 | 1,052 | 61 |
| 1970 to 1979 | 684 | 10,846 | 12,536 | 15.9 | 865 | 61 |
| 1980 to 1989 | 915 | 15,185 | 17,468 | 16.6 | 869 | 65 |
| 1990 to 1999 | 845 | 13,803 | 13,432 | 16.3 | 1,028 | 68 |
| 2000 to 2003 | 375 | 7,215 | 7,471 | 19.2 | 966 | 66 |
| 2004 to 2007 | 347 | 6,524 | 5,993 | 18.8 | 1,089 | 69 |
| 2008 to 2012 | 303 | 5,726 | 5,552 | 18.9 | 1,031 | 76 |

– Represents zero. X Not applicable. [1] For explanation of mean, see Guide to Tabular Presentation.

Source: U.S. Energy Information Administration, "2012 CBECS Survey Data," <http://www.eia.gov/consumption/commercial/data/2012/>, accessed March 2015.

# Section 21
# Manufactures

This section presents summary data for manufacturing as a whole and more detailed information for major industry groups and selected products. The types of measures shown at the different levels include data for establishments, employment and payroll, value and quantity of production and shipments, value added by manufacture, inventories, and various indicators of financial status.

The principal source of these data is the U.S. Census Bureau's Annual Survey of Manufactures . Reports on current activities of industries or current movements of individual commodities are also compiled by such government agencies as the Bureau of Economic Analysis; Bureau of Labor Statistics; the Department of Commerce, International Trade Administration; and by private research or trade associations.

The Census Bureau's *Quarterly Financial Report* publishes up-to-date aggregate statistics on the financial results and position of U.S. corporations. Based upon a sample survey, the QFR presents estimated statements of income and retained earnings, balance sheets, and related financial and operating ratios for manufacturing corporations with assets of $250,000 or over, and mining, wholesale trade and retail trade corporations with assets of $50 million and over or above industry-specific receipt cut-off values. These statistical data are classified by industry and by asset size.

Several private trade associations provide industry coverage for certain sections of the economy.

**Censuses and annual surveys**—The first census of manufactures covered the year 1809. Between 1809 and 1963, a census was conducted at periodic intervals. Since 1967, it has been conducted every 5 years for years ending in "2" and "7". Results from the 2012 census are presented in this section utilizing the North American Industry Classification System (NAICS). Release of data from the 2012 Economic Census was completed in 2016. The 2017 Economic Census is being released on a flow basis between September 2019 and December 2021. Census data, either directly reported or estimated from administrative records, are obtained for every manufacturing plant with one or more paid employees. For additional information see text, Section 15, Business Enterprise, and the Census Bureau website at <https://www.census.gov/programs-surveys/economic-census.html>.

The Annual Survey of Manufactures (ASM), conducted for the first time in 1949, collects data for the years between censuses for the more general measure of manufacturing activity covered in detail by the censuses. The annual survey data are estimates derived from a scientifically selected sample of establishments. The ASM is a sample survey of approximately 50,000 establishments conducted annually, except for years ending in 2 and 7, at which time ASM statistics are included in the manufacturing sector of the Economic Census. In 2012, there were approximately 294,600 active manufacturing establishments. For sample efficiency and cost considerations, the manufacturing population is partitioned into two groups: (1) establishments eligible to be mailed a questionnaire, defined as the mail stratum, which is comprised of larger single-location manufacturing companies and all manufacturing establishments of multi-location companies, supplemented annually with new large single-location companies from IRS data and new multi-location companies from the Company Organization Survey; and (2) establishments not eligible to be mailed a questionnaire, defined as the nonmail stratum, which includes small- and medium-sized single establishment companies.

**Establishments and classification**—Each of the establishments covered in the 2012 Economic Census– Manufacturing was classified in accordance with the industry definitions in the 2012 NAICS manual. In NAICS, an industry is generally defined as a group of establishments that have similar production processes. To the extent practical, the system uses supply-based or production-oriented concepts in defining industries. The resulting group of establishments must be significant in terms of number, value added by manufacture, value of shipments, and number of employees. Establishments frequently make products classified both in their industry (primary products) and other industries (secondary products). Industry statistics (employment, payroll, value added by manufacture, value of shipments, etc.) reflect the activities of the establishments, which may make both primary and secondary products. Product statistics, however, represent the output of all establishments without regard for the classification of the producing establishment. For this reason, when relating the industry statistics, especially the value of shipments, to the product statistics, the composition of the industry's output should be considered.

**Establishment**—An establishment is a single physical location where business is conducted or where services or industrial operations are performed. Data in this sector includes those establishments where manufacturing is performed. A separate report is required for each manufacturing establishment (plant) with one employee or more that is in operation at any time during the year. An establishment not in operation for any portion of the year is requested to return the report form with the proper notation in the "Operational Status" section of the form. In addition, the establishment is requested to report data on any employees, capital expenditures, inventories, or shipment from inventories during the year.

**Durable goods**—Items with a normal life expectancy of 3 years or more. Automobiles, furniture, household appliances, and mobile homes are common examples.

**Nondurable goods**—Items which generally last for only a short time (3 years or less). Food, beverages, clothing, shoes, and gasoline are common examples.

**Statistical reliability**—For a discussion of statistical collection and estimation, sampling procedures, and measures of statistical reliability applicable to Census Bureau data, see Appendix III.

# Table 1038. Manufacturing—Contribution to Gross Domestic Product in Current and Real (2012) Dollars by Industry: 2000 to 2018

[In billions of dollars (10,252.3 represents $10,252,300,000,000). Value added GDP is the contribution of each industry's labor and capital to its gross output and to the overall gross domestic product (GDP) of the United States. Value added is equal to an industry's gross output (sales or receipts and other operating income, commodity taxes, and inventory change) minus its intermediate inputs (consumption of goods and services purchased from other industries or imported). Current-dollar value added is calculated as the sum of distributions by an industry to its labor and capital which are derived from the components of gross domestic income]

| Industry | NAICS code [1] | 2000 | 2010 | 2015 | 2016 | 2017 | 2018 |
|---|---|---|---|---|---|---|---|
| **CURRENT DOLLARS** | | | | | | | |
| **Gross domestic product, total [2]** | (X) | **10,252.3** | **14,992.1** | **18,219.3** | **18,707.2** | **19,485.4** | **20,494.1** |
| Private industries | (X) | 8,929.3 | 12,884.1 | 15,878.8 | 16,319.4 | 17,031.7 | 17,989.4 |
| **Manufacturing** | **31–33** | **1,550.2** | **1,797.0** | **2,123.0** | **2,085.2** | **2,179.6** | **2,334.6** |
| Durable goods | 33, 321, 327 | 924.8 | 964.3 | 1,182.7 | 1,182.0 | 1,226.6 | 1,300.6 |
| Wood products | 321 | 28.3 | 23.3 | 32.3 | 35.0 | 38.1 | 40.4 |
| Nonmetallic mineral products | 327 | 42.6 | 38.4 | 54.0 | 57.5 | 59.5 | 61.6 |
| Primary metals | 331 | 47.0 | 50.9 | 60.3 | 56.9 | 59.8 | 64.5 |
| Fabricated metal products | 332 | 121.3 | 119.9 | 146.2 | 144.6 | 151.9 | 162.0 |
| Machinery | 333 | 113.1 | 127.2 | 154.0 | 143.7 | 150.4 | 162.5 |
| Computer and electronic products | 334 | 225.4 | 239.8 | 267.6 | 270.7 | 281.1 | 295.8 |
| Electrical equipment, appliances, and components | 335 | 45.7 | 50.7 | 62.9 | 57.6 | 58.5 | 61.9 |
| Motor vehicles, bodies and trailers, and parts | 3361–63 | 137.5 | 88.7 | 145.6 | 153.6 | 158.9 | 169.2 |
| Other transportation equipment | 3364–66, 69 | 71.1 | 120.6 | 148.6 | 145.7 | 148.1 | 157.9 |
| Furniture and related products | 337 | 33.5 | 21.8 | 29.0 | 30.2 | 31.3 | 32.6 |
| Miscellaneous manufacturing | 339 | 59.2 | 83.0 | 82.1 | 86.6 | 88.9 | 92.4 |
| Nondurable goods | 31, 32 (except 321 and 327) | 625.4 | 832.7 | 940.3 | 903.1 | 953.0 | 1,034.0 |
| Food and beverage and tobacco products | 311, 312 | 163.2 | 223.2 | 259.4 | 261.3 | 269.7 | 279.2 |
| Textile mills and textile product mills | 313, 314 | 28.0 | 15.5 | 17.8 | 18.0 | 18.5 | 19.0 |
| Apparel and leather and allied products | 315, 316 | 22.2 | 10.4 | 9.7 | 9.4 | 9.3 | 9.2 |
| Paper products | 322 | 62.2 | 56.3 | 59.2 | 57.7 | 58.9 | 60.9 |
| Printing and related support activities | 323 | 43.7 | 39.4 | 40.0 | 40.0 | 39.2 | 39.8 |
| Petroleum and coal products | 324 | 52.7 | 123.4 | 144.9 | 89.6 | 120.7 | 165.5 |
| Chemical products | 325 | 187.9 | 302.6 | 331.9 | 346.7 | 354.0 | 373.9 |
| Plastics and rubber products | 326 | 65.5 | 61.8 | 77.6 | 80.5 | 82.8 | 86.5 |
| **CHAINED (2012) DOLLARS** | | | | | | | |
| **Gross domestic product, total [2]** | (X) | **13,131.0** | **15,598.8** | **17,386.7** | **17,659.2** | **18,050.7** | **18,566.4** |
| Private industries | (X) | 11,384.0 | 13,467.3 | 15,140.2 | 15,387.5 | 15,718.2 | 16,188.9 |
| **Manufacturing** | **31–33** | **1,678.8** | **1,932.6** | **2,016.7** | **1,993.1** | **2,041.8** | **2,133.6** |
| Durable goods | 33, 321, 327 | 753.1 | 967.7 | 1,110.6 | 1,105.3 | 1,140.1 | 1,201.4 |
| Wood products | 321 | 25.4 | 22.9 | 25.7 | 27.2 | 28.8 | 28.0 |
| Nonmetallic mineral products | 327 | 49.2 | 38.7 | 45.4 | 45.5 | 46.1 | 46.0 |
| Primary metals | 331 | 61.7 | 50.9 | 73.6 | 77.4 | 68.6 | 62.6 |
| Fabricated metal products | 332 | 156.0 | 125.5 | 132.1 | 127.4 | 137.9 | 145.8 |
| Machinery | 333 | 130.1 | 132.1 | 134.8 | 122.2 | 128.9 | 139.5 |
| Computer and electronic products | 334 | 67.6 | 226.8 | 281.5 | 292.7 | 302.7 | 320.7 |
| Electrical equipment, appliances, and components | 335 | 54.5 | 52.7 | 60.0 | 55.1 | 56.5 | 57.9 |
| Motor vehicles, bodies and trailers, and parts | 3361–63 | 99.7 | 87.0 | 120.0 | 123.8 | 128.7 | 145.0 |
| Other transportation equipment | 3364–66, 69 | 95.4 | 124.3 | 138.0 | 133.7 | 134.5 | 143.1 |
| Furniture and related products | 337 | 40.1 | 22.6 | 26.8 | 27.2 | 28.5 | 29.5 |
| Miscellaneous manufacturing | 339 | 61.0 | 84.1 | 77.6 | 80.8 | 83.3 | 86.9 |
| Nondurable goods | 31, 32 (except 321 and 327) | 967.0 | 972.3 | 906.0 | 887.4 | 901.0 | 931.4 |
| Food and beverage and tobacco products | 311, 312 | 225.1 | 233.3 | 228.5 | 219.4 | 233.1 | 243.4 |
| Textile mills and textile product mills | 313, 314 | 30.9 | 16.6 | 16.9 | 16.6 | 17.3 | 17.5 |
| Apparel and leather and allied products | 315, 316 | 20.0 | 10.6 | 9.1 | 8.7 | 8.5 | 8.3 |
| Paper products | 322 | 71.0 | 55.8 | 53.3 | 51.9 | 50.6 | 51.5 |
| Printing and related support activities | 323 | 37.7 | 37.5 | 37.2 | 36.9 | 36.2 | 36.9 |
| Petroleum and coal products | 324 | 184.7 | 212.7 | 195.8 | 176.4 | 178.2 | 190.2 |
| Chemical products | 325 | 289.4 | 346.5 | 298.5 | 301.7 | 297.5 | 303.0 |
| Plastics and rubber products | 326 | 77.3 | 67.6 | 71.8 | 73.7 | 77.0 | 78.5 |

X Not applicable. [1] North American Industry Classification System; see text, Section 15. [2] Includes industries, not shown separately. For additional industries, see Table 699.

Source: U.S. Bureau of Economic Analysis, Industry Data, Gross Domestic Product by Industry, "Value Added by Industry," <http://www.bea.gov/industry/gdpbyind_data.htm>, accessed May 2019.

# Table 1039. Manufacturing—Selected Industry Statistics by State: 2012

[11,214 represents 11,214,000. Based on the 2012 Economic Census and the 2012 Nonemployer Statistics. See Appendix III]

| State | Employers | | | | Nonemployers | |
|---|---|---|---|---|---|---|
| | Number of establishments | Number of employees (1,000) | Annual payroll (mil. dol.) | Sales, shipments, receipts or revenue (mil. dol.) | Number of establishments | Sales, shipments, receipts or revenue (mil. dol.) |
| United States........ | 297,191 | 11,214 | 593,397 | 5,696,730 | 344,658 | 16,164 |
| Alabama.............. | 4,283 | 233 | 11,099 | 124,810 | 4,472 | 185 |
| Alaska................. | 527 | 12 | 515 | (D) | 1,130 | 38 |
| Arizona............... | 4,269 | 132 | 8,193 | 51,243 | 6,897 | 302 |
| Arkansas............. | 2,688 | 154 | 6,291 | 62,713 | 2,733 | 118 |
| California............. | 38,741 | 1,163 | 69,317 | 512,303 | 45,927 | 2,640 |
| Colorado.............. | 4,898 | 115 | 6,230 | 50,447 | 7,324 | 293 |
| Connecticut.......... | 4,350 | 164 | 10,546 | 55,160 | 3,646 | 230 |
| Delaware............. | 573 | 26 | 1,393 | 22,597 | 643 | 39 |
| District of Columbia.... | 113 | 1 | 61 | 310 | 267 | 10 |
| Florida................ | 12,890 | 277 | 14,270 | 96,924 | 21,526 | 1,057 |
| Georgia............... | 7,456 | 334 | 15,317 | 155,837 | 10,179 | 453 |
| Hawaii................. | 796 | 11 | 465 | (D) | 2,163 | 89 |
| Idaho................. | 1,759 | 52 | 2,445 | 20,201 | 2,674 | 89 |
| Illinois............... | 13,868 | 542 | 28,414 | 281,038 | 10,978 | 493 |
| Indiana............... | 8,141 | 453 | 23,041 | 242,764 | 6,995 | 322 |
| Iowa.................. | 3,598 | 204 | 10,021 | 116,669 | 3,053 | 115 |
| Kansas............... | 2,875 | 152 | 7,578 | 86,076 | 2,891 | 124 |
| Kentucky............. | 3,782 | 214 | 10,140 | 129,284 | 3,860 | 182 |
| Louisiana............. | 3,308 | 136 | 8,489 | 271,191 | 4,413 | 195 |
| Maine................. | 1,650 | 49 | 2,424 | 16,045 | 2,608 | 91 |
| Maryland.............. | 3,096 | 100 | 5,909 | 39,533 | 4,517 | 180 |
| Massachusetts........ | 6,806 | 234 | 14,395 | 81,928 | 6,073 | 322 |
| Michigan.............. | 12,444 | 514 | 27,611 | 238,892 | 12,399 | 582 |
| Minnesota............ | 7,313 | 298 | 15,823 | 123,076 | 7,623 | 300 |
| Mississippi............ | 2,252 | 133 | 5,919 | 66,442 | 2,497 | 95 |
| Missouri.............. | 6,097 | 243 | 11,921 | 111,535 | 6,237 | 283 |
| Montana.............. | 1,237 | 16 | 715 | 11,535 | 2,108 | 71 |
| Nebraska............. | 1,844 | 92 | 4,003 | 57,499 | 1,620 | 54 |
| Nevada............... | 1,706 | 38 | 1,979 | 14,719 | 2,301 | 134 |
| New Hampshire........ | 1,851 | 67 | 3,924 | 18,896 | 2,274 | 110 |
| New Jersey........... | 7,758 | 231 | 14,095 | 108,855 | 6,676 | 430 |
| New Mexico........... | 1,389 | 27 | 1,349 | 29,102 | 3,173 | 91 |
| New York.............. | 16,475 | 427 | 22,073 | 148,880 | 18,373 | 876 |
| North Carolina....... | 8,953 | 404 | 18,191 | 202,345 | 10,352 | 384 |
| North Dakota.......... | 745 | 24 | 1,043 | 14,427 | 640 | 25 |
| Ohio.................. | 14,482 | 627 | 33,135 | 313,630 | 13,302 | 677 |
| Oklahoma............. | 3,610 | 133 | 6,416 | 74,295 | 4,012 | 193 |
| Oregon............... | 5,289 | 152 | 8,122 | 51,350 | 7,193 | 289 |
| Pennsylvania.......... | 13,988 | 544 | 28,058 | 231,396 | 14,067 | 744 |
| Rhode Island.......... | 1,509 | 40 | 2,076 | 11,262 | 1,184 | 51 |
| South Carolina........ | 3,854 | 207 | 10,082 | 99,161 | 4,152 | 180 |
| South Dakota........ | 1,025 | 42 | 1,765 | 16,883 | 968 | 31 |
| Tennessee............ | 5,823 | 294 | 14,181 | 139,960 | 6,300 | 292 |
| Texas................. | 19,782 | 767 | 42,530 | 702,603 | 32,514 | 1,557 |
| Utah.................. | 3,163 | 108 | 5,763 | 50,046 | 4,024 | 160 |
| Vermont............... | 1,013 | 31 | 1,594 | 9,315 | 1,890 | 55 |
| Virginia............... | 5,101 | 228 | 11,586 | 96,390 | 5,610 | 212 |
| Washington........... | 6,992 | 248 | 14,462 | 131,531 | 8,816 | 338 |
| West Virginia.......... | 1,245 | 49 | 2,604 | 24,553 | 1,295 | 44 |
| Wisconsin............. | 8,995 | 437 | 21,879 | 177,729 | 7,127 | 330 |
| Wyoming.............. | 553 | 10 | 631 | 10,784 | 962 | 33 |
| Puerto Rico........... | 1,653 | 84 | 2,875 | 76,575 | (NA) | (NA) |

NA Not available. D Withheld to avoid disclosing data on individual companies.

Source: U.S. Census Bureau, "2012 Economic Census, EC1200A1: All sectors: Geographic Area Series: Economy-Wide Key Statistics: 2012," <http://factfinder.census.gov/>, accessed September 2015. See also <http://www.census.gov/econ/census/>.

## Table 1040. Manufacturing—Establishments, Employees, and Annual Payroll by Industry: 2015 and 2016

[124,086 represents 124,086,000. Excludes most government employees, railroad employees, and self-employed persons. See Appendix III]

| Industry | NAICS code [1] | Establishments | | Employees (1,000) [2] | | Payroll (mil. dol.) | |
|---|---|---|---|---|---|---|---|
| | | 2015 | 2016 | 2015 | 2016 | 2015 | 2016 |
| All industries, total.......................... | (X) | 7,663,938 | 7,757,807 | 124,086 | 126,752 | 6,253,488 | 6,435,142 |
| Manufacturing, total..................... | 31–33 | 292,825 | 291,543 | 11,606 | 11,590 | 656,771 | 663,734 |
| Percent of all industries................. | (X) | 3.82 | 3.76 | 9.35 | 9.14 | 10.50 | 10.31 |
| Food.......................................... | 311 | 26,819 | 27,138 | 1,486 | 1,507 | 62,392 | 65,278 |
| Beverage and tobacco products............ | 312 | 8,002 | 8,465 | 185 | 198 | 9,632 | 10,243 |
| Textile mills................................ | 313 | 2,210 | 2,151 | 103 | 102 | 4,333 | 4,145 |
| Textile product mills....................... | 314 | 6,195 | 6,031 | 114 | 113 | 4,128 | 4,109 |
| Apparel manufacturing.................... | 315 | 7,087 | 6,262 | 104 | 97 | 2,863 | 2,733 |
| Leather and allied products................ | 316 | 1,180 | 1,203 | 26 | 26 | 944 | 954 |
| Wood products.............................. | 321 | 14,071 | 14,251 | 378 | 391 | 15,243 | 16,044 |
| Paper........................................ | 322 | 4,217 | 4,091 | 351 | 348 | 21,481 | 21,282 |
| Printing and related support activities...... | 323 | 25,688 | 25,521 | 448 | 446 | 20,240 | 20,379 |
| Petroleum and coal products.............. | 324 | 2,133 | 2,167 | 102 | 105 | 10,446 | 10,938 |
| Chemical..................................... | 325 | 13,182 | 13,480 | 759 | 767 | 60,805 | 62,345 |
| Plastics and rubber products............. | 326 | 12,276 | 12,083 | 740 | 750 | 35,063 | 35,971 |
| Nonmetallic mineral products.............. | 327 | 14,731 | 14,969 | 370 | 383 | 19,231 | 20,130 |
| Primary metal............................... | 331 | 4,533 | 4,464 | 399 | 376 | 24,204 | 22,738 |
| Fabricated metal products................. | 332 | 54,767 | 54,968 | 1,447 | 1,406 | 73,683 | 72,346 |
| Machinery................................... | 333 | 23,794 | 23,509 | 1,078 | 1,031 | 64,579 | 62,268 |
| Computer and electronic products.......... | 334 | 12,677 | 12,378 | 796 | 786 | 65,423 | 64,976 |
| Electrical equipment, appliance and components................................ | 335 | 5,671 | 5,657 | 345 | 344 | 19,984 | 20,126 |
| Transportation equipment................. | 336 | 11,880 | 11,683 | 1,478 | 1,504 | 97,124 | 100,524 |
| Furniture and related products............. | 337 | 15,098 | 15,031 | 359 | 369 | 14,729 | 15,348 |
| Miscellaneous............................... | 339 | 26,614 | 26,041 | 539 | 541 | 30,247 | 30,857 |

X Not applicable. [1] Data based on North American Industry Classification System (NAICS) 2012; see text, Section 15. [2] Covers full- and part-time employees who are on the payroll in the pay period including March 12.

Source: U.S. Census Bureau, County Business Patterns, "Geography Area Series: County Business Patterns," <https://factfinder.census.gov/>, accessed April 2018. See also <https://www.census.gov/programs-surveys/cbp.html>.

## Table 1041. Manufacturing—Establishments, Employees, and Annual Payroll by State: 2016

[11,590 represents 11,590,000. Excludes most government employees, railroad employees, and self-employed persons. Data are for North American Industry Classification System (NAICS) 2012, codes 31–33. See Appendix III]

| State | Establishments | Employees (1,000) [1] | Payroll (mil. dol.) | State | Establishments | Employees (1,000) [1] | Payroll (mil. dol.) |
|---|---|---|---|---|---|---|---|
| United States....... | 291,543 | 11,590 | 663,734 | Missouri............. | 5,833 | 260 | 14,055 |
| Alabama.............. | 4,109 | 250 | 12,666 | Montana............. | 1,291 | 18 | 877 |
| Alaska................ | 532 | 13 | 582 | Nebraska............ | 1,772 | 92 | 4,412 |
| Arizona............... | 4,291 | 144 | 8,752 | Nevada.............. | 1,838 | 43 | 2,372 |
| Arkansas............. | 2,561 | 154 | 6,910 | New Hampshire..... | 1,799 | 69 | 4,476 |
| California............. | 38,103 | 1,154 | 77,026 | New Jersey.......... | 7,341 | 219 | 14,228 |
| Colorado............. | 5,027 | 121 | 7,418 | New Mexico......... | 1,352 | 26 | 1,297 |
| Connecticut.......... | 4,070 | 156 | 11,375 | New York............ | 15,728 | 419 | 23,381 |
| Delaware............. | 564 | 27 | 1,621 | North Carolina....... | 8,739 | 433 | 21,199 |
| District of Columbia.. | 113 | 1 | 56 | North Dakota........ | 727 | 24 | 1,163 |
| Florida................ | 13,323 | 307 | 16,605 | Ohio................. | 14,000 | 662 | 36,622 |
| Georgia............... | 7,478 | 368 | 18,586 | Oklahoma............ | 3,416 | 130 | 6,575 |
| Hawaii................ | 779 | 13 | 566 | Oregon.............. | 5,493 | 164 | 8,906 |
| Idaho................. | 1,794 | 60 | 3,172 | Pennsylvania........ | 13,578 | 540 | 30,391 |
| Illinois................ | 13,381 | 536 | 31,783 | Rhode Island........ | 1,370 | 40 | 2,273 |
| Indiana............... | 8,023 | 500 | 26,900 | South Carolina....... | 3,783 | 228 | 12,314 |
| Iowa.................. | 3,485 | 209 | 10,975 | South Dakota....... | 1,035 | 44 | 1,998 |
| Kansas................ | 2,791 | 160 | 8,869 | Tennessee........... | 5,724 | 320 | 16,890 |
| Kentucky............. | 3,696 | 235 | 12,424 | Texas................ | 19,649 | 769 | 47,064 |
| Louisiana............. | 3,209 | 118 | 8,196 | Utah................. | 3,340 | 121 | 6,822 |
| Maine................. | 1,660 | 50 | 2,564 | Vermont............. | 1,015 | 30 | 1,665 |
| Maryland............. | 2,947 | 97 | 6,288 | Virginia.............. | 4,999 | 240 | 13,071 |
| Massachusetts....... | 6,528 | 221 | 15,641 | Washington.......... | 6,998 | 265 | 17,272 |
| Michigan............. | 12,351 | 580 | 33,480 | West Virginia........ | 1,163 | 47 | 2,635 |
| Minnesota............ | 7,252 | 306 | 17,635 | Wisconsin............ | 8,791 | 453 | 24,400 |
| Mississippi........... | 2,141 | 143 | 6,668 | Wyoming............. | 561 | 9 | 618 |

[1] Covers full- and part-time employees who are on the payroll in the pay period including March 12.

Source: U.S. Census Bureau, County Business Patterns, "Geography Area Series: County Business Patterns," <https://factfinder.census.gov>, accessed April 2018. See also <https://www.census.gov/programs-surveys/cbp.html>.

# Table 1042. Manufactures—Summary by Selected Industry: 2016

[Employee data in thousands (11,112.8 represents 11,112,800); financial data in millions of dollars (643,406 represents $643,406,000,000), except as noted. Based on data from the 2016 Annual Survey of Manufactures]

| Industry based on shipments | 2012 NAICS code [1] | All employees | | | Production workers [2] (1,000) | Value added by manufactures [3] (mil. dol.) | Value of shipments [4] (mil. dol.) |
| | | Number [2] (1,000) | Payroll | | | | |
| | | | Total (mil. dol.) | Per employee (dol.) | | | |
|---|---|---|---|---|---|---|---|
| **Manufacturing, total [5]** | 31–33 | **11,112.8** | **643,406** | **57,898** | **7,733.2** | **2,408,996** | **5,354,694** |
| Food [5] | 311 | 1,417.0 | 62,772 | 44,298 | 1,118.0 | 292,824 | 764,787 |
| Grain and oil seed milling | 3112 | 52.7 | 3,227 | 61,193 | 38.2 | 25,161 | 87,657 |
| Sugar and confectionery products | 3113 | 73.7 | 3,552 | 48,171 | 53.9 | 16,775 | 35,899 |
| Fruit and vegetable preserving and specialty food | 3114 | 160.6 | 7,217 | 44,952 | 133.4 | 33,567 | 71,946 |
| Dairy products | 3115 | 135.8 | 7,424 | 54,659 | 102.9 | 34,183 | 111,284 |
| Animal slaughtering and processing | 3116 | 479.5 | 17,737 | 36,989 | 418.2 | 63,520 | 207,660 |
| Bakeries and tortilla | 3118 | 252.2 | 10,417 | 41,303 | 176.8 | 41,516 | 70,913 |
| Beverage and tobacco products | 312 | 166.6 | 9,921 | 59,569 | 94.6 | 95,980 | 154,864 |
| Beverage | 3121 | 153.5 | 9,067 | 59,052 | 84.8 | 61,613 | 112,245 |
| Textile mills | 313 | 97.1 | 4,068 | 41,918 | 78.9 | 11,370 | 28,129 |
| Textile product mills | 314 | 110.3 | 4,172 | 37,840 | 84.9 | 11,172 | 24,736 |
| Apparel [5] | 315 | 81.3 | 2,541 | 31,256 | 64.6 | 5,682 | 10,513 |
| Cut and sew apparel | 3152 | 63.5 | 2,005 | 31,594 | 50.0 | 4,610 | 8,399 |
| Leather and allied products | 316 | 24.2 | 911 | 37,601 | 18.2 | 1,991 | 4,919 |
| Wood products [5] | 321 | 378.5 | 16,072 | 42,466 | 302.1 | 44,245 | 102,047 |
| Sawmills and wood preservation | 3211 | 77.2 | 3,742 | 48,477 | 64.8 | 11,663 | 30,556 |
| Paper | 322 | 332.9 | 20,689 | 62,145 | 258.2 | 84,464 | 181,667 |
| Pulp, paper, and paperboard mills | 3221 | 99.0 | 7,640 | 77,136 | 78.0 | 41,418 | 76,435 |
| Converted paper products | 3222 | 233.9 | 13,049 | 55,796 | 180.2 | 43,046 | 105,232 |
| Printing and related support activities | 323 | 416.5 | 20,801 | 49,946 | 295.1 | 49,169 | 82,693 |
| Petroleum and coal products | 324 | 104.3 | 10,741 | 103,001 | 67.0 | 85,966 | 430,329 |
| Chemical [5] | 325 | 744.6 | 57,556 | 77,299 | 438.8 | 400,333 | 723,271 |
| Basic chemical | 3251 | 148.4 | 13,046 | 87,917 | 89.5 | 98,500 | 207,884 |
| Pharmaceutical and medicine | 3254 | 256.0 | 21,189 | 82,762 | 132.1 | 155,009 | 219,868 |
| Soap, cleaning compound, and toilet preparation | 3256 | 87.4 | 5,548 | 63,454 | 54.1 | 52,588 | 83,781 |
| Plastics and rubber products | 326 | 741.2 | 35,446 | 47,821 | 571.9 | 118,271 | 235,711 |
| Plastics products | 3261 | 613.7 | 28,787 | 46,909 | 474.0 | 97,809 | 193,239 |
| Rubber product | 3262 | 127.5 | 6,659 | 52,208 | 97.9 | 20,462 | 42,472 |
| Nonmetallic mineral products | 327 | 371.9 | 19,589 | 52,678 | 284.1 | 71,428 | 123,230 |
| Glass and glass product | 3272 | 90.5 | 4,754 | 52,528 | 72.0 | 15,873 | 26,231 |
| Cement and concrete products | 3273 | 165.6 | 8,616 | 52,039 | 128.2 | 31,291 | 57,215 |
| Primary metal [5] | 331 | 364.2 | 22,508 | 61,800 | 283.6 | 79,866 | 206,603 |
| Iron and steel mills and ferroalloy | 3311 | 91.9 | 7,027 | 76,447 | 73.5 | 29,077 | 79,606 |
| Foundries | 3315 | 115.5 | 6,065 | 52,507 | 92.7 | 16,736 | 29,549 |
| Fabricated metal products [5] | 332 | 1,327.6 | 71,417 | 53,792 | 959.8 | 182,988 | 335,756 |
| Forging and stamping | 3321 | 106.8 | 5,697 | 53,340 | 79.6 | 14,668 | 31,351 |
| Architectural and structural metals | 3323 | 326.4 | 17,127 | 52,477 | 230.3 | 42,837 | 84,860 |
| Machine shops, turned product and screw, nut, and bolt | 3327 | 348.4 | 18,700 | 53,670 | 256.8 | 39,521 | 62,781 |
| Coating, engraving, heat treating, and allied activities | 3328 | 120.1 | 5,768 | 48,046 | 92.9 | 15,712 | 25,682 |
| Machinery [5] | 333 | 988.7 | 60,429 | 61,120 | 615.7 | 171,559 | 348,446 |
| Agriculture, construction, and mining machinery | 3331 | 173.0 | 10,099 | 58,380 | 110.7 | 30,767 | 75,306 |
| Industrial machinery | 3332 | 98.2 | 7,239 | 73,683 | 52.6 | 17,028 | 31,042 |
| HVAC and commercial refrigeration equipment | 3334 | 126.9 | 6,229 | 49,090 | 90.1 | 21,924 | 43,117 |
| Metalworking machinery | 3335 | 143.5 | 8,472 | 59,024 | 97.2 | 18,276 | 29,850 |
| Computer and electronic products [5] | 334 | 768.7 | 61,712 | 80,286 | 351.7 | 170,600 | 293,587 |
| Computer and peripheral equipment | 3341 | 36.1 | 2,751 | 76,136 | 14.5 | 11,199 | 24,410 |
| Communications equipment | 3342 | 95.3 | 8,456 | 88,691 | 37.0 | 19,949 | 36,197 |
| Semiconductor and other electronic component | 3344 | 250.3 | 17,890 | 71,483 | 148.9 | 46,344 | 87,252 |
| Navigational, measuring, medical, and control instruments | 3345 | 364.9 | 31,421 | 86,118 | 139.5 | 90,041 | 140,233 |
| Electrical equipment, appliance, and component [5] | 335 | 330.9 | 19,157 | 57,887 | 218.9 | 61,489 | 124,181 |
| Electrical equipment | 3353 | 108.7 | 6,463 | 59,452 | 67.5 | 17,321 | 36,383 |
| Other electrical equipment and component | 3359 | 134.1 | 8,191 | 61,093 | 85.7 | 26,158 | 52,942 |
| Transportation equipment [5] | 336 | 1,478.9 | 98,049 | 66,297 | 1,050.1 | 330,589 | 949,275 |
| Motor vehicle | 3361 | 197.7 | 14,770 | 74,723 | 170.8 | 82,224 | 344,359 |
| Motor vehicle parts | 3363 | 539.9 | 29,407 | 54,469 | 416.4 | 84,120 | 260,812 |
| Aerospace product and parts | 3364 | 420.9 | 36,599 | 86,946 | 234.1 | 117,256 | 234,798 |
| Ship and boat building | 3366 | 130.6 | 7,642 | 58,501 | 85.1 | 20,520 | 33,372 |
| Furniture and related products [5] | 337 | 353.9 | 15,370 | 43,433 | 263.8 | 41,094 | 74,685 |
| Miscellaneous [5] | 339 | 513.6 | 29,486 | 57,411 | 313.3 | 97,920 | 155,267 |
| Medical equipment and supplies | 3391 | 256.8 | 16,594 | 64,622 | 156.7 | 60,538 | 91,990 |

[1] North American Industrial Classification System, 2012; see text, Section 15. [2] Includes all full-time and part-time employees on payrolls of operating manufacturing establishments. All employees represents the average of production workers plus all other employees for the payroll period ended nearest the 12th of March. [3] Adjusted value added; takes into account (a) value added by merchandising operations (that is, difference between the sales value and cost of merchandise sold without further manufacture, processing, or assembly), plus (b) net change in finished goods and work-in-process inventories between beginning and end of year. [4] This item covers the received or receivable net selling values, "free on board" (FOB) plant (exclusive of freight and taxes), of all products shipped as well as all miscellaneous receipts. In the case of multiunit companies, the manufacturer was requested to report the value of products transferred to other establishments of the same company at full economic or commercial value. [5] Includes industries not shown separately.

Source: U.S. Census Bureau, Annual Survey of Manufactures, "Geographic Area Statistics: Statistics for All Manufacturing by State: 2016 and 2015," December 2017, <http://factfinder.census.gov/>, accessed May 2018. See also <https://www.census.gov/programs-surveys/asm.html>.

# Table 1043. Manufactures—Summary by State: 2016

[Employment data in thousands (11,112.8 represents 11,112,800); financial data in millions of dollars (643,406 represents $643,406,000,000). Based on data from the 2016 Annual Survey of Manufactures. Data are for North American Industry Classification System (NAICS) 2012 codes 31–33. Sum of state totals may not add to U.S. total due to independent rounding. See Appendix III]

| State | All employees [1] | | | Production workers [1] | | Value added by manufactures [2] | | Value of shipments [3] (mil. dol.) |
| | Number (1,000) | Payroll Total (mil. dol.) | Payroll Per employee (dol.) | Number (1,000) | Wages (mil. dol.) | Total (mil. dol.) | Per production worker (dol.) | |
|---|---|---|---|---|---|---|---|---|
| United States............. | 11,112.8 | 643,406 | 57,898 | 7,733.2 | 364,985 | 2,408,996 | 311,515 | 5,354,694 |
| Alabama...................... | 234.8 | 12,256 | 52,195 | 176.7 | 7,884 | 46,264 | 261,855 | 131,012 |
| Alaska........................ | 12.2 | 590 | 48,431 | 10.2 | 442 | 2,212 | 217,420 | 6,003 |
| Arizona....................... | 136.9 | 9,142 | 66,753 | 82.4 | 3,990 | 29,122 | 353,384 | 55,065 |
| Arkansas.................... | 145.7 | 6,657 | 45,679 | 116.8 | 4,721 | 25,096 | 214,939 | 55,731 |
| California.................... | 1,119.9 | 73,011 | 65,194 | 706.4 | 34,022 | 255,636 | 361,891 | 493,165 |
| Colorado..................... | 121.1 | 7,373 | 60,896 | 79.1 | 3,713 | 26,020 | 329,156 | 50,853 |
| Connecticut................. | 155.1 | 10,968 | 70,731 | 88.0 | 4,730 | 32,663 | 371,311 | 56,376 |
| Delaware.................... | 25.4 | 1,455 | 57,216 | 17.9 | 816 | 5,870 | 327,905 | 16,558 |
| District of Columbia........ | 1.3 | 58 | 46,270 | 0.8 | 34 | 213 | 262,593 | 330 |
| Florida........................ | 270.2 | 15,473 | 57,271 | 180.0 | 7,959 | 57,038 | 316,950 | 104,865 |
| Georgia....................... | 352.0 | 18,119 | 51,482 | 265.7 | 11,282 | 71,133 | 267,687 | 166,678 |
| Hawaii........................ | 11.5 | 568 | 49,359 | 7.1 | 312 | 2,093 | 292,744 | 5,686 |
| Idaho......................... | 55.8 | 3,186 | 57,123 | 41.2 | 1,945 | 9,195 | 223,155 | 20,968 |
| Illinois........................ | 538.2 | 30,952 | 57,511 | 371.0 | 17,266 | 111,573 | 300,764 | 252,503 |
| Indiana....................... | 476.4 | 26,341 | 55,290 | 357.5 | 17,133 | 102,353 | 286,302 | 241,539 |
| Iowa.......................... | 203.8 | 10,913 | 53,538 | 148.0 | 6,563 | 43,511 | 294,086 | 105,663 |
| Kansas....................... | 154.7 | 8,626 | 55,762 | 110.9 | 5,318 | 33,892 | 305,605 | 83,920 |
| Kentucky..................... | 230.8 | 12,487 | 54,110 | 178.6 | 8,550 | 45,084 | 252,440 | 128,159 |
| Louisiana.................... | 113.9 | 8,008 | 70,298 | 80.1 | 4,925 | 47,821 | 596,800 | 156,874 |
| Maine........................ | 49.7 | 2,657 | 53,453 | 36.0 | 1,734 | 8,093 | 224,915 | 15,169 |
| Maryland..................... | 91.8 | 6,051 | 65,923 | 56.3 | 2,754 | 22,769 | 404,720 | 41,214 |
| Massachusetts.............. | 224.0 | 15,416 | 68,821 | 131.0 | 6,678 | 46,717 | 356,565 | 84,735 |
| Michigan..................... | 555.0 | 32,361 | 58,307 | 398.9 | 19,868 | 103,771 | 260,112 | 261,293 |
| Minnesota................... | 297.8 | 16,961 | 56,961 | 197.1 | 8,984 | 56,929 | 288,836 | 117,397 |
| Mississippi.................. | 130.5 | 6,329 | 48,483 | 103.1 | 4,324 | 21,760 | 211,095 | 56,801 |
| Missouri...................... | 245.4 | (S) | (NA) | 182.9 | 9,029 | 50,314 | 275,121 | 118,828 |
| Montana...................... | 16.7 | 888 | 53,170 | 11.2 | 522 | 3,175 | 282,553 | 9,396 |
| Nebraska..................... | 92.9 | 4,496 | 48,367 | 70.7 | 2,986 | 19,005 | 268,741 | 53,112 |
| Nevada....................... | 41.4 | 2,311 | 55,887 | 27.8 | 1,312 | 8,702 | 313,493 | 16,682 |
| New Hampshire.............. | 65.6 | 4,137 | 63,109 | 39.5 | 1,845 | 11,562 | 292,986 | 20,658 |
| New Jersey................... | 210.3 | 13,237 | 62,946 | 139.9 | 6,818 | 45,823 | 327,608 | 90,605 |
| New Mexico.................. | 21.7 | 1,253 | 57,626 | 14.7 | 707 | 4,936 | 335,788 | 12,674 |
| New York..................... | 395.1 | 23,105 | 58,474 | 261.2 | 12,404 | 79,496 | 304,332 | 148,469 |
| North Carolina.............. | 411.1 | 20,701 | 50,362 | 303.8 | 12,424 | 109,824 | 361,536 | 210,018 |
| North Dakota................ | 22.9 | 1,181 | 51,672 | 16.9 | 752 | 4,923 | 291,086 | 13,050 |
| Ohio.......................... | 642.9 | 36,033 | 56,044 | 460.8 | 22,047 | 129,554 | 281,162 | 312,532 |
| Oklahoma.................... | 121.2 | 6,469 | 53,370 | 89.1 | 4,024 | 22,705 | 254,923 | 56,775 |
| Oregon....................... | 160.1 | 9,543 | 59,598 | 108.9 | 5,222 | 27,846 | 255,597 | 57,315 |
| Pennsylvania................ | 522.2 | 29,380 | 56,260 | 362.0 | 17,290 | 105,636 | 291,806 | 217,753 |
| Rhode Island................ | 36.1 | 2,148 | 59,526 | 23.7 | 1,145 | 5,607 | 236,153 | 11,344 |
| South Carolina.............. | 213.1 | 11,641 | 54,638 | 159.8 | 7,513 | 44,029 | 275,528 | 109,000 |
| South Dakota................ | 44.1 | 2,040 | 46,256 | 32.5 | 1,263 | 7,882 | 242,575 | 17,441 |
| Tennessee................... | 309.0 | 16,329 | 52,852 | 228.5 | 10,236 | 66,937 | 292,939 | 149,126 |
| Texas......................... | 725.3 | 44,620 | 61,523 | 493.7 | 24,678 | 216,626 | 438,788 | 523,118 |
| Utah.......................... | 114.5 | 6,541 | 57,124 | 75.8 | 3,562 | 23,250 | 306,881 | 48,428 |
| Vermont...................... | 27.4 | 1,542 | 56,230 | 18.6 | 864 | 4,205 | 225,578 | 8,788 |
| Virginia....................... | 222.8 | 12,504 | 56,118 | 156.9 | 7,374 | 57,359 | 365,564 | 99,131 |
| Washington.................. | 253.5 | 16,567 | 65,362 | 165.5 | 9,067 | 60,007 | 362,491 | 142,700 |
| West Virginia................ | 44.9 | 2,594 | 57,750 | 32.0 | 1,623 | 11,341 | 354,612 | 23,851 |
| Wisconsin.................... | 435.9 | 23,662 | 54,280 | 310.1 | 13,931 | 78,972 | 254,671 | 168,601 |
| Wyoming..................... | 8.4 | 603 | 71,954 | 6.1 | 403 | 2,452 | 404,175 | 6,742 |

NA Not available. S Withheld because estimate did not meet publication standards. [1] Includes all full-time and part-time employees on the payrolls of operating manufacturing establishments during the pay period that included March 12. Included are employees on paid sick leave, paid holidays, and paid vacations; not included are proprietors and partners of unincorporated businesses. [2] Value added is derived by subtracting the cost of materials, supplies, containers, fuel, purchased electricity, and contract work from the value of shipments (products manufactured plus receipts for services rendered). The result of this calculation is adjusted by the addition of value added by merchandising operations (i.e., the difference between the sales value and the cost of merchandise sold without further manufacture, processing, or assembly) plus the net change in finished goods and work-in-process between the beginning and end of year inventories. [3] Includes extensive and unmeasurable duplication from shipments between establishments in the same industry classification.

Source: U.S. Census Bureau, Annual Survey of Manufactures, "Geographic Area Statistics for All Manufacturing by State: 2016 and 2015," December 2017, <http://factfinder.census.gov/>, accessed August 2018. See also <https://www.census.gov/programs-surveys/asm.html>.

# Table 1044. Manufacturing Industries—Employees by Industry: 1990 to 2018

[Annual averages of monthly figures (132,024 represents 132,024,000). Covers all full- and part-time employees who worked during, or received pay for, any part of the pay period including the 12th of the month. Minus sign (-) indicates decrease. See also head note, Table 657]

| Industry | 2017 NAICS code [1] | All employees (1,000) | | | | | Percent change | | |
|---|---|---|---|---|---|---|---|---|---|
| | | 2000 | 2010 | 2016 | 2017 | 2018 | 1990-2000 | 2000-2010 | 2010-2018 |
| **All industries**........................ | (X) | **132,024** | **130,362** | **144,352** | **146,624** | **149,074** | **20.5** | **-1.3** | **14.4** |
| **Manufacturing**........................ | 31–33 | **17,263** | **11,528** | **12,354** | **12,439** | **12,689** | **-2.4** | **-33.2** | **10.1** |
| Percent of all industries................ | (X) | 13.1 | 8.8 | 8.6 | 8.5 | 8.5 | -19.1 | -32.4 | -3.7 |
| Durable goods............................ | (X) | 10,877 | 7,064 | 7,714 | 7,741 | 7,945 | 1.3 | -35.1 | 12.5 |
| Wood products [2]........................ | 321 | 615 | 342 | 393 | 397 | 406 | 13.3 | -44.4 | 18.8 |
| Sawmills & wood preservation............ | 3211 | 134 | 82 | 92 | 92 | 93 | -9.6 | -38.5 | 12.8 |
| Nonmetallic mineral products [2]............ | 327 | 554 | 371 | 406 | 410 | 415 | 4.9 | -33.1 | 11.9 |
| Cement & concrete products............ | 3273 | 234 | 170 | 191 | 192 | 192 | 20.1 | -27.4 | 13.1 |
| Primary metals [2]........................ | 331 | 622 | 362 | 375 | 371 | 378 | -9.7 | -41.7 | 4.3 |
| Iron & steel mills & ferroalloy production...... | 3311 | 135 | 87 | 83 | 82 | 83 | -27.7 | -35.9 | -4.3 |
| Steel products from purchased steel........... | 3312 | 73 | 52 | 55 | 56 | 57 | 4.0 | -28.7 | 9.8 |
| Alumina & aluminum production............ | 3313 | 101 | 54 | 58 | 58 | 58 | -7.3 | -46.3 | 7.6 |
| Foundries........................ | 3315 | 217 | 112 | 118 | 117 | 120 | 1.4 | -48.4 | 7.1 |
| Fabricated metal products [2]................ | 332 | 1,753 | 1,282 | 1,422 | 1,425 | 1,467 | 8.9 | -26.9 | 14.4 |
| Architectural & structural metals............ | 3323 | 428 | 321 | 370 | 373 | 390 | 20.0 | -25.0 | 21.5 |
| Machine shops & threaded products............ | 3327 | 365 | 313 | 352 | 353 | 362 | 18.4 | -14.4 | 15.7 |
| Coating, engraving, & heat treating metals.... | 3328 | 175 | 122 | 136 | 136 | 140 | 22.7 | -30.0 | 14.8 |
| Machinery [2]........................ | 333 | 1,457 | 996 | 1,077 | 1,079 | 1,120 | 3.3 | -31.6 | 12.4 |
| Agricultural, construction, & mining machinery........................ | 3331 | 222 | 208 | 206 | 206 | 220 | -2.8 | -6.4 | 5.8 |
| HVAC & commercial refrigeration equipment........................ | 3334 | 194 | 125 | 129 | 130 | 133 | 17.7 | -35.9 | 7.0 |
| Metalworking machinery................ | 3335 | 274 | 155 | 180 | 180 | 182 | 2.5 | -43.3 | 17.2 |
| Turbine & power transmission equipment...... | 3336 | 111 | 92 | 99 | 97 | 99 | -2.4 | -17.6 | 7.8 |
| Other general purpose machinery............ | 3339 | 344 | 226 | 260 | 261 | 272 | 2.4 | -34.4 | 20.3 |
| Computer & electronic products [2]................ | 334 | 1,820 | 1,095 | 1,048 | 1,039 | 1,055 | -4.3 | -39.9 | -3.6 |
| Computer & peripheral equipment............ | 3341 | 302 | 158 | 163 | 156 | 156 | -17.8 | -47.8 | -0.8 |
| Communications equipment................ | 3342 | 239 | 117 | 86 | 87 | 86 | 7.0 | -50.8 | -27.0 |
| Semiconductors & electronic components..... | 3344 | 676 | 369 | 367 | 362 | 369 | 17.8 | -45.4 | 0.0 |
| Electronic instruments........................ | 3345 | 488 | 406 | 397 | 401 | 410 | -23.2 | -16.7 | 0.9 |
| Electrical equipment & appliances [2]............ | 335 | 591 | 360 | 383 | 386 | 399 | -6.7 | -39.2 | 11.0 |
| Electrical equipment................ | 3353 | 210 | 136 | 139 | 138 | 141 | -13.9 | -35.1 | 3.7 |
| Other electrical equipment & components..... | 3359 | 191 | 119 | 132 | 137 | 145 | -2.3 | -37.8 | 22.5 |
| Transportation equipment [2]................ | 336 | 2,057 | 1,333 | 1,630 | 1,643 | 1,702 | 3.6 | -35.2 | 27.7 |
| Motor vehicles........................ | 3361 | 291 | 153 | 212 | 219 | 234 | 7.4 | -47.6 | 53.1 |
| Motor vehicle bodies & trailers................ | 3362 | 183 | 107 | 151 | 155 | 165 | 40.8 | -41.4 | 54.3 |
| Motor vehicle parts........................ | 3363 | 840 | 419 | 581 | 589 | 597 | 28.6 | -50.1 | 42.5 |
| Aerospace products & parts................ | 3364 | 517 | 478 | 490 | 488 | 509 | -38.5 | -7.5 | 6.6 |
| Ship & boat building................ | 3366 | 154 | 125 | 136 | 135 | 139 | -11.3 | -19.1 | 11.9 |
| Furniture & related products [2]................ | 337 | 680 | 357 | 390 | 395 | 395 | 13.0 | -47.5 | 10.5 |
| Household & institutional furniture............ | 3371 | 441 | 223 | 246 | 249 | 249 | 10.7 | -49.3 | 11.5 |
| Miscellaneous manufacturing................ | 339 | 728 | 567 | 591 | 595 | 608 | 6.2 | -22.1 | 7.2 |
| Medical equipment & supplies............ | 3391 | 305 | 303 | 308 | 311 | 317 | 7.7 | -0.7 | 4.8 |
| Other miscellaneous manufacturing............ | 3399 | 423 | 264 | 283 | 284 | 291 | 5.1 | -37.6 | 10.1 |
| Nondurable goods........................ | (X) | 6,386 | 4,464 | 4,640 | 4,699 | 4,743 | -8.2 | -30.1 | 6.3 |
| Food manufacturing [2]........................ | 311 | 1,553 | 1,451 | 1,557 | 1,598 | 1,620 | 3.0 | -6.6 | 11.7 |
| Fruit & vegetable preserving & specialty....... | 3114 | 197 | 173 | 172 | 174 | 172 | -9.5 | -12.6 | -0.2 |
| Dairy products........................ | 3115 | 136 | 130 | 141 | 146 | 149 | -5.9 | -4.2 | 14.4 |
| Animal slaughtering & processing............ | 3116 | 507 | 489 | 496 | 513 | 521 | 18.6 | -3.5 | 6.5 |
| Bakeries & tortilla manufacturing............ | 3118 | 306 | 277 | 305 | 311 | 313 | 4.9 | -9.7 | 12.9 |
| Textile mills [2]........................ | 313 | 378 | 119 | 115 | 113 | 113 | -23.1 | -68.5 | -5.3 |
| Fabric mills........................ | 3132 | 192 | 53 | 54 | 53 | 53 | -29.0 | -72.2 | -0.6 |
| Textile product mills [2]........................ | 314 | 230 | 119 | 116 | 116 | 116 | -2.5 | -48.2 | -2.4 |
| Textile furnishings mills................ | 3141 | 129 | 57 | 53 | 52 | 52 | 1.3 | -55.7 | -8.3 |
| Apparel [2]........................ | 315 | 484 | 157 | 131 | 119 | 113 | -46.4 | -67.6 | -28.1 |
| Cut & sew apparel........................ | 3152 | 380 | 124 | 106 | 96 | 91 | -49.3 | -67.4 | -27.0 |
| Paper & paper products........................ | 322 | 605 | 395 | 371 | 366 | 367 | -6.6 | -34.7 | -7.0 |
| Pulp, paper, & paperboard mills................ | 3221 | 191 | 112 | 100 | 97 | 95 | -19.7 | -41.3 | -15.3 |
| Converted paper products................ | 3222 | 413 | 282 | 271 | 269 | 272 | 1.1 | -31.7 | -3.8 |
| Printing & related support activities................ | 323 | 807 | 488 | 448 | 440 | 431 | -0.2 | -39.6 | -11.6 |
| Petroleum & coal products................ | 324 | 123 | 114 | 113 | 115 | 116 | -19.4 | -7.5 | 1.5 |
| Chemicals [2]........................ | 325 | 980 | 787 | 812 | 824 | 838 | -5.3 | -19.8 | 6.5 |
| Basic chemicals........................ | 3251 | 188 | 142 | 149 | 151 | 153 | -24.4 | -24.5 | 7.2 |
| Pharmaceuticals & medicines................ | 3254 | 274 | 277 | 286 | 293 | 296 | 32.4 | 0.9 | 6.8 |
| Soaps, cleaning compounds, and toiletries.... | 3256 | 129 | 102 | 106 | 107 | 110 | -2.4 | -20.6 | 7.8 |
| Plastics & rubber products [2]................ | 326 | 951 | 625 | 702 | 717 | 731 | 15.3 | -34.3 | 17.0 |
| Plastics products........................ | 3261 | 737 | 502 | 569 | 581 | 593 | 19.2 | -31.9 | 18.3 |
| Rubber products........................ | 3262 | 214 | 123 | 134 | 136 | 138 | 3.5 | -42.5 | 11.8 |
| Miscellaneous nondurable goods manufacturing [2]........................ | 312,6 | 276 | 211 | 277 | 291 | 300 | -21.4 | -23.5 | 42.0 |
| Beverages........................ | 3121 | 175 | 167 | 235 | 251 | 261 | 1.2 | -4.5 | 56.4 |

X Not applicable. [1] Based on the North American Industry Classification System, 2017 (NAICS); see text, this section and Section 15. [2] Includes other industries, not shown separately.

Source: U.S. Bureau of Labor Statistics, Current Employment Statistics, "Employment, Hours, and Earnings—National," <http://www.bls.gov/ces/data.htm>, accessed July 2019.

# Table 1045. Manufacturing—Value of Imports and Exports by Commodity: 2016

[In thousands of dollars (22,933,334 represents $22,933,334,000). Values are based on manufacturing data from the Annual Survey of Manufacturers and administrative records from official U.S. import and export merchandise trade statistics]

| Commodity description | Product code [1] | Value of product shipments [2] | Total export value of goods [3] | General import value of goods [4] |
|---|---|---|---|---|
| Food manufacturing: | | | | |
| Dog and cat food................................ | 311111 | 22,933,334 | 1,315,436 | 750,587 |
| Other animal food............................... | 311119 | 32,310,895 | 1,633,277 | 552,029 |
| Soybean and other oilseed products................ | 311224 | 31,282,491 | 6,470,490 | 6,770,328 |
| Fruit and vegetable canning products............... | 311421 | 25,481,320 | 2,992,732 | 5,659,242 |
| Fluid milk products.............................. | 311511 | 33,320,569 | 259,924 | 59,719 |
| Cheese products................................ | 311513 | 40,139,943 | 1,209,024 | 1,259,170 |
| Animal (except poultry) slaughtering products....... | 311611 | 87,629,077 | 14,721,102 | 8,533,537 |
| Meat processed from carcasses................... | 311612 | 50,661,463 | (NA) | 75,688 |
| Poultry processing products...................... | 311615 | 61,740,224 | 3,892,349 | 519,487 |
| Commercial bakery products...................... | 311812 | 30,589,439 | (NA) | (NA) |
| Beverage and tobacco product manufacturing: | | | | |
| Soft drinks..................................... | 312111 | 35,464,262 | 1,042,512 | 2,817,168 |
| Brewery products............................... | 312120 | 30,518,887 | 2,779,377 | 4,940,274 |
| Tobacco products............................... | 312230 | 41,360,631 | 1,155,877 | 1,413,967 |
| Wood product manufacturing: | | | | |
| Sawmill products................................ | 321113 | 22,332,560 | 3,594,972 | 6,821,382 |
| Paper manufacturing: | | | | |
| Paper (except newsprint) mill products.............. | 322121 | 38,387,992 | 2,387,662 | 3,523,186 |
| Paperboard mill products......................... | 322130 | 28,456,285 | 4,749,078 | 1,974,937 |
| Corrugated and solid fiber boxes.................. | 322211 | 37,137,108 | 1,541,479 | 456,034 |
| Paper bags and coated and treated paper........... | 322220 | 20,496,725 | 5,066,946 | 3,499,012 |
| Printing and related support activities manufacturing: | | | | |
| Commercial printing products (except screen and books).. | 323111 | 63,006,196 | 2,975,117 | 3,448,871 |
| Petroleum and coal products manufacturing: | | | | |
| Petroleum refinery products...................... | 324110 | 367,379,559 | 66,138,901 | 41,757,855 |
| Chemical manufacturing: | | | | |
| Petrochemicals................................. | 325110 | 49,724,229 | 1,962,962 | 1,161,965 |
| Other basic inorganic chemicals.................. | 325180 | 27,160,725 | 12,087,142 | 9,063,331 |
| Ethyl alcohol................................... | 325193 | 25,171,720 | 2,052,938 | 474,199 |
| All other basic organic chemical manufacturing...... | 325199 | 71,734,847 | 30,009,159 | 32,781,551 |
| Plastics materials and resins..................... | 325211 | 75,842,384 | 27,410,887 | 12,529,935 |
| Pharmaceutical preparations..................... | 325412 | 151,058,524 | 28,369,122 | 76,867,073 |
| Biological products (except diagnostic)............. | 325414 | 27,776,154 | 19,053,878 | 20,053,806 |
| Paints and coatings............................. | 325510 | 27,445,132 | 2,688,799 | 1,043,696 |
| Soaps and other detergents...................... | 325611 | 22,433,822 | 1,474,230 | 1,005,264 |
| Toilet preparations.............................. | 325620 | 36,599,913 | 9,059,348 | 8,408,216 |
| Plastics and rubber products manufacturing: | | | | |
| All other plastics products....................... | 326199 | 91,168,720 | 11,139,675 | 19,174,669 |
| Nonmetallic mineral product manufacturing: | | | | |
| Ready-mix concrete............................. | 327320 | 28,910,513 | 4,133 | 1,188 |
| Primary metal manufacturing: | | | | |
| Iron and steel mill products and ferroalloys......... | 331110 | 75,671,972 | 11,693,601 | 24,284,212 |
| Fabricated metal product manufacturing: | | | | |
| Fabricated structural metal products............... | 332312 | 27,415,851 | 1,022,136 | 3,990,190 |
| Machine shops................................. | 332710 | 35,017,553 | (NA) | (NA) |
| Machinery manufacturing: | | | | |
| Farm machinery and equipment................... | 333111 | 22,568,333 | 6,607,460 | 7,145,733 |
| Construction machinery.......................... | 333120 | 24,010,377 | 10,958,135 | 16,189,841 |
| Air-conditioning and warm air heating equipment and commercial and industrial refrigeration equipment.. | 333415 | 31,113,498 | 5,513,311 | 10,004,731 |
| Other engine equipment......................... | 333618 | 23,203,303 | 10,431,523 | 11,859,221 |
| Computer and electronic product manufacturing: | | | | |
| Semiconductors and related devices............... | 334413 | 45,729,550 | 42,932,709 | 45,535,817 |
| Electromedical and electrotherapeutic apparatus.... | 334510 | 26,291,936 | 10,217,928 | 10,747,574 |
| Search, detection, navigation, guidance, aeronautical, and nautical systems and instruments............ | 334511 | 40,690,878 | 3,958,648 | 7,571,485 |
| Transportation equipment manufacturing: | | | | |
| Automobiles.................................... | 336111 | 123,557,447 | 47,654,237 | 168,796,384 |
| Light truck and utility vehicles.................... | 336112 | 190,316,687 | 9,834,772 | 18,359,171 |
| Heavy duty trucks............................... | 336120 | 26,779,308 | 5,259,339 | 10,645,150 |
| Motor vehicle gasoline engines and engine parts.... | 336310 | 31,209,958 | 9,731,596 | 18,415,781 |
| Motor vehicle electrical and electronic equipment.... | 336320 | 23,457,092 | 7,035,692 | 20,087,287 |
| Motor vehicle transmission and power train parts.... | 336350 | 39,919,280 | 2,901,242 | 8,637,523 |
| Motor vehicle seating and interior trim............. | 336360 | 31,773,837 | 2,451,721 | 7,802,656 |
| Motor vehicle metal stampings.................... | 336370 | 35,529,192 | 1,587,182 | 665,764 |
| Other motor vehicle parts........................ | 336390 | 65,150,150 | 16,318,203 | 36,476,598 |
| Aircraft........................................ | 336411 | 120,974,701 | 4,546,595 | 13,844,272 |
| Aircraft engines and engine parts................. | 336412 | 39,652,987 | 2,267,804 | 19,039,796 |
| Other aircraft parts and auxiliary equipment........ | 336413 | 40,570,416 | 5,983,217 | 16,508,498 |
| Guided missiles and space vehicles............... | 336414 | 23,130,420 | 1,509,744 | 2,264 |
| Ships and ship repair........................... | 336611 | 23,417,674 | 1,366,634 | 493,378 |
| Miscellaneous manufacturing: | | | | |
| Surgical and medical instruments................. | 339112 | 41,039,499 | 16,998,378 | 13,476,651 |
| Surgical appliances and supplies................. | 339113 | 30,630,740 | 11,014,731 | 14,101,341 |

NA Not available. [1] Based on North American Industry Classification (NAICS) product codes. [2] Includes total value of all products produced and shipped by all producers. For selected products, this can represent value of receipts, value of production, or value of work done. [3] Exports measure total physical movement of merchandise out of the U.S. to foreign countries whether such merchandise is exported from within the U.S. Customs territory, from a U.S. Customs bonded warehouse, or a U.S. Foreign Trade Zone. [4] Imports include commodities of foreign origin as well as goods of domestic origin returned to the U.S. with no change in condition or after having been processed and/or assembled in other countries.

Source: U.S. Census Bureau, *Manufacturing and International Trade Report: 2016*, February 2018. See also <https://www.census.gov/foreign-trade/index.html>.

## Table 1046. Manufacturing Industries—Average Weekly Hours and Average Weekly Overtime Hours of Production Workers: 2000 to 2018

[Covers all full- and part-time employees who worked during, or received pay for, any part of the pay period including the 12th of the month]

| Industry | 2017 NAICS code [1] | Average weekly hours of production workers | | | | | Average weekly overtime hours of production workers | | | | |
|---|---|---|---|---|---|---|---|---|---|---|---|
| | | 2000 | 2010 | 2015 | 2017 | 2018 | 2000 | 2010 | 2015 | 2017 | 2018 |
| Total................. | 31–33 | 41.3 | 41.1 | 41.8 | 41.9 | 42.2 | 4.7 | 3.8 | 4.3 | 4.3 | 4.6 |
| Durable goods..................... | (X) | 41.8 | 41.4 | 42.1 | 42.3 | 42.5 | 4.8 | 3.8 | 4.3 | 4.4 | 4.7 |
| Wood products..................... | 321 | 41.0 | 39.1 | 41.3 | 42.1 | 41.9 | 4.1 | 3.0 | 4.1 | 4.6 | 5.0 |
| Nonmetallic mineral products..... | 327 | 41.6 | 41.7 | 42.4 | 42.9 | 44.2 | 6.1 | 4.7 | 4.9 | 5.6 | 6.2 |
| Primary metals..................... | 331 | 44.2 | 43.7 | 43.8 | 43.1 | 44.6 | 6.5 | 5.7 | 6.5 | 5.7 | 6.7 |
| Fabricated metal products......... | 332 | 41.9 | 41.4 | 42.3 | 42.2 | 42.2 | 4.9 | 3.8 | 4.3 | 4.2 | 4.4 |
| Machinery.......................... | 333 | 42.3 | 42.1 | 41.9 | 42.7 | 42.7 | 5.1 | 3.9 | 4.0 | 4.5 | 4.7 |
| Computer and electronic products................. | 334 | 41.4 | 40.9 | 40.9 | 41.2 | 40.9 | 4.6 | 2.9 | 3.0 | 3.3 | 3.2 |
| Electrical equipment and appliances.................. | 335 | 41.6 | 41.1 | 42.2 | 43.1 | 42.6 | 3.7 | 3.6 | 4.2 | 4.6 | 4.5 |
| Transportation equipment......... | 336 | 43.3 | 42.9 | 43.7 | 43.9 | 44.4 | 5.6 | 4.7 | 5.3 | 5.4 | 5.8 |
| Furniture and related products.... | 337 | 39.2 | 38.5 | 39.8 | 39.3 | 39.3 | 3.5 | 2.3 | 3.1 | 2.7 | 2.6 |
| Miscellaneous manufacturing..... | 339 | 39.0 | 38.7 | 40.1 | 39.9 | 39.5 | 3.1 | 2.7 | 3.1 | 3.0 | 3.2 |
| Nondurable goods................. | (X) | 40.3 | 40.8 | 41.4 | 41.3 | 41.6 | 4.5 | 3.8 | 4.3 | 4.2 | 4.4 |
| Food manufacturing................ | 311 | 40.1 | 40.7 | 41.0 | 41.7 | 42.0 | 4.9 | 4.5 | 4.5 | 4.8 | 4.9 |
| Textile mills....................... | 313 | 41.4 | 41.2 | 42.5 | 40.6 | 42.3 | 4.8 | 3.3 | 5.2 | 3.8 | 5.0 |
| Textile product mills............... | 314 | 38.7 | 39.0 | 37.0 | 38.4 | 39.3 | 3.4 | 2.4 | 2.5 | 2.3 | 2.6 |
| Apparel............................ | 315 | 35.7 | 36.6 | 38.2 | 36.5 | 37.7 | 2.1 | 1.1 | 2.0 | 2.1 | 2.6 |
| Paper and paper products......... | 322 | 42.8 | 42.9 | 43.0 | 42.5 | 43.1 | 5.7 | 4.9 | 4.8 | 5.1 | 5.6 |
| Printing and related support activities................. | 323 | 39.2 | 38.2 | 39.8 | 39.5 | 39.3 | 3.7 | 2.2 | 3.1 | 2.9 | 3.1 |
| Petroleum and coal products...... | 324 | 42.7 | 43.0 | 45.2 | 45.0 | 45.6 | 6.5 | 6.4 | 7.8 | 8.1 | 9.9 |
| Chemicals......................... | 325 | 42.2 | 42.2 | 42.6 | 41.7 | 42.1 | 5.0 | 3.6 | 4.5 | 3.6 | 3.8 |
| Plastics and rubber products...... | 326 | 40.8 | 41.9 | 42.4 | 42.6 | 42.1 | 3.9 | 4.0 | 4.5 | 4.2 | 4.3 |
| Misc. nondurable manufacturing.. | 329 | 40.5 | 37.8 | 38.0 | 37.2 | 37.7 | 5.4 | 2.3 | 3.2 | 2.9 | 2.6 |

X Not applicable. [1] Based on the North American Industry Classification System (NAICS), 2017; see text, this section and Section 15.

Source: U.S. Bureau of Labor Statistics, Current Employment Statistics, "Employment, Hours, and Earnings — National," <https://www.bls.gov/ces/data/home.htm>, accessed July 2019.

## Table 1047. Indexes of Employment and Hours of All Persons in Manufacturing: 2010 to 2018

[2007=100. Based on Current Employment Statistics and supplemented with Current Population Survey. Employment and hours of all persons include those of paid employees, the self employed (partners and proprietors), and unpaid family workers. See text, Section 12]

| Industry | NAICS code [1] | Employment | | | | | Hours | | | | |
|---|---|---|---|---|---|---|---|---|---|---|---|
| | | 2010 | 2015 | 2016 | 2017 | 2018 | 2010 | 2015 | 2016 | 2017 | 2018 |
| Food manufacturing.............. | 311 | 97.4 | 102.6 | 104.9 | 108.5 | 109.9 | 97.6 | 103.2 | 106.8 | 110.1 | 112.9 |
| Beverage and tobacco products......................... | 312 | 93.2 | 115.5 | 125.0 | 135.8 | 136.6 | 87.0 | 109.1 | 118.1 | 126.0 | 132.6 |
| Textile mills........................ | 313 | 71.3 | 68.8 | 66.3 | 64.2 | 65.0 | 73.2 | 72.1 | 66.9 | 63.6 | 67.3 |
| Textile product mills.............. | 314 | 72.5 | 74.0 | 76.0 | 74.2 | 71.7 | 76.6 | 71.5 | 74.8 | 77.1 | 73.8 |
| Apparel manufacturing.......... | 315 | 72.4 | 63.9 | 60.0 | 55.1 | 51.0 | 72.3 | 64.9 | 57.8 | 53.3 | 50.8 |
| Leather and allied products...... | 316 | 83.2 | 84.2 | 84.7 | 86.8 | 79.0 | 82.8 | 86.2 | 83.0 | 81.6 | 78.5 |
| Wood product manufacturing. .. | 321 | 66.6 | 72.9 | 75.0 | 76.8 | 79.3 | 67.7 | 76.1 | 78.6 | 80.8 | 83.6 |
| Paper and paper products....... | 322 | 86.4 | 81.4 | 81.0 | 80.3 | 80.6 | 87.2 | 81.9 | 81.1 | 79.8 | 80.9 |
| Printing and related support activities....................... | 323 | 79.7 | 71.8 | 70.7 | 70.0 | 68.0 | 79.0 | 72.6 | 71.1 | 71.2 | 68.8 |
| Petroleum and coal products.... | 324 | 99.0 | 98.1 | 98.5 | 99.3 | 101.4 | 95.7 | 100.3 | 100.7 | 100.5 | 105.4 |
| Chemical manufacturing......... | 325 | 91.5 | 94.2 | 94.6 | 96.5 | 98.2 | 92.6 | 94.5 | 93.3 | 95.2 | 97.2 |
| Plastics and rubber products.... | 326 | 82.2 | 90.7 | 92.6 | 94.4 | 96.1 | 82.8 | 93.1 | 94.2 | 96.9 | 97.7 |
| Nonmetallic mineral products. .. | 327 | 75.2 | 80.0 | 82.3 | 83.0 | 82.3 | 74.4 | 78.2 | 79.6 | 82.3 | 84.4 |
| Primary metal products.......... | 331 | 79.7 | 86.5 | 81.9 | 81.3 | 82.8 | 81.8 | 88.4 | 83.6 | 82.4 | 87.1 |
| Fabricated metal products....... | 332 | 82.4 | 92.9 | 90.8 | 90.7 | 93.1 | 81.3 | 94.1 | 91.5 | 91.3 | 93.5 |
| Machinery manufacturing........ | 333 | 83.6 | 94.1 | 90.2 | 90.4 | 93.6 | 84.2 | 93.2 | 90.1 | 91.8 | 94.5 |
| Computer and electronic products......................... | 334 | 86.2 | 82.4 | 82.6 | 81.6 | 82.7 | 87.6 | 84.0 | 84.0 | 83.1 | 83.0 |
| Electrical equipment and appliances..................... | 335 | 83.8 | 88.9 | 89.4 | 91.1 | 93.0 | 83.9 | 91.0 | 92.0 | 94.9 | 95.2 |
| Transportation equipment....... | 336 | 78.1 | 93.5 | 94.9 | 96.3 | 99.5 | 79.2 | 96.8 | 98.9 | 99.6 | 103.5 |
| Furniture and related products.. | 337 | 67.7 | 72.2 | 72.2 | 74.4 | 74.7 | 66.5 | 73.4 | 74.2 | 75.2 | 75.6 |
| Miscellaneous manufacturing. .. | 339 | 87.2 | 91.9 | 90.8 | 91.1 | 92.3 | 87.5 | 95.0 | 96.6 | 95.0 | 95.4 |

[1] North American Industry Classification System; see text, Section 15.

Source: U.S. Bureau of Labor Statistics, Labor Productivity and Costs, "LPC Tables and Charts," <http://www.bls.gov/lpc/tables.htm>, accessed July 2019.

## Table 1048. Average Hourly Earnings of Production Workers in Manufacturing Industries by State: 2015 to 2018

[In dollars. Data are based on the North American Industry Classification System (NAICS), 2017. Based on the Current Employment Statistics Program. Covers full- and part-time employees who received pay for any part of the pay period including the 12th of the month. Excludes proprietors, self-employed, unpaid family or volunteer workers, farm workers, and domestic workers. See source, and Appendix III]

| State | 2015 | 2016 | 2017 | 2018 | State | 2015 | 2016 | 2017 | 2018 |
|---|---|---|---|---|---|---|---|---|---|
| **United States**........ | **19.91** | **20.44** | **20.90** | **21.54** | Montana................. | 18.01 | 18.70 | 19.23 | 20.80 |
| Alabama................ | 18.79 | 19.38 | 19.89 | 20.11 | Nebraska.............. | 17.73 | 17.79 | 19.16 | 19.47 |
| Alaska................. | 22.60 | 22.18 | 21.61 | 20.18 | Nevada................ | 17.48 | 19.13 | 19.51 | 19.75 |
| Arizona................ | 17.95 | 17.60 | 17.50 | 19.49 | New Hampshire....... | 19.74 | 20.67 | 21.57 | 21.64 |
| Arkansas.............. | 16.19 | 15.84 | 16.11 | 17.44 | New Jersey........... | 20.03 | 21.26 | 21.69 | 22.29 |
| California.............. | 21.37 | 21.90 | 22.75 | 23.45 | New Mexico........... | 16.56 | 16.87 | 17.31 | 17.89 |
| Colorado.............. | 26.54 | 28.66 | 27.52 | 26.90 | New York............. | 19.40 | 19.51 | 20.55 | 22.04 |
| Connecticut........... | 25.68 | 26.72 | 25.01 | 26.60 | North Carolina........ | 16.98 | 17.39 | 17.74 | 18.27 |
| Delaware.............. | 17.25 | 17.61 | 19.17 | 19.14 | North Dakota......... | 19.96 | 20.61 | 20.29 | 19.97 |
| Florida................ | 20.02 | 21.01 | 21.47 | 21.76 | Ohio.................. | 19.85 | 20.59 | 21.11 | 21.49 |
| Georgia............... | 18.02 | 18.14 | 18.42 | 18.90 | Oklahoma............. | 18.47 | 18.62 | 18.94 | 19.00 |
| Hawaii................ | 20.14 | 21.40 | 20.49 | 20.63 | Oregon............... | 19.67 | 19.96 | 20.65 | 21.73 |
| Idaho................. | 22.18 | 19.75 | 18.57 | 18.86 | Pennsylvania......... | 18.95 | 19.29 | 20.34 | 20.78 |
| Illinois................ | 19.78 | 20.25 | 20.22 | 21.30 | Rhode Island......... | 17.69 | 18.22 | 19.00 | 19.15 |
| Indiana............... | 18.91 | 18.88 | 19.90 | 21.09 | South Carolina....... | 18.84 | 19.23 | 19.07 | 19.29 |
| Iowa.................. | 19.03 | 18.66 | 19.37 | 19.68 | South Dakota........ | 18.01 | 18.59 | 18.75 | 18.80 |
| Kansas................ | 18.87 | 19.00 | 19.15 | 19.95 | Tennessee............ | 17.48 | 18.59 | 19.41 | 19.83 |
| Kentucky.............. | 20.33 | 20.41 | 20.30 | 20.44 | Texas................ | 21.67 | 22.66 | 23.13 | 23.54 |
| Louisiana............. | 22.07 | 22.11 | 21.88 | 22.01 | Utah................. | 19.05 | 20.11 | 20.61 | 20.81 |
| Maine................. | 20.89 | 21.28 | 22.18 | 22.48 | Vermont.............. | 18.93 | 20.15 | 21.09 | 21.17 |
| Maryland.............. | 18.87 | 19.10 | 20.61 | 21.13 | Virginia.............. | 19.97 | 19.55 | 19.41 | 19.64 |
| Massachusetts........ | 21.79 | 22.78 | 23.71 | 24.56 | Washington........... | 25.52 | 26.42 | 27.38 | 28.43 |
| Michigan.............. | 20.81 | 20.50 | 20.74 | 21.31 | West Virginia......... | 19.19 | 19.83 | 21.14 | 21.38 |
| Minnesota............. | 20.22 | 20.03 | 20.76 | 21.71 | Wisconsin............ | 19.32 | 19.62 | 20.25 | 20.56 |
| Mississippi............ | 18.30 | 20.33 | 20.58 | 20.54 | Wyoming............. | 21.58 | 21.99 | 22.78 | 23.95 |
| Missouri............... | 19.62 | 20.26 | 22.38 | 22.04 | Puerto Rico........... | 13.03 | 12.27 | 12.60 | 12.38 |

Source: U.S. Bureau of Labor Statistics, Current Employment Statistics, "Employment, Hours, and Earnings – National," <http://www.bls.gov/ces/data.htm>; and "Employment, Hours, and Earnings – State and Metro Area," <http://www.bls.gov/sae/data.htm>; accessed July 2019.

## Table 1049. Manufacturing Full–Time Equivalent (FTE) Employees and Wages by Industry: 2000 to 2018

[123,384 represents 123,384,000. Based on National Income and Product Account tables. Full-time equivalent employees equals the number of employees on full-time schedules plus the number of employees for part-time schedules converted to full-time basis]

| Industry | 2012 NAICS code [1] | Full-time equivalent (FTE) employees (1,000) | | | | Wage and salary accruals per FTE worker (dol.) | | | |
|---|---|---|---|---|---|---|---|---|---|
| | | 2000 | 2010 | 2017 | 2018 | 2000 | 2010 | 2017 | 2018 |
| **Domestic industries, total**........... | (X) | **123,384** | **120,519** | **136,483** | **138,889** | **39,166** | **52,939** | **62,095** | **64,090** |
| **Manufacturing**............................. | **31–33** | **16,948** | **11,223** | **12,181** | **12,391** | **43,957** | **59,997** | **69,418** | **71,281** |
| Percent of all industries................... | (X) | 13.7 | 9.3 | 8.9 | 8.9 | 112.2 | 113.3 | 111.8 | 111.2 |
| Durable goods............................. | (X) | 10,713 | 6,900 | 7,601 | 7,795 | 46,573 | 63,311 | 73,614 | 75,630 |
| Wood products........................... | 321 | 602 | 333 | 387 | 398 | 30,351 | 38,149 | 46,668 | 48,106 |
| Nonmetallic mineral products........... | 327 | 549 | 357 | 402 | 412 | 39,021 | 50,628 | 60,073 | 61,191 |
| Primary metals........................... | 331 | 611 | 353 | 360 | 371 | 45,836 | 61,058 | 70,851 | 73,554 |
| Fabricated metal products.............. | 332 | 1,735 | 1,249 | 1,387 | 1,433 | 37,766 | 51,445 | 58,794 | 60,242 |
| Machinery................................ | 333 | 1,427 | 975 | 1,058 | 1,094 | 46,612 | 62,656 | 72,397 | 74,104 |
| Computer and electronic products...... | 334 | 1,779 | 1,079 | 1,029 | 1,039 | 70,449 | 96,001 | 123,161 | 127,709 |
| Electrical equipment, appliances, and components............................... | 335 | 583 | 351 | 383 | 391 | 40,241 | 59,438 | 69,169 | 70,180 |
| Motor vehicles, bodies and trailers, and parts.................................. | 3361–3363 | 1,301 | 666 | 961 | 990 | 48,754 | 57,922 | 62,787 | 64,608 |
| Other transportation equipment......... | 3364–3365 | 740 | 645 | 669 | 691 | 53,294 | 79,421 | 93,945 | 96,818 |
| Furniture and related products.......... | 337 | 671 | 345 | 384 | 384 | 29,571 | 39,980 | 47,178 | 48,351 |
| Miscellaneous manufacturing........... | 339 | 715 | 547 | 579 | 591 | 38,744 | 56,903 | 67,386 | 69,099 |
| Nondurable goods......................... | (X) | 6,235 | 4,322 | 4,579 | 4,596 | 39,464 | 54,706 | 62,454 | 63,904 |
| Food and beverage and tobacco products................................. | 311–312 | 1,728 | 1,561 | 1,789 | 1,814 | 33,956 | 44,711 | 51,123 | 52,284 |
| Textile mills and textile product mills... | 313–314 | 588 | 230 | 222 | 220 | 29,013 | 39,110 | 46,198 | 47,089 |
| Apparel and leather and allied products................................. | 315 | 539 | 179 | 145 | 137 | 24,198 | 38,244 | 44,394 | 45,719 |
| Paper products........................... | 322 | 598 | 382 | 360 | 354 | 45,834 | 61,586 | 69,487 | 71,384 |
| Printing and related support activities.. | 323 | 757 | 472 | 431 | 418 | 39,142 | 45,783 | 51,001 | 52,878 |
| Petroleum and coal products............ | 324 | 120 | 109 | 112 | 112 | 62,998 | 97,162 | 115,105 | 119,340 |
| Chemical products....................... | 325 | 967 | 775 | 815 | 820 | 61,314 | 84,813 | 97,093 | 98,787 |
| Plastics and rubber products............ | 326 | 938 | 615 | 705 | 720 | 35,624 | 47,778 | 55,041 | 56,139 |

X Not applicable. [1] North American Industry Classification System, 2012; see text, Section 15.

Source: U.S. Bureau of Economic Analysis, National Income and Product Accounts, "Table 6.5D. Full-Time Equivalent Employees by Industry," and "Table 6.6D. Wages and Salaries Per Full-Time Equivalent Employee by Industry," <http://bea.gov/itable/>, accessed August 2019.

# Table 1050. Manufacturers' Shipments, Inventories, and New Orders: 1995 to 2018

[In billions of dollars (3,480 represents $3,480,000,000,000), except ratio. Data are not seasonally adjusted, except ratios as noted. Based on the Manufacturers' Shipments, Inventories, and Orders (M3) survey. See source for details]

| Year | Shipments | Inventories (December 31) [1] | Ratio of inventories to shipments [2] | New orders | Unfilled orders (December 31) |
|---|---|---|---|---|---|
| 1995 | 3,480 | 415 | 1.41 | 3,427 | 443 |
| 1996 | 3,597 | 421 | 1.40 | 3,567 | 485 |
| 1997 | 3,835 | 433 | 1.36 | 3,780 | 508 |
| 1998 | 3,900 | 439 | 1.37 | 3,808 | 492 |
| 1999 | 4,032 | 453 | 1.34 | 3,957 | 501 |
| 2000 | 4,209 | 470 | 1.37 | 4,161 | 545 |
| 2001 | 3,970 | 417 | 1.33 | 3,869 | 506 |
| 2002 | 3,915 | 412 | 1.30 | 3,823 | 476 |
| 2003 | 4,015 | 398 | 1.20 | 3,976 | 503 |
| 2004 | 4,309 | 429 | 1.17 | 4,289 | 555 |
| 2005 | 4,742 | 461 | 1.14 | 4,764 | 652 |
| 2006 | 5,016 | 509 | 1.22 | 5,090 | 796 |
| 2007 | 5,319 | 547 | 1.22 | 5,397 | 946 |
| 2008 | 5,469 | 529 | 1.42 | 5,452 | 995 |
| 2009 | 4,424 | 491 | 1.29 | 4,206 | 825 |
| 2010 | 4,911 | 538 | 1.28 | 4,896 | 870 |
| 2011 | 5,492 | 589 | 1.29 | 5,512 | 953 |
| 2012 | 5,697 | 607 | 1.30 | 5,710 | 1,015 |
| 2013 | 5,810 | 612 | 1.29 | 5,827 | 1,077 |
| 2014 | 5,888 | 623 | 1.34 | 5,926 | 1,162 |
| 2015 | 5,519 | 619 | 1.44 | 5,439 | 1,130 |
| 2016 | 5,355 | 615 | 1.37 | 5,293 | 1,115 |
| 2017 | 5,605 | 643 | 1.36 | 5,579 | 1,136 |
| 2018 | 6,000 | 666 | 1.35 | 5,994 | 1,180 |

[1] Inventories are stated at current cost. [2] Ratio based on December seasonally adjusted inventory data.

Source: U.S. Census Bureau, Manufacturers' Shipments, Inventories, and Orders, "Historical Data," <http://www.census.gov/manufacturing/m3/historical_data/index.html>, accessed July 2019.

# Table 1051. Ratios of Manufacturers' Inventories to Shipments and Unfilled Orders to Shipments by Industry Group: 2000 to 2018

[Based on the Manufacturers' Shipments, Inventories, and Orders (M3) survey. Ratio based on December seasonally adjusted inventory and unfilled orders data. See source for details]

| Industry | 2012 NAICS code [1] | 2000 | 2010 | 2014 | 2015 | 2016 | 2017 | 2018 |
|---|---|---|---|---|---|---|---|---|
| INVENTORIES-TO-SHIPMENTS RATIO | | | | | | | | |
| **All manufacturing industries** | (X) | **1.37** | **1.28** | **1.34** | **1.44** | **1.37** | **1.36** | **1.35** |
| Durable goods | (X) | 1.56 | 1.62 | 1.64 | 1.75 | 1.66 | 1.64 | 1.61 |
| Wood products | 321 | 1.41 | 1.39 | 1.33 | 1.33 | 1.27 | 1.26 | 1.37 |
| Nonmetallic mineral products | 327 | 1.26 | 1.52 | 1.32 | 1.28 | 1.28 | 1.27 | 1.35 |
| Primary metals | 331 | 1.77 | 1.58 | 1.75 | 1.92 | 1.71 | 1.70 | 1.69 |
| Fabricated metals | 332 | 1.56 | 1.58 | 1.61 | 1.72 | 1.65 | 1.61 | 1.62 |
| Machinery | 333 | 2.05 | 1.86 | 2.06 | 2.21 | 2.16 | 2.07 | 2.14 |
| Computers and electronic products | 334 | 1.47 | 1.59 | 1.69 | 1.75 | 1.65 | 1.66 | 1.57 |
| Electrical equipment, appliances, and components | 335 | 1.41 | 1.47 | 1.57 | 1.65 | 1.59 | 1.67 | 1.73 |
| Transportation equipment | 336 | 1.42 | 1.64 | 1.54 | 1.72 | 1.58 | 1.59 | 1.45 |
| Furniture and related products | 337 | 1.36 | 1.18 | 1.09 | 1.14 | 1.17 | 1.22 | 1.20 |
| Miscellaneous products | 339 | 1.83 | 1.72 | 1.70 | 1.67 | 1.79 | 1.67 | 1.76 |
| Nondurable goods | (X) | 1.13 | 0.99 | 1.05 | 1.12 | 1.09 | 1.08 | 1.08 |
| Food products | 311 | 0.86 | 0.79 | 0.80 | 0.85 | 0.83 | 0.82 | 0.80 |
| Beverages and tobacco products | 312 | 1.50 | 1.65 | 1.67 | 1.78 | 1.85 | 2.00 | 1.99 |
| Textile mills | 313 | 1.54 | 1.24 | 1.24 | 1.33 | 1.26 | 1.29 | 1.39 |
| Textile product mills | 314 | 1.87 | 1.65 | 1.52 | 1.70 | 1.58 | 1.57 | 1.49 |
| Apparel | 315 | 1.91 | 1.63 | 2.01 | 2.31 | 2.14 | 2.04 | 1.98 |
| Leather and allied products | 316 | 1.88 | 1.77 | 1.98 | 2.12 | 1.77 | 1.83 | 1.98 |
| Paper products | 322 | 1.11 | 0.97 | 1.01 | 1.03 | 1.04 | 0.99 | 1.01 |
| Printing | 323 | 0.78 | 0.77 | 0.82 | 0.78 | 0.81 | 0.81 | 0.84 |
| Petroleum and coal products | 324 | 0.68 | 0.74 | 0.81 | 0.86 | 0.77 | 0.76 | 0.74 |
| Basic chemicals | 325 | 1.35 | 1.23 | 1.29 | 1.37 | 1.39 | 1.36 | 1.36 |
| Plastics and rubber products | 326 | 1.24 | 1.21 | 1.28 | 1.27 | 1.27 | 1.31 | 1.38 |
| UNFILLED ORDERS-TO-SHIPMENTS RATIO | | | | | | | | |
| **All manufacturing industries** | (X) | **4.02** | **6.11** | **6.93** | **7.32** | **7.07** | **6.77** | **6.57** |
| Durable goods | (X) | 4.02 | 6.11 | 6.93 | 7.32 | 7.07 | 6.77 | 6.57 |
| Primary metals | 331 | 1.52 | 1.91 | 1.49 | 1.58 | 1.46 | 1.45 | 1.46 |
| Fabricated metals | 332 | 2.13 | 2.81 | 2.62 | 2.72 | 2.66 | 2.60 | 2.61 |
| Machinery | 333 | 2.66 | 3.81 | 3.55 | 3.54 | 3.64 | 3.52 | 3.59 |
| Computers and electronic products | 334 | 4.24 | 5.93 | 5.89 | 5.74 | 5.87 | 5.46 | 5.38 |
| Electrical equipment, appliances, and components | 335 | 1.83 | 1.95 | 2.03 | 2.01 | 1.97 | 1.96 | 1.85 |
| Transportation equipment | 336 | 8.06 | 13.92 | 15.61 | 16.52 | 15.46 | 15.30 | 14.31 |
| Furniture and related products | 337 | 1.29 | 1.40 | 1.41 | 1.54 | 1.51 | 1.51 | 1.48 |

X Not applicable. [1] Based on the North American Industry Classification System, 2012; see text, this section and Section 15.

Source: U.S. Census Bureau, Manufacturers' Shipments, Inventories, and Orders, "Historical Data," <http://www.census.gov/manufacturing/m3/historical_data/index.html>, accessed June 2019.

# Table 1052. Value of Manufacturers' Shipments, Inventories, and New Orders by Industry: 2000 to 2017

[In billions of dollars (4,209 represents $4,209,000,000,000). Data are not seasonally adjusted. Based on the Manufacturers' Shipments, Inventories, and Orders (M3) survey. See source for details]

| Industry | 2007 NAICS code [1] | 2000 | 2010 | 2014 | 2015 | 2016 | 2017 |
|---|---|---|---|---|---|---|---|
| **SHIPMENTS** | | | | | | | |
| **All manufacturing industries** | (X) | **4,209** | **4,911** | **5,888** | **5,519** | **5,355** | **5,605** |
| Durable goods | (X) | 2,374 | 2,281 | 2,797 | 2,772 | 2,713 | 2,814 |
| Wood products | 321 | 94 | 69 | 95 | 98 | 102 | 109 |
| Nonmetallic mineral products | 327 | 97 | 90 | 113 | 118 | 123 | 126 |
| Primary metals | 331 | 157 | 231 | 265 | 228 | 207 | 222 |
| Fabricated metals | 332 | 268 | 295 | 357 | 349 | 336 | 361 |
| Machinery | 333 | 292 | 316 | 404 | 378 | 348 | 369 |
| Computers and electronic products | 334 | 511 | 328 | 302 | 299 | 294 | 304 |
| Electrical equipment, appliances, and components | 335 | 125 | 110 | 126 | 125 | 124 | 128 |
| Transportation equipment | 336 | 640 | 636 | 912 | 949 | 949 | 959 |
| Furniture and related products | 337 | 75 | 60 | 70 | 74 | 75 | 76 |
| Miscellaneous products | 339 | 115 | 145 | 152 | 153 | 155 | 159 |
| Nondurable goods | (X) | 1,835 | 2,631 | 3,091 | 2,747 | 2,642 | 2,791 |
| Food products | 311 | 435 | 654 | 794 | 774 | 765 | 797 |
| Beverages and tobacco products | 312 | 112 | 130 | 147 | 155 | 155 | 148 |
| Textile mills | 313 | 52 | 30 | 31 | 29 | 28 | 29 |
| Textile product mills | 314 | 34 | 21 | 25 | 25 | 25 | 25 |
| Apparel | 315 | 60 | 13 | 11 | 11 | 11 | 11 |
| Leather and allied products | 316 | 10 | 5 | 5 | 5 | 5 | 5 |
| Paper products | 322 | 165 | 172 | 187 | 185 | 182 | 184 |
| Printing | 323 | 104 | 83 | 82 | 81 | 83 | 78 |
| Petroleum and coal products | 324 | 235 | 628 | 786 | 508 | 430 | 537 |
| Basic chemicals | 325 | 449 | 705 | 787 | 737 | 723 | 744 |
| Plastics and rubber products | 326 | 178 | 189 | 234 | 237 | 236 | 233 |
| **INVENTORIES** **(as of December 31)** | | | | | | | |
| **All manufacturing industries** | (X) | **470** | **538** | **623** | **619** | **615** | **643** |
| Durable goods | (X) | 298 | 313 | 378 | 381 | 370 | 386 |
| Wood products | 321 | 10 | 8 | 11 | 11 | 11 | 12 |
| Nonmetallic mineral products | 327 | 10 | 11 | 12 | 13 | 13 | 14 |
| Primary metals | 331 | 22 | 31 | 38 | 33 | 30 | 33 |
| Fabricated metals | 332 | 34 | 40 | 48 | 47 | 46 | 50 |
| Machinery | 333 | 49 | 52 | 66 | 64 | 61 | 65 |
| Computers and electronic products | 334 | 63 | 42 | 40 | 41 | 39 | 41 |
| Electrical equipment, appliances, and components | 335 | 15 | 14 | 16 | 16 | 16 | 17 |
| Transportation equipment | 336 | 69 | 90 | 119 | 128 | 122 | 124 |
| Furniture and related products | 337 | 8 | 6 | 7 | 7 | 7 | 8 |
| Miscellaneous products | 339 | 18 | 20 | 21 | 22 | 22 | 23 |
| Nondurable goods | (X) | 172 | 225 | 246 | 238 | 246 | 256 |
| Food products | 311 | 32 | 44 | 53 | 53 | 54 | 54 |
| Beverages and tobacco products | 312 | 14 | 18 | 21 | 23 | 24 | 24 |
| Textile mills | 313 | 6 | 3 | 3 | 3 | 3 | 3 |
| Textile product mills | 314 | 5 | 3 | 3 | 3 | 3 | 3 |
| Apparel | 315 | 9 | 2 | 2 | 2 | 2 | 2 |
| Leather and allied products | 316 | 2 | 1 | 1 | 1 | 1 | 1 |
| Paper products | 322 | 15 | 14 | 16 | 16 | 16 | 16 |
| Printing | 323 | 6 | 5 | 5 | 5 | 5 | 5 |
| Petroleum and coal products | 324 | 13 | 43 | 37 | 28 | 32 | 38 |
| Basic chemicals | 325 | 52 | 73 | 80 | 80 | 82 | 85 |
| Plastics and rubber products | 326 | 18 | 19 | 25 | 24 | 24 | 25 |
| **NEW ORDERS** | | | | | | | |
| **All manufacturing industries** | (X) | **4,161** | **4,896** | **5,926** | **5,439** | **5,293** | **5,579** |
| Durable goods | (X) | 2,327 | 2,265 | 2,835 | 2,692 | 2,651 | 2,788 |
| Wood products | 321 | 94 | (NA) | (NA) | (NA) | (NA) | (NA) |
| Nonmetallic mineral products | 327 | 97 | (NA) | (NA) | (NA) | (NA) | (NA) |
| Primary metals | 331 | 154 | 244 | 266 | 223 | 206 | 224 |
| Fabricated metals | 332 | 270 | 304 | 359 | 345 | 336 | 366 |
| Machinery | 333 | 295 | 334 | 403 | 370 | 349 | 375 |
| Computers and electronic products | 334 | 436 | 270 | 249 | 251 | 248 | 260 |
| Electrical equipment, appliances, and components | 335 | 126 | 110 | 128 | 124 | 124 | 129 |
| Transportation equipment | 336 | 663 | 638 | 1,001 | 935 | 932 | 963 |
| Furniture and related products | 337 | 75 | 60 | 69 | 75 | 75 | 76 |
| Miscellaneous products | 339 | 117 | (NA) | (NA) | (NA) | (NA) | (NA) |
| Nondurable goods | (X) | 1,835 | (NA) | (NA) | (NA) | (NA) | (NA) |

NA Not available. X Not applicable. [1] Based on the North American Industry Classification System, 2007; see text, this section and Section 15.

Source: U.S. Census Bureau, Manufacturers' Shipments, Inventories, and Orders, "Annual Benchmark Data and Benchmark Procedures," <http://www.census.gov/manufacturing/m3/index.html>, and "Historical Data," <http://www.census.gov /manufacturing/m3/historical_data/index.html>; accessed July 2018.

# Table 1053. Value of Manufacturers' Shipments, Inventories, and New Orders by Market Grouping: 2000 to 2018

[In billions of dollars (4,209 represents $4,209,000,000,000). Data are not seasonally adjusted. Based on the Manufacturers' Shipments, Inventories, and Orders (M3) survey. See source for details]

| Market grouping | 2000 | 2010 | 2013 | 2014 | 2015 | 2016 | 2017 | 2018 |
|---|---|---|---|---|---|---|---|---|
| **SHIPMENTS** | | | | | | | | |
| **All manufacturing industries** | **4,209** | **4,911** | **5,810** | **5,888** | **5,519** | **5,355** | **5,605** | **6,000** |
| Consumer goods | 1,501 | 2,059 | 2,496 | 2,508 | 2,256 | 2,184 | 2,331 | 2,528 |
| Consumer durable goods | 391 | 323 | 403 | 436 | 462 | 477 | 476 | 513 |
| Consumer nondurable goods | 1,109 | 1,735 | 2,093 | 2,072 | 1,795 | 1,708 | 1,855 | 2,015 |
| Aircraft and parts | 112 | 147 | 197 | 211 | 210 | 208 | 209 | 217 |
| Defense aircraft and parts | 25 | 63 | 59 | 58 | 55 | 50 | 53 | 55 |
| Nondefense aircraft and parts | 87 | 84 | 138 | 153 | 155 | 158 | 156 | 163 |
| Construction materials and supplies | 445 | 444 | 524 | 547 | 554 | 555 | 582 | 615 |
| Motor vehicles and parts | 471 | 401 | 546 | 600 | 638 | 647 | 652 | 707 |
| Computers and related products | 110 | 42 | 29 | 27 | 26 | 24 | 23 | 22 |
| Information technology industries | 400 | 270 | 271 | 263 | 258 | 255 | 270 | 294 |
| Nondefense capital goods | 808 | 728 | 892 | 906 | 878 | 833 | 870 | 928 |
| Excluding aircraft | 758 | 675 | 799 | 804 | 774 | 728 | 767 | 816 |
| Defense capital goods | 67 | 130 | 116 | 111 | 110 | 112 | 125 | 140 |
| **INVENTORIES** (as of December 31) | | | | | | | | |
| **All manufacturing industries** | **470** | **538** | **612** | **623** | **619** | **615** | **643** | **666** |
| Consumer goods | 128 | 169 | 187 | 181 | 179 | 185 | 193 | 194 |
| Consumer durable goods | 26 | 21 | 25 | 27 | 28 | 27 | 28 | 29 |
| Consumer nondurable goods | 102 | 148 | 162 | 155 | 152 | 158 | 165 | 165 |
| Aircraft and parts | 36 | 55 | 69 | 72 | 79 | 75 | 76 | 77 |
| Defense aircraft and parts | 9 | 12 | 12 | 12 | 12 | 11 | 13 | 13 |
| Nondefense aircraft and parts | 27 | 43 | 57 | 60 | 67 | 63 | 63 | 64 |
| Construction materials and supplies | 49 | 52 | 60 | 64 | 62 | 63 | 67 | 73 |
| Motor vehicles and parts | 22 | 22 | 30 | 33 | 34 | 33 | 34 | 36 |
| Computers and related products | 8 | 4 | 4 | 4 | 4 | 3 | 4 | 4 |
| Information technology industries | 51 | 36 | 37 | 35 | 36 | 35 | 37 | 38 |
| Nondefense capital goods | 127 | 135 | 159 | 166 | 172 | 163 | 168 | 176 |
| Excluding aircraft | 107 | 100 | 113 | 117 | 116 | 112 | 117 | 123 |
| Defense capital goods | 17 | 21 | 20 | 20 | 21 | 21 | 23 | 23 |
| **NEW ORDERS** | | | | | | | | |
| **All manufacturing industries** | **4,161** | **4,896** | **5,827** | **5,926** | **5,439** | **5,293** | **5,579** | **5,994** |
| Consumer goods | 1,502 | 2,059 | 2,496 | 2,508 | 2,256 | 2,185 | 2,331 | 2,528 |
| Consumer durable goods | 393 | 323 | 403 | 436 | 462 | 477 | 476 | 513 |
| Consumer nondurable goods | 1,109 | 1,735 | 2,093 | 2,072 | 1,795 | 1,708 | 1,855 | 2,015 |
| Aircraft and parts | 131 | 155 | 277 | 291 | 200 | 193 | 215 | 232 |
| Defense aircraft and parts | 31 | 63 | 54 | 56 | 51 | 55 | 54 | 64 |
| Nondefense aircraft and parts | 99 | 91 | 223 | 235 | 149 | 137 | 161 | 168 |
| Construction materials and supplies | 447 | 451 | 524 | 547 | 554 | 556 | 586 | 620 |
| Motor vehicles and parts | 468 | 403 | 546 | 605 | 639 | 648 | 654 | 708 |
| Computers and related products | 108 | 40 | 29 | 27 | 27 | 25 | 24 | 22 |
| Information technology industries | 410 | 273 | 256 | 257 | 255 | 257 | 272 | 297 |
| Nondefense capital goods | 831 | 748 | 970 | 977 | 858 | 810 | 883 | 935 |
| Excluding aircraft | 768 | 685 | 804 | 805 | 761 | 727 | 774 | 821 |
| Defense capital goods | 80 | 137 | 92 | 108 | 105 | 120 | 122 | 151 |

Source: U.S. Census Bureau, Manufacturers' Shipments, Inventories, and Orders, "Historical Data," <http://www.census.gov/manufacturing/m3/historical_data/index.html>, accessed June 2019.

# Table 1054. Finances and Profits of Manufacturing Corporations: 2005 to 2018

[In billions of dollars (5,411 represents $5,411,000,000,000). Data exclude estimates for corporations with less than $250,000 in assets at time of sample selection]

| Item | 2005 [1] | 2010 [2] | 2011 [2] | 2012 [3] | 2013 [3] | 2014 [3] | 2015 [3] | 2016 [3] | 2017 [4] | 2018 [4] |
|---|---|---|---|---|---|---|---|---|---|---|
| Net sales | 5,411 | 5,756 | 6,486 | 6,668 | 6,743 | 6,903 | 6,433 | 6,249 | 6,552 | 7,006 |
| Net operating profit | 359 | 420 | 479 | 508 | 497 | 538 | 516 | 502 | 530 | 579 |
| Net profit: | | | | | | | | | | |
| Before taxes | 524 | 584 | 722 | 676 | 722 | 745 | 612 | 649 | 681 | 735 |
| After taxes | 401 | 478 | 594 | 564 | 601 | 609 | 506 | 541 | 549 | 649 |
| Cash dividends | 179 | 180 | 184 | 212 | 242 | 259 | 275 | 276 | 290 | 316 |
| Net income retained in business | 222 | 298 | 410 | 353 | 359 | 350 | 231 | 265 | 259 | 334 |

[1] Based on the North American Industry Classification System, 2002. [2] Based on the North American Industry Classification System, 2007. [3] Based on the North American Industry Classification System, 2012. [4] Based on the North American Industry Classification System, 2017.

Source: U.S. Census Bureau, *Quarterly Financial Report for Manufacturing, Mining, Trade, and Selected Service Industries*. See also <http://www.census.gov/econ/qfr>.

## Table 1055. Manufacturing Corporations—Assets and Profits by Asset Size: 2000 to 2018

[In millions of dollars (4,852,106 represents $4,852,106,000,000). Corporations and assets as of end of 4th quarter; profits for entire year. Through 2000, based on Standard Industrial Classification code (SIC); beginning 2001, based on the North American Industry Classification System; see text, Section 15. For corporations above a certain asset value based on complete canvass. The asset value for complete canvass was raised in 1988 to $50 million and in 1995 to $250 million. Asset sizes less than these values are sampled, except as noted. For details regarding survey description, data analysis, and methodology, see source, 4th quarter report. Minus sign (-) indicates loss]

| Year | Total | Under $10 million [1] | $10 to $25 million | $25 to $50 million | $50 to $100 million | $100 to $250 million | $250 million to $1 billion | $1 billion and over |
|---|---|---|---|---|---|---|---|---|
| **Assets:** | | | | | | | | |
| 2000 | 4,852,106 | 171,666 | 85,482 | 72,122 | 90,866 | 149,714 | 389,537 | 3,892,720 |
| 2002 | 4,823,219 | 166,191 | 82,369 | 62,654 | 81,667 | 134,821 | 407,423 | 3,888,095 |
| 2003 | 5,162,852 | 161,462 | 80,681 | 62,592 | 77,205 | 126,826 | 392,192 | 4,261,894 |
| 2004 | 5,538,113 | 163,072 | 80,085 | 71,674 | 81,741 | 126,950 | 414,144 | 4,600,447 |
| 2005 | 5,828,716 | 165,195 | 85,785 | 68,731 | 87,818 | 142,900 | 423,917 | 4,854,370 |
| 2006 | 6,179,142 | 168,537 | 93,786 | 72,494 | 91,877 | 146,651 | 418,501 | 5,187,295 |
| 2007 | 6,891,131 | 180,319 | 98,348 | 80,400 | 93,017 | 144,254 | 433,634 | 5,861,160 |
| 2008 | 6,819,681 | 180,025 | 99,430 | 80,757 | 98,478 | 137,907 | 420,104 | 5,802,981 |
| 2009 | 6,942,972 | 166,590 | 106,773 | 71,642 | 76,308 | 126,202 | 413,856 | 5,981,600 |
| 2010 | 7,432,384 | 165,598 | 105,661 | 74,081 | 82,713 | 130,428 | 405,113 | 6,468,791 |
| 2011 | 7,907,376 | 169,045 | 114,818 | 76,809 | 86,452 | 130,488 | 435,889 | 6,893,876 |
| 2012 | 8,331,651 | 173,043 | 112,237 | 81,304 | 90,724 | 130,768 | 440,070 | 7,303,505 |
| 2013 | 8,838,478 | 173,571 | 116,199 | 88,598 | 86,532 | 138,222 | 439,357 | 7,795,999 |
| 2014 | 9,088,807 | 174,633 | 118,458 | 94,843 | 85,856 | 134,269 | 456,857 | 8,023,891 |
| 2015 | 9,632,509 | 174,895 | 121,807 | 88,342 | 90,246 | 153,601 | 446,889 | 8,556,729 |
| 2016 | 10,249,316 | 178,231 | 116,255 | 91,577 | 93,597 | 138,825 | 452,800 | 9,178,030 |
| 2017 | 10,820,109 | 172,717 | 127,152 | 93,230 | 95,998 | 149,252 | 425,288 | 9,756,472 |
| 2018 | 10,992,312 | 169,521 | 140,440 | 89,973 | 111,077 | 169,520 | 447,062 | 9,864,719 |
| **Net profit:** [2] | | | | | | | | |
| 2000 | 275,313 | 16,578 | 6,820 | 3,403 | 2,742 | 3,510 | 15,121 | 227,136 |
| 2002 | 134,686 | 10,003 | 2,784 | 807 | 1,699 | 3,356 | -1,227 | 117,262 |
| 2003 | 237,041 | 9,821 | 3,374 | 2,005 | 2,256 | 2,973 | 4,115 | 212,497 |
| 2004 | 348,151 | 14,970 | 5,745 | 3,858 | 3,080 | 5,140 | 12,787 | 302,571 |
| 2005 | 401,344 | 17,357 | 6,057 | 4,066 | 3,781 | 7,678 | 15,967 | 346,438 |
| 2006 | 470,282 | 22,301 | 8,685 | 5,260 | 4,601 | 8,901 | 21,405 | 399,131 |
| 2007 | 442,734 | 22,930 | 9,006 | 4,402 | 6,518 | 8,400 | 17,565 | 373,915 |
| 2008 | 266,346 | 18,182 | 7,472 | 5,820 | 3,739 | 3,403 | 2,239 | 225,492 |
| 2009 | 286,491 | 9,692 | 5,979 | 4,617 | 2,500 | 2,723 | 2,653 | 258,310 |
| 2010 | 477,884 | 16,637 | 7,670 | 4,181 | 5,880 | 5,390 | 19,494 | 417,121 |
| 2011 | 594,335 | 20,357 | 9,257 | 5,209 | 5,730 | 6,808 | 17,568 | 529,406 |
| 2012 | 564,191 | 23,042 | 11,500 | 6,452 | 6,727 | 5,820 | 19,727 | 490,924 |
| 2013 | 601,368 | 24,740 | 10,202 | 6,468 | 6,141 | 6,982 | 21,000 | 525,835 |
| 2014 | 608,722 | 26,754 | 12,012 | 5,782 | 5,841 | 6,676 | 18,976 | 532,680 |
| 2015 | 506,008 | 25,663 | 11,056 | 5,858 | 6,079 | 6,577 | 15,602 | 435,174 |
| 2016 | 541,206 | 24,819 | 10,870 | 6,664 | 6,674 | 6,363 | 21,020 | 464,797 |
| 2017 | 549,253 | 28,798 | 10,866 | 6,489 | 4,665 | 7,271 | 20,761 | 470,403 |
| 2018 | 649,659 | 29,896 | 14,203 | 4,750 | 2,502 | 7,665 | 18,933 | 571,710 |

[1] Excludes estimates for corporations with less than $250,000 in assets at time of sample selection. [2] After taxes.

Source: U.S. Census Bureau, *Quarterly Financial Report for Manufacturing, Mining, Trade, and Selected Service Industries*. See also <http://www.census.gov/econ/qfr>.

## Table 1056. Manufacturing Corporations—Selected Finances: 2000 to 2018

[In billions of dollars (4,548 represents $4,548,000,000,000). Data are not necessarily comparable from year to year due to changes in accounting procedures, industry classifications, sampling procedures, etc.; for details, see source. Through 2000 based on Standard Industrial Classification code; beginning 2001, based on North American Industry Classification System; see text, Section 15. Minus sign (-) indicates loss]

| Year | All manufacturing corporations | | | Durable goods | | | Nondurable goods | | |
|---|---|---|---|---|---|---|---|---|---|
| | Sales | Profits [1] Before taxes | After taxes | Sales | Profits [1] Before taxes | After taxes | Sales | Profits [1] Before taxes | After taxes |
| 2000 | 4,548 | 381 | 275 | 2,457 | 191 | 132 | 2,091 | 190 | 144 |
| 2001 [2] | 4,295 | 83 | 36 | 2,321 | -69 | -76 | 1,974 | 152 | 112 |
| 2002 | 4,217 | 196 | 135 | 2,261 | 45 | 21 | 1,955 | 149 | 113 |
| 2003 | 4,397 | 306 | 237 | 2,283 | 118 | 88 | 2,114 | 188 | 149 |
| 2004 | 4,934 | 447 | 348 | 2,537 | 200 | 157 | 2,397 | 248 | 192 |
| 2005 | 5,411 | 524 | 401 | 2,731 | 211 | 161 | 2,681 | 313 | 240 |
| 2006 | 5,783 | 605 | 470 | 2,910 | 249 | 193 | 2,873 | 356 | 278 |
| 2007 | 6,060 | 603 | 443 | 3,016 | 247 | 159 | 3,044 | 356 | 283 |
| 2008 | 6,374 | 388 | 266 | 2,970 | 98 | 43 | 3,405 | 290 | 223 |
| 2009 | 5,110 | 361 | 286 | 2,427 | 84 | 55 | 2,683 | 276 | 232 |
| 2010 | 5,756 | 584 | 478 | 2,708 | 287 | 232 | 3,048 | 297 | 245 |
| 2011 | 6,486 | 722 | 594 | 2,927 | 335 | 284 | 3,558 | 387 | 310 |
| 2012 | 6,668 | 676 | 564 | 3,102 | 303 | 260 | 3,567 | 373 | 304 |
| 2013 | 6,743 | 722 | 601 | 3,178 | 358 | 294 | 3,566 | 365 | 308 |
| 2014 | 6,903 | 745 | 609 | 3,342 | 378 | 308 | 3,561 | 367 | 301 |
| 2015 | 6,433 | 612 | 506 | 3,367 | 324 | 265 | 3,065 | 289 | 241 |
| 2016 | 6,249 | 649 | 541 | 3,320 | 333 | 273 | 2,929 | 316 | 268 |
| 2017 | 6,552 | 681 | 549 | 3,403 | 373 | 273 | 3,149 | 308 | 276 |
| 2018 | 7,006 | 735 | 650 | 3,639 | 403 | 359 | 3,367 | 332 | 290 |

[1] Beginning 1998, profits before and after income taxes reflect inclusion of minority stockholders' interest in net income before and after income taxes. [2] Beginning 2001, data reported based on the North American Industry Classification System.

Source: U.S. Census Bureau, *Quarterly Financial Report for Manufacturing, Mining, Trade, and Selected Service Industries*. See also <http://www.census.gov/econ/qfr>.

# Table 1057. Motor Vehicle Manufactures—Summary by Selected Industry: 2016

[50,494 represents $50,494,000,000. Based on the Annual Survey of Manufactures; see Appendix III]

| Industry | 2012 NAICS code [1] | All employees [2] | | | Production workers [2] | Value of product shipments [3] (mil. dol.) |
| | | Number | Payroll | | | |
| | | | Total (mil. dol.) | Payroll per employee (dol.) | | |
|---|---|---|---|---|---|---|
| **Motor vehicle manufacturing, total**.................... | **3361-3363** | **869,871** | **50,494** | **58,047** | **692,125** | **647,147** |
| Motor vehicle, total........................................ | 3361 | 197,666 | 14,770 | 74,723 | 170,775 | 344,359 |
| Automobile and light duty motor vehicle.................. | 33611 | 169,006 | 13,074 | 77,356 | 148,312 | 317,519 |
| Automobile............................................ | 336111 | 82,360 | 6,383 | 77,498 | 71,122 | 129,996 |
| Light truck and utility vehicle...................... | 336112 | 86,647 | 6,691 | 77,221 | 77,190 | 187,523 |
| Heavy duty truck........................................ | 33612 | 28,660 | 1,696 | 59,192 | 22,464 | 26,840 |
| Motor vehicle body and trailer............................... | 3362 | 132,327 | 6,317 | 47,736 | 104,992 | 41,975 |
| Motor vehicle body...................................... | 336211 | 47,875 | 2,260 | 47,211 | 36,098 | 14,565 |
| Truck trailer............................................ | 336212 | 28,961 | 1,324 | 45,725 | 24,126 | 9,262 |
| Motor home............................................ | 336213 | 10,501 | 550 | 52,347 | 8,228 | 4,660 |
| Travel trailer and camper............................. | 336214 | 44,990 | 2,183 | 48,513 | 36,540 | 13,488 |
| Motor vehicle parts........................................ | 3363 | 539,878 | 29,407 | 54,469 | 416,358 | 260,812 |
| Motor vehicle gasoline engine and engine parts.......... | 33631 | 54,664 | 3,779 | 69,140 | 43,942 | 33,879 |
| Motor vehicle electrical and electronic equipment........ | 33632 | 57,238 | 2,971 | 51,907 | 42,832 | 24,869 |
| Motor vehicle steering and suspension................... | 33633 | 36,039 | 1,900 | 52,716 | 26,172 | 14,732 |
| Motor vehicle brake system............................. | 33634 | 22,245 | 1,100 | 49,471 | 17,101 | 11,237 |
| Motor vehicle transmission and power train parts........ | 33635 | 66,848 | 4,317 | 64,576 | 51,444 | 37,902 |
| Motor vehicle seating and interior trim................... | 33636 | 68,074 | 3,085 | 45,323 | 51,922 | 32,795 |
| Motor vehicle metal stamping........................... | 33637 | 97,120 | 5,499 | 56,624 | 77,127 | 36,712 |
| Other motor vehicle parts.............................. | 33639 | 137,651 | 6,754 | 49,069 | 105,817 | 68,687 |

[1] North American Industry Classification System, 2012; see text, Section 15. [2] Includes all full-time and part-time employees on the payrolls of operating manufacturing establishments during any part of the pay period that included the 12th of the month specified on the report form. Included are employees on paid sick leave, paid holidays, and paid vacations; not included are proprietors and partners of unincorporated businesses. [3] Includes extensive and unmeasurable duplication from shipments between establishments in the same industry classification.

Source: U.S. Census Bureau, Annual Survey of Manufactures, "General Statistics: Statistics for Industry Groups and Industries: 2016 and 2015," <http://www.factfinder.census.gov/>, accessed July 2018.

# Table 1058. Motor Vehicle Manufactures—Employees, Payroll, and Shipments by Major Producing State: 2016

[14,770,141 represents $14,770,141,000. Industry based on the 2012 North American Industry Classification System (NAICS); see text, Section 15. See footnote 3, Table 1057 for information regarding shipments. Based on the Annual Survey of Manufactures; see Appendix III]

| State | Motor vehicle manufacturing (NAICS 3361) | | | Motor vehicle parts manufacturing (NAICS 3363) | | |
| | Employees | Payroll ($1,000) | Value of shipments ($1,000) | Employees | Payroll ($1,000) | Value of shipments ($1,000) |
|---|---|---|---|---|---|---|
| **United States [1]**................ | **197,666** | **14,770,141** | **344,360,096** | **539,878** | **29,406,642** | **260,812,268** |
| Alabama......................... | 11,221 | 930,298 | 29,538,857 | 27,427 | 1,266,510 | 16,777,419 |
| Arizona.......................... | 80 | 7,093 | (D) | 2,240 | 129,737 | 2,790,091 |
| Arkansas........................ | (4) | (D) | (D) | 4,858 | 214,338 | 1,742,582 |
| California....................... | 7,203 | 679,296 | 5,971,811 | 14,479 | 770,921 | 6,436,684 |
| Colorado........................ | 41 | 3,375 | (D) | 1,324 | 96,253 | 336,653 |
| Florida.......................... | 1,235 | 76,618 | 432,609 | 3,423 | 173,457 | 1,184,213 |
| Georgia......................... | (8) | (D) | (D) | 14,904 | 723,335 | 8,898,694 |
| Illinois.......................... | 9,860 | 647,386 | (D) | 30,189 | 1,440,266 | 10,489,757 |
| Indiana.......................... | 17,179 | 1,272,255 | 36,133,016 | 54,670 | 3,145,356 | 24,544,473 |
| Iowa............................ | 56 | 3,410 | 45,968 | 4,665 | 225,117 | 1,396,331 |
| Kentucky........................ | 24,050 | 1,784,246 | 32,012,789 | 33,993 | 1,691,990 | 16,397,671 |
| Maryland........................ | (3) | (D) | (D) | 625 | 48,253 | 292,905 |
| Massachusetts.................. | (3) | (D) | (D) | 989 | 58,016 | 438,633 |
| Michigan........................ | 36,707 | 2,830,551 | 66,265,067 | 112,573 | 6,695,090 | 54,312,932 |
| Minnesota....................... | (7) | (D) | (D) | 2,164 | 103,025 | 760,695 |
| Mississippi...................... | (9) | (D) | (D) | 5,166 | 244,611 | 2,540,537 |
| Missouri......................... | 13,662 | 1,106,336 | (D) | 11,642 | 539,784 | 4,813,210 |
| Nebraska........................ | (3) | (D) | 35,445 | 3,946 | 200,365 | 1,300,132 |
| New Hampshire.................. | (NA) | (NA) | (NA) | 1,699 | 71,783 | 395,470 |
| New Jersey...................... | 32 | 2,529 | (D) | 801 | 43,351 | 300,165 |
| New York........................ | 32 | 1,849 | 20,793 | 9,435 | 805,371 | 5,322,539 |
| North Carolina................... | (8) | (D) | (D) | 17,247 | 893,800 | 9,605,501 |
| North Dakota.................... | (4) | (D) | (D) | 821 | 40,724 | 200,471 |
| Ohio............................ | 21,361 | 1,539,530 | 43,240,528 | 69,830 | 4,162,332 | 33,863,209 |
| Oregon.......................... | (6) | (D) | (D) | 1,400 | 71,024 | 421,552 |
| Pennsylvania.................... | (7) | (D) | (D) | 8,240 | 363,153 | 3,311,449 |
| South Carolina.................. | (9) | (D) | (D) | 14,315 | 839,611 | 9,042,030 |
| South Dakota.................... | (5) | (D) | (D) | 775 | 35,025 | 222,918 |
| Tennessee....................... | 8,348 | 640,678 | 15,815,996 | 40,142 | 2,063,339 | 21,614,749 |
| Texas........................... | 8,415 | 675,798 | 28,401,053 | 15,282 | 744,214 | 7,799,885 |
| Utah............................ | (2) | (D) | (D) | 3,995 | 174,184 | 2,141,784 |
| Virginia......................... | (7) | (D) | (D) | 5,094 | 243,350 | 1,494,564 |
| Washington...................... | (5) | (D) | (D) | 2,588 | 122,846 | 924,603 |
| West Virginia.................... | (4) | (D) | (D) | 2,859 | 155,844 | 3,076,616 |
| Wisconsin....................... | (8) | (D) | (D) | 9,644 | 463,819 | 3,520,006 |

D Withheld to avoid disclosing data on individual companies. [1] Includes states not shown separately. [2] Employee class size of 0 to 19. [3] Employee class size of 20 to 99. [4] Employee class size of 100 to 249. [5] Employee class size of 250 to 499. [6] Employee class size of 500 to 999. [7] Employee class size of 1,000 to 2,499. [8] Employee class size of 2,500 to 4,999. [9] Employee class size of 5,000 to 9,999.

Source: U.S. Census Bureau, Annual Survey of Manufactures, "Geographic Area Statistics: Statistics for All Manufacturing by State: 2016 and 2015," December 2017, <http://factfinder.census.gov/>, accessed July 2018.

## Table 1059. General Aviation Airplane Shipments and Billings: 1990 to 2018

[2,008 represents $2,008,000,000. Data are for U.S. manufactured airplanes. Totals may not add up due to rounding]

| Type of airplane | 1990 | 2000 | 2010 | 2014 | 2015 | 2016 | 2017 | 2018 |
|---|---|---|---|---|---|---|---|---|
| **Airplane units shipped (number)** | **1,144** | **2,816** | **1,334** | **1,631** | **1,592** | **1,531** | **1,599** | **1,746** |
| Total piston | 695 | 1,913 | 746 | 788 | 783 | 718 | 786 | 829 |
| Single-engine | 608 | 1,810 | 679 | 716 | 740 | 685 | 745 | 771 |
| Multi-engine | 87 | 103 | 67 | 72 | 43 | 33 | 41 | 58 |
| Total turbine | 449 | 903 | 588 | 843 | 809 | 813 | 813 | 917 |
| Turboprop | 281 | 315 | 224 | 468 | 420 | 411 | 409 | 444 |
| Business jet | 168 | 588 | 364 | 375 | 389 | 402 | 404 | 473 |
| **Factory net billings (mil. dol.)** | **2,008** | **8,558** | **7,875** | **11,688** | **11,982** | **11,560** | **10,641** | **11,598** |
| Total piston | 92 | 446 | 368 | 484 | 477 | 511 | 557 | 691 |
| Single-engine | 68 | (NA) | (NA) | (NA) | (NA) | (NA) | (NA) | (NA) |
| Multi-engine | 24 | (NA) | (NA) | (NA) | (NA) | (NA) | (NA) | (NA) |
| Total turbine | 1,916 | 8,112 | 7,506 | 11,204 | 11,506 | 11,049 | 10,085 | 10,907 |
| Turboprop | 644 | 934 | 724 | 1,316 | 1,282 | 1,180 | 1,032 | 1,151 |
| Business jet | 1,272 | 7,178 | 6,782 | 9,888 | 10,224 | 9,869 | 9,053 | 9,756 |

NA Not available.

Source: General Aviation Manufacturers Association, *2018 Annual Report* ©, 2019, and earlier reports. See also <www.gama.aero>.

## Table 1060. Pharmaceutical Preparations—Value of Shipments: 2010 to 2016

[In millions of dollars (117,282 represents $117,282,000,000). Data are from the Annual Survey of Manufactures (ASM) and based on the North American Industry Classification System (NAICS). The ASM is conducted annually, except for years ending in 2 and 7, at which time ASM data are included in the manufacturing sector of the Economic Census]

| Product description | Product code | 2010 | 2011 | 2012 | 2013 | 2014 | 2015 | 2016 |
|---|---|---|---|---|---|---|---|---|
| Pharmaceutical preparations | 325412 | 117,282 | 128,060 | 115,776 | 120,032 | 137,663 | 146,661 | 151,059 |
| Affecting neoplasms, endocrine system, and metabolic disease | 3254121 | 27,335 | 28,181 | 24,432 | 27,019 | 26,101 | 25,888 | 27,429 |
| Acting on the central nervous system and sense organs | 3254124 | 27,102 | 28,500 | 24,154 | 25,334 | 27,966 | 30,889 | 33,614 |
| Acting on the cardiovascular system | 3254127 | 10,537 | 11,205 | 7,796 | 12,317 | 13,807 | 13,492 | 15,798 |
| Acting on the respiratory system | 325412A | 14,237 | 20,525 | 19,241 | 13,108 | 13,705 | 13,751 | 12,464 |
| Acting on the digestive system or genito-urinary system | 325412D | 8,633 | 8,197 | 7,500 | 4,581 | 5,286 | 5,318 | 4,786 |
| Acting on the skin | 325412G | 4,160 | 3,601 | 2,986 | 2,624 | 2,771 | 4,531 | 4,343 |
| Vitamin, nutrient, and hematinic preparations | 325412L | 8,669 | 9,796 | 9,298 | 8,103 | 10,665 | 10,995 | 11,958 |
| Affecting parasitic and infective diseases (excl. diagnostic) | 325412P | 8,464 | 8,978 | 8,355 | 15,634 | 28,032 | 33,215 | 30,451 |
| Preparations for veterinary use (excl. diagnostic) [1] | 325412T | 2,698 | 2,883 | 2,920 | 2,411 | 2,328 | 1,582 | 1,540 |
| In vivo diagnostic substances | 325412V | 1,951 | 2,309 | 2,692 | 2,504 | 1,259 | 1,318 | 2,018 |
| Other pharmaceutical preparation manufacturing [2] | 325412W | 3,494 | 3,885 | 6,402 | 6,397 | 5,744 | 5,682 | 6,659 |
| In-vitro diagnostic substances manufacturing | 325413 | 11,133 | 11,468 | 11,580 | 11,978 | 11,180 | 11,742 | 11,884 |
| Biological product (excl. diagnostic) manufacturing | 325414 | 23,793 | 23,372 | 23,959 | 23,987 | 23,075 | 26,729 | 27,776 |
| Blood and blood derivatives, for human use | 3254141 | 2,664 | 2,785 | 6,238 | 6,746 | 5,297 | 5,093 | 5,403 |
| Vaccines, toxoids, and antigens, excluding allergens, for human use | 3254144 | 9,114 | 7,245 | 6,344 | 6,355 | 6,987 | 8,114 | 8,484 |
| Other biologics (excl. diagnostic) for human use | 3254147 | 7,576 | 8,799 | 6,619 | 5,785 | 5,573 | 6,336 | 6,375 |
| Biological products (excl. diagnostic) for veterinary, industrial, and all other miscellaneous uses | 325414A | 4,063 | 3,912 | 4,326 | 4,599 | 4,672 | 6,546 | 6,881 |
| Biological product (excl. diagnostic) manufacturing, total [2] | 325414W | 376 | 631 | 433 | 501 | 546 | 640 | 633 |

[1] Including medicinal premixes and medicated pet care products; excluding pet flea and tick products. [2] Not specified by kind.

Source: U.S. Census Bureau, Annual Survey of Manufactures, "Value of Products Shipments: Value of Shipments for Product Classes: 2016 and 2015," <http://factfinder.census.gov>, accessed April 2018, and earlier releases.

## Table 1061. Household Appliances Manufacturing—Value of Shipments: 2010 to 2016

[In millions of dollars (3,676 represents $3,676,000,000). Data are from the Annual Survey of Manufacturers (ASM) and are based on the North American Industry Classification System (NAICS). The ASM is conducted annually, except for years ending in 2 and 7, at which time ASM data are included in the manufacturing sector of the Economic Census]

| Product description | Product code | 2010 | 2011 | 2012 | 2013 | 2014 | 2015 | 2016 |
|---|---|---|---|---|---|---|---|---|
| Household cooking appliance manufacturing | 335221 | 3,676 | 3,729 | 4,369 | 4,419 | 4,472 | 4,768 | 4,865 |
| Electric household ranges, ovens, and surface cooking units & equipment | 3352211 | 1,839 | 1,836 | 2,494 | 2,376 | 2,452 | 2,618 | 2,601 |
| Gas household ranges, ovens, and surface cooking units & equipment | 3352213 | 1,131 | 1,168 | 1,156 | 1,223 | 975 | 1,039 | 1,111 |
| Other household ranges and cooking equipment | 3352215 | 698 | 719 | 700 | 801 | 1,012 | 1,069 | 1,121 |
| Other household cooking appliance manufacturing | 335221W | 7 | 6 | 18 | 19 | 33 | 41 | 32 |
| Household refrigerator and home freezer manufacturing | 335222 | 3,495 | 3,530 | 3,497 | 3,364 | 3,824 | 4,095 | 4,451 |
| Household refrigerators (incl. combination refrigerator-freezers) | 3352221 | (D) | 2,884 | 2,966 | 2,931 | (D) | 3,751 | (D) |
| Household laundry equipment manufacturing | 335224 | 3,491 | 3,531 | 3,553 | 3,529 | 3,497 | 3,526 | 3,845 |
| Other major household appliance manufacturing | 335228 | 3,729 | 3,902 | 4,385 | 4,318 | 4,610 | 4,882 | 4,854 |
| Household water heaters, electric, for permanent installation | 3352281 | 611 | 671 | 957 | 815 | 898 | 861 | 1,116 |
| Household water heaters, except electric | 3352283 | 964 | 1,064 | 1,251 | 1,144 | 1,253 | 1,433 | 1,293 |
| All other misc. household appliances (including parts) | 3352285 | 2,139 | 2,152 | 2,161 | 2,317 | 2,437 | 2,587 | 2,445 |
| Other major household appliance manufacturing [1] | 335228W | 15 | 15 | 16 | 42 | 22 | – | – |

D Data withheld to avoid disclosing data of individual companies. – Rounds to zero. [1] Not specified by kind.

Source: U.S. Census Bureau, Annual Survey of Manufactures, "Value of Products Shipments: Value of Shipments for Product Classes: 2016 and 2015," <http://factfinder.census.gov>, accessed April 2018, and earlier releases.

# Table 1062. Communications Equipment Manufacturing—Value of Shipments: 2010 to 2016

[In millions of dollars (8,793 represents $8,793,000,000). Data are from the Annual Survey of Manufacturers (ASM) and are based on the North American Industry Classification System (NAICS). The ASM is conducted annually, except for years ending in 2 and 7, at which time ASM data are included in the manufacturing sector of the Economic Census]

| Product description | Product code | 2010 | 2011 | 2012 | 2013 | 2014 | 2015 | 2016 |
|---|---|---|---|---|---|---|---|---|
| Telephone apparatus manufacturing................................ | 334210 | 8,793 | 8,590 | 7,171 | 7,539 | 6,535 | 6,384 | 5,722 |
| Telephone switching and switchboard equipment............. | 3342101 | 1,366 | 1,161 | 654 | 1,368 | 1,333 | 1,355 | 1,207 |
| Carrier line equipment and non-consumer modems........... | 3342104 | 2,521 | 2,802 | 2,310 | 1,728 | 1,860 | 1,966 | 2,062 |
| Wireline voice and data network equipment.................... | 3342107 | 4,179 | 3,889 | 3,348 | 3,621 | 2,530 | 2,293 | 1,738 |
| Other telephone apparatus manufacturing..................... | 334210W | 728 | 739 | 859 | 822 | 812 | 771 | 715 |
| Radio and television broadcast and wireless communications equipment.......................... | 334220 | 27,592 | 27,161 | 26,345 | 26,379 | 23,066 | 22,565 | 22,316 |
| Broadcast, studio, and related electronic equipment........... | 3342202 | 3,484 | 3,205 | 2,335 | 2,025 | 1,923 | 2,028 | 1,892 |
| Wireless networking equipment.................................. | 3342203 | 2,224 | 1,728 | 2,093 | 2,262 | 1,528 | 1,430 | 2,304 |
| Radio station equipment......................................... | 3342205 | 12,210 | 11,309 | 9,761 | 9,936 | 9,140 | 8,729 | 8,721 |
| Other communications systems and equipment............... | 3342209 | 8,556 | 9,545 | 10,571 | 10,582 | 9,142 | 9,094 | 8,170 |
| Other radio and television broadcast and wireless communications equipment......................... | 334220W | (S) | (S) | 1,586 | 1,574 | 1,334 | 1,283 | 1,229 |
| Other communications equipment manufacturing............... | 334290 | 4,871 | 5,008 | 4,663 | 4,909 | 4,923 | 3,922 | 3,496 |
| Alarm systems (incl. electric sirens and horns)............... | 3342901 | 1,394 | 1,561 | 2,015 | 2,177 | 1,951 | 1,606 | 1,516 |
| Vehicular and pedestrian traffic control equipment............ | 3342902 | 2,585 | 2,543 | 1,595 | 1,739 | 1,995 | 1,522 | 1,242 |
| Intercommunications systems (incl. inductive paging systems)....................................................... | 3342903 | 358 | 342 | 562 | 465 | 450 | 321 | 337 |
| Other communications equipment [2].......................... | 334290W | 534 | 563 | 491 | 528 | 527 | 473 | 401 |
| External modems, consumer..................................... | 3344184 | 637 | 597 | 232 | 260 | 180 | [1] 112 | 97 |

S Estimates do not meet publication standards. [1] Sampling error exceeds 40 percent. [2] Not specified by kind.

Source: U.S. Census Bureau, Annual Survey of Manufactures, "Value of Products Shipments: Value of Shipments for Product Classes: 2016 and 2015," <https://factfinder.census.gov>, accessed April 2018, and earlier releases.

# Table 1063. Computers and Peripheral Equipment Manufacturing—Value of Shipments: 2010 to 2016

[In millions of dollars (17,731 represents $17,731,000,000). Data are from the Annual Survey of Manufacturers (ASM) and are based on the North American Industry Classification System (NAICS). The ASM is conducted annually, except for years ending in 2 and 7, at which time ASM data are included in the manufacturing sector of the Economic Census]

| Product description | Product code | 2010 | 2012 | 2013 | 2014 | 2015 | 2016 |
|---|---|---|---|---|---|---|---|
| Electronic computers manufacturing................................. | 334111 | 17,731 | 8,116 | 7,878 | 8,918 | 9,172 | 8,951 |
| Host computers, multiusers (mainframes, servers, etc.)........... | 3341111 | 12,443 | 4,769 | 4,559 | 5,464 | 5,724 | 5,372 |
| Single user computers, microprocessor-based................... | 3341117 | 4,584 | 2,550 | 2,534 | 2,531 | 2,557 | 2,678 |
| Other computers (array, analog, hybrid, and special-use computers)........ | 334111D | 426 | 456 | 446 | 517 | 380 | 389 |
| Other electronic computer [2]................................... | 334111W | [1] 278 | 341 | 340 | 407 | 511 | 511 |
| Computer storage devices manufacturing......................... | 334112 | 8,425 | 8,619 | 9,072 | 8,138 | 7,441 | 6,631 |
| Computer storage devices [3].................................... | 3341121 | 7,697 | 6,948 | 7,092 | 6,359 | 5,962 | 5,258 |
| Parts, attachments, and accessories for computer storage devices.......... | 3341124 | 649 | 1,616 | 1,920 | 1,699 | 1,417 | 1,302 |
| Other computer storage device manufacturing [2].............. | 334112W | 79 | 56 | 60 | 80 | 63 | 71 |
| Computer terminal and other computer peripheral equipment manufacturing.................................................. | 334118 | (NA) | 10,634 | 10,691 | 8,974 | 8,350 | 7,180 |
| Computer terminals (excluding point-of-sale and funds-transfer devices, parts, attachments, and accessories)............... | 3341181 | (NA) | 353 | 514 | 579 | 664 | 556 |
| Parts, attachments, and accessories for computer terminals (excluding point-of-sale and funds-transfer devices)............ | 3341182 | (NA) | 20 | 22 | 70 | 96 | 127 |
| All other miscellaneous computer peripheral (input/output) equipment [3]..... | 3341183 | (NA) | 7,041 | 6,232 | 4,721 | 3,992 | 3,452 |
| Parts, subassemblies, and accessories for computer peripheral equipment [3]................................... | 3341184 | (NA) | 1,445 | 2,287 | 2,412 | 2,417 | 1,855 |
| Point-of-sale terminals and fund-transfer devices................ | 3341185 | (NA) | 906 | 855 | 592 | 568 | 541 |
| Parts and attachments for point-of-sale terminals and fund-transfer devices........................................... | 3341186 | (NA) | 284 | 135 | 97 | 80 | 82 |
| Other computer terminal and other computer peripheral equipment [2]........ | 334118W | (NA) | 585 | 645 | 503 | 534 | 567 |
| Magnetic and optical recording media........................... | 334613 | 532 | 321 | [1] 233 | 452 | 446 | 345 |
| Software and other prerecorded compact disc, tape, and record reproducing.................................................. | 334614 | (NA) | 2,670 | 2,525 | 2,291 | 2,301 | 2,144 |
| Software reproducing............................................ | 3346141 | (NA) | 684 | 649 | 648 | 613 | 665 |
| Reproduction of recording media................................ | 3346142 | (NA) | 1,904 | 1,749 | 1,554 | 1,596 | 1,364 |

NA Not available. [1] Sampling error exceeds 40 percent. [2] Not specified by kind. [3] Excluding parts, attachments, digital cameras, accessories, etc.

Source: U.S. Census Bureau, Annual Survey of Manufactures, "Value of Products Shipments: Value of Shipments for Product Classes: 2016 and 2015," <http://factfinder.census.gov>, accessed April 2018, and earlier releases.

## Table 1064. Semiconductors, Electronic Components, and Other Electronic Component Manufacturing Equipment—Value of Shipments: 2010 to 2016

[In millions of dollars (9,083 represents $9,083,000,000). Data are from the Annual Survey of Manufacturers (ASM) and are based on the North American Industry Classification System (NAICS). The ASM is conducted annually, except for years ending in 2 and 7, at which time ASM data are included in the manufacturing sector of the Economic Census]

| Product description | Product code | 2010 | 2012 | 2013 | 2014 | 2015 | 2016 |
|---|---|---|---|---|---|---|---|
| Semiconductor machinery manufacturing | 333242 | (NA) | 9,765 | 8,795 | 6,970 | 5,816 | 5,412 |
| Semiconductor machinery manufacturing | 333295 | 9,083 | (NA) | (NA) | (NA) | (NA) | (NA) |
| Electron tube manufacturing | 334411 | 1,287 | (NA) | (NA) | (NA) | (NA) | (NA) |
| Bare printed circuit board manufacturing | 334412 | 4,977 | 4,773 | 4,449 | 4,121 | 4,166 | 3,867 |
| Semiconductors and related device manufacturing | 334413 | 58,474 | 47,211 | 43,411 | 45,443 | 45,810 | 45,730 |
| Integrated circuit packages | 3344131 | 39,784 | 33,611 | 29,360 | 31,073 | 30,693 | 32,017 |
| Transistors | 3344134 | 637 | 542 | 539 | 285 | 317 | 422 |
| Diodes and rectifiers | 3344137 | 398 | 286 | 215 | 243 | 291 | 316 |
| Other semiconductor devices (incl. chips, wafers, & heat sinks) | 334413A | 14,875 | 10,524 | 11,316 | 12,517 | 13,077 | 11,582 |
| Other semiconductor and related device [1] | 334413W | 2,780 | 2,249 | 1,981 | 1,325 | 1,431 | 1,392 |
| Electronic capacitor manufacturing | 334414 | 916 | (NA) | (NA) | (NA) | (NA) | (NA) |
| Electronic resistor manufacturing | 334415 | 563 | (NA) | (NA) | (NA) | (NA) | (NA) |
| Capacitor, resistor, coil, transformer, and other inductor manufacturing | 334416 | 1,743 | 3,522 | 3,323 | 3,343 | 3,458 | 3,433 |
| Capacitors for electronic circuitry | 3344161 | (NA) | 1,025 | 916 | 946 | 1,160 | 1,174 |
| Resistors for electronic circuitry | 3344162 | (NA) | 433 | 382 | 402 | 340 | 279 |
| Electronic coils, transformers, and other inductors | 3344163 | (NA) | 1,977 | 1,936 | 1,889 | 1,847 | 1,882 |
| Other capacitor, resistor, coil, transformer, & other inductor [1] | 334416W | (NA) | 86 | 90 | 106 | 112 | 98 |
| Electronic connector manufacturing | 334417 | 4,639 | 5,393 | 5,488 | 5,157 | 5,536 | 5,432 |
| Printed circuit assembly, electronic assembly manufacturing | 334418 | 18,497 | 16,383 | 16,947 | 15,820 | 16,912 | 15,688 |
| External modems, consumer | 3344184 | 637 | 232 | 260 | 180 | [2] 112 | 97 |
| Printed circuit assemblies, loaded boards and modules | 334418B | 16,673 | 15,134 | 15,757 | 14,776 | 15,852 | 14,631 |
| Other printed circuit assembly, electronic assembly | 334418W | 1,188 | 1,017 | 930 | 864 | 948 | 960 |
| Other electronic component manufacturing | 334419 | 9,072 | 10,717 | 10,684 | 11,340 | 11,648 | 10,435 |
| Crystals, filters, piezoelectric, & other related electronic devices | 3344191 | 879 | 992 | 937 | 880 | 932 | 703 |
| Electron tubes and parts, excluding glass blanks | 3344192 | (NA) | 1,154 | 927 | 952 | 905 | 774 |
| Transducers, incl. electrical-electronic input/output transducers | 3344194 | 1,177 | 626 | 789 | 943 | 904 | 710 |
| Switches, mechanical, for electronic circuitry | 3344197 | 1,121 | 981 | 973 | 997 | 993 | 934 |
| Microwave components and devices (excl. antennae, tubes, etc.) | 334419A | 1,248 | 1,807 | 1,684 | 1,707 | 1,663 | 1,605 |
| All other miscellaneous electronic components | 334419E | 3,856 | 4,212 | 4,508 | 4,840 | 5,182 | 4,729 |
| Other electronic component manufacturing [1] | 334419W | 791 | 946 | 866 | 1,022 | 1,069 | 980 |

NA Not available. [1] Not specified by kind. [2] Sampling error exceeds 40 percent.

Source: U.S. Census Bureau, Annual Survey of Manufactures, "Value of Products Shipments: Value of Shipments for Product Classes: 2016 and 2015," <http://factfinder.census.gov>, accessed April 2018, and earlier releases.

## Table 1065. Beverage Manufacturing Industry—Brewery, Distillery, and Winery Establishments and Employment: 2008 to 2017

[Beverage manufacturer data are from the Quarterly Census of Employment and Wages (QCEW)]

| Industry characteristic | 2008 | 2009 | 2010 | 2011 | 2012 | 2013 | 2014 | 2015 | 2016 | 2017 |
|---|---|---|---|---|---|---|---|---|---|---|
| **Establishments (number):** | | | | | | | | | | |
| Breweries | 454 | 482 | 527 | 638 | 843 | 1,167 | 1,616 | 2,190 | 2,843 | 3,509 |
| Wineries | 2,311 | 2,456 | 2,616 | 2,771 | 2,978 | 3,201 | 3,560 | 3,848 | 4,083 | 4,343 |
| Distilleries | 117 | 132 | 145 | 184 | 243 | 306 | 424 | 558 | 675 | 805 |
| Soft drink and ice manufacturing | 1,886 | 1,854 | 1,845 | 1,808 | 1,802 | 1,830 | 1,864 | 1,858 | 1,969 | 2,053 |
| **Employment (number):** | | | | | | | | | | |
| Breweries | 26,380 | 25,058 | 24,864 | 26,707 | 29,309 | 34,519 | 40,101 | 48,401 | 58,580 | 68,148 |
| Wineries | 40,160 | 40,100 | 40,830 | 42,231 | 45,351 | 48,386 | 52,879 | 57,003 | 60,436 | 64,212 |
| Distilleries | 7,107 | 7,189 | 7,252 | 7,625 | 8,001 | 8,872 | 10,579 | 11,075 | 12,207 | 13,759 |
| Soft drink and ice manufacturing | 101,254 | 96,018 | 94,225 | 92,889 | 94,576 | 93,854 | 93,333 | 94,334 | 102,793 | 104,743 |
| **Average weekly wages (in dollars):** | | | | | | | | | | |
| Breweries | 2,025 | 1,401 | 1,321 | 1,266 | 1,226 | 1,140 | 1,129 | 1,163 | 969 | 906 |
| Wineries | 778 | 770 | 773 | 792 | 808 | 789 | 803 | 833 | 846 | 861 |
| Distilleries | 1,328 | 1,311 | 1,352 | 1,417 | 1,550 | 1,430 | 1,415 | 1,462 | 1,362 | 1,300 |
| Soft drink and ice manufacturing | 876 | 884 | 938 | 962 | 955 | 952 | 980 | 1,020 | 1,028 | 1,044 |

Source: U.S. Bureau of Labor Statistics, Quarterly Census of Employment and Wages, QCEW Databases, "State and County Wages," <http://www.bls.gov/cew/home.htm>, accessed April 2019; and Spotlight on Statistics, "Industry on Tap: Breweries," <https://www.bls.gov/spotlight/2017/industry-on-tap-breweries/home.htm>, accessed September 2018.

# Wholesale and Retail Trade

This section presents statistics relating to the distributive trades, specifically wholesale trade and retail trade. Data shown for the trades are classified by kind of business and cover sales, establishments, employees, payrolls, and other items. The principal sources of these data are from the U.S. Census Bureau and include the *2007* and *2012 Economic Censuses*, annual and monthly surveys, and the *County Business Patterns* program. These data are supplemented by several tables from trade associations, such as the National Automobile Dealers Association.

Data on wholesale and retail trade also appear in several other sections. For instance, labor force employment and earnings data appear in Section 12, Labor Force, Employment, and Earnings; gross domestic product of the industry (Table 699) appears in Section 13, Income, Expenditures, Poverty, and Wealth; and financial data (several tables) from the quarterly *Statistics of Income Bulletin*, published by the Internal Revenue Service, appear in Section 15, Business Enterprise.

**Censuses**—Censuses of wholesale trade and retail trade have been taken at various intervals since 1929. Beginning with the *1967 Economic Census*, legislation provides for a census to be conducted every 5 years (for years ending in "2" and "7"). The industries covered in the censuses and surveys of business are defined in the North American Industry Classification System (NAICS). Retail trade refers to places of business primarily engaged in retailing merchandise to the general public; and wholesale trade, to establishments primarily engaged in selling goods to other businesses and normally operating from a warehouse or office that have little or no display of merchandise. Census Bureau tables in this section primarily utilize the 2012 or 2017 NAICS codes. NAICS codes are reviewed every 5 years to identify areas for revision, so that the classification system can keep pace with the changing economy. For information on this system and how it affects the comparability of wholesale and retail statistics historically, see text, Section 15, Business Enterprise, and especially the Census Bureau Web site at <http://www.census.gov/eos/www/naics>.

The *2007* and *2012 Economic Censuses* have three series of publications for these two sectors: 1) subject series with reports such as product lines and establishment and firm sizes, 2) geographic reports with individual reports for each state, and 3) industry series with individual reports for industry groups. Release of data from the *2012 Economic Census* was completed in 2016. Data from the *2017 Economic Census* will be released on a flow basis between September 2019 and December 2021. For information on these series, see the Census Bureau Web site at <https://www.census.gov/programs-surveys/economic-census.html>.

**Current surveys**—Current sample surveys conducted by the Census Bureau cover various aspects of wholesale and retail trade. Its *Monthly Retail Trade and Food Services* release at <http://www.census.gov/retail/index.html> contains monthly estimates of sales, inventories, and inventory/sales ratios for the United States, by kind of business. Annual figures on retail sales, year-end inventories, purchases, accounts receivable, and gross margins by kind of business are located on the Census Bureau Web site at <https://www.census.gov/programs-surveys/arts.html>.

Statistics from the Census Bureau's monthly wholesale trade survey include national estimates of sales, inventories, and inventory/sales ratios for merchant wholesalers excluding manufacturers' sales branches and offices. Data are presented by major summary groups "durable and nondurable," and 4-digit NAICS industry groups. Merchant wholesalers excluding manufacturers' sales branches and offices are those wholesalers who take title to the goods they sell (e.g., jobbers, exporters, importers, industrial distributors). These data, based on reports submitted by a sample of firms, appear in the *Monthly Wholesale Trade Report*. This report, along with monthly sales, inventories, and inventories/sales ratios, also provides data on annual sales, inventories, and year-end inventories/sales ratios. The *Annual Wholesale Trade Survey* provides data on merchant wholesalers excluding manufacturer sales branches and offices as well as summary data for all merchant wholesalers. This report also provides separate data for manufacturer sales branches and offices, and electronic markets, agents, brokers, and commission merchants. Included in the *Annual Wholesale Trade Report* are data on annual sales, year-end inventories, inventories/sales ratios, operating expenses, purchases, and gross margins. Data are presented by major summary groups "durable and nondurable" and 4-digit NAICS industry groups. These reports are available on the Census Bureau Web site at <https://www.census.gov/econ/wholesale.html>.

**E-commerce**—Electronic commerce (or e-commerce) is the sale of goods and services over the internet and extranet, electronic data interchange (EDI) network, electronic mail, or other online systems. Payment may or may not be made online. E-commerce data are collected in four separate Census Bureau surveys. These surveys use different measures of economic activity such as shipments for manufacturing, sales for wholesale and retail trade, and revenues for service industries. Data can be found at <http://www.census.gov/programs-surveys/e-stats.html>. Consequently, measures of total economic and e-commerce activity vary by economic sector, are conceptually and definitionally different, and therefore, are not additive. This edition has several tables on e-commerce sales, such as Tables 1069, 1079, and 1080 in this section; and Table 1306 in Section 27, Accommodation, Food Services, and Other Services.

**Statistical reliability**—For a discussion of statistical collection and estimation, sampling procedures, and measures of statistical reliability applicable to Census Bureau data, see Appendix III.

## Table 1066. Wholesale and Retail Trade—Establishments, Sales, Payroll, and Employees: 2007 and 2012

[435 represents 435,000. Covers establishments with payroll. Based on data from the Economic Census; see Appendix III]

| Kind of business | 2007 NAICS code [1] | Establishments (1,000) | | Sales (bil. dol.) | | Annual payroll (bil. dol.) | | Paid employees (1,000) | |
|---|---|---|---|---|---|---|---|---|---|
| | | 2007 | 2012 | 2007 | 2012 | 2007 | 2012 | 2007 | 2012 |
| **Wholesale trade**................................. | **42** | **435** | **419** | **6,516** | **7,900** | **336** | **362** | **6,227** | **5,882** |
| Wholesale trade, durable goods..................... | 423 | 255 | 245 | 2,898 | 3,152 | 207 | 217 | 3,619 | 3,355 |
| Wholesale trade, nondurable goods................. | 424 | 135 | 131 | 2,991 | 4,108 | 116 | 132 | 2,320 | 2,244 |
| Wholesale electronic markets and agents and brokers......................... | 425 | 45 | 43 | 627 | 639 | 13 | 14 | 289 | 283 |
| **Retail trade**........................................ | **44–45** | **1,128** | **1,062** | **3,918** | **4,220** | **363** | **369** | **15,515** | **14,704** |
| Motor vehicle and parts dealers.................. | 441 | 127 | 116 | 891 | 869 | 73 | 70 | 1,914 | 1,710 |
| Furniture and home furnishings stores............... | 442 | 65 | 52 | 108 | 89 | 15 | 11 | 557 | 425 |
| Electronics and appliance stores.................... | 443 | 51 | 47 | 109 | 101 | 11 | 10 | 486 | 416 |
| Building material and garden equipment and supplies dealers................................ | 444 | 91 | 78 | 318 | 279 | 38 | 34 | 1,331 | 1,145 |
| Food and beverage stores........................... | 445 | 146 | 148 | 539 | 620 | 55 | 61 | 2,827 | 2,865 |
| Health and personal care stores..................... | 446 | 88 | 91 | 234 | 270 | 28 | 31 | 1,068 | 1,002 |
| Gasoline stations.................................. | 447 | 119 | 114 | 450 | 554 | 15 | 16 | 891 | 857 |
| Clothing and clothing accessories stores...... | 448 | 156 | 148 | 216 | 234 | 27 | 28 | 1,644 | 1,664 |
| Sporting goods, hobby, book, and music stores..... | 451 | 57 | 48 | 81 | 79 | 9 | 9 | 619 | 535 |
| General merchandise stores.......................... | 452 | 46 | 49 | 577 | 641 | 54 | 58 | 2,763 | 2,773 |
| Miscellaneous store retailers....................... | 453 | 122 | 107 | 104 | 98 | 14 | 14 | 792 | 713 |
| Nonstore retailers.................................. | 454 | 59 | 64 | 290 | 386 | 23 | 27 | 621 | 600 |

[1] North American Industrial Classification System, 2007; see text, Section 15.

Source: U.S. Census Bureau, 2012 Economic Census, "EC1200CCOMP1: All sectors: Core Business Statistics Series: Comparative Statistics for the U.S. (2007 NAICS Basis): 2012 and 2007," <http://factfinder.census.gov>, accessed July 2016.

## Table 1067. Wholesale Trade—Nonemployer Firms and Receipts by Industry Type: 2017

[37,568,130 represents $37,568,130,000. Includes only firms subject to federal income tax. Nonemployers are businesses with no paid employees. Each distinct business income tax return filed by a nonemployer business is counted as a firm]

| Industry type | 2017 NAICS code [1] | Firms | | | | Receipts ($1,000) |
|---|---|---|---|---|---|---|
| | | Total | Corporations [2] | Individual proprietorships [3] | Partnerships [4] | |
| **Wholesale trade, total**.......................... | **42** | **399,261** | **69,949** | **300,821** | **28,491** | **37,568,130** |
| **Durable goods merchant wholesalers**................. | **423** | **191,849** | **37,480** | **139,758** | **14,611** | **19,210,870** |
| Motor vehicle and motor vehicle parts and supplies merchant wholesalers................ | 4231 | 17,276 | 3,481 | 12,689 | 1,106 | 2,394,103 |
| Furniture and home furnishing merchant wholesalers.............. | 4232 | 12,680 | 1,967 | 9,891 | 822 | 1,083,561 |
| Lumber and other construction materials merchant wholesalers................ | 4233 | 7,000 | 1,390 | 4,954 | 656 | 847,962 |
| Professional and commercial equipment and supplies merchant wholesalers................ | 4234 | 10,820 | 2,252 | 7,591 | 977 | 1,182,562 |
| Metal and mineral (except petroleum) merchant wholesalers...... | 4235 | 2,686 | 652 | 1,824 | 210 | 381,298 |
| Household appliance and electrical and electronic goods merchant wholesalers................ | 4236 | 9,393 | 2,823 | 5,714 | 856 | 1,142,354 |
| Hardware and plumbing and heating equipment and supplies merchant wholesalers................ | 4237 | 4,177 | 998 | 2,796 | 383 | 454,799 |
| Machinery, equipment, and supplies merchant wholesalers................ | 4238 | 17,609 | 4,900 | 11,059 | 1,650 | 2,393,318 |
| Miscellaneous durable goods merchant wholesalers.......... | 4239 | 110,208 | 19,017 | 83,240 | 7,951 | 9,330,913 |
| **Nondurable goods merchant wholesalers**................. | **424** | **148,775** | **24,954** | **112,617** | **11,204** | **13,868,755** |
| Paper and paper product merchant wholesalers............ | 4241 | 4,916 | 910 | 3,713 | 293 | 465,500 |
| Drugs and druggists' sundries merchant wholesalers.............. | 4242 | 2,922 | 651 | 1,986 | 285 | 269,614 |
| Apparel, piece goods, and notions merchant wholesalers.......... | 4243 | 27,566 | 3,924 | 21,837 | 1,805 | 1,844,300 |
| Grocery and related products merchant wholesalers.......... | 4244 | 28,048 | 5,421 | 20,471 | 2,156 | 4,055,867 |
| Farm product raw material merchant wholesalers.......... | 4245 | 5,894 | 573 | 4,964 | 357 | 623,036 |
| Chemical and allied products merchant wholesalers.............. | 4246 | 3,285 | 983 | 1,940 | 362 | 420,913 |
| Petroleum and petroleum products merchant wholesalers......... | 4247 | 2,290 | 474 | 1,579 | 237 | 313,272 |
| Beer, wine, and distilled alcoholic beverage merchant wholesalers................ | 4248 | 6,101 | 914 | 4,235 | 952 | 544,038 |
| Miscellaneous nondurable goods merchant wholesalers.......... | 4249 | 67,753 | 11,104 | 51,892 | 4,757 | 5,332,215 |
| **Wholesale electronic markets and agents and brokers**.......... | **425** | **58,637** | **7,515** | **48,446** | **2,676** | **4,488,505** |
| Business to business electronics markets........................... | 42511 | 9,216 | 1,277 | 7,440 | 499 | 833,899 |
| Wholesale trade agents and brokers.................... | 42512 | 49,421 | 6,238 | 41,006 | 2,177 | 3,654,606 |

[1] North American Industry Classification System, 2017; see text, Section 15. [2] A legally incorporated business under state laws. [3] Also referred to as "sole proprietorship," an unincorporated business with a sole owner. Includes self-employed persons. [4] An unincorporated business where two or more persons join to carry on a trade or business with each having a shared financial interest in the business.

Source: U.S. Census Bureau, Nonemployer Statistics, "NES Datasets," <https://www.census.gov/programs-surveys/nonemployer-statistics/data/datasets.html>, accessed July 2019.

## Table 1068. Wholesale Trade—Establishments, Employees, and Payroll: 2015 and 2016

[413.4 represents 413,400. Covers establishments with payroll. Excludes self-employed individuals, employees of private households, railroad employees, agricultural production employees, and most government employees. For statement on methodology, see Appendix III]

| Kind of business | 2012 NAICS code [1] | Establishments (1,000) | | Employees [2] (1,000) | | Payroll (bil. dol.) | |
|---|---|---|---|---|---|---|---|
| | | 2015 | 2016 | 2015 | 2016 | 2015 | 2016 |
| Wholesale trade, total........................ | 42 | **413.4** | **412.5** | **6,076** | **6,111** | **423.1** | **427.9** |
| **Merchant wholesalers, durable goods**.......................... | **423** | **237.5** | **237.8** | **3,441** | **3,464** | **251.8** | **257.6** |
| Motor vehicle and motor vehicle parts and supply merchant wholesalers............. | 4231 | 24.1 | 23.9 | 389 | 398 | 21.3 | 22.1 |
| Furniture and home furnishing merchant wholesalers.......... | 4232 | 12.1 | 12.0 | 151 | 153 | 9.0 | 9.3 |
| Lumber and other construction materials merchant wholesalers............. | 4233 | 16.8 | 17.1 | 217 | 234 | 12.5 | 13.8 |
| Professional and commercial equipment and supplies merchant wholesalers.............. | 4234 | 34.1 | 35.0 | 643 | 654 | 60.2 | 61.9 |
| Metal and mineral (except petroleum) merchant wholesalers............. | 4235 | 10.0 | 9.8 | 157 | 151 | 9.7 | 9.4 |
| Household appliances and electrical and electronic goods merchant wholesalers......... | 4236 | 29.2 | 30.4 | 547 | 550 | 55.4 | 57.4 |
| Hardware, plumbing and heating equipment and supplies merchant wholesalers............. | 4237 | 19.1 | 19.0 | 235 | 241 | 15.1 | 15.6 |
| Machinery, equipment, and supplies merchant wholesalers............. | 4238 | 57.6 | 57.2 | 769 | 760 | 50.8 | 50.1 |
| Miscellaneous durable goods merchant wholesalers.......... | 4239 | 34.3 | 33.4 | 334 | 323 | 17.8 | 18.0 |
| **Merchant wholesalers, nondurable goods**.................... | **424** | **130.4** | **129.1** | **2,334** | **2,341** | **155.4** | **153.9** |
| Paper and paper product merchant wholesalers............... | 4241 | 10.1 | 9.5 | 147 | 148 | 8.8 | 9.0 |
| Drugs and druggists' sundries merchant wholesalers.......... | 4242 | 10.1 | 10.1 | 307 | 299 | 38.6 | 34.7 |
| Apparel, piece goods and notions merchant wholesalers...... | 4243 | 16.1 | 15.6 | 200 | 199 | 12.1 | 12.2 |
| Grocery and related product merchant wholesalers............ | 4244 | 35.3 | 35.4 | 815 | 818 | 43.2 | 44.0 |
| Farm product raw material merchant wholesalers.............. | 4245 | 6.3 | 6.2 | 65 | 65 | 3.7 | 3.6 |
| Chemical and allied products merchant wholesalers............ | 4246 | 12.5 | 12.5 | 158 | 158 | 11.9 | 12.2 |
| Petroleum and petroleum products merchant wholesalers..... | 4247 | 6.7 | 6.6 | 103 | 100 | 7.8 | 7.6 |
| Beer, wine, and distilled alcoholic beverages.................... | 4248 | 4.5 | 4.5 | 198 | 202 | 12.5 | 12.5 |
| Miscellaneous nondurable goods merchant wholesalers...... | 4249 | 28.8 | 28.6 | 340 | 352 | 16.9 | 18.1 |
| **Wholesale electronic markets and agents and brokers**..... | **425** | **45.5** | **45.6** | **302** | **306** | **16.0** | **16.4** |

[1] North American Industry Classification System (NAICS), 2012. See text, Section 15. [2] Covers full- and part-time employees who are on the payroll in the pay period including March 12.

Source: U.S. Census Bureau, County Business Patterns, "Geography Area Series: County Business Patterns," <http://factfinder.census.gov/>, accessed May 2018. See also <https://www.census.gov/programs-surveys/cbp.html>.

## Table 1069. Merchant Wholesale Trade Sales—Total and E-Commerce: 2016

[5,225,877 represents $5,225,877,000,000. Covers only businesses with paid employees. Excludes manufacturers' sales branches and offices. Based on the Annual Wholesale Trade Survey; see Appendix III]

| Kind of business | 2012 NAICS code [1] | Value of sales (mil. dol.) | | E-commerce as percent of total sales | Percent distribution of E-commerce sales |
|---|---|---|---|---|---|
| | | Total | E-commerce | | |
| Total merchant wholesale trade.................................. | 42 | 5,225,877 | 1,420,907 | 27.2 | 100.0 |
| Durable goods............................................ | 423 | 2,501,625 | 583,911 | 23.3 | 41.1 |
| Motor vehicles, parts and supplies............................... | 4231 | 425,577 | 184,261 | 43.3 | 13.0 |
| Furniture and home furnishings.................................. | 4232 | 83,187 | 17,604 | 21.2 | 1.2 |
| Lumber and other construction materials......................... | 4233 | 126,072 | (S) | (S) | (S) |
| Professional and commercial equipment and supplies................. | 4234 | 460,334 | 120,064 | 26.1 | 8.4 |
| Computers and peripheral equipment and software.............. | 42343 | 233,809 | 55,263 | 23.6 | 3.9 |
| Medical, dental, and hospital equipment and supplies.............. | 42345 | 134,716 | 49,808 | 37.0 | 3.5 |
| Metals and minerals (except petroleum)........................ | 4235 | 137,419 | 10,895 | 7.9 | 0.8 |
| Household appliances and electrical and electronic goods............ | 4236 | 538,521 | 143,041 | 26.6 | 10.1 |
| Hardware, plumbing and heating equipment................... | 4237 | 133,823 | 18,551 | 13.9 | 1.3 |
| Machinery, equipment and supplies............................ | 4238 | 387,379 | 44,747 | 11.6 | 3.1 |
| Miscellaneous durable goods................................. | 4239 | 209,313 | (S) | (S) | (S) |
| Nondurable goods....................................... | 424 | 2,724,252 | 836,996 | 30.7 | 58.9 |
| Paper and paper products..................................... | 4241 | 96,621 | 32,255 | 33.4 | 2.3 |
| Drugs and druggists' sundries................................. | 4242 | 644,159 | (S) | (S) | (S) |
| Apparel, piece goods and notions.............................. | 4243 | 160,646 | 38,924 | 24.2 | 2.7 |
| Groceries and related products................................ | 4244 | 630,444 | 170,920 | 27.1 | 12.0 |
| Farm product raw materials................................... | 4245 | 205,038 | 23,729 | 11.6 | 1.7 |
| Chemical and allied products.................................. | 4246 | 113,266 | 11,230 | 9.9 | 0.8 |
| Petroleum and petroleum products............................. | 4247 | 475,679 | (S) | (S) | (S) |
| Beer, wine, and distilled alcoholic beverages.................... | 4248 | 143,747 | 10,558 | 7.3 | 0.7 |
| Miscellaneous nondurable goods.............................. | 4249 | 254,652 | 43,205 | 17.0 | 3.0 |

S Figure does not meet publication standards. [1] North American Industry Classification System, 2012. See text, Section 15.

Source: U.S. Census Bureau, "Annual Report for Wholesale Trade: 2016," <https://www.census.gov/programs-surveys/awts/data/tables.html>; and "2016 E-Commerce Multi-sector Data Tables," <http://www.census.gov/programs-surveys/e-stats/data/tables.html>; accessed June 2018.

# Table 1070. Merchant Wholesalers' Sales and Inventories by Kind of Business: 2010 to 2017

[In billions of dollars (4,337.4 represents $4,337,400,000,000), except ratios. Inventories and inventories/sales ratios, as of December, not seasonally adjusted. Excludes manufacturers' sales branches and offices. Data adjusted using final results of the 2012 Economic Census. Based on data from the Annual Wholesale Trade Survey and the Monthly Wholesale Trade Survey; see Appendix III]

| Kind of business | 2012 NAICS code [1] | 2010 | 2012 | 2013 | 2014 | 2015 | 2016 | 2017 |
|---|---|---|---|---|---|---|---|---|
| **SALES** | | | | | | | | |
| **Merchant wholesalers**............................ | **42** | **4,337.4** | **5,208.0** | **5,370.6** | **5,564.2** | **5,292.4** | **5,228.5** | **5,557.9** |
| **Durable goods**............................ | **423** | **1,999.2** | **2,389.6** | **2,461.0** | **2,556.6** | **2,520.1** | **2,506.0** | **2,677.5** |
| Motor vehicles, parts, and supplies................. | 4231 | 303.0 | 393.6 | 401.6 | 415.0 | 430.2 | 425.8 | 448.1 |
| Furniture and home furnishings..................... | 4232 | 57.4 | 67.5 | 71.6 | 76.7 | 79.6 | 83.3 | 88.3 |
| Lumber and other construction materials............ | 4233 | 86.5 | 94.1 | 105.0 | 111.5 | 117.6 | 126.9 | 137.4 |
| Professional, commercial equipment and supplies......... | 4234 | 397.8 | 412.6 | 425.5 | 437.9 | 449.3 | 460.0 | 482.3 |
| Computer, peripheral equipment and software............ | 42343 | 220.1 | 217.9 | 224.6 | 228.8 | 231.9 | 231.7 | 246.7 |
| Medical, dental, and hospital equipment and supplies.... | 42345 | (NA) | (NA) | (NA) | (NA) | 126.4 | 134.7 | 138.9 |
| Metals and minerals (except petroleum)............... | 4235 | 138.4 | 180.6 | 173.8 | 184.7 | 156.7 | 137.7 | 159.6 |
| Household appliances and electrical and electronic goods...... | 4236 | 391.2 | 476.0 | 510.9 | 535.8 | 549.1 | 543.1 | 583.6 |
| Hardware, plumbing, heating equipment and supplies..... | 4237 | 96.1 | 112.3 | 117.3 | 124.5 | 129.1 | 134.3 | 140.5 |
| Machinery, equipment, and supplies................. | 4238 | 305.3 | 394.4 | 404.2 | 421.3 | 398.2 | 386.8 | 409.7 |
| Miscellaneous durable goods.................... | 4239 | 223.7 | 258.4 | 251.1 | 249.4 | 210.2 | 208.4 | 228.1 |
| **Nondurable goods**.................... | **424** | **2,338.1** | **2,818.4** | **2,909.5** | **3,007.5** | **2,772.3** | **2,722.4** | **2,880.4** |
| Paper and paper products..................... | 4241 | 86.0 | 90.2 | 92.0 | 95.9 | 95.8 | 96.1 | 97.1 |
| Drugs and druggists' sundries................... | 4242 | 415.9 | 462.6 | 486.8 | 540.1 | 604.4 | 645.3 | 663.6 |
| Apparel, piece goods, and notions................ | 4243 | 137.0 | 148.9 | 156.2 | 162.4 | 165.5 | 161.4 | 161.2 |
| Grocery and related products................... | 4244 | 491.3 | 556.3 | 576.8 | 611.5 | 629.1 | 631.5 | 653.1 |
| Farm product raw materials.................... | 4245 | 188.3 | 254.5 | 270.7 | 254.9 | 219.1 | 203.0 | 196.6 |
| Chemical and allied products................... | 4246 | 102.7 | 122.4 | 124.4 | 128.8 | 117.8 | 112.4 | 122.8 |
| Petroleum and petroleum products................ | 4247 | 591.0 | 811.6 | 818.5 | 834.5 | 552.5 | 477.4 | 582.0 |
| Beer, wine, and distilled alcoholic beverages............ | 4248 | 111.3 | 122.0 | 130.0 | 130.7 | 136.5 | 143.7 | 148.7 |
| Miscellaneous nondurable goods................. | 4249 | 214.5 | 249.9 | 254.1 | 248.7 | 251.6 | 251.6 | 255.3 |
| **INVENTORIES** | | | | | | | | |
| **Merchant wholesalers**............................ | **42** | **445.1** | **526.6** | **547.1** | **579.8** | **587.4** | **597.6** | **617.2** |
| **Durable goods**............................ | **423** | **257.4** | **312.0** | **327.4** | **350.0** | **350.9** | **349.9** | **365.8** |
| Motor vehicles, parts, and supplies................. | 4231 | 40.5 | 48.5 | 50.1 | 54.2 | 61.5 | 62.2 | 62.8 |
| Furniture and home furnishings..................... | 4232 | 8.6 | 9.8 | 10.7 | 11.3 | 11.9 | 12.3 | 12.5 |
| Lumber and other construction materials............ | 4233 | 10.6 | 11.7 | 13.1 | 14.0 | 15.0 | 15.0 | 16.1 |
| Professional, commercial equipment and supplies......... | 4234 | 33.4 | 37.9 | 40.1 | 43.9 | 43.4 | 45.3 | 47.7 |
| Computer, peripheral equipment and software............ | 42343 | 13.5 | 14.5 | 15.6 | 17.3 | 16.6 | 17.0 | 18.6 |
| Medical, dental, and hospital equipment and supplies.... | 42345 | (NA) | (NA) | (NA) | (NA) | 15.8 | 16.4 | 17.2 |
| Metals and minerals (except petroleum)............... | 4235 | 22.8 | 29.5 | 29.3 | 32.8 | 26.8 | 25.3 | 29.1 |
| Household appliances and electrical and electronic goods...... | 4236 | 35.4 | 43.8 | 45.7 | 47.6 | 50.0 | 49.4 | 52.6 |
| Hardware, plumbing, heating equipment and supplies..... | 4237 | 16.7 | 18.9 | 19.3 | 21.1 | 21.9 | 22.3 | 23.7 |
| Machinery, equipment, and supplies................. | 4238 | 64.5 | 83.8 | 90.3 | 96.1 | 92.9 | 89.6 | 92.4 |
| Miscellaneous durable goods.................... | 4239 | 24.9 | 28.1 | 28.8 | 29.1 | 27.4 | 28.5 | 28.9 |
| **Nondurable goods**.................... | **424** | **187.7** | **214.6** | **219.8** | **229.8** | **236.5** | **247.8** | **251.4** |
| Paper and paper products..................... | 4241 | 7.4 | 7.9 | 8.2 | 8.5 | 8.5 | 8.6 | 8.9 |
| Drugs and druggists' sundries................... | 4242 | 38.7 | 42.8 | 48.4 | 56.6 | 63.3 | 65.5 | 65.2 |
| Apparel, piece goods, and notions................ | 4243 | 20.1 | 22.9 | 24.0 | 25.5 | 27.7 | 26.6 | 26.2 |
| Grocery and related products................... | 4244 | 27.3 | 32.2 | 32.6 | 35.5 | 36.9 | 38.1 | 39.3 |
| Farm product raw materials.................... | 4245 | 28.3 | 31.2 | 27.5 | 27.7 | 24.4 | 26.7 | 28.3 |
| Chemical and allied products................... | 4246 | 9.3 | 11.3 | 11.4 | 11.8 | 11.5 | 11.8 | 12.5 |
| Petroleum and petroleum products................ | 4247 | 23.0 | 26.2 | 25.4 | 19.4 | 18.2 | 23.3 | 22.1 |
| Beer, wine, and distilled alcoholic beverages............ | 4248 | 10.7 | 12.4 | 13.4 | 14.1 | 14.2 | 15.1 | 15.9 |
| Miscellaneous nondurable goods................. | 4249 | 22.9 | 27.7 | 28.9 | 30.7 | 31.8 | 32.1 | 32.9 |
| **INVENTORIES/SALES RATIO** | | | | | | | | |
| **Merchant wholesalers**............................ | **42** | **1.03** | **1.01** | **1.02** | **1.04** | **1.11** | **1.14** | **1.11** |
| **Durable goods**............................ | **423** | **1.29** | **1.31** | **1.33** | **1.37** | **1.39** | **1.40** | **1.37** |
| Motor vehicles, parts, and supplies................. | 4231 | 1.34 | 1.23 | 1.25 | 1.31 | 1.43 | 1.46 | 1.40 |
| Furniture and home furnishings..................... | 4232 | 1.50 | 1.45 | 1.49 | 1.47 | 1.50 | 1.48 | 1.42 |
| Lumber and other construction materials............ | 4233 | 1.22 | 1.25 | 1.25 | 1.25 | 1.28 | 1.18 | 1.17 |
| Professional, commercial equipment and supplies......... | 4234 | 0.84 | 0.92 | 0.94 | 1.00 | 0.97 | 0.99 | 0.99 |
| Computer, peripheral equipment and software............ | 42343 | 0.62 | 0.67 | 0.69 | 0.76 | 0.72 | 0.73 | 0.75 |
| Medical, dental, and hospital equipment and supplies.... | 42345 | (NA) | (NA) | (NA) | (NA) | 1.2 | 1.2 | 1.2 |
| Metals and minerals (except petroleum)............... | 4235 | 1.65 | 1.63 | 1.69 | 1.78 | 1.71 | 1.84 | 1.82 |
| Household appliances and electrical and electronic goods...... | 4236 | 0.90 | 0.92 | 0.89 | 0.89 | 0.91 | 0.91 | 0.90 |
| Hardware, plumbing, heating equipment and supplies..... | 4237 | 1.74 | 1.68 | 1.64 | 1.69 | 1.70 | 1.66 | 1.69 |
| Machinery, equipment, and supplies................. | 4238 | 2.11 | 2.12 | 2.23 | 2.28 | 2.33 | 2.32 | 2.26 |
| Miscellaneous durable goods.................... | 4239 | 1.11 | 1.09 | 1.15 | 1.17 | 1.30 | 1.37 | 1.27 |
| **Nondurable goods**.................... | **424** | **0.80** | **0.76** | **0.76** | **0.76** | **0.85** | **0.91** | **0.87** |
| Paper and paper products..................... | 4241 | 0.86 | 0.88 | 0.89 | 0.89 | 0.88 | 0.90 | 0.91 |
| Drugs and druggists' sundries................... | 4242 | 0.93 | 0.93 | 0.99 | 1.05 | 1.05 | 1.01 | 0.98 |
| Apparel, piece goods, and notions................ | 4243 | 1.47 | 1.54 | 1.53 | 1.57 | 1.67 | 1.65 | 1.63 |
| Grocery and related products................... | 4244 | 0.55 | 0.58 | 0.57 | 0.58 | 0.59 | 0.60 | 0.60 |
| Farm product raw materials.................... | 4245 | 1.50 | 1.22 | 1.02 | 1.09 | 1.12 | 1.32 | 1.44 |
| Chemical and allied products................... | 4246 | 0.90 | 0.93 | 0.92 | 0.92 | 0.98 | 1.05 | 1.02 |
| Petroleum and petroleum products................ | 4247 | 0.39 | 0.32 | 0.31 | 0.23 | 0.33 | 0.49 | 0.38 |
| Beer, wine, and distilled alcoholic beverages............ | 4248 | 0.96 | 1.01 | 1.03 | 1.08 | 1.04 | 1.05 | 1.07 |
| Miscellaneous nondurable goods................. | 4249 | 1.07 | 1.11 | 1.14 | 1.24 | 1.26 | 1.28 | 1.29 |

NA Not available. [1] North American Industry Classification System, 2012. See text, Section 15.

Source: U.S. Census Bureau, "Annual Report for Wholesale Trade: 2017," <https://www.census.gov/programs-surveys/awts.html>, accessed March 2019.

# Table 1071. Wholesale and Retail Trade—Establishments, Employees, and Payroll by State: 2015 and 2016

[6,076 represents 6,076,000. Covers establishments with payroll. Excludes self-employed individuals, employees of private households, railroad employees, agricultural production employees, and most government employees. Data based on 2012 North American Industry Classification System (NAICS). See text, Section 15. For statement on methodology, see Appendix III]

| State | Wholesale trade (NAICS 42) | | | | | | Retail trade (NAICS 44, 45) | | | | | |
|---|---|---|---|---|---|---|---|---|---|---|---|---|
| | Establishments | | Employees [1] (1,000) | | Annual payroll (mil. dol.) | | Establishments | | Employees [1] (1,000) | | Annual payroll (mil. dol.) | |
| | 2015 | 2016 | 2015 | 2016 | 2015 | 2016 | 2015 | 2016 | 2015 | 2016 | 2015 | 2016 |
| U.S......... | 413,437 | 412,526 | 6,076 | 6,111 | 423,133 | 427,859 | 1,070,209 | 1,069,096 | 15,704 | 15,968 | 428,218 | 437,654 |
| AL.......... | 5,315 | 5,275 | 71 | 73 | 3,942 | 4,048 | 18,043 | 18,097 | 232 | 237 | 5,820 | 5,997 |
| AK.......... | 729 | 739 | 9 | 9 | 588 | 573 | 2,514 | 2,478 | 35 | 35 | 1,105 | 1,132 |
| AZ.......... | 6,488 | 6,467 | 92 | 94 | 5,856 | 5,998 | 18,103 | 18,027 | 314 | 321 | 8,788 | 8,958 |
| AR.......... | 3,418 | 3,396 | 44 | 47 | 2,421 | 2,522 | 10,908 | 10,851 | 143 | 148 | 3,555 | 3,757 |
| CA.......... | 59,353 | 59,111 | 854 | 843 | 72,916 | 70,786 | 108,542 | 108,331 | 1,690 | 1,711 | 51,641 | 52,902 |
| CO.......... | 7,219 | 7,303 | 100 | 103 | 7,367 | 7,837 | 18,734 | 18,790 | 273 | 281 | 7,953 | 8,260 |
| CT.......... | 4,261 | 4,219 | 73 | 73 | 5,724 | 6,071 | 12,524 | 12,590 | 184 | 187 | 5,476 | 5,551 |
| DE.......... | 1,117 | 1,173 | 16 | 17 | 1,250 | 1,389 | 3,656 | 3,716 | 55 | 56 | 1,472 | 1,498 |
| DC.......... | 419 | 505 | 4 | 5 | 384 | 402 | 1,751 | 1,801 | 22 | 22 | 635 | 649 |
| FL.......... | 31,221 | 31,147 | 314 | 319 | 17,877 | 18,821 | 74,533 | 75,181 | 1,071 | 1,089 | 29,166 | 29,671 |
| GA.......... | 12,928 | 13,050 | 205 | 212 | 13,010 | 13,812 | 34,041 | 34,109 | 469 | 485 | 12,091 | 12,525 |
| HI.......... | 1,661 | 1,677 | 19 | 19 | 958 | 1,003 | 4,602 | 4,615 | 72 | 71 | 2,074 | 2,073 |
| ID.......... | 2,064 | 2,118 | 30 | 31 | 1,855 | 1,980 | 6,004 | 6,043 | 82 | 84 | 2,206 | 2,307 |
| IL.......... | 18,539 | 18,383 | 316 | 322 | 23,812 | 24,321 | 39,165 | 38,732 | 627 | 632 | 16,258 | 16,283 |
| IN.......... | 7,668 | 7,657 | 129 | 118 | 8,440 | 6,984 | 21,426 | 21,232 | 318 | 326 | 7,974 | 8,140 |
| IA.......... | 4,974 | 4,970 | 68 | 69 | 3,602 | 3,678 | 11,736 | 11,613 | 185 | 187 | 4,457 | 4,630 |
| KS.......... | 4,459 | 4,457 | 63 | 63 | 3,760 | 3,738 | 10,327 | 10,197 | 150 | 154 | 3,712 | 3,827 |
| KY.......... | 4,293 | 4,284 | 72 | 72 | 4,113 | 4,046 | 15,187 | 15,061 | 207 | 214 | 5,176 | 5,404 |
| LA.......... | 5,463 | 5,455 | 78 | 76 | 4,400 | 4,255 | 16,525 | 16,554 | 238 | 240 | 6,099 | 6,152 |
| ME.......... | 1,581 | 1,570 | 18 | 18 | 939 | 997 | 6,281 | 6,262 | 82 | 84 | 2,163 | 2,240 |
| MD.......... | 5,581 | 5,657 | 88 | 91 | 6,235 | 6,487 | 18,273 | 18,201 | 290 | 294 | 7,992 | 8,252 |
| MA.......... | 7,763 | 7,679 | 140 | 144 | 12,416 | 12,361 | 24,101 | 24,345 | 366 | 373 | 10,599 | 10,964 |
| MI.......... | 11,053 | 10,938 | 177 | 180 | 11,813 | 12,293 | 34,711 | 34,493 | 466 | 471 | 12,037 | 12,398 |
| MN.......... | 8,032 | 8,035 | 135 | 138 | 10,144 | 10,867 | 18,974 | 19,008 | 300 | 307 | 8,087 | 8,248 |
| MS.......... | 2,756 | 2,748 | 37 | 37 | 1,838 | 1,878 | 11,587 | 11,608 | 143 | 146 | 3,392 | 3,471 |
| MO.......... | 7,705 | 7,655 | 126 | 126 | 6,990 | 7,072 | 21,177 | 21,028 | 316 | 325 | 8,145 | 8,427 |
| MT.......... | 1,594 | 1,594 | 16 | 17 | 805 | 843 | 4,791 | 4,769 | 60 | 60 | 1,587 | 1,604 |
| NE.......... | 3,209 | 3,205 | 42 | 42 | 2,495 | 2,434 | 7,352 | 7,253 | 113 | 113 | 2,835 | 2,901 |
| NV.......... | 2,969 | 2,992 | 35 | 37 | 2,086 | 2,182 | 8,682 | 8,708 | 147 | 146 | 4,077 | 4,141 |
| NH.......... | 1,839 | 1,853 | 25 | 24 | 1,807 | 1,778 | 6,050 | 5,997 | 99 | 101 | 2,753 | 2,802 |
| NJ.......... | 14,060 | 13,970 | 255 | 264 | 23,102 | 24,844 | 31,557 | 31,446 | 461 | 465 | 13,465 | 13,584 |
| NM.......... | 1,847 | 1,838 | 21 | 21 | 1,105 | 1,074 | 6,536 | 6,478 | 97 | 97 | 2,537 | 2,570 |
| NY.......... | 31,785 | 31,436 | 371 | 363 | 26,208 | 26,120 | 78,832 | 78,851 | 937 | 945 | 27,245 | 27,406 |
| NC.......... | 11,602 | 11,632 | 180 | 191 | 12,344 | 13,366 | 34,527 | 34,752 | 482 | 496 | 12,293 | 12,652 |
| ND.......... | 1,723 | 1,742 | 24 | 23 | 1,408 | 1,296 | 3,259 | 3,248 | 52 | 51 | 1,502 | 1,447 |
| OH.......... | 14,035 | 13,856 | 236 | 233 | 14,334 | 14,257 | 36,339 | 36,020 | 565 | 574 | 14,592 | 14,782 |
| OK.......... | 4,026 | 4,618 | 61 | 58 | 3,287 | 3,206 | 13,305 | 13,168 | 184 | 186 | 4,743 | 4,788 |
| OR.......... | 5,352 | 5,358 | 82 | 84 | 6,077 | 6,271 | 14,159 | 14,102 | 203 | 209 | 5,743 | 6,043 |
| PA.......... | 14,628 | 14,471 | 249 | 248 | 17,891 | 17,705 | 43,399 | 43,216 | 665 | 667 | 17,338 | 17,377 |
| RI.......... | 1,328 | 1,337 | 21 | 20 | 1,504 | 1,460 | 3,748 | 3,776 | 50 | 49 | 1,398 | 1,448 |
| SC.......... | 4,915 | 4,896 | 74 | 73 | 4,165 | 4,165 | 17,599 | 17,638 | 237 | 245 | 5,899 | 5,991 |
| SD.......... | 1,507 | 1,514 | 19 | 19 | 997 | 995 | 3,941 | 3,920 | 53 | 54 | 1,373 | 1,408 |
| TN.......... | 6,779 | 6,754 | 114 | 116 | 6,957 | 7,124 | 22,643 | 22,733 | 317 | 330 | 8,357 | 8,751 |
| TX.......... | 33,380 | 33,467 | 524 | 521 | 35,987 | 35,464 | 80,298 | 80,652 | 1,280 | 1,304 | 34,965 | 35,852 |
| UT.......... | 3,702 | 3,722 | 55 | 58 | 3,337 | 3,445 | 9,546 | 9,842 | 151 | 156 | 4,177 | 4,359 |
| VT.......... | 824 | 815 | 12 | 12 | 629 | 687 | 3,351 | 3,280 | 40 | 40 | 1,099 | 1,105 |
| VA.......... | 7,073 | 7,203 | 103 | 106 | 6,744 | 7,174 | 27,188 | 26,895 | 424 | 430 | 11,182 | 11,344 |
| WA.......... | 9,283 | 9,328 | 131 | 134 | 8,636 | 9,227 | 21,778 | 21,701 | 331 | 337 | 10,082 | 10,485 |
| WV.......... | 1,486 | 1,475 | 22 | 18 | 1,109 | 911 | 6,150 | 6,041 | 86 | 87 | 2,071 | 2,076 |
| WI.......... | 6,987 | 6,954 | 117 | 120 | 6,950 | 7,138 | 19,114 | 19,002 | 309 | 314 | 7,934 | 8,160 |
| WY.......... | 844 | 828 | 9 | 8 | 524 | 474 | 2,640 | 2,645 | 32 | 31 | 900 | 860 |

[1] Covers full- and part-time employees who are on the payroll in the pay period including March 12.

Source: U.S. Census Bureau, County Business Patterns, "Geography Area Series: County Business Patterns," <https://factfinder.census.gov/>, accessed May 2018. See also <https://www.census.gov/programs-surveys/cbp.html>.

# Table 1072. Retail Trade—Establishments, Employees, and Payroll: 2015 and 2016

[1,070.2 represents 1,070,200. Covers establishments with payroll. Excludes self-employed individuals, employees of private households, railroad employees, agricultural production employees, and most government employees. For statement on methodology, see Appendix III]

| Kind of business | 2012 NAICS code [1] | Establishments (1,000) | | Employees (1,000) [2] | | Payroll (bil. dol.) | |
|---|---|---|---|---|---|---|---|
| | | 2015 | 2016 | 2015 | 2016 | 2015 | 2016 |
| **Retail trade, total** | **44–45** | **1,070.2** | **1,069.1** | **15,704** | **15,968** | **428.2** | **437.7** |
| Motor vehicle and parts dealers | 441 | 118.2 | 118.2 | 1,908 | 1,972 | 86.7 | 90.1 |
| Automobile dealers | 4411 | 46.5 | 46.8 | 1,247 | 1,299 | 65.8 | 68.2 |
| New car dealers | 44111 | 21.4 | 21.4 | 1,105 | 1,150 | 59.9 | 62.0 |
| Used car dealers | 44112 | 25.1 | 25.4 | 142 | 149 | 5.9 | 6.2 |
| Other motor vehicle dealers | 4412 | 13.8 | 13.7 | 138 | 144 | 6.0 | 6.3 |
| Recreational vehicle dealers | 44121 | 2.6 | 2.6 | 39 | 42 | 2.0 | 2.2 |
| Motorcycle and boat and other motor vehicle dealers [3] | 44122 | 11.2 | 11.1 | 100 | 102 | 4.0 | 4.1 |
| Motorcycle, ATV, and all other motor vehicle dealers | 441228 | 6.8 | 6.8 | 68 | 70 | 2.6 | 2.7 |
| Automotive parts, accessories, and tire stores | 4413 | 57.8 | 57.7 | 523 | 529 | 14.9 | 15.6 |
| Automotive parts and accessories stores | 44131 | 37.2 | 37.3 | 347 | 351 | 8.7 | 9.0 |
| Tire dealers | 44132 | 20.7 | 20.5 | 177 | 179 | 6.2 | 6.6 |
| Furniture and home furnishing stores | 442 | 50.3 | 50.0 | 445 | 453 | 13.6 | 14.3 |
| Furniture stores | 4421 | 23.4 | 23.3 | 202 | 210 | 7.5 | 7.9 |
| Home furnishings stores | 4422 | 27.0 | 26.8 | 243 | 243 | 6.1 | 6.4 |
| Floor covering stores | 44221 | 10.6 | 11.0 | 65 | 69 | 2.7 | 3.0 |
| Other home furnishings stores [3] | 44229 | 16.4 | 15.7 | 178 | 174 | 3.4 | 3.4 |
| Window treatment stores | 442291 | 2.2 | 1.9 | 7 | 7 | 0.2 | 0.3 |
| Electronics and appliance stores | 443 | 46.7 | 40.5 | 407 | 379 | 11.8 | 11.0 |
| Household appliance stores | 443141 | 7.6 | 7.5 | 60 | 62 | 2.0 | 2.2 |
| Electronics stores | 443142 | 39.1 | 33.0 | 347 | 316 | 9.8 | 8.8 |
| Building material & garden equipment & supplies dealers | 444 | 76.6 | 75.7 | 1,280 | 1,331 | 38.6 | 41.1 |
| Building material & supplies dealers [3] | 4441 | 58.9 | 58.1 | 1,131 | 1,175 | 33.9 | 36.3 |
| Home centers | 44411 | 6.5 | 6.6 | 686 | 722 | 16.5 | 18.3 |
| Hardware stores | 44413 | 15.4 | 15.3 | 143 | 146 | 3.6 | 3.7 |
| Lawn & garden equipment & supplies stores [3] | 4442 | 17.7 | 17.6 | 149 | 155 | 4.7 | 4.8 |
| Nursery, garden center, and farm supply stores | 44422 | 13.9 | 13.8 | 124 | 129 | 3.8 | 3.8 |
| Food & beverage stores | 445 | 152.5 | 152.8 | 3,130 | 3,176 | 68.3 | 70.7 |
| Grocery stores | 4451 | 95.5 | 95.4 | 2,800 | 2,830 | 61.2 | 63.2 |
| Supermarkets & grocery (except convenience) stores | 44511 | 66.3 | 65.4 | 2,667 | 2,691 | 58.8 | 60.6 |
| Convenience stores | 44512 | 29.2 | 30.0 | 133 | 139 | 2.3 | 2.5 |
| Specialty food stores | 4452 | 23.3 | 23.4 | 167 | 179 | 3.4 | 3.7 |
| Beer, wine, & liquor stores [4] | 4453 | 33.7 | 34.0 | 162 | 167 | 3.7 | 3.8 |
| Health & personal care stores [3] | 446 | 92.8 | 96.8 | 1,041 | 1,057 | 34.9 | 33.8 |
| Pharmacies & drug stores | 44611 | 44.1 | 48.2 | 713 | 708 | 26.2 | 24.8 |
| Cosmetics, beauty supplies, & perfume stores | 44612 | 16.3 | 16.6 | 140 | 155 | 2.7 | 3.0 |
| Optical goods stores | 44613 | 11.9 | 12.0 | 78 | 82 | 2.3 | 2.3 |
| Gasoline stations | 447 | 111.6 | 111.1 | 922 | 948 | 18.2 | 19.1 |
| Gasoline stations with convenience stores | 44711 | 97.0 | 96.9 | 775 | 797 | 14.6 | 15.3 |
| Other gasoline stations | 44719 | 14.6 | 14.2 | 147 | 151 | 3.6 | 3.8 |
| Clothing & clothing accessories stores | 448 | 146.7 | 143.9 | 1,711 | 1,738 | 31.4 | 31.4 |
| Clothing stores [3] | 4481 | 98.5 | 96.5 | 1,348 | 1,373 | 22.9 | 23.1 |
| Men's clothing stores | 44811 | 7.0 | 6.9 | 53 | 52 | 1.5 | 1.5 |
| Women's clothing stores | 44812 | 35.3 | 33.7 | 330 | 340 | 5.5 | 5.5 |
| Children's & infants' clothing stores | 44813 | 7.2 | 7.1 | 74 | 69 | 1.1 | 1.0 |
| Family clothing stores | 44814 | 28.9 | 29.0 | 720 | 737 | 11.4 | 11.6 |
| Shoe stores | 4482 | 25.0 | 24.7 | 234 | 238 | 4.1 | 4.0 |
| Jewelry, luggage, & leather goods stores [3] | 4483 | 23.2 | 22.7 | 129 | 127 | 4.4 | 4.3 |
| Jewelry stores | 44831 | 22.2 | 21.7 | 123 | 121 | 4.1 | 4.1 |
| Sporting goods, hobby, musical instrument, & book stores | 451 | 46.2 | 45.9 | 579 | 569 | 10.4 | 10.4 |
| Sporting goods/hobby/musical instrument stores [3] | 4511 | 38.2 | 38.4 | 479 | 477 | 8.9 | 8.8 |
| Sporting goods stores | 45111 | 21.9 | 22.0 | 271 | 273 | 5.5 | 5.4 |
| Hobby, toy, and game stores | 45112 | 8.1 | 8.3 | 141 | 136 | 2.1 | 2.2 |
| Book stores and news dealers [3] | 4512 | 8.0 | 7.5 | 100 | 91 | 1.5 | 1.5 |
| Book stores | 451211 | 6.9 | 6.4 | 91 | 83 | 1.3 | 1.3 |
| General merchandise stores | 452 | 53.0 | 54.5 | 2,902 | 2,927 | 67.6 | 68.5 |
| Department stores | 4521 | 7.9 | 7.9 | 1,017 | 970 | 21.0 | 19.8 |
| Other general merchandise stores | 4529 | 45.1 | 46.6 | 1,886 | 1,957 | 46.6 | 48.7 |
| Warehouse clubs & superstores | 45291 | 5.6 | 5.6 | 1,502 | 1,557 | 40.3 | 42.0 |
| All other general merchandise stores | 45299 | 39.6 | 41.0 | 384 | 401 | 6.3 | 6.7 |
| Miscellaneous store retailers [3] | 453 | 108.5 | 109.5 | 758 | 781 | 16.5 | 16.9 |
| Florists | 4531 | 13.4 | 13.2 | 60 | 60 | 1.1 | 1.1 |
| Office supplies, stationery, and gift stores | 4532 | 28.8 | 28.7 | 231 | 227 | 4.4 | 4.3 |
| Office supplies and stationery stores | 45321 | 6.5 | 6.1 | 80 | 75 | 1.7 | 1.6 |
| Gift, novelty, and souvenir stores | 45322 | 22.4 | 22.6 | 151 | 152 | 2.7 | 2.7 |
| Used merchandise stores | 4533 | 20.1 | 20.1 | 198 | 209 | 3.7 | 3.8 |
| Other miscellaneous store retailers [3] | 4539 | 46.2 | 47.5 | 269 | 286 | 7.3 | 7.7 |
| Pet and pet supplies stores | 45391 | 9.4 | 9.8 | 111 | 117 | 2.3 | 2.4 |
| Nonstore retailers [3] | 454 | 67.1 | 70.1 | 620 | 637 | 30.5 | 30.4 |
| Electronic shopping & mail-order houses | 4541 | 34.6 | 37.2 | 414 | 435 | 22.0 | 22.3 |
| Direct selling establishments | 4543 | 28.8 | 29.2 | 172 | 167 | 7.3 | 7.0 |
| Fuel dealers | 45431 | 8.3 | 8.2 | 73 | 72 | 3.5 | 3.4 |

[1] Data based on North American Industry Classification System (NAICS), 2012. See text, Section 15. [2] Covers full- and part-time employees who are on the payroll in the pay period including March 12. [3] Includes other kinds of business, not shown separately. [4] Includes government employees.

Source: U.S. Census Bureau, County Business Patterns, "Geography Area Series: County Business Patterns," <https://factfinder.census.gov>, accessed May 2018. See also <https://www.census.gov/programs-surveys/cbp.html>.

# Table 1073. Retail Trade—Nonemployer Firms and Receipts by Industry Type: 2017

[90,616,627 represents $90,616,627,000. See headnote, Table 1067]

| Industry type | 2017 NAICS code [1] | Firms | | | | Receipts ($1,000) |
|---|---|---|---|---|---|---|
| | | Total | Corpora- tions [2] | Individual proprietor- ships [3] | Partner- ships [4] | |
| Retail trade, total.......................... | 44–45 | 2,093,459 | 119,590 | 1,895,219 | 78,650 | 90,616,627 |
| Motor vehicle & parts dealers................ | 441 | 165,778 | 15,785 | 143,004 | 6,989 | 17,928,445 |
| Furniture & home furnishings stores........... | 442 | 38,997 | 4,827 | 31,410 | 2,760 | 2,485,591 |
| Electronics and appliance stores.............. | 443 | 23,544 | 3,190 | 19,230 | 1,124 | 1,320,930 |
| Building material & garden equipment & supplies dealers...... | 444 | 35,793 | 3,653 | 30,395 | 1,745 | 2,412,500 |
| Building material & supplies dealers............ | 4441 | 24,321 | 2,903 | 20,111 | 1,307 | 1,861,751 |
| Food & beverage stores.................... | 445 | 98,849 | 11,586 | 80,248 | 7,015 | 7,465,981 |
| Grocery stores........................ | 4451 | 37,814 | 4,822 | 30,865 | 2,127 | 3,223,473 |
| Specialty food stores..................... | 4452 | 50,692 | 4,973 | 41,953 | 3,766 | 2,731,346 |
| Health & personal care stores............... | 446 | 171,947 | 7,507 | 160,475 | 3,965 | 4,395,271 |
| Gasoline stations...................... | 447 | 7,791 | 1,720 | 5,391 | 680 | 1,083,483 |
| Clothing & clothing accessories stores........... | 448 | 187,757 | 10,296 | 167,828 | 9,633 | 6,835,019 |
| Clothing stores........................ | 4481 | 140,892 | 7,426 | 125,269 | 8,197 | 4,933,135 |
| Jewelry, luggage, and leather goods stores....... | 4483 | 41,750 | 2,380 | 38,198 | 1,172 | 1,606,157 |
| Sporting goods, hobby, musical instrument, & book stores..... | 451 | 76,580 | 5,099 | 66,967 | 4,514 | 3,366,734 |
| Book stores and news dealer............... | 4512 | 13,230 | 674 | 12,014 | 542 | 453,123 |
| General merchandise stores................ | 452 | 33,737 | 2,023 | 30,350 | 1,364 | 1,565,025 |
| Miscellaneous store retailers............... | 453 | 268,022 | 20,877 | 231,808 | 15,337 | 12,697,170 |
| Office supplies, stationery, and gift stores....... | 4532 | 46,097 | 3,490 | 39,956 | 2,651 | 1,761,856 |
| Nonstore retailers...................... | 454 | 984,538 | 33,027 | 927,987 | 23,524 | 29,056,916 |
| Electronic shopping & mail-order houses....... | 4541 | 164,867 | 11,437 | 145,158 | 8,272 | 8,911,730 |
| Direct selling establishments............... | 4543 | 802,376 | 19,957 | 768,554 | 13,865 | 19,470,595 |

[1] North American Industry Classification System, 2017; see text, Section 15. [2] A legally incorporated business under state laws. [3] Also referred to as "sole proprietorship," an unincorporated business with a sole owner. Includes self-employed persons. [4] An unincorporated business where two or more persons join to carry on a trade or business with each having a shared financial interest in the business.

Source: U.S. Census Bureau, Nonemployer Statistics, "NES Datasets," <https://www.census.gov/programs-surveys/nonemployer-statistics/data/datasets.html>, accessed July 2019.

# Table 1074. Retail Industries—Employees, Average Weekly Hours, and Average Hourly Earnings: 2010 to 2018

[Annual averages of monthly figures (14,446 represents 14,446,000). Covers all full- and part-time employees who worked during, or received pay for, any part of the pay period including the 12th of the month]

| Industry | 2017 NAICS code [1] | Employees (1,000) | | | Average weekly hours [2] | | | Average hourly earnings [2] (dol.) | | |
|---|---|---|---|---|---|---|---|---|---|---|
| | | 2010 | 2015 | 2018 | 2010 | 2015 | 2018 | 2010 | 2015 | 2018 |
| Retail trade, total [3]...................... | 44,45 | 14,446 | 15,611 | 15,833 | 30.2 | 30.1 | 30.4 | 13.25 | 14.83 | 15.91 |
| Motor vehicle and parts dealers [3].............. | 441 | 1,629 | 1,929 | 2,021 | 36.5 | 37.5 | 36.9 | 17.06 | 18.93 | 20.24 |
| Automobile dealers....................... | 4411 | 1,012 | 1,239 | 1,299 | 36.7 | 37.6 | 37.2 | 18.22 | 20.34 | 21.87 |
| Auto parts, accessories, and tire stores.......... | 4413 | 489 | 545 | 563 | 36.9 | 37.7 | 36.8 | 14.54 | 15.88 | 16.45 |
| Furniture and home furnishings stores............ | 442 | 438 | 467 | 481 | 29.1 | 30.7 | 30.1 | 15.25 | 16.79 | 18.59 |
| Electronics and appliance stores [3]............. | 443 | 523 | 523 | 488 | 31.6 | 37.4 | 35.5 | 16.84 | 21.91 | 22.65 |
| Electronics stores................... [4] | 443142 | 466 | 466 | 439 | 31.3 | 37.8 | 35.6 | 17.04 | 22.67 | 23.00 |
| Building material and garden supply stores [3]....... | 444 | 1,133 | 1,235 | 1,307 | 33.9 | 32.0 | 31.9 | 14.12 | 15.15 | 16.56 |
| Building material and supplies dealers........... | 4441 | 1,006 | 1,085 | 1,147 | 34.2 | 31.7 | 31.7 | 14.14 | 15.21 | 16.62 |
| Lawn and garden equip. and supplies stores..... | 4442 | 127 | 150 | 160 | 31.6 | 34.0 | 33.7 | 13.98 | 14.73 | 16.10 |
| Food and beverage stores [3].................. | 445 | 2,808 | 3,062 | 3,087 | 29.0 | 28.4 | 28.7 | 12.03 | 12.71 | 13.41 |
| Grocery stores......................... | 4451 | 2,461 | 2,682 | 2,698 | 29.0 | 28.5 | 28.7 | 12.12 | 12.76 | 13.39 |
| Supermarkets and other grocery stores......... | 44511 | 2,323 | 2,523 | 2,537 | 28.9 | 28.4 | 28.7 | 12.27 | 12.91 | 13.54 |
| Convenience stores..................... | 44512 | 138 | 159 | 161 | 31.3 | 30.8 | 30.3 | 9.43 | 10.41 | 10.96 |
| Specialty food stores.................... | 4452 | 211 | 227 | 229 | 29.7 | 27.8 | 28.3 | 11.13 | 12.42 | 13.49 |
| Beer, wine, and liquor stores.............. | 4453 | 136 | 153 | 161 | 27.2 | 26.1 | 27.7 | 11.89 | 12.02 | 13.67 |
| Health and personal care stores [3]............. | 446 | 981 | 1,034 | 1,061 | 29.4 | 28.8 | 29.5 | 16.99 | 17.31 | 18.99 |
| Pharmacies and drug stores................ | 44611 | 715 | 721 | 709 | 29.3 | 28.9 | 29.2 | 17.59 | 17.87 | 20.39 |
| Gasoline stations [3]...................... | 447 | 819 | 905 | 934 | 30.7 | 30.7 | 30.9 | 10.25 | 10.99 | 11.66 |
| Gasoline stations with convenience stores........ | 44711 | 719 | 799 | 830 | 30.4 | 30.5 | 30.8 | 9.99 | 10.76 | 11.45 |
| Clothing and clothing accessories stores [3]......... | 448 | 1,353 | 1,354 | 1,366 | 21.2 | 21.7 | 21.9 | 11.59 | 12.87 | 14.87 |
| Clothing stores......................... | 4481 | 1,040 | 1,006 | 1,028 | 20.1 | 20.2 | 20.6 | 10.91 | 12.12 | 14.06 |
| Shoe stores........................... | 4482 | 182 | 212 | 202 | 23.3 | 24.0 | 23.7 | 11.80 | 14.01 | 15.35 |
| Jewelry, luggage, and leather goods stores....... | 4483 | 131 | 136 | 136 | 28.1 | 30.0 | 30.2 | 15.56 | 15.46 | 18.91 |
| Sporting goods, hobby, book, and music stores [3].... | 451 | 579 | 623 | 576 | 23.4 | 24.5 | 25.5 | 11.69 | 13.74 | 14.97 |
| Sporting goods and musical instrument stores.... | 4511 | 459 | 538 | 500 | 23.8 | 24.6 | 26.3 | 11.82 | 13.92 | 15.02 |
| Book stores and news dealers............... | 4512 | 120 | 86 | 76 | 22.0 | 24.0 | 20.4 | 11.10 | 12.58 | 14.53 |
| General merchandise stores.................. | 452 | 2,998 | 3,131 | 3,105 | 31.7 | 29.3 | 30.9 | 10.98 | 12.03 | 13.76 |
| Miscellaneous store retailers [3]................ | 453 | 762 | 828 | 834 | 28.0 | 28.9 | 27.4 | 12.50 | 13.75 | 14.03 |
| Florists............................... | 4531 | 69 | 63 | 60 | 22.4 | 27.4 | 24.6 | 11.05 | 11.66 | 13.23 |
| Office supplies, stationary, and gift stores........ | 4532 | 303 | 281 | 249 | 27.1 | 27.8 | 25.4 | 13.06 | 15.31 | 14.27 |
| Used merchandise stores.................. | 4533 | 125 | 171 | 175 | 29.5 | 30.1 | 28.0 | 10.72 | 11.20 | 12.49 |
| Other miscellaneous store retailers........... | 4539 | 264 | 314 | 349 | 29.8 | 29.4 | 29.1 | 13.07 | 14.34 | 14.79 |
| Pet and pet supplies stores.............. | 45391 | 99 | 114 | 124 | 27.4 | 28.8 | 29.1 | 12.83 | 14.09 | 13.60 |
| Nonstore retailers [3]..................... | 454 | 425 | 519 | 573 | 36.3 | 36.5 | 34.5 | 17.83 | 22.42 | 20.01 |
| Electronic shopping and mail-order houses....... | 4541 | 250 | 346 | 399 | 35.9 | 36.5 | 33.4 | 18.34 | 23.92 | 19.72 |

[1] Based on the North American Industry Classification System (NAICS), 2017; see text, this section and Section 15. [2] Data shown for production and nonsupervisory employees. [3] Includes other kind of businesses, not shown separately.

Source: U.S. Bureau of Labor Statistics, Current Employment Statistics, "Employment, Hours, and Earnings—National," <http://www.bls.gov/ces/data.htm>, accessed March 2019.

## Table 1075. Retail Trade—Sales by Kind of Business: 2000 to 2017

[In billions of dollars (2,983.3 represents $2,983,300,000,000). Data have been adjusted using final results of the 2012 Economic Census]

| Kind of business | 2012 NAICS code [1] | 2000 | 2010 | 2013 | 2014 | 2015 | 2016 | 2017 |
|---|---|---|---|---|---|---|---|---|
| **Retail sales, total**............................. | **44, 45** | **2,983.3** | **3,818.0** | **4,458.5** | **4,639.4** | **4,726.0** | **4,851.8** | **5,046.9** |
| GAFO, total [2].................................. | (X) | 862.7 | 1,114.4 | 1,212.5 | 1,238.7 | 1,258.2 | 1,262.1 | 1,269.1 |
| Motor vehicle and parts dealers.................... | 441 | 796.2 | 742.9 | 959.3 | 1,020.9 | 1,094.1 | 1,142.3 | 1,174.4 |
| Automobile dealers............................ | 4411 | 687.8 | 621.2 | 819.3 | 875.6 | 940.5 | 982.4 | 1,009.5 |
| New car dealers............................ | 44111 | 630.1 | 549.5 | 735.4 | 785.1 | 842.1 | 876.6 | 898.9 |
| Used car dealers........................... | 44112 | 57.7 | 71.7 | 83.9 | 90.4 | 98.3 | 105.8 | 110.6 |
| Other motor vehicle dealers.................. | 4412 | 45.0 | 43.8 | 55.0 | 59.5 | 64.4 | 69.3 | 74.1 |
| Auto parts, accessories, and tire stores......... | 4413 | 63.4 | 77.9 | 85.0 | 85.8 | 89.3 | 90.6 | 90.8 |
| Furniture and home furnishings stores............. | 442 | 91.2 | 85.2 | 95.3 | 99.7 | 106.6 | 110.7 | 113.8 |
| Furniture stores............................. | 4421 | 50.6 | 46.7 | 50.9 | 53.3 | 57.3 | 59.0 | 59.9 |
| Home furnishings stores....................... | 4422 | 40.6 | 38.5 | 44.5 | 46.4 | 49.3 | 51.7 | 53.9 |
| Electronics and appliance stores [3]................. | 443 | 90.4 | 99.6 | 104.7 | 105.2 | 103.7 | 99.3 | 99.4 |
| Electronics stores........................... | 443142 | 77.8 | 84.1 | 87.6 | 88.1 | 86.5 | 82.0 | 82.9 |
| Building materials, garden equipment, and supply stores............................. | 444 | 229.0 | 260.6 | 301.8 | 318.4 | 331.6 | 349.4 | 365.7 |
| Food and beverage stores [3]...................... | 445 | 444.8 | 580.5 | 640.8 | 669.2 | 685.4 | 699.4 | 725.9 |
| Grocery stores.............................. | 4451 | 402.5 | 520.8 | 574.5 | 599.6 | 613.2 | 624.1 | 648.5 |
| Supermarkets and other grocery (except convenience) stores............................ | 44511 | 381.4 | 498.0 | 549.1 | 573.8 | 587.8 | 597.2 | 620.0 |
| Beer, wine and liquor stores................... | 4453 | 28.5 | 41.4 | 46.1 | 48.3 | 50.6 | 53.1 | 55.2 |
| Health and personal care stores [3]................ | 446 | 155.2 | 260.4 | 281.8 | 299.3 | 315.2 | 327.0 | 333.2 |
| Pharmacies and drug stores................... | 44611 | 130.9 | 222.2 | 235.5 | 250.5 | 263.5 | 272.3 | 277.6 |
| Gasoline stations.............................. | 447 | 249.8 | 448.3 | 549.6 | 538.8 | 444.0 | 418.7 | 452.9 |
| Clothing and clothing accessory stores [3].......... | 448 | 167.7 | 213.3 | 244.7 | 250.4 | 255.8 | 259.8 | 258.5 |
| Clothing stores [3]............................ | 4481 | 118.1 | 158.3 | 179.0 | 183.1 | 187.1 | 189.7 | 189.1 |
| Shoe stores................................ | 4482 | 22.9 | 27.2 | 32.5 | 33.5 | 34.5 | 36.2 | 35.5 |
| Jewelry, luggage, and leather goods stores..... | 4483 | 26.7 | 27.8 | 33.2 | 33.8 | 34.1 | 34.0 | 33.9 |
| Sporting goods, hobby, musical instrument, and book stores [3]............................ | 451 | 67.6 | 78.2 | 82.9 | 83.8 | 85.7 | 86.6 | 84.3 |
| Sporting goods stores........................ | 45111 | 25.3 | 37.4 | 44.4 | 44.7 | 46.3 | 47.3 | 45.2 |
| Hobby, toy, and game stores.................. | 45112 | 16.9 | 15.8 | 16.9 | 17.4 | 18.0 | 18.3 | 18.0 |
| General merchandise stores [3].................... | 452 | 404.2 | 603.8 | 651.9 | 667.2 | 674.9 | 675.4 | 683.9 |
| Department stores........................... | 4521 | 232.5 | 184.8 | 170.2 | 168.1 | 164.0 | 152.6 | 144.7 |
| Discount department stores................. | 452112 | 136.2 | 119.9 | 109.6 | 107.5 | 105.1 | 97.9 | 94.4 |
| Other general merchandise stores............ | 4529 | 171.8 | 419.0 | 481.7 | 499.1 | 510.9 | 522.8 | 539.2 |
| Warehouse clubs and supercenters........... | 45291 | 139.6 | 368.0 | 419.4 | 433.3 | 441.7 | 449.9 | 461.7 |
| Miscellaneous store retailers [3].................. | 453 | 106.7 | 104.2 | 112.4 | 115.9 | 119.4 | 121.7 | 125.5 |
| Office supplies, stationery, and gift stores........ | 4532 | 41.7 | 34.3 | 33.0 | 32.4 | 31.5 | 30.3 | 29.3 |
| Office supplies and stationery stores........... | 45321 | 22.7 | 18.8 | 16.6 | 15.8 | 14.7 | 13.5 | 12.6 |
| Used merchandise stores...................... | 4533 | 9.8 | 11.8 | 15.4 | 16.2 | 17.0 | 17.4 | 18.4 |
| Nonstore retailers [3]........................... | 454 | 180.5 | 341.0 | 433.1 | 470.9 | 509.7 | 561.6 | 629.6 |
| Electronic shopping and mail-order houses...... | 4541 | 113.8 | 263.5 | 350.5 | 386.1 | 434.0 | 488.6 | 552.2 |
| Fuel dealers............................... | 45431 | 26.7 | 35.5 | 37.7 | 39.6 | 29.8 | 24.0 | 26.7 |

X Not applicable. [1] North American Industry Classification System, 2012; see text, Section 15. [2] GAFO (General Merchandise, Apparel, Furniture, and Office Supplies) represents stores classified in the following NAICS codes: 442, 443, 448, 451, 452, and 4532. [3] Includes other kinds of businesses, not shown separately.

Source: U.S. Census Bureau, "Annual Retail Trade Survey (ARTS) Tables," <https://www.census.gov/programs-surveys/arts/data/tables.html>, accessed April 2019.

## Table 1076. Retail Trade Corporations—Sales, Net Profit, and Profit Per Dollar of Sales: 2017 and 2018

[2,917 represents $2,917,000,000,000. Represents 2017 North American Industry Classification System (NAICS) groups 44 and 45. Profit rates are averages of quarterly figures at annual rates. Covers corporations with assets of $50,000,000 or more]

| Item | Unit | Total retail trade | | Food and beverage stores (NAICS 445) | | Clothing & general merchandise stores (NAICS 448, 452) | | All other retail stores | |
|---|---|---|---|---|---|---|---|---|---|
| | | 2017 | 2018 | 2017 | 2018 | 2017 | 2018 | 2017 | 2018 |
| Sales....................................... | Bil. dol. | 2,917 | 3,068 | 470 | 473 | 944 | 981 | 1,503 | 1,614 |
| Net profit: | | | | | | | | | |
| Before income taxes.................. | Bil. dol. | 115.2 | 113.6 | 8.7 | 8.8 | 39.8 | 34.1 | 66.7 | 70.7 |
| After income taxes.................... | Bil. dol. | 88.6 | 88.9 | 7.7 | 6.8 | 30.6 | 24.7 | 50.3 | 57.3 |
| Profits per dollar of sales: | | | | | | | | | |
| Before income taxes.................. | Cents | 3.9 | 3.7 | 1.8 | 1.9 | 4.2 | 3.4 | 4.4 | 4.4 |
| After income taxes.................... | Cents | 3.0 | 2.9 | 1.6 | 1.4 | 3.2 | 2.5 | 3.3 | 3.6 |
| Profits on stockholders' equity: | | | | | | | | | |
| Before income taxes.................. | Percent | 23.1 | 20.9 | 14.1 | 13.2 | 23.0 | 19.2 | 25.2 | 23.9 |
| After income taxes.................... | Percent | 17.7 | 16.4 | 12.5 | 10.2 | 17.6 | 13.9 | 19.0 | 19.4 |

Source: U.S. Census Bureau, *Quarterly Financial Report for Manufacturing, Mining, Trade, and Selected Service Industries*. See also <http://www.census.gov/econ/qfr/>.

## Table 1077. Retail Trade—Estimated Per Capita Sales by Selected Kind of Business: 2000 to 2017

[Estimates are shown in dollars and are based on data from the Annual Retail Trade Survey and the Census Bureau's Population Estimates Program. Based on estimated resident population estimates as of July 1. Data have been adjusted using final results of the 2012 Economic Census. For additional information, see source and Appendix III]

| Kind of business | 2012 NAICS code [1] | 2000 | 2005 | 2010 | 2014 | 2015 | 2016 | 2017 |
|---|---|---|---|---|---|---|---|---|
| **Retail, total.** | **44–45** | **10,573** | **12,484** | **12,343** | **14,572** | **14,735** | **15,018** | **15,522** |
| *Total excluding motor vehicle and parts dealers* | *44–45, ex 441* | 7,751 | 9,478 | 9,941 | 11,365 | 11,323 | 11,482 | 11,910 |
| Motor vehicle and parts dealers | 441 | 2,822 | 3,006 | 2,402 | 3,206 | 3,411 | 3,536 | 3,612 |
| Furniture and home furnishings stores | 442 | 323 | 369 | 275 | 313 | 332 | 343 | 350 |
| Electronics and appliance stores | 443 | 320 | 359 | 322 | 330 | 323 | 307 | 306 |
| Building material and garden equipment and supplies dealers | 444 | 812 | 1,086 | 842 | 1,000 | 1,034 | 1,081 | 1,125 |
| Food and beverage stores | 445 | 1,576 | 1,721 | 1,877 | 2,102 | 2,137 | 2,165 | 2,233 |
| Health and personal care stores | 446 | 550 | 711 | 842 | 940 | 983 | 1,012 | 1,025 |
| Gasoline stations | 447 | 885 | 1,282 | 1,449 | 1,692 | 1,384 | 1,296 | 1,393 |
| Clothing and clothing accessories stores | 448 | 594 | 680 | 690 | 786 | 798 | 804 | 795 |
| Sporting goods, hobby, musical instrument, and book stores | 451 | 240 | 255 | 253 | 263 | 267 | 268 | 259 |
| General merchandise stores | 452 | 1,433 | 1,788 | 1,952 | 2,095 | 2,104 | 2,090 | 2,103 |
| Miscellaneous store retailers | 453 | 378 | 363 | 337 | 364 | 372 | 377 | 386 |
| Nonstore retailers | 454 | 640 | 865 | 1,102 | 1,479 | 1,589 | 1,738 | 1,936 |

[1] North American Industry Classification System, 2012; see text, Section 15.

Source: U.S. Census Bureau, "Annual Retail Trade Survey (ARTS) Tables," <https://www.census.gov/programs-surveys/arts/data/tables.html>, accessed April 2019.

## Table 1078. Retail Trade—Merchandise Inventories and Inventory/Sales Ratios by Kind of Business: 2015 to 2018

[Inventories in billions of dollars (587.9 represents $587,900,000,000). As of Dec. 31. Estimates exclude food services. Includes warehouses. Adjusted for seasonal variations. Sales data also adjusted for holiday and trading-day differences. Based on data from the Monthly Retail Trade Survey, Annual Retail Trade Survey, and administrative records; see Appendix III]

| Kind of business | 2012 NAICS code [1] | Inventories | | | | Inventory/sales ratio | | | |
|---|---|---|---|---|---|---|---|---|---|
| | | 2015 | 2016 | 2017 | 2018 | 2015 | 2016 | 2017 | 2018 |
| **Retail inventories, total [2]** | **44–45** | **587.9** | **612.0** | **626.5** | **652.9** | **1.48** | **1.48** | **1.43** | **1.47** |
| Total excluding motor vehicle and parts dealers | 44–45 ex 441 | 390.4 | 398.0 | 406.6 | 411.7 | 1.28 | 1.27 | 1.21 | 1.21 |
| Motor vehicle and parts dealers | 441 | 197.5 | 214.0 | 219.9 | 241.2 | 2.13 | 2.15 | 2.16 | 2.31 |
| Furniture, home furnishings, electronics, and appliance stores | 442, 443 | 27.6 | 27.4 | 28.1 | 27.9 | 1.57 | 1.59 | 1.55 | 1.55 |
| Building material and garden equipment and supplies dealers | 444 | 50.6 | 52.7 | 54.7 | 58.7 | 1.75 | 1.77 | 1.67 | 1.78 |
| Food and beverage stores | 445 | 45.4 | 46.9 | 48.8 | 49.1 | 0.79 | 0.80 | 0.79 | 0.79 |
| Clothing and clothing accessories stores | 448 | 51.9 | 52.3 | 51.5 | 51.8 | 2.43 | 2.40 | 2.33 | 2.26 |
| General merchandise stores | 452 | 83.3 | 82.2 | 81.1 | 81.3 | 1.47 | 1.47 | 1.38 | 1.36 |
| Department stores | 4521 | 28.9 | 27.3 | 25.8 | 24.5 | 2.12 | 2.19 | 2.07 | 2.02 |

[1] North American Industry Classification System, 2012; see text, Section 15. [2] Includes other kind of businesses, not shown separately.

Source: U.S. Census Bureau, Monthly Retail Trade Report, "Retail Inventories and Inventories/Sales Ratios," <http://www.census.gov/retail/index.html>, accessed April 2019.

## Table 1079. Retail Trade Sales—Total and E-Commerce by Kind of Business: 2016

[4,856,334 represents $4,856,334,000,000. Covers retailers with and without payroll. Based on the Annual Retail Trade Survey; see Appendix III]

| Kind of business | 2012 NAICS code [1] | Value of sales (mil. dol.) | | E-commerce as percent of total sales | Percent distribution of E-commerce sales |
|---|---|---|---|---|---|
| | | Total | E-commerce | | |
| **Retail trade, total.** | **44-45** | **4,856,334** | **389,111** | **8.0** | **100.0** |
| Motor vehicle and parts dealers | 441 | 1,144,419 | 32,016 | 2.8 | 8.2 |
| Furniture and home furnishings stores | 442 | 111,468 | 1,076 | 1.0 | 0.3 |
| Electronics and appliance stores | 443 | 98,780 | 2,186 | 2.2 | 0.6 |
| Building material and garden equipment and supplies stores | 444 | 349,285 | 2,251 | 0.6 | 0.6 |
| Food and beverage stores | 445 | 700,816 | 2,463 | 0.4 | 0.6 |
| Health and personal care stores | 446 | 326,879 | (D) | (D) | (D) |
| Gasoline stations | 447 | 418,700 | (D) | (D) | (D) |
| Clothing and clothing accessories stores | 448 | 259,617 | 7,843 | 3.0 | 2.0 |
| Sporting goods, hobby, book, and music stores | 451 | 86,596 | 2,219 | 2.6 | 0.6 |
| General merchandise stores | 452 | 676,554 | 318 | (Z) | 0.1 |
| Miscellaneous store retailers | 453 | 122,467 | 3,723 | 3.0 | 1.0 |
| Nonstore retailers | 454 | 560,753 | 334,197 | 59.6 | 85.9 |
| Electronic shopping and mail-order houses | 4541 | 487,782 | 332,681 | 68.2 | 85.5 |

Z Less than 0.05 percent. D Withheld to avoid disclosing individual company data. [1] North American Industry Classification System, 2012; see text, Section 15.

Source: U.S. Census Bureau, "2016 E-Commerce Multi-sector Data Tables," <http://www.census.gov/programs-surveys/e-stats/data/tables.html>, accessed June 2018.

## Table 1080. Electronic Shopping and Mail-Order Houses—Total and E-Commerce Sales by Merchandise Line: 2015 and 2016

[433,987 represents $433,987,000,000. Represents 2012 North American Industry Classification System code 4541, which comprises establishments primarily engaged in retailing all types of merchandise using nonstore means, including catalogs, toll-free telephone numbers, or electronic media, such as interactive television or computer. Covers businesses with and without paid employees. Based on the Annual Retail Survey; see Appendix III]

| Merchandise lines | 2015 | | | 2016 | | |
|---|---|---|---|---|---|---|
| | Value of sales (million dollars) | | E-commerce as percent of total sales | Value of sales (million dollars) | | E-commerce as percent of total sales |
| | Total | E-commerce | | Total | E-commerce | |
| **Total** | **433,987** | **287,333** | **66.2** | **487,782** | **332,681** | **68.2** |
| Books (includes audio books and e-books) | 13,966 | 12,233 | 87.6 | 14,732 | 13,100 | 88.9 |
| Clothing and clothing accessories (includes footwear) | 61,876 | 52,258 | 84.5 | 68,281 | 59,135 | 86.6 |
| Computer and communications equipment & related products (includes cell phones) | 22,275 | 15,302 | 68.7 | 23,595 | 18,686 | 79.2 |
| Computer software (including video game) | 9,299 | 8,292 | 89.2 | 11,834 | 10,550 | 89.1 |
| Drugs, health aids, beauty aids | 116,187 | 24,226 | 20.9 | 129,459 | 29,692 | 22.9 |
| Electronics and appliances | 38,514 | 34,316 | 89.1 | 43,993 | 39,433 | 89.6 |
| Food, beer, and wine | 9,285 | 7,062 | 76.1 | 11,371 | 9,129 | 80.3 |
| Furniture and home furnishings | 37,110 | 32,728 | 88.2 | 44,077 | 39,510 | 89.6 |
| Jewelry | 9,053 | 6,542 | 72.3 | 9,192 | 6,882 | 74.9 |
| Audio and video recordings [1] | 8,665 | 7,780 | 89.8 | 9,558 | 8,665 | 90.7 |
| Office equipment and supplies | 9,265 | 9,070 | 97.9 | 10,688 | 9,069 | 84.9 |
| Sporting goods | 13,697 | 11,737 | 85.7 | 15,730 | 13,389 | 85.1 |
| Toys, hobby goods, and games | 15,486 | 12,482 | 80.6 | 17,439 | 14,332 | 82.2 |
| Other merchandise [2] | 57,005 | 44,524 | 78.1 | 64,703 | 51,512 | 79.6 |
| Nonmerchandise receipts [3] | 12,304 | 8,781 | 71.4 | 13,130 | 9,597 | 73.1 |

[1] Includes purchased downloads. [2] Includes other merchandise such as collectibles, souvenirs, auto parts and accessories, hardware, and lawn and garden equipment and supplies. [3] Includes auction commissions, shipping and handling, customer training, customer support, and advertising.

Source: U.S. Census Bureau, "2016 E-Commerce Multi-sector Data Tables," <https://www.census.gov/programs-surveys/e-stats/data/tables.html>, accessed June 2018.

## Table 1081. Franchised New Car Dealerships—Summary: 2000 to 2018

[In units as indicated (8.8 represents 8,800,000)]

| Item | Unit | 2000 | 2005 | 2010 | 2012 | 2013 | 2014 | 2015 | 2016 | 2017 | 2018 |
|---|---|---|---|---|---|---|---|---|---|---|---|
| Dealerships [1] | Number | 20,490 | 19,898 | 16,181 | 16,125 | 16,170 | 16,396 | 16,545 | 16,708 | 16,802 | 16,753 |
| Sales [2] | Bil. dol. | (NA) | (NA) | (NA) | (NA) | (NA) | (NA) | (NA) | 996 | 1,003 | 1,026 |
| New light duty vehicle sales | Millions | (NA) | 16.9 | 11.6 | 14.4 | 15.5 | 16.4 | 17.4 | 17.5 | 17.1 | 17.2 |
| New cars sold | Millions | 8.8 | 7.7 | 5.6 | 7.2 | 7.6 | 7.7 | 7.5 | 6.9 | 6.1 | 5.3 |
| New light trucks sold | Millions | (NA) | 9.3 | 5.9 | 7.2 | 7.9 | 8.7 | 9.9 | 10.6 | 11.1 | 11.9 |
| Average retail new vehicle selling price | Dollars | (NA) | (NA) | 30,079 | 31,194 | 32,035 | 32,824 | 33,456 | 34,449 | 34,670 | 35,608 |
| Used vehicles sold | Millions | 20.5 | 19.7 | 15.3 | 17.1 | 17.4 | (NA) | (NA) | 15.0 | (NA) | (NA) |
| Employment | 1,000 | 1,114 | 1,138 | 892 | 963 | 1,009 | 1,056 | 1,111 | 1,132 | 1,136 | 1,137 |
| Annual payroll | Bil. dol. | 46.1 | 51.5 | 42.4 | 51.6 | 53.7 | 58.1 | 62.6 | 64.9 | 65.3 | 66.5 |
| Average dealer pretax profits as percent of sales [2] | Percent | (NA) | (NA) | (NA) | (NA) | (NA) | 2.6 | 2.7 | 2.5 | 2.3 | 2.2 |
| Inventory: [3] | | | | | | | | | | | |
| Domestic: [4] | | | | | | | | | | | |
| Total | 1,000 | 3,183 | 2,991 | 1,687 | (NA) | (NA) | (NA) | 2,868 | 2,056 | 1,923 | 2,085 |
| Days' supply | Days | 68 | 70 | 60 | 62 | 66 | (NA) | 65 | 74 | 70 | 76 |
| Imported: [4] | | | | | | | | | | | |
| Total | 1,000 | 468 | 566 | 494 | (NA) | (NA) | (NA) | 656 | 1,853 | 1,866 | 1,836 |
| Days' supply | Days | 50 | 52 | 55 | 52 | 58 | (NA) | 55 | 54 | 56 | 54 |

NA Not available. [1] Light-duty new vehicle dealerships, as of December 31. [2] Beginning 2016, new methodology for calculating sales was implemented. [3] Annual average. [4] Classification based on location of automobile production (i.e., automobiles manufactured by foreign companies but produced in the U.S., Canada, and Mexico are classified as domestic).

Source: National Automobile Dealers Association, <www.nada.org>. NADA Data 2018: Annual Financial Profile of America's Franchised New-Car Dealerships, annual ©.

## Table 1082. New Motor Vehicle Sales and Car Production: 1990 to 2018

[In thousands (14,137 represents 14,137,000). Data are primarily from "Ward's Automotive Reports" published by Ward's Communications, Southfield, MI]

| Type of vehicle | 1990 | 2000 | 2010 | 2012 | 2013 | 2014 | 2015 | 2016 | 2017 | 2018 |
|---|---|---|---|---|---|---|---|---|---|---|
| **New motor vehicle sales** | **14,137** | **17,812** | **11,773** | **14,779** | **15,883** | **16,860** | **17,846** | **17,866** | **17,551** | **17,701** |
| New-car sales | 9,300 | 8,778 | 5,636 | 7,245 | 7,586 | 7,708 | 7,517 | 6,873 | 6,081 | 5,304 |
| Domestic | 6,897 | 6,762 | 3,791 | 5,120 | 5,433 | 5,610 | 5,595 | 5,146 | 4,593 | 4,087 |
| Import | 2,403 | 2,016 | 1,844 | 2,125 | 2,153 | 2,098 | 1,922 | 1,727 | 1,488 | 1,217 |
| New-truck sales | 4,837 | 9,034 | 6,137 | 7,534 | 8,296 | 9,152 | 10,329 | 10,993 | 11,470 | 12,398 |
| Light | 4,560 | 8,572 | 5,919 | 7,188 | 7,944 | 8,744 | 9,879 | 10,592 | 11,055 | 11,910 |
| Domestic | 3,957 | 7,720 | 5,020 | 6,127 | 6,704 | 7,384 | 8,097 | 8,436 | 8,652 | 9,159 |
| Import | 603 | 852 | 899 | 1,061 | 1,239 | 1,360 | 1,782 | 2,156 | 2,404 | 2,751 |
| Heavy | 278 | 462 | 218 | 346 | 353 | 408 | 449 | 401 | 415 | 488 |
| **Domestic-car production** | **6,231** | **5,471** | **2,731** | **4,109** | **4,369** | **4,253** | **4,163** | **3,917** | **3,033** | **2,795** |

Source: U.S. Bureau of Economic Analysis, National Economic Accounts, "Supplemental Information & Additional Data: Motor Vehicles," <https://www.bea.gov/data/gdp/gross-domestic-product#supp>, accessed March 2019.

# Table 1083. Food and Alcoholic Beverage Expenditures by Sales Outlet: 2000 to 2017

[In millions of dollars (295,883 represents $295,883,000,000). In constant dollars (1988=100). Includes taxes and tips. Data are shown for final purchasers including individuals and households, government (food assistance programs, Medicare/Medicaid inpatient meals, expensed meals), and businesses (expensed meals) for final use by individuals and households (including food assistance programs)]

| Sales outlet | 2000 | 2005 | 2010 | 2013 | 2014 | 2015 | 2016 | 2017 |
|---|---|---|---|---|---|---|---|---|
| Food at home................................ | 295,883 | 324,394 | 330,912 | 337,703 | 342,936 | 343,424 | 354,098 | 365,057 |
| Grocery stores................................ | 199,081 | 198,339 | 195,127 | 195,560 | 199,625 | 202,184 | 208,626 | 213,135 |
| Convenience stores............................ | 7,167 | 5,625 | 5,588 | 6,402 | 6,334 | 6,151 | 6,655 | 7,271 |
| Other food stores............................ | 7,825 | 8,448 | 8,016 | 8,238 | 8,465 | 8,525 | 8,880 | 9,513 |
| Warehouse clubs and supercenters........ | 31,354 | 58,072 | 70,292 | 73,055 | 73,731 | 74,315 | 76,811 | 79,472 |
| Mass merchandisers........................ | 6,516 | 6,585 | 6,085 | 5,261 | 5,043 | 4,873 | 4,599 | 4,539 |
| Other stores and foodservice.............. | 30,338 | 33,589 | 33,525 | 36,470 | 36,495 | 33,975 | 34,452 | 36,383 |
| Mail order and home delivery.............. | 10,648 | 10,891 | 9,355 | 9,571 | 9,791 | 9,739 | 10,354 | 11,035 |
| Direct selling by farmers, manufacturers, and wholesalers.... | 2,187 | 1,800 | 1,905 | 2,243 | 2,543 | 2,794 | 2,842 | 2,825 |
| Home production and donations........... | 767 | 1,044 | 1,019 | 904 | 908 | 868 | 880 | 883 |
| Food away from home (FAFH).............. | 287,811 | 326,391 | 332,026 | 357,837 | 367,232 | 382,636 | 391,579 | 393,851 |
| Full-service restaurants..................... | 100,586 | 115,925 | 114,118 | 125,632 | 131,627 | 137,786 | 139,824 | 140,925 |
| Limited-service restaurants................ | 93,964 | 110,908 | 114,508 | 123,323 | 127,103 | 136,007 | 141,909 | 142,276 |
| Drinking places............................. | 1,461 | 1,828 | 1,999 | 2,011 | 1,979 | 1,911 | 2,017 | 2,284 |
| Hotels and motels........................... | 15,568 | 13,383 | 12,172 | 14,610 | 15,136 | 15,646 | 16,010 | 16,483 |
| Retail stores and vending.................. | 13,396 | 15,323 | 16,151 | 17,852 | 17,752 | 16,580 | 16,221 | 16,490 |
| Recreational places......................... | 12,245 | 12,412 | 11,224 | 12,440 | 12,765 | 13,308 | 13,712 | 14,052 |
| Schools and colleges....................... | 23,510 | 27,911 | 33,082 | 32,510 | 31,264 | 31,444 | 31,406 | 30,990 |
| Other FAFH sales, not elsewhere classified.................................. | 9,117 | 10,169 | 9,670 | 9,675 | 9,845 | 10,112 | 10,432 | 10,089 |
| Food furnished and donated............... | 17,964 | 18,533 | 19,102 | 19,783 | 19,761 | 19,842 | 20,048 | 20,263 |
| Alcohol at home.............................. | 41,685 | 44,951 | 49,620 | 55,325 | 57,005 | 57,567 | 58,915 | 60,568 |
| Liquor stores................................ | 18,093 | 20,008 | 22,743 | 24,749 | 25,774 | 26,944 | 28,161 | 28,756 |
| Food stores................................ | 11,546 | 12,187 | 13,396 | 15,331 | 15,853 | 16,125 | 16,386 | 16,758 |
| All other.................................... | 12,045 | 12,757 | 13,481 | 15,244 | 15,378 | 14,497 | 14,367 | 15,054 |
| Alcohol away from home.................... | 32,755 | 34,070 | 32,889 | 36,249 | 37,525 | 38,929 | 40,194 | 41,964 |
| Eating and drinking places................. | 26,059 | 27,689 | 26,834 | 29,418 | 30,462 | 31,589 | 32,619 | 34,056 |
| Hotels and motels........................... | 3,500 | 3,066 | 2,917 | 3,483 | 3,628 | 3,779 | 3,895 | 4,022 |
| All other.................................... | 3,195 | 3,316 | 3,138 | 3,348 | 3,435 | 3,560 | 3,680 | 3,887 |

Source: U.S. Department of Agriculture, Economic Research Service, "Food Expenditure Series," <https://www.ers.usda.gov/data-products/food-expenditure-series/>, accessed January 2019.

# Section 23
# Transportation

This section presents data on civil air transportation, both passenger and cargo, and on water transportation, including inland waterways, oceanborne commerce, the merchant marine, cargo, and vessel tonnages.

This section also presents statistics on revenues, passenger and freight traffic volume, and employment in various revenue-producing modes of the transportation industry, including motor vehicles, trains, and pipelines. Data are also presented on highway mileage and finances, motor vehicle travel, accidents, and registrations; and characteristics of public transit, railroads, and pipelines.

The principal source of transportation data is the annual *National Transportation Statistics* publication of the U.S. Bureau of Transportation Statistics. Principal sources of water transportation data is the annual *Waterborne Commerce of the United States* issued by the Corps of Engineers of the Department of Army. In addition, the U.S. Census Bureau in its Commodity Flow Survey (part of the Economic Census, taken every 5 years through 2012, for years ending in "2" and "7") provides data on the type, weight, and value of commodities shipped by manufacturing establishments in the United States, by means of transportation, origin, and destination. Release of data from the 2012 Economic Census was completed in 2016. This census was conducted in accordance with the 2012 North American Industry Classification System (NAICS). The 2017 Economic Census is being released on a flow basis between September 2019 and December 2021. See text, Section 15, Business Enterprise, for a discussion of the Economic Census and NAICS.

The Bureau of Transportation Statistics (BTS) was established within the U.S. Department of Transportation (DOT) in 1992 to collect, report, and analyze transportation data. BTS products include reports to Congress, the Secretary of Transportation, and stakeholders in the nation's transportation community. These stakeholders include: federal agencies, state and local governments, metropolitan planning organizations, universities, the private sector, and the general public. Congress requires, by congressional mandate laid out in 49 U.S.C. 111 (1), the BTS to report on transportation statistics to the President and Congress. *The Transportation Statistics Annual Report* (TSAR), provides a data overview of U.S. transportation issues. As required by Congress, each TSAR has two essential components: a review of the state of transportation statistics with recommendations for improvements, and a presentation of the data. The BTS publication *National Transportation Statistics* (NTS), a companion report to the TSAR, has more comprehensive and longer time-series data. NTS presents information on the U.S. transportation system, including its physical components, safety record, economic performance, energy use, and environmental impacts. The BTS publication *State Transportation Statistics* presents a statistical profile of transportation in the 50 states and the District of Columbia. This profile includes infrastructure, freight movement and passenger travel, system safety, vehicles, transportation-related economy and finance, energy usage, and the environment.

The principal compiler of data on public roads and on operation of motor vehicles is the U.S. Department of Transportation's (DOT) Federal Highway Administration (FHWA). These data appear in FHWA's annual *Highway Statistics* and other publications.

The U.S. National Highway Traffic Safety Administration (NHTSA), through its *Traffic Safety Facts FARS/GES Annual Report*, presents descriptive statistics about traffic crashes of all severities, from those that result in property damage to those that result in the loss of life. This report compiles motor vehicle crash data from the Fatality Analysis Reporting System (FARS) and the General Estimates System (GES). Other publications and reports can be found at the National Center for Statistics and Analysis (NCSA), Publications and Data Request, located on the internet at <https://crashstats.nhtsa.dot.gov/#/>. DOT's Federal Railroad Administration (FRA), Office of Safety Analysis presents railroad safety information, including accidents and incidents, inspections, and highway-rail crossing data at its "Safety Database" located at <http://safetydata.fra.dot.gov/officeofsafety>.

**Civil aviation**—Federal promotion and regulation of civil aviation have been carried out by the Federal Aviation Administration (FAA) and the Civil Aeronautics Board (CAB). The CAB promoted and regulated the civil air transportation industry within the United States and between the United States and foreign countries. The Board granted licenses to provide air transportation service, approved or disapproved proposed rates and fares, and approved or disapproved proposed agreements and corporate relationships involving air carriers. In December 1984, the CAB ceased to exist as an agency. Some of its functions were transferred to the DOT, as outlined below. The responsibility for investigation of aviation accidents resides with the National Transportation Safety Board.

The Office of the Secretary, DOT aviation activities include: negotiation of international air transportation rights, selection of U.S. air carriers to serve capacity controlled international markets, oversight of international rates and fares, maintenance of essential air service to small communities, and consumer affairs. DOT's Bureau of Transportation Statistics (BTS) handles aviation information functions formerly assigned to CAB. Prior to BTS, the Research and Special Programs Administration handled these functions.

The principal activities of the FAA include: the promotion of air safety; controlling the use of navigable airspace; prescribing regulations dealing with the competency of airmen, airworthiness of aircraft, and air traffic control; operation of air route traffic control centers, airport traffic control towers, and flight service stations; the design, construction, maintenance, and inspection of navigation, traffic control, and communications equipment; and the development of general aviation.

The CAB published monthly and quarterly financial and traffic statistical data for the certificated route air carriers. BTS continues these publications, including both certificated and noncertificated (commuter) air carriers. The FAA annually publishes data on the use of airway facilities; data related to the location of airmen, aircraft, and airports; the volume of activity in the field of nonair carrier (general aviation) flying; and aircraft production and registration.

General aviation comprises all civil flying (including such commercial operations as small demand air taxis, agriculture application, powerline patrol, etc.) but excludes certificated route air carriers, supplemental operators, large-aircraft commercial operators, and commuter airlines.

**Air carriers and service**—The CAB previously issued "certificates of public convenience and necessity" under Section 401 of the Federal Aviation Act of 1958 for scheduled and nonscheduled (charter) passenger services and cargo services. It also issued certificates under Section 418 of the Act to cargo air carriers for domestic all-cargo service only. The DOT Office of the Secretary now issues the certificates under a "fit, willing, and able" test of air carrier operations. Carriers operating only a 60-seat-or-less aircraft are given exemption authority to carry passengers, cargo, and mail in scheduled and nonscheduled service under Part 298 of the DOT (formerly CAB) regulations. Exemption authority carriers who offer scheduled passenger service to an essential air service point must meet the "fit, willing, and able" test.

**Vessel shipments, entrances, and clearances**—Shipments by dry cargo vessels comprise shipments on all types of watercraft, except tanker vessels; shipments by tanker vessels comprise all types of cargo, liquid and dry, carried by tanker vessels. A vessel is reported as entered only at the first port which it enters in the United States, whether or not cargo is unloaded at that port.

A vessel is reported as cleared only at the last port at which clearance is made to a foreign port, whether or not it takes on cargo. Army and Navy vessels entering or clearing without commercial cargo are not included in the figures.

**Units of measurement**—Cargo (or freight) tonnage and shipping weight both represent the gross weight of the cargo including the weight of containers, wrappings, crates, etc. However, shipping weight excludes lift and cargo vans and similar substantial outer containers. Other tonnage figures generally refer to stowing capacity of vessels, 100 cubic feet being called 1 ton. Gross tonnage comprises the space within the frames and the ceiling of the hull, together with those closed-in spaces above deck available for cargo, stores, passengers, or crew, with certain minor exceptions. Net or registered tonnage is the gross tonnage less the spaces occupied by the propelling machinery, fuel, crew quarters, master's cabin, and navigation spaces. Substantially, it represents space available for cargo and passengers. The net tonnage capacity of a ship may bear little relation to weight of cargo. Deadweight tonnage is the weight in long tons required to depress a vessel from light water line (that is, with only the machinery and equipment on board) to load line. It is, therefore, the weight of the cargo, fuel, etc., which a vessel is designed to carry with safety.

**Federal-aid highway systems**—The Intermodal Surface Transportation Efficiency Act (ISTEA) of 1991 eliminated the historical Federal-Aid Highway Systems and created the National Highway System (NHS) and other federal-aid highway categories. The final NHS was approved by Congress in December of 1995 under the National Highway System Designation Act.

**Functional systems**—Roads and streets are assigned to groups according to the character of service intended. The functional systems are (1) arterial highways that generally handle the long trips, (2) collector facilities that collect and disperse traffic between the arterials and the lower systems, and (3) local roads and streets that primarily serve direct access to residential areas, farms, and other local areas.

**Regulatory bodies**—The Federal Energy Regulatory Commission (FERC) is an independent agency that regulates the interstate transmission of electricity, natural gas, and oil. FERC also reviews proposals to build liquefied natural gas (LNG) terminals and interstate natural gas pipelines as well as licenses hydropower projects. The Energy Policy Act of 2005 gave FERC additional responsibilities such as regulating the transmission and wholesale sales of electricity in interstate commerce.

The Surface Transportation Board (STB) was created in the Interstate Commerce Commission Termination Act of 1995, Pub. L. No.104-88, 109 Stat. 803 (1995) (ICCTA), and is the successor agency to the Interstate Commerce Commission. The STB is an economic regulatory agency that Congress charged with the fundamental missions of resolving railroad rate and service disputes and reviewing proposed railroad mergers. The STB makes decisions independently, although it is administratively affiliated with the Department of Transportation.

The STB serves as both an adjudicatory and a regulatory body. The agency has jurisdiction over railroad rate and service issues and rail restructuring transactions (mergers, line sales, line construction, and line abandonment); certain trucking company, moving van, and noncontiguous ocean shipping company rate matters; certain intercity passenger bus company structure, financial, and operational matters; and rates and services of certain pipelines not regulated by the Federal Energy Regulatory Commission. Other ICC regulatory functions were either eliminated or transferred to the Federal Highway Administration or the Bureau of Transportation Statistics within DOT.

Class I Railroads are regulated by the STB and subject to the Uniform System of Accounts and required to file annual and periodic reports. Railroads are classified based on their annual operating revenues. The class to which a carrier belongs is determined by comparing its adjusted operating revenues for 3 consecutive years to the following scale: Class I, $250 million or more; Class II, $20 million to $250 million; and Class III, $0 to $20 million. Operating revenue dollar ranges are indexed for inflation.

**Postal Service**—The U.S. Postal Service provides mail processing and delivery services within the United States. The Postal Accountability and Enhancement Act of 2006 was the first major legislative change to the Postal Service since 1971 when the Postal Reorganization Act of 1970 created the Postal Service as an independent establishment of the Federal Executive Branch. The Act of 2006 changed the way the U.S. Postal Service operates and conducts business. Now annual rate increases for market dominant products are linked to the Consumer Price Index and the Postal Service has more flexibility for pricing competitive products, enabling it to respond to dynamic market conditions and changing customer needs.

Revenue and cost analysis describes the Postal Service's system of attributing revenues and costs to classes of mail and service. This system draws primarily upon probability sampling techniques to develop estimates of revenues, volumes, and weights, as well as costs by class of mail and special service. The costs attributed to classes of mail and special services are primarily incremental costs which vary in response to changes in volume; they account for roughly 60 percent of the total costs of the Postal Service. The balance represents "institutional costs." Statistics on revenues, volume of mail, and distribution of expenditures are presented in the Postal Service's annual reports *Cost and Revenue Analysis* and *Annual Report to Congress*.

**Statistical reliability**—For a discussion of statistical collection and estimation, sampling procedures, and measures of statistical reliability applicable to Census Bureau data, see Appendix III.

## Table 1084. Transportation-Related Components of U.S. Gross Domestic Product: 2005 to 2017

[In billions of dollars (1,242.7 represents $1,242,700,000,000), except percent. For explanation of chained dollars, see text, Section 13. Minus sign (-) indicates a decrease]

| Item | 2005 | 2010 | 2014 | 2015 | 2016 | 2017 |
|---|---|---|---|---|---|---|
| **CURRENT DOLLARS** | | | | | | |
| **Total transportation-related final demand** [1] | **1,242.7** | **1,344.7** | **1,696.2** | **1,670.2** | **1,666.2** | **1,718.1** |
| Total gross domestic product (GDP) | 13,036.6 | 14,992.1 | 17,521.7 | 18,219.3 | 18,707.2 | 19,485.4 |
| Transportation as a percent of GDP | 9.5 | 9.0 | 9.7 | 9.2 | 8.9 | 8.8 |
| Personal consumption of transportation | 955.3 | 961.8 | 1,202.4 | 1,162.7 | 1,160.4 | 1,225.2 |
| Motor vehicles and parts | 410.0 | 344.5 | 442.3 | 473.9 | 483.7 | 498.2 |
| Motor vehicle fuels, lubricants, and fluids | 261.4 | 312.1 | 376.9 | 289.5 | 258.9 | 290.0 |
| Transportation services | 283.9 | 305.2 | 383.2 | 399.3 | 417.8 | 437.0 |
| Gross private domestic investment | 186.7 | 145.7 | 284.4 | 318.5 | 303.6 | 299.1 |
| Transportation structures | 7.1 | 9.9 | 12.2 | 13.6 | 13.1 | 14.8 |
| Transportation equipment | 179.6 | 135.8 | 272.2 | 304.9 | 290.5 | 284.3 |
| Net exports of transportation-related goods and service [2] | -133.2 | -75.9 | -113.4 | -143.1 | -142.1 | -145.7 |
| Exports (+) | 206.9 | 255.6 | 363.6 | 359.1 | 355.9 | 367.2 |
| Civilian aircraft, engines, and parts | 55.9 | 71.9 | 113.1 | 119.5 | 120.9 | 121.0 |
| Automotive vehicles, engines, and parts | 98.4 | 112.0 | 159.8 | 151.9 | 150.3 | 157.6 |
| Transport | 52.6 | 71.7 | 90.7 | 87.7 | 84.7 | 88.6 |
| Imports (-) | 340.1 | 331.5 | 477.0 | 502.2 | 498.0 | 512.9 |
| Civilian aircraft, engines, and parts | 25.8 | 31.3 | 53.3 | 55.2 | 50.0 | 51.4 |
| Automotive vehicles, engines, and parts | 238.7 | 225.6 | 329.5 | 350.0 | 351.1 | 359.8 |
| Transport | 75.6 | 74.6 | 94.2 | 97.0 | 96.9 | 101.7 |
| Government transportation-related purchases | 236.8 | 301.3 | 313.5 | 321.4 | 325.3 | 328.4 |
| Federal purchases [3] | 29.9 | 38.5 | 39.4 | 40.7 | 41.0 | 42.9 |
| State and local purchases [3] | 191.0 | 238.1 | 259.6 | 267.5 | 271.1 | 272.0 |
| Defense-related purchases [4] | 15.9 | 24.7 | 14.5 | 13.2 | 13.2 | 13.5 |
| **CHAINED (2012) DOLLARS** | | | | | | |
| **Total transportation-related final demand** [1] | **1,584.5** | **1,497.0** | **1,686.5** | **1,755.6** | **1,778.6** | **1,777.9** |
| Total gross domestic product (GDP) | 14,912.5 | 15,598.8 | 16,899.8 | 17,386.7 | 17,659.2 | 18,050.7 |
| Transportation as a percent of GDP | 10.6 | 9.6 | 10.0 | 10.1 | 10.1 | 9.8 |
| Personal consumption of transportation | 1,206.3 | 1,086.8 | 1,217.7 | 1,282.5 | 1,315.1 | 1,345.7 |
| Motor vehicles and parts | 435.1 | 360.0 | 439.8 | 471.4 | 486.5 | 507.2 |
| Motor vehicle fuels, lubricants, and fluids | 419.5 | 406.0 | 403.2 | 421.6 | 424.4 | 420.9 |
| Transportation services | 351.7 | 320.8 | 374.7 | 389.5 | 404.2 | 417.6 |
| Gross private domestic investment | 200.3 | 151.7 | 276.1 | 304.2 | 286.3 | 277.5 |
| Transportation structures | 8.2 | 10.2 | 11.7 | 12.8 | 12.0 | 13.3 |
| Transportation equipment | 192.1 | 141.5 | 264.4 | 291.4 | 274.3 | 264.2 |
| Net exports of transportation-related goods and service [2] | -147.5 | -80.9 | -118.9 | -154.1 | -158.2 | -166.5 |
| Exports (+) | 248.5 | 272.3 | 355.1 | 353.1 | 352.0 | 357.4 |
| Civilian aircraft, engines, and parts | 73.2 | 76.6 | 107.6 | 110.7 | 110.3 | 106.2 |
| Automotive vehicles, engines, and parts | 106.7 | 115.9 | 158.0 | 150.4 | 150.0 | 156.9 |
| Transport | 68.6 | 79.8 | 89.5 | 92.0 | 91.7 | 94.3 |
| Imports (-) | 396.0 | 353.2 | 474.0 | 507.2 | 510.2 | 523.9 |
| Civilian aircraft, engines, and parts | 36.9 | 36.1 | 51.6 | 52.8 | 47.5 | 48.2 |
| Automotive vehicles, engines, and parts | 264.5 | 237.0 | 332.8 | 360.7 | 364.5 | 375.1 |
| Transport | 94.6 | 80.1 | 89.6 | 93.7 | 98.2 | 100.6 |
| Government transportation-related purchases | 328.6 | 327.1 | 302.2 | 312.2 | 316.1 | 309.8 |
| Federal purchases [3] | 35.1 | 39.9 | 38.1 | 38.8 | 38.7 | 39.6 |
| State and local purchases [3] | 273.8 | 260.3 | 250.1 | 260.3 | 264.0 | 256.6 |
| Defense-related purchases [4] | 19.7 | 26.9 | 14.0 | 13.1 | 13.4 | 13.6 |

[1] Sum of total personal consumption of transportation, total gross private domestic investment, net exports of transportation-related goods and services, and total government transportation-related purchases. [2] Exports minus imports. [3] Federal purchases and state and local purchases are the sum of consumption expenditures and gross investment. [4] Defense-related purchases are the sum of transportation of material and travel.

Source: U.S. Bureau of Transportation Statistics, "National Transportation Statistics," <https://www.bts.gov/product/national-transportation-statistics>, accessed July 2019.

## Table 1085. Employment in Transportation and Warehousing: 2000 to 2018

[In thousands (4,414 represents 4,414,000). Annual average of monthly figures. Based on Current Employment Statistics program; see Appendix III]

| Industry | NAICS code [1] | 2000 | 2010 | 2012 | 2013 | 2014 | 2015 | 2016 | 2017 | 2018 |
|---|---|---|---|---|---|---|---|---|---|---|
| **Transportation and warehousing** | **48–49** | **4,414** | **4,196** | **4,421** | **4,504** | **4,667** | **4,877** | **5,020** | **5,195** | **5,419** |
| Air transportation | 481 | 614 | 458 | 459 | 444 | 444 | 459 | 478 | 492 | 501 |
| Rail transportation | 482 | 232 | 216 | 231 | 231 | 236 | 241 | 217 | 215 | 214 |
| Water transportation | 483 | 56 | 62 | 64 | 65 | 67 | 66 | 66 | 65 | 65 |
| Truck transportation | 484 | 1,406 | 1,251 | 1,350 | 1,383 | 1,418 | 1,453 | 1,448 | 1,457 | 1,492 |
| Transit and ground passenger | 485 | 372 | 430 | 440 | 449 | 467 | 478 | 484 | 489 | 488 |
| Pipeline transportation | 486 | 46 | 42 | 44 | 45 | 47 | 50 | 50 | 49 | 49 |
| Scenic and sightseeing | 487 | 28 | 27 | 28 | 29 | 31 | 33 | 35 | 35 | 34 |
| Support activities | 488 | 537 | 543 | 580 | 598 | 626 | 652 | 667 | 690 | 712 |
| Couriers and messengers | 492 | 605 | 528 | 534 | 544 | 577 | 613 | 645 | 676 | 725 |
| Warehousing and storage | 493 | 518 | 638 | 692 | 716 | 755 | 834 | 932 | 1,027 | 1,140 |

[1] North American Industry Classification System 2017, see text, Sections 12 and 15.

Source: U.S. Bureau of Labor Statistics, Current Employment Statistics, "Employment, Hours, and Earnings—National," <http://www.bls.gov/ces/data.htm/>, accessed July 2019.

# Table 1086. Transportation and Warehousing—Establishments, Employees, and Payroll by Kind of Business: 2015 and 2016

[Employment in thousands (4,616.6 represents 4,616,600); payroll in millions of dollars ($222,018.3 represents $222,018,300,000). Covers establishments with payroll. Excludes self-employed individuals, railroad employees, and most government employees. For statement on methodology, see Appendix III. County Business Patterns excludes rail transportation (NAICS 482) and the National Postal Service (NAICS 491)]

| Industry | NAICS code [1] | Establishments | | Paid employees (1,000) [2] | | Annual payroll (mil. dol.) | |
|---|---|---|---|---|---|---|---|
| | | 2015 | 2016 | 2015 | 2016 | 2015 | 2016 |
| **Transportation & warehousing** | **48–49** | **228,382** | **230,994** | **4,616.6** | **4,729.7** | **222,018.3** | **229,162.6** |
| Air transportation | 481 | 4,877 | 4,522 | 453.4 | 466.4 | 32,614.3 | 35,365.5 |
| Scheduled air transportation | 4811 | 2,516 | 2,230 | 416.2 | 428.3 | 29,444.3 | 32,045.3 |
| Scheduled passenger air transportation | 481111 | 2,089 | 1,800 | 405.6 | 416.7 | 28,656.2 | 31,174.3 |
| Scheduled freight air transportation | 481112 | 427 | 430 | 10.7 | 11.6 | 788.1 | 871.0 |
| Nonscheduled air transportation | 4812 | 2,361 | 2,292 | 37.1 | 38.1 | 3,170.0 | 3,320.2 |
| Water transportation | 483 | 1,710 | 1,677 | 67.9 | 65.1 | 5,495.9 | 5,228.4 |
| Deep sea, coastal, & Great Lakes water transportation | 4831 | 1,141 | 1,134 | 45.3 | 42.7 | 3,789.7 | 3,609.2 |
| Inland water transportation | 4832 | 569 | 543 | 22.6 | 22.4 | 1,706.3 | 1,619.1 |
| Inland water freight transportation | 483211 | 359 | 355 | 20.3 | 20.1 | 1,584.4 | 1,492.2 |
| Inland water passenger transportation | 483212 | 210 | 188 | 2.3 | 2.3 | 121.9 | 126.9 |
| Truck transportation | 484 | 121,653 | 124,320 | 1,448.6 | 1,460.6 | 68,039.8 | 68,761.2 |
| General freight trucking | 4841 | 74,098 | 75,637 | 955.3 | 977.1 | 45,046.4 | 46,481.6 |
| General freight trucking, local | 48411 | 29,884 | 30,560 | 195.9 | 196.5 | 8,202.1 | 8,292.6 |
| General freight trucking, long distance | 48412 | 44,214 | 45,077 | 759.3 | 780.6 | 36,844.4 | 38,189.0 |
| Specialized freight trucking | 4842 | 47,555 | 48,683 | 493.4 | 483.5 | 22,993.4 | 22,279.6 |
| Used household & office goods moving | 48421 | 7,933 | 8,183 | 96.9 | 99.3 | 3,474.2 | 3,541.8 |
| Specialized freight (except used goods) trucking, local | 48422 | 29,163 | 29,459 | 217.1 | 207.2 | 10,341.6 | 9,834.8 |
| Specialized freight (except used goods) trucking, long-distance | 48423 | 10,459 | 11,041 | 179.4 | 176.9 | 9,177.5 | 8,903.0 |
| Transit & ground passenger transportation | 485 | 20,249 | 20,247 | 492.6 | 516.0 | 13,614.8 | 14,560.8 |
| Urban transit systems | 4851 | 794 | 784 | 53.5 | 54.3 | 2,462.6 | 2,548.0 |
| Mixed mode systems | 485111 | 27 | 22 | 0.7 | 0.7 | 27.6 | 29.0 |
| Commuter rail | 485112 | 14 | 13 | 3.4 | 3.3 | 303.2 | 299.4 |
| Bus and other motor vehicle mode systems | 485113 | 708 | 702 | 47.5 | 48.2 | 2,002.7 | 2,080.4 |
| Other | 485119 | 45 | 47 | 2.0 | 2.1 | 129.1 | 139.2 |
| Interurban & rural bus transportation | 4852 | 467 | 465 | 12.5 | 13.3 | 477.2 | 468.9 |
| Taxi & limousine service | 4853 | 8,553 | 8,386 | 77.5 | 77.6 | 2,452.8 | 2,799.1 |
| Taxi service | 48531 | 3,348 | 3,315 | 35.1 | 36.7 | 1,276.6 | 1,643.9 |
| Limousine service | 48532 | 5,205 | 5,071 | 42.4 | 40.9 | 1,176.2 | 1,155.2 |
| School & employee bus transportation | 4854 | 4,302 | 4,168 | 227.1 | 241.7 | 4,921.2 | 5,190.7 |
| Charter bus industry | 4855 | 1,315 | 1,287 | 34.0 | 34.3 | 1,010.1 | 1,070.3 |
| Other transit & ground passenger transportation | 4859 | 4,818 | 5,157 | 87.9 | 94.9 | 2,290.9 | 2,483.9 |
| Special needs transportation | 485991 | 3,085 | 3,192 | 66.6 | 71.6 | 1,758.4 | 1,889.8 |
| Pipeline transportation | 486 | 3,671 | 3,695 | 52.2 | 53.7 | 5,909.3 | 6,021.9 |
| Pipeline transportation of crude oil | 4861 | 796 | 785 | 13.9 | 14.2 | 1,614.0 | 1,526.0 |
| Pipeline transportation of natural gas | 4862 | 2,179 | 2,218 | 30.3 | 30.7 | 3,376.1 | 3,501.2 |
| Other pipeline transportation | 4869 | 696 | 692 | 8.0 | 8.8 | 919.2 | 994.2 |
| Scenic & sightseeing transportation | 487 | 2,744 | 2,846 | 26.5 | 29.1 | 968.1 | 1,060.4 |
| Scenic & sightseeing transportation, land | 4871 | 715 | 753 | 11.2 | 11.9 | 352.7 | 371.3 |
| Scenic & sightseeing transportation, water | 4872 | 1,803 | 1,867 | 13.0 | 14.5 | 508.8 | 554.0 |
| Scenic & sightseeing transportation, other | 4879 | 226 | 226 | 2.3 | 2.7 | 107.6 | 135.1 |
| Support activities for transportation | 488 | 43,495 | 43,627 | 674.5 | 692.8 | 34,248.2 | 34,877.9 |
| Support activities for air transportation | 4881 | 5,762 | 5,829 | 175.0 | 184.8 | 7,595.6 | 7,893.9 |
| Airport operations | 48811 | 2,076 | 2,063 | 94.9 | 100.7 | 2,923.5 | 3,014.9 |
| Air traffic control | 488111 | 191 | 182 | 1.4 | 1.3 | 96.0 | 90.4 |
| Other support activities for air transportation | 48819 | 3,686 | 3,766 | 80.1 | 84.1 | 4,672.1 | 4,879.0 |
| Support activities for rail transportation | 4882 | 1,403 | 1,347 | 39.4 | 41.7 | 2,026.2 | 2,009.0 |
| Support activities for water transportation | 4883 | 2,556 | 2,555 | 97.4 | 93.4 | 6,423.2 | 6,432.1 |
| Port and harbor operations | 48831 | 337 | 332 | 7.9 | 8.0 | 434.2 | 424.4 |
| Marine cargo handling | 48832 | 492 | 492 | 66.4 | 62.7 | 4,335.0 | 4,392.4 |
| Navigational services to shipping | 48833 | 889 | 877 | 11.9 | 12.5 | 923.3 | 920.5 |
| Other support activities for water transportation | 48839 | 838 | 854 | 11.2 | 10.3 | 730.7 | 695.0 |
| Support activities for road transportation | 4884 | 11,497 | 11,362 | 91.8 | 89.5 | 3,087.1 | 3,044.1 |
| Motor vehicle towing | 48841 | 8,878 | 8,994 | 57.6 | 59.2 | 2,022.7 | 2,107.9 |
| Freight transportation arrangement | 4885 | 20,606 | 20,780 | 253.9 | 266.2 | 14,530.2 | 14,876.3 |
| Other support activities for transportation | 4889 | 1,671 | 1,754 | 17.1 | 17.2 | 585.9 | 622.4 |
| Couriers & messengers | 492 | 14,853 | 14,665 | 591.4 | 611.9 | 25,661.5 | 26,796.7 |
| Couriers | 4921 | 10,402 | 10,198 | 553.2 | 566.4 | 24,435.2 | 25,369.6 |
| Local messengers & local delivery | 4922 | 4,451 | 4,467 | 38.2 | 45.6 | 1,226.3 | 1,427.1 |
| Warehousing & storage | 493 | 15,130 | 15,395 | 809.4 | 834.1 | 35,465.4 | 36,489.8 |

[1] Based on 2012 North American Industry Classification System (NAICS). See text, Section 15. [2] Covers full- and part-time employees who are on the payroll in the pay period including March 12.

Source: U.S. Census Bureau, County Business Patterns, "Geography Area Series: County Business Patterns," <https://factfinder.census.gov/>, accessed April 2018. See also <https://www.census.gov/programs-surveys/cbp.html>.

## Table 1087. Transportation Sector—Estimated Revenue by Kind of Business: 2010 to 2017

[In millions of dollars (660,440 represents $660,440,000,000). For taxable employer firms. Estimates have been adjusted to results of the 2012 Economic Census. Based on the Service Annual Survey; see Appendix III]

| Kind of business | NAICS code [1] | 2010 | 2014 | 2015 | 2016 | 2017 |
|---|---|---|---|---|---|---|
| Transportation and warehousing (excl. 482 and 491)............ | 4849y | 660,440 | 859,178 | 876,498 | 879,216 | 917,458 |
| Air transportation [2]................................ | 481 | 148,419 | 199,009 | 200,161 | 199,411 | 209,752 |
| Scheduled passenger air transportation........................ | 481111 | 126,902 | 173,250 | 174,099 | 172,268 | 180,421 |
| Nonscheduled chartered passenger air transportation........... | 481211 | 10,499 | 13,285 | 13,709 | 13,785 | 14,514 |
| Water transportation [2]............................... | 483 | 37,392 | 45,132 | 44,003 | 42,806 | 42,187 |
| Deep sea freight transportation............................ | 483111 | 9,281 | 9,215 | 8,443 | 7,656 | 6,167 |
| Deep sea passenger transportation......................... | 483112 | 14,393 | 17,985 | 18,593 | 19,692 | 21,370 |
| Coastal and great lakes freight transportation................... | 483113 | 6,254 | 7,909 | 7,509 | 6,872 | 6,505 |
| Inland water freight transportation......................... | 483211 | 6,879 | 9,281 | 8,652 | 7,742 | 7,186 |
| Truck transportation.................................. | 484 | 197,963 | 263,875 | 263,249 | 259,531 | 271,389 |
| General freight trucking, local........................... | 48411 | 19,902 | 26,222 | 26,426 | 26,453 | 27,750 |
| General freight trucking, long-distance, truckload....... | 484121 | 77,474 | 101,178 | 101,884 | 101,243 | 106,940 |
| General freight trucking, long-distance, less than truckload...... | 484122 | 31,698 | 41,378 | 41,221 | 40,739 | 43,210 |
| Used household and office goods moving................... | 48421 | 12,361 | 15,366 | 15,897 | 16,169 | 16,237 |
| Specialized freight (except used goods) trucking, local..... | 48422 | 28,465 | 40,873 | 38,828 | 37,399 | 39,564 |
| Specialized freight (except used goods) trucking, long-distance.. | 48423 | 28,063 | 38,858 | 38,993 | 37,528 | 37,688 |
| Transit and ground passenger transportation [2] | 485 | 26,900 | 32,969 | 34,031 | 35,754 | 38,062 |
| Urban transit systems.................................. | 4851 | 4,460 | 5,443 | 5,596 | 5,873 | 6,001 |
| Interurban and rural bus transportation................... | 4852 | 1,037 | 1,188 | 1,146 | 1,154 | 1,161 |
| Taxi service........................................ | 48531 | 2,225 | 2,640 | 2,678 | (S) | (S) |
| Limousine service..................................... | 48532 | 3,554 | 4,572 | 4,564 | 4,338 | 4,186 |
| School and employee bus transportation................... | 4854 | 8,628 | 10,355 | 10,939 | 11,482 | 12,528 |
| Charter bus industry.................................. | 4855 | 2,888 | 3,273 | 3,439 | 3,509 | 3,654 |
| Pipeline transportation [2].............................. | 486 | 33,069 | 41,852 | 43,764 | 44,459 | 46,666 |
| Pipeline transportation of crude oil........................ | 4861 | 5,004 | 9,029 | 10,004 | 10,158 | 10,565 |
| Pipeline transportation of natural gas...................... | 4862 | 21,831 | 25,097 | 25,230 | 25,612 | 27,321 |
| Pipeline transportation of refined petroleum products.............. | 48691 | 5,993 | 7,451 | 8,227 | 8,403 | 8,510 |
| Scenic and sightseeing transportation [2].................... | 487 | 2,545 | 3,368 | 3,666 | 3,581 | 3,523 |
| Scenic and sightseeing transportation, land................. | 4871 | 903 | 1,027 | 1,084 | 1,121 | 1,142 |
| Scenic and sightseeing transportation, water................ | 4872 | 1,236 | 1,727 | 1,906 | 1,767 | 1,633 |
| Support activities for transportation [2]..................... | 488 | 125,423 | 167,478 | 177,816 | 177,631 | 182,448 |
| Airport operations.................................... | 48811 | 5,699 | 7,709 | 7,936 | 8,296 | 8,357 |
| Other support activities for air transportation................. | 48819 | 15,072 | 16,723 | 16,826 | 17,731 | (S) |
| Support activities for rail transportation.................... | 4882 | 3,945 | 5,238 | 5,781 | 6,299 | 6,358 |
| Port and harbor operations............................. | 48831 | 1,856 | 2,625 | 2,809 | 2,915 | (S) |
| Marine cargo handling................................. | 48832 | 7,572 | 10,034 | 10,782 | 10,080 | 10,116 |
| Navigational services to shipping......................... | 48833 | 2,886 | 3,426 | 3,503 | 3,499 | 3,616 |
| Motor vehicle towing.................................. | 48841 | 5,040 | 5,795 | 6,016 | 6,174 | 6,617 |
| Freight transportation arrangement........................ | 4885 | 77,359 | 108,392 | 116,044 | 113,709 | 117,133 |
| Couriers and messengers.............................. | 492 | 63,855 | 75,118 | 78,424 | 82,976 | 88,780 |
| Couriers and express delivery services.................... | 4921 | 60,917 | 71,280 | 74,117 | 78,110 | 82,771 |
| Local messengers and local delivery...................... | 4922 | 2,938 | 3,838 | 4,307 | 4,866 | 6,009 |
| Warehousing and storage.............................. | 493 | 24,874 | 30,377 | 31,384 | 33,067 | 34,651 |
| General warehousing and storage........................ | 49311 | 15,966 | 18,864 | 19,486 | 20,615 | 21,739 |
| Refrigerated warehousing and storage.................... | 49312 | 4,083 | 4,310 | (S) | (S) | 4,931 |
| Farm product warehousing and storage.................... | 49313 | 698 | 726 | 786 | 798 | 811 |
| Other warehousing and storage.......................... | 49319 | 4,127 | 6,477 | 6,698 | 6,995 | 7,170 |

S Estimate does not meet publication standards. [1] 2010 data are based on 2007 North American Industry Classification System (NAICS). Beginning 2013, data are based on 2012 NAICS; see text, this section and Section 15. [2] Includes other kinds of business not shown separately.

Source: U.S. Census Bureau, Service Annual Survey, "Service Annual Survey Latest Data (NAICS-basis): 2017," <https://www.census.gov/programs-surveys/sas/data.html>, accessed November 2018.

## Table 1088. Transportation and Warehousing—Establishments, Revenue, Payroll, and Employees by Industry: 2012

[730,541 represents $730,541,000,000. For establishments with payroll. Based on the 2012 Economic Censuses. Paid employees for pay period including March 12. See Appendix III]

| Industry type | NAICS code [1] | Number of establish- ments | Revenue (mil. dol.) | Annual payroll (mil. dol.) | Paid employees (1,000) |
|---|---|---|---|---|---|
| **Transportation and warehousing total**.................... | **48–49** | **213,809** | **730,541** | **183,841** | **4,305.5** |
| Air transportation................................. | 481 | 4,979 | 181,273 | 26,236 | 444.6 |
| Water transportation............................... | 483 | 1,496 | 41,709 | 4,802 | 67.4 |
| Truck transportation............................... | 484 | 111,899 | 238,003 | 57,861 | 1,363.1 |
| Transit and ground passenger transportation.................. | 485 | 18,735 | 28,687 | 11,275 | 495.1 |
| Pipeline transportation............................ | 486 | 3,391 | 36,483 | 5,086 | 47.4 |
| Scenic and sightseeing transportation.................... | 487 | 2,573 | 3,092 | 832 | 27.9 |
| Support activities for transportation........................ | 488 | 42,489 | 103,439 | 28,435 | 617.7 |
| Couriers and messengers.......................... | 492 | 13,799 | 69,362 | 21,157 | 529.5 |
| Warehousing and storage.......................... | 493 | 14,448 | 28,494 | 28,157 | 712.8 |

[1] Data based on the 2007 North American Industry Classification System (NAICS); see text, Section 15.

Source: U.S. Census Bureau, 2012 Economic Census, Table EC1200CCOMP1, "All Sectors: Core Business Statistics Series: Comparative Statistics for the U.S. (2007 NAICS Basis): 2012 and 2007," <http://factfinder.census.gov/>, accessed September 2016.

## Table 1089. Transportation and Warehousing—Nonemployer Establishments and Receipts by Kind of Business: 2010 to 2017

[1,021.2 represents 1,021,200. Includes only firms subject to federal income tax. Nonemployers are businesses with no paid employees. Data originate chiefly from administrative records of the Internal Revenue Service; see Appendix III]

| Kind of business | NAICS code [1] | Establishments (1,000) | | | Receipts (mil. dol.) | | |
|---|---|---|---|---|---|---|---|
| | | 2010 | 2016 | 2017 | 2010 | 2016 | 2017 |
| **Transportation and warehousing**............ | **48–49** | **1,021.2** | **1,865.0** | **2,205.6** | **60,746** | **86,974** | **99,482** |
| Air transportation................................ | 481 | 19.1 | 20.6 | 22.4 | 1,219 | 1,355 | 1,486 |
| Water transportation............................. | 483 | 6.6 | 6.6 | 7.0 | 490 | 519 | 590 |
| Truck transportation.............................. | 484 | 490.3 | 587.0 | 621.4 | 42,485 | 55,343 | 62,357 |
| General freight trucking........................ | 4841 | 445.1 | 539.7 | 572.1 | 39,277 | 51,796 | 58,575 |
| General freight trucking, local............. | 48411 | 168.7 | 187.9 | 194.9 | 12,144 | 15,855 | 17,386 |
| General freight trucking, long-distance......... | 48412 | 276.4 | 351.8 | 377.2 | 27,133 | 35,941 | 41,189 |
| Specialized freight trucking.................... | 4842 | 45.2 | 47.3 | 49.3 | 3,207 | 3,547 | 3,782 |
| Transit and ground passenger transportation.... | 485 | 218.4 | 869.1 | 1,099.6 | 7,463 | 17,990 | 21,938 |
| Urban transit system.......................... | 4851 | 1.1 | 2.3 | 2.6 | 39 | 48 | 71 |
| Interurban and rural bus transportation......... | 4852 | 1.5 | 2.3 | 2.4 | 67 | 76 | 80 |
| Taxi and limousine service.................... | 4853 | 176.4 | 700.6 | 973.8 | 6,107 | 14,821 | 19,137 |
| School and employee bus transportation........ | 4854 | 6.9 | 6.8 | 6.9 | 191 | 200 | 201 |
| Charter bus industry........................... | 4855 | 3.8 | 4.4 | 4.3 | 172 | 192 | 209 |
| Other transit and ground passenger transportation........................ | 4859 | 28.7 | 152.8 | 109.8 | 887 | 2,653 | 2,240 |
| Pipeline transportation........................... | 486 | 0.9 | 1.2 | 1.3 | 76 | 80 | 91 |
| Scenic and sightseeing transportation............ | 487 | 4.9 | 6.0 | 6.3 | 163 | 219 | 236 |
| Support activities for transportation.............. | 488 | 105.2 | 165.4 | 169.6 | 4,624 | 6,506 | 7,070 |
| Couriers and messengers......................... | 492 | 166.6 | 197.4 | 262.1 | 3,772 | 4,388 | 5,085 |
| Warehousing and storage......................... | 493 | 9.2 | 11.7 | 15.9 | 455 | 575 | 628 |

[1] 2010 data based on the 2007 North American Industry Classification System (NAICS); 2016 data based on 2012 NAICS; and 2017 data based on 2017 NAICS.

Source: U.S. Census Bureau, Nonemployer Statistics, "NES Datasets," <https://www.census.gov/programs-surveys/nonemployer-statistics/data/datasets.html>, accessed July 2019.

## Table 1090. Transportation System Mileage Within the United States: 1985 to 2017

[3,864 represents 3,864,000. Numbers, except where indicated]

| System | Unit | 1985 | 1990 | 1995 | 2000 | 2005 | 2010 | 2015 | 2016 | 2017 |
|---|---|---|---|---|---|---|---|---|---|---|
| Highway [1]....................... | 1,000 | 3,864 | 3,867 | 3,912 | 3,936 | 3,996 | 4,067 | 4,155 | 4,140 | 4,165 |
| Class 1 rail [2].................... | Number | 145,764 | 119,758 | 108,264 | 99,250 | 95,664 | 95,573 | 93,527 | 93,239 | 93,058 |
| Amtrak [2]......................... | Number | 24,000 | 24,000 | 24,000 | 23,000 | 22,007 | 21,178 | 21,358 | 21,358 | 21,407 |
| Transit: [3] | | | | | | | | | | |
| Commuter rail [4].............. | Number | 3,574 | 4,132 | 4,160 | 5,209 | 7,118 | 7,630 | 7,697 | 7,745 | 7,815 |
| Heavy rail [5]................... | Number | 1,293 | 1,351 | 1,458 | 1,558 | 1,622 | 1,617 | 1,643 | 1,646 | 1,653 |
| Light rail [6]..................... | Number | 384 | 483 | 568 | 834 | 1,188 | 1,497 | 1,893 | 1,958 | 2,030 |
| Navigable channels [7].......... | Number | 25,000 | 25,000 | 25,000 | 25,000 | 25,000 | 25,000 | 25,000 | 25,000 | 25,000 |
| Oil pipeline [8]................... | Number | (NA) | (NA) | (NA) | (NA) | 166,760 | 181,986 | 208,618 | 212,105 | 215,736 |
| Gas pipeline [9]................. | 1,000 | 1,641 | 1,871 | 2,028 | 2,115 | 2,287 | 2,427 | 2,509 | 2,529 | 2,542 |

NA Not available. [1] All public road and street mileage in the 50 states and the District of Columbia. Beginning in 1998, approximately 43,000 miles of Bureau of Land Management Roads are excluded. [2] Data represent miles of road owned (aggregate length of road, excluding yard tracks, sidings, and parallel lines). Portions of Class I freight railroads, Amtrak, and Commuter rail networks share common trackage. Amtrak data represent miles of road operated. [3] Transit system length is measured in directional route-miles; see source. [4] Urban passenger train service for short-distance travel between a central city and adjacent suburb. Does not include rapid rail transit or light rail service. [5] Also known as subway, elevated (railway), or metropolitan railway (metro). [6] A streetcar-type vehicle operated on city streets. Beginning in 2011, "Light rail" includes light rail, street car rail, and hybrid rail. [7] Estimated sums of domestic waterways which include rivers, bays, channels, and the inner route of the Southeast Alaskan Islands, but does not include the Great Lakes or deep ocean traffic. Beginning in 2007, includes waterways connecting the Great Lakes and the St. Lawrence Seaway inside the U.S. [8] Includes trunk and gathering lines for crude-oil pipeline. Oil pipeline data has been discontinued for years prior to 2001. [9] Excludes service pipelines.

Source: U.S. Bureau of Transportation Statistics, "National Transportation Statistics," <https://www.bts.gov/content/system-mileage-within-united-states>, accessed July 2019.

## Table 1091. U.S. Aircraft, Vehicles, and Other Conveyances: 2000 to 2017

[Number, or in thousands (225,821 represents 225,821,000), as indicated]

| Mode | 2000 | 2010 | 2011 | 2012 | 2013 | 2014 | 2015 | 2016 | 2017 |
|---|---|---|---|---|---|---|---|---|---|
| **AIR** | | | | | | | | | |
| Air carrier [1] | 7,826 | 7,185 | 7,168 | 6,914 | 6,740 | 6,761 | 6,876 | 7,039 | 7,141 |
| General aviation [2] (active fleet) | 217,533 | 223,370 | 222,250 | 209,034 | 199,927 | 204,408 | 210,030 | 211,793 | 211,757 |
| **HIGHWAY, REGISTERED VEHICLES (1,000s)** | | | | | | | | | |
| Total registered vehicles | 225,821 | 250,070 | 253,216 | 253,639 | 255,877 | 260,351 | 263,610 | 268,799 | 272,481 |
| Light duty vehicle, short wheel base [3] | (NA) | 190,203 | 183,523 | 183,172 | 184,497 | 187,555 | 189,618 | 192,775 | 193,672 |
| Passenger cars [3] | 133,621 | (NA) | (NA) | (NA) | (NA) | (NA) | (NA) | (NA) | (NA) |
| Motorcycle | 4,346 | 8,010 | 8,438 | 8,455 | 8,405 | 8,418 | 8,601 | 8,679 | 8,715 |
| Light duty vehicle, long wheel base [4] | (NA) | 40,242 | 50,319 | 50,589 | 51,513 | 52,600 | 53,299 | 54,870 | 56,881 |
| Other 2-axle 4-tire vehicles [4] | 79,085 | (NA) | (NA) | (NA) | (NA) | (NA) | (NA) | (NA) | (NA) |
| Trucks [5] | 5,926 | 8,217 | 7,819 | 8,190 | 8,126 | 8,329 | 8,456 | 8,747 | 9,337 |
| Truck, combination | 2,097 | 2,553 | 2,452 | 2,469 | 2,471 | 2,577 | 2,747 | 2,752 | 2,892 |
| Bus | 746 | 846 | 666 | 765 | 865 | 872 | 889 | 976 | 983 |
| **TRANSIT** | | | | | | | | | |
| Motor bus | 58,578 | 63,108 | 61,127 | 61,245 | 66,823 | 62,449 | 63,573 | 63,270 | 63,759 |
| Light rail cars [6] | 1,306 | 2,096 | 2,284 | 2,348 | 2,842 | 2,444 | 2,478 | 2,553 | 2,557 |
| Heavy rail cars [7] | 10,311 | 11,510 | 14,942 | 10,469 | 10,380 | 10,551 | 10,737 | 10,775 | 10,705 |
| Trolley bus | 652 | 571 | 479 | 570 | 560 | 537 | 611 | 601 | 539 |
| Commuter rail cars and locomotives | 5,497 | 6,768 | 6,971 | 6,938 | 7,150 | 7,177 | 7,151 | 7,190 | 7,129 |
| Demand responsive | 22,087 | 33,555 | 31,846 | 31,929 | 31,433 | 31,359 | 32,490 | 33,225 | 33,012 |
| Other [8] | 7,705 | 18,066 | 18,965 | 16,996 | 17,793 | 17,994 | 18,601 | 17,042 | 18,104 |
| **RAIL** | | | | | | | | | |
| Class I, freight cars | 560,154 | 397,730 | 380,699 | 380,641 | 373,838 | 371,642 | 330,996 | 315,227 | 306,268 |
| Class I, locomotive | 20,028 | 23,893 | 24,250 | 24,707 | 25,033 | 25,916 | 26,574 | 26,716 | 26,547 |
| Nonclass I freight cars | 132,448 | 101,755 | 95,972 | 92,742 | 88,122 | (NA) | (NA) | (NA) | (NA) |
| Car companies' and shippers' freight cars | 688,194 | 809,544 | 806,554 | 842,802 | 873,679 | (NA) | (NA) | (NA) | (NA) |
| Amtrak, passenger train car | 1,894 | 1,274 | 1,301 | 2,090 | 1,447 | 1,419 | 1,428 | 1,402 | 1,405 |
| Amtrak, locomotive | 378 | 282 | 287 | 485 | 418 | 428 | 423 | 434 | 419 |
| **WATER** | | | | | | | | | |
| Non-self-propelled vessels [9] | 31,360 | 31,412 | 31,498 | 31,550 | 31,081 | 31,043 | 31,748 | 33,212 | 33,128 |
| Self-propelled vessels [10] | 8,202 | 9,100 | 9,023 | 8,980 | 8,918 | 9,039 | 9,043 | 9,462 | 9,411 |
| Ocean-going self-propelled vessels (1,000 gross tons and over) [11] | 282 | 221 | 214 | 198 | 187 | 179 | 170 | 169 | 176 |
| Recreational boats (1,000s) | 12,782 | 12,439 | 12,174 | 12,102 | 12,013 | 11,804 | 11,867 | 11,862 | 11,962 |

NA Not available. [1] Air carrier aircraft are those carrying passengers or cargo for hire under 14 CFR 121 and 14 CFR 135. [2] Includes air taxi aircraft. [3] Data for 2000-06 are for passenger cars. Beginning 2007, data are for Light Duty Vehicles Short Wheel Base—passenger cars, light trucks, vans and sport utility vehicles with a wheelbase of 121 inches or less. [4] Data for 2000-06 are for 2-axle, 4-tire vehicles other than passenger cars, motorcycles, and buses. Beginning 2007, data are for Light Duty Vehicles Long Wheel Base—large passenger cars, vans, pickup trucks, and sport/utility vehicles with wheelbases larger than 121 inches. [5] Includes trucks on a single frame with at least 2 axles and 6 tires. [6] Fixed rail streetcar or trolley, for example. [7] Metro, subway, or rapid transit, for example. [8] Includes Alaska railroad, automated guideway transit, cable car, ferry boat, inclined plane, monorail, and vanpool. [9] Includes dry-cargo barges, tank barges, and railroad-car floats. [10] Includes dry-cargo and/or passenger, offshore supply vessels, railroad-car ferries, tankers, and towboats. [11] 2000-06 data include private and government owned vessels of 1,000 gross tons or more. Beginning 2007, data are reported only for privately owned vessels of 1,000 gross tons or more. 2009 data include privately owned vessels of 10,000 deadweight tons or more, not including the Great Lakes vessels.

Source: U.S. Bureau of Transportation Statistics, "National Transportation Statistics," <https://www.bts.gov/topics/national-transportation-statistics>, accessed August 2019.

## Table 1092. Transportation Shipments by Mode: 2012 to 2045

[16,996 represents 16,996,000,000. All truck, rail, water, and pipeline movements that involve more than one mode, including exports and imports that change mode at international gateways, are included in multiple modes & mail to avoid double counting. Data do not include imports and exports that pass through the United States from a foreign origin to a foreign destination by any mode]

| Mode | 2012 | | | | 2016 [1] | | | | 2045 [2] | | | |
|---|---|---|---|---|---|---|---|---|---|---|---|---|
| | Total | Do-mestic | Ex-ports | Im-ports | Total | Do-mestic | Ex-ports | Im-ports | Total | Do-mestic | Ex-ports | Im-ports |
| **WEIGHT (millions of tons)** | | | | | | | | | | | | |
| **Total** | **16,996** | **14,895** | **933** | **1,169** | **17,686** | **15,762** | **887** | **1,037** | **25,521** | **20,932** | **2,330** | **2,259** |
| Truck | 10,098 | 9,893 | 115 | 90 | 11,086 | 10,882 | 101 | 103 | 14,836 | 14,226 | 304 | 306 |
| Rail | 1,625 | 1,481 | 57 | 87 | 1,575 | 1,418 | 66 | 90 | 1,926 | 1,588 | 112 | 226 |
| Water | 959 | 502 | 77 | 380 | 798 | 519 | 131 | 148 | 1,186 | 609 | 203 | 373 |
| Air, air and truck | 11 | 2 | 5 | 4 | 11 | 2 | 4 | 4 | 41 | 4 | 19 | 18 |
| Multiple modes and mail [3] | 1,361 | 309 | 627 | 425 | 1,354 | 322 | 505 | 528 | 2,941 | 431 | 1,482 | 1,028 |
| Pipeline | 2,901 | 2,672 | 50 | 179 | 2,823 | 2,589 | 72 | 162 | 4,559 | 4,058 | 205 | 296 |
| Other and unknown | 42 | 37 | 2 | 3 | 39 | 29 | 9 | 1 | 32 | 16 | 5 | 11 |
| **VALUE (billions of 2012 dollars)** | | | | | | | | | | | | |
| **Total** | **17,729** | **13,965** | **1,545** | **2,219** | **18,142** | **14,341** | **1,542** | **2,259** | **37,064** | **22,469** | **6,511** | **8,084** |
| Truck | 10,929 | 10,251 | 366 | 311 | 11,225 | 10,532 | 347 | 347 | 18,682 | 16,219 | 1,244 | 1,219 |
| Rail | 582 | 411 | 63 | 109 | 621 | 445 | 65 | 111 | 1,080 | 646 | 157 | 278 |
| Water | 631 | 270 | 73 | 288 | 527 | 279 | 98 | 151 | 1,031 | 340 | 281 | 411 |
| Air, air and truck | 1,067 | 135 | 461 | 472 | 1,081 | 132 | 447 | 502 | 5,221 | 324 | 2,544 | 2,354 |
| Multiple modes and mail [3] | 3,246 | 1,746 | 552 | 947 | 3,315 | 1,784 | 487 | 1,044 | 8,981 | 3,393 | 2,123 | 3,465 |
| Pipeline | 1,233 | 1,150 | 13 | 70 | 1,282 | 1,169 | 31 | 81 | 1,744 | 1,546 | 88 | 110 |
| Other and unknown | 40 | 1 | 17 | 22 | 91 | 1 | 67 | 23 | 325 | – | 76 | 248 |

– Represents zero. [1] The 2016 data are provisional estimates that are based on selected modal and economic trend data. [2] Freight Analysis Framework forecasts. [3] Multiple modes and mail also includes some air movements.

Source: U.S. Department of Transportation, Bureau of Transportation Statistics, *Transportation Statistics Annual Report 2018*, February 2019. See also <https://www.bts.gov/TSAR>.

## Table 1093. Shipment Characteristics by Mode of Transportation: 2012 and 2017

[13,852,143 represents $13,852,143,000,000, unless otherwise noted. For business establishments in mining, manufacturing, wholesale trade, and selected retail and services industries. 2017 industries classified by the 2012 North American Industry Classification System (NAICS). 2012 industries classified by 2007 NAICS. Selected auxiliary establishments are also included. Based on the Commodity Flow Survey, conducted as part of the Economic Census; see Appendix III]

| Mode of transportation | Value (mil. dol.) | | Tons (1,000) | | Ton-miles (mil.) | | Average miles per shipment | |
|---|---|---|---|---|---|---|---|---|
| | 2012 | 2017 | 2012 | 2017 | 2012 | 2017 | 2012 | 2017 |
| All modes.................... | 13,852,143 | 14,366,611 | 11,299,409 | 12,478,849 | 2,969,506 | 3,130,697 | 630 | 633 |
| Single modes.................. | 11,900,364 | 11,642,939 | 10,905,518 | 11,496,515 | 2,697,418 | 2,399,208 | 262 | 222 |
| Truck [1]............................. | 10,132,229 | 10,490,038 | 8,060,166 | 8,925,313 | 1,247,717 | 1,301,054 | 227 | 188 |
| For-hire truck.............. | 6,504,636 | 7,257,437 | 4,298,693 | 5,568,811 | 1,050,942 | 1,142,613 | 508 | 325 |
| Private truck.............. | 3,627,592 | 3,232,602 | 3,761,472 | 3,356,501 | 196,775 | 158,441 | 58 | 46 |
| Rail................................. | 473,070 | 203,432 | 1,628,537 | 1,156,760 | 1,211,481 | 842,716 | 805 | 554 |
| Water................................. | 301,554 | 145,179 | 575,996 | 561,634 | 192,866 | 175,829 | 908 | 225 |
| Great Lakes.............. | 218,927 | 59,246 | 424,542 | 288,697 | 118,742 | 119,297 | 275 | 256 |
| Inland water.............. | 59,878 | 80,426 | 72,987 | 202,146 | 22,130 | 28,337 | 1,157 | 215 |
| Deep sea.................... | 424 | 733 | 31,403 | 55,564 | 10,959 | 20,778 | 347 | 290 |
| Multiple waterways.......... | (NA) | 4,774 | (NA) | 15,228 | (NA) | 7,417 | (NA) | (S) |
| Air (includes truck and air)..... | 450,575 | 408,772 | 4,845 | 5,745 | 5,810 | 6,853 | 1,295 | 1,437 |
| Pipeline [2]......................... | 542,936 | 395,517 | 635,975 | 847,063 | (S) | (S) | (S) | (S) |
| Multiple modes................ | 1,950,753 | 2,720,518 | 357,047 | 856,355 | 271,832 | 731,363 | 922 | 890 |
| Parcel, U.S. Postal Service or courier.......................... | 1,688,242 | 2,037,533 | 28,490 | 36,040 | 22,716 | 27,182 | 922 | 890 |
| Truck and rail.................. | 224,833 | 459,933 | 213,814 | 650,615 | 169,524 | 577,100 | 988 | 1,140 |
| Truck and water................. | 29,035 | 178,624 | 56,720 | 81,063 | 48,568 | 43,228 | 1,562 | 994 |
| Rail and water.................. | 7,976 | 21,485 | 55,570 | 75,996 | 29,170 | 70,177 | 1,073 | 1,306 |
| Other multiple modes........... | 668 | 22,944 | 2,452 | 12,642 | 1,853 | 13,676 | (S) | 1,429 |
| Other and unknown modes.. | 1,026 | 3,153 | 36,844 | 125,979 | 256 | 126 | (S) | 1 |

NA Not available. S Data do not meet publication standards due to high sampling variability or other reasons. [1] Truck as a single mode includes shipments that went by private truck only, for-hire truck only, or a combination of private truck and for-hire truck. [2] Commodity Flow Survey data exclude shipments of crude oil.

Source: U.S. Department of Transportation, Bureau of Transportation Statistics, and U.S. Census Bureau, Commodity Flow Survey, "CFS Preliminary Report: Shipment Characteristics by Mode of Transportation: 2017," <http://factfinder.census.gov>, accessed August 2019. See also <https://www.census.gov/programs-surveys/cfs.html>.

## Table 1094. Hazardous Shipments—Value, Tons, and Ton-Miles: 2007 and 2012

[1,448,218 represents $1,448,218,000,000. For business establishments in mining, manufacturing, wholesale trade, and selected retail industries. 2012 data cover industries classified by the 2007 North American Industry Classification System (NAICS). 2007 data cover industries classified by 2002 NAICS. Also includes auxiliary establishments of multi-establishment companies. Based on the Commodity Flow Survey, conducted as part of the Economic Census; see Appendix III]

| Mode of transportation and class of material | Value (mil. dol.) | | Tons (1,000) | | Ton-miles (mil.) | | Average miles per shipment | |
|---|---|---|---|---|---|---|---|---|
| | 2007 | 2012 | 2007 | 2012 | 2007 | 2012 | 2007 | 2012 |
| All modes........................ | 1,448,218 | 2,334,425 | 2,231,133 | 2,580,153 | 323,457 | 307,524 | 96 | 114 |
| Single modes...................... | 1,370,615 | 2,304,743 | 2,111,022 | 2,552,808 | 279,105 | 275,628 | 85 | 88 |
| Truck [1]............................. | 837,074 | 1,466,021 | 1,202,825 | 1,531,405 | 103,997 | 96,559 | 59 | 56 |
| For-hire truck.................... | 358,792 | 870,893 | 495,077 | 882,288 | 63,288 | 62,018 | 214 | 150 |
| Private truck.................... | 478,282 | 595,128 | 707,748 | 649,117 | 40,709 | 34,541 | 32 | 33 |
| Rail................................. | 69,213 | 79,222 | 129,743 | 110,988 | 92,169 | 84,850 | 578 | 808 |
| Water................................. | 69,186 | 217,816 | 149,794 | 283,561 | 37,064 | 54,902 | 383 | 212 |
| Air (includes truck and air)............ | 1,735 | 4,380 | (S) | 261 | (S) | 271 | 1,095 | 1,120 |
| Pipeline [2]......................... | 393,408 | 537,304 | 628,905 | 626,652 | (S) | (S) | (S) | (S) |
| Multiple modes [3]................. | 71,069 | 29,682 | 111,022 | 27,285 | 42,886 | 31,896 | 834 | 654 |
| Parcel, U.S. Postal Service or courier............. | 7,675 | 10,294 | 236 | 305 | 151 | 178 | 836 | 650 |
| Other and unknown modes.................. | 6,534 | (NA) | 8,489 | (NA) | 1,466 | (NA) | 58 | (NA) |
| Class of Material........................ | 1,448,218 | 2,334,425 | 2,231,133 | 2,580,153 | 323,457 | 307,524 | 96 | 114 |
| Class 1, Explosives.................... | 11,754 | 18,397 | 3,047 | 4,045 | 911 | 1,012 | 738 | 840 |
| Class 2, Gases........................ | 131,810 | 125,054 | 250,506 | 164,794 | 55,260 | 33,157 | 51 | 57 |
| Class 3, Flammable and combustible liquid...... | 1,170,455 | 2,016,681 | 1,752,814 | 2,203,490 | 181,615 | 204,573 | 91 | 93 |
| Class 4, Flammable solid; spontaneously combustible material; dangerous when wet material.............. | 4,067 | 5,415 | 20,408 | 11,321 | 5,547 | 5,804 | 309 | 565 |
| Class 5, Oxidizers and organic peroxides........ | 6,695 | 7,562 | 14,959 | 12,025 | 7,024 | 5,479 | 361 | 437 |
| Class 6, Toxic materials and infectious substances................ | 21,198 | 15,196 | 11,270 | 7,612 | 5,667 | 3,607 | 467 | 513 |
| Class 7, Radioactive materials.................... | 20,633 | 12,288 | 515 | (S) | 37 | 39 | (S) | 34 |
| Class 8, Corrosive materials.................... | 51,475 | 75,850 | 114,441 | 125,287 | 44,395 | 37,784 | 208 | 264 |
| Class 9, Miscellaneous hazardous material...... | 30,131 | 57,981 | 63,173 | 51,006 | 23,002 | 16,068 | 484 | 530 |

NA Not available. S Data do not meet publication standards. [1] Truck as a single mode includes shipments that went by private truck only, for-hire truck only, or a combination of private truck and for-hire truck. [2] Commodity Flow Survey Data exclude shipments of crude oil. [3] Includes other modes not shown. Multimode data for 2012 and 2007 are not comparable due to methodological changes; see source.

Source: U.S. Department of Transportation, Bureau of Transportation Statistics, and U.S. Census Bureau, *United States: 2012, Hazardous Materials*, February 2015; and 2012 Commodity Flow Survey, CF1200H01, "Hazardous Materials Series: HazMat Shipment Characteristics by Mode," and CF1200H02, "Hazardous Materials Series: HazMat Shipment Characteristics by Hazardous Class," <http://factfinder.census.gov>, accessed February 2015. See also <https://www.census.gov/programs-surveys/cfs.html>.

# Table 1095. Transportation Accidents, Deaths, and Injuries: 2000 to 2017

[Number, except in thousands (6,394 represents 6,394,000) as indicated. See source for more information]

| Mode | Accidents 2000 | 2005 | 2010 | 2016 | 2017 | Deaths 2000 | 2005 | 2010 | 2016 | 2017 | Injuries 2000 | 2005 | 2010 | 2016 | 2017 |
|---|---|---|---|---|---|---|---|---|---|---|---|---|---|---|---|
| Air | 1,985 | 1,782 | 1,507 | 1,336 | 1,316 | 764 | 603 | 477 | 413 | 346 | 359 | 305 | 278 | 238 | 232 |
| Air carrier [1] | 56 | 40 | 30 | 31 | 32 | 92 | 22 | 2 | – | 1 | 31 | 14 | 17 | 19 | 18 |
| Commuter [2] | 12 | 6 | 6 | 8 | 8 | 5 | – | – | 8 | – | 7 | – | 2 | 11 | 11 |
| On-demand [3] | 80 | 65 | 30 | 30 | 43 | 71 | 18 | 17 | 19 | 15 | 12 | 20 | 3 | 9 | 4 |
| General aviation | 1,837 | 1,671 | 1,441 | 1,267 | 1,233 | 596 | 563 | 458 | 386 | 330 | 309 | 271 | 256 | 199 | 210 |
| Land: | | | | | | | | | | | | | | | |
| Highway crashes (1,000) [4] | 6,394 | 6,159 | 5,419 | 7,277 | (NA) | 41.9 | 43.5 | 33.0 | 37.8 | 37.1 | 3,189 | 2,699 | 2,239 | 3,061 | 2,746 |
| Passenger car occupants | 4,926 | 4,499 | 5,350 | 7,200 | (NA) | 20.7 | 18.5 | 12.5 | 13.5 | 13.4 | 2,052 | 1,573 | 1,253 | 1,690 | 1,529 |
| Motorcyclists | 69 | 101 | 96 | 129 | (NA) | 2.9 | 4.6 | 4.5 | 5.3 | 5.2 | 58 | 87 | 82 | 104 | 89 |
| Light truck occupants | 3,208 | 3,382 | 3,775 | 5,010 | (NA) | 11.5 | 13.0 | 9.8 | 10.4 | 10.2 | 887 | 872 | 733 | 1,035 | 937 |
| Large truck occupants | 438 | 423 | 276 | 502 | (NA) | 0.8 | 0.1 | 0.5 | 0.7 | 0.8 | 31 | 27 | 20 | 37 | 40 |
| Bus occupants | 56 | 50 | 54 | 71 | (NA) | – | 0.1 | – | – | – | 18 | 11 | 17 | 24 | 12 |
| Pedestrians | (NA) | (NA) | (NA) | (NA) | (NA) | 4.8 | 4.9 | 4.3 | 6.1 | 6.0 | 78 | 64 | 70 | 87 | 71 |
| Pedalcyclists | (NA) | (NA) | (NA) | (NA) | (NA) | 0.7 | 0.8 | 0.6 | 0.9 | 0.8 | 51 | 45 | 52 | 64 | 50 |
| Other | (NA) | (NA) | (NA) | (NA) | (NA) | 0.6 | 0.8 | 0.7 | 0.9 | 0.8 | 15 | 18 | 13 | 20 | 17 |
| Railroad [5] | 14,024 | 11,816 | 10,032 | 9,875 | 10,140 | 937 | 884 | 735 | 760 | 822 | 11,643 | 9,550 | 8,379 | 8,695 | 8,830 |
| Highway-rail grade crossing [6] | 607 | 571 | 453 | 528 | 498 | 425 | 359 | 261 | 255 | 271 | 1,219 | 1,053 | 888 | 852 | 844 |
| Transit [7] | 24,261 | 8,151 | 3,492 | 6,878 | (NA) | 295 | 149 | 222 | 257 | 239 | 56,697 | 19,039 | 25,376 | 24,405 | 22,829 |
| Waterborne [8] | 13,143 | 9,946 | 9,889 | 7,679 | 6,817 | 701 | 829 | 821 | 737 | 706 | (NA) | 4,125 | 3,770 | 3,044 | (NA) |
| Recreational boating [9] | 7,740 | 4,969 | 4,604 | 4,463 | 4,291 | 701 | 697 | 672 | 701 | 658 | 4,355 | 3,451 | 3,153 | 2,903 | 2,629 |
| Pipeline | 380 | 719 | 586 | 633 | 650 | 38 | 17 | 22 | 16 | 20 | 81 | 47 | 108 | 87 | 38 |
| Hazard liquid | 146 | 369 | 350 | 420 | 415 | 1 | 2 | 1 | 3 | 1 | 4 | 2 | 3 | 9 | 1 |
| Gas | 234 | 350 | 236 | 213 | 235 | 37 | 15 | 21 | 19 | 19 | 77 | 45 | 105 | 78 | 37 |

– Represents or rounds to zero. NA Not available. [1] See footnote 1, Table 1103. Injuries classified as serious. [2] See footnote 2, Table 1103. Injuries classified as serious. [3] See footnote 3, Table 1103. Injuries classified as serious. [4] Highway crashes often involve more than one motor vehicle, and hence "total highway crashes" is smaller than the sum of the components. Data on deaths are from U.S. National Highway Traffic Safety Administration and are based on deaths within 30 days of the accident. Includes only police reported crashes. For more details, see Table 1137. [5] Accidents and incidents resulting from freight and passenger rail operations including commuter rail. Grade crossing accidents are also included when classified as a train accident. Deaths and injuries exclude those in highway-rail grade crossing accidents involving motor vehicles. Injury figures also include occupational illness. [6] Accidents and incidents occurring at highway-rail crossings resulting from freight and passenger rail operations including commuter rail. Public highway-rail grade crossing incidents, fatalities, and injuries involving motor vehicles are excluded and counted under Highway. Highway-rail grade crossing injuries, except train occupants, are also counted under Highway. [7] Includes motor bus, commuter rail, heavy rail, light rail, demand response, van pool, and automated guideway. Starting with 2002, only injuries requiring immediate medical treatment away from the scene now qualify as reportable. [8] To include vessel-related deaths and injuries include those involving damage to vessels, such as collisions or groundings. Totals include deaths and injuries not related to vessel casualties, not shown separately. [9] Covers occurrences involving a vessel or its equipment that results in 1) a death; 2) an injury that requires medical treatment beyond first aid; 3) damage to a vessel and other property, totaling to more than $2,000 or complete loss of a vessel; or 4) the disappearance of the vessel under circumstances that indicate death or injury. Federal regulations (33 CFR 173-4) require the operator of any vessel that is numbered or used for recreational purposes to submit an accident report.

Source: U.S. Bureau of Transportation Statistics, "National Transportation Statistics," <https://www.bts.gov/topics/national-transportation-statistics>, accessed August 2019.

## Table 1096. U.S. Scheduled Airline Industry—Summary: 2007 to 2014

[In units as indicated (769.6 represents $769,600,000). For calendar years or as of December 31. For domestic and international operations. Covers carriers certificated under Section 401 of the Federal Aviation Act. Minus sign (-) indicates loss]

| Item | Unit | 2007 | 2008 | 2009 | 2010 | 2011 | 2012 | 2013 | 2014 |
|---|---|---|---|---|---|---|---|---|---|
| SCHEDULED SERVICE | | | | | | | | | |
| Revenue passengers enplaned.... | Mil. | 769.6 | 743.3 | 703.9 | 720.5 | 730.8 | 736.7 | 743.2 | 762.1 |
| Revenue passenger miles.......... | Bil. | 829.4 | 812.4 | 769.5 | 798.0 | 814.4 | 823.2 | 840.4 | 862.1 |
| Available seat miles................. | Bil. | 1,037.7 | 1,021.3 | 957.2 | 972.6 | 992.7 | 994.5 | 1,011.2 | 1,033.8 |
| Revenue passenger load factor.... | Percent | 79.9 | 79.5 | 80.4 | 82.1 | 82.0 | 82.8 | 83.1 | 83.4 |
| Mean passenger trip length [1]....... | Miles | 1,078 | 1,093 | 1,093 | 1,108 | 1,114 | 1,117 | 1,131 | 1,131 |
| Cargo ton miles.................... | Mil. | 29,571 | 28,119 | 24,970 | 27,885 | 28,123 | 27,790 | 26,441 | 27,236 |
| Aircraft departures................. | 1,000 | 11,399 | 10,897 | 10,145 | 10,095 | 10,058 | 9,864 | 9,745 | 9,536 |
| FINANCES | | | | | | | | | |
| **Total operating revenue [2]**........ | **Mil. dol.** | **174,696** | **186,087** | **155,051** | **174,677** | **193,041** | **196,105** | **200,245** | **207,708** |
| Passenger revenue.................. | Mil. dol. | 107,678 | 111,511 | 91,443 | 103,978 | 114,299 | 115,975 | 120,642 | 126,706 |
| Cargo revenue...................... | Mil. dol. | 24,002 | 29,192 | 23,014 | 17,622 | 1,589 | 889 | 1,023 | 1,140 |
| Charter revenue.................... | Mil. dol. | 5,544 | 4,338 | 3,841 | 3,254 | 604 | 976 | 877 | 930 |
| Other revenue...................... | Mil. dol. | 37,472 | 41,047 | 36,753 | 49,824 | 76,548 | 78,265 | 77,703 | 78,932 |
| Total operating expense............ | Mil. dol. | 165,353 | 189,437 | 152,716 | 164,160 | 186,005 | 188,592 | 187,726 | 191,029 |
| Operating profit (or loss)........... | Mil. dol. | 9,344 | -3,350 | 2,335 | 10,517 | 7,036 | 7,513 | 12,519 | 16,678 |
| Interest income (or expense)....... | Mil. dol. | -3,915 | -3,743 | -4,214 | -4,215 | -3,970 | -3,740 | -3,334 | -3,005 |
| Net profit (or loss)................. | Mil. dol. | 7,691.4 | -23,749.8 | -2,610.3 | 3,666.0 | 1,392.2 | 363.7 | 12,710.6 | 8,514.3 |
| Passenger revenue per passenger mile................................. | Cents | 13.0 | 13.7 | 11.9 | 13.0 | 14.0 | 14.1 | 14.4 | 14.7 |
| Operating profit margin.............. | Percent | 5.3 | -1.8 | 1.5 | 6.0 | 3.6 | 3.8 | 6.3 | 8.0 |
| Net profit margin................... | Percent | 4.4 | -12.8 | -1.7 | 2.1 | 0.7 | 0.2 | 6.3 | 4.1 |
| EMPLOYEES | | | | | | | | | |
| **Average full-time equivalents....** | **1,000** | **613.9** | **608.9** | **573.9** | **564.4** | **577.3** | **584.5** | **584.0** | **589.1** |

[1] For definition of mean, see Guide to Tabular Presentation. [2] Includes other types of revenues, not shown separately.

Source: Airlines for America, ©; and Bureau of Transportation Statistics, <http://www.transtats.bts.gov/>, accessed June 2015.

## Table 1097. On-Time Flight Arrivals and Departures at Major U.S. Airports: 2018

[In percent. Quarterly, based on gate arrival and departure times for domestic scheduled operations of U.S. major airlines. All U.S. airlines with 1 percent or more of total U.S. domestic scheduled airline passenger revenues are required to report on-time data. A flight is considered on time if it operated within 15 minutes of the scheduled time shown in the carrier's computerized reservation system. See source for data on individual airlines]

| Airport | Code | On-time arrivals | | | | On-time departures | | | |
|---|---|---|---|---|---|---|---|---|---|
| | | 1st quarter | 2nd quarter | 3rd quarter | 4th quarter | 1st quarter | 2nd quarter | 3rd quarter | 4th quarter |
| **Total, all airports [1]**........................ | **(X)** | **80.0** | **79.1** | **77.7** | **80.9** | **80.4** | **79.8** | **78.9** | **82.2** |
| Atlanta, Hartsfield-Jackson Intl............... | ATL | 84.9 | 82.5 | 83.5 | 83.9 | 82.4 | 79.7 | 80.8 | 83.3 |
| Baltimore/Washington Intl..................... | BWI | 83.9 | 79.0 | 75.7 | 84.4 | 80.2 | 75.4 | 73.3 | 80.7 |
| Boston, Logan Intl............................. | BOS | 74.3 | 75.5 | 70.0 | 76.5 | 74.1 | 76.3 | 75.2 | 79.9 |
| Charlotte, Douglas............................ | CLT | 81.6 | 80.0 | 79.2 | 83.6 | 80.4 | 76.6 | 75.4 | 82.3 |
| Chicago, Midway Intl.......................... | MDW | 78.7 | 77.9 | 79.6 | 82.1 | 70.3 | 65.9 | 68.3 | 72.0 |
| Chicago, O'Hare.............................. | ORD | 79.3 | 74.8 | 75.6 | 79.5 | 78.8 | 75.6 | 75.7 | 80.2 |
| Dallas Fort Worth Intl......................... | DFW | 81.0 | 81.4 | 75.7 | 78.1 | 80.9 | 79.0 | 73.9 | 77.8 |
| Denver Intl.................................... | DEN | 83.6 | 81.2 | 80.3 | 83.7 | 81.7 | 79.3 | 78.2 | 81.8 |
| Detroit, Metro Wayne County.................. | DTW | 81.4 | 84.5 | 83.8 | 87.1 | 80.9 | 84.8 | 83.5 | 87.6 |
| Fort Lauderdale-Hollywood Intl................ | FLL | 79.7 | 76.1 | 76.3 | 78.8 | 76.9 | 75.2 | 76.4 | 80.9 |
| Houston, George Bush Intercontinental..... | IAH | 83.1 | 84.2 | 79.2 | 78.9 | 85.2 | 85.6 | 81.5 | 83.1 |
| Las Vegas, McCarran Intl..................... | LAS | 82.2 | 80.1 | 79.4 | 83.4 | 79.8 | 77.7 | 77.3 | 82.4 |
| Los Angeles Intl.............................. | LAX | 79.7 | 79.9 | 82.2 | 81.9 | 80.4 | 81.1 | 82.2 | 82.3 |
| Miami Intl..................................... | MIA | 84.5 | 78.3 | 76.5 | 81.6 | 84.6 | 76.0 | 74.5 | 83.3 |
| Minneapolis-St. Paul Intl...................... | MSP | 83.2 | 82.7 | 84.4 | 86.7 | 83.2 | 84.1 | 84.7 | 87.9 |
| New York, JFK Intl............................ | JFK | 76.8 | 76.4 | 69.8 | 80.5 | 76.9 | 79.5 | 75.0 | 83.8 |
| New York, La Guardia......................... | LGA | 70.6 | 74.7 | 68.9 | 74.1 | 73.2 | 77.8 | 73.9 | 79.1 |
| Newark Intl.................................... | EWR | 68.8 | 66.6 | 62.7 | 68.2 | 74.5 | 74.7 | 69.7 | 76.7 |
| Orlando Intl................................... | MCO | 80.2 | 76.6 | 73.7 | 79.5 | 80.1 | 76.3 | 73.3 | 79.9 |
| Philadelphia Intl.............................. | PHL | 78.2 | 74.6 | 71.6 | 81.8 | 77.6 | 76.4 | 73.4 | 83.7 |
| Phoenix, Sky Harbor Intl...................... | PHX | 74.2 | 83.8 | 80.1 | 82.8 | 78.0 | 82.3 | 78.9 | 82.3 |
| Portland Intl.................................. | PDX | 85.2 | 82.9 | 81.7 | 84.8 | 87.3 | 86.8 | 85.0 | 87.2 |
| Salt Lake City Intl............................ | SLC | 84.3 | 85.6 | 85.8 | 87.1 | 85.1 | 86.7 | 85.3 | 87.9 |
| San Diego Intl................................ | SAN | 80.9 | 81.7 | 81.3 | 82.3 | 80.4 | 82.1 | 81.8 | 83.0 |
| San Francisco Intl............................ | SFO | 74.8 | 72.2 | 73.0 | 74.4 | 80.3 | 77.5 | 77.3 | 78.5 |
| Seattle-Tacoma Intl........................... | SEA | 84.9 | 81.9 | 76.8 | 76.9 | 87.9 | 86.2 | 80.2 | 82.8 |
| Tampa, Tampa Intl............................ | TPA | 81.4 | 77.5 | 75.2 | 80.0 | 81.3 | 77.6 | 75.8 | 82.0 |
| Washington, Reagan National................. | DCA | 77.1 | 77.2 | 74.8 | 82.1 | 77.4 | 78.9 | 78.1 | 83.4 |
| Washington/Dulles............................ | IAD | 85.2 | 79.2 | 75.9 | 83.0 | 85.1 | 82.0 | 80.2 | 86.2 |

X Not applicable. [1] Includes other airports not shown separately.

Source: U.S. Department of Transportation, Bureau of Transportation Statistics, "TranStats," <http://www.transtats.bts.gov>, accessed September 2019.

## Table 1098. Airline Fuel Consumption and Fuel Costs: 2000 to 2018

[20,373 represents 20,373,000,000. Data are shown aggregated for scheduled and unscheduled service on U.S. carriers with over $20 million in revenue per year]

| Year | Total fuel consumption (million gallons) | Total fuel cost (million dollars) | Cost per gallon (dollars) | Domestic service Consumption (million gallons) | Cost (million dollars) | Cost per gallon (dollars) | International service Consumption (million gallons) | Cost (million dollars) | Cost per gallon (dollars) |
|---|---|---|---|---|---|---|---|---|---|
| 2000 | 20,373 | 16,448 | 0.81 | 14,865 | 11,708 | 0.79 | 5,508 | 4,739 | 0.86 |
| 2005 | 19,950 | 33,175 | 1.66 | 13,976 | 22,951 | 1.64 | 5,975 | 10,224 | 1.71 |
| 2010 | 17,298 | 39,350 | 2.27 | 11,257 | 25,571 | 2.27 | 6,042 | 13,779 | 2.28 |
| 2015 | 17,349 | 32,196 | 1.86 | 10,929 | 20,006 | 1.83 | 6,421 | 12,190 | 1.90 |
| 2016 | 17,668 | 25,742 | 1.46 | 11,374 | 16,636 | 1.46 | 6,295 | 9,106 | 1.45 |
| 2017 | 18,029 | 30,630 | 1.70 | 11,588 | 19,728 | 1.70 | 6,441 | 10,902 | 1.69 |
| 2018 | 18,731 | 40,504 | 2.16 | 12,148 | 26,121 | 2.15 | 6,599 | 14,383 | 2.18 |

Source: U.S. Bureau of Transportation Statistics, "Airline Fuel Cost and Consumption," <https://www.transtats.bts.gov/fuel.asp>, accessed August 2019.

## Table 1099. Top 50 Airports in 2017—Passengers Enplaned: 2016 and 2017

[In thousands (946,330 represents 946,330,000), except rank. For calendar year. Intl = international. Airports ranked by total passengers enplaned on U.S. carrier scheduled domestic and international service and foreign carrier scheduled international service from the U.S.]

| Airport city and code | 2016 Rank | 2016 Total | 2017 Rank | 2017 Total | Airport city and code | 2016 Rank | 2016 Total | 2017 Rank | 2017 Total |
|---|---|---|---|---|---|---|---|---|---|
| All U.S. airports | (X) | 946,330 | (X) | 979,521 | San Diego, CA (SAN) | 27 | 10,513 | 25 | 11,140 |
| Total, top 50 [1] | (X) | 718,050 | (X) | 726,259 | Washington, DC (IAD) | 26 | 10,640 | 26 | 11,023 |
| Atlanta, GA (ATL) | 1 | 50,882 | 1 | 50,252 | Chicago, IL (MDW) | 24 | 11,306 | 27 | 10,908 |
| Los Angeles, CA (LAX) | 2 | 40,185 | 2 | 41,232 | Honolulu, HI (HNL) | 28 | 9,733 | 28 | 9,730 |
| Chicago, IL (ORD) | 3 | 37,755 | 3 | 38,593 | Tampa, FL (TPA) | 29 | 9,320 | 29 | 9,548 |
| Dallas/Fort Worth, TX (DFW) | 4 | 31,442 | 4 | 31,817 | Portland, OR (PDX) | 30 | 9,109 | 30 | 9,435 |
| Denver, CO (DEN) | 6 | 28,642 | 5 | 29,809 | Dallas, TX (DAL) | 31 | 7,882 | 31 | 7,593 |
| New York, NY (JFK) | 5 | 29,336 | 6 | 29,529 | St. Louis, MO (STL) | 33 | 7,010 | 32 | 7,195 |
| San Francisco, CA (SFO) | 7 | 25,868 | 7 | 26,900 | Nashville, TN (BNA) | 34 | 6,541 | 33 | 6,902 |
| Las Vegas, NV (LAS) | 8 | 23,051 | 8 | 23,209 | Austin-Bergstrom, TX (AUS) | 36 | 6,239 | 34 | 6,813 |
| Seattle-Tacoma, WA (SEA) | 9 | 21,978 | 9 | 22,644 | Houston, TX (HOU) | 35 | 6,511 | 35 | 6,539 |
| Charlotte-Douglas, NC (CLT) | 10 | 21,790 | 10 | 22,011 | Oakland, CA (OAK) | 37 | 6,095 | 36 | 6,414 |
| Newark, NJ (EWR) | 15 | 19,976 | 11 | 21,571 | San Jose, CA (SJC) | 42 | 5,406 | 37 | 6,131 |
| Orlando, FL (MCO) | 13 | 20,407 | 12 | 21,565 | New Orleans, LA (MSY) | 39 | 5,692 | 38 | 6,022 |
| Phoenix, AZ (PHX) | 11 | 21,389 | 13 | 21,185 | Raleigh, NC (RDU) | 41 | 5,454 | 39 | 5,691 |
| Miami, FL (MIA) | 12 | 20,917 | 14 | 20,709 | Kansas City, MO (MCI) | 40 | 5,546 | 40 | 5,629 |
| Houston, TX (IAH) | 14 | 20,162 | 15 | 19,604 | Sacramento, CA (SMF) | 44 | 5,063 | 41 | 5,342 |
| Boston, MA (BOS) | 17 | 17,811 | 16 | 18,759 | Santa Ana, CA (SNA) | 43 | 5,276 | 42 | 5,083 |
| Minneapolis-St. Paul, MN (MSP) | 16 | 18,248 | 17 | 18,409 | Cleveland, OH (CLE) | 50 | 4,120 | 43 | 4,446 |
| Detroit, MI (DTW) | 18 | 16,927 | 18 | 17,036 | San Antonio, TX (SAT) | 49 | 4,275 | 44 | 4,382 |
| Fort Lauderdale, FL (FLL) | 21 | 14,364 | 19 | 15,817 | Fort Myers, FL (RSW) | 48 | 4,277 | 45 | 4,364 |
| New York, NY (LGA) | 19 | 14,777 | 20 | 14,607 | Indianapolis, IN (IND) | 47 | 4,288 | 46 | 4,344 |
| Philadelphia, PA (PHL) | 20 | 14,644 | 21 | 14,271 | Pittsburgh, PA (PIT) | 51 | 4,035 | 47 | 4,327 |
| Baltimore, MD (BWI) | 22 | 12,620 | 22 | 12,976 | San Juan, PR (SJU) | 45 | 4,396 | 48 | 4,164 |
| Salt Lake City, UT (SLT) | 25 | 11,187 | 23 | 11,616 | Cincinnati, OH (CVG) | 59 | 3,289 | 49 | 3,792 |
| Washington, DC (DCA) | 23 | 11,498 | 24 | 11,506 | Columbus, OH (CMH) | 54 | 3,620 | 50 | 3,677 |

X Not applicable. [1] The 2016 totals for the top 50 airports will not sum to total top 50 because some top 50 airports in 2017 were not in the top 50 in those years.

Source: U.S. Bureau of Transportation Statistics, "National Transportation Statistics," <https://www.bts.gov/topics/national-transportation-statistics>, accessed July 2019.

## Table 1100. Consumer Complaints Filed Against U.S. Airlines: 2000 to 2018

[Calendar year data. Represents complaints filed by consumers to the U.S. Department of Transportation (DOT), Aviation Consumer Protection Division, regarding service problems with air carriers. See source for data on individual airlines]

| Complaint category | 2000 | 2005 | 2010 | 2013 | 2014 | 2015 | 2016 | 2017 | 2018 |
|---|---|---|---|---|---|---|---|---|---|
| Total | 20,564 | 6,900 | 10,988 | 13,176 | 15,539 | 20,175 | 17,908 | 18,156 | 15,541 |
| Flight problems [1] | 8,698 | 1,942 | 3,337 | 3,980 | 4,974 | 6,434 | 6,179 | 6,078 | 4,516 |
| Baggage | 2,753 | 1,586 | 1,938 | 2,134 | 2,667 | 3,133 | 2,770 | 2,745 | 2,728 |
| Ticketing/boarding [2] | 1,405 | 679 | 1,510 | 1,900 | 2,256 | 2,695 | 2,115 | 2,194 | 1,907 |
| Customer service [3] | 4,074 | 800 | 1,345 | 1,836 | 1,708 | 2,276 | 1,934 | 1,781 | 1,614 |
| Refunds | 803 | 530 | 730 | 920 | 1,156 | 1,573 | 1,361 | 1,359 | 1,328 |
| Fares [4] | 708 | 219 | 465 | 503 | 916 | 1,813 | 1,363 | 2,022 | 1,546 |
| Disability [5] | 612 | 430 | 572 | 683 | 784 | 944 | 865 | 850 | 828 |
| Oversales [6] | 759 | 284 | 544 | 426 | 514 | 648 | 597 | 511 | 409 |
| Discrimination [7] | (NA) | 100 | 143 | 80 | 68 | 65 | 95 | 98 | 96 |
| Advertising | 42 | 45 | 77 | 96 | 130 | 163 | 124 | 80 | 57 |
| Animals | 1 | 3 | 8 | 6 | 2 | 3 | 1 | 1 | 2 |
| Other [8] | 684 | 282 | 319 | 612 | 364 | 428 | 504 | 437 | 510 |

NA Not available. [1] Cancellations, delays, and other deviations from schedule. [2] Errors in reservations and ticketing; and problems in making reservations, obtaining tickets, and boarding (except oversales). Prior to 1998, includes disability complaints. [3] Unhelpful employees, inadequate meals or cabin service, treatment of delayed passengers. [4] Incorrect or incomplete information about fares, discount fare conditions, and availability, etc. [5] Civil rights complaints by air travelers with disabilities. Prior to 2000, included in ticketing/boarding. [6] All bumping problems, whether or not airline complied with DOT regulations. [7] Civil rights complaints by air travelers (other than disability) based on factors such as race, religion, national origin or sex. [8] Frequent flyer, smoking, tours credit, cargo problems, security, airport facilities, claims for bodily injury, and others not classified above.

Source: U.S. Department of Transportation, Aviation Consumer Protection Division, *Air Travel Consumer Report*, February 2019, and earlier reports. See also <https://www.transportation.gov/airconsumer>.

# Table 1101. U.S. Airline Carrier Delays, Cancellations, and Diversions: 2000 to 2018

[5,683.0 represents 5,683,000. For calendar year. See headnote, Table 1097]

| Item | 2000 | 2010 | 2011 | 2012 | 2013 | 2014 | 2015 | 2016 | 2017 | 2018 |
|---|---|---|---|---|---|---|---|---|---|---|
| Total operations........ | 5,683.0 | 6,450.1 | 6,085.3 | 6,096.8 | 6,369.5 | 5,819.8 | 5,819.1 | 5,617.7 | 5,674.6 | 7,213.4 |
| NUMBER (1,000) | | | | | | | | | | |
| Delayed departures [1]..... | 1,131.7 | 1,111.9 | 1,042.4 | 991.8 | 1,229.3 | 1,193.2 | 1,055.5 | 952.2 | 1,012.5 | 1,304.2 |
| Delayed arrivals [2].......... | 1,356.0 | 1,174.9 | 1,109.9 | 1,015.2 | 1,269.3 | 1,240.5 | 1,063.4 | 964.2 | 1,029.5 | 1,352.7 |
| Cancellations [3]............. | 187.5 | 113.3 | 116.0 | 78.9 | 96.0 | 127.0 | 89.9 | 65.9 | 82.7 | 116.6 |
| Diversions [4]................ | 14.3 | 15.5 | 14.4 | 12.5 | 14.2 | 14.4 | 15.2 | 13.7 | 12.5 | 17.9 |
| PERCENT | | | | | | | | | | |
| Delayed departures [1]..... | 19.9 | 17.2 | 17.1 | 16.3 | 19.3 | 20.5 | 18.1 | 17.0 | 17.8 | 18.1 |
| Delayed arrivals [2].......... | 23.9 | 18.2 | 18.2 | 16.7 | 19.9 | 21.3 | 18.3 | 17.2 | 18.1 | 18.8 |
| Cancellations [3]............. | 3.3 | 1.8 | 1.9 | 1.3 | 1.5 | 2.2 | 1.5 | 1.2 | 1.5 | 1.6 |
| Diversions [4]................ | 0.3 | 0.2 | 0.2 | 0.2 | 0.2 | 0.2 | 0.3 | 0.2 | 0.2 | 0.2 |

[1] Late departures departed 15 minutes or more after the scheduled departure time. [2] Late arrivals arrived 15 minutes or more after the scheduled arrival time. [3] A cancelled flight is one that was not operated, but was listed in a carrier's computer reservation system within seven days of the scheduled departure. [4] A diverted flight is one that left from the scheduled departure airport but flew to a destination point other than the scheduled destination point.

Source: U.S. Bureau of Transportation Statistics, "National Transportation Statistics," <https://www.bts.gov/topics/national-transportation-statistics>, accessed August 2019.

# Table 1102. Commuter/Regional Airline Operations Summary: 2010 to 2017

[In units as indicated (164.1 represents 164,100,000). Calendar year data. Commuter/regional airlines primarily operate aircraft of 75 passengers or less and 18,000 pounds of payload capacity serving short haul and small community markets. Represents operations within all of North America by U.S. regional carriers. As of 2014, "operating carriers" is defined as those certificate holders operating scheduled passenger service under 14 CFR Parts 135 or 121 with capacities of fewer than 100 seats. As of 2015, Part 380 public charter operations are excluded. Averages are means. For definition of mean, see Guide to Tabular Presentation]

| Item | Unit | 2010 | 2013 | 2014 | 2015 | 2016 | 2017 |
|---|---|---|---|---|---|---|---|
| Passenger certificated carriers operating............. | Number | 66 | 63 | 65 | 64 | 67 | 65 |
| Passengers enplaned.................................... | Millions | 164.1 | 159.1 | 157.6 | 156.6 | 154.9 | 153.3 |
| Average passengers enplaned per carrier............. | 1,000 | 2,486.4 | 2,525.9 | 2,424.0 | 2,446.3 | 2,312.2 | 2,357.7 |
| Revenue passenger miles (RPM)...................... | Billions | 76.6 | 74.9 | 75.1 | 74.8 | 75.5 | 74.5 |
| Average RPMs per carrier.............................. | Millions | 1,160.9 | 1,189.5 | 1,155.5 | 1,168.0 | 1,126.3 | 1,146.0 |
| Available seat miles.................................... | Billions | 100.1 | 95.7 | 94.0 | 92.8 | 94.8 | 94.6 |
| Average load factor..................................... | Percent | 76.6 | 78.3 | 79.9 | 80.6 | 79.6 | 78.8 |
| Departures completed................................... | Millions | 4.69 | 4.34 | 4.11 | 3.87 | 3.81 | 3.68 |
| Airports served.......................................... | Number | 673 | 614 | 607 | 615 | 622 | 619 |
| Average trip length...................................... | Miles | 467 | 471 | 477 | 478 | 488 | 487 |
| Average seating capacity (seats)...................... | Number | 56 | 56 | 58 | 61 | 62 | 64 |
| Fleet flying hours....................................... | 1,000 | 5,048 | 4,782 | 4,522 | 4,302 | 4,255 | 4,137 |

Source: Regional Airline Association, *2018 Annual Report* ©, and previous editions. See also <http://www.raa.org/>.

# Table 1103. U.S. Air Carrier Aircraft Accidents: 2000 to 2017

[For years ending December 31. See source for more details]

| Item | Unit | 2000 | 2010 | 2013 | 2014 | 2015 | 2016 | 2017 (P) |
|---|---|---|---|---|---|---|---|---|
| Air carrier accidents, all services [1]........... | Number | 56 | 30 | 23 | 32 | 29 | 31 | 32 |
| Fatal accidents............................. | Number | 3 | 1 | 2 | – | – | – | – |
| Fatalities.................................... | Number | 92 | 2 | 9 | – | – | – | – |
| Aboard....................................... | Number | 92 | 2 | 9 | – | – | – | – |
| Rates per 100,000 flight hours: | | | | | | | | |
| Accidents.................................... | Rate | 0.31 | 0.17 | 0.13 | 0.18 | 0.16 | 0.17 | 0.17 |
| Fatal accidents.............................. | Rate | 0.02 | 0.01 | – | – | – | – | – |
| Commuter air carrier accidents [2]............ | Number | 12 | 6 | 6 | 3 | 4 | 8 | 8 |
| Fatal accidents............................. | Number | 1 | – | 2 | – | 1 | 2 | 1 |
| Fatalities.................................... | Number | 5 | – | 5 | – | 1 | 8 | 1 |
| Aboard....................................... | Number | 5 | – | 5 | – | 1 | 6 | 1 |
| Rates per 100,000 flight hours: | | | | | | | | |
| Accidents.................................... | Rate | 3.25 | 1.91 | 1.85 | 0.84 | 1.07 | 2.07 | 2.00 |
| Fatal accidents.............................. | Rate | 0.27 | – | 0.6 | – | 0.27 | 0.52 | 0.25 |
| On-demand air taxi accidents [3].............. | Number | 80 | 30 | 45 | 35 | 39 | 30 | 43 |
| Fatal accidents............................. | Number | 22 | 6 | 10 | 8 | 7 | 7 | 7 |
| Fatalities.................................... | Number | 71 | 17 | 25 | 20 | 27 | 19 | 15 |
| Aboard....................................... | Number | 68 | 17 | 25 | 20 | 27 | 19 | 15 |
| Rates per 100,000 flight hours: | | | | | | | | |
| Accidents.................................... | Rate | 2.04 | 0.96 | 1.33 | 0.96 | 1.09 | 0.86 | 1.23 |
| Fatal accidents.............................. | Rate | 0.56 | 0.19 | 0.30 | 0.22 | 0.20 | 0.20 | 0.20 |
| General aviation accidents [4]................. | Number | 1,837 | 1,441 | 1,223 | 1,224 | 1,211 | 1,267 | 1,233 |
| Fatal accidents............................. | Number | 345 | 271 | 221 | 256 | 230 | 213 | 203 |
| Fatalities.................................... | Number | 596 | 458 | 390 | 423 | 378 | 386 | 330 |
| Aboard....................................... | Number | 585 | 455 | 386 | 413 | 375 | 379 | 330 |
| Rates per 100,000 flight hours: | | | | | | | | |
| Accidents.................................... | Rate | 6.57 | 6.63 | 6.26 | 6.24 | 5.85 | 5.93 | 5.67 |
| Fatal accidents.............................. | Rate | 1.21 | 1.24 | 1.12 | 1.31 | 1.10 | 0.98 | 0.93 |

– Represents zero. P Preliminary. [1] U.S. air carriers operating aircraft with 10 or more seats, under 14 CFR 121. [2] All scheduled service of U.S. air carriers operating aircraft with fewer than 10 seats, under 14 CFR 135. [3] All nonscheduled service of U.S. air carriers operating aircraft with fewer than 10 seats, under 14 CFR 135. [4] U.S. civil registered aircraft not operated under 14 CFR 121 or 135.

Source: U.S. National Transportation Safety Board, Investigations Data and Stats, "Review of Accident Data—2017 Preliminary Aviation Statistics," <https://www.ntsb.gov/investigations/data/Pages/Data_Stats.aspx>, accessed December 2018.

# Table 1104. Airports, Aircraft, and Airmen: 1990 to 2018

[As of December 31 or for years ending December 31]

| Item | 1990 | 2000 | 2010 | 2014 | 2015 | 2016 | 2017 | 2018 |
|---|---|---|---|---|---|---|---|---|
| **AIRPORTS** | | | | | | | | |
| **Airports, total [1]** | **17,490** | **19,281** | **19,802** | **19,299** | **(NA)** | **19,536** | **19,655** | **19,636** |
| Public [1] | 5,589 | 5,317 | 5,175 | 5,145 | (NA) | 5,136 | 5,104 | 5,087 |
| Percent with lighted runways | 71.4 | 75.9 | (NA) | (NA) | (NA) | (NA) | (NA) | (NA) |
| Percent with paved runways | 70.7 | 74.3 | (NA) | (NA) | (NA) | (NA) | (NA) | (NA) |
| Private | 11,901 | 13,964 | 14,353 | 13,863 | (NA) | 14,112 | 14,263 | 14,549 |
| Percent with lighted runways | 7.0 | 7.2 | (NA) | (NA) | (NA) | (NA) | (NA) | (NA) |
| Percent with paved runways | 31.5 | 32.0 | (NA) | (NA) | (NA) | (NA) | (NA) | (NA) |
| Military | (NA) | (NA) | 274 | 286 | (NA) | 288 | 288 | 305 |
| Certificated [2] | 680 | 651 | 551 | 537 | (NA) | 531 | 526 | 523 |
| General aviation | 16,810 | 18,630 | 19,251 | 18,762 | (NA) | 19,005 | 19,129 | 19,125 |
| **AIRCRAFT** | | | | | | | | |
| **Active air carrier fleet [3]** | **6,083** | **7,826** | **7,185** | **6,761** | **6,876** | **7,039** | **7,141** | **(NA)** |
| Fixed wing | 6,072 | 8,010 | (NA) | (NA) | (NA) | (NA) | (NA) | (NA) |
| Helicopter [4] | 11 | 39 | (NA) | (NA) | (NA) | (NA) | (NA) | (NA) |
| **General aviation fleet [5]** | **198,000** | **217,533** | **223,370** | **204,408** | **210,030** | **211,793** | **211,757** | **(NA)** |
| Fixed-wing | 184,500 | 183,276 | 176,272 | 161,321 | 164,293 | 166,167 | 167,082 | (NA) |
| Turbojet | 4,100 | 7,001 | 11,484 | 12,362 | 13,440 | 13,751 | 14,217 | (NA) |
| Turboprop | 5,300 | 5,762 | 9,369 | 9,777 | 9,712 | 9,779 | 9,949 | (NA) |
| Piston | 175,200 | 170,513 | 155,419 | 139,182 | 141,141 | 142,638 | 142,916 | (NA) |
| Rotorcraft | 6,900 | 7,150 | 10,102 | 9,966 | 10,506 | 10,577 | 10,511 | (NA) |
| Other | 6,600 | 6,700 | 5,684 | 4,699 | 4,941 | 4,986 | 4,692 | (NA) |
| Gliders | (X) | 2,041 | 1,899 | 1,791 | 1,870 | 1,789 | 1,747 | (NA) |
| Lighter than air | (X) | 4,660 | 3,785 | 2,908 | 3,071 | 3,197 | 2,945 | (NA) |
| Experimental | (X) | 20,407 | 29,662 | 26,191 | 27,922 | 27,585 | 26,921 | (NA) |
| **AIRMAN CERTIFICATES HELD** | | | | | | | | |
| **Pilot, total** | **702,659** | **625,581** | **627,588** | **593,499** | **590,039** | **584,362** | **609,306** | **633,317** |
| Female | 40,515 | 35,607 | 42,218 | 39,322 | 39,287 | 39,187 | 42,694 | 46,463 |
| Student [6] | 128,663 | 93,064 | 119,119 | 120,546 | 122,729 | 128,501 | 149,121 | 167,804 |
| Recreational | 87 | 340 | 212 | 220 | 190 | 175 | 153 | 144 |
| Sport | (X) | (X) | 3,682 | 5,157 | 5,482 | 5,889 | 6,097 | 6,246 |
| Airplane: | | | | | | | | |
| Private | 299,111 | 251,561 | 202,020 | 174,883 | 170,718 | 162,313 | 162,455 | 163,695 |
| Commercial | 149,666 | 121,858 | 123,705 | 104,322 | 101,164 | 96,081 | 98,161 | 99,880 |
| Air transport | 107,732 | 141,596 | 142,198 | 152,933 | 154,730 | 157,894 | 159,825 | 162,145 |
| Rotorcraft only | 9,567 | 7,775 | 15,377 | 15,511 | 15,566 | 15,518 | 15,355 | 15,033 |
| Glider only | 7,833 | 9,387 | 21,275 | 19,927 | 19,460 | 17,991 | 18,139 | 18,370 |
| Flight instructor certificates | 63,775 | 80,931 | 96,473 | 100,993 | 102,628 | 104,382 | 106,692 | 108,564 |
| Instrument ratings | 297,073 | 311,944 | 318,001 | 306,066 | 304,329 | 302,572 | 306,652 | 311,017 |
| Remote pilots [7] | (NA) | (NA) | (NA) | (NA) | (NA) | 20,362 | 69,166 | 106,321 |
| **Nonpilot [8]** | **492,237** | **547,453** | **686,717** | **717,399** | **728,329** | **652,943** | **671,222** | **688,002** |
| Mechanic | 344,282 | 344,434 | 331,989 | 341,409 | 342,528 | 279,435 | 286,268 | 292,002 |
| Repairmen | (X) | 38,208 | 41,267 | 39,566 | 39,363 | 34,411 | 35,040 | 35,382 |
| Parachute rigger | 10,094 | 10,477 | 8,407 | 8,702 | 8,846 | 5,851 | 6,192 | 6,430 |
| Ground instructor | 66,882 | 72,326 | 75,205 | 71,755 | 70,957 | 65,053 | 66,423 | 67,784 |
| Dispatcher | 11,002 | 16,340 | 20,691 | 23,113 | 23,754 | 19,758 | 20,664 | 21,465 |
| Flight navigator | 1,290 | 570 | 174 | 115 | 102 | 67 | 64 | 58 |
| Flight attendant | (X) | (X) | 159,946 | 188,936 | 200,319 | 212,607 | 222,037 | 231,355 |
| Flight engineer | 58,687 | 65,098 | 49,038 | 43,803 | 42,460 | 35,761 | 34,534 | 33,526 |

NA Not available. X Not applicable. [1] Includes civil and joint-use civil-military airports, heliports, STOL (short takeoff and landing) ports, and seaplane bases in the U.S. and its territories. Sole-use military airports are included beginning in 2007. Public airports are under public agency control; private airports are owned by a private individual or corporation. [2] Certificated airports serve air-carriers with aircraft seating more than 9 passengers. As of 2005, the Federal Aviation Administration (FAA) no longer certificates military airports. [3] Air-carrier aircraft carry passengers or cargo for hire under 14 CFR 121 (large aircraft—more than 30 seats) and 14 CFR 135 (small aircraft—30 seats or fewer). Beginning in 1990, the number of aircraft is the monthly average reported in use for the last three months of the year. Prior to 1990, it was the number of aircraft reported in use during December of a given year. [4] 2000 change in helicopters due to estimating methods. [5] Beginning 1995, excludes commuters. [6] Beginning 2010, duration of validity for student pilot certificates for pilots under age 40 increased from 36 to 60 months. [7] Remote pilot certification started in August 2016. These numbers are not included in the pilot totals. [8] All certificates on record. No medical examination required.

Source: Prior to 2000: *FAA Statistical Handbook of Aviation*, annual. Thereafter: U.S. Bureau of Transportation Statistics, "National Transportation Statistics," <https://www.bts.gov/topics/national-transportation-statistics>, accessed August 2019. U.S. Federal Aviation Administration, "U.S. Civil Airmen Statistics," and "General Aviation and Air Tax (Part 135) Activity Surveys," <http://www.faa.gov/data_research/aviation_data_statistics/>, accessed August 2019.

## Table 1105. Passenger Airline Revenues from Fares, Fees, and Services; and Expenses and Profits: 2016 to 2018

[In millions of dollars (169,158 represents $169,158,000,000). Data shown for U.S. scheduled passenger airlines. Data for 2016-2017 are compiled from 23 reporting airlines; 2018 data are compiled from 21 airlines]

| Item | 2016 | 2017 | 2018 (P) | Item | 2016 | 2017 | 2018 (P) |
|---|---|---|---|---|---|---|---|
| **Total operating revenue** [1] | **169,158** | **175,337** | **187,474** | Landing fees | 2,977 | 3,056 | 3,211 |
| Passenger fares, | | | | | | | |
| scheduled/charter | 125,916 | 130,491 | 139,005 | Maintenance materials | 2,500 | 2,438 | 2,208 |
| Cargo | 2,629 | 2,985 | 3,522 | Transport-related [2] | 17,995 | 19,009 | 21,493 |
| Baggage fees | 4,321 | 4,576 | 4,895 | Other [4] | 30,272 | 31,656 | 33,760 |
| Reservation change fees | 2,906 | 2,856 | 2,700 | **Operating profit** | **25,366** | **21,444** | **17,646** |
| Transport-related [2] | 28,095 | 28,694 | 28,824 | Operating margin (percent) [5] | 15 | 12 | 9 |
| Other [3] | 5,291 | 5,735 | 8,529 | Nonoperating income/expense [6] | -3,331 | -2,298 | -2,483 |
| **Total operating expenses** | **143,792** | **153,893** | **169,828** | Pre-tax income | 22,035 | 19,146 | 15,163 |
| Fuel | 22,549 | 26,241 | 34,460 | Income tax benefit/expense | -7,989 | -3,851 | -3,388 |
| Labor | 49,948 | 53,556 | 56,104 | Other income/expense | – | – | – |
| Rentals | 8,777 | 8,887 | 9,098 | Net income | 14,047 | 15,295 | 11,775 |
| Depreciation and amortization | 8,773 | 9,051 | 9,495 | Net margin (percent) [7] | 8 | 9 | 6 |

P Preliminary – Represents or rounds to zero. [1] Based on U.S. Department of Transportation accounting standards. Total operating revenues are overstated by code share revenues, which are included in both mainline transport-related revenues and code share passenger revenues. Code share revenues are expensed out in the mainline transport-related expense to allow a true operating profit (loss). This reporting may understate all components of operating revenue, including passenger revenue, as a percent of total operating revenue. [2] Includes in-flight onboard sales, code share revenues, and revenues and expenses from associated businesses (aircraft maintenance, fuel sales, restaurants, vending machines). [3] Includes pet transportation, sale of frequent flyer award miles to airline business partners, standby passenger fees, and public service revenues subsidy. [4] Includes purchase of materials such as passenger food and purchase of services such as advertising, communication, insurance, outside flight equipment maintenance, and traffic commissions. [5] Operating profit or loss as a percent of operating revenue. [6] Interest on long-term debt and capital leases, other interest expense, foreign exchange gains and losses, capital gains and losses, and other income and expenses. [7] Net income or loss as a percent of operating revenue.

Source: U.S. Department of Transportation, Bureau of Transportation Statistics, "2018 Annual and 4th Quarter U.S. Airline Financial Data," and earlier releases, <https://www.bts.gov/statistical-releases> accessed May 2019.

## Table 1106. Worldwide Airline Accidents and Fatalities by World Region: 2018

[Number, except departures in thousands (38,087 represents 38,087,000). Regions are Regional Aviation Safety Group (RASG) regions]

| Region | Departures (1,000) | Accidents | Accident rates [1] | Fatal accidents | Fatalities |
|---|---|---|---|---|---|
| **World** | **38,087** | **98** | **2.6** | **11** | **514** |
| Africa (AFI) | 1,441 | 4 | 2.8 | 2 | 21 |
| Asia and Pacific (APAC) | 12,445 | 20 | 1.6 | 3 | 241 |
| Europe (EUR) [2] | 9,299 | 26 | 2.8 | 2 | 72 |
| Middle East (MID) | 1,327 | 3 | 2.3 | 1 | 66 |
| Americas (PA) | 13,576 | 45 | 3.3 | 3 | 114 |

– Represents zero. [1] Number of accidents per million departures of scheduled commercial operations that involve the transportation of passengers, cargo and mail for remuneration or hire. [2] RASG EUR includes Algeria, Morocco, and Tunisia.

Source: International Civil Aviation Organization, Montreal, Canada, *State of Global Aviation Safety, ICAO Safety Report 2019 Edition* ©, <http://www.icao.int/safety/Pages/Safety-Report.aspx>.

## Table 1107. Water Transportation System Summary: 2000 to 2016

[12.8 represents 12,800,000. Data compiled from U.S. Army Corps of Engineers, Department of Homeland Security/Coast Guard, and Bureau of Transportation Statistics publications; see source for details]

| Item or characteristic | Unit | 2000 | 2010 | 2013 | 2014 | 2016 |
|---|---|---|---|---|---|---|
| U.S.-flag privately owned merchant fleet [1] | Number | 282 | 221 | 187 | 179 | (NA) |
| Recreational boats | Millions | 12.8 | 12.4 | 12.0 | 11.8 | 11.9 |
| Lock chambers | Number | 276 | 239 | 239 | 239 | 239 |
| Lock sites | Number | 230 | 193 | 193 | 193 | 193 |
| Average age of locks | Years | 50.2 | 59.5 | 62.5 | 63.5 | (NA) |
| Waterway facilities (including cargo handling docks) | Number | 9,309 | 8,060 | 8,231 | 8,229 | 8,227 |
| Ports (handling over 250,000 tons) | Number | 197 | 178 | 182 | 183 | 181 |
| Miles of navigable waterways | Number | 25,000 | 25,000 | 25,000 | 25,000 | 25,000 |
| U.S. flag vessels: | | | | | | |
| Total vessels [2] | Number | 41,354 | 40,512 | 39,999 | 40,082 | 41,328 |
| Barge/non-self-propelled vessels | Number | 33,152 | 31,412 | 31,081 | 31,043 | 32,354 |
| Self-propelled vessels | Number | 8,202 | 9,078 | 8,918 | 9,039 | 8,974 |
| U.S. flag vessels by age: | | | | | | |
| Under 6 years old | Percent | 19.6 | 18.5 | 19.3 | 17.7 | (NA) |
| 6 to 10 years old | Percent | 9.2 | 11.5 | 12.1 | 14.1 | (NA) |
| 11 to 15 years old | Percent | 5.1 | 17.0 | 14.3 | 12.4 | (NA) |
| 16 to 20 years old | Percent | 19.6 | 8.7 | 13.6 | 15.1 | (NA) |
| 21 to 25 years old | Percent | 18.3 | 4.2 | 7.7 | 8.3 | (NA) |
| 25 years old and over | Percent | 27.7 | 39.3 | 32.6 | 31.9 | (NA) |

NA Not available. [1] Includes only oceangoing self-propelled, cargo-carrying vessels of 1,000 gross tons and above. [2] Includes unclassified vessels.

Source: U.S. Department of Transportation, Bureau of Transportation Statistics, *Transportation Statistics Annual Report 2018*, February 2019. See also <https://www.bts.dot.gov/product/transportation-statistics-annual-report>.

## Table 1108. Ferry Operators, Vessels, Terminals, Route Distance, and Boarding Counts by State and Island Area: 2015

[Data from the 2016 National Census of Ferry Operators (NCFO). States without ferry operations are omitted. Ferry operations included within the scope of the NCFO were those providing itinerant, fixed route, common carrier passenger and/or vehicle ferry service; and railroad car float operations. Also includes operations providing international services to or from at least one U.S. terminal. Not included within the scope of the ferry census were operations that were exclusively nonitinerant, such as excursion services (e.g. whale watches, casino boats, day cruises, dinner cruises, etc.)]

| State and area | Business operators | Vessels in service | Terminals | Route segment distance (nautical miles) [1] | Boarding counts Passengers | Boarding counts Vehicles |
|---|---|---|---|---|---|---|
| **Total**........................ | **163** | **609** | **560** | **20,042.4** | **118,868,511** | **25,000,034** |
| U.S. total..................... | 157 | 585 | 537 | 19,358.2 | 118,311,065 | 24,796,601 |
| Alabama....................... | 1 | 3 | 4 | 11.4 | 248,166 | 80,782 |
| Alaska......................... | 6 | 18 | 41 | 12,492.5 | 906,851 | 268,862 |
| Arizona........................ | – | – | 1 | 3.1 | – | |
| Arkansas...................... | 1 | 5 | 1 | 0.7 | 34,502 | 17,250 |
| California...................... | 12 | 54 | 47 | 1,048.6 | 8,923,100 | 566,073 |
| Connecticut................... | 4 | 15 | 9 | 83.9 | 2,034,954 | 776,343 |
| Delaware...................... | 1 | 1 | 3 | 14.2 | 400,000 | 189,160 |
| Florida......................... | 6 | 19 | 18 | 23.4 | 798,570 | 248,276 |
| Georgia........................ | 3 | 9 | 8 | 55.3 | 899,972 | – |
| Hawaii......................... | 1 | 4 | 3 | 32.0 | – | – |
| Illinois......................... | 6 | 29 | 16 | 19.3 | 2,136,032 | 801,717 |
| Iowa........................... | – | – | 3 | 6.5 | 32,844 | 2,831 |
| Kentucky...................... | 5 | 11 | 15 | 5.9 | 428,053 | 463,752 |
| Louisiana...................... | 3 | 15 | 16 | 6.0 | 1,978,521 | 905,425 |
| Maine.......................... | 7 | 23 | 32 | 324.9 | 1,730,675 | 278,884 |
| Maryland....................... | 4 | 22 | 21 | 91.2 | 898,914 | 250,000 |
| Massachusetts................ | 9 | 45 | 23 | 439.0 | 5,681,996 | 638,158 |
| Michigan....................... | 10 | 22 | 31 | 1,461.7 | 1,065,364 | 1,147,176 |
| Minnesota..................... | 1 | 2 | 1 | 270.0 | 5,639 | – |
| Mississippi.................... | 2 | 5 | 4 | 22.4 | 61,304 | 910 |
| Missouri....................... | 3 | 5 | 6 | 252.3 | 60,508 | 103,777 |
| Montana....................... | 2 | 3 | 6 | 0.5 | 3,473 | 4,022 |
| New Hampshire............... | 1 | 1 | 2 | 13.0 | 10,000 | – |
| New Jersey.................... | 6 | 48 | 14 | 87.0 | 5,035,614 | 140,000 |
| New York...................... | 12 | 53 | 60 | 335.7 | 43,557,550 | 1,733,475 |
| North Carolina................ | 6 | 37 | 29 | 252.1 | 2,500,990 | 821,244 |
| Ohio........................... | 2 | 8 | 7 | 125.4 | 1,467,807 | 28,983 |
| Oklahoma..................... | 1 | 3 | 4 | 16.1 | 10,338 | |
| Oregon........................ | 2 | 3 | 7 | 2.2 | 1,065,475 | 412,522 |
| Pennsylvania.................. | 1 | 2 | 2 | (NA) | 2,319 | 600 |
| Rhode Island.................. | 5 | 10 | 11 | 189.3 | 201,634 | 26,024 |
| South Carolina................ | 1 | 2 | 5 | 53.0 | 358,785 | – |
| Tennessee..................... | 1 | 6 | 4 | 1.7 | 93,440 | 73,000 |
| Texas.......................... | 4 | 17 | 8 | 9.3 | 6,393,436 | 2,259,084 |
| Utah........................... | 1 | 1 | 2 | 7.7 | 7,022 | 2,546 |
| Vermont....................... | 2 | 13 | 4 | 13.5 | (D) | (D) |
| Virginia........................ | 6 | 12 | 17 | 76.2 | 2,649,150 | 955,233 |
| Washington................... | 12 | 44 | 40 | 1,345.3 | 26,081,154 | 11,145,634 |
| Wisconsin..................... | 7 | 15 | 12 | 165.9 | 546,913 | 454,858 |
| Puerto Rico................... | 1 | 9 | 5 | 82.0 | – | – |
| Virgin Islands................. | 5 | 15 | 14 | 434.0 | 287,046 | 79,755 |
| British Columbia.............. | (X) | (X) | 3 | 167.2 | 236,638 | 74,671 |
| Ontario........................ | (X) | (X) | 1 | 1.0 | 33,762 | 49,007 |

X Not applicable. NA Not available. D Data withheld to avoid individual disclosure. – Represents zero. [1] Interstate segment route nautical miles are assigned to the state of the origin terminal.

Source U.S. Department of Transportation, Bureau of Transportation Statistics, *2016 Highlights of Ferry Operations in the United States*, October 2017. See also <https://www.bts.gov/NCFO>.

## Table 1109. Freight Carried on Major U.S. Waterways: 2000 to 2017

[In millions of short tons (3.1 represents 3,100,000). One short ton equals 2,000 pounds]

| Waterway | 2000 | 2005 | 2010 | 2013 | 2014 | 2015 | 2016 | 2017 |
|---|---|---|---|---|---|---|---|---|
| Atlantic Intracoastal Waterway........... | 3.1 | 2.7 | 2.9 | 2.9 | 2.4 | 2.6 | 2.3 | 2.3 |
| Great Lakes.................................. | 187.5 | 169.4 | 129.5 | 127.6 | 132.3 | 123.7 | 118.2 | 125.4 |
| Gulf Intracoastal Waterway............... | 113.8 | 116.1 | 116.2 | 115.4 | 126.1 | 118.9 | 111.7 | 111.2 |
| Mississippi River system [1]............... | 715.5 | 678.0 | 663.2 | 670.0 | 718.6 | 684.4 | 680.9 | (NA) |
| Mississippi River main stem............. | 515.6 | 464.6 | 483.2 | 493.7 | 536.2 | 521.1 | 526.3 | 552.3 |
| Ohio River system [2]...................... | 274.4 | 280.1 | 245.2 | 239.4 | 246.0 | 223.2 | 204.7 | 202.2 |
| Columbia River.............................. | 55.2 | 51.5 | 54.7 | 55.3 | 61.7 | 54.7 | 61.3 | 63.4 |
| Snake River................................. | 6.7 | 5.3 | 3.4 | 3.7 | 4.4 | 3.6 | 3.4 | 3.5 |

NA Not available. [1] Main channels and all tributaries of the Mississippi, Illinois, Missouri, and Ohio Rivers. [2] Main channels and all navigable tributaries and embayments of the Ohio, Tennessee, and Cumberland Rivers.

Source: U.S. Army Corps of Engineers, *Waterborne Commerce of the United States, 2017*, December 2018, and earlier reports. See also <https://www.iwr.usace.army.mil/About/Technical-Centers/WCSC-Waterborne-Commerce-Statistics-Center/>.

# Table 1110. Waterborne Commerce by Type of Commodity: 2000 to 2016

[In millions of short tons (2,424.6 represents 2,424,600,000). One short ton is equal to 2,000 pounds. Domestic trade includes all commercial movements between United States ports and on inland rivers, the Great Lakes, canals, and connecting channels of the United States and its territories and possessions. Foreign commerce is waterborne import, export, and in-transit traffic between the United States, Puerto Rico and the Virgin Islands, and any foreign country; these statistics do not include traffic between any foreign country and selected United States territories and possessions (American Samoa, Guam, Northern Mariana Islands and U.S. outlying islands)]

| Commodity | 2000 | 2005 | 2010 | 2013 | 2014 | 2015 | 2016 Total | 2016 Domestic | 2016 Foreign imports | 2016 Foreign exports |
|---|---|---|---|---|---|---|---|---|---|---|
| Total | 2,424.6 | 2,527.6 | 2,334.4 | 2,274.8 | 2,345.8 | 2,278.8 | 2,292.0 | 876.6 | 755.6 | 659.8 |
| Coal | 297.0 | 316.6 | 309.6 | 312.3 | 292.2 | 233.9 | 197.7 | 133.2 | 9.2 | 55.3 |
| Petroleum and petroleum products | 1,044.0 | 1,111.4 | 1,018.8 | 927.5 | 906.0 | 917.3 | 953.8 | 337.5 | 396.6 | 219.7 |
| Crude petroleum | 571.4 | 602.7 | 508.5 | 418.9 | 396.8 | 382.7 | 387.3 | 89.5 | 280.2 | 17.6 |
| Petroleum products [1] | 472.4 | 508.8 | 510.4 | 508.6 | 509.1 | 534.6 | 566.5 | 248.0 | 116.4 | 202.1 |
| Gasoline | 125.2 | 156.1 | 137.8 | 124.6 | 118.7 | 131.4 | 125.5 | 67.5 | 27.0 | 31.0 |
| Distillate fuel oil | 91.7 | 141.1 | 185.4 | 198.7 | 192.7 | 191.6 | 194.9 | 65.2 | 56.1 | 73.5 |
| Residual fuel oil | 131.6 | 96.1 | 81.1 | 65.3 | 62.2 | 64.5 | 61.3 | 51.1 | 6.5 | 3.6 |
| Chemicals and related products | 172.4 | 174.9 | 180.1 | 180.5 | 180.4 | 181.8 | 186.2 | 74.4 | 47.5 | 64.3 |
| Fertilizers | 35.1 | 34.5 | 35.8 | 39.9 | 43.5 | 42.3 | 42.1 | 19.6 | 13.7 | 8.9 |
| Other chemicals and related products | 137.3 | 140.4 | 144.3 | 140.6 | 136.9 | 139.5 | 144.1 | 54.8 | 33.8 | 55.4 |
| Crude material, inedible | 380.3 | 386.0 | 307.0 | 331.4 | 354.3 | 347.6 | 327.2 | 173.2 | 80.6 | 73.5 |
| Forest products, wood and chips | 33.1 | 29.4 | 20.8 | 28.9 | 30.3 | 29.0 | 31.1 | 5.5 | 5.2 | 20.4 |
| Pulp and waste paper | 13.6 | 18.7 | 21.4 | 24.0 | 23.5 | 23.4 | 24.5 | – | 2.5 | 22.0 |
| Soil, sand, gravel, rock, and stone [1] | 165.0 | 177.9 | 120.3 | 126.2 | 134.1 | 140.9 | 138.3 | 101.4 | 35.2 | 1.7 |
| Limestone | 67.4 | 73.5 | 61.3 | 59.9 | 64.7 | 69.9 | 65.3 | 46.6 | 17.7 | 1.0 |
| Phosphate rock | 3.4 | 6.0 | 4.6 | 5.8 | 5.6 | 4.3 | 3.0 | 1.3 | 1.7 | – |
| Sand & gravel | 79.0 | 80.2 | 46.3 | 51.8 | 54.8 | 57.4 | 59.4 | 49.7 | 9.1 | 0.6 |
| Iron ore and scrap | 97.9 | 85.7 | 82.0 | 85.4 | 85.8 | 74.2 | 76.8 | 50.4 | 6.7 | 19.6 |
| Marine shells | 0.3 | – | 0.1 | 0.1 | 0.1 | 0.1 | – | – | – | – |
| Nonferrous ores and scrap | 29.2 | 29.2 | 23.9 | 29.5 | 29.5 | 29.0 | 19.0 | 4.6 | 10.0 | 4.4 |
| Sulphur, clay, and salt | 11.3 | 8.7 | 6.3 | 7.6 | 7.9 | 7.9 | 27.1 | 8.0 | 14.0 | 5.0 |
| Slag | 4.0 | 6.0 | 4.3 | 5.0 | 5.2 | 5.2 | 5.6 | 1.8 | 3.8 | – |
| Other nonmetal minerals | 25.9 | 30.4 | 27.8 | 24.6 | 38.0 | 37.9 | 4.8 | 1.5 | 3.0 | 0.3 |
| Primary manufactured goods | 153.0 | 166.4 | 103.7 | 117.1 | 135.2 | 129.8 | 124.7 | 32.0 | 78.8 | 13.9 |
| Papers products | 12.1 | 13.7 | 13.7 | 13.1 | 12.8 | 12.8 | 13.3 | 0.7 | 5.5 | 7.1 |
| Lime, cement, and glass | 55.9 | 62.4 | 27.6 | 29.8 | 31.6 | 33.9 | 36.1 | 14.5 | 20.6 | 1.1 |
| Primary iron and steel products | 57.1 | 52.1 | 33.5 | 49.7 | 64.5 | 57.2 | 49.8 | 15.6 | 32.5 | 1.6 |
| Primary nonferrous metal products | 25.5 | 33.5 | 26.7 | 22.3 | 24.0 | 23.3 | 22.7 | 1.3 | 17.4 | 4.0 |
| Primary wood products | 2.5 | 4.8 | 2.2 | 2.1 | 2.3 | 2.7 | 2.9 | – | 2.7 | 0.2 |
| Food and farm products | 283.3 | 251.3 | 300.1 | 270.1 | 319.4 | 312.9 | 346.8 | 103.1 | 46.4 | 197.3 |
| Fish | 2.4 | 3.0 | 3.1 | 3.2 | 3.2 | 3.2 | 3.5 | 0.3 | 2.0 | 1.1 |
| Grain [1] | 145.2 | 124.0 | 131.8 | 100.6 | 131.0 | 120.3 | 135.8 | 47.1 | 2.8 | 85.9 |
| Wheat | 43.4 | 36.4 | 38.4 | 49.7 | 35.9 | 30.6 | 33.6 | 8.8 | 0.9 | 23.9 |
| Corn | 88.2 | 75.2 | 81.8 | 41.7 | 80.5 | 70.1 | 88.7 | 35.8 | 0.9 | 52.1 |
| Oilseeds [1] | 57.6 | 47.2 | 76.9 | 73.2 | 89.2 | 91.3 | 109.0 | 41.4 | 0.9 | 66.8 |
| Soybeans | 47.3 | 40.8 | 67.4 | 62.5 | 80.3 | 79.5 | 97.0 | 37.1 | 0.5 | 59.4 |
| Vegetables products | 8.9 | 8.3 | 12.9 | 13.1 | 12.7 | 12.5 | 13.2 | 1.4 | 6.4 | 5.3 |
| Processed grain and animal feed | 23.1 | 18.4 | 20.6 | 22.1 | 27.0 | 30.0 | 26.6 | 7.0 | 1.2 | 18.4 |
| Other agricultural products | 46.1 | 50.5 | 54.9 | 57.8 | 56.2 | 55.7 | 58.9 | 6.0 | 33.1 | 19.8 |
| All manufactured equipment, machinery, and products | 83.6 | 110.3 | 104.1 | 121.0 | 132.5 | 133.6 | 133.3 | 20.8 | 87.2 | 25.3 |
| Waste and scrap, not elsewhere classified | 4.3 | 2.0 | 1.3 | 1.3 | 1.3 | 1.2 | 1.5 | 1.5 | – | – |
| Unknown or not elsewhere classified | 6.8 | 8.7 | 9.6 | 13.7 | 24.4 | 20.6 | 20.7 | 0.7 | 9.4 | 10.6 |

– Represents or rounds to zero. [1] Includes commodities not shown separately.

Source: U.S. Army Corps of Engineers, *Waterborne Commerce of the United States, 2016*, November 2017, and earlier editions. See also <https://www.iwr.usace.army.mil/About/Technical-Centers/WCSC-Waterborne-Commerce-Statistics-Center/>.

## Table 1111. Top 30 U.S. Ports by Tons of Traffic: 2017

[In thousands of short tons (45,475 represents 45,475,000), except rank. One short ton equals 2,000 lbs. For calendar year. Represents tons of cargo shipped from or received by the specified port. Excludes cargo carried on general ferries; coal and petroleum products loaded from shore facilities directly onto bunkers of vessels for fuel; and amounts of less than 100 tons of government-owned equipment in support of Corps of Engineers projects]

| Port name | Rank | Total | Domestic | Foreign Total | Inbound | Outbound |
|---|---|---|---|---|---|---|
| Baltimore, MD............. | 14 | 45,475 | 6,539 | 38,936 | 13,653 | 25,283 |
| Baton Rouge, LA............. | 8 | 77,013 | 45,672 | 31,341 | 5,723 | 25,618 |
| Beaumont, TX............. | 5 | 89,437 | 35,744 | 53,694 | 27,534 | 26,159 |
| Charleston, SC............. | 26 | 26,981 | 2,180 | 24,801 | 16,313 | 8,488 |
| Cincinnati-Northern KY, Ports of.......... | 15 | 42,677 | 42,677 | – | – | – |
| Corpus Christi, TX............. | 6 | 87,323 | 27,074 | 60,248 | 22,225 | 38,023 |
| Duluth-Superior, MN and WI............. | 19 | 34,783 | 26,305 | 8,478 | 595 | 7,883 |
| Houston, TX............. | 2 | 260,071 | 86,860 | 173,211 | 72,386 | 100,825 |
| Huntington-Tristate [1]............. | 20 | 34,151 | 34,151 | – | – | – |
| Lake Charles, LA............. | 13 | 54,317 | 27,845 | 26,471 | 16,241 | 10,231 |
| Long Beach, CA............. | 7 | 85,997 | 11,827 | 74,170 | 51,569 | 22,601 |
| Los Angeles, CA............. | 10 | 65,827 | 6,901 | 58,926 | 38,636 | 20,290 |
| Mobile, AL............. | 11 | 58,157 | 22,595 | 35,562 | 19,834 | 15,728 |
| New Orleans, LA............. | 4 | 96,342 | 50,686 | 45,655 | 18,827 | 26,829 |
| New York, NY and NJ............. | 3 | 135,875 | 46,980 | 88,895 | 69,144 | 19,751 |
| Pascagoula, MS............. | 28 | 25,645 | 8,641 | 17,004 | 9,059 | 7,945 |
| Philadelphia, PA............. | 23 | 28,524 | 12,232 | 16,292 | 14,840 | 1,452 |
| Pittsburgh, PA............. | 27 | 26,023 | 26,023 | – | – | – |
| Plaquemines, LA, Port of............. | 12 | 54,466 | 31,357 | 23,109 | 4,757 | 18,352 |
| Port Arthur, TX............. | 17 | 39,203 | 9,855 | 29,348 | 10,084 | 19,265 |
| Port Everglades, FL............. | 30 | 24,901 | 13,927 | 10,974 | 7,563 | 3,411 |
| Richmond, CA............. | 25 | 27,773 | 9,049 | 18,724 | 13,912 | 4,811 |
| Savannah, GA............. | 16 | 39,866 | 1,521 | 38,344 | 21,089 | 17,255 |
| Seattle, WA............. | 29 | 25,207 | 5,803 | 19,404 | 8,999 | 10,405 |
| South Louisiana, LA, Port of............. | 1 | 275,064 | 140,193 | 134,871 | 41,286 | 93,586 |
| St. Louis, MO and IL............. | 22 | 33,068 | 33,068 | – | – | – |
| Tampa, FL............. | 21 | 33,120 | 21,116 | 12,004 | 6,789 | 5,214 |
| Texas City, TX............. | 18 | 37,751 | 15,582 | 22,169 | 10,979 | 11,190 |
| Valdez, AK............. | 24 | 27,972 | 27,707 | 265 | – | 265 |
| Virginia, VA, Port of............. | 9 | 67,252 | 5,592 | 61,659 | 12,254 | 49,405 |

– Represents or rounds to zero. [1] The Port of Huntington is the largest inland shipping port in the United States. Port operations occur in Ashland, KY; Ironton, OH; and Huntington, WV.

Source: U.S. Army Corps of Engineers, Waterborne Commerce Statistics Center, "Tonnage for Selected U.S. Ports in 2017," <https://www.iwr.usace.army.mil/About/Technical-Centers/WCSC-Waterborne-Commerce-Statistics-Center/>, accessed January 2019.

## Table 1112. Top 30 U.S. Ports/Waterways Ranked by Container Traffic: 2017

[In thousands of twenty-foot equivalent units (TEUs) (38,222.3 represents 38,222,300). For calendar year. For the 30 leading ports/waterways in total TEUs. A TEU is a measure of containerized cargo capacity equal to one standard 20-foot length by 8-foot width by 8-foot, 6 inch height container. Does not include empty foreign containers]

| Port/waterway name | Rank | Total loaded | Domestic loaded Total [1] | Inbound | Outbound | Foreign loaded Total | Inbound |
|---|---|---|---|---|---|---|---|
| **Total U.S.** [2]............. | (X) | 38,222.3 | 5,263.5 | 2,003.9 | 2,003.9 | 34,214.6 | 22,183.2 |
| Anchorage, AK............. | 19 | 274.1 | 340.8 | 204.4 | 69.6 | 0.1 | 0.1 |
| Baltimore, MD............. | 15 | 724.8 | 33.9 | 15.3 | 10.3 | 699.2 | 465.2 |
| Boston, MA............. | 21 | 209.5 | – | – | – | 209.5 | 130.7 |
| Camden-Gloucester, NJ............. | 27 | 110.4 | 49.8 | 11.4 | 25.1 | 73.9 | 72.9 |
| Charleston, SC............. | 8 | 1,719.1 | – | – | – | 1,719.1 | 941.1 |
| Chester, PA............. | 26 | 128.5 | – | – | – | 128.5 | 92.8 |
| Gulfport, MS............. | 24 | 145.4 | – | – | – | 145.4 | 90.8 |
| Honolulu, HI............. | 11 | 814.0 | 1,067.1 | 482.9 | 300.9 | 30.1 | 20.5 |
| Houston, TX............. | 6 | 2,016.1 | – | – | – | 2,016.1 | 1,072.9 |
| Jacksonville, FL............. | 12 | 802.0 | 498.2 | 77.0 | 375.6 | 349.4 | 231.8 |
| Juneau, AK............. | 28 | 91.0 | 127.4 | 70.2 | 20.7 | – | – |
| Kahului, HI............. | 30 | 86.6 | 138.0 | 72.7 | 13.9 | – | – |
| Ketchikan, AK............. | 29 | 87.0 | 132.7 | 21.6 | 65.4 | – | – |
| Long Beach, CA............. | 2 | 5,241.6 | 249.5 | 30.2 | 174.4 | 5,037.0 | 3,821.2 |
| Los Angeles, CA............. | 1 | 6,272.7 | 145.0 | 12.3 | 132.7 | 6,127.8 | 4,544.9 |
| Miami, FL............. | 14 | 765.8 | – | – | – | 765.8 | 415.8 |
| Mobile, AL............. | 20 | 250.3 | – | – | – | 250.3 | 117.7 |
| New Orleans, LA............. | 17 | 406.4 | – | – | – | 406.4 | 110.0 |
| New York (NJ-NY), NY............. | 3 | 4,853.4 | 115.4 | 50.5 | 50.5 | 4,752.4 | 3,389.7 |
| Oakland, CA............. | 7 | 1,782.0 | 194.7 | 30.2 | 97.7 | 1,654.2 | 876.3 |
| Palm Beach, FL............. | 25 | 141.1 | – | – | – | 141.1 | 25.3 |
| Philadelphia, PA............. | 18 | 374.3 | 39.1 | 13.1 | 11.7 | 349.6 | 263.9 |
| Port Everglades, FL............. | 13 | 771.0 | – | – | – | 771.0 | 352.3 |
| Port of Virginia, VA............. | 5 | 2,221.9 | 41.4 | 12.5 | 18.8 | 2,190.6 | 1,236.1 |
| San Juan, PR............. | 16 | 699.8 | 552.0 | 403.3 | 89.7 | 206.8 | 175.7 |
| Savannah, GA............. | 4 | 3,154.7 | – | – | – | 3,154.7 | 1,855.3 |
| Seattle, WA............. | 10 | 1,198.2 | 350.0 | 61.9 | 145.8 | 990.4 | 575.6 |
| Tacoma, WA............. | 9 | 1,531.0 | 348.7 | 73.1 | 208.8 | 1,249.1 | 774.8 |
| Wilmington, DE............. | 22 | 195.5 | – | – | – | 195.5 | 172.3 |
| Wilmington, NC............. | 23 | 178.9 | – | – | – | 178.9 | 75.6 |

– Represents or rounds to zero. X Not applicable. [1] Includes empty TEUs, not shown separately. [2] Includes other ports/waterways not shown separately.

Source: U.S. Army Corps of Engineers, Navigation Data Center, Waterborne Commerce Statistics Center, "U.S. Waterborne Container Traffic by Port/Waterway in 2017," <https://www.iwr.usace.army.mil/About/Technical-Centers/WCSC-Waterborne-Commerce-Statistics-Center/>, accessed January 2019.

## Table 1113. Highway Mileage—Urban and Rural by Ownership: 1990 to 2017

[In thousands (3,880 represents 3,880,000). As of December 31. Includes Puerto Rico beginning 2000]

| Type and control of roadways | 1990 | 2000 | 2005 | 2010 | 2013 | 2014 | 2015 | 2016 | 2017 |
|---|---|---|---|---|---|---|---|---|---|
| **Total mileage** [1] | **3,880** | **3,951** | **4,012** | **4,084** | **4,132** | **4,194** | **4,171** | **4,157** | **4,184** |
| Urban mileage | 757 | 859 | 1,023 | 1,103 | 1,192 | 1,215 | 1,223 | 1,226 | 1,235 |
| Under state control | 96 | 112 | 144 | (NA) | 160 | 172 | 174 | 173 | 172 |
| Under local control [1] | 661 | 746 | 874 | (NA) | 1,021 | 1,036 | 1,042 | 1,044 | 1,054 |
| Under federal control [2] | (NA) | (NA) | 4 | (NA) | 11 | 8 | 7 | 8 | 8 |
| Rural mileage | 3,123 | 3,092 | 2,989 | 2,980 | 2,941 | 2,978 | 2,949 | 2,931 | 2,949 |
| Under state control | 703 | 664 | 637 | (NA) | 625 | 616 | 612 | 612 | 613 |
| Under local control [1] | 2,242 | 2,311 | 2,228 | (NA) | 2,174 | 2,209 | 2,198 | 2,186 | 2,180 |
| Under federal control [2] | 178 | 117 | 123 | (NA) | 141 | 154 | 139 | 133 | 156 |

NA Not available. [1] Includes state park, state toll, other state agency, other local agency and other roadways not identified by ownership. [2] Includes roadways in federal parks, forest, and reservations that are not part of the state and local highway system.

Source: U.S. Federal Highway Administration, "Highway Statistics 2017," and earlier reports, <http://www.fhwa.dot.gov/policyinformation/statistics.cfm>, accessed February 2019.

## Table 1114. Highway Mileage—Functional Systems and Urban/Rural Status by State: 2017

[As of December 31. For definition of functional systems, see text, this section]

| State | Total | Functional systems | | | | | Urban | Rural |
|---|---|---|---|---|---|---|---|---|
| | | Interstate | Other freeways and expressways | Arterial | Collector | Local | | |
| **United States** | **4,183,707** | **48,556** | **18,797** | **404,334** | **817,579** | **2,894,441** | **1,235,011** | **2,948,696** |
| Alabama | 101,097 | 1,004 | 29 | 9,689 | 22,273 | 68,103 | 28,692 | 72,405 |
| Alaska | 15,535 | 1,080 | – | 1,570 | 3,288 | 9,596 | 2,854 | 12,681 |
| Arizona | 66,558 | 1,169 | 233 | 5,973 | 8,256 | 50,928 | 26,358 | 40,200 |
| Arkansas | 102,603 | 749 | 174 | 7,407 | 21,156 | 73,116 | 17,180 | 85,422 |
| California | 176,214 | 2,456 | 1,920 | 27,205 | 32,386 | 112,248 | 104,665 | 71,549 |
| Colorado | 88,818 | 952 | 352 | 8,904 | 16,210 | 62,400 | 20,698 | 68,120 |
| Connecticut | 21,544 | 346 | 279 | 2,724 | 3,405 | 14,790 | 15,853 | 5,691 |
| Delaware | 6,452 | 41 | 56 | 627 | 1,133 | 4,595 | 3,648 | 2,804 |
| District of Columbia | 1,514 | 12 | 16 | 270 | 156 | 1,060 | 1,514 | – |
| Florida | 122,848 | 1,495 | 750 | 12,990 | 15,552 | 92,061 | 86,368 | 36,481 |
| Georgia | 128,355 | 1,247 | 177 | 14,328 | 22,798 | 89,805 | 52,264 | 76,091 |
| Hawaii | 4,476 | 55 | 34 | 791 | 761 | 2,836 | 2,810 | 1,666 |
| Idaho | 52,437 | 611 | 141 | 4,223 | 11,040 | 36,422 | 6,222 | 46,215 |
| Illinois | 145,936 | 2,185 | 165 | 14,162 | 22,734 | 106,689 | 49,736 | 96,200 |
| Indiana | 96,790 | 1,262 | 325 | 8,664 | 22,692 | 63,845 | 30,105 | 66,685 |
| Iowa | 114,637 | 786 | – | 9,907 | 31,582 | 72,363 | 12,648 | 101,989 |
| Kansas | 142,054 | 874 | 595 | 8,568 | 33,998 | 98,019 | 14,235 | 127,820 |
| Kentucky | 80,054 | 842 | 566 | 5,565 | 16,963 | 56,118 | 15,096 | 64,958 |
| Louisiana | 61,411 | 938 | 97 | 5,952 | 10,353 | 44,072 | 17,610 | 43,801 |
| Maine | 22,000 | 300 | 18 | 2,112 | 5,962 | 14,401 | 3,406 | 19,454 |
| Maryland | 32,211 | 480 | 380 | 3,616 | 5,396 | 22,339 | 18,640 | 13,571 |
| Massachusetts | 36,723 | 575 | 335 | 6,435 | 4,560 | 24,818 | 30,529 | 6,193 |
| Michigan | 122,036 | 1,251 | 700 | 14,325 | 24,620 | 81,140 | 37,962 | 84,075 |
| Minnesota | 139,449 | 913 | 255 | 13,301 | 30,661 | 94,318 | 22,231 | 117,218 |
| Mississippi | 77,445 | 822 | 64 | 7,577 | 15,844 | 53,139 | 13,048 | 64,397 |
| Missouri | 131,879 | 1,380 | 1,620 | 8,914 | 25,184 | 94,783 | 24,348 | 107,531 |
| Montana | 73,566 | 1,192 | – | 6,163 | 16,142 | 50,069 | 4,229 | 69,337 |
| Nebraska | 95,163 | 483 | 462 | 7,711 | 20,848 | 65,658 | 7,879 | 87,284 |
| Nevada | 48,234 | 602 | 53 | 3,515 | 6,052 | 38,011 | 10,154 | 38,080 |
| New Hampshire | 16,156 | 225 | 83 | 1,661 | 2,642 | 11,545 | 5,064 | 11,092 |
| New Jersey | 38,896 | 432 | 488 | 5,900 | 4,435 | 27,640 | 33,452 | 5,443 |
| New Mexico | 77,205 | 1,000 | 12 | 5,646 | 8,809 | 61,739 | 11,099 | 66,106 |
| New York | 113,559 | 1,744 | 997 | 13,600 | 20,698 | 76,521 | 49,686 | 63,874 |
| North Carolina | 106,975 | 1,272 | 911 | 10,103 | 17,332 | 77,357 | 41,284 | 65,691 |
| North Dakota | 87,688 | 571 | – | 5,992 | 12,304 | 68,821 | 2,873 | 84,816 |
| Ohio | 122,987 | 1,574 | 910 | 10,590 | 23,308 | 86,605 | 47,489 | 75,498 |
| Oklahoma | 112,865 | 933 | 207 | 8,360 | 25,735 | 77,630 | 18,398 | 94,467 |
| Oregon | 79,275 | 730 | 64 | 7,022 | 18,724 | 52,734 | 15,054 | 64,221 |
| Pennsylvania | 120,521 | 1,861 | 909 | 12,921 | 20,004 | 84,826 | 47,762 | 72,759 |
| Rhode Island | 6,027 | 70 | 92 | 855 | 894 | 4,117 | 4,685 | 1,342 |
| South Carolina | 77,364 | 851 | 129 | 7,368 | 14,946 | 54,071 | 21,322 | 56,042 |
| South Dakota | 82,584 | 679 | 309 | 6,126 | 19,004 | 56,466 | 3,421 | 79,163 |
| Tennessee | 95,986 | 1,201 | 187 | 9,338 | 18,552 | 66,708 | 31,788 | 64,199 |
| Texas | 314,319 | 3,459 | 1,532 | 33,093 | 66,866 | 209,369 | 108,817 | 205,503 |
| Utah | 49,290 | 937 | 58 | 3,810 | 8,366 | 36,119 | 11,175 | 38,115 |
| Vermont | 14,255 | 320 | 18 | 1,339 | 3,154 | 9,424 | 1,501 | 12,753 |
| Virginia | 75,238 | 1,119 | 447 | 8,876 | 15,676 | 49,120 | 26,543 | 48,695 |
| Washington | 80,429 | 764 | 1,034 | 7,503 | 17,308 | 53,820 | 24,179 | 56,250 |
| West Virginia | 38,854 | 555 | 15 | 3,482 | 8,641 | 26,161 | 6,652 | 32,202 |
| Wisconsin | 115,547 | 877 | 543 | 12,273 | 23,546 | 78,308 | 23,852 | 91,695 |
| Wyoming | 30,430 | 913 | 3 | 3,681 | 12,941 | 12,892 | 2,768 | 27,662 |
| Puerto Rico | 18,359 | 301 | 56 | 1,609 | 1,688 | 14,705 | 15,168 | 3,191 |

– Represents zero.

Source: U.S. Federal Highway Administration, "Highway Statistics 2017," <http://www.fhwa.dot.gov/policyinformation/statistics.cfm>, accessed February 2019.

# Table 1115. Bridge Inventory—Total, Area, and Condition: 2012 to 2018, and by State, 2018

[Based on the National Bridge Inventory program; for details, see source]

| State and year | Number of bridges | Bridge deck area (square meters) | Bridge condition [1] | | | | | |
|---|---|---|---|---|---|---|---|---|
| | | | Number | | | Percent | | |
| | | | Good | Fair | Poor | Good | Fair | Poor |
| 2012 | 607,380 | 358,547,072 | 287,194 | 262,878 | 57,049 | 47.3 | 43.3 | 9.4 |
| 2013 | 607,751 | 362,428,004 | 287,581 | 265,456 | 54,492 | 47.3 | 43.7 | 9.0 |
| 2014 | 610,749 | 365,542,771 | 287,701 | 269,734 | 52,905 | 47.1 | 44.2 | 8.7 |
| 2015 | 611,845 | 369,109,088 | 289,158 | 271,690 | 50,917 | 47.3 | 44.4 | 8.3 |
| 2016 | 614,387 | 371,463,919 | 291,412 | 274,306 | 48,559 | 47.4 | 44.6 | 7.9 |
| 2017 | 615,002 | 374,362,285 | 288,030 | 279,270 | 47,619 | 46.8 | 45.4 | 7.7 |
| **U.S. total, 2018** | **616,096** | **390,438,601** | **283,316** | **285,676** | **47,054** | **46.0** | **46.4** | **7.6** |
| Alabama | 16,130 | 9,760,735 | 6,838 | 8,603 | 689 | 42.4 | 53.3 | 4.3 |
| Alaska | 1,592 | 743,788 | 711 | 725 | 155 | 44.7 | 45.5 | 9.7 |
| Arizona | 8,294 | 5,846,176 | 5,068 | 3,076 | 150 | 61.1 | 37.1 | 1.8 |
| Arkansas | 12,892 | 6,708,589 | 6,816 | 5,488 | 588 | 52.9 | 42.6 | 4.6 |
| California | 25,737 | 30,067,631 | 14,779 | 9,146 | 1,812 | 57.4 | 35.5 | 7.0 |
| Colorado | 8,786 | 5,024,622 | 3,694 | 4,618 | 473 | 42.0 | 52.6 | 5.4 |
| Connecticut | 4,270 | 3,414,833 | 1,238 | 2,724 | 308 | 29.0 | 63.8 | 7.2 |
| Delaware | 863 | 1,000,357 | 195 | 634 | 34 | 22.6 | 73.5 | 3.9 |
| District of Columbia | 244 | 569,296 | 62 | 174 | 8 | 25.4 | 71.3 | 3.3 |
| Florida | 12,435 | 17,516,213 | 8,389 | 3,717 | 328 | 67.5 | 29.9 | 2.6 |
| Georgia | 14,879 | 10,082,064 | 6,303 | 8,082 | 494 | 42.4 | 54.3 | 3.3 |
| Hawaii | 1,137 | 1,324,180 | 355 | 704 | 78 | 31.2 | 61.9 | 6.9 |
| Idaho | 4,482 | 1,756,871 | 1,259 | 2,907 | 315 | 28.1 | 64.9 | 7.0 |
| Illinois | 26,809 | 13,524,885 | 13,438 | 11,098 | 2,273 | 50.1 | 41.4 | 8.5 |
| Indiana | 19,280 | 8,197,646 | 7,959 | 10,114 | 1,203 | 41.3 | 52.5 | 6.2 |
| Iowa | 24,123 | 8,806,907 | 9,180 | 10,263 | 4,675 | 38.1 | 42.5 | 19.4 |
| Kansas | 24,906 | 8,680,998 | 13,594 | 10,024 | 1,288 | 54.6 | 40.2 | 5.2 |
| Kentucky | 14,368 | 6,509,802 | 5,239 | 8,111 | 1,016 | 36.5 | 56.5 | 7.1 |
| Louisiana | 12,899 | 16,587,147 | 6,484 | 4,733 | 1,678 | 50.3 | 36.7 | 13.0 |
| Maine | 2,473 | 1,264,519 | 786 | 1,362 | 325 | 31.8 | 55.1 | 13.1 |
| Maryland | 5,357 | 5,426,511 | 1,757 | 3,326 | 274 | 32.8 | 62.1 | 5.1 |
| Massachusetts | 5,215 | 4,119,863 | 1,370 | 3,364 | 481 | 26.3 | 64.5 | 9.2 |
| Michigan | 11,228 | 6,445,678 | 4,479 | 5,548 | 1,196 | 39.9 | 49.4 | 10.7 |
| Minnesota | 13,358 | 7,132,639 | 8,259 | 4,431 | 668 | 61.8 | 33.2 | 5.0 |
| Mississippi | 17,071 | 9,940,070 | 10,711 | 4,757 | 1,603 | 62.7 | 27.9 | 9.4 |
| Missouri | 24,512 | 10,701,764 | 10,579 | 11,817 | 2,116 | 43.2 | 48.2 | 8.6 |
| Montana | 5,265 | 2,084,807 | 1,605 | 3,270 | 390 | 30.5 | 62.1 | 7.4 |
| Nebraska | 15,349 | 4,340,537 | 7,985 | 6,003 | 1,358 | 52.0 | 39.1 | 8.8 |
| Nevada | 1,979 | 1,791,492 | 978 | 974 | 27 | 49.4 | 49.2 | 1.4 |
| New Hampshire | 2,494 | 1,130,225 | 1,323 | 947 | 224 | 53.0 | 38.0 | 9.0 |
| New Jersey | 6,746 | 7,002,430 | 1,819 | 4,383 | 544 | 27.0 | 65.0 | 8.1 |
| New Mexico | 4,010 | 2,080,960 | 1,519 | 2,259 | 232 | 37.9 | 56.3 | 5.8 |
| New York | 17,521 | 13,089,606 | 6,400 | 9,364 | 1,757 | 36.5 | 53.4 | 10.0 |
| North Carolina | 18,377 | 9,994,006 | 7,186 | 9,313 | 1,871 | 39.1 | 50.7 | 10.2 |
| North Dakota | 4,355 | 1,320,937 | 2,341 | 1,545 | 469 | 53.8 | 35.5 | 10.8 |
| Ohio | 27,277 | 13,956,582 | 15,974 | 9,785 | 1,518 | 58.6 | 35.9 | 5.6 |
| Oklahoma | 23,116 | 8,738,610 | 10,304 | 10,268 | 2,540 | 44.6 | 44.4 | 11.0 |
| Oregon | 8,161 | 5,060,329 | 2,881 | 4,858 | 422 | 35.3 | 59.5 | 5.2 |
| Pennsylvania | 22,737 | 13,945,241 | 6,985 | 11,979 | 3,770 | 30.7 | 52.7 | 16.6 |
| Rhode Island | 780 | 793,527 | 134 | 466 | 180 | 17.2 | 59.7 | 23.1 |
| South Carolina | 9,401 | 6,985,851 | 4,225 | 4,381 | 795 | 44.9 | 46.6 | 8.5 |
| South Dakota | 5,824 | 1,803,770 | 1,906 | 2,945 | 973 | 32.7 | 50.6 | 16.7 |
| Tennessee | 20,177 | 10,275,911 | 9,221 | 10,084 | 871 | 45.7 | 50.0 | 4.3 |
| Texas | 54,131 | 50,368,715 | 28,020 | 25,411 | 695 | 51.8 | 46.9 | 1.3 |
| Utah | 3,061 | 1,948,005 | 1,659 | 1,336 | 66 | 54.2 | 43.6 | 2.2 |
| Vermont | 2,778 | 884,043 | 1,473 | 1,239 | 66 | 53.0 | 44.6 | 2.4 |
| Virginia | 13,931 | 10,125,635 | 4,786 | 8,499 | 646 | 34.4 | 61.0 | 4.6 |
| Washington | 8,278 | 7,224,042 | 4,317 | 3,579 | 382 | 52.2 | 43.2 | 4.6 |
| West Virginia | 7,269 | 3,811,742 | 1,978 | 3,844 | 1,444 | 27.2 | 52.9 | 19.9 |
| Wisconsin | 14,275 | 7,006,791 | 7,383 | 5,838 | 1,054 | 51.7 | 40.9 | 7.4 |
| Wyoming | 3,129 | 1,339,545 | 926 | 1,946 | 257 | 29.6 | 62.2 | 8.2 |
| Puerto Rico | 2,325 | 2,180,690 | 444 | 1,608 | 273 | 19.1 | 69.2 | 11.7 |

[1] Good: pavement and bridge infrastructure that is free of significant defects, and has a condition that does not adversely affect its performance. Fair: pavement and bridge infrastructure that has isolated surface defects or functional deficiencies on pavements; or minor deterioration of bridge elements. Poor: pavement and bridge infrastructure that is exhibiting advanced deterioration and conditions that impact structural capacity.

Source: U.S. Federal Highway Administration, Office of Bridges and Structures, "Bridge Condition by Highway System 2018," and earlier editions, <https://www.fhwa.dot.gov/bridge/britab.cfm>, accessed April 2019.

## Table 1116. Funding for Highways and Disposition of Highway–User Revenue: 1990 to 2016

[In millions of dollars (75,444 represents $75,444,000,000). Data compiled from reports of state and local authorities]

| Type | 1990 | 2000 | 2010 | 2011 | 2012 | 2013 | 2014 | 2015 | 2016 |
|---|---|---|---|---|---|---|---|---|---|
| **Total receipts** | **75,444** | **131,115** | **220,977** | **204,939** | **216,561** | **(NA)** | **252,642** | **241,063** | **267,941** |
| Current income | 69,880 | 119,815 | 187,960 | 177,861 | 195,307 | (NA) | 222,515 | 218,812 | 248,789 |
| Highway-user revenues | 44,346 | 81,335 | 93,830 | 95,138 | 105,153 | (NA) | 106,423 | 113,454 | 111,296 |
| Other taxes and fees | 19,827 | 31,137 | 80,220 | 66,968 | 69,273 | (NA) | 97,838 | 85,434 | 118,366 |
| Investment income, other receipts | 5,707 | 7,342 | 13,910 | 15,754 | 20,881 | (NA) | 18,253 | 19,924 | 19,126 |
| Bond issue proceeds [1] | 5,564 | 11,301 | 33,017 | 27,078 | 21,254 | (NA) | 30,127 | 22,251 | 19,152 |
| Funds drawn from or placed in reserves [2] | -36 | -8,418 | -15,664 | 1,501 | 4,758 | (NA) | -14,213 | -5,868 | -48,940 |
| Total funds available | 75,408 | 122,697 | 205,313 | 206,440 | 221,319 | (NA) | 238,429 | 235,195 | 219,001 |
| **Total disbursements** | **75,408** | **122,697** | **205,313** | **206,440** | **221,319** | **(NA)** | **238,429** | **235,195** | **219,001** |
| Current disbursements | 72,457 | 117,592 | 193,034 | 192,727 | 198,670 | (NA) | 204,976 | 207,537 | 204,617 |
| Capital outlay | 35,151 | 61,323 | 100,175 | 101,612 | 105,199 | (NA) | 105,452 | 106,539 | 106,780 |
| Maintenance and traffic services | 20,365 | 30,636 | 48,773 | 46,311 | 47,990 | (NA) | 51,593 | 51,817 | 49,749 |
| Administration and research | 6,501 | 10,020 | 16,165 | 16,590 | 16,023 | (NA) | 16,137 | 16,930 | 19,706 |
| Highway law enforcement and safety | 7,235 | 11,031 | 18,080 | 17,374 | 17,847 | (NA) | 19,629 | 20,165 | 17,850 |
| Interest on debt | 3,205 | 4,583 | 9,842 | 10,840 | 11,611 | (NA) | 12,164 | 12,087 | 10,532 |
| Bond retirement [1] | 2,951 | 5,105 | 12,279 | 13,713 | 22,649 | (NA) | 33,453 | 27,658 | 14,384 |

NA Not available. [1] Proceeds and redemptions of short-term notes and refunding issues are excluded. [2] Negative numbers indicate that funds were placed in reserves.

Source: U.S. Federal Highway Administration, "Highway Statistics 2016," and earlier reports, <http://www.fhwa.dot.gov/policyinformation/statistics.cfm>, accessed December 2018.

## Table 1117. State Motor Fuel Tax and Related Receipts, 2014 to 2017; and Gasoline Tax Rates, 2017

[645 represents $645,000,000. Federal tax rate is 18.4 cents a gallon. This table includes revenues from state taxes on all motor-vehicle fuels and related receipts due to motor-fuel taxation and administration. In many states, however, the tax on special fuels (fuels other than gasoline and gasohol) is applicable only to the amount used on the highways. For the states that apply the tax to all fuel sold, the revenue and refunds covering the nonhighway portion of these special fuels have been excluded]

| State | Adjusted total receipts (million dollars) | | | | Tax rate, [1] 2017 | State | Adjusted total receipts (million dollars) | | | | Tax rate, [1] 2017 |
|---|---|---|---|---|---|---|---|---|---|---|---|
| | 2014 | 2015 | 2016 | 2017 | | | 2014 | 2015 | 2016 | 2017 | |
| AL | 645 | 667 | 670 | 672 | 18.00 | MO | 668 | 680 | 698 | 700 | 17.00 |
| AK | 32 | 32 | 30 | 29 | 8.00 | MT | 201 | 210 | 208 | 193 | 32.25 |
| AZ | 635 | 657 | 689 | 718 | 18.00 | NE | 331 | 332 | 349 | 357 | 27.90 |
| AR | 431 | 437 | 486 | 473 | 21.50 | NV | 511 | 579 | 624 | 665 | 24.00 |
| CA | 5,724 | 5,485 | 4,809 | 4,587 | 41.70 | NH | 146 | 180 | 184 | 185 | 23.83 |
| CO | 586 | 606 | 649 | 670 | 22.00 | NJ | 539 | 542 | 560 | 545 | 37.10 |
| CT | 786 | 869 | 746 | 719 | 25.00 | NM | 275 | 284 | 284 | 290 | 17.00 |
| DE | 113 | 117 | 124 | 129 | 23.00 | NY | 1,632 | 1,654 | 1,639 | 1,653 | 24.25 |
| DC | 23 | 25 | 25 | 26 | 23.50 | NC | 1,904 | 1,913 | 1,924 | 1,914 | 34.55 |
| FL | 2,345 | 2,452 | 2,586 | 2,685 | 17.40 | ND | 223 | 207 | 195 | 190 | 23.00 |
| GA [2] | 970 | 1,026 | 1,605 | 1,740 | 26.30 | OH | 1,777 | 1,819 | 1,837 | 1,871 | 28.00 |
| HI | 84 | 84 | 85 | 82 | 16.00 | OK | 451 | 455 | 138 | 161 | 17.00 |
| ID | 231 | 238 | 309 | 324 | 33.00 | OR | 586 | 601 | 620 | 629 | 30.00 |
| IL | 1,219 | 1,215 | 1,260 | 1,251 | 19.00 | PA | 2,252 | 2,991 | 3,344 | 3,533 | 58.20 |
| IN | 810 | 828 | 837 | 848 | 29.00 | RI | 139 | 144 | 151 | 150 | 33.00 |
| IA | 436 | 491 | 656 | 705 | 31.50 | SC | 551 | 566 | 597 | 606 | 18.00 |
| KS | 451 | 447 | 454 | 448 | 24.00 | SD | 140 | 171 | 187 | 187 | 30.00 |
| KY | 881 | 849 | 748 | 759 | 24.60 | TN | 843 | 863 | 900 | 914 | 24.00 |
| LA | 589 | 595 | 616 | 629 | 20.00 | TX | 3,339 | 3,445 | 3,490 | 3,560 | 20.00 |
| ME | 287 | 243 | 244 | 252 | 30.00 | UT | 359 | 362 | 418 | 482 | 29.40 |
| MD | 803 | 911 | 996 | 1,063 | 33.80 | VT | 122 | 122 | 117 | 119 | 30.73 |
| MA | 732 | 755 | 766 | 764 | 24.00 | VA | 702 | 773 | 889 | 927 | 16.20 |
| MI | 942 | 987 | 993 | 1,342 | 26.30 | WA | 1,198 | 1,198 | 1,419 | 1,632 | 49.40 |
| MN | 881 | 879 | 912 | 923 | 28.50 | WV | 386 | 383 | 359 | 358 | 35.70 |
| MS | 401 | 398 | 433 | 425 | 18.40 | WI | 980 | 993 | 1,017 | 1,034 | 30.90 |
| | | | | | | WY | 169 | 168 | 162 | 168 | 24.00 |

[1] State gasoline tax rates in cents per gallon. In effect July 1. Includes other miscellaneous tax (environmental, etc.). [2] Beginning 2014, Georgia receipts includes special fuel and use tax.

Source: U.S. Federal Highway Administration, "Highway Statistics 2017," and earlier reports, <http://www.fhwa.dot.gov/policyinformation/statistics.cfm>, accessed August 2019.

## Table 1118. Public Obligations for Highways—Changes in Indebtedness During the Year: 2000 to 2017

[In millions of dollars (56,264 represents $56,264,000,000). Table summarizes state indebtedness from all state bond issues, including the toll facility issues and the state issues for local roads. This table is compiled from reports of state authorities. Table also summarizes the change in status of the highway obligations of local governments including toll authorities]

| Item | 2000 | 2005 | 2010 | 2013 | 2014 | 2015 | 2016 | 2017 |
|---|---|---|---|---|---|---|---|---|
| STATE GOVERNMENT | | | | | | | | |
| Obligations outstanding, beginning of year......... | 56,264 | 82,476 | 138,798 | 181,075 | 201,462 | 211,692 | 216,516 | 217,090 |
| Obligations issued.................................. | 9,067 | 19,784 | 26,895 | 27,163 | 30,402 | 29,155 | 20,103 | 34,186 |
| Obligations retired................................. | 3,897 | 14,072 | 11,143 | 15,783 | 19,311 | 22,909 | 16,991 | 23,355 |
| Obligations outstanding, end of year................ | 61,434 | 88,187 | 154,550 | 192,455 | 212,553 | 217,938 | 219,628 | 227,921 |
| LOCAL GOVERNMENT [1,2] | | | | | | | | |
| Obligations outstanding, beginning of year......... | 34,904 | 44,406 | 65,679 | 83,776 | (NA) | 51,377 | 78,923 | (NA) |
| Bonds outstanding, beginning of year............. | 34,229 | 43,403 | 63,891 | 81,461 | (NA) | 48,262 | 75,524 | (NA) |
| Bonds outstanding, end of year................... | 34,949 | 46,168 | 67,707 | 70,415 | (NA) | 49,189 | 75,867 | (NA) |
| Obligations outstanding, end of year.............. | 35,557 | 47,170 | 69,794 | 72,108 | (NA) | 52,579 | 79,552 | (NA) |

NA Not available. [1] Short-term notes data not shown. The data are included in beginning and ending year obligations. [2] The number of local government data estimated varied year to year.

Source: U.S. Federal Highway Administration, "Highway Statistics 2017," and earlier reports, <https://www.fhwa.dot.gov/policyinformation/statistics.cfm>, accessed September 2019.

## Table 1119. State Disbursements for Highways by State: 2000 to 2017

[In millions of dollars (89,832 represents $89,832,000,000). Comprises disbursements from current revenues or loans for construction, maintenance, interest and principal payments on highway bonds, transfers to local units, and miscellaneous. Includes transactions by state toll authorities. Data exclude amounts allocated for collection expenses, nonhighway purposes, and mass transit]

| State | 2000 | 2005 | 2010 | 2013 | 2014 | 2015 | 2016 | 2017 |
|---|---|---|---|---|---|---|---|---|
| **United States............** | **89,832** | **116,517** | **145,944** | **152,179** | **164,620** | **168,242** | **162,673** | **168,666** |
| Alabama..................... | 1,246 | 1,519 | 1,781 | 1,988 | 2,285 | 2,281 | 1,948 | 1,963 |
| Alaska....................... | 501 | 643 | 756 | 991 | 1,173 | 1,185 | 1,277 | (NA) |
| Arizona...................... | 2,040 | 2,458 | 2,663 | 3,125 | 2,388 | 3,388 | 2,574 | 3,158 |
| Arkansas.................... | 817 | 1,078 | 1,376 | 1,783 | 2,022 | 1,473 | 1,535 | 1,901 |
| California................... | 6,750 | 8,308 | 19,961 | 12,337 | 14,350 | 12,162 | 11,620 | 11,001 |
| Colorado.................... | 1,392 | 1,652 | 2,249 | 2,580 | 2,571 | 2,632 | 2,975 | 2,081 |
| Connecticut................. | 1,304 | 1,434 | 1,761 | 1,982 | 1,943 | 2,097 | 2,325 | 1,975 |
| Delaware.................... | 595 | 1,104 | 1,353 | 1,368 | 1,291 | 984 | 1,984 | 1,717 |
| District of Columbia......... | 244 | 327 | 582 | 432 | 386 | 413 | 384 | 607 |
| Florida...................... | 4,208 | 7,369 | 7,867 | 9,547 | 8,538 | 9,635 | 11,231 | 10,390 |
| Georgia..................... | 1,567 | 2,070 | 2,926 | 2,679 | 2,743 | 3,017 | 3,223 | 4,796 |
| Hawaii...................... | 272 | 506 | 460 | 463 | 397 | 568 | 402 | 702 |
| Idaho....................... | 492 | 608 | 959 | 791 | 808 | 853 | 965 | 790 |
| Illinois...................... | 3,447 | 4,201 | (NA) | 5,711 | 6,331 | 6,783 | 6,907 | 6,350 |
| Indiana..................... | 1,932 | 2,235 | 2,839 | 2,825 | 2,613 | 2,636 | 2,684 | 3,360 |
| Iowa........................ | 1,494 | 1,392 | 1,888 | 1,837 | 2,025 | 2,183 | 2,181 | 2,341 |
| Kansas..................... | 1,206 | 1,394 | 1,571 | 1,419 | 1,727 | 1,806 | 1,573 | 1,200 |
| Kentucky................... | 1,651 | 1,723 | 2,528 | 2,537 | 2,946 | 3,013 | 3,232 | 2,525 |
| Louisiana................... | 1,301 | 1,387 | 2,457 | 2,079 | 1,774 | 2,698 | 1,865 | 2,177 |
| Maine....................... | 488 | 616 | 684 | (NA) | (NA) | 988 | 1,052 | 1,159 |
| Maryland.................... | 1,599 | 2,049 | 2,255 | 2,483 | 2,785 | 3,395 | 3,052 | 3,673 |
| Massachusetts.............. | 3,524 | 3,196 | 2,923 | (NA) | (NA) | (NA) | (NA) | 4,364 |
| Michigan.................... | 2,748 | 3,561 | 3,484 | 3,022 | 3,419 | 3,111 | 3,883 | 3,659 |
| Minnesota.................. | 1,692 | 2,131 | 2,625 | 2,840 | 2,997 | 3,486 | 3,365 | 3,071 |
| Mississippi................. | 1,039 | 1,081 | 1,345 | 1,414 | 1,413 | 1,200 | 1,209 | 1,365 |
| Missouri.................... | 1,818 | 2,069 | 2,814 | 2,408 | 3,421 | 2,364 | 2,248 | 2,422 |
| Montana.................... | 474 | 664 | 778 | 723 | 764 | 783 | 763 | 698 |
| Nebraska................... | 745 | 876 | 1,409 | 1,508 | 1,555 | 1,595 | 1,770 | 1,721 |
| Nevada..................... | 651 | 865 | 1,007 | 1,064 | 779 | 867 | 1,218 | 1,250 |
| New Hampshire............. | 387 | 389 | 793 | (NA) | 722 | 858 | 609 | 642 |
| New Jersey................. | 4,503 | 7,119 | 5,201 | 7,492 | (NA) | 7,146 | 6,423 | 8,545 |
| New Mexico................. | 1,162 | 911 | 1,163 | 1,296 | 1,018 | 1,142 | 885 | 956 |
| New York.................... | 5,307 | 9,638 | 7,711 | (NA) | 11,391 | 9,821 | 9,926 | 9,735 |
| North Carolina.............. | 2,621 | 3,698 | 3,646 | 4,505 | 4,414 | 4,324 | 4,424 | 5,334 |
| North Dakota................ | 385 | 456 | 559 | 1,022 | 880 | 950 | 800 | 838 |
| Ohio........................ | 3,351 | 4,040 | 4,520 | 4,835 | 5,151 | 5,838 | 5,529 | 5,343 |
| Oklahoma................... | 1,417 | 1,163 | 2,040 | 1,818 | 2,005 | 2,669 | 3,318 | 3,018 |
| Oregon...................... | 1,010 | 1,628 | 1,522 | 1,263 | 2,223 | 2,265 | 1,372 | 2,571 |
| Pennsylvania............... | 4,517 | 4,567 | 8,835 | 7,134 | 8,200 | 8,592 | 9,930 | 10,091 |
| Rhode Island............... | 256 | 407 | 540 | 511 | (NA) | (NA) | 611 | 473 |
| South Carolina.............. | 970 | 1,360 | 1,899 | 1,523 | 1,864 | 1,555 | 1,441 | 1,709 |
| South Dakota............... | 466 | 466 | 532 | 677 | 651 | 625 | 579 | 541 |
| Tennessee.................. | 1,440 | 1,718 | 2,076 | 2,187 | 1,987 | 1,879 | 1,899 | 1,959 |
| Texas....................... | 5,665 | 8,918 | 9,365 | 15,024 | 19,682 | 21,222 | 15,105 | 15,372 |
| Utah........................ | 1,072 | 986 | 2,303 | 1,608 | 1,482 | 1,622 | 1,412 | 1,571 |
| Vermont.................... | 287 | 310 | 436 | 518 | 532 | 568 | 536 | 552 |
| Virginia..................... | 2,678 | 3,384 | 3,334 | 4,487 | 5,316 | 5,235 | 5,761 | 5,691 |
| Washington................. | 1,871 | 2,625 | 4,149 | 6,491 | 4,802 | 5,489 | 4,407 | 5,159 |
| West Virginia............... | 1,170 | 1,425 | 1,327 | 1,275 | 1,315 | 1,227 | 1,413 | 1,295 |
| Wisconsin................... | 1,663 | 2,363 | 2,702 | 3,071 | 3,316 | 3,547 | 3,409 | 3,071 |
| Wyoming.................... | 396 | 429 | 605 | 568 | 594 | 635 | 515 | 506 |

NA Not available.

Source: U.S. Federal Highway Administration, "Highway Statistics 2017," and earlier reports, <https://www.fhwa.dot.gov/policyinformation/statistics.cfm>, accessed August 2019.

## Table 1120. Federal Highway Trust Fund-Receipts, Expenditures, and Balance: 1960 to 2017

[In billions of dollars (2.54 represents $2,540,000,000). For fiscal year ending September 30. Established as part of the Federal Aid Highway Act of 1956]

| Year | Receipts | Expend-itures | Balance | Year | Receipts | Expend-itures | Balance |
|---|---|---|---|---|---|---|---|
| 1960............ | 2.54 | 2.94 | 0.12 | 2008............. | 39.36 | 37.01 | 10.03 |
| 1970............ | 5.47 | 4.38 | 2.61 | 2009............. | 37.32 | 37.57 | 8.88 |
| 1980............ | 7.65 | 9.21 | 11.00 | 2010............. | 44.89 | 32.01 | 20.74 |
| 1990............ | 13.45 | 14.38 | 9.63 | 2011............. | 32.01 | 37.32 | 14.32 |
| 2000............ | 30.35 | 27.00 | 22.55 | 2012............. | 37.64 | 41.15 | 9.73 |
| 2003............ | 28.96 | 32.11 | 12.99 | 2013............. | 37.70 | 42.92 | 3.77 |
| 2004............ | 29.79 | 31.97 | 10.81 | 2014............. | 52.50 | 43.79 | 11.38 |
| 2005............ | 32.91 | 33.12 | 10.59 | 2015............. | 41.83 | 42.95 | 9.04 |
| 2006............ | 33.70 | 33.91 | 9.01 | 2016............. | 88.27 | 44.79 | 51.44 |
| 2007............ | 34.31 | 34.98 | 8.11 | 2017............. | 36.11 | 44.98 | 41.44 |

Source: U.S. Federal Highway Administration, "Highway Statistics 2017," <https://www.fhwa.dot.gov/policyinformation/statistics.cfm>, accessed August 2019.

## Table 1121. Federal Highway Trust Fund Receipts from Highway Users by State: 2017

[In thousands of dollars (41,019,165 represents $41,019,165,000). For fiscal year ending September 30. Federal Highway Trust Fund receipts are reported by the U.S. Department of the Treasury. Payments into the Fund attributable to highway users in each State are estimated by the Federal Highway Administration]

| State | Total | Highway account | | | | | | Mass transit account | |
|---|---|---|---|---|---|---|---|---|---|
| | | Motor fuel | | | Other | | | | |
| | | Motor fuel, total | Gasoline | Special fuels | Federal use tax | Trucks and trailers | Tires | Gasoline | Special fuels |
| Total............... | 41,019,165 | 30,934,314 | 22,097,131 | 8,837,184 | 1,206,147 | 3,117,447 | 475,597 | 4,109,724 | 1,175,931 |
| Alabama........... | 843,895 | 626,530 | 449,423 | 198,045 | 27,030 | 69,863 | 10,658 | 83,586 | 26,353 |
| Alaska.............. | 90,573 | 66,121 | 41,254 | 24,830 | 3,389 | 8,759 | 1,336 | 7,673 | 3,304 |
| Arizona............. | 828,891 | 624,088 | 442,286 | 181,257 | 24,739 | 63,941 | 9,755 | 82,258 | 24,119 |
| Arkansas........... | 502,765 | 367,311 | 229,975 | 137,154 | 18,720 | 48,383 | 7,381 | 42,772 | 18,251 |
| California........... | 3,951,069 | 3,050,673 | 2,367,042 | 680,199 | 92,837 | 239,950 | 36,607 | 440,233 | 90,512 |
| Colorado........... | 656,480 | 497,384 | 360,935 | 136,141 | 18,581 | 48,026 | 7,327 | 67,128 | 18,116 |
| Connecticut........ | 376,788 | 293,559 | 234,725 | 58,478 | 7,981 | 20,629 | 3,147 | 43,655 | 7,781 |
| Delaware........... | 112,766 | 88,900 | 73,808 | 14,974 | 2,044 | 5,282 | 806 | 13,727 | 1,993 |
| Dist. of Columbia. .. | 27,819 | 22,074 | 18,696 | 3,348 | 457 | 1,181 | 180 | 3,477 | 446 |
| Florida.............. | 2,176,524 | 1,689,890 | 1,335,901 | 351,996 | 48,042 | 124,172 | 18,944 | 248,457 | 46,839 |
| Georgia............. | 1,362,182 | 1,031,490 | 746,764 | 283,670 | 38,717 | 100,069 | 15,267 | 138,886 | 37,747 |
| Hawaii.............. | 103,703 | 83,048 | 72,288 | 10,637 | 1,452 | 3,752 | 572 | 13,444 | 1,415 |
| Idaho............... | 246,882 | 181,545 | 116,382 | 64,653 | 8,824 | 22,807 | 3,479 | 21,645 | 8,603 |
| Illinois.............. | 1,458,022 | 1,091,254 | 756,464 | 335,448 | 45,784 | 118,334 | 18,053 | 140,691 | 44,637 |
| Indiana............. | 1,042,743 | 767,371 | 495,885 | 270,996 | 36,987 | 95,598 | 14,584 | 92,227 | 36,060 |
| Iowa................ | 565,609 | 416,109 | 268,529 | 147,316 | 20,106 | 51,968 | 7,928 | 49,942 | 19,603 |
| Kansas............. | 416,229 | 309,737 | 209,639 | 99,865 | 13,630 | 36,220 | 5,375 | 30,990 | 13,209 |
| Kentucky........... | 691,801 | 514,508 | 347,424 | 166,699 | 22,752 | 58,806 | 8,971 | 64,615 | 22,182 |
| Louisiana........... | 661,028 | 495,875 | 346,485 | 148,975 | 20,333 | 52,553 | 8,018 | 64,441 | 19,824 |
| Maine.............. | 210,697 | 162,371 | 109,520 | 41,351 | 5,644 | 14,587 | 2,225 | 20,369 | 5,502 |
| Maryland........... | 700,765 | 543,512 | 448,704 | 114,720 | 15,658 | 40,469 | 6,174 | 83,452 | 15,265 |
| Massachusetts...... | 686,647 | 539,149 | 442,005 | 96,448 | 13,164 | 34,024 | 5,191 | 82,206 | 12,834 |
| Michigan............ | 1,212,639 | 935,678 | 724,404 | 210,248 | 28,696 | 74,168 | 11,315 | 134,728 | 27,977 |
| Minnesota.......... | 761,135 | 571,270 | 399,976 | 170,813 | 23,313 | 60,257 | 9,193 | 74,389 | 22,729 |
| Mississippi......... | 571,313 | 421,027 | 273,701 | 147,052 | 20,070 | 51,875 | 7,914 | 50,904 | 19,568 |
| Missouri............ | 966,870 | 723,216 | 499,666 | 222,967 | 30,432 | 78,655 | 12,000 | 92,930 | 29,669 |
| Montana............ | 190,083 | 136,833 | 79,978 | 56,799 | 7,752 | 20,037 | 3,057 | 14,875 | 7,558 |
| Nebraska........... | 331,437 | 238,248 | 138,295 | 99,860 | 13,629 | 35,227 | 5,374 | 25,721 | 13,288 |
| Nevada............. | 333,719 | 251,601 | 179,219 | 72,157 | 9,848 | 25,455 | 3,883 | 33,332 | 9,602 |
| New Hampshire. ... | 162,965 | 128,729 | 107,533 | 21,022 | 2,869 | 7,416 | 1,131 | 20,000 | 2,797 |
| New Jersey......... | 1,106,164 | 853,066 | 659,187 | 192,835 | 26,319 | 68,025 | 10,378 | 122,599 | 25,660 |
| New Mexico........ | 368,150 | 262,766 | 147,223 | 115,459 | 15,759 | 40,730 | 6,214 | 27,381 | 15,364 |
| New York........... | 1,566,059 | 1,188,120 | 866,355 | 320,637 | 43,762 | 113,109 | 17,256 | 161,129 | 42,666 |
| North Carolina...... | 1,265,605 | 968,810 | 729,609 | 238,194 | 32,510 | 84,026 | 12,819 | 135,696 | 31,696 |
| North Dakota....... | 183,384 | 128,943 | 66,614 | 61,761 | 8,430 | 21,787 | 3,324 | 12,389 | 8,218 |
| Ohio................ | 1,510,200 | 1,133,230 | 792,754 | 339,525 | 46,340 | 119,772 | 18,273 | 147,440 | 45,179 |
| Oklahoma........... | 671,703 | 488,090 | 298,182 | 189,661 | 25,886 | 66,906 | 10,207 | 55,457 | 25,237 |
| Oregon............. | 492,599 | 365,456 | 244,307 | 120,885 | 16,499 | 42,644 | 6,506 | 45,437 | 16,086 |
| Pennsylvania....... | 1,448,653 | 1,089,780 | 769,774 | 319,063 | 43,547 | 112,554 | 17,171 | 143,166 | 42,457 |
| Rhode Island....... | 88,210 | 69,551 | 57,771 | 11,688 | 1,595 | 4,123 | 629 | 10,745 | 1,555 |
| South Carolina...... | 818,378 | 616,843 | 435,902 | 169,106 | 23,081 | 59,655 | 9,101 | 81,071 | 22,502 |
| South Dakota....... | 170,586 | 123,417 | 73,888 | 49,472 | 6,752 | 17,452 | 2,662 | 13,742 | 6,583 |
| Tennessee.......... | 976,836 | 737,974 | 531,172 | 207,169 | 28,276 | 73,082 | 11,149 | 98,790 | 27,567 |
| Texas............... | 4,557,014 | 3,372,223 | 2,230,498 | 1,139,198 | 155,484 | 401,869 | 61,309 | 414,838 | 151,589 |
| Utah................ | 390,019 | 286,377 | 187,142 | 103,919 | 14,183 | 36,659 | 5,593 | 34,805 | 13,828 |
| Vermont............ | 82,410 | 63,148 | 47,728 | 15,354 | 2,096 | 5,416 | 826 | 8,877 | 2,043 |
| Virginia............. | 1,126,835 | 858,058 | 634,169 | 223,042 | 30,442 | 78,682 | 12,004 | 117,946 | 29,679 |
| Washington......... | 758,794 | 579,386 | 435,164 | 145,778 | 19,897 | 51,425 | 7,845 | 80,934 | 19,398 |
| West Virginia....... | 253,148 | 188,189 | 126,847 | 61,202 | 8,353 | 21,590 | 3,294 | 23,592 | 8,144 |
| Wisconsin........... | 757,168 | 567,148 | 393,986 | 172,696 | 23,571 | 60,921 | 9,294 | 73,275 | 22,980 |
| Wyoming............ | 183,211 | 124,638 | 51,953 | 72,422 | 9,885 | 25,548 | 3,898 | 9,662 | 9,637 |

Source: U.S. Federal Highway Administration, "Highway Statistics 2017," <http://www.fhwa.dot.gov/policyinformation/statistics.cfm>, accessed September 2019.

## Table 1122. Motor Vehicle Distance Traveled by Type of Vehicle: 1970 to 2017

[1,110 represents 1,110,000,000,000. The travel data by vehicle type and stratification of trucks are estimated by the Federal Highway Administration (FHWA)]

| Year | Vehicle miles of travel (bil.) [1] | | | | | Average miles traveled per vehicle (1,000) [1] | | | | |
|---|---|---|---|---|---|---|---|---|---|---|
| | Total [2] | Light duty vehicle short WB [3] | Buses [4] | Light duty vehicle long WB [3] | Trucks [5,6] | Total [2] | Light duty vehicle short WB [3] | Buses [4] | Light duty vehicle long WB [3] | Trucks [5,6] |
| 1970........ | 1,110 | 920 | 4.5 | 123 | 62 | 10.0 | 10.0 | 12.0 | 8.7 | 13.6 |
| 1975........ | 1,328 | 1,040 | 6.1 | 201 | 81 | 9.6 | 9.3 | 13.1 | 9.8 | 15.2 |
| 1980........ | 1,527 | 1,122 | 6.1 | 291 | 108 | 9.5 | 8.8 | 11.5 | 10.4 | 18.7 |
| 1985........ | 1,775 | 1,256 | 4.5 | 391 | 124 | 10.0 | 9.4 | 7.5 | 10.5 | 20.6 |
| 1990........ | 2,144 | 1,418 | 5.7 | 575 | 146 | 11.1 | 10.3 | 9.1 | 11.9 | 23.6 |
| 1995........ | 2,423 | 1,438 | 6.4 | 790 | 178 | 11.8 | 11.2 | 9.4 | 12.0 | 26.5 |
| 2000........ | 2,747 | 1,967 | 14.8 | 491 | 262 | 12.2 | 11.0 | 19.8 | 14.6 | 29.1 |
| 2001........ | 2,796 | 1,987 | 13.0 | 512 | 272 | 11.9 | 10.7 | 17.3 | 14.7 | 28.9 |
| 2002........ | 2,856 | 2,036 | 13.3 | 520 | 276 | 12.2 | 11.1 | 17.5 | 14.3 | 29.4 |
| 2003........ | 2,890 | 2,051 | 13.4 | 528 | 286 | 12.2 | 11.1 | 17.2 | 14.8 | 30.3 |
| 2004........ | 2,965 | 2,083 | 13.5 | 569 | 284 | 12.2 | 11.0 | 17.0 | 15.2 | 29.7 |
| 2005........ | 2,989 | 2,096 | 13.2 | 581 | 285 | 12.1 | 11.0 | 16.3 | 14.8 | 28.8 |
| 2006........ | 3,014 | 2,048 | 14.0 | 633 | 301 | 12.0 | 10.5 | 17.1 | 16.3 | 29.1 |
| 2007........ | 3,031 | 2,104 | 14.5 | 587 | 304 | 11.9 | 10.7 | 17.4 | 15.0 | 28.3 |
| 2008........ | 2,977 | 2,025 | 14.8 | 605 | 311 | 11.6 | 10.3 | 17.6 | 15.3 | 28.6 |
| 2009........ | 2,957 | 2,016 | 14.4 | 617 | 288 | 11.6 | 10.4 | 17.1 | 15.3 | 26.3 |
| 2010........ | 2,967 | 2,026 | 13.8 | 623 | 287 | 11.9 | 10.7 | 16.3 | 15.5 | 26.6 |
| 2011........ | 2,950 | 2,046 | 13.8 | 604 | 268 | 11.7 | 11.2 | 20.7 | 12.0 | 26.1 |
| 2012........ | 2,969 | 2,063 | 14.8 | 601 | 269 | 11.7 | 11.3 | 19.3 | 11.9 | 25.3 |
| 2013........ | 2,988 | 2,074 | 15.2 | 603 | 275 | 11.7 | 11.2 | 17.5 | 11.7 | 26.0 |
| 2014........ | 3,026 | 2,072 | 16.0 | 638 | 279 | 11.6 | 11.0 | 18.3 | 12.1 | 25.6 |
| 2015........ | 3,095 | 2,148 | 16.2 | 632 | 280 | 11.7 | 11.3 | 18.3 | 11.9 | 25.0 |
| 2016........ | 3,174 | 2,192 | 16.3 | 658 | 288 | 11.8 | 11.4 | 16.7 | 12.0 | 25.0 |
| 2017........ | 3,212 | 2,221 | 17.2 | 657 | 298 | 11.8 | 11.5 | 17.5 | 11.5 | 24.3 |

[1] Beginning with 2000 data, FHWA updated data using an enhanced methodology implemented in March 2011. Prior to 2000, "Light Duty Vehicles Short WB" were categorized as "Cars"; and "Light Duty Vehicles Long WB" were categorized as "Vans, pickups, sport utility vehicles." [2] Motorcycles included with "Cars" through 1994; thereafter in total, not shown separately. [3] Light Duty Vehicles Short WB—passenger cars, light trucks, vans and sport utility vehicles with a wheelbase (WB) equal to or less than 121 inches. Light Duty Vehicles Long WB—large passenger cars, vans, pickup trucks, and sport/utility vehicles with WB larger than 121 inches. [4] Includes school buses. [5] Includes combination trucks. [6] Beginning in 2000: Single-Unit—single frame trucks that have 2-axles and at least 6 tires or a gross vehicle weight rating exceeding 10,000 lbs.

Source: U.S. Federal Highway Administration, "Highway Statistics 2017," and earlier reports, <http://www.fhwa.dot.gov/policyinformation/statistics.cfm>, accessed August 2019.

## Table 1123. Licensed Drivers, Total and as a Percent of Age Group, by Age: 2000 to 2017

[Licensed drivers in thousands (190,625 represents 190,625,000). Percentages are computed using Census Bureau data]

| Age or range | Licensed drivers (1,000) | | | | | | | Licensed drivers as percent of age group [1] | | |
|---|---|---|---|---|---|---|---|---|---|---|
| | 2000 | 2010 | 2013 | 2014 | 2015 | 2016 | 2017 | 2010 | 2016 | 2017 |
| Total.................. | 190,625 | 210,115 | 212,160 | 214,092 | 218,084 | 221,712 | 225,346 | 83.5 | 83.2 | 85.1 |
| Under 16 years old [2]..... | 27 | 398 | 62 | 62 | 65 | 63 | 77 | 4.7 | 0.8 | 1.9 |
| 16 years old............. | 1,470 | 1,213 | 1,169 | 1,022 | 1,065 | 1,121 | 1,100 | 28.1 | 26.2 | 26.0 |
| 17 years old............. | 2,331 | 2,028 | 2,010 | 1,881 | 1,920 | 1,973 | 1,990 | 46.1 | 46.9 | 46.3 |
| 18 years old............. | 2,839 | 2,731 | 2,680 | 2,540 | 2,550 | 2,619 | 2,629 | 60.7 | 62.0 | 62.0 |
| 19 years old............. | 3,077 | 3,187 | 3,061 | 2,986 | 2,990 | 3,040 | 3,049 | 69.5 | 71.6 | 71.6 |
| 20 to 24 years old........ | 15,966 | 17,468 | 17,668 | 17,579 | 17,630 | 17,710 | 17,611 | 80.9 | 79.1 | 79.6 |
| 20 years old............. | 3,140 | 3,426 | 3,294 | 3,221 | 3,224 | 3,250 | 3,253 | 75.8 | 75.8 | 76.1 |
| 21 years old............. | 3,172 | 3,474 | 3,435 | 3,341 | 3,368 | 3,390 | 3,365 | 79.8 | 77.3 | 77.9 |
| 22 years old............. | 3,182 | 3,483 | 3,576 | 3,536 | 3,532 | 3,547 | 3,528 | 81.7 | 79.2 | 79.8 |
| 23 years old............. | 3,247 | 3,515 | 3,689 | 3,683 | 3,688 | 3,691 | 3,667 | 83.7 | 81.1 | 81.2 |
| 24 years old............. | 3,225 | 3,571 | 3,675 | 3,799 | 3,818 | 3,832 | 3,797 | 84.0 | 81.9 | 82.8 |
| 25 to 29 years old....... | 17,586 | 18,431 | 18,341 | 18,710 | 19,266 | 19,723 | 20,076 | 87.3 | 86.0 | 85.9 |
| 30 to 34 years old....... | 19,155 | 17,849 | 18,357 | 18,651 | 19,120 | 19,472 | 19,755 | 89.4 | 89.1 | 89.9 |
| 35 to 39 years old....... | 21,059 | 18,161 | 17,274 | 17,512 | 18,088 | 18,649 | 19,194 | 90.0 | 89.6 | 90.4 |
| 40 to 44 years old....... | 21,093 | 19,178 | 18,745 | 18,351 | 18,107 | 17,852 | 17,897 | 91.8 | 90.5 | 91.1 |
| 45 to 49 years old....... | 19,154 | 20,814 | 19,299 | 18,910 | 18,988 | 19,221 | 19,345 | 91.7 | 91.7 | 92.2 |
| 50 to 54 years old....... | 16,868 | 20,628 | 20,608 | 20,587 | 20,488 | 20,186 | 19,831 | 92.5 | 92.4 | 92.7 |
| 55 to 59 years old....... | 12,760 | 18,440 | 19,399 | 19,750 | 20,068 | 20,304 | 20,502 | 93.8 | 92.3 | 93.2 |
| 60 to 64 years old....... | 9,915 | 15,858 | 16,657 | 17,102 | 17,647 | 18,076 | 18,677 | 94.3 | 92.7 | 93.4 |
| 65 to 69 years old....... | 8,386 | 11,468 | 13,227 | 14,014 | 14,788 | 15,417 | 15,626 | 92.2 | 91.6 | 92.8 |
| 70 to 74 years old....... | 7,468 | 8,231 | 9,307 | 9,818 | 10,232 | 10,653 | 11,705 | 88.7 | 90.2 | 91.1 |
| 75 to 79 years old....... | 5,911 | 6,158 | 6,420 | 6,634 | 6,834 | 7,151 | 7,581 | 84.1 | 85.4 | 86.7 |
| 80 to 84 years old....... | 3,511 | 4,464 | 4,399 | 4,405 | 4,521 | 4,606 | 4,723 | 77.7 | 78.5 | 79.2 |
| 85 and over.............. | 2,050 | 3,411 | 3,477 | 3,577 | 3,716 | 3,877 | 3,980 | 62.1 | 60.8 | 61.5 |

[1] Calculated based on Census Bureau population estimates for the population aged 14 and over, see <https://www.census.gov/data/datasets/2017/demo/popest/nation-detail.html>. [2] Percent of age group data based on Census Bureau population estimates for 14- and 15-year olds.

Source: U.S. Federal Highway Administration, "Highway Statistics 2017," and earlier reports, <https://www.fhwa.dot.gov/policyinformation/statistics.cfm>, accessed September 2019.

## Table 1124. State Motor Vehicle Registrations, 1990 to 2017; and Motorcycle Registrations and Licensed Drivers, 2017

[In thousands (188,798 represents 188,798,000). Motor vehicle registrations cover publicly, privately, and commercially owned vehicles. Some states did not provide complete current registration data. Table displays estimates by FHWA, transaction data, or previous year data; see source and earlier editions for more information. For uniformity, data have been adjusted to a calendar-year basis as registration years in states differ; figures represent net numbers where possible, excluding reregistrations and nonresident registrations. See also Table 1125]

| State | Motor vehicle registrations [1] | | | | | | 2017 | | Motor-cycle registra-tions [2], in 2017 | Licensed drivers in 2017 |
| | 1990 | 2000 | 2010 | 2014 | 2015 | 2016 | Total | Auto-mobile | | |
|---|---|---|---|---|---|---|---|---|---|---|
| U.S. | 188,798 | 221,475 | 242,061 | 251,933 | 255,009 | 260,120 | 263,766 | 111,177 | 8,686 | 225,346 |
| AL | 3,744 | 3,960 | 4,654 | 5,251 | 5,285 | 5,359 | 4,944 | 2,065 | 111 | 3,954 |
| AK | 477 | 594 | 710 | 768 | 783 | 763 | 773 | 173 | 32 | [3] 535 |
| AZ | 2,825 | 3,795 | 4,320 | 5,407 | 5,470 | 5,620 | 5,800 | 2,392 | 164 | 5,165 |
| AR | 1,448 | 1,840 | 2,073 | 2,686 | 2,680 | 2,717 | 2,744 | 927 | 89 | 2,417 |
| CA | 21,926 | 27,698 | 31,014 | 27,873 | 28,595 | 29,379 | 29,953 | 14,861 | 828 | 26,777 |
| CO | 3,155 | 3,626 | 4,180 | 4,632 | 4,814 | 4,926 | 5,070 | 1,785 | 190 | 4,156 |
| CT | 2,623 | 2,853 | 3,082 | 2,777 | 2,755 | 2,755 | 2,736 | 1,302 | 90 | 2,587 |
| DE | 526 | 630 | 799 | 927 | 936 | 976 | 943 | 419 | 28 | 771 |
| DC | 262 | 242 | 212 | 330 | 319 | 333 | 342 | 208 | 4 | 521 |
| FL | 10,950 | 11,781 | 14,373 | 14,947 | 15,532 | 16,018 | 16,373 | 7,778 | 584 | 15,076 |
| GA | 5,489 | 7,155 | 7,702 | 7,956 | 7,937 | 8,037 | 8,238 | 3,536 | 203 | 7,060 |
| HI | 771 | 738 | 904 | 1,350 | 1,209 | 1,201 | 1,224 | 512 | 35 | 951 |
| ID | 1,054 | 1,178 | 1,325 | 1,696 | 1,788 | 1,776 | 1,773 | 550 | 63 | 1,190 |
| IL | 7,873 | 8,973 | 10,079 | 10,042 | 10,249 | 9,962 | 10,557 | 4,656 | 334 | 8,529 |
| IN | 4,366 | 5,571 | 5,698 | 5,790 | 5,822 | 5,917 | 5,919 | 2,261 | 251 | 4,554 |
| IA | 2,632 | 3,106 | 3,313 | 3,409 | 3,447 | 3,484 | 3,555 | 1,269 | 194 | 2,247 |
| KS | 2,012 | 2,296 | 2,436 | 2,446 | 2,539 | 2,553 | 2,622 | 987 | 96 | 2,030 |
| KY | 2,909 | 2,826 | 3,589 | 4,038 | 4,041 | 4,118 | 4,192 | 1,691 | 101 | 3,019 |
| LA | 2,995 | 3,557 | 4,086 | 3,773 | 3,787 | 3,791 | 3,793 | 1,389 | 114 | 3,426 |
| ME | 977 | 1,024 | 1,054 | 1,143 | 1,049 | 1,055 | 1,043 | 387 | 51 | 1,033 |
| MD | 3,607 | 3,848 | 4,557 | 3,927 | 4,009 | 4,055 | 4,239 | 2,007 | 118 | 4,330 |
| MA | 3,726 | 5,265 | 5,334 | 4,869 | 4,902 | 4,902 | 4,896 | 2,208 | 169 | 4,935 |
| MI | 7,209 | 8,436 | 9,286 | 7,868 | 8,037 | 8,076 | 8,260 | 3,257 | 258 | 7,096 |
| MN | 3,508 | 4,630 | 4,848 | 4,986 | 5,033 | 5,129 | 5,441 | 2,146 | 242 | 3,395 |
| MS | 1,875 | 2,289 | 2,016 | 2,039 | 2,041 | 2,039 | 2,029 | 823 | 28 | 2,054 |
| MO | 3,905 | 4,580 | 5,153 | 5,179 | 5,406 | 5,531 | 5,430 | 2,141 | 138 | 4,275 |
| MT | 783 | 1,026 | 926 | 1,402 | 1,448 | 1,504 | 1,557 | 441 | 257 | 807 |
| NE | 1,384 | 1,619 | 1,802 | 1,895 | 1,925 | 1,896 | 1,909 | 677 | 56 | [3] 1,404 |
| NV | 853 | 1,220 | 1,362 | 2,169 | 2,242 | 2,324 | 2,379 | 1,048 | 76 | 1,918 |
| NH | 946 | 1,052 | 1,203 | 1,234 | 1,222 | 1,244 | 1,240 | 505 | 79 | 1,104 |
| NJ | 5,652 | 6,390 | 6,628 | 6,724 | 5,786 | 5,790 | 5,905 | 2,799 | 153 | 6,301 |
| NM | 1,301 | 1,529 | 1,612 | 1,866 | 1,760 | 1,762 | 1,682 | 609 | 58 | 1,473 |
| NY | 10,196 | 10,235 | 10,255 | 10,557 | 10,284 | 10,730 | 10,465 | 4,563 | 392 | 12,185 |
| NC | 5,162 | 6,223 | 5,743 | 7,682 | 7,740 | 8,075 | 7,882 | 3,318 | 189 | 7,389 |
| ND | 630 | 694 | 736 | 833 | 852 | 856 | 1,005 | 277 | 52 | 562 |
| OH | 8,410 | 10,467 | 9,801 | 10,049 | 10,152 | 10,278 | 10,399 | 4,605 | 410 | 8,012 |
| OK | 2,649 | 3,014 | 3,357 | 3,388 | 2,859 | 3,601 | 3,608 | 1,338 | 136 | 2,506 |
| OR | 2,445 | 3,022 | 3,050 | 3,330 | 3,479 | 3,675 | 3,961 | 1,542 | 142 | 2,911 |
| PA | 7,971 | 9,260 | 9,991 | 10,108 | 10,205 | 10,356 | 10,312 | 4,463 | 376 | 8,965 |
| RI | 672 | 760 | 782 | 833 | 843 | 845 | 842 | 420 | 31 | 753 |
| SC | 2,521 | 3,095 | 3,661 | 3,903 | 4,046 | 4,206 | 4,286 | 1,808 | 118 | 3,811 |
| SD | 704 | 793 | 926 | 943 | 906 | 1,132 | 1,141 | 353 | 117 | 629 |
| TN | 4,444 | 4,820 | 5,114 | 5,331 | 5,446 | 5,542 | 5,635 | 2,325 | 164 | 5,378 |
| TX | 12,800 | 14,070 | 17,194 | 20,432 | 21,478 | 21,391 | 21,766 | 8,177 | 364 | 17,099 |
| UT | 1,206 | 1,628 | 2,655 | 2,076 | 2,150 | 2,235 | 2,272 | 925 | 84 | 1,995 |
| VT | 462 | 515 | 567 | 582 | 624 | 585 | 591 | 222 | 31 | 560 |
| VA | 4,938 | 6,046 | 6,149 | 6,965 | 7,046 | 7,109 | 7,321 | 3,251 | 193 | 5,926 |
| WA | 4,257 | 5,116 | 4,683 | 6,176 | 6,489 | 6,812 | 7,025 | 2,926 | 231 | 5,768 |
| WV | 1,225 | 1,442 | 1,436 | 1,496 | 1,555 | 1,644 | 1,631 | 563 | 59 | 1,149 |
| WI | 3,815 | 4,366 | 4,968 | 5,059 | 5,142 | 5,229 | 5,272 | 2,093 | 324 | 4,235 |
| WY | 528 | 586 | 663 | 789 | 784 | 825 | 790 | 194 | 29 | 422 |

[1] Automobiles, trucks, and buses (excludes motorcycles). Excludes vehicles owned by military services. [2] Private and commercial, excluding publicly-owned. [3] State did not provide current data; data shown are for 2016.

Source: U.S. Federal Highway Administration, "Highway Statistics 2017," and earlier reports, <http://www.fhwa.dot.gov/policyinformation/statistics.cfm>, accessed August 2019.

## Table 1125. State Motor Vehicle Registrations: 2000 to 2017

[In thousands (221,475 represents 221,475,000). Information obtained from state authorities, see source. For motorcycles; see Table 1124]

| Type | 2000 | 2010 | 2012 | 2013 | 2014 | 2015 | 2016 | 2017 |
|---|---|---|---|---|---|---|---|---|
| All motor vehicles | 221,475 | 242,061 | 245,184 | 247,417 | 251,933 | 255,009 | 260,120 | 263,766 |
| Private and commercial | 217,567 | 237,784 | 241,457 | 243,487 | 247,849 | 250,967 | 255,972 | 259,623 |
| Publicly owned | 3,908 | 4,277 | 3,728 | 3,985 | 4,084 | 4,042 | 4,148 | 4,142 |
| Automobiles | 133,621 | 130,892 | 111,290 | 113,676 | 113,899 | 112,864 | 112,961 | 111,177 |
| Private and commercial | 132,247 | 129,434 | 109,834 | 112,128 | 112,261 | 111,412 | 111,491 | 109,750 |
| Publicly owned | 1,374 | 1,458 | 1,456 | 1,548 | 1,638 | 1,453 | 1,471 | 1,427 |
| Buses | 746 | 846 | 765 | 865 | 872 | 889 | 976 | 983 |
| Private and commercial | 314 | 347 | 301 | 361 | 467 | 466 | 568 | 572 |
| Publicly owned | 432 | 499 | 464 | 503 | 405 | 423 | 409 | 411 |
| Trucks [1] | 87,108 | 110,322 | 133,130 | 132,931 | 137,162 | 141,256 | 146,182 | 151,605 |
| Private and commercial | 85,005 | 108,003 | 131,322 | 130,998 | 135,121 | 139,090 | 143,913 | 149,301 |
| Publicly owned | 2,103 | 2,319 | 1,808 | 1,934 | 2,041 | 2,166 | 2,269 | 2,304 |

[1] Includes panel, delivery, personal, passenger vans, minivans, pickups, and utility vehicles.

Source: U.S. Federal Highway Administration, "Highway Statistics 2017," and earlier reports, <http://www.fhwa.dot.gov/policyinformation/statistics.cfm>, accessed July 2019.

## Table 1126. Domestic Motor Fuel Consumption by Type of Vehicle: 1970 to 2017

[Consumption in billions (92.3 represents 92,300,000,000 gallons). See Table 1122. Comprises all fuel types used for propulsion of vehicles under state motor fuels laws. Excludes federal purchases for military use. Minus sign (-) indicates decrease]

| Year | Annual fuel consumption (bil. gal.) [1] | | | | | | Average miles per gallon [1] | | | | | |
|---|---|---|---|---|---|---|---|---|---|---|---|---|
| | All vehicles [2] | Annual percent change [3] | Light duty vehicle short WB [4] | Buses [5] | Light duty vehicle long WB [4] | Trucks [6,7] | All vehicles [2] | Light duty vehicle short WB [4] | Buses [5] | Light duty vehicle long WB [4] | Trucks [6,7] | |
| 1970...... | 92.3 | 4.8 | 67.8 | 0.8 | 12.3 | 11.3 | 12.0 | 13.5 | 5.5 | 10.0 | 5.5 | |
| 1980...... | 115.0 | -5.9 | 70.2 | 1.0 | 23.8 | 20.0 | 13.3 | 16.0 | 6.0 | 12.2 | 5.4 | |
| 1990...... | 130.8 | -0.8 | 69.8 | 0.9 | 35.6 | 24.5 | 16.4 | 20.3 | 6.4 | 16.1 | 6.0 | |
| 2000...... | 162.5 | 0.7 | 88.9 | 2.2 | 28.9 | 42.0 | 16.9 | 22.1 | 6.7 | 17.0 | 6.2 | |
| 2001...... | 163.5 | 0.6 | 87.8 | 1.9 | 30.1 | 43.0 | 17.1 | 22.6 | 6.8 | 17.0 | 6.3 | |
| 2002...... | 168.7 | 3.2 | 91.5 | 1.9 | 30.8 | 43.3 | 17.0 | 22.3 | 6.9 | 16.9 | 6.4 | |
| 2003...... | 170.0 | 0.8 | 91.6 | 1.9 | 31.3 | 44.8 | 17.0 | 22.4 | 7.1 | 16.9 | 6.4 | |
| 2004...... | 173.5 | 2.1 | 93.4 | 1.9 | 33.8 | 44.4 | 17.1 | 22.3 | 7.1 | 16.9 | 6.4 | |
| 2005...... | 174.8 | 0.7 | 93.2 | 1.9 | 34.4 | 44.5 | 17.2 | 22.5 | 7.1 | 16.9 | 6.4 | |
| 2006...... | 175.0 | 0.1 | 88.6 | 2.0 | 37.0 | 46.4 | 17.2 | 23.1 | 7.1 | 17.1 | 6.5 | |
| 2007...... | 176.2 | 0.7 | 89.6 | 2.0 | 36.9 | 47.2 | 17.2 | 22.9 | 7.2 | 17.1 | 6.4 | |
| 2008...... | 170.8 | -3.1 | 85.6 | 2.1 | 34.9 | 47.7 | 17.4 | 23.7 | 7.2 | 17.3 | 6.5 | |
| 2009...... | 168.1 | -1.6 | 85.7 | 2.0 | 35.7 | 44.3 | 17.6 | 23.5 | 7.2 | 17.3 | 6.5 | |
| 2010...... | 170.4 | 1.4 | 86.8 | 1.9 | 36.3 | 45.0 | 17.4 | 23.3 | 7.2 | 17.2 | 6.4 | |
| 2011...... | 168.5 | -1.1 | 88.4 | 1.9 | 35.3 | 42.4 | 17.5 | 23.2 | 7.1 | 17.1 | 6.3 | |
| 2012...... | 168.6 | 0.1 | 88.6 | 2.1 | 35.1 | 42.4 | 17.6 | 23.3 | 7.2 | 17.1 | 6.4 | |
| 2013...... | 169.7 | 0.6 | 88.6 | 2.1 | 35.2 | 46.8 | 17.6 | 23.4 | 7.2 | 17.2 | 6.4 | |
| 2014...... | 173.3 | 2.2 | 89.3 | 2.2 | 37.3 | 44.0 | 17.5 | 23.2 | 7.2 | 17.1 | 6.3 | |
| 2015...... | 172.9 | -0.2 | 90.0 | 2.2 | 36.4 | 43.7 | 17.9 | 23.9 | 7.3 | 17.3 | 6.4 | |
| 2016...... | 176.9 | 2.3 | 91.5 | 2.2 | 37.8 | 44.9 | 17.9 | 24.0 | 7.3 | 17.4 | 6.4 | |
| 2017...... | 178.0 | 0.6 | 91.7 | 2.4 | 37.5 | 46.0 | 18.1 | 24.2 | 7.3 | 17.5 | 6.5 | |

[1] See footnote 1, Table 1122. [2] Motorcycles included with Light Duty Vehicles Short WB through 1994; thereafter in total, not shown separately. [3] Change from immediate prior year. [4] Light Duty Vehicles Short WB—passenger cars, light trucks, vans and sport utility vehicles with a wheelbase (WB) equal to or less than 121 inches. Light Duty Vehicles Long WB—large passenger cars, vans, pickup trucks, and sport/utility vehicles with WB larger than 121 inches. [5] Includes school buses. [6] Includes combination trucks. [7] Beginning 2000: Single-Unit—single frame trucks that have 2-axles and at least 6 tires or a gross vehicle weight rating over 10,000 lbs.

Source: U.S. Federal Highway Administration, "Highway Statistics 2017," and earlier reports, <http://www.fhwa.dot.gov/policyinformation/statistics.cfm>, accessed August 2019.

## Table 1127. Alternative Fuel Vehicles—Models Available and Refueling Stations by Vehicle Fuel Type: 1995 to 2018

[Data gathered as close to September 30 as possible. The Energy Policy Act of 1992 defines alternative fuels and allows the U.S. Department of Energy (DOE) to add to the list of alternative fuels if the fuel is substantially nonpetroleum, yields substantial energy security benefits, and offers substantial environmental benefits]

| Fuel type | 1995 | 2000 | 2005 | 2010 | 2015 | 2016 | 2017 | 2018 (P) |
|---|---|---|---|---|---|---|---|---|
| MODELS AVAILABLE | | | | | | | | |
| Total........................ | 13 | 37 | 29 | 36 | 141 | 115 | 111 | 128 |
| Propane [1]...................... | – | 2 | – | – | 10 | 5 | 9 | 7 |
| Compressed natural gas (CNG) [1]...... | 10 | 15 | 5 | 1 | 17 | 12 | 8 | 9 |
| Ethanol (E85)...................... | – | 8 | 24 | 34 | 84 | 66 | 45 | 54 |
| Methanol (M85)...................... | 2 | – | – | – | – | – | – | – |
| Electric vehicle [2]................. | 1 | 12 | – | 1 | 27 | 29 | 46 | 56 |
| Hydrogen...................... | – | – | – | – | 3 | 3 | 3 | 2 |
| REFUELING STATIONS | | | | | | | | |
| Total........................ | 4,677 | 5,205 | 5,164 | 6,912 | 39,963 | 51,398 | 60,053 | 70,562 |
| Propane...................... | 3,299 | 3,268 | 2,995 | 2,647 | 3,594 | 3,665 | 3,541 | 3,341 |
| Compressed Natural Gas (CNG)...... | 1,065 | 1,217 | 787 | 841 | 1,563 | 1,725 | 1,697 | 1,659 |
| LNG (Liquid Natural Gas)............. | (NA) | 44 | 40 | 39 | 111 | 140 | 131 | 137 |
| Biodiesel [3]...................... | – | 2 | 304 | 644 | 721 | 697 | 702 | 681 |
| Ethanol (E85)...................... | 37 | 113 | 436 | 2,142 | 2,990 | 3,091 | 3,322 | 3,617 |
| Methanol (M85)...................... | 88 | 3 | – | – | – | – | – | – |
| Electric vehicle [4]................. | 188 | 558 | 588 | 541 | 30,945 | 42,029 | 50,627 | 61,067 |
| Hydrogen...................... | (NA) | (NA) | 14 | 58 | 39 | 54 | 64 | 60 |

P Preliminary. – Represents zero. NA Not available. [1] Dedicated and bi-fuel vehicles. [2] Electric vehicles include plug-in hybrid-electric vehicles but do not include neighborhood electric vehicles, low-speed electric vehicles, or two-wheeled electric vehicles. [3] Stations selling biodiesel blends less than B20 are only included in the 2005-2007 station counts. [4] Beginning 2011, electric stations are counted by the plug rather than by the geographical location. This is different from the other fuels, which count only the geographical location regardless of how many dispensers or nozzles are on site.

Source: U.S. Department of Energy, Office of Energy Efficiency and Renewable Energy, *Transportation Energy Data Book*, Edition 37, April 2019. See also <http://cta.ornl.gov/data>.

## Table 1128. Traffic Fatalities—Number and Rate by State: 2000 to 2017

[For deaths within 30 days of the accident]

| State | 2000 | 2010 | 2016 | 2017 | Fatality rate [1] 2010 | 2017 | State | 2000 | 2010 | 2016 | 2017 | Fatality rate [1] 2010 | 2017 |
|---|---|---|---|---|---|---|---|---|---|---|---|---|---|
| U.S..... | 41,945 | 32,999 | 37,806 | 37,133 | 1.11 | 1.16 | MO...... | 1,157 | 821 | 947 | 930 | 1.16 | 1.23 |
| AL........ | 996 | 862 | 1,083 | 948 | 1.34 | 1.34 | MT...... | 237 | 189 | 190 | 186 | 1.69 | 1.47 |
| AK........ | 106 | 56 | 84 | 79 | 1.17 | 1.43 | NE...... | 276 | 190 | 218 | 228 | 0.98 | 1.09 |
| AZ........ | 1,036 | 759 | 952 | 1,000 | 1.27 | 1.54 | NV...... | 323 | 257 | 329 | 309 | 1.16 | 1.12 |
| AR........ | 652 | 571 | 561 | 493 | 1.70 | 1.35 | NH...... | 126 | 128 | 136 | 102 | 0.98 | 0.75 |
| CA........ | 3,753 | 2,720 | 3,837 | 3,602 | 0.84 | 1.05 | NJ...... | 731 | 556 | 602 | 624 | 0.76 | 0.81 |
| CO...... | 681 | 450 | 608 | 648 | 0.96 | 1.21 | NM...... | 432 | 349 | 405 | 379 | 1.38 | 1.28 |
| CT........ | 341 | 320 | 304 | 278 | 1.02 | 0.88 | NY...... | 1,460 | 1,201 | 1,041 | 999 | 0.92 | 0.81 |
| DE........ | 123 | 101 | 119 | 119 | 1.13 | 1.14 | NC...... | 1,557 | 1,320 | 1,450 | 1,412 | 1.29 | 1.18 |
| DC........ | 48 | 24 | 27 | 31 | 0.67 | 0.83 | ND...... | 86 | 105 | 113 | 115 | 1.27 | 1.18 |
| FL........ | 2,999 | 2,444 | 3,176 | 3,112 | 1.25 | 1.42 | OH...... | 1,366 | 1,080 | 1,132 | 1,179 | 0.97 | 0.99 |
| GA........ | 1,541 | 1,247 | 1,556 | 1,540 | 1.12 | 1.23 | OK...... | 650 | 668 | 687 | 655 | 1.40 | 1.33 |
| HI........ | 132 | 113 | 120 | 107 | 1.13 | 1.00 | OR...... | 451 | 317 | 498 | 437 | 0.94 | 1.19 |
| ID........ | 276 | 209 | 253 | 244 | 1.32 | 1.41 | PA...... | 1,520 | 1,324 | 1,188 | 1,137 | 1.32 | 1.12 |
| IL........ | 1,418 | 927 | 1,078 | 1,097 | 0.88 | 1.02 | RI...... | 80 | 67 | 51 | 83 | 0.81 | 1.04 |
| IN........ | 886 | 754 | 829 | 914 | 1.00 | 1.12 | SC...... | 1,065 | 809 | 1,020 | 988 | 1.65 | 1.78 |
| IA........ | 445 | 390 | 402 | 330 | 1.24 | 0.99 | SD...... | 173 | 140 | 116 | 129 | 1.58 | 1.34 |
| KS........ | 461 | 431 | 429 | 461 | 1.44 | 1.43 | TN...... | 1,307 | 1,032 | 1,037 | 1,040 | 1.47 | 1.26 |
| KY........ | 820 | 760 | 834 | 782 | 1.58 | 1.59 | TX...... | 3,779 | 3,023 | 3,797 | 3,722 | 1.29 | 1.36 |
| LA........ | 938 | 721 | 757 | 760 | 1.59 | 1.54 | UT...... | 373 | 253 | 281 | 273 | 0.95 | 0.87 |
| ME........ | 169 | 161 | 160 | 172 | 1.11 | 1.17 | VT...... | 76 | 71 | 62 | 69 | 0.98 | 0.93 |
| MD...... | 588 | 496 | 522 | 550 | 0.88 | 0.92 | VA...... | 929 | 740 | 760 | 839 | 0.90 | 0.98 |
| MA...... | 433 | 347 | 387 | 350 | 0.64 | 0.56 | WA...... | 631 | 460 | 536 | 565 | 0.80 | 0.92 |
| MI........ | 1,382 | 942 | 1,065 | 1,030 | 0.97 | 1.01 | WV...... | 411 | 315 | 269 | 303 | 1.64 | 1.59 |
| MN...... | 625 | 411 | 392 | 357 | 0.73 | 0.60 | WI...... | 799 | 572 | 607 | 613 | 0.96 | 0.94 |
| MS...... | 949 | 641 | 687 | 690 | 1.61 | 1.69 | WY...... | 152 | 155 | 112 | 123 | 1.66 | 1.26 |

[1] Deaths per 100 million vehicle miles traveled.

Source: U.S. National Highway Traffic Safety Administration, "Traffic Safety Facts Annual Report Tables," <https://cdan.nhtsa.gov/tsftables/tsfar.htm>, accessed June 2019; and "Fatality Analysis Reporting System," <http://www.nhtsa.gov/FARS>, accessed July 2019.

## Table 1129. Motor Vehicle Occupants and Nonoccupants Killed and Injured: 1990 to 2017

[Injuries in thousands (3,231 represents 3,231,000). For deaths within 30 days of the accident. Beginning 2016, data for persons injured are not comparable to previous years due to a new data collection system. The National Automotive Sampling System (NASS) GES (General Estimates System) was replaced with the Crash Report Sampling System (CRSS). See <https://crashstats.nhtsa.dot.gov/Api/Public/ViewPublication/812509> for details]

| Year | Total | Occupants Total | Passenger cars | Light trucks [1] | Large trucks [1] | Buses | Other/unknown [2] | Motorcycle occupants [3] | Nonoccupants Total | Pedestrian | Pedalcyclist | Other/unknown [2] |
|---|---|---|---|---|---|---|---|---|---|---|---|---|
| **KILLED** | | | | | | | | | | | | |
| 1990............... | 44,599 | 33,890 | 24,092 | 8,601 | 705 | 32 | 460 | 3,244 | 7,465 | 6,482 | 859 | 124 |
| 2000............... | 41,945 | 33,451 | 20,699 | 11,526 | 754 | 22 | 450 | 2,897 | 5,597 | 4,763 | 693 | 141 |
| 2005............... | 43,510 | 33,070 | 18,512 | 13,037 | 804 | 58 | 659 | 4,576 | 5,864 | 4,892 | 786 | 186 |
| 2006............... | 42,708 | 32,119 | 17,925 | 12,761 | 805 | 27 | 601 | 4,837 | 5,752 | 4,795 | 772 | 185 |
| 2007............... | 41,259 | 30,527 | 16,614 | 12,458 | 805 | 36 | 614 | 5,174 | 5,558 | 4,699 | 701 | 158 |
| 2008............... | 37,423 | 26,791 | 14,646 | 10,816 | 682 | 67 | 580 | 5,312 | 5,320 | 4,414 | 718 | 188 |
| 2009............... | 33,883 | 24,526 | 13,135 | 10,312 | 499 | 26 | 554 | 4,469 | 4,888 | 4,109 | 628 | 151 |
| 2010............... | 32,999 | 23,371 | 12,491 | 9,782 | 530 | 44 | 524 | 4,518 | 5,110 | 4,302 | 623 | 185 |
| 2011............... | 32,479 | 22,510 | 12,014 | 9,302 | 640 | 55 | 499 | 4,630 | 5,339 | 4,457 | 682 | 200 |
| 2012............... | 33,782 | 23,017 | 12,361 | 9,418 | 697 | 39 | 502 | 4,986 | 5,779 | 4,818 | 734 | 227 |
| 2013............... | 32,893 | 22,483 | 12,037 | 9,186 | 695 | 54 | 511 | 4,692 | 5,718 | 4,779 | 749 | 190 |
| 2014............... | 32,744 | 22,307 | 11,947 | 9,103 | 656 | 44 | 557 | 4,594 | 5,843 | 4,910 | 729 | 204 |
| 2015............... | 35,484 | 23,899 | 12,763 | 9,878 | 665 | 49 | 544 | 5,029 | 6,556 | 5,494 | 829 | 233 |
| 2016............... | 37,806 | 25,276 | 13,508 | 10,369 | 725 | 64 | 610 | 5,337 | 7,193 | 6,080 | 852 | 261 |
| 2017............... | 37,133 | 24,973 | 13,363 | 10,188 | 841 | 44 | 537 | 5,172 | 6,988 | 5,977 | 783 | 228 |
| **INJURED (1,000)** | | | | | | | | | | | | |
| 1990............... | 3,231 | 2,960 | 2,376 | 505 | 42 | 33 | 4 | 84 | 187 | 105 | 75 | 7 |
| 2000............... | 3,189 | 2,997 | 2,052 | 887 | 31 | 18 | 10 | 58 | 134 | 78 | 51 | 5 |
| 2005............... | 2,699 | 2,494 | 1,573 | 872 | 27 | 11 | 10 | 87 | 118 | 64 | 45 | 8 |
| 2006............... | 2,575 | 2,375 | 1,475 | 857 | 23 | 10 | 11 | 88 | 112 | 61 | 44 | 7 |
| 2007............... | 2,491 | 2,264 | 1,379 | 841 | 23 | 12 | 8 | 103 | 124 | 70 | 43 | 10 |
| 2008............... | 2,346 | 2,120 | 1,304 | 768 | 23 | 15 | 9 | 96 | 130 | 69 | 52 | 9 |
| 2009............... | 2,217 | 2,011 | 1,216 | 759 | 17 | 12 | 7 | 90 | 116 | 59 | 51 | 7 |
| 2010............... | 2,239 | 2,027 | 1,253 | 733 | 20 | 17 | 5 | 82 | 130 | 70 | 52 | 8 |
| 2011............... | 2,217 | 2,010 | 1,240 | 728 | 23 | 13 | 6 | 81 | 126 | 69 | 48 | 9 |
| 2012............... | 2,362 | 2,134 | 1,328 | 762 | 25 | 12 | 6 | 93 | 136 | 76 | 49 | 10 |
| 2013............... | 2,313 | 2,099 | 1,296 | 750 | 24 | 23 | 5 | 88 | 125 | 66 | 48 | 11 |
| 2014............... | 2,338 | 2,121 | 1,292 | 782 | 27 | 14 | 6 | 92 | 125 | 65 | 50 | 10 |
| 2015............... | 2,443 | 2,230 | 1,378 | 803 | 30 | 12 | 8 | 88 | 125 | 70 | 45 | 10 |
| 2016 [4]........... | 3,061 | 2,790 | 1,690 | 1,035 | 37 | 24 | 5 | 104 | 166 | 87 | 64 | 15 |
| 2017 [4]........... | 2,746 | 2,524 | 1,529 | 937 | 40 | 12 | 5 | 89 | 133 | 71 | 50 | 12 |

[1] See footnotes 2 and 3, Table 1131. [2] Includes combination trucks. [3] Includes mopeds, three wheel motorcycles, off-road motorcycles, etc. [4] Beginning 2016, data are not comparable to previous years due to a new data collection system. Numbers are not actual counts but estimates of actual counts.

Source: U.S. National Highway Traffic Safety Administration, "Traffic Safety Facts Annual Report Tables," <https://cdan.nhtsa.gov/tsftables/tsfar.htm>, accessed June 2019. See also <https://www.nhtsa.gov/research-data>.

# Table 1130. Fatal Motor Vehicle Accidents—National Summary: 2000 to 2017

[Based on data from the Fatality Analysis Reporting System (FARS). FARS gathers data on accidents that result in loss of human life. FARS is operated and maintained by National Highway Traffic Safety Administration's (NHTSA), National Center for Statistics and Analysis (NCSA). FARS data are gathered on motor vehicle accidents that occurred on a roadway customarily open to the public, resulting in the death of a person within 30 days of the accident. Collection of these data depend on the use of police, hospital, medical examiner/coroner, and Emergency Medical Services reports; state vehicle registration, driver licensing, and highway department files; and vital statistics documents and death certificates. See source for further detail]

| Item | 2000 | 2010 | 2012 | 2013 | 2014 | 2015 | 2016 | 2017 |
|---|---|---|---|---|---|---|---|---|
| **Fatal crashes, total** | **37,526** | **30,296** | **31,006** | **30,202** | **30,056** | **32,538** | **34,748** | **34,247** |
| One vehicle involved | 21,117 | 18,221 | 18,824 | 18,156 | 17,930 | 18,902 | 20,264 | 19,531 |
| Two or more vehicles involved | 16,409 | 12,075 | 12,182 | 12,046 | 12,126 | 13,636 | 14,484 | 14,716 |
| Occupants involved | 94,325 | 69,184 | 69,982 | 67,903 | 67,102 | 74,270 | 78,454 | 77,103 |
| Drivers involved | 57,280 | 44,599 | 45,664 | 44,803 | 44,671 | 49,163 | 52,399 | 52,274 |
| **Persons killed in fatal crashes** [1] | **41,945** | **32,999** | **33,782** | **32,893** | **32,744** | **35,484** | **37,806** | **37,133** |
| Occupants | 33,451 | 23,371 | 23,017 | 22,483 | 22,307 | 23,899 | 25,276 | 24,973 |
| Drivers | 22,914 | 16,864 | 16,838 | 16,520 | 16,470 | 17,615 | 18,717 | 18,726 |
| Passengers | 10,451 | 6,451 | 6,106 | 5,896 | 5,766 | 6,213 | 6,485 | 6,174 |
| Other | 86 | 56 | 73 | 67 | 71 | 71 | 74 | 73 |
| Motorcyclists | 2,897 | 4,518 | 4,986 | 4,692 | 4,594 | 5,029 | 5,337 | 5,172 |
| Nonoccupants | 5,597 | 5,110 | 5,779 | 5,718 | 5,843 | 6,556 | 7,193 | 6,988 |
| Pedestrians | 4,763 | 4,302 | 4,818 | 4,779 | 4,910 | 5,494 | 6,080 | 5,977 |
| Pedalcyclists | 693 | 623 | 734 | 749 | 729 | 829 | 852 | 783 |
| Other | 141 | 185 | 227 | 190 | 204 | 233 | 261 | 228 |
| Occupants killed by vehicle type: | | | | | | | | |
| Passenger cars | 20,699 | 12,491 | 12,361 | 12,037 | 11,947 | 12,763 | 13,508 | 13,363 |
| Mini-compact (95 inches) | 1,113 | 171 | 192 | (NA) | (NA) | 135 | 140 | 144 |
| Subcompact (95 to 99 inches) | 3,660 | 1,259 | 1,168 | (NA) | (NA) | 1,018 | 943 | 928 |
| Compact (100 to 104 inches) | 7,022 | 3,977 | 3,866 | (NA) | (NA) | 3,532 | 3,669 | 3,435 |
| Intermediate (105 to 109) inches | 5,204 | 4,244 | 4,088 | (NA) | (NA) | 4,621 | 4,966 | 5,099 |
| Full-size (110 to 114) inches | 2,287 | 1,993 | 2,106 | (NA) | (NA) | 2,353 | 2,549 | 2,466 |
| Largest (115 inches and over) | 897 | 685 | 754 | (NA) | (NA) | 796 | 876 | 903 |
| Unknown | 516 | 162 | 187 | (NA) | (NA) | 308 | 365 | 388 |
| Motorcycles and other motorized cycles | 2,897 | 4,518 | 4,986 | 4,692 | 4,594 | 5,029 | 5,337 | 5,172 |
| Motorcycles | 2,783 | 4,281 | 4,652 | 4,356 | 4,270 | 4,696 | 4,971 | 4,731 |
| Other motorized cycles | 114 | 237 | 334 | 336 | 324 | 333 | 366 | 441 |
| Light trucks [2] | 11,526 | 9,782 | 9,418 | 9,186 | 9,103 | 9,878 | 10,369 | 10,188 |
| Pickup | 6,003 | 4,486 | 4,343 | 4,175 | 4,249 | 4,470 | 4,534 | 4,356 |
| Utility | 3,358 | 3,942 | 3,885 | 3,831 | 3,800 | 4,213 | 4,462 | 4,598 |
| Van | 2,129 | 1,346 | 1,167 | 1,142 | 1,021 | 1,128 | 1,240 | 1,168 |
| Other | 36 | 8 | 23 | 38 | 33 | 67 | 133 | 66 |
| Large trucks [3] | 754 | 530 | 697 | 695 | 656 | 665 | 725 | 841 |
| Buses | 22 | 44 | 39 | 54 | 44 | 49 | 64 | 44 |
| Other/unknown vehicles | 450 | 524 | 502 | 511 | 557 | 544 | 610 | 537 |
| Persons killed, and distribution by highest driver BAC in the crash [6] | 41,945 | 32,999 | 33,782 | 32,893 | 32,744 | 35,484 | 37,806 | 37,133 |
| 0.00 percent | 62 | 64 | 64 | 63 | 64 | 65 | 65 | 65 |
| 0.01 to 0.07 percent | 6 | 5 | 5 | 6 | 5 | 5 | 5 | 5 |
| 0.08 percent and over | 32 | 31 | 31 | 31 | 30 | 29 | 29 | 29 |
| Drivers in fatal crashes by BAC [6] | 57,280 | 44,599 | 45,664 | 44,803 | 44,671 | 49,163 | 52,399 | 52,274 |
| 0.00 percent | 42,643 | 33,190 | 34,193 | 33,478 | 33,438 | 37,529 | 39,994 | 40,021 |
| 0.01 to 0.07 percent | 2,376 | 1,812 | 1,791 | 1,850 | 1,837 | 1,964 | 2,037 | 1,909 |
| 0.08 percent and over | 12,261 | 9,598 | 9,680 | 9,475 | 9,396 | 9,670 | 10,368 | 10,344 |
| Fatalities per 100,000 resident population: | | | | | | | | |
| Under 5 years old | 3.70 | 2.00 | 2.03 | 1.98 | 1.71 | 1.90 | 2.01 | 2.00 |
| 5 to 9 years old | 3.55 | 1.74 | 1.70 | 1.67 | 1.72 | 1.73 | 1.88 | 1.57 |
| 10 to 15 years old | 5.65 | 2.71 | 2.49 | 2.37 | 2.27 | 2.46 | 2.65 | 2.47 |
| 16 to 20 years old | 29.38 | 15.43 | 14.89 | 13.85 | 14.12 | 14.85 | 15.20 | 14.56 |
| 21 to 24 years old | 27.02 | 19.49 | 19.13 | 18.13 | 17.84 | 18.89 | 20.10 | 18.56 |
| 25 to 34 years old | 17.29 | 13.47 | 14.03 | 13.44 | 13.40 | 14.41 | 15.50 | 14.88 |
| 35 to 44 years old | 15.08 | 11.09 | 11.26 | 10.86 | 10.48 | 11.63 | 12.40 | 12.37 |
| 45 to 54 years old | 13.79 | 11.32 | 11.80 | 11.34 | 11.32 | 12.31 | 12.50 | 12.56 |
| 55 to 64 years old | 13.61 | 10.94 | 11.22 | 11.11 | 11.00 | 11.90 | 12.60 | 12.72 |
| 65 to 74 years old | 15.29 | 10.96 | 11.30 | 10.93 | 10.42 | 11.41 | 12.00 | 11.03 |
| 75 years old and over | 23.29 | 16.80 | 15.12 | 15.22 | 15.01 | 15.33 | 16.50 | 16.58 |
| Fatalities per 100 million VMT [4] | 1.53 | 1.11 | 1.14 | 1.10 | 1.08 | 1.15 | 1.19 | 1.16 |
| Fatalities per 100,000 licensed drivers | 22.00 | 15.71 | 15.95 | 15.50 | 15.29 | 16.27 | 17.05 | 16.48 |
| VMT per registered vehicle [4] | 12,657 | 11,531 | 11,176 | 11,096 | 11,011 | 11,002 | 11,020 | 11,061 |
| Fatalities per 100,000 registered vehicles | 19.33 | 12.82 | 12.72 | 12.21 | 11.92 | 12.61 | 13.13 | 12.79 |
| Fatal crashes per 100 million VMT [4] | 1.37 | 1.02 | 1.04 | 1.01 | 0.99 | 1.05 | 1.09 | 1.07 |
| Fatalities per 100,000 resident population | 14.87 | 10.67 | 10.76 | 10.40 | 10.28 | 11.05 | 11.69 | 11.40 |
| Vehicle miles traveled (VMT) (bil.) | 2,747 | 2,967 | 2,969 | 2,988 | 3,026 | 3,095 | 3,174 | 3,212 |
| Licensed drivers (1,000) | 190,625 | 210,115 | 211,815 | 212,160 | 214,092 | 218,084 | 221,712 | 225,346 |
| Registered vehicles (1,000) [5] | 217,028 | 257,312 | 265,647 | 269,294 | 274,805 | 281,312 | 288,034 | 290,387 |

NA Not available. [1] Deaths within 30 days of the accident. Starting with 1995, total does not include motorcyclist data. [2] Trucks with a gross vehicle weight rating of 10,000 pounds or less, including pickups, vans, truck-based station wagons, and utility vehicles. [3] Trucks with a gross vehicle weight rating of over 10,000 pounds. [4] VMT = vehicle miles of travel. [5] Data on motor vehicle registrations for 2011 and beyond are not strictly comparable to data for prior years due to methodology changes. See source for details. [6] BAC = blood alcohol concentration. NHTSA estimates alcohol involvement when test results are unknown. Includes crashes in which there was no driver present.

Source: National Highway Traffic Safety Administration, *Traffic Safety Facts, 2017*, and earlier reports; "Traffic Safety Facts Annual Report Tables," <https://cdan.nhtsa.gov/tsftables/tsfar.htm> accessed September 2019; and "Fatality Analysis Reporting System," <http://www.nhtsa.gov/FARS>, accessed September 2019.

# Table 1131. Vehicles Involved in Crashes by Vehicle Type, Rollover Occurrence, and Crash Severity: 2017

[Excludes motorcycles. Beginning 2016, data for injury and property damage only crashes are not comparable to previous years due to a new data collection system. The National Automotive Sampling System (NASS) General Estimates System (GES) was replaced with the Crash Report Sampling System (CRSS). See <https://crashstats.nhtsa.dot.gov/Api/Public/ViewPublication/812509> for details]

| Crash severity by vehicle type | Total | Rollover occurrence | | | |
|---|---|---|---|---|---|
| | | Yes | | No | |
| | Number | Number | Percent | Number | Percent |
| **Vehicles involved in all crashes [1]** | **11,431,000** | **246,000** | **2.2** | **11,185,000** | **97.8** |
| Passenger cars | 6,331,000 | 97,000 | 1.5 | 6,235,000 | 98.5 |
| Light trucks: [2] | | | | | |
| Pickup | 1,496,000 | 49,000 | 3.2 | 1,448,000 | 96.8 |
| Utility | 2,423,000 | 69,000 | 2.8 | 2,354,000 | 97.2 |
| Van | 590,000 | 9,000 | 1.5 | 581,000 | 98.5 |
| Other | 34,000 | 1,000 | 2.1 | 33,000 | 97.9 |
| Large truck [3] | 475,000 | 21,000 | 4.4 | 454,000 | 95.6 |
| Bus | 67,000 | (Z) | 0.2 | 67,000 | 99.8 |
| Other/unknown | 16,000 | 2,000 | 9.4 | 14,000 | 90.6 |
| **Fatal crashes** | **47,319** | **8,076** | **17.1** | **39,243** | **82.9** |
| Passenger cars | 21,031 | 2,753 | 13.1 | 18,278 | 86.9 |
| Light trucks: [2] | | | | | |
| Pickup | 8,768 | 1,980 | 22.6 | 6,788 | 77.4 |
| Utility | 8,893 | 2,138 | 24.0 | 6,755 | 76.0 |
| Van | 2,197 | 320 | 14.6 | 1,877 | 85.4 |
| Other | 128 | 28 | 21.9 | 100 | 78.1 |
| Large truck [3] | 4,657 | 591 | 12.7 | 4,066 | 87.3 |
| Bus | 232 | 14 | 6.0 | 218 | 94.0 |
| Other/unknown | 1,413 | 252 | 17.8 | 1,161 | 82.2 |
| **Injury crashes** | **3,417,000** | **143,000** | **4.2** | **3,274,000** | **95.8** |
| Passenger cars | 1,956,000 | 59,000 | 3.0 | 1,897,000 | 97.0 |
| Light trucks: [2] | | | | | |
| Pickup | 425,000 | 26,000 | 6.2 | 399,000 | 93.8 |
| Utility | 725,000 | 41,000 | 5.7 | 683,000 | 94.3 |
| Van | 177,000 | 5,000 | 2.8 | 172,000 | 97.2 |
| Other | 8,000 | 1,000 | 9.1 | 7,000 | 90.9 |
| Large truck [3] | 107,000 | 10,000 | 9.1 | 97,000 | 90.9 |
| Bus | 15,000 | (Z) | 0.6 | 14,000 | 99.4 |
| Other/unknown | 6,000 | 1,000 | 14.5 | 5,000 | 85.5 |

Z less than 500 or 0.05 percent. [1] Includes property-only crashes, not shown separately. [2] Light trucks of 10,000 pounds gross vehicle weight rating or less, including pickups, vans, truck-based station wagons and utility vehicles. [3] Large trucks over 10,000 pounds gross vehicle weight rating.

Source: U.S. National Highway Traffic Safety Administration, "Traffic Safety Facts Annual Report Tables," <https://cdan.nhtsa.gov/tsftables/tsfar.htm>, accessed June 2019. See also <https://www.nhtsa.gov/research-data>.

# Table 1132. Distracted Drivers—Crashes, Road Fatalities, and Injuries: 2010 to 2017

["Distraction" is defined as a specific type of inattention that occurs when drivers divert their attention from the driving task to focus on some other activity instead. "Distraction" is a subset of "inattention" (which also includes fatigue and physical and emotional conditions of the driver). For more information, including revision in coding of "distracted driving," see appendix in source report]

| Description | 2010 | 2012 | 2013 | 2014 | 2015 | 2016 | 2017 |
|---|---|---|---|---|---|---|---|
| **FATAL CRASHES [1]** | | | | | | | |
| Total | 30,196 | 31,006 | 30,202 | 30,056 | 32,539 | 34,439 | 34,247 |
| Drivers involved | 44,440 | 45,337 | 44,574 | 44,583 | 48,613 | 51,914 | 52,274 |
| Fatalities | 32,885 | 33,561 | 32,719 | 32,675 | 35,092 | 37,461 | 37,133 |
| **Crashes involving driver distraction [2]** | **2,993** | **3,098** | **2,923** | **2,972** | **3,242** | **3,157** | **2,935** |
| Percent | 10 | 10 | 10 | 10 | 10 | 9 | 9 |
| Involving cell phone use | 366 | 380 | 411 | 387 | 453 | 444 | 401 |
| Percent | 12 | 12 | 14 | 13 | 14 | 14 | 14 |
| Drivers involved | 2,912 | 3,119 | 2,959 | 3,000 | 3,263 | 3,210 | 2,994 |
| Percent | 7 | 7 | 7 | 7 | 7 | 6 | 6 |
| Fatalities | 3,092 | 3,328 | 3,154 | 3,179 | 3,477 | 3,450 | 3,166 |
| Percent | 9 | 10 | 10 | 10 | 10 | 9 | 9 |
| **INJURY CRASHES (ESTIMATED) [3]** | | | | | | | |
| Total | 1,542,000 | 1,634,000 | 1,591,000 | 1,648,000 | 1,715,000 | (NA) | (NA) |
| People injured | 2,239,000 | 2,362,000 | 2,313,000 | 2,338,000 | 2,443,000 | (NA) | (NA) |
| In crashes involving driver distraction | 416,000 | 421,000 | 424,000 | 431,000 | 391,000 | (NA) | (NA) |
| Percent of total | 19 | 18 | 18 | 18 | 16 | (NA) | (NA) |
| In crashes involving cell phone use | 24,000 | 28,000 | 34,000 | 33,000 | 30,000 | (NA) | (NA) |
| Percent of total distracted | 6 | 7 | 8 | 8 | 8 | (NA) | (NA) |

NA Not available. [1] Data from NHTSA's Fatality Analysis Reporting System (FARS). [2] For multiple-vehicle crashes, the crash was reported as a distracted-driving crash if at least one driver was reported as distracted. In some of these multiple-vehicle crashes, multiple drivers were reported as distracted. [3] Data from National Automotive Sampling System (NASS) General Estimates System (GES).

Source: U.S. National Highway Traffic Safety Administration, *Distracted Driving in Fatal Crashes, 2017*, April 2019, and earlier reports. See also <https://crashstats.nhtsa.dot.gov> and <https://www.nhtsa.gov/risky-driving/distracted-driving>.

# Table 1133. Traffic Fatalities by State and Highest Driver Blood Alcohol Concentration (BAC) in the Crash: 2017

[A crash is a police-reported event that produces injury and/or property damage, involves a vehicle in transport and occurs on a trafficway or while the vehicle is in motion after running off the trafficway. A positive blood alcohol concentration (BAC level of .01 grams per deciliter and higher) indicates that alcohol was consumed by the person tested, and the incident is alcohol related or alcohol involved; a BAC level of .08 g/dL or more indicates that the person was alcohol impaired]

| State | Traffic fatalities, total [1] | Traffic fatalities not involving alcohol (BAC=.00) | | Alcohol involved driving fatalities (BAC=.01–.07) | | Alcohol impaired driving fatalities (BAC=.08 or more) | | Total fatalities involving alcohol (BAC=.01 or more) | |
|---|---|---|---|---|---|---|---|---|---|
| | | Number | Percent | Number | Percent | Number | Percent | Number | Percent |
| United States [2]..... | 37,133 | 24,280 | 65 | 1,873 | 5 | 10,874 | 29 | 12,747 | 34 |
| Alabama............... | 948 | 629 | 66 | 48 | 5 | 268 | 28 | 317 | 33 |
| Alaska................. | 79 | 55 | 70 | 2 | 2 | 22 | 28 | 24 | 30 |
| Arizona............... | 1,000 | 641 | 64 | 59 | 6 | 278 | 28 | 337 | 34 |
| Arkansas............. | 493 | 336 | 68 | 17 | 3 | 140 | 28 | 157 | 32 |
| California............. | 3,602 | 2,275 | 63 | 196 | 5 | 1,120 | 31 | 1,316 | 37 |
| Colorado............. | 648 | 439 | 68 | 31 | 5 | 177 | 27 | 208 | 32 |
| Connecticut.......... | 278 | 142 | 51 | 14 | 5 | 120 | 43 | 134 | 48 |
| Delaware............. | 119 | 82 | 69 | 5 | 4 | 32 | 27 | 37 | 31 |
| District of Columbia... | 31 | 15 | 47 | 0 | 1 | 16 | 51 | 16 | 53 |
| Florida................ | 3,112 | 2,126 | 68 | 135 | 4 | 839 | 27 | 974 | 31 |
| Georgia............... | 1,540 | 1,102 | 72 | 68 | 4 | 366 | 24 | 435 | 28 |
| Hawaii................ | 107 | 58 | 54 | 8 | 7 | 42 | 39 | 50 | 46 |
| Idaho................. | 244 | 168 | 69 | 15 | 6 | 60 | 24 | 74 | 30 |
| Illinois................ | 1,097 | 677 | 62 | 70 | 6 | 349 | 32 | 418 | 38 |
| Indiana............... | 914 | 658 | 72 | 36 | 4 | 220 | 24 | 256 | 28 |
| Iowa.................. | 330 | 226 | 68 | 15 | 5 | 88 | 27 | 103 | 31 |
| Kansas................ | 461 | 349 | 76 | 10 | 2 | 102 | 22 | 112 | 24 |
| Kentucky.............. | 782 | 563 | 72 | 32 | 4 | 181 | 23 | 213 | 27 |
| Louisiana............. | 760 | 490 | 65 | 52 | 7 | 212 | 28 | 264 | 35 |
| Maine................. | 172 | 113 | 65 | 10 | 6 | 50 | 29 | 60 | 35 |
| Maryland.............. | 550 | 343 | 62 | 20 | 4 | 186 | 34 | 206 | 37 |
| Massachusetts........ | 350 | 213 | 61 | 16 | 4 | 120 | 34 | 136 | 39 |
| Michigan.............. | 1,030 | 656 | 64 | 60 | 6 | 311 | 30 | 371 | 36 |
| Minnesota............ | 357 | 253 | 71 | 19 | 5 | 85 | 24 | 104 | 29 |
| Mississippi............ | 690 | 517 | 75 | 25 | 4 | 148 | 21 | 173 | 25 |
| Missouri............... | 930 | 622 | 67 | 51 | 5 | 254 | 27 | 304 | 33 |
| Montana.............. | 186 | 121 | 65 | 7 | 4 | 56 | 30 | 63 | 34 |
| Nebraska............. | 228 | 153 | 67 | 6 | 2 | 67 | 29 | 73 | 32 |
| Nevada............... | 309 | 207 | 67 | 12 | 4 | 89 | 29 | 101 | 33 |
| New Hampshire....... | 102 | 70 | 69 | 5 | 5 | 27 | 26 | 32 | 31 |
| New Jersey............ | 624 | 460 | 74 | 39 | 6 | 125 | 20 | 165 | 26 |
| New Mexico........... | 379 | 234 | 62 | 24 | 6 | 120 | 32 | 145 | 38 |
| New York.............. | 999 | 657 | 66 | 47 | 5 | 295 | 30 | 342 | 34 |
| North Carolina........ | 1,412 | 933 | 66 | 64 | 5 | 413 | 29 | 477 | 34 |
| North Dakota.......... | 115 | 61 | 53 | 4 | 4 | 46 | 40 | 50 | 44 |
| Ohio.................. | 1,179 | 794 | 67 | 48 | 4 | 333 | 28 | 381 | 32 |
| Oklahoma............. | 655 | 462 | 71 | 27 | 4 | 165 | 25 | 193 | 29 |
| Oregon................ | 437 | 278 | 64 | 23 | 5 | 137 | 31 | 160 | 36 |
| Pennsylvania.......... | 1,137 | 777 | 68 | 43 | 4 | 314 | 28 | 357 | 31 |
| Rhode Island.......... | 83 | 46 | 55 | 1 | 1 | 34 | 41 | 35 | 42 |
| South Carolina........ | 988 | 615 | 62 | 60 | 6 | 313 | 32 | 374 | 38 |
| South Dakota......... | 129 | 82 | 64 | 12 | 9 | 35 | 27 | 47 | 36 |
| Tennessee............. | 1,040 | 730 | 70 | 59 | 6 | 251 | 24 | 310 | 30 |
| Texas................. | 3,722 | 2,003 | 54 | 248 | 7 | 1,468 | 39 | 1,715 | 46 |
| Utah.................. | 273 | 213 | 78 | 7 | 3 | 53 | 19 | 61 | 22 |
| Vermont............... | 69 | 48 | 69 | 3 | 5 | 18 | 26 | 21 | 31 |
| Virginia............... | 839 | 560 | 67 | 33 | 4 | 246 | 29 | 279 | 33 |
| Washington........... | 565 | 355 | 63 | 32 | 6 | 178 | 32 | 211 | 37 |
| West Virginia.......... | 303 | 218 | 72 | 13 | 4 | 72 | 24 | 85 | 28 |
| Wisconsin............. | 613 | 380 | 62 | 42 | 7 | 190 | 31 | 232 | 38 |
| Wyoming.............. | 123 | 78 | 63 | 1 | 1 | 44 | 36 | 45 | 37 |
| Puerto Rico........... | 290 | 169 | 58 | 23 | 8 | 96 | 33 | 119 | 41 |

[1] Total fatalities include those in which there was no driver or motorcycle rider present. [2] U.S. total excludes Puerto Rico.

Source: U.S. National Highway Traffic Safety Administration, "Traffic Safety Facts Annual Report Tables," <https://cdan.nhtsa.gov/tsftables/tsfar.htm>, accessed June 2019. See also <https://www.nhtsa.gov/research-data>.

## Table 1134. Alcohol Involvement for Drivers in Fatal Crashes: 2000 to 2017

[BAC = blood alcohol concentration. See headnote, Table 1133. NHTSA estimates alcohol involvement when alcohol test results are unknown, see source for more information]

| Age, sex, and vehicle type | 2000 Total drivers in fatal crashes | 2000 Percent with .08% BAC or greater | 2010 Total drivers in fatal crashes | 2010 Percent with .08% BAC or greater | 2015 Total drivers in fatal crashes | 2015 Percent with .08% BAC or greater | 2016 Total drivers in fatal crashes | 2016 Percent with .08% BAC or greater | 2017 Total drivers in fatal crashes | 2017 Percent with .08% BAC or greater |
|---|---|---|---|---|---|---|---|---|---|---|
| **Total drivers involved in fatal crashes [1]** | **57,280** | **21** | **44,599** | **22** | **49,163** | **20** | **52,399** | **20** | **52,274** | **20** |
| Drivers by age group: | | | | | | | | | | |
| Under 16 years old | 320 | 10 | 159 | 6 | 155 | 9 | 178 | 10 | 145 | 7 |
| 16 to 20 years old | 8,024 | 18 | 4,505 | 18 | 4,258 | 16 | 4,453 | 15 | 4,278 | 15 |
| 21 to 24 years old | 5,950 | 32 | 4,608 | 34 | 5,014 | 28 | 5,284 | 27 | 5,007 | 27 |
| 25 to 34 years old | 11,739 | 28 | 8,567 | 30 | 9,994 | 27 | 10,913 | 27 | 10,876 | 26 |
| 35 to 44 years old | 11,132 | 26 | 7,333 | 25 | 7,768 | 23 | 8,179 | 22 | 8,217 | 23 |
| 45 to 54 years old | 8,234 | 18 | 7,517 | 21 | 7,915 | 19 | 8,023 | 19 | 8,118 | 19 |
| 55 to 64 years old | 4,766 | 12 | 5,577 | 14 | 6,525 | 14 | 7,037 | 14 | 7,271 | 15 |
| 65 to 74 years old | 3,134 | 8 | 2,902 | 8 | 3,794 | 9 | 4,155 | 9 | 4,107 | 9 |
| 75 years old and over | 3,147 | 4 | 2,688 | 4 | 2,762 | 6 | 3,014 | 5 | 3,120 | 6 |
| Drivers by sex: | | | | | | | | | | |
| Male | 41,795 | 24 | 32,079 | 24 | 35,850 | 22 | 37,941 | 21 | 37,654 | 21 |
| Female | 14,790 | 13 | 11,859 | 15 | 12,382 | 14 | 13,376 | 14 | 13,555 | 14 |
| Drivers by vehicle type: | | | | | | | | | | |
| Passenger cars | 27,661 | 24 | 17,710 | 24 | 19,689 | 21 | 20,965 | 21 | 20,895 | 21 |
| Light trucks [2] | 20,393 | 22 | 17,385 | 22 | 18,762 | 21 | 20,112 | 20 | 19,847 | 20 |
| Large trucks [3] | 4,948 | 1 | 3,456 | 1 | 4,020 | 2 | 4,193 | 2 | 4,600 | 3 |
| Motorcycles | 2,971 | 32 | 4,647 | 28 | 5,126 | 26 | 5,460 | 26 | 5,316 | 27 |

[1] Includes age and sex unknown, and other and unknown types of vehicles. [2] See footnote 2, Table 1131. [3] See footnote 3, Table 1131.

Source: U.S. National Highway Traffic Safety Administration, "Traffic Safety Facts Annual Report Tables," <https://cdan.nhtsa.gov/tsftables/tsfar.htm> accessed June 2019. See also <https://www.nhtsa.gov/research-data>.

## Table 1135. Fatalities by Highest Driver Blood Alcohol Concentration (BAC) in the Crash: 2000 to 2017

[A motor vehicle crash is alcohol impaired if at least one driver involved in the crash is determined to have a BAC of .08 gram per deciliter (g/dl) or higher. Thus, any fatality that occurs in an alcohol impaired crash is considered an alcohol impaired driving fatality. A person is considered to be legally impaired with a BAC of .08 g/dl or more. See source for more information]

| Item | 2000 | 2005 | 2010 | 2013 | 2014 | 2015 | 2016 | 2017 |
|---|---|---|---|---|---|---|---|---|
| **Total fatalities [1]** | **41,945** | **43,510** | **32,999** | **32,893** | **32,744** | **35,484** | **37,806** | **37,133** |
| BAC=.00 | | | | | | | | |
| Number | 26,082 | 27,423 | 21,005 | 20,865 | 20,913 | 23,165 | 24,732 | 24,280 |
| Percent | 62.2 | 63.0 | 63.7 | 63.4 | 63.9 | 65.3 | 65.4 | 65.4 |
| BAC=.01–.07 | | | | | | | | |
| Number | 2,422 | 2,404 | 1,771 | 1,834 | 1,800 | 1,930 | 1,985 | 1,873 |
| Percent | 5.8 | 5.5 | 5.4 | 5.6 | 5.5 | 5.4 | 5.3 | 5.0 |
| Alcohol impaired driving fatalities: | | | | | | | | |
| BAC=.08 or more | | | | | | | | |
| Number | 13,324 | 13,582 | 10,136 | 10,084 | 9,943 | 10,280 | 10,996 | 10,874 |
| Percent | 31.8 | 31.2 | 30.7 | 30.7 | 30.4 | 29.0 | 29.1 | 29.3 |

[1] Total fatalities include those in which there was no driver or motorcycle rider present.

Source: U.S. National Highway Traffic Safety Administration, "Traffic Safety Facts Annual Report Tables," <https://cdan.nhtsa.gov/tsftables/tsfar.htm>, accessed June 2019. See also <https://www.nhtsa.gov/research-data>.

## Table 1136. Motor Vehicle Crashes by Crash Severity: 2000 to 2017

[6,394 represents 6,394,000. A crash is a police-reported event that produces injury and/or property damage, involves a vehicle in transport, and occurs on a trafficway or while the vehicle is in motion after running off the trafficway. A fatal crash involves at least 1 person dying within 30 days of the crash. Beginning 2016, data for injury and property damage crashes are not comparable to previous years due to a new data collection system. The National Automotive Sampling System (NASS) General Estimates System (GES) was replaced with the Crash Report Sampling System (CRSS). See <https://crashstats.nhtsa.dot.gov/Api/Public/ViewPublication/812509> for details]

| Item | 2000 | 2010 | 2011 | 2012 | 2013 | 2014 | 2015 | 2016 [1] | 2017 [1] |
|---|---|---|---|---|---|---|---|---|---|
| **Crashes (1,000)** | **6,394** | **5,419** | **5,338** | **5,615** | **5,687** | **6,064** | **6,296** | **6,821** | **6,452** |
| Fatal | 37.5 | 30.3 | 29.9 | 31.0 | 30.2 | 30.1 | 32.5 | 34.7 | 34.2 |
| Nonfatal injury | 2,070 | 1,542 | 1,530 | 1,634 | 1,591 | 1,648 | 1,715 | 2,116 | 1,889 |
| Property damage only | 4,286 | 3,847 | 3,778 | 3,950 | 4,066 | 4,387 | 4,548 | 4,670 | 4,530 |
| Percent of total crashes: | | | | | | | | | |
| Fatal | 0.6 | 0.6 | 0.6 | 0.6 | 0.5 | 0.5 | 0.5 | 0.5 | 0.5 |
| Nonfatal injury | 32.4 | 28.5 | 28.7 | 29.1 | 28.0 | 27.2 | 27.2 | 31.0 | 29.3 |
| Property damage only | 67.0 | 71.0 | 70.8 | 70.3 | 71.5 | 72.3 | 72.2 | 68.5 | 70.2 |

[1] Beginning 2016, injury and property damage only data are not comparable to previous years due to a new data collection system. Numbers are not actual counts but estimates of actual counts.

Source: U.S. National Highway Traffic Safety Administration, "Traffic Safety Facts Annual Report Tables," <https://cdan.nhtsa.gov/tsftables/tsfar.htm>, accessed June 2019. See also <https://www.nhtsa.gov/research-data>.

## Table 1137. Motor Vehicle Crashes—Number and Deaths: 2000 to 2017

[6,394 represents 6,394,000. Beginning 2016, data for injury and property damage crashes are not comparable to previous years due to a new data collection system. The National Automotive Sampling System (NASS) General Estimates System (GES) was replaced with the Crash Report Sampling System (CRSS). See <https://crashstats.nhtsa.dot.gov/Api/Public/ViewPublication/812509> for details]

| Item | Unit | 2000 | 2010 | 2012 | 2013 | 2014 | 2015 | 2016 | 2017 |
|---|---|---|---|---|---|---|---|---|---|
| CRASHES | | | | | | | | | |
| **Total [1,2]** | **1,000** | **6,394** | **5,419** | **5,615** | **5,687** | **6,064** | **6,296** | **6,821** | **6,452** |
| Fatal. | 1,000 | 37.5 | 30.3 | 31.0 | 30.2 | 30.1 | 32.5 | 34.7 | 34.2 |
| Injury [2] | 1,000 | 2,070 | 1,542 | 1,634 | 1,591 | 1,648 | 1,715 | 2,116 | 1,889 |
| Property damage only [2] | 1,000 | 4,286 | 3,847 | 3,950 | 4,066 | 4,387 | 4,548 | 4,670 | 4,530 |
| DEATHS | | | | | | | | | |
| **Deaths within 30 days of crash** | **1,000** | **41.9** | **33.0** | **33.8** | **32.9** | **32.7** | **35.5** | **37.8** | **37.1** |
| Occupants | 1,000 | 33.5 | 23.4 | 23.0 | 22.5 | 22.3 | 23.9 | 25.3 | 25.0 |
| Passenger cars | 1,000 | 20.7 | 12.5 | 12.4 | 12.0 | 11.9 | 12.8 | 13.5 | 13.4 |
| Light trucks [3] | 1,000 | 11.5 | 9.8 | 9.4 | 9.2 | 9.1 | 9.9 | 10.4 | 10.2 |
| Large trucks [3] | 1,000 | 0.8 | 0.5 | 0.7 | 0.7 | 0.7 | 0.7 | 0.7 | 0.8 |
| Buses | 1,000 | (Z) | (Z) | (Z) | 0.1 | (Z) | (Z) | 0.1 | (Z) |
| Other/unknown | 1,000 | 0.5 | 0.5 | 0.5 | 0.5 | 0.6 | 0.5 | 0.6 | 0.5 |
| Motorcycle riders [4] | 1,000 | 2.9 | 4.5 | 5.0 | 4.7 | 4.6 | 5.0 | 5.3 | 5.2 |
| Nonoccupants | 1,000 | 5.6 | 5.1 | 5.8 | 5.7 | 5.8 | 6.6 | 7.2 | 7.0 |
| Pedestrians | 1,000 | 4.8 | 4.3 | 4.8 | 4.8 | 4.9 | 5.5 | 6.1 | 6.0 |
| Pedalcyclist | 1,000 | 0.7 | 0.6 | 0.7 | 0.7 | 0.7 | 0.8 | 0.9 | 0.8 |
| Other/unknown | 1,000 | 0.1 | 0.2 | 0.2 | 0.2 | 0.2 | 0.2 | 0.3 | 0.2 |
| TRAFFIC DEATH RATES [5] | | | | | | | | | |
| Per 100 million vehicle miles | Rate | 1.5 | 1.1 | 1.1 | 1.1 | 1.1 | 1.2 | 1.2 | 1.2 |
| Per 100,000 licensed drivers | Rate | 22.0 | 15.7 | 16.0 | 15.5 | 15.3 | 16.3 | 17.1 | 16.5 |
| Per 100,000 registered vehicles | Rate | 19.3 | 12.8 | 12.7 | 12.2 | 11.9 | 12.6 | 13.1 | 12.8 |
| Per 100,000 resident population | Rate | 14.9 | 10.7 | 10.8 | 10.4 | 10.3 | 11.1 | 11.7 | 11.4 |

Z Represents less than 50 deaths. [1] Covers police-reported accidents in which at least one person dies within 30 days of the crash; or no one dies but at least one person is injured; or no one is injured but property damage has occurred. [2] Beginning 2016, injury and property damage only data are not comparable to previous years due to a new data collection system. Numbers are not actual counts but estimates of actual counts. [3] See footnotes 2 and 3 in Table 1131. [4] Includes motor scooters, minibikes, and mopeds. [5] Based on 30-day definition of traffic deaths.

Source: U.S. National Highway Traffic Safety Administration, "Traffic Safety Facts Annual Report Tables," <https://cdan.nhtsa.gov/tsftables/tsfar.htm>, accessed June 2019. See also <https://www.nhtsa.gov/research-data>.

## Table 1138. Licensed Drivers and Number in Fatal Accidents by Age and Sex: 2017

[111,401 represents 111,401,000]

| Age group | Licensed drivers (1,000) | | | Drivers in fatal accidents | | | Accident rates per number of drivers [2] | |
|---|---|---|---|---|---|---|---|---|
| | Total | Male | Female | Total [1] | Male | Female | Male | Female |
| **Total** | **225,346** | **111,401** | **113,945** | **52,274** | **37,654** | **13,555** | **33.8** | **11.9** |
| 19 years old and under | 8,843 | 4,484 | 4,360 | 3,317 | 2,313 | 1,002 | 51.4 | 22.9 |
| Under 16 years old | 77 | 38 | 39 | 145 | 107 | 38 | 263.0 | 90.7 |
| 16 years old | 1,100 | 544 | 555 | 445 | 288 | 156 | 52.9 | 28.1 |
| 17 years old | 1,990 | 999 | 991 | 671 | 453 | 218 | 45.3 | 22.0 |
| 18 years old | 2,629 | 1,342 | 1,286 | 992 | 696 | 295 | 51.9 | 22.9 |
| 19 years old | 3,049 | 1,560 | 1,489 | 1,064 | 769 | 295 | 49.3 | 19.8 |
| 20 to 24 years old | 17,611 | 8,924 | 8,687 | 6,113 | 4,442 | 1,669 | 49.8 | 19.2 |
| 20 years old | 3,253 | 1,661 | 1,593 | 1,106 | 787 | 318 | 47.4 | 20.0 |
| 21 years old | 3,365 | 1,708 | 1,657 | 1,249 | 885 | 363 | 51.8 | 21.9 |
| 22 years old | 3,528 | 1,788 | 1,740 | 1,214 | 863 | 351 | 48.3 | 20.2 |
| 23 years old | 3,667 | 1,850 | 1,817 | 1,244 | 929 | 315 | 50.2 | 17.3 |
| 24 years old | 3,797 | 1,917 | 1,880 | 1,300 | 978 | 322 | 51.0 | 17.1 |
| 25 to 29 years old | 20,076 | 10,038 | 10,038 | 5,973 | 4,378 | 1,595 | 43.6 | 15.9 |
| 30 to 34 years old | 19,755 | 9,835 | 9,921 | 4,903 | 3,620 | 1,279 | 36.8 | 12.9 |
| 35 to 39 years old | 19,194 | 9,518 | 9,677 | 4,387 | 3,239 | 1,147 | 34.0 | 11.9 |
| 40 to 44 years old | 17,897 | 8,885 | 9,011 | 3,830 | 2,847 | 981 | 32.0 | 10.9 |
| 45 to 49 years old | 19,345 | 9,628 | 9,717 | 4,114 | 3,074 | 1,038 | 31.9 | 10.7 |
| 50 to 54 years old | 19,831 | 9,850 | 9,981 | 4,004 | 3,015 | 989 | 30.6 | 9.9 |
| 55 to 59 years old | 20,502 | 10,100 | 10,402 | 4,025 | 3,060 | 964 | 30.3 | 9.3 |
| 60 to 64 years old | 18,677 | 9,138 | 9,540 | 3,246 | 2,474 | 771 | 27.1 | 8.1 |
| 65 to 69 years old | 15,626 | 7,609 | 8,017 | 2,316 | 1,695 | 621 | 22.3 | 7.7 |
| 70 to 74 years old | 11,705 | 5,690 | 6,015 | 1,791 | 1,267 | 524 | 22.3 | 8.7 |
| 75 to 79 years old | 7,581 | 3,637 | 3,944 | 1,292 | 891 | 401 | 24.5 | 10.2 |
| 80 to 84 years old | 4,723 | 2,238 | 2,485 | 934 | 642 | 292 | 28.7 | 11.8 |
| 85 and over | 3,980 | 1,828 | 2,152 | 894 | 627 | 267 | 34.3 | 12.4 |

[1] Total includes unknown/unreported instances. [2] Per 100,000 male or female licensed drivers. Rates for drivers 19 years old and under are likely overstated because of a higher proportion of unlicensed drivers.

Source: U.S. Federal Highway Administration, "Highway Statistics 2017," <https://www.fhwa.dot.gov/policyinformation/>; and National Highway Traffic Safety Administration, "Fatality Analysis Reporting System," <http://www.nhtsa.gov/FARS>; accessed September 2019.

# Table 1139. Speeding-Related Traffic Fatalities by Road Type and State: 2017

[Speeding consists of exceeding the posted speed limit or driving too fast for the road conditions or any speed-related violation charged (racing, driving above speed limit, speed greater than reasonable, exceeding special speed limit)]

| State | Traffic fatalities, total | Speeding-related fatalities by roadway function class | | | | | | | |
|---|---|---|---|---|---|---|---|---|---|
| | | Total [2] | Interstate | | Non-interstate | | | | |
| | | | Rural | Urban | Freeway and expressway | Other principal arterial | Minor arterial | Collector | Local |
| **United States [1]** | **37,133** | **9,717** | **517** | **776** | **455** | **2,429** | **1,896** | **1,896** | **1,638** |
| Alabama | 948 | 257 | 20 | 8 | – | 35 | 57 | 104 | 33 |
| Alaska | 79 | 26 | 4 | 3 | – | 6 | 2 | 5 | 6 |
| Arizona | 1,000 | 299 | 36 | 32 | 22 | 81 | 45 | 38 | 45 |
| Arkansas | 493 | 116 | 14 | 9 | – | 23 | 21 | 35 | 14 |
| California | 3,602 | 1,070 | 44 | 117 | 157 | 273 | 230 | 154 | 93 |
| Colorado | 648 | 230 | 7 | 19 | 10 | 79 | 43 | 42 | 29 |
| Connecticut | 278 | 88 | 1 | 12 | 7 | 15 | 30 | 10 | 13 |
| Delaware | 119 | 33 | – | – | 2 | 3 | 10 | 7 | 9 |
| District of Columbia | 31 | 17 | – | – | – | – | – | – | 17 |
| Florida | 3,112 | 299 | 9 | 14 | 8 | 72 | 53 | 41 | 40 |
| Georgia | 1,540 | 248 | 9 | 36 | 2 | 53 | 47 | 54 | 47 |
| Hawaii | 107 | 50 | – | 2 | – | 32 | 13 | 1 | 2 |
| Idaho | 244 | 48 | 5 | 3 | – | 11 | 5 | 5 | 1 |
| Illinois | 1,097 | 462 | 28 | 68 | 2 | 116 | 101 | 101 | 44 |
| Indiana | 914 | 208 | 13 | 11 | 1 | 40 | 49 | 52 | 42 |
| Iowa | 330 | 70 | 6 | – | – | 16 | 6 | 21 | 21 |
| Kansas | 461 | 104 | 8 | 6 | 2 | 21 | 9 | 9 | 49 |
| Kentucky | 782 | 138 | 4 | 8 | 2 | 24 | 29 | 39 | 32 |
| Louisiana | 760 | 177 | 6 | 21 | 2 | 18 | 43 | 52 | 35 |
| Maine | 172 | 49 | – | 1 | 1 | 10 | 10 | 18 | 9 |
| Maryland | 550 | 160 | 1 | 20 | 9 | 43 | 30 | 34 | 20 |
| Massachusetts | 350 | 98 | 2 | 17 | 3 | 25 | 25 | 8 | 18 |
| Michigan | 1,030 | 241 | 2 | 17 | 5 | 52 | 61 | 56 | 47 |
| Minnesota | 357 | 89 | 8 | 8 | 2 | 19 | 22 | 13 | 17 |
| Mississippi | 690 | 59 | 4 | 4 | – | 18 | 7 | 20 | 6 |
| Missouri | 930 | 346 | 12 | 36 | 14 | 52 | 66 | 107 | 59 |
| Montana | 186 | 59 | 12 | – | – | 15 | 4 | 12 | 16 |
| Nebraska | 228 | 37 | 1 | – | 2 | 13 | 7 | 5 | 9 |
| Nevada | 309 | 95 | 4 | 9 | 5 | 23 | 30 | 11 | 12 |
| New Hampshire | 102 | 58 | 4 | 6 | – | 15 | 3 | 15 | 15 |
| New Jersey | 624 | 120 | – | 3 | 8 | 44 | 16 | 23 | 24 |
| New Mexico | 379 | 141 | 14 | 9 | – | 55 | 19 | 23 | 20 |
| New York | 999 | 308 | 15 | 7 | 19 | 72 | 25 | 18 | 152 |
| North Carolina | 1,412 | 423 | 23 | 27 | 1 | 257 | 1 | 10 | 104 |
| North Dakota | 115 | 28 | 1 | 1 | 1 | 13 | 1 | 2 | 8 |
| Ohio | 1,179 | 252 | 4 | 19 | 15 | 28 | 44 | 96 | 44 |
| Oklahoma | 655 | 143 | 7 | 6 | 2 | 25 | 24 | 46 | 33 |
| Oregon | 437 | 119 | 2 | 7 | – | 51 | 22 | 26 | 11 |
| Pennsylvania | 1,137 | 468 | 31 | 24 | 16 | 104 | 98 | 98 | 97 |
| Rhode Island | 83 | 41 | 3 | 6 | 6 | 9 | 3 | – | 14 |
| South Carolina | 988 | 416 | 37 | 10 | 13 | 104 | 182 | 26 | 44 |
| South Dakota | 129 | 31 | 5 | – | – | 5 | 2 | 14 | 5 |
| Tennessee | 1,040 | 166 | 8 | 8 | 5 | 36 | 35 | 39 | 35 |
| Texas | 3,722 | 1,029 | 56 | 105 | 98 | 232 | 211 | 213 | 111 |
| Utah | 273 | 78 | 7 | 7 | – | 30 | 10 | 12 | 11 |
| Vermont | 69 | 31 | 3 | – | 3 | 7 | 8 | 2 | 8 |
| Virginia | 839 | 219 | 10 | 14 | 4 | 37 | 50 | 64 | 37 |
| Washington | 565 | 172 | 9 | 21 | 4 | 42 | 33 | 46 | 15 |
| West Virginia | 303 | 84 | 2 | 7 | – | 15 | 22 | 25 | 11 |
| Wisconsin | 613 | 180 | 10 | 6 | 2 | 50 | 24 | 41 | 46 |
| Wyoming | 123 | 37 | 6 | 2 | – | 10 | 8 | 3 | 8 |
| Puerto Rico | 290 | 77 | 11 | 6 | 1 | 24 | 17 | 16 | 2 |

– Represents zero. [1] U.S. totals do not include Puerto Rico. [2] Includes fatalities that occurred on roads for which the type was unknown.

Source: U.S. National Highway Traffic Safety Administration, "Traffic Safety Facts Annual Report Tables," <https://cdan.nhtsa.gov/tsftables/tsfar.htm> accessed June 2019. See also <https://www.nhtsa.gov/research-data>.

# Table 1140. Roadway Traffic Congestion by Urbanized Area: 2014

[15,142 represents 15,142,000. Various federal, state, and local information sources were used to develop the database with the primary source being the Federal Highway Administration's Highway Performance Monitoring System]

| Urbanized area | Daily vehicle miles of travel (1,000) | | Annual person hours of delay | | Annual congestion cost [1] | | |
|---|---|---|---|---|---|---|---|
| | Freeway | Arterial streets | Total hours (1,000) | Per auto commuter [2] | Delay and fuel cost (million dollars) | Per person (dollars) [2] | Fuel wasted (gal. per person) [2] |
| **U.S., average** | **15,142** | **14,786** | **59,767** | **52** | **1,371** | **1,189** | **23** |
| Akron, OH | 5,847 | 4,493 | 12,283 | 27 | 284 | 634 | 15 |
| Albany-Schenectady, NY | 7,273 | 5,623 | 20,409 | 42 | 479 | 991 | 21 |
| Albuquerque, NM | 4,736 | 7,834 | 20,452 | 36 | 501 | 886 | 19 |
| Allentown, PA-NJ | 5,427 | 5,231 | 17,114 | 30 | 393 | 694 | 15 |
| Atlanta, GA | 51,003 | 46,002 | 148,666 | 52 | 3,214 | 1,130 | 20 |
| Austin, TX | 13,273 | 11,237 | 51,116 | 52 | 1,140 | 1,159 | 22 |
| Baltimore, MD | 28,412 | 19,258 | 87,620 | 47 | 2,075 | 1,115 | 21 |
| Birmingham, AL | 10,059 | 7,473 | 19,385 | 34 | 501 | 891 | 16 |
| Boston, MA-NH-RI | 41,097 | 36,127 | 153,994 | 64 | 3,363 | 1,388 | 30 |
| Bridgeport-Stamford, CT-NY | 10,030 | 5,649 | 37,119 | 49 | 898 | 1,174 | 22 |
| Buffalo, NY | 6,709 | 9,164 | 26,851 | 40 | 620 | 918 | 21 |
| Charleston-North, Charleston, SC | 3,971 | 6,141 | 18,422 | 41 | 470 | 1,047 | 20 |
| Charlotte, NC-SC | 12,776 | 10,348 | 34,153 | 43 | 770 | 963 | 17 |
| Chicago, IL-IN | 57,279 | 79,284 | 302,609 | 61 | 7,222 | 1,445 | 29 |
| Cincinnati, OH-KY-IN | 18,088 | 15,593 | 48,485 | 41 | 1,159 | 989 | 21 |
| Cleveland, OH | 18,297 | 13,364 | 45,051 | 38 | 1,046 | 887 | 22 |
| Colorado Springs, CO | 4,652 | 5,366 | 16,058 | 35 | 356 | 772 | 17 |
| Columbus OH | 16,360 | 11,421 | 40,025 | 41 | 921 | 933 | 20 |
| Dallas-Fort, Worth-Arlington, TX | 64,411 | 41,713 | 186,535 | 53 | 4,202 | 1,185 | 22 |
| Dayton, OH | 7,006 | 5,280 | 14,604 | 25 | 346 | 590 | 13 |
| Denver-Aurora, CO | 21,709 | 21,048 | 91,479 | 49 | 2,061 | 1,101 | 24 |
| Detroit, MI | 33,441 | 44,627 | 155,358 | 52 | 3,514 | 1,183 | 25 |
| El Paso, TX-NM | 5,777 | 5,633 | 19,127 | 33 | 439 | 760 | 16 |
| Fresno, CA | 3,160 | 7,289 | 11,823 | 23 | 251 | 495 | 11 |
| Grand Rapids, MI | 5,617 | 7,539 | 21,536 | 39 | 470 | 854 | 19 |
| Hartford, CT | 11,022 | 7,073 | 28,296 | 45 | 656 | 1,038 | 21 |
| Honolulu, HI | 6,066 | 3,252 | 27,672 | 50 | 616 | 1,125 | 26 |
| Houston, TX | 51,673 | 39,211 | 203,173 | 61 | 4,924 | 1,490 | 29 |
| Indianapolis, IN | 12,735 | 16,382 | 46,435 | 43 | 1,142 | 1,060 | 23 |
| Jackson, MS | 4,602 | 6,208 | 12,287 | 38 | 282 | 878 | 15 |
| Jacksonville, FL | 11,801 | 9,189 | 29,680 | 38 | 659 | 842 | 15 |
| Kansas City, MO-KS | 22,986 | 12,479 | 45,570 | 39 | 1,085 | 933 | 18 |
| Las Vegas -Henderson, NV | 11,297 | 14,267 | 63,693 | 46 | 1,375 | 984 | 21 |
| Los Angeles-Long Beach-Anaheim, CA | 121,603 | 119,049 | 622,509 | 80 | 13,318 | 1,711 | 25 |
| Louisville-Jefferson Co., KY-IN | 12,020 | 9,178 | 35,622 | 43 | 860 | 1,048 | 22 |
| Memphis, TN-MS-AR | 9,339 | 13,122 | 37,824 | 43 | 939 | 1,080 | 21 |
| Miami, FL | 40,928 | 49,525 | 195,946 | 52 | 4,444 | 1,169 | 24 |
| Milwaukee, WI | 11,170 | 14,241 | 37,659 | 38 | 984 | 987 | 22 |
| Minneapolis-St Paul, MN-WI | 30,259 | 26,451 | 99,710 | 47 | 2,196 | 1,035 | 18 |
| Nashville-Davidson, TN | 16,339 | 11,781 | 38,977 | 45 | 1,013 | 1,168 | 22 |
| New Haven, CT | 7,820 | 3,929 | 16,430 | 40 | 384 | 932 | 19 |
| New Orleans, LA | 5,422 | 8,239 | 39,159 | 45 | 1,014 | 1,161 | 22 |
| New York-Newark, NY-NJ-CT | 122,655 | 110,098 | 628,241 | 74 | 14,712 | 1,739 | 35 |
| Oklahoma City, OK | 11,088 | 13,287 | 45,652 | 49 | 1,030 | 1,110 | 23 |
| Omaha, NE-IA | 5,369 | 5,978 | 18,224 | 32 | 407 | 707 | 17 |
| Orlando, FL | 12,928 | 17,251 | 52,723 | 46 | 1,207 | 1,044 | 21 |
| Oxnard, CA | 2,093 | 3,255 | 6,282 | 23 | 134 | 494 | 8 |
| Philadelphia, PA-NJ-DE-MD | 36,224 | 45,884 | 157,183 | 48 | 3,669 | 1,112 | 23 |
| Phoenix-Mesa, AZ | 29,548 | 39,686 | 155,730 | 51 | 3,641 | 1,201 | 25 |
| Pittsburgh, PA | 9,093 | 14,740 | 44,758 | 39 | 1,030 | 889 | 21 |
| Portland, OR-WA | 13,874 | 13,882 | 72,341 | 52 | 1,763 | 1,273 | 29 |
| Providence, RI-MA | 11,302 | 10,286 | 37,809 | 43 | 846 | 951 | 21 |
| Raleigh, NC | 8,588 | 10,138 | 23,128 | 34 | 504 | 734 | 13 |
| Richmond, VA | 11,719 | 9,492 | 26,104 | 34 | 558 | 729 | 14 |
| Riverside-San Bernardino, CA | 32,679 | 17,079 | 99,058 | 59 | 2,201 | 1,316 | 18 |
| Sacramento, CA | 16,200 | 17,371 | 60,220 | 43 | 1,334 | 958 | 19 |
| Salt Lake City-West Valley City, UT | 8,600 | 8,400 | 26,925 | 37 | 779 | 1,059 | 22 |
| San Antonio, TX | 21,270 | 12,956 | 64,328 | 44 | 1,462 | 1,002 | 20 |
| San Diego, CA | 39,817 | 22,543 | 79,412 | 42 | 1,658 | 887 | 11 |
| San Francisco-Oakland, CA | 28,137 | 24,086 | 146,013 | 78 | 3,143 | 1,675 | 33 |
| San Jose, CA | 27,553 | 17,794 | 104,559 | 67 | 2,230 | 1,422 | 28 |
| Seattle, WA | 28,010 | 27,708 | 139,842 | 63 | 3,294 | 1,491 | 28 |
| St Louis, MO-IL | 31,260 | 19,537 | 69,350 | 43 | 1,637 | 1,020 | 21 |
| Tampa-St Petersburg, FL | 14,418 | 27,894 | 71,628 | 41 | 1,589 | 907 | 18 |
| Toledo, OH-MI | 4,332 | 4,729 | 15,905 | 38 | 381 | 920 | 20 |
| Tucson, AZ | 3,826 | 11,760 | 35,993 | 47 | 856 | 1,128 | 23 |
| Tulsa, OK | 8,036 | 9,129 | 30,341 | 44 | 682 | 984 | 20 |
| Virginia Beach, VA | 13,003 | 15,875 | 48,274 | 45 | 1,020 | 953 | 19 |
| Washington, DC-VA-MD | 39,071 | 45,433 | 204,375 | 82 | 4,560 | 1,834 | 35 |
| Worcester, MA | 6,107 | 5,243 | 13,143 | 38 | 302 | 865 | 18 |

[1] Value of extra time (delay) and the extra fuel consumed by vehicles traveling at slower speeds. Fuel cost per gallon is the average price for each state. [2] Per auto commuter data are based on estimated commuters in the urban area.

Source: Texas A&M Transportation Institute, College Station, Texas, *2015 Urban Mobility Report*, August 2015 ©. See also <http://mobility.tamu.edu/ums/>.

# Table 1141. Commuting to Work by Transportation Method and State: 2017

[In percent, except as indicated. Workers in thousands (152,803 represents 152,803,000). For workers 16 years old and over. The American Community Survey universe includes the household population and the population living in institutions, college dormitories, and other group quarters. Based on a sample and subject to sampling variability; see Appendix III]

| State | Total workers (1,000) | Car, truck, or van | | Public transpor- tation [1] | Walking | Taxi, motorcycle, bicycle or other means | Working at home | Mean travel time to work (minutes) |
|---|---|---|---|---|---|---|---|---|
| | | Drove alone | Car- pooled | | | | | |
| U.S............ | 152,803 | 76.4 | 8.9 | 5.0 | 2.7 | 1.8 | 5.2 | 26.9 |
| AL.............. | 2,042 | 85.7 | 8.5 | 0.4 | 1.2 | 1.0 | 3.4 | 24.6 |
| AK.............. | 351 | 69.3 | 11.8 | 1.7 | 7.4 | 5.3 | 4.6 | 19.6 |
| AZ.............. | 3,086 | 76.5 | 11.0 | 1.8 | 2.0 | 2.4 | 6.3 | 25.6 |
| AR.............. | 1,282 | 83.3 | 9.9 | 0.3 | 1.8 | 1.0 | 3.7 | 21.6 |
| CA.............. | 18,321 | 73.9 | 10.0 | 5.0 | 2.6 | 2.5 | 6.0 | 29.8 |
| CO.............. | 2,887 | 74.9 | 8.6 | 3.2 | 2.7 | 2.2 | 8.5 | 25.9 |
| CT.............. | 1,778 | 78.3 | 7.9 | 4.7 | 2.8 | 1.3 | 5.1 | 26.4 |
| DE.............. | 431 | 82.0 | 7.1 | 2.2 | 2.2 | 1.2 | 5.2 | 26.5 |
| DC.............. | 375 | 34.4 | 5.2 | 32.7 | 12.7 | 7.7 | 7.4 | 30.8 |
| FL.............. | 9,355 | 79.4 | 9.1 | 1.7 | 1.4 | 2.3 | 6.1 | 27.8 |
| GA.............. | 4,783 | 78.7 | 9.9 | 2.1 | 1.6 | 1.9 | 5.8 | 28.8 |
| HI.............. | 704 | 67.6 | 13.3 | 6.1 | 5.5 | 3.2 | 4.4 | 27.0 |
| ID.............. | 774 | 79.1 | 10.2 | 0.6 | 2.3 | 2.2 | 5.7 | 21.0 |
| IL.............. | 6,129 | 73.0 | 7.8 | 9.6 | 2.9 | 1.8 | 4.9 | 29.1 |
| IN.............. | 3,126 | 82.4 | 8.7 | 0.9 | 2.1 | 1.5 | 4.3 | 23.6 |
| IA.............. | 1,597 | 81.4 | 8.0 | 0.9 | 3.2 | 1.4 | 5.1 | 19.4 |
| KS.............. | 1,431 | 82.4 | 8.7 | 0.4 | 2.3 | 1.4 | 4.7 | 19.1 |
| KY.............. | 1,949 | 82.0 | 9.4 | 1.1 | 2.1 | 1.5 | 3.9 | 23.3 |
| LA.............. | 2,003 | 82.7 | 9.2 | 1.1 | 1.7 | 2.0 | 3.3 | 25.3 |
| ME.............. | 658 | 78.6 | 9.4 | 0.6 | 4.1 | 1.5 | 5.9 | 24.0 |
| MD.............. | 3,061 | 73.7 | 9.1 | 8.5 | 2.1 | 1.6 | 4.9 | 33.3 |
| MA.............. | 3,526 | 70.0 | 7.2 | 10.4 | 4.8 | 2.2 | 5.3 | 29.8 |
| MI.............. | 4,561 | 82.5 | 8.7 | 1.3 | 2.2 | 1.2 | 4.2 | 24.3 |
| MN.............. | 2,909 | 78.0 | 8.2 | 3.7 | 2.6 | 1.6 | 5.9 | 23.8 |
| MS.............. | 1,215 | 85.5 | 9.1 | 0.3 | 1.4 | 1.5 | 2.3 | 24.9 |
| MO.............. | 2,882 | 82.2 | 8.4 | 1.3 | 1.9 | 1.1 | 5.1 | 23.7 |
| MT.............. | 509 | 76.5 | 8.9 | 0.8 | 4.9 | 2.3 | 6.5 | 18.1 |
| NE.............. | 997 | 81.7 | 9.1 | 0.7 | 2.7 | 1.1 | 4.7 | 18.5 |
| NV.............. | 1,403 | 78.5 | 9.8 | 3.1 | 1.9 | 2.4 | 4.3 | 24.2 |
| NH.............. | 713 | 80.9 | 8.3 | 0.7 | 2.4 | 1.4 | 6.2 | 27.3 |
| NJ.............. | 4,410 | 71.0 | 7.9 | 11.8 | 2.9 | 1.8 | 4.6 | 32.1 |
| NM.............. | 867 | 79.4 | 10.6 | 1.1 | 2.0 | 1.8 | 5.1 | 22.3 |
| NY.............. | 9,428 | 53.1 | 6.3 | 28.1 | 6.2 | 2.0 | 4.3 | 33.7 |
| NC.............. | 4,780 | 81.1 | 8.9 | 1.0 | 1.7 | 1.3 | 6.1 | 24.9 |
| ND.............. | 105 | 81.6 | 8.2 | 0.6 | 3.8 | 1.2 | 1.6 | 16.5 |
| OH.............. | 5,477 | 83.3 | 7.7 | 1.5 | 2.1 | 1.2 | 4.2 | 23.6 |
| OK.............. | 1,745 | 82.3 | 9.8 | 0.3 | 1.9 | 1.4 | 4.3 | 21.9 |
| OR.............. | 1,953 | 71.7 | 9.7 | 4.5 | 3.7 | 3.1 | 7.4 | 24.3 |
| PA.............. | 6,056 | 76.2 | 8.5 | 5.3 | 3.5 | 1.5 | 5.0 | 27.1 |
| RI.............. | 522 | 79.4 | 9.4 | 2.2 | 3.6 | 0.9 | 4.5 | 25.1 |
| SC.............. | 2,260 | 81.8 | 9.5 | 0.5 | 2.1 | 1.4 | 4.7 | 24.6 |
| SD.............. | 436 | 81.2 | 7.8 | 0.7 | 3.4 | 1.0 | 5.8 | 17.3 |
| TN.............. | 3,079 | 83.2 | 8.8 | 0.6 | 1.3 | 1.2 | 4.9 | 25.1 |
| TX.............. | 13,051 | 80.6 | 9.8 | 1.4 | 1.5 | 1.6 | 5.1 | 26.5 |
| UT.............. | 1,487 | 76.1 | 10.7 | 2.3 | 2.4 | 1.7 | 6.8 | 22.0 |
| VT.............. | 319 | 74.9 | 9.2 | 1.5 | 5.7 | 1.6 | 7.1 | 23.2 |
| VA.............. | 4,195 | 77.4 | 8.7 | 4.2 | 2.6 | 1.8 | 5.4 | 28.6 |
| WA.............. | 3,567 | 71.7 | 10.2 | 6.5 | 3.4 | 1.8 | 6.3 | 27.9 |
| WV.............. | 712 | 82.8 | 9.0 | 0.9 | 2.9 | 1.1 | 3.3 | 26.0 |
| WI.............. | 2,939 | 81.1 | 7.6 | 1.8 | 3.0 | 1.6 | 4.9 | 22.2 |
| WY.............. | 279 | 77.9 | 10.2 | 0.6 | 3.6 | 2.4 | 5.3 | 17.6 |
| PR.............. | 979 | 83.9 | 7.5 | 1.8 | 2.8 | 1.8 | 2.2 | 28.5 |

[1] Excluding taxicabs.

Source: U.S. Census Bureau, 2017 American Community Survey, B08006, "Sex of Workers by Means of Transportation to Work" and GCT0801, "Mean Travel Time to Work of Workers 16 Years Old and Over Who Did Not Work At Home (Minutes)," <http://factfinder.census.gov>, accessed November 2018.

# Table 1142. Use of Ride Hailing Services by Age Group: 2017

[Data from the 2017 National Household Travel Survey. Approximately 8% of the U.S. population used a ride-hailing service (services such as Uber and Lyft) at least once in the last 30 days. Age groups are based on Pew Research Center definitions]

| Item | Millennials, aged 21 to 36 | Generation X, aged 37 to 52 | Baby Boomers, aged 53 to 71 | Matures, aged 72 and over |
|---|---|---|---|---|
| Used ride-hailing service (percent)..................... | 19 | 10 | 5 | 2 |
| **Total respondents (millions)** [2]..................... | **8.6** | **6.3** | **6.9** | **1.4** |
| Used public transit and ride hailing................... | 4.8 | 2.1 | 1.1 | 0.1 |
| Used public transit but not ride hailing.............. | 3.8 | 4.2 | 5.8 | 1.3 |

[1] Data shown for metropolitan statistical areas with populations of 3 million or more people.

Source: U.S. Department of Transportation, Federal Highway Administration, *Changing Attitudes and Transportation Choices, 2017 National Household Travel Survey*, February 2019. See also <https://nhts.ornl.gov/>.

## Table 1143. Passenger Transit Industry—Summary: 1990 to 2017

[16,053 represents $16,053,000,000. Includes Puerto Rico. Includes aggregate information for all transit systems in the United States. Excludes nontransit services such as taxicab, school bus, unregulated jitney (a small bus or automobile that transports passengers on a route for a small fare), sightseeing bus, intercity bus, and special application mass transportation systems (e.g., amusement parks, airports, island, and urban park ferries). Includes active vehicles only]

| Item | Unit | 1990 | 2000 | 2010 | 2014 | 2015 | 2016 | 2017 |
|---|---|---|---|---|---|---|---|---|
| Operating systems............ | Number | 5,078 | 6,000 | 7,088 | 6,817 | 6,752 | (NA) | 6,770 |
| Motor bus systems........... | Number | 2,688 | 2,262 | 1,206 | 1,223 | 1,163 | (NA) | 1,226 |
| Revenue vehicles, active......... | Number | 93,430 | 131,089 | 174,425 | 181,847 | 183,601 | 179,021 | 181,652 |
| Motor bus.................. | Number | 58,714 | 75,013 | 66,239 | 71,066 | 72,075 | 71,956 | 72,338 |
| Commuter rail............[1] | Number | 4,982 | 5,498 | 6,927 | 7,387 | 7,271 | 7,405 | 7,345 |
| Demand response [1]........ | Number | 16,471 | 33,080 | 68,621 | 71,359 | 71,299 | 68,059 | 69,316 |
| Heavy rail.................. | Number | 10,567 | 10,311 | 11,510 | 10,551 | 10,737 | 10,775 | 10,705 |
| Surface rail (light rail, street car)........ | Number | 910 | 1,327 | 2,104 | 2,394 | 2,423 | 2,498 | 2,502 |
| Trolley bus................. | Number | 610 | 652 | 571 | 537 | 611 | 601 | 539 |
| Other.................. | Number | 1,176 | 5,208 | 18,453 | 18,553 | 19,185 | 17,727 | 18,907 |
| Operating funding, total........... | Mil. dol. | 16,053 | 24,243 | 39,117 | 48,311 | 48,367 | 50,634 | 50,807 |
| Agency funds............. | Mil. dol. | 6,786 | 11,004 | 14,675 | 17,332 | 18,105 | 18,394 | 18,457 |
| Passenger funding......... | Mil. dol. | 5,891 | 8,746 | 12,556 | 15,465 | 15,727 | 15,848 | 15,929 |
| Other.................. | Mil. dol. | 895 | 2,258 | 2,119 | 1,867 | 2,378 | 2,546 | 2,528 |
| Government funds [2]......... | Mil. dol. | 9,267 | 13,239 | 24,442 | 30,979 | 30,262 | 32,240 | 32,350 |
| Directly generated [3]......... | Mil. dol. | ( [4] ) | 1,959 | 2,549 | 3,336 | 3,242 | 3,418 | 3,484 |
| Local................... | Mil. dol. | 5,327 | 5,319 | 8,458 | 11,224 | 11,812 | 12,491 | 12,866 |
| State................... | Mil. dol. | 2,971 | 4,967 | 9,761 | 12,277 | 11,197 | 12,274 | 11,673 |
| Federal................. | Mil. dol. | 970 | 994 | 3,675 | 4,142 | 4,011 | 4,057 | 4,327 |
| Operating expense............. | Mil. dol. | 15,742 | 22,646 | 37,755 | 44,425 | 45,353 | 47,409 | 47,544 |
| Vehicle operations............ | Mil. dol. | 6,653 | 10,111 | 17,009 | 19,335 | 19,388 | 19,998 | 19,902 |
| Maintenance............... | Mil. dol. | 4,631 | 6,445 | 9,797 | 12,036 | 12,237 | 13,017 | 13,327 |
| General administration........... | Mil. dol. | 3,450 | 3,329 | 5,731 | 6,992 | 7,300 | 7,909 | 7,543 |
| Purchased transportation........... | Mil. dol. | 1,008 | 2,761 | 5,218 | 6,062 | 6,427 | 6,484 | 6,772 |
| Capital expenditures............. | Mil. dol. | (NA) | 9,587 | 17,824 | 18,466 | 19,696 | 19,943 | 20,185 |
| Vehicle-miles operated........... | Million | 3,242 | 4,081 | 5,455 | 5,468 | 5,509 | 5,654 | 5,696 |
| Motor bus.................. | Million | 2,130 | 2,315 | 2,413 | 2,434 | 2,428 | 2,483 | 2,502 |
| Trolley bus................. | Million | 14 | 15 | 12 | 11 | 11 | 12 | 11 |
| Heavy rail.................. | Million | 537 | 595 | 666 | 676 | 695 | 696 | 704 |
| Surface rail (light rail, street car)........ | Million | 24 | 53 | 94 | 105 | 108 | 114 | 120 |
| Commuter rail............... | Million | 213 | 271 | 345 | 371 | 374 | 376 | 378 |
| Demand response [1]............ | Million | 306 | 759 | 1,694 | 1,595 | 1,617 | 1,692 | 1,705 |
| Other.................. | Million | 18 | 74 | 232 | 276 | 277 | 282 | 277 |
| Trips taken................. | Million | 8,799 | 9,363 | 10,218 | 10,750 | 10,599 | 10,459 | 10,152 |
| Motor bus.................. | Million | 5,677 | 5,678 | 5,256 | 5,274 | 5,199 | 5,054 | 4,793 |
| Trolley bus................. | Million | 126 | 122 | 99 | 96 | 90 | 94 | 83 |
| Heavy rail.................. | Million | 2,346 | 2,632 | 3,550 | 3,928 | 3,860 | 3,848 | 3,816 |
| Surface rail (light rail, street car)........ | Million | 175 | 320 | 457 | 531 | 529 | 550 | 555 |
| Commuter rail............... | Million | 328 | 413 | 464 | 490 | 495 | 504 | 503 |
| Demand response [1]............ | Million | 68 | 105 | 190 | 233 | 223 | 211 | 207 |
| Other.................. | Million | 79 | 93 | 202 | 198 | 204 | 199 | 195 |
| Avg. fare per trip............. | Dollars | 0.67 | 0.93 | 1.23 | 1.44 | 1.50 | 1.52 | 1.56 |
| Employees, number (avg.) [5]......... | 1,000 | 273 | 360 | 394 | 416 | 433 | 436 | 432 |
| Salaries and wages, employee........... | Mil. dol. | 7,226 | 10,400 | 14,286 | 15,396 | 15,913 | 16,739 | 16,688 |
| Fringe benefits, employee............... | Mil. dol. | 3,986 | 5,413 | 10,342 | 11,712 | 11,992 | 13,034 | 12,729 |

NA Not available. [1] This operation (also called paratransit or dial-a-ride) is comprised of passenger cars, vans or small buses operating in response to calls from passengers or their agents to the transit operator, who then dispatches a vehicle to pick up the passengers and transport them to their destinations. [2] Represents the sum of federal, state, and local assistance, and that portion of directly generated funds that accrue from tax collections, toll transfers from other sectors of operations, and bond proceeds. [3] These are any funds generated from taxes controlled by the transit agency. [4] Funds data are included in local government data through 1993. [5] Through 1990, represents employee equivalents of 2,080 hours = one employee; beginning 1995, equals actual employees.

Source: American Public Transportation Association, Washington, DC, *Public Transportation Fact Book*, annual ©. See also <https://www.apta.com/research-technical-resources/research-reports>.

## Table 1144. Top Twenty Cities—Public Transit Savings for Daily Commuters: 2019

[Individuals who use public transportation for their daily commute can save on average $10,037 annually based on the June 24, 2019 national average gas price and the national unreserved monthly parking rate. On a per month basis, transit riders can save on average $836 per month versus driving. See source report and other monthly "Transit Savings" releases for information and methodology on how savings are calculated. The cities with the highest transit ridership are ranked in order of their transit savings based on the purchase of a monthly public transit pass and factoring in local gas prices and the local monthly unreserved parking rate]

| City | Savings (dollars) Monthly | Savings (dollars) Annual | City | Savings (dollars) Monthly | Savings (dollars) Annual |
|---|---|---|---|---|---|
| New York................. | 1,237 | 14,846 | Minneapolis.................. | 874 | 10,488 |
| San Francisco.............. | 1,124 | 13,486 | Denver ................. | 856 | 10,269 |
| Boston................. | 1,083 | 12,999 | Baltimore................. | 855 | 10,261 |
| Chicago................. | 1,009 | 12,104 | Washington, DC............. | 839 | 10,068 |
| Seattle................. | 1,007 | 12,090 | Pittsburgh................. | 827 | 9,924 |
| Philadelphia.............. | 1,005 | 12,061 | Cleveland................. | 823 | 9,873 |
| Honolulu................. | 977 | 11,727 | Las Vegas................. | 792 | 9,499 |
| Los Angeles.............. | 966 | 11,595 | Atlanta................. | 789 | 9,472 |
| San Diego................. | 919 | 11,027 | Miami................. | 784 | 9,403 |
| Portland................. | 898 | 10,775 | Dallas................. | 778 | 9,334 |

Source: American Public Transportation Association, Media Center, Press Releases ©. See also <https://www.publictransportation.org/tools/transitsavings/>.

# Table 1145. Characteristics of Rail Transit by Transit Authority: 2017

[9,296.1 represents $9,296,100,000]

| Mode and transit agency | Metro area served | Directional route–miles [1,2] | Number of high-way rail cross-ings [1] | Number of stations | Fare revenues earned (mil. dol.) | Total operating expenses (mil. dol.) | Unlinked passenger trips (million) |
|---|---|---|---|---|---|---|---|
| Total [3] | (X) | 12,570.3 | 7,708 | 3,399 | 9,296.1 | 17,238.9 | 4,875.9 |
| Heavy rail | (X) | 1,659.8 | 27 | 1,054 | 5,510.6 | 8,711.2 | 3,816.3 |
| Chicago Transit Authority | Chicago | 207.8 | 25 | 145 | 294.5 | 604.1 | 230.2 |
| Greater Cleveland Regional Transit Authority | Cleveland | 38.1 | – | 18 | 7.3 | 37.0 | 5.9 |
| Los Angeles County Metropolitan Transportation Authority, Metro | Los Angeles | 31.9 | – | 16 | 35.6 | 161.6 | 45.6 |
| Maryland Transit Administration | Baltimore | 29.4 | – | 14 | 12.2 | 51.8 | 10.5 |
| Massachusetts Bay Transportation Authority | Boston | 76.3 | – | 54 | 228.7 | 355.1 | 164.1 |
| Metropolitan Atlanta Rapid Transit Authority | Atlanta | 96.1 | – | 38 | 76.5 | 189.9 | 68.3 |
| Miami-Dade Transit | Miami | 49.8 | – | 23 | 16.1 | 101.5 | 20.0 |
| MTA New York City Transit | New York | 493.7 | – | 472 | 3,500.4 | 4,788.2 | 2,699.5 |
| Port Authority Trans-Hudson Corporation | New York | 28.6 | 2 | 13 | 191.2 | 423.4 | 92.9 |
| Port Authority Transit Corporation | Philadelphia | 31.5 | – | 13 | 26.7 | 51.3 | 10.8 |
| San Francisco Bay Area Rapid Transit District | San Francisco | 218.3 | – | 45 | 479.3 | 618.7 | 131.8 |
| Southeastern Pennsylvania Transportation Authority | Philadelphia | 74.9 | – | 75 | 101.7 | 202.1 | 93.9 |
| Staten Island Rapid Transit Operating Authority, MTA Staten Island Railway | New York | 28.6 | – | 21 | 8.8 | 70.5 | 8.3 |
| Washington Metropolitan Area Transit Authority | Washington | 234.2 | – | 91 | 521.8 | 992.6 | 227.1 |
| Alternativa de Transporte Integrado ATI | San Juan, PR | 20.6 | – | 16 | 9.8 | 63.4 | 7.4 |
| Light rail | (X) | 1,572.1 | 2,326 | 885 | 517.5 | 2,143.0 | 498.1 |
| Missouri-Illinois Metropolitan District Metro | St. Louis | 91.1 | 25 | 37 | 15.4 | 76.3 | 14.9 |
| Central Puget Sound Regional Transit Authority | Seattle | 40.4 | 37 | 16 | 38.0 | 91.2 | 23.0 |
| Charlotte Area Transit System | Charlotte | 18.6 | 20 | 15 | 3.6 | 14.3 | 4.8 |
| Greater Cleveland Regional Transit Authority | Cleveland | 30.4 | 25 | 34 | 3.0 | 12.7 | 2.1 |
| Dallas Area Rapid Transit | Dallas | 182.4 | 171 | 64 | 27.7 | 175.2 | 30.0 |
| Denver Regional Transportation District | Denver | 115.2 | 77 | 54 | 38.2 | 115.2 | 24.6 |
| Los Angeles County Metropolitan Transportation Authority, Metro | Los Angeles | 171.9 | 181 | 79 | 52.6 | 366.4 | 67.8 |
| Maryland Transit Administration (MTA) | Baltimore | 57.6 | 52 | 33 | 7.2 | 42.6 | 7.3 |
| Massachusetts Bay Transportation Authority | Boston | 51.0 | 65 | 74 | 83.2 | 187.1 | 62.3 |
| Metro Transit | Minneapolis | 44.3 | 104 | 37 | 24.1 | 70.9 | 23.8 |
| Harris County, Texas (Metro) | Houston | 43.6 | 165 | 39 | 6.0 | 65.2 | 18.3 |
| New Jersey Transit Corporation | Newark | 46.5 | 48 | 41 | 20.7 | 112.4 | 21.0 |
| Niagara Frontier Transportation Authority | Buffalo | 12.4 | 8 | 14 | 5.6 | 23.9 | 4.7 |
| Port Authority of Allegheny County | Pittsburgh | 49.6 | 42 | 30 | 9.2 | 63.0 | 7.8 |
| Sacramento Regional Transit District | Sacramento | 84.9 | 137 | 41 | 14.8 | 67.8 | 11.4 |
| San Diego Metropolitan Transit System | San Diego | 108.4 | 96 | 53 | 39.0 | 82.5 | 37.6 |
| San Francisco Municipal Railway | San Francisco | 64.4 | 335 | 9 | 39.2 | 213.8 | 51.0 |
| Santa Clara Valley Transportation Authority | San Jose | 81.0 | 168 | 64 | 8.1 | 106.0 | 9.1 |
| Hampton Roads Transit | Hampton | 14.8 | 22 | 11 | 1.4 | 11.6 | 1.4 |
| Metropolitan Transportation District of Oregon | Portland | 118.9 | 212 | 44 | 49.4 | 138.8 | 39.7 |
| Utah Transit Authority | Salt Lake City | 93.9 | 144 | 56 | 18.0 | 64.7 | 18.8 |
| Valley Metro Rail, Inc | Phoenix | 50.8 | 192 | 40 | 13.4 | 41.5 | 16.5 |
| Commuter rail [3] | (X) | 8,871.8 | 3,490 | 1,273 | 3,217.6 | 6,088.9 | 497.9 |
| Alaska Railroad Corporation | Anchorage | 959.9 | 136 | 11 | 23.3 | 46.4 | 0.2 |
| Altamont Corridor Express | San Jose | 172.0 | 92 | 10 | 8.9 | 21.6 | 1.3 |
| Central Florida Commuter Rail | Orlando | 63.5 | 94 | 12 | 2.0 | 34.1 | 0.9 |
| Central Puget Sound Regional Transit Authority | Seattle | 163.8 | 63 | 12 | 15.0 | 45.5 | 4.4 |
| Connecticut Department of Transportation | Hartford | 101.2 | – | 9 | 2.5 | 30.1 | 0.8 |
| Dallas Area Rapid Transit | Dallas | 72.3 | 44 | 10 | 8.9 | 28.3 | 2.1 |
| Denver Regional Transportation District | Denver | 58.7 | 12 | 9 | 20.3 | 39.2 | 7.0 |
| Maryland Transit Administration | Baltimore | 400.4 | 40 | 42 | 52.6 | 142.6 | 9.2 |
| Massachusetts Bay Transportation Authority | Boston | 776.1 | 247 | 138 | 218.4 | 399.0 | 33.9 |
| Metro Transit | Minneapolis | 77.9 | 36 | 7 | 2.5 | 15.3 | 0.8 |
| Metro-North Commuter Railroad Company, MTA Metro-North Railroad | New York | 545.7 | 158 | 112 | 737.4 | 1,220.2 | 86.4 |
| MTA Long Island Rail Road | New York | 638.2 | 329 | 124 | 733.0 | 1,362.0 | 103.6 |
| New Jersey Transit Corporation | New York | 1,001.8 | 335 | 166 | 578.6 | 971.3 | 88.6 |
| North County Transit District | San Diego | 82.2 | 31 | 8 | 5.9 | 18.0 | 1.5 |
| Northeast Illinois Regional Commuter Railroad Corporation | Chicago | 975.0 | 565 | 241 | 355.3 | 742.7 | 70.6 |
| Northern Indiana Commuter Transportation District | Chicago | 179.8 | 134 | 19 | 22.2 | 48.5 | 3.5 |
| Northern New England Passenger Rail Authority | Boston | 287.6 | 103 | 12 | 8.9 | 21.8 | 0.5 |
| Peninsula Corridor Joint Powers Board: Caltrain | San Francisco | 153.7 | 54 | 32 | 92.4 | 127.3 | 18.6 |
| Pennsylvania Department of Transportation | Philadelphia | 144.4 | 1 | 12 | 44.0 | 51.2 | 1.5 |
| Regional Transportation Authority | Nashville | 62.8 | 35 | 6 | 0.9 | 4.3 | 0.3 |
| Rio Metro Regional Transit District | Albuquerque | 193.1 | 86 | 14 | 2.2 | 28.4 | 0.8 |
| South Florida Regional Transportation Authority | Miami | 142.2 | 73 | 18 | 12.8 | 90.9 | 4.3 |
| Southeastern Pennsylvania Transportation Authority | Philadelphia | 446.9 | 287 | 155 | 137.0 | 269.6 | 33.2 |
| Southern California Regional Rail Authority | Los Angeles | 824.4 | 450 | 59 | 83.4 | 222.0 | 14.4 |
| Utah Transit Authority | Salt Lake City | 174.5 | 65 | 16 | 7.2 | 34.4 | 4.9 |
| Virginia Railway Express | Washington | 173.6 | 20 | 19 | 42.3 | 74.0 | 4.7 |

– Represents zero. X Not applicable. [1] Vehicles operated in maximum services (VOMS) include directly operated (DO) and Purchase Transportation (PT) by mode. [2] The mileage in each direction over which public transportation vehicles travel while in revenue service. The mileage is computed without regard to the number of traffic lanes or rail tracks existing in the right-of-way. [3] Excludes commuter-type services operated independently by Amtrak.

Source: U.S. Department of Transportation, Federal Transit Administration, National Transit Database, Annual Data Tables, "Transit Way Mileage," "Service," "Metrics," and "Transit Stations," <https://www.transit.dot.gov/ntd/ntd-data>, accessed September 2019.

## Table 1146. Household Daily Travel Trips and Trip Length by Trip Purpose: 1969 to 2017

[Data based on the National Household Travel Survey (NHTS), which asks each participating household to report all travel by household members on a randomly assigned 24-hour single travel day using any mode of transportation including walking. Data for 2017 may not be comparable to previous years due to change in survey methodology; see source for details]

| Trip characteristic | 1969 | 1977 | 1983 | 1990 | 1995 | 2001 | 2009 | 2017 |
|---|---|---|---|---|---|---|---|---|
| Daily person trips per person | 2.0 | 2.9 | 2.9 | 3.8 | 4.3 | 4.1 | 3.8 | 3.4 |
| Daily person miles of travel (PMT) per person | 19.5 | 26.0 | 25.1 | 34.9 | 38.7 | 36.9 | 36.1 | 39.0 |
| Daily vehicle trips per driver | 2.3 | 2.3 | 2.4 | 3.3 | 3.6 | 3.4 | 3.0 | 2.7 |
| Daily vehicle miles of travel (VMT) per driver | 20.6 | 19.5 | 18.7 | 28.5 | 32.1 | 32.7 | 29.0 | 28.5 |
| Average person trip length (miles) | 9.7 | 8.9 | 8.7 | 9.5 | 9.1 | 10.0 | 9.8 | 11.6 |
| Average vehicle trip length (miles) | 8.9 | 8.3 | 7.9 | 8.9 | 9.1 | 9.9 | 9.7 | 10.5 |
| **AVERAGE ANNUAL PERSON TRIPS PER HOUSEHOLD BY TRIP PURPOSE** | | | | | | | | |
| All purposes | (NA) | (NA) | 2,628 | 3,262 | 3,828 | 3,581 | 3,466 | 3,140 |
| To/from work | (NA) | (NA) | 537 | 539 | 676 | 565 | 541 | 546 |
| Work related business | (NA) | (NA) | 62 | 38 | 100 | 109 | 106 | 51 |
| Shopping | (NA) | (NA) | 474 | 630 | 775 | 707 | 725 | 580 |
| Other family/personal errands | (NA) | (NA) | 456 | 854 | 981 | 863 | 748 | 628 |
| School/church | (NA) | (NA) | 310 | 304 | 337 | 351 | 333 | 341 |
| Social/recreation | (NA) | (NA) | 728 | 874 | 953 | 952 | 952 | 866 |
| Other | (NA) | (NA) | 61 | 22 | 6 | 30 | 61 | 128 |
| **AVERAGE PERSON TRIP LENGTH BY TRIP PURPOSE (miles)** | | | | | | | | |
| All purposes | (NA) | (NA) | 8.7 | 9.5 | 9.1 | 10.0 | 9.7 | 11.6 |
| To/from work | (NA) | (NA) | 8.5 | 10.7 | 11.6 | 12.1 | 11.8 | 12.2 |
| Work related business | (NA) | (NA) | 21.8 | 28.2 | 20.3 | 28.3 | 20.0 | 27.4 |
| Shopping | (NA) | (NA) | 5.4 | 5.4 | 6.1 | 7.0 | 6.5 | 7.9 |
| Other family/personal errands | (NA) | (NA) | 7.3 | 8.6 | 7.6 | 7.8 | 7.0 | 7.9 |
| School/church | (NA) | (NA) | 4.9 | 5.4 | 6.0 | 6.0 | 6.3 | 7.0 |
| Social/recreation | (NA) | (NA) | 12.3 | 13.2 | 11.3 | 11.4 | 10.7 | 11.4 |
| Other | (NA) | (NA) | 8.2 | 10.3 | 22.8 | 43.1 | 51.5 | 50.4 |
| **AVERAGE ANNUAL VEHICLE TRIPS PER HOUSEHOLD** | | | | | | | | |
| All purposes | 1,396 | 1,442 | 1,486 | 2,077 | 2,321 | 2,171 | 2,068 | 1,865 |
| To/from work | 445 | 423 | 414 | 448 | 553 | 479 | 457 | 450 |
| Shopping | 213 | 268 | 297 | 431 | 501 | 459 | 468 | 372 |
| Other family/personal errands | 195 | 215 | 272 | 579 | 626 | 537 | 500 | 434 |
| Social/recreation | 312 | 320 | 335 | 460 | 427 | 441 | 436 | 410 |
| **AVERAGE VEHICLE TRIP LENGTH (miles)** | | | | | | | | |
| All purposes | 8.9 | 8.4 | 7.9 | 8.9 | 9.1 | 9.9 | 9.7 | 10.5 |
| To/from work | 9.4 | 9.0 | 8.6 | 11.0 | 11.8 | 12.1 | 12.2 | 12.8 |
| Shopping | 4.4 | 5.0 | 5.3 | 5.1 | 5.6 | 6.7 | 6.4 | 7.9 |
| Other family/personal errands | 6.5 | 6.7 | 6.7 | 7.4 | 6.9 | 7.5 | 7.1 | 7.7 |
| Social/recreation | 13.1 | 10.3 | 10.6 | 11.8 | 11.2 | 11.9 | 11.2 | 11.8 |

NA Not available.

Source: U.S. Department of Transportation, Federal Highway Administration, *Summary of Travel Trends 2017, National Household Travel Survey*, July 2018. See also <https://nhts.ornl.gov/>.

## Table 1147. Federal Transit Administration (FTA) Funding Allocations by State: 2018 and 2019

[In millions of dollars (9,903.0 represents $9,903,000,000). For fiscal years ending September 30. Data shown are apportionments and allocations for formula and discretionary programs]

| State | 2018 | 2019 | State | 2018 | 2019 | State | 2018 | 2019 | State | 2018 | 2019 |
|---|---|---|---|---|---|---|---|---|---|---|---|
| **Total [1]** | **9,903.0** | **9,964.3** | ID | 27.0 | 29.3 | MO | 106.7 | 108.6 | PA | 460.9 | 456.7 |
| AL | 58.8 | 60.5 | IL | 634.9 | 630.1 | MT | 23.2 | 24.3 | RI | 41.1 | 42.7 |
| AK | 58.0 | 57.9 | IN | 95.4 | 97.9 | NE | 28.1 | 29.0 | SC | 53.4 | 54.8 |
| AZ | 126.2 | 129.5 | IA | 43.6 | 45.3 | NV | 67.3 | 69.6 | SD | 18.4 | 19.1 |
| AR | 35.5 | 36.6 | KS | 38.2 | 39.3 | NH | 19.2 | 19.7 | TN | 93.6 | 96.5 |
| CA | 1,467.5 | 1,462.5 | KY | 57.2 | 59.3 | NJ | 656.1 | 658.3 | TX | 461.4 | 477.3 |
| CO | 128.3 | 132.1 | LA | 68.5 | 70.1 | NM | 54.6 | 55.4 | UT | 84.8 | 89.2 |
| CT | 189.6 | 189.8 | ME | 35.0 | 35.7 | NY | 1,608.6 | 1,592.2 | VT | 11.3 | 11.9 |
| DE | 28.2 | 29.0 | MD | 268.3 | 270.9 | NC | 130.6 | 133.6 | VA | 175.6 | 181.7 |
| DC | 218.6 | 210.6 | MA | 404.1 | 402.8 | ND | 16.7 | 18.0 | WA | 274.3 | 276.6 |
| FL | 400.3 | 404.3 | MI | 142.8 | 149.4 | OH | 198.6 | 200.5 | WV | 28.2 | 29.0 |
| GA | 209.6 | 211.0 | MN | 123.3 | 124.8 | OK | 52.5 | 53.5 | WI | 88.9 | 90.6 |
| HI | 47.0 | 47.2 | MS | 31.8 | 33.1 | OR | 116.7 | 119.1 | WY | 13.9 | 14.5 |

[1] Includes data for Island Areas of the U.S. and unallocated funds, not shown separately. Does not include oversight funds.

Source: U.S. Department of Transportation, Federal Transit Administration, Office of Budget and Policy, "FTA Allocations for Formula and Discretionary Programs by State FY1998-2019," <https://www.transit.dot.gov/funding/apportionments/funding-state>, accessed August 2019.

## Table 1148. Commuters by Commuting Time to Work for Top Metropolitan Statistical Areas: 2017

[144,808 represents 144,808,000, except percent. For workers 16 years and over who did not work at home. Covers any mode of travel. Based on a sample, subject to sampling variability]

| Metropolitan Statistical Area | Total commuters (1,000) | Percent over 35 minutes | Commuters by commuting time | | | | | | | | |
|---|---|---|---|---|---|---|---|---|---|---|---|
| | | | Less than 10 minutes | 10 to 14 minutes | 15 to 19 minutes | 20 to 24 minutes | 25 to 29 minutes | 30 to 34 minutes | 35 to 44 minutes | 45 to 59 minutes | 60 or more minutes |
| **United States** | **144,808** | **24.7** | **17,685** | **19,201** | **21,891** | **20,912** | **9,404** | **19,998** | **10,160** | **12,061** | **13,496** |
| Atlanta-Sandy Springs-Roswell, GA | 2,660 | 35.5 | 179 | 251 | 331 | 362 | 161 | 432 | 231 | 325 | 386 |
| Baltimore-Columbia-Towson, MD | 1,337 | 32.8 | 100 | 123 | 180 | 185 | 90 | 220 | 122 | 141 | 175 |
| Boston-Cambridge-Newton, MA-NH | 2,435 | 35.4 | 218 | 246 | 291 | 303 | 141 | 375 | 230 | 286 | 345 |
| Charlotte-Concord-Gastonia, NC-SC | 1,153 | 25.7 | 104 | 146 | 178 | 177 | 83 | 168 | 101 | 111 | 84 |
| Chicago-Naperville-Elgin, IL-IN-WI | 4,416 | 36.3 | 359 | 443 | 511 | 542 | 276 | 682 | 426 | 554 | 622 |
| Dallas-Ft. Worth-Arlington, TX | 3,449 | 28.7 | 293 | 370 | 470 | 493 | 244 | 588 | 294 | 373 | 325 |
| Denver-Aurora-Lakewood, CO | 1,429 | 27.1 | 114 | 152 | 200 | 225 | 103 | 247 | 131 | 145 | 112 |
| Detroit-Warren-Dearborn, MI | 1,902 | 25.4 | 178 | 231 | 278 | 291 | 155 | 286 | 171 | 177 | 135 |
| Houston-The Woodlands-Sugar Land, TX | 3,049 | 31.3 | 229 | 318 | 411 | 415 | 187 | 534 | 262 | 354 | 339 |
| Los Angeles-Long Beach-Anaheim, CA | 6,066 | 31.6 | 422 | 645 | 836 | 829 | 339 | 1,079 | 467 | 623 | 826 |
| Miami-Ft. Lauderdale-West Palm Beach, FL | 2,741 | 29.8 | 180 | 263 | 346 | 418 | 193 | 524 | 238 | 288 | 290 |
| Minneapolis-St. Paul-Bloomington, MN-WI | 1,826 | 22.3 | 183 | 219 | 282 | 305 | 155 | 274 | 154 | 149 | 105 |
| New York-Newark-Jersey City, NY-NJ-PA | 9,382 | 43.7 | 642 | 824 | 929 | 1,043 | 472 | 1,374 | 834 | 1,153 | 2,111 |
| Orlando-Kissimmee-Sanford, FL | 1,130 | 28.9 | 80 | 101 | 148 | 177 | 88 | 209 | 110 | 129 | 88 |
| Philadelphia-Camden-Wilmington, PA-NJ-DE-MD | 2,761 | 31.9 | 249 | 288 | 352 | 383 | 186 | 421 | 252 | 303 | 327 |
| Phoenix-Mesa-Scottsdale, AZ | 2,035 | 24.5 | 197 | 237 | 294 | 315 | 169 | 326 | 168 | 181 | 149 |
| Pittsburgh, PA | 1,082 | 27.0 | 125 | 137 | 152 | 150 | 72 | 154 | 97 | 103 | 91 |
| Portland-Vancouver-Hillsboro, OR-WA | 1,150 | 26.7 | 116 | 132 | 168 | 172 | 81 | 173 | 92 | 116 | 98 |
| Riverside-San Bernardino-Ontario, CA | 1,806 | 31.8 | 167 | 223 | 252 | 245 | 98 | 248 | 114 | 152 | 308 |
| St. Louis, MO-IL | 1,308 | 22.5 | 143 | 152 | 197 | 209 | 104 | 209 | 110 | 110 | 74 |
| San Diego-Carlsbad, CA | 1,535 | 22.1 | 121 | 194 | 247 | 272 | 111 | 252 | 112 | 118 | 109 |
| San Francisco-Oakland-Hayward, CA | 2,211 | 40.2 | 149 | 211 | 265 | 263 | 116 | 318 | 202 | 289 | 397 |
| Seattle-Tacoma-Bellevue, WA | 1,872 | 33.8 | 140 | 185 | 228 | 258 | 130 | 298 | 183 | 220 | 230 |
| Tampa-St. Petersburg-Clearwater, FL | 1,299 | 26.9 | 119 | 154 | 193 | 196 | 83 | 204 | 105 | 130 | 115 |
| Washington-Arlington-Alexandria, DC-VA-MD-WV | 3,123 | 42.4 | 184 | 253 | 342 | 358 | 187 | 476 | 328 | 450 | 546 |

Source: U.S. Census Bureau, 2017 American Community Survey, B08134, "Means of Transportation to Work by Travel Time to Work," <https://factfinder.census.gov/>, accessed November 2018.

## Table 1149. Commuters Who Ride Bicycles or Walk to Work—Selected Large Cities: 2016

[Covers cities with the highest percent of commuters who walk or bike to work, based on the American Community Survey. Data are weighted 5-year averages for 2012-2016]

| | Walking | | | | Bicycling | | |
|---|---|---|---|---|---|---|---|
| Leading cities | Percent of commuters who walk to work | Percent male | Percent female | Leading cities | Percent of commuters who bike to work | Percent male | Percent female |
| Boston | 14.8 | 47.3 | 52.7 | Portland, OR | 6.5 | 64.0 | 36.0 |
| Washington, DC | 13.3 | 50.1 | 49.9 | Minneapolis | 4.3 | 65.3 | 34.7 |
| San Francisco | 10.6 | 52.2 | 47.8 | Washington, DC | 4.3 | 61.0 | 39.0 |
| Seattle | 10.1 | 56.9 | 43.1 | San Francisco | 4.1 | 68.7 | 31.3 |
| New York City | 10.0 | 48.5 | 51.5 | Seattle | 3.8 | 70.2 | 29.8 |
| Philadelphia | 8.2 | 46.4 | 53.6 | Oakland | 3.1 | 62.3 | 37.7 |
| Minneapolis | 7.2 | 52.7 | 47.3 | Tucson | 2.9 | 67.5 | 32.5 |
| Baltimore | 6.7 | 47.2 | 52.8 | Denver | 2.3 | 70.7 | 29.3 |
| Chicago | 6.7 | 49.8 | 50.2 | Boston | 2.1 | 71.5 | 28.5 |
| Portland, OR | 6.0 | 52.8 | 47.2 | Philadelphia | 2.1 | 62.9 | 37.1 |
| Cleveland | 5.3 | 55.8 | 44.2 | Sacramento | 2.1 | 64.8 | 35.2 |
| Milwaukee | 5.0 | 47.7 | 52.3 | Chicago | 1.6 | 71.5 | 28.5 |
| Atlanta | 4.6 | 59.0 | 41.0 | Albuquerque | 1.5 | 73.4 | 26.6 |
| Denver | 4.5 | 55.8 | 44.2 | Austin | 1.4 | 70.7 | 29.3 |
| Miami | 4.2 | 52.9 | 47.1 | Los Angeles | 1.2 | 80.1 | 19.9 |
| Oakland | 4.0 | 45.8 | 54.2 | Fresno | 1.1 | 75.0 | 25.0 |
| Detroit | 3.7 | 53.5 | 46.5 | New York City | 1.1 | 73.5 | 26.5 |
| Los Angeles | 3.5 | 51.2 | 48.8 | Long Beach | 1.0 | 71.3 | 28.7 |
| Tucson | 3.3 | 56.2 | 43.8 | Miami | 1.0 | 77.0 | 23.0 |
| Sacramento | 3.1 | 51.7 | 48.3 | Milwaukee | 1.0 | 70.0 | 30.0 |
| San Diego | 3.1 | 60.4 | 39.6 | San Diego | 1.0 | 75.4 | 24.6 |
| Columbus, OH | 3.0 | 55.7 | 44.3 | Mesa | 0.9 | 70.7 | 29.3 |
| Virginia Beach | 2.6 | 66.4 | 33.6 | San Jose | 0.9 | 76.0 | 24.0 |
| Long Beach | 2.5 | 49.1 | 50.9 | Atlanta | 0.8 | 80.2 | 19.8 |
| Austin | 2.3 | 53.7 | 46.3 | Baltimore | 0.8 | 72.2 | 27.8 |

Source: League of American Bicyclists, *Bicycling and Walking in the United States: 2018 Benchmarking Report* ©. See also <http://bikeleague.org/benchmarking-report/>.

## Table 1150. Truck Transportation—Revenue and Equipment Inventory: 2013 to 2017

[In millions of dollars (245,520 represents $245,520,000,000), except where noted. For all employer firms regardless of tax status. Covers NAICS 484. Estimates have been adjusted to the results of the 2012 Economic Census. Data are based on the 2012 North American Industry Classification System (NAICS); see text, this section and Section 15]

| Item | 2013 | 2014 | 2015 | 2016 | 2017 |
|---|---|---|---|---|---|
| **Total operating revenue** | **245,520** | **263,875** | **263,249** | **259,531** | **271,389** |
| Total motor carrier revenue | (NA) | (NA) | 244,353 | 240,542 | 251,509 |
| Revenue by commodities handled: | | | | | |
|   Agricultural products | (NA) | (NA) | 27,820 | 28,879 | 27,925 |
|   Grains, alcohol, and tobacco products | (NA) | (NA) | 9,531 | 9,636 | 9,928 |
|   Stone, nonmetallic minerals, and metallic ores | (NA) | (NA) | 17,853 | 17,386 | 19,359 |
|   Coal and petroleum products | (NA) | (NA) | 15,720 | 14,568 | 13,620 |
|   Pharmaceutical and chemical products | (NA) | (NA) | 12,693 | 12,111 | 12,581 |
|   Wood products, textiles, and leathers | (NA) | (NA) | 15,981 | 15,920 | 18,211 |
|   Base metal and machinery | (NA) | (NA) | 24,029 | 22,294 | 23,388 |
|   Electronic, motorized vehicles, and precision instruments | (NA) | (NA) | 11,789 | 11,361 | 13,067 |
|   Used household and office goods | (NA) | (NA) | 12,732 | 13,109 | 13,568 |
|   New furniture and miscellaneous manufactured products | (NA) | (NA) | 17,543 | 17,225 | 18,383 |
|   Other goods | (NA) | (NA) | 78,662 | 78,053 | 81,479 |
| Hazardous materials | (NA) | (NA) | 16,469 | 15,562 | 15,545 |
| Inventory of revenue-generating equipment (1,000): | | | | | |
|   Trucks | 223 | 228 | 165 | 171 | 188 |
|   Owned and/or leased with drivers | 201 | 203 | 149 | 154 | 170 |
|   Leased without drivers | (S) | (S) | 16 | 17 | 18 |
|   Truck-tractors | 761 | 817 | 569 | 579 | 625 |
|   Owned and/or leased with drivers | 666 | 717 | 493 | 503 | 544 |
|   Leased without drivers | 95 | 100 | 76 | 76 | 81 |
|   Trailers | 1,772 | 1,858 | 1,426 | 1,468 | 1,498 |
|   Owned and/or leased with drivers | 1,577 | 1,677 | 1,268 | 1,299 | 1,362 |
|   Leased without drivers | 195 | 181 | 158 | 169 | 136 |

S Estimate does not meet publication standards. NA Not available.

Source: U.S. Census Bureau, Service Annual Survey, "Service Annual Survey Latest Data (NAICS-basis): 2017," <https://www.census.gov/programs-surveys/sas/data.html>, accessed November 2018.

## Table 1151. Crude Oil, Fuel Ethanol and Biodiesel Movements by Rail: 2010 to 2018

[In thousands of barrels (23,788 represents 23,788,000). Crude oil movements on railroads to and from Canada, within the 50 States and the District of Columbia (including interstate and intrastate). Estimates based on data from the Surface Transportation Board and other information]

| Item | 2010 | 2011 | 2012 | 2013 | 2014 | 2015 | 2016 | 2017 | 2018 |
|---|---|---|---|---|---|---|---|---|---|
| Crude oil | 23,788 | 42,370 | 152,047 | 296,064 | 382,034 | 318,782 | 175,701 | 139,805 | 200,860 |
|   Intra-U.S. movements | 23,712 | 41,371 | 138,024 | 259,194 | 316,276 | 275,218 | 142,587 | 87,190 | 113,568 |
|   U.S. exports to Canada | 55 | 256 | 6,217 | 7,391 | 12,605 | 4,414 | – | 102 | 180 |
|   U.S. imports from Canada | 21 | 743 | 7,807 | 29,479 | 53,153 | 39,149 | 33,114 | 52,513 | 87,112 |
| Fuel ethanol | 208,061 | 219,324 | 207,870 | 202,412 | 211,692 | 220,877 | 237,193 | 253,874 | 258,954 |
| Biodiesel | 2,606 | 6,387 | 7,855 | 7,950 | 9,473 | 8,332 | 12,226 | 11,706 | 13,653 |

– Represents zero.

Source: U.S. Energy Information Administration, Petroleum & Other Liquids, "Movements of Crude Oil and Selected Products by Rail," <http://www.eia.gov/petroleum/data.cfm>, accessed September 2019.

## Table 1152. Petroleum Pipeline Companies—Characteristics: 1980 to 2017

[173 represents 173,000. Covers pipeline companies operating in interstate commerce and subject to the jurisdiction of the Federal Energy Regulatory Commission]

| Item | Unit | 1980 | 1990 | 2000 | 2010 | 2013 | 2014 | 2015 | 2016 | 2017 |
|---|---|---|---|---|---|---|---|---|---|---|
| Miles of pipeline, total | 1,000 | 173 | 168 | 152 | 148 | 152 | 161 | 165 | 166 | 168 |
|   Gathering lines | 1,000 | 36 | 32 | 18 | 10 | 15 | 15 | 16 | 15 | 15 |
|   Trunk lines | 1,000 | 136 | 136 | 134 | 138 | 137 | 146 | 149 | 152 | 154 |
| Total deliveries | Mil. barrel | 10,600 | 11,378 | 14,450 | 13,518 | 14,594 | 16,170 | 18,148 | 18,504 | 19,331 |
|   Crude oil | Mil. barrel | 6,405 | 6,563 | 6,923 | 7,204 | 8,122 | 9,289 | 10,865 | 10,730 | 11,421 |
|   Products | Mil. barrel | 4,195 | 4,816 | 7,527 | 6,314 | 6,471 | 6,881 | 7,283 | 7,785 | 7,911 |
| Total trunk line traffic | Bil. barrel miles | 3,405 | 3,500 | 3,508 | 3,565 | 3,800 | 4,193 | 4,589 | 4,771 | 5,135 |
|   Crude oil | Bil. barrel miles | 1,948 | 1,891 | 1,602 | 1,634 | 1,760 | 2,059 | 2,339 | 2,499 | 2,775 |
|   Products | Bil. barrel miles | 1,458 | 1,609 | 1,906 | 1,931 | 2,053 | 2,134 | 2,250 | 2,272 | 2,359 |
| Carrier property value | Mil. dol. | 19,752 | 25,828 | 29,648 | 45,380 | 67,890 | 84,910 | 93,485 | 99,565 | 111,862 |
| Operating revenues | Mil. dol. | 6,356 | 7,149 | 7,483 | 11,219 | 15,734 | 19,281 | 22,019 | 23,100 | 25,427 |
| Net income | Mil. dol. | 1,912 | 2,340 | 2,705 | 4,582 | 6,981 | 9,573 | 6,689 | 10,542 | 13,856 |

Source: PennWell Publishing Co., Houston, TX, *Oil & Gas Journal*, annual ©. See also <http://www.ogj.com/>.

## Table 1153. Pipelines—Mileage and Incident Summary: 2005 to 2017

[In miles except where indicated (1,245,463 represents $1,245,463,000)]

| Year | Pipeline mileage | | | | | | | | Pipeline incidents [2] | |
|------|------------------|--|--|--|--|--|--|--|-------------------------|--|
| | Natural gas systems | | | Hazardous liquid or carbon dioxide systems | | | | | | |
| | Distri-bution [1] | Trans-mission | Gathering | Total [3] | Petro-leum/ refined products | Highly volatile liquids | Crude oil | CO2 or other | Number of incidents | Total cost as reported ($1,000) |
| 2005........ | 1,962,351 | 300,468 | 23,754 | 166,760 | 62,899 | 51,284 | 48,732 | 3,846 | 719 | 1,245,463 |
| 2006........ | 2,022,474 | 300,324 | 20,898 | 166,719 | 61,905 | 52,533 | 48,453 | 3,827 | 639 | 151,984 |
| 2007........ | 2,025,731 | 301,066 | 20,042 | 169,846 | 62,091 | 54,382 | 49,488 | 3,884 | 611 | 153,904 |
| 2008........ | 2,075,191 | 303,181 | 20,663 | 173,789 | 61,599 | 57,024 | 50,963 | 4,203 | 660 | 565,532 |
| 2009........ | 2,086,689 | 304,560 | 20,376 | 175,965 | 61,803 | 57,233 | 52,737 | 4,192 | 627 | 179,070 |
| 2010........ | 2,102,431 | 304,803 | 19,621 | 181,986 | 64,800 | 57,980 | 54,631 | 4,560 | 586 | 1,692,502 |
| 2011........ | 2,121,253 | 305,063 | 19,277 | 183,580 | 64,130 | 58,599 | 56,100 | 4,735 | 588 | 426,129 |
| 2012........ | 2,137,909 | 303,391 | 16,532 | 186,221 | 64,042 | 59,861 | 57,463 | 4,840 | 571 | 229,843 |
| 2013........ | 2,149,767 | 302,878 | 17,377 | 192,412 | 63,351 | 62,768 | 61,087 | 5,190 | 618 | 368,910 |
| 2014........ | 2,169,316 | 301,822 | 17,530 | 199,793 | 61,766 | 65,792 | 66,943 | 5,276 | 706 | 321,320 |
| 2015........ | 2,190,147 | 301,164 | 17,776 | 208,618 | 62,634 | 67,673 | 73,055 | 5,241 | 712 | 349,959 |
| 2016........ | 2,210,303 | 300,378 | 17,858 | 212,105 | 62,461 | 68,725 | 75,710 | 5,195 | 633 | 328,330 |
| 2017........ | 2,223,106 | 300,650 | 18,137 | 215,625 | 62,349 | 68,943 | 79,082 | 5,237 | 649 | 273,429 |

[1] Includes main and estimated service mileage. [2] Includes serious and significant incidents. Serious incidents include a fatality or injury requiring in-patient hospitalization. Significant incidents include serious incidents; those with $50,000 or more in total costs; highly volatile liquid releases of 5 barrels or more, or other liquid releases of 50 barrels or more; and liquid releases resulting in an unintentional fire or explosion. [3] Beginning 2010, includes fuel grade ethanol, not shown separately.

Source: U.S. Department of Transportation, Pipeline and Hazardous Materials Safety Administration, "Pipeline Mileage and Facilities" and "Pipeline Incidents: 20 Year Trends," <https://www.phmsa.dot.gov/data-and-statistics/pipeline/data-and-statistics-overview>, accessed January 2019.

## Table 1154. U.S. Postal Service Rates for Letters and Postcards: 1991 to 2019

[In dollars. For 1st class retail mail. Prior to 2013, international rates exclude Canada and Mexico]

| Domestic mail date of rate change | Letters | | Post-cards | Express mail— first 1/2 pound [1] | International air mail date of rate change | Letters | Post-cards |
|-----------------------------------|---------|--|-----------|-----------------------------------|---------------------------------------------|---------|-----------|
| | First ounce | Each added ounce | | | | | |
| 1991 (Feb. 3)................ | 0.29 | 0.23 | 0.19 | 9.95 | **First 1/2 ounce** | | |
| 1995 (Jan. 1)................ | 0.32 | 0.23 | 0.20 | 10.75 | 1991 (Feb. 3)............. | 0.50 | 0.40 |
| 1999 (Jan. 10)................ | 0.33 | 0.22 | 0.20 | 11.75 | 1995 (July 9)............. | 0.60 | 0.40 |
| 2001 (Jan. 7)................ | 0.34 | 0.21 | 0.20 | 12.25 | 1999 (Jan. 10)............. | 0.60 | 0.50 |
| 2001 (July 1)................ | 0.34 | 0.23 | 0.21 | 12.45 | **First ounce** [2] | | |
| 2002 (June 30)................ | 0.37 | 0.23 | 0.23 | 13.65 | 2001 (Jan. 7)............. | 0.80 | 0.70 |
| 2006 (Jan. 8)................ | 0.39 | 0.24 | 0.24 | 14.40 | 2006 (Jan. 8)............. | 0.84 | 0.75 |
| 2007 (May 14)................ | 0.41 | 0.17 | 0.26 | 16.25 | 2007 (May 14)............. | 0.90 | 0.90 |
| 2008 (May 12)................ | 0.42 | 0.17 | 0.27 | [3] 12.60 | 2008 (May 12)............. | 0.94 | 0.94 |
| 2009 (May 11)................ | 0.44 | 0.17 | 0.28 | [4] 13.05 | 2009 (May 11)............. | 0.98 | 0.98 |
| 2010 (Jan. 4)................ | 0.44 | 0.17 | 0.28 | [5] 13.65 | 2010 (no change)........ | 0.98 | 0.98 |
| 2011 (Apr. 17)................ | 0.44 | 0.20 | 0.29 | [6] 13.25 | 2011 (no change)........ | 0.98 | 0.98 |
| 2012 (Jan. 22)................ | 0.45 | 0.20 | 0.32 | [7] 12.95 | 2012 (Jan. 22)............. | 1.05 | 1.05 |
| 2013 (Jan. 27)................ | 0.46 | 0.20 | 0.33 | [8] 14.10 | 2013 (Jan. 27)............. | 1.10 | 1.10 |
| 2014 (Jan. 26)................ | 0.49 | 0.21 | 0.34 | [9] 16.95 | 2014 (Jan. 26)............. | 1.15 | 1.15 |
| 2015 (May 31)................ | 0.49 | 0.22 | 0.35 | [9] 16.95 | 2015 (May 31)............. | 1.20 | 1.20 |
| 2016 (Apr. 10)................ | 0.47 | 0.21 | 0.34 | [10] 22.95 | 2016 (Apr. 10)............. | 1.15 | 1.15 |
| 2017 (Jan. 22)................ | 0.49 | 0.21 | 0.34 | [11] 23.75 | 2017 (no change)........ | 1.15 | 1.15 |
| 2018 (Jan. 21)................ | 0.50 | 0.21 | 0.35 | [12] 24.70 | 2018 (no change)........ | 1.15 | 1.15 |
| 2019 (Jan. 27)................ | 0.55 | 0.15 | 0.35 | [13] 25.50 | 2019 (no change)........ | 1.15 | 1.15 |

[1] On May 12, 2008, the Postal Service initiated a zoned pricing structure for Express Mail. [2] International letter prices after the first ounce vary according to the price group that is applicable to each destination country. [3] Prices increased on May 12, 2008. Prices range from $12.60 to zones 1 and 2 to $19.50 to zone 8. [4] Prices increased on January 18, 2009. Prices range from $13.05 to zones 1 and 2 to $21.20 to zone 8. [5] Prices range from $13.65 to zones 1 and 2 to $22.20 to zone 8. [6] Prices changed on January 2, 2011. Prices range from $13.25 to zones 1 and 2 to $26.65 to zone 8. [7] Prices range from $12.95 to zones 1 and 2 to $28.00 to zone 8. [8] Prices range from $14.10 to zones 1 and 2 to $30.60 to zone 8. [9] Beginning January 2014, the Postal Service implemented a Zone 9. Prices range from $16.95 to zones 1 and 2 to $38.05 to zone 9. [10] Prices range from $22.95 to zones 1 and 2 to $38.05 to zone 9. [11] Prices range from $23.75 to zones 1 and 2 to $39.40 to zone 9. [12] Prices range from $24.70 to zones 1 and 2 to $40.95 to zone 9. [13] Prices range from $25.50 to zones 1 and 2 to $47.70 to zone 9.

Source: U.S. Postal Service, *Domestic Rate History*, July 2009; and "Price List Notice 123," and previous editions, <http://pe.usps.com/text/dmm300/Notice123.htm>, accessed January 2019.

## Table 1155. U.S. Postal Service—Summary: 1990 to 2018

[166,301 represents 166,301,000,000 except as indicated. For years ending September 30. Includes Puerto Rico and all Island Areas]

| Item | 1990 | 2000 | 2010 | 2015 | 2016 | 2017 | 2018 |
|---|---|---|---|---|---|---|---|
| **Offices, stations, and branches** | **40,067** | **38,060** | **36,222** | **35,520** | **35,423** | **35,005** | **34,772** |
| Number of post offices | 28,959 | 27,876 | 27,077 | 26,615 | 26,611 | 26,410 | 26,365 |
| Number of stations and branches | 11,108 | 10,184 | 9,145 | 8,905 | 8,812 | 8,595 | 8,407 |
| **Delivery points (mil.)** | **(NA)** | **135.9** | **150.9** | **155.0** | **156.1** | **157.3** | **158.6** |
| Residential | (NA) | 123.9 | 137.5 | 142.1 | 143.3 | 144.5 | 145.8 |
| City | (NA) | 76.1 | 80.5 | 82.0 | 82.4 | 82.9 | 83.3 |
| P.O. Box | (NA) | 15.9 | 15.7 | 15.9 | 15.9 | 16.0 | 16.0 |
| Rural/highway contract | (NA) | 31.9 | 41.2 | 44.2 | 44.9 | 45.7 | 46.6 |
| Business | (NA) | 12.1 | 13.3 | 12.8 | 12.8 | 12.8 | 12.8 |
| **Pieces of mail handled (mil.)** | **166,301** | **207,882** | **170,859** | **154,321** | **154,342** | **149,590** | **146,402** |
| First-class mail [1,2] | 89,270 | 103,526 | 77,592 | 62,599 | 61,240 | 58,834 | 56,714 |
| Periodicals (formerly 2nd class) | 10,680 | 10,365 | 7,269 | 5,838 | 5,586 | 5,301 | 4,993 |
| Marketing Mail (formerly Standard A) [2] | 63,725 | 90,057 | 81,841 | 80,030 | 80,885 | 78,329 | 77,269 |
| U.S. Postal Service | 538 | 363 | 438 | 356 | 422 | 322 | 291 |
| Free for the blind | 35 | 47 | 68 | 46 | 45 | 45 | 42 |
| Shipping and package services [2,3,6] | (X) | (X) | 3,057 | 4,539 | 5,159 | 5,758 | 6,152 |
| Express mail [2,3,5] | 59 | 71 | 43 | 36 | 33 | 30 | 28 |
| Package services (formerly Standard B) | 663 | 1,128 | 657 | 566 | 591 | 620 | 640 |
| Priority mail [2,3,4] | 518 | 1,223 | 779 | 1,007 | 1,029 | 1,045 | 1,089 |
| International economy mail (surface) [3] | 166 | 79 | (3) | (3) | (3) | (3) | (3) |
| International, airmail or total [3,7] | 632 | 1,021 | 594 | 913 | 1,005 | 1,001 | 941 |
| **Employees, total (1,000)** | **843** | **901** | **672** | **622** | **640** | **644** | **634** |
| **Career** | **761** | **788** | **584** | **492** | **509** | **503** | **497** |
| Headquarters | 2 | 2 | 3 | 3 | 3 | 3 | 3 |
| Headquarters support | 6 | 6 | 5 | 4 | 4 | 4 | 3 |
| Inspection Service | 4 | 4 | 2 | 2 | 2 | 2 | 2 |
| Inspector General | (X) | 1 | 1 | 1 | 1 | 1 | 1 |
| Field Career | 749 | 775 | 573 | 482 | 499 | 493 | 487 |
| Postmasters | 27 | 26 | 23 | 15 | 14 | 14 | 14 |
| Supervisors/managers | 43 | 39 | 28 | 24 | 25 | 25 | 26 |
| Professional, administrative, and technical | 10 | 10 | 6 | 4 | 5 | 5 | 5 |
| Clerks | 290 | 282 | 157 | 126 | 130 | 128 | 122 |
| Mail handlers | 51 | 61 | 49 | 38 | 39 | 39 | 38 |
| City carriers | 236 | 241 | 192 | 164 | 171 | 167 | 168 |
| Motor vehicle operators | 7 | 9 | 7 | 7 | 8 | 8 | 8 |
| Rural carriers | 42 | 57 | 67 | 67 | 68 | 69 | 71 |
| Special delivery messengers | 2 | (X) | (X) | (X) | (X) | (X) | (X) |
| Building and equipment maintenance | 33 | 42 | 37 | 31 | 32 | 31 | 30 |
| Vehicle maintenance | 5 | 6 | 5 | 5 | 5 | 5 | 5 |
| Other [8] | 1 | 2 | (X) | (X) | (X) | (X) | (X) |
| **Non-career** | **83** | **114** | **88** | **130** | **131** | **141** | **137** |
| Casuals | 27 | 30 | 7 | 2 | 2 | 1 | 1 |
| Transitional | (X) | 13 | 16 | – | – | – | – |
| Rural part-time | 43 | 58 | 52 | 51 | 53 | 60 | 59 |
| Relief/leave replacements | 12 | 12 | 11 | 5 | 4 | 2 | 2 |
| Non-bargaining temporary | (Z) | 1 | 2 | (Z) | (Z) | (Z) | (Z) |
| Compensation and employee benefits (mil. dol.) | 34,214 | 49,532 | 48,909 | 47,278 | 48,441 | 49,108 | 50,004 |
| Avg. salary per employee (dol.) [9] | 37,570 | 50,103 | 72,099 | (NA) | (NA) | (NA) | (NA) |
| Pieces of mail per employee (1,000) | 197 | 231 | 254 | 248 | 241 | 232 | 231 |
| **Operating postal revenue** | **39,201** | **64,476** | **67,052** | **68,928** | **71,498** | **69,636** | **70,660** |
| **Mail revenue** | **37,891** | **62,285** | **63,262** | **65,548** | **67,868** | **65,876** | **66,940** |
| First-class mail [1,2] | 24,023 | 35,516 | 32,111 | 28,412 | 27,508 | 25,689 | 24,976 |
| Periodicals (formerly 2nd class) | 1,509 | 2,171 | 1,879 | 1,589 | 1,507 | 1,375 | 1,277 |
| Marketing Mail (formerly Standard A) [2] | 8,082 | 15,193 | 16,728 | 17,646 | 17,622 | 16,626 | 16,512 |
| Shipping and Package Services [2,3,6] | (X) | (X) | 10,156 | 15,061 | 17,427 | 19,529 | 21,507 |
| Express mail [2,3,5] | 630 | 996 | 829 | 779 | 809 | 766 | 751 |
| Package Services (formerly Standard B) | 919 | 1,912 | 1,531 | 810 | 800 | 803 | 828 |
| Priority mail [2,3,4] | 1,555 | 4,837 | 5,455 | 7,664 | 8,206 | 8,717 | 9,387 |
| International economy mail (surface) [3] | 222 | 180 | (3) | (3) | (3) | (3) | (3) |
| International, airmail or total [3,7] | 941 | 1,477 | 2,388 | 2,702 | 2,674 | 2,614 | 2,630 |
| **Service revenue** | **1,310** | **2,191** | **3,790** | **3,380** | **3,630** | **3,760** | **3,720** |
| Certified [10] | 310 | 385 | 791 | 669 | 672 | 672 | 614 |
| Insurance [10] | 47 | 109 | 128 | 90 | 79 | 74 | 79 |
| Money orders | 155 | 235 | 182 | 159 | 153 | 147 | 147 |
| Other [10] | 592 | 1,342 | 2,635 | 2,462 | 2,726 | 2,863 | 2,880 |
| **Operating expenses (million dollars) [11]** | **40,490** | **62,992** | **75,426** | **73,641** | **77,121** | **72,436** | **74,696** |

– Represents zero. NA Not available. X Not applicable. Z Fewer than 500. [1] Items mailed at 1st class rates and weighing 11 ounces or less. [2] Beginning 2010, Express Mail, Priority Mail, First-Class Parcels, and Standard Parcels are not included in Mail categories but reclassified under Shipping and Package Services. [3] "Volume" and "Mailing & Shipping Revenue" restructured for the "Postal Accountability and Enhancement Act (PAEA) of 2006." Some categories eliminated. [4] Provides 2 to 3 day delivery service. [5] Overnight delivery of packages weighing up to 70 pounds. [6] Beginning 2010, also includes Package Services. [7] Airmail only, for 2005 and earlier. Beginning 2010, total international, including all international revenues and pieces formerly included in First-Class Mail, Standard Mail, and Package Services. [8] Includes discontinued operations, area offices, and nurses. Beginning 2010, nurses are included with clerks, and not "other" employment is reported. [9] For career bargaining unit employees. Includes fringe benefits. [10] Beginning 2000, return receipt revenue broken out from registry, certified, and insurance and included in "other." [11] Shown in year in which obligation was incurred.

Source: U.S. Postal Service, *FY2018 Annual Report to Congress,* 2019, and earlier reports, and unpublished data. See also <https://about.usps.com/strategic-planning/future-postal-service/publications.htm>.

# Information and Communications

This section presents statistics on the various information and communications media: publishing, including newspapers, periodicals, books, and software; motion pictures, sound recordings, broadcasting, and telecommunications; computers, and internet access and use: and information services, such as libraries.

**Information industry**—The U.S. Census Bureau's *Service Annual Survey* provides estimates of revenues and expenses of firms in the information sector. Data are based on the North American Industry Classification System (NAICS). The information sector comprises establishments engaged in the following: (1) producing and distributing information and cultural products, (2) providing the means to transmit or distribute these products as well as data or communications, and 3) processing data.

The main components of the information sector include the publishing industries, including software publishing, and both traditional publishing and publishing exclusively on the internet; the motion picture and sound recording industries; the broadcasting industries, including traditional broadcasting and broadcasting exclusively over the internet; the telecommunications industries; and web search portals, data processing industries, and information services.

Telecommunications encompasses wired (including broadband internet service), wireless (including mobile), and satellite telecommunications. Broadcasting covers radio, television, and cable and other subscription programming. Internet publishing and broadcasting, and web search portals are grouped together.

Service Annual Survey data from 1998 to 2003 are based on the 1997 NAICS; 2004 to 2012 data are based variously on 2002 and 2007 NAICS; beginning in 2013, data are all based on 2012 NAICS, with data for various previous years revised to accommodate the new NAICS codes. Major revisions in many communications industries affect the comparability of these data. For detailed information about NAICS, see <http://www.census.gov/eos/www/naics/>. See also the text in Section 15, Business Enterprise.

The 1997 Economic Census was the first to cover the new information sector of the economy. The census, conducted every 5 years, for the years ending in "2" and "7," provides information on the number of establishments, receipts, payroll, and paid employees for the United States and various geographic levels in the U.S., including the U.S. territories. Data covered in this edition of the *Statistical Abstract of the U.S.* come from the 2012 Economic Census. Data from the 2017 Economic Census will be released on a flow basis between September 2019 and December 2021.

The Bureau of Economic Analysis recently began producing statistics to measure the digital economy. The BEA is developing a digital economy satellite account to provide economic measures on the infrastructure that enables a digital economy, electronic commerce transactions, and the content that users of the digital economy create and access (digital media). Currently, the BEA covers only services that are primarily digital, and excludes goods and services that have a non-digital component. Thus, a service such as ride-sharing, which uses the internet to connect services, is not included since a major component (the ride) is not digital. The BEA is working on expanding coverage of the digital economy.

The Federal Communications Commission (FCC), established in 1934, regulates interstate and international communications by radio, television, wire, satellite, and cable across the entire U.S. Large carriers and holding companies file annual financial reports, which are publicly available. The FCC has jurisdiction over interstate and foreign communication services but not over intrastate or local services. Also, the gross operating revenues of the telephone carriers reporting publicly available data annually to the FCC are estimated to cover about 90 percent of the revenues of all U.S. telephone companies. Data are not comparable with Census Bureau's *Service Annual Survey* because of coverage and different accounting practices for those telephone companies which report to the FCC.

Reports filed by the broadcasting industry cover all radio and television stations operating in the United States. Private radio services represent the largest and most diverse group of licensees regulated by the FCC. These services provide voice, data communications, point-to-point, and point-to-multipoint radio communications for fixed and mobile communicators. Major users of these services are small businesses, the aviation industry, the maritime trades, the land transportation industry, the manufacturing industry, state and local public safety and governmental authorities, emergency medical service providers, amateur radio operators, and personal radio operations (CB and the General Mobile Radio Service). The FCC also licenses entities as private and common carriers. Private and common carriers provide fixed and land mobile communications service on a for-profit basis.

Statistics on publishing are available from the Census Bureau and various private agencies. Editor & Publisher Co., Irvine, CA, provides annual data on the number and circulation of daily and Sunday newspapers in its *Data Book*. Data on public libraries are from the Institute of Museums and Library Services. The Pew Research Center in Washington D.C. collects data on media use, including the internet and social media, and of mobile electronic devices, among the general public. MRI-Simmons (launched as a joint venture under GfK in 2019) also collects data on internet use, and use of other traditional media.

**Statistical reliability**—For a discussion of statistical collection and estimation, sampling procedures, and measures of statistical reliability applicable to Census Bureau data, see Appendix III.

## Table 1156. Information Industries—Type of Establishment, Employees, and Payroll: 2016

[Employees in thousands (3,448.0 represents 3,448,000); payroll in millions of dollars (317,501 represents $317,501,000,000). Excludes self-employed individuals, employees of private households, railroad employees, agricultural production employees, and most government employees. For more information, see source and Appendix III]

| Industry | 2012 NAICS code [1] | Establishments | | | | Employees [6] (1,000) | Annual payroll (mil. dol.) |
| | | Total [2] | Corporations [3] | Sole proprietorships [4] | Non-profits [5] | | |
| --- | --- | --- | --- | --- | --- | --- | --- |
| **Information industries**.............................. | **51** | **146,407** | **78,876** | **5,127** | **5,190** | **3,448.0** | **317,501** |
| Publishing industries (except internet)............... | 511 | 27,486 | 13,070 | 1,363 | 723 | 916.6 | 106,190 |
| Newspaper, periodical, book, and directory......... | 5111 | 17,256 | 6,676 | 1,102 | 706 | 370.4 | 22,408 |
| Newspaper publishers................................. | 51111 | 7,496 | 3,755 | 513 | 165 | 180.6 | 8,142 |
| Periodical publishers................................. | 51112 | 5,584 | 1,723 | 334 | 297 | 90.6 | 7,335 |
| Book publishers...................................... | 51113 | 2,574 | 769 | 160 | 214 | 64.1 | 5,020 |
| Directory and mailing list publishers............... | 51114 | 786 | 248 | 33 | 6 | 15.3 | 1,110 |
| Other publishers..................................... | 51119 | 816 | 181 | 62 | 24 | 19.7 | 801 |
| Greeting card publishers........................... | 511191 | 99 | 29 | 11 | (NA) | 13.8 | 473 |
| All other publishers................................ | 511199 | 717 | 152 | 51 | 24 | 5.9 | 327 |
| Software publishers.................................... | 5112 | 10,230 | 6,394 | 261 | 17 | 546.2 | 83,782 |
| Motion picture and sound recording industries....... | 512 | 25,497 | 6,220 | 1,263 | 599 | 447.6 | 17,411 |
| Motion picture and video industries................. | 5121 | 21,936 | 5,445 | 1,001 | 526 | 424.6 | 15,412 |
| Motion picture and video production............... | 51211 | 14,259 | 2,804 | 596 | 266 | 242.7 | 11,189 |
| Motion picture and video distribution............. | 51212 | 357 | 110 | 19 | 14 | 3.1 | 267 |
| Motion picture and video exhibition................ | 51213 | 4,620 | 1,996 | 272 | 233 | 151.7 | 1,906 |
| Motion picture theaters (except drive-ins)........ | 512131 | 4,414 | 1,962 | 221 | 232 | 150.5 | 1,882 |
| Drive-in motion picture theaters.................. | 512132 | 206 | 34 | 51 | 1 | 1.2 | 24 |
| Postproduction and other motion picture and video industries............................. | 51219 | 2,700 | 535 | 114 | 13 | 27.1 | 2,050 |
| Teleproduction and other postproduction services............................. | 512191 | 2,468 | 478 | 100 | 8 | 25.7 | 1,945 |
| Other motion picture and video industries........ | 512199 | 232 | 57 | 14 | 5 | 1.4 | 105 |
| Sound recording industries............................. | 5122 | 3,561 | 775 | 262 | 73 | 22.9 | 1,999 |
| Record production.................................... | 51221 | 353 | 65 | 16 | 3 | 1.0 | 70 |
| Integrated record production/distribution.......... | 51222 | 397 | 136 | 18 | 8 | 9.0 | 1,033 |
| Music publishers..................................... | 51223 | 705 | 184 | 71 | 5 | 5.2 | 464 |
| Sound recording studios............................. | 51224 | 1,703 | 304 | 138 | 12 | 5.1 | 293 |
| Other sound recording industries.................... | 51229 | 403 | 86 | 19 | 45 | 2.7 | 139 |
| Broadcasting (except internet)........................ | 515 | 8,311 | 3,504 | 293 | 1,203 | 267.1 | 22,328 |
| Radio and television broadcasting.................... | 5151 | 7,598 | 3,164 | 263 | 1,037 | 217.3 | 15,721 |
| Radio broadcasting................................... | 51511 | 5,413 | 1,960 | 210 | 758 | 92.1 | 5,196 |
| Radio networks.................................... | 515111 | 859 | 306 | 26 | 196 | 11.5 | 919 |
| Radio stations.................................... | 515112 | 4,554 | 1,654 | 184 | 562 | 80.6 | 4,277 |
| Television broadcasting.............................. | 51512 | 2,185 | 1,204 | 53 | 279 | 125.2 | 10,524 |
| Cable and other subscription programming......... | 5152 | 713 | 340 | 30 | 166 | 49.8 | 6,607 |
| Telecommunications................................... | 517 | 59,236 | 44,827 | 1,031 | 264 | 1,070.8 | 82,244 |
| Wired telecommunications carriers................... | 5171 | 36,257 | 33,689 | 202 | 241 | 753.3 | 59,529 |
| Wireless telecommunications carriers (except satellite)...................................... | 5172 | 15,845 | 9,048 | 299 | 6 | 244.7 | 16,866 |
| Satellite telecommunications........................ | 5174 | 463 | 172 | 23 | 2 | 8.2 | 887 |
| Other telecommunications............................ | 5179 | 6,671 | 1,918 | 507 | 15 | 64.6 | 4,962 |
| Telecommunications resellers...................... | 517911 | 2,148 | 573 | 111 | 4 | 25.7 | 1,654 |
| All other telecommunications...................... | 517919 | 4,523 | 1,345 | 396 | 11 | 38.9 | 3,308 |
| Data processing, hosting, and related services........................................... | 518 | 13,566 | 7,017 | 419 | 145 | 462.4 | 44,059 |
| Other information services........................... | 519 | 12,311 | 4,238 | 758 | 2,256 | 283.5 | 45,269 |
| News syndicates...................................... | 51911 | 451 | 328 | 8 | 16 | 7.9 | 685 |
| Libraries and archives............................... | 51912 | 2,223 | 86 | 49 | 2,011 | 26.3 | 857 |
| Internet publishing and broadcasting and web search portals.................................. | 51913 | 8,065 | 3,500 | 390 | 182 | 236.5 | 42,882 |
| All other information services....................... | 51919 | 1,572 | 324 | 311 | 47 | 12.9 | 845 |

NA Not available. [1] 2012 North American Industry Classification System; see text, this section and Section 15. [2] Includes other types of establishments, not shown separately. [3] An incorporated business that is granted a charter recognizing it as a separate legal entity having its own privileges, and liabilities distinct from those of its members. [4] An unincorporated business with a sole owner. [5] An organization that does not distribute surplus funds to its owners or shareholders, but instead uses surplus funds to help pursue its goals. Most non-profit organizations are exempt from income taxes. [6] For employees on the payroll for the pay period including March 12.

Source: U.S. Census Bureau, County Business Patterns, "Geography Area Series: County Business Patterns by Legal Form of Organization," <http://factfinder.census.gov>, accessed April 2018.

# Table 1157. Information Industries—Establishments, Revenue, Payroll, and Employees by Kind of Business: 2012

[1,238,463 represents $1,238,463,000,000. For establishments with payroll. Based on the 2012 Economic Census; see Appendix III]

| Kind of business | 2012 NAICS code [1] | Establish-ments | Receipts [2] (mil. dol.) | Annual payroll (mil. dol.) | Paid employees (1,000) |
|---|---|---|---|---|---|
| **Information industries**............... | **51** | **138,341** | **1,238,463** | **269,070** | **3,321** |
| Publishing industries (except internet)..................... | 511 | 27,788 | 272,152 | 80,426 | 876 |
| Newspaper, periodical, book, & directory publishers............... | 5111 | 18,940 | 101,076 | 25,050 | 466 |
| Software publishers.................. | 5112 | 8,848 | 171,075 | 55,376 | 411 |
| Motion picture & sound recording industries.......................... | 512 | 25,018 | 91,974 | 16,252 | 304 |
| Motion picture & video industries.................. | 5121 | 21,264 | 80,762 | 14,299 | 281 |
| Sound recording industries........................ | 5122 | 3,754 | 11,212 | 1,953 | 24 |
| Broadcasting (except internet)........................... | 515 | 9,597 | 126,723 | 20,332 | 278 |
| Radio broadcasting........................ | 51511 | 6,735 | 18,000 | 5,182 | 104 |
| Television broadcasting.................. | 51512 | 2,090 | 45,126 | 8,934 | 119 |
| Cable & other subscription programming........................ | 5152 | 772 | 63,596 | 6,217 | 56 |
| Telecommunications........................ | 517 | 50,698 | 545,594 | 75,895 | 1,134 |
| Wired telecommunications carriers.................. | 5171 | 32,688 | 285,663 | 54,232 | 781 |
| Wireless telecommunications carriers (except satellite)........... | 5172 | 13,458 | 225,397 | 17,041 | 293 |
| Satellite telecommunications....................... | 5174 | 535 | 6,802 | 859 | 10 |
| Other telecommunications........................ | 5179 | 4,017 | 27,732 | 3,763 | 51 |
| Data processing, hosting, and related services...................... | 518 | 14,689 | 107,994 | 41,126 | 497 |
| Other information services......................... | 519 | 10,551 | 94,026 | 35,038 | 231 |

[1] North American Industry Classification System, 2012; see text, this section and Section 15. [2] Includes value of sales, shipments, receipts, revenue, or business done.

Source: U.S. Census Bureau, 2012 Economic Census, "Table EC1200A1: All Sectors: Geographic Area Series: Economy-Wide Key Statistics: 2012," <http://factfinder.census.gov/>, accessed April 2016.

# Table 1158. Information Industries—Establishments, Employees, and Payroll by State: 2016

[Annual payroll in millions of dollars (317,501 represents $317,501,000,000). Based on Census Bureau's County Business Patterns and Nonemployer Statistics programs. Data based on North American Industry Classification System (NAICS) 2012 code 51]

| State | Establish-ments | Annual payroll (mil. dol.) | Paid employ-ees [1] | Non-employer establish-ments | State | Establish-ments | Annual payroll (mil. dol.) | Paid employ-ees [1] | Non-employer establish-ments |
|---|---|---|---|---|---|---|---|---|---|
| **U.S.**......... | **146,407** | **317,501** | **3,447,950** | **337,194** | MO......... | 2,559 | 3,866 | 58,009 | 4,467 |
| AL........... | 1,658 | 1,870 | 32,984 | 2,970 | MT......... | 663 | 428 | 8,503 | 1,032 |
| AK........... | 408 | 425 | 6,759 | 512 | NE......... | 915 | 1,149 | 19,203 | 1,338 |
| AZ........... | 2,272 | 3,175 | 48,161 | 6,006 | NV......... | 1,353 | 1,089 | 16,913 | 3,359 |
| AR........... | 1,085 | 1,375 | 25,303 | 1,711 | NH......... | 728 | 1,203 | 14,148 | 1,448 |
| CA........... | 23,830 | 88,840 | 711,680 | 63,372 | NJ......... | 3,821 | 8,951 | 86,792 | 10,448 |
| CO........... | 3,347 | 7,239 | 86,918 | 7,566 | NM......... | 776 | 543 | 15,080 | 1,654 |
| CT........... | 1,749 | 3,490 | 37,781 | 3,983 | NY......... | 11,836 | 31,469 | 296,728 | 31,642 |
| DE........... | 571 | 435 | 6,766 | 1,043 | NC......... | 3,743 | 5,942 | 83,205 | 8,505 |
| DC........... | 775 | 2,557 | 22,834 | 1,488 | ND......... | 345 | 453 | 7,274 | 434 |
| FL........... | 8,835 | 12,575 | 167,490 | 23,135 | OH......... | 4,035 | 6,104 | 84,760 | 8,799 |
| GA........... | 4,385 | 10,715 | 120,699 | 11,187 | OK......... | 1,493 | 1,478 | 27,919 | 2,676 |
| HI........... | 516 | 511 | 8,202 | 1,159 | OR......... | 2,167 | 2,629 | 38,361 | 5,105 |
| ID........... | 703 | 675 | 13,103 | 1,560 | PA......... | 5,229 | 9,457 | 111,248 | 10,403 |
| IL........... | 5,640 | 10,019 | 123,156 | 11,511 | RI......... | 476 | 486 | 7,035 | 951 |
| IN........... | 2,207 | 2,709 | 44,335 | 4,548 | SC......... | 1,494 | 2,178 | 36,207 | 3,599 |
| IA........... | 1,530 | 1,596 | 29,739 | 2,131 | SD......... | 453 | 324 | 7,208 | 632 |
| KS........... | 1,431 | 2,080 | 30,674 | 2,123 | TN......... | 2,696 | 2,896 | 48,714 | 7,117 |
| KY........... | 1,599 | 1,420 | 32,140 | 2,676 | TX......... | 9,677 | 19,255 | 241,572 | 24,140 |
| LA........... | 1,520 | 1,273 | 30,111 | 3,366 | UT......... | 1,539 | 3,257 | 46,034 | 4,048 |
| ME........... | 808 | 643 | 11,872 | 1,315 | VT......... | 507 | 422 | 7,041 | 860 |
| MD........... | 2,573 | 4,216 | 52,412 | 6,929 | VA......... | 4,016 | 8,245 | 87,084 | 8,022 |
| MA........... | 3,722 | 12,674 | 114,607 | 8,083 | WA......... | 3,528 | 20,946 | 132,733 | 7,443 |
| MI........... | 3,983 | 4,530 | 65,937 | 8,258 | WV......... | 689 | 493 | 10,492 | 842 |
| MN........... | 2,679 | 4,383 | 58,844 | 5,404 | WI......... | 2,486 | 4,003 | 55,771 | 4,115 |
| MS........... | 970 | 628 | 13,464 | 1,447 | WY......... | 387 | 184 | 3,945 | 632 |

[1] Number of paid employees for pay period including March 12.

Source: U.S. Census Bureau, County Business Patterns, "Geography Area Series: County Business Patterns, 2016"; and Nonemployer Statistics, "Geographic Area Series: Nonemployer Statistics for the U.S."; <http://factfinder.census.gov/>, accessed June 2018. See also <https://www.census.gov/programs-surveys/cbp.html> and <https://www.census.gov/programs-surveys/nonemployer-statistics.html>.

## Table 1159. Digital Economy—Value Added, Gross Output, and Employment by Industry: 2010 to 2017

[In billions of dollars (944.7 represents $944,700,000,000), except as noted. Estimates are preliminary and are based on goods and services that are primarily digital. BEA includes in its definition of the digital economy: (1) the digital-enabling infrastructure needed for an interconnected computer network to exist and operate, (2) the digital transactions that take place using that system ("e-commerce"), and (3) the content that digital economy users create and access ("digital media"). Industries are based on 2012 North American Classification System (NAICS). For discussion of defining and measuring the digital economy, see <https://www.bea.gov/data/special-topics/digital-economy>]

| Industry | Value added (bil. dol.) [1] | | | Gross output (bil. dol.) [1] | | | Employees (1,000s) | | |
|---|---|---|---|---|---|---|---|---|---|
| | 2010 | 2016 | 2017 | 2010 | 2016 | 2017 | 2010 | 2016 | 2017 |
| **All industries** | **944.7** | **1,277.0** | **1,351.3** | **1,512.2** | **1,949.6** | **2,050.1** | **4,282** | **4,979** | **5,077** |
| **Private industries** | **931.1** | **1,264.2** | **1,338.1** | **1,498.4** | **1,936.6** | **2,036.7** | **4,184** | **4,898** | **4,995** |
| Agriculture and mining | 0.1 | 0.2 | 0.1 | 0.1 | 0.2 | 0.1 | (Z) | (Z) | (Z) |
| Utilities | 0.4 | 0.5 | 0.5 | 0.4 | 0.5 | 0.5 | 1 | 1 | 1 |
| Construction | 0.2 | 0.3 | 0.4 | 0.2 | 0.3 | 0.4 | 1 | 1 | 2 |
| Manufacturing | 132.8 | 121.8 | 129.8 | 206.3 | 167.0 | 176.7 | 615 | 534 | 551 |
| Wholesale trade | 23.2 | 28.0 | 30.7 | 28.2 | 33.5 | 35.9 | 155 | 138 | 140 |
| Retail trade | 39.9 | 81.0 | 89.2 | 52.3 | 110.3 | 122.3 | 155 | 285 | 310 |
| Transportation and warehousing | 0.7 | 0.8 | 0.8 | 0.7 | 0.8 | 0.8 | 3 | 4 | 4 |
| Information | 501.3 | 686.1 | 720.3 | 869.4 | 1,163.9 | 1,209.7 | 1,494 | 1,583 | 1,585 |
| Publishing, except internet (includes software) | 103.3 | 167.0 | 177.9 | 150.7 | 207.0 | 221.3 | 281 | 401 | 411 |
| Motion picture and sound recording | 8.1 | 9.8 | 9.6 | 11.4 | 15.7 | 16.0 | 26 | 41 | 41 |
| Broadcasting and telecommunications | 317.5 | 358.5 | 359.6 | 590.0 | 725.7 | 731.7 | 970 | 861 | 837 |
| Data processing, internet publishing, and other information services | 72.5 | 150.8 | 173.2 | 117.2 | 215.4 | 240.7 | 217 | 279 | 296 |
| Finance, insurance, real estate, rental, and leasing | 6.1 | 7.1 | 7.4 | 6.1 | 7.1 | 7.4 | 20 | 19 | 19 |
| Professional and business services | 209.0 | 317.6 | 337.7 | 310.3 | 423.7 | 453.0 | 1,521 | 2,101 | 2,156 |
| Educational services, health care, and social assistance | 11.5 | 14.3 | 14.9 | 15.5 | 19.0 | 19.9 | 149 | 151 | 150 |
| Arts, entertainment, recreation, accommodation, and food services | 0.3 | 0.4 | 0.4 | 0.3 | 0.4 | 0.4 | 3 | 3 | 3 |
| Other services, except government | 5.5 | 6.1 | 5.9 | 8.6 | 10.0 | 9.5 | 67 | 78 | 75 |
| Government | 13.6 | 12.7 | 13.2 | 13.8 | 13.0 | 13.4 | 98 | 82 | 82 |
| Federal | 6.2 | 5.1 | 5.3 | 6.1 | 5.1 | 5.3 | 28 | 21 | 21 |
| State and local | 7.4 | 7.6 | 7.8 | 7.7 | 7.9 | 8.1 | 70 | 60 | 61 |
| Private goods-producing industries | 133.1 | 122.3 | 130.4 | 206.6 | 167.5 | 177.3 | 616 | 536 | 553 |
| Private services-producing industries | 798.0 | 1,141.9 | 1,207.7 | 1,291.9 | 1,769.1 | 1,859.4 | 3,568 | 4,362 | 4,442 |

Z Less than 500 employees. [1] These estimates are based on data valued in producers' prices and exclude transportation costs and wholesale and retail trade markups, with the exception of retail trade markups associated with e-commerce transactions.

Source: U.S. Bureau of Economic Analysis, Special Topics: Digital Economy, "Data for 1997-2017," <https://www.bea.gov/data/special-topics/digital-economy>, accessed April 2019.

## Table 1160. Digital Economy—Value Added and Gross Output by Commodity: 2005 to 2017

[In billions of dollars (13,036.6 represents $13,036,600,000,000). Estimates are preliminary and are based on goods and services that are primarily digital. BEA includes in its definition of the digital economy: (1) the digital-enabling infrastructure needed for an interconnected computer network to exist and operate, (2) the digital transactions that take place using that system ("e-commerce"), and (3) the content that digital economy users create and access ("digital media"). See headnote, Table 1159]

| Commodity | Value added (GDP) [1,2] | | | | Gross output [2] | | | |
|---|---|---|---|---|---|---|---|---|
| | 2005 | 2010 | 2016 | 2017 | 2005 | 2010 | 2016 | 2017 |
| BILLION DOLLARS | | | | | | | | |
| Total U.S. economy | 13,036.6 | 14,992.1 | 18,707.2 | 19,485.4 | 23,512.9 | 26,422.4 | 32,776.4 | 34,445.6 |
| **Digital economy, total** | **755.9** | **944.7** | **1,277.0** | **1,351.3** | **1,329.5** | **1,512.2** | **1,949.6** | **2,050.1** |
| Digital-enabling infrastructure | 696.4 | 840.6 | 1,087.7 | 1,143.4 | 1,234.0 | 1,354.4 | 1,658.6 | 1,734.6 |
| Hardware | 99.3 | 102.2 | 88.0 | 96.3 | 210.5 | 150.8 | 120.5 | 126.5 |
| Software | 116.2 | 151.7 | 224.9 | 239.0 | 167.4 | 194.4 | 260.3 | 277.3 |
| Telecommunications | 286.4 | 304.1 | 341.8 | 339.6 | 551.0 | 576.3 | 675.4 | 682.8 |
| Support services | 194.4 | 282.6 | 433.1 | 468.5 | 305.0 | 432.8 | 602.4 | 647.9 |
| E-commerce and digital media | 59.5 | 104.0 | 189.2 | 207.8 | 95.5 | 157.9 | 291.0 | 315.6 |
| *Addendum:* | | | | | | | | |
| Digital goods | 128.6 | 128.4 | 116.6 | 124.1 | 281.6 | 201.8 | 161.8 | 171.0 |
| Digital services | 627.3 | 816.3 | 1,160.3 | 1,227.2 | 1,047.9 | 1,310.4 | 1,787.8 | 1,879.1 |
| PERCENT | | | | | | | | |
| Total U.S. economy | 100.0 | 100.0 | 100.0 | 100.0 | 100.0 | 100.0 | 100.0 | 100.0 |
| **Digital economy, total** | **5.8** | **6.3** | **6.8** | **6.9** | **5.7** | **5.7** | **5.9** | **6.0** |
| Digital-enabling infrastructure | 5.3 | 5.6 | 5.8 | 5.9 | 5.2 | 5.1 | 5.1 | 5.0 |
| Hardware | 0.8 | 0.7 | 0.5 | 0.5 | 0.9 | 0.6 | 0.4 | 0.4 |
| Software | 0.9 | 1.0 | 1.2 | 1.2 | 0.7 | 0.7 | 0.8 | 0.8 |
| Telecommunications | 2.2 | 2.0 | 1.8 | 1.7 | 2.3 | 2.2 | 2.1 | 2.0 |
| Support services | 1.5 | 1.9 | 2.3 | 2.4 | 1.3 | 1.6 | 1.8 | 1.9 |
| E-commerce and digital media | 0.5 | 0.7 | 1.0 | 1.1 | 0.4 | 0.6 | 0.9 | 0.9 |
| *Addendum:* | | | | | | | | |
| Digital goods | 1.0 | 0.9 | 0.6 | 0.6 | 1.2 | 0.8 | 0.5 | 0.5 |
| Digital services | 4.8 | 5.4 | 6.2 | 6.3 | 4.5 | 5.0 | 5.5 | 5.5 |

[1] Value added by commodity is prepared by (1) calculating ratios of commodity output to total industry output for each industry and digital commodity, (2) applying these ratios to each industry's value added, and (3) aggregating the result by digital commodity. [2] These estimates are based on data valued in producers' prices and exclude transportation costs and wholesale and retail trade markups, with the exception of retail trade markups associated with e-commerce transactions.

Source: U.S. Bureau of Economic Analysis, Special Topics: Digital Economy, "Data for 1997-2017," <https://www.bea.gov/data/special-topics/digital-economy>, accessed April 2019.

## Table 1161. Information Sector Services—Estimated Revenue and Expenses: 2015 to 2017

[In millions of dollars (1,405,882 represents $1,405,882,000,000). For all employer firms regardless of tax status. Estimates have been adjusted to the results of the 2012 Economic Census and are based on the 2012 North American Industry Classification System (NAICS). Based on the Service Annual Survey and administrative data; see Appendix III]

| Industry | NAICS code | Operating revenue | | | Operating expenses | | |
|---|---|---|---|---|---|---|---|
| | | 2015 | 2016 | 2017 | 2015 | 2016 | 2017 |
| **Information industries**..................... | **51** | **1,405,882** | **1,493,592** | **1,533,690** | **1,076,897** | **1,130,936** | **1,172,687** |
| Publishing industries (except internet)........... | 511 | 293,771 | 308,489 | 317,850 | 208,458 | 218,323 | 227,721 |
| Newspaper publishers.................... | 51111 | 26,550 | 25,264 | 25,204 | 24,950 | 23,650 | 24,022 |
| Periodical publishers..................... | 51112 | 28,314 | 28,237 | 28,258 | 23,026 | 23,123 | 23,390 |
| Book publishers......................... | 51113 | 27,676 | 27,744 | 27,478 | 17,587 | 17,267 | 17,578 |
| Directory and mailing list publishers..... | 51114 | 8,214 | 7,777 | 7,533 | 7,301 | 6,674 | 6,419 |
| Greeting card publishers................. | 511191 | 3,457 | 3,351 | 3,705 | 2,486 | (S) | (S) |
| All other publishers..................... | 511199 | 1,219 | 1,318 | 1,310 | 707 | 790 | 781 |
| Software publishers...................... | 5112 | 198,341 | 214,798 | 224,362 | 132,401 | 144,662 | 153,281 |
| Motion picture and sound recording industries........... | 512 | 98,982 | 103,120 | 103,886 | 69,571 | 73,049 | 74,399 |
| Motion picture and video production and distribution [1]... | 5121x | 64,434 | 66,761 | 64,941 | 44,582 | 46,833 | 46,202 |
| Motion picture and video exhibition..... | 51213 | 15,787 | 16,536 | 17,526 | 12,349 | 13,050 | 14,244 |
| Teleproduction and other postproduction services....... | 512191 | 5,500 | 5,885 | 6,001 | 4,872 | 4,823 | 4,912 |
| Other motion picture and video industries.............. | 512199 | 398 | 407 | 425 | 265 | 294 | 277 |
| Record production....................... | 51221 | 392 | 387 | 385 | 325 | 299 | 289 |
| Integrated record production/distribution.................. | 51222 | 5,765 | 6,229 | 7,207 | 3,883 | 4,316 | 4,781 |
| Music publishers........................ | 51223 | 5,054 | 5,250 | 5,754 | 2,024 | 2,144 | 2,401 |
| Sound recording studios................. | 51224 | 1,086 | 1,097 | 1,073 | 835 | 865 | 845 |
| Other sound recording industries......... | 51229 | 566 | 568 | 574 | 436 | 425 | 448 |
| Broadcasting (except internet)............ | 515 | 148,462 | 159,227 | 160,879 | 103,858 | 111,121 | 111,631 |
| Radio networks.......................... | 515111 | 6,509 | 7,089 | 7,641 | 5,017 | 5,296 | 5,623 |
| Radio stations........................... | 515112 | 12,445 | 12,807 | 12,360 | 10,034 | 10,343 | 10,236 |
| Television broadcasting.................. | 51512 | 50,577 | 57,823 | 57,551 | 42,448 | 47,131 | 46,103 |
| Cable and other subscription programming........ | 5152 | 78,931 | 81,508 | 83,327 | 46,359 | 48,351 | 49,669 |
| Telecommunications...................... | 517 | 601,970 | 628,045 | 617,160 | 454,759 | 484,584 | 484,605 |
| Wired telecommunications carriers....... | 5171 | 306,384 | 326,119 | 315,343 | 239,533 | 262,993 | 262,254 |
| Wireless telecommunications carriers (except satellite)... | 5172 | 254,406 | 259,321 | 257,845 | 184,527 | 188,983 | 189,136 |
| Satellite telecommunications............. | 5174 | 6,926 | 7,208 | 6,947 | 5,316 | 5,634 | 5,432 |
| Telecommunications resellers............ | 517911 | 18,708 | 19,078 | 19,524 | 12,413 | 12,973 | 12,785 |
| All other telecommunications............ | 517919 | 15,546 | 16,319 | 17,501 | 12,970 | 14,001 | 14,998 |
| Data processing, hosting, and related services............ | 518 | 129,957 | 139,715 | 155,934 | 124,777 | 119,866 | 131,713 |
| Other information services................ | 519 | 132,740 | 154,996 | 177,981 | 115,474 | 123,993 | 142,618 |
| News syndicates........................ | 51911 | 2,042 | 2,091 | 1,854 | 1,692 | 1,691 | 1,490 |
| Libraries and archives................... | 51912 | 2,514 | 2,454 | 2,756 | 2,352 | 2,445 | 2,615 |
| Internet publishing and broadcasting, and Web search portals............... | 51913 | 125,868 | 148,039 | 170,781 | 109,619 | 117,929 | 136,426 |
| Other information services............... | 51919 | 2,316 | 2,412 | 2,590 | 1,811 | 1,928 | 2,087 |

S Data does not meet publication standards. [1] Includes NAICS 51211 (Motion Picture and Video Production) and NAICS 51212 (Motion Picture and Video Distribution).

Source: U.S. Census Bureau, Service Annual Survey, "Service Annual Survey Latest Data (NAICS-basis): 2017," <https://www.census.gov/programs-surveys/sas/data.html>, accessed December 2018.

## Table 1162. Audience Use of Media by Type—Summary: 2018

[In percent, except total population (247,786 represents 247,786,000). As of Fall 2018. For persons age 18 and over. Represents the percent of persons using each media type during an average week, except as noted. Based on a sample and subject to sampling error]

| Item | Total population (1,000) | TV viewing | TV prime time viewing | Cable/ pay TV viewing [1] | Radio listening | Newspaper reading [2] | Internet use |
|---|---|---|---|---|---|---|---|
| **Total**.................... | **247,786** | **89.01** | **77.69** | **78.52** | **85.25** | **38.25** | **84.38** |
| 18 to 24 years old.............. | 29,586 | 78.06 | 58.55 | 76.07 | 87.17 | 27.35 | 96.86 |
| 25 to 34 years old.............. | 44,467 | 82.60 | 68.36 | 72.91 | 87.68 | 29.92 | 95.82 |
| 35 to 44 years old.............. | 40,296 | 87.75 | 76.88 | 77.63 | 90.33 | 33.16 | 95.20 |
| 45 to 54 years old.............. | 42,301 | 91.70 | 81.98 | 79.34 | 91.00 | 38.44 | 89.06 |
| 55 to 64 years old.............. | 41,563 | 93.81 | 84.36 | 79.72 | 84.84 | 41.73 | 78.74 |
| 65 years old and over.......... | 49,573 | 96.00 | 88.91 | 84.03 | 73.22 | 53.29 | 58.61 |
| Male........................ | 119,610 | 88.71 | 76.57 | 78.70 | 86.42 | 38.39 | 83.81 |
| Female...................... | 128,176 | 89.28 | 78.74 | 78.35 | 84.15 | 38.12 | 84.91 |
| White only.................. | 180,848 | 89.44 | 79.09 | 79.79 | 85.68 | 39.18 | 85.52 |
| Black only.................. | 30,171 | 91.49 | 77.48 | 80.64 | 84.68 | 44.11 | 79.35 |
| Other races/multiple classifications. .. | 36,767 | 84.87 | 71.01 | 70.55 | 83.57 | 28.88 | 82.89 |
| Employed: | | | | | | | |
| Full time.................... | 122,371 | 88.20 | 76.18 | 79.20 | 90.69 | 35.77 | 93.86 |
| Part time.................... | 29,623 | 84.92 | 71.64 | 76.67 | 86.82 | 37.92 | 89.62 |
| Not employed................ | 95,792 | 91.31 | 81.50 | 78.23 | 77.81 | 41.53 | 70.65 |
| Household income: | | | | | | | |
| Less than $50,000............ | 86,674 | 88.07 | 76.52 | 69.59 | 79.31 | 37.47 | 70.69 |
| $50,000 to $74,999........... | 42,964 | 88.80 | 76.07 | 80.77 | 86.25 | 39.87 | 86.55 |
| $75,000 to $149,999.......... | 77,946 | 89.76 | 79.73 | 82.97 | 89.66 | 38.17 | 92.39 |
| $150,000 or more............ | 40,202 | 89.80 | 78.01 | 86.72 | 88.43 | 38.35 | 96.05 |

[1] In the past 7 days. [2] One or more issues over a 28-day period.

Source: © Fall 2018, MRI Survey of the American Consumer. Courtesy of MRI-Simmons. See also <https://www.mrisimmons.com/>.

# Table 1163. Utilization and Number of Selected Media: 2000 to 2017

[100.2 represents 100,200,000]

| Media | Unit | 2000 | 2005 | 2010 | 2011 | 2012 | 2013 | 2014 | 2015 | 2016 | 2017 |
|---|---|---|---|---|---|---|---|---|---|---|---|
| Households with— | | | | | | | | | | | |
| Telephones [1] | Millions | 100.2 | 107.0 | 114.0 | 114.4 | 116.9 | 118.4 | 119.9 | 122.2 | 122.6 | 122.1 |
| Telephone service [1] | Percent | 94.1 | 92.9 | 95.5 | 95.6 | 95.8 | 95.7 | 96.1 | 96.3 | 96.3 | 95.8 |
| Landline households with wireless telephone [2] | Percent | (X) | 42.4 | 58.1 | 55.0 | 52.5 | 49.5 | 44.7 | 41.6 | 40.2 | 37.8 |
| Wireless-only [2] | Percent | (X) | 7.3 | 26.6 | 31.6 | 35.8 | 39.4 | 44.0 | 47.4 | 49.3 | 52.5 |
| Total broadcast stations [3,4] | Number | (NA) | 27,354 | 30,630 | 30,411 | 30,470 | 30,432 | 30,592 | 31,032 | 32,397 | 33,006 |
| Radio stations | Number | (NA) | 13,660 | 14,619 | 14,952 | 15,196 | 15,358 | 15,432 | 15,480 | 15,516 | 15,503 |
| AM stations | Number | 4,685 | 4,757 | 4,782 | 4,766 | 4,738 | 4,727 | 4,705 | 4,684 | 4,669 | 4,639 |
| FM commercial | Number | 5,892 | 6,231 | 6,526 | 6,542 | 6,598 | 6,612 | 6,652 | 6,701 | 6,746 | 6,744 |
| FM educational | Number | (NA) | 2,672 | 3,311 | 3,644 | 3,860 | 4,019 | 4,075 | 4,095 | 4,101 | 4,120 |
| Television stations [3] | Number | 1,663 | 1,750 | 1,781 | 1,783 | 1,781 | 1,784 | 1,785 | 1,782 | 1,778 | 1,767 |
| Commercial | Number | 1,288 | 1,370 | 1,390 | 1,387 | 1,386 | 1,388 | 1,390 | 1,387 | 1,384 | 1,377 |
| VHF TV band | Number | 567 | 588 | 368 | 360 | 358 | 358 | 358 | 356 | 351 | 364 |
| UHF TV band | Number | 721 | 782 | 1,022 | 1,027 | 1,028 | 1,030 | 1,032 | 1,031 | 1,033 | 1,013 |
| Educational | Number | (NA) | 380 | 391 | 396 | 395 | 396 | 395 | 395 | 394 | 390 |
| VHF TV band | Number | (NA) | 126 | 107 | 107 | 107 | 107 | 106 | 106 | 105 | 114 |
| UHF TV band | Number | (NA) | 254 | 284 | 289 | 288 | 289 | 289 | 289 | 289 | 276 |
| Broadband subscribers: [5,9] | | | | | | | | | | | |
| Total fixed broadband [6] | Millions | 6.8 | 47.8 | 84.5 | 88.3 | 92.5 | 96.0 | 98.2 | 102.2 | 105.7 | 106.3 |
| 25 Mbps/3 Mbps [7] | Millions | (NA) | (NA) | (NA) | (NA) | (NA) | (NA) | 42.7 | 54.3 | 62.9 | 68.0 |
| Mobile wireless [8] | Millions | (NA) | (NA) | 97.5 | 141.9 | 170.1 | 197.4 | 240.0 | 273.7 | 299.3 | 302.6 |
| Residential fixed broadband [6] | Millions | 5.2 | 44.0 | 76.9 | 80.7 | 84.4 | 87.6 | 89.5 | 93.4 | 96.6 | 97.1 |
| 25 Mbps/3 Mbps [7] | Millions | (NA) | (NA) | (NA) | (NA) | (NA) | (NA) | 40.9 | 51.8 | 59.5 | 64.3 |
| Residential mobile wireless | Millions | (NA) | (NA) | 72.5 | 105.8 | 131.4 | 159.2 | 201.2 | 229.1 | 253.0 | 256.0 |

NA Not available. X Not applicable. [1] As of November. Based on Current Population Survey. Source: Federal Communications Commission, prior to 2011, *Telephone Subscribership in the United States*, December 2011, and earlier reports. Beginning 2012, *Universal Service Monitoring Report, 2018,* and earlier reports. See also <https://www.fcc.gov/general/federal-state-joint-board-monitoring-reports>. [2] For January to June. Based on National Health Interview Survey. For families living in the same housing unit. Source: U.S. National Center for Health Statistics, *Wireless Substitution: Early Release of Estimates From the National Health Interview Survey, January–June 2018,* December 2018, and earlier reports. [3] As of December 31. Source: Federal Communications Commission Encyclopedia, "Broadcast Station Totals," <https://www.fcc.gov/media/radio/radio-lists>, accessed June 2019. [4] Includes Class A, Low Power TV, UHF and VHF Translators; FM Translators and Boosters; and Low Power FM stations. [5] As of December. Internet access over 200 kilobits per second in at least one direction. Based on FCC Form 477. Source: Federal Communications Commission, Wireline Competition Bureau, *Internet Access Services: Status as of December 31, 2016,* February 2018, and previous reports, and *Internet Access Services: Status as of June 30, 2017,* November 2018. [6] Includes aDSL, sDSL, cable modem, fiber-to-the-premises, satellite, fixed wireless, and power line/other. [7] Internet download and upload speeds, measured in megabits per second (Mbps). [8] Data prior to 2008 not shown due to reporting instruction changes on FCC Form 477. [9] For 2017, data for the following items under broadband internet subscribers are as of June 2017.

Source: Compiled from sources mentioned in footnotes.

# Table 1164. Publishing Industries—Estimated Revenue by Source and Media Type: 2010 to 2017

[In millions of dollars (260,795 represents $260,795,000,000). 2010 data based on the 2007 North American Industry Classification System (NAICS); beginning 2013, data based on 2012 NAICS. See text, this section and Section 15, and Appendix III]

| Source of revenue and media type | 2010 | 2014 | 2015 | 2016 | 2017 |
|---|---|---|---|---|---|
| **Publishing industries (except internet), NAICS 511 [1]** | **260,795** | **291,575** | **293,771** | **308,489** | **317,850** |
| Newspaper publishers, NAICS 51111 | 33,360 | 28,112 | 26,550 | 25,264 | 25,204 |
| Subscription and sales | 8,491 | 8,040 | 8,873 | 8,848 | 8,852 |
| Advertising space | 20,378 | 15,667 | 14,734 | 13,648 | 13,438 |
| Printing services | 1,214 | 1,454 | 1,109 | 1,081 | 1,067 |
| Distribution services | 1,268 | 1,052 | 614 | 547 | 533 |
| All other operating revenue | 2,009 | 1,899 | 1,220 | 1,140 | 1,314 |
| Print newspapers | 26,973 | 20,421 | 19,033 | 17,775 | 17,270 |
| Online newspapers | 1,614 | 2,901 | 4,534 | 4,680 | 4,961 |
| Other media newspapers | 282 | 385 | (S) | (S) | 59 |
| Periodical publishers, NAICS 51112 | 31,876 | 29,378 | 28,314 | 28,237 | 28,258 |
| Subscription and sales | 10,764 | 10,435 | 10,108 | 9,861 | (S) |
| Advertising space | 13,938 | 12,475 | 14,496 | 14,425 | (S) |
| All other operating revenue | 5,499 | 5,005 | 2,573 | 2,831 | 2,601 |
| Print periodicals | 20,587 | 17,790 | 16,818 | 16,550 | (S) |
| Online periodicals | 3,402 | 4,433 | 6,569 | 6,582 | 6,886 |
| Other media periodicals | 713 | 687 | (S) | (S) | (S) |
| Book publishers, NAICS 51113 [1] | 27,735 | 26,891 | 27,676 | 27,744 | 27,478 |
| Textbooks | 8,596 | 8,616 | 11,707 | 11,121 | 10,869 |
| Children's books | 3,189 | 3,234 | 1,900 | 1,911 | 1,981 |
| General reference books | 637 | 625 | (S) | (S) | (S) |
| Professional, technical, and scholarly books | 5,131 | 4,369 | 6,426 | 7,007 | (S) |
| Adult trade books | 6,626 | 5,551 | 5,176 | 5,425 | 5,378 |
| Print books | 19,890 | 17,127 | 16,636 | 16,569 | 16,109 |
| Online books | 3,297 | 4,274 | 7,513 | 7,760 | (S) |
| Other media books | 992 | 994 | 1,389 | 1,431 | (S) |
| Directory and mailing list publishers, NAICS 51114 [1] | 11,987 | 8,602 | 8,214 | 7,777 | 7,533 |
| Subscription and sales | 2,067 | 3,436 | 2,997 | 2,980 | 3,192 |
| Advertising space | 9,226 | 4,707 | 4,320 | 3,758 | 3,342 |
| Print directories, databases, and other information collections | 7,360 | 4,387 | 3,179 | 2,613 | (S) |
| Online directories, databases, and other information collections | 3,507 | 3,425 | 3,644 | 3,596 | 3,314 |
| Greeting card publishers operating revenue, NAICS 511191 | 3,829 | 3,501 | 3,457 | 3,351 | 3,705 |

S Figure does not meet publication standards. [1] Includes other industries or revenue sources not shown separately.

Source: U.S. Census Bureau, Service Annual Survey, "Service Annual Survey Latest Data (NAICS-basis): 2017" and "Service Annual Survey Historical Tables," <https://www.census.gov/programs-surveys/sas/data.html>, accessed December 2018.

## Table 1165. Daily and Sunday Newspapers—Number and Circulation: 1970 to 2018

[Circulation in millions (62.1 represents 62,100,000). Number of newspapers as of February 1 the following year, except as noted. Circulation figures as of 6-month period ended primarily September 30 of year shown. Covers all 50 States and D.C. For English language newspapers only]

| Type | 1970 | 1980 | 1990 | 2000 | 2005 | 2010 | 2013[3] | 2014[3] | 2015[3] | 2016[3] | 2017[3] | 2018[3] |
|---|---|---|---|---|---|---|---|---|---|---|---|---|
| **NUMBER** | | | | | | | | | | | | |
| **Total daily newspapers** [1] | **1,748** | **1,745** | **1,611** | **1,480** | **1,452** | **(NA)** | **1,395** | **1,331** | **1,338** | **1,286** | **1,277** | **1,279** |
| Morning | 334 | 387 | 559 | 766 | 817 | (NA) | 980 | 953 | 972 | 939 | 947 | 925 |
| Evening | 1,429 | 1,388 | 1,084 | 727 | 645 | (NA) | 444 | 402 | 389 | 369 | 356 | 354 |
| Sunday newspapers | 586 | 736 | 863 | 917 | 914 | (NA) | 934 | 923 | 904 | 866 | 857 | 840 |
| **NET PAID CIRCULATION (mil.)** | | | | | | | | | | | | |
| Total daily newspapers [1] | 62.1 | 62.2 | 62.3 | 55.8 | 53.3 | (NA) | 40.7 | 40.4 | 34.9 | 33.4 | 29.2 | 25.7 |
| Morning | 25.9 | 29.4 | 41.3 | 46.8 | 46.1 | (NA) | 37.0 | 36.8 | 31.6 | 30.4 | 26.2 | 23.0 |
| Evening | 36.2 | 32.8 | 21.0 | 9.0 | 7.2 | (NA) | 3.7 | 3.7 | 3.3 | 3.1 | 3.0 | 2.7 |
| Sunday newspapers | 49.2 | 54.7 | 62.6 | 59.4 | 55.3 | (NA) | 43.3 | 42.8 | 40.0 | 37.8 | 33.2 | 29.3 |
| **PER CAPITA CIRCULATION** [2] | | | | | | | | | | | | |
| Total daily newspapers [1] | 0.30 | 0.27 | 0.25 | 0.20 | 0.18 | (NA) | 0.13 | 0.13 | 0.11 | 0.10 | 0.09 | 0.08 |
| Morning | 0.13 | 0.13 | 0.17 | 0.17 | 0.16 | (NA) | 0.12 | 0.12 | 0.10 | 0.09 | 0.08 | 0.07 |
| Evening | 0.18 | 0.14 | 0.08 | 0.03 | 0.02 | (NA) | 0.01 | 0.01 | 0.01 | 0.01 | 0.01 | 0.01 |
| Sunday newspapers | 0.24 | 0.24 | 0.25 | 0.21 | 0.19 | (NA) | 0.14 | 0.13 | 0.12 | 0.12 | 0.10 | 0.09 |

NA Not available. [1] All-day newspapers are counted in both morning and evening rows but only once in total. Circulation is divided equally between morning and evening. [2] Based on U.S. Census Bureau estimated resident population as of July 1 of year shown. [3] Number of newspapers as of January 1 of following year.

Source: Editor & Publisher, 18475 Bandilier Circle, Fountain Valley, CA 92708, *Editor & Publisher Newspaper DataBook* ©, annual. See also <http://www.editorandpublisher.com/>.

## Table 1166. Daily and Sunday Newspapers—Number and Circulation: Total, 1997 to 2018, and by State, 2018

[Circulation in thousands (56,728 represents 56,728,000). Number of newspapers as of February 1 the following year, except as noted. Circulation as of 6-month period ended primarily September 30 of year shown. Covers the 50 states and D.C. For English language newspapers only]

| State | Daily Number | Daily Circulation [1] Net paid (1,000) | Daily Circulation [1] Per capita [2] | Sunday Number | Sunday Net paid circulation [1] (1,000) | State | Daily Number | Daily Circulation [1] Net paid (1,000) | Daily Circulation [1] Per capita [2] | Sunday Number | Sunday Net paid circulation [1] (1,000) |
|---|---|---|---|---|---|---|---|---|---|---|---|
| 1997 | 1,509 | 56,728 | 0.21 | 903 | 60,484 | IN | 67 | 719 | 0.11 | 29 | 777 |
| 1998 | 1,489 | 56,182 | 0.20 | 898 | 60,066 | IA | 33 | 321 | 0.10 | 13 | 305 |
| 1999 | 1,483 | 55,979 | 0.20 | 905 | 59,894 | KS | 30 | 219 | 0.08 | 11 | 170 |
| 2000 | 1,480 | 55,773 | 0.20 | 917 | 59,421 | KY | 21 | 284 | 0.06 | 14 | 307 |
| 2001 | 1,468 | 55,578 | 0.19 | 913 | 59,090 | LA | 18 | 232 | 0.05 | 13 | 254 |
| 2002 | 1,457 | 55,186 | 0.19 | 913 | 58,780 | ME | 7 | 108 | 0.08 | 5 | 95 |
| 2003 | 1,456 | 55,185 | 0.19 | 917 | 58,495 | MD | 9 | 213 | 0.04 | 8 | 340 |
| 2004 | 1,457 | 54,626 | 0.19 | 915 | 57,753 | MA | 30 | 633 | 0.09 | 16 | 651 |
| 2005 | 1,452 | 53,345 | 0.18 | 914 | 55,270 | MI | 47 | 670 | 0.07 | 24 | 744 |
| 2006 | 1,437 | 52,329 | 0.18 | 907 | 53,175 | MN | 22 | 586 | 0.10 | 14 | 787 |
| 2007 | 1,422 | 50,742 | 0.17 | 907 | 51,246 | MS | 17 | 161 | 0.05 | 15 | 163 |
| 2008 | 1,408 | 48,598 | 0.16 | 902 | 49,115 | MO | 36 | 388 | 0.06 | 16 | 388 |
| 2009 | 1,397 | 46,278 | 0.15 | 919 | 46,895 | MT | 11 | 133 | 0.13 | 8 | 153 |
| 2010 | (NA) | (NA) | (NA) | (NA) | (NA) | NE | 15 | 218 | 0.11 | 6 | 196 |
| 2011 | 1,381 | 44,243 | 0.14 | 899 | 48,301 | NV | 5 | 241 | 0.08 | 5 | 276 |
| 2012 | 1,425 | 43,154 | 0.14 | 980 | 44,612 | NH | 10 | 105 | 0.08 | 7 | 108 |
| 2013[3] | 1,395 | 40,712 | 0.13 | 934 | 43,292 | NJ | 17 | 460 | 0.05 | 16 | 652 |
| 2014[3] | 1,331 | 40,420 | 0.13 | 923 | 42,751 | NM | 14 | 157 | 0.07 | 10 | 161 |
| 2015[3] | 1,338 | 34,901 | 0.11 | 904 | 40,014 | NY | 55 | 3,366 | 0.17 | 39 | 3,936 |
| 2016[3] | 1,286 | 33,419 | 0.10 | 866 | 37,771 | ND | 44 | 579 | 0.06 | 36 | 651 |
| 2017[3] | 1,277 | 29,185 | 0.09 | 857 | 33,160 | ND | 10 | 103 | 0.14 | 7 | 102 |
| | | | | | | OH | 81 | 1,113 | 0.10 | 46 | 1,231 |
| **Total, 2018** [3] | **1,279** | **25,705** | **0.08** | **840** | **29,273** | OK | 33 | 309 | 0.08 | 26 | 330 |
| AL | 22 | 186 | 0.04 | 16 | 214 | OR | 16 | 293 | 0.07 | 11 | 310 |
| AK | 8 | 98 | 0.13 | 4 | 89 | PA | 70 | 1,167 | 0.09 | 41 | 1,386 |
| AZ | 12 | 285 | 0.04 | 10 | 403 | RI | 5 | 77 | 0.07 | 2 | 79 |
| AR | 25 | 253 | 0.08 | 14 | 256 | SC | 16 | 268 | 0.05 | 14 | 315 |
| CA | 69 | 2,178 | 0.06 | 49 | 2,846 | SD | 11 | 84 | 0.10 | 4 | 55 |
| CO | 28 | 418 | 0.07 | 14 | 503 | TN | 25 | 424 | 0.06 | 18 | 466 |
| CT | 18 | 279 | 0.08 | 14 | 357 | TX | 66 | 1,100 | 0.04 | 64 | 1,562 |
| DE | 2 | 73 | 0.08 | 2 | 89 | UT | 6 | 174 | 0.05 | 6 | 274 |
| DC | 3 | 473 | 0.67 | 2 | 483 | VT | 8 | 52 | 0.08 | 4 | 37 |
| FL | 37 | 1,159 | 0.05 | 33 | 1,598 | VA | 20 | 2,174 | 0.26 | 17 | 1,415 |
| GA | 29 | 435 | 0.04 | 23 | 494 | WA | 20 | 534 | 0.07 | 16 | 657 |
| HI | 6 | 183 | 0.13 | 5 | 198 | WV | 17 | 175 | 0.10 | 11 | 174 |
| ID | 12 | 130 | 0.07 | 9 | 213 | WI | 32 | 470 | 0.08 | 20 | 525 |
| IL | 56 | 1,183 | 0.09 | 27 | 1,437 | WY | 8 | 62 | 0.11 | 6 | 61 |

NA Not available. [1] Circulation figures based on the principal community served by a newspaper, which is not necessarily the same location as the publisher's office. [2] Per capita based on estimated resident population as of July 1 of year shown. [3] Number of newspapers as of January 1 of following year.

Source: Editor & Publisher, 18475 Bandilier Circle, Fountain Valley, CA 92708, *Editor & Publisher Newspaper DataBook* ©, annual. See also <http://www.editorandpublisher.com/>.

## Table 1167. Software Publishers—Estimated Revenue, Expenses, and Inventories by Type: 2013 to 2017

[In millions of dollars (181,734 represents $181,734,000,000). For all employer firms regardless of tax status. Data are based on the 2012 North American Industry Classification System (NAICS), and cover NAICS 5112. Estimates are adjusted to the 2012 Economic Census where applicable. See text, this section, and Section 15, Business Enterprise. See also Appendix III]

| Item | 2013 | 2014 | 2015 | 2016 | 2017 |
|---|---|---|---|---|---|
| **Operating revenue** | **181,734** | **193,822** | **198,341** | **214,798** | **224,362** |
| By source: | | | | | |
| System software publishing [1] | 59,447 | 61,352 | 55,269 | 57,728 | 59,253 |
| Operating system software | 19,813 | 19,127 | 18,991 | 19,897 | 21,247 |
| Network software | 17,614 | 18,163 | 12,894 | 14,243 | 15,044 |
| Database management software | 12,737 | 13,364 | 13,838 | 13,913 | 14,294 |
| Development tools and programming languages software | 4,185 | 4,264 | 2,366 | 2,297 | 2,403 |
| Application software publishing [1] | 68,088 | 75,125 | 88,934 | 95,850 | 100,568 |
| General business productivity and home use applications | 32,173 | 35,803 | 41,504 | 44,993 | 49,203 |
| Cross-industry application software | 17,973 | 18,713 | 25,074 | 26,746 | 26,227 |
| Vertical market application software | 9,726 | 11,350 | 11,186 | 12,293 | 13,745 |
| Utilities application software | 3,142 | 3,164 | 2,327 | 2,604 | 2,526 |
| Other services [1] | (NA) | 57,345 | 54,138 | 61,220 | 64,541 |
| Custom application design and development | 6,192 | 5,667 | 3,483 | 3,814 | 3,884 |
| Information technology technical consulting services | 6,560 | 6,516 | 6,170 | 7,318 | 9,025 |
| Resale of computer hardware and software | 6,602 | 8,609 | 8,145 | 8,792 | 8,398 |
| Information technology-related training services | 2,004 | 1,947 | 2,958 | 3,558 | 3,427 |
| By software sales type: | | | | | |
| System software | 59,447 | 61,352 | 55,269 | 57,728 | 59,253 |
| Personal computer software | 16,119 | 15,469 | 14,738 | 15,601 | 16,021 |
| Enterprise or network software | 26,096 | 26,651 | 24,020 | 26,265 | 26,328 |
| Mainframe computer software | 12,205 | 13,485 | 9,883 | 9,851 | 11,466 |
| Other system software | 5,027 | 5,747 | 6,628 | 6,011 | 5,438 |
| Application software | 68,088 | 75,125 | 88,934 | 95,850 | 100,568 |
| Personal computer software | 22,360 | 23,107 | 22,300 | 24,814 | 25,708 |
| Enterprise or network software | 34,937 | 38,555 | 44,270 | 46,420 | 49,281 |
| Mainframe computer software | 1,541 | 1,619 | 5,014 | 5,124 | 4,505 |
| Other application software | (S) | (S) | 17,350 | 19,492 | 21,074 |
| **Operating expenses, total** [1] | **117,706** | **128,835** | **132,401** | **144,662** | **153,281** |
| Gross annual payroll | 57,018 | 61,307 | 60,595 | 64,684 | 70,495 |
| Health insurance | 4,863 | 5,029 | 5,306 | 5,760 | 6,333 |
| Defined benefit pension plans | (S) | 104 | 22 | 31 | 36 |
| Defined contribution plans | 1,367 | 1,649 | 1,829 | 2,081 | 2,308 |
| Payroll taxes, employer paid insurance premiums (except health), and other employer benefits | 7,840 | 8,528 | 9,120 | 9,563 | 10,404 |
| Temporary staff and leased employee expense | 3,663 | 3,922 | 3,240 | 3,699 | 4,009 |
| Expensed equipment | 931 | 804 | 797 | 865 | (S) |
| Expensed purchases of software | 956 | 1,222 | 1,537 | 1,932 | 2,092 |
| Purchased electricity | 241 | 258 | 252 | 260 | 276 |
| Purchased fuels (except motor fuels) | (S) | (S) | 11 | 12 | (S) |
| Lease and rental payments | 2,348 | 2,602 | 2,757 | 2,954 | 3,384 |
| Purchased advertising and promotional services | 7,481 | 8,466 | 8,165 | 8,404 | 8,409 |
| Depreciation and amortization charges | 7,011 | 7,856 | 8,718 | 10,076 | 10,138 |
| Governmental taxes and license fees | 916 | 1,369 | 1,444 | 1,246 | 1,432 |
| **Inventories at end of year, total** | **(S)** | **3,961** | **3,697** | **3,551** | **3,397** |
| Finished goods | (S) | 1,912 | 2,388 | 2,303 | 2,123 |
| Works-in-process | (S) | 1,273 | 932 | 859 | 930 |
| Materials, supplies, fuel, etc. | (S) | (S) | 377 | 389 | (S) |

NA Not available. S Data do not meet publication standards. [1] Includes other sources of revenue and types of expenses, not shown separately.

Source: U.S. Census Bureau, Service Annual Survey, "Service Annual Survey Latest Data (NAICS-basis): 2017," <https://www.census.gov/programs-surveys/sas/data.html>, accessed December 2018.

## Table 1168. Internet Publishing and Broadcasting, and Web Search Portals—Estimated Revenue and Expenses: 2010 to 2017

[In millions of dollars (54,976 represents $54,976,000,000). For all employer firms regardless of tax status. Data for 2010 are based on the 2007 North American Industry Classification System (NAICS); beginning 2013, data are based on the 2012 NAICS. Covers NAICS 51913. Estimates are adjusted to the 2012 Economic Census. See text, Section 15, and Appendix III]

| Item | 2010 | 2013 | 2014 | 2015 | 2016 | 2017 |
|---|---|---|---|---|---|---|
| **Operating revenue** | **54,976** | **96,951** | **109,414** | **125,868** | **148,039** | **170,781** |
| Source of revenue: | | | | | | |
| Publishing and broadcasting of content on the internet | 19,238 | 30,765 | 34,079 | 33,763 | 37,948 | 42,806 |
| Licensing of rights to use intellectual property | 1,320 | 3,782 | 4,133 | 3,590 | 4,125 | 4,317 |
| Online advertising space | 27,406 | 49,805 | 54,670 | 75,266 | 90,288 | 105,190 |
| All other operating revenue | (S) | 12,599 | 16,532 | 13,249 | 15,678 | 18,468 |
| Revenue by type of customer: | | | | | | |
| Household consumers and individual users | (S) | 25,125 | 31,741 | 38,968 | 44,870 | 51,386 |
| Business firms, not-for-profit organizations, and government | (S) | 71,826 | 77,673 | 86,900 | 103,169 | 119,395 |
| **Operating expenses** | **40,417** | **76,765** | **94,306** | **109,619** | **117,929** | **136,426** |

S Data do not meet publication standards.

Source: U.S. Census Bureau, Service Annual Survey, "Service Annual Survey Latest Data (NAICS-basis): 2017" and "Service Annual Survey Historical Tables," <https://www.census.gov/programs-surveys/sas/data.html>, accessed December 2018.

# Table 1169. Motion Picture and Sound Recording Industries—Estimated Revenue and Sources of Revenue: 2010 to 2017

[In millions of dollars (90,108 represents $90,108,000,000). For all employer firms regardless of tax status. Data for 2010 are based on the 2007 North American Industry Classification System (NAICS); beginning 2013, data are based on the 2012 NAICS. Covers NAICS 512. Estimates have been adjusted to the results of the 2012 Economic Census. See text, this section, and Section 15, Business Enterprise. See also Appendix III]

| Kind of business and revenue source | 2010 | 2014 | 2015 | 2016 | 2017 |
|---|---|---|---|---|---|
| **Operating revenue, total**............................ | **90,108** | **94,745** | **98,982** | **103,120** | **103,886** |
| **Motion picture and video industries**.................. | **77,520** | **83,054** | **86,119** | **89,589** | **88,893** |
| Motion picture and video production and distribution [1,2].... | 59,411 | 62,831 | 64,434 | 66,761 | 64,941 |
| Domestic licensing of rights to motion picture films.... | 13,113 | 12,156 | 15,235 | 14,403 | 13,973 |
| Domestic licensing of rights to television programs.... | 10,767 | 13,225 | 13,093 | 13,971 | 13,347 |
| International licensing of rights to motion picture films.... | 8,623 | 6,897 | 7,958 | 7,814 | 6,705 |
| International licensing of rights to television programs.... | 3,010 | 4,828 | 3,647 | 3,795 | 3,435 |
| Sale of audiovisual works for wholesale, retail, and rental markets.... | 10,619 | 6,395 | 7,474 | 6,983 | 5,810 |
| Motion picture and video exhibition, NAICS 51213 [1].... | 12,869 | 14,563 | 15,787 | 16,536 | 17,526 |
| Admissions to feature film exhibitions.... | 8,731 | 9,316 | 9,597 | 10,026 | 10,621 |
| Food and beverage sales.... | 3,615 | 4,388 | 4,940 | 5,306 | 5,652 |
| Postproduction services and other motion picture and video industries, NAICS 51219 [1].... | 5,240 | 5,660 | 5,898 | 6,292 | 6,426 |
| Audiovisual postproduction services.... | 3,125 | 3,674 | 3,410 | 3,713 | 3,707 |
| Motion picture film laboratory services.... | 428 | 166 | (S) | (S) | 86 |
| Duplication and copying services.... | 1,158 | 1,050 | 235 | 247 | (S) |
| **Sound recording industries**........................ | **11,803** | **10,811** | **11,905** | **12,576** | **14,034** |
| Integrated record production and distribution, NAICS 51222 [1].... | 6,991 | 5,077 | 5,765 | 6,229 | 7,207 |
| Licensing revenue.... | (NA) | 559 | 642 | 692 | 798 |
| Sales of recordings.... | 5,475 | 3,890 | 4,457 | 4,778 | 5,522 |
| Music publishers, NAICS 51223 [1].... | 3,964 | 4,732 | 5,054 | 5,250 | 5,754 |
| Licensing of rights to use musical compositions.... | 3,205 | 3,753 | 4,274 | 4,420 | 4,756 |
| Print music.... | 280 | 242 | 268 | 263 | 303 |
| Sound recording studios, NAICS 51224 [1].... | 848 | 1,002 | 1,086 | 1,097 | 1,073 |
| Studio recording.... | 627 | 644 | 765 | 742 | 659 |

NA Not available. S Data do not meet publication standards. [1] Includes other sources of revenue not shown separately. [2] Includes NAICS 51211 (Motion Picture and Video Production) and NAICS 51212 (Motion Picture and Video Distribution).

Source: U.S. Census Bureau, Service Annual Survey, "Service Annual Survey Latest Data (NAICS-basis): 2017" and "Service Annual Survey Historical Tables," <https://www.census.gov/programs-surveys/sas/data.html>, accessed December 2018.

# Table 1170. Recorded Music Industry—Shipments and Value: 2000 to 2018

[1,079.2 represents 1,079,200,000. Data are net after returns. Formats with no retail value equivalent included at wholesale value. Based on reports of Recording Industry Association of America member companies who distribute about 85 percent of the music sold in the U.S.]

| Medium | 2000 | 2005 | 2010 | 2013 | 2014 | 2015 | 2016 | 2017 | 2018 |
|---|---|---|---|---|---|---|---|---|---|
| **UNIT SHIPMENTS (mil.)** | | | | | | | | | |
| **Total [1]**.... | **1,079.2** | **1,301.9** | **1,739.5** | **1,691.2** | **1,458.2** | **1,255.5** | **970.1** | **742.6** | **532.3** |
| **Physical [2]**.... | **1,079.2** | **748.8** | **267.7** | **188.9** | **154.6** | **135.1** | **115.5** | **105.7** | **70.5** |
| Compact disk, album [3].... | 942.5 | 705.4 | 253.0 | 173.8 | 138.7 | 117.1 | 97.6 | 87.7 | 52.0 |
| Compact disk, single.... | 34.2 | 2.8 | 1.0 | 0.6 | 0.9 | 0.4 | 0.1 | 0.1 | (Z) |
| Vinyl LP/EP (long play/extended play).... | 2.2 | 1.0 | 4.2 | 9.4 | 10.3 | 13.7 | 14.8 | 15.6 | 16.7 |
| Vinyl single.... | 4.8 | 2.3 | 0.3 | 0.3 | 0.5 | 0.5 | 0.4 | 0.4 | 0.3 |
| Music video [4].... | 18.2 | 33.8 | 9.1 | 4.8 | 4.1 | 3.1 | 2.5 | 1.9 | 1.4 |
| **Digital [5]**.... | **(NA)** | **554.4** | **1,473.3** | **1,508.5** | **1,311.4** | **1,131.2** | **877.3** | **672.2** | **512.0** |
| Download single.... | (NA) | 366.9 | 1,177.4 | 1,332.8 | 1,154.4 | 986.3 | 743.0 | 553.5 | 399.8 |
| Download album.... | (NA) | 13.6 | 85.8 | 118.0 | 114.2 | 106.8 | 85.1 | 66.4 | 49.7 |
| Mobile [6].... | (NA) | 170.0 | 188.5 | 39.4 | 26.6 | 21.9 | 22.6 | 14.3 | 10.0 |
| Paid subscription [7].... | (NA) | 1.3 | 1.5 | 6.2 | 7.7 | 10.8 | 22.7 | 35.3 | 50.2 |
| **VALUE (mil. dol.) [13]** | | | | | | | | | |
| **Total**.... | **14,323.7** | **12,289.9** | **7,013.8** | **7,034.6** | **6,694.7** | **6,710.8** | **7,578.7** | **8,796.6** | **9,846.1** |
| **Physical [2]**.... | **14,323.7** | **11,195.0** | **3,663.7** | **2,463.8** | **2,121.8** | **1,862.2** | **1,552.3** | **1,495.5** | **1,154.8** |
| Compact disk, album [3].... | 13,214.5 | 10,520.2 | 3,389.4 | 2,140.9 | 1,776.2 | 1,445.0 | 1,130.8 | 1,057.3 | 698.4 |
| Compact disk, single.... | 142.7 | 10.9 | 2.9 | 2.4 | 3.6 | 1.2 | 0.3 | 1.5 | 0.2 |
| Vinyl LP/EP (long play/extended play).... | 27.7 | 14.2 | 88.9 | 210.7 | 243.8 | 333.4 | 355.4 | 388.5 | 419.2 |
| Vinyl single.... | 26.3 | 13.2 | 2.3 | 3.0 | 5.5 | 5.8 | 4.9 | 6.1 | 5.3 |
| Music video [4].... | 281.9 | 602.2 | 177.6 | 106.3 | 89.7 | 70.4 | 56.9 | 38.6 | 27.6 |
| **Digital [5]**.... | **(NA)** | **1,094.9** | **3,161.4** | **4,381.1** | **4,383.2** | **4,645.7** | **5,811.5** | **7,069.0** | **8,405.8** |
| Download single.... | (NA) | 363.3 | 1,336.4 | 1,573.4 | 1,355.3 | 1,185.2 | 900.2 | 678.5 | 490.4 |
| Download album.... | (NA) | 135.7 | 872.4 | 1,232.1 | 1,117.9 | 1,064.4 | 868.6 | 668.5 | 499.7 |
| Mobile [6].... | (NA) | 421.6 | 448.0 | 98.0 | 66.3 | 54.6 | 56.3 | 35.5 | 25.0 |
| Paid subscription [7].... | (NA) | 149.2 | 212.4 | 643.3 | 770.3 | 1,156.7 | 2,244.2 | 3,500.6 | 4,656.0 |
| Limited tier paid subscription [8].... | (NA) | (NA) | (NA) | (NA) | (NA) | (NA) | 263.4 | 591.6 | 747.1 |
| SoundExchange distributions [9].... | (NA) | 20.4 | 249.2 | 590.4 | 773.4 | 802.6 | 883.9 | 652.0 | 952.8 |
| On-demand streaming [10].... | (NA) | (NA) | (NA) | 220.9 | 283.8 | 372.0 | 489.4 | 658.6 | 759.5 |
| Other ad-supported streaming [11].... | (NA) | (NA) | (NA) | (NA) | (NA) | (NA) | 81.3 | 261.8 | 251.4 |
| **Synchronization royalties [12]**.... | **(NA)** | **(NA)** | **188.7** | **189.7** | **189.7** | **202.9** | **214.8** | **232.1** | **285.5** |

Z Represents less than 500. NA Not available. [1] Total unit shipments exclude paid digital subscriptions. [2] Includes other media (DVD audio, super audio CD, and cassettes), not shown separately. [3] Prior to 2006, includes DualDisc. [4] Includes DVD video. [5] Includes kiosks, music video downloads, and, beginning 2016, value for other digital music licensing, not shown separately. [6] Master ringtones and ringbacks; prior to 2013, also included music videos, full length downloads, and other mobile. [7] Streaming, tethered, and other paid subscription services not operating under statutory licenses. Volume is annual average number of subscribers. [8] Includes streaming services with interactivity limitations by availability, device restriction, catalog limitations, on demand access, or other factors. [9] SoundExchange is a nonprofit organization that collects and distributes digital performance royalties on behalf of recording artists and master rights owners. [10] Advertising supported audio and music video services not operating under statutory licenses. [11] Includes revenues from services paid directly that are not distributed by SoundExchange and not included in other streaming categories. [12] Include fees and royalties from synchronization of sound recordings with other media. [13] In 2016, accounting standards updated.

Source: Recording Industry Association of America, Washington, D.C., Facts & Research, *2018 RIAA Shipment and Revenue Statistics* ©, <https://www.riaa.com/reports/>, accessed March 2019.

## Table 1171. Radio and Television Broadcasting—Estimated Revenue and Expenses: 2013 to 2017

[In millions of dollars (5,703 represents $5,703,000,000). For all employer firms regardless of tax status. Based on the 2012 North American Industry Classification System (NAICS). See text, this section, and Section 15, Business Enterprise]

| Item | 2013 | 2014 | 2015 | 2016 | 2017 |
|---|---|---|---|---|---|
| **RADIO NETWORKS (NAICS 515111)** | | | | | |
| **Total operating revenue** | **5,703** | **6,011** | **6,509** | **7,089** | **7,641** |
| National/regional/local air time | 961 | 1,005 | 1,467 | 1,596 | 1,801 |
| Public and non-commercial programming services | 421 | 427 | 367 | 395 | 415 |
| All other operating revenue | 4,321 | 4,579 | 4,675 | 5,098 | 5,425 |
| **RADIO STATIONS (NAICS 515112)** | | | | | |
| **Total operating revenue** | **12,523** | **12,397** | **12,445** | **12,807** | **12,360** |
| National/regional/local air time | 10,558 | 10,437 | 10,611 | 11,001 | 10,553 |
| Public and non-commercial programming services | 689 | 685 | 711 | 660 | 749 |
| All other operating revenue | 1,276 | 1,275 | 1,123 | 1,146 | 1,058 |
| **TELEVISION BROADCASTING (NAICS 51512)** | | | | | |
| **Total operating revenue** | **44,782** | **49,911** | **50,577** | **57,823** | **57,551** |
| National/regional/local air time | 34,240 | 37,274 | 35,706 | 39,435 | 37,105 |
| Public and non-commercial programming services | 2,121 | 2,246 | 2,117 | 2,175 | 2,004 |
| All other operating revenue | 8,421 | 10,391 | 12,754 | 16,213 | 18,442 |
| **RADIO AND TELEVISION BROADCASTING (NAICS 5151)** | | | | | |
| **Operating expenses, total** | **50,697** | **54,214** | **57,499** | **62,770** | **61,962** |
| Gross annual payroll | 13,621 | 14,610 | 14,514 | 14,848 | 15,069 |
| Health insurance | 841 | 931 | 1,113 | 1,175 | 1,270 |
| Other personnel costs [1] | 2,094 | 2,184 | 2,363 | 2,210 | 1,384 |
| Expensed equipment | 116 | 136 | 112 | 155 | 142 |
| Expensed purchases of other materials, parts, and supplies | 243 | 263 | 291 | 307 | 322 |
| Expensed purchases of software | 197 | 202 | 234 | 249 | 242 |
| Purchased electricity and fuels (except motor fuel) | (NA) | (NA) | 376 | 379 | 379 |
| Lease and rental payments | 966 | 1,033 | 1,024 | 1,090 | 1,127 |
| Purchased repair and maintenance | 338 | 376 | 313 | 331 | 320 |
| Purchased advertising and promotional services | 1,720 | 1,902 | 2,057 | 2,249 | 2,404 |
| Broadcast rights and music license fees | 15,028 | 15,608 | 16,391 | 14,090 | 14,431 |
| Network compensation fees (networks only) | 588 | 818 | 1,612 | 2,090 | 2,364 |
| Depreciation and amortization charges | 2,817 | 3,360 | 3,236 | 3,356 | 3,474 |
| Governmental taxes and license fees | 378 | 285 | 256 | 269 | 294 |
| Data processing and other purchased computer services | 227 | 284 | 213 | 244 | 213 |
| Purchased communication services | 410 | 407 | 360 | 380 | 390 |
| Water, sewer, refuse removal, and other utility payments | 32 | 37 | 69 | 70 | (S) |
| Purchased professional and technical services | 1,052 | 1,002 | 988 | 1,113 | 1,215 |
| All other operating expenses | 9,627 | 10,335 | 11,977 | 18,165 | 16,224 |

NA Not available. S Figure does not meet publication standards. [1] Includes costs for defined benefit and defined contribution plans, payroll taxes/insurance premiums (except health)/other benefits, and temporary employees.

Source: U.S. Census Bureau, Service Annual Survey, "Service Annual Survey Latest Data (NAICS-basis): 2017," <https://www.census.gov/programs-surveys/sas/data.html>, accessed December 2018.

## Table 1172. Cable and Other Subscription Programming—Estimated Revenue and Expenses: 2013 to 2017

[In millions of dollars (68,405 represents $68,405,000,000). For all employer firms regardless of tax status. Based on the 2012 North American Industry Classification System. Covers NAICS 5152. See text, this section and Section 15, and Appendix III]

| Item | 2013 | 2014 | 2015 | 2016 | 2017 |
|---|---|---|---|---|---|
| **Operating revenue, total** | **68,405** | **72,473** | **78,931** | **81,508** | **83,327** |
| Source of revenue: | | | | | |
| Advertising and program revenue [1] | 39,273 | 42,266 | 48,811 | 50,715 | 52,160 |
| Air time | 24,734 | 26,039 | 26,264 | 26,745 | 26,907 |
| All other operating services revenue | 4,398 | 4,168 | 3,856 | 4,048 | 4,260 |
| **Operating expenses, total [2]** | **40,731** | **44,080** | **46,359** | **48,351** | **49,669** |
| Gross annual payroll | 5,966 | 6,151 | 6,979 | 7,265 | 7,566 |
| Health insurance | 387 | 504 | 528 | 537 | 616 |
| Defined benefit pension plans | 136 | 91 | 141 | 127 | (S) |
| Defined contribution plans | 230 | 249 | 223 | 251 | 317 |
| Payroll taxes, employer paid insurance premiums (except health), and other employer benefits | 447 | 464 | 503 | 519 | 616 |
| Temporary staff and leased employee expense | 225 | 277 | 238 | 272 | 306 |
| Expensed equipment | 80 | 80 | 82 | 76 | 94 |
| Expensed purchases of other materials, parts, and supplies | 63 | 72 | 63 | 69 | 83 |
| Expensed purchases of software | 109 | 126 | 153 | 178 | 220 |
| Purchased electricity | 64 | 65 | 63 | 60 | 43 |
| Lease and rental payments | 672 | 709 | 713 | 711 | 720 |
| Purchased repairs and maintenance | 130 | 129 | 167 | 176 | 151 |
| Purchased advertising and promotional services | 2,632 | 2,828 | 3,143 | 3,228 | 3,350 |
| Program and production costs | 20,799 | 21,778 | 23,100 | 24,493 | 24,348 |
| Depreciation and amortization charges | 4,445 | 4,911 | 4,957 | 4,983 | 5,667 |
| Governmental taxes and license fees | 92 | 106 | 853 | 861 | 921 |
| Data processing and other purchased computer services | 54 | 53 | 40 | 52 | 59 |
| Purchased communication services | 96 | 102 | 102 | 106 | 116 |
| Purchased professional and technical services | 597 | 642 | 613 | 661 | 701 |

S Estimate does not meet publication standards. [1] Licensing of rights to broadcast specialty programming protected by copyright. [2] Includes items not shown separately.

Source: U.S. Census Bureau, Service Annual Survey, "Service Annual Survey Latest Data (NAICS-basis): 2017," <https://www.census.gov/programs-surveys/sas/data.html>, accessed December 2018.

# Table 1173. Wired and Wireless Telecommunications Carriers—Estimated Revenue: 2010 to 2017

[In millions of dollars (281,149 represents $281,149,000,000). For all employer firms regardless of tax status. Data for 2010-2012 are based on the 2007 North American Industry Classification System (NAICS); beginning 2013, data are based on the 2012 NAICS. Covers NAICS 5171 Wired Telecommunications Carriers and NAICS 5172 Wireless Telecommunications Carriers (except satellite). Estimates have been adjusted to the results of the 2012 Economic Census. See text, this section and Section 15, and Appendix III]

| Item | 2010 | 2011 | 2012 | 2013 | 2014 | 2015 | 2016 | 2017 |
|---|---|---|---|---|---|---|---|---|
| **Wired telecommunications carriers operating revenue** | **281,149** | **284,810** | **285,663** | **288,647** | **296,792** | **306,384** | **326,119** | **315,343** |
| Fixed local telephony | 43,765 | 39,546 | 35,990 | 31,201 | 30,395 | 26,782 | 27,386 | 25,075 |
| Fixed long-distance telephony | 19,964 | 20,155 | 18,068 | 16,447 | 15,478 | 10,576 | 10,820 | (S) |
| Fixed all distance | 2,640 | 2,539 | 1,894 | 1,249 | 1,131 | 2,004 | 1,952 | 1,587 |
| Carrier services | 18,183 | 18,742 | 17,663 | 16,386 | 18,588 | 21,489 | (S) | 13,252 |
| Private network services | 21,069 | 20,942 | 20,496 | 19,929 | 19,429 | 17,463 | 17,607 | (S) |
| Internet access services | 51,588 | 57,208 | 63,069 | 70,146 | 73,048 | 78,350 | 87,250 | 88,699 |
| Internet telephony | 9,874 | 11,614 | 12,530 | 12,976 | 13,013 | 11,710 | 11,291 | 10,243 |
| Telecommunications network installation services | 503 | 401 | 399 | 504 | 654 | 897 | 818 | 842 |
| Reselling services for telecommunications equipment, retail | 1,696 | 1,637 | 1,273 | 1,305 | 1,143 | 1,628 | 1,476 | 1,465 |
| Rental of telecommunications equipment | 687 | 537 | 472 | 484 | 592 | 563 | 1,701 | 4,457 |
| Repair and maintenance services for telecommunications equipment | 373 | (S) | 538 | 566 | 904 | 974 | (S) | 858 |
| Subscriber line charges | 3,239 | 4,098 | 3,988 | 3,555 | 3,430 | 3,230 | 3,222 | 2,896 |
| Basic programming package | 52,634 | 53,220 | 55,594 | 58,569 | 60,034 | 61,090 | 63,659 | 59,724 |
| Premium programming package | 20,367 | 22,042 | 21,752 | 21,181 | 21,124 | 23,258 | 24,394 | 22,975 |
| Pay-per-view | 3,303 | 3,164 | 3,200 | (S) | 3,086 | 2,894 | 2,898 | 2,782 |
| Air time (advertising and program content) | 4,843 | 4,849 | (S) | (S) | 5,021 | 5,722 | 6,345 | 5,606 |
| Rental and reselling services for program distribution equipment | 7,840 | 8,874 | 10,707 | 11,558 | 12,132 | 14,221 | 13,862 | 12,047 |
| Installation services for connections to program distribution networks | 1,081 | 1,076 | 1,245 | 1,360 | 1,658 | (S) | (S) | (S) |
| Website hosting services | 291 | 275 | 140 | 134 | 178 | 568 | (S) | (S) |
| All other operating revenue | 17,159 | 13,299 | 12,058 | 13,345 | 15,754 | 20,765 | 31,271 | 33,539 |
| **Wireless telecommunications carrier operating revenue [1]** | **199,235** | **214,361** | **225,397** | **233,123** | **251,766** | **254,406** | **259,321** | **257,845** |
| Messaging (paging) services | 921 | 908 | 554 | (S) | (S) | 3,714 | 2,956 | (S) |
| Mobile telephony | 58,238 | 57,060 | 54,716 | 62,015 | 59,890 | 46,384 | 45,659 | (S) |
| Mobile long distance | 3,387 | 3,309 | (D) | (D) | 4,184 | 2,910 | 2,441 | 2,525 |
| Mobile all distance | (S) | 62,596 | 65,493 | 59,666 | 54,093 | 46,995 | (S) | 37,643 |
| Internet access services | (S) | (S) | 62,878 | 66,274 | 77,373 | 90,755 | 97,296 | 96,058 |
| Telecommunication network installation services | (S) | (S) | 172 | 196 | 207 | 207 | 242 | 191 |
| Reselling services for telecommunications equipment, retail | 18,754 | 21,341 | 23,682 | 24,690 | 35,483 | 41,284 | 44,367 | 46,670 |
| Rental of telecommunications equipment | 333 | 362 | 342 | 433 | 489 | (S) | (S) | 4,705 |
| Repair and maintenance services for telecommunications equipment | 1,219 | 1,374 | (D) | (D) | 2,232 | 2,303 | 2,338 | 1,857 |
| All other operating revenue | 11,492 | 13,144 | 12,694 | 13,723 | 17,277 | 16,318 | 17,484 | 18,655 |

S Data do not meet publication standards. D Estimate in table is withheld to avoid disclosing data of individual companies; data are included in higher level totals. [1] Excludes satellite telecommunications.

Source: U.S. Census Bureau, Service Annual Survey, "Service Annual Survey Latest Data (NAICS-basis): 2017" and "Service Annual Survey Historical Tables," <https://www.census.gov/programs-surveys/sas/data.html>, accessed December 2018.

Information and Communications    731

# Table 1174. Telecommunications Industry Revenue by Service Type: 2010 to 2017

[Revenue in millions of dollars (446,386 represents $446,386,000,000). Data are based on carrier Form 499-A filings to the Federal Communications Commission, and are the basis for establishing Universal Service Fund (USF) program collections]

| Category | Revenue (mil. dol.) | | | | | | |
|---|---|---|---|---|---|---|---|
| | 2010 | 2012 | 2013 | 2014 | 2015 | 2016 | 2017 |
| Total reported revenue................................. | 446,386 | 479,729 | 494,981 | 496,892 | 515,598 | 509,679 | 504,516 |
| **Total telecommunications revenue................** | **273,158** | **255,242** | **243,088** | **228,631** | **214,477** | **198,276** | **182,918** |
| Non-telecommunications revenue..................... | 173,228 | 224,487 | 251,892 | 268,260 | 301,121 | 311,404 | 321,597 |
| **Local service and payphone revenue............** | **102,847** | **95,422** | **93,105** | **90,994** | **90,495** | **87,162** | **83,572** |
| Local exchange Federal/State USF support.......... | 56,993 | 50,598 | 49,016 | 47,495 | 46,515 | 46,314 | 43,539 |
| Pay telephone......................................... | 197 | 362 | 359 | 327 | 286 | 271 | 269 |
| Local private line.................................... | 26,809 | 29,101 | 29,632 | 31,194 | 32,191 | 30,472 | 30,272 |
| Other local............................................ | 3,032 | 2,408 | 1,746 | 1,456 | 1,493 | 1,510 | 1,749 |
| Subscriber line charges.............................. | 7,481 | 6,195 | 5,968 | 5,507 | 5,175 | 4,787 | 4,431 |
| Access................................................. | 8,336 | 6,759 | 6,384 | 5,016 | 4,836 | 3,809 | 3,312 |
| **Mobile service revenue.............................** | **111,643** | **105,183** | **98,160** | **86,998** | **75,263** | **65,636** | **56,952** |
| **Toll service revenue................................** | **50,006** | **44,624** | **42,837** | **41,555** | **39,678** | **36,342** | **34,075** |
| Operator............................................... | 3,585 | 3,092 | 3,064 | 2,785 | 2,351 | 1,876 | 1,844 |
| Non-operator switched toll........................... | 27,132 | 25,340 | 23,345 | 22,518 | 21,499 | 18,297 | 15,609 |
| Long distance private line........................... | 14,344 | 12,262 | 12,542 | 12,362 | 12,778 | 13,353 | 13,316 |
| Other long distance.................................. | 4,945 | 3,929 | 3,886 | 3,891 | 3,050 | 2,816 | 3,306 |

Source: U.S. Federal Communications Commission, *Universal Service Monitoring Report, 2018,* May 2019. See also <https://www.fcc.gov/general/federal-state-joint-board-monitoring-reports>.

# Table 1175. Data Processing, Hosting, and Related Services—Estimated Revenue and Expenses: 2013 to 2017

[In millions of dollars (116,040 represents $116,040,000,000). For all employer firms regardless of tax status. Data are based on the 2012 North American Industry Classification System (NAICS), and cover NAICS 518. Estimates have been adjusted to the results of the 2012 Economic Census. See text, Section 15, and Appendix III]

| Item | 2013 | 2014 | 2015 | 2016 | 2017 |
|---|---|---|---|---|---|
| **Total operating revenue.........................** | **116,040** | **120,450** | **129,957** | **139,715** | **155,934** |
| Data processing, information technology infrastructure provisioning, and hosting services............................. | 85,252 | 86,546 | (S) | 98,525 | 111,038 |
| Information technology design and development services.................... | 3,223 | 4,141 | 6,730 | 6,538 | (S) |
| Information technology technical support services......................... | 3,311 | 4,023 | 4,347 | 4,287 | 4,445 |
| Information technology technical consulting services..................... | 5,214 | 5,421 | 3,806 | 3,909 | (S) |
| Information and document transformation services..................... | 3,020 | 2,827 | 2,473 | (S) | 2,693 |
| Software publishing.................................. | (S) | (S) | 2,800 | (S) | (S) |
| Reselling of computer hardware and software.......... | (S) | (S) | 2,557 | 2,574 | 3,203 |
| All other operating revenue........................... | 13,178 | 14,138 | 18,969 | 18,705 | (S) |
| **Total operating expenses........................** | **105,746** | **112,703** | **124,777** | **119,866** | **131,713** |
| Gross annual payroll.................................. | 41,928 | 46,752 | 46,209 | 49,166 | 54,428 |
| Health insurance...................................... | 2,599 | 3,003 | (S) | 3,313 | 3,752 |
| Defined benefit pension plans......................... | 146 | 141 | (S) | 193 | (S) |
| Defined contribution plans............................ | 630 | 628 | (S) | 819 | 930 |
| Payroll taxes, employer paid insurance premiums (except health), and other employer benefits......... | 3,645 | 4,400 | (S) | 5,289 | 5,659 |
| Temporary staff and leased employee expense.......... | 3,262 | 3,372 | (S) | 2,407 | (S) |
| Expensed equipment.................................. | 927 | 1,048 | (S) | 752 | 836 |
| Expensed purchases of other materials, parts, and supplies................. | 2,960 | 3,080 | (S) | 2,298 | (S) |
| Expensed purchases of software....................... | 2,854 | 3,361 | (S) | 2,997 | 3,465 |
| Purchased electricity................................. | 663 | 714 | (S) | 760 | 980 |
| Purchased fuels (except motor fuels).................. | (S) | (S) | (S) | (S) | (S) |
| Lease and rental payments for machinery, equipment, and other tangible items......................... | 762 | 762 | (S) | 657 | 793 |
| Lease and rental payments for land, buildings, structures, store spaces, and offices......................... | 2,739 | 2,925 | (S) | 2,430 | 2,712 |
| Purchased repairs and maintenance to machinery and equipment........... | 887 | 952 | (S) | 934 | 968 |
| Purchased repairs and maintenance to buildings, structures, and offices.... | 319 | 335 | 243 | 197 | 228 |
| Purchased advertising and promotional services......... | 2,376 | 2,609 | (S) | 4,251 | 4,813 |
| Depreciation and amortization charges................. | 9,173 | 9,478 | (S) | 11,271 | 13,735 |
| Governmental taxes and license fees.................. | 687 | 780 | (S) | 920 | 873 |
| Data processing and other purchased computer services.................... | 2,901 | 2,873 | (S) | 3,411 | 3,455 |
| Purchased communication services.................... | 1,484 | 1,584 | (S) | 1,182 | (S) |
| Water, sewer, refuse removal, and other utility payments..................... | 80 | 86 | (S) | 65 | 74 |
| Purchased professional and technical services............................ | 5,610 | 4,599 | (S) | 5,937 | (S) |
| All other operating expenses.......................... | 19,102 | 19,203 | 26,100 | 20,612 | 21,554 |

S Data do not meet publication standards.

Source: U.S. Census Bureau, Service Annual Survey, "Service Annual Survey Latest Data (NAICS-basis): 2017," <https://www.census.gov/programs-surveys/sas/data.html>, accessed December 2018.

# Table 1176. Cellular Telecommunications Industry: 2000 to 2018

[In units as indicated (109.5 represents 109,500,000). Calendar year data, except as noted. Based on a survey sent to facilities-based commercial mobile radio service providers, including cellular, personal communications services, advanced wireless service, mobile WiMAX, and enhanced special mobile radio (ESMR) systems. The number of operational systems beginning 2000 differs from that reported for previous periods as a result of the consolidated operation of ESMR systems in a broader service area instead of by a city-to-city basis]

| Item | Unit | 2000 | 2005 | 2010 | 2014 | 2015 | 2016 | 2017 | 2018 |
|---|---|---|---|---|---|---|---|---|---|
| Wireless subscriber connections [1] | Millions | 109.5 | 207.9 | 296.3 | 355.4 | 377.9 | 395.9 | 400.2 | 421.8 |
| Wireless penetration [2] | Percent | 38.0 | 69.0 | 94.2 | 109.7 | 115.7 | 120.6 | 120.7 | 126.6 |
| Cell sites [3] | Number | 104,288 | 183,689 | 253,086 | 298,055 | 307,626 | 308,334 | 323,448 | 349,344 |
| Employees | Number | 184,449 | 233,067 | 250,393 | 232,169 | 235,818 | 216,537 | 207,324 | 205,855 |
| Service revenue | Mil. dol. | 52,466 | 113,538 | 159,930 | 187,848 | 191,949 | 188,524 | 179,091 | 182,779 |
| Capital investment [4] | Mil. dol. | 89,624 | 199,025 | 310,015 | 430,624 | 462,605 | 488,997 | 514,625 | 542,033 |
| Average monthly revenue per unit [5] | Dollars | 48.55 | 50.65 | 47.53 | 46.64 | 44.65 | 41.50 | 38.66 | 37.85 |
| Voice minutes, annual reported | Billions | 258.9 | 1,495.5 | 2,241.3 | 2,454.9 | 2,881.0 | 2,751.0 | 2,180.0 | 2,389.3 |
| Voice minutes, monthly [6] | Minutes | 248.0 | 716.0 | 683.0 | 610.0 | 670.0 | 606.0 | 471.0 | 495.0 |
| Wireless data usage (megabytes), annual | Billions | (NA) | (NA) | 388.0 | 4,060.7 | 9,649.9 | 13,719.0 | 15,678.3 | 28,584.7 |
| Number of text messages [7] | Billions | (Z) | 9.8 | 187.7 | 169.3 | 156.7 | 132.7 | 128.5 | 141.0 |
| Number of MMS [7, 8] | Billions | (NA) | 0.2 | 4.3 | 15.4 | 19.8 | 25.7 | 26.0 | 31.0 |

NA Not available. Z Entry less than half the unit of measurement shown. [1] Number of active wireless devices. Does not represent individual subscribers. [2] Number of active wireless devices divided by total U.S. population (including U.S. territories). [3] The basic geographic unit for wireless telecommunications coverage. [4] Beginning 2005, cumulative capital investment figure reached by summing the incremental capital investment in year shown with cumulative capital investment of prior year. [5] As of December 31. [6] Derived, based on minutes divided by reported devices. [7] Number of messages in final month of survey (December). [8] Multimedia Messaging Service.

Source: CTIA-The Wireless Association, Washington, DC, *Annual Wireless Industry Survey* ©.

# Table 1177. Landline and Wireless Telephone Status of Households and Adults: 2010 to 2018

[In percent. Data cover 6-month period from January to June. Estimates are preliminary. Based on in-person interviews of a sample of the civilian noninstitutionalized population, conducted for the National Health Interview Survey (NHIS). A new sample design was implemented with the 2016 NHIS]

| Telephone status and characteristics | 2010 | 2011 | 2012 | 2013 | 2014 | 2015 | 2016 | 2017 | 2018 |
|---|---|---|---|---|---|---|---|---|---|
| **HOUSEHOLDS** | | | | | | | | | |
| Landline with wireless | 58.1 | 55.0 | 52.5 | 49.5 | 44.7 | 41.6 | 40.2 | 37.8 | 36.3 |
| Landline without wireless | 12.9 | 11.2 | 9.4 | 8.5 | 8.5 | 7.6 | 7.2 | 5.9 | 5.4 |
| Wireless only | 26.6 | 31.6 | 35.8 | 39.4 | 44.0 | 47.4 | 49.3 | 52.5 | 54.9 |
| Without any telephone | 2.0 | 2.0 | 2.1 | 2.3 | 2.6 | 3.4 | 3.1 | 3.7 | 3.3 |
| Other [1] | 0.3 | 0.3 | 0.2 | 0.1 | 0.1 | 0.1 | 0.1 | 0.2 | 0.1 |
| **ADULTS** | | | | | | | | | |
| Landline with wireless | 62.2 | 58.8 | 56.1 | 52.8 | 47.3 | 43.9 | 42.1 | 39.6 | 37.4 |
| Wireless mostly [2] | 17.7 | 18.2 | 17.6 | 17.7 | 16.6 | 16.3 | 16.6 | 16.3 | 16.8 |
| Landline without wireless | 10.9 | 9.0 | 7.8 | 6.9 | 7.0 | 6.2 | 5.8 | 4.8 | 4.1 |
| Wireless only | 24.9 | 30.2 | 34.0 | 38.0 | 43.1 | 46.7 | 49.0 | 52.0 | 55.2 |
| Without any telephone | 1.7 | 1.8 | 1.9 | 2.2 | 2.4 | 3.1 | 2.9 | 3.4 | 3.2 |
| Other [1] | 0.3 | 0.2 | 0.2 | 0.1 | 0.2 | 0.1 | 0.1 | 0.1 | 0.1 |
| **ADULTS IN WIRELESS ONLY HOUSEHOLDS** | | | | | | | | | |
| Sex: | | | | | | | | | |
| Male | 26.2 | 31.4 | 35.2 | 39.7 | 44.3 | 48.2 | 50.3 | 53.2 | 56.4 |
| Female | 23.7 | 29.1 | 32.9 | 36.5 | 41.9 | 45.3 | 47.8 | 51.0 | 54.1 |
| Age: | | | | | | | | | |
| 18 to 24 years | 39.9 | 46.8 | 49.5 | 54.3 | 57.8 | 59.4 | 62.7 | 64.2 | 65.0 |
| 25 to 29 years | 51.3 | 58.1 | 60.1 | 65.6 | 69.3 | 71.3 | 72.1 | 73.3 | 77.3 |
| 30 to 34 years | 40.4 | 46.2 | 55.1 | 59.9 | 64.9 | 67.8 | 69.8 | 74.4 | 77.3 |
| 35 to 44 years | 27.0 | 34.3 | 39.1 | 44.5 | 52.5 | 56.6 | 60.0 | 63.9 | 65.7 |
| 45 to 64 years | 16.9 | 21.6 | 25.8 | 29.8 | 35.7 | 40.8 | 43.3 | 47.1 | 50.7 |
| 65 and over years | 5.4 | 7.9 | 10.5 | 12.6 | 15.7 | 19.3 | 21.1 | 23.9 | 29.2 |
| Race/ethnicity: | | | | | | | | | |
| White only, non-Hispanic | 22.7 | 27.6 | 30.4 | 35.1 | 39.6 | 43.2 | 45.0 | 48.0 | 51.6 |
| Black only, non-Hispanic | 28.5 | 32.5 | 37.7 | 39.4 | 44.9 | 48.1 | 49.2 | 52.5 | 55.6 |
| Asian only, non-Hispanic | 18.8 | 27.7 | 33.4 | 35.2 | 41.3 | 47.9 | 51.4 | 53.1 | 53.8 |
| Multiple race, non-Hispanic | 36.0 | 39.3 | 40.2 | 46.2 | 52.5 | 53.6 | 53.9 | 58.7 | 55.8 |
| Hispanic or Latino, any race | 34.7 | 40.8 | 46.5 | 49.9 | 56.1 | 59.2 | 63.7 | 66.3 | 69.1 |
| Education: | | | | | | | | | |
| Some high school or less | 28.6 | 32.1 | 36.4 | 41.7 | 46.6 | 49.0 | 52.1 | 54.8 | 58.7 |
| High school graduate or GED [3] | 23.6 | 30.8 | 33.9 | 37.2 | 44.3 | 46.7 | 48.4 | 51.5 | 56.5 |
| Some post-high school, no degree | 26.5 | 31.8 | 36.7 | 40.6 | 45.6 | 49.0 | 50.8 | 55.1 | 56.0 |
| 4-year college degree or higher | 22.7 | 26.9 | 30.1 | 34.5 | 39.0 | 43.5 | 46.5 | 48.6 | 51.9 |
| Household poverty status: [4] | | | | | | | | | |
| Poor | 39.3 | 46.8 | 51.8 | 54.7 | 59.1 | 59.3 | 63.1 | 67.5 | 67.1 |
| Near poor | 32.9 | 38.1 | 42.3 | 47.5 | 50.8 | 54.4 | 54.0 | 61.6 | 62.8 |
| Not poor | 21.7 | 27.7 | 30.7 | 35.3 | 40.8 | 45.7 | 48.2 | 50.3 | 53.4 |
| Home ownership status: | | | | | | | | | |
| Owned or home being bought | 15.5 | 20.6 | 23.2 | 27.2 | 32.9 | 37.2 | 39.0 | 42.9 | 46.8 |
| Renting | 47.1 | 52.5 | 58.2 | 61.5 | 64.6 | 67.0 | 69.7 | 70.7 | 74.4 |
| Other arrangement | 34.9 | 38.4 | 37.7 | 42.6 | 52.2 | 52.8 | 52.0 | 64.8 | 60.0 |

[1] Other includes unknown cellular telephone status, with and without a landline telephone. [2] Wireless mostly is for adults living in households with both landline and cellular telephones but in which all families receive all or almost all calls on cell phones. [3] GED is General Educational Development high school equivalency diploma. [4] Based on household income and household size using the U.S. Census Bureau's poverty thresholds. "Poor" persons have incomes below the poverty threshold. "Near poor" persons have incomes of 100% to less than 200% of the poverty threshold. "Not poor" persons have incomes of 200% of the poverty threshold or greater.

Source: U.S. National Center for Health Statistics, *Wireless Substitution: Early Release of Estimates From the National Health Interview Survey, January–June 2018*, December 2018, and earlier reports. See also <http://www.cdc.gov/nchs/nhis/releases.htm#wireless>.

## Table 1178. Average Annual Telephone Service Expenditures by All Consumer Units: 2001 to 2017

[In dollars except percent distribution. Based on the Consumer Expenditure Survey. Expenditures reported are direct out-of-pocket expenditures. A consumer unit is defined as members of a household related by blood, marriage, adoption, or some other legal arrangement; a single person living alone or sharing a household with others, but who is financially independent; or two or more persons living together who share responsibility for at least two out of the three major types of expenses: food, housing, and other expenses]

| Year | Average annual telephone service (dollars) | | | | Percent distribution | | | |
|---|---|---|---|---|---|---|---|---|
| | Total telephone services | Residential and other telephone services [1] | Cellular phone service | Other services [2] | Total telephone services | Residential and other telephone services [1] | Cellular phone service | Other services [2] |
| 2001 | 914 | 686 | 210 | 19 | 100.0 | 75.1 | 23.0 | 2.1 |
| 2002 | 957 | 641 | 294 | 22 | 100.0 | 67.0 | 30.7 | 2.3 |
| 2003 | 956 | 620 | 316 | 20 | 100.0 | 64.9 | 33.1 | 2.1 |
| 2004 | 990 | 592 | 378 | 20 | 100.0 | 59.8 | 38.2 | 2.0 |
| 2005 | 1,048 | 570 | 455 | 23 | 100.0 | 54.4 | 43.4 | 2.2 |
| 2006 | 1,087 | 542 | 524 | 21 | 100.0 | 49.9 | 48.2 | 1.9 |
| 2007 | 1,110 | 482 | 608 | 20 | 100.0 | 43.4 | 54.8 | 1.8 |
| 2008 | 1,127 | 467 | 643 | 17 | 100.0 | 41.4 | 57.0 | 1.5 |
| 2009 | 1,162 | 434 | 712 | 17 | 100.0 | 37.3 | 61.2 | 1.4 |
| 2010 | 1,178 | 401 | 760 | 17 | 100.0 | 34.1 | 64.5 | 1.4 |
| 2011 | 1,226 | 381 | 826 | 20 | 100.0 | 31.1 | 67.3 | 1.6 |
| 2012 | 1,239 | 359 | 862 | 19 | 100.0 | 28.9 | 69.6 | 1.5 |
| 2013 | 1,271 | 358 | 913 | (NA) | 100.0 | 28.2 | 71.8 | (NA) |
| 2014 | 1,315 | 353 | 963 | (NA) | 100.0 | 26.8 | 73.2 | (NA) |
| 2015 | 1,347 | 324 | 1,023 | (NA) | 100.0 | 24.1 | 75.9 | (NA) |
| 2016 | 1,431 | 307 | 1,124 | (NA) | 100.0 | 21.5 | 78.5 | (NA) |
| 2017 | 1,356 | 238 | 1,118 | (NA) | 100.0 | 17.6 | 82.4 | (NA) |

NA Not available. [1] Beginning 2013, data are shown for residential telephone, phone cards, VoIP (Voice over Internet Protocol), and pay phone services combined. Prior to 2013, data are shown for residential and pay telephone services only. [2] Phone cards, pager services, and for 2007-2012, VoIP.

Source: U.S. Bureau of Labor Statistics, Consumer Expenditure Survey, unpublished data; and "Annual Calendar Year Tables," <http://www.bls.gov/cex/home.htm>, accessed December 2018.

## Table 1179. Electronic Device Ownership by Device Type and Owner Characteristics: 2019

[In percent. Based on a January 8-February 7, 2019 survey of 1,502 adults age 18 and older. Surveys are conducted in English and Spanish, on landline and cellular telephones]

| Owner characteristic | Any cellular telephone | Smart-phone | Cellphone, not smart-phone | Tablet computer | Computer [1] |
|---|---|---|---|---|---|
| **Total** | **96** | **81** | **15** | **52** | **74** |
| SEX | | | | | |
| Men | 98 | 84 | 14 | 50 | **76** |
| Women | 95 | 79 | 16 | 54 | 73 |
| RACE/ETHNICITY | | | | | |
| White, non-Hispanic | 96 | 82 | 14 | 53 | 82 |
| Black, non-Hispanic | 98 | 80 | 17 | 58 | 58 |
| Hispanic | 96 | 79 | 17 | 43 | 57 |
| AGE | | | | | |
| 18 to 29 years | 99 | 96 | 4 | 46 | 80 |
| 30 to 49 years | 99 | 92 | 6 | 57 | 78 |
| 50 to 64 years | 95 | 79 | 17 | 55 | 75 |
| 65 years and older | 91 | 53 | 39 | 42 | 62 |
| EDUCATION | | | | | |
| Less than high school | 92 | 66 | 25 | 33 | 36 |
| High school graduate | 96 | 72 | 24 | 43 | 60 |
| Some college | 96 | 85 | 11 | 56 | 82 |
| College or higher | 98 | 91 | 7 | 61 | 93 |
| HOUSEHOLD INCOME | | | | | |
| Less than $30,000 | 95 | 71 | 23 | 36 | 54 |
| $30,000 to $49,999 | 96 | 78 | 18 | 51 | 74 |
| $50,000 to $74,999 | 98 | 90 | 8 | 52 | 89 |
| $75,000 and over | 100 | 95 | 5 | 68 | 92 |
| METRO STATUS | | | | | |
| Urban | 97 | 83 | 13 | 49 | 73 |
| Suburban | 96 | 83 | 13 | 58 | 80 |
| Rural | 95 | 71 | 24 | 49 | 69 |

[1] Desktop or laptop computer.

Source: Pew Research Center ©, "Mobile Fact Sheet," <http://www.pewinternet.org/fact-sheet/mobile/>, accessed August 2019; and unpublished data.

# Table 1180. Computer and Internet Use by Selected Characteristics: 2017

[In thousands (276,477 represents 276,477,000), except percent. Based on the American Community Survey. Data are based on a sample and are subject to sampling variability. Due to changes in the ACS questionnaire, use caution when comparing data on computer and internet use before and after 2016. For more information, see <https://www.census.gov/programs-surveys/acs/methodology/content-test.html>]

| Characteristic | Population with computer in household [1] | | | | No computer in household | |
| | With broadband internet subscription [2] | | No internet subscription [3] | | | |
| | Number | Percent | Number | Percent | Number | Percent |
|---|---|---|---|---|---|---|
| **Total household population** | **276,477** | **87.0** | **21,915** | **6.9** | **18,532** | **5.8** |
| AGE | | | | | | |
| Under 18 years | 66,328 | 90.3 | 5,013 | 6.8 | 2,037 | 2.8 |
| 18 to 64 years | 173,686 | 89.1 | 13,128 | 6.7 | 7,819 | 4.0 |
| 65 years and over | 36,463 | 74.0 | 3,773 | 7.7 | 8,677 | 17.6 |
| RACE AND ETHNICITY | | | | | | |
| White alone | 202,411 | 87.9 | 14,278 | 6.2 | 12,932 | 5.6 |
| Black or African American alone | 31,739 | 80.2 | 4,266 | 10.8 | 3,543 | 8.9 |
| American Indian and Alaska Native alone | 1,949 | 73.9 | 351 | 13.3 | 330 | 12.5 |
| Asian alone | 16,690 | 93.4 | 702 | 3.9 | 452 | 2.5 |
| Native Hawaiian/Other Pacific Islander alone | 484 | 82.1 | 60 | 10.2 | 43 | 7.3 |
| Some other race alone | 13,644 | 83.8 | 1,714 | 10.5 | 915 | 5.6 |
| Two or more races | 9,559 | 91.6 | 544 | 5.2 | 316 | 3.0 |
| Hispanic or Latino origin [4] | 48,573 | 84.1 | 5,782 | 10.0 | 3,345 | 5.8 |
| White alone, not Hispanic or Latino | 170,990 | 88.7 | 10,483 | 5.4 | 10,659 | 5.5 |
| EDUCATIONAL ATTAINMENT | | | | | | |
| Household population age 25 and over | 185,426 | 85.6 | 14,850 | 6.9 | 15,819 | 7.3 |
| Less than high school graduate | 17,147 | 67.7 | 3,163 | 12.5 | 4,952 | 19.5 |
| High school graduate/some college [5] | 101,823 | 84.1 | 9,345 | 7.7 | 9,500 | 7.8 |
| Bachelor's degree or higher | 66,456 | 94.5 | 2,342 | 3.3 | 1,367 | 1.9 |
| EMPLOYMENT STATUS | | | | | | |
| Civilian population age 16 and over | 217,168 | 86.2 | 17,373 | 6.9 | 16,679 | 6.6 |
| In labor force | 147,099 | 90.7 | 9,873 | 6.1 | 5,045 | 3.1 |
| Employed | 139,861 | 90.9 | 9,124 | 5.9 | 4,609 | 3.0 |
| Unemployed | 7,238 | 85.8 | 749 | 8.9 | 436 | 5.2 |
| Not in labor force | 70,069 | 78.2 | 7,500 | 8.4 | 11,634 | 13.0 |

[1] Includes desktop or laptop; smartphone; tablet or other portable wireless computer; or some other type of computer. [2] Paid internet access services via cable, fiber optic, or DSL; a cellular data plan (mobile phone); satellite; or a fixed wireless subscription. [3] Includes those who accessed the internet without a subscription and also those with no internet access at all. [4] Persons of Hispanic or Latino origin may be of any race. [5] Includes persons with high school equivalency, and with associate's degree.

Source: U.S. Census Bureau, 2017 American Community Survey, S2802 "Types of Internet Subscriptions by Selected Characteristics," <https://factfinder.census.gov/>, accessed December 2018.

# Table 1181. Percent of Households with a Computer and Paid Internet Subscription by State: 2017

[In percent. Survey respondents could select more than one type of computer and more than one type of Internet subscription. Household computer can include desktop or laptop; smartphone; tablet or other portable wireless computer; or some other type of computer. Based on the American Community Survey. Please note that although the ACS includes people living in group quarters, computer and internet use data were not collected from group quarters. See also headnote Table 1180]

| State | Total households with computer | Type of internet subscription | | | State | Total households with computer | Type of internet subscription | | |
| | | Dial-up internet service | Broadband internet service [1] | No paid internet service [2] | | | Dial-up internet service | Broadband internet service [1] | No paid internet service [2] |
|---|---|---|---|---|---|---|---|---|---|
| **U.S.** | **90.8** | **0.3** | **91.2** | **8.4** | MO | 89.7 | 0.4 | 89.7 | 9.9 |
| AL | 86.1 | 0.4 | 89.7 | 9.9 | MT | 88.7 | 0.7 | 91.0 | 8.4 |
| AK | 94.2 | 0.3 | 90.9 | 8.8 | NE | 90.8 | 0.5 | 92.3 | 7.2 |
| AZ | 92.2 | 0.4 | 92.1 | 7.6 | NV | 93.3 | 0.3 | 88.8 | 11.0 |
| AR | 86.3 | 0.3 | 83.7 | 16.0 | NH | 93.7 | 0.4 | 93.9 | 5.7 |
| CA | 93.5 | 0.3 | 93.1 | 6.7 | NJ | 92.6 | 0.3 | 92.9 | 6.8 |
| CO | 94.2 | 0.4 | 93.1 | 6.5 | NM | 86.6 | 0.6 | 87.3 | 12.0 |
| CT | 90.9 | 0.4 | 93.2 | 6.4 | NY | 90.1 | 0.3 | 91.6 | 8.1 |
| DE | 92.9 | 0.3 | 92.2 | 7.5 | NC | 89.4 | 0.4 | 90.5 | 9.1 |
| DC | 91.9 | 0.1 | 89.3 | 10.6 | ND | 90.5 | 0.3 | 88.6 | 11.1 |
| FL | 91.9 | 0.2 | 89.8 | 10.0 | OH | 89.6 | 0.4 | 92.0 | 7.6 |
| GA | 90.9 | 0.2 | 90.0 | 9.8 | OK | 89.2 | 0.3 | 88.7 | 11.0 |
| HI | 91.3 | 0.3 | 92.0 | 7.7 | OR | 93.2 | 0.3 | 92.7 | 7.0 |
| ID | 91.3 | 0.6 | 89.9 | 9.5 | PA | 88.0 | 0.6 | 91.7 | 7.7 |
| IL | 90.3 | 0.3 | 91.7 | 7.9 | RI | 89.7 | 0.3 | 94.6 | 5.1 |
| IN | 88.8 | 0.5 | 90.5 | 9.0 | SC | 88.8 | 0.3 | 88.4 | 11.4 |
| IA | 89.5 | 0.6 | 90.7 | 8.7 | SD | 88.4 | 0.4 | 90.3 | 9.3 |
| KS | 90.7 | 0.4 | 90.7 | 9.0 | TN | 87.4 | 0.2 | 89.9 | 9.9 |
| KY | 86.3 | 0.3 | 90.2 | 9.5 | TX | 91.8 | 0.2 | 90.0 | 9.7 |
| LA | 86.0 | 0.2 | 86.9 | 12.9 | UT | 95.5 | 0.3 | 91.7 | 8.1 |
| ME | 89.7 | 1.0 | 90.6 | 8.4 | VT | 89.5 | 0.5 | 90.0 | 9.5 |
| MD | 93.0 | 0.2 | 93.7 | 6.1 | VA | 91.8 | 0.3 | 91.8 | 7.9 |
| MA | 91.2 | 0.2 | 94.3 | 5.5 | WA | 94.2 | 0.4 | 94.1 | 5.6 |
| MI | 90.0 | 0.4 | 91.0 | 8.6 | WV | 84.6 | 0.3 | 88.6 | 11.1 |
| MN | 92.1 | 0.5 | 92.6 | 6.8 | WI | 89.5 | 0.6 | 92.3 | 7.1 |
| MS | 84.6 | 0.3 | 85.6 | 14.1 | WY | 91.7 | 0.3 | 90.4 | 9.3 |

[1] Broadband internet service includes access via cable, fiber optic, or DSL; a cellular data plan; satellite; or a fixed wireless subscription. [2] Includes households accessing the internet without a subscription and also households with no internet access.

Source: U.S. Census Bureau, 2017 American Community Survey, B28003, "Presence of a Computer and Type of Internet Subscription in Household," <http://factfinder.census.gov>, accessed December 2018.

## Table 1182. Internet Access by Location and Selected User Characteristics: 2018

[In percent, except as noted (247,786 represents 247,786,000). For persons aged 18 and over. As of Fall 2018. Based on sample and subject to sampling error]

| Characteristic | Total adults (1,000) | Accessed the internet (percent) | | | | | |
|---|---|---|---|---|---|---|---|
| | | At home | At work | At school or library | At another place | Using a cellphone or smart-phone | Using WiFi or wireless connection outside of home |
| Total adults [1] | 247,786 | 82.9 | 45.4 | 12.5 | 38.0 | 79.1 | 26.2 |
| Age: | | | | | | | |
| 18 to 34 years old | 74,053 | 91.9 | 56.1 | 22.8 | 48.6 | 95.3 | 35.1 |
| 35 to 54 years old | 82,596 | 89.3 | 60.9 | 11.6 | 42.4 | 90.1 | 30.1 |
| 55 years old and over | 91,137 | 69.8 | 22.8 | 4.8 | 25.4 | 56.0 | 15.5 |
| Sex: | | | | | | | |
| Male | 119,610 | 82.4 | 48.7 | 11.0 | 38.1 | 78.1 | 26.5 |
| Female | 128,176 | 83.4 | 42.4 | 13.9 | 37.9 | 80.1 | 26.0 |
| Census region: [2] | | | | | | | |
| Northeast | 44,147 | 85.1 | 48.9 | 12.9 | 46.6 | 80.2 | 27.7 |
| South | 94,063 | 80.8 | 44.0 | 12.0 | 33.6 | 77.9 | 24.9 |
| Midwest | 52,196 | 80.9 | 42.7 | 11.2 | 33.5 | 75.1 | 21.6 |
| West | 57,380 | 86.6 | 47.6 | 14.0 | 42.5 | 83.9 | 31.5 |
| Household size: | | | | | | | |
| 1 to 2 persons | 114,902 | 77.2 | 37.4 | 8.7 | 33.2 | 68.5 | 22.3 |
| 3 to 4 persons | 90,598 | 87.5 | 53.8 | 15.1 | 43.2 | 87.4 | 30.0 |
| 5 or more persons | 42,286 | 88.9 | 49.5 | 17.2 | 39.7 | 90.2 | 28.8 |
| Presence of child in household | 95,243 | 89.6 | 55.8 | 15.7 | 42.9 | 91.8 | 30.0 |
| Marital status: | | | | | | | |
| Never married | 70,688 | 86.7 | 49.5 | 21.9 | 44.6 | 87.9 | 31.9 |
| Married | 131,271 | 86.0 | 48.6 | 9.2 | 38.2 | 80.7 | 26.2 |
| Other [3] | 53,738 | 71.7 | 34.0 | 8.6 | 29.8 | 65.9 | 19.0 |
| Education: | | | | | | | |
| Graduated college plus | 77,932 | 94.1 | 64.8 | 15.8 | 49.1 | 90.1 | 40.4 |
| Attended college | 70,912 | 88.4 | 47.4 | 16.3 | 40.9 | 84.5 | 27.9 |
| Did not attend college | 98,942 | 70.2 | 28.8 | 7.1 | 27.1 | 66.6 | 13.9 |
| Employment status: | | | | | | | |
| Employed full-time | 122,371 | 90.4 | 77.9 | 11.1 | 44.3 | 91.6 | 32.8 |
| Employed part-time | 29,623 | 87.8 | 55.9 | 25.7 | 42.5 | 86.3 | 31.4 |
| Occupation of employed: | | | | | | | |
| Professional | 36,196 | 95.6 | 88.4 | 21.7 | 52.6 | 95.4 | 44.2 |
| Management/business/financial | 25,519 | 94.7 | 90.1 | 10.6 | 48.1 | 94.8 | 41.7 |
| Sales/office | 32,488 | 91.4 | 77.9 | 14.2 | 41.5 | 91.7 | 30.9 |
| Natural resources/construction/maintenance | 14,216 | 81.6 | 52.6 | 4.7 | 34.4 | 83.4 | 19.2 |
| Other | 43,575 | 83.8 | 55.4 | 12.2 | 39.2 | 85.6 | 22.9 |
| Sector of employment: | | | | | | | |
| Business | 81,118 | 90.0 | 73.8 | 11.1 | 45.4 | 90.9 | 31.2 |
| Government | 21,435 | 93.0 | 84.1 | 26.8 | 47.8 | 93.2 | 38.3 |
| Other | 37,332 | 87.2 | 64.3 | 10.5 | 38.4 | 87.3 | 31.1 |
| Household income: | | | | | | | |
| Less than $50,000 | 86,674 | 69.1 | 22.9 | 11.4 | 26.6 | 64.1 | 15.5 |
| $50,000 to $74,999 | 42,964 | 86.1 | 42.0 | 12.5 | 36.0 | 78.6 | 24.0 |
| $75,000 to $149,999 | 77,946 | 90.7 | 60.1 | 12.8 | 44.2 | 88.7 | 31.0 |
| $150,000 or more | 40,202 | 94.3 | 69.3 | 14.2 | 52.6 | 93.6 | 42.5 |

[1] Includes other labor force status not shown separately. [2] For composition of regions, see map inside front cover. [3] Includes separated, divorced, and widowed, and also persons engaged to be married.

Source: © Fall 2018, MRI Survey of the American Consumer. Courtesy of MRI-Simmons. See also <https://www.mrisimmons.com/>.

## Table 1183. Internet Activities by Selected Characteristics: 2017

[In percent. Covers population age 15 and over. Based on the November 2017 Computer and Internet Use supplement to the Current Population Survey, for the National Telecommunications and Information Administration's Digital Nation research project]

| Activity conducted online or via the internet | Total | By sex | | By age | | | |
|---|---|---|---|---|---|---|---|
| | | Male | Female | 15 to 24 years old | 25 to 44 years old | 45 to 64 years old | 65 years and over |
| Uses the internet, any location | 79.4 | 79.3 | 79.5 | 85.1 | 85.4 | 80.2 | 63.1 |
| Interact with household equipment | 11.0 | 11.9 | 10.2 | 6.5 | 14.8 | 11.4 | 6.5 |
| Offer services for sale | 6.0 | 6.6 | 5.5 | 5.1 | 7.6 | 6.1 | 3.2 |
| Video or voice calls, or conferencing | 46.6 | 45.4 | 47.7 | 60.5 | 55.0 | 40.1 | 25.5 |
| Post or upload blog posts, videos, or other original content | 16.9 | 16.7 | 17.2 | 26.0 | 20.7 | 13.0 | 6.4 |
| Request services provided by other people | 25.9 | 26.6 | 25.3 | 25.3 | 34.0 | 23.3 | 14.0 |
| Search for a job | 20.8 | 20.7 | 21.0 | 34.5 | 26.6 | 15.1 | 4.4 |
| Shop, make travel reservations, or use other consumer services | 68.5 | 66.4 | 70.5 | 62.9 | 74.2 | 69.4 | 60.2 |
| Stream or download music, radio, podcasts, etc. | 52.6 | 54.2 | 51.1 | 73.6 | 63.4 | 43.6 | 23.3 |
| Take class or participate in job training | 19.1 | 18.8 | 19.3 | 28.4 | 22.5 | 16.4 | 6.3 |
| Telecommute | 22.6 | 24.7 | 20.5 | 10.4 | 31.4 | 26.8 | 7.3 |
| Use email | 90.8 | 90.0 | 91.6 | 91.0 | 93.4 | 90.5 | 85.5 |
| Use financial services such as banking, investing, paying bills | 65.9 | 65.2 | 66.5 | 53.2 | 76.5 | 66.6 | 54.6 |
| Use social networks | 74.4 | 70.8 | 77.8 | 88.2 | 83.8 | 67.5 | 52.0 |
| Use text messaging or instant messaging | 90.2 | 89.8 | 90.5 | 95.7 | 96.4 | 89.7 | 70.8 |
| Use internet to sell goods | 11.3 | 12.2 | 10.5 | 10.9 | 14.6 | 10.4 | 6.4 |
| Watch videos | 69.5 | 71.5 | 67.7 | 86.4 | 81.7 | 61.2 | 40.2 |

Source: U.S. Department of Commerce, National Telecommunications and Information Administration, "Digital Nation Data Explorer," <https://www.ntia.doc.gov/category/data-central>, accessed June 2018.

## Table 1184. Home Internet Access—Broadband and Smartphone Only Service by Selected Characteristics: 2016 to 2019

[In percent. Based on a survey of 4,535 adults conducted in April and November 2016 (sampling error plus or minus 1.7 percentage points); a survey of 2,002 adults conducted in January 2018; and a survey of 1,502 adults conducted January 8-February 7, 2019 (sampling error plus or minus 2.8 percentage points). Surveys were conducted in English and Spanish on landline and cellular telephones]

| Characteristic | Internet broadband service in the home | | | Internet via smartphone only [1] | | |
|---|---|---|---|---|---|---|
| | 2016 | 2018 | 2019 | 2016 | 2018 | 2019 |
| **Total** | **72** | **65** | **73** | **12** | **20** | **17** |
| SEX | | | | | | |
| Male | 74 | 66 | 73 | 12 | 20 | 17 |
| Female | 70 | 64 | 73 | 12 | 19 | 16 |
| RACE/ETHNICITY | | | | | | |
| White, non-Hispanic | 77 | 72 | 79 | 9 | 14 | 12 |
| Black, non-Hispanic | 65 | 57 | 66 | 15 | 24 | 23 |
| Hispanic | 55 | 47 | 61 | 23 | 35 | 25 |
| AGE | | | | | | |
| 18 to 29 years | 78 | 67 | 77 | 17 | 28 | 22 |
| 30 to 49 years | 80 | 70 | 77 | 13 | 24 | 18 |
| 50 to 64 years | 72 | 68 | 79 | 11 | 16 | 14 |
| 65 years and older | 51 | 50 | 59 | 7 | 10 | 12 |
| EDUCATION | | | | | | |
| Less than high school graduate | 30 | 24 | 46 | 27 | 39 | 32 |
| High school graduate | 61 | 56 | 59 | 15 | 22 | 24 |
| Some college | 80 | 68 | 77 | 12 | 21 | 16 |
| College graduate | 90 | 85 | 93 | 5 | 10 | 4 |
| HOUSEHOLD INCOME | | | | | | |
| Less than $30,000 | 52 | 45 | 56 | 21 | 31 | 26 |
| $30,000 to $49,999 | 72 | 67 | 72 | 12 | 22 | 20 |
| $50,000 to $74,999 | 82 | 79 | 87 | 10 | 14 | 10 |
| $75,0000 and over | 92 | 87 | 92 | 5 | 9 | 6 |
| METRO STATUS | | | | | | |
| Urban | 73 | 67 | 75 | 12 | 22 | 17 |
| Suburban | 74 | 70 | 79 | 12 | 17 | 13 |
| Rural | 62 | 58 | 63 | 14 | 17 | 20 |
| PARENTAL STATUS | | | | | | |
| Parent of minor child | 79 | (NA) | (NA) | 12 | (NA) | (NA) |
| Not parent of minor child | 69 | (NA) | (NA) | 12 | (NA) | (NA) |

NA Not available. [1] Persons without traditional home broadband internet service who own a smartphone that can access the internet.

Source: Pew Research Center ©, "Internet/Broadband Fact Sheet," <http://www.pewinternet.org/fact-sheet/internet-broadband/>, accessed June 2019; and unpublished data.

## Table 1185. Adult Internet Users and Home Internet Connection by Selected Characteristics: 2000 to 2019

[In percent. Covers persons age 18 and over who use the internet at a workplace, school, home, or anywhere else, on at least an occasional basis. Based on telephone surveys of persons with landline telephones unless otherwise noted. Beginning 2011, surveys include interviews conducted in English and Spanish. Data for 2019 are from January-February 2019 interviews of 1,502 persons, including 1,200 cellphone users. Data for 2018 are from January 2018 interviews of 2,002 persons, including 1,502 cellphone users. Data for 2016 are from November 2016 interviews with 3,015 persons, including 2,258 cellphone users. Data for 2015 are from July 2015 interviews with 2,001 persons, including 1,300 cellphone users. Data for 2010 are from interviews with 2,252 persons, including 744 cellphone users]

| Characteristic | Adult internet users | | | | | | | All adults, by type of home connection, 2019 | |
|---|---|---|---|---|---|---|---|---|---|
| | 2000 | 2005 | 2010 | 2015 | 2016 | 2018 | 2019 | Broadband | Dial-up |
| **Total adults** | **53** | **69** | **79** | **87** | **90** | **89** | **90** | **73** | **2** |
| Sex: | | | | | | | | | |
| Male | 56 | 70 | 79 | 87 | 90 | 89 | 90 | 73 | 2 |
| Female | 51 | 67 | 79 | 87 | 90 | 88 | 91 | 73 | 1 |
| Race/ethnicity: | | | | | | | | | |
| White, non-Hispanic | 55 | 70 | 80 | 87 | 90 | 89 | 92 | 79 | 1 |
| Black, non-Hispanic | 42 | 54 | 71 | 84 | 86 | 87 | 85 | 66 | 1 |
| Hispanic | 48 | 73 | 82 | 84 | 90 | 88 | 86 | 61 | 2 |
| Age: | | | | | | | | | |
| 18 to 29 years old | 72 | 82 | 95 | 97 | 99 | 98 | 100 | 77 | 1 |
| 30 to 49 years old | 62 | 80 | 87 | 97 | 96 | 97 | 97 | 77 | 1 |
| 50 to 64 years old | 48 | 68 | 78 | 80 | 89 | 87 | 88 | 79 | 1 |
| 65 years old and over | 15 | 28 | 42 | 65 | 67 | 66 | 73 | 59 | 3 |
| Education: | | | | | | | | | |
| Less than high school | 19 | 35 | 52 | 68 | 71 | 65 | 71 | 46 | 1 |
| High school graduate [1] | 41 | 59 | 67 | 77 | 84 | 84 | 84 | 59 | 2 |
| Some college | 69 | 80 | 90 | 93 | 94 | 93 | 95 | 77 | 1 |
| College graduate or higher | 79 | 88 | 96 | 97 | 98 | 97 | 98 | 93 | 1 |
| Annual household income: | | | | | | | | | |
| Less than $30,000 | 35 | 50 | 63 | 78 | 81 | 81 | 82 | 56 | 2 |
| $30,000 to $49,999 | 61 | 74 | 84 | 87 | 91 | 93 | 93 | 72 | 1 |
| $50,000 to $74,999 | 74 | 86 | 89 | 94 | 96 | 97 | 97 | 87 | 2 |
| $75,000 or more | 81 | 91 | 95 | 97 | 98 | 98 | 98 | 92 | 1 |

[1] Includes those with a GED certificate.

Source: Pew Research Center, Pew Internet & American Life Project Surveys © conducted September-December 2000, September and December of 2005, May 2010, July 2015, November 2016, January 2018, and January-February 2019. See also <http://www.pewinternet.org>.

## Table 1186. Teen Electronic Device Ownership and Social Media Use by Selected Characteristics: 2018

[In percent. Based on responses from 1,058 parents of teenagers and 743 teenagers age 13 to 17 participating in a survey conducted by NORC at the University of Chicago, March 7 to April 10, 2018. Margin of error for results at 95% level of confidence for parents is 4.5 percentage points and for teens 5.0 percentage points. Multiple responses were allowed]

| Characteristic | Device ownership [1] | | | | Online/social media platform use | | | | |
|---|---|---|---|---|---|---|---|---|---|
| | Smart-phone | Cellphone but not smart-phone | Desktop or laptop | Gaming console | YouTube | Instagram | Snapchat | Facebook | Twitter |
| **Total**.................... | **95** | **29** | **88** | **84** | **85** | **72** | **69** | **51** | **32** |
| SEX | | | | | | | | | |
| Male.......................... | 93 | 27 | 89 | 92 | 89 | 69 | 67 | 49 | 33 |
| Female....................... | 97 | 31 | 88 | 75 | 81 | 75 | 72 | 53 | 32 |
| RACE/ETHNICITY | | | | | | | | | |
| White, non-Hispanic......... | 94 | 25 | 90 | 87 | 86 | 73 | 72 | 48 | 33 |
| Black, non-Hispanic......... | 94 | 32 | 89 | 78 | 79 | 72 | 77 | 57 | 29 |
| Hispanic [2]................. | 95 | 34 | 82 | 81 | 85 | 72 | 64 | 58 | 36 |
| AGE | | | | | | | | | |
| 13 to 14 years.............. | 94 | 26 | 88 | 86 | 84 | 63 | 63 | 47 | 24 |
| 15 to 17 years.............. | 95 | 30 | 88 | 82 | 86 | 78 | 74 | 54 | 38 |
| HOUSEHOLD INCOME | | | | | | | | | |
| Less than $30,000........... | 93 | 38 | 75 | 85 | 86 | 74 | 77 | 70 | 40 |
| $30,000 to $74,999.......... | 93 | 28 | 89 | 82 | 84 | 72 | 71 | 56 | 30 |
| $75,000 and over............ | 97 | 24 | 96 | 84 | 85 | 71 | 64 | 36 | 30 |

[1] Percent of US teens who say they have or have access at home to the listed device. [2] Persons of Hispanic origin may be of any race.

Source: Pew Research Center, *Teens, Social Media & Technology 2018*, May 2018 ©. See also <http://www.pewinternet.org>.

## Table 1187. Households Using Electronics, Internet Devices, and Cell Phones by Type and Household Income: 2015

[In millions (118.2 represents 118,200,000). Based on the Residential Energy Consumption Survey. Includes single-family homes, units in multifamily buildings, and mobile homes. Excludes secondary homes, vacant, seasonal and vacation homes, group quarters, and common areas of apartment buildings. Data may not sum to totals due to rounding]

| Item | Total | Households by income (millions) | | | | | | | |
|---|---|---|---|---|---|---|---|---|---|
| | | Less than $20,000 | $20,000 to $39,999 | $40,000 to $59,999 | $60,000 to $79,999 | $80,000 to $99,000 | $100,000 to $119,999 | $120,000 to $139,999 | $140,000 or more |
| **Total households**.............. | **118.2** | **22.5** | **27.2** | **18.6** | **15.4** | **9.7** | **8.1** | **5.4** | **11.2** |
| TELEVISION AND VIDEO | | | | | | | | | |
| Number of televisions: | | | | | | | | | |
| 0............................ | 3.1 | 0.9 | 1.0 | 0.4 | 0.3 | (B) | (B) | (B) | (B) |
| 1............................ | 30.0 | 8.7 | 7.0 | 4.2 | 3.8 | 1.5 | 1.7 | 0.9 | 2.2 |
| 2............................ | 39.1 | 7.5 | 9.6 | 6.4 | 4.9 | 3.4 | 2.5 | 1.8 | 2.9 |
| 3 or more.................... | 46.0 | 5.4 | 9.6 | 7.6 | 6.4 | 4.5 | 3.8 | 2.7 | 6.0 |
| Hours TV used per weekday: [1] | | | | | | | | | |
| Less than 1 hour............. | 3.7 | 0.9 | 0.8 | 0.5 | 0.5 | 0.2 | 0.3 | (B) | 0.5 |
| 1 to 3 hours................. | 29.7 | 4.2 | 5.7 | 4.3 | 4.4 | 2.6 | 2.7 | 1.9 | 4.0 |
| 4 to 6 hours................. | 43.0 | 6.6 | 9.2 | 6.9 | 6.0 | 4.1 | 3.1 | 2.4 | 4.6 |
| 7 to 10 hours................ | 21.5 | 4.6 | 5.8 | 3.9 | 2.4 | 1.7 | 1.3 | 0.6 | 1.3 |
| More than 10 hours........... | 17.2 | 5.4 | 4.7 | 2.6 | 1.9 | 0.9 | 0.6 | 0.4 | 0.6 |
| Hours TV used per weekend day: [1] | | | | | | | | | |
| Less than 1 hour............. | 3.1 | 1.0 | 0.8 | 0.4 | 0.4 | (B) | 0.2 | (B) | (B) |
| 1 to 3 hours................. | 20.2 | 3.7 | 4.0 | 2.6 | 3.0 | 1.9 | 1.5 | 1.1 | 2.6 |
| 4 to 6 hours................. | 38.4 | 5.7 | 8.6 | 5.9 | 5.0 | 3.4 | 3.0 | 2.1 | 4.7 |
| 7 to 10 hours................ | 30.4 | 5.3 | 7.0 | 5.4 | 4.1 | 2.6 | 2.3 | 1.3 | 2.4 |
| More than 10 hours........... | 23.0 | 6.1 | 5.7 | 4.0 | 2.7 | 1.6 | 1.0 | 0.7 | 1.2 |
| Number of cable or satellite TV boxes: [2] | | | | | | | | | |
| 1............................ | 34.0 | 4.2 | 6.8 | 6.3 | 4.7 | 3.3 | 2.8 | 1.8 | 4.2 |
| 2 or more.................... | 20.0 | 1.6 | 3.3 | 3.0 | 2.9 | 2.5 | 1.9 | 1.7 | 3.1 |
| Number of internet streaming devices: | | | | | | | | | |
| 1............................ | 24.9 | 3.0 | 4.6 | 4.1 | 3.7 | 2.2 | 2.5 | 1.3 | 3.5 |
| 2 or more.................... | 9.0 | 0.5 | 1.4 | 1.5 | 1.1 | 1.2 | 0.7 | 0.8 | 1.8 |
| COMPUTERS AND PHONES | | | | | | | | | |
| Number of desktop computers: | | | | | | | | | |
| 1............................ | 41.3 | 5.2 | 9.2 | 6.7 | 5.4 | 3.8 | 3.3 | 2.6 | 5.0 |
| 2 or more.................... | 8.0 | (NA) | 1.1 | (NA) | (NA) | (NA) | (NA) | (NA) | 1.5 |
| Number of laptop computers: | | | | | | | | | |
| 1............................ | 44.6 | 6.2 | 10.1 | 8.2 | 6.7 | 4.6 | 3.3 | 1.7 | 3.8 |
| 2............................ | 21.2 | 1.8 | 3.3 | 3.2 | 3.6 | 2.1 | 2.1 | 1.9 | 3.3 |
| 3 or more.................... | 9.6 | 0.7 | 0.9 | 0.9 | 1.1 | 0.8 | 1.2 | 0.9 | 3.0 |
| Number of tablets and e-readers: | | | | | | | | | |
| 1............................ | 38.2 | 5.2 | 9.1 | 6.9 | 5.5 | 3.9 | 2.8 | 1.8 | 3.0 |
| 2............................ | 19.1 | 1.6 | 2.6 | 2.9 | 2.7 | 1.9 | 2.0 | 1.5 | 3.8 |
| 3 or more.................... | 10.5 | 0.4 | 1.1 | 1.1 | 1.7 | 1.1 | 1.3 | 1.1 | 2.5 |
| Number of smartphones: | | | | | | | | | |
| 1............................ | 28.4 | 5.8 | 8.0 | 5.6 | 3.7 | 2.1 | 1.4 | 0.8 | 1.1 |
| 2............................ | 37.6 | 4.0 | 6.5 | 6.3 | 5.9 | 4.1 | 3.3 | 2.6 | 4.9 |
| 3 or more.................... | 23.9 | 2.5 | 3.6 | 3.1 | 3.2 | 2.4 | 2.7 | 1.7 | 4.6 |

B Data withheld due to relative standard error being greater than 50 percent or fewer than 10 cases responded. NA Not available. [1] Data shown for primary television. [2] Cable and satellite boxes with digital video recorder (DVR).

Source: U.S. Energy Information Administration, Residential Energy Consumption Survey—2015 Data, "Table HC4.5 Electronics in U.S. Homes by Household Income, 2015," <https://www.eia.gov/consumption/residential/data/2015/>, accessed June 2017.

## Table 1188. Social Media—Use of Social Networking Sites Among Adult Internet Users: 2019

[In percent. Based on a survey of 1,502 adults age 18 and older living in all 50 states and DC, conducted January 8-February 7, 2019 in English and Spanish on landline and cellular telephones. Margin of error for results for the total sample is plus or minus 2.85 percentage points]

| Characteristic | Social media platform | | | | | | | |
|---|---|---|---|---|---|---|---|---|
| | Facebook | Instagram | LinkedIn | Pinterest | Snapchat | Twitter | WhatsApp | YouTube |
| **Total**................. | **69** | **37** | **27** | **28** | **24** | **22** | **20** | **73** |
| SEX | | | | | | | | |
| Male........................ | 63 | 31 | 29 | 15 | 24 | 24 | 21 | 78 |
| Female....................... | 75 | 43 | 24 | 42 | 24 | 21 | 19 | 68 |
| RACE/ETHNICITY | | | | | | | | |
| White, non-Hispanic.................. | 70 | 33 | 28 | 33 | 22 | 21 | 13 | 71 |
| Black, non-Hispanic.................. | 70 | 40 | 24 | 27 | 28 | 24 | 24 | 77 |
| Hispanic origin [1]..................... | 69 | 51 | 16 | 22 | 29 | 25 | 42 | 78 |
| AGE | | | | | | | | |
| 18 to 29 years...................... | 79 | 67 | 28 | 34 | 62 | 38 | 23 | 91 |
| 30 to 49 years...................... | 79 | 47 | 37 | 35 | 25 | 26 | 31 | 87 |
| 50 to 64 years...................... | 68 | 23 | 24 | 27 | 9 | 17 | 16 | 70 |
| 65 years and over.................... | 46 | 8 | 11 | 15 | 3 | 7 | 3 | 38 |
| EDUCATION | | | | | | | | |
| High school graduate or less......... | 61 | 33 | 9 | 19 | 22 | 13 | 18 | 64 |
| Some college.......................... | 75 | 37 | 26 | 32 | 29 | 24 | 14 | 79 |
| College graduate or higher........... | 74 | 43 | 51 | 38 | 20 | 32 | 28 | 80 |
| INCOME | | | | | | | | |
| Under $30,000....................... | 69 | 35 | 10 | 18 | 27 | 20 | 19 | 68 |
| $30,000 to $74,999.................... | 72 | 39 | 26 | 27 | 26 | 20 | 16 | 75 |
| $75,000 and over..................... | 74 | 42 | 49 | 41 | 22 | 31 | 25 | 83 |
| METRO STATUS | | | | | | | | |
| Urban................................ | 73 | 46 | 33 | 30 | 29 | 26 | 24 | 77 |
| Suburban............................. | 69 | 35 | 30 | 30 | 20 | 22 | 19 | 74 |
| Rural................................. | 66 | 21 | 10 | 26 | 20 | 13 | 10 | 64 |

[1] Persons of Hispanic origin may be of any race.

Source: Pew Research Center, Fact Tank, "Share of U.S. adults using social media, including Facebook, is mostly unchanged since 2018," April 2019 ©. See also <http://www.pewinternet.org/>.

## Table 1189. Public Libraries—Selected Characteristics: 2017

[Total operating income in thousands of dollars (13,236,542 represents $13,236,542,000). Data are generally for the fiscal year ending in June; see source for reporting periods. Based on a census of all public libraries in the 50 states and the District of Columbia. See source for details]

| Population of service area | Number of— | | Operating income | | | Paid staff [4] | | Avg. number of public use internet computers per stationary outlet [6] |
|---|---|---|---|---|---|---|---|---|
| | Public libraries [1] | Stationary outlets [2] | Total [3] ($1,000) | Source (percent) | | Total FTE | Librarians with ALA-MLS [5] | |
| | | | | State government | Local government | | | |
| **Total**................... | **9,045** | **16,557** | **13,236,542** | **6.7** | **85.9** | **142,131** | **33,620** | **18.1** |
| Less than 1,000........ | 935 | 940 | 39,592 | 7.0 | 76.5 | 715 | 42 | 4.6 |
| 1,000 to 2,499.......... | 1,461 | 1,477 | 123,355 | 5.2 | 78.0 | 2,090 | 155 | 6.4 |
| 2,500 to 4,999.......... | 1,263 | 1,299 | 207,312 | 5.5 | 79.1 | 3,191 | 394 | 8.2 |
| 5,000 to 9,999.......... | 1,494 | 1,638 | 493,074 | 6.5 | 83.4 | 6,832 | 1,267 | 12.3 |
| 10,000 to 24,999........ | 1,757 | 2,230 | 1,336,468 | 5.9 | 86.6 | 16,316 | 3,945 | 15.8 |
| 25,000 to 49,999....... | 989 | 1,755 | 1,583,276 | 6.3 | 86.9 | 17,874 | 4,567 | 18.8 |
| 50,000 to 99,999....... | 578 | 1,576 | 1,642,031 | 7.4 | 86.4 | 17,987 | 4,477 | 22.1 |
| 100,000 to 249,999.... | 366 | 2,024 | 2,036,440 | 7.3 | 86.3 | 22,510 | 5,180 | 22.7 |
| 250,000 to 499,999.... | 112 | 1,186 | 1,563,570 | 7.1 | 87.5 | 16,295 | 3,935 | 25.3 |
| 500,000 to 999,999.... | 55 | 1,071 | 1,900,057 | 7.2 | 85.8 | 18,184 | 4,234 | 29.4 |
| 1,000,000 or more..... | 35 | 1,361 | 2,311,366 | 5.7 | 85.0 | 20,136 | 5,424 | 33.3 |

[1] A public library is the administrative entity, the agency, that provides public library services. Of the 9,045 public libraries in the 50 States and DC, 7,320 were single-outlet and 1,725 were multiple-outlet libraries. There are 8,870 central library outlets, 7,687 branch library outlets, and 672 bookmobiles. [2] The sum of central and branch libraries. [3] Total includes income from the federal government (0.4%) and other sources (7.1%), not shown separately. [4] Full-time equivalents. Forty hours per week equals 1 FTE. [5] Librarians with master's degrees from a graduate library education program accredited by the American Library Association (ALA). Total librarians, including those without ALA-MLS, is 49,576. [6] The average per stationary outlet was calculated by dividing the total number of public use internet computers in central and branch outlets by the total number of such outlets.

Source: Institute of Museum and Library Services, Public Libraries Survey, *Supplementary Tables, Public Libraries Survey, Fiscal Year 2017,* June 2019. See also <https://www.imls.gov/research-evaluation/data-collection/public-libraries-survey>.

# Table 1190. Number of Public Libraries and Library Services by State: 2017

[1,317,654 represents 1,317,654,000. Data are generally for the fiscal year ending in June; see source documentation for reporting periods. Based on a census of all public libraries that meet the definition of a Federal State Cooperative System (FSCS) Public Library, which can have one or more outlets (central, branch, bookmobile, or books-by-mail-only) that provide direct service to the public]

| State | Number of public libraries [1] | Visits — Library visits (1,000s) | Visits — Per capita visits [2] | Circulation — Total circulation (1,000s) | Circulation — Per capita circulation of materials [2] | Circulation — Children's circulation (1,000s) | Children's circulation as percent of total circulation | Average number of public use internet computers [3] |
|---|---|---|---|---|---|---|---|---|
| **United States** | **9,045** | **1,317,654** | **4.2** | **2,163,539** | **6.9** | **766,459** | **35.4** | **18.1** |
| Alabama | 218 | 14,578 | 3.2 | 19,919 | 4.3 | 6,766 | 34.0 | 17.4 |
| Alaska | 61 | 3,364 | 5.2 | 4,680 | 7.3 | 1,490 | 31.8 | 11.7 |
| Arizona | 90 | 24,589 | 3.5 | 45,352 | 6.6 | 12,427 | 27.3 | 33.3 |
| Arkansas | 60 | 10,358 | 3.9 | 13,900 | 5.3 | 3,919 | 28.1 | 12.0 |
| California | 184 | 151,059 | 3.8 | 208,171 | 5.3 | 85,182 | 40.9 | 20.9 |
| Colorado | 113 | 31,976 | 5.9 | 62,439 | 11.5 | 21,350 | 34.2 | 24.6 |
| Connecticut | 181 | 20,036 | 5.9 | 24,804 | 7.6 | 9,132 | 35.3 | 18.7 |
| Delaware | 21 | 4,118 | 4.3 | 5,546 | 5.8 | 1,775 | 32.0 | 32.7 |
| District of Columbia | 1 | 3,593 | 5.2 | 4,293 | 6.2 | 1,519 | 35.4 | 38.5 |
| Florida | 81 | 66,753 | 3.3 | 99,660 | 4.9 | 31,821 | 31.9 | 31.5 |
| Georgia | 63 | 28,816 | 2.7 | 35,453 | 3.4 | 15,921 | 44.9 | 24.1 |
| Hawaii | 1 | 4,135 | 2.9 | 5,906 | 4.1 | 2,359 | 39.9 | 11.3 |
| Idaho | 102 | 8,029 | 5.6 | 15,618 | 11.0 | 6,557 | 42.0 | 13.4 |
| Illinois | 622 | 66,175 | 5.7 | 107,710 | 9.3 | 41,948 | 38.8 | 20.2 |
| Indiana | 236 | 31,849 | 5.2 | 70,761 | 11.6 | 21,293 | 30.1 | 19.7 |
| Iowa | 535 | 17,233 | 5.6 | 25,213 | 8.3 | 9,060 | 35.8 | 9.1 |
| Kansas | 319 | 13,734 | 5.5 | 24,534 | 9.8 | 9,574 | 39.0 | 10.1 |
| Kentucky | 119 | 17,909 | 4.0 | 29,539 | 6.7 | 9,271 | 31.4 | 24.6 |
| Louisiana | 67 | 17,211 | 3.7 | 21,469 | 4.6 | 4,739 | 22.1 | 17.0 |
| Maine | 228 | 6,673 | 5.8 | 8,467 | 7.3 | 3,109 | 36.7 | 7.9 |
| Maryland | 24 | 26,090 | 4.4 | 56,357 | 9.5 | 23,038 | 40.9 | 27.3 |
| Massachusetts | 368 | 40,456 | 6.0 | 54,673 | 8.1 | 20,050 | 36.7 | 14.4 |
| Michigan | 397 | 46,053 | 4.7 | 77,583 | 7.9 | 25,017 | 32.2 | 19.0 |
| Minnesota | 137 | 23,357 | 4.2 | 48,990 | 8.9 | 19,489 | 39.7 | 16.0 |
| Mississippi | 52 | 8,582 | 2.9 | 7,189 | 2.4 | 2,314 | 32.2 | 11.8 |
| Missouri | 148 | 26,129 | 4.8 | 51,981 | 9.5 | 17,157 | 33.0 | 13.5 |
| Montana | 82 | 4,215 | 4.3 | 5,973 | 6.0 | 1,998 | 33.5 | 11.1 |
| Nebraska | 235 | 7,726 | 4.9 | 12,395 | 7.9 | 5,783 | 46.6 | 11.4 |
| Nevada | 22 | 9,685 | 3.3 | 18,414 | 6.2 | 6,038 | 32.8 | 16.4 |
| New Hampshire | 222 | 7,016 | 5.3 | 10,425 | 7.9 | 3,613 | 34.6 | 6.7 |
| New Jersey | 286 | 41,874 | 4.8 | 51,596 | 6.0 | 20,391 | 39.4 | 19.6 |
| New Mexico | 87 | 7,019 | 4.7 | 9,321 | 6.2 | 2,658 | 28.5 | 15.2 |
| New York | 756 | 100,012 | 5.2 | 127,223 | 6.6 | 41,037 | 32.3 | 19.7 |
| North Carolina | 81 | 32,621 | 3.2 | 49,231 | 4.9 | 21,643 | 44.0 | 19.6 |
| North Dakota | 74 | 2,159 | 3.2 | 3,592 | 5.3 | 1,342 | 37.3 | 9.4 |
| Ohio | 251 | 71,896 | 6.3 | 170,443 | 14.9 | 52,515 | 30.7 | 20.0 |
| Oklahoma | 119 | 13,491 | 4.2 | 23,661 | 7.3 | 6,686 | 28.3 | 15.0 |
| Oregon | 131 | 20,260 | 5.7 | 54,031 | 15.2 | 12,182 | 22.6 | 13.8 |
| Pennsylvania | 453 | 42,252 | 3.4 | 61,830 | 5.0 | 22,272 | 35.9 | 13.1 |
| Rhode Island | 48 | 5,669 | 5.4 | 6,049 | 5.7 | 1,847 | 30.5 | 20.9 |
| South Carolina | 42 | 14,568 | 3.1 | 23,924 | 5.1 | 8,705 | 36.4 | 22.0 |
| South Dakota | 111 | 3,700 | 4.7 | 5,929 | 7.6 | 2,422 | 40.5 | 7.9 |
| Tennessee | 186 | 19,397 | 3.0 | 26,992 | 4.2 | 9,394 | 34.8 | 19.9 |
| Texas | 540 | 70,302 | 2.8 | 117,268 | 4.6 | 46,981 | 40.0 | 25.2 |
| Utah | 74 | 15,327 | 5.1 | 33,801 | 11.4 | 15,072 | 44.2 | 17.8 |
| Vermont | 162 | 3,585 | 6.2 | 3,932 | 7.4 | 1,732 | 40.3 | 6.7 |
| Virginia | 92 | 34,563 | 4.2 | 65,985 | 7.9 | 24,967 | 37.8 | 21.6 |
| Washington | 62 | 37,988 | 5.3 | 84,405 | 11.7 | 26,610 | 31.5 | 20.1 |
| West Virginia | 97 | 5,231 | 2.8 | 6,510 | 3.5 | 2,030 | 31.2 | 8.0 |
| Wisconsin | 381 | 30,877 | 5.3 | 55,712 | 9.6 | 20,416 | 36.7 | 13.8 |
| Wyoming | 23 | 3,367 | 5.8 | 4,691 | 8.0 | 1,846 | 39.4 | 12.0 |

[1] A public library is the administrative entity, the agency, that provides public library services. Of the 9,045 public libraries in the 50 States and DC, 7,320 were single-outlet libraries and 1,725 were multiple-outlet libraries. There are 8,870 central library outlets, 7,687 branch library outlets, and 672 bookmobiles. Excludes 168 libraries that do not meet the criteria in the FSCS public library definition but that qualify as public libraries under state law. [2] Per capita rate based on total unduplicated population of legal service area given by the state library agency of each state. [3] The average per stationary outlet was calculated by dividing the total number of public use Internet computers in central and branch outlets by the total number of such outlets.

Source: Institute of Museum and Library Services, Public Libraries Survey, *Supplementary Tables, Public Libraries Survey, Fiscal Year 2017*, June 2019. See also <https://www.imls.gov/research-evaluation/data-collection/public-libraries-survey>.

# Table 1191. Public Library Holdings by Type by State: 2017

[In thousands (715,019 represents 715,019,000). Data are generally for the fiscal year ending in June; see source for reporting periods. Based on a census of all public libraries conducted by Institute of Museum and Library Services. Covers only libraries that meet the definition of a Federal State Cooperative System (FSCS) public library. State data comparisons should be made with caution because of differences in reporting periods and adherence to survey definitions. Data are not subject to sampling error; census results may contain nonsampling error]

| State | Print | | Electronic materials | | Audio | | Video | |
|---|---|---|---|---|---|---|---|---|
| | Print materials [1] | Current print serial subscriptions | Electronic books [2] | Electronic collections [3] | Physical units | Downloadable units [4] | Physical units | Downloadable units [4] |
| **United States, total....** | **715,019** | **1,574.2** | **463,489** | **417.4** | **43,568** | **258,582** | **65,904** | **16,140** |
| Alabama.................. | 8,808 | 8.5 | 4,460 | 14.4 | 435 | 1,590 | 674 | 113 |
| Alaska................... | 2,083 | 4.2 | 1,056 | 3.3 | 113 | 823 | 276 | 15 |
| Arizona.................. | 7,586 | 17.4 | 4,378 | 3.6 | 592 | 4,535 | 1,049 | 285 |
| Arkansas................. | 6,079 | 9.3 | 1,426 | 3.5 | 257 | 1,488 | 526 | 75 |
| California............... | 62,110 | 86.7 | 13,595 | 4.1 | 3,329 | 17,262 | 5,317 | 723 |
| Colorado................. | 9,517 | 21.4 | 2,815 | 15.2 | 811 | 2,277 | 1,407 | 216 |
| Connecticut.............. | 12,942 | 18.8 | 2,026 | 8.4 | 776 | 1,079 | 1,159 | 23 |
| Delaware................. | 1,434 | 3.6 | 497 | 0.2 | 114 | 122 | 254 | 18 |
| District of Columbia...... | 1,049 | 2.7 | 29 | 0.1 | 21 | 13 | 85 | 1 |
| Florida.................. | 28,148 | 42.6 | 5,202 | 7.2 | 1,880 | 18,368 | 3,509 | 371 |
| Georgia.................. | 16,219 | 13.3 | 772 | 4.1 | 534 | 300 | 1,022 | 123 |
| Hawaii................... | 2,922 | 2.7 | 82 | 0.1 | 114 | 27 | 170 | – |
| Idaho.................... | 4,221 | 5.0 | 515 | 5.4 | 227 | 323 | 358 | 1 |
| Illinois................. | 39,946 | 91.3 | 21,831 | 15.2 | 2,836 | 7,855 | 3,582 | 492 |
| Indiana.................. | 21,370 | 43.3 | 8,637 | 23.8 | 1,445 | 2,948 | 2,177 | 224 |
| Iowa..................... | 11,698 | 26.1 | 14,590 | 8.4 | 658 | 6,748 | 1,116 | 23 |
| Kansas................... | 8,780 | 13.2 | 32,882 | 20.8 | 500 | 7,712 | 964 | 55 |
| Kentucky................. | 8,919 | 14.8 | 12,955 | 6.9 | 519 | 2,867 | 932 | 275 |
| Louisiana................ | 11,737 | 22.1 | 3,164 | 4.3 | 472 | 1,588 | 1,208 | 205 |
| Maine.................... | 5,921 | 8.8 | 2,091 | 13.8 | 239 | 1,240 | 417 | 74 |
| Maryland................. | 10,729 | 19.0 | 1,550 | 1.0 | 918 | 1,150 | 1,080 | 127 |
| Massachusetts............ | 29,788 | 42.6 | 18,452 | 25.6 | 1,532 | 5,220 | 2,098 | 518 |
| Michigan................. | 27,948 | 45.4 | 8,404 | 2.1 | 1,946 | 4,830 | 2,669 | 493 |
| Minnesota................ | 13,773 | 24.9 | 5,230 | 7.7 | 841 | 901 | 1,094 | 4 |
| Mississippi.............. | 5,484 | 4.7 | 626 | 2.7 | 201 | 95 | 377 | 32 |
| Missouri................. | 15,700 | 25.6 | 4,119 | 2.6 | 936 | 1,311 | 1,264 | 144 |
| Montana.................. | 2,505 | 3.8 | 1,432 | 0.2 | 114 | 968 | 213 | 8 |
| Nebraska................. | 5,475 | 9.9 | 4,423 | 6.2 | 234 | 2,473 | 370 | 8 |
| Nevada................... | 3,915 | 5.6 | 655 | 1.3 | 301 | 803 | 591 | 62 |
| New Hampshire............ | 5,660 | 10.2 | 4,774 | 5.1 | 283 | 3,887 | 494 | 47 |
| New Jersey............... | 25,712 | 313.5 | 6,243 | 10.0 | 1,573 | 4,214 | 2,303 | 1,017 |
| New Mexico............... | 4,083 | 6.4 | 685 | 4.7 | 207 | 415 | 359 | 59 |
| New York................. | 68,129 | 134.7 | 28,446 | 26.0 | 3,533 | 6,074 | 5,320 | 262 |
| North Carolina........... | 15,527 | 20.3 | 6,418 | 7.6 | 667 | 1,003 | 844 | 153 |
| North Dakota............. | 2,188 | 3.5 | 885 | 2.1 | 92 | 800 | 132 | 33 |
| Ohio..................... | 39,581 | 90.0 | 81,436 | 21.1 | 3,368 | 33,758 | 5,487 | 3,882 |
| Oklahoma................. | 6,423 | 73.1 | 3,456 | 4.2 | 371 | 792 | 577 | 58 |
| Oregon................... | 8,940 | 13.6 | 7,071 | 4.2 | 637 | 4,349 | 949 | 106 |
| Pennsylvania............. | 24,238 | 47.1 | 26,462 | 15.4 | 2,115 | 46,996 | 2,037 | 3,296 |
| Rhode Island............. | 3,461 | 4.7 | 2,594 | 2.0 | 152 | 878 | 260 | 33 |
| South Carolina........... | 8,637 | 25.9 | 1,722 | 2.5 | 437 | 1,530 | 735 | 80 |
| South Dakota............. | 2,752 | 4.0 | 1,244 | 6.5 | 129 | 510 | 156 | 9 |
| Tennessee................ | 11,262 | 31.6 | 21,178 | 14.8 | 565 | 9,472 | 769 | 575 |
| Texas.................... | 38,322 | 40.8 | 10,300 | 35.8 | 1,946 | 5,661 | 3,114 | 499 |
| Utah..................... | 6,404 | 9.4 | 1,647 | 4.5 | 616 | 1,663 | 667 | 133 |
| Vermont.................. | 2,613 | 4.9 | 226 | 8.6 | 126 | 113 | 210 | – |
| Virginia................. | 16,308 | 20.9 | 9,780 | 4.1 | 951 | 5,201 | 1,305 | 299 |
| Washington............... | 12,696 | 37.5 | 3,852 | 2.3 | 1,055 | 1,359 | 1,504 | 151 |
| West Virginia............ | 4,947 | 5.5 | 3,799 | 1.7 | 198 | 14,230 | 345 | 220 |
| Wisconsin................ | 18,084 | 36.0 | 62,895 | 20.1 | 1,492 | 18,498 | 2,156 | 503 |
| Wyoming.................. | 2,246 | 3.3 | 482 | 1.9 | 159 | 263 | 221 | 17 |

– Rounds to zero. [1] Includes books, and non-serial government documents. [2] E-books include digital documents digitized by the library, licensed or not; and non-serial government documents. [3] An electronic collection is a collection of electronically stored data or unit records (facts, bibliographic data, abstracts, texts, photographs, music, video, etc.) with a common user interface and software for the retrieval and use of the data. Electronic collections do not have a circulation period. [4] Downloadable units are items for which permanent or temporary access rights have been acquired. For items with a finite number of simultaneous users, the number of units equals the number of simultaneous users (equivalent to purchasing multiple copies of a single title). For items with unlimited simultaneous users, the number of units equals the number of titles acquired.

Source: Institute of Museum and Library Services, Public Libraries Survey, *Supplementary Tables, Public Libraries Survey, Fiscal Year 2017*, June 2019. See also <https://www.imls.gov/research-evaluation/data-collection/public-libraries-survey>.

# Table 1192. Use of Public Libraries, Library Websites, and Library Mobile Applications by Demographic Characteristics: 2016

[In percent. Covers visits or use in past 12 months. Based on interviews with 3,015 adults conducted September 29 to November 6, 2016, in English and Spanish on landline and cellular telephones. Margin of sampling error plus or minus 2.0 percentage points]

| Characteristics | Visited library or book-mobile | Used library website | Used library mobile app | Characteristics | Visited library or book-mobile | Used library website | Used library mobile app |
|---|---|---|---|---|---|---|---|
| **Total**............................ | **46** | **31** | **8** | EDUCATION | | | |
| SEX | | | | Less than high school............ | 30 | 12 | 4 |
| Male............................... | 39 | 24 | 5 | High school graduate............. | 40 | 23 | 6 |
| Female............................ | 54 | 37 | 11 | Some college....................... | 49 | 35 | 6 |
| RACE/ETHNICITY | | | | College graduate or higher...... | 56 | 40 | 14 |
| White, non-Hispanic............ | 45 | 29 | 8 | | | | |
| Black, non-Hispanic............ | 50 | 35 | 11 | HOUSEHOLD INCOME | | | |
| Hispanic.......................... | 43 | 27 | 5 | Less than $30,000................ | 42 | 28 | 7 |
| AGE | | | | $30,000 to $74,999............... | 50 | 32 | 7 |
| 18 to 29 years.................... | 56 | 43 | 7 | $75,000 to $99,999................ | 48 | 34 | 11 |
| 30 to 49 years.................... | 46 | 35 | 10 | $100,000 to $149,000............ | 49 | 35 | 11 |
| 50 to 64 years.................... | 43 | 25 | 9 | $150,000 and over............... | 46 | 32 | 11 |
| 65 years and older.............. | 39 | 15 | 6 | METRO STATUS | | | |
| PARENTAL STATUS | | | | Urban.............................. | 46 | 32 | 10 |
| Parent of minor child............ | 54 | 38 | 11 | Suburban.......................... | 48 | 30 | 7 |
| Not a parent of minor child..... | 43 | 27 | 7 | Rural............................... | 42 | 27 | 7 |

Source: Pew Research Center ©, unpublished data. See also <http://www.pewinternet.org>.

# Banking, Finance, and Insurance

This section presents data on the nation's finances, various types of financial institutions, money and credit, securities, insurance, and real estate. The primary sources of these data are publications of several departments of the federal government, especially the U.S. Treasury Department, and independent agencies such as the Federal Deposit Insurance Corporation, the Board of Governors of the Federal Reserve System, and the Securities and Exchange Commission. National data on insurance are available primarily from private organizations, such as the American Council of Life Insurers and the National Association of Insurance Commissioners.

**Financial Accounts of the United States**—The Federal Reserve Board brings together statistics on all of the major forms of financial instruments to present an economy-wide view of asset and liability relationships in the Financial Accounts of the United States. The accounts relate borrowing and lending to one another and to the nonfinancial activities that generate income and production. Each claim outstanding is included simultaneously as an asset of the lender and as a liability of the debtor. The accounts also indicate the balance between asset totals and liability totals over the economy as a whole. Several publications of the Federal Reserve Board contain information on these financial accounts: Summary data on flows and outstandings in the statistical release *Financial Accounts of the United States* (quarterly); and concepts and organization of the accounts in *Financial Accounts Guide* <http://www.federalreserve.gov/apps/fof/>. Data are also available on the Federal Reserve Board's website at <http://www.federalreserve.gov/releases/z1/>.

**Survey of Consumer Finances (SCF)**—The Federal Reserve Board, in cooperation with the Treasury Department, sponsors this survey, which is conducted every 3 years to provide detailed information on the finances of U.S. families. Among the topics covered are the balance sheet, pension, income, and other demographic characteristics of U.S. families. The survey also gathers information on the use of financial institutions. Since 1992, data for the SCF have been collected by the National Organization for Research at the University of Chicago. Data and information on the survey are available on the Federal Reserve Board's website at <https://www.federalreserve.gov/econres/scfindex.htm>.

**Banking system**—Banks in this country are organized under the laws of both the states and the federal government and are regulated by several bank supervisory agencies. National banks are supervised by the Comptroller of the Currency. *Reports of Condition and Income*, commonly known as call reports, have been collected from national banks since 1863. Summaries of these reports are published in the Comptroller's *Annual Report*, which also presents data on the structure of the national banking system.

The Federal Reserve System was established in 1913 to exercise central banking functions, some of which are shared with the U.S. Treasury. It includes national banks and state banks that voluntarily join the system. Statements of state bank members are consolidated by the Federal Reserve Board with data for national banks collected by the Comptroller of the Currency into totals for all member banks of the system. Balance sheet data for member banks and other commercial banks are available on the Federal Reserve Board's website at <www.federalreserve.gov/data.htm>.

The Federal Deposit Insurance Corporation (FDIC), established in 1933, insures each depositor up to $250,000. Major item balance sheet and income data for all insured financial institutions are published in the *FDIC Quarterly Banking Profile*. This publication is also available on the internet at <https://www.fdic.gov/bank/analytical/qbp/>. Quarterly financial information for individual institutions is available through the FDIC and Federal Financial Institutions Examination Council websites at <http://www.fdic.gov> and <http://www.ffiec.gov>.

**Credit unions**—Federally chartered credit unions are under the supervision of the National Credit Union Administration. State-chartered credit unions are supervised by the respective state supervisory authorities. The administration publishes comprehensive program and statistical information on all federal and federally insured state credit unions in the *Annual Report of the National Credit Union Administration*.

**Other credit agencies**—Insurance companies, finance companies dealing primarily in installment sales financing, and personal loan companies represent important sources of funds for the credit market. Statistics on loans, investments, cash, etc., of life insurance companies are published principally by the American Council of Life Insurers in its *Life Insurers Fact Book*. Consumer credit data are available on the Federal Reserve Board's website at <www.federalreserve.gov/data.htm>. Government corporations and credit agencies make available credit of specified types or to specified groups of private borrowers, either by lending directly or by insuring or guaranteeing loans made by private lending institutions. Data on operations of government credit agencies, along with other government corporations, are available in reports of individual agencies.

**Securities**—The Securities and Exchange Commission (SEC) was established in 1934 to protect the interests of the public and investors against malpractices in the securities and financial markets and to provide the fullest possible disclosure of information regarding securities to the investing public.

Data on the securities industry and securities transactions are also available from a number of private sources. The Securities Industry and Financial Markets Association (SIFMA), New York, NY, <http://www.sifma.org/>, publishes the *SIFMA Fact Book*. The Investment Company Institute, Washington, DC, <http://www.ici.org/>, publishes a reference book, research newsletters, and a variety of research reports that examine the industry, its shareholders, or industry issues. The annual *Investment Company Fact Book* is a guide to trends and statistics observed in the investment company industry. Institute research reports provide a detailed examination of shareholder demographics and other aspects of fund ownership.

Among the many sources of data on stock and bond prices and sales are the New York Stock Exchange, New York, NY, <http://www.nyse.com/>; NASDAQ, Washington, DC, <http://www.nasdaq.com/>; and Global Financial Data, Los Angeles, CA, <http://www.globalfinancialdata.com/>.

**Insurance**—Insuring companies, which are regulated by the various states or the District of Columbia, are classified as either life or property. Both life and property insurance companies may underwrite health insurance. Insuring companies, other than those classified as life, are permitted to underwrite one or more property lines provided they are so licensed and have the necessary capital or surplus. There are a number of published sources for statistics on the various classes of insurance—life, health, fire, marine, and casualty. Organizations representing certain classes of insurers publish reports for these classes. The American Council of Life Insurers publishes statistics on life insurance purchases, ownership, benefit payments, and assets in its *Life Insurers Fact Book*.

**Statistical reliability**—For a discussion of statistical collection, estimation, and sampling procedures and measures of reliability applicable to data from the Census Bureau and the Federal Reserve Board's Survey of Consumer Finances, see Appendix III.

## Table 1193. Gross Domestic Product in Finance, Insurance, Real Estate, Rental and Leasing Industries in Current and Chained (2012) Dollars: 2000 to 2018

[In billions of dollars, except percent (743 represents $743,000,000,000). Represents value added by industry. For definition of gross domestic product and explanation of chained dollars, see text, Section 13, Income]

| Industry | 2012 NAICS code [1] | Current dollars | | | | Chained (2012) dollars | | | |
|---|---|---|---|---|---|---|---|---|---|
| | | 2000 | 2010 | 2017 | 2018 | 2000 | 2010 | 2017 | 2018 |
| **Finance & insurance, total**............... | 52 | **743** | **1,004** | **1,466** | **1,514** | **905** | **1,078** | **1,164** | **1,128** |
| Percent of gross domestic product...... | (X) | 7.2 | 6.7 | 7.5 | 7.4 | 6.9 | 6.9 | 6.5 | 6.1 |
| Federal Reserve banks, credit inter- mediation, and related activities.......... | 521, 522 | 320 | 418 | 617 | 643 | 362 | 444 | 434 | 419 |
| Securities, commodity contracts, & investments.................................... | 523 | 133 | 196 | 291 | 289 | 173 | 232 | 217 | 200 |
| Insurance carriers & related activities...... | 524 | 275 | 373 | 541 | 565 | 341 | 385 | 515 | 513 |
| Funds, trusts, & other financial vehicles. ... | 525 | 15 | 17 | 17 | 18 | 18 | 20 | 12 | 12 |
| **Real estate & rental & leasing, total....** | **53** | **1,232** | **1,939** | **2,591** | **2,725** | **1,546** | **1,987** | **2,285** | **2,342** |
| Percent of gross domestic product...... | (X) | 12.0 | 12.9 | 13.3 | 13.3 | 11.8 | 12.7 | 12.7 | 12.6 |
| Real estate................................... | 531 | 1,096 | 1,779 | 2,368 | 2,490 | 1,374 | 1,823 | 2,057 | 2,108 |
| Rental & leasing services and lessors of intangible assets................ | 532, 533 | 136 | 160 | 224 | 235 | 175 | 164 | 231 | 237 |

X Not applicable. [1] Data based on the 2012 North American Industry Classification System (NAICS). See text, Section 15.

Source: U.S. Bureau of Economic Analysis, "Value Added by Industry" and "Real Value Added by Industry," <http://www.bea.gov/iTable/indcx_industry_gdpIndy.cfm>, accessed May 2019.

## Table 1194. Finance, Insurance, Real Estate, and Rental and Leasing—Establishments, Revenue, Payroll, and Employees by Kind of Business: 2007 and 2012

[3,669 represents $3,669,000,000,000. For establishments with payroll. Based on the 2007 and 2012 Economic Censuses; see Appendix III]

| Kind of business | 2007 NAICS code [1] | Establishments (number) | | Revenue (bil. dol.) | | Annual payroll (bil. dol.) | | Paid employees (1,000) | |
|---|---|---|---|---|---|---|---|---|---|
| | | 2007 | 2012 | 2007 | 2012 | 2007 | 2012 | 2007 | 2012 |
| **Finance & insurance** [2]......................... | **52** | **501,713** | **468,183** | **3,669** | **3,636** | **502.4** | **523.6** | **6,608** | **6,041** |
| Monetary authorities—central bank............. | 521 | 47 | 56 | 45 | 100 | 1.3 | 1.7 | 19 | 17 |
| Credit intermediation & related activities........ | 522 | 231,439 | 196,147 | 1,343 | 1,095 | 180.9 | 184.2 | 3,280 | 2,815 |
| Security, commodity contracts, & like activity... | 523 | 85,475 | 95,906 | 612 | 515 | 166.3 | 168.4 | 885 | 904 |
| Insurance carriers & related activities........... | 524 | 184,752 | 176,074 | 1,669 | 1,925 | 153.9 | 169.2 | 2,423 | 2,304 |
| **Real estate & rental & leasing**................ | **53** | **384,297** | **354,106** | **485** | **488** | **84.8** | **85.3** | **2,188** | **1,924** |
| Real estate........................................... | 531 | 316,730 | 295,780 | 330 | 325 | 61.3 | 60.9 | 1,529 | 1,403 |
| Rental & leasing services............................ | 532 | 65,120 | 55,795 | 122 | 129 | 21.1 | 21.3 | 630 | 485 |
| Lessors of other nonfinancial intangible assets.......................................... | 533 | 2,447 | 2,531 | 33 | 33 | 2.3 | 3.1 | 29 | 36 |

[1] Based on the North American Industry Classification System (NAICS); see text, Section 15. [2] Total does not include NAICS 525, Funds, trusts, and other financial vehicles.

Source: U.S. Census Bureau, 2012 Economic Census, EC1253A2, "Geographic Area Series: Comparative Statistics for the U.S. (2007 NAICS Basis): 2012 and 2007," <http://factfinder.census.gov/>, accessed June 2016.

## Table 1195. Finance and Insurance—Nonemployer Establishments and Receipts by Kind of Business: 2010 to 2017

[716.8 represents 716,800. Includes only firms subject to federal income tax. Nonemployers are businesses with no paid employees. Data originate chiefly from administrative records of the Internal Revenue Service; see Appendix III]

| Kind of business | NAICS code [1] | Establishments (1,000) | | | Receipts (mil. dol.) | | |
|---|---|---|---|---|---|---|---|
| | | 2010 | 2015 | 2017 | 2010 | 2015 | 2017 |
| **Finance and insurance**............................ | **52** | **716.8** | **718.5** | **732.2** | **50,626** | **55,329** | **58,376** |
| Credit intermediation & related activities.......... | 522 | 53.3 | 45.8 | 45.4 | 2,790 | 3,134 | 3,239 |
| Depository credit intermediation.................... | 5221 | 6.2 | 5.9 | 6.2 | 181 | 214 | 243 |
| Nondepository credit intermediation............... | 5222 | 21.8 | 22.1 | 21.7 | 1,554 | 1,864 | 1,902 |
| Activities related to credit intermediation.......... | 5223 | 25.3 | 17.8 | 17.5 | 1,056 | 1,056 | 1,093 |
| Securities, commodity contracts, & related activities........... | 523 | 273.4 | 272.2 | 282.1 | 29,202 | 30,204 | 32,223 |
| Securities & commodity contracts intermediation and brokerage............................... | 5231 | 29.8 | 27.6 | 27.0 | 4,969 | 4,812 | 5,183 |
| Investment banking and securities dealing.................... | 52311 | 7.2 | 7.4 | 7.7 | 1,748 | 1,389 | 1,526 |
| Securities brokerage............................. | 52312 | 18.6 | 17.0 | 16.2 | 2,589 | 2,914 | 3,131 |
| Commodity contracts dealing...................... | 52313 | 1.1 | 1.0 | 1.0 | 236 | 175 | 230 |
| Commodity contracts brokerage.................... | 52314 | 2.9 | 2.2 | 2.1 | 397 | 334 | 296 |
| Securities & commodity exchanges.................. | 5232 | 1.9 | 1.8 | 1.3 | 660 | 354 | 271 |
| Other financial investment activities.................. | 5239 | 241.7 | 242.7 | 253.8 | 23,573 | 25,038 | 26,769 |
| Insurance carriers & related activities................. | 524 | 390.1 | 400.5 | 404.8 | 18,634 | 21,991 | 22,914 |
| Insurance carriers.................................... | 5241 | 2.7 | 1.8 | 1.8 | 185 | 172 | 171 |
| Agencies & other insurance-related activities.................. | 5242 | 387.4 | 398.7 | 403.0 | 18,449 | 21,819 | 22,742 |
| Insurance agencies & brokerages.................... | 52421 | 270.5 | 279.0 | 284.8 | 13,854 | 16,340 | 16,853 |
| Other insurance related activities.................... | 52429 | 116.9 | 119.8 | 118.2 | 4,595 | 5,479 | 5,890 |

[1] Data for 2010 are based on 2007 North American Industry Classification System (NAICS); data for 2015 are based on 2012 NAICS; and beginning 2017, data based on 2017 NAICS. For more information, see text, Section 15.

Source: U.S. Census Bureau, Nonemployer Statistics, "NES Datasets," <https://www.census.gov/programs-surveys/nonemployer-statistics/data/datasets.html>, accessed July 2019.

## Table 1196. Finance and Insurance—Establishments, Employees, and Payroll: 2015 and 2016

[470.1 represents 470,100. Covers establishments with payroll. Employees are for the week including March 12. Excludes most government employees, railroad employees, and self-employed persons. For statement on methodology, see Appendix III]

| Kind of business | NAICS code [1] | Establishments (1,000) | | Employees (1,000) | | Payroll (bil. dol.) | |
|---|---|---|---|---|---|---|---|
| | | 2015 | 2016 | 2015 | 2016 | 2015 | 2016 |
| **Finance & insurance, total** [2] | **52** | **470.1** | **477.0** | **6,136** | **6,337** | **595.8** | **611.7** |
| Monetary authorities—central bank | 521 | 0.1 | 0.1 | 19 | 19 | 2.1 | 2.3 |
| Credit intermediation & related activities | 522 | 191.7 | 192.1 | 2,761 | 2,838 | 212.5 | 220.8 |
| Depository credit intermediation [2] | 5221 | 119.4 | 118.9 | 1,910 | 1,954 | 140.5 | 144.1 |
| Commercial banking | 52211 | 91.8 | 91.6 | 1,512 | 1,552 | 118.3 | 120.9 |
| Savings institutions | 52212 | 9.0 | 8.7 | 125 | 121 | 8.5 | 8.6 |
| Credit unions | 52213 | 18.6 | 18.5 | 271 | 279 | 13.4 | 14.4 |
| Nondepository credit intermediation [2] | 5222 | 43.3 | 44.6 | 580 | 597 | 51.9 | 55.0 |
| Real estate credit | 522292 | 13.2 | 14.7 | 243 | 259 | 23.3 | 26.1 |
| Activities related to credit intermediation | 5223 | 29.0 | 28.7 | 271 | 287 | 20.2 | 21.8 |
| Security, commodity contracts & like activity [2] | 523 | 98.5 | 102.0 | 896 | 907 | 187.0 | 184.1 |
| Security & commodity contracts intermediation & brokerage [2] | 5231 | 42.7 | 44.6 | 405 | 410 | 86.1 | 84.3 |
| Securities brokerage | 52312 | 37.1 | 39.3 | 294 | 298 | 50.3 | 49.9 |
| Other financial investment activities [2] | 5239 | 55.7 | 57.4 | 486 | 490 | 99.8 | 98.5 |
| Portfolio management | 52392 | 23.6 | 23.6 | 279 | 282 | 73.9 | 72.2 |
| Insurance carriers & related activities | 524 | 178.7 | 181.5 | 2,453 | 2,565 | 193.0 | 203.5 |
| Insurance carriers [2] | 5241 | 32.8 | 35.3 | 1,491 | 1,574 | 131.6 | 138.6 |
| Direct life insurance carriers | 524113 | 8.5 | 8.3 | 360 | 366 | 37.7 | 37.5 |
| Direct health & medical insurance carriers | 524114 | 5.4 | 6.7 | 491 | 567 | 38.9 | 44.7 |
| Direct property & casualty insurance carriers | 524126 | 14.0 | 15.2 | 551 | 548 | 46.8 | 47.7 |
| Agencies & other insurance-related activities [2] | 5242 | 145.9 | 146.2 | 963 | 991 | 61.4 | 64.9 |
| Insurance agencies & brokerages | 52421 | 134.1 | 134.4 | 685 | 711 | 44.9 | 47.6 |

[1] Data based on North American Industry Classification System (NAICS) 2012. See text, Section 15. [2] Includes other kinds of businesses, not shown separately.

Source: U.S. Census Bureau, County Business Patterns, "Geography Area Series: County Business Patterns," <http://factfinder.census.gov/>, accessed April 2018. See also <https://www.census.gov/programs-surveys/cbp.html>.

## Table 1197. Revenues of Finance and Insurance Industries: 2010 to 2017

[In billions of dollars (3,495.7 represents $3,495,700,000,000). Covers taxable employer firms only. Based on Service Annual Survey. Estimates have been adjusted to the results of the 2012 Economic Census. See Appendix III]

| Kind of business | NAICS code [1] | 2010 | 2013 | 2014 | 2015 | 2016 | 2017 |
|---|---|---|---|---|---|---|---|
| **Finance & insurance, total** | **52** | **3,495.7** | **3,728.1** | **3,948.4** | **4,101.7** | **4,262.3** | **4,498.1** |
| Monetary authorities—central bank | 521 | 88.2 | 90.4 | 114.2 | 113.5 | 112.2 | 116.8 |
| Credit intermediation & related activities | 522 | 1,161.3 | 1,085.1 | 1,075.0 | 1,104.8 | 1,163.3 | 1,234.8 |
| Commercial banking | 52211 | 407.9 | 383.3 | 384.7 | 391.5 | 422.4 | 450.2 |
| Savings institutions | 52212 | 48.2 | 35.8 | (D) | (D) | 38.7 | 41.8 |
| Credit unions | 52213 | 47.7 | 49.8 | 49.9 | 53.4 | 58.5 | 64.1 |
| Other depository credit intermediation | 52219 | 0.9 | 0.9 | (D) | (D) | 1.0 | 1.1 |
| Credit card issuing | 52221 | 81.5 | 87.4 | 83.6 | 85.1 | 89.5 | 95.7 |
| Sales financing | 52222 | 89.5 | 89.9 | 97.3 | 104.9 | 112.7 | 120.9 |
| Other nondepository credit intermediation | 52229 | 416.6 | 354.0 | 338.3 | 342.0 | 346.0 | 360.7 |
| Mortgage & nonmortgage loan brokers | 52231 | 6.3 | 8.1 | 7.2 | 9.5 | 11.1 | 11.9 |
| Financial transactions processing, reserve, and clearinghouse activities | 52232 | 52.7 | 61.7 | 62.4 | 65.0 | 67.4 | 72.0 |
| Other activities related to credit intermediation | 52239 | 9.8 | 14.3 | 15.3 | 16.3 | 16.1 | 16.4 |
| Securities, commodity contracts, and other financial investment activities | 523 | 497.6 | 547.1 | 582.5 | 586.5 | 594.8 | 634.6 |
| Investment banking and securities dealing | 52311 | 119.6 | 104.1 | 105.9 | 107.3 | 108.8 | 116.5 |
| Securities brokerage | 52312 | 114.8 | 126.9 | 136.5 | 135.6 | 137.0 | 146.7 |
| Commodity contracts dealing | 52313 | 6.9 | 7.2 | 7.8 | 7.9 | 7.2 | 6.9 |
| Commodity contracts brokerage | 52314 | 6.2 | 5.0 | 5.3 | 5.1 | 5.0 | 5.0 |
| Securities and commodity exchanges | 5232 | 10.1 | 9.8 | 10.0 | 10.5 | 11.4 | 11.1 |
| Miscellaneous intermediation | 52391 | 17.2 | 20.1 | 22.2 | 22.5 | 23.2 | 26.1 |
| Portfolio management | 52392 | 172.3 | 213.1 | 227.2 | 227.2 | 228.4 | 247.2 |
| Investment advice | 52393 | 25.7 | 36.2 | 40.8 | 44.3 | 45.8 | 47.5 |
| All other financial investment activities | 52399 | 24.9 | 24.7 | 26.6 | 26.0 | 28.0 | 27.6 |
| Insurance carriers & related activities | 524 | 1,748.6 | 2,005.6 | 2,176.9 | 2,296.9 | 2,392.0 | 2,512.0 |
| Direct life, health, medical insurance carriers | 52411 | 1,060.7 | 1,174.7 | 1,298.9 | 1,378.8 | 1,434.8 | 1,502.7 |
| Other direct insurance carriers | 52412 | 441.6 | 493.1 | 521.2 | 544.3 | 561.4 | 585.8 |
| Reinsurance carriers | 52413 | 45.7 | 52.2 | 55.0 | 55.8 | 58.4 | 62.3 |
| Insurance agencies & brokerages | 52421 | 98.4 | 115.0 | 120.1 | 130.0 | 134.2 | 137.8 |
| Other insurance-related activities | 52429 | 102.1 | 170.5 | 181.6 | 188.0 | 203.2 | 223.4 |

D Estimate in table is withheld to avoid disclosing data of individual companies; data are included in higher level totals. [1] Data for 2010 are based on the 2007 North American Industry Classification System (NAICS); beginning 2013, data are based on 2012 NAICS. See text, this section and Section 15 for more information.

Source: U.S. Census Bureau, Service Annual Survey, "Service Annual Survey Latest Data (NAICS-basis): 2017" and "Service Annual Survey Historical Survey Tables," <https://www.census.gov/programs-surveys/sas/data.html>, accessed November 2018.

# Table 1198. Financial Accounts of the United States—Financial Assets of Financial and Nonfinancial Institutions by Holder Sector: 2000 to 2018

[In billions of dollars (94,661 represents $94,661,000,000,000). As of Dec. 31]

| Sector | 2000 | 2005 | 2010 | 2012 | 2013 | 2014 | 2015 | 2016 | 2017 | 2018 |
|---|---|---|---|---|---|---|---|---|---|---|
| All sectors | 94,661 | 134,206 | 166,590 | 183,101 | 200,202 | 212,117 | 215,609 | 226,789 | 244,481 | 244,051 |
| Households[1] | 34,570 | 47,028 | 55,632 | 61,543 | 68,642 | 72,920 | 74,132 | 78,294 | 85,135 | 84,657 |
| Nonfinancial business | 11,272 | 14,562 | 17,815 | 19,380 | 20,857 | 22,313 | 24,194 | 26,079 | 27,490 | 28,063 |
| Nonfinancial corporations | 9,799 | 11,965 | 14,087 | 15,153 | 16,325 | 17,339 | 18,822 | 20,162 | 21,158 | 21,309 |
| Nonfinancial noncorporate | 1,473 | 2,597 | 3,728 | 4,227 | 4,531 | 4,974 | 5,372 | 5,917 | 6,332 | 6,754 |
| Federal government | 565 | 655 | 1,638 | 1,530 | 1,733 | 1,883 | 2,133 | 2,344 | 2,300 | 2,604 |
| State and local government | 1,661 | 2,379 | 2,820 | 2,817 | 2,935 | 2,998 | 3,007 | 3,114 | 3,176 | 3,060 |
| Monetary authority | 636 | 879 | 2,452 | 3,339 | 4,217 | 4,918 | 4,821 | 4,734 | 4,731 | 4,236 |
| Private depository institutions | 7,496 | 11,092 | 13,644 | 14,963 | 15,777 | 16,804 | 17,265 | 17,963 | 18,834 | 19,193 |
| U.S.-chartered depository institutions | 6,323 | 9,435 | 11,443 | 12,225 | 12,681 | 13,597 | 14,114 | 14,820 | 15,318 | 15,633 |
| Foreign banking offices in U.S. | 691 | 889 | 1,244 | 1,690 | 1,999 | 2,041 | 1,900 | 1,798 | 2,085 | 2,050 |
| Banks in U.S.-affiliated areas | 62 | 107 | 78 | 82 | 80 | 88 | 85 | 92 | 88 | 91 |
| Credit unions | 421 | 661 | 876 | 971 | 1,016 | 1,078 | 1,166 | 1,254 | 1,342 | 1,419 |
| Property-casualty insurance companies | 1,059 | 1,718 | 1,868 | 1,987 | 2,064 | 2,134 | 2,142 | 2,224 | 2,388 | 2,411 |
| Life insurance companies | 3,250 | 4,631 | 5,635 | 6,320 | 6,551 | 6,929 | 6,895 | 7,248 | 7,747 | 7,566 |
| Private pension funds | 4,283 | 5,391 | 6,604 | 7,243 | 8,398 | 8,675 | 8,567 | 9,004 | 9,752 | 9,381 |
| Defined benefit plans | 1,785 | 2,251 | 2,836 | 3,019 | 3,415 | 3,427 | 3,400 | 3,419 | 3,421 | 3,407 |
| Defined contribution plans | 2,497 | 3,140 | 3,768 | 4,224 | 4,984 | 5,248 | 5,167 | 5,585 | 6,332 | 5,975 |
| Federal government retirement funds | 2,028 | 2,504 | 3,165 | 3,391 | 3,550 | 3,641 | 3,741 | 3,830 | 3,949 | 4,017 |
| State and local government employee retirement funds | 3,322 | 4,695 | 6,169 | 6,502 | 7,438 | 7,776 | 8,086 | 8,364 | 8,728 | 9,015 |
| Money market mutual funds[2] | 1,845 | 2,027 | 2,804 | 2,693 | 2,733 | 2,749 | 2,742 | 2,731 | 2,848 | 3,038 |
| Mutual funds[2] | 5,119 | 6,865 | 9,030 | 10,364 | 12,333 | 13,151 | 12,897 | 13,616 | 15,899 | 14,670 |
| Closed-end funds | 143 | 276 | 238 | 264 | 279 | 289 | 263 | 265 | 277 | 251 |
| Exchange-traded funds | 66 | 301 | 992 | 1,337 | 1,675 | 1,975 | 2,101 | 2,524 | 3,401 | 3,371 |
| Government-sponsored enterprises (GSE)[3] | 1,965 | 2,822 | 6,722 | 6,275 | 6,361 | 6,400 | 6,488 | 6,685 | 6,819 | 6,923 |
| Agency- and GSE-backed mortgage pools[4] | 2,493 | 3,548 | 1,147 | 1,443 | 1,574 | 1,649 | 1,775 | 1,933 | 2,127 | 2,293 |
| Asset-backed securities issuers | 1,509 | 3,499 | 2,343 | 1,843 | 1,510 | 1,423 | 1,347 | 1,231 | 1,169 | 1,161 |
| Finance companies[5] | 1,229 | 1,875 | 1,794 | 1,720 | 1,696 | 1,728 | 1,600 | 1,532 | 1,494 | 1,492 |
| Real estate investment trusts | 65 | 306 | 302 | 594 | 663 | 725 | 659 | 675 | 754 | 821 |
| Security brokers and dealers | 2,020 | 3,569 | 3,504 | 3,706 | 3,408 | 3,255 | 3,044 | 3,022 | 3,097 | 3,359 |
| Holding companies[6] | 841 | 1,500 | 2,894 | 3,717 | 3,623 | 3,745 | 3,608 | 3,853 | 3,858 | 3,841 |
| Funding corporations[7] | 984 | 1,297 | 1,129 | 969 | 918 | 918 | 1,020 | 1,267 | 1,343 | 1,430 |
| Rest of the world | 6,241 | 10,788 | 16,249 | 19,161 | 21,267 | 23,121 | 23,083 | 24,258 | 27,166 | 27,198 |

[1] Includes nonprofit organizations. [2] Open-end investment companies. Includes funding vehicles for variable annuities. [3] Federal Home Loan Banks, Federal National Mortgage Association (Fannie Mae), Federal Home Loan Mortgage Corporation (Freddie Mac), Federal Agriculture Mortgage Corporation, Farm Credit System, the Financing Corporation, and the Resolution Funding Corporation. The Student Loan Marketing Association (Sallie Mae), was included until it was fully privatized in 2004. [4] Government National Mortgage Association, Federal National Mortgage Association, Federal Home Loan Mortgage Corporation, Federal Agriculture Mortgage Corporation, and Farmers Home Administration pools. Also includes agency- and GSE-backed mortgage pool securities which are used as collateral for agency- and GSE-backed collateralized mortgage obligations (CMOs) and privately issued CMOs. Excludes Federal Financing Bank holdings of pool securities, which are included with federal government mortgages and other loans and advances. [5] Includes retail captive finance companies and mortgage companies. [6] Parent-only bank holding companies, savings and loan holding companies, and security holding companies that file Federal Reserve Board form FR Y-9LP, FR Y-9SP, or FR 2320. [7] Funding subsidiaries, custodial accounts for reinvested collateral of securities lending operations, Federal Reserve lending facilities, and funds associated with the Public-Private Investment Program (PPIP).

Source: Board of Governors of the Federal Reserve System, "Financial Accounts of the United States, Z.1," <https://www.federalreserve.gov/data.htm>, accessed July 2019.

## Table 1199. Financial Accounts of the United States—Debt Securities and Debt Loans Outstanding By Sector: 2000 to 2018

[In billions of dollars (28,632 represents $28,632,000,000,000). As of December 31. Represents credit market debt owed by sectors shown. Some sectors only borrow/lend through debt securities or loans, but not both]

| Item | 2000 | 2005 | 2010 | 2012 | 2013 | 2014 | 2015 | 2016 | 2017 | 2018 |
|---|---|---|---|---|---|---|---|---|---|---|
| Total debt outstanding............... | 28,632 | 43,494 | 55,255 | 58,079 | 59,779 | 62,033 | 63,676 | 66,195 | 69,113 | 72,095 |
| Total debt securities [1]................ | 16,418 | 24,787 | 33,951 | 36,619 | 37,758 | 39,085 | 40,056 | 41,637 | 43,204 | 45,020 |
| Domestic nonfinancial............. | 8,137 | 11,452 | 17,951 | 20,767 | 21,850 | 22,866 | 24,019 | 25,180 | 25,941 | 27,404 |
| Nonprofit and household sector.......... | 138 | 217 | 271 | 249 | 235 | 228 | 220 | 216 | 218 | 216 |
| Nonfinancial corporate business......... | 2,721 | 3,010 | 3,966 | 4,524 | 4,819 | 5,143 | 5,571 | 5,860 | 6,175 | 6,284 |
| Federal government................. | 4,090 | 5,585 | 10,529 | 12,848 | 13,705 | 14,441 | 15,166 | 16,008 | 16,455 | 17,865 |
| State and local governments [2]......... | 1,189 | 2,639 | 3,186 | 3,146 | 3,092 | 3,054 | 3,063 | 3,095 | 3,093 | 3,039 |
| Financial sectors................. | 7,577 | 12,126 | 13,924 | 13,286 | 13,258 | 13,352 | 13,284 | 13,656 | 13,958 | 14,289 |
| U.S.-chartered depository institutions......... | 99 | 134 | 585 | 478 | 350 | 314 | 301 | 277 | 223 | 243 |
| Foreign banking offices in U.S............. | 2 | 1 | 88 | 68 | 57 | 46 | 43 | 49 | 38 | 40 |
| Government-sponsored enterprises (GSE)... | 1,826 | 2,592 | 6,435 | 6,093 | 6,200 | 6,276 | 6,369 | 6,563 | 6,716 | 6,797 |
| Agency- and GSE-backed mortgage pools... | 2,493 | 3,548 | 1,147 | 1,443 | 1,574 | 1,649 | 1,775 | 1,933 | 2,127 | 2,293 |
| Asset-backed securities issuers......... | 1,516 | 3,503 | 2,343 | 1,843 | 1,510 | 1,423 | 1,347 | 1,231 | 1,169 | 1,161 |
| Finance companies................. | 743 | 966 | 1,188 | 1,084 | 1,078 | 1,080 | 953 | 886 | 835 | 879 |
| Real estate investment trusts......... | 65 | 217 | 145 | 179 | 355 | 403 | 396 | 417 | 439 | 470 |
| Brokers and dealers................ | 41 | 62 | 130 | 90 | 112 | 124 | 131 | 129 | 186 | 184 |
| Holding companies................ | 290 | 482 | 1,241 | 1,416 | 1,403 | 1,394 | 1,213 | 1,376 | 1,449 | 1,402 |
| Funding corporations.............. | 503 | 620 | 622 | 591 | 618 | 644 | 755 | 793 | 776 | 821 |
| Rest of the world................. | 703 | 1,209 | 2,076 | 2,566 | 2,649 | 2,867 | 2,753 | 2,801 | 3,305 | 3,327 |
| Total loans [3]................ | 12,214 | 18,708 | 21,304 | 21,460 | 22,021 | 22,948 | 23,619 | 24,558 | 25,910 | 27,075 |
| Domestic nonfinancial.............. | 10,981 | 16,989 | 19,538 | 19,617 | 19,939 | 20,600 | 21,167 | 22,000 | 23,336 | 24,454 |
| Financial sectors................. | 1,099 | 1,602 | 1,596 | 1,585 | 1,761 | 1,934 | 1,978 | 2,052 | 2,038 | 2,027 |
| Rest of the world................. | 134 | 116 | 170 | 259 | 321 | 415 | 474 | 506 | 536 | 594 |

[1] Includes open market paper, Treasury securities, agency- and GSE-backed securities, municipal securities, and corporate and foreign bonds. [2] Excludes employee retirement funds. [3] Includes depository loans not elsewhere classified, other loans and advances, mortgages, and consumer credit.

Source: Board of Governors of the Federal Reserve System, "Financial Accounts of the United States, Z.1," <https://www.federalreserve.gov/data.htm>, accessed July 2019.

## Table 1200. Financial Accounts of the United States—Financial Assets and Liabilities of Foreign Sector: 2000 to 2018

[In billions of dollars (6,241 represents $6,241,000,000,000). As of December 31. Minus sign (-) indicates loss]

| Type of instrument | 2000 | 2005 | 2010 | 2012 | 2013 | 2014 | 2015 | 2016 | 2017 | 2018 |
|---|---|---|---|---|---|---|---|---|---|---|
| Total financial assets................ | 6,241 | 10,788 | 16,249 | 19,161 | 21,267 | 23,121 | 23,083 | 24,258 | 27,166 | 27,198 |
| Special Drawing Rights allocations............. | 6 | 7 | 54 | 54 | 54 | 51 | 49 | 47 | 50 | 49 |
| Net interbank assets............. | 49 | -42 | -68 | 24 | 292 | 258 | 198 | 54 | 158 | 192 |
| U.S. checkable deposits and currency......... | 236 | 300 | 390 | 541 | 591 | 674 | 707 | 767 | 848 | 925 |
| U.S. time deposits............... | 226 | 223 | 308 | 394 | 445 | 499 | 480 | 551 | 572 | 594 |
| Money market fund shares............. | 11 | 23 | 70 | 97 | 106 | 105 | 108 | 96 | 91 | 104 |
| Security repurchase agreements............. | 91 | 705 | 582 | 671 | 705 | 811 | 665 | 713 | 756 | 672 |
| Debt securities, excluding negotiable certificates of deposit............ | 2,335 | 4,980 | 8,252 | 9,365 | 9,587 | 10,174 | 10,337 | 10,661 | 11,408 | 11,166 |
| Open market (commercial) paper............. | 114 | 157 | 102 | 103 | 101 | 108 | 104 | 141 | 136 | 124 |
| Treasury securities............. | 1,021 | 1,984 | 4,459 | 5,571 | 5,793 | 6,158 | 6,146 | 6,003 | 6,285 | 6,265 |
| Agency- and GSE-backed securities [1]........ | 348 | 1,006 | 1,096 | 1,001 | 884 | 900 | 916 | 992 | 1,011 | 1,078 |
| Municipal securities............. | 8 | 29 | 72 | 72 | 76 | 81 | 87 | 94 | 101 | 101 |
| U.S. corporate bonds............. | 843 | 1,804 | 2,523 | 2,618 | 2,733 | 2,928 | 3,083 | 3,432 | 3,874 | 3,598 |
| Nonfinancial business loans............. | 117 | 163 | 162 | 144 | 140 | 171 | 208 | 203 | 376 | 733 |
| U.S. corporate equities............. | 1,483 | 2,118 | 3,213 | 3,953 | 5,205 | 5,921 | 5,501 | 5,781 | 7,031 | 6,479 |
| Mutual fund shares............. | 149 | 163 | 263 | 495 | 553 | 617 | 601 | 693 | 830 | 870 |
| Trade receivables............. | 70 | 122 | 203 | 222 | 224 | 237 | 247 | 254 | 301 | 332 |
| Life insurance reserves............. | – | 1 | 6 | 8 | 4 | 11 | 6 | 17 | 20 | 10 |
| Pension entitlements............. | – | – | 1 | 3 | 2 | 5 | 3 | 4 | 4 | 15 |
| Foreign direct investment in U.S. [2]............. | 1,459 | 2,007 | 2,791 | 3,159 | 3,321 | 3,553 | 3,935 | 4,377 | 4,670 | 4,995 |
| Miscellaneous assets (insurance receivables)............. | 7 | 19 | 22 | 32 | 36 | 36 | 39 | 40 | 50 | 59 |
| Total liabilities............. | 3,419 | 6,079 | 9,208 | 10,289 | 10,497 | 11,247 | 11,086 | 11,459 | 12,740 | 12,979 |
| U.S. official reserve assets [3]............. | 57 | 54 | 121 | 139 | 133 | 119 | 106 | 106 | 112 | 115 |
| U.S. private deposits............. | 803 | 1,165 | 1,304 | 919 | 951 | 828 | 591 | 501 | 759 | 872 |
| Security repurchase agreements............. | – | 381 | 664 | 801 | 692 | 709 | 789 | 905 | 873 | 915 |
| Debt securities............. | 703 | 1,209 | 2,076 | 2,566 | 2,649 | 2,867 | 2,753 | 2,801 | 3,305 | 3,327 |
| Commercial paper............. | 121 | 87 | 173 | 199 | 266 | 275 | 329 | 270 | 362 | 368 |
| Bonds............. | 582 | 1,122 | 1,903 | 2,367 | 2,384 | 2,592 | 2,424 | 2,531 | 2,943 | 2,958 |
| Loans............. | 134 | 116 | 170 | 259 | 321 | 415 | 474 | 506 | 536 | 594 |
| Depository institution loans n.e.c. [4,5]........ | 84 | 85 | 149 | 229 | 289 | 381 | 441 | 475 | 483 | 548 |
| Other loans and advances............. | 50 | 31 | 21 | 30 | 32 | 34 | 34 | 32 | 53 | 46 |
| Trade credit and advances............. | 47 | 46 | 65 | 74 | 71 | 66 | 66 | 69 | 77 | 79 |
| Life insurance reserves............. | 22 | 49 | 68 | 55 | 52 | 48 | 51 | 75 | 98 | 67 |
| Pension entitlements............. | 6 | 16 | 33 | 29 | 28 | 21 | 21 | 15 | 19 | 78 |
| U.S. direct investment abroad [2]............. | 1,551 | 2,827 | 4,388 | 5,124 | 5,296 | 5,879 | 5,934 | 6,252 | 6,706 | 6,661 |
| Miscellaneous liabilities............. | 96 | 215 | 319 | 323 | 303 | 297 | 299 | 228 | 255 | 273 |

– Represents or rounds to zero. [1] GSE = Government-sponsored enterprises. [2] Direct investment is valued on a current-cost basis. [3] Excludes monetary gold. [4] N.e.c. = not elsewhere classified. [5] Beginning with 2010, includes loans to foreign non-depository financial institutions.

Source: Board of Governors of the Federal Reserve System, "Financial Accounts of the United States, Z.1," <https://www.federalreserve.gov/data.htm>, accessed July 2019.

## Table 1201. Financial Accounts of the United States—Assets of Households and Nonprofit Organizations: 2000 to 2018

[In billions of dollars (34,570 represents $34,570,000,000,000). As of December 31. See also Table 753]

| Type of instrument | Total (billion dollars) | | | | | | | Percent distribution | | |
|---|---|---|---|---|---|---|---|---|---|---|
| | 2000 | 2005 | 2010 | 2015 | 2016 | 2017 | 2018 | 2000 | 2010 | 2018 |
| Total financial assets................ | 34,570 | 47,028 | 55,632 | 74,132 | 78,294 | 85,135 | 84,657 | 100.0 | 100.0 | 100.0 |
| Foreign deposits........................... | 48 | 64 | 67 | 32 | 26 | 39 | 45 | 0.1 | 0.1 | 0.1 |
| Checkable deposits and currency......... | 405 | 372 | 480 | 1,220 | 1,142 | 1,344 | 1,558 | 1.2 | 0.9 | 1.8 |
| Time and savings deposits................ | 3,068 | 4,882 | 6,464 | 8,432 | 9,107 | 9,285 | 9,701 | 8.9 | 11.6 | 11.5 |
| Money market fund shares................ | 1,296 | 1,262 | 1,658 | 1,551 | 1,557 | 1,615 | 1,798 | 3.7 | 3.0 | 2.1 |
| Debt securities.......................... | 2,047 | 3,220 | 5,226 | 4,705 | 4,608 | 4,620 | 5,587 | 5.9 | 9.4 | 6.6 |
| Treasury securities..................... | 536 | 283 | 1,093 | 1,074 | 1,196 | 1,212 | 1,940 | 1.6 | 2.0 | 2.3 |
| Agency and GSE-backed securities [1].... | 574 | 385 | 194 | 463 | 402 | 481 | 647 | 1.7 | 0.3 | 0.8 |
| Municipal securities..................... | 475 | 1,699 | 1,912 | 1,885 | 1,861 | 1,870 | 1,842 | 1.4 | 3.4 | 2.2 |
| Corporate and foreign bonds............. | 463 | 853 | 2,026 | 1,283 | 1,148 | 1,058 | 1,158 | 1.3 | 3.6 | 1.4 |
| Loans [2]................................ | 558 | 759 | 955 | 985 | 973 | 900 | 876 | 1.6 | 1.7 | 1.0 |
| Mortgages............................. | 96 | 127 | 132 | 99 | 92 | 83 | 73 | 0.3 | 0.2 | 0.1 |
| Consumer credit (student loans)......... | – | – | 71 | 45 | 41 | 35 | 30 | – | 0.1 | – |
| Corporate equities [3]................... | 7,119 | 8,017 | 8,517 | 13,128 | 14,853 | 17,544 | 15,565 | 20.6 | 15.3 | 18.4 |
| Mutual fund shares...................... | 2,558 | 3,401 | 4,686 | 6,944 | 7,295 | 8,657 | 7,920 | 7.4 | 8.4 | 9.4 |
| Trade receivables....................... | 124 | 153 | 184 | 241 | 251 | 261 | 269 | 0.4 | 0.3 | 0.3 |
| Life insurance reserves.................. | 839 | 1,136 | 1,273 | 1,511 | 1,568 | 1,627 | 1,659 | 2.4 | 2.3 | 2.0 |
| Pension entitlements [4]................. | 11,052 | 14,546 | 18,325 | 23,483 | 24,361 | 25,801 | 25,669 | 32.0 | 32.9 | 30.3 |
| Equity in noncorporate business.......... | 5,019 | 8,470 | 6,891 | 10,819 | 11,413 | 12,251 | 12,766 | 14.5 | 12.4 | 15.1 |
| Miscellaneous assets.................... | 437 | 744 | 905 | 1,082 | 1,139 | 1,192 | 1,243 | 1.3 | 1.6 | 1.5 |

– Represents or rounds to zero. [1] GSE = government-sponsored enterprises. [2] Includes other instruments not shown separately [3] Directly held corporate equities, including closed-end fund, exchange-traded fund, and real estate investment trust shares. [4] Includes public and private defined benefit and defined contribution plans and annuities, including those in IRAs and at life insurance companies. Excludes social security.

Source: Board of Governors of the Federal Reserve System, "Financial Accounts of the United States, Z.1," <https://www.federalreserve.gov /data.htm>, accessed July 2019.

## Table 1202. Financial Assets Held by Families by Type of Asset: 2013 and 2016

[Median value in thousands of constant 2016 dollars (21.9 represents $21,900). All dollar figures are adjusted to 2016 dollars using the "current methods" version of the consumer price index for all urban consumers published by U.S. Bureau of Labor Statistics. Families include one-person units; for definition of family, see text, Section 1. Based on Survey of Consumer Finances; see Appendix III]

| Age of family head and family income | Any financial asset [1] | Trans- action accounts [2] | Certifi- cates of deposit | Savings bonds | Stocks [3] | Pooled invest- ment funds [4] | Retire- ment accounts [5] | Life insur- ance [6] | Other man- aged [7] |
|---|---|---|---|---|---|---|---|---|---|
| PERCENT OF FAMILIES OWNING ASSET | | | | | | | | | |
| 2013, total.................. | 94.5 | 93.2 | 7.8 | 10.0 | 13.8 | 8.2 | 49.2 | 19.2 | 5.2 |
| 2016, total.................. | 98.5 | 98.0 | 6.5 | 8.6 | 13.9 | 10.0 | 52.1 | 19.4 | 5.5 |
| Under 35 years old.......... | 98.1 | 97.7 | 2.4 | 5.8 | 10.0 | 4.8 | 42.2 | 9.3 | 1.4 |
| 35 to 44 years old........... | 97.9 | 97.3 | 4.7 | 10.2 | 11.4 | 6.9 | 56.7 | 12.6 | 1.7 |
| 45 to 54 years old........... | 99.0 | 98.5 | 4.6 | 9.3 | 14.6 | 9.9 | 59.8 | 18.4 | 2.6 |
| 55 to 64 years old........... | 98.6 | 98.0 | 6.7 | 8.6 | 15.5 | 12.6 | 59.3 | 23.4 | 6.4 |
| 65 to 74 years old........... | 98.9 | 98.6 | 10.5 | 9.7 | 15.2 | 13.3 | 49.8 | 29.7 | 12.5 |
| 75 years old and over........ | 98.4 | 97.8 | 14.5 | 9.1 | 19.6 | 15.6 | 40.8 | 29.5 | 12.6 |
| Percentiles of income: [8] | | | | | | | | | |
| Less than 20................. | 95.2 | 94.2 | 2.9 | 2.7 | 3.9 | 1.6 | 11.3 | 12.2 | 2.1 |
| 20 to 39.9................... | 97.4 | 96.3 | 5.1 | 5.1 | 6.0 | 3.2 | 33.6 | 15.9 | 3.9 |
| 40 to 59.9................... | 99.7 | 99.4 | 6.3 | 8.6 | 10.5 | 5.4 | 53.1 | 19.5 | 3.7 |
| 60 to 79.9................... | 100.0 | 99.9 | 6.7 | 11.3 | 13.8 | 12.5 | 75.2 | 22.7 | 6.7 |
| 80 to 89.9................... | 100.0 | 99.8 | 11.5 | 15.0 | 25.1 | 17.6 | 82.2 | 22.3 | 8.6 |
| 90 to 100................... | 100.0 | 100.0 | 11.5 | 15.8 | 45.9 | 37.3 | 91.9 | 31.0 | 13.3 |
| MEDIAN VALUE [9] | | | | | | | | | |
| 2013, total.................. | 21.9 | 4.2 | 16.5 | 1.0 | 27.8 | 82.5 | 60.8 | 8.2 | 103.1 |
| 2016, total.................. | 23.5 | 4.5 | 20.0 | 1.0 | 25.0 | 114.0 | 60.0 | 8.5 | 110.0 |
| Under 35 years old.......... | 6.0 | 2.6 | 4.0 | 0.5 | 5.0 | 10.3 | 12.3 | 3.0 | 50.0 |
| 35 to 44 years old........... | 17.0 | 3.8 | 7.7 | 0.6 | 12.0 | 55.9 | 37.0 | 6.0 | 22.0 |
| 45 to 54 years old........... | 35.0 | 4.1 | 10.0 | 0.8 | 25.0 | 100.0 | 82.6 | 9.6 | 70.0 |
| 55 to 64 years old........... | 59.3 | 5.4 | 20.0 | 2.0 | 45.0 | 270.0 | 120.0 | 15.0 | 165.0 |
| 65 to 74 years old........... | 59.5 | 8.0 | 25.0 | 1.0 | 55.0 | 300.0 | 126.0 | 9.6 | 140.0 |
| 75 years old and over........ | 63.0 | 10.0 | 40.0 | 4.8 | 70.0 | 155.0 | 120.0 | 7.5 | 100.0 |

[1] Includes other types of financial assets, not shown separately. [2] Checking, savings, and money market deposit accounts, money market mutual funds, call or cash accounts at brokerages, and prepaid debit cards. [3] Covers only publicly traded stocks that are directly held by families—that is, corporate equities not held as part of a managed investment account or mutual fund. [4] Excludes money market mutual funds and indirectly held mutual funds and includes all other types of directly held pooled investment funds, such as traditional open-ended and closed-end mutual funds, real estate investment trusts, and hedge funds. [5] The tax-deferred retirement accounts consist of IRAs, Keogh accounts, and certain employer-sponsored accounts. Employer-sponsored accounts include 401(k), 403(b), and thrift saving accounts from current or past jobs; other current job plans from which loans or withdrawals can be made; and accounts from past jobs from which the family expects to receive the account balance in the future. [6] The value of such policies according to their current cash value, not their death benefit. [7] Includes personal annuities and trusts with an equity interest and managed investment accounts. [8] Percentiles of income distribution in 2016 dollars: 20th: $25,300; 40th: $43,500; 60th: $69,500; 80th: $111,400; 90th: $177,100. Percentile: A value on a scale of zero to 100 that indicates the percent of a distribution that is equal to or below it. [9] Median value of financial asset for families holding such assets.

Source: Board of Governors of the Federal Reserve System, 2016 Survey of Consumer Finances, *Changes in U.S. Family Finances From 2013 to 2016: Evidence from the Survey of Consumer Finances*, Federal Reserve Bulletin, Vol. 103, No. 3, September 2017. See also <http://www.federalreserve.gov/econres/scfindex.htm>.

## Table 1203. Financial Accounts of the United States—Liabilities of Households and Nonprofit Organizations: 2000 to 2018

[In billions of dollars (7,407 represents $7,407,000,000,000). As of December 31. Minus sign (-) indicates decrease. See also Table 753]

| Type of instrument | Total (billion dollars) | | | | | | | Percent distribution | | |
|---|---|---|---|---|---|---|---|---|---|---|
| | 2000 | 2005 | 2010 | 2015 | 2016 | 2017 | 2018 | 2000 | 2010 | 2018 |
| **Total liabilities** | **7,407** | **12,260** | **14,037** | **14,527** | **14,977** | **15,555** | **16,045** | **100.0** | **100.0** | **100.0** |
| Debt securities (municipal securities) | 138 | 217 | 271 | 220 | 216 | 218 | 216 | 1.9 | 1.9 | 1.3 |
| Loans | 7,102 | 11,817 | 13,467 | 13,934 | 14,370 | 14,926 | 15,396 | 95.9 | 95.9 | 96.0 |
| Home mortgages [1] | 4,817 | 8,941 | 9,994 | 9,567 | 9,760 | 10,054 | 10,331 | 65.0 | 71.2 | 64.4 |
| Consumer credit | 1,741 | 2,321 | 2,647 | 3,411 | 3,644 | 3,828 | 4,009 | 23.5 | 18.9 | 25.0 |
| Depository institution loans, not elsewhere classified [2] | 61 | 36 | 214 | 281 | 291 | 299 | 327 | 0.8 | 1.5 | 2.0 |
| Other loans and advances | 354 | 352 | 414 | 437 | 427 | 488 | 463 | 4.8 | 3.0 | 2.9 |
| Commercial mortgages | 129 | 168 | 198 | 239 | 248 | 257 | 266 | 1.7 | 1.4 | 1.7 |
| Trade payables | 148 | 203 | 274 | 341 | 359 | 378 | 397 | 2.0 | 2.0 | 2.5 |
| Deferred and unpaid life insurance premiums | 20 | 23 | 25 | 32 | 31 | 33 | 35 | 0.3 | 0.2 | 0.2 |

[1] Includes loans made under home equity lines of credit and home equity loans secured by junior liens. [2] Includes loans extended by the Federal Reserve to financial institutions such as domestic hedge funds through the Term Asset-Backed Securities Loan Facility (TALF).

Source: Board of Governors of the Federal Reserve System, "Financial Accounts of the United States, Z.1," <https://www.federalreserve.gov/data.htm>, accessed July 2019.

## Table 1204. Financial Debt Held by Families by Type of Debt: 2013 and 2016

[Median debt in thousands of constant 2016 dollars (62.3 represents $62,300). See headnote, Table 1202]

| Age and race of family head and family income | Any debt | Secured by residential property | | Installment loans [2] | Credit card balances [3] | Lines of credit not secured by residential property | Other [4] |
|---|---|---|---|---|---|---|---|
| | | Primary residence [1] | Other | | | | |
| **PERCENT OF FAMILIES HOLDING DEBT** | | | | | | | |
| 2013, total | 74.5 | 42.9 | 5.2 | 47.2 | 38.1 | 1.9 | 6.6 |
| **2016, total** | **77.1** | **41.9** | **5.6** | **50.2** | **43.9** | **1.8** | **5.4** |
| Under 35 years old | 81.0 | 28.3 | 2.3 | 67.5 | 45.4 | 1.9 | 4.0 |
| 35 to 44 years old | 86.2 | 50.1 | 6.7 | 64.2 | 49.1 | 2.6 | 5.9 |
| 45 to 54 years old | 86.6 | 53.5 | 6.4 | 55.2 | 52.3 | 2.2 | 8.2 |
| 55 to 64 years old | 77.1 | 49.0 | 8.8 | 44.9 | 41.4 | 1.9 | 7.0 |
| 65 to 74 years old | 70.1 | 38.8 | 5.8 | 33.7 | 42.1 | 1.1 | 3.7 |
| 75 years old and over | 49.8 | 26.5 | 2.7 | 19.3 | 26.2 | (B) | 1.5 |
| White, non-Hispanic | 77.5 | 46.4 | 6.5 | 49.3 | 42.1 | 1.8 | 5.1 |
| Black or African-American, non-Hispanic | 77.1 | 31.9 | 2.7 | 54.2 | 47.8 | 2.5 | 5.9 |
| Hispanic or Latino | 74.0 | 31.5 | 3.3 | 46.0 | 49.6 | (B) | 4.7 |
| Other or multiple race | 77.9 | 37.8 | 6.2 | 53.8 | 44.1 | 1.9 | 7.1 |
| Percentiles of income: [5] | | | | | | | |
| Less than 20 | 57.9 | 14.1 | 0.7 | 35.8 | 29.0 | 1.2 | 2.5 |
| 20 to 39.9 | 70.4 | 26.1 | 1.6 | 44.4 | 41.7 | 1.4 | 3.3 |
| 40 to 59.9 | 84.3 | 40.7 | 2.5 | 57.1 | 53.0 | 2.1 | 5.3 |
| 60 to 79.9 | 88.2 | 59.3 | 7.0 | 60.3 | 52.8 | 2.4 | 7.0 |
| 80 to 89.9 | 89.0 | 70.9 | 12.2 | 61.3 | 51.5 | 1.7 | 8.4 |
| 90 to 100 | 80.6 | 67.3 | 19.9 | 45.5 | 34.4 | 2.3 | 9.0 |
| **MEDIAN DEBT [6]** | | | | | | | |
| 2013, total | 62.3 | 118.6 | 92.8 | 15.1 | 2.4 | 4.5 | 4.1 |
| **2016, total** | **59.8** | **111.0** | **100.0** | **17.1** | **2.3** | **3.0** | **5.0** |
| Under 35 years old | 39.3 | 119.0 | 37.0 | 21.0 | 1.4 | 0.6 | 2.0 |
| 35 to 44 years old | 93.7 | 140.0 | 127.5 | 20.5 | 2.5 | 5.0 | 4.0 |
| 45 to 54 years old | 89.9 | 125.0 | 85.0 | 17.8 | 2.8 | 5.0 | 7.0 |
| 55 to 64 years old | 69.0 | 96.1 | 110.0 | 13.8 | 2.8 | 3.5 | 8.0 |
| 65 to 74 years old | 42.0 | 79.0 | 96.0 | 12.4 | 2.5 | 1.2 | 5.0 |
| 75 years old and over | 20.6 | 50.1 | 100.0 | 9.8 | 2.1 | (B) | 9.0 |
| White, non-Hispanic | 74.1 | 115.0 | 116.0 | 17.0 | 2.7 | 3.0 | 7.5 |
| Black or African-American, non-Hispanic | 31.1 | 78.9 | 19.2 | 18.6 | 1.4 | 0.9 | 2.5 |
| Hispanic or Latino | 30.0 | 99.0 | 55.8 | 15.7 | 1.7 | (B) | 2.0 |
| Other or multiple race | 56.7 | 150.0 | 78.5 | 16.3 | 2.3 | 1.2 | 7.0 |

B Base figure too small. [1] Debt secured by residential property consists of first-lien and junior-lien mortgages and home equity lines of credit secured by the primary residence. [2] Consumer loans that typically have fixed payments and a fixed term. Examples are automobile loans, student loans, and loans for furniture, appliances, and other durable consumer goods. [3] Balances exclude purchases made after the most recent bill was paid. [4] Includes loans on insurance policies, loans against pension accounts, borrowing on margin accounts, and unclassified loans. [5] See footnote 8, Table 1202. [6] Median amount of financial debt for families holding such debts.

Source: Board of Governors of the Federal Reserve System, 2016 Survey of Consumer Finances, *Changes in U.S. Family Finances From 2013 to 2016: Evidence from the Survey of Consumer Finances*, Federal Reserve Bulletin, Vol. 103, No. 3, September 2017. See also <http://www.federalreserve.gov/econres/scfindex.htm>.

## Table 1205. Debt Held by Families—Percent Distribution by Type and Purpose of Debt: 2010 to 2016

[See headnote, Table 1202]

| Type and purpose of debt | 2010 | 2013 | 2016 | Type and purpose of debt | 2010 | 2013 | 2016 |
|---|---|---|---|---|---|---|---|
| **TYPE OF DEBT** | | | | **PURPOSE OF DEBT** | | | |
| Total.......................... | **100.0** | **100.0** | **100.0** | Total............................... | **100.0** | **100.0** | **100.0** |
| Secured by residential property: | | | | Primary residence: | | | |
| Primary residence................... | 74.1 | 73.8 | 69.4 | Purchase............................ | 69.5 | 70.5 | 66.7 |
| Other............................ | 9.8 | 9.0 | 9.4 | Improvement....................... | 1.9 | 1.7 | 1.5 |
| Lines of credit not secured | | | | Other residential property........... | 10.5 | 10.2 | 10.3 |
| by residential property.............. | 1.0 | 0.7 | 1.1 | Investments, except real estate..... | 2.0 | 1.0 | 1.5 |
| Installment loans...................... | 11.1 | 13.1 | 16.0 | Vehicles............................ | 4.7 | 5.1 | 6.3 |
| Credit card balances................. | 2.9 | 2.4 | 2.6 | Goods and services................. | 5.7 | 4.4 | 4.9 |
| Other.................................. | 1.1 | 1.1 | 1.5 | Education.......................... | 5.2 | 6.6 | 8.2 |
| | | | | Other................................. | 0.4 | 0.5 | 0.5 |

Source: Board of Governors of the Federal Reserve System, 2016 Survey of Consumer Finances, *Changes in U.S. Family Finances From 2013 to 2016: Evidence from the Survey of Consumer Finances*, Federal Reserve Bulletin, Vol. 103, No. 3, September 2017. See also <http://www.federalreserve.gov/econres/scfindex.htm>.

## Table 1206. Ratios of Debt Payments to Family Income: 2010 to 2016

[In percent. See headnote, Table 1202]

| Family characteristic | Ratio of debt payments to family income | | | | | | Percent of debtors with— | | | | | |
|---|---|---|---|---|---|---|---|---|---|---|---|---|
| | Aggregate [1] | | | Median for debtors [2] | | | Ratios above 40 percent | | | Any payment 60 days or more past due | | |
| | 2010 | 2013 | 2016 | 2010 | 2013 | 2016 | 2010 | 2013 | 2016 | 2010 | 2013 | 2016 |
| **All families...............** | **14.7** | **12.0** | **10.8** | **18.2** | **15.9** | **14.7** | **13.9** | **11.0** | **9.1** | **10.8** | **9.3** | **7.5** |
| Under 35 years old.......... | 17.0 | 14.9 | 14.1 | 16.4 | 13.7 | 13.1 | 11.6 | 8.1 | 8.5 | 10.4 | 11.6 | 10.6 |
| 35 to 44 years old........... | 18.4 | 13.6 | 15.2 | 20.9 | 16.1 | 16.0 | 16.4 | 9.8 | 8.7 | 15.7 | 11.4 | 10.5 |
| 45 to 54 years old........... | 16.2 | 13.9 | 11.7 | 19.2 | 18.6 | 16.2 | 15.6 | 12.0 | 8.5 | 12.6 | 12.0 | 6.9 |
| 55 to 64 years old........... | 12.5 | 11.1 | 9.1 | 17.6 | 16.4 | 15.1 | 13.1 | 14.0 | 10.9 | 8.4 | 6.4 | 5.7 |
| 65 to 74 years old........... | 11.3 | 8.8 | 7.9 | 17.0 | 14.2 | 13.7 | 12.1 | 12.2 | 8.5 | 6.1 | 4.7 | 4.5 |
| 75 years old and over....... | 6.8 | 5.8 | 6.0 | 14.1 | 10.6 | 12.5 | 11.9 | 10.0 | 9.9 | 3.2 | 2.7 | 2.8 |
| Percentiles of income: [3] | | | | | | | | | | | | |
| Less than 20.................... | 23.5 | 15.5 | 16.2 | 16.3 | 12.8 | 11.9 | 26.1 | 23.2 | 21.6 | 21.2 | 16.1 | 13.9 |
| 20 to 39.9.................... | 16.9 | 14.8 | 14.6 | 17.5 | 15.3 | 15.6 | 18.7 | 18.4 | 13.3 | 15.2 | 14.3 | 11.1 |
| 40 to 59.9.................... | 19.5 | 16.2 | 15.3 | 20.0 | 16.4 | 14.4 | 15.5 | 11.1 | 8.3 | 10.2 | 10.0 | 9.1 |
| 60 to 79.9.................... | 19.3 | 16.7 | 15.7 | 20.4 | 17.9 | 16.1 | 11.0 | 6.1 | 4.2 | 8.8 | 7.3 | 4.4 |
| 80 to 89.9.................... | 18.1 | 16.5 | 15.4 | 19.3 | 18.5 | 16.3 | 5.4 | 3.9 | 4.2 | 5.4 | 4.1 | 2.9 |
| 90 to 100.................... | 9.4 | 7.3 | 6.2 | 13.1 | 11.8 | 11.3 | 2.9 | 1.8 | 1.5 | 2.1 | 1.0 | 0.8 |
| Percentiles of net worth: [3] | | | | | | | | | | | | |
| Less than 25.................... | 19.2 | 16.7 | 13.2 | 13.6 | 12.2 | 9.9 | 14.9 | 12.3 | 8.3 | 22.2 | 21.1 | 16.7 |
| 25 to 49.9.................... | 19.3 | 16.9 | 16.1 | 21.3 | 18.0 | 17.2 | 15.4 | 13.8 | 10.7 | 13.3 | 10.4 | 8.9 |
| 50 to 74.9.................... | 19.2 | 16.8 | 16.9 | 20.8 | 17.8 | 17.7 | 14.1 | 10.2 | 9.9 | 6.8 | 5.0 | 3.9 |
| 75 to 89.9.................... | 15.9 | 14.1 | 13.3 | 16.7 | 15.4 | 14.9 | 11.0 | 7.7 | 7.8 | 2.0 | 1.8 | 1.9 |
| 90 to 100.................... | 8.8 | 6.4 | 5.5 | 13.4 | 11.3 | 11.2 | 11.0 | 7.9 | 6.3 | 1.2 | 1.0 | 0.4 |
| Owner occupied............. | 16.1 | 13.1 | 11.7 | 22.2 | 19.7 | 18.9 | 17.1 | 14.0 | 11.5 | 8.7 | 6.5 | 5.0 |
| Renter occupied or other. .. | 7.0 | 6.6 | 6.7 | 6.8 | 6.8 | 6.5 | 5.0 | 4.2 | 3.9 | 16.6 | 15.9 | 13.1 |

[1] The aggregate measure is the ratio of total debt payments to total income for all families. [2] The median is the median of the distribution of ratios calculated for individual families with debt. [3] Percentiles of income distribution in 2016 dollars: 20th: $25,300; 40th: $43,500; 60th: $69,500; 80th: $111,400; 90th: $177,100. Percentiles of distribution of net worth in 2016 dollars: 25th: $10,300; 50th: $97,300; 75th: $369,100; 90th: $1,186,300.

Source: Board of Governors of the Federal Reserve System, 2016 Survey of Consumer Finances, *Changes in U.S. Family Finances From 2013 to 2016: Evidence from the Survey of Consumer Finances*, Federal Reserve Bulletin, Vol. 103, No. 3, September 2017. See also <http://www.federalreserve.gov/econres/scfindex.htm>.

## Table 1207. Household Debt-Service Payments and Financial Obligations as a Percent of Disposable Personal Income: 1990 to 2018

[As of end of year, seasonally adjusted. Mortgage debt service ratio (DSR) is defined as the total quarterly required mortgage payments divided by total quarterly disposable personal income. The consumer DSR is defined as the total quarterly required consumer debt payments divided by total quarterly disposable personal income. The financial obligations ratio adds automobile lease payments, rental payments on tenant-occupied property, homeowners' insurance, and property tax payments to the debt service ratio]

| Year | Financial obligations ratio | Household debt service ratio | | | Year | Financial obligations ratio | Household debt service ratio | | |
|---|---|---|---|---|---|---|---|---|---|
| | | Total | Mortgage | Consumer | | | Total | Mortgage | Consumer |
| 1990........... | 16.96 | 11.60 | 6.18 | 5.42 | 2012........... | 14.90 | 9.84 | 4.95 | 4.89 |
| 2000........... | 17.06 | 12.06 | 5.72 | 6.34 | 2013........... | 15.37 | 10.08 | 4.87 | 5.21 |
| 2005........... | 17.26 | 12.59 | 6.49 | 6.10 | 2014........... | 15.26 | 9.88 | 4.57 | 5.31 |
| 2008........... | 17.87 | 12.82 | 6.96 | 5.86 | 2015........... | 15.53 | 9.93 | 4.48 | 5.45 |
| 2009........... | 17.15 | 11.96 | 6.55 | 5.41 | 2016........... | 15.66 | 10.04 | 4.39 | 5.66 |
| 2010........... | 16.08 | 10.98 | 5.95 | 5.03 | 2017........... | 15.47 | 9.95 | 4.29 | 5.66 |
| 2011........... | 15.64 | 10.45 | 5.44 | 5.01 | 2018........... | 15.33 | 9.88 | 4.25 | 5.63 |

Source: Board of Governors of the Federal Reserve System, "Household Debt Service and Financial Obligations Ratios," <https://www.federalreserve.gov/data.htm>, accessed May 2019.

## Table 1208. FDIC-Insured Financial Institutions—Number and Assets by State and Island Area: 2018

[In billions of dollars, except as indicated (18,034.4 represents $18,034,400,000,000). As of December 31. Includes data from U.S. banks and U.S. branches of foreign banks that have insured deposits. Information is obtained primarily from the Federal Financial Institutions Examination Council (FFIEC) Call Reports and the Office of Thrift Supervision's Thrift Financial Reports. Data are based on the location of each reporting institution's main office. Reported data may include assets located outside of the reporting institution's home state]

| State or Island Area | Number of institutions | Assets by asset size of bank | | | | State or Island Area | Number of institutions | Assets by asset size of bank | | | |
|---|---|---|---|---|---|---|---|---|---|---|---|
| | | Total | Less than $100 mil. | $100 mil. to $1 bil. | Greater than $1 bil. | | | Total | Less than $100 mil. | $100 mil. to $1 bil. | Greater than $1 bil. |
| Total....... | 5,415 | 18,034.4 | 75.9 | 1,108.6 | 16,849.9 | NE.......... | 170 | 77.9 | 3.4 | 29.0 | 45.5 |
| AL.......... | 119 | 272.3 | 1.8 | 23.6 | 246.9 | NV.......... | 19 | 271.6 | 0.1 | 4.2 | 267.3 |
| AK.......... | 5 | 6.5 | – | 1.3 | 5.2 | NH.......... | 17 | 11.3 | – | 7.9 | 3.4 |
| AZ.......... | 15 | 27.3 | 0.2 | 4.0 | 23.1 | NJ.......... | 75 | 161.2 | 0.1 | 19.3 | 141.8 |
| AR.......... | 93 | 107.6 | 1.4 | 18.8 | 87.4 | NM.......... | 37 | 13.5 | 0.2 | 9.4 | 3.9 |
| CA.......... | 155 | 804.5 | 0.7 | 37.5 | 766.3 | NY.......... | 145 | 1,131.1 | 0.4 | 33.8 | 1,096.9 |
| CO.......... | 79 | 64.9 | 0.9 | 12.3 | 51.8 | NC.......... | 47 | 2,068.6 | 0.6 | 9.6 | 2,058.4 |
| CT.......... | 38 | 113.5 | 0.1 | 9.9 | 103.5 | ND.......... | 75 | 31.9 | 1.7 | 10.3 | 19.9 |
| DE.......... | 22 | 1,078.0 | 0.1 | 2.7 | 1,075.2 | OH.......... | 182 | 3,171.7 | 3.4 | 34.0 | 3,134.3 |
| DC.......... | 3 | 1.3 | – | 1.3 | – | OK.......... | 201 | 119.2 | 4.3 | 37.2 | 77.7 |
| FL.......... | 117 | 202.0 | 1.3 | 29.2 | 171.4 | OR.......... | 17 | 32.2 | 0.2 | 5.1 | 26.9 |
| GA.......... | 168 | 321.5 | 2.0 | 33.5 | 286.0 | PA.......... | 149 | 260.7 | 0.8 | 37.0 | 222.8 |
| HI.......... | 8 | 54.1 | – | 1.4 | 52.7 | RI.......... | 8 | 140.2 | 0.1 | 0.4 | 139.7 |
| ID.......... | 13 | 6.6 | – | 3.8 | 2.8 | SC.......... | 50 | 37.5 | 0.8 | 14.0 | 22.6 |
| IL.......... | 436 | 515.6 | 7.7 | 73.5 | 434.4 | SD.......... | 63 | 3,161.1 | 1.2 | 11.0 | 3,148.8 |
| IN.......... | 104 | 97.3 | 1.0 | 22.7 | 73.5 | TN.......... | 144 | 136.2 | 1.4 | 36.0 | 98.7 |
| IA.......... | 288 | 86.9 | 5.0 | 50.7 | 31.2 | TX.......... | 438 | 508.1 | 6.1 | 96.6 | 405.4 |
| KS.......... | 235 | 72.7 | 5.6 | 33.1 | 34.0 | UT.......... | 41 | 726.5 | 0.3 | 7.3 | 719.0 |
| KY.......... | 148 | 59.0 | 1.6 | 30.1 | 27.2 | VT.......... | 11 | 5.2 | 0.1 | 4.1 | 1.0 |
| LA.......... | 117 | 80.9 | 1.3 | 29.7 | 49.9 | VA.......... | 74 | 742.8 | 0.4 | 18.5 | 723.9 |
| ME.......... | 26 | 28.7 | 0.3 | 5.8 | 22.7 | WA.......... | 42 | 81.0 | 0.4 | 8.2 | 72.5 |
| MD.......... | 46 | 45.6 | 0.2 | 13.0 | 32.4 | WV.......... | 51 | 32.4 | 0.6 | 9.4 | 22.5 |
| MA.......... | 120 | 407.0 | 0.4 | 36.9 | 369.7 | WI.......... | 201 | 116.2 | 2.7 | 47.1 | 66.5 |
| MI.......... | 93 | 84.6 | 1.1 | 21.1 | 62.4 | WY.......... | 31 | 8.8 | 0.3 | 8.5 | – |
| MN.......... | 292 | 73.0 | 6.9 | 41.7 | 24.4 | GU.......... | 3 | 2.4 | – | 0.5 | 1.9 |
| MS.......... | 73 | 102.7 | 0.7 | 17.0 | 85.0 | FM.......... | 1 | 0.2 | – | 0.2 | – |
| MO.......... | 256 | 167.3 | 4.5 | 48.2 | 114.6 | PR.......... | 5 | 65.9 | – | – | 65.9 |
| MT.......... | 48 | 37.4 | 1.4 | 7.0 | 29.0 | VI.......... | 1 | 0.2 | – | 0.2 | – |

– Represents or round zero. GU—Guam, FM—Federated States of Micronesia, PR—Puerto Rico, VI—Virgin Islands.

Source: U.S. Federal Deposit Insurance Corporation, "Statistics on Depository Institutions (SDI)," <https://www.fdic.gov/bank/statistical/index.html>, accessed August 2019.

## Table 1209. FDIC-Insured Financial Institutions—Income and Selected Measures of Financial Condition: 2000 to 2018

[In billions of dollars, except as indicated (511.9 represents $511,900,000,000). Includes Island Areas. Includes foreign branches of U.S. banks. Minus sign (-) indicates decrease]

| Item | 2000 | 2005 | 2010 | 2013 | 2014 | 2015 | 2016 | 2017 | 2018 |
|---|---|---|---|---|---|---|---|---|---|
| **INCOME** | | | | | | | | | |
| Interest income........................ | 511.9 | 522.2 | 536.9 | 470.4 | 469.8 | 478.5 | 515.8 | 572.3 | 661.0 |
| Interest expense....................... | 276.6 | 205.1 | 106.9 | 53.3 | 47.1 | 46.9 | 54.4 | 73.3 | 119.8 |
| Net interest income.................. | 235.3 | 317.0 | 430.0 | 417.1 | 422.7 | 431.6 | 461.4 | 499.0 | 541.2 |
| Provisions for loan losses........... | 32.1 | 29.8 | 158.0 | 32.4 | 29.8 | 37.1 | 48.1 | 51.1 | 50.0 |
| Noninterest income................... | 165.6 | 223.4 | 235.7 | 252.5 | 247.9 | 253.3 | 253.6 | 255.3 | 266.2 |
| Noninterest expense.................. | 242.3 | 317.4 | 391.8 | 416.8 | 422.8 | 416.9 | 423.3 | 442.5 | 459.3 |
| Income taxes.......................... | 43.6 | 64.6 | 38.4 | 70.0 | 68.2 | 70.6 | 76.0 | 98.0 | 61.1 |
| Net income attributable to bank.... | 81.5 | 133.8 | 85.5 | 154.3 | 152.2 | 163.4 | 170.7 | 164.3 | 236.7 |
| **PERFORMANCE RATIOS** | | | | | | | | | |
| Return on assets (percent)[1]....... | 1.14 | 1.28 | 0.65 | 1.07 | 1.01 | 1.04 | 1.04 | 0.97 | 1.35 |
| Return on equity (percent)[2]....... | 13.53 | 12.43 | 5.85 | 9.54 | 9.01 | 9.29 | 9.29 | 8.61 | 11.98 |
| Net interest margin (percent)[3].... | 3.77 | 3.47 | 3.76 | 3.26 | 3.14 | 3.07 | 3.13 | 3.25 | 3.40 |
| Net charge-offs (bil. dol.)[4]...... | 26.32 | 31.59 | 187.64 | 53.54 | 39.56 | 37.28 | 42.42 | 46.80 | 47.48 |
| Net charge-offs to loans and leases, total (percent)................. | 0.59 | 0.49 | 2.55 | 0.69 | 0.49 | 0.44 | 0.47 | 0.50 | 0.48 |
| Net charge-off rate, credit card loans (percent)................. | 4.36 | 4.74 | 10.08 | 3.35 | 3.12 | 2.92 | 3.16 | 3.61 | 3.75 |
| **CONDITION RATIOS** | | | | | | | | | |
| Equity capital to assets (percent)................. | 8.49 | 10.28 | 11.15 | 11.15 | 11.15 | 11.24 | 11.10 | 11.22 | 11.25 |
| Noncurrent assets plus other real estate owned to assets (percent)[5]..... | 0.71 | 0.50 | 3.11 | 1.63 | 1.20 | 0.97 | 0.86 | 0.72 | 0.60 |

[1] Net income (including securities transactions and nonrecurring items) as a percentage of average total assets. [2] Net income as a percentage of average total equity capital. [3] Interest income less interest expense as a percentage of average earning assets (i.e. the profit margin a bank earns on its loans and investments). [4] Total loans and leases charged off (removed from balance sheet because of uncollectibility), less amounts recovered on loans and leases previously charged off. [5] Noncurrent assets: the sum of loans, leases, debt securities and other assets that are 90 days or more past due, or in nonaccrual status, plus other real estate owned, primarily foreclosed property.

Source: U.S. Federal Deposit Insurance Corporation, *Quarterly Banking Profile*, Fourth Quarter 2018, and earlier reports; and "QBP Time Series Spreadsheets, Annual Income," <https://www.fdic.gov/bank/analytical/qbp/>, accessed May 2019.

## Table 1210. FDIC-Insured Financial Institutions—Number, Assets, and Liabilities: 2000 to 2018

[In billions of dollars, except as indicated (7,463 represents $7,463,000,000,000). As of December 31. Includes Island Areas. Excludes insured branches of foreign banks. Includes foreign branches of U.S. banks]

| Item | 2000 | 2005 | 2010 | 2013 | 2014 | 2015 | 2016 | 2017 | 2018 |
|---|---|---|---|---|---|---|---|---|---|
| Commercial bank offices, total................ | 73,231 | 81,136 | 89,165 | 88,582 | 87,597 | 86,881 | 85,201 | 84,081 | (NA) |
| Number of main offices...................... | 8,315 | 7,523 | 6,519 | 5,847 | 5,607 | 5,338 | 5,112 | 4,918 | 4,715 |
| Number of branches......................... | 64,916 | 73,613 | 82,646 | 82,735 | 81,990 | 81,541 | 80,089 | 79,163 | (NA) |
| Savings institutions, total.................... | 1,589 | 1,310 | 1,139 | 965 | 902 | 844 | 801 | 752 | 691 |
| **COMMERCIAL BANKS AND SAVINGS INSTITUTIONS** | | | | | | | | | |
| **Number of financial institutions** | | | | | | | | | |
| **reporting** [1]............................... | **9,904** | **8,833** | **7,658** | **6,812** | **6,509** | **6,182** | **5,913** | **5,670** | **5,406** |
| **Assets, total** [1]............................ | **7,463** | **10,879** | **13,319** | **14,731** | **15,554** | **15,968** | **16,780** | **17,415** | **17,943** |
| Net loans and leases [1]..................... | 4,572 | 6,641 | 7,144 | 7,757 | 8,187 | 8,721 | 9,183 | 9,597 | 10,027 |
| Real estate loans [1]...................... | 2,396 | 4,140 | 4,267 | 4,066 | 4,171 | 4,375 | 4,603 | 4,774 | 4,888 |
| 1-4 family residential mortgages.......... | 1,340 | 2,042 | 1,900 | 1,830 | 1,842 | 1,904 | 1,995 | 2,064 | 2,119 |
| Nonfarm nonresidential.................. | 525 | 826 | 1,071 | 1,109 | 1,150 | 1,232 | 1,324 | 1,391 | 1,445 |
| Construction and development............ | 197 | 450 | 321 | 210 | 238 | 275 | 313 | 338 | 350 |
| Home equity loans...................... | 151 | 534 | 637 | 510 | 492 | 465 | 434 | 411 | 376 |
| Multifamily residential real estate......... | 117 | 188 | 213 | 263 | 297 | 344 | 383 | 404 | 430 |
| Commercial and industrial loans............. | 1,086 | 1,086 | 1,184 | 1,567 | 1,715 | 1,837 | 1,932 | 2,009 | 2,165 |
| Loans to individuals [1]...................... | 672 | 949 | 1,316 | 1,353 | 1,418 | 1,498 | 1,589 | 1,678 | 1,743 |
| Credit cards and related plans............. | 266 | 396 | 702 | 691 | 718 | 756 | 800 | 865 | 903 |
| Other loans to individuals................ | 406 | 553 | 614 | 662 | 700 | 741 | 790 | 813 | 839 |
| Auto loans.......................... | (NA) | (NA) | (NA) | 353 | 385 | 415 | 442 | 450 | 455 |
| Loans to depository institutions............ | 118 | 162 | 109 | 114 | 101 | 98 | 88 | 87 | 84 |
| Lease financing receivables............... | 167 | 139 | 102 | 111 | 114 | 116 | 127 | 130 | 133 |
| Less: Reserve for losses................. | 71 | 77 | 231 | 136 | 123 | 119 | 122 | 124 | 125 |
| Securities................................. | 1,361 | 1,893 | 2,668 | 3,002 | 3,219 | 3,354 | 3,560 | 3,632 | 3,723 |
| Domestic office assets..................... | 6,702 | 9,825 | 11,693 | 12,948 | 13,866 | 14,408 | 15,177 | 15,714 | 16,150 |
| Foreign office assets...................... | 760 | 1,054 | 1,626 | 1,782 | 1,688 | 1,560 | 1,603 | 1,702 | 1,793 |
| **Liabilities and capital, total** [1]............ | **7,463** | **10,879** | **13,319** | **14,731** | **15,554** | **15,968** | **16,780** | **17,415** | **17,943** |
| Deposits................................... | 4,915 | 7,141 | 9,423 | 11,192 | 11,764 | 12,190 | 12,895 | 13,399 | 13,866 |
| Foreign office deposits.................... | 707 | 921 | 1,550 | 1,401 | 1,393 | 1,282 | 1,246 | 1,318 | 1,253 |
| Domestic office deposits................... | 4,208 | 6,221 | 7,873 | 9,791 | 10,371 | 10,908 | 11,649 | 12,081 | 12,613 |
| Interest-bearing deposits................. | 3,437 | 5,004 | 6,184 | 7,180 | 7,518 | 7,908 | 8,497 | 8,832 | 9,478 |
| Noninterest-bearing deposits.............. | 771 | 1,217 | 1,689 | 2,612 | 2,852 | 3,000 | 3,152 | 3,250 | 3,135 |
| Equity capital............................. | 633 | 1,119 | 1,511 | 1,654 | 1,741 | 1,801 | 1,869 | 1,958 | 2,023 |

NA Not available. [1] Includes other items not shown separately.

Source: U.S. Federal Deposit Insurance Corporation, "FDIC Quarterly Banking Profile," and "Statistics At A Glance," <https://www.fdic.gov/bank/analytical/qbp/>; and "Historical Statistics on Banking," <http://www5.fdic.gov/hsob>; accessed September 2019.

## Table 1211. FDIC-Insured Financial Institutions by Asset Size: 2018

[16,728.1 represents $16,728,100,000,000. Includes Island Areas. Includes foreign branches of U.S. banks]

| Item | Unit | Total | Less than $100 mil. | $100 mil. to $1 bil. | $1 bil. to $10 bil. | Greater than $10 bil. |
|---|---|---|---|---|---|---|
| **COMMERCIAL BANKS** | | | | | | |
| Institutions reporting.............................. | Number | 4,715 | 1,133 | 2,941 | 518 | 123 |
| Assets, total...................................... | Billion dollars | 16,728.1 | 67.4 | 954.1 | 1,386.0 | 14,320.6 |
| Deposits.......................................... | Billion dollars | 12,898.5 | 56.6 | 802.3 | 1,121.2 | 10,918.3 |
| Net income attributable to bank.................... | Billion dollars | 222.1 | 0.7 | 11.6 | 18.6 | 191.2 |
| Percentage of banks losing money................. | Percent | 2.91 | 7.06 | 1.87 | 0.39 | (NA) |
| Return on assets................................. | Percent | 1.35 | 1.00 | 1.25 | 1.39 | 1.36 |
| Return on equity................................. | Percent | 11.99 | 7.86 | 11.31 | 11.95 | 12.06 |
| Net charge-offs to loans and leases............... | Percent | 0.46 | 0.20 | 0.14 | 0.22 | 0.52 |
| Noncurrent assets plus other real estate owned to assets................. | Percent | 0.58 | 0.96 | 0.74 | 0.66 | 0.56 |
| Equity capital to assets........................... | Percent | 11.29 | 12.90 | 11.20 | 11.84 | 11.24 |
| **SAVINGS INSTITUTIONS** | | | | | | |
| Institutions reporting.............................. | Number | 691 | 145 | 412 | 120 | 14 |
| Assets, total...................................... | Billion dollars | 1,214.9 | 8.5 | 154.5 | 348.8 | 703.1 |
| Deposits.......................................... | Billion dollars | 967.7 | 6.3 | 121.9 | 267.9 | 571.7 |
| Net income attributable to bank.................... | Billion dollars | 14.7 | 0.1 | 1.7 | 3.6 | 9.3 |
| Percentage of banks losing money................. | Percent | 6.51 | 17.93 | 4.61 | (NA) | (NA) |
| Return on assets................................. | Percent | 1.27 | 1.14 | 1.07 | 1.07 | 1.41 |
| Return on equity................................. | Percent | 11.74 | 6.09 | 8.16 | 8.88 | 14.92 |
| Net charge-offs to loans and leases............... | Percent | 0.81 | 0.05 | 0.24 | 0.10 | 1.61 |
| Noncurrent assets plus other real estate owned to assets................. | Percent | 0.91 | 1.01 | 0.66 | 0.54 | 1.15 |
| Equity capital to assets........................... | Percent | 10.74 | 18.90 | 13.36 | 12.21 | 9.34 |

NA Not available.

Source: U.S. Federal Deposit Insurance Corporation, "Statistics on Depository Institutions," <https://www5.fdic.gov/sdi/main.asp>, accessed July 2019.

## Table 1212. FDIC-Insured Financial Institutions—Deposit Insurance Fund (DIF) Indicators: 2009 to 2018

[In billions of dollars, except as indicated (8,021 represents $8,021,000,000,000). As of December 31. Includes Island Areas. Includes insured branches of foreign banks. Minus sign (-) indicates decrease]

| Item | 2009 | 2010 | 2011 | 2012 | 2013 | 2014 | 2015 | 2016 | 2017 | 2018 |
|---|---|---|---|---|---|---|---|---|---|---|
| Number of institutions reporting.......... | 8,021 | 7,667 | 7,366 | 7,092 | 6,821 | 6,518 | 6,191 | 5,922 | 5,679 | 5,415 |
| Domestic deposits, total [1].............. | 7,705 | 7,888 | 8,782 | 9,475 | 9,825 | 10,408 | 10,953 | 11,693 | 12,130 | 12,659 |
| Estimated insured deposits [2] | 5,408 | 6,302 | 6,973 | 7,405 | 5,998 | 6,196 | 6,519 | 6,918 | 7,158 | 7,523 |
| DIF balance.......................... | -21 | -7 | 12 | 33 | 47 | 63 | 73 | 83 | 93 | 103 |
| Reserve ratio [3]....................... | -0.39 | -0.12 | 0.17 | 0.45 | 0.79 | 1.01 | 1.11 | 1.20 | 1.30 | 1.36 |
| Number of problem institutions........... | 702 | 884 | 813 | 651 | 467 | 291 | 183 | 123 | 95 | 60 |
| Assets of problem institutions............ | 402.8 | 390.0 | 319.4 | 232.7 | 152.7 | 86.7 | 46.8 | 27.6 | 13.9 | 48.5 |
| Number of assisted institutions.......... | 8 | – | – | – | – | – | – | – | – | – |
| Assets of assisted institutions............ | 1,917.5 | – | – | – | – | – | – | – | – | – |
| Number of failed institutions............. | 140 | 157 | 92 | 51 | 24 | 18 | 8 | 5 | 8 | – |
| Assets of assisted institutions.......... | 169.7 | 92.1 | 34.9 | 11.6 | 6.0 | 2.9 | 6.7 | 0.3 | 5.1 | – |

– Represents zero. [1] Excludes foreign office deposits, which are uninsured. [2] In general, insured deposits are total domestic deposits minus estimated uninsured deposits. Prior to September 30, 2009, insured deposits included deposits in accounts of $100,000 or less. Beginning September 30, 2009, insured deposits include deposits in accounts of $100,000 to $250,000 that are covered by a temporary increase in the FDIC's standard maximum deposit insurance amount. The Dodd-Frank Wall Street Reform and Consumer Protection Act of July 21, 2010 (Dodd-Frank) made permanent the standard maximum deposit insurance amount of $250,000. The Dodd-Frank Act also provided unlimited coverage for noninterest bearing transaction accounts for two years beginning December 31, 2010, and ending December 31, 2012. [3] DIF balance as percent of DIF-insured deposits.

Source: U.S. Federal Deposit Insurance Corporation, *Quarterly Banking Profile*, Fourth Quarter 2018, and earlier reports. See also <https://www.fdic.gov/bank/analytical/qbp/index.html>.

## Table 1213. FDIC-Insured Financial Institutions—Number of Offices and Deposits by State: 2018

[12,308 represents $12,308,000,000,000. As of June 30. Includes insured U.S. branches of foreign banks. The term "offices" includes both main offices and branches. "Banking office" is defined to include all offices and facilities that actually hold deposits, and does not include loan production offices, computer centers, and other nondeposit installations, such as automated teller machines (ATMs). Several institutions have designated home offices that do not accept deposits; these have been included to provide a more complete listing of all offices. The figures for each geographical area only include deposits of offices located within that area. Based on the Summary of Deposits survey]

| State | Number of offices | Total deposits (bil. dol.) | State | Number of offices | Total deposits (bil. dol.) | State | Number of offices | Total deposits (bil. dol.) |
|---|---|---|---|---|---|---|---|---|
| Total [1]..... | 88,070 | 12,308 | IA............. | 1,518 | 87 | NC............. | 2,313 | 366 |
| | | | KS............. | 1,439 | 75 | ND............. | 427 | 28 |
| U.S........... | 87,699 | 12,227 | KY............. | 1,634 | 82 | OH............. | 3,598 | 343 |
| AL............. | 1,466 | 101 | LA............. | 1,469 | 104 | OK............. | 1,345 | 87 |
| AK............. | 123 | 12 | ME............. | 472 | 29 | OR............. | 972 | 78 |
| AZ............. | 1,177 | 132 | MD............. | 1,490 | 145 | PA............. | 4,123 | 395 |
| AR............. | 1,344 | 67 | MA............. | 2,156 | 397 | RI............. | 251 | 35 |
| CA............. | 6,839 | 1,397 | MI............. | 2,515 | 218 | SC............. | 1,226 | 86 |
| CO............. | 1,482 | 138 | MN............. | 1,682 | 231 | SD............. | 462 | 603 |
| CT............. | 1,159 | 136 | MS............. | 1,142 | 54 | TN............. | 2,054 | 155 |
| DE............. | 268 | 399 | MO............. | 2,291 | 163 | TX............. | 6,419 | 840 |
| DC............. | 216 | 51 | MT............. | 379 | 24 | UT............. | 523 | 524 |
| FL............. | 4,982 | 587 | NE............. | 1,073 | 64 | VT............. | 236 | 13 |
| GA............. | 2,312 | 250 | NV............. | 495 | 274 | VA............. | 2,294 | 323 |
| HI............. | 270 | 45 | NH............. | 418 | 34 | WA............. | 1,716 | 161 |
| ID............. | 490 | 26 | NJ............. | 2,886 | 334 | WV............. | 618 | 33 |
| IL............. | 4,306 | 483 | NM............. | 467 | 31 | WI............. | 1,971 | 150 |
| IN............. | 2,012 | 131 | NY............. | 4,960 | 1,691 | WY............. | 219 | 16 |

[1] Includes outlying areas not shown separately.

Source: U.S. Federal Deposit Insurance Corporation, "Summary of Deposits, Reference Tables," <https://www5.fdic.gov/sod/sodSummary.asp?barItem=3>, accessed July 2019.

## Table 1214. U.S. Banking Offices of Foreign Banks—Summary: 2000 to 2018

[In billions of dollars (1,358 represents $1,358,000,000,000), except as indicated. As of December. The U.S. offices of foreign banking organizations consist of U.S. branches and agencies of foreign banks and bank subsidiaries of foreign banking organizations. Foreign-owned institutions are those owned by a bank located outside of the United States and its affiliated insular areas. Bank subsidiaries of foreign banking organizations are U.S. commercial banks of which more than 25 percent are owned by a foreign banking organization or where the relationship is reported as being a controlling relationship by the filer of the FR Y-10 (Report of Changes in Organizational Structure) report form. Covers the U.S. offices of foreign banking organizations that are located in the 50 states and the District of Columbia; excludes offices located in Puerto Rico, American Samoa, Guam, the Virgin Islands and other U.S.-affiliated insular areas]

| Item | 2000 | 2005 | 2010 | 2014 | 2015 | 2016 | 2017 | 2018 | Share [1] | | |
|---|---|---|---|---|---|---|---|---|---|---|---|
| | | | | | | | | | 2000 | 2010 | 2018 |
| Assets...................... | 1,358 | 2,123 | 2,838 | 3,730 | 3,539 | 3,515 | 3,776 | 3,737 | 18.9 | 20.4 | 19.6 |
| Loans, total................ | 557 | 802 | 960 | 1,335 | 1,416 | 1,444 | 1,484 | 1,558 | 13.5 | 13.7 | 15.2 |
| Business loans............ | 308 | 276 | 326 | 519 | 580 | 584 | 568 | 599 | 25.0 | 25.1 | 24.5 |
| Deposits.................... | 770 | 1,162 | 1,752 | 2,149 | 2,029 | 1,962 | 2,032 | 2,036 | 16.5 | 18.3 | 14.7 |

[1] Foreign owned banks plus U.S. branches and offices of foreign banks as percent of all banks in the United States.

Source: Board of Governors of the Federal Reserve System, "Share Data for U.S. Offices of Foreign Banks," December 2018, <http://www.federalreserve.gov/Releases/iba/fboshr.htm>, accessed June 2019.

## Table 1215. Federal and State-Chartered Credit Unions—Summary: 2000 to 2018

[43,883 represents 43,883,000. As of December 31. Federal data include District of Columbia, Puerto Rico, Guam, and Virgin Islands. Excludes state-insured, privately insured, and noninsured state-chartered credit unions and corporate central credit unions, which have mainly other credit unions as members]

| Year | Operating credit unions | | Number of failed institutions [1] | Members (1,000) | | Assets (mil. dol.) | | Loans outstanding (mil. dol.) | | Savings (mil. dol.) | |
|---|---|---|---|---|---|---|---|---|---|---|---|
| | Federal | State | | Federal | State | Federal | State | Federal | State | Federal | State |
| 2000........ | 6,336 | 3,980 | 29 | 43,883 | 33,705 | 242,881 | 195,363 | 163,851 | 137,485 | 210,188 | 169,053 |
| 2008........ | 4,847 | 2,959 | 19 | 49,130 | 39,453 | 447,124 | 364,132 | 309,277 | 256,720 | 373,366 | 307,762 |
| 2009........ | 4,714 | 2,840 | 31 | 49,604 | 40,333 | 482,684 | 402,069 | 311,154 | 261,285 | 408,832 | 343,835 |
| 2010........ | 4,589 | 2,750 | 29 | 50,081 | 40,447 | 500,075 | 414,395 | 306,276 | 258,555 | 427,603 | 358,877 |
| 2011........ | 4,447 | 2,647 | 16 | 50,743 | 41,093 | 525,633 | 436,121 | 308,845 | 262,640 | 449,316 | 378,093 |
| 2012........ | 4,272 | 2,547 | 22 | 51,797 | 42,043 | 557,119 | 464,612 | 322,675 | 275,066 | 474,903 | 402,948 |
| 2013........ | 4,105 | 2,449 | 17 | 52,499 | 43,762 | 571,326 | 490,588 | 343,780 | 301,440 | 485,500 | 424,587 |
| 2014........ | 3,927 | 2,346 | 15 | 53,355 | 45,870 | 596,145 | 525,942 | 373,387 | 338,938 | 499,683 | 451,107 |
| 2015........ | 3,764 | 2,257 | 16 | 54,284 | 48,369 | 628,012 | 576,266 | 404,729 | 382,288 | 522,109 | 493,892 |
| 2016........ | 3,608 | 2,177 | 14 | 56,599 | 50,205 | 670,124 | 622,354 | 444,516 | 424,591 | 559,825 | 532,759 |
| 2017........ | 3,499 | 2,074 | 10 | 59,037 | 52,261 | 718,287 | 660,530 | 490,119 | 467,188 | 594,662 | 564,807 |
| 2018........ | 3,376 | 1,999 | 8 | 61,281 | 54,896 | 753,559 | 699,873 | 532,715 | 510,879 | 625,456 | 594,271 |

[1] A failed institution is defined as a credit union which has ceased operation because it was involuntarily liquidated or merged with assistance from the National Credit Union Share Insurance Fund.

Source: National Credit Union Administration, *National Credit Union Administration 2018 Annual Report,* February 2019, and earlier reports; and "5300 Call Report Aggregate Financial Performance Report," December 2018, <https://www.ncua.gov/analysis/credit-union-corporate-call-report-data>. See also <https://www.ncua.gov/news/annual-reports>.

## Table 1216. Noncash Debit and Credit Payments by Method of Payment: 2016 and 2017

[112.2 represents 112,200,000,000. Estimates are based on survey data from the Federal Reserve Payments Survey, which is conducted every three years and updated with a smaller supplemental annual data collection between the triennial studies. The Study combines information gathered in three related survey efforts. Some estimates are based on data collected in the Depository and Financial Institutions Payments Survey (DFIPS), which was sent to a nationally representative, stratified random sample of depository and financial institutions. Other estimates are based on data collected in the Networks, Processors, and Issuers Payments Surveys (NPIPS) through a set of surveys of payment networks, processors, and card issuers. Finally, some estimates are from data collected in the Check Sample Survey (CSS), which are based on the information from a random sample of checks processed by a selected number of large commercial banks. ATM withdrawals are excluded]

| Method of payment [1] | Transactions (billions) | | Value (trillion dollars) | | Average value per transaction (dollars) | |
|---|---|---|---|---|---|---|
| | 2016 | 2017 | 2016 | 2017 | 2016 | 2017 |
| Total card payments........................... | 112.2 | 123.5 | 0.0 | 0.5 | 53 | 52 |
| Debit cards.................................... | 74.8 | 82.6 | 2.7 | 2.9 | 36 | 35 |
| Non-prepaid................................... | 63.0 | 69.6 | 2.4 | 2.6 | 38 | 37 |
| In person.................................... | 52.1 | 55.9 | 1.7 | 1.7 | 32 | 31 |
| Chip......................................... | 8.3 | 22.8 | 0.4 | 0.9 | 42 | 38 |
| No chip...................................... | 43.8 | 33.1 | 1.3 | 0.8 | 30 | 26 |
| Remote....................................... | 10.9 | 13.7 | 0.8 | 0.9 | 69 | 63 |
| Prepaid...................................... | 11.8 | 13.1 | 0.3 | 0.3 | 25 | 23 |
| General purpose [2]........................... | 4.4 | 5.3 | 0.2 | 0.2 | 34 | 30 |
| In person.................................... | 3.6 | 4.1 | 0.1 | 0.1 | 28 | 26 |
| Chip......................................... | 0.1 | 0.5 | (Z) | (Z) | 39 | 29 |
| No chip...................................... | 3.5 | 3.6 | 0.1 | 0.1 | 28 | 25 |
| Remote....................................... | 0.8 | 1.2 | (Z) | 0.1 | 59 | 46 |
| Private label [3]............................. | 4.9 | 5.4 | 0.1 | 0.1 | 15 | 15 |
| Electronic benefits transfer (EBT)............ | 2.5 | 2.4 | 0.1 | 0.1 | 28 | 27 |
| Credit cards.................................. | 37.3 | 40.8 | 3.3 | 3.6 | 88 | 88 |
| General purpose [2]........................... | 34.3 | 37.7 | 3.0 | 3.3 | 88 | 88 |
| In person.................................... | 23.4 | 24.8 | 1.4 | 1.4 | 58 | 58 |
| Chip......................................... | 6.6 | 12.1 | 0.5 | 0.8 | 71 | 65 |
| No chip...................................... | 16.8 | 12.8 | 0.9 | 0.6 | 53 | 50 |
| Remote....................................... | 10.9 | 12.9 | 1.6 | 1.9 | 151 | 147 |
| Private label [3]............................. | 3.1 | 3.1 | 0.3 | 0.3 | 90 | 89 |
| General purpose cards [1,4]................... | 101.7 | 112.6 | 5.6 | 6.1 | 55 | 54 |
| In person.................................... | 79.1 | 84.8 | 3.1 | 3.3 | 39 | 38 |
| Chip......................................... | 15.0 | 35.3 | 0.8 | 1.7 | 55 | 47 |
| No chip...................................... | 64.1 | 49.5 | 2.3 | 1.6 | 36 | 32 |
| Remote....................................... | 22.6 | 27.8 | 2.4 | 2.8 | 108 | 101 |

Z Less than $50 billion. [1] ATM withdrawals are not included in the data. [2] Cards issued by depository institutions and processed over card networks. They carry a network brand from one of the four major card networks or from smaller or regional networks and can be used wherever that network card is accepted, regardless of merchant or merchant type. [3] Cards issued by merchants and processed over proprietary networks. They are accepted only by the sponsoring merchant. [4] General-purpose cards include general-purpose credit, non-prepaid debit, and general-purpose prepaid debit card payments.

Source: Board of Governors of the Federal Reserve System *The 2016 Federal Reserve Payments Study: Recent Developments in Consumer and Business Payment Choices,* June 2017; and *The Federal Reserve Payments Study 2018 Annual Supplement,* January 2019. See also <https://www.federalreserve.gov/paymentsystems/fr-payments-study.htm>.

## Table 1217. Debit Cards: Holders, Number, Transactions, and Volume: 2000 and 2010, and Projections, 2018

[160 represents 160,000,000]

| Type of debit card | Cardholders (mil.) | | | Number of cards (mil.) | | | Number of point-of-sale transactions (mil.) | | | Purchase volume (bil. dol.) | | |
|---|---|---|---|---|---|---|---|---|---|---|---|---|
| | 2000 | 2010 | 2018 (P) | 2000 | 2010 | 2018 (P) | 2000 | 2010 | 2018 (P) | 2000 | 2010 | 2018 (P) |
| Total [1].................... | 160 | 185 | 209 | 235 | 4,008 | 5,357 | 9,571 | 49,281 | 84,585 | 342 | 1,825 | 3,321 |
| Bank [2]...................... | 137 | 164 | 192 | 137 | 516 | 752 | 5,290 | 36,879 | 62,717 | 210 | 1,387 | 2,452 |
| EFT networks [3]............ | 159 | 184 | 206 | 223 | 281 | 321 | 2,979 | 7,239 | 14,313 | 100 | 262 | 569 |
| Private label prepaid [4]..... | (NA) | (NA) | (NA) | (NA) | 3,447 | 5,004 | 1,280 | 5,125 | 7,284 | 31 | 172 | 283 |
| ACH network [5]............. | 11 | 13 | 31 | 11 | 13 | 32 | 22 | 39 | 270 | 1 | 3 | 17 |

NA Not available. P Projected. [1] Cardholders may hold more than one type of card. Bank cards and electronic funds transfer (EFT) cards are the same pieces of plastic that carry multiple brands. The total card figure shown does not include any duplication. [2] Visa and MasterCard debit cards, including prepaid cards. Beginning 2006, includes Interlink & MasterCard PIN debit. [3] Cards issued by financial institution members of regional and national switches such as Star, Interlink (for 2000), Pulse, Nyce, etc. EFT = Electronic funds transfer. [4] Prepaid cards without the Visa, MasterCard, American Express, or Discover logos. [5] ACH = Automated clearing house. Retail cards such as those issued by Target, Nordstrom, etc.

Source: The Nilson Report, Carpinteria, CA, twice-monthly newsletter. © Used by permission.

## Table 1218. Credit Cards: Holders, Number, Purchase Volume, and Debt: 2000 and 2010, and Projections, 2018

[159 represents 159,000,000]

| Type of credit card | Cardholders (mil.) | | | Number of cards (mil.) | | | Credit card purchase volume (bil. dol.) | | | Credit card debt outstanding (bil. dol.) | | |
|---|---|---|---|---|---|---|---|---|---|---|---|---|
| | 2000 | 2010 | 2018 (P) | 2000 | 2010 | 2018 (P) | 2000 | 2010 | 2018 (P) | 2000 | 2010 | 2018 (P) |
| Total [1].................... | 159 | 152 | 180 | 1,425 | 877 | 1,123 | 1,242 | 2,061 | 3,936 | 680 | 811 | 1,125 |
| Visa........................ | 93 | 100 | 124 | 255 | 240 | 338 | 487 | 809 | 1,956 | 268 | 332 | 471 |
| MasterCard................ | 86 | 75 | 97 | 200 | 171 | 231 | 281 | 479 | 811 | 212 | 240 | 310 |
| Store....................... | 114 | 95 | 110 | 597 | 318 | 392 | 120 | 138 | 182 | 92 | 92 | 131 |
| Oil company............... | 76 | 38 | 27 | 98 | 35 | 32 | 45 | 47 | 56 | 5 | 6 | 6 |
| Discover................... | 36 | 41 | 44 | 50 | 55 | 57 | 69 | 106 | 139 | 48 | 50 | 73 |
| American Express........ | 23 | 34 | 36 | 33 | 49 | 54 | 221 | 476 | 772 | 50 | 90 | 120 |
| The rest [2]................. | 7 | 6 | 16 | 192 | 9 | 19 | 18 | 5 | 20 | 5 | 1 | 15 |

P Projected. [1] Cardholders may hold more than one type of card. [2] Includes Universal Air Travel Plan (UATP), medical cards, automobile rental, and miscellaneous cards.

Source: The Nilson Report, Carpinteria, CA, twice-monthly newsletter. © Used by permission.

## Table 1219. Consumer Credit by Type of Holder: 2000 to 2018

[In billions of dollars (1,741 represents $1,741,000,000,000). As of December 31. Not seasonally adjusted]

| Type of holder | 2000 | 2005 | 2010 | 2012 | 2013 | 2014 | 2015 | 2016 | 2017 | 2018 |
|---|---|---|---|---|---|---|---|---|---|---|
| Total........................... | 1,741 | 2,321 | 2,647 | 2,914 | 3,091 | 3,313 | 3,411 | 3,644 | 3,828 | 4,009 |
| Nonprofit organizations [1].................... | – | – | 71 | 58 | 52 | 48 | 45 | 41 | 35 | 30 |
| Nonfinancial corporate business............... | 81 | 60 | 44 | 45 | 39 | 39 | 38 | 40 | 39 | 39 |
| Federal government [2].................... | 60 | 90 | 364 | 622 | 736 | 846 | 950 | 1,049 | 1,146 | 1,236 |
| U.S.-chartered depository institutions.......... | 616 | 816 | 1,186 | 1,215 | 1,271 | 1,343 | 1,428 | 1,532 | 1,612 | 1,682 |
| Credit unions................... | 184 | 229 | 226 | 244 | 266 | 303 | 342 | 380 | 418 | 469 |
| Asset-backed securities issuers.................. | 528 | 610 | 50 | 50 | 49 | 50 | 46 | 53 | 38 | 18 |
| Finance companies............................. | 234 | 517 | 705 | 680 | 679 | 684 | 561 | 549 | 541 | 534 |
| Memo: | | | | | | | | | | |
| Credit card loans [3]............................ | 702 | 857 | 839 | 840 | 855 | 888 | 907 | 968 | 1,022 | 1,053 |
| Auto loans..................... | 581 | 823 | 713 | 809 | 878 | 957 | 1,000 | 1,075 | 1,113 | 1,153 |
| Student loans [4]................... | – | – | 855 | 1,055 | 1,146 | 1,236 | 1,320 | 1,408 | 1,490 | 1,568 |
| Other consumer credit [5]........................ | 458 | 641 | 239 | 209 | 213 | 231 | 184 | 193 | 203 | 234 |

– Represents or rounds to zero. [1] Student loans originated under the Federal Family Education Loan Program. Asset of the households and nonprofit organizations sector. [2] Includes loans originated by the Department of Education under the Federal Direct Loan Program and Perkins Loans; as well as Federal Family Education Loan Program loans that the government purchased from depository institutions, finance companies, and nonprofit and educational institutions; and loans in default. [3] Revolving credit that also includes overdraft plans on checking accounts and other loans without a fixed repayment schedule. [4] Includes student loans held by nonprofit organizations, the federal government, depository institutions, and finance companies. Data begin in 2006. [5] Prior to 2006, includes student loans.

Source: Board of Governors of the Federal Reserve System, "Financial Accounts of the United States, Z.1," <https://www.federalreserve.gov/data.htm>, accessed July 2019.

## Table 1220. Consumer Credit Outstanding and Finance Rates: 2000 to 2018

[In billions of dollars (1,717 represents $1,717,000,000,000), except percent. Covers most short- and intermediate-term credit extended to individuals, excluding loans secured by real estate. Estimated amounts of seasonally adjusted credit outstanding as of end of year; finance rates, annual averages]

| Type of credit | 2000 | 2005 | 2010 | 2012 | 2013 | 2014 | 2015 | 2016 | 2017 | 2018 |
|---|---|---|---|---|---|---|---|---|---|---|
| **Total** | **1,717** | **2,291** | **2,647** | **2,914** | **3,091** | **3,313** | **3,411** | **3,644** | **3,828** | **4,009** |
| Revolving | 683 | 830 | 839 | 840 | 855 | 888 | 907 | 968 | 1,022 | 1,053 |
| Nonrevolving [1] | 1,034 | 1,461 | 1,808 | 2,073 | 2,237 | 2,424 | 2,504 | 2,676 | 2,806 | 2,956 |
| FINANCE RATES (percent) | | | | | | | | | | |
| Commercial banks: | | | | | | | | | | |
| New automobiles (48 months) | 9.34 | 7.07 | 6.21 | 4.91 | 4.43 | 4.24 | 4.19 | 4.30 | 4.61 | 5.03 |
| Personal loans (24 months) | 13.90 | 12.06 | 10.87 | 10.71 | 10.20 | 10.23 | 9.75 | 9.69 | 10.13 | 10.32 |
| Credit card plans, all accounts | 15.78 | 12.51 | 13.78 | 12.06 | 11.91 | 11.87 | 12.09 | 12.35 | 12.89 | 14.22 |
| Credit card plans, accounts assessed interest | 14.92 | 14.55 | 14.26 | 12.96 | 12.95 | 13.19 | 13.66 | 13.56 | 14.44 | 16.05 |
| Finance companies: | | | | | | | | | | |
| New automobiles [2] | (NA) | (NA) | 4.70 | 4.63 | 4.67 | 4.88 | 5.12 | 5.05 | 5.36 | 6.13 |

NA Not available. [1] Comprises automobile loans and all other loans not included in revolving credit, such as loans for mobile homes, education, boats, trailers, or vacations. These loans may be secured or unsecured. [2] Covers most of the captive and non-captive finance companies. Amount of finance weighted.

Source: Board of Governors of the Federal Reserve System, Data Releases, Household Finances, "Consumer Credit-G.19" <http://www.federalreserve.gov/econresdata/statisticsdata.htm>, accessed May 2019.

## Table 1221. Bank Account Status of Households by Selected Characteristics: 2015 and 2017

[In percent, except total households (127,538 represents 127,538,000). A household is 'unbanked' if no one in the household has a checking or savings account at an insured bank. An 'underbanked' household is one that had a bank account but also used the following products or services from an alternative financial services (AFS) provider in the past 12 months: money orders, check cashing, international remittances, payday loans, refund anticipation loans, rent-to-own services, pawn shop loans, or auto title loans. A 'fully banked' household is one that has a bank account and has not used an AFS in the past 12 months. Data collected through a Federal Deposit Insurance Corporation (FDIC)-sponsored supplement to the Current Population Survey]

| Characteristic | Total households (1,000) | | Unbanked households | | Banked households | | | | | |
|---|---|---|---|---|---|---|---|---|---|---|
| | | | | | Underbanked | | Fully banked | | Underbanked status unknown | |
| | 2015 | 2017 | 2015 | 2017 | 2015 | 2017 | 2015 | 2017 | 2015 | 2017 |
| **Total households** | **127,538** | **129,276** | **7.0** | **6.5** | **19.9** | **18.7** | **68.0** | **68.4** | **5.0** | **6.3** |
| RACE/ETHNICITY [1] | | | | | | | | | | |
| White | 85,428 | 85,599 | 3.1 | 3.0 | 15.6 | 14.1 | 76.6 | 77.1 | 4.7 | 5.7 |
| Black | 17,961 | 18,201 | 18.2 | 16.9 | 31.1 | 30.4 | 45.5 | 45.8 | 5.2 | 6.9 |
| Asian | 6,275 | 6,792 | 4.0 | 2.5 | 21.0 | 17.5 | 67.2 | 69.2 | 7.8 | 10.8 |
| Hispanic | 16,106 | 16,655 | 16.2 | 14.0 | 29.3 | 28.9 | 48.9 | 49.7 | 5.6 | 7.4 |
| Other | 1,767 | 2,030 | (NA) | 12.8 | (NA) | 28.0 | (NA) | 55.8 | (NA) | 3.3 |
| AGE | | | | | | | | | | |
| 15 to 24 years | 6,648 | 6,625 | 13.1 | 10.0 | 29.4 | 29.3 | 52.1 | 56.5 | 5.5 | 4.2 |
| 25 to 34 years | 21,005 | 20,997 | 10.6 | 8.5 | 24.5 | 23.1 | 60.8 | 62.5 | 4.0 | 5.9 |
| 35 to 44 years | 21,640 | 21,532 | 8.9 | 7.8 | 22.7 | 22.2 | 63.1 | 63.6 | 5.3 | 6.5 |
| 45 to 54 years | 23,773 | 23,277 | 6.7 | 6.9 | 21.1 | 19.3 | 67.5 | 67.1 | 4.8 | 6.7 |
| 55 to 64 years | 23,981 | 24,484 | 5.8 | 5.9 | 18.5 | 17.8 | 70.9 | 70.3 | 4.8 | 6.0 |
| 65 years or more | 30,491 | 32,361 | 3.1 | 3.9 | 13.0 | 11.6 | 78.1 | 77.5 | 5.8 | 7.0 |
| EDUCATION | | | | | | | | | | |
| No high school diploma | 13,802 | 12,461 | 23.2 | 22.4 | 25.9 | 24.3 | 46.4 | 46.3 | 4.5 | 7.0 |
| High school diploma | 33,239 | 33,334 | 9.7 | 9.4 | 22.2 | 20.3 | 62.9 | 63.7 | 5.3 | 6.5 |
| Some college | 37,512 | 37,355 | 5.5 | 5.1 | 22.0 | 20.8 | 67.7 | 67.8 | 4.8 | 6.3 |
| College degree | 42,985 | 46,127 | 1.1 | 1.3 | 14.5 | 14.4 | 79.1 | 78.3 | 5.2 | 6.1 |
| EMPLOYMENT STATUS | | | | | | | | | | |
| Employed | 78,152 | 79,436 | 5.0 | 4.5 | 21.4 | 20.4 | 68.7 | 68.8 | 5.0 | 6.3 |
| Unemployed | 3,869 | 3,433 | 23.0 | 19.9 | 24.8 | 23.9 | 48.6 | 51.4 | 3.7 | 4.8 |
| Not in labor force | 45,517 | 46,407 | 9.2 | 9.0 | 17.1 | 15.4 | 68.5 | 69.0 | 5.3 | 6.6 |
| FAMILY INCOME | | | | | | | | | | |
| Less than $15,000 | 18,046 | 15,997 | 25.6 | 25.7 | 24.3 | 20.9 | 45.1 | 47.7 | 4.9 | 5.7 |
| $15,000 to $30,000 | 21,392 | 19,842 | 11.8 | 12.3 | 23.6 | 22.4 | 59.5 | 58.3 | 5.1 | 7.0 |
| $30,000 to $50,000 | 25,336 | 25,610 | 5.0 | 5.1 | 23.7 | 22.8 | 66.2 | 65.4 | 5.1 | 6.8 |
| $50,000 to $75,000 | 23,003 | 23,763 | 1.6 | 1.5 | 20.2 | 19.7 | 73.0 | 72.8 | 5.1 | 6.0 |
| At least $75,000 | 39,761 | 44,064 | 0.5 | 0.6 | 13.4 | 13.3 | 81.3 | 79.9 | 4.9 | 6.2 |
| DISABILITY STATUS | | | | | | | | | | |
| Disabled, age 25 to 64 | 11,497 | 11,297 | 17.6 | 18.1 | 28.4 | 24.7 | 49.7 | 52.2 | 4.3 | 5.0 |
| Not disabled, age 25 to 64 | 78,902 | 78,993 | 6.5 | 5.7 | 20.6 | 19.9 | 68.1 | 68.0 | 4.8 | 6.4 |
| HOUSING TENURE | | | | | | | | | | |
| Homeowner | 80,685 | 82,241 | 2.3 | 2.3 | 15.4 | 14.2 | 77.4 | 77.2 | 4.9 | 6.3 |
| Non-homeowner | 46,853 | 47,035 | 15.2 | 14.0 | 27.7 | 26.5 | 51.8 | 53.1 | 5.3 | 6.4 |
| REGION | | | | | | | | | | |
| Northeast | 22,699 | 22,776 | 6.3 | 6.0 | 19.3 | 17.9 | 67.9 | 69.0 | 6.4 | 7.2 |
| Midwest | 27,625 | 27,719 | 5.7 | 5.4 | 17.5 | 15.8 | 72.5 | 73.3 | 4.3 | 5.5 |
| South | 48,382 | 49,360 | 8.7 | 7.7 | 21.6 | 21.0 | 65.0 | 65.1 | 4.7 | 6.2 |
| West | 28,832 | 29,420 | 5.9 | 6.0 | 19.9 | 18.2 | 68.9 | 69.1 | 5.3 | 6.7 |

NA Not available. [1] Households are categorized into racial/ethnic classification as follows: if the householder is black, the household is classified as "black" regardless of whether the householder is also Hispanic or any other race. If the householder is not identified as black and is identified as Hispanic, the household is classified as "Hispanic." If the householder is identified as white and not any other race and not Hispanic, then the household is classified as "white." If the householder is identified as Asian and not black or Hispanic, then the household is classified as "Asian." All other households are listed as "other".

Source: Federal Deposit Insurance Corporation, Division of Depositor and Consumer Protection, *2017 FDIC National Survey of Unbanked and Underbanked Households*, October 2018. See also <https://www.economicinclusion.gov/surveys/>.

# Table 1222. Mortgage Debt Outstanding by Type of Property and Holder: 2000 to 2018

[In billions of dollars (6,767 represents $6,767,000,000,000). As of December 31]

| Type of property and holder | 2000 | 2005 | 2010 | 2012 | 2013 | 2014 | 2015 | 2016 | 2017 | 2018 |
|---|---|---|---|---|---|---|---|---|---|---|
| **MORTGAGES BY TYPE** | | | | | | | | | | |
| Total | 6,767 | 12,117 | 13,897 | 13,336 | 13,345 | 13,491 | 13,860 | 14,325 | 14,891 | 15,441 |
| Home [1] | 5,125 | 9,450 | 10,525 | 10,050 | 9,959 | 9,939 | 10,064 | 10,273 | 10,584 | 10,878 |
| Multifamily residential | 404 | 675 | 866 | 893 | 933 | 993 | 1,095 | 1,201 | 1,309 | 1,411 |
| Commercial | 1,152 | 1,887 | 2,352 | 2,220 | 2,267 | 2,362 | 2,493 | 2,625 | 2,760 | 2,901 |
| Farm | 85 | 105 | 154 | 173 | 185 | 197 | 209 | 226 | 238 | 251 |
| Total liabilities | 6,767 | 12,117 | 13,897 | 13,336 | 13,345 | 13,491 | 13,860 | 14,325 | 14,891 | 15,441 |
| Household sector | 4,946 | 9,109 | 10,192 | 9,777 | 9,703 | 9,684 | 9,805 | 10,007 | 10,310 | 10,597 |
| Nonfinancial business | 1,737 | 2,862 | 3,529 | 3,365 | 3,428 | 3,576 | 3,819 | 4,081 | 4,339 | 4,618 |
| Nonfinancial corporate business | 356 | 769 | 676 | 455 | 441 | 404 | 469 | 463 | 516 | 585 |
| Nonfinancial noncorporate business | 1,381 | 2,093 | 2,853 | 2,910 | 2,986 | 3,172 | 3,350 | 3,618 | 3,822 | 4,033 |
| Real estate investment trusts | 84 | 145 | 176 | 194 | 214 | 231 | 235 | 236 | 242 | 226 |
| Total assets | 6,767 | 12,117 | 13,897 | 13,336 | 13,345 | 13,491 | 13,860 | 14,325 | 14,891 | 15,441 |
| Household sector | 96 | 127 | 132 | 125 | 122 | 113 | 99 | 92 | 83 | 73 |
| Nonfinancial corporate business | 44 | 68 | 28 | 26 | 27 | 29 | 31 | 31 | 56 | 80 |
| Nonfinancial noncorporate business | 23 | 36 | 42 | 34 | 35 | 34 | 42 | 40 | 43 | 46 |
| Federal government | 76 | 77 | 107 | 111 | 115 | 117 | 116 | 120 | 121 | 125 |
| State and local governments | 136 | 174 | 225 | 219 | 227 | 227 | 231 | 233 | 229 | 214 |
| U.S.-chartered depository institutions | 2,350 | 4,055 | 4,195 | 4,026 | 3,983 | 4,091 | 4,297 | 4,538 | 4,698 | 4,819 |
| Foreign banking offices in U.S | 17 | 21 | 35 | 31 | 31 | 38 | 51 | 68 | 77 | 77 |
| Banks in U.S.-affiliated areas | 16 | 35 | 36 | 34 | 32 | 30 | 26 | 26 | 26 | 24 |
| Credit unions | 120 | 226 | 317 | 328 | 346 | 372 | 405 | 439 | 481 | 523 |
| Property-casualty insurance companies | 2 | 3 | 4 | 6 | 8 | 10 | 13 | 15 | 18 | 20 |
| Life insurance companies | 236 | 286 | 319 | 347 | 366 | 388 | 431 | 465 | 507 | 568 |
| Private pension funds | 12 | 10 | 26 | 23 | 22 | 24 | 22 | 23 | 23 | 23 |
| State and local government retirement funds | 22 | 11 | 11 | 10 | 6 | 8 | 8 | 15 | 4 | 3 |
| Government-sponsored enterprises (GSE) | 264 | 589 | 5,021 | 4,824 | 4,878 | 4,870 | 4,920 | 5,027 | 5,194 | 5,332 |
| Agency- and GSE-backed mortgage pools | 2,493 | 3,548 | 1,147 | 1,443 | 1,574 | 1,649 | 1,775 | 1,933 | 2,127 | 2,293 |
| Asset-backed securities issuers | 604 | 2,163 | 1,963 | 1,506 | 1,201 | 1,094 | 1,016 | 895 | 846 | 852 |
| Finance companies | 238 | 541 | 244 | 179 | 157 | 148 | 159 | 138 | 124 | 115 |
| Real estate investment trusts | 18 | 147 | 45 | 64 | 215 | 247 | 218 | 228 | 235 | 254 |
| **HOME MORTGAGES [1]** | | | | | | | | | | |
| Total liabilities | 5,125 | 9,450 | 10,525 | 10,050 | 9,959 | 9,939 | 10,064 | 10,273 | 10,584 | 10,878 |
| Household sector | 4,817 | 8,941 | 9,994 | 9,564 | 9,481 | 9,455 | 9,567 | 9,760 | 10,054 | 10,331 |
| Nonfinancial corporate business | 14 | 31 | 14 | 10 | 10 | 11 | 13 | 15 | 16 | 17 |
| Nonfinancial noncorporate business | 294 | 477 | 518 | 476 | 469 | 472 | 484 | 498 | 514 | 530 |
| Total assets | 5,125 | 9,450 | 10,525 | 10,050 | 9,959 | 9,939 | 10,064 | 10,273 | 10,584 | 10,878 |
| Household sector | 87 | 118 | 124 | 118 | 112 | 102 | 91 | 80 | 70 | 59 |
| Nonfinancial corporate business | 21 | 41 | 17 | 15 | 16 | 17 | 19 | 19 | 33 | 48 |
| Nonfinancial noncorporate business | 9 | 13 | 15 | 12 | 13 | 13 | 15 | 14 | 16 | 17 |
| Federal government | 16 | 13 | 24 | 25 | 26 | 27 | 28 | 30 | 29 | 29 |
| State and local governments | 69 | 89 | 116 | 113 | 117 | 117 | 119 | 120 | 118 | 110 |
| U.S.-chartered depository institutions | 1,556 | 2,730 | 2,616 | 2,501 | 2,386 | 2,390 | 2,434 | 2,510 | 2,557 | 2,585 |
| Foreign banking offices in U.S | – | – | 1 | 2 | 1 | 3 | 2 | 1 | 1 | 1 |
| Banks in U.S.-affiliated areas | 9 | 16 | 20 | 20 | 19 | 17 | 16 | 15 | 15 | 14 |
| Credit unions | 120 | 226 | 317 | 328 | 346 | 372 | 405 | 439 | 481 | 523 |
| Life insurance companies | 7 | 7 | 9 | 11 | 12 | 15 | 19 | 23 | 25 | 31 |
| Private pension funds | 8 | 1 | 2 | 2 | 1 | 1 | 1 | 1 | 1 | 1 |
| State and local government retirement funds | 7 | 4 | 4 | 4 | 2 | 3 | 3 | 5 | 1 | 1 |
| Government-sponsored enterprises (GSE) | 210 | 454 | 4,691 | 4,476 | 4,546 | 4,538 | 4,571 | 4,645 | 4,775 | 4,882 |
| Agency- and GSE-backed mortgage pools | 2,426 | 3,446 | 1,075 | 1,327 | 1,424 | 1,475 | 1,569 | 1,685 | 1,826 | 1,949 |
| Asset-backed securities issuers | 385 | 1,671 | 1,315 | 938 | 793 | 700 | 603 | 518 | 475 | 467 |
| Finance companies | 187 | 490 | 170 | 133 | 115 | 105 | 123 | 107 | 95 | 87 |
| Real estate investment trusts | 8 | 128 | 9 | 26 | 31 | 44 | 46 | 60 | 65 | 73 |
| Memo: | | | | | | | | | | |
| Home equity loans included above [2] | 408 | 918 | 929 | 772 | 703 | 673 | 642 | 601 | 570 | 533 |
| U.S.-chartered depository institutions | 308 | 701 | 783 | 655 | 596 | 568 | 533 | 495 | 460 | 420 |
| Credit unions | 41 | 76 | 88 | 76 | 72 | 74 | 76 | 78 | 84 | 89 |
| Asset-backed securities issuers | 10 | 43 | 23 | 15 | 12 | 10 | 8 | 6 | 6 | 6 |
| Finance companies | 49 | 98 | 34 | 27 | 23 | 21 | 25 | 21 | 19 | 17 |

– Represents zero. [1] Mortgages on one- to four-family properties, including mortgages on farm houses. [2] Loans made under home equity lines of credit and home equity loans secured by junior liens. Excludes home equity loans held by individuals.

Source: Board of Governors of the Federal Reserve System, "Financial Accounts of the United States, Z.1," <https://www.federalreserve.gov/data.htm>, accessed July 2019.

# Table 1223. Mortgage Originations and Delinquency and Foreclosure Rates: 2000 to 2018

[In percent, except as indicated (1,139 represents $1,139,000,000,000). Covers one- to four-family residential nonfarm mortgage loans. Mortgage origination is the making of a new mortgage, including all steps taken by a lender to attract and qualify a borrower, process the mortgage loan, and place it on the lender's books. Based on the National Delinquency Survey, which covers 45 million loans on one- to four-unit properties, representing between 80 to 85 percent of all 'first-lien' residential mortgage loans outstanding. Loans surveyed were reported by approximately 120 lenders, including mortgage bankers, commercial banks, and thrifts]

| Item | 2000 | 2005 | 2010 | 2012 | 2013 | 2014 | 2015 | 2016 | 2017 | 2018 |
|---|---|---|---|---|---|---|---|---|---|---|
| MORTGAGE ORIGINATIONS | | | | | | | | | | |
| Total (bil. dol.) | 1,139 | 2,908 | 1,698 | 2,044 | 1,845 | 1,261 | 1,679 | 2,051 | 1,710 | 1,250 |
| Purchase (bil. dol.) | 905 | 1,512 | 530 | 588 | 734 | 759 | 903 | 1,052 | 1,110 | 873 |
| Refinance (bil. dol.) | 234 | 1,397 | 1,168 | 1,456 | 1,111 | 502 | 776 | 999 | 600 | 377 |
| DELINQUENCY RATES [1] | | | | | | | | | | |
| Total | 4.4 | 4.5 | 9.3 | 7.4 | 6.7 | 5.9 | 5.1 | 4.7 | 4.8 | 4.4 |
| Conventional loans [2] | (NA) | 3.6 | 8.8 | 6.6 | 5.9 | 5.1 | 4.4 | 3.9 | 3.9 | 3.5 |
| Prime conventional loans | 2.3 | 2.3 | 6.5 | 4.6 | 3.9 | 3.4 | 3.0 | 2.8 | (NA) | (NA) |
| Subprime conventional loans | 11.9 | 10.8 | 25.9 | 20.6 | 21.0 | 19.1 | 16.5 | 14.9 | (NA) | (NA) |
| Federal Housing Administration loans | 9.1 | 12.5 | 12.8 | 11.6 | 10.6 | 9.7 | 9.0 | 8.6 | 9.0 | 8.8 |
| Veterans Administration loans | 6.8 | 7.0 | 7.5 | 6.4 | 5.8 | 5.2 | 4.5 | 4.1 | 4.1 | 4.0 |
| FORECLOSURE RATES | | | | | | | | | | |
| Total loans in foreclosure process [3] | 1.2 | 1.0 | 4.6 | 4.1 | 3.2 | 2.5 | 2.0 | 1.6 | 1.3 | 1.0 |
| Conventional loans [2] | (NA) | 0.9 | 4.8 | 4.2 | 3.2 | 2.4 | 1.9 | 1.5 | 1.2 | 0.9 |
| Prime conventional loans | 0.4 | 0.4 | 3.5 | 3.0 | 2.2 | 1.5 | 1.2 | 0.9 | (NA) | (NA) |
| Subprime conventional loans | 9.4 | 3.3 | 14.5 | 13.0 | 11.1 | 9.8 | 8.3 | 7.2 | (NA) | (NA) |
| Federal Housing Administration loans | 1.7 | 2.3 | 3.5 | 4.0 | 3.6 | 2.8 | 2.6 | 2.2 | 1.8 | 1.7 |
| Veterans Administration loans | 1.2 | 1.1 | 2.4 | 2.3 | 5.8 | 1.5 | 1.4 | 1.2 | 1.0 | 0.9 |
| Loans entering foreclosure process [4] | 1.5 | 1.6 | 5.0 | 3.5 | 2.5 | 1.8 | 1.6 | 1.3 | 1.1 | 1.0 |
| Conventional loans [2] | (NA) | 1.5 | 5.1 | 3.4 | 2.3 | 1.6 | 1.4 | 1.1 | 0.9 | 0.8 |
| Prime conventional loans | 0.6 | 0.7 | 4.0 | 2.6 | 1.6 | 1.1 | 1.0 | 0.7 | (NA) | (NA) |
| Subprime conventional loans | 9.2 | 5.6 | 12.9 | 9.5 | 8.2 | 6.1 | 5.2 | 4.7 | (NA) | (NA) |
| Federal Housing Administration loans | 2.3 | 3.4 | 4.7 | 4.5 | 3.3 | 2.5 | 2.5 | 2.2 | 1.9 | 2.0 |
| Veterans Administration loans | 1.5 | 1.5 | 3.3 | 2.2 | 1.9 | 1.4 | 1.4 | 1.3 | 1.1 | 1.1 |

NA Not available. [1] Number of loans delinquent 30 days or more as a percent of mortgage loans serviced in survey. Annual average of quarterly figures, not seasonally adjusted. Delinquency rate does not include loans in the process of foreclosure. [2] Conventional loans include any non-government (FHA or VA) loans. The prime and subprime criteria used in the National Delinquency Survey are based on survey participants' reporting of what they consider to be their prime or subprime servicing portfolio, since internal servicing guidelines vary. Participants who service both prime and subprime loans report the results of each separately for maximum precision in the classification. [3] Percent of loans in the foreclosure process at year-end, not seasonally adjusted. [4] Percent of loans entering foreclosure process at year-end, not seasonally adjusted.

Source: Mortgage Bankers Association of America, Washington, DC, "MBA Mortgage Originations Estimates," and National Delinquency Survey, <http://www.mortgagebankers.org/>; and unpublished data ©.

# Table 1224. Delinquency Rates and Charge-Off Rates on Loans at Insured Commercial Banks: 2000 to 2018

[In percent. Annual averages of quarterly figures, not seasonally adjusted. Delinquent loans are those past due 30 days or more and still accruing interest as well as those in nonaccrual status. They are measured as a percentage of end-of-period loans. Charge-offs, which are the value of loans removed from the books and charged against loss reserves, are measured, net of recoveries, as a percentage of average loans and annualized. Includes only U.S.-chartered commercial banks]

| Type of loan | 2000 | 2005 | 2010 | 2013 | 2014 | 2015 | 2016 | 2017 | 2018 |
|---|---|---|---|---|---|---|---|---|---|
| DELINQUENCY RATES | | | | | | | | | |
| Total loans | 2.20 | 1.57 | 6.96 | 3.96 | 3.00 | 2.34 | 2.10 | 1.85 | 1.62 |
| Real estate | 1.87 | 1.37 | 9.69 | 6.44 | 4.83 | 3.62 | 2.80 | 2.31 | 1.97 |
| Residential [1,2] | 2.08 | 1.55 | 10.81 | 8.97 | 7.20 | 5.64 | 4.46 | 3.71 | 3.12 |
| Commercial [2,3] | 1.48 | 1.07 | 8.53 | 3.06 | 1.87 | 1.23 | 0.90 | 0.77 | 0.72 |
| Consumer | 3.55 | 2.81 | 4.15 | 2.45 | 2.22 | 2.00 | 2.07 | 2.23 | 2.29 |
| Credit cards | 4.51 | 3.70 | 4.90 | 2.50 | 2.23 | 2.14 | 2.26 | 2.48 | 2.52 |
| Other | 2.98 | 2.23 | 3.32 | 2.41 | 2.21 | 1.88 | 1.90 | 1.99 | 2.07 |
| Leases | 1.62 | 1.28 | 1.89 | 0.87 | 0.75 | 0.77 | 1.01 | 1.00 | 1.01 |
| Business | 2.30 | 1.51 | 3.46 | 1.00 | 0.80 | 0.87 | 1.57 | 1.34 | 1.03 |
| Agricultural production | 2.54 | 1.30 | 3.04 | 1.15 | 0.91 | 0.84 | 1.22 | 1.53 | 1.70 |
| Farmland [2] | 2.30 | 1.59 | 3.57 | 2.24 | 1.71 | 1.55 | 1.75 | 2.01 | 2.15 |
| CHARGE-OFF RATES | | | | | | | | | |
| Total loans | 0.66 | 0.54 | 2.66 | 0.69 | 0.49 | 0.42 | 0.46 | 0.47 | 0.46 |
| Real estate | 0.09 | 0.06 | 2.15 | 0.48 | 0.20 | 0.13 | 0.06 | 0.03 | 0.01 |
| Residential [1,2] | 0.12 | 0.08 | 2.11 | 0.65 | 0.29 | 0.21 | 0.10 | 0.04 | (-Z) |
| Commercial [2,3] | 0.05 | 0.05 | 2.34 | 0.26 | 0.07 | 0.04 | 0.01 | 0.02 | 0.01 |
| Consumer | 2.32 | 2.74 | 5.90 | 2.17 | 1.92 | 1.75 | 1.91 | 2.18 | 2.24 |
| Credit cards | 4.30 | 4.83 | 9.43 | 3.48 | 3.16 | 2.93 | 3.15 | 3.56 | 3.64 |
| Other | 1.13 | 1.38 | 2.05 | 0.86 | 0.77 | 0.68 | 0.78 | 0.90 | 0.88 |
| Leases | 0.31 | 0.58 | 0.72 | 0.15 | 0.08 | 0.18 | 0.24 | 0.17 | 0.17 |
| Business | 0.76 | 0.26 | 1.71 | 0.30 | 0.22 | 0.24 | 0.43 | 0.35 | 0.28 |
| Agricultural production | 0.27 | 0.07 | 0.77 | 0.05 | 0.04 | 0.05 | 0.21 | 0.21 | 0.23 |
| Farmland [2] | 0.04 | 0.04 | 0.43 | 0.07 | 0.04 | 0.01 | 0.03 | 0.05 | 0.04 |

Z Represents less than .005%. [1] Residential real estate loans include loans secured by one- to four-family properties, including home equity lines of credit. [2] Booked in domestic offices only. [3] Commercial real estate loans include construction and land development loans, loans secured by multifamily residences, and loans secured by nonfarm, nonresidential real estate, only.

Source: Board of Governors of the Federal Reserve, Data Releases, Bank Assets and Liabilities, "Charge-Off and Delinquency Rates on Loans and Leases at Commercial Banks," <http://www.federalreserve.gov/releases/chargeoff/>, accessed February 2019.

## Table 1225. Money Stock: 2000 to 2018

[In billions of dollars (1,089 represents $1,089,000,000,000). As of December. Seasonally adjusted averages of daily figures]

| Item | 2000 | 2005 | 2010 | 2012 | 2013 | 2014 | 2015 | 2016 | 2017 | 2018 |
|---|---|---|---|---|---|---|---|---|---|---|
| **M1, total** | **1,089** | **1,375** | **1,838** | **2,461** | **2,664** | **2,940** | **3,095** | **3,342** | **3,599** | **3,781** |
| Currency [1] | 531 | 725 | 919 | 1,091 | 1,161 | 1,253 | 1,340 | 1,421 | 1,526 | 1,626 |
| Travelers' checks [2] | 8.3 | 7.2 | 4.7 | 3.8 | 3.5 | 2.9 | 2.5 | 2.2 | 1.9 | 1.7 |
| Demand deposits [3] | 310 | 325 | 518 | 927 | 1,034 | 1,200 | 1,239 | 1,372 | 1,478 | 1,522 |
| Other checkable deposits [4] | 239 | 319 | 396 | 439 | 466 | 484 | 514 | 546 | 593 | 632 |
| **M2, total** | **4,914** | **6,667** | **8,789** | **10,446** | **11,016** | **11,671** | **12,338** | **13,210** | **13,837** | **14,455** |
| M1 | 1,089 | 1,375 | 1,838 | 2,461 | 2,664 | 2,940 | 3,095 | 3,342 | 3,599 | 3,781 |
| Non-M1 components of M2 | 3,826 | 5,292 | 6,952 | 7,985 | 8,352 | 8,731 | 9,243 | 9,869 | 10,238 | 10,674 |
| Retail money funds | 900 | 697 | 687 | 655 | 652 | 631 | 654 | 692 | 705 | 832 |
| Savings deposits (including money market deposit accounts) | 1,880 | 3,601 | 5,331 | 6,684 | 7,130 | 7,577 | 8,178 | 8,826 | 9,123 | 9,284 |
| Commercial banks | 1,425 | 2,777 | 4,412 | 5,728 | 6,110 | 6,500 | 7,034 | 7,566 | 7,824 | 7,942 |
| Thrift institutions | 454 | 825 | 919 | 956 | 1,020 | 1,078 | 1,145 | 1,260 | 1,299 | 1,342 |
| Small time deposits [5] | 1,046 | 994 | 935 | 646 | 570 | 522 | 411 | 350 | 410 | 558 |
| Commercial banks | 701 | 647 | 664 | 469 | 426 | 390 | 301 | 250 | 300 | 440 |
| Thrift institutions | 345 | 347 | 271 | 177 | 144 | 132 | 110 | 101 | 110 | 118 |

[1] Currency outside U.S. Treasury, Federal Reserve Banks and the vaults of depository institutions. [2] Outstanding amount of U.S. dollar-denominated travelers' checks of nonbank issuers. Travelers' checks issued by depository institutions are included in demand deposits. [3] Demand deposits at domestically chartered commercial banks, U.S. branches and agencies of foreign banks, and Edge Act corporations (excluding those amounts held by depository institutions, the U.S. government, and foreign banks and official institutions) less cash items in the process of collection and Federal Reserve float. [4] Negotiable order of withdrawal (NOW) and automatic transfer service (ATS) balances at domestically chartered commercial banks, U.S. branches and agencies of foreign banks, Edge Act corporations, and thrift institutions, credit union share draft balances, and demand deposits at thrift institutions. [5] Small-denomination time deposits are those issued in amounts of less than $100,000. All Individual Retirement Account (IRA) and Keogh account balances at commercial banks and thrift institutions are subtracted from small time deposits.

Source: Board of Governors of the Federal Reserve System, Data Releases, Money Stock and Reserve Balances, "Money Stock Measures – H.6," weekly releases, <http://www.federalreserve.gov/releases/h6/>, accessed January 2019.

## Table 1226. Volume of Debt Markets by Type of Security: 2000 to 2018

[In billions of dollars (2,552 represents $2,552,000,000,000). Covers debt markets as represented by the source]

| Type of security | 2000 | 2005 | 2010 | 2014 | 2015 | 2016 | 2017 | 2018 |
|---|---|---|---|---|---|---|---|---|
| **NEW ISSUE VOLUME [1]** | | | | | | | | |
| **Total** | **2,552** | **5,776** | **7,309** | **6,385** | **6,802** | **7,440** | **7,541** | **7,426** |
| Municipal | 198 | 407 | 433 | 339 | 405 | 446 | 448 | 338 |
| U.S. Treasury securities [2] | 312 | 746 | 2,320 | 2,215 | 2,122 | 2,169 | 2,224 | 2,685 |
| Federal agency debt [3] | 447 | 635 | 1,362 | 559 | 645 | 928 | 731 | 649 |
| Mortgage-backed securities [4] | 780 | 2,764 | 2,013 | 1,440 | 1,801 | 2,044 | 1,935 | 1,899 |
| Asset-backed securities [5] | 240 | 474 | 126 | 393 | 333 | 325 | 550 | 517 |
| Corporate debt [6] | 575 | 750 | 1,055 | 1,438 | 1,495 | 1,528 | 1,652 | 1,338 |
| **AVERAGE DAILY TRADING VOLUME** | | | | | | | | |
| **Total** | **357.6** | **918.6** | **893.7** | **729.2** | **728.8** | **775.5** | **763.7** | **817.0** |
| Municipal | 8.8 | 16.9 | 13.3 | 9.9 | 8.6 | 10.6 | 10.8 | 11.6 |
| U.S. Treasury securities [2] | 206.5 | 554.5 | 528.2 | 504.2 | 490.1 | 519.1 | 505.2 | 547.8 |
| Federal agency debt [3,7] | 72.8 | 78.8 | 11.2 | 5.3 | 4.5 | 5.4 | 4.1 | 3.4 |
| Mortgage-backed securities [4,7] | 69.5 | 251.8 | 320.6 | 178.0 | 193.0 | 206.6 | 209.1 | 219.0 |
| Non-agency mortgaged-back securities [8] | (NA) | (NA) | (NA) | 3.7 | 3.1 | 2.9 | 2.5 | 2.5 |
| Corporate [6] | (NA) | 16.6 | 20.5 | 26.7 | 27.9 | 29.6 | 30.6 | 31.2 |
| Asset-backed securities [5] | (NA) | (NA) | (NA) | 1.5 | 1.4 | 1.3 | 1.4 | 1.4 |
| **VOLUME OF SECURITIES OUTSTANDING** | | | | | | | | |
| **Total** | **16,191** | **24,621** | **34,073** | **37,296** | **38,303** | **39,603** | **40,804** | **42,685** |
| Municipal [9] | 1,489 | 3,027 | 4,123 | 3,592 | 3,607 | 3,722 | 3,658 | 3,675 |
| U.S. Treasury securities [2] | 2,952 | 4,170 | 8,853 | 12,505 | 13,192 | 13,908 | 14,469 | 15,608 |
| Federal agency debt [3] | 1,854 | 2,616 | 2,539 | 2,029 | 1,995 | 1,972 | 1,935 | 1,842 |
| Mortgage-backed securities [4] | 4,119 | 7,218 | 9,258 | 8,842 | 8,895 | 9,023 | 9,305 | 9,732 |
| Asset-backed securities [5] | 702 | 1,281 | 1,508 | 1,349 | 1,377 | 1,392 | 1,458 | 1,616 |
| Money market instruments [10] | 1,614 | 1,644 | 1,058 | 930 | 941 | 885 | 966 | 996 |
| Corporate debt [11] | 3,461 | 4,665 | 6,734 | 8,048 | 8,296 | 8,701 | 9,015 | 9,216 |

NA Not available. [1] Covers only long-term issuance. [2] Marketable public debt. [3] Beginning with 2004, Sallie Mae (Student Loan Marketing Association) has been excluded due to privatization. [4] Includes Government National Mortgage Association (GNMA), Federal National Mortgage Association (FNMA), and Federal Home Loan Mortgage Corporation (FHLMC) mortgage-backed securities (MBS), and collateralized mortgage obligations (CMOs), and CMBS, and private-label MBS/CMOs. [5] Excludes mortgage-backed assets. Includes auto, credit card, home equity loans, manufacturing, student loan and other. Collateralized debt obligations are included. [6] Includes nonconvertible corporate debt, Yankee bonds, and MTNs (Medium-Term Notes), but excludes federal agency debt and certificates of deposit. [7] Primary dealer trading volume through March 2010 for federal agency debt and through May 2011 for mortgage-backed securities. After those dates, data from FINRA Trace. [8] Includes mortgage securities issued by private institutions, such as subsidiaries of investment banks, banks, financial institutions, non-bank mortgage lenders, and home builders. [9] Due to the change in underlying sourcing from the Federal Reserve, municipal securities outstanding has been restated from 2004 onward and revised upward by about $840 billion. [10] Commercial paper, bankers acceptances, and large time deposits. [11] Debt obligations of U.S. financial and nonfinancial corporations including bonds, notes, debentures, mandatory convertible securities, long-term debt, private mortgage-backed securities, and unsecured debt. Includes bonds issued both in the United States and in foreign countries, but not bonds issued in foreign countries by foreign subsidiaries of U.S. corporations. Recorded at book value.

Source: The Securities Industry and Financial Markets Association, New York, NY ©. Based on data supplied by Bloomberg, Dealogic, Thomson Reuters Eikon, Thomson Reuters SDC, U.S. Treasury, Fannie Mae (FNMA), Freddie Mac (FHLMC), Ginnie Mae (GNMA), Farmer Mac, Farm Credit, FHLB, Federal Reserve Bank of New York, Municipal Securities Rulemaking Board, and FINRA Trace (Financial Industry Regulatory Authority Trade Reporting and Compliance Engine). See also <https://www.sifma.org/>.

## Table 1227. Bond Yields: 2000 to 2018

[Percent per year. Annual averages of daily figures]

| Type | 2000 | 2005 | 2010 | 2012 | 2013 | 2014 | 2015 | 2016 | 2017 | 2018 |
|---|---|---|---|---|---|---|---|---|---|---|
| U.S. Treasury, constant maturities: [1] | | | | | | | | | | |
| 1-year | 6.11 | 3.62 | 0.32 | 0.17 | 0.13 | 0.12 | 0.32 | 0.61 | 1.20 | 2.33 |
| 2-year | 6.26 | 3.85 | 0.70 | 0.28 | 0.31 | 0.46 | 0.69 | 0.83 | 1.40 | 2.53 |
| 3-year | 6.22 | 3.93 | 1.11 | 0.38 | 0.54 | 0.90 | 1.02 | 1.00 | 1.58 | 2.63 |
| 5-year | 6.16 | 4.05 | 1.93 | 0.76 | 1.17 | 1.64 | 1.53 | 1.33 | 1.91 | 2.75 |
| 7-year | 6.20 | 4.15 | 2.62 | 1.22 | 1.74 | 2.14 | 1.89 | 1.63 | 2.16 | 2.85 |
| 10-year | 6.03 | 4.29 | 3.22 | 1.80 | 2.35 | 2.54 | 2.14 | 1.84 | 2.33 | 2.91 |
| 20-year | 6.23 | 4.64 | 4.03 | 2.54 | 3.12 | 3.07 | 2.55 | 2.22 | 2.65 | 3.02 |
| High-grade municipal bonds (Standard & Poor's) [2] | 5.77 | 4.29 | 4.16 | 3.14 | 3.96 | 3.78 | 3.48 | 3.07 | 3.36 | 3.53 |

[1] Yields on actively traded non-inflation-indexed issues adjusted to constant maturities. Yields are based on closing indicative prices quoted by secondary market participants. [2] Source: U.S. Council of Economic Advisors, *Economic Indicators*, monthly, <https://www.gpo.gov/fdsys/browse/collection.action?collectionCode=ECONI>, accessed March 2019.

Source: Except as noted, Board of Governors of the Federal Reserve System, "H15, Selected Interest Rates," <https://www.federalreserve.gov/releases/h15/>, accessed March 2019.

## Table 1228. Securities Industry—Financial Summary: 2000 to 2016

[In billions of dollars, except as indicated (349.5 represents $349,500,000,000). Minus sign (-) indicates loss]

| Type | 2000 | 2005 | 2010 | 2011 | 2012 | 2013 | 2014 | 2015 | 2016 |
|---|---|---|---|---|---|---|---|---|---|
| Number of firms | 7,258 | 6,016 | 4,907 | 4,708 | 4,761 | 4,555 | 4,380 | 4,247 | 4,135 |
| **Revenues, total** | **349.5** | **332.5** | **262.0** | **245.8** | **264.4** | **272.5** | **279.4** | **275.7** | **278.7** |
| Commissions | 54.1 | 46.8 | 47.0 | 47.7 | 40.6 | 40.1 | 39.5 | 37.3 | 34.3 |
| Trading/investment gains | 70.8 | 30.7 | 31.2 | 10.2 | 26.9 | 21.2 | 21.6 | 16.4 | 21.8 |
| Underwriting profits | 18.7 | 19.9 | 24.4 | 22.9 | 27.9 | 32.0 | 33.5 | 30.7 | 26.9 |
| Margin interest | 24.5 | 13.3 | 5.0 | 6.2 | 7.2 | 7.1 | 8.2 | 8.4 | 8.9 |
| Mutual fund sales | 19.4 | 20.7 | 18.8 | 19.4 | 20.1 | 21.6 | 22.8 | 22.1 | 20.4 |
| Other | 161.9 | 201.2 | 135.5 | 139.3 | 141.7 | 150.4 | 153.9 | 160.7 | 166.5 |
| **Expenses, total** | **310.4** | **311.3** | **224.0** | **228.9** | **229.9** | **243.8** | **253.9** | **250.9** | **251.2** |
| Interest expense | 131.9 | 140.2 | 22.4 | 20.3 | 20.6 | 16.6 | 15.9 | 16.1 | 23.7 |
| Compensation | 95.2 | 88.8 | 102.1 | 102.4 | 104.7 | 110.0 | 114.5 | 115.8 | 113.9 |
| Commissions/clearance paid | 15.5 | 18.6 | 24.0 | 25.4 | 24.2 | 25.1 | 25.7 | 25.1 | 23.1 |
| Other | 67.8 | 63.6 | 75.5 | 80.8 | 80.4 | 92.2 | 97.7 | 93.8 | 90.5 |
| **Net income, pretax** | **39.1** | **21.2** | **38.0** | **16.8** | **34.6** | **28.6** | **25.6** | **24.8** | **27.5** |
| Pre-tax profit margin (percent) | 11.2 | 6.4 | 14.5 | 6.9 | 13.1 | 10.5 | 9.2 | 9.0 | 9.9 |
| Pre-tax return on equity (percent) | 31.1 | 13.1 | 17.1 | 7.5 | 14.7 | 12.0 | 10.5 | 10.2 | 11.3 |
| Assets | 2,866 | 5,215 | 4,757 | 4,662 | 4,892 | 4,591 | 4,440 | 4,051 | 3,906 |
| Liabilities | 2,728 | 5,051 | 4,526 | 4,444 | 4,658 | 4,348 | 4,197 | 3,806 | 3,665 |
| Ownership equity | 138 | 164 | 231 | 218 | 234 | 243 | 243 | 245 | 241 |

Source: U.S. Securities and Exchange Commission, "Select Market Data Fiscal 2017," and earlier reports, <https://www.sec.gov/reports>, accessed September 2018.

## Table 1229. Total Returns of Stocks, Bonds, and Treasury Bills: 1980 to 2018

[Average annual percent change. Stock return data are based on the Standard & Poor's 500 index. Minus sign (-) indicates loss]

| Period | Stocks | | | | Treasury bills, total return | Bonds (10-year), total return |
|---|---|---|---|---|---|---|
| | Total return before inflation | Capital gains | Dividends and reinvestment | Total return after inflation | | |
| 1980 to 1989 | 17.55 | 12.59 | 4.40 | 11.85 | 9.13 | 13.01 |
| 1990 to 1999 | 18.21 | 15.31 | 2.51 | 14.85 | 4.95 | 8.02 |
| 2000 to 2009 | -0.45 | -2.73 | 2.27 | -3.39 | 2.74 | 6.63 |
| 2001 | -11.89 | -13.04 | 1.32 | -13.68 | 3.32 | 5.53 |
| 2002 | -22.10 | -23.37 | 1.65 | -23.91 | 1.61 | 15.37 |
| 2003 | 28.68 | 26.38 | 1.82 | 26.31 | 1.03 | 0.46 |
| 2004 | 10.88 | 8.99 | 1.73 | 7.38 | 1.43 | 4.61 |
| 2005 | 4.91 | 3.00 | 1.85 | 1.45 | 3.30 | 3.09 |
| 2006 | 15.80 | 13.62 | 1.91 | 11.97 | 4.97 | 2.21 |
| 2007 | 5.49 | 3.53 | 1.89 | 1.35 | 4.52 | 10.54 |
| 2008 | -37.00 | -38.49 | 1.88 | -37.10 | 1.24 | 20.23 |
| 2009 | 26.25 | 23.45 | 2.44 | 23.11 | 0.15 | -9.50 |
| 2010 | 15.06 | 12.78 | 2.02 | 13.36 | 0.03 | 7.26 |
| 2011 | 2.96 | 0.00 | 2.96 | 0.83 | 0.06 | 16.89 |
| 2012 | 16.00 | 13.41 | 2.29 | 14.02 | 0.08 | 2.77 |
| 2013 | 32.39 | 29.60 | 2.15 | 30.43 | 0.05 | -8.56 |
| 2014 | 13.69 | 11.39 | 2.06 | 12.83 | 0.03 | 10.74 |
| 2015 | 1.32 | -0.73 | 2.05 | 0.58 | 0.06 | 11.27 |
| 2016 | 11.96 | 9.53 | 2.22 | 9.68 | 0.33 | -5.40 |
| 2017 | 21.83 | 19.41 | 2.03 | 19.30 | 0.95 | 2.81 |
| 2018 | -4.38 | -6.24 | 1.98 | -6.37 | 2.00 | 0.34 |

Source: Global Financial Data, Los Angeles, CA, "GFD Guide to Total Returns," <www.globalfinancialdata.com> and unpublished data ©.

## Table 1230. New Security Issues of Corporations by Type of Offering: 2010 to 2018

[In billions of dollars (1,025 represents $1,025,000,000,000). Represents gross proceeds of issues maturing in more than one year. Figures are the principal amount or the number of units multiplied by the offering price. Excludes secondary offerings, employee stock plans, investment companies other than closed-end, intracorporate transactions, Yankee bonds, and private placements listed. Stock data include ownership securities issued by limited partnerships]

| Type of offering | 2010 | 2015 | 2017 | 2018 | Type of offering | 2010 | 2015 | 2017 | 2018 |
|---|---|---|---|---|---|---|---|---|---|
| **Total** [1] | **1,025** | **1,664** | **1,844** | **1,549** | Nonfinancial............ | 498 | 888 | 912 | 651 |
| | | | | | Financial............... | 396 | 723 | 896 | 876 |
| Bonds, total................ | 894 | 1,611 | 1,808 | 1,526 | Stocks, total [2]......... | 131 | 174 | 144 | 131 |
| Sold in the U.S.............. | 880 | 1,511 | 1,715 | 1,489 | Nonfinancial.......... | 61 | 111 | 89 | 88 |
| Sold abroad................. | 14 | 100 | 93 | 38 | Financial............... | 70 | 63 | 55 | 44 |

[1] Total reflects the sum of the gross issuance of bonds and the gross proceeds of stocks in the domestic market. [2] Gross proceeds of stocks in all markets.

Source: Board of Governors of the Federal Reserve System, "New Security Issues, U.S. Corporations," <https://www.federalreserve.gov/data/corpsecure/current.htm>, April 2019.

## Table 1231. Equities, Corporate Bonds, and Municipal and Treasury Securities—Holdings and Net Purchases by Type of Investor: 2000 to 2018

[In billions of dollars (18,261 represents $18,261,000,000,000). Holdings as of December 31. Minus sign (-) indicates net sales]

| Type of investor | Holdings | | | | | Net purchases | | | | |
|---|---|---|---|---|---|---|---|---|---|---|
| | 2000 | 2010 | 2015 | 2017 | 2018 | 2000 | 2010 | 2015 | 2017 | 2018 |
| **EQUITIES** [1] | | | | | | | | | | |
| **Total** [2]................ | **18,261** | **24,074** | **36,661** | **47,557** | **42,810** | **5.6** | **23.2** | **-122.4** | **237.8** | **-197.3** |
| Household sector [3].......... | 7,119 | 8,517 | 13,128 | 17,544 | 15,565 | -401.3 | -230.0 | -133.8 | 184.7 | -76.4 |
| State and local governments........ | 97 | 132 | 210 | 275 | 249 | 6.0 | 2.0 | 1.7 | -1.7 | -6.3 |
| Property-casualty insurance companies........ | 195 | 224 | 334 | 411 | 391 | 1.1 | -5.2 | -1.5 | 9.8 | 20.1 |
| Life insurance companies................ | 338 | 408 | 546 | 623 | 542 | -5.6 | 43.3 | 27.0 | -5.9 | -40.2 |
| Private pension funds.......... | 1,823 | 1,778 | 2,220 | 2,682 | 2,361 | 64.4 | 38.7 | -29.3 | -81.6 | -71.4 |
| Federal government retirement funds. .. | 57 | 145 | 240 | 324 | 303 | 5.2 | 6.1 | – | 6.4 | -10.5 |
| State and local government retirement funds.......... | 1,299 | 1,723 | 2,250 | 2,677 | 2,459 | 11.6 | -67.4 | 22.6 | -89.6 | -51.5 |
| Mutual funds................. | 3,911 | 5,873 | 8,625 | 10,820 | 9,657 | 233.3 | 69.0 | 58.1 | -133.6 | -124.2 |
| Exchange-traded funds.......... | 66 | 753 | 1,710 | 2,776 | 2,669 | 42.4 | 80.1 | 173.5 | 347.3 | 210.4 |
| Brokers and dealers.......... | 77 | 117 | 167 | 183 | 148 | 9.6 | -18.5 | -10.3 | -21.3 | -10.9 |
| Rest of the world [4]......... | 1,483 | 3,213 | 5,501 | 7,031 | 6,479 | 197.1 | 129.6 | -191.4 | 125.2 | 34.8 |
| **CORPORATE & FOREIGN BONDS** | | | | | | | | | | |
| **Total** [2]................ | **4,770** | **11,115** | **11,855** | **13,127** | **12,816** | **358.5** | **-20.7** | **295.2** | **585.5** | **281.5** |
| Household sector [3].......... | 463 | 2,026 | 1,283 | 1,058 | 1,158 | 108.8 | -210.5 | -204.8 | -49.7 | -44.0 |
| U.S.-chartered depository institutions.... | 312 | 551 | 507 | 493 | 452 | 46.9 | -98.2 | -12.0 | -16.1 | -37.7 |
| Foreign banking offices in U.S............ | 55 | 238 | 173 | 160 | 151 | 7.6 | -9.4 | -10.8 | -0.5 | 0.7 |
| Property-casualty insurance companies........ | 192 | 348 | 452 | 482 | 532 | 7.4 | 24.3 | 19.2 | 12.2 | 54.3 |
| Life insurance companies................ | 1,189 | 2,074 | 2,429 | 2,735 | 2,709 | 54.2 | 85.8 | 92.4 | 73.6 | 121.6 |
| Private pension funds.......... | 263 | 446 | 691 | 745 | 724 | -76.9 | 27.6 | 5.8 | 27.8 | 26.1 |
| State and local government retirement funds.......... | 314 | 427 | 558 | 546 | 502 | 4.2 | 12.0 | 37.2 | 22.6 | 41.2 |
| Mutual funds................. | 361 | 1,224 | 1,737 | 2,038 | 2,017 | -39.2 | 211.5 | 55.8 | 139.4 | 115.2 |
| Exchange-traded funds.......... | – | 78 | 242 | 404 | 420 | – | 18.7 | 37.2 | 89.3 | 33.6 |
| Rest of the world [4]......... | 843 | 2,523 | 3,083 | 3,874 | 3,598 | 168.3 | -36.8 | 334.9 | 320.9 | -10.0 |
| **MUNICIPAL SECURITIES** [5] | | | | | | | | | | |
| **Total** [2]................ | **1,472** | **3,797** | **4,036** | **4,102** | **3,955** | **23.6** | **110.9** | **14.6** | **13.4** | **-59.8** |
| Household sector [3].......... | 475 | 1,912 | 1,885 | 1,870 | 1,842 | 16.9 | 74.1 | -41.2 | -39.3 | -8.6 |
| U.S.-chartered depository institutions.... | 117 | 255 | 508 | 573 | 499 | 3.4 | 30.3 | 45.4 | 21.1 | -40.9 |
| Property-casualty insurance companies........ | 189 | 370 | 358 | 339 | 294 | -13.8 | -24.0 | 10.2 | -9.9 | -35.4 |
| Money market mutual funds.............. | 242 | 388 | 236 | 134 | 143 | 32.5 | -53.1 | -28.8 | -19.9 | 8.4 |
| Mutual funds................. | 273 | 490 | 604 | 688 | 694 | -20.5 | 33.0 | 16.2 | 40.0 | 22.1 |
| **TREASURY SECURITIES** | | | | | | | | | | |
| **Total** [2]................ | **4,018** | **10,549** | **15,289** | **16,456** | **17,760** | **-274.0** | **1,645.3** | **724.4** | **447.0** | **1,411.2** |
| Household sector [3].......... | 536 | 1,093 | 1,074 | 1,212 | 1,940 | -207.7 | 295.6 | 322.3 | 12.5 | 652.2 |
| State and local governments............ | 317 | 636 | 680 | 690 | 660 | 6.4 | 18.7 | 22.9 | -27.1 | -30.3 |
| Monetary authority............ | 512 | 1,021 | 2,676 | 2,633 | 2,338 | 33.7 | 244.9 | -15.6 | -21.7 | -243.3 |
| U.S.-chartered depository institutions.... | 97 | 218 | 435 | 484 | 570 | -36.4 | 93.0 | 14.8 | -43.2 | 87.3 |
| Life insurance companies................ | 60 | 161 | 206 | 228 | 205 | -6.4 | 20.7 | 7.2 | -0.8 | -27.6 |
| Private pension funds.......... | 111 | 202 | 287 | 324 | 365 | -9.3 | 46.0 | -13.1 | 25.1 | 45.4 |
| Federal government retirement funds. .. | 739 | 1,277 | 1,715 | 1,730 | 2,039 | 22.9 | 77.2 | 91.6 | -84.3 | 309.3 |
| State and local governments retirement funds.......... | 179 | 154 | 175 | 277 | 349 | -19.8 | 3.4 | -22.2 | 59.6 | 45.7 |
| Money market mutual funds.............. | 94 | 342 | 486 | 703 | 873 | -13.2 | -72.4 | 53.4 | -94.7 | 170.6 |
| Mutual funds................. | 113 | 417 | 827 | 1,088 | 1,100 | 7.5 | 129.8 | 155.3 | 186.6 | 26.4 |
| Rest of the world [4]......... | 1,021 | 4,459 | 6,146 | 6,285 | 6,265 | -75.2 | 740.4 | 42.7 | 306.8 | 115.6 |

– Represents or rounds to zero. [1] Includes shares of exchange-traded funds, closed-end funds, and real estate investment trusts. Excludes mutual fund shares of open-end investment companies; see Table 1237. [2] Includes other types, not shown separately. [3] Includes nonprofit organizations. [4] Holdings and net purchases of U.S. issues by foreign residents. [5] Includes loans.

Source: Board of Governors of the Federal Reserve System, "Financial Accounts of the United States, Z.1," <https://www.federalreserve.gov/data.htm>, accessed July 2019.

## Table 1232. Foreign Securities Held by U.S. Residents: 2010 to 2017

[In billions of dollars (6,763 represents $6,763,000,000,000). Estimates for end of calendar year. See also Table 1312]

| Country | Total | | | Equities | | | Long-term and short-term debt | | |
|---|---|---|---|---|---|---|---|---|---|
| | 2010 | 2015 | 2017 | 2010 | 2015 | 2017 | 2010 | 2015 | 2017 |
| **Total holdings [1]** | **6,763** | **9,455** | **12,409** | **4,647** | **6,756** | **9,118** | **2,116** | **2,699** | **3,291** |
| Australia | 323 | 296 | 355 | 150 | 139 | 197 | 174 | 157 | 158 |
| Belgium | 35 | 68 | 72 | 29 | 56 | 56 | 7 | 12 | 17 |
| Bermuda | 160 | 217 | 263 | 134 | 187 | 229 | 25 | 30 | 34 |
| Brazil | 235 | 116 | 182 | 194 | 66 | 148 | 41 | 50 | 34 |
| Canada | 695 | 705 | 996 | 409 | 325 | 512 | 287 | 380 | 484 |
| Cayman Islands | 366 | 1,217 | 1,767 | 166 | 915 | 1,362 | 200 | 302 | 405 |
| China [2] | 102 | 108 | 162 | 101 | 103 | 158 | 2 | 5 | 4 |
| Curacao [3] | (NA) | 70 | 73 | (NA) | 67 | 70 | (NA) | 3 | 3 |
| France | 366 | 474 | 605 | 244 | 327 | 442 | 122 | 146 | 163 |
| Germany | 299 | 378 | 494 | 207 | 283 | 400 | 92 | 95 | 94 |
| Hong Kong | 135 | 136 | 164 | 133 | 129 | 155 | 2 | 7 | 8 |
| India | 91 | 130 | 194 | 86 | 120 | 181 | 5 | 10 | 14 |
| Ireland | 132 | 498 | 495 | 101 | 422 | 421 | 31 | 77 | 74 |
| Israel | 64 | 80 | 66 | 45 | 63 | 49 | 19 | 17 | 17 |
| Italy | 66 | 107 | 140 | 51 | 73 | 97 | 14 | 34 | 43 |
| Japan | 519 | 822 | 1,132 | 450 | 690 | 902 | 69 | 131 | 230 |
| Jersey | 42 | 92 | 123 | 21 | 80 | 108 | 21 | 12 | 16 |
| Korea, South | 148 | 171 | 263 | 122 | 139 | 242 | 26 | 32 | 21 |
| Luxembourg | 100 | 128 | 146 | 33 | 41 | 72 | 68 | 87 | 73 |
| Mexico | 109 | 148 | 163 | 77 | 56 | 67 | 32 | 91 | 96 |
| Netherlands | 233 | 404 | 538 | 120 | 250 | 345 | 112 | 154 | 193 |
| Norway | 56 | 58 | 71 | 23 | 22 | 36 | 33 | 36 | 36 |
| Russia | 62 | 40 | 69 | 56 | 32 | 56 | 7 | 8 | 13 |
| Singapore | 64 | 99 | 171 | 56 | 81 | 143 | 8 | 18 | 28 |
| South Africa | 78 | 63 | 115 | 70 | 54 | 101 | 8 | 9 | 14 |
| Spain | 87 | 115 | 158 | 66 | 90 | 125 | 22 | 25 | 33 |
| Sweden | 122 | 138 | 172 | 63 | 86 | 107 | 59 | 51 | 65 |
| Switzerland | 327 | 420 | 506 | 319 | 407 | 477 | 8 | 13 | 29 |
| Taiwan | 95 | 108 | 178 | 94 | 108 | 178 | (Z) | (Z) | (Z) |
| United Kingdom | 1,001 | 1,240 | 1,473 | 626 | 897 | 1,091 | 375 | 343 | 382 |

NA Not available. Z Less than $500 million. [1] Includes other countries, not shown separately. [2] Excludes Hong Kong, Macau, and Taiwan. [3] Separate reporting for Curacao began with the 2013 survey. In previous years, data were reported as part of Netherlands Antilles.

Source: U.S. Department of Treasury, "Securities (c): Annual Cross-U.S. Border Portfolio Holdings, PART B: U.S. Residents' Portfolio Holdings of Foreign Securities," <http://www.treasury.gov/resource-center/data-chart-center/tic/Pages/fpis.aspx#usclaims>, accessed February 2019.

## Table 1233. U.S. Securities Held by Foreign Residents: 2010 and 2018

[In billions of dollars (10,691 represents $10,691,000,000,000). Estimates as of June. Long-term securities include all forms of equity and all debt securities with an original term-to-maturity of over one year]

| Region and country | U.S. securities, total [1] | | U.S. equities [2] | | U.S Treasury long-term securities | | Long-term corporate debt | |
|---|---|---|---|---|---|---|---|---|
| | 2010 | 2018 | 2010 | 2018 | 2010 | 2018 | 2010 | 2018 |
| **Total [3]** | **10,691** | **19,400** | **2,814** | **8,139** | **3,343** | **5,467** | **2,493** | **3,790** |
| Australia | 118 | 303 | 74 | 223 | 14 | 31 | 22 | 35 |
| Belgium | 408 | 739 | 19 | 54 | 31 | 138 | 342 | 512 |
| Bermuda | 249 | 317 | 44 | 102 | 42 | 43 | 91 | 123 |
| Brazil | 169 | 310 | 2 | 6 | 132 | 294 | 2 | 1 |
| British Virgin Islands | 85 | 175 | 42 | 114 | 4 | 25 | 22 | 22 |
| Canada | 424 | 1,210 | 298 | 928 | 29 | 87 | 80 | 171 |
| Cayman Islands | 743 | 1,757 | 290 | 1,038 | 36 | 86 | 303 | 487 |
| China, mainland [4] | 1,611 | 1,607 | 127 | 217 | 1,108 | 1,188 | 11 | 17 |
| Denmark | 49 | 123 | 26 | 87 | 5 | 16 | 14 | 19 |
| France | 194 | 329 | 115 | 166 | 15 | 76 | 52 | 64 |
| Germany | 195 | 456 | 57 | 239 | 46 | 64 | 65 | 142 |
| Hong Kong | 293 | 364 | 33 | 113 | 60 | 154 | 16 | 44 |
| India | 41 | 152 | 1 | 4 | 21 | 141 | 3 | 1 |
| Ireland | 356 | 1,149 | 77 | 393 | 27 | 247 | 130 | 328 |
| Israel | 37 | 92 | 13 | 55 | 8 | 26 | 3 | 6 |
| Italy | 41 | 90 | 13 | 33 | 21 | 38 | 3 | 15 |
| Japan | 1,393 | 2,044 | 224 | 543 | 737 | 970 | 130 | 208 |
| Korea, South | 122 | 316 | 13 | 125 | 34 | 94 | 9 | 36 |
| Kuwait | 80 | 269 | 45 | 185 | 13 | 39 | 7 | 17 |
| Luxembourg | 622 | 1,494 | 172 | 617 | 49 | 169 | 302 | 568 |
| Mexico | 84 | 117 | 17 | 58 | 31 | 33 | 12 | 3 |
| Netherlands | 247 | 413 | 152 | 280 | 22 | 41 | 57 | 70 |
| Norway | 136 | 370 | 90 | 277 | 14 | 49 | 25 | 43 |
| Saudi Arabia | 125 | 233 | 36 | 57 | 68 | 110 | 9 | 8 |
| Singapore | 176 | 353 | 91 | 180 | 47 | 116 | 28 | 41 |
| Sweden | 81 | 216 | 49 | 164 | 14 | 46 | 11 | 7 |
| Switzerland | 397 | 813 | 162 | 452 | 87 | 206 | 110 | 113 |
| Taiwan | 228 | 577 | 12 | 65 | 149 | 161 | 18 | 99 |
| United Arab Emirates | 86 | 156 | 44 | 89 | 17 | 49 | 8 | 7 |
| United Kingdom | 798 | 1,598 | 324 | 924 | 72 | 229 | 369 | 390 |

[1] Includes short-term debt and other long-term debt. [2] Includes common and preferred stock, all types of investment company shares (open-end funds, closed-end funds, money market mutual funds, and hedge funds), interests in limited partnerships, and other equity interests that may not involve stocks or shares. [3] Includes other countries not shown separately. [4] Excludes Hong Kong, Macau, and Taiwan.

Source: U.S. Department of Treasury, "Securities (c): Annual Cross-U.S. Border Portfolio Holdings, PART A: Foreign Residents' Portfolio Holdings of U.S. Securities," <http://www.treasury.gov/resource-center/data-chart-center/tic/Pages/fpis.aspx>, accessed May 2019.

# Table 1234. Stock Prices and Yields: 2000 to 2018

[Closing values as of end of December, except as noted]

| Index | 2000 | 2005 | 2010 | 2015 | 2016 | 2017 | 2018 |
|---|---|---|---|---|---|---|---|
| STOCK PRICES | | | | | | | |
| Standard & Poor's indices: [1] | | | | | | | |
| S&P 500 composite (1941–43 = 10)........... | 1,320 | 1,248 | 1,257 | 2,044 | 2,239 | 2,674 | 2,507 |
| S&P 400 MidCap Index (1982 = 100)........... | 517 | 738 | 907 | 1,399 | 1,661 | 1,901 | 1,663 |
| S&P 600 SmallCap Index (Dec. 31, 1993 = 100)........... | 220 | 351 | 416 | 672 | 838 | 936 | 845 |
| S&P 500 Citigroup Value Index (Dec. 31, 1974 = 35)........... | 636 | 648 | 590 | 876 | 1,001 | 1,127 | 1,000 |
| S&P 500 Citigroup Growth Index (Dec. 31, 1974 = 35)........... | 688 | 597 | 659 | 1,164 | 1,223 | 1,533 | 1,512 |
| Russell indices: [2] | | | | | | | |
| Russell 1000 (Dec. 31, 1986 = 130)........... | 700 | 679 | 697 | 1,132 | 1,242 | 1,482 | 1,384 |
| Russell 2000 (Dec. 31, 1986 = 135)........... | 484 | 673 | 784 | 1,136 | 1,357 | 1,536 | 1,349 |
| Russell 3000 (Dec. 31, 1986 = 140)........... | 726 | 723 | 749 | 1,206 | 1,332 | 1,583 | 1,472 |
| N.Y. Stock Exchange common stock index: | | | | | | | |
| Composite (Dec. 31, 2002 = 5000)........... | 6,946 | 7,754 | 7,964 | 10,143 | 11,057 | 12,809 | 11,374 |
| Yearly high........... | 7,165 | 7,868 | 7,983 | 11,255 | 11,688 | 12,886 | 11,378 |
| Yearly low........... | 6,095 | 6,903 | 6,356 | 9,510 | 8,938 | 12,809 | 11,272 |
| American Stock Exchange Composite Index | | | | | | | |
| (Dec. 29, 1995 = 550)........... | 898 | 1,759 | 2,208 | 2,149 | 2,308 | 2,662 | 2,292 |
| NASDAQ Composite Index (Feb. 5, 1971 = 100)........... | 2,471 | 2,205 | 2,653 | 5,007 | 5,383 | 6,903 | 6,635 |
| Nasdaq-100 (Jan. 31, 1985 = 125)........... | 2,342 | 1,645 | 2,218 | 4,593 | 4,864 | 6,396 | 6,330 |
| Industrial (Feb. 5, 1971 = 100)........... | 1,483 | 1,860 | 2,184 | 4,101 | 4,445 | 5,514 | 5,401 |
| Banks (Feb. 5, 1971 = 100)........... | 1,939 | 3,078 | 1,847 | 2,853 | 3,852 | 3,988 | 3,274 |
| Computers (Oct. 29, 1993 = 200)........... | 1,295 | 992 | 1,372 | 2,606 | 2,926 | 4,060 | 3,911 |
| Transportation (Feb. 5, 1971 = 100)........... | 1,160 | 2,438 | 2,562 | 3,334 | 4,063 | 5,075 | 4,605 |
| Telecommunications (Oct. 29, 1993 = 200)........... | 463 | 184 | 226 | 251 | 288 | 339 | 349 |
| Biotech (Oct. 29, 1993 = 200)........... | 1,085 | 790 | 970 | 3,540 | 2,773 | 3,357 | 3,044 |
| Dow Jones Averages: | | | | | | | |
| Composite (65 stocks)........... | 3,317 | 3,638 | 4,033 | 5,978 | 6,902 | 8,310 | 7,710 |
| Industrial (30 stocks)........... | 10,787 | 10,718 | 11,578 | 17,425 | 19,763 | 24,719 | 23,327 |
| Transportation (20 stocks)........... | 2,947 | 4,196 | 5,107 | 7,509 | 9,044 | 10,612 | 9,170 |
| Utility (15 stocks)........... | 412 | 405 | 405 | 578 | 660 | 723 | 713 |
| COMMON STOCK YIELDS (percent) | | | | | | | |
| Standard & Poor's Composite Index (500 stocks): [3] | | | | | | | |
| Dividend-price ratio [4]........... | 1.15 | 1.83 | 1.98 | 2.2 | 2.11 | 1.84 | 2.20 |
| Earnings-price ratio [5]........... | 3.63 | 5.36 | 6.04 | 4.64 | 3.89 | 3.89 | 4.60 |

[1] Standard & Poor's Indices are market-value weighted and are chosen for market size, liquidity, and industry group representation. The S&P 500 index represents 500 large publicly-traded companies. The S&P MidCap Index tracks mid-cap companies. The S&P SmallCap Index consists of 600 domestic small-cap stocks. [2] The Russell 1000 and 3000 indices show respectively the 1000 and 3000 largest capitalization stocks in the United States. The Russell 2000 index shows the 2000 largest capitalization stocks in the United States after the first 1000. [3] Source: U.S. Council of Economic Advisors, *Economic Indicators*, monthly. [4] Aggregate cash dividends (based on latest known annual rate) divided by aggregate market value based on Wednesday closing prices. Averages of monthly figures. [5] Averages of quarterly ratios which are ratio of earnings (after taxes) for 4 quarters ending with particular quarter- to-price index for last day of that quarter.

Source: Except as noted, Global Financial Data, Los Angeles, CA, <http://www.globalfinancialdata.com/> ©.

# Table 1235. Stock Ownership by Age of Head of Family and Family Income: 2010 to 2016

[Median value in thousands of constant (2016) dollars (32.1 represents $32,100). All dollar figures are adjusted to 2016 dollars using the "current methods" version of the consumer price index for all urban consumers published by U.S. Bureau of Labor Statistics. Families include one-person units; for definition of family, see text, Section 1. Based on Survey of Consumer Finance; see Appendix III. For definition of median, see Guide to Tabular Presentation]

| Age of family head and family income (constant (2016) dollars) | Families having direct or indirect stock holdings [1] (percent) | | | Median value among families with holdings | | | Stock holdings share of group's financial assets (percent) | | |
|---|---|---|---|---|---|---|---|---|---|
| | 2010 | 2013 | 2016 | 2010 | 2013 | 2016 | 2010 | 2013 | 2016 |
| All families........... | 49.9 | 48.8 | 51.9 | 32.1 | 37.1 | 40.0 | 47.0 | 51.7 | 53.4 |
| Under 35 years old........... | 39.8 | 38.6 | 41.1 | 7.7 | 7.3 | 7.8 | 39.3 | 46.5 | 40.2 |
| 35 to 44 years old........... | 50.1 | 53.9 | 55.7 | 21.9 | 24.2 | 21.9 | 50.5 | 53.7 | 50.0 |
| 45 to 54 years old........... | 58.0 | 54.9 | 57.4 | 41.8 | 45.4 | 50.8 | 48.6 | 56.2 | 55.0 |
| 55 to 64 years old........... | 59.7 | 57.2 | 57.5 | 61.9 | 61.1 | 80.0 | 48.3 | 51.6 | 56.0 |
| 65 to 74 years old........... | 45.6 | 49.2 | 50.4 | 85.0 | 121.1 | 94.5 | 44.2 | 49.2 | 50.2 |
| 75 years old and over........... | 42.0 | 34.5 | 48.9 | 60.8 | 82.7 | 100.0 | 44.6 | 50.3 | 54.2 |
| Percentiles of income: [2] | | | | | | | | | |
| Less than 20........... | 12.5 | 11.4 | 11.6 | 5.9 | 6.2 | 6.0 | 40.5 | 31.7 | 39.8 |
| 20 to 39.9........... | 30.5 | 26.4 | 32.5 | 7.8 | 10.7 | 10.0 | 31.3 | 33.2 | 33.1 |
| 40 to 59.9........... | 51.7 | 49.7 | 51.8 | 13.2 | 14.4 | 15.0 | 37.5 | 41.7 | 38.3 |
| 60 to 79.9........... | 68.1 | 69.5 | 73.6 | 24.6 | 28.9 | 32.4 | 41.6 | 43.9 | 45.3 |
| 80 to 89.9........... | 82.6 | 81.6 | 85.3 | 64.0 | 71.1 | 81.2 | 44.4 | 49.7 | 49.3 |
| 90 to 100........... | 90.6 | 93.0 | 94.7 | 295.7 | 290.4 | 363.4 | 50.9 | 56.1 | 57.9 |

[1] Indirect holdings are those in pooled investment trusts, retirement accounts and other managed assets. [2] See footnote 8, Table 1202.

Source: Board of Governors of the Federal Reserve System, 2016 Survey of Consumer Finances, *Changes in U.S. Family Finances From 2013 to 2016: Evidence from the Survey of Consumer Finances*, Federal Reserve Bulletin, Vol. 103, No. 3, September 2017. See also <http://www.federalreserve.gov/econres/scfindex.htm>.

## Table 1236. Transaction Activity in Equities, Options, and Security Futures, 2000 to 2016, and by Exchange, 2016

[In billions of dollars (36,275 represents $36,275,000,000,000). Market value of all sales of equities and options listed on an exchange or subject to last-sale reporting. Also reported are the value of such options that were exercised and the value of single-stock futures that were delivered. Excludes options and futures on indexes]

| Year and exchange | Market value of sales | | | Option exercises and futures deliveries |
|---|---|---|---|---|
| | Total | Equity trading | Option trading | |
| 2000. | 36,275 | 35,557 | 485 | 233 |
| 2004. | 27,876 | 27,158 | 223 | 495 |
| 2005. | 34,568 | 33,223 | 350 | 995 |
| 2006. | 43,941 | 41,798 | 531 | 1,611 |
| 2007. | 66,136 | 63,064 | 861 | 2,211 |
| 2008. | 82,012 | 78,653 | 1,096 | 2,264 |
| 2009. | 59,850 | 57,566 | 710 | 1,574 |
| 2010. | 64,008 | 61,146 | 725 | 2,137 |
| 2011. | 70,100 | 66,683 | 923 | 2,494 |
| 2012. | 59,371 | 55,620 | 938 | 2,813 |
| 2013. | 62,899 | 59,515 | 752 | 2,633 |
| 2014. | 69,979 | 66,354 | 762 | 2,863 |
| 2015. | 74,148 | 70,790 | 720 | 2,638 |
| **2016, total.** | **72,494** | **69,264** | **647** | **2,583** |
| BATS (Better Alternative Trading System) Exchange, Inc. | 5,067 | 4,743 | 65 | 260 |
| BATS Y-Exchange, Inc. | 2,522 | 2,522 | – | – |
| BOX Options Exchange LLC. | 79 | – | 16 | 63 |
| C2 Options Exchange, Inc. | 50 | – | 10 | 40 |
| Chicago Board Options Exchange, Inc. | 504 | – | 102 | 402 |
| The Chicago Stock Exchange, Inc. | 583 | 583 | – | – |
| EDGA Exchange, Inc. | 1,611 | 1,611 | – | – |
| EDGX Exchange, Inc. | 4,836 | 4,808 | 6 | 22 |
| FINRA, Inc. [1] | 23,783 | 23,783 | – | – |
| International Securities Exchange, LLC. | 453 | – | 91 | 362 |
| Investors' Exchange LLC. | 406 | 406 | – | – |
| ISE Mercury, LLC. | 4 | – | 1 | 3 |
| Miami International Securities Exchange, LLC. | – | – | – | – |
| Securities Exchange, LLC. | 172 | – | 34 | 138 |
| NASDAQ OMX BX. | 1,660 | 1,637 | 5 | 19 |
| NASDAQ OMX PHLX. | 1,342 | 719 | 125 | 498 |
| The Nasdaq Stock Market LLC. | 11,313 | 11,081 | 47 | 185 |
| National Stock Exchange. | 8 | 8 | – | – |
| New York Stock Exchange, Inc. | 8,621 | 8,621 | – | – |
| NYSE Amex LLC. | 345 | 36 | 63 | 246 |
| NYSE Arca, Inc. | 9,053 | 8,707 | 70 | 277 |
| OneChicago, LLC. | 19 | – | – | 19 |

– Represents or rounds to zero. [1] Financial Industry Regulatory Authority.

Source: U.S. Securities and Exchange Commission, "Select SEC and Market Data, Fiscal 2017," <http://www.sec.gov/about.shtml>, accessed September 2018.

## Table 1237. Mutual Fund Shares—Holdings and Net Purchases by Type of Investor: 2000 to 2018

[In billions of dollars (5,119.4 represents $5,119,400,000,000). Holdings as of Dec. 31. A mutual fund is an open-end investment company that continuously issues and redeems shares that represent an interest in a pool of financial assets. Excludes money market mutual funds and exchange-traded funds. Minus sign (-) indicates net sales]

| Type of investor | Holdings | | | | | Net purchases | | | | |
|---|---|---|---|---|---|---|---|---|---|---|
| | 2000 | 2010 | 2015 | 2017 | 2018 | 2000 | 2010 | 2015 | 2017 | 2018 |
| **Total.** | **5,119.4** | **9,029.8** | **12,897.2** | **15,899.0** | **14,669.8** | **295.2** | **395.9** | **98.9** | **318.8** | **-67.3** |
| Households, nonprofit organizations | 2,557.9 | 4,686.3 | 6,944.1 | 8,656.9 | 7,920.0 | 82.1 | 257.1 | 92.8 | 330.1 | -70.4 |
| Nonfinancial corporate business. | 118.0 | 185.7 | 248.2 | 303.1 | 271.0 | 0.3 | 7.5 | 12.3 | 7.6 | -9.9 |
| State and local governments. | 32.2 | 61.4 | 79.2 | 94.9 | 84.8 | 1.1 | 4.1 | 0.9 | -0.9 | -3.2 |
| U.S.-chartered depository institutions. | 15.0 | 45.0 | 53.0 | 64.8 | 52.1 | 2.5 | -5.8 | -0.9 | (Z) | -5.9 |
| Credit unions. | 2.3 | 1.5 | 1.9 | 2.3 | 2.5 | -0.7 | -0.3 | -0.1 | 0.1 | 0.3 |
| Property-casualty insurance companies. | 3.0 | 11.4 | 19.1 | 24.4 | 21.4 | 0.5 | -0.7 | 0.7 | 1.2 | -1.0 |
| Life insurance companies. | 632.8 | 1,117.4 | 1,397.4 | 1,572.3 | 1,398.7 | 57.6 | 28.2 | -30.8 | -75.9 | -91.3 |
| Private pension funds. | 1,246.1 | 2,220.2 | 3,088.1 | 3,845.4 | 3,567.5 | 106.9 | 55.4 | -8.6 | 25.3 | 2.4 |
| State and local government retirement funds. | 362.5 | 438.4 | 465.6 | 505.1 | 481.5 | 51.5 | -6.1 | 30.8 | -4.2 | 12.7 |
| Rest of the world. | 149.5 | 262.5 | 600.6 | 829.9 | 870.4 | -6.7 | 56.5 | 1.8 | 35.4 | 99.1 |

Z Less than $50 million.

Source: Board of Governors of the Federal Reserve System, "Financial Accounts of the United States, Z.1," <https://www.federalreserve.gov/data.htm>, accessed July 2019.

## Table 1238. Household Ownership of Mutual Funds by Age and Income: 2008 and 2018

[In percent. Ownership includes money market, stock, bond, and hybrid mutual funds, variable annuities, and mutual funds owned through Individual Retirement Accounts (IRAs), Keoghs, and employer-sponsored retirement plans. In 2018, an estimated 56,000,000 households own mutual funds. A mutual fund is an open-end investment company that continuously issues and redeems shares that represent an interest in a pool of financial assets]

| Age of household head [1] | Percent distribution of all households owning mutual funds, 2018 [3] | As a percent of all households within each group | | Household income [2] | Percent distribution of all households owning mutual funds, 2018 [3] | As a percent of all households within each group | |
|---|---|---|---|---|---|---|---|
| | | 2008 | 2018 [3] | | | 2008 | 2018 [3] |
| Total.......................... | 100 | 47 | 44 | Less than $25,000...... | 4 | 10 | 9 |
| Less than 35 years old...... | 17 | 38 | 36 | $25,000 to $34,999.... | 4 | 24 | 20 |
| 35 to 44 years old............ | 19 | 54 | 49 | $35,000 to $49,999.... | 8 | 41 | 29 |
| 45 to 54 years old............ | 22 | 58 | 54 | $50,000 to $74,999.... | 16 | 58 | 42 |
| 55 to 64 years old............ | 21 | 52 | 48 | $75,000 to $99,999.... | 17 | 75 | 59 |
| 65 years old and over........ | 21 | 35 | 37 | $100,000 and over..... | 51 | 83 | 76 |

[1] Age is based on the sole or co-decision maker for household saving and investing. [2] Total reported is household income before taxes in prior year. [3] Starting in 2014, the survey was revised to include a dual frame random digit dial (RDD) sample design of landline and cellular telephone numbers. See source for details.

Source: Holden, Sarah, Daniel Schrass, and Michael Bogdan. 2018. "Ownership of Mutual Funds, Shareholder Sentiment, and Use of the Internet, 2018." ICI Research Perspective 24, no. 8 (November). See also <www.ici.org/pdf/per24-08.pdf>.

## Table 1239. Characteristics of Mutual Fund Owners: 2018

[In percent, except as indicated. The 2018 data are based on responses from 2,196 households owning mutual funds. Interviews were conducted with the person most knowledgeable about the household's investments and savings. Prior to 2014, the annual mutual fund shareholder survey was conducted via landline telephones only; starting in 2014, the survey was expanded and is based on a dual frame sample of landline and cellular telephone numbers. Mutual fund ownership includes holdings of money market, stock, bond, and hybrid mutual funds; and funds owned through variable annuities, Individual Retirement Accounts (IRAs), Keoghs, and employer-sponsored retirement plans. A mutual fund is an open-end investment company that continuously issues and redeems shares that represent an interest in a pool of financial assets. For definition of median, see Guide to Tabular Presentation]

| Characteristic | Total | Age [1] | | | | Household income [2] | | | |
|---|---|---|---|---|---|---|---|---|---|
| | | Under 35 years | 35 to 54 years | 55 to 64 years | 65 years and over | Less than $50,000 | $50,000 to $99,000 | $100,000 to $149,000 | $150,000 or more |
| Median age [1] (years)........................ | 51 | 29 | 45 | 59 | 72 | 55 | 52 | 51 | 50 |
| Median household income [2] (dol.)............ | 100,000 | 87,500 | 103,700 | 100,200 | 80,000 | 34,900 | 75,000 | 120,000 | 200,000 |
| Median household financial assets [3] (dol.)... | 250,000 | 60,000 | 200,000 | 400,000 | 400,000 | 50,200 | 150,000 | 300,000 | 500,000 |
| Own an IRA............................................ | 61 | 49 | 59 | 65 | 69 | 55 | 55 | 64 | 68 |
| Household with defined contribution retirement plan(s) [4]............................ | 84 | 86 | 88 | 86 | 70 | 69 | 83 | 86 | 91 |
| 401(k) plan.......................................... | 73 | 78 | 80 | 78 | 50 | 55 | 68 | 78 | 84 |
| 403(b), state, local, or federal government plan.................................. | 33 | 28 | 33 | 34 | 34 | 29 | 34 | 31 | 36 |
| Median mutual fund assets (dol.).............. | 150,000 | 30,000 | 150,000 | 300,000 | 250,000 | 30,000 | 75,000 | 175,000 | 400,000 |
| Own: | | | | | | | | | |
| Equity funds....................................... | 88 | 86 | 89 | 88 | 87 | 76 | 85 | 89 | 95 |
| Bond funds......................................... | 44 | 35 | 46 | 45 | 47 | 30 | 36 | 49 | 56 |

[1] See Table 1238, footnote 1. [2] See Table 1238, footnote 2. [3] Includes assets in employer-sponsored retirement plans but excludes value of primary residence. [4] For definition of defined contribution plan, see headnote, Table 577.

Source: Schrass, Daniel, and Michael Bogdan. 2018. "Profile of Mutual Fund Shareholders, 2018." ICI Research Report (December) ©. Washington, DC: Investment Company Institute. See also <https://www.ici.org/pdf/rpt_18_profiles18.pdf>.

## Table 1240. Mutual Funds—Summary: 2000 to 2018

[6,956 represents $6,956,000,000,000. Number of funds and assets as of December 31. A mutual fund is an open-end investment company that continuously issues and redeems shares that represent an interest in a pool of financial assets. Excludes data for funds that invest in other mutual funds. Minus sign (-) indicates net redemptions]

| Type of fund | Unit | 2000 | 2005 | 2010 | 2013 | 2014 | 2015 | 2016 | 2017 | 2018 |
|---|---|---|---|---|---|---|---|---|---|---|
| **Number of funds, total.....................** | **Number** | **8,134** | **7,967** | **7,546** | **7,721** | **7,934** | **8,121** | **8,073** | **7,965** | **8,078** |
| Equity funds..................................... | Number | 4,359 | 4,566 | 4,508 | 4,538 | 4,647 | 4,762 | 4,751 | 4,706 | 4,753 |
| Hybrid funds.................................... | Number | 506 | 480 | 495 | 613 | 674 | 726 | 727 | 738 | 783 |
| Bond funds...................................... | Number | 2,232 | 2,052 | 1,891 | 2,015 | 2,086 | 2,152 | 2,174 | 2,139 | 2,174 |
| Money market funds, taxable [1]........... | Number | 703 | 592 | 442 | 382 | 364 | 336 | 319 | 299 | 287 |
| Money market funds, tax-exempt [2]......... | Number | 334 | 277 | 210 | 173 | 163 | 145 | 102 | 83 | 81 |
| **Net assets, total..............................** | **Bil. dol.** | **6,956** | **8,889** | **11,831** | **15,049** | **15,877** | **15,658** | **16,353** | **18,764** | **17,707** |
| Equity funds..................................... | Bil. dol. | 3,933 | 4,885 | 5,596 | 7,763 | 8,314 | 8,150 | 8,577 | 10,306 | 9,225 |
| Hybrid funds.................................... | Bil. dol. | 361 | 621 | 842 | 1,285 | 1,379 | 1,341 | 1,400 | 1,545 | 1,383 |
| Bond funds...................................... | Bil. dol. | 817 | 1,356 | 2,589 | 3,284 | 3,459 | 3,412 | 3,648 | 4,065 | 4,062 |
| Money market funds, taxable [1]........... | Bil. dol. | 1,611 | 1,690 | 2,474 | 2,447 | 2,464 | 2,500 | 2,598 | 2,716 | 2,892 |
| Money market funds, tax-exempt [2]......... | Bil. dol. | 234 | 336 | 330 | 271 | 261 | 255 | 130 | 131 | 145 |
| **Net new cash flow:..........................** | **Bil. dol.** | **390** | **254** | **-281** | **178** | **106** | **-98** | **-223** | **179** | **-191** |
| Equity funds..................................... | Bil. dol. | 315 | 124 | -24 | 159 | 25 | -76 | -258 | -159 | -261 |
| Hybrid funds.................................... | Bil. dol. | -37 | 43 | 36 | 75 | 30 | -19 | -42 | -28 | -91 |
| Bond funds...................................... | Bil. dol. | -48 | 25 | 232 | -71 | 44 | -25 | 107 | 260 | 2 |
| Money market funds........................... | Bil. dol. | 159 | 62 | -525 | 15 | 6 | 21 | -30 | 107 | 159 |

[1] Funds invest in short-term, high-grade securities sold in the money market. [2] Funds invest in municipal securities with relatively short maturities.

Source: Investment Company Institute. 2019. 2019 Investment Company Fact Book: A Review of Trends and Activities in the U.S. Investment Company Industry. © Washington, DC: Investment Company Institute. See also <www.icifactbook.org>.

## Table 1241. Retirement Assets by Type of Asset: 2000 to 2018

[In billions of dollars, except as indicated (11,556 represents $11,556,000,000,000). As of December 31]

| Item | 2000 | 2005 | 2010 | 2014 | 2015 | 2016 | 2017 | 2018 |
|---|---|---|---|---|---|---|---|---|
| **Retirement assets, total**.................... | **11,556** | **14,386** | **17,951** | **23,944** | **23,975** | **25,344** | **28,250** | **27,132** |
| IRA assets [1]................................. | 2,629 | 3,425 | 5,029 | 7,292 | 7,477 | 8,015 | 9,105 | 8,715 |
| Bank and thrift deposits [2]............... | 250 | 278 | 461 | 506 | 523 | 561 | 548 | 568 |
| Life insurance companies [3]............. | 202 | 301 | 311 | 378 | 394 | 410 | 431 | 441 |
| Mutual funds............................... | 1,263 | 1,781 | 2,420 | 3,526 | 3,495 | 3,710 | 4,282 | 3,989 |
| Other assets [1,4]......................... | 914 | 1,065 | 1,838 | 2,882 | 3,065 | 3,334 | 3,844 | 3,716 |
| Traditional [1]............................. | 2,407 | 3,034 | 4,340 | 6,225 | 6,387 | 6,824 | 7,742 | 7,392 |
| Roth [1].................................. | 78 | 156 | 355 | 600 | 625 | 697 | 820 | 810 |
| SEP and SAR-SEP [1,5].................. | 134 | 193 | 265 | 367 | 364 | 382 | 420 | 395 |
| SIMPLE [1,6].............................. | 10 | 42 | 69 | 100 | 101 | 112 | 123 | 118 |
| Defined contribution plans............... | 2,958 | 3,739 | 4,767 | 6,510 | 6,465 | 6,929 | 7,812 | 7,538 |
| 401(k) plans.............................. | 1,738 | 2,393 | 3,119 | 4,406 | 4,377 | 4,741 | 5,400 | 5,200 |
| Other private-sector defined contribution plans [7].......... | 500 | 413 | 464 | 514 | 483 | 498 | 540 | 500 |
| 403(b) plans.............................. | 519 | 622 | 724 | 889 | 884 | 913 | 993 | 959 |
| Thrift Savings Plan [8].................... | 92 | 168 | 272 | 440 | 458 | 495 | 557 | 570 |
| 457 plans................................. | 110 | 143 | 189 | 261 | 263 | 282 | 321 | 309 |
| Private-sector defined benefit plans..... | 2,020 | 2,262 | 2,481 | 3,003 | 2,861 | 2,935 | 3,169 | 2,947 |
| State and local government defined benefit plans........... | 2,340 | 2,761 | 2,946 | 3,730 | 3,679 | 3,819 | 4,279 | 4,101 |
| Federal defined benefit plans [9]........ | 705 | 912 | 1,168 | 1,445 | 1,519 | 1,603 | 1,695 | 1,796 |
| Annuities [10]............................ | 904 | 1,287 | 1,559 | 1,965 | 1,973 | 2,042 | 2,190 | 2,035 |
| Memo: | | | | | | | | |
| Mutual fund retirement assets........... | 2,547 | 3,661 | 4,927 | 7,227 | 7,129 | 7,559 | 8,825 | 8,174 |
| Percent of total retirement assets....... | 22 | 25 | 27 | 30 | 30 | 30 | 31 | 30 |
| Percent of all mutual funds.............. | 37 | 41 | 42 | 46 | 46 | 46 | 47 | 46 |

[1] Data for 2017 and 2018 are estimated. [2] Includes Keogh deposits. [3] Annuities held by IRAs, excluding variable annuity mutual fund IRA assets, which are included in mutual funds. [4] Excludes mutual fund assets held through brokerage accounts, which are included in mutual funds. [5] Simplified Employee Pension (SEP) IRAs and salary reduction (SAR) IRAs. [6] Savings Incentive Match Plan for Employees (SIMPLE) IRAs. [7] Includes Keoghs and other defined contribution plans (profit-sharing, thrift-savings, stock bonus, and money purchase) without 401(k) features. [8] Federal Employees Retirement System (FERS) Thrift Savings Plan (TSP) as reported by the Federal Reserve Board. [9] Federal pension plans include U.S. Treasury security holdings of the civil service retirement and disability fund, the military retirement fund, the judicial retirement funds, the Railroad Retirement Board, and the foreign service retirement and disability fund. These plans also include securities held in the National Railroad Retirement Investment Trust. [10] Annuities include all fixed and variable annuities held outside of retirement plans and IRAs.

Source: Investment Company Institute. 2019. "The US Retirement Market, First Quarter 2019" (June) ©. For the most up-to-date figures about the fund industry, please visit <https://www.ici.org/research/stats>.

## Table 1242. Pension Funds—Summary: 2000 to 2018

[In billions of dollars (9,633 represents $9,633,000,000,000). As of end of year. Covers private pension funds, state and local government employee retirement funds, and federal government retirement funds in defined benefit plans and defined contribution plans (including 401(k) type plans). Excludes social security trust funds; see Table 572]

| Item | 2000 | 2005 | 2010 | 2013 | 2014 | 2015 | 2016 | 2017 | 2018 |
|---|---|---|---|---|---|---|---|---|---|
| **Total financial assets [1]**................................ | **9,633** | **12,591** | **15,938** | **19,386** | **20,092** | **20,393** | **21,197** | **22,429** | **22,413** |
| Money market fund shares................................. | 104 | 143 | 195 | 212 | 211 | 208 | 225 | 212 | 202 |
| Debt securities [1]........................................ | 2,058 | 2,371 | 2,927 | 3,479 | 3,764 | 3,792 | 3,952 | 4,018 | 4,397 |
| Treasury securities [2]................................. | 1,029 | 1,225 | 1,633 | 1,998 | 2,127 | 2,176 | 2,335 | 2,331 | 2,753 |
| Agency- and GSE (government-sponsored enterprises)-backed securities......................... | 374 | 514 | 334 | 264 | 290 | 268 | 276 | 292 | 326 |
| Corporate and foreign bonds............................ | 578 | 583 | 881 | 1,127 | 1,257 | 1,262 | 1,243 | 1,305 | 1,239 |
| Corporate equities........................................ | 3,178 | 3,931 | 3,646 | 4,708 | 4,808 | 4,711 | 4,908 | 5,684 | 5,124 |
| Mutual fund shares........................................ | 1,609 | 2,213 | 2,659 | 3,415 | 3,620 | 3,554 | 3,768 | 4,350 | 4,049 |
| Miscellaneous assets [1]................................. | 2,464 | 3,794 | 6,399 | 7,449 | 7,555 | 7,998 | 8,203 | 7,897 | 8,533 |
| Unallocated insurance contracts [3]................... | 462 | 533 | 626 | 676 | 672 | 652 | 684 | 712 | 707 |
| Contributions receivable............................... | 73 | 45 | 91 | 79 | 76 | 91 | 95 | 101 | 110 |
| Claims of pension fund on sponsor [4].................. | 1,755 | 2,991 | 5,017 | 5,902 | 5,981 | 6,444 | 6,517 | 6,112 | 6,728 |
| **Pension entitlements (liabilities) [5]**................... | **9,720** | **12,684** | **16,081** | **19,569** | **20,284** | **20,571** | **21,344** | **22,562** | **22,542** |
| Memo: | | | | | | | | | |
| *Defined benefit plan funded status:* | | | | | | | | | |
| **Pension entitlements, total**.............................. | **6,820** | **8,985** | **11,566** | **13,691** | **14,115** | **14,470** | **14,826** | **15,181** | **15,524** |
| Funded by assets [6]..................................... | 5,065 | 5,994 | 6,549 | 7,790 | 8,134 | 8,025 | 8,309 | 9,069 | 8,796 |
| Unfunded.................................................. | 1,755 | 2,991 | 5,017 | 5,902 | 5,981 | 6,444 | 6,517 | 6,112 | 6,728 |
| **Household retirement assets, total [7]**.................. | **13,456** | **17,627** | **22,956** | **28,655** | **29,939** | **30,450** | **31,913** | **34,436** | **33,994** |
| Defined benefit plans..................................... | 6,820 | 8,985 | 11,566 | 13,691 | 14,115 | 14,470 | 14,826 | 15,181 | 15,524 |
| Defined contribution plans............................... | 2,901 | 3,699 | 4,515 | 5,877 | 6,169 | 6,101 | 6,519 | 7,381 | 7,018 |
| Individual retirement plans (IRAs) [8]................... | 2,629 | 3,425 | 5,029 | 6,819 | 7,292 | 7,477 | 8,080 | 9,200 | 8,806 |
| Annuities at life insurance companies [9].............. | 1,106 | 1,518 | 1,846 | 2,267 | 2,363 | 2,402 | 2,488 | 2,675 | 2,646 |

[1] Includes other types of assets not shown separately. [2] Includes both marketable and nonmarketable government securities. [3] Assets of pension plans held at life insurance companies. [4] Unfunded defined benefit pension entitlements. [5] Actuarial value of accrued pension entitlements in defined benefit plans and assets of defined contribution plans. These liabilities are assets of the household sector. [6] Total defined benefit financial assets plus nonfinancial assets less claims of pension fund on sponsor. [7] Households' retirement assets in tax-deferred accounts, including employer sponsored pension plans, individual retirement accounts (IRAs), Roth IRAs, and annuities. [8] IRA assets are not included in above assets or entitlements. [9] Excludes annuities held in IRAs at life insurance companies.

Source: Board of Governors of the Federal Reserve System, "Financial Accounts of the United States, Z.1," <https://www.federalreserve.gov/data.htm>, accessed July 2019.

## Table 1243. Private Pension Fund Assets by Type, and Liabilities: 2000 to 2018

[In billions of dollars (4,283 represents $4,283,000,000,000). As of December 31. Covers private defined benefit plans and defined contribution plans (including 401(k) type plans). Minus sign (-) indicates overfunding]

| Type of instrument | 2000 | 2005 | 2010 | 2013 | 2014 | 2015 | 2016 | 2017 | 2018 |
|---|---|---|---|---|---|---|---|---|---|
| **Total financial assets** [1] | **4,283** | **5,391** | **6,604** | **8,398** | **8,675** | **8,567** | **9,004** | **9,752** | **9,381** |
| Money market fund shares | 84 | 90 | 142 | 155 | 156 | 153 | 159 | 156 | 152 |
| Debt securities [1] | 596 | 665 | 867 | 1,087 | 1,210 | 1,176 | 1,224 | 1,286 | 1,311 |
| Treasury securities | 111 | 111 | 202 | 281 | 305 | 287 | 303 | 324 | 365 |
| Agency and GSE-backed securities [2] | 194 | 245 | 181 | 156 | 168 | 158 | 167 | 180 | 188 |
| Corporate and foreign bonds | 263 | 286 | 446 | 608 | 694 | 691 | 715 | 745 | 724 |
| Corporate equities | 1,823 | 2,288 | 1,778 | 2,244 | 2,284 | 2,220 | 2,327 | 2,682 | 2,361 |
| Mutual fund shares | 1,246 | 1,727 | 2,220 | 3,008 | 3,175 | 3,088 | 3,326 | 3,845 | 3,567 |
| Miscellaneous assets [1] | 387 | 518 | 1,524 | 1,831 | 1,768 | 1,853 | 1,890 | 1,705 | 1,916 |
| Unallocated insurance contracts [3] | 362 | 405 | 466 | 525 | 527 | 506 | 545 | 563 | 548 |
| **Pension entitlements (liabilities)** [4] | **4,323** | **5,430** | **6,641** | **8,435** | **8,711** | **8,603** | **9,040** | **9,789** | **9,418** |
| Funded status of defined benefit plans: | | | | | | | | | |
| Pension entitlements | 1,826 | 2,290 | 2,872 | 3,451 | 3,464 | 3,436 | 3,456 | 3,457 | 3,443 |
| Funded by assets [5] | 2,020 | 2,321 | 2,435 | 2,859 | 2,959 | 2,827 | 2,887 | 3,117 | 2,899 |
| Unfunded | -193 | -30 | 437 | 592 | 504 | 609 | 569 | 340 | 545 |
| Defined benefit plan assets | 1,785 | 2,251 | 2,836 | 3,415 | 3,427 | 3,400 | 3,419 | 3,421 | 3,407 |
| Defined contribution plan assets | 2,497 | 3,140 | 3,768 | 4,984 | 5,248 | 5,167 | 5,585 | 6,332 | 5,975 |

[1] Includes other types of assets not shown separately. [2] GSE=Government-sponsored enterprises. [3] Assets of private pension plans held at life insurance companies (e.g., GICs, variable annuities). [4] Actuarial value of accrued pension entitlements in defined benefit plans and assets of defined contribution plans. [5] Total defined benefit financial assets plus nonfinancial assets less claims of pension fund on sponsor.

Source: Board of Governors of the Federal Reserve System, "Financial Accounts of the United States, Z.1," <https://www.federalreserve.gov/data.htm>, accessed July 2019.

## Table 1244. Public Employee Retirement Systems—Assets and Liabilities: 2000 to 2018

[In billions of dollars (3,322 represents $3,322,000,000,000). As of December 31. Includes claims of sponsor (unfunded pension entitlements). Minus sign (-) indicates overfunding]

| Type of instrument | 2000 | 2005 | 2010 | 2013 | 2014 | 2015 | 2016 | 2017 | 2018 |
|---|---|---|---|---|---|---|---|---|---|
| **STATE AND LOCAL GOVERNMENT EMPLOYEE RETIREMENT PLANS** | | | | | | | | | |
| **Total financial assets** [1] | **3,322** | **4,695** | **6,169** | **7,438** | **7,776** | **8,086** | **8,364** | **8,728** | **9,015** |
| Debt securities [1] | 721 | 740 | 765 | 836 | 910 | 881 | 891 | 978 | 1,025 |
| Treasury securities | 179 | 163 | 154 | 181 | 199 | 175 | 218 | 277 | 349 |
| Agency and GSE-backed securities [2] | 179 | 261 | 144 | 99 | 113 | 101 | 100 | 103 | 129 |
| Corporate and foreign bonds | 314 | 289 | 427 | 507 | 551 | 558 | 514 | 546 | 502 |
| Corporate equities | 1,299 | 1,530 | 1,723 | 2,247 | 2,284 | 2,250 | 2,321 | 2,677 | 2,459 |
| Mutual fund shares | 363 | 486 | 438 | 407 | 445 | 466 | 442 | 505 | 481 |
| Miscellaneous assets [1] | 846 | 1,852 | 3,150 | 3,842 | 4,031 | 4,381 | 4,582 | 4,473 | 4,967 |
| Claims of pension fund on sponsor [3] | 717 | 1,596 | 2,855 | 3,533 | 3,721 | 4,072 | 4,217 | 4,054 | 4,532 |
| **Pension entitlements (liabilities)** [4] | **3,369** | **4,749** | **6,275** | **7,584** | **7,932** | **8,227** | **8,474** | **8,824** | **9,107** |
| Funded status of defined benefit plans: | | | | | | | | | |
| Pension entitlements | 3,058 | 4,358 | 5,801 | 7,087 | 7,450 | 7,751 | 8,036 | 8,333 | 8,634 |
| Funded by assets [5] | 2,340 | 2,761 | 2,946 | 3,554 | 3,730 | 3,679 | 3,819 | 4,279 | 4,101 |
| Unfunded [3] | 717 | 1,596 | 2,855 | 3,533 | 3,721 | 4,072 | 4,217 | 4,054 | 4,532 |
| Defined benefit plan assets | 3,011 | 4,304 | 5,695 | 6,941 | 7,294 | 7,610 | 7,925 | 8,236 | 8,541 |
| Defined contribution plan assets | 311 | 391 | 474 | 497 | 482 | 476 | 438 | 492 | 473 |
| **FEDERAL GOVERNMENT EMPLOYEE RETIREMENT FUNDS** | | | | | | | | | |
| **Total financial assets** [1] | **2,028** | **2,504** | **3,165** | **3,550** | **3,641** | **3,741** | **3,830** | **3,949** | **4,017** |
| Debt securities [1] | 740 | 966 | 1,295 | 1,556 | 1,644 | 1,736 | 1,837 | 1,754 | 2,061 |
| Treasury securities [6] | 739 | 951 | 1,277 | 1,536 | 1,623 | 1,715 | 1,814 | 1,730 | 2,039 |
| Corporate equities | 57 | 113 | 145 | 217 | 240 | 240 | 261 | 324 | 303 |
| Claims of pension fund on sponsor [7] | 1,231 | 1,425 | 1,725 | 1,776 | 1,756 | 1,764 | 1,731 | 1,718 | 1,651 |
| **Pension entitlements (liabilities)** [8] | **2,028** | **2,504** | **3,165** | **3,550** | **3,641** | **3,741** | **3,830** | **3,949** | **4,017** |
| Funded status of defined benefit plans: | | | | | | | | | |
| Pension entitlements | 1,936 | 2,336 | 2,893 | 3,153 | 3,201 | 3,282 | 3,334 | 3,391 | 3,447 |
| Funded by assets [9] | 705 | 912 | 1,168 | 1,377 | 1,445 | 1,519 | 1,603 | 1,673 | 1,796 |
| Unfunded [7] | 1,231 | 1,425 | 1,725 | 1,776 | 1,756 | 1,764 | 1,731 | 1,718 | 1,651 |
| Defined benefit plan assets [10] | 1,936 | 2,336 | 2,893 | 3,153 | 3,201 | 3,282 | 3,334 | 3,391 | 3,447 |
| Defined contribution plan assets [11] | 92 | 168 | 272 | 397 | 440 | 458 | 495 | 557 | 570 |

[1] Includes other types of instruments not shown separately. [2] GSE=Government sponsored enterprises. [3] Unfunded defined benefit pension entitlements. [4] Actuarial value of accrued defined benefit pension entitlements. [5] Total defined benefit financial assets plus nonfinancial assets less claims of pension fund on sponsor. [6] Comprised primarily of nonmarketable Treasury securities. [7] Unfunded defined benefit pension entitlements and suspended investments in the Thrift Savings Plan G Fund by the Treasury. [8] Actuarial value of accrued pension entitlements in defined benefit plans and assets of defined contribution plans, including suspended investments in the Thrift Savings Plan G Fund. [9] Total defined benefit financial assets less defined benefit claims of pension fund on sponsor. [10] Includes the Civil Service Retirement and Disability Fund, Railroad Retirement Board, judicial retirement fund, Military Retirement Fund, Foreign Service Retirement and Disability Fund, and National Railroad Retirement Investment Trust. [11] Thrift Savings Plan.

Source: Board of Governors of the Federal Reserve System, "Financial Accounts of the United States, Z.1," <https://www.federalreserve.gov/data.htm>, accessed July 2019.

# Table 1245. Life Insurance in Force and Purchases in the United States—Summary: 1990 to 2018

[389 represents 389,000,000. As of December 31 or calendar year, as applicable. Covers life insurance with life insurance companies, and beginning in 2003, also with fraternal benefit societies. Data represents all life insurance in force on lives of U.S. residents whether issued by U.S. or foreign companies]

| Year | Number of policies, total (millions) | Life insurance in force — Value (bil. dol.) | | | Life insurance purchases [1] — Number (1,000) | | | Life insurance purchases [1] — Amount (bil. dol.) | | |
|---|---|---|---|---|---|---|---|---|---|---|
| | | Total [2] | Individual | Group | Total | Individual | Group | Total | Individual | Group |
| 1990........ | 389 | 9,393 | 5,391 | 3,754 | 28,791 | 14,199 | 14,592 | 1,529 | 1,070 | 459 |
| 2000........ | 369 | 15,953 | 9,376 | 6,376 | 34,882 | 13,345 | 21,537 | 2,515 | 1,594 | 921 |
| 2005........ | 373 | 18,399 | 9,970 | 8,263 | 34,519 | 11,407 | 23,112 | 2,836 | 1,796 | 1,040 |
| 2010........ | 284 | 18,426 | 10,484 | 7,831 | 28,621 | 10,123 | 18,498 | 2,809 | 1,673 | 1,135 |
| 2013........ | 275 | 19,662 | 11,365 | 8,215 | 25,264 | 9,929 | 15,336 | 2,779 | 1,640 | 1,139 |
| 2014........ | 278 | 20,115 | 11,826 | 8,209 | 27,147 | 9,440 | 17,707 | 2,759 | 1,590 | 1,168 |
| 2015........ | 281 | 20,779 | 12,342 | 8,361 | 28,315 | 10,305 | 18,010 | 2,877 | 1,647 | 1,229 |
| 2016........ | 291 | 20,316 | 11,992 | 8,246 | 27,523 | 11,005 | 16,518 | 2,874 | 1,685 | 1,190 |
| 2017........ | 289 | 20,416 | 11,927 | 8,411 | 28,035 | 10,478 | 17,557 | 3,027 | 1,712 | 1,316 |
| 2018........ | 267 | 19,571 | 12,120 | 7,367 | 27,748 | 10,289 | 17,459 | 2,972 | 1,728 | 1,244 |

[1] Excludes revivals, increases, dividend additions, and reinsurance acquired. Includes long-term credit insurance (life insurance on loans of more than 10 years' duration). [2] Includes other types of policies not shown separately such as credit.

Source: American Council of Life Insurers, Washington, DC, *Life Insurers Fact Book*, annual ©.

# Table 1246. U.S. Life Insurance Companies—Summary: 2000 to 2018

[811.5 represents $811,500,000,000. As of December 31 or calendar year, as applicable. Covers domestic and foreign business of U.S. companies. Includes annual statement data for companies that primarily are health insurance companies. Beginning in 2005, includes also fraternal benefit societies]

| Item | Unit | 2000 | 2005 | 2010 | 2013 | 2014 | 2015 | 2016 | 2017 | 2018 |
|---|---|---|---|---|---|---|---|---|---|---|
| U.S. companies [1]............ | Number | 1,269 | 1,119 | 917 | 850 | 830 | 814 | 797 | 781 | 773 |
| Income [2]............ | Bil. dol. | 811.5 | 779.0 | 862.6 | 906.7 | 999.4 | 1,064.7 | 985.8 | 973.4 | 1,008.2 |
| Life insurance premiums........ | Bil. dol. | 130.6 | 142.3 | 104.6 | 130.6 | 138.3 | 155.9 | 119.3 | 141.8 | 150.2 |
| Annuity considerations [3]........ | Bil. dol. | 306.7 | 277.1 | 293.6 | 287.7 | 361.6 | 333.0 | 326.8 | 294.9 | 279.3 |
| Health insurance premiums........ | Bil. dol. | 105.6 | 118.3 | 172.7 | 175.1 | 158.4 | 159.9 | 164.0 | 170.5 | 185.4 |
| Investment and other [4]........ | Bil. dol. | 268.5 | 241.4 | 291.6 | 313.4 | 341.1 | 416.0 | 375.7 | 366.3 | 393.3 |
| Payments under life insurance and annuity contracts........ | Bil. dol. | 375.2 | 365.7 | 365.6 | 411.6 | 443.8 | 447.7 | 443.0 | 490.1 | 536.9 |
| Payments to life insurance beneficiaries........ | Bil. dol. | 44.1 | 53.0 | 58.4 | 64.3 | 67.9 | 74.3 | 76.0 | 77.1 | 79.7 |
| Surrender values under life insurance [5]........ | Bil. dol. | 27.2 | 39.2 | 35.8 | 28.7 | 27.8 | 28.8 | 30.2 | 33.2 | 35.3 |
| Surrender values under annuity contracts [5, 6]........ | Bil. dol. | 214.0 | 190.3 | 184.1 | 222.8 | 256.7 | 247.2 | 238.0 | 279.4 | 319.1 |
| Policyholder dividends........ | Bil. dol. | 20.0 | 17.9 | 15.9 | 16.0 | 16.7 | 18.5 | 18.4 | 17.7 | 18.4 |
| Annuity payments [6]........ | Bil. dol. | 68.7 | 63.9 | 70.1 | 78.8 | 73.8 | 77.8 | 79.1 | 81.6 | 83.4 |
| Matured endowments........ | Bil. dol. | 0.6 | 0.6 | 0.6 | 0.4 | 0.4 | 0.4 | 0.4 | 0.5 | 0.4 |
| Other payments........ | Bil. dol. | 0.6 | 0.7 | 0.7 | 0.7 | 0.7 | 0.7 | 0.7 | 0.6 | 0.7 |
| Health insurance benefit payments........ | Bil. dol. | 78.8 | 79.6 | 122.5 | 127.5 | 113.6 | 115.3 | 119.8 | 126.7 | 132.2 |
| **BALANCE SHEET** | | | | | | | | | | |
| Assets........ | Bil. dol. | 3,182 | 4,482 | 5,311 | 6,150 | 6,406 | 6,478 | 6,772 | 7,183 | 6,993 |
| Mortgage-backed securities........ | Bil. dol. | (NA) | (NA) | 631 | 562 | 567 | 556 | 568 | 568 | 576 |
| Government bonds........ | Bil. dol. | 364 | 590 | 413 | 464 | 479 | 496 | 522 | 547 | 475 |
| Corporate securities........ | Bil. dol. | 2,238 | 3,136 | 3,271 | 3,978 | 4,133 | 4,150 | 4,313 | 4,627 | 4,441 |
| Bonds........ | Bil. dol. | 1,241 | 1,850 | 1,700 | 1,974 | 2,061 | 2,150 | 2,257 | 2,365 | 2,441 |
| Stocks........ | Bil. dol. | 997 | 1,285 | 1,570 | 2,004 | 2,072 | 2,001 | 2,056 | 2,262 | 2,000 |
| Mortgages........ | Bil. dol. | 237 | 295 | 327 | 374 | 395 | 437 | 472 | 514 | 565 |
| Real estate........ | Bil. dol. | 36 | 33 | 28 | 31 | 32 | 44 | 47 | 43 | 39 |
| Policy loans........ | Bil. dol. | 102 | 110 | 127 | 132 | 133 | 135 | 135 | 137 | 137 |
| Other........ | Bil. dol. | 204 | 319 | 515 | 610 | 666 | 659 | 715 | 749 | 760 |
| Interest earned on assets [7]........ | Percent | 7.05 | 4.90 | 4.33 | 4.20 | 4.61 | 4.81 | 4.50 | 4.28 | 4.72 |
| Obligations and surplus funds [8]........ | Bil. dol. | 3,182 | 4,482 | 5,311 | 6,150 | 6,406 | 6,478 | 6,772 | 7,183 | 6,993 |
| Policy reserves........ | Bil. dol. | 2,712 | 3,360 | 4,098 | 4,780 | 4,956 | 5,025 | 5,232 | 5,542 | 5,375 |
| Annuities [9]........ | Bil. dol. | 1,875 | 2,189 | 2,660 | 3,186 | 3,299 | 3,320 | 3,467 | 3,701 | 3,554 |
| Group........ | Bil. dol. | 960 | 758 | 863 | 1,029 | 1,050 | 1,022 | 1,053 | 1,129 | 1,079 |
| Individual........ | Bil. dol. | 881 | 1,415 | 1,780 | 2,137 | 2,228 | 2,276 | 2,391 | 2,548 | 2,449 |
| Supplementary contracts [10]........ | Bil. dol. | 34 | 16 | 17 | 20 | 22 | 23 | 23 | 24 | 25 |
| Life insurance........ | Bil. dol. | 742 | 1,029 | 1,224 | 1,365 | 1,423 | 1,463 | 1,500 | 1,563 | 1,574 |
| Health insurance........ | Bil. dol. | 96 | 141 | 214 | 228 | 234 | 242 | 264 | 279 | 247 |
| Liabilities for deposit-type contracts [11]........ | Bil. dol. | 21 | 456 | 420 | 450 | 468 | 470 | 495 | 530 | 524 |
| Capital and surplus........ | Bil. dol. | 188 | 256 | 319 | 348 | 368 | 383 | 398 | 413 | 419 |

NA Not available. [1] Includes life insurance companies that sell accident and health insurance. [2] Premiums are net of reinsurance business and fluctuate with reinsurance activities as well as sale changes. [3] Beginning 2005, excludes certain deposit-type funds from income due to codification. [4] Investment represents gross investment income. [5] "Surrender values" include annuity withdrawals of funds. [6] Beginning 2005, excludes payments under deposit-type contracts. [7] Net rate. [8] Includes other obligations not shown separately. [9] Beginning 2005, excludes reserves for guaranteed interest contracts (GICs). [10] Data for 2000 include reserves for contracts with and without life contingencies; beginning 2005, includes only reserves for contracts with life contingencies. [11] Policyholder dividend accumulations for all years. Beginning 2005, also includes liabilities for guaranteed interest contracts, supplementary contracts without life contingencies, and premium and other deposits.

Source: American Council of Life Insurers, Washington, DC, *Life Insurers Fact Book*, annual ©.

## Table 1247. Property and Casualty Insurance—Summary: 2005 to 2016

[In billions of dollars (427.6 represents $427,600,000,000). Minus sign (-) indicates loss]

| Item | 2005 | 2010 | 2012 | 2013 | 2014 | 2015 | 2016 |
|---|---|---|---|---|---|---|---|
| Premiums, net written [1] | 427.6 | 425.9 | 460.5 | 481.5 | 502.8 | 520.1 | 533.5 |
| Automobile, private [2] | 159.6 | 160.3 | 168.0 | 174.9 | 183.5 | 192.8 | 207.4 |
| Automobile, commercial [2] | 26.8 | 21.1 | 22.1 | 23.9 | 25.7 | 27.6 | 28.3 |
| Fire | 7.9 | 10.2 | 10.8 | 11.2 | 11.5 | 11.4 | 11.0 |
| Homeowners' multiple peril | 53.0 | 61.7 | 67.8 | 72.8 | 77.9 | 79.9 | 81.2 |
| Commercial multiple peril | 29.7 | 28.9 | 31.5 | 33.2 | 34.4 | 34.7 | 33.9 |
| Marine, inland and ocean | 11.2 | 11.2 | 12.3 | 13.0 | 13.9 | 14.2 | 14.0 |
| Workers' compensation | 39.7 | 31.6 | 38.7 | 41.1 | 43.8 | 45.4 | 45.6 |
| Other liability [3] | 39.4 | 35.8 | 38.3 | 42.1 | 44.2 | 45.6 | 44.6 |
| Reinsurance | 6.6 | 11.4 | 14.7 | 12.5 | 11.5 | 12.4 | 11.6 |
| Losses and expenses | 421.4 | 430.4 | 462.1 | 449.6 | 473.3 | 494.6 | 525.9 |
| Underwriting gain/loss | -5.6 | -10.5 | -15.4 | 15.2 | 12.2 | 8.9 | -4.7 |
| Investment income earned | 49.7 | 47.6 | 48.0 | 47.3 | 46.4 | 47.2 | 46.3 |
| Net income after taxes | 44.2 | 35.2 | 35.1 | 63.4 | 55.9 | 56.8 | 42.6 |

[1] Excludes state funds, after reinsurance transactions. Includes other lines of insurance not shown separately. [2] Includes premiums for automobile liability and physical damage. [3] Coverages protecting against legal liability resulting from negligence, carelessness, or failure to act.

Source: Insurance Information Institute, New York, NY. *The Insurance Fact Book, 2018* ©, and previous reports. See also <http://www.iii.org>.

## Table 1248. Automobile Insurance—Average Expenditures Per Insured Vehicle by State: 2015 and 2016

[In dollars. Average expenditure equals total premiums written divided by liability car-years. A car-year is equal to 365 days of insured coverage for a single vehicle. The average expenditures for automobile insurance in a state are affected by a number of factors, including the underlying rate structure, the coverages purchased, the deductibles and limits selected, the types of vehicles insured, and the distribution of driver characteristics. The National Association of Insurance Commissioners does not rank state average expenditures and does not endorse any conclusions drawn from these data]

| State | 2015 | 2016 | State | 2015 | 2016 | State | 2015 | 2016 | State | 2015 | 2016 |
|---|---|---|---|---|---|---|---|---|---|---|---|
| U.S. | 889 | 935 | ID | 574 | 600 | MO | 745 | 791 | PA | 878 | 918 |
| AL | 723 | 769 | IL | 804 | 837 | MT | 692 | 707 | RI | 1,147 | 1,194 |
| AK | 872 | 859 | IN | 667 | 692 | NE | 682 | 708 | SC | 854 | 923 |
| AZ | 844 | 891 | IA | 599 | 628 | NV | 990 | 1,026 | SD | 616 | 648 |
| AR | 736 | 772 | KS | 698 | 714 | NH | 775 | 802 | TN | 737 | 760 |
| CA | 841 | 893 | KY | 802 | 839 | NJ | 1,266 | 1,309 | TX | 934 | 1,009 |
| CO | 858 | 935 | LA | 1,232 | 1,302 | NM | 762 | 781 | UT | 784 | 824 |
| CT | 1,049 | 1,086 | ME | 618 | 650 | NY | 1,235 | 1,302 | VT | 680 | 692 |
| DE | 1,146 | 1,160 | MD | 1,017 | 1,077 | NC | 655 | 700 | VA | 751 | 786 |
| DC | 1,202 | 1,247 | MA | 1,059 | 1,097 | ND | 638 | 639 | WA | 884 | 924 |
| FL | 1,185 | 1,260 | MI | 1,231 | 1,271 | OH | 703 | 727 | WV | 855 | 870 |
| GA | 896 | 966 | MN | 788 | 808 | OK | 826 | 851 | WI | 665 | 688 |
| HI | 763 | 782 | MS | 827 | 859 | OR | 828 | 877 | WY | 657 | 678 |

Source: National Association of Insurance Commissioners (NAIC), Kansas City, MO, *Auto Insurance Database Report*, annual ©. Reprinted with permission of the NAIC. Further reprint or distribution strictly prohibited without prior written permission of the NAIC.

## Table 1249. Renters and Homeowners Insurance—Average Premiums by State: 2016

[In dollars. Average premium equals premiums divided by exposure per house-years. A house-year is equal to 365 days of insured coverage for a single dwelling and is the standard measurement for homeowners insurance. The National Association of Insurance Commissioners does not rank state average expenditures and does not endorse any conclusions drawn from these data]

| State | Renters [1] | Home-owners [2] | State | Renters [1] | Home-owners [2] | State | Renters [1] | Home-owners [2] | State | Renters [1] | Home-owners [2] |
|---|---|---|---|---|---|---|---|---|---|---|---|
| U.S. | 185 | 1,192 | ID | 150 | 703 | MO | 181 | 1,280 | PA | 157 | 927 |
| AL | 245 | 1,386 | IL | 167 | 1,042 | MT | 145 | 1,130 | RI | 180 | 1,496 |
| AK | 148 | 974 | IN | 179 | 1,003 | NE | 141 | 1,402 | SC | 188 | 1,285 |
| AZ | 181 | 803 | IA | 141 | 945 | NV | 182 | 742 | SD | 114 | 1,125 |
| AR | 223 | 1,348 | KS | 177 | 1,548 | NH | 154 | 965 | TN | 207 | 1,185 |
| CA | 200 | 1,000 | KY | 169 | 1,085 | NJ | 163 | 1,174 | TX [3] | 241 | 1,937 |
| CO | 156 | 1,446 | LA | 252 | 1,967 | NM | 198 | 996 | UT | 141 | 664 |
| CT | 196 | 1,455 | ME | 151 | 866 | NY | 198 | 1,309 | VT | 158 | 898 |
| DE | 159 | 816 | MD | 161 | 1,022 | NC | 157 | 1,098 | VA | 151 | 966 |
| DC | 163 | 1,225 | MA | 198 | 1,451 | ND | 113 | 1,239 | WA | 157 | 822 |
| FL | 181 | 1,918 | MI | 197 | 952 | OH | 182 | 850 | WV | 196 | 917 |
| GA | 230 | 1,200 | MN | 142 | 1,340 | OK | 247 | 1,875 | WI | 132 | 762 |
| HI | 154 | 1,026 | MS | 275 | 1,525 | OR | 159 | 659 | WY | 150 | 1,120 |

[1] Based on the HO-4 renters insurance policy for tenants. Includes broad named-peril coverage for the personal property of tenants. [2] Based on the HO-3 homeowner package policy for owner-occupied dwellings, 1–4 family units. Provides "all risks" coverage (except those specifically excluded in the policy) on buildings, broad named-peril coverage on personal property, and is the most common package written. [3] The Texas Insurance Commissioner promulgates residential policy forms which are similar but not identical to the standard forms.

Source: National Association of Insurance Commissioners (NAIC), Kansas City, MO, *Dwelling Fire, Homeowners Owner-Occupied, and Homeowners Tenant and Condominium/Cooperative Unit Owners Insurance* ©. Reprinted with permission of the NAIC. Further reprint or distribution strictly prohibited without prior written permission of the NAIC.

## Table 1250. Real Estate and Rental and Leasing—Nonemployer Establishments and Receipts by Kind of Business: 2010 to 2017

[2,343.1 represents 2,343,100. Includes only firms subject to federal income tax. Nonemployers are businesses with no paid employees. Data originate chiefly from administrative records of the Internal Revenue Service; see Appendix III]

| Kind of business | NAICS code [1] | Establishments (1,000) | | | Receipts (mil. dol.) | | |
|---|---|---|---|---|---|---|---|
| | | 2010 | 2015 | 2017 | 2010 | 2015 | 2017 |
| **Real estate & rental & leasing, total**............ | **53** | **2,343.1** | **2,635.8** | **2,784.8** | **209,549** | **259,768** | **279,569** |
| Real estate............ | 531 | 2,262.2 | 2,552.5 | 2,702.6 | 203,065 | 252,450 | 272,040 |
| Lessors of real estate............ | 5311 | 989.3 | 1,156.2 | 1,192.8 | 135,015 | 158,624 | 166,644 |
| Offices of real estate agents & brokers............ | 5312 | 641.6 | 694.7 | 764.4 | 25,502 | 38,904 | 44,123 |
| Activities related to real estate............ | 5313 | 631.3 | 701.6 | 745.5 | 42,549 | 54,922 | 61,273 |
| Rental & leasing services............ | 532 | 78.9 | 80.2 | 79.5 | 6,288 | 7,024 | 7,237 |
| Automotive equipment rental & leasing............ | 5321 | 18.3 | 18.6 | 19.8 | 990 | 1,171 | 1,233 |
| Consumer goods rental............ | 5322 | 18.3 | 19.1 | 16.9 | 779 | 887 | 770 |
| General rental centers............ | 5323 | 4.8 | 6.5 | 6.9 | 409 | 519 | 588 |
| Commercial/industrial equipment rental & leasing............ | 5324 | 37.5 | 36.0 | 35.7 | 4,109 | 4,448 | 4,642 |
| Lessors of other nonfinancial intangible assets............ | 533 | 2.0 | 3.1 | 2.7 | 197 | 293 | 292 |

[1] Data for 2010 based on 2007 North American Industry Classification System (NAICS); data for 2015 based on 2012 NAICS; data for 2017 based on 2017 NAICS. For more information, see text, Section 15.

Source: U.S. Census Bureau, Nonemployer Statistics, "NES Datasets," <https://www.census.gov/programs-surveys/nonemployer-statistics/data/datasets.html>, accessed July 2019.

## Table 1251. Real Estate and Rental and Leasing—Establishments, Employees, and Payroll: 2015 and 2016

[377.6 represents 377,600. Covers establishments with payroll. Data based on the North American Industry Classification System (NAICS) 2012; see text, section 15, Business Enterprise. Employees are for the week including March 12. Most government employees are excluded. For statement on methodology, see Appendix III]

| Kind of business | NAICS code | Establishments (1,000) | | Employees (1,000) | | Payroll (bil. dol.) | |
|---|---|---|---|---|---|---|---|
| | | 2015 | 2016 | 2015 | 2016 | 2015 | 2016 |
| **Real estate & rental & leasing, total**............ | **53** | **377.6** | **390.5** | **2,065.4** | **2,111.4** | **106.3** | **110.5** |
| Real estate............ | 531 | 321.9 | 334.3 | 1,522.2 | 1,563.0 | 78.2 | 82.5 |
| Lessors of real estate............ | 5311 | 125.6 | 127.1 | 573.3 | 576.6 | 26.1 | 26.7 |
| Offices of real estate agents & brokers............ | 5312 | 102.8 | 110.9 | 281.8 | 306.5 | 18.4 | 20.4 |
| Activities related to real estate [1]............ | 5313 | 93.5 | 96.3 | 667.1 | 679.9 | 33.7 | 35.4 |
| Residential property managers............ | 531311 | 47.1 | 49.4 | 427.3 | 439.4 | 17.7 | 18.8 |
| Rental & leasing services............ | 532 | 53.2 | 53.7 | 508.8 | 512.4 | 24.4 | 24.3 |
| Automotive equipment rental & leasing............ | 5321 | 15.8 | 16.4 | 164.9 | 167.1 | 6.8 | 7.0 |
| Passenger car rental & leasing............ | 53211 | 10.3 | 10.7 | 102.2 | 101.2 | 3.8 | 3.9 |
| Truck, utility trailer & RV rental & leasing............ | 53212 | 5.5 | 5.7 | 62.7 | 65.9 | 3.0 | 3.2 |
| Consumer goods rental [1]............ | 5322 | 20.0 | 19.6 | 143.7 | 146.2 | 5.1 | 5.1 |
| Video tape & disc rental............ | 53223 | 2.1 | 2.0 | 15.3 | 14.7 | 0.4 | 0.4 |
| Home health equipment rental............ | 532291 | 3.2 | 3.1 | 32.0 | 30.7 | 1.3 | 1.2 |
| General rental centers............ | 5323 | 2.8 | 2.8 | 10.8 | 19.6 | 0.8 | 0.8 |
| Commercial/industrial equipment rental & leasing [1]............ | 5324 | 14.7 | 14.9 | 181.4 | 179.5 | 11.8 | 11.4 |
| Construction, transportation, and mining equipment............ | 53241 | 5.2 | 5.1 | 69.4 | 62.7 | 5.2 | 4.6 |
| Lessors of other nonfinancial intangible assets............ | 533 | 2.5 | 2.6 | 34.5 | 36.0 | 3.7 | 3.7 |

[1] Includes industries not shown separately.

Source: U.S. Census Bureau, County Business Patterns, "Geography Area Series: County Business Patterns," <http://factfinder.census.gov>, accessed April 2018. See also <https://www.census.gov/programs-surveys/cbp.html>.

## Table 1252. Real Estate and Rental and Leasing Services—Revenue by Kind of Business: 2012 to 2017

[In millions of dollars (487,656 represents $487,656,000,000). Covers taxable and tax-exempt employer firms. Data for 2012 are based on the 2007 North American Industry Classification System (NAICS); beginning 2013, data are based on 2012 NAICS. See text, this section and Section 15. Estimates have been adjusted using the results of the 2012 Economic Census. Based on Service Annual Survey; see Appendix III]

| Kind of business | NAICS code | 2012 | 2013 | 2014 | 2015 | 2016 | 2017 |
|---|---|---|---|---|---|---|---|
| **Real estate and rental and leasing, total**............ | **53** | **487,656** | **523,255** | **564,613** | **602,846** | **633,974** | **663,749** |
| Real estate [1]............ | 531 | 325,339 | 351,972 | 380,860 | 410,457 | 437,996 | 459,322 |
| Lessors of residential buildings and dwellings............ | 53111 | 85,980 | 91,448 | 98,130 | 105,318 | 111,345 | 114,349 |
| Lessors of nonresidential buildings (excl. miniwarehouses)... | 53112 | 96,132 | 100,759 | 107,747 | 114,499 | 119,521 | 123,924 |
| Offices of real estate agents and brokers............ | 5312 | 65,094 | 75,928 | 84,199 | 92,869 | 102,487 | 108,233 |
| Real estate property managers............ | 53131 | 47,179 | 50,670 | 55,574 | 59,429 | 64,316 | 69,485 |
| Offices of real estate appraisers............ | 53132 | 5,824 | 5,734 | 5,464 | 5,881 | 6,402 | 6,303 |
| Rental and leasing services [1]............ | 532 | 129,336 | 135,753 | 145,799 | 152,544 | 154,823 | 159,931 |
| Passenger car rental............ | 532111 | 25,033 | 25,957 | 27,295 | 28,194 | 29,976 | 30,560 |
| Passenger car leasing............ | 532112 | 7,714 | 8,136 | 8,610 | 9,050 | 9,506 | 10,157 |
| Truck, trailer, and recreational vehicle rental and leasing..... | 53212 | 15,667 | 15,941 | 16,933 | 18,082 | 18,634 | 19,356 |
| Consumer electronics and appliances rental............ | 53221 | 6,667 | 6,809 | 7,462 | 7,991 | 8,049 | 8,098 |
| Construction/transportation/mining equipment rental and leasing............ | 53241 | 30,480 | 32,837 | 36,285 | 36,201 | 34,475 | 37,755 |
| Lessors of other nonfinancial intangible assets............ | 533 | 32,981 | 35,530 | 37,954 | 39,845 | 41,155 | 44,496 |

[1] Includes other kinds of business, not shown separately.

Source: U.S. Census Bureau, Service Annual Survey, "Service Annual Survey Latest Data (NAICS-basis): 2017," <https://www.census.gov/programs-surveys/sas/data.html>, accessed November 2018.

# Section 26
# Arts, Recreation, and Travel

This section presents data on the arts, entertainment, and recreation economic sector of the economy, and personal recreational activities, the arts and humanities, and domestic and foreign travel.

**Arts, entertainment, and recreation industry**—The U.S. Census Bureau surveys—*County Business Patterns*, *Economic Census*, *Nonemployer Statistics*, and *Service Annual Survey*—provide data on the arts, entertainment, and recreation sector. The *County Business Patterns*' annual data include number of establishments, number of employees, first quarter and annual payrolls, and number of establishments by employment size class. The *Economic Census*, conducted every five years for the years ending in '2' and '7', provides information on the number of establishments, receipts, payroll, and paid employees for the United States and various geographic levels. Data from the 2012 Economic Census have been fully released as of September 2016 through the Census Bureau's American FactFinder® service on the Census Bureau website at <factfinder.census.gov>. Data from the 2017 Economic Census will be released on a flow basis between September 2019 and December 2021. *Nonemployer Statistics* is an annual tabulation of economic data by industry for active businesses without paid employees that are subject to federal income tax. The *Service Annual Survey* provides estimates of operating revenue of taxable firms and revenues and expenses of firms exempt from federal taxes for industries in this sector of the economy. See Appendix III for more details.

**Recreation and leisure activities**—Data on the participation in various recreation and leisure time activities are based on several sample surveys. Data on the public's involvement with arts events and activities are published by the National Endowment for Arts (NEA). The NEA's *Survey of Public Participation in the Arts* remains the largest periodic study of arts participation in the United States. The most recent data are from the 2012 survey. Data on participation in fishing, hunting, and other forms of wildlife associated recreation are published periodically by the U.S. Department of Interior, Fish and Wildlife Service in *The National Survey of Fishing, Hunting, and Wildlife-Associated Recreation*. The most recent data are from the 2016 survey. Data on participation in various sports recreation activities are published by the National Sporting Goods Association. MRI-Simmons (launched as joint venture under GfK in 2019) also conducts periodic surveys on sports and leisure activities, as well as other topics.

**Parks and recreation**—The Department of the Interior has responsibility for administering the national parks. The National Park Service publishes information on visits to national park areas in its annual report, *National Park Statistical Abstract*. Additional data regarding acreage and visits for each area administered by the service, plus certain "related" areas can be found at <https://irma.nps.gov/Stats/>. Statistics for state parks are compiled by the National Association of State Park Directors in its annual *Statistical Report of State Park Operations.*

**Travel**—Statistics on arrivals and departures to the United States, cities and states visited by overseas travelers, and tourism sales and employment are reported by the International Trade Administration (ITA), Office of Travel & Tourism Industries (OTTI). Data on domestic travel and travel expenditures are published by the research department of the U.S. Travel Association. Other data on household transportation characteristics are in Section 23, Transportation.

**Statistical reliability**—For a discussion of statistical collection and estimation, sampling procedures, and measures of statistical reliability applicable to Census Bureau data, see Appendix III.

## Table 1253. Arts, Entertainment, and Recreation Services—Estimated Revenue: 2010 to 2017

[In millions of dollars (188,117 represents $188,117,000,000). For taxable and tax-exempt employer firms. Data for 2010 are based on the 2007 North American Industry Classification System (NAICS); beginning 2013, data are based on 2012 NAICS. Selected estimates have been adjusted using the results of the 2012 Economic Census. Based on the Service Annual Survey, see Appendix III]

| Kind of business | NAICS Code | 2010 | 2013 | 2014 | 2015 | 2016 | 2017 |
|---|---|---|---|---|---|---|---|
| Arts, entertainment, and recreation............ | 71 | 188,117 | 211,292 | 223,154 | 237,482 | 249,608 | 265,506 |
| Performing arts, spectator sports, and related industries......................... | 711 | 80,461 | 90,200 | 96,483 | 104,698 | 110,564 | 118,366 |
| Performing arts companies......................... | 7111 | 13,814 | 13,769 | 14,332 | 15,263 | 15,988 | 16,955 |
| Spectator sports............................... | 7112 | 31,737 | 34,977 | 37,264 | 40,095 | 42,415 | 45,466 |
| Sports teams and clubs........................ | 711211 | 21,442 | 24,145 | 26,668 | 28,979 | 31,192 | 33,977 |
| Racetracks....................................... | 711212 | 6,951 | 7,421 | 7,238 | 7,596 | 7,560 | 7,788 |
| Other spectator sports....................... | 711219 | 3,344 | 3,411 | 3,358 | 3,520 | 3,663 | 3,701 |
| Promoters of performing arts, sports, and similar events............................. | 7113 | 16,312 | 19,916 | 22,020 | 24,538 | 26,473 | 28,331 |
| Agents and managers for artists, athletes, entertainers and other public figures............. | 7114 | 5,358 | 6,208 | 6,674 | 7,322 | 7,883 | 8,193 |
| Independent artists, writers, and performers....... | 7115 | 13,240 | 15,330 | 16,193 | 17,480 | 17,805 | 19,421 |
| Museums, historical sites, and similar institutions. .. | 712 | 14,241 | 15,080 | 15,900 | 15,168 | 15,210 | 17,175 |
| Amusement, gambling, and recreation industries. .. | 713 | 93,415 | 106,012 | 110,771 | 117,616 | 123,834 | 129,965 |
| Amusement parks and arcades.................... | 7131 | 11,832 | 15,168 | 16,374 | 18,075 | 19,145 | 20,250 |
| Amusement and theme parks................... | 71311 | 10,205 | 13,524 | 14,694 | 16,252 | 17,144 | 17,945 |
| Amusement arcades............................. | 71312 | 1,627 | 1,644 | 1,680 | 1,823 | 2,001 | 2,305 |
| Gambling industries.............................. | 7132 | 23,432 | 25,698 | 26,607 | 27,923 | 29,257 | 30,310 |
| Casinos (except casino hotels)................... | 71321 | 15,367 | 16,617 | 17,094 | 18,323 | 18,965 | 19,460 |
| Other gambling industries....................... | 71329 | 8,065 | 9,081 | 9,513 | 9,600 | 10,292 | 10,850 |
| Other amusement and recreation industries........ | 7139 | 58,151 | 65,146 | 67,790 | 71,618 | 75,432 | 79,405 |
| Golf courses and country clubs.................... | 71391 | 19,788 | 20,918 | 21,224 | 21,821 | 22,445 | 22,902 |
| Skiing facilities................................... | 71392 | 2,265 | 2,433 | 2,530 | 2,571 | 2,823 | 3,262 |
| Marinas.......................................... | 71393 | 3,604 | 3,999 | 4,203 | 4,291 | 4,382 | 4,608 |
| Fitness and recreational sports centers............ | 71394 | 22,311 | 25,649 | 26,673 | 28,319 | 30,162 | 32,315 |
| Bowling centers.................................. | 71395 | 3,007 | 3,224 | 3,403 | 3,629 | 3,787 | 3,894 |
| All other amusement and recreation industries. .. | 71399 | 7,176 | 8,923 | 9,757 | 10,987 | 11,833 | 12,424 |

Source: U.S. Census Bureau, Service Annual Survey, "Service Annual Survey Latest Data (NAICS-basis): 2017," <https://www.census.gov/programs-surveys/sas/data.html>, accessed December 2018.

## Table 1254. Arts, Entertainment, and Recreation—Establishments, Revenue, Payroll, and Employees by Kind of Business: 2007 and 2012

[189,417 represents $189,417,000,000. For establishments with payroll only. Definition of paid employees varies among NAICS sectors. Data are based on the 2007 and 2012 Economic Censuses which are subject to nonsampling error. For details on survey methodology, sampling and nonsampling errors, see Appendix III]

| Kind of business | 2007 NAICS code [1] | Number of establishments | | Revenue (mil. dol.) | | Annual payroll (mil. dol.) | | Paid employees (1,000) | |
|---|---|---|---|---|---|---|---|---|---|
| | | 2007 | 2012 | 2007 | 2012 | 2007 | 2012 | 2007 | 2012 |
| Arts, entertainment, and recreation, total........ | 71 | 124,620 | 124,591 | 189,417 | 201,193 | 58,359 | 64,052 | 2,061 | 2,082 |
| Performing arts, spectator sports, and related industries [2]........ | 711 | 43,868 | 45,612 | 77,773 | 86,421 | 27,839 | 31,545 | 438 | 434 |
| Performing arts companies......................... | 7111 | 8,838 | 8,508 | 13,574 | 13,857 | 3,980 | 3,950 | 128 | 119 |
| Spectator sports................................. | 7112 | 4,237 | 4,164 | 30,403 | 33,298 | 14,136 | 16,653 | 121 | 118 |
| Promoters of performing arts, sports and similar events........ | 7113 | 6,647 | 6,846 | 16,122 | 18,474 | 2,957 | 3,211 | 121 | 137 |
| Agents and managers for artists, athletes, entertainers and other public figures............. | 7114 | 3,534 | 3,716 | 4,919 | 5,832 | 1,694 | 1,886 | 19 | 18 |
| Museums, historical sites, and similar institutions [2]........ | 712 | 7,125 | 7,319 | 13,285 | 13,726 | 3,662 | 4,197 | 130 | 135 |
| Amusement, gambling, and recreation industries [2]........ | 713 | 73,627 | 71,660 | 98,359 | 101,046 | 26,859 | 28,310 | 1,494 | 1,513 |
| Amusement parks and arcades.................. | 7131 | 3,145 | 3,299 | 13,544 | 14,302 | 2,802 | 3,386 | 134 | 155 |
| Gambling industries............................. | 7132 | 2,327 | 2,886 | 25,135 | 24,385 | 4,566 | 4,272 | 170 | 149 |
| Other amusement and recreation services........ | 7139 | 68,155 | 65,475 | 59,680 | 62,359 | 19,490 | 20,652 | 1,190 | 1,208 |

[1] Based on 2007 North American Industry Classification System (NAICS); see text, this section and section 15. [2] Includes other industries not shown separately.

Source: U.S. Census Bureau, 2012 Economic Census, EC1271A2, "Arts, Entertainment, and Recreation: Geographic Area Series: Comparative Statistics for the U.S. (2007 NAICS Basis): 2012 and 2007," <http://factfinder.census.gov/>, accessed September 2016.

## Table 1255. Arts, Entertainment, and Recreation—Nonemployer Establishments and Receipts by Kind of Business (NAICS Basis): 2010 to 2017

[Firms in thousands (1,154.0 represents 1,154,000); receipts in millions of dollars (26,756 represents $26,756,000,000). Includes only firms subject to federal income tax. Nonemployers are businesses with no paid employees but with annual receipts of $1,000 or more]

| Kind of business | NAICS code [1] | Firms (1,000) | | | Receipts (mil. dol.) | | |
|---|---|---|---|---|---|---|---|
| | | 2010 | 2016 | 2017 | 2010 | 2016 | 2017 |
| **Arts, entertainment, and recreation** | **71** | **1,154.0** | **1,383.8** | **1,436.2** | **26,756** | **35,407** | **37,396** |
| Performing arts, spectator sports, and related industries | 711 | 1,004.9 | 1,221.6 | 1,275.3 | 21,053 | 28,428 | 30,206 |
| Performing arts companies | 7111 | 61.2 | 94.0 | 87.2 | 1,249 | 1,893 | 1,895 |
| Spectator sports | 7112 | 151.9 | 181.9 | 200.9 | 2,515 | 3,381 | 3,613 |
| Promoters of performing arts, sports, and similar events | 7113 | 45.0 | 58.9 | 64.7 | 1,699 | 2,499 | 2,675 |
| Agents/managers for artists, athletes, and other public figures | 7114 | 36.3 | 37.6 | 36.7 | 1,300 | 1,702 | 1,802 |
| Independent artists, writers, and performers | 7115 | 710.3 | 849.2 | 885.9 | 14,290 | 18,954 | 20,221 |
| Museums, historical sites, and similar institutions | 712 | 5.8 | 6.5 | 6.3 | 95 | 125 | 123 |
| Amusement, gambling, and recreation industries | 713 | 143.4 | 155.8 | 154.5 | 5,607 | 6,854 | 7,067 |
| Amusement parks and arcades | 7131 | 4.7 | 4.3 | 4.2 | 251 | 254 | 254 |
| Gambling industries | 7132 | 10.2 | 10.9 | 11.0 | 1,185 | 1,360 | 1,421 |
| Other amusement and recreation services | 7139 | 128.5 | 140.6 | 139.3 | 4,171 | 5,240 | 5,392 |

[1] Data for 2010 are based on 2007 North American Industry Classification System; 2016 data are based on the 2012 NAICS; 2017 data are based on the 2017 NAICS. See text, Section 15.

Source: U.S. Census Bureau, Nonemployer Statistics, "NES Datasets," <https://www.census.gov/programs-surveys/nonemployer-statistics/data/datasets.html>, accessed July 2019.

## Table 1256. Arts, Entertainment, and Recreation—Establishments, Employees, and Payroll by Kind of Business (NAICS Basis): 2015 and 2016

[Employees in thousands (2,230.8 represents 2,230,800); payroll in millions of dollars (76,799 represents $76,799,000,000). Covers establishments with paid employees. Excludes self-employed individuals, employees of private households, railroad employees, agricultural production employees, and most government employees. For statement on methodology, see Appendix III]

| Kind of business | 2012 NAICS code [1] | Establishments | | Employees [2] (1,000) | | Payroll (mil. dol.) | |
|---|---|---|---|---|---|---|---|
| | | 2015 | 2016 | 2015 | 2016 | 2015 | 2016 |
| **Arts, entertainment, & recreation** | **71** | **133,610** | **137,210** | **2,230.8** | **2,311.4** | **76,799** | **81,124** |
| Performing arts, spectator sports | 711 | 50,239 | 52,235 | 483.3 | 503.8 | 38,070 | 41,041 |
| Performing arts companies | 7111 | 8,908 | 9,149 | 124.1 | 128.1 | 4,607 | 4,748 |
| Theater companies & dinner theaters | 71111 | 3,355 | 3,378 | 69.1 | 71.3 | 2,258 | 2,326 |
| Dance companies | 71112 | 668 | 724 | 9.9 | 10.5 | 278 | 288 |
| Musical groups & artists | 71113 | 4,522 | 4,678 | 38.5 | 39.6 | 1,819 | 1,878 |
| Other performing arts companies | 71119 | 363 | 369 | 6.6 | 6.8 | 252 | 257 |
| Spectator sports | 7112 | 4,315 | 4,357 | 128.3 | 135.9 | 19,491 | 20,981 |
| Sports teams & clubs | 711211 | 1,004 | 1,032 | 68.9 | 74.9 | 17,182 | 18,626 |
| Racetracks | 711212 | 639 | 600 | 42.7 | 43.8 | 1,300 | 1,386 |
| Other spectator sports | 711219 | 2,672 | 2,725 | 16.7 | 17.1 | 919 | 970 |
| Promoters of performing arts, sports, & similar events | 7113 | 7,600 | 7,770 | 163.9 | 172.6 | 4,410 | 5,366 |
| Promoters of performing arts, sports, & similar events with facilities | 71131 | 3,228 | 3,271 | 133.7 | 139.8 | 2,849 | 3,302 |
| Promoters of performing arts, sports, & similar events without facilities | 71132 | 4,372 | 4,499 | 30.2 | 32.8 | 1,561 | 2,064 |
| Agents/managers for artists, athletes, and other public figures | 7114 | 4,211 | 4,100 | 20.2 | 20.5 | 2,451 | 2,428 |
| Independent artists, writers, & performers | 7115 | 25,205 | 26,859 | 46.8 | 46.6 | 7,111 | 7,518 |
| Museums, historical sites, & similar institutions | 712 | 7,594 | 7,655 | 146.0 | 151.3 | 4,835 | 5,067 |
| Museums | 71211 | 5,125 | 5,137 | 93.3 | 96.1 | 3,141 | 3,287 |
| Historical sites | 71212 | 1,139 | 1,157 | 10.5 | 10.7 | 280 | 292 |
| Zoos & botanical gardens | 71213 | 632 | 647 | 35.2 | 36.8 | 1,164 | 1,217 |
| Nature parks & other similar institutions | 71219 | 698 | 714 | 7.1 | 7.6 | 250 | 271 |
| Amusement, gambling, & recreation industries | 713 | 75,777 | 77,320 | 1,601.5 | 1,656.4 | 33,895 | 35,016 |
| Amusement parks & arcades | 7131 | 3,280 | 3,388 | 196.9 | 200.9 | 4,513 | 4,752 |
| Amusement & theme parks | 71311 | 523 | 579 | 155.9 | 157.3 | 3,965 | 4,158 |
| Amusement arcades | 71312 | 2,757 | 2,809 | 41.0 | 43.6 | 548 | 594 |
| Gambling industries | 7132 | 2,828 | 2,817 | 152.9 | 148.4 | 5,208 | 5,091 |
| Casinos (except casino hotels) | 71321 | 338 | 344 | 99.0 | 94.8 | 3,407 | 3,262 |
| Other gambling industries | 71329 | 2,490 | 2,473 | 53.9 | 53.6 | 1,801 | 1,829 |
| Other amusement & recreation services | 7139 | 69,669 | 71,115 | 1,251.7 | 1,307.1 | 24,174 | 25,173 |
| Golf courses & country clubs | 71391 | 11,280 | 11,037 | 295.2 | 311.1 | 8,958 | 9,100 |
| Skiing facilities | 71392 | 373 | 370 | 73.2 | 73.7 | 821 | 859 |
| Marinas | 71393 | 3,881 | 3,826 | 27.0 | 27.5 | 1,036 | 1,081 |
| Fitness & recreational sports centers | 71394 | 32,712 | 33,980 | 658.8 | 685.9 | 9,493 | 9,973 |
| Bowling centers | 71395 | 3,820 | 3,698 | 69.2 | 70.0 | 1,026 | 1,065 |
| All other amusement & recreation industries | 71399 | 17,603 | 18,204 | 128.2 | 139.0 | 2,840 | 3,094 |

[1] Data based on 2012 North American Industry Classification System (NAICS) see text, this section and Section 15. [2] For employees on the payroll for the period including March 12.

Source: U.S. Census Bureau, County Business Patterns, "Geography Area Series: County Business Patterns," <http://factfinder.census.gov/>, accessed April 2018. See also <https://www.census.gov/programs-surveys/cbp.html>.

## Table 1257. Arts and Culture Production—Real Value Added In Chained (2009) Dollars and Employment by Industry: 2010 to 2016

[In millions of dollars (650,432 represents $650,432,000,000); employment in thousands (4,676 represents 4,676,000)]

| Industry | 2010 | 2012 | 2013 | 2014 | 2015 | 2016 |
|---|---|---|---|---|---|---|
| REAL VALUE ADDED, CHAINED (2009) DOLLARS | | | | | | |
| **Total** | **650,432** | **657,402** | **674,412** | **676,547** | **713,109** | **733,940** |
| **Core arts and cultural production** | **119,946** | **125,603** | **127,647** | **135,334** | **137,288** | **139,719** |
| Performing arts | 41,694 | 42,823 | 43,430 | 46,269 | 45,164 | 45,640 |
| Performing arts companies | 16,654 | 15,599 | 15,343 | 16,155 | 16,234 | 16,707 |
| Promoters of performing arts and similar events | 5,973 | 6,961 | 7,807 | 8,552 | 7,970 | 8,035 |
| Agents/managers for artists | 1,747 | 1,976 | 1,971 | 2,105 | 1,862 | 1,999 |
| Independent artists, writers, and performers | 17,367 | 18,314 | 18,309 | 19,483 | 19,170 | 18,971 |
| Museums | 4,068 | 4,522 | 4,777 | 4,948 | 4,563 | 4,835 |
| Design services [1] | 67,004 | 71,403 | 72,619 | 77,329 | 80,773 | 82,420 |
| Advertising | 24,822 | 28,914 | 29,312 | 30,708 | 31,817 | 33,151 |
| Architectural services | 14,472 | 13,974 | 14,062 | 15,036 | 16,349 | 16,838 |
| Landscape architectural services | 2,619 | 2,411 | 2,526 | 2,673 | 2,772 | 2,837 |
| Interior design services | 6,807 | 6,475 | 6,750 | 7,584 | 8,082 | 7,917 |
| Industrial design services | 1,325 | 1,429 | 1,476 | 1,575 | 1,658 | 1,524 |
| Graphic design services | 7,148 | 6,602 | 6,656 | 7,172 | 7,505 | 7,738 |
| Computer systems design | 2,180 | 2,831 | 2,892 | 3,123 | 3,398 | 3,600 |
| Photography and photofinishing services | 7,112 | 8,141 | 8,419 | 8,759 | 8,547 | 8,264 |
| Fine arts education | 2,942 | 2,516 | 2,500 | 2,570 | 2,632 | 2,693 |
| Education services | 4,232 | 4,408 | 4,321 | 4,353 | 4,395 | 4,391 |
| **Supporting arts and cultural production** | **508,918** | **507,862** | **523,944** | **518,123** | **551,467** | **569,948** |
| Art support services [1] | 96,119 | 93,668 | 93,782 | 94,467 | 94,823 | 96,405 |
| Rental and leasing | 5,396 | 5,480 | 5,491 | 5,668 | 6,092 | 6,822 |
| Grant-making and giving services | 494 | 484 | 517 | 528 | 558 | 632 |
| Unions | 1,017 | 1,154 | 1,156 | 1,180 | 1,172 | 1,266 |
| Government | 88,786 | 86,099 | 86,162 | 86,631 | 86,563 | 87,274 |
| Information services [1] | 314,128 | 320,985 | 335,663 | 329,754 | 360,915 | 373,415 |
| Publishing | 75,605 | 78,373 | 77,653 | 75,267 | 82,306 | 84,974 |
| Motion pictures | 92,036 | 92,583 | 93,922 | 90,712 | 96,433 | 96,358 |
| Sound recording | 14,475 | 16,095 | 15,404 | 15,318 | 18,792 | 21,624 |
| Broadcasting | 107,264 | 107,938 | 115,264 | 110,958 | 117,039 | 120,455 |
| Manufacturing [1] | 17,291 | 14,809 | 14,297 | 14,406 | 13,371 | 13,508 |
| Jewelry and silverware manufacturing | 3,297 | 2,095 | 1,338 | 1,700 | 1,292 | 1,314 |
| Printed goods manufacturing | 8,661 | 8,386 | 8,372 | 8,317 | 7,714 | 7,789 |
| Musical instruments manufacturing | 980 | 786 | 721 | 756 | 764 | 775 |
| Custom architectural woodwork & metalwork manufacturing | 2,057 | 1,893 | 1,874 | 1,969 | 2,011 | 1,866 |
| Construction | 16,747 | 9,540 | 8,575 | 8,322 | 8,636 | 9,026 |
| Wholesale and transportation industries | 24,455 | 27,019 | 28,614 | 27,115 | 28,374 | 29,076 |
| Retail industries | 40,398 | 41,857 | 43,013 | 44,152 | 46,327 | 49,676 |
| **All other industries** | **21,572** | **23,910** | **22,820** | **23,173** | **24,404** | **24,356** |
| EMPLOYMENT | | | | | | |
| **Total** | **4,676** | **4,682** | **4,750** | **4,813** | **4,914** | **5,039** |
| **Core arts and cultural production** | **930** | **961** | **988** | **1,033** | **1,057** | **1,085** |
| Performing arts | 229 | 236 | 246 | 262 | 262 | 273 |
| Performing arts companies | 101 | 101 | 102 | 105 | 105 | 107 |
| Promoters of performing arts and similar events | 73 | 77 | 84 | 93 | 94 | 100 |
| Agents/managers for artists | 21 | 22 | 23 | 24 | 24 | 28 |
| Independent artists, writers, and performers | 35 | 37 | 38 | 40 | 39 | 38 |
| Museums | 116 | 121 | 126 | 132 | 134 | 139 |
| Design services [1] | 457 | 466 | 473 | 490 | 507 | 515 |
| Advertising | 124 | 135 | 139 | 147 | 149 | 150 |
| Architectural services | 104 | 103 | 105 | 111 | 117 | 121 |
| Landscape architectural services | 22 | 22 | 22 | 23 | 24 | 24 |
| Interior design services | 18 | 19 | 20 | 22 | 24 | 25 |
| Industrial design services | 24 | 25 | 28 | 28 | 34 | 35 |
| Graphic design services | 61 | 61 | 62 | 63 | 63 | 64 |
| Computer systems design | 16 | 18 | 19 | 20 | 21 | 22 |
| Photography and photofinishing services | 85 | 81 | 76 | 74 | 72 | 71 |
| Fine arts education | 39 | 43 | 47 | 50 | 52 | 55 |
| Education services | 90 | 94 | 95 | 98 | 101 | 102 |
| **Supporting arts and cultural production** | **3,561** | **3,515** | **3,566** | **3,581** | **3,648** | **3,745** |
| Art support services [1] | 1,229 | 1,178 | 1,193 | 1,194 | 1,198 | 1,209 |
| Rental and leasing | 54 | 42 | 40 | 38 | 39 | 43 |
| Grant-making and giving services | 4 | 6 | 6 | 6 | 6 | 6 |
| Unions | 17 | 20 | 23 | 22 | 24 | 23 |
| Government | 1,150 | 1,108 | 1,121 | 1,124 | 1,125 | 1,133 |
| Information services [1] | 1,156 | 1,166 | 1,175 | 1,181 | 1,208 | 1,243 |
| Publishing | 348 | 341 | 333 | 327 | 328 | 327 |
| Motion pictures | 357 | 365 | 369 | 372 | 396 | 427 |
| Sound recording | 13 | 13 | 13 | 13 | 13 | 13 |
| Broadcasting | 397 | 400 | 409 | 415 | 412 | 411 |
| Manufacturing [1] | 191 | 176 | 175 | 177 | 172 | 178 |
| Jewelry and silverware manufacturing | 27 | 26 | 26 | 26 | 24 | 24 |
| Printed goods manufacturing | 106 | 95 | 93 | 92 | 90 | 91 |
| Musical instruments manufacturing | 8 | 8 | 8 | 8 | 8 | 8 |
| Custom architectural woodwork & metalwork manufacturing | 29 | 30 | 30 | 31 | 32 | 33 |
| Construction | 124 | 89 | 95 | 101 | 110 | 118 |
| Wholesale and transportation industries | 176 | 193 | 198 | 189 | 196 | 202 |
| Retail industries | 686 | 711 | 730 | 740 | 764 | 796 |
| **All other industries** | **185** | **205** | **197** | **199** | **209** | **209** |

[1] Includes other services or goods manufacturing, not shown separately.

Source: U.S. Bureau of Economic Analysis, "Arts and Cultural Production—Satellite Account," <https://www.bea.gov/data/special-topics/arts-and-culture>, accessed March 2019.

# Table 1258. Arts and Cultural Production—Summary by State: 2016

[In millions of dollars (804,197 represents $804,197,000,000); except employment (5,039 represents 5,039,000). Arts and cultural production is defined narrowly to include creative artistic activity; the goods and services produced by it; the goods and services produced in the support of it; and the construction of buildings in which it is taking place]

| State | Total arts and cultural production industries | | | Core arts and cultural production industries | | | Supporting arts and cultural production industries | | |
|---|---|---|---|---|---|---|---|---|---|
| | Value added (mil. dol.) [1] | Employ-ment (1,000) | Compen-sation (mil. dol.) | Value added (mil. dol.) [1] | Employ-ment (1,000) | Compen-sation (mil. dol.) | Value added (mil. dol.) [1] | Employ-ment (1,000) | Compen-sation (mil. dol.) |
| Total............. | 804,197 | 5,039 | 386,213 | 154,344 | 1,085 | 80,643 | 622,371 | 3,745 | 291,507 |
| Alabama........... | 4,642 | 47 | 2,400 | 658 | 7 | 359 | 3,652 | 36 | 1,882 |
| Alaska............ | 1,355 | 12 | 895 | 118 | 1 | 71 | 1,179 | 10 | 794 |
| Arizona........... | 9,346 | 92 | 4,944 | 1,642 | 16 | 858 | 7,230 | 72 | 3,839 |
| Arkansas.......... | 2,911 | 34 | 1,568 | 461 | 5 | 247 | 2,244 | 27 | 1,224 |
| California.......... | 185,517 | 738 | 83,410 | 36,711 | 161 | 17,701 | 145,617 | 553 | 63,900 |
| Colorado.......... | 14,538 | 103 | 7,239 | 2,649 | 22 | 1,410 | 11,408 | 78 | 5,579 |
| Connecticut....... | 9,178 | 57 | 4,746 | 1,712 | 13 | 926 | 7,031 | 41 | 3,607 |
| Delaware.......... | 1,025 | 9 | 492 | 201 | 2 | 105 | 733 | 6 | 340 |
| Dist. of Columbia... | 10,998 | 53 | 7,363 | 2,575 | 14 | 1,450 | 8,295 | 38 | 5,831 |
| Florida............ | 35,048 | 259 | 15,641 | 7,746 | 59 | 3,604 | 25,746 | 187 | 11,293 |
| Georgia........... | 22,075 | 140 | 10,175 | 4,078 | 27 | 2,019 | 17,173 | 107 | 7,749 |
| Hawaii............ | 2,577 | 23 | 1,350 | 591 | 7 | 340 | 1,877 | 15 | 959 |
| Idaho............. | 1,942 | 22 | 1,015 | 241 | 3 | 136 | 1,596 | 18 | 826 |
| Illinois............ | 27,207 | 211 | 14,485 | 6,797 | (D) | (D) | 19,179 | 151 | 10,167 |
| Indiana............ | 8,286 | 96 | 4,616 | 1,277 | (D) | (D) | 6,455 | 77 | 3,661 |
| Iowa.............. | 4,009 | 42 | 2,200 | 630 | 8 | 361 | 3,090 | 32 | 1,707 |
| Kansas............ | 4,234 | 46 | 2,502 | 586 | 7 | 339 | 3,393 | 37 | 2,046 |
| Kentucky.......... | 4,950 | 53 | 2,689 | 688 | 8 | 364 | 3,926 | 42 | 2,164 |
| Louisiana.......... | 6,687 | 55 | 2,834 | 826 | 9 | 439 | 5,501 | 43 | 2,235 |
| Maine............. | 1,520 | 17 | 830 | 338 | 3 | 179 | 1,084 | 12 | 602 |
| Maryland.......... | 11,135 | 79 | 5,858 | 2,146 | 17 | 1,208 | 8,494 | 59 | 4,398 |
| Massachusetts..... | 22,215 | 137 | 11,859 | 4,625 | 40 | 2,869 | 16,817 | 92 | 8,552 |
| Michigan.......... | 13,958 | 130 | 7,724 | 3,029 | 33 | 1,802 | 10,066 | 90 | 5,487 |
| Minnesota......... | 12,064 | 99 | 6,523 | 2,490 | 22 | 1,381 | 8,979 | 73 | 4,841 |
| Mississippi........ | 2,458 | 26 | 1,181 | 242 | 3 | 124 | 2,039 | 21 | 979 |
| Missouri........... | 9,900 | 94 | 5,086 | 2,155 | (D) | (D) | 7,242 | 69 | 3,662 |
| Montana.......... | 1,518 | 16 | 822 | 250 | 3 | 126 | 1,194 | 12 | 663 |
| Nebraska.......... | 2,732 | 28 | 1,481 | 537 | 6 | 303 | 2,014 | 20 | 1,098 |
| Nevada........... | 7,019 | 41 | 3,050 | 2,429 | 9 | 986 | 4,388 | 30 | 1,950 |
| New Hampshire. .. | 2,499 | 22 | 1,399 | 403 | 4 | 239 | 1,970 | 16 | 1,093 |
| New Jersey........ | 21,545 | 136 | 11,264 | 3,755 | 27 | 1,991 | 16,882 | 103 | 8,802 |
| New Mexico........ | 2,908 | 27 | 1,483 | 326 | 4 | 186 | 2,462 | 22 | 1,238 |
| New York.......... | 119,857 | 467 | 47,709 | 27,021 | 141 | 13,897 | 90,970 | 313 | 32,709 |
| North Carolina..... | 14,352 | 120 | 7,523 | 2,507 | 24 | 1,413 | 11,065 | 89 | 5,733 |
| North Dakota....... | 1,437 | 14 | 794 | 137 | 2 | 77 | 1,225 | 12 | 679 |
| Ohio.............. | 18,287 | 179 | 10,007 | 3,775 | (D) | (D) | 13,491 | 133 | 7,436 |
| Oklahoma......... | 4,280 | 42 | 2,188 | 758 | 6 | 403 | 3,223 | 34 | 1,659 |
| Oregon............ | 7,848 | 67 | 4,304 | 1,569 | 15 | 894 | 5,950 | 50 | 3,238 |
| Pennsylvania...... | 24,041 | 176 | 11,228 | 4,420 | 48 | 2,675 | 18,450 | 119 | 7,963 |
| Rhode Island....... | 1,931 | 18 | 1,052 | 358 | 4 | 217 | 1,485 | 13 | 789 |
| South Carolina..... | 5,273 | 52 | 2,767 | 944 | (D) | (D) | 3,998 | 38 | 2,100 |
| South Dakota...... | 1,189 | 14 | 674 | 146 | 2 | 83 | 969 | 11 | 558 |
| Tennessee......... | 14,182 | 87 | 5,677 | 3,464 | (D) | (D) | 10,196 | 61 | 3,732 |
| Texas............. | 45,114 | 367 | 22,963 | 8,138 | 66 | 4,410 | 34,590 | 284 | 17,345 |
| Utah.............. | 6,913 | 63 | 3,430 | 1,072 | 12 | 569 | 5,606 | 48 | 2,750 |
| Vermont........... | 996 | 11 | 564 | 234 | 3 | 145 | 714 | 7 | 394 |
| Virginia............ | 16,998 | 120 | 8,015 | 2,674 | 24 | 1,502 | 13,618 | 91 | 6,149 |
| Washington........ | 41,079 | 178 | 20,944 | 2,445 | 23 | 1,472 | 37,928 | 150 | 19,158 |
| West Virginia....... | 1,604 | 18 | 920 | 111 | 2 | 63 | 1,380 | 16 | 804 |
| Wisconsin......... | 9,749 | 94 | 5,591 | 1,548 | 16 | 855 | 7,638 | 73 | 4,480 |
| Wyoming.......... | 1,071 | 11 | 739 | 110 | 1 | 57 | 918 | 10 | 661 |

D Withheld to avoid disclosing data on individual companies. [1] Nominal; not adjusted for inflation.

Source: U.S. Bureau of Economic Analysis, "Arts and Cultural Production Satellite Account," <https://www.bea.gov/data/special-topics/arts-and-culture>, accessed March 2019.

# Table 1259. Broadway Shows and Tours—Selected Data: 1990 to 2019

[In units, as indicated (282 represents $282,000,000). For season ending in year shown, except as indicated]

| Item | Unit | 1990 | 1995 | 2000 | 2005 | 2010 | 2015 | 2016 | 2017 | 2018 | 2019 |
|---|---|---|---|---|---|---|---|---|---|---|---|
| Broadway shows: | | | | | | | | | | | |
| New productions.................... | Number | 39 | 34 | 36 | 39 | 39 | 37 | 39 | 45 | 33 | 38 |
| Attendance..................... | Millions | 8.0 | 9.0 | 11.4 | 11.5 | 11.9 | 13.1 | 13.3 | 13.3 | 13.8 | 14.8 |
| Playing weeks [1, 2].................. | Number | 1,070 | 1,120 | 1,464 | 1,494 | 1,464 | 1,626 | 1,648 | 1,580 | 1,624 | 1,737 |
| Gross ticket sales................. | Mil. dol. | 282 | 406 | 603 | 769 | 1,020 | 1,365 | 1,373 | 1,449 | 1,697 | 1,829 |
| Broadway road tours: [3] | | | | | | | | | | | |
| Attendance..................... | Millions | 11.1 | 9.9 | 11.4 | 12.9 | 15.9 | 13.7 | 14.0 | 13.9 | 17.0 | 18.5 |
| Playing weeks.................... | Number | 944 | 882 | 854 | 1,027 | 1,250 | 953 | 1,014 | 983 | 1,125 | 1,188 |
| Gross ticket sales................. | Mil. dol. | 367 | 547 | 553 | 706 | 947 | 957 | 981 | 1,007 | 1,416 | 1,633 |

NA Not available. [1] All shows (new productions and holdovers from previous seasons). [2] Eight performances constitute one playing week. [3] North American Tours include U.S. and Canadian companies.

Source: The Broadway League, New York, NY ©. See also <http://www.broadwayleague.com>.

## Table 1260. Arts and Humanities—Selected Federal Aid Programs: 1990 to 2018

[In millions of dollars (170.8 represents $170,800,000), except as indicated. For fiscal year ending September 30. FY2010 includes funds from the American Recovery and Reinvestment Act]

| Type of fund and program | 1990 | 1995 | 2000 | 2005 | 2010 | 2015 | 2016 | 2017 | 2018 |
|---|---|---|---|---|---|---|---|---|---|
| **National Endowment for the Arts:** | | | | | | | | | |
| Funds available [1] | 170.8 | 152.1 | 85.2 | 108.8 | 153.1 | 127.1 | 132.7 | 129.5 | 124.3 |
| Program appropriation [2] | 152.3 | 138.1 | 79.6 | 99.5 | 138.7 | 116.6 | 118.4 | 119.2 | 120.7 |
| Grants awarded (number) [3] | 4,252 | 3,534 | 1,906 | 2,161 | 2,731 | 2,346 | 2,446 | 2,509 | 2,306 |
| Funds obligated [4,5] | 157.6 | 147.9 | 83.5 | 104.4 | 141.1 | 118.4 | 124.4 | 128 | 121.7 |
| **National Endowment for the Humanities:** | | | | | | | | | |
| Funds available [1] | 140.6 | 152.3 | 102.6 | 119.8 | 146.6 | 129.8 | 130.1 | 128.7 | 134.4 |
| Program appropriation | 114.2 | 125.7 | 82.7 | 99.9 | 125.7 | 108.1 | 109.8 | 111.2 | 113.4 |
| Matching funds [6] | 26.3 | 25.7 | 15.1 | 15.9 | 14.3 | 10.9 | 10.9 | 10.7 | 11.3 |
| Grants awarded (number) [3] | 2,195 | 1,871 | 1,230 | 1,174 | 1,204 | 822 | 920 | 813 | 697 |
| Funds obligated [4,5] | 141.0 | 151.8 | 100.0 | 117.8 | 142.7 | 121.5 | 121.9 | 120.7 | 116.1 |
| Education programs | 16.3 | 19.2 | 13.0 | 14.6 | 16.0 | 13.8 | 13.5 | 13.3 | 10.3 |
| State partnership | 29.6 | 32.0 | 30.6 | 36.9 | 49.1 | 42.6 | 43.9 | 46.5 | 47.2 |
| Research grants | 22.5 | 22.2 | 6.9 | 7.1 | 12.5 | 10.1 | 10.1 | 10.1 | 9.4 |
| Fellowships | 15.3 | 16.5 | 6.1 | 8.9 | 6.8 | 7.0 | 5.8 | 5.8 | 5.9 |
| Challenge [7] | 14.6 | 13.8 | 10.8 | 12.7 | 10.5 | 7.8 | 8.8 | 6.9 | 4.8 |
| Public programs | 25.4 | 25.8 | 11.8 | 14.4 | 19.4 | 17.6 | 13.9 | 14.4 | 13.4 |
| Digital Humanities | (NA) | (NA) | (NA) | (NA) | 4.9 | 4.7 | 4.7 | 4.7 | 4.8 |
| Preservation and access | 17.5 | 22.2 | 20.7 | 22.4 | 22.6 | 17.1 | 15.7 | 15.4 | 20.3 |

NA Not available. [1] Includes other program funds not shown separately. Excludes administrative funds. [2] FY1990–FY1996 include Regular Program Funds, Treasury Funds, Challenge Grant Funds, and Policy, Planning, and Research Funds. FY1997 includes Regular Program Funds, Matching Grant Funds, and Policy, Research and Technology Funds. FY1998–FY 2000 includes Regular Program Funds and Matching Grant Funds. [3] Excludes cooperative agreements and interagency agreements. [4] Includes obligations for new grants, supplemental awards on previous years' grants, cooperative agreements, and interagency agreements. Excludes obligations funded with administrative funds. [5] Beginning with 1997 data, the grantmaking structure changed from discipline-based categories to thematic ones. [6] Represents federal funds obligated only upon receipt or certification by endowment of matching nonfederal gifts. Funds for matching grants are not allocated by program area because they are awarded on a grant-by-grant basis. [7] Program designed to stimulate new sources and higher levels of giving to institutions for the purpose of guaranteeing long-term stability and financial independence. Program currently requires a match of at least 3 private dollars to each federal dollar.

Source: U.S. National Endowment for the Arts, unpublished data; and U.S. National Endowment for the Humanities, unpublished data.

## Table 1261. State Arts Agency Legislative Appropriations: 2018 to 2019

[In thousands of dollars (353,228 represents $353,228,000). For fiscal year ending June 30 in most states. The National Assembly of State Arts Agencies (NASAA) is the membership organization of the nations' state and jurisdictional arts agencies. Legislative appropriations include funds designated to the state arts agency by state legislatures. These include line items, which are not controlled by the agency but passed through to designated entities. State arts agencies also receive monies from other sources including other state funds, the federal government (primarily the National Endowment for the Arts), private funds, and legislative earmarks. Minus sign (-) indicates decrease in spending]

| State | Legislative appropriations including line items 2018, revised | Legislative appropriations including line items 2019, enacted | Percent change, 2018 to 2019 | State | Legislative appropriations including line items 2018, revised | Legislative appropriations including line items 2019, enacted | Percent change, 2018 to 2019 | State | Legislative appropriations including line items 2018, revised | Legislative appropriations including line items 2019, enacted | Percent change, 2018 to 2019 |
|---|---|---|---|---|---|---|---|---|---|---|---|
| **U.S.** | **353,228** | **360,495** | **2.1** | LA | 2,130 | 2,131 | 0.1 | OR | 2,701 | 2,449 | -9.3 |
| AL | 4,809 | 5,459 | 13.5 | ME | 923 | 947 | 2.5 | PA [4] | 10,429 | 10,429 | – |
| AK | 693 | 693 | – | MD | 20,086 | 21,747 | 8.3 | RI | 2,023 | 3,165 | 56.4 |
| AZ [1] | 1,500 | 2,000 | 33.3 | MA | 13,951 | 16,155 | 15.8 | SC | 3,358 | 4,216 | 25.5 |
| AR | 1,492 | 1,426 | -4.4 | MI | 10,000 | 10,000 | – | SD | 904 | 957 | 6.0 |
| CA | 18,490 | 27,295 | 47.6 | MN | 33,904 | 39,275 | 15.8 | TN | 7,141 | 7,176 | 0.5 |
| CO | 2,000 | 2,000 | – | MS | 1,595 | 1,595 | – | TX | 5,037 | 5,043 | 0.1 |
| CT | 4,411 | 5,219 | 18.3 | MO | 6,451 | 6,459 | 0.1 | UT [5] | 3,171 | 3,327 | 4.9 |
| DE | 3,207 | 3,206 | – | MT | 456 | 516 | 13.1 | VT | 675 | 718 | 6.3 |
| DC | 28,978 | 31,367 | 8.2 | NE | 1,538 | 1,477 | -4.0 | VA | 3,468 | 3,704 | 6.8 |
| FL [2] | 25,653 | 7,404 | -71.1 | NV | 1,807 | 1,826 | 1.0 | WA | 1,479 | 1,633 | 10.4 |
| GA [3] | 1,112 | 1,211 | 9.0 | NH | 406 | 402 | -1.0 | WV | 698 | 880 | 26.0 |
| HI | 5,462 | 6,027 | 10.3 | NJ | 16,405 | 16,405 | – | WI [6] | 917 | 763 | -16.8 |
| ID | 811 | 841 | 3.8 | NM | 1,315 | 1,322 | 0.5 | WY | 1,039 | 1,039 | – |
| IL | 9,901 | 11,326 | 14.4 | NY | 45,334 | 45,334 | – | AS [7] | 85 | 121 | 42.4 |
| IN | 4,000 | 4,000 | – | NC | 8,258 | 9,103 | 10.2 | GU [7] | 451 | 361 | -20.0 |
| IA | 1,217 | 1,267 | 4.1 | ND | 782 | 782 | – | MP [7,8] | 586 | 586 | – |
| KS | 189 | 189 | – | OH | 14,654 | 14,654 | – | PR [7] | 9,424 | 8,034 | -14.7 |
| KY | 2,628 | 1,709 | -35.0 | OK | 2,795 | 2,799 | 0.1 | VI [7] | 299 | 325 | 8.6 |

– Represents zero. [1] Since FY2012, the legislature has not appropriated funding to the state arts agency from the general fund. The SAA's FY2018 and FY2019 appropriations were drawn from interest on the state's rainy-day fund and were nonrecurring. [2] Funding for the division suffered a 71.1% reduction for FY2019 due to the state legislature's decision to not fund a large portion of designated grants for organizations. [3] The Georgia Council for the Arts appropriation includes one-time funding of $150,000 in FY2018 and $100,000 in FY2019. [4] Total legislative appropriation includes an administrative allocation for the Pennsylvania Council on the Arts. [5] The agency's appropriation does not include state support for the Fine Arts Outreach POPS program and the Beverley Taylor Sorenson Arts Learning Program, which are administered by agencies other than the SAA. [6] In Wisconsin, the FY2019 legislative appropriation figure does not include an additional $35,900 to match Partnership Agreement funds from the NEA. The additional appropriation was pending legislative action at the time of data collection. [7] AS—American Samoa, GU—Guam, MP—Northern Marianas, PR—Puerto Rico, VI—Virgin Islands. [8] Due to the significant damage from Typhoon Yutu in October 2018, NASAA did not collect data from the Commonwealth Council for Arts and Culture. Tables display level funding for the agency in FY2018.

Source: National Assembly of State Arts Agencies, *State Arts Agency Revenues, Fiscal Year 2019* ©, February 2019. See also <http://www.nasaa-arts.org>.

## Table 1262. Personal Participation in Various Arts or Creative Activities by Selected Characteristics: 2012

[In percent, except as indicated (235.0 represents 235,000,000). For persons 18 years old and over. Represents creating or performing at least once in the prior 12 months]

| Item | Adult population (millions) | Music | Dance | Films/ videos | Photos | Visual Arts | Pottery/ jewelry | Weaving/ sewing [1] | Creative writing |
|---|---|---|---|---|---|---|---|---|---|
| Total.......................... | **235.0** | **5.0** | **1.3** | **2.8** | **12.4** | **5.7** | **4.5** | **13.2** | **5.9** |
| Sex: | | | | | | | | | |
| Male......................... | 113.1 | 5.6 | 0.9 | 3.6 | 11.5 | 4.7 | 2.1 | 2.4 | 5.6 |
| Female....................... | 121.9 | 4.5 | 1.6 | 2.1 | 13.2 | 6.7 | 6.8 | 23.2 | 6.2 |
| Race and ethnicity: | | | | | | | | | |
| White alone................. | 155.7 | 5.3 | 1.1 | 2.9 | 14.3 | 6.4 | 5.1 | 14.8 | 6.7 |
| African American alone...... | 26.8 | 4.3 | 1.7 | 3.0 | 8.0 | 3.4 | 4.2 | 9.5 | 4.3 |
| Hispanic..................... | 35.0 | 4.1 | 1.5 | 2.2 | 7.9 | 3.7 | 2.5 | 9.4 | 4.1 |
| Other alone................. | 17.5 | 5.5 | 1.2 | 3.2 | 10.9 | 6.9 | 4.5 | 11.9 | 5.2 |
| Age: | | | | | | | | | |
| 18 to 24 years old........... | 30.4 | 8.6 | 2.7 | 4.5 | 13.4 | 9.3 | 7.1 | 9.8 | 10.2 |
| 25 to 34 years old........... | 41.0 | 5.0 | 1.0 | 3.6 | 15.4 | 6.0 | 4.2 | 10.6 | 6.4 |
| 35 to 44 years old........... | 39.6 | 4.2 | 1.4 | 4.2 | 14.0 | 5.6 | 4.4 | 10.8 | 6.4 |
| 45 to 54 years old........... | 43.7 | 5.3 | 1.0 | 2.5 | 12.4 | 5.0 | 4.6 | 13.5 | 4.3 |
| 55 to 64 years old........... | 38.3 | 4.4 | 0.9 | 2.0 | 11.9 | 5.7 | 4.6 | 15.5 | 5.3 |
| 65 to 74 years old........... | 23.8 | 3.0 | 1.2 | 1.2 | 10.0 | 4.0 | 3.6 | 19.0 | 4.1 |
| 75 years old and older....... | 18.1 | 3.8 | 0.5 | 0.5 | 5.3 | 3.3 | 2.3 | 16.5 | 4.6 |

[1] Includes weaving, crocheting, knitting, quilting, needlepoint, and sewing.

Source: U.S. National Endowment for the Arts, *A Decade of Arts Engagement: Findings From the Survey of Public Participation in the Arts, 2002–2012*, January 2015. See also <http://arts.gov/publications/decade-arts-engagement-findings-survey-public-participation-arts-2002-2012>.

## Table 1263. Attendance/Participation Rates for Various Arts Activities by Selected Characteristics: 2012

[In percent, except as indicated (235.0 represents 235,000,000). For persons 18 years old and over. Represents attendance at least once in the prior twelve months. Excludes elementary and high school performances]

| Item | Adult population (million) | Jazz concert | Classical music concert | Musicals | Non- musical plays | Art muse- ums/ galleries | Craft/ visual art festivals | Parks/ historic build- ings [1] | Live book reading or story- telling [2] |
|---|---|---|---|---|---|---|---|---|---|
| Total................. | **235.0** | **8.1** | **8.8** | **15.2** | **8.3** | **21.0** | **22.4** | **23.9** | **4.1** |
| Sex: | | | | | | | | | |
| Male......................... | 113.1 | 7.9 | 8.0 | 12.9 | 7.3 | 18.7 | 18.2 | 23.1 | 3.0 |
| Female....................... | 121.9 | 8.3 | 9.5 | 17.3 | 9.2 | 23.1 | 26.4 | 24.6 | 5.1 |
| Race and ethnicity: | | | | | | | | | |
| White alone................. | 155.7 | 8.4 | 11.0 | 18.4 | 10.1 | 24.1 | 26.2 | 28.3 | 4.2 |
| African American alone...... | 26.8 | 11.2 | 4.0 | 9.3 | 6.2 | 11.9 | 12.0 | 13.1 | 5.2 |
| Hispanic..................... | 35.0 | 5.0 | 3.3 | 7.3 | 3.6 | 14.3 | 16.8 | 13.8 | 2.5 |
| Other alone................. | 17.5 | 7.4 | 7.3 | 11.2 | 4.9 | 21.2 | 16.3 | 21.2 | 4.7 |
| Age: | | | | | | | | | |
| 18 to 24 years old........... | 30.4 | 9.2 | 6.7 | 13.0 | 6.4 | 18.3 | 18.3 | 20.5 | 4.6 |
| 25 to 34 years old........... | 41.0 | 8.0 | 7.3 | 13.6 | 7.5 | 22.0 | 21.6 | 25.1 | 5.2 |
| 35 to 44 years old........... | 39.6 | 7.8 | 6.4 | 12.9 | 7.3 | 21.2 | 22.0 | 23.3 | 4.8 |
| 45 to 54 years old........... | 43.7 | 7.9 | 8.2 | 16.9 | 9.5 | 22.0 | 24.6 | 26.2 | 3.3 |
| 55 to 64 years old........... | 38.3 | 10.0 | 11.0 | 19.0 | 9.0 | 22.5 | 25.8 | 26.5 | 4.0 |
| 65 to 74 years old........... | 23.8 | 7.9 | 13.9 | 17.7 | 10.6 | 22.4 | 26.1 | 25.5 | 3.6 |
| 75 years old and older....... | 18.1 | 3.9 | 10.9 | 11.9 | 7.8 | 15.5 | 15.0 | 15.0 | 2.2 |
| Education: | | | | | | | | | |
| Grade school................. | 9.9 | 0.9 | 0.9 | 1.6 | 0.3 | 3.6 | 5.9 | 3.9 | 1.2 |
| Some high school............ | 19.0 | 1.3 | 1.6 | 2.9 | 1.8 | 4.3 | 8.0 | 5.9 | 1.5 |
| High school graduate........ | 70.9 | 4.5 | 3.1 | 8.3 | 3.9 | 9.9 | 16.3 | 13.3 | 1.8 |
| Some college................ | 68.7 | 8.2 | 7.3 | 14.6 | 7.8 | 19.7 | 23.6 | 25.0 | 4.2 |
| College graduate............. | 43.0 | 13.1 | 15.9 | 26.7 | 14.6 | 37.2 | 32.9 | 38.4 | 6.6 |
| Graduate school............. | 23.5 | 17.9 | 26.0 | 32.1 | 20.0 | 49.3 | 36.9 | 48.8 | 9.2 |
| Income: | | | | | | | | | |
| Less than $20,000........... | 40.9 | 4.8 | 3.9 | 6.2 | 3.8 | 10.2 | 12.3 | 12.1 | 3.0 |
| $20,000 to $50,000........... | 76.0 | 5.3 | 5.6 | 9.6 | 5.8 | 14.0 | 17.9 | 16.2 | 3.5 |
| $50,000 to $75,000.......... | 43.9 | 8.2 | 9.2 | 16.8 | 7.9 | 22.1 | 24.5 | 25.1 | 4.4 |
| $75,000 to $100,000........ | 27.6 | 10.2 | 10.3 | 20.1 | 11.6 | 26.5 | 28.9 | 30.1 | 5.4 |
| $100,000 to $150,000........ | 27.1 | 12.6 | 15.1 | 24.6 | 13.5 | 33.8 | 30.5 | 38.8 | 4.7 |
| $150,000 and over......... | 19.6 | 16.3 | 19.4 | 32.4 | 16.6 | 43.2 | 36.4 | 46.6 | 5.5 |

[1] Visiting historic parks or monuments or touring buildings or neighborhoods for the historic or design value. [2] Examples include author readings, poetry, or storytelling events.

Source: U.S. National Endowment for the Arts, *A Decade of Arts Engagement: Findings From the Survey of Public Participation in the Arts, 2002–2012*, January 2015. See also <http://arts.gov/publications/decade-arts-engagement-findings-survey-public-participation-arts-2002-2012>.

# Table 1264. Outdoor Recreation Sector Gross Output by Activity: 2012 to 2016

[In millions of current dollars (679,386 represents $679,386,000,000)]

| Activity | 2012 | 2013 | 2014 | 2015 | 2016 |
|---|---|---|---|---|---|
| **Total outdoor recreation**..... | **679,386** | **700,298** | **714,396** | **716,073** | **731,364** |
| **Total core outdoor recreation**..... | **341,132** | **363,246** | **372,266** | **380,293** | **392,987** |
| Conventional outdoor recreation..... | 208,496 | 225,248 | 232,546 | 234,153 | 243,145 |
| Bicycling..... | 3,411 | 3,322 | 3,360 | 3,330 | 3,480 |
| Boating/fishing..... | 31,501 | 33,023 | 34,234 | 36,903 | 38,199 |
| Canoeing..... | 117 | 115 | 126 | 131 | 135 |
| Kayaking..... | 499 | 459 | 512 | 521 | 556 |
| Fishing (excludes boating)..... | 4,810 | 5,283 | 5,532 | 6,522 | 6,360 |
| Sailing..... | 1,896 | 1,974 | 2,121 | 2,185 | 2,419 |
| Other boating..... | 24,178 | 25,191 | 25,942 | 27,544 | 28,729 |
| Climbing/hiking/tent camping..... | 6,536 | 6,913 | 7,182 | 7,619 | 7,756 |
| Equestrian..... | 9,017 | 9,614 | 10,664 | 10,454 | 11,108 |
| Hunting/shooting/trapping..... | 9,496 | 11,723 | 11,821 | 13,682 | 14,546 |
| Motorcycling/ATVing..... | 18,970 | 18,717 | 19,047 | 18,062 | 19,537 |
| Recreational flying..... | 4,335 | 4,452 | 4,583 | 4,154 | 3,932 |
| RVing..... | 26,688 | 28,428 | 30,236 | 30,077 | 30,831 |
| Snow activities..... | 10,470 | 10,578 | 10,847 | 10,560 | 10,643 |
| Skiing..... | 2,829 | 2,878 | 3,094 | 3,314 | 3,378 |
| Snowboarding..... | 2,420 | 2,498 | 2,646 | 2,835 | 2,986 |
| Other snow activities (includes snowmobiling) [1]..... | 5,221 | 5,202 | 5,107 | 4,412 | 4,279 |
| Other conventional outdoor recreation activities..... | 17,065 | 17,497 | 17,272 | 16,038 | 16,591 |
| Multi-use apparel and accessories (conventional) [2]..... | 71,009 | 80,981 | 83,300 | 83,274 | 86,520 |
| Other outdoor recreation..... | 132,635 | 137,998 | 139,721 | 146,140 | 149,842 |
| Amusement parks/water parks..... | 14,807 | 15,628 | 16,555 | 18,067 | 19,228 |
| Festivals/sporting events/concerts..... | 22,122 | 23,058 | 24,235 | 25,697 | 26,481 |
| Field sports..... | 6,186 | 7,010 | 7,099 | 7,552 | 7,778 |
| Game areas (includes golfing and tennis)..... | 31,622 | 32,775 | 31,756 | 33,942 | 36,266 |
| Guided tours/outfitted travel..... | 27,256 | 28,222 | 29,713 | 29,326 | 27,543 |
| Productive activities (includes gardening)..... | 10,104 | 10,516 | 9,538 | 9,728 | 9,932 |
| Other outdoor recreation activities [3]..... | 14,839 | 14,997 | 15,362 | 16,254 | 16,698 |
| Multi-use apparel and accessories (other) [2]..... | 5,700 | 5,792 | 5,464 | 5,575 | 5,917 |
| **Supporting outdoor recreation**..... | 338,254 | 337,052 | 342,130 | 335,780 | 338,378 |
| Construction..... | 9,527 | 9,423 | 9,930 | 11,503 | 12,363 |
| Local trips [4]..... | 72,385 | 73,049 | 72,934 | 65,371 | 63,502 |
| Travel and tourism [5]..... | 224,902 | 222,369 | 226,474 | 225,330 | 227,959 |
| Food and beverages..... | 37,646 | 31,711 | 33,238 | 35,730 | 37,696 |
| Lodging..... | 46,673 | 48,652 | 48,565 | 52,150 | 54,307 |
| Shopping and souvenirs..... | 44,365 | 45,513 | 47,433 | 47,416 | 48,549 |
| Transportation..... | 96,219 | 96,493 | 97,240 | 90,035 | 87,407 |
| Government expenditures..... | 31,439 | 32,211 | 32,791 | 33,576 | 34,553 |
| Federal Government..... | 3,947 | 4,247 | 4,011 | 4,036 | 4,247 |
| State and local government..... | 27,492 | 27,965 | 28,779 | 29,540 | 30,306 |

[1] Dog mushing, sleighing, snowmobiling, snow shoeing, and snow tubing. [2] Backpacks, bug spray, coolers, general outdoor clothing, GPS equipment, hydration equipment, lighting, sports racks, sunscreen, watches, and other miscellaneous gear and equipment. [3] Agritourism, augmented reality games, beachgoing, disc golf, hot springs soaking, kite flying, model airplane/rocket/UAV, paintball, photography, stargazing/astronomy, swimming, therapeutic programs, water polo, and yard sports. [4] Trip expenses less than 50 miles away from home, including food and beverages, lodging, shopping and souvenirs, and transportation. [5] Expenses for travel at least 50 miles away from home.

Source: U.S. Bureau of Economic Analysis, Satellite Accounts, *Outdoor Recreation Satellite Account: Updated Statistics for 2012-2016*, September 2018. See also <https://www.bea.gov/data/special-topics/outdoor-recreation>.

# Table 1265. Personal Consumption Expenditures for Recreation: 1990 to 2018

[In billions of dollars (314.7 represents $314,700,000,000), except percent. Represents market value of purchases of goods and services by individuals and nonprofit institutions]

| Type of product or service | 1990 | 2000 | 2005 | 2010 | 2016 | 2017 | 2018 |
|---|---|---|---|---|---|---|---|
| **Total recreation expenditures**..... | **314.7** | **633.7** | **805.2** | **884.4** | **1,103.6** | **1,157.0** | **1,203.5** |
| Percent of total personal consumption [1]..... | 8.3 | 9.4 | 9.2 | 8.7 | 8.7 | 8.7 | 8.6 |
| Video and audio equipment, computers, and related services.... | 81.1 | 181.2 | 240.0 | 275.5 | 332.1 | 345.1 | 359.2 |
| Video and audio equipment..... | 43.7 | 79.9 | 101.4 | 83.2 | 78.6 | 80.7 | 84.2 |
| Information processing equipment..... | 9.6 | 44.1 | 68.4 | 95.0 | 121.0 | 134.0 | 142.1 |
| Services related to video and audio goods and computers...... | 27.8 | 57.2 | 70.2 | 97.3 | 132.5 | 130.4 | 132.9 |
| Sports and recreational goods and related services..... | 74.2 | 146.0 | 184.1 | 177.4 | 237.9 | 247.8 | 250.4 |
| Sports and recreational vehicles..... | 16.6 | 34.9 | 49.1 | 35.8 | 56.1 | 60.3 | 61.3 |
| Other sporting and recreational goods..... | 55.4 | 106.8 | 130.0 | 137.2 | 176.0 | 181.5 | 182.7 |
| Maintenance and repair of recreational vehicles and sports equipment..... | 2.1 | 4.2 | 4.9 | 4.4 | 5.7 | 6.0 | 6.3 |
| Membership clubs, sports centers, parks, theaters, and museums..... | 49.7 | 91.9 | 117.9 | 146.1 | 187.4 | 199.5 | 211.0 |
| Membership clubs and participant sports centers..... | 14.3 | 26.4 | 34.3 | 40.9 | 52.0 | 54.7 | 57.0 |
| Amusement parks, campgrounds, and related services..... | 19.2 | 31.1 | 33.6 | 40.1 | 57.8 | 61.8 | 65.8 |
| Admissions to specified spectator amusements..... | 14.4 | 30.6 | 43.7 | 58.7 | 69.1 | 73.6 | 78.8 |
| Motion picture theaters..... | 5.1 | 8.6 | 9.7 | 12.3 | 13.9 | 14.7 | 15.7 |
| Live entertainment, excluding sports..... | 4.5 | 10.4 | 18.3 | 26.7 | 30.7 | 32.8 | 35.4 |
| Spectator sports..... | 4.8 | 11.6 | 15.7 | 19.7 | 24.5 | 26.1 | 27.6 |
| Museums and libraries..... | 1.9 | 3.8 | 6.4 | 6.5 | 8.5 | 9.3 | 9.5 |
| Magazines, newspapers, books, and stationery..... | 47.3 | 81.0 | 85.0 | 74.8 | 83.1 | 89.0 | 95.1 |
| Gambling..... | 23.7 | 67.6 | 96.1 | 109.4 | 131.3 | 135.9 | 142.6 |
| Pets, pet products, and related services..... | 18.8 | 39.7 | 57.2 | 76.2 | 104.8 | 111.1 | 114.9 |
| Photographic goods and services..... | 16.7 | 19.7 | 17.7 | 15.2 | 15.9 | 16.2 | 16.7 |
| Package tours [2]..... | 3.2 | 6.7 | 7.2 | 9.8 | 11.3 | 12.5 | 13.7 |

[1] See Table 707. [2] Consists of tour operators' and travel agents' margins. Purchases of travel and accommodations included in tours are accounted for separately in other personal consumption expenditures categories.

Source: U.S. Bureau of Economic Analysis, National Income and Product Accounts Tables, "Table 2.5.5. Personal Consumption Expenditures by Function," <http://www.bea.gov/iTable/index_nipa.cfm>, accessed July 2019.

# Table 1266. Expenditures Per Consumer Unit for Entertainment and Reading: 1985 to 2017

[Data are annual averages. In dollars, except as indicated. Based on the Consumer Expenditure Survey (CES). For description of survey, see text, Section 13; also see headnote, Table 716. For composition of regions, see map, inside front cover]

| Year and characteristic | Entertainment and reading | | Entertainment | | | | Reading |
|---|---|---|---|---|---|---|---|
| | Total | Percent of total expenditures | Total | Fees and admissions | Audio and visual equipment and services | Other supplies, equipment & services [1] | |
| 1985. | 1,311 | 5.6 | 1,170 | 320 | 371 | 479 | 141 |
| 1990. | 1,575 | 5.6 | 1,422 | 371 | 454 | 597 | 153 |
| 1995. | 1,775 | 5.5 | 1,612 | 433 | 542 | 637 | 163 |
| 2000. | 2,009 | 5.3 | 1,863 | 515 | 622 | 727 | 146 |
| 2001. | 2,094 | 5.3 | 1,953 | 526 | 660 | 767 | 141 |
| 2002. | 2,218 | 5.5 | 2,079 | 542 | 692 | 845 | 139 |
| 2003. | 2,187 | 5.4 | 2,060 | 494 | 730 | 835 | 127 |
| 2004. | 2,348 | 5.4 | 2,218 | 528 | 788 | 903 | 130 |
| 2005. | 2,514 | 5.4 | 2,388 | 588 | 888 | 912 | 126 |
| 2006. | 2,493 | 5.2 | 2,376 | 606 | 906 | 863 | 117 |
| 2007. | 2,816 | 5.7 | 2,698 | 658 | 987 | 1,053 | 118 |
| 2008. | 2,951 | 5.8 | 2,835 | 616 | 1,036 | 1,183 | 116 |
| 2009. | 2,803 | 5.7 | 2,693 | 628 | 975 | 1,090 | 110 |
| 2010. | 2,604 | 5.4 | 2,504 | 581 | 954 | 970 | 100 |
| 2011. | 2,687 | 5.4 | 2,572 | 594 | 977 | 1,001 | 115 |
| 2012. | 2,714 | 5.3 | 2,605 | 614 | 979 | 1,011 | 109 |
| 2013. | 2,584 | 5.1 | 2,482 | 569 | 964 | 949 | 102 |
| 2014. | 2,831 | 5.3 | 2,728 | 636 | 1,051 | 1,041 | 103 |
| 2015. | 2,956 | 5.3 | 2,842 | 652 | 1,084 | 1,106 | 114 |
| 2016. | 3,031 | 5.3 | 2,913 | 681 | 1,085 | 1,146 | 118 |
| **2017, total.** | **3,313** | **5.5** | **3,203** | **750** | **985** | **1,468** | **110** |
| Age of reference person: | | | | | | | |
| Under 25 years old. | 1,530 | 4.5 | 1,488 | 333 | 542 | 612 | 42 |
| 25 to 34 years old. | 2,705 | 4.9 | 2,644 | 619 | 826 | 1,200 | 61 |
| 35 to 44 years old. | 4,116 | 6.0 | 4,001 | 1,090 | 1,031 | 1,880 | 115 |
| 45 to 54 years old. | 4,176 | 5.7 | 4,064 | 1,056 | 1,161 | 1,847 | 112 |
| 55 to 64 years old. | 3,563 | 5.5 | 3,444 | 655 | 1,093 | 1,696 | 119 |
| 65 years old and older. | 2,783 | 5.6 | 2,636 | 560 | 954 | 1,122 | 147 |
| 65 to 74 years old. | 3,463 | 6.3 | 3,327 | 683 | 1,067 | 1,578 | 136 |
| 76 years old and over. | 1,921 | 4.4 | 1,857 | 388 | 794 | 475 | 164 |
| Hispanic or Latino origin of reference person: | | | | | | | |
| Hispanic. | 1,926 | 3.9 | 1,878 | 404 | 830 | 644 | 48 |
| Non-Hispanic. | 3,529 | 5.7 | 3,409 | 804 | 1,010 | 1,595 | 120 |
| Race of reference person: | | | | | | | |
| White, and all other races [2] | 3,596 | 5.8 | 3,475 | 782 | 1,021 | 1,672 | 121 |
| Asian. | 2,894 | 4.0 | 2,797 | 1,400 | 772 | 625 | 97 |
| Black. | 1,690 | 3.9 | 1,643 | 313 | 848 | 482 | 47 |
| Region of residence: | | | | | | | |
| Northeast. | 3,256 | 5.1 | 3,133 | 925 | 1,000 | 1,208 | 123 |
| Midwest. | 3,451 | 6.0 | 3,341 | 708 | 960 | 1,672 | 110 |
| South. | 2,930 | 5.3 | 2,832 | 610 | 967 | 1,255 | 98 |
| West. | 3,883 | 5.7 | 3,763 | 890 | 1,031 | 1,842 | 120 |
| Size of consumer unit: | | | | | | | |
| One person. | 1,740 | 4.8 | 1,660 | 354 | 667 | 640 | 80 |
| Two or more persons. | 3,949 | 5.7 | 3,827 | 910 | 1,114 | 1,803 | 122 |
| Two persons. | 3,877 | 6.0 | 3,750 | 787 | 1,086 | 1,877 | 127 |
| Three persons. | 3,505 | 4.9 | 3,378 | 836 | 1,117 | 1,426 | 127 |
| Four persons. | 4,598 | 5.7 | 4,465 | 1,251 | 1,157 | 2,056 | 133 |
| Five persons or more. | 4,048 | 5.5 | 3,962 | 1,020 | 1,152 | 1,790 | 86 |
| Income before taxes: | | | | | | | |
| Quintiles of income: | | | | | | | |
| Lowest 20 percent. | 1,318 | 5.1 | 1,270 | 214 | 555 | 501 | 48 |
| Second 20 percent. | 1,935 | 4.9 | 1,873 | 278 | 763 | 830 | 62 |
| Third 20 percent. | 2,619 | 5.2 | 2,517 | 509 | 934 | 1,074 | 102 |
| Fourth 20 percent. | 3,600 | 5.3 | 3,470 | 796 | 1,113 | 1,560 | 130 |
| Highest 20 percent. | 7,097 | 6.1 | 6,889 | 1,955 | 1,562 | 3,372 | 208 |
| Education: | | | | | | | |
| Less than a high school graduate. | 1,137 | 3.8 | 1,117 | 89 | 538 | 491 | 20 |
| High school graduate. | 1,806 | 4.8 | 1,751 | 201 | 773 | 778 | 55 |
| High school graduate with some college. | 2,778 | 5.7 | 2,708 | 385 | 948 | 1,375 | 70 |
| Associate's degree. | 3,068 | 5.6 | 2,992 | 469 | 990 | 1,533 | 76 |
| Bachelor's degree. | 4,080 | 5.7 | 3,929 | 1,027 | 1,114 | 1,789 | 151 |
| Master's, professional, or doctoral degree. | 5,411 | 5.6 | 5,201 | 1,817 | 1,239 | 2,145 | 210 |

[1] Includes pets, toys, hobbies, and playground equipment, and other entertainment supplies, equipment, and services. [2] All other races includes Native Hawaiian or other Pacific Islander, American Indian or Alaska Native, and approximately 1 percent reporting more than one race.

Source: U.S. Bureau of Labor Statistics, Consumer Expenditure Survey, "Annual Calendar Year Tables, 2017," <https://www.bls.gov/cex/tables.htm#annual>, accessed February 2019.

# Table 1267. Attendance at/Participation in Various Leisure Activities Including Reading by Selected Characteristics: 2012

[In percent, except as indicated (235.0 represents 235,000,000). See headnote, Table 1262]

| Item | Adult population (mil.) | Attendance at— | | | Participation in— | | Reading— | | |
|---|---|---|---|---|---|---|---|---|---|
| | | Movies | Sports events [1] | Film festival | Exercise/ playing sports | Book club/ reading group | Fiction books | Non-fiction books | Literature [2] |
| **Total**............ | **235.0** | **59.4** | **30.3** | **2.4** | **45.7** | **3.5** | **44.4** | **42.7** | **47.0** |
| Sex: | | | | | | | | | |
| Male.................... | 113.1 | 58.2 | 34.7 | 2.4 | 47.5 | 1.9 | 33.3 | 36.8 | 37.0 |
| Female................. | 121.9 | 60.4 | 26.4 | 2.5 | 44.0 | 5.1 | 54.5 | 48.2 | 56.1 |
| Race and ethnicity: | | | | | | | | | |
| White alone............. | 155.7 | 61.6 | 34.0 | 2.6 | 49.3 | 3.8 | 59.2 | 47.0 | 52.3 |
| African American alone..... | 26.8 | 53.3 | 21.9 | 1.6 | 37.7 | 5.0 | 36.8 | 38.0 | 40.2 |
| Hispanic................. | 35.0 | 54.8 | 24.3 | 2.2 | 38.5 | 1.4 | 26.9 | 29.0 | 31.0 |
| Other alone............. | 17.5 | 57.5 | 21.4 | 3.1 | 40.8 | 2.9 | 37.9 | 38.6 | 41.7 |
| Age: | | | | | | | | | |
| 18 to 24 years old........ | 30.4 | 75.7 | 40.7 | 3.0 | 58.5 | 2.8 | 45.3 | 39.2 | 47.9 |
| 25 to 34 years old........ | 41.0 | 68.5 | 36.2 | 3.0 | 52.8 | 3.0 | 45.0 | 41.3 | 47.9 |
| 35 to 44 years old........ | 39.6 | 68.3 | 35.2 | 2.2 | 49.3 | 3.7 | 42.6 | 41.3 | 45.1 |
| 45 to 54 years old........ | 43.7 | 59.9 | 32.2 | 2.6 | 44.9 | 4.0 | 43.0 | 41.9 | 44.7 |
| 55 to 64 years old........ | 38.3 | 50.6 | 24.5 | 2.4 | 40.8 | 3.8 | 45.4 | 45.4 | 48.2 |
| 65 to 74 years old........ | 23.8 | 44.1 | 20.8 | 2.0 | 37.2 | 4.6 | 48.8 | 48.6 | 51.9 |
| 75 years old and older....... | 18.1 | 30.6 | 11.2 | 1.2 | 24.1 | 3.0 | 40.4 | 42.6 | 43.8 |
| Education: | | | | | | | | | |
| Grade school............. | 9.9 | 21.6 | 7.8 | 1.0 | 12.2 | 1.7 | 12.1 | 19.2 | 16.9 |
| Some high school......... | 19.0 | 36.7 | 13.6 | 0.4 | 24.1 | 0.4 | 21.5 | 21.2 | 22.9 |
| High school graduate........ | 70.9 | 48.6 | 22.0 | 0.9 | 35.0 | 2.2 | 33.1 | 31.0 | 36.9 |
| Some college.............. | 68.7 | 64.9 | 33.1 | 2.6 | 49.2 | 2.8 | 49.1 | 45.7 | 50.3 |
| College graduate........... | 43.0 | 75.3 | 44.4 | 3.9 | 62.6 | 5.6 | 60.5 | 57.3 | 63.0 |
| Graduate school............. | 23.5 | 76.8 | 42.2 | 6.0 | 68.8 | 9.2 | 65.8 | 68.8 | 69.5 |
| Income: | | | | | | | | | |
| Less than $20,000.......... | 40.9 | 39.4 | 14.5 | 1.7 | 31.3 | 2.3 | 34.3 | 35.3 | 36.5 |
| $20,000 to $50,000......... | 76.0 | 50.3 | 32.9 | 1.8 | 35.4 | 2.4 | 37.6 | 36.7 | 42.2 |
| $50,000 to $75,000......... | 43.9 | 65.3 | 33.0 | 3.1 | 48.9 | 4.2 | 46.6 | 44.8 | 47.7 |
| $75,000 to $100,000....... | 27.6 | 74.8 | 42.4 | 3.1 | 56.1 | 3.9 | 41.9 | 39.7 | 52.8 |
| $100,000 to $150,000...... | 27.1 | 73.0 | 43.9 | 2.4 | 63.3 | 5.3 | 56.8 | 51.2 | 57.0 |
| $150,000 and over........... | 19.6 | 77.9 | 49.9 | 3.7 | 69.4 | 6.1 | 61.3 | 58.6 | 63.3 |

[1] Includes amateur or professional sports events. [2] Includes plays, poetry, novels, or short stories.

Source: U.S. National Endowment for the Arts, *A Decade of Arts Engagement: Findings From the Survey of Public Participation in the Arts, 2002–2012*, January 2015. See also <http://arts.gov/publications/decade-arts-engagement-findings-survey-public-participation-arts-2002-2012>.

# Table 1268. Household Pet Ownership: 2011

[In percent, except as indicated (69.9 represents 69,900,000). Based on a sample survey of 50,347 households in 2012]

| Item | Unit | Dogs | Cats | Birds | Horses |
|---|---|---|---|---|---|
| **Total companion pet population** [1]................... | **Million** | **69.9** | **74.1** | **8.3** | **4.9** |
| Number of households owning pets................... | Million | 43.3 | 36.1 | 3.7 | 1.8 |
| Percent of households owning companion pets [1]............ | Percent | 36.5 | 30.4 | 3.1 | 1.5 |
| Average number owned per household.................. | Number | 1.6 | 2.1 | 2.3 | 2.7 |
| PERCENT OF HOUSEHOLDS OWNING PETS | | | | | |
| Annual household income: | | | | | |
| Under $20,000.................... | Percent | 34.5 | 34.1 | 4.3 | 1.4 |
| $20,000 to $34,999................... | Percent | 40.0 | 36.8 | 4.0 | 2.1 |
| $35,000 to $54,999................... | Percent | 42.4 | 35.6 | 3.9 | 1.9 |
| $55,000 to $84,999................... | Percent | 43.8 | 34.0 | 3.3 | 1.9 |
| $85,000 and over.................... | Percent | 43.9 | 31.7 | 3.1 | 1.9 |
| Household size: [1] | | | | | |
| One person..................... | Percent | 26.8 | 29.8 | 2.6 | 1.3 |
| Two persons.................... | Percent | 40.1 | 34.6 | 3.2 | 1.8 |
| Three persons................... | Percent | 50.0 | 38.3 | 4.2 | 2.2 |
| Four persons.................... | Percent | 53.7 | 34.9 | 4.3 | 2.0 |
| Five or more persons............... | Percent | 54.2 | 38.1 | 6.8 | 2.6 |
| VETERINARY CARE AND EXPENDITURES | | | | | |
| Households obtaining veterinary care [2]................... | Percent | 81.3 | 55.1 | 12.4 | 53.8 |
| Average visits per household per year................ | Number | 2.6 | 1.6 | 0.3 | 1.9 |
| Expenditures per household per year (mean)................ | Dollars | 378 | 191 | 33 | 373 |
| Expenditures per animal (mean)................. | Dollars | 227 | 90 | 14 | 133 |

[1] As of December 31, 2011. [2] During the year.

Source: American Veterinary Medical Association, Schaumburg, IL, *U.S. Pet Ownership and Demographics Sourcebook, 2012*, ©. See also <http://www.avma.org/reference/marketstats/sourcebook.asp>.

# Table 1269. Adult Participation in Selected Leisure Activities by Frequency: 2018

[In thousands (18,215 represents 18,215,000), except percent. For Fall 2018. Percent is based on total projected population of 247,786,000. Based on sample and subject to sampling error; see source]

| Activity | Participated in the last 12 months [1] Number (1,000) | Percent | Two or more times a week Number (1,000) | Percent | Once a week Number (1,000) | Percent | Two to three times a month Number (1,000) | Percent | Once a month Number (1,000) | Percent |
|---|---|---|---|---|---|---|---|---|---|---|
| Adult education courses | 18,215 | 7.4 | 3,957 | 1.6 | 1,864 | 0.8 | 1,241 | 0.5 | 1,638 | 0.7 |
| Aquarium attendance | 12,760 | 5.2 | 147 | 0.1 | 118 | 0.1 | 190 | 0.1 | 337 | 0.1 |
| Attend a state or county fair | 30,829 | 12.4 | 222 | 0.1 | 678 | 0.3 | 398 | 0.2 | 679 | 0.3 |
| Attend art galleries or shows | 17,772 | 7.2 | 92 | (Z) | 203 | 0.1 | 553 | 0.2 | 2,148 | 0.9 |
| Attend auto shows | 14,092 | 5.7 | 127 | 0.1 | 153 | 0.1 | 308 | 0.1 | 1,120 | 0.5 |
| Attend classical music/opera performances | 9,536 | 3.9 | 101 | (Z) | 247 | 0.1 | 397 | 0.2 | 951 | 0.4 |
| Attend country music performances | 15,399 | 6.2 | 92 | (Z) | 67 | (Z) | 228 | 0.1 | 470 | 0.2 |
| Attend dance performances | 10,399 | 4.2 | 54 | (Z) | 34 | (Z) | 325 | 0.1 | 362 | 0.2 |
| Attend other music performances [2] | 27,984 | 11.3 | 130 | 0.1 | 618 | 0.3 | 1,170 | 0.5 | 2,275 | 0.9 |
| Attend rock music performances | 22,920 | 9.3 | 96 | (Z) | 170 | 0.1 | 394 | 0.2 | 1,382 | 0.6 |
| Baking | 53,277 | 21.5 | 7,195 | 2.9 | 6,609 | 2.7 | 11,100 | 4.5 | 8,539 | 3.5 |
| Barbecuing | 63,911 | 25.8 | 7,116 | 2.9 | 9,030 | 3.6 | 13,262 | 5.4 | 9,488 | 3.8 |
| Billiards/pool | 14,999 | 6.1 | 462 | 0.2 | 928 | 0.4 | 737 | 0.3 | 1,966 | 0.8 |
| Bird watching | 10,294 | 4.2 | 4,192 | 1.7 | 782 | 0.3 | 558 | 0.2 | 810 | 0.3 |
| Board games | 38,614 | 15.6 | 2,054 | 0.8 | 4,141 | 1.7 | 6,701 | 2.7 | 7,198 | 2.9 |
| Chess | 8,518 | 3.4 | 705 | 0.3 | 512 | 0.2 | 1,040 | 0.4 | 722 | 0.3 |
| Cooking for fun | 46,279 | 18.7 | 17,053 | 6.9 | 7,094 | 2.9 | 6,184 | 2.5 | 3,947 | 1.6 |
| Crossword puzzles | 22,329 | 9.0 | 8,877 | 3.6 | 1,995 | 0.8 | 2,263 | 0.9 | 1,525 | 0.6 |
| Dance/go dancing | 18,157 | 7.3 | 2,055 | 0.8 | 1,417 | 0.6 | 1,688 | 0.7 | 1,864 | 0.8 |
| Dining out | 125,222 | 50.5 | 23,323 | 9.4 | 26,763 | 10.8 | 29,555 | 11.9 | 16,278 | 6.6 |
| Entertain friends or relatives at home | 75,503 | 30.5 | 5,990 | 2.4 | 9,249 | 3.7 | 14,194 | 5.7 | 15,939 | 6.4 |
| Fantasy sports league | 11,143 | 4.5 | 2,318 | 0.9 | 2,124 | 0.9 | 374 | 0.2 | 676 | 0.3 |
| Furniture refinishing | 8,847 | 3.6 | 282 | 0.1 | 232 | 0.1 | 282 | 0.1 | 814 | 0.3 |
| Genealogy | 9,680 | 3.9 | 1,056 | 0.4 | 628 | 0.3 | 719 | 0.3 | 1,119 | 0.5 |
| Go to bars/night clubs | 41,204 | 16.6 | 2,312 | 0.9 | 3,459 | 1.4 | 6,635 | 2.7 | 6,270 | 2.5 |
| Go to beach | 68,887 | 27.8 | 2,994 | 1.2 | 2,521 | 1.0 | 4,834 | 2.0 | 6,446 | 2.6 |
| Go to live theater | 28,086 | 11.3 | 278 | 0.1 | 500 | 0.2 | 1,219 | 0.5 | 2,932 | 1.2 |
| Go to museums | 35,790 | 14.4 | 400 | 0.2 | 1,103 | 0.5 | 1,182 | 0.5 | 3,886 | 1.6 |
| Home decoration and furnishing | 23,579 | 9.5 | 1,408 | 0.6 | 700 | 0.3 | 2,152 | 0.9 | 4,232 | 1.7 |
| Karaoke | 9,358 | 3.8 | 451 | 0.2 | 1,905 | 0.8 | 628 | 0.3 | 547 | 0.2 |
| Painting, drawing | 17,338 | 7.0 | 2,879 | 1.2 | 1,263 | 0.5 | 1,584 | 0.6 | 2,205 | 0.9 |
| PC/computer games (play offline with software) | 17,164 | 6.9 | 9,196 | 3.7 | 1,971 | 0.8 | 1,022 | 0.4 | 628 | 0.3 |
| PC/computer games (play online) | 27,940 | 11.3 | 16,914 | 6.8 | 856 | 0.4 | 1,771 | 0.7 | 790 | 0.3 |
| Photo album/scrap book | 10,075 | 4.1 | 727 | 0.3 | 3,129 | 1.3 | 917 | 0.4 | 1,126 | 0.5 |
| Photography | 20,798 | 8.4 | 5,153 | 2.1 | 497 | 0.2 | 3,102 | 1.3 | 2,350 | 1.0 |
| Picnic | 20,941 | 8.5 | 487 | 0.2 | 979 | 0.4 | 1,264 | 0.5 | 2,231 | 0.9 |
| Play bingo | 11,065 | 4.5 | 968 | 0.4 | 3,821 | 1.5 | 622 | 0.3 | 644 | 0.3 |
| Play cards | 39,552 | 16.0 | 3,954 | 1.6 | 2,057 | 0.8 | 5,474 | 2.2 | 5,998 | 2.4 |
| Play musical instrument | 16,580 | 6.7 | 6,036 | 2.4 | 7,173 | 2.9 | 1,390 | 0.6 | 1,375 | 0.6 |
| Reading books | 76,932 | 31.1 | 40,928 | 16.5 | 1,988 | 0.8 | 6,596 | 2.7 | 5,088 | 2.1 |
| Sudoku puzzles | 20,564 | 8.3 | 7,220 | 2.9 | 101 | (Z) | 1,962 | 0.8 | 1,791 | 0.7 |
| Tailgating | 9,492 | 3.8 | 206 | 0.1 | 1,587 | 0.6 | 282 | 0.1 | 616 | 0.3 |
| Trivia games | 15,017 | 6.1 | 3,653 | 1.5 | 2,118 | 0.9 | 1,360 | 0.6 | 1,572 | 0.6 |
| Video/electronic games (console) | 22,042 | 8.9 | 9,678 | 3.9 | 627 | 0.3 | 2,063 | 0.8 | 950 | 0.4 |
| Video/electronic games (portable) | 10,435 | 4.2 | 4,944 | 2.0 | 812 | 0.3 | 727 | 0.3 | 535 | 0.2 |
| Woodworking | 10,970 | 4.4 | 1,728 | 0.7 | 2,367 | 1.0 | 1,505 | 0.6 | 1,679 | 0.7 |
| Word games | 23,627 | 9.5 | 10,956 | 4.4 | 100 | (Z) | 1,846 | 0.7 | 1,273 | 0.5 |
| Zoo attendance | 28,162 | 11.4 | 231 | 0.1 | | | 535 | 0.2 | 1,831 | 0.7 |

Z Represents less than 0.05. [1] Includes those participating less than once a month, not shown separately. [2] Excluding country and rock.

Source: MRI Survey of the American Consumer.© Courtesy of MRISimmons. See also <https://www.mrisimmons.com/>.

## Table 1270. Selected Recreational Activities: 1990 to 2018

[18,719 represents 18,719,000]

| Activity | Unit | 1990 | 2000 | 2005 | 2010 | 2014 | 2015 | 2016 | 2017 | 2018 |
|---|---|---|---|---|---|---|---|---|---|---|
| Golf facilities [1] | Number | 12,846 | 15,489 | 16,052 | 15,890 | 15,372 | 15,204 | 15,014 | 14,794 | 14,613 |
| Tennis players: [2] | 1,000 | (NA) | (NA) | (NA) | 18,719 | 17,904 | 17,963 | 18,079 | 17,683 | 17,841 |
| Skiing: [3] | | | | | | | | | | |
|   Skier & snowboarder visits [4] | Million | 50.0 | 52.2 | 56.9 | 59.8 | 56.5 | 53.6 | 52.8 | 54.8 | 53.3 |
|   Operating resorts | Number | 591 | 503 | 492 | 471 | 470 | 470 | 463 | 481 | 472 |

NA Not available. [1] Source: National Golf Foundation, Jupiter, FL. [2] Source: Tennis Industry Association, Hilton Head Island, SC. Based on a nationwide telephone survey of households, in which all household members ages 6 and up are enumerated, with data on tennis participation collected for each person. Data prior to 2007 is not available due to new methodology being implemented after 2007. [3] Source: National Ski Areas Association, Lakewood, CO. ©. [4] Represents one person visiting a ski area for all or any part of a day or night, and includes full-and half-day, night, complimentary, adult, child, season, and other types of tickets. Data are estimated and are for the season ending in the year shown.

Source: Compiled from sources listed in footnotes.

## Table 1271. Amusement Park Attendance at Top 15 U.S. Facilities: 2010 to 2018

[In thousands (16,972 represents 16,972,000). Covers gated (entry ticket required) commercial theme and amusement parks with annual attendance of one million or more. Ranked for top 15 parks in 2018. Excludes water parks]

| Park name | Location | Attendance | | | | |
|---|---|---|---|---|---|---|
| | | 2010 | 2015 | 2016 | 2017 | 2018 |
| Magic Kingdom, Walt Disney World | Lake Buena Vista, FL | 16,972 | 20,492 | 20,395 | 20,450 | 20,859 |
| Disneyland | Anaheim, CA | 15,980 | 18,278 | 17,943 | 18,300 | 18,666 |
| Disney's Animal Kingdom | Lake Buena Vista, FL | 9,886 | 10,922 | 10,844 | 12,500 | 13,750 |
| EPCOT, Walt Disney World | Lake Buena Vista, FL | 10,825 | 11,798 | 11,712 | 12,200 | 12,444 |
| Disney's Hollywood Studios | Lake Buena Vista, FL | 9,603 | 10,828 | 10,776 | 10,722 | 11,258 |
| Universal Studios at Universal Orlando | Orlando, FL | 5,925 | 9,585 | 9,998 | 10,198 | 10,708 |
| Disney's California Adventure | Anaheim, CA | 6,278 | 9,383 | 9,295 | 9,574 | 9,861 |
| Universal's Islands of Adventure at Universal Orlando | Orlando, FL | 5,949 | 8,792 | 9,362 | 9,549 | 9,788 |
| Universal Studios Hollywood | Universal City, CA | 5,040 | 7,097 | 8,086 | 9,056 | 9,147 |
| SeaWorld Orlando | Orlando, FL | 5,100 | 4,777 | 4,402 | 3,962 | 4,594 |
| Busch Gardens | Tampa, FL | 4,200 | 4,252 | 4,169 | 3,961 | 4,139 |
| Knott's Berry Farm | Buena Park, CA | 3,600 | 3,867 | 4,014 | 4,034 | 4,115 |
| SeaWorld San Diego | San Diego, CA | 3,800 | 3,528 | 3,600 | 3,100 | 3,723 |
| Cedar Point | Sandusky, OH | 3,051 | 3,507 | 3,604 | 3,604 | 3,676 |
| Six Flags Magic Mountain | Valencia, CA | 2,600 | 3,104 | 3,332 | 3,500 | 3,592 |

Source: Themed Entertainment Association and AECOM, *2018 Theme Index and Museum Index: The Global Attractions Attendance Report* ©, and previous reports. See also <https://www.aecom.com/theme-index/> and <http://www.teaconnect.org/Resources/Theme-Index/index.cfm>.

## Table 1272. Reading in Print, Electronic, and Audio Formats Among Adults: 2016 and 2019

[In percent. Data shown for adults aged 18 years and older who read at least one book in the formats shown during the previous 12 months. Based on telephone surveys conducted March 7-April 4, 2016 among a nationally representative sample of 1,520 adults, and January 8-February 7, 2019 among a nationally representative sample of 1,502 adults]

| Characteristic | 2016 | | | | 2019 | | | |
|---|---|---|---|---|---|---|---|---|
| | Total | Print | E-book | Audio-book | Total | Print | E-book | Audio-book |
| **Total** | **73** | **65** | **28** | **14** | **72** | **65** | **25** | **20** |
| SEX | | | | | | | | |
| Male | 68 | 61 | 27 | 14 | 67 | 60 | 24 | 17 |
| Female | 77 | 70 | 29 | 14 | 76 | 70 | 27 | 22 |
| RACE/ETHNICITY | | | | | | | | |
| White, non-Hispanic | 76 | 70 | 31 | 15 | 76 | 70 | 27 | 22 |
| Black, non-Hispanic | 69 | 63 | 23 | 11 | 65 | 58 | 19 | 13 |
| Hispanic | 58 | 48 | 18 | 12 | 59 | 54 | 20 | 15 |
| AGE | | | | | | | | |
| 18 to 29 years | 80 | 72 | 35 | 16 | 81 | 73 | 34 | 23 |
| 30 to 49 years | 73 | 65 | 32 | 15 | 72 | 76 | 28 | 27 |
| 50 to 64 years | 70 | 64 | 24 | 15 | 67 | 74 | 22 | 16 |
| 65 years and older | 67 | 61 | 19 | 9 | 68 | 65 | 17 | 8 |
| EDUCATION | | | | | | | | |
| Less than high school | 45 | 38 | 11 | 12 | 32 | 25 | 5 | 6 |
| High school graduate | 62 | 55 | 19 | 9 | 61 | 55 | 15 | 12 |
| Some college | 81 | 74 | 32 | 14 | 75 | 70 | 26 | 17 |
| College graduate | 86 | 79 | 41 | 20 | 90 | 82 | 41 | 34 |
| HOUSEHOLD INCOME | | | | | | | | |
| Less than $30,000 | 65 | 59 | 19 | 9 | 62 | 56 | 18 | 14 |
| $30,000 to $49,000 | 74 | 68 | 26 | 16 | 67 | 63 | 19 | 13 |
| $50,000 to $74,999 | 75 | 69 | 33 | 19 | 78 | 71 | 28 | 27 |
| $75,000 and higher | 81 | 73 | 40 | 16 | 86 | 78 | 38 | 30 |
| METRO STATUS | | | | | | | | |
| Urban | 75 | 69 | 29 | 17 | 75 | 68 | 27 | 23 |
| Suburban | 73 | 64 | 30 | 14 | 74 | 68 | 27 | 19 |
| Rural | 66 | 61 | 22 | 10 | 66 | 58 | 20 | 18 |

Source: Pew Research Center, *Book Reading 2016*, September 2016 ©; and unpublished data. See also <http://www.pewinternet.org/>.

# Table 1273. Leisure Time Use on Weekends and Holidays by Type of Activity and Selected Demographic Characteristics: 2018

[Data are based on interviews of approximately 9,600 individuals age 15 years and over who reported their activities for a single 24-hour period. Respondents engaging in more than one activity at a time reported only their primary activity; except for child care, secondary activities were not reported]

| Selected characteristics | Average hours per day spent on all leisure and sports activities | | | Percent distribution of leisure time on weekends and holidays | | | | | | |
|---|---|---|---|---|---|---|---|---|---|---|
| | All days (hours) | Weekdays (hours) | Weekends and holidays (hours) | Sports, exercise, recreation | Socializing, communicating | Watching TV | Reading | Relaxing, thinking | Playing games, using computers for leisure | Other [1] |
| **Total, 15 years old and over** | **5.27** | **4.72** | **6.56** | **5.2** | **14.9** | **51.8** | **4.4** | **5.2** | **8.7** | **9.8** |
| Sex: | | | | | | | | | | |
| Men | 5.69 | 5.09 | 7.09 | 6.5 | 12.8 | 52.3 | 3.7 | 4.7 | 10.6 | 9.3 |
| Women | 4.87 | 4.37 | 6.06 | 3.6 | 17.3 | 51.5 | 5.1 | 5.6 | 6.6 | 10.1 |
| Age: | | | | | | | | | | |
| 15 to 19 years | 5.79 | 5.28 | 7.07 | 7.9 | 15.0 | 39.5 | 1.1 | 3.1 | 21.9 | 11.3 |
| 20 to 24 years | 5.02 | 4.26 | 6.79 | 8.1 | 15.8 | 38.3 | 1.8 | 1.9 | 20.3 | 14.0 |
| 25 to 34 years | 4.22 | 3.54 | 5.77 | 5.9 | 19.1 | 46.3 | 2.3 | 4.7 | 10.4 | 11.1 |
| 35 to 44 years | 4.08 | 3.51 | 5.42 | 6.5 | 19.2 | 49.6 | 2.8 | 5.0 | 4.8 | 12.0 |
| 45 to 54 years | 4.54 | 3.80 | 6.21 | 5.3 | 13.0 | 57.2 | 3.1 | 6.0 | 6.0 | 9.3 |
| 55 to 64 years | 5.49 | 4.90 | 6.90 | 4.1 | 14.6 | 56.8 | 4.8 | 6.2 | 5.4 | 8.1 |
| 65 to 74 years | 7.17 | 6.93 | 7.73 | 3.5 | 11.9 | 59.5 | 7.9 | 5.2 | 4.9 | 7.2 |
| 75 years and over | 7.75 | 7.61 | 8.09 | 1.5 | 9.8 | 58.7 | 11.3 | 7.5 | 5.1 | 6.2 |
| Race/ethnicity: | | | | | | | | | | |
| White | 5.28 | 4.70 | 6.62 | 5.4 | 15.4 | 51.2 | 4.8 | 4.8 | 8.6 | 9.7 |
| Black | 5.73 | 5.30 | 6.76 | 3.4 | 12.7 | 61.0 | 2.1 | 6.5 | 6.1 | 8.3 |
| Asian | 4.00 | 3.58 | 5.02 | 5.2 | 14.9 | 41.5 | 5.2 | 5.8 | 13.2 | 14.1 |
| Hispanic origin [2] | 4.82 | 4.35 | 5.95 | 4.5 | 19.3 | 48.2 | 1.7 | 6.4 | 9.6 | 10.1 |
| Employment status: | | | | | | | | | | |
| Employed | 4.22 | 3.49 | 5.96 | 6.0 | 16.6 | 48.8 | 3.7 | 4.9 | 8.7 | 11.1 |
| Full-time workers | 4.03 | 3.25 | 5.83 | 6.4 | 16.5 | 49.7 | 3.3 | 5.2 | 7.7 | 11.3 |
| Part-time workers | 4.96 | 4.38 | 6.46 | 5.1 | 16.6 | 46.1 | 5.3 | 4.3 | 12.2 | 10.4 |
| Not employed | 7.06 | 6.84 | 7.56 | 4.0 | 12.8 | 55.8 | 5.3 | 5.6 | 8.7 | 7.9 |
| Weekly earnings: [3] | | | | | | | | | | |
| $0 to $630 | 4.39 | 3.70 | 5.93 | 5.1 | 17.9 | 47.6 | 1.5 | 3.7 | 12.8 | 11.3 |
| $631 to $960 | 4.11 | 3.39 | 5.92 | 7.1 | 13.3 | 57.1 | 1.9 | 3.9 | 6.3 | 10.3 |
| $961 to $1,530 | 4.05 | 3.23 | 5.98 | 5.4 | 15.9 | 52.7 | 3.0 | 6.0 | 7.7 | 9.4 |
| $1,531 and higher | 3.82 | 2.90 | 6.08 | 7.2 | 17.3 | 44.9 | 5.3 | 5.9 | 6.1 | 13.3 |
| Presence and age of children: | | | | | | | | | | |
| No household children under age 18 | 5.83 | 5.28 | 7.13 | 4.8 | 13.3 | 53.7 | 5.2 | 5.1 | 8.4 | 9.4 |
| Household children under age 18 | 4.23 | 3.68 | 5.52 | 6.2 | 18.7 | 47.6 | 2.4 | 5.3 | 9.2 | 10.5 |
| Children age 13 to 17, none younger | 4.79 | 4.23 | 6.12 | 4.9 | 14.2 | 53.6 | 2.5 | 5.2 | 11.1 | 8.3 |
| Children age 6 to 12, none younger | 4.34 | 3.83 | 5.61 | 5.7 | 18.0 | 47.2 | 2.7 | 5.5 | 9.8 | 10.9 |
| Youngest child under age 6 | 3.76 | 3.16 | 5.07 | 7.3 | 22.9 | 43.4 | 2.2 | 5.1 | 7.5 | 11.8 |
| Educational attainment, age 25 and over: | | | | | | | | | | |
| Less than a high school diploma | 6.34 | 6.14 | 6.75 | 2.8 | 15.0 | 59.9 | 1.8 | 8.6 | 5.5 | 6.5 |
| High school graduates, no college | 5.77 | 5.28 | 6.93 | 3.6 | 13.6 | 59.7 | 2.7 | 6.2 | 6.2 | 7.9 |
| Some college or associate degree | 5.20 | 4.69 | 6.49 | 4.8 | 14.2 | 54.7 | 5.4 | 5.6 | 6.2 | 9.1 |
| Bachelor's degree and higher | 4.59 | 3.92 | 6.10 | 5.9 | 16.4 | 48.4 | 7.4 | 4.6 | 6.6 | 10.8 |

[1] Includes other leisure and sports activities, not elsewhere classified, and travel related to leisure and sports activities. [2] People of Hispanic origin may be of any race. [3] These values are based on usual weekly earnings. The earnings data are limited to wage and salary workers (both incorporated and unincorporated self-employed workers are excluded). Each earnings range represents approximately 25 percent of full-time wage and salary workers who held only one job.

Source: U.S. Bureau of Labor Statistics, *American Time Use Survey, 2018*, Bulletin USDL 19-1003, June 2019. See also <http://www.bls.gov/tus/>.

# Table 1274. Characteristics of Selected Spectator Sports: 1990 to 2018

[54,824 represents 54,824,000]

| Sport | Unit | 1990 | 1995 | 2000 | 2005 | 2010 | 2015 | 2016 | 2017 | 2018 |
|---|---|---|---|---|---|---|---|---|---|---|
| Baseball, major leagues: [1] | | | | | | | | | | |
| Regular season attendance........ | 1,000 | 54,824 | 50,469 | 72,749 | 74,926 | 73,054 | 73,760 | 73,159 | 72,670 | 69,625 |
| National League.............. | 1,000 | 24,492 | 25,110 | 39,851 | 41,644 | 40,890 | 38,903 | 38,114 | 38,307 | 37,251 |
| American League......... | 1,000 | 30,332 | 25,359 | 32,898 | 33,282 | 32,164 | 34,857 | 35,045 | 34,364 | 32,375 |
| Playoffs attendance [2] | 1,000 | 479 | 533 | 1,314 | 1,191 | 1,210 | 1,420 | 1,275 | 1,399 | 1,258 |
| World Series attendance........... | 1,000 | 209 | 286 | 277 | 168 | 244 | 215 | 278 | 347 | 239 |
| Basketball: [3, 4] | | | | | | | | | | |
| NCAA—Men's college: | | | | | | | | | | |
| Teams........................ | Number | 768 | 866 | 937 | 984 | 1,027 | 1,067 | 1,075 | 1,068 | 1,071 |
| Attendance................. | 1,000 | 28,741 | 28,225 | 28,949 | 30,940 | 32,632 | 32,382 | 31,859 | 32,781 | 31,277 |
| NCAA—Women's college: | | | | | | | | | | |
| Teams........................ | Number | 782 | 864 | 958 | 1,018 | 1,048 | 1,084 | 1,089 | 1,092 | 1,093 |
| Attendance [5]................ | 1,000 | 2,777 | 4,962 | 8,825 | 9,903 | 11,160 | 11,367 | 11,346 | 11,496 | 11,514 |
| NCAA—Men's college football: [4] | | | | | | | | | | |
| Teams........................ | Number | 534 | 600 | 624 | 618 | 644 | 666 | 668 | 666 | 669 |
| Attendance................. | 1,000 | 35,330 | 35,638 | 39,059 | 43,487 | 49,671 | 49,058 | 49,316 | 47,622 | 46,985 |
| National Hockey League: [6] | | | | | | | | | | |
| Regular season attendance...... | 1,000 | 12,580 | 9,234 | 18,800 | (NA) | 20,996 | 21,533 | 21,615 | 21,545 | 22,174 |
| Playoffs attendance............ | 1,000 | 1,356 | 1,329 | 1,525 | (NA) | 1,702 | 1,701 | 1,685 | 1,606 | 1,518 |
| Professional rodeo: [7] | | | | | | | | | | |
| Rodeos........................ | Number | 754 | 739 | 688 | 662 | 570 | 624 | 618 | 650 | 644 |
| Performances.................... | Number | 2,159 | 2,217 | 2,081 | 1,940 | 1,671 | 1,663 | 1,639 | 1,711 | 1,682 |
| Members........................ | Number | 5,693 | 6,894 | 6,255 | 6,127 | 5,323 | 4,782 | 4,692 | 4,885 | 4,618 |
| Permit-holders.................. | Number | 3,290 | 3,835 | 3,249 | 2,701 | 1,881 | 1,784 | 1,748 | 1,734 | 1,694 |
| Total prize money................. | Mil. dol. | 18.2 | 24.5 | 32.3 | 36.6 | 39.9 | 46.3 | 45.1 | 48.2 | 49.0 |

NA Not available. [1] Source: Major League Baseball (previously, The National League of Professional Baseball Clubs), New York, NY, National League Green Book ©; and The American League of Professional Baseball Clubs, New York, NY, American League Red Book ©. [2] Beginning 1995, two rounds of playoffs were played. Prior years had one round. [3] Season beginning in year shown. [4] Source: National Collegiate Athletic Association, Indianapolis, IN ©. [5] Attendance for women's basketball includes doubleheaders with men's teams beginning with the 1997 season, if attendance was taken by halftime of the women's game. [6] For season ending in year shown. Source: National Hockey League, Montreal, Quebec ©. In September 2004, franchise owners locked out their players upon the expiration of the collective bargaining agreement. The entire season was cancelled in February 2005. [7] Source: Professional Rodeo Cowboys Association, Colorado Springs, CO, Official Professional Rodeo Media Guide, annual ©.

Source: Compiled from sources listed in footnotes.

# Table 1275. Adult Attendance at Sports Events by Frequency: 2018

[In thousands (156 represents 156,000), except percent. For Fall 2018. Percent is based on total projected population 247,786,000. Data not comparable to previous years. Pro is professional. Based on a survey and subject to sampling error; see source]

| Event | Attend regularly | | Attend on occasion [1] | | Event | Attend regularly | | Attend on occasion [1] | |
|---|---|---|---|---|---|---|---|---|---|
| | Number (1,000) | Percent | Number (1,000) | Percent | | Number (1,000) | Percent | Number (1,000) | Percent |
| Alpine skiing and ski jumping... | 156 | 0.06 | 421 | 0.17 | Other golf..................... | 111 | 0.04 | 334 | 0.13 |
| Auto racing – NASCAR......... | 324 | 0.13 | 1,361 | 0.55 | Gymnastics................... | 424 | 0.17 | 968 | 0.39 |
| Auto racing – other............. | 281 | 0.11 | 1,362 | 0.55 | High school sports............. | 3,085 | 1.24 | 5,684 | 2.29 |
| Baseball: | | | | | Horse racing (track or OTB)... | 200 | 0.08 | 1,205 | 0.49 |
| College.......................... | 333 | 0.13 | 1,240 | 0.50 | Ice hockey: | | | | |
| Pro (MLB) regular season.... | 1,404 | 0.57 | 10,748 | 4.34 | NHL regular season.......... | 495 | 0.20 | 3,570 | 1.44 |
| Pro (MLB) playoffs/ | | | | | NHL playoffs and Stanley | | | | |
| World Series................. | 431 | 0.2 | 1798 | 0.7 | Cup finals.................. | 296 | 0.12 | 625 | 0.25 |
| Basketball: | | | | | Lacrosse (MLL)................ | 193 | 0.08 | 449 | 0.18 |
| College.......................... | 921 | 0.37 | 3,995 | 1.61 | Marathon, triathlon & other | | | | |
| NCAA tournament............... | 221 | 0.09 | 646 | 0.26 | endurance events............. | 200 | 0.08 | 825 | 0.33 |
| Pro (NBA) regular season.... | 400 | 0.16 | 3,974 | 1.60 | Mixed martial arts (other)...... | 200 | 0.08 | 484 | 0.20 |
| Pro (NBA) playoffs............. | 262 | 0.11 | 955 | 0.39 | Motorcycle racing............. | 137 | 0.06 | 476 | 0.19 |
| Pro (WNBA)..................... | 70 | 0.03 | 446 | 0.18 | Olympics – Summer........... | 165 | 0.07 | 381 | 0.15 |
| Bicycle racing................... | 281 | 0.11 | 759 | 0.31 | Olympics – Winter............. | 149 | 0.06 | 452 | 0.18 |
| Bowling......................... | 212 | 0.09 | 867 | 0.35 | Poker.......................... | 79 | 0.03 | 424 | 0.17 |
| Boxing.......................... | 115 | 0.05 | 494 | 0.20 | Rodeo.......................... | 396 | 0.16 | 1,158 | 0.47 |
| Bull riding (Pro)................. | 175 | 0.07 | 773 | 0.31 | Soccer: | | | | |
| Equestrian events.............. | 305 | 0.12 | 687 | 0.28 | MLS.......................... | 472 | 0.19 | 1,545 | 0.62 |
| Extreme sports – Summer..... | 277 | 0.11 | 425 | 0.17 | World Cup.................... | 139 | 0.06 | 538 | 0.22 |
| Extreme sports – Winter........ | 115 | 0.05 | 349 | 0.14 | Tennis: | | | | |
| Figure skating.................. | 64 | 0.03 | 358 | 0.14 | Men's........................ | 150 | 0.06 | 457 | 0.18 |
| Fishing......................... | 446 | 0.18 | 1,080 | 0.44 | Women's..................... | 128 | 0.05 | 416 | 0.17 |
| Football: | | | | | Track & field.................... | 250 | 0.10 | 678 | 0.27 |
| College.......................... | 2,300 | 0.93 | 7,199 | 2.91 | Truck and tractor | | | | |
| Pro (NFL) Monday, Thursday | | | | | pull/mud racing.............. | 231 | 0.09 | 650 | 0.26 |
| or Sunday night games...... | 844 | 0.34 | 3,676 | 1.48 | Ultimate Fighting | | | | |
| NFL weekend games.......... | 1,049 | 0.42 | 4,260 | 1.72 | Championship (UFC)......... | 137 | 0.06 | 378 | 0.15 |
| NFL playoffs/Super Bowl...... | 452 | 0.18 | 1,565 | 0.63 | Volleyball (Pro beach)......... | 158 | 0.06 | 420 | 0.17 |
| Golf: | | | | | Wrestling: | | | | |
| PGA............................ | 242 | 0.10 | 991 | 0.40 | WWE......................... | 128 | 0.05 | 764 | 0.31 |
| LPGA........................... | 124 | 0.05 | 294 | 0.12 | Other Pro..................... | 60 | 0.02 | 287 | 0.12 |

[1] Attended at least once during last 12 months.

Source: MRI Survey of the American Consumer. © Courtesy of MRISimmons. See also <https://www.mrisimmons.com/>.

# Table 1276. Participation in NCAA Sports by Sex: 2017 to 2018

[For the academic year ending in 2018]

| Sport | Males | | | Females | | |
|---|---|---|---|---|---|---|
| | Teams | Athletes | Average squad | Teams | Athletes | Average squad |
| **Total** | **9,279** | **281,928** | **(X)** | **10,695** | **218,805** | **(X)** |
| Baseball | 953 | 35,460 | 37.2 | (X) | (X) | (X) |
| Basketball | 1,087 | 18,816 | 17.3 | 1,103 | 16,614 | 15.1 |
| Bowling [2] | 2 | 22 | 11.0 | 80 | 739 | 9.2 |
| Cross country [1] | 992 | 14,270 | 14.4 | 1,071 | 15,632 | 14.6 |
| Equestrian [1,2,3] | 6 | 14 | 2.3 | 45 | 1,381 | 30.7 |
| Fencing [1] | 35 | 675 | 19.3 | 45 | 706 | 15.7 |
| Field hockey | (X) | (X) | (X) | 275 | 6,103 | 22.2 |
| Football | 671 | 73,557 | 109.6 | (X) | (X) | (X) |
| Golf [1] | 835 | 8,609 | 10.3 | 685 | 5,375 | 7.8 |
| Gymnastics | 16 | 343 | 21.4 | 83 | 1,547 | 18.6 |
| Ice hockey | 148 | 4,229 | 28.6 | 102 | 2,400 | 23.5 |
| Lacrosse | 380 | 14,310 | 37.7 | 505 | 12,061 | 23.9 |
| Rifle [1] | 22 | 154 | 7.0 | 30 | 196 | 6.5 |
| Rowing [2] | 55 | 2,246 | 40.8 | 145 | 7,277 | 50.2 |
| Rugby [2,3] | 3 | 154 | 51.3 | 17 | 480 | 28.2 |
| Sailing [1,2] | 21 | 391 | 18.6 | (X) | (X) | (X) |
| Sand volleyball | (X) | (X) | (X) | 68 | 1,165 | 17.1 |
| Skiing [1] | 33 | 426 | 12.9 | 34 | 392 | 11.5 |
| Soccer | 832 | 25,072 | 30.1 | 1,038 | 27,811 | 26.8 |
| Softball | (X) | (X) | (X) | 1,001 | 20,316 | 20.3 |
| Squash [2,3] | 33 | 487 | 14.8 | 31 | 436 | 14.1 |
| Swimming/diving [1] | 439 | 9,697 | 22.1 | 555 | 12,848 | 23.1 |
| Synchronized swimming [3] | (X) | (X) | (X) | 3 | 47 | 15.7 |
| Tennis | 750 | 7,838 | 10.5 | 908 | 8,608 | 9.5 |
| Track, indoor [1] | 724 | 26,011 | 35.9 | 818 | 27,883 | 34.1 |
| Track, outdoor [1] | 818 | 28,698 | 35.1 | 907 | 30,018 | 33.1 |
| Volleyball | 135 | 2,163 | 16.0 | 1,071 | 17,471 | 16.3 |
| Water polo | 48 | 1,047 | 21.8 | 62 | 1,216 | 19.6 |
| Wrestling | 241 | 7,239 | 30.0 | (X) | (X) | (X) |

X Not applicable. [1] Co-ed sport. [2] Sport recognized by the NCAA but does not have an NCAA men's championship. [3] Sport recognized by the NCAA as an emerging sport for women.

Source: The National Collegiate Athletic Association (NCAA), Indianapolis, IN, *NCAA Sports Sponsorship and Participation Rates Report* ©, October 2018. See also <http://www.ncaapublications.com/>.

# Table 1277. Participation in High School Athletic Programs by Sex: 1980 to 2019

[For academic years. Data based on number of state associations reporting and may underrepresent the number of schools with and participants in athletic programs]

| Year | Participants [1] | | Sex and sport | Most popular sports, 2018–2019 [2] | |
|---|---|---|---|---|---|
| | Males | Females | | Schools | Participants |
| 1980 to 1981 | 3,503,124 | 1,853,789 | MALE | | |
| 1985 to 1986 | 3,344,275 | 1,807,121 | Football (11-player) | 14,247 | 1,006,013 |
| 1990 to 1991 | 3,406,355 | 1,892,316 | Track & field (outdoor) | 17,052 | 605,354 |
| 1995 to 1996 | 3,634,052 | 2,367,936 | Basketball | 18,617 | 540,769 |
| 2000 to 2001 | 3,921,069 | 2,784,154 | Baseball | 16,170 | 482,740 |
| 2002 to 2003 | 3,988,738 | 2,856,358 | Soccer | 12,552 | 459,077 |
| 2003 to 2004 | 4,038,253 | 2,865,299 | Cross country | 15,632 | 269,295 |
| 2004 to 2005 | 4,110,319 | 2,908,390 | Wrestling | 10,843 | 247,441 |
| 2005 to 2006 | 4,206,549 | 2,953,355 | Tennis | 9,809 | 159,314 |
| 2006 to 2007 | 4,321,103 | 3,021,807 | Golf | 13,590 | 143,200 |
| 2007 to 2008 | 4,372,115 | 3,057,266 | Swimming & diving | 7,704 | 136,638 |
| 2008 to 2009 | 4,422,662 | 3,114,091 | FEMALE | | |
| 2009 to 2010 | 4,455,740 | 3,172,637 | Track & field (outdoor) | 17,012 | 488,267 |
| 2010 to 2011 | 4,494,406 | 3,173,549 | Volleyball | 16,572 | 452,808 |
| 2011 to 2012 | 4,484,987 | 3,207,533 | Basketball | 18,210 | 399,067 |
| 2012 to 2013 | 4,490,854 | 3,222,723 | Soccer | 12,107 | 394,105 |
| 2013 to 2014 | 4,527,994 | 3,267,664 | Softball (fast pitch) | 15,877 | 362,038 |
| 2014 to 2015 | 4,519,312 | 3,287,735 | Cross country | 15,435 | 219,345 |
| 2015 to 2016 | 4,541,959 | 3,324,306 | Tennis | 10,290 | 189,436 |
| 2016 to 2017 | 4,563,238 | 3,400,297 | Swimming & diving | 8,007 | 173,088 |
| 2017 to 2018 | 4,565,580 | 3,415,306 | Competitive spirit squads | 7,214 | 161,358 |
| 2018 to 2019 | 4,534,758 | 3,402,733 | Lacrosse | 2,877 | 99,750 |

[1] Participants are counted in each sport in which they participate. [2] Ten most popular sports for each gender, ranked by number of participants.

Source: National Federation of State High School Associations, Indianapolis, IN, *The 2018–19 High School Athletics Participation Survey* ©. Reprinted with permission of the National Federation of State High School Associations. See also <http://www.nfhs.org/>.

# Table 1278. Participants in Selected Sports Activities: 2016

[In thousands (293,474 represents 293,474,000). Data are based on an online survey of 34,000 individuals. The questionnaire asked the heads of households and up to three other household members who were at least seven years of age to indicate their age, the sports in which they participated in 2016, and the number of days of participation in 2016. A participant is defined as an individual seven years of age or older who participates in a sport more than once a year; selected fitness activities required participation of 6 or more days during the year. See source for methodology]

| Activity | Total (number) | Sex | | Age (years) | | | | | | | | Household income (dollars) | | | | | | |
|---|---|---|---|---|---|---|---|---|---|---|---|---|---|---|---|---|---|---|
| | | Male | Female | 7–17 | 18–24 | 25–34 | 35–44 | 45–54 | 55–64 | 65–74 | 75 and over | Under 25,000 | 25,000–34,999 | 35,000–49,999 | 50,000–74,999 | 75,000–99,999 | 100,000–149,999 | 150,000 and over |
| **Total persons age 7 and older** | **293,474** | **143,950** | **149,524** | **45,700** | **31,220** | **44,137** | **40,590** | **43,188** | **40,878** | **36,135** | **11,625** | **64,858** | **29,347** | **37,271** | **49,010** | **35,510** | **41,380** | **36,097** |
| Aerobic exercising [1] | 45,591 | 16,413 | 29,179 | 3,616 | 4,680 | 9,548 | 7,736 | 6,823 | 6,440 | 5,671 | 1,077 | 7,350 | 3,768 | 5,144 | 8,336 | 5,728 | 7,607 | 7,659 |
| Archery, target | 8,311 | 5,274 | 3,037 | 2,618 | 1,340 | 1,266 | 1,190 | 988 | 623 | 252 | 36 | 1,930 | 531 | 921 | 1,314 | 924 | 1,262 | 1,428 |
| Backpacking [2] | 12,555 | 7,600 | 4,955 | 2,354 | 1,713 | 2,873 | 2,419 | 1,918 | 906 | 321 | 53 | 2,387 | 1,206 | 1,137 | 1,972 | 1,759 | 2,111 | 1,985 |
| Baseball | 12,179 | 9,501 | 2,678 | 5,811 | 1,382 | 2,113 | 1,489 | 920 | 342 | 122 | – | 1,084 | 576 | 1,100 | 1,867 | 2,498 | 2,840 | 2,214 |
| Basketball | 24,762 | 18,621 | 6,142 | 9,569 | 4,452 | 4,494 | 3,404 | 1,912 | 726 | 206 | – | 4,012 | 1,965 | 2,879 | 4,010 | 3,689 | 4,731 | 3,478 |
| Bicycle riding [1] | 36,188 | 21,007 | 15,181 | 10,458 | 2,955 | 4,923 | 5,138 | 5,193 | 4,521 | 2,548 | 452 | 5,828 | 2,723 | 3,919 | 6,414 | 4,594 | 6,489 | 6,221 |
| Billiards/pool | 21,250 | 13,966 | 7,284 | 2,120 | 3,497 | 5,011 | 3,870 | 3,272 | 2,211 | 996 | 274 | 4,319 | 1,977 | 2,503 | 3,956 | 2,536 | 2,887 | 3,071 |
| Boating, motor/power | 14,412 | 7,998 | 6,414 | 2,003 | 1,560 | 1,889 | 2,180 | 2,496 | 2,466 | 1,577 | 241 | 1,837 | 1,036 | 1,517 | 2,534 | 2,069 | 2,441 | 2,978 |
| Bowling | 34,691 | 18,666 | 16,024 | 7,818 | 4,309 | 6,881 | 5,725 | 5,089 | 2,939 | 1,472 | 458 | 6,312 | 3,175 | 4,287 | 6,057 | 3,768 | 5,400 | 5,693 |
| Camping [3] | 40,410 | 21,865 | 18,545 | 7,989 | 4,281 | 7,927 | 7,354 | 5,923 | 4,255 | 2,287 | 395 | 7,261 | 4,132 | 5,094 | 7,234 | 5,719 | 6,752 | 4,218 |
| Cheerleading | 3,709 | 559 | 3,150 | 2,553 | 483 | 409 | 125 | 139 | – | – | – | 414 | 262 | 326 | 863 | 575 | 538 | 730 |
| Dart throwing | 9,504 | 6,017 | 3,487 | 1,114 | 1,398 | 2,071 | 1,950 | 1,710 | 895 | 271 | 95 | 1,759 | 862 | 1,165 | 1,775 | 1,220 | 911 | 1,811 |
| Exercise walking [1] | 105,700 | 46,028 | 59,672 | 7,688 | 8,918 | 15,373 | 15,705 | 19,772 | 18,365 | 15,339 | 4,540 | 22,568 | 10,378 | 13,438 | 18,537 | 12,054 | 14,704 | 14,022 |
| Exercise with equipment [1] | 57,100 | 27,710 | 29,390 | 4,035 | 6,984 | 10,920 | 8,862 | 9,801 | 7,920 | 6,773 | 1,805 | 9,055 | 4,960 | 7,247 | 10,976 | 6,936 | 8,229 | 9,699 |
| Fishing, fresh water | 28,921 | 19,614 | 9,306 | 5,095 | 2,671 | 3,469 | 4,580 | 5,720 | 3,650 | 3,047 | 689 | 5,615 | 3,422 | 4,105 | 5,241 | 3,321 | 3,220 | 3,997 |
| Fishing, salt water | 9,116 | 6,658 | 2,458 | 1,254 | 574 | 1,658 | 1,420 | 1,611 | 1,489 | 816 | 294 | 1,372 | 849 | 1,157 | 1,339 | 1,293 | 1,675 | 1,430 |
| Football, tackle | 7,899 | 7,157 | 742 | 4,580 | 999 | 1,190 | 782 | 263 | 85 | – | – | 1,116 | 480 | 701 | 1,220 | 1,565 | 1,835 | 983 |
| Golf | 18,472 | 13,757 | 4,715 | 1,517 | 1,209 | 2,751 | 3,198 | 3,188 | 3,234 | 2,568 | 808 | 1,516 | 797 | 1,798 | 2,922 | 2,718 | 4,065 | 4,656 |
| Gymnastics | 6,115 | 1,645 | 4,469 | 3,722 | 612 | 877 | 462 | 218 | 70 | 142 | 13 | 407 | 325 | 619 | 1,041 | 1,138 | 1,535 | 1,049 |
| Hiking [1] | 42,927 | 21,694 | 21,234 | 5,394 | 4,683 | 8,618 | 7,297 | 7,380 | 5,743 | 3,350 | 462 | 6,994 | 3,524 | 5,344 | 8,021 | 5,237 | 6,832 | 6,975 |
| Hockey, ice | 3,366 | 2,680 | 686 | 1,065 | 512 | 772 | 511 | 318 | 189 | – | – | 290 | 59 | 259 | 616 | 787 | 552 | 803 |
| Hunting with bow & arrow | 5,843 | 4,188 | 1,655 | 768 | 781 | 1,513 | 1,240 | 824 | 502 | 197 | 19 | 1,506 | 390 | 689 | 978 | 772 | 766 | 740 |
| Hunting with firearms | 18,027 | 14,815 | 3,212 | 1,657 | 1,740 | 2,902 | 3,309 | 3,808 | 2,663 | 1,646 | 302 | 3,229 | 1,777 | 2,673 | 3,123 | 1,938 | 2,464 | 2,822 |
| In-line roller skating | 4,600 | 2,024 | 2,576 | 2,303 | 602 | 847 | 466 | 251 | 112 | 19 | – | 548 | 390 | 675 | 822 | 688 | 753 | 725 |
| Kayaking | 9,617 | 4,533 | 5,084 | 1,505 | 1,205 | 2,187 | 1,514 | 1,300 | 1,297 | 513 | 97 | 1,138 | 323 | 1,122 | 1,712 | 1,316 | 1,954 | 2,052 |
| Lacrosse | 2,947 | 1,933 | 1,014 | 1,540 | 419 | 500 | 254 | 179 | 55 | – | – | 190 | 281 | 254 | 369 | 833 | 383 | 638 |
| Mountain biking, off road | 5,741 | 4,119 | 1,622 | 919 | 652 | 1,602 | 1,212 | 807 | 398 | 152 | – | 1,131 | 229 | 452 | 980 | 931 | 1,047 | 971 |
| Muzzleloading | 2,727 | 2,405 | 322 | 226 | 463 | 439 | 342 | 593 | 320 | 307 | 37 | 579 | 228 | 436 | 510 | 371 | 257 | 345 |
| Paintball games | 5,320 | 3,832 | 1,488 | 2,004 | 1,070 | 1,145 | 826 | 234 | 41 | – | – | 473 | 430 | 574 | 820 | 1,040 | 918 | 1,064 |
| Running/jogging [1] | 44,946 | 23,808 | 21,137 | 8,873 | 7,378 | 10,513 | 8,482 | 5,323 | 2,913 | 1,204 | 261 | 6,510 | 3,375 | 5,383 | 8,041 | 6,586 | 8,096 | 6,957 |
| Skateboarding | 5,400 | 3,802 | 1,598 | 2,797 | 1,115 | 944 | 351 | 119 | 73 | – | – | 626 | 463 | 555 | 987 | 755 | 1,064 | 950 |
| Skiing, alpine | 5,791 | 3,492 | 2,299 | 1,299 | 630 | 1,065 | 779 | 880 | 825 | 313 | – | 277 | 167 | 453 | 574 | 869 | 940 | 2,512 |
| Skiing, cross country | 2,335 | 1,338 | 998 | 354 | 284 | 467 | 409 | 341 | 372 | 107 | – | 437 | 1 | 240 | 130 | 408 | 450 | 671 |
| Snowboarding | 4,000 | 2,575 | 1,425 | 1,032 | 685 | 1,399 | 474 | 236 | 153 | 22 | – | 428 | 168 | 373 | 810 | 676 | 696 | 850 |
| Soccer | 14,053 | 9,263 | 4,790 | 7,670 | 1,930 | 2,302 | 1,452 | 484 | 191 | 24 | – | 1,007 | 720 | 1,582 | 2,347 | 2,587 | 3,466 | 2,346 |
| Softball | 9,634 | 5,130 | 4,504 | 4,007 | 988 | 1,468 | 1,305 | 1,005 | 618 | 243 | – | 740 | 708 | 890 | 1,429 | 1,681 | 1,832 | 2,355 |
| Swimming [1] | 45,618 | 21,679 | 23,939 | 12,763 | 3,840 | 5,894 | 6,321 | 5,840 | 5,541 | 4,318 | 1,102 | 5,179 | 3,579 | 5,747 | 7,834 | 6,360 | 8,303 | 8,616 |
| Table tennis/ping pong | 10,242 | 5,708 | 4,534 | 2,319 | 1,570 | 2,208 | 1,344 | 1,296 | 804 | 582 | 119 | 1,083 | 772 | 708 | 1,638 | 1,693 | 2,132 | 2,217 |
| Target shooting, live ammunition | 20,446 | 14,392 | 6,055 | 1,790 | 1,965 | 4,557 | 3,686 | 3,392 | 2,888 | 1,862 | 307 | 2,764 | 1,691 | 2,945 | 3,804 | 2,806 | 3,343 | 3,094 |
| Target shooting, airgun | 5,033 | 3,949 | 1,084 | 1,148 | 752 | 1,028 | 681 | 703 | 342 | 310 | 70 | 609 | 497 | 672 | 942 | 765 | 876 | 671 |
| Tennis | 12,643 | 6,776 | 5,867 | 2,750 | 1,614 | 2,601 | 2,382 | 1,627 | 1,003 | 551 | 115 | 971 | 811 | 920 | 2,135 | 2,233 | 2,690 | 2,884 |
| Volleyball [1] | 10,697 | 4,604 | 6,093 | 4,696 | 1,631 | 1,943 | 1,259 | 822 | 270 | 76 | – | 957 | 759 | 936 | 1,568 | 2,246 | 2,732 | 1,499 |
| Water skiing | 3,571 | 1,882 | 1,688 | 914 | 550 | 889 | 633 | 354 | 192 | 39 | – | 348 | 103 | 301 | 305 | 580 | 841 | 1,092 |
| Weightlifting [1] | 35,569 | 23,153 | 12,416 | 2,901 | 5,182 | 7,939 | 6,549 | 5,729 | 4,033 | 2,746 | 489 | 5,318 | 2,926 | 4,346 | 6,939 | 4,632 | 5,740 | 5,668 |
| Workout at club [1] | 37,800 | 17,846 | 19,954 | 2,773 | 5,623 | 8,590 | 5,783 | 5,743 | 4,339 | 3,928 | 1,021 | 4,838 | 2,639 | 4,200 | 6,900 | 5,033 | 6,565 | 7,616 |
| Wrestling | 2,984 | 2,381 | 604 | 1,463 | 451 | 626 | 244 | 184 | 17 | – | – | 520 | 122 | 322 | 540 | 650 | 401 | 428 |
| Yoga | 30,320 | 7,227 | 23,093 | 2,294 | 4,757 | 8,187 | 5,481 | 4,341 | 3,059 | 1,822 | 378 | 6,057 | 2,083 | 4,023 | 5,239 | 3,614 | 4,478 | 4,825 |

– Represents zero.  [1] Participant engaged in activity at least six times in the year.  [2] Includes wilderness camping.  [3] Vacation/overnight.

Source: National Sporting Goods Association, Mt. Prospect, IL, *Sports Participation in the United States, 2017 Edition* ©. See also <https://www.nsga.org/research/nsga-research-offerings/>.

## Table 1279. Consumer Purchases of Sporting Goods by Consumer Characteristics: 2016

[Shown as percent of dollar purchases. Data are based on an online survey of over 15,000 households]

| Characteristic | Total | Footwear | | | | | Equipment | | | | |
|---|---|---|---|---|---|---|---|---|---|---|---|
| | | Cross-train/ fitness shoes | Gym shoes/ sneak-ers | Hiking shoes/ boots | Jog-ging/ running shoes | Walking shoes | Bi-cycles | Fitness trackers/ pedo-meters | Golf club sets | Hand-guns | Rod/ reel combi-nation |
| Total | 100.0 | 100.0 | 100.0 | 100.0 | 100.0 | 100.0 | 100.0 | 100.0 | 100.0 | 100.0 | 100.0 |
| Age of user: | | | | | | | | | | | |
| Under 14 years old | 17.7 | 4.4 | 11.2 | 3.2 | 4.2 | 3.5 | 9.4 | 1.4 | 1.1 | – | 2.7 |
| 14 to 17 years old | 5.2 | 4.4 | 8.3 | 4.5 | 5.4 | 3.4 | 5.7 | 1.5 | 2.3 | 0.4 | 2.7 |
| 18 to 24 years old | 9.7 | 10.9 | 12.7 | 5.5 | 9.9 | 5.2 | 7.1 | 9.1 | 3.9 | 3.5 | 6.5 |
| 25 to 34 years old | 13.7 | 20.2 | 17.0 | 12.5 | 17.4 | 11.6 | 16.3 | 18.1 | 14.0 | 16.0 | 14.3 |
| 35 to 44 years old | 12.6 | 18.8 | 14.0 | 20.0 | 21.7 | 15.6 | 13.9 | 16.5 | 24.0 | 15.5 | 16.2 |
| 45 to 64 years old | 26.2 | 32.3 | 23.5 | 40.0 | 32.6 | 35.4 | 42.7 | 41.6 | 38.0 | 40.1 | 36.6 |
| 65 years old and over | 14.9 | 9.0 | 13.3 | 14.3 | 8.8 | 25.3 | 4.9 | 11.8 | 16.7 | 24.5 | 21.0 |
| Sex of user: | | | | | | | | | | | |
| Male | 49.2 | 48.2 | 43.7 | 62.4 | 52.9 | 45.9 | 60.3 | 38.5 | 85.0 | 83.7 | 81.5 |
| Female | 50.8 | 51.8 | 56.3 | 37.6 | 47.1 | 54.1 | 39.7 | 61.5 | 15.0 | 16.3 | 18.5 |
| Annual household income: | | | | | | | | | | | |
| Under $15,000 | 11.6 | 4.9 | 5.3 | 6.6 | 5.2 | 7.4 | 3.3 | 5.2 | 3.2 | 3.7 | 6.3 |
| $15,000 to $24,999 | 10.5 | 3.7 | 6.5 | 5.5 | 3.9 | 6.7 | 4.2 | 4.0 | 0.5 | 3.2 | 6.8 |
| $25,000 to $34,999 | 10.0 | 5.8 | 9.0 | 6.3 | 5.1 | 8.3 | 4.4 | 5.6 | 6.5 | 7.0 | 11.6 |
| $35,000 to $49,999 | 12.7 | 9.2 | 11.1 | 11.0 | 8.5 | 10.6 | 5.3 | 8.0 | 4.9 | 11.6 | 11.6 |
| $50,000 to $74,999 | 16.7 | 16.2 | 17.5 | 13.2 | 16.9 | 17.2 | 11.9 | 18.8 | 20.2 | 17.1 | 18.7 |
| $75,000 to $99,999 | 12.1 | 16.0 | 13.1 | 13.1 | 15.0 | 13.9 | 14.0 | 15.3 | 14.9 | 14.8 | 12.8 |
| $100,000 to $149,999 | 14.1 | 21.8 | 17.3 | 19.6 | 20.3 | 20.2 | 23.2 | 20.6 | 37.1 | 16.8 | 13.6 |
| $150,000 and over | 12.3 | 22.4 | 20.2 | 24.7 | 25.1 | 15.7 | 33.7 | 22.5 | 12.7 | 25.8 | 18.6 |
| Education of household head: | | | | | | | | | | | |
| Less than high school | 11.7 | 1.1 | 1.2 | 0.7 | 0.8 | 1.4 | 0.5 | 0.9 | 0.7 | 0.5 | 1.8 |
| High school | 29.0 | 9.7 | 13.4 | 9.2 | 9.8 | 12.8 | 10.7 | 7.3 | 7.8 | 11.0 | 20.2 |
| Some college | 28.6 | 19.8 | 30.2 | 21.8 | 22.5 | 24.3 | 18.3 | 21.4 | 18.1 | 25.8 | 29.4 |
| College graduate | 30.7 | 69.4 | 55.2 | 68.3 | 66.9 | 61.5 | 70.5 | 70.4 | 73.4 | 62.7 | 48.6 |

– Represents or rounds to zero.

Source: National Sporting Goods Association, Mt. Prospect, IL, *Sporting Goods Market: 2017 Edition* ©. See also <https://www.nsga.org/research/nsga-research-offerings/>.

## Table 1280. National Park Service—Summary: 1990 to 2018

[In units as indicated (986 represents $986,000,000). For year ending September 30, except as noted. Covers all States, the District of Columbia, and the U.S. territories of American Samoa, Guam, Puerto Rico, and the U.S. Virgin Islands]

| Item | 1990 | 1995 | 2000 | 2005 | 2010 | 2016 | 2017 | 2018 |
|---|---|---|---|---|---|---|---|---|
| FINANCES (mil. dol.): [1] | | | | | | | | |
| Expenditures reported | 986 | 1,445 | 1,833 | 2,451 | 3,239 | 2,964 | 3,119 | 3,245 |
| Salaries and wages | 459 | 633 | 799 | 984 | 1,237 | 1,196 | 1,197 | 1,195 |
| Improvements, maintenance | 160 | 234 | 299 | 361 | 531 | 559 | 588 | 606 |
| Construction | 109 | 192 | 215 | 381 | 443 | 182 | 223 | 228 |
| Other | 259 | 386 | 520 | 725 | 1,028 | 1,022 | 1,111 | 1,227 |
| Funds available | 1,506 | 2,225 | 3,316 | 4,218 | 5,402 | 5,228 | 5,559 | 6,366 |
| Appropriations | 1,053 | 1,325 | 1,881 | 2,425 | 2,848 | 3,233 | 3,343 | 3,804 |
| Other [2] | 453 | 900 | 1,435 | 1,793 | 2,554 | 1,995 | 2,152 | 2,515 |
| Revenue from operations | 79 | 106 | 234 | 286 | 387 | 548 | 546 | 551 |
| RECREATION VISITS (millions): [3] | | | | | | | | |
| All areas | 258.7 | 269.6 | 285.9 | 273.5 | 281.3 | 331.0 | 330.9 | 318.2 |
| National parks [4] | 57.7 | 64.8 | 66.1 | 63.5 | 64.6 | 82.9 | 85.5 | 85.9 |
| National monuments | 23.9 | 23.5 | 23.8 | 20.9 | 23.0 | 25.7 | 26.3 | 22.2 |
| National historical, commemorative, archaeological [5] | 57.5 | 56.9 | 72.2 | 74.9 | 80.0 | 99.5 | 96.5 | 93.2 |
| National parkways | 29.1 | 31.3 | 34.0 | 31.7 | 28.6 | 32.8 | 31.4 | 29.8 |
| National recreation areas [4] | 47.2 | 53.7 | 50.0 | 46.8 | 49.0 | 50.3 | 52.1 | 51.0 |
| National seashores and lakeshores | 23.3 | 22.5 | 22.5 | 21.7 | 22.2 | 24.1 | 23.3 | 21.0 |
| National Capital Parks [6] | 7.5 | 5.5 | 5.4 | 4.3 | 3.0 | 3.0 | 3.3 | 3.2 |
| Recreation overnight stays (millions) | 17.6 | 16.8 | 15.4 | 13.5 | 14.4 | 15.3 | 14.8 | 14.0 |
| In commercial lodgings [7] | 3.9 | 3.8 | 3.7 | 3.4 | 3.5 | 4.6 | 4.9 | 4.5 |
| In Park Service campgrounds | 7.9 | 7.1 | 5.9 | 5.2 | 5.5 | 6.4 | 6.2 | 6.0 |
| In backcountry | 1.7 | 2.2 | 1.9 | 1.7 | 1.8 | 2.2 | 2.1 | 1.9 |
| Other [8] | 4.2 | 3.7 | 3.8 | 3.2 | 3.7 | 2.2 | 1.6 | 1.6 |
| LAND (1,000 acres): [9] | | | | | | | | |
| Total | 76,362 | 77,355 | 78,153 | 79,048 | 80,527 | 80,726 | 81,008 | 81,041 |
| Parks | 46,089 | 49,307 | 49,785 | 49,910 | 50,662 | 50,748 | 50,749 | 50,752 |
| Recreation areas | 3,344 | 3,353 | 3,388 | 3,391 | 3,418 | 3,399 | 3,400 | 3,425 |
| Other | 26,929 | 24,695 | 24,980 | 25,747 | 26,447 | 26,579 | 26,859 | 26,864 |
| Acquisition, net | 21 | 27 | 186 | 17 | 23 | 125 | 282 | 33 |

[1] Financial data are those associated with the National Park System. Certain other functions of the National Park Service (principally the activities absorbed from the former Heritage Conservation and Recreation Service in 1981) are excluded. [2] Includes funds carried over from prior years. [3] For calendar year. Includes other types of areas, not shown separately. [4] For 1990, combined data for North Cascades National Park and two adjacent National Recreation Areas are included in National Parks total. [5] Includes National Battlefields, National Battlefield Parks, National Historic Sites, National Historical Parks, National Memorials, National Military Parks, National Preserves, and National Reserves. [6] For 1990 to 1996, data are for National Capital Parks combined. Beginning 1997, data are summed for National Capital Parks East and National Capital Parks Central (also known as National Mall and Memorial Parks). [7] Beginning in 2011, includes concessioner lodging and campgrounds. [8] Prior to 2011, includes concessioner campgrounds. [9] Federal land only, as of December 31. Federal land acreages, in addition to National Park Service administered lands, also include lands within national park system area boundaries but under the administration of other agencies. Year-to-year changes in the federal lands figures includes changes in the acreages of these other lands and hence often differ from "net acquisition."

Source: U.S. National Park Service, *National Park Statistical Abstract 2018*, April 2019, and earlier reports; unpublished data; and "National Park Service Visitor Use Statistics," <https://irma.nps.gov/Stats/Reports/National>, accessed May 2019.

## Table 1281. National Park Service (NPS) Visits and Acreage by State: 2018

| State | Recreation visits [1] | Gross area acres | Federal land — NPS fee acres [2] | Federal land — NPS less than fee acres [3] | Federal land — Other federal fee acres [4] | Nonfederal land — Other public acres [5] | Nonfederal land — Private acres |
|---|---|---|---|---|---|---|---|
| Total [6]................ | 318,211,832 | 85,051,196 | 79,978,472 | 351,511 | 710,914 | 1,392,439 | 2,617,860 |
| Alabama................. | 1,020,975 | 22,746 | 17,540 | 203 | 13 | 3,288 | 1,702 |
| Alaska................... | 2,920,249 | 54,653,962 | 52,455,308 | 103,493 | 8 | 372,315 | 1,722,838 |
| Arizona................. | 12,850,196 | 2,947,211 | 2,658,113 | 94 | 75,949 | 56,833 | 156,222 |
| Arkansas............... | 3,175,612 | 104,980 | 98,346 | 3,428 | 20 | 2,749 | 437 |
| California.............. | 39,908,521 | 8,170,938 | 7,612,899 | 22,427 | 12,487 | 349,948 | 173,177 |
| Colorado............... | 7,565,055 | 738,389 | 665,260 | 4,276 | 42,456 | 303 | 26,094 |
| Connecticut............ | 35,382 | 7,781 | 5,846 | 1,055 | – | 874 | 6 |
| Delaware............... | (NA) | 904 | 890 | 6 | – | 2 | 6 |
| District of Columbia..... | 40,159,092 | 8,626 | 8,476 | 8 | 6 | 134 | 2 |
| Florida.................. | 9,646,727 | 2,638,606 | 2,469,214 | 1,350 | 44,486 | 101,444 | 22,112 |
| Georgia................. | 7,519,835 | 64,844 | 39,954 | 167 | 1,461 | 17,381 | 5,881 |
| Hawaii.................. | 4,838,838 | 371,494 | 360,111 | 1 | 22 | 11,228 | 132 |
| Idaho................... | 745,544 | 806,297 | 511,963 | 1,226 | 273,488 | 9,058 | 10,562 |
| Illinois.................. | 197,717 | 114 | 12 | – | – | 17 | 85 |
| Indiana................. | 2,011,116 | 15,574 | 10,772 | 538 | – | 3,425 | 839 |
| Iowa.................... | 193,663 | 2,714 | 2,708 | – | – | 5 | 1 |
| Kansas................. | 110,191 | 11,624 | 462 | 271 | – | 56 | 10,835 |
| Kentucky............... | 1,742,439 | 97,504 | 94,483 | 137 | – | 838 | 2,046 |
| Louisiana.............. | 611,240 | 26,999 | 21,145 | – | – | 2,779 | 3,075 |
| Maine................... | 3,549,576 | 182,005 | 156,205 | 11,204 | 24 | 10,646 | 3,926 |
| Maryland............... | 6,006,443 | 74,246 | 41,532 | 5,797 | 480 | 23,791 | 2,646 |
| Massachusetts......... | 9,646,316 | 59,501 | 33,336 | 1,029 | 44 | 21,920 | 3,172 |
| Michigan............... | 2,745,670 | 718,190 | 632,302 | 671 | 46 | 58,515 | 26,656 |
| Minnesota.............. | 1,186,406 | 301,330 | 139,789 | 3,193 | 142 | 98,663 | 59,543 |
| Mississippi............. | 6,863,047 | 118,590 | 104,369 | 5,229 | – | 72 | 8,920 |
| Missouri................ | 3,622,004 | 83,546 | 54,569 | 9,168 | – | 14,070 | 5,739 |
| Montana................ | 5,547,379 | 1,274,134 | 1,214,193 | 1,850 | 6,137 | 1,464 | 50,490 |
| Nebraska............... | 287,996 | 66,569 | 5,898 | 485 | 845 | 435 | 58,906 |
| Nevada................. | 5,837,312 | 801,173 | 797,613 | – | 2,508 | 44 | 1,008 |
| New Hampshire........ | 35,218 | 21,191 | 13,696 | 1,556 | 5,772 | 162 | 5 |
| New Jersey............. | 4,488,754 | 99,598 | 35,683 | 140 | 3,208 | 59,050 | 1,517 |
| New Mexico............ | 2,113,807 | 480,863 | 468,970 | 5 | 1,076 | 4,656 | 6,156 |
| New York............... | 19,291,389 | 97,415 | 34,106 | 3,903 | 148 | 19,988 | 39,270 |
| North Carolina......... | 18,121,305 | 410,021 | 366,889 | 12,272 | 20,782 | 3,289 | 6,789 |
| North Dakota........... | 774,622 | 72,569 | 71,192 | 256 | 151 | 123 | 847 |
| Ohio.................... | 2,511,418 | 34,550 | 20,290 | 1,462 | 84 | 8,463 | 4,251 |
| Oklahoma.............. | 1,491,343 | 10,241 | 10,011 | 9 | 189 | 5 | 27 |
| Oregon................. | 1,279,046 | 203,385 | 196,197 | 1,404 | 4,976 | 295 | 513 |
| Pennsylvania........... | 9,708,439 | 116,510 | 53,460 | 3,043 | 387 | 19,592 | 40,028 |
| Rhode Island........... | 60,709 | 331 | 5 | – | – | – | 326 |
| South Carolina......... | 1,612,758 | 32,728 | 32,339 | 63 | 16 | 51 | 259 |
| South Dakota.......... | 4,386,898 | 296,585 | 148,010 | 122,324 | – | 78 | 26,173 |
| Tennessee............. | 9,256,335 | 388,125 | 359,197 | 1,714 | 9,665 | 4,196 | 13,353 |
| Texas.................. | 5,310,767 | 1,255,705 | 1,206,489 | 88 | 1,013 | 10,785 | 37,330 |
| Utah.................... | 15,125,729 | 2,117,689 | 2,097,896 | 833 | 1,142 | 12,819 | 4,999 |
| Vermont................ | 63,886 | 23,236 | 9,836 | 3,927 | 8,809 | 544 | 120 |
| Virginia................. | 22,171,017 | 371,374 | 306,393 | 7,138 | 24,866 | 7,144 | 25,833 |
| Washington............ | 8,375,784 | 1,967,559 | 1,834,633 | 2,165 | 100,222 | 12,798 | 17,741 |
| West Virginia........... | 1,627,458 | 92,697 | 65,567 | 370 | 386 | 6,893 | 19,481 |
| Wisconsin.............. | 615,244 | 133,758 | 61,835 | 11,353 | 802 | 47,671 | 12,097 |
| Wyoming............... | 7,662,402 | 2,396,431 | 2,345,619 | 177 | 48,462 | 497 | 1,676 |

– Represents or rounds to zero. [1] See footnote 1, Table 1282. [2] See footnote 2, Table 1282. [3] See footnote 3, Table 1282. [4] See footnote 4, Table 1282. [5] See footnote 5, Table 1282. [6] Includes Island Areas of the U.S., not shown separately.

Source: U.S. National Park Service, Land Resources Division, unpublished data; and "National Park Service Visitor Use Statistics," <https://irma.nps.gov/Stats/Reports/National>, accessed May 2019.

## Table 1282. National Park Service (NPS) Visits and Acreage by Type of Area: 2018

[Includes data for four areas in Virgin Islands, and one area in each Puerto Rico, American Samoa, and Guam]

| Type of area | Recreation visits [1] | Gross area acres | Federal land — NPS fee acres [2] | Federal land — NPS less than fee acres [3] | Federal land — Other federal fee acres [4] | Non-federal land — Other public acres [5] | Non-federal land — Private acres |
|---|---|---|---|---|---|---|---|
| Total [6]........................... | 318,211,833 | 85,051,196 | 79,978,473 | 351,513 | 710,912 | 1,392,436 | 2,617,862 |
| National historic sites.......... | 8,664,509 | 34,568 | 22,351 | 856 | 42 | 373 | 10,946 |
| National historical parks....... | 33,161,620 | 192,194 | 139,535 | 4,139 | 550 | 29,206 | 18,764 |
| National memorials............. | 38,111,959 | 10,543 | 9,664 | 3 | 24 | 60 | 792 |
| National monuments........... | 22,180,695 | 2,136,723 | 1,970,351 | 14,790 | 24,582 | 8,531 | 118,469 |
| National parks.................. | 85,878,500 | 52,206,654 | 50,484,451 | 222,008 | 45,760 | 567,122 | 887,313 |
| National parkways............. | 29,846,041 | 182,027 | 162,103 | 9,123 | 214 | 404 | 10,183 |
| National recreation areas....... | 51,022,484 | 3,707,917 | 3,156,194 | 23,786 | 244,827 | 111,824 | 171,286 |
| National seashores............. | 18,325,744 | 596,931 | 404,612 | 14,947 | 61,226 | 106,820 | 9,326 |

[1] Recreation visit represents the entry of a person onto lands or waters administered by the NPS for recreational purposes, excluding government personnel, through traffic, tradespeople, and persons residing within park boundaries. [2] Complete Federal ownership of all rights in the land. [3] Federal ownership of some rights in the land. [4] Tracts under the administration of another federal agency (e.g., U.S. Forest Service, Department of the Army, etc.). Bureau of Land Management tracts are also identified as Other Fee (Federal) until they are withdrawn for NPS use; then status changes to Fee (Federal). [5] Non-federal tracts owned by the state, county, and/or other municipalities, including quasi-public entities. [6] Includes other types of areas, not shown separately.

Source: U.S. National Park Service, Land Resources Division, unpublished data; and "National Park Service Visitor Use Statistics," <https://irma.nps.gov/Stats/Reports/National>, accessed May 2019.

# Table 1283. State Parks and Recreation Areas by State: 2018

[In units as indicated (18,553 represents 18,553,000). For year ending June 30. Data are shown as reported by state park directors. In some states, the park agency has forests, fish and wildlife areas, and/or other areas under its control. In other states, the park agency is responsible for state parks only]

| State | Acreage (1,000) | Visitors (1,000) [1] | Total revenue generated ($1,000) | Operating expenditures ($1,000) | Revenue share of operating expenditures |
|---|---|---|---|---|---|
| United States.......................... | 18,553 | 813,216 | 1,391,600 | 2,849,225 | 48.8 |
| Alabama............................... | 48 | 4,815 | 38,195 | 41,663 | 91.7 |
| Alaska................................. | 3,387 | 3,686 | 3,809 | 13,393 | 28.4 |
| Arizona................................ | 64 | 3,190 | 20,362 | 22,298 | 91.3 |
| Arkansas.............................. | 55 | 7,108 | 28,389 | 63,432 | 44.8 |
| California............................. | 1,647 | 81,043 | 132,154 | 617,211 | 21.4 |
| Colorado.............................. | 1,580 | 14,777 | 85,246 | 63,105 | 135.1 |
| Connecticut........................... | 210 | 9,134 | 5,230 | 16,296 | 32.1 |
| Delaware.............................. | 26 | 5,893 | 19,730 | 28,432 | 69.4 |
| Florida................................. | 721 | 28,179 | 66,068 | 82,520 | 80.1 |
| Georgia............................... | 83 | 9,003 | 33,664 | 49,311 | 68.3 |
| Hawaii................................. | 33 | 11,348 | 4,321 | 12,650 | 34.2 |
| Idaho.................................. | 59 | 5,696 | 11,794 | 18,057 | 65.3 |
| Illinois................................. | 483 | 38,527 | 7,221 | 49,840 | 14.5 |
| Indiana................................ | 171 | 16,765 | 66,757 | 62,969 | 106.0 |
| Iowa................................... | 116 | 14,492 | 5,310 | 19,940 | 26.6 |
| Kansas................................ | 33 | 6,884 | 10,689 | 13,970 | 76.5 |
| Kentucky.............................. | 44 | 6,505 | 52,713 | 87,915 | 60.0 |
| Louisiana.............................. | 43 | 1,772 | 10,916 | 29,033 | 37.6 |
| Maine.................................. | 98 | 2,804 | 5,348 | 9,106 | 58.7 |
| Maryland.............................. | 140 | 14,095 | 11,971 | 65,813 | 18.2 |
| Massachusetts........................ | 354 | 27,292 | 17,568 | 84,025 | 20.9 |
| Michigan.............................. | 303 | 31,277 | 64,370 | 67,532 | 95.3 |
| Minnesota............................ | 284 | 9,737 | 29,319 | 100,784 | 29.1 |
| Mississippi............................ | 24 | 1,200 | 9,798 | 13,970 | 70.1 |
| Missouri............................... | 160 | 22,142 | 14,507 | 54,673 | 26.5 |
| Montana............................... | 46 | 2,663 | 2,469 | 10,667 | 23.1 |
| Nebraska.............................. | 170 | 10,894 | 35,286 | 25,961 | 135.9 |
| Nevada................................ | 151 | 3,888 | 6,576 | 18,569 | 35.4 |
| New Hampshire....................... | 232 | 1,177 | 25,077 | 23,182 | 108.2 |
| New Jersey............................ | 455 | 17,438 | 13,989 | 40,450 | 34.6 |
| New Mexico........................... | 192 | 5,010 | 6,124 | 16,053 | 38.1 |
| New York.............................. | 4,318 | 72,032 | 107,004 | 225,675 | 47.4 |
| North Carolina........................ | 235 | 19,078 | 11,043 | 43,967 | 25.1 |
| North Dakota.......................... | 35 | 1,497 | 3,867 | 17,062 | 22.7 |
| Ohio................................... | 175 | 42,831 | 32,026 | 73,690 | 43.5 |
| Oklahoma............................. | 62 | 9,903 | 22,905 | 28,518 | 80.3 |
| Oregon................................ | 113 | 54,421 | 31,261 | 65,612 | 47.6 |
| Pennsylvania.......................... | 295 | 38,338 | 25,917 | 105,761 | 24.5 |
| Rhode Island.......................... | 10 | 8,928 | 5,444 | 11,872 | 45.9 |
| South Carolina........................ | 77 | 8,731 | 30,684 | 31,112 | 98.6 |
| South Dakota......................... | 103 | 7,734 | 27,865 | 22,944 | 121.5 |
| Tennessee............................ | 226 | 40,477 | 42,924 | 96,391 | 44.5 |
| Texas.................................. | 640 | 8,772 | 49,995 | 81,724 | 61.2 |
| Utah................................... | 153 | 5,728 | 25,368 | 19,764 | 128.4 |
| Vermont............................... | 74 | 987 | 11,491 | 7,289 | 157.7 |
| Virginia................................ | 74 | 9,443 | 24,818 | 45,781 | 54.2 |
| Washington........................... | 122 | 36,745 | 49,852 | 74,250 | 67.1 |
| West Virginia.......................... | 151 | 6,865 | 22,701 | 43,176 | 52.6 |
| Wisconsin............................. | 158 | 17,749 | 18,487 | 21,375 | 86.5 |
| Wyoming.............................. | 120 | 4,525 | 2,979 | 10,438 | 28.5 |

[1] Includes day and overnight visitors.

Source: National Association of State Park Directors, Raleigh NC, *Statistical Report of State Park Operations: 2017-2018, Annual Information Exchange for the Period of July 1, 2017 through June 30, 2018* ©, September 2019. See also <http://www.stateparks.org/>.

## Table 1284. Participants in Wildlife-Related Recreation Activities: 2016

[In thousands (39,553 represents 39,553,000). For persons 16 years old and over engaging in activity at least once in 2016. Based on survey and subject to sampling error; see source for details]

| Participant | Number | Days of participation | Trips | Participant | Number | Days of participation |
|---|---|---|---|---|---|---|
| **Total sportspersons** [1] | **39,553** | **643,362** | **530,167** | **Wildlife watchers** [1] | **86,042** | (X) |
| Total anglers | 35,754 | 459,341 | 383,296 | Away from home [2] | 23,720 | 386,045 |
| Freshwater | 30,137 | 383,192 | 322,266 | Observe wildlife | 19,583 | 308,769 |
| Excluding Great Lakes | 29,490 | 372,660 | 311,237 | Photograph wildlife | 13,721 | 151,559 |
| Great Lakes | 1,824 | 13,440 | 11,029 | Feed wildlife | 4,869 | 70,846 |
| Saltwater | 8,320 | 75,392 | 61,030 | Around the home [3] | 81,128 | (X) |
| | | | | Observe wildlife | 43,829 | (X) |
| Total hunters | 11,453 | 184,021 | 146,871 | Photograph wildlife | 30,473 | (X) |
| Big game | 9,208 | 132,665 | 88,561 | Feed wildlife | 59,083 | (X) |
| Small game | 3,505 | 38,306 | 31,772 | Visit public parks | 11,359 | (X) |
| Migratory birds | 2,353 | 15,621 | 14,548 | Maintain plantings or | | |
| Other animals | 1,315 | 13,275 | 11,989 | natural areas | 11,024 | (X) |

X Not applicable. [1] Detail does not add to total due to multiple responses and nonresponse. [2] Persons taking a trip of at least 1 mile from home for activity. [3] Activity within 1 mile of home.

Source: U.S. Fish and Wildlife Service, *2016 National Survey of Fishing, Hunting, and Wildlife Associated Recreation*, April 2018. See also <https://wsfrprograms.fws.gov/Subpages/NationalSurvey/2016_Survey.html>.

## Table 1285. Expenditures for Wildlife-Related Recreation Activities: 2016

[46,115 represents $46,115,000,000. For persons 16 years old and over. Based on survey and subject to sampling error; see source]

| Expenditure item | Fishing | | | Hunting | | | Wildlife watching | | |
|---|---|---|---|---|---|---|---|---|---|
| | | Spenders | | | Spenders | | | Spenders | |
| | Expendi-tures (mil. dol.) | Number (1,000) | Percent of anglers | Expendi-tures (mil. dol.) | Number (1,000) | Percent of hunters | Expendi-tures [1] (mil. dol.) | Number (1,000) | Percent [2] |
| **Total, all items** [3] | **46,115** | **32,511** | **91** | **26,190** | **10,992** | **96** | **75,867** | **63,578** | **74** |
| Total trip-related | 21,730 | 31,260 | 87 | 9,196 | 9,984 | 87 | 11,588 | 20,235 | 85 |
| Food and lodging | 7,849 | 27,127 | 76 | 3,114 | 9,065 | 79 | 6,068 | 17,058 | 72 |
| Food | 4,759 | 26,867 | 75 | 2,507 | 9,053 | 79 | 3,810 | 16,955 | 71 |
| Lodging | 3,090 | 8,625 | 24 | 607 | 1,775 | 16 | 2,258 | 6,331 | 27 |
| Transportation | 5,049 | 26,337 | 74 | 3,184 | 9,047 | 79 | 4,229 | 19,018 | 80 |
| Public | 543 | 2,852 | 8 | 193 | 912 | 8 | 1,233 | 3,052 | 13 |
| Private | 4,506 | 25,622 | 72 | 2,991 | 8,937 | 78 | 2,996 | 17,766 | 75 |
| Other trip costs | 8,832 | 26,212 | 73 | 2,898 | 3,664 | 32 | 1,291 | 8,609 | 36 |
| Equipment expenditures: | | | | | | | | | |
| Equipment | 7,431 | 22,393 | 63 | 7,384 | 8,413 | 73 | 64,279 | 57,496 | 67 |
| Auxiliary equipment | 3,164 | 4,522 | 13 | 2,019 | 4,436 | 39 | 1,044 | 6,669 | 8 |
| Special equipment [4] | 10,483 | 2,291 | 6 | [5] 3,353 | [5] 396 | [5] 3 | 41,934 | 3,037 | 4 |
| Other expenditures: | | | | | | | | | |
| Magazines and books | 147 | 3,142 | 9 | 166 | 1,130 | 10 | 237 | 7,022 | 8 |
| Land leasing and ownership | 2,359 | 1,019 | 3 | 2,899 | 1,845 | 16 | 4,196 | 1,195 | 1 |
| Membership dues and contributions | 214 | 1,741 | 5 | 182 | 1,403 | 12 | 3,817 | 10,076 | 12 |
| Plantings | (X) | (X) | (X) | [5] 165 | [5] 1,020 | [5] 9 | 946 | 7,289 | 8 |
| Licenses, stamps, tags, and permits | 587 | 15,647 | 44 | 826 | 8,668 | 76 | (X) | (X) | (X) |

X Not applicable. [1] Information on trip-related expenditures for wildlife watching was collected for away-from-home participants only. Equipment and other expenditures for wildlife watching are base on information collected from both away-from-home and around-the-home participants. [2] Based on away-from-home participants for trip-related expenditures. For equipment and other expenditures the percent of wildlife-watching participants is based on total participants. [3] Total not adjusted for multiple responses or nonresponse. [4] Special equipment includes boats, campers, cabins, trail bikes, etc. [5] Estimate based on a sample size of 10 to 29.

Source: U.S. Fish and Wildlife Service, *2016 National Survey of Fishing, Hunting, and Wildlife Associated Recreation*, April 2018. See also <https://wsfrprograms.fws.gov/Subpages/NationalSurvey/2016_Survey.html>.

## Table 1286. Tribal Gaming Revenues: 2010 to 2018

[Revenue in millions of dollars (26,503 represents $26,503,000,000). For year ending September 30]

| Region | 2010 | | 2015 | | 2016 | | 2017 | | 2018 | |
|---|---|---|---|---|---|---|---|---|---|---|
| | Operations (number) | Revenue | Operations (number) | Revenue | Operations (number) | Revenue | Operations (number) | Revenue | Operations (number) | Revenue |
| **Total** [1] | **422** | **26,503** | **474** | **29,882** | **484** | **31,196** | **494** | **32,404** | **501** | **33,720** |
| Portland | 50 | 2,655 | 52 | 3,022 | 53 | 3,177 | 52 | 3,384 | 55 | 3,663 |
| Sacramento | 62 | 6,794 | 71 | 7,881 | 70 | 8,381 | 74 | 8,996 | 73 | 9,279 |
| Phoenix | 48 | 2,539 | 53 | 2,808 | 57 | 2,932 | 59 | 3,038 | 59 | 3,141 |
| St. Paul [2] | 119 | 4,452 | 134 | 4,829 | 93 | 4,511 | 92 | 4,587 | 95 | 4,796 |
| Rapid City [3] | (X) | (X) | (X) | (X) | 39 | 373 | 39 | 363 | 36 | 369 |
| Tulsa | 65 | 1,769 | 68 | 2,207 | 69 | 2,295 | 72 | 2,391 | 73 | 2,466 |
| Oklahoma City | 51 | 1,583 | 65 | 2,142 | 66 | 2,265 | 69 | 2,312 | 72 | 2,480 |
| Washington DC | 27 | 6,711 | 31 | 6,994 | 37 | 7,261 | 37 | 7,333 | 38 | 7,525 |

X Not applicable. [1] Regions formerly were numbered I to VI, as follows: Portland (Region I): Alaska, Idaho, Oregon, and Washington. Sacramento (Region II): California, and Northern Nevada. Phoenix (Region III): Arizona, Colorado, New Mexico, and Southern Nevada. St Paul (Region IV): Iowa, Michigan, Minnesota, Montana, North Dakota, Nebraska, South Dakota, Wisconsin, and Wyoming. Tulsa (Eastern part of Region V): Kansas, and Eastern Oklahoma. Oklahoma City (Western part of Region V): Western Oklahoma, and Texas. Washington (Region VI): Alabama, Connecticut, Florida, Louisiana, Mississippi, North Carolina, and New York. See footnote 2 regarding St. Paul region. [2] Through FY2015, St. Paul region covers Iowa, Michigan, Minnesota, Montana, North Dakota, Nebraska, South Dakota, Wisconsin, and Wyoming. Beginning FY2016, St. Paul region covers Indiana, Iowa, Michigan, Minnesota, Nebraska, and Wisconsin. Also known as Region IV. [3] Rapid City region data begins with data for FY2016, and covers North Dakota, South Dakota, Montana, and Wyoming.

Source: National Indian Gaming Commission, *Gross Gaming Revenues 2014-2018*, September 2019, and earlier reports; and *Gross Gaming Revenues by Region 2017 and 2018*, September 2019, and earlier reports.

## Table 1287. Real Tourism Output: 2005 to 2017

[In millions of dollars (681,024 represents $681,024,000,000)]

| Commodity | Direct output (current dollars) | | | Real output (chained 2009 dollars) | | |
|---|---|---|---|---|---|---|
| | 2005 | 2010 | 2017 | 2005 | 2010 | 2017 |
| **Total**........................................ | **681,024** | **701,356** | **940,894** | **752,607** | **678,716** | **839,619** |
| Traveler accommodations........................ | 121,924 | 129,651 | 189,263 | 133,129 | 130,757 | 162,187 |
| Food services and drinking places.............. | 101,965 | 105,700 | 139,087 | 118,378 | 104,448 | 115,614 |
| Domestic passenger air transportation services.... | 79,398 | 80,094 | 105,543 | 87,937 | 74,679 | 89,103 |
| International passenger air transportation services.... | 30,371 | 43,096 | 49,676 | 30,477 | 38,785 | 42,578 |
| Passenger rail transportation services.......... | 1,460 | 1,862 | 2,311 | 1,726 | 1,847 | 1,815 |
| Passenger water transportation services......... | 9,883 | 10,976 | 14,795 | 8,746 | 10,852 | 14,253 |
| Interurban bus transportation................... | 1,636 | 1,370 | 1,532 | 1,953 | 1,310 | 1,192 |
| Interurban charter bus transportation........... | 1,764 | 1,625 | 2,086 | 2,107 | 1,550 | 1,622 |
| Urban transit systems and other transportation services...... | 4,298 | 4,227 | 5,804 | 4,965 | 4,060 | 4,638 |
| Taxi service.................................... | 3,983 | 4,090 | 4,934 | 4,573 | 3,934 | 3,945 |
| Scenic and sightseeing transportation services.... | 2,496 | 2,467 | 3,489 | 2,767 | 2,459 | 3,081 |
| Automotive rental.............................. | 26,940 | 28,007 | 38,070 | 34,863 | 28,234 | 45,238 |
| Other vehicle rental............................ | 762 | 763 | 1,009 | 853 | 747 | 1,037 |
| Automotive repair services..................... | 13,913 | 12,390 | 14,505 | 16,362 | 12,156 | 12,655 |
| Parking lots and garages....................... | 2,168 | 2,322 | 2,702 | 2,649 | 2,248 | 2,053 |
| Highway tolls.................................. | 679 | 702 | 872 | 837 | 664 | 767 |
| Travel arrangement and reservation services..... | 31,665 | 36,771 | 52,748 | 33,766 | 36,765 | 51,226 |
| Motion pictures and performing arts............. | 14,736 | 14,040 | 18,758 | 16,700 | 13,855 | 15,948 |
| Spectator sports............................... | 6,732 | 5,179 | 4,400 | 7,910 | 5,071 | 3,490 |
| Participant sports.............................. | 12,183 | 10,073 | 10,844 | 13,045 | 10,171 | 9,915 |
| Gambling...................................... | 37,721 | 41,286 | 52,243 | 41,452 | 40,614 | 45,730 |
| All other recreation and entertainment.......... | 13,955 | 12,110 | 12,090 | 15,749 | 12,004 | 11,322 |
| Gasoline...................................... | 54,926 | 61,592 | 84,412 | 56,865 | 51,958 | 79,260 |
| Nondurable PCE [1] commodities other than gasoline.......... | 105,467 | 90,962 | 129,720 | 116,065 | 89,976 | 119,457 |

[1] Personal consumption expenditures.

Source: U.S. Bureau of Economic Analysis, Satellite Accounts Data, "Travel and tourism data files," <https://www.bea.gov/data/special-topics/travel-and-tourism>, accessed July 2018.

## Table 1288. Travel Forecast Summary: 2016 to 2022

[In units as indicated (18,707 represents $18,707,000,000,000)]

| Indicator | Unit | 2016 | 2017 | 2018 | 2019 (P) | 2020 (P) | 2021 (P) | 2022 (P) |
|---|---|---|---|---|---|---|---|---|
| Real GDP.................................. | Bil. dol. | 18,707 | 19,485 | 20,494 | 21,357 | 22,115 | 22,955 | 23,857 |
| Unemployment rate......................... | Percent | 4.9 | 4.4 | 3.9 | 3.6 | 3.5 | 3.7 | 3.8 |
| Consumer price index (CPI) [1].............. | Percent | 240.0 | 245.1 | 251.1 | 256.3 | 261.1 | 265.9 | 271.2 |
| Travel price index (TPI) [1]................. | Percent | 273.1 | 279.4 | 286.5 | 289.0 | 293.2 | 298.5 | 303.8 |
| Total travel expenditures in U.S............ | Bil. dol. | 994.1 | 1,037.7 | 1,089.0 | 1,118.7 | 1,160.6 | 1,209.4 | 1,257.7 |
| U.S. residents............................ | Bil. dol. | 838.5 | 881.9 | 932.7 | 959.7 | 996.3 | 1,038.3 | 1,079.6 |
| International visitors [2].................... | Bil. dol. | 155.6 | 155.8 | 156.3 | 159.0 | 164.4 | 171.1 | 178.1 |
| Total international visitors to the United States................... | Millions | 76.4 | 76.9 | 79.6 | 79.8 | 82.2 | 84.9 | 87.8 |
| Overseas arrivals to the United States [3]... | Millions | 38.1 | 38.9 | 39.9 | 40.6 | 42.0 | 43.5 | 45.0 |
| Total domestic person trips [4]............... | Millions | 2,206.6 | 2,247.9 | 2,291.1 | 2,330.8 | 2,369.2 | 2,411.2 | 2,457.5 |
| Business.................................. | Millions | 454.7 | 456.3 | 463.6 | 470.4 | 477.0 | 484.9 | 493.7 |
| Leisure................................... | Millions | 1,751.9 | 1,791.5 | 1,827.5 | 1,860.5 | 1,892.2 | 1,926.3 | 1,963.8 |

P Projected. [1] 1982-1984=100. [2] Excludes international traveler spending on medical, educational, and cross-border/seasonal work-related activities or international passenger fares on U.S. airlines. [3] Subject to revision as updated visitation statistics are released by the Department of Commerce. [4] One person on one trip 50 miles or more, one way, away from home or including one or more nights away from home.

Source: U.S. Travel Association, *Travel Forecast Summary Table*, July 2019 ©. See also <https://www.ustravel.org/research>.

## Table 1289. Chain-Type Price Indexes for Direct Tourism Output: 2000 to 2017

[Index numbers, 2009=100. For explanation of chain-type price indexes, see text, Section 13]

| Tourism goods and services group | 2000 | 2005 | 2010 | 2011 | 2012 | 2013 | 2014 | 2015 | 2016 | 2017 |
|---|---|---|---|---|---|---|---|---|---|---|
| **All tourism goods and services**....... | **79.0** | **90.5** | **103.3** | **108.6** | **111.6** | **112.2** | **113.5** | **112.6** | **110.3** | **111.5** |
| Traveler accommodations.................. | 80.1 | 91.6 | 99.2 | 100.9 | 103.9 | 104.7 | 110.1 | 114.5 | 117.5 | 116.7 |
| Transportation........................... | 77.7 | 91.6 | 107.5 | 117.4 | 120.7 | 120.4 | 119.8 | 113.4 | 105.2 | 107.9 |
| Passenger air transportation.............. | 79.3 | 93.2 | 108.6 | 116.6 | 122.1 | 122.3 | 123.1 | 120.7 | 117.7 | 117.7 |
| All other transportation-related commodities............................ | 76.5 | 90.4 | 106.7 | 117.9 | 119.9 | 119.2 | 117.7 | 108.9 | 97.7 | 102.0 |
| Food services and drinking places......... | 74.8 | 86.1 | 101.2 | 103.6 | 106.8 | 109.1 | 111.7 | 112.4 | 116.9 | 120.3 |
| Recreation, entertainment, and shopping.... | 82.5 | 90.5 | 101.1 | 103.6 | 106.0 | 106.3 | 107.9 | 110.8 | 110.7 | 109.6 |
| Recreation and entertainment............. | 78.5 | 90.1 | 101.2 | 103.0 | 105.2 | 106.9 | 108.8 | 112.8 | 112.5 | 110.8 |
| Shopping................................. | 85.7 | 90.9 | 101.1 | 104.2 | 106.6 | 107.4 | 107.0 | 109.3 | 109.4 | 108.6 |

Source: U.S. Department of Commerce, Bureau of Economic Analysis, *Survey of Current Business, U.S. Travel and Tourism Satellite Account for 2015–2017*, June 2018, <https://www.bea.gov/scb/2018/06-june/0618-us-travel-tourism-satellite-account.htm>.

## Table 1290. Tourism Sales and Employment by Industry Segment: 2000 to 2017

[Sales in billions of dollars (580.3 represents $580,300,000,000); employment in thousands (5,926 represents 5,926,000). Direct tourism-related sales comprise all output purchased directly by visitors (e.g., traveler accommodations, passenger air transportation, souvenirs). Direct tourism-related employment comprises all jobs where the workers are engaged in the production of direct tourism-related sales (output), such as hotel staff, airline pilots, and souvenir sellers]

| Tourism commodity group | 2000 | 2005 | 2010 | 2011 | 2012 | 2013 | 2014 | 2015 | 2016 | 2017 |
|---|---|---|---|---|---|---|---|---|---|---|
| **DIRECT TOURISM SALES (OUTPUT) (bil. dol.)** | | | | | | | | | | |
| **All tourism goods and services** | **580.3** | **681.0** | **701.4** | **780.7** | **812.8** | **839.4** | **875.0** | **901.9** | **913.7** | **940.9** |
| Traveler accommodations | 106.3 | 121.9 | 129.7 | 137.8 | 146.3 | 154.0 | 166.6 | 176.0 | 182.0 | 189.3 |
| Transportation | 231.1 | 266.3 | 292.4 | 338.8 | 353.5 | 373.6 | 386.2 | 382.3 | 372.7 | 384.5 |
| Passenger air transportation | 100.6 | 109.8 | 123.2 | 136.4 | 138.1 | 145.1 | 151.4 | 152.1 | 150.7 | 155.2 |
| All other transportation-related commodities | 130.5 | 156.6 | 169.2 | 202.4 | 215.4 | 228.5 | 234.8 | 230.3 | 222.0 | 229.3 |
| Food services and drinking places | 87.4 | 102.0 | 105.7 | 114.0 | 118.7 | 105.9 | 112.5 | 127.8 | 136.8 | 139.1 |
| Recreation, entertainment, and shopping | 155.5 | 190.8 | 173.7 | 190.0 | 194.3 | 206.0 | 209.7 | 215.8 | 222.2 | 228.1 |
| Recreation and entertainment | 62.9 | 85.3 | 82.7 | 86.8 | 91.1 | 90.2 | 89.5 | 92.1 | 95.1 | 98.3 |
| Shopping | 92.6 | 105.5 | 91.0 | 103.2 | 103.2 | 115.7 | 120.2 | 123.7 | 127.0 | 129.7 |
| **DIRECT TOURISM EMPLOYMENT (1,000)** | | | | | | | | | | |
| **All tourism industries** | **5,926** | **5,589** | **4,925** | **5,107** | **5,176** | **5,064** | **5,174** | **5,380** | **5,573** | **5,509** |
| Traveler accommodations | 1,386 | 1,324 | 1,268 | 1,300 | 1,328 | 1,338 | 1,374 | 1,405 | 1,429 | 1,459 |
| Transportation | 1,377 | 1,154 | 996 | 1,020 | 1,030 | 1,045 | 1,063 | 1,113 | 1,155 | 1,099 |
| Air transportation services | 569 | 474 | 424 | 436 | 440 | 434 | 440 | 458 | 475 | 454 |
| All other transportation-related industries | 809 | 680 | 572 | 584 | 591 | 611 | 623 | 656 | 681 | 646 |
| Food services and drinking places | 1,658 | 1,690 | 1,551 | 1,625 | 1,660 | 1,481 | 1,530 | 1,612 | 1,712 | 1,742 |
| Recreation, entertainment, and shopping | 1,257 | 1,197 | 932 | 969 | 957 | 983 | 987 | 1,014 | 1,034 | 986 |
| Recreation and entertainment | 590 | 621 | 505 | 520 | 527 | 522 | 515 | 513 | 513 | 503 |
| Shopping | 668 | 576 | 428 | 449 | 429 | 460 | 472 | 501 | 521 | 483 |
| All other industries | 247 | 224 | 178 | 193 | 201 | 210 | 213 | 228 | 235 | 216 |

Source: U.S. Department of Commerce, Bureau of Economic Analysis, *Survey of Current Business*, July 2018; and Satellite Accounts Data, "Travel and tourism data files," <https://www.bea.gov/data/special-topics/travel-and-tourism>, accessed July 2018.

## Table 1291. Top States and Cities Visited by Overseas Travelers: 2000 to 2017

[25,975 represents 25,975,000. Includes travelers for business and pleasure, international travelers in transit through the United States, and students. Excludes travel by international personnel and international businessmen employed in the United States. Starting with the 2006 data, the statistical policy for visitation estimates of international visitation requires a minimum sample of 400 respondents. States and cities are ranked by the latest overseas visitors data]

| State and other area | Overseas visitors [1] (1,000) | | | | City | Overseas visitors [1] (1,000) | | | |
|---|---|---|---|---|---|---|---|---|---|
| | 2000 | 2010 | 2015 | 2017 | | 2000 | 2010 | 2015 | 2017 |
| **Total overseas travelers [2,3]** | **25,975** | **26,363** | **38,392** | **38,906** | New York, NY [4] | 5,714 | 8,462 | 10,132 | 10,084 |
| New York | 5,922 | 8,647 | 10,385 | 10,287 | Miami, FL | 2,935 | 3,111 | 5,509 | 5,101 |
| Florida | 6,026 | 5,826 | 9,667 | 9,481 | Los Angeles-Long Beach, CA | 3,533 | 3,348 | 4,857 | 4,766 |
| California | 6,364 | 5,615 | 8,139 | 8,178 | Orlando, FL | 3,013 | 2,715 | 4,718 | 4,653 |
| Hawaiian Islands | 2,727 | 2,135 | 3,021 | 3,319 | San Francisco, CA | 2,831 | 2,636 | 3,632 | 3,443 |
| Nevada | 2,364 | 2,504 | 3,505 | 3,023 | Las Vegas, NV | 2,260 | 2,425 | 3,409 | 2,937 |
| Massachusetts | 1,429 | 1,292 | 1,789 | 1,817 | Honolulu, HI | 2,234 | 1,634 | 2,380 | 2,677 |
| Texas | 1,169 | 1,028 | 1,789 | 1,739 | Washington, DC | 1,481 | 1,740 | 2,135 | 2,128 |
| Guam | 1,325 | 1,318 | 1,505 | 1,681 | Boston, MA | 1,325 | 1,186 | 1,609 | 1,650 |
| Illinois | 1,377 | 1,186 | 1,708 | 1,638 | Chicago, IL | 1,351 | 1,134 | 1,620 | 1,537 |
| New Jersey | 909 | 975 | 994 | 1,093 | San Diego, CA | 701 | 765 | 1,159 | 1,027 |
| Arizona | 883 | 765 | 1,044 | 1,035 | Fort Lauderdale, FL | (X) | (X) | 902 | 903 |
| Pennsylvania | 649 | 923 | 1,029 | 1,004 | Houston, TX | 442 | 448 | 864 | 875 |
| Georgia | 805 | 817 | 998 | 879 | Atlanta, GA | 701 | 712 | 837 | 735 |
| Washington | 468 | 501 | 852 | 798 | Seattle, WA | 416 | 475 | 783 | 731 |
| Utah | (B) | 475 | 595 | 634 | Anaheim-Santa Ana, CA | 494 | 369 | 610 | 665 |
| North Carolina | 416 | 343 | 491 | 525 | Flagstaff, AZ [5] | (B) | 501 | 672 | 650 |
| Louisiana | (X) | (X) | 518 | 506 | Philadelphia, PA | 390 | 633 | 680 | 622 |
| Colorado | 519 | 343 | 461 | 459 | San Jose, CA | 494 | 290 | 499 | 611 |

B Figure too small to meet statistical standards for reliability of a derived figure. X Not applicable (not ranked). [1] Excludes visitors from Canada and Mexico. [2] A person is counted in each area visited, but only once in the total. [3] Includes other states and cities, not shown separately. [4] Data include New York City-White Plains-Wayne, NY-NJ grouped together. [5] Data include Flagstaff, Grand Canyon, and Sedona grouped together.

Source: U.S. Department of Commerce, International Trade Administration, National Travel and Tourism Office, "2017 U.S. Travel and Tourism Statistics (Inbound), Overseas Visitation Estimates," <https://travel.trade.gov/outreachpages/inbound.general_information.inbound_overview.asp>, accessed April 2019.

## Table 1292. Domestic and International Travel Expenditures by State: 2017

[In millions of dollars (1,037,677 represents $1,037,677,000,000). Shows aggregate spending by foreign visitors and by U.S. residents on domestic overnight trips and day trips of 50 miles or more, one way, away from home]

| State | Total (mil. dol.) | Percent distribution | Rank | State | Total (mil. dol.) | Percent distribution | Rank | State | Total (mil. dol.) | Percent distribution | Rank |
|---|---|---|---|---|---|---|---|---|---|---|---|
| U.S. total..... | 1,037,677 | 100.0 | (X) | KS......... | 7,662 | 0.7 | 35 | ND........ | 2,914 | 0.3 | 46 |
| | | | | KY......... | 9,711 | 0.9 | 31 | OH........ | 20,375 | 2.0 | 16 |
| AL......... | 9,761 | 0.9 | 30 | LA......... | 12,691 | 1.2 | 25 | OK........ | 8,122 | 0.8 | 34 |
| AK......... | 2,727 | 0.3 | 48 | ME........ | 4,166 | 0.4 | 43 | OR........ | 12,330 | 1.2 | 26 |
| AZ......... | 20,257 | 2.0 | 17 | MD........ | 17,703 | 1.7 | 20 | PA........ | 26,393 | 2.5 | 8 |
| AR......... | 7,058 | 0.7 | 37 | MA........ | 22,870 | 2.2 | 13 | RI......... | 2,160 | 0.2 | 51 |
| CA......... | 139,940 | 13.5 | 1 | MI......... | 22,291 | 2.1 | 14 | SC........ | 14,640 | 1.4 | 22 |
| CO......... | 20,129 | 1.9 | 18 | MN........ | 14,588 | 1.4 | 23 | SD........ | 2,855 | 0.3 | 47 |
| CT......... | 11,822 | 1.1 | 27 | MS........ | 6,467 | 0.6 | 38 | TN........ | 20,771 | 2.0 | 15 |
| DE......... | 2,202 | 0.2 | 50 | MO........ | 14,665 | 1.4 | 21 | TX........ | 72,483 | 7.0 | 4 |
| DC......... | 13,201 | 1.3 | 24 | MT........ | 4,573 | 0.4 | 41 | UT........ | 9,148 | 0.9 | 32 |
| FL......... | 98,578 | 9.5 | 2 | NE........ | 5,141 | 0.5 | 39 | VT........ | 2,557 | 0.2 | 49 |
| GA......... | 29,619 | 2.9 | 7 | NV........ | 41,485 | 4.0 | 5 | VA........ | 25,639 | 2.5 | 10 |
| HI......... | 25,926 | 2.5 | 9 | NH........ | 4,209 | 0.4 | 42 | WA........ | 19,140 | 1.8 | 19 |
| ID......... | 4,789 | 0.5 | 40 | NJ........ | 23,060 | 2.2 | 12 | WV........ | 4,021 | 0.4 | 44 |
| IL......... | 39,733 | 3.8 | 6 | NM........ | 7,181 | 0.7 | 36 | WI........ | 11,822 | 1.1 | 27 |
| IN......... | 11,737 | 1.1 | 29 | NY........ | 79,133 | 7.6 | 3 | WY........ | 3,392 | 0.3 | 45 |
| IA......... | 8,706 | 0.8 | 33 | NC........ | 24,928 | 2.4 | 11 | Other [1].... | 10,207 | 1.0 | (X) |

X Not applicable. [1] This category includes foreign visitor spending in U.S. territories, and Canadian and Mexican visitor spending in the U.S. Those dollars are not represented in state totals.

Source: U.S. Travel Association, Washington, DC, *Impact of Travel on State Economies 2018* ©, March 2019. See also <http://www.ustravel.org/research>.

## Table 1293. Average Cost of Airfare for Domestic Routes: 1995 to 2018

[In dollars, except percent. Fares based on domestic itinerary fares. Itinerary fares consist of round-trip fares unless the customer does not purchase a return trip. In that case, the one-way fare is included. Fares are based on the total ticket value which consists of the price charged by the airlines plus any additional taxes and fees levied by an outside entity at the time of purchase. Fares include only the price paid at the time of the ticket purchase and do not include other fees paid at the airport or onboard the aircraft. Averages do not include frequent-flyer or "zero fares" or a few abnormally high reported fares]

| Year | Current dollars | | | Constant (2018) dollars [1] | | |
|---|---|---|---|---|---|---|
| | | Percent change | | | Percent change | |
| | Average fare | From previous year | Cumulative from 1995 | Average fare | From previous year | Cumulative from 1995 |
| 1995..................... | 292 | (NA) | (NA) | 481 | (NA) | (NA) |
| 2000..................... | 339 | 4.7 | 16.0 | 494 | 1.3 | 2.7 |
| 2005..................... | 307 | 0.6 | 5.2 | 395 | -2.7 | -17.9 |
| 2010..................... | 336 | 8.3 | 15.0 | 387 | 6.5 | -19.6 |
| 2011..................... | 364 | 8.3 | 24.5 | 406 | 4.9 | -15.6 |
| 2012..................... | 375 | 3.0 | 28.3 | 410 | 0.9 | -14.9 |
| 2013..................... | 382 | 1.9 | 30.7 | 412 | 0.5 | -14.5 |
| 2014..................... | 392 | 2.5 | 34.1 | 416 | 0.9 | -13.7 |
| 2015..................... | 377 | -3.8 | 29.0 | 399 | -3.9 | -17.0 |
| 2016..................... | 349 | -7.4 | 19.5 | 365 | -8.5 | -24.1 |
| 2017..................... | 348 | -0.4 | 19.0 | 356 | -2.5 | -26.0 |
| 2018..................... | 350 | 0.6 | 19.7 | 350 | -1.8 | -27.4 |

NA Not available. [1] Rate calculated using Bureau of Labor Statistics Consumer Price Index.

Source: U.S. Department of Transportation, Bureau of Transportation Statistics, Air Fares, "National Level Fares since 1995—Annual," <https://www.bts.gov/air-fares>, accessed April 2019.

## Table 1294. Top 20 U.S. Gateway Airports for Nonstop International Air Travel Passengers: 2018

[238,605 represents 238,605,000. International passengers are residents of any country traveling nonstop to and from the United States on U.S. and foreign carriers. The data cover all passengers arriving and departing from U.S. airports on nonstop commercial international flights with 60 seats or more]

| Gateway airport | Airport code | Passengers, (1,000) | Gateway airport | Airport code | Passengers, (1,000) |
|---|---|---|---|---|---|
| **Total, all airports**....................... | (X) | **238,605** | Fort Lauderdale, FL....................... | FLL | 8,455 |
| Total, top 20 airports....................... | (X) | 210,648 | Dallas-Ft. Worth, TX....................... | DFW | 8,390 |
| Top 20, percentage of total............... | (X) | 88.3 | Washington (Dulles), DC............... | IAD | 7,865 |
| | | | Boston, MA............................... | BOS | 7,243 |
| New York (JFK), NY....................... | JFK | 33,302 | Orlando, FL............................... | MCO | 6,401 |
| Los Angeles, CA....................... | LAX | 25,824 | Honolulu, HI............................... | HNL | 5,332 |
| Miami, FL............................... | MIA | 21,078 | Seattle-Tacoma, WA....................... | SEA | 5,275 |
| San Francisco, CA....................... | SFO | 13,965 | Philadelphia, PA....................... | PHL | 3,861 |
| Newark, NJ............................... | EWR | 13,792 | Detroit, MI............................... | DTW | 3,751 |
| Chicago (O'Hare), IL....................... | ORD | 13,600 | Las Vegas, NV............................... | LAS | 3,618 |
| Atlanta, GA............................... | ATL | 12,318 | Charlotte, NC............................... | CLT | 3,125 |
| Houston (G. Bush), TX....................... | IAH | 10,485 | Minneapolis-St. Paul, MN............... | MSP | 2,968 |

X Not applicable.

Source: U.S. Department of Transportation, Research and Innovative Technology Administration, Bureau of Transportation Statistics, Office of Airline Information, "T-100 International Segment data," <http://www.transtats.bts.gov/Fields.asp?Table_ID=261>, accessed June 2019.

# Table 1295. International Travel: 2005 to 2017

[In thousands (63,502 represents 63,502,000), except percent. U.S. travelers cover residents of the United States, its territories and possessions. International travelers to the U.S. include travelers for business and pleasure, and excludes travel by international personnel and international businessmen employed in the United States. Some traveler data revised since originally issued]

| Item and area | 2005 | 2010 | 2011 | 2012 | 2013 | 2014 | 2015 | 2016 | 2017 |
|---|---|---|---|---|---|---|---|---|---|
| U.S. TRAVELERS TO FOREIGN COUNTRIES BY WORLD REGION OF DESTINATION [1] | | | | | | | | | |
| Total.......................... | 63,502 | 61,061 | 59,209 | 60,697 | 61,344 | 68,185 | 74,191 | 80,226 | 87,703 |
| Canada........................ | 14,390 | 11,871 | 11,597 | 11,887 | 11,478 | 11,523 | 12,669 | 13,895 | 14,326 |
| Mexico......................... | 20,325 | 20,683 | 20,589 | 20,308 | 20,851 | 25,882 | 28,733 | 31,194 | 35,050 |
| Total overseas [2]............. | 28,787 | 28,507 | 27,023 | 28,502 | 29,015 | 30,780 | 32,789 | 35,137 | 38,327 |
| Percent of overseas travelers to... | | | | | | | | | |
| Europe..................... | 41.6 | 34.4 | 35.8 | 35.8 | 34.6 | 35.1 | 34.7 | 35.7 | 37.8 |
| South America............ | 8.2 | 8.4 | 7.3 | 7.0 | 7.3 | 7.4 | 7.2 | 7.2 | 6.5 |
| Central America.......... | 6.1 | 6.7 | 7.2 | 7.3 | 6.9 | 7.7 | 7.9 | 7.9 | 7.2 |
| Caribbean.................. | 18.0 | 21.7 | 22.7 | 23.5 | 24.8 | 24.0 | 23.9 | 23.2 | 23.3 |
| Asia......................... | 21.1 | 19.7 | 18.9 | 19.0 | 18.8 | 18.5 | 18.5 | 18.8 | 18.0 |
| Middle East................ | 3.8 | 6.4 | 6.5 | 6.1 | 5.9 | 5.6 | 5.8 | 5.0 | 4.8 |
| Oceania.................... | 2.9 | 2.1 | 1.8 | 1.8 | 1.9 | 1.9 | 2.0 | 2.0 | 2.0 |
| Africa....................... | 2.0 | 3.4 | 3.3 | 3.1 | 3.1 | 2.9 | 2.9 | 2.8 | 2.7 |
| INTERNATIONAL TRAVELERS TO U.S. BY VISITOR REGION OF RESIDENCE | | | | | | | | | |
| Total.......................... | 49,206 | 60,010 | 63,477 | 66,967 | 71,643 | 75,379 | 77,774 | 76,407 | 76,941 |
| Canada........................ | 14,862 | 20,176 | 21,337 | 22,697 | 23,407 | 23,014 | 20,699 | 19,287 | 20,212 |
| Mexico......................... | 12,665 | 13,472 | 13,601 | 14,199 | 14,547 | 17,070 | 18,374 | 18,991 | 17,824 |
| Total overseas [2]............. | 21,679 | 26,363 | 28,540 | 30,071 | 33,689 | 35,296 | 38,700 | 38,129 | 38,906 |
| Europe..................... | (NA) | (NA) | (NA) | (NA) | (NA) | (NA) | 15,790 | 14,831 | 14,974 |
| Asia......................... | (NA) | (NA) | (NA) | (NA) | (NA) | (NA) | 10,946 | 11,538 | 12,137 |
| South America............ | (NA) | (NA) | (NA) | (NA) | (NA) | (NA) | 5,699 | 5,407 | 5,556 |
| Caribbean.................. | (NA) | (NA) | (NA) | (NA) | (NA) | (NA) | 1,479 | 1,587 | 1,671 |
| Oceania.................... | (NA) | (NA) | (NA) | (NA) | (NA) | (NA) | 1,768 | 1,661 | 1,632 |
| Central America.......... | (NA) | (NA) | (NA) | (NA) | (NA) | (NA) | 1,077 | 1,187 | 1,168 |
| Middle East................ | (NA) | (NA) | (NA) | (NA) | (NA) | (NA) | 1,369 | 1,342 | 1,182 |
| Africa....................... | (NA) | (NA) | (NA) | (NA) | (NA) | (NA) | 573 | 576 | 586 |

NA Not available. [1] A person is counted in each area visited but only once in the total. [2] "Overseas" excludes Canada and Mexico.

Source: U.S. Department of Commerce, International Trade Administration, National Travel and Tourism Office, "2017 U.S. Travel and Tourism Statistics (U.S. Resident Outbound)," <https://travel.trade.gov/outreachpages/outbound.general_information.outbound_overview.asp>; and "Monthly-Quarterly-Annual 1-94 Arrival Statistics," <https://travel.trade.gov/research/monthly/arrivals/index.asp>, accessed April 2019.

# Table 1296. International Travel Payments: 2000 to 2017

[In millions of dollars (86,184 represents $86,184,000,000)]

| Year | Travel and passenger fare (mil. dol.) | | | | | | U.S. net travel and passenger receipts (mil. dol.) |
|---|---|---|---|---|---|---|---|
| | Payments by U.S. travelers | | | Receipts from international visitors | | | |
| | Total | Travel payments [1,2] | Air transport [3] | Total | Travel receipts [1,2] | Air transport [3] | |
| 2000............. | 86,184 | 65,787 | 20,397 | 120,384 | 100,187 | 20,197 | 34,200 |
| 2005............. | 101,419 | 79,988 | 21,431 | 122,079 | 101,470 | 20,609 | 20,660 |
| 2010............. | 110,049 | 86,623 | 23,426 | 167,997 | 137,010 | 30,987 | 57,948 |
| 2011............. | 116,447 | 89,700 | 26,747 | 187,630 | 150,867 | 36,763 | 71,183 |
| 2012............. | 129,903 | 100,338 | 29,565 | 200,996 | 161,632 | 39,364 | 71,093 |
| 2013............. | 130,149 | 98,120 | 32,029 | 218,497 | 177,484 | 41,013 | 88,348 |
| 2014............. | 140,558 | 105,668 | 34,890 | 235,989 | 191,918 | 44,071 | 95,431 |
| 2015............. | 150,042 | 114,548 | 35,494 | 249,183 | 206,936 | 42,247 | 99,141 |
| 2016............. | 160,936 | 123,569 | 37,367 | 246,173 | 206,902 | 39,271 | 85,237 |
| 2017............. | 173,921 | 135,024 | 38,897 | 251,360 | 210,747 | 40,613 | 77,439 |

[1] Covers purchases of goods and services by U.S. persons traveling abroad and by foreign travelers in the United States for business or personal reasons. These goods and services include food, lodging, recreation, gifts, entertainment, local transportation in the country of travel, and other items incidental to a foreign visit. [2] Covers business travel, including expenditures by border, seasonal, and other short-term workers; and personal travel, including health-related and education-related travel, along with spending on day-trips (less than one night). [3] Fares received for the transport of nonresidents by U.S. air carriers between the United States and foreign countries and between two foreign points, and the transport of U.S. residents by foreign air carriers between the United States and foreign countries.

Source: U.S. Department of Commerce, International Trade Administration, National Travel and Tourism Office, "Annual Visitor Spending (1960-Present)," <https://travel.trade.gov/research/reports/recpay/index.asp>, accessed May 2019.

## Table 1297. Inbound Crossings for Top 5 U.S.-Canadian and U.S.-Mexican Border Land Passenger Gateways: 2018

[26,905 represents 26,905,000]

| Item and gateway | Entering the U.S. (1,000) | Item and gateway | Entering the U.S. (1,000) |
|---|---|---|---|
| **All U.S.-Canadian land gateways:** [1] | | **All U.S.-Mexican land gateways:** [1] | |
| Personal vehicles.................................. | 26,905 | Personal vehicles.................................. | 76,916 |
| Personal vehicle passengers.................... | 51,461 | Personal vehicle passengers.................... | 144,960 |
| Buses.................................................. | 78 | Buses.................................................. | 164 |
| Bus passengers.................................... | 1,796 | Bus passengers.................................... | 1,838 |
| Train passengers.................................. | 289 | Train passengers.................................. | 10 |
| Pedestrians.......................................... | 486 | Pedestrians.......................................... | 46,174 |
| **Top five gateways:** | | **Top five gateways:** | |
| Personal vehicles: | | Personal vehicles: | |
| Buffalo-Niagara Falls, NY....................... | 4,972 | El Paso, TX.......................................... | 12,383 |
| Blaine, WA........................................... | 4,132 | Otay Mesa, CA...................................... | 7,708 |
| Detroit, MI........................................... | 4,012 | Laredo, TX........................................... | 5,158 |
| Port Huron, MI...................................... | 1,525 | Brownsville, TX..................................... | 4,742 |
| Champlain-Rouses Point, NY................... | 1,019 | Calexico, CA......................................... | 4,558 |
| Personal vehicle passengers: | | Personal vehicle passengers: | |
| Buffalo-Niagara Falls, NY....................... | 10,676 | San Ysidro, CA...................................... | 25,182 |
| Blaine, WA........................................... | 8,135 | El Paso, TX.......................................... | 22,226 |
| Detroit, MI........................................... | 6,717 | Otay Mesa, CA...................................... | 13,318 |
| Port Huron, MI...................................... | 3,086 | Laredo, TX........................................... | 10,598 |
| Champlain-Rouses Point, NY................... | 2,284 | Brownsville, TX..................................... | 10,043 |
| Pedestrians: | | Pedestrians: | |
| Buffalo-Niagara Falls, NY....................... | 359 | San Ysidro, CA...................................... | 9,436 |
| Sumas, WA........................................... | 48 | El Paso, TX.......................................... | 7,218 |
| Point Roberts, WA................................. | 27 | Calexico, CA......................................... | 4,015 |
| Detroit, MI........................................... | 14 | Laredo, TX........................................... | 3,701 |
| International Falls-Ranier, MN.................. | 11 | Nogales, AZ.......................................... | 3,423 |

[1] Data reflect all personal vehicles and buses, passengers, and pedestrians entering the U.S.-Canadian border and U.S.-Mexican border, regardless of nationality.

Source: U.S. Department of Transportation, Bureau of Transportation Statistics, "Border Crossing / Entry Data," <https://www.bts.gov/content/border-crossingentry-data>, accessed May 2019.

## Table 1298. Foreign Tourists Admitted by Country of Citizenship: 2000 to 2017

[In thousands (30,511 represents 30,511,000). For years ending September 30. Represents non-U.S. citizens admitted to the country for a temporary period of time, for pleasure (tourists). Includes nonimmigrant admission classes B2 (temporary visitors for pleasure), GMT (Commonwealth of the Northern Marianas Islands visa waiver program–temporary visitors for pleasure, Guam or Northern Mariana Islands), and WT (visa waiver program–temporary visitors for pleasure)]

| Country and region | 2000 [1] | 2010 | 2015 | 2017 | Country and region | 2000 [1] | 2010 | 2015 | 2017 |
|---|---|---|---|---|---|---|---|---|---|
| **All countries** [2]............... | **30,511** | **35,131** | **61,017** | **61,600** | Thailand....................... | 76 | 48 | 72 | 75 |
| **Europe** [3]........................ | **11,806** | **11,741** | **13,552** | **13,934** | Turkey.......................... | 93 | 74 | 143 | 137 |
| Austria......................... | 182 | 166 | 181 | 179 | United Arab Emirates...... | 36 | 8 | 28 | 25 |
| Belgium........................ | 254 | 227 | 244 | 241 | **Africa** [3]...................... | **327** | **274** | **540** | **546** |
| Czechia........................ | 44 | 58 | 87 | 105 | Egypt........................... | 44 | 34 | 73 | 66 |
| Denmark....................... | 150 | 244 | 281 | 292 | Nigeria......................... | 27 | 62 | 170 | 174 |
| Finland......................... | 95 | 106 | 128 | 130 | South Africa.................. | 114 | 63 | 99 | 95 |
| France [4]...................... | 1,113 | 1,371 | 1,658 | 1,662 | **Oceania** [3].................... | **748** | **1,047** | **1,545** | **1,632** |
| Germany....................... | 1,925 | 1,599 | 1,786 | 1,790 | Australia....................... | 535 | 843 | 1,245 | 1,302 |
| Greece......................... | 60 | 54 | 57 | 68 | New Zealand.................. | 170 | 191 | 281 | 313 |
| Hungary........................ | 58 | 49 | 68 | 82 | **North America** [3, 6]......... | **6,501** | **12,754** | **30,038** | **29,153** |
| Iceland......................... | 27 | 35 | 48 | 60 | Canada [7]..................... | 277 | 87 | 9,977 | 9,758 |
| Ireland......................... | 325 | 406 | 402 | 446 | Mexico......................... | 3,972 | 11,010 | 17,904 | 16,786 |
| Italy............................ | 626 | 924 | 1,052 | 1,090 | **Caribbean**................... | **1,404** | **999** | **1,226** | **1,484** |
| Netherlands [4]............... | 559 | 598 | 596 | 639 | Bahamas, The............... | 24 | 250 | 229 | 281 |
| Norway......................... | 144 | 197 | 273 | 262 | Dominican Republic........ | 195 | 219 | 295 | 410 |
| Poland......................... | 116 | 103 | 146 | 162 | Haiti............................ | 72 | 90 | 126 | 143 |
| Portugal....................... | 86 | 120 | 151 | 162 | Jamaica........................ | 240 | 180 | 249 | 291 |
| Russia......................... | 74 | 134 | 242 | 254 | Trinidad and Tobago...... | 133 | 129 | 163 | 172 |
| Spain........................... | 370 | 692 | 846 | 929 | **Central America**........... | **792** | **657** | **930** | **1,124** |
| Sweden........................ | 321 | 330 | 505 | 487 | Costa Rica.................... | 172 | 143 | 202 | 275 |
| Switzerland................... | 400 | 315 | 409 | 383 | El Salvador................... | 175 | 105 | 150 | 182 |
| United Kingdom [4]........... | 4,671 | 3,768 | 3,991 | 4,077 | Guatemala.................... | 177 | 159 | 209 | 244 |
| **Asia** [3, 5]....................... | **7,853** | **6,254** | **9,826** | **10,721** | Honduras...................... | 87 | 101 | 156 | 199 |
| China [5]....................... | 656 | 482 | 1,950 | 2,216 | Nicaragua..................... | 47 | 38 | 56 | 64 |
| India........................... | 253 | 490 | 921 | 980 | Panama........................ | 106 | 94 | 136 | 135 |
| Indonesia...................... | 62 | 44 | 84 | 88 | **South America** [3].......... | **2,867** | **2,785** | **5,484** | **5,558** |
| Israel........................... | 319 | 253 | 340 | 353 | Argentina...................... | 515 | 375 | 713 | 1,030 |
| Japan........................... | 4,946 | 3,252 | 3,350 | 3,294 | Bolivia......................... | 48 | 31 | 55 | 66 |
| Korea, South.................. | 606 | 896 | 1,564 | 2,149 | Brazil.......................... | 706 | 976 | 2,222 | 1,848 |
| Malaysia....................... | 64 | 37 | 59 | 57 | Chile........................... | 194 | 119 | 298 | 365 |
| Pakistan....................... | 47 | 39 | 87 | 90 | Colombia...................... | 411 | 455 | 854 | 855 |
| Philippines.................... | 163 | 179 | 255 | 306 | Ecuador....................... | 122 | 169 | 351 | 414 |
| Saudi Arabia.................. | 67 | 36 | 138 | 98 | Peru........................... | 190 | 162 | 269 | 289 |
| Singapore..................... | 131 | 72 | 97 | 94 | Uruguay....................... | 66 | 35 | 70 | 74 |
| Taiwan......................... | (NA) | 183 | 344 | 374 | Venezuela..................... | 570 | 423 | 560 | 511 |

[1] Due to the expiration of the Visa Waiver Program during May-October 2000, data for business and pleasure not available separately. [2] Total includes visitors of unknown country of citizenship. [3] Total includes other countries, not shown separately. [4] As of 2005, includes overseas territories; see source for details. [5] Prior to 2005, data for China includes Taiwan. As of 2005, data for China includes Hong Kong and Macau. [6] The majority of short-term admissions from Canada and Mexico are excluded. [7] Beginning in 2014, the number of admissions greatly exceeds totals reported in previous years due to a more complete count of Canadian air and sea admissions.

Source: U.S. Department of Homeland Security, Office of Immigration Statistics, "2017 Yearbook of Immigration Statistics," and earlier reports, <https://www.dhs.gov/immigration-statistics/yearbook>, accessed November 2018.

# Section 27
# Accommodation, Food Services, and Other Services

This section presents statistics relating to services other than those covered in the previous sections on wholesale and retail trade, transportation, communications, financial services, and recreation services. Data shown for services are classified by kind of business and cover sales or receipts, establishments, employees, payrolls, and other items.

The principal sources of these data are from the U.S. Census Bureau and include the 2007 and 2012 Economic Censuses, Service Annual Survey, and the County Business Patterns program.

Data on these services also appear in several other sections. For instance, labor force employment and earnings data appear in Section 12, Labor Force, Employment, and Earnings; gross domestic product of the industry (Table 699) appears in Section 13, Income, Expenditures, Poverty, and Wealth; and financial data (several tables) from the quarterly *Statistics of Income Bulletin*, published by the Internal Revenue Service, appear in Section 15, Business Enterprise.

**Censuses**—Limited coverage of the service industries started in 1933. Beginning with the 1967 Economic Census, legislation provides for a census to be conducted every 5 years (for years ending in "2" and "7"). For more information on the most current census, see the Census Bureau's *Economic Census* website at <https://www.census.gov/programs-surveys/economic-census.html>. The industries covered in the censuses and surveys of business are defined in the North American Industry Classification System (NAICS). For information on NAICS, see the Census website at <www.census.gov/eos/www/naics/>.

In general, the 2007 and 2012 Economic Censuses have three series of publications for these sectors: 1) subject series with reports such as product lines, and establishment and firm sizes, 2) geographic reports with individual reports for each state, and 3) industry series with individual reports for industry groups.

Release of data from the 2012 Economic Census was completed in 2016. Data from the 2017 Economic Census will be released on a flow basis between September 2019 and December 2021.

**Current surveys**—The Service Annual Survey provides annual estimates of nationwide receipts for selected personal, business, leasing and repair, amusement and entertainment, social and health, and other professional service industries in the United States. For selected social, health, and other professional service industries, separate estimates are developed for receipts of taxable firms and revenue and expenses for firms and organizations exempt from federal income taxes. Several service sectors from this survey are covered in other sections of this publication. The estimates for tax exempt firms in these industries are derived from a sample of employer firms only. Estimates obtained from annual and monthly surveys are based on sample data and are not expected to agree exactly with results that would be obtained from a complete census of all establishments. Data include estimates for sampling units not reporting. Data are released in the *Quarterly Services Report* and the *Annual Services Report* at <http://www.census.gov/services/index.html>.

**Statistical reliability**—For a discussion of statistical collection and estimation, sampling procedures, and measures of statistical reliability applicable to Census Bureau data, see Appendix III.

# Table 1299. Selected Service-Related Industries—Establishments, Sales, Payroll, and Employees by Kind of Business: 2012

[1,480,277,061 represents $1,480,277,061,000. Covers only establishments with payroll. Based on the 2012 Economic Census; for statement on methodology, see Appendix III]

| Kind of business | 2012 NAICS code [1] | Establish- ments, (number) | Sales or receipts ($1,000) | Annual payroll (1,000) | Paid employ- ees [2] (number) |
|---|---|---|---|---|---|
| **Professional, scientific, and technical services**......... | **54** | **856,463** | **1,480,277,061** | **581,406,127** | **8,203,735** |
| Professional, scientific, and technical services............ | 541 | 856,463 | 1,480,277,061 | 581,406,127 | 8,203,735 |
| **Management of companies and enterprises**................ | **55** | **53,765** | **115,513,632** | **308,764,261** | **3,082,292** |
| **Administrative and support and waste management and remediation services**........................ | **56** | **386,387** | **673,036,536** | **329,013,077** | **9,774,262** |
| Administrative and support services................ | 561 | 363,188 | 593,837,306 | 311,056,595 | 9,405,895 |
| Waste management and remediation services............ | 562 | 23,199 | 79,199,230 | 17,956,482 | 368,367 |
| **Accommodation and food services**........................ | **72** | **662,489** | **708,138,598** | **196,103,341** | **12,007,689** |
| Accommodation.................................. | 721 | 63,833 | 195,858,388 | 50,120,659 | 1,950,081 |
| Food services and drinking places.................. | 722 | 598,656 | 512,280,210 | 145,982,682 | 10,057,608 |
| **Other services (except public administration)**............ | **81** | **529,691** | **426,693,675** | **108,185,736** | **3,430,711** |
| Repair and maintenance........................... | 811 | 210,151 | 143,943,567 | 41,273,746 | 1,194,122 |
| Personal and laundry services..................... | 812 | 212,568 | 87,031,329 | 28,674,529 | 1,349,371 |
| Religious, grantmaking, civic, professional, and similar organizations........................... | 813 | 106,972 | 195,718,779 | 38,237,461 | 887,218 |

[1] North American Industrial Classification System, 2012; see text, Section 15. [2] For employees on the payroll during the pay period including March 12.

Source: U.S. Census Bureau, 2012 Economic Census, "EC1200A1: All sectors: Geographic Area Series: Economy-Wide Key Statistics: 2012," <http://factfinder.census.gov>, accessed July 2016.

# Table 1300. Selected Service-Related Industries—Nonemployer Establishments and Receipts by Kind of Business: 2015 to 2017

[3,411 represents 3,411,000. Includes only firms subject to federal income tax. Nonemployers are businesses with no paid employees. Data originate chiefly from administrative records of the Internal Revenue Service; see Appendix III]

| Kind of business | NAICS code [1] | Firms (1,000) | | | Receipts (mil. dol.) | | |
|---|---|---|---|---|---|---|---|
| | | 2015 | 2016 | 2017 | 2015 | 2016 | 2017 |
| **Professional, scientific, and technical services**.......... | **54** | **3,411** | **3,441** | **3,535** | **157,584** | **159,177** | **166,944** |
| Professional, scientific, and technical services [2]........ | 541 | 3,411 | 3,441 | 3,535 | 157,584 | 159,177 | 166,944 |
| Legal services..................................... | 5411 | 290 | 286 | 290 | 19,565 | 19,566 | 20,432 |
| Accounting, tax preparation, bookkeeping, and payroll services................................. | 5412 | 374 | 370 | 373 | 10,083 | 10,146 | 10,428 |
| Architectural, engineering, and related services........ | 5413 | 230 | 227 | 230 | 11,635 | 11,475 | 11,924 |
| Specialized design services........................ | 5414 | 228 | 231 | 238 | 8,721 | 8,779 | 9,171 |
| Computer systems design and related services........ | 5415 | 305 | 303 | 309 | 14,955 | 14,931 | 15,306 |
| Management, scientific and technical consulting......... | 5416 | 729 | 758 | 800 | 35,925 | 36,820 | 39,543 |
| Scientific research and development services........... | 5417 | 39 | 43 | 48 | 1,420 | 1,492 | 1,575 |
| Advertising, public relations, and related services....... | 5418 | 147 | 150 | 158 | 8,071 | 8,273 | 8,700 |
| **Administrative and support and waste management and remediation services**........................... | **56** | **2,069** | **2,083** | **2,143** | **46,393** | **47,214** | **50,102** |
| Administrative and support services [2]............... | 561 | 2,050 | 2,064 | 2,124 | 44,870 | 45,726 | 48,497 |
| Office administrative services..................... | 5611 | 233 | 245 | 266 | 4,132 | 4,336 | 4,748 |
| Business support services........................ | 5614 | 218 | 221 | 215 | 6,193 | 6,220 | 6,334 |
| Services to buildings and dwellings................ | 5617 | 1,277 | 1,270 | 1,301 | 25,442 | 25,946 | 27,540 |
| Waste management and remediation services........... | 562 | 19 | 18 | 19 | 1,523 | 1,488 | 1,605 |
| **Accommodation and food services**........................ | **72** | **371** | **383** | **403** | **17,658** | **17,628** | **18,580** |
| Accommodation.................................... | 721 | 66 | 73 | 79 | 3,826 | 3,875 | 4,077 |
| Food services and drinking places.................... | 722 | 306 | 310 | 323 | 13,832 | 13,753 | 14,503 |
| Special food services............................. | 7223 | 183 | 189 | 200 | 5,113 | 5,248 | 5,555 |
| Drinking places (alcoholic beverages)................ | 7224 | 25 | 25 | 25 | 1,671 | 1,591 | 1,600 |
| Restaurants and other eating places................ | 7225 | 97 | 97 | 98 | 7,048 | 6,914 | 7,348 |
| Full-service restaurants........................ | 722511 | 43 | 42 | 43 | 3,373 | 3,363 | 3,603 |
| Limited-service eating places.................... | 722513 | 36 | 35 | 34 | 3,129 | 2,967 | 3,053 |
| **Other services (except public administration)**............. | **81** | **3,695** | **3,680** | **3,740** | **98,971** | **100,380** | **104,780** |
| Repair and maintenance [2]........................ | 811 | 756 | 747 | 753 | 29,004 | 28,948 | 29,895 |
| Automotive repair and maintenance................. | 8111 | 328 | 329 | 331 | 14,856 | 14,878 | 15,269 |
| Personal and household goods repair and maintenance..... | 8114 | 330 | 324 | 331 | 9,759 | 9,784 | 10,319 |
| Personal and laundry services [2]................... | 812 | 2,727 | 2,721 | 2,776 | 66,573 | 68,042 | 71,490 |
| Personal care services........................... | 8121 | 1,352 | 1,334 | 1,335 | 31,051 | 31,963 | 33,487 |
| Hair, nail, and skin care services................ | 81211 | 1,104 | 1,088 | 1,098 | 26,118 | 26,909 | 28,270 |
| Beauty salons................................ | 812112 | 746 | 731 | 733 | 16,280 | 16,588 | 17,214 |
| Death care services.............................. | 8122 | 17 | 17 | 17 | 913 | 906 | 900 |
| Drycleaning and laundry services................... | 8123 | 31 | 30 | 29 | 1,789 | 1,748 | 1,739 |
| Other personal services.......................... | 8129 | 1,327 | 1,340 | 1,395 | 32,820 | 33,425 | 35,365 |
| Religious, grantmaking, civic, professional, and similar organizations........................... | 813 | 212 | 212 | 211 | 3,394 | 3,391 | 3,395 |

[1] Data for 2015 and 2016, based on North American Industry Classification System (NAICS), 2012; data for 2017, based on NAICS 2017. See text, Section 15. [2] Includes other kinds of business not shown separately.

Source: U.S. Census Bureau, Nonemployer Statistics, "NES Datasets," <https://www.census.gov/programs-surveys/nonemployer-statistics/data/datasets.html>, accessed July 2019.

## Table 1301. Selected Service-Related Industries—Establishments, Employees, and Payroll by Industry: 2015 and 2016

[In thousands (896.0 represents 896,000); payroll in billions of dollars (704.4 represents $704,400,000,000). Covers establishments with paid employees. Excludes self-employed individuals, employees of private households, railroad employees, agricultural production employees, and most government employees; see source for NAICS and other exclusions. For statement on methodology, see Appendix III]

| Industry | 2012 NAICS code [1] | Establishments (1,000) | | Employees [2] (1,000) | | Annual payroll (bil. dol.) | |
|---|---|---|---|---|---|---|---|
| | | 2015 | 2016 | 2015 | 2016 | 2015 | 2016 |
| **Professional, scientific, & technical services**........ | **54** | **896.0** | **903.5** | **8,798.3** | **8,799.9** | **704.4** | **720.3** |
| Professional, scientific, & technical services............. | 541 | 896.0 | 903.5 | 8,798.3 | 8,799.9 | 704.4 | 720.3 |
| Legal services............................... | 5411 | 186.2 | 185.3 | 1,139.3 | 1,137.5 | 100.3 | 103.1 |
| Offices of lawyers........................ | 54111 | 172.8 | 172.1 | 1,060.5 | 1,056.5 | 95.9 | 98.6 |
| Accounting, tax preparation, bookkeeping, and payroll services................. | 5412 | 132.9 | 133.0 | 1,453.8 | 1,233.3 | 74.3 | 66.9 |
| Offices of certified public accountants........... | 541211 | 56.5 | 56.2 | 481.2 | 498.4 | 36.3 | 38.1 |
| Tax preparation services................... | 541213 | 31.4 | 31.4 | 193.7 | 192.5 | 2.4 | 2.4 |
| Architectural, engineering, & related services [3].... | 5413 | 111.6 | 111.0 | 1,438.0 | 1,431.7 | 119.5 | 119.6 |
| Architectural services..................... | 54131 | 21.5 | 21.6 | 163.2 | 170.4 | 12.9 | 13.6 |
| Engineering services..................... | 54133 | 60.9 | 60.2 | 1,029.4 | 1,015.8 | 91.9 | 91.0 |
| Specialized design services [3]................ | 5414 | 31.5 | 32.3 | 113.0 | 119.7 | 6.6 | 7.1 |
| Graphic design services.................. | 54143 | 15.3 | 15.5 | 52.8 | 55.4 | 3.0 | 3.2 |
| Computer systems design & related services [3].... | 5415 | 138.8 | 142.1 | 1,687.6 | 1,811.1 | 163.5 | 173.2 |
| Custom computer programming services...... | 541511 | 67.0 | 67.3 | 784.7 | 834.9 | 75.1 | 79.2 |
| Computer systems design services......... | 541512 | 53.0 | 56.1 | 653.1 | 718.9 | 64.0 | 69.6 |
| Management, scientific, & technical consulting services [3]................. | 5416 | 168.8 | 171.1 | 1,183.7 | 1,224.9 | 95.6 | 101.1 |
| Management consulting services........... | 54161 | 134.1 | 137.1 | 976.5 | 1,014.6 | 79.9 | 85.2 |
| Environmental consulting services......... | 54162 | 10.0 | 9.9 | 78.9 | 79.5 | 5.2 | 5.3 |
| Scientific research & development services....... | 5417 | 19.0 | 19.3 | 710.1 | 732.6 | 84.5 | 85.8 |
| Research & development in the physical engineering & life sciences............... | 54171 | 17.0 | 17.3 | 671.7 | 695.8 | 81.8 | 82.9 |
| Advertising & related services [3]............ | 5418 | 37.5 | 37.9 | 462.2 | 472.2 | 32.5 | 33.8 |
| Advertising agencies..................... | 54181 | 13.4 | 13.4 | 188.8 | 194.8 | 16.4 | 17.2 |
| Public relations agencies................. | 54182 | 8.5 | 8.5 | 55.1 | 58.5 | 5.4 | 5.6 |
| Other professional, scientific, & technical services.... | 5419 | 69.8 | 71.6 | 610.7 | 636.9 | 27.6 | 29.8 |
| Veterinary services...................... | 54194 | 31.0 | 31.2 | 338.7 | 353.7 | 12.4 | 13.2 |
| **Management of companies and enterprises**........ | **55** | **53.9** | **55.4** | **3,308.8** | **3,380.4** | **367.0** | **367.2** |
| **Administrative and support and waste management and remediation services**........ | **56** | **404.3** | **409.5** | **11,112.5** | **11,628.5** | **428.2** | **460.4** |
| Administrative & support services [3].......... | 561 | 380.4 | 384.9 | 10,728.6 | 11,236.0 | 407.0 | 438.0 |
| Employment services................... | 5613 | 51.5 | 52.0 | 6,023.6 | 6,439.0 | 240.6 | 263.7 |
| Temporary help services................. | 56132 | 34.7 | 35.5 | 3,320.0 | 3,463.1 | 98.4 | 107.6 |
| Business support services [3]............. | 5614 | 32.8 | 32.5 | 787.2 | 792.4 | 26.6 | 27.2 |
| Telephone call centers.................. | 56142 | 5.2 | 5.2 | 449.0 | 454.5 | 11.8 | 12.2 |
| Collection agencies..................... | 56144 | 4.2 | 4.0 | 124.3 | 120.1 | 4.9 | 4.8 |
| Travel arrangement & reservation services.... | 5615 | 23.4 | 21.4 | 229.9 | 222.6 | 12.7 | 13.8 |
| Travel agencies....................... | 56151 | 16.8 | 14.8 | 119.0 | 109.0 | 6.8 | 7.4 |
| Investigation & security services........... | 5616 | 25.7 | 25.7 | 910.3 | 933.1 | 26.0 | 27.6 |
| Investigation, guard, & armored car services.... | 56161 | 14.8 | 14.9 | 779.4 | 798.5 | 19.7 | 20.9 |
| Security systems services............... | 56162 | 10.9 | 10.8 | 130.9 | 134.6 | 6.3 | 6.7 |
| Services to buildings & dwellings [3]......... | 5617 | 189.1 | 194.6 | 1,805.8 | 1,881.6 | 49.8 | 53.5 |
| Landscaping services................... | 56173 | 98.7 | 101.6 | 587.0 | 632.0 | 21.9 | 23.8 |
| Waste management & remediation services...... | 562 | 23.9 | 24.6 | 383.9 | 392.5 | 21.2 | 22.4 |
| Waste collection....................... | 5621 | 10.9 | 11.4 | 199.8 | 206.1 | 10.9 | 11.7 |
| Waste treatment & disposal.............. | 5622 | 2.6 | 2.6 | 51.3 | 54.0 | 3.3 | 3.5 |
| Remediation & other waste management services.... | 5629 | 10.4 | 10.6 | 132.7 | 132.4 | 7.0 | 7.1 |
| **Accommodation & food services**............... | **72** | **687.6** | **703.5** | **13,196.9** | **13,704.0** | **245.2** | **261.3** |
| Accommodation............................ | 721 | 66.0 | 66.8 | 2,032.0 | 2,067.4 | 57.8 | 59.6 |
| Traveler accommodation [3]............... | 7211 | 56.6 | 57.3 | 1,977.1 | 2,011.0 | 56.1 | 57.8 |
| Hotels (except casino hotels) & motels....... | 72111 | 51.7 | 52.4 | 1,540.0 | 1,569.0 | 41.5 | 42.8 |
| RV (recreational vehicle) parks & recreational camps..... | 7212 | 7.4 | 7.4 | 43.4 | 44.7 | 1.4 | 1.5 |
| Rooming & boarding houses.............. | 7213 | 2.1 | 2.1 | 11.6 | 11.6 | 0.3 | 0.3 |
| Food services & drinking places.............. | 722 | 621.6 | 636.7 | 11,164.9 | 11,636.6 | 187.5 | 201.7 |
| Drinking places (alcoholic beverages)....... | 7224 | 40.7 | 40.6 | 367.6 | 378.1 | 6.1 | 6.5 |
| Restaurants and other eating places........ | 7225 | 542.0 | 553.1 | 10,081.0 | 10,472.7 | 166.3 | 177.8 |
| Full-service restaurants................. | 722511 | 243.1 | 246.9 | 5,253.9 | 5,431.1 | 97.9 | 104.2 |
| Limited-service restaurants.............. | 722513 | 233.4 | 237.9 | 4,043.2 | 4,227.4 | 56.6 | 61.0 |
| Cafeterias, grill buffets, and buffets....... | 722514 | 6.0 | 6.0 | 123.1 | 107.5 | 1.7 | 1.6 |
| Snack and nonalcoholic beverage bars...... | 722515 | 59.5 | 62.3 | 660.8 | 706.7 | 10.0 | 11.0 |
| **Other services (except public administration)**.... | **81** | **746.0** | **754.2** | **5,401.2** | **5,499.2** | **168.7** | **174.9** |
| Repair & maintenance [3]................... | 811 | 213.5 | 214.8 | 1,244.7 | 1,265.0 | 49.4 | 50.9 |
| Automotive repair & maintenance.......... | 8111 | 158.8 | 159.9 | 865.1 | 892.0 | 30.3 | 31.7 |
| Personal & household goods repair & maintenance.... | 8114 | 20.8 | 21.1 | 69.9 | 71.4 | 2.3 | 2.3 |
| Personal & laundry services [3]............. | 812 | 225.6 | 230.3 | 1,398.1 | 1,441.3 | 33.7 | 35.2 |
| Personal care services.................. | 8121 | 125.9 | 129.4 | 669.9 | 699.7 | 13.9 | 14.9 |
| Death care services.................... | 8122 | 20.8 | 20.8 | 139.3 | 140.4 | 5.0 | 5.0 |
| Drycleaning & laundry services........... | 8123 | 34.7 | 34.3 | 294.7 | 293.0 | 7.8 | 8.0 |
| Religious/grantmaking/civic/professional [4].... | 813 | 307.0 | 309.2 | 2,758.4 | 2,792.9 | 85.6 | 88.8 |
| Religious organizations.................. | 8131 | 184.2 | 184.7 | 1,679.6 | 1,687.0 | 35.6 | 36.5 |
| Grantmaking & giving services............ | 8132 | 19.7 | 20.4 | 186.9 | 196.8 | 10.9 | 11.6 |
| Social advocacy organizations............ | 8133 | 17.3 | 18.0 | 165.1 | 169.3 | 7.7 | 8.0 |
| Civic & social organizations.............. | 8134 | 26.3 | 26.6 | 238.8 | 246.4 | 5.1 | 5.3 |
| Business/professional/labor/political [4]...... | 8139 | 59.5 | 59.4 | 487.9 | 493.4 | 26.3 | 27.3 |
| Labor unions [4]....................... | 81393 | 14.2 | 14.0 | 149.0 | 148.3 | 5.5 | 5.6 |

[1] North American Industry Classification System (NAICS), 2012. See text, section 15. [2] Includes employees on the payroll for the pay period including March 12. [3] Includes other kinds of business, not shown separately. [4] Also includes other similar organizations.

Source: U.S. Census Bureau, County Business Patterns, "Geography Area Series: County Business Patterns," <https://factfinder.census.gov/>, accessed May 2018. See also <https://www.census.gov/programs-surveys/cbp.html>.

# Table 1302. Employed Persons in Service Industries by Sex, Race, and Hispanic Origin and by Industry: 2018

[18,950 represents 18,950,000. Civilian noninstitutionalized population 16 years and older. Based on the Current Population Survey (CPS); see text, Section 1, and Appendix III. For information on employees in other sectors, see Table 641 and Table 659]

| Industry | 2012 NAICS code [1] | Total employed (1,000) | Percent of total | | | | |
|---|---|---|---|---|---|---|---|
| | | | Female | White | Black [2] | Asian [2] | Hispanic or Latino [3] |
| **Professional and business services**............... | **54-56** | **18,950** | **41.5** | **78.1** | **9.9** | **9.0** | **15.9** |
| **Professional and technical services**.................. | **54** | **12,105** | **42.2** | **79.0** | **6.6** | **12.1** | **8.7** |
| Legal services.................................. | 5411 | 1,673 | 56.2 | 87.5 | 6.4 | 4.0 | 10.9 |
| Accounting, tax preparation, bookkeeping, and payroll services......................... | 5412 | 1,131 | 60.0 | 81.0 | 7.9 | 8.6 | 8.7 |
| Architectural, engineering, and related services......... | 5413 | 1,767 | 25.5 | 84.8 | 5.9 | 6.9 | 9.0 |
| Specialized design services....................... | 5414 | 405 | 57.7 | 84.9 | 3.4 | 7.7 | 13.1 |
| Computer systems design and related services......... | 5415 | 3,339 | 27.2 | 67.1 | 7.0 | 23.6 | 6.6 |
| Management, scientific, and technical consulting services..................................... | 5416 | 1,686 | 43.2 | 79.8 | 7.6 | 10.7 | 7.9 |
| Scientific research and development services........... | 5417 | 616 | 45.6 | 75.6 | 8.3 | 13.8 | 8.3 |
| Advertising, public relations, and related services....... | 5418 | 629 | 47.5 | 85.0 | 5.0 | 8.5 | 10.0 |
| Veterinary services............................. | 54194 | 404 | 84.3 | 92.3 | 2.5 | 2.3 | 9.0 |
| Other professional, scientific, and technical services [4].. | 5419 | 456 | 55.6 | 83.2 | 6.8 | 7.1 | 11.6 |
| **Management, administrative, and waste services**..... | **55-56** | **6,845** | **40.3** | **76.7** | **15.7** | **3.4** | **28.8** |
| Management of companies and enterprises............ | 55 | 212 | 43.5 | 83.8 | 8.1 | 5.6 | 12.6 |
| Employment services............................ | 5613 | 954 | 55.3 | 70.3 | 21.2 | 4.9 | 19.4 |
| Business support services........................ | 5614 | 705 | 64.6 | 70.4 | 20.8 | 3.8 | 18.8 |
| Travel arrangement and reservation services........... | 5615 | 290 | 61.4 | 77.1 | 11.5 | 9.1 | 15.4 |
| Investigations and security services................. | 5616 | 839 | 24.5 | 65.5 | 27.0 | 3.3 | 15.3 |
| Services to buildings and dwellings [5]............... | 5617 | 1,604 | 55.8 | 77.5 | 14.7 | 2.6 | 40.8 |
| Landscaping services........................... | 56173 | 1,418 | 10.6 | 87.9 | 6.8 | 1.1 | 44.2 |
| Other administrative and support services............. | 5611,2,9 | 345 | 51.6 | 78.7 | 9.8 | 6.5 | 18.8 |
| Waste management and remediation services.......... | 562 | 480 | 16.1 | 77.4 | 17.5 | 2.1 | 23.0 |
| **Accommodation and food services**.................. | **72** | **10,905** | **53.6** | **73.3** | **14.0** | **7.4** | **25.9** |
| Accommodation.................................. | 721 | 1,467 | 58.2 | 70.4 | 16.6 | 8.0 | 27.9 |
| Traveler accommodation......................... | 7211 | 1,350 | 59.6 | 68.7 | 17.6 | 8.4 | 29.5 |
| Recreational vehicle parks and camps, and rooming and board houses..................... | 7212,3 | 117 | 41.3 | 90.9 | 5.0 | 2.8 | 9.6 |
| Food services and drinking places.................. | 722 | 9,438 | 52.9 | 73.8 | 13.6 | 7.3 | 25.6 |
| Restaurants and other food services [6]............. | 722, excl. 7224 | 9,190 | 52.9 | 73.6 | 13.7 | 7.4 | 26.0 |
| Drinking places, alcoholic beverages................ | 7224 | 248 | 52.6 | 82.9 | 9.9 | 1.7 | 10.2 |
| **Other services**................................... | **81** | **7,742** | **53.6** | **77.5** | **10.8** | **8.4** | **20.3** |
| Other services (except private households)............. | 81 | 6,965 | 49.1 | 76.9 | 11.0 | 9.0 | 17.7 |
| Repair and maintenance.......................... | 811 | 2,189 | 12.5 | 84.7 | 8.1 | 3.3 | 27.2 |
| Automotive repair and maintenance [7]............... | 8111 | 1,342 | 9.7 | 85.2 | 8.1 | 2.8 | 28.1 |
| Car washes.................................. | 811192 | 194 | 15.7 | 73.3 | 16.9 | 5.7 | 35.5 |
| Electronic and precision equipment repair and maintenance................................. | 8112 | 107 | 21.6 | 77.4 | 8.2 | 9.0 | 20.7 |
| Commercial and industrial machinery and equipment repair and maintenance....................... | 8113 | 328 | 8.0 | 88.5 | 5.9 | 1.1 | 26.8 |
| Personal and household goods repair and maintenance [8]............................... | 8114 | 210 | 30.2 | 89.8 | 2.9 | 5.5 | 18.9 |
| Footwear and leather goods repair.................. | 81143 | 7 | (Z) | (Z) | (Z) | (Z) | (Z) |
| Personal and laundry services..................... | 812 | 2,676 | 74.1 | 67.5 | 12.6 | 16.8 | 17.0 |
| Barber shops............................... | 812111 | 123 | 23.8 | 61.4 | 30.8 | 5.9 | 28.1 |
| Beauty salons............................... | 812112 | 1,092 | 90.5 | 73.5 | 13.4 | 10.2 | 16.6 |
| Nail salons and other personal care services.......... | 812113, 81219 | 585 | 78.0 | 42.6 | 7.2 | 47.2 | 8.4 |
| Drycleaning and laundry services................... | 8123 | 301 | 50.5 | 70.7 | 12.4 | 11.4 | 37.6 |
| Funeral homes, cemeteries, and crematories.......... | 8122 | 122 | 38.8 | 84.5 | 13.5 | 0.8 | 12.8 |
| Other personal services......................... | 8129 | 454 | 68.1 | 80.2 | 12.4 | 4.5 | 13.6 |
| Membership associations and organizations............ | 813 | 2,101 | 55.6 | 80.6 | 12.0 | 4.9 | 8.8 |
| Religious organizations.......................... | 8131 | 1,043 | 47.7 | 83.7 | 10.1 | 4.3 | 6.8 |
| Civic, social, advocacy organizations, grantmaking and giving services........................... | 8132,3,4 | 815 | 67.1 | 74.7 | 15.8 | 6.1 | 10.5 |
| Labor unions................................ | 81393 | 71 | 40.8 | 85.0 | 7.4 | 6.1 | 18.2 |
| Business, professional, political, and similar organizations [9]...................... | 8139 | 171 | 54.5 | 88.0 | 7.5 | 2.5 | 9.0 |
| Private households............................... | 814 | 777 | 93.2 | 83.2 | 9.4 | 3.0 | 43.6 |

Z Base less than 50,000. [1] Based on the North American Industry Classification System, 2012; see Section 15. [2] The Current Population Survey (CPS) allows respondents to choose more than one race. Data represent persons who selected this race group only and exclude persons reporting more than one race. See also comments on race in text for Section 1. [3] Persons of Hispanic origin may be of any race. [4] Excludes NAICS 54194 (veterinary services). [5] Excludes NAICS 56173 (landscaping services). [6] Excludes NAICS 7224 (drinking places, alcoholic beverages). [7] Excludes NAICS 811192 (car washes). [8] Excludes NAICS 81143 (footwear and leather goods repair). [9] Excludes NAICS 81393 (labor unions).

Source: U.S. Bureau of Labor Statistics, CPS Tables, "Employed persons by detailed industry, sex, race, and Hispanic or Latino ethnicity," <http://www.bls.gov/cps/tables.htm>, accessed February 2019.

# Table 1303. Selected Service-Related Industries—Establishments, Employees, and Annual Payroll by State: 2016

[Employees in thousands (8,800 represents 8,800,000); payroll in millions of dollars (720,299 represents $720,299,000,000). Covers establishments with paid employees. Excludes most government employees, railroad employees, and self-employed persons. Data are from Census Bureau's County Business Patterns program. For statement on methodology, see Appendix III]

| State | Professional, scientific, and technical services (NAICS 54) [1] | | | Administrative and support and waste management and remediation services (NAICS 56) [1] | | | Accommodation and food services (NAICS 72) [1] | | |
|---|---|---|---|---|---|---|---|---|---|
| | Establish-ments | Employ-ees [2] (1,000) | Annual payroll (mil. dol.) | Establish-ments | Employ-ees [2] (1,000) | Annual payroll (mil. dol.) | Establish-ments | Employ-ees [2] (1,000) | Annual payroll (mil. dol.) |
| **United States** | **903,534** | **8,800** | **720,299** | **409,518** | **11,629** | **460,419** | **703,528** | **13,704** | **261,261** |
| Alabama | 9,404 | 100 | 6,896 | 4,424 | 151 | 4,201 | 8,819 | 179 | 2,673 |
| Alaska | 1,960 | 19 | 1,381 | 1,128 | 17 | 860 | 2,156 | 29 | 776 |
| Arizona | 17,614 | 148 | 10,534 | 8,370 | 271 | 9,373 | 12,546 | 290 | 5,359 |
| Arkansas | 5,847 | 38 | 2,141 | 2,704 | 64 | 1,553 | 5,750 | 106 | 1,542 |
| California | 124,806 | 1,191 | 113,612 | 44,211 | 1,458 | 68,650 | 86,057 | 1,671 | 36,607 |
| Colorado | 25,832 | 194 | 16,341 | 8,988 | 256 | 12,002 | 13,569 | 282 | 5,569 |
| Connecticut | 9,186 | 106 | 9,858 | 5,320 | 86 | 3,636 | 8,580 | 146 | 3,124 |
| Delaware | 2,951 | 30 | 2,777 | 1,518 | 29 | 1,072 | 2,120 | 41 | 761 |
| District of Columbia | 5,684 | 103 | 12,669 | 1,148 | 33 | 1,485 | 2,639 | 72 | 2,034 |
| Florida | 78,248 | 500 | 33,892 | 35,779 | 1,708 | 75,934 | 40,350 | 936 | 18,459 |
| Georgia | 29,398 | 264 | 19,725 | 12,536 | 380 | 13,512 | 20,291 | 421 | 6,921 |
| Hawaii | 3,341 | 23 | 1,523 | 1,846 | 55 | 1,956 | 3,777 | 108 | 3,166 |
| Idaho | 4,589 | 33 | 1,839 | 2,346 | 40 | 1,237 | 3,681 | 62 | 973 |
| Illinois | 38,929 | 390 | 34,744 | 17,033 | 541 | 19,069 | 28,470 | 528 | 10,193 |
| Indiana | 12,944 | 129 | 9,178 | 7,402 | 216 | 6,312 | 13,369 | 277 | 4,296 |
| Iowa | 6,364 | 55 | 3,313 | 3,713 | 78 | 2,515 | 7,143 | 121 | 1,843 |
| Kansas | 7,146 | 65 | 4,126 | 3,705 | 82 | 2,761 | 6,126 | 115 | 1,709 |
| Kentucky | 8,199 | 75 | 3,588 | 4,113 | 121 | 3,054 | 8,046 | 174 | 2,611 |
| Louisiana | 11,948 | 97 | 6,218 | 4,741 | 105 | 3,850 | 9,548 | 218 | 3,848 |
| Maine | 3,516 | 23 | 1,439 | 2,205 | 25 | 757 | 4,174 | 52 | 1,150 |
| Maryland | 20,764 | 277 | 24,118 | 8,403 | 195 | 7,884 | 11,793 | 231 | 4,539 |
| Massachusetts | 21,630 | 284 | 30,854 | 10,827 | 201 | 9,859 | 17,450 | 300 | 6,713 |
| Michigan | 21,565 | 267 | 20,700 | 11,588 | 338 | 11,070 | 19,952 | 386 | 6,437 |
| Minnesota | 16,780 | 183 | 14,410 | 7,641 | 166 | 6,154 | 11,708 | 243 | 4,311 |
| Mississippi | 4,654 | 30 | 1,579 | 2,254 | 55 | 1,412 | 5,542 | 128 | 2,106 |
| Missouri | 13,971 | 157 | 11,053 | 7,609 | 174 | 5,457 | 12,596 | 260 | 4,306 |
| Montana | 3,748 | 21 | 975 | 1,797 | 24 | 751 | 3,524 | 52 | 888 |
| Nebraska | 4,683 | 40 | 2,444 | 2,709 | 125 | 4,971 | 4,493 | 77 | 1,145 |
| Nevada | 8,922 | 60 | 3,740 | 4,447 | 117 | 3,891 | 6,548 | 321 | 9,543 |
| New Hampshire | 3,733 | 32 | 2,287 | 2,361 | 56 | 2,604 | 3,702 | 57 | 1,144 |
| New Jersey | 29,233 | 328 | 29,347 | 14,106 | 326 | 13,162 | 20,953 | 311 | 6,410 |
| New Mexico | 4,646 | 58 | 4,225 | 1,881 | 32 | 1,065 | 4,276 | 90 | 1,530 |
| New York | 61,607 | 648 | 60,827 | 27,130 | 594 | 31,939 | 53,199 | 786 | 19,325 |
| North Carolina | 24,280 | 220 | 16,467 | 12,694 | 382 | 12,838 | 20,809 | 419 | 6,782 |
| North Dakota | 1,848 | 16 | 966 | 1125 | 14 | 516 | 2,110 | 38 | 650 |
| Ohio | 23,929 | 251 | 17,053 | 13,576 | 397 | 13,171 | 24,115 | 482 | 7,359 |
| Oklahoma | 9,618 | 74 | 4,561 | 4,525 | 103 | 3,750 | 8,006 | 154 | 2,329 |
| Oregon | 12,381 | 91 | 6,705 | 5,919 | 103 | 3,442 | 11,387 | 177 | 3,383 |
| Pennsylvania | 29,780 | 324 | 25,552 | 15,745 | 332 | 11,701 | 28,515 | 476 | 7,982 |
| Rhode Island | 3,048 | 24 | 1,515 | 1,764 | 25 | 938 | 3,092 | 48 | 959 |
| South Carolina | 10,479 | 89 | 5,848 | 5,916 | 172 | 5,718 | 10,428 | 221 | 3,633 |
| South Dakota | 1,943 | 12 | 597 | 1,135 | 12 | 401 | 2,441 | 40 | 668 |
| Tennessee | 11,258 | 118 | 7,722 | 7,079 | 252 | 7,533 | 12,967 | 280 | 4,769 |
| Texas | 68,751 | 708 | 57,607 | 28,165 | 980 | 37,543 | 54,188 | 1,177 | 20,650 |
| Utah | 10,519 | 89 | 5,037 | 4,393 | 134 | 4,821 | 5,708 | 116 | 1,906 |
| Vermont | 2,144 | 13 | 858 | 1,161 | 8 | 277 | 1,929 | 33 | 622 |
| Virginia | 31,252 | 460 | 41,840 | 10,716 | 245 | 10,157 | 17,778 | 353 | 6,306 |
| Washington | 21,773 | 202 | 16,719 | 9,846 | 156 | 7,284 | 17,150 | 280 | 6,064 |
| West Virginia | 2,852 | 25 | 1,260 | 1,458 | 33 | 1,014 | 3,547 | 68 | 1,082 |
| Wisconsin | 11,551 | 107 | 7,118 | 7,275 | 155 | 5,089 | 14,599 | 238 | 3,537 |
| Wyoming | 2,286 | 10 | 523 | 1,043 | 6 | 222 | 1,812 | 28 | 571 |

[1] North American Industry Classification System, 2012. See text, section 15. [2] For employees on the payroll for the pay period including March 12.

Source: U.S. Census Bureau, County Business Patterns, "Geography Area Series: County Business Patterns," <https://factfinder.census.gov/>, accessed May 2018. See also <https://www.census.gov/programs-surveys/cbp.html>.

# Table 1304. Professional, Scientific, and Technical Services—Estimated Revenue by Kind of Business: 2010 to 2017

[In millions of dollars (1,293,795 represents $1,293,795,000,000). For taxable employer firms. Estimates have been adjusted to the results of the 2012 Economic Census. Based on the Service Annual Survey and administrative data; see Appendix III]

| Kind of business | NAICS code [1] | 2010 | 2013 | 2014 | 2015 | 2016 | 2017 |
|---|---|---|---|---|---|---|---|
| **Professional, scientific, and technical services (except notaries) [2], [3]** | **54** | **1,293,795** | **1,471,255** | **1,549,333** | **1,605,848** | **1,689,633** | **1,790,587** |
| Offices of lawyers | 54111 | 231,608 | 245,031 | 251,745 | 260,956 | 267,823 | 286,879 |
| Other legal services | 54119 | 11,228 | 14,121 | 13,193 | 14,092 | 14,753 | 15,430 |
| Offices of certified public accountants | 541211 | 68,702 | 79,715 | 84,586 | 91,321 | 97,590 | 101,493 |
| Tax preparation services | 541213 | 5,740 | 6,276 | 6,657 | 7,099 | 7,011 | 7,253 |
| Payroll services | 541214 | 25,748 | 31,020 | 32,803 | 35,097 | 38,543 | 38,572 |
| Other accounting services | 541219 | 15,742 | 19,126 | 20,733 | 22,498 | 23,900 | 25,561 |
| Architectural services | 54131 | 26,849 | 28,865 | 31,967 | 34,864 | 37,489 | 39,921 |
| Landscape architectural services | 54132 | 3,021 | 3,018 | 3,211 | 3,357 | 3,560 | 3,794 |
| Engineering services | 54133 | 191,660 | 205,874 | 217,178 | 225,517 | 231,515 | 247,672 |
| Drafting services | 54134 | 602 | 931 | 1,046 | 1,134 | 1,132 | 1,204 |
| Building inspection services | 54135 | 1,856 | 2,114 | 2,416 | 2,590 | 2,680 | 2,856 |
| Surveying and mapping services [4] | 5413z | 7,534 | 9,083 | 9,871 | 9,130 | 8,356 | 8,922 |
| Testing laboratories | 54138 | 14,057 | 16,146 | 16,257 | 17,190 | 17,203 | 17,435 |
| Interior design services | 54141 | 6,594 | 8,172 | 9,479 | 10,351 | 10,537 | 10,753 |
| Industrial design services | 54142 | 1,308 | 1,690 | 1,827 | 1,941 | 1,839 | 1,878 |
| Graphic design services | 54143 | 7,378 | 7,497 | 8,157 | 8,761 | 9,348 | 9,691 |
| Other specialized design services | 54149 | 945 | 1,301 | 1,506 | 1,562 | 1,553 | 1,468 |
| Computer systems design and related services | 5415 | 283,362 | 331,025 | 347,637 | 348,245 | 371,736 | 399,117 |
| Management consulting services [5] | 54161 | 138,955 | 180,646 | 193,290 | 199,868 | 211,368 | 216,947 |
| Environmental consulting services | 54162 | 12,554 | 13,409 | 13,018 | 12,789 | 12,884 | 12,732 |
| Other scientific and technical consulting services | 54169 | 18,779 | 25,714 | 27,821 | 29,409 | 29,977 | 31,323 |
| Research and development in physical, engineering and life sciences | 54171 | 73,067 | 80,564 | 86,013 | 92,803 | 100,644 | 114,885 |
| Research and development in social sciences and humanities | 54172 | 1,848 | 2,142 | 2,293 | 2,168 | 2,230 | 2,227 |
| Advertising agencies | 54181 | 30,870 | 35,473 | 37,563 | 39,815 | 42,792 | 44,989 |
| Public relations agencies | 54182 | 9,515 | 10,633 | 11,405 | 11,863 | 13,564 | 12,478 |
| Media buying agencies | 54183 | 5,107 | 6,939 | 7,165 | 7,503 | 7,918 | 7,381 |
| Media representatives | 54184 | 2,992 | 3,153 | 3,311 | 3,296 | 3,342 | 3,206 |
| Outdoor advertising | 54185 | 7,089 | 7,104 | 7,159 | 7,248 | 7,299 | 7,485 |
| Direct mail advertising | 54186 | 10,140 | 10,033 | 10,226 | 10,126 | 10,611 | 10,308 |
| Advertising material distribution services | 54187 | 3,616 | 3,102 | 3,475 | 3,976 | 3,957 | 3,812 |
| Other services related to advertising | 54189 | 11,964 | 12,820 | 13,369 | 13,630 | 14,616 | 15,184 |
| Marketing research and public opinion polling | 54191 | 16,531 | 16,450 | 17,695 | 17,769 | 18,841 | 19,019 |
| Photography studios, portrait | 541921 | 4,180 | 3,676 | 3,952 | 4,109 | 4,042 | 3,986 |
| Commercial photography | 541922 | 1,590 | 1,934 | 1,908 | 1,757 | 1,821 | 1,839 |
| Translation and interpretation services | 54193 | 3,740 | 3,797 | 3,654 | 3,627 | 3,927 | 4,204 |
| Veterinary services | 54194 | 27,033 | 30,825 | 33,390 | 35,421 | 39,797 | 43,385 |
| All other professional, scientific, and technical services | 54199 | 10,291 | 11,836 | 12,357 | 12,966 | 13,435 | 15,298 |

[1] Data for 2010 are based on the 2007 North American Industry Classification System (NAICS); beginning 2013, data are based on 2012 NAICS. See text Section 15 for more information. [2] Data prior to 2011 have been restated to reflect comparable data on the 2007 NAICS basis for more detailed levels within this aggregate. [3] Excludes NAICS 54112 (Offices of Notaries). [4] Includes NAICS 54136 (Geophysical Surveying and Mapping Services) and NAICS 54137 (Surveying and Mapping Services, except Geophysical Services). [5] A portion of NAICS 54161 (Management Consulting Services) moved to NAICS 56131 (Employment Placement Agencies and Executive Search Services) with the 2007 NAICS update. Data prior to 2011 have been restated to reflect comparable data on the 2007 NAICS basis.

Source: U.S. Census Bureau, Service Annual Survey, "Service Annual Survey Latest Data (NAICS-basis): 2017" and "Service Annual Historical Survey Tables," <https://www.census.gov/programs-surveys/sas/data.html>, accessed December 2018.

# Table 1305. Administrative and Support and Waste Management and Remediation Services—Estimated Revenue by Kind of Business: 2010 to 2017

[In millions of dollars (614,178 represents $614,178,000,000). For taxable and tax-exempt employer firms. Estimates have been adjusted to results of the 2012 Economic Census. Based on the Service Annual Survey and administrative data; see Appendix III]

| Kind of business | NAICS code [1] | 2010 | 2013 | 2014 | 2015 | 2016 | 2017 |
|---|---|---|---|---|---|---|---|
| **Administrative and support and waste management and remediation services [2]** | **56** | **614,178** | **701,050** | **769,796** | **816,393** | **870,553** | **929,684** |
| Administrative and support services [2] | **561** | **535,359** | **619,716** | **683,527** | **728,883** | **778,178** | **832,981** |
| Office administrative services | 5611 | 39,193 | 45,580 | 49,552 | 50,806 | 50,903 | 51,074 |
| Facilities support services | 5612 | 25,592 | 24,895 | 25,773 | 27,218 | 28,213 | 29,775 |
| Employment placement agencies & executive search svcs [3] | 56131 | 14,336 | 16,825 | 18,236 | 19,186 | 20,943 | 22,396 |
| Temporary help services | 56132 | 99,329 | 125,193 | 136,727 | 153,477 | 158,672 | 166,353 |
| Professional employer organizations | 56133 | 90,081 | 110,241 | 135,918 | 146,510 | 163,919 | 185,192 |
| Document preparation services | 56141 | 3,130 | 3,361 | 3,320 | 3,400 | 3,713 | 3,972 |
| Telephone answering services | 561421 | 2,167 | 1,911 | 1,982 | 2,086 | 2,241 | 2,387 |
| Telemarketing bureaus and other contact centers | 561422 | 14,729 | 17,252 | 18,269 | 18,626 | 19,867 | 19,601 |
| Private mail centers | 561431 | 2,107 | 2,327 | 2,491 | 2,626 | 2,831 | 3,195 |
| Other business service centers (including copy shops) | 561439 | 6,619 | 5,907 | 5,920 | 5,896 | 6,508 | 6,705 |
| Collection agencies | 56144 | 11,660 | 12,362 | 11,945 | 11,537 | 11,548 | 11,683 |
| Credit bureaus | 56145 | 6,604 | 7,443 | 8,084 | 9,330 | 10,180 | 11,136 |
| Repossession services | 561491 | 844 | 674 | 760 | 769 | 878 | 975 |
| Court reporting and stenotype services | 561492 | 2,252 | 2,097 | 2,175 | 2,240 | 2,379 | 2,497 |
| All other business support services | 561499 | 8,199 | 6,804 | 6,997 | 7,018 | 7,442 | 8,148 |
| Travel agencies | 56151 | 12,203 | 13,405 | 14,313 | 15,052 | 16,366 | 18,347 |
| Tour operators | 56152 | 5,125 | 5,649 | 5,826 | 6,084 | 6,128 | 6,751 |
| Convention and visitors bureaus | 561591 | 1,387 | 1,710 | 1,876 | 2,010 | 2,192 | 2,364 |
| All other travel arrangement and reservation services | 561599 | 12,846 | 15,397 | 16,393 | 17,640 | 18,307 | 20,260 |
| Investigation services | 561611 | 4,404 | 5,170 | 5,133 | 5,323 | 5,617 | 5,905 |
| Security guards and patrol services | 561612 | 20,820 | 23,589 | 23,604 | 24,012 | 26,113 | 28,092 |
| Armored car services | 561613 | 2,291 | 2,326 | 2,191 | 2,247 | 2,387 | 2,362 |
| Security systems services (except locksmiths) | 561621 | 13,833 | 15,888 | 17,861 | 19,045 | 20,683 | 22,123 |
| Locksmiths | 561622 | 1,542 | 1,659 | 1,767 | 1,803 | 1,963 | 2,124 |
| Exterminating and pest control services | 56171 | 9,444 | 10,972 | 11,525 | 11,929 | 12,713 | 14,239 |
| Janitorial services | 56172 | 34,559 | 37,885 | 40,015 | 41,676 | 43,935 | 44,570 |
| Landscaping services | 56173 | 47,674 | 55,609 | 63,570 | 67,549 | 75,061 | 80,477 |
| Carpet and upholstery cleaning services | 56174 | 2,746 | 3,193 | 3,446 | 3,537 | 3,795 | 4,120 |
| Other services to buildings and dwellings | 56179 | 4,758 | 6,040 | 6,609 | 7,141 | 7,746 | 8,145 |
| Packaging and labeling services | 56191 | 5,397 | 6,490 | 6,875 | 7,474 | 7,773 | 8,512 |
| Convention and trade show organizers | 56192 | 10,016 | 12,127 | 12,920 | 13,050 | 14,109 | 14,609 |
| All other support services | 56199 | 19,472 | 19,735 | 21,454 | 22,586 | 23,053 | 24,892 |
| **Waste management and remediation services** | **562** | **78,819** | **81,334** | **86,269** | **87,510** | **92,375** | **96,703** |
| Solid waste collection | 562111 | 36,431 | 37,435 | 39,409 | 39,503 | 41,949 | 44,320 |
| Hazardous waste collection | 562112 | 2,096 | 2,618 | 2,899 | 3,225 | 3,475 | 3,511 |
| Other waste collection | 562119 | 1,271 | 1,377 | 1,508 | 1,703 | 1,707 | 1,760 |
| Hazardous waste treatment and disposal | 562211 | 6,221 | 6,491 | 8,019 | 7,915 | 8,507 | 9,046 |
| Solid waste landfill | 562212 | 4,798 | 5,667 | 5,782 | 5,778 | 6,013 | (S) |
| Solid waste combustors and incinerators | 562213 | (S) | 2,520 | 2,517 | (S) | (S) | (S) |
| Other nonhazardous waste treatment and disposal | 562219 | 481 | 528 | 480 | 509 | 378 | 440 |
| Remediation services | 56291 | 16,422 | 14,500 | 14,940 | 15,532 | 16,844 | 17,780 |
| Materials recovery facilities | 56292 | 5,092 | 5,570 | 5,722 | 5,285 | 5,351 | 5,825 |
| Septic tank and related services | 562991 | 2,351 | 2,847 | 3,101 | 3,563 | 4,065 | 4,320 |
| All other miscellaneous waste management services | 562998 | 1,442 | 1,781 | 1,892 | 1,947 | 1,716 | 1,871 |

S Figure does not meet publication standards. [1] Data for 2010 are based on the 2007 North American Industry Classification System (NAICS); beginning 2013, data are based on 2012 NAICS. See text Section 15 for more information. [2] Data prior to 2011 have been restated to reflect comparable data on the 2007 NAICS basis for more detailed levels within this aggregate. [3] Includes 2002 NAICS 561310 (Employment Placement Agencies) and a portion of 2002 NAICS 541612 (Human Resources and Executive Search Consulting Services).

Source: U.S. Census Bureau, Service Annual Survey, "Service Annual Survey Latest Data (NAICS-basis): 2017" and "Service Annual Survey Historical Survey Tables," <https://www.census.gov/programs-surveys/sas/data.html>, accessed December 2018.

Accommodation, Food Services, and Other Services   805

## Table 1306. Selected Service Industries—E-Commerce Revenue: 2015 and 2016

[557,607 represents $557,607,000,000. Includes data only for businesses with paid employees, except for accommodation and food services, which also includes businesses with and without paid employees. Except as noted, based on the Service Annual Survey. E-commerce is defined as the value of goods and services sold online. The term "online" includes the use of the internet, intranet, extranet, as well as proprietary networks that run systems such as Electronic Data Interchange (EDI)]

| Kind of business | NAICS code [1] | E-commerce revenue (mil. dol.) | | E-commerce as percent of total revenue | | E-commerce revenue, percent distribution | |
|---|---|---|---|---|---|---|---|
| | | 2015 | 2016 | 2015 | 2016 | 2015 | 2016 |
| Selected service industries, total [2] | (X) | 557,607 | 608,718 | 4.0 | 4.2 | 100.0 | 100.0 |
| Utilities [3] | 22 | 4,238 | 4,382 | 0.7 | 0.8 | 0.8 | 0.7 |
| Selected transportation and warehousing [4] | 4849y | 110,842 | 113,880 | 12.6 | 13.0 | 19.9 | 18.7 |
| Air transportation | 481 | 58,632 | 60,654 | 29.3 | 30.5 | 10.5 | 10.0 |
| Water transportation | 483 | 7,698 | 7,640 | 17.5 | 17.8 | 1.4 | 1.3 |
| Truck transportation | 484 | 17,639 | 17,907 | 6.7 | 6.9 | 3.2 | 2.9 |
| Transit and ground passenger transportation | 485 | 772 | 854 | 2.3 | 2.4 | 0.1 | 0.1 |
| Pipeline transportation | 486 | 3,697 | 3,735 | 8.4 | 8.4 | 0.7 | 0.6 |
| Scenic and sightseeing transportation | 487 | 379 | 422 | 10.3 | 11.8 | 0.1 | 0.1 |
| Support activities for transportation | 488 | 16,031 | 15,859 | 9.0 | 9.0 | 2.9 | 2.6 |
| Information | 51 | 147,656 | 165,237 | 10.5 | 11.0 | 26.5 | 27.1 |
| Publishing industries (except internet) | 511 | 77,595 | 85,272 | 26.4 | 27.7 | 13.9 | 14.0 |
| Motion picture and sound recording industries | 512 | 5,697 | 6,053 | 5.8 | 5.8 | 1.0 | 1.0 |
| Broadcasting (except internet) | 515 | 2,340 | 2,316 | 1.6 | 1.5 | 0.4 | 0.4 |
| Telecommunications | 517 | 8,886 | 9,540 | 1.5 | 1.5 | 1.6 | 1.6 |
| Data processing, hosting, and related services | 518 | (S) | (S) | (S) | (S) | (S) | (S) |
| Other information services | 519 | 37,101 | 44,942 | 28.0 | 29.2 | 6.7 | 7.4 |
| Finance and insurance [5] | 52 | 127,714 | 142,782 | 3.1 | 3.3 | 22.9 | 23.5 |
| Activities related to credit intermediation | 5223 | 14,177 | 15,224 | 15.6 | 16.1 | 2.5 | 2.5 |
| Securities and commodity contracts intermediation and brokerage | 5231 | 17,160 | 16,457 | 6.7 | 6.2 | 3.1 | 2.7 |
| Real estate and rental and leasing | 53 | 25,878 | 27,987 | 4.3 | 4.4 | 4.6 | 4.6 |
| Rental and leasing services | 532 | 19,734 | 21,321 | 12.9 | 13.8 | 3.5 | 3.5 |
| Selected professional, scientific, and technical services [6] | 54 | 43,570 | 47,009 | 2.6 | 2.7 | 7.8 | 7.7 |
| Computer systems design and related services | 5415 | 13,565 | 14,486 | 3.9 | 3.9 | 2.4 | 2.4 |
| Administrative and support and waste management and remediation services | 56 | 29,221 | 31,648 | 3.6 | 3.6 | 5.2 | 5.2 |
| Travel arrangement and reservation services | 5615 | 14,708 | 16,435 | 36.1 | 38.2 | 2.6 | 2.7 |
| Educational services [7] | 61 | 6,715 | 7,508 | 10.8 | 11.7 | 1.2 | 1.2 |
| Health care and social assistance | 62 | 1,649 | 1,828 | 0.1 | 0.1 | 0.3 | 0.3 |
| Arts, entertainment, and recreation | 71 | 9,385 | 10,931 | 4.0 | 4.4 | 1.7 | 1.8 |
| Accommodation and food services [8] | 72 | 36,725 | 40,592 | 4.4 | 4.6 | 6.6 | 6.7 |
| Other services (except public administration) [9] | 81 | 14,014 | 14,934 | 2.8 | 2.9 | 2.5 | 2.5 |
| Repair and maintenance | 811 | 1,200 | 1,182 | 0.7 | 0.7 | 0.2 | 0.2 |
| Personal and laundry services | 812 | 3,969 | 4,378 | 3.9 | 4.1 | 0.7 | 0.7 |
| Religious, grantmaking, civic, professional, and similar organizations | 813 | 8,845 | 9,374 | 3.8 | 3.9 | 1.6 | 1.5 |

X Not applicable. S Data do not meet publication standards. [1] North American Industry Classification System (NAICS), 2012; see text Section 15. [2] Includes other kinds of business, not shown separately. [3] Excludes government owned utilities. [4] Excludes NAICS 482 (Rail Transportation) and NAICS 491 (Postal Service). [5] Excludes NAICS 525 (Funds, Trusts, and Other Financial Vehicles). [6] Excludes NAICS 54112 (Offices of Notaries). [7] Excludes NAICS 6111 (Elementary and Secondary Schools), NAICS 6112 (Junior Colleges), and NAICS 6113 (Colleges, Universities, and Professional Schools). [8] Prior to 2016, NAICS sector 72 was collected and published by the Annual Retail Trade Report. [9] Excludes NAICS 81311 (Religious Organizations), NAICS 81393 (Labor Unions and Similar Labor Organizations), NAICS 81394 (Political Organizations), and NAICS 814 (Private Households).

Source: U.S. Census Bureau, "2016 E-Commerce Multi-sector Data Tables," <http://www.census.gov/programs-surveys/e-stats/data/tables.html>, accessed June 2018.

## Table 1307. Accommodation and Food Services Revenue by Kind of Business: 2013 to 2017

[In millions of dollars (737,177 represents $737,177,000,000). Based on data from the Service Annual Survey, see headnote Table 1305. Prior to 2016, data collected and published by the Annual Retail Trade Report; see <https://www.census.gov//programs-surveys/arts/data/tables.html>]

| Kind of business | NAICS code [1] | 2013 | 2014 | 2015 | 2016 | 2017 |
|---|---|---|---|---|---|---|
| Accommodation and food services, total | 72 | 737,177 | 781,828 | 840,745 | 885,702 | 929,087 |
| Accommodation | 721 | 205,978 | 218,444 | 231,082 | 241,905 | 250,120 |
| Hotels (except casino hotels) and motels | 72111 | 142,890 | 153,699 | 164,964 | 173,822 | 179,892 |
| Casino hotels | 72112 | 54,981 | 56,133 | 57,010 | 58,561 | 60,068 |
| Other traveler accommodations | 72119 | 1,823 | 2,037 | 2,264 | 2,337 | 2,472 |
| RV (recreation vehicle) parks and recreational camps | 7212 | 4,942 | 5,128 | 5,413 | 5,777 | 6,243 |
| Rooming and boarding houses | 7213 | 1,342 | 1,447 | 1,431 | 1,408 | 1,445 |
| Food services and drinking places | 722 | 531,199 | 563,384 | 609,663 | 643,797 | 678,967 |
| Food services contractors | 72231 | 37,685 | 39,271 | 42,049 | 44,681 | 46,391 |
| Caterers | 72232 | 7,459 | 7,652 | 8,191 | 8,668 | 9,462 |
| Mobile food services | 72233 | 822 | 986 | 1,138 | 1,403 | 1,613 |
| Drinking places (alcoholic beverages) | 7224 | 19,796 | 19,956 | 20,971 | 23,400 | 25,669 |
| Full-service restaurants | 722511 | 232,900 | 250,216 | 269,741 | 279,948 | 290,894 |
| Limited-service restaurants | 722513 | 193,009 | 202,213 | 219,699 | 233,907 | 249,858 |
| Cafeterias, grill buffets, and buffets | 722514 | 6,401 | 6,230 | 7,043 | 7,377 | 7,819 |
| Snack and nonalcoholic beverage bars | 722515 | 33,127 | 36,860 | 40,831 | 44,413 | 47,261 |

[1] North American Industry Classification System (NAICS), 2012; see text, Section 15.

Source: U.S. Census Bureau, Service Annual Survey, "Service Annual Survey Latest Data (NAICS-basis): 2017," <https://www.census.gov/programs-surveys/sas/data.html>, accessed December 2018.

## Table 1308. Other Services—Estimated Revenue for Employer Firms by Kind of Business: 2013 to 2017

[In millions of dollars (450,492 represents $450,492,000,000). For taxable and tax exempt employer firms. Estimates have been adjusted to results of the 2012 Economic Census. Based on the Service Annual Survey; see Appendix III]

| Kind of business | NAICS code [1] | 2013 | 2014 | 2015 | 2016 | 2017 |
|---|---|---|---|---|---|---|
| **Other services (except public administration) [2]** | **81** | **450,492** | **482,548** | **498,951** | **517,246** | **556,573** |
| Repair and maintenance | 811 | 148,202 | 157,449 | 162,955 | 170,040 | 175,901 |
| General automotive repair | 811111 | 42,602 | 46,655 | 47,718 | 49,954 | 51,511 |
| Automotive exhaust system repair | 811112 | 710 | 727 | 774 | 788 | 802 |
| Automotive transmission repair | 811113 | 2,262 | 2,369 | 2,313 | 2,319 | 2,332 |
| Other automotive mechanical and electrical repair and maintenance | 811118 | 1,932 | 2,053 | 2,054 | 2,136 | 2,139 |
| Automotive body, paint, interior repair and maintenance | 811121 | 29,345 | 30,244 | 32,009 | 34,943 | 37,107 |
| Automotive glass replacement shops | 811122 | 3,415 | 3,729 | 4,196 | 4,591 | 4,654 |
| Automotive oil change and lubrication shops | 811191 | 4,979 | 5,122 | 5,336 | 5,721 | 6,013 |
| Car washes | 811192 | 7,264 | 7,609 | 8,031 | 8,747 | 9,204 |
| All other automotive repair and maintenance | 811198 | 1,727 | 1,916 | 1,964 | 2,103 | 2,333 |
| Consumer electronics repair and maintenance | 811211 | 1,704 | 1,640 | 1,653 | 1,611 | 1,598 |
| Computer and office machine repair and maintenance | 811212 | 4,960 | 5,014 | 4,962 | 5,065 | 4,850 |
| Communication equipment repair and maintenance | 811213 | 2,670 | 3,015 | 3,145 | 3,348 | 3,271 |
| Other electronic and precision equipment repair and maintenance | 811219 | 6,365 | 6,727 | 7,187 | 7,199 | 7,302 |
| Commercial and industrial machinery and equipment (except automotive and electronic) repair and maintenance | 8113 | 31,539 | 33,679 | 34,270 | 33,807 | 35,003 |
| Home and garden equipment and appliance repair and maintenance | 81141 | 2,623 | 2,780 | 2,808 | 2,937 | 2,846 |
| Reupholstery and furniture repair | 81142 | 1,053 | 1,085 | 1,173 | 1,205 | 1,161 |
| Footwear and leather goods repair | 81143 | 211 | 217 | 230 | 230 | 221 |
| Other personal and household goods repair and maintenance | 81149 | 2,841 | 2,868 | 3,132 | 3,336 | 3,554 |
| Personal and laundry services | 812 | 91,165 | 96,608 | 101,406 | 105,976 | 111,323 |
| Barber shops | 812111 | 590 | 692 | 748 | 818 | 953 |
| Beauty shops | 812112 | 19,947 | 20,866 | 21,348 | 22,093 | 22,406 |
| Nail salons | 812113 | 3,393 | 3,834 | 4,415 | 5,032 | 5,703 |
| Diet and weight reducing centers | 812191 | 1,710 | 1,569 | 1,456 | 1,533 | 1,628 |
| Other personal care services | 812199 | 5,441 | 6,033 | 6,661 | 7,420 | 8,256 |
| Funeral homes and funeral services | 81221 | 13,542 | 13,733 | 14,476 | 14,790 | 15,085 |
| Cemeteries and crematories | 81222 | 3,425 | 3,646 | 3,782 | 3,996 | 4,053 |
| Coin-operated laundries and drycleaners | 81231 | 3,844 | 4,003 | 4,021 | 4,149 | 4,286 |
| Dry-cleaning and laundry services (except coin-operated) | 81232 | 7,708 | 7,956 | 7,908 | 7,842 | 8,110 |
| Linen supply | 812331 | 5,259 | 5,610 | 6,075 | 6,177 | 6,250 |
| Industrial launders | 812332 | 7,304 | 7,718 | 7,982 | 8,494 | 8,645 |
| Pet care (except veterinary) services | 81291 | 3,707 | 4,206 | 4,768 | 5,339 | 6,108 |
| Photofinishing | 81292 | 1,680 | 1,839 | 1,844 | 1,788 | 1,849 |
| Parking lots and garages | 81293 | 7,741 | 8,315 | 9,033 | 9,088 | 9,749 |
| All other personal services | 81299 | 5,874 | 6,588 | 6,889 | 7,417 | 8,242 |
| Religious, grantmaking, civic, professional, and similar organizations [3] | 813 | 211,125 | 228,491 | 234,590 | 241,230 | 269,349 |
| Grantmaking and giving services | 8132 | 102,359 | 114,180 | 117,547 | 118,764 | 137,191 |
| Social advocacy organizations | 8133 | 25,470 | 28,253 | 28,693 | 30,716 | 32,764 |
| Civic and social organizations | 8134 | 16,759 | 17,143 | 17,864 | 18,332 | 19,814 |
| Business, professional, labor, political, and similar organizations [4] | 8139 | 66,537 | 68,915 | 70,486 | 73,418 | 79,580 |

[1] Data based on 2012 NAICS. See section 15, Business Enterprise. [2] Excludes NAICS 8131 (Religious Organizations), NAICS 81393 (Labor Unions and Similar Labor Organizations), NAICS 81394 (Political Organizations), and NAICS 814 (Private Households). [3] Excludes NAICS 8131 (Religious Organizations), NAICS 81393 (Labor Unions and Similar Labor Organizations), and NAICS 81394 (Political Organizations). [4] Excludes NAICS 81393 (Labor Unions and Similar Labor Organizations) and NAICS 81394 (Political Organizations).

Source: U.S. Census Bureau, Service Annual Survey, "Service Annual Survey Latest Data (NAICS-basis): 2017," <https://www.census.gov/programs-surveys/sas/data.html>, accessed December 2018.

## Table 1309. National Nonprofit Associations—Number by Type: 1980 to 2019

[Data compiled during last few months of year previous to year shown and the beginning months of year shown]

| Type | 1980 | 1990 | 2000 | 2005 | 2010 [1] | 2015 | 2017 | 2018 | 2019 |
|---|---|---|---|---|---|---|---|---|---|
| **Total** | **14,726** | **22,289** | **21,840** | **22,720** | **23,983** | **23,891** | **24,102** | **24,146** | **24,242** |
| Trade, business, commercial | 3,118 | 3,918 | 3,880 | 3,789 | 3,761 | 3,487 | 3,521 | 3,576 | 3,571 |
| Agriculture and environment | 677 | 940 | 1,103 | 1,170 | 1,442 | 1,421 | 1,415 | 1,393 | 1,441 |
| Legal, governmental, public admin., military | 529 | 792 | 790 | 868 | 913 | 894 | 912 | 958 | 977 |
| Scientific, engineering, technical | 1,039 | 1,417 | 1,302 | 1,354 | 1,563 | 1,507 | 1,553 | 1,567 | 1,570 |
| Educational | [2] 2,376 | 1,291 | 1,297 | 1,318 | 1,444 | 1,344 | 1,368 | 1,365 | 1,436 |
| Cultural | ([2]) | 1,886 | 1,786 | 1,733 | 1,717 | 1,610 | 1,681 | 1,655 | 1,658 |
| Social welfare | 994 | 1,705 | 1,829 | 2,072 | 2,673 | 3,166 | 3,067 | 3,018 | 2,950 |
| Health, medical | 1,413 | 2,227 | 2,495 | 2,982 | 3,481 | 4,069 | 4,274 | 4,350 | 4,283 |
| Public affairs | 1,068 | 2,249 | 1,776 | 1,854 | 1,734 | 1,601 | 1,513 | 1,509 | 1,459 |
| Fraternal, nationality, ethnic | 435 | 573 | 525 | 550 | 461 | 398 | 411 | 405 | 405 |
| Religious | 797 | 1,172 | 1,123 | 1,147 | 1,056 | 964 | 970 | 968 | 992 |
| Veteran, hereditary, patriotic | 208 | 462 | 835 | 774 | 585 | 545 | 543 | 541 | 550 |
| Hobby, avocational | 910 | 1,475 | 1,330 | 1,433 | 1,374 | 1,287 | 1,274 | 1,268 | 1,353 |
| Athletic sports | 504 | 840 | 717 | 762 | 946 | 899 | 892 | 884 | 863 |
| Labor unions | 235 | 253 | 232 | 208 | 188 | 162 | 163 | 160 | 215 |
| Chambers of Commerce [3] | 105 | 168 | 143 | 135 | 142 | 125 | 126 | 116 | 106 |
| Greek and non-Greek letter societies | 318 | 340 | 296 | 349 | 305 | 294 | 316 | 316 | 317 |
| Fan clubs | (NA) | 581 | 381 | 314 | 198 | 118 | 103 | 97 | 96 |

NA Not available. [1] Beginning in 2007, there was an increase in the number of associations due to an increase in newly discovered and established associations. [2] Data for cultural associations included with educational associations. [3] National and binational. Includes trade and tourism organizations.

Source: Gale, Cengage Learning. *Encyclopedia of Associations: National Organizations* © 2019 Gale, a part of Cengage, Inc. Reproduced by permission. See <www.cengage.com/permissions>.

# Foreign Commerce and Aid

This section presents data on the flow of goods, services, and capital between the United States and other countries; changes in official reserve assets of the United States; international investments; and foreign assistance programs.

The Bureau of Economic Analysis publishes current figures on U.S. international transactions and the U.S. international investment position in its monthly *Survey of Current Business* and in an interactive database on the internet at <https://apps.bea.gov/itable/index.cfm>. Statistics for the foreign aid programs are presented by the Agency for International Development (USAID) in its annual *U.S. Overseas Loans and Grants*.

The principal source of merchandise import and export data is the U.S. Census Bureau. Current data are presented monthly in *U.S. International Trade in Goods and Services Report* Series FT 900, as well as in the "USA Trade Online" database, at <https://usatrade.census.gov/>. The *Guide to Foreign Trade Statistics*, found on the Census Bureau website at <http://www.census.gov/foreign-trade/guide/index.html>, lists the Census Bureau's monthly and annual products and services in this field. In addition, the International Trade Administration and the Bureau of Economic Analysis present summary as well as selected commodity and country data for U.S. foreign trade on their websites: <http://www.trade.gov/mas/ian/tradestatistics/> and <https://www.bea.gov/data/economic-accounts/international>, respectively. The merchandise trade data published by the Bureau of Economic Analysis in the *Survey of Current Business* and on the web include balance of payments adjustments to the Census Bureau data. The U.S. Treasury Department's *Monthly Treasury Statement of Receipts and Outlays of the United States Government* contains information on import duties. The International Trade Commission, U.S. Department of Agriculture (agricultural products), U.S. Department of Energy (mineral fuels, like petroleum and coal), and the U.S. Geological Survey (minerals) release various reports and specialized products on U.S. trade.

**International accounts**—The international transactions tables (Tables 1310, 1313, and 1314) show, for given time periods, the transfer of goods, services, grants, and financial assets and liabilities between the United States and the rest of the world. The international investment position table (Table 1312) presents, for specific dates, the value of U.S. investments abroad and of foreign investments in the United States. The movement of foreign and U.S. capital as presented in the balance of payments is not the only factor affecting the total value of foreign investments. Among the other factors are changes in the valuation of assets or liabilities, including changes in prices of securities, defaults, expropriations, and write-offs.

Direct investment abroad means the ownership or control, directly or indirectly, by one person of 10 percent or more of the voting securities of an incorporated business enterprise or an equivalent interest in an unincorporated business enterprise. Direct investment position is the value of U.S. parents' claims on the equity of and receivables due from

foreign affiliates, less foreign affiliates' receivables due from their U.S. parents. Income consists of parents' shares in the earnings of their affiliates plus net interest received by parents on intercompany accounts, less withholding taxes on dividends and interest.

**Foreign aid**—Foreign assistance is divided into three major categories—grants (military supplies and services and other grants), credits, and other assistance (through net accumulation of foreign currency claims from the sale of agricultural commodities). *Grants* are transfers for which no payment is expected (other than a limited percentage of the foreign currency "counterpart" funds generated by the grant), or which at most involve an obligation on the part of the receiver to extend aid to the United States or other countries to achieve a common objective. *Credits* are loan disbursements or transfers under other agreements which give rise to specific obligations to repay, over a period of years, usually with interest. All known returns to the U.S. government stemming from grants and credits (reverse grants, returns of grants, and payments of principal) are taken into account in net grants and net credits, but no allowance is made for interest or commissions. *Other assistance* represents the transfer of U.S. farm products in exchange for foreign currencies (plus, since enactment of Public Law 87-128, currency claims from principal and interest collected on credits extended under the farm products program), less the government's disbursements of the currencies as grants, credits, or for purchases. The net acquisition of currencies represents net transfers of resources to foreign countries under the agricultural programs, in addition to those classified as grants or credits.

**Exports**—Export statistics consist of goods valued at more than $2,500 per commodity shipped by individuals and organizations (including exporters, freight forwarders, and carriers) from the U.S. to other countries. The Census Bureau compiles export data primarily from three sources: Shipper's Export Declaration documents filed with Customs and Border Protection and sent to the Census Bureau (3 percent of all transactions), data in electronic form submitted directly by exporters and their agents (63 percent); and special computer tapes from Canada for U.S. exports to Canada (34 percent). Estimates are made for low-value exports by country of destination, and based on bilateral trade patterns. They include U.S. exports under mutual security programs and exclude shipments to U.S. Armed Forces for their own use.

The value reported in the export statistics is generally equivalent to a free alongside ship (f.a.s.) value at the U.S. port of export, based on the transaction price, including inland freight, insurance, and other charges incurred in placing the merchandise alongside the carrier at the U.S. port of exportation. This value, as defined, excludes the cost of loading merchandise aboard the exporting carrier and also excludes freight, insurance, and any other charges or transportation and other costs beyond the U.S. port of exportation. The country of destination is defined as the country of ultimate destination or country where the merchandise is to be consumed, further processed, or manufactured, as known to the shipper at the time of exportation. When ultimate destination is not known, the shipment is statistically credited to the last country to which the shipper knows the merchandise will be shipped in the same form as exported.

Statistics for U.S. exports to Canada are based on import documents filed with Canadian agencies and forwarded to the U.S. Census Bureau under a 1987 data exchange agreement. Under this agreement, each country eliminated most cross-border export documents; maintains detailed statistics on cross-border imports; exchanges monthly files of cross-border import statistics; and publishes exchanged statistics in place of previously compiled export statistics.

Prior to 1989, exports were based on Schedule B, Statistical Classification of Domestic and Foreign Commodities Exported from the United States. Beginning in 1989, Schedule B classifications are based on the Harmonized System and coincide with the Standard International Trade Classification, Revision 3. This revision will affect the comparability of most export series beginning with the 1989 data for commodities.

**Imports**—Import statistics consist of goods valued at more than $2,000 per commodity shipped by individuals and organizations (including importers and customs brokers) into the U.S. from other countries. The Census Bureau compiles import data from records filed with Customs and Border Protection, usually within 10 days after the merchandise enters the United States. Estimates are made for low-value shipments by country of origin, based on previous bilateral trade patterns and periodically updated. Country of origin is defined as country where the merchandise was grown, mined, or manufactured. If country of origin is unknown, country of shipment is reported. Statistics for over 95 percent of all commodity transactions are compiled from records filed electronically with Customs and forwarded as computer tape files to the U.S. Census Bureau. Statistics for other transactions are compiled from

hard-copy documents filed with Customs and forwarded on a flow basis for U.S. Census Bureau processing.

Data on import values are presented on two valuations bases in this section: the c.i.f. (cost, insurance, and freight) and the customs import value (as appraised by the U.S. Customs Service in accordance with legal requirements of the Tariff Act of 1930, as amended). This latter valuation, primarily used for collection of import duties, frequently does not reflect the actual transaction value.

Imports are classified either as "General imports" or "Imports for consumption." *General imports* are a combination of entries for immediate consumption, entries into customs bonded warehouses, and entries into U.S. Foreign Trade Zones, thus generally reflecting total arrivals of merchandise. *Imports for consumption* are a combination of entries for immediate consumption, withdrawals from warehouses for consumption, and entries of merchandise into U.S. customs territory from U.S. Foreign Trade Zones, thus generally reflecting the total of the commodities entered into U.S. consumption channels.

Beginning in 1989, import statistics are based on the Harmonized Tariff Schedule of the United States, which coincides with import Standard International Trade Classification, Revision 3. This revision will affect the comparability of most import series beginning with the 1989 data.

**Area coverage**—Except as noted, the geographic area covered by the export and import trade statistics is the United States Customs area (includes the 50 states, the District of Columbia, and Puerto Rico), the U.S. Virgin Islands (effective January 1981), and U.S. Foreign Trade Zones (effective July 1982).

**Statistical reliability**—For a discussion of statistical collection and estimation, sampling procedures, and measures of statistical reliability applicable to Census Bureau data, see Appendix III.

# Table 1310. U.S. International Transactions by Type of Transaction: 2000 to 2018

[In millions of dollars (1,469,648 represents $1,469,648,000,000). Minus sign (-) indicates debits. N.i.e. is not indicated elsewhere]

| Type of transaction | 2000 | 2005 | 2010 | 2012 | 2013 | 2014 | 2015 | 2016 | 2017 | 2018 |
|---|---|---|---|---|---|---|---|---|---|---|
| **Exports of goods and services and income receipts** | 1,469,648 | 1,885,833 | 2,623,991 | 3,095,038 | 3,212,991 | 3,341,768 | 3,207,288 | 3,188,508 | 3,444,824 | 3,735,684 |
| Exports of goods and services | 1,075,321 | 1,286,022 | 1,853,038 | 2,218,354 | 2,294,199 | 2,376,657 | 2,266,691 | 2,215,839 | 2,352,546 | 2,501,310 |
| Goods | 784,940 | 913,016 | 1,290,279 | 1,562,630 | 1,593,708 | 1,635,563 | 1,511,381 | 1,457,393 | 1,553,589 | 1,674,330 |
| General merchandise | 778,718 | 906,104 | 1,271,972 | 1,524,790 | 1,559,363 | 1,612,611 | 1,489,795 | 1,436,552 | 1,531,835 | 1,652,113 |
| Foods, feeds, and beverages | 47,871 | 58,955 | 107,719 | 133,049 | 136,163 | 143,721 | 127,721 | 130,515 | 132,736 | 133,176 |
| Industrial supplies and materials | 171,108 | 236,812 | 388,561 | 483,232 | 492,422 | 500,677 | 418,141 | 387,600 | 456,223 | 534,649 |
| Capital goods except automotive | 357,000 | 358,426 | 447,839 | 527,459 | 534,757 | 551,758 | 539,805 | 520,001 | 533,485 | 563,156 |
| Automotive vehicles, parts, and engines | 80,356 | 98,406 | 112,008 | 146,158 | 152,661 | 159,812 | 151,894 | 150,398 | 157,865 | 158,839 |
| Consumer goods except food and automotive | 89,305 | 115,228 | 164,909 | 180,994 | 188,093 | 198,398 | 197,318 | 193,258 | 197,168 | 205,471 |
| Other general merchandise | 33,078 | 38,276 | 50,938 | 53,898 | 55,268 | 58,246 | 54,917 | 54,781 | 54,359 | 56,821 |
| Net exports of goods under merchanting | 159 | 1,330 | 411 | 552 | 461 | 299 | 261 | 300 | 210 | 270 |
| Nonmonetary gold | 6,063 | 5,582 | 17,896 | 37,289 | 33,883 | 22,654 | 21,325 | 20,542 | 21,544 | 21,947 |
| Services | 290,381 | 373,006 | 562,759 | 655,724 | 700,491 | 741,094 | 755,310 | 758,446 | 798,957 | 826,980 |
| Maintenance and repair services n.i.e. | 5,011 | 7,624 | 14,549 | 17,186 | 18,568 | 21,149 | 23,384 | 25,132 | 26,880 | 30,968 |
| Transport [1] | 45,758 | 52,622 | 71,656 | 83,944 | 86,776 | 90,729 | 87,725 | 84,749 | 88,836 | 92,852 |
| Travel (for all purposes including education) [2] | 100,187 | 101,470 | 137,010 | 161,632 | 177,484 | 191,918 | 206,936 | 206,650 | 210,655 | 214,680 |
| Insurance services | 3,631 | 7,566 | 14,397 | 16,790 | 16,696 | 17,333 | 16,248 | 16,819 | 18,015 | 17,466 |
| Financial services | 22,117 | 39,878 | 72,348 | 76,692 | 95,131 | 106,949 | 102,435 | 99,074 | 109,203 | 112,015 |
| Charges for the use of intellectual property n.i.e. | 51,808 | 74,448 | 107,521 | 124,440 | 128,034 | 129,716 | 124,769 | 124,387 | 126,523 | 128,748 |
| Telecommunications, computer, and information services | 12,215 | 15,515 | 25,038 | 32,510 | 34,419 | 34,691 | 36,578 | 38,245 | 42,001 | 43,196 |
| Other business services | 40,497 | 58,302 | 101,029 | 120,382 | 121,530 | 128,915 | 137,148 | 144,614 | 157,190 | 165,821 |
| Government goods and services n.i.e. [3,4] | 9,156 | 15,582 | 19,210 | 22,148 | 21,852 | 19,693 | 20,087 | 18,777 | 19,653 | 21,235 |
| Primary income receipts | 356,706 | 534,215 | 680,159 | 767,972 | 792,819 | 824,543 | 810,073 | 835,509 | 933,307 | 1,084,183 |
| Investment income | 352,311 | 529,419 | 674,228 | 761,670 | 786,206 | 818,040 | 803,494 | 829,180 | 927,182 | 1,077,515 |
| Compensation of employees | 4,395 | 4,796 | 5,931 | 6,302 | 6,613 | 6,503 | 6,578 | 6,329 | 6,125 | 6,668 |
| Secondary income (current transfer) receipts [5] | 37,621 | 65,595 | 90,733 | 108,711 | 125,973 | 140,567 | 130,525 | 137,160 | 158,970 | 150,191 |
| **Imports of goods and services and income payments** | 1,873,098 | 2,631,067 | 3,055,256 | 3,521,871 | 3,561,792 | 3,706,967 | 3,615,053 | 3,616,858 | 3,884,470 | 4,226,662 |
| Imports of goods and services | 1,447,837 | 2,000,267 | 2,348,263 | 2,755,762 | 2,755,334 | 2,866,241 | 2,765,216 | 2,718,821 | 2,902,669 | 3,128,989 |
| Goods | 1,231,722 | 1,695,820 | 1,938,950 | 2,303,749 | 2,294,247 | 2,385,480 | 2,273,249 | 2,207,195 | 2,358,789 | 2,561,667 |
| General merchandise | 1,225,780 | 1,691,201 | 1,924,446 | 2,284,535 | 2,276,499 | 2,370,016 | 2,260,659 | 2,189,041 | 2,346,585 | 2,551,105 |
| Foods, feeds, and beverages | 46,489 | 69,072 | 92,492 | 111,127 | 116,003 | 126,805 | 128,762 | 131,014 | 138,811 | 148,364 |
| Industrial supplies and materials | 303,768 | 533,686 | 610,268 | 734,803 | 686,673 | 675,567 | 492,483 | 441,793 | 511,359 | 583,344 |
| Capital goods except automotive | 347,706 | 382,833 | 450,406 | 551,777 | 558,971 | 598,759 | 607,160 | 593,614 | 642,887 | 695,939 |
| Automotive vehicles, parts, and engines | 194,954 | 238,715 | 225,641 | 298,498 | 309,573 | 329,498 | 350,049 | 350,847 | 359,189 | 373,123 |
| Consumer goods except food and automotive | 284,634 | 412,734 | 485,121 | 518,821 | 532,876 | 558,700 | 596,417 | 584,900 | 603,580 | 649,096 |
| Other general merchandise | 48,229 | 54,161 | 60,519 | 69,503 | 72,402 | 80,688 | 85,789 | 86,876 | 90,759 | 101,237 |
| Nonmonetary gold | 5,942 | 4,518 | 14,504 | 19,214 | 17,748 | 15,464 | 12,590 | 18,154 | 12,204 | 10,562 |
| Services | 216,115 | 304,448 | 409,313 | 452,013 | 461,087 | 480,761 | 491,966 | 511,627 | 543,880 | 567,322 |
| Maintenance and repair services n.i.e. | 2,569 | 3,015 | 6,909 | 8,015 | 7,420 | 7,520 | 9,013 | 8,764 | 8,400 | 8,718 |
| Transport [1] | 57,606 | 75,343 | 74,628 | 84,985 | 90,634 | 94,188 | 97,006 | 96,982 | 101,756 | 108,202 |
| Travel (for all purposes including education) [2] | 65,787 | 79,988 | 86,623 | 100,338 | 98,120 | 105,668 | 114,548 | 123,549 | 134,868 | 144,463 |
| Insurance services | 11,284 | 28,710 | 61,478 | 55,513 | 53,420 | 51,011 | 47,420 | 50,144 | 50,599 | 42,485 |
| Financial services | 10,936 | 12,126 | 15,502 | 16,703 | 21,545 | 24,883 | 25,769 | 25,710 | 28,957 | 31,298 |
| Charges for the use of intellectual property n.i.e. | 16,606 | 25,577 | 32,551 | 38,661 | 38,860 | 41,983 | 40,608 | 46,987 | 53,440 | 56,117 |
| Telecommunications, computer, and information services | 12,397 | 15,975 | 29,015 | 32,779 | 35,034 | 36,502 | 36,704 | 37,418 | 39,628 | 41,190 |
| Other business services | 24,414 | 35,960 | 70,646 | 87,157 | 90,714 | 94,771 | 99,368 | 100,570 | 104,185 | 111,874 |
| Government goods and services n.i.e. [3,6] | 14,516 | 27,454 | 31,960 | 27,861 | 25,341 | 24,236 | 21,531 | 21,503 | 22,047 | 22,975 |
| Primary income payments | 338,637 | 480,317 | 511,948 | 560,497 | 586,842 | 606,152 | 606,464 | 636,855 | 707,508 | 830,198 |
| Investment income | 327,682 | 464,409 | 497,986 | 545,551 | 570,816 | 589,093 | 588,809 | 618,123 | 688,524 | 810,618 |
| Compensation of employees | 10,955 | 15,909 | 13,962 | 14,946 | 16,026 | 17,059 | 17,656 | 18,732 | 18,985 | 19,580 |
| Secondary income (current transfer) payments [5] | 86,624 | 150,482 | 195,045 | 205,611 | 219,616 | 234,574 | 243,372 | 261,181 | 274,293 | 267,475 |
| **Capital transfer receipts and other credits** | 35 | 15,462 | 157 | 7,668 | 412 | 45 | 42 | 152 | 19,154 | 3,247 |
| **Capital transfer payments and other debits** | 36 | 2,346 | – | 764 | – | – | – | – | 204 | 12 |
| **Net U.S. acquisition of financial assets [7]** | 587,682 | 562,983 | 958,703 | 176,764 | 649,587 | 866,523 | 202,208 | 353,036 | 1,167,447 | 310,827 |
| Direct investment assets | 186,371 | 52,591 | 349,829 | 377,239 | 392,796 | 387,528 | 307,058 | 318,317 | 384,574 | -78,457 |
| Equity | 170,011 | 42,287 | 338,294 | 321,228 | 334,706 | 344,914 | 297,440 | 341,999 | 357,856 | -151,614 |

See footnotes at end of table.

# Table 1310. U.S. International Transactions by Type of Transaction: 2000 to 2018-Continued.

See headnote on page 811.

| Type of transaction | 2000 | 2005 | 2010 | 2012 | 2013 | 2014 | 2015 | 2016 | 2017 | 2018 |
|---|---|---|---|---|---|---|---|---|---|---|
| Debt instruments | 16,360 | 10,304 | 11,535 | 56,011 | 58,090 | 42,614 | 9,618 | -23,683 | 26,718 | 73,157 |
| Portfolio investment assets | 159,713 | 267,290 | 199,620 | 248,760 | 481,298 | 582,676 | 160,410 | 36,283 | 569,376 | 334,033 |
| Equity and investment fund shares | 106,714 | 186,684 | 79,150 | 103,974 | 287,432 | 431,625 | 196,922 | 21,743 | 139,940 | 194,087 |
| Debt securities [8] | 52,999 | 80,606 | 120,469 | 144,786 | 193,866 | 151,051 | 151,051 | 14,541 | 429,437 | 139,945 |
| Other investment assets | 241,308 | 257,196 | 407,420 | -453,695 | -221,408 | -100,099 | -258,968 | -3,654 | 215,187 | 50,262 |
| Currency and deposits | (NA) | 82,879 | 150,249 | -521,922 | -126,959 | -160,480 | -191,472 | -91,319 | 169,239 | 71,792 |
| Loans | (NA) | 173,031 | 251,128 | 67,538 | -104,254 | 66,204 | -65,793 | 86,762 | 40,240 | -22,423 |
| Insurance technical reserves | (NA) | (NA) | (NA) | (NA) | (NA) | (NA) | (NA) | (NA) | (NA) | (NA) |
| Trade credit and advances | 680 | 1,286 | 6,043 | 689 | 9,805 | -5,824 | -1,702 | 903 | 5,708 | 893 |
| Reserve assets | 290 | -14,094 | 1,835 | 4,460 | -3,099 | -3,583 | -6,292 | 2,090 | -1,690 | 4,989 |
| Special drawing rights | 722 | -4,511 | 31 | 37 | 22 | 23 | 9 | 684 | 78 | 156 |
| Reserve position in the International Monetary Fund | -2,308 | -10,200 | 1,293 | 4,032 | -3,438 | -3,849 | -6,485 | 1,348 | -1,812 | 4,824 |
| Other reserve assets | 1,876 | 617 | 511 | 391 | 317 | 243 | 185 | 58 | 44 | 10 |
| Currency and deposits | (NA) | 224 | 55 | 24 | 3 | 5 | -20 | -56 | (Z) | (Z) |
| Securities | (NA) | 309 | 439 | 365 | 313 | 234 | 205 | 114 | 44 | 10 |
| Other claims | (NA) | 84 | 17 | 3 | 1 | 4 | (Z) | (Z) | (Z) | (Z) |
| **Net U.S. incurrence of liabilities [7]** | 1,066,074 | 1,277,056 | 1,391,042 | 632,034 | 1,052,068 | 1,109,443 | 501,121 | 742,905 | 1,549,024 | 735,583 |
| Direct investment liabilities | 349,124 | 142,345 | 264,039 | 250,343 | 288,131 | 251,857 | 509,087 | 494,438 | 354,651 | 258,392 |
| Equity | 258,438 | 116,476 | 207,842 | 211,419 | 211,769 | 146,073 | 423,974 | 387,582 | 308,228 | 357,164 |
| Debt instruments | 90,686 | 25,869 | 56,197 | 38,925 | 76,362 | 105,784 | 85,114 | 106,856 | 46,423 | -98,773 |
| Portfolio investment liabilities | 441,966 | 832,037 | 820,434 | 747,017 | 511,987 | 697,607 | 213,910 | 231,349 | 792,523 | 315,676 |
| Equity and investment fund shares | 193,600 | 89,258 | 178,952 | 239,065 | -62,642 | 154,311 | -187,306 | -139,700 | 149,633 | 142,396 |
| Debt securities [8] | 248,366 | 742,779 | 641,481 | 507,952 | 574,629 | 543,296 | 401,216 | 371,049 | 642,889 | 173,280 |
| Other investment liabilities | 274,984 | 302,673 | 306,569 | -365,327 | 251,949 | 159,979 | -221,876 | 17,118 | 401,851 | 161,515 |
| Currency and deposits | (NA) | -124,782 | 115,678 | -246,001 | 202,838 | 61,076 | -35,103 | 18,695 | 217,750 | 32,320 |
| Loans | (NA) | 415,824 | 172,256 | -130,307 | 41,333 | 87,870 | -264,970 | -7,574 | 168,871 | 114,066 |
| Insurance technical reserves | (NA) | (NA) | (NA) | (NA) | (NA) | (NA) | (NA) | (NA) | (NA) | (NA) |
| Trade credit and advances | (NA) | (NA) | (NA) | (NA) | 7,778 | 11,033 | 7,991 | 5,997 | 15,231 | 15,129 |
| Special drawing rights allocations | 10,375 | 11,632 | 18,635 | 10,981 | — | — | — | — | — | — |
| **Financial derivatives, net [9]** | (NA) | (NA) | -14,076 | 7,064 | 2,222 | -54,335 | -27,035 | 7,827 | 23,998 | -20,721 |
| **Statistical discrepancy [10]** | -74,941 | 18,045 | -14,992 | -28,277 | -51,046 | 67,989 | 81,859 | 46,460 | 63,117 | 42,266 |
| **Balance on current account (exports less imports)** | -403,450 | -745,234 | -431,265 | -426,832 | -348,801 | -365,199 | -407,764 | -428,349 | -439,646 | -490,978 |
| Balance on goods and services | -372,517 | -714,245 | -495,225 | -537,408 | -461,135 | -489,584 | -498,525 | -502,982 | -550,123 | -627,679 |
| Balance on goods | -446,783 | -782,804 | -648,671 | -741,119 | -700,539 | -749,917 | -761,868 | -749,801 | -805,200 | -887,338 |
| Balance on services | 74,266 | 68,558 | 153,446 | 203,711 | 239,404 | 260,333 | 263,343 | 246,819 | 255,077 | 259,659 |
| Balance on primary income | 18,069 | 53,898 | 168,221 | 207,475 | 205,977 | 218,391 | 203,608 | 198,654 | 225,799 | 253,985 |
| Balance on secondary income | -49,003 | -84,887 | -104,261 | -96,900 | -93,643 | -94,006 | -112,848 | -124,022 | -115,322 | -117,284 |
| **Balance on capital account** | -1 | 13,116 | -157 | 6,904 | -412 | -45 | -42 | -152 | 18,950 | 3,235 |
| **Net lending/borrowing from current- and capital-account transactions [11]** | -403,451 | -732,118 | -431,422 | -419,928 | -349,213 | -365,244 | -407,807 | -428,502 | -420,696 | -487,743 |
| **Net lending/borrowing from financial-account transactions [11, 12]** | -478,392 | -714,073 | -446,415 | -448,205 | -400,259 | -297,255 | -325,948 | -382,042 | -357,579 | -445,477 |

— Represents zero. NA Not available. Z Transactions between zero and +/- $500,000. [1] Includes passenger fares. [2] All travel purposes include 1) business travel, including expenditures by border, seasonal, and other short-term workers and 2) personal travel, including health-related and education-related travel. [3] Includes goods and services supplied by and to embassies, consulates, and military bases; goods and services acquired from the host economy by diplomatic and military personnel; and services supplied by and to governments that are not included in other service categories. [4] Includes transfers under U.S. military sales contracts. [5] Secondary income (current transfer) receipts and payments include U.S. government and private transfers, such as U.S. government grants and pensions, fines and penalties, withholding taxes, personal transfers (remittances), insurance-related transfers, and other current transfers. [6] Includes direct defense expenditures. [7] Excluding financial derivatives. [8] Includes transactions in U.S. Treasury and other U.S. securities. [9] Transactions for financial derivatives are only available as a net value equal to transactions for assets less transactions for liabilities. A positive value represents net U.S. cash payments arising from derivatives contracts, and a negative value represents net U.S. cash receipts. [10] The statistical discrepancy is the difference between total debits and total credits recorded in the current, capital, and financial accounts. In the current and capital account, an acquisition of an asset or a repayment of a liability is a debit, and an incurrence of a liability or a disposal of an asset is a credit. [11] Net lending means that U.S. residents are net suppliers of funds to foreign residents, and net borrowing means the opposite. Net lending or net borrowing can be computed from current- and capital-account transactions or from financial-account transactions. The two amounts differ by the statistical discrepancy. [12] Net lending or net borrowing from financial-account transactions is the net U.S. acquisition of financial assets excluding financial derivatives plus financial derivatives less net U.S. incurrence of liabilities excluding financial derivatives other than reserves.

Source: U.S. Bureau of Economic Analysis, International Economic Accounts, "Table 1.2. U.S. International Transactions, Expanded Detail," <http://www.bea.gov/international/index.htm>, accessed July 2019.

## Table 1311. U.S. Government Reserve Assets: 1990 to 2017

[In billions of dollars (83.3 represents $83,300,000,000). As of end of year]

| Type | 1990 | 2000 | 2009 | 2010 | 2011 | 2012 | 2013 | 2014 | 2015 | 2016 | 2017 |
|---|---|---|---|---|---|---|---|---|---|---|---|
| **Total** | **83.3** | **67.6** | **130.8** | **132.4** | **148.0** | **150.2** | **144.6** | **130.1** | **117.6** | **117.3** | **123.3** |
| Gold stock | 11.1 | 11.0 | 11.0 | 11.0 | 11.0 | 11.0 | 11.0 | 11.0 | 11.0 | 11.0 | 11.0 |
| Special drawing rights | 11.0 | 10.5 | 57.8 | 56.8 | 55.0 | 55.1 | 55.2 | 51.9 | 49.7 | 48.9 | 51.9 |
| Reserve position in IMF [1] | 52.2 | 14.8 | 11.4 | 12.5 | 30.1 | 34.2 | 30.8 | 25.2 | 17.6 | 18.4 | 17.6 |
| Foreign currencies | 9.1 | 31.2 | 50.5 | 52.1 | 51.9 | 49.9 | 47.6 | 41.9 | 39.2 | 39.0 | 42.8 |

[1] International Monetary Fund.

Source: Data prior to 2005, U.S. Department of the Treasury, *Treasury Bulletin*. Beginning in 2005, Board of Governors of the Federal Reserve System, "International Summary Statistics," February 2019 and earlier releases, <https://www.federalreserve.gov/data.htm>.

## Table 1312. U.S. International Investment Position by Type of Investment: 2010 to 2018

[In billions of dollars (-2,512 represents -$2,512,000,000,000). Estimates as of end of 4th quarter. Minus sign (-) indicates loss or deficit]

| Type of investment | 2010 | 2013 | 2014 | 2015 | 2016 | 2017 | 2018 |
|---|---|---|---|---|---|---|---|
| **U.S. net international investment position** | **-2,512** | **-5,369** | **-6,945** | **-7,462** | **-8,192** | **-7,743** | **-9,555** |
| Net international investment position excluding financial derivatives | -2,622 | -5,446 | -7,031 | -7,516 | -8,250 | -7,781 | -9,592 |
| Financial derivatives other than reserves, net | 110 | 78 | 86 | 54 | 58 | 38 | 38 |
| **U.S. assets** | **21,768** | **24,145** | **24,883** | **23,431** | **24,060** | **27,773** | **25,241** |
| Assets excluding financial derivatives | 18,116 | 21,128 | 21,631 | 20,987 | 21,839 | 26,212 | 23,749 |
| Financial derivatives other than reserves, gross positive fair value | 3,652 | 3,017 | 3,252 | 2,443 | 2,220 | 1,561 | 1,492 |
| By functional category: | | | | | | | |
| Direct investment at market value | 5,486 | 7,121 | 7,242 | 7,057 | 7,422 | 8,910 | 7,504 |
| Equity | 4,621 | 6,054 | 6,060 | 5,812 | 6,201 | 7,646 | 6,184 |
| Debt instruments | 866 | 1,066 | 1,183 | 1,245 | 1,221 | 1,264 | 1,320 |
| Portfolio investment | 7,160 | 9,206 | 9,704 | 9,570 | 10,011 | 12,571 | 11,491 |
| Equity and investment fund shares | 4,900 | 6,473 | 6,771 | 6,756 | 7,146 | 9,118 | 7,996 |
| Debt securities | 2,260 | 2,733 | 2,934 | 2,814 | 2,865 | 3,453 | 3,495 |
| Financial derivatives other than reserves, gross positive fair value | 3,652 | 3,017 | 3,252 | 2,443 | 2,220 | 1,561 | 1,492 |
| Over-the-counter contracts | 3,622 | 2,980 | 3,182 | 2,400 | 2,184 | 1,497 | 1,434 |
| Exchange-traded contracts | 31 | 37 | 70 | 44 | 37 | 64 | 58 |
| Other investment | 4,980 | 4,353 | 4,250 | 3,976 | 3,999 | 4,281 | 4,305 |
| Currency and deposits | 2,767 | 1,976 | 1,807 | 1,633 | 1,572 | 1,775 | 1,826 |
| Loans | 2,162 | 2,323 | 2,396 | 2,299 | 2,381 | 2,454 | 2,426 |
| Trade credit and advances | 51 | 53 | 47 | 45 | 45 | 52 | 52 |
| Reserve assets | 489 | 448 | 434 | 384 | 407 | 450 | 449 |
| Monetary gold | 368 | 315 | 315 | 277 | 301 | 338 | 334 |
| Special drawing rights | 57 | 55 | 52 | 50 | 49 | 52 | 51 |
| Reserve position in the International Monetary Fund | 12 | 31 | 25 | 18 | 18 | 18 | 22 |
| Other reserve assets | 52 | 47 | 42 | 39 | 39 | 43 | 42 |
| **U.S. liabilities** | **24,280** | **29,513** | **31,828** | **30,892** | **32,252** | **35,516** | **34,796** |
| Liabilities excluding financial derivatives | 20,738 | 26,574 | 28,662 | 28,503 | 30,090 | 33,993 | 33,342 |
| Financial derivatives other than reserves, gross negative fair value | 3,542 | 2,940 | 3,167 | 2,389 | 2,162 | 1,523 | 1,455 |
| By functional category: | | | | | | | |
| Direct investment at market value | 4,099 | 5,815 | 6,379 | 6,729 | 7,596 | 8,925 | 8,483 |
| Equity | 2,928 | 4,443 | 4,896 | 5,110 | 5,851 | 7,133 | 6,797 |
| Debt instruments | 1,171 | 1,372 | 1,483 | 1,619 | 1,745 | 1,793 | 1,686 |
| Portfolio investment | 11,869 | 15,541 | 16,922 | 16,646 | 17,360 | 19,398 | 18,716 |
| Equity and investment fund shares | 3,546 | 5,865 | 6,643 | 6,209 | 6,570 | 7,942 | 7,420 |
| Debt securities | 8,323 | 9,677 | 10,279 | 10,437 | 10,790 | 11,457 | 11,296 |
| Financial derivatives other than reserves, gross negative fair value | 3,542 | 2,940 | 3,167 | 2,389 | 2,162 | 1,523 | 1,455 |
| Over-the-counter contracts | 3,512 | 2,903 | 3,101 | 2,346 | 2,122 | 1,461 | 1,395 |
| Exchange-traded contracts | 30 | 37 | 66 | 43 | 40 | 62 | 60 |
| Other investment | 4,769 | 5,218 | 5,361 | 5,128 | 5,133 | 5,669 | 6,142 |
| Currency and deposits | 2,365 | 2,674 | 2,891 | 2,947 | 2,967 | 3,228 | 3,255 |
| Loans | 2,238 | 2,345 | 2,264 | 1,970 | 1,950 | 2,207 | 2,639 |
| Trade credit and advances | 112 | 144 | 155 | 162 | 168 | 184 | 199 |
| Special drawing rights allocations | 54 | 54 | 51 | 49 | 47 | 50 | 49 |

Source: U.S. Bureau of Economic Analysis, International Economic Accounts, International Investment Position, "Table 1.2 U.S. Net International Investment Position at the End of the Period, Expanded Detail," <http://www.bea.gov/iTable/index_ita.cfm>, accessed July 2019. See also <http://www.bea.gov/international/Index.htm>.

# Table 1313. International Service Transactions by Selected Type of Service and Selected Country: 2000 to 2018

[In millions of dollars (290,381 represents $290,381,000,000). Country data are based on information available from U.S. reporting sources. In some instances, the statistics may not necessarily reflect the ultimate foreign transactor. N.i.e. is not included elsewhere]

| Type of service and country | Exports | | | | Imports | | | |
|---|---|---|---|---|---|---|---|---|
| | 2000 | 2010 | 2017 | 2018 | 2000 | 2010 | 2017 | 2018 |
| Services, total.......................... | 290,381 | 562,759 | 798,957 | 826,980 | 216,115 | 409,313 | 543,880 | 567,322 |
| TYPE OF SERVICE | | | | | | | | |
| Maintenance and repair services n.i.e. [1].......... | 5,011 | 14,549 | 26,880 | 30,968 | 2,569 | 6,909 | 8,400 | 8,718 |
| Transport................................ | 45,758 | 71,656 | 88,836 | 92,852 | 57,606 | 74,628 | 101,756 | 108,202 |
| Sea transport........................ | 11,554 | 15,905 | 18,707 | 19,514 | 21,787 | 29,496 | 37,058 | 39,014 |
| Air transport [2]...................... | 31,267 | 51,579 | 65,505 | 68,188 | 32,678 | 41,377 | 60,821 | 65,329 |
| Passenger........................ | 20,197 | 30,987 | 40,889 | 41,465 | 20,397 | 23,426 | 38,892 | 42,043 |
| Other modes of transport [3]......... | 2,938 | 4,172 | 4,625 | 5,149 | 3,141 | 3,755 | 3,877 | 3,860 |
| Travel.................................. | 100,187 | 137,010 | 210,655 | 214,680 | 65,787 | 86,623 | 134,868 | 144,463 |
| Business............................ | 42,664 | 39,523 | 39,294 | 38,814 | 22,640 | 21,274 | 16,641 | 16,411 |
| Expenditures by border, seasonal, and other short-term workers................. | 5,975 | 6,344 | 8,161 | 8,401 | 366 | 1,065 | 1,396 | 1,444 |
| Other business travel............. | 36,689 | 33,179 | 31,133 | 30,413 | 22,274 | 20,209 | 15,244 | 14,967 |
| Personal............................ | 57,523 | 97,487 | 171,361 | 175,866 | 43,147 | 65,349 | 118,227 | 128,052 |
| Health related.................... | 1,501 | 2,876 | 3,925 | 4,097 | 155 | 1,019 | 2,316 | 2,606 |
| Education related................. | 10,348 | 20,937 | 42,395 | 44,715 | 2,032 | 5,468 | 8,118 | 8,661 |
| Other personal travel............. | 45,674 | 73,674 | 125,041 | 127,054 | 40,960 | 58,862 | 107,793 | 116,785 |
| Insurance services.................... | 3,631 | 14,397 | 18,015 | 17,466 | 11,284 | 61,478 | 50,599 | 42,485 |
| Direct insurance.................... | 628 | 4,029 | 1,839 | 1,887 | 1,683 | 4,374 | 3,778 | 3,453 |
| Reinsurance........................ | 3,002 | 8,981 | 14,466 | 14,308 | 9,601 | 55,660 | 45,111 | 37,241 |
| Auxiliary insurance services [4]....... | (NA) | 1,387 | 1,710 | 1,270 | (NA) | 1,444 | 1,711 | 1,792 |
| Financial services [2]................... | 22,117 | 72,348 | 109,203 | 112,015 | 10,936 | 15,502 | 28,957 | 31,298 |
| Financial management, financial advisory, and custody services............ | (NA) | 27,319 | 53,553 | 53,335 | (NA) | 4,105 | 12,192 | 12,651 |
| Credit card and other credit-related services..... | (NA) | 10,460 | 22,852 | 25,766 | (NA) | 3,702 | 8,149 | 9,378 |
| Charges for the use of intellectual property n.i.e. [2]............................ | 51,808 | 107,521 | 126,523 | 128,748 | 16,606 | 32,551 | 53,440 | 56,117 |
| Industrial processes.................. | (NA) | 36,333 | 45,506 | 45,287 | (NA) | 18,847 | 24,934 | 25,069 |
| Computer software [5]................. | (NA) | 36,008 | 36,423 | 37,642 | (NA) | 5,228 | 9,969 | 10,333 |
| Trademarks and franchise fees......... | (NA) | 19,131 | 22,636 | 23,997 | (NA) | 4,635 | 4,564 | 4,170 |
| Audio-visual and related products....... | (NA) | 15,886 | 21,867 | 21,750 | (NA) | 3,627 | 13,804 | 16,396 |
| Telecommunications, computer, and information services................ | 12,215 | 25,038 | 42,001 | 43,196 | 12,397 | 29,015 | 39,628 | 41,190 |
| Telecommunications services......... | 5,266 | 10,911 | 10,828 | 9,354 | 6,167 | 7,986 | 5,329 | 5,747 |
| Computer services.................. | 4,358 | 8,991 | 22,864 | 24,455 | 5,934 | 19,407 | 31,764 | 32,864 |
| Information services................. | 2,591 | 5,137 | 8,309 | 9,386 | 295 | 1,622 | 2,536 | 2,579 |
| Other business services............... | 40,497 | 101,029 | 157,190 | 165,821 | 24,414 | 70,646 | 104,185 | 111,874 |
| Research and development services...... | 7,116 | 22,446 | 42,232 | 42,555 | 3,346 | 22,170 | 35,231 | 34,618 |
| Professional and management consulting services.......................... | 17,621 | 46,749 | 78,940 | 86,828 | 10,648 | 27,690 | 42,156 | 47,612 |
| Technical, trade-related, and other business services [6]................ | 15,760 | 31,834 | 36,019 | 36,439 | 10,420 | 20,786 | 26,799 | 29,644 |
| Government goods and services n.i.e. [7].......... | 9,156 | 19,210 | 19,653 | 21,235 | 14,516 | 31,960 | 22,047 | 22,975 |
| AREA AND COUNTRY | | | | | | | | |
| Europe................................. | 107,416 | 214,164 | 298,772 | 311,510 | 97,718 | 172,108 | 233,891 | 236,447 |
| European Union...................... | 93,485 | 179,237 | 244,297 | 253,593 | 84,215 | 143,615 | 192,597 | 198,621 |
| Euro Area [8]........................ | 56,433 | 110,572 | 155,701 | 160,270 | 52,511 | 90,824 | 122,716 | 123,847 |
| France.......................... | 10,351 | 16,761 | 19,605 | 21,136 | 10,842 | 15,820 | 18,073 | 18,507 |
| Germany........................ | 15,848 | 24,896 | 32,516 | 34,764 | 15,822 | 28,397 | 35,440 | 33,613 |
| Italy............................ | 5,706 | 8,452 | 9,360 | 9,995 | 6,824 | 9,552 | 12,373 | 13,362 |
| Netherlands...................... | 7,052 | 12,990 | 17,305 | 17,874 | 5,978 | 8,061 | 11,311 | 12,645 |
| United Kingdom.................... | 31,706 | 53,568 | 70,010 | 74,064 | 27,238 | 42,307 | 57,020 | 60,717 |
| Canada.............................. | 24,808 | 53,126 | 58,237 | 64,057 | 18,239 | 27,351 | 33,201 | 35,859 |
| Latin America, other Western Hemisphere......... | 54,194 | 106,293 | 155,009 | 157,172 | 38,752 | 87,596 | 103,422 | 107,142 |
| Brazil............................... | 6,494 | 18,405 | 26,911 | 28,250 | 1,530 | 5,143 | 7,116 | 6,124 |
| Mexico.............................. | 15,780 | 24,614 | 32,545 | 33,804 | 11,200 | 13,966 | 25,481 | 25,799 |
| Asia and Pacific....................... | 83,301 | 153,455 | 238,591 | 242,959 | 48,509 | 95,203 | 144,788 | 154,835 |
| Australia............................ | 5,719 | 15,690 | 21,968 | 21,856 | 2,637 | 5,269 | 7,745 | 8,190 |
| China............................... | 5,099 | 22,500 | 56,009 | 57,140 | 3,202 | 10,609 | 17,454 | 18,341 |
| Hong Kong.......................... | 3,652 | 5,775 | 10,619 | 12,818 | 4,017 | 6,419 | 9,727 | 10,480 |
| India................................ | 2,789 | 10,322 | 23,647 | 25,200 | 1,909 | 14,711 | 28,201 | 29,586 |
| Japan............................... | 36,862 | 43,259 | 45,987 | 45,197 | 16,326 | 24,589 | 33,287 | 34,727 |
| Korea, South........................ | 6,661 | 15,451 | 23,874 | 22,302 | 5,699 | 9,334 | 10,859 | 12,330 |
| Singapore........................... | 6,358 | 10,380 | 21,189 | 21,733 | 1,995 | 4,279 | 7,701 | 9,395 |
| Taiwan.............................. | 5,380 | 9,742 | 9,885 | 10,027 | 3,693 | 5,865 | 8,049 | 8,262 |
| Middle East............................ | 9,101 | 21,148 | 31,386 | 33,303 | 5,234 | 18,049 | 18,605 | 20,508 |
| Africa.................................. | 6,184 | 11,997 | 14,710 | 15,719 | 3,710 | 7,934 | 9,715 | 10,817 |
| International organizations and unallocated....... | 5,377 | 2,576 | 2,252 | 2,260 | 3,954 | 1,071 | 259 | 1,714 |

NA Not available. [1] Covers maintenance and repair services by residents of country on goods owned by residents of another country. Excludes transportation equipment, construction, and computer maintenance and repair. [2] Includes other types not shown separately. [3] Includes freight services performed by truck, rail, pipeline, in space, and port services for rail and water transport. [4] Includes agents' commissions, brokerage services, insurance consulting services, actuarial services, and other insurance services. [5] Includes receipts and payments for rights to reproduce and distribute. Excludes licenses for use; these licenses are included under computer services. [6] Includes construction, architectural and engineering services, waste treatment, operational leasing, trade-related, and other business services. [7] See footnote 3, Table 1310. Exports include transfers under U.S. military sales contracts; imports include direct defense expenditures. [8] Euro area refers to European Union member countries that have adopted the Euro as the common currency. Data for each year cover only member countries in that year.

Source: U.S. Bureau of Economic Analysis, International Economic Accounts, International Transactions, "Table 3.1. U.S. International Trade in Services," and "Table 3.3. U.S. International Trade in Services by Area and Country, Not Seasonally Adjusted Detail," <http://www.bea.gov/international/index.htm>, accessed July 2019.

# Table 1314. U.S. Balances on International Transactions by Area and Selected Country: 2017 and 2018

[In millions of dollars (-439,646 represents -$439,646,000,000). Country data are based on information available from U.S. reporting sources. In some instances, the statistics may not necessarily reflect the ultimate foreign transactor. With the June 2017 data release, the Bureau of Economic Analysis has incorporated a new data source, an improved estimation methodology, newly available and revised source data, and updated seasonal adjustments beginning with statistics for 1999. Data here are not comparable to data presented in previous editions; for details see <https://www.bea.gov/newsreleases/international/transactions/transnewsrelease.htm>. Minus sign (-) indicates debits]

| Area or country | 2017, balance on— | | | | 2018, balance on— | | | |
|---|---|---|---|---|---|---|---|---|
| | Current account | Goods | Services | Primary income [1] | Current account | Goods | Services | Primary income [1] |
| **All areas** | **-439,646** | **-805,200** | **255,077** | **225,799** | **-490,978** | **-887,338** | **259,659** | **253,985** |
| Europe | 1,825 | -174,776 | 64,881 | 117,687 | -3,558 | -202,474 | 75,063 | 124,568 |
| European Union | 14,815 | -152,880 | 51,700 | 108,136 | 3,890 | -169,597 | 54,973 | 112,009 |
| Euro Area [2] | -23,859 | -134,010 | 32,985 | 76,588 | -46,733 | -152,758 | 36,423 | 68,335 |
| Germany | -65,756 | -63,965 | -2,924 | -4,283 | -80,426 | -68,523 | 1,151 | -13,391 |
| Italy | -32,542 | -31,637 | -3,014 | 2,742 | -33,569 | -32,087 | -3,367 | 2,548 |
| Netherlands | 97,929 | 23,285 | 5,993 | 68,516 | 105,855 | 23,839 | 5,230 | 76,667 |
| United Kingdom | 53,259 | 2,655 | 12,991 | 30,715 | 65,735 | 5,282 | 13,347 | 43,268 |
| Canada | 13,818 | -22,222 | 25,036 | 12,138 | 15,364 | -24,559 | 28,198 | 12,919 |
| Latin America, other Western Hemisphere | 69,505 | -39,067 | 51,587 | 88,493 | 71,863 | -44,183 | 50,030 | 99,030 |
| Brazil | 33,341 | 9,366 | 19,796 | 4,352 | 36,831 | 9,615 | 22,126 | 3,909 |
| Mexico | -81,480 | -74,471 | 7,064 | 856 | -93,729 | -86,584 | 8,004 | -294 |
| Asia and Pacific | -503,861 | -558,192 | 93,803 | -3,964 | -542,451 | -598,650 | 88,124 | 5,746 |
| Australia | 38,988 | 14,432 | 14,223 | 11,696 | 39,519 | 15,257 | 13,666 | 11,407 |
| China | -358,080 | -375,758 | 38,554 | -16,633 | -404,246 | -419,603 | 38,799 | -19,165 |
| Hong Kong | 38,100 | 32,855 | 892 | 4,278 | 38,855 | 31,424 | 2,337 | 4,892 |
| India | -34,226 | -22,960 | -4,554 | 5,074 | -32,348 | -20,894 | -4,386 | 4,768 |
| Japan | -78,397 | -69,911 | 12,700 | -25,125 | -80,144 | -68,451 | 10,470 | -24,152 |
| Korea, South | -12,072 | -22,527 | 13,015 | -665 | -9,581 | -17,394 | 9,973 | -653 |
| Singapore | 44,909 | 9,992 | 13,489 | 21,250 | 49,498 | 5,979 | 12,337 | 31,131 |
| Taiwan | -27,425 | -16,149 | 1,836 | -11,784 | -26,300 | -14,519 | 1,765 | -12,231 |
| Middle East | -3,042 | 391 | 12,781 | -4,662 | -13,094 | -7,703 | 12,795 | -6,283 |
| Africa | -18,864 | -11,544 | 4,995 | 5,456 | -18,985 | -10,039 | 4,902 | 6,349 |
| International organizations and unallocated | 974 | 210 | 1,993 | 10,652 | -117 | 270 | 546 | 11,656 |

[1] Primary income consists of investment income and compensation of employees. [2] Euro area refers to European Union member countries that have adopted the Euro as the common currency. For the 2017 and 2018 data, this includes the countries that had adopted the Euro as of January 1, 2017: Austria, Belgium, Cyprus, Estonia, Finland, France, Germany, Greece, Ireland, Italy, Latvia, Luxembourg, Malta, Netherlands, Portugal, Slovakia, Slovenia, and Spain.

Source: U.S. Bureau of Economic Analysis, International Transactions (ITA), "Table 1.1. U.S. International Transactions" and "Table 1.3. U.S. International Transactions, Expanded Detail by Area and Country," <https://apps.bea.gov/iTable/index_ita.cfm>, accessed July 2019.

# Table 1315. Employment of Majority-Owned U.S. Affiliates of Foreign Companies by State: 2010 to 2016

[In thousands (5,435.4 represents 5,435,400). Covers full-time and part-time employees on the payroll, generally at the end of the fiscal year. A U.S. majority-owned affiliate is a U.S. business enterprise in which a foreign entity has a direct or indirect voting interest greater than 50 percent]

| State and other area | 2010 | 2014 | 2015 | 2016 | State and other area | 2010 | 2014 | 2015 | 2016 |
|---|---|---|---|---|---|---|---|---|---|
| **Total** | **5,435.4** | **6,613.3** | **6,822.8** | **7,087.9** | Montana | 6.3 | 7.2 | 6.8 | 7.2 |
| | | | | | Nebraska | 23.9 | 32.6 | 31.4 | 32.1 |
| Alabama | 81.9 | 93.0 | 104.6 | 109.1 | Nevada | 39.0 | 51.2 | 47.8 | 48.1 |
| Alaska | 14.1 | 17.9 | 16.3 | 17.2 | New Hampshire | 39.3 | 43.6 | 41.2 | 43.3 |
| Arizona | 77.0 | 95.7 | 104.4 | 108.9 | New Jersey | 222.9 | 265.6 | 270.7 | 283.6 |
| Arkansas | 35.9 | 47.0 | 46.1 | 47.0 | New Mexico | 15.3 | 20.8 | 16.9 | 18.0 |
| California | 584.0 | 689.2 | 734.2 | 769.2 | New York | 398.9 | 448.1 | 477.9 | 499.1 |
| Colorado | 80.9 | 100.6 | 105.0 | 107.4 | North Carolina | 194.7 | 242.0 | 252.6 | 260.4 |
| Connecticut | 100.9 | 102.5 | 102.6 | 105.3 | North Dakota | 11.5 | 13.5 | 13.0 | 12.6 |
| Delaware | 26.7 | 26.5 | 25.2 | 25.0 | Ohio | 210.2 | 254.2 | 257.7 | 267.5 |
| District of Columbia | 22.4 | 23.5 | 23.5 | 24.3 | Oklahoma | 38.6 | 48.8 | 49.6 | 51.8 |
| Florida | 232.9 | 312.7 | 331.2 | 348.8 | Oregon | 43.0 | 59.1 | 60.6 | 65.3 |
| Georgia | 189.5 | 218.4 | 228.9 | 239.2 | Pennsylvania | 261.3 | 296.0 | 291.4 | 301.0 |
| Hawaii | 26.8 | 37.2 | 36.7 | 37.2 | Rhode Island | 26.1 | 30.9 | 25.5 | 26.5 |
| Idaho | 13.4 | 17.3 | 15.6 | 15.4 | South Carolina | 108.4 | 129.0 | 134.6 | 140.4 |
| Illinois | 252.7 | 313.8 | 321.7 | 340.5 | South Dakota | 7.2 | 13.3 | 11.9 | 12.1 |
| Indiana | 136.0 | 186.2 | 189.7 | 193.0 | Tennessee | 117.2 | 152.5 | 164.2 | 177.1 |
| Iowa | 44.9 | 55.4 | 59.9 | 60.3 | Texas | 451.4 | 559.9 | 588.5 | 596.9 |
| Kansas | 54.5 | 57.3 | 56.1 | 58.0 | Utah | 31.4 | 40.8 | 42.6 | 47.8 |
| Kentucky | 89.2 | 112.4 | 120.2 | 129.4 | Vermont | 11.1 | 12.3 | 11.0 | 11.1 |
| Louisiana | 56.1 | 67.7 | 67.5 | 67.7 | Virginia | 147.8 | 173.3 | 180.6 | 187.2 |
| Maine | 30.3 | 33.4 | 34.3 | 34.2 | Washington | 94.4 | 109.1 | 113.3 | 115.5 |
| Maryland | 101.6 | 113.0 | 116.9 | 118.3 | West Virginia | 28.7 | 28.7 | 29.4 | 28.9 |
| Massachusetts | 187.3 | 216.2 | 203.0 | 213.7 | Wisconsin | 77.5 | 96.4 | 97.3 | 98.6 |
| Michigan | 145.4 | 238.4 | 243.3 | 250.3 | Wyoming | 7.8 | 8.5 | 7.2 | 7.3 |
| Minnesota | 90.7 | 107.8 | 113.9 | 119.7 | Puerto Rico | 21.9 | 24.4 | 24.0 | 25.0 |
| Mississippi | 26.8 | 37.3 | 37.4 | 37.9 | Other U.S. areas | 13.9 | 23.8 | 24.2 | 23.5 |
| Missouri | 81.7 | 105.0 | 109.8 | 119.2 | Foreign | 2.3 | 2.3 | ([1]) | ([1]) |

[1] 2,500 to 4,999 employees.

Source: U.S. Bureau of Economic Analysis, International Economic Accounts, "Direct Investment and Multinational Enterprises (MNEs)," <http://www.bea.gov/iTable/index_MNC.cfm>, accessed December 2018.

## Table 1316. New Foreign Direct Investment in the U.S. by Industry of U.S. Business Enterprise and Country of Ultimate Beneficial Owner: 2017 and 2018

[In millions of dollars (272,756 represents $272,756,000,000). Data shown are first year expenditures by foreign direct investors to acquire, establish, or expand U.S. businesses. First year expenditures include those expenditures in the calendar year in which the transaction occurred. A U.S. business enterprise is categorized as "acquired" if a foreign entity acquired a 10 percent or more voting interest in an incorporated U.S. business, or an equivalent interest of an unincorporated U.S. business, either directly or indirectly through an existing U.S. affiliate. A U.S. business enterprise is categorized as "established" if a foreign entity or existing U.S. affiliate of a foreign entity establishes a new legal entity in the U.S. in which the foreign entity owns 10 percent or more of the new business enterprise's voting interest, or an equivalent interest if unincorporated. An existing U.S. affiliate is categorized as "expanded" if it expands its operations to include a new facility where business is conducted and the expansion has a projected total cost of more than $3 million]

| Industry and country | 2017 | | | | 2018 | | | |
|---|---|---|---|---|---|---|---|---|
| | Total | U.S. businesses acquired | U.S. businesses established | U.S. businesses expanded | Total | U.S. businesses acquired | U.S. businesses established | U.S. businesses expanded |
| **Total** [1] | 272,756 | 261,455 | 6,044 | 5,257 | 296,368 | 287,260 | 5,331 | 3,777 |
| **INDUSTRY** [2] | | | | | | | | |
| Manufacturing | 106,259 | 103,805 | 540 | 1,914 | 199,744 | 197,132 | 1,170 | 1,441 |
| Wholesale trade | 6,607 | 6,328 | 135 | 144 | 5,668 | 5,560 | 102 | 6 |
| Retail trade | 10,096 | 9,974 | (D) | (D) | 14,298 | 14,261 | 35 | 2 |
| Information | 26,663 | 26,306 | (D) | (D) | 16,349 | 16,046 | (D) | (D) |
| Finance and insurance | 16,485 | 15,489 | 940 | 56 | 7,501 | 7,064 | 271 | 166 |
| Real estate and rental and leasing | 19,678 | 17,206 | 2,317 | 156 | 22,077 | 19,511 | (D) | (D) |
| Professional, scientific, and technical services | 16,008 | 15,790 | 181 | 37 | 8,442 | 7,645 | 763 | 34 |
| Other industries | 70,960 | 66,558 | 1,706 | 2,695 | 22,289 | 20,042 | (D) | (D) |
| **COUNTRY** [3] | | | | | | | | |
| Canada | 69,414 | 67,714 | 384 | 1,316 | 32,466 | 30,063 | (D) | (D) |
| Europe [1] | 115,745 | 111,454 | 1,662 | 2,629 | 221,445 | 217,904 | 1,755 | 1,785 |
| France | 24,444 | 24,031 | 84 | 329 | 19,924 | 18,963 | (D) | (D) |
| Germany | 12,103 | 11,565 | 301 | 237 | (D) | (D) | 125 | 96 |
| Ireland | 7,654 | 7,601 | 7 | 46 | (D) | (D) | 2 | 4 |
| Netherlands | 5,940 | 5,323 | 17 | 599 | 4,759 | (D) | 11 | (D) |
| Switzerland | 5,740 | 5,192 | 501 | 47 | 22,426 | 22,355 | 67 | 3 |
| United Kingdom | 45,851 | 45,578 | 118 | 155 | 16,712 | 16,537 | (D) | (D) |
| Latin America/other Western Hemisphere | 4,750 | 4,415 | (D) | (D) | (D) | (D) | (D) | (D) |
| South and Central America [1] | 869 | (D) | (D) | (D) | (D) | (D) | (D) | – |
| Other Western Hemisphere [1] | 3,881 | (D) | 101 | (D) | 13,005 | (D) | 48 | – |
| Bermuda | (D) | (D) | (D) | (D) | (D) | (D) | (Z) | (D) |
| Caribbean Islands (British) | 3,138 | 3,033 | (D) | (D) | (D) | (D) | (D) | (D) |
| Africa | (D) | (D) | 31 | – | – | – | – | (D) |
| Middle East | 2,059 | 1,442 | 614 | 3 | 1,998 | 1,802 | 194 | 3 |
| Asia and Pacific [1] | 73,080 | 69,451 | 2,546 | 1,083 | 25,771 | 23,138 | 2,223 | 410 |
| Australia | 4,134 | 4,052 | (D) | (D) | 1,951 | 1,917 | 33 | (Z) |
| China | 14,994 | 14,570 | 377 | 47 | 1,791 | (D) | (D) | (D) |
| Hong Kong | 463 | (D) | 77 | (D) | 2,077 | 2,053 | 24 | – |
| Japan | 34,410 | 32,004 | 1,668 | 738 | 12,810 | 11,601 | 909 | 299 |
| South Korea | (D) | (D) | (D) | (D) | 993 | 869 | (D) | (D) |
| Singapore | 9,697 | 9,557 | (D) | (D) | 3,835 | (D) | (D) | – |

– Represents zero. D Suppressed to avoid disclosure of data of individual companies. Z Less than $500,000. [1] Includes other countries not shown separately. [2] Based on 2012 North American Industry Classification System (NAICS); see text, Section 15. [3] Country of ultimate beneficial owner (UBO). The UBO is the entity proceeding up a U.S. affiliate's ownership chain, beginning with the foreign parents, which is not owned more than 50 percent by another entity.

Source: U.S. Bureau of Economic Analysis, International Economic Accounts, "Direct Investment and Multinational Enterprises," <http://www.bea.gov/iTable/index_MNC.cfm>, accessed July 2019.

# Table 1317. Foreign Direct Investment Position in the United States on a Historical-Cost Basis: by Selected Country, 2000 to 2018, and by Industry, 2018

[In millions of dollars (1,256,867 represents $1,256,867,000,000). Foreign direct investment is defined as the ownership or control, directly or indirectly, by one foreign entity of 10 percent or more of the voting interest of a U.S. business enterprise. As used here, "entity" is synonymous with "person," used in a broad legal sense that includes any individual, branch, partnership, association, trust, corporation, or government. Data are based on surveys of U.S. affiliates of foreign companies]

| Country | All industries total | | | | 2018 | | | |
|---|---|---|---|---|---|---|---|---|
| | 2000 | 2010 | 2015 | 2017 | Total [1] | Manufacturing | Wholesale trade | Finance and insurance [2] |
| All countries............... | 1,256,867 | 2,280,044 | 3,354,907 | 4,025,492 | 4,344,610 | 1,771,552 | 446,387 | 527,345 |
| Canada........... | 114,309 | 192,463 | 323,207 | 453,127 | 511,176 | 135,836 | 57,848 | 74,748 |
| Europe [3]............. | 887,014 | 1,659,774 | 2,306,254 | 2,731,290 | 2,957,427 | 1,365,939 | 208,865 | 353,392 |
| Austria................ | 3,007 | 4,532 | 7,159 | 12,303 | 12,638 | 5,223 | (D) | 3 |
| Belgium............... | 14,787 | 69,565 | 88,121 | 103,451 | 100,166 | 55,126 | 2,677 | 6 |
| Denmark............. | 4,025 | 7,772 | 14,509 | 17,974 | 20,108 | 5,382 | 7,824 | 2 |
| Finland.............. | 8,875 | 4,943 | 6,471 | 6,507 | 13,409 | 8,004 | 2,506 | (Z) |
| France............... | 125,740 | 189,763 | 233,547 | 275,470 | 292,721 | 142,340 | 18,822 | 52,668 |
| Germany............. | 122,412 | 203,077 | 281,295 | 310,190 | 324,151 | 119,529 | 36,891 | 38,287 |
| Ireland............... | 25,523 | 24,097 | 55,861 | 147,834 | 235,701 | 98,456 | 1,756 | 16,343 |
| Italy.............. | 6,576 | 20,142 | 27,709 | 29,285 | 31,256 | 10,736 | 1,733 | 152 |
| Luxembourg.......... | 58,930 | 170,309 | 350,772 | 410,729 | 356,015 | 195,651 | 33,565 | (D) |
| Netherlands.......... | 138,894 | 234,408 | 298,782 | 367,145 | 479,039 | 266,399 | 27,181 | 48,995 |
| Norway.............. | 2,665 | 10,478 | 20,641 | 26,035 | 29,941 | (D) | (D) | 122 |
| Spain............... | 5,068 | 43,095 | 67,349 | 74,716 | 78,481 | 11,439 | 739 | (D) |
| Sweden.............. | 21,991 | 38,780 | 44,961 | 50,902 | 50,115 | 42,629 | -1,815 | 839 |
| Switzerland........... | 64,719 | 180,642 | 241,008 | 309,363 | 309,673 | 150,145 | 25,618 | 71,160 |
| United Kingdom....... | 277,613 | 400,435 | 522,954 | 540,922 | 560,914 | 230,407 | 23,458 | 89,027 |
| Latin America and other Western Hemisphere......... | 53,691 | 62,130 | 123,846 | 124,862 | 131,381 | 39,367 | (D) | (D) |
| South and Central America [3]..... | 13,384 | 17,943 | 25,261 | 26,060 | 28,510 | 11,143 | (D) | (D) |
| Brazil................ | 882 | 1,357 | 142 | -2,025 | -2,468 | -381 | -2,849 | 671 |
| Mexico............... | 7,462 | 10,970 | 15,262 | 18,011 | 18,693 | 5,324 | 1,735 | 212 |
| Venezuela............ | 792 | 3,122 | 4,186 | 4,519 | 5,481 | (D) | 23 | -1 |
| Other Western Hemisphere [3].... | 40,307 | 44,187 | 98,585 | 98,803 | 102,871 | 28,224 | 5,508 | 760 |
| Curacao............. | (X) | (X) | 1,630 | 1,339 | 1,408 | 34 | (D) | 16 |
| Netherlands Antilles............. | 3,807 | 2,819 | (X) | (X) | (X) | (X) | (X) | (X) |
| U.K. Islands, Caribbean........ | 15,191 | 38,477 | 101,725 | 87,409 | 88,481 | 15,705 | 9,986 | 16,421 |
| Africa.................. | 2,700 | 2,265 | 4,310 | 5,591 | 5,591 | 2,074 | 129 | 8 |
| Middle East [3]............... | 6,506 | 16,808 | 17,582 | 26,025 | 28,442 | 9,299 | (D) | (D) |
| Israel................ | 3,012 | 8,714 | 6,865 | 11,940 | 13,602 | 9,253 | 474 | (D) |
| Asia and Pacific [3]............... | 192,647 | 346,605 | 579,708 | 684,598 | 710,593 | 219,038 | 165,620 | 96,631 |
| Australia............. | 18,775 | 35,632 | 65,259 | 66,736 | 66,250 | 19,403 | 1,776 | 4,979 |
| China............... | 277 | 3,300 | 14,714 | 39,518 | 39,473 | 13,641 | 623 | 446 |
| Hong Kong........... | 1,493 | 4,440 | 10,981 | 11,022 | 15,716 | 1,727 | 3,194 | -35 |
| India................ | 96 | 4,102 | 9,639 | 9,819 | 9,623 | 2,334 | 167 | (D) |
| Japan................ | 159,690 | 255,012 | 401,835 | 469,047 | 484,392 | 161,809 | 111,188 | 81,423 |
| Korea, South.......... | 3,110 | 15,746 | 39,784 | 51,770 | 58,315 | 6,528 | 44,716 | 568 |
| Singapore............ | 5,087 | 21,517 | 21,585 | 22,360 | 19,665 | 7,851 | 270 | (D) |
| Taiwan.............. | 3,174 | 4,642 | 6,889 | 8,058 | 10,592 | 4,371 | 2,019 | (D) |

D Suppressed to avoid disclosure of data of individual companies. X Not applicable. Z Between -$500,000 and +$500,000. [1] Includes other industries, not shown separately. [2] Excludes depository institutions. [3] Includes other countries, not shown separately.

Source: U.S. Bureau of Economic Analysis, International Economic Accounts, "Direct Investment and Multinational Enterprises," <http://www.bea.gov/iTable/index_MNC.cfm>, accessed August 2019.

# Table 1318. U.S. Majority-Owned Affiliates of Foreign Companies—Assets, Sales, Employment, Value, Exports, and Imports by Industry of Affiliate: 2015

[In billions of dollars (13,318 represents $13,318,000,000,000), except as indicated. A majority-owned U.S. affiliate is a U.S. business enterprise in which a foreign entity ("entity" is used here in a broad legal sense including any individual, branch, partnership, association, trust, corporation, or government) has a direct or indirect voting interest greater than 50 percent]

| Industry | NAICS code [2] | Total assets | Sales | Employment (1,000) | Employee compensation | Gross property, plant, and equipment | Merchandise exports | Merchandise imports |
|---|---|---|---|---|---|---|---|---|
| All industries...................... | (X) | 13,318 | 3,994 | 6,823 | 549 | 2,256 | 369 | 693 |
| Manufacturing [1]........................ | 31-33 | 2,485 | 1,668 | 2,425 | 221 | 958 | 212 | 289 |
| Petroleum and coal products.................... | 324 | 261 | 217 | 46 | 12 | 259 | 22 | 34 |
| Chemicals........................ | 325 | 822 | 353 | 343 | 45 | 179 | 42 | 59 |
| Machinery....................... | 333 | 149 | 101 | 217 | 22 | 27 | 19 | 16 |
| Transportation equipment..................... | 336 | 362 | 393 | 506 | 40 | 179 | 59 | 109 |
| Wholesale trade...................... | 42 | 904 | 1,113 | 670 | 60 | 352 | 145 | 383 |
| Retail trade...................... | 44-45 | 111 | 178 | 594 | 21 | 69 | 1 | 16 |
| Information....................... | 51 | 404 | 150 | 295 | 27 | 102 | 1 | (Z) |
| Finance and insurance..................... | 52 | 7,934 | 347 | 400 | 73 | 110 | (D) | (Z) |
| Real estate and rental and leasing............... | 53 | 209 | 33 | 64 | 4 | 145 | (D) | (D) |
| Professional, scientific, and technical services........................ | 54 | 217 | 127 | 359 | 39 | 21 | 1 | (Z) |
| Other industries................................. | (X) | 1,055 | 379 | 2,018 | 103 | 499 | 9 | (D) |

D Suppressed to avoid disclosure of data of individual companies. X Not applicable. Z Less than $500,000,000. [1] Includes other industries not shown separately. [2] Based on the North American Industry Classification System (NAICS); see text, Section 15.

Source: U.S. Bureau of Economic Analysis, International Economic Accounts, "Foreign Direct Investment in the United States," <http://www.bea.gov/international/di1fdiop.htm>, accessed December 2018.

# Table 1319. U.S. Direct Investment Position Abroad, Capital Outflows, and Income by Industry of Foreign Affiliates: 2000 to 2018

[In millions of dollars (1,316,247 represents $1,316,247,000,000). U.S. investment abroad is the ownership or control by one U.S. person (in the broad legal sense to include any individual, partnership, corporation, or other form of organization) of 10 percent or more of the voting securities of an incorporated foreign business enterprise or an equivalent interest in an unincorporated foreign business enterprise]

| Industry | 2000 | 2005 | 2010 | 2015 | 2016 | 2017 | 2018 |
|---|---|---|---|---|---|---|---|
| **DIRECT INVESTMENT POSITION ON A HISTORICAL-COST BASIS** | | | | | | | |
| **All industries, total [1]** | **1,316,247** | **2,241,656** | **3,741,910** | **5,289,071** | **5,586,030** | **6,013,335** | **5,950,991** |
| Mining | 72,111 | 109,280 | 172,819 | 180,418 | 169,643 | 159,493 | 156,795 |
| Manufacturing [1] | 343,899 | 430,737 | 518,321 | 693,847 | 735,648 | 870,099 | 902,555 |
| Food | 23,497 | 27,638 | 47,704 | 81,914 | 76,596 | 86,403 | 90,879 |
| Chemicals | 75,807 | 106,975 | 111,327 | 151,369 | 165,242 | 213,110 | 203,002 |
| Primary and fabricated metals | 21,644 | 23,013 | 18,674 | 34,506 | 33,687 | 40,289 | 45,100 |
| Machinery | 22,229 | 26,433 | 41,285 | 45,932 | 56,221 | 62,286 | 63,981 |
| Computer and electronic products | 59,909 | 50,773 | 72,935 | 97,641 | 98,246 | 126,402 | 152,302 |
| Electrical equipment, appliances, and components | 10,005 | 15,449 | 19,941 | 17,591 | 15,029 | 17,296 | 18,027 |
| Transportation equipment | 49,887 | 50,739 | 49,636 | 62,087 | 73,112 | 84,912 | 86,189 |
| Other manufacturing | (NA) | 129,716 | 156,819 | 202,807 | 217,516 | 239,401 | 243,073 |
| Wholesale trade | 93,936 | 132,915 | 168,722 | 225,217 | 238,213 | 253,645 | 221,683 |
| Information | 52,345 | 102,848 | 126,063 | 198,689 | 207,182 | 226,576 | 286,330 |
| Depository institutions (banking) | 40,152 | 66,707 | 118,585 | 118,271 | 119,325 | 117,437 | 124,479 |
| Finance and insurance | 217,086 | 463,981 | 734,859 | 719,608 | 738,837 | 826,391 | 904,858 |
| Professional, scientific, and technical services | 32,868 | 57,164 | 81,874 | 117,646 | 124,342 | 127,093 | 138,790 |
| Holding companies (nonbank) | (NA) | 710,386 | 1,584,903 | 2,686,477 | 2,864,411 | 2,996,212 | 2,779,549 |
| **FINANCIAL OUTFLOWS [INFLOWS(-)] WITHOUT CURRENT-COST ADJUSTMENT** | | | | | | | |
| **All industries, total [1]** | **142,627** | **15,369** | **277,779** | **264,359** | **289,261** | **300,378** | **-90,623** |
| Mining | 2,174 | 12,015 | 11,884 | 416 | -4,488 | -16,672 | -4,259 |
| Manufacturing [1] | 43,002 | 28,121 | 33,320 | 43,502 | 52,609 | 77,073 | 50,911 |
| Food | 2,014 | 1,171 | 5,341 | 4,449 | 3,059 | 5,330 | 2,034 |
| Chemicals | 3,812 | 3,911 | 7,614 | 6,470 | 14,945 | 15,639 | 17,852 |
| Primary and fabricated metals | 1,233 | -703 | 546 | 503 | -923 | 4,809 | 2,025 |
| Machinery | 2,659 | 2,077 | 4,229 | 3,110 | 4,151 | 4,284 | 2,495 |
| Computer and electronic products | 17,303 | 3,607 | 6,772 | 6,440 | 12,427 | 16,218 | 13,123 |
| Electrical equipment, appliances, and components | 2,100 | 1,662 | 1,743 | 1,545 | 196 | 1,649 | 824 |
| Transportation equipment | 7,814 | -250 | -380 | 11,282 | 7,446 | 9,160 | 3,376 |
| Other manufacturing | (NA) | 16,645 | 7,456 | 9,704 | 11,307 | 19,984 | 9,182 |
| Wholesale trade | 11,938 | 12,517 | 15,487 | 9,495 | 16,629 | 11,628 | -17,785 |
| Information | 16,531 | 2,831 | 8,777 | 13,488 | 21,503 | 19,997 | 51,810 |
| Depository institutions | -1,274 | -4,751 | -4,811 | -6,448 | 2,503 | -4,445 | 5,887 |
| Finance and insurance | 21,659 | 13,079 | 21,887 | 15,632 | 13,705 | 46,542 | 110,519 |
| Professional, scientific, and technical services | 5,441 | -2,055 | 2,774 | 5,121 | 9,759 | 176 | 10,292 |
| Holding companies (nonbank) | (NA) | -66,351 | 169,743 | 161,310 | 146,599 | 125,603 | -318,841 |
| **INCOME WITHOUT CURRENT-COST ADJUSTMENT [2]** | | | | | | | |
| **All industries, total [1]** | **133,692** | **271,877** | **417,605** | **433,333** | **427,542** | **470,933** | **531,010** |
| Mining | 13,164 | 24,559 | 29,138 | 3,541 | 3,157 | 9,819 | 14,932 |
| Manufacturing [1] | 42,230 | 46,896 | 61,240 | 67,102 | 72,037 | 81,077 | 79,791 |
| Food | 2,681 | 3,558 | 4,322 | 4,149 | 3,509 | 4,180 | 4,057 |
| Chemicals | 11,552 | 13,056 | 14,088 | 18,114 | 22,280 | 24,246 | 20,039 |
| Primary and fabricated metals | 1,536 | 1,815 | 1,349 | 1,721 | 2,147 | 1,861 | 2,635 |
| Machinery | 2,257 | 2,253 | 4,465 | 3,495 | 3,922 | 4,973 | 6,458 |
| Computer and electronic products | 8,860 | 7,714 | 11,440 | 10,868 | 13,936 | 13,609 | 18,356 |
| Electrical equipment, appliances, and components | 1,079 | 1,703 | 1,653 | 1,461 | 1,041 | 1,538 | 1,373 |
| Transportation equipment | 4,107 | 1,936 | 6,471 | 10,632 | 7,699 | 9,937 | 7,991 |
| Other manufacturing | (NA) | 14,862 | 17,452 | 16,662 | 17,504 | 20,733 | 18,881 |
| Wholesale trade | 14,198 | 24,494 | 24,538 | 19,129 | 20,873 | 21,652 | 26,656 |
| Information | -964 | 10,832 | 12,229 | 14,756 | 17,485 | 17,566 | 16,781 |
| Depository institutions | 2,191 | 164 | 1,328 | 3,521 | 7,165 | 7,090 | 9,141 |
| Finance and insurance | 15,210 | 27,911 | 35,143 | 45,760 | 39,226 | 47,174 | 57,372 |
| Professional, scientific, and technical services | 3,548 | 9,272 | 8,856 | 11,145 | 13,511 | 13,909 | 9,577 |
| Holding companies (nonbank) | (NA) | 109,566 | 220,101 | 233,272 | 216,381 | 230,655 | 278,233 |

NA Not available. [1] Includes other industries, not shown separately. [2] Prior to 2006, income is shown net of withholding taxes. Beginning 2006, income is shown gross of withholding taxes.

Source: U.S. Bureau of Economic Analysis, International Economic Accounts, "Direct Investment and Multinational Enterprises," <http://www.bea.gov/iTable/index_MNC.cfm>, accessed July 2019.

# Table 1320. U.S. Direct Investment Position Abroad on a Historical-Cost Basis by Selected Country: 2000 to 2018

[In millions of dollars (1,316,247 represents $1,316,247,000,000). U.S. investment abroad is the ownership or control by one U.S. person (in the broad legal sense to include any individual, partnership, corporation, or other form of organization) of 10 percent or more of the voting securities of an incorporated foreign business enterprise or an equivalent interest in an unincorporated foreign business enterprise. Negative position can occur when a U.S. parent company's liabilities to the foreign affiliate are greater than its equity in and loans to the foreign affiliate]

| Country | 2000 | 2005 | 2010 | 2014 | 2015 | 2016 | 2017 | 2018 |
|---|---|---|---|---|---|---|---|---|
| All countries................... | 1,316,247 | 2,241,656 | 3,741,910 | 5,108,835 | 5,289,071 | 5,586,030 | 6,013,335 | 5,950,991 |
| Canada............................ | 132,472 | 231,836 | 295,206 | 370,220 | 361,954 | 365,375 | 391,208 | 401,874 |
| Europe [1]...................... | 687,320 | 1,210,679 | 2,034,559 | 2,901,039 | 3,075,567 | 3,309,782 | 3,553,429 | 3,610,432 |
| Austria........................ | 2,872 | 11,236 | 11,485 | 10,171 | 6,508 | 6,871 | 7,819 | 8,579 |
| Belgium........................ | 17,973 | 49,306 | 43,975 | 48,242 | 48,096 | 51,589 | 54,954 | 64,051 |
| Czechia........................ | 1,228 | 2,729 | 5,268 | 6,183 | 6,343 | 4,888 | 5,406 | 6,737 |
| Denmark....................... | 5,270 | 6,914 | 11,802 | 16,497 | 15,794 | 17,018 | 13,873 | 13,205 |
| Finland........................ | 1,342 | 1,950 | 1,597 | 2,765 | 1,258 | 3,200 | 3,318 | 2,482 |
| France......................... | 42,628 | 60,526 | 78,320 | 77,738 | 81,274 | 80,739 | 85,572 | 86,863 |
| Germany....................... | 55,508 | 100,473 | 103,319 | 114,421 | 120,519 | 133,696 | 136,128 | 140,331 |
| Greece......................... | 795 | 1,884 | 1,775 | -54 | 1,007 | 1,042 | 1,224 | 1,415 |
| Hungary........................ | 1,920 | 2,795 | 4,237 | 5,582 | 7,625 | 7,223 | 7,131 | 7,811 |
| Ireland........................ | 35,903 | 55,173 | 158,851 | 273,247 | 337,831 | 391,264 | 446,383 | 442,167 |
| Italy........................... | 23,484 | 24,528 | 27,137 | 30,154 | 30,869 | 30,922 | 30,708 | 38,479 |
| Luxembourg.................... | 27,849 | 79,937 | 272,206 | 596,105 | 599,001 | 640,646 | 676,418 | 713,829 |
| Netherlands................... | 115,429 | 240,205 | 514,689 | 753,546 | 829,693 | 898,495 | 936,728 | 883,188 |
| Norway......................... | 4,379 | 8,533 | 28,541 | 34,808 | 31,697 | 29,230 | 29,187 | 27,913 |
| Poland......................... | 3,884 | 5,575 | 13,152 | 13,122 | 11,872 | 11,863 | 12,604 | 12,977 |
| Portugal....................... | 2,664 | 2,138 | 2,612 | 2,067 | 1,971 | 1,985 | 2,060 | 2,825 |
| Russia......................... | 1,147 | 9,363 | 10,040 | 9,764 | 10,259 | 14,520 | 13,881 | 14,795 |
| Spain.......................... | 21,236 | 50,197 | 52,390 | 35,253 | 36,075 | 33,484 | 33,128 | 36,962 |
| Sweden......................... | 25,959 | 30,153 | 23,275 | 33,516 | 32,593 | 31,723 | 34,622 | 39,307 |
| Switzerland.................... | 55,377 | 100,692 | 119,891 | 142,886 | 171,342 | 187,048 | 249,968 | 278,044 |
| Turkey......................... | 1,826 | 2,563 | 4,155 | 3,718 | 3,798 | 3,852 | 4,266 | 4,656 |
| United Kingdom............... | 230,762 | 351,513 | 501,247 | 631,666 | 632,327 | 686,048 | 747,571 | 757,781 |
| **Latin America and other Western Hemisphere**....... | 266,576 | 379,582 | 752,788 | 898,460 | 902,642 | 929,459 | 1,008,080 | 932,320 |
| South America [1]............. | 84,220 | 73,311 | 136,598 | 144,592 | 129,303 | 135,681 | 133,972 | 140,016 |
| Argentina.................... | 17,488 | 10,103 | 11,747 | 14,727 | 14,624 | 14,057 | 14,907 | 15,196 |
| Brazil........................ | 36,717 | 30,882 | 66,963 | 69,548 | 56,847 | 66,418 | 68,272 | 70,878 |
| Chile......................... | 10,052 | 11,127 | 30,747 | 28,843 | 28,134 | 28,959 | 25,884 | 26,146 |
| Colombia..................... | 3,693 | 4,292 | 6,181 | 8,280 | 7,750 | 7,467 | 7,222 | 7,737 |
| Ecuador...................... | 832 | 941 | 1,283 | 971 | 913 | 1,036 | 779 | 898 |
| Peru.......................... | 3,130 | 5,542 | 7,196 | 8,097 | 7,573 | 5,742 | 6,370 | 6,403 |
| Venezuela.................... | 10,531 | 8,934 | 10,255 | 10,803 | 9,825 | 7,364 | 6,632 | 6,478 |
| Central America [1].......... | 73,841 | 82,496 | 97,752 | 105,731 | 112,690 | 111,723 | 121,695 | 126,571 |
| Costa Rica................... | 1,716 | 1,598 | 1,827 | 1,608 | 1,642 | 1,349 | 1,567 | 1,625 |
| Honduras..................... | 399 | 821 | 936 | 848 | 1,274 | 1,283 | 1,405 | 504 |
| Mexico....................... | 39,352 | 73,687 | 85,751 | 94,482 | 101,326 | 100,734 | 109,671 | 114,877 |
| Panama....................... | 30,758 | 4,826 | 5,156 | 4,510 | 4,447 | 4,301 | 4,706 | 5,050 |
| Other Western Hemisphere [1]..... | 108,515 | 223,775 | 518,438 | 648,137 | 660,650 | 682,056 | 752,413 | 665,733 |
| Barbados..................... | 2,141 | 3,881 | 7,524 | 14,242 | 14,084 | 20,194 | 20,368 | 33,276 |
| Bermuda...................... | 60,114 | 113,222 | 265,524 | 283,019 | 303,244 | 314,853 | 346,804 | 249,386 |
| Dominican Republic.......... | 1,143 | 815 | 1,432 | 880 | 1,079 | 1,226 | 2,140 | 2,020 |
| U.K. Islands, Caribbean....... | 33,451 | 83,164 | 191,680 | 304,005 | 303,438 | 306,512 | 331,391 | 334,477 |
| **Africa [1]**................... | 11,891 | 22,756 | 54,816 | 69,029 | 52,004 | 51,689 | 50,285 | 47,796 |
| Egypt......................... | 1,998 | 5,475 | 12,599 | (D) | 14,068 | 12,561 | 9,352 | 8,384 |
| Nigeria....................... | 470 | 1,105 | 5,058 | 4,884 | 5,872 | 4,349 | 5,774 | 5,630 |
| South Africa.................. | 3,562 | 3,969 | 6,017 | 7,346 | 6,926 | 6,659 | 7,334 | 7,621 |
| **Middle East [1]**.............. | 10,863 | 21,115 | 34,431 | 55,467 | 49,802 | 48,593 | 69,132 | 72,236 |
| Israel......................... | 3,735 | 7,978 | 9,464 | 10,387 | 10,251 | 10,325 | 26,667 | 27,144 |
| Saudi Arabia.................. | 3,661 | 3,830 | 7,436 | 8,800 | 10,025 | 10,585 | 11,085 | 11,379 |
| United Arab Emirates......... | 683 | 2,285 | 4,935 | 17,466 | 16,205 | 13,568 | 16,785 | 17,303 |
| **Asia and Pacific [1]**......... | 207,125 | 375,689 | 570,111 | 814,620 | 847,102 | 881,132 | 941,202 | 886,333 |
| Australia...................... | 34,838 | 75,669 | 125,421 | 177,420 | 160,061 | 166,430 | 168,855 | 162,983 |
| China......................... | 11,140 | 19,016 | 58,996 | 82,244 | 92,150 | 97,287 | 107,556 | 116,518 |
| Hong Kong.................... | 27,447 | 36,415 | 41,264 | 64,741 | 69,367 | 68,944 | 81,234 | 82,546 |
| India......................... | 2,379 | 7,162 | 24,666 | 33,241 | 35,361 | 38,634 | 44,458 | 45,984 |
| Indonesia.................... | 8,904 | 8,603 | 10,558 | 15,674 | 15,717 | 14,944 | 15,171 | 11,140 |
| Japan......................... | 57,091 | 81,175 | 113,523 | 104,130 | 106,932 | 124,550 | 129,064 | 125,488 |
| Korea, South................. | 8,968 | 19,760 | 26,233 | 37,454 | 38,608 | 38,493 | 41,602 | 41,532 |
| Malaysia...................... | 7,910 | 11,097 | 11,791 | 14,642 | 15,765 | 14,606 | 15,080 | 13,581 |
| New Zealand.................. | 4,271 | 5,191 | 6,724 | 9,011 | 11,427 | 11,948 | 11,938 | 11,289 |
| Philippines................... | 3,638 | 6,522 | 5,399 | 4,073 | 5,992 | 6,325 | 7,116 | 7,645 |
| Singapore..................... | 24,133 | 76,390 | 102,778 | 229,189 | 253,277 | 255,344 | 274,260 | 218,835 |
| Taiwan........................ | 7,836 | 14,356 | 22,188 | 15,942 | 15,295 | 15,935 | 17,031 | 17,530 |
| Thailand...................... | 5,824 | 10,252 | 12,999 | 18,143 | 17,942 | 18,021 | 15,006 | 17,667 |

D Suppressed to avoid disclosure of data of individual companies. [1] Includes other countries, not shown separately.

Source: U.S. Bureau of Economic Analysis, International Economic Accounts, "Direct Investment and Multinational Enterprises," <http://www.bea.gov/iTable/index_MNC.cfm>, accessed July 2019.

# Table 1321. U.S. Foreign Economic and Military Aid by Major Recipient Country: 2000 to 2017

[In millions of dollars (17,111.9 represents $17,111,900,000). For years ending September 30. Annual figures are for obligations. Total aid may not add due to rounding]

| Region/country | 2000 | 2010 | 2015 | 2016 | 2017 Total | 2017 Economic aid | 2017 Military aid |
|---|---|---|---|---|---|---|---|
| Total [1] | 17,111.9 | 48,398.0 | 49,471.6 | 49,936.6 | 49,868.3 | 35,100.4 | 14,768.0 |
| **Middle East & North Africa [1]** | **6,799.2** | **8,829.2** | **10,679.1** | **13,462.7** | **13,631.9** | **5,500.6** | **8,131.3** |
| Egypt | 2,076.1 | 1,603.1 | 1,567.3 | 1,239.2 | 1,475.6 | 173.3 | 1,302.3 |
| Iraq | 1.2 | 2,092.4 | 1,547.6 | 5,281.6 | 3,712.0 | 734.5 | 2,977.5 |
| Israel | 3,863.4 | 2,837.6 | 3,293.3 | 3,113.3 | 3,191.1 | 16.1 | 3,175.0 |
| Jordan | 448.3 | 765.8 | 1,512.6 | 1,218.8 | 1,489.5 | 1,015.6 | 473.9 |
| Lebanon | 35.0 | 158.7 | 506.9 | 418.3 | 505.4 | 418.6 | 86.8 |
| Morocco | 51.1 | 56.4 | 108.6 | 126.5 | 490.1 | 478.0 | 12.1 |
| Syria | – | 22.4 | 913.6 | 916.4 | 891.0 | 891.0 | |
| Tunisia | 7.1 | 21.2 | 123.2 | 145.8 | 194.2 | 96.7 | 97.5 |
| West Bank/Gaza [2] | 122.0 | 686.9 | 556.8 | 416.7 | 399.0 | 399.0 | |
| Yemen | 57.2 | 122.4 | 176.8 | 305.1 | 595.2 | 594.9 | 0.3 |
| **Sub-Saharan Africa [1]** | **2,025.1** | **8,434.7** | **11,358.7** | **12,582.5** | **12,686.3** | **12,187.1** | **499.2** |
| Angola | 105.4 | 99.9 | 58.3 | 67.1 | 75.6 | 75.1 | 0.5 |
| Botswana | 0.9 | 52.0 | 44.1 | 57.3 | 40.8 | 40.0 | 0.8 |
| Burkina Faso | 18.1 | 33.3 | 34.0 | 75.4 | 81.9 | 81.3 | 0.7 |
| Chad | 4.1 | 184.4 | 108.7 | 117.4 | 116.4 | 111.4 | 5.0 |
| Congo, Democratic Republic of | 32.6 | 366.2 | 469.4 | 454.2 | 493.9 | 489.7 | 4.2 |
| Ethiopia | 277.6 | 832.1 | 808.9 | 1,111.3 | 1,103.0 | 1,102.3 | 0.6 |
| Ghana | 66.8 | 110.1 | 290.2 | 711.7 | 184.3 | 179.9 | 4.4 |
| Kenya | 93.5 | 573.3 | 938.8 | 1,144.2 | 1,060.4 | 1,026.2 | 34.2 |
| Lesotho | 2.1 | 33.3 | 29.2 | 73.4 | 52.3 | 52.3 | – |
| Liberia | 22.4 | 179.8 | 770.9 | 474.2 | 212.4 | 203.0 | 9.4 |
| Madagascar | 27.4 | 58.2 | 155.6 | 103.3 | 112.7 | 112.4 | 0.3 |
| Malawi | 44.4 | 173.2 | 244.0 | 420.7 | 304.1 | 303.6 | 0.5 |
| Mali | 43.7 | 125.6 | 206.5 | 257.4 | 230.5 | 228.9 | 1.6 |
| Mozambique | 82.1 | 299.0 | 339.0 | 514.0 | 580.0 | 579.4 | 0.6 |
| Namibia | 15.5 | 89.4 | 43.4 | 53.7 | 53.8 | 53.6 | 0.1 |
| Nigeria | 112.6 | 408.5 | 592.9 | 718.7 | 851.9 | 848.4 | 3.5 |
| Rwanda | 39.0 | 173.6 | 246.5 | 268.9 | 169.8 | 168.9 | 0.9 |
| Senegal | 37.4 | 657.0 | 118.5 | 100.1 | 196.9 | 185.5 | 11.4 |
| Somalia | 13.9 | 156.2 | 252.7 | 277.0 | 583.8 | 461.1 | 122.7 |
| South Africa [3] | 56.8 | 467.2 | 355.1 | 597.2 | 511.5 | 510.6 | 0.9 |
| South Sudan [3] | – | – | 848.7 | 717.3 | 924.0 | 913.3 | 10.7 |
| Sudan | 51.0 | 893.9 | 233.7 | 239.5 | 269.3 | 269.3 | |
| Tanzania | 44.5 | 422.6 | 592.0 | 629.3 | 626.5 | 619.7 | 6.8 |
| Uganda | 76.2 | 423.8 | 588.1 | 742.7 | 740.8 | 739.7 | 1.1 |
| Zambia | 35.4 | 264.5 | 244.9 | 445.7 | 418.6 | 418.1 | 0.5 |
| Zimbabwe | 20.9 | 217.4 | 188.4 | 261.4 | 194.1 | 194.1 | |
| **Latin America & Caribbean [1]** | **2,301.2** | **4,347.6** | **3,943.6** | **2,158.0** | **2,535.3** | **2,227.0** | **308.3** |
| Bolivia | 241.1 | 91.7 | 56.0 | 1.4 | 2.3 | 2.3 | – |
| Colombia | 1,168.6 | 795.4 | 839.5 | 324.6 | 517.6 | 405.6 | 112.0 |
| El Salvador | 34.9 | 62.2 | 331.9 | 74.8 | 118.2 | 108.9 | 9.4 |
| Guatemala | 71.8 | 153.5 | 137.7 | 296.6 | 257.3 | 224.2 | 33.2 |
| Haiti | 84.5 | 1,366.2 | 502.0 | 376.7 | 306.8 | 305.1 | 1.8 |
| Honduras | 41.8 | 39.7 | 133.5 | 127.4 | 180.9 | 160.7 | 20.3 |
| Mexico | 43.9 | 718.2 | 581.5 | 86.7 | 289.9 | 238.8 | 51.1 |
| Peru | 204.2 | 203.7 | 301.7 | 95.6 | 122.5 | 103.5 | 19.0 |
| **Asia [1]** | **1,163.2** | **15,178.4** | **11,291.8** | **7,969.2** | **8,690.0** | **3,819.9** | **4,870.1** |
| Afghanistan | 54.1 | 10,873.2 | 8,131.3 | 5,060.1 | 5,730.5 | 1,309.9 | 4,420.6 |
| Bangladesh | 78.3 | 184.6 | 225.2 | 263.4 | 260.9 | 257.6 | 3.3 |
| Cambodia | 27.5 | 72.2 | 84.3 | 103.7 | 95.8 | 94.5 | 1.3 |
| India | 188.0 | 117.2 | 101.9 | 179.6 | 104.9 | 103.8 | 1.1 |
| Indonesia | 242.3 | 309.3 | 219.7 | 221.5 | 277.1 | 260.4 | 16.6 |
| Mongolia | 25.8 | 38.1 | 12.3 | 14.1 | 23.9 | 19.5 | 4.4 |
| Nepal | 22.6 | 66.8 | 263.5 | 194.3 | 192.8 | 190.3 | 2.5 |
| Pakistan | 23.8 | 2,681.7 | 1,139.9 | 779.8 | 836.8 | 555.8 | 281.0 |
| Philippines | 82.2 | 200.9 | 262.4 | 290.6 | 153.8 | 92.5 | 61.3 |
| Sri Lanka | 10.5 | 81.5 | 30.6 | 24.0 | 76.0 | 74.6 | 1.4 |
| **Oceania [1]** | **164.7** | **209.7** | **229.3** | **310.7** | **229.1** | **228.4** | **0.7** |
| Micronesia, Federated States of | 81.0 | 90.1 | 112.8 | 140.6 | 125.1 | 125.1 | – |
| **Central Asia [1]** | **1,461.9** | **2,143.2** | **1,141.2** | **884.6** | **1,067.2** | **726.9** | **340.3** |
| Armenia | 104.2 | 54.6 | 52.3 | 22.2 | 31.5 | 29.9 | 1.6 |
| Georgia | 112.4 | 229.4 | 108.9 | 96.4 | 93.4 | 53.3 | 40.1 |
| Kazakhstan | 53.4 | 331.4 | 106.3 | 34.3 | 29.4 | 17.5 | 11.9 |
| Kyrgyzstan | 47.3 | 128.3 | 61.4 | 41.2 | 61.8 | 60.9 | 0.9 |
| Moldova | 48.6 | 294.0 | 47.7 | 26.0 | 49.0 | 35.3 | 13.7 |
| Russia | 708.6 | 505.7 | 314.9 | 19.0 | 167.8 | 167.8 | – |
| Ukraine | 199.5 | 314.7 | 268.7 | 510.6 | 506.7 | 256.4 | 250.3 |
| **Eastern Europe [1]** | **1,045.3** | **707.5** | **316.6** | **366.0** | **468.0** | **341.4** | **126.6** |
| Kosovo | – | 35.0 | 52.2 | 46.0 | 101.2 | 95.8 | 5.4 |
| Poland | 84.8 | 221.2 | 11.1 | 12.6 | 11.2 | 3.0 | 8.2 |
| **Western Europe** | **24.0** | **78.6** | **117.9** | **164.3** | **199.1** | **193.9** | **5.2** |

– Represents zero. [1] Includes other countries, not shown separately, and aid not assigned to specific countries within their parent regions. [2] See footnote 6, Table 1362. [3] South Sudan seceded from Sudan in July 2011.

Source: U.S. Agency for International Development, *U.S. Overseas Loans and Grants: Obligations and Loan Authorizations, July 1, 1945–September 30, 2017*, and earlier reports. See also <https://explorer.usaid.gov/reports.html>.

## Table 1322. U.S. Foreign Economic and Military Aid Programs: 1980 to 2017

[In millions of dollars (9,682 represents $9,682,000,000). For years ending September 30. Total foreign aid programs are the sum of economic and military assistance. Major components in recent years include U.S. Agency for International Development (USAID), U.S. Department of Agriculture (USDA), U.S. Department of State, and U.S. Department of Treasury. Annual figures are in obligations]

| Year and world region | Total foreign assistance | Military assistance | Economic assistance, by funding agency | | | | | |
| --- | --- | --- | --- | --- | --- | --- | --- | --- |
| | | | Total | USAID | USDA | State Department | Treasury Department | Other U.S. agencies |
| 1980............................... | 9,682 | 2,110 | 7,572 | 4,062 | 1,437 | 459 | 1,478 | 137 |
| 1985............................... | 18,107 | 5,780 | 12,327 | 8,132 | 2,052 | 431 | 1,548 | 164 |
| 1990............................... | 16,003 | 4,959 | 11,044 | 6,964 | 1,643 | 590 | 1,469 | 377 |
| 1995............................... | 15,556 | 4,290 | 11,266 | 7,281 | 1,284 | 132 | 1,781 | 788 |
| 2000............................... | 17,112 | 5,149 | 11,963 | 5,907 | 1,936 | 2,278 | 1,110 | 731 |
| 2005............................... | 35,461 | 9,071 | 26,390 | 14,160 | 2,208 | 4,674 | 1,240 | 4,108 |
| 2006............................... | 37,255 | 12,889 | 24,366 | 11,389 | 1,983 | 5,270 | 1,127 | 4,596 |
| 2007............................... | 39,726 | 13,973 | 25,754 | 10,371 | 1,806 | 5,594 | 1,476 | 6,507 |
| 2008............................... | 46,747 | 16,457 | 30,290 | 9,800 | 2,755 | 8,969 | 1,217 | 7,550 |
| 2009............................... | 46,643 | 14,801 | 31,842 | 11,810 | 2,614 | 11,263 | 1,638 | 4,518 |
| 2010............................... | 48,398 | 14,853 | 33,546 | 12,056 | 2,562 | 11,558 | 2,245 | 5,124 |
| 2011............................... | 48,976 | 18,621 | 30,355 | 10,396 | 1,999 | 10,612 | 2,034 | 5,314 |
| 2012............................... | 50,078 | 17,861 | 32,217 | 11,304 | 2,028 | 12,628 | 2,829 | 3,429 |
| 2013............................... | 45,674 | 13,808 | 31,866 | 11,772 | 1,675 | 11,191 | 2,672 | 4,556 |
| 2014............................... | 43,110 | 10,485 | 32,625 | 10,853 | 1,728 | 13,924 | 2,735 | 3,385 |
| 2015............................... | 49,472 | 14,993 | 34,479 | 13,179 | 1,679 | 13,405 | 2,642 | 3,574 |
| 2016............................... | 49,937 | 15,498 | 34,439 | 12,414 | 1,979 | 14,025 | 2,286 | 3,735 |
| **2017, total**............... | **49,868** | **14,768** | **35,100** | **14,441** | **2,072** | **13,624** | **1,846** | **3,117** |
| Asia................................. | 8,690 | 4,870 | 3,820 | 2,240 | 76 | 1,145 | 106 | 253 |
| Eurasia............................ | 1,067 | 340 | 727 | 411 | 16 | 121 | (Z) | 179 |
| Eastern Europe................ | 468 | 127 | 341 | 233 | (Z) | 52 | – | 56 |
| Latin America and Caribbean... | 2,535 | 308 | 2,227 | 1,156 | 75 | 821 | 30 | 146 |
| Middle East and North Africa... | 13,632 | 8,131 | 5,501 | 2,966 | 288 | 1,597 | (Z) | 650 |
| Oceania........................... | 229 | 1 | 228 | 25 | – | 9 | – | 194 |
| Sub-Saharan Africa.............. | 12,686 | 499 | 12,187 | 3,721 | 1,552 | 5,895 | 253 | 767 |
| Western Europe................. | 199 | 5 | 194 | 41 | (Z) | 151 | – | 2 |
| Canada............................ | 30 | – | 30 | (Z) | (Z) | – | – | 30 |
| World, not specified............. | 10,331 | 486 | 9,845 | 3,649 | 65 | 3,833 | 1,458 | 839 |

– Represents zero. Z indicates a value less than $500,000.

Source: U.S. Agency for International Development, *U.S. Overseas Loans and Grants: Obligations and Loan Authorizations, July 1, 1945–September 30, 2017*, and earlier reports. See also <https://explorer.usaid.gov/reports.html>.

## Table 1323. U.S. International Trade in Goods by Related Parties: 2010 to 2018

[In millions of dollars (1,900,587 represents $1,900,587,000,000). "Related party trade" is trade by U.S. companies with their subsidiaries abroad as well as trade by U.S. subsidiaries of foreign companies with their parent companies]

| Country and commodity | NAICS code [2] | 2010 | 2015 | 2016 | 2017 | 2018 |
| --- | --- | --- | --- | --- | --- | --- |
| IMPORTS FOR CONSUMPTION | | | | | | |
| Total imports........................ | (X) | 1,900,587 | 2,227,237 | 2,172,183 | 2,327,360 | 2,552,407 |
| **Related party trade, imports, total [1]**........... | (X) | **922,340** | **1,113,211** | **1,070,589** | **1,140,997** | **1,249,855** |
| Mexico.............................. | (X) | 135,989 | 207,923 | 206,163 | 215,136 | 240,202 |
| Canada.............................. | (X) | 138,210 | 148,471 | 139,077 | 153,484 | 163,413 |
| China................................ | (X) | 107,007 | 131,390 | 114,521 | 123,756 | 125,826 |
| Japan................................ | (X) | 94,001 | 101,753 | 103,159 | 107,557 | 112,549 |
| Germany............................ | (X) | 54,005 | 83,616 | 76,968 | 79,413 | 87,926 |
| Ireland.............................. | (X) | 27,980 | 35,350 | 37,555 | 43,832 | 49,968 |
| Transportation equipment........ | 336 | 179,675 | 276,328 | 281,216 | 290,909 | 300,278 |
| Computer & electronic products... | 334 | 203,829 | 221,761 | 214,425 | 214,702 | 217,483 |
| Chemicals........................... | 325 | 134,018 | 152,484 | 142,603 | 155,289 | 185,199 |
| Machinery, except electrical........ | 333 | 53,722 | 81,871 | 77,484 | 86,520 | 99,647 |
| Oil & gas........................... | 211 | 80,046 | 53,351 | 41,119 | 53,977 | 69,752 |
| Electrical equipment, appliances & components......... | 335 | 33,496 | 50,007 | 49,410 | 53,467 | 58,136 |
| EXPORTS | | | | | | |
| Total exports....................... | (X) | 1,122,567 | 1,286,172 | 1,226,926 | 1,307,698 | 1,413,447 |
| **Related party trade, domestic exports, total [1]**....... | (X) | **311,693** | **382,910** | **378,842** | **409,055** | **449,150** |
| Canada.............................. | (X) | 85,861 | 91,863 | 88,885 | 97,066 | 103,349 |
| Mexico.............................. | (X) | 49,612 | 78,123 | 75,110 | 75,486 | 81,525 |
| China................................ | (X) | 13,396 | 22,196 | 25,231 | 28,344 | 27,095 |
| Netherlands........................ | (X) | 15,032 | 17,309 | 17,644 | 19,456 | 23,854 |
| Japan................................ | (X) | 16,690 | 17,702 | 16,787 | 18,579 | 21,557 |
| United Kingdom................... | (X) | 11,200 | 13,798 | 14,248 | 14,945 | 18,285 |
| Transportation equipment........ | 336 | 55,466 | 86,973 | 90,404 | 93,527 | 94,068 |
| Chemicals........................... | 325 | 64,361 | 79,695 | 77,025 | 77,798 | 83,819 |
| Machinery, except electrical........ | 333 | 32,318 | 34,338 | 31,367 | 36,710 | 39,757 |
| Computer & electronic products... | 334 | 42,795 | 38,524 | 37,012 | 37,526 | 39,508 |
| Petroleum & coal products........ | 324 | 23,367 | 24,271 | 22,393 | 29,350 | 33,464 |
| Oil & gas........................... | 211 | 4,316 | 5,362 | 7,441 | 17,350 | 33,080 |

X Not applicable. [1] Includes other countries and other commodities, not shown separately. [2] Based on the North American Industry Classification System (NAICS); see text, Section 15.

Source: U.S. Census Bureau, "NAICS Related Party Database," <https://relatedparty.ftd.census.gov/>, accessed September 2019. See also <https://www.census.gov/foreign-trade/index.html>.

# Table 1324. U.S. International Trade in Goods and Services: 2000 to 2018

[In millions of dollars (-372,517 represents -$372,517,000,000). Data are presented on a balance of payments basis and will not agree with the following merchandise trade tables in this section. Minus sign (-) indicates deficit]

| Category | 2000 | 2005 | 2010 | 2015 | 2016 | 2017 | 2018 |
|---|---|---|---|---|---|---|---|
| **TRADE BALANCE** | | | | | | | |
| **Total** | **-372,517** | **-714,245** | **-495,225** | **-498,525** | **-502,001** | **-552,277** | **-622,106** |
| Goods | -446,783 | -782,804 | -648,671 | -761,868 | -751,051 | -807,495 | -891,320 |
| Services | 74,266 | 68,558 | 153,446 | 263,343 | 249,050 | 255,219 | 269,214 |
| Maintenance and repair services, n.i.e. [1] | 2,442 | 4,609 | 7,640 | 14,371 | 16,273 | 18,093 | 21,320 |
| Transport [2] | -11,848 | -23,021 | -2,972 | -9,281 | -12,260 | -13,146 | -16,001 |
| Travel for all purposes [3] | 34,400 | 21,482 | 50,387 | 92,388 | 83,333 | 75,723 | 70,313 |
| Insurance services | -7,653 | -21,144 | -47,081 | -31,172 | -32,833 | -32,618 | -19,064 |
| Financial services | 11,181 | 27,752 | 56,846 | 76,666 | 73,632 | 80,711 | 82,253 |
| Charges for the use of intellectual property, n.i.e. [1,4] | 35,202 | 48,871 | 74,970 | 84,161 | 78,157 | 77,080 | 76,700 |
| Telecommunications, computer, and information services | -182 | -460 | -3,977 | -126 | 1,157 | 2,165 | 3,542 |
| Other business services [5] | 16,083 | 22,342 | 30,383 | 37,780 | 44,292 | 49,928 | 52,925 |
| Government goods and services, n.i.e. [1,6] | -5,360 | -11,872 | -12,750 | -1,444 | -2,702 | -2,718 | -2,776 |
| **EXPORTS** | | | | | | | |
| **Total** | **1,075,321** | **1,286,022** | **1,853,038** | **2,266,691** | **2,215,844** | **2,351,072** | **2,500,756** |
| Goods | 784,940 | 913,016 | 1,290,279 | 1,511,381 | 1,456,957 | 1,553,383 | 1,672,331 |
| Services | 290,381 | 373,006 | 562,759 | 755,310 | 758,888 | 797,690 | 828,425 |
| Maintenance and repair services, n.i.e. [1] | 5,011 | 7,624 | 14,549 | 23,384 | 25,004 | 26,430 | 30,041 |
| Transport [2] | 45,758 | 52,622 | 71,656 | 87,725 | 84,679 | 88,598 | 92,304 |
| Travel for all purposes [3] | 100,187 | 101,470 | 137,010 | 206,936 | 206,902 | 210,747 | 214,469 |
| Insurance services | 3,631 | 7,566 | 14,397 | 16,248 | 17,067 | 18,047 | 19,164 |
| Financial services | 22,117 | 39,878 | 72,348 | 102,435 | 99,384 | 109,642 | 113,043 |
| Charges for the use of intellectual property, n.i.e. [1,4] | 51,808 | 74,448 | 107,521 | 124,769 | 124,734 | 128,364 | 130,451 |
| Telecommunications, computer, and information services | 12,215 | 15,515 | 25,038 | 36,578 | 38,548 | 42,219 | 43,959 |
| Other business services [5] | 40,497 | 58,302 | 101,029 | 137,148 | 143,768 | 154,313 | 164,790 |
| Government goods and services, n.i.e. [1,6] | 9,156 | 15,582 | 19,210 | 20,087 | 18,801 | 19,329 | 20,202 |
| **IMPORTS** | | | | | | | |
| **Total** | **1,447,837** | **2,000,267** | **2,348,263** | **2,765,216** | **2,717,846** | **2,903,349** | **3,122,862** |
| Goods | 1,231,722 | 1,695,820 | 1,938,950 | 2,273,249 | 2,208,008 | 2,360,878 | 2,563,651 |
| Services | 216,115 | 304,448 | 409,313 | 491,966 | 509,838 | 542,471 | 559,211 |
| Maintenance and repair services, n.i.e. [1] | 2,569 | 3,015 | 6,909 | 9,013 | 8,731 | 8,337 | 8,721 |
| Transport [2] | 57,606 | 75,643 | 74,628 | 97,006 | 96,939 | 101,744 | 108,305 |
| Travel for all purposes [3] | 65,787 | 79,988 | 86,623 | 114,548 | 123,569 | 135,024 | 144,156 |
| Insurance services | 11,284 | 28,710 | 61,478 | 47,420 | 49,900 | 50,665 | 38,228 |
| Financial services | 10,936 | 12,126 | 15,502 | 25,769 | 25,752 | 28,931 | 30,790 |
| Charges for the use of intellectual property, n.i.e. [1,4] | 16,606 | 25,577 | 32,551 | 40,608 | 46,577 | 51,284 | 53,751 |
| Telecommunications, computer, and information services | 12,397 | 15,975 | 29,015 | 36,704 | 37,391 | 40,054 | 40,417 |
| Other business services [5] | 24,414 | 35,960 | 70,646 | 99,368 | 99,476 | 104,385 | 111,865 |
| Government goods and services, n.i.e. [1,6] | 14,516 | 27,454 | 31,960 | 21,531 | 21,503 | 22,047 | 22,978 |

[1] N.i.e. means not included elsewhere. [2] Includes passenger fares. [3] All travel purposes include 1) business travel, including expenditures by border, seasonal, and other short-term workers and 2) personal travel, including health-related and education-related travel. [4] Includes charges for the use of proprietary rights, such as patents, trademarks, and copyrights, and charges for licenses to use, reproduce, distribute, and sell or purchase intellectual property. [5] Consists of research and development services, professional and management consulting services (including advertising and market research), and technical, trade-related, and other business services. [6] Includes goods and services supplied by and to embassies, consulates, and military bases; goods and services acquired by diplomatic and military personnel in the host economy; and services supplied by and to governments not included in other categories of services.

Source: U.S. Bureau of Economic Analysis, "International Economic Accounts: Trade in Goods and Services," <http://www.bea.gov/international/index.htm#trade>, accessed May 2019.

## Table 1325. U.S. Freight Gateways—Value of Shipments: 2018

[In billions of dollars (4,206.8 represents $4,206,800,000,000), except as indicated. For the top 40 gateways ranked by value of shipments]

| Port | Rank | Total trade | Exports | Imports | Exports as a percent of total |
|---|---|---|---|---|---|
| **Total U.S. merchandise trade**........... | (X) | **4,206.8** | **1,666.0** | **2,540.8** | **39.6** |
| Top 40 gateways............... | (X) | 3,326.7 | 1,373.4 | 2,154.0 | 41.3 |
| As a percent of total............. | (X) | 79.1 | 82.4 | 84.8 | (X) |
| Los Angeles, CA................. | 1 | 298.4 | 35.8 | 262.6 | 12.0 |
| Laredo, TX...................... | 2 | 234.6 | 100.4 | 134.2 | 42.8 |
| Chicago, IL..................... | 3 | 210.5 | 52.2 | 158.3 | 24.8 |
| Newark, NJ..................... | 4 | 194.9 | 16.6 | 178.3 | 8.5 |
| JFK International Airport, NY........ | 5 | 194.8 | 93.7 | 101.0 | 48.1 |
| Houston, TX.................... | 6 | 159.4 | 89.9 | 69.5 | 56.4 |
| Detroit, MI..................... | 7 | 150.1 | 78.9 | 71.2 | 52.6 |
| New Orleans, LA................ | 8 | 137.4 | 67.5 | 69.8 | 49.2 |
| Los Angeles International Airport, CA... | 9 | 120.7 | 58.1 | 62.6 | 48.1 |
| Long Beach, CA................. | 10 | 109.1 | 34.1 | 75.0 | 31.3 |
| Port Huron, MI.................. | 11 | 105.3 | 50.4 | 54.9 | 47.9 |
| Savannah, GA................... | 12 | 102.6 | 28.2 | 74.4 | 27.5 |
| Charleston, SC.................. | 13 | 84.4 | 34.2 | 50.2 | 40.5 |
| El Paso, TX..................... | 14 | 81.4 | 31.9 | 49.5 | 39.2 |
| Buffalo-Niagara Falls, NY........... | 15 | 81.1 | 42.2 | 38.9 | 52.0 |
| Norfolk-Newport News, VA.......... | 16 | 73.7 | 24.6 | 49.1 | 33.4 |
| San Francisco International Airport, CA.. | 17 | 66.4 | 29.9 | 36.5 | 45.0 |
| Anchorage, AK.................. | 18 | 65.3 | 21.2 | 44.1 | 32.5 |
| Cleveland, OH.................. | 19 | 64.4 | 36.5 | 27.9 | 56.7 |
| Miami International Airport, FL........ | 20 | 61.7 | 36.4 | 25.3 | 59.0 |
| Baltimore, MD.................. | 21 | 59.7 | 16.8 | 42.9 | 28.1 |
| Atlanta, GA..................... | 22 | 56.8 | 20.7 | 36.1 | 36.5 |
| Dallas-Fort Worth, TX............. | 23 | 55.1 | 23.7 | 31.4 | 43.0 |
| Oakland, CA.................... | 24 | 49.8 | 19.9 | 29.9 | 39.9 |
| Tacoma, WA.................... | 25 | 49.0 | 8.9 | 40.1 | 18.1 |
| Otay Mesa, CA.................. | 26 | 48.0 | 17.3 | 30.7 | 36.1 |
| New York, NY................... | 27 | 43.7 | 34.1 | 9.6 | 77.9 |
| Hidalgo, TX..................... | 28 | 35.4 | 12.4 | 23.0 | 35.1 |
| Seattle-Tacoma International Airport, WA.. | 29 | 30.8 | 20.4 | 10.5 | 66.0 |
| Corpus Christi, TX................ | 30 | 30.4 | 23.2 | 7.2 | 76.5 |
| Eagle Pass, TX.................. | 31 | 30.3 | 8.3 | 22.0 | 27.5 |
| Seattle, WA.................... | 32 | 30.2 | 9.1 | 21.1 | 30.2 |
| Philadelphia, PA................. | 33 | 29.4 | 4.7 | 24.7 | 15.8 |
| Champlain-Rouses Point, NY........ | 34 | 27.4 | 10.8 | 16.6 | 39.4 |
| Blaine, WA..................... | 35 | 27.2 | 15.2 | 11.9 | 56.2 |
| Santa Teresa, NM................ | 36 | 26.0 | 11.7 | 14.3 | 44.8 |
| Miami, FL...................... | 37 | 25.9 | 9.8 | 16.0 | 38.0 |
| Jacksonville, FL................. | 38 | 25.7 | 6.5 | 19.2 | 25.3 |
| Pembina, ND................... | 39 | 25.1 | 13.2 | 11.9 | 52.6 |
| Nogales, AZ.................... | 40 | 24.9 | 9.8 | 15.1 | 39.4 |

X Not applicable.

Source: U.S. Census Bureau, Foreign Trade Division, "USA Trade Online," <https://usatrade.census.gov/>, accessed June 2019.

## Table 1326. U.S. Agricultural Exports by State: 2000 to 2017

[In millions of dollars (51,265 represents $51,265,000,000). Calendar year. Export estimates based on U.S. farm cash receipts. Export values are calibrated such that the sum of state export estimates for a commodity equals the total U.S. export value for the commodity]

| State | 2000 | 2010 | 2015 | 2016 | 2017 | State | 2000 | 2010 | 2015 | 2016 | 2017 |
|---|---|---|---|---|---|---|---|---|---|---|---|
| **U.S.**........ | **51,265** | **115,820** | **133,034** | **134,650** | **138,152** | MO......... | 1,348 | 3,486 | 3,613 | 3,554 | 4,027 |
| | | | | | | MT......... | 504 | 1,080 | 1,187 | 1,260 | 1,226 |
| AL.......... | 575 | 1,132 | 1,199 | 1,208 | 1,272 | NE......... | 2,301 | 5,338 | 6,467 | 6,677 | 6,397 |
| AK.......... | 6 | 11 | 16 | 17 | 17 | NV......... | 66 | 111 | 142 | 120 | 133 |
| AZ.......... | 486 | 1,070 | 1,391 | 1,454 | 1,683 | NH......... | 33 | 65 | 81 | 74 | 76 |
| AR.......... | 1,306 | 3,190 | 3,143 | 3,007 | 3,183 | NJ......... | 246 | 399 | 525 | 522 | 531 |
| CA.......... | 6,853 | 15,353 | 22,897 | 21,860 | 23,050 | NM......... | 322 | 682 | 740 | 711 | 762 |
| CO.......... | 893 | 1,510 | 1,591 | 1,541 | 1,702 | NY......... | 501 | 1,224 | 1,454 | 1,416 | 1,423 |
| CT.......... | 132 | 213 | 264 | 249 | 248 | NC......... | 1,840 | 3,382 | 3,573 | 3,389 | 3,625 |
| DE.......... | 131 | 242 | 259 | 258 | 268 | ND......... | 1,233 | 3,705 | 3,823 | 4,629 | 4,535 |
| FL.......... | 1,883 | 2,963 | 3,434 | 3,317 | 3,225 | OH......... | 1,461 | 3,408 | 3,688 | 3,660 | 3,634 |
| GA.......... | 1,301 | 2,584 | 2,819 | 2,882 | 2,804 | OK......... | 818 | 1,542 | 1,508 | 1,566 | 1,813 |
| HI.......... | 151 | 308 | 356 | 366 | 371 | OR......... | 800 | 1,354 | 1,862 | 1,808 | 1,866 |
| ID.......... | 718 | 1,490 | 1,818 | 1,872 | 1,993 | PA......... | 697 | 1,610 | 2,016 | 1,942 | 2,020 |
| IL.......... | 3,116 | 7,474 | 8,039 | 8,305 | 8,158 | RI......... | 13 | 32 | 34 | 34 | 35 |
| IN.......... | 1,710 | 4,298 | 4,673 | 4,499 | 4,600 | SC......... | 397 | 805 | 792 | 684 | 751 |
| IA.......... | 3,476 | 9,369 | 9,962 | 10,970 | 10,295 | SD......... | 1,212 | 2,969 | 3,700 | 3,952 | 3,596 |
| KS.......... | 1,955 | 4,676 | 4,165 | 4,721 | 4,831 | TN......... | 553 | 1,243 | 1,522 | 1,371 | 1,487 |
| KY.......... | 1,275 | 1,516 | 2,099 | 2,059 | 2,140 | TX......... | 2,695 | 6,321 | 5,953 | 6,057 | 7,195 |
| LA.......... | 615 | 1,512 | 1,562 | 1,326 | 1,477 | UT......... | 162 | 328 | 418 | 385 | 418 |
| ME.......... | 143 | 236 | 253 | 247 | 263 | VT......... | 49 | 140 | 194 | 196 | 201 |
| MD.......... | 338 | 565 | 656 | 647 | 654 | VA......... | 539 | 871 | 1,031 | 991 | 1,017 |
| MA.......... | 106 | 198 | 172 | 164 | 171 | WA......... | 1,313 | 2,801 | 3,645 | 3,746 | 4,005 |
| MI.......... | 911 | 2,355 | 2,857 | 2,844 | 2,710 | WV......... | 59 | 114 | 141 | 143 | 150 |
| MN.......... | 2,207 | 6,112 | 6,297 | 6,991 | 6,869 | WI......... | 921 | 2,412 | 2,844 | 2,861 | 2,937 |
| MS.......... | 750 | 1,786 | 1,858 | 1,811 | 2,005 | WY......... | 147 | 235 | 300 | 289 | 304 |

Source: U.S. Department of Agriculture, Economic Research Service, "State Export Data," <https://www.ers.usda.gov/data-products/state-export-data/>, accessed November 2018.

# Table 1327. U.S. Exports and General Imports of Merchandise by Customs District: 2010 to 2018

[In billions of dollars (1,278.5 represents $1,278,500,000,000). Exports are f.a.s. (free alongside ship) value basis; imports are on customs-value basis. General imports are a combination of entries for immediate consumption, entries into customs bonded warehouses, and entries into U.S. Foreign Trade Zones. General imports are a combination of entries for immediate consumption, entries into customs bonded warehouses, and entries into U.S. Foreign Trade Zones. These data may differ from those in Table 1323, Table 1330, and Table 1331. For methodology, see Foreign Trade Statistics in Appendix III]

| Customs district | Exports | | | | | General imports | | | | |
|---|---|---|---|---|---|---|---|---|---|---|
| | 2010 | 2015 | 2016 | 2017 | 2018 | 2010 | 2015 | 2016 | 2017 | 2018 |
| Total [1] | 1,278.5 | 1,503.3 | 1,451.5 | 1,546.5 | 1,666.0 | 1,913.9 | 2,248.8 | 2,186.8 | 2,339.9 | 2,540.8 |
| Anchorage, AK | 14.5 | 18.7 | 18.8 | 19.8 | 21.8 | 16.2 | 16.9 | 16.8 | 17.2 | 19.3 |
| Baltimore, MD | 14.7 | 15.6 | 14.2 | 16.3 | 17.3 | 28.8 | 36.8 | 36.7 | 38.9 | 43.4 |
| Boston, MA | 8.2 | 7.4 | 7.7 | 8.8 | 9.1 | 19.2 | 25.2 | 21.8 | 21.7 | 24.1 |
| Buffalo, NY | 40.6 | 47.3 | 47.2 | 42.5 | 42.2 | 39.2 | 41.6 | 40.1 | 40.0 | 40.1 |
| Charleston, SC | 19.5 | 31.7 | 33.3 | 31.1 | 34.5 | 29.4 | 47.2 | 43.3 | 44.9 | 49.0 |
| Chicago, IL | 35.8 | 46.6 | 45.7 | 48.0 | 52.5 | 125.6 | 155.2 | 152.6 | 175.5 | 199.5 |
| Cleveland, OH | 25.4 | 34.1 | 36.6 | 41.1 | 46.5 | 69.2 | 95.8 | 95.2 | 101.6 | 105.8 |
| Columbia-Snake, OR | 12.3 | 12.1 | 13.2 | 14.2 | 15.2 | 12.2 | 12.3 | 14.7 | 13.7 | 14.3 |
| Dallas-Fort Worth, TX | 18.1 | 21.9 | 22.5 | 24.3 | 24.5 | 38.4 | 52.0 | 46.8 | 51.3 | 52.6 |
| Detroit, MI | 113.2 | 120.5 | 118.9 | 129.8 | 132.7 | 106.0 | 124.7 | 129.1 | 134.5 | 137.6 |
| Duluth, MN | 2.6 | 5.0 | 4.6 | 4.7 | 5.0 | 6.8 | 8.9 | 8.6 | 9.1 | 11.0 |
| El Paso, TX | 29.3 | 41.9 | 42.5 | 40.5 | 43.8 | 44.1 | 56.9 | 59.3 | 61.4 | 67.3 |
| Great Falls, MT | 17.4 | 14.3 | 9.6 | 13.1 | 14.2 | 26.9 | 24.2 | 22.3 | 26.2 | 28.8 |
| Honolulu, HI | 7.4 | 13.9 | 10.3 | 11.8 | 12.0 | 4.6 | 4.1 | 3.1 | 3.8 | 4.4 |
| Houston-Galveston, TX | 94.5 | 109.2 | 91.7 | 109.0 | 141.4 | 116.9 | 86.2 | 69.8 | 83.0 | 92.6 |
| Laredo, TX | 81.4 | 121.7 | 118.4 | 126.1 | 134.1 | 104.2 | 163.5 | 164.4 | 176.5 | 192.7 |
| Los Angeles, CA | 105.1 | 114.1 | 118.7 | 128.5 | 130.2 | 242.7 | 279.5 | 279.2 | 302.4 | 325.7 |
| Miami, FL | 58.9 | 58.6 | 56.1 | 59.2 | 61.6 | 36.6 | 48.2 | 48.3 | 48.5 | 49.8 |
| Milwaukee, WI | 0.1 | 0.3 | 0.5 | 0.4 | 0.4 | 0.9 | 1.0 | 0.9 | 1.0 | 1.3 |
| Minneapolis, MN | 2.6 | 2.6 | 2.1 | 2.1 | 2.1 | 13.6 | 12.6 | 12.3 | 14.4 | 14.5 |
| Mobile, AL | 8.7 | 10.6 | 10.1 | 10.6 | 10.3 | 20.8 | 22.8 | 23.2 | 22.9 | 24.1 |
| New Orleans, LA | 69.1 | 84.1 | 83.5 | 95.4 | 107.5 | 125.3 | 115.2 | 109.8 | 122.0 | 131.0 |
| New York, NY | 136.3 | 143.8 | 136.3 | 136.3 | 145.1 | 190.6 | 226.5 | 220.1 | 227.8 | 247.3 |
| Nogales, AZ | 8.9 | 14.9 | 13.1 | 12.4 | 12.7 | 17.4 | 21.7 | 21.9 | 21.0 | 19.9 |
| Norfolk, VA | 21.1 | 28.8 | 26.1 | 27.1 | 24.7 | 23.9 | 34.4 | 33.8 | 34.0 | 35.3 |
| Ogdensburg, NY | 16.2 | 17.2 | 16.1 | 16.5 | 19.0 | 27.8 | 29.3 | 29.3 | 27.8 | 29.6 |
| Pembina, ND | 21.3 | 25.7 | 22.4 | 27.7 | 30.1 | 14.7 | 17.3 | 15.5 | 17.1 | 20.5 |
| Philadelphia, PA | 14.3 | 15.8 | 15.7 | 16.8 | 18.5 | 56.9 | 56.0 | 53.8 | 57.8 | 60.0 |
| Port Arthur, TX | 6.5 | 12.2 | 10.3 | 17.6 | 26.2 | 26.4 | 14.3 | 10.2 | 13.2 | 16.1 |
| Portland, ME | 4.4 | 4.3 | 4.7 | 5.1 | 5.1 | 9.8 | 14.0 | 10.9 | 12.7 | 13.8 |
| Providence, RI | 0.3 | 0.2 | 0.2 | 0.3 | 0.4 | 5.8 | 8.6 | 7.7 | 8.5 | 8.9 |
| San Diego, CA | 16.2 | 22.7 | 24.1 | 23.3 | 25.8 | 32.4 | 47.4 | 46.2 | 45.8 | 48.3 |
| San Francisco, CA | 47.1 | 47.8 | 50.8 | 54.7 | 55.6 | 60.6 | 70.0 | 68.9 | 78.2 | 86.8 |
| San Juan, PR | 19.7 | 17.3 | 15.8 | 13.0 | 14.0 | 19.4 | 20.1 | 21.8 | 18.7 | 26.8 |
| Savannah, GA | 41.0 | 47.6 | 45.8 | 49.1 | 54.2 | 68.0 | 101.1 | 98.0 | 106.7 | 119.0 |
| Seattle, WA | 58.5 | 87.9 | 82.7 | 79.8 | 78.7 | 52.6 | 66.9 | 64.6 | 69.3 | 76.5 |
| St. Albans, VT | 3.3 | 2.1 | 2.2 | 2.2 | 1.3 | 6.9 | 9.3 | 7.6 | 7.8 | 8.4 |
| St. Louis, MO | 1.0 | 1.6 | 1.8 | 2.0 | 1.3 | 6.5 | 17.3 | 15.2 | 16.6 | 19.3 |
| Tampa, FL | 14.4 | 14.7 | 11.9 | 11.0 | 11.9 | 16.4 | 25.6 | 26.5 | 29.0 | 30.2 |
| Virgin Islands, U.S. | 1.9 | 0.1 | 0.3 | 1.0 | 0.9 | 10.5 | 0.1 | 0.6 | 1.2 | 1.5 |
| Washington, DC | 6.0 | 5.1 | 5.0 | 5.9 | 7.4 | 8.2 | 7.1 | 7.7 | 6.9 | 8.3 |
| Wilmington, NC | 5.3 | 5.1 | 5.6 | 6.0 | 7.5 | 12.8 | 13.6 | 11.5 | 11.8 | 17.1 |

[1] Totals include the following special districts, not shown separately: vessels under their own power or afloat, low valued imports and exports, and mail shipments. Totals may also include data for two or more Customs Districts that have been combined and published under an arbitrary designation, as a solution to disclosure situations.

Source: U.S. Census Bureau, U.S. Foreign Trade Division, "USA Trade Online," <https://usatrade.census.gov/>, accessed July 2019.

# Table 1328. U.S. Exports of Goods by State of Origin: 2005 to 2018

[In millions of dollars (901,082 represents $901,082,000,000), except as indicated. Data are on a Census Basis. Exports are on a f.a.s. (free alongside ship) value basis and are based on origin of movement]

| State [1] | 2005 | 2009 | 2010 | 2011 | 2012 | 2013 | 2014 | 2015 | 2016 | 2017 | 2018 Total | 2018 Rank |
|---|---|---|---|---|---|---|---|---|---|---|---|---|
| Total [1] | 901,082 | 1,056,043 | 1,278,495 | 1,482,508 | 1,545,821 | 1,578,517 | 1,621,874 | 1,503,328 | 1,451,460 | 1,546,473 | 1,665,992 | (X) |
| United States | 853,292 | 1,000,269 | 1,208,081 | 1,416,625 | 1,478,314 | 1,509,865 | 1,551,164 | 1,436,224 | 1,385,513 | 1,481,005 | 1,595,412 | (X) |
| Alabama | 10,879 | 12,355 | 15,495 | 17,928 | 19,577 | 19,301 | 19,450 | 19,322 | 20,471 | 21,797 | 21,417 | 23 |
| Alaska | 3,613 | 3,270 | 4,155 | 5,259 | 4,543 | 4,528 | 5,111 | 4,620 | 4,350 | 4,941 | 4,840 | 40 |
| Arizona | 14,947 | 14,023 | 15,721 | 17,885 | 18,405 | 19,478 | 21,247 | 22,654 | 22,004 | 20,916 | 22,509 | 21 |
| Arkansas | 3,871 | 5,267 | 5,219 | 5,611 | 7,615 | 7,161 | 6,866 | 5,871 | 5,722 | 6,234 | 6,447 | 37 |
| California | 116,690 | 120,080 | 143,208 | 159,421 | 161,757 | 168,192 | 173,869 | 165,360 | 163,261 | 171,916 | 178,181 | 2 |
| Colorado | 6,773 | 5,867 | 6,726 | 7,338 | 8,170 | 8,545 | 8,364 | 7,950 | 7,569 | 8,054 | 8,329 | 33 |
| Connecticut | 9,750 | 13,979 | 16,029 | 16,233 | 15,871 | 16,427 | 15,963 | 15,242 | 14,394 | 14,791 | 17,403 | 25 |
| Delaware | 2,535 | 4,312 | 4,945 | 5,516 | 5,114 | 5,327 | 5,267 | 5,408 | 4,517 | 4,565 | 4,714 | 41 |
| District of Columbia | 823 | 1,091 | 1,483 | 1,041 | 2,014 | 2,708 | 940 | 1,088 | 1,331 | 1,483 | 2,725 | 46 |
| Florida | 33,444 | 46,888 | 55,399 | 65,010 | 66,223 | 60,482 | 58,439 | 53,903 | 52,036 | 54,895 | 57,237 | 8 |
| Georgia | 20,657 | 23,743 | 28,899 | 34,863 | 36,039 | 37,578 | 39,413 | 38,596 | 35,673 | 37,221 | 40,613 | 11 |
| Hawaii | 1,032 | 563 | 684 | 884 | 732 | 599 | 1,447 | 1,896 | 795 | 952 | 660 | 51 |
| Idaho | 3,273 | 3,877 | 5,157 | 5,913 | 6,120 | 5,789 | 5,138 | 4,302 | 4,877 | 3,863 | 4,022 | 42 |
| Illinois | 36,169 | 41,626 | 50,061 | 64,903 | 68,158 | 66,213 | 68,394 | 63,369 | 59,862 | 65,291 | 65,491 | 6 |
| Indiana | 21,594 | 22,907 | 28,764 | 32,332 | 34,399 | 34,216 | 35,589 | 33,819 | 34,653 | 37,746 | 39,330 | 12 |
| Iowa | 7,373 | 9,042 | 10,880 | 13,317 | 14,622 | 13,903 | 15,112 | 13,238 | 12,330 | 13,422 | 14,377 | 28 |
| Kansas | 6,736 | 8,917 | 9,900 | 11,623 | 11,684 | 12,459 | 12,022 | 10,689 | 10,155 | 11,244 | 11,587 | 31 |
| Kentucky | 14,961 | 17,650 | 19,346 | 20,119 | 22,132 | 25,412 | 27,757 | 27,637 | 29,192 | 30,915 | 31,810 | 17 |
| Louisiana | 19,404 | 32,616 | 41,371 | 54,971 | 62,869 | 63,247 | 64,770 | 48,679 | 48,367 | 56,826 | 67,297 | 5 |
| Maine | 2,332 | 2,231 | 3,162 | 3,422 | 3,048 | 2,687 | 2,811 | 2,762 | 2,863 | 2,711 | 2,837 | 45 |
| Maryland | 7,138 | 9,225 | 10,167 | 10,863 | 11,745 | 11,747 | 12,228 | 10,052 | 9,656 | 9,317 | 12,102 | 29 |
| Massachusetts | 22,052 | 23,593 | 26,305 | 27,871 | 25,514 | 26,812 | 27,384 | 25,289 | 25,893 | 27,563 | 27,158 | 18 |
| Michigan | 37,849 | 32,655 | 44,851 | 51,064 | 57,051 | 59,400 | 57,573 | 53,945 | 54,752 | 59,921 | 58,035 | 7 |
| Minnesota | 14,736 | 15,532 | 18,904 | 20,732 | 20,327 | 20,760 | 21,398 | 20,013 | 19,201 | 20,692 | 22,677 | 20 |
| Mississippi | 4,021 | 6,316 | 8,224 | 10,939 | 11,794 | 12,415 | 11,485 | 10,849 | 10,505 | 10,988 | 11,630 | 30 |
| Missouri | 10,514 | 9,522 | 12,925 | 14,161 | 13,903 | 12,958 | 14,190 | 13,647 | 13,935 | 14,289 | 14,531 | 26 |
| Montana | 715 | 1,053 | 1,393 | 1,592 | 1,576 | 1,506 | 1,545 | 1,404 | 1,360 | 1,616 | 1,666 | 48 |
| Nebraska | 3,003 | 4,873 | 5,821 | 7,588 | 7,455 | 7,393 | 7,890 | 6,664 | 6,381 | 7,210 | 7,952 | 35 |
| Nevada | 3,941 | 5,672 | 5,913 | 7,990 | 10,261 | 8,701 | 7,692 | 8,667 | 9,766 | 12,162 | 11,094 | 32 |
| New Hampshire | 2,557 | 3,061 | 4,368 | 4,307 | 3,488 | 3,511 | 4,233 | 4,001 | 4,143 | 5,148 | 5,306 | 39 |
| New Jersey | 21,107 | 27,244 | 32,131 | 38,172 | 37,286 | 36,612 | 36,587 | 32,063 | 31,164 | 34,258 | 35,354 | 13 |
| New Mexico | 2,543 | 1,270 | 1,543 | 2,096 | 2,958 | 2,726 | 3,802 | 3,782 | 3,616 | 3,601 | 3,657 | 43 |
| New York | 51,841 | 58,743 | 69,685 | 84,999 | 81,338 | 86,407 | 88,834 | 83,125 | 76,691 | 78,190 | 84,683 | 3 |
| North Carolina | 19,507 | 21,793 | 24,918 | 27,067 | 28,839 | 29,347 | 31,420 | 30,202 | 30,183 | 32,620 | 32,762 | 15 |
| North Dakota | 1,192 | 2,193 | 2,532 | 3,393 | 4,310 | 4,402 | 5,513 | 4,027 | 5,294 | 5,846 | 7,894 | 36 |
| Ohio | 35,110 | 34,104 | 41,505 | 46,458 | 48,819 | 51,048 | 52,641 | 51,262 | 49,330 | 50,070 | 54,404 | 9 |
| Oklahoma | 4,322 | 4,415 | 5,354 | 6,228 | 6,579 | 6,920 | 6,308 | 5,251 | 5,046 | 5,364 | 6,108 | 38 |
| Oregon | 12,407 | 14,907 | 17,684 | 18,317 | 18,388 | 18,634 | 20,889 | 20,057 | 21,772 | 21,894 | 22,335 | 22 |
| Pennsylvania | 22,334 | 28,381 | 34,943 | 41,103 | 38,852 | 41,181 | 40,411 | 39,439 | 36,453 | 38,669 | 41,193 | 10 |
| Rhode Island | 1,268 | 1,496 | 1,949 | 2,289 | 2,366 | 2,164 | 2,388 | 2,133 | 2,278 | 2,391 | 2,407 | 47 |
| South Carolina | 13,960 | 16,488 | 20,336 | 24,733 | 25,115 | 26,341 | 29,773 | 31,021 | 31,324 | 32,201 | 34,629 | 14 |
| South Dakota | 948 | 1,011 | 1,259 | 1,462 | 1,557 | 1,582 | 1,578 | 1,421 | 1,218 | 1,356 | 1,437 | 49 |
| Tennessee | 19,174 | 20,484 | 25,948 | 30,016 | 31,143 | 32,474 | 33,251 | 32,617 | 31,476 | 33,233 | 32,711 | 16 |
| Texas | 129,346 | 162,995 | 206,992 | 251,104 | 264,665 | 277,716 | 285,559 | 248,780 | 231,527 | 264,789 | 315,939 | 1 |
| Utah | 6,067 | 10,337 | 13,808 | 18,968 | 19,260 | 16,111 | 12,224 | 13,308 | 12,078 | 11,583 | 14,389 | 27 |
| Vermont | 4,672 | 3,219 | 4,278 | 4,275 | 4,139 | 4,027 | 3,670 | 3,176 | 2,993 | 2,776 | 2,920 | 44 |
| Virginia | 12,238 | 15,052 | 17,169 | 18,125 | 18,277 | 17,896 | 19,391 | 17,801 | 16,311 | 16,508 | 18,353 | 24 |
| Washington | 33,078 | 51,851 | 53,345 | 64,800 | 75,654 | 81,630 | 90,558 | 86,375 | 79,562 | 76,351 | 77,968 | 4 |
| West Virginia | 3,161 | 4,826 | 6,443 | 9,039 | 11,407 | 8,732 | 7,597 | 5,833 | 5,045 | 7,110 | 8,217 | 34 |
| Wisconsin | 14,961 | 16,725 | 19,800 | 22,069 | 23,119 | 23,110 | 23,426 | 22,442 | 21,036 | 22,305 | 22,721 | 19 |
| Wyoming | 671 | 926 | 983 | 1,219 | 1,439 | 1,351 | 1,757 | 1,175 | 1,099 | 1,196 | 1,357 | 50 |

X Not applicable. [1] Includes other areas, not shown separately, and exports with an unknown state or area of origin.

Source: U.S. Census Bureau, Foreign Trade Division, "USA Trade Online," <https://usatrade.census.gov/>, accessed June 2019. See also <http://www.census.gov/foreign-trade/data/index.html>.

# Table 1329. Value of State Exports to Top Trading Countries by State: 2018

[In millions of dollars (1,665,992 represents $1,665,992,000,000). Data are on a f.a.s. (free alongside ship) value basis. Exports are based on origin of movement]

| | Total | Canada | Mexico | China | Japan | United Kingdom | Germany | South Korea | Nether-lands |
|---|---|---|---|---|---|---|---|---|---|
| **United States** [1] | **1,665,992** | **299,769** | **265,443** | **120,148** | **75,229** | **66,313** | **57,753** | **56,507** | **48,703** |
| Alabama | 21,417 | 4,092 | 2,602 | 3,017 | 832 | 288 | 2,547 | 517 | 355 |
| Alaska | 4,840 | 647 | 33 | 1,018 | 797 | 21 | 209 | 907 | 263 |
| Arizona | 22,509 | 2,245 | 7,652 | 1,193 | 755 | 929 | 746 | 371 | 618 |
| Arkansas | 6,447 | 1,208 | 870 | 307 | 167 | 204 | 122 | 231 | 104 |
| California | 178,181 | 17,698 | 30,763 | 16,339 | 13,030 | 5,266 | 6,592 | 9,975 | 6,429 |
| Colorado | 8,329 | 1,445 | 1,254 | 577 | 456 | 220 | 301 | 494 | 305 |
| Connecticut | 17,403 | 1,963 | 948 | 942 | 628 | 1,484 | 2,332 | 423 | 770 |
| Delaware | 4,714 | 720 | 156 | 381 | 176 | 404 | 239 | 196 | 129 |
| District of Columbia | 2,725 | 9 | 23 | 3 | 8 | 457 | 43 | 2 | 8 |
| Florida | 57,237 | 3,789 | 3,334 | 2,075 | 1,012 | 2,103 | 2,294 | 782 | 1,124 |
| Georgia | 40,613 | 6,317 | 3,908 | 2,978 | 1,480 | 1,591 | 2,295 | 1,038 | 1,315 |
| Hawaii | 660 | 19 | 1 | 35 | 72 | 9 | 2 | 233 | 19 |
| Idaho | 4,022 | 928 | 229 | 418 | 215 | 189 | 58 | 108 | 94 |
| Illinois | 65,491 | 17,729 | 10,191 | 3,458 | 1,982 | 1,913 | 3,304 | 1,196 | 1,781 |
| Indiana | 39,330 | 13,375 | 5,416 | 1,967 | 2,066 | 1,191 | 1,531 | 697 | 1,008 |
| Iowa | 14,377 | 4,283 | 2,336 | 627 | 975 | 333 | 458 | 388 | 185 |
| Kansas | 11,587 | 1,948 | 2,106 | 657 | 1,008 | 528 | 475 | 413 | 121 |
| Kentucky | 31,810 | 7,775 | 2,274 | 2,233 | 1,063 | 2,962 | 1,164 | 501 | 1,316 |
| Louisiana | 67,297 | 3,568 | 9,226 | 3,015 | 2,478 | 1,766 | 585 | 3,973 | 3,356 |
| Maine | 2,837 | 1,428 | 50 | 205 | 87 | 49 | 66 | 67 | 60 |
| Maryland | 12,102 | 1,652 | 422 | 592 | 1,121 | 504 | 591 | 200 | 596 |
| Massachusetts | 27,158 | 3,028 | 2,512 | 2,639 | 1,487 | 1,102 | 1,952 | 1,239 | 1,351 |
| Michigan | 58,035 | 23,903 | 12,290 | 3,556 | 1,432 | 908 | 1,971 | 1,387 | 363 |
| Minnesota | 22,677 | 4,830 | 2,343 | 2,260 | 1,515 | 621 | 1,073 | 1,042 | 464 |
| Mississippi | 11,630 | 2,230 | 1,170 | 638 | 525 | 136 | 205 | 137 | 492 |
| Missouri | 14,531 | 5,590 | 2,610 | 780 | 532 | 323 | 439 | 336 | 196 |
| Montana | 1,666 | 692 | 39 | 115 | 57 | 30 | 20 | 292 | 18 |
| Nebraska | 7,952 | 1,718 | 1,774 | 424 | 833 | 64 | 147 | 483 | 166 |
| Nevada | 11,094 | 1,188 | 589 | 917 | 247 | 183 | 355 | 145 | 160 |
| New Hampshire | 5,306 | 668 | 420 | 368 | 217 | 181 | 692 | 94 | 178 |
| New Jersey | 35,354 | 7,060 | 2,956 | 1,573 | 1,435 | 2,405 | 1,525 | 1,030 | 1,425 |
| New Mexico | 3,657 | 120 | 1,420 | 1,102 | 241 | 25 | 63 | 121 | 28 |
| New York | 84,683 | 16,788 | 3,516 | 3,436 | 1,912 | 6,431 | 2,964 | 1,183 | 1,321 |
| North Carolina | 32,762 | 6,678 | 3,775 | 2,317 | 1,602 | 971 | 1,014 | 621 | 1,046 |
| North Dakota | 7,894 | 6,943 | 228 | 22 | 36 | 36 | 60 | 14 | 8 |
| Ohio | 54,404 | 21,189 | 6,868 | 3,635 | 1,671 | 2,199 | 1,619 | 971 | 963 |
| Oklahoma | 6,108 | 1,647 | 783 | 203 | 296 | 157 | 612 | 94 | 246 |
| Oregon | 22,335 | 3,212 | 464 | 4,742 | 2,215 | 302 | 469 | 1,721 | 347 |
| Pennsylvania | 41,193 | 10,839 | 4,219 | 2,565 | 2,152 | 2,145 | 1,375 | 1,005 | 1,714 |
| Rhode Island | 2,407 | 513 | 199 | 144 | 64 | 56 | 123 | 63 | 17 |
| South Carolina | 34,629 | 3,978 | 2,771 | 5,638 | 1,636 | 2,416 | 3,768 | 665 | 319 |
| South Dakota | 1,437 | 586 | 339 | 48 | 66 | 36 | 47 | 21 | 9 |
| Tennessee | 32,711 | 7,878 | 4,866 | 2,504 | 1,945 | 1,129 | 994 | 748 | 1,366 |
| Texas | 315,939 | 27,541 | 109,688 | 16,627 | 12,108 | 8,436 | 4,193 | 13,128 | 9,239 |
| Utah | 14,389 | 1,791 | 725 | 576 | 811 | 5,096 | 404 | 402 | 447 |
| Vermont | 2,920 | 1,270 | 46 | 168 | 37 | 88 | 77 | 186 | 66 |
| Virginia | 18,353 | 3,167 | 1,110 | 1,213 | 506 | 1,059 | 1,054 | 445 | 678 |
| Washington | 77,968 | 9,268 | 2,226 | 15,918 | 6,091 | 4,042 | 823 | 4,581 | 1,442 |
| West Virginia | 8,217 | 1,302 | 235 | 484 | 284 | 208 | 228 | 273 | 675 |
| Wisconsin | 22,721 | 7,039 | 3,455 | 1,633 | 735 | 792 | 814 | 592 | 448 |
| Wyoming | 1,357 | 235 | 35 | 53 | 62 | 19 | 10 | 65 | 4 |

[1] Total includes data for Puerto Rico and the Virgin Islands, not shown separately. Total also includes exports to unknown partners.

Source: U.S. Census Bureau, Foreign Trade Division, "USA Trade Online," <https://usatrade.census.gov/>, accessed July 2019. See also <https://www.census.gov/foreign-trade/statistics/state/index.html>.

# Table 1330. U.S. Exports, Imports, and Trade Balance by Country: 2005 to 2018

[In millions of dollars (901,082 represents $901,082,000,000). Data reflect trade between foreign countries and the U.S., Puerto Rico, the U.S. Virgin Islands, and U.S. Foreign Trade Zones. Data are shown on a Census Basis. Country totals include exports of special category commodities, if any. For methodology, see Foreign Trade Statistics in Appendix III. Minus sign (-) denotes an excess of imports over exports]

| Country | Exports, domestic and foreign | | | | | General imports | | | | | Merchandise trade balance | | | | |
|---|---|---|---|---|---|---|---|---|---|---|---|---|---|---|---|
| | 2005 | 2010 | 2015 | 2017 | 2018 | 2005 | 2010 | 2015 | 2017 | 2018 | 2005 | 2010 | 2015 | 2017 | 2018 |
| Total [1] | 901,082 | 1,278,495 | 1,503,328 | 1,546,473 | 1,665,992 | 1,673,455 | 1,913,857 | 2,248,811 | 2,339,884 | 2,540,806 | -772,373 | -635,362 | -745,483 | -793,411 | -874,814 |
| Afghanistan | 262 | 2,151 | 479 | 942 | 1,227 | 67 | 85 | 24 | 14 | 29 | 195 | 2,066 | 455 | 928 | 1,198 |
| Algeria | 1,106 | 1,194 | 1,876 | 1,062 | 1,261 | 10,446 | 14,518 | 3,372 | 3,811 | 4,618 | -9,340 | -13,324 | -1,496 | -2,749 | -3,357 |
| Angola | 929 | 1,293 | 1,166 | 809 | 525 | 8,484 | 11,940 | 2,806 | 2,604 | 2,698 | -7,555 | -10,646 | -1,640 | -1,794 | -2,173 |
| Antigua and Barbuda | 190 | 158 | 678 | 426 | 513 | 4 | 5 | 7 | 12 | 5 | 186 | 153 | 671 | 414 | 508 |
| Argentina | 4,122 | 7,392 | 9,362 | 9,602 | 9,927 | 4,584 | 3,803 | 3,951 | 4,785 | 4,833 | -462 | 3,589 | 5,411 | 4,817 | 5,094 |
| Armenia | 65 | 113 | 50 | 55 | 47 | 46 | 75 | 62 | 68 | 53 | 19 | 38 | -12 | -13 | -7 |
| Aruba | 559 | 540 | 1,168 | 968 | 602 | 2,920 | 19 | 55 | 35 | 31 | -2,361 | 521 | 1,113 | 932 | 571 |
| Australia | 15,589 | 21,805 | 25,032 | 24,518 | 25,310 | 7,342 | 8,583 | 10,886 | 10,049 | 10,124 | 8,246 | 13,222 | 14,147 | 14,469 | 15,186 |
| Austria | 2,544 | 2,429 | 4,024 | 4,275 | 3,564 | 6,103 | 6,835 | 11,312 | 11,727 | 13,429 | -3,558 | -4,407 | -7,288 | -7,452 | -9,865 |
| Azerbaijan | 132 | 253 | 478 | 355 | 314 | 45 | 1,989 | 507 | 212 | 505 | 87 | -1,736 | -29 | 143 | -191 |
| Bahamas, The | 1,787 | 3,178 | 2,387 | 3,058 | 3,002 | 700 | 815 | 453 | 459 | 245 | 1,087 | 2,363 | 1,934 | 2,600 | 2,557 |
| Bahrain | 351 | 1,235 | 1,271 | 898 | 2,042 | 432 | 420 | 902 | 996 | 991 | -81 | 815 | 368 | -98 | 1,051 |
| Bangladesh | 320 | 576 | 943 | 1,474 | 2,081 | 2,693 | 4,294 | 5,950 | 5,687 | 6,103 | -2,373 | -3,718 | -5,048 | -4,213 | -4,021 |
| Barbados | 395 | 397 | 595 | 525 | 597 | 32 | 43 | 68 | 49 | 55 | 363 | 355 | 527 | 477 | 542 |
| Belarus | 35 | 133 | 59 | 73 | 132 | 345 | 175 | 158 | 278 | 395 | -310 | -41 | -99 | -205 | -263 |
| Belgium | 18,691 | 25,458 | 34,174 | 29,924 | 31,427 | 13,023 | 15,552 | 19,487 | 14,980 | 17,182 | 5,668 | 9,906 | 14,687 | 14,944 | 14,245 |
| Belize | 218 | 289 | 285 | 295 | 407 | 98 | 120 | 75 | 278 | 226 | 119 | 169 | 210 | 17 | 180 |
| Benin | 72 | 463 | 631 | 250 | 254 | 1 | (Z) | 5 | 18 | 19 | 72 | 462 | 626 | 232 | 235 |
| Bermuda | 490 | 637 | 601 | 694 | 611 | 87 | 22 | 109 | 33 | 18 | 403 | 614 | 492 | 660 | 593 |
| Bolivia | 219 | 508 | 932 | 595 | 562 | 293 | 680 | 1,006 | 567 | 486 | -74 | -172 | -75 | 28 | 76 |
| Botswana | 67 | 48 | 39 | 93 | 82 | 178 | 170 | 212 | 772 | 461 | -111 | -121 | -173 | -679 | -379 |
| Brazil | 15,372 | 35,418 | 31,641 | 37,331 | 39,560 | 24,436 | 23,958 | 27,474 | 29,450 | 31,104 | -9,064 | 11,460 | 4,167 | 7,880 | 8,456 |
| British Virgin Islands | 125 | 146 | 260 | 399 | 823 | 34 | 19 | 16 | 7 | 20 | 91 | 127 | 243 | 392 | 803 |
| Brunei | 50 | 124 | 133 | 121 | 266 | 563 | 12 | 19 | 23 | 98 | -513 | 112 | 114 | 98 | 168 |
| Bulgaria | 268 | 171 | 289 | 381 | 370 | 454 | 260 | 598 | 659 | 986 | -186 | -89 | -308 | -277 | -616 |
| Cambodia | 70 | 154 | 391 | 400 | 446 | 1,767 | 2,301 | 3,026 | 3,063 | 3,818 | -1,697 | -2,147 | -2,635 | -2,663 | -3,372 |
| Cameroon | 117 | 132 | 225 | 159 | 193 | 158 | 297 | 68 | 118 | 220 | -41 | -165 | 93 | 41 | -26 |
| Canada | 211,899 | 249,256 | 280,855 | 282,473 | 299,769 | 290,384 | 277,637 | 296,305 | 299,090 | 318,824 | -78,486 | -28,380 | -15,450 | -16,618 | -19,056 |
| Chad | 54 | 90 | 57 | 31 | 53 | 1,498 | 2,044 | 1,303 | 526 | 479 | -1,444 | -1,954 | -1,247 | -494 | -427 |
| Chile | 5,134 | 10,907 | 15,449 | 13,633 | 15,377 | 6,664 | 7,017 | 8,777 | 10,550 | 11,387 | -1,531 | 3,889 | 6,672 | 3,082 | 3,989 |
| China | 41,192 | 91,911 | 115,873 | 129,798 | 120,148 | 243,470 | 364,953 | 483,202 | 505,220 | 539,676 | -202,278 | -273,042 | -367,328 | -375,423 | -419,527 |
| Colombia | 5,462 | 12,068 | 16,302 | 13,375 | 15,158 | 8,849 | 15,659 | 14,079 | 13,552 | 13,783 | -3,387 | -3,592 | 2,223 | -178 | 1,375 |
| Congo, Rep. of | 104 | 254 | 249 | 117 | 100 | 1,623 | 3,316 | 304 | 128 | 433 | -1,519 | -3,062 | -55 | -11 | -332 |
| Congo, Dem. Rep. of | 65 | 93 | 136 | 76 | 78 | 264 | 528 | 154 | 85 | 50 | -199 | -434 | -18 | -9 | 28 |
| Costa Rica | 3,599 | 5,178 | 6,045 | 6,146 | 6,497 | 3,415 | 8,697 | 4,489 | 4,564 | 4,881 | 183 | -3,519 | 1,556 | 1,582 | 1,617 |
| Cote d'Ivoire | 124 | 163 | 266 | 322 | 309 | 1,198 | 1,177 | 1,028 | 1,216 | 1,247 | -1,074 | -1,014 | -761 | -894 | -937 |
| Croatia | 159 | 312 | 332 | 446 | 615 | 364 | 336 | 577 | 436 | 466 | -206 | -24 | -245 | 10 | 150 |
| Cuba [2] | 369 | 363 | 186 | 291 | 276 | (Z) | (X) | (Z) | (Z) | | 369 | 363 | 186 | 291 | 275 |
| Curacao [2] | (X) | (X) | 521 | 702 | 704 | (X) | (X) | 335 | 151 | 105 | (X) | (X) | 186 | 552 | 599 |
| Cyprus | 84 | 134 | 102 | 82 | 132 | 31 | 11 | 32 | 47 | 68 | 54 | 123 | 70 | 35 | 65 |
| Czechia | 1,054 | 1,411 | 1,977 | 2,274 | 3,003 | 2,193 | 2,450 | 4,489 | 4,589 | 5,000 | -1,139 | -1,039 | -2,512 | -2,315 | -1,997 |
| Denmark | 1,918 | 2,132 | 2,203 | 2,211 | 2,589 | 5,144 | 6,012 | 7,760 | 7,691 | 8,858 | -3,226 | -3,879 | -5,557 | -5,480 | -6,268 |
| Djibouti | 48 | 123 | 145 | 157 | 113 | 1 | 3 | 35 | 34 | 48 | 46 | 120 | 109 | 123 | 65 |
| Dominican Republic | 4,719 | 6,579 | 7,115 | 7,850 | 8,947 | 4,604 | 3,672 | 4,668 | 4,744 | 5,306 | 115 | 2,908 | 2,447 | 3,106 | 3,642 |
| Ecuador | 1,964 | 5,409 | 5,818 | 4,832 | 5,897 | 5,759 | 7,451 | 7,467 | 6,379 | 6,740 | -3,795 | -2,042 | -1,649 | -1,547 | -843 |
| Egypt | 3,159 | 6,833 | 4,759 | 3,990 | 5,051 | 2,091 | 2,238 | 1,406 | 1,637 | 2,430 | 1,068 | 4,594 | 3,353 | 2,353 | 2,570 |
| El Salvador | 1,854 | 2,434 | 3,249 | 3,072 | 3,399 | 1,989 | 2,206 | 2,532 | 2,464 | 2,511 | -134 | 228 | 717 | 608 | 888 |
| Equatorial Guinea | 281 | 272 | 162 | 112 | 139 | 1,561 | 2,214 | 163 | 356 | 580 | -1,280 | -1,942 | -1 | -244 | -441 |
| Ethiopia | 456 | 773 | 1,555 | 877 | 1,308 | 62 | 128 | 310 | 291 | 445 | 394 | 645 | 1,245 | 586 | 863 |
| Fiji | 28 | 44 | 57 | 67 | 105 | 169 | 179 | 200 | 221 | 221 | -141 | -135 | -146 | -156 | -116 |
| Finland | 2,254 | 2,180 | 1,560 | 1,510 | 1,877 | 4,342 | 3,884 | 4,510 | 5,893 | 7,164 | -2,088 | -1,704 | -2,951 | -4,383 | -5,287 |
| France | 22,259 | 26,970 | 30,026 | 33,595 | 36,617 | 33,842 | 38,355 | 47,809 | 48,912 | 52,432 | -11,583 | -11,386 | -17,782 | -15,317 | -15,815 |
| French Polynesia | 112 | 122 | 120 | 120 | 288 | 60 | 53 | 43 | 49 | 36 | 52 | 69 | 77 | 71 | 252 |

See footnotes at end of table.

# Table 1330. U.S. Exports, Imports, and Trade Balance by Country: 2005 to 2018-Continued.

See headnote on page 827.

| Country | Exports, domestic and foreign 2005 | 2010 | 2015 | 2017 | 2018 | General imports 2005 | 2010 | 2015 | 2017 | 2018 | Merchandise trade balance 2005 | 2010 | 2015 | 2017 | 2018 |
|---|---|---|---|---|---|---|---|---|---|---|---|---|---|---|---|
| Gabon | 99 | 243 | 204 | 89 | 113 | 2,816 | 2,212 | 337 | 199 | 288 | -2,716 | -1,969 | -133 | -110 | -175 |
| Georgia | 214 | 301 | 340 | 383 | 478 | 194 | 198 | 181 | 131 | 190 | 20 | 103 | 159 | 252 | 287 |
| Germany | 34,184 | 48,155 | 49,979 | 53,961 | 57,753 | 84,751 | 82,450 | 124,888 | 117,548 | 125,849 | -50,567 | -34,295 | -74,909 | -63,587 | -68,096 |
| Ghana | 337 | 989 | 950 | 860 | 769 | 158 | 273 | 309 | 750 | 581 | 179 | 716 | 641 | 109 | 187 |
| Gibraltar | 163 | 1,494 | 1,979 | 1,140 | 1,328 | 5 | 1 | 2 | 1 | (Z) | 159 | 1,493 | 1,978 | 1,139 | 1,328 |
| Greece | 1,192 | 1,106 | 726 | 954 | 1,084 | 884 | 798 | 1,357 | 1,257 | 1,606 | 309 | 309 | -631 | -303 | -522 |
| Grenada | 82 | 71 | 90 | 103 | 119 | 6 | 8 | 9 | 12 | 15 | 77 | 64 | 81 | 91 | 104 |
| Guatemala | 2,835 | 4,477 | 5,821 | 6,864 | 6,657 | 3,137 | 3,523 | 4,121 | 4,014 | 4,209 | -302 | 954 | 1,700 | 2,850 | 2,448 |
| Guyana | 177 | 291 | 368 | 377 | 541 | 120 | 299 | 431 | 314 | 253 | 57 | -8 | -63 | 64 | 288 |
| Haiti | 710 | 1,209 | 1,141 | 1,423 | 1,392 | 447 | 551 | 950 | 919 | 991 | 262 | 658 | 190 | 504 | 401 |
| Honduras | 3,254 | 4,606 | 5,216 | 5,069 | 5,585 | 3,749 | 3,933 | 4,760 | 4,575 | 4,696 | -495 | 673 | 457 | 493 | 889 |
| Hong Kong | 16,351 | 26,570 | 37,183 | 39,855 | 37,310 | 8,892 | 4,296 | 6,802 | 7,372 | 6,286 | 7,459 | 22,274 | 30,381 | 32,483 | 31,024 |
| Hungary | 1,023 | 1,290 | 1,715 | 1,888 | 1,753 | 2,561 | 2,491 | 5,719 | 5,078 | 5,072 | -1,538 | -1,201 | -4,004 | -3,190 | -3,319 |
| Iceland | 512 | 325 | 415 | 399 | 655 | 269 | 201 | 317 | 412 | 430 | 243 | 124 | 99 | -13 | 226 |
| India | 7,919 | 19,249 | 21,453 | 25,648 | 33,503 | 18,804 | 29,533 | 44,783 | 48,550 | 54,349 | -10,886 | -10,284 | -23,330 | -22,901 | -20,846 |
| Indonesia | 3,054 | 6,948 | 7,118 | 6,863 | 8,172 | 12,014 | 16,478 | 19,605 | 20,206 | 20,842 | -8,960 | -9,530 | -12,487 | -13,343 | -12,670 |
| Iran | 96 | 211 | 282 | 136 | 426 | 174 | 95 | 11 | 63 | 70 | -79 | 117 | 271 | 73 | 356 |
| Iraq | 1,374 | 1,643 | 1,973 | 1,205 | 1,312 | 9,054 | 12,143 | 4,353 | 10,754 | 11,872 | -7,680 | -10,500 | -2,380 | -9,550 | -10,560 |
| Ireland | 8,447 | 7,276 | 8,931 | 10,708 | 10,725 | 28,733 | 33,848 | 39,351 | 48,861 | 57,454 | -20,286 | -26,572 | -30,421 | -38,154 | -46,729 |
| Israel | 9,737 | 11,295 | 13,539 | 12,548 | 13,707 | 16,830 | 20,985 | 24,495 | 21,945 | 21,771 | -7,093 | -9,690 | -10,956 | -9,397 | -8,064 |
| Italy | 11,524 | 14,220 | 16,212 | 18,391 | 22,798 | 31,009 | 28,514 | 44,221 | 49,888 | 54,744 | -19,485 | -14,294 | -28,008 | -31,497 | -31,946 |
| Jamaica | 1,701 | 1,661 | 1,716 | 2,111 | 2,611 | 376 | 328 | 306 | 337 | 379 | 1,325 | 1,334 | 1,410 | 1,774 | 2,232 |
| Japan | 54,681 | 60,472 | 62,388 | 67,585 | 75,229 | 138,004 | 120,552 | 131,445 | 136,418 | 142,425 | -83,323 | -60,080 | -69,058 | -68,833 | -67,196 |
| Jordan | 644 | 1,172 | 1,360 | 1,921 | 1,581 | 1,267 | 974 | 1,492 | 1,687 | 1,814 | -623 | 198 | -132 | 234 | -232 |
| Kazakhstan | 538 | 730 | 510 | 552 | 729 | 1,101 | 1,872 | 816 | 791 | 1,387 | -563 | -1,142 | -306 | -239 | -658 |
| Kenya | 573 | 375 | 943 | 454 | 366 | 348 | 311 | 573 | 572 | 643 | 225 | 64 | 370 | -118 | -278 |
| Korea, South | 27,572 | 38,821 | 43,484 | 48,350 | 56,507 | 43,781 | 48,875 | 71,775 | 71,416 | 74,264 | -16,210 | -10,055 | -28,291 | -23,066 | -17,757 |
| Kuwait | 1,975 | 2,775 | 2,741 | 5,098 | 2,983 | 4,335 | 5,382 | 4,685 | 2,926 | 2,088 | -2,360 | -2,607 | -1,944 | -2,172 | 895 |
| Kyrgyzstan | 31 | 79 | 32 | 26 | 17 | 5 | 4 | 16 | 6 | 7 | 27 | 76 | 16 | 20 | 10 |
| Laos | 10 | 13 | 25 | 26 | 16 | 4 | 59 | 45 | 96 | 142 | 6 | -46 | -21 | -71 | -126 |
| Latvia | 178 | 345 | 267 | 382 | 510 | 362 | 193 | 303 | 453 | 727 | -185 | 152 | -36 | -71 | -217 |
| Lebanon | 466 | 2,009 | 1,286 | 1,221 | 1,328 | 86 | 84 | 93 | 129 | 109 | 379 | 1,925 | 1,193 | 1,093 | 1,220 |
| Liberia | 69 | 191 | 136 | 138 | 197 | 91 | 180 | 45 | 91 | 62 | -22 | 11 | 91 | 47 | 135 |
| Libya | 84 | 666 | 231 | 135 | 244 | 1,590 | 2,117 | 155 | 1,372 | 1,404 | -1,506 | -1,451 | 76 | -1,237 | -1,160 |
| Liechtenstein | 20 | 35 | 35 | 28 | 49 | 296 | 213 | 310 | 289 | 304 | -276 | -183 | -274 | -261 | -255 |
| Lithuania | 390 | 628 | 528 | 609 | 706 | 634 | 637 | 1,060 | 1,497 | 1,268 | -244 | -9 | -532 | -888 | -562 |
| Luxembourg | 711 | 1,440 | 1,394 | 1,078 | 1,084 | 389 | 451 | 639 | 494 | 553 | 323 | 989 | 755 | 585 | 531 |
| Macau | 102 | 225 | 542 | 502 | 602 | 1,249 | 141 | 122 | 95 | 102 | -1,147 | 84 | 420 | 407 | 500 |
| Macedonia | 32 | 33 | 31 | 41 | 41 | 48 | 37 | 203 | 255 | 353 | -17 | -4 | -173 | -214 | -311 |
| Madagascar | 28 | 116 | 55 | 53 | 114 | 324 | 108 | 320 | 743 | 892 | -295 | 8 | -265 | -690 | -778 |
| Malawi | 28 | 37 | 37 | 28 | 17 | 116 | 72 | 61 | 62 | 57 | -87 | -35 | -24 | -34 | -39 |
| Malaysia | 10,461 | 14,079 | 12,278 | 12,873 | 13,012 | 33,685 | 25,901 | 33,972 | 37,370 | 39,356 | -23,224 | -11,821 | -21,694 | -24,498 | -26,344 |
| Malta | 194 | 457 | 491 | 293 | 201 | 283 | 262 | 241 | 163 | 197 | -89 | 196 | 249 | 130 | 4 |
| Marshall Islands | 75 | 91 | 54 | 557 | 290 | 17 | 12 | 29 | 35 | 21 | 58 | 79 | 25 | 522 | 269 |
| Martinique | 35 | 297 | 133 | 167 | 247 | 22 | 23 | 37 | 6 | 12 | 13 | 274 | 95 | 162 | 235 |
| Mauritania | 86 | 84 | 126 | 128 | 88 | 1 | 53 | 1 | 61 | 13 | 85 | 31 | 125 | 66 | 75 |
| Mexico | 120,248 | 163,665 | 236,460 | 243,508 | 265,443 | 170,109 | 229,986 | 296,433 | 312,809 | 346,101 | -49,861 | -66,321 | -59,973 | -69,301 | -80,658 |
| Mongolia | 22 | 116 | 69 | 82 | 121 | 144 | 12 | 17 | 9 | 10 | -122 | 104 | 52 | 73 | 111 |
| Morocco | 481 | 1,948 | 1,625 | 2,218 | 3,011 | 446 | 686 | 1,012 | 1,237 | 1,553 | 35 | 1,262 | 613 | 982 | 1,458 |
| Mozambique | 63 | 224 | 264 | 177 | 184 | 12 | 65 | 96 | 146 | 112 | 51 | 159 | 168 | 32 | 72 |
| Namibia | 112 | 110 | 128 | 115 | 210 | 130 | 195 | 85 | 119 | 120 | -17 | -85 | 42 | -4 | 90 |
| Nepal | 25 | 28 | 36 | 76 | 55 | 111 | 61 | 87 | 92 | 99 | -87 | -32 | -51 | -16 | -43 |
| Netherlands | 26,468 | 34,740 | 40,212 | 41,475 | 48,703 | 14,862 | 19,055 | 16,844 | 17,808 | 24,504 | 11,606 | 15,685 | 23,368 | 23,667 | 24,199 |
| New Zealand | 2,592 | 2,820 | 3,631 | 3,924 | 4,061 | 3,155 | 2,764 | 4,293 | 4,161 | 4,189 | -563 | 57 | -662 | -238 | -127 |
| Nicaragua | 625 | 981 | 1,267 | 1,587 | 1,629 | 1,181 | 2,008 | 3,189 | 3,256 | 3,583 | -555 | -1,026 | -1,921 | -1,669 | -1,954 |
| Niger | 79 | 49 | 72 | 44 | 62 | 66 | 27 | 4 | 7 | 29 | 13 | 22 | 67 | 37 | 32 |
| Nigeria | 1,620 | 4,061 | 3,431 | 2,173 | 2,686 | 24,239 | 30,516 | 1,916 | 7,050 | 5,617 | -22,620 | -26,455 | 1,516 | -4,877 | -2,930 |

See footnotes at end of table.

# Table 1330. U.S. Exports, Imports, and Trade Balance by Country: 2005 to 2018-Continued.

See headnote on page 827.

| Country | Exports, domestic and foreign | | | | | General imports | | | | | Merchandise trade balance | | | | |
|---|---|---|---|---|---|---|---|---|---|---|---|---|---|---|---|
| | 2005 | 2010 | 2015 | 2017 | 2018 | 2005 | 2010 | 2015 | 2017 | 2018 | 2005 | 2010 | 2015 | 2017 | 2018 |
| Norway | 1,942 | 3,100 | 3,570 | 5,451 | 5,414 | 6,776 | 6,950 | 4,763 | 5,051 | 6,786 | -4,834 | -3,850 | -1,192 | 400 | -1,373 |
| Oman | 571 | 1,105 | 2,355 | 1,984 | 2,415 | 555 | 773 | 907 | 1,066 | 1,275 | 16 | 332 | 1,448 | 918 | 1,140 |
| Pakistan | 1,252 | 1,901 | 1,838 | 2,808 | 2,849 | 3,253 | 3,509 | 3,701 | 3,574 | 3,709 | -2,002 | -1,608 | -1,863 | -766 | -860 |
| Panama | 2,162 | 6,066 | 7,669 | 6,290 | 6,838 | 327 | 381 | 408 | 442 | 421 | 1,835 | 5,685 | 7,261 | 5,847 | 6,417 |
| Papua New Guinea | 55 | 186 | 208 | 106 | 87 | 58 | 97 | 91 | 121 | 90 | -3 | 89 | 117 | -15 | -3 |
| Paraguay | 896 | 1,810 | 1,492 | 2,713 | 2,257 | 52 | 62 | 163 | 125 | 131 | 844 | 1,748 | 1,329 | 2,588 | 2,126 |
| Peru | 2,309 | 6,750 | 8,724 | 8,668 | 9,724 | 5,119 | 5,243 | 5,056 | 7,282 | 7,888 | -2,810 | 1,506 | 3,668 | 1,386 | 1,837 |
| Philippines | 6,895 | 7,377 | 7,903 | 8,450 | 8,720 | 9,250 | 7,982 | 10,232 | 11,623 | 12,597 | -2,355 | -605 | -2,329 | -3,173 | -3,877 |
| Poland | 1,268 | 2,983 | 3,715 | 4,523 | 5,352 | 1,949 | 2,964 | 5,611 | 7,103 | 8,036 | -681 | 19 | -1,896 | -2,580 | -2,684 |
| Portugal | 1,132 | 1,058 | 942 | 1,192 | 1,573 | 2,329 | 2,142 | 3,271 | 3,503 | 3,885 | -1,197 | -1,084 | -2,328 | -2,310 | -2,312 |
| Qatar | 987 | 3,160 | 4,222 | 3,124 | 4,428 | 448 | 466 | 1,354 | 1,197 | 1,571 | 539 | 2,693 | 2,868 | 1,927 | 2,857 |
| Romania | 609 | 730 | 754 | 954 | 1,114 | 1,208 | 1,008 | 2,150 | 2,198 | 2,610 | -599 | -278 | -1,396 | -1,244 | -1,496 |
| Russia | 3,962 | 5,994 | 7,087 | 7,003 | 6,659 | 15,307 | 25,691 | 16,372 | 17,058 | 20,875 | -11,344 | -19,697 | -9,286 | -10,055 | -14,216 |
| Rwanda | 11 | 31 | 14 | 66 | 25 | 6 | 21 | 46 | 21 | 67 | 4 | 9 | -31 | 22 | -42 |
| Saudi Arabia | 6,805 | 11,506 | 19,792 | 16,355 | 13,601 | 27,193 | 31,413 | 22,083 | 18,871 | 24,062 | -20,387 | -19,907 | -2,292 | -2,516 | -10,461 |
| Senegal | 141 | 219 | 199 | 208 | 289 | 4 | 5 | 72 | 72 | 127 | 138 | 214 | 127 | 136 | 162 |
| Serbia | (X) | 104 | 126 | 126 | 166 | (X) | 164 | 273 | 292 | 322 | (X) | -60 | -146 | -167 | -157 |
| Sierra Leone | 38 | 61 | 77 | 79 | 71 | 9 | 29 | 40 | 30 | 57 | 29 | 32 | 38 | 49 | 15 |
| Singapore | 20,466 | 29,009 | 28,481 | 29,649 | 32,747 | 15,110 | 17,428 | 18,272 | 19,368 | 26,612 | 5,356 | 11,581 | 10,209 | 10,281 | 6,135 |
| Sint Maarten [2] | (X) | (X) | 741 | 549 | 673 | (X) | (X) | 52 | 71 | 96 | (X) | (X) | 690 | 478 | 577 |
| Slovakia | 150 | 256 | 380 | 442 | 289 | 961 | 1,073 | 2,300 | 3,049 | 4,163 | -811 | -817 | -1,920 | -2,607 | -3,874 |
| Slovenia | 234 | 328 | 346 | 372 | 322 | 413 | 465 | 678 | 760 | 847 | -179 | -137 | -332 | -389 | -525 |
| South Africa | 3,907 | 5,632 | 5,457 | 5,051 | 5,517 | 5,886 | 8,220 | 7,323 | 7,735 | 8,468 | -1,979 | -2,589 | -1,866 | -2,685 | -2,950 |
| Spain | 6,839 | 10,355 | 10,310 | 11,071 | 13,086 | 8,615 | 8,554 | 14,133 | 15,672 | 17,205 | -1,776 | 1,802 | -3,823 | -4,601 | -4,124 |
| Sri Lanka | 198 | 179 | 362 | 336 | 372 | 2,083 | 1,748 | 2,891 | 2,843 | 2,675 | -1,885 | -1,569 | -2,529 | -2,506 | -2,303 |
| Suriname | 246 | 362 | 444 | 360 | 388 | 165 | 191 | 146 | 67 | 87 | 80 | 171 | 297 | 292 | 301 |
| Sweden | 3,715 | 4,740 | 3,939 | 3,735 | 4,469 | 13,821 | 10,497 | 9,910 | 10,750 | 10,992 | -10,106 | -5,757 | -5,971 | -7,015 | -6,523 |
| Switzerland | 10,718 | 20,704 | 22,154 | 21,695 | 22,172 | 13,000 | 19,137 | 31,431 | 35,974 | 41,092 | -2,282 | 1,567 | -9,277 | -14,279 | -18,920 |
| Syria | 155 | 503 | 3 | 7 | 51 | 324 | 429 | 7 | 7 | 6 | -169 | 74 | -3 | (-Z) | 45 |
| Taiwan | 21,614 | 26,050 | 25,826 | 25,736 | 30,560 | 34,826 | 35,847 | 40,911 | 42,426 | 45,756 | -13,211 | -9,797 | -15,085 | -16,690 | -15,196 |
| Tajikistan | 29 | 57 | 19 | 18 | 14 | 241 | 2 | 31 | 1 | 1 | -212 | 56 | -12 | 17 | 14 |
| Tanzania | 96 | 163 | 173 | 145 | 332 | 34 | 43 | 105 | 124 | 97 | 63 | 121 | 68 | 22 | 235 |
| Thailand | 7,257 | 8,976 | 11,229 | 11,023 | 12,448 | 19,890 | 22,694 | 28,622 | 31,116 | 31,873 | -12,633 | -13,717 | -17,393 | -20,093 | -19,424 |
| Togo | 28 | 158 | 312 | 456 | 642 | 6 | 9 | 14 | 15 | 13 | 21 | 149 | 298 | 442 | 629 |
| Trinidad and Tobago | 1,417 | 1,925 | 2,512 | 1,817 | 2,116 | 7,891 | 6,613 | 4,320 | 3,318 | 3,668 | -6,474 | -4,688 | -1,808 | -1,501 | -1,552 |
| Tunisia | 261 | 573 | 602 | 544 | 598 | 264 | 405 | 546 | 461 | 650 | -3 | 167 | 56 | 83 | -52 |
| Turkey | 4,239 | 10,538 | 9,520 | 9,772 | 10,261 | 5,182 | 4,207 | 7,886 | 9,387 | 10,334 | -943 | 6,331 | 1,633 | 385 | -73 |
| Turkmenistan | 215 | 40 | 81 | 282 | 31 | 135 | 48 | 56 | 14 | 12 | 80 | -8 | 25 | 268 | 19 |
| Uganda | 63 | 94 | 88 | 108 | 87 | 26 | 58 | 64 | 79 | 69 | 37 | 36 | 24 | 29 | 19 |
| Ukraine | 533 | 1,349 | 862 | 1,789 | 2,486 | 1,098 | 1,078 | 852 | 1,020 | 1,353 | -565 | 271 | 11 | 769 | 1,134 |
| United Arab Emirates | 8,120 | 11,662 | 23,001 | 20,079 | 19,511 | 1,468 | 1,145 | 2,474 | 4,243 | 5,002 | 6,651 | 10,517 | 20,527 | 15,836 | 14,510 |
| United Kingdom | 38,568 | 48,410 | 56,095 | 56,257 | 66,313 | 51,033 | 49,805 | 58,057 | 53,282 | 60,783 | -12,465 | -1,395 | -1,962 | 2,975 | 5,530 |
| Uruguay | 357 | 975 | 1,295 | 1,588 | 1,386 | 732 | 235 | 605 | 584 | 508 | -376 | 740 | 690 | 1,004 | 878 |
| Uzbekistan | 74 | 101 | 138 | 136 | 297 | 96 | 68 | 10 | 14 | 18 | -22 | 33 | 128 | 122 | 278 |
| Venezuela | 6,421 | 10,645 | 8,344 | 4,127 | 6,120 | 33,978 | 32,707 | 15,564 | 12,344 | 13,172 | -27,557 | -22,063 | -7,221 | -8,217 | -7,052 |
| Vietnam | 1,193 | 3,706 | 7,101 | 8,134 | 9,675 | 6,631 | 14,868 | 38,015 | 46,477 | 49,174 | -5,438 | -11,162 | -30,914 | -38,343 | -39,498 |
| Yemen | 219 | 398 | 158 | 199 | 191 | 279 | 181 | 48 | 10 | 2 | -60 | 216 | 110 | 189 | 189 |
| Zambia | 29 | 56 | 84 | 85 | 195 | 32 | 30 | 47 | 68 | 189 | -3 | 27 | 37 | 17 | 6 |
| Zimbabwe | 46 | 68 | 38 | 40 | 34 | 94 | 59 | 67 | 47 | 75 | -49 | 9 | -29 | -7 | -42 |

X Not applicable. Z Entry would amount to less than half the unit of measurement: shown. [1] Includes additional countries, not shown separate y. [2] The Netherlands Antilles dissolved on October 10, 2010. Curacao and Sint Maarten became autonomous territories of the Kingdom of the Netherlands.

Source: U.S. Census Bureau, "USA Trade Online," <https://usatrade.census.gov/>, accessed July 2019. See also U.S. *International Trade in Goods and Services*, Series FT-900, <http://www.census.gov/foreign-trade/Press-Release/ft900_index.html>.

## Table 1331. U.S. Exports and General Imports by Selected Commodity Groups: 2016 to 2018

[In millions of dollars (1,451,460 represents $1,451,460,000,000). All data are presented on a Census basis. For methodology, see Foreign Trade Statistics in Appendix III]

| Selected commodity | Exports | | | General imports | | |
|---|---|---|---|---|---|---|
| | 2016 | 2017 | 2018 | 2016 | 2017 | 2018 |
| Total [1] | 1,451,460 | 1,546,473 | 1,665,992 | 2,186,786 | 2,339,884 | 2,540,806 |
| Manufactured goods [2] | 1,049,629 | 1,095,702 | 1,159,740 | 1,911,335 | 2,019,639 | 2,182,385 |
| Agricultural commodities [2] | 134,672 | 138,151 | 139,586 | 114,406 | 120,986 | 128,807 |
| Food and live animals [3] | 95,995 | 99,051 | 103,882 | 99,905 | 105,874 | 113,338 |
| Live animals other than fish | 722 | 906 | 955 | 2,789 | 2,812 | 2,746 |
| Meat and preparations | 16,260 | 18,026 | 18,958 | 8,556 | 8,870 | 9,253 |
| Cereals and preparations | 22,834 | 22,452 | 24,927 | 9,013 | 9,600 | 10,669 |
| Vegetables and fruits | 21,683 | 22,516 | 22,064 | 32,635 | 34,519 | 36,726 |
| Coffee, tea, cocoa, and spices | 3,070 | 3,025 | 3,028 | 13,367 | 14,042 | 13,117 |
| Feeding stuff for animals | 11,288 | 11,032 | 12,540 | 2,771 | 2,877 | 3,294 |
| Crude materials except fuels [3] | 71,305 | 76,464 | 77,188 | 29,577 | 33,883 | 36,747 |
| Hides, skins, and furskins, raw | 1,921 | 1,888 | 1,460 | 165 | 100 | 56 |
| Oil seeds and oleaginous fruits | 24,705 | 23,269 | 19,388 | 1,026 | 1,046 | 1,022 |
| Crude rubber | 2,452 | 2,727 | 2,710 | 2,693 | 3,320 | 3,146 |
| Cork and wood | 6,707 | 7,536 | 7,608 | 8,018 | 8,662 | 8,800 |
| Pulp and waste paper | 8,280 | 8,605 | 9,227 | 3,010 | 3,160 | 3,739 |
| Textile fibers including waste | 5,879 | 7,711 | 8,471 | 1,280 | 1,286 | 1,398 |
| Crude fertilizers | 2,290 | 2,751 | 3,016 | 2,231 | 2,607 | 3,287 |
| Metalliferous ores and metal scrap | 16,146 | 18,865 | 21,932 | 5,862 | 7,982 | 9,174 |
| Mineral fuels and lubricants [3] | 92,971 | 137,431 | 191,213 | 153,800 | 194,786 | 232,801 |
| Coal, coke, and briquettes | 4,597 | 10,183 | 12,482 | 996 | 966 | 871 |
| Petroleum products and preparations | 74,921 | 104,611 | 150,206 | 142,920 | 181,667 | 219,548 |
| Gas, natural and manufactured | 13,260 | 22,451 | 28,133 | 7,692 | 9,887 | 10,129 |
| Animal and vegetable oils [3] | 2,619 | 2,744 | 2,535 | 6,052 | 6,803 | 6,705 |
| Animal oil and fat | 637 | 689 | 692 | 243 | 269 | 307 |
| Fixed vegetable fats and oil, crude | 1,715 | 1,814 | 1,596 | 5,624 | 6,331 | 6,152 |
| Chemicals and related products [3] | 185,736 | 194,664 | 209,068 | 217,282 | 221,558 | 258,555 |
| Organic chemicals | 31,257 | 34,028 | 38,524 | 47,154 | 43,805 | 51,261 |
| Inorganic chemicals | 10,100 | 11,298 | 11,516 | 10,938 | 10,553 | 12,123 |
| Dyeing, tanning, and coloring materials | 7,137 | 7,568 | 7,670 | 3,761 | 4,019 | 4,466 |
| Medicinal and pharmaceutical products | 46,498 | 45,040 | 47,681 | 95,497 | 99,807 | 119,511 |
| Fertilizers | 2,955 | 3,002 | 3,110 | 5,333 | 5,593 | 6,644 |
| Plastics in primary forms | 30,852 | 32,897 | 36,194 | 14,244 | 15,497 | 17,678 |
| Plastics in nonprimary forms | 12,599 | 13,256 | 13,818 | 9,467 | 10,455 | 11,675 |
| Manufactured goods by material | 102,021 | 106,573 | 110,901 | 232,159 | 255,525 | 277,398 |
| Leather and leather manufactures | 1,116 | 1,026 | 927 | 1,411 | 1,431 | 1,504 |
| Rubber manufactures | 8,390 | 8,979 | 9,429 | 20,044 | 20,840 | 22,697 |
| Cork and wood manufactures | 2,068 | 2,007 | 2,008 | 10,829 | 11,558 | 12,845 |
| Paper and paperboard | 14,603 | 15,474 | 16,081 | 16,052 | 16,128 | 17,760 |
| Textile yarn, fabric | 11,888 | 12,182 | 12,350 | 27,467 | 28,315 | 30,480 |
| Nonmetallic mineral manufactures | 13,428 | 13,180 | 12,858 | 45,800 | 45,635 | 48,605 |
| Iron and steel | 12,624 | 14,730 | 14,115 | 27,330 | 36,885 | 39,333 |
| Nonferrous metals | 13,476 | 14,293 | 16,848 | 33,463 | 41,995 | 45,246 |
| Manufactures of metals | 24,428 | 24,703 | 26,284 | 49,763 | 52,739 | 58,928 |
| Machinery and transport equipment | 493,825 | 502,058 | 518,833 | 953,589 | 1,013,276 | 1,071,951 |
| Power generating machinery | 33,907 | 34,776 | 35,948 | 64,528 | 68,357 | 74,928 |
| Specialized industrial machinery | 38,215 | 44,991 | 48,135 | 42,464 | 49,151 | 54,603 |
| Metalworking machinery | 4,734 | 4,880 | 5,304 | 9,317 | 10,406 | 11,383 |
| General industrial machinery | 58,715 | 59,354 | 62,212 | 89,868 | 97,989 | 108,742 |
| Office machinery | 19,351 | 19,636 | 19,426 | 110,536 | 123,906 | 137,419 |
| Telecommunications equipment | 20,736 | 21,560 | 21,011 | 157,879 | 167,530 | 163,407 |
| Electrical machinery | 78,015 | 78,247 | 80,049 | 168,078 | 175,487 | 189,686 |
| Road vehicles | 111,956 | 116,907 | 116,585 | 276,969 | 286,049 | 296,359 |
| Transport equipment | 128,195 | 121,707 | 130,163 | 33,951 | 34,401 | 35,424 |
| Miscellaneous manufactured articles [3] | 117,765 | 119,790 | 126,595 | 366,150 | 380,517 | 405,296 |
| Prefabricated buildings | 2,509 | 2,357 | 2,527 | 13,149 | 13,780 | 14,927 |
| Furniture | 6,263 | 6,297 | 6,325 | 47,165 | 49,982 | 53,765 |
| Travel goods | 613 | 635 | 715 | 10,646 | 10,854 | 11,525 |
| Apparel and clothing accessories | 3,082 | 3,008 | 3,223 | 88,170 | 88,206 | 91,918 |
| Footwear | 788 | 859 | 985 | 25,632 | 25,636 | 26,547 |
| Scientific and controlling equipment | 46,771 | 47,173 | 51,057 | 53,424 | 56,690 | 61,362 |
| Photographic equipment | 6,111 | 6,390 | 6,537 | 14,167 | 14,459 | 15,004 |
| Miscellaneous commodities [4] | 58,205 | 62,565 | 66,783 | 104,406 | 102,693 | 111,565 |
| Re-exports | 224,534 | 238,775 | 252,545 | (X) | (X) | (X) |

X Not applicable. [1] Total exports including re-exports (exports of foreign merchandise). [2] Manufactured goods is based on the North American Industry Classification System (NAICS) and Agricultural commodities is based on the Harmonized System commodities specified by the U.S. Department of Agriculture definition. All other commodity detail is based on Standard International Trade Classification (SITC). [3] Includes other commodities, not shown separately. [4] Includes special transactions, coin, nonmonetary gold, and the low value estimate.

Source: U.S. Census Bureau, *U.S. International Trade in Goods and Services, Annual Revision for 2018*, Series FT-900, June 2019. See also <http://www.census.gov/foreign-trade/Press-Release/ft900_index.html>.

# Table 1332. Domestic Exports and Imports for Consumption of Merchandise by Selected NAICS Product Category: 2005 to 2018

[In millions of dollars (799,957 represents $799,957,000,000). Includes nonmonetary gold. For methodology, see Foreign Trade Statistics in Appendix III. NAICS = North American Industry Classification System; see text, Section 15. N.e.c. = Not elsewhere classified]

| Product category | 2005 | 2010 | 2015 | 2016 | 2017 | 2018 |
|---|---|---|---|---|---|---|
| **Domestic exports, total** | **799,957** | **1,122,567** | **1,286,172** | **1,226,926** | **1,307,698** | **1,413,447** |
| Agricultural, forestry, and fishery products | 37,109 | 65,753 | 69,766 | 73,987 | 75,838 | 74,325 |
| Agricultural products, total | 30,683 | 58,023 | 60,200 | 64,796 | 65,908 | 64,377 |
| Livestock and livestock products | 1,118 | 1,539 | 2,032 | 1,804 | 1,825 | 1,922 |
| Forestry products, n.e.c. | 1,686 | 2,181 | 2,354 | 2,336 | 2,636 | 2,712 |
| Fish, fresh or chilled, and other marine products | 3,622 | 4,011 | 5,180 | 5,051 | 5,469 | 5,314 |
| Mining, total | 12,629 | 26,394 | 34,188 | 34,404 | 62,463 | 97,009 |
| Oil and gas | 4,547 | 9,248 | 19,802 | 22,661 | 44,539 | 75,898 |
| Minerals and ores | 8,082 | 17,146 | 14,386 | 11,743 | 17,924 | 21,111 |
| Manufacturing, total | 708,205 | 952,360 | 1,110,979 | 1,049,629 | 1,095,702 | 1,159,740 |
| Food and kindred products | 28,937 | 50,902 | 61,982 | 60,172 | 62,616 | 64,893 |
| Beverages and tobacco products | 3,423 | 5,339 | 8,476 | 7,436 | 7,141 | 7,796 |
| Textiles and fabrics | 8,483 | 7,833 | 9,001 | 8,318 | 8,435 | 8,656 |
| Textile mill products | 2,344 | 2,583 | 2,793 | 2,676 | 2,791 | 2,761 |
| Apparel and accessories | 4,075 | 3,070 | 3,104 | 2,881 | 2,827 | 3,046 |
| Leather and allied products | 2,300 | 2,421 | 3,041 | 2,887 | 2,930 | 2,977 |
| Wood products | 4,463 | 5,075 | 6,812 | 6,817 | 7,583 | 7,665 |
| Paper products | 16,640 | 22,962 | 23,321 | 22,198 | 23,522 | 24,585 |
| Printed, publishing, & similar products | 5,526 | 6,021 | 5,088 | 4,846 | 4,799 | 4,633 |
| Petroleum and coal products | 17,979 | 61,010 | 78,168 | 66,057 | 83,053 | 103,519 |
| Chemicals | 114,821 | 171,365 | 182,411 | 173,319 | 181,537 | 195,095 |
| Plastics and rubber products [1] | 18,784 | 24,262 | 29,970 | 28,865 | 29,908 | 31,341 |
| Nonmetallic mineral products [1] | 6,663 | 9,226 | 10,699 | 10,529 | 11,048 | 11,393 |
| Primary metal products | 27,455 | 49,725 | 51,694 | 46,057 | 52,184 | 54,174 |
| Fabricated metal products | 23,370 | 32,690 | 41,602 | 39,057 | 39,431 | 41,790 |
| Machinery, except electrical | 97,001 | 126,023 | 123,736 | 108,883 | 116,761 | 124,517 |
| Computers and electronic products [1] | 122,744 | 121,121 | 119,879 | 115,260 | 114,611 | 115,902 |
| Electrical equipment, appliances, and components [1] | 26,457 | 31,035 | 46,671 | 42,555 | 44,175 | 46,161 |
| Transportation equipment [1] | 144,985 | 176,337 | 252,299 | 252,307 | 251,090 | 258,283 |
| Furniture and fixtures | 2,844 | 3,979 | 4,960 | 4,607 | 4,695 | 4,820 |
| Miscellaneous manufactured commodities | 28,909 | 39,381 | 45,271 | 43,901 | 44,564 | 45,733 |
| Newspapers, books, & other published matter, n.e.c. | 960 | 851 | – | – | – | – |
| Special classification provisions | 41,055 | 77,210 | 71,239 | 68,905 | 73,695 | 82,374 |
| Waste and scrap | 10,389 | 29,420 | 17,548 | 16,724 | 18,186 | 20,537 |
| Used or second-hand merchandise | 2,570 | 4,711 | 12,432 | 12,131 | 13,033 | 15,516 |
| Goods returned or reimported | 65 | 30 | 32 | 25 | 49 | 35 |
| Special classification provision, n.e.c. | 28,030 | 43,049 | 41,228 | 40,025 | 42,427 | 46,287 |
| **Imports for consumption, total** | **1,664,625** | **1,900,587** | **2,227,237** | **2,172,183** | **2,327,360** | **2,552,407** |
| Agricultural, forestry, and fishery products | 30,761 | 42,686 | 56,308 | 57,970 | 62,345 | 63,353 |
| Agricultural products, total | 15,818 | 24,017 | 33,435 | 35,139 | 37,193 | 37,039 |
| Livestock and livestock products | 3,277 | 4,116 | 6,124 | 5,818 | 6,180 | 6,317 |
| Forestry products, n.e.c. | 2,250 | 3,356 | 2,380 | 2,220 | 2,729 | 2,610 |
| Fish, fresh or chilled, and other marine products | 9,416 | 11,198 | 14,369 | 14,793 | 16,244 | 16,486 |
| Mining, total | 192,115 | 235,401 | 115,949 | 92,848 | 124,815 | 150,935 |
| Oil and gas | 185,621 | 228,066 | 109,006 | 87,632 | 119,130 | 144,348 |
| Minerals and ores | 6,494 | 7,335 | 6,943 | 5,216 | 5,685 | 6,587 |
| Manufacturing, total | 1,372,004 | 1,550,204 | 1,948,837 | 1,916,851 | 2,029,564 | 2,212,919 |
| Food and kindred products | 29,779 | 41,039 | 58,434 | 57,911 | 60,858 | 67,289 |
| Beverages and tobacco products | 12,849 | 15,515 | 21,201 | 22,358 | 23,558 | 25,029 |
| Textiles and fabrics | 7,450 | 6,525 | 8,570 | 8,179 | 8,114 | 8,761 |
| Textile mill products | 13,508 | 15,825 | 20,752 | 20,567 | 21,587 | 23,123 |
| Apparel and accessories | 74,478 | 75,411 | 89,281 | 83,974 | 84,092 | 89,050 |
| Leather and allied products | 26,559 | 30,859 | 40,163 | 37,849 | 37,740 | 39,573 |
| Wood products | 23,654 | 11,364 | 17,107 | 18,770 | 20,166 | 21,518 |
| Paper products | 22,094 | 21,029 | 20,304 | 19,538 | 19,788 | 22,107 |
| Printed, publishing, & similar products | 5,599 | 5,324 | 5,532 | 5,473 | 5,554 | 5,872 |
| Petroleum and coal products | 81,359 | 102,169 | 67,950 | 55,162 | 63,851 | 81,227 |
| Chemicals | 131,936 | 187,576 | 217,099 | 215,141 | 221,446 | 256,813 |
| Plastics and rubber products | 28,072 | 34,364 | 49,836 | 49,161 | 52,320 | 58,563 |
| Nonmetallic mineral products | 18,445 | 16,075 | 21,799 | 21,646 | 22,994 | 25,368 |
| Primary metal products | 64,666 | 79,617 | 85,118 | 79,760 | 91,817 | 96,474 |
| Fabricated metal products | 41,026 | 46,712 | 67,397 | 65,351 | 68,858 | 77,519 |
| Machinery, except electrical | 109,619 | 104,832 | 156,908 | 150,372 | 168,592 | 188,608 |
| Computers and electronic products | 269,921 | 324,379 | 372,260 | 372,609 | 398,802 | 421,119 |
| Electrical equipment, appliances, and components | 55,179 | 68,465 | 101,912 | 102,018 | 110,925 | 123,753 |
| Transportation equipment | 251,386 | 239,870 | 375,354 | 375,215 | 385,266 | 405,401 |
| Furniture and fixtures | 25,096 | 25,702 | 36,874 | 38,419 | 41,874 | 45,619 |
| Miscellaneous manufactured commodities | 79,329 | 97,554 | 114,987 | 117,378 | 121,362 | 130,133 |
| Newspapers, books, & other published matter, n.e.c. | 128 | 35 | – | – | – | – |
| Special classification provisions | 69,617 | 72,261 | 106,143 | 104,514 | 110,636 | 125,200 |
| Waste and scrap | 3,207 | 5,261 | 5,089 | 4,672 | 6,230 | 6,874 |
| Used or second-hand merchandise | 6,026 | 6,403 | 13,159 | 11,460 | 11,710 | 13,113 |
| Goods returned or reimported | 37,024 | 40,992 | 66,960 | 68,142 | 71,104 | 82,779 |
| Special classification provision, n.e.c. | 23,359 | 19,605 | 20,935 | 20,241 | 21,593 | 22,434 |

– Represents zero or rounds to less than half the unit of measurement shown. [1] Beginning 2009, export statistics for certain commodity classifications related to the aircraft industry are subject to suppression and have been aggregated in a manner that prevents the disclosure of confidential information.

Source: U.S. Census Bureau, Foreign Trade Division, USA Trade Online, <https://usatrade.census.gov/>, accessed July 2019. See also U.S. International Trade in Goods and Services, Series FT-900, <http://www.census.gov/foreign-trade/data/index.html>.

# Table 1333. High-technology Products Exports and Imports by World Region and Country: 2007 to 2016

[In billions of dollars (1,833.8 represents $1,833,800,000,000). High-technology products include those technology-intensive products that consist of aerospace; communications; computers; pharmaceuticals; semiconductors; and testing, measuring, and control instruments. Data primarily from IHS Global Insight, special tabulations (2017) of the World Trade Service database]

| Region and country | 2007 | 2008 | 2009 | 2010 | 2011 | 2012 | 2013 | 2014 | 2015 | 2016 |
|---|---|---|---|---|---|---|---|---|---|---|
| **EXPORTS** | | | | | | | | | | |
| **World** | **1,833.8** | **1,919.4** | **1,718.9** | **2,089.2** | **2,248.0** | **2,308.6** | **2,404.5** | **2,480.0** | **2,465.5** | **2,555.1** |
| North America [1] | 283.5 | 279.9 | 259.3 | 278.7 | 288.8 | 307.9 | 315.2 | 326.3 | 328.7 | 330.7 |
| **United States** | **260.9** | **254.6** | **236.1** | **252.0** | **261.0** | **280.3** | **287.4** | **297.7** | **301.8** | **303.3** |
| Central and South America [1] | 23.5 | 25.9 | 26.5 | 33.0 | 37.3 | 41.8 | 40.8 | 34.6 | 24.7 | 26.8 |
| Europe | | | | | | | | | | |
| European Union [1,2] | 335.6 | 363.7 | 325.3 | 361.3 | 405.6 | 410.8 | 429.8 | 437.9 | 419.9 | 423.9 |
| France | 59.3 | 69.1 | 62.2 | 70.2 | 73.9 | 75.5 | 77.9 | 76.8 | 70.9 | 68.8 |
| Germany | 83.3 | 88.3 | 78.9 | 87.6 | 102.3 | 109.7 | 119.0 | 123.0 | 117.4 | 113.8 |
| United Kingdom | 45.4 | 48.5 | 44.7 | 47.3 | 49.3 | 50.9 | 52.7 | 52.6 | 51.6 | 49.1 |
| Other Europe [1] | 79.4 | 93.9 | 87.5 | 95.8 | 117.2 | 122.2 | 126.7 | 131.1 | 123.4 | 138.5 |
| Russia | 3.4 | 4.7 | 3.8 | 4.1 | 6.3 | 6.7 | 7.4 | 6.9 | 6.3 | 6.4 |
| Switzerland | 62.3 | 74.1 | 69.4 | 76.7 | 94.4 | 96.5 | 100.6 | 105.6 | 99.9 | 114.3 |
| Middle East [1] | 25.4 | 30.0 | 24.4 | 30.4 | 33.3 | 33.3 | 36.0 | 31.6 | 35.3 | 36.8 |
| Israel | 15.0 | 17.1 | 18.3 | 20.5 | 22.1 | 22.7 | 23.5 | 21.0 | 23.9 | 23.9 |
| Africa | 6.0 | 7.0 | 5.9 | 5.7 | 7.0 | 7.2 | 7.0 | 8.6 | 9.1 | 9.4 |
| Asia [1] | | | | | | | | | | |
| China [3] | 365.8 | 404.4 | 364.3 | 489.0 | 539.7 | 545.4 | 564.2 | 600.6 | 597.2 | 615.1 |
| India | 10.0 | 12.9 | 15.0 | 17.4 | 22.6 | 23.1 | 25.9 | 26.7 | 28.4 | 31.2 |
| Japan | 152.3 | 154.0 | 124.4 | 153.2 | 156.1 | 151.0 | 133.8 | 129.2 | 118.8 | 122.4 |
| Malaysia | 80.6 | 71.7 | 71.7 | 83.8 | 85.0 | 80.3 | 81.0 | 86.5 | 83.5 | 85.3 |
| Philippines | 33.7 | 30.7 | 22.9 | 32.5 | 27.5 | 28.7 | 28.8 | 32.7 | 33.3 | 36.9 |
| Singapore | 91.7 | 96.2 | 77.9 | 109.0 | 117.4 | 117.7 | 121.0 | 121.8 | 119.1 | 124.0 |
| South Korea | 118.3 | 116.2 | 106.5 | 133.7 | 132.5 | 131.8 | 143.3 | 148.4 | 143.6 | 140.3 |
| Taiwan | 153.0 | 150.7 | 130.3 | 168.3 | 177.6 | 192.2 | 224.7 | 233.9 | 251.1 | 274.5 |
| Thailand | 47.9 | 52.6 | 48.2 | 58.8 | 57.2 | 56.5 | 55.0 | 58.0 | 58.8 | 60.6 |
| Vietnam | 3.0 | 4.3 | 4.6 | 7.8 | 13.8 | 29.5 | 42.1 | 42.7 | 57.2 | 63.4 |
| Australia | 7.7 | 8.2 | 7.8 | 8.5 | 9.8 | 10.0 | 9.2 | 9.0 | 8.3 | 10.0 |
| All others | 5.8 | 5.2 | 5.6 | 6.2 | 7.3 | 7.4 | 8.9 | 9.1 | 13.5 | 13.3 |
| **IMPORTS** | | | | | | | | | | |
| **World** | **1,833.8** | **1,919.4** | **1,718.9** | **2,089.2** | **2,248.0** | **2,308.6** | **2,404.5** | **2,480.0** | **2,465.5** | **2,555.1** |
| North America [1] | 355.4 | 367.1 | 331.8 | 391.0 | 418.0 | 424.7 | 431.1 | 450.8 | 461.6 | 463.7 |
| **United States** | **288.8** | **291.0** | **263.4** | **306.0** | **326.6** | **331.9** | **333.1** | **353.6** | **365.3** | **364.6** |
| Central and South America [1] | 71.2 | 90.0 | 80.5 | 97.6 | 112.5 | 115.0 | 116.6 | 112.3 | 103.5 | 97.6 |
| Europe | | | | | | | | | | |
| European Union [1,2] | 388.6 | 407.8 | 356.2 | 416.9 | 435.3 | 416.9 | 417.7 | 426.6 | 417.7 | 435.9 |
| France | 48.1 | 51.4 | 48.1 | 52.0 | 55.8 | 57.1 | 58.0 | 56.3 | 57.9 | 60.3 |
| Germany | 94.6 | 98.0 | 87.5 | 105.5 | 110.8 | 102.0 | 99.9 | 107.0 | 103.4 | 107.9 |
| United Kingdom | 51.0 | 51.3 | 43.4 | 54.1 | 57.4 | 52.3 | 50.5 | 53.0 | 54.9 | 56.8 |
| Other Europe [1] | 113.0 | 126.6 | 104.9 | 124.1 | 146.5 | 150.5 | 159.7 | 153.5 | 134.8 | 142.8 |
| Russia | 29.5 | 36.1 | 25.4 | 34.3 | 40.9 | 47.3 | 47.2 | 42.4 | 31.5 | 31.6 |
| Switzerland | 36.0 | 38.1 | 34.7 | 37.6 | 43.4 | 43.8 | 47.2 | 48.1 | 44.5 | 46.7 |
| Middle East [1] | 63.6 | 68.8 | 66.8 | 75.6 | 85.3 | 93.8 | 105.9 | 112.5 | 117.8 | 123.2 |
| Israel | 9.4 | 9.7 | 8.1 | 8.8 | 10.0 | 10.6 | 10.5 | 11.2 | 11.7 | 12.6 |
| Africa | 40.3 | 50.5 | 43.7 | 48.0 | 50.6 | 49.5 | 52.7 | 59.3 | 56.9 | 58.2 |
| Asia [1] | | | | | | | | | | |
| China [3] | 295.8 | 301.2 | 281.7 | 367.2 | 393.2 | 421.7 | 456.9 | 482.3 | 500.6 | 522.2 |
| India | 29.8 | 30.3 | 30.8 | 34.6 | 38.6 | 37.5 | 40.0 | 40.3 | 40.5 | 41.1 |
| Japan | 103.3 | 106.0 | 94.1 | 118.3 | 127.9 | 140.1 | 138.7 | 139.3 | 130.3 | 132.6 |
| Malaysia | 50.5 | 44.7 | 39.3 | 54.6 | 52.1 | 53.0 | 54.8 | 55.7 | 51.4 | 54.5 |
| Philippines | 23.6 | 22.3 | 16.6 | 21.7 | 18.8 | 21.9 | 22.9 | 23.4 | 22.9 | 26.9 |
| Singapore | 86.2 | 86.2 | 72.5 | 93.3 | 94.6 | 97.8 | 103.4 | 102.3 | 97.1 | 98.6 |
| South Korea | 64.4 | 65.6 | 57.1 | 71.3 | 77.3 | 78.0 | 81.3 | 89.4 | 93.1 | 102.4 |
| Taiwan | 54.4 | 50.0 | 44.6 | 59.7 | 63.2 | 63.6 | 66.0 | 72.4 | 72.3 | 80.9 |
| Thailand | 29.7 | 29.4 | 26.7 | 33.8 | 36.9 | 40.9 | 41.7 | 40.1 | 40.3 | 41.8 |
| Vietnam | 6.1 | 7.0 | 8.6 | 10.5 | 14.8 | 21.8 | 29.2 | 33.3 | 40.6 | 44.7 |
| Australia | 27.4 | 31.1 | 29.7 | 34.2 | 39.8 | 38.4 | 36.3 | 36.1 | 34.3 | 35.0 |
| All others | 14.9 | 12.6 | 12.3 | 9.6 | 12.4 | 10.9 | 12.2 | 12.1 | 11.8 | 13.2 |

[1] Includes other countries not shown separately. [2] Data are not available for EU member Luxembourg. [3] Includes Hong Kong.

Source: National Science Foundation, *Science and Engineering Indicators, 2018*, NSB-2018-1, January 2018. See also <http://www.nsf.gov/statistics/seind/>.

# Table 1334. Exporting Firms and Revenue, Employees, and Payroll by Country and Area of Export Destination: 2014

[33,036,935 represents $33,036,935,000,000. Covers nonfarm employer firms with paid employees. A company or firm is a business consisting of one or more domestic establishments that the reporting firm specified under its ownership or control. Data were compiled from two Census Bureau data products, the 2014 Profile of U.S. Importing and Exporting Companies and the 2014 Annual Survey of Entrepreneurs. Excludes firms without reported sales, payroll, and employment; non-employer firms; firms operating primarily in out of scope industries, such as crop and animal production; and firms located in Puerto Rico and other Island Areas]

| Export destination | Firms (number) | Revenue (mil. dol.) | Export revenue (mil. dol.) | Paid employees (1,000) | Annual payroll (mil. dol.) |
|---|---|---|---|---|---|
| All firms with and without exports | 5,437,782 | 33,036,935 | 1,593,012 | 115,129 | 5,640,983 |
| **Firms with exports** [1] | **183,439** | **18,726,634** | **1,593,012** | **41,367** | **2,585,583** |
| Australia | 26,047 | 9,094,380 | 23,459 | 15,029 | 1,122,439 |
| Austria | 4,964 | 3,912,745 | 20,918 | 6,166 | 525,658 |
| Belgium | 9,791 | 6,544,309 | 26,297 | 9,608 | 774,267 |
| Brazil | 14,863 | 8,379,882 | 39,861 | 14,073 | 1,025,895 |
| Canada | 70,936 | 14,797,648 | 290,071 | 30,821 | 1,918,882 |
| Chile | 12,245 | 7,890,198 | 15,062 | 13,099 | 908,350 |
| China | 27,292 | 9,687,754 | 160,409 | 17,262 | 1,188,211 |
| Colombia | 11,344 | 7,767,439 | 24,397 | 11,806 | 860,604 |
| France | 17,692 | 7,736,831 | 48,623 | 13,941 | 1,009,770 |
| Germany | 25,540 | 9,578,466 | 47,619 | 17,453 | 1,244,802 |
| Hong Kong | 19,953 | 8,121,675 | 44,700 | 14,027 | 1,044,024 |
| India | 14,637 | 8,155,963 | 14,623 | 14,264 | 1,050,460 |
| Italy | 15,060 | 7,419,636 | 21,455 | 11,788 | 881,439 |
| Japan | 22,405 | 9,462,453 | 66,592 | 16,533 | 1,189,041 |
| Malaysia | 10,916 | 6,255,066 | 13,018 | 9,902 | 747,884 |
| Mexico | 43,314 | 11,728,934 | 226,835 | 21,095 | 1,404,870 |
| Netherlands | 15,804 | 8,361,018 | 38,331 | 14,065 | 1,021,324 |
| Saudi Arabia | 8,930 | 5,836,188 | 15,475 | 9,289 | 686,547 |
| Singapore | 17,096 | 7,879,007 | 26,101 | 13,030 | 993,388 |
| South Korea | 18,217 | 7,932,405 | 37,525 | 12,914 | 956,678 |
| Spain | 10,474 | 6,236,271 | 32,233 | 10,168 | 770,541 |
| Switzerland | 9,465 | 5,223,332 | 22,487 | 9,536 | 748,359 |
| Taiwan | 14,659 | 7,414,200 | 26,664 | 11,058 | 852,190 |
| United Arab Emirates | 13,470 | 7,390,577 | 17,975 | 12,820 | 878,927 |
| United Kingdom | 35,249 | 10,440,985 | 52,405 | 19,219 | 1,452,752 |
| APEC (Asia-Pacific Economic Cooperation) | 138,425 | 17,311,670 | 986,037 | 37,172 | 2,349,030 |
| ASEAN (Association of Southeast Asian Nations) | 31,462 | 9,984,971 | 69,936 | 18,661 | 1,277,471 |
| European Union | 72,662 | 14,004,167 | 319,520 | 27,367 | 1,886,698 |
| LAFTA (Latin American Free Trade Area) | 62,793 | 12,959,214 | 347,289 | 24,719 | 1,637,559 |
| OECD [2] | 147,350 | 17,794,292 | 1,025,069 | 38,594 | 2,429,459 |
| OPEC [3] | 29,286 | 10,020,895 | 63,620 | 17,862 | 1,201,791 |

[1] Includes other countries, not shown separately. [2] Organisation for Economic Cooperation and Development. [3] Organization of Petroleum Exporting Countries.

Source: U.S. Census Bureau, Annual Survey of Entrepreneurs (ASE), "U.S. Exporting Firms: 2014 Tables," <https://www.census.gov/programs-surveys/ase/data/tables.2014.html>, accessed May 2018. See also <https://www.census.gov/programs-surveys/ase/about.html>

# Table 1335. U.S. Exporting and Importing Companies by Employment-Size Class: 2010 and 2016

[Value in millions of dollars (1,140,406 represents $1,140,406,000,000). Data include all companies that can be linked to import and/or export transactions. Trade values are taken from the transactions used to compile the official U.S. Trade statistics; company information is taken from the Business Register. For information on data limitations, see Technical Documentation in source]

| Employment-size class and company type | Number | | Known value [1] (mil. dol.) | | Percent of— | | | |
|---|---|---|---|---|---|---|---|---|
| | | | | | Number | | Known value | |
| | 2010 | 2016 | 2010 | 2016 | 2010 | 2016 | 2010 | 2016 |
| **EXPORTERS** | | | | | | | | |
| **All companies, total** | **293,988** | **287,314** | **1,140,406** | **1,290,213** | **100.0** | **100.0** | **100.0** | **100.0** |
| By employment-size: | | | | | | | | |
| 1 to 19 employees | 112,572 | 104,590 | 82,739 | 77,938 | 38.3 | 36.4 | 7.3 | 6.0 |
| 20 to 49 employees | 30,984 | 29,989 | 45,037 | 44,063 | 10.5 | 10.4 | 3.9 | 3.4 |
| 50 to 99 employees | 15,179 | 14,999 | 43,710 | 38,033 | 5.2 | 5.2 | 3.8 | 2.9 |
| 100 to 249 employees | 11,581 | 11,880 | 59,349 | 87,050 | 3.9 | 4.1 | 5.2 | 6.7 |
| 250 to 499 employees | 4,336 | 4,637 | 46,254 | 69,529 | 1.5 | 1.6 | 4.1 | 5.4 |
| 500 or more employees | 6,490 | 7,085 | 755,466 | 860,961 | 2.2 | 2.5 | 66.2 | 66.7 |
| Unknown [2] | 112,846 | 114,134 | 107,851 | 112,639 | 38.4 | 39.7 | 9.5 | 8.7 |
| **IMPORTERS** | | | | | | | | |
| **All companies, total** | **181,648** | **211,335** | **1,679,522** | **1,911,184** | **100.0** | **100.0** | **100.0** | **100.0** |
| By employment-size: | | | | | | | | |
| 1 to 19 employees | 77,796 | 87,203 | 112,664 | 137,773 | 42.8 | 41.3 | 6.7 | 7.2 |
| 20 to 49 employees | 18,487 | 21,230 | 71,093 | 73,422 | 10.2 | 10.0 | 4.2 | 3.8 |
| 50 to 99 employees | 9,472 | 10,914 | 58,075 | 67,691 | 5.2 | 5.2 | 3.5 | 3.5 |
| 100 to 249 employees | 7,820 | 8,944 | 96,080 | 104,148 | 4.3 | 4.2 | 5.7 | 5.4 |
| 250 to 499 employees | 3,174 | 3,706 | 69,812 | 103,617 | 1.7 | 1.8 | 4.2 | 5.4 |
| 500 or more employees | 5,013 | 5,725 | 1,148,183 | 1,293,417 | 2.8 | 2.7 | 68.4 | 67.7 |
| Unknown [2] | 59,886 | 73,613 | 123,616 | 131,117 | 33.0 | 34.8 | 7.4 | 6.9 |

[1] Known value is defined as the portion of U.S. total exports and general imports that could be matched to specific companies. Export values are on f.a.s. or "free alongside ship basis." [2] Includes missing employment data, nonemployers, and companies that reported annual payroll but did not report any employees on their payroll.

Source: U.S. Census Bureau, *Profile of U.S. Importing and Exporting Companies 2015-2016*, April 2018, and earlier reports. See also <http://www.census.gov/foreign-trade/statistics/press-release/>.

## Table 1336. Export and Import Value Indexes—Selected Countries: 2013 to 2017

[Indexes in U.S. dollars, 2000=100. Values are the current value of exports/imports converted to U.S. dollars and expressed as a percentage of the average for the base period]

| Country | Export value index | | | | | Import value index | | | | |
|---|---|---|---|---|---|---|---|---|---|---|
| | 2013 | 2014 | 2015 | 2016 | 2017 | 2013 | 2014 | 2015 | 2016 | 2017 |
| **United States**........ | **202.1** | **207.3** | **192.2** | **185.6** | **197.8** | **185.0** | **191.6** | **183.9** | **178.7** | **191.3** |
| Australia............. | 396.1 | 375.7 | 293.9 | 301.4 | 361.8 | 338.5 | 331.3 | 291.6 | 274.2 | 319.6 |
| Belgium.............. | 249.4 | 251.3 | 211.2 | 211.9 | 228.9 | 255.0 | 256.2 | 212.1 | 214.1 | 229.5 |
| Canada.............. | 165.7 | 172.2 | 148.2 | 141.1 | 152.2 | 194.4 | 193.8 | 175.4 | 168.8 | 180.6 |
| France.............. | 177.7 | 177.7 | 154.9 | 153.4 | 163.7 | 201.5 | 200.8 | 169.5 | 169.2 | 184.6 |
| Germany............ | 261.6 | 271.5 | 240.9 | 242.4 | 263.1 | 237.9 | 243.4 | 211.9 | 212.8 | 235.3 |
| Greece.............. | 309.1 | 307.2 | 244.9 | 240.3 | 278.3 | 186.9 | 192.2 | 144.7 | 146.4 | 169.8 |
| Ireland.............. | 151.0 | 156.8 | 159.7 | 169.5 | 177.4 | 141.7 | 161.1 | 151.2 | 159.2 | 173.8 |
| Italy................ | 215.4 | 220.3 | 190.0 | 192.0 | 210.5 | 200.8 | 198.7 | 172.1 | 170.4 | 189.4 |
| Japan............... | 149.1 | 144.0 | 130.4 | 134.6 | 145.7 | 219.3 | 214.0 | 170.7 | 160.1 | 177.0 |
| Korea, South........ | 324.9 | 332.4 | 305.8 | 287.6 | 333.0 | 321.3 | 327.5 | 272.0 | 253.1 | 298.2 |
| Netherlands......... | 288.8 | 289.1 | 245.3 | 245.5 | 280.2 | 270.9 | 270.8 | 235.2 | 231.8 | 264.1 |
| Norway.............. | 259.8 | 240.9 | 172.8 | 149.0 | 173.3 | 261.1 | 260.1 | 222.1 | 218.1 | 241.1 |
| Spain............... | 276.3 | 282.3 | 245.5 | 252.2 | 278.4 | 218.7 | 230.4 | 200.2 | 199.6 | 226.1 |
| Sweden............. | 192.7 | 189.4 | 161.1 | 160.3 | 176.2 | 220.9 | 223.1 | 190.4 | 193.6 | 211.9 |
| Switzerland......... | 444.5 | 386.6 | 360.0 | 376.3 | (NA) | 389.6 | 334.1 | 306.7 | 327.3 | (NA) |
| United Kingdom..... | 189.7 | 177.2 | 161.4 | 143.7 | 154.9 | 190.1 | 198.7 | 180.4 | 183.4 | 185.5 |

NA Not available.

Source: World Bank, "World Development Indicators" database ©, <http://data.worldbank.org/>, accessed August 2019.

## Table 1337. U.S. Trade with China—Leading Commodity Imports and Exports: 2010 to 2018

[In billions of dollars (365.0 represents $365,000,000,000), except as noted]

| Commodity | NAICS code [1] | 2010 | 2015 | 2016 | 2017 | 2018 | 2017-2018 percent change |
|---|---|---|---|---|---|---|---|
| **IMPORTS FROM CHINA** | | | | | | | |
| **Total imports [2]**........................ | (X) | **365.0** | **483.2** | **462.4** | **505.2** | **539.7** | **6.8** |
| Communications equipment......................... | 3342 | 33.0 | 67.4 | 65.7 | 78.2 | 77.5 | -1.0 |
| Computer equipment............................... | 3341 | 57.2 | 57.8 | 52.2 | 58.5 | 59.8 | 2.2 |
| Misc. manufactured commodities.................... | 3399 | 34.2 | 35.3 | 34.4 | 35.9 | 38.0 | 5.9 |
| Apparel........................................... | 3152 | 26.6 | 27.9 | 25.5 | 24.6 | 24.8 | 0.8 |
| Semiconductors and other electronic components..... | 3344 | 18.3 | 19.6 | 18.9 | 23.2 | 24.5 | 5.6 |
| Furniture and kitchen cabinets..................... | 3371 | 11.6 | 15.9 | 16.6 | 18.2 | 19.8 | 8.3 |
| Household appliances and misc. machines............ | 3352 | 10.0 | 15.0 | 14.0 | 14.5 | 16.5 | 13.8 |
| Plastics products................................. | 3261 | 7.2 | 12.1 | 12.4 | 13.7 | 16.1 | 17.4 |
| Motor vehicle parts............................... | 3363 | 6.7 | 13.3 | 13.1 | 13.5 | 15.4 | 14.0 |
| Electrical equipment and components............... | 3359 | 7.1 | 11.3 | 11.1 | 12.7 | 15.2 | 19.4 |
| **EXPORTS TO CHINA** | | | | | | | |
| **Total exports [2]**........................ | (X) | **85.8** | **107.2** | **107.0** | **119.9** | **109.6** | **-8.6** |
| Aerospace products and parts...................... | 3364 | 5.7 | 15.1 | 14.2 | 15.7 | 17.7 | 12.9 |
| Oil and gas....................................... | 2111 | (Z) | 1.0 | 1.4 | 6.7 | 7.0 | 5.4 |
| Motor vehicles.................................... | 3361 | 3.2 | 8.3 | 8.3 | 9.5 | 6.0 | -36.7 |
| Semiconductors and other electronic components..... | 3344 | 6.1 | 5.3 | 5.3 | 4.9 | 5.6 | 15.2 |
| Navigational, measuring, electromedical, and control instruments............... | 3345 | 3.5 | 4.8 | 4.8 | 4.8 | 5.2 | 9.4 |
| Basic chemicals................................... | 3251 | 4.1 | 4.4 | 4.5 | 4.8 | 4.7 | -1.9 |
| Industrial machinery.............................. | 3332 | 2.0 | 2.2 | 2.5 | 3.2 | 4.3 | 32.1 |
| Resin, synthetic rubber, artificial and synthetic fibers and filaments.................... | 3252 | 4.3 | 3.7 | 3.5 | 4.1 | 4.2 | 2.8 |
| Oilseeds and grains............................... | 1111 | 11.3 | 13.0 | 15.5 | 13.6 | 3.8 | -72.0 |
| Waste and scrap.................................. | 9100 | 8.6 | 6.0 | 5.2 | 5.6 | 3.4 | -39.1 |

Z Less than $500,000. X Not applicable. [1] Based on the North American Industry Classification System (NAICS); see text, Section 15. [2] Includes items not shown separately.

Source: U.S. International Trade Commission, "Interactive Tariff and Trade DataWeb," <http://dataweb.usitc.gov/>, accessed August 2019.

# Table 1338. U.S. Trade with Canada and Mexico—Leading Commodity Imports and Exports: 2010 to 2018

[In billions of dollars (277.6 represents $277,600,000,000), except as noted]

| Commodity | NAICS code [1] | 2010 | 2015 | 2016 | 2017 | 2018 | 2017-2018 percent change |
|---|---|---|---|---|---|---|---|
| **IMPORTS FROM CANADA** | | | | | | | |
| **Total imports [2]** | (X) | **277.6** | **296.3** | **277.7** | **299.1** | **318.8** | **6.6** |
| Oil & gas | 2111 | 66.3 | 55.0 | 42.9 | 58.8 | 69.4 | 18.0 |
| Motor vehicles | 3361 | 36.5 | 43.4 | 46.3 | 44.6 | 40.9 | -8.4 |
| Motor vehicle parts | 3363 | 12.1 | 14.4 | 13.8 | 13.1 | 14.1 | 7.7 |
| Petroleum & coal products | 3241 | 14.5 | 12.0 | 8.4 | 11.1 | 12.4 | 11.3 |
| Aerospace products & parts | 3364 | 6.4 | 10.7 | 8.7 | 8.6 | 9.3 | 8.3 |
| Nonferrous metal (except aluminum) production and processing | 3314 | 10.3 | 9.4 | 9.4 | 8.7 | 9.0 | 3.5 |
| Basic chemicals | 3251 | 7.4 | 6.4 | 5.9 | 6.4 | 7.0 | 8.3 |
| Alumina and aluminum production and processing | 3313 | 6.2 | 5.9 | 5.5 | 6.9 | 6.7 | -3.9 |
| Pulp, paper, & paperboard mill products | 3221 | 8.0 | 6.3 | 5.5 | 5.4 | 6.0 | 10.7 |
| Sawmill & wood products | 3211 | 3.0 | 4.9 | 6.0 | 6.2 | 5.9 | -5.1 |
| **EXPORTS TO CANADA** | | | | | | | |
| **Total exports [2]** | (X) | **206.8** | **234.1** | **221.0** | **233.9** | **247.7** | **5.9** |
| Motor vehicles | 3361 | 20.7 | 25.0 | 25.8 | 27.8 | 27.8 | 0.0 |
| Motor vehicle parts | 3363 | 19.5 | 17.1 | 18.2 | 19.1 | 18.0 | -5.6 |
| Petroleum & coal products | 3241 | 5.9 | 10.1 | 8.7 | 9.2 | 12.9 | 39.2 |
| Oil & gas | 2111 | 5.2 | 10.5 | 7.4 | 9.6 | 12.7 | 33.4 |
| Aerospace products & parts | 3364 | 4.7 | 7.2 | 6.3 | 7.1 | 8.1 | 13.3 |
| Agriculture, construction, and mining machinery | 3331 | 7.4 | 6.9 | 5.6 | 7.2 | 8.0 | 11.0 |
| Other general purpose machinery | 3339 | 6.2 | 6.4 | 6.3 | 6.6 | 7.3 | 9.6 |
| Motor vehicle bodies & trailers | 3362 | 2.5 | 6.4 | 6.5 | 6.5 | 7.1 | 9.8 |
| Basic chemicals | 3251 | 6.1 | 6.3 | 5.9 | 6.4 | 6.6 | 3.9 |
| Resin, synthetic rubber, and artificial and synthetic fibers and filaments | 3252 | 5.8 | 5.9 | 5.6 | 6.1 | 6.4 | 5.7 |
| **IMPORTS FROM MEXICO** | | | | | | | |
| **Total imports [2]** | (X) | **230.0** | **296.4** | **293.5** | **312.8** | **346.1** | **10.6** |
| Motor vehicles | 3361 | 27.5 | 50.0 | 49.3 | 57.5 | 64.5 | 12.2 |
| Motor vehicle parts | 3363 | 23.6 | 43.9 | 45.9 | 45.2 | 49.8 | 10.2 |
| Computer & peripheral equipment | 3341 | 13.2 | 17.1 | 18.2 | 20.2 | 26.6 | 31.8 |
| Oil & gas | 2111 | 29.7 | 12.5 | 7.6 | 10.1 | 14.2 | 41.0 |
| Electrical equipment | 3353 | 6.8 | 10.5 | 10.4 | 10.9 | 11.8 | 8.9 |
| Communications equipment | 3342 | 14.1 | 13.3 | 14.5 | 12.5 | 11.6 | -7.2 |
| Audio & video equipment | 3343 | 16.5 | 14.5 | 12.5 | 12.1 | 11.2 | -7.6 |
| Navigational, measuring, electromedical, and control instruments | 3345 | 5.0 | 8.4 | 8.7 | 9.0 | 9.4 | 4.3 |
| Other electrical equipment and components | 3359 | 4.2 | 6.5 | 6.7 | 8.0 | 9.1 | 13.3 |
| Household appliances | 3352 | 4.6 | 6.5 | 6.6 | 6.6 | 7.1 | 7.1 |
| **EXPORTS TO MEXICO** | | | | | | | |
| **Total exports [2]** | (X) | **131.8** | **186.0** | **176.7** | **187.1** | **204.0** | **9.0** |
| Petroleum & coal products | 3241 | 12.0 | 15.4 | 16.0 | 21.7 | 29.1 | 34.4 |
| Motor vehicle parts | 3363 | 12.6 | 17.6 | 16.3 | 16.0 | 16.4 | 2.0 |
| Basic chemicals | 3251 | 7.0 | 8.3 | 7.8 | 9.2 | 10.1 | 9.7 |
| Resin, synthetic rubber, artificial and synthetic fibers and filaments | 3252 | 6.2 | 7.9 | 7.6 | 7.9 | 8.7 | 10.2 |
| Engines, turbines, & power transmission equipment | 3336 | 3.3 | 5.2 | 5.0 | 6.4 | 7.4 | 16.5 |
| Plastics products | 3261 | 4.2 | 6.5 | 6.5 | 6.4 | 6.7 | 4.9 |
| Oilseeds & grains | 1111 | 4.5 | 4.9 | 5.2 | 5.6 | 6.0 | 7.1 |
| Other electrical equipment and components | 3359 | 2.9 | 5.7 | 5.4 | 5.4 | 5.6 | 5.4 |
| Oil & gas | 2111 | 2.0 | 3.0 | 3.3 | 4.6 | 5.4 | 16.2 |
| Other fabricated metal products | 3329 | 3.1 | 4.8 | 4.7 | 4.7 | 5.0 | 7.5 |

X Not applicable. [1] Based on the North American Industry Classification System (NAICS); see text, Section 15. [2] Includes items not shown separately.

Source: U.S. International Trade Commission, "Interactive Tariff and Trade DataWeb," <http://dataweb.usitc.gov/>, accessed August 2019.

# Table 1339. U.S. Trade in Processed Foods By Commodity: 2000 to 2018

[Includes Puerto Rico, U.S. territories, and shipments under foreign aid programs. Metric ton = 1.102 short tons or .984 long tons]

| Product category | Units | 2000 | 2010 | 2015 | 2017 | 2018 |
|---|---|---|---|---|---|---|
| **Processed foods imports, total [1, 2]** | **Metric tons** | **11,054,749** | **16,834,276** | **20,871,014** | **22,970,147** | **24,293,054** |
| Beer and wine | Kiloliters | 2,771,174 | 4,078,532 | 4,752,894 | 5,214,575 | 5,296,925 |
| Beer | Kiloliters | 2,331,185 | 3,146,395 | 3,658,196 | 4,021,036 | 4,164,249 |
| Wine | Kiloliters | 439,989 | 932,137 | 1,094,698 | 1,193,539 | 1,132,676 |
| Distilled spirits and other alcoholic beverages | Kiloliters | 47,708 | 36,640 | 96,825 | 109,771 | 117,974 |
| Chocolate and confectionery [2] | Metric tons | 858,136 | 1,362,569 | 1,445,896 | 1,619,326 | 1,638,207 |
| Chocolate | Metric tons | 525,437 | 820,017 | 857,595 | 983,054 | 957,592 |
| Sugar confectionery | Metric tons | 293,105 | 499,236 | 552,216 | 601,062 | 646,297 |
| Condiments and sauces | Metric tons | 351,000 | 569,652 | 688,589 | 753,319 | 814,045 |
| Fats and oils [2] | Metric tons | 1,698,793 | 3,518,341 | 4,518,987 | 5,125,233 | 5,147,269 |
| Olive oil | Metric tons | 203,960 | 275,435 | 312,317 | 317,085 | 339,619 |
| Soybean oil | 1,000 kilograms | 35,949 | 53,697 | 141,979 | 137,792 | 164,973 |
| Vegetable oils (excl. soybean) | Metric tons | 1,427,711 | 3,075,082 | 3,911,059 | 4,456,935 | 4,407,391 |
| Food preparations [2] | Metric tons | 1,111,342 | 2,052,605 | 2,610,736 | 2,866,442 | 3,010,982 |
| Baking inputs, mixes, and types of dough [3] | Metric tons | 682,340 | 1,097,081 | 1,449,035 | 1,613,319 | 1,725,809 |
| Non-alcoholic beverages [2] | Kiloliters | 3,689,991 | 5,552,744 | 6,316,792 | 6,864,836 | 7,268,074 |
| Bottled drinks [4] | Kiloliters | 555,954 | 1,222,531 | 1,853,009 | 2,200,372 | 2,122,226 |
| Juices | Kiloliters | 3,134,037 | 4,330,213 | 4,463,783 | 4,664,464 | 5,145,847 |
| Pasta and processed cereals [2] | Metric tons | 517,471 | 881,572 | 1,117,843 | 1,119,309 | 1,444,127 |
| Breakfast cereals and other breakfast products | Metric tons | 113,024 | 277,763 | 345,427 | 304,180 | 711,172 |
| Pasta | Metric tons | 316,886 | 367,974 | 453,293 | 462,579 | 474,176 |
| Prepared/preserved meats | Metric tons | 197,083 | 143,248 | 183,471 | 189,284 | 196,410 |
| Prepared/preserved seafood | Metric tons | 876,402 | 1,283,775 | 1,302,087 | 1,409,399 | 1,451,198 |
| Processed fruit | Metric tons | 865,350 | 1,422,793 | 2,013,971 | 1,905,572 | 2,082,127 |
| Processed vegetables and pulses [2] | Metric tons | 1,695,961 | 2,455,785 | 2,814,411 | 3,111,678 | 3,266,498 |
| Frozen potato products [5] | Metric tons | 527,642 | 725,033 | 836,770 | 993,589 | 1,054,714 |
| Processed/prepared dairy products [2] | Metric tons | 245,530 | 230,269 | 332,609 | 354,391 | 357,430 |
| Cheese | Metric tons | 188,707 | 138,539 | 197,768 | 182,401 | 176,211 |
| Cream & powdered/condensed milk | Metric tons | 18,897 | 33,250 | 43,062 | 59,935 | 49,342 |
| Ice cream | Metric tons | 9,151 | 30,263 | 24,253 | 25,919 | 29,232 |
| Yogurt and dairy drinks | Liters | 23,060 | 11,197 | 766,532 | 1,114,268 | 938,472 |
| Snack foods | Metric tons | 627,030 | 1,126,307 | 1,392,480 | 1,800,787 | 1,940,466 |
| Baked snack foods [6] | Metric tons | 480,515 | 899,781 | 1,203,116 | 1,563,502 | 1,718,210 |
| Mixes of nuts and fruit [7] | Metric tons | 92,782 | 156,182 | 97,200 | 115,149 | 108,795 |
| Potato chips | Metric tons | 23,758 | 40,569 | 49,443 | 49,537 | 56,862 |
| Prepared peanuts and peanut butter | Metric tons | 29,976 | 29,774 | 42,721 | 72,599 | 56,599 |
| Spices | Metric tons | 192,577 | 300,902 | 373,529 | 405,263 | 412,214 |
| Syrups and sweeteners [2] | Metric tons | 1,106,543 | 866,613 | 1,109,099 | 1,039,163 | 1,259,022 |
| Fructose and fructose syrup | Metric tons | 66,513 | 92,496 | 128,660 | 91,181 | 96,269 |
| Glucose and glucose syrup | Metric tons | 113,647 | 217,058 | 250,667 | 219,223 | 254,391 |
| **Processed foods exports, total [2]** | **Metric tons** | **10,908,071** | **17,719,580** | **19,634,075** | **19,922,462** | **20,180,257** |
| Beer and wine | Kiloliters | 526,828 | 703,995 | 1,037,531 | 1,024,230 | 1,036,424 |
| Beer | Kiloliters | 262,305 | 320,694 | 623,417 | 685,776 | 695,378 |
| Wine | Kiloliters | 264,523 | 383,301 | 414,114 | 338,453 | 341,046 |
| Distilled spirits and other alcoholic beverages | Kiloliters | 23,884 | 23,969 | 47,166 | 41,641 | 33,059 |
| Chocolate and confectionery [2] | Metric tons | 302,600 | 420,212 | 507,548 | 518,634 | 515,865 |
| Chocolate | Metric tons | 192,742 | 303,757 | 359,697 | 368,183 | 360,221 |
| Sugar confectionery | Metric tons | 98,043 | 108,527 | 139,194 | 143,972 | 147,829 |
| Condiments and sauces | Metric tons | 363,963 | 638,943 | 1,035,365 | 1,029,316 | 958,508 |
| Fats and oils [2] | Metric tons | 1,998,801 | 3,356,665 | 2,388,023 | 2,531,935 | 2,322,748 |
| Soybean oil | 1,000 kilograms | 586,786 | 1,656,926 | 957,404 | 1,067,426 | 1,105,362 |
| Vegetable oils (excl. soybean) | Metric tons | 1,044,199 | 1,066,611 | 916,581 | 844,389 | 672,831 |
| Food preparations [2] | Metric tons | 2,492,061 | 3,397,278 | 4,475,534 | 4,424,610 | 4,963,149 |
| Baking inputs, mixes, and types of dough [3] | Metric tons | 1,904,460 | 2,280,017 | 3,247,709 | 3,150,038 | 3,730,523 |
| Non-alcoholic beverages [2] | Kiloliters | 1,661,547 | 1,617,263 | 1,540,424 | 1,253,137 | 1,129,603 |
| Bottled drinks [4] | Kiloliters | 487,448 | 636,964 | 752,004 | 625,454 | 615,979 |
| Juices | Kiloliters | 1,174,098 | 980,299 | 788,420 | 627,683 | 513,624 |
| Pasta and processed cereals [2] | Metric tons | 683,017 | 983,674 | 812,351 | 766,981 | 743,021 |
| Breakfast cereals and other breakfast products | Metric tons | 265,399 | 568,666 | 447,769 | 423,433 | 418,237 |
| Pasta | Metric tons | 102,295 | 181,765 | 208,630 | 173,012 | 174,090 |
| Prepared/preserved meats | Metric tons | 313,841 | 643,614 | 733,100 | 766,053 | 757,642 |
| Prepared/preserved seafood | Metric tons | 434,173 | 457,886 | 499,510 | 477,313 | 462,951 |
| Processed fruit | Metric tons | 388,844 | 571,165 | 619,759 | 592,775 | 512,839 |
| Processed vegetables and pulses [2] | Metric tons | 1,272,076 | 1,679,157 | 2,376,787 | 2,476,510 | 2,387,604 |
| Frozen potato products [5] | Metric tons | 568,709 | 344,807 | 475,906 | 614,237 | 585,431 |
| Processed/prepared dairy products [2] | Metric tons | 398,655 | 1,179,545 | 1,441,155 | 1,616,394 | 1,765,825 |
| Cheese | Metric tons | 47,760 | 173,327 | 316,885 | 340,267 | 348,653 |
| Cream & powdered/condensed milk | Metric tons | 114,847 | 466,853 | 612,493 | 650,176 | 776,960 |
| Ice cream | Metric tons | 41,652 | 35,680 | 69,668 | 67,997 | 74,781 |
| Snack foods | Metric tons | 490,079 | 784,168 | 1,026,988 | 980,355 | 1,010,473 |
| Baked snack foods [6] | Metric tons | 274,577 | 476,137 | 658,300 | 640,965 | 662,762 |
| Mixes of nuts and fruit [7] | Metric tons | 72,748 | 160,303 | 187,305 | 146,742 | 159,129 |
| Potato chips | Metric tons | 106,040 | 86,510 | 90,800 | 94,413 | 93,211 |
| Prepared peanuts and peanut butter | Metric tons | 36,713 | 61,218 | 90,583 | 98,235 | 95,371 |
| Soups | 1,000 kilograms | 97,212 | 140,420 | 172,054 | 174,623 | 192,044 |
| Syrups and sweeteners [2] | Metric tons | 726,427 | 2,525,583 | 2,386,299 | 2,418,924 | 2,342,620 |
| Fructose and fructose syrup | Metric tons | 322,904 | 1,395,278 | 1,339,450 | 1,413,264 | 1,382,958 |
| Glucose and glucose syrup | Metric tons | 209,686 | 738,966 | 521,434 | 474,418 | 458,281 |
| Molasses | Kiloliters | 199,070 | 203,841 | 61,713 | 106,345 | 28,197 |

[1] Imports for consumption. Excludes merchandise entered into bonded warehouses of Foreign Trade Zones under Customs custody; see source for details. [2] Includes commodities not shown separately. [3] Includes pudding. [4] Includes soda, juice mixes, beer, milk-based drinks, etc. [5] Includes French fries. [6] Pastries, pretzels, corn chips, etc. [7] Includes packaged and microwaveable popcorn.

Source: U.S. Department of Agriculture, Foreign Agricultural Service, "Global Agricultural Trade System," <http://www.fas.usda.gov/gats>, accessed August 2019.

# Puerto Rico and the Island Areas

This section presents summary economic and social statistics for Puerto Rico, the U.S. Virgin Islands, Guam, American Samoa, and the Northern Mariana Islands. Primary sources include the decennial censuses of population and housing and the annual Puerto Rico Community Survey conducted by the U.S. Census Bureau; County Business Patterns and other Census Bureau publications and databases; other U.S. government publications, such as the *National Vital Statistics Reports* (NSVR) series, issued by the National Center for Health Statistics; and the annual *Economic Report for the Governor and Legislative Assembly* of the Puerto Rico Planning Board.

**Jurisdiction**—The United States gained jurisdiction over these areas as follows: the islands of Puerto Rico and Guam, surrendered by Spain in December 1898, were ceded to the United States by the Treaty of Paris, ratified in 1899. Puerto Rico became a commonwealth on July 25, 1952, thereby achieving a high degree of local autonomy under its own constitution. The U.S. Virgin Islands, comprising approximately 50 islands and cays, was purchased by the United States from Denmark in 1917. American Samoa, a group of seven islands, was acquired in accordance with a convention among the United States, Great Britain, and Germany, ratified in 1900 (Swains Island was annexed in 1925). By an agreement approved by the United Nations Security Council and the United States, the Northern Mariana Islands, previously under Japanese mandate, was administered by the United States between 1947 and 1986 under the United Nations trusteeship system. The Northern Mariana Islands became a U.S. commonwealth in 1986.

**Censuses**—Because characteristics of Puerto Rico and the Island Areas differ, the presentation of census data for them is not uniform. The 1960 Census of Population covered all the territories listed above except the Northern Mariana Islands (their census was conducted in April 1958 by the Office of the High Commissioner of the Trust Territory of the Pacific Islands), while the 1960 Census of Housing excluded American Samoa. The 1970, 1980, 1990, 2000, and 2010 censuses of population and housing covered all five areas. Beginning in 1967, Congress authorized the Economic Censuses, to be taken at 5-year intervals, for years ending in "2" and "7." Prior economic censuses were conducted in Puerto Rico for 1949, 1954, 1958, and 1963 and in Guam and the U.S. Virgin Islands for 1958 and 1963. In 1967, the census of construction industries was added for the first time in Puerto Rico; in 1972, the U.S. Virgin Islands and Guam were covered; and in 1982, the Economic Census was taken for the first time for the Northern Mariana Islands. Agricultural censuses have been conducted with increasing regularity in Puerto Rico since 1910, in the U.S. Virgin Islands since 1917, and in Guam and American Samoa since 1920; the first agricultural census in the Northern Mariana Islands was conducted in 1970.

**Puerto Rico Community Survey**—The Puerto Rico Community Survey (PRCS) began in 2005 and was an important element in the Census Bureau's re-engineered 2010 census plan. The American Community Survey (ACS) is the equivalent of the PRCS for the United States (50 states and District of Columbia). The PRCS collects and produces population and housing information every year instead of every 10 years. About 36,000 households are surveyed each year from across every municipio in Puerto Rico.

**Information in other sections**—In addition to the statistics presented in this section, other data on Puerto Rico and the island areas are included in many tables showing distribution by states in various sections of the *Abstract*. See "Puerto Rico" and "Island Areas of the U.S." in the Index.

# Selected Island Areas of the United States

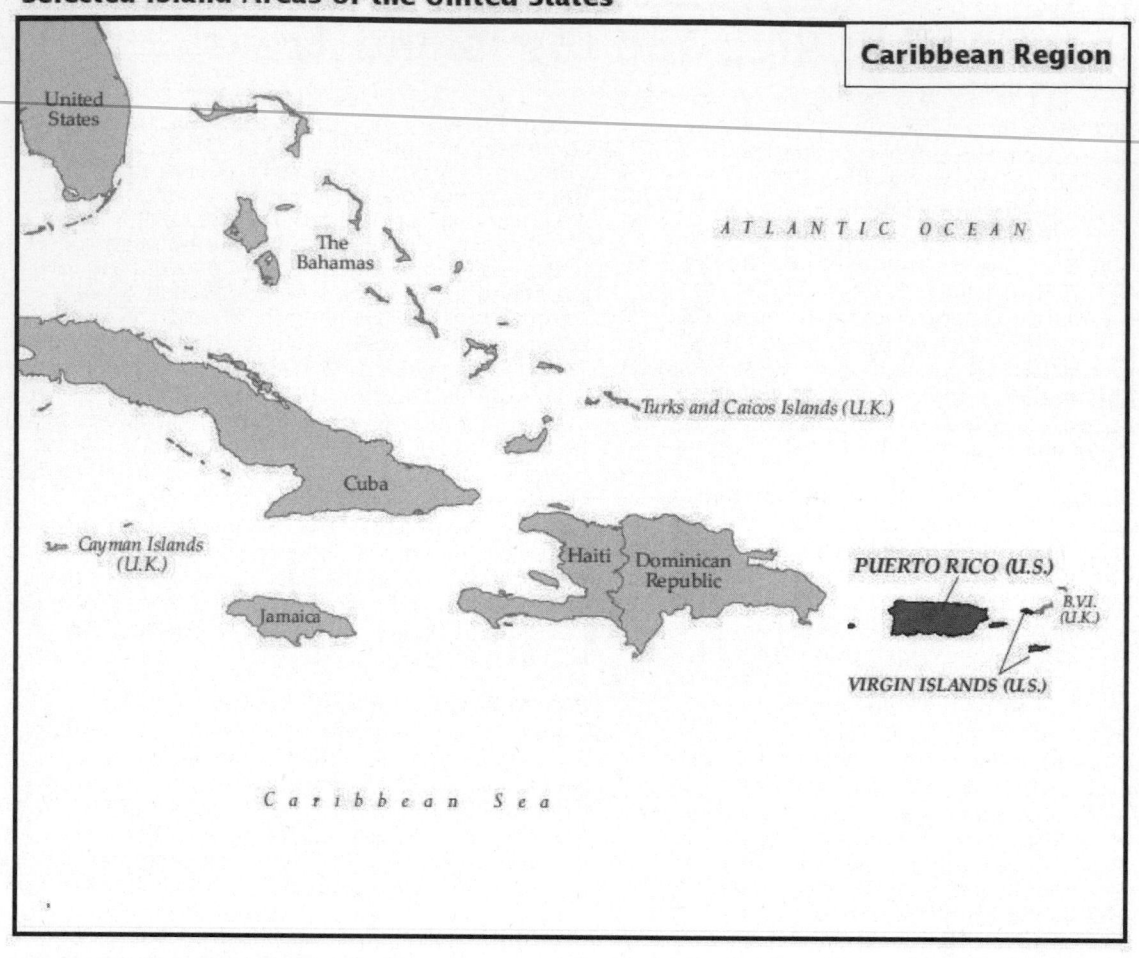

## Caribbean Region

United States

ATLANTIC OCEAN

The Bahamas

Turks and Caicos Islands (U.K.)

Cuba

Cayman Islands (U.K.)

Haiti

Dominican Republic

PUERTO RICO (U.S.)

B.V.I. (U.K.)

VIRGIN ISLANDS (U.S.)

Jamaica

Caribbean Sea

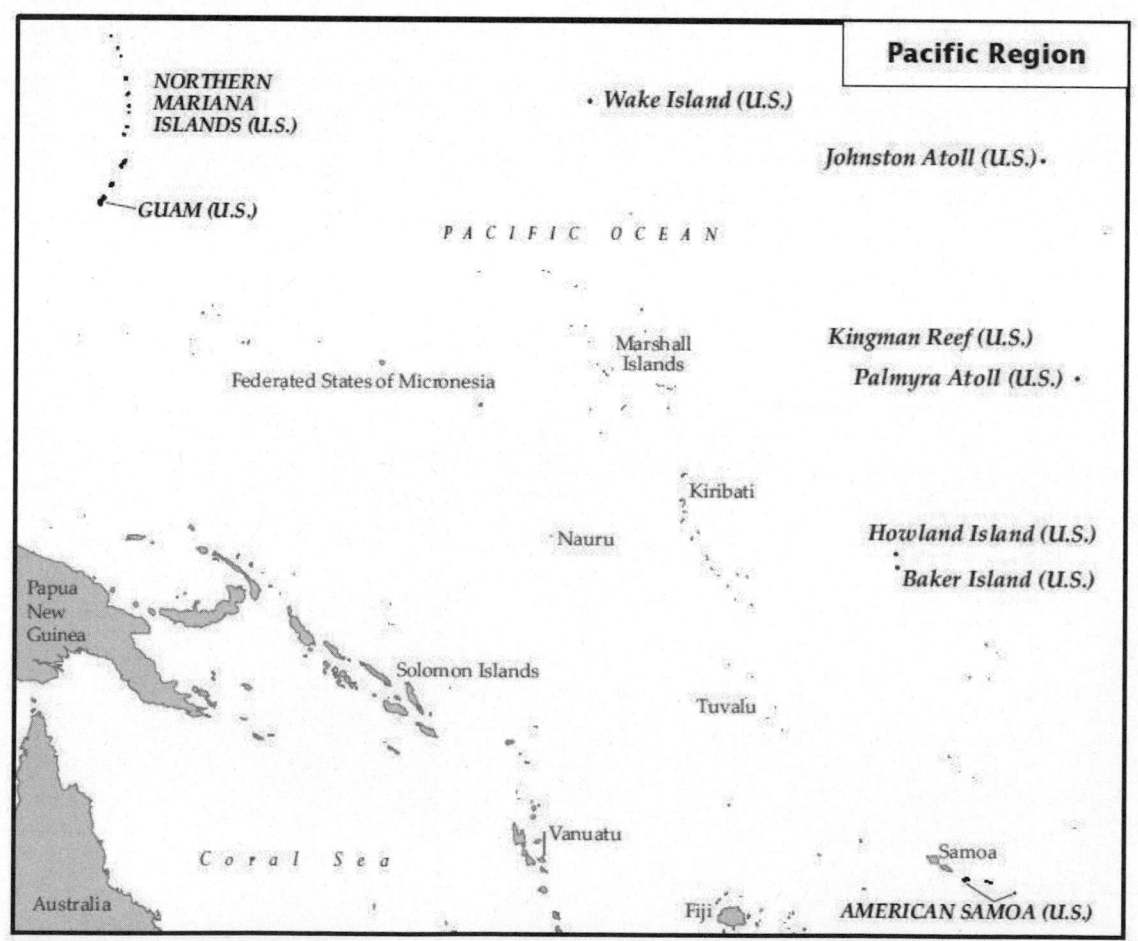

## Pacific Region

NORTHERN MARIANA ISLANDS (U.S.)

Wake Island (U.S.)

Johnston Atoll (U.S.)

GUAM (U.S.)

PACIFIC OCEAN

Kingman Reef (U.S.)

Marshall Islands

Palmyra Atoll (U.S.)

Federated States of Micronesia

Kiribati

Howland Island (U.S.)

Nauru

Baker Island (U.S.)

Papua New Guinea

Solomon Islands

Tuvalu

Vanuatu

Samoa

Coral Sea

Australia

Fiji

AMERICAN SAMOA (U.S.)

# Table 1340. Estimated and Projected Resident Population of Puerto Rico and Island Areas: 2000 to 2035

[In thousands (58 represents 58,000). Population as of July 1. Population data generally are de facto figures for the present territory. Data are adjusted to the 2010 Census of Population. See text, Section 30, for general comments regarding the data. For details of methodology, coverage, and reliability, see source]

| Area | 2000 | 2005 | 2010 | 2015 | 2016 | 2017 | 2018 | Projected | | |
| --- | --- | --- | --- | --- | --- | --- | --- | --- | --- | --- |
| | | | | | | | | 2025 | 2030 | 2035 |
| American Samoa............... | 58 | 57 | 56 | 53 | 52 | 52 | 51 | 46 | 43 | 39 |
| Guam........................ | 155 | 160 | 163 | 166 | 167 | 167 | 168 | 170 | 169 | 168 |
| Northern Mariana Islands...... | 70 | 68 | 55 | 53 | 53 | 52 | 52 | 50 | 48 | 47 |
| Puerto Rico.................. | 3,811 | 3,822 | 3,722 | 3,473 | 3,411 | 3,352 | 3,295 | 2,980 | 2,809 | 2,631 |
| Virgin Islands................. | 109 | 108 | 108 | 108 | 108 | 107 | 107 | 104 | 100 | 95 |

Source: U.S. Census Bureau, "International Data Base (IDB)," <https://www.census.gov/data-tools/demo/idb/informationGateway.php>, accessed August 2019.

# Table 1341. Births, Deaths, and Infant Deaths for Puerto Rico and the Island Areas: 2000 to 2017

[Births, deaths, and infant deaths by place of residence. Rates for 2000 and 2010 based on population enumerated as of April 1; for other years, on population estimated as of July 1]

| Area and year | Births | | Deaths | | Infant deaths | |
| --- | --- | --- | --- | --- | --- | --- |
| | Number | Rate [1] | Number | Rate [2] | Number | Rate [3] |
| Puerto Rico: | | | | | | |
| 2000............. | 59,333 | 15.6 | 28,365 | 7.4 | 574 | 9.7 |
| 2010............. | 42,153 | 11.3 | 29,153 | 7.8 | 341 | 8.1 |
| 2015............. | 31,157 | 9.0 | 28,085 | 8.1 | 218 | 7.0 |
| 2016............. | 28,257 | 8.3 | 29,338 | 8.6 | 214 | 7.6 |
| 2017............. | 24,310 | 7.3 | 30,777 | 9.2 | 163 | 6.7 |
| Guam: | | | | | | |
| 2000............. | 3,766 | 24.2 | 648 | 4.2 | 22 | 5.8 |
| 2010............. | 3,416 | 21.4 | 857 | 5.4 | 48 | 14.1 |
| 2015............. | 3,366 | 20.8 | 985 | 6.1 | 47 | 14.0 |
| 2016............. | 3,432 | 20.6 | 998 | 6.0 | 43 | 12.5 |
| 2017............. | 3,297 | 19.7 | 990 | 5.9 | 24 | 7.3 |
| Virgin Islands: | | | | | | |
| 2000............. | 1,564 | 14.4 | 641 | 5.9 | 21 | 13.4 |
| 2010............. | 1,600 | 15.1 | 715 | 6.7 | 13 | (B) |
| 2015............. | 1,325 | 12.8 | 673 | 6.5 | 4 | (B) |
| 2016............. | 1,187 | 11.0 | 632 | 5.9 | 3 | (B) |
| 2017............. | (NA) | (NA) | 707 | 6.6 | 10 | (B) |
| American Samoa: | | | | | | |
| 2000............. | 1,731 | 30.0 | 219 | 3.8 | 11 | (B) |
| 2010............. | 1,234 | 22.2 | 224 | 4.0 | 14 | (B) |
| 2015............. | 1,078 | 19.8 | 303 | 5.6 | 10 | (B) |
| 2016............. | 1,012 | 19.4 | 278 | 5.3 | 14 | (B) |
| 2017............. | 977 | 19.0 | 304 | 5.9 | 12 | (B) |
| Northern Marianas: | | | | | | |
| 2000............. | 1,431 | 20.5 | 136 | 2.0 | 11 | (B) |
| 2010............. | 1,072 | 20.0 | 174 | 3.3 | 4 | (B) |
| 2015............. | 427 | 8.2 | 223 | 4.3 | 5 | (B) |
| 2016............. | 416 | 7.9 | 220 | 4.2 | 8 | (B) |
| 2017............. | 363 | 6.9 | 232 | 4.4 | 8 | (B) |

B Base figure too small to meet statistical standards of reliability. NA Not available. [1] Birth rates are births per 1,000 women of child-bearing age. [2] Death rates are deaths per 1,000 population. [3] Infant death rates are infant deaths (under 1 year old) per 1,000 live births.

Source: U.S. National Center for Health Statistics, National Vital Statistics Reports (NVSR), *Births: Final Data for 2017*, Vol. 67, No. 8, November 2018, and earlier reports; and *Deaths: Final Data for 2017*, Vol. 68, No. 9, June 2019, and earlier reports. See also <http://www.cdc.gov/nchs/nvss.htm>.

# Table 1342. Public Elementary and Secondary Schools by Island Area: 2016

[Enrollment and staff are for Fall of year shown. Revenues and expenditures are for school year ending in year shown]

| Item | Puerto Rico | Guam | U.S. Virgin Islands | American Samoa | Northern Marianas |
| --- | --- | --- | --- | --- | --- |
| Enrollment............ | 365,181 | 30,758 | 13,194 | [1] 16,400 | [2] 10,638 |
| Elementary (pre-kindergarten to grade 8, and elementary ungraded)................. | 251,197 | 20,621 | 9,037 | [1] 11,763 | [2] 7,340 |
| Secondary (grades 9 to 12, and secondary ungraded)......... | 113,984 | 10,137 | 4,157 | [1] 4,637 | [2] 3,298 |
| Total staff (Fall)........ | 41,012 | 3,954 | 2,377 | [1] 1,869 | [2] 876 |
| School district staff............. | 2,004 | 434 | 139 | [1] 186 | [2] 98 |
| School staff............. | 32,643 | 3,301 | 1,744 | [1] 1,364 | [2] 679 |
| Teachers............. | 28,899 | 2,289 | 1,154 | [1] 971 | [2] 417 |
| Student support staff............. | 1,725 | 123 | 63 | [1] 218 | [2] 22 |
| Other support services staff............. | 4,640 | 96 | 431 | [1] 101 | [2] 77 |
| Revenues, total [4] ($1,000)....... | 2,876,676 | 321,973 | 186,961 | 70,851 | 74,136 |
| Current expenditures [5] ($1,000)....... | 2,970,386 | 309,238 | 160,559 | 58,675 | 75,562 |
| Per pupil [5] (dollars)............. | 7,821 | 10,033 | 11,631 | [1] 3,481 | [3] 5,886 |

[1] 2006 data. [2] 2013 data. [3] 2014 data. [4] Includes federal, territorial, local, and private revenues. [5] Includes current expenditures only, and excludes capital expenditures, interest on school debt, community services, private school programs, adult education, and other expenditures not directly allocable to public school operations.

Source: U.S. National Center for Education Statistics, *Digest of Education Statistics*, "Advance Release of Selected 2018 Digest Tables," <http://www.nces.ed.gov/programs/digest/>, accessed June 2019.

## Table 1343. Puerto Rico—Selected Social, Demographic, and Housing Characteristics: 2010 and 2017

[The Puerto Rico Community Survey universe includes the household population and the population living in institutions, college dormitories, and other group quarters. Based on a sample and subject to sampling variability; see text, this section and Appendix III]

| Characteristic | 2010 Number | 2010 Percent | 2017 Number | 2017 Percent |
|---|---|---|---|---|
| **Total population** | **3,722,133** | **100.0** | **3,337,177** | **100.0** |
| SEX | | | | |
| Male | 1,785,266 | 48.0 | 1,591,997 | 47.7 |
| Female | 1,936,867 | 52.0 | 1,745,180 | 52.3 |
| AGE | | | | |
| Under 5 years | 223,247 | 6.0 | 146,699 | 4.4 |
| 5 to 9 years | 236,531 | 6.4 | 172,834 | 5.2 |
| 10 to 14 years | 268,378 | 7.2 | 205,425 | 6.2 |
| 15 to 19 years | 284,254 | 7.6 | 231,633 | 6.9 |
| 20 to 24 years | 264,790 | 7.1 | 236,911 | 7.1 |
| 25 to 34 years | 482,756 | 13.0 | 396,657 | 11.9 |
| 35 to 44 years | 487,539 | 13.1 | 427,844 | 12.8 |
| 45 to 54 years | 486,273 | 13.1 | 430,603 | 12.9 |
| 55 to 59 years | 219,460 | 5.9 | 217,142 | 6.5 |
| 60 to 64 years | 223,184 | 6.0 | 212,674 | 6.4 |
| 65 to 74 years | 313,604 | 8.4 | 368,874 | 11.1 |
| 75 to 84 years | 170,712 | 4.6 | 215,153 | 6.4 |
| 85 years and over | 61,405 | 1.6 | 74,728 | 2.2 |
| MARITAL STATUS | | | | |
| **Males 15 years and over** | **1,410,023** | **100.0** | **1,314,422** | **100.0** |
| Never married | 566,489 | 40.2 | 583,563 | 44.4 |
| Married, not separated | 610,584 | 43.3 | 499,234 | 38.0 |
| Separated | 39,169 | 2.8 | 30,303 | 2.3 |
| Widowed | 39,752 | 2.8 | 48,149 | 3.7 |
| Divorced | 154,029 | 10.9 | 153,173 | 11.7 |
| **Females 15 years and over** | **1,583,954** | **100.0** | **1,497,797** | **100.0** |
| Never married | 523,558 | 33.1 | 551,459 | 36.8 |
| Married, not separated | 601,632 | 38.0 | 498,477 | 33.3 |
| Separated | 50,458 | 3.2 | 44,219 | 3.0 |
| Widowed | 171,416 | 10.8 | 167,941 | 11.2 |
| Divorced | 236,890 | 15.0 | 235,701 | 15.7 |
| HOUSEHOLDS | | | | |
| **Total households** | **1,319,448** | **100.0** | **1,191,305** | **100.0** |
| Family households (families) | 966,123 | 73.2 | 805,573 | 67.6 |
| With own children under 18 years | 405,933 | 30.8 | 271,408 | 22.8 |
| Married-couple families | 557,851 | 42.3 | 447,425 | 37.6 |
| With own children under 18 years | 200,406 | 15.2 | 115,073 | 9.7 |
| Male householder, no wife present | 82,129 | 6.2 | 79,185 | 6.6 |
| With own children under 18 years | 39,285 | 3.0 | 32,143 | 2.7 |
| Female householder, no husband present | 326,143 | 24.7 | 278,963 | 23.4 |
| With own children under 18 years | 166,242 | 12.6 | 124,192 | 10.4 |
| Nonfamily households | 353,325 | 26.8 | 385,732 | 32.4 |
| Householder living alone | 306,036 | 23.2 | 341,739 | 28.7 |
| 65 years and over | 125,754 | 9.5 | 160,026 | 13.4 |
| Average household size | 2.79 | (X) | 2.77 | (X) |
| Average family size | 3.28 | (X) | 3.45 | (X) |
| DISABILITY STATUS | | | | |
| **Total civilian noninstitutionalized population** | **3,695,636** | **100.0** | **3,309,977** | **100.0** |
| With a disability | 726,334 | 19.7 | 713,475 | 21.6 |

X Not applicable.

Source: U.S. Census Bureau, 2017 Puerto Rico Community Survey, DP02PR, "Selected Social Characteristics in Puerto Rico," and DP05, "Demographic and Housing Estimates," <http://factfinder.census.gov>, accessed May 2019. See also <http://census.gov/programs-surveys/acs/about/puerto-rico-community-survey.html>.

## Table 1344. Puerto Rico—Owner and Renter Occupied Housing by Household Type: 2017

[The Puerto Rico Community Survey universe includes the household population and the population living in institutions, college dormitories, and other group quarters. Based on a sample and subject to sampling variability; see text, this section and Appendix III]

| Household type | Owner occupied | Renter occupied | Household type | Owner occupied | Renter occupied |
|---|---|---|---|---|---|
| **Total households** | **802,024** | **389,281** | | | |
| **Family households** | **566,212** | **239,361** | Householder 15 to 34 years | 10,291 | 43,783 |
| Married-couple family | 366,162 | 81,263 | Householder 35 to 64 years | 88,211 | 71,232 |
| Householder 15 to 34 years | 15,219 | 20,713 | Householder 65 years and over | 54,382 | 11,064 |
| Householder 35 to 64 years | 210,804 | 45,553 | **Nonfamily households** | **235,812** | **149,920** |
| Householder 65 years and over | 140,139 | 14,997 | Householder living alone | 213,278 | 128,461 |
| Other family | 200,050 | 158,098 | Householder 15 to 34 years | 6,082 | 16,150 |
| Male householder, no wife present | 47,166 | 32,019 | Householder 35 to 64 years | 91,106 | 68,375 |
| Householder 15 to 34 years | 5,119 | 9,636 | Householder 65 years and over | 116,090 | 43,936 |
| Householder 35 to 64 years | 27,233 | 18,394 | Householder not living alone | 22,534 | 21,459 |
| Householder 65 years and over | 14,814 | 3,989 | Householder 15 to 34 years | 1,689 | 8,824 |
| Female householder, | | | Householder 35 to 64 years | 13,410 | 10,835 |
| no husband present | 152,884 | 126,079 | Householder 65 years and over | 7,435 | 1,800 |

Source: U.S. Census Bureau, 2017 Puerto Rico Community Survey, B25011, "Tenure by Household Type and Age of Householder," <http://factfinder.census.gov>, accessed May 2019. See also <http://census.gov/programs-surveys/acs/about/puerto-rico-community-survey.html>.

# Table 1345. Puerto Rico—Socioeconomic Summary: 1990 to 2018

[3,512 represents 3,512,000]

| Item | Unit | 1990 | 2000 | 2005 | 2010 | 2015 | 2016 | 2017 | 2018 (P) |
|---|---|---|---|---|---|---|---|---|---|
| **POPULATION** | | | | | | | | | |
| Total [1] | 1,000 | 3,512 | 3,808 | 3,824 | 3,731 | 3,504 | 3,440 | 3,366 | 3,260 |
| Persons per family | Number | 3.7 | 3.4 | 3.3 | 3.0 | 2.9 | 2.8 | 2.8 | 2.8 |
| **LABOR FORCE** | | | | | | | | | |
| Total [2] | 1,000 | 1,124 | 1,303 | 1,357 | 1,285 | 1,121 | 1,121 | 1,109 | 1,082 |
| Employed [3] | 1,000 | 963 | 1,159 | 1,213 | 1,075 | 977 | 989 | 982 | 971 |
| Agriculture [4] | 1,000 | 36 | 24 | 25 | 18 | 16 | 16 | 18 | 16 |
| Manufacturing | 1,000 | 168 | 159 | 135 | 101 | 81 | 84 | 79 | 89 |
| Trade | 1,000 | 185 | 239 | 256 | 238 | 237 | 235 | 228 | 235 |
| Government | 1,000 | 222 | 249 | 268 | 256 | 197 | 188 | 197 | 192 |
| Unemployed | 1,000 | 161 | 143 | 144 | 209 | 144 | 132 | 127 | 111 |
| Unemployment rate [5] | Rate | 14.0 | 11.0 | 10.6 | 16.3 | 12.8 | 11.8 | 11.5 | 10.3 |
| Compensation of employees | Mil. dol. | 13,639 | 23,504 | 29,372 | 29,870 | 28,874 | 28,572 | 28,464 | 27,672 |
| Average compensation | Dollar | 14,854 | 20,280 | 24,214 | 27,786 | 29,554 | 28,890 | 28,986 | 28,499 |
| Salary and wages | Mil. dol. | 13,639 | 23,504 | 25,393 | 25,793 | 24,768 | 24,347 | 24,269 | 23,851 |
| **INCOME [6]** | | | | | | | | | |
| Personal income: | | | | | | | | | |
| Current dollars | Mil. dol. | 21,105 | 38,856 | 49,929 | 59,983 | 63,756 | 63,601 | 64,599 | 67,726 |
| Constant (1954) dollars | Mil. dol. | 5,551 | 8,491 | 10,030 | 9,958 | 9,726 | 9,529 | 9,362 | 9,692 |
| Disposable personal income: | | | | | | | | | |
| Current dollars | Mil. dol. | 19,914 | 36,239 | 46,597 | 57,111 | 61,238 | 61,359 | 62,392 | 65,522 |
| Constant (1954) dollars | Mil. dol. | 5,238 | 7,919 | 9,173 | 9,481 | 9,342 | 9,193 | 9,042 | 9,377 |
| Average family income: | | | | | | | | | |
| Current dollars | Dollar | 22,232 | 34,693 | 43,086 | 48,231 | 52,766 | 51,769 | 53,738 | 58,170 |
| Constant (1954) dollars | Dollar | 5,847 | 7,581 | 8,655 | 8,007 | 8,050 | 7,756 | 7,787 | 8,324 |
| **TOURISM [6]** | | | | | | | | | |
| Number of visitors | 1,000 | 3,426 | 4,566 | 5,073 | 4,379 | 5,051 | 5,002 | 4,927 | 4,260 |
| Visitor expenditures | Mil. dol. | 1,366 | 2,388 | 3,239 | 3,211 | 3,825 | 3,974 | 3,848 | 3,282 |
| Average per visitor | Dollar | 399 | 523 | 638 | 733 | 757 | 794 | 781 | 770 |
| Net income from tourism | Mil. dol. | 383 | 615 | 771 | (NA) | (NA) | (NA) | (NA) | (NA) |

P Preliminary. NA Not available. [1] 1990 and 2000 enumerated as of April 1; for all other years the population is the average of population estimates at the beginning and the end of the fiscal year. [2] For population 16 years old and over. [3] Includes employment in other industries, not shown separately. [4] Includes forestry and fisheries. [5] Unemployed as percent of the labor force. [6] For fiscal years.

Source: Puerto Rico Planning Board, San Juan, PR, *Informe Económico al Gobernador Puerto Rico: Economic Report for the Governor 2018*, March 2019, and earlier reports. See also <http://jp.gobierno.pr/plan-econ-y-social>.

# Table 1346. Puerto Rico—School Enrollment and Educational Attainment by Level: 2005 to 2017

[The Puerto Rico Community Survey universe includes the household population and the population living in institutions, college dormitories, and other group quarters. Based on a sample and subject to sampling variability; see text, this section and Appendix III]

| Item | 2005 | 2010 | 2013 | 2014 | 2015 | 2016 | 2017 |
|---|---|---|---|---|---|---|---|
| **EDUCATIONAL ENROLLMENT** | | | | | | | |
| Population 3 years and over enrolled in school | 1,138,768 | 995,743 | 942,530 | 921,168 | 892,872 | 846,874 | 804,711 |
| Nursery school, preschool | 69,731 | 55,298 | 55,475 | 55,250 | 52,792 | 48,916 | 45,061 |
| Kindergarten | 52,261 | 45,366 | 42,217 | 37,899 | 37,989 | 36,227 | 33,751 |
| Elementary school (grades 1-8) | 486,546 | 414,233 | 376,924 | 362,625 | 340,580 | 320,223 | 307,128 |
| High school (grades 9-12) | 242,548 | 213,581 | 199,044 | 187,227 | 189,446 | 179,748 | 168,446 |
| College or graduate school | 287,682 | 267,265 | 268,870 | 278,167 | 272,065 | 261,760 | 250,325 |
| **EDUCATIONAL ATTAINMENT** | | | | | | | |
| Population 25 years and over | 2,431,653 | 2,444,933 | 2,417,418 | 2,400,677 | 2,382,526 | 2,372,197 | 2,343,675 |
| Less than 9th grade | 547,055 | 484,138 | 419,215 | 398,760 | 391,558 | 370,922 | 370,702 |
| 9th to 12th grade, no diploma | 269,039 | 262,682 | 234,868 | 229,019 | 210,220 | 207,689 | 188,871 |
| High school graduate (includes equivalency) | 588,130 | 623,709 | 653,505 | 669,936 | 647,581 | 657,523 | 653,789 |
| Some college, no degree | 290,283 | 317,797 | 291,031 | 292,524 | 314,431 | 298,426 | 285,018 |
| Associate's degree | 231,848 | 212,186 | 233,730 | 223,726 | 228,508 | 237,746 | 242,776 |
| Bachelor's degree | 377,437 | 389,954 | 416,877 | 417,133 | 424,255 | 433,120 | 428,558 |
| Graduate or professional degree | 127,861 | 154,467 | 168,192 | 169,579 | 165,973 | 166,771 | 173,961 |
| Percent high school graduate or higher | 66.4 | 69.5 | 72.9 | 73.8 | 74.7 | 75.6 | 76.1 |
| Percent bachelor's degree or higher | 20.8 | 22.3 | 24.2 | 24.4 | 24.8 | 25.3 | 25.7 |

Source: U.S. Census Bureau, 2017 Puerto Rico Community Survey, DP02PR, "Selected Social Characteristics in Puerto Rico," <http://factfinder.census.gov>, accessed May 2019. See also <http://census.gov/programs-surveys/acs/about/puerto-rico-community-survey.html>.

## Table 1347. Puerto Rico—Gross Product and Net Income: 1990 to 2018

[In millions of dollars (21,619 represents $21,619,000,000). For fiscal years ending June 30. Minus sign (-) indicates decrease]

| Item | 1990 | 2000 | 2010 | 2015 | 2016 | 2017 | 2018 (P) |
|---|---|---|---|---|---|---|---|
| **Gross product** | **21,619** | **41,419** | **64,295** | **69,602** | **69,985** | **70,000** | **68,049** |
| Agriculture | 434 | 407 | 822 | 855 | 841 | 847 | 792 |
| Manufacturing | 12,126 | 24,489 | 46,577 | 49,520 | 50,544 | 50,424 | 47,835 |
| Contract construction and mining [1] | 720 | 2,157 | 1,518 | 1,034 | 890 | 831 | 889 |
| Transportation, warehousing, and utilities | 2,468 | 2,579 | 2,923 | 3,131 | 3,025 | 3,275 | 3,077 |
| Trade (wholesale and retail) | 4,728 | 6,093 | 7,466 | 7,702 | 7,854 | 7,997 | 8,010 |
| Finance, insurance, and real estate | 3,896 | 10,511 | 19,026 | 19,919 | 20,252 | 20,087 | 20,578 |
| Services [2] | 3,015 | 9,987 | 11,993 | 13,581 | 14,013 | 14,118 | 13,991 |
| Government | 3,337 | 5,478 | 8,350 | 7,264 | 7,236 | 7,145 | 6,439 |
| Commonwealth | 2,884 | 4,601 | 6,862 | 5,741 | 5,686 | 5,596 | 4,927 |
| Municipalities | 453 | 877 | 1,488 | 1,523 | 1,550 | 1,549 | 1,512 |
| Rest of the world | -8,985 | -20,283 | -34,087 | -33,774 | -34,352 | -34,251 | -33,082 |
| Statistical discrepancy | -121 | 585 | -294 | 371 | -318 | -473 | -478 |
| **Net income** | **17,941** | **32,610** | **50,246** | **55,995** | **56,192** | **55,981** | **54,097** |
| Agriculture | 486 | 385 | 824 | 860 | 846 | 851 | 796 |
| Manufacturing | 11,277 | 22,627 | 43,292 | 45,893 | 46,640 | 46,302 | 43,751 |
| Mining [1] | 26 | 34 | 21 | 20 | 19 | 18 | 19 |
| Contract construction | 679 | 1,764 | 1,206 | 850 | 750 | 694 | 759 |
| Transportation, warehousing, and utilities | 1,778 | 1,961 | 2,128 | 2,195 | 2,016 | 2,188 | 2,008 |
| Trade (wholesale and retail) | 3,420 | 4,995 | 6,155 | 6,498 | 6,688 | 6,775 | 6,803 |
| Finance, insurance, and real estate | 3,280 | 8,175 | 13,099 | 15,324 | 15,367 | 15,143 | 15,534 |
| Services [2] | 2,643 | 7,475 | 9,257 | 10,865 | 10,982 | 11,115 | 11,072 |
| Government | 3,337 | 5,478 | 8,350 | 7,264 | 7,236 | 7,145 | 6,439 |
| Rest of the world | -8,985 | -20,283 | -34,087 | -33,774 | -34,352 | -34,251 | -33,082 |

P Preliminary. [1] Mining includes only quarries. [2] Includes all other services not elsewhere classified.

Source: Puerto Rico Planning Board, San Juan, PR, *Informe Económico al Gobernador: Economic Report to the Governor 2018*, March 2019, and earlier reports. See also <http://jp.gobierno.pr/plan-econ-y-social>.

## Table 1348. Puerto Rico—Transfer Payments: 2000 to 2018

[In millions of dollars (8,659 represents $8,659,000,000). Data represent transfer payments between federal and state governments and other nonresidents]

| Item | 2000 | 2005 | 2010 | 2015 | 2016 | 2017 | 2018 (P) |
|---|---|---|---|---|---|---|---|
| **Total receipts** | **8,659** | **10,551** | **16,504** | **18,017** | **18,077** | **19,322** | **22,049** |
| Federal government | 7,966 | 9,673 | 15,585 | 17,091 | 17,148 | 18,534 | 21,298 |
| Transfers to individuals [1] | 7,868 | 9,547 | 15,352 | 16,863 | 16,907 | 18,295 | 21,053 |
| Veterans benefits | 491 | 491 | 733 | 1,416 | 1,230 | 1,762 | 1,170 |
| Medicare | 1,196 | 1,825 | 2,529 | 4,467 | 4,511 | 5,430 | 6,562 |
| Social security | 3,863 | 5,118 | 7,074 | 7,718 | 7,820 | 7,875 | 7,202 |
| Nutritional assistance | 1,193 | 1,306 | 1,605 | 1,846 | 1,908 | 1,894 | 2,282 |
| Industry subsidies | 98 | 127 | 233 | 228 | 241 | 239 | 245 |
| U.S. state governments | 15 | 15 | 29 | 34 | 34 | 30 | 38 |
| Other nonresidents | 679 | 863 | 890 | 892 | 896 | 757 | 714 |
| **Total payments** | **2,763** | **3,583** | **3,804** | **3,961** | **4,019** | **4,207** | **4,320** |
| Federal government | 2,693 | 3,516 | 3,586 | 3,844 | 3,889 | 4,029 | 4,184 |
| Transfers from individuals [1] | 1,326 | 1,792 | 1,862 | 1,984 | 1,976 | 2,068 | 2,181 |
| Contribution to Medicare | 191 | 303 | 392 | 464 | 443 | 532 | 645 |
| Employee contributions to social security | 1,133 | 1,483 | 1,467 | 1,516 | 1,530 | 1,533 | 1,532 |
| Transfers from industries | 51 | 74 | 93 | 133 | 137 | 143 | 145 |
| Unemployment insurance | 234 | 221 | 207 | 248 | 283 | 322 | 364 |
| Employer contributions to social security | 1,081 | 1,429 | 1,424 | 1,479 | 1,493 | 1,496 | 1,495 |
| Other nonresidents [2] | 70 | 67 | 218 | 117 | 131 | 179 | 135 |
| **Net balance** | **5,897** | **6,968** | **12,700** | **14,056** | **14,058** | **15,115** | **17,730** |
| Federal government | 5,273 | 6,157 | 11,999 | 13,247 | 13,259 | 14,505 | 17,113 |
| U.S. state governments | 10 | 10 | 26 | 31 | 31 | 28 | 35 |
| Other nonresidents | 614 | 801 | 675 | 778 | 768 | 581 | 582 |

P Preliminary. [1] Includes other receipts and payments not shown separately. [2] Includes U.S. state governments.

Source: Puerto Rico Planning Board, San Juan, PR, *Informe Económico al Gobernador: Economic Report to the Governor 2018*, March 2019, and earlier reports. See also <http://jp.gobierno.pr/plan-econ-y-social>.

## Table 1349. Puerto Rico—Merchandise Imports and Exports: 1980 to 2018

[In millions of dollars (9,018 represents $9,018,000,000). Data shown is trade for the San Juan, Puerto Rico Customs District. Imports are imports for consumption; see text, Section 28]

| Item | 1980 | 1990 | 2000 | 2010 | 2011 | 2012 | 2013 | 2014 | 2015 | 2016 | 2017 | 2018 |
|---|---|---|---|---|---|---|---|---|---|---|---|---|
| Imports | 9,018 | 16,200 | 27,006 | 39,766 | 44,736 | 45,407 | 43,811 | 42,768 | 42,288 | 45,833 | 41,920 | 52,902 |
| From U.S. | 5,345 | 10,792 | 15,172 | 20,641 | 20,346 | 19,808 | 20,314 | 20,848 | 22,882 | 25,151 | 23,160 | 26,994 |
| From other | 3,673 | 5,408 | 11,834 | 19,125 | 24,391 | 25,599 | 23,497 | 21,920 | 19,406 | 20,682 | 18,759 | 25,909 |
| Exports | 6,576 | 20,402 | 43,191 | 67,347 | 56,767 | 58,646 | 61,632 | 66,746 | 70,621 | 71,978 | 64,278 | 62,570 |
| To U.S. | 5,643 | 17,915 | 38,335 | 47,630 | 40,942 | 42,308 | 44,229 | 49,194 | 53,281 | 56,136 | 51,287 | 48,508 |
| To other | 933 | 2,487 | 4,856 | 19,717 | 15,825 | 16,337 | 17,404 | 17,552 | 17,339 | 15,842 | 12,992 | 14,062 |

Source: U.S. Census Bureau, Foreign Trade Division, *U.S. Trade with Puerto Rico and U.S. Possessions* (FT 895), 2018 and earlier reports; *U.S. Merchandise Trade: Selected Highlights* (FT 920), December 2011 and earlier reports; and "USA Trade Online," <https://usatrade.census.gov/>, accessed May 2019.

## Table 1350. Puerto Rico—Agricultural Summary: 2007 and 2012

[1 cuerda = 0.97 acre]

| All farms | Unit | 2007 | 2012 |
|---|---|---|---|
| Farms | Number | 15,745 | 13,159 |
| Farm land | Cuerdas | 557,530 | 584,988 |
| Average size of farm | Cuerdas | 35.4 | 44.5 |
| Approximate land area | Cuerdas | 2,254,365 | 2,254,365 |
| Proportion in farms | Percent | 24.7 | 25.9 |
| Farms by size: | | | |
| Less than 10 cuerdas | Number | 7,502 | 5,129 |
| 10 to 19 cuerdas | Number | 3,545 | 2,859 |
| 20 to 49 cuerdas | Number | 2,680 | 2,872 |
| 50 to 99 cuerdas | Number | 865 | 940 |
| 100 to 174 cuerdas | Number | 524 | 563 |
| 175 to 259 cuerdas | Number | 207 | 401 |
| 260 cuerdas or more | Number | 422 | 395 |
| Tenure of operator: | | | |
| Operators | Number | 15,745 | 13,159 |
| Full owners | Number | 11,402 | 9,362 |
| Part owners | Number | 1,918 | 1,069 |

| All farms | Unit | 2007 | 2012 |
|---|---|---|---|
| Tenants | Number | 2,425 | 2,728 |
| Farms by type of organization: | | | |
| Individual or family | Number | 13,958 | 11,938 |
| Partnership | Number | 49 | 117 |
| Corporation | Number | 575 | 738 |
| Other | Number | 1,163 | 366 |
| Farms by value of sales: | | | |
| Less than $1,000 | Number | 4,442 | 1,837 |
| $1,000 to $2,499 | Number | 2,771 | 2,015 |
| $2,500 to $4,499 | Number | 2,428 | 1,986 |
| $5,000 to $7,499 | Number | 1,206 | 1,209 |
| $7,500 to $9,999 | Number | 882 | 771 |
| $10,000 to $19,999 | Number | 1,497 | 1,521 |
| $20,000 to $39,999 | Number | 1,030 | 968 |
| $40,000 to $59,999 | Number | 281 | 394 |
| $60,000 or more | Number | 1,208 | 1,322 |

Source: U.S. Department of Agriculture, National Agricultural Statistics Service (NASS), *2012 Census of Agriculture: Puerto Rico, Island and Municipio Data*, Geographic Area Series, Volume 1: Part 52, June 2014. See also <https://www.nass.usda.gov/Publications/AgCensus/2012/index.php>.

## Table 1351. Puerto Rico—Farms and Market Value of Agricultural Products Sold: 2012

[For market value, 547,629 represents $547,629,000]

| Type of product | Number of farms | Market value ($1,000) | Average value per farm (dol.) |
|---|---|---|---|
| Total | 13,159 | 547,629 | 41,616 |
| Crops | 9,367 | 271,320 | (NA) |
| Coffee | 4,478 | 29,273 | 6,537 |
| Pineapples | 42 | 1,906 | 45,375 |
| Plantains | 3,628 | 80,505 | 22,190 |
| Bananas | 1,474 | 12,106 | 8,213 |
| Grains | 781 | 8,539 | 10,934 |
| Root crops or tubers | 1,242 | 8,192 | 6,596 |
| Fruits and coconuts | 1,926 | 31,541 | 16,377 |
| Vegetables and melons [1] | 1,528 | 47,135 | 30,848 |

| Type of product | Number of farms | Market value ($1,000) | Average value per farm (dol.) |
|---|---|---|---|
| Horticultural specialties | 657 | 37,534 | 57,129 |
| Grasses and other crops | 532 | 14,589 | 27,422 |
| Livestock, poultry, and their products | 4,119 | 276,309 | 67,081 |
| Cattle and calves | 2,911 | 33,606 | 11,544 |
| Poultry and poultry products | 706 | 40,376 | 57,189 |
| Dairy products | 318 | 189,425 | 595,677 |
| Hogs and pigs | 532 | 8,019 | 15,074 |
| Aquaculture | 51 | 688 | 13,490 |
| Other | 630 | 4,195 | 6,659 |

NA Not available. [1] Includes hydroponic crops.

Source: U.S. Department of Agriculture, National Agricultural Statistics Service (NASS), *2012 Census of Agriculture: Puerto Rico, Island and Municipio Data*, Geographic Area Series, Volume 1: Part 52, June 2014. See also <https://www.nass.usda.gov/Publications/AgCensus/2012/index.php>.

## Table 1352. Guam, Virgin Islands, Northern Mariana Islands, and American Samoa—Economic Summary by Sector: 2012

[Sales and payroll in millions of dollars (7,737 represents $7,737,000,000). Data for establishments with annual payroll. Based on the 2012 Economic Census of Island Areas; see Appendix III]

| Kind of business | Guam | Virgin Islands | Northern Mariana Islands | American Samoa |
|---|---|---|---|---|
| Total: [1] | | | | |
| Establishments | 3,099 | 2,414 | 1,339 | 377 |
| Sales | 7,737 | 6,831 | 1,324 | 1,154 |
| Annual payroll | 1,287 | 1,129 | 208 | 114 |
| Paid employees [2] | 53,579 | 32,465 | 14,215 | 7,070 |
| Construction: | | | | |
| Establishments | 320 | 161 | 62 | 20 |
| Sales | 750 | 238 | 37 | 31 |
| Annual payroll | 167 | 58 | 8 | 5 |
| Paid employees [2] | 6,722 | 1,729 | 821 | 432 |
| Manufacturing: | | | | |
| Establishments | 54 | 57 | 39 | 25 |
| Sales | 123 | 1,963 | 21 | (D) |
| Annual payroll | 28 | 168 | 7 | (D) |
| Paid employees [2] | 1,282 | 1,984 | 592 | (3) |
| Wholesale trade: | | | | |
| Establishments | 177 | 64 | 74 | 16 |
| Sales | 982 | 221 | 247 | 275 |
| Annual payroll | 66 | 25 | 11 | 5 |

| Kind of business | Guam | Virgin Islands | Northern Mariana Islands | American Samoa |
|---|---|---|---|---|
| Paid employees [2] | 2,505 | 686 | 716 | 253 |
| Retail trade: | | | | |
| Establishments | 630 | 560 | 284 | 136 |
| Sales | 1,980 | 1,318 | 314 | 210 |
| Annual payroll | 184 | 142 | 31 | 17 |
| Paid employees [2] | 8,879 | 6,596 | 2,463 | 1,435 |
| Professional, scientific, & technical services: | | | | |
| Establishments | 241 | 232 | 105 | 22 |
| Sales | 294 | 307 | 29 | 20 |
| Annual payroll | 105 | 95 | 10 | 5 |
| Paid employees [2] | 2,737 | 2,108 | 602 | 254 |
| Accommodation & food services: | | | | |
| Establishments | 450 | 279 | 142 | 36 |
| Sales | 790 | 539 | 180 | 29 |
| Annual payroll | 189 | 161 | 38 | 6 |
| Paid employees [2] | 12,575 | 6,864 | 3,195 | 574 |

D Withheld to avoid disclosing data for individual companies; data are included in higher level totals. [1] Includes other industries, not shown separately. [2] For pay period including March 12. [3] 1,000 to 2,499 employees.

Source: U.S. Census Bureau, 2012 Economic Census of the Island Areas, Geographic Area Series, "General Statistics by Kind of Business," <http://factfinder.census.gov/>, accessed July 2014. See also <https://www.census.gov/programs-surveys/economic-census/about/island-areas.html>.

## Table 1353. Puerto Rico—Business Summary by Industry: 2015 and 2016

[Payroll in millions of dollars (17,256.3 represents $17,256,300,000). Covers establishments with payroll. Excludes self-employed individuals, employees of private households, railroad employees, agricultural production employees, and most government employees. For statement on methodology, see Appendix III]

| Industry | NAICS code [1] | Establishments | | Paid employees [2] | | Annual payroll (mil. dol.) | |
|---|---|---|---|---|---|---|---|
| | | 2015 | 2016 | 2015 | 2016 | 2015 | 2016 |
| **Total, all industries**............... | (X) | **43,325** | **43,620** | **672,399** | **677,974** | **17,256.3** | **17,315.9** |
| Agriculture, forestry, fishing and hunting.......... | 11 | 14 | 14 | 99 | 172 | 0.9 | 1.4 |
| Mining, quarrying, and oil and gas extraction..... | 21 | 44 | 43 | 511 | 516 | 10.1 | 10.7 |
| Utilities............. | 22 | 27 | 26 | 314 | 344 | 19.4 | 21.7 |
| Construction............. | 23 | 1,707 | 1,773 | 21,924 | 24,510 | 488.1 | 527.9 |
| Manufacturing............. | 31–33 | 1,703 | 1,730 | 72,437 | 73,706 | 2,910.2 | 2,885.2 |
| Wholesale trade............. | 42 | 1,968 | 1,986 | 29,342 | 29,568 | 1,106.8 | 1,129.0 |
| Retail trade............. | 44–45 | 9,313 | 9,569 | 131,644 | 130,558 | 2,451.0 | 2,388.4 |
| Transportation and warehousing.............. | 48–49 | 969 | 988 | 14,849 | 14,312 | 423.0 | 414.8 |
| Information............. | 51 | 714 | 681 | 17,928 | 18,019 | 747.6 | 749.7 |
| Finance and insurance............. | 52 | 1,785 | 1,814 | 30,463 | 31,708 | 1,418.4 | 1,432.4 |
| Real estate and rental and leasing............. | 53 | 1,589 | 1,581 | 11,402 | 10,414 | 275.6 | 257.5 |
| Professional, scientific, and technical services.. | 54 | 4,405 | 4,327 | 32,525 | 32,389 | 1,236.6 | 1,218.9 |
| Management of companies and enterprises...... | 55 | 104 | 102 | 7,003 | 7,129 | 346.1 | 341.3 |
| Administrative, support, waste management and remediation services......................... | 56 | 1,963 | 1,928 | 73,889 | 77,062 | 1,383.4 | 1,469.2 |
| Educational services............. | 61 | 902 | 920 | 42,242 | 40,866 | 828.9 | 853.9 |
| Health care and social assistance.............. | 62 | 7,563 | 7,646 | 82,836 | 84,261 | 2,046.5 | 2,065.3 |
| Arts, entertainment, and recreation.............. | 71 | 455 | 452 | 4,023 | 3,543 | 81.2 | 71.4 |
| Accommodation and food services.............. | 72 | 4,508 | 4,434 | 80,101 | 79,246 | 1,115.1 | 1,100.3 |
| Other services (except public administration). ... | 81 | 3,286 | 3,313 | 18,501 | 18,841 | 359.9 | 363.8 |
| Industries not classified............. | 99 | 306 | 293 | 366 | 810 | 7.6 | 12.9 |

X Not applicable. [1] Based on the 2012 North American Industry Classification System. See text, Section 15. [2] Covers full- and part-time employees who are on the payroll in the pay period including March 12.

Source: U.S. Census Bureau, County Business Patterns, "Geography Area Series: County Business Patterns for Puerto Rico and the Island Areas," <http://factfinder.census.gov/>, accessed April 2018. See also <https://www.census.gov/programs-surveys/cbp.html>.

## Table 1354. Virgin Islands—Business Summary by Industry: 2015 and 2016

[Payroll in thousands of dollars (969,738 represents $969,738,000). Covers establishments with payroll. Excludes self-employed individuals, employees of private households, railroad employees, agricultural production employees, and most government employees. For statement on methodology, see Appendix III]

| Industry | NAICS code [1] | Establishments | | Paid employees [2] | | Annual payroll ($1,000) | |
|---|---|---|---|---|---|---|---|
| | | 2015 | 2016 | 2015 | 2016 | 2015 | 2016 |
| **Total, all industries**............... | (X) | **2,572** | **2,528** | **29,118** | **29,598** | **969,738** | **986,079** |
| Agriculture, forestry, fishing and hunting............... | 11 | 2 | 1 | ([3]) | ([3]) | (D) | (D) |
| Mining, quarrying, and oil and gas extraction........... | 21 | 2 | 3 | ([3]) | ([3]) | (D) | (D) |
| Utilities............. | 22 | 6 | 5 | 37 | 47 | 2,498 | 2,841 |
| Construction............. | 23 | 160 | 154 | 1,293 | 1,348 | 47,089 | 50,231 |
| Manufacturing............. | 31-33 | 49 | 46 | 602 | 585 | 27,131 | 26,002 |
| Wholesale trade............. | 42 | 58 | 60 | 771 | 630 | 44,001 | 27,245 |
| Retail trade............. | 44-45 | 535 | 508 | 6,086 | 6,262 | 136,588 | 137,206 |
| Transportation and warehousing............... | 48-49 | 108 | 113 | 1,677 | 1,749 | 53,187 | 54,015 |
| Information............. | 51 | 41 | 45 | 775 | 720 | 38,667 | 34,554 |
| Finance and insurance............. | 52 | 116 | 119 | 1,082 | 1,118 | 69,927 | 67,835 |
| Real estate and rental and leasing............... | 53 | 196 | 204 | 1,002 | 1,127 | 39,465 | 44,865 |
| Professional, scientific, and technical services........ | 54 | 240 | 225 | 979 | 918 | 52,316 | 54,375 |
| Management of companies and enterprises........... | 55 | 8 | 7 | 126 | 84 | 5,503 | 5,343 |
| Administrative, support, waste management and remediation services................................ | 56 | 165 | 155 | 2,132 | 2,142 | 78,406 | 86,377 |
| Educational services............. | 61 | 33 | 33 | 673 | 643 | 18,636 | 18,595 |
| Health care and social assistance...................... | 62 | 259 | 248 | 3,152 | 3,116 | 136,423 | 140,516 |
| Arts, entertainment, and recreation.................... | 71 | 55 | 51 | 676 | 609 | 15,625 | 14,455 |
| Accommodation and food services.................... | 72 | 297 | 305 | 6,966 | 7,239 | 175,918 | 182,638 |
| Other services (except public administration).......... | 81 | 214 | 222 | 1,015 | 1,200 | 27,112 | 36,372 |
| Industries not classified................................ | 99 | 28 | 24 | 56 | 46 | 888 | 918 |

X Not applicable. D Withheld to avoid disclosing data for individual companies; data are included in total. [1] Based on the 2012 North American Industry Classification System. See text, Section 15. [2] Covers full- and part-time employees who are on the payroll in the pay period including March 12. [3] 0 to 19 employees.

Source: U.S. Census Bureau, County Business Patterns, "Geography Area Series: County Business Patterns for Puerto Rico and the Island Areas," <http://factfinder.census.gov/>, accessed April 2018. See also <https://www.census.gov/programs-surveys/cbp.html>.

## Table 1355. Guam—Business Summary by Industry: 2015 and 2016

[Payroll in thousands of dollars (1,494,258 represents $1,494,258,000). Covers establishments with payroll. Excludes self-employed individuals, employees of private households, railroad employees, agricultural production employees, and most government employees. For statement on methodology, see Appendix III]

| Industry | NAICS code [1] | Establishments | | Paid employees [2] | | Annual payroll ($1,000) | |
|---|---|---|---|---|---|---|---|
| | | 2015 | 2016 | 2015 | 2016 | 2015 | 2016 |
| Total, all industries.............................. | (X) | 3,475 | 3,504 | 57,902 | 59,032 | 1,494,258 | 1,522,834 |
| Agriculture, forestry, fishing and hunting........ | 11 | 2 | 3 | ( [3] ) | ( [3] ) | (D) | 78 |
| Mining, quarrying, and oil and gas extraction... | 21 | 1 | 1 | ( [3] ) | ( [3] ) | (D) | (D) |
| Utilities............................................ | 22 | 5 | 4 | 61 | 66 | 3,216 | 2,863 |
| Construction....................................... | 23 | 346 | 357 | 6,380 | 5,696 | 164,934 | 141,633 |
| Manufacturing..................................... | 31-33 | 57 | 52 | 911 | 885 | 22,040 | 22,090 |
| Wholesale trade................................... | 42 | 200 | 205 | 2,849 | 3,007 | 80,587 | 80,716 |
| Retail trade........................................ | 44-45 | 684 | 683 | 9,801 | 9,930 | 217,246 | 230,025 |
| Transportation and warehousing................. | 48-49 | 99 | 92 | 2,782 | 2,649 | 106,025 | 100,471 |
| Information........................................ | 51 | 52 | 50 | 1,227 | 1,247 | 46,167 | 46,428 |
| Finance and insurance............................ | 52 | 128 | 127 | 2,230 | 2,161 | 89,093 | 95,677 |
| Real estate and rental and leasing.............. | 53 | 263 | 278 | 2,083 | 2,188 | 52,006 | 57,487 |
| Professional, scientific, and technical services........................................... | 54 | 262 | 261 | 2,646 | 2,718 | 111,557 | 117,701 |
| Management of companies and enterprises.... | 55 | 9 | 8 | 68 | 75 | 3,340 | 3,263 |
| Administrative, support, waste managment and remediation services....................... | 56 | 172 | 166 | 4,479 | 4,314 | 93,001 | 92,250 |
| Educational services.............................. | 61 | 60 | 63 | 1,255 | 1,249 | 26,390 | 27,130 |
| Health care and social assistance............... | 62 | 204 | 211 | 3,758 | 4,363 | 163,813 | 175,057 |
| Arts, entertainment, and recreation............. | 71 | 69 | 71 | 1,174 | 1,209 | 21,243 | 22,005 |
| Accommodation and food services.............. | 72 | 518 | 522 | 13,496 | 14,643 | 231,928 | 247,552 |
| Other services (except public administration)... | 81 | 293 | 284 | 2,500 | 2,411 | 58,624 | 57,266 |
| Industries not classified.......................... | 99 | 51 | 66 | 196 | 214 | 2,715 | 3,002 |

X Not applicable. D Withheld to avoid disclosing data for individual companies; data are included in total. [1] Based on the 2012 North American Industry Classification System. See text, Section 15. [2] Covers full- and part-time employees who are on the payroll in the pay period including March 12. [3] 0 to 19 employees.

Source: U.S. Census Bureau, County Business Patterns, "Geography Area Series: County Business Patterns for Puerto Rico and the Island Areas," <http://factfinder.census.gov/>, accessed April 2018. See also <https://www.census.gov/programs-surveys/cbp.html>.

## Table 1356. Northern Marianas—Business Summary by Industry: 2015 and 2016

[Payroll in thousands of dollars (301,267 represents $301,267,000). Covers establishments with payroll. Excludes self-employed individuals, employees of private households, railroad employees, agricultural production employees, and most government employees. For statement on methodology, see Appendix III]

| Industry | NAICS code [1] | Establishments | | Paid employees [2] | | Annual payroll ($1,000) | |
|---|---|---|---|---|---|---|---|
| | | 2015 | 2016 | 2015 | 2016 | 2015 | 2016 |
| Total, all industries.............................. | (X) | 1,724 | 1,759 | 16,276 | 18,374 | 301,267 | 362,360 |
| Agriculture, forestry, fishing and hunting........ | 11 | 2 | 1 | ( [3] ) | ( [3] ) | (D) | (D) |
| Mining, quarrying, and oil and gas extraction... | 21 | 1 | 1 | ( [4] ) | ( [4] ) | (D) | (D) |
| Utilities............................................ | 22 | 4 | 4 | ( [5] ) | ( [5] ) | (D) | (D) |
| Construction....................................... | 23 | 80 | 96 | 842 | 1,399 | 14,618 | 29,205 |
| Manufacturing..................................... | 31-33 | 48 | 45 | 442 | 550 | 7,562 | 9,255 |
| Wholesale trade................................... | 42 | 83 | 92 | 681 | 762 | 12,208 | 13,230 |
| Retail trade........................................ | 44-45 | 346 | 349 | 2,475 | 2,577 | 40,571 | 42,260 |
| Transportation and warehousing................. | 48-49 | 48 | 53 | 1,038 | 1,057 | 18,614 | 20,754 |
| Information........................................ | 51 | 23 | 22 | 409 | 397 | 11,928 | 10,967 |
| Finance and insurance............................ | 52 | 47 | 48 | 277 | 285 | 7,468 | 8,009 |
| Real estate and rental and leasing.............. | 53 | 163 | 161 | 563 | 662 | 8,355 | 9,665 |
| Professional, scientific, and technical services........................................... | 54 | 102 | 110 | 556 | 534 | 11,868 | 13,306 |
| Management of companies and enterprises.... | 55 | 5 | 6 | 24 | 37 | 689 | 977 |
| Administrative, support, waste management and remediation services....................... | 56 | 147 | 162 | 1,646 | 1,655 | 24,453 | 25,422 |
| Educational services.............................. | 61 | 68 | 61 | 340 | 391 | 5,905 | 7,235 |
| Health care and social assistance............... | 62 | 45 | 45 | 1,042 | 1,016 | 34,101 | 36,553 |
| Arts, entertainment, and recreation............. | 71 | 53 | 57 | 459 | 500 | 7,302 | 8,158 |
| Accommodation and food services.............. | 72 | 195 | 202 | 4,203 | 5,255 | 69,733 | 102,829 |
| Other services (except public administration)... | 81 | 166 | 162 | 651 | 636 | 9,570 | 9,729 |
| Industries not classified.......................... | 99 | 98 | 82 | 217 | 202 | 2,267 | 2,363 |

X Not applicable. D Withheld to avoid disclosing data for individual companies; data are included in total. [1] Based on the 2012 North American Industry Classification System. See text, Section 15. [2] Covers full- and part-time employees who are on the payroll in the pay period including March 12. [3] 0 to 19 employees. [4] 20 to 99 employees. [5] 250 to 499 employees.

Source: U.S. Census Bureau, County Business Patterns, "Geography Area Series: County Business Patterns for Puerto Rico and the Island Areas," <http://factfinder.census.gov/>, accessed April 2018. See also <https://www.census.gov/programs-surveys/cbp.html>.

## Table 1357. American Samoa—Business Summary by Industry: 2015 and 2016

[Payroll in thousands of dollars (140,751 represents $140,751,000). Covers establishments with payroll. Excludes self-employed individuals, employees of private households, railroad employees, agricultural production employees, and most government employees. For statement on methodology, see Appendix III]

| Industry | NAICS code [1] | Establishments | | Paid employees [2] | | Annual payroll ($1,000) | |
|---|---|---|---|---|---|---|---|
| | | 2015 | 2016 | 2015 | 2016 | 2015 | 2016 |
| **Total, all industries**............... | (X) | **486** | **504** | **8,156** | **8,506** | **140,751** | **144,226** |
| Agriculture, forestry, fishing and hunting.......... | 11 | 1 | 2 | ([3]) | ([3]) | (D) | (D) |
| Construction.......................... | 23 | 30 | 33 | 500 | 502 | 9,113 | 8,512 |
| Manufacturing....................... | 31-33 | 38 | 40 | 3,160 | 3,190 | 50,943 | 51,017 |
| Wholesale trade..................... | 42 | 25 | 26 | 264 | 268 | 4,784 | 5,785 |
| Retail trade.......................... | 44-45 | 170 | 172 | 1,465 | 1,515 | 20,655 | 21,398 |
| Transportation and warehousing................... | 48-49 | 27 | 27 | 326 | 343 | 4,649 | 4,893 |
| Information........................... | 51 | 6 | 7 | 168 | 185 | 4,024 | 4,253 |
| Finance and insurance.......................... | 52 | 10 | 11 | 110 | 109 | 2,735 | 2,685 |
| Real estate and rental and leasing... | 53 | 13 | 15 | 67 | 80 | 878 | 1,270 |
| Professional, scientific, and technical services... | 54 | 26 | 26 | 199 | 169 | 5,788 | 5,355 |
| Management of companies and enterprises..... | 55 | 2 | 2 | ([3]) | ([3]) | (D) | (D) |
| Administrative, support, waste management and remediation services.......................... | 56 | 24 | 21 | 116 | 119 | 1,679 | 1,868 |
| Educational services....................... | 61 | 4 | 5 | 127 | 168 | 1,760 | 1,994 |
| Health care and social assistance................. | 62 | 15 | 16 | ([4]) | ([4]) | (D) | (D) |
| Arts, entertainment, and recreation............... | 71 | 1 | 1 | ([3]) | ([3]) | (D) | (D) |
| Accommodation and food services.................. | 72 | 40 | 44 | 448 | 576 | 6,335 | 7,176 |
| Other services (except public administration).... | 81 | 45 | 47 | 399 | 384 | 4,627 | 4,982 |
| Industries not classified............................ | 99 | 9 | 9 | 26 | 29 | 269 | 306 |

X Not applicable. D Withheld to avoid disclosing data for individual companies; data are included in total. [1] Based on the 2012 North American Industry Classification System. See text, Section 15. [2] Covers full- and part-time employees who are on the payroll in the pay period including March 12. [3] 0 to 19 employees. [4] 500 to 999 employees.

Source: U.S. Census Bureau, County Business Patterns, "Geography Area Series: County Business Patterns for Puerto Rico and the Island Areas," <http://factfinder.census.gov/>, accessed April 2018. See also <https://www.census.gov/programs-surveys/cbp.html>.

## Table 1358. Occupational Employment and Average Annual Wages in Guam, Puerto Rico, and Virgin Islands: 2018

[The Occupational Employment Survey (OES) program conducts a semiannual mail survey designed to produce estimates of employment and wages for specific occupations. Excludes self-employed persons. For more details on the survey, see <https://www.bls.gov/oes/oes_emp.htm>]

| Selected occupation | SOC code [1] | Guam | | Puerto Rico | | Virgin Islands | |
|---|---|---|---|---|---|---|---|
| | | Employ-ment | Average annual wages [2] | Employ-ment | Average annual wages [2] | Employ-ment | Average annual wages [2] |
| **Total, all occupations [3]**............................ | (X) | **60,170** | **36,550** | **846,010** | **29,460** | **32,290** | **42,870** |
| Management occupations.............................. | 11 | 4,950 | 69,890 | 37,080 | 75,540 | 3,080 | 82,810 |
| Business and financial operations.................... | 13 | 2,240 | 53,510 | 42,300 | 39,730 | 1,360 | 56,810 |
| Computer and mathematical occupations........... | 15 | 600 | 51,660 | 11,070 | 43,470 | 320 | 58,860 |
| Architecture and engineering......................... | 17 | 940 | 60,330 | 14,230 | 54,440 | 210 | 60,360 |
| Life, physical, and social sciences................... | 19 | 390 | 55,820 | 6,000 | 47,680 | 260 | 52,360 |
| Community and social services....................... | 21 | 710 | 46,370 | 15,290 | 29,300 | 420 | 45,450 |
| Legal occupations...................................... | 23 | 250 | 73,170 | 4,620 | 67,170 | 480 | 90,160 |
| Education, training, and library occupations......... | 25 | 4,530 | 45,390 | 65,300 | 35,130 | 2,000 | 45,620 |
| Arts, design, entertainment, sports, and media..... | 27 | 550 | 37,180 | 6,670 | 35,660 | 180 | 42,130 |
| Healthcare practitioner and technical occupations.......................................... | 29 | 2,200 | 69,790 | 50,910 | 36,300 | 1,260 | 69,230 |
| Healthcare support..................................... | 31 | 960 | 27,620 | 9,840 | 20,830 | 380 | 31,330 |
| Protective service occupations........................ | 33 | 2,420 | 37,610 | 56,630 | 24,990 | 2,280 | 35,350 |
| Food preparation and serving related occupations.......................................... | 35 | 6,810 | 21,300 | 64,890 | 18,990 | 3,040 | 26,350 |
| Buildings and grounds cleaning and maintenance.......................................... | 37 | 3,180 | 21,350 | 39,520 | 20,290 | 1,510 | 25,970 |
| Personal care and service occupations.............. | 39 | 1,370 | 22,810 | 13,500 | 19,750 | 970 | 26,820 |
| Sales and related occupations........................ | 41 | 5,080 | 24,680 | 98,120 | 23,090 | 3,030 | 32,090 |
| Office and administrative support..................... | 43 | 10,850 | 29,640 | 153,920 | 25,040 | 5,460 | 34,570 |
| Farming, fishing, and forestry......................... | 45 | 70 | 28,200 | 1,690 | 22,260 | (NA) | (NA) |
| Construction and extraction........................... | 47 | 4,010 | 31,630 | 27,630 | 22,040 | 1,780 | 44,440 |
| Installation, maintenance, and repair................. | 49 | 2,960 | 33,950 | 28,800 | 26,820 | 1,350 | 38,760 |
| Production occupations................................ | 51 | 1,500 | 31,150 | 55,240 | 24,240 | 730 | 43,790 |
| Transportation and material moving.................. | 53 | 3,590 | 30,030 | 42,780 | 22,860 | 2,170 | 32,610 |

X Not applicable. NA Not available. [1] Office of Management and Budget's Standard Occupational Classification (SOC) is used to define occupations. SOC categorizes workers into one of over 800 detailed occupations, which are classified into 23 major occupational groups. [2] Annual wages have been calculated by multiplying the hourly mean wage by a "year-round, full-time" hours figure of 2,080 hours; for those occupations where there is not an hourly mean wage published, the annual wage has been directly calculated from the reported survey data. [3] Estimates do not sum to the total because the total may include data for occupations not shown separately. See source for more information.

Source: U.S. Bureau of Labor Statistics, "Occupational Employment Statistics," <http://www.bls.gov/oes/current/oessrcst.htm>, accessed May 2019.

# Section 30
# International Statistics

This section presents statistics for the world as a whole and for many countries on a comparative basis with the United States. Data are shown for population, births and deaths, social and economic indicators, finances, agriculture, energy, climate, science and technology, communications, and military affairs.

Statistics for individual countries may be found primarily in official national publications, generally in the form of yearbooks, issued by most countries in their own national languages and expressed in their own customary units of measure. For a listing of selected publications, see Appendix I table under international statistical abstracts from a foreign agency.

For international comparisons, the United Nations Statistics Division compiles data as submitted by member countries and issues a number of summary publications, generally in English and French. Among these are the annual *Statistical Yearbook; Demographic Yearbook; Population and Vital Statistics Report; International Trade Statistics Yearbook; Energy Statistics Yearbook; Industrial Commodity Statistics Yearbook; National Accounts Statistics;* and the *Monthly Bulletin of Statistics*. Specialized agencies of the United Nations also issue international summary publications on various topics, including agricultural, labor, health, and trade statistics. Among these are *Food Outlook* and the *Statistical Pocketbook* issued by the Food and Agriculture Organization (FAO); *World Employment and Social Outlook* issued by the International Labor Organization (ILO); *World Health Statistics* issued by the World Health Organization (WHO); and the *Handbook of Statistics* issued by the Conference on Trade and Development (UNCTAD).

The U.S. Census Bureau publishes estimates and projections of key demographic measures for countries and regions of the world in its International Data Base at <https://www.census.gov/programs-surveys/international-programs.html>.

The International Monetary Fund (IMF), the World Bank, and the Organisation for Economic Co-operation and Development (OECD) also compile international statistics. The IMF publishes a series of reports related to financial data. These include *World Economic Outlook, Global Financial Stability Report*, and *Fiscal Monitor*. The World Bank publishes many reports on a wide range of topics related to international development. Three of their flagship statistical publications are *World Development Report, World Development Indicators*, and *Global Economic Prospects*. The OECD also produces numerous statistical publications in fields including economics, health, and education. Among these are the *Economic Outlook; National Accounts of OECD Countries; Science, Technology and Innovation Outlook; International Migration Outlook; Employment Outlook*; and *Education at a Glance*.

**Statistical coverage and country classifications—** Problems of space and availability of data limit the number of countries and the extent of statistical coverage shown. The lists of countries and territories included in individual tables are generally based on source publications and databases, as cited.

In the last quarter-century, several important changes took place in the status of the world's nations. In 1991, the Soviet Union broke up into 15 independent countries: Armenia, Azerbaijan, Belarus, Estonia, Georgia, Kazakhstan, Kyrgyzstan, Latvia, Lithuania, Moldova, Russia, Tajikistan, Turkmenistan, Ukraine, and Uzbekistan.

Germany was reunified in 1990, when the German Democratic Republic (former East Germany) joined the Federal Republic of Germany (former West Germany) to form a single country. On January 1, 1993, Czechoslovakia was succeeded by two independent countries: the Czech Republic and Slovakia. The Czech Republic is now known as Czechia.

Following the breakup of the Socialist Federal Republic of Yugoslavia in 1992, the United States recognized Bosnia and Herzegovina, Croatia, Slovenia, and Macedonia as independent countries. Serbia and Montenegro, both former republics of Yugoslavia, became independent of one another on May 31, 2006. This separation is reflected in the population estimates of Table 1362. On February 17, 2008, Kosovo declared its independence from Serbia.

The Treaty of Maastricht created the European Union (EU) in 1992 with 12 member countries. The EU is not a state intended to replace existing states, but it is more than just an international organization. Its member states have set up common institutions to which they delegate some of their sovereignty so that decisions on specific matters of joint interest can be made democratically at a European level. This pooling of sovereignty is also called "European integration." The EU has grown in size with successive waves of accessions in 1995, 2004, 2007, and 2013. The 28 current members of the EU are: Austria, Belgium, Bulgaria, Croatia, Cyprus, Czechia, Denmark, Estonia, Finland, France, Germany, Greece, Hungary, Ireland, Italy, Latvia, Lithuania, Luxembourg, Malta, the Netherlands, Poland, Portugal, Romania, Slovakia, Slovenia, Spain, Sweden, and the United Kingdom. In June 2016, the electorate of the United Kingdom voted to withdraw from the EU. Negotiations for the exit have begun, but withdrawal is not expected to be complete until late 2019. Until that time, the UK remains a full member of the EU.

In 1992, the EU decided to establish an economic and monetary union (EMU), with the introduction of a single European currency managed by a European Central Bank. The single currency—the euro—became a reality on January 1, 2002, when euro notes and coins replaced national currencies in 12 of the then 15 countries of the European Union (Austria, Belgium, Finland, France, Germany, Greece, Ireland, Italy, Luxembourg, the Netherlands, Portugal, and Spain). Since then, 13 additional countries have acceded to EU membership, but Cyprus, Estonia, Latvia, Lithuania, Malta, Slovakia, and Slovenia have been the only new members of the EU to adopt the euro as the national currency. In total, the euro is the official currency of 19 of the 28 EU member countries.

Elsewhere in the world, Eritrea announced its independence from Ethiopia in April 1993 and was subsequently recognized as an independent nation by the United States. In the South Pacific, the Marshall Islands, Micronesia, and Palau gained independence from the United States in 1991. In May of 2002, Timor-Leste won independence from Indonesia. The Netherlands Antilles dissolved on October 10, 2010. As a result, Curaçao and Sint Maarten became autonomous territories of the Netherlands. As of July 2011, Sudan and South Sudan became separate countries. And, in 2018, Swaziland was officially renamed Eswatini.

The population estimates and projections used in Tables 1359 through 1362, 1364, and 1365 were prepared by the U.S. Census Bureau. For each country, available data on population by age and sex, fertility, mortality, and international migration were evaluated and, where necessary, adjusted for inconsistencies and errors in the data. Comprehensive population projections were made by the cohort-component method based on an assessment of probable future trends.

**Economic associations**—The Organisation for European Economic Co–operation (OEEC) was originally a regional grouping of Western European countries established in 1948 for the purpose of harmonizing national economic policies and conditions. It was succeeded on September 30, 1961 by the Organisation for Economic Co-operation and Development (OECD). As of 2019, the 36 member nations of the OECD are Australia, Austria, Belgium, Canada, Chile, Czechia, Denmark, Estonia, Finland, France, Germany, Greece, Hungary, Iceland, Ireland, Israel, Italy, Japan, Latvia, Lithuania, Luxembourg, Mexico, the Netherlands, New Zealand, Norway, Poland, Portugal, Slovak Republic, Slovenia, South Korea, Spain, Sweden, Switzerland, Turkey, the United Kingdom, and the United States. Additionally, Colombia has been invited to join and its accession is imminent.

**Quality and comparability of the data**—The quality and comparability of the data presented here are affected by a number of factors:

1 The year for which data are presented may not be the same for all subjects for a particular country or for a given subject for different countries, though the data shown are the most recent available. All such variations have been noted. The data shown are for calendar years except as otherwise specified.

2 The statistical bases, methods of estimating, methods of data collection, extent of coverage, precision of definition, scope of territory, and margins of error may vary for different items within a particular country, and for like items for different countries. Footnotes and headnotes to the tables describe some of the major coverage qualifications attached to the figures; considerably more detail is presented in the source publications. Many of the measures shown are merely rough indicators of magnitude.

3 Figures shown in this section for the United States may not always agree with figures shown in the preceding sections. Discrepancies may be attributable to the use of differing original sources, differences in the definition of geographic limits (the 50 states, continental U.S. only, or the U.S. including certain outlying areas and possessions), or to possible adjustments made to the U.S. figures in order to make them more comparable with figures from other countries.

**International comparisons of national accounts data**—To compare national accounts data for different countries, it is necessary to convert each country's data into a common unit of currency, usually the U.S. dollar. The market exchange rates, which often are used in converting national currencies, do not necessarily reflect the relative purchasing power in the various countries. It is necessary that the goods and services produced in different countries be valued consistently if the differences observed are meant to reflect real differences in the volumes of goods and services produced. The use of purchasing power parities (see Tables 1373, 1374, and 1380) instead of exchange rates is intended to achieve this objective.

The method used to present the data shown in Table 1380 is to construct volume measures directly by revaluing the goods and services sold in different countries at a common set of international prices. By dividing the ratio of the gross domestic products of two countries expressed in their own national currencies by the corresponding ratio calculated at constant international prices, it is possible to derive the implied purchasing power parity (PPP) between the two currencies concerned. PPPs show how many units of currency are needed in one country to buy the same amount of goods and services that one unit of currency will buy in the other country. For further information, see *National Accounts of OECD Countries, Main Aggregates*, issued annually by the Organisation for Economic Co-operation and Development (OECD), Paris, France.

**International Standard Industrial Classification**—The original version of the International Standard Industrial Classification of All Economic Activities (ISIC) was adopted in 1948. A number of countries have utilized ISIC as the basis for devising their industrial classification schemes. Substantial comparability has been attained among the industrial classification schemes of many countries, including the United States, by ensuring that national classification categories correspond to ISIC categories. The United Nations, the International Labour Organization, the Food and Agriculture Organization, and other international bodies use ISIC in publishing and analyzing statistical data. Revisions of ISIC were issued in 1958, 1968, 1989, 2002, and 2008.

**International Maps**—A series of regional world maps is provided within this section. References are included in Table 1362 for easy location of individual countries on the maps. Map projection will be distorted due to being portrayed on a flat surface. For additional information and maps see the Central Intelligence Agency's *The World Factbook*, at <https://www.cia.gov/library/publications/the-world-factbook/docs/refmaps.html>.

Scale: 1:36,000,000

Lambert Conformal Conic Projection,
standard parallels 25°N and 77°N

803541AI(G00694)6-12

Scale 1: 12,500,000

Lambert Conformal Conic Projection,
standard parallels 7° N and 24° N

Boundary representation is not necessarily authoritative.

803538AI (G00800) 6-12

HONDURAS
Tegucigalpa
Isla de Providencia (COLOMBIA)
Caribbean Sea
Martinique (FRANCE)
ST. LUCIA
ST. VINCENT AND THE GRENADINES
BARBADOS
NICARAGUA
Managua
Aruba (NETH.)
Curaçao (NETH.)
GRENADA
Isla de San Andrés (COLOMBIA)
Barranquilla
Maracaibo
Caracas
Port of Spain
TRINIDAD AND TOBAGO
San José
Panama City
Cartagena
Valencia
Barcelona
North Atlantic Ocean
COSTA RICA
PANAMA
Cúcuta
San Cristóbal
VENEZUELA
Ciudad Guayana
Georgetown
Paramaribo
Medellín
Bucaramanga
Río Orinoco
GUYANA
Cayenne
Pereira
Ibagué
Bogotá
SURINAME
French Guiana (FRANCE)
Isla de Malpelo (COLOMBIA)
Cali
COLOMBIA
Boa Vista
Macapá
Equator
Quito
Río Negro
Amazon
Belém
São Luís
ECUADOR
Guayaquil
Manaus
Santarém
Fortaleza
Cuenca
Iquitos
Teresina
Natal
Piura
Río Madeira
BRAZIL
João Pessoa
Chiclayo
Pucallpa
Recife
Trujillo
Río Branco
Pôrto Velho
Maceió
Huánuco
Aracajú
PERU
Salvador
Lima
Huancayo
Cusco
South Pacific Ocean
Ica
Trinidad
Brasília
Arequipa
La Paz
BOLIVIA
Goiânia
Cochabamba
Santa Cruz
Contagem
Arica
Sucre
Potosí
Uberlândia
Belo Horizonte
Iquique
Campo Grande
Vitória
Tropic of Capricorn
Antofagasta
PARAGUAY
Río Paraná
Londrina
Campinas
Rio de Janeiro
Isla San Félix (CHILE)
Isla San Ambrosio (CHILE)
Salta
Asunción
São Paulo
Santos
San Miguel de Tucumán
Ciudad del Este
Curitiba
Joinvile
Resistencia
Florianópolis
CHILE
Córdoba
Santa Fe
Porto Alegre
ARCHIPIÉLAGO JUAN FERNÁNDEZ (CHILE)
Valparaíso
Mendoza
Rosario
Salto
URUGUAY
Santiago
Buenos Aires
Montevideo
La Plata
South Atlantic Ocean
Concepción
ARGENTINA
Bahía Blanca
Mar del Plata
Temuco
Puerto Montt
San Carlos de Bariloche
Comodoro Rivadavia
Scale 1:35,000,000
Azimuthal Equal-Area Projection
Río Gallegos
Stanley
Falkland Islands (Islas Malvinas)
(administered by U.K., claimed by ARGENTINA)
South Georgia and South Sandwich Islands
(administered by U.K., claimed by ARGENTINA)
0    500 Kilometers
0    500 Miles
Strait of Magellan
Punta Arenas
Ushuaia
Cape Horn
Boundary representation is not necessarily authoritative.

803543AI (G00186) 6-12

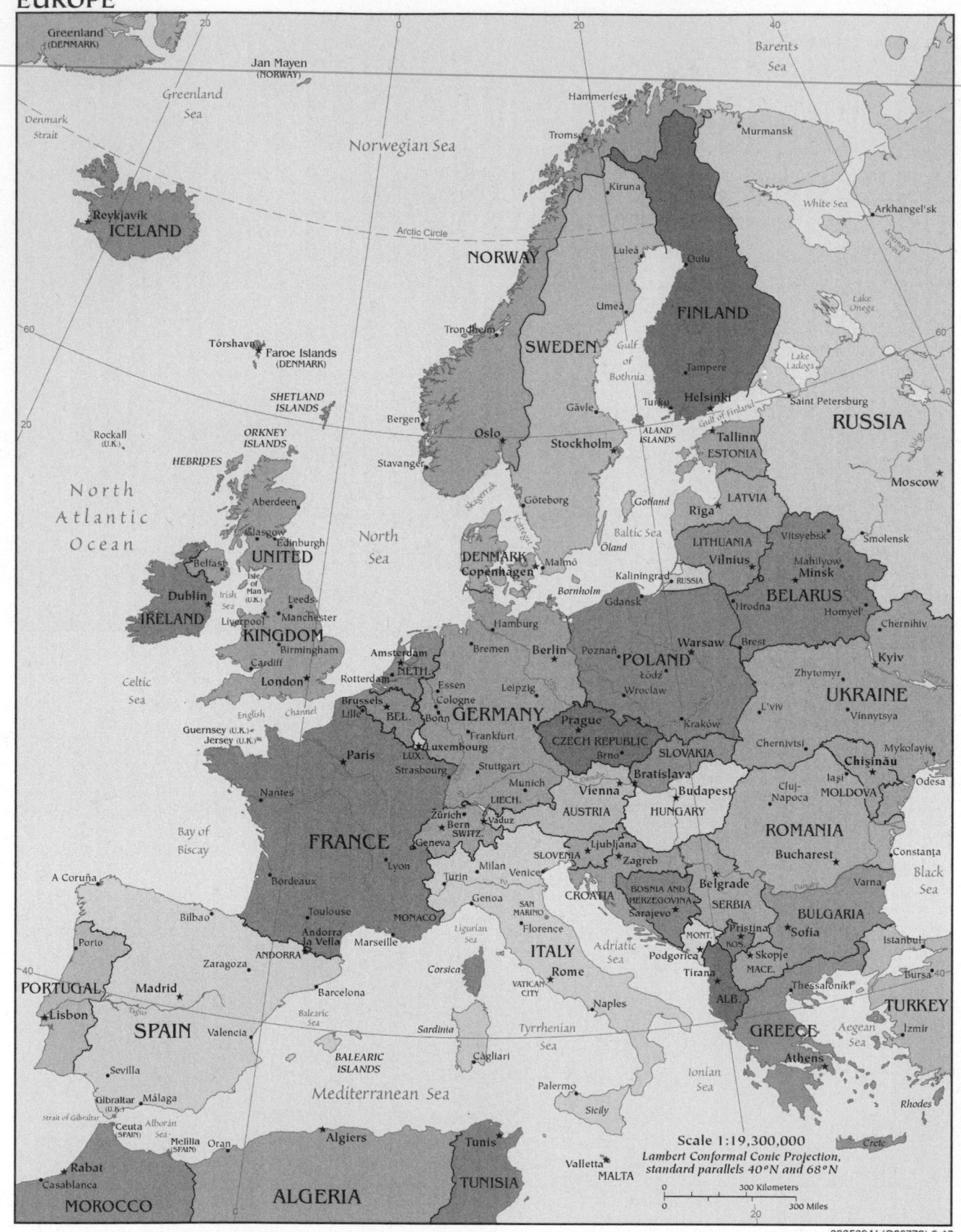

Scale 1:19,300,000
Lambert Conformal Conic Projection,
standard parallels 40°N and 68°N

803539AI (G00772) 6-12

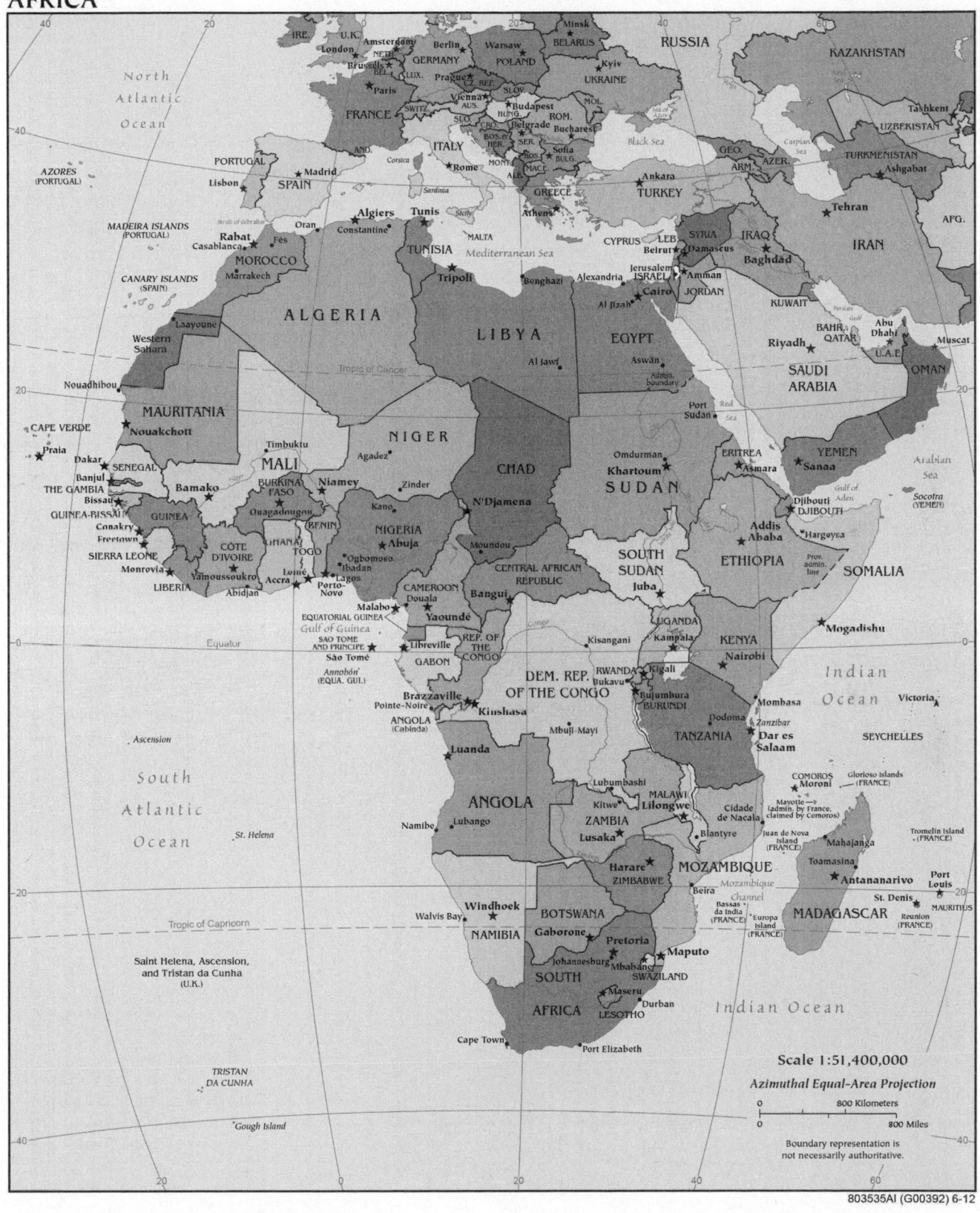

Scale 1:51,400,000

Azimuthal Equal-Area Projection

0    800 Kilometers

0    800 Miles

Boundary representation is
not necessarily authoritative.

803535AI (G00392) 6-12

ROM.
Bucharest ★
Sofia ★
BULGARIA
Varna
Black Sea
Sevastopol'
Constanţa
Krasnodar
Sochi
RUSSIA
KAZAKHSTAN
Aqtaū
(Aktau)
Aral
Sea
KAZAKHSTAN
Nukus
UZBEKISTAN
Dasoguz
Thessaloniki
Istanbul
Bosporus
Samsun
Trabzon
Sokhumi
Bat'umi
GEORGIA
Tbilisi ★
Caspian
Sea
Türkmenbaşy
Amu
TURKMENISTAN
Buxoro
Aegean
Sea
GREECE
İzmir
Athens
Denizli
Dardanelles
Ankara ★
TURKEY
Kayseri
Konya
Erzurum
ARMENIA
Yerevan ★
AZERBAIJAN
Baku ★
Sumqayit
Balkanabat
Turkmenabat
Ashgabat ★
Mary
Crete
Antalya
İçel
(Mersin)
Adana
Gaziantep
Diyarbakır
Van
Lake
Van
Tabrīz
Lake
Urmia
Rasht
Zanjān
Qazvin
Tehran ★
Qom
Mashhad
Herāt
AFG.
Nicosia ★
CYPRUS
Mediterranean Sea
Latakia
Aleppo
Homs
SYRIA
Beirut ★
LEBANON
Damascus ★
ISRAEL
Golan
Heights
Tel Aviv-
Yafo
Mosul
Erbil
Kirkuk
Baghdad ★
IRAQ
Kermānshāh
Arāk
Eşfahān
Esfahan
IRAN
Kermān
Zāhedān
PAK.
Alexandria
Port
Said
Jerusalem ★
West Bank
Amman ★
JORDAN
Dead Sea
Gaza Strip
An Nāşirīyah
Ahvāz
Abādān
Al Başrah
Suez
Cairo ★
Al Jīzah
Al
'Aqabah
Tabūk
Hā'il
Hafar
al Bāţin
Kuwait
City
KUWAIT
Bandar
Būshehr
Bandar
'Abbās
Strait of
Hormuz
OMAN
EGYPT
Asyūţ
Gulf of
Aqaba
Luxor
Aswān
Yanbu'
al Bahr
Medina
Buraydah
Al Jubayl
Ad Dammām
Dhahran
BAHRAIN
Manama ★
QATAR
Doha ★
Abu
Dhabi ★
Dubai
Gulf of
Oman
Muscat ★
Administrative
boundary
Halā'ib
SAUDI
Jeddah
Mecca
Riyadh ★
Persian
Gulf
UNITED ARAB
EMIRATES
ARABIA
OMAN
Red
Sea
Port Sudan
Abhā
Jizan
Al Ghaydah
SUDAN
Omdurman
Khartoum ★
Kassala
Wad
Medani
ERITREA
Asmara ★
Massawa
Sanaa ★
Al Hudaydah
YEMEN
Ta'izz
Aden
Al Mukallā
Arabian Sea
Socotra
(YEMEN)
Scale 1:21,000,000
Lambert Conformal Conic Projection,
standard parallels 12°N and 38°N
0       300 Kilometers
0       300 Miles
Boundary representation is
not necessarily authoritative.
T'ana
Hāyk'
Desē
DJIBOUTI
★ Djibouti
Bab el
Mandeb
Gulf of Aden
Boosaaso
Berbera
Addis Ababa ★
Dirē
Dawa
Hargeysa
SOMALIA
ETHIOPIA
Provisional
administrative line

Golan Heights is Israeli-occupied Syria.

West Bank is Israeli-occupied with current status subject to
the Israeli-Palestinian Interim Agreement; permanent status
to be determined through further negotiation.

The status of the Gaza Strip is a final status issue to be
resolved through negotiations.

Israel proclaimed Jerusalem as its capital in 1950, but the
US, like nearly all other countries, maintains its Embassy in
Tel Aviv-Yafo.

803540AI (G00412) 6-12

Scale 1:48,000,000

Azimuthal Equal-Area Projection

0 ——— 800 Kilometers

0 ——— 800 Miles

Boundary representation is
not necessarily authoritative.

803537AI (G00543) 6-12

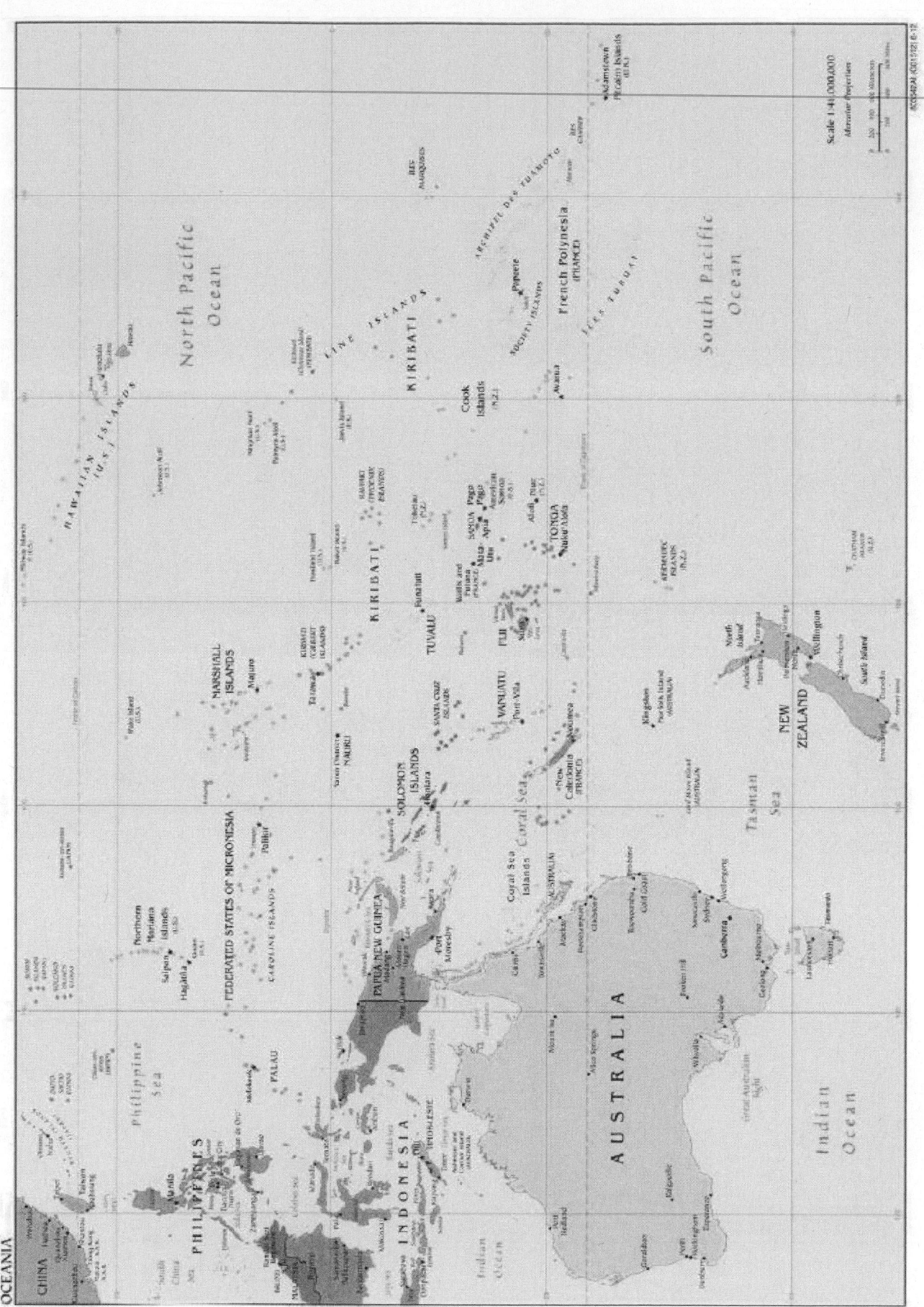

## Table 1359. Total World Population and Population Projections: 1980 to 2050

[4,445.4 represents 4,445,400,000. As of midyear]

| Year | Population (mil.) | Average annual [1] Growth rate (percent) | Average annual [1] Population change (mil.) | Year | Population (mil.) | Average annual [1] Growth rate (percent) | Average annual [1] Population change (mil.) |
|---|---|---|---|---|---|---|---|
| 1980............ | 4,445.4 | 1.83 | 81.35 | 2020............ | 7,659.4 | 0.99 | 76.13 |
| 1990............ | 5,286.8 | 1.58 | 83.29 | 2025............ | 8,030.1 | 0.88 | 70.97 |
| 2000............ | 6,086.1 | 1.26 | 76.66 | 2030............ | 8,373.5 | 0.78 | 65.31 |
| 2005............ | 6,471.4 | 1.22 | 79.09 | 2035............ | 8,690.0 | 0.69 | 60.28 |
| 2010............ | 6,872.7 | 1.14 | 78.54 | 2040............ | 8,981.8 | 0.62 | 55.38 |
| 2015............ | 7,267.0 | 1.08 | 78.75 | 2045............ | 9,248.6 | 0.54 | 50.13 |
| **2018**............ | **7,503.8** | **1.04** | **78.28** | 2050............ | 9,488.2 | (NA) | (NA) |

NA Not available. [1] Represents change from year shown to immediate succeeding year.

Source: U.S. Census Bureau, "International Data Base (IDB)," <https://www.census.gov/programs-surveys/international-programs/data/tools.html>, accessed September 2019.

## Table 1360. Population by Continent: 1980 to 2050

[In millions, except percent (4,445.4 represents 4,445,400,000). As of midyear. For geographic classification of individual countries, see source]

| Year | World | Africa | North America [1] | South America | Asia | Europe | Oceania |
|---|---|---|---|---|---|---|---|
| 1980.............................. | 4,445.4 | 479.4 | 370.8 | 239.7 | 2,637.7 | 695.2 | 22.5 |
| 1990.............................. | 5,286.8 | 631.7 | 423.0 | 295.4 | 3,184.5 | 725.8 | 26.4 |
| 2000.............................. | 6,086.1 | 807.2 | 485.7 | 346.3 | 3,686.1 | 730.4 | 30.4 |
| 2010.............................. | 6,872.7 | 1,039.9 | 539.2 | 391.3 | 4,127.1 | 740.2 | 34.9 |
| **2018**.............................. | **7,503.8** | **1,264.3** | **579.8** | **422.2** | **4,451.0** | **748.1** | **38.4** |
| 2020.............................. | 7,659.4 | 1,325.5 | 589.8 | 429.3 | 4,526.1 | 749.5 | 39.3 |
| 2030.............................. | 8,373.5 | 1,658.1 | 635.6 | 460.2 | 4,829.6 | 747.0 | 43.0 |
| 2040.............................. | 8,981.8 | 2,025.5 | 670.9 | 480.9 | 5,022.5 | 736.0 | 46.1 |
| 2050.............................. | 9,488.2 | 2,412.7 | 696.8 | 490.1 | 5,122.9 | 717.3 | 48.4 |
| **PERCENT DISTRIBUTION** | | | | | | | |
| 1980.............................. | 100.0 | 10.8 | 8.3 | 5.4 | 59.3 | 15.6 | 0.5 |
| 1990.............................. | 100.0 | 11.9 | 8.0 | 5.6 | 60.2 | 13.7 | 0.5 |
| 2000.............................. | 100.0 | 13.3 | 8.0 | 5.7 | 60.6 | 12.0 | 0.5 |
| 2010.............................. | 100.0 | 15.1 | 7.8 | 5.7 | 60.1 | 10.8 | 0.5 |
| **2018**.............................. | **100.0** | **16.8** | **7.7** | **5.6** | **59.3** | **10.0** | **0.5** |
| 2020.............................. | 100.0 | 17.3 | 7.7 | 5.6 | 59.1 | 9.8 | 0.5 |
| 2030.............................. | 100.0 | 19.8 | 7.6 | 5.5 | 57.7 | 8.9 | 0.5 |
| 2040.............................. | 100.0 | 22.6 | 7.5 | 5.4 | 55.9 | 8.2 | 0.5 |
| 2050.............................. | 100.0 | 25.4 | 7.3 | 5.2 | 54.0 | 7.6 | 0.5 |

[1] Data for North America include Central America and Caribbean area.

Source: U.S. Census Bureau, "International Data Base (IDB)," <https://www.census.gov/programs-surveys/international-programs/data/tools.html>, accessed September 2019.

## Table 1361. Population and Population Change by Development Status: 1950 to 2050

[2,557.6 represents 2,557,600,000. As of midyear. Minus sign (-) indicates decrease. "Less developed" countries include all of Africa, all of Asia except Japan, the Transcaucasian and Central Asian republics, all of Latin America and the Caribbean, and all of Oceania except Australia and New Zealand. For details on classification of individual countries, see source]

| Year | Number (millions) World | Number (millions) Less developed countries | Number (millions) More developed countries | Percent of world Less developed countries | Percent of world More developed countries |
|---|---|---|---|---|---|
| **POPULATION** | | | | | |
| 1950........................... | 2,557.6 | 1,750.6 | 807.1 | 68.4 | 31.6 |
| 1960........................... | 3,043.0 | 2,132.3 | 910.8 | 70.1 | 29.9 |
| 1970........................... | 3,713.4 | 2,709.8 | 1,003.6 | 73.0 | 27.0 |
| 1980........................... | 4,445.4 | 3,363.6 | 1,081.7 | 75.7 | 24.3 |
| 1990........................... | 5,286.8 | 4,139.6 | 1,147.2 | 78.3 | 21.7 |
| 2000........................... | 6,086.1 | 4,892.7 | 1,193.4 | 80.4 | 19.6 |
| 2010........................... | 6,872.7 | 5,635.9 | 1,236.8 | 82.0 | 18.0 |
| **2018**........................... | **7,503.8** | **6,236.3** | **1,267.5** | **83.1** | **16.9** |
| 2020........................... | 7,659.4 | 6,384.9 | 1,274.6 | 83.4 | 16.6 |
| 2030........................... | 8,373.5 | 7,076.7 | 1,296.8 | 84.5 | 15.5 |
| 2040........................... | 8,981.8 | 7,678.1 | 1,303.7 | 85.5 | 14.5 |
| 2050........................... | 9,488.2 | 8,189.9 | 1,298.3 | 86.3 | 13.7 |
| **POPULATION CHANGE** | | | | | |
| 1950 to 1960.............. | 485.4 | 381.7 | 103.7 | 78.6 | 21.4 |
| 1960 to 1970.............. | 670.4 | 577.6 | 92.9 | 86.1 | 13.9 |
| 1970 to 1980.............. | 732.0 | 653.8 | 78.1 | 89.3 | 10.7 |
| 1980 to 1990.............. | 841.4 | 775.9 | 65.5 | 92.2 | 7.8 |
| 1990 to 2000.............. | 799.3 | 753.1 | 46.2 | 94.2 | 5.8 |
| 2000 to 2010.............. | 786.5 | 743.2 | 43.4 | 94.5 | 5.5 |
| 2010 to 2020.............. | 786.7 | 749.0 | 37.7 | 95.2 | 4.8 |
| 2020 to 2030.............. | 714.1 | 691.8 | 22.3 | 96.9 | 3.1 |
| 2030 to 2040.............. | 608.3 | 601.4 | 6.9 | 98.9 | 1.1 |
| 2040 to 2050.............. | 506.3 | 511.8 | -5.4 | 101.1 | -1.1 |

Source: U.S. Census Bureau, "International Data Base (IDB)," <https://www.census.gov/programs-surveys/international-programs/data/tools.html>, accessed September 2019.

# Table 1362. Population and Land Area by Country or Territory: 2000 to 2020

[6,086,149 represents 6,086,149,000. Covers countries or territories with populations of 5,000 or more in 2018. Population estimates were derived from information available as of September 2018. See text of this section for general comments concerning the data. For details of methodology, coverage, and reliability, see source. Minus sign (-) indicates decrease]

| Country or territory | Map reference [1] | Mid-year population (1,000) | | | | Population rank, 2018 | Annual growth rate [2], 2010 to 2020 | Population per sq. mile, 2018 | Land area [3], (sq. mile) |
|---|---|---|---|---|---|---|---|---|---|
| | | 2000 | 2010 | 2018 | 2020 (P) | | | | |
| **World**................ | (X) | **6,086,149** | **6,872,671** | **7,503,828** | **7,659,420** | (X) | **1.08** | **148** | **50,855,386** |
| Afghanistan................. | S7 | 22,461 | 29,121 | 34,941 | 36,644 | 39 | 2.30 | 139 | 251,827 |
| Albania..................... | S4 | 3,158 | 2,987 | 3,057 | 3,075 | 136 | 0.29 | 289 | 10,578 |
| Algeria..................... | S5 | 30,638 | 35,950 | 41,657 | 42,973 | 34 | 1.78 | 45 | 919,595 |
| Andorra..................... | S4 | 65 | 85 | 86 | 86 | 200 | 0.13 | 474 | 181 |
| Angola...................... | S5 | 15,657 | 22,641 | 30,356 | 32,522 | 45 | 3.62 | 63 | 481,354 |
| Antigua and Barbuda....... | S2 | 75 | 87 | 96 | 98 | 197 | 1.24 | 561 | 171 |
| Argentina................... | S3 | 37,336 | 41,358 | 44,694 | 45,479 | 31 | 0.95 | 42 | 1,056,642 |
| Armenia..................... | S6 | 3,100 | 3,072 | 3,038 | 3,021 | 137 | -0.17 | 279 | 10,889 |
| Australia................... | S8 | 19,053 | 21,516 | 23,470 | 23,939 | 56 | 1.07 | 8 | 2,966,153 |
| Austria..................... | S4 | 8,113 | 8,448 | 8,793 | 8,859 | 96 | 0.48 | 276 | 31,832 |
| Azerbaijan.................. | S6 | 8,463 | 9,302 | 10,047 | 10,206 | 90 | 0.93 | 315 | 31,903 |
| Bahamas, The............... | S2 | 283 | 310 | 333 | 338 | 179 | 0.84 | 86 | 3,865 |
| Bahrain..................... | S6 | 655 | 1,180 | 1,443 | 1,505 | 154 | 2.43 | 4,916 | 293 |
| Bangladesh.................. | S7 | 128,735 | 146,616 | 159,453 | 162,651 | 8 | 1.04 | 3,173 | 50,259 |
| Barbados.................... | S2 | 274 | 286 | 293 | 295 | 180 | 0.31 | 1,766 | 166 |
| Belarus..................... | S4 | 10,033 | 9,680 | 9,528 | 9,478 | 94 | -0.21 | 122 | 78,340 |
| Belgium..................... | S4 | 10,264 | 10,866 | 11,571 | 11,721 | 77 | 0.76 | 990 | 11,690 |
| Belize...................... | S2 | 252 | 327 | 386 | 400 | 177 | 2.01 | 44 | 8,805 |
| Benin....................... | S5 | 6,619 | 9,056 | 11,341 | 11,956 | 79 | 2.78 | 266 | 42,711 |
| Bhutan...................... | S7 | 606 | 700 | 766 | 782 | 165 | 1.11 | 52 | 14,824 |
| Bolivia..................... | S3 | 8,195 | 9,947 | 11,306 | 11,640 | 80 | 1.57 | 27 | 418,265 |
| Bosnia and Herzegovina..... | S4 | 3,806 | 3,885 | 3,850 | 3,836 | 128 | -0.13 | 195 | 19,763 |
| Botswana.................... | S5 | 1,655 | 1,978 | 2,249 | 2,317 | 144 | 1.58 | 10 | 218,816 |
| Brazil...................... | S3 | 174,315 | 195,834 | 208,847 | 211,716 | 5 | 0.78 | 65 | 3,227,096 |
| Brunei...................... | S8 | 325 | 395 | 451 | 464 | 174 | 1.62 | 222 | 2,033 |
| Bulgaria.................... | S4 | 7,909 | 7,391 | 7,058 | 6,967 | 104 | -0.59 | 168 | 41,888 |
| Burkina Faso................ | S5 | 11,430 | 15,634 | 19,743 | 20,835 | 61 | 2.87 | 187 | 105,715 |
| Burma....................... | S7 | 46,641 | 51,415 | 55,623 | 56,590 | 24 | 0.96 | 220 | 252,321 |
| Burundi..................... | S5 | 6,716 | 9,121 | 11,845 | 12,632 | 76 | 3.26 | 1,195 | 9,915 |
| Cabo Verde.................. | S5 | 430 | 509 | 568 | 583 | 173 | 1.37 | 365 | 1,557 |
| Cambodia.................... | S7 | 12,351 | 14,454 | 16,450 | 16,927 | 69 | 1.58 | 241 | 68,153 |
| Cameroon.................... | S5 | 15,818 | 20,822 | 25,641 | 26,969 | 53 | 2.59 | 140 | 182,514 |
| Canada...................... | S1 | 31,100 | 33,760 | 35,882 | 36,387 | 38 | 0.75 | 10 | 3,511,023 |
| Central African Republic... | S5 | 3,980 | 4,845 | 5,745 | 5,991 | 116 | 2.12 | 24 | 240,535 |
| Chad........................ | S5 | 8,118 | 11,990 | 15,833 | 16,877 | 71 | 3.42 | 33 | 486,180 |
| Chile....................... | S3 | 15,175 | 16,760 | 17,925 | 18,187 | 65 | 0.82 | 62 | 287,187 |
| China....................... | S7 | 1,268,302 | 1,336,681 | 1,384,689 | 1,394,016 | 1 | 0.42 | 385 | 3,600,947 |
| Colombia.................... | S3 | 38,910 | 44,205 | 48,169 | 49,085 | 30 | 1.05 | 120 | 401,044 |
| Comoros..................... | S5 | 545 | 706 | 821 | 846 | 163 | 1.81 | 952 | 863 |
| Congo, Republic of......... | S5 | 2,939 | 4,238 | 5,062 | 5,293 | 122 | 2.22 | 38 | 131,854 |
| Congo, Democratic Republic. | S5 | 52,445 | 69,851 | 85,281 | 89,250 | 16 | 2.45 | 97 | 875,312 |
| Costa Rica.................. | S2 | 3,883 | 4,516 | 4,987 | 5,098 | 123 | 1.21 | 253 | 19,714 |
| Cote d'Ivoire.............. | S5 | 16,686 | 21,719 | 26,261 | 27,481 | 51 | 2.35 | 214 | 122,782 |
| Croatia..................... | S4 | 4,390 | 4,417 | 4,270 | 4,228 | 127 | -0.44 | 198 | 21,612 |
| Cuba........................ | S2 | 11,147 | 11,262 | 11,116 | 11,059 | 82 | -0.18 | 262 | 42,402 |
| Cyprus...................... | S6 | 920 | 1,103 | 1,237 | 1,267 | 158 | 1.39 | 347 | 3,568 |
| Czechia..................... | S4 | 10,269 | 10,551 | 10,686 | 10,702 | 85 | 0.14 | 358 | 29,825 |
| Denmark..................... | S4 | 5,337 | 5,547 | 5,810 | 5,869 | 115 | 0.57 | 355 | 16,384 |
| Djibouti.................... | S5 | 669 | 741 | 884 | 922 | 162 | 2.19 | 99 | 8,950 |
| Dominica.................... | S2 | 71 | 73 | 74 | 74 | 202 | 0.19 | 255 | 290 |
| Dominican Republic......... | S2 | 8,231 | 9,433 | 10,299 | 10,500 | 88 | 1.07 | 552 | 18,656 |
| Ecuador..................... | S3 | 12,446 | 14,791 | 16,499 | 16,905 | 68 | 1.34 | 154 | 106,889 |
| Egypt....................... | S5 | 65,504 | 81,239 | 99,413 | 104,124 | 14 | 2.48 | 259 | 384,345 |
| El Salvador................. | S2 | 5,850 | 6,052 | 6,187 | 6,217 | 109 | 0.27 | 773 | 8,000 |
| Equatorial Guinea.......... | S5 | 491 | 651 | 797 | 836 | 164 | 2.51 | 74 | 10,831 |
| Eritrea..................... | S5 | 3,884 | 5,365 | 5,971 | 6,081 | 113 | 1.25 | 153 | 38,996 |
| Estonia..................... | S4 | 1,380 | 1,303 | 1,244 | 1,229 | 157 | -0.59 | 76 | 16,366 |
| Eswatini.................... | S5 | 1,032 | 1,019 | 1,087 | 1,104 | 160 | 0.80 | 164 | 6,643 |
| Ethiopia.................... | S5 | 64,365 | 86,043 | 108,386 | 114,640 | 12 | 2.87 | 281 | 386,102 |
| Fiji........................ | S8 | 805 | 876 | 926 | 936 | 161 | 0.66 | 131 | 7,056 |
| Finland..................... | S4 | 5,169 | 5,355 | 5,537 | 5,572 | 117 | 0.40 | 47 | 117,304 |
| France...................... | S4 | 61,255 | 64,941 | 67,364 | 67,848 | 21 | 0.44 | 272 | 247,270 |
| Gabon....................... | S5 | 1,199 | 1,628 | 2,119 | 2,231 | 145 | 3.15 | 21 | 99,486 |
| Gambia, The................ | S5 | 1,357 | 1,755 | 2,093 | 2,174 | 148 | 2.14 | 536 | 3,907 |
| Georgia..................... | S6 | 4,819 | 4,903 | 4,926 | 4,930 | 124 | 0.06 | 183 | 26,911 |
| Germany..................... | S4 | 82,184 | 81,644 | 80,458 | 80,160 | 19 | -0.18 | 598 | 134,623 |
| Ghana....................... | S5 | 18,981 | 23,571 | 28,102 | 29,340 | 49 | 2.19 | 320 | 87,851 |
| Greece...................... | S4 | 10,559 | 10,750 | 10,762 | 10,742 | 84 | -0.01 | 213 | 50,443 |
| Grenada..................... | S2 | 102 | 108 | 112 | 113 | 190 | 0.48 | 845 | 133 |
| Guatemala................... | S2 | 11,283 | 14,209 | 16,581 | 17,153 | 67 | 1.88 | 401 | 41,374 |
| Guinea...................... | S5 | 7,780 | 9,571 | 11,855 | 12,527 | 75 | 2.69 | 125 | 94,872 |
| Guinea-Bissau............... | S5 | 1,208 | 1,516 | 1,833 | 1,927 | 153 | 2.40 | 169 | 10,857 |
| Guyana...................... | S3 | 785 | 746 | 741 | 750 | 166 | 0.06 | 10 | 76,004 |
| Haiti....................... | S2 | 8,279 | 9,553 | 10,788 | 11,068 | 83 | 1.47 | 1,014 | 10,641 |
| Honduras.................... | S2 | 6,359 | 7,989 | 9,183 | 9,465 | 95 | 1.69 | 213 | 43,201 |
| Hungary..................... | S4 | 10,147 | 9,992 | 9,826 | 9,772 | 92 | -0.22 | 284 | 34,598 |
| Iceland..................... | S1 | 281 | 318 | 344 | 351 | 178 | 0.98 | 9 | 38,707 |
| India....................... | S7 | 1,006,300 | 1,173,108 | 1,296,834 | 1,326,093 | 2 | 1.23 | 1,130 | 1,147,956 |
| Indonesia................... | S8 | 214,091 | 243,423 | 262,787 | 267,026 | 4 | 0.93 | 376 | 699,451 |
| Iran........................ | S6 | 66,482 | 75,035 | 83,025 | 84,923 | 17 | 1.24 | 140 | 591,352 |

See footnotes at end of table.

| Country or territory | Map refer- ence [1] | Mid-year population (1,000) | | | | Popula- tion rank, 2018 | Annual growth rate [2], 2010 to 2020 | Popula- tion per sq. mile, 2018 | Land area [3], (sq. mile) |
|---|---|---|---|---|---|---|---|---|---|
| | | 2000 | 2010 | 2018 | 2020 (P) | | | | |
| Iraq | S6 | 23,128 | 30,526 | 40,194 | 42,213 | 36 | 3.24 | 238 | 168,868 |
| Ireland | S4 | 3,822 | 4,623 | 5,068 | 5,177 | 121 | 1.13 | 191 | 26,596 |
| Israel | S6 | 6,097 | 7,368 | 8,425 | 8,675 | 98 | 1.63 | 1,073 | 7,849 |
| Italy | S4 | 57,784 | 60,749 | 62,247 | 62,403 | 23 | 0.27 | 548 | 113,568 |
| Jamaica | S2 | 2,811 | 2,839 | 2,812 | 2,809 | 139 | -0.11 | 672 | 4,182 |
| Japan | S7 | 126,776 | 127,579 | 126,168 | 125,507 | 10 | -0.16 | 897 | 140,728 |
| Jordan | S6 | 4,785 | 6,800 | 10,458 | 10,821 | 86 | 4.64 | 305 | 34,287 |
| Kazakhstan | S7 | 15,687 | 17,085 | 18,745 | 19,092 | 63 | 1.11 | 18 | 1,042,360 |
| Kenya | S5 | 30,606 | 40,843 | 48,398 | 49,858 | 29 | 1.99 | 220 | 219,746 |
| Kiribati | S8 | 85 | 99 | 109 | 112 | 191 | 1.17 | 349 | 313 |
| Korea, North | S7 | 22,785 | 24,326 | 25,381 | 25,643 | 54 | 0.53 | 546 | 46,490 |
| Korea, South | S7 | 46,841 | 49,258 | 51,418 | 51,835 | 27 | 0.51 | 1,374 | 37,421 |
| Kosovo | S4 | 1,700 | 1,815 | 1,908 | 1,933 | 151 | 0.63 | 454 | 4,203 |
| Kuwait | S6 | 1,972 | 2,543 | 2,916 | 2,994 | 138 | 1.63 | 424 | 6,880 |
| Kyrgyzstan | S6 | 4,937 | 5,410 | 5,849 | 5,965 | 114 | 0.98 | 79 | 74,055 |
| Laos | S7 | 5,397 | 6,368 | 7,234 | 7,447 | 101 | 1.57 | 81 | 89,112 |
| Latvia | S4 | 2,368 | 2,115 | 1,924 | 1,881 | 150 | -1.17 | 80 | 24,034 |
| Lebanon | S6 | 3,834 | 4,492 | 6,100 | 5,470 | 110 | 1.97 | 1,544 | 3,950 |
| Lesotho | S5 | 1,916 | 1,920 | 1,962 | 1,969 | 149 | 0.26 | 167 | 11,720 |
| Liberia | S5 | 2,847 | 3,817 | 4,810 | 5,073 | 125 | 2.84 | 129 | 37,189 |
| Libya | S5 | 5,025 | 6,110 | 6,755 | 6,943 | 107 | 1.28 | 10 | 679,362 |
| Liechtenstein | S4 | 33 | 36 | 39 | 39 | 213 | 0.80 | 624 | 62 |
| Lithuania | S4 | 3,489 | 3,089 | 2,793 | 2,731 | 141 | -1.23 | 115 | 24,201 |
| Luxembourg | S4 | 438 | 509 | 606 | 628 | 171 | 2.10 | 607 | 998 |
| Macedonia | S4 | 2,017 | 2,080 | 2,119 | 2,126 | 146 | 0.22 | 216 | 9,820 |
| Madagascar | S5 | 15,712 | 20,847 | 25,684 | 26,956 | 52 | 2.57 | 114 | 224,534 |
| Malawi | S5 | 11,129 | 15,183 | 19,843 | 21,197 | 60 | 3.34 | 546 | 36,324 |
| Malaysia | S8 | 23,151 | 28,275 | 31,810 | 32,652 | 42 | 1.44 | 251 | 126,895 |
| Maldives | S7 | 300 | 396 | 392 | 392 | 176 | -0.10 | 3,411 | 115 |
| Mali | S5 | 10,844 | 14,514 | 18,430 | 19,553 | 64 | 2.98 | 39 | 471,118 |
| Malta | S4 | 394 | 417 | 449 | 457 | 175 | 0.92 | 3,680 | 122 |
| Marshall Islands | S8 | 53 | 66 | 76 | 78 | 201 | 1.68 | 1,083 | 70 |
| Mauritania | S5 | 2,501 | 3,205 | 3,840 | 4,005 | 129 | 2.23 | 10 | 397,955 |
| Mauritius | S5 | 1,186 | 1,294 | 1,364 | 1,379 | 155 | 0.64 | 1,741 | 784 |
| Mexico | S1 | 99,775 | 114,061 | 125,959 | 128,650 | 11 | 1.20 | 168 | 750,561 |
| Micronesia, Federated States of | S8 | 108 | 107 | 104 | 102 | 194 | -0.45 | 382 | 271 |
| Moldova | S4 | 4,180 | 3,732 | 3,438 | 3,364 | 132 | -1.04 | 271 | 12,699 |
| Monaco | S4 | 32 | 31 | 31 | 31 | 217 | 0.12 | 39,791 | 1 |
| Mongolia | S7 | 2,461 | 2,783 | 3,103 | 3,168 | 135 | 1.29 | 5 | 599,831 |
| Montenegro | S4 | 623 | 623 | 614 | 610 | 169 | -0.21 | 118 | 5,194 |
| Morocco | S5 | 28,113 | 31,627 | 34,314 | 34,956 | 40 | 1.00 | 199 | 172,317 |
| Mozambique | S5 | 17,997 | 22,417 | 27,234 | 28,603 | 50 | 2.44 | 90 | 303,623 |
| Namibia | S5 | 1,878 | 2,183 | 2,533 | 2,630 | 142 | 1.86 | 8 | 317,874 |
| Nauru | S8 | 10 | 9 | 10 | 10 | 223 | 0.54 | 1,195 | 8 |
| Nepal | S7 | 23,487 | 26,664 | 29,718 | 30,328 | 47 | 1.29 | 537 | 55,348 |
| Netherlands | S4 | 15,930 | 16,574 | 17,151 | 17,280 | 66 | 0.42 | 1,311 | 13,086 |
| New Zealand | S8 | 3,802 | 4,252 | 4,546 | 4,615 | 126 | 0.82 | 45 | 102,138 |
| Nicaragua | S2 | 4,866 | 5,604 | 6,085 | 6,203 | 111 | 1.02 | 131 | 46,328 |
| Niger | S5 | 10,725 | 15,270 | 19,866 | 21,151 | 59 | 3.26 | 41 | 489,076 |
| Nigeria | S5 | 125,581 | 165,905 | 203,453 | 214,028 | 7 | 2.55 | 579 | 351,649 |
| Norway | S4 | 4,492 | 4,891 | 5,372 | 5,467 | 120 | 1.11 | 46 | 117,484 |
| Oman | S6 | 2,432 | 2,968 | 3,494 | 3,635 | 131 | 2.03 | 29 | 119,499 |
| Pakistan | S6 | 152,429 | 184,405 | 207,863 | 213,719 | 6 | 1.48 | 698 | 297,637 |
| Palau | S8 | 19 | 21 | 22 | 22 | 219 | 0.38 | 121 | 177 |
| Panama | S2 | 2,900 | 3,411 | 3,801 | 3,894 | 130 | 1.33 | 132 | 28,703 |
| Papua New Guinea | S8 | 4,813 | 6,065 | 7,027 | 7,259 | 105 | 1.80 | 40 | 174,850 |
| Paraguay | S3 | 5,418 | 6,376 | 7,026 | 7,192 | 106 | 1.20 | 46 | 153,399 |
| Peru | S3 | 25,797 | 28,948 | 31,331 | 31,915 | 44 | 0.98 | 63 | 494,209 |
| Philippines | S7 | 76,452 | 93,137 | 105,893 | 109,181 | 13 | 1.59 | 920 | 115,124 |
| Poland | S4 | 38,654 | 38,616 | 38,421 | 38,282 | 37 | -0.09 | 327 | 117,474 |
| Portugal | S4 | 10,361 | 10,663 | 10,355 | 10,303 | 87 | -0.34 | 293 | 35,317 |
| Qatar | S6 | 640 | 1,719 | 2,364 | 2,444 | 143 | 3.52 | 528 | 4,473 |
| Romania | S4 | 22,447 | 21,959 | 21,457 | 21,303 | 58 | -0.30 | 242 | 88,761 |
| Russia | S7 | 147,054 | 142,527 | 142,123 | 141,722 | 9 | -0.06 | 22 | 6,323,482 |
| Rwanda | S5 | 8,047 | 9,923 | 12,187 | 12,712 | 74 | 2.48 | 1,280 | 9,524 |
| Saint Kitts and Nevis | S2 | 46 | 50 | 53 | 54 | 208 | 0.76 | 527 | 101 |
| Saint Lucia | S2 | 153 | 161 | 166 | 166 | 187 | 0.34 | 707 | 234 |
| Saint Vincent and the Grenadines | S2 | 108 | 104 | 102 | 101 | 195 | -0.28 | 678 | 150 |
| Samoa | S8 | 176 | 192 | 201 | 204 | 185 | 0.60 | 185 | 1,089 |
| San Marino | S4 | 27 | 31 | 34 | 34 | 215 | 0.84 | 1,434 | 24 |
| Sao Tome and Principe | S5 | 141 | 176 | 204 | 211 | 184 | 1.83 | 549 | 372 |
| Saudi Arabia | S6 | 21,362 | 27,963 | 33,091 | 34,173 | 41 | 2.01 | 40 | 830,000 |
| Senegal | S5 | 9,469 | 12,323 | 15,021 | 15,736 | 72 | 2.44 | 202 | 74,336 |
| Serbia | S4 | 7,604 | 7,345 | 7,078 | 7,012 | 103 | -0.46 | 237 | 29,913 |
| Seychelles | S5 | 79 | 88 | 95 | 96 | 198 | 0.83 | 539 | 176 |
| Sierra Leone | S5 | 3,809 | 5,246 | 6,312 | 6,625 | 108 | 2.33 | 228 | 27,653 |
| Singapore | S8 | 4,063 | 5,140 | 5,996 | 6,210 | 112 | 1.89 | 21,903 | 274 |
| Slovakia | S4 | 5,400 | 5,426 | 5,445 | 5,441 | 118 | 0.03 | 293 | 18,573 |
| Slovenia | S4 | 2,011 | 2,084 | 2,102 | 2,103 | 147 | 0.09 | 270 | 7,780 |
| Solomon Islands | S8 | 434 | 559 | 660 | 685 | 167 | 2.03 | 61 | 10,805 |
| Somalia | S5 | 7,501 | 9,768 | 11,259 | 11,757 | 81 | 1.85 | 46 | 242,216 |
| South Africa | S5 | 44,913 | 51,123 | 55,380 | 56,464 | 26 | 0.99 | 118 | 468,909 |

See footnotes at end of table.

**Table 1362. Population and Land Area by Country or Territory: 2000 to 2020**-Continued.

See headnote on page 858.

| Country or territory | Map refer- ence [1] | Mid-year population (1,000) | | | | Popula- tion rank, 2018 | Annual growth rate [2], 2010 to 2020 | Popula- tion per sq. mile, 2018 | Land area [3], (sq. mile) |
|---|---|---|---|---|---|---|---|---|---|
| | | 2000 | 2010 | 2018 | 2020 (P) | | | | |
| South Sudan [4] | S5 | 6,366 | 9,765 | 10,205 | 10,561 | 89 | 0.78 | 41 | 248,777 |
| Spain | S4 | 40,589 | 46,506 | 49,331 | 50,016 | 28 | 0.73 | 256 | 192,657 |
| Sri Lanka | S7 | 19,041 | 21,084 | 22,577 | 22,889 | 57 | 0.82 | 905 | 24,954 |
| Sudan [4] | S5 | 27,634 | 34,984 | 43,121 | 45,562 | 33 | 2.64 | 60 | 718,723 |
| Suriname | S3 | 464 | 546 | 598 | 610 | 172 | 1.10 | 10 | 60,232 |
| Sweden | S4 | 8,924 | 9,432 | 10,041 | 10,202 | 91 | 0.78 | 63 | 158,431 |
| Switzerland | S4 | 7,277 | 7,770 | 8,293 | 8,404 | 99 | 0.78 | 537 | 15,443 |
| Syria | S6 | 16,514 | 21,766 | 19,454 | 22,346 | 62 | 0.26 | 274 | 70,900 |
| Taiwan | S7 | 22,185 | 23,127 | 23,546 | 23,603 | 55 | 0.20 | 1,890 | 12,456 |
| Tajikistan | S7 | 6,230 | 7,487 | 8,605 | 8,874 | 97 | 1.70 | 157 | 54,637 |
| Tanzania | S5 | 33,193 | 44,288 | 55,451 | 58,553 | 25 | 2.79 | 162 | 342,009 |
| Thailand | S7 | 62,902 | 66,720 | 68,616 | 68,977 | 20 | 0.33 | 348 | 197,256 |
| Timor-Leste | S8 | 767 | 1,088 | 1,322 | 1,384 | 156 | 2.41 | 230 | 5,743 |
| Togo | S5 | 4,992 | 6,587 | 8,176 | 8,608 | 100 | 2.68 | 389 | 20,998 |
| Tonga | S8 | 100 | 106 | 106 | 106 | 193 | 0.04 | 384 | 277 |
| Trinidad and Tobago | S2 | 1,252 | 1,229 | 1,216 | 1,209 | 159 | -0.16 | 614 | 1,980 |
| Tunisia | S5 | 9,546 | 10,526 | 11,516 | 11,721 | 78 | 1.08 | 192 | 59,985 |
| Turkey | S6 | 65,970 | 74,687 | 81,257 | 82,018 | 18 | 0.94 | 273 | 297,157 |
| Turkmenistan | S6 | 4,385 | 4,941 | 5,411 | 5,529 | 119 | 1.12 | 30 | 181,441 |
| Tuvalu | S8 | 10 | 10 | 11 | 11 | 222 | 0.80 | 1,110 | 10 |
| Uganda | S5 | 22,916 | 31,507 | 40,854 | 43,518 | 35 | 3.23 | 537 | 76,101 |
| Ukraine | S4 | 49,014 | 45,768 | 43,952 | 43,923 | 32 | -0.41 | 196 | 223,681 |
| United Arab Emirates | S6 | 3,231 | 8,380 | 9,701 | 9,992 | 93 | 1.76 | 301 | 32,278 |
| United Kingdom | S4 | 59,140 | 62,348 | 65,105 | 65,761 | 22 | 0.53 | 697 | 93,410 |
| **United States** | **S1** | **282,162** | **309,338** | **329,256** | **334,503** | **3** | **0.78** | **93** | **3,532,315** |
| Uruguay | S3 | 3,220 | 3,301 | 3,369 | 3,388 | 133 | 0.26 | 50 | 67,574 |
| Uzbekistan | S6 | 25,042 | 27,866 | 30,024 | 30,565 | 46 | 0.92 | 183 | 164,248 |
| Vanuatu | S8 | 191 | 245 | 288 | 298 | 182 | 1.96 | 61 | 4,706 |
| Venezuela | S3 | 24,249 | 28,481 | 31,689 | 32,442 | 43 | 1.30 | 93 | 340,561 |
| Vietnam | S7 | 79,178 | 89,571 | 97,040 | 98,721 | 15 | 0.97 | 811 | 119,719 |
| Yemen | S6 | 17,236 | 23,210 | 28,667 | 29,884 | 48 | 2.53 | 141 | 203,850 |
| Zambia | S5 | 9,984 | 13,042 | 16,445 | 17,427 | 70 | 2.90 | 57 | 287,028 |
| Zimbabwe | S5 | 12,047 | 12,722 | 14,030 | 14,546 | 73 | 1.34 | 94 | 149,362 |
| **TERRITORIES AND DEPENDENCIES** | | | | | | | | | |
| American Samoa | S8 | 58 | 56 | 51 | 49 | 211 | -1.16 | 665 | 76 |
| Anguilla | S1 | 11 | 15 | 17 | 18 | 220 | 2.03 | 496 | 35 |
| Aruba | S1 | 90 | 105 | 117 | 119 | 189 | 1.33 | 1,677 | 69 |
| Bermuda | S1 | 63 | 68 | 71 | 72 | 203 | 0.50 | 3,414 | 21 |
| Cayman Islands | S1 | 38 | 50 | 60 | 62 | 205 | 2.10 | 585 | 102 |
| Cook Islands | S8 | 16 | 11 | 9 | 9 | 224 | -2.93 | 99 | 91 |
| Curacao [5] | S2 | 134 | 143 | 150 | 151 | 188 | 0.54 | 876 | 171 |
| Faroe Islands | S4 | 46 | 49 | 51 | 52 | 210 | 0.51 | 95 | 538 |
| French Polynesia | S8 | 236 | 269 | 290 | 295 | 181 | 0.93 | 197 | 1,478 |
| Gaza Strip [6] | S6 | 1,128 | 1,503 | 1,837 | 1,918 | 152 | 2.44 | 13,214 | 139 |
| Gibraltar | S4 | 27 | 29 | 29 | 30 | 218 | 0.24 | 10,901 | 3 |
| Greenland | S1 | 57 | 58 | 58 | 58 | 206 | (Z) | (Z) | 836,330 |
| Guam | S8 | 155 | 163 | 168 | 168 | 186 | 0.31 | 800 | 210 |
| Guernsey | S4 | 62 | 65 | 67 | 67 | 204 | 0.35 | 2,215 | 30 |
| Hong Kong | S7 | 6,656 | 7,029 | 7,213 | 7,250 | 102 | 0.31 | 17,411 | 414 |
| Isle of Man | S4 | 76 | 84 | 89 | 90 | 199 | 0.76 | 405 | 221 |
| Jersey | S4 | 87 | 93 | 100 | 101 | 196 | 0.79 | 2,224 | 45 |
| Macau | S7 | 432 | 568 | 606 | 614 | 170 | 0.79 | 56,086 | 11 |
| Montserrat | S2 | 4 | 5 | 5 | 5 | 228 | 0.49 | 135 | 39 |
| New Caledonia | S8 | 211 | 252 | 283 | 290 | 183 | 1.39 | 40 | 7,056 |
| Northern Mariana Islands | S8 | 70 | 55 | 52 | 51 | 209 | -0.69 | 285 | 182 |
| Puerto Rico | S2 | 3,811 | 3,722 | 3,295 | 3,189 | 134 | -1.54 | 962 | 3,424 |
| Saint Barthelemy | S2 | 7 | 7 | 7 | 7 | 226 | -0.39 | 742 | 10 |
| Saint Helena | S5 | 7 | 8 | 8 | 8 | 225 | 0.25 | 66 | 119 |
| Saint Martin | S2 | 28 | 30 | 32 | 33 | 216 | 0.74 | 1,548 | 21 |
| Saint Pierre and Miquelon | S1 | 6 | 6 | 5 | 5 | 227 | -1.06 | 59 | 93 |
| Sint Maarten [5] | S2 | 31 | 38 | 43 | 44 | 212 | 1.46 | 3,251 | 13 |
| Turks and Caicos Islands | S2 | 19 | 43 | 54 | 56 | 207 | 2.58 | 147 | 366 |
| Virgin Islands, British | S2 | 23 | 30 | 36 | 37 | 214 | 2.32 | 614 | 58 |
| Virgin Islands, U.S. | S2 | 109 | 108 | 107 | 106 | 192 | -0.20 | 796 | 134 |
| Wallis and Futuna | S8 | 15 | 15 | 16 | 16 | 221 | 0.33 | 288 | 55 |
| West Bank [6] | S6 | 1,947 | 2,404 | 2,798 | 2,900 | 140 | 1.87 | 1,285 | 2,178 |
| Western Sahara | S5 | 336 | 492 | 620 | 652 | 168 | 2.83 | 6 | 102,703 |

P Projected. X Not applicable. Z Less than 0.05 percent or less than 1 person per square mile. [1] See maps for geographic locations, as indicated. [2] Computed by the exponential method. For explanation of average annual percent change, see Guide to Tabular Presentation. [3] Data converted from square kilometers to square miles. [4] Sudan and South Sudan became separate countries in July 2011. [5] The Netherlands Antilles dissolved on October 10, 2010. Curacao and Sint Maarten became autonomous territories of the Kingdom of the Netherlands. [6] The Gaza Strip and West Bank are Israeli occupied with interim status subject to Israeli/Palestinian negotiations. The final status is yet to be determined.

Source: U.S. Census Bureau, "International Data Base (IDB)," <https://www.census.gov/programs-surveys/international-programs/about/idb.html>, accessed September 2019.

## Table 1363. Foreign or Foreign-Born Population in Selected OECD Countries: 2000 to 2017

[28,052 represents 28,052,000. In Australia, Mexico, and the United States, the data refer to residents who are foreign born. In the European countries, Japan, and South Korea, data represent the legal nationality or citizenship status of residents. Data are based on censuses, population registers, and residence permits. For details about data methodology for individual countries, see source]

| Country | 2000 | 2005 | 2010 | 2012 | 2013 | 2014 | 2015 | 2016 | 2017 |
|---|---|---|---|---|---|---|---|---|---|
| **United States** | **28,052** | **34,258** | **38,453** | **40,382** | **40,738** | **41,344** | **42,391** | **43,290** | **43,739** |
| Australia | 4,369 | 4,753 | 5,730 | 6,018 | 6,210 | 6,399 | 6,558 | 6,711 | 6,873 |
| Austria | 694 | 774 | 884 | 951 | 1,004 | 1,066 | 1,146 | 1,268 | 1,342 |
| Belgium | 897 | 871 | 1,058 | 1,169 | 1,257 | 1,268 | 1,277 | 1,333 | 1,367 |
| Denmark | 259 | 268 | 330 | 359 | 375 | 397 | 423 | 463 | 485 |
| France | 3,259 | (NA) | 3,821 | 3,981 | 4,084 | 4,200 | 4,351 | 4,400 | (NA) |
| Germany | 7,344 | 6,717 | 6,695 | 6,931 | 7,214 | 7,634 | 8,153 | 9,108 | 10,039 |
| Greece | 274 | 533 | 840 | 757 | 768 | 687 | 707 | 686 | 538 |
| Italy | 1,341 | 2,402 | 3,648 | 4,052 | 4,388 | 4,921 | 5,014 | 5,027 | 5,047 |
| Japan | 1,556 | 1,974 | 2,185 | 2,079 | 2,034 | 2,066 | 2,122 | 2,232 | 2,383 |
| Korea, South | 210 | 511 | 1,003 | 933 | 986 | 1,092 | 1,143 | 1,162 | (NA) |
| Mexico | (NA) | (NA) | 886 | 967 | 974 | 991 | 940 | 1,007 | (NA) |
| Netherlands | 652 | 699 | 735 | 786 | 796 | 816 | 847 | 901 | 972 |
| Spain | 924 | 3,731 | 5,403 | 5,236 | 5,073 | 4,677 | 4,454 | 4,418 | 4,424 |
| Sweden | 482 | 481 | 603 | 655 | 667 | 695 | 739 | 783 | 852 |
| Switzerland | 1,369 | 1,495 | 1,680 | 1,772 | 1,825 | 1,887 | 1,947 | 1,994 | 2,030 |
| United Kingdom | 2,208 | 2,857 | 4,524 | 4,788 | 4,941 | 5,154 | 5,592 | 5,951 | 6,137 |

NA Not available.

Source: Organisation for Economic Co-operation and Development (OECD), 2019, "International Migration Database," OECD International Migration Statistics (database) ©, <http://dx.doi.org/10.1787/data-00342-en>, accessed July 2019.

## Table 1364. Youth and Elderly Population Distribution by Country: 2018 and 2020

[Percent of total population, as of mid-year. Covers countries with 11 million or more population in 2018]

| Country | 2018 Under 15 years old | 2018 65 years old and over | 2020 (P) Under 15 years old | 2020 (P) 65 years old and over | Country | 2018 Under 15 years old | 2018 65 years old and over | 2020 (P) Under 15 years old | 2020 (P) 65 years old and over |
|---|---|---|---|---|---|---|---|---|---|
| **World** | **25.3** | **9.1** | **25.0** | **9.5** | Korea, South | 13.0 | 14.6 | 12.8 | 15.9 |
| Afghanistan | 40.9 | 2.6 | 40.6 | 2.7 | Madagascar | 39.5 | 3.4 | 38.9 | 3.5 |
| Algeria | 29.5 | 5.8 | 29.0 | 6.2 | Malawi | 46.2 | 2.7 | 45.9 | 2.7 |
| Angola | 48.1 | 2.3 | 47.8 | 2.3 | Malaysia | 27.5 | 6.3 | 26.8 | 6.9 |
| Argentina | 24.4 | 11.8 | 24.0 | 12.1 | Mali | 48.0 | 3.0 | 47.7 | 3.0 |
| Australia | 17.7 | 16.4 | 17.6 | 17.0 | Mexico | 26.6 | 7.3 | 26.0 | 7.7 |
| Bangladesh | 27.3 | 6.4 | 26.5 | 6.8 | Morocco | 25.5 | 7.0 | 24.9 | 7.5 |
| Belgium | 17.2 | 18.8 | 17.2 | 19.2 | Mozambique | 44.5 | 2.9 | 44.1 | 2.9 |
| Benin | 42.3 | 2.9 | 41.5 | 2.9 | Nepal | 29.5 | 5.3 | 28.4 | 5.7 |
| Bolivia | 31.3 | 5.4 | 30.3 | 5.7 | Netherlands | 16.3 | 19.1 | 16.1 | 19.8 |
| Brazil | 21.9 | 8.6 | 21.1 | 9.2 | Niger | 48.7 | 2.6 | 47.9 | 2.7 |
| Burkina Faso | 44.3 | 3.2 | 43.6 | 3.2 | Nigeria | 42.5 | 3.3 | 41.7 | 3.3 |
| Burma | 26.6 | 5.7 | 26.0 | 6.0 | Pakistan | 30.8 | 4.6 | 29.7 | 4.8 |
| Burundi | 45.5 | 2.7 | 45.3 | 2.8 | Peru | 26.0 | 7.6 | 25.4 | 8.0 |
| Cambodia | 30.8 | 4.4 | 30.2 | 4.6 | Philippines | 33.1 | 4.6 | 32.4 | 4.9 |
| Cameroon | 42.1 | 3.2 | 41.6 | 3.3 | Poland | 14.8 | 17.5 | 14.8 | 18.7 |
| Canada | 15.4 | 19.1 | 15.4 | 20.1 | Romania | 14.3 | 16.8 | 14.1 | 17.6 |
| Chad | 48.1 | 2.4 | 47.4 | 2.4 | Russia | 17.2 | 14.7 | 17.2 | 15.5 |
| Chile | 20.0 | 11.1 | 19.8 | 11.8 | Rwanda | 41.0 | 2.5 | 40.0 | 2.6 |
| China | 17.2 | 11.3 | 17.3 | 12.3 | Saudi Arabia | 25.7 | 3.3 | 24.8 | 3.6 |
| Colombia | 23.9 | 7.7 | 23.3 | 8.4 | Senegal | 41.2 | 3.0 | 40.4 | 3.1 |
| Congo, Dem. Rep. | 41.3 | 2.7 | 40.3 | 2.7 | Somalia | 42.9 | 2.2 | 42.4 | 2.3 |
| Cote d'Ivoire | 39.6 | 2.8 | 38.5 | 2.8 | South Africa | 28.2 | 5.8 | 27.9 | 6.1 |
| Cuba | 16.4 | 15.2 | 16.3 | 15.8 | Spain | 15.3 | 18.1 | 15.0 | 18.5 |
| Ecuador | 26.6 | 7.7 | 25.8 | 8.1 | Sri Lanka | 23.7 | 10.0 | 23.1 | 10.6 |
| Egypt | 33.4 | 4.3 | 33.6 | 4.4 | Sudan [1] | 43.1 | 3.0 | 42.0 | 3.0 |
| Ethiopia | 43.2 | 3.0 | 42.7 | 3.0 | Syria | 31.4 | 4.3 | 30.8 | 4.5 |
| France | 18.5 | 19.8 | 18.4 | 20.5 | Taiwan | 12.7 | 14.4 | 12.4 | 15.7 |
| Germany | 12.8 | 22.4 | 12.9 | 23.0 | Tanzania | 43.4 | 3.0 | 42.7 | 3.1 |
| Ghana | 37.8 | 4.3 | 37.4 | 4.4 | Thailand | 16.7 | 11.0 | 16.4 | 11.8 |
| Guatemala | 34.6 | 4.5 | 33.7 | 4.7 | Tunisia | 25.3 | 8.2 | 25.3 | 8.9 |
| Guinea | 41.4 | 3.9 | 41.2 | 3.9 | Turkey | 24.3 | 7.8 | 23.4 | 8.4 |
| Haiti | 32.3 | 4.2 | 31.2 | 4.3 | Uganda | 47.8 | 2.0 | 47.4 | 1.9 |
| India | 27.0 | 6.4 | 26.3 | 6.7 | Ukraine | 15.9 | 16.5 | 16.2 | 17.0 |
| Indonesia | 24.6 | 7.3 | 23.9 | 7.8 | United Kingdom | 17.6 | 18.2 | 17.6 | 18.5 |
| Iran | 24.2 | 5.5 | 24.1 | 5.9 | **United States** | **18.6** | **16.0** | **18.4** | **16.9** |
| Iraq | 39.0 | 3.6 | 38.1 | 3.8 | Uzbekistan | 23.6 | 5.4 | 23.2 | 5.9 |
| Italy | 13.6 | 21.7 | 13.4 | 22.1 | Venezuela | 27.0 | 7.4 | 26.4 | 8.0 |
| Japan | 12.7 | 28.4 | 12.5 | 29.2 | Vietnam | 23.3 | 6.4 | 22.6 | 6.9 |
| Kazakhstan | 26.1 | 7.9 | 26.1 | 8.4 | Yemen | 39.2 | 2.8 | 37.7 | 2.9 |
| Kenya | 39.0 | 3.1 | 36.8 | 3.3 | Zambia | 45.9 | 2.3 | 45.7 | 2.3 |
| Korea, North | 20.6 | 9.5 | 20.5 | 9.7 | Zimbabwe | 38.6 | 4.5 | 38.3 | 4.5 |

P Projected. [1] Data for Sudan exclude South Sudan, which became an independent country in July 2011.

Source: U.S. Census Bureau, "International Data Base (IDB)," <https://www.census.gov/programs-surveys/international-programs/about/idb.html>, accessed September 2019.

# Table 1365. Births, Deaths, and Life Expectancy by Country or Territory: 2018 and 2020

[Covers countries with 12 million or more population in 2018]

| Country or territory | Crude birth rate [1] | | Crude death rate [2] | | Expectation of life at birth (years) | | Infant mortality rate [3] | | Total fertility rate per woman [4] | |
|---|---|---|---|---|---|---|---|---|---|---|
| | 2018 | 2020 (P) | 2018 | 2020 (P) | 2018 | 2020 (P) | 2018 | 2020 (P) | 2018 | 2020 (P) |
| **World** | **18.2** | **17.7** | **7.7** | **7.7** | **69.8** | **70.3** | **32.0** | **30.5** | **2.42** | **2.39** |
| Afghanistan | 37.5 | 36.7 | 13.2 | 12.7 | 52.1 | 52.8 | 108.5 | 104.3 | 5.02 | 4.82 |
| Algeria | 21.5 | 20.0 | 4.3 | 4.4 | 77.2 | 77.5 | 18.9 | 17.6 | 2.66 | 2.59 |
| Angola | 43.7 | 42.7 | 9.0 | 8.5 | 60.6 | 61.3 | 65.8 | 62.3 | 6.09 | 5.96 |
| Argentina | 16.5 | 16.0 | 7.5 | 7.4 | 77.5 | 77.8 | 9.5 | 9.0 | 2.25 | 2.21 |
| Australia | 12.0 | 11.9 | 7.3 | 7.5 | 82.4 | 82.5 | 4.2 | 4.1 | 1.77 | 1.76 |
| Bangladesh | 18.6 | 18.1 | 5.4 | 5.5 | 73.7 | 74.2 | 30.5 | 28.3 | 2.15 | 2.11 |
| Brazil | 13.9 | 13.6 | 6.7 | 6.9 | 74.3 | 74.7 | 16.9 | 15.9 | 1.75 | 1.73 |
| Burkina Faso | 36.9 | 35.1 | 8.7 | 8.2 | 61.8 | 62.7 | 54.7 | 52.0 | 4.77 | 4.51 |
| Burma | 17.7 | 17.0 | 7.3 | 7.2 | 68.6 | 69.3 | 34.4 | 31.7 | 2.13 | 2.07 |
| Cambodia | 22.5 | 21.3 | 7.4 | 7.3 | 65.2 | 65.9 | 46.1 | 43.7 | 2.47 | 2.39 |
| Cameroon | 35.0 | 34.2 | 9.4 | 9.0 | 59.4 | 60.3 | 49.8 | 47.6 | 4.58 | 4.46 |
| Canada | 10.2 | 10.1 | 8.8 | 9.0 | 82.0 | 82.2 | 4.5 | 4.4 | 1.60 | 1.61 |
| Chad | 43.0 | 41.7 | 10.5 | 10.0 | 57.5 | 58.3 | 71.7 | 68.6 | 5.90 | 5.68 |
| Chile | 13.4 | 13.1 | 6.3 | 6.5 | 79.1 | 79.4 | 6.4 | 6.2 | 1.79 | 1.77 |
| China | 12.1 | 11.6 | 8.0 | 8.2 | 75.8 | 76.1 | 11.8 | 11.4 | 1.60 | 1.60 |
| Colombia | 15.8 | 15.4 | 5.5 | 5.6 | 76.2 | 76.6 | 13.2 | 12.3 | 1.98 | 1.94 |
| Congo, Dem. Rep. | 32.8 | 31.3 | 9.4 | 9.1 | 58.1 | 58.8 | 66.7 | 63.6 | 4.26 | 3.99 |
| Cote d'Ivoire | 30.1 | 29.1 | 8.4 | 7.9 | 60.1 | 61.3 | 62.6 | 59.1 | 3.83 | 3.67 |
| Ecuador | 17.6 | 17.0 | 5.1 | 5.2 | 77.1 | 77.5 | 15.9 | 15.0 | 2.15 | 2.09 |
| Egypt | 28.8 | 27.2 | 4.5 | 4.4 | 73.2 | 73.7 | 18.3 | 17.1 | 3.41 | 3.29 |
| Ethiopia | 36.0 | 35.2 | 7.5 | 7.2 | 63.0 | 63.7 | 48.3 | 45.6 | 4.91 | 4.75 |
| France | 12.1 | 11.9 | 9.4 | 9.6 | 82.0 | 82.2 | 3.2 | 3.2 | 2.06 | 2.06 |
| Germany | 8.6 | 8.6 | 11.8 | 12.1 | 80.9 | 81.1 | 3.4 | 3.3 | 1.46 | 1.47 |
| Ghana | 30.2 | 29.6 | 6.8 | 6.6 | 67.4 | 68.2 | 34.1 | 32.1 | 3.96 | 3.90 |
| Guatemala | 24.6 | 23.3 | 5.0 | 4.9 | 71.8 | 72.4 | 23.3 | 21.8 | 2.87 | 2.72 |
| India | 18.7 | 18.2 | 7.3 | 7.3 | 69.1 | 69.7 | 37.8 | 35.4 | 2.40 | 2.35 |
| Indonesia | 15.9 | 15.4 | 6.5 | 6.6 | 73.2 | 73.7 | 21.9 | 20.4 | 2.08 | 2.04 |
| Iran | 17.4 | 16.3 | 5.3 | 5.3 | 74.2 | 74.5 | 15.5 | 14.9 | 1.96 | 1.94 |
| Iraq | 30.0 | 29.1 | 3.8 | 3.8 | 74.9 | 74.9 | 37.5 | 37.5 | 3.94 | 3.82 |
| Italy | 8.5 | 8.4 | 10.5 | 10.7 | 82.4 | 82.5 | 3.2 | 3.2 | 1.45 | 1.47 |
| Japan | 7.5 | 7.3 | 9.9 | 10.2 | 85.5 | 86.0 | 2.0 | 1.9 | 1.42 | 1.43 |
| Kazakhstan | 17.5 | 16.4 | 8.2 | 8.2 | 71.4 | 72.0 | 19.0 | 17.9 | 2.22 | 2.16 |
| Kenya | 22.6 | 20.8 | 6.7 | 6.6 | 64.6 | 65.1 | 36.1 | 34.0 | 2.81 | 2.57 |
| Korea, North | 14.6 | 14.5 | 9.3 | 9.4 | 71.0 | 71.6 | 21.4 | 20.0 | 1.94 | 1.92 |
| Korea, South | 8.3 | 8.2 | 6.3 | 6.8 | 82.5 | 82.6 | 3.0 | 3.0 | 1.27 | 1.29 |
| Madagascar | 31.0 | 29.9 | 6.4 | 6.2 | 66.6 | 67.3 | 40.1 | 37.8 | 3.95 | 3.78 |
| Malawi | 40.7 | 40.1 | 7.7 | 7.2 | 62.2 | 63.2 | 42.1 | 39.5 | 5.43 | 5.31 |
| Malaysia | 18.8 | 18.3 | 5.2 | 5.3 | 75.4 | 75.9 | 12.1 | 11.4 | 2.48 | 2.43 |
| Mali | 43.2 | 42.2 | 9.6 | 9.0 | 60.8 | 61.6 | 67.6 | 64.0 | 5.90 | 5.72 |
| Mexico | 18.1 | 17.6 | 5.4 | 5.4 | 76.3 | 76.7 | 11.3 | 10.7 | 2.22 | 2.19 |
| Morocco | 17.5 | 16.9 | 4.9 | 5.0 | 77.0 | 77.7 | 21.1 | 19.5 | 2.09 | 2.07 |
| Mozambique | 37.8 | 37.2 | 11.4 | 10.9 | 54.1 | 54.8 | 64.0 | 60.5 | 5.02 | 4.90 |
| Nepal | 19.1 | 18.1 | 5.6 | 5.7 | 71.3 | 71.8 | 26.9 | 25.1 | 2.07 | 1.96 |
| Netherlands | 10.9 | 11.0 | 9.0 | 9.2 | 81.5 | 81.7 | 3.5 | 3.5 | 1.78 | 1.77 |
| Niger | 43.6 | 42.5 | 11.5 | 11.0 | 56.3 | 57.1 | 79.4 | 76.1 | 6.35 | 6.08 |
| Nigeria | 35.2 | 34.6 | 9.6 | 9.1 | 59.3 | 60.4 | 63.3 | 59.8 | 4.85 | 4.72 |
| Pakistan | 21.6 | 20.7 | 6.3 | 6.2 | 68.4 | 69.0 | 50.4 | 47.2 | 2.55 | 2.42 |
| Peru | 17.6 | 17.0 | 6.1 | 6.2 | 74.2 | 74.7 | 17.8 | 16.7 | 2.10 | 2.04 |
| Philippines | 23.4 | 22.9 | 6.1 | 6.0 | 69.6 | 70.0 | 20.9 | 20.0 | 2.99 | 2.92 |
| Poland | 9.3 | 8.9 | 10.5 | 10.6 | 77.9 | 78.3 | 4.4 | 4.3 | 1.36 | 1.38 |
| Romania | 8.7 | 8.5 | 12.0 | 12.0 | 75.6 | 76.0 | 9.2 | 8.7 | 1.36 | 1.38 |
| Russia | 10.7 | 10.0 | 13.4 | 13.4 | 71.3 | 71.9 | 6.7 | 6.5 | 1.61 | 1.60 |
| Rwanda | 29.8 | 27.9 | 6.3 | 6.1 | 64.5 | 65.1 | 29.1 | 28.0 | 3.75 | 3.52 |
| Saudi Arabia | 15.6 | 14.7 | 3.3 | 3.4 | 75.7 | 76.2 | 12.1 | 11.3 | 2.04 | 1.95 |
| Senegal | 32.9 | 31.8 | 7.9 | 7.6 | 62.5 | 63.2 | 48.0 | 45.7 | 4.20 | 4.04 |
| South Africa | 19.9 | 19.2 | 9.3 | 9.3 | 64.1 | 64.8 | 29.9 | 27.8 | 2.26 | 2.22 |
| Spain | 9.0 | 8.7 | 9.2 | 9.3 | 81.8 | 82.0 | 3.3 | 3.2 | 1.50 | 1.51 |
| Sri Lanka | 14.8 | 14.2 | 6.3 | 6.5 | 77.1 | 77.5 | 8.2 | 7.8 | 2.05 | 2.01 |
| Sudan | 34.2 | 33.8 | 6.7 | 6.5 | 65.8 | 66.5 | 44.2 | 41.8 | 4.85 | 4.72 |
| Syria | 20.7 | 19.7 | 4.0 | 4.0 | 75.2 | 75.6 | 14.4 | 13.7 | 2.44 | 2.34 |
| Taiwan | 8.2 | 8.0 | 7.6 | 7.9 | 80.4 | 80.6 | 4.3 | 4.2 | 1.13 | 1.14 |
| Tanzania | 35.3 | 34.6 | 7.5 | 7.1 | 63.1 | 63.9 | 38.7 | 36.4 | 4.71 | 4.59 |
| Thailand | 11.0 | 10.7 | 8.1 | 8.3 | 75.1 | 75.6 | 9.0 | 8.6 | 1.52 | 1.54 |
| Turkey | 15.4 | 14.8 | 6.0 | 6.1 | 75.3 | 75.7 | 16.9 | 15.8 | 2.00 | 1.96 |
| Uganda | 42.4 | 41.4 | 9.9 | 9.4 | 56.3 | 57.2 | 54.6 | 51.8 | 5.62 | 5.44 |
| Ukraine | 10.1 | 9.6 | 14.3 | 14.0 | 72.4 | 72.9 | 7.7 | 7.4 | 1.55 | 1.56 |
| United Kingdom | 12.0 | 11.9 | 9.4 | 9.5 | 80.9 | 81.1 | 4.2 | 4.1 | 1.88 | 1.86 |
| **United States** | **12.4** | **12.4** | **8.2** | **8.3** | **80.1** | **80.4** | **5.7** | **5.6** | **1.87** | **1.87** |
| Uzbekistan | 16.6 | 16.1 | 5.4 | 5.4 | 74.3 | 74.8 | 17.4 | 16.3 | 1.75 | 1.74 |
| Venezuela | 18.5 | 17.9 | 5.3 | 5.4 | 76.2 | 76.6 | 11.9 | 11.3 | 2.30 | 2.26 |
| Vietnam | 15.2 | 14.5 | 5.9 | 6.0 | 73.9 | 74.4 | 16.7 | 15.7 | 1.79 | 1.77 |
| Yemen | 27.6 | 25.8 | 5.9 | 5.6 | 66.2 | 66.9 | 44.6 | 41.9 | 3.48 | 3.20 |
| Zambia | 41.1 | 40.4 | 12.0 | 11.6 | 53.0 | 53.6 | 59.3 | 56.0 | 5.58 | 5.49 |
| Zimbabwe | 34.0 | 33.6 | 9.9 | 9.3 | 61.1 | 62.3 | 31.9 | 30.3 | 3.97 | 3.93 |

P Projection. [1] Number of births during 1 year per 1,000 persons (based on midyear population). [2] Number of deaths during 1 year per 1,000 persons (based on midyear population). [3] Number of deaths of children under 1 year of age per 1,000 live births in a calendar year. [4] Average number of children that would be born if all women lived to the end of childbearing age, based on birth rates for each specified year.

Source: U.S. Census Bureau, "International Data Base (IDB)," <https://www.census.gov/programs-surveys/international-programs/about/idb.html>, accessed September 2019.

# Table 1366. Life Expectancy at Birth and at Age 65 by Sex—Selected Countries: 2010 and 2017

| Country | Life expectancy at birth (years) | | | | Life expectancy at age 65 (years) | | | |
|---|---|---|---|---|---|---|---|---|
| | Females | | Males | | Females | | Males | |
| | 2010 | 2017 | 2010 | 2017 | 2010 | 2017 | 2010 | 2017 |
| **United States**............ | **81.0** | **81.1** | **76.2** | **76.1** | **20.3** | **20.6** | **17.7** | **18.1** |
| Australia.................. | 84.0 | 84.6 | 79.5 | 80.5 | 21.8 | 22.3 | 18.9 | 19.7 |
| Austria................... | 83.5 | 84.0 | 77.8 | 79.4 | 21.4 | 21.5 | 17.9 | 18.5 |
| Belgium.................. | 83.0 | 83.9 | 77.5 | 79.2 | 21.3 | 21.9 | 17.6 | 18.5 |
| Brazil.................... | 77.6 | 79.3 | 70.1 | 72.1 | 19.2 | [1] 19.8 | 16.4 | [1] 16.7 |
| Canada.................. | 83.3 | 84.0 | 78.8 | 79.9 | 21.5 | 22.1 | 18.4 | 19.3 |
| Czechia.................. | 80.9 | 82.0 | 74.5 | 76.1 | 19.0 | 19.8 | 15.5 | 16.2 |
| Denmark................. | 81.4 | 83.1 | 77.2 | 79.2 | 19.7 | 20.8 | 17.0 | 18.2 |
| Finland.................. | 83.5 | 84.5 | 76.9 | 78.9 | 21.5 | 22.1 | 17.5 | 18.4 |
| France................... | 85.3 | 85.6 | 78.3 | 79.6 | 23.4 | 23.6 | 18.9 | 19.6 |
| Germany................. | 83.0 | 83.4 | 78.0 | 78.7 | 20.9 | 21.2 | 17.8 | 18.1 |
| Greece................... | 83.3 | 83.9 | 78.0 | 78.8 | 21.0 | 21.4 | 18.2 | 18.6 |
| Hungary................. | 78.6 | 79.3 | 70.7 | 72.5 | 18.2 | 18.4 | 14.1 | 14.5 |
| Iceland.................. | 84.1 | 84.3 | 79.8 | 81.1 | 21.5 | 21.4 | 18.3 | 19.8 |
| Ireland.................. | 83.1 | 84.0 | 78.5 | 80.4 | 20.8 | 21.4 | 17.7 | 19.0 |
| Israel [2]................ | 83.6 | 84.6 | 79.7 | 80.6 | 21.2 | 21.9 | 18.9 | 19.3 |
| Italy..................... | 84.7 | 85.2 | 79.5 | 80.8 | 22.1 | 22.4 | 18.3 | 19.2 |
| Japan.................... | 86.3 | 87.3 | 79.6 | 81.1 | 23.8 | 24.4 | 18.7 | 19.6 |
| Korea, South............. | 83.6 | 85.7 | 76.8 | 79.7 | 21.2 | 22.7 | 16.8 | 18.6 |
| Mexico................... | 77.0 | 77.9 | 71.1 | 72.9 | 18.5 | 18.7 | 16.6 | 16.8 |
| Netherlands.............. | 83.0 | 83.4 | 78.9 | 80.2 | 21.0 | 21.2 | 17.7 | 18.7 |
| New Zealand............. | 82.7 | [3] 83.6 | 78.9 | [3] 80.2 | 21.0 | [3] 21.7 | 18.5 | [3] 19.6 |
| Norway.................. | 83.3 | 84.3 | 79.0 | 81.0 | 21.2 | 21.6 | 18.0 | 19.3 |
| Poland................... | 80.7 | 81.8 | 72.2 | 73.9 | 19.5 | 20.2 | 15.1 | 15.9 |
| Portugal................. | 83.2 | 84.6 | 76.8 | 78.4 | 21.0 | 22.1 | 17.2 | 18.3 |
| Russia................... | 74.9 | 77.6 | 63.1 | 67.5 | 16.5 | 18.0 | 12.1 | 13.7 |
| Slovenia................. | 83.1 | 84.0 | 76.4 | 78.2 | 21.0 | 21.7 | 16.8 | 17.6 |
| Spain.................... | 85.5 | 86.1 | 79.2 | 80.6 | 22.9 | 23.4 | 18.6 | 19.3 |
| Sweden.................. | 83.6 | 84.1 | 79.6 | 80.8 | 21.2 | 21.5 | 18.3 | 19.2 |
| Switzerland.............. | 84.9 | 85.6 | 80.3 | 81.6 | 22.5 | 22.8 | 19.0 | 20.0 |
| Turkey................... | 76.8 | 80.8 | 71.8 | 75.3 | 16.0 | 19.2 | 14.0 | 16.0 |
| United Kingdom.......... | 82.6 | 83.1 | 78.6 | 79.5 | 20.8 | 21.1 | 18.2 | 18.8 |

[1] Data are for 2015. [2] The statistical data for Israel are supplied by and under the responsibility of the relevant Israeli authorities. The use of such data by the OECD is without prejudice to the status of the Golan Heights, East Jerusalem and Israeli settlements in the West Bank under the terms of international law. [3] Provisional.

Source: Organisation for Economic Co-operation and Development (OECD), 2019, "OECD Health Data: Health Status," OECD Health Statistics (database) ©, <http://dx.doi.org/10.1787/data-00546-en>, accessed July 2019.

# Table 1367. Percent of the Adult Population Considered to Be Obese: 2000 to 2017

[Obesity rates are defined as the percentage of the population with a Body Mass Index (BMI) over 30 kg/m $^2$. The BMI is a single number that evaluates an individual's weight status in relation to height (weight/height $^2$). Obesity estimates derived from health examinations are generally higher and more reliable than those coming from self-reports because they preclude any misreporting of people's height and weight. However, health examinations are only conducted regularly in a few countries. For more information on methods, see source]

| Country | 2000 | 2005 | 2010 | 2013 | 2014 | 2015 | 2016 | 2017 |
|---|---|---|---|---|---|---|---|---|
| **OBESITY, MEASURED** | | | | | | | | |
| **United States**................... | **30.9** | **(NA)** | **36.1** | **(NA)** | **[1] 38.2** | **(NA)** | **40.0** | **(NA)** |
| Australia........................ | (NA) | (NA) | (NA) | (NA) | [1] 27.9 | (NA) | (NA) | 30.4 |
| Canada......................... | (NA) | 23.7 | 25.4 | 25.8 | (NA) | [1] 28.1 | (NA) | 26.3 |
| Colombia........................ | (NA) | 13.8 | 16.5 | (NA) | (NA) | 18.7 | (NA) | (NA) |
| Czechia......................... | 14.0 | 17.0 | 21.0 | (NA) | (NA) | (NA) | (NA) | (NA) |
| Finland......................... | 22.5 | (NA) | (NA) | (NA) | (NA) | (NA) | (NA) | 26.8 |
| Ireland......................... | (NA) | (NA) | (NA) | (NA) | (NA) | 23.0 | (NA) | 23.0 |
| Japan.......................... | 2.9 | 3.9 | 3.5 | 3.7 | 3.9 | 3.7 | 4.2 | 4.4 |
| Korea, South.................... | (NA) | 3.5 | 4.1 | 4.7 | 4.3 | 5.3 | 5.5 | 5.4 |
| Luxembourg..................... | 16.3 | 18.6 | 22.5 | 22.7 | 22.6 | (NA) | (NA) | (NA) |
| Mexico......................... | 24.2 | 30.2 | (NA) | (NA) | (NA) | (NA) | 33.3 | (NA) |
| New Zealand.................... | (NA) | (NA) | (NA) | 30.8 | 29.9 | 30.7 | 31.6 | 32.2 |
| United Kingdom................. | 21.2 | 23.2 | 26.1 | 24.9 | 25.6 | 26.9 | 26.2 | 28.7 |
| **OBESITY, SELF-REPORTED** | | | | | | | | |
| **United States**................... | **21.7** | **25.1** | **28.1** | **28.7** | **29.5** | **30.1** | **30.2** | **31.0** |
| Brazil.......................... | (NA) | (NA) | 15.0 | 17.5 | 16.8 | 17.0 | 18.9 | 18.9 |
| Canada......................... | (NA) | 15.2 | 17.5 | 18.2 | 19.6 | [1] 19.2 | 19.7 | 19.8 |
| Denmark........................ | 9.5 | 11.4 | 13.4 | 14.2 | 14.9 | (NA) | (NA) | 16.8 |
| Finland......................... | 11.2 | 14.1 | 15.6 | 15.7 | 18.3 | [1] 18.8 | 19.0 | 19.0 |
| France.......................... | 9.0 | (NA) | 12.9 | (NA) | 15.3 | (NA) | (NA) | (NA) |
| Germany........................ | (NA) | 13.6 | (NA) | 15.7 | 16.4 | (NA) | (NA) | 16.3 |
| Iceland......................... | (NA) | (NA) | 21.0 | (NA) | (NA) | [1] 19.0 | (NA) | [1] 26.6 |
| Israel [2]....................... | (NA) | (NA) | 15.7 | 15.7 | 17.8 | (NA) | [1] 16.6 | 14.7 |
| Italy........................... | 8.6 | 9.9 | 10.3 | 10.3 | 10.3 | 9.8 | 10.4 | 10.6 |
| Korea, South.................... | (NA) | (NA) | 2.0 | 2.4 | 2.6 | 2.8 | 3.2 | 3.4 |
| Netherlands..................... | 9.4 | 10.7 | 11.4 | 11.1 | [1] 13.3 | 12.8 | 13.6 | 13.4 |
| Russia.......................... | (NA) | (NA) | 19.3 | 21.7 | [1] 22.3 | 21.6 | 21.4 | 22.3 |
| Sweden......................... | 9.2 | 10.9 | 11.3 | 11.7 | 12.2 | 12.3 | 13.0 | 13.1 |
| Turkey.......................... | (NA) | (NA) | 16.9 | (NA) | 19.9 | (NA) | 19.6 | (NA) |

NA Not available. [1] Break in series. [2] See footnote 2, Table 1366.

Source: Organisation for Economic Co-operation and Development (OECD), 2019, "OECD Health Data: Non-medical Determinants of Health," OECD Health Statistics (database) ©, <http://dx.doi.org/10.1787/data-00546-en>, accessed July 2019.

## Table 1368. Daily Tobacco Consumption by Country and Sex: 2000 to 2017

[Daily smokers as percent of population aged over 15. Covers only tobacco forms consumed by smoking]

| Country | Total | | | | Females | | | | Males | | | |
|---|---|---|---|---|---|---|---|---|---|---|---|---|
| | 2000 | 2010 | 2016 | 2017 | 2000 | 2010 | 2016 | 2017 | 2000 | 2010 | 2016 | 2017 |
| **United States**...... | 19.1 | 15.1 | 11.8 | 10.5 | 17.3 | 13.6 | 10.5 | 9.5 | 21.2 | 16.7 | 13.2 | 11.5 |
| Australia............ | (NA) | 15.4 | 12.4 | (NA) | (NA) | 14.1 | 10.8 | (NA) | (NA) | 16.7 | 14.0 | (NA) |
| Brazil.............. | (NA) | 14.1 | 10.2 | 10.1 | (NA) | 11.7 | 8.0 | 7.5 | (NA) | 16.8 | 12.7 | 13.2 |
| Canada............. | (NA) | 16.3 | 12.5 | 12.0 | (NA) | 13.7 | 10.8 | 10.0 | (NA) | 19.0 | 14.2 | 14.2 |
| Czechia............ | (NA) | 22.8 | 19.6 | 18.4 | (NA) | 16.5 | 15.6 | 14.5 | (NA) | 29.3 | 23.8 | 22.6 |
| Denmark........... | 30.5 | ¹ 20.9 | (NA) | 16.9 | 29.0 | ¹ 19.3 | (NA) | 15.4 | 32.0 | ¹ 22.7 | (NA) | 18.5 |
| Finland............. | 23.4 | 19.0 | 15.0 | 13.0 | 20.3 | 15.7 | 15.0 | 12.0 | 27.3 | 23.2 | 16.0 | 15.0 |
| Ireland............. | (NA) | (NA) | 19.0 | 18.0 | (NA) | (NA) | 17.0 | 17.0 | (NA) | (NA) | 21.0 | 20.0 |
| Israel ²............ | 24.1 | 18.5 | ¹ 19.6 | 16.9 | 15.4 | 12.6 | ¹ 14.1 | 12.8 | 34.0 | 24.8 | ¹ 25.3 | 21.3 |
| Italy............... | 24.4 | 23.1 | 20.0 | 19.9 | 17.4 | 17.1 | 15.3 | 15.0 | 31.9 | 29.6 | 25.1 | 25.1 |
| Japan.............. | 27.0 | 19.5 | 18.3 | 17.7 | 11.5 | 8.4 | 8.2 | 7.2 | 47.4 | 32.2 | 30.2 | 29.4 |
| Korea.............. | (NA) | 22.9 | 18.4 | 17.5 | (NA) | 5.2 | 4.1 | 3.5 | (NA) | 40.8 | 32.9 | 31.6 |
| Luxembourg........ | (NA) | 18.3 | 14.9 | 16.0 | (NA) | 15.7 | 12.6 | 14.0 | (NA) | 20.9 | 17.3 | 18.1 |
| Mexico............. | ¹ 12.4 | (NA) | (NA) | ¹ 7.6 | ¹ 6.4 | (NA) | (NA) | ¹ 3.6 | ¹ 20.5 | (NA) | (NA) | ¹ 12.0 |
| Netherlands........ | 32.0 | ¹ 20.9 | 18.0 | 16.8 | 29.0 | ¹ 18.8 | 15.2 | 14.1 | 35.0 | ¹ 23.1 | 20.9 | 19.5 |
| New Zealand....... | 25.0 | (NA) | 14.2 | 13.8 | 25.0 | (NA) | 12.9 | 12.6 | 25.0 | (NA) | 15.6 | 15.1 |
| Norway............ | 32.0 | 19.0 | 12.0 | 11.0 | 32.0 | 19.0 | 11.0 | 10.0 | 31.0 | 19.0 | 13.0 | 12.0 |
| Russia............. | 34.9 | (NA) | ¹ 30.3 | (NA) | 12.6 | (NA) | ¹ 14.4 | (NA) | 62.2 | (NA) | ¹ 49.5 | (NA) |
| Sweden............ | 18.9 | 13.6 | 10.9 | 10.4 | 21.0 | 12.5 | 11.2 | 10.3 | 16.8 | 14.7 | 10.6 | 10.5 |
| United Kingdom..... | 27.0 | 20.0 | 16.1 | 17.2 | 25.0 | 20.0 | 14.5 | 15.5 | 29.0 | 21.0 | 17.7 | 19.1 |

NA Not available. ¹ Break in series or difference in methodology. ² See footnote 2, Table 1366.

Source: Organisation for Economic Co-operation and Development (OECD), 2019, "OECD Health Data: Non-medical Determinants of Health," OECD Health Statistics (database) ©, <http://dx.doi.org/10.1787/data-00546-en>, accessed July 2019.

## Table 1369. Road Traffic Fatalities by Country: 2000 to 2017

[Fatalities include any person killed immediately or dying within 30 days as a result of an injury accident. For countries that do not apply the threshold of 30 days, conversion coefficients are estimated so that comparisons on the basis of the 30 day-definition can be made]

| Country | 2000 | 2005 | 2010 | 2015 | 2017 | Country | 2000 | 2005 | 2010 | 2015 | 2017 |
|---|---|---|---|---|---|---|---|---|---|---|---|
| **United States**..... | **41,945** | **43,510** | **32,999** | **35,092** | ² **37,150** | Japan............. | 10,410 | 7,997 | 5,828 | 4,885 | 4,431 |
| Argentina.......... | (NA) | (NA) | 5,094 | (NA) | ² 5,420 | Korea, South...... | 10,236 | 6,376 | 5,505 | 4,621 | 4,185 |
| Armenia............ | 214 | 310 | ² 294 | 346 | 279 | Latvia............. | 588 | 442 | 218 | 188 | 136 |
| Australia........... | 1,817 | 1,627 | 1,353 | 1,205 | (NA) | Lithuania.......... | 641 | 773 | 299 | 242 | 191 |
| Austria............. | 976 | 768 | 552 | 479 | (NA) | Mexico............ | 5,224 | 4,710 | 5,032 | 3,490 | 2,919 |
| Belgium............ | 1,470 | 1,131 | 850 | 762 | 615 | Moldova........... | 406 | 391 | 452 | 300 | 301 |
| Bulgaria............ | 1,012 | 957 | 776 | 708 | 682 | Netherlands....... | 1,166 | 817 | 640 | 621 | 613 |
| Canada............ | 2,904 | 2,898 | 2,238 | 1,860 | (NA) | New Zealand...... | 462 | 405 | 375 | 319 | 378 |
| China.............. | (NA) | 98,738 | 65,225 | 58,022 | (NA) | Norway........... | 341 | 224 | 208 | 117 | 106 |
| Croatia............ | 655 | 597 | 426 | 348 | 331 | Poland............ | 6,294 | 5,444 | 3,907 | 2,938 | 2,831 |
| Czechia............ | 1,486 | 1,286 | 802 | 738 | 577 | Portugal........... | 1,857 | 1,247 | 937 | 593 | (NA) |
| Finland............ | 396 | 379 | 272 | 270 | ² 230 | Romania........... | 2,499 | 2,641 | 2,377 | 1,893 | 1,951 |
| France............. | 8,079 | 5,318 | 3,992 | 3,461 | 3,448 | Russia............ | 29,594 | 33,957 | 26,567 | 23,114 | 19,088 |
| Georgia............ | 500 | 581 | 685 | 602 | 517 | Serbia............ | 1,048 | 841 | 656 | 601 | 578 |
| Germany........... | 7,503 | 5,361 | 3,648 | 3,459 | 3,180 | Slovakia........... | 648 | 600 | 353 | 310 | 276 |
| Greece............ | 2,037 | 1,658 | 1,258 | 793 | ² 732 | Slovenia.......... | 313 | 258 | 138 | 120 | 104 |
| Hungary........... | 1,200 | 1,278 | 740 | 644 | 625 | Spain............. | 5,776 | 4,442 | 2,478 | 1,689 | (NA) |
| Iceland............ | 32 | 19 | 8 | 16 | 16 | Sweden........... | 591 | 440 | ¹ 266 | 259 | 253 |
| India.............. | 78,911 | 94,968 | 134,513 | 146,133 | 147,913 | Switzerland........ | 592 | 409 | 327 | 253 | 230 |
| Ireland............. | 415 | 396 | 212 | ² 162 | ² 157 | Turkey............ | 5,510 | 4,505 | 4,045 | ¹ 7,530 | 7,427 |
| Italy............... | 7,061 | 5,818 | 4,114 | 3,428 | 3,378 | United Kingdom... | 3,580 | 3,336 | 1,905 | 1,804 | 1,856 |

NA Not available. ¹ Break in series. ² Estimated or provisional.

Source: International Transport Forum (ITF) / Organisation for Economic Co-operation and Development (OECD), 2019, "Road accidents," Transport Statistics ©, <https://doi.org/10.1787/g2g55585-en>, accessed July 2019. See also <https://www.itf-oecd.org/>.

## Table 1370. Suicide Rates by Sex and Country: 2016

[Deaths due to intentional self-harm per 100,000 persons. Rates are standardized]

| Country | Total | Men | Women | Country | Total | Men | Women |
|---|---|---|---|---|---|---|---|
| **United States**............ | **13.9** | **22.2** | **6.2** | Israel ².................... | 5.4 | 9.4 | 1.8 |
| Australia................. | 11.9 | 18.2 | 5.8 | Italy ¹.................... | 5.7 | 9.4 | 2.4 |
| Austria.................. | 12.2 | 19.9 | 5.8 | Japan.................... | 15.2 | 22.1 | 8.6 |
| Belgium.................. | 15.9 | 23.6 | 8.8 | Korea, South............. | 24.6 | 37.4 | 14.1 |
| Brazil ¹.................. | 6.0 | 9.9 | 2.4 | Lithuania................. | 26.7 | 50.9 | 7.1 |
| Canada ¹................. | 11.8 | 17.8 | 6.1 | Luxembourg.............. | 7.2 | 11.0 | 3.5 |
| Chile.................... | 10.7 | 18.8 | 3.5 | Mexico.................. | 5.4 | 9.5 | 1.8 |
| Colombia ¹............... | 5.2 | 9.0 | 1.9 | Netherlands.............. | 10.5 | 14.6 | 6.6 |
| Czechia.................. | 11.7 | 19.9 | 4.5 | Norway.................. | 11.6 | 15.8 | 7.4 |
| Denmark ¹................ | 9.4 | 13.4 | 5.6 | Poland.................. | 11.6 | 21.4 | 2.8 |
| Estonia.................. | 13.0 | 23.5 | 4.6 | Portugal................. | 8.1 | 13.8 | 3.4 |
| Finland.................. | 13.9 | 22.2 | 6.0 | Russia ³................. | 17.9 | 33.7 | 5.7 |
| France ¹................. | 13.1 | 21.8 | 5.8 | Spain................... | 6.8 | 10.7 | 3.4 |
| Germany................. | 10.2 | 16.3 | 4.9 | Sweden................. | 11.1 | 15.4 | 6.8 |
| Greece.................. | 4.0 | 7.0 | 1.4 | Switzerland.............. | 11.2 | 17.3 | 5.6 |
| Hungary................. | 16.2 | 27.5 | 7.3 | Turkey.................. | 2.6 | 4.1 | 1.1 |
| Iceland.................. | 12.1 | 21.5 | 2.4 | United Kingdom.......... | 7.3 | 11.4 | 3.3 |

¹ 2015 data. ² See footnote 2, Table 1366. ³ 2014 data.

Source: Organisation for Economic Co-operation and Development (OECD), 2019, "Health Status," OECD Health Statistics database ©, <http://dx.doi.org/10.1787/data-00540-en>, accessed July 2019.

# Table 1371. Health Expenditures by Country: 1990 to 2018

[In percent. GDP = gross domestic product]

| Country | Total expenditures on health (percent of GDP) | | | | | Public (government) expenditures on health (percent of total) | | | | |
|---|---|---|---|---|---|---|---|---|---|---|
| | 1990 | 2000 | 2010 | 2017 | 2018 [1] | 1990 | 2000 | 2010 | 2017 | 2018 [1] |
| **United States** | **11.3** | **12.5** | **16.4** | **17.1** | **16.9** | **40.2** | **44.2** | **48.4** | **84.5** | **84.5** |
| Australia | 6.5 | 7.6 | 8.4 | 9.2 | 9.3 | 66.2 | 68.4 | 68.6 | 68.9 | 69.3 |
| Austria | 7.7 | 9.2 | 10.2 | 10.4 | 10.3 | 74.4 | 75.5 | 74.6 | 74.0 | 74.7 |
| Belgium | 7.1 | 7.9 | 10.0 | 10.3 | 10.4 | (NA) | 74.6 | 77.8 | 77.2 | 77.3 |
| Canada | 8.4 | 8.2 | 10.7 | 10.7 | 10.7 | 74.3 | 70.0 | 70.3 | 69.8 | 69.7 |
| Czechia | 3.7 | 5.7 | 6.9 | 7.2 | 7.5 | 97.1 | 89.8 | 83.3 | 82.1 | 82.5 |
| Denmark | 8.0 | 8.1 | 10.3 | 10.1 | 10.5 | 82.4 | 83.1 | 83.9 | 84.0 | 84.4 |
| Finland | 7.2 | 6.8 | 8.9 | 9.2 | 9.1 | 80.0 | 71.5 | 74.5 | 75.2 | 75.2 |
| France | 8.0 | 9.6 | 11.2 | 11.3 | 11.2 | 76.0 | 78.9 | 76.3 | 83.4 | 83.4 |
| Germany [2] | 8.0 | 9.8 | 11.0 | 11.2 | 11.2 | 75.4 | 78.2 | 83.4 | 84.4 | 84.5 |
| Greece | 6.1 | 7.2 | 9.6 | 8.0 | 7.8 | 54.1 | 61.6 | 69.1 | 60.8 | 60.3 |
| Iceland | 7.4 | 9.0 | 8.5 | 8.3 | 8.3 | 86.2 | 80.6 | 80.4 | 81.8 | 82.1 |
| Ireland | 5.6 | 5.9 | 10.5 | 7.2 | 7.0 | 73.2 | 77.5 | 76.2 | 73.3 | 73.6 |
| Israel [3] | 6.5 | 6.8 | 7.0 | 7.4 | 7.5 | (NA) | 63.1 | 62.8 | 63.6 | 63.8 |
| Italy | 7.0 | 7.6 | 9.0 | 8.8 | 8.8 | 81.3 | 72.6 | 78.5 | 73.9 | 74.2 |
| Japan | 5.8 | 7.2 | 9.2 | 10.9 | 10.9 | 77.6 | 80.4 | 81.9 | 84.1 | 84.1 |
| Korea, South | 3.7 | 4.0 | 6.2 | 7.6 | 8.1 | 40.1 | 53.9 | 60.6 | 58.9 | 59.8 |
| Luxembourg | 5.1 | 5.9 | 7.0 | 5.4 | 5.4 | 93.1 | 82.0 | 84.9 | 83.8 | 84.0 |
| Mexico | (NA) | 4.4 | 6.0 | 5.5 | 5.5 | (NA) | 45.2 | 48.6 | 51.5 | 51.5 |
| Netherlands | 7.0 | 7.7 | 10.2 | 10.1 | 9.9 | 71.2 | 69.0 | 83.4 | 81.5 | 82.1 |
| New Zealand | 6.7 | 7.5 | 9.6 | 9.1 | 9.3 | 82.4 | 78.0 | 81.2 | 78.6 | 79.2 |
| Norway | 7.1 | 7.7 | 8.9 | 10.4 | 10.2 | 82.8 | 81.7 | 84.7 | 85.5 | 85.5 |
| Poland | 4.3 | 5.3 | 6.4 | 6.5 | 6.3 | 90.9 | 68.9 | 71.7 | 69.5 | 71.8 |
| Portugal | 5.5 | 8.4 | 9.8 | 9.0 | 9.1 | 64.9 | 70.5 | 69.8 | 66.3 | 66.5 |
| Slovak Republic | (NA) | 5.3 | 7.8 | 6.7 | 6.7 | (NA) | 89.2 | 71.9 | 79.9 | 80.1 |
| Spain | 6.1 | 6.8 | 9.0 | 8.9 | 8.9 | 78.4 | 71.4 | 74.8 | 70.6 | 70.5 |
| Sweden | 7.2 | 7.4 | 8.5 | 11.0 | 11.0 | 79.6 | 85.5 | 81.9 | 83.7 | 83.9 |
| Switzerland | 7.9 | 9.8 | 10.7 | 12.3 | 12.2 | (NA) | 55.6 | 61.8 | 63.6 | 63.7 |
| Turkey | 2.5 | 4.6 | 5.1 | 4.2 | 4.2 | 59.9 | 61.7 | 78.0 | 77.7 | 78.0 |
| United Kingdom | 5.1 | 6.0 | 8.4 | 9.6 | 9.8 | 84.3 | 79.3 | 83.1 | 78.8 | 77.1 |

NA Not available. [1] Data are estimated or provisional. [2] Data prior to 1991 are for former West Germany. [3] See footnote 3, Table 1372.

Source: Organisation for Economic Co-operation and Development (OECD), 2019, "Health expenditure and financing: Health expenditure indicators," OECD Health Statistics (database) ©, <http://dx.doi.org/10.1787/data-00349-en>, accessed July 2019.

# Table 1372. Physicians and Inpatient Hospital Care—Selected Countries: 2000 to 2017

| Country | Practicing physicians per 1,000 population | | | | Acute (curative) inpatient hospital care | | | | | | | |
|---|---|---|---|---|---|---|---|---|---|---|---|---|
| | | | | | Beds per 1,000 population | | | | Average length of stay (days) | | | |
| | 2000 | 2010 | 2015 | 2017 | 2000 | 2010 | 2015 | 2017 | 2000 | 2010 | 2015 | 2017 |
| **United States** | **2.3** | **2.4** | **2.6** | **2.6** | **3.0** | **2.7** | **2.5** | **(NA)** | **5.8** | **5.4** | **5.5** | **(NA)** |
| Australia | 2.5 | (NA) | [1] 3.5 | [1] 3.7 | (NA) | (NA) | (NA) | (NA) | 6.1 | 5.0 | [2] 4.2 | (NA) |
| Austria | 3.9 | 4.8 | 5.1 | 5.2 | 6.9 | 6.2 | 5.7 | 5.5 | 7.6 | 6.6 | 6.5 | 6.4 |
| Belgium | 2.8 | 2.9 | 3.0 | 3.1 | [2] 6.2 | [2] 5.7 | [2] 5.2 | [2] 5.0 | 8.2 | 7.2 | 6.8 | 6.6 |
| Canada | [1] 2.0 | [1] 2.3 | [1] 2.6 | [1] 2.7 | 3.5 | 2.1 | 2.0 | 2.0 | 7.2 | 7.7 | 7.4 | 7.4 |
| Czechia | 3.4 | 3.6 | (NA) | (NA) | [2] 5.8 | [2] 4.8 | 4.2 | 4.1 | 7.9 | 6.6 | 5.9 | 5.8 |
| Denmark | 2.9 | 3.7 | 3.9 | (NA) | [2] 4.3 | [2] 3.4 | 2.5 | 2.5 | 3.8 | (NA) | (NA) | (NA) |
| Estonia | 3.1 | 3.2 | 3.4 | 3.5 | [2] 6.0 | 3.8 | 3.7 | 3.5 | 7.3 | 5.5 | 6.0 | 6.1 |
| Finland | 2.5 | [1] 3.0 | (NA) | (NA) | [2] 3.9 | 3.4 | 3.1 | 2.8 | [2] 6.9 | 7.0 | 6.6 | 6.4 |
| France | [1] 3.0 | [1] 3.0 | 3.1 | 3.2 | 4.1 | 3.5 | 3.2 | 3.1 | 5.6 | 5.8 | 5.7 | (NA) |
| Germany | 3.3 | 3.7 | 4.1 | 4.3 | 6.8 | 6.2 | 6.1 | 6.0 | 10.1 | 8.1 | 7.6 | 7.5 |
| Hungary | [1,2] 2.7 | [2] 2.9 | [2] 3.1 | 3.3 | [1] 6.2 | 4.5 | 4.3 | 4.3 | 7.1 | 5.8 | 5.6 | 5.5 |
| Ireland | (NA) | (NA) | [1] 2.9 | [1] 3.1 | 2.8 | 2.5 | [2] 2.8 | 2.8 | 6.4 | 6.0 | 6.1 | 6.0 |
| Israel [3] | 3.5 | 3.3 | 3.1 | 3.1 | 2.9 | 2.4 | 2.3 | 2.2 | 9.0 | 5.2 | 5.2 | 5.1 |
| Italy | 3.4 | 3.8 | 3.8 | 4.0 | [2] 4.2 | 3.0 | 2.6 | 2.6 | 7.0 | 6.7 | 6.9 | 6.9 |
| Japan | 1.9 | 2.2 | (NA) | (NA) | 9.8 | 8.1 | 7.9 | 7.8 | 24.8 | 18.2 | 16.5 | 16.2 |
| Korea, South | 1.3 | 2.0 | 2.2 | 2.3 | 4.6 | 6.4 | 7.0 | 7.1 | 11.0 | 10.0 | 7.8 | 7.5 |
| Mexico | 1.6 | 2.0 | 2.4 | 2.4 | [2] 1.8 | [2] 1.6 | 1.4 | 1.4 | (NA) | (NA) | (NA) | (NA) |
| Netherlands | (NA) | (NA) | 3.5 | 3.6 | 3.1 | [2] 2.9 | 3.0 | [1] 2.9 | 9.0 | 5.6 | 5.0 | [1] 5.0 |
| New Zealand | 2.2 | 2.6 | [1] 3.0 | [1] 3.3 | (NA) | [2] 2.8 | [2] 2.7 | [2] 2.7 | 4.3 | 6.1 | 5.3 | (NA) |
| Norway | 3.4 | 4.1 | [2] 4.4 | 4.7 | [2] 3.8 | [2] 3.8 | [2] 3.4 | [2] 3.2 | 6.0 | 6.3 | [2] 6.2 | 6.0 |
| Poland | 2.2 | 2.2 | 2.3 | 2.4 | 5.2 | [2] 5.0 | 4.9 | 4.9 | (NA) | 7.3 | 6.9 | 6.6 |
| Portugal | (NA) | (NA) | (NA) | (NA) | 3.7 | 3.3 | 3.2 | 3.3 | 7.8 | 7.0 | 7.2 | 7.3 |
| Russia | 4.6 | 5.0 | 3.9 | 4.0 | (NA) | (NA) | (NA) | (NA) | 13.5 | 10.8 | 9.7 | 9.3 |
| Slovak Republic | 3.2 | (NA) | (NA) | (NA) | 6.4 | 5.4 | 4.9 | 4.9 | 8.4 | 6.6 | 6.9 | 6.8 |
| Slovenia | 2.2 | 2.4 | 2.8 | 3.1 | [2] 5.2 | [2] 4.3 | [2] 4.2 | [2] 4.2 | 7.1 | 5.5 | 6.5 | 6.6 |
| Spain | 3.1 | 3.8 | 3.9 | 3.9 | 2.9 | 2.5 | 2.4 | [1] 2.4 | 7.1 | 6.3 | 5.9 | [1] 5.9 |
| Sweden | 3.1 | 3.9 | 4.3 | (NA) | [2] 3.1 | [2] 2.5 | [2] 2.3 | [2] 2.0 | 6.6 | 5.8 | 5.7 | 5.5 |
| Switzerland | (NA) | 3.8 | 4.2 | 4.3 | 5.3 | [2] 3.9 | 3.6 | 3.6 | 9.3 | [2] 6.6 | 5.7 | 5.5 |
| Turkey | (NA) | (NA) | (NA) | (NA) | (NA) | 2.7 | 2.7 | 2.8 | 5.6 | 4.0 | 3.9 | 4.1 |
| United Kingdom | 2.0 | 2.7 | [2] 2.8 | [1] 2.8 | (NA) | (NA) | (NA) | 2.1 | (NA) | 6.1 | 6.0 | 5.9 |

NA Not available. [1] Estimated. [2] Break in series or difference in methodology. [3] The statistical data for Israel are supplied by and under the responsibility of the relevant Israeli authorities. The use of such data by the OECD is without prejudice as to the status of the Golan Heights, East Jerusalem and Israeli settlements in the West Bank under the terms of international law.

Source: Organisation for Economic Co-Operation and Development (OECD), 2019, "Health care resources," OECD Health Statistics (database) ©, <http://dx.doi.org/10.1787/data-00541-en>; and "Health care utilisation," OECD Health Statistics (database) ©, <http://dx.doi.org/10.1787/data-00542-en>; accessed July 2019.

# Table 1373. Gross National Income (GNI) by Country: 2010 and 2018

[For total GNI, 65,150,154 represents $65,150,154,000,000. GNI is the sum of value added by all resident producers, plus any product taxes (less subsidies) not included in the valuation of output, plus net receipts of primary income from abroad]

| Country | Gross national income [1] | | | | GNI on purchasing power parity basis [2] | | | |
|---|---|---|---|---|---|---|---|---|
| | Total (mil. dol.) | | Per capita (dol.) | | Total (mil. dol.) | | Per capita (dol.) | |
| | 2010 | 2018 | 2010 | 2018 | 2010 | 2018 | 2010 | 2018 |
| World [3] | 65,150,154 | 84,303,095 | 9,411 | 11,101 | 88,648,240 | 135,966,755 | 12,805 | 17,904 |
| United States | 15,154,199 | 20,562,616 | 48,990 | 62,850 | 15,126,736 | 20,738,399 | 48,900 | 63,390 |
| Algeria | 161,081 | 171,618 | 4,480 | 4,060 | 454,250 | 648,219 | 12,630 | 15,350 |
| Angola | 75,764 | 103,840 | 3,240 | 3,370 | 131,474 | 189,617 | 5,630 | 6,150 |
| Argentina | 378,241 | 550,333 | 9,270 | 12,370 | 729,853 | 882,055 | 17,890 | 19,820 |
| Australia | 1,027,321 | 1,329,354 | 46,630 | 53,190 | 832,728 | 1,247,801 | 37,800 | 49,930 |
| Austria | 414,883 | 435,694 | 49,610 | 49,250 | 354,252 | 495,047 | 42,360 | 55,960 |
| Bangladesh | 118,314 | 282,036 | 800 | 1,750 | 393,544 | 736,277 | 2,670 | 4,560 |
| Belgium | 522,087 | 518,957 | 47,920 | 45,430 | 450,144 | 587,846 | 41,310 | 51,470 |
| Brazil | 1,890,906 | 1,915,275 | 9,660 | 9,140 | 2,720,412 | 3,314,555 | 13,900 | 15,820 |
| Bulgaria | 51,608 | 62,262 | 6,980 | 8,860 | 108,146 | (NA) | 14,620 | (NA) |
| Canada | 1,512,385 | 1,662,414 | 44,480 | 44,860 | 1,336,868 | 1,752,268 | 39,310 | 47,280 |
| Chile | 183,354 | 274,752 | 10,750 | 14,670 | 288,017 | 454,119 | 16,880 | 24,250 |
| China | 5,801,888 | 13,184,125 | 4,340 | 9,470 | 12,392,344 | 25,266,121 | 9,260 | 18,140 |
| Colombia | 253,663 | 307,421 | 5,610 | 6,190 | 467,571 | 719,579 | 10,340 | 14,490 |
| Czechia | 201,913 | 215,196 | 19,280 | 20,250 | 268,404 | 402,376 | 25,620 | 37,870 |
| Denmark | 339,645 | 348,663 | 61,220 | 60,140 | 242,450 | 333,201 | 43,700 | 57,470 |
| Dominican Republic | 51,785 | 78,283 | 5,340 | 7,370 | 104,077 | 180,205 | 10,730 | 16,960 |
| Ecuador | 65,933 | 104,511 | 4,390 | 6,120 | 134,777 | 194,963 | 8,980 | 11,410 |
| Egypt | 196,207 | 275,407 | 2,370 | 2,800 | 796,047 | 1,188,987 | 9,620 | 12,080 |
| Ethiopia | 33,248 | 86,667 | 380 | 790 | 91,917 | 219,041 | 1,050 | 2,010 |
| Finland | 264,586 | 263,875 | 49,330 | 47,820 | 210,577 | 267,594 | 39,260 | 48,490 |
| France | 2,851,169 | 2,751,423 | 43,850 | 41,070 | 2,388,529 | 3,141,674 | 36,730 | 46,900 |
| Germany | 3,662,448 | 3,934,666 | 44,790 | 47,450 | 3,267,763 | 4,627,202 | 39,960 | 55,800 |
| Ghana | 30,540 | 63,356 | 1,230 | 2,130 | 72,239 | 138,279 | 2,920 | 4,650 |
| Greece | 307,604 | 209,586 | 27,660 | 19,540 | 306,635 | 317,556 | 27,570 | 29,600 |
| Guatemala | 39,587 | 76,007 | 2,710 | 4,410 | 93,663 | 143,266 | 6,400 | 8,310 |
| Hong Kong, China | 236,168 | 374,870 | 33,620 | 50,310 | 338,010 | 504,414 | 48,120 | 67,700 |
| Hungary | 131,673 | 142,534 | 13,170 | 14,590 | 205,401 | 291,009 | 20,540 | 29,790 |
| India | 1,505,735 | 2,733,523 | 1,220 | 2,020 | 5,323,989 | 10,391,783 | 4,310 | 7,680 |
| Indonesia | 612,254 | 1,026,760 | 2,530 | 3,840 | 1,950,129 | 3,386,415 | 8,060 | 12,650 |
| Iraq | 136,158 | 193,510 | 4,580 | 5,030 | 387,625 | 664,345 | 13,030 | 17,290 |
| Ireland | 204,817 | 288,118 | 44,910 | 59,360 | 165,411 | 324,264 | 36,270 | 66,810 |
| Israel | 225,987 | 362,899 | 29,640 | 40,850 | 215,703 | 362,437 | 28,290 | 40,800 |
| Italy | 2,234,110 | 2,028,073 | 37,690 | 33,560 | 2,071,050 | 2,567,974 | 34,940 | 42,490 |
| Japan | 5,562,858 | 5,231,267 | 43,440 | 41,340 | 4,596,531 | 5,693,329 | 35,890 | 45,000 |
| Kazakhstan | 121,371 | 143,090 | 7,440 | 7,830 | 279,262 | 442,768 | 17,110 | 24,230 |
| Kenya | 40,445 | 83,063 | 960 | 1,620 | 99,915 | 176,420 | 2,380 | 3,430 |
| Korea, South | 1,053,302 | 1,580,109 | 21,260 | 30,600 | 1,506,237 | 2,088,780 | 30,400 | 40,450 |
| Kuwait | 126,114 | 139,398 | 42,150 | 33,690 | 237,047 | 344,992 | 79,230 | 83,390 |
| Malaysia | 232,945 | 329,881 | 8,260 | 10,460 | 562,742 | 964,892 | 19,950 | 30,600 |
| Mexico | 1,031,499 | 1,157,971 | 9,040 | 9,180 | 1,720,422 | 2,453,500 | 15,080 | 19,440 |
| Morocco | 96,295 | 113,123 | 2,930 | 3,090 | 204,722 | 307,918 | 6,240 | 8,410 |
| Myanmar | 42,923 | 70,246 | 850 | 1,310 | 182,777 | 348,268 | 3,610 | 6,480 |
| Netherlands | 895,636 | 883,575 | 53,900 | 51,280 | 750,559 | 988,728 | 45,170 | 57,380 |
| New Zealand | 129,155 | 199,422 | 29,690 | 40,820 | 129,216 | 196,618 | 29,700 | 40,250 |
| Nigeria | 339,100 | 384,803 | 2,140 | 1,960 | 747,158 | 1,117,358 | 4,710 | 5,700 |
| Norway | 433,000 | 429,345 | 88,560 | 80,790 | 286,431 | 352,806 | 58,580 | 66,390 |
| Oman | 55,258 | 72,998 | 18,170 | 15,110 | 126,816 | 199,130 | 41,700 | 41,230 |
| Pakistan | 184,123 | 335,619 | 1,030 | 1,580 | 742,921 | 1,238,656 | 4,140 | 5,840 |
| Panama | 26,053 | 60,024 | 7,150 | 14,370 | 50,665 | 98,209 | 13,910 | 23,510 |
| Peru | 127,971 | 208,920 | 4,410 | 6,530 | 265,434 | 441,730 | 9,140 | 13,810 |
| Philippines | 231,619 | 408,840 | 2,460 | 3,830 | 619,361 | 1,143,475 | 6,590 | 10,720 |
| Poland | 484,234 | 537,573 | 12,730 | 14,150 | 772,076 | 1,181,684 | 20,290 | 31,110 |
| Portugal | 242,730 | 222,950 | 22,960 | 21,680 | 279,022 | 341,312 | 26,390 | 33,200 |
| Puerto Rico | 62,977 | 67,412 | 16,920 | 21,100 | 80,819 | 84,860 | 21,720 | 26,560 |
| Qatar | 118,091 | 170,210 | 63,620 | 61,190 | 195,585 | 345,285 | 105,360 | 124,130 |
| Romania | 174,370 | 219,925 | 8,610 | 11,290 | 338,278 | (NA) | 16,710 | (NA) |
| Russia | 1,425,184 | 1,501,659 | 9,980 | 10,230 | 2,836,589 | 3,886,717 | 19,860 | 26,470 |
| Saudi Arabia | 514,152 | 725,984 | 18,750 | 21,540 | 1,236,492 | 1,875,396 | 45,090 | 55,650 |
| Singapore | 228,092 | 331,373 | 44,930 | 58,770 | 359,396 | 532,875 | 70,790 | 94,500 |
| Slovak Republic | 92,967 | 99,824 | 17,240 | 18,330 | 131,564 | 183,019 | 24,400 | 33,600 |
| South Africa | 317,112 | 330,751 | 6,190 | 5,720 | 587,872 | 764,275 | 11,480 | 13,230 |
| Spain | 1,496,362 | 1,376,131 | 32,130 | 29,450 | 1,466,034 | 1,908,426 | 31,480 | 40,840 |
| Sri Lanka | 48,796 | 87,896 | 2,410 | 4,060 | 166,922 | 283,554 | 8,240 | 13,090 |
| Sudan [4] | 55,350 | 65,214 | 1,260 | 1,560 | 135,121 | 184,812 | 3,070 | 4,420 |
| Sweden | 505,173 | 560,773 | 53,870 | 55,070 | 401,175 | 549,781 | 42,780 | 53,990 |
| Switzerland | 606,981 | 711,812 | 77,570 | 83,580 | 439,637 | 589,517 | 56,180 | 69,220 |
| Thailand | 308,010 | 458,655 | 4,580 | 6,610 | 850,675 | 1,261,084 | 12,660 | 18,160 |
| Turkey | 754,130 | 854,315 | 10,430 | 10,380 | 1,249,722 | 2,335,892 | 17,280 | 28,380 |
| Ukraine | 136,703 | 112,498 | 2,980 | 2,660 | 346,378 | 381,130 | 7,550 | 9,020 |
| United Arab Emirates | 285,525 | 394,968 | 33,390 | 41,010 | 463,508 | 725,234 | 54,210 | 75,300 |
| United Kingdom | 2,590,722 | 2,747,844 | 41,280 | 41,330 | 2,261,925 | 3,035,742 | 36,040 | 45,660 |
| Uzbekistan | 38,335 | 66,513 | 1,340 | 2,020 | 122,243 | 238,335 | 4,280 | 7,230 |
| Vietnam | 110,302 | 229,435 | 1,250 | 2,400 | 367,460 | 671,245 | 4,180 | 7,030 |

NA Not available. [1] Gross national income calculated using the World Bank Atlas conversion factor; for details, see source. [2] For explanation of purchasing power parity (PPP), see headnote, Table 1374. [3] Includes other countries not shown separately. [4] Sudan and South Sudan became separate countries in July 2011. Data for 2018 exclude South Sudan.

Source: The World Bank, Washington, DC, "World Development Indicators" database ©, <https://data.worldbank.org/data-catalog/world-development-indicators>, accessed August 2019.

# Table 1374. Real Gross Domestic Product (GDP) Per Capita and Per Employed Persons by Country: 1960 to 2018

[U.S. figures based on the System of National Income and Product Accounts (NIPA) from the Bureau of Economic Analysis. Data for all other countries are based on the 1993 or 2008 United Nations System of National Accounts (SNA). Per capita data based on total resident population. Real GDP is a macroeconomic measure of the size of an economy adjusted for price changes and inflation. Employment data include people serving in the armed forces. Real dollars are calculated based on 2018 Purchasing Power Parities (PPPs). PPPs are currency conversion rates used to convert GDP expressed in different currencies to a common value (U.S. dollars in this case). A PPP for a given country is the number of national currency units needed to buy the specific basket of goods and services that one dollar will buy in the United States. See text, this section]

| Country | 1960 | 1970 | 1980 | 1990 | 2000 | 2005 | 2010 | 2013 | 2014 | 2015 | 2016 | 2017 | 2018 |
|---|---|---|---|---|---|---|---|---|---|---|---|---|---|
| **REAL GDP PER CAPITA (2018 U.S. dollars)** | | | | | | | | | | | | | |
| **United States** | **19,917** | **26,653** | **32,763** | **41,330** | **51,264** | **55,588** | **55,547** | **57,466** | **58,439** | **59,685** | **60,202** | **60,878** | **62,117** |
| Canada | 16,303 | 22,446 | 30,130 | 35,153 | 42,008 | 45,401 | 45,594 | 47,468 | 48,336 | 48,279 | 48,307 | 49,151 | 49,369 |
| Australia | 17,925 | 24,234 | 27,935 | 33,167 | 41,555 | 46,101 | 48,542 | 50,366 | 50,950 | 51,452 | 52,004 | 52,415 | 53,048 |
| Japan | 6,920 | 16,863 | 23,310 | 34,368 | 38,075 | 40,091 | 40,389 | 41,967 | 42,193 | 42,777 | 43,109 | 44,013 | 44,451 |
| South Korea | 1,844 | 3,258 | 6,185 | 13,087 | 23,352 | 28,706 | 34,146 | 36,617 | 37,603 | 38,449 | 39,397 | 40,440 | 41,351 |
| Singapore | 6,281 | 12,071 | 24,631 | 38,669 | 57,708 | 64,625 | 80,194 | 87,997 | 89,858 | 90,369 | 91,215 | 93,074 | 94,366 |
| Austria | 13,547 | 20,257 | 28,595 | 35,111 | 43,515 | 46,247 | 48,547 | 49,631 | 49,570 | 49,575 | 50,042 | 50,963 | 51,883 |
| Belgium | 13,819 | 21,091 | 28,757 | 34,182 | 41,478 | 44,394 | 45,721 | 45,744 | 46,113 | 46,634 | 47,089 | 47,702 | 48,076 |
| Czechia | (NA) | 13,795 | 19,452 | 22,359 | 23,680 | 28,306 | 31,679 | 31,709 | 32,536 | 34,196 | 34,967 | 36,392 | 37,354 |
| Denmark | 17,305 | 24,913 | 30,125 | 36,908 | 46,250 | 48,687 | 48,064 | 48,683 | 49,221 | 50,019 | 50,821 | 51,638 | 51,973 |
| Finland | 11,861 | 18,232 | 24,651 | 32,196 | 38,859 | 43,569 | 44,335 | 43,917 | 43,459 | 43,533 | 44,612 | 45,688 | 46,585 |
| France | 13,487 | 20,803 | 27,312 | 33,058 | 38,952 | 40,341 | 41,351 | 41,946 | 42,073 | 42,390 | 42,775 | 43,606 | 44,078 |
| Germany [1] | 17,266 | 24,288 | 31,626 | 35,693 | 41,903 | 42,973 | 46,117 | 48,155 | 49,000 | 49,422 | 50,124 | 51,014 | 51,507 |
| Ireland | 8,921 | 12,915 | 17,792 | 24,619 | 44,621 | 52,793 | 49,300 | 51,198 | 55,298 | 59,404 | 61,666 | 65,404 | 69,049 |
| Italy | 12,540 | 20,599 | 27,870 | 34,576 | 40,565 | 41,751 | 40,193 | 37,993 | 37,689 | 38,074 | 38,566 | 39,240 | 39,592 |
| Netherlands | 17,538 | 25,327 | 31,121 | 36,534 | 47,517 | 49,567 | 52,137 | 51,744 | 52,292 | 53,080 | 53,956 | 55,176 | 56,300 |
| Norway | 18,808 | 26,180 | 39,267 | 48,751 | 66,095 | 71,583 | 70,997 | 71,619 | 72,214 | 72,908 | 73,126 | 73,975 | 74,339 |
| Spain | 6,666 | 13,714 | 19,972 | 26,163 | 33,709 | 37,010 | 36,566 | 34,509 | 35,090 | 36,397 | 37,520 | 38,548 | 39,509 |
| Sweden | 17,278 | 25,568 | 29,509 | 34,942 | 41,627 | 46,554 | 48,493 | 49,095 | 49,875 | 51,550 | 52,273 | 52,659 | 53,338 |
| United Kingdom | 15,138 | 18,855 | 23,122 | 30,219 | 37,556 | 42,110 | 41,359 | 42,596 | 43,530 | 44,201 | 44,652 | 45,158 | 45,466 |
| **REAL GDP PER EMPLOYED PERSON (2018 U.S. dollars)** | | | | | | | | | | | | | |
| **United States** | **51,816** | **65,932** | **72,943** | **84,684** | **104,169** | **115,081** | **121,970** | **124,473** | **125,533** | **127,303** | **127,359** | **128,223** | **130,140** |
| Canada | 44,148 | 58,826 | 66,393 | 72,848 | 85,935 | 89,514 | 90,019 | 92,882 | 94,985 | 94,757 | 94,793 | 95,768 | 96,278 |
| Australia | 45,164 | 56,671 | 64,918 | 71,701 | 88,646 | 93,855 | 95,700 | 101,374 | 103,043 | 103,403 | 104,523 | 104,561 | 104,677 |
| Japan | 13,667 | 32,162 | 46,181 | 65,725 | 73,663 | 78,219 | 78,644 | 81,261 | 81,085 | 81,734 | 81,450 | 82,220 | 81,219 |
| South Korea | 6,702 | 10,924 | 17,234 | 31,021 | 5?,886 | 60,518 | 71,010 | 72,988 | 73,686 | 74,930 | 76,449 | 77,860 | 79,647 |
| Singapore | 21,256 | 38,556 | 54,345 | 81,337 | 11?,004 | 131,664 | 135,172 | 140,220 | 140,686 | 141,178 | 143,737 | 149,668 | 153,412 |
| Austria | 27,932 | 46,633 | 61,963 | 76,170 | 93,389 | 98,827 | 99,654 | 100,316 | 100,028 | 100,566 | 101,306 | 102,159 | 103,197 |
| Belgium | 36,041 | 54,555 | 75,002 | 88,607 | 103,502 | 109,342 | 111,618 | 112,459 | 113,376 | 114,302 | 114,537 | 114,884 | 115,106 |
| Czechia | (NA) | 26,361 | 38,069 | 44,855 | 49,859 | 59,615 | 65,462 | 65,467 | 66,875 | 69,434 | 70,022 | 71,952 | 72,894 |
| Denmark | 37,561 | 50,710 | 61,359 | 72,033 | 89,635 | 94,804 | 95,841 | 98,811 | 99,544 | 100,490 | 101,384 | 101,989 | 101,605 |
| Finland | 23,913 | 36,873 | 50,038 | 64,723 | 87,518 | 94,817 | 95,841 | 94,802 | 94,658 | 95,261 | 97,458 | 98,875 | 98,542 |
| France | 31,176 | 50,669 | 66,480 | 81,368 | 92,534 | 97,847 | 99,934 | 101,732 | 102,164 | 103,086 | 103,552 | 104,674 | 105,169 |
| Germany [1] | 33,819 | 50,202 | 64,099 | 71,497 | 86,244 | 90,058 | 91,801 | 93,148 | 94,391 | 95,141 | 96,002 | 96,683 | 96,817 |
| Ireland | 22,864 | 34,547 | 49,980 | 71,115 | 99,961 | 111,734 | 119,750 | 125,418 | 132,930 | 139,282 | 140,938 | 146,897 | 151,350 |
| Italy | 29,986 | 55,281 | 73,378 | 86,499 | 100,377 | 98,823 | 96,244 | 94,128 | 94,170 | 94,426 | 94,222 | 94,624 | 94,627 |
| Netherlands | 42,676 | 59,032 | 72,764 | 80,313 | 92,251 | 96,993 | 98,677 | 99,567 | 101,077 | 102,086 | 103,187 | 103,896 | 104,043 |
| Norway | 44,016 | 61,837 | 82,315 | 100,438 | 127,960 | 140,607 | 133,989 | 134,110 | 135,116 | 137,228 | 138,606 | 139,832 | 139,686 |
| Spain | 16,554 | 34,581 | 59,232 | 73,128 | 82,949 | 82,677 | 87,797 | 91,190 | 91,540 | 92,264 | 92,812 | 93,200 | 93,597 |
| Sweden | 35,360 | 51,999 | 57,298 | 65,029 | 85,878 | 96,666 | 101,115 | 100,891 | 102,083 | 105,079 | 105,936 | 105,688 | 106,221 |
| United Kingdom | 32,819 | 42,421 | 51,904 | 64,655 | 80,822 | 88,543 | 89,197 | 91,313 | 91,834 | 92,395 | 92,689 | 93,456 | 93,645 |

NA Not available. [1] Prior to 1991, data are for the former West Germany.

Source: The Conference Board, Inc., "Total Economy Database™", April 2019 (original version). Reproduced with permission from The Conference Board, Inc. © 2019 The Conference Board, Inc.

# Table 1375. Sectoral Contributions to Gross Value Added: 2010 and 2018

[In percent. According to the 2008 System of National Accounts (SNA) and the International Standard Industrial Classification (ISIC), Revision 4 (2008), with some exceptions, value added is estimated at basic prices and includes financial intermediation services indirectly measured (FISIM). Value added represents an industry's contribution to national GDP and is calculated as the difference between production and intermediate inputs. Value added comprises labor costs, consumption of fixed capital, indirect taxes less subsidies, and net operating surplus and mixed income. Selected data are estimated or provisional; see source for details]

| Country | Agriculture [1] | | Industry [2] | | | | Services | |
|---|---|---|---|---|---|---|---|---|
| | | | Total | | Manufacturing | | | |
| | 2010 | 2018 | 2010 | 2018 | 2010 | 2018 | 2010 | 2018 |
| United States [3] | 1.1 | [5] 0.9 | 16.4 | [5] 14.7 | 12.4 | [5] 11.6 | 78.9 | [5] 80.2 |
| Australia | 2.4 | [5] 2.8 | 20.4 | [5] 17.7 | 7.9 | [5] 6.2 | 69.3 | [5] 71.5 |
| Austria | 1.4 | 1.3 | 22.2 | 22.0 | 18.5 | 18.5 | 69.9 | 70.2 |
| Belgium | 0.9 | 0.8 | 17.6 | 16.7 | 14.7 | (NA) | 76.0 | 77.2 |
| Chile [4] | 3.9 | 4.0 | 32.3 | 25.6 | 11.7 | 11.6 | 57.3 | 63.3 |
| China [4] | 9.6 | 7.5 | 40.1 | 33.9 | 32.2 | (NA) | 43.7 | 51.7 |
| Czechia | 1.7 | 2.2 | 29.9 | 30.2 | 23.4 | 25.6 | 61.5 | 62.0 |
| Denmark | 1.4 | 1.2 | 18.4 | 18.0 | 12.7 | 14.5 | 75.8 | 75.0 |
| Estonia | 3.2 | 2.6 | 22.0 | 20.8 | 15.7 | 15.4 | 68.8 | 68.9 |
| Finland | 2.7 | 2.9 | 23.5 | 21.4 | 19.5 | 17.7 | 67.3 | 68.4 |
| France | 1.8 | 1.8 | 13.8 | 13.4 | 11.5 | 11.1 | 78.4 | 79.2 |
| Germany | 0.7 | 0.8 | 25.9 | 25.8 | 22.2 | 23.1 | 69.1 | 68.2 |
| Greece | 3.3 | 4.3 | 11.2 | 15.0 | 8.2 | 11.0 | 81.1 | 78.2 |
| Hungary | 3.5 | 4.3 | 25.7 | 25.9 | 21.5 | 23.1 | 66.6 | 64.5 |
| Ireland | 1.0 | 1.0 | 24.1 | 36.5 | 21.4 | 34.6 | 73.3 | 59.7 |
| Italy | 2.0 | 2.1 | 18.7 | 19.4 | 15.8 | 16.7 | 73.7 | 73.8 |
| Japan [6] | 1.1 | [5] 1.2 | 23.7 | [5] 23.5 | 20.9 | [5] 20.8 | 70.4 | [5] 69.5 |
| Korea | 2.5 | [5] 2.2 | 33.1 | [5] 33.6 | 30.7 | [5] 30.4 | 59.3 | [5] 58.3 |
| Latvia | 4.4 | 3.8 | 18.4 | 16.1 | 13.5 | 12.0 | 72.2 | 73.0 |
| Netherlands | 2.0 | 1.8 | 16.7 | 15.2 | 11.7 | 12.4 | 76.1 | 78.1 |
| Norway | 1.8 | 2.1 | 33.7 | 28.8 | 8.1 | 6.4 | 59.2 | 62.6 |
| Poland | 2.9 | 2.8 | 24.7 | 25.6 | 17.7 | 19.4 | 63.9 | 63.5 |
| Portugal | 2.2 | 2.3 | 16.8 | 18.5 | 13.2 | 14.4 | 75.2 | 75.2 |
| Slovak Republic | 2.8 | 3.3 | 26.3 | 26.2 | 20.8 | 22.3 | 62.0 | 61.8 |
| Slovenia | 2.0 | 2.2 | 24.2 | 27.2 | 20.2 | 23.7 | 67.4 | 64.6 |
| South Africa | 2.6 | 2.4 | 26.3 | 25.1 | 14.4 | 13.2 | 67.2 | 68.5 |
| Spain | 2.6 | 2.9 | 17.2 | 17.7 | 13.3 | 14.0 | 71.4 | 72.9 |
| Sweden | 1.6 | 1.2 | 23.0 | 19.2 | 18.6 | 15.6 | 69.5 | 73.2 |
| Switzerland | 0.7 | 0.7 | 21.6 | 20.5 | 19.5 | 18.9 | 72.7 | 73.5 |
| United Kingdom | 0.7 | 0.6 | 14.3 | 14.1 | 9.9 | 10.0 | 79.4 | 79.2 |

NA Not available. [1] Includes forestry, fishing, and hunting sectors. [2] Includes energy. [3] Value added is estimated at factor cost for U.S. [4] Value added is estimated at producer's prices. [5] Data is for 2017. [6] Value added is estimated approximately at market prices for Japan.

Source: Organisation for Economic Co-operation and Development (OECD), 2019, "National Accounts at a Glance," OECD National Accounts Statistics (database) ©, <http://dx.doi.org/10.1787/data-00369-en>, accessed July 2019.

# Table 1376. Index of Industrial Production by Country: 2000 to 2018

[Annual averages of monthly data. Industrial production indexes generally measure output in the manufacturing, mining, electric, gas, and water utilities sectors. Minus sign (-) indicates decrease]

| Country | Index (2015=100) | | | | | | | Annual percent change | | | | |
|---|---|---|---|---|---|---|---|---|---|---|---|---|
| | 2000 | 2005 | 2010 | 2015 | 2016 | 2017 | 2018 | 2010 to 2011 | 2014 to 2015 | 2015 to 2016 | 2016 to 2017 | 2017 to 2018 |
| United States | 91.5 | 95.6 | 90.4 | 100.0 | 98.0 | 100.3 | 104.3 | 3.1 | -1.0 | -2.0 | 2.3 | 3.9 |
| Australia | 75.0 | 80.1 | 89.0 | 100.0 | 101.9 | 103.0 | 106.7 | 0.8 | 1.6 | 1.9 | 1.1 | 3.7 |
| Austria | 70.1 | 82.2 | 90.6 | 100.0 | 102.6 | 107.8 | 112.1 | 5.9 | 2.2 | 2.6 | 5.1 | 4.0 |
| Belgium | 71.8 | 84.3 | 97.1 | 100.0 | 104.4 | 107.3 | 108.5 | 4.8 | -1.1 | 4.4 | 2.9 | 1.1 |
| Brazil | 83.8 | 97.8 | 112.2 | 100.0 | 93.6 | 95.9 | 97.0 | 0.4 | -8.2 | -6.4 | 2.5 | 1.1 |
| Canada | 96.8 | 100.0 | 89.9 | 100.0 | 99.9 | 105.4 | 109.3 | 4.8 | -0.4 | -0.1 | 5.5 | 3.7 |
| Chile | 70.2 | 87.8 | 88.6 | 100.0 | 100.2 | 99.3 | 101.8 | 5.4 | 0.6 | 0.2 | -1.0 | 2.5 |
| Czechia | 60.5 | 78.9 | 87.1 | 100.0 | 103.4 | 110.1 | 113.5 | 5.9 | 4.3 | 3.4 | 6.5 | 3.0 |
| Denmark | 109.8 | 115.7 | 98.6 | 100.0 | 104.2 | 106.3 | 108.4 | 1.1 | 0.1 | 4.2 | 2.0 | 2.0 |
| Finland | 99.9 | 105.6 | 106.6 | 100.0 | 104.2 | 107.5 | 110.9 | 1.7 | -0.9 | 4.1 | 3.2 | 3.1 |
| France | 109.3 | 110.5 | 100.1 | 100.0 | 100.6 | 102.6 | 103.0 | 2.5 | 1.7 | 0.6 | 2.0 | 0.4 |
| Germany | 80.4 | 85.9 | 90.4 | 100.0 | 101.5 | 104.5 | 105.7 | 8.5 | 1.1 | 1.5 | 2.9 | 1.2 |
| Greece | 140.2 | 135.2 | 113.2 | 100.0 | 102.6 | 107.5 | 108.8 | -5.9 | 1.0 | 2.6 | 4.8 | 1.2 |
| Hungary | 58.2 | 76.1 | 82.2 | 99.7 | 100.4 | 105.8 | 109.9 | 5.6 | 7.0 | 0.8 | 5.3 | 3.9 |
| India | 42.9 | [2] 57.8 | 87.9 | 100.0 | 105.2 | 108.9 | 114.5 | 4.8 | 2.5 | 5.2 | 3.5 | 5.2 |
| Ireland | 42.9 | 57.2 | 63.0 | 100.0 | 101.8 | 99.5 | 99.4 | -0.4 | 36.9 | 1.8 | -2.2 | -0.1 |
| Italy | 127.7 | 121.8 | 107.8 | 99.7 | 101.7 | 105.5 | 106.1 | 0.8 | 1.0 | 2.1 | 3.7 | 0.5 |
| Japan | 106.1 | 108.9 | 102.8 | 100.0 | 100.2 | 102.8 | 103.9 | -2.8 | -1.2 | 0.2 | 2.6 | 1.0 |
| Korea, South | 49.4 | 66.5 | 92.5 | 100.0 | 102.2 | 104.7 | 106.1 | 6.0 | -0.3 | 2.2 | 2.5 | 1.3 |
| Mexico [1] | 92.5 | 96.8 | 100.0 | 109.8 | 109.6 | [3] 109.1 | (NA) | (NA) | (NA) | (NA) | (NA) | (NA) |
| Netherlands | 95.9 | 100.2 | 106.9 | 100.0 | 101.4 | 102.5 | 103.1 | -0.5 | -3.4 | 1.4 | 1.1 | 0.7 |
| New Zealand | 87.0 | 98.4 | 97.2 | 100.0 | 101.3 | 103.6 | 104.5 | -2.8 | 1.6 | 1.3 | 2.3 | 0.8 |
| Norway | 121.6 | 116.4 | 102.5 | 100.0 | 98.8 | 98.5 | 96.7 | -5.0 | 1.5 | -1.2 | -0.3 | -1.8 |
| Poland | 47.4 | 62.0 | 83.4 | 100.0 | 102.8 | 109.6 | 116.1 | 6.7 | 4.9 | 2.8 | 6.6 | 5.9 |
| Russia | 61.6 | 81.5 | 89.1 | 100.0 | 102.4 | 104.7 | 107.7 | 5.1 | -0.7 | 2.4 | 2.2 | 2.9 |
| Spain | 124.0 | 127.1 | 105.6 | 100.0 | 101.9 | 105.1 | 105.4 | -1.5 | 3.2 | 1.9 | 3.2 | 0.3 |
| Sweden | 101.2 | 110.0 | 102.6 | 100.0 | 101.8 | 106.2 | 108.8 | 2.7 | 3.7 | 1.8 | 4.3 | 2.4 |
| Switzerland | 77.8 | 79.1 | 94.4 | 100.0 | 100.0 | 105.0 | (NA) | 3.6 | -2.5 | 0.0 | 5.0 | (NA) |
| Turkey | 43.8 | 59.6 | 69.4 | 100.0 | 103.4 | 112.8 | 114.0 | 15.4 | 6.1 | 3.4 | 9.1 | 1.1 |
| United Kingdom | 113.5 | 109.5 | 101.4 | 100.0 | 101.0 | 102.1 | 103.1 | -0.6 | 1.2 | 1.0 | 1.1 | 1.0 |

NA Not available. [1] Including construction. [2] Break in series. [3] Estimated.

Source: Organisation for Economic Co-operation and Development (OECD), 2019, "Key short-term indicators," Main Economic Indicators (database) ©, <http://dx.doi.org/10.1787/data-00039-en>, accessed July 2019.

# Table 1377. Selected Indexes of Manufacturing Productivity, Unit Labor Costs, Employment, and Hours Worked by Country: 2000 to 2017

[2010=100. Data for all countries are prepared according to the System of National Accounts (SNA) 2008 or its European counterpart, the European System of Accounts 2010 (ESA 2010). Data refer to all employed persons (including employees, self-employed, and unpaid family workers). Minus sign (-) indicates decrease]

| Index | United States | Aus-tralia | Canada | France | Ger-many | Italy | Japan | Nether-lands | South Korea | Swe-den | United King-dom |
|---|---|---|---|---|---|---|---|---|---|---|---|
| **REAL VALUED ADDED PER HOUR WORKED (PRODUCTIVITY)** | | | | | | | | | | | |
| 2000 | 59.1 | 84.3 | 92.9 | 74.6 | 78.5 | 90.6 | 75.6 | 76.0 | 48.4 | 62.0 | 70.1 |
| 2010 | 100.0 | 100.0 | 100.0 | 100.0 | 100.0 | 100.0 | 100.0 | 100.0 | 100.0 | 100.0 | 100.0 |
| 2015 | 97.4 | 103.5 | 109.7 | 111.9 | 107.1 | 109.3 | 109.5 | 109.2 | 110.1 | 100.9 | 100.8 |
| 2016 | 97.8 | 100.5 | 111.0 | 114.4 | 110.1 | 108.3 | 111.6 | 111.1 | 114.4 | 103.9 | 101.6 |
| 2017 | 98.6 | 102.5 | 112.7 | 117.2 | 113.2 | 108.9 | 115.6 | 115.0 | 122.1 | 107.2 | 104.2 |
| Average annual percent change: | | | | | | | | | | | |
| 2000-2007 | 6.1 | 1.9 | 1.7 | 3.9 | 4.2 | 1.5 | 3.9 | 4.4 | 9.0 | 6.4 | 4.7 |
| 2010-2017 | 0.5 | 0.7 | 1.9 | 2.7 | 3.5 | 2.5 | 3.3 | 2.4 | 3.3 | 3.3 | 1.2 |
| 2016-2017 | 0.9 | 2.0 | 1.6 | 2.5 | 2.8 | 0.5 | 3.6 | 3.5 | 6.8 | 3.1 | 2.6 |
| **HOURLY LABOR COSTS (national currency basis)** | | | | | | | | | | | |
| 2000 | 72.2 | 66.2 | 74.7 | 72.9 | 82.1 | 71.9 | 101.8 | 74.6 | 44.9 | 69.6 | 62.2 |
| 2010 | 100.0 | 100.0 | 100.0 | 100.0 | 100.0 | 100.0 | 100.0 | 100.0 | 100.0 | 100.0 | 100.0 |
| 2015 | 109.3 | 114.9 | 114.9 | 110.6 | 111.7 | 111.5 | 103.9 | 110.6 | 118.1 | 115.7 | 110.6 |
| 2016 | 110.2 | 112.9 | 116.7 | 111.8 | 115.2 | 110.2 | 105.0 | 113.3 | 125.1 | 117.8 | 111.8 |
| 2017 | 113.0 | 114.1 | 117.2 | 114.2 | 117.8 | 110.6 | 105.3 | 116.0 | 130.7 | 121.6 | 116.0 |
| Average annual percent change: | | | | | | | | | | | |
| 2000-2007 | 4.0 | 4.4 | 3.8 | 3.2 | 2.2 | 3.0 | -0.5 | 3.5 | 9.9 | 4.7 | 5.3 |
| 2010-2017 | 1.7 | 1.8 | 1.9 | 2.1 | 2.2 | 1.7 | 0.5 | 1.3 | 4.0 | 2.2 | 2.3 |
| 2016-2017 | 2.5 | 1.1 | 0.4 | 2.2 | 2.3 | 0.3 | 0.3 | 2.4 | 4.5 | 3.2 | 3.7 |
| **REAL HOURLY COMPENSATION, CPI DEFLATED (national currency basis)** | | | | | | | | | | | |
| 2000 | 91.4 | 89.0 | 91.2 | 86.4 | 95.8 | 89.1 | 99.2 | 91.1 | 61.4 | 80.7 | 75.8 |
| 2010 | 100.0 | 100.0 | 100.0 | 100.0 | 100.0 | 100.0 | 100.0 | 100.0 | 100.0 | 100.0 | 100.0 |
| 2015 | 100.6 | 102.5 | 105.7 | 104.8 | 104.5 | 103.7 | 100.3 | 101.3 | 107.6 | 111.7 | 99.6 |
| 2016 | 100.1 | 99.5 | 105.9 | 105.7 | 107.2 | 102.6 | 101.4 | 103.4 | 112.9 | 112.6 | 99.8 |
| 2017 | 100.5 | 98.7 | 104.7 | 106.9 | 107.8 | 101.7 | 101.2 | 104.4 | 115.7 | 114.2 | 100.9 |
| Average annual percent change: | | | | | | | | | | | |
| 2000-2007 | 1.2 | 1.1 | 1.4 | 1.4 | 0.6 | 0.7 | -0.2 | 1.3 | 6.8 | 3.1 | 3.6 |
| 2010-2017 | (Z) | -0.4 | 0.3 | 1.1 | 0.9 | 0.4 | 0.1 | -0.1 | 2.0 | 1.3 | 0.2 |
| 2016-2017 | 0.4 | -0.8 | -1.2 | 1.1 | 0.6 | -0.9 | -0.2 | 1.0 | 2.5 | 1.4 | 1.1 |
| **UNIT LABOR COSTS, (national currency basis)** | | | | | | | | | | | |
| 2000 | 122.3 | 78.5 | 80.4 | 97.8 | 104.6 | 79.4 | 134.6 | 98.2 | 92.7 | 112.3 | 88.8 |
| 2010 | 100.0 | 100.0 | 100.0 | 100.0 | 100.0 | 100.0 | 100.0 | 100.0 | 100.0 | 100.0 | 100.0 |
| 2015 | 112.3 | 111.0 | 104.7 | 98.8 | 104.3 | 102.0 | 94.9 | 101.2 | 107.3 | 114.7 | 109.7 |
| 2016 | 112.7 | 112.4 | 105.1 | 97.7 | 104.6 | 101.7 | 94.1 | 102.0 | 109.4 | 113.3 | 110.1 |
| 2017 | 114.6 | 111.4 | 103.9 | 97.4 | 104.1 | 101.5 | 91.1 | 100.9 | 107.1 | 113.5 | 111.3 |
| Average annual percent change: | | | | | | | | | | | |
| 2000-2007 | -2.0 | 2.4 | 2.0 | -0.7 | -1.9 | 1.5 | -4.3 | -0.9 | 0.9 | -1.6 | 0.6 |
| 2010-2017 | 1.2 | 1.1 | (Z) | -0.5 | -1.3 | -0.8 | -2.8 | -1.1 | 0.7 | -1.0 | 1.0 |
| 2016-2017 | 1.7 | -0.9 | -1.1 | -0.3 | -0.5 | -0.2 | -3.2 | -1.1 | -2.2 | 0.1 | 1.1 |
| **REAL VALUE ADDED PER EMPLOYED PERSON** | | | | | | | | | | | |
| 2000 | 59.2 | 86.2 | 95.5 | 75.3 | 81.4 | 97.9 | 76.4 | 77.1 | 51.8 | 62.1 | 71.3 |
| 2010 | 100.0 | 100.0 | 100.0 | 100.0 | 100.0 | 100.0 | 100.0 | 100.0 | 100.0 | 100.0 | 100.0 |
| 2015 | 98.5 | 102.2 | 112.5 | 112.1 | 108.6 | 108.6 | 110.4 | 110.4 | 106.8 | 98.9 | 101.5 |
| 2016 | 99.0 | 98.5 | 113.6 | 114.9 | 110.7 | 109.1 | 112.3 | 112.4 | 109.8 | 102.2 | 102.7 |
| 2017 | 99.8 | 101.1 | 114.5 | 117.2 | 113.1 | 110.6 | 116.9 | 116.0 | 115.1 | 104.1 | 104.4 |
| Average annual percent change: | | | | | | | | | | | |
| 2000-2007 | 5.9 | 1.6 | 1.5 | 3.6 | 3.9 | 1.3 | 4.4 | 4.1 | 7.8 | 6.3 | 4.6 |
| 2010-2017 | 1.0 | 0.7 | 2.3 | 2.9 | 4.0 | 2.8 | 4.1 | 2.8 | 2.8 | 3.3 | 1.4 |
| 2016-2017 | 0.9 | 2.6 | 0.8 | 2.1 | 2.2 | 1.4 | 4.1 | 3.2 | 4.8 | 1.9 | 1.6 |
| **ALL EMPLOYED PERSONS** | | | | | | | | | | | |
| 2000 | 148.8 | 107.6 | 128.7 | 125.8 | 109.7 | 109.8 | 114.7 | 118.9 | 102.5 | 121.6 | 151.8 |
| 2010 | 100.0 | 100.0 | 100.0 | 100.0 | 100.0 | 100.0 | 100.0 | 100.0 | 100.0 | 100.0 | 100.0 |
| 2015 | 106.7 | 91.5 | 96.0 | 95.2 | 105.3 | 92.0 | 94.9 | 95.8 | 111.5 | 91.9 | 101.1 |
| 2016 | 106.7 | 92.4 | 95.6 | 94.3 | 105.6 | 92.7 | 95.0 | 96.1 | 110.9 | 91.4 | 100.8 |
| 2017 | 107.8 | 90.8 | 97.9 | 93.7 | 106.4 | 93.3 | 95.6 | 97.0 | 110.4 | 92.9 | 101.7 |
| Average annual percent change: | | | | | | | | | | | |
| 2000-2007 | -2.7 | 0.1 | -0.9 | -1.4 | -0.8 | (-Z) | -1.2 | -1.4 | 0.3 | -0.9 | -4.1 |
| 2010-2017 | 0.6 | -1.3 | -0.3 | -1.4 | 0.5 | -1.3 | -0.7 | -0.8 | 1.9 | -1.1 | -0.1 |
| 2016-2017 | 1.0 | -1.8 | 2.5 | -0.6 | 0.7 | 0.7 | 0.6 | 0.9 | -0.5 | 1.6 | 0.9 |
| **HOURS WORKED OF ALL EMPLOYED PERSONS** | | | | | | | | | | | |
| 2000 | 149.3 | 110.0 | 132.2 | 127.0 | 113.8 | 118.7 | 115.9 | 120.6 | 109.6 | 121.8 | 154.5 |
| 2010 | 100.0 | 100.0 | 100.0 | 100.0 | 100.0 | 100.0 | 100.0 | 100.0 | 100.0 | 100.0 | 100.0 |
| 2015 | 107.9 | 90.3 | 98.4 | 95.3 | 106.8 | 91.4 | 95.7 | 96.8 | 108.1 | 90.1 | 101.8 |
| 2016 | 108.0 | 90.6 | 97.8 | 94.7 | 106.2 | 93.3 | 95.6 | 97.3 | 106.6 | 89.9 | 101.9 |
| 2017 | 109.1 | 89.6 | 99.5 | 93.7 | 106.4 | 94.8 | 96.7 | 97.8 | 104.1 | 90.3 | 101.9 |
| Average annual percent change: | | | | | | | | | | | |
| 2000-2007 | -2.8 | -0.3 | -1.1 | -1.7 | -1.0 | -0.2 | -0.8 | -1.7 | -0.7 | -1.0 | -4.2 |
| 2010-2017 | 1.1 | -1.3 | 0.1 | -1.2 | 1.0 | -1.0 | 0.1 | -0.4 | 1.4 | -1.1 | 0.1 |
| 2016-2017 | 1.0 | -1.2 | 1.7 | -1.0 | 0.2 | 1.6 | 1.1 | 0.6 | -2.3 | 0.4 | (Z) |

Z less than 0.05 percent.

Source: The Conference Board, Inc., International Labor Comparisons program, "International Comparisons of Manufacturing Productivity and Unit Labor Cost Trends - Data," July 2018, <https://www.conference-board.org/llcprogram>. Reproduced with permission from The Conference Board, Inc. © 2019 The Conference Board, Inc.

## Table 1378. Indexes of Hourly Compensation Costs for Employees in Manufacturing by Country: 2000 to 2016

[United States=100. Compensation costs include pay for time worked (base wages and salaries, overtime pay, bonuses and premiums paid each pay period, and cost of living adjustments), directly-paid benefits (pay for leave time, irregular bonuses, and pay in kind), employer social insurance expenditures (legally required, private, and contractual social benefit costs), and labor-related taxes (minus subsidies). Data are adjusted for exchange rates. Regional averages are trade-weighted to account for differences in countries' relative importance to total world trade in manufactured goods. See source for details]

| Area or country | 2000 | 2010 | 2014 | 2015 | 2016 | Area or country | 2000 | 2010 | 2014 | 2015 | 2016 |
|---|---|---|---|---|---|---|---|---|---|---|---|
| United States | 100 | 100 | 100 | 100 | 100 | Hungary | 12 | 24 | 26 | 22 | 22 |
| | | | | | | Ireland | 66 | 117 | 117 | 95 | 93 |
| ILC economies [1] | 78 | 90 | 93 | 82 | 80 | Israel | 49 | 55 | 62 | 58 | 58 |
| OECD [2] | 82 | 96 | 97 | 85 | 84 | Italy | 67 | 97 | 102 | 86 | 83 |
| Europe | 82 | 103 | 108 | 91 | 88 | Japan [6] | 100 | 91 | 73 | 62 | 68 |
| Euro Area [3] | 83 | 112 | 118 | 98 | 95 | Mexico | 14 | 13 | 13 | 12 | 10 |
| Eastern Europe [4] | 13 | 28 | 29 | 25 | 25 | Netherlands | 85 | 111 | 114 | 93 | 89 |
| East Asia ex-Japan [5] | 35 | 44 | 54 | 51 | 50 | New Zealand | 36 | 59 | 73 | 61 | 61 |
| Argentina [6] | 33 | 37 | 48 | 53 | 43 | Norway | 98 | 165 | 170 | 135 | 125 |
| Australia | 67 | 114 | 124 | 102 | 98 | Philippines | 4 | 5 | 6 | 6 | 5 |
| Austria | 88 | 115 | 123 | 103 | 101 | Poland | 14 | 24 | 27 | 23 | 22 |
| Belgium | 105 | 146 | 152 | 127 | 121 | Portugal | 24 | 35 | 34 | 29 | 28 |
| Brazil | 17 | 29 | 28 | 20 | 20 | Singapore | 47 | 56 | 72 | 68 | 69 |
| Canada | 73 | 99 | 93 | 81 | 77 | Slovakia | 10 | 31 | 35 | 29 | 30 |
| Czechia | 14 | 33 | 32 | 27 | 27 | South Korea | 39 | 51 | 64 | 60 | 59 |
| Denmark | 89 | 139 | 143 | 118 | 116 | Spain | 50 | 77 | 76 | 62 | 60 |
| Estonia | 10 | 27 | 34 | 29 | 30 | Sweden | 94 | 123 | 135 | 110 | 107 |
| Finland | 79 | 116 | 122 | 102 | 99 | Switzerland | 108 | 147 | 175 | 161 | 155 |
| France | 85 | 112 | 119 | 99 | 97 | Taiwan [6] | 29 | 24 | 26 | 25 | 25 |
| Germany | 101 | 126 | 134 | 112 | 111 | Turkey | (NA) | 18 | 17 | 15 | 16 |
| Greece | 40 | 65 | 52 | 42 | 40 | United Kingdom | 83 | 83 | 89 | 82 | 73 |

NA Not available. [1] ILC (International Labor Comparisons) economies refers to the 35 national economies included in ILC compensation comparisons, excluding China and India that are not strictly comparable with each other or with data for other countries. Data for 2000 excludes Turkey. [2] Organisation for Economic Co-operation and Development; see text, this section. Includes only those countries that are also ILC economies. [3] Euro Area includes Austria, Belgium, Estonia, Finland, France, Germany, Greece, Ireland, Italy, the Netherlands, Portugal, Slovakia and Spain. [4] Czechia, Estonia, Hungary, Poland, and Slovakia. [5] South Korea, Philippines, Singapore, and Taiwan. Excludes Japan. [6] Except for Argentina, Japan, and Taiwan, data relate to manufacturing as defined by the International Standard Industrial Classification of All Economic Activities (ISIC) Revision 4.

Source: The Conference Board, Inc., International Labor Comparisons program, "International Comparisons of Hourly Compensation Costs in Manufacturing, 2016," April 2018, <https://www.conference-board.org/ilcprogram/compensation>. Reproduced with permission from The Conference Board, Inc. © 2019 The Conference Board, Inc.

## Table 1379. Annual Percent Change in Labor Productivity and Hours Worked by Country: 2002 to 2018

[Annual percent change for period shown. Labor productivity growth refers to the growth in gross domestic product (GDP) per hour worked. Data are derived from The Conference Board Total Economy Database. Regional labor productivity growth rates are aggregated using shares in nominal PPP converted GDP; regional hours growth is weighted using total hours shares. Growth rates are the averages of yearly growth rates. Minus sign (-) indicates decrease]

| Country | Labor productivity | | Total hours worked | | Country | Labor productivity | | Total hours worked | |
|---|---|---|---|---|---|---|---|---|---|
| | 2002-2007 | 2010-2018 | 2002-2007 | 2010-2018 | | 2002-2007 | 2010-2018 | 2002-2007 | 2010-2018 |
| Advanced economies [1] | 1.9 | 1.1 | 0.7 | 0.8 | Czechia | 4.3 | 1.5 | 0.5 | 0.8 |
| United States | 2.2 | 0.8 | 0.6 | 1.5 | Estonia | 6.0 | 2.4 | 1.7 | 1.2 |
| Japan | 1.3 | 1.0 | 0.1 | 0.4 | Hungary | 3.9 | 1.2 | -0.3 | 1.2 |
| | | | | | Latvia | 8.1 | 3.2 | 1.2 | -0.4 |
| European Union (EU-15, old) [2] | 1.3 | 0.8 | 0.9 | 0.5 | Lithuania | 6.4 | 3.0 | 1.8 | 0.4 |
| Austria | 2.0 | 0.9 | 0.4 | 0.7 | Malta | 1.7 | 2.8 | 0.8 | 2.7 |
| Belgium | 1.7 | 0.5 | 0.7 | 0.9 | Poland | 3.5 | 3.4 | 1.0 | 0.1 |
| Denmark | 1.4 | 1.3 | 0.3 | 0.2 | Romania | 8.4 | 4.0 | -1.9 | -1.0 |
| Finland | 2.3 | 0.9 | 0.9 | 0.3 | Slovak Republic | 5.8 | 2.6 | 1.0 | 0.5 |
| France | 1.2 | 0.9 | 0.6 | 0.5 | Slovenia | 4.0 | 1.9 | 0.6 | -0.1 |
| Germany | 1.3 | 1.1 | 0.0 | 0.9 | European Union (EU-28, enlarged) [4] | 1.6 | 1.1 | 0.8 | 0.4 |
| Greece | 2.2 | -0.8 | 1.8 | -1.7 | Addenda: | | | | |
| Ireland | 2.3 | 3.6 | 2.9 | 1.2 | Other advanced economies [1] | 2.9 | 1.8 | 1.1 | 1.2 |
| Italy | 0.0 | 0.4 | 1.1 | -0.2 | Australia | 1.3 | 1.1 | 2.2 | 1.6 |
| Luxembourg | 1.4 | 0.2 | 2.8 | 2.6 | Canada | 1.0 | 0.9 | 1.6 | 1.2 |
| Netherlands | 1.4 | 0.7 | 0.5 | 0.7 | Hong Kong | 4.5 | 2.5 | 1.1 | 0.8 |
| Portugal | 1.3 | 0.6 | -0.2 | -0.1 | Iceland | 4.4 | 0.9 | 0.8 | 2.0 |
| Spain | 0.5 | 1.0 | 3.0 | -0.2 | Israel | 1.6 | 1.4 | 2.0 | 2.4 |
| Sweden | 2.8 | 1.1 | 0.4 | 1.5 | New Zealand | 1.5 | 0.5 | 2.3 | 2.3 |
| United Kingdom | 2.0 | 0.5 | 0.7 | 1.4 | Norway | 0.9 | 0.6 | 1.5 | 0.9 |
| European Union (EU-13, new) [3] | 4.7 | 2.8 | 0.4 | 0.0 | Singapore | 4.6 | 3.3 | 2.6 | 1.9 |
| Bulgaria | 3.9 | 2.9 | 2.5 | -0.7 | South Korea | 4.9 | 2.6 | 0.0 | 0.7 |
| Croatia | 2.8 | 2.0 | 2.0 | -1.2 | Switzerland | 1.4 | 0.9 | 1.0 | 1.0 |
| Cyprus | 1.8 | 0.8 | 2.5 | -0.1 | Taiwan | 4.0 | 1.8 | 1.6 | 1.6 |

[1] "Advanced" includes the U.S., EU-15, Japan, and "other advanced" economies. [2] Referring to membership of the European Union until April 30, 2004. [3] Referring to membership of the European Union as of January 1, 2007. [4] Referring to all 28 current members of the European Union. See text, this section.

Source: The Conference Board, New York, NY, "The Conference Board Total Economy Database™," April 2019 (original version). Reproduced with permission from The Conference Board, Inc. © 2019 The Conference Board, Inc.

# Table 1380. Comparative Price Levels—Selected OECD Countries: May 2019

[Purchasing power parities (PPPs) are rates of currency conversion that eliminate the differences in price levels between countries. Comparative price levels are defined as the ratios of PPPs to exchange rates. The PPPs are given in national currency units per U.S. dollar. This table should be read vertically. Each column shows the number of specified monetary units needed in each of the countries listed to buy the same representative basket of consumer goods and services. In each case the representative basket costs a hundred units in the country whose currency is specified. For example, in May 2019, an item that costs $1.00 in the United States would cost $0.96 (U.S. dollars) in Japan]

| Country | United States (USD) | Australia (AUD) | Canada (CAD) | Chile (Chilean peso) | France (EUR) | Germany (EJR) | Italy (EUR) | Japan (JPY) | Korea (KRW) | Mexico (MXN) | Spain (EUR) | Turkey (TRY) | United Kingdom (GBP) |
|---|---|---|---|---|---|---|---|---|---|---|---|---|---|
| United States | 100 | 95 | 100 | 150 | 107 | 112 | 117 | 104 | 126 | 181 | 127 | 284 | 99 |
| Australia [1] | 105 | 100 | 106 | 158 | 113 | 118 | 124 | 110 | 133 | 191 | 134 | 299 | 104 |
| Austria | 93 | 88 | 93 | 139 | 100 | 105 | 109 | 97 | 117 | 169 | 118 | 264 | 92 |
| Belgium | 95 | 90 | 95 | 142 | 102 | 107 | 112 | 99 | 120 | 173 | 121 | 270 | 94 |
| Canada | 100 | 95 | 100 | 149 | 107 | 112 | 117 | 104 | 126 | 181 | 127 | 283 | 99 |
| Chile | 67 | 63 | 67 | 100 | 72 | 75 | 79 | 70 | 84 | 121 | 85 | 190 | 66 |
| Czechia | 61 | 58 | 61 | 91 | 65 | 68 | 71 | 63 | 76 | 110 | 77 | 172 | 60 |
| Denmark | 117 | 111 | 117 | 174 | 125 | 131 | 137 | 122 | 147 | 211 | 148 | 330 | 115 |
| Estonia | 69 | 65 | 69 | 103 | 73 | 77 | 81 | 72 | 86 | 125 | 87 | 195 | 68 |
| Finland | 104 | 98 | 104 | 155 | 111 | 116 | 122 | 108 | 130 | 188 | 131 | 294 | 103 |
| France | 93 | 89 | 94 | 140 | 100 | 105 | 110 | 98 | 118 | 170 | 119 | 265 | 92 |
| Germany | 89 | 85 | 89 | 133 | 95 | 100 | 105 | 93 | 112 | 162 | 113 | 253 | 88 |
| Greece | 72 | 68 | 72 | 107 | 77 | 80 | 84 | 75 | 90 | 130 | 91 | 203 | 71 |
| Hungary | 53 | 50 | 53 | 79 | 57 | 60 | 62 | 55 | 67 | 96 | 67 | 150 | 52 |
| Iceland | 127 | 121 | 128 | 190 | 136 | 143 | 149 | 133 | 160 | 231 | 161 | 361 | 126 |
| Ireland | 107 | 102 | 107 | 160 | 115 | 120 | 126 | 112 | 135 | 194 | 136 | 304 | 106 |
| Israel [2] | 116 | 110 | 116 | 173 | 124 | 130 | 136 | 121 | 146 | 210 | 147 | 328 | 115 |
| Italy | 85 | 81 | 85 | 127 | 91 | 96 | 100 | 89 | 107 | 155 | 108 | 242 | 84 |
| Japan | 96 | 91 | 96 | 143 | 102 | 108 | 112 | 100 | 121 | 174 | 121 | 272 | 95 |
| Korea, South | 79 | 75 | 80 | 119 | 85 | 89 | 93 | 83 | 100 | 144 | 101 | 225 | 79 |
| Latvia | 64 | 61 | 64 | 96 | 68 | 72 | 75 | 67 | 81 | 116 | 81 | 181 | 63 |
| Lithuania | 56 | 54 | 57 | 84 | 60 | 63 | 66 | 59 | 71 | 102 | 72 | 160 | 56 |
| Luxembourg | 108 | 102 | 108 | 161 | 115 | 121 | 127 | 113 | 136 | 196 | 137 | 306 | 107 |
| Mexico | 55 | 52 | 55 | 82 | 59 | 62 | 65 | 58 | 69 | 100 | 70 | 156 | 55 |
| Netherlands | 97 | 92 | 97 | 145 | 103 | 109 | 114 | 101 | 122 | 176 | 123 | 274 | 96 |
| New Zealand [1] | 104 | 98 | 104 | 155 | 111 | 116 | 122 | 108 | 130 | 188 | 131 | 294 | 102 |
| Norway | 124 | 117 | 124 | 185 | 132 | 139 | 145 | 129 | 156 | 225 | 157 | 351 | 123 |
| Poland | 48 | 46 | 49 | 72 | 52 | 54 | 57 | 51 | 61 | 88 | 61 | 137 | 48 |
| Portugal | 73 | 69 | 73 | 109 | 78 | 82 | 85 | 76 | 92 | 132 | 92 | 206 | 72 |
| Slovak Republic | 61 | 58 | 61 | 91 | 65 | 68 | 71 | 64 | 77 | 110 | 77 | 173 | 60 |
| Slovenia | 72 | 69 | 72 | 108 | 77 | 81 | 85 | 75 | 91 | 131 | 92 | 205 | 72 |
| Spain | 79 | 75 | 79 | 118 | 84 | 89 | 93 | 82 | 99 | 143 | 100 | 224 | 78 |
| Sweden | 97 | 92 | 97 | 145 | 104 | 109 | 114 | 101 | 122 | 176 | 123 | 275 | 96 |
| Switzerland | 133 | 126 | 133 | 199 | 142 | 149 | 156 | 139 | 167 | 241 | 168 | 377 | 131 |
| Turkey | 35 | 33 | 35 | 53 | 38 | 40 | 41 | 37 | 44 | 64 | 45 | 100 | 35 |
| United Kingdom | 101 | 96 | 101 | 151 | 108 | 113 | 119 | 106 | 127 | 183 | 128 | 287 | 100 |

[1] Estimates based on quarterly consumer prices. [2] The statistical data for Israel are supplied by and under the responsibility of the relevant Israeli authorities. The use of such data by the OECD is without prejudice to the status of the Golan Heights, East Jerusalem and Israeli settlements in the West Bank under the terms of international law.

Source: Organisation for Economic Co-operation and Development (OECD), 2019 "Prices: Comparative Price Levels," Main Economic Indicators (database) ©, <http://dx.doi.org/10.1787/data-00536-en>, accessed July 2019.

# Table 1381. Indexes of Living Costs Abroad by Selected City: 2019

[As of January 2019. Washington, DC=100. Indexes compare the costs in dollars of representative goods and services (excluding housing and education) purchased at the foreign location and the cost of comparable goods and services in the Washington, DC area. The indexes are place-to-place comparisons at specific times and currency exchange rates. They cannot be used for measuring cost changes over time at a foreign location. Since the indexes reflect only the expenditure pattern and living costs of American families, they are not comparable to the living costs of foreign nationals living in their own country. Survey dates show month/day/year]

| Country/territory | City | Survey date | Local index [1] | Country/territory | City | Survey date | Local index [1] |
|---|---|---|---|---|---|---|---|
| Algeria | Algiers | 12/13/2015 | 88 | Kyrgyzstan | Bishkek | 4/26/2016 | 112 |
| Angola | Luanda | 9/27/2015 | 184 | Laos | Vientiane | 1/15/2016 | 127 |
| Argentina | Buenos Aires | 6/14/2017 | 143 | Latvia | Riga | 5/11/2014 | 143 |
| Armenia | Yerevan | 11/22/2015 | 140 | Lebanon | Beirut | 12/17/2014 | 130 |
| Australia | Canberra | 4/16/2015 | 147 | Liberia | Monrovia | 10/31/2017 | 155 |
| Austria | Vienna | 12/3/2013 | 176 | Libya | Tripoli | 1/5/2007 | 116 |
| Azerbaijan | Baku | 1/5/2015 | 156 | Lithuania | Vilnius | 12/7/2017 | 105 |
| Bahamas | Nassau | 4/11/2016 | 160 | Luxembourg | (X) | 6/8/2015 | 140 |
| Bangladesh | Dhaka | 7/1/2015 | 130 | Macedonia | Skopje | 7/8/2015 | 82 |
| Belarus | Minsk | 11/2/2016 | 84 | Madagascar | Antananarivo | 1/13/2016 | 156 |
| Belgium | Brussels | 3/23/2015 | 132 | Malawi | Lilongwe | 3/12/2014 | 132 |
| Belize | Belmopan | 3/20/2014 | 131 | Malaysia | Kuala Lumpur | 12/29/2016 | 93 |
| Bolivia | La Paz | 6/7/2017 | 122 | Mali | Bamako | 2/12/2014 | 154 |
| Bosnia-Herzegovina | Sarajevo | 2/23/2015 | 102 | Mauritania | Nouakchott | 4/4/2018 | 119 |
| Botswana | Gaborone | 11/5/2014 | 129 | Mexico | Mexico City | 2/24/2018 | 105 |
| Brazil | Sao Paulo | 3/19/2018 | 162 | Moldova | Chisinau | 5/1/2012 | 122 |
| Bulgaria | Sofia | 8/11/2017 | 138 | Mongolia | Ulaanbaatar | 4/6/2014 | 141 |
| Burma | Rangoon | 12/1/2015 | 90 | Montenegro | Podgorica | 9/14/2015 | 116 |
| Burundi | Bujumbura | 12/2/2014 | 128 | Morocco | Casablanca | 12/27/2017 | 121 |
| Cambodia | Phnom Penh | 2/15/2016 | 121 | Mozambique | Maputo | 5/17/2017 | 122 |
| Cameroon | Yaounde | 5/11/2015 | 143 | Nepal | Kathmandu | 3/17/2014 | 109 |
| Canada | Ottawa | 9/26/2017 | 139 | Netherlands | The Hague | 4/21/2014 | 159 |
| Chad | Ndjamena | 7/20/2017 | 137 | New Zealand | Wellington | 2/8/2016 | 126 |
| Chile | Santiago | 9/7/2015 | 134 | Nicaragua | Managua | 2/1/2017 | 122 |
| China | Beijing | 5/26/2016 | 139 | Niger | Niamey | 5/16/2016 | 135 |
| Colombia | Bogota | 12/15/2014 | 138 | Nigeria | Abuja | 5/9/2016 | 153 |
| Costa Rica | San Jose | 1/26/2016 | 146 | Norway | Oslo | 1/25/2016 | 153 |
| Cote d'Ivoire | Abidjan | 2/23/2015 | 142 | Oman | Muscat | 1/22/2017 | 116 |
| Croatia | Zagreb | 6/15/2016 | 108 | Pakistan | Islamabad | 11/14/2016 | 96 |
| Cuba | Havana | 12/26/2014 | 137 | Panama | Panama City | 12/31/2015 | 127 |
| Cyprus | Nicosia | 9/17/2014 | 148 | Papua New Guinea | Port Moresby | 1/22/2015 | 170 |
| Czechia | Prague | 3/31/2017 | 101 | Paraguay | Asuncion | 11/26/2015 | 116 |
| Dem. Rep. of Congo | Kinshasa | 7/20/2016 | 178 | Peru | Lima | 6/5/2015 | 138 |
| Denmark | Copenhagen | 5/4/2015 | 160 | Philippines | Manila | 4/19/2015 | 115 |
| Djibouti | Djibouti City | 2/11/2014 | 155 | Poland | Warsaw | 7/31/2012 | 131 |
| Dominican Republic | Santo Domingo | 4/20/2017 | 134 | Portugal | Lisbon | 2/9/2018 | 127 |
| Ecuador | Quito | 4/13/2016 | 157 | Qatar | Doha | 9/9/2015 | 133 |
| Egypt | Cairo | 3/13/2006 | 96 | Romania | Bucharest | 1/10/2018 | 100 |
| El Salvador | San Salvador | 11/1/2016 | 119 | Russia | Moscow | 2/6/2017 | 155 |
| Equatorial Guinea | Malabo | 8/24/2016 | 136 | Rwanda | Kigali | 8/16/2017 | 142 |
| Eritrea | Asmara | 4/12/2015 | 184 | Samoa | (X) | 6/20/2011 | 137 |
| Estonia | Tallinn | 7/21/2015 | 138 | Saudi Arabia | Riyadh | 6/2/2014 | 141 |
| Ethiopia | Addis Ababa | 11/30/2016 | 149 | Senegal | Dakar | 9/17/2014 | 179 |
| Fiji | Suva | 2/6/2017 | 121 | Serbia | Belgrade | 3/28/2016 | 97 |
| Finland | Helsinki | 2/3/2015 | 133 | Sierra Leone | Freetown | 5/14/2014 | 155 |
| France | Paris | 2/19/2015 | 162 | Singapore | (X) | 11/7/2016 | 127 |
| Gabon | Libreville | 10/21/2015 | 153 | Slovakia | Bratislava | 7/27/2016 | 116 |
| Georgia | Tbilisi | 7/27/2014 | 130 | Slovenia | Ljubljana | 3/18/2016 | 139 |
| Germany | Berlin | 3/1/2017 | 135 | South Africa | Pretoria | 10/23/2014 | 128 |
| Ghana | Accra | 7/26/2017 | 127 | Spain | Madrid | 3/2/2017 | 123 |
| Greece | Athens | 10/22/2013 | 150 | Sri Lanka | Colombo | 3/4/2015 | 98 |
| Guatemala | Guatemala City | 2/10/2014 | 125 | Sudan | Khartoum | 10/11/2017 | 141 |
| Guyana | Georgetown | 9/29/2017 | 139 | Sweden | Stockholm | 5/13/2010 | 185 |
| Haiti | Port-au-Prince | 3/23/2016 | 147 | Switzerland | Geneva | 11/17/2015 | 169 |
| Honduras | Tegucigalpa | 3/14/2017 | 126 | Syria | Damascus | 10/13/2010 | 116 |
| Hong Kong | (X) | 8/1/2017 | 142 | Taiwan | Taipei | 12/29/2015 | 126 |
| Hungary | Budapest | 11/22/2017 | 102 | Tajikistan | Dushanbe | 4/7/2016 | 117 |
| Iceland | Reykjavik | 6/12/2017 | 150 | Tanzania | Dar es Salaam | 10/14/2014 | 147 |
| India | New Delhi | 4/21/2016 | 105 | Thailand | Bangkok | 3/10/2015 | 122 |
| Indonesia | Jakarta | 11/17/2015 | 107 | Tunisia | Tunis | 1/9/2014 | 121 |
| Iraq | Baghdad | 7/21/2004 | 74 | Turkey | Istanbul | 3/9/2014 | 129 |
| Ireland | Dublin | 12/4/2014 | 147 | Uganda | Kampala | 2/8/2017 | 114 |
| Israel | Tel Aviv | 3/4/2014 | 153 | Ukraine | Kyiv | 10/28/2015 | 130 |
| Italy | Rome | 11/8/2016 | 146 | United Arab Emirates | Dubai | 3/15/2018 | 130 |
| Jamaica | Kingston | 3/31/2016 | 118 | United Kingdom | London | 9/11/2014 | 220 |
| Japan | Tokyo City | 2/18/2014 | 180 | Uruguay | Montevideo | 10/19/2017 | 132 |
| Jordan | Amman | 3/12/2013 | 140 | Uzbekistan | Tashkent | 2/15/2017 | 143 |
| Kazakhstan | Astana | 4/3/2018 | 108 | Venezuela | Caracas | 9/4/2014 | 173 |
| Kenya | Nairobi | 5/4/2017 | 120 | Vietnam | Hanoi | 2/28/2017 | 98 |
| Korea, South | Seoul | 10/24/2017 | 145 | Yemen | Sanaa | 4/25/2009 | 92 |
| Kosovo | Pristina | 8/16/2009 | 129 | Zambia | Lusaka | 6/15/2014 | 143 |
| Kuwait | Kuwait City | 3/26/2017 | 113 | Zimbabwe | Harare | 10/12/2017 | 154 |

X Not applicable. [1] The local index measures living costs for private American citizens and excludes special price advantages available only to U.S. government employees. The local index is a comparison of prices at the foreign post and in Washington, DC, with the price ratios weighted by the expenditure pattern of American employees living at the foreign post. This is the index most appropriate for use by business firms and other private organizations to establish cost-of-living allowances for their American employees stationed abroad.

Source: U.S. Department of State, Bureau of Administration, "Indexes of Living Costs Abroad, Quarters Allowances, and Hardship Differentials," January 2019, <https://aoprals.state.gov/content.asp?content_id=186&menu_id=81>.

## Table 1382. Percent of Consumer Expenditures Spent on Food, Alcohol, and Tobacco Consumed at Home by Selected Country: 2018

| Country/territory | Food [1] | Alcoholic beverages and tobacco | Country/territory | Food [1] | Alcoholic beverages and tobacco | Country/territory | Food [1] | Alcoholic beverages and tobacco |
|---|---|---|---|---|---|---|---|---|
| **United States** | **6.4** | **1.7** | France | 13.2 | 3.7 | Nigeria | 59.0 | 1.0 |
| Algeria | 37.3 | 1.0 | Georgia | 32.3 | 3.4 | Norway | 11.7 | 4.1 |
| Argentina | 28.3 | 1.9 | Germany | 10.7 | 3.2 | Pakistan | 39.5 | 1.1 |
| Australia | 9.3 | 3.5 | Ghana | 41.3 | 1.0 | Peru | 26.3 | 2.4 |
| Austria | 9.8 | 3.2 | Greece | 17.1 | 4.9 | Philippines | 42.0 | 1.4 |
| Azerbaijan | 38.6 | 1.6 | Guatemala | 41.2 | 1.6 | Poland | 16.7 | 5.7 |
| Bahrain | 13.2 | 0.4 | Honduras | 32.8 | 4.7 | Portugal | 16.6 | 3.2 |
| Bangladesh | 53.5 | 1.9 | Hong Kong | 14.7 | 1.2 | Romania | 27.3 | 5.7 |
| Belarus | 32.3 | 7.2 | Hungary | 18.2 | 7.3 | Russia | 28.0 | 7.4 |
| Belgium | 13.4 | 4.3 | India | 29.8 | 2.4 | Saudi Arabia | 20.6 | 0.6 |
| Bolivia | 29.1 | 2.1 | Indonesia | 31.7 | 7.2 | Serbia | 25.6 | 7.0 |
| Bosnia-Herzegovina | 30.7 | 9.2 | Iran | 27.9 | 0.6 | Singapore | 6.9 | 1.9 |
| Brazil | 15.7 | 1.5 | Iraq | 30.1 | 4.2 | Slovakia | 18.4 | 5.0 |
| Bulgaria | 19.3 | 5.0 | Ireland | 9.0 | 5.8 | Slovenia | 14.6 | 5.1 |
| Cambodia | 42.3 | 2.2 | Israel | 16.2 | 2.9 | South Africa | 21.4 | 4.9 |
| Canada | 9.1 | 3.3 | Italy | 14.2 | 4.1 | South Korea | 13.8 | 2.7 |
| Chile | 16.0 | 2.9 | Japan | 16.0 | 2.3 | Spain | 12.1 | 3.5 |
| China | 21.6 | 2.5 | Jordan | 29.6 | 4.6 | Sweden | 12.4 | 3.4 |
| Colombia | 19.2 | 3.0 | Kazakhstan | 44.9 | 1.7 | Switzerland | 9.2 | 3.6 |
| Costa Rica | 25.7 | 1.2 | Kenya | 52.9 | 4.1 | Taiwan | 14.7 | 2.3 |
| Croatia | 23.0 | 2.3 | Kuwait | 19.2 | 0.2 | Thailand | 24.3 | 3.4 |
| Czechia | 16.3 | 8.0 | Latvia | 17.3 | 7.9 | Tunisia | 21.9 | 3.2 |
| Denmark | 11.5 | 3.4 | Lebanon | 20.7 | 1.2 | Turkey | 21.8 | 3.4 |
| Dominican Republic | 26.8 | 3.8 | Lithuania | 21.2 | 5.9 | Ukraine | 42.2 | 7.7 |
| Ecuador | 26.2 | 0.8 | Malaysia | 21.5 | 1.8 | United Arab Emirates | 13.7 | 0.4 |
| Egypt | 33.3 | 4.7 | Mexico | 23.4 | 2.8 | United Kingdom | 8.1 | 3.2 |
| El Salvador | 26.5 | 0.5 | Morocco | 34.0 | 1.4 | Uruguay | 18.6 | 1.3 |
| Ethiopia | 56.6 | 3.8 | Netherlands | 11.4 | 3.3 | Venezuela | 19.1 | 3.8 |
| Finland | 11.5 | 4.3 | New Zealand | 13.4 | 4.8 | Vietnam | 38.8 | 2.3 |

[1] Includes nonalcoholic beverages.

Source: U.S. Department of Agriculture, Economic Research Service, International Consumer and Food Industry Trends, "Data on expenditures on food and alcoholic beverages in selected countries," <https://www.ers.usda.gov/topics/international-markets-us-trade/international-consumer-and-food-industry-trends/>, accessed July 2019.

## Table 1383. Gross Public Debt, Expenditures, and Receipts as Percent of GDP by Country: 2000 to 2020

[Percent of nominal gross domestic product. Gross debt, expenditures, and receipts refer to the general government sector, which is a consolidation of accounts for the central, state, and local governments plus social security. Expenditures, or total outlays, are defined as current outlays plus capital outlays. Receipts cover current receipts, but exclude capital receipts. Nontax receipts consist of property income (including dividends and other transfers from public enterprises), fees, charges, sales, fines, and capital transfers received by the general government, etc.]

| Country | Gross debt 2000 | Gross debt 2010 | Gross debt 2020 (P) | Expenditures 2000 | Expenditures 2010 | Expenditures 2020 (P) | Receipts 2000 | Receipts 2010 | Receipts 2020 (P) |
|---|---|---|---|---|---|---|---|---|---|
| **United States** | **52.9** | **95.2** | **113.4** | **34.5** | **43.4** | **38.1** | **34.8** | **30.8** | **31.4** |
| Australia | 25.3 | 24.9 | 40.2 | 35.2 | 36.4 | 35.0 | 36.2 | 32.3 | 35.4 |
| Austria | 70.9 | 96.3 | 91.9 | 50.9 | 52.9 | 47.2 | 48.5 | 48.4 | 47.5 |
| Belgium | 120.5 | 108.0 | 118.3 | 49.0 | 53.3 | 52.2 | 49.0 | 49.3 | 50.8 |
| Canada | 84.4 | 86.6 | 92.9 | 40.6 | 43.1 | 40.9 | 43.2 | 38.3 | 40.7 |
| Czechia | 24.4 | 46.2 | 37.4 | 40.9 | 43.6 | 41.2 | 37.4 | 39.4 | 41.6 |
| Denmark | 60.5 | 53.4 | 46.6 | 52.7 | 56.7 | 50.2 | 54.6 | 54.0 | 50.4 |
| Estonia | 6.8 | 12.0 | 17.5 | 36.4 | 40.5 | 39.3 | 36.3 | 40.7 | 39.1 |
| Finland | 50.9 | 55.9 | 70.9 | 48.0 | 54.8 | 51.6 | 54.9 | 52.1 | 51.7 |
| France | 72.4 | 100.1 | 124.5 | 51.6 | 56.9 | 54.4 | 50.3 | 50.0 | 52.1 |
| Germany | 59.5 | 86.4 | 64.7 | 44.7 | 47.4 | 44.2 | 45.6 | 43.1 | 44.9 |
| Greece | 111.8 | 129.2 | 178.3 | 46.3 | 52.3 | 45.3 | 42.3 | 41.2 | 45.6 |
| Hungary | 61.5 | 86.4 | 83.9 | 47.1 | 49.3 | 45.7 | 44.1 | 44.8 | 43.6 |
| Iceland | 40.1 | 88.0 | 61.4 | 41.0 | 47.8 | 43.0 | 42.2 | 38.3 | 42.8 |
| Ireland | 38.3 | 84.6 | 65.7 | 30.9 | 65.1 | 24.8 | 35.8 | 33.0 | 25.2 |
| Israel [1] | 79.6 | 70.7 | 62.5 | 45.5 | 41.1 | 40.2 | 44.2 | 37.4 | 36.8 |
| Italy | 118.8 | 126.2 | 151.9 | 46.5 | 49.9 | 50.0 | 44.1 | 45.7 | 47.1 |
| Japan | 130.9 | 186.6 | 225.7 | 37.5 | 39.3 | 38.2 | 30.2 | 30.1 | 36.1 |
| Korea | (NA) | 33.5 | 44.9 | 24.8 | 31.1 | 36.6 | 29.2 | 32.0 | 37.2 |
| Latvia | 14.5 | 53.3 | 44.1 | 37.3 | 45.4 | 37.5 | 34.5 | 36.8 | 36.7 |
| Luxembourg | 17.3 | 28.4 | 29.5 | 37.8 | 44.1 | 43.7 | 43.7 | 43.5 | 45.5 |
| Netherlands | 61.1 | 68.7 | 60.2 | 42.2 | 47.9 | 41.8 | 43.3 | 42.6 | 42.6 |
| New Zealand | 36.2 | 37.0 | 36.5 | 34.3 | 44.3 | 38.3 | 36.0 | 37.3 | 38.4 |
| Norway | 32.2 | 48.4 | (NA) | 42.0 | 44.9 | 48.3 | 57.1 | 55.9 | 56.1 |
| Poland | 45.1 | 60.9 | 63.8 | 42.2 | 45.8 | 43.8 | 39.2 | 38.5 | 42.8 |
| Portugal | 62.0 | 104.1 | 135.0 | 42.6 | 51.8 | 42.5 | 39.4 | 40.6 | 42.2 |
| Slovak Republic | 57.9 | 47.4 | 52.4 | 52.0 | 42.1 | 40.2 | 40.0 | 34.7 | 40.1 |
| Slovenia | (NA) | 47.8 | 79.0 | 46.1 | 49.3 | 41.6 | 42.5 | 43.6 | 42.6 |
| Spain | 65.2 | 66.8 | 111.7 | 39.2 | 45.6 | 40.8 | 38.1 | 36.2 | 39.4 |
| Sweden | 57.5 | 46.4 | 44.3 | 53.3 | 50.9 | 49.6 | 56.5 | 50.8 | 50.6 |
| Switzerland | 54.5 | 42.8 | 39.5 | 33.9 | 33.0 | 33.7 | 34.2 | 33.4 | 34.8 |
| United Kingdom | 44.9 | 86.7 | 112.0 | 35.4 | 47.6 | 41.0 | 36.8 | 38.3 | 39.0 |

NA Not available. P Projection. [1] See footnote 2, Table 1380.

Source: Organisation for Economic Co-operation and Development (OECD), 2019, "OECD Economic Outlook No. 105 (Edition 2019/1)," OECD Economic Outlook: Statistics and Projections (database) ©, <https://www.oecd-ilibrary.org/economics/data/oecd-economic-outlook-statistics-and-projections_eo-data-en>, accessed July 2019.

## Table 1384. Percent Distribution of Tax Receipts by Country and Tax Type: 2010 to 2017

| Country | Total [1] | Taxes on income and profits [2] | | | Social security contributions | | | Taxes on goods and services [5] | | |
|---|---|---|---|---|---|---|---|---|---|---|
| | | Total [3] | Individual | Corporate | Total [4] | Employ-ees | Employ-ers | Total [3] | General consump-tion taxes [6] | Taxes on specific goods, services [7] |
| United States: | | | | | | | | | | |
| 2010........... | 100.0 | 42.4 | 34.8 | 7.6 | 26.1 | 11.6 | 13.1 | 18.3 | 8.4 | 7.0 |
| 2017 [8]........... | 100.0 | 45.7 | 38.6 | 7.1 | 23.1 | 10.3 | 11.5 | 15.9 | 7.3 | 6.1 |
| Australia: | | | | | | | | | | |
| 2010........... | 100.0 | 56.5 | 38.6 | 17.9 | 0.0 | 0.0 | 0.0 | 29.0 | 13.8 | 11.9 |
| 2016 [9]........... | 100.0 | 57.2 | 40.8 | 16.5 | 0.0 | 0.0 | 0.0 | 27.1 | 13.2 | 10.0 |
| Canada: | | | | | | | | | | |
| 2010........... | 100.0 | 46.6 | 35.0 | 10.5 | 14.9 | 5.9 | 8.4 | 24.0 | 14.0 | 8.5 |
| 2017 [8]........... | 100.0 | 47.6 | 35.9 | 10.6 | 14.3 | 5.7 | 8.1 | 24.0 | 14.4 | 7.7 |
| Chile: | | | | | | | | | | |
| 2010........... | 100.0 | 38.1 | 6.8 | 20.4 | 6.8 | 6.6 | 0.3 | 51.2 | 38.5 | 9.8 |
| 2017 [8]........... | 100.0 | 34.5 | 9.7 | 21.1 | 7.3 | 7.0 | 0.2 | 54.8 | 41.6 | 9.7 |
| Czechia: | | | | | | | | | | |
| 2010........... | 100.0 | 20.2 | 10.2 | 10.0 | 44.8 | 9.1 | 28.2 | 33.2 | 20.5 | 10.8 |
| 2017 [8]........... | 100.0 | 22.2 | 11.6 | 10.6 | 43.0 | 8.9 | 27.5 | 32.9 | 22.0 | 9.3 |
| France: | | | | | | | | | | |
| 2010........... | 100.0 | 22.6 | 17.0 | 5.5 | 38.2 | 9.2 | 25.9 | 24.8 | 16.7 | 7.4 |
| 2017 [8]........... | 100.0 | 23.6 | 18.5 | 5.1 | 36.4 | 9.5 | 24.3 | 24.4 | 15.6 | 8.1 |
| Germany: | | | | | | | | | | |
| 2010........... | 100.0 | 28.5 | 24.3 | 4.3 | 39.2 | 17.2 | 18.5 | 29.5 | 20.0 | 8.4 |
| 2017 [8]........... | 100.0 | 32.6 | 27.2 | 5.4 | 37.9 | 17.0 | 17.6 | 26.2 | 18.4 | 6.8 |
| Greece: | | | | | | | | | | |
| 2010........... | 100.0 | 22.0 | 12.4 | 7.9 | 34.2 | 18.4 | 15.8 | 38.3 | 22.8 | 11.9 |
| 2016 [9]........... | 100.0 | 23.5 | 15.2 | 6.5 | 28.5 | 17.1 | 11.4 | 39.6 | 21.6 | 12.4 |
| Italy: | | | | | | | | | | |
| 2010........... | 100.0 | 32.6 | 26.8 | 5.5 | 31.1 | 5.6 | 21.5 | 26.3 | 14.5 | 9.1 |
| 2017 [8]........... | 100.0 | 31.7 | 25.7 | 5.0 | 30.4 | 5.6 | 20.3 | 28.4 | 14.9 | 10.1 |
| Japan: | | | | | | | | | | |
| 2010........... | 100.0 | 30.2 | 18.6 | 11.6 | 41.1 | 17.8 | 18.6 | 18.7 | 9.6 | 7.2 |
| 2016 [9]........... | 100.0 | 30.6 | 18.6 | 12.0 | 40.4 | 17.8 | 18.5 | 20.4 | 13.3 | 5.7 |
| Korea, South: | | | | | | | | | | |
| 2010........... | 100.0 | 28.0 | 14.2 | 13.8 | 23.3 | 9.5 | 10.4 | 33.7 | 17.5 | 15.1 |
| 2017 [8]........... | 100.0 | 32.1 | 17.9 | 14.2 | 25.7 | 11.0 | 11.6 | 27.7 | 16.0 | 10.1 |
| Turkey: | | | | | | | | | | |
| 2010........... | 100.0 | 21.3 | 14.0 | 7.3 | 24.9 | 9.4 | 13.7 | 47.7 | 21.7 | 24.1 |
| 2017 [8]........... | 100.0 | 21.4 | 14.5 | 6.8 | 29.3 | 11.2 | 16.6 | 43.4 | 20.1 | 21.9 |
| United Kingdom: | | | | | | | | | | |
| 2010........... | 100.0 | 37.6 | 28.7 | 8.9 | 19.0 | 7.5 | 10.9 | 30.9 | 18.7 | 10.7 |
| 2017 [8]........... | 100.0 | 35.9 | 27.4 | 8.5 | 19.2 | 7.4 | 11.3 | 31.5 | 20.4 | 10.0 |

[1] Includes property taxes, employer payroll taxes other than social security contributions, and miscellaneous taxes not shown separately. [2] Includes taxes on capital gains. [3] Includes other taxes, not shown separately. [4] Includes contributions of self-employed persons, not shown separately. [5] Taxes on the production, extraction, sale, transfer, leasing or delivery of goods, and the rendering of services. [6] Primarily value-added and sales taxes. [7] For example, excise taxes on alcohol, tobacco, and gasoline. [8] Data are provisional/estimates. [9] Data for 2017 are not available.

Source: Organisation for Economic Co-operation and Development (OECD), 2019, "Revenue Statistics: Comparative tables," OECD Tax Statistics (database) ©, <http://dx.doi.org/10.1787/data-00262-en>, accessed July 2019.

## Table 1385. Household Tax Burden by Country: 2018

[As percent of gross wage earnings of the average worker. The tax burden reflects income tax plus employee social security contributions less cash benefits]

| Country | Single person without children | One-earner married couple with two children | Country | Single person without children | One-earner married couple with two children |
|---|---|---|---|---|---|
| OECD average [1]........... | 25.48 | 20.14 | Italy........... | 31.42 | 24.70 |
| | | | Japan........... | 22.34 | 20.96 |
| United States........... | 23.77 | 11.74 | Korea, South........... | 14.95 | 12.72 |
| Australia........... | 24.65 | 24.65 | Latvia........... | 28.39 | 20.31 |
| Austria........... | 32.80 | 30.60 | Lithuania........... | 22.11 | 22.11 |
| Belgium........... | 39.83 | 28.42 | Luxembourg........... | 29.50 | 18.19 |
| Canada........... | 23.02 | 18.38 | Mexico........... | 10.23 | 10.23 |
| Chile........... | 7.01 | 7.00 | Netherlands........... | 30.45 | 28.99 |
| Czechia........... | 24.62 | 5.93 | New Zealand........... | 18.44 | 18.44 |
| Denmark........... | 35.84 | 31.80 | Norway........... | 27.47 | 27.47 |
| Estonia........... | 15.00 | 10.03 | Poland........... | 25.20 | 20.07 |
| Finland........... | 29.96 | 29.96 | Portugal........... | 26.63 | 15.74 |
| France [2]........... | 28.72 | 21.44 | Slovak Republic........... | 23.86 | 13.59 |
| Germany........... | 39.71 | 21.67 | Slovenia........... | 34.11 | 25.76 |
| Greece........... | 26.13 | 26.63 | Spain........... | 21.26 | 14.13 |
| Hungary........... | 33.50 | 23.35 | Sweden........... | 25.17 | 25.17 |
| Iceland........... | 28.71 | 21.65 | Switzerland........... | 17.40 | 10.82 |
| Ireland........... | 25.40 | 15.46 | Turkey........... | 28.17 | 26.22 |
| Israel [3]........... | 18.08 | 18.08 | United Kingdom........... | 23.40 | 22.80 |

[1] As of 2018, the Organisation for Economic Co-operation and Development (OECD) was comprised of the 36 member countries shown. See text, this section. [2] Figures correspond to tax calculations that are based on the tax legislation relating to the income earned in the selected year. [3] See footnote 2, Table 1380.

Source: Organisation for Economic Co-operation and Development (OECD), 2019, "Taxing Wages: Comparative tables," OECD Tax Statistics (database) ©, <http://dx.doi.org/10.1787/data-00265-en>, accessed July 2019.

# Table 1386. Household Net Saving Rates by Country: 2000 to 2017

[As a percentage of household disposable income. Household savings are estimated by subtracting household consumption expenditure from household disposable income, plus the change in net equity of households in pension funds. Households include households plus nonprofit institutions serving households. Net saving rates are measured after deducting consumption of fixed capital (depreciation), with respect to assets used in enterprises operated by households, as well as owner-occupied dwellings. The household saving rate is calculated as the ratio of household savings to household disposable income (plus the change in net equity of households in pension funds). Minus sign (-) indicates an excess of expenditures over income]

| Country | 2000 | 2005 | 2010 | 2011 | 2012 | 2013 | 2014 | 2015 | 2016 | 2017 |
|---|---|---|---|---|---|---|---|---|---|---|
| United States............... | 5.0 | 3.3 | 6.8 | 7.4 | 9.1 | 6.6 | 7.6 | 7.8 | 6.9 | 6.9 |
| EU-28 [1]............ | 6.8 | 5.6 | 6.1 | 5.2 | 4.9 | 4.9 | 4.8 | 4.7 | 4.4 | 3.2 |
| Australia [2]................ | 2.0 | 0.3 | 8.4 | 8.8 | 7.5 | 7.9 | 7.9 | 6.0 | 4.9 | 3.5 |
| Austria.................. | 10.6 | 11.1 | 9.6 | 7.9 | 8.9 | 7.1 | 7.3 | 6.8 | 7.8 | 6.8 |
| Belgium................... | 10.4 | 8.5 | 8.1 | 6.5 | 5.7 | 5.1 | 5.1 | 4.3 | 3.9 | 4.0 |
| Canada.................. | 5.3 | 1.5 | 4.4 | 4.3 | 4.8 | 5.3 | 3.6 | 4.2 | 1.3 | 1.8 |
| Chile...................... | (NA) | 12.1 | 7.8 | 9.3 | 10.6 | 10.7 | 10.6 | 9.6 | 10.7 | 10.2 |
| Denmark.................. | -5.7 | -4.3 | 1.8 | 0.8 | 0.1 | 2.3 | -2.9 | 3.9 | 4.5 | 6.2 |
| Finland................... | 3.0 | 1.0 | 3.2 | 1.3 | 0.7 | 1.5 | -0.1 | -0.5 | -1.4 | -1.7 |
| France.................... | 8.7 | 8.5 | 10.5 | 9.9 | 10.0 | 8.5 | 8.9 | 8.4 | [3] 8.2 | [3] 8.5 |
| Germany.................. | 9.0 | 10.1 | 10.0 | 9.6 | 9.3 | 8.9 | 9.5 | 9.7 | 9.8 | 9.9 |
| Greece [3]............... | -1.4 | -2.9 | -6.9 | -8.9 | -10.9 | -16.4 | -13.8 | -15.5 | -17.0 | -16.9 |
| Hungary.................. | 6.5 | 8.0 | 6.1 | 7.0 | 5.2 | 7.1 | 8.0 | 6.2 | 8.1 | 7.3 |
| Ireland................... | -3.9 | 1.5 | 8.2 | 4.2 | 7.0 | 5.2 | 3.6 | 4.2 | 3.8 | 6.6 |
| Italy...................... | 7.4 | 9.1 | 4.2 | 3.7 | 2.0 | 3.6 | 3.9 | 3.2 | 3.2 | 2.3 |
| Japan..................... | 8.9 | 3.7 | 3.9 | 4.2 | 2.9 | 0.6 | 0.1 | 1.4 | 3.1 | 2.7 |
| Latvia.................... | -9.8 | -6.5 | -1.3 | -15.9 | -15.0 | -15.3 | -12.7 | -8.1 | -4.0 | -5.8 |
| Lithuania................. | (NA) | -0.2 | 4.1 | 0.9 | -2.0 | -1.2 | -3.6 | -3.4 | -3.6 | -5.2 |
| Mexico................... | (NA) | 6.0 | 14.5 | 15.8 | 14.6 | 12.2 | 14.1 | 15.1 | 15.4 | (NA) |
| New Zealand [2]........... | -2.5 | -5.5 | 2.0 | 2.4 | 0.8 | 0.6 | -0.6 | -0.3 | 0.3 | [3] -1.4 |
| Norway................... | 4.3 | 9.7 | 4.0 | 5.9 | 7.1 | 7.4 | 8.2 | 10.3 | 7.3 | 6.7 |
| Poland.................... | 11.0 | 2.2 | 2.4 | -1.1 | -1.1 | -0.1 | -0.4 | -0.4 | 1.5 | [3] -0.9 |
| Portugal.................. | 3.5 | 1.8 | 1.3 | -0.9 | -0.5 | -0.2 | -3.3 | -3.2 | -3.7 | -4.1 |
| Spain..................... | 5.8 | 3.2 | 3.7 | 4.6 | 2.3 | 3.8 | 3.5 | 2.9 | 1.8 | [3] -0.8 |
| Sweden................... | 4.4 | 5.4 | 11.8 | 12.5 | 14.4 | 15.0 | 16.4 | 15.0 | 16.0 | 15.1 |
| Switzerland............... | 14.0 | 12.8 | 15.7 | 16.8 | 17.4 | [3] 17.5 | [3] 18.9 | [3] 17.6 | [3] 18.8 | (NA) |
| United Kingdom............ | 5.7 | 2.8 | 6.5 | 4.5 | 4.5 | 3.7 | 3.6 | 4.6 | 1.6 | 0.9 |

NA Not available. [1] See footnote 3, Table 1396 for list of EU 28 countries. [2] Data refer to fiscal year. [3] Data are estimates.

Source: Organisation for Economic Co-operation and Development (OECD), 2019, "National Accounts at a Glance," OECD National Accounts Statistics (database) ©, <http://dx.doi.org/10.1787/data-00369-en>, accessed July 2019.

# Table 1387. Insurance and Pensions by Country: 2017

[5,592,566 represents $5,592,566,000,000]

| Country | Insurance | | | | | Pensions [2] | |
|---|---|---|---|---|---|---|---|
| | Investment assets (mil. U.S. dollars) [1] | Direct gross premiums (percent of GDP) | Total gross premiums (mil. U.S. dollars) | | Gross claims payments (mil. U.S. dollars) | Investment assets (mil. U.S. dollars) | Benefits paid (percent of GDP) |
| | | | Life | Non-life | | | |
| United States............... | 5,592,566 | 11.2 | 1,009,291 | 1,827,002 | 1,646,030 | 28,168,971 | (NA) |
| Australia.................. | 192,553 | 4.4 | 37,668 | 34,671 | 61,603 | 1,760,107 | 6.4 |
| Austria.................... | 149,069 | 4.6 | 6,477 | 13,957 | 17,007 | (NA) | 0.2 |
| Belgium................... | 369,662 | 6.1 | 16,506 | 14,257 | 30,449 | (NA) | 0.2 |
| Chile..................... | 66,411 | 4.6 | 8,930 | 3,930 | 8,250 | 210,512 | 1.1 |
| Czechia................... | 19,346 | 2.9 | 2,451 | 3,951 | 3,881 | 20,920 | 0.5 |
| Denmark.................. | 527,790 | 11.0 | 25,945 | 11,604 | 24,022 | 721,674 | 0.8 |
| Estonia................... | 2,032 | 3.5 | 251 | 671 | 509 | 4,839 | (Z) |
| Finland................... | 90,301 | 3.9 | 5,103 | 4,956 | 8,353 | 162,380 | 1.5 |
| France.................... | 3,066,513 | 10.6 | 173,177 | 140,366 | 277,873 | (NA) | (NA) |
| Germany.................. | 1,998,781 | 6.3 | 99,523 | 210,917 | 173,383 | 270,728 | 0.2 |
| Greece.................... | 18,510 | 2.1 | 2,120 | 2,083 | (NA) | 1,605 | (NA) |
| Hungary.................. | 10,295 | 2.5 | 1,679 | 1,804 | 2,165 | 8,770 | 0.1 |
| Iceland................... | (NA) | 2.5 | 54 | 556 | 426 | 40,256 | 5.3 |
| Ireland................... | 328,432 | 13.6 | 37,438 | 7,955 | 39,676 | 126,571 | (NA) |
| Israel [3]................. | 135,300 | 4.9 | 9,368 | 8,059 | 10,445 | 215,030 | (NA) |
| Italy..................... | 945,366 | 7.6 | 112,705 | 37,654 | 106,946 | 200,850 | 0.4 |
| Japan.................... | 3,788,141 | 7.4 | 293,005 | 97,090 | 315,183 | 1,623,545 | (NA) |
| Latvia.................... | 735 | 2.4 | 163 | 564 | 407 | 4,448 | 0.1 |
| Lithuania................. | 1,514 | 1.9 | 261 | 633 | 513 | 3,613 | 0.1 |
| Luxembourg............... | 223,617 | 38.8 | 22,262 | 1,991 | 14,690 | 1,941 | 0.2 |
| Mexico................... | 58,674 | 2.3 | 11,421 | 15,148 | 13,392 | 185,638 | 0.3 |
| Netherlands............... | 392,783 | 9.5 | 14,618 | 64,658 | 87,371 | 1,627,799 | (NA) |
| Norway................... | 201,067 | 5.1 | 11,313 | 9,094 | 12,966 | (NA) | 0.2 |
| Poland.................... | 51,859 | 3.0 | 6,499 | 10,000 | 10,542 | 57,642 | (NA) |
| Portugal.................. | 58,331 | 5.6 | 7,562 | 5,347 | 10,798 | 26,430 | 0.4 |
| Slovenia.................. | 8,084 | 4.7 | 581 | 2,009 | 1,773 | 3,591 | 0.2 |
| Spain..................... | 345,597 | 5.2 | 33,180 | 40,878 | 55,508 | 189,361 | 0.4 |
| Sweden................... | 561,683 | 8.0 | 33,761 | 10,621 | 16,730 | 505,464 | (NA) |
| Switzerland............... | 461,858 | 8.6 | 30,486 | 37,287 | 52,032 | (NA) | 5.2 |
| United Kingdom............ | 287,090 | 12.8 | 269,258 | 124,843 | 417,974 | 2,903,324 | (NA) |

NA Not available or not applicable. Z Less than 0.05 percent. [1] Includes total investment assets of direct insurance companies (excludes re-insurance). [2] Includes public and private autonomous pension funds of all types (occupational and personal, mandatory and voluntary). [3] See footnote 2, Table 1380.

Source: Organisation for Economic Co-operation and Development (OECD), 2019, Insurance Statistics (database) ©, <http://www.oecd.org/daf/fin/insurance/oecdinsurancestatistics.htm>; and Global Pension Statistics (database) ©, <http://www.oecd.org/daf/fin/private-pensions/globalpensionstatistics.htm>; accessed September 2019.

## Table 1388. Inflation—Annual Percent Changes in Consumer Prices by Country: 2010 to 2018

[Percent change from previous year. Inflation as measured by the consumer price index reflects the annual percentage change in the cost to the average consumer of acquiring a basket of goods and services that may be fixed or adjusted at specified intervals, such as yearly. For general comments concerning the data, see text, this section. For additional qualifications of the data for individual countries, see source. Minus sign (-) indicates decrease]

| Country | 2010 | 2015 | 2016 | 2017 | 2018 | Country | 2010 | 2015 | 2016 | 2017 | 2018 |
|---|---|---|---|---|---|---|---|---|---|---|---|
| **World** [1] | **3.3** | **1.4** | **1.4** | **2.2** | **2.5** | Kenya | 4.0 | 6.6 | 6.3 | 8.0 | 4.7 |
| **United States** | **1.6** | **0.1** | **1.3** | **2.1** | **2.4** | Korea, South | 2.9 | 0.7 | 1.0 | 1.9 | 1.5 |
| Afghanistan | 2.2 | -0.7 | 4.4 | 5.0 | (NA) | Malaysia | 1.6 | 2.1 | 2.1 | 3.9 | 0.9 |
| Australia | 2.9 | 1.5 | 1.3 | 1.9 | 1.9 | Mexico | 4.2 | 2.7 | 2.8 | 6.0 | 4.9 |
| Austria | 1.8 | 0.9 | 0.9 | 2.1 | 2.0 | Mongolia | 10.1 | 6.6 | 1.1 | 4.1 | 6.8 |
| Bangladesh | 8.1 | 6.2 | 5.5 | 5.7 | 5.5 | Morocco | 1.0 | 1.6 | 1.6 | 0.8 | 1.9 |
| Belarus | 7.7 | 13.5 | 11.8 | 6.0 | 4.9 | Netherlands | 1.3 | 0.6 | 0.3 | 1.4 | 1.7 |
| Brazil | 5.0 | 9.0 | 8.7 | 3.4 | 3.7 | New Zealand | 2.3 | 0.3 | 0.6 | 1.9 | 1.6 |
| Cambodia | 4.0 | 1.2 | 3.0 | 2.9 | (NA) | Nigeria | 13.7 | 9.0 | 15.7 | 16.5 | 12.1 |
| China | 3.2 | 1.4 | 2.0 | 1.6 | 2.1 | Norway | 2.4 | 2.2 | 3.6 | 1.9 | 2.8 |
| Colombia | 2.3 | 5.0 | 7.5 | 4.3 | 3.2 | Pakistan | 13.9 | 2.5 | 3.8 | 4.1 | 5.1 |
| Croatia | 1.0 | -0.5 | -1.1 | 1.1 | 1.5 | Peru | 1.5 | 3.5 | 3.6 | 2.8 | 1.3 |
| Czechia | 1.5 | 0.3 | 0.7 | 2.5 | 2.1 | Philippines | 3.8 | 0.7 | 1.3 | 2.9 | 5.2 |
| Denmark | 2.3 | 0.5 | 0.2 | 1.1 | 0.8 | Poland | 2.6 | -0.9 | -0.7 | 2.1 | 1.8 |
| Egypt | 11.3 | 10.4 | 13.8 | 29.5 | (NA) | Romania | 6.1 | -0.6 | -1.5 | 1.3 | 4.6 |
| Ethiopia | 8.1 | 10.1 | 7.3 | 9.8 | (NA) | Russia | 6.8 | 15.5 | 7.0 | 3.7 | 2.9 |
| France | 1.5 | (Z) | 0.2 | 1.0 | 1.9 | Saudi Arabia | 5.3 | 1.2 | 2.1 | -0.8 | 2.5 |
| Germany | 1.1 | 0.5 | 0.5 | 1.5 | 1.7 | Singapore | 2.8 | -0.5 | -0.5 | 0.6 | 0.4 |
| Ghana | 10.7 | 17.1 | 17.5 | 12.4 | 9.8 | South Africa | 4.1 | 4.5 | 6.6 | 5.2 | 4.5 |
| Greece | 4.7 | -1.7 | -0.8 | 1.1 | 0.6 | Spain | 1.8 | -0.5 | -0.2 | 2.0 | 1.7 |
| Haiti | 5.7 | 9.0 | 13.8 | 14.7 | (NA) | Sri Lanka | 6.2 | 3.8 | 4.0 | 7.7 | 2.1 |
| Honduras | 4.7 | 3.2 | 2.7 | 3.9 | 4.3 | Sweden | 1.2 | (Z) | 1.0 | 1.8 | 2.0 |
| India | 12.0 | 5.9 | 4.9 | 2.5 | 4.9 | Switzerland | 0.7 | -1.1 | -0.4 | 0.5 | 0.9 |
| Indonesia | 5.1 | 6.4 | 3.5 | 3.8 | 3.2 | Thailand | 3.2 | -0.9 | 0.2 | 0.7 | 1.1 |
| Iran | 10.1 | 13.7 | 8.7 | 10.0 | (NA) | Tunisia | -30.9 | 4.4 | 3.6 | 5.3 | 7.3 |
| Ireland | -0.9 | -0.3 | (Z) | 0.3 | 0.5 | Turkey | 8.6 | 7.7 | 7.8 | 11.1 | 16.3 |
| Israel | 2.7 | -0.6 | -0.5 | 0.2 | 0.8 | Ukraine | 9.4 | 48.7 | 13.9 | 14.4 | 11.0 |
| Italy | 1.5 | (Z) | -0.1 | 1.2 | 1.1 | United Kingdom | 2.5 | 0.4 | 1.0 | 2.6 | 2.3 |
| Japan | -0.7 | 0.8 | -0.1 | 0.5 | 1.0 | Venezuela | 28.2 | 121.7 | 254.9 | (NA) | (NA) |
| Jordan | 4.8 | -0.9 | -0.8 | 3.3 | 4.5 | Vietnam | 8.9 | 0.9 | 3.2 | 3.5 | 3.5 |

NA Not available. Z Less than 0.05 percent. [1] Includes other countries not shown separately.

Source: The World Bank, Washington, DC, World Development Indicators database, "Inflation, consumer prices (annual %)" ©, <http://data.worldbank.org/data-catalog/world-development-indicators>, accessed July 2019.

## Table 1389. Unemployment Rates by Country: 2000 to 2018

[Annual averages. The standardized unemployment rates shown here are calculated as the number of unemployed persons as a percentage of the civilian labor force. The unemployed are persons of working age who, in the reference period, are without work, are available for work, and have taken specific steps to find work]

| Country | 2000 | 2005 | 2010 | 2011 | 2012 | 2013 | 2014 | 2015 | 2016 | 2017 | 2018 |
|---|---|---|---|---|---|---|---|---|---|---|---|
| OECD, total [1] | (NA) | 6.6 | 8.3 | 7.9 | 7.9 | 7.9 | 7.4 | 6.8 | 6.3 | 5.8 | 5.3 |
| EU-28 [2] | (NA) | 8.9 | 9.5 | 9.6 | 10.4 | 10.8 | 10.2 | 9.4 | 8.5 | 7.6 | 6.8 |
| **United States** | **4.0** | **5.1** | **9.6** | **9.0** | **8.1** | **7.4** | **6.2** | **5.3** | **4.9** | **4.4** | **3.9** |
| Australia | 6.3 | 5.0 | 5.2 | 5.1 | 5.2 | 5.7 | 6.1 | 6.1 | 5.7 | 5.6 | 5.3 |
| Austria | 3.5 | 5.6 | 4.8 | 4.6 | 4.9 | 5.3 | 5.6 | 5.7 | 6.0 | 5.5 | 4.8 |
| Belgium | 7.0 | 8.4 | 8.3 | 7.1 | 7.5 | 8.4 | 8.5 | 8.5 | 7.8 | 7.1 | 5.9 |
| Canada | 6.8 | 6.8 | 8.1 | 7.5 | 7.3 | 7.1 | 6.9 | 6.9 | 7.0 | 6.3 | 5.8 |
| Chile | 9.7 | 9.2 | 8.2 | 7.1 | 6.4 | 5.9 | 6.4 | 6.2 | 6.5 | 6.7 | 7.0 |
| Czechia | 8.8 | 7.9 | 7.3 | 6.7 | 7.0 | 7.0 | 6.1 | 5.0 | 4.0 | 2.9 | 2.2 |
| Denmark | 4.6 | 4.8 | 7.5 | 7.6 | 7.5 | 7.0 | 6.6 | 6.2 | 6.2 | 5.7 | 5.0 |
| Estonia | 14.6 | 8.0 | 16.7 | 12.3 | 10.0 | 8.6 | 7.4 | 6.2 | 6.8 | 5.8 | 5.4 |
| Finland | 9.8 | 8.4 | 8.4 | 7.8 | 7.7 | 8.2 | 8.7 | 9.4 | 8.8 | 8.6 | 7.4 |
| France | (NA) | 8.5 | 8.9 | 8.8 | 9.4 | 9.9 | 10.3 | 10.4 | 10.1 | 9.4 | 9.1 |
| Germany | 7.8 | 11.2 | 7.0 | 5.8 | 5.4 | 5.2 | 5.0 | 4.6 | 4.1 | 3.7 | 3.4 |
| Greece | 11.4 | 10.0 | 12.7 | 17.9 | 24.4 | 27.5 | 26.5 | 24.9 | 23.5 | 21.5 | 19.3 |
| Hungary | 6.4 | 7.2 | 11.2 | 11.0 | 11.0 | 10.2 | 7.7 | 6.8 | 5.1 | 4.2 | 3.7 |
| Iceland | (NA) | 2.5 | 7.5 | 7.0 | 6.0 | 5.4 | 4.9 | 4.0 | 3.0 | 2.7 | 2.7 |
| Ireland | 4.3 | 4.3 | 14.5 | 15.4 | 15.4 | 13.7 | 11.9 | 9.9 | 8.4 | 6.7 | 5.7 |
| Israel [3] | 8.8 | 9.0 | 6.6 | 5.6 | 6.9 | 6.2 | 5.9 | 5.2 | 4.8 | 4.2 | 4.0 |
| Italy | 10.6 | 7.7 | 8.4 | 8.4 | 10.7 | 12.1 | 12.7 | 11.9 | 11.7 | 11.2 | 10.6 |
| Japan | 4.7 | 4.4 | 5.1 | 4.6 | 4.4 | 4.0 | 3.6 | 3.4 | 3.1 | 2.8 | 2.4 |
| Korea, South | 4.4 | 3.8 | 3.7 | 3.4 | 3.2 | 3.1 | 3.5 | 3.6 | 3.7 | 3.7 | 3.8 |
| Latvia | (NA) | 10.0 | 19.5 | 16.2 | 15.1 | 11.9 | 10.8 | 9.9 | 9.6 | 8.7 | 7.4 |
| Lithuania | (NA) | 8.3 | 17.8 | 15.4 | 13.4 | 11.8 | 10.7 | 9.1 | 7.9 | 7.1 | 6.2 |
| Luxembourg | (NA) | 4.5 | 4.4 | 4.9 | 5.1 | 5.8 | 5.9 | 6.7 | 6.3 | 5.5 | 5.6 |
| Mexico | 2.5 | 3.6 | 5.3 | 5.2 | 4.9 | 4.9 | 4.8 | 4.3 | 3.9 | 3.4 | 3.3 |
| Netherlands | 2.9 | 5.9 | 5.0 | 5.0 | 5.8 | 7.2 | 7.4 | 6.9 | 6.0 | 4.8 | 3.8 |
| New Zealand | 6.2 | 3.8 | 6.2 | 6.0 | 6.4 | 5.8 | 5.4 | 5.4 | 5.1 | 4.7 | 4.3 |
| Norway | 3.3 | 4.4 | 3.5 | 3.2 | 3.1 | 3.4 | 3.5 | 4.3 | 4.7 | 4.2 | 3.8 |
| Poland | 16.1 | 17.8 | 9.6 | 9.6 | 10.1 | 10.3 | 9.0 | 7.5 | 6.2 | 4.9 | 3.8 |
| Portugal | 4.0 | 7.6 | 10.8 | 12.7 | 15.5 | 16.2 | 13.9 | 12.4 | 11.1 | 8.9 | 7.0 |
| Slovak Republic | 18.8 | 16.3 | 14.4 | 13.6 | 14.0 | 14.2 | 13.2 | 11.5 | 9.7 | 8.1 | 6.5 |
| Spain | 13.9 | 9.2 | 19.9 | 21.4 | 24.8 | 26.1 | 24.4 | 22.1 | 19.6 | 17.2 | 15.3 |
| Sweden | (NA) | 7.5 | 8.6 | 7.8 | 8.0 | 8.1 | 8.0 | 7.4 | 7.0 | 6.7 | 6.3 |
| Switzerland | (NA) | (NA) | 4.8 | 4.4 | 4.5 | 4.7 | 4.8 | 4.8 | 4.9 | 4.8 | 4.7 |
| Turkey | (NA) | (NA) | 10.7 | 8.8 | 8.2 | 8.7 | 9.9 | 10.2 | 10.8 | 10.8 | 10.9 |
| United Kingdom | 5.6 | 4.7 | 7.8 | 8.0 | 7.9 | 7.5 | 6.1 | 5.3 | 4.8 | 4.3 | 4.0 |

NA Not available. [1] For OECD membership listing, see Section 30 introduction. [2] See footnote 3, Table 1396. [3] See footnote 2, Table 1380.

Source: Organisation for Economic Co-operation and Development (OECD), 2019, "Labour Force Statistics: Summary tables," OECD Employment and Labour Market Statistics (database) ©, <http://dx.doi.org/10.1787/data-00286-en>, accessed July 2019.

# Table 1390. Labor Force, Employment, and Unemployment by Country: 1990 to 2018

[Labor force and employment in thousands (125,840 represent 125,840,000)]

| Country and indicator | 1990 | 2000 | 2005 | 2010 | 2011 | 2012 | 2013 | 2014 | 2015 | 2016 | 2017 | 2018 |
|---|---|---|---|---|---|---|---|---|---|---|---|---|
| **LABOR FORCE (1,000s)** | | | | | | | | | | | | |
| **United States** | 125,840 | 142,583 | 149,321 | 153,889 | 153,616 | 154,975 | 155,389 | 155,922 | 157,130 | 159,187 | 160,319 | 162,075 |
| Australia | 8,443 | 9,495 | 10,400 | 11,626 | 11,813 | 11,976 | 12,145 | 12,275 | 12,517 | 12,691 | 12,971 | 13,283 |
| Canada | 14,048 | 15,634 | 17,054 | 18,177 | 18,350 | 18,551 | 18,776 | 18,857 | 19,011 | 19,173 | 19,384 | 19,526 |
| France | (NA) | (NA) | 26,957 | 27,925 | 27,926 | 28,294 | 28,376 | 28,367 | 28,442 | 28,596 | 28,775 | 28,767 |
| Germany | (NA) | 38,342 | 39,724 | 40,586 | 41,045 | 41,151 | 41,536 | 41,778 | 41,987 | 42,867 | 43,017 | 43,085 |
| Italy | (NA) | (NA) | 24,027 | 24,305 | 24,425 | 24,957 | 25,014 | 25,247 | 25,248 | 25,508 | 25,684 | 25,727 |
| Japan | (NA) | (NA) | (NA) | 65,526 | 65,106 | 64,731 | 64,913 | 65,154 | 65,320 | 65,856 | 66,395 | 67,477 |
| Netherlands | (NA) | (NA) | 8,269 | 8,677 | 8,674 | 8,812 | 8,886 | 8,846 | 8,884 | 8,920 | 8,994 | 9,097 |
| Sweden | (NA) | (NA) | (NA) | 4,931 | 4,999 | 5,040 | 5,093 | 5,161 | 5,204 | 5,253 | 5,355 | 5,435 |
| United Kingdom | (NA) | 28,962 | 30,224 | 31,637 | 31,883 | 32,173 | 32,435 | 32,705 | 32,983 | 33,288 | 33,452 | 33,729 |
| **EMPLOYMENT LEVEL (1,000s)** | | | | | | | | | | | | |
| **United States** | 118,793 | 136,891 | 141,730 | 139,064 | 139,869 | 142,469 | 143,929 | 146,305 | 148,834 | 151,436 | 153,337 | 155,761 |
| Australia | 7,856 | 8,899 | 9,877 | 11,021 | 11,213 | 11,350 | 11,457 | 11,531 | 11,760 | 11,967 | 12,247 | 12,580 |
| Canada | 12,961 | 14,683 | 16,035 | 16,889 | 17,153 | 17,371 | 17,630 | 17,741 | 17,889 | 18,026 | 18,357 | 18,588 |
| France | (NA) | (NA) | 24,636 | 25,421 | 25,436 | 25,617 | 25,537 | 25,528 | 25,560 | 25,789 | 26,146 | 26,227 |
| Germany | (NA) | 35,338 | 35,328 | 37,757 | 38,644 | 38,926 | 39,355 | 39,688 | 40,038 | 41,092 | 41,397 | 41,615 |
| Italy | (NA) | (NA) | 22,157 | 22,256 | 22,351 | 22,262 | 21,948 | 22,031 | 22,210 | 22,502 | 22,763 | 22,964 |
| Japan | (NA) | (NA) | (NA) | 62,431 | 62,372 | 62,245 | 62,715 | 63,170 | 63,463 | 64,120 | 64,782 | 66,088 |
| Netherlands | (NA) | (NA) | 7,779 | 8,241 | 8,241 | 8,296 | 8,239 | 8,186 | 8,270 | 8,381 | 8,556 | 8,747 |
| Sweden | (NA) | (NA) | (NA) | 4,511 | 4,614 | 4,643 | 4,688 | 4,756 | 4,823 | 4,894 | 5,003 | 5,096 |
| United Kingdom | (NA) | 27,375 | 28,760 | 29,140 | 29,289 | 29,501 | 29,961 | 30,679 | 31,202 | 31,655 | 31,976 | 32,349 |
| **UNEMPLOYMENT LEVEL (1,000s)** | | | | | | | | | | | | |
| **United States** | 7,047 | 5,692 | 7,591 | 14,825 | 13,747 | 12,506 | 11,460 | 9,617 | 8,296 | 7,751 | 6,982 | 6,314 |
| Australia | 587 | 596 | 523 | 605 | 600 | 626 | 688 | 744 | 757 | 724 | 724 | 703 |
| Canada | 1,087 | 951 | 1,019 | 1,288 | 1,197 | 1,180 | 1,146 | 1,116 | 1,122 | 1,147 | 1,027 | 938 |
| France | 1,890 | 2,136 | 2,321 | 2,504 | 2,490 | 2,677 | 2,839 | 2,839 | 2,882 | 2,807 | 2,629 | 2,540 |
| Germany | (NA) | 3,004 | 4,396 | 2,829 | 2,401 | 2,225 | 2,181 | 2,090 | 1,949 | 1,775 | 1,620 | 1,470 |
| Italy | (NA) | (NA) | 1,870 | 2,049 | 2,074 | 2,695 | 3,066 | 3,216 | 3,038 | 3,006 | 2,921 | 2,763 |
| Japan | 1,282 | 2,916 | 2,479 | 3,095 | 2,734 | 2,486 | 2,198 | 1,984 | 1,857 | 1,736 | 1,613 | 1,389 |
| Netherlands | (NA) | (NA) | 490 | 436 | 433 | 516 | 647 | 660 | 614 | 539 | 438 | 350 |
| Sweden | (NA) | (NA) | (NA) | 420 | 385 | 397 | 405 | 405 | 381 | 359 | 352 | 339 |
| United Kingdom | (NA) | 1,587 | 1,464 | 2,497 | 2,594 | 2,572 | 2,474 | 2,026 | 1,781 | 1,633 | 1,476 | 1,380 |
| **UNEMPLOYMENT RATE (percent)** | | | | | | | | | | | | |
| **United States** | 5.6 | 4.0 | 5.1 | 9.6 | 8.9 | 8.1 | 7.4 | 6.2 | 5.3 | 4.9 | 4.4 | 3.9 |
| Australia | 6.9 | 6.3 | 5.0 | 5.2 | 5.1 | 5.2 | 5.7 | 6.1 | 6.1 | 5.7 | 5.6 | 5.3 |
| Canada | 7.7 | 6.1 | 6.0 | 7.1 | 6.5 | 6.4 | 6.1 | 5.9 | 5.9 | 6.0 | 5.3 | 4.8 |
| France | (NA) | (NA) | 8.6 | 9.0 | 8.9 | 9.5 | 10.0 | 10.0 | 10.1 | 9.8 | 9.1 | 8.8 |
| Germany | (NA) | 7.8 | 11.1 | 7.0 | 5.8 | 5.4 | 5.3 | 5.0 | 4.6 | 4.1 | 3.8 | 3.4 |
| Italy | (NA) | (NA) | 7.8 | 8.4 | 8.5 | 10.8 | 12.3 | 12.7 | 12.0 | 11.8 | 11.4 | 10.7 |
| Japan | (NA) | (NA) | (NA) | 4.7 | 4.2 | 3.8 | 3.4 | 3.0 | 2.8 | 2.6 | 2.4 | 2.1 |
| Netherlands | (NA) | (NA) | 5.9 | 5.0 | 5.0 | 5.9 | 7.3 | 7.5 | 6.9 | 6.0 | 4.9 | 3.8 |
| Sweden | (NA) | (NA) | (NA) | 8.5 | 7.7 | 7.9 | 8.0 | 7.8 | 7.3 | 6.8 | 6.6 | 6.2 |
| United Kingdom | (NA) | 5.5 | 4.8 | 7.9 | 8.1 | 8.0 | 7.6 | 6.2 | 5.4 | 4.9 | 4.4 | 4.1 |

NA Not available.

Source: The Conference Board, Inc., *Business Cycle Indicators*, 2019. Reproduced with permission from The Conference Board, Inc. © The Conference Board 2019. For more information see <https://www.conference-board.org/data/bci.cfm>.

## Table 1391. Youth Educational Enrollment and Employment Status by Country: 2008 and 2018

[Percent of total youth population for selected age groups]

| Country | 2008 15 to 29 year olds — In education, total | 2008 15 to 29 year olds — Not in education, Employed | 2008 15 to 29 year olds — Not in education, Not employed | 2008 20 to 24 year olds — In education, total | 2008 20 to 24 year olds — Not in education, Employed | 2008 20 to 24 year olds — Not in education, Not employed | 2018 15 to 29 year olds — In education, total | 2018 15 to 29 year olds — Not in education, Employed | 2018 15 to 29 year olds — Not in education, Not employed | 2018 20 to 24 year olds — In education, total | 2018 20 to 24 year olds — Not in education, Employed | 2018 20 to 24 year olds — Not in education, Not employed |
|---|---|---|---|---|---|---|---|---|---|---|---|---|
| OECD average.... | 45.6 | 41.1 | 13.4 | 41.5 | 43.2 | 15.3 | 46.9 | 39.9 | 13.2 | 44.9 | 39.8 | 15.3 |
| United States..... | 45.0 | 40.2 | 14.7 | 36.9 | 45.9 | 17.2 | 44.1 | 43.2 | 12.7 | 38.5 | 46.7 | 14.8 |
| Australia..... | 44.4 | 45.2 | 10.4 | 39.3 | 50.0 | 10.7 | 47.4 | 41.7 | 10.8 | 46.4 | 41.7 | 11.9 |
| Canada....... | 43.6 | 44.5 | 11.9 | 38.6 | 48.1 | 13.3 | 43.2 | 44.8 | 11.9 | 42.8 | 43.8 | 13.4 |
| Denmark..... | 54.3 | 38.8 | 6.9 | 51.3 | 40.6 | 8.2 | 56.5 | 32.7 | 10.8 | 56.8 | 31.3 | 11.9 |
| Finland....... | 56.2 | 34.0 | 9.9 | 50.5 | 37.5 | 12.0 | 53.6 | 34.5 | 11.9 | 49.8 | 36.0 | 14.2 |
| France........ | 45.8 | 40.2 | 14.0 | 42.2 | 41.2 | 16.6 | 47.8 | 36.1 | 16.1 | 42.2 | 37.5 | 20.3 |
| Germany..... | 52.3 | 36.1 | 11.6 | 46.7 | 39.3 | 14.0 | 53.1 | 37.7 | 9.2 | 54.7 | 35.0 | 10.4 |
| Greece....... | 44.7 | 39.3 | 16.0 | 49.2 | 34.1 | 16.7 | 53.2 | 25.3 | 21.5 | 57.8 | 19.4 | 22.9 |
| Hungary...... | 47.2 | 36.5 | 16.3 | 48.4 | 33.2 | 18.4 | 42.1 | 44.4 | 13.5 | 39.6 | 45.0 | 15.4 |
| Iceland....... | 48.1 | 46.4 | 5.6 | 48.3 | 46.5 | 5.2 | 47.1 | 46.9 | 6.1 | 44.6 | 49.0 | 6.5 |
| Ireland........ | 36.1 | 51.1 | 12.8 | 30.2 | 55.3 | 14.6 | 50.8 | 37.5 | 11.7 | 45.9 | 40.5 | 13.6 |
| Israel......... | 42.1 | 30.3 | 27.5 | 28.9 | 33.6 | 37.5 | 43.3 | 43.4 | 13.4 | 27.5 | 55.4 | 17.0 |
| Italy......... | 45.3 | 35.5 | 19.2 | 42.6 | 35.4 | 22.0 | 48.1 | 28.1 | 23.9 | 44.4 | 27.2 | 28.4 |
| Lithuania..... | 56.0 | 32.6 | 11.4 | 51.4 | 32.7 | 15.9 | 49.6 | 39.9 | 10.5 | 51.4 | 34.0 | 14.6 |
| Mexico....... | 33.3 | 43.2 | 23.4 | 24.8 | 49.3 | 25.9 | 37.8 | 41.4 | 20.9 | 30.6 | 46.3 | 23.2 |
| Netherlands.. | 54.3 | 40.6 | 5.1 | 52.1 | 42.3 | 5.6 | 56.0 | 37.1 | 7.0 | 58.3 | 34.0 | 7.7 |
| Norway....... | 44.1 | 49.2 | 6.7 | 39.3 | 53.6 | 7.0 | 46.6 | 44.7 | 8.7 | 46.0 | 43.8 | 10.3 |
| Poland........ | 52.5 | 33.8 | 13.7 | 56.8 | 27.6 | 15.6 | 43.2 | 44.1 | 12.7 | 43.3 | 42.2 | 14.5 |
| Portugal...... | 40.1 | 47.6 | 12.2 | 36.5 | 50.0 | 13.5 | 49.2 | 39.2 | 11.6 | 43.7 | 39.6 | 16.8 |
| Slovenia...... | 57.1 | 34.5 | 8.5 | 60.6 | 29.2 | 10.3 | 54.7 | 35.7 | 9.7 | 58.5 | 29.4 | 12.0 |
| Spain........ | 35.6 | 47.7 | 16.7 | 34.4 | 46.5 | 19.0 | 51.1 | 29.8 | 19.1 | 51.8 | 26.2 | 22.0 |
| Sweden...... | 51.3 | 39.9 | 8.7 | 39.5 | 47.5 | 12.9 | 49.2 | 42.0 | 8.9 | 45.9 | 44.1 | 10.0 |
| Switzerland... | 46.0 | 44.5 | 9.6 | 42.7 | 48.2 | 9.1 | 48.4 | 43.6 | 8.1 | 45.4 | 44.6 | 10.0 |
| Turkey........ | 23.4 | 34.6 | 42.0 | 20.0 | 33.9 | 46.1 | 42.4 | 31.1 | 26.5 | 34.7 | 34.1 | 31.2 |
| United Kingdom.... | 38.2 | 47.1 | 14.8 | 28.3 | 53.4 | 18.3 | 36.1 | 51.3 | 12.6 | 34.3 | 51.5 | 14.2 |

Source: Organisation for Economic Co-operation and Development (OECD), 2019, "Indicator A2: Transition from education to work: Where are today's youth," Education at a Glance 2019: OECD Indicators, OECD Publishing ©, <https://doi.org/10.1787/0a164991-en>, accessed September 2019.

## Table 1392. Educational Performance and Attainment by Country: 2015 and 2018

| Country | 2015 Student mean scores in reading, science, and mathematics proficiency [1] — Reading scale | 2015 — Mathematics scale | 2015 — Science scale | 2018 Educational attainment of adult population 25 to 64 years old (percent) — Below upper secondary | 2018 — Upper secondary and vocational | 2018 — Tertiary [2] |
|---|---|---|---|---|---|---|
| United States................... | 496.9 | 469.6 | 496.2 | 9.2 | 43.4 | 47.4 |
| Australia......................... | 502.9 | 493.9 | 510.0 | 18.1 | 36.2 | 45.7 |
| Austria.......................... | 484.9 | 496.7 | 495.0 | 14.7 | 52.6 | 32.7 |
| Belgium.......................... | 498.5 | 507.0 | 502.0 | 21.8 | 37.6 | 40.6 |
| Canada.......................... | 526.7 | 515.6 | 527.7 | 8.4 | 33.7 | 57.9 |
| Chile............................. | 458.6 | 422.7 | 447.0 | [4] 32.6 | [4] 42.3 | [4] 25.2 |
| Czechia.......................... | 487.3 | 492.3 | 492.8 | 6.1 | 69.6 | 24.3 |
| Denmark......................... | 499.8 | 511.1 | 501.9 | 19.1 | 42.9 | 38.1 |
| France........................... | 499.3 | 492.9 | 495.0 | 20.6 | 42.5 | 36.9 |
| Germany......................... | 509.1 | 506.0 | 509.1 | 13.3 | 57.6 | 29.1 |
| Greece........................... | 467.0 | 453.6 | 454.8 | 26.6 | 41.6 | 31.7 |
| Ireland........................... | 520.8 | 503.7 | 502.6 | 16.8 | 36.2 | 46.9 |
| Israel [3]......................... | 479.0 | 469.7 | 466.6 | [4] 12.6 | [4] 36.5 | [4] 50.9 |
| Italy.............................. | 484.8 | 489.7 | 480.5 | 38.3 | 42.4 | 19.3 |
| Japan............................ | 516.0 | 532.4 | 538.4 | (NA) | (NA) | [5] 51.9 |
| Korea, South..................... | 517.4 | 524.1 | 515.8 | 11.8 | 39.2 | 49.0 |
| Mexico........................... | 423.3 | 408.0 | 415.7 | 60.9 | 21.2 | 18.0 |
| Netherlands...................... | 503.0 | 512.3 | 508.6 | 21.0 | 40.7 | 38.3 |
| New Zealand..................... | 509.3 | 495.2 | 513.3 | 19.5 | 41.2 | 39.3 |
| Norway........................... | 513.2 | 501.7 | 498.5 | 17.5 | 38.9 | 43.6 |
| Poland........................... | 505.7 | 504.5 | 501.4 | 7.6 | 61.5 | 30.9 |
| Portugal.......................... | 498.1 | 491.6 | 501.1 | 50.2 | 24.8 | 25.0 |
| Spain............................ | 495.6 | 485.8 | 492.8 | 39.9 | 22.9 | 37.3 |
| Sweden.......................... | 500.2 | 493.9 | 493.4 | 16.8 | 39.9 | 43.3 |
| Switzerland....................... | 492.2 | 521.3 | 505.5 | 11.6 | 44.7 | 43.7 |
| Turkey........................... | 428.3 | 420.5 | 425.5 | 59.8 | 19.5 | 20.8 |
| United Kingdom.................. | 498.0 | 492.5 | 509.2 | 20.7 | 33.5 | 45.8 |

NA Not available. [1] Proficiency scores are based on the Program for International Student Assessment (PISA), an international standardized test which takes place in three-year cycles. PISA tests are administered to a nationally representative sample of fifteen-year-old students in each country. [2] Tertiary education entails completion of an advanced course of study or research program leading to an associate's, bachelor's, master's, or doctorate degree, usually 2 years or longer in duration. [3] See footnote 2, Table 1380. [4] 2017 data. [5] Includes data from another category.

Source: Organisation for Economic Co-operation and Development (OECD), 2019, "Education at a glance: Educational Attainment and Labour-force Status," OECD Education Statistics (database) ©, <http://dx.doi.org/10.1787/889e8641-en>; and "Annex B1. Results (tables)" in PISA 2015 Results (Volume 1), OECD Publishing ©, <http://dx.doi.org/10.1787/9789264266490-en>; accessed September 2019.

# Table 1393. World Supply and Utilization of Major Crops and Livestock: 2010 to 2019

[In millions of units (225.8 represents 225,800,000). For major crops, data are for marketing or trade year ending in year shown, unless otherwise indicated. For livestock and dairy, data are for calendar year]

| Commodity | 2010 | 2013 | 2014 | 2015 | 2016 | 2017 | 2018 | 2019 [1] |
|---|---|---|---|---|---|---|---|---|
| **Wheat:** | | | | | | | | |
| Area harvested (hectares) | 225.8 | 216.2 | 220.0 | 221.4 | 224.0 | 222.3 | 218.3 | 215.4 |
| Production (metric tons) | 688.2 | 660.4 | 716.6 | 730.4 | 738.2 | 756.3 | 761.9 | 731.7 |
| Exports (metric tons) | 135.3 | 147.2 | 162.5 | 162.0 | 172.0 | 182.3 | 183.0 | 176.5 |
| Consumption (metric tons) | 651.0 | 688.1 | 691.2 | 700.5 | 713.1 | 734.8 | 741.1 | 734.6 |
| Ending stocks (metric tons) | 204.1 | 179.6 | 197.7 | 222.8 | 244.8 | 262.1 | 280.9 | 276.6 |
| **Corn:** | | | | | | | | |
| Area harvested (hectares) | 158.8 | 183.7 | 187.9 | 188.9 | 187.8 | 194.6 | 192.0 | 191.1 |
| Production (metric tons) | 834.1 | 898.1 | 1,026.2 | 1,056.9 | 1,014.2 | 1,125.2 | 1,078.0 | 1,120.5 |
| Exports (metric tons) | 92.7 | 100.7 | 130.8 | 128.4 | 145.0 | 142.2 | 152.3 | 167.5 |
| Consumption (metric tons) | 832.3 | 880.9 | 949.8 | 974.7 | 1,001.2 | 1,060.6 | 1,091.3 | 1,125.7 |
| Ending stocks (metric tons) | 131.7 | 144.7 | 214.4 | 279.3 | 311.7 | 351.5 | 339.3 | 325.4 |
| **Rice, milled:** | | | | | | | | |
| Area harvested (hectares) | 155.9 | 159.9 | 162.2 | 162.1 | 160.3 | 162.8 | 162.1 | 163.6 |
| Production (metric tons) | 441.0 | 475.8 | 481.2 | 482.4 | 476.7 | 491.1 | 494.9 | 499.1 |
| Exports (metric tons) | 31.8 | 39.5 | 44.2 | 42.7 | 40.2 | 48.1 | 47.5 | 47.0 |
| Consumption (metric tons) | 435.5 | 462.1 | 472.2 | 472.8 | 467.2 | 477.3 | 482.1 | 488.6 |
| Ending stocks (metric tons) | 96.6 | 122.9 | 127.6 | 135.0 | 142.3 | 149.6 | 162.1 | 170.2 |
| **Coarse grains:** [2] | | | | | | | | |
| Area harvested (hectares) | 307.8 | 320.5 | 331.0 | 333.2 | 326.1 | 338.3 | 329.0 | 327.3 |
| Production (metric tons) | 1,124.3 | 1,159.0 | 1,313.5 | 1,346.2 | 1,303.7 | 1,418.0 | 1,360.1 | 1,394.7 |
| Exports (metric tons) | 118.8 | 132.3 | 165.2 | 173.9 | 185.0 | 182.1 | 188.7 | 200.4 |
| Consumption (metric tons) | 1,124.7 | 1,139.6 | 1,237.9 | 1,281.2 | 1,270.4 | 1,382.1 | 1,376.9 | 1,411.9 |
| Ending stocks (metric tons) | 183.3 | 175.9 | 251.5 | 316.5 | 349.8 | 385.7 | 368.8 | 351.7 |
| **Oilseeds:** | | | | | | | | |
| Area harvested (hectares) | 235.6 | 256.5 | 260.7 | 267.2 | 264.9 | 267.8 | 280.5 | 282.0 |
| Production (metric tons) | 447.0 | 474.8 | 503.7 | 538.4 | 524.1 | 575.0 | 580.7 | 601.4 |
| Exports (metric tons) | 107.6 | 118.1 | 133.8 | 147.2 | 153.4 | 170.6 | 176.2 | 172.8 |
| Consumption (metric tons) | 425.4 | 471.1 | 494.4 | 520.5 | 526.1 | 554.6 | 572.7 | 584.3 |
| Ending stocks (metric tons) | 77.6 | 72.4 | 81.5 | 95.8 | 93.9 | 109.9 | 116.0 | 130.4 |
| **Coffee, green:** | | | | | | | | |
| Production (60 kg bags) | 129.8 | 158.0 | 160.1 | 153.8 | 152.9 | 161.7 | 158.7 | 174.5 |
| Exports (60 kg bags) | 106.3 | 122.8 | 128.9 | 123.6 | 133.4 | 133.5 | 131.1 | 137.9 |
| Consumption (60 kg bags) | 138.3 | 142.1 | 142.4 | 145.6 | 152.7 | 153.8 | 159.5 | 163.9 |
| Ending stocks (60 kg bags) | 28.8 | 35.4 | 41.2 | 43.1 | 34.4 | 35.3 | 31.0 | 36.3 |
| **Sugar, centrifugal:** | | | | | | | | |
| Production (metric tons) | 153.2 | 177.8 | 176.0 | 177.6 | 164.9 | 174.0 | 191.6 | 178.0 |
| Exports (metric tons) | 48.3 | 55.7 | 58.0 | 55.0 | 54.0 | 58.7 | 64.5 | 56.4 |
| Consumption (metric tons) | 154.1 | 165.3 | 165.7 | 168.0 | 169.5 | 170.8 | 173.6 | 174.0 |
| Ending stocks (metric tons) | 28.0 | 42.3 | 44.8 | 48.8 | 44.1 | 42.2 | 52.2 | 50.9 |
| **Cotton:** | | | | | | | | |
| Area harvested (hectares) | 30.2 | 34.1 | 32.6 | 33.9 | 30.8 | 29.8 | 33.6 | 33.2 |
| Production (480 lb. bales) | 103.1 | 123.9 | 120.4 | 119.2 | 96.2 | 106.7 | 123.8 | 118.9 |
| Exports (480 lb. bales) | 35.8 | 46.4 | 41.0 | 35.9 | 34.7 | 37.9 | 41.0 | 42.1 |
| Consumption (480 lb. bales) | 119.5 | 107.9 | 110.0 | 112.5 | 113.5 | 116.4 | 123.2 | 122.6 |
| Ending stocks (480 lb. bales) | 46.2 | 89.3 | 99.9 | 106.7 | 90.2 | 80.3 | 80.9 | 77.5 |
| **Beef:** | | | | | | | | |
| Beef cow beginning stocks (head) | 204.6 | 208.2 | 209.9 | 202.4 | 203.6 | 207.1 | 208.2 | 209.7 |
| Production (metric tons) [3] | 59.0 | 59.9 | 60.1 | 59.2 | 59.7 | 60.7 | 62.2 | 62.6 |
| Exports (metric tons) [3] | 7.8 | 9.3 | 10.0 | 9.6 | 9.4 | 10.0 | 10.6 | 10.8 |
| Consumption (metric tons) [3] | 58.0 | 58.2 | 58.0 | 57.3 | 57.9 | 58.7 | 60.3 | 60.7 |
| Ending stocks (metric tons) [3] | 0.6 | 0.7 | 0.6 | 0.6 | 0.6 | 0.5 | 0.5 | 0.5 |
| **Pork:** | | | | | | | | |
| Sow beginning stocks (head) | 79.3 | 79.5 | 78.9 | 76.3 | 74.5 | 74.1 | 73.0 | 67.6 |
| Production (metric tons) [3] | 103.5 | 109.9 | 112.0 | 112.0 | 111.4 | 112.1 | 113.1 | 108.5 |
| Exports (metric tons) [3] | 6.0 | 7.0 | 7.0 | 7.2 | 8.4 | 8.3 | 8.4 | 9.1 |
| Consumption (metric tons) [3] | 103.4 | 109.5 | 111.3 | 111.5 | 111.1 | 111.6 | 112.5 | 108.2 |
| Ending stocks (metric tons) [3] | 0.6 | 0.6 | 0.7 | 0.7 | 0.6 | 0.7 | 0.7 | 0.7 |
| **Chicken (meat):** [4] | | | | | | | | |
| Beginning stocks (metric tons) | 0.5 | 0.7 | 0.6 | 0.6 | 0.7 | 0.7 | 0.8 | 0.7 |
| Production (metric tons) | 78.2 | 85.1 | 87.9 | 91.4 | 92.3 | 93.6 | 95.5 | 98.4 |
| Exports (metric tons) | 8.9 | 10.3 | 10.5 | 10.3 | 10.7 | 11.0 | 11.2 | 11.6 |
| Consumption (metric tons) | 76.7 | 83.3 | 86.0 | 89.7 | 90.9 | 91.9 | 93.6 | 96.5 |
| Ending stocks (metric tons) | 0.5 | 0.6 | 0.6 | 0.7 | 0.7 | 0.8 | 0.7 | 0.8 |
| **Dairy:** | | | | | | | | |
| Dairy cows beginning stocks (head) | 233.6 | 242.4 | 247.2 | 247.0 | 247.8 | 249.0 | 251.8 | 253.3 |
| Milk production (metric tons) [5] | 513.8 | 546.0 | 565.1 | 577.5 | 584.3 | 596.0 | 605.8 | 616.9 |
| Milk exports (metric tons) [5] | 0.7 | 1.1 | 1.4 | 1.6 | 1.9 | 1.8 | 1.7 | 1.8 |
| Milk consumption (metric tons) [5] | 513.5 | 545.6 | 564.7 | 576.9 | 583.7 | 595.5 | 605.3 | 616.4 |

[1] Preliminary. [2] Coarse grains include corn, barley, sorghum, oats, rye, millet, and mixed grains but exclude trade in barley malt, millet, and mixed grains. [3] Carcass weight equivalent (CWE). [4] Weight in ready-to-eat equivalent meat. [5] Includes milk from cows as well as other bovines.

Source: U.S. Department of Agriculture, Foreign Agricultural Service, "Production, Supply and Distribution Online," <http://www.fas.usda.gov/psdonline/>, accessed June 2019.

## Table 1394. World Crop Production Summary: 2017 to 2019

[In millions of metric tons (761.9 represents 761,900,000). Data are for marketing or trade year. Data for 2018-2019 are preliminary]

| Country | Wheat | | Coarse grains [1] | | Rice (milled) | | Oilseeds [2] | | Cotton | |
|---|---|---|---|---|---|---|---|---|---|---|
| | 2017–2018 | 2018–2019 | 2017–2018 | 2018–2019 | 2017–2018 | 2018–2019 | 2017–2018 | 2018–2019 | 2017–2018 | 2018–2019 |
| **World** | **761.9** | **731.7** | **1,360.1** | **1,394.7** | **494.9** | **499.1** | **580.7** | **601.4** | **123.8** | **118.9** |
| Total foreign | 714.5 | 680.4 | 975.7 | 1,014.8 | 489.2 | 492.0 | 449.2 | 467.5 | 102.9 | 100.5 |
| **United States** | **47.4** | **51.3** | **384.4** | **379.9** | **5.7** | **7.1** | **131.5** | **133.9** | **20.9** | **18.4** |
| Canada | 30.0 | 31.8 | 26.2 | 26.2 | – | – | 29.1 | 28.5 | – | – |
| Mexico | 3.5 | 3.0 | 33.2 | 32.5 | 0.2 | 0.2 | 1.3 | 1.2 | 1.6 | 1.7 |
| Russia | 85.2 | 71.7 | 41.7 | 35.0 | 0.6 | 0.7 | 15.5 | 18.7 | – | – |
| Ukraine | 27.0 | 25.1 | 34.1 | 44.5 | – | – | 19.8 | 22.3 | – | – |
| European Union | (3) | (3) | (3) | (3) | (3) | (3) | (3) | (3) | 1.5 | 1.7 |
| China | 134.3 | 131.4 | 266.8 | 265.4 | 148.9 | 148.5 | 59.5 | 59.9 | 27.5 | 27.8 |
| India | 98.5 | 99.9 | 46.9 | 43.4 | 112.8 | 115.6 | 35.4 | 36.3 | 29.0 | 26.0 |
| Indonesia | – | – | 11.9 | 12.6 | 37.0 | 37.1 | 13.8 | 14.1 | – | – |
| Pakistan | 26.6 | 25.1 | 6.2 | 6.6 | 7.5 | 7.4 | 4.0 | 3.8 | 8.2 | 7.7 |
| Thailand | – | – | 5.1 | 5.4 | 20.6 | 20.7 | 1.0 | 1.0 | – | – |
| Argentina | 18.5 | 19.5 | 39.3 | 56.6 | 0.9 | 0.8 | 42.5 | 61.5 | 0.8 | 1.1 |
| Brazil | 4.3 | 5.4 | 85.1 | 104.3 | 8.2 | 7.3 | 125.8 | 121.9 | 9.2 | 12.8 |
| Australia | 20.9 | 17.3 | 12.2 | 10.9 | 0.5 | 0.1 | 5.4 | 3.0 | 4.8 | 2.4 |
| South Africa | 1.5 | 1.9 | 13.6 | 12.1 | – | – | 2.6 | 2.0 | 0.2 | 0.2 |
| Turkey | 21.0 | 19.0 | 12.3 | 13.7 | 0.5 | 0.6 | 3.2 | 3.5 | 4.0 | 3.7 |
| All others | 243.2 | 229.4 | 341.1 | 345.6 | 151.6 | 152.9 | 90.5 | 89.9 | 16.1 | 15.4 |

– Represents zero. [1] Includes corn, barley, sorghum, oats, rye, millet, and mixed grains. [2] Includes soybean, cottonseed, peanut (in shell), sunflower seed, and rapeseed for individual countries. Copra and palm kernel are added to world totals. [3] Indicates no reported or insignificant production.

Source: U.S. Department of Agriculture, Foreign Agricultural Service, *World Agricultural Production*, June 2019. See also <http://www.fas.usda.gov/data/world-agricultural-production>.

## Table 1395. Meat Production by Type and Country: 2017 and 2018

[In thousands of metric tons (60,651 represents 60,651,000). Carcass weight equivalent basis for beef, veal, and pork. Chicken weight based on ready-to-cook equivalent meat]

| Country | Beef and veal [1] | | Country | Pork | | Country | Chicken [2] | |
|---|---|---|---|---|---|---|---|---|
| | 2017 | 2018 | | 2017 | 2018 | | 2017 | 2018 |
| **World** | **60,651** | **62,193** | **World** | **112,114** | **113,081** | **World** | **93,622** | **95,500** |
| **United States** | **11,943** | **12,253** | China | 54,518 | 54,040 | **United States** | **18,938** | **19,361** |
| Brazil | 9,550 | 9,900 | EU-28 [3] | 23,660 | 24,300 | Brazil | 13,612 | 13,355 |
| EU-28 [3] | 7,869 | 8,030 | **United States** | **11,611** | **11,942** | EU-28 [3] | 11,912 | 12,200 |
| China | 6,346 | 6,440 | Brazil | 3,725 | 3,763 | China | 11,600 | 11,700 |
| India | 4,250 | 4,300 | Russia | 2,990 | 3,155 | Russia | 4,617 | 4,872 |
| Argentina | 2,840 | 3,050 | Vietnam | 2,741 | 2,801 | India | 4,640 | 4,855 |
| Australia | 2,149 | 2,306 | Canada | 1,959 | 1,930 | Mexico | 3,400 | 3,485 |
| Mexico | 1,925 | 1,980 | Philippines | 1,563 | 1,602 | Thailand | 2,990 | 3,170 |
| Pakistan | 1,780 | 1,800 | Korea, South | 1,280 | 1,329 | Turkey | 2,188 | 2,225 |
| Turkey | 1,399 | 1,400 | Mexico | 1,267 | 1,321 | Argentina | 2,150 | 2,110 |
| Others | 10,600 | 10,734 | Others | 6,800 | 6,898 | Others | 17,575 | 18,167 |

[1] May include meat of other bovines. [2] Excludes chicken paws. [3] See footnote 3, Table 1396.

Source: U.S. Department of Agriculture, Foreign Agricultural Service, "Production, Supply and Distribution Online," <http://apps.fas.usda.gov/psdonline>, accessed June 2019.

## Table 1396. Meat Consumption by Type and Country: 2017 and 2018

[In thousands of metric tons (58,679 represents 58,679,000). Carcass weight equivalent basis for beef, veal, and pork. Chicken weight based on ready-to-cook equivalent meat]

| Country | Beef and veal [1] | | Country | Pork | | Country | Chicken [2] | |
|---|---|---|---|---|---|---|---|---|
| | 2017 | 2018 | | 2017 | 2018 | | 2017 | 2018 |
| **World** | **58,679** | **60,258** | **World** | **111,642** | **112,472** | **World** | **91,853** | **93,629** |
| **United States** | **12,052** | **12,179** | China | 55,930 | 55,398 | **United States** | **15,823** | **16,185** |
| EU-28 [3] | 7,838 | 8,049 | EU-28 [3] | 20,816 | 21,380 | China | 11,475 | 11,595 |
| China | 7,313 | 7,910 | **United States** | **9,542** | **9,749** | EU-28 [3] | 11,279 | 11,474 |
| Brazil | 7,750 | 7,865 | Russia | 3,327 | 3,197 | Brazil | 9,768 | 9,671 |
| India | 2,401 | 2,744 | Brazil | 2,941 | 3,035 | Russia | 4,718 | 4,947 |
| Argentina | 2,547 | 2,544 | Vietnam | 2,703 | 2,786 | India | 4,638 | 4,852 |
| Mexico | 1,841 | 1,872 | Japan | 2,731 | 2,775 | Mexico | 4,198 | 4,301 |
| Russia | 1,800 | 1,805 | Mexico | 2,180 | 2,331 | Japan | 2,688 | 2,761 |
| Pakistan | 1,722 | 1,741 | Korea, South | 1,926 | 2,001 | Thailand | 2,226 | 2,345 |
| Turkey | 1,424 | 1,496 | Philippines | 1,803 | 1,887 | Argentina | 1,978 | 1,997 |
| Others | 11,991 | 12,053 | Others | 7,743 | 7,933 | Others | 23,062 | 23,501 |

[1] May include meat of other bovines. [2] Excludes chicken paws. [3] European Union-28: Austria, Belgium, Bulgaria, Croatia, Cyprus, Czechia, Denmark, Estonia, Finland, France, Germany, Greece, Hungary, Ireland, Italy, Latvia, Lithuania, Luxembourg, Malta, Netherlands, Poland, Portugal, Romania, Slovakia, Slovenia, Spain, Sweden, and United Kingdom.

Source: U.S. Department of Agriculture, Foreign Agricultural Service, "Production, Supply and Distribution Online," <http://apps.fas.usda.gov/psdonline>, accessed June 2019.

## Table 1397. Wheat, Rice, and Corn—Exports and Imports of Leading Countries: 2010 to 2019

[In thousands of metric tons (18,556 represents 18,556,000). Wheat data represent trade years ending in June of year shown; corn data represent trade years ending in September of year shown; rice data represent trade years ending in December of year shown. Countries listed are the ten leading exporters or importers in 2019]

| Leading country | Exports | | | Leading country | Imports | | |
|---|---|---|---|---|---|---|---|
| | 2010 | 2018 | 2019 (P) | | 2010 | 2018 | 2019 (P) |
| **WHEAT** | | | | **WHEAT** | | | |
| Russia | 18,556 | 41,419 | 36,000 | Egypt | 10,500 | 12,407 | 12,500 |
| **United States** | **24,143** | **23,067** | **26,800** | Indonesia | 5,364 | 10,516 | 11,200 |
| Canada | 18,992 | 21,989 | 24,200 | Brazil | 6,691 | 6,702 | 7,700 |
| European Union [1] | 22,293 | 23,289 | 24,000 | Algeria | 5,167 | 8,172 | 7,000 |
| Ukraine | 9,337 | 17,775 | 16,200 | Philippines | 3,197 | 5,987 | 7,000 |
| Argentina | 5,255 | 13,945 | 12,500 | Japan | 5,502 | 5,876 | 5,800 |
| Australia | 13,764 | 15,512 | 9,800 | Turkey | 3,218 | 5,916 | 5,800 |
| Kazakhstan | 7,871 | 8,600 | 8,500 | European Union [1] | 5,358 | 5,824 | 5,500 |
| Turkey | 4,363 | 6,218 | 6,400 | Mexico | 3,196 | 5,245 | 5,100 |
| China | 892 | 1,000 | 1,200 | Bangladesh | 3,353 | 6,150 | 5,000 |
| **RICE** | | | | **RICE** | | | |
| India | 2,228 | 11,791 | 12,000 | China | 366 | 4,500 | 3,500 |
| Thailand | 9,047 | 11,056 | 9,800 | Philippines | 2,400 | 2,500 | 3,000 |
| Vietnam | 6,734 | 6,590 | 6,500 | Nigeria | 2,000 | 2,100 | 2,200 |
| Pakistan | 4,000 | 3,913 | 4,000 | European Union [1] | 1,235 | 1,921 | 2,000 |
| **United States** | **3,868** | **2,763** | **3,000** | Cote d'Ivoire | 840 | 1,500 | 1,600 |
| Burma | 700 | 2,750 | 2,800 | Saudi Arabia | 1,069 | 1,300 | 1,350 |
| China | 619 | 2,058 | 2,800 | Iraq | 1,188 | 1,200 | 1,300 |
| Brazil | 430 | 1,245 | 800 | Senegal | 685 | 1,100 | 1,250 |
| Uruguay | 808 | 799 | 800 | Iran | 1,520 | 1,250 | 1,200 |
| Guyana | 298 | 414 | 500 | South Africa | 733 | 1,071 | 1,100 |
| **CORN** | | | | **CORN** | | | |
| **United States** | **49,696** | **63,636** | **55,000** | European Union [1] | 2,758 | 18,465 | 23,500 |
| Brazil | 8,623 | 25,142 | 33,000 | Mexico | 8,298 | 16,129 | 17,500 |
| Argentina | 16,973 | 24,200 | 30,000 | Japan | 15,971 | 15,668 | 15,500 |
| Ukraine | 5,072 | 18,036 | 29,500 | Korea, South | 8,461 | 10,018 | 10,200 |
| European Union [1] | 1,569 | 1,749 | 2,500 | Vietnam | 1,600 | 9,400 | 10,200 |
| Paraguay | 1,359 | 1,476 | 2,200 | Egypt | 5,832 | 9,464 | 9,700 |
| Canada | 186 | 1,973 | 2,000 | Iran | 4,300 | 8,900 | 9,500 |
| South Africa | 1,586 | 2,361 | 1,600 | Colombia | 3,651 | 5,201 | 5,500 |
| Burma | 300 | 1,350 | 1,400 | China | 1,296 | 3,456 | 5,000 |
| Mexico | 642 | 958 | 800 | Saudi Arabia | 1,872 | 3,983 | 5,000 |

P Preliminary. [1] See footnote 3, Table 1396.

Source: U.S. Department of Agriculture, Foreign Agricultural Service, "Production, Supply and Distribution Online," <http://www.fas.usda.gov/psdonline>, accessed June 2019.

## Table 1398. World Production of Major Mineral Commodities: 2014 to 2017

[Units are as noted. Th. represents thousand, mil. represents million, and bil. represents billion]

| Commodity | Unit | 2014 | 2015 | 2016 | 2017 | Leading producers, 2017 |
|---|---|---|---|---|---|---|
| **MINERAL FUELS** | | | | | | |
| Coal | mil. short tons | 8,981 | 8,737 | 8,150 | (NA) | China, India, United States [4] |
| Dry natural gas | bil. cubic feet | 122,340 | 124,611 | 125,740 | 130,751 | United States, Russia, Iran |
| Natural gas plant liquids | mil. barrels [1] | 3,590 | 3,695 | 3,762 | 3,871 | United States, Saudi Arabia, Canada |
| Petroleum, crude | mil. barrels [1] | 28,602 | 29,476 | 29,507 | 29,600 | Russia, Saudi Arabia, United States |
| **NONMETALLIC MINERALS** | | | | | | |
| Cement, hydraulic | mil. metric tons | 4,190 | 4,100 | 4,140 | 4,050 | China, India, United States |
| Diamond, gem and industrial | mil. carats | 125 | 127 | 134 | (NA) | Russia, Congo (Dem. Rep. of), Botswana [4] |
| Nitrogen in ammonia | mil. metric tons | 141 | 147 | 144 | 142 | China, Russia, United States |
| Phosphate rock, marketable | mil. metric tons | 237 | 263 | 255 | 269 | China, Morocco/Western Sahara, United States, |
| Potash, marketable | mil. metric tons | 41 | 41 | 39 | 41 | Canada, Russia, Belarus |
| Salt | mil. metric tons | 275 | 277 | 274 | 288 | China, United States, India |
| Sulfur | mil. metric tons | 71 | 74 | 74 | 80 | China, United States, Russia |
| **METALS** | | | | | | |
| Aluminum | mil. metric tons | 54 | 58 | 59 | 59 | China, Russia, Canada |
| Bauxite, gross weight | mil. metric tons | 258 | 299 | 270 | 309 | Australia, China, Guinea |
| Chromium (chromite), gross weight | th. metric tons | 30,500 | 31,200 | 30,400 | 35,700 | South Africa, Turkey, Kazakhstan |
| Copper, metal content [2] | th. metric tons | 18,400 | 19,100 | 20,100 | 20,000 | Chile, Peru, China |
| Gold, metal content | metric tons | 3,030 | 3,090 | 3,120 | 3,230 | China, Australia, Russia |
| Iron ore, gross weight [3] | mil. metric tons | 2,340 | 2,320 | 2,350 | 2,430 | Australia, Brazil, China |
| Lead, metal content [2] | th. metric tons | 5,440 | 4,950 | 4,710 | 4,580 | China, Australia, United States |
| Manganese ore, metal content | th. metric tons | 16,400 | 17,000 | 15,700 | 17,300 | South Africa, Australia, Gabon |
| Nickel, metal content [2] | th. metric tons | 2,170 | 2,180 | 2,040 | 2,160 | Philippines, Indonesia, New Caledonia |
| Steel, raw | mil. metric tons | 1,670 | 1,620 | 1,630 | 1,690 | China, Japan, India |
| Tin, metal content [2] | th. metric tons | 288 | 341 | 288 | 313 | China, Indonesia, Burma |
| Zinc, metal content | th. metric tons | 13,600 | 13,500 | 12,600 | 12,500 | China, Peru, Australia |

NA Not available. [1] 42-gallon barrels. [2] Mine output. [3] Includes iron ore concentrates and iron ore agglomerates. [4] Leading producers in 2016.

Source: Mineral fuels, U.S. Energy Information Administration, Open Data, "International Energy Data", <www.eia.gov/opendata/>, accessed August 2019. Nonmetallic minerals and metals, U.S. Geological Survey, *Minerals Yearbook*, annual; *Mineral Commodity Summaries*, annual; and "Historical Statistics for Mineral and Material Commodities in the United States," <https://minerals.usgs.gov/minerals/pubs/historical-statistics/>, accessed August 2019. See also <https://minerals.usgs.gov/minerals/pubs/>.

## Table 1399. Net Electricity Generation by Energy Source and Country: 2016

[23,765.8 represents 23,765,800,000,000. kWh = kilowatt hours. Ranked for top 40 countries]

| Country | Total [1] (bil. kWh) | Amount | | | | Percent distribution | | | |
|---|---|---|---|---|---|---|---|---|---|
| | | Fossil fuels [2] | Hydro-electricity | Nuclear | Non-hydro renew-ables [3] | Fossil fuels [2] | Hydro-electricity | Nuclear | Non-hydro renew-ables [3] |
| **World, total [4]**.......... | **23,765.8** | **15,367.3** | **4,000.9** | **2,468.8** | **1,967.2** | **64.7** | **16.8** | **10.4** | **8.3** |
| China.................. | 5,882.9 | 4,157.3 | 1,150.9 | 197.8 | 388.6 | 70.7 | 19.6 | 3.4 | 6.6 |
| **United States**........... | 4,095.5 | 2,654.5 | 267.8 | 805.7 | 374.2 | 64.8 | 6.5 | 19.7 | 9.1 |
| India................. | 1,386.4 | 1,127.5 | 121.3 | 35.0 | 102.6 | 81.3 | 8.7 | 2.5 | 7.4 |
| Russia................ | 1,031.3 | 661.9 | 182.8 | 184.1 | 3.5 | 64.2 | 17.7 | 17.8 | 0.3 |
| Japan................. | 989.3 | 790.0 | 78.6 | 9.3 | 114.2 | 79.8 | 7.9 | 0.9 | 11.5 |
| Canada................ | 649.6 | 124.4 | 383.3 | 95.7 | 46.4 | 19.2 | 59.0 | 14.7 | 7.1 |
| Germany............... | 612.8 | 339.7 | 20.2 | 80.1 | 174.7 | 55.4 | 3.3 | 13.1 | 28.5 |
| Brazil................ | 567.9 | 91.7 | 377.1 | 15.0 | 84.2 | 16.1 | 66.4 | 2.6 | 14.8 |
| France................ | 529.1 | 45.0 | 59.3 | 386.5 | 40.2 | 8.5 | 11.2 | 73.0 | 7.6 |
| Korea, South.......... | 526.0 | 356.3 | 2.8 | 154.3 | 13.6 | 67.7 | 0.5 | 29.3 | 2.6 |
| Saudi Arabia.......... | 324.1 | 324.1 | – | – | – | 100.0 | – | – | – |
| United Kingdom........ | 318.2 | 166.1 | 5.3 | 65.1 | 82.6 | 52.2 | 1.7 | 20.5 | 26.0 |
| Mexico................ | 302.7 | 245.1 | 29.7 | 10.3 | 17.5 | 81.0 | 9.8 | 3.4 | 5.8 |
| Italy................. | 275.3 | 166.1 | 42.0 | – | 67.9 | 60.3 | 15.2 | – | 24.7 |
| Iran.................. | 272.3 | 249.8 | 16.3 | 5.9 | 0.3 | 91.8 | 6.0 | 2.2 | 0.1 |
| Turkey................ | 261.9 | 172.4 | 66.7 | – | 22.8 | 65.8 | 25.5 | – | 8.7 |
| Spain................. | 258.6 | 100.8 | 35.8 | 56.1 | 67.3 | 39.0 | 13.8 | 21.7 | 26.0 |
| Taiwan................ | 246.1 | 203.5 | 6.5 | 30.5 | 6.1 | 82.7 | 2.6 | 12.4 | 2.5 |
| Australia............. | 243.0 | 206.0 | 15.1 | – | 22.1 | 84.8 | 6.2 | – | 9.1 |
| Indonesia............. | 235.4 | 203.8 | 19.2 | – | 12.5 | 86.6 | 8.1 | – | 5.3 |
| South Africa.......... | 234.5 | 213.1 | 0.7 | 15.2 | 7.1 | 90.9 | 0.3 | 6.5 | 3.0 |
| Egypt................. | 183.5 | 167.9 | 13.3 | – | 2.2 | 91.5 | 7.3 | – | 1.2 |
| Thailand.............. | 181.5 | 152.5 | 6.9 | – | 22.1 | 84.0 | 3.8 | – | 12.2 |
| Vietnam............... | 158.2 | 94.4 | 63.5 | – | 0.3 | 59.7 | 40.1 | – | 0.2 |
| Poland................ | 156.9 | 134.5 | 2.1 | – | 20.6 | 85.7 | 1.3 | – | 13.1 |
| Ukraine............... | 153.6 | 68.3 | 7.6 | 76.1 | 1.6 | 44.5 | 4.9 | 49.5 | 1.0 |
| Sweden................ | 152.9 | 1.9 | 61.6 | 60.6 | 28.7 | 1.3 | 40.3 | 39.7 | 18.8 |
| Malaysia.............. | 148.3 | 127.4 | 19.8 | – | 1.1 | 85.9 | 13.4 | – | 0.7 |
| Norway................ | 147.7 | 2.6 | 143.0 | – | 2.6 | 1.8 | 96.8 | – | 1.7 |
| Argentina............. | 131.9 | 92.9 | 29.4 | 7.7 | 2.3 | 70.4 | 22.3 | 5.8 | 1.7 |
| United Arab Emirates... | 121.8 | 121.5 | – | – | 0.4 | 99.7 | – | – | 0.3 |
| Pakistan.............. | 109.7 | 66.6 | 36.3 | 5.4 | 1.4 | 60.7 | 33.0 | 5.0 | 1.3 |
| Venezuela............. | 109.3 | 42.2 | 67.0 | – | 0.1 | 38.7 | 61.3 | – | 0.1 |
| Netherlands........... | 109.3 | 88.9 | 0.1 | 3.8 | 16.5 | 81.3 | 0.1 | 3.4 | 15.1 |
| Kazakhstan............ | 100.8 | 89.0 | 11.5 | – | 0.4 | 88.2 | 11.4 | – | 0.4 |
| Philippines........... | 86.6 | 64.7 | 8.0 | – | 13.9 | 74.7 | 9.3 | – | 16.0 |
| Belgium............... | 79.8 | 23.4 | 0.4 | 41.4 | 14.9 | 29.4 | 0.5 | 51.9 | 18.7 |
| Czechia............... | 77.4 | 45.5 | 2.0 | 22.7 | 7.5 | 58.8 | 2.6 | 29.4 | 9.7 |
| Chile................. | 76.1 | 42.3 | 22.8 | – | 11.0 | 55.6 | 30.0 | – | 14.4 |
| Iraq.................. | 75.5 | 72.1 | 3.3 | – | 0.1 | 95.5 | 4.4 | – | 0.1 |

– Represents or rounds to zero. [1] Electricity generated from fossil fuels, and hydroelectric, nuclear, geothermal, solar, wind, tidal, biomass, and waste energy resources. Includes negative values from hydroelectric pumped storage. [2] Electricity generated from coal, oil, and gas resources. [3] Electricity generated from geothermal, solar, wind, tidal and wave, biomass, and waste resources. [4] Includes countries not shown separately.

Source: U.S. Energy Information Administration, Open Data, "International Energy Data," <https://www.eia.gov/opendata/>, accessed April 2019.

## Table 1400. World Primary Energy Production by Region and Type: 1980 to 2016

[In quadrillion Btu (294.9 represents 294,900,000,000,000,000). Btu = British thermal unit. For Btu conversion factors, see source]

| Region and type | 1980 | 1990 | 1995 | 2000 | 2005 | 2010 | 2014 | 2015 | 2016 |
|---|---|---|---|---|---|---|---|---|---|
| **World total**........................ | **294.9** | **358.7** | **367.4** | **399.2** | **461.0** | **520.2** | **566.0** | **570.2** | **564.8** |
| REGION | | | | | | | | | |
| North America......................... | 83.0 | 91.5 | 95.8 | 98.5 | 98.5 | 102.0 | 116.9 | 117.0 | 112.8 |
| **United States** [1]................... | **67.2** | **70.7** | **71.2** | **71.3** | **69.4** | **74.9** | **87.8** | **88.2** | **84.3** |
| Central and South America............. | 12.1 | 16.9 | 21.5 | 26.2 | 28.3 | 31.3 | 33.6 | 33.7 | 33.6 |
| Europe.[2]............................ | 41.5 | 48.7 | 49.2 | 50.6 | 48.9 | 46.0 | 43.8 | 44.0 | 43.6 |
| Eurasia [2]........................... | 61.6 | 77.7 | 54.7 | 55.8 | 68.1 | 72.6 | 76.5 | 76.9 | 77.7 |
| Middle East........................... | 42.3 | 40.9 | 48.3 | 57.5 | 66.3 | 72.2 | 79.4 | 83.0 | 87.8 |
| Africa................................ | 17.4 | 21.8 | 24.2 | 27.7 | 34.5 | 37.1 | 33.8 | 33.1 | 32.2 |
| Asia and Oceania...................... | 37.0 | 61.1 | 73.7 | 83.0 | 116.5 | 159.0 | 181.9 | 182.5 | 177.2 |
| TYPE OF FUEL | | | | | | | | | |
| Petroleum [3]......................... | 133.1 | 136.2 | 141.8 | 156.4 | 169.8 | 173.1 | 182.3 | 187.5 | 188.5 |
| Dry natural gas....................... | 54.8 | 75.7 | 80.3 | 89.3 | 102.1 | 116.9 | 127.0 | 129.6 | 130.9 |
| Coal.................................. | 78.7 | 100.2 | 92.1 | 95.8 | 125.6 | 156.2 | 174.3 | 169.6 | 158.2 |
| Hydroelectric power................... | 17.9 | 22.3 | 25.3 | 26.8 | 29.1 | 33.3 | 36.7 | 35.8 | 36.9 |
| Nuclear electric power................ | 7.6 | 20.4 | 23.3 | 25.7 | 27.3 | 27.4 | 25.1 | 25.4 | 25.7 |
| Non-hydroelectric renewables [4]....... | 0.3 | 1.6 | 2.1 | 2.8 | 4.3 | 8.3 | 14.6 | 16.3 | 18.4 |

[1] Includes biomass, geothermal, and solar energy produced in the United States and not used for generating electricity. [2] Prior to 1992, data were for the former U.S.S.R. [3] Includes crude oil, lease condensate, and natural gas plant liquids. [4] Including geothermal, solar, wind, tidal and wave, biomass, and waste resources.

Source: U.S. Energy Information Administration, Open Data, "International Energy Data," <http://www.eia.gov/opendata/>, accessed April 2019.

## Table 1401. World Primary Energy Consumption by Region and Type: 1980 to 2016

[In quadrillion Btu (289.5 represents 289,500,000,000,000,000). Btu = British thermal unit. For Btu conversion factors, see source]

| Region and type | 1980 | 1990 | 1995 | 2000 | 2005 | 2010 | 2013 | 2014 | 2015 | 2016 |
|---|---|---|---|---|---|---|---|---|---|---|
| **World, total**............... | **289.5** | **359.9** | **369.3** | **403.9** | **467.3** | **526.4** | **565.1** | **570.8** | **573.4** | **576.4** |
| REGION | | | | | | | | | | |
| North America................... | 91.4 | 100.4 | 109.4 | 119.0 | 121.9 | 120.4 | 121.4 | 122.6 | 121.7 | 121.8 |
| United States [1]................... | **78.1** | **84.9** | **91.8** | **99.8** | **101.0** | **99.1** | **98.9** | **100.2** | **99.2** | **99.2** |
| Central and South America......... | 11.1 | 14.8 | 17.6 | 21.1 | 23.5 | 27.2 | 29.4 | 29.9 | 29.6 | 28.9 |
| Europe............................ | 75.1 | 79.6 | 77.3 | 81.3 | 86.1 | 84.6 | 81.5 | 79.4 | 80.7 | 81.8 |
| Eurasia [2]......................... | 51.7 | 66.1 | 44.2 | 40.5 | 43.1 | 45.3 | 46.5 | 46.5 | 45.5 | 45.4 |
| Middle East....................... | 5.9 | 11.0 | 13.8 | 17.8 | 23.5 | 30.2 | 33.9 | 35.2 | 36.3 | 36.4 |
| Africa............................. | 6.8 | 9.9 | 11.0 | 12.3 | 14.9 | 17.1 | 18.7 | 19.4 | 19.4 | 19.8 |
| Asia and Oceania................. | 47.5 | 78.0 | 96.2 | 111.9 | 154.2 | 201.5 | 233.7 | 237.9 | 240.1 | 242.2 |
| TYPE OF FUEL | | | | | | | | | | |
| Petroleum [3]....................... | 128.1 | 137.0 | 142.9 | 158.3 | 173.2 | 180.6 | 187.3 | 190.4 | 194.3 | 196.7 |
| Dry natural gas.................... | 53.9 | 75.1 | 81.3 | 89.6 | 102.6 | 119.4 | 127.7 | 128.1 | 130.1 | 132.7 |
| Coal............................... | 79.4 | 101.5 | 92.2 | 98.7 | 128.6 | 154.8 | 173.8 | 173.1 | 168.8 | 163.4 |
| Nuclear, renewables, and other..... | 28.2 | 46.3 | 52.9 | 57.4 | 62.8 | 71.5 | 76.3 | 79.2 | 80.3 | 83.7 |

[1] Includes biomass, geothermal, and solar energy consumed in the United States and not used for generating electricity. [2] Prior to 1992, data were for the former U.S.S.R. [3] Includes all refined petroleum products.

Source: U.S. Energy Information Administration, Open Data, "International Energy Data," <http://www.eia.gov/opendata/>, accessed April 2019.

## Table 1402. Energy Consumption by Country: 2010 to 2016

[In quadrillion Btu (526.39 represents 526,390,000,000,000,000). Btu = British thermal units. Total primary energy consumption includes the consumption of petroleum, dry natural gas, coal, and net nuclear, hydroelectric, and non-hydroelectric renewable electricity. See text of this section for general comments about the data. For data qualifications for countries and Btu conversion factors, see source]

| Country | Total (quad. Btu) | | | | Country | Total (quad. Btu) | | | |
|---|---|---|---|---|---|---|---|---|---|
| | 2010 | 2014 | 2015 | 2016 | | 2010 | 2014 | 2015 | 2016 |
| **World, total [1]**........ | **526.39** | **570.84** | **573.43** | **576.44** | Kuwait.................... | 1.49 | 1.57 | 1.71 | 1.60 |
| **United States**......... | **99.05** | **100.15** | **99.23** | **99.16** | Libya.................... | 0.91 | 0.78 | 0.68 | 0.65 |
| Algeria................. | 1.79 | 2.29 | 2.34 | 2.36 | Malaysia................ | 2.97 | 3.43 | 3.28 | 3.31 |
| Argentina.............. | 3.57 | 3.79 | 3.82 | 3.69 | Mexico................. | 7.52 | 7.65 | 7.77 | 7.94 |
| Australia.............. | 5.26 | 5.74 | 5.81 | 5.99 | Morocco................ | 0.68 | 0.79 | 0.78 | 0.78 |
| Austria................ | 1.51 | 1.45 | 1.45 | 1.48 | Netherlands............ | 4.38 | 3.90 | 3.93 | 3.97 |
| Azerbaijan............. | 0.59 | 0.59 | 0.63 | 0.61 | New Zealand........... | 0.84 | 0.89 | 0.89 | 0.90 |
| Bahrain................ | 0.59 | 0.68 | 0.70 | 0.69 | Nigeria................ | 0.83 | 1.41 | 1.44 | 1.59 |
| Bangladesh............ | 0.95 | 1.16 | 1.27 | 1.37 | Norway................ | 1.84 | 1.91 | 1.91 | 1.95 |
| Belarus................ | 1.12 | 1.12 | 0.96 | 0.95 | Oman.................. | 0.89 | 1.17 | 1.17 | 1.17 |
| Belgium................ | 2.83 | 2.48 | 2.54 | 2.68 | Pakistan................ | 2.60 | 2.81 | 2.91 | 3.11 |
| Brazil.................. | 11.72 | 13.14 | 12.86 | 12.48 | Paraguay............... | 0.44 | 0.45 | 0.46 | 0.52 |
| Bulgaria............... | 0.74 | 0.75 | 0.79 | 0.76 | Peru................... | 0.86 | 1.01 | 1.06 | 1.10 |
| Burma (Myanmar)...... | 0.24 | 0.41 | 0.46 | 0.51 | Philippines............. | 1.21 | 1.43 | 1.58 | 1.63 |
| Canada................ | 13.81 | 14.80 | 14.73 | 14.68 | Poland................. | 4.03 | 3.90 | 4.00 | 4.13 |
| Chile.................. | 1.26 | 1.35 | 1.40 | 1.48 | Portugal................ | 1.11 | 1.04 | 1.04 | 1.09 |
| China.................. | 109.36 | 136.90 | 137.18 | 136.09 | Qatar.................. | 1.26 | 2.12 | 2.11 | 1.85 |
| Colombia.............. | 1.36 | 1.70 | 1.70 | 1.77 | Romania................ | 1.45 | 1.37 | 1.37 | 1.37 |
| Czechia............... | 1.79 | 1.69 | 1.68 | 1.66 | Russia................. | 30.87 | 31.97 | 31.57 | 31.49 |
| Denmark.............. | 0.82 | 0.73 | 0.72 | 0.74 | Saudi Arabia........... | 8.81 | 10.36 | 10.90 | 10.83 |
| Ecuador............... | 0.59 | 0.71 | 0.70 | 0.69 | Serbia................. | 0.68 | 0.58 | 0.64 | 0.66 |
| Egypt.................. | 3.48 | 3.71 | 3.74 | 3.82 | Singapore.............. | 2.93 | 3.23 | 3.32 | 3.51 |
| Finland................ | 1.30 | 1.18 | 1.20 | 1.23 | Slovakia............... | 0.78 | 0.69 | 0.71 | 0.71 |
| France................. | 11.00 | 10.27 | 10.31 | 10.15 | South Africa........... | 5.89 | 6.00 | 5.95 | 6.07 |
| Germany............... | 14.09 | 13.65 | 13.82 | 13.86 | Spain.................. | 6.20 | 5.60 | 5.64 | 5.74 |
| Greece................. | 1.32 | 1.12 | 1.13 | 1.12 | Sweden................ | 2.22 | 2.11 | 2.15 | 2.17 |
| Hong Kong............. | 1.34 | 1.17 | 1.28 | 1.33 | Switzerland............ | 1.31 | 1.24 | 1.21 | 1.18 |
| Hungary............... | 1.03 | 0.94 | 0.98 | 1.00 | Syria.................. | 1.03 | 0.50 | 0.45 | 0.44 |
| India.................. | 21.66 | 27.54 | 28.49 | 29.04 | Taiwan................. | 4.64 | 4.69 | 4.68 | 4.76 |
| Indonesia.............. | 6.41 | 6.81 | 6.95 | 7.25 | Thailand............... | 4.41 | 5.16 | 5.23 | 5.42 |
| Iran................... | 9.21 | 10.63 | 10.77 | 11.26 | Trinidad and Tobago. .. | 0.96 | 1.01 | 0.98 | 0.89 |
| Iraq................... | 1.37 | 1.93 | 1.82 | 1.90 | Turkey................. | 4.51 | 5.21 | 5.75 | 5.97 |
| Ireland................ | 0.63 | 0.57 | 0.60 | 0.63 | Turkmenistan........... | 1.04 | 1.45 | 1.79 | 1.77 |
| Israel.................. | 0.95 | 0.98 | 1.02 | 1.04 | Ukraine................ | 5.17 | 4.40 | 3.87 | 3.89 |
| Italy.................. | 7.68 | 6.70 | 6.77 | 6.72 | United Arab Emirates... | 3.63 | 4.23 | 4.63 | 4.71 |
| Japan.................. | 21.51 | 19.90 | 19.55 | 19.65 | United Kingdom........ | 9.19 | 8.27 | 8.35 | 8.77 |
| Kazakhstan............ | 3.19 | 3.29 | 3.25 | 3.47 | Uzbekistan............. | 1.97 | 2.15 | 2.01 | 1.76 |
| Korea, North.......... | 0.69 | 0.43 | 0.33 | 0.38 | Venezuela.............. | 3.19 | 3.31 | 3.10 | 2.75 |
| Korea, South.......... | 11.23 | 12.08 | 12.39 | 12.96 | Vietnam................ | 1.96 | 2.59 | 2.83 | 3.20 |

[1] Includes countries not shown separately.

Source: U.S. Energy Information Administration, Open Data, "International Energy Data," <http://www.eia.gov/open/data>, accessed April 2019.

## Table 1403. World Energy Consumption by Region and Energy Source: 2015, and Projections, 2020 to 2050

[In quadrillion Btu (575.4 represents 575,400,000,000,000,000). Btu = British thermal units. For Btu conversion factors, see source. Energy totals include net imports of coal coke and electricity generated from biomass in the United States. The electricity portion of the national consumption values consists of generation for domestic use plus an adjustment for electricity trade based on a fuel's share of total generation in the exporting country. OECD = Organisation for Economic Co-operation and Development; see text, this section]

| Region and energy source | 2015 | Projections 2020 | 2025 | 2030 | 2035 | 2040 | 2045 | 2050 | Average annual percent change 2015-2050 |
|---|---|---|---|---|---|---|---|---|---|
| **World, total** | **575.4** | **604.9** | **634.9** | **663.2** | **697.3** | **736.5** | **775.2** | **813.7** | **1.00** |
| OECD, total | 239.9 | 244.0 | 247.8 | 250.3 | 254.8 | 261.8 | 268.3 | 276.6 | 0.40 |
| OECD Americas | 121.9 | 124.4 | 125.5 | 124.8 | 126.3 | 129.5 | 133.0 | 136.9 | 0.30 |
| **United States** | **97.5** | **100.2** | **100.7** | **99.1** | **99.5** | **101.6** | **104.1** | **106.9** | **0.30** |
| OECD Europe | 79.8 | 80.5 | 81.0 | 83.0 | 84.8 | 87.2 | 88.8 | 91.4 | 0.40 |
| OECD Asia | 38.3 | 39.1 | 41.3 | 42.5 | 43.7 | 45.1 | 46.5 | 48.3 | 0.70 |
| Non-OECD, total | 335.5 | 360.9 | 387.1 | 413.0 | 442.4 | 474.7 | 506.9 | 537.1 | 1.40 |
| Non-OECD Europe and Eurasia | 47.7 | 47.5 | 47.4 | 47.6 | 48.4 | 48.7 | 48.6 | 48.7 | 0.10 |
| Non-OECD Asia | 200.1 | 221.8 | 241.8 | 260.3 | 280.0 | 302.3 | 324.5 | 344.6 | 1.60 |
| China | 133.1 | 146.4 | 155.9 | 161.2 | 166.8 | 172.5 | 177.9 | 181.6 | 0.90 |
| India | 28.4 | 33.3 | 38.0 | 44.3 | 51.9 | 60.7 | 69.2 | 76.5 | 2.90 |
| Middle East | 33.9 | 36.4 | 39.0 | 41.8 | 45.4 | 49.3 | 53.5 | 57.2 | 1.50 |
| Africa | 22.7 | 24.2 | 25.5 | 27.9 | 31.0 | 34.2 | 37.5 | 41.1 | 1.70 |
| Non-OECD Americas | 31.1 | 31.0 | 33.4 | 35.4 | 37.6 | 40.2 | 42.8 | 45.6 | 1.10 |
| Liquids | 190.6 | 200.0 | 203.9 | 208.1 | 216.0 | 226.0 | 235.8 | 244.9 | 0.70 |
| Natural gas | 128.9 | 131.7 | 143.4 | 154.3 | 168.6 | 184.0 | 200.9 | 218.2 | 1.50 |
| Coal | 158.2 | 161.9 | 161.9 | 158.8 | 159.3 | 160.5 | 162.5 | 164.6 | 0.10 |
| Nuclear | 26.0 | 28.5 | 30.9 | 33.5 | 35.4 | 37.9 | 38.7 | 39.4 | 1.20 |
| Other | 71.7 | 82.7 | 94.8 | 108.4 | 117.9 | 128.0 | 137.3 | 146.6 | 2.10 |

Source: U.S. Energy Information Administration, *International Energy Outlook 2017*, September 2017. See also <http://www.eia.gov/forecasts/ieo/index.cfm>.


## Table 1404. World Daily Crude Oil Production by Major Producing Country: 1980 to 2018

[In thousands of barrels per day (59,558 barrels represents 59,558,000 barrels). Includes lease condensate. Ranked for top 40 countries, as of current year]

| Country | 1980 | 1990 | 2000 | 2005 | 2010 | 2014 | 2015 | 2016 | 2017 | 2018 |
|---|---|---|---|---|---|---|---|---|---|---|
| **World, total** [1] | **59,558** | **60,498** | **68,527** | **73,869** | **74,887** | **78,362** | **80,755** | **80,842** | **81,092** | **82,854** |
| **United States** | **8,597** | **7,355** | **5,822** | **5,184** | **5,478** | **8,759** | **9,431** | **8,831** | **9,352** | **10,950** |
| Russia | (X) | (X) | 6,479 | 9,043 | 9,694 | 10,107 | 10,253 | 10,551 | 10,580 | 10,759 |
| Saudi Arabia | 9,900 | 6,410 | 8,404 | 9,550 | 8,900 | 9,735 | 10,168 | 10,461 | 10,134 | 10,425 |
| Iraq | 2,514 | 2,040 | 2,571 | 1,878 | 2,399 | 3,368 | 4,045 | 4,444 | 4,454 | 4,613 |
| Canada | 1,435 | 1,553 | 1,977 | 2,369 | 2,741 | 3,613 | 3,677 | 3,679 | 3,977 | 4,263 |
| Iran | 1,662 | 3,088 | 3,696 | 4,139 | 4,080 | 3,239 | 3,293 | 4,151 | 4,469 | 4,254 |
| China | 2,114 | 2,774 | 3,249 | 3,609 | 4,078 | 4,208 | 4,278 | 3,983 | 3,821 | 3,773 |
| United Arab Emirates | 1,709 | 2,117 | 2,368 | 2,535 | 2,570 | 3,010 | 3,149 | 3,243 | 3,174 | 3,216 |
| Kuwait | 1,656 | 1,175 | 2,079 | 2,529 | 2,300 | 2,642 | 2,784 | 2,905 | 2,753 | 2,807 |
| Brazil | 182 | 631 | 1,269 | 1,634 | 2,055 | 2,255 | 2,437 | 2,515 | 2,622 | 2,593 |
| Nigeria | 2,055 | 1,810 | 2,165 | 2,627 | 2,408 | 2,347 | 2,171 | 1,871 | 1,946 | 1,991 |
| Mexico | 1,936 | 2,553 | 3,104 | 3,423 | 2,621 | 2,469 | 2,302 | 2,187 | 1,981 | 1,869 |
| Kazakhstan | (X) | (X) | 718 | 1,288 | 1,525 | 1,632 | 1,653 | 1,595 | 1,777 | 1,856 |
| Angola | 150 | 475 | 746 | 1,239 | 1,909 | 1,742 | 1,802 | 1,770 | 1,666 | 1,594 |
| Norway | 486 | 1,630 | 3,222 | 2,698 | 1,871 | 1,562 | 1,610 | 1,648 | 1,618 | 1,517 |
| Venezuela | 2,168 | 2,137 | 3,155 | 2,565 | 2,410 | 2,500 | 2,500 | 2,277 | 2,007 | 1,484 |
| Qatar | 472 | 406 | 742 | 978 | 1,451 | 1,537 | 1,498 | 1,496 | 1,500 | 1,464 |
| Algeria | 1,106 | 1,180 | 1,214 | 1,692 | 1,540 | 1,420 | 1,429 | 1,348 | 1,306 | 1,259 |
| Libya | 1,787 | 1,375 | 1,410 | 1,651 | 1,710 | 530 | 484 | 466 | 897 | 1,042 |
| United Kingdom | 1,622 | 1,820 | 2,275 | 1,649 | 1,233 | 787 | 893 | 933 | 911 | 1,000 |
| Oman | 282 | 685 | 970 | 774 | 865 | 943 | 982 | 1,007 | 970 | 979 |
| Colombia | 126 | 440 | 691 | 526 | 786 | 988 | 1,003 | 886 | 854 | 863 |
| Azerbaijan | (X) | (X) | 280 | 433 | 1,035 | 847 | 848 | 834 | 789 | 793 |
| Indonesia | 1,577 | 1,462 | 1,428 | 1,059 | 945 | 789 | 786 | 832 | 802 | 772 |
| India | 182 | 660 | 646 | 665 | 751 | 767 | 761 | 735 | 734 | 709 |
| Malaysia | 283 | 619 | 690 | 726 | 638 | 603 | 654 | 667 | 648 | 647 |
| Egypt | 595 | 873 | 768 | 623 | 636 | 645 | 686 | 654 | 630 | 638 |
| Ecuador | 204 | 285 | 395 | 532 | 486 | 556 | 543 | 548 | 531 | 517 |
| Argentina | 491 | 483 | 761 | 704 | 626 | 532 | 532 | 511 | 479 | 489 |
| Congo, Republic of | 65 | 165 | 280 | 229 | 340 | 233 | 238 | 198 | 244 | 342 |
| Australia | 380 | 575 | 722 | 456 | 479 | 353 | 322 | 290 | 263 | 291 |
| Turkmenistan | (X) | (X) | 142 | 183 | 178 | 239 | 243 | 231 | 245 | 243 |
| Vietnam | – | 50 | 316 | 358 | 299 | 307 | 333 | 302 | 271 | 242 |
| Thailand | – | 44 | 110 | 183 | 242 | 233 | 248 | 258 | 240 | 228 |
| Gabon | 175 | 270 | 315 | 266 | 246 | 220 | 213 | 211 | 199 | 196 |
| Equatorial Guinea | – | – | 168 | 363 | 298 | 260 | 250 | 227 | 188 | 172 |
| Ghana | 2 | – | 7 | 6 | 7 | 105 | 102 | 98 | 151 | 168 |
| Chad | – | – | – | 177 | 123 | 121 | 123 | 114 | 128 | 132 |
| South Sudan | (X) | (X) | (X) | (X) | (X) | 148 | 153 | 152 | 150 | 126 |
| Denmark | 6 | 121 | 363 | 377 | 245 | 165 | 156 | 141 | 137 | 115 |

X Not applicable. – Represents zero or rounds to zero. [1] Includes countries not shown separately.

Source: U.S. Energy Information Administration, Open Data, "International Energy Data," <http://www.eia.gov/opendata/>, accessed April 2019.

## Table 1405. World Dry Natural Gas Production by Major Producing Country: 1980 to 2017

[In billions of cubic feet (53,378 represents 53,378,000,000,000). Ranked for top 30 countries, as of current year]

| Country | Dry natural gas production | | | | | | | | |
|---|---|---|---|---|---|---|---|---|---|
| | 1980 | 1990 | 2000 | 2005 | 2010 | 2014 | 2015 | 2016 | 2017 |
| **World, total** [1] | **53,378** | **73,387** | **86,770** | **98,598** | **113,085** | **122,340** | **124,611** | **125,740** | **130,751** |
| **United States** | **19,403** | **17,810** | **19,182** | **18,051** | **21,316** | **25,890** | **27,065** | **26,592** | **27,291** |
| Russia | (X) | (X) | 19,335 | 21,224 | 21,458 | 21,468 | 21,531 | 21,750 | 23,508 |
| Iran | 250 | 818 | 2,127 | 3,655 | 5,161 | 6,162 | 6,526 | 7,083 | 7,577 |
| Qatar | 184 | 222 | 1,028 | 1,617 | 4,121 | 5,650 | 5,794 | 5,869 | 5,875 |
| Canada | 2,759 | 3,849 | 6,470 | 6,561 | 5,390 | 5,349 | 5,489 | 5,554 | 5,618 |
| China | 505 | 508 | 962 | 1,763 | 3,334 | 4,360 | 4,692 | 4,794 | 5,152 |
| Norway | 917 | 976 | 1,867 | 3,072 | 3,756 | 3,843 | 4,139 | 4,115 | 4,375 |
| Saudi Arabia | 334 | 1,077 | 1,759 | 2,516 | 3,096 | 3,547 | 3,614 | 3,739 | 3,859 |
| Australia | 313 | 723 | 1,159 | 1,266 | 1,859 | 2,212 | 2,373 | 3,068 | 3,717 |
| Algeria | 411 | 1,787 | 2,940 | 3,151 | 2,988 | 2,942 | 2,933 | 3,312 | 3,302 |
| Turkmenistan | (X) | (X) | 1,642 | 2,225 | 1,466 | 2,684 | 2,831 | 2,692 | 2,735 |
| Indonesia | 654 | 1,602 | 2,237 | 2,001 | 2,917 | 2,594 | 2,571 | 2,533 | 2,546 |
| Malaysia | 56 | 501 | 1,465 | 1,977 | 2,171 | 2,310 | 2,240 | 2,214 | 2,454 |
| United Arab Emirates | 200 | 780 | 1,355 | 1,659 | 1,811 | 1,916 | 2,125 | 2,157 | 2,190 |
| Uzbekistan | (X) | (X) | 1,992 | 2,108 | 2,123 | 2,099 | 1,967 | 1,823 | 1,840 |
| Egypt | 30 | 286 | 646 | 1,501 | 2,166 | 1,723 | 1,565 | 1,497 | 1,796 |
| Netherlands | 3,398 | 2,687 | 2,572 | 2,773 | 3,126 | 2,471 | 1,907 | 1,840 | 1,601 |
| Nigeria | 38 | 131 | 440 | 791 | 1,024 | 1,548 | 1,594 | 1,475 | 1,571 |
| United Kingdom | 1,323 | 1,754 | 3,826 | 3,118 | 2,111 | 1,370 | 1,460 | 1,471 | 1,487 |
| Argentina | 280 | 630 | 1,321 | 1,611 | 1,416 | 1,254 | 1,285 | 1,387 | 1,445 |
| Pakistan | 286 | 482 | 856 | 1,088 | 1,400 | 1,380 | 1,388 | 1,379 | 1,379 |
| Thailand | – | 208 | 658 | 837 | 1,278 | 1,487 | 1,406 | 1,384 | 1,363 |
| Trinidad and Tobago | 81 | 177 | 493 | 1,094 | 1,499 | 1,486 | 1,389 | 1,274 | 1,297 |
| Mexico | 900 | 903 | 1,297 | 1,513 | 1,769 | 1,567 | 1,426 | 1,296 | 1,115 |
| India | 51 | 399 | 719 | 1,056 | 1,848 | 1,158 | 1,103 | 1,092 | 1,114 |
| Oman | 28 | 99 | 322 | 705 | 957 | 1,091 | 1,057 | 1,076 | 1,103 |
| Bangladesh | 50 | 162 | 343 | 494 | 711 | 844 | 949 | 1,039 | 1,043 |
| Venezuela | 517 | 761 | 961 | 828 | 697 | 773 | 918 | 972 | 956 |
| Brazil | 42 | 97 | 257 | 345 | 445 | 719 | 721 | 740 | 846 |
| Kazakhstan | (X) | (X) | 314 | 428 | 621 | 712 | 749 | 751 | 791 |

X Not applicable. – Represents zero. [1] Includes countries not shown separately.

Source: U.S. Energy Information Administration, Open Data, "International Energy Data," <https://www.eia.gov/opendata/>, accessed August 2019.

## Table 1406. World Coal Production by Major Producing Country: 1980 to 2016

[In thousands of short tons (4,158,802 represents 4,158,802,000). Coal includes anthracite, bituminous, subbituminous, metallurgical and lignite. Ranked for top 30 countries, as of current year]

| Country | Coal production | | | | | | | | |
|---|---|---|---|---|---|---|---|---|---|
| | 1980 | 1990 | 2000 | 2005 | 2010 | 2013 | 2014 | 2015 | 2016 |
| **World, total** [1] | **4,158,802** | **5,280,388** | **5,126,951** | **6,644,162** | **8,154,991** | **9,057,094** | **8,981,213** | **8,736,740** | **8,149,802** |
| China | 683,587 | 1,189,725 | 1,525,800 | 2,607,124 | 3,779,212 | 4,380,935 | 4,270,260 | 4,129,851 | 3,708,155 |
| **United States** | **829,700** | **1,029,076** | **1,073,612** | **1,131,498** | **1,084,368** | **984,842** | **1,000,049** | **896,941** | **728,364** |
| India | 127,989 | 239,035 | 372,518 | 481,825 | 578,216 | 671,435 | 713,454 | 747,074 | 761,662 |
| Australia | 115,196 | 225,491 | 338,103 | 408,505 | 467,823 | 521,124 | 555,812 | 556,120 | 554,764 |
| Indonesia | 627 | 11,628 | 87,498 | 187,989 | 358,251 | 522,904 | 504,965 | 508,789 | 502,653 |
| Russia | (X) | (X) | 264,912 | 311,823 | 329,258 | 385,818 | 393,765 | 409,701 | 423,095 |
| South Africa | 126,898 | 192,684 | 247,138 | 270,055 | 280,403 | 282,780 | 288,695 | 278,003 | 277,952 |
| Germany | (X) | (X) | 226,047 | 226,993 | 202,286 | 210,493 | 205,597 | 203,612 | 193,593 |
| Poland | 253,517 | 237,082 | 178,247 | 174,987 | 146,257 | 156,875 | 150,374 | 149,147 | 143,996 |
| Kazakhstan | (X) | (X) | 82,548 | 91,258 | 122,278 | 131,808 | 125,647 | 118,299 | 113,620 |
| Colombia | 4,590 | 22,562 | 42,044 | 65,107 | 82,021 | 94,247 | 97,640 | 94,300 | 99,772 |
| Turkey | 20,531 | 52,280 | 69,741 | 64,309 | 80,908 | 72,877 | 75,094 | 67,025 | 80,473 |
| Canada | 40,442 | 75,323 | 76,239 | 72,582 | 74,835 | 75,958 | 76,079 | 68,267 | 67,606 |
| Czechia | (X) | (X) | 71,829 | 68,372 | 60,857 | 53,990 | 51,651 | 51,168 | 49,949 |
| Vietnam | 5,732 | 5,100 | 12,797 | 37,581 | 49,422 | 43,712 | 45,290 | 45,927 | 42,469 |
| Serbia | (X) | (X) | (X) | (X) | 41,861 | 44,420 | 33,081 | 41,696 | 42,373 |
| Ukraine | (X) | (X) | 68,787 | 66,537 | 63,558 | 71,019 | 50,630 | 37,990 | 39,261 |
| Mongolia | 5,818 | 7,889 | 5,715 | 8,285 | 27,793 | 36,752 | 26,951 | 26,616 | 39,157 |
| Greece | 25,571 | 57,205 | 70,423 | 76,498 | 62,303 | 59,441 | 56,047 | 50,977 | 35,977 |
| Bulgaria | 33,304 | 34,916 | 29,136 | 27,222 | 32,413 | 31,549 | 34,467 | 39,528 | 34,426 |
| Korea, North | 33,367 | 36,542 | 24,802 | 26,522 | 35,452 | 33,005 | 33,985 | 30,303 | 34,238 |
| Romania | 38,762 | 42,090 | 32,281 | 34,288 | 34,312 | 27,250 | 25,976 | 28,101 | 25,344 |
| Thailand | 1,681 | 13,711 | 19,605 | 23,014 | 20,126 | 19,964 | 19,821 | 16,701 | 18,716 |
| Mexico | 3,405 | 7,642 | 12,505 | 14,854 | 16,870 | 16,741 | 16,961 | 16,831 | 13,853 |
| Philippines | 363 | 1,370 | 1,491 | 3,487 | 8,088 | 7,940 | 9,280 | 9,009 | 13,324 |
| Hungary | 28,688 | 19,654 | 15,469 | 10,549 | 10,045 | 10,536 | 10,528 | 10,208 | 10,159 |
| Kosovo | (X) | (X) | (X) | (X) | 9,534 | 9,060 | 7,941 | 9,084 | 9,701 |
| Brazil | 5,778 | 5,065 | 7,502 | 6,895 | 5,969 | 9,473 | 8,749 | 8,850 | 7,722 |
| Bosnia and Herzegovina | (X) | (X) | 8,200 | 6,356 | 7,047 | 6,875 | 6,798 | 6,666 | 7,167 |
| Mozambique | – | – | 26 | 36 | 39 | 6,702 | 7,551 | 7,274 | 6,819 |

– Represents zero. X Not applicable. [1] Includes countries not shown separately.

Source: U.S. Energy Information Administration, Open Data, "International Energy Data," <http://www.eia.gov/opendata/>, accessed April 2019.

## Table 1407. Carbon Dioxide Emissions From Consumption of Fossil Fuels by Country: 1980 to 2016

[In millions of metric tons of carbon dioxide (19,450 represents 19,450,000,000). Ranked for top 25 countries, as of current year. Includes carbon dioxide emissions from the consumption of petroleum, natural gas, coal, and the flaring of natural gas]

| Region/country | 1980 | 1990 | 2000 | 2005 | 2010 | 2013 | 2014 | 2015 | 2016 |
|---|---|---|---|---|---|---|---|---|---|
| **World, total** [1] | **19,450** | **22,920** | **24,478** | **28,941** | **32,688** | **35,869** | **36,023** | **35,972** | **35,811** |
| China | 1,665 | 2,667 | 3,523 | 6,106 | 8,779 | 10,802 | 10,744 | 10,604 | 10,593 |
| **United States** | **4,788** | **5,057** | **5,886** | **6,014** | **5,598** | **5,512** | **5,555** | **5,415** | **5,317** |
| India | 275 | 557 | 918 | 1,161 | 1,614 | 1,951 | 2,089 | 2,151 | 2,155 |
| Russia | (X) | (X) | 1,566 | 1,644 | 1,761 | 1,789 | 1,811 | 1,802 | 1,767 |
| Japan | 960 | 1,086 | 1,200 | 1,252 | 1,159 | 1,271 | 1,238 | 1,200 | 1,203 |
| Germany | (X) | (X) | 821 | 822 | 802 | 856 | 824 | 826 | 826 |
| Korea, South | 150 | 265 | 464 | 518 | 616 | 719 | 716 | 732 | 771 |
| Saudi Arabia | 177 | 208 | 291 | 405 | 516 | 582 | 629 | 662 | 657 |
| Iran | 119 | 215 | 322 | 452 | 568 | 615 | 644 | 642 | 639 |
| Canada | 443 | 451 | 545 | 589 | 568 | 632 | 639 | 642 | 633 |
| Indonesia | 85 | 160 | 273 | 325 | 438 | 478 | 488 | 504 | 513 |
| South Africa | 243 | 351 | 419 | 474 | 504 | 511 | 507 | 503 | 511 |
| Brazil | 186 | 244 | 355 | 380 | 474 | 530 | 556 | 541 | 493 |
| United Kingdom | 633 | 608 | 574 | 591 | 547 | 516 | 476 | 459 | 481 |
| Mexico | 240 | 304 | 386 | 424 | 454 | 450 | 438 | 454 | 453 |
| Australia | 202 | 283 | 342 | 374 | 395 | 396 | 395 | 403 | 412 |
| Turkey | 64 | 127 | 205 | 232 | 267 | 309 | 332 | 352 | 366 |
| Italy | 375 | 418 | 446 | 473 | 422 | 366 | 350 | 359 | 356 |
| France | 507 | 378 | 410 | 423 | 389 | 384 | 352 | 355 | 354 |
| Thailand | 34 | 84 | 158 | 237 | 280 | 327 | 334 | 338 | 342 |
| Taiwan | 70 | 119 | 238 | 267 | 272 | 310 | 318 | 318 | 326 |
| Poland | 351 | 317 | 270 | 278 | 299 | 300 | 294 | 300 | 307 |
| United Arab Emirates | 30 | 79 | 116 | 140 | 218 | 255 | 259 | 286 | 289 |
| Spain | 204 | 233 | 319 | 383 | 310 | 279 | 278 | 290 | 286 |
| Kazakhstan | (X) | (X) | 172 | 218 | 267 | 291 | 275 | 269 | 279 |

X Not applicable. [1] Includes other countries not shown separately.

Source: U.S. Energy Information Administration, Open Data, "International Energy Data," <http://www.eia.gov/countries/data.cfm>, accessed April 2019.

## Table 1408. Average Temperatures and Precipitation—Selected International Cities

[In degrees Fahrenheit, except as noted. Data are generally based on a standard 30-year period; for details, see source. Minus sign (-) indicates degrees below zero]

| City | January Average high | January Average low | January Warm-est | January Coldest | January Average precipitation (inches) | July Average high | July Average low | July Warm-est | July Coldest | July Average precipitation (inches) |
|---|---|---|---|---|---|---|---|---|---|---|
| Amsterdam, Netherlands | 41 | 34 | 57 | 3 | 3.1 | 69 | 55 | 90 | 39 | 2.9 |
| Athens, Greece | 55 | 44 | 70 | 28 | 1.9 | 89 | 73 | 108 | 61 | 0.2 |
| Baghdad, Iraq | 58 | 38 | 75 | 25 | 1.1 | 110 | 78 | 122 | 61 | – |
| Bangkok, Thailand | 89 | 71 | 95 | 54 | 0.4 | 90 | 78 | 99 | 72 | 6.2 |
| Beijing, China | 34 | 17 | 54 | 1 | 0.2 | 86 | 72 | 104 | 63 | 8.8 |
| Berlin, Germany | 35 | 26 | 58 | -11 | (NA) | 73 | 56 | 95 | 41 | (NA) |
| Bogota, Colombia | 66 | 43 | 84 | 27 | 1.9 | 64 | 47 | 82 | 32 | 1.8 |
| Brasilia, Brazil | 81 | 64 | 95 | 54 | (NA) | 79 | 52 | 97 | 37 | (NA) |
| Buenos Aires, Argentina | 85 | 64 | 104 | 44 | 4.2 | 58 | 41 | 88 | 23 | 2.3 |
| Cairo, Egypt | 65 | 49 | 86 | 32 | 0.2 | 93 | 72 | 108 | 63 | – |
| Frankfurt, Germany | 38 | 30 | 56 | -4 | 1.8 | 75 | 57 | 97 | 38 | 2.4 |
| Geneva, Switzerland | 39 | 29 | 57 | -2 | 2.2 | 77 | 56 | 96 | 41 | 2.8 |
| Hong Kong, China | 67 | 58 | 79 | 43 | 1.1 | 89 | 81 | 97 | 70 | 14.3 |
| Istanbul, Turkey | 46 | 37 | 64 | 16 | 3.7 | 82 | 66 | 100 | 50 | 0.7 |
| Jakarta, Indonesia | 83 | 75 | 92 | 72 | (NA) | 88 | 74 | 92 | 67 | (NA) |
| Karachi, Pakistan | 76 | 55 | 93 | 39 | 0.3 | 89 | 83 | 109 | 68 | 3.5 |
| Lagos, Nigeria | 82 | 79 | 93 | 64 | (NA) | 79 | 76 | 88 | 70 | (NA) |
| London, England | 45 | 36 | 61 | 15 | 2.4 | 72 | 56 | 93 | 45 | 1.8 |
| Madrid, Spain | 51 | 32 | 68 | 14 | 1.8 | 90 | 61 | 104 | 46 | 0.4 |
| Manila, Philippines | 86 | 71 | 95 | 61 | 0.8 | 88 | 76 | 99 | 70 | 15.9 |
| Mexico City, Mexico | 70 | 45 | 86 | 26 | 0.3 | 74 | 56 | 86 | 37 | 5.1 |
| Montreal, Canada | 21 | 7 | 52 | -31 | 2.8 | 79 | 61 | 93 | 43 | 3.4 |
| Moscow, Russia | 21 | 11 | 46 | -33 | 1.4 | 71 | 55 | 95 | 41 | 3.2 |
| Nairobi, Kenya | 77 | 58 | 88 | 45 | 1.8 | 71 | 54 | 85 | 43 | 0.5 |
| New Delhi, India | 68 | 48 | 85 | 32 | 0.9 | 93 | 81 | 111 | 70 | 7.9 |
| Paris, France | 43 | 34 | 59 | 1 | (NA) | 75 | 58 | 95 | 41 | (NA) |
| Rio De Janeiro, Brazil | 91 | 74 | 109 | 64 | 5.3 | 81 | 64 | 102 | 52 | 1.8 |
| Rome, Italy | 55 | 39 | 64 | 19 | 3.2 | 83 | 66 | 100 | 55 | 0.6 |
| Seoul, Korea | 33 | 21 | 55 | -1 | (NA) | 82 | 71 | 97 | 55 | (NA) |
| Singapore, Singapore | 85 | 73 | 100 | 66 | 9.4 | 86 | 76 | 99 | 70 | 5.9 |
| Sydney, Australia | 79 | 65 | 109 | 49 | 4.0 | 62 | 44 | 80 | 32 | 2.5 |
| Tel Aviv, Israel | 62 | 46 | 84 | 32 | (NA) | 87 | 69 | 100 | 50 | (NA) |
| Tokyo, Japan | 48 | 35 | 66 | 25 | 2.0 | 82 | 71 | 95 | 55 | 5.3 |
| Toronto, Canada | 28 | 15 | 59 | -24 | 1.9 | 79 | 60 | 99 | 45 | 2.8 |

– Represents zero. NA Not available.

Source: U.S. National Oceanic and Atmospheric Administration, *Climates of the World*. See also <https://library.noaa.gov/Research-Tools/Subject-Guides/weathersites>.

# Table 1409. Telephones, Cellular Phones, and Internet Use by Country: 2017

[For data qualifications for individual countries, see source]

| Country | Fixed telephone subscriptions per 100 people [1] | Cell phone subscriptions per 100 people [2] | Internet users (as percent of population) [3] | Country | Fixed telephone subscriptions per 100 people [1] | Cell phone subscriptions per 100 people [2] | Internet users (as percent of population) [3] |
|---|---|---|---|---|---|---|---|
| **United States....** | **37.0** | **120.7** | **75.2** | Jordan............ | 3.4 | 100.0 | 66.8 |
| Afghanistan....... | 0.3 | 67.4 | 11.4 | Kenya............ | 0.1 | 86.1 | 17.8 |
| Argentina......... | 22.0 | 139.8 | 75.8 | Korea, South..... | 52.7 | 124.9 | 95.1 |
| Australia......... | 34.6 | 112.7 | 86.5 | Malaysia......... | 20.8 | 133.9 | 80.1 |
| Azerbaijan....... | 17.2 | 103.0 | 79.0 | Mexico.......... | 16.1 | 88.5 | 63.9 |
| Bangladesh....... | 0.4 | 91.7 | 18.0 | Morocco.......... | 5.7 | 122.9 | 61.8 |
| Brazil............ | 19.5 | 113.0 | 67.5 | Myanmar......... | 1.0 | 89.8 | 30.7 |
| Canada........... | 39.5 | 86.5 | 92.7 | Netherlands...... | 38.5 | 120.5 | 93.2 |
| China............ | 13.7 | 104.3 | 54.3 | Nigeria.......... | 0.1 | 75.9 | 27.7 |
| Croatia........... | 33.5 | 103.0 | 67.1 | Pakistan......... | 1.5 | 73.4 | 15.5 |
| Cuba............ | 11.7 | 40.2 | 49.1 | Panama......... | 15.8 | 126.7 | 57.9 |
| Egypt............ | 6.8 | 105.5 | 45.0 | Poland.......... | 19.4 | 132.2 | 76.0 |
| France........... | 59.5 | 106.2 | 80.5 | Russia.......... | 22.2 | 157.9 | 76.0 |
| Germany......... | 54.1 | 133.6 | 84.4 | Saudi Arabia..... | 11.0 | 122.1 | 82.1 |
| Greece.......... | 46.4 | 115.9 | 69.9 | South Africa...... | 8.5 | 156.0 | 56.2 |
| Haiti............ | 0.1 | 57.4 | 12.3 | Spain........... | 42.5 | 113.3 | 84.6 |
| Hong Kong....... | 57.7 | 249.8 | 89.4 | Switzerland...... | 43.1 | 130.8 | 93.7 |
| India............ | 1.7 | 87.3 | 34.5 | Syria........... | 14.9 | 84.2 | 34.3 |
| Indonesia........ | 4.2 | 164.9 | 32.3 | Thailand......... | 5.0 | 176.0 | 52.9 |
| Iran............ | 38.4 | 107.2 | 60.4 | Turkey.......... | 14.0 | 96.4 | 64.7 |
| Iraq............ | 8.5 | 87.3 | 49.4 | Ukraine.......... | 17.2 | 133.5 | 57.1 |
| Israel........... | 38.9 | 126.7 | 81.6 | United Kingdom.. | 50.1 | 119.5 | 94.6 |
| Italy............ | 34.9 | 141.3 | 61.3 | Venezuela........ | 18.5 | 78.5 | 64.3 |
| Japan........... | 50.2 | 135.5 | 90.9 | Vietnam......... | 4.6 | 125.6 | 49.6 |

[1] Refers to the sum of active number of analogue fixed telephone lines, voice-over-IP (VoIP) subscriptions, fixed wireless local loop (WLL) subscriptions, ISDN voice-channel equivalents and fixed public payphones. [2] Subscriptions to a public mobile telephone service that provide access to the public switched telephone network (PSTN) using cellular technology. Includes number of postpaid subscriptions and active prepaid accounts. Applies to all mobile cellular subscriptions that offer voice communications. Excludes subscriptions via data cards or USB modems, subscriptions to public mobile data services, private trunked mobile radio, telepoint, radio paging, and telemetry services. [3] Internet users are individuals who have used the internet (from any location) in the last 3 months. The internet can be used via a computer, mobile phone, personal digital assistant, games machine, digital TV etc.

Source: The World Bank, Washington, DC, "World Development Indicators" database ©, <http://data.worldbank.org/data-catalog/world-development-indicators>, accessed July 2019.

# Table 1410. Global Telecommunications Indicators: 2000 to 2017

[975 represents 975,000,000]

| Indicators | 2000 | 2005 | 2010 | 2012 | 2013 | 2014 | 2015 | 2016 | 2017 |
|---|---|---|---|---|---|---|---|---|---|
| **NUMBER (million)** | | | | | | | | | |
| Fixed telephone subscriptions [1]....................... | 975 | 1,244 | 1,229 | 1,179 | 1,142 | 1,095 | 1,046 | 1,009 | 982 |
| Mobile cellular subscriptions [1]....................... | 738 | 2,206 | 5,296 | 6,261 | 6,662 | 6,999 | 7,183 | 7,505 | 7,764 |
| Fixed broadband internet subscriptions [2]............. | (NA) | 220 | 532 | 649 | 692 | 730 | 839 | 916 | 1,025 |
| **PERCENT OF POPULATION** | | | | | | | | | |
| Internet users [1]..................................... | 6.7 | 15.7 | 28.7 | 34.2 | 36.7 | 39.8 | 43.0 | 45.7 | 48.6 |
| **PER 100 INHABITANTS** | | | | | | | | | |
| Fixed telephone subscriptions [1]....................... | 15.9 | 19.4 | 17.7 | 16.6 | 15.8 | 15.0 | 14.2 | 13.5 | 13.0 |
| Mobile cellular subscriptions [1]....................... | 12.1 | 33.8 | 76.1 | 87.9 | 92.4 | 96.0 | 97.4 | 100.6 | 103.0 |
| Fixed broadband internet subscriptions [2]............. | (NA) | 3.7 | 7.8 | 9.4 | 9.8 | 10.2 | 11.5 | 12.4 | 13.7 |

NA Not available. [1] See footnotes, Table 1409. [2] Refers to fixed subscriptions to high-speed access to the public internet (a TCP/IP connection), at downstream speeds equal to, or greater than, 256 kbit/s. Including cable modem, DSL, fiber-to-the-home/building, other fixed (wired)-broadband subscriptions, satellite broadband and terrestrial fixed wireless broadband. Excludes subscriptions that have access to data communications (including the internet) via mobile-cellular networks.

Source: The World Bank, Washington, DC, "World Development Indicators" database ©, <http://data.worldbank.org/data-catalog/world-development-indicators>, accessed July 2019.

# Table 1411. Patents by Country: 2017

[Includes only U.S. patents granted to residents of areas outside of the United States and its territories. For information on types of patents, see <http://www.uspto.gov/web/offices/ac/ido/oeip/taf/patdesc.htm>. Countries are in rank order. See also Table 808 and Table 809]

| Country | Total [1] | Utility (inventions) | Designs | Country | Total [1] | Utility (inventions) | Designs |
|---|---|---|---|---|---|---|---|
| **Total.....................** | **182,196** | **167,880** | **13,331** | Netherlands............ | 3,138 | 2,721 | 149 |
| | | | | Switzerland............. | 3,015 | 2,749 | 262 |
| Japan..................... | 51,952 | 49,677 | 2,147 | Australia................ | 1,988 | 1,673 | 255 |
| Korea, South............. | 22,823 | 20,717 | 2,058 | Finland................. | 1,729 | 1,598 | 125 |
| Germany.................. | 18,190 | 16,846 | 1,219 | Austria................. | 1,625 | 1,520 | 104 |
| China.................... | 14,853 | 13,243 | 1,604 | Belgium................ | 1,404 | 1,312 | 75 |
| Taiwan................... | 12,558 | 11,580 | 970 | Denmark............... | 1,248 | 1,106 | 85 |
| Canada.................. | 7,690 | 6,934 | 738 | Singapore.............. | 1,037 | 998 | 38 |
| United Kingdom.......... | 7,686 | 6,635 | 991 | Spain.................. | 974 | 857 | 104 |
| France................... | 7,393 | 6,816 | 530 | Hong Kong............. | 911 | 706 | 204 |
| Israel.................... | 4,310 | 4,092 | 179 | Norway................ | 639 | 618 | 18 |
| India.................... | 4,262 | 4,163 | 98 | Ireland................ | 594 | 562 | 30 |
| Sweden.................. | 3,308 | 3,019 | 285 | Saudi Arabia........... | 578 | 571 | 6 |
| Italy..................... | 3,262 | 2,718 | 532 | Other countries......... | 5,029 | 4,449 | 525 |

[1] Includes patents for botanical plants and reissues, not shown separately.

Source: U.S. Patent and Trademark Office, "General Patent Statistics Reports Available for Viewing," <http://www.uspto.gov/web/offices/ac/ido/oeip/taf/reports_stco.htm>, accessed September 2018; and unpublished data.

# Table 1412. Foreign Stock Market Indices: 1980 to 2018

[As of year end. The DAX-30 index is a total return index which includes dividends, whereas the other foreign indices are price indices which exclude dividends]

| Year | London FTSE 100 | Tokyo Nikkei 225 | Hong Kong Hang Seng | Germany DAX-30 | Paris CAC-40 | Dow Jones Europe STOXX 50 |
|---|---|---|---|---|---|---|
| 1980 | 647 | 7,116 | 1,477 | 481 | (X) | (X) |
| 1985 | 1,413 | 13,113 | 1,752 | 1,366 | (X) | (X) |
| 1990 | 2,144 | 23,849 | 3,025 | 1,398 | 1,518 | 835 |
| 1995 | 3,689 | 19,868 | 10,073 | 2,254 | 1,872 | 1,538 |
| 2000 | 6,223 | 13,786 | 15,096 | 6,434 | 5,926 | 4,557 |
| 2005 | 5,619 | 16,111 | 14,876 | 5,408 | 4,715 | 3,349 |
| 2010 | 5,900 | 10,229 | 23,035 | 6,914 | 3,805 | 2,586 |
| 2013 | 6,749 | 16,291 | 23,306 | 9,552 | 4,296 | 2,919 |
| 2014 | 6,566 | 17,451 | 23,605 | 9,806 | 4,273 | 3,004 |
| 2015 | 6,242 | 19,034 | 21,914 | 10,743 | 4,637 | 3,100 |
| 2016 | 7,143 | 19,114 | 22,001 | 11,481 | 4,862 | 3,011 |
| 2017 | 7,688 | 22,765 | 29,919 | 12,918 | 5,313 | 3,178 |
| 2018 | 6,728 | 20,015 | 25,846 | 10,559 | 4,731 | 2,760 |

X Not applicable.

Source: Global Financial Data, Los Angeles, CA ©, <http://www.globalfinancialdata.com>.

# Table 1413. Research and Development (R&D) Expenditures by Sector and Country: 2017

[Total and per capita expenditures in millions of dollars (1,360,044 represents $1,360,044,000,000). Gross domestic expenditure on R&D (GERD) may include financing from abroad. Selected data are preliminary or estimated. For methodological information for individual countries, see source. GDP = gross domestic product]

| Country | Gross domestic expenditure on R&D (GERD) | | | Percent of GERD performed by: | | | |
|---|---|---|---|---|---|---|---|
| | Total (million current PPP U.S. dollars) [1] | Per capita (million current PPP U.S. dollars) [1] | Percent of GDP | Government sector | Business enterprise sector | Higher education sector | Private non-profit sector |
| OECD total [2] | 1,360,044 | 1,050 | 2.4 | 9.9 | 70.5 | 17.2 | 2.4 |
| EU-28 [2] | 430,121 | 839 | 2.0 | 11.3 | 65.8 | 22.1 | 0.9 |
| EU-15 [3] | 397,754 | 975 | 2.1 | 11.1 | 66.0 | 21.9 | 1.0 |
| **United States [4]** | **543,249** | **1,666** | **2.8** | **9.7** | **73.1** | **13.0** | **4.1** |
| Argentina | 5,024 | 114 | 0.5 | 48.2 | 25.0 | 26.0 | 0.9 |
| Australia [5] | 21,152 | 888 | 1.9 | 12.7 | 53.4 | 30.6 | 3.2 |
| Austria | 14,966 | 1,702 | 3.2 | 7.1 | 70.2 | 22.2 | 0.5 |
| Belgium | 15,189 | 1,338 | 2.7 | 9.4 | 70.2 | 19.8 | 0.6 |
| Canada | 27,163 | 743 | 1.6 | 6.8 | 51.8 | 41.1 | 0.4 |
| Chile | 1,591 | 86 | 0.4 | 13.1 | 34.2 | 45.8 | 6.8 |
| China | 495,981 | 357 | 2.1 | 15.2 | 77.6 | 7.2 | (NA) |
| Czechia | 7,213 | 681 | 1.8 | 17.2 | 62.9 | 19.6 | 0.3 |
| Denmark | 9,545 | 1,655 | 3.0 | 3.0 | 64.7 | 32.1 | 0.3 |
| Estonia | 568 | 432 | 1.3 | 11.8 | 47.2 | 39.6 | 1.4 |
| Finland | 7,038 | 1,278 | 2.8 | 8.5 | 65.3 | 25.4 | 0.8 |
| France | 64,672 | 964 | 2.2 | 12.7 | 65.0 | 20.7 | 1.7 |
| Germany | 132,004 | 1,597 | 3.0 | 13.5 | 69.1 | 17.4 | (NA) |
| Greece | 3,477 | 323 | 1.1 | 22.1 | 48.8 | 28.3 | 0.8 |
| Iceland | 400 | 1,164 | 2.1 | 4.2 | 64.3 | 31.5 | (NA) |
| Ireland [5] | 3,840 | 818 | 1.2 | 4.4 | 71.8 | 23.8 | (NA) |
| Israel [6] | 15,392 | 1,767 | 4.5 | 1.6 | 86.1 | 11.4 | 0.9 |
| Italy | 33,543 | 554 | 1.4 | 12.7 | 61.4 | 24.2 | 1.7 |
| Japan | 170,901 | 1,349 | 3.2 | 7.8 | 78.8 | 12.0 | 1.4 |
| Korea, South | 90,980 | 1,768 | 4.6 | 10.7 | 79.4 | 8.5 | 1.4 |
| Latvia | 281 | 145 | 0.5 | 26.1 | 27.2 | 46.7 | (NA) |
| Lithuania | 845 | 299 | 0.9 | 27.9 | 36.8 | 35.3 | (NA) |
| Mexico [5] | 11,670 | 97 | 0.5 | 37.9 | 30.0 | 26.8 | 5.4 |
| Netherlands | 18,564 | 1,084 | 2.0 | 11.4 | 58.8 | 29.8 | (NA) |
| New Zealand | 2,648 | 548 | 1.4 | 20.1 | 55.2 | 24.7 | (NA) |
| Norway | 6,869 | 1,302 | 2.1 | 13.7 | 52.6 | 33.7 | (NA) |
| Poland | 11,758 | 306 | 1.0 | 2.3 | 64.5 | 32.9 | 0.3 |
| Portugal | 4,454 | 432 | 1.3 | 5.5 | 50.4 | 42.5 | 1.6 |
| Romania | 2,625 | 134 | 0.5 | 32.4 | 56.7 | 10.6 | 0.3 |
| Russia | 41,868 | 285 | 1.1 | 30.4 | 60.1 | 9.0 | 0.4 |
| Slovak Republic | 1,554 | 286 | 0.9 | 20.8 | 54.1 | 24.7 | 0.4 |
| Slovenia | 1,392 | 674 | 1.9 | 13.8 | 74.7 | 11.2 | 0.3 |
| South Africa [5] | 5,817 | 106 | 0.8 | 24.0 | 42.7 | 30.5 | 2.8 |
| Spain | 21,932 | 471 | 1.2 | 17.7 | 55.0 | 27.1 | 0.2 |
| Sweden | 17,562 | 1,746 | 3.4 | 3.6 | 71.3 | 24.9 | 0.1 |
| Switzerland | 18,900 | 2,236 | 3.4 | 0.8 | 69.4 | 27.6 | 2.2 |
| Taiwan | 39,296 | 1,667 | 3.3 | 12.1 | 78.7 | 8.9 | 0.2 |
| Turkey | 21,729 | 271 | 1.0 | 9.6 | 56.9 | 33.5 | (NA) |
| United Kingdom | 49,345 | 747 | 1.7 | 6.5 | 67.6 | 23.7 | 2.2 |

NA Not available or not applicable. [1] Purchasing power parities (PPPs) are currency conversion rates used to convert different currencies to a common value (U.S. dollars in this case). See introductory text, this section. [2] For full membership listing of the Organisation for Economic Co-operation and Development (OECD) and the European Union-28, see introductory text, this section. [3] European Union-15: Austria, Belgium, Denmark, Finland, France, Germany, Greece, Ireland, Italy, Luxembourg, Netherlands, Portugal, Spain, Sweden, and United Kingdom. [4] Excludes all or most capital expenditures. [5] 2015 data. [6] Excludes defense expenditures. The statistical data for Israel are supplied by and under the responsibility of the relevant Israeli authorities. The use of such data by the OECD is without prejudice to the status of the Golan Heights, East Jerusalem and Israeli settlements in the West Bank under the terms of international law.

Source: Organisation for Economic Co-cooperation and Development (OECD), 2019, "Main Science and Technology Indicators," OECD Science, Technology and R&D Statistics (database) ©, <http://dx.doi.org/10.1787/data-00182-en>, accessed September 2019.

# Table 1414. Development Assistance Outlays by Donor Country: 2017

[147,160 represents $147,160,000,000 except percent. Official development assistance (ODA) includes concessional loans and grants made by donor governments to developing countries and to multilateral institutions such as the United Nations or the World Bank]

| Country | Official development assistance (ODA) | | | Multilateral ODA (mil. current U.S. dol.) | Net private grants (mil. current U.S. dol.) |
| | Net disbursements (mil. current U.S. dollars) | Percent of GNI [1] | Percent of total DAC [2] ODA | | |
|---|---|---|---|---|---|
| DAC countries, total [2]......... | **147,160** | **0.31** | **100.0** | **41,600** | **41,762** |
| United States..................... | **34,732** | **0.18** | **23.6** | **4,726** | **35,122** |
| Australia........................ | 3,036 | 0.23 | 2.1 | 624 | (NA) |
| Austria.......................... | 1,251 | 0.30 | 0.9 | 651 | (NA) |
| Belgium......................... | 2,196 | 0.45 | 1.5 | 901 | (NA) |
| Canada.......................... | 4,305 | 0.26 | 2.9 | 1,178 | 2,949 |
| Czechia......................... | 304 | 0.15 | 0.2 | 224 | (NA) |
| Denmark......................... | 2,448 | 0.74 | 1.7 | 727 | 125 |
| Finland.......................... | 1,084 | 0.42 | 0.7 | 486 | (NA) |
| France........................... | 11,331 | 0.43 | 7.7 | 4,682 | (NA) |
| Germany........................ | 25,005 | 0.67 | 17.0 | 5,187 | 1,490 |
| Greece.......................... | 314 | 0.16 | 0.2 | 229 | (NA) |
| Hungary......................... | 149 | 0.11 | 0.1 | 109 | (NA) |
| Iceland.......................... | 68 | 0.28 | – | 14 | (NA) |
| Ireland.......................... | 838 | 0.32 | 0.6 | 345 | 364 |
| Italy............................. | 5,858 | 0.30 | 4.0 | 2,881 | 64 |
| Japan........................... | 11,463 | 0.23 | 7.8 | 3,382 | 475 |
| Korea, South.................... | 2,201 | 0.14 | 1.5 | 586 | 406 |
| Luxembourg..................... | 424 | 1.00 | 0.3 | 120 | (NA) |
| Netherlands..................... | 4,958 | 0.60 | 3.4 | 1,425 | 86 |
| New Zealand.................... | 450 | 0.23 | 0.3 | 79 | 122 |
| Norway.......................... | 4,125 | 0.99 | 2.8 | 998 | (NA) |
| Poland.......................... | 679 | 0.13 | 0.5 | 457 | (NA) |
| Portugal......................... | 381 | 0.18 | 0.3 | 266 | 11 |
| Slovak Republic................. | 119 | 0.13 | 0.1 | 84 | (NA) |
| Slovenia......................... | 76 | 0.16 | 0.1 | 51 | (NA) |
| Spain........................... | 2,560 | 0.19 | 1.7 | 1,877 | (NA) |
| Sweden......................... | 5,563 | 1.02 | 3.8 | 1,736 | (NA) |
| Switzerland...................... | 3,138 | 0.46 | 2.1 | 808 | 548 |
| United Kingdom................. | 18,103 | 0.70 | 12.3 | 6,768 | (NA) |

– Represents or rounds to zero. NA Not available. [1] Gross national income. See headnote, Table 1373. [2] Development Assistance Committee (DAC) of the Organisation for Economic Co-operation and Development (OECD) is comprised of 29 developed countries, as shown above, and European Union institutions, not shown separately.

Source: Organisation for Economic Co-operation and Development (OECD), 2019, "Detailed aid statistics: Official and private flows," OECD International Development Statistics (database) ©, <http://dx.doi.org/10.1787/data-00072-en>, accessed September 2019.

# Table 1415. Net Flow of Financial Resources to Developing Countries and Multilateral Organizations by Donor Country: 2000 to 2017

[134,228 represents $134,228,000,000. Net flow covers official and private loans, grants, development assistance, and technical assistance, minus amortization on loans. Military flows are excluded. GNI = gross national income. For explanation of GNI, see headnote, Table 1373]

| Country | Amount (million dollars) | | | | Percent of GNI | | | |
| | 2000 | 2010 | 2015 | 2017 | 2000 | 2010 | 2015 | 2017 |
|---|---|---|---|---|---|---|---|---|
| DAC countries total [1]............... | **134,228** | **512,792** | **315,651** | **429,090** | **0.54** | **1.25** | **0.72** | **0.91** |
| United States...................... | **25,252** | **216,950** | **38,520** | **172,871** | **0.25** | **1.48** | **0.21** | **0.88** |
| Australia.......................... | 1,891 | 14,531 | 13,840 | 266 | 0.51 | 1.23 | 1.15 | 0.02 |
| Austria........................... | 1,135 | 6,372 | 4,692 | 2,105 | 0.61 | 1.70 | 1.25 | 0.50 |
| Belgium.......................... | 2,281 | 7,896 | 3,635 | 7,728 | 1.00 | 1.68 | 0.79 | 1.57 |
| Canada........................... | 6,483 | 22,642 | 3,718 | 4,348 | 0.95 | 1.46 | 0.24 | 0.27 |
| Czechia.......................... | 16 | 228 | 263 | 124 | 0.03 | 0.13 | 0.16 | 0.06 |
| Denmark.......................... | 2,176 | 4,794 | 2,931 | 5,980 | 1.39 | 1.52 | 0.97 | 1.80 |
| Finland........................... | 1,087 | 4,312 | -48 | 3,704 | 0.91 | 1.78 | -0.02 | 1.45 |
| France............................ | 5,557 | 35,198 | 1,234 | 23,120 | 0.41 | 1.35 | 0.05 | 0.87 |
| Germany.......................... | 12,331 | 41,637 | 47,627 | 49,517 | 0.66 | 1.24 | 1.39 | 1.32 |
| Greece........................... | 229 | 761 | -85 | 364 | 0.20 | 0.26 | -0.04 | 0.18 |
| Hungary.......................... | (NA) | 114 | 156 | -184 | (NA) | 0.09 | 0.13 | -0.14 |
| Iceland........................... | 9 | 29 | 40 | 83 | 0.10 | 0.26 | 0.24 | 0.35 |
| Ireland........................... | 740 | 2,695 | 1,228 | 1,202 | 0.93 | 1.57 | 0.54 | 0.46 |
| Italy.............................. | 10,846 | 9,608 | 15,621 | 14,791 | 1.01 | 0.47 | 0.86 | 0.76 |
| Japan............................ | 11,423 | 48,249 | 37,908 | 37,699 | 0.24 | 0.86 | 0.83 | 0.75 |
| Korea............................ | 44 | 11,834 | 12,318 | 10,882 | 0.01 | 1.17 | 0.89 | 0.71 |
| Luxembourg....................... | 129 | 411 | 363 | 424 | 0.73 | 1.07 | 0.95 | 1.00 |
| Netherlands....................... | 6,947 | 13,013 | 68,160 | 35,700 | 1.85 | 1.67 | 8.91 | 4.35 |
| New Zealand...................... | 142 | 426 | 621 | 648 | 0.32 | 0.32 | 0.37 | 0.33 |
| Norway........................... | 1,437 | 5,876 | 4,565 | 4,001 | 0.87 | 1.41 | 1.12 | 0.96 |
| Poland........................... | 29 | 378 | 499 | 1,114 | 0.02 | 0.08 | 0.11 | 0.22 |
| Portugal.......................... | 4,622 | 162 | 128 | 2,149 | 4.45 | 0.07 | 0.07 | 1.01 |
| Slovak Republic................... | 6 | 74 | 85 | 119 | 0.03 | 0.09 | 0.10 | 0.13 |
| Slovenia.......................... | (NA) | 59 | 156 | 23 | (NA) | 0.13 | 0.37 | 0.05 |
| Spain............................ | 23,471 | 10,340 | 22,041 | 8,721 | 4.25 | 0.74 | 1.84 | 0.66 |
| Sweden........................... | 3,952 | 5,127 | 10,365 | 7,041 | 1.76 | 1.10 | 2.05 | 1.29 |
| Switzerland........................ | 1,765 | 23,444 | 6,518 | 16,813 | 0.64 | 4.01 | 0.95 | 2.45 |
| United Kingdom................... | 10,230 | 25,632 | 18,553 | 17,735 | 0.72 | 1.12 | 0.70 | 0.68 |

NA Not available. [1] The OECD Development Assistance Committee (DAC) is comprised of the above-listed member countries plus the European Union.

Source: Organisation for Economic Co-operation and Development (OECD), 2019, "Detailed aid statistics: Official and private flows," OECD International Development Statistics (database) ©, <http://dx.doi.org/10.1787/data-00072-en>, accessed September 2019.

## Table 1416. External Debt by Developing Country: 2000 to 2017

[In millions of U.S. dollars (9,763 represents $9,763,000,000). Total external debt is debt owed to nonresidents repayable in foreign currency, goods, or services. Total external debt is the sum of public, publicly guaranteed, and private nonguaranteed long-term debt, use of International Monetary Fund (IMF) credit, and short-term debt. Short-term debt includes all debt having an original maturity of one year or less and interest in arrears on long-term debt]

| Country | 2000 | 2010 | 2015 | 2017 | Country | 2000 | 2010 | 2015 | 2017 |
|---|---|---|---|---|---|---|---|---|---|
| Angola | 9,763 | 16,949 | 27,991 | 37,201 | Lebanon | 10,073 | 47,699 | 67,612 | 73,526 |
| Azerbaijan | 1,585 | 7,279 | 13,758 | 15,254 | Mexico | 152,558 | 245,906 | 426,905 | 455,058 |
| Bangladesh | 15,603 | 26,881 | 36,305 | 47,155 | Mongolia | 960 | 5,928 | 21,940 | 28,199 |
| Belarus | 2,620 | 28,412 | 38,258 | 39,584 | Morocco | 20,790 | 27,259 | 43,059 | 49,752 |
| Bosnia and Herzegovina | 2,791 | 14,289 | 13,771 | 14,495 | Myanmar | 6,239 | 10,187 | 14,848 | 16,139 |
| Brazil | 242,512 | 352,364 | 543,397 | 542,980 | Nigeria | 32,374 | 15,484 | 28,943 | 40,238 |
| Bulgaria | 12,009 | 50,635 | 40,115 | 40,438 | Pakistan | 33,022 | 62,801 | 65,818 | 84,523 |
| China | 145,666 | 734,465 | 1,325,868 | 1,710,235 | Papua New Guinea | 2,325 | 5,987 | 20,494 | 17,367 |
| Colombia | 34,409 | 64,228 | 113,177 | 124,364 | Paraguay | 3,106 | 15,903 | 16,125 | 16,063 |
| Costa Rica | 4,692 | 8,154 | 23,589 | 25,615 | Peru | 28,834 | 42,154 | 67,185 | 68,083 |
| Cote d'Ivoire | 12,060 | 11,704 | 11,374 | 13,433 | Philippines | 58,456 | 65,358 | 76,448 | 73,080 |
| Dominican Republic | 4,618 | 13,499 | 26,659 | 29,772 | Romania | 11,259 | 115,393 | 96,448 | 109,354 |
| Ecuador | 17,113 | 15,046 | 27,310 | 39,536 | Russia | 146,665 | 417,852 | 467,699 | 492,763 |
| Egypt | 29,233 | 36,776 | 48,340 | 82,886 | Serbia [1] | 11,573 | 32,907 | 31,291 | 34,549 |
| El Salvador | 4,535 | 11,496 | 15,556 | 16,699 | South Africa | 25,435 | 108,392 | 138,078 | 176,335 |
| Ethiopia | 5,516 | 7,286 | 21,021 | 26,562 | Sri Lanka | 9,250 | 21,684 | 43,925 | 50,142 |
| Georgia | 1,826 | 8,790 | 14,375 | 15,756 | Sudan [2] | 16,076 | 22,323 | 21,429 | 21,754 |
| Ghana | 6,743 | 9,110 | 20,633 | 22,022 | Tanzania | 7,188 | 8,892 | 15,451 | 18,242 |
| Guatemala | 3,948 | 15,043 | 20,378 | 22,993 | Thailand | 79,830 | 106,358 | 129,654 | 129,765 |
| India | 101,131 | 290,428 | 478,875 | 513,209 | Tunisia | 11,355 | 22,472 | 27,184 | 32,152 |
| Indonesia | 144,032 | 198,269 | 306,201 | 354,352 | Turkey | 116,799 | 300,869 | 399,966 | 454,725 |
| Jamaica | 4,828 | 14,193 | 14,113 | 14,722 | Ukraine | 13,910 | 124,297 | 117,182 | 113,281 |
| Jordan | 11,063 | 17,073 | 25,739 | 30,036 | Uzbekistan | 4,948 | 7,802 | 14,802 | 17,708 |
| Kazakhstan | 12,890 | 119,145 | 153,395 | 167,485 | Venezuela | 42,753 | 101,766 | 124,386 | 105,598 |
| Kenya | 6,148 | 8,848 | 19,764 | 26,424 | Vietnam | 12,785 | 44,902 | 77,806 | 104,079 |
| Laos | 2,531 | 6,554 | 11,664 | 14,498 | Zambia | 5,811 | 4,384 | 11,754 | 16,309 |

[1] Data from 2000 to 2005 are for Serbia and Montenegro. In June 2006, Serbia and Montenegro became separate countries; beginning 2006, data exclude Montenegro. Data from 2008 onward exclude Kosovo, which declared independence that year. [2] South Sudan declared independence July 2011. Data are shown separately for South Sudan where available.

Source: The World Bank, Washington, DC, "External debt stocks, total," World Development Indicators (database) ©, <http://data.worldbank.org/data-catalog/world-development-indicators>, accessed August 2019.

## Table 1417. Foreign Direct Investment Flows in Selected Countries: 2010 to 2018

[In millions of dollars (210,554 represents $210,554,000,000). Data are converted to U.S. dollars using the yearly average exchange rate]

| Country | Inflows | | | | | Outflows | | | | |
|---|---|---|---|---|---|---|---|---|---|---|
| | 2010 | 2015 | 2016 | 2017 | 2018 | 2010 | 2015 | 2016 | 2017 | 2018 |
| United States | 210,544 | 481,502 | 486,022 | 291,898 | 268,441 | 296,334 | 279,471 | 309,901 | 321,822 | -68,407 |
| Australia | 36,442 | 20,466 | 47,753 | 46,363 | (NA) | 19,803 | -20,059 | 2,321 | 4,881 | (NA) |
| Austria | -21,694 | -7,577 | -34,863 | 11,547 | 6,374 | -14,065 | -1,783 | -32,782 | 11,800 | -3,837 |
| Belgium | 43,233 | 23,536 | 50,971 | -5,765 | 4,873 | -8,313 | 39,896 | 20,968 | 24,208 | 6,909 |
| Brazil | 77,687 | 49,514 | 52,751 | 67,583 | 61,223 | 22,060 | -7,686 | -5,934 | 16,678 | -13,036 |
| Canada | 28,399 | 43,853 | 35,992 | 24,826 | 42,231 | 34,721 | 67,467 | 69,948 | 79,802 | 49,593 |
| Chile | 15,033 | 20,011 | 11,942 | 6,856 | 7,160 | 8,474 | 14,886 | 6,801 | 6,175 | 3,027 |
| China | 243,703 | 242,489 | 174,750 | 166,084 | 203,492 | 57,954 | 174,391 | 216,424 | 138,293 | 96,472 |
| Czechia | 6,147 | 465 | 9,814 | 9,518 | 9,477 | 1,168 | 2,488 | 2,182 | 7,557 | 5,277 |
| Denmark | -12,559 | 2,237 | 6,992 | 1,893 | 2,007 | -1,407 | 7,536 | 17,173 | 7,421 | -2,983 |
| Estonia | 1,509 | 36 | 1,095 | 1,713 | 1,470 | 167 | 183 | 538 | 744 | 58 |
| Finland | 7,359 | 1,484 | 9,247 | 1,613 | 1,366 | 10,189 | -16,587 | 26,072 | 2,094 | 1,943 |
| France | 13,891 | 45,355 | 23,055 | 29,812 | 37,286 | 48,158 | 53,206 | 64,785 | 41,271 | 102,408 |
| Germany | 65,646 | 30,563 | 12,614 | 33,190 | 11,917 | 125,453 | 99,023 | 60,344 | 88,075 | 63,280 |
| Greece | 330 | 1,268 | 2,762 | 3,612 | 4,256 | 1,558 | 1,578 | -1,665 | 581 | 848 |
| Hungary | -37,264 | -28,427 | 47,804 | 1,244 | -78,501 | -41,146 | -31,219 | 44,969 | -831 | -83,502 |
| Iceland | (NA) | 670 | -402 | -3,058 | -317 | (NA) | -29 | -1,122 | -3,224 | 148 |
| Indonesia | 13,771 | 16,641 | 3,921 | 20,579 | 21,810 | 2,664 | 5,937 | -12,215 | 2,077 | 8,157 |
| Ireland | 42,807 | 215,829 | 39,377 | 52,722 | -28,073 | 22,350 | 168,359 | 30,055 | -2,043 | 723 |
| Italy | 9,179 | 19,631 | 28,441 | 21,976 | 24,273 | 32,657 | 22,314 | 17,746 | 25,681 | 20,573 |
| Japan | -1,252 | -2,251 | 19,357 | 10,976 | 9,856 | 56,276 | 128,698 | 155,923 | 164,658 | 143,142 |
| Korea, South | 9,497 | 3,076 | 7,415 | 12,699 | (NA) | 28,280 | 18,490 | 30,508 | 51,044 | (NA) |
| Latvia | 379 | 708 | 175 | 733 | 877 | 20 | 68 | 149 | 140 | 151 |
| Lithuania | 799 | 871 | 264 | 653 | 905 | -6 | 85 | 108 | 33 | 838 |
| Luxembourg | 222,023 | 652,012 | 262,724 | 140,894 | -373,306 | 205,556 | 740,284 | 240,470 | 205,041 | -353,902 |
| Netherlands | 135,774 | 329,916 | 210,740 | 82,615 | -276,218 | 210,620 | 397,500 | 221,048 | 132,054 | -265,203 |
| New Zealand | -61 | -311 | 3,069 | 2,538 | 1,534 | 716 | -59 | 7 | -222 | 457 |
| Norway | 17,043 | -2,515 | -3,900 | -5,922 | (NA) | 23,238 | 30,947 | 3,092 | -7,415 | (NA) |
| Poland | 12,799 | 11,819 | 17,329 | 8,667 | 11,354 | 6,148 | 1,928 | 13,122 | 2,305 | 196 |
| Portugal | 2,424 | 6,926 | 6,309 | 6,947 | 4,894 | -9,783 | 5,575 | 2,714 | -2,410 | 271 |
| Russia | 31,668 | 11,858 | 37,176 | 25,954 | 13,228 | 41,116 | 27,090 | 26,951 | 34,153 | 35,820 |
| Slovak Republic | 1,770 | 106 | 805 | 2,277 | 475 | 946 | 6 | 95 | 350 | 234 |
| Slovenia | 106 | 1,675 | 1,245 | 896 | 1,368 | -19 | 267 | 290 | 338 | 267 |
| Spain | (NA) | 11,913 | 27,650 | 20,925 | 41,603 | (NA) | 40,271 | 43,608 | 39,977 | 30,567 |
| Sweden | 141 | 8,470 | 17,624 | 12,167 | 9,962 | 20,364 | 12,922 | 4,520 | 22,769 | 19,668 |
| Switzerland | 28,750 | 80,407 | 60,688 | 38,999 | -87,210 | 85,718 | 87,512 | 88,554 | -34,916 | 26,927 |
| Turkey | 9,086 | 18,903 | 13,707 | 11,478 | 12,942 | 1,469 | 4,812 | 2,892 | 2,634 | 3,606 |
| United Kingdom | 58,180 | 39,189 | 196,034 | 101,290 | 64,476 | 48,075 | -66,827 | -22,505 | 117,605 | 49,872 |

NA Not available.

Source: Organisation for Economic Co-operation and Development (OECD), 2018, "Benchmark definition, 4th edition (BMD4): Foreign direct investment: financial flows, main aggregates," OECD International Direct Investment Statistics (database) ©, <http://dx.doi.org/10.1787/data-00741-en>, accessed July 2019.

# Table 1418. International Transaction Balances, Reserve Assets, and Trade in Relation to Gross Domestic Product (GDP) by Country: 2017 and 2018

[In millions of U.S. dollars (-449,137 represents -$449,137,000,000), except as noted. Minus sign (-) indicates deficit]

| Country | Current account balance | | Reserve assets [1] | | Goods and services trade balance | | Exports as percent of GDP | | Imports as percent of GDP | |
|---|---|---|---|---|---|---|---|---|---|---|
| | 2017 | 2018 | 2017 | 2018 | 2017 | 2018 | 2017 | 2018 | 2017 | 2018 |
| United States......... | -449,137 | -488,480 | 112,252 | 114,757 | -578,421 | (NA) | 12.1 | (NA) | 15.0 | (NA) |
| Albania................. | -981 | -1,008 | 3,524 | 3,829 | -1,960 | -2,079 | 31.6 | 31.7 | 46.6 | 45.5 |
| Argentina.............. | -31,598 | -28,003 | 53,031 | 63,964 | -17,596 | -10,179 | 11.2 | 14.4 | 14.0 | 16.4 |
| Australia............... | -35,758 | -30,508 | 63,561 | 51,048 | 8,184 | 5,263 | 21.2 | 21.7 | 20.6 | 21.3 |
| Austria................. | 7,996 | 10,801 | 9,894 | 11,653 | 12,882 | 16,390 | 53.7 | 54.5 | 50.6 | 51.0 |
| Azerbaijan............. | 1,685 | 6,051 | 6,680 | 6,666 | 2,735 | 7,779 | 48.5 | 54.3 | 41.9 | 37.7 |
| Belgium................ | 3,567 | -6,819 | 16,673 | 17,487 | 5,763 | 1,151 | 85.8 | 87.9 | 84.6 | 87.7 |
| Bolivia................. | -1,871 | -1,990 | 8,474 | 7,178 | -2,587 | -2,068 | 24.9 | 26.0 | 31.8 | 31.1 |
| Brazil.................. | -7,235 | -14,509 | 371,151 | 371,934 | 20,586 | 9,878 | 12.6 | 14.8 | 11.6 | 14.3 |
| Bulgaria............... | 1,847 | 2,959 | 26,693 | 27,045 | 2,132 | 552 | 67.4 | 64.5 | 63.7 | 63.6 |
| Cabo Verde............ | -114 | -87 | 617 | 606 | -368 | -375 | 46.1 | 48.9 | 66.9 | 67.7 |
| Cambodia.............. | -1,743 | -2,773 | 11,262 | 13,373 | -759 | -419 | 60.7 | 61.6 | 64.1 | 63.3 |
| Canada................ | -46,388 | -45,461 | 86,678 | 83,926 | -38,255 | -36,255 | 31.1 | 31.9 | 33.4 | 34.0 |
| Chile.................. | -5,965 | -9,157 | 38,971 | 39,849 | 3,835 | 276 | 28.5 | 28.8 | 27.1 | 28.7 |
| China.................. | 195,117 | 49,092 | 3,158,877 | 3,091,881 | 215,696 | 106,623 | 20.0 | 19.5 | 18.2 | 18.7 |
| Colombia.............. | -10,296 | -12,661 | 46,699 | 47,359 | -15,822 | -16,523 | 15.1 | 15.9 | 20.2 | 20.9 |
| Costa Rica............ | -1,815 | -1,878 | 7,150 | 7,501 | 35 | 382 | 33.1 | 33.7 | 33.0 | 33.1 |
| Croatia................ | 2,997 | 1,459 | 18,818 | 19,991 | 1,241 | 831 | 51.1 | 51.2 | 48.8 | 49.9 |
| Cyprus................. | -1,852 | -1,685 | 308 | 351 | -777 | -421 | 64.8 | 64.3 | 68.3 | 66.0 |
| Czechia................ | 3,148 | 860 | 147,583 | 142,151 | 16,244 | 15,179 | 79.7 | 78.8 | 72.2 | 72.6 |
| Denmark............... | 26,270 | 20,406 | 72,470 | 68,200 | 23,409 | 18,767 | 54.5 | 54.7 | 47.4 | 49.3 |
| Ecuador............... | -481 | -1,358 | 1,678 | 1,896 | -789 | -246 | 20.8 | 22.8 | 21.6 | 23.0 |
| El Salvador............ | -465 | -1,242 | 3,510 | 3,512 | -4,111 | -5,136 | 29.0 | 28.9 | 45.5 | 48.6 |
| Estonia................ | 861 | 524 | 335 | 745 | 1,212 | 1,067 | 76.5 | 75.2 | 72.0 | 71.7 |
| Finland................ | -706 | -5,190 | 8,458 | 8,284 | 734 | -1,563 | 38.5 | 39.0 | 38.2 | 39.5 |
| France................. | -13,307 | -9,247 | 54,781 | 66,103 | -27,370 | -21,484 | 30.8 | 31.3 | 31.9 | 32.1 |
| Georgia................ | -1,331 | -1,249 | 3,039 | 3,289 | -1,807 | -1,880 | 50.3 | 55.1 | 62.2 | 66.7 |
| Germany............... | 296,172 | 291,440 | 59,357 | 59,173 | 279,235 | 270,514 | 47.0 | 47.0 | 39.5 | 40.2 |
| Greece................. | -3,325 | -6,370 | 3,096 | 2,918 | -2,071 | -570 | 33.0 | 36.1 | 34.0 | 36.4 |
| Guatemala............. | 1,189 | 638 | 11,478 | 12,299 | -6,099 | -7,504 | 18.8 | 18.1 | 26.9 | 27.7 |
| Honduras.............. | -409 | -1,003 | 4,679 | 4,741 | -3,340 | -4,421 | 43.4 | 41.8 | 57.9 | 60.4 |
| Hong Kong, China.... | 15,885 | 15,625 | 431,355 | 424,534 | 3,708 | 292 | 188.8 | 188.0 | 187.7 | 188.0 |
| Hungary................ | 3,848 | 806 | 27,874 | 30,068 | 10,572 | 7,443 | 88.2 | 86.5 | 80.7 | 81.7 |
| Iceland................ | 899 | 756 | 6,483 | 6,239 | 1,000 | 799 | 46.1 | 47.2 | 42.0 | 44.1 |
| Indonesia.............. | -16,196 | -31,060 | 126,857 | 117,425 | 10,300 | -11,363 | 20.2 | 21.0 | 19.2 | 22.1 |
| Iraq................... | 14,892 | 35,270 | 45,571 | 60,595 | 5,184 | 13,576 | 38.4 | 43.6 | 35.7 | 37.6 |
| Ireland................ | 29,099 | 34,638 | 4,162 | 4,975 | 100,617 | 117,393 | 119.9 | 120.5 | 89.5 | 89.3 |
| Israel.................. | 9,968 | 10,797 | 113,010 | 115,266 | 5,924 | (NA) | 29.2 | (NA) | 27.6 | (NA) |
| Italy................... | 51,595 | 50,559 | 48,919 | 51,331 | 56,687 | 51,890 | 31.2 | 31.8 | 28.3 | 29.3 |
| Japan.................. | 201,639 | 174,719 | 1,232,244 | 1,238,935 | 45,435 | (NA) | 17.8 | (NA) | 16.8 | (NA) |
| Korea, South.......... | 75,231 | 76,409 | 384,453 | 398,780 | 82,702 | 81,236 | 43.1 | 44.0 | 37.7 | 39.0 |
| Lithuania.............. | 463 | 817 | 4,207 | 5,531 | 1,327 | 1,400 | 80.9 | 82.3 | 78.1 | 79.7 |
| Luxembourg............ | 3,067 | 3,426 | 785 | 847 | 20,745 | 23,659 | 223.1 | 224.8 | 189.8 | 190.7 |
| Mexico................. | -19,401 | -22,186 | 170,458 | 171,445 | -20,922 | -22,965 | 37.6 | 39.2 | 39.4 | 41.1 |
| Moldova............... | -562 | -1,187 | 2,800 | 2,992 | -2,267 | -2,923 | 31.1 | 30.4 | 54.5 | 56.3 |
| Mongolia............... | -1,155 | -2,207 | 2,839 | 2,780 | 270 | -424 | 59.8 | 60.3 | 57.4 | 63.5 |
| Montenegro............ | -760 | -943 | 1,077 | 1,261 | -1,136 | -1,317 | 41.1 | 43.2 | 64.5 | 67.4 |
| Morocco............... | -3,677 | -6,445 | 25,268 | 23,550 | -10,432 | -12,469 | 37.1 | 38.3 | 46.6 | 48.8 |
| Namibia............... | -689 | -312 | 2,432 | 2,150 | -1,236 | -899 | 37.5 | 38.7 | 46.6 | 44.9 |
| Netherlands............ | 87,393 | 98,507 | 12,893 | 13,195 | 89,146 | 97,016 | 83.0 | 83.0 | 72.2 | 72.4 |
| New Zealand.......... | -5,870 | -7,396 | 20,684 | 17,657 | 1,798 | (NA) | 27.6 | (NA) | 26.7 | (NA) |
| Nicaragua.............. | -675 | 83 | 2,758 | 2,261 | -1,885 | -1,219 | 41.2 | 42.0 | 54.8 | 51.3 |
| Norway................. | 22,367 | 35,182 | 65,924 | 63,145 | 12,600 | 23,931 | 36.2 | 38.1 | 33.1 | 32.5 |
| Pakistan............... | -16,251 | -18,250 | 15,765 | 9,175 | -28,413 | -34,102 | 8.2 | 8.5 | 17.6 | 19.4 |
| Philippines............ | -2,143 | -7,879 | 73,228 | 71,040 | -30,889 | -41,995 | 31.0 | 31.7 | 40.9 | 44.4 |
| Poland................. | 602 | -3,929 | 108,975 | 111,656 | 22,014 | 20,034 | 54.3 | 55.3 | 50.2 | 51.9 |
| Portugal............... | 1,167 | -1,508 | 10,153 | 9,159 | 1,758 | 357 | 42.7 | 43.6 | 41.9 | 43.4 |
| Romania................ | -6,755 | -10,757 | 40,107 | 37,856 | -4,496 | -7,692 | 41.5 | 41.6 | 43.7 | 44.9 |
| Russia................. | 33,156 | 113,811 | 356,084 | 381,575 | 84,351 | 165,288 | 26.1 | 30.7 | 20.7 | 20.8 |
| Saudi Arabia.......... | 10,464 | 72,337 | 495,990 | 496,156 | 37,947 | 100,403 | 34.9 | 39.7 | 29.3 | 26.8 |
| Serbia................. | -2,322 | -2,630 | 11,099 | 12,033 | -2,908 | -4,225 | 50.5 | 50.9 | 57.1 | 59.3 |
| Singapore............. | 53,913 | 63,910 | 279,690 | 287,466 | 84,632 | 96,730 | 171.4 | 176.4 | 146.4 | 149.8 |
| Slovenia............... | 3,483 | 3,785 | 758 | 802 | 4,712 | 5,140 | 82.9 | 85.2 | 73.2 | 75.7 |
| South Africa........... | -8,908 | -13,381 | 45,499 | 46,478 | 4,766 | 1,266 | 29.8 | 30.1 | 28.4 | 29.7 |
| Spain.................. | 25,008 | 12,924 | 57,663 | 59,030 | 38,304 | 27,858 | 34.3 | 34.3 | 31.4 | 32.3 |
| Sudan................. | -4,611 | -4,679 | 178 | (NA) | -2,613 | -857 | 9.7 | 10.2 | 11.8 | 12.3 |
| Sweden................ | 15,015 | 10,643 | 56,951 | 55,386 | 19,739 | 17,355 | 45.3 | 47.0 | 41.7 | 43.9 |
| Switzerland............ | 45,360 | 72,186 | 767,680 | 744,167 | 72,721 | 85,196 | 64.9 | 65.5 | 54.2 | 53.4 |
| Thailand............... | 50,211 | 35,159 | 196,121 | 199,296 | 62,964 | 52,167 | 68.2 | 66.8 | 54.3 | 56.5 |
| Turkey................. | -47,347 | -27,115 | 84,115 | 72,867 | -38,435 | -9,029 | 24.8 | 29.6 | 29.3 | 30.8 |
| Uganda................ | -1,491 | -2,565 | 3,721 | 3,359 | -1,874 | -2,431 | 18.1 | 19.5 | 25.3 | 28.3 |
| Ukraine................ | -2,442 | -4,510 | 17,748 | 19,818 | -8,627 | -11,250 | 48.0 | 45.2 | 55.7 | 53.8 |
| United Kingdom....... | -87,895 | -108,745 | 137,924 | 159,872 | -30,802 | -41,315 | 30.1 | 29.9 | 31.3 | 31.4 |
| Uruguay............... | 465 | -374 | 15,955 | 15,552 | 1,748 | 1,202 | 21.4 | 21.0 | 18.3 | 19.0 |
| Zambia................ | -1,006 | -708 | 2,082 | 1,569 | 351 | -218 | 35.2 | 37.4 | 33.8 | 38.2 |

NA Not available. [1] Reserve assets are comprised of special drawing rights and reserve position in International Monetary Fund (IMF), and foreign exchange holdings. Gold holdings are excluded.

Source: The World Bank, Washington, DC, "World Development Indicators" database ©, <http://data.worldbank.org/data-catalog/world-development-indicators>, accessed August 2019.

## Table 1419. International Tourism Arrivals, Expenditures, and Receipts—Leading Countries: 2000 to 2017

[Arrivals at national borders in thousands of non-resident tourists (677,387 represents 677,387,000). Expenditures and receipts in millions of current U.S. dollars (451,766 represents $451,766,000,000). Receipts are money spent by foreign tourists while traveling inside the country shown and include prepayment for goods or services in destination country. Expenditures are money spent by tourists from a given country of origin while traveling outside their home country. Data exclude receipts and expenditures for international transport. Ranked for top 50 countries in tourist arrivals as of 2017. Sources and collection methods differ, thus caution should be used in comparing data across countries]

| Country | Arrivals (1,000) | | | | | Expenditures (mil. dol.) | | | | | Receipts (mil. dol.) | | | | |
|---|---|---|---|---|---|---|---|---|---|---|---|---|---|---|---|
| | 2000 | 2005 | 2010 | 2015 | 2017 | 2000 | 2005 | 2010 | 2015 | 2017 | 2000 | 2005 | 2010 | 2015 | 2017 |
| World [1] | 677,387 | 808,774 | 956,372 | 1,206,216 | 1,341,457 | 451,766 | 663,327 | 874,868 | 1,193,823 | 1,309,900 | 498,628 | 714,016 | 965,630 | 1,215,027 | 1,338,751 |
| France | 77,190 | 74,988 | 76,647 | 84,452 | 86,861 | 22,533 | 31,354 | 38,304 | 39,508 | 41,600 | 32,855 | 43,947 | 46,466 | 58,307 | 61,020 |
| Spain | 46,403 | 55,914 | 52,677 | 68,175 | 81,786 | 5,922 | 15,175 | 16,930 | 17,347 | 22,321 | 29,802 | 49,565 | 54,305 | 56,532 | 68,437 |
| United States | 51,238 | 49,206 | 60,010 | 77,774 | 76,941 | 67,860 | 79,990 | 86,623 | 114,550 | 135,023 | 100,716 | 101,469 | 137,010 | 206,936 | 210,748 |
| China | 31,229 | 46,809 | 55,664 | 56,886 | 60,740 | 13,114 | 21,759 | 54,880 | 249,831 | 257,733 | 16,231 | 29,296 | 45,814 | 44,969 | 32,617 |
| Italy | 41,181 | 36,513 | 43,626 | 50,732 | 58,253 | 15,683 | 22,370 | 26,908 | 24,417 | 27,883 | 27,494 | 35,318 | 38,438 | 39,420 | 44,548 |
| Mexico | 20,641 | 21,915 | 23,290 | 32,093 | 39,291 | 5,499 | 7,600 | 7,255 | 10,098 | 10,840 | 8,294 | 11,803 | 11,992 | 17,734 | 21,336 |
| United Kingdom | 23,212 | 28,039 | 28,295 | 34,436 | 37,651 | 38,262 | 62,837 | 62,790 | 74,010 | 71,671 | 21,769 | 32,032 | 33,971 | 50,242 | 51,474 |
| Turkey | 9,586 | 20,273 | 31,364 | 39,478 | 37,601 | 1,713 | 3,104 | 5,194 | 5,368 | 4,823 | 7,636 | 19,191 | 22,585 | 26,616 | 22,478 |
| Germany | 18,983 | 21,500 | 26,875 | 34,970 | 37,452 | 52,824 | 74,190 | 77,580 | 77,445 | 89,677 | 18,611 | 29,122 | 34,564 | 36,883 | 39,953 |
| Thailand | 9,579 | 11,567 | 15,936 | 29,923 | 35,592 | 2,772 | 3,803 | 5,627 | 7,718 | 9,593 | 7,483 | 9,576 | 20,104 | 44,922 | 57,477 |
| Austria | 17,982 | 19,952 | 22,004 | 26,728 | 29,460 | 6,232 | 9,316 | 10,122 | 9,327 | 10,761 | 9,899 | 16,243 | 18,758 | 18,287 | 20,323 |
| Japan | 4,757 | 6,728 | 8,611 | 19,737 | 28,691 | 31,884 | 37,565 | 27,950 | 15,974 | 18,177 | 3,373 | 12,430 | 13,224 | 24,968 | 34,065 |
| Hong Kong, China | 8,814 | 14,773 | 20,085 | 26,686 | 27,884 | 12,502 | 13,305 | 17,357 | 23,059 | 25,388 | 5,868 | 10,179 | 21,689 | 35,574 | 31,682 |
| Greece | 13,096 | 14,765 | 15,007 | 23,599 | 27,194 | 4,558 | 3,039 | 2,854 | 2,259 | 2,155 | 5,219 | 13,334 | 12,479 | 15,662 | 16,864 |
| Malaysia | 10,222 | 16,431 | 24,577 | 25,721 | 25,948 | 2,075 | 3,711 | 8,324 | 10,708 | 10,699 | 5,011 | 8,846 | 18,152 | 17,666 | 18,352 |
| Russia | 21,169 | 22,201 | 22,281 | 33,729 | 24,390 | 8,848 | 16,972 | 26,693 | 34,932 | 31,058 | 3,429 | 5,870 | 8,830 | 8,420 | 8,945 |
| Canada | 19,627 | 18,771 | 16,219 | 17,971 | 20,798 | 12,438 | 18,021 | 29,727 | 30,263 | 31,816 | 10,778 | 13,651 | 15,829 | 16,527 | 20,404 |
| Poland | 17,400 | 15,200 | 12,470 | 16,728 | 18,258 | 3,315 | 5,547 | 8,570 | 7,939 | 8,876 | 5,677 | 6,304 | 9,576 | 10,474 | 12,772 |
| Netherlands | 10,003 | 10,012 | 10,883 | 15,007 | 17,924 | 12,191 | 13,724 | 19,044 | 18,038 | 19,513 | 7,197 | 8,770 | 11,653 | 13,171 | 15,827 |
| Macao, China | 5,197 | 9,014 | 11,926 | 14,308 | 17,255 | (NA) | 412 | 800 | 1,227 | 1,244 | (NA) | 6,924 | 22,276 | 30,981 | 35,726 |
| Saudi Arabia | 6,585 | 8,037 | 10,850 | 17,994 | 16,109 | (NA) | 9,087 | 21,135 | 19,346 | 17,312 | (NA) | 4,626 | 6,712 | 10,130 | 12,056 |
| Croatia | 5,831 | 7,743 | 9,111 | 12,683 | 15,593 | 568 | 754 | 832 | 755 | 1,369 | 2,758 | 7,370 | 8,069 | 8,833 | 10,915 |
| India | 2,649 | 3,919 | 5,776 | 13,284 | 15,543 | 2,690 | 6,187 | 10,490 | 14,838 | 18,443 | 3,460 | 7,493 | 14,490 | 21,013 | 27,365 |
| Portugal | 5,599 | 5,769 | 6,756 | 11,723 | 15,432 | 2,228 | 3,050 | 3,906 | 4,005 | 4,854 | 5,243 | 7,676 | 10,006 | 12,692 | 17,276 |
| Ukraine | 6,431 | 17,631 | 21,203 | 12,428 | 14,230 | 470 | 2,805 | 3,742 | 5,101 | 7,128 | 394 | 3,125 | 3,788 | 1,082 | 1,261 |
| Indonesia | 5,064 | 5,002 | 7,003 | 10,407 | 14,040 | 3,197 | 3,584 | 6,395 | 7,292 | 8,289 | 4,975 | 4,522 | 6,958 | 10,761 | 12,520 |
| Singapore | 6,062 | 7,079 | 9,161 | 12,051 | 13,903 | 4,535 | 10,070 | 18,700 | 23,702 | 24,543 | 5,142 | 6,209 | 14,178 | 16,617 | 19,707 |
| Korea, South | 5,322 | 6,023 | 8,798 | 13,232 | 13,336 | 7,132 | 15,406 | 18,766 | 25,270 | 30,600 | 6,834 | 5,806 | 10,328 | 15,214 | 13,427 |
| Vietnam | 2,140 | 3,477 | 5,050 | 7,944 | 12,922 | (NA) | (NA) | (NA) | (NA) | (NA) | (NA) | (NA) | (NA) | (NA) | (NA) |
| Denmark | 3,535 | 9,587 | 9,425 | 10,424 | 11,743 | 4,669 | 6,850 | 9,082 | 8,918 | 9,640 | 3,671 | 5,293 | 5,704 | 6,685 | 7,969 |
| Bahrain | 3,869 | 6,313 | 11,952 | 9,670 | 11,370 | 224 | 414 | 506 | 822 | 1,791 | 573 | 920 | 1,362 | 1,574 | 3,642 |
| Morocco | 4,278 | 5,843 | 9,288 | 10,177 | 11,349 | 425 | 612 | 1,203 | 1,402 | 1,793 | 2,039 | 4,610 | 6,702 | 6,260 | 7,494 |
| Belarus | 60 | 91 | 119 | 4,386 | 11,060 | 216 | 448 | 622 | 901 | 983 | 93 | 253 | 440 | 729 | 801 |
| Romania | 5,264 | 5,839 | 7,498 | 9,331 | 10,926 | 425 | 923 | 1,637 | 2,059 | 3,491 | 359 | 1,051 | 1,136 | 1,711 | 2,539 |
| Ireland | 6,646 | 7,333 | 7,134 | 9,528 | 10,338 | 2,525 | 6,074 | 7,071 | 5,694 | 6,612 | 2,615 | 4,782 | 4,086 | 4,785 | 5,657 |
| South Africa | 5,872 | 7,369 | 8,074 | 8,904 | 10,285 | 2,085 | 3,374 | 5,595 | 2,998 | 3,256 | 2,677 | 7,516 | 9,085 | 8,259 | 8,810 |
| Czechia | 4,773 | 6,336 | 6,334 | 8,707 | 10,160 | 1,276 | 2,405 | 4,252 | 4,772 | 5,451 | 2,973 | 4,813 | 7,172 | 6,056 | 6,968 |
| Switzerland | 7,821 | 7,229 | 8,628 | 9,305 | 9,889 | 5,419 | 8,801 | 11,173 | 16,293 | 17,081 | 6,652 | 10,047 | 14,721 | 16,428 | 17,032 |
| Bulgaria | 2,785 | 4,837 | 6,047 | 7,099 | 8,883 | 538 | 1,309 | 826 | 1,116 | 1,695 | 1,074 | 2,412 | 3,343 | 3,154 | 4,114 |
| Australia | 4,931 | 5,499 | 5,790 | 7,450 | 8,815 | 6,388 | 11,749 | 22,558 | 23,734 | 34,251 | 9,375 | 16,750 | 28,472 | 28,892 | 41,754 |
| Belgium | 6,457 | 6,747 | 7,186 | 8,355 | 8,385 | 9,429 | 14,948 | 18,866 | 18,922 | 20,814 | 6,592 | 9,845 | 11,395 | 11,964 | 12,506 |
| Egypt | 5,116 | 8,244 | 14,051 | 9,139 | 8,157 | 1,072 | 1,629 | 2,240 | 3,442 | 2,160 | 4,345 | 6,851 | 12,528 | 6,065 | 7,775 |
| Kazakhstan | 1,683 | 4,365 | 4,097 | 6,430 | 7,701 | 408 | 753 | 1,273 | 1,979 | 1,791 | 356 | 701 | 1,005 | 1,534 | 1,781 |
| Sweden | 3,828 | 4,883 | 5,183 | 6,482 | 7,054 | 8,048 | 10,014 | 12,126 | 14,410 | 17,097 | 4,064 | 6,554 | 8,336 | 11,307 | 14,205 |
| Tunisia | 5,058 | 6,378 | 7,828 | 5,359 | 7,052 | 263 | 374 | 547 | 696 | 795 | 1,682 | 2,143 | 2,645 | 1,381 | 1,305 |
| Argentina | 2,909 | 3,823 | 5,325 | 5,736 | 6,720 | 4,425 | 2,790 | 4,951 | 6,982 | 10,506 | 2,904 | 2,729 | 4,989 | 4,927 | 5,060 |
| Philippines | 1,992 | 2,623 | 3,520 | 5,361 | 6,621 | 1,642 | 3,018 | 5,487 | 11,343 | 12,194 | 2,156 | 2,287 | 2,645 | 5,273 | 6,988 |
| Brazil | 5,313 | 5,358 | 5,161 | 6,306 | 6,589 | 3,894 | 4,720 | 15,965 | 17,357 | 19,002 | 1,810 | 3,861 | 5,261 | 5,844 | 5,809 |
| Georgia | 387 | 560 | 2,032 | 5,256 | 6,483 | 110 | 169 | 199 | 330 | 464 | 97 | 241 | 659 | 1,868 | 2,704 |
| Chile | 1,742 | 2,027 | 2,801 | 4,478 | 6,450 | 620 | 810 | 1,313 | 1,963 | 2,316 | 819 | 1,001 | 1,552 | 2,481 | 3,634 |

NA Not available. [1] Includes other countries not shown separately.

Source: The World Bank, Washington, DC, "World Development Indicators" database ©, <http://data.worldbank.org/data-catalog/world-development-indicators>, accessed July 2019.

# Table 1420. Military Expenditures as a Percent of GDP by Country: Selected Years 2016 to 2019

[Military expenditures compares spending on defense programs for the most recent year available as a percent of gross domestic product (GDP), calculated on an exchange rate basis]

| Country | Data as of year | Expenditures (percent of GDP) | Rank [1] | Country | Data as of year | Expenditures (percent of GDP) | Rank [1] |
|---|---|---|---|---|---|---|---|
| **United States**............ | **2016** | **3.3** | **24** | Kazakhstan................ | 2017 | 0.8 | 129 |
| Afghanistan................ | 2017 | 0.9 | 122 | Kenya.................... | 2019 | 1.3 | 91 |
| Albania.................... | 2019 [2] | 1.3 | 94 | Korea, South.............. | 2017 | 2.7 | 37 |
| Algeria.................... | 2017 | 5.8 | 5 | Lebanon.................. | 2017 | 2.9 | 32 |
| Angola.................... | 2016 | 3.0 | 31 | Lithuania................. | 2018 | 2.0 | 54 |
| Argentina.................. | 2016 | 1.0 | 117 | Malaysia................. | 2017 | 1.1 | 108 |
| Armenia................... | 2018 | 4.2 | 14 | Mexico................... | 2017 | 0.5 | 147 |
| Australia.................. | 2016 | 2.0 | 51 | Montenegro............... | 2019 [2] | 1.7 | 70 |
| Austria................... | 2018 | 0.6 | 142 | Morocco.................. | 2017 | 3.2 | 25 |
| Azerbaijan................ | 2016 | 3.6 | 17 | Nepal.................... | 2017 | 1.6 | 77 |
| Bangladesh............... | 2017 | 1.4 | 79 | Netherlands.............. | 2018 | 1.4 | 89 |
| Brazil.................... | 2017 | 1.4 | 82 | New Zealand............. | 2017 | 1.1 | 109 |
| Bulgaria.................. | 2018 | 1.6 | 76 | Nigeria.................. | 2018 | 0.5 | 146 |
| Cambodia................. | 2017 | 2.1 | 48 | North Macedonia.......... | 2018 | 1.2 | 101 |
| Canada................... | 2017 | 1.3 | 92 | Norway.................. | 2018 | 1.6 | 71 |
| Chile..................... | 2016 | 1.9 | 57 | Oman.................... | 2017 | 12.1 | 1 |
| China.................... | 2017 | 2.0 | 52 | Pakistan................. | 2017 | 3.5 | 21 |
| Colombia.................. | 2018 [2] | 3.5 | 19 | Peru..................... | 2017 | 0.9 | 126 |
| Congo, Republic of the. .. | 2016 | 7.2 | 4 | Philippines............... | 2017 | 1.4 | 83 |
| Czechia.................. | 2018 | 1.1 | 107 | Poland................... | 2018 [2] | 2.0 | 55 |
| Denmark.................. | 2018 | 1.2 | 99 | Romania................. | 2018 | 1.9 | 56 |
| Ecuador.................. | 2017 | 1.7 | 67 | Russia................... | 2017 | 4.2 | 13 |
| Egypt.................... | 2016 | 1.7 | 69 | Saudi Arabia............. | 2016 | 9.9 | 3 |
| France................... | 2017 | 1.8 | 62 | South Africa............. | 2016 | 1.1 | 110 |
| Georgia.................. | 2018 | 2.1 | 47 | Spain.................... | 2018 | 0.9 | 121 |
| Germany................. | 2018 | 1.2 | 97 | Sri Lanka................ | 2017 | 2.1 | 46 |
| Ghana................... | 2017 | 0.4 | 148 | Tanzania................. | 2016 | 1.1 | 104 |
| Greece................... | 2017 | 2.4 | 41 | Thailand................. | 2017 | 1.5 | 78 |
| India.................... | 2016 | 2.5 | 40 | Tunisia.................. | 2017 | 2.0 | 50 |
| Indonesia................ | 2017 | 0.8 | 128 | Turkey................... | 2018 | 2.9 | 33 |
| Iran..................... | 2017 | 5.0 | 8 | Uganda.................. | 2017 | 1.7 | 68 |
| Iraq..................... | 2016 | 3.6 | 18 | Ukraine.................. | 2017 | 3.5 | 22 |
| Ireland.................. | 2017 | 0.4 | 149 | United Arab Emirates..... | 2017 | 4.9 | 9 |
| Israel.................... | 2017 | 5.6 | 6 | United Kingdom........... | 2016 | 2.2 | 43 |
| Italy..................... | 2017 | 1.1 | 105 | Vietnam.................. | 2017 | 2.2 | 45 |
| Japan.................... | 2016 | 0.9 | 120 | Zambia.................. | 2018 | 1.3 | 96 |
| Jordan................... | 2017 | 4.8 | 11 | Zimbabwe................ | 2016 | 2.2 | 44 |

[1] Based on a list of 156 countries for which data is available. Not all countries are shown. [2] Data are estimated.

Source: Central Intelligence Agency, *The World Factbook*, <https://www.cia.gov/library/publications/the-world-factbook/index.html>, accessed August 2019.

# Table 1421. Terrorism Attacks, Fatalities, Injuries, and Hostages Taken for Top 10 Countries and Perpetrator Groups: 2016 and 2017

[Data shown for top 10 countries and perpetrator groups of attacks in 2017. Based on data collected by the National Consortium for the Study of Terrorism and Responses to Terrorism (START) and maintained in the Global Terrorism Database (GTD). Any assessments and descriptions, including those regarding the nature of the incidents or the factual circumstances thereof, are offered only as part of the analytic work product of the National Consortium START and may not reflect the views of the U.S. Government]

| Country and perpetrator group | 2016 | | | | 2017 | | | |
|---|---|---|---|---|---|---|---|---|
| | Attacks | Fatalities [1] | Injuries [1] | Kidnapped/ hostages taken | Attacks | Fatalities [1] | Injuries [1] | Kidnapped/ hostages taken |
| **Worldwide total**............................. | **11,150** | **25,722** | **33,932** | **15,664** | **8,584** | **18,753** | **19,461** | **8,937** |
| By country: | | | | | | | | |
| Iraq.................................. | 2,969 | 9,782 | 13,317 | 8,598 | 1,951 | 4,269 | 4,077 | 1,960 |
| Afghanistan.......................... | 1,343 | 4,578 | 5,057 | 1,694 | 1,171 | 4,672 | 5,023 | 835 |
| India................................ | 931 | 344 | 636 | 317 | 860 | 380 | 601 | 224 |
| Pakistan............................. | 739 | 957 | 1,729 | 452 | 574 | 851 | 1,827 | 106 |
| Philippines........................... | 484 | 272 | 416 | 218 | 483 | 327 | 298 | 408 |
| Nigeria.............................. | 467 | 1,832 | 919 | 265 | 411 | 1,532 | 852 | 245 |
| Somalia............................. | 367 | 735 | 943 | 391 | 370 | 1,469 | 1,093 | 286 |
| Nepal............................... | 43 | 5 | 15 | 1 | 247 | 4 | 94 | 10 |
| Egypt............................... | 262 | 293 | 376 | 27 | 169 | 655 | 481 | 37 |
| Syria [2]............................. | 365 | 2,119 | 2,726 | 1,406 | 141 | 1,096 | 1,055 | 267 |
| By perpetrator: | | | | | | | | |
| Islamic State of Iraq and Syria (ISIS) [3].... | 1,153 | 9,180 | 7,786 | 8,391 | 857 | 4,350 | 3,262 | 2,180 |
| Taliban.............................. | 851 | 3,620 | 3,572 | 1,501 | 703 | 3,654 | 3,205 | 705 |
| Al-Shabaab.......................... | 342 | 736 | 927 | 393 | 353 | 1,464 | 1,049 | 316 |
| Maoists/Communist Party of India-Maoist......................... | 338 | 177 | 141 | 171 | 295 | 206 | 212 | 125 |
| Boko Haram/ISIS West Africa.............. | 200 | 1,090 | 1,121 | 232 | 276 | 1,287 | 949 | 235 |

[1] Includes perpetrators. [2] Given the limitations of media coverage in Syria, the data presented here are conservative estimates of terrorism in Syria. Consistent with START's practice of including in the GTD only those attacks that have been verified by at least one well-regarded source, these statistics represent those incidents that were reported by independent news outlets. [3] Excludes attacks attributed to branches of ISIS or ISIS-inspired individuals.

Source: U.S. State Department, Bureau of Counterterrorism, *Annex of Statistical Information: Country Reports on Terrorism 2017*, September 2018. See also <http://www.state.gov/j/ct/rls/crt/index.htm>.

# Guide to Sources of Statistics, State Statistical Abstracts, and Foreign Statistical Abstracts

Alphabetically arranged, this guide contains references to important primary sources of statistical information for the United States and other countries. Secondary sources have been included if the information contained in them is presented in a particularly convenient form or if primary sources are not readily available. Nonrecurrent publications presenting compilations or estimates for years later than 2005, or types of data not available in regular series, are also included. Data are also available in press releases.

Valuable information may also be found in state reports and foreign statistical abstracts, which are included at the end of this appendix, and in reports for particular commodities, industries, or similar segments of our economic and social structures, many of which are not included here.

Publications listed under each subject are divided into two main groups: "U.S. Government" and "Nongovernment." The location of the publisher of each report is given except for federal agencies located in Washington, DC. Most federal publications may be purchased from the Superintendent of Documents, U.S. Government Printing Office, Washington, DC, tel. 1-866-512-1800, or at <http://bookstore.gpo.gov>. In some cases, federal publications may be obtained from the issuing agency.

## Appendix I Table: Sources of Statistics, State Statistical Abstracts, and Foreign Statistical Abstracts

| Title | Frequency | Paper | Internet | |
|---|---|---|---|---|
| | | | PDF | Other *Formats* |
| **U.S. GOVERNMENT** | | | | |
| **Administrative Office of the United States Courts** | | | | |
| http://www.uscourts.gov | | | | |
| Calendar Year Reports on Authorized Wiretaps (state and federal) | Annual | | X | X |
| Federal Court Management Statistics | Quarterly | | X | X |
| Federal Judicial Caseload Statistics | Annual | | | X |
| Judicial Business of the United States Courts | Annual | | X | X |
| Statistical Tables for the Federal Judiciary | Semiannual | | X | |
| **Agency for International Development** | | | | |
| http://www.usaid.gov | | | | |
| U.S. Overseas Loans and Grants: Obligations and Loan Authorizations | Annual | | X | X |
| **Army Corps of Engineers** | | | | |
| http://www.usace.army.mil | | | | |
| Waterborne Commerce of the United States Waterways and Harbors (in five parts) | Annual | | X | X |
| **Board of Governors of the Federal Reserve System** | | | | |
| http://www.federalreserve.gov | | | | |
| Assets and Liabilities of Commercial Banks in the United States H.8 | Weekly | | X | X |
| Consumer Credit G.19 | Monthly | | X | X |
| Federal Reserve Bulletin | Periodic | X | X | X |
| Financial Accounts of the United States Z.1 | Quarterly | X | X | X |
| Foreign Exchange Rates H.10 | Weekly | | | X |
| Industrial Production and Capacity Utilization G.17 | Monthly | | X | X |
| Money Stock Measures H.6 | Weekly | | X | X |
| Survey of Consumer Finances | Triennial | | X | X |
| **Bureau of Economic Analysis** | | | | |
| http://www.bea.gov | | | | |
| Arts and Cultural Production Satellite Accounts | Ongoing | | X | X |
| Health Care Satellite Account | Ongoing | | X | X |
| Industry Economic Accounts: Digital Economy | Ongoing | | X | X |
| International Economic Accounts | Ongoing | | X | X |
| National Economic Accounts | Ongoing | | X | X |
| Regional Economic Accounts | Ongoing | | X | X |
| Survey of Current Business | Monthly | X | X | X |
| Travel and Tourism Satellite Accounts | Ongoing | | X | X |
| **Bureau of Justice Statistics** | | | | |
| http://www.bjs.gov/ | | | | |
| 2018 Update On Prisoner Recidivism: A 9-Year Follow-Up Period (2005-2014) | Periodic | | X | X |
| Background Checks for Firearm Transfers | Annual | | X | X |
| Capital Punishment | Annual | | X | X |
| Census of Problem-Solving Courts | Periodic | | X | X |
| Census of Publicly Funded Forensic Crime Laboratories, 2009, August 2012 | Periodic | | X | X |
| Census of State and Federal Correctional Facilities, 2005, October 2008 | Periodic | | X | X |
| Civil Rights Complaints in U.S. District Courts, 1990-2006, August 2008 | Periodic | X | X | X |
| Civil Trial Cases and Verdicts in Large Counties, 2005, September 2009 | Periodic | X | X | X |
| Compendium of Federal Justice Statistics, 2009, December 2011 | Periodic | X | X | X |
| Crimes Against the Elderly, 2003-2013, November 2014 | Periodic | | X | X |
| Criminal Victimization | Annual | | X | X |
| Family Violence Statistics | Periodic | X | X | X |
| Federal Law Enforcement Officers, 2008, June 2012 | Periodic | | X | X |
| Felony Defendants in Large Urban Counties, 2009, December 2013 | Biennial | | X | X |
| HIV in Prisons, 2015, August 2017 | Periodic | | X | X |

See footnotes at end of table.

| Title | Frequency | Paper | Internet PDF | Internet Other Formats |
|---|---|---|---|---|
| Homicide in the U.S. Known to Law Enforcement, 1992 to 2011, December 2013 | Periodic | | X | X |
| Immigration Offenders in the Federal Criminal Justice System, 2010, July 2012 | Periodic | | X | X |
| Indicators of School Crime and Safety, 2017, March 2018 | Annual | | X | X |
| Intimate Partner Violence, 1993-2011, November 2013 | Periodic | X | X | X |
| Jail Inmates at Midyear, 2016, February 2018 | Annual | | X | X |
| Jails in Indian Country, 2016, December 2017 | Annual | | X | |
| Justice Expenditure and Employment Extract Series, 2015, June 2018 | Annual | | | X |
| Local Police Departments, 2013: Personnel, Policies, and Practices, May 2015 | Periodic | | X | X |
| Prisoners in 2016, January 2018 | Annual | | X | X |
| Probation and Parole in the United States, 2016, April 2018 | Annual | | X | X |
| Publicly Funded Forensic Crime Laboratories: Resources and Services, 2014, November 2016 | Periodic | | X | X |
| Prosecutors in State Courts, 2007, December 2011 | Biennial | | X | X |
| Rape and Sexual Assault Victimization Among College-Age Females, 1995-2013 | Periodic | | X | X |
| Sheriffs' Offices Personnel, 1993-2013, June 2016 | Periodic | X | X | X |
| Sourcebook of Criminal Justice Statistics | Periodic | | X | X |
| Survey of State Criminal History Information Systems, 2014, December 2015 | Biennial | X | X | X |
| Survey of State Procedures Related to Firearm Sales, 2005, November 2006 | Periodic | X | X | X |
| Tribal Crime Data Collection Activities, 2016-2018, July 2018 | Annual | | X | X |
| Victims of Identity Theft, 2014, September 2015 | Periodic | | X | X |
| **Bureau of Labor Statistics** http://www.bls.gov | | | | |
| 100 Years of U.S. Consumer Spending: Data for the Nation, New York City, and Boston, Report 991 | Periodic | X | X | |
| College Enrollment and Work Activity of High School Graduates | Annual | | X | X |
| Compensation and Working Conditions | Periodic | | X | X |
| Consumer Expenditure Survey, Integrated Diary and Interview Survey data | Annual | | X | X |
| Consumer Price Index (CPI) Detailed Report | Monthly | | X | X |
| Consumer Prices | Monthly | | X | X |
| Contingent and Alternative Employment Arrangements | Periodic | | X | X |
| Employer Costs for Employee Compensation | Quarterly | | X | X |
| Employment and Earnings | Monthly | | X | X |
| Employment and Wages | Annual | | X | X |
| Employment Characteristics of Families | Annual | | X | X |
| Employment Cost Index | Quarterly | | X | X |
| The Employment Situation | Monthly | | X | X |
| Geographic Profile of Employment and Unemployment | Annual | | X | X |
| Metropolitan Area Employment and Unemployment | Monthly | | X | X |
| Monthly Labor Review | Monthly | | X | X |
| National Compensation Survey | Annual | | X | X |
| Occupational Employment and Wages | Annual | | X | X |
| Occupational Injuries and Illnesses | Annual | | X | X |
| Occupational Projections Data | Biennial | | X | X |
| Producer Price Index (PPI) Detailed Report | Monthly | | X | X |
| Productivity and Costs by Industry | Annual | | X | X |
| Real Earnings | Monthly | | X | X |
| Regional and State Employment and Unemployment | Monthly | | X | X |
| Relative Importance of Components in the Consumer Price Indexes | Annual | | X | X |
| U.S. Import and Export Price Indexes | Monthly | | X | X |
| Union Membership | Annual | | X | X |
| Usual Weekly Earnings of Wage and Salary Workers | Quarterly | | X | X |
| Work Experience of the Population | Annual | | X | X |
| **Bureau of Land Management** http://www.blm.gov | | | | |
| Public Land Statistics | Annual | | X | |
| **Census Bureau** http://www.census.gov | | | | |
| 2012 Economic Census, Bridge Between 2012 NAICS and 2007 NAICS Report | Quinquennial | | | X |
| 2012 Economic Census, Company Statistics Series, Survey of Business Owners | Quinquennial | | | X |
| 2012 Economic Census, Company Statistics Series, Survey of Business Owners: American Indian- and Alaska Native-Owned Firms | Quinquennial | | | X |
| 2012 Economic Census, Company Statistics Series, Survey of Business Owners: Asian-Owned Firms | Quinquennial | | | X |
| 2012 Economic Census, Company Statistics Series, Survey of Business Owners: Black-Owned Firms | Quinquennial | | | X |
| 2012 Economic Census, Company Statistics Series, Survey of Business Owners: Hispanic-Owned Firms | Quinquennial | | | X |
| 2012 Economic Census, Company Statistics Series, Survey of Business Owners: Native Hawaiian- and other Pacific Islander-Owned Firms | Quinquennial | | | X |
| 2012 Economic Census, Comparative Statistics | Quinquennial | | | X |
| 2012 Economic Census, Industry/Geography | Quinquennial | | | X |
| America's Families and Living Arrangements: 2017 | Annual | | | X |
| Annual Revision of Monthly Retail and Food Services: Sales and Inventories | Annual | | X | X |
| Annual Survey of Entrepreneurs | Annual | | X | X |
| Annual Revision of Monthly Wholesale Distributors: Sales and Inventories | Annual | | X | X |
| Annual Survey of Manufactures | Annual | | X | |
| Census of Governments | Quinquennial | | X | |
| Census of Population and Housing Decennial (2010, most recent) | Decennial | X | X | X |
| Computer and Internet Access in the United States: 2016 | Biennial | | X | X |
| Consumer Income and Poverty, P60, and Household Economic Studies, P70 | Periodic | X | X | |
| County Business Patterns | Annual | | X | X |
| Current Construction Reports: New Residential Construction and New Residential Sales | Monthly | | X | X |

See footnotes at end of table.

# Appendix I Table: Sources of Statistics, State Statistical Abstracts, and Foreign Statistical Abstracts-Continued.

See headnote on page 895.

| Title | Frequency | Paper | Internet PDF | Internet Other Formats |
|---|---|---|---|---|
| Current Construction Reports: Value of Construction Put in Place, C30 | Monthly | | X | X |
| Current Housing Reports, American Housing Survey for Selected Metropolitan Areas, H170 | Biennial | | | X |
| Current Housing Reports, American Housing Survey for the United States, H150 | Biennial | | | X |
| Current Housing Reports, Housing Vacancies and Homeownership, H111 | Quarterly | | | X |
| Current Housing Reports, Survey of Market Absorption of New Multifamily Units (SOMA) | Quarterly | | X | X |
| Current Housing Reports, Who Can Afford to Buy a Home in 2009, H121 | Periodic | X | X | X |
| Current Population Reports (Series P20 and P23) | Periodic | | X | X |
| Economic Census of Island Areas | Quinquennial | | | X |
| Fertility of American Women in the United States | Annual | | | X |
| Health Insurance Coverage in the United States | Annual | | X | X |
| Income and Poverty in the United States | Annual | | X | X |
| International Data Base | Annual | | | X |
| International Population Reports (Series P95) | Periodic | | X | |
| Manufacturing and International Trade Report: 2016 | Annual | | X | X |
| Manufacturer's Shipments, Inventories, and Orders | Monthly | | X | X |
| Manufacturer's Shipments, Inventories, and Orders: 1992-2018 | Annual | | | X |
| New York City Housing and Vacancy Survey, 2014 | Triennial | | | X |
| Nonemployer Statistics | Annual | | | X |
| Population Estimates and Projections | Annual | | | X |
| Quarterly Financial Report for Manufacturing, Mining, and Trade Corporations | Quarterly | | X | X |
| Service Annual Survey Report | Annual | | | X |
| Survey of Plant Capacity Utilization | Quarterly | | | X |
| U.S. International Trade in Goods and Services (FT900) | Annual | | X | X |
| U.S. Trade with Puerto Rico and U.S. Possessions (FT 895) | Annual | | X | |

**Centers for Disease Control and Prevention, Atlanta, Georgia**
http://www.cdc.gov

| Title | Frequency | Paper | Internet PDF | Internet Other Formats |
|---|---|---|---|---|
| Morbidity and Mortality Weekly Report | Weekly | X | X | X |
| National Health Interview Survey | Ongoing | | X | X |
| National Immunization Survey (NIS) – Children (19-35 months) | Annual | | X | X |
| Surveillance for Foodborne Disease Outbreaks | Annual | | X | |

**Centers for Medicare and Medicaid Services (CMS)**
http://www.cms.gov

| Title | Frequency | Paper | Internet PDF | Internet Other Formats |
|---|---|---|---|---|
| CMS Program Statistics | Annual | | X | X |
| Trustees Report | Annual | X | X | X |

**Central Intelligence Agency**
http://www.cia.gov

| Title | Frequency | Paper | Internet PDF | Internet Other Formats |
|---|---|---|---|---|
| World Factbook | Annual | | X | X |

**Coast Guard (See Department of Homeland Security)**

**Council of Economic Advisers**
http://www.whitehouse.gov/cea

| Title | Frequency | Paper | Internet PDF | Internet Other Formats |
|---|---|---|---|---|
| Economic Indicators | Monthly | X | X | X |
| Economic Report of the President | Annual | X | X | X |

**Department of Agriculture, Economic Research Service**
http://www.ers.usda.gov

| Title | Frequency | Paper | Internet PDF | Internet Other Formats |
|---|---|---|---|---|
| Amber Waves | Monthly | | X | X |
| America's Diverse Family Farms | Annual | X | X | X |
| Cotton and Wool Yearbook | Annual | | | X |
| Feed Grains Yearbook | Annual | | X | X |
| Food Availability (Per Capita) Data System | Ongoing | | | X |
| Food Expenditures | Annual | | | X |
| Fruit and Tree Nut Yearbook | Annual | | X | X |
| Household Food Security in the United States | Annual | | X | X |
| Oil Crops Yearbook | Annual | | X | X |
| Rice Yearbook | Annual | | | X |
| Situation and Outlook Reports. Issued for: agricultural exports, feed, fruit and tree nuts, livestock and poultry, oil crops, rice, sugar and sweeteners, vegetables, wheat, and world agriculture | Periodic | X | X | X |
| Structure and Finances of U.S. Farms: Family Farm Report | Periodic | X | X | X |
| Sugar and Sweeteners Yearbook | Annual | | | X |
| Vegetable and Pulses Yearbook | Annual | | X | X |
| World Agricultural Supply and Demand Estimates | Monthly | X | X | X |

**Department of Agriculture, Food and Nutrition Service**
http://www.fns.usda.gov/fns/

| Title | Frequency | Paper | Internet PDF | Internet Other Formats |
|---|---|---|---|---|
| Characteristics of Supplemental Nutrition Assistance Program Households | Annual | X | X | |
| WIC Participant and Program Characteristics | Biennial | X | X | |

**Department of Agriculture, Foreign Agricultural Service**
http://www.fas.usda.gov

| Title | Frequency | Paper | Internet PDF | Internet Other Formats |
|---|---|---|---|---|
| Livestock and Poultry World Markets and Trade | Semiannual | X | X | |

**Department of Agriculture, National Agricultural Statistics Service**
http://www.nass.usda.gov

| Title | Frequency | Paper | Internet PDF | Internet Other Formats |
|---|---|---|---|---|
| Agricultural Chemical Usage | Periodic | | | X |
| Agricultural Statistics | Annual | X | X | X |
| Catfish Production | Semiannual | X | X | X |
| Cattle | Semiannual | X | X | X |
| Census of Agriculture | Quinquennial | X | X | X |
| Census of Agriculture: Organic Survey 2014 | Periodic | | X | X |
| Cherry Production | Annual | X | X | X |
| Chickens and Eggs | Monthly | X | X | X |
| Citrus Fruits | Annual | X | X | X |

See footnotes at end of table.

# Appendix I Table: Sources of Statistics, State Statistical Abstracts, and Foreign Statistical Abstracts-Continued.

See headnote on page 895.

| Title | Frequency | Paper | Internet | |
|---|---|---|---|---|
| | | | PDF | Other *Formats* |
| Cranberries | Annual | X | X | X |
| Crop Production | Monthly | X | X | X |
| Crop Progress | Weekly | X | X | X |
| Crop Values | Annual | X | X | X |
| Dairy Products | Monthly | X | X | X |
| Farm Labor | Semiannual | X | X | X |
| Farms and Land in Farms | Annual | X | X | X |
| Floriculture Crops | Annual | X | X | X |
| Agricultural Land Values | Annual | X | X | X |
| Livestock Slaughter | Monthly | X | X | X |
| Meat Animals Production, Disposition, and Income | Annual | X | X | X |
| Milk Production | Monthly | X | X | X |
| Milk Production, Disposition, and Income | Annual | X | X | X |
| Noncitrus Fruits and Nuts | Semiannual | X | X | X |
| Poultry Yearbook | Annual | X | X | X |
| Stock Reports. Stocks of grain, peanuts, potatoes, and rice | Periodic | X | X | X |
| Trout Production | Annual | X | X | X |
| Turkey Hatchery | Monthly | X | X | X |
| Turkeys Raised | Annual | X | X | X |
| Usual Planting and Harvesting Dates | Periodic | X | X | X |
| Vegetables | Periodic | X | X | X |
| Weekly Weather and Crop Bulletin | Weekly | X | X | |
| Winter Wheat and Rye Seedlings | Annual | X | X | X |
| Winter Wheat Seedlings | Annual | X | X | X |
| **Department of Agriculture, Natural Resources Conservation Service**<br>http://www.nrcs.usda.gov | | | | |
| National Resources Inventory | Periodic | | X | X |
| **Department of Defense**<br>http://www.dod.gov/ | | | | |
| Base Structure Report<br> A Summary of the Real Property Inventory | Annual | | X | X |
| Demographics Report, Profile of the Military Community | Annual | | X | X |
| **Department of Defense, Defense Manpower Data Center**<br>https://www.dmdc.osd.mil/appj/dwp/dwp_reports.jsp | | | | |
| Personnel Statistics | Periodic | | X | X |
| **Department of Defense, Defense Security Cooperation Agency**<br>http://www.dsca.mil/resources/dsca-historical-facts-book-fiscal-year-series | | | | |
| Historical Facts Book & Fiscal Year Series | Annual | | X | |
| **Department of Education**<br>http://www.ed.gov | | | | |
| Annual Report for Federal Student Aid | Annual | | X | |
| Annual Report on Teacher Quality | Annual | | X | |
| Federal Campus-Based Programs Data Book | Annual | | | X |
| Federal Pell Grant Program, End of Year Report | Annual | | X | X |
| **Department of Energy**<br>https://energy.gov/ | | | | |
| Transportation Energy Data Book | Annual | | X | X |
| **Department of Health and Human Services**<br>http://www.hhs.gov | | | | |
| Health Care Fraud and Abuse Control Program Annual Report | Annual | X | X | |
| Profile of Older Americans | Annual | X | X | X |
| **Department of Homeland Security**<br>https://www.dhs.gov/ | | | | |
| Budget in Brief | Annual | X | X | |
| Entry/Exit Overstay Report | Annual | | X | |
| **Department of Homeland Security, Coast Guard**<br>https://www.uscg.mil/ | | | | |
| State of the Coast Guard | Annual | X | X | |
| **Department of Homeland Security, Office of Immigration Statistics**<br>http://www.dhs.gov/immigration-statistics | | | | |
| Yearbook of Immigration Statistics | Annual | X | X | X |
| **Department of Housing and Urban Development**<br>http://www.hud.gov | | | | |
| National Housing Market Summary | Quarterly | | X | X |
| **Department of Justice**<br>https://www.justice.gov | | | | |
| Asset Forfeiture Fund Report to Congress | Annual | | X | X |
| **Department of Justice, Bureau of Alcohol, Tobacco, Firearms and Explosives**<br>http://www.atf.gov/ | | | | |
| Firearms Commerce in the U.S. [Annual Firearms Manufacturing and Export Report] | Annual | | X | |
| Firearms Trace Data (by State) | Annual | | X | |
| **Department of Labor**<br>http://www.dol.gov | | | | |
| Agency Financial Report | Annual | X | X | |
| Annual Performance Report | Annual | X | X | |
| Health Insurance Coverage Bulletin | Annual | | X | X |
| Retirement Bulletins | Periodic | | X | X |

See footnotes at end of table.

# Appendix I Table: Sources of Statistics, State Statistical Abstracts, and Foreign Statistical Abstracts-Continued.

See headnote on page 895.

| Title | Frequency | Paper | Internet PDF | Internet Other Formats |
|---|---|---|---|---|
| **Department of State** | | | | |
| http://www.state.gov | | | | |
| Country Reports on Terrorism | Annual | | X | X |
| United States Contributions to International Organizations | Annual | | X | X |
| Annex of Statistical Information: Country Reports on Terrorism | Annual | | X | X |
| **Department of Transportation** | | | | |
| http://www.dot.gov | | | | |
| Air Travel Consumer Report | Monthly | X | X | |
| Annual U.S Domestic Average Itinerary Fare in Current and Constant Dollars | Annual | | | X |
| National Transportation Statistics | Quarterly | | X | X |
| Transportation Statistics Annual Report | Annual | X | X | |
| U.S. International Air Passenger and Freight Statistics | Quarterly | X | X | X |
| **Department of the Treasury, Alcohol and Tobacco Tax and Trade Bureau** | | | | |
| http://www.ttb.gov | | | | |
| Tobacco Products Monthly Statistical Releases | Monthly | X | X | |
| **Department of the Treasury, Bureau of the Fiscal Service** | | | | |
| https://www.fiscal.treasury.gov/ | | | | |
| Combined Statement of Receipts, Outlays, and Balances | Annual | X | X | X |
| Financial Report of the United States Government | Annual | X | X | X |
| Monthly Statement of the Public Debt of the United States | Monthly | X | X | X |
| Monthly Treasury Statement of Receipts and Outlays of the United States Government | Monthly | X | X | X |
| Treasury Bulletin | Quarterly | X | X | X |
| **Department of Veterans Affairs** | | | | |
| http://www.va.gov | | | | |
| Annual Benefits Report | Annual | | X | |
| Annual Performance Plan and Report | Annual | | X | |
| Compensation and Pension Data by County | Annual | | | X |
| **Employment and Training Administration** | | | | |
| http://www.doleta.gov | | | | |
| Unemployment Insurance Weekly Claims | Weekly | | X | X |
| **Energy Information Administration** | | | | |
| http://www.eia.gov | | | | |
| Annual Coal Report | Annual | | X | X |
| Annual Energy Outlook | Annual | X | X | X |
| Electric Power Annual | Annual | | X | X |
| Electric Power Monthly | Monthly | | X | X |
| Electric Sales, Revenue and Average Price | Annual | | X | X |
| International Energy Outlook | Annual | X | X | X |
| International Energy Statistics portal | Ongoing | | X | X |
| Monthly Energy Review | Monthly | | X | X |
| Petroleum Marketing Monthly | Monthly | | X | X |
| Petroleum Supply Annual | Annual | | X | X |
| Petroleum Supply Monthly | Monthly | | X | X |
| Quarterly Coal Report | Quarterly | | X | X |
| Residential Energy Consumption Survey | Quadrennial | | X | X |
| State Electricity Profiles | Annual | | X | X |
| State Energy Data System Reports | Annual | | X | X |
| U.S. Crude Oil and Natural Gas Proved Reserves | Annual | | X | X |
| Weekly Coal Production | Weekly | | | X |
| **Environmental Protection Agency** | | | | |
| http://www.epa.gov | | | | |
| Air Quality Statistics Report | Annual | | X | X |
| Clean Watersheds Needs Survey | Quadrennial | | X | |
| Drinking Water Infrastructure Needs Survey and Assessment | Quadrennial | | X | |
| National Water Quality Inventory Report to Congress | Periodic | | | X |
| Toxics Release Inventory National Analysis | Annual | | X | X |
| UST Performance Measures | Semi-Annual | | X | |
| **Export-Import Bank of the United States** | | | | |
| http://www.exim.gov | | | | |
| Annual Report | Annual | X | X | |
| Report to the U.S. Congress on Global Export Credit Competition and the Export-Import Bank of the United States | Annual | X | X | |
| **Farm Credit Administration** | | | | |
| https://www.fca.gov/ | | | | |
| Annual Report on the Farm Credit System | Annual | X | X | |
| **Federal Bureau of Investigation** | | | | |
| https://ucr.fbi.gov/ | | | | |
| Crime in the United States | Annual | | X | X |
| Hate Crime Statistics | Annual | | X | X |
| Law Enforcement Officers Killed and Assaulted | Annual | | X | X |
| **Federal Communications Commission** | | | | |
| http://www.fcc.gov | | | | |
| Annual Assessment of the Status of Competition in the Market for the Delivery of Video Programming | Annual | | X | X |
| International Telecommunications Traffic and Revenue Data Report | Annual | | X | X |
| Internet Access Services | Semi-Annual | | X | X |
| Quarterly Report on Informal Consumer Inquiries and Complaints | Quarterly | | X | X |
| Report on Cable Industry Prices | Periodically | | X | X |
| Voice Telephone Services Report | Semi-Annual | | X | X |

See footnotes at end of table.

# Appendix I Table: Sources of Statistics, State Statistical Abstracts, and Foreign Statistical Abstracts-Continued.

See headnote on page 895.

| Title | Frequency | Paper | Internet PDF | Internet Other Formats |
|---|---|---|---|---|
| **Federal Deposit Insurance Corporation** | | | | |
| http://www.fdic.gov | | | | |
| Annual Report | Annual | X | X | X |
| FDIC Survey of Unbanked and Underbanked Households | Biennial | | X | X |
| FDIC Quarterly | Quarterly | X | X | X |
| Historical Bank Data | Annual | | | X |
| Quarterly Banking Profile | Quarterly | | X | X |
| Statistics on Banking | Quarterly | | | X |
| Summary of Deposits | Annual | | | X |
| **Federal Highway Administration** | | | | |
| http://www.fhwa.dot.gov | | | | |
| Highway Statistics | Annual | X | X | X |
| **Federal Railroad Administration** | | | | |
| http://safetydata.fra.dot.gov/OfficeofSafety/default.aspx | | | | |
| Railroad Safety Statistics | Annual | X | X | |
| **Fish and Wildlife Service** | | | | |
| http://www.fws.gov | | | | |
| National Survey of Fishing, Hunting, and Wildlife Associated Recreation | Quinquennial | X | X | |
| **Forest Service** | | | | |
| http://www.fs.fed.us | | | | |
| An Analysis of the Timber Situation in the United States 1952-2050 | Periodic | X | X | |
| Land Areas of the National Forest System | Annual | X | X | X |
| RPA Assessment Tables | Periodic | X | X | X |
| U.S. Timber Production, Trade, Consumption, and Price Statistics | Biennial | X | X | |
| **General Services Administration** | | | | |
| http://www.gsa.gov | | | | |
| Federal Real Property Profile | Annual | | X | X |
| **Geological Survey** | | | | |
| http://www.usgs.gov/ | | | | |
| Estimated Use of Water in the United States | Quinquennial | X | X | X |
| Mineral Commodity Summaries | Annual | X | X | |
| Mineral Industry Surveys | Monthly/ Quarterly | | X | X |
| Minerals Yearbook | Annual | X | X | X |
| **Internal Revenue Service** | | | | |
| https://www.irs.gov/statistics | | | | |
| Corporation Income Tax Returns | Annual | X | X | X |
| Individual Income Tax Returns | Annual | X | X | X |
| IRS Data Book | Annual | X | X | X |
| Statistics of Income Bulletin | Quarterly | X | X | X |
| **International Trade Administration, National Travel and Tourism Office** | | | | |
| https://travel.trade.gov/ | | | | |
| U.S. Travel and Tourism Statistics | Annual | | X | X |
| **International Trade Commission** | | | | |
| http://www.usitc.gov | | | | |
| Interactive Tariff and Trade Dataweb | Ongoing | | | X |
| Recent Trends in U.S. Services Trade | Annual | X | X | |
| **Library of Congress** | | | | |
| http://www.loc.gov | | | | |
| Annual Report | Annual | X | X | |
| **Maritime Administration** | | | | |
| http://www.marad.dot.gov | | | | |
| Annual Report to Congress | Annual | X | X | |
| Fleet Statistics | Annual | | | X |
| U.S. Waterborne Foreign Trade | Annual | | | X |
| Vessel Calls | Annual | | X | X |
| **Mine Safety and Health Administration** | | | | |
| http://www.msha.gov | | | | |
| Informational Reports by Mining Industry: Coal, Metallic Minerals, Nonmetallic Minerals (except stone and coal), Sand and Gravel, and Stone | Annual | | X | X |
| Mine Injuries and Worktime | Quarterly | X | X | X |
| **National Aeronautics and Space Administration** | | | | |
| http://www.nasa.gov | | | | |
| Annual Procurement Report | Annual | X | X | |
| **National Center for Education Statistics** | | | | |
| http://nces.ed.gov | | | | |
| After the Post-9/11 GI Bill: A Profile of Military Service Members and Veterans Enrolled in Undergraduate and Graduate Education | Periodic | | X | X |
| Career and Technical Education Programs in Public School Districts | Annual | X | X | X |
| Characteristics of Private Schools in the United States | Annual | X | X | X |
| The Condition of Education | Annual | X | X | X |
| Digest of Education Statistics | Annual | X | X | X |
| Enrollment in Postsecondary Institutions, Graduation Rates, and Financial Statistics | Annual | | X | X |
| Indicators of School Crime and Safety | Annual | X | X | X |
| National Teacher and Principal Survey | Periodic | | X | X |
| Profile and Financial Aid Estimates of Graduate Students | Quadrennial | | X | X |
| Programs and Services for High School English Learners in Public School Districts | Annual | | X | X |

See footnotes at end of table.

## Appendix I Table: Sources of Statistics, State Statistical Abstracts, and Foreign Statistical Abstracts-Continued.

See headnote on page 895.

| Title | Frequency | Paper | Internet PDF | Internet Other Formats |
|---|---|---|---|---|
| The Nation's Report Card: Civics | Periodic | X | X | |
| The Nation's Report Card: Economics | Periodic | X | X | |
| The Nation's Report Card: Geography | Periodic | X | X | |
| The Nation's Report Card: U.S. History | Periodic | X | X | |
| The Nation's Report Card: Mathematics | Periodic | X | X | |
| The Nation's Report Card: Reading | Periodic | X | X | |
| The Nation's Report Card: Science | Periodic | X | X | |
| The Nation's Report Card: Writing | Periodic | X | X | |
| Trends in Undergraduate Nonfederal Grant and Scholarship Aid by Demographic and Enrollment Characteristics | Quadrennial | | X | X |
| Trends in Pell Grant Receipt and the Characteristics of Pell Grant Recipients | Quadrennial | | X | X |
| Projections of Education Statistics | Annual | X | X | X |
| Status and Trends in the Education of Racial and Ethnic Groups | Irregular | X | X | X |
| Trends in High School Dropout and Completion Rates in the United States | Annual | | X | X |
| **National Center for Health Statistics** http://www.cdc.gov/nchs/ | | | | |
| Health, United States | Annual | X | X | X |
| National Health Statistics Reports | Periodic | X | X | |
| National Vital Statistics Reports | Periodic | X | X | |
| Vital and Health Statistics: | | | | |
| Series 3: Analytical and Epidemiological Studies | Irregular | X | X | |
| Series 11: Health and Nutrition Examination Survey Statistics | Irregular | X | X | |
| Series 13: Data on Health Resources Utilization | Irregular | X | X | |
| Series 20: Data on Mortality | Irregular | X | X | |
| Series 21: Data on Natality, Marriage, and Divorce | Irregular | X | X | |
| Series 23: Data from the National Survey of Family Growth | Irregular | X | X | |
| **National Credit Union Administration** http://www.ncua.gov | | | | |
| Annual Report | Annual | X | X | |
| Call Report Quarterly Summary Reports | Quarterly | | X | |
| **National Endowment for the Arts** https://www.arts.gov/ | | | | |
| Annual Report | Annual | X | X | |
| Appropriations Request | Annual | X | X | |
| **National Endowment for the Humanities** http://www.neh.gov | | | | |
| Annual Report | Annual | X | X | |
| Appropriations Request | Annual | X | X | |
| **National Guard Bureau** http://www.nationalguard.mil/ | | | | |
| Posture Statement | Annual | | X | |
| **National Highway Traffic Safety Administration** http://www.nhtsa.gov | | | | |
| Traffic Safety Facts | Annual | X | X | |
| **National Oceanic and Atmospheric Administration** http://www.noaa.gov | | | | |
| Climatic Data for the World | Monthly | | | X |
| Comparative Climatic Data | Annual | | X | X |
| Daily Normals of Temperature, Precipitation, Heating Degree Days (HDD), and Cooling Degree Days (CDD) | Periodic | | | X |
| Fisheries of the United States | Annual | X | X | |
| Hourly Precipitation Data. Monthly with annual summary; for each state | Monthly | | X | X |
| Local Climatological Data. Monthly with annual summary; for major cities | Monthly | | X | X |
| Monthly Normals of Temperature, Precipitation, Heating Degree Days (HDD), and Cooling Degree Days (CDD) | Periodic | | | X |
| Our Living Oceans | Periodic | X | X | |
| Storm Data | Monthly | | X | |
| Tornado Summaries | Monthly | | | X |
| U.S. Climate Normals | Decennial | X | X | X |
| **National Park Service** http://www.nps.gov | | | | |
| National Park Statistical Abstract | Annual | X | X | |
| **National Science Foundation** http://www.nsf.gov/statistics | | | | |
| Academic Institutional Profiles | Annual | | | X |
| Academic Research and Development Expenditures | Annual | | X | X |
| Characteristics of Doctoral Scientists and Engineers in the United States | Biennial | | X | X |
| Characteristics of Recent Science/Engineering Graduates | Biennial | | X | X |
| Doctorate Recipients from U.S. Universities | Annual | | X | X |
| Federal Funds for Research and Development | Annual | | X | X |
| Federal Research and Development Funding by Budget Function | Annual | | X | |
| Federal Science and Engineering Support to Universities, Colleges, and Nonprofit Institutions | Annual | | X | X |
| Graduate Students and Postdoctorates in Science and Engineering | Annual | | X | X |
| National Patterns of Research and Development Resources | Annual | | X | X |
| Research and Development in Industry | Annual | | X | X |
| Science and Engineering Degrees | Biennial | | X | X |
| Science and Engineering Degrees, by Race/Ethnicity of Recipients | Biennial | | X | X |
| Science and Engineering Doctorate Awards | Annual | | X | X |
| Science and Engineering Indicators | Biennial | X | X | X |

See footnotes at end of table.

| Title | Frequency | Paper | Internet PDF | Internet Other Formats |
|---|---|---|---|---|
| Science and Engineering State Profiles | Annual | | | X |
| Science Resources Statistics Info Briefs (various topics) | Frequent | X | X | X |
| Scientific and Engineering Research Facilities at Universities and Colleges | Biennial | | X | X |
| Women, Minorities, and Persons with Disabilities in Science and Engineering | Biennial | | X | X |
| **National Transportation Safety Board** http://www.ntsb.gov | | | | |
| Review of U.S. Civil Aviation Accidents | Annual | | X | X |
| **Office of Juvenile Justice and Delinquency Prevention** http://ojjdp.gov | | | | |
| Highlights of the National Youth Gang Survey | Annual | X | X | X |
| Juvenile Arrests | Annual | X | X | X |
| Juvenile Offenders and Victims | Periodic | X | X | X |
| **Office of Management and Budget** http://www.whitehouse.gov/omb | | | | |
| The Budget of the United States Government | Annual | X | X | X |
| **Office of Personnel Management** http://www.opm.gov | | | | |
| Common Characteristics of the Government | Annual | | X | |
| Demographic Profile of the Federal Workforce | Biennial | | X | |
| Executive Branch Retirement Statistics | Annual | | X | |
| **Office of the Clerk, U.S. House of Representatives** http://clerk.house.gov | | | | |
| Statistics of the Presidential and Congressional Election | Biennial | X | X | |
| **Patent and Trademark Office** http://www.uspto.gov | | | | |
| All Technologies (Utility Patents) | Annual | X | X | X |
| Patent Counts by Country/State and Year | Annual | X | | X |
| Patenting Trends in the United States | Annual | X | | X |
| **Railroad Retirement Board** https://secure.rrb.gov/ | | | | |
| Annual Report | Annual | X | X | |
| Quarterly Benefit Statistics | Quarterly | X | X | |
| **Securities and Exchange Commission** http://www.sec.gov/about.shtml | | | | |
| Select SEC and Market Data | Annual | | X | |
| **Small Business Administration** http://www.sba.gov | | | | |
| Loan Program Performance Reports | Annual | | X | |
| Quarterly Bulletin | Quarterly | | X | X |
| Small Business Lending in the United States | Annual | X | X | X |
| Small Business Economy | Annual | | X | X |
| Small Business Profiles for States and Territories | Annual | | X | |
| **Social Security Administration** http://www.ssa.gov | | | | |
| Annual Statistical Report on the Social Security Disability Insurance Program | Annual | X | X | X |
| Annual Statistical Supplement to the Social Security Bulletin | Annual | X | X | X |
| Congressional Statistics | Annual | X | X | X |
| Fast Facts & Figures about Social Security | Annual | X | X | X |
| Income of the Population 55 and over | Biennially | X | X | X |
| OASDI Beneficiaries by State and County | Annual | X | X | X |
| Social Security Bulletin | Quarterly | X | X | X |
| SSI Annual Statistical Report | Annual | X | X | X |
| SSI Recipients by State and County | Annual | X | X | X |
| **Substance Abuse and Mental Health Services Administration** http://www.samhsa.gov | | | | |
| Behavioral Health Barometer, United States | Annual | X | X | |
| National Mental Health Services Survey (N-MHSS) | Annual | X | X | X |
| National Survey on Drug Use and Health (NSDUH) | Annual | X | X | |
| National Survey on Substance Abuse Treatment Services (N-SSATS) | Annual | X | X | X |
| **U.S. Copyright Office** http://www.copyright.gov/ | | | | |
| Annual Report | Annual | X | X | |
| **U.S. Equal Employment Opportunity Commission** https://www.eeoc.gov | | | | |
| Enforcement and Litigation Statistics | Ongoing | | X | X |
| **U.S. Health Resources & Services Administration** https://www.hrsa.gov/ | | | | |
| Health Center Data Program | Ongoing | | X | X |
| **U.S. Sentencing Commission** https://www.ussc.gov/ | | | | |
| 2017 Sourcebook of Federal Sentencing Statistics | Annual | | X | X |
| **NONGOVERNMENT** | | | | |
| **Aerospace Industries Association, Arlington, VA** http://www.aia-aerospace.org | | | | |
| Aerospace Industry Year-End Review and Forecast | Annual | | X | |
| Economic Impact Study of the U.S. Aerospace and Defense Industry | Annual | | X | |

See footnotes at end of table.

# Appendix I Table: Sources of Statistics, State Statistical Abstracts, and Foreign Statistical Abstracts-Continued.

See headnote on page 895.

| Title | Frequency | Paper | Internet PDF | Internet Other Formats |
|---|---|---|---|---|
| Quarterly Trade Bulletin | Quarterly | | X | |
| U.S. Aerospace Manufacturing Update | Quarterly | | X | |
| **Airlines for America, Washington, DC** http://www.airlines.org | | | | |
| **American Council of Life Insurers, Washington, DC** http://www.acli.com | | | | |
| Life Insurers Fact Book | Annual | | X | |
| **American Dental Association, Chicago, IL** http://www.ada.org | | | | |
| Survey of Dental Practice | Annual | | | X |
| **American Forest and Paper Association, Washington, DC** http://www.afandpa.org | | | | |
| Monthly Exports/Imports Report | Monthly | | X | |
| Monthly Statistics of Paper, Paperboard and Wood Pulp | Monthly | | X | X |
| Paper Industry Annual Capacity and Fiber Consumption | Annual | | X | |
| Paper Industry Annual Statistical Summary | Annual | | X | |
| **American Gas Association, Washington, DC** http://www.aga.org | | | | |
| Gas Facts | Annual | X | X | |
| **American Iron and Steel Institute, Washington, DC** http://www.steel.org | | | | |
| Annual Statistical Report | Annual | X | X | |
| **American Medical Association, Chicago, IL** http://www.ama-assn.org | | | | |
| State Medical Licensure Statistics and License Requirements | Annual | X | | X |
| **American Osteopathic Association, Chicago, IL** http://www.osteopathic.org/ | | | | |
| Osteopathic Medical Profession Report | Annual | | X | |
| **American Public Transportation Association, Washington, DC** http://www.apta.com | | | | |
| Public Transportation Fact Book | Annual | | X | X |
| **American Society for Aesthetic Plastic Surgery** https://www.surgery.org/ | | | | |
| 2017 Cosmetic Surgery National Data Bank Statistics | Annual | | X | |
| **Association of American Medical Colleges** https://www.aamc.org | | | | |
| Physician Specialty Data Report | Biennial | X | X | |
| State Physician Workforce Data Book | Biennial | X | X | |
| **Association of American Railroads, Washington, DC** http://www.aar.org | | | | |
| Analysis of Class I Railroads | Annual | X | X | X |
| Freight Commodity Statistics | Annual | X | X | X |
| Railroad Facts | Annual | X | X | |
| **Berman Jewish Data Bank, Storrs, CT** http://www.jewishdatabank.org | | | | |
| Jewish Population in the United States | Annual | | X | X |
| **Bloomberg BNA, Washington, DC** https://www.bloombergindustry.com/ | | | | |
| BNA's Labor and Employment Outlook Report | Annual | X | | |
| BNA's Job Absence and Turnover Report | Quarterly | X | | |
| Directory of U.S. Labor Organizations | Annual | X | | |
| Source Book on Collective Bargaining | Annual | X | | |
| Union Membership and Earnings Data Book | Annual | X | | |
| **Brookings Institution, Washington, DC** https://www.brookings.edu/ | | | | |
| Vital Statistics on Congress | Biennial | | X | X |
| **Chronicle of Higher Education, Inc., Washington, DC** http://chronicle.com | | | | |
| Almanac of Higher Education | Annual | X | | X |
| **College Board, New York, NY** https://www.collegeboard.org/ | | | | |
| College-Bound Seniors Total Group Profile Report | Annual | | X | |
| **cmdty® by barchart, Chicago, IL** https://www.barchart.com/cmdty | | | | |
| Commodity Indexes | Ongoing | | X | X |
| cmdty Yearbook® | Annual | X | | X |
| CRB Infotech CD | Monthly | | | X |
| CRB TrendTrader | Daily | | X | X |
| Final Markets | Daily | | | X |
| **Conference Board, New York, NY** http://www.conference-board.org | | | | |
| Business Cycle Indicators | Monthly | | X | X |
| Corporate Contributions Report | Annual | | X | |
| International Comparisons of Annual Labor Force Statistics | Annual | | X | X |
| International Comparisons of Hourly Compensation | | | | |

See footnotes at end of table.

# Appendix I Table: Sources of Statistics, State Statistical Abstracts, and Foreign Statistical Abstracts—Continued.

See headnote on page 895.

| Title | Frequency | Paper | Internet PDF | Internet Other Formats |
|---|---|---|---|---|
| Costs for Production Workers in Manufacturing International Comparisons of Manufacturing | Annual | | X | X |
| Productivity and Unit Labor Cost Trends | Annual | | X | X |
| Performance: Productivity, Employment, and Growth in the World's Economies | Irregular | | X | |
| **Congressional Quarterly (CQ) Press, Washington, DC** https://us.sagepub.com/en-us/nam/cqpress | | | | |
| America Votes | Biennial | X | | |
| **Consumer Technology Association, Arlington, VA** https://www.cta.tech/ | | | | |
| U.S. Consumer Technology Sales and Forecasts | Semiannual | | X | |
| **Council of State Governments, Lexington, KY** http://www.csg.org | | | | |
| Book of the States | Annual | X | X | |
| **Credit Union National Association, Madison, WI** http://www.cuna.org | | | | |
| Operating Ratios and Spreads | Quarterly | X | X | |
| **Dodge Data & Analytics, New York, NY** https://www.construction.com | | | | |
| Construction Potentials Bulletin | Monthly | | X | |
| **Dow Jones and Company, New York, NY** http://www.dowjones.com/ | | | | |
| Wall Street Journal | Daily | X | | X |
| **Duncan McIntosh Company, Inc., Irvine, CA** http://www.editorandpublisher.com | | | | |
| Editor and Publisher | Monthly | X | | X |
| Newspaper Databook | Annual | X | | X |
| **Edison Electric Institute, Washington, DC** http://www.eei.org | | | | |
| Statistical Yearbook of the Electric Power Industry | Annual | X | X | X |
| **Euromonitor International, London, England** http://www.euromonitor.com | | | | |
| Consumer Lifestyles in the US | Annual | X | X | |
| **Federal National Mortgage Association, Washington, DC** http://www.fanniemae.com | | | | |
| Annual Report on Form 10-K | Annual | | X | |
| **Food and Agriculture Organization of the United Nations, Rome, Italy** http://www.fao.org | | | | |
| World Fertilizer Trends and Outlook | Annual | | X | |
| FAO Statistical Yearbook: World Food and Agriculture | Annual | X | X | |
| FAO Yearbook: Fishery and Aquaculture Statistics | Periodic | X | X | X |
| Yearbook of Forest Products | Annual | X | X | |
| **General Aviation Manufacturers Association, Washington, DC** http://www.gama.aero | | | | |
| General Aviation Aircraft Shipment Report | Quarterly | | X | |
| General Aviation Statistical Databook & Industry Outlook | Annual | | X | |
| **Giving USA Foundation, Chicago, IL** http://www.givingusa.org/ | | | | |
| Giving USA | Annual | X | X | X |
| **Guttmacher Institute, New York, NY** http://www.guttmacher.org | | | | |
| Perspectives on Sexual and Reproductive Health | Quarterly | | X | |
| **Health Forum, an American Hospital Association Company, Chicago, IL** http://www.ahadataviewer.com/ | | | | |
| AHA Annual Survey Data Base | Annual | | | X |
| AHA Hospital Statistics | Annual | X | | X |
| **IHS Global, Inc., Englewood, CO** http://www.janes.com | | | | |
| IHS Jane's All the World's Aircraft: Development & Production | Annual | X | | X |
| IHS Jane's Defence: C4ISR & Mission Systems | Annual | X | | X |
| IHS Jane's Fighting Ships | Annual | X | | X |
| IHS Jane's Flight Avionics | Annual | X | | X |
| IHS Jane's Land Warfare Platforms: Armoured Fighting Vehicles | Annual | X | | X |
| IHS Jane's Land Warfare Platforms: Logistics, Support & Unmanned | Annual | X | | X |
| IHS Jane's Simulation & Training Systems | Annual | X | | X |
| IHS Jane's Space Systems & Industry | Annual | X | | X |
| IHS Jane's Weapons: Air-Launched | Annual | X | | X |
| IHS Jane's Weapons: Infantry | Annual | X | | X |
| **Independent Petroleum Association of America, Washington, DC** http://www.ipaa.org | | | | |
| IPAA Oil & Gas Producing Industry in Your State | Annual | X | X | |
| U.S. Petroleum Statistics | Annual | X | X | |
| **Infobase Publishing, New York, NY** http://www.worldalmanac.com | | | | |
| The World Almanac and Book of Facts | Annual | X | | |
| **Information Today, Inc., Medford, NJ** | | | | |

See footnotes at end of table.

# Appendix I Table: Sources of Statistics, State Statistical Abstracts, and Foreign Statistical Abstracts-Continued.

See headnote on page 895.

| Title | Frequency | Paper | Internet PDF | Internet Other Formats |
|---|---|---|---|---|
| http://www.infotoday.com | | | | |
| American Library Directory | Annual | X | | X |
| Library and Book Trade Almanac (formerly The Bowker Annual) | Annual | X | | |
| **Institute for Criminal Justice Ethics, New York, NY** | | | | |
| https://www.jjay.cuny.edu/institute-criminal-justice-ethics | | | | |
| Criminal Justice Ethics | Thrice yearly | X | X | |
| **Insurance Information Institute, New York, NY** | | | | |
| http://www.iii.org | | | | |
| The I.I.I. Insurance Fact Book | Annual | X | X | X |
| **Inter-American Development Bank, Washington, DC** | | | | |
| http://www.iadb.org | | | | |
| Annual Report | Annual | X | X | |
| Development in the Americas | Periodic | X | X | X |
| **International Air Transport Association, Montreal, Canada and Geneva, Switzerland** | | | | |
| http://www.iata.org | | | | |
| World Air Transport Statistics | Annual | X | X | X |
| **International City Management Association, Washington, DC** | | | | |
| http://www.icma.org | | | | |
| ICMA Chief Administrative Officers Salary & Compensation Survey | Annual | | X | |
| Municipal Year Book | Annual | | X | |
| **International Labour Organization, Geneva, Switzerland** | | | | |
| http://www.ilo.org | | | | |
| Yearbook of Labour Statistics | Annual | X | | X |
| **International Monetary Fund, Washington, DC** | | | | |
| http://www.imf.org | | | | |
| Annual Report | Annual | X | X | X |
| Balance of Payments Statistics | Monthly | X | X | X |
| Direction of Trade Statistics | Quarterly | X | | X |
| Government Finance Statistics Yearbook | Annual | X | X | X |
| International Financial Statistics | Monthly | X | X | X |
| **International Telecommunication Union, Geneva, Switzerland** | | | | |
| http://www.itu.int/home/index.html | | | | |
| ITU Yearbook of Statistics | Annual | X | X | |
| World Telecommunication/ICT Indicators | Annual | X | X | X |
| **Investment Company Institute, Washington, DC** | | | | |
| http://www.ici.org | | | | |
| Investment Company Fact Book | Annual | | X | X |
| **Joint Center for Housing Studies of Harvard University, Cambridge, MA** | | | | |
| http://www.jchs.harvard.edu/ | | | | |
| The State of the Nation's Housing | Annual | | X | X |
| **Media Source, Inc., New York, NY** | | | | |
| https://www.mediasourceinc.com/ | | | | |
| Library Journal | Semimonthly | X | | X |
| School Library Journal | Monthly | X | | X |
| **National Academy of Social Insurance, Washington, DC** | | | | |
| http://www.nasi.org/ | | | | |
| Workers Compensation: Benefits, Coverage, and Costs | Annual | X | X | |
| **National Association of Home Builders, Washington, DC** | | | | |
| http://www.nahb.org | | | | |
| HousingEconomics.com (online subscription) | Ongoing | | | X |
| **National Association of Latino Elected and Appointed Officials, Los Angeles, CA** | | | | |
| http://www.naleo.org | | | | |
| National Directory of Latino Elected Officials | Annual | | X | X |
| **National Association of Realtors, Chicago, IL** | | | | |
| https://www.nar.realtor/ | | | | |
| Economist's Outlook | Daily | | | X |
| Investment and Vacation Home Buyers Survey | Annual | X | X | |
| NAR Member Profile | Annual | X | X | X |
| NAR Profile of Home Buyer and Sellers | Annual | X | X | |
| **National Association of State Budget Officers, Washington, DC** | | | | |
| http://www.nasbo.org | | | | |
| Fiscal Survey of the States | Semiannual | X | X | |
| State Expenditure Report | Annual | X | X | |
| **National Association of State Park Directors, Raleigh, NC** | | | | |
| https://www.stateparks.org/ | | | | |
| Statistical Report of State Park Operations: Annual Information Exchange | Annual | X | X | |
| **National Catholic Educational Association, Arlington, VA** | | | | |
| http://www.ncea.org | | | | |
| The Annual Financial Report | Biennial | X | X | |
| U.S. Catholic Elementary and Secondary Schools: The Annual Statistical Report on Schools, Enrollment and Staffing | Annual | X | X | |
| **National Education Association, Washington, DC** | | | | |
| http://www.nea.org | | | | |
| Rankings & Estimates: Rankings of the States and Estimates of School Statistics | Annual | X | X | |
| **National Fire Protection Association, Quincy, MA** | | | | |

See footnotes at end of table.

# Appendix I Table: Sources of Statistics, State Statistical Abstracts, and Foreign Statistical Abstracts-Continued.

See headnote on page 895.

| Title | Frequency | Paper | Internet PDF | Internet Other Formats |
|---|---|---|---|---|
| http://www.nfpa.org | | | | |
| National Fire Protection Association (NFPA) Journal | Bimonthly | X | | X |
| **National Golf Foundation, Jupiter, FL** | | | | |
| http://www.ngf.org | | | | |
| Golf Facilities in the U.S. | Annual | X | X | |
| **National Restaurant Association, Washington, DC** | | | | |
| http://www.restaurant.org | | | | |
| Restaurant Industry 2020 | Recurring | | X | |
| Restaurant Industry Pocket Factbook | Annual | X | X | X |
| Restaurant Operations Report | Recurring | X | X | |
| Restaurant Performance Index | Monthly | | X | |
| Restaurant Trendmapper (online subscription) | Ongoing | | | X |
| State of the Industry | Annual | X | X | |
| **National Safety Council, Itasca, IL** | | | | |
| http://www.nsc.org | | | | |
| Injury Facts | Annual | X | X | |
| **National Sporting Goods Association, Mount Prospect, IL** | | | | |
| http://www.nsga.org | | | | |
| Sporting Goods Market | Annual | X | X | |
| Sports Participation in the U.S. | Annual | X | X | |
| **Organisation for Economic Cooperation and Development, Paris, France** | | | | |
| http://www.oecd-ilibrary.org/ | | | | |
| CO2 Emissions From Fuel Combustion | Annual | X | X | X |
| Coal Information | Annual | X | X | X |
| Digital Economy Outlook | Biennial | X | X | X |
| Education at a Glance: OECD Indicators | Annual | X | X | X |
| Electricity Information | Annual | X | X | X |
| Energy Prices and Taxes | Quarterly | X | X | X |
| Environmental Outlook | Periodic | X | X | X |
| Financial Accounts | Annual | X | X | X |
| Financial Balance Sheets | Annual | X | X | X |
| General Government Accounts | Annual | X | X | X |
| Geographical Distribution of Financial Flows to Developing Countries | Annual | X | X | X |
| International Migration Outlook | Annual | X | X | X |
| International Trade by Commodity Statistics | Ongoing | X | X | X |
|   Issue 1: Main Aggregates | Annual | X | X | X |
|   Issue 2: Detailed Tables | Annual | X | X | X |
| ITF Transport Outlook | Annual | X | X | X |
| Main Economic Indicators | Monthly | X | X | X |
| Main Science and Technology Indicators | Semiannual | X | X | X |
| National Accounts at a Glance | Annual | X | X | X |
| National Accounts of OECD Countries | Annual | X | X | X |
| Natural Gas Information | Annual | X | X | X |
| Nuclear Energy Data | Annual | X | X | X |
| OECD Communications Outlook | Biennial | X | X | X |
| OECD Economic Outlook | Semiannual | X | X | X |
| OECD Economic Surveys | Periodic | X | X | X |
| OECD Employment Outlook | Annual | X | X | X |
| OECD Factbook | Annual | X | X | X |
| OECD-FAO Agricultural Outlook | Annual | X | X | X |
| OECD Health Statistics | Annual | | | X |
| OECD Insurance Statistics | Annual | X | X | X |
| OECD International Development Statistics | Annual | | | X |
| OECD Quarterly International Trade Statistics | Quarterly | X | X | X |
| OECD Review of Fisheries: Policies and Summary Statistics | Annual | X | X | X |
| OECD Science, Technology, and Innovation Outlook | Biennial | X | X | X |
| OECD Science, Technology and R&D Statistics | Ongoing | | | X |
| OECD Society at a Glance | Biennial | X | X | X |
| OECD Territorial Reviews | Periodic | X | X | X |
| Oil Information | Annual | X | X | |
| Oil, Gas, Coal, and Electricity Quarterly Statistics | Quarterly | X | X | X |
| Pensions at a Glance | Biennial | X | X | X |
| PISA (OECD Programme for International Student Assessment) | Periodic | X | X | X |
| Quarterly National Accounts | Quarterly | X | X | X |
| Revenue Statistics | Ongoing | | | X |
| Taxing Wages | Annual | X | X | X |
| Uranium: Resources Production and Demand | Biennial | X | X | X |
| World Energy Balances | Annual | X | X | |
| World Energy Outlook | Annual | X | X | |
| World Energy Statistics | Annual | X | X | |
| **PennWell Corporation, Tulsa, OK** | | | | |
| http://www.pennwell.com | | | | |
| Offshore | Monthly | X | X | X |
| Oil and Gas Journal | Weekly | X | X | X |
| **Pew Research Center** | | | | |
| http://www.pewinternet.org | | | | |
| Book Reading | Periodic | | X | X |
| Home Broadband | Periodic | | X | X |
| Libraries and Learning | Periodic | | X | X |
| Social Media Update | Periodic | | X | X |
| Technology Device Ownership | Periodic | | X | X |

See footnotes at end of table.

# Appendix I Table: Sources of Statistics, State Statistical Abstracts, and Foreign Statistical Abstracts-Continued.

See headnote on page 895.

| Title | Frequency | Paper | Internet PDF | Internet Other Formats |
|---|---|---|---|---|
| Teens, Social Media & Technology | Periodic | | X | X |
| **Puerto Rico Planning Board, San Juan, PR** http://www.jp.gobierno.pr | | | | |
| Construction Industry | Periodic | X | | |
| Economic Report to the Governor | Annual | X | X | X |
| External Trade Statistics | Annual | X | X | |
| Income and Production | Annual | X | X | |
| Statistical Appendix-Economic Report to the Governor | Annual | X | X | X |
| **PWxyz, LLC, New York, NY** http://www.publishersweekly.com | | | | |
| Publishers Weekly | Weekly | X | | X |
| **Radio Advertising Bureau, Dallas, TX** http://www.rab.com | | | | |
| Why Radio: Fact Sheets | Ongoing | | | X |
| **Regional Airline Association, Washington, DC** http://www.raa.org | | | | |
| Regional Airlines Association Annual Report | Annual | | X | |
| **Securities Industry and Financial Markets Association, New York, NY** http://www.sifma.org | | | | |
| SIFMA Fact Book | Annual | X | | X |
| U.S. Foreign Activity Report | Quarterly | | X | X |
| **Standard and Poor's Financial Services LLC, New York, NY** http://www.standardandpoors.com | | | | |
| Analyst's Handbook | Monthly | X | | X |
| Corporation Records: Corporate Description | Monthly | X | X | X |
| Corporation Records: Daily News | Daily | X | X | X |
| Daily Stock Price Records | Quarterly | | | X |
| **United Nations Conference on Trade and Development, Geneva, Switzerland** http://www.unctad.org | | | | |
| Development and Globalization: Facts and Figures | Periodic | X | X | X |
| Handbook of Statistics | Annual | X | X | X |
| **United Nations Statistics Division, New York, NY** https://unstats.un.org/home/ | | | | |
| Demographic Yearbook (Series R) | Annual | X | X | |
| Energy Balances and Electricity Profiles (Series W) | Annual | X | X | |
| Energy Statistics Yearbook (Series J) | Annual | X | X | |
| Industrial Commodity Statistics Yearbook: Production Statistics | Annual | X | X | |
| International Trade Statistics Yearbook (Series G) | Annual | X | X | |
| Monthly Bulletin of Statistics (Series Q) | Monthly | X | X | |
| National Accounts Statistics: Analysis of Main Aggregates | Annual | X | | |
| National Accounts Statistics (Series X) | Annual | X | X | |
| Population and Vital Statistics Report (Series A) | Quarterly | X | X | |
| Statistical Yearbook | Annual | X | X | |
| World Statistics Pocketbook (Series V) | Annual | X | X | |
| The World's Women: Progress in Statistics | Quinquennial | X | X | |
| **University of Michigan, Institute for Social Research, Inter-University Consortium for Political and Social Research, Ann Arbor, MI** http://www.icpsr.umich.edu/icpsrweb/ICPSR/studies/8475 | | | | |
| American National Election Studies Cumulative Data File | Biennial | | | X |
| **Warren Communications News, Washington, DC** http://www.warren-news.com | | | | |
| Television and Cable Factbook | Ongoing | | | X |
| **World Bank Group, Washington, DC** http://www.worldbank.org | | | | |
| Atlas of Global Development | Periodic | X | X | |
| Global Development Finance | Annual | X | X | X |
| The Little Data Book | Annual | X | X | |
| World Development Indicators | Annual | X | | X |
| **World Health Organization, Geneva, Switzerland** http://www.who.int/en/ | | | | |
| World Health Statistics Report | Annual | X | X | |
| **World Trade Organization, Geneva, Switzerland** http://www.wto.org | | | | |
| World Trade Statistical Review | Annual | X | X | X |
| **STATE STATISTICAL ABSTRACTS FROM UNIVERSITIES** | | | | |
| **Pennsylvania State University, Pennsylvania State Data Center, Middletown, PA** http://pasdc.hbg.psu.edu/ | | | | |
| Pennsylvania Abstract: A Statistical Fact Book | Annual | X | X | X |
| **State University of New York: Nelson A. Rockefeller Institute of Government, Nelson A. Rockefeller Institute of Government, Albany, NY** http://www.rockinst.org/ | | | | |
| New York State Statistical Yearbook | Annual | X | X | X |
| **University of Florida: Bureau of Economic and Business Research, Gainesville, FL** http://www.bebr.ufl.edu/ | | | | |
| Florida Statistical Dashboards | Ongoing | | | X |
| **University of Georgia: Selig Center for Economic Growth, Athens, GA** | | | | |

See footnotes at end of table.

| Title | Frequency | Paper | Internet PDF | Internet Other Formats |
|---|---|---|---|---|
| http://www.terry.uga.edu/selig/ Georgia Economic Outlook | Annual | X | X | X |
| **University of Kansas: Institute for Policy and Social Research, Lawrence, KS** http://www.ipsr.ku.edu/ksdata/ksah/ Kansas Statistical Abstract | Annual | | X | X |
| **University of Missouri-Columbia: Economic and Policy Analysis Research Center, Columbia, MO** http://eparc.missouri.edu/ Missouri Statistical Data Archive (online) | Ongoing | | X | |
| **University of Oklahoma: Center for Economic and Management Research, Norman, OK** http://www.ou.edu/content/price/centersresearch/cemr/cemr_publications.html Oklahoma Statistical Abstract | Annual | X | | |
| STATE STATISTICAL ABSTRACT FROM AN ASSOCIATION | | | | |
| **Texas State Historical Association, Austin, TX** http://texasalmanac.com/ Texas Almanac | Biennial | X | X | X |
| STATE STATISTICAL ABSTRACTS FROM STATE AGENCIES | | | | |
| **Hawaii State Department of Business, Economic Development & Tourism, Honolulu, HI** http://dbedt.hawaii.gov/economic/databook/ State of Hawaii Data Book | Annual | | X | X |
| **Maryland State Data Center, Maryland Department of Planning, Baltimore, MD** http://www.mdp.state.md.us/msdc/ Maryland Statistical Abstract | Annual | | X | |
| Maryland Statistical Handbook | Periodic | | X | |
| **Mississippi Secretary of State** http://www.sos.ms.gov/ 2016-2020 Mississippi Blue Book | Quadrennial | X | X | |
| **South Carolina, Revenue and Fiscal Affairs Office, Columbia, SC** http://abstract.sc.gov/ South Carolina Statistical Abstract | Ongoing | | | X |
| INTERNATIONAL STATISTICAL ABSTRACTS FROM A FOREIGN AGENCY | | | | |
| **Australia** **Australian Bureau of Statistics, Canberra** http://www.abs.gov.au/ Year Book Australia, 2012 (Discontinued) | Annual | X | X | X |
| **Austria** **Statistik Austria, Vienna** http://www.statistik.at/web_en/ Statistisches Jahrbuch Österreichs | Annual | X | X | X |
| **Belgium** **Statistics Belgium, Brussels** http://statbel.fgov.be/en Key Figures: Statistical Overview of Belgium | Annual | X | X | X |
| **Canada** **Statistics Canada, Ottawa** https://www150.statcan.gc.ca/n1/en/catalogue/11-402-X Canada Year Book (Discontinued) | Annual | | X | X |
| **Czechia** **Czech Statistical Office, Praha** http://www.czso.cz Statistical Yearbook of the Czech Republic, 2017 | Annual | X | X | X |
| **Denmark** **Statistics Denmark, Copenhagen** http://www.dst.dk/en Statistical Yearbook | Annual | | X | |
| **Finland** **Statistics Finland, Helsinki** http://www.stat.fi/index_en.html Statistical Yearbook of Finland | Annual | X | | |
| **France** **National Institute of Statistics and Economic Studies, Paris** http://www.insee.fr/en/ Tableaux de l'Economie Francaise | Annual | | X | X |
| **Germany** **Statistisches Bundesamt, Wiesbaden** https://www.destatis.de/EN/Homepage.html Statistisches Jahrbuch: Deutschland und Internationales | Annual | | X | |
| **Greece** **Hellenic Statistical Authority, Pireus** http://www.statistics.gr/en/home/ Statistical Yearbook of Greece | Annual | X | X | |
| **Hungary** | | | | |

See footnotes at end of table.

# Appendix I Table: Sources of Statistics, State Statistical Abstracts, and Foreign Statistical Abstracts-Continued.

See headnote on page 895.

| Title | Frequency | Paper | Internet PDF | Internet Other Formats |
|---|---|---|---|---|
| **Hungarian Central Statistical Office, Budapest** http://www.ksh.hu/ Statistical Yearbook of Hungary | Annual | X | X | X |
| **Iceland** **Statistics Iceland, Reykjavik** http://www.statice.is/ Statistical Yearbook of Iceland, 2015 (Discontinued) | Annual | X | X | X |
| **Ireland** **Central Statistics Office, Cork** http://www.cso.ie/en/ Statistical Yearbook of Ireland | Annual | | | X |
| **Italy** **Italian National Institute of Statistics, Rome** http://www.istat.it/en/ Annuario Statistico Italiano | Annual | X | X | X |
| **Japan** **Statistics Bureau, Ministry of Internal Affairs and Communications, Tokyo** http://www.stat.go.jp/english/data/index.html Japan Statistical Yearbook | Annual | X | X | X |
| **Korea, South** **Statistics Korea, Daejeon** http://kostat.go.kr/eng/ Korea Statistical Yearbook | Annual | X | | |
| **Luxembourg** **Service Central de la Statistique et des Etudes Economiques, Luxembourg** http://www.statistiques.public.lu/fr/acteurs/statec/index.html Annuaire statistique du Luxembourg | Annual | X | X | |
| **Mexico** **Instituto Nacional de Estadistica y Geografia, Aguascalientes** http://www.inegi.org.mx/ Anuario Estadistico de los Estados Unidos Mexicanos, 2016 | Annual | | X | X |
| **Netherlands** **Statistics Netherlands, The Hague** https://www.cbs.nl/nl-nl Statistical Yearbook of the Netherlands | Annual | | X | X |
| **New Zealand** **Statistics New Zealand, Wellington** http://www.stats.govt.nz/ New Zealand Official Yearbook | Biennial | | X | X |
| **Norway** **Statistics Norway, Oslo** https://www.ssb.no/en/ Statistical Yearbook of Norway (Discontinued) | Annual | | X | |
| **Poland** **Central Statistical Office of Poland, Warsaw** http://stat.gov.pl/en/intrastat Concise Statistical Yearbook of Poland Statistical Yearbook of the Republic of Poland | Annual Annual | X X | X X | |
| **Portugal** **Statistics Portugal, Lisbon** https://www.ine.pt/ Statistical Yearbook of Portugal | Annual | X | X | X |
| **Russia** **Russian Federation Federal State Statistics Service, Moscow** http://www.gks.ru/ Russia in Figures | Annual | | | X |
| **Slovakia** **Statistical Office of the Slovak Republic, Bratislava** http://slovak.statistics.sk/ Statistical Yearbook of the Slovak Republic | Annual | X | X | X |
| **Spain** **Instituto Nacional de Estadistica, Madrid** http://www.ine.es/en/welcome_en.htm Statistical Yearbook of Spain | Annual | X | X | |
| **Sweden** **Statistics Sweden, Stockholm** http://www.scb.se/en/ Statistical Yearbook of Sweden, 2014 (Discontinued) | Annual | X | X | X |
| **Switzerland** **Federal Statistical Office, Neuchâtel** https://www.bfs.admin.ch/bfs/en/home.html Statistisches Jahrbuch der Schweiz | Annual | X | | |
| **Turkey** **Turkish Statistical Institute, Ankara** http://www.turkstat.gov.tr Turkey's Statistical Yearbook | Annual | X | X | X |

See footnotes at end of table.

# Appendix I Table: Sources of Statistics, State Statistical Abstracts, and Foreign Statistical Abstracts-Continued.

See headnote on page 895.

| Title | Frequency | Paper | Internet | |
|---|---|---|---|---|
| | | | PDF | Other *Formats* |
| Turkey in Statistics | Annual | X | X | X |
| **United Kingdom** **Office for National Statistics, London** http://www.ons.gov.uk Annual Abstract of Statistics, 2011 (Discontinued) | Annual | | X | |

Source: ProQuest research.

# Guide to State Statistical Abstracts

This bibliography includes the most recent statistical abstracts for states published since 2008, plus those that will be issued in 2019. For some states, a near equivalent has been listed in substitution for, or in addition to, a statistical abstract. All sources contain statistical tables on a variety of subjects for the state as a whole, its component parts, or both. Internet sites also contain statistical data.

## Alabama

University of Alabama, Center for Business and Economic Research, Box 870221, Tuscaloosa, AL 35487-0221. 205-348-6191. Fax: 205-348-2951. Internet site <http://cber.culverhouse.ua.edu>.
*Alabama Economic Outlook.* Annual. Print.

## Alaska

Department of Commerce, Community and Economic Development, P.O. Box 110804, Juneau, AK 99811. 907-465-2510. Fax: 907-465-3767. Internet site <http://commerce.alaska.gov/web/ded/>.
*The Alaska Economic Performance Report, 2013.* Online.
*Alaska's Economic Report.* Quarterly. Online.

## Arizona

University of Arizona, Economic and Business Research Center, Eller College of Management, 1130 East Helen Street, McClelland Hall, Room 103, P.O. Box 210108, Tucson, AZ 85721-0108. 520-621-2155. Internet site <https://azeconomy.org/>.
*Arizona's Economy.* Quarterly. Online.

## Arkansas

University of Arkansas at Little Rock, Arkansas Economic Development Institute, 2801 South University Avenue, Little Rock, AR 72204-1099. 501-569-8519. Internet site <http://youraedi.com/>.
*Arkansas State and County Economic Data, 2017.* Annual. Print and Online.
*Arkansas Personal Income Handbook.* Annual. Print and Online.

## California

Department of Finance, 915 L Street, Sacramento, CA 95814. 916-445-3878. Internet site <http://www.dof.ca.gov/>.
*Finance Bulletin.* Monthly. Online.

## Colorado

Colorado Department of Local Affairs, Division of Local Government, State Demography Office, 1313 Sherman Street, Room 521, Denver, CO 80203. 303-864-7720. Fax: 303-353-0751. Internet site <http://dola.colorado.gov/demog-cms/content/region-profiles>.
*2017 Region Profiles and Reports.* Online.

## Connecticut

Connecticut Department of Economic and Community Development, 450 Columbus Boulevard, Hartford, CT 06103. 860-500-2300. Internet site <http://profiles.ctdata.org/>.
*Connecticut Town Profiles, 2018.* Recurring. Online.

## Delaware

Delaware Economic Development Office, 99 Kings Highway, Dover, DE 19901-7305. 302-739-4271. Fax: 302-739-5749. Internet site <http://business.delaware.gov>.
*Delaware Data Book, 2017.* Online.

## District of Columbia

Office of the City Administrator, John A. Wilson Building, 1350 Pennsylvania Avenue, NW, Suite 521, Washington, DC 20004. 202-478-9200. Fax: 202-727-9878. Internet site <http://opendata.dc.gov/>.
*Open Data Catalog.* Online.

## Florida

University of Florida, Bureau of Economic and Business Research, P.O. Box 117148, Gainesville, FL 32611. 352-392-0171. Fax: 888-534-2404. Internet site <http://bebr.ufl.edu/data>.
*Florida Statistical Dashboards.* Online.

## Georgia

University of Georgia, Terry College of Business, Selig Center for Economic Growth, E201 Ivester Hall, 650 S. Lumpkin St., Athens, GA 30602-6269. 706-542-5073. Internet site <http://www.terry.uga.edu/about/centers-institutes/selig>.
*Georgia Economic Outlook, 2019.* Annual. Online.

University of Georgia, Carl Vinson Institute of Government, 201 N. Milledge Avenue, Athens, GA 30602. 706-542-2736. Fax: 706-542-9301. Internet site <https://cviog.uga.edu/>.
*The Georgia County Guide, 2019.* Annual. Print.

## Hawaii

Hawaii State Department of Business, Economic Development & Tourism, Research and Economic Analysis Division, Statistics and Data Support Branch, P.O. Box 2359, Honolulu, HI 96804. 808-586-2355. Internet site <http://dbedt.hawaii.gov/economic/databook/>.
*2018 State of Hawaii Data Book.* Annual. Online.

## Idaho

University of Idaho Extension, 875 Perimeter Drive. MS 2338, Moscow, ID 83844-2338. 208-885-5883. Internet site <http://indicatorsidaho.org/>.
*Indicators Idaho.* Online.

## Illinois

University of Illinois, Institute of Government and Public Affairs, 1007 W. Nevada Street, Urbana, IL 61801, MC-037. 217-333-3340. Fax: 217-244-4817. Internet site <http://igpa.uillinois.edu/>.

## Indiana

Indiana University, Kelley School of Business, Indiana Business Research Center, 1309 E. 10th Street, Suite 4048, Bloomington, IN 47405. 812-855-5507. Internet site <http://stats.indiana.edu/>.
*STATS Indiana.* Online.

## Iowa

Iowa State University of Science and Technology: Community Indicators Program, 17 East Hall, Ames, IA 50010. 515-294-9903. Fax: 515-294-0592. Internet site <http://icip.iastate.edu/>.
*Community Indicators.* Online.

State Library of Iowa, State Data Center, Ola Babcock Miller Building, 1112 East Grand, Des Moines, IA 50319-0233. 800-248-4483. Fax: 515-242-6543. Internet site <http://iowadatacenter.org>.

## Kansas

University of Kansas, Institute for Policy and Social Research, 1541 Lilac Lane, 607 Blake Hall, Lawrence, KS 66045-3129. 785-864-3701. Fax: 785-864-3683. Internet site <http://ipsr.ku.edu/ksdata/ksah/>.
*Kansas Statistical Abstract, 2018.* Online.

## Kentucky

Kentucky Cabinet for Economic Development, Old Capitol Annex, 300 West Broadway, Frankfort, KY 40601. 800-626-2930. Fax:502-564-3256. Internet site <http://thinkkentucky.com/>.

## Louisiana

Louisiana State Census Data Center, Office of Electronic Services, 1201 N. Third Street, Suite 7-210, Baton Rouge, LA 70802. 225-342-7000. Internet site <https://louisiana.gov/demographics-and-geography/>.

## Maine

Department of Administrative and Financial Services, 78 State House Station, Augusta, ME 04333. 207-624-7800. Fax: 207-624-7804. Internet site <http://maine.gov/portal/about_me/statistics.html>.

## Maryland

Maryland Department of Planning, 301 W. Preston Street, Suite 1101, Baltimore, MD 21201. 410-767-3219. Internet site <http://mdp.state.md.us/msdc/>.
*2017 Maryland Statistical Handbook.* Annual. Online.

## Massachusetts

MassCHIP, Massachusetts Department of Public Health, 250 Washington Street, Boston, MA 02108-4619. 617-624-5670. Internet site <http://mass.gov/dph/masschip>. Instant Topics. Online.

## Michigan

Michigan Economic Development Corporation, 300 N. Washington Square, Lansing, MI 48913. 1-888-522-0103. Internet site <http://michiganbusiness.org>.

## Minnesota

Minnesota Department of Employment and Economic Development, 1st National Bank Building, 332 Minnesota Street, Suite E200, Saint Paul, MN 55101-1351. 800-657-3858. Internet site <mn.gov/deed/data/>.
*Compare Minnesota: Profiles of Minnesota's Economy & Population.* Online.

Minnesota State Demographic Center, 658 Cedar Street, Room 300, Saint Paul, MN 55155. 651-296-2557. Internet site <http://demography.state.mn.us/>.

## Mississippi

Mississippi Secretary of State, 401 Mississippi Street, Jackson, MS 39201. 601-359-1350. Internet site <http://sos.ms.gov/Education-Publications/Pages/Blue-Book-2016-2020.aspx>.
*2016-2020 Mississippi Blue Book.* Quadrennial. Online.

## Missouri

University of Missouri—Columbia, Economic and Policy Analysis Research Center, 10 Professional Building, Columbia, MO 65211. 573-882-4805. Fax: 573-882-5563. Internet site <http://eparc.missouri.edu/>.
*Missouri Statistical Data Archive.* Online.

## Montana

Montana Department of Commerce, Census and Economic Information Center, 301 S. Park Avenue, Helena, MT 59620-0533. 406-841-2742. Fax: 406-841-2871. Internet site <http://ceic.mt.gov/>.

## Nebraska

Nebraska Department of Economic Development, P.O. Box 94666, 301 Centennial Mall South, Lincoln, NE 68509-4666. 800-426-6505. Fax: 402-471-3778. Internet site <https://opportunity.nebraska.gov/>.

## Nevada

Nevada Department of Administration, Budget Division, 209 East Musser Street, Room 200, Carson City, NV 89701-4298. 775-684-0222. Fax: 775-684-0260. Internet site <http://budget.nv.gov/>.

## New Hampshire

New Hampshire State Data Center, Governor Hugh J. Gallen State Office Park, Johnson Hall, 3rd Floor, 107 Pleasant Street, Concord, NH 03301-8501. 603-271-2155. Fax: 603-271-2615. Internet site <https://nh.gov/osi/data-center/>.

## New Jersey

State of New Jersey Department of Labor and Workforce Development, Bureau of Labor Market Information, 1 John Fitch Plaza, P.O. Box 110, Trenton, NJ 08625-0110. 609-292-2582. Fax: 609-633-9240. Internet site <http://lwd.dol.state.nj.us/labor/lpa/LMI_index.html>.
*Labor Market Information.* Online.

## New Mexico

University of New Mexico, Bureau of Business and Economic Research, 400 Cornell Dr NE, Albuquerque, NM 87106. 505-277-6626. Fax: 505-277-2773. Internet site <http://bber.unm.edu/>.
*New Mexico's Economy: Current Situation and Outlook.* Annual. Online. FOR-UNM Bulletin. Quarterly. Online.

## New York

Nelson A. Rockefeller Institute of Government, 411 State Street, Albany, NY 12203-1003. 518-443-5522. Fax: 518-443-5788. Internet site <rockinst.org/>.
*New York State Statistical Yearbook, 2015.* Annual. Print and Online.

## North Carolina

Office of State Budget and Management, MSC 20320, Raleigh, NC 27699-0320. 919-807-4700. Internet site <http://osbm.nc.gov/>.
*State Comparisons.* Online.

## North Dakota

University of North Dakota, Nistler College of Business and Public Administration, Gamble Hall Room 110, 293 Centennial Drive, Stop 8098, Grand Forks, ND 58202-8098. 701-777-2135. Fax: 701-777-2019. Internet site <http://business.und.edu/>.

## Ohio

Office of Research, Ohio Development Services Agency, 77 South High Street, Columbus, OH 43215-6130. 614-466-2116. Internet site <https://development.ohio.gov>.
*Research Products and Services.* Updated continuously. *Ohio County Trends.* Online.

## Oklahoma

University of Oklahoma, Center for Economic and Management Research, Michael F. Price College of Business, 307 West Brooks, Room 3, Norman, OK 73019-4004. 405-325-2931. Fax: 405-325-7688. Internet site <http://ou.edu/price/centersresearch/cemr.html>.
*Statistical Abstract of Oklahoma, Annual.* Print.

## Oregon

Secretary of State, Archives Division, Archives Bldg., 800 Summer Street NE, Salem, OR 97310. 503-373-0701 ext.1. Fax: 503-378-4118. Internet site <http://arcweb.sos.state.or.us/>.
*Oregon Blue Book. 2019-2020.* Biennial. Online.

## Pennsylvania

Pennsylvania State Data Center, Institute of State and Regional Affairs, Penn State Harrisburg, 777 West Harrisburg Pike, Middletown, PA 17057-4898. 717-948-6336. Fax: 717-948-6754. Internet site <http://pasdc.hbg.psu.edu>.
*Pennsylvania Statistical Abstract, 2019.* Print and electronic.

## Rhode Island

Rhode Island Department of Labor and Training, Labor Market Information, 1511 Pontiac Avenue, Cranston, RI 02920. 401-462-8740. Fax: 401-462-8766. Internet site <http://dlt.ri.gov/lmi/>.
*State of the State: A Statistical Profile of Rhode Island's Cities and Towns.* Online.

## South Carolina

South Carolina Revenue and Fiscal Affairs Offices, Health and Demographics Section, 1000 Assembly Street, Suite 402, Columbia, SC 29201. 803-898-9940. Internet site <http://abstract.sc.gov>.
*South Carolina Statistical Abstract.* Ongoing. Online.

## South Dakota

South Dakota State University, Rural Life and Census Data Center, Box 504, Brookings, SD 57007. 605-688-4899. Internet site <http://sdstate.edu/soc/rlcdc/index.cfm>.
*Preliminary Population Projections 2010-2035.* Online.
*South Dakota State and Demographic Profiles 2008.* Online.

## Tennessee

Tennessee State Data Center, 916 Volunteer Blvd., 716 Stokely Management Center, Knoxville, TN 37996-0570. 865-974-6070. Fax: 865-974-3100. Internet site <http://tndata.utk.edu/>.

## Texas

Texas State Historical Association, 3001 Lake Austin Blvd., Suite 3.116, Austin, TX 78703. 512-471-2600. Fax: 512-473-8691. Internet site <http://www.tshaonline.org/publications/books/3196>.
*Texas Almanac, 2018-2019.* Biennial. Print and Online.

Texas State Data Center and Office of the State Demographer, Institute for Demographic and Socioeconomic Research (IDSER), 501 W. César E. Chavez Blvd., San Antonio, TX 78207-4415. 210-458-6543. Fax: 210-458-6541. Internet site <https://texasalmanac.com/>.

## Utah

The University of Utah, Thomas S. Monson Center, 411 East South Temple Street, Salt Lake City, UT 84111. 801-585-5618. Internet site <gardner.utah.edu/economics-and-public-policy/economic-report-to-the-governor/>.
*2019 Economic Report to the Governor.* Annual. Online.

## Vermont

Department of Labor, Labor Market Information, P.O. Box 488, Montpelier, VT 05601-0488. 802-828-4202. Fax: 802-828-4050. Internet site <http://vtlmi.info/>.
*Vermont Economic-Demographic Profile, 2019.* Annual. Online.

## Virginia

University of Virginia, Weldon Cooper Center for Public Service, 2400 Old Ivy Road, P.O. Box 400206, Charlottesville, VA 22904-4206. 434-982-5522. Fax: 434-982-5524. Internet site <http://coopercenter.org/>.
*Virginia Population Estimates.* Online.
*Virginia Population Projections.* Online.

## Washington

Washington State Office of Financial Management, Forecasting Division, P.O. Box 43113, Olympia, WA 98504-3113. 360-902-0599. Internet site <ofm.wa.gov/>.
*Washington State Data Book, 2017*. Biennial. Online.

## West Virginia

West Virginia University, John Chambers College of Business and Economics, Bureau of Business and Economic Research, P.O. Box 6527, Morgantown, WV 26506-6025. 304-293-7831. Internet site <http://be.wvu.edu/bber/index.htm >.
*West Virginia County Data Profile 2017*. Annual. Online.
*West Virginia Economic Outlook, 2019-2023*. Annual. Online.

## Wisconsin

Wisconsin Legislative Reference Bureau, One East Main Street, Suite 200, Madison, WI 53703. 608-266-0341. Internet site <http://legis.wisconsin.gov/lrb/>.
*2017-2018 Wisconsin Blue Book*. Biennial. Online.

## Wyoming

Department of Administration and Information, Economic Analysis Division, 2800 Central Avenue, Cheyenne, WY 82002-0060. 307-777-7504. Fax: 307-632-1819. Internet site <http://eadiv.state.wy.us/>.
*The Equality State Almanac, 2010*. Annual. Online.
*Wyoming and County Profiles, 2018*. Annual. Online.

# Metropolitan and Micropolitan Statistical Areas: Concepts, Components, and Population

The United States Office of Management and Budget (OMB) defines metropolitan and micropolitan statistical areas according to published standards that are applied to U.S. Census Bureau data. The general concept of a metropolitan or micropolitan statistical area is that of a core area containing a substantial population nucleus, together with adjacent communities having a high degree of economic and social integration with that core. Currently defined metropolitan and micropolitan statistical areas are based on application of 2010 standards (which appeared in the Federal Register on June 28, 2010) to 2010 decennial census data. Current metropolitan and micropolitan statistical area definitions were announced by OMB effective September 2018.

Standard definitions of metropolitan areas were first issued in 1949 by the then Bureau of the Budget (predecessor of OMB), under the designation "standard metropolitan area" (SMA). The term was changed to "standard metropolitan statistical area" (SMSA) in 1959 and to "metropolitan statistical area" (MSA) in 1983. The term "metropolitan area" (MA) was adopted in 1990 and referred collectively to metropolitan statistical areas (MSAs), consolidated metropolitan statistical areas (CMSAs), and primary metropolitan statistical areas (PMSAs). The term "core-based statistical area" (CBSA) became effective in 2000 and refers collectively to metropolitan and micropolitan statistical areas.

OMB has been responsible for the official metropolitan areas since they were first defined, except for the period 1977 to 1981, when they were the responsibility of the Office of Federal Statistical Policy and Standards, U.S. Department of Commerce. The standards for defining metropolitan areas were modified in 1958, 1971, 1975, 1980, 1990, 2000, and 2010.

**Defining Metropolitan and Micropolitan Statistical Areas**—The 2010 standards provide that each CBSA must contain at least one urban area of 10,000 or more population. Each metropolitan statistical area must have at least one urbanized area of 50,000 or more inhabitants. Each micropolitan statistical area must have at least one urban cluster of at least 10,000 but less than 50,000 population.

Under the standards, the county (or counties) in which at least 50 percent of the population resides within urban areas of 10,000 or more population, or that contain at least 5,000 people residing within a single urban area of 10,000 or more population, is identified as a "central county" (counties). Additional "outlying counties" are included in the CBSA if they meet specific requirements of commuting to or from the central counties. Counties or equivalent entities form the geographic "building blocks" for metropolitan and micropolitan statistical areas throughout the United States and Puerto Rico.

If specific criteria are met, a metropolitan statistical area containing a single core with a population of 2.5 million or more may be subdivided to form smaller groupings of counties referred to as "metropolitan divisions."

As of September 2018, there are 384 metropolitan statistical areas and 542 micropolitan statistical areas in the United States. In addition, there are 8 metropolitan statistical areas and 4 micropolitan statistical areas in Puerto Rico.

**Principal Cities and Metropolitan and Micropolitan Statistical Area Titles**—The largest city in each metropolitan or micropolitan statistical area is designated a "principal city." Additional cities qualify if specific requirements are met concerning population size and employment. The title of each metropolitan or micropolitan statistical area consists of the names of up to three of its principal cities in order of descending population size and the name of each state into which the metropolitan or micropolitan statistical area extends. Titles of metropolitan divisions also typically are based on principal city names, but in certain cases consist of county names.

**Defining New England City and Town Areas**—Cities and towns are the primary units of local government in the six New England states, where counties, unlike elsewhere, have little or no official governmental functions. The 2010 standards provide for a set of geographic areas that are defined using cities and towns in the New England states. The New England city and town areas (NECTAs) are defined using the same criteria as metropolitan and micropolitan statistical areas and are identified as either metropolitan or micropolitan, based, respectively, on the presence of either an urbanized area of 50,000 or more population or an urban cluster of at least 10,000 but less than 50,000 population. If the specific criteria are met, a NECTA containing a single core with a population of at least 2.5 million may be subdivided to form smaller groupings of cities and towns referred to as New England city and town area divisions.

**Changes in Definitions Over Time**—Changes in the definitions of these statistical areas since the 1950 census have consisted chiefly of (1) the recognition of new areas as they reached the minimum required city or urbanized area population and (2) the addition of counties (or cities and towns in New England) to existing areas as new decennial census data showed them to qualify.

In some instances, formerly separate areas have been merged, components of an area have been transferred from one area to another, or components have been dropped from an area. The large majority of changes have taken place on the basis of decennial census data. However, Census Bureau data serve as the basis for intercensal updates in specific circumstances.

Because of these historical changes in geographic definitions, users must be cautious in comparing data for these statistical areas from different dates. For some purposes, comparisons of data for areas as defined at given dates may be appropriate; for other purposes, it may be preferable to maintain consistent area definitions. Historical metropolitan area definitions are available for 1950, 1960, 1963, 1970, 1973, 1981, 1983, 1990, 1993, and 1999.

Excluding Tables 21 through 23 in the Population section; Table 620 in the Labor Force section; Table 713 in the Income section, and the tables that follow in this appendix, the tables presenting data for metropolitan areas in this edition of the Statistical Abstract may be based on earlier metropolitan area definitions. See the Census Bureau website at <https://www.census.gov/programs-surveys/metro-micro.html> for information on historical delineations and component counties.

# Table A. Metropolitan Statistical Areas and Components—Population: 2018

[In thousands (171 represents 171,000). Population as of July 2018. Metropolitan Statistical Areas defined by the U.S. Office of Management and Budget as of September 2018. All Metropolitan Statistical Areas are arranged alphabetically]

| Metropolitan Statistical Area<br>~~Metropolitan Division<br>~~~~Component county | Population, 2018 (1,000) |
|---|---|
| **Abilene, TX** | **171** |
| Callahan County, TX | 14 |
| Jones County, TX | 20 |
| Taylor County, TX | 138 |
| **Akron, OH** | **705** |
| Portage County, OH | 163 |
| Summit County, OH | 542 |
| **Albany, GA** | **153** |
| Baker County, GA | 3 |
| Dougherty County, GA | 91 |
| Lee County, GA | 30 |
| Terrell County, GA | 9 |
| Worth County, GA | 20 |
| **Albany, OR** | **127** |
| Linn County, OR | 127 |
| **Albany-Schenectady-Troy, NY** | **883** |
| Albany County, NY | 307 |
| Rensselaer County, NY | 159 |
| Saratoga County, NY | 230 |
| Schenectady County, NY | 155 |
| Schoharie County, NY | 31 |
| **Albuquerque, NM** | **916** |
| Bernalillo County, NM | 679 |
| Sandoval County, NM | 145 |
| Torrance County, NM | 16 |
| Valencia County, NM | 76 |
| **Alexandria, LA** | **153** |
| Grant Parish, LA | 22 |
| Rapides Parish, LA | 131 |
| **Allentown-Bethlehem-Easton, PA-NJ** | **843** |
| Warren County, NJ | 106 |
| Carbon County, PA | 64 |
| Lehigh County, PA | 368 |
| Northampton County, PA | 305 |
| **Altoona, PA** | **122** |
| Blair County, PA | 122 |
| **Amarillo, TX** | **266** |
| Armstrong County, TX | 2 |
| Carson County, TX | 6 |
| Oldham County, TX | 2 |
| Potter County, TX | 120 |
| Randall County, TX | 136 |
| **Ames, IA** | **98** |
| Story County, IA | 98 |
| **Anchorage, AK** | **399** |
| Anchorage Municipality, AK | 292 |
| Matanuska-Susitna Borough, AK | 108 |
| **Ann Arbor, MI** | **371** |
| Washtenaw County, MI | 371 |
| **Anniston-Oxford-Jacksonville, AL** | **114** |
| Calhoun County, AL | 114 |
| **Appleton, WI** | **238** |
| Calumet County, WI | 50 |
| Outagamie County, WI | 187 |
| **Asheville, NC** | **460** |
| Buncombe County, NC | 259 |
| Haywood County, NC | 62 |
| Henderson County, NC | 117 |
| Madison County, NC | 22 |
| **Athens-Clarke County, GA** | **211** |
| Clarke County, GA | 127 |
| Madison County, GA | 30 |
| Oconee County, GA | 39 |
| Oglethorpe County, GA | 15 |
| **Atlanta-Sandy Springs-Roswell, GA** | **5,950** |
| Barrow County, GA | 81 |
| Bartow County, GA | 106 |
| Butts County, GA | 24 |
| Carroll County, GA | 118 |
| Cherokee County, GA | 254 |
| Clayton County, GA | 290 |
| Cobb County, GA | 757 |
| Coweta County, GA | 146 |
| Dawson County, GA | 25 |
| DeKalb County, GA | 757 |
| Douglas County, GA | 145 |
| Fayette County, GA | 113 |
| Forsyth County, GA | 237 |
| Fulton County, GA | 1,050 |
| Gwinnett County, GA | 928 |
| Haralson County, GA | 30 |
| Heard County, GA | 12 |
| Henry County, GA | 230 |
| Jasper County, GA | 14 |
| Lamar County, GA | 19 |
| Meriwether County, GA | 21 |
| Morgan County, GA | 19 |
| Newton County, GA | 110 |
| Paulding County, GA | 164 |
| Pickens County, GA | 32 |
| Pike County, GA | 19 |
| Rockdale County, GA | 91 |
| Spalding County, GA | 66 |
| Walton County, GA | 94 |
| **Atlantic City-Hammonton, NJ** | **265** |
| Atlantic County, NJ | 265 |
| **Auburn-Opelika, AL** | **164** |
| Lee County, AL | 164 |
| **Augusta-Richmond County, GA-SC** | **604** |
| Burke County, GA | 22 |
| Columbia County, GA | 154 |
| Lincoln County, GA | 8 |
| McDuffie County, GA | 22 |
| Richmond County, GA | 202 |
| Aiken County, SC | 169 |
| Edgefield County, SC | 27 |
| **Austin-Round Rock, TX** | **2,168** |
| Bastrop County, TX | 87 |
| Caldwell County, TX | 43 |
| Hays County, TX | 223 |
| Travis County, TX | 1,249 |
| Williamson County, TX | 667 |
| **Bakersfield, CA** | **897** |
| Kern County, CA | 897 |
| **Baltimore-Columbia-Towson, MD** | **2,803** |
| Anne Arundel County, MD | 576 |
| Baltimore County, MD | 828 |
| Carroll County, MD | 168 |
| Harford County, MD | 254 |
| Howard County, MD | 323 |
| Queen Anne's County, MD | 50 |
| Baltimore city, MD | 602 |
| **Bangor, ME** | **151** |
| Penobscot County, ME | 151 |
| **Barnstable Town, MA** | **213** |
| Barnstable County, MA | 213 |
| **Baton Rouge, LA** | **831** |
| Ascension Parish, LA | 125 |
| East Baton Rouge Parish, LA | 441 |
| East Feliciana Parish, LA | 19 |
| Iberville Parish, LA | 33 |
| Livingston Parish, LA | 140 |
| Pointe Coupee Parish, LA | 22 |
| St. Helena Parish, LA | 10 |
| West Baton Rouge Parish, LA | 26 |
| West Feliciana Parish, LA | 15 |
| **Battle Creek, MI** | **134** |
| Calhoun County, MI | 134 |
| **Bay City, MI** | **104** |
| Bay County, MI | 104 |
| **Beaumont-Port Arthur, TX** | **410** |
| Hardin County, TX | 57 |
| Jefferson County, TX | 255 |
| Newton County, TX | 14 |
| Orange County, TX | 84 |
| **Beckley, WV** | **117** |
| Fayette County, WV | 43 |
| Raleigh County, WV | 74 |
| **Bellingham, WA** | **226** |
| Whatcom County, WA | 226 |
| **Bend-Redmond, OR** | **192** |
| Deschutes County, OR | 192 |
| **Billings, MT** | **172** |
| Carbon County, MT | 11 |
| Golden Valley County, MT | 1 |
| Yellowstone County, MT | 160 |
| **Binghamton, NY** | **240** |
| Broome County, NY | 192 |
| Tioga County, NY | 49 |
| **Birmingham-Hoover, AL** | **1,152** |
| Bibb County, AL | 22 |
| Blount County, AL | 58 |
| Chilton County, AL | 44 |
| Jefferson County, AL | 659 |
| St. Clair County, AL | 89 |
| Shelby County, AL | 216 |
| Walker County, AL | 64 |
| **Bismarck, ND** | **133** |
| Burleigh County, ND | 95 |
| Morton County, ND | 31 |
| Oliver County, ND | 2 |
| Sioux County, ND | 4 |
| **Blacksburg-Christiansburg-Radford, VA** | **184** |
| Floyd County, VA | 16 |
| Giles County, VA | 17 |
| Montgomery County, VA | 99 |
| Pulaski County, VA | 34 |
| Radford city, VA | 18 |
| **Bloomington, IL** | **189** |
| De Witt County, IL | 16 |
| McLean County, IL | 173 |
| **Bloomington, IN** | **168** |
| Monroe County, IN | 147 |
| Owen County, IN | 21 |
| **Bloomsburg-Berwick, PA** | **84** |
| Columbia County, PA | 65 |
| Montour County, PA | 18 |
| **Boise City, ID** | **730** |
| Ada County, ID | 470 |
| Boise County, ID | 8 |
| Canyon County, ID | 223 |
| Gem County, ID | 18 |
| Owyhee County, ID | 12 |
| **Boston-Cambridge-Newton, MA-NH** | **4,875** |
| **Boston, MA** | **2,031** |
| Norfolk County, MA | 705 |
| Plymouth County, MA | 518 |
| Suffolk County, MA | 807 |
| **Cambridge-Newton-Framingham, MA** | **2,405** |
| Essex County, MA | 791 |
| Middlesex County, MA | 1,615 |
| **Rockingham County-Strafford County, NH** | **439** |
| Rockingham County, NH | 309 |
| Strafford County, NH | 130 |
| **Boulder, CO** | **326** |
| Boulder County, CO | 326 |
| **Bowling Green, KY** | **177** |
| Allen County, KY | 21 |
| Butler County, KY | 13 |
| Edmonson County, KY | 12 |
| Warren County, KY | 131 |
| **Bremerton-Silverdale, WA** | **270** |
| Kitsap County, WA | 270 |
| **Bridgeport-Stamford-Norwalk, CT** | **944** |
| Fairfield County, CT | 944 |
| **Brownsville-Harlingen, TX** | **424** |
| Cameron County, TX | 424 |
| **Brunswick, GA** | **118** |
| Brantley County, GA | 19 |
| Glynn County, GA | 85 |
| McIntosh County, GA | 14 |
| **Buffalo-Cheektowaga-Niagara Falls, NY** | **1,130** |
| Erie County, NY | 920 |
| Niagara County, NY | 210 |
| **Burlington, NC** | **166** |
| Alamance County, NC | 166 |
| **Burlington-South Burlington, VT** | **221** |

See footnotes at end of table.

# Table A. Metropolitan Statistical Areas and Components—Population: 2018-Continued.

See headnote on page 917.

| Metropolitan Statistical Area ~~Metropolitan Division ~~~~Component county | Population, 2018 (1,000) |
|---|---|
| Chittenden County, VT | 165 |
| Franklin County, VT | 49 |
| Grand Isle County, VT | 7 |
| **California-Lexington Park, MD** | **113** |
| St. Mary's County, MD | 113 |
| **Canton-Massillon, OH** | **399** |
| Carroll County, OH | 27 |
| Stark County, OH | 372 |
| **Cape Coral-Fort Myers, FL** | **755** |
| Lee County, FL | 755 |
| **Cape Girardeau, MO-IL** | **97** |
| Alexander County, IL | 6 |
| Bollinger County, MO | 12 |
| Cape Girardeau County, MO | 79 |
| **Carbondale-Marion, IL** | **124** |
| Jackson County, IL | 57 |
| Williamson County, IL | 67 |
| **Carson City, NV** | **55** |
| Carson City, NV | 55 |
| **Casper, WY** | **79** |
| Natrona County, WY | 79 |
| **Cedar Rapids, IA** | **272** |
| Benton County, IA | 26 |
| Jones County, IA | 21 |
| Linn County, IA | 226 |
| **Chambersburg-Waynesboro, PA** | **155** |
| Franklin County, PA | 155 |
| **Champaign-Urbana, IL** | **240** |
| Champaign County, IL | 210 |
| Ford County, IL | 13 |
| Piatt County, IL | 16 |
| **Charleston, WV** | **211** |
| Boone County, WV | 22 |
| Clay County, WV | 9 |
| Kanawha County, WV | 180 |
| **Charleston-North Charleston, SC** | **788** |
| Berkeley County, SC | 221 |
| Charleston County, SC | 406 |
| Dorchester County, SC | 161 |
| **Charlotte-Concord-Gastonia, NC-SC** | **2,569** |
| Cabarrus County, NC | 211 |
| Gaston County, NC | 223 |
| Iredell County, NC | 178 |
| Lincoln County, NC | 84 |
| Mecklenburg County, NC | 1,094 |
| Rowan County, NC | 141 |
| Union County, NC | 236 |
| Chester County, SC | 32 |
| Lancaster County, SC | 95 |
| York County, SC | 274 |
| **Charlottesville, VA** | **235** |
| Albemarle County, VA | 109 |
| Buckingham County, VA | 17 |
| Fluvanna County, VA | 27 |
| Greene County, VA | 20 |
| Nelson County, VA | 15 |
| Charlottesville city, VA | 48 |
| **Chattanooga, TN-GA** | **561** |
| Catoosa County, GA | 67 |
| Dade County, GA | 16 |
| Walker County, GA | 69 |
| Hamilton County, TN | 364 |
| Marion County, TN | 29 |
| Sequatchie County, TN | 15 |
| **Cheyenne, WY** | **99** |
| Laramie County, WY | 99 |
| **Chicago-Naperville-Elgin, IL-IN-WI** | **9,499** |
| **Chicago-Naperville-Arlington Heights, IL** | **7,289** |
| Cook County, IL | 5,180 |
| DuPage County, IL | 929 |
| Grundy County, IL | 51 |
| Kendall County, IL | 128 |
| McHenry County, IL | 309 |
| Will County, IL | 692 |
| **Elgin, IL** | **638** |
| DeKalb County, IL | 104 |
| Kane County, IL | 534 |
| **Gary, IN** | **701** |

| Metropolitan Statistical Area ~~Metropolitan Division ~~~~Component county | Population, 2018 (1,000) |
|---|---|
| Jasper County, IN | 33 |
| Lake County, IN | 484 |
| Newton County, IN | 14 |
| Porter County, IN | 170 |
| **Lake County-Kenosha County, IL-WI** | **870** |
| Lake County, IL | 701 |
| Kenosha County, WI | 169 |
| **Chico, CA** | **231** |
| Butte County, CA | 231 |
| **Cincinnati, OH-KY-IN** | **2,190** |
| Dearborn County, IN | 50 |
| Ohio County, IN | 6 |
| Union County, IN | 7 |
| Boone County, KY | 132 |
| Bracken County, KY | 8 |
| Campbell County, KY | 93 |
| Gallatin County, KY | 9 |
| Grant County, KY | 25 |
| Kenton County, KY | 166 |
| Pendleton County, KY | 15 |
| Brown County, OH | 44 |
| Butler County, OH | 382 |
| Clermont County, OH | 205 |
| Hamilton County, OH | 817 |
| Warren County, OH | 232 |
| **Clarksville, TN-KY** | **292** |
| Christian County, KY | 72 |
| Trigg County, KY | 15 |
| Montgomery County, TN | 206 |
| **Cleveland, TN** | **124** |
| Bradley County, TN | 107 |
| Polk County, TN | 17 |
| **Cleveland-Elyria, OH** | **2,057** |
| Cuyahoga County, OH | 1,244 |
| Geauga County, OH | 94 |
| Lake County, OH | 231 |
| Lorain County, OH | 309 |
| Medina County, OH | 179 |
| **Coeur d'Alene, ID** | **162** |
| Kootenai County, ID | 162 |
| **College Station-Bryan, TX** | **262** |
| Brazos County, TX | 227 |
| Burleson County, TX | 18 |
| Robertson County, TX | 17 |
| **Colorado Springs, CO** | **739** |
| El Paso County, CO | 714 |
| Teller County, CO | 25 |
| **Columbia, MO** | **180** |
| Boone County, MO | 180 |
| **Columbia, SC** | **833** |
| Calhoun County, SC | 15 |
| Fairfield County, SC | 22 |
| Kershaw County, SC | 66 |
| Lexington County, SC | 295 |
| Richland County, SC | 415 |
| Saluda County, SC | 21 |
| **Columbus, GA-AL** | **305** |
| Russell County, AL | 58 |
| Chattahoochee County, GA | 11 |
| Harris County, GA | 34 |
| Marion County, GA | 8 |
| Muscogee County, GA | 194 |
| **Columbus, IN** | **83** |
| Bartholomew County, IN | 83 |
| **Columbus, OH** | **2,107** |
| Delaware County, OH | 205 |
| Fairfield County, OH | 156 |
| Franklin County, OH | 1,310 |
| Hocking County, OH | 28 |
| Licking County, OH | 176 |
| Madison County, OH | 44 |
| Morrow County, OH | 35 |
| Perry County, OH | 36 |
| Pickaway County, OH | 58 |
| Union County, OH | 58 |
| **Corpus Christi, TX** | **453** |
| Aransas County, TX | 24 |
| Nueces County, TX | 362 |
| San Patricio County, TX | 67 |
| **Corvallis, OR** | **92** |
| Benton County, OR | 92 |

| Metropolitan Statistical Area ~~Metropolitan Division ~~~~Component county | Population, 2018 (1,000) |
|---|---|
| **Crestview-Fort Walton Beach-Destin, FL** | **279** |
| Okaloosa County, FL | 207 |
| Walton County, FL | 71 |
| **Cumberland, MD-WV** | **98** |
| Allegany County, MD | 71 |
| Mineral County, WV | 27 |
| **Dallas-Fort Worth-Arlington, TX** | **7,540** |
| **Dallas-Plano-Irving, TX** | **5,007** |
| Collin County, TX | 1,005 |
| Dallas County, TX | 2,638 |
| Denton County, TX | 859 |
| Ellis County, TX | 179 |
| Hunt County, TX | 96 |
| Kaufman County, TX | 129 |
| Rockwall County, TX | 101 |
| **Fort Worth-Arlington, TX** | **2,533** |
| Hood County, TX | 61 |
| Johnson County, TX | 171 |
| Parker County, TX | 138 |
| Somervell County, TX | 9 |
| Tarrant County, TX | 2,085 |
| Wise County, TX | 68 |
| **Dalton, GA** | **144** |
| Murray County, GA | 40 |
| Whitfield County, GA | 104 |
| **Danville, IL** | **77** |
| Vermilion County, IL | 77 |
| **Daphne-Fairhope-Foley, AL** | **218** |
| Baldwin County, AL | 218 |
| **Davenport-Moline-Rock Island, IA-IL** | **381** |
| Henry County, IL | 49 |
| Mercer County, IL | 16 |
| Rock Island County, IL | 143 |
| Scott County, IA | 173 |
| **Dayton, OH** | **807** |
| Greene County, OH | 168 |
| Miami County, OH | 106 |
| Montgomery County, OH | 532 |
| **Decatur, AL** | **152** |
| Lawrence County, AL | 33 |
| Morgan County, AL | 119 |
| **Decatur, IL** | **105** |
| Macon County, IL | 105 |
| **Deltona-Daytona Beach-Ormond Beach, FL** | **660** |
| Flagler County, FL | 112 |
| Volusia County, FL | 548 |
| **Denver-Aurora-Lakewood, CO** | **2,932** |
| Adams County, CO | 512 |
| Arapahoe County, CO | 651 |
| Broomfield County, CO | 69 |
| Clear Creek County, CO | 10 |
| Denver County, CO | 716 |
| Douglas County, CO | 343 |
| Elbert County, CO | 26 |
| Gilpin County, CO | 6 |
| Jefferson County, CO | 580 |
| Park County, CO | 19 |
| **Des Moines-West Des Moines, IA** | **655** |
| Dallas County, IA | 90 |
| Guthrie County, IA | 11 |
| Madison County, IA | 16 |
| Polk County, IA | 487 |
| Warren County, IA | 51 |
| **Detroit-Warren-Dearborn, MI** | **4,326** |
| **Detroit-Dearborn-Livonia, MI** | **1,754** |
| Wayne County, MI | 1,754 |
| **Warren-Troy-Farmington Hills, MI** | **2,573** |
| Lapeer County, MI | 88 |
| Livingston County, MI | 191 |
| Macomb County, MI | 875 |
| Oakland County, MI | 1,259 |
| St. Clair County, MI | 159 |
| **Dothan, AL** | **148** |
| Geneva County, AL | 26 |
| Henry County, AL | 17 |

See footnotes at end of table.

# Table A. Metropolitan Statistical Areas and Components—Population: 2018-Continued.

See headnote on page 917.

| Metropolitan Statistical Area ~~Metropolitan Division ~~~~Component county | Popu-lation, 2018 (1,000) |
|---|---|
| Houston County, AL | 105 |
| **Dover, DE** | **179** |
| Kent County, DE | 179 |
| **Dubuque, IA** | **97** |
| Dubuque County, IA | 97 |
| **Duluth, MN-WI** | **279** |
| Carlton County, MN | 36 |
| St. Louis County, MN | 200 |
| Douglas County, WI | 43 |
| **Durham-Chapel Hill, NC** | **575** |
| Chatham County, NC | 73 |
| Durham County, NC | 317 |
| Orange County, NC | 146 |
| Person County, NC | 40 |
| **East Stroudsburg, PA** | **170** |
| Monroe County, PA | 170 |
| **Eau Claire, WI** | **169** |
| Chippewa County, WI | 64 |
| Eau Claire County, WI | 105 |
| **El Centro, CA** | **182** |
| Imperial County, CA | 182 |
| **Elizabethtown-Fort Knox, KY** | **153** |
| Hardin County, KY | 110 |
| Larue County, KY | 14 |
| Meade County, KY | 29 |
| **Elkhart-Goshen, IN** | **206** |
| Elkhart County, IN | 206 |
| **Elmira, NY** | **84** |
| Chemung County, NY | 84 |
| **El Paso, TX** | **846** |
| El Paso County, TX | 841 |
| Hudspeth County, TX | 5 |
| **Enid, OK** | **61** |
| Garfield County, OK | 61 |
| **Erie, PA** | **272** |
| Erie County, PA | 272 |
| **Eugene, OR** | **380** |
| Lane County, OR | 380 |
| **Evansville, IN-KY** | **316** |
| Posey County, IN | 26 |
| Vanderburgh County, IN | 181 |
| Warrick County, IN | 63 |
| Henderson County, KY | 46 |
| **Fairbanks, AK** | **99** |
| Fairbanks North Star Borough, AK | 99 |
| **Fargo, ND-MN** | **245** |
| Clay County, MN | 64 |
| Cass County, ND | 182 |
| **Farmington, NM** | **125** |
| San Juan County, NM | 125 |
| **Fayetteville, NC** | **387** |
| Cumberland County, NC | 332 |
| Hoke County, NC | 55 |
| **Fayetteville-Springdale-Rogers, AR-MO** | **549** |
| Benton County, AR | 273 |
| Madison County, AR | 16 |
| Washington County, AR | 237 |
| McDonald County, MO | 23 |
| **Flagstaff, AZ** | **143** |
| Coconino County, AZ | 143 |
| **Flint, MI** | **407** |
| Genesee County, MI | 407 |
| **Florence, SC** | **205** |
| Darlington County, SC | 67 |
| Florence County, SC | 138 |
| **Florence-Muscle Shoals, AL** | **147** |
| Colbert County, AL | 55 |
| Lauderdale County, AL | 92 |
| **Fond du Lac, WI** | **103** |
| Fond du Lac County, WI | 103 |
| **Fort Collins, CO** | **351** |
| Larimer County, CO | 351 |
| **Fort Smith, AR-OK** | **282** |
| Crawford County, AR | 63 |
| Sebastian County, AR | 128 |
| Le Flore County, OK | 50 |
| Sequoyah County, OK | 41 |
| **Fort Wayne, IN** | **438** |

| Metropolitan Statistical Area ~~Metropolitan Division ~~~~Component county | Popu-lation, 2018 (1,000) |
|---|---|
| Allen County, IN | 375 |
| Wells County, IN | 28 |
| Whitley County, IN | 34 |
| **Fresno, CA** | **994** |
| Fresno County, CA | 994 |
| **Gadsden, AL** | **103** |
| Etowah County, AL | 103 |
| **Gainesville, FL** | **288** |
| Alachua County, FL | 270 |
| Gilchrist County, FL | 18 |
| **Gainesville, GA** | **202** |
| Hall County, GA | 202 |
| **Gettysburg, PA** | **103** |
| Adams County, PA | 103 |
| **Glens Falls, NY** | **125** |
| Warren County, NY | 64 |
| Washington County, NY | 61 |
| **Goldsboro, NC** | **123** |
| Wayne County, NC | 123 |
| **Grand Forks, ND-MN** | **102** |
| Polk County, MN | 32 |
| Grand Forks County, ND | 71 |
| **Grand Island, NE** | **85** |
| Hall County, NE | 62 |
| Hamilton County, NE | 9 |
| Howard County, NE | 6 |
| Merrick County, NE | 8 |
| **Grand Junction, CO** | **153** |
| Mesa County, CO | 153 |
| **Grand Rapids-Wyoming, MI** | **1,069** |
| Barry County, MI | 61 |
| Kent County, MI | 654 |
| Montcalm County, MI | 64 |
| Ottawa County, MI | 290 |
| **Grants Pass, OR** | **87** |
| Josephine County, OR | 87 |
| **Great Falls, MT** | **82** |
| Cascade County, MT | 82 |
| **Greeley, CO** | **314** |
| Weld County, CO | 314 |
| **Green Bay, WI** | **322** |
| Brown County, WI | 263 |
| Kewaunee County, WI | 20 |
| Oconto County, WI | 38 |
| **Greensboro-High Point, NC** | **768** |
| Guilford County, NC | 534 |
| Randolph County, NC | 143 |
| Rockingham County, NC | 91 |
| **Greenville, NC** | **180** |
| Pitt County, NC | 180 |
| **Greenville-Anderson-Mauldin, SC** | **907** |
| Anderson County, SC | 200 |
| Greenville County, SC | 514 |
| Laurens County, SC | 67 |
| Pickens County, SC | 125 |
| **Gulfport-Biloxi-Pascagoula, MS** | **397** |
| Hancock County, MS | 47 |
| Harrison County, MS | 207 |
| Jackson County, MS | 143 |
| **Hagerstown-Martinsburg, MD-WV** | **268** |
| Washington County, MD | 151 |
| Berkeley County, WV | 117 |
| **Hammond, LA** | **134** |
| Tangipahoa Parish, LA | 134 |
| **Hanford-Corcoran, CA** | **151** |
| Kings County, CA | 151 |
| **Harrisburg-Carlisle, PA** | **575** |
| Cumberland County, PA | 251 |
| Dauphin County, PA | 277 |
| Perry County, PA | 46 |
| **Harrisonburg, VA** | **135** |
| Rockingham County, VA | 81 |
| Harrisonburg city, VA | 54 |
| **Hartford-West Hartford-East Hartford, CT** | **1,206** |
| Hartford County, CT | 893 |
| Middlesex County, CT | 163 |

| Metropolitan Statistical Area ~~Metropolitan Division ~~~~Component county | Popu-lation, 2018 (1,000) |
|---|---|
| Tolland County, CT | 151 |
| **Hattiesburg, MS** | **149** |
| Forrest County, MS | 75 |
| Lamar County, MS | 62 |
| Perry County, MS | 12 |
| **Hickory-Lenoir-Morganton, NC** | **368** |
| Alexander County, NC | 37 |
| Burke County, NC | 90 |
| Caldwell County, NC | 82 |
| Catawba County, NC | 159 |
| **Hilton Head Island-Bluffton-Beaufort, SC** | **218** |
| Beaufort County, SC | 189 |
| Jasper County, SC | 29 |
| **Hinesville, GA** | **80** |
| Liberty County, GA | 61 |
| Long County, GA | 19 |
| **Homosassa Springs, FL** | **148** |
| Citrus County, FL | 148 |
| **Hot Springs, AR** | **99** |
| Garland County, AR | 99 |
| **Houma-Thibodaux, LA** | **209** |
| Lafourche Parish, LA | 98 |
| Terrebonne Parish, LA | 111 |
| **Houston-The Woodlands-Sugar Land, TX** | **6,997** |
| Austin County, TX | 30 |
| Brazoria County, TX | 370 |
| Chambers County, TX | 42 |
| Fort Bend County, TX | 788 |
| Galveston County, TX | 338 |
| Harris County, TX | 4,699 |
| Liberty County, TX | 86 |
| Montgomery County, TX | 591 |
| Waller County, TX | 53 |
| **Huntington-Ashland, WV-KY-OH** | **353** |
| Boyd County, KY | 47 |
| Greenup County, KY | 35 |
| Lawrence County, OH | 60 |
| Cabell County, WV | 93 |
| Lincoln County, WV | 21 |
| Putnam County, WV | 57 |
| Wayne County, WV | 40 |
| **Huntsville, AL** | **463** |
| Limestone County, AL | 96 |
| Madison County, AL | 367 |
| **Idaho Falls, ID** | **149** |
| Bonneville County, ID | 117 |
| Butte County, ID | 3 |
| Jefferson County, ID | 29 |
| **Indianapolis-Carmel-Anderson, IN** | **2,049** |
| Boone County, IN | 67 |
| Brown County, IN | 15 |
| Hamilton County, IN | 330 |
| Hancock County, IN | 76 |
| Hendricks County, IN | 167 |
| Johnson County, IN | 156 |
| Madison County, IN | 130 |
| Marion County, IN | 955 |
| Morgan County, IN | 70 |
| Putnam County, IN | 38 |
| Shelby County, IN | 45 |
| **Iowa City, IA** | **173** |
| Johnson County, IA | 151 |
| Washington County, IA | 22 |
| **Ithaca, NY** | **103** |
| Tompkins County, NY | 103 |
| **Jackson, MI** | **159** |
| Jackson County, MI | 159 |
| **Jackson, MS** | **580** |
| Copiah County, MS | 29 |
| Hinds County, MS | 237 |
| Madison County, MS | 106 |
| Rankin County, MS | 154 |
| Simpson County, MS | 27 |
| Yazoo County, MS | 28 |
| **Jackson, TN** | **129** |

See footnotes at end of table.

# Table A. Metropolitan Statistical Areas and Components—Population: 2018-Continued.

See headnote on page 917.

| Metropolitan Statistical Area<br>~~Metropolitan Division<br>~~~~Component county | Population, 2018 (1,000) |
|---|---|
| Chester County, TN................ | 17 |
| Crockett County, TN............... | 14 |
| Madison County, TN............... | 98 |
| **Jacksonville, FL.................** | **1,535** |
| Baker County, FL................. | 28 |
| Clay County, FL.................. | 216 |
| Duval County, FL................. | 950 |
| Nassau County, FL................ | 86 |
| St. Johns County, FL............. | 254 |
| **Jacksonville, NC.................** | **198** |
| Onslow County, NC................ | 198 |
| **Janesville-Beloit, WI...........** | **163** |
| Rock County, WI.................. | 163 |
| **Jefferson City, MO..............** | **152** |
| Callaway County, MO.............. | 45 |
| Cole County, MO.................. | 77 |
| Moniteau County, MO.............. | 16 |
| Osage County, MO................. | 14 |
| **Johnson City, TN...............** | **203** |
| Carter County, TN................ | 56 |
| Unicoi County, TN................ | 18 |
| Washington County, TN............ | 129 |
| **Johnstown, PA..................** | **132** |
| Cambria County, PA............... | 132 |
| **Jonesboro, AR..................** | **133** |
| Craighead County, AR............. | 109 |
| Poinsett County, AR.............. | 24 |
| **Joplin, MO.....................** | **179** |
| Jasper County, MO................ | 121 |
| Newton County, MO................ | 58 |
| **Kahului-Wailuku-Lahaina, HI....** | **167** |
| Kalawao County, HI............... | (Z) |
| Maui County, HI.................. | 167 |
| **Kalamazoo-Portage, MI..........** | **340** |
| Kalamazoo County, MI............. | 265 |
| Van Buren County, MI............. | 75 |
| **Kankakee, IL...................** | **110** |
| Kankakee County, IL.............. | 110 |
| **Kansas City, MO-KS.............** | **2,144** |
| Johnson County, KS............... | 598 |
| Leavenworth County, KS........... | 81 |
| Linn County, KS.................. | 10 |
| Miami County, KS................. | 34 |
| Wyandotte County, KS............. | 165 |
| Bates County, MO................. | 16 |
| Caldwell County, MO.............. | 9 |
| Cass County, MO.................. | 105 |
| Clay County, MO.................. | 246 |
| Clinton County, MO............... | 20 |
| Jackson County, MO............... | 700 |
| Lafayette County, MO............. | 33 |
| Platte County, MO................ | 103 |
| Ray County, MO................... | 23 |
| **Kennewick-Richland, WA.........** | **296** |
| Benton County, WA................ | 202 |
| Franklin County, WA.............. | 94 |
| **Killeen-Temple, TX.............** | **452** |
| Bell County, TX.................. | 356 |
| Coryell County, TX............... | 75 |
| Lampasas County, TX.............. | 21 |
| **Kingsport-Bristol-Bristol,<br>TN-VA.........................** | **307** |
| Hawkins County, TN............... | 57 |
| Sullivan County, TN.............. | 158 |
| Scott County, VA................. | 22 |
| Washington County, VA............ | 54 |
| Bristol city, VA................. | 16 |
| **Kingston, NY...................** | **179** |
| Ulster County, NY................ | 179 |
| **Knoxville, TN..................** | **883** |
| Anderson County, TN.............. | 76 |
| Blount County, TN................ | 131 |
| Campbell County, TN.............. | 40 |
| Grainger County, TN.............. | 23 |
| Knox County, TN.................. | 465 |
| Loudon County, TN................ | 53 |
| Morgan County, TN................ | 22 |
| Roane County, TN................. | 53 |
| Union County, TN................. | 20 |
| **Kokomo, IN....................** | **82** |
| Howard County, IN................ | 82 |
| **La Crosse-Onalaska, WI-MN.....** | **137** |
| Houston County, MN............... | 19 |

| Metropolitan Statistical Area<br>~~Metropolitan Division<br>~~~~Component county | Population, 2018 (1,000) |
|---|---|
| La Crosse County, WI............. | 118 |
| **Lafayette, LA..................** | **489** |
| Acadia Parish, LA................ | 62 |
| Iberia Parish, LA................ | 71 |
| Lafayette Parish, LA............. | 243 |
| St. Martin Parish, LA............ | 54 |
| Vermilion Parish, LA............. | 60 |
| **Lafayette-West Lafayette, IN....** | **222** |
| Benton County, IN................ | 9 |
| Carroll County, IN............... | 20 |
| Tippecanoe County, IN............ | 193 |
| **Lake Charles, LA...............** | **210** |
| Calcasieu Parish, LA............. | 203 |
| Cameron Parish, LA............... | 7 |
| **Lake Havasu City-Kingman,<br>AZ............................** | **210** |
| Mohave County, AZ................ | 210 |
| **Lakeland-Winter Haven, FL......** | **708** |
| Polk County, FL.................. | 708 |
| **Lancaster, PA..................** | **544** |
| Lancaster County, PA............. | 544 |
| **Lansing-East Lansing, MI.......** | **482** |
| Clinton County, MI............... | 79 |
| Eaton County, MI................. | 110 |
| Ingham County, MI................ | 293 |
| **Laredo, TX.....................** | **276** |
| Webb County, TX.................. | 276 |
| **Las Cruces, NM.................** | **218** |
| Doña Ana County, NM.............. | 218 |
| **Las Vegas-Henderson-<br>Paradise, NV..................** | **2,232** |
| Clark County, NV................. | 2,232 |
| **Lawrence, KS...................** | **121** |
| Douglas County, KS............... | 121 |
| **Lawton, OK....................** | **126** |
| Comanche County, OK.............. | 120 |
| Cotton County, OK................ | 6 |
| **Lebanon, PA...................** | **141** |
| Lebanon County, PA............... | 141 |
| **Lewiston, ID-WA................** | **63** |
| Nez Perce County, ID............. | 40 |
| Asotin County, WA................ | 23 |
| **Lewiston-Auburn, ME............** | **108** |
| Androscoggin County, ME.......... | 108 |
| **Lexington-Fayette, KY..........** | **517** |
| Bourbon County, KY............... | 20 |
| Clark County, KY................. | 36 |
| Fayette County, KY............... | 324 |
| Jessamine County, KY............. | 54 |
| Scott County, KY................. | 56 |
| Woodford County, KY.............. | 27 |
| **Lima, OH......................** | **103** |
| Allen County, OH................. | 103 |
| **Lincoln, NE...................** | **335** |
| Lancaster County, NE............. | 317 |
| Seward County, NE................ | 17 |
| **Little Rock-North Little<br>Rock-Conway, AR...............** | **741** |
| Faulkner County, AR.............. | 125 |
| Grant County, AR................. | 18 |
| Lonoke County, AR................ | 74 |
| Perry County, AR................. | 10 |
| Pulaski County, AR............... | 393 |
| Saline County, AR................ | 121 |
| **Logan, UT-ID..................** | **141** |
| Franklin County, ID.............. | 14 |
| Cache County, UT................. | 127 |
| **Longview, TX..................** | **219** |
| Gregg County, TX................. | 124 |
| Rusk County, TX.................. | 54 |
| Upshur County, TX................ | 41 |
| **Longview, WA..................** | **109** |
| Cowlitz County, WA............... | 109 |
| **Los Angeles-Long<br>Beach-Anaheim, CA............** | **13,291** |
| **Anaheim-Santa Ana-Irvine,<br>CA............................** | **3,186** |
| Orange County, CA................ | 3,186 |
| **Los Angeles-Long<br>Beach-Glendale, CA............** | **10,106** |
| Los Angeles County, CA........... | 10,106 |

| Metropolitan Statistical Area<br>~~Metropolitan Division<br>~~~~Component county | Population, 2018 (1,000) |
|---|---|
| **Louisville/Jefferson County,<br>KY-IN.........................** | **1,297** |
| Clark County, IN................. | 117 |
| Floyd County, IN................. | 78 |
| Harrison County, IN.............. | 40 |
| Scott County, IN................. | 24 |
| Washington County, IN............ | 28 |
| Bullitt County, KY............... | 81 |
| Henry County, KY................. | 16 |
| Jefferson County, KY............. | 771 |
| Oldham County, KY................ | 66 |
| Shelby County, KY................ | 49 |
| Spencer County, KY............... | 19 |
| Trimble County, KY............... | 9 |
| **Lubbock, TX...................** | **319** |
| Crosby County, TX................ | 6 |
| Lubbock County, TX............... | 307 |
| Lynn County, TX.................. | 6 |
| **Lynchburg, VA.................** | **263** |
| Amherst County, VA............... | 32 |
| Appomattox County, VA............ | 16 |
| Bedford County, VA............... | 79 |
| Campbell County, VA.............. | 55 |
| Lynchburg city, VA............... | 82 |
| **Macon-Bibb County, GA.........** | **230** |
| Bibb County, GA.................. | 153 |
| Crawford County, GA.............. | 12 |
| Jones County, GA................. | 29 |
| Monroe County, GA................ | 28 |
| Twiggs County, GA................ | 8 |
| **Madera, CA....................** | **158** |
| Madera County, CA................ | 158 |
| **Madison, WI...................** | **660** |
| Columbia County, WI.............. | 57 |
| Dane County, WI.................. | 542 |
| Green County, WI................. | 37 |
| Iowa County, WI.................. | 24 |
| **Manchester-Nashua, NH.........** | **415** |
| Hillsborough County, NH.......... | 415 |
| **Manhattan, KS.................** | **98** |
| Pottawatomie County, KS.......... | 24 |
| Riley County, KS................. | 74 |
| **Mankato-North Mankato, MN....** | **102** |
| Blue Earth County, MN............ | 67 |
| Nicollet County, MN.............. | 34 |
| **Mansfield, OH.................** | **121** |
| Richland County, OH.............. | 121 |
| **McAllen-Edinburg-Mission,<br>TX............................** | **866** |
| Hidalgo County, TX............... | 866 |
| **Medford, OR...................** | **220** |
| Jackson County, OR............... | 220 |
| **Memphis, TN-MS-AR.............** | **1,351** |
| Crittenden County, AR............ | 48 |
| Benton County, MS................ | 8 |
| DeSoto County, MS................ | 182 |
| Marshall County, MS.............. | 35 |
| Tate County, MS.................. | 29 |
| Tunica County, MS................ | 10 |
| Fayette County, TN............... | 41 |
| Shelby County, TN................ | 936 |
| Tipton County, TN................ | 62 |
| **Merced, CA....................** | **275** |
| Merced County, CA................ | 275 |
| **Miami-Fort Lauderdale-West<br>Palm Beach, FL...............** | **6,199** |
| **Fort Lauderdale-Pompano<br>Beach-Deerfield Beach, FL....** | **1,951** |
| Broward County, FL............... | 1,951 |
| **Miami-Miami Beach-Kendall,<br>FL............................** | **2,762** |
| Miami-Dade County, FL............ | 2,762 |
| **West Palm Beach-Boca<br>Raton-Delray Beach, FL.......** | **1,486** |
| Palm Beach County, FL............ | 1,486 |
| **Michigan City-La Porte, IN.......** | **110** |
| LaPorte County, IN............... | 110 |
| **Midland, MI...................** | **83** |
| Midland County, MI............... | 83 |
| **Midland, TX...................** | **178** |
| Martin County, TX................ | 6 |

See footnotes at end of table.

| Metropolitan Statistical Area ~~Metropolitan Division ~~~~Component county | Population, 2018 (1,000) |
|---|---|
| Midland County, TX | 173 |
| **Milwaukee-Waukesha-West Allis, WI** | **1,576** |
| Milwaukee County, WI | 948 |
| Ozaukee County, WI | 89 |
| Washington County, WI | 136 |
| Waukesha County, WI | 403 |
| **Minneapolis-St. Paul-Bloomington, MN-WI** | **3,629** |
| Anoka County, MN | 354 |
| Carver County, MN | 104 |
| Chisago County, MN | 56 |
| Dakota County, MN | 425 |
| Hennepin County, MN | 1,259 |
| Isanti County, MN | 40 |
| Le Sueur County, MN | 28 |
| Mille Lacs County, MN | 26 |
| Ramsey County, MN | 550 |
| Scott County, MN | 147 |
| Sherburne County, MN | 96 |
| Sibley County, MN | 15 |
| Washington County, MN | 259 |
| Wright County, MN | 136 |
| Pierce County, WI | 43 |
| St. Croix County, WI | 90 |
| **Missoula, MT** | **119** |
| Missoula County, MT | 119 |
| **Mobile, AL** | **414** |
| Mobile County, AL | 414 |
| **Modesto, CA** | **550** |
| Stanislaus County, CA | 550 |
| **Monroe, LA** | **177** |
| Ouachita Parish, LA | 154 |
| Union Parish, LA | 22 |
| **Monroe, MI** | **150** |
| Monroe County, MI | 150 |
| **Montgomery, AL** | **373** |
| Autauga County, AL | 56 |
| Elmore County, AL | 82 |
| Lowndes County, AL | 10 |
| Montgomery County, AL | 226 |
| **Morgantown, WV** | **140** |
| Monongalia County, WV | 106 |
| Preston County, WV | 34 |
| **Morristown, TN** | **119** |
| Hamblen County, TN | 65 |
| Jefferson County, TN | 54 |
| **Mount Vernon-Anacortes, WA** | **128** |
| Skagit County, WA | 128 |
| **Muncie, IN** | **115** |
| Delaware County, IN | 115 |
| **Muskegon, MI** | **174** |
| Muskegon County, MI | 174 |
| **Myrtle Beach-Conway-North Myrtle Beach, SC-NC** | **481** |
| Brunswick County, NC | 137 |
| Horry County, SC | 344 |
| **Napa, CA** | **139** |
| Napa County, CA | 139 |
| **Naples-Immokalee-Marco Island, FL** | **378** |
| Collier County, FL | 378 |
| **Nashville-Davidson-Murfreesboro-Franklin, TN** | **1,931** |
| Cannon County, TN | 14 |
| Cheatham County, TN | 40 |
| Davidson County, TN | 693 |
| Dickson County, TN | 53 |
| Hickman County, TN | 25 |
| Macon County, TN | 24 |
| Maury County, TN | 94 |
| Robertson County, TN | 71 |
| Rutherford County, TN | 325 |
| Smith County, TN | 20 |
| Sumner County, TN | 187 |
| Trousdale County, TN | 11 |
| Williamson County, TN | 232 |
| Wilson County, TN | 141 |
| **New Bern, NC** | **125** |
| Craven County, NC | 103 |

| Metropolitan Statistical Area ~~Metropolitan Division ~~~~Component county | Population, 2018 (1,000) |
|---|---|
| Jones County, NC | 10 |
| Pamlico County, NC | 13 |
| **New Haven-Milford, CT** | **858** |
| New Haven County, CT | 858 |
| **New Orleans-Metairie, LA** | **1,270** |
| Jefferson Parish, LA | 434 |
| Orleans Parish, LA | 391 |
| Plaquemines Parish, LA | 23 |
| St. Bernard Parish, LA | 47 |
| St. Charles Parish, LA | 53 |
| St. James Parish, LA | 21 |
| St. John the Baptist Parish, LA | 43 |
| St. Tammany Parish, LA | 258 |
| **New York-Newark-Jersey City, NY-NJ-PA** | **19,979** |
| **Dutchess County-Putnam County, NY** | **393** |
| Dutchess County, NY | 294 |
| Putnam County, NY | 99 |
| **Nassau County-Suffolk County, NY** | **2,839** |
| Nassau County, NY | 1,358 |
| Suffolk County, NY | 1,481 |
| **Newark, NJ-PA** | **2,505** |
| Essex County, NJ | 800 |
| Hunterdon County, NJ | 125 |
| Morris County, NJ | 494 |
| Somerset County, NJ | 331 |
| Sussex County, NJ | 141 |
| Union County, NJ | 558 |
| Pike County, PA | 56 |
| **New York-Jersey City-White Plains, NY-NJ** | **14,243** |
| Bergen County, NJ | 937 |
| Hudson County, NJ | 676 |
| Middlesex County, NJ | 830 |
| Monmouth County, NJ | 621 |
| Ocean County, NJ | 602 |
| Passaic County, NJ | 503 |
| Bronx County, NY | 1,432 |
| Kings County, NY | 2,583 |
| New York County, NY | 1,629 |
| Orange County, NY | 382 |
| Queens County, NY | 2,279 |
| Richmond County, NY | 476 |
| Rockland County, NY | 326 |
| Westchester County, NY | 968 |
| **Niles-Benton Harbor, MI** | **154** |
| Berrien County, MI | 154 |
| **North Port-Sarasota-Bradenton, FL** | **822** |
| Manatee County, FL | 395 |
| Sarasota County, FL | 427 |
| **Norwich-New London, CT** | **267** |
| New London County, CT | 267 |
| **Ocala, FL** | **360** |
| Marion County, FL | 360 |
| **Ocean City, NJ** | **93** |
| Cape May County, NJ | 93 |
| **Odessa, TX** | **162** |
| Ector County, TX | 162 |
| **Ogden-Clearfield, UT** | **675** |
| Box Elder County, UT | 55 |
| Davis County, UT | 352 |
| Morgan County, UT | 12 |
| Weber County, UT | 256 |
| **Oklahoma City, OK** | **1,396** |
| Canadian County, OK | 144 |
| Cleveland County, OK | 282 |
| Grady County, OK | 56 |
| Lincoln County, OK | 35 |
| Logan County, OK | 47 |
| McClain County, OK | 40 |
| Oklahoma County, OK | 793 |
| **Olympia-Tumwater, WA** | **286** |
| Thurston County, WA | 286 |
| **Omaha-Council Bluffs, NE-IA** | **942** |
| Harrison County, IA | 14 |
| Mills County, IA | 15 |
| Pottawattamie County, IA | 94 |

| Metropolitan Statistical Area ~~Metropolitan Division ~~~~Component county | Population, 2018 (1,000) |
|---|---|
| Cass County, NE | 26 |
| Douglas County, NE | 567 |
| Sarpy County, NE | 184 |
| Saunders County, NE | 21 |
| Washington County, NE | 21 |
| **Orlando-Kissimmee-Sanford, FL** | **2,573** |
| Lake County, FL | 356 |
| Orange County, FL | 1,381 |
| Osceola County, FL | 368 |
| Seminole County, FL | 468 |
| **Oshkosh-Neenah, WI** | **171** |
| Winnebago County, WI | 171 |
| **Owensboro, KY** | **119** |
| Daviess County, KY | 101 |
| Hancock County, KY | 9 |
| McLean County, KY | 9 |
| **Oxnard-Thousand Oaks-Ventura, CA** | **851** |
| Ventura County, CA | 851 |
| **Palm Bay-Melbourne-Titusville, FL** | **597** |
| Brevard County, FL | 597 |
| **Panama City, FL** | **201** |
| Bay County, FL | 185 |
| Gulf County, FL | 16 |
| **Parkersburg-Vienna, WV** | **90** |
| Wirt County, WV | 6 |
| Wood County, WV | 84 |
| **Pensacola-Ferry Pass-Brent, FL** | **495** |
| Escambia County, FL | 316 |
| Santa Rosa County, FL | 179 |
| **Peoria, IL** | **368** |
| Marshall County, IL | 12 |
| Peoria County, IL | 181 |
| Stark County, IL | 5 |
| Tazewell County, IL | 132 |
| Woodford County, IL | 38 |
| **Philadelphia-Camden-Wilmington, PA-NJ-DE-MD** | **6,096** |
| **Camden, NJ** | **1,244** |
| Burlington County, NJ | 445 |
| Camden County, NJ | 507 |
| Gloucester County, NJ | 291 |
| **Montgomery-Bucks-Chester, PA** | **1,979** |
| Bucks County, PA | 628 |
| Chester County, PA | 522 |
| Montgomery County, PA | 829 |
| **Philadelphia, PA** | **2,149** |
| Delaware County, PA | 565 |
| Philadelphia County, PA | 1,584 |
| **Wilmington, DE-MD-NJ** | **725** |
| New Castle County, DE | 559 |
| Cecil County, MD | 103 |
| Salem County, NJ | 63 |
| **Phoenix-Mesa-Scottsdale, AZ** | **4,858** |
| Maricopa County, AZ | 4,411 |
| Pinal County, AZ | 447 |
| **Pine Bluff, AR** | **90** |
| Cleveland County, AR | 8 |
| Jefferson County, AR | 68 |
| Lincoln County, AR | 13 |
| **Pittsburgh, PA** | **2,325** |
| Allegheny County, PA | 1,218 |
| Armstrong County, PA | 65 |
| Beaver County, PA | 165 |
| Butler County, PA | 188 |
| Fayette County, PA | 130 |
| Washington County, PA | 207 |
| Westmoreland County, PA | 351 |
| **Pittsfield, MA** | **126** |
| Berkshire County, MA | 126 |
| **Pocatello, ID** | **87** |
| Bannock County, ID | 87 |
| **Portland-South Portland, ME** | **535** |
| Cumberland County, ME | 294 |
| Sagadahoc County, ME | 36 |
| York County, ME | 206 |

See footnotes at end of table.

# Table A. Metropolitan Statistical Areas and Components—Population: 2018-Continued.

See headnote on page 917.

| Metropolitan Statistical Area ~~Metropolitan Division ~~~~Component county | Population, 2018 (1,000) |
|---|---|
| **Portland-Vancouver-Hillsboro, OR-WA** | **2,479** |
| Clackamas County, OR | 416 |
| Columbia County, OR | 52 |
| Multnomah County, OR | 812 |
| Washington County, OR | 598 |
| Yamhill County, OR | 107 |
| Clark County, WA | 482 |
| Skamania County, WA | 12 |
| **Port St. Lucie, FL** | **482** |
| Martin County, FL | 161 |
| St. Lucie County, FL | 321 |
| **Prescott, AZ** | **232** |
| Yavapai County, AZ | 232 |
| **Providence-Warwick, RI-MA** | **1,621** |
| Bristol County, MA | 564 |
| Bristol County, RI | 49 |
| Kent County, RI | 164 |
| Newport County, RI | 83 |
| Providence County, RI | 636 |
| Washington County, RI | 126 |
| **Provo-Orem, UT** | **634** |
| Juab County, UT | 12 |
| Utah County, UT | 622 |
| **Pueblo, CO** | **168** |
| Pueblo County, CO | 168 |
| **Punta Gorda, FL** | **185** |
| Charlotte County, FL | 185 |
| **Racine, WI** | **197** |
| Racine County, WI | 197 |
| **Raleigh, NC** | **1,363** |
| Franklin County, NC | 68 |
| Johnston County, NC | 203 |
| Wake County, NC | 1,092 |
| **Rapid City, SD** | **149** |
| Custer County, SD | 9 |
| Meade County, SD | 28 |
| Pennington County, SD | 112 |
| **Reading, PA** | **420** |
| Berks County, PA | 420 |
| **Redding, CA** | **180** |
| Shasta County, CA | 180 |
| **Reno, NV** | **470** |
| Storey County, NV | 4 |
| Washoe County, NV | 466 |
| **Richmond, VA** | **1,306** |
| Amelia County, VA | 13 |
| Caroline County, VA | 31 |
| Charles City County, VA | 7 |
| Chesterfield County, VA | 349 |
| Dinwiddie County, VA | 29 |
| Goochland County, VA | 23 |
| Hanover County, VA | 107 |
| Henrico County, VA | 329 |
| King William County, VA | 17 |
| New Kent County, VA | 22 |
| Powhatan County, VA | 29 |
| Prince George County, VA | 38 |
| Sussex County, VA | 11 |
| Colonial Heights city, VA | 18 |
| Hopewell city, VA | 23 |
| Petersburg city, VA | 32 |
| Richmond city, VA | 229 |
| **Riverside-San Bernardino-Ontario, CA** | **4,622** |
| Riverside County, CA | 2,451 |
| San Bernardino County, CA | 2,172 |
| **Roanoke, VA** | **314** |
| Botetourt County, VA | 33 |
| Craig County, VA | 5 |
| Franklin County, VA | 56 |
| Roanoke County, VA | 94 |
| Roanoke city, VA | 100 |
| Salem city, VA | 26 |
| **Rochester, MN** | **220** |
| Dodge County, MN | 21 |
| Fillmore County, MN | 21 |
| Olmsted County, MN | 156 |
| Wabasha County, MN | 22 |
| **Rochester, NY** | **1,071** |
| Livingston County, NY | 63 |
| Monroe County, NY | 742 |
| Ontario County, NY | 110 |

| Metropolitan Statistical Area ~~Metropolitan Division ~~~~Component county | Population, 2018 (1,000) |
|---|---|
| Orleans County, NY | 41 |
| Wayne County, NY | 90 |
| Yates County, NY | 25 |
| **Rockford, IL** | **338** |
| Boone County, IL | 54 |
| Winnebago County, IL | 284 |
| **Rocky Mount, NC** | **146** |
| Edgecombe County, NC | 52 |
| Nash County, NC | 94 |
| **Rome, GA** | **98** |
| Floyd County, GA | 98 |
| **Sacramento-Roseville-Arden-Arcade, CA** | **2,345** |
| El Dorado County, CA | 191 |
| Placer County, CA | 393 |
| Sacramento County, CA | 1,541 |
| Yolo County, CA | 220 |
| **Saginaw, MI** | **191** |
| Saginaw County, MI | 191 |
| **St. Cloud, MN** | **200** |
| Benton County, MN | 41 |
| Stearns County, MN | 159 |
| **St. George, UT** | **172** |
| Washington County, UT | 172 |
| **St. Joseph, MO-KS** | **126** |
| Doniphan County, KS | 8 |
| Andrew County, MO | 18 |
| Buchanan County, MO | 89 |
| DeKalb County, MO | 13 |
| **St. Louis, MO-IL [1]** | **2,805** |
| Bond County, IL | 17 |
| Calhoun County, IL | 5 |
| Clinton County, IL | 38 |
| Jersey County, IL | 22 |
| Macoupin County, IL | 45 |
| Madison County, IL | 264 |
| Monroe County, IL | 34 |
| St. Clair County, IL | 261 |
| Franklin County, MO | 104 |
| Jefferson County, MO | 224 |
| Lincoln County, MO | 58 |
| St. Charles County, MO | 399 |
| St. Louis County, MO | 997 |
| Warren County, MO | 35 |
| St. Louis city, MO | 303 |
| **Salem, OR** | **432** |
| Marion County, OR | 347 |
| Polk County, OR | 85 |
| **Salinas, CA** | **436** |
| Monterey County, CA | 436 |
| **Salisbury, MD-DE** | **410** |
| Sussex County, DE | 229 |
| Somerset County, MD | 26 |
| Wicomico County, MD | 103 |
| Worcester County, MD | 52 |
| **Salt Lake City, UT** | **1,223** |
| Salt Lake County, UT | 1,153 |
| Tooele County, UT | 70 |
| **San Angelo, TX** | **120** |
| Irion County, TX | 2 |
| Tom Green County, TX | 118 |
| **San Antonio-New Braunfels, TX** | **2,518** |
| Atascosa County, TX | 50 |
| Bandera County, TX | 23 |
| Bexar County, TX | 1,986 |
| Comal County, TX | 148 |
| Guadalupe County, TX | 164 |
| Kendall County, TX | 46 |
| Medina County, TX | 51 |
| Wilson County, TX | 50 |
| **San Diego-Carlsbad, CA** | **3,343** |
| San Diego County, CA | 3,343 |
| **San Francisco-Oakland-Hayward, CA** | **4,729** |
| **Oakland-Hayward-Berkeley, CA** | **2,817** |
| Alameda County, CA | 1,667 |
| Contra Costa County, CA | 1,150 |

| Metropolitan Statistical Area ~~Metropolitan Division ~~~~Component county | Population, 2018 (1,000) |
|---|---|
| **San Francisco-Redwood City-South San Francisco, CA** | **1,653** |
| San Francisco County, CA | 883 |
| San Mateo County, CA | 770 |
| **San Rafael, CA** | **260** |
| Marin County, CA | 260 |
| **San Jose-Sunnyvale-Santa Clara, CA** | **1,999** |
| San Benito County, CA | 62 |
| Santa Clara County, CA | 1,938 |
| **San Luis Obispo-Paso Robles-Arroyo Grande, CA** | **284** |
| San Luis Obispo County, CA | 284 |
| **Santa Cruz-Watsonville, CA** | **274** |
| Santa Cruz County, CA | 274 |
| **Santa Fe, NM** | **150** |
| Santa Fe County, NM | 150 |
| **Santa Maria-Santa Barbara, CA** | **447** |
| Santa Barbara County, CA | 447 |
| **Santa Rosa, CA** | **500** |
| Sonoma County, CA | 500 |
| **Savannah, GA** | **389** |
| Bryan County, GA | 38 |
| Chatham County, GA | 289 |
| Effingham County, GA | 62 |
| **Scranton-Wilkes-Barre-Hazleton, PA** | **555** |
| Lackawanna County, PA | 211 |
| Luzerne County, PA | 318 |
| Wyoming County, PA | 27 |
| **Seattle-Tacoma-Bellevue, WA** | **3,939** |
| **Seattle-Bellevue-Everett, WA** | **3,048** |
| King County, WA | 2,233 |
| Snohomish County, WA | 815 |
| **Tacoma-Lakewood, WA** | **891** |
| Pierce County, WA | 891 |
| **Sebastian-Vero Beach, FL** | **157** |
| Indian River County, FL | 157 |
| **Sebring, FL** | **105** |
| Highlands County, FL | 105 |
| **Sheboygan, WI** | **115** |
| Sheboygan County, WI | 115 |
| **Sherman-Denison, TX** | **134** |
| Grayson County, TX | 134 |
| **Shreveport-Bossier City, LA** | **436** |
| Bossier Parish, LA | 127 |
| Caddo Parish, LA | 243 |
| De Soto Parish, LA | 27 |
| Webster Parish, LA | 39 |
| **Sierra Vista-Douglas, AZ** | **127** |
| Cochise County, AZ | 127 |
| **Sioux City, IA-NE-SD** | **169** |
| Plymouth County, IA | 25 |
| Woodbury County, IA | 103 |
| Dakota County, NE | 20 |
| Dixon County, NE | 6 |
| Union County, SD | 16 |
| **Sioux Falls, SD** | **266** |
| Lincoln County, SD | 59 |
| McCook County, SD | 6 |
| Minnehaha County, SD | 193 |
| Turner County, SD | 8 |
| **South Bend-Mishawaka, IN-MI** | **322** |
| St. Joseph County, IN | 271 |
| Cass County, MI | 52 |
| **Spartanburg, SC** | **341** |
| Spartanburg County, SC | 314 |
| Union County, SC | 27 |
| **Spokane-Spokane Valley, WA** | **573** |
| Pend Oreille County, WA | 14 |
| Spokane County, WA | 515 |
| Stevens County, WA | 45 |
| **Springfield, IL** | **208** |
| Menard County, IL | 12 |
| Sangamon County, IL | 195 |
| **Springfield, MA** | **632** |

See footnotes at end of table.

# Table A. Metropolitan Statistical Areas and Components—Population: 2018-Continued.

See headnote on page 917.

| Metropolitan Statistical Area ~~Metropolitan Division ~~~~Component county | Population, 2018 (1,000) |
|---|---|
| Hampden County, MA | 470 |
| Hampshire County, MA | 161 |
| **Springfield, MO** | **467** |
| Christian County, MO | 87 |
| Dallas County, MO | 17 |
| Greene County, MO | 292 |
| Polk County, MO | 32 |
| Webster County, MO | 39 |
| **Springfield, OH** | **135** |
| Clark County, OH | 135 |
| **State College, PA** | **163** |
| Centre County, PA | 163 |
| **Staunton-Waynesboro, VA** | **123** |
| Augusta County, VA | 75 |
| Staunton city, VA | 25 |
| Waynesboro city, VA | 23 |
| **Stockton-Lodi, CA** | **753** |
| San Joaquin County, CA | 753 |
| **Sumter, SC** | **107** |
| Sumter County, SC | 107 |
| **Syracuse, NY** | **651** |
| Madison County, NY | 71 |
| Onondaga County, NY | 462 |
| Oswego County, NY | 118 |
| **Tallahassee, FL** | **385** |
| Gadsden County, FL | 46 |
| Jefferson County, FL | 14 |
| Leon County, FL | 293 |
| Wakulla County, FL | 32 |
| **Tampa-St. Petersburg-Clearwater, FL** | **3,143** |
| Hernando County, FL | 191 |
| Hillsborough County, FL | 1,437 |
| Pasco County, FL | 540 |
| Pinellas County, FL | 975 |
| **Terre Haute, IN** | **170** |
| Clay County, IN | 26 |
| Sullivan County, IN | 21 |
| Vermillion County, IN | 15 |
| Vigo County, IN | 107 |
| **Texarkana, TX-AR** | **150** |
| Little River County, AR | 12 |
| Miller County, AR | 44 |
| Bowie County, TX | 94 |
| **The Villages, FL** | **129** |
| Sumter County, FL | 129 |
| **Toledo, OH** | **603** |
| Fulton County, OH | 42 |
| Lucas County, OH | 430 |
| Wood County, OH | 131 |
| **Topeka, KS** | **233** |
| Jackson County, KS | 13 |
| Jefferson County, KS | 19 |
| Osage County, KS | 16 |
| Shawnee County, KS | 177 |
| Wabaunsee County, KS | 7 |
| **Trenton, NJ** | **370** |
| Mercer County, NJ | 370 |
| **Tucson, AZ** | **1,039** |
| Pima County, AZ | 1,039 |
| **Tulsa, OK** | **994** |
| Creek County, OK | 72 |
| Okmulgee County, OK | 38 |
| Osage County, OK | 47 |
| Pawnee County, OK | 16 |
| Rogers County, OK | 92 |
| Tulsa County, OK | 648 |
| Wagoner County, OK | 80 |
| **Tuscaloosa, AL** | **244** |
| Hale County, AL | 15 |
| Pickens County, AL | 20 |
| Tuscaloosa County, AL | 209 |

| Metropolitan Statistical Area ~~Metropolitan Division ~~~~Component county | Population, 2018 (1,000) |
|---|---|
| **Twin Falls, ID** | **110** |
| Jerome County, ID | 24 |
| Twin Falls County, ID | 86 |
| **Tyler, TX** | **230** |
| Smith County, TX | 230 |
| **Urban Honolulu, HI** | **980** |
| Honolulu County, HI | 980 |
| **Utica-Rome, NY** | **291** |
| Herkimer County, NY | 62 |
| Oneida County, NY | 230 |
| **Valdosta, GA** | **146** |
| Brooks County, GA | 16 |
| Echols County, GA | 4 |
| Lanier County, GA | 10 |
| Lowndes County, GA | 116 |
| **Vallejo-Fairfield, CA** | **447** |
| Solano County, CA | 447 |
| **Victoria, TX** | **100** |
| Goliad County, TX | 8 |
| Victoria County, TX | 92 |
| **Vineland-Bridgeton, NJ** | **151** |
| Cumberland County, NJ | 151 |
| **Virginia Beach-Norfolk-Newport News, VA-NC** | **1,729** |
| Currituck County, NC | 27 |
| Gates County, NC | 12 |
| Gloucester County, VA | 37 |
| Isle of Wight County, VA | 37 |
| James City County, VA | 76 |
| Mathews County, VA | 9 |
| York County, VA | 68 |
| Chesapeake city, VA | 243 |
| Hampton city, VA | 134 |
| Newport News city, VA | 179 |
| Norfolk city, VA | 244 |
| Poquoson city, VA | 12 |
| Portsmouth city, VA | 95 |
| Suffolk city, VA | 91 |
| Virginia Beach city, VA | 450 |
| Williamsburg city, VA | 15 |
| **Visalia-Porterville, CA** | **466** |
| Tulare County, CA | 466 |
| **Waco, TX** | **272** |
| Falls County, TX | 17 |
| McLennan County, TX | 255 |
| **Walla Walla, WA** | **65** |
| Columbia County, WA | 4 |
| Walla Walla County, WA | 61 |
| **Warner Robins, GA** | **194** |
| Houston County, GA | 155 |
| Peach County, GA | 27 |
| Pulaski County, GA | 11 |
| **Washington-Arlington-Alexandria, DC-VA-MD-WV** | **6,250** |
| **Silver Spring-Frederick-Rockville, MD** | **1,308** |
| Frederick County, MD | 256 |
| Montgomery County, MD | 1,053 |
| **Washington-Arlington-Alexandria, DC-VA-MD-WV** | **4,942** |
| District of Columbia, DC | 702 |
| Calvert County, MD | 92 |
| Charles County, MD | 162 |
| Prince George's County, MD | 909 |
| Arlington County, VA | 238 |
| Clarke County, VA | 15 |
| Culpeper County, VA | 52 |
| Fairfax County, VA | 1,151 |
| Fauquier County, VA | 71 |
| Loudoun County, VA | 407 |
| Prince William County, VA | 468 |
| Rappahannock County, VA | 7 |

| Metropolitan Statistical Area ~~Metropolitan Division ~~~~Component county | Population, 2018 (1,000) |
|---|---|
| Spotsylvania County, VA | 134 |
| Stafford County, VA | 150 |
| Warren County, VA | 40 |
| Alexandria city, VA | 161 |
| Fairfax city, VA | 25 |
| Falls Church city, VA | 15 |
| Fredericksburg city, VA | 29 |
| Manassas city, VA | 42 |
| Manassas Park city, VA | 17 |
| Jefferson County, WV | 57 |
| **Waterloo-Cedar Falls, IA** | **170** |
| Black Hawk County, IA | 132 |
| Bremer County, IA | 25 |
| Grundy County, IA | 12 |
| **Watertown-Fort Drum, NY** | **112** |
| Jefferson County, NY | 112 |
| **Wausau, WI** | **135** |
| Marathon County, WI | 135 |
| **Weirton-Steubenville, WV-OH** | **117** |
| Jefferson County, OH | 66 |
| Brooke County, WV | 22 |
| Hancock County, WV | 29 |
| **Wenatchee, WA** | **120** |
| Chelan County, WA | 77 |
| Douglas County, WA | 43 |
| **Wheeling, WV-OH** | **140** |
| Belmont County, OH | 68 |
| Marshall County, WV | 31 |
| Ohio County, WV | 42 |
| **Wichita, KS** | **645** |
| Butler County, KS | 67 |
| Harvey County, KS | 34 |
| Kingman County, KS | 7 |
| Sedgwick County, KS | 514 |
| Sumner County, KS | 23 |
| **Wichita Falls, TX** | **151** |
| Archer County, TX | 9 |
| Clay County, TX | 10 |
| Wichita County, TX | 132 |
| **Williamsport, PA** | **114** |
| Lycoming County, PA | 114 |
| **Wilmington, NC** | **294** |
| New Hanover County, NC | 232 |
| Pender County, NC | 62 |
| **Winchester, VA-WV** | **140** |
| Frederick County, VA | 88 |
| Winchester city, VA | 28 |
| Hampshire County, WV | 23 |
| **Winston-Salem, NC** | **671** |
| Davidson County, NC | 167 |
| Davie County, NC | 43 |
| Forsyth County, NC | 379 |
| Stokes County, NC | 45 |
| Yadkin County, NC | 38 |
| **Worcester, MA-CT** | **948** |
| Windham County, CT | 117 |
| Worcester County, MA | 831 |
| **Yakima, WA** | **251** |
| Yakima County, WA | 251 |
| **York-Hanover, PA** | **448** |
| York County, PA | 448 |
| **Youngstown-Warren-Boardman, OH-PA** | **539** |
| Mahoning County, OH | 230 |
| Trumbull County, OH | 199 |
| Mercer County, PA | 111 |
| **Yuba City, CA** | **175** |
| Sutter County, CA | 97 |
| Yuba County, CA | 78 |
| **Yuma, AZ** | **212** |
| Yuma County, AZ | 212 |

Z Represents less than 500. [1] The portion of Sullivan city in Crawford County, Missouri, is legally part of the St. Louis, MO-IL Metropolitan Statistical Area. The estimate shown here for the St. Louis, MO-IL Metropolitan Statistical Area does not include this area.

Source: U.S. Census Bureau, 2018 Population Estimates, <https://www.census.gov/programs-surveys/metro-micro/data/tables.html>.

# Table B. Micropolitan Statistical Areas and Components—Population: 2018

[In thousands (43 represents 43,000). Population as of July 2018. Micropolitan Statistical Areas defined by the U.S. Office of Management and Budget as of September 2018. All Micropolitan Statistical Areas are arranged alphabetically]

| Micropolitan Statistical Area ~~Component county | Population, 2018 (1,000) |
|---|---|
| **Aberdeen, SD** | **43** |
| Brown County, SD | 39 |
| Edmunds County, SD | 4 |
| **Aberdeen, WA** | **74** |
| Grays Harbor County, WA | 74 |
| **Ada, OK** | **38** |
| Pontotoc County, OK | 38 |
| **Adrian, MI** | **98** |
| Lenawee County, MI | 98 |
| **Alamogordo, NM** | **67** |
| Otero County, NM | 67 |
| **Albemarle, NC** | **62** |
| Stanly County, NC | 62 |
| **Albert Lea, MN** | **30** |
| Freeborn County, MN | 30 |
| **Albertville, AL** | **96** |
| Marshall County, AL | 96 |
| **Alexander City, AL** | **40** |
| Tallapoosa County, AL | 40 |
| **Alexandria, MN** | **38** |
| Douglas County, MN | 38 |
| **Alice, TX** | **41** |
| Jim Wells County, TX | 41 |
| **Alma, MI** | **41** |
| Gratiot County, MI | 41 |
| **Alpena, MI** | **28** |
| Alpena County, MI | 28 |
| **Altus, OK** | **25** |
| Jackson County, OK | 25 |
| **Americus, GA** | **35** |
| Schley County, GA | 5 |
| Sumter County, GA | 30 |
| **Amsterdam, NY** | **49** |
| Montgomery County, NY | 49 |
| **Andrews, TX** | **18** |
| Andrews County, TX | 18 |
| **Angola, IN** | **35** |
| Steuben County, IN | 35 |
| **Arcadia, FL** | **37** |
| DeSoto County, FL | 37 |
| **Ardmore, OK** | **48** |
| Carter County, OK | 48 |
| **Arkadelphia, AR** | **22** |
| Clark County, AR | 22 |
| **Arkansas City-Winfield, KS** | **35** |
| Cowley County, KS | 35 |
| **Ashland, OH** | **54** |
| Ashland County, OH | 54 |
| **Ashtabula, OH** | **97** |
| Ashtabula County, OH | 97 |
| **Astoria, OR** | **40** |
| Clatsop County, OR | 40 |
| **Atchison, KS** | **16** |
| Atchison County, KS | 16 |
| **Athens, OH** | **66** |
| Athens County, OH | 66 |
| **Athens, TN** | **53** |
| McMinn County, TN | 53 |
| **Athens, TX** | **82** |
| Henderson County, TX | 82 |
| **Atmore, AL** | **37** |
| Escambia County, AL | 37 |
| **Auburn, IN** | **43** |
| DeKalb County, IN | 43 |
| **Auburn, NY** | **77** |
| Cayuga County, NY | 77 |
| **Augusta-Waterville, ME** | **122** |
| Kennebec County, ME | 122 |
| **Austin, MN** | **40** |
| Mower County, MN | 40 |
| **Bainbridge, GA** | **27** |
| Decatur County, GA | 27 |
| **Baraboo, WI** | **64** |
| Sauk County, WI | 64 |
| **Bardstown, KY** | **46** |
| Nelson County, KY | 46 |
| **Barre, VT** | **58** |
| Washington County, VT | 58 |
| **Bartlesville, OK** | **52** |
| Washington County, OK | 52 |
| **Bastrop, LA** | **25** |
| Morehouse Parish, LA | 25 |
| **Batavia, NY** | **58** |
| Genesee County, NY | 58 |
| **Batesville, AR** | **38** |
| Independence County, AR | 38 |
| **Bay City, TX** | **37** |
| Matagorda County, TX | 37 |
| **Beatrice, NE** | **21** |
| Gage County, NE | 21 |
| **Beaver Dam, WI** | **88** |
| Dodge County, WI | 88 |
| **Bedford, IN** | **46** |
| Lawrence County, IN | 46 |
| **Beeville, TX** | **33** |
| Bee County, TX | 33 |
| **Bellefontaine, OH** | **45** |
| Logan County, OH | 45 |
| **Bemidji, MN** | **47** |
| Beltrami County, MN | 47 |
| **Bennettsville, SC** | **26** |
| Marlboro County, SC | 26 |
| **Bennington, VT** | **36** |
| Bennington County, VT | 36 |
| **Berlin, NH-VT** | **38** |
| Coos County, NH | 32 |
| Essex County, VT | 6 |
| **Big Rapids, MI** | **44** |
| Mecosta County, MI | 44 |
| **Big Spring, TX** | **38** |
| Glasscock County, TX | 1 |
| Howard County, TX | 36 |
| **Big Stone Gap, VA** | **57** |
| Dickenson County, VA | 15 |
| Wise County, VA | 38 |
| Norton city, VA | 4 |
| **Blackfoot, ID** | **46** |
| Bingham County, ID | 46 |
| **Bluefield, WV-VA** | **100** |
| Tazewell County, VA | 41 |
| Mercer County, WV | 59 |
| **Blytheville, AR** | **41** |
| Mississippi County, AR | 41 |
| **Bogalusa, LA** | **47** |
| Washington Parish, LA | 47 |
| **Bonham, TX** | **35** |
| Fannin County, TX | 35 |
| **Boone, IA** | **26** |
| Boone County, IA | 26 |
| **Boone, NC** | **56** |
| Watauga County, NC | 56 |
| **Borger, TX** | **21** |
| Hutchinson County, TX | 21 |
| **Bozeman, MT** | **112** |
| Gallatin County, MT | 112 |
| **Bradford, PA** | **41** |
| McKean County, PA | 41 |
| **Brainerd, MN** | **94** |
| Cass County, MN | 30 |
| Crow Wing County, MN | 65 |
| **Branson, MO** | **88** |
| Stone County, MO | 32 |
| Taney County, MO | 56 |
| **Breckenridge, CO** | **31** |
| Summit County, CO | 31 |
| **Brenham, TX** | **35** |
| Washington County, TX | 35 |
| **Brevard, NC** | **34** |
| Transylvania County, NC | 34 |
| **Brookhaven, MS** | **34** |
| Lincoln County, MS | 34 |
| **Brookings, OR** | **23** |
| Curry County, OR | 23 |
| **Brookings, SD** | **35** |
| Brookings County, SD | 35 |
| **Brownsville, TN** | **17** |
| Haywood County, TN | 17 |
| **Brownwood, TX** | **38** |
| Brown County, TX | 38 |
| **Bucyrus, OH** | **42** |
| Crawford County, OH | 42 |
| **Burley, ID** | **45** |
| Cassia County, ID | 24 |
| Minidoka County, ID | 21 |
| **Burlington, IA-IL** | **46** |
| Henderson County, IL | 7 |
| Des Moines County, IA | 39 |
| **Butte-Silver Bow, MT** | **35** |
| Silver Bow County, MT | 35 |
| **Cadillac, MI** | **49** |
| Missaukee County, MI | 15 |
| Wexford County, MI | 33 |
| **Calhoun, GA** | **58** |
| Gordon County, GA | 58 |
| **Cambridge, MD** | **32** |
| Dorchester County, MD | 32 |
| **Cambridge, OH** | **39** |
| Guernsey County, OH | 39 |
| **Camden, AR** | **29** |
| Calhoun County, AR | 5 |
| Ouachita County, AR | 24 |
| **Campbellsville, KY** | **26** |
| Taylor County, KY | 26 |
| **Cañon City, CO** | **48** |
| Fremont County, CO | 48 |
| **Canton, IL** | **35** |
| Fulton County, IL | 35 |
| **Carlsbad-Artesia, NM** | **58** |
| Eddy County, NM | 58 |
| **Carroll, IA** | **20** |
| Carroll County, IA | 20 |
| **Cedar City, UT** | **53** |
| Iron County, UT | 53 |
| **Cedartown, GA** | **42** |
| Polk County, GA | 42 |
| **Celina, OH** | **41** |
| Mercer County, OH | 41 |
| **Central City, KY** | **31** |
| Muhlenberg County, KY | 31 |
| **Centralia, IL** | **38** |
| Marion County, IL | 38 |
| **Centralia, WA** | **80** |
| Lewis County, WA | 80 |
| **Charleston-Mattoon, IL** | **62** |
| Coles County, IL | 51 |
| Cumberland County, IL | 11 |
| **Chillicothe, OH** | **77** |
| Ross County, OH | 77 |
| **Claremont-Lebanon, NH-VT** | **217** |
| Grafton County, NH | 90 |
| Sullivan County, NH | 43 |
| Orange County, VT | 29 |
| Windsor County, VT | 55 |
| **Clarksburg, WV** | **93** |
| Doddridge County, WV | 8 |
| Harrison County, WV | 68 |
| Taylor County, WV | 17 |
| **Clarksdale, MS** | **23** |
| Coahoma County, MS | 23 |
| **Clearlake, CA** | **64** |
| Lake County, CA | 64 |
| **Cleveland, MS** | **31** |
| Bolivar County, MS | 31 |
| **Clewiston, FL** | **42** |
| Hendry County, FL | 42 |
| **Clinton, IA** | **47** |
| Clinton County, IA | 47 |
| **Clovis, NM** | **49** |
| Curry County, NM | 49 |
| **Coffeyville, KS** | **32** |
| Montgomery County, KS | 32 |
| **Coldwater, MI** | **44** |
| Branch County, MI | 44 |
| **Columbus, MS** | **59** |
| Lowndes County, MS | 59 |
| **Columbus, NE** | **33** |
| Platte County, NE | 33 |
| **Concord, NH** | **151** |
| Merrimack County, NH | 151 |
| **Connersville, IN** | **23** |
| Fayette County, IN | 23 |
| **Cookeville, TN** | **113** |
| Jackson County, TN | 12 |
| Overton County, TN | 22 |
| Putnam County, TN | 79 |

See footnotes at end of table.

# Table B. Microplitan Statistical Areas and Components—Population: 2018-Continued.

See headnote on page 924.

| Microplitan Statistical Area ~~Component county | Population, 2018 (1,000) |
|---|---|
| **Coos Bay, OR** | **64** |
| Coos County, OR | 64 |
| **Cordele, GA** | **23** |
| Crisp County, GA | 23 |
| **Corinth, MS** | **37** |
| Alcorn County, MS | 37 |
| **Cornelia, GA** | **45** |
| Habersham County, GA | 45 |
| **Corning, NY** | **96** |
| Steuben County, NY | 96 |
| **Corsicana, TX** | **50** |
| Navarro County, TX | 50 |
| **Cortland, NY** | **48** |
| Cortland County, NY | 48 |
| **Coshocton, OH** | **37** |
| Coshocton County, OH | 37 |
| **Craig, CO** | **13** |
| Moffat County, CO | 13 |
| **Crawfordsville, IN** | **38** |
| Montgomery County, IN | 38 |
| **Crescent City, CA** | **28** |
| Del Norte County, CA | 28 |
| **Crossville, TN** | **60** |
| Cumberland County, TN | 60 |
| **Cullman, AL** | **83** |
| Cullman County, AL | 83 |
| **Cullowhee, NC** | **43** |
| Jackson County, NC | 43 |
| **Danville, KY** | **55** |
| Boyle County, KY | 30 |
| Lincoln County, KY | 25 |
| **Danville, VA** | **102** |
| Pittsylvania County, VA | 61 |
| Danville city, VA | 41 |
| **Dayton, TN** | **33** |
| Rhea County, TN | 33 |
| **Decatur, IN** | **36** |
| Adams County, IN | 36 |
| **Defiance, OH** | **38** |
| Defiance County, OH | 38 |
| **Del Rio, TX** | **49** |
| Val Verde County, TX | 49 |
| **Deming, NM** | **24** |
| Luna County, NM | 24 |
| **DeRidder, LA** | **37** |
| Beauregard Parish, LA | 37 |
| **Dickinson, ND** | **31** |
| Stark County, ND | 31 |
| **Dixon, IL** | **34** |
| Lee County, IL | 34 |
| **Dodge City, KS** | **34** |
| Ford County, KS | 34 |
| **Douglas, GA** | **43** |
| Coffee County, GA | 43 |
| **Dublin, GA** | **57** |
| Johnson County, GA | 10 |
| Laurens County, GA | 47 |
| **DuBois, PA** | **79** |
| Clearfield County, PA | 79 |
| **Dumas, TX** | **21** |
| Moore County, TX | 21 |
| **Duncan, OK** | **43** |
| Stephens County, OK | 43 |
| **Dunn, NC** | **134** |
| Harnett County, NC | 134 |
| **Durango, CO** | **56** |
| La Plata County, CO | 56 |
| **Durant, OK** | **47** |
| Bryan County, OK | 47 |
| **Dyersburg, TN** | **37** |
| Dyer County, TN | 37 |
| **Eagle Pass, TX** | **58** |
| Maverick County, TX | 58 |
| **Easton, MD** | **37** |
| Talbot County, MD | 37 |
| **Edwards, CO** | **55** |
| Eagle County, CO | 55 |
| **Effingham, IL** | **34** |
| Effingham County, IL | 34 |
| **El Campo, TX** | **42** |
| Wharton County, TX | 42 |
| **El Dorado, AR** | **39** |
| Union County, AR | 39 |
| **Elizabeth City, NC** | **64** |
| Camden County, NC | 11 |
| Pasquotank County, NC | 40 |
| Perquimans County, NC | 13 |
| **Elk City, OK** | **22** |
| Beckham County, OK | 22 |
| **Elkins, WV** | **29** |
| Randolph County, WV | 29 |
| **Elko, NV** | **54** |
| Elko County, NV | 52 |
| Eureka County, NV | 2 |
| **Ellensburg, WA** | **47** |
| Kittitas County, WA | 47 |
| **Emporia, KS** | **33** |
| Lyon County, KS | 33 |
| **Enterprise, AL** | **52** |
| Coffee County, AL | 52 |
| **Escanaba, MI** | **36** |
| Delta County, MI | 36 |
| **Española, NM** | **39** |
| Rio Arriba County, NM | 39 |
| **Eufaula, AL-GA** | **27** |
| Barbour County, AL | 25 |
| Quitman County, GA | 2 |
| **Eureka-Arcata-Fortuna, CA** | **136** |
| Humboldt County, CA | 136 |
| **Evanston, WY** | **20** |
| Uinta County, WY | 20 |
| **Fairfield, IA** | **18** |
| Jefferson County, IA | 18 |
| **Fairmont, MN** | **20** |
| Martin County, MN | 20 |
| **Fairmont, WV** | **56** |
| Marion County, WV | 56 |
| **Fallon, NV** | **24** |
| Churchill County, NV | 24 |
| **Faribault-Northfield, MN** | **67** |
| Rice County, MN | 67 |
| **Farmington, MO** | **67** |
| St. Francois County, MO | 67 |
| **Fergus Falls, MN** | **59** |
| Otter Tail County, MN | 59 |
| **Fernley, NV** | **56** |
| Lyon County, NV | 56 |
| **Findlay, OH** | **76** |
| Hancock County, OH | 76 |
| **Fitzgerald, GA** | **17** |
| Ben Hill County, GA | 17 |
| **Forest City, NC** | **67** |
| Rutherford County, NC | 67 |
| **Forrest City, AR** | **25** |
| St. Francis County, AR | 25 |
| **Fort Dodge, IA** | **36** |
| Webster County, IA | 36 |
| **Fort Leonard Wood, MO** | **52** |
| Pulaski County, MO | 52 |
| **Fort Madison-Keokuk, IA-IL-MO** | **59** |
| Hancock County, IL | 18 |
| Lee County, IA | 34 |
| Clark County, MO | 7 |
| **Fort Morgan, CO** | **29** |
| Morgan County, CO | 29 |
| **Fort Payne, AL** | **71** |
| DeKalb County, AL | 71 |
| **Fort Polk South, LA** | **49** |
| Vernon Parish, LA | 49 |
| **Frankfort, IN** | **32** |
| Clinton County, IN | 32 |
| **Frankfort, KY** | **73** |
| Anderson County, KY | 23 |
| Franklin County, KY | 51 |
| **Fredericksburg, TX** | **27** |
| Gillespie County, TX | 27 |
| **Freeport, IL** | **45** |
| Stephenson County, IL | 45 |
| **Fremont, NE** | **37** |
| Dodge County, NE | 37 |
| **Fremont, OH** | **59** |
| Sandusky County, OH | 59 |
| **Gaffney, SC** | **57** |
| Cherokee County, SC | 57 |
| **Gainesville, TX** | **41** |
| Cooke County, TX | 41 |
| **Galesburg, IL** | **50** |
| Knox County, IL | 50 |
| **Gallup, NM** | **72** |
| McKinley County, NM | 72 |
| **Garden City, KS** | **41** |
| Finney County, KS | 37 |
| Kearny County, KS | 4 |
| **Gardnerville Ranchos, NV** | **48** |
| Douglas County, NV | 48 |
| **Georgetown, SC** | **62** |
| Georgetown County, SC | 62 |
| **Gillette, WY** | **46** |
| Campbell County, WY | 46 |
| **Glasgow, KY** | **54** |
| Barren County, KY | 44 |
| Metcalfe County, KY | 10 |
| **Glenwood Springs, CO** | **78** |
| Garfield County, CO | 60 |
| Pitkin County, CO | 18 |
| **Gloversville, NY** | **54** |
| Fulton County, NY | 54 |
| **Grand Rapids, MN** | **45** |
| Itasca County, MN | 45 |
| **Grants, NM** | **27** |
| Cibola County, NM | 27 |
| **Great Bend, KS** | **26** |
| Barton County, KS | 26 |
| **Greeneville, TN** | **69** |
| Greene County, TN | 69 |
| **Greenfield Town, MA** | **71** |
| Franklin County, MA | 71 |
| **Greensburg, IN** | **27** |
| Decatur County, IN | 27 |
| **Greenville, MS** | **45** |
| Washington County, MS | 45 |
| **Greenville, OH** | **51** |
| Darke County, OH | 51 |
| **Greenwood, MS** | **39** |
| Carroll County, MS | 10 |
| Leflore County, MS | 29 |
| **Greenwood, SC** | **95** |
| Abbeville County, SC | 25 |
| Greenwood County, SC | 71 |
| **Grenada, MS** | **21** |
| Grenada County, MS | 21 |
| **Guymon, OK** | **20** |
| Texas County, OK | 20 |
| **Hailey, ID** | **29** |
| Blaine County, ID | 23 |
| Camas County, ID | 1 |
| Lincoln County, ID | 5 |
| **Hannibal, MO** | **39** |
| Marion County, MO | 29 |
| Ralls County, MO | 10 |
| **Harrison, AR** | **45** |
| Boone County, AR | 37 |
| Newton County, AR | 8 |
| **Hastings, NE** | **32** |
| Adams County, NE | 32 |
| **Hays, KS** | **29** |
| Ellis County, KS | 29 |
| **Heber, UT** | **33** |
| Wasatch County, UT | 33 |
| **Helena, MT** | **81** |
| Jefferson County, MT | 12 |
| Lewis and Clark County, MT | 69 |
| **Helena-West Helena, AR** | **18** |
| Phillips County, AR | 18 |
| **Henderson, NC** | **45** |
| Vance County, NC | 45 |
| **Hereford, TX** | **19** |
| Deaf Smith County, TX | 19 |
| **Hermiston-Pendleton, OR** | **89** |
| Morrow County, OR | 11 |
| Umatilla County, OR | 78 |
| **Hillsdale, MI** | **46** |
| Hillsdale County, MI | 46 |
| **Hilo, HI** | **201** |
| Hawaii County, HI | 201 |

See footnotes at end of table.

# Table B. Micropolitan Statistical Areas and Components—Population: 2018-Continued.

See headnote on page 924.

| Micropolitan Statistical Area ~~Component county | Population, 2018 (1,000) |
|---|---|
| **Hobbs, NM** | **70** |
| Lea County, NM | 70 |
| **Holland, MI** | **117** |
| Allegan County, MI | 117 |
| **Hood River, OR** | **23** |
| Hood River County, OR | 23 |
| **Hope, AR** | **30** |
| Hempstead County, AR | 22 |
| Nevada County, AR | 8 |
| **Houghton, MI** | **38** |
| Houghton County, MI | 36 |
| Keweenaw County, MI | 2 |
| **Hudson, NY** | **60** |
| Columbia County, NY | 60 |
| **Huntingdon, PA** | **45** |
| Huntingdon County, PA | 45 |
| **Huntington, IN** | **36** |
| Huntington County, IN | 36 |
| **Huntsville, TX** | **87** |
| Trinity County, TX | 15 |
| Walker County, TX | 72 |
| **Huron, SD** | **19** |
| Beadle County, SD | 19 |
| **Hutchinson, KS** | **62** |
| Reno County, KS | 62 |
| **Hutchinson, MN** | **36** |
| McLeod County, MN | 36 |
| **Indiana, PA** | **85** |
| Indiana County, PA | 85 |
| **Indianola, MS** | **26** |
| Sunflower County, MS | 26 |
| **Ionia, MI** | **64** |
| Ionia County, MI | 64 |
| **Iron Mountain, MI-WI** | **30** |
| Dickinson County, MI | 25 |
| Florence County, WI | 4 |
| **Jackson, OH** | **32** |
| Jackson County, OH | 32 |
| **Jackson, WY-ID** | **35** |
| Teton County, ID | 12 |
| Teton County, WY | 23 |
| **Jacksonville, IL** | **39** |
| Morgan County, IL | 34 |
| Scott County, IL | 5 |
| **Jacksonville, TX** | **53** |
| Cherokee County, TX | 53 |
| **Jamestown, ND** | **21** |
| Stutsman County, ND | 21 |
| **Jamestown-Dunkirk-Fredonia, NY** | **128** |
| Chautauqua County, NY | 128 |
| **Jasper, IN** | **55** |
| Dubois County, IN | 43 |
| Pike County, IN | 12 |
| **Jefferson, GA** | **70** |
| Jackson County, GA | 70 |
| **Jennings, LA** | **32** |
| Jefferson Davis Parish, LA | 32 |
| **Jesup, GA** | **30** |
| Wayne County, GA | 30 |
| **Junction City, KS** | **33** |
| Geary County, KS | 33 |
| **Juneau, AK** | **32** |
| Juneau City and Borough, AK | 32 |
| **Kalispell, MT** | **102** |
| Flathead County, MT | 102 |
| **Kapaa, HI** | **72** |
| Kauai County, HI | 72 |
| **Kearney, NE** | **56** |
| Buffalo County, NE | 50 |
| Kearney County, NE | 7 |
| **Keene, NH** | **76** |
| Cheshire County, NH | 76 |
| **Kendallville, IN** | **48** |
| Noble County, IN | 48 |
| **Kennett, MO** | **29** |
| Dunklin County, MO | 29 |
| **Kerrville, TX** | **52** |
| Kerr County, TX | 52 |
| **Ketchikan, AK** | **14** |
| Ketchikan Gateway Borough, AK | 14 |
| **Key West, FL** | **75** |

| Micropolitan Statistical Area ~~Component county | Population, 2018 (1,000) |
|---|---|
| Monroe County, FL | 75 |
| **Kill Devil Hills, NC** | **41** |
| Dare County, NC | 37 |
| Tyrrell County, NC | 4 |
| **Kingsville, TX** | **32** |
| Kenedy County, TX | (Z) |
| Kleberg County, TX | 31 |
| **Kinston, NC** | **56** |
| Lenoir County, NC | 56 |
| **Kirksville, MO** | **30** |
| Adair County, MO | 25 |
| Schuyler County, MO | 5 |
| **Klamath Falls, OR** | **68** |
| Klamath County, OR | 68 |
| **Laconia, NH** | **61** |
| Belknap County, NH | 61 |
| **La Grande, OR** | **26** |
| Union County, OR | 26 |
| **LaGrange, GA** | **70** |
| Troup County, GA | 70 |
| **Lake City, FL** | **71** |
| Columbia County, FL | 71 |
| **Lamesa, TX** | **13** |
| Dawson County, TX | 13 |
| **Laramie, WY** | **39** |
| Albany County, WY | 39 |
| **Las Vegas, NM** | **28** |
| San Miguel County, NM | 28 |
| **Laurel, MS** | **85** |
| Jasper County, MS | 16 |
| Jones County, MS | 68 |
| **Laurinburg, NC** | **35** |
| Scotland County, NC | 35 |
| **Lawrenceburg, TN** | **44** |
| Lawrence County, TN | 44 |
| **Lebanon, MO** | **36** |
| Laclede County, MO | 36 |
| **Levelland, TX** | **23** |
| Hockley County, TX | 23 |
| **Lewisburg, PA** | **45** |
| Union County, PA | 45 |
| **Lewisburg, TN** | **34** |
| Marshall County, TN | 34 |
| **Lewistown, PA** | **46** |
| Mifflin County, PA | 46 |
| **Lexington, NE** | **26** |
| Dawson County, NE | 24 |
| Gosper County, NE | 2 |
| **Liberal, KS** | **22** |
| Seward County, KS | 22 |
| **Lincoln, IL** | **29** |
| Logan County, IL | 29 |
| **Lock Haven, PA** | **39** |
| Clinton County, PA | 39 |
| **Logan, WV** | **33** |
| Logan County, WV | 33 |
| **Logansport, IN** | **38** |
| Cass County, IN | 38 |
| **London, KY** | **128** |
| Knox County, KY | 31 |
| Laurel County, KY | 61 |
| Whitley County, KY | 36 |
| **Los Alamos, NM** | **19** |
| Los Alamos County, NM | 19 |
| **Ludington, MI** | **29** |
| Mason County, MI | 29 |
| **Lufkin, TX** | **87** |
| Angelina County, TX | 87 |
| **Lumberton, NC** | **132** |
| Robeson County, NC | 132 |
| **Macomb, IL** | **30** |
| McDonough County, IL | 30 |
| **Madison, IN** | **32** |
| Jefferson County, IN | 32 |
| **Madisonville, KY** | **45** |
| Hopkins County, KY | 45 |
| **Magnolia, AR** | **24** |
| Columbia County, AR | 24 |
| **Malone, NY** | **50** |
| Franklin County, NY | 50 |
| **Malvern, AR** | **34** |
| Hot Spring County, AR | 34 |

| Micropolitan Statistical Area ~~Component county | Population, 2018 (1,000) |
|---|---|
| **Manitowoc, WI** | **79** |
| Manitowoc County, WI | 79 |
| **Marietta, OH** | **60** |
| Washington County, OH | 60 |
| **Marinette, WI-MI** | **63** |
| Menominee County, MI | 23 |
| Marinette County, WI | 40 |
| **Marion, IN** | **66** |
| Grant County, IN | 66 |
| **Marion, NC** | **46** |
| McDowell County, NC | 46 |
| **Marion, OH** | **65** |
| Marion County, OH | 65 |
| **Marquette, MI** | **67** |
| Marquette County, MI | 67 |
| **Marshall, MN** | **26** |
| Lyon County, MN | 26 |
| **Marshall, MO** | **23** |
| Saline County, MO | 23 |
| **Marshall, TX** | **67** |
| Harrison County, TX | 67 |
| **Marshalltown, IA** | **40** |
| Marshall County, IA | 40 |
| **Martin, TN** | **33** |
| Weakley County, TN | 33 |
| **Martinsville, VA** | **64** |
| Henry County, VA | 51 |
| Martinsville city, VA | 13 |
| **Maryville, MO** | **22** |
| Nodaway County, MO | 22 |
| **Mason City, IA** | **50** |
| Cerro Gordo County, IA | 43 |
| Worth County, IA | 7 |
| **Mayfield, KY** | **37** |
| Graves County, KY | 37 |
| **Maysville, KY** | **17** |
| Mason County, KY | 17 |
| **McAlester, OK** | **44** |
| Pittsburg County, OK | 44 |
| **McComb, MS** | **52** |
| Amite County, MS | 12 |
| Pike County, MS | 40 |
| **McMinnville, TN** | **41** |
| Warren County, TN | 41 |
| **McPherson, KS** | **29** |
| McPherson County, KS | 29 |
| **Meadville, PA** | **85** |
| Crawford County, PA | 85 |
| **Menomonie, WI** | **45** |
| Dunn County, WI | 45 |
| **Meridian, MS** | **101** |
| Clarke County, MS | 16 |
| Kemper County, MS | 10 |
| Lauderdale County, MS | 75 |
| **Merrill, WI** | **28** |
| Lincoln County, WI | 28 |
| **Mexico, MO** | **25** |
| Audrain County, MO | 25 |
| **Miami, OK** | **31** |
| Ottawa County, OK | 31 |
| **Middlesborough, KY** | **27** |
| Bell County, KY | 27 |
| **Milledgeville, GA** | **53** |
| Baldwin County, GA | 45 |
| Hancock County, GA | 8 |
| **Mineral Wells, TX** | **29** |
| Palo Pinto County, TX | 29 |
| **Minot, ND** | **76** |
| McHenry County, ND | 6 |
| Renville County, ND | 2 |
| Ward County, ND | 68 |
| **Mitchell, SD** | **23** |
| Davison County, SD | 20 |
| Hanson County, SD | 3 |
| **Moberly, MO** | **25** |
| Randolph County, MO | 25 |
| **Montrose, CO** | **42** |
| Montrose County, CO | 42 |
| **Morehead City, NC** | **70** |
| Carteret County, NC | 70 |
| **Morgan City, LA** | **50** |
| St. Mary Parish, LA | 50 |

See footnotes at end of table.

| Micropolitan Statistical Area ~~Component county | Population, 2018 (1,000) | Micropolitan Statistical Area ~~Component county | Population, 2018 (1,000) | Micropolitan Statistical Area ~~Component county | Population, 2018 (1,000) |
|---|---|---|---|---|---|
| **Moscow, ID** | **40** | Payette County, ID | 24 | **Pontiac, IL** | **36** |
| Latah County, ID | 40 | Malheur County, OR | 31 | Livingston County, IL | 36 |
| **Moses Lake, WA** | **97** | **Opelousas, LA** | **83** | **Poplar Bluff, MO** | **43** |
| Grant County, WA | 97 | St. Landry Parish, LA | 83 | Butler County, MO | 43 |
| **Moultrie, GA** | **46** | **Orangeburg, SC** | **87** | **Portales, NM** | **19** |
| Colquitt County, GA | 46 | Orangeburg County, SC | 87 | Roosevelt County, NM | 19 |
| **Mountain Home, AR** | **42** | **Oskaloosa, IA** | **22** | **Port Angeles, WA** | **77** |
| Baxter County, AR | 42 | Mahaska County, IA | 22 | Clallam County, WA | 77 |
| **Mountain Home, ID** | **27** | **Othello, WA** | **20** | **Port Clinton, OH** | **41** |
| Elmore County, ID | 27 | Adams County, WA | 20 | Ottawa County, OH | 41 |
| **Mount Airy, NC** | **72** | **Ottawa, KS** | **26** | **Port Lavaca, TX** | **22** |
| Surry County, NC | 72 | Franklin County, KS | 26 | Calhoun County, TX | 22 |
| **Mount Pleasant, MI** | **71** | **Ottawa-Peru, IL** | **148** | **Portsmouth, OH** | **76** |
| Isabella County, MI | 71 | Bureau County, IL | 33 | Scioto County, OH | 76 |
| **Mount Pleasant, TX** | **33** | LaSalle County, IL | 109 | **Pottsville, PA** | **142** |
| Titus County, TX | 33 | Putnam County, IL | 6 | Schuylkill County, PA | 142 |
| **Mount Sterling, KY** | **47** | **Ottumwa, IA** | **44** | **Price, UT** | **20** |
| Bath County, KY | 12 | Davis County, IA | 9 | Carbon County, UT | 20 |
| Menifee County, KY | 6 | Wapello County, IA | 35 | **Prineville, OR** | **24** |
| Montgomery County, KY | 28 | **Owatonna, MN** | **37** | Crook County, OR | 24 |
| **Mount Vernon, IL** | **38** | Steele County, MN | 37 | **Pullman, WA** | **50** |
| Jefferson County, IL | 38 | **Owosso, MI** | **68** | Whitman County, WA | 50 |
| **Mount Vernon, OH** | **62** | Shiawassee County, MI | 68 | **Quincy, IL-MO** | **76** |
| Knox County, OH | 62 | **Oxford, MS** | **55** | Adams County, IL | 66 |
| **Murray, KY** | **39** | Lafayette County, MS | 55 | Lewis County, MO | 10 |
| Calloway County, KY | 39 | **Oxford, NC** | **60** | **Raymondville, TX** | **22** |
| **Muscatine, IA** | **43** | Granville County, NC | 60 | Willacy County, TX | 22 |
| Muscatine County, IA | 43 | **Ozark, AL** | **49** | **Red Bluff, CA** | **64** |
| **Muskogee, OK** | **68** | Dale County, AL | 49 | Tehama County, CA | 64 |
| Muskogee County, OK | 68 | **Paducah, KY-IL** | **97** | **Red Wing, MN** | **46** |
| **Nacogdoches, TX** | **66** | Massac County, IL | 14 | Goodhue County, MN | 46 |
| Nacogdoches County, TX | 66 | Ballard County, KY | 8 | **Rexburg, ID** | **52** |
| **Natchez, MS-LA** | **51** | Livingston County, KY | 9 | Fremont County, ID | 13 |
| Concordia Parish, LA | 20 | McCracken County, KY | 65 | Madison County, ID | 39 |
| Adams County, MS | 31 | **Pahrump, NV** | **45** | **Richmond, IN** | **66** |
| **Natchitoches, LA** | **39** | Nye County, NV | 45 | Wayne County, IN | 66 |
| Natchitoches Parish, LA | 39 | **Palatka, FL** | **74** | **Richmond-Berea, KY** | **109** |
| **Newberry, SC** | **39** | Putnam County, FL | 74 | Madison County, KY | 92 |
| Newberry County, SC | 39 | **Palestine, TX** | **58** | Rockcastle County, KY | 17 |
| **New Castle, IN** | **48** | Anderson County, TX | 58 | **Rio Grande City, TX** | **65** |
| Henry County, IN | 48 | **Pampa, TX** | **22** | Starr County, TX | 65 |
| **New Castle, PA** | **86** | Gray County, TX | 22 | **Riverton, WY** | **40** |
| Lawrence County, PA | 86 | **Paragould, AR** | **45** | Fremont County, WY | 40 |
| **New Philadelphia-Dover, OH** | **92** | Greene County, AR | 45 | **Roanoke Rapids, NC** | **70** |
| Tuscarawas County, OH | 92 | **Paris, TN** | **32** | Halifax County, NC | 51 |
| **Newport, OR** | **49** | Henry County, TN | 32 | Northampton County, NC | 20 |
| Lincoln County, OR | 49 | **Paris, TX** | **50** | **Rochelle, IL** | **51** |
| **Newport, TN** | **36** | Lamar County, TX | 50 | Ogle County, IL | 51 |
| Cocke County, TN | 36 | **Parsons, KS** | **20** | **Rockingham, NC** | **45** |
| **Newton, IA** | **37** | Labette County, KS | 20 | Richmond County, NC | 45 |
| Jasper County, IA | 37 | **Payson, AZ** | **54** | **Rock Springs, WY** | **43** |
| **New Ulm, MN** | **25** | Gila County, AZ | 54 | Sweetwater County, WY | 43 |
| Brown County, MN | 25 | **Pecos, TX** | **16** | **Rolla, MO** | **45** |
| **Nogales, AZ** | **47** | Reeves County, TX | 16 | Phelps County, MO | 45 |
| Santa Cruz County, AZ | 47 | **Pella, IA** | **33** | **Roseburg, OR** | **110** |
| **Norfolk, NE** | **49** | Marion County, IA | 33 | Douglas County, OR | 110 |
| Madison County, NE | 35 | **Peru, IN** | **36** | **Roswell, NM** | **65** |
| Pierce County, NE | 7 | Miami County, IN | 36 | Chaves County, NM | 65 |
| Stanton County, NE | 6 | **Picayune, MS** | **55** | **Ruidoso, NM** | **20** |
| **North Platte, NE** | **36** | Pearl River County, MS | 55 | Lincoln County, NM | 20 |
| Lincoln County, NE | 35 | **Pierre, SD** | **22** | **Russellville, AR** | **86** |
| Logan County, NE | 1 | Hughes County, SD | 18 | Pope County, AR | 64 |
| McPherson County, NE | (Z) | Stanley County, SD | 3 | Yell County, AR | 22 |
| **North Vernon, IN** | **28** | Sully County, SD | 1 | **Ruston, LA** | **47** |
| Jennings County, IN | 28 | **Pinehurst-Southern Pines, NC** | **99** | Lincoln Parish, LA | 47 |
| **North Wilkesboro, NC** | **69** | Moore County, NC | 99 | **Rutland, VT** | **59** |
| Wilkes County, NC | 69 | **Pittsburg, KS** | **39** | Rutland County, VT | 59 |
| **Norwalk, OH** | **59** | Crawford County, KS | 39 | **Safford, AZ** | **38** |
| Huron County, OH | 59 | **Plainview, TX** | **34** | Graham County, AZ | 38 |
| **Oak Harbor, WA** | **84** | Hale County, TX | 34 | **St. Marys, GA** | **54** |
| Island County, WA | 84 | **Platteville, WI** | **52** | Camden County, GA | 54 |
| **Ogdensburg-Massena, NY** | **108** | Grant County, WI | 52 | **St. Marys, PA** | **30** |
| St. Lawrence County, NY | 108 | **Plattsburgh, NY** | **81** | Elk County, PA | 30 |
| **Oil City, PA** | **51** | Clinton County, NY | 81 | **Salem, OH** | **103** |
| Venango County, PA | 51 | **Plymouth, IN** | **46** | Columbiana County, OH | 103 |
| **Okeechobee, FL** | **42** | Marshall County, IN | 46 | **Salina, KS** | **60** |
| Okeechobee County, FL | 42 | **Point Pleasant, WV-OH** | **57** | Ottawa County, KS | 6 |
| **Olean, NY** | **77** | Gallia County, OH | 30 | Saline County, KS | 54 |
| Cattaraugus County, NY | 77 | Mason County, WV | 27 | **Sandpoint, ID** | **45** |
| **Oneonta, NY** | **60** | **Ponca City, OK** | **44** | Bonner County, ID | 45 |
| Otsego County, NY | 60 | Kay County, OK | 44 | **Sandusky, OH** | **75** |
| **Ontario, OR-ID** | **54** | | | Erie County, OH | 75 |

# Table B. Microplitan Statistical Areas and Components—Population: 2018-Continued.

See headnote on page 924.

| Micropolitan Statistical Area ~~Component county | Popu-lation, 2018 (1,000) | Micropolitan Statistical Area ~~Component county | Popu-lation, 2018 (1,000) | Micropolitan Statistical Area ~~Component county | Popu-lation, 2018 (1,000) |
|---|---|---|---|---|---|
| **Sanford, NC** | **61** | **Sulphur Springs, TX** | **37** | Warren County, MS | 46 |
| Lee County, NC | 61 | Hopkins County, TX | 37 | **Vidalia, GA** | **36** |
| **Sault Ste. Marie, MI** | **38** | **Summerville, GA** | **25** | Montgomery County, GA | 9 |
| Chippewa County, MI | 38 | Chattooga County, GA | 25 | Toombs County, GA | 27 |
| **Sayre, PA** | **61** | **Summit Park, UT** | **42** | **Vincennes, IN** | **37** |
| Bradford County, PA | 61 | Summit County, UT | 42 | Knox County, IN | 37 |
| **Scottsbluff, NE** | **38** | **Sunbury, PA** | **91** | **Vineyard Haven, MA** | **17** |
| Banner County, NE | 1 | Northumberland County, PA | 91 | Dukes County, MA | 17 |
| Scotts Bluff County, NE | 36 | **Susanville, CA** | **31** | **Wabash, IN** | **31** |
| Sioux County, NE | 1 | Lassen County, CA | 31 | Wabash County, IN | 31 |
| **Scottsboro, AL** | **52** | **Sweetwater, TX** | **15** | **Wahpeton, ND-MN** | **22** |
| Jackson County, AL | 52 | Nolan County, TX | 15 | Wilkin County, MN | 6 |
| **Searcy, AR** | **79** | **Tahlequah, OK** | **49** | Richland County, ND | 16 |
| White County, AR | 79 | Cherokee County, OK | 49 | **Wapakoneta, OH** | **46** |
| **Sedalia, MO** | **43** | **Talladega-Sylacauga, AL** | **91** | Auglaize County, OH | 46 |
| Pettis County, MO | 43 | Coosa County, AL | 11 | **Warren, PA** | **39** |
| **Selinsgrove, PA** | **41** | Talladega County, AL | 80 | Warren County, PA | 39 |
| Snyder County, PA | 41 | **Taos, NM** | **33** | **Warrensburg, MO** | **54** |
| **Selma, AL** | **38** | Taos County, NM | 33 | Johnson County, MO | 54 |
| Dallas County, AL | 38 | **Taylorville, IL** | **33** | **Warsaw, IN** | **79** |
| **Seneca, SC** | **78** | Christian County, IL | 33 | Kosciusko County, IN | 79 |
| Oconee County, SC | 78 | **The Dalles, OR** | **27** | **Washington, IN** | **33** |
| **Seneca Falls, NY** | **34** | Wasco County, OR | 27 | Daviess County, IN | 33 |
| Seneca County, NY | 34 | **Thomaston, GA** | **26** | **Washington, NC** | **47** |
| **Sevierville, TN** | **98** | Upson County, GA | 26 | Beaufort County, NC | 47 |
| Sevier County, TN | 98 | **Thomasville, GA** | **44** | **Washington Court House,** | |
| **Seymour, IN** | **44** | Thomas County, GA | 44 | **OH** | **29** |
| Jackson County, IN | 44 | **Tiffin, OH** | **55** | Fayette County, OH | 29 |
| **Shawano, WI** | **45** | Seneca County, OH | 55 | **Watertown, SD** | **28** |
| Menominee County, WI | 5 | **Tifton, GA** | **41** | Codington County, SD | 28 |
| Shawano County, WI | 41 | Tift County, GA | 41 | **Watertown-Fort Atkinson, WI** | **85** |
| **Shawnee, OK** | **73** | **Toccoa, GA** | **26** | Jefferson County, WI | 85 |
| Pottawatomie County, OK | 73 | Stephens County, GA | 26 | **Wauchula, FL** | **27** |
| **Shelby, NC** | **98** | **Torrington, CT** | **181** | Hardee County, FL | 27 |
| Cleveland County, NC | 98 | Litchfield County, CT | 181 | **Waycross, GA** | **55** |
| **Shelbyville, TN** | **49** | **Traverse City, MI** | **150** | Pierce County, GA | 19 |
| Bedford County, TN | 49 | Benzie County, MI | 18 | Ware County, GA | 36 |
| **Shelton, WA** | **66** | Grand Traverse County, MI | 93 | **Weatherford, OK** | **29** |
| Mason County, WA | 66 | Kalkaska County, MI | 18 | Custer County, OK | 29 |
| **Sheridan, WY** | **30** | Leelanau County, MI | 22 | **West Plains, MO** | **40** |
| Sheridan County, WY | 30 | **Troy, AL** | **33** | Howell County, MO | 40 |
| **Show Low, AZ** | **110** | Pike County, AL | 33 | **West Point, MS** | **19** |
| Navajo County, AZ | 110 | **Truckee-Grass Valley, CA** | **100** | Clay County, MS | 19 |
| **Sidney, OH** | **49** | Nevada County, CA | 100 | **Whitewater-Elkhorn, WI** | **104** |
| Shelby County, OH | 49 | **Tullahoma-Manchester, TN** | **104** | Walworth County, WI | 104 |
| **Sikeston, MO** | **38** | Coffee County, TN | 56 | **Williston, ND** | **35** |
| Scott County, MO | 38 | Franklin County, TN | 42 | Williams County, ND | 35 |
| **Silver City, NM** | **27** | Moore County, TN | 6 | **Willmar, MN** | **43** |
| Grant County, NM | 27 | **Tupelo, MS** | **141** | Kandiyohi County, MN | 43 |
| **Snyder, TX** | **17** | Itawamba County, MS | 24 | **Wilmington, OH** | **42** |
| Scurry County, TX | 17 | Lee County, MS | 85 | Clinton County, OH | 42 |
| **Somerset, KY** | **65** | Pontotoc County, MS | 32 | **Wilson, NC** | **81** |
| Pulaski County, KY | 65 | **Ukiah, CA** | **88** | Wilson County, NC | 81 |
| **Somerset, PA** | **74** | Mendocino County, CA | 88 | **Winnemucca, NV** | **17** |
| Somerset County, PA | 74 | **Union City, TN-KY** | **36** | Humboldt County, NV | 17 |
| **Sonora, CA** | **55** | Fulton County, KY | 6 | **Winona, MN** | **51** |
| Tuolumne County, CA | 55 | Obion County, TN | 30 | Winona County, MN | 51 |
| **Spearfish, SD** | **26** | **Urbana, OH** | **39** | **Wisconsin Rapids-Marshfield,** | |
| Lawrence County, SD | 26 | Champaign County, OH | 39 | **WI** | **73** |
| **Spencer, IA** | **16** | **Uvalde, TX** | **27** | Wood County, WI | 73 |
| Clay County, IA | 16 | Uvalde County, TX | 27 | **Woodward, OK** | **20** |
| **Spirit Lake, IA** | **17** | **Valley, AL** | **34** | Woodward County, OK | 20 |
| Dickinson County, IA | 17 | Chambers County, AL | 34 | **Wooster, OH** | **116** |
| **Starkville, MS** | **50** | **Van Wert, OH** | **28** | Wayne County, OH | 116 |
| Oktibbeha County, MS | 50 | Van Wert County, OH | 28 | **Worthington, MN** | **22** |
| **Statesboro, GA** | **77** | **Vermillion, SD** | **14** | Nobles County, MN | 22 |
| Bulloch County, GA | 77 | Clay County, SD | 14 | **Yankton, SD** | **23** |
| **Steamboat Springs, CO** | **26** | **Vernal, UT** | **35** | Yankton County, SD | 23 |
| Routt County, CO | 26 | Uintah County, UT | 35 | **Zanesville, OH** | **86** |
| **Stephenville, TX** | **42** | **Vernon, TX** | **13** | Muskingum County, OH | 86 |
| Erath County, TX | 42 | Wilbarger County, TX | 13 | **Zapata, TX** | **14** |
| **Sterling, CO** | **22** | **Vicksburg, MS** | **55** | Zapata County, TX | 14 |
| Logan County, CO | 22 | Claiborne County, MS | 9 | | |
| **Sterling, IL** | **56** | | | | |
| Whiteside County, IL | 56 | | | | |
| **Stevens Point, WI** | **71** | | | | |
| Portage County, WI | 71 | | | | |
| **Stillwater, OK** | **82** | | | | |
| Payne County, OK | 82 | | | | |
| **Storm Lake, IA** | **20** | | | | |
| Buena Vista County, IA | 20 | | | | |
| **Sturgis, MI** | **61** | | | | |
| St. Joseph County, MI | 61 | | | | |

Z Represents less than 500.

Source: U.S. Census Bureau, 2018 Population Estimates, <https://www.census.gov/programs-surveys/metro-micro/data/tables.html>.

# Appendix III
# Limitations of the Data

**Introduction**—The data presented in this *Statistical Abstract* come from not only federal statistical bureaus and other organizations that collect and issue statistics as their principal activity, but also governmental administrative and regulatory agencies, private research bodies, trade associations, insurance companies, health associations, private organizations, and philanthropic foundations. Consequently, the data vary considerably as to reference periods, definitions of terms and, for ongoing series, the number and frequency of time periods for which data are available.

The statistics presented were obtained and tabulated by various methods. Some statistics are based on complete enumerations or censuses while others are based on samples. Some information is extracted from records kept for administrative or regulatory purposes (school enrollment, hospital records, securities registration, financial accounts, social security records, income tax returns, etc.), while other information is obtained explicitly for statistical purposes through surveys.

Each set of data relates to a group of individuals or units of interest referred to as the *target universe,* or *target population*, or simply as the *universe* or *population*. Tables may present data obtained for all population units, *a census*, or data obtained for only a portion, or *sample*, of the population units.

Prior to data collection, the target universe is clearly defined. For example, if data are to be collected for the universe of households in the United States, it is necessary to define a "household." The target universe may not be completely tractable. Cost and other considerations may restrict data collection to a *survey universe* based on an available list. This list is called a *survey frame, sampling frame*, or *survey sample.*

When data are based on a sample, the sample is usually a scientifically selected *probability sample.* This is a sample selected from a list or sampling frame in such a way that every possible sample has a known chance of selection and usually each unit selected can be assigned a number, greater than zero and less than or equal to one, representing its likelihood or probability of selection.

For large-scale sample surveys, the probability sample of units is often selected as a multistage sample. The first stage of a multistage sample is the selection of a probability sample of large groups of population members, referred to as primary sampling units (PSUs). For example, in a national multistage household sample, PSUs are often counties or groups of counties. The second stage of a multistage sample is the selection, within each PSU selected at the first stage, of smaller groups of population units, referred to as secondary sampling units. In subsequent stages of selection, smaller and smaller nested groups are chosen until the ultimate sample of population units is obtained. To qualify a multistage sample as a probability sample, all stages of sampling must be carried out using probability sampling methods.

Prior to selection at each stage of a multistage (or a single stage) sample, a list of the sampling units or sampling frame for that stage must be obtained. For example, for the first stage of selection of a national household sample, a list of the counties and county groups that form the PSUs must be compiled. For the final stage of selection, lists of households, and sometimes persons within the households, have to be compiled in the field. For surveys of economic entities and for the economic censuses, the U.S. Census Bureau generally uses a frame constructed from the Bureau's Business Register. The Business Register contains all establishments with payroll in the United States, including small single-establishment firms as well as larger firms with multiple establishments.

Wherever the quantities in a table refer to an entire universe, but are constructed from data collected in a sample survey, the table quantities are referred to as *sample estimates*. In constructing a sample estimate, an attempt is made to come as close as is feasible to the corresponding universe quantity that would be obtained from a complete census of the universe. Estimates based on a sample will, however, generally differ from the hypothetical census figures. Two classifications of errors are associated with estimates based on sample surveys:

1 *Sampling error*  the error arising from the use of a sample, rather than a census, to estimate population quantities and

2 *Nonsampling error*—those errors arising from nonsampling sources. Nonsampling errors can include mistakes made in data collection or data processing, misunderstandings of the interviewer or the respondent, and data entry errors. As discussed below, the magnitude of the sampling error for an estimate can usually be estimated from the sample data. However, the magnitude of the nonsampling error for an estimate can rarely be estimated. Consequently, actual error in an estimate exceeds the error that can be estimated.

The particular sample used in a survey is only one of a large number of possible samples of the same size which could have been selected using the same sampling procedure. Estimates derived from the different samples would, in general, differ from each other. The *standard error* (SE) is a measure of the variation among the estimates derived from all possible samples. The standard error is the most commonly used measure of the sampling error of an estimate. Valid estimates of the standard errors of survey estimates can usually be calculated from the data collected in a probability sample. For convenience, the standard error is sometimes expressed as a percent of the estimate and is called the relative standard error or *coefficient of variation* (CV). For example, an estimate of 200 units with an estimated standard error of 10 units has an estimated CV of 5 percent.

A sample estimate and an estimate of its standard error or CV can be used to construct interval estimates that have a prescribed confidence that the interval includes the average of the estimates derived from all possible samples with a known probability. To illustrate, if all possible samples were selected under essentially the same general conditions, and using the same sample design, and if an estimate and its estimated standard error were calculated from each sample, then: 1) approximately 68 percent of the intervals from one standard error below the estimate to one standard error above the estimate would include the average estimate derived from all possible samples; 2) approximately 90 percent of the intervals from 1.6 standard errors below the estimate to 1.6 standard errors above the estimate would include the average estimate derived from all possible samples; and 3) approximately 95 percent of the intervals from two standard errors below the estimate to two standard errors above the estimate would include the average estimate derived from all possible samples.

Thus, for a particular sample, one can say with the appropriate level of confidence (e.g., 90 percent or 95 percent) that the average of all possible samples is included in the constructed interval. Example of a confidence interval: an estimate is 200 units with a standard error of 10 units. An approximately 90 percent confidence interval (plus or minus 1.6 standard errors) is from 184 to 216.

All surveys and censuses are subject to nonsampling errors. Nonsampling errors arise from a variety of factors, including total nonresponse (no usable data obtained for a sampled unit), partial or item nonresponse (only a portion of a response may be usable), inability or unwillingness on the part of respondents to provide correct information, difficulty interpreting questions, mistakes in recording or keying data, errors of collection or processing, and coverage problems (overcoverage and undercoverage of the target universe). Nonresponse errors usually, but not always, result in an understatement of sampling errors and thus an overstatement of the precision of survey estimates. Estimating the magnitude of nonsampling errors would require special experiments or access to independent data. Organizations seldom attempt to measure nonsampling errors.

Nearly all types of nonsampling errors that affect surveys also occur in complete censuses. Since surveys can be conducted on a smaller scale than censuses, nonsampling errors can presumably be controlled more tightly. Relatively more funds and effort can perhaps be expended toward eliciting responses, detecting and correcting response error, and reducing processing errors. As a result, survey results can sometimes be more accurate than census results.

To reduce nonsampling errors, most surveys use computer-assisted telephone or personal interviewing (CATI or CAPI). The computer-assisted data collection method employs computer software and programs that guide the interviewer through the questionnaire to keep the survey consistent across all respondents, and can automatically route the interviewer to appropriate questions based on answers to previous questions. Often the computer program determines if responses are within an allowable range, and checks for consistency against other data collected during the interview. Capturing a survey on a computer also aids in the complete and accurate transfer of data to the organization's data system. Once collected, survey organizations run automated reviews and edits of data, and impute and weight data items.

Adjustments of sample estimates are often made, frequently for nonresponse, both total and partial. These adjustments are *imputations*. Imputation for total nonresponse is usually made by substituting for the questionnaire responses of the nonrespondents the "average" questionnaire responses of the respondents. These imputations usually are made separately within various groups of sample members, formed by attempting to place respondents and nonrespondents together that have similar characteristics. Imputation for item nonresponse is usually made by substituting for a missing item the response to that item of a respondent having characteristics that are similar to those of the nonrespondent.

For an estimate calculated from a sample survey, the *total error* in the estimate is composed of the sampling error, which can usually be estimated from the sample, and the nonsampling error, which usually cannot be estimated from the sample. The total error present in a population quantity obtained from a complete census is composed of only nonsampling errors. Ideally, estimates of the total error associated with data presented in the *Statistical Abstract* tables would be available; however, due to the unavailability of estimates of nonsampling errors, only estimates of the levels of sampling errors, in terms of estimated standard errors or coefficients of variation, are available. To obtain estimates of the estimated standard errors from the sample of interest, see the source cited at the end of each table.

*Source of Additional Material:* The Federal Committee on Statistical Methodology (FCSM) is an interagency committee dedicated to improving the quality of federal statistics, online at <https://nces.ed.gov/FCSM/index.asp>. See also information available on the Census Bureau website at <https://www.census.gov/about/policies/quality/guidelines.html>.

**Principal data sources**—Beginning below are brief descriptions of over 30 of the sample surveys and censuses that provide a substantial portion of the data contained in this *Abstract*.

# U.S. DEPARTMENT OF AGRICULTURE, National Agricultural Statistics Service

## Census of Agriculture

*Universes, Frequency, and Types of Data*: Complete count of U.S. farms and ranches conducted once every 5 years, with data at the national, state, and county level. The survey includes any place from which $1,000 or more of agricultural products were produced and sold, or normally would have been sold, during the census year. The census collects data on all commodities produced in the U.S. as well as detailed information on land use and ownership, operator characteristics (such as race, gender, age, tenure on farm, and operating arrangement), production practices, and income and expenditures.

*Type of Data Collection Operation*: Data collection is by mailing questionnaires to all farmers and ranchers. Producers can return their forms by mail or utilize a census form online. Nonrespondents are contacted by telephone and correspondence follow-ups. Collection is supplemented by electronic data reporting on the internet, and personal enumeration for special classes of records in census operations. Personal enumeration (interviewing) involves the use of both Computer-Assisted Telephone Interview (CATI) and Computer-Assisted Personal Interview (CAPI) data collection instruments. The response rate for the 2012 Census was 74.6 percent, and for the 2017 Census, 71.8 percent.

*Imputation Procedures*: Computer editing determined the best value to impute for reported responses that were deemed unreasonable and for required responses that were absent. If an item could not be calculated directly from other current responses, the edit determined whether acreage, production, or inventory items had been reported for that farm on a recent NASS crop or livestock survey. For producers who had not changed in five years, demographics such as race and gender were taken from the previous census. Administrative data from the Farm Service Agency were used for a few items, such as Conservation Reserve Program acreage. When deterministic edit logic and previously reported data sources were unable to provide a current value, data from a reporting farm of similar type, size, and location were considered. In cases where automated imputation was unable to provide a consistent report, the record was referred to an analyst for resolution.

*Estimates of Sampling Error*: NASS uses statistical methodology to correct for undercoverage (farms not reached in the original mailing), nonresponse (people not returning their census questionnaires), and misclassification (whether an operation is correctly classified as a farm or not). The uncertainty these adjustments introduce causes the exact numbers to be unknown; however, the uncertainty can be quantified. This measure of relative reliability is known as the coefficient of variation. In the 2017 Census results, NASS is publishing a measure of uncertainty with all estimates at the national, state, and county level, increasing transparency and data usability.

*Nonsampling Errors:* Nonsampling errors are imbedded in the census process that cannot be directly measured as part of the design of the census but must be contained to ensure an accurate count. Extensive efforts were made to compile a complete and accurate mail list for the census, to elicit response to the census, to design an understandable report form with clear instructions, to minimize processing errors through the use of quality control measures, to reduce matching error associated with the capture-recapture estimation process, and to minimize error associated with identification of a respondent as a farm operation (referred to as classification error). The weight adjustment and tabulation processes recognize the presence of nonsampling errors; however, it is assumed that these errors are small and that, in total, the net effect is zero. The positive errors cancel the negative errors.

*Sources of Additional Material*: U.S. Department of Agriculture (NASS), 2017 Census of Agriculture, Appendix A Census of Agriculture Methodology, and Appendix B General Explanation and Census of Agriculture Report Form, at <https://www.nass.usda.gov/Publications/AgCensus/2017/index.php>

and <https://www.nass.usda.gov/Surveys/Guide_to_NASS_Surveys/Census_of_Agriculture/index.php>.

## June Area Survey

*Universe, Frequency, and Types of Data:* The annual June Area survey utilizes an area sampling frame, and is designed to account for every acre of land, all agricultural activities, and land uses within segment boundaries. Data are collected annually from all states (except Alaska), on crop acreage, grain stocks, cattle inventory, hog inventory, sheep inventory, poultry inventory, land values, cash rents, farm numbers, and sales. The survey also serves to measure list incompleteness and is subsampled for multiple frame surveys.

*Data Collection and Imputation Procedures:* Stratified probability sample of about 11,000 land area units of about 1 sq. mile (range from 0.1 sq. mile in cities to several sq. miles in open grazing areas). All farm operators within the boundaries of selected segments are interviewed. The JAS typically conducts over 35,000 interviews each year. Approximately 20 percent of the sample is replaced annually. Data collection for the June Area survey is completed entirely by personal interview during the 1st two weeks in June. Imputation is based on enumerator observation or data reported by respondents having similar agricultural characteristics.

*Estimates of Sampling Error:* Estimated CVs range from 1 to 2 percent for regional estimates and 3 to 6 percent for state estimates of major crop acres and livestock inventories.

*Nonsampling Errors:* Steps taken to minimize nonsampling errors include comprehensive interviewer training, validation, and verification of processing systems, application of detailed computer edits, and evaluation of the data via analysis tools.

*Sources of Additional Material:* U.S. Department of Agriculture, National Agricultural Statistics Service, *Area Frame Design for Agricultural Surveys*, June 2009, online at <https://www.nass.usda.gov/Publications/Methodology_and_Data_Quality/index.php>; and <https://www.nass.usda.gov/Surveys/Guide_to_NASS_Surveys/June_Area/index.php>.

## Objective Yield Surveys

*Universe, Frequency, and Types of Data:* Monthly forecasts and end-of-season estimates of planted and harvested acres, yield, and production of winter wheat, corn for grain, soybeans, fall potatoes, and upland cotton. All acres for harvest as grain in the leading producing states are eligible for this survey. Survey samples are selected from participants in the March Crops/Stocks Survey or the June Agricultural Survey, and include only the top producing states that together produce the majority of a given crop in the U.S.

*Data Collection Operation:* Random location of plots in probability sample. Field work begins April 25 for winter wheat and July 25 for all the other crops. Sample units are visited at the end of each month during the growing season. Enumerators count and measure plant characteristics in sample fields. Production is measured from plots at harvest. Harvest loss is measured from post harvest gleanings.

*Estimates of Sampling Error:* CVs for national estimates of production are about 2 to 3 percent.

*Nonsampling Errors:* In addition to above, replicated sampling procedures are used to monitor effects of changes in survey procedures.

*Sources of Additional Material:* U.S. Department of Agriculture, National Agricultural Statistics Service, Statistical Methods Branch, *The Yield Forecasting Program of NASS,* May 2012, online at <https://www.nass.usda.gov/Publications/Methodology_and_Data_Quality/index.php>.

# U.S. BUREAU OF JUSTICE STATISTICS (BJS)

## National Crime Victimization Survey (NCVS)

*Universe, Frequency, and Types of Data:* Annual survey of U.S. household members age 12 and older to obtain data on criminal victimization for compilation of annual estimates. The 2017 NCVS data file includes 145,508 household interviews; 76% of eligible households completed an interview. Within participating households, 239,541 persons completed an interview in 2017, representing an 84% response rate among eligible persons from responding households. Survey excludes victimizations occurring outside of the U.S. The NCVS covers violent and property crime victimization, and the characteristics of crimes and victims. Violent crimes include rape or sexual assault, robbery, aggravated and simple assault, and personal larceny (purse-snatching, pick-pocketing). Property crimes include household burglary, motor vehicle theft, and other theft. The survey covers crimes that are both reported and not reported to the police. The survey excludes homicide, arson, and commercial crimes.

*Data Collection and Imputation Procedures:* Eligible household members age 12 and older are interviewed every 6 months for a total of 7 interviews. Households stay in the sample for about 3 1/2 years. New households rotate into the sample on an ongoing basis. Personal interviews are used in the first interview; subsequent interviews are conducted either in person or by telephone. Survey respondents provide information about their crime victimization experiences during the past 6 months, and their personal characteristics. NCVS data include both person and household weights to provide estimates of the population and households represented by each person and each household in the sample. Weights are designed to adjust data to known population totals and compensate for survey nonresponse and other aspects of the complex sample design.

The 2017 NCVS utilizes new household weighting adjustments, resulting in the 2017 NCVS household estimate being about 8 percent lower than the 2016 NCVS household estimate. The number of households affected by property crime is also about 8 percent lower. Comparisons of the number of property crime victimizations between 2016 and 2017 are not appropriate due to the change in weighting methodology.

*Estimates of Sampling Error:* To generate standard errors around victimization and incidence estimates from the NCVS, the U.S. Census Bureau produces generalized variance function (GVF) parameters for BJS. To generate standard errors around prevalence estimates, BJS used direct variance estimation methods. The GVFs and direct variance estimation methods take into account aspects of the NCVS complex sample design and represent the curve fitted to a selection of individual standard errors based on the Balanced Repeated Replication (BRR) technique. The BJS determined that the estimated 2017 victimization rate per 1,000 persons age 12 and older for violent crime has a standard error of 1.03, and for property crime a standard error of 1.86. The source report provides standard errors by detailed type of crime and victim characteristics.

*Nonsampling Errors:* Respondent recall errors, including reporting incidents for other than the reference period; interviewer coding and processing errors; and possible mistaken reporting or classifying of events.

*Sources of Additional Material:* U.S. Bureau of Justice Statistics, *Criminal Victimization, 2017,* and the BJS website.

# U.S. BUREAU OF LABOR STATISTICS

## Consumer Expenditure Survey (CE)

*Universe, Frequency and Types of Data:* The Consumer Expenditure Survey (CE) is a nationwide household survey on family expenditures for goods and services. The CE also collects information on amount and sources of family income, changes in assets and liabilities, and demographic and economic characteristics of family members. The CE has two components: a quarterly interview survey, and a weekly diary survey. Estimates covering 12-month periods are released twice a year. Samples are national probability samples of households that are representative of the civilian noninstitutional population. The CE interviews approximately 16,800 households each year.

*Type of Data Collection Operation:* Both the Interview Survey and the Diary survey are conducted primarily by personal visit, with some telephone interviewing. The Interview Survey is a panel rotation survey. Each panel is interviewed for four quarters and then dropped from the survey. The measurement unit is the set of eligible individuals constituting a consumer unit (CU). The CU is defined as 1) all members in a housing unit who make up a family (includes foster children); 2) a person living alone or sharing a household with others, or living as a roomer in a private home or other lodging (includes hotel or motel), but who is financially independent; or 3) two or more unrelated persons living together who pool their income to make joint expenditure decisions. Students living in university-sponsored housing are also included in the sample as separate consumer units. The Census Bureau selects a sample of approximately 12,000 addresses per year to participate in the Diary Survey; approximately 6,900 households provide usable diaries (two 1-week diaries per household). For the Interview Survey, approximately 12,000 addresses are contacted each quarter. One-fourth of the addresses that are contacted each quarter are new to the survey. Approximately 6,900 households provide usable interviews.

*Data Collection and Imputation Procedures:* For the Interview Survey, data are collected by personal interview with each consumer unit interviewed once per quarter. The Interview Survey is designed to collect information that respondents can recall for the past 3 months or longer regarding large or recurring expenditures. For the Diary Survey, respondents record all their expenditures in a self-reporting diary for two consecutive 1-week periods. The Diary Survey is designed to pick up small, frequently purchased items which can be difficult to recall over a long period of time. These items include food, beverages, and household and personal care products and services. Missing or invalid attributes, expenditures, or incomes are imputed. Assets and liabilities are not imputed. Beginning with 2014 data, the CES imputes federal and state income taxes. The U.S. Census Bureau collects the data for the Bureau of Labor Statistics.

*Estimates of Sampling Error:* Standard errors measure the uncertainty in the survey estimates caused by the fact that a random sample of consumer units from across the United States is used instead of every consumer unit in the nation. Beginning with the release of 2012 data, separate standard error tables are no longer issued; standard errors are included in the combined expenditure, share, and standard error tables.

*Nonsampling Errors:* Nonsampling errors can be attributed to many sources, such as differences in the interpretation of questions, inability or unwillingness of the respondent to provide correct information, mistakes in recording or coding the data obtained, and other errors of collection, response, processing, coverage, and estimation for missing data. The full extent of nonsampling error is unknown.

*Sources of Additional Material:* Bureau of Labor Statistics website <http://www.bls.gov/cex>; and "BLS Handbook of Methods," <http://www.bls.gov/opub/hom/cex/home.htm>.

## Consumer Price Index (CPI)

*Universe, Frequency, and Types of Data:* The Consumer Price Index (CPI) is a measure of the average change over time in the prices paid by urban consumers for a market basket of consumer goods and services. The CPI is derived from a monthly survey. The CPI reflects spending patterns of two population groups: all urban consumers (CPI-U), and urban wage earners and clerical workers (CPI-W). The all urban consumer group represents approximately 93 percent of the total U.S. population. The CPI-W population represents about 29 percent of the total U.S. population and is a subset of the CPI-U population. Not included in the CPI are the spending patterns of people living in rural non-metropolitan areas, farm families, Armed Forces personnel, and those in institutions such as prisons and mental hospitals. The BLS calculates CPI indexes for the U.S., the census regions and divisions, urban areas by population size, and selected metropolitan and local areas. The CPI covers over 200 item categories of consumer purchases in eight major groups (food and beverages, housing, apparel, transportation, medical care, recreation, education and communication, and other goods and services). Included within these major groups are various government-charged user fees, such as water and sewerage charges, auto registration fees, and vehicle tolls.

*Data Collection Operation:* BLS data collectors, called economic assistants, visit or call thousands of retail stores, service establishments, rental units, and doctors' offices, all over the United States, to obtain information on the prices of thousands of items used for the CPI. Prices are collected each month for approximately 80,000 items in 75 urban areas across the country from about 5,000 housing units and approximately 23,000 retail establishments. The BLS also collects rents from about 43,000 landlords and tenants; rent information is collected every 6 months. The CPI also covers price quotes from a small percentage of online outlets (8 percent in 2017).

*Imputation Procedures:* The CPI uses imputation for missing information, which can be due to refusals of responses, inability to collect data for some other reason (the item may be out of season), and the inability to make a satisfactory estimate of the quality change. For noncomparable substitutions, an estimate of constant-quality price change is made by imputation.

*Estimates of Sampling Error:* The CPI is a statistical estimate that is subject to sampling error because it is based upon a sample of retail prices and not the complete universe of all prices. BLS calculates and publishes estimates of the 1-month, 2-month, 6-month, and 12-month percent change standard errors annually for the CPI-U. These standard error estimates can be used to construct confidence intervals for hypothesis testing. For the latest data, including information on how to use the estimates of standard error, see <https://www.bls.gov/cpi/tables/variance-estimates/home.htm>.

*Nonsampling Errors:* The total nonsampling error of the CPI results from errors in the type of data collected, the methods of collection, the data processing routines, and the estimation processes. The cumulative nonsampling error can be much greater than the sampling error. These errors occur for a variety of reasons, including logistical lags in conducting surveys, and difficulties in defining basic concepts and their operational implementation. Highly trained personnel ensure the comparability of quality of items from period to period; collection procedures are extensively documented, and recurring audits are conducted. The CPI program has an ongoing research and evaluation program in order to identify and implement improvements in the index.

*Sources of Additional Material:* U.S. Bureau of Labor Statistics, <https://www.bls.gov/cpi/overview.htm>; and "BLS Handbook of Methods," Chapter 17, <https://www.bls.gov/opub/hom/pdf/cpihom.pdf>.

## Current Employment Statistics (CES) Program

*Universe, Frequency, and Types of Data:* Monthly survey of approximately 142,000 businesses and government agencies representing approximately 689,000 worksites drawn from a sampling frame of Unemployment Insurance (UI) tax accounts covering roughly 10.0 million establishments, about 97 percent of all employment within the scope of the CES. The active CES sample includes approximately one-third of all nonfarm payroll employees in the

50 states and the District of Columbia. A semiannual update is performed each summer to select units from the population of business openings and other units not previously eligible for selection. The CES collects data on employment, hours, and earnings at detailed industry levels. The CES series are estimates of nonfarm wage and salary jobs, not of employed persons; an individual with 2 jobs is counted twice by the payroll survey. The CES excludes employees in agriculture and private households, and the self-employed.

*Type of Data Collection Operation:* The BLS uses various collection techniques. Data collection centers (DCCs) perform initial enrollment of each firm via telephone, collect the data for several months via Computer Assisted Telephone Interviewing (CATI), and, where possible, transfer respondents to a self-reporting mode such as touch-tone data entry (TDE), facsimile, or internet collection. Very large, multi-establishment firms are often enrolled via personal visit, and thereafter report data via electronic data interchange (EDI). These firms provide electronic files to BLS that include data from all their worksites. All firms with 1,000 or more employees are asked to participate in the survey, as is a sample of firms across all employment sizes. When firms are rotated into the sample, they are retained for 2 years or more.

*Data Collection and Imputation Procedures:* Each month, respondents extract the employment, hours, and earnings data from their payroll records and submit it to the BLS. Data are collected for the pay period that includes the 12th of each month. BLS staff prepare national estimates of employment, hours, and earnings. State agencies cooperate with the BLS to develop state and metropolitan area estimates.

*Estimates of Sampling Errors:* The magnitude of sampling error, or variance, is directly related to the size of the sample and the percentage of universe coverage achieved by the sample. The establishment survey sample covers over one-third of total universe employment; this yields a relatively small variance on the total nonfarm estimates. Information on measurements of error associated with sample estimates are available online under "CES Technical Notes" at <http://www.bls.gov/ces/home.htm>.

*Total Error:* The benchmark error is used as a proxy measure of total error for the CES survey, and it represents the difference between two employment estimates derived from separate statistical processes (the CES sample process, and the Unemployment Insurance administrative process), and thus reflects the sum of the errors present in each program. For total nonfarm employment over the past 10 years, absolute percentage benchmark error has averaged 0.2 percent, with an absolute range from less than 0.05 percent to 0.7 percent.

*Sources of Additional Material:* U.S. Bureau of Labor Statistics, "BLS Handbook of Methods," Chapter 2, <https://www.bls.gov/opub/hom/pdf/ces-20110307.pdf>; and Current Employment Statistics, "Technical Notes," <http://www.bls.gov/web/empsit/cestn.htm>.

## National Compensation Survey (NCS)

*Universe, Frequency, and Types of Data:* The NCS is an establishment-based survey that provides comprehensive measures of 1) employer costs for employee compensation, including wages and salaries, and benefits, 2) compensation trends, and 3) the availability of and/or employee participation in employer-provided benefits, with an emphasis on health insurance and retirement benefits. The NCS includes establishments in private industry and in state and local government; major exclusions are workers in federal and quasi-federal agencies, military personnel, agricultural workers, workers in private households, the self-employed, and unpaid workers. The NCS releases data through the quarterly Employment Cost Index and the Employer Costs for Employee Compensation, and annual reports on employee benefits, by various employer and/or employee characteristics, including industry, occupational group, labor union status, and other characteristics.

*Sample Selection:* The total sample is selected in two stages, one for establishments, and one for occupations within the sample of establishments. The establishment sample has three rotation groups, one for private industry, one for state and local government, and one for the aerospace industry. Government establishments are rotated approximately every 10 years, and all others are rotated every 3 years (except during the government rotation year). Field economists use a probability selection of occupations method to select jobs to sample, then match employees with those jobs, and classify workers according to their duties rather than specific job title. NCS data releases include the number of establishments and occupations covered in the survey.

*Data Collection and Imputation Procedures:* BLS field economists use personal visits, mail, telephone, and email, to obtain data from NCS survey respondents; they do not use paper and online surveys, but rather use conversational interviews and descriptive documents. Updated data are collected quarterly. Imputation is done for individual benefits. To address the problems of nonresponse and missing data, the NCS adjusts the weights of the remaining establishments and imputes missing values; missing values for an initially responding establishment are replaced by values from the original interview; missing values for an item are replaced by values derived from establishments with similar characteristics.

*Estimates of Sampling Error:* NCS uses standard errors to evaluate published series. A discussion of sampling and nonsampling errors, as well as links to more detailed data on the reliability of estimates from the NCS, are available at <https://www.bls.gov/opub/hom/ncs/calculation.htm>.

*Nonsampling Errors:* Data collection and processing errors are mitigated primarily through quality assurance programs that include the use of data collection reinterviews, observed interviews, computer edits of the data, and a systematic professional review of the data.

*Sources of Additional Material:* Bureau of Labor Statistics, Handbook of Methods, "National Compensation Measures," <https://www.bls.gov/opub/hom/ncs/home.htm>.

## Producer Price Index (PPI)

*Universe, Frequency, and Types of Data:* Monthly survey of producing companies to determine price changes of all commodities and services produced in the United States for sale in commercial transactions. Price changes are from the perspective of the seller. Covers nearly all industries in the goods-producing sectors, including agriculture, fishing, forestry, mining, and manufacturing, and over 70 percent of the service sector's output as measured by revenue reported in the Economic Census. Domestic production of goods for the military is included, as are goods shipped between establishments owned by the same company. The BLS releases each month about 10,000 PPIs for individual products and groups of products. PPIs are organized into three main sets: (1) Final demand-Intermediate demand (FD-ID) indexes, (2) commodity indexes, and (3) indexes for the net output of industries and their products.

*Type of Data Collection Operation:* PPIs are based on selling prices reported by establishments of all sizes selected by probability sampling, with the probability of selection proportionate to employment size. Individual items and services from these firms are chosen by disaggregation, a process to select items based on their proportionate value to the manufacturer's overall revenue; further steps involve the item's characteristics. BLS periodically updates the PPI sample of survey respondents to reflect current conditions when the structure, membership, technology, or product mix of an industry shifts significantly, and to spread reporting burden among smaller firms. Results of these resampling efforts are incorporated into the PPI with the release of data for January and July. Participation in the PPI program is voluntary. The BLS encourages companies to supply actual transaction prices at the time of shipment to minimize the use of list prices. Each month approximately 100,000 prices are solicited from roughly 25,000 reporters. Establishments report prices via a secure website.

*Data Collection and Imputation Procedures:* Prices are effective on the Tuesday of the week containing the 13th day of the month. Missing prices are estimated by those received for similar products or services. The current standard base period for most commodity-oriented PPI series is 1982, but many indexes that began after 1982 are based on the month of their introduction. The FD-ID indexes typically have a reference base of November 2009 = 100. All unadjusted PPIs are routinely subject to revision only once, 4 months after their original publication, to reflect late reports and corrections by company respondents. Once revised, indexes are considered final.

*Estimates of Sampling Error:* The Producer Price Index (PPI) program began publishing variance estimates in 2016 based on data for 2015. PPI intends to publish variance estimates on an annual basis. The median absolute value of the percent change is provided as the reference statistic and the corresponding median standard error is provided as the measure of variance. A report on variance estimates for PPI price changes is available online at <https://www.bls.gov/ppi/ppi_variance_methodology.htm>.

*Nonsampling Errors:* Nonsampling error occurs in many forms, but whatever the form, nonsampling error does not affect the spread of the sample estimates. Nonsampling error can, however, cause the estimate to be consistently higher (or lower) than the true population estimate. When this occurs, it is called the bias of a sample estimate. The PPI program, along with other programs at BLS, analyzes estimates for the presence of bias and mitigates nonsampling error by conducting research into the population of interest, by clearly documenting data collection procedures, and by performing quality checks throughout the collection process.

*Sources of Additional Material:* U.S. Bureau of Labor Statistics, PPI overview available online at <https://www.bls.gov/ppi/ppiover.htm>, methodology online at <http://www.bls.gov/ppi/methodology.htm>; and more information at <https://www.bls.gov/ppi/ppi_variance_methodology.htm>.

# BOARD OF GOVERNORS OF THE FEDERAL RESERVE SYSTEM

## Survey of Consumer Finances (SCF)

*Universe, Frequency, and Types of Data:* Triennial sample survey of families on their finances. The 2016 Survey of Consumer Finances is the most recent survey available. The survey collects detailed data on the composition of family balance sheets, pensions, income, the terms of loans, and relationships with financial institutions. It also gathers information on the employment history and pension rights of the survey respondent and the spouse or partner of the respondent. Data include respondent demographic characteristics. In this survey a given household is divided into a primary economic unit (the family), and everyone else in the household. The primary economic unit is the economically dominant single person or couple (married or cohabitating) and all other persons in the household who are financially interdependent with the economically dominant person or couple. The primary economic unit is used as the reference family. To stay up-to-date with new developments in family finances, the SCF underwent a redesign in 2016. Despite the changes, the core questionnaire remains comparable with earlier surveys. The goals of the redesign were to improve the collection of data on new developments key to family finances, improve coordination and integration with other household surveys and administrative data sources, reduce respondent burden, and generally improve upon the quality of data collected.

*Type of Data Collection Operation:* The SCF employs a sample design consisting of two parts: a standard, geographically based random sample and a special list sample that oversamples relatively wealthy families under strict rules to provide confidentiality and give potential respondents the right to refuse participation. Weights are used to combine information from the two samples to make estimates for the full population. In the 2016 survey, 6,254 families were interviewed, and in the 2013 survey, 6,026 were interviewed. Of the 6,254 interviews completed for the 2016 SCF, 4,754 were from the area-probability sample, and 1,500 were from the list sample; for 2013, 4,568 were from the area-probability sample, and 1,458 were from the list sample. In both the 2013 and 2016 surveys, about 65 percent of the households selected for the area-probability sample and about a third of the list sample completed interviews.

*Data Collection and Imputation Procedures:* National Opinion Research Center (NORC) at the University of Chicago has collected data for the survey since 1992. The majority of interviews for the SCF are conducted in person. Interviews are conducted via telephone if more convenient for respondents. Adjustments for nonresponse are made through multiple imputation of unanswered questions and through weighting adjustments based on data used in the sample design for families that refused participation.

*Estimates of Sampling Error:* The SCF attempts to reduce sampling error by designing the sample to reduce important sources of variability. Sampling error is estimated using replication methods. Replication methods draw samples, called replicates, from the set of actual respondents, and compute weights for all cases in each of the replicates.

*Nonsampling Errors:* Proper training and monitoring of interviewers, careful design of questionnaires, and systematic editing of the resulting data were used to control for nonsampling errors.

*Sources of Additional Material:* Board of Governors of the Federal Reserve System, "Changes in U.S. Family Finances from 2013 to 2016: Evidence from the Survey of Consumer Finances," *Federal Reserve Bulletin*, September 2017, <https://www.federalreserve.gov/econres/scfindex.htm>.

# U.S. CENSUS BUREAU

## 2012 Economic Census

*Universe, Frequency, and Types of Data:* Conducted every 5 years to obtain data on number of establishments, number of employees, payroll, total sales/receipts/revenue, and other industry-specific statistics. The universe is all establishments with paid employees, excluding agriculture, forestry, fishing and hunting, and government. (Nonemployer Statistics, discussed separately, covers establishments without paid employees.) For the 2012 Economic Census, 3.9 million businesses received economic census forms. The 2007 Economic Census used a cutoff of 5,000 population or jobs to identify the economic places valid for publication. The 2012 Economic Census reduced the cutoff to 2,500, resulting in nearly 5,000 new places to be published in the Census. See also <https://www.census.gov/programs-surveys/economic-census/about.html>.

*Type of Data Collection Operation:* For most economic census sectors and programs, all large- and medium-size firms and all multi-establishment firms were sent report forms to be completed for each of their establishments. For most sectors and programs, report forms were also mailed to a sample of small employers (those with paid employees). This sample consists of single-establishment firms with payroll below a specified cut-off. The cut-off and sampling rate varies by economic census sector, industry, and geography. Data for firms with no paid employees were obtained from administrative records of other federal agencies.

*Data Collection and Imputation Procedures:* Mail questionnaires were used, with both mail and telephone follow-ups for nonrespondents. Businesses also had the option to respond electronically. Data for nonrespondents and for small employer firms not mailed a questionnaire

were obtained from administrative records of other federal agencies, or imputed.

*Estimates of Sampling Error:* No measures of sampling variability are provided for sample-based estimates derived from the economic census, except for the construction sector. For additional information about sampling errors, see the methodology text for the sector of interest. Estimates of sampling error for construction industries are included with the data as published on the Census Bureau website.

*Nonsampling Errors:* Nonsampling errors may be attributed to an inability to identify all cases in the actual universe; definition and classification difficulties; differences in interpretation of questions; errors in recording or coding data; and other errors of collection, response, coverage, processing, and estimation for missing or misreported data. Nonsampling error is not measured, but the Census Bureau employs quality control measures to reduce the effects of errors.

*Sources of Additional Material:* U.S. Census Bureau, see website <https://www.census.gov/EconomicCensus>.

## American Community Survey (ACS)

*Universe, Frequency, and Types of Data:* Nationwide survey of approximately 3.54 million households in the U.S. and 36,000 households in Puerto Rico, per year, to obtain data about demographic, social, economic, and housing characteristics of housing units and the people residing in them. It covers the household population and, beginning in 2006, also includes the group quarter population living in correctional facilities, skilled-nursing homes, military barracks, college residence halls, and other group quarters. Sampling frames are drawn from the Census Bureau's Master Address File.

*Sample Selection:* Housing unit address sampling is performed twice a year in both August and January. First-phase of sampling defines the universe for the second stage of sampling through two steps. First, all addresses that were eligible for the second-phase sampling within the past four years are excluded from eligibility. This ensures that no address is in sample more than once in any 5-year period. The second step is to select a 20 percent systematic sample of "new" units, i.e. those units that have never appeared on a previous Master Address File (MAF) extract. All new addresses are systematically assigned to either the current year or to one of four back-samples. This procedure maintains five equal partitions of the universe. The second-phase sampling is done on the current year's partition and results in approximately 3,540,000 housing unit addresses in the U.S. and 36,000 in Puerto Rico (PR).

Group quarter sampling is performed separately from the housing unit sampling. The sampling begins with separating the small (15 persons or fewer) and the large (more than 15 persons) group quarters. The target sampling rate for both groups is a 2.5% sample of the group quarters population. Data are collected from approximately 20,000 group quarters and 195,000 sample residents per year.

*Data Collection Procedures:* The American Community Survey is conducted every month on independent samples. The data collection operation for housing units (HUs) consists of four modes: internet, mail, telephone, and personal visit. For most housing units, the first phase includes a mailed request to respond by internet, followed later by an option to complete a paper questionnaire and return it by mail. If no response is received by mail or internet, the Census Bureau follows up with computer-assisted telephone interviewing (CATI) when a telephone number is available. If a telephone interview is not successful, then the ACS attempts a personal visit and interview. Mailable addresses with neither a response to the mail-out nor a telephone interview are sampled at a rate of 1 in 2, 2 in 5, or 1 in 3 based on the expected rate of completed interviews at the tract level. Unmailable addresses are sampled at a rate of 2 in 3. Those addresses selected through this process are assigned to field representatives (FRs), who visit the addresses, verify their existence, determine their occupancy status, and conduct interviews.

Collection of group quarters data is conducted primarily through FR interviews. Field representatives' methods include completing the questionnaire while speaking to the resident in person or over the telephone, or leaving paper questionnaires for residents to complete for themselves and then pick up later. This last option is used for data collection in federal prisons. If needed, a personal interview can be conducted with a proxy, such as a relative or guardian.

*Imputation Procedures:* The Census Bureau uses two principal methods to impute missing or inconsistent data: assignment and allocation. Assignment involves looking at other data as reported by the respondent to fill in missing responses. For example, if sex is unknown but the respondent reported giving birth, the assignment is female. Hot deck allocation uses a statistical method to supply missing or inconsistent responses from other housing units or survey respondents with similar characteristics.

*Estimates of Sampling Error:* The data in the ACS products are estimates and can vary from the actual values that would have been obtained by conducting a census of the entire population. The estimates from the chosen sample addresses can also vary from those that would have been obtained from a different set of addresses. This variation causes uncertainty, which can be measured using statistics such as standard errors, margins of error, and confidence intervals. All ACS estimates are accompanied by margins of errors or confidence intervals to assist users.

*Nonsampling Errors:* Other types of errors may occur during any of the various complex operations used to select, collect and process survey data. An important goal of the ACS is to minimize the amount of nonsampling error introduced through coverage issues in the sample list, nonresponse from sample housing units, and transcribing or editing data. One way of accomplishing this is by finding additional sources of addresses, following up on nonrespondents, and maintaining quality control systems.

*Sources of Additional Material:* U.S. Census Bureau, American Community Survey, online at <http://www.census.gov/programs-surveys/acs/>; and American Community Survey Accuracy of the

Data documents available on the internet at <http://www.census.gov/programs-surveys/acs/methodology.html>.

## American Housing Survey (AHS)

*Universe, Frequency, and Types of Data:* Conducted biennially in odd numbered years to obtain data on occupied or vacant housing units in the United States (group quarters are excluded). The AHS provides information on a wide range of "core" housing subjects, including size and composition of the nation's housing inventory, vacancies, fuel usage, physical condition of housing units, characteristics of occupants, equipment breakdowns, home improvements, mortgages and other housing costs, persons eligible for and beneficiaries of assisted housing, home values, and characteristics of recent movers. Beginning 2011, the AHS includes topical supplements. For the 2017 survey, the AHS topics include commuting to work, evictions, delinquent payment and notices, and emergency and disaster preparedness. In 2015 AHS, the Department of Housing and Urban Development (HUD) and the Census Bureau selected a integrated national sample that includes a representative sample of the nation, and oversamples of the top 15 metro areas and HUD-assisted housing units. Beginning in 2015, the total sample size is about 115,000 housing units. The 2017 AHS sample comprised of 114,860 housing units, including 45,285 units in top 15 metropolitan areas, 29,981 housing units in an additional 10 metropolitan areas, and 5,202 units in a subsidized-renter oversample.

*Type of Data Collection Operation:* Census Bureau interviewers visit or telephone the household occupying each housing unit in the sample. For unoccupied units, they obtain information from landlords, rental agents, or neighbors. The 2015 American Housing Survey underwent a major redesign – a new sample was redrawn, the questionnaire was redesigned, variables were dropped, added or modified, recodes and imputation methods were streamlined, and weighting methodology changed. Tables were redesigned and some estimates may not be comparable with previous years. Information is available online at <https://www.census.gov/programs-surveys/ahs/tech-documentation/def-errors-changes.2015.html>.

*Data Collection:* Housing units participating in the AHS are scientifically selected to represent a cross section of all housing in the nation. The same basic sample of housing units is interviewed every two years until a new sample is selected. The U.S. Census Bureau updates the sample by adding newly constructed housing units and units discovered through coverage improvement efforts. Each housing unit in the AHS sample represents itself and between 450 to 4,000 other units.

*Estimates of Sampling Error:* Error from sampling reflects how estimates from a sample vary from the actual value if all housing units had been interviewed under the same conditions. The AHS provides documentation for users to use to calculate sampling errors. See source website under Technical Documentation, "Accuracy of the Data."

*Nonsampling Errors:* These may arise from a variety of factors, including errors in coverage, nonresponse, missing response, and inaccurate responses, and processing errors. The AHS takes numerous steps to minimize these types of errors.

*Sources of Additional Material:* U.S. Census Bureau, "American Housing Survey, Methodology and other Technical Documentation," <https://www.census.gov/programs-surveys/ahs/tech-documentation.html>; and <https://www.census.gov/programs-surveys/ahs/about/methodology.html>.

## Annual Survey of Public Employment and Payroll, and Census of Governments

*Universe, Frequency, and Types of Data:* A sample survey is conducted annually except in years ending in '2' and '7', when a census of all state and local governments is done. Covers employees of all agencies of the 50 state governments, the District of Columbia, and about 90,000 local governments (i.e., counties, municipalities, townships, special districts, and school districts). The survey measures the number of state and local government employees and their gross payrolls for the pay period including March 12. The annual survey provides state and local government data on full-time and part-time employment, part-time hours worked, full-time equivalent employment, and payroll statistics by governmental function. The census obtains data on how governments are organized, employment and payroll, and government finances. The Census Bureau collected and published annual survey data on federal government employees and payroll through the year 2014. The 2012 Census of Governments includes civilian employment and payroll for the federal government (except for the central, national security, and defense intelligence agencies), as well as for state and local government; the 2017 census covers employment at the state and local government level only.

*Type of Data Collection Operations:* Census Bureau staff compiled Federal Government data from records of the U.S. Office of Personnel Management. Most state governments provide data from central payroll records for all or most of their agencies/institutions. Data for agencies and institutions for the remaining state governments were obtained by mail canvass questionnaires. Local governments were also canvassed using a mail questionnaire. However, elementary and secondary school system data in Delaware, Florida, and North Dakota were supplied by special arrangements with the state education agency in each of these states. All respondents receiving the mail questionnaire had the option of completing the survey online.

*Editing Procedures:* Editing ensures survey data are accurate, complete, and consistent. Efforts are made at all phases of collection, processing, and tabulation to minimize errors. Although some edits are built into the internet data collection instrument and the data entry programs, the majority of edits are performed after the case has been loaded into the Census Bureau's database. Edits consist primarily of two types: consistency, and a ratio of the current years reported value to the prior year's value. Additional checks are made by comparing data from the Annual Finance Survey to data reported on the Annual Survey of Public Employment and Payroll to verify that employees reported on the Annual Survey of Public Employment and Payroll at a particular function

have a corresponding expenditure on the Finance Survey. The edit results are reviewed by analysts and adjusted when needed. When the analyst is unable to resolve or accept the edit failure, contact is made with the respondent to verify or correct data.

*Imputation Procedures:* For general purpose governments, school districts, and special districts, imputations were based on recent historical data from either a prior year annual survey or the most recent Census of Governments, as available. These data were adjusted by a growth rate that was determined by the growth of units that were similar (in size, geography, and type of government) to the nonrespondent. If no recent historical data were available, imputations were based on the data from a randomly selected donor that was similar to the nonrespondent.

*Estimates of Sampling Error:* Census data are not subject to sampling and do not contain sampling error. Data from the annual survey are subject to sampling error. The estimated coefficients of variation (CVs), which are provided for each estimate in data tables available online, are an estimate of this sampling variability. The CVs are expressed as percentages. The CV is the ratio of the standard error to the expectation of the estimate. State government employment and payroll data are not subject to sampling error. Consequently, state and local government aggregates for individual states are more reliable statistically than the local government only estimates.

*Nonsampling Errors:* Sample data are subject to nonsampling errors such as inability to obtain data for every variable from all units in the sample, inaccuracies in classification, response errors, misinterpretation of questions, mistakes in keying and coding, and coverage errors. These same errors may be evident in census collections and may affect the Census of Governments data used to adjust the sample during the estimation phase and used in the imputation process.

*Sources of Additional Material:* Census Bureau, Annual Survey of Public Employment and Payroll (ASPEP), <https://www.census.gov/programs-surveys/apes/technical-documentation.html>.

## Annual Survey of State and Local Government Finances

*Universe, Frequency, and Types of Data*: In the years ending in "2" and "7," the Census Bureau conducts a census of the entire universe of all 50 state governments, the District of Columbia, and approximately 90,000 local governments (counties, cities, townships, special districts, and school districts). In intervening years, the Bureau conducts an annual survey of a sample of state and local governments. The survey collects data on government revenue (including taxes, charges, interest, and other earnings), expenditures by function and accounting category, debt, and financial assets by type. Data are published about 20 months after data collection. Revisions are made for the next 2 years.

*Type of Data Collection Operations:* Data are collected via mail canvass, internet, and central collection from State sources. Collection methods vary by state and type of government. Reviews of government accounting records provide data for most state government agencies and some of the largest and most complex county and municipal governments. Twenty-seven states have central collection arrangements with the Census Bureau; these states get special mailings for all or specific types of government units within that state. In some cases, data could be obtained from state Comprehensive Annual Financial Reports. Data edits were built into the internet data collection instrument and data entry programs, and include consistency edits, historical and current year ratio edits, and balance checks.

*Imputation Procedures:* Imputations for nonresponding general purpose governments are based on recently reported historical data from either a prior year annual survey or the most recent census, adjusted by a growth rate. If no historical data are available, or the unit has not responded in over five years, data from a randomly selected similar unit are adjusted by the ratio of the populations of the non-responding and randomly selected donor governments. The imputations for non-responding special districts are done similarly. If prior year reported data are available, the prior year data for the non-respondent are adjusted by a growth rate that is determined from reporting units that are similar to the non-respondent.

*Estimates of Sampling Error:* State government financial statistics result from a complete canvass of all state government agencies, and therefore do not have an associated measure of sampling error. Data from local governments come from a sample of local governments, and are subject to sampling variability. Data files include the coefficients of variation that can be used to derive the standard error of the estimates.

*Nonsampling Errors:* The estimates are subject to inaccuracies in classification, response, and processing. Efforts were made at all phases of collection, processing, and tabulation to minimize errors. Data are also subject to errors from imputations for missing data, errors from misreported data, errors from miscoding, and difficulties in identifying every unit that should be included in the report. Every effort was made to keep such errors to a minimum through examining, editing, and tabulating the data reported by government officials.

*Sources of Additional Material:* Census Bureau, State and Local Government Finances, <https://www.census.gov/programs-surveys/gov-finances/technical-documentation.html>.

## Annual Survey of Manufactures (ASM)

*Universe, Frequency, and Types of Data:* The Annual Survey of Manufactures is a sample survey of approximately 50,000 establishments conducted annually, except for years ending in '2' and '7' when the survey is included in the Economic Census, for all manufacturing establishments having one or more paid employees. Sample selection is currently made from the 2012 Economic Census - Manufacturing universe, which contains approximately 294,600 active manufacturing establishments. The purpose of the ASM is to provide key intercensal measures of manufacturing activity, products, and location for the public and private sectors. The ASM provides statistics on employment, payroll, worker hours, payroll supplements, cost of materials, value added by manufacturing, capital expenditures, inventories, and energy consumption. It also provides estimates of value of shipments for 1,390 seven-digit NAICS product classes.

*Type of Data Collection Operation:* The ASM is conducted by mail with telephone and mail follow-ups of nonrespondents. The ASM surveys approximately 50,000 establishments; about 15,600 establishments are selected with certainty, and the remaining establishments are selected with probability proportional to a composite measure of establishment size. The sample universe is updated from two sources: Internal Revenue Service administrative records are used to include new single-establishment manufacturers, and the Company Organization Survey identifies new establishments of companies with multiple establishments.

*Imputation Procedures:* Imputation (for all nonresponse items) is based on previous year reports, or for new establishments in the survey, on industry averages.

*Estimates of Sampling Error:* Statistics for the industry groups and industries, and product shipments include estimated relative standard errors. Relative standard errors vary by industry and product category.

*Nonsampling Errors:* Includes errors due to collection, reporting, and transcription errors, many of which are corrected through computer and clerical checks.

*Sources of Additional Material:* Census Bureau, Annual Survey of Manufactures Methodology, <http://www.census.gov/programs-surveys/asm/technical-documentation/methodology.html>.

## Census of Population and Housing

*Universe, Frequency, and Types of Data:* Complete count of the U.S. population conducted every 10 years since 1790. Data obtained on number and characteristics of people in the United States, U.S. outlying territories, and Federally affiliated Americans overseas.

*Data Collection and Imputation Procedures:* In 1980, 1990, and 2000, mail questionnaires were used extensively with personal interviews in the remainder. Extensive telephone and personal follow-up for nonrespondents was done in the censuses. For the 2010 Census, 130 million households received a census form. Questionnaires were mailed and hand-delivered, and for nonresponding households, census workers made personal visits to conduct a census count. Imputations, which were needed most often when an entry for a given item was missing, included three general procedures known as assignments, allocations, and substitution, which all in one form or another use values or entries that were consistent for the person or housing unit in question.

*Estimates of Sampling Error:* Sampling errors for data are estimated for all items collected by sample and vary by characteristic and geographic area. The coefficients of variation (CVs) for national and state estimates are generally very small.

*Nonsampling Errors:* Since 1950, evaluation programs have been conducted to provide information on the magnitude of some sources of nonsampling errors such as response bias and undercoverage in each census. Results from the evaluation program for the 1990 census indicated that the estimated net undercoverage amounted to about 1.61 percent of the total resident population. Census 2000 had a national overcount of 0.49 percent (0.20 percent standard error) for the household population. For the 2010 Census, the Census Coverage Measurement Program found a net overcount of 0.01 percent (0.14 percent standard error) of the resident population.

*Sources of Additional Material:* U.S. Census Bureau, *The Coverage of Population in the 1980 Census,* PHC80-E4; *Content Reinterview Study: Accuracy of Data for Selected Population and Housing Characteristics as Measured by Reinterview,* PHC80-E2; *1980 Census of Population,* Vol. 1, (PC80-1), Appendixes B, C, and D. *Content Reinterview Survey: Accuracy of Data for Selected Population and Housing Characteristics as Measured by Reinterview,* 1990, CPH-E-1; *Effectiveness of Quality Assurance, CPH-E-2; Programs to Improve Coverage in the 1990 Census,* 1990, CPH-E-3. Documentation regarding the 2010 Census is available online at <https://www.census.gov/newsroom/releases/archives/2010_census/press-kits/> and <https://www.census.gov/programs-surveys/decennial-census/technical-documentation.html>.

## County Business Patterns

*Universe, Frequency, and Types of Data:* County Business Patterns is an annual series that contains data on number of establishments, number of employees, and first quarter and annual payrolls, by detailed industry and geographic level. Data cover over 6 million single-unit establishments and 1.8 million multi-unit establishments, and are available by geographic area (state, county, and metropolitan areas), 6-digit NAICS industry, legal form of organization (U.S. and state only), and employment size class. Most industries are covered; excluded are crop and animal production; rail transportation; U.S. Postal Service; pension, health, welfare, and vacation funds; trusts, estates, and agency accounts; private households; and public administration. CBP also excludes most establishments reporting government employees.

*Type of Data Collection Operation:* Most basic data items are extracted from the Census Bureau's Business Register, a database of all known employer companies. The Company Organization Survey provides individual establishment data for companies that operate 2 or more units (multi-establishment companies). Data for single establishment companies are obtained from various Census Bureau programs, such as the Economic Census, Annual Survey of Manufactures, and Current Business Surveys, as well as from administrative records of the Internal Revenue Service, the Social Security Administration, and the Bureau of Labor Statistics.

*Estimates of Sampling Error:* Payroll and employment data are not subject to sampling error.

*Nonsampling Errors:* The data are subject to nonsampling errors, such as inability to identify all cases in the universe; definition and classification difficulties; differences in interpretation of questions; errors in recording or coding the data obtained; and estimation of employers who

reported too late to be included in the tabulations and for records with missing or misreported data. Employment data are missing from approximately 6.5 percent of incoming administrative payroll records. Missing employment and payroll data are imputed by examining employment and payroll patterns for various time periods.

*Sources of Additional Material:* U. S. Census Bureau, County Business Patterns, <http://www.census.gov/programs-surveys/cbp/about.html> and internet site <http://www.census.gov/programs-surveys/cbp/technical-documentation/methodology.html>.

## Current Population Survey (CPS)

*Universe, Frequency, and Types of Data:* Nationwide monthly sample of approximately 60,000 households designed primarily to produce national and state estimates of labor force and other characteristics of the civilian noninstitutionalized population 15 years of age and older, including sex, age, race, marital status, educational attainment, and family structure. In addition to the monthly survey, each March the CPS produces the Annual Social and Economic (ASEC) Supplement, which contains the basic monthly demographic and labor force data covered by the CPS, plus additional data on work experience, income, health insurance coverage, poverty, receipt of noncash benefits, and migration.

*Type of Data Collection Operation:* Multistage probability sample that currently includes 60,000 households from 824 sample areas. Sample size increased in some states to improve data reliability for those areas on an average annual basis. A continual sample rotation system is used. Households are in sample for 4 months, out for 8 months, and in for 4 more. The CPS questionnaire is a computerized document that is administered by Census Bureau field representatives across the country through both personal and telephone interviews. One person, usually the person who owns or rents the housing unit, generally responds for all eligible members in a household regarding activities during the prior week (the week including the 12th of the month).

*Imputation Procedures:* The CPS makes imputations for missing and inconsistent data items. The CPS uses 3 imputation methods for item nonresponse: relational imputation, which infers the missing value from other characteristics on the person's record or within the household; longitudinal edits for most of the labor force edits, as appropriate; and "hot deck" allocation, a method of assigning a missing value from a record with similar characteristics, which is the hot deck. Hot decks are defined by variables such as age, race, and sex.

*Estimates of Sampling Error:* Sufficient sample is allocated to maintain, at most, a 1.9 percent coefficient of variation on national monthly estimates of unemployment, assuming a 6 percent unemployment rate. This translates into a change of 0.2 percentage point in the unemployment rate being significant at a 90 percent confidence level. For each of the 50 States and for the District of Columbia, the design maintains a coefficient of variation of at most 8 percent on the annual average estimate of unemployment, assuming a 6 percent unemployment rate.

*Nonsampling Errors:* Nonsampling errors in surveys can be attributed to many sources. The full extent of nonsampling error is unknown, but special studies have been conducted to quantify some sources of nonsampling error in the CPS. The CPS employs numerous measures to reduce nonsampling error.

*Sources of Additional Material:* U.S. Census Bureau and Bureau of Labor Statistics, *Current Population Survey: Design and Methodology*, (Technical Paper 66), online at <http://www.census.gov/prod/2006pubs/tp-66.pdf>; and internet site <http://www.census.gov/programs-surveys/cps/technical-documentation.html>.

## Foreign Trade—Export Statistics

*Universe, Frequency, and Types of Data:* Export statistics cover goods valued at more than $2,500 per commodity shipped by individuals and organizations (including exporters, freight forwarders, and carriers) from the U.S. to other countries. Data are compiled in terms of commodity classification, quantities, values, shipping weights, method of transportation (air or vessel), state of (movement) origin, customs district, customs port, country of destination, and whether contents are domestic goods or reexports. Data are continuously compiled and processed. Documents are collected as shipments depart, and processed on a flow basis. Reports summarize shipments made during calendar months, quarters, and years. Statistics are reported monthly approximately 35 days after the end of the reference month and on a year-to-date basis.

*Type of Data Collection Operation:* A full compilation (i.e., a "census") of commodity exports, plus U.S. Census Bureau estimates of low-valued exports and Bureau of Economic Analysis (BEA) estimates of trade in services. Statistics for exported goods transactions are compiled from three sources: Shipper's Export Declaration documents filed with Customs and Border Protection (CBP) and sent to the U.S. Census Bureau (3 percent of all transactions), comparable data in electronic form submitted directly by exporters and their agents (63 percent), and special computer tapes from Canada for U.S. exports to Canada (34 percent). Estimates are made for low-value exports by country of destination, and based on bilateral trade patterns. Statistics for U.S. exports to Canada are based on import documents filed with Canadian agencies and forwarded to the U.S. Census Bureau under a 1987 data exchange agreement. Under this agreement, each country eliminated most cross-border export documents; maintains detailed statistics on cross-border imports; exchanges monthly files of cross-border import statistics; and publishes exchanged statistics in place of previously compiled export statistics.

*Estimates of Sampling Error:* Not applicable.

*Nonsampling Errors:* The goods data are a complete enumeration of electronic export information (EEI) reported in the automated export system (AES) and are not subject to sampling errors, but they are subject to several types of nonsampling errors. Quality assurance procedures are performed at every stage of collection, processing and tabulation; however the data are still subject to several types of nonsampling errors. The most significant of these include reporting errors, undocumented shipments, timeliness, data capture errors, and errors in the estimation of low-valued transactions.

*Sources of Additional Material:* Foreign Trade Statistics Overview, <http://www.census.gov/foreign-trade/about/index.html>.

## Foreign Trade—Import Statistics

*Universe, Frequency, and Types of Data:* The import statistics consist of goods valued at more than $2,000 per commodity shipped by individuals and organizations (including importers and customs brokers) into the U.S. from other countries. Data are compiled in terms of commodity classification, quantities, values, shipping weights, methods of transportation (air or vessel), duties collected, unit prices, and market share, country of origin, customs district, customs port, import charges and duties. Data are continuously compiled and processed. Documents are collected as shipments arrive and processed on a flow basis. Reports summarize shipments made during calendar months and years. Statistics are reported monthly approximately 35 days after the end of the reference month and on a year-to-date basis.

*Type of Data Collection Operation:* A full compilation (i.e., a census) is taken of import shipments, plus U.S. Census Bureau estimates of low-valued imports and Bureau of Economic Analysis (BEA) estimates of trade in services. Statistics for imported goods shipments are compiled from the records filed with Customs and Border Protection (CBP), usually within 10 days after the merchandise enters the United States. Estimates are made for low-value shipments by country of origin, based on previous bilateral trade patterns and periodically updated. Statistics for over 95 percent of all commodity transactions are compiled from records filed electronically with CBP and forwarded as computer tape files to the U.S. Census Bureau. Statistics for other transactions are compiled from hard-copy documents filed with CBP and forwarded on a flow basis for U.S. Census Bureau processing.

*Estimates of Sampling Error:* Not applicable.

*Nonsampling Errors:* The goods data are a complete enumeration of documents collected by the U.S. Customs and Border Protection and are not subject to sampling errors, but they are subject to several types of nonsampling errors. The most significant of these include reporting errors, undocumented shipments, timeliness, data capture errors, and errors in the estimation of low-valued transactions. Quality assurance procedures are performed at every stage of collection, processing, and tabulation.

*Sources of Additional Material:* Foreign Trade Statistics Overview, online at <http://www.census.gov/foreign-trade/about/index.html>.

## Monthly and Annual Retail Trade Survey

*Universe, Frequency, and Types of Data:* The size of the Monthly Retail Trade Survey (MRTS) sample is approximately 13,000 employer firms. Data cover sales at retail stores, and inventories held by retail stores. Statistics are available at the national level only. The Annual Retail Trade Survey (ARTS) uses a sample of approximately 16,500 employer firms in the retail trade sector and electronic commerce sales, and requests data on sales, sales taxes, inventories, purchases, operating expenses, and other financial items. Annual data are published at the industry level, using the North American Industry Classifcation System.

*Data Collection and Imputation Procedures:* Firms for the retail trade surveys come from the Economic Census and the Census Bureau's Business Register. Data are collected by mail questionnaire and the internet, with telephone follow-ups for nonrespondents. Imputation is made for each nonresponse item and each item failing edit checks. For both unit and item nonresponse, a missing value is replaced by a predicted value obtained from an appropriate model for nonresponse. This imputation uses survey data and administrative data as input. In any given month, imputed data amount to about 31 percent of the total monthly retail and food services sales estimate and about 33 percent of the total retail end-of-month inventory estimate. For the annual survey, imputed data amount to about 8 percent of the total retail sales and food services estimate and about 10 percent of the total retail end-of-year inventory estimate. Additional information about the imputation rates for published estimates are available upon request.

*Estimates of Sampling Error:* Estimated CVs and standard errors are included in monthly reports available online at <http://www.census.gov/retail/index.html#mrts>. ARTS data releases include measures of sampling variability.

*Nonsampling Errors:* Nonsampling errors are difficult to measure and can be attributed to many sources: the inclusion of erroneous units in the survey (overcoverage), the exclusion of eligible units from the survey (undercoverage), nonresponse, misreporting, mistakes in recording and coding responses, misinterpretation of questions, and other errors of collection, response, coverage, or processing. Although nonsampling errors are not measured directly, the Census Bureau employs quality control procedures throughout the process to minimize these types of errors.

*Sources of Additional Material:* Census Bureau, Monthly and Annual Retail Trade, <http://www.census.gov/retail/index.html>, <http://www.census.gov/retail/how_surveys_are_collected.html>, and <https://www.census.gov/programs-surveys/arts/technical-documentation/methodology.html>.

## Survey of Construction

*Universe, Frequency, and Types of Data:* The Survey of Construction provides current national and regional statistics on starts, completions, and characteristics of new, privately-owned single-family and multifamily housing units and on sales of new single-family houses. Data collected include start and completion dates, sales date, sales price (single-family houses only), and the physical characteristics of housing units. Survey data are available monthly and annually for housing starts since 1959, for new home sales since 1963, and for completions since 1968. Reported data are for building or sales activity taking place during the applicable reference period. Monthly data collection begins the first day after the reference month and continues through the 7th working day.

*Type of Data Collection Operation:* A multistage probability sample of approximately 900 permit-issuing jurisdictions in the U.S. was selected.

Each month in each of these permit offices, field representatives list and select a sample of permits for which to collect data. To obtain data in areas where building permits are not required, a multistage probability sample of over 70 land areas (census tracts or subsections of census tracts) is selected. All roads in these areas are canvassed and data are collected on all new residential construction found. Sampled buildings are followed up until they are completed (and sold, if for sale), or abandoned. Permits for 1- to 4-unit buildings are sampled at an overall rate of 1 in 50. All permits authorizing buildings with 5 or more housing units in the sampled permit offices are selected.

*Data Collection and Imputation Procedures:* Data are obtained by telephone and/or field visit each month. Contact continues until the project is either completed or abandoned. If a single-family home is not sold by the time of completion, the project is followed until the sale occurs. Each month, interviews are required for about half of the buildings currently being followed up. Nonresponse/undercoverage adjustment factors are used to account for late reported data. Each month, housing starts, completions, and sales estimates derived from this survey are adjusted by the total numbers of authorized housing units (obtained from the Building Permits Survey) to develop national and regional estimates. Estimates are adjusted to reflect variations by region and type of construction, and to account for late reports and houses started or sold before a permit has been issued. Reported data are seasonally adjusted.

*Estimates of Sampling Error:* Data are subject to sampling errors. Estimates of the standard errors have been computed from the sample data for selected statistics. They are presented in the source tables in the form of average relative standard errors (RSEs). The relative standard error equals the standard error divided by the estimated value to which it refers.

*Nonsampling Errors:* Nonsampling errors are attributable to definition problems, differences in interpretation of questions, incorrect reporting, inability to obtain information about all cases in the sample, and processing errors. Although not measured directly, the Census Bureau employs quality control procedures to minimize nonsampling errors.

*Sources of Additional Material:* Census Bureau, Survey of Construction, online at <https://www.census.gov/econ/overview/co0400.html>.

## Nonemployer Statistics

*Universe, Frequency, and Types of Data:* Nonemployer statistics are an annual tabulation of economic data by industry for active businesses without paid employees or payroll, that are subject to federal income taxes, and that have receipts of $1,000 or more ($1 or more for the construction sector). Excluded are corporations and partnerships with over $1 million in receipts (except for service-type industries, maximum is $2 million). Maximum receipts for sole proprietorships depends on industry classification. Data showing the number of firms and receipts by industry are available for the U.S., states, counties, and metropolitan areas. Most types of businesses covered by the Census Bureau's economic statistics programs are included in the nonemployer statistics. Tax-exempt and agricultural-production businesses are excluded from nonemployer statistics.

*Type of Data Collection Operation:* The universe of nonemployer firms is created annually as a byproduct of the Census Bureau's Business Register processing for employer establishments. If a business is active but without paid employees, then it becomes part of the potential nonemployer universe. Industry classification and receipts are available for each potential nonemployer business. These data are obtained primarily from the annual business income tax returns of the Internal Revenue Service (IRS). The potential nonemployer universe undergoes a series of complex processing, editing, and analytical review procedures at the Census Bureau to distinguish nonemployers from employers, and to correct and complete data items used in creating the data tables.

*Estimates of Sampling Error:* Data are tabulated from administrative records, and are not subject to sampling error.

*Nonsampling Errors:* The data are subject to nonsampling errors, such as inability to identify all cases that should be included, difficulties with definitions and classification, errors in recording or coding data, and other coverage and processing errors. The improper inclusion of possible employer establishments in the nonemployer universe is a primary source of nonsampling error. The Census Bureau takes several steps to identify and remove these establishments from the nonemployer universe.

*Sources of Additional Material:* U. S. Census Bureau, Nonemployer Statistics, <https://www.census.gov/programs-surveys/nonemployer-statistics/technical-documentation.html>.

## Service Annual Survey (SAS)

*Universe, Frequency, and Types of Data:* The U.S. Census Bureau conducts the Service Annual Survey (SAS) to provide nationwide estimates of revenues and expenses for most traditional service industries. Estimates are summarized by industry classification based on the North American Industry Classification System (NAICS). Service industries covered by the Service Annual Survey include all or part of the following NAICS sectors: Utilities (NAICS 22); Transportation and Warehousing (NAICS 48-49); Information (NAICS 51); Finance and Insurance (NAICS 52); Real Estate and Rental and Leasing (NAICS 53); Professional, Scientific, and Technical Services (NAICS 54); Administrative and Support and Waste Management and Remediation Services (NAICS 56); Educational Services (NAICS 61); Health Care and Social Assistance (NAICS 62); Arts, Entertainment, and Recreation (NAICS 71); Accommodation and Food Services (NAICS 72); and Other Services, except Public Administration (NAICS 81). Covers taxable firms and firms exempt from Federal income taxes.

*Type of Data Collection Operation:* Questionnaires are mailed in January and request annual data for the prior year. Estimates are published approximately 12 months after the initial survey mailing. The Service Annual Survey estimates are developed from a probability sample of approximately 72,000 employer firms, and administrative records for nonemployers. Service Annual Survey uses a probability sample that is periodically reselected from a universe of firms having paid employees.

The sample includes firms of all sizes and covers both taxable firms and firms exempt from federal income taxes. Updates to the sample are made on a quarterly basis to account for new and closed businesses. Firms without paid employees, or nonemployers, are included in the estimates through imputation and/or administrative records data provided by other federal agencies.

*Estimates of Sampling Error:* Estimates are based on a sample and subject to sampling error. The most recent Service Annual Survey results, including coefficients of variations (CVs), can be found on the internet at <https://www.census.gov/programs-surveys/sas/data/tables.html>. Additional information regarding sampling error may also be found online at <https://www.census.gov/programs-surveys/sas/technical-documentation/methodology.html>.

*Nonsampling Errors:* For both unit and item nonresponse, a missing value is replaced by a predicted value obtained from an appropriate model for nonresponse. The imputation uses survey data and administrative data as input.

*Sources of Additional Material:* U.S. Census Bureau, "Service Annual Survey," <https://www.census.gov/programs-surveys/sas/about.html>.

## Survey of Business Owners (SBO)

*Universe, Frequency, and Types of Data:* The Survey of Business Owners (SBO), conducted every 5 years since 1972 in the years ending in "2" and "7," provides statistics that describe the composition of U.S. businesses by owner characteristics. Data are presented for nonfarm businesses by sex, detailed ethnic and Hispanic group, and veteran status of the owner with 51 percent or more of stock or equity in the business. All U.S. firms with receipts of $1,000 or more, with and without paid employees, which are classified by the North American Industry Classification System (NAICS) codes 11 through 99, are represented, except for the following: NAICS 111, 112, 482, 491, 521, 525, 813, 814, and 92. The SBO collects data on the number of firms, sales and receipts, employment, and annual payroll. Data are presented by industry classifications, detailed geographic area, and size of firm (employment and receipts). Please note that businesses can be tabulated in more than one racial group if the owners report more than one race; Hispanic owned firms may be of any race.

*Type of Data Collection Operation:* The Survey of Business Owners (SBO) sends letters to a random sample of businesses asking recipients to respond to the survey electronically. The list of all firms (or universe) is compiled from a combination of business tax returns and data collections for other economic census reports. The Survey of Business Owners (SBO) is conducted on a company or firm basis rather than an establishment basis. Several methodology changes were made for the 2012 SBO, in comparison to the previous 2007 SBO. The Census Bureau expanded the use of direct data substitution from existing sources, such as the American Community Survey and the decennial Census, to reduce the 2012 SBO sample size to 1.75 million firms from 2.3 million in 2007. The small sample size yielded sufficient quality, reduced overall respondent burden, and reduced costs associated with conducting a mail survey.

Approximately half of the 2012 SBO sample was asked to respond to the survey electronically.

*Data Collection and Imputation Procedures*: The Census Bureau conducted follow-up mailings to nonrespondents, including sending letters to prompt electronic responses and paper forms. For the most recent SBO, responses came from approximately 66.2 percent of the 1.75 million businesses included in the SBO. For 2012 nonrespondents, 2007 data were substituted if available. For other nonrespondents, the Bureau used administrative data, and also imputed gender, ethnicity, race, and veteran status from donor respondents in the same sampling frame with similar characteristics. Imputed data account for approximately 24 percent of the firm count estimates by gender, ethnicity, race, and veteran status, and approximately 21 percent for the estimates of sales.

*Estimates of Sampling Error*: Sampling error is present in these estimates because they are based on the results of a sample survey and not on an enumeration of the entire universe. Relative standard errors for select data items are included in the data tables.

*Nonsampling Errors*: These stem from many sources: inability to obtain information for all cases in the universe, adjustments to the weights of respondents to compensate for nonrespondents, imputation for missing data, data errors and biases, mistakes in recording or keying data, errors in collection or processing, and coverage problems. Explicit measures of the effects of these nonsampling errors are not available. The Census Bureau detects and corrects most operational and data errors through an automated data edit designed to review the data for reasonableness and consistency. Quality control techniques were used to verify that operating procedures were carried out as specified.

*Sources of Additional Materials*: U.S. Census Bureau, Survey of Business Owners, <https://www.census.gov/programs-surveys/sbo/about.html> and <https://www.census.gov/programs-surveys/sbo/technical-documentation.html>

## Annual Survey of Entrepreneurs (ASE)

*Universe, Frequency, and Types of Data*: The Annual Survey of Entrepreneurs (ASE) collects statistics on the characteristics of businesses and their owners with 51 percent or more of stock or equity in the business. The ASE includes all nonfarm businesses with paid employees filing Internal Revenue Service tax forms as individual proprietorships, partnerships, or any type of corporation, with receipts of $1,000 or more. The ASE samples approximately 290,000 employer businesses in operation any time during the survey year. The ASE is conducted on a company or firm basis rather than an establishment basis. The survey produces estimates on the number of firms, sales and receipts, annual payroll, and employment. Data are presented by gender, ethnicity, race, and veteran status of business owners by industry and other business characteristics. The survey covers 20 NAICS industries except for crop and animal production; rail transportation; postal service; monetary authorities-central bank; funds, trusts, and other financial vehicles; religious, grantmaking, civic, professional, and similar organizations;

private households; and public administration. The annual survey is a supplement to the Survey of Business Owners (SBO), which is conducted every 5 years.

*Data Collection and Imputation Procedures*: Businesses selected for the survey receive an initial letter informing the recipients of their requirement to complete the survey as well as instructions on accessing the survey; data collection is electronic only. The ASE does not directly collect receipts, payroll, or employment; payroll and employment figures are derived from administrative sources. Approximately 64.7 percent of the 289,937 businesses in the 2016 ASE sample responded to the survey. Among nonrespondents, if they had participated in the most recent Survey of Business Owners, or a recent ASE, their previous survey response data were substituted in for current data. For the remaining nonrespondents, information was imputed from donor respondents in the same sampling frame with similar characteristics (industry, legal form of organization, geography). Imputed data in the 2016 ASE accounted for approximately 17.7 percent of the firm count estimates by gender, ethnicity, race, and veteran status, and approximately 24.4 percent of the estimates of sales.

*Estimates of Sampling Error*: The estimated relative standard errors and estimated standard errors are included in the data tables; they estimate the sampling variability, and thus measure the precision with which an estimate from the particular sample selected for this survey approximates the average result of all possible samples. Relative standard errors and standard errors are applicable only to those published cells in which sample cases are tabulated. A relative standard error is an expression of the standard error as a percent of the quantity being estimated.

*Nonsampling Errors*: Nonsampling errors are attributable to various sources, including the inability to obtain information for all cases in the universe, imputation for missing data, data errors and biases, mistakes in recording or keying data, errors in collection or processing, and coverage problems. While explicit measures of the effects of these nonsampling errors are not available, adjustments are made to the published relative standard errors to account for errors associated with imputation of missing data. It is believed that most of the important operational and data errors were detected and corrected through an automated data edit designed to review the data for reasonableness and consistency. Quality control techniques were used to verify that operating procedures were carried out as specified.

*Sources of Additional Materials*: U.S. Census Bureau, Annual Survey of Entrepreneurs Methodology online at <https://www.census.gov/programs-surveys/ase/technical-documentation/methodology.html>.

# U.S. DEPARTMENT OF EDUCATION National Center for Education Statistics

## Integrated Postsecondary Education Data Survey (IPEDS), Completions

*Universe, Frequency, and Types of Data:* The IPEDS collects institution-level data from postsecondary institutions across the U.S. on tuition and fees, number and types of degrees and certificates conferred, number of students applying and enrolled, number of employees, financial statistics, graduation rates, student financial aid, and academic libraries. The survey consists of 12 components which are administered across the fall, winter, and spring reporting seasons. Submission of data to IPEDS is mandatory for any institution that participates in or is an applicant for participation in any federal financial assistance program authorized by Title IV of the Higher Education Act of 1965. IPEDS response rates for each component are nearly 100 percent. Close to 7,000 institutions participate in the annual survey.

*Type of Data Collection Operation:* The IPEDS collects data via the internet. As respondents enter data online, the data collection system automatically calculates totals, averages, and percentages, and compares the responses with the previous year's submission for the same institution to ensure the data are consistent. The system also compares data with other related values to ensure consistency of reporting within each survey component and across the data collection program. If data are still missing, analysts conduct imputations to complete the database.

*Imputation Procedures:* Missing data are imputed by using data of similar institutions. With the exception of the Institutional Characteristics component, all items collected in each component were eligible for imputation. Within the Institutional Characteristics component, only cost of attendance and other institutional charges data were eligible for imputation. IPEDS applies a single imputation method for both unit and item nonresponse. The Nearest Neighbor procedure identifies data related to the key statistics of interest for each component (the distance measure), then uses those data to identify a responding institution similar to the nonresponding institution and uses the respondent's data as a substitute for the nonrespondent's missing items.

*Estimates of Sampling Error:* Not applicable.

*Edit Procedures:* The internet-based survey instrument contained edit checks to detect major reporting errors. The system automatically generated percentages and totals for each collection component and compared current responses to data reported the previous year. As edit checks ran, they prompted survey respondents to correct any errors detected by the system. If accurate data failed the edit checks, the survey respondents either confirmed the response or had to explain why the data appeared to be out of the expected data range. The system required all edit checks to be confirmed or explained. In some cases, respondents could contact IPEDS for assistance. IPEDS staff also reviewed data for additional errors and contacted respondents for verification.

*Sources of Additional Material:* U.S. Department of Education, National Center for Education Statistics, IPEDS Technical/Methodological reports, online at <http://nces.ed.gov/pubsearch/getpubcats.asp?sid=010>.

## National Household Education Surveys (NHES) Program

*Universe, Frequency, and Types of Data:* The National Household Education Surveys Program is a system of surveys of the noninstitutionalized civilian population of the United States. NHES surveys have been conducted periodically since 1991 and have varying universes of interest depending on the particular survey. Some surveys are recurring, others are fielded as 1-time surveys. Currently, the four main topics NHES surveys cover are young children's care and education before school, participation in adult training and education, parent involvement in their children's education, and homeschooling. Specific topics covered by each survey are at the NHES website <http://nces.ed.gov/nhes>. Surveys fielded as part of NHES, each universe, and the years they were fielded include:

1  Early Childhood Program Participation—Surveys of parents of a representative sample of children from birth through grade 3, with the specific age groups varying by survey year (1991, 1995, 1999, 2001, 2005, 2012, and 2016).

2  School Readiness—Interviews with parents of a representative sample of 3-7 year-old children (1993 and 1999) and of 3-6 year old children, not yet in kindergarten (2007).

3  Before- and After-School Programs and Activities—Interviews with parents of a representative sample of students in grades K through 8 (1999, 2001, and 2005).

4  School Safety and Discipline—Interviews with a representative sample of students in grades 6-12, their parents, and the parents of a representative sample of students in grades 3-12 (1993).

5  Parent and Family Involvement in Education—Surveys of parents of a representative sample of children age three through grade 12 or in grades K through 12 depending on the survey year (1996, 1999, 2003, 2007, 2012, and 2016). Separate questionnaires are administered for children enrolled in public and private schools, and for children who are home schooled.

6  Adult Education—Interviews with a representative sample of civilian, noninstitutionalized persons aged 16 and older who were not enrolled in grade 12 or below (1991, 1995, 1999, 2001, 2003, and 2005).

7  Civic Involvement—Interviews with representative samples of parents, youth, and adults (1996 and 1999).

8  Household Library Use—Interviews with a representative sample of U.S. households (1996).

9  Adult training and education-survey of adults age 16 to 65 who are not enrolled in high school, focusing on nondegree credentials and work experience programs (2016).

*Data Collection Operation:* NHES typically fields 2 to 3 topical surveys at a time, although the number has varied across its administrations. Surveys are administered in English and in Spanish. From 1991 to 2007, the NHES used telephone interviews to collect data. In 2012, the NHES switched to a mail survey, and samples were developed using household address information for all 50 states and the District of Columbia. The NHES 2016 sample was selected using a 2-stage address-based sampling frame. Black and Hispanic American households were sampled at a higher rate than other households. Data were collected using printed questionnaires mailed to sampled respondents. In order to assess using the internet for future surveys, 35,000 of the 206,000 sampled households in 2016 were ask to complete the survey online. The 2016 NHES received 47,744 responses to the Adult Training and Education survey; responses for the Early Childhood Program Participation Survey covering 5,837 children age 5 and under; and 1,803 responses to the Parent and Family Involvement in Education Survey.

*Estimates of Sampling Error:* Reports presenting NHES data include tables on standard errors.

*Nonsampling Errors:* For each NHES survey, efforts were made to prevent nonsampling errors and errors from bias from occurring and to compensate for them, where possible. For instance, during the survey design phase, cognitive interviews are conducted to assess respondents' knowledge of the survey topics, their comprehension of questions and terms, and the sensitivity of items. Data from the 2016 NHES went through a series of processing procedures to reduce nonsampling errors and also several strategies to assess and reduce the effects of bias.

*Sources of Additional Material:* Please see the NHES website at <http://nces.ed.gov/nhes>; and technical notes and related methodological information in individual NHES reports available online at <https://nces.ed.gov/pubsearch/getpubcats.asp?sid=004>.

# U.S. DEPARTMENT OF JUSTICE, FEDERAL BUREAU OF INVESTIGATION

## Uniform Crime Reporting (UCR) Program

*Universe, Frequency, and Types of Data:* Monthly reports on the number of criminal offenses that become known to law enforcement agencies. More than 18,000 city, university and college, county, state, tribal, and federal law enforcement agencies are eligible to contribute data to the FBI. The UCR Program collects information regarding the violent crimes of murder and nonnegligent manslaughter, rape, robbery, and aggravated assault as well as the property crimes of burglary, larceny-theft, motor vehicle theft, and arson. (Although the FBI classifies arson as a property crime, it does not estimate arson data because of variations in the level of participation by the reporting agencies. Consequently, arson is not included in the property crime estimate.) The program also collects arrest data for the offenses listed above plus 20 offenses that include all other crimes except traffic violations.

*Type of Data Collection Operation:* The UCR Program consists of four data collections: The National Incident-Based Reporting System (NIBRS), the Summary Reporting System (SRS), the Law Enforcement Officers Killed and Assaulted (LEOKA) Program, and the Hate Crime Statistics Program. Crime statistics are based on reports of crime data submitted either directly to the FBI by contributing law enforcement agencies or through cooperating state UCR Programs. States with UCR programs collect data directly from individual law enforcement agencies and forward reports, prepared in accordance with UCR standards, to the FBI. UCR program participation is voluntary. Beginning with the 2013 data collections, all data must be submitted electronically, and after July 2013, the UCR Program no longer accepted paper submissions or the electronic submission of documents (i.e., Portable Document Format files).

*Data Quality Procedures:* The FBI's Crime Statistics Management Unit staff initially review the data to determine adherence to UCR policy, conformance to UCR definitions and principles, and consistency with established statistical methodologies and norms. Before the information is entered into the national database, the CSMU staff use edit functions to ensure that the data meet established standards. If staff find errors or anomalies, they obtain verification and/or correction from the submitting agency/state UCR Program. After the data pass through this first series of checks, the data are uploaded into the national database. Data then undergo a series of multi-layered processes to check for reasonableness, quality, and validity. FBI staff contact data contributors to clarify data submissions that do not pass data quality checks.

*Estimates of Sampling Error:* Not applicable.

*Nonsampling Errors:* Due to computer problems, changes in records management systems, personnel shortages, or a number of other reasons, some agencies cannot provide data for publication.

*Sources of Additional Material:* U.S. Department of Justice, Federal Bureau of Investigation, <https://www.fbi.gov/services/cjis/ucr>; and *Crime in the United States*, annual, *Hate Crime Statistics*, annual, and *Law Enforcement Officers Killed and Assaulted*, annual, <https://www.fbi.gov/services/cjis/ucr/publications>.

# U.S. INTERNAL REVENUE SERVICE, TAX STATISTICS

## Corporation Income Tax Returns

*Universe, Frequency, and Types of Data:* Annual study of unaudited corporation income tax returns, Forms 1120, 1120-F, 1120-L, 1120-PC, 1120-REIT, 1120-RIC, and 1120S, filed by corporations or businesses legally defined as corporations. The IRS Statistics of Income (SOI) Division collects data on corporations by size, industry, total assets, business receipts, deductions, liabilities, net income, income tax liability, tax credits, and other financial data. SOI aggregates these data for C corporations and passthrough entities, such as S corporations. The target population consists of all returns of active corporations organized for profit that are required to file one of the 1120 forms that are part of the SOI study.

*Type of Data Collection Operation:* For the 2014 tax year, the target sample was approximately 117,000 corporate tax returns (including inactive and non-eligible corporations), allocated to sample classes which are based on type of return, and either size of total assets alone or both size of total assets and a measure of income. Sampling rates for sample classes varied from 0.25 percent to 100 percent. The total realized sample for 2014, including inactive and noneligible corporations, is 120,196 returns.

*Data Collection and Imputation Procedures:* Data processing for SOI begins with information already extracted for IRS administrative purposes; over 100 items available from the Business Master File system are checked and corrected as necessary. SOI extracts some 2,500 additional data items from corporate tax returns during processing. After data capture, data go through hundreds of tests for consistency and error resolution. If missing data items are from the balance sheet, then imputation procedures are used. If data for a whole return are missing because the return is unavailable to SOI during the data capture process, imputation procedures are also used in certain cases. Beginning with the Tax Year 2012 sample, only the largest returns with incomplete balance sheets are subject to a balance sheet imputation procedure. The IRS's Statistics of Income (SOI) division performs imputation on an ad hoc basis only.

*Estimates of Sampling Error:* Statistics of Income reports do not directly present the standard error. Instead, the ratio of the standard error to the estimate itself is presented in percentage form. This ratio is called the coefficient of variation (CV). The user of SOI data may multiply an estimate by its CV to recreate the standard error and to construct confidence intervals. Estimated CVs for are published in the Statistics of Income, *Corporation Complete Report.*

*Nonsampling Errors:* These may include coverage errors, processing errors, and nonresponse errors.

*Sources of Additional Material:* U.S. Internal Revenue Service, Statistics of Income, *Corporation Income Tax Returns*, <http://www.irs.gov/uac/SOI-Tax-Stats-Corporation-Tax-Statistics>.

## Individual Income Tax Returns

*Universe, Frequency, and Types of Data:* Annual study of unaudited individual income tax returns, Forms 1040, 1040A, and 1040EZ, filed by U.S. citizens and residents. Data provided on various financial characteristics by size of adjusted gross income, marital status, and by taxable and nontaxable returns.

*Type of Data Collection Operation:* For 2016 tax year, data cover a stratified probability sample of 351,049 returns selected from a total of 151,014,093 returns received during the calendar year 2017. These are mostly returns filed for the 2016 tax year, but might they also include a few for other tax years that the IRS received during the 2017 calendar year. The sample is classified into sample strata based on the larger of total income or total loss amounts, the size of business plus farm receipts, and other criteria such as the potential usefulness of the return for tax policy modeling. Sampling rates for sample strata varied from 0.10 percent to 100 percent.

*Data Collection and Imputation Procedures:* Computer selection of sample of tax return records. Data adjusted and imputed during editing for incorrect, missing, or inconsistent entries to ensure consistency with other entries on return. Adjustments and imputations are based on prior-year data and other available information.

*Estimates of Sampling Error:* Coefficients of variation are available from source tables available at the website indicated below.

*Nonsampling Errors:* Processing errors and errors can arise from the use of tolerance checks for the data.

*Sources of Additional Material:* U.S. Internal Revenue Service, Statistics of Income, *Individual Income Tax Returns* (Publication 1304), annual, <https://www.irs.gov/statistics/soi-tax-stats-individual-income-tax-returns-publication-1304-complete-report>.

## Partnership Income Tax Returns

*Universe, Frequency, and Types of Data:* Annual study of unaudited income tax returns of active partnerships related to financial and tax-related activity and reported on Forms 1065 and 1065B to the IRS. Data are provided by industry, based on the NAICS industry coding used by IRS.

*Type of Data Collection Operation:* Statistics for the 2016 tax year are estimates based on a stratified probability sample of 38,921 returns received during the 2017 calendar year from an overall active population of over 3.76 million. Statistics of Income (SOI) stratified the population into classes based on industry, type of return, size of total assets, and size of certain receipt or income amounts from both ordinary business income (loss) and portfolio income (loss). From these classes, SOI selected returns at various probabilities (from 0.01 percent to 100 percent) and weighted them to represent the total population.

*Data Collection and Imputation Procedures:* The sample of tax return records are selected via computer after data are transcribed by IRS and placed on an administrative file. Data are manually adjusted during editing for incorrect, missing, or inconsistent entries to ensure consistency with other entries on return. Data not available due to regulations are handled with weighting adjustments.

*Estimates of Sampling Error:* Some of the estimated coefficients of variation (the estimated standard error of the total divided by the estimated total) for tax year 2016: number of partnerships, 0.90 percent; number of partners, 2.13 percent; total assets, 0.13 percent; total income, 0.23 percent; total deductions, 0.24 percent; and business receipts, 0.80 percent. For more information, see source below.

*Nonsampling Errors:* The potential exists for coverage error due to unavailable returns; processing errors; and taxpayer reporting errors.

*Sources of Additional Material:* U.S. Internal Revenue Service, Statistics of Income, *Partnership Returns,* <https://www.irs.gov/statistics/soi-tax-stats-partnership-soi-bulletin-articles>; and <https://www.irs.gov/statistics/soi-tax-stats-partnership-statistics>.

## Sole Proprietorship Income Tax Returns

*Universe, Frequency, and Types of Data:* Annual study of unaudited income tax returns of nonfarm sole proprietorships, Form 1040 with business schedules. Data provided on various financial characteristics by industry.

*Type of Data Collection Operation:* Stratified probability sample of 93,107 returns from sole proprietorships for tax year 2016. The sample is classified based on presence or absence of certain business schedules; the larger of total income or loss; size of business plus farm receipts, and other criteria such as the potential usefulness of the return for tax policy modeling. Sampling rates vary from 0.1 percent to 100 percent.

*Data Collection and Imputation Procedures:* Computer selection of sample of tax return records. Data adjusted during editing for incorrect, missing, or inconsistent entries to ensure consistency with other entries on return.

*Estimates of Sampling Error:* Coefficients of variation for tax year 2016 are available in source documentation. In brief, CVs for sole proprietorships, all nonfarm industries are: total business receipts, 0.63 percent; total business deductions, 0.72; depreciation, 1.63 percent; and net income, 0.74 percent.

*Nonsampling Errors:* Processing errors and errors arising from the use of tolerance checks for the data.

*Sources of Additional Material:* U.S. Internal Revenue Service, Statistics of Income, Nonfarm Sole Proprietorship Statistics, <https://www.irs.gov/statistics/soi-tax-stats-nonfarm-sole-proprietorship-statistics>.

# U.S. NATIONAL CENTER FOR HEALTH STATISTICS (NCHS)

## National Health Interview Survey (NHIS)

*Universe, Frequency, and Types of Data:* Since 1957, the NHIS has been a continuous data collection covering the civilian noninstitutional population to obtain information on demographic characteristics, health conditions, injuries, impairments, use of health services, health behaviors, and other health topics. Excluded are persons in long-term care institutions, correctional facilities, and U.S. nationals living abroad; active-duty armed forces personnel are also excluded unless at least one other family member is a civilian eligible for the survey. The NHIS aims to have a sample size (completed interviews) of approximately 35,000 households containing about 87,500 persons. The annual response rate is approximately 70 percent of eligible households in the sample.

*Type of Data Collection Operation:* Trained interviewers from the U.S. Census Bureau visit each selected household and administer the NHIS in person using computer assisted personal interviewing. Follow-up interviews may be conducted via telephone. The core questionnaire remains largely the same each year and has 4 main components: the Household Composition section, the Family Core, the Sample Child Core, and the Sample Adult Core. The Household component collects limited demographic information on all of the individuals living in the household. The Family component collects additional demographic information on each member from each family in the house and collects data on topics such as health status and limitations, injuries, healthcare access and utilization, and health insurance. From each family, one sample adult and one sample child (if any children are present) are randomly selected for data collection. Because some health issues are different for children and adults, the Sample Child Core and the Sample Adult Core questionnaires differ in some items but both collect basic information on health status, health care services, and health behaviors. All eligible adults in a family had the same chance of being selected as the sample adult. A feature of the current sample design is that adults age 65 and older who are black, Hispanic, or Asian have an increased chance of being selected as the sample adult, relative to adults under age 65 and adults age 65 and older who are not black, Hispanic, or Asian. Core questions remain consistent. The NHIS also uses supplements to ask questions on current health topics that change.

*Imputation Procedures:* The computer assisted personal interviewing program incorporated range

and consistency checks of the data. Some missing data items (e.g., race, ethnicity) are imputed using a hot deck imputation value. Sequential regression models are used to create multiple imputation files for family income. Unit nonresponse is compensated for by an adjustment to the survey weights. Since 2004, imputation has been performed for injury and poisoning episodes for which the respondent did not provide sufficient information to determine a month, day, and year of occurrence.

*Estimates of Sampling Error:* Because NHIS data are based on a sample of the population, they are subject to sampling error. Standard errors appear with the data to indicate the reliability of the estimates. Analysts at NCHS generally use the software package SUDAAN® with Taylor series linearization methods to produce standard error estimates and hypothesis test results (such as p values).

*Nonsampling Errors:* Nonsampling errors such as response errors, defective sample frames, nonresponse, and undercoverage, are difficult quantities to measure, but every effort is made to minimize such errors at each step of the NHIS operation.

*Sources of Additional Material:* National Center for Health Statistics, National Health Interview Survey, online at <http://www.cdc.gov/nchs/nhis/about_nhis.htm>. See also <http://www.cdc.gov/nchs/nhis/methods.htm>, and <http://www.cdc.gov/nchs/nhis/data-questionnaires-documentation.htm>.

## National Survey of Family Growth (NSFG)

*Universe, Frequency, and Types of Data:* The National Survey of Family Growth (NSFG) gathers information on family life and planning, marriage and divorce, pregnancy, infertility, use of contraception, and general and reproductive health. The NSFG also collects data on sexual behavior and attraction, and sexual orientation. The NSFG began in 1973 as a periodic survey of women age 15-44 among the civilian noninstitutionalized population. In 2002, the NSFG included men age 15-44. In 2015 the age range covered became 15-49. Beginning 2006, the program switched from periodic surveys to continuous interviewing. The 2011-2013 NSFG conducted in-person interviews with 5,601 women and 4,815 men. The response rates were 72.8 percent for all respondents, 73.4 percent for women, and 72.1 percent for men. The 2013-2015 NSFG included 5,699 interviews with women and 4,506 interviews with men; response rates were 71.2 percent for women and 67.1 percent for men.

*Type of Data Collection Operation:* Survey participation is voluntary. Only one person is interviewed in a selected household. Signed consent is required for minors age 15-17. The NSFG collects data by employing female interviewers to conduct personal interviews using computer-assisted personal interviewing (CAPI). Selected data items are also collected using audio computer-assisted self-interviewing (ACASI). In ACASI, the respondent listens to the questions through headphones, reads them on the screen, or both, and enters the response directly into the computer. This method avoids asking the respondent to give his or her answers to the interviewer, and it has been found to yield more complete reporting of sensitive behaviors.

*Imputation Procedures:* Imputation is the process of assigning answers to cases with missing data. In the NSFG, item imputation is performed on approximately 600 "recoded variables," or "recodes," rather than all of the thousands of variables in the data set. The purposes of imputation are to make the data more complete, more consistent, easier to use, and to reduce bias caused by differential failure to respond. Imputation is done in two ways for the 2013-2015 NSFG, logical and regression imputation. Regression imputation uses a regression equation to estimate a value for a case with missing data. Regression imputation was used to assign most of the imputed values. Logical imputation uses a subject-matter expert to assign a value based on the value of other variables for the case with missing data. For nearly all the recoded variables for which imputation is done in the continuous NSFG, less than 2 percent of the cases received an imputed value.

*Data Quality:* Standard errors are generally released along with data in NCHS reports. The NSFG utilizes the following to maintain high quality data: 1) questionnaire design work, 2) consistency checks built into the interview to enable the interviewer to resolve problems in the field, 3) evaluation of monthly data files to find and correct survey instrument problems, and 4) extensive interviewer training. The source website has numerous documents discussing the survey sample design and collection methods, sample error estimation design, examples of variance estimation, and other methodological issues under National Survey of Family Growth, "Questionnaires, Datasets, and Related Documentation," for each cycle of the NSFG online at <https://www.cdc.gov/nchs/nsfg/nsfg_questionnaires.htm>

*Sources of Additional Material:* National Center for Health Statistics, National Survey of Family Growth, online at <http://www.cdc.gov/nchs/nsfg/about_nsfg.htm>. See also materials available online at <https://www.cdc.gov/nchs/nsfg/nsfg_questionnaires.htm>.

## National Vital Statistics System

*Universe, Frequency, and Types of Data:* Annual data on births, deaths, marriages, divorces, and fetal deaths in the United States. Legal authority for the registration of these events resides individually with the 50 States, 2 cities (Washington, DC, and New York City), and 5 territories (Puerto Rico, the Virgin Islands, Guam, American Samoa, and the Commonwealth of the Northern Mariana Islands). These jurisdictions are responsible for maintaining registries of vital events and for issuing copies of birth, marriage, divorce, and death certificates.

*Type of Data Collection Operation:* Mortality data based on complete file of death records, except 1972, based on 50 percent sample. Natality statistics 1951-1971, based on 50 percent sample of birth certificates, except a 20 percent to 50 percent sample in 1967, received by NCHS.

*Data Collection and Imputation Procedures:* Reports based on records from registration offices of the jurisdictions listed above. Data pertaining to causes of death are classified and coded according to the International Classification of Diseases (ICD).

*Estimates of Sampling Error:* For recent years, there is no sampling for these files; the files are based on 100 percent of certificates registered. Generally more than 99 percent of the births and deaths occurring in this country are registered.

*Nonsampling Errors:*The NCHS checks electronic files for completeness, valid coding of items, inconsistencies in data items, and other problems or errors. The NCHS investigates items that effect the quality and completeness of data, and registration areas are asked to verify counts or determine the nature of data discrepancies, in order to resolve and correct data.

*Sources of Additional Material:* U.S. National Center for Health Statistics, *Vital Statistics of the United States*, Vol. I and Vol. II, annual, and the *National Vital Statistics Reports*. See the NCHS website at <http://www.cdc.gov/nchs/nvss/index.htm>.

# National Highway Traffic Safety Administration (NHTSA)

## Fatality Analysis Reporting System (FARS)

*Universe, Frequency, and Types of Data:* FARS is a census of all fatal motor vehicle traffic crashes that occur throughout the United States, including the District of Columbia and Puerto Rico, on roadways customarily open to the public. The crash must be reported to the state/jurisdiction, and is classified as fatal if a directly related fatality occurs within thirty days of the crash.

*Data Collection and Imputation Procedures:* NHTSA has a cooperative agreement with an agency in each State government to provide specific information in a standard format on fatal crashes occurring in the State. State analysts extract data from state documents and enter the data into a standardized electronic database. State documents include police accident reports, death certificates, state vehicle registration files, coroner/medical examiner reports, vital statistics, and other records. Computerized edit checks monitor the accuracy, consistency, and completeness of the data. The FARS incorporates a sophisticated mathematical multiple imputation procedure to develop a probability distribution of missing blood alcohol concentration (BAC) levels in the database for drivers, pedestrians, and cyclists.

*Estimates of Sampling Error:* Since this is census data, there are no sampling errors.

*Nonsampling Errors:* FARS represents a census of all police-reported crashes and captures all data reported at the state level. FARS data undergo a rigorous quality control process to prevent inaccurate reporting. However, these data are highly dependent on the accuracy of the police accident reports. Errors or omissions within police accident reports may not be detected.

*Sources of Additional Material:* Fatality Analysis Reporting System (FARS), online at <http://www.nhtsa.gov/FARS>.

# Weights and Measures

## U.S. Customary/Metric Conversion Table
[Conversions provided in the table are approximate]

| Symbol | When you know U.S. customary | Multiply by | To find metric | Symbol |
|---|---|---|---|---|
| in | inches | 2.54 | centimeters | cm |
| ft | feet | 30.48 | centimeters | cm |
| yd | yards | 0.91 | meters | m |
| mi | miles | 1.61 | kilometers | km |
| $in^2$ | square inches | 6.45 | square centimeters | $cm^2$ |
| $ft^2$ | square feet | 0.09 | square meters | $m^2$ |
| $yd^2$ | square yards | 0.84 | square meters | $m^2$ |
| $mi^2$ | square miles | 2.59 | square kilometers | $km^2$ |
| | acre | 0.41 | hectare | ha |
| oz | ounces | 28.35 | grams | g |
| lb | pounds | 0.45 | kilograms | kg |
| oz (troy) | troy ounces | 31.1 | grams | g |
| | short tons (2,000 lb) | 0.91 | metric tons | t |
| | long tons (2,240 lb) | 1.02 | metric tons | t |
| fl oz | fluid ounces | 29.57 | mililiters | mL |
| c | cups | 0.24 | liters | L |
| pt | pints | 0.47 | liters | L |
| qt | quarts | 0.95 | liters | L |
| gal | gallons | 3.79 | liters | L |
| $ft^3$ | cubic feet | 0.03 | cubic meters | $m^3$ |
| $yd^3$ | cubic yards | 0.76 | cubic meters | $m^3$ |
| °F | degrees Fahrenheit (subtract 32) | 0.55 | degrees Celsius | °C |

| Symbol | When you know metric | Multiply by | To find U.S. customary | Symbol |
|---|---|---|---|---|
| cm | centimeters | 0.39 | inches | in |
| cm | centimeters | 0.03 | feet | ft |
| m | meters | 1.09 | yards | yd |
| km | kilometers | 0.62 | miles | mi |
| $cm^2$ | square centimeters | 0.16 | square inches | $in^2$ |
| $cm^2$ | square centimeters | 10.76 | square feet | $ft^2$ |
| $m^2$ | square meters | 1.2 | square yards | $yd^2$ |
| $km^2$ | square kilometers | 0.39 | square miles | $mi^2$ |
| ha | hectare | 2.47 | acre | |
| g | grams | 0.04 | ounces | oz |
| kg | kilograms | 2.20 | pounds | lb |
| g | grams | 0.04 | troy ounces | oz (troy) |
| t | metric tons | 1.1 | short tons (2,000 lb) | |
| t | metric tons | 0.98 | long tons (2,240 lb) | |
| mL | mililiters | 0.03 | fluid ounces | fl oz |
| L | liters | 4.23 | cups | c |
| L | liters | 2.11 | pints | pt |
| L | liters | 1.06 | quarts | qt |
| L | liters | 0.26 | gallons | gal |
| $m^3$ | cubic meters | 35.31 | cubic feet | $ft^3$ |
| $m^3$ | cubic meters | 1.31 | cubic yards | $yd^3$ |
| °C | degrees Celsius (after multiplying, add 32) | 1.8 | degrees Fahrenheit | °F |

Source: National Institute of Standards and Technology (NIST), Weights and Measures Division. See <https://www.nist.gov/pml/weights-and-measures/metric-si/unit-conversion>

# Index

[NOTE: Index citations refer to **table** numbers, not **page** numbers]

Agricultural science, 321, 323, 839, 844
Agriculture (see also Farms):
    Employees, 628, 641
    Foreign trade, 770, 880, 881, 882, 883, 884, 885,
      886, 887, 888, 889, 1326, 1331, 1332
    Government payments, 474, 505, 872, 873, 874
    Value added, 873
Agriculture, construction, and mining machinery
    manufacturing (see also Machine tools, and
    Machinery manufacturing), 659, 667, 1042, 1044
Agriculture, forestry, and fishing industry:
    Capital, 789, 811, 813
    Earnings, 670, 798, 799, 800, 801, 802, 803, 804,
      913
    Employees, 648, 665, 787, 790, 798, 799, 800, 801,
      802, 803, 804, 913
    Establishments, 665, 784, 786, 787, 789, 790, 805,
      913
    Finances, 775, 778, 1347
    Gross domestic product, 699, 915
    Occupational safety, 688, 690
    Profits, 822
    Sales, 775, 778, 784, 804
Aid to families with dependent children. (See
    Temporary Assistance for Needy Families.)
AIDS (Acquired Immuno- Deficiency Syndrome), 125,
    201, 202, 203, 204
Air conditioning, homes with, 1019
Air Force, personnel, 535
Air pollution:
    Air pollution control equipment, 421
    Emissions, 413, 414, 415, 422, 423, 424, 964, 1407
    Greenhouse gases, 416, 417
    Toxic chemicals, 422, 423, 424
Air transportation:
    Accidents and deaths, 1095, 1103, 1106
    Airfare costs and fees, 1105, 1293
    Airports, 1097, 1099, 1104, 1294
    Carrier delays, cancellations, 1101
    Civil aviation, 1104
    Consumer complaints, 1100
    Employees, 496, 1085, 1096, 1104
    Expenditures of State and local government, 478
    Federal outlays, 505
    Finances, 1096, 1105
    Fleet size, 1091, 1104
    Freight, 1096, 1325
    Fuel consumption and costs, 961, 1098
    Price indexes, 758, 768
    Regional airlines, 1102
    Revenue, 1087, 1105
    Traffic carried, 1096, 1102, 1294
Air transportation industry:
    Capital, 811
    Earnings, 659, 1088
    Employees, 659, 1086, 1088, 1290
    Establishments, 1086, 1088, 1089
    Foreign trade, 1092
    Finances, 1096
    Gross domestic product, 699
    Productivity, 667
    Profits, 1096
    Revenues, 1087, 1089, 1096, 1290
    Shipments, 1092, 1093
Aircraft manufacturing. (See Aerospace industry.)

Airline operations (see also Air transportation), 1096,
    1098, 1101, 1102, 1105
Airplanes, 1059
Airports or airfields, 1104
    Federal aid to state and local government, 474
    Serving regional airlines, 1102
    Traffic, 1097, 1099, 1294
Alaska Native. (See American Indian, Alaska
    Native population.)
Alcoholic beverages (see also individual types, and
    Beer, wine, and liquor stores):
    Alcoholism treatment, 219
    Consumer expenditures, 707, 716, 719, 720, 1083
    Consumption, 220, 221, 1382
    Price indexes, 758, 767
    Sales, 1069, 1083
Alcohol- induced deaths, 123
Alcohol involvement in fatal crashes, 1130, 1133,
    1134, 1135
Alcoholism treatment, 219
Aleut population. (See American Indian, Alaska
    Native population.)
Algeria (See Foreign countries.)
Aliens, illegal, 49, 357, 551, 556, 557, 558
Alimony, 520
Allergies, 209, 232
Almonds, 875, 897, 898, 901
Alternative medicine, 208
Alternative minimum tax, 516
Altitudes, geographical, 407
Aluminum:
    Consumption, 938
    Employment, 938
    Foreign trade, 771, 772, 938, 942
    Prices, 767, 771, 772
    Production, 936, 937, 938
    Recycling, 419, 420
    World production, 941, 1398
Alzheimer's disease, 121, 122, 123, 124, 125,
    126, 179, 206
Ambulatory health care services industry:
    Capital, 811
    Earnings, 171, 659, 783
    Employees, 173, 659, 783
    Establishments, 783
    Gross domestic product, 699
    Sales, receipts, 783
American College Testing Program (ACT), 283
American Indian, Alaska Native population, 5, 7, 9,
    10, 11, 13, 20, 43, 44, 72
    Age and/or sex, 7, 9, 10, 11
    AIDS, 204
    Births, birth rates, 5, 84, 85, 89, 90, 91, 95
    Business owners, 797, 804
    Children, 9, 10, 11, 598
    College costs, 302, 304
    College enrollment, 293, 326
    Criminal victimizations, 340
    Deaths, death rates, 5, 114, 115, 116, 122, 127,
      130, 134, 340
    Degrees conferred, 320, 843
    Educational attainment, 36, 72
    Elderly, 9, 10, 11

**Note**: Index citations refer to **table** numbers, not **page** numbers

                                        

Note: Index citations refer to **table** numbers, not **page** numbers

Establishments, 665, 783, 784, 786, 787, 789, 790, 805, 1254, 1255, 1256
Finances, 775, 778, 1253
Gaming, 1286
Gross domestic product, 699
Hires and separations, 663, 664
Hours, 657
Nonemployers, 784, 1255
Occupational safety, 688
Payroll, 1256
Productivity, 667
Profits, 822
Receipts, revenue, 775, 778, 783, 784, 798, 799, 800, 801, 802, 803, 804, 1253, 1254, 1255
Value added, 1257, 1258, 1264
Asbestos, 937, 938, 941
Asia. (See Foreign countries.)
Asian and Pacific Islander population (see also Asian population):
Births, 84, 85, 89, 90
Business owners, 797, 802, 803
Consumer expenditures, 719
Criminal victimizations, 340
Deaths, death rates, 114, 115, 116, 122, 127, 130, 134, 340
Degrees conferred, 320
Educational attainment, 256, 257
Heart disease, deaths, 122, 127
Income, 723, 724, 729, 730, 734, 737
Jail inmates, 385
Language, 55, 57, 261
Poverty, 742, 743, 746
Suicides, deaths, 122, 130, 540
Asian population, 5, 7, 9, 10, 11, 13, 20, 36, 42
Adoption, 598
Age and/or sex, 7, 9, 10, 11
AIDS, 204
Births, 5, 91, 95, 96
Bullying, 333, 334
Child care, 595, 599
Business owners, 797, 802, 803
Children, 9, 10, 11, 68, 240
College costs, 302, 304
College enrollment, 293, 294, 295, 326, 621
Congress, members of, 457
Deaths, 5
Degrees conferred, 843
Disabled students, 299
Educational attainment, 36, 256, 257, 258, 259
Elderly, 9, 10, 11
Family type, 66
Food stamp participants, 568, 594
Foster care, 598
Grandparents living with grandchildren, 66, 69
Health and dental care visits, 185, 186, 229
Health insurance coverage, 157, 163, 167
Households, 61, 72
Housing tenure, 36, 72
Immunization of children, 238
Income, 36, 723, 724, 726, 728, 729, 730, 734, 737, 738
Labor force, 612, 613, 614, 618, 621, 625, 633, 635, 641, 648, 674, 679, 693
Class of worker, 630

Displaced workers, 637
Earnings, 259, 674, 679, 681
Educational attainment, 618, 621, 647, 654
Industry, 648, 1302
Job search, 650
Multiple job holders, 633
Occupation, 36, 641, 647
Public assistance, 594
Teachers, 276, 277
Unemployment, 613, 614, 621, 649, 650, 654
Union membership, 693
Leisure time use, 1273
Marital status, 58, 72
Minimum wage workers, 679
Migration, 5
Occupation, 36, 641, 647
Physical activity, 227
Poverty, 36, 742, 743, 744, 746, 747
Public assistance, 568, 600
School enrollment, 270, 293, 294, 295
States, 20
Veterans, 550
Voter registration and turnout, 444, 446
Weapons in schools, 331
Asparagus, 245, 896
Assaults, 213, 328, 336, 337, 338, 339, 342, 343, 345, 346, 364
Asset- backed securities, 781, 1198, 1199, 1219, 1226
Asset forfeiture, 361
Assets, personal, 748, 751, 752, 753, 1202
Assisted reproduction, 109
Assistance, public. (See Public aid, assistance.)
Associations, national, nonprofit, 606, 607, 608, 609, 665, 1309
Asthma, 123, 209, 239
Astronomy, 844
Athletic goods. (See Sporting and athletic goods.)
Attention deficit hyperactivity disorder (ADHD), 233
Audio and video equipment, 768, 1187, 1265
Auditing. (See Accounting, tax preparation, bookkeeping, and payroll services.)
Audits, 511
Australia. (See Foreign countries.)
Austria. (See Foreign countries.)
Authors, 641
Autism, 234, 236
Automobile dealers:
Earnings, 659, 1074
Employees, 659, 1072, 1074, 1081
Establishments, 1072, 1081
Inventories, 1078, 1081
Productivity, 667
Sales, 1075, 1078, 1081
Automobile Insurance, 1248
Automobile loans, 1220
Automobile rentals and leasing. (See Automotive equipment rental and leasing, and Rental and leasing services.)
Automobiles (see also Motor vehicles):
Alternative fuel, 1127
Consumer expenditures, 707, 716, 717, 719, 720, 721
Energy consumption, 961
Foreign trade, 1331
Imports, 1082
Lease, 758

**Note**: Index citations refer to **table** numbers, not **page** numbers

Delivery characteristics, 87, 88, 92, 93, 94
Education, 95, 98, 99
First births, 97
Foreign countries, 1365
Hispanic population, 5, 84, 85, 86, 87, 89, 90,
   91, 94, 95, 96, 97
Household income, 100
Induction of labor, 93
Island areas of the U.S., 85, 1341
Life expectancy, 110, 111, 112, 1366
Native Hawaiian, Other Pacific Islander, 5, 85, 89,
   90, 91, 95
Poverty, 95, 99
Premature, 94
Race, 5, 84, 85, 86, 87, 89, 90, 91, 94, 95, 96, 97
States, 16, 85, 92, 99
Twin and multiple, 86
Births, businesses, 795
Birth control, 101, 104
Birth weight, 92
Bismuth, 938
Black, African American population, 5, 7, 9, 10, 11,
   13, 20, 36, 40
Abortions, 105, 106
Adoption, 598
Age and/or sex, 7, 9, 10, 11
AIDS, 204
Birth and birth rates, 5, 84, 85, 86, 87, 89, 90,
   91, 94, 95, 96
   Births to teenage mothers, 90, 91, 95, 96, 97
   Births to unmarried women, 91, 95, 96, 97
Body weight, 225, 226
Breastfeeding, 108
Bullying, 333, 334
Business owners, 797, 801
Cancer, 199, 200
Child care, 595, 599
Children, 9, 10, 11, 68
   Obesity, 240
   Poverty, 743, 744
Cigarette smoking and tobacco use, 217, 242
Congress, members of, 457
Consumer expenditures, 719
Contraceptive use, 101, 104
Criminal victimizations, 340, 341, 343, 348, 350
Deaths and death rates, 5, 114, 115, 116, 119, 120,
   122, 127, 130, 132, 134
Degrees conferred, 320, 843
Disabled persons, 299
Educational attainment, 36, 256, 257, 258, 259
Elderly, 9, 10, 11, 744
Families, characteristics, 36, 66
Food stamp participants, 568, 594
Foster care, children in, 598
Grandparents living with grandchildren, 66, 69
Hate crimes, 348
Health and dental care visits, 185, 186, 189, 229
Health insurance coverage, 157, 163, 165, 167
Heart disease, deaths, 122, 127
HIV disease, 204
Homeschooled, 275
Homicides, 122, 340, 341
Households, characteristics, 61, 72
Housing, 36, 1022, 1026, 1029, 1032
Immunization of children, 238

Income, 36, 567, 723, 724, 726, 728, 729, 730,
   734, 737, 738
Infant deaths, 119, 120
Internet access/use, 1180, 1184, 1185, 1188
Jail inmates, 385, 386
Job search, 650
Labor force, 612, 613, 614, 618, 621, 625, 674, 693
   Class of worker, 630
   Displaced workers, 637
   Earnings, 259, 498, 674, 679, 681
   Educational attainment, 618, 621, 634, 647, 654
   Employed, 498, 613, 633, 634, 635, 641, 647, 648
   Industry, 648, 1302
   Multiple job holders, 633
   Unemployed, 613, 614, 621, 649, 650, 654
Leisure time use, 1273
Life expectancy, 110, 111, 112, 113
Living arrangements, 68, 78
Marital status, 58, 62, 72
Migration, 5
Minimum wage workers, 679
Nurses, 641
Occupations, 36, 641, 647
Physical activity, 227
Poverty, 36, 742, 743, 744, 746, 747
Property owners, 1022, 1026, 1029, 1032
Public assistance, 567, 568, 594, 600
Recreation activities, 1263, 1267
Schools and education:
   American College Testing Program (ACT), 283
   College costs, 302, 304
   College enrollment, 270, 288, 290, 291, 293, 294,
      295, 326
   Degrees conferred, 843
   Enrollment, 253, 262, 270, 288, 290, 293, 294,
      295, 621
   High school dropouts, 270, 286, 287, 288
   High school graduates, 270, 288, 291
   Parent participation, 269
   Teachers, 276, 277, 641
   Weapons in school, 331
Sexual activity and orientation, 101, 102, 103, 104
States, 20
Suicides, 122, 130, 540
Union membership, 693
Veterans, 550
Voter registration and turnout, 444, 446
Black lung benefit program, 583, 584
Blackberries, 897
Blast furnace and basic steel products. (See Iron
   and steel products.)
Blind persons, 160, 206, 236, 585
Blood alcohol concentration, 1130, 1133, 1134, 1135
Blood poisoning (See Septicemia.)
Blueberries, 245, 875, 897, 901
Boats and boating (see also Ships), 1091, 1095, 1107
Body Mass Index (BMI), 226
Bolivia. (See Foreign countries.)
Bolts, nuts, etc. (See Iron and steel products.)
Bonds:
   Foreign, 1232
   Holdings by sector, 753, 1200, 1201, 1231, 1232,
      1233
   Life insurance companies, 1231, 1246
   New issues, 1230
   Prices, yields, sales, and issues, 1227, 1229
   U.S. savings, 1202

---

**Note**: Index citations refer to **table** numbers, not **page** numbers

Note: Index citations refer to **table** numbers, not **page** numbers

# C

Cabbage, 245, 896, 901
Cable/pay television services, 758, 1162
Cable and other subscription programming:
    Earnings, 659, 1156
    Employees, 659, 1156, 1157
    Establishments, 1156, 1157
    Finances, 1161, 1172
    Revenue, 1157, 1161, 1172
Cadmium, 938, 941
Cafeterias. (See Food services and drinking places.)
California. (See State data.)
Calves, 875, 903, 904, 907
Cambodia. (See Foreign countries.)
Cameroon. (See Foreign countries.)
Campaigns, fundraising, 467, 468, 469
Camping, 1278
Campylobacteriosis, 201, 244
Canada, (see also Foreign countries), 401, 404
Cancer (malignancies), 199, 200
   Deaths, 121, 122, 123, 124, 125, 126, 129
Candy, 758
Cantaloupes, 875, 896
Capacity utilization, index, 819
Cape Verde. (See Foreign countries.)
Capital (see also individual industries):
    Banking, 1209, 1210
    Expenditures, 812, 813, 814, 824
    New security issues, 1230
    Residential, 1016
    Services, 666
    Stocks, 811
    Utilities, 985, 990
Capital equipment, producer price indexes, 767
Capital gains, 514, 515
Capital punishment, 387, 388, 389
Carbon dioxide emissions, 416, 417, 964, 1407
Cardiovascular disease. (See Heart disease.)
Carpal tunnel syndrome, 691
Carrots, 245, 875, 896, 901
Cars. (See Automobiles.)
Casualty insurance, 1247
Catalog and mail order sales, 1073, 1075, 1079, 1080
Catfish, 931
Catholic population. (See Religion.)
Cat ownership, 1268
Cattle:
    Dairy cows, 902, 905, 908, 909
    Farm marketings, sales, 875, 876, 902
    Imports, 883
    Number on farms, 902, 904, 905, 907, 908
    Prices, 767, 904
    Production, 904, 907
    Slaughter, 907
    Value on farms, 904
Cauliflower, 245, 896
Celery, 245, 896
Cellular and other wireless telecommunications, 1156, 1161, 1173, 1174, 1176, 1177
Cellular telephones, 1176, 1177, 1178, 1179, 1182, 1184, 1186, 1187, 1409, 1410
Cement (see also Nonmetallic mineral product manufacturing), 937, 938, 941
    Earnings, 659

Employment, 659, 938
Prices, 767, 938
Productivity, 667
World production, 1398
Central African Republic. (See Foreign countries.)
Central America. (See Foreign countries.)
Central and South American population (see also Hispanic or Latino origin population), 37
Cereal and bakery products:
   Expenditures, prices, 716, 719, 720, 758
   Per capita consumption, 246
Cerebrovascular diseases, 121, 122, 123, 124, 125, 126, 128, 211
Certificates of deposit, 1202
Certification and license status of workers, 681
Cesarean section deliveries, 87
Chad. (See Foreign countries.)
Charitable contributions (see also Philanthropy), 519, 521, 606, 607, 608, 609, 610
Charter schools, 280, 281
Cheerleading, 1277, 1278
Cheese (see also Dairy products), 246, 763, 909
Chemical engineering, degrees conferred, 844
Chemical products:
   Foreign trade, 881, 1323, 1331, 1332, 1337, 1338
   Price indexes, 767, 771, 772
   Production, 818
Chemicals manufacturing (see also individual chemicals):
   Capital, 811
   Earnings, 659, 1042, 1049
   Employees, 659, 1040, 1042, 1044, 1049
   Establishments, 1040
   Finances, 823
   Foreign trade, 771, 772, 1045, 1332
   Gross domestic product, 699, 1038
   Industrial production index, 818
   Inventories, 1051, 1052
   Multinational companies, 825, 826, 827
   Productivity, 667
   Profits, 823
   Research and development, 834
   Shipments, 1042, 1045, 1051, 1052
   Toxic chemical releases, 422, 423
   Waterborne commerce, 1110
Chemistry (see also Physical sciences):
   Degrees conferred, 843, 844
   Employment, 641
   Salary offers, 318
Cherries, 245, 875, 897
Chicken pox, 201, 237, 238
Chickens. (See Poultry.)
Chikungunya virus, 201
Child abuse, 382, 383
Child care, 595, 599, 641, 758
   Expenditures for, 599, 722
   Tax credit, 522
Child day care services, 595, 599, 602, 641, 659
Child support, 567, 596, 597
Children (see also Births, Deaths, Marriages, Divorces, and Population):
   Adopted, 46, 76, 77, 598
   Age and/or sex, 6, 8, 9, 10, 11, 17, 76, 78
   Aid, social welfare programs, 565, 567, 568, 570, 587, 588, 590, 591, 593, 594, 596, 597, 600, 602

---

**Note**: Index citations refer to **table** numbers, not **page** numbers

---

**Note**: Index citations refer to **table** numbers, not **page** numbers

**Note**: Index citations refer to **table** numbers, not **page** numbers

---

**Note**: Index citations refer to **table** numbers, not **page** numbers

**Note**: Index citations refer to **table** numbers, not **page** numbers

**Note**: Index citations refer to **table** numbers, not **page** numbers

**Note**: Index citations refer to **table** numbers, not **page** numbers

(Education, continued)

**Note**: Index citations refer to **table** numbers, not **page** numbers

**Note**: Index citations refer to **table** numbers, not **page** numbers

**Note**: Index citations refer to **table** numbers, not **page** numbers

Note: Index citations refer to **table** numbers, not **page** numbers

---

**Note**: Index citations refer to **table** numbers, not **page** numbers

Immigrant population, 49, 1363
Immigration to U.S., 42, 51, 52, 53
Insurance, 1387
Income taxes, 1384, 1385
Infant mortality, 1365
Inpatient care, 1372
Insurance premiums, 1387
International transactions, balances, 1313, 1314, 1417, 1418
Internet users, 1409, 1410
Investment in U.S., 1200, 1233, 1312, 1315, 1316, 1317
Kidnappings, 560
Labor costs, 1377, 1378
Labor force, 1390
Labor productivity, 1377, 1379
Life expectancy, 1365, 1366
Living costs, 1381
Manufacturing, 1375, 1377, 1378
Meat, 1393, 1395, 1396
Military aid of U.S., 1321, 1322
Military expenditures, 1420
Military personnel, U.S., on active duty, 534, 539
Military sales, 542, 543, 544
Minerals, 1398
Multinational companies, 827
Natural gas, 1400, 1401, 1403, 1405
Net savings, households, 1386
Nuclear power, 1399, 1400, 1403
Obesity, 1367
Oil, 970, 1404
Oilseeds, 1393, 1394
Orphans adopted, 46
Patents, 808, 1411
Pensions, 1387
Petroleum production and consumption, 1400, 1401, 1403, 1404
Physicians, 1372
Population, 1362, 1363, 1364
Poultry, 887, 1393, 1395, 1396
Precipitation, in cities, 1408
Prices, 1380
Production:
    Crops, 885, 1393, 1394
    Industrial, 1376
    Meat, 1395
    Minerals, 941, 1398
Productivity, labor, 1377, 1379
Purchasing power parity, 1373
Rainfall in cities, 1408
Refugees, admitted to U.S., 45, 53
Research and development expenditures, 829, 1413
Rice, 885, 1393, 1394, 1397
Savings rates, households, 1386
Social security contributions, 1384
Soybean, 887
Stocks and bonds, 1232, 1233, 1412
Suicide, 1370
Tax burden, 1384, 1385
Tax revenues, 1383, 1384
Telephones, 1409
Temperature (cities), 1408
Terrorism, 560, 1421
Tobacco, 1368, 1382

Tourism, 1419
Trade with United States, 887, 889, 1330, 1333
Traffic fatalities, 1369
Travelers and expenditures, 1291, 1295, 1296
Unemployment, 1389, 1390, 1391
U.S. investment abroad, 1232, 1320
Visa overstays, 559
Visitors from, 559, 1295, 1298
Vital statistics, 1365
Weather, 1408
Wheat, 885, 887, 1393, 1394, 1397
Young adults, 1391
Foreign investments, 1200, 1315, 1316, 1317, 1319
Foreign languages:
    Degrees conferred, 321, 322, 323, 324
    Persons speaking, 55, 56, 57, 261
    Students enrolled, 297
Foreign sales and assistance by U.S. government, 542, 543, 1321, 1322
Foreign students, college, 296, 839
Foreign trade (see also Foreign aid, Foreign countries, and individual commodities), 1045, 1323, 1326, 1327, 1328, 1329, 1330, 1331, 1332, 1333, 1334, 1335, 1336, 1337, 1338
    Aerospace products, 1045, 1337, 1338
    Agricultural products, 880, 881, 882, 883, 884, 885, 886, 887, 888, 889, 898, 1326, 1331, 1332
    Aircraft and aircraft parts, 1045
    Automobiles, 1045, 1331
    Balance of trade, 1310, 1313, 1314, 1324, 1330, 1418
    Chemicals, 881, 1045, 1323, 1331, 1332, 1338
    China- U.S. trade, 1337
    Coal, 951, 968, 969, 1338
    Companies exporting, 1334, 1335
    Computer and electronic products, 1045, 1323, 1332, 1337, 1338
    Countries, 1329, 1330, 1333, 1334
    Crude oil, 944, 969, 970, 971, 1338
    Customs districts, 1327
    Electrical equipment, appliances and components, 1045, 1323, 1331, 1332, 1337, 1338
    Freight, 1092, 1325
    Fishery products, 928
    High- technology products, 1333
    Indexes, unit value, 1336
    Industry, 1332
    International transactions, balances, U.S., 1310, 1313, 1314, 1324
    Mineral imports, 942, 1332
    Oil and gas, 944, 968, 969, 1323, 1331, 1332
    Petroleum products, 944, 968, 969, 1045, 1323, 1331, 1338
    Price indexes, 769, 770, 771, 772
    Processed food, 1045, 1339
    Puerto Rico, 1349
    Related party trade, 1323
    Services, 1310
    Timber products, 922, 923, 1332
    Transportation equipment, 1045, 1323, 1331, 1332
    U.S. affiliates of foreign countries, 1318

---

**Note**: Index citations refer to **table** numbers, not **page** numbers

---

**Note**: Index citations refer to **table** numbers, not **page** numbers

Gemstones, 938
Gender identity, 348, 349
General merchandise stores:
    Earnings, 659, 783, 1074
    Electronic commerce, 1079
    Employees, 659, 783, 1066, 1072, 1074
    Establishments, 783, 1066, 1072, 1073
    Finances, 823
    Inventories, 1078
    Productivity, 667
    Profits, 823
    Sales, 783, 1066, 1073, 1075, 1077, 1078, 1079
Geography and cartography. (See Land.)
Genetically engineered crops, 869
Georgia. (See Foreign countries, and State data.)
Geothermal energy, 962, 976, 977, 978
Germanium, 938
German stock market index (DAX), 1412
Germany. (See Foreign countries.)
Ghana. (See Foreign countries.)
Giardiasis, 201
Gift and estate taxes, 491, 510
Glass, 418, 419, 420, 767
Gold:
    Consumption, 938
    Employment, 938
    Foreign trade, 938, 1331
    Prices, 767, 772, 938, 939
    Production and value, 936, 937, 938, 941, 1398
    Reserve assets, 1311
Golf, 1270, 1275, 1276, 1277, 1278, 1279
Golf courses, industry, 1253, 1256
Gonorrhea, 201
Government (see also Expenditures of U.S.
    government, Receipts, and individual
    governmental units):
    Buildings, 529
    Capital stock, 754
    Consumer credit holdings, 1219
    Earnings, 500, 657, 670, 672
    Employees, 498, 657, 658, 659, 672, 847
        Benefits, 497
        Characteristics, 525
        Federal, civilian, 495, 525, 526, 527, 528
        Hours, 657
        Local government, 495, 496, 499, 500
        Retirement, 528
        Retirement systems, 506, 528, 567, 575
        State government, 495, 496, 499, 500
    Employment cost index, 677, 764
    Expenditures:
        Capital outlays, 477, 478
        Consumption, 706, 769
        Federal, 501, 503, 504, 505, 506, 509
            Agriculture, 872, 873, 874
            Aid to state and local government, 473, 474,
              475
        Local government, 477, 478, 494
        State and local government, 475, 476, 477,
            478, 481, 483
        State government, 476, 477, 478, 488, 489, 492
        Transfer payments, 564, 565, 566, 1348
    Federally owned land, 529
    Flow of funds, 1198

Freedom of Information Act, 367
Highways, 483, 492, 494, 1090, 1113, 1114,
    1116, 1117, 1118, 1119, 1120, 1121
Hires and separations, 663, 664
Hospitals, 194, 483
Insurance. (See Social insurance.)
Land. (See Public lands.)
Local government:
    Employees, 495, 496, 499, 500, 672
    Finances, 493, 494
    Number, by type, 470, 471
    Payroll, 495, 496, 500
Number of units, by type of government, 470, 471
Occupational safety, 688, 690
Payrolls, 495, 496
Purchases of goods and services, 696, 697
Reserve assets, 1311
Salaries and wages (see also Income, and
    individual industries):
    Federal, 670, 672
    State and local government employees, 265,
        498, 500, 670, 672
Securities, 480, 1227
State and local government:
    Benefits, 497
    Employees, 495, 496, 498
    Federal aid, 473, 474
    Finances, 475, 476, 477, 478, 479, 481, 482,
        483
    Payroll, 495, 496, 500
    Revenue from pari-mutuel and amusement taxes
        and lotteries, 486
State government, 488, 490, 491, 492, 672
Government National Mortgage Association loans,
    1222
Governors, 461, 462
Graduates:
    College, 319, 320, 321, 324, 325, 842, 843,
        844, 846
    High school, 250, 285, 288, 291
Grain (see also individual classes):
    Consumption, 246, 1393
    Farm marketings, sales, 867, 875, 901
    Foreign trade, 880, 883, 885, 886, 888, 1393
    Prices, 878
    Production, 873, 885, 901, 1393, 1394
Grandparents, living with grandchildren, 66, 69, 77
Grants, by foundations, 606, 607, 608
Grapefruit, 245, 763, 875, 897
Grapes, 245, 763, 875, 897, 901
Graphite, 938
Great Britain. (See Foreign countries.)
Great Lakes, 27, 28, 400, 401, 402, 1109
Greece. (See Foreign countries.)
Greenhouse gases, 416, 417
Grocery stores (see also Food and beverage stores),
    659, 667, 1072, 1073, 1074, 1075
Gross domestic product (GDP):
    Components, annual growth rates, 696, 697,
        698, 1084
    Foreign countries, 1374
    Foreign trade, 1418
    Industry, 699

---

**Note**: Index citations refer to **table** numbers, not **page** numbers

**Note**: Index citations refer to **table** numbers, not **page** numbers

Note: Index citations refer to **table** numbers, not **page** numbers

HIV (see also AIDS), 123, 124, 125, 201, 202, 203, 204
Hockey, ice, 1274, 1275, 1276, 1278
Hogs, 767, 875, 902, 903, 904, 905, 906
Home appliances. (See Appliances.)
Home equity loans/lines of credit, 1029, 1204, 1210, 1222
Home furnishings stores, 659, 667, 1072, 1075
Home health care, 160, 172, 179, 641, 645, 646
Home health care services:
  Earnings, 659
  Employees, 173, 645, 646, 659
  Expenditures, 140, 142, 143
  Finances, 171, 172
  Medicare program, 153
Home remodeling, 1035
Homeland Security, Department of (see also National Security):
  Employees, 552
  Expenditures, 552
  Grants by program, 555
  Grants by state, 553
  Grants by urban area, 554
  Outlays, 504
Homeless, persons and assistance, 603, 604
Homeowners' insurance, 1247, 1249
Homes. (See Housing and housing units.)
Homeschooling, 275
Homicides, 122, 123, 124, 125, 335, 336, 337, 338, 339, 340, 341, 538
Homosexuality:
  Anti- gay crimes, 331, 348, 349
  Households, same- sex couples, 72, 74
  Sexual attraction and orientation, 103
  Sexual experiences, 102
  Worker benefits for partners, 683
Honduras. (See Foreign countries.)
Honey, 246, 875, 899
Hong Kong. (See Foreign countries.)
Hong Kong Hang Seng stock market index, 1412
Horses, 1268, 1275
Horticultural specialty crops, 892
Hospice services, 153, 179, 190
Hospitals:
  Average daily patient care, 194, 196
  Beds, 180, 190, 194, 196, 1372
  Capital, 811
  Charges and personal expenditure for, 140, 142, 143, 144, 147, 160
  Construction, 995, 997, 998
  Consumer price index, 148
  Cost to hospital per patient, 196, 197
  Earnings, 659, 783
  Emergency departments, 188, 189, 192, 194
  Employees, 173, 194, 496, 499, 648, 659, 665, 783
  Establishments, 190, 194, 196, 665, 783
  Finances, 171, 172, 194
  Gross domestic product, 699
  Medicare program, 152, 153, 155, 156, 162, 190
  Mental hospitals, 171, 173, 180, 181, 182, 194, 195
  National expenditures, 140, 141, 142, 143, 144, 147
  Outpatient visits, 189, 194, 195, 196
  Patients, 180, 182, 192, 193, 194, 196, 197
  Prices, 758, 768

Public expenditures, 141, 142, 143, 145, 147, 194, 493
  Local governments, 477
  State governments, 477, 486, 489
Receipts, 171, 172, 783
States, 196
Surgery, 198, 205
Use, admissions, and patient days, 185, 188, 192, 193, 194, 195, 196, 244, 1372
Hotels and other lodging places (see also Accommodation and food services):
  Buildings and floor space, 1037
  Earnings, 659, 788
  Employees, 659, 788
  Establishments, 788
  New construction, 997
  Prices, 758
  Productivity, 667
  Revenue, 1307
House of Representatives, 452, 453, 454, 455, 456, 457, 458, 459
Households or families (see also Housing and housing units), 61, 63, 64, 65, 66, 72
  Adoption, 76, 77, 598
  Age of householder, 64, 65, 725, 731
  American Indian, Alaska Native population, 36, 72
  Asian population, 36, 61, 66, 72, 723, 726, 728
  Assets, 753, 1198, 1199, 1201, 1202, 1231, 1237
  Balance sheet, 753
  Banking status, 1221
  Black, African American population, 36, 61, 62, 66, 72, 723, 726, 728
  Characteristics, 61, 63, 64, 65, 66, 72, 74, 78, 725
  Children under 18 years, 65, 66, 67, 68, 72, 73, 76, 77, 722, 733
  Computer use, 1180, 1182
  Consumer credit, 1201, 1203, 1204
  Consumer expenditures, 716, 717, 719, 720, 721
  Criminal victimization, 344, 350, 351
  Debt, 753, 1199, 1204, 1205, 1206, 1207
  Division of labor, 682
  Educational attainment, 725, 731
  Elderly, 34, 64, 73, 725
  Energy consumption and expenditures, 1033
  Energy insecurity, 1034
  Employment of parents, 626, 639
  Female householder, 61, 63, 64, 65, 66, 73, 74
  Finances, financial services, 1198, 1199, 1201, 1202, 1222, 1231, 1237, 1238, 1239
  Flow of funds, 1198, 1201
  Food costs, 762, 879
  Food insecurity, 215
  Food stamp program, 593, 594
  Foreign- born population, 40
  Foster care, 77, 598
  Hispanic origin population, 36, 37, 61, 62, 66, 72, 723, 726, 728
  Hunger, 215
  Income, 36, 37, 72, 723, 724, 725, 726, 728, 729, 730, 731, 732, 733, 1034, 1202, 1204, 1238, 1239
  Individual retirement accounts (IRAs), 574, 578, 579
  Internet access, 1162, 1180, 1184
  Interracial married couples, 62
  Language spoken at home, 261, 269
  Leisure time use, 682, 1273
  Living arrangements, 34, 60, 68, 75, 78

**Note**: Index citations refer to **table** numbers, not **page** numbers

Male householder, 61, 63, 64, 65, 66, 73, 74
Marital status, 61, 63, 65, 72
Married couples with or without own children, 61, 62, 65, 72
Media users, 1162
Mobility (geographic) status, 30
Mortgages, 1029, 1203, 1204, 1205
Mutual fund ownership, 1238, 1239
Net worth, 751, 752, 753
Native Hawaiian, Other Pacific Islander, 36, 72
Nonfamily, 61, 63
Participation in education, 269
Persons living alone (one- person households), 34, 60, 61, 63, 64
Pets, 1268
Poverty, 36, 746, 747
Production value, 704
Public assistance to families, 568
Race, 36, 61, 66, 72
Region of householder, 725, 731
Same- sex couple, 72, 74
Savings rate, 1386
Single parent, 61, 65, 66
Size, 40, 61, 64
Stay- at- home parents, 67
Stock ownership, 1202, 1235
Telephones, 1163, 1177
Tenure, 36, 72, 725
Travel trips, 1146
Unmarried partners, 72, 73, 74
Wealth, 751, 752
Household work, 682
Housekeeping supplies expenditures, 719, 720
Housing and household operations, price indexes, 758, 768
Housing and housing units (see also Households or families):
Age of housing stocks, 1019
Amenities, 1000, 1032
Apartments, 1002, 1010, 1011
Appliances, 758
Building permit value, 994
Capital, 1016
Coastal counties, 28
Condominiums, 1010
Construction:
    Apartments completed and rented, 1002, 1011
    New units, 994, 999, 1000, 1003
    Time to completion, 1003
    Value, 993, 995, 997, 998
Consumer expenditures, 707, 716, 717, 719, 720, 721
Consumer price indexes, 756, 757, 758
Costs, 1025, 1026, 1027
Deficiencies, 1032
Elderly, 1013, 1023, 1026, 1032
Energy, 960, 962, 963, 965, 967, 979, 983, 1000, 1033, 1034
Fires, and property loss, 394
Floor space, 1000, 1033
Government expenditures, 475, 476, 483, 505, 506
Heating equipment used, 1000, 1019, 1031
Heating fuel used, 1000, 1031, 1033
Homeless, 603, 604
Hurricanes, 403

Improvements, 1035
Kitchen equipment, 1019
Loans and mortgages, 1005, 1029, 1030, 1036, 1222, 1223, 1224
Lot size, 1021
Maintenance and repair expenditures, 719, 720
Metropolitan area data, 1009, 1018
Mobile homes, 1007, 1019, 1020, 1029
New privately owned homes, characteristics, 1000
Ownership, 29, 36, 40, 725, 1012, 1013, 1014, 1015, 1017, 1018, 1019, 1021, 1022, 1023, 1024, 1025, 1026, 1027
Plumbing, 1019
Price indexes, 756, 757, 758, 759, 1004
Prices, or costs, 1004, 1005, 1006, 1007, 1008, 1009, 1010, 1025, 1026, 1027
Puerto Rico, 1344
Remodeling, 1035
Rent, rental value, 1011, 1025, 1026, 1028
Rooms, 1021
Sales, 1005, 1008, 1010
Shelters, 603
Square footage, 1021
State data, 1015, 1017, 1020, 1024, 1027, 1028
Structural type, 1014, 1019, 1020
Subsidized, 1002
Supportive, 603
Tenure, 29, 36, 40, 725, 751, 752, 1012, 1013, 1014, 1015, 1017, 1018, 1019, 1021, 1022, 1023, 1024, 1025, 1026, 1027, 1028, 1033, 1034, 1344
Transitional, 603
Vacancies, 1012, 1014, 1015, 1017, 1018, 1019, 1021
Value, 751, 753, 1027
Year built, 1019, 1033
Housing assistance, 568, 603, 604
Human immunodeficiency virus (HIV) (see also AIDS), 123, 124, 125, 201, 202, 203, 204
Human services, 603
Hungary. (See Foreign countries.)
Hunger, 215
Hunting and fishing, 913, 1278, 1284
Hurricanes, 403, 429, 432
Hydrocarbon gas liquids, 944
Hydroelectric power, 962, 986
    Capacity, 976
    Consumption, 958, 962, 963
    Net generation, 976, 977, 980, 986
    Net summer capacity, 976, 978
    Production, 958, 976, 1399, 1400
Hypertension, 93, 122, 123, 124, 211

I

Ice cream, 246, 763, 909
Ice hockey, 1274, 1275, 1276, 1278
Iceland. (See Foreign countries.)
Idaho. (See State data.)
Identity theft, 352, 353
Illegal aliens, 49, 357, 551, 556, 557, 558
Illinois. (See State data.)
Immigrants (see also Foreign- born population):
    Class of admission, 47, 50, 51
    Country of birth, 46, 49, 51, 52, 53
    Deferred Action for Childhood Arrivals, 551

**Note**: Index citations refer to **table** numbers, not **page** numbers

Note: Index citations refer to **table** numbers, not **page** numbers

Influenza and pneumonia, 121, 122, 123, 124, 125, 126, 201
Inhalants, persons using, 220
Injuries (see also Accidents, and Occupational safety), 213, 214, 397, 429, 1095, 1129
    Crime victimization, 342
    Industrial, 687, 688, 690, 691, 935
Inmates (see also Prisoners), 384, 385, 386
Installment loans (see also Loans and mortgages), 1204, 1205, 1220
Institutional care facilities (see also Hospitals, and Nursing and residential care facilities), 70, 153, 179, 190, 191, 194, 195
Instruments and related products, manufacturing:
    Earnings, 659
    Employees, 659
    Foreign trade, 771, 772, 1331, 1332
    Productivity, 667
Insurance. (See individual forms of insurance.)
Insurance agents, brokers, and services:
    Earnings, 1196
    Employees, 1196
    Establishments, 1196
    Finances, 1197, 1231, 1247
    Foreign countries, 1387
    Gross domestic product, 1193
    Prices, 758
Insurance carriers:
    Capital, 811
    Earnings, 659, 1194, 1196
    Employees, 659, 1194, 1196
    Establishments, 1194, 1195, 1196
    Finances, 1197, 1198, 1247
    Gross domestic product, 1193
    Nonemployers, 1195
    Profits, 1247
    Receipts, 1194, 1195
Insurance, government. (See Social insurance.)
Insurance, medical care, 141, 142, 145, 146
Intellectual property, 563, 706, 754
Intentional self- harm. (See Suicide.)
Interest:
    Payments, federal government, 505
    Persons receiving income, 567
    Receipts, by source:
        Individual income tax returns, 513
        National and personal income component, 708
Intermediate goods, price indexes, producer, 766
Internal revenue collections (see also Tax receipts), 510
Internal waterways, traffic, 1109
International affairs:
    Charitable organizations, 606
    Commerce, 1327, 1330, 1333, 1336, 1349
    Development aid, 1414, 1415
    Federal outlays, 505
    Foreign investments in U.S., 1233, 1312, 1315, 1316, 1317
    International transactions, U.S., 1310, 1311, 1312, 1313, 1314
    U.S. government aid, 1321, 1322
    U.S. investments, 1232, 1310, 1319, 1320
International data (See Foreign countries, or World summary statistics.)

International investment position, U.S., 1310, 1312, 1319, 1320
International mail (U.S. postal), 1154, 1155
Internet access and use, 1162, 1163, 1180, 1181, 1182, 1183, 1184, 1187, 1188, 1269, 1409, 1410
    Connection type, 1180, 1181, 1184, 1185
Internet publishing and broadcasting:
    Earnings, 659, 1156
    Employees, 659, 1156
    Establishments, 1156
    Finances, 1161, 1168
    Revenue, 1161, 1168
Internet service providers, Web search portals, data processing:
    Earnings, 659, 783, 1156
    Employees, 659, 783, 1156
    Establishments, 783, 1156
    Finances, 1161, 1175
    Revenue, 783, 1161, 1175
Interracial married couples, 62
Inventories (see also commodities), 696, 1050, 1051, 1052, 1053, 1070, 1078, 1081
Investments (see also Capital stocks, and Securities):
    Foreign, in U.S., 1233, 1312, 1315, 1316, 1317
    Private domestic, gross, 696, 697, 701, 769, 814
    U.S. government obligations, 1210
    U.S. international, 1232, 1310, 1312, 1319, 1320
Iodine, 938
Iowa. (See State data.)
Iran. (See Foreign countries.)
Iraq. (See Foreign countries.)
Ireland. (See Foreign countries.)
Iron (see also Steel):
    Foreign trade, 938, 942, 1331
    Mining industry, 667, 936
    Prices, 767, 936, 938
    Production, 937, 938, 941, 1398
Iron and steel mills (see also Primary metal manufacturing):
    Earnings, 659, 1042
    Employees, 659, 1042, 1044
    Shipments, 1042
Iron and steel products, 771, 772, 936, 937, 938, 941, 942, 1331
Irrigation, 412
Islamic population. (See Religions.)
Island Areas of the U.S.:
    Agriculture, 1350, 1351
    Aid by U.S. government, 1348
    Area, 399
    Births, 85, 1341
    Climate (Puerto Rico), 434, 435, 436, 437
    Commerce, 1347, 1349
    Deaths, 120, 1341
    Economic summary, 1352, 1353
    Education, 1342, 1346
    Employees, 1345, 1352, 1353, 1354, 1355, 1356, 1357, 1358
    Establishments, 1352, 1353, 1354, 1355, 1356, 1357
    Finances, 1347, 1348
    Foreign investment, 1315

---

**Note**: Index citations refer to **table** numbers, not **page** numbers

**Note**: Index citations refer to **table** numbers, not **page** numbers

Lebanon. (See Foreign countries.)
Legal assistants, 641
Legal services:
   Capital, 811
   Earnings, 659
   Employees, 659, 1301, 1302
   Establishments, 1300, 1301
   Finances, 775
   Gross domestic product, 699
   Prices, 758
   Receipts, 775, 1300, 1304
Legionellosis, 201
Legislatures, state party composition, 463, 464
Leisure activities, 1267, 1269, 1273
Leisure and hospitality industry:
   Earnings, 659, 671
   Employees, 648, 658, 659
   Hires and separations, 663, 664
   Occupational safety, 690
   Union membership, 693
Lemons, 245, 763, 875, 897
Lesotho. (See Foreign countries.)
Letters (postal), 1154, 1155
Lettuce, 245, 763, 875, 896, 901
Liberal arts degrees conferred, 321, 322, 324
Liberia. (See Foreign countries.)
Libraries and librarians, 1156, 1161, 1189, 1190,
   1191, 1192
   Colleges and universities, 327
   Degrees conferred, 322, 323, 324
   Employees, 327, 496, 641, 1189
   Internet access/use, 1189, 1190, 1192
   Library visits, 1190, 1192
   Resources and services, 1189, 1190, 1191, 1192
Libya. (See Foreign countries.)
Liechtenstein. (See Foreign countries.)
Life expectancy, 110, 111, 112, 113, 1365, 1366
Life insurance:
   Capital, 1246
   Cash value, 1202
   Consumer expenditures, 707, 716, 719, 720
   Establishments, 1246
   Finances, 1198, 1222, 1231, 1237, 1246
   Foreign countries, 1387
   Flow of funds, 1231
   In force, 1245
   Individual Retirement Accounts (IRAs), 1241
   Mortgage loans outstanding, 1222
   Purchases, policies, 1245
   Reserves, 753, 1200, 1201, 1246
   Sales, 1245, 1246
Life sciences, 321, 324, 831, 836, 843, 844, 847
Life tables, 110, 111, 112, 113
Light and power. (See Electric light and power
   industry.)
Lightning, 429
Lime, mineral, 937, 938
Liposuction, 198
Liquor stores. (See Beer, wine, and liquor stores.)
Liquors and beverages:
   Alcoholism treatment, 219
   Consumption, 220
   Government revenues, 475, 476, 482, 489, 490,
   493
   Manufacturing industry, 1065

Listeriosis, 201
Literacy, comparative, 1392
Lithium, 938
Lithuania. (See Foreign countries.)
Liver disease, 122, 123, 124, 125, 210
Livestock and livestock products (see also Animals
   domestic, and individual classes):
   Consumption, 246, 903, 1351, 1393
   Farm marketings, sales, 867, 873, 875, 877, 902,
   1351
   Foreign trade, 883, 886, 888, 903, 1331, 1332,
   1393
   Number on farms, 902, 904, 905, 906, 907, 908
   Prices, 765, 771, 772, 878, 904
   Production, 903, 904, 906, 907, 908, 1393, 1395
   Purchases, 873
   Supply, 903
   Value on farms, 904
Living cost. (See Consumer price indexes and Prices.)
Loans and mortgages (see also Debt):
   Automobile loans, 1205, 1220
   Banks, commercial, 1210, 1224
   Consumer credit, 1201, 1203, 1204, 1205, 1207,
   1210, 1218, 1219, 1220, 1224
   Credit market, flow of funds, 1201
   Credit unions, 1215
   Delinquency rates, 1223, 1224
   Farms. (See Farm mortgage loans.)
   Federal Housing Administration (FHA), 1223
   Foreclosure rates, 1223
   Gross assets, 748
   Home mortgage/equity loans, 748, 1029, 1030,
   1204, 1205, 1207, 1222
     Applications, denials, 1030
     Delinquency, 1223, 1224
     Home improvement, 1036
   Installment loans, 1204, 1205
   Life insurance, 1245, 1246
   Minority- operated small businesses, 796
   Mortgage- backed securities, 1226
   Personal loans, 1220
   Savings institutions, 1215
   Student loan debt, 306
   Veterans Administration (VA), 1223
Lobsters, 930, 932
Local and suburban transit. (See Passenger
   transit industry.)
Local government. (See State and local government, and
   individual governmental units.)
Locks, water navigation, 1107
Lodging industries. (See Hotels and other
   lodging places.)
London FTSE 100 stock market index, 1412
Long- term care facilities, 179
Lotteries, 486, 487
Louisiana. (See State data.)
Low birth weight, 92
Lumber (see also Forest products, and Wood
   products manufacturing):
   Consumption, 922, 924
   Foreign trade, 922, 923
   Prices, 767, 926
   Production, 922, 924
   Waterborne commerce, 1110

**Note**: Index citations refer to **table** numbers, not **page** numbers

**Note**: Index citations refer to **table** numbers, not **page** numbers

**Note**: Index citations refer to **table** numbers, not **page** numbers

Note: Index citations refer to **table** numbers, not **page** numbers

Motorcycles, 1091, 1124, 1137
   Accidents and deaths, 1095, 1129, 1130, 1137
   Racing, 1275
Mountain biking, 1278
Movie theaters, 1169, 1267
Mozambique. (See Foreign countries.)
Multinational companies, 824, 825, 826, 827, 1319
Multiple births, 86
Multiple job holders, 633, 669
Mumps, 201
Municipal and state bonds, 779, 780, 781, 1201, 1227, 1229
Municipal waste, 418, 419, 420, 976
Municipalities. (See Cities and Metropolitan areas.)
Murders, 328, 336, 337, 338, 339
Museums, 1257, 1263
Museums, historical sites:
   Earnings, 659, 783
   Employees, 659, 665, 783, 1256
   Establishments, 665, 783, 1255, 1256
   Federal aid, 1260
   Nonemployers, 1255
   Receipts, revenue, 783, 1253, 1255
Mushrooms, 245, 875
Music:
   Electronic commerce sales, 1080
   Industry shipments and value, 1170
   Listening to, 1262, 1263
Musicians and composers, 641
Muslim population. (See Religions.)
Mutton (see also Meat and meat products), 903
Mutual funds, 780, 781, 1198, 1200, 1201, 1202, 1228, 1231, 1237, 1238, 1239, 1240, 1241

# N

National Association of Securities Dealers (NASDAQ) stock prices, 1234, 1236
National College Athletic Association (NCAA) sports participation, 1276
National debt. (See Debt.)
National forests. (See Forests.)
National health expenditures, 140, 141, 142, 143, 144, 145, 146, 147
National income (see also Gross domestic product), 696, 697, 698, 700, 709
National Park Service, 1280, 1281, 1282
National Security. (See, Defense, Department of; Homeland Security, Department of; and individual military services.)
Native Hawaiian, Other Pacific Islander, 5, 7, 9, 10, 11, 13, 20, 72
   Adoption, 78
   Age and/or sex, 7, 9, 10
   AIDS, 204
   Births, 5, 85, 89, 90, 95
   Business owners, 797, 803
   Children, 9, 10, 11
   College costs, 302, 304
   Deaths, 5
   Educational attainment, 36, 72
   Elderly, 9, 10, 11
   Grandparents, living with grandchildren, 69
   Head Start, 600

Health and dental care visits, 185, 186
Housing tenure, 36
Income, 36, 72
Marital status, 72
Migration, 5
Occupation, 36
Physical activity, 227
Poverty, 36
Veterans, 550
Weapons in school, 331
Natural disasters. (See Disasters, natural.)
Natural gas:
   Coalbed methane, 949
   Consumption, 948, 958, 959, 961, 963, 977, 1401, 1403
   Electricity generation, 978, 980
   Emissions, 417
   Expenditures, 965
   Foreign trade, 944, 959, 968, 969, 1331
   Pipelines, 1153
   Prices, 758, 760, 948
   Production, 937, 944, 945, 946, 948, 949, 958, 959
      World, 941, 948, 1398, 1400, 1405
   Reserves, 947, 948, 949
   Shale gas, 949
   Unconventional dry, 949
   Vehicles and fuel stations, 1127
Natural gas distribution industry, 659, 667, 818, 956, 957
Natural gas plant liquids, 943, 944, 945, 949
Natural resources (see also Forest products, Minerals and mineral products, Paper and paperboard products, Timber, Wood products manufacturing, and individual resources and minerals):
   Federal outlays, 505, 832
   Fisheries and fish products (see also Aquaculture): 928, 929, 930, 931, 932, 933
   Forests and timberland, 918, 919, 920, 921
   Governmental finances, 475, 476
      Aid to state and local governments, 474
      Government employment and payrolls, 496
      Governmental revenue, 476
      State and local governments, 475, 476, 477, 483
      State governments, 489
   Minerals, 939
      Coal, 950, 951, 952
      Employment, 934, 938
      Mining, 935, 936
      Natural gas, 943, 945, 946, 947, 948, 949, 955
      Petroleum, 943, 946, 947, 954
      Price, 938, 939
      Production, 937, 938, 940, 941, 1398
      Products, 939
      Trade, 938, 942
      Uranium, 953, 975
   Paper products, 923, 925, 926, 927
   Wood products, 922, 923, 924, 925, 926
Natural resource- related industry (see also Mining industry, Oil and gas extraction, and individual industries):
   Employment, 496, 659, 663, 664, 671, 913, 914
   Establishments, 913, 914
   Gross domestic product, 915

---

**Note**: Index citations refer to **table** numbers, not **page** numbers

Mineral industry, 934
  Oil and gas extraction, 934, 954, 955
  Payroll and earnings, 659, 913, 914
  Petroleum industry, 943
  Sales and revenue, 914
  Timber- related industry, 916, 917
Naturalized citizens, 37, 40, 42, 48, 446
Nauru. (See Foreign countries.)
Navy, personnel, 535
Nebraska. (See State data.)
Nectarines, 245, 897
Neonatal deaths (see also Deaths and death rates), 119
Nepal. (See Foreign countries.)
Nephritis, nephrotic syndrome, and nephrosis (see also Kidney disease), 121, 122, 123, 124, 125, 210
Netherlands. (See Foreign countries.)
Neurologists, 174
Nevada. (See State data.)
New Hampshire. (See State data.)
New Jersey. (See State data.)
New Mexico. (See State data.)
New York. (See State data.)
New York Stock Exchange, 1234, 1236
New Zealand. (See Foreign countries.)
Newspaper, book, and directory publishers:
  Earnings, 659, 1156
  Employees, 659, 1156, 1157
  Establishments, 1156, 1157
  Finances, 1161, 1164
  Productivity, 667
  Revenue, 1157, 1161, 1164
Newspapers (see also Publishing industry):
  Number and circulation, 1165, 1166
  Reading, 1162
  Recycling, 420
Newsprint, 926, 927
Nicaragua. (See Foreign countries.)
Nickel:
  Consumption, 938
  Employment, 938
  Foreign trade, 938, 942
  Prices, 938, 939
  Production and value, 937, 938, 941
  World production, 941, 1398
Niger. (See Foreign countries.)
Nigeria. (See Foreign countries.)
Niobium, 938, 942
Nitrogen in ammonia, 938, 941, 1398
Nonalcoholic beverages, 719, 720
Nonemployer establishments, 601, 784, 1039, 1067, 1073, 1089, 1158, 1195, 1250, 1255, 1300
Nonmetallic mineral mining and quarrying, except fuels, 811, 913, 934
Nonmetallic mineral product manufacturing (see also Metals and metal products):
  Earnings, 659, 1042, 1049
  Employees, 659, 1040, 1042, 1044, 1049
  Establishments, 1040
  Foreign trade, 1045, 1331, 1332
  Gross domestic product, 699, 1038
  Productivity, 667, 818
  Profits, 823

  Shipments, receipts, 1042, 1045, 1051, 1052
  Toxic chemical releases, 423
Nonprofit organizations, 606, 607, 608, 609, 659, 665, 1308, 1309
North Carolina. (See State data.)
North Dakota. (See State data.)
North Korea. (See Foreign countries.)
Northern Mariana Islands. (See Island areas of the U.S.)
Norway. (See Foreign countries.)
Notifiable diseases, 201
Nuclear power, 973, 974, 975, 977, 978
  Capacity, 973, 974
  Consumption, 958, 959, 963, 1403
  Production, 958, 959, 973, 974, 977, 978, 980, 1399, 1400
  Reactors, 973, 974
  State data, 974, 980
Nursing and residential care facilities:
  Capital, 811
  Earnings, 659, 783
  Employees, 173, 659, 783
  Establishments, 190, 191, 783
  Expenditures, 140, 142, 143, 144, 147, 150
  Gross domestic product, 699
  Medicare utilization, 153
  Population, 70, 191
  Receipts, 171, 172, 783
Nursing personnel, 176, 184, 641, 643, 645
Nutritional deficiencies, deaths, 123
Nuts, 246, 875, 886, 888, 897, 898

## O

Obesity, 226, 228, 240, 1367
Obstetricians (see also Physicians), 174, 184
Occupational safety, 687, 688, 690, 935
Occupations (see also individual occupations):
  American Indian, Alaska Native population, 36
  Asian population, 36, 641, 647
  Black, African American population, 36, 641, 647
  Earnings, 643, 674, 676
  Employment, 36, 641, 643, 644, 647, 676
  Employment cost index, 677, 764
  Hispanic origin population, 36, 641, 647
  Island areas of the U.S., 1358
  Mobility (geographic) status, 29
  Native Hawaiian, Other Pacific Islander population, 36
  Retirement and health plan benefits, 685
  Self- employed, 631
  Science and engineering, 845, 846, 847, 850
  Women, 641
Office buildings. (See Commercial buildings.)
Office equipment, 1080
Office supplies, stationery, and gift stores, 659, 667, 1072, 1073, 1074, 1075
Ohio. (See State data.)
Oil. (See Petroleum and products.)
Oil and gas extraction industry:
  Capital, 811
  Earnings, 659, 783, 913, 914, 934
  Employees, 645, 659, 783, 913, 914, 934, 954, 955

Note: Index citations refer to **table** numbers, not **page** numbers

**Note**: Index citations refer to **table** numbers, not **page** numbers

---

**Note**: Index citations refer to **table** numbers, not **page** numbers

---

**Note**: Index citations refer to **table** numbers, not **page** numbers

Note: Index citations refer to **table** numbers, not **page** numbers

Note: Index citations refer to **table** numbers, not **page** numbers

# Q

Qatar. (See Foreign countries.)
Quarries. (See Mining industries.)
Quicksilver (mercury), 938, 941

# R

Rabies, 201
Race (See individual race categories.)
Radio broadcasting industry (see also Broadcasting, and Telecommunications):
   Earnings, 659, 1156, 1157
   Employees, 659, 1156, 1157
   Establishments, 1156, 1157
   Finances, 1161, 1171
   Productivity, 667
   Revenue, 1157, 1161, 1171
   Stations, 1163
Radiologists, 174
Radio listening, 1162
Rail transportation industry (see also Railroads):
   Capital, 811
   Earnings, 659
   Employees, 659, 1085, 1086
   Establishments, 1086
   Foreign trade, 1092
   Gross domestic product, 699
   Shipments, 1092, 1093, 1151
Railroad employees' retirement funds, 565
Railroads:
   AMTRAK, 1090, 1091
   Energy consumption, 961
   Mileage owned and operated, 1090
   Occupational safety, 1095
   Passenger traffic and revenue, 1145, 1297
   Shipments, 1092, 1093, 1151
   Vehicles, 1091
Rainfall, selected cities, 1408
Rankings:
   Airport traffic, 1099, 1294
   Amusement parks, 1271
   Cities:
      Commuting, 1149
      Population, 21, 24, 39
      Residential property tax, 485
      Science and engineering employment, 848
   Countries:
      Agricultural exports and imports, 1397
      Consumption of beef, pork, poultry, 1396
      Population, 1362
   Federal R&D obligations to higher education, 837
   Freight gateways, 1325
   Port traffic, 1111, 1112
   State:
      Exports, 1328
      Farm marketings, 877
      Foreign trade, 1328
      Personal income per capita, 711
      Population, 15, 21
      Public elementary/secondary school finances, 264
      Travel expenditures, 1292

Rape, 328, 336, 337, 338, 339, 342, 343, 345, 362, 363, 541
Raspberries, 875, 897
Raw materials. (See Crude materials.)
Reading (see also Books, and Libraries), 716, 719, 720, 1266, 1267, 1269, 1272, 1273
   E- book readers, 1272
   Literacy, 1392
Real estate (see also Housing), 749
Real estate and rental and leasing industry:
   Capital, 789, 811, 813
   Earnings, 657, 659, 670, 783, 788, 798, 799, 800, 801, 802, 803, 804, 1194, 1251, 1252
   Electronic commerce, 1306
   Employees, 641, 648, 657, 659, 665, 783, 787, 788, 790, 798, 799, 800, 801, 802, 803, 804, 1194, 1251
   Establishments, 665, 783, 784, 786, 787, 789, 790, 805, 1194, 1250, 1251
   Finances, 775, 778
   Gross domestic product, 699, 703, 1193
   Hires and separations, 663, 664
   Hours, 657
   Multinational companies, 825, 826
   Nonemployers, 784, 1250
   Occupational safety, 688
   Productivity, 667
   Profits, 822
   Sales, receipts, 775, 778, 783, 784, 798, 799, 800, 801, 802, 803, 804, 1194, 1250
Real estate investment trust (REITs), 1198, 1222
Receipts (see also Tax receipts, and individual industries):
   American Indian, Alaska Native- owned businesses, 797, 804
   Asian- owned businesses, 797, 802
   Black- owned businesses, 797, 801
   Corporations, partnerships, and proprietorships, 773, 774, 775, 776, 777, 778, 782, 1067
   Hispanic- or Latino- owned businesses, 797, 800
   International transactions, 1310
   Minority- owned businesses, 797, 799, 800, 801, 802, 803, 804
   Native Hawaiian, Other Pacific Islander- owned businesses, 797, 798
Revenue, government (see also individual governmental units):
   Local governments, 476, 493
   State and local governments combined, 472, 475, 476, 481, 482
   State governments, 476, 489, 490
   Tax collections, 491
   United States government, 475, 501, 507, 510
Recreation (see also Arts, recreation, and travel, and Sports):
   Activities, 227, 1259, 1263, 1267, 1269, 1270, 1271, 1273, 1278, 1280, 1283
   Art, 1262, 1263
   Building construction, value, 995, 997, 998
   Consumer expenditures, 707, 1265, 1266, 1279, 1285
   Consumer price indexes, 758, 768
   Employment and expenditures, government, 496, 499, 505
   Leisure, 1267, 1269, 1273

---

Note: Index citations refer to **table** numbers, not **page** numbers

Note: Index citations refer to **table** numbers, not **page** numbers

**Note**: Index citations refer to **table** numbers, not **page** numbers

**Note**: Index citations refer to **table** numbers, not **page** numbers

Social services, 659
Social welfare (see also Public aid, and individual programs):
  Charitable contributions, 606
  Employees (government), 496, 499
  Federal government outlays, 505, 506
  Program participation, 568
  State and local government, 475, 476, 483
  State government, 489, 492, 494
  Volunteers, 605
Social workers, 278
Sodium carbonate, 937, 938
Soft drinks (see also Beverages), 758, 767, 1065
Softball, 1276, 1277, 1278
Software publishing industry (see also Publishing):
  Earnings, 659, 1156, 1157
  Employees, 659, 1156, 1157
  Establishments, 1156, 1157
  Finances, 1157, 1161, 1167
  Productivity, 667
  Research and development, 834
  Revenue, 1161, 1167
Solar energy, 958, 962, 976, 977, 978, 986
Solid waste:
  Disposal, 407, 418, 419, 420
  Expenditures, 478, 483, 492, 494
  Industry, 421
  Landfills, 418, 419, 420
  Recycling, 418, 419, 420
Solomon Islands. (See Foreign countries.)
Somalia. (See Foreign countries.)
South Africa. (See Foreign countries.)
South Carolina. (See State data.)
South Dakota. (See State data.)
South Korea. (See Foreign countries.)
Soybeans:
  Acreage, 894, 901
  Farm marketings, sales, 875, 876, 901
  Foreign trade, 885, 887, 888, 1331
  Genetically engineered, 869
  Prices, 767, 894
  Production, 885, 894, 901
Space industry, commercial, 852
Space research and technology, federal outlays, 505, 851
Spain. (See Foreign countries.)
Spanish speakers, 55, 57, 261
Special education, 235, 236
Specialty trade contractors, 659, 992
Speeding, 1139
Spices, 758
Spinach, 245, 896, 901
Sporting and athletic goods, 214, 758, 767, 1080, 1279
Sporting goods, hobby, book, and music stores:
  Earnings, 659, 783, 1066, 1074
  Electronic commerce, 1079
  Employees, 659, 783, 1066, 1072, 1074
  Establishments, 783, 1066, 1072, 1073
  Nonemployers, 1073
  Productivity, 667
  Sales, 783, 1066, 1073, 1075, 1077, 1079

Sports (see also Sporting and athletic goods), 1269, 1270, 1273, 1274, 1275, 1276, 1277
  NCAA, 1274, 1275, 1276
  Volunteers, 605
Sports associations, 1309
Sports industry, 1253, 1255, 1256
Spot market price index, 765
Spotted fever, 201
Squash (NCAA), 1276
Squash (vegetable), 245, 896, 901
Squid, 930
Sri Lanka. (See Foreign countries.)
Standard & Poor's (S&P), 1234
Startups, firms, 794
State and local governments, combined data (see also individual governmental units):
  Debt, 475, 476, 479, 483
  Highways, 477, 478, 1118
  Employees, 495, 496, 499, 500
    Benefits, 497
  Employer costs, 684
  Expenditures, 313, 472, 475, 476, 477, 478, 480, 481, 483, 706
    By type, 475, 476, 477, 483
    Capital outlay, 477, 478
    Construction, value, 998
    Hospitals and medical care, 144, 146, 194, 483
  Federal aid, 473, 474, 503
  Finances, 472, 474, 475, 476, 481, 482
  Flow of funds, 1198, 1199
  Governmental units, 470
  Gross domestic product, 699
  Hospitals, 194, 197
  Mortgage holdings, 1222
  Payrolls, 495, 496
  Purchases of goods and services, 696, 697, 698
  Receipts by source, 472, 475, 476, 482
  Retirement systems, 575, 1198, 1231, 1237, 1241, 1242
  Securities issued, 480
  Treasury securities holdings, 1231
  Women holding public office, 465
State and regional data:
  Abortion, 107
  Agriculture, 855, 860, 874, 876, 877
  AIDS, 202
  Alcohol use, 221
  Altitudes, 407
  American Indian, Alaska Native population, 20
  Area, 399
  Arts, funding and production, 1258, 1261
  Asian population, 20
  Asset forfeiture, 361
  Automobile insurance expenditures, 1248
  Average pay, 673
  Bankruptcies, 807
  Births and birth rates, 16, 85, 92, 99
  Black, African American population, 20
  Blood alcohol concentration (BAC), 1133
  Border crossings, 1297
  Border lengths, 404
  Bridge inventory and condition, 1115
  Building permits, 994
  Buildings, federally owned, 529
  Charter schools, 281

---

**Note**: Index citations refer to **table** numbers, not **page** numbers

**Note**: Index citations refer to **table** numbers, not **page** numbers

**Note**: Index citations refer to **table** numbers, not **page** numbers

**Note**: Index citations refer to **table** numbers, not **page** numbers

---

**Note**: Index citations refer to **table** numbers, not **page** numbers

Note: Index citations refer to **table** numbers, not **page** numbers

Turkmenistan. (See Foreign countries.)
Turks and Caicos Islands. (See Foreign countries.)
Tuvalu. (See Foreign countries.)
Typhoid fever, 201

# U

Uganda (See Foreign countries.)
Ukraine (See Foreign countries.)
Ulcers, 210
Unemployment. (See Labor force, unemployed workers.)
Unemployment insurance:
  Beneficiaries, 567, 581, 582, 656
  Coverage, workers and earnings, 581, 582
  Governmental finances, 475, 489, 507, 508
  Payments, 564, 565, 566, 581, 582
Union membership, 692, 693, 694
United Arab Emirates. (See Foreign countries.)
United Kingdom. (See Foreign countries.)
United States securities (see also Debt), 1199, 1200, 1201, 1210, 1226, 1227, 1231, 1233
Universities. (See Education, higher education institutions.)
Unpaid work, 627, 682, 704
Uranium (see also Nuclear power), 937, 953, 975
Urban population (see also Cities, and Metropolitan statistical areas), 26, 81
Urban transit systems, 1086, 1090, 1144
Uruguay. (See Foreign countries.)
Utah. (See State data.)
Utilities (see also Electric light and power industry, and Gas utility industry.):
  Capital, 811, 813, 988, 990
  Consumer expenditures, 707, 716
  Customers and bills, 984, 988, 989
  Earnings, 657, 659, 670, 783, 798, 799, 800, 801, 802, 803, 804, 956, 957
  Electric, 976, 981
  Employees, 648, 657, 659, 783, 790, 798, 799, 800, 801, 802, 803, 804, 956, 957, 991
  Establishments, 783, 784, 790, 957
  Expense, 985
  Finances, 775, 778, 990
  Gross domestic product, 699
  Gas, 988, 989, 990
  Government employees and payroll, 496
  Hours, 657
  Income, 985
  Industrial production index, 818
  Industry, 783, 956, 957, 981
  Investor owned, 985
  Multinational companies, 825, 826
  Net generation, 981, 984
  Net summer capacity, 976, 980, 981
  Nonemployers, 784
  Occupational safety, 688, 690
  Price indexes, 757, 758
  Productivity, 667
  Profits, 821, 822
  Revenue, 956, 984, 985, 988, 989
  Sales, receipts, 775, 778, 783, 784, 798, 799, 800, 801, 802, 803, 804, 989
  Sewage treatment, 957, 991
  State and local government expenditures, 476, 477, 478, 483, 489, 492, 494

States, 980, 982, 983
Water, 957
Uzbekistan. (See Foreign countries.)

# V

Vacancy rates, housing, 1012, 1014, 1015, 1017, 1018, 1021
Vaccination, 237, 238
Vanadium, 937, 941, 942
Vanuatu. (See Foreign countries.)
Vaping (Electronic cigarette use), 242
Veal (see also Beef, and Meat and meat products), 246, 767, 903, 1395, 1396
Vegetable oils. (See Oils.)
Vegetables (see also individual commodities):
  Acreage, 896, 901
  Consumer expenditures, 716, 719, 720
  Consumption, 245, 900
  Farm marketings, sales, 867, 873, 875, 901
  Foreign trade, 880, 883, 886, 888, 900, 1331
  Organic, 901
  Prices, 758, 767, 771, 772, 878
  Production, 896, 900, 901
Vehicles. (See Motor vehicles.)
Veneer, wood products, 913, 916, 917
Venezuela. (See Foreign countries.)
Vermiculite, 937, 938
Vermont. (See State data.)
Vessels. (See Ships.)
Veterans:
  Business owners, 797
  Characteristics, 548, 549, 550
  Employment, 525, 615
  Number, 545, 547, 548
  Pensions and other benefits:
    Service- connected compensation, 546, 547
    Disbursements, 530, 547, 565, 566
    Federal aid to state and local governments, 474
    Federal payments, 505, 506, 564, 565, 566
    Veterans or dependents receiving, 546, 547, 567
Veterans Affairs, Dept. of:
  Expenditures, 141, 144, 147, 546, 547, 564, 565, 566
  Home loans, 1223
  Mental health treatment facilities, 180, 181
Veterinary services, 1268, 1301, 1302, 1304
Vetoed bills, Congressional, 460
Victimizations, criminal, 342, 343, 344, 346, 347, 348, 349, 350, 351, 354, 355
Vietnam. (See Foreign countries.)
Violent crime, (see also Crime), 328, 336, 337, 338, 339, 340, 341, 342, 347, 354, 355, 362, 363
Virgin Islands. (See Island areas of the U.S.)
Virginia. (See State data.)
Visa holders, doctorates, 840
Visa overstays, 559
Visual and performing arts, degrees, 321, 322, 323, 324
Vital statistics. (See Births and birth rates, Deaths and death rates, Divorces, and Marriages.)
Vocational rehabilitation, 141, 602
Volleyball, 1275, 1276, 1277, 1278
Volunteer activities, 269, 605

---

**Note**: Index citations refer to **table** numbers, not **page** numbers

**Note**: Index citations refer to **table** numbers, not **page** numbers

**Note**: Index citations refer to **table** numbers, not **page** numbers

**Note**: Index citations refer to **table** numbers, not **page** numbers